W9-AQW-121

Readers' Guide to
Periodical Literature

MARCH 1970—FEBRUARY 1971

READERS' GUIDE TO
PERIODICAL LITERATURE

Cumulated Volumes

READERS' GUIDE TO PERIODICAL LITERATURE

An Author and Subject Index

MARCH 1970—FEBRUARY 1971

Edited by
ZADA LIMERICK

Assistant Editor
LINDA LACK HOY

Indexers
ANN F. DIETZ
ANNE W. FURNESS
MARY HUMPHREY
LOVISA J. JENKINS
MURIEL M. PHILLIPS
BERTA PISCIOTTANO

THE H. W. WILSON COMPANY
NEW YORK   1971

ACKNOWLEDGMENTS

In addition to the staff members whose names appear
on the title page we wish to acknowledge the contributions of Virginia Turrell who indexed for this volume.

Z. L.

PREFATORY NOTE

The READERS' GUIDE TO PERIODICAL LITERATURE is a cumulative author subject index to periodicals of general interest published in the United States.

The Committee on Wilson Indexes of the American Library Association's Reference Services Division advises the publisher on indexing and editorial policy by means of in-depth contents studies conducted at intervals of several years. The Committee as part of its study prepares a list of periodicals, representative of all subject areas included in the Index, for consideration by the subscribers.

Selection of periodicals for indexing is accomplished by subscriber vote. In voting their preferences subscribers are asked to place primary emphasis on the reference value of the periodicals under consideration. They are also asked to give particular consideration to subject balance in order to insure that no important field be overlooked in proportion to overall index coverage.

Suggestions for additions or deletions of titles should be brought to the attention of the Committee in care of The H. W. Wilson Company.

SUGGESTIONS FOR THE USE OF THE
READERS' GUIDE TO PERIODICAL LITERATURE

Arrangement

Authors and subjects are arranged in one alphabet. Under authors and subjects, titles are arranged also in alphabetical order by the first word, initial articles being disregarded. Under personal names titles *by* author precede those *about* him. Subdivisions of a subject are arranged alphabetically under the subject. Geographical subheads follow the other subdivisions in a separate alphabet.

Cross References

See references are made from various forms of personal names and subject headings to the most generally accepted forms appearing in the first issue, after made, and thereafter in but one quarterly issue, until the annual volume. They are also made from titles of dramas, operas, and stories to names of authors and composers.

See also references are made from a subject to related subjects under which additional material may be found.

Dramas

Dramas are indexed under the dramatist's name with a *see* reference from the title of the drama; titles are also listed under the heading—Dramas—Criticisms, plots, etc.—Single works.

Fiction

Novels and short stories are indexed under the author's name with a *see* reference from the title to the author. Subject entries are made for selected types of fiction, e.g. Historical fiction; Christmas stories; etc.

Moving Pictures

Moving picture plays are indexed only under the headings Moving picture plays—Criticisms, plots, etc.—Single works, or Moving pictures—Documentary films—Criticisms, plots, etc. No title references are made.

Musical comedies, revues, etc.

Musical comedies, revues, etc. are indexed under the heading Musical comedies, revues, etc.—Criticisms, plots, etc. with a *see* reference from the title of the work.

Operas, Operettas

Operas, Operettas are indexed under the composer's name with a *see* reference from the title of the opera or operetta; titles are also listed under the headings Operas—Criticisms, plots, etc., or Operettas—Criticisms, plots, etc.

Sample entry: PHOTOGRAPHY
For better holiday pictures: open your mind first. K. Poli. il Pop Phot 66:78-9+ Ja '70

An illustrated article on the subject PHOTOGRAPHY entitled "For better holiday pictures: open your mind first," by K. Poli, will be found in volume 66 of Popular Photography, pages 78-9 (continued on later pages of the same issue) the January 1970 number

PERIODICALS INDEXED

March 1970—February 1971

All data as of latest issue received

Aging—$2. m Aging, Superintendent of Documents, U.S. Government Printing Office, Washington, D.C. 20402

America—$10. w (bi-w Jl, Ag and year-end issue) America Press, 106 W 56th St, New York 10019

American Artist—$10. m (Ag-Je) American Artist, 2160 Patterson St, Cincinnati, Ohio 45214

The American City—$15. m The American City Magazine, Buttenheim Publishing Corp, Berkshire Common, Pittsfield, Mass. 01201

American Education—$4.50. m (bi-m Ja, Ag) American Education, Superintendent of Documents, U.S. Government Printing Office, Washington, D.C. 20402

American Forests—$7.50. m American Forestry Association, 919 17th St, NW, Washington, D.C. 20006

*American Heritage—$20. bi-m American Heritage, 383 W Center St, Marion, Ohio 43302

The American Historical Review—$20. free to members of the American Historical Association, 5 times a yr (O, D, F, Ap, Je) American Historical Association, 400 A St, SE, Washington, D.C. 20003

American Home—$4. m American Home, Flushing, New York 11357

American Imago—$10. q Wayne State Univ. Press, 5980 Cass Av, Detroit, Mich. 48202

American Libraries—available only to members. m (bi-m Jl-Ag) American Library Association, 50 E Huron St, Chicago 60611

The American Record Guide—$4.50. m American Record Guide, P.O. Box 319, Radio City Station, New York 10019

The American Scholar—$5. q United Chapters of Phi Beta Kappa, 1811 Q St, NW, Washington, D.C. 20009

The American West—$9. bi-m American West Pub. Co, 599 College Av, Palo Alto, Calif. 94306

Américas—$5. m General Secretariat of the Organization of American states, Washington, D.C. 20006

The Annals of the American Academy of Political and Social Science—$12. free to members. bi-m American Academy of Political and Social Science, 3937 Chestnut St, Philadelphia 19104

Antiques—$14. m Straight Enterprises, Inc, 551 5th Av, New York 10017

The Architectural Forum—$12. m (bi-m Ja, Jl) The Architectural Forum, 130 E 59th St, New York 10022

Architectural Record—$7.50. m (semi-m My) Architectural Record, P.O. Box 430, Hightstown, N.J. 08520

Art in America—$15. bi-m Art in America, 115 Tenth St, Des Moines, Ia. 50304

Art News—$13. m (S-Je) Art News, 444 Madison Av, New York 10022

*The Atlantic—$9.50. m Atlantic, 125 Garden St, Marion, Ohio 43302

Audubon—$8.50. bi-m National Audubon Society, 1130 5th Av, New York 10028

Aviation Week & Space Technology—$15. w Aviation Week, P.O. Box 430, Hightstown, N.J. 08520

Better Homes and Gardens—$4. m Better Homes and Gardens, 1716 Locust St, Des Moines, Ia. 50303

Bulletin of the Atomic Scientists—$8.50. m (S-Je) Bulletin of the Atomic Scientists, 935 E 60th St, Chicago 60637

Business Week—$12. w Business Week, P.O. Box 430, Highstown, N.J. 08520

Camping Magazine—$7.50. free to members of the American Camping Association, m (Ja-Je, bi-m S-D) Camping Magazine, 5 Mountain Av, N Plainfield, N.J. 07060

The Catholic World—$8. m Catholic World, 400 Sette Drive, Paramus, N.J. 07652

Ceramics Monthly—$6. m (S-Je) Ceramics Monthly, P.O. Box 4548, Columbus, Ohio 43212

*Changing Times—$6. m Changing Times, The Kiplinger Magazine, Editors Park, Md. 20782

Chemistry—$6. m (bi-m Jl-Ag) American Chemical Society, 1155 16th St, NW, Washington, D.C. 20036

The Christian Century continuing New Christian—$8.50. w Christian Century Foundation, 407 S Dearborn St, Chicago 60605

Christianity Today—$6. fortn. Christianity Today, 1014 Washington Building, Washington, D.C. 20005

The Clearing House—$5. m (S-My) The Clearing House, 205 Lexington Av, Sweet Springs, Missouri 65351

Commentary—$10. m American Jewish Committee, 165 E 56th St, New York 10022

Commonweal—$12. w (bi-w year-end issue, Je-mid-S) Commonweal Pub. Co, Inc, 232 Madison Av, New York 10016

Congressional Digest—$12.50. m (bi-m Je, Ag) Congressional Digest Corp, 3231 P St, NW, Washington, D.C. 20007

Conservationist (Albany)–$2. bi-m The New York State Conservationist, Circulation Dept, New York State Conservation Department, Albany, N.Y. 12201

*Consumer Bulletin–$8. m Consumers' Research, Inc, Washington, N.J. 07882

*Consumer Reports–$8. m Consumers Union of U.S. Inc, 256 Washington St, Mount Vernon, N.Y. 10550

Craft Horizons–$10. bi-m American Craftsmen's Council, 44 W 53d St, New York 10019

Current–$10. m (except Jl) Current, Plainfield, Vermont 05667

Current History–$9.50. m Current History, Inc, 1822 Ludlow St, Philadelphia 19103

Dance Magazine–$10. m Dance Magazine, 268 W 47th St, New York 10036

The Department of State Bulletin–$16. w Department of State Bulletin, Superintendent of Documents, U.S. Government Printing Office, Washington, D.C. 20402

Design–$7. bi-m (S-Je) Design Magazine, 1100 Waterway Blvd, Indianapolis, Ind. 46202

Dun's–$7. m Dun & Bradstreet Pub. Corp, P.O. Box 3088, Grand Central Station, New York 10017

*Ebony–$8. m Johnson Pub. Co, Inc, 1820 S Michigan Av, Chicago 60616

The Education Digest–$6. m (S-My) Prakken Publications, Inc, 416 Longshore Drive, Ann Arbor, Michigan 48107

Electronics World–$7. m Electronics World, P.O. Box 1093 Flushing, New York 11352

English Journal–$10. m (S-My) National Council of Teachers of English, 508 S Sixth St, Champaign, Illinois 61820

Environment–$8.50. 10 issues a yr Environment, 438 N Skinker Blvd, St Louis, Missouri 63130

Esquire–$7.50. m Esquire, Portland Pl, Boulder, Colo. 80301

*Farm Journal (Central edition)–$2. m Farm Journal, Inc, 230 W Washington Sq, Philadelphia 19105

Field & Stream–$5. m Holt, Rinehart and Winston, Inc, 383 Madison Av, New York 10017

Film Quarterly–$5. q University of California Press, Berkeley, Calif. 94720

Flying–$7. m P.O. Box 1094, Flushing, New York 11352

Focus–$3.50. m (S-Je) American Geographical Society, Broadway at 156th St, New York 10032

Forbes–$9.50. semi-m Forbes, 60 Fifth Av, New York 10011

*Foreign Affairs–$8. q Council on Foreign Relations, Inc, 58 E 68th St, New York 10021

Fortune–$16. m Fortune, 541 N Fairbanks Court, Chicago 60611

*Good Housekeeping–$5. m Good Housekeeping, Box 517, New York 10019

Harper's Bazaar–$7. m Harper's Bazaar, P.O. Box 552, New York 10019

*Harper's Magazine–$8.50. m Harper's Magazine, 381 W Center St, Marion, Ohio 43302

Harvard Business Review–$12. bi-m Harvard Business Review, 108 10th St, Des Moines, Ia. 50305

*Harvest Years–$6. m Harvest Years, 104 E 40th St, New York 10016

*High Fidelity and Musical America (2 sects)–$14. m High Fidelity, 2160 Patterson St, Cincinnati, Ohio 45214

Hobbies–$5. m Lightner Pub. Corp, 1006 S Michigan Av, Chicago 60605

*Holiday–$7. m Holiday, 1255 Portland Pl, Boulder, Colo. 80302

Home Garden & Flower Grower–$7. m Home Garden, Portland Pl, Boulder, Colo. 80302

*Horizon–$20. q Horizon, 379 W Center St, Marion, Ohio 43302

The Horn Book Magazine–$7.50. bi-m Horn Book, Inc, 585 Boylston St, Boston 02116

Horticulture–$6. m Horticulture, 125 Garden St, Marion, Ohio 43302

Hot Rod–$7.50. m Petersen Pub. Co, 8490 Sunset Blvd, Los Angeles 90069

House & Garden incorporating Living for Young Homemakers–$7. m House & Garden, Box 5202, Boulder, Colo. 80302

House Beautiful–$7. m House Beautiful, P.O. Box 560, New York 10019

International Conciliation–$2.75. 5 times a yr (S, N, Ja, Mr, My) Carnegie Endowment for International Peace, 345 E 46th St, New York 10017

*Ladies' Home Journal–$4. m Ladies' Home Journal, Flushing, New York 11357

Library Journal–$12. semi-m (m Jl-Ag) R. R. Bowker Co, 1180 Avenue of the Americas, New York 10036

Life–$10. w (except one issue at the beginning and one issue at the year end) Life, 541 N Fairbanks Court, Chicago 60611

The Living Wilderness–$7.50. q The Wilderness Society, 729 15th St, NW, Washington, D.C. 20005

*Look–$3. bi-w Look, Box 857 Des Moines, Ia. 50304

McCall's–$3.95. m McCall's, P.O. Box 986, Dayton, Ohio 45401

Mademoiselle–$6. m Mademoiselle, P.O. Box 2204, Boulder, Colo. 80302

Mechanix Illustrated–$4. m Fawcett Publications, Inc, Fawcett Pl, Greenwich, Conn. 06830

Mental Hygiene–$10. q National Association for Mental Health, 10 Columbus Circle, New York 10019

Modern Photography–$7. m Modern Photography, 2160 Patterson St, Cincinnati, Ohio 45214

Monthy Labor Review–$9. m Superintendent of Documents, U.S. Government Printing Office, Washington, D.C. 20402

*Sports Illustrated—$12. w (except one issue at year end) Sports Illustrated, 541 N Fairbanks Court, Chicago 60611

Successful Farming (Midwest edition)—$2. m (semi-m F, Mr, bi-m Je-Jl, N-D) Successful Farming, 1716 Locust St, Des Moines, Ia. 50303

Sunset (Central edition)—$4. in Calif, Ore, Wash, Idaho, Ariz, Nev, Utah, Hawaii, Alaska. $5 in other states m Sunset Magazine, Menlo Park, Calif. 94025

Time—$15. w Time, 541 N Fairbanks Court, Chicago 60611

Today's Education—available only to members. m (S-My) National Education Association of the United States, 1201 16th St, NW, Washington, D.C. 20036

*Today's Health—$5. m Today's Health, 535 N Dearborn St, Chicago 60610

Trans-Action—$9.75. m (bi-m Jl-Ag) Transaction, Box A, Rutgers—The State University, New Brunswick, N.J. 08903

Travel—$8.50. m Travel, Travel Bldg, Floral Park, N.Y. 11001

Travel & Camera—$7.50. m (bi-m Jl-Ag, D-Ja) Travel & Camera, Box 562, Des Moines, Ia. 50302

UN Monthly Chronicle—$7. m (except in Ag) United Nations Publications, Room LX-2300, New York 10017

The UNESCO Courier—$5. m (bi-m Ag-S) UNESCO Pub. Center, Box 433, New York 10016

U.S. News & World Report—$12. w U.S. News & World Report, 435 Parker Av, Dayton, Ohio 45401

Vital Speeches of the Day—$10. semi-m City News Pub. Co, Inc, Box 606, Southold, N.Y. 11971

Vogue—$10. semi-m (m My-Jl, D) Vogue, Box 5201, Boulder, Colo. 80302

Weatherwise—$7. bi-m American Meteorological Society, 45 Beacon St, Boston, Mass. 02108

Wilson Library Bulletin—$9. m (S-Je) The H. W. Wilson Co, 950 University Av, Bronx, N.Y. 10452

*The Writer—$7. m The Writer, Inc, 8 Arlington St, Boston 02116

Writer's Digest—$4. m Writer's Digest, 22 E 12th St, Cincinnati, Ohio 45210

Yachting—$7. m Yachting Pub. Corp, 50 W 44th St, New York 10036

The Yale Review—$6. q Yale Review, 28 Hillhouse Av, New Haven, Conn. 06520

* Available for blind and other physically handicapped readers on talking books, in braille, or on magnetic tape. For information address Division for the Blind and Physically Handicapped, Library of Congress, Washington, D.C. 20542

ABBREVIATIONS OF PERIODICALS INDEXED

For full information, consult pages IX-XII

Aging—Aging
Am Artist—American Artist
Am City—American City
Am Ed—American Education
Am For—American Forests
*Am Heritage—American Heritage
Am Hist R—American Historical Review
Am Home—American Home
Am Imago—American Imago
Am Lib—American Libraries
Am Rec G—American Record Guide
Am Scholar—American Scholar
Am West—American West
America—America
Américas—Américas
Ann Am Acad—Annals of the American Academy of Political and Social Science
Antiques—Antiques
Arch Forum—Architectural Forum
Arch Rec—Architectural Record
Art in Am—Art in America
Art N—Art News
*Atlan—Atlantic
Audubon—Audubon
Aviation W—Aviation Week & Space Technology

Bet Hom & Gard—Better Homes and Gardens
Bsns W—Business Week
Bul Atom Sci—Bulletin of the Atomic Scientists

Camp Mag—Camping Magazine
Cath World—Catholic World
Ceram Mo—Ceramics Monthly
*Changing T—Changing Times
Chem—Chemistry
Chr Cent—Christian Century continuing New Christian
Chr Today—Christianity Today
Clear House—Clearing House
Commentary—Commentary
Commonweal—Commonweal
Cong Digest—Congressional Digest
Cons—Conservationist (Albany)
*Consumer Bul—Consumer Bulletin
*Consumer Rep—Consumer Reports
Craft Horiz—Craft Horizons
Cur—Current
Cur Hist—Current History

Dance Mag—Dance Magazine
Dept State Bul—Department of State Bulletin
Design—Design
Duns—Dun's

*Ebony—Ebony
Ed Digest—Education Digest
Electr World—Electronics World
Engl J—English Journal
Environ—Environment
Esquire—Esquire

*Farm J—Farm Journal (Central edition)
Field & S—Field & Stream
Film Q—Film Quarterly
Flying—Flying
Focus—Focus
*For Affairs—Foreign Affairs
Forbes—Forbes
Fortune—Fortune

*Good H—Good Housekeeping

*Har Yrs—Harvest Years
Harp Baz—Harper's Bazaar
*Harper—Harper's Magazine
Harvard Bsns R—Harvard Business Review
*Hi Fi—High Fidelity and Musical America (sections I and II)
Hobbies—Hobbies
*Holiday—Holiday
Home Gard—Home Garden & Flower Grower
*Horizon—Horizon
Horn Bk—Horn Book Magazine
Horticulture—Horticulture
Hot Rod—Hot Rod
House & Gard—House & Garden incorporating Living for Young Homemakers
House B—House Beautiful

Int Concil—International Conciliation

*Ladies Home J—Ladies' Home Journal
Library J—Library Journal
    Includes School Library Journal
Life—Life
Liv Wildn—Living Wilderness
*Look—Look

McCalls—McCall's
Mech Illus—Mechanix Illustrated
Ment Hy—Mental Hygiene
Mlle—Mademoiselle
Mo Labor R—Monthly Labor Review
Mod Phot—Modern Photography
Motor B—Motor Boating & Sailing
Motor T—Motor Trend
Mus Q—Musical Quarterly

N Y Times Mag—New York Times Magazine
*Nat Geog—National Geographic Magazine
Nat Parks & Con Mag—National Parks & Conservation Magazine
Nat R—National Review (44p issues only, pub. in alternate weeks)
Nat Wildlife—National Wildlife
Nation—Nation
Nations Bsns—Nation's Business
*Natur Hist—Natural History
Negro Hist Bul—Negro History Bulletin
New Repub—New Republic
New Yorker—New Yorker
*Newsweek—Newsweek

Opera N—Opera News
Org Gard & Farm—Organic Gardening & Farming
Outdoor Life—Outdoor Life

PTA Mag—PTA Magazine
Parents Mag—Parents' Magazine & Better Family Living
Parks & Rec—Parks & Recreation
Phys Today—Physics Today
Plays—Plays
Poetry—Poetry
Pop Electr—Popular Electronics
*Pop Mech—Popular Mechanics
Pop Phot—Popular Photography
Pop Sci—Popular Science Monthly
Pub W—Publishers' Weekly

R Pop Astron—Review of Popular Astronomy
    Discontinued publication Ag '69
Radio-Electr—Radio-Electronics
Ramp Mag—Ramparts Magazine
*Read Digest—Reader's Digest
Redbook—Redbook

*Sat R—Saturday Review
Sch & Soc—School and Society
Sch Arts—School Arts

Schol Teach—Scholastic Teacher
    Bound in Senior Scholastic
Schol Teach Jr/Sr High—Scholastic Teacher Junior/Senior High Teacher's Edition
Schol Teach Sec Teach Sup—Scholastic Teacher Secondary Teachers' Supplement
    Continued as Scholastic Teacher Junior/Senior High Teacher's Edition S 21 '70
School Library Journal. See Library Journal
*Sci Am—Scientific American
Sci Digest—Science Digest
Sci N—Science News
Science—Science
Sea Front—Sea Frontiers
*Seventeen—Seventeen
Sky & Tel—Sky and Telescope
Space World—Space World
*Sports Illus—Sports Illustrated
Sr Schol—Senior Scholastic (Teacher edition)
Suc Farm—Successful Farming (Midwest edition)
Sunset—Sunset (Central edition)

Time—Time
Todays Ed—Today's Education
*Todays Health—Today's Health
Trans-Action—Trans-Action
Travel—Travel
Travel & Camera—Travel & Camera

UN Mo Chron—UN Monthly Chronicle
UNESCO Courier—UNESCO Courier
U S News—U.S. News & World Report

Vital Speeches—Vital Speeches of the Day
Vogue—Vogue

Weatherwise—Weatherwise
Wilson Lib Bul—Wilson Library Bulletin
*Writer—Writer
Writers Digest—Writer's Digest

Yachting—Yachting
Yale R—Yale Review

* Available for blind and other physically handicapped readers on talking books, in braille, or on magnetic tape. For information address Division for the Blind and Physically Handicapped, Library of Congress, Washington, D.C. 20542

ABBREVIATIONS

*	following name entry, a printer's device		jr	junior
			jt auth	joint author
+	continued on later pages of same issue		ltd	limited
abp	archbishop		m	monthly
abr	abridged		Mr	March
Ag	August		My	**May**
Ap	April			
arch	architect		N	November
assn	association		no	number
Aut	Autumn			
av	avenue		O	October
bart	baronet		por	portrait
bibliog	bibliography		pseud	pseudonym
bibliog f	bibliographical foot-notes		pt	part
			pub	published, publisher, publishing
bi-m	bimonthly			
bi-w	biweekly			
bldg	building		q	quarterly
bp	bishop			
			rev	revised
co	company			
comp	compiled, compiler		S	September
cond	condensed		sec	section
cont	continued		semi-m	semimonthly
corp	corporation		soc	society
			Spr	Spring
D	December		sq	square
dept	department		sr	senior
ed	edited, edition, editor		st	street
			Sum	Summer
F	February		sup	supplement
			supt	superintendent
Hon	Honorable			
il	illustrated, illustration, illustrator		tr	translated, translation, translator
inc	incorporated			
introd	introduction, introductory		v	volume
			w	weekly
Ja	January		Wint	Winter
Je	June			
Jl	July		yr	year

READERS' GUIDE TO
PERIODICAL LITERATURE

MARCH 1970—FEBRUARY 1971

A Quaker action group. See Friends, Society of

AAAS. See American association for the advancement of science

AACA. See Antique automobile club of America

AADC. See Association of American dance companies

AAES. See American association of evangelical students

AAHA. See American association of homes for the aging

AAP. See Association of American publishers

AAPT. See American association of physics teachers

AARP. See American association of retired persons

AASA. See American association of school administrators

AASCU. See American association of state colleges and universities

AASL. See American association of school librarians

AAU. See Amateur athletic union of the United States

AAUP. See American association of university professors; Association of American university presses

AAVSO. See American association of variable star observers

A and P company. See Great Atlantic and Pacific tea company

ABA. See American bar association; American booksellers association

ABC. See American broadcasting companies

ABCC. See Atomic bomb casualty commission

ABM (anti-ballistic missile) See Guided missiles—Defenses

ABPC. See American book publishers council

ABT. See American ballet theatre

ABUP (Association of Boston urban priests) See Priests—Associations, institutions, etc.

A. C. Nielsen company. See Nielsen, A. C, company

ACA. See American camping association

ACC. See United Nations—Administrative committee on co-ordination

ACCC. See American council of Christian churches

ACDA. See United States—Arms control and disarmament agency

ACE. See American council on education

ACHE. See Acetylcholinesterase

ACLU. See American civil liberties union

ACP. See Associated church press (organization)

ACT. See Action for children's television (organization)

ACTH
Radioreceptor assay of adrenocorticotropic hormone: new approach to assay of polypeptide hormones in plasma. R. J. Lefkowitz and others. bibliog il Science 170: 633-5 N 6 '70

ACV. See Air cushion vehicles

ACWA. See Amalgamated clothing workers of America

A. D. 1970 (periodical) See Catholic press

ADF (automatic direction finder) See Airplanes—Radio equipment

ADR. See Applied data research, inc.

AEA. See Great Britain—Atomic energy authority

AEC. See United States—Atomic energy commission

AEF. See Art emergency fund

AEPi. See American educational publishers institute

AEW. See American education week

AFA. See American forestry association

AFDC (aid to families with dependent children) See Child welfare—United States

AFGE. See American federation of government employees

AFL. See American football league

AFL-CIO. See American federation of labor and Congress of industrial organizations

AFSE. See Association for social economics

AFT. See American federation of teachers

AFVN. See American forces Vietnam radio-television network

A. G. Schoonmaker company. See Schoonmaker, A. G, company

AHA. See American historical association

AHP. See American home products corporation

AHRA (American hot rod association) springnationals. See Automobile racing

AHRA (American hot rod association) summernationals. See Automobile racing

AI. See Artificial insemination

AIA. See American institute of architects

AIA-Sunset Western home awards. See Western home awards

AICPA. See American institute of certified public accountants

AID. See United States—Agency for international development

AIFS. See American institute for foreign study

AIG. See American insurance group

AIM. See Association for the integration of management

AIP. See American institute of physics

AIR (automatic infrared rangefinder) See View finders

ALA. See American library association

ALA bulletin
Decade of letters; a study of letters to the editor. E. M. Parker. il Am Lib 1:614-15 Je '70
See also
American libraries (periodical)

ALEA. See Air line employees association, International

ALPA. See Air line pilots association, International

ALSEP (Apollo lunar surface experiments package) See Moon—Exploration—Equipment

ALTA. See American library trustee association

AMA. See American management association; American medical association

AMK corporation. See United brands company

AMP. See Adenosine monophosphate; Another mother for peace (organization)

ANCA. See American national cattlemen's association

AP. See Associated press

APA. See American psychiatric association; American psychological association

APS. See American physical society

APWA. See American public works associations

AQAG (A Quaker action group) See Friends, Society of

ARC. See United States—Appalachian regional commission

ARENA (Adoption resource exchange of North America) See Adoption

ARL. See Association of research libraries

ARVN (army of the Republic of Vietnam) See Vietnam (Republic)—Army

ASA. See American scientific affiliation

ASCD. See Association for supervision and curriculum development

ASFTA. See American Shakespeare festival theatre and academy, Stratford, Conn.

ASIS. See American society for information science

ASMP. See American society of magazine photographers

ASNLH. See Association for the study of Negro life and history

ASTA. See American society of travel agents

AT and T. See American telephone and telegraph company

ATA. See Air transport association of America

ATC satellites. See Artificial satellites—Air traffic control applications

ATP. See Adenosine triphosphate

ATS (applications technology satellites) See Artificial satellites

ATV (all-terrain vehicles) See Motor vehicles, Amphibious

ATV racing. See Motor vehicle racing

AWACS (airborne warning and control system) See Airplanes, Military—Radar equipment

AWOL cases. See United States—Armed forces —Desertions

AACH, Herb
Materials of art versus the art of materials (cont) il Craft Horiz 30:40-1+ Mr '70
New York season. il Craft Horiz 30:49-51+ Ag '70

AAMODT, Kim
Book notes and reviews. See issues of Yachting

AARON, Chloe
Women in league for better education. Am Ed 6:32-3 Mr '70

AARON, Henry, 1934–
Henry raps one for history. W. Leggett. il pors Sports Illus 32:30-2+ My 25 '70 *

AARON, Jonathan
Cooking an omelette; poem. New Yorker 46:40 Ap 4 '70
Three poems; Death of the sports-car driver; Night driving; Her own feelings. Yale R 59:359-7 Mr '70

AARON, Sam
Choosing wines for dinner parties; excerpts from How to eat better for less money. House & Gard 137:86+ F '70
—See Beard, J. A. jt. auth.

AARONSON, Terri
Mystery. bibliog il Environ 12:2-10 My '70
Out of the frying pan. bibliog il Environ 12:26-31 Je '70
Problems underfoot. bibliog il Environ 12:16-29 N '70

AASENG, Rolf E.
Male and female created he them. Chr Today 15:5-6 N 20 '70

ABACO ISLANDS. See Bahama Islands

ABACUS
Abacus: primitive but effective digital computer. M. Gardner. il Sci Am 222:124-7 Ja '70

ABAKANOWICZ, Magdalena
Magdalena Abakanowicz. D. Wroblewska. il por Craft Horiz 30:18-23 O '70 *

ABALONE fisheries. See Shellfish fisheries

ABANDONED cars. See Automobiles—Wrecking

ABANDONED towns
Between Reno and Vegas: ghosts. il Sunset 145:28-9 S '70
Ghost towns: for sale! Bumble Bee, Ariz. B. Thomas. il Travel 134:34-9 O '70

Photographs
Taken by the wind; excerpt from Nevada ghost towns and mining camps. S. W. Paher. il Am West 7:9-17 My '70

ABANO TERME, Italy
Anatomy of a special Abano cure, decidedly Italian. D. Messinesi. Vogue 156:60 S 15 '70

ABBEY, Edward
Appalachian pictures; excerpt from Appalachian wilderness. il Audubon 72:4-13 S '70
Hallelujah, on the bum. il Am West 7:11-14 Jl '70
Let us now praise mountain lions. il Life 68:52B-54+ Mr 13 '70

ABBOTT, Berenice
Gallery; photographs. Life 69:8-9 D 11 '70

ABBOTT, Bernard C. See Paster, Z. jt. auth.

ABBOTT, John A.
Freud's repressed feelings about Athena on the Acropolis. bibliog Am Imago 26:355-63 Wint '69

ABBOTT, William L.
Right to strike in Hawaii. Nation 210:756 Je 22 '70

ABBREVIATIONS
See also
Acronyms

ABEGGLEN, James C.
Economic growth of Japan; with biographical sketch. bibliog il Sci Am 222:25, 31-7 bibliog (p 146) Mr '70

ABEL, I. W.
Steelworkers talk tough. por Bsns W p68 O 3 '70

ABEL, Lionel
What is society? bibliog f Commentary 50:45-55 S '70

ABEL, Péter
Running the gamut from Kipling to Zoltán Zelk. Pub W 198:pt2 182-3 S 21 '70

ABELL, Paul I. and others
Organic analysis of the returned lunar sample. bibliog il Science 167:757-9 Ja 30 '70

ABERCROMBIE, Thomas J.
Kansai: Japan's historic heartland. il Nat Geog 137:295-339 Mr '70

ABERNATHEY, Harold
Amateur scientist. il Sci Am 222:135-6 Mr '70

ABERNATHY, Ralph David
Encounter in Recife. B. Tyson. il pors Chr Cent 87:720-2 Je 10 '70 *
Ralph D. Abernathy: editor at large. Chr Cent 87:749 Je 17 '70 *
Two-continent visit on behalf of the poor. il pors Ebony 25:54-6+ Je '70 *

ABHAU, Elliot
Of Orléans; poem. Am Scholar 39:471 Sum '70

ABILENE Christian college, Abilene, Tex.
Abilene Christian: the Margarett and Herman Brown library. il Library J 95:4144 D 1 '70

ABILITY
See also
Creative ability
Executive ability
Great men

ABILITY, Influence of age on
Improvement of learning in the aged by modification of autonomic nervous system activity. C. Eisdorfer and others. bibliog il Science 170:1327-9 D 18 '70

ABILITY grouping in education
Ability grouping: out or in? with study-discussion program, by C. Smallenburg and H. Smallenburg. G. Rinehart. bibliog il PTA Mag 65:10-12, 33-4 N '70

ABILITY tests
See also
Intelligence tests

ABINGTON, Pa.

Education
Discipline in the innovative school. J. F. McCaffery and D. S. Turner. Clear House 44:491-6 Ap '70

ABNORMALITIES (animals)
Biology of the way out. J. Eastman. Natur Hist 79:24-9 My '70
Teratogenic evaluation of 2,4,5-T. K. D. Courtney and others. bibliog il Science 168:864-6 My 15 '70
Teratogenicity of vitamin B_3 deficiency: omphalocele, skeletal and neural defects, and splenic hypoplasia. S. D. Davis and others. bibliog il Science 169:1329-30 S 25 '70

ABNORMALITIES (man) See Deformities

ABOLITIONISTS
Black freedom: the nonviolent abolitionists from 1830 through the Civil war, by C. Mabee. Review
Nation 210:533-4 My 4 '70. C. Cohen

ABORIGINES, Australian. See Australia—Native races

ABORTION
Abortion. Nat R 22:658-9 Je 30 '70
Abortion: a startling proposal. M. J. Halberstam. Redbook 134:78-9+ Ap '70
Abortion comes out of the shadows; with an anonymous interview, ed. by F. von Moschzisker. il Life 68:20B-29 F 27 '70
Abortion in New York. il Newsweek 76:52 O 5 '70
Abortion in New York. il Time 96:48 S 7 '70
Abortion on request; Hawaii. Time 95:34 Mr 9 '70
Abortion: the academic angle. Mlle 72:145 D '70
Abortion unlimited. Newsweek 75:46 Mr 9 '70
Abortion without surgery? using prostaglandin F² alpha. Time 95:39-40 F 9 '70
Abortions on demand. il Newsweek 76:60 Jl 13 '70
Catholics and abortion. W. F. Buckley jr. Nat R 22:1366-7 D 15 '70

---

* Printer's device

ABORTION—*Continued*

Constitutional question: is there a right to abortion? L. J. Greenhouse. il N Y Times Mag p30-1+ Ja 25 '70; Discussion. p 14+ F 22 '70

How doctors perform abortions. D. R. Zimmerman. Ladies Home J 87:38+ N '70

How men feel about abortion. C. Karpel. Mlle 71:142-3+ Je '70

Legal abortion mess; Women's medical group, New York. A. Barry. McCalls 98:30+ Ja '71

Let us be born, by R. Joyce and M. Joyce. Review
　　Cath World 212:218 Ja '71. P. Marx

Not fit to print? New York bishops' pastoral letter. S. J. Adamo. America 123:568-70 D 26 '70

Number one method. Nation 210:69-70 Ja 26 '70

Open letter to American doctors. America 122:490-1 My 9 '70

Right not to be born; refusal to grant therapeutic abortion in case of rubella baby. M. K. Sanders. il Harper 240:92-9 Ap '70

Right to live. J. R. Quinn. America 123:56-7 Ag 8 '70

Talk with two abortionists; interview. ed. by B. Buresh. Newsweek 75:61 Ap 13 '70

Victims; interviews. il Ramp Mag 9:23-5 Ag '70

Who shall live? ed. by K. Vaux. Review
　　America 122:424-5 Ap 18 '70. R. A. McCormick

Whole world off her back; the Dorene Falk case. il Newsweek 75:54-5 Ap 13 '70

Bibliography

Abortion: new studies. Commonweal 93:76-7 O 16 '70

Laws and legislation

Abortion and responsibility. America 122:400 Ap 18 '70

Abortion and the changing law. il Newsweek 75:53-6+ Ap 13 '70

Abortion and the courts. Sci Am 222:50+ Ja '70

Abortion comes out of the shadows. il Life 68:20B-29 F 27 '70

Abortion counseling in legal trouble; Rabbi Ticktin on conspiracy charges. Chr Cent 87: 68 Ja 21 '70

Abortion debate. Commonweal 92:131-2 Ap 24 '70

Abortion: law, choice and morality, by D. Callahan. Review
　　America il 123:20-3 Jl 11 '70. J. J. Diamond and R. A. McCormick. Reply. D. Callahan. 123:143 S 12 '70
　　Commonweal 93:72-5 O 16 '70. D. Little

Abortion legislation: a fundamental challenge. L. Massett. il Sci N 97:75-6 Ja 17 '70

Abortion made easier. Chr Today 14:36 Mr 27 '70

Abortion: new and old issues. America 122: 666-7 Je 27 '70

Abortion on demand; New York and Hawaii. il Time 96:34 Jl 6 '70

Abortion reform. Time 95:46 Ap 20 '70

Abortion reform: the new tokenism; excerpt from Notes (from the second year) radical feminism (May 1970) Ramp Mag 9:19-21 Ag '70

Abortion tumult. Sr Schol 96:7-8 My 4 '70

Abortion veto; legislation vetoed by Maryland's Governor Marvin Mandel. New Repub 162:8 Je 13 '70

After abortion reform. America 122:449 Ap 25 '70

After July 1, an abortion should be as simple to have as a tonsillectomy, but—. L. Greenhouse. il N Y Times Mag p7+ Je 28 '70

Anti-abortion lobby; Catholic resistance to New York state's bill. J. Deedy. Commonweal 92:154 My 1 '70; Discussion. 92: 255 My 22 '70

Crime of abortion; address, April 9, 1970. B. F. Brown. Vital Speeches 36:549-53 Jl 1 '70

Easier abortion. Sci Am 222:47-8 Je '70

Fathers and sons; liberalization of New York state law. Newsweek 75:77 Ap 20 '70

Is abortion a right? symposium. il Chr Cent 87:624-31 My 20 '70; Discussion. 87:972-3 Ag 12 '70

Letters to editor. Cath World 212:173-4 Ja '71

National guide to legal abortion. L. Lader. il Ladies Home J 87:73 Jl '70

New abortion laws: how are they working? T. Irwin. il Todays Health 48:20-3+ Mr '70

Only her doctor knows. Chr Today 14:35-6 Ap 24 '70

Perverse observations on abortion. P. J. Weber. il Cath World 212:74-7 N '70

Reforming the abortion laws: a doctor looks at the case. D. Cavanagh. il America 122: 406-11 Ap 18 '70; Discussion. 122:571 My 30 '70

Should abortion laws be liberalized? interviews. ed. by C. Remsberg and B. Remsberg. L. Beebe; J. G. Fleming. pors Good H 170:92-3+ Mr '70

State of the abortion question. R. F. Drinan. Commonweal 92:108-9 Ap 17 '70; Reply with rejoinder. E. MacNeil. 92:283+ Je 12 '70

Two books on abortion and the questions they raise. C. B. Luce. Nat R 23:27-8+ Ja 12 '71

Veto for abortion; Maryland. Newsweek 75: 51-2 Je 8 '70

What every woman should know about abortion. G. M. Landau. Parents Mag 46:42-3+ Ja '71

When abortion is made easier. U S News 68:83 Je 8 '70

Great Britain

Britain's abortion act: inquiry requested. T. Beeson. Chr Cent 87:984-5 Ag 19 '70

Moral and religious aspects

Abortion: law, choice and morality. by D. Callahan. Review
　　America il 123:20-3 Jl 11 '70. J. J. Diamond and R. A. McCormick. Reply. D. Callahan. 123:143 S 12 '70
　　Commonweal 93:72-5 O 16 '70. D. Little

Christian choices in a liberal abortion climate. R. F. R. Gardner. Chr Today 14: 6-8 My 22 '70

Crime of abortion; address, April 9, 1970. B. F. Brown. Vital Speeches 36:549-53 Jl 1 '70

Is abortion a right? symposium. il Chr Cent 87:624-31 My 20 '70; Discussion. 87:972-3 Ag 12 '70

Morality of abortion; views of D. Callahan. K. L. Woodward. por Newsweek 75:64-5 Je 8 '70

Papal fallibility. Chr Cent 87:1309 N 4 '70; Discussion. 88:21 Ja 6 '71

Perverse observations on abortion. P. J. Weber. il Cath World 212:74-7 N '70

State of the abortion question. R. F. Drinan. Commonweal 92:108-9 Ap 17 '70; Reply with rejoinder. E. MacNeil. 92:283+ Je 12 '70

Two books on abortion and the questions they raise. C. B. Luce. Nat R 23:27-8+ Ja 12 '71

War on the womb. Chr Today 14:24-5 Je 5 '70

ABRAHAM, Farid F.
Orientation order of dipole molecules in the surface of embryonic droplets. bibliog il Science 168:833-5 My 15 '70

ABRAHAM, George
How to get more mileage from house plants. il Horticulture 48:30-1+ O '70

Still time to sow a tossed salad. il Home Gard 57:36-7 Ag '70

Worth their salt, home-grown tomatoes. il Home Gard 57:52-3 My '70

Your kitchen is a garden center! il Org Gard & Farm 17:41-3 F '70

ABRAMS, Al. See Abrams, C. jt. auth.

ABRAMS, Carol, and Abrams, Al
Our life on a border kibbutz. il pors Nat Geog 138:364-91 S '70

ABRAMS, Charles
Charles Abrams, 1901-1970. L. C. Campbell. por Arch Forum 132:62-3 Ap '70 *

ABRAMS, Rita
Happy sound in Mill Valley. il pors Life 69:50-2 S 25 '70 *

Pet teacher. il por Newsweek 76:86-7 Jl 20 '70 *

ABRAMS, Sam
Big Sur storm. il Natur Hist 79:8-10+ Ag '70

When to thee; poem. Nation 210:732 Je 15 '70

ABRAMSON, Martin
Singing Lennon sisters. il pors Good H 170: 42+ Je '70

ABRAMSON, Ruth K. and others
Homozygous Hb J Tongariki: evidence for only one alpha chain structural locus in Melanesians. bibliog il Science 169:194-6 Jl 10 '70

ABRUZZI, William
Rock doctor tells about 985 freakouts; ed. by R. Stokes. il por Life 69:37 Ag 14 '70

ABSCISIC acid
Phenotypic reversion of flacca, a wilty mutant of tomato, by abscisic acid. D. Imber and M. Tal. bibliog il Science 169:592-3 Ag 7 '70

ABSE, Dannie
New diary; poem. Am Scholar 40:122 Wint '70

ABSENT voting. See Voting, Absent
ABSENTEEISM
  Absenteeism just won't quit. Bsns W p66
    Jl 25 '70
ABSORPTION spectra. See Spectrum—Absorption spectra
ABSTINENCE. See Fasting
ABSTRACT art. See Art, Abstract
ABSTRACT expressionism
  Art world; M. Rothko. H. Rosenberg. New
    Yorker 46:90+ Mr 28 '70
ABSTRACT films. See Moving pictures—Abstract films
ABSTRACT photography. See Photography, Artistic
ABSURD, Theater of the. See Theater, Experimental
ABU DHABI
  Tilling the desert under plastic skies; integrated power-water-food system. il Bsns W
    p92+ My 9 '70
ABU Lotuf
  Hidden leader of the Arab guerrillas; interview; ed. by O. Fallaci. il Look 34:24-6 Je
    30 '70
ABUNDANCE. See Prosperity
ABUSE. See Invective
ABUTILON. See Flowering maples
ABYSSINIAN church. See Ethiopic church
ABZUG, Bella
  Bella. il por Newsweek 76:28-9 O 5 '70 •
ACADEMIC achievement. See Student achievements
ACADEMIC degrees. See Degrees, Academic
ACADEMIC evaluation. See Grading and marking (students)
ACADEMIC freedom
  Academic freedom and responsibility. Sch &
    Soc 98:138-41 Mr '70
  Academic freedom in evangelical perspective.
    Chr Today 14:20-1 Jl 3 '70
  Davis affair. il por Newsweek 75:78 Je 22 '70
  Guarding your freedom to teach. il Todays
    Ed 59:20-3 N '70
  Hardly the last word; case of A. Davis at
    UCLA. por Time 95:45 Je 29 '70
  Muzzling atheists. Chr Today 14:35 Je 19 '70
  Realism in education; by W. O. Martin. Review
    Nat R 22:844 Ag 11 '70. R. Kirk
  Responsible professors. T. H. Clancy. America
    124:45 Ja 16 '71
  Revival of heresy; speakers on campuses
    listed by Congress. Nation 211:450-1 N 9 '70
  Rights of a gadfly; M. Zeitlin case. Nation
    211:165 S 7 '70
  St John's: four years after. J. A. Scimecca;
    discussion. Commonweal 91:419+, 523+ Ja
    16, F 13 '70
  South Africa: university system follows
    apartheid pattern; government enforces
    limits on academic dissenters. D. S.
    Greenberg. il Science 169:260-4+ Jl 17 '70
  Teachers, students, and selfishness in the
    seventies. V. R. Mollenkott. Chr Today 14:
    6-8+ Ap 10 '70 (to be cont)
  What the Warren court decided; excerpts
    from The Warren court and the public
    schools. H. C. Hudgins, jr. Ed Digest 36:
    44-7 N '70
  Whither Angela Davis? Chr Today 14:22 Jl
    17 '70
    See also
  Colleges and universities—Administration
  Colleges and universities—Political control
  Tennessee evolution controversy
ACADEMIC tenure. See College professors and instructors—Tenure
ACADÉMIE française. See French academy
ACADEMY awards (moving pictures)
  Mocking the mockery. il Time 95:72 Ap 20 '70
  Whose Oscar? M. S. Dworkin. il Cath World
    212:40-2 O '70
ACADEMY of motion picture arts and sciences
    See also
  Academy awards (moving pictures)
ACADIA NATIONAL PARK
  Oil threatens Acadia. F. Davisson. il Nat
    Parks & Con Mag 44:4-7 D '70
ACADIANS in Louisiana
  Exploring the Cajun country. L. L. King.
    il Holiday 47:70-3 My '70
  My most unforgettable character; U. Veazey
    of the Louisiana Cajuns. G. Veazey. il
    Read Digest 97:145-6+ N '70
ACANTHASTER planci. See Starfishes
ACAPULCO, Mexico
  Resort luxury at a bargain. F. Somers. Redbook 135:162 O '70
  Rich way to make a getaway; Tres Vidas
    country club. E. Shrake. il por Sports
    Illus 33:26-33 Ag 31 '70

Two faces of Acapulco. il Bsns W p69+ Mr
  21 '70
Who said the big boom was over in Acapulco? It's just beginning. H. Sutton. il
  Holiday 48:12-15 Jl '70
    Hotels, restaurants, etc.
Let's travel: on a honeymoon; las Brisas. il
  Mlle 70:40-2 Ja '70
ACCARDO, Carl A.
  March eclipse rocket program at Wallops
    Island. il Sky & Tel 39:344-9 Je '70
ACCELERATION in education. See Educational acceleration
ACCELERATION of particles. See Particles
  (nuclear physics)—Acceleration
ACCELERATORS (electrons, etc)
  Accelerator accelerated; Batavia, Ill. Sci
    Am 223:44 Ag '70
  Action and diplomacy. Sci N 97:479 My 16
    '70
  Atom smasher. il por Newsweek 75:56 Je
    22 '70
  Batavia accelerator, startup a year early? H.
    L. Davis. il Phys Today 23:29-32 Je '70
  Batavia participation loses out. W. Kornberg.
    il Sci N 97:380 Ap 11 '70
  Brookhaven's emperors survey nuclear realm.
    G. B. Lubkin. il Phys Today 23:19-20 N '70
  CERN proposes missing magnets and 150 GeV
    for new machine. G. B. Lubkin. Phys Today
    23:56-7 Jl '70
  CERN: rumors but no decision on site. D. S.
    Greenberg. Science 167:1231 F 27 '70
  CERN's new accelerator; Germans insist on
    a site in Germany. D. S. Greenberg. Science
    167:358-9 Ja 23 '70
  Europe's maxiaccelerator. Sci N 98:445 D 12
    '70
  Experimenters vie for first crack at Batavia.
    G. B. Lubkin. Phys Today 23:17-18 S '70
  Flexibility for Batavia. Sci N 97:408 Ap 25 '70
  High-energy accelerator panic. il Sci N 97:
    239 Mr 7 '70
  High-energy physics suffers a setback: lack
    of federal funds. D. E. Thomsen. il Sci N
    97:298-9 Mr 21 '70
  Japan builds first GeV-class synchrotron in
    Asia. H. L. Davis. Phys Today 23:63 D '70
  Meson factories and the two-nucleon problem. M. J. Moravcsik. bibliog il Phys Today 23:40-4+ O '70
  More power sooner for Batavia. il Sci N 98:
    111-13 Ag 8 '70
  Principle for a pi-pi collision device proposed; precetron. G. B. Lubkin. Phys Today
    23:57 Jl '70
  Progress report on the big accelerators;
    Batavia and CERN. P. M. Boffey; D. S.
    Greenberg. il Science 168:1071-7 My 29 '70
  Saving space with superconductors; Stanford
    linear acccelerator. il Sci N 98:317 O 17 '70
  Surprises at Serpukhov. D. E. Thomsen. il
    Sci N 97:437-8 My 2 '70
  Tandem Van de Graaff accelerators. P. H.
    Rose and A. B. Wittkower. il Sci Am
    223:24-33 Ag '70
  Twilight for a workhorse; Princeton-Penn accelerator. D. E. Thomsen. il Sci N 97:327-8
    Mr 28 '70
  Uncertainty at CERN. Sci N 98:94 Ag 1 '70
  Your preview of the world's mightiest atom
    smasher; proton synchrotron at Weston, Ill.
    A. P. Armagnac. il Pop Sci 197:56-8+ O '70
    See also
  National accelerator laboratory
ACCESS to the press. See Press law
ACCESSORIES, Dress. See Dress accessories
ACCESSORIES, Household. See Household furnishings
ACCIDENT law
  Illness and injury: the legal steps you must
    know about. L. M. Brown. Bet Hom &
    Gard 48:38 Je '70
ACCIDENT litigation. See Actions and defenses
ACCIDENTAL war. See Atomic weapons—Accidents
ACCIDENTS
  Beware those holiday accidents. J. H. Winchester. Read Digest 96:155-8 Ja '70
  Fourteen camp accidents which could have
    been avoided. Camp Mag 42:16+ Ja '70
    See also
  Burns and scalds
  Electricity, Injuries from
  Fires
  First aid in illness and injury
  Rescue work
  Shipwrecks
  Sprains
  Traffic accidents
  Traumatism
    also subhead Accidents or Accidents and
    injuries under various subjects, e.g. Football—Accidents and injuries

ACCIDENTS—*Continued*
Laws and legislation
See Accident law
Prevention
Caution! These products can kill! household and garden products. il Changing T 24:27-30 F '70
Is living safely popular? Consumer Bul 53: 14-15 Mr '70
Preventing injury to young children in the home. il Good H 172:127 Ja '71
See also
Aviation—Safety devices and measures
Fire protection
Safety education
ACCIDENTS, Industrial
Industrial accidents. Mo Labor R 93:2 D '70
See also
Industrial safety
Insurance, Workmens compensation
Prevention
See Industrial safety
ACCIDENTS, Liability for. See Liability (law)
ACCION international
Peace corps for Latin slums. il Bsns W p48 Ja 17 '70
ACCLIMATIZATION
See also
Altitude, Influence on
ACCOMPLICES
Vicarious murder; ruling of California supreme court in A. Taylor case. Time 96: 61 D 21 '70
ACCOUNTABILITY. See Responsibility
ACCOUNTABILITY in education. See Performance contracts (education)
ACCOUNTING
Fat maverick stirs up the accounting profession. A. M. Louis. il Fortune 82:96-9+ D '70
See also
Auditing
Business consolidations and mergers—Accounting
Cash flow
Contracts, Government—Accounting
Corporations—Accounting
Cost accounting
Financial statements
Mechanical aids
See also
Computers—Business use
ACCOUNTING, Household. See Budget, Household; Domestic finance
ACCOUNTING principles board. See American institute of certified public accountants
ACCOUNTS, Collecting of. See Collecting of accounts
ACCREDITATION of library schools. See Library schools and education
ACCREDITED library schools. See Library schools and education
ACE, Goodman
Top of my head. See issues of Saturday review
ACETALDEHYDE
Blood concentrations of acetaldehyde and ethanol in chronic alcoholics. E. Majchrowicz and J. H. Mendelson. bibliog il Science 168:1100-2 My 29 '70
ACETATES
Phenylthioacetate: a useful substrate for the histochemical and colorimetric detection of cholinesterase. G. M. Booth and R. L. Metcalf. bibliog il Science 170:455-7 O 23 '70
Sex pheromones of the southern armyworm moth: isolation, identification, and synthesis. M. Jacobson and others. bibliog il Science 170:542-4 O 30 '70
ACETYLAMINOFLUORENE. See Fluorenylacetamide
ACETYLATION
Puffing and histone acetylation in polytene chromosomes. U. Clever and E. G. Ellgaard. bibliog il Science 169:373-4 Jl 24 '70
ACETYLCHOLINE
Acetylcholine concentrations in rat brain: diurnal oscillation. I. Hanin and others. bibliog il Science 170:341-2 O 16 '70
Acetylcholine sensitivity and distribution on mouse neuroblastoma cells. A. J. Harris and M. J. Dennis. bibliog il Science 167: 1253-5 F 27 '70
Vesicular and synaptoplasmic synthesis of acetylcholine. A. K. Ritchie and A. M. Goldberg. bibliog il Science 169:489-90 Jl 31 '70

ACETYLCHOLINESTERASE
Price of convenience; breakdown of acetylcholine-ACHE system by DDVP and other organic phosphates. bibliog il Environ 12:7-15+ O '70
ACETYLMETHADOL
New heroin substitute. il Sci Digest 67:56 Je '70
ACETYLSALICYLIC acid. See Aspirin
ACETYLTRANSFERASE. See Transferases
ACHESON, Dean Gooderham
God in striped pants. P. Seaburg. Trans-Action 7:56-8 Je '70 *
Mr Secretary. M. Cunliffe. Commentary 49: 109-12 My '70 *
Peripatetic reviewer. E. Weeks. Atlan 225:99 Ja '70
ACHIEVEMENT motivation. See Motivation (education)
ACHIEVEMENTS, Student. See Student achievements
ACIDS
Bronsted-Lowry acid-base theory, a brief survey. D. L. Morris. por Chem 43:18-19 Mr '70
See also names of acids and acid groups, e.g. Trisparic acid; Fulvic acids
ACIDS, Fatty
Enzyme specificity as a factor in regulation of fatty acid chain length in escherichia coli. M. D. Greenspan and others. bibliog il Science 170:1203-4 D 11 '70
See also
Prostaglandins
ACKERLY, Robert L.
Controlling student conduct. Ed Digest 35: 12-15 Ap '70
ACKERMAN, Nathan W.
To treat a disturbed person, treat his family. S. Davidson. il por N Y Times Mag p 10-11+ Ag 16 '70; Reply. K. DeCrow. p22 S 13 '70
What happened to the family? Ment Hy 54: 459-63 Jl '70
about
To treat a disturbed person, treat his family. S. Davidson. il por N Y Times Mag p 10-11+ Ag 16 '70 *
ACKERMAN, Page, and others
New directions; excerpts from report, ed. by G. R. Shields. Am Lib 1:1021-2 D '70
ACKLEY, Gardner
Inflation control; address, December 5, 1969. Vital Speeches 36:200-3 Ja 15 '70
ACKWORTH, Robert
Is it for real? story. Redbook 135:75 Ag '70
ACNE
Acne: who gets it, and why. Vogue 156:131+ Ag 1 '70
If your child has acne. S. L. Englebardt. Parents Mag 45:64-5+ O '70
ACONDA. See American library association—Committee on new directions
ACONITASE. See Enzymes
ACOSTA, Mary J.
Drawing with erasers. il Design 71:27 Sum '70
Mimeographics. il Design 71:38-40 Spr '70
Rubber band & string prints. il Design 71:22-3 Fall '69
Wire drawings. il Design 71:37 Wint '69
ACOSTA SOLIS, Misael
Feast of the sun. il Américas 22:24-30 O '70
ACOUSTIC phenomena in nature
See also
Singing sands
ACOUSTIC research, inc.
Fruits of industry, or What AR hath wrought. O. Daniel. Sat R 53:47-8 D 26 '70
ACOUSTICS, Architectural
See also
Orchestra shells
Soundproofing
ACQUISITIONS, College library. See College libraries—Acquisitions
ACROBATS and acrobatism
Smell of death was in the air; K. Wallenda's walk across Tallulah Gorge, Ga. M. Kram. il pors Sports Illus 33:18+ Jl 27 '70
Wallenda is at it again; Tallulah Gorge, Ga. high wire walk. il pors Life 69:39-40 Jl 31 '70
See also
Stunt women
ACRONYMS
Agonies of Acronymania. il Time 96:58+ Jl 20 '70
ACTIN. See Muscle—Proteins
ACTING
Actors' search for a self. W. E. Henry and J. H. Sims. il Trans-Action 7:57-62 S '70
Bruce Davison: hope for the future; interview, ed. by E. Miller. B. Davison. il por Seventeen 29:166-7+ Ap '70

ACTING—*Continued*
Essence of Barbara; interview, ed. by E. Miller. B. Hershey. il pors Seventeen 29: 132-3+ F '70
Irishman with impact; interview, ed. by E. Miller. R. Harris. pors Seventeen 29:152-3+ Mr '70
Sir says; interview, ed by H. Ehrlich. L. Olivier. il pors Look 34:22-6 Ja 27 '70
They hardly ever make passes at Glenda Jackson. H. Ehrlich. il pors Look 34:36-41 D 29 '70

Study and teaching
Three-ring classroom; a look at circus arts. J. Marks. il Mlle 72:184-5+ N '70

ACTINIDE elements
Isotopic abundances of actinide elements in lunar material. P. R. Fields and others. bibliog il Science 167:499-501 Ja 30 '70
See also
Plutonium

ACTION for children's television (organization)
Act with ACT. R. L. Shayon. Sat R 53:22 Mr 7 '70
Caveat pre-emptor; ACT's request for free time to expose overstated toy commercials. R. L. Shayon. Sat R 54:37 Ja 9 '71
Kidvid ghetto; reactions to proposal to ban commercials from children's programs. R. L. Shayon. Sat R 53:21 Je 20 '70

ACTION in art
See also
Mobiles

ACTIONS and defenses
Butler sues former producer of Aerostar. Aviation W 94:66 Ja 11 '71
Environmental degradation and legal action. A. A. D'Amato. Bul Atom Sci 26:24-6 Mr '70
Fifteenth amendment and the white primary. Negro Hist Bul 33:88-9 Ap '70
Journalist sues Viking, Esquire, over Calley story. Pub W 198:30 O 19 '70
Pollution politics; IRS clampdown to stop environmentalists' class action suits. New Repub 163:5-6 O 31 '70
Tax-exempt litigation; IRS curbs draw widespread opposition. R. J. Bazell. Science 170: 716-17 N 13 '70
When should you sue? D. Green. il Mech Illus 66:46-8+ Ja '70
See also
Damages
Injunctions
Libel and slander

ACTIVATED sludge method. See Sewage disposal—Activated sludge method

ACTIVATION analysis. See Radioactivation analysis

ACTIVE handicapped (periodical)
Active handicapped. America 122:118 F 7 '70

ACTIVITIES, Student. See Student activities

ACTIVITIES committee on new directions. See American library association—Committee on new directions

ACTOMYOSIN
Actomyosin from physarum polycephalum; electron microscopy of myosin-enriched preparations. V. T. Nachmias and W. C. Ingram. bibliog il Science 170:743-5 N 13 '70

ACTORS and actresses
Actors' search for a self. W. E. Henry and J. H. Sims. il Trans-Action 7:57-62 S '70
Commercial successes. il Newsweek 76:100 O 19 '70
Five young beauties & how they get that way. il Mlle 72:135-41 N '70
Futures, great. pors Vogue 156:90-3 Jl '70
Player's the thing; current London theater. C. Porterfield. il Time 96:46 S 14 '70
Real names of Edison cylinder performers. J. Walsh. il Hobbies 75:37-9 Je '70
See also
Acting
Comedians
Moving pictures actors and actresses
Negro actors and actresses
Strikes—United States—Actors and actresses
Theatrical agencies
also names of actors and actresses
e.g. M. Smith

ACTRESSES. See Actors and actresses

ADAIR, E. Ross
Excerpt from debate, September 16, 1969. Cong Digest 49:20 Ja '70

ADAM, Adolphe Charles
Giselle, all of it for the first time on records. C. J. Luten. por Am Rec G 36:868-9 Jl '70 *

ADAMO, N. J. and Ratner, A.
Monosodium glutamate; lack of effects on brain and reproductive function in rats. bibliog il Science 169:673-4 Ag 14 '70

ADAMO, S. J.
Press. See issues of America

ADAMS, A. Paul, and Spendlove, J. C.
Coliform aerosols emitted by sewage treatment plants. bibliog il Science 169:1218-20 S 18 '70

ADAMS, Alice
Propitiation of witches; story. Redbook 134: 60-1 F '70

ADAMS, Bill
Rigging for lakers. il Field & S 74:78-9+ Ap '70

ADAMS, Brockman
Excerpt from debate, July 31, 1970. Cong Digest 49:250+ O '70

ADAMS, Carolyn
Brief biography. S. Goodman. pors Dance Mag 44:60-1 N '70 *

ADAMS, Charles W.
Letting the genie out of the bottle. il por Nations Bsns 58:64-5 Ja '70

ADAMS, Henry
In search of innocence. L. Auchincloss. il pors Am Heritage 21:28-33 Je '70 *
Never leave me, never leave me. L. Auchincloss. il pors Am Heritage 21:20-2+ F '70 *

ADAMS, John B. and Jones, R. L.
Spectral reflectivity of lunar samples. bibliog il Science 167:737-9 Ja 30 '70

ADAMS, John Clarke
Then the music. il Opera N 34:25+ F 7 '70

ADAMS, John F.
Super-segmental chukar-checker. il Field & S 75:56-7+ S '70

ADAMS, John Quincy
Portraits of John Quincy Adams. S. B. Sherrill. por Antiques 98:492+ O '70 *

ADAMS, John Quincy, family
Portraits of John Quincy Adams and his wife; excerpts. A. Oliver. pors Antiques 98:748-53 N '70

ADAMS, Kaywynne
Semantikos/rejectementa; poem. Poetry 116: 96 My '70

ADAMS, Phoebe Lou
Short reviews: books. See issues of Atlantic

ADAMS, Russell B. See Hart, J. F. jt. auth.

ADAMS, Ruth C.
Years we began using garbage. Org Gard & Farm 17:67 Ja '70

ADAMS, Sam
Sun also sets. il Sports Illus 32:56-60+ Je 29 '70

ADAMS, Samuel
Samuel Adams; architect of Revolution. por Sr Schol 95:16 S 29 '69 *

ADAMS, Thomas B.
Collecting for Clio. il Sat R 53:16-17 Je 20 '70

ADAMSON, June
Mary. Chr Cent 87:175-6 F 11 '70

ADAPTABLITY
My problem and how I solved it; fear of a change. il Good H 171:12+ S '70

ADAPTABILITY (psychology)
Adaptation under extreme environmental conditions. G. E. Ruff. bibliog f il Ann Am Acad 389:19-26 My '70

ADAPTATION (biology)
Adaptation under extreme environmental conditions. G. E. Ruff. bibliog f il Ann Am Acad 389:19-26 My '70
Physiology of high altitude. R. J. Hock. il Sci Am 222:52-8+ F '70

ADAPTATION, Social. See Adjustment, Social

ADAPTATION, Visual. See Eye—Accommodation and refraction

ADAPTERS, Radio. See Radio apparatus

ADAPTIVE control systems
See also
Feedback control systems

ADDICOTT, F. L.
Leaf-dropping hormone isolated. il Horticulture 48:40 F '70

ADDICTS, Drug. See Narcotic addicts

ADDING machines
Converting England; the Addmaster. T. J. Murray. Duns 97:53-4 Ja '71
Inexpensive tape-printing adding machines. il Consumer Bul 53:25-8 Mr '70

ADDINGTON, L. F.
Kingfisher repays her debt. il Nat Wildlife 8: 36-7 D '69

ADDITION, Mental. See Arithmetic, Mental

ADDITIONS, House. See Houses, Remodeled

ADDITIVES. See Gasoline—Additives

ADDITIVES, Food. See Food additives

ADDONIZIO, Hugh Joseph
Double jeopardy in Newark. il por Time 95: 20 Je 15 '70 *
Let us enjoy our victory. il pors Newsweek 75:16-19 Je 29 '70 *
Newark; the price of the past. por Newsweek 76:18 Ag 3 '70 *

ADDONIZIO trial. See Trials (extortion)

ADDRESS, Forms of. See Forms of address

ADELA. See Atlantic community development group for Latin America

ADELMAN, Maurice, jr
Biography (cont) America 122:479-80; 123: 466-8 My 2, N 28 '70

ADELSEN, Charles E.
Love affair: James Baldwin and Istanbul. il pors Ebony 25:40-2+ Mr '70

ADELSON, Alan M.
Subpoena siege: have the news media become too big to fight? il Sat R 53:106-8 Mr 14 '70

ADELSON, Joseph
What generation gap? il N Y Times Mag p 10-11+ Ja 18 '70

ADENOHYPOPHYSIS. See Pituitary body

ADENOSINE monophosphate
Adenosine 3', 5'-monophosphate, adreno-corticotropic hormone, and adrenocortical cytosol protein synthesis. M. F. Grower and E. D. Bransome, jr. bibliog il Science 168:483-5 Ap 24 '70
Adenosine 3',5'-monophosphate in rat pineal gland: increase induced by light. M. S. Ebadi and others. bibliog il Science 170: 188-90 O 9 '70
Cell communication, calcium ion, and cyclic adenosine monophosphate. H. Rasmussen. bibliog il Science 170:404-12 O 23 '70
Cyclic adenosine monophosphate: andromimetic action on seminal vesicular enzymes. R. L. Singhal and others. bibliog il Science 168:261-3 Ap 10 '70
Cyclic adenosine monophosphate in bacteria. I. Pastan and R. Perlman. bibliog il Science 169:339-44 Jl 24 '70
Cyclic adenosine monophosphate: potassium-dependent action on vascular smooth muscle membrane potential. A. V. Somlyo and others. bibliog il Science 169:490-1 Jl 31 '70
Divergent biological effects of adenosine and dibutyryl adenosine 3',5'-monophosphate on the isolated fat cell. S. S. Solomon and others. bibliog il Science 169:387-8 Jl 24 '70
Pineal gland: dibutyryl cyclic adenosine monophosphate stimulation of labeled melatonin production. D. C. Klein and others. bibliog il Science 167:1738-50 Mr 27 '70
Prostaglandin receptor site: evidence for an essential role in the action of luteinizing hormone. F. A. Kuehl, jr. and others. bibliog il Science 169:883-6 Ag 28 '70
Second messenger; cyclic AMP. B. J. Culliton. il Sci N 98:450-1 D 12 '70
Steroid hormones: effects on adenyl cyclase activity and adenosine 3',5'-monophosphate in target tissues. M. G. Rosenfeld and B. W. O'Malley. bibliog il Science 168:253-5 Ap 10 '70

ADENOSINE triphosphate
Brain adenosine triphosphate: decreased concentration precedes convulsions. A. P. Sanders and others. bibliog il Science 169: 206-8 Jl 10 '70; Reply with rejoinder. R. C. Collins and others. 170:1430-1 D 25 '70

ADENOVIRUSES
Nucleotide sequence of an RNA from cells infected with adenovirus. K. Ohe and S. M. Weissman. bibliog il Science 167:879-81 F 6 '70

ADENYL cyclase. See Enzymes

ADHESION
Adhesion. Chem 43:27 My '70

ADHESIVE hooks. See Hooks

ADHESIVE tape
Double-face tape: inadequacies. il Consumer Bul 53:14 Ap '70
Masking tapes. il Consumer Rep 35:558-9 S '70
Nonskid tapes. il Consumer Rep 35:480-1 Ag '70
Now sticky tapes stick everything. il Changing T 24:10 F '70
Transparent tapes. Consumer Rep 35:418-19 Jl '70
See also
Mending tape

ADHESIVES
Barnacle glue. R. L. Amey. bibliog il por Chem 43:44-6 Jl '70
See also
Cements, Adhesive
Epoxy adhesives
Glue

ADIRONDACK MOUNTAINS
Escape from pollution; the Adirondacks; address. June 3, 1969. V. J. Schaefer. il Cons 24:8-11 F '70
Impact of man on the Adirondack high country. E. H. Ketchledge and R. E. Leonard. il Cons 25:14-18 O '70

New York state's most spectacular environment: the Adirondack high country. E. H. Ketchledge. il Cons 25:16-20 Ag '70

ADIRONDACK MOUNTAINS in art
Wilderness and the Adirondacks, an historical view. W. K. Verner. il Liv Wildn 33: 27-46 Wint '69

ADISESHIAH, Malcolm S.
Crisis in development. il UNESCO Courier 23: 4-14 O '70
Tasks for the International education year. Sch & Soc 98:296-8 Sum '70

ADJUSTMENT (biology) See Adaptation (biology)

ADJUSTMENT (psychology)
Signs of emotional adjustment and disturbance. B. Spock. Redbook 135:22+ Je '70
See also
Adaptability (psychology)
Conflict (psychology)

ADJUSTMENT, Social
Social adequacy of state mental hospital patients. C. Bentinck and others. bibliog Ment Hy 54:421-4 Jl '70
See also
Aged—Activities
Aged—Adjustment problems
College students—Adjustment
Individual and society
School children—Adjustment
Widows—Adjustment

ADLER, Bill
Dear baby doctor: excerpt from Mothers write funny letters to baby doctors. il Todays Health 48:24-6 S; 75-6 O '70

ADLER, Isidore, and others
Electron microprobe analysis of lunar samples. il Science 167:590-2 Ja 30 '70

ADLER, Keith
Rotary print washer anyone can build. il Pop Mech 134:146 S '70

ADLER, Les K. and Paterson, T. G.
Red fascism: the merger of Nazi Germany and Soviet Russia in the American image of totalitarianism, 1930's-1950's. bibliog f Am Hist R 75:1046-64, 2159-64 Ap, D '70

ADLER, Norman T. and Zoloth, S. R.
Copulatory behavior can inhibit pregnancy in female rats. bibliog il Science 168:1480-2 Je 19 '70

ADLER, Renata
Collect calls; story. New Yorker 46:46-54 O 24 '70
Radicalism and the skipped generation; excerpt from Toward a radical middle: fourteen pieces of reporting and criticism. Atlan 225:53-7 F '70
Reporter at large. New Yorker 46:40-4+ O 3 '70
about
Films: film critic for the New York times. J. Brackman. Esquire 73:26+ Mr '70 *
Liberated, all liberated. il pors Vogue 155: 114-15 Je '70 *
Movie critic on movie critics. R. Schickel. Harper 240:97-9 Ja '70
Peculiar experience. R. A. Sokolov. por Newsweek 75:80A+ F 2 '70
Perils of Renata, pearls of Pauline. R. Corliss. Nat R 22:369-70 Ap 7 '70 *

ADMAN, R. and Pious, D. A.
Isoantigenic variants: isolation from human diploid cells in culture. bibliog il Science 168:370-2 Ap 17 '70

ADMINISTRATION, Public
See also
Bureaucracy

ADMINISTRATIVE ability. See Executive ability

ADMINISTRATIVE and budgetary committee. See United Nations—Administrative and budgetary committee

ADMINISTRATIVE and political divisions
See also
Independent regulatory commissions

ADMINISTRATIVE assistants to the president. See Public officers

ADMINISTRATIVE committee on co-ordination. See United States—Administrative committee on co-ordination

ADMINISTRATIVE communication. See Communication in management

ADMINISTRATIVE efficiency. See Efficiency, Administrative

ADMINISTRATORS, College. See College officials

ADMINISTRATORS and executors. See Executors and administrators

ADOBE buildings. See Building, Adobe

ADOFF, Arnold
New new poets in old old America. por Pub W 198:86-8 Jl 13 '70

ADOLESCENCE
Booster shots for personality: with study-discussion program. by C. Smallenburg and H. Smallenburg. W. G. Hollister. bibliog il PTA Mag 64:16-19. 36 Ja '70
Bouquet for Miss Benson; excerpt from Growing pains: the autobiography of a young boy. P. Villiard. il Read Digest 97:119-21 Jl '70
Learning and maturation in middle school age youth. H. Thornburg. bibliog Clear House 45:150-5 N '70
   See also
Boys
High school students
Puberty
Youth

        Psychology
Telephonitis, the teen-age hangup. H. Arnstein. il Todays Health 48:40-1+ F '70
ADOLESCENT clinics. See Health clinics
ADOLESCENT literature. See Young adults literature
ADOLESCENT medicine. See Youth—Health and hygiene
ADOPTION
ARENA breaks the adoption barrier. E. M. Wylie. il Read Digest 97:19-20+ N '70
Can atheists be parents? case of John and Cynthia Burke of Newark, N.J. Time 96:71 D 7 '70
Children without parents. Trans-Action 7:14+ Jl '70
In the matter of the adoption of E. J. Burke and D. Burke. Chr Cent 88:36 Ja 13 '71
It's easier to adopt today. H. H. King. il Ebony 26:120-2+ D '70
Mom, Michael & the five little Indians; adoption of Navahos by newlyweds Lynn and Mike Milot. W. J. McKean. il Look 34:76-80 Je 30 '70
Must babies wear religious tags? A. Lake. il Good H 171:78-9+ N '70
Of fathers, sons and love; adopted Negro baby of B. Bridges. J. Barthel. il pors Life 68:61-2+ My 15 '70
What adoption means to a child. B. Bettelheim. Ladies Home J 87:18+ O '70
Woman alone; racially mixed child adopted by single woman. E. Keiffer. il pors Good H 171:84-5+ Jl '70
   See also
Children, Adopted
ADOPTION resource exchange of North America. See Adoption
ADRENAL glands
Genetic variation of cholesterol ester content in mouse adrenals. C. H. Doering and others. bibliog il Science 170:1220-2 D 11 '70
In vivo conversion of ^{3}H-L-tryptophan into ^{3}H-serotonin in brain areas of adrenalectomized rats. E. C. Azmitia, jr. and others. bibliog il Science 169:201-3 Jl 10 '70
   See also
ACTH
ADRENOCORTICOTROPIC hormone. See ACTH
ADSORPTION
   See also
Adhesion
ADULT education
ABE and the twentieth century pioneers; adult basic education classes in Berlin, N.H. D. Lamoureux. il Todays Ed 59:60-1 Ja '70
Adult school trends in course offerings; the evening high school. G.N. Gardiner. Clear House 45:15-17 S '70
Allen asks educators' views on U.S. center of lifelong learning. Aging 183:14 Ja '70
Breaking the diploma barrier; J. L. Smith's program in Kansas City, Mo. il por Time 96:49 S 7 '70
Needed: more adult education. America 123:167 S 19 '70; Reply. L. J. Losoncy. 123:275 O 17 '70
New directory for continuing education. J. A. McCrossan. Am Lib 1:88 Ja '70
Partners for literacy; Literacy volunteers, inc. R. Cohen. il Am Ed 6:36 Je '70
   See also
Aged—Education
Education of women
Executives—Training
Illiteracy
Labor and laboring classes—Education
Self culture
Vocational education

        Library participation
Our other customers; symposium. bibliog il Wilson Lib Bul 45:465-93 Ja '71

ADULT reading. See Books and reading
ADULT-youth relationship. See Youth-adult relationship
ADVANCED research and technology, Office of. See United States—National aeronautics and space administration—Advanced research and technology, Office of
ADVANCEMENT schools. See Schools, Experimental
ADVENT
Who's in charge of history? Chr Cent 87:1439 D 2 '70
ADVENTISTS, Seventh day. See Seventh-day Adventists
ADVENTURE; story. See Barthelme, D.
ADVENTURE and adventurers
Have buckler, will swash; chronicle of Colonel Blood. M. Bishop. por Horizon 11:76-7 Aut '69
ADVENTURE stories
Writing the teenage adventure novel. L. Duncan. il Writers Digest 50:33-5 Je '70
ADVENTURE tours. See Travel
ADVERTISEMENT writers. See Advertising copy writers
ADVERTISEMENT writing. See Advertising copy
ADVERTISEMENTS. See Advertising
ADVERTISING
Admen suffer from overkill. il Bsns W D 132+ O 17 '70
Better results from retail advertising. J. O. Whitney. il Harvard Bsns R 48:111-20 My '70
Boost the boss; executives featured in advertisements. Time 95:94 Je 15 '70
It's a tough life. il por Time 95:78 Je 22 '70
Madison avenue. W. Weir. il Sat R 53:78 F 14; 113 Mr 14 '70
Matter of taste. il Time 95:84+ F 16 '70
News behind the ads. See issues of Changing times
Opinion: working freaks. A. Frazer. Mlle 71:34+ Jl '70
Percentage power. Time 96:80 O 12 '70
Promoting nature's friends; antipollution ads. il Time 96:58+ Ag 17 '70
Sweet smell of value. il Time 95:83 My 18 '70
   See also
Bank advertising
Marketing
Photography in advertising
Posters
Publicity
Radio advertising
Salesmen and salesmanship
Slogans
Television advertising
   also subhead Advertising under various subjects, e.g. Steel industry and trade—Advertising

        Bibliography
Books in communications. S. W. Little. See issues of Saturday review

        Copy
   See Advertising copy

        International aspects
Madison avenue goes multinational. il Bsns W p48-51+ S 12 '70

        Laws and regulations
Burden of proof: now on advertisers. Newsweek 75:88 My 18 '70

        Moral aspects
   See Advertising ethics

        Prize contests
Prize snafu in the Coke game. Bsns W p32 Jl 18 '70
Things go wrong for Coca-Cola; FTC moves on Big name bingo contest. Consumer Rep 35:578 O '70

        Social aspects
Developing responsible promotion; consumer information policies; address, October 15, 1970. E. L. Bond, jr. Vital Speeches 37:124-8 D 1 '70
Morality (?) of advertising. T. Levitt. il Harvard Bsns R 48:84-92 Jl '70

        Testimonials
Celebrity commercials industry. S. W. Little. il Sat R 53:55-6+ Ap 11 '70
ADVERTISING, Direct mail
Direct sales of books in America; excerpts from address. G. R. Smith. Pub W 197:51-4 Je 15 '70; Reply. H. M. Levin. 198:15-18 Ag 10 '70

ADVERTISING, Fraudulent
Big balloon caper: Chevron's controversial ad. Newsweek 75:80+ Ap 27 '70
Excedrin's headache. New Repub 163:7 Ag 15 '70
Few words of advice; earn money at home schemes. A. Herman. il Har Yrs 10:34-6 S '70
FTC ties a can to a Zerex ad; antifreeze commercial. Bsns W p30+ D 5 '70
Pollution: puffery or progress? FTC investigation into anti-pollution claims. il Newsweek 76:49-51 D 28 '70

ADVERTISING, Industrial
Industrial ads: the view from the top. il Bsns W p92-3+ My 30 '70
Industrial advertising pays off. J. E. Morrill. il Harvard Bsns R 48:4-6+ Mr '70

ADVERTISING, Institutional
Buying an image on public TV. Z. B. Grant. New Repub 163:13 N 14 '70
Making good guy ads work; Chinook bookshop. J. Noyes. il Pub W 197:147-9 Je 8 '70

ADVERTISING, Outdoor
See also
Billboards

ADVERTISING, Political
Madison avenue against the war. il Time 96:67 Jl 27 '70
Morning after. Nation 211:547-8 N 30 '70
Reshaping Teddy's image; advertisements prepared by three advertising agencies. il pors Esquire 73:87-99 Je '70
See also
Political campaigns
Television in politics

ADVERTISING, Public service
SR's eighteenth annual advertising awards. R. L. Tobin. il Sat R 53:59-63 Ap 11 '70

ADVERTISING agencies
Ad game. W. Weir. il Sat R 53:78 F 14 '70
Advertisers do it themselves. il Bsns W p66 Jl 18 '70
Beyond the frontiers. il Time 96:54-5 S 7 '70
Case of indigestion; Alka-Seltzer account switched. il Newsweek 76:81 D 21 '70
Europe's creative new breed. il por Time 95:90 Mr 16 '70
International network; Benson Needham Univas. il Time 95:68 F 2 '70
Is the agency in trouble? H. D. Maneloveg. Sat R 53:73-4 N 14 '70
Little agency that could; Keye, Donna & Pearlstein taking over Peace corps advertising. Time 95:84 F 23 '70
Madison avenue. W. Weir. Sat R 52:72 D 13 '69; 53:65-6 Ja 17 '70
Mammon tabernacle choir; jingles of Pepper & Tanner. Time 96:42+ D 21 '70
Nice work, you're fired; Doyle Dane Bernbach lose Alka-Seltzer account to Wells, Rich, Greene. Time 96:66 D 21 '70
See also
Negro advertising agencies
also names of advertising agencies, e.g. Thompson, J. Walter, company

Foreign business
J. Walter Thompson is alive and well in thirty countries. I. Ross. il Fortune 82:102-5+ O '70
Madison avenue goes multinational. il Bsns W p48-51+ S 12 '70

ADVERTISING and Negroes
Brown is beautiful; Negro selling suntan lotion. il Newsweek 75:92 Mr 23 '70
See also
Negro advertising agencies

ADVERTISING and women
Liberating women. il Time 95:93 Je 15 '70

ADVERTISING art
Paul Rand, commercial artist. P. Seitlin. il por Am Artist 34:48-53 O '70

ADVERTISING as a profession
Opinion: working freaks. A. Frazer. Mlle 71:34+ Jl '70

ADVERTISING campaigns
Mea culpa campaign; General telephone commercials. Time 96:67 Jl 27 '70
Roarin' rockets! It's Brand-rex. il Bsns W p44 Jl 11 '70

ADVERTISING characters
Parting shots: two bears named Smokey. S. Mahoney. il Life 68:72-4 Ap 3 '70

ADVERTISING copy
Advertising copywriting. T. Murphy. Writers Digest 51:32-3 Ja '71
Writing personalized newspaper ads for small businesses. F. H. Drewes. il Writers Digest 50:23 S '70

ADVERTISING copy writers
Jobless admen live on hope. il Bsns W p68 Ag 22 '70

ADVERTISING ethics
Matter of taste. il Time 95:84+ F 16 '70
You can take Salem out of the country, but—. J. H. Bowden. Chr Cent 87:1562-3 D 30 '70
See also
Advertising, Fraudulent

ADVERTISING in politics. See Advertising, Political

ADVERTISING mediums

Moving pictures
You've seen the movie, now read the ad. il Time 96:80 O 12 '70

Periodicals
Another look. Newsweek 75:64 My 4 '70
Auto strike costs magazines a bundle. Bsns W p27 S 26 '70
Hot magazines aim at special targets. il Bsns W p64-5+ My 2 '70
Telling it to Africa; advertising in Jeune Afrique. il Bsns W p84-5 O 31 '70

Telephone directories
Going astray in the yellow pages. Consumer Rep 35:74 F '70

ADVERTISING models. See Models (persons)

ADVERTISING policy
See also
Newspapers—Advertising policy

ADVERTISING research
Industrial advertising pays off. J. E. Morrill. il Harvard Bsns R 48:4-6+ Mr '70

ADVERTISING signs. See Billboards

ADVICE columns. See Newspapers—Advice columns

ADVISERS, Presidential. See Public officers

ADVISORY commission on civil disorders. See United States—National advisory commission on civil disorders

ADVISORY commissions. See United States—Federal commissions

ADVISORY committee on public opinion. See United States—State, Department of—Advisory committee on public opinion

ADVISORY council on African affairs. See United States—State, Department of—Advisory council on African affairs

ADVISORY council on executive organization. See United States— President's advisory council on executive organization

ADVISORY council on management improvement. See United States—President's advisory council on management improvement

AEDES aegypti. See Mosquitoes

AEGEAN ISLANDS
Off-season is in-season on these islands. S. Wiedel. Travel & Camera 33:53-4 O '70
See also
Cyclades (islands)

AEKEN, Hieronymus van. See Bosch, H.

AERIAL cableways. See Cableways

AERIAL gunnery
See also
Fire control (aerial gunnery)

AERIAL maps. See Maps, Aerial

AERIAL navigation. See Navigation, Aerial

AERIAL photography. See Photography, Aerial

AERIAL reconnaissance
Eyes in the sky over the Suez. il Newsweek 76:35 Ag 31 '70
Spy race in the sky. il U S News 69:24-6 O 12 '70
Watch on the Suez: intelligence gaps. il Time 96:27 Ag 31 '70

AERIAL tramways. See Cableways

AERIAL walkways. See Sidewalks, Elevated

AERO design and engineering company. See Butler aviation international, inc.

AEROBATIC airplanes. See Airplanes, Aerobatic

AEROBATICS. See Aviation—Stunt flying

AEROBIC sewage treatment. See Sewage disposal—Aeration

AEROBICS. See Exercise

AEROBIOLOGY. See Air microbiology

AERODYNAMICS
Aerodynamic whistles. R. C. Chanaud. il Sci Am 222:40-6 biblig(p 146) Ja '70
Formation flight of birds. P. B. S. Lissaman and C. A. Shollenberger. il Science 168:1003-5 My 22 '70
Those terrible downwind turns. P. Garrison. Flying 86:58-9 Ap '70
See also
Airfoils
Turbulence

AEROFLOT (airline) See Airlines—Russia

AEROJET-General corporation
Aerojet uses aerospace methods to build test surface effect ship. Aviation W 92:52-3 Ap 20 '70

AERONAUTIC education. See Aeronautics—Study and teaching

AERONAUTIC engineering
See also
Computers—Aeronautic use

AERONAUTIC exhibitions. See Aviation—Exhibitions

AERONAUTIC instruments
Flight directors. R. Blodget. il Flying 87:74-7+ O '70
New instrumentation concepts. Aviation W 92:46-8+ Mr 23; 48-9+ Mr 30 '70
Product news (cont of) New products. See issues of Flying
See also
Airplanes—Instrument boards
Airplanes—Radio equipment
Airplanes, Supersonic—Instrument boards
Altimeters
Automatic pilot (airplanes)
Detectors, Infrared
Inertial guidance systems
Navigation, Aerial—Aids and devices
Proximity warning indicators
Radio beacons

Display systems
Anti-collision display tested. il Aviation W 93:46-7 Jl 20 '70
Avionics displays gain acceptance. K. J. Stein. il Aviation W 92:48-9+ Mr 30 '70
Display exhibits added versatility; electronic attitude director indicator. il Aviation W 92:49+ My 4 '70
EADI leads surge into new phase. K. J. Stein. il Aviation W 92:46-8+ Mr 23 '70
F-14 uses digital display method; integrated vertical and head-up display system. B. M. Elson. il Aviation W 93:45-6 Jl 20 '70

Maintenance and repair
Checked your localizer lately? R. Blodget. Flying 86:10+ Ap '70

AERONAUTIC meteorology. See Meteorology, Aeronautic

AERONAUTIC research
See also
Airplanes, Experimental
United States—Langley research center
United States—National aeronautics and space administration—Advanced research and technology, Office of
United States—Naval air propulsion test center

AERONAUTICS
See also
Airfoils
Airplanes
Aviation
Balloon ascensions

Exhibitions
See Aviation—Exhibitions

History
Editorial: 50th anniversary of the flight service station system. R. B. Parke. Flying 86:35 Je '70
First to fly, by S. Harris. Review
Sat R il 53:37 Je 6 '70. A. R. Dodd
First to fly; excerpt. S. Harris. il Am Heritage 21:60-9 Je '70
Return of the Rockford. R. E. Carlin. il por Flying 87:52-7 N '70
World war I aircraft fly again in Rhinebeck's rickety rendezvous. H. Arden. il por Nat Geog 138:578-87 O '70
See also
Airplanes in business—History

Study and teaching
Aerospace education takes off. C. H. Harrison. il Schol Teach Sec Teach Sup 10-11 Ap 6 '70
See also
Air pilots—Training

AERONAUTICS, Commercial
See also
Air freight service
Air travel

International aspects
See Aviation—International aspects

Africa
League of fourteen African nations raises airport, airway fees. Aviation W 92:41 Ja 26 '70

Australia
See also
Airlines—Australia

Europe, Western
See also
Air freight service—Europe, Western

Great Britain
British intercity V/STOL effort faces indefinite postponement. H. J. Coleman. Aviation W 92:18 F 16 '70
British veto BAC 311, A-300B-7. H. J. Coleman. Aviation W 93:16-17 D 7 '70
U.K. postpones A-300B talks; decision expected on BAC 311. H. J. Coleman. Aviation W 93:27 N 9 '70
See also
Airlines—Great Britain

Iran
See also
Airlines—Iran

Latin America
South American market on threshold of growth. E. J. Bulban. il Aviation W 93:67-9 O 26 '70

United States
CAB chairman terms airlines overly pessimistic on industry. Aviation W 92:26 My 11 '70
Power fight snarls air leadership. L. Doty. Aviation W 93:16-17 N 9 '70
See also
Airlines—United States
Airplane industry and trade—United States

AERONAUTICS, Military
See also
Air defenses
Airplanes, Military
Gliders (aeronautics)—Military applications
Helicopters—Military use

Cambodia
See also
Cambodian-Vietnamese conflict—Aerial operations

France
See also
Airplanes, Military—France

Great Britain
U.K. cuts defense estimates; drops consideration of C-5A. Aviation W 93:18 N 2 '70

Iran
Air power pivotal to Iran's diplomacy. E. H. Kolcum. Aviation W 93:21-2 N 23 '70

Israel
See also
Israeli-Arab war, 1967- —Aerial operations

Italy
See also
Airplanes, Military—Italy

Japan
Japan drafts five-year force plan. C. Brownlow. il Aviation W 92:37+ F 9 '70

Libya
Arab pilots to train at Wheelus. E. H. Kolcum. il Aviation W 92:14-16 Mr 23 '70
Libya faces problems of obtaining qualified pilots for fifty Mirages. Aviation W 92:67+ Ja 26 '70

Middle East
Soviet, Arab aircraft strength in Mideast tops Israel's 4 to 1. il Aviation W 92:16-17 Je 1 '70

Russia
Soviets press strategic military expansion. D. C. Winston. il Aviation W 92:46-7 Mr 9 '70
See also
Airplanes, Military—Russia

Sweden
See also
Airplanes, Military—Sweden

Switzerland
Swiss military fights Parliament on new support aircraft analysis. Aviation W 92:19 Je 29 '70
See also
Airplanes, Military—Switzerland

United States
See also
United States—Air force

AFFILIATE artists, inc.
I am an Affiliate artist. C. Forbes. il
Hi Fi 20:secII 10-11+ Je '70
AFFINITY chromatography. See Chromato-
graphic analysis
AFFRO-arts theater. See Chicago—Theater
AFGHANISTAN
Antiquities
Ghar-i-Mordeh Gusfand (Cave of the dead
sheep): a new Mousterian locality in north
Afghanistan. L. Dupree and others. bibliog
il Science 167:1610-12 Mr 20 '70
AFRICA
Africa: a new constellation in history. il
Negro Hist Bul 32:4-6 D '69
See also
Aeronautics, Commercial—Africa
Arts and crafts—Africa
Economic assistance in Africa
Evangelistic work—Africa
Folklore—Africa
Foreign students in Africa
Investments, Foreign (in Africa)
Negroes in Africa
Periodicals—Africa
Religious conferences—Africa
Science—Africa
Technical assistance in Africa
Tourist trade—Africa
Wildlife conservation—Africa
Women—Africa
Zoology—Africa

Description and travel
Smiling through Africa. D. Ardrey. il pors
Esquire 73:94-6+ F '70
Travel notes. R. Joseph. Esquire 73:28+ F;
74:18-20 Jl '70

Economic conditions
ECA and the paradox of African cooperation.
J. S. Magee. bibliog f por Int Concil 580:5-
64 N '70
New Africa. G. Hunter. For Affairs 48:
712-25 Jl '70

Foreign relations
Africa, 1970; symposium. bibliog f il Cur Hist
58:129-69+ Mr '70
United States
See United States—Foreign relations—
Africa
History
Bibliography
Articles and other books received; comp. by
D. E. Gardinier. See issues of American
historical review
Maps
Africa. Sr Schol 95:20 S 22 '69; 97:13 S 21 '70

Native races
See also
Kenya—Native races

Politics
Africa, 1970; symposium. bibliog f il Cur Hist
58:129-69+ Mr '70
Africa: year of the handshake. Sr Schol 97:12
S 21 '70
Cross over Africa. C. Morris. Chr Cent 87:
688-91 Je 3 '70
New Africa. G. Hunter. For Affairs 48:
712-25 Jl '70
Rhodesia; U.S. foreign policy? address,
March 12, 1970. J. R. Rarick. Vital Speech-
es 36:434-7 My 1 '70
Shaping of African institutions and national
life; address, May 27, 1970. D. D. Newsom.
Dept State Bul 62:778-81 Je 22 '70
Up from chaos: black Africa after ten
years of freedom. A. J. Meyers. il U S
News 69:52-5 Jl 6 '70
See also
African and Malagasy common organization
Organization of African unity
Pan-Africanism

Race problems
See also subhead Race problems under
names of African countries, e.g. South
Africa—Race problems

Religious institutions and affairs
See also
Catholic church in Africa
Christians in Africa

Social conditions
Letter from Lagos; conferences of West African universities. J. B. Schuyler. il America 123:204-6 S 26 '70

Union (proposed)
Africa: year of the handshake. Sr Schol 97:12
S 21 '70
AFRICA, CENTRAL
See also
Chad
Congo (Democratic Republic)—Politics and
government
AFRICA, EAST
See also
Automobile racing—Africa, East
Colleges and universities—Africa, East
Evangelistic work—Africa, East
Kenya
Wildlife conservation—Africa, East
Zoology—Africa, East

Description and travel
Safari for commuters. il Esquire 74:66-71
Jl '70
Shooting big game with a camera. C. Pur-
cell. il por Pop Phot 66:98-101+ My '70
Travel: camera with cross hairs. il Time 95:
68-72 F 16 '70

Native races
See also
Mozambique—Native races
AFRICA, NORTH
One Arab area still friendly to U.S. F. C.
Painton. il U S News 68:52-4 F 9 '70
Soviet Mediterranean push deepens; with edi-
torial comment. E. H. Kolcum. il Aviation
W 92:9, 14-18 Mr 30 '70
See also
Morocco
Sahara Desert
AFRICA, NORTHEAST
Storm clouds over the African Horn. K.
Irvine. il Cur Hist 58:142-7+ Mr '70
AFRICA, NORTHWEST
See also
Gambia
Spanish Sahara
AFRICA, SOUTHERN
See also
Lesotho
United Nations—Africa, Southern

Race problems
Cross over Africa. C. Morris. Chr Cent 87:
688-91 Je 3 '70
Lusaka manifesto; excerpts from statement
by the Organization of African unity; April
14-16, 1969. Cur Hist 58:173-5 Mr '70
On violence in Africa; British council of
churches report. Chr Cent 87:1441 D 2 '70
AFRICA, WEST
See also
Ghana
Ivory Coast
Portuguese Guinea
Togo
AFRICA in literature
Africa in medieval Spanish literature: its
appearance in el Caballero Cifar. M. Samp-
son. bibliog il Negro Hist Bul 32:14-19 D '69
AFRICAN and Malagasy common organization
League of fourteen African nations raises
airport, airway fees. Aviation W 92:41 Ja 26
'70
AFRICAN art. See Art, African
AFRICAN authors. See Authors, African
AFRICAN daisies (dimorphotheca) See Cape
marigolds
AFRICAN dancing. See Dancing, African
AFRICAN dolls. See Dolls
AFRICAN languages
See also
Zulu language
AFRICAN literature
West African literature in English in the
sixties. B. Lindfors. Negro Hist Bul 33:80-1
Mr '70
AFRICAN philosophy. See Philosophy, African
AFRICAN RIVIERA. See Seaside resorts—
Ivory Coast
AFRICAN sculpture. See Sculpture, African
AFRICAN students in the United States. See
Foreign students in the United States
AFRICAN theology. See Negroes in Africa—
Religion
AFRICAN violets
African violet society favorites. il Home Gard
57:34 Ap '70
African violets; fertilizing and propagating.
H. Van Zele. il Horticulture 48:30-2 N '70
African-violets that bloom and bloom! il
Home Gard 57:28-9 S '70
Victorian nosegay in a neat ruff of green
leaves. il Sunset 144:178-9 F '70
Your garden indoors. F. S. David. il Home
Gard 57:30 My '70

AFRICAN wild dogs. See Wild dogs

AFRICAN wood sculpture. See Wood carving

AFRO-AMERICAN culture. See Negroes—Culture

AFRO-AMERICAN literature. See Negro literature

AFRO-AMERICAN students. See Negro students

AFRO-AMERICAN studies
Acceptance of minority studies. Sch & Soc 98:265-6 Sum '70
Answering the black's Who am I? K. Branan and M. K. Murphy. Schol Teach Sec Teach Sup p4-6+ Ja 5 '70
Black studies: a painful birth. il por Time 95:50+ Ja 26 '70
Black studies: a practical alternative. L. L. Leslie and R. C. Bigelow. bibliog f Clear House 44:479-82 Ap '70
Black studies at Cornell: the troubled path to understanding. C. Childs. il Life 68:56-60+ Ap 17 '70
Black studies bandwagon. W. W. Brickman. Sch & Soc 98:140-1 Mr '70
Black studies: fuse or pacifier? America 122:548-9 My 23 '70
Black studies in glass houses; Amistad I. R. Whittemore. New Repub 162:25-7 My 9 '70
Black studies in Illinois; with directory of institutions offering black studies. C. J. Evans. Negro Hist Bul 33:43-4 F '70
Black studies in the schools. Sch & Soc 98:400+ N '70
Black studies in trouble. Time 95:40 F 16 '70
Black studies: more than soul courses. S. V. Roberts. Commonweal 91:478-9 Ja 30 '70
Black studies: time for restructuring. B. Kurtz. Clear House 45:201-3 D '70
Harvard's Afro-American studies. por Negro Hist Bul 33:20 Ja '70
Kids will decide and more power to them. P. Wilcox. il por Ebony 25:134-7 Ag '70
Learn baby learn; address, May 24, 1970. M. T. Bowie. Vital Speeches 36:604-6 Jl 15 '70
NYU institute of Afro-American affairs. por Sch & Soc 98:146-7 Mr '70
Teaching black history in America: what are the problems; address, December 28, 1969. M. Drimmer. Negro Hist Bul 33:32-4 F '70
Think tank for black scholars. A. Poinsett. il por Ebony 25:46-8+ F '70
What white students think of black studies. il Life 68:34 My 8 '70
White faces and black studies. M. L. Dillon. Commonweal 91:476-9 Ja 30 '70
White faces and white studies; courses in Afro-American history. S. Synnestvedt. Commonweal 92:182-3 My 8 '70
Why black studies? R. B. Bailey. Ed Digest 35:46-8 My '70

AFRO-AMERICANS. See Negroes

AFRO-ASIAN institute for labor studies and cooperation
Letter from Israel: technical cooperation: Israel's way in the third world and administered territories. N. Levin. il Bul Atom Sci 26:46-52 Ap '70

AFTER-baby blues. See Depression, Mental

AFTER images
See also
Eidetic imagery
Phosphenes

AFTERNOON teas
Teatime for the United Nations. il McCalls 97:94-5+ F '70

AGA KHAN, Yasmin. See Yasmin, princess

AGAM, Yaacov
Living wall. il Time 95:66-7 My 18 '70 *

AGAPANTHUS
New dwarf agapanthus. il Sunset 144:255 Mr '70

AGAVES
Desert exotic for northern homes and gardens; century plant. M. M. Gunn. il Org Gard & Farm 17:80-2 Jl '70

AGE
See also
Aging
Longevity
Middle age
Old age

AGE (insects)
Senescence and genetic load: evidence from tribolium. R. R. Sokal. bibliog il Science 167:1733-4 Mr 27 '70

AGE (plants)
Senescence in detached betel leaves: role of the petiole. S. D. Mishra and B. K. Gaur. bibliog il Science 167:387-8 Ja 23 '70

AGE, Voting. See Suffrage; Suffrage—United States

AGE and ability. See Ability, Influence of age on

AGE and employment
Ability is ageless; San Antonio, Tex. K. Davis. il Har Yrs 10:46-7 My '70
California group finds jobs for 3,000 men and women sixty plus. Aging 190:18 Ag '70
NCOA Senior community service aides extended through June 30, 1971. il Aging 191:10-11 S '70
Penalizing the oldsters' earnings. B. L. Masse. America 122:119 F 7 '70; Reply. H. S. Ryan. 122:360 Ap 4 '70
Retire to a part-time job? il Changing T 24:21-3 F '70
Should Congress flunk the retirement test? raising earning power under social security. G. Town. Har Yrs 10:30-1 Ja '70
Where you have to be retired to be hired. C. Stevenson. Read Digest 96:21-4+ Je '70
See also
Green thumb, inc.
Mature Temps, inc.

AGE and sex. See Aged—Sexual behavior; Sex relations

AGE for marrying. See Marriage

AGED
Caroline Van Hook Bean; exhibition of World war I paintings at the Chapellier galleries. C. V. Bean. New Yorker 46:34 Ap 18 '70
Growing old gracefully. America 122:516 My 16 '70
Learned Cuban, 85, continues studies in Miami, seeking job. Aging 193:17 N '70
Let my dad go home. J. N. Bell. Good H 170:65+ Je '70
Nonagenarian: S. H. Gottscho. New Yorker 46:34 Ap 4 '70
Old in the country of the young. il Time 96:49-52+ Ag 3 '70
Quotations from the commissioner. J. B. Martin. Aging 182:10 D '69
Well-bread woman: Anna N. Walberg baking Swedish rye bread at age of ninety. D. S. Hansen. Har Yrs 10:31 Ja '70
See also
Ability, influence of age on
Aging
Christmas gifts for the aged
Church work with the aged
Gerontology
Libraries—Services to aged
Old age
Old age assistance
Retirement
Retirement income
Senior citizens month
Telephone in service to the aged
United States—Aging, Administration on

Activities

Today is what you make it. K. Hillyard. por Har Yrs 10:30-1 N '70
Your 1970 activities almanac. K. Hillyard .il Har Yrs 10:23-9 Ja '70

Adjustment problems

How well do you understand elderly people? il Changing T 24:37-9 Ag '70
People, places. Har Yrs 10:20-2 Mr '70
Stay put? Or move out? Har Yrs 10:24-6+ Mr '70
What we want from the time we spend. P. A. Dickinson. il Har Yrs 10:19-23 O '70
When your parents grow old. E. McLaughlin. il Parents Mag 45:66-7+ O '70

Bibliography

Publications. See issues of Aging

Care and hygiene

AoA backs aging visibility in planning for model cities; excerpts from interviews. J. B. Martin. Aging 182:11 D '69
Doctor, I have a question; questions and answers. M. A. Hinrichs. See issues of Harvest years
Homemakers prove their value in Nevada state program. il Aging 193:12-13 N '70
Idaho telephone plan named ECHO sends aid on calls to 522-HELP. Aging 183:15 Ja '70
Magic of exercise. C. Coiro. bibliog il Har Yrs 10:14-18 My '70
Martin hails Texas, Oklahoma programs. Aging 182:12 D '69
Ohio to relocate 3,000 elderly patients in new geriatric centers. il Aging 183:14 Ja '70
Psychiatric training program for high school students assigned to a geriatric service. J. H. Friedman and A. R. Spada. bibliog Ment Hy 54:427-9 Jl '70

AGED—Care and hygiene—*Continued*

Six-point program urged in New York state for dependent aging. Aging 182:16 D '69

Unpaid N.Y. County council clearing house for elderly; Ulster County. Aging 193:16 N '70

See also
Aged—Housing
Nursing homes

Clubs

See Recreation for the aged

Economic conditions

Easier living on less money. F. C. Weed. il Har Yrs 10:19-23 D '70

Society stupid in attitude toward aging, expert asserts. Aging 182:8 D '69

Education

Grandma was a dropout. E. Reed. il Har Yrs 10:38-9 Ja '70

Oklahoma adult education has 800 enrollees; started with 135. Aging 190:20 Ag '70

Employment

See Age and employment

Federal aid

See Old age assistance

Health

See Aged—Care and hygiene

Housing

Housing for the elderly, Wayne, Mich. il Arch Rec 147:90-1 Mid-My '70

Housing: problems and solutions. I. Ladimer. il Har Yrs 10:38-42 F '70

Needed: more housing for the elderly; Quincy, Mass. B. Baharian. il por Am City 85:91-2 Ap '70

1,800-member Florida center plans retirees housing project. il Aging 191:19 S '70

People, people, people. L. Jaquith. il Har Yrs 10:32-3+ My '70

Pre-retirement plan; Sun City resort-retirement communities. il Travel 134:26 Ag '70

Senate committee holds hearing on rural aged. il Aging 182:6-7 D '69

$3.4 million Galena park facility for elderly under way in Illinois. il Aging 187:9 My '70

See also
Old age homes
Retirement. Places of
Sun City, Ariz.

Income

See Income

Medical care

Doctor, I have a question; questions and answers. M. A. Hinrichs. See issues of Harvest years

Nutrition

Baltimore Meals on wheels ten years old and still growing. il Aging 193:10-11 N '70

Denver seniors served food with friendship. il Aging 184:11-14 F '70

Gerontologist publishes guide to aid nutrition practitioners. Aging 184:15 F '70

Meals plus offered by Detroit project. il Aging 184:16-18 F '70

San Francisco elderly enjoy big $1 senior meals, 5¢ fare. il Aging 83:10 Ja '70

San Francisco senior plate at $1 in second year still going strong. Aging 191:15 S '70

Seattle's Columbia club reaches out to serve isolated elderly. il Aging 184:9-10 F '70

White House conference urges nutritional aids for elderly. Aging 184:19 F '70

White House panel, AoA, chart moves on nutrition for aging. Aging 191:16 S '70

Political activities

Senior power breaks the barriers. C. Coiro. il Har Yrs 10:6-12 O '70

Senior power; pressure groups. Newsweek 76:101 O 12 '70

So you're not a politician! E. W. Chandler. Har Yrs 10:13-14 O '70

Radio programs

See Radio broadcasting—Programs

Recreation

See Recreation for the aged

Sexual behavior

It takes two. F. Bean; C. Lewis. Har Yrs 10:34-7 F '70

Love in the later years. H. Alpert. il Har Yrs 10:6-10 Je '70

Statistics

Of every 100 older persons. il Aging 187:18-27 My '70

Transportation

Chicago YMCA senior transport serves 1606, aids 48 agencies. il Aging 186:7-8 Ap '70

500,000 older New Yorkers get ½ fare; OFTA has paper. Aging 182:13 D '69

Pittsburgh inaugurates reduced senior fares with 61,000 enrolled. Aging 186:8 Ap '70

Policy on aged, handicapped, inserted in mass transit bill. Aging 193:7 N '70

San Francisco elderly enjoy big $1 senior meals, 5¢ fare. il Aging 183:10 Ja '70

Transport for elderly problem now and for future, Martin says; excerpts from testimony. J. B. Martin. Aging 186:6 Ap '70

Transportation for older Americans starts in Prince Georges County. il Aging 186:4-5 Ap '70

See also
Local transit—Fares

Denmark

Thanks to Doug Crutchfield Fru Nilsen can dance again. il pors Ebony 25:86-91 Ap '70

AGED, Homes for the. See Old age homes

AGED as consumers. See Old age market

AGEE, James
Unfathomably mysterious: Let us now praise famous men. L. Betts. bibliog f Engl J 59: 44-7+ Ja '70

AGEE, Kate Keffer
Think three. il Design 72:22-3 Fall '70

AGENCIES, Advertising. See Advertising agencies

AGENCIES, Employment. See Employment agencies

AGENCIES, Federal. See United States—Executive departments

AGENCIES, Regulatory. See Independent regulatory commissions

AGENCIES, Social. See Social agencies

AGENCIES, Travel. See Travel agencies and agents

AGENCY for international development. See United States—Agency for international development

AGENTS. See Literary agents

AGFACHROME films. See Photography—Films

AGGREGATES (building materials)
Streets of glass; Toledo, Ohio. W. R. Malisch and others. il Am City 85:104+ Jl '70

AGGRESSION (international law)
See also
United Nations—Special committee on the question of defining aggression

AGGRESSIVENESS (psychology)
Aggression and its control in childhood; excerpts from Decent and indecent. B. Spock. Redbook 134:32+ F '70

Is aggression natural? with study-discussion program, by M. M. Conant. J. L. Hymes, jr. bibliog il PTA Mag 65:2-4, 34 O '70

On killing members of one's own species; tr. by H. Zeisel. K. Lorenz. il por Bul Atom Sci 26:2-5+ O '70

Psychologists report new therapy for aggressive children. Todays Health 48:70 Jl '70

Tooth and claw. L. Berkowitz. Trans-Action 7:59-60 Je '70

Understanding man's aggressiveness. D. Behrman. il UNESCO Courier 23:4-18+ Ag '70

War is not in our genes. S. Carrighar. il UNESCO Courier 23:40-5 Ag '70

See also
Hostility (psychology)
Violence

AGHAJANIAN, George K. and others
Serotonin-containing neurons in brain: depression of firing by monoamine oxidase inhibitors. bibliog il Science 169:1100-2 S 11 '70

AGING

At my age? C. L. Miller. il Harp Baz 103: 180-3 Mr '70

Cicero on growing older. A. E. Everett. Har Yrs 10:25 S '70

If you lie about your age. T. I. Rubin. por Ladies Home J 87:68 Ap '70

Lying about your age. K. Gordon. Harp Baz 103:228 Mr '70

Mathematics of cancer; steady-state theory. Sci N 98:270 S 26 '70

Old in the country of the young. il Time 96:49-52+ Ag 3 '70

On aging; excerpt from La vieillesse, tr. by J. Oringer and D. Kolodney. S. de Beauvoir. il Ramp Mag 9:19-24 S '70

On the theory of aging. Chem 43:25-6 My '70

AGING—*Continued*
Sense and nonsense about growing older. M. Rudolph. Read Digest 97:23-4+ S '70
Why some women never seem to grow old. il Good H 170:197 Mr '70
Why we must grow old. I. Asimov. por Sci Digest 68:76-7 D '70
Why women panic about age. R. Blackmon. Vogue 155:98-9+ F 15 '70
Your kids may live to be 100+. W. Hartley and E. Hartley. il Sci Digest 68:38-42 S '70

See also
Gerontology
United States—President's task force on aging
AGING, Administration on.   See United States—Aging, Administration on
AGING, Conferences on
Conference calendar. See issues of Aging
Conference explores prospects for older people in the 1970s. il Aging 191:4-7 S '70
Fourth ISCA congress meeting in Japan studies problems, seeks world peace. il Aging 193:9 N '70
Future of protective services discussed at San Diego conference. il Aging 188:5-7 Je '70
Gerontological society Toronto session has record attendance. il Aging 193:6 N '70
July 2-7, 1972, date set for gerontologist meeting in Soviet Union. Aging 193:7 N '70

See also
National council on the aging
White House conference on aging, 1971 (proposed)
AGING, Councils on
See also
Mississippi council on aging
AGING of insects. See Age (insects)
AGING of plants. See Age (plants)
AGNELLI, Giovanni, 1921-
Industrial and commercial relations; address, October 12, 1970. Vital Speeches 37:93-6 N 15 '70
AGNELLI, Susanna
To a man: the terrain of love. por Vogue 156:112-13+ N 15 '70
AGNESE, Rita
On the boards. W. Como. il por Dance Mag 44:24 Ja '70
AGNEW, H. W. Jr. See Webb, W. B. jt. auth.
AGNEW, Spiro Theodore
Agnew explains the president's welfare plan; excerpts from address, March 9, 1970. il por U S News 68:84-5 Mr 23 '70
Agnew speaks out on terrorists vs. law and order; excerpts from address, September 2, 1970. por U S News 69:49 S 14 '70
Agnew talks about those Agnew speeches; interview. por U S News 69:34-6 Ag 24 '70
Enough of government by street carnival! excerpt from address, October 30, 1969. Read Digest 96:85-8 F '70
How to roast a marshmallow; address, April 1970. por Time 95:20 My 11 '70
Say it again, Sprio; excerpts from address, 1970. Nat R 22:608-9 Je 16 '70
Senate shift toward President's viewpoints; interview. por U S News 69:31-2 N 16 '70
Vice President Agnew meets with Asian leaders; text of remarks and statements, August 22-September 1, 1970. Dept State Bul 63:379-87 O 5 '70
Vice president Agnew on Agnew; interview, ed. by H. Sidey and J. Stacks. il por Time 96:25 O 26 '70
Vice President on major issues; excerpts from addresses. por U S News 68:38-9 Je 8 '70
—and others
Agnew's talk with five students; text of television debate. il pors U S News 69:86-8+ O 12 '70

about
Agnew and red meat. J. Osborne. New Repub 163:10-12 Jl 25 '70 *
Agnew on the road; prelude to political campaigning. J. Osborne. por New Repub 163:8-10 S 19 '70 *
Agnew on the warpath. B. Brower. il pors Life 69:26-31 O 16 '70 *
Agnew: profile in conflict, by J. G. Lucas. Review
    Nat R 22:1060-1+ O 6 '70. H. V. Jaffa *
Agnew: purging the GOP? il pors Newsweek 76:36 O 12 '70 *
Agnew: the local image is cool. por Bsns W p43 O 17 '70 *
Agnew words pay off, in funds. por U S News 68:38-9 Je 8 '70 *
Agnews. New Yorker 46:19-20 Ag 1 '70 *

Agnew's effect; attack on news media. J. Osborne. New Repub 162:13-15 F 28 '70 *
Agnew's elastic list; radical-liberals. por Time 96:8-9 S 28 '70 *
Agnew's hour. il por Newsweek 75:24 F 23 '70 *
Agnew's pungent quotient. il por Time 95:12 Je 29 '70 *
Agnew's task, and task force. por U S News 69:21 S 14 '70 *
Agony lingers on. H. Brandon. Sat R 53:4+ Mr 14 '70 *
Amazing success story of "Spiro who?" A. Schlesinger, jr. il por N Y Times Mag p5-7+ Jl 26 '70 *
And now, the Spiro and Martha show. J. Austin. il pors Time 96:10 N 23 '70 *
As Muskie opens fire on Agnew . . . pors U S News 69:33 S 28 '70 *
Brilliance of Spiro Agnew. M. Mayer. pors Esquire 73:117-19+ My '70 *
Culture and counterculture in U.S. politics. G. W. Schwartzkopf. il America 123:396-8 N 14 '70 *
Diagnosis of the anti-Spiro jitters by a former chairman of ADA. J. P. Roche. Nat R 22:878 Ag 25 '70 *
Don Quixote rides again in New York; S. T. Agnew vs C. E. Goodell. P. J. Lavin. America 123:279 O 17 '70 *
Don't get Agnew wrong. B. Brower. il pors Life 68:64-6+ My 8 '70 *
First round to Agnew. M. L. Stein. Nation 211:178-81 S 7 '70 *
Frank Merrivell's way. Sedulus. New Repub 162:30-2 Je 20 '70 *
Ghost hunt. por Newsweek 75:26 Je 8 '70 *
Great debate; on TV with students; campaign tour. il por Newsweek 76:26-7 O 5 '70 *
Happy days. il Newsweek 76:32 S 14 '70 *
Heart of the racial crisis. B. L. Masse. America 122:547 My 23 '70 *
Idea is to cool it a little. il pors Time 96:9-10 Jl 27 '70 *
I'm an ordinary man. . . J. M. Naughton. il pors N Y Times Mag p8-9+ D 27 '70 *
Is Agnew washed up? J. Osborne. New Repub 163:11-12 N 14 '70 *
Language and violence. America 123:281 O 17 '70 *
Leaves from a lurid lexicon. il Newsweek 76:24 S 28 '70 *
Making of a campaigner 1970. il por Newsweek 76:14-15 Ag 31 '70 *
Middle America's Mr America. il pors Newsweek 76:23-7 S 28 '70 *
Missiles from the Michelle Ann. il pors Time 96:14-16 S 21 '70 *
Mr Agnew and the future of the GOP. W. F. Buckley, jr. Nat R 22:324-5 Mr 24 '70 *
Notes and comment. New Yorker 46:35-7 O 10 '70 *
Notes on a new style for Agnew. W. K. Zinsser. Life 69:29 O 16 '70 *
Open letter to Spiro T. Agnew. R. M. Brown. Chr Cent 87:1213-17 O 14 '70; Discussion. 87:1320, 1423 N 4, 25 '70 *
Our Sharpeville. J. Deedy. Commonweal 92:234 My 22 '70 *
Perils of Spiro. il por Newsweek 76:20-1 Jl 20 '70 *
Politics and the name game; Time essay. M. Ways. il por Time 96:14-15 N 2 '70 *
Press monopoly: Mr Agnew's oversights. S. R. Barnett. Nation 210:72-5 Ja '70 *
Rally round, radiclibs. P. Steinfels. Commonweal 93:191 N 20 '70 *
Role of the mass media; symposium. Cur 114:41-54 Ja '70 *
Secret of Spiro T. S. Alsop. Newsweek 76:104 S 28 '70 *
Showing up Agnew. New Repub 163:7 S 5 '70 *
Slammin' Spiro. il por Newsweek 75:30 Je 1 '70 *
Spiro Agnew and the '70 campaign; with excerpts from his statements and replies from his critics. por Sr Schol 97:17-18 O 12 '70 *
Spiro Agnew on the defensive. il por Time 96:10-11 D 28 '70 *
Spiro Agnew vs. the radic-libs. il por Newsweek 76:35-6 S 21 '70 *
Spiro Agnew's candles. M. Mintz. New Repub 162:13-15 Ja 17 '70 *
Spiro grooves; long-playing records. Newsweek 76:103A D 14 '70 *
Spiro of '76? il por Time 95:10 F 2 '70 *
Spiro T. Agnew: vice president extraordinary. F. Van Der Linden. por Read Digest 97:123-7 O '70 *
State of broadcast journalism. F. W. Friendly. Cur 114:49-54 Ja '70 *

AGNEW, Spiro Theodore—about—*Continued*
Sun Valley days. il por Newsweek 76:16-17 D 28 '70 *

Talking back. New Repub 163:7-8 O 10 '70 *

They answer Agnew. K. Crawford. Newsweek 76:31 Ag 31 '70 *

TRB from Washington: coming, boss. New Repub 163:6 N 7 '70 *

Vice President and the senator. Nat R 22: 1096-7 O 20 '70 *

Who's kidding whom? Agnew's near-psychopathic crusade against Goodell. Commonweal 93:83-4 O 23 '70

Year after Des Moines. Nation 211:549 N 30 '70 *

Caricatures and cartoons
First in war, first in peace, first in the hearts of his country club. Atlan 225:64-5 F '70

Visit to Asia
How did it go, Spiro? il por Time 95:13 Ja 26 '70

On the Asian trail with Agnew. il por U S News 68:9 Ja 19 '70

Vice President Agnew visits Asia; text of remarks and statements, December 29, 1969-January 20, 1970. S. T. Agnew. Dept State Bul 62:189-202 F 23 '70 *

What Agnew found in Asia; support for U.S. role there. il U S News 68:13 Ja 26 '70

Visit to southeast Asia, 1970
Agnew in Asia: the rainy season. il pors Newsweek 76:15-16 S 7 '70

At home and abroad; itinerary. il por Time 96:10-11 Ag 31 '70

Here comes the aggernaut. H. Sidey. Life 69: 2 Ag 28 '70

Palace-to-palace salesmanship. il por Time 96:10-11 S 7 '70

Vice President Agnew meets with Asian leaders; text of remarks and statements, August 22-September 1, 1970. R. M. Nixon; S. T. Agnew. Dept State Bul 63:379-87 O 5 '70

AGNON, Samuel Joseph
On Lea Goldberg & S. Y. Agnon. bibliog f Commentary 49:83-6 My '70 *

Seeing into the hidden interior of things. C. Leviant. por Sat R 53:27-30+ My 16 '70 *

AGNON, Shmuel Yosef. See Agnon, S. J.

AGOCS, Carol
Social indicators: selected readings. Ann Am Acad 388:127-32 Mr '70

AGREE, Rose
(ed) See Lionni, L. Lionni's artichokes: an interview

AGREEMENTS, International. See Treaties

AGREEMENTS, Trade. See Trade agreements

AGRELL, S. O. and others
Mineralogy and petrology of some lunar samples. bibliog il Science 167:583-6 Ja 30 '70

AGRICULTURAL administration

Canada
Great wheat glut. il Newsweek 75:71 Ja 26 '70

How Canada stays cholera-free. R. Wilmore. Farm J 93:H8-9+ O '69

Cuba
Castro's time running out? il U S News 68: 48-50 Mr 9 '70

Great Britain
U.S. and U.K. discuss impact of new U.K. agricultural program; statement, November 4, 1970. J. King. Dept State Bul 63:677 N 30 '70

India
View from New Delhi, by C. Bowles. Review Sat R 53:38-9+ Ap 25 '70. L. J. Walinsky

Russia
Prospects for Soviet agriculture. M. E. Bradley. bibliog f Cur Hist 59:226-31+ O '70

Russia tries incentive farming. il U S News 69:65 Ag 3 '70

United States
Agribusiness in California. A. V. Krebs, jr. Commonweal 93:45-7 O 9 '70

Co-ops face two-year tax fight. C. W. Gifford. Farm J 94:50L Mr '70

Diet for fat cats? subsidy bill. Newsweek 76:52+ Ag 3 '70

Dividing the farmers. New Repub 162:8 My 23 '70

Do farmers care about farm programs? W. E. Swegle. Suc Farm 69:20 Ja '71

Farm bill makes superficial cuts. il Bsns W p22 Ag 15 '70

Farm payments. J. Schnittker. New Repub 162:11 Je 27 '70

Farm programs don't help the rural poor. B. L. Masse. America 122:623 Je 13 '70

Hardin's hybrid plan for farm support. Bsns W p 122 My 9 '70

How farmers would change PCAs and land banks. C. W. Gifford. il Farm J 93:28+ D '69

How those new farm plans would work. L. Palmer. Farm J 93:23-4 N '69

Is the NFO changing directions? interview, ed. by L. Palmer. O. L. Staley. il por Farm J 93:28-9+ O '69

Last minute report straight from Washington. See issues of Farm journal

New drive to cut subsidies for giant farms. il U S News 69:54-5 Jl 27 '70

Parting shots; farm subsidies. il Life 69:73-6 N 6 '70

Thought for food. Fortune 81:80 Mr '70

Time for a new strategy. il Farm J 94:46 Je '70

Time to say no to big-farm subsidies. E. H. Methvin. Read Digest 96:78-82 My '70

TRB from Washington; farm subsidies. New Repub 162:8 Ap 18 '70

What big farmers will do about those payment limits. C. E. Ball. Farm J 94:25 N '70

What to do with diverted acres; to comply with Feed-grain program. R. Krumme. il Suc Farm 68:no4 37 Mr '70

What's in that new farm law. C. W. Gifford. Farm J 94:17+ N '70

Who will get what in new farm plan. il U S News 69:49 D 7 '70

Who'll win the farm bill fight? C. W. Gifford. Farm J 94:22 Je '70

See also
United States—Agriculture, Department of

AGRICULTURAL airplanes. See Airplanes in agriculture

AGRICULTURAL assistance in Vietnam. See Technical assistance in Vietnam

AGRICULTURAL associations. See Agricultural societies

AGRICULTURAL chemicals
Sales pressure keeps the chemicals coming. R. Rodale. Org Gard & Farm 17:23-5 Ag '70

See also
Herbicides
Pesticides

Packaging
See Packaging

AGRICULTURAL chemistry
See also
Plants—Chemical analysis

AGRICULTURAL clubs. See Agricultural societies

AGRICULTURAL contracts. See Contracts, Agricultural

AGRICULTURAL cooperation, International. See Agriculture—International aspects

AGRICULTURAL cooperatives. See Cooperative associations

AGRICULTURAL credit
Credit and the farm of the future: family owned or corporation; address, March 17, 1970. J. P. Campbell. Vital Speeches 36: 431-3 My 1 '70

How to figure corn and soybean loan rates. R. Reiman. il Suc Farm 68:A6-7 Je '70

New source of money: AG credit corporations. R. Krumme. il Suc Farm 68:no4 C6 Mr '70

Where to get a loan. il Suc Farm 68:40-1 S '70

See also
Farm finance
Federal land banks
United States—Farm credit administration

AGRICULTURAL economics. See Agriculture—Economic aspects

AGRICULTURAL education
College students, too, learn by doing; two-year area vocational training centers. R. J. Fee. il Suc Farm 68:no4 D16 Mr '70

Tech schools; survey of training in feedlots and livestock technology. W. Kester. il Farm J 94:B8-9+ Ag '70

They're out to revamp vo-ag. J. D. Boyd. il Farm J 93:26-7+ D '69

Three cheers for the boys in blue. Farm J 94:106 F '70

AGRICULTURAL exhibitions
Americana by the acre; Orleans County fair, Vermont. E. Hoagland. il Harper 241:109-14+ O '70
   See also
Livestock shows

AGRICULTURAL experiment stations
How to get an experiment station to test organic gardening. J. Olds. Org Gard & Farm 17:100-1 N '70

AGRICULTURAL experimentation. See Agricultural research

AGRICULTURAL forecasts
Farmcast. See issues of Farm Journal
How you'll do in 1970. C. W. Gifford. Farm J 94:19+ Ja '70
Let's make them better; USDA estimates. Farm J 93:66 O '69
1971 farm outlook. R. Krumme and R. Reiman. il Suc Farm 68:8-9 N '70
Those USDA crop reports: how good are they? C. W. Gifford. il Farm J 94:18-19+ D '70

AGRICULTURAL history. See Agriculture—History

AGRICULTURAL land. See Land

AGRICULTURAL laws and legislation
Farm bill outlook. Suc Farm 68:no2 9 F '70

AGRICULTURAL literature
Journey down a Roman road. A. S. Taormina. il Cons 24:5-7 Ag '69

AGRICULTURAL machinery
Big machinery; slower speed? Suc Farm 68:G8 Ap '70
Fantastic new farm machines. M. Lamm. il Pop Mech 133:118-23 Ja '70
Four machinery ideas from Europe. G. W. Wormley. il Farm J 94:28 Jl '70
From Europe: new machinery ideas. il Farm J 94:32-3 My '70
How to be fair when you share machinery. Farm J 94:50J Mr '70
How to calibrate your granular applicator. L. D. Rawson. il Suc Farm 68:D12 Ap '70
Machinery management (cont of) What's new. P. Jones. See issues of Successful farming
Machinery management; symposium. il Suc Farm 68:no2 31-43+ F '70
Machinery parade; photographs. See issues of Farm Journal
Machinery preview for 1970. G. W. Wormley. il Farm J 94:22-7 Ja '70
More power, big machines in Europe, too. G. W. Wormley. il Farm J 94:19 Je '70
Seven ways to speed up spring work. G. Earle. il Suc Farm 68:no5 20-1 Mr '70
   See also
Cultivators
Fertilizer spreaders
Grain handling
Harvesting machinery
Irrigation machinery
Planters (farm machines)
Plows
Tractors

Cost
How to make a $20,000 machinery decision. R. Krumme. il Suc Farm 68:no2 32-3 F '70
Keep machine costs down. Suc Farm 68:G11 S '70

Cost of operation
How to reduce combine costs. Suc Farm 68:B8 O '70
Thumb rules to figure machinery costs. il Suc Farm 68:no2 34-5 F '70

Depreciation
See Depreciation

Equipment
These monitors watch your equipment. il Suc Farm 68:B8 Ap '70

Maintenance and repair
Machinery maintenance; plows, disks, cultivators. il Suc Farm 67:B1 Ja '70
Machinery maintenance; spreaders and sprayers. il Suc Farm 68:B16 Ja '70
This shop makes service fast and easy. P. B. Jones. il Suc Farm 68:32-3 Ja '70
Tools to save planting time. G. L. Earle. il Suc Farm 68:38-9 Ap '70

Prices
Machinery prices: a let-up in the cost squeeze. G. W. Wormley. il Farm J 93:23 O '69

Safety devices and measures
Planting time safety tips. G. L. Earle. il Suc Farm 68:no4 38 Mr '70

Storage
Straight talk about machinery storage. P. B. Jones. il Suc Farm 68:26-7 My '70

AGRICULTURAL machinery industry and trade
Drought in farm machinery. il Bsns W p80-1 Jl 4 '70
   See also
Collective bargaining—Agricultural machinery industry
Deere and company
International harvester company

AGRICULTURAL mechanization. See Farm mechanization

AGRICULTURAL museums
Where the past lives again; farm museums. J. D. Boyd. il Farm J 94:50B-50C My '70

AGRICULTURAL organizations. See Agricultural societies

AGRICULTURAL pests
Watch for these pests in 1970. C. E. Sommers. il Suc Farm 68:no5 B18 Mr '70
   See also
Birds, Injurious and beneficial
Pest control
Prairie dogs
Weeds
   also subhead Diseases and pests under names of crops. e.g. Corn—Diseases and pests; *also* names of Agricultural pests. e.g. Armyworms

AGRICULTURAL planning. See Farm management

AGRICULTURAL production. See Production, Agricultural

AGRICULTURAL products. See Farm produce

AGRICULTURAL research
Green revolution. UNESCO Courier 23:31-2 F '70
On the life sciences; address, March 5, 1970. J. Mayer. Vital Speeches 36:402-7 Ap 15 '70
   See also
Agricultural experiment stations
Artificial satellites—Agricultural use
Field experiments (agriculture)

AGRICULTURAL research service. See United States—Agricultural research service

AGRICULTURAL societies
Coming: a new kind of organic gardening club; San Antonio Family farms organic growers' association. R. Rodale. il Org Gard & Farm 17:28-31 Ap '70
Speak with one voice? Farm J 93:58 D '69
   See also
American farm bureau federation
Future farmers of America
National farmers organization

AGRICULTURAL subsidies. See Agricultural administration —United States

AGRICULTURE
Human food production as a process in the biosphere. L. R. Brown. il Sci Am 223:160-70 bibliog(p265) S '70
J. Russell Smith's great organic idea; tree-crops partnership. R. Rodale. il Org Gard & Farm 17:28-33 S '70
   See also
Airplanes in agriculture
Chemical industries—Agricultural operations
Country life
Crops
Dairying
Electronics in agriculture
Farm management
Farmers
Food and agriculture organization of the United Nations
Food supply
Irrigation farming
Livestock
Part time farming
Tillage
Viticulture
   also headings beginning Agricultural; Farm; Soil

Economic aspects
Can farmers ease through a recession? C. W. Gifford. il Farm J 94:14-15 Jl '70
Eleven reasons why you are no. 1. Farm J 94:62 O '70
Farm business. See issues of Farm Journal
Farmcast. See issues of Farm Journal
Farming at a crossroads? Suc Farm 68:no4 C10 Mr '70
Money management (cont of) What's new; money management. R. Krumme. See issues of Successful farming
What it'll cost you ... L. D. Rawson. Suc Farm 68:42-3 Ap '70
Why farmers are concerned. il U S News 68:84-5 F 16 '70
Will Congress plug the farm loss loophole? L. Palmer. Farm J 93:17+ D '69
   See also
Agricultural credit

AGRICULTURE—*Continued*

Exhibitions
See Agricultural exhibitions

Federal aid
See Agricultural administration—United States

History
Origins of agriculture. C. D. Darlington. il Natur Hist 79:46-57 My '70
See also
Agricultural literature
Agricultural museums
Agriculture—France—History
Agriculture, Prehistoric

International aspects
Agriculture and foreign economic policy; address, November 19, 1969. N. Samuels. Dept State Bul 61:559-72 D 15 '69

Periodicals
See also
Farm journal
Successful farming (periodical)

Public relations
City folks love you, but! Farm J 94:46 Ag '70

Statistics
Can you rely on government crop reports? R. Reiman. il Suc Farm 68:18 Ag '70
Those USDA crop reports: how good are they? C. W. Gifford. il Farm J 94:18-19+ D '70

Study and teaching
For Latin Americans: Shell Italy's agricultural studies center. il Américas 22:28-30 Ja '70
See also
Agricultural education
Forestry schools and education

California
Agribusiness in California. A. V. Krebs, jr. Commonweal 93:45-7 O 9 '70
From Dustbowl to Saigon: the "Peoples bank" builds an empire. M. Sweeney. il por Ramp Mag 9:24-5+ N '70

France
History
Obstacles to agricultural growth in eighteenth-century France. R. Forster. bibliog f Am Hist R 75:1600-15 O '70

Great Britain
Rototandem target: one man, 120 cows per hour. T. Fellows. il Farm J 93:D12 D '69

India
Ironies of India's green revolution. W. Ladejinsky. For Affairs 48:758-68 Jl '70

Rome
Journey down a Roman road. A. S. Taormina. il Cons 24:5-7 Ag '69

Russia
Russian farmer's big joke on communism. S. Ostrander and L. Schroeder. Farm J 93:30A O '69
Russian grain expert visits U.S. il por Suc Farm 68:no2 A12 F '70

Southern states
Whatever happened to the Black Muslims? Negroes building farm empire. il U S News 69:83-4 S 21 '70

Underdeveloped areas
See Underdeveloped areas—Agriculture

United States
Agriculture and foreign economic policy; address, November 19, 1969. N. Samuels. Dept State Bul 61:569-72 D 15 '69
Credit and the farm of the future: family owned or corporation; address, March 17, 1970. J. R. Campbell. Vital Speeches 36:431-3 My 1 '70
Crisis in agriculture. R. Steffen. Org Gard & Farm 17:52-5 Ag '70
Down on the farm. Trans-Action 7:10 Ap '70
Farmcast. See issues of Farm journal
How you'll do in 1970. C. W. Gifford. Farm J 94:19+ Ja '70
Is there any future in grain farming? R. Krumme. il Suc Farm 68:no5 19 Mr '70
Last minute report straight from Washington. See issues of Farm journal

Revolution in American agriculture. J. B. Billard. il Nat Geog 137:147-85 F '70; Same abr. with title Farming's fantastic new look. Read Digest 96:216-18+ Je '70
Social significance of organic foods. J. Olds. Org Gard & Farm 17:48-51 Ag '70
See also
Agricultural administration—United States
Agricultural experiment stations
Food supply—United States
Irrigation—United States
United States—Agriculture, Department of

Vietnam (Republic)
Success story in war-torn Vietnam. il U S News 69:22-3 O 26 '70

Wisconsin
Who will be farming here ten years from now? neighborhood near Sun Prairie. J. Carlson. il Farm J 93:20-1+ D '69

AGRICULTURE, Cooperative
See also
Collective settlements
Contracts, Agricultural
Dairying, Cooperative

AGRICULTURE, Prehistoric
Creativity of ancient man. E. Keller and J. Zimmerman. il Chem 43:20-1 Jl '70
Early farming village in Turkey; Çayönü Tepesi. H. Çambel and R. J. Braidwood. il Sci Am 222:51-6 Mr '70
World's first farmers. Sci Digest 67:68 Ap '70
See also
Indians—Agriculture

AGRICULTURE census. See Farm census—United States

AGUALLO, Thomaline
Bummer; story. Seventeen 29:128-9 Je '70
This day of joy; story. Good H 171:82-3 Jl '70
When Eric loved me; story. Good H 171:98-9 S '70

AGUARUNA Indians. See Indians of South America

AGUILAR publishers. See Publishers and publishing—Spain

AGUIRRE SAMANIEGO, Manuel Bernardo
President Nixon greets Mexico-U.S. interparliamentary conference; exchange of remarks, May 5, 1970. Dept State Bul 62:656-7 My 25 '70

AHLBORN, Richard E.
Saints and brothers. il Américas 22:6-13 S '70

AHLERS, Conrad
Ahlers affair. por Newsweek 75:68-9 F 23 '70 *

AHLFELD, Kathy
Montessori revival. Ed Digest 35:18-21 Ap '70

AHLSTROM, Sydney E.
Radical turn in theology and ethics: why it occurred in the 1960's. bibliog f Ann Am Acad 387:1-13 Ja '70

AHMAD, Aijaz
(tr) See Ghalib. Ghazals

AHWAHNEE (hotel) See Hotels, taverns, etc.—United States

AID to dependent children (program) See Child welfare—United States

AIDA; opera. See Verdi, G.

AIDES, Nurses. See Nurses aides

AIDES, Psychiatric hospital. See Hospitals, Psychiatric—Staff

AIDES, Teachers. See Teachers aides

AIDS in teaching. See Teaching—Aids and devices

AIKEN, Conrad
Voyagers; poem. Am Scholar 39:253-4 Spr '70

AIKEN, George David
Wildflower expert speaks his mind; interview. House & Gard 138:56-7 N '70

AIKEN, William
In a Provincetown bar; poem. Chr Cent 87:207 F 18 '70

AIKIDO. See Self defense

AIKMAN, Lonnelle
Lights are up at Ford's theatre. il Nat Geog 137:392-401 Mr '70

AILANTHUS
Our local correspondents; ailanthus altissima; or, the tree of heaven. E. Kinkead. New Yorker 46:143-6+ O 24 '70

AILEEN, inc.
Knit-picking for profits. R. Levy. por Duns 96:67-8 N '70

AILES, Roger E.
How Nixon changed his TV image; interview. il pors U S News 68:68-71 F 2 '70

AILEY, Alvin
Dance me a river. H. Saal. il Newsweek 76:86 Jl 6 '70 *

AILEY, Alvin, dance theatre.   See Alvin Ailey
    American dance theater
AIMS in education. See Education—Aims and
    objectives
AINSWORTH, Norma Ruedi
    Aladdin lamp for editors and authors. Writer
    83:28-30 Ap '70
AIR
    Medieval uses of air. L. White, jr. il Sci
    Am 223:92-100 Ag '70
        See also
    Aerodynamics
    Fog
                    Analysis
    Atmospheric oxygen in 1967 to 1970. L.
    Machta and E. Hughes. bibliog il Science
    168:1582-4 Je 26 '70
        See also
    Air pollution—Measurement
    Air sampling
AIR, Compressed. See Compressed air
AIR agreements. See Aviation—International
    aspects
AIR America, Inc.
    Air America: anything goes. il Newsweek 75:
    37 Ap 6 '70
    Air America: flying the U.S. into Laos. P. D.
    Scott. por Ramp Mag 8:39-42+ F '70
    Clandestine militarism; Air America and the
    CIA. Nation 210:452 Ap 20 '70
AIR analysis. See Air—Analysis
AIR bases
    After one community lost a military base;
    Olmstead air force base. il U S News 68:33
    F 16 '70
AIR buildings. See Air-supported structures
AIR buses. See Airplanes, Jet
AIR California (airline)
    PSA merger voted by Air California. Avia-
    tion W 92:31 Ap 13 '70
AIR circus. See Aviation—Stunt flying
AIR circus pilots. See Air pilots
AIR cleaners. See Air filters
AIR compressors
        See also
    Superchargers
AIR conditioning
    Case for central air conditioning. J. Hand.
    il Pop Sci 196:67-9+ My '70
    Climate control. Bet Hom & Gard 48:90+ F
    '70
    How to cool it this summer; central sys-
    tems. J. H. Ingersoll. House B 112:120+
    Mr '70
    Two-house home has natural air condition-
    ing. il Sunset 145:60-1 S '70
    What the systems approach means to air
    conditioning (cont) R. E. Fischer and F. J.
    Walsh. Arch Rec 147:153-60 Ap '70
        See also subhead Air conditioning under
    various subjects, e.g. Automobiles—Air
    conditioning
AIR conditioning equipment
    Air-conditioners. il Consumer Rep 35:345-51
    Je '70
    1970 story on air conditioners; room units.
    il Mech Illus 66:46-8+ My '70
    Room air-conditioners. il Consumer Rep 34:
    133-6 D '69
    Window air conditioners. il Consumer Bul 53:
    4+ Jl '70
        See also
    Dehumidifiers
    Humidifiers
    Trane company
                    Installation
    Two new airconditioners for problem win-
    dows; casement or sliding windows. H.
    Wicks. il Pop Mech 134:158-9 Jl '70

            Maintenance and repair
    Frustrating facts of life about air conditioner
    service. D. F. Daly. il Consumer Bul 53:17-
    19 S '70
AIR conditioning from central stations
    Buying chill air from cool utilities. Bsns W
    p69 Ja 31 '70
AIR currents. See Winds
AIR-cushion landing system. See Airplanes—
    Landing gear
AIR cushion vehicles
    Aerojet uses aerospace methods to build test
    surface effect ship. Aviation W 92:52-3 Ap
    20 '70
    Air-cushion train airport link studied. Avia-
    tion W 92:36 Ja 26 '70
    Air cushion train effort quickens. H. Dyck-
    off. il Aviation W 92:47-51 F 2 '70
    Air cushion utility vehicle tested. E. J.
    Bulban. il Aviation W 93:51-3 Ag 3 '70

Amazing Air cycle. E. H. Arctander. il Pop
    Sci 196:53-5 Mr '70
Flying railroad; magnetic train. il Time 96:
    39 Ag 24 '70
Four-track crawler with hoverpads. D. Scott.
    il por Pop Sci 196:58-9+ My '70
France's 200-mph train; aerotrain. il Mech
    Illus 66:67 Ag '70
Leading international ground effect machines;
    tables (cont) Aviation W 92:131 Mr 9 '70
Supermagnets to speed tomorrow's transit.
    il Radio-Electr 41:2+ N '70
Your second car/boat: a Hovercraft? E. H.
    Arctander. il Pop Sci 196:30 Ja '70
AIR defenses
    World air defense market grows; automated
    command/control systems. B. Miller. il Avia-
    tion W 94:38-42 Ja 4 '71
AIR drop. See Airdrop
AIR filters
    Breathe easier with a home air cleaner. il Pop
    Mech 133:182-3 F '70
    Build a transcipitor; electrostatic air cleaner.
    W. T. Boyd. il Pop Electr 32:31-5+ Je '70
    Cleaning the air we breathe. J. Frye. Electr
    World 84:58-9 S '70
AIR force academy. See United States air force
    academy, Colorado Springs
AIR force football. See Football
AIR force pilots. See Air pilots
AIR France. See Airlines—France
AIR freight containerization. See Containeriza-
    tion (freight)
AIR freight forwarders. See Forwarding com-
    panies
AIR freight forwarders association
    Forwarders attack small parcel problem. il
    Aviation W 93:32-4 O 26 '70
AIR freight handling. See Freight handling
AIR freight service
    Air cargo at the crossroads; symposium with
    editorial comment. il Aviation W 93:11, 26-
    34+ O 26 '70
    Air cargo seen stumbling on the ground. E.
    H. Kolcum. il Aviation W 93:27-8 S 28 '70
    Faster small package service by airlines cuts
    shipping time. R. S. Kahn. Aviation W 93:
    30-1 N 30 '70
    General aviation operators divided on cargo
    carrier role. Aviation W 93:79 S 21 '70
    Lockheed mass cargo system (cont) D. A.
    Brown. il Aviation W 92:32-4 Ja 19 '70
        See also
    Airlift international, inc.
    Animals—Transportation
    Computers—Air freight service use
    Flying Tiger line, inc.
    Hawaii air cargo shippers association

            International aspects
    Cargo looming larger in global air transport.
    L. Doty. il Aviation W 93:26-8 O 26 '70
    Foreign trade by air up; U.S. carrier share
    slips. Aviation W 94:27 Ja 4 '71
    Lufthansa's cargo marketing emphasizes U.S.-
    German traffic. Aviation W 93:36 N 16 '70

            Laws and regulations
        See Aviation—Laws and regulations

                    Rates
    Airlines, CAB grapple with cargo tariffs.
    H. D. Watkins. il Aviation W 93:39+ O 26
    '70
    Board to investigate air express tariffs. Avia-
    tion W 93:32 S 28 '70
    Broad freight tariff increases anticipated.
    Aviation W 92:36 My 25 '70
    CAB approves some cargo rate increases.
    Aviation W 94:27 Ja 11 '71

                    Statistics
    Growth in North Atlantic air cargo and mail,
    year 1969 over 1968; table. Aviation W 93:38
    Jl 6 '70
    North Atlantic air cargo and mail data, first
    six months of 1970; table. Aviation W 93:
    52-3 O 26 '70
    North Atlantic air cargo and mail data, year
    1969; table. Aviation W 93:42-3 Jl 6 '70
    U.S. airline mail and cargo carried, twelve
    months ending June 30, 1970; table. Avia-
    tion W 93:54 O 26 '70
    U.S. airline mail and cargo revenues; table.
    Aviation W 93:40 O 26 '70

            Europe, Western
    Cargo revenues climbing in Europe. E. H.
    Kolcum. il Aviation W 93:59+ O 26 '70
AIR inter (airline) See Airlines—France
AIR layering of plants. See Plant propagation

AIR line employees association, International
Agreement reached in airline strike. U S
News 68:64 Je 1 '70
AIR line pilots association, International
ALPA committee scores FAA all-weather
landing program. B. M. Elson. Aviation W
93:27 Jl 27 '70
Added benefits sought by pilots. L. Doty.
Aviation W 93:22-3 Ag 24 '70
Captains capricious. Time 97:70 Ja 4 '71
United-pilots dispute grows; Eastern, Air
West threatened. Aviation W 93:25 Ag 17
'70
AIR mail service
CAB reduces rates on non-priority mail.
Aviation W 92:48 Ap 27 '70
Intense struggle foreseen over air mail rate
level. Aviation W 93:143 O 26 '70
Post office reviews ruling on first class.
Aviation W 92:30 Je 1 '70
    See also
Rocket mail
        Statistics
Growth in North Atlantic air cargo and mail,
year 1969 over 1968; table. Aviation W 93:
38 Jl 6 '70
North Atlantic air cargo and mail data, first
six months of 1970; table. Aviation W 93:
52-3 O 26 '70
North Atlantic air cargo and mail data, year
1969; table. Aviation W 93:42-3 Jl 6 '70
U.S. airline mail and cargo carried, twelve
months ending June 30, 1970; table. Avia-
tion W 93:54 O 26 '70
U.S. airline mail and cargo revenues; table.
Aviation W 93:40 O 26 '70
AIR microbiology
Life in the clouds. por Time 96:42 N 2 '70
Life in the clouds; theories of B. C. Parker.
Newsweek 76:57 O 5 '70
Life in the sky. B. C. Parker. il Natur Hist
79:54-9 O '70
Mechanism for the water-to-air transfer and
concentration of bacteria. D. C. Blanchard
and L. Syzdek. bibliog il Science 170:626-8
N 6 '70
AIR New Zealand. See Airlines—New Zealand
AIR pilots
Look, ma, no hands; air circus pilots. W.
Johnson. il Sports Illus 33:106-10+ S 14 '70
Silver-barred prison. R. Bach. il Flying 86:
8-9 Ap '70
    See also
Air line pilots association, International
Airlines—Captains
Airplane crews
Airplanes—Piloting
Aviation—Physiological aspects
International federation of air line pilots as-
sociations
National pilots association
Negro air pilots
Women as air pilots

    Anecdotes, facetiae, satire, etc.
Say again everything after ATC clears. . .
R. Peterson. il Flying 88:62-4 Ja '71

    Psychology
Up-tight pilot. T. H. Block. il Flying 87:76-
7+ S '70

    Recruiting
Eastern starts pilot recruiting program. H. D.
Watkins. Aviation W 93:32 Ag 3 '70

    Salaries, allowances, etc.
    See also
Collective bargaining—Air pilots

    Supply and demand
    See also
Air pilots—Recruiting

    Training
Arab pilots to train at Wheelus. E. H.
Kolcum. il Aviation W 92:14-16 Mr 23 '70
Business study expected to aid pilot careers.
il Aviation W 93:85-6 S 21 '70
Concepts for pilots range studied; electronic
air combat maneuvering range. B. Miller.
il Aviation W 93:42-4 S 28 '70
Follow me through. R. Blodget. See issues of
Flying
How to get a multi-engine rating in eight
days without a nervous breakdown, and
why. R. Peterson. il Flying 86:64-70+ Je '70
Increased training standards expected. il
Aviation W 93:80-1+ S 21 '70
Learning curve. R. B. Parke. il Flying 86:34
My; 87:28 Ag '70

Libya faces problems of obtaining qualified
pilots for fifty Mirages. Aviation W 92:67+
Ja 26 '70
    See also
Aviation schools
Flight simulators
AIR piracy. See Airplane hijacking
AIR pollution
Age of eternal twilight. R. Rienow and L. T.
Rienow. il Audubon 72:4-8 Jl '70
Air pollution and rubber. Chem 43:21 D '70
Air pollution and the temperature inversion.
R. E. Falconer. il Cons 25:21-7 O '70
Auto exhaust, pollution and weather pat-
terns; adaptation of testimony before sub-
committee on air and water pollution,
March, 1970. V. J. Schaefer. Bul Atom Sci
26:31-3 O '70
Carriers seek alternatives to turbojet fuel
dumping. H. D. Watkins. Aviation W 93:
27-8 N 2 '70
Clean air? Color it black! H. Higdon. il To-
days health 48:38-41+ S '70
Coming: ice-free Arctic? Sci Digest 67:39 Ja
'70
Escape from pollution; the Adirondacks; ad-
dress, June 3, 1969. V. J. Schaefer. il Cons
24:8-11 F '70
Fly-ash-by-night conspiracy. R. Guffey. il
Audubon 72:147-8 N '70
Man and his home; address, April 28, 1970.
A. J. Haagen-Smit. Vital Speeches 36:572-6
Jl 1 '70; Same. Liv Wildn 34:38-46 Sum '70
Perspectives on polluted air, 1970. R. S.
Berry. il Bul Atom Sci 26:2+ Ap '70
Poisons in the air. il Sr Schol 97:14-15 N 2
'70
Some burning questions about combustion.
T. Alexander. il Fortune 81:130-1+ F '70
Teacher tips; air pollution and the tempera-
ture inversion. J. A. Weeks. il Cons 25:32-3
O '70
Who has seen the wind? D. Lambert. Nat
Parks & Con Mag 44:19 D '70
Will the SST pollute the stratosphere? Science
168:1562 Je 26 '70
You can sample the air around you. A. Hul-
strunk. il Cons 25:48+ Ag '70
    See also
Automobile engines—Exhaust
Jet airplane engines—Exhaust
Plants, Effect of air pollution on
Plants, Effect of ozone on
Smog
    also subhead Air pollution under names
of cities, e.g. San Francisco—Air pollution

        Control
Air pollution. D. R. Newman. Cur Hist 59:18-
22 Jl '70
Air pollution control news. See issues of
American city
Copper men see red over pollution. il Bsns
W p31 Je 13 '70
Driving with methane. E. Gross. il Sci N 97:
73-4 Ja 17 '70
Fill 'er up with antismog gasoline. il Bsns
W p24 F 7 '70
Get the lead out: pollution remedy? il Sr
Schol 97:5 O 12 '70
Getting the lead out. J. B. Sullivan and
A. J. Fritsh. New Repub 163:9-10 N 21 '70
Grime doesn't pay, but clean air does. Na-
tions Bsns 58:15 F '70
How to prevent air pollution indoors. il Good
H 170:183 Ap '70
Less pollution from automobiles? U S News
68:12 F 16 '70
New engineering; priorities for the 70's; ad-
dress, January 14, 1970. E. N. Cole. Vital
Speeches 36:236-40 F 1 '70
New York's fight against pollution. N. Cou-
sins. il Sat R 53:53-4+ Mr 7 '70
Planning Philadelphia's air; three-state Phi-
ladelphia air quality control region. Sci N
9:243 Mr 7 '70
Pollution. G. Lorang. il Farm J 94:20-1+ Ag
'70
Precision controlled flames fight air pollu-
tion; New York harbor. R. G. Burns and
R. E. Newton. il Am City 85:98+ My '70
Progress in abating air pollution. P. H.
Abelson. Science 167:1567 Mr 20 '70
Sulfur oxide control: a grim future; findings
of National research council study. R. Gil-
luly. il Sci N 98:187-8 Ag 22 '70
Wanted: a pulp mill deodorant. Bsns W p 102
F 21 '70
Wind up car. K. Hohenemser and J. McCaull.
il Environ 12:14-21+ Je '70
    See also
Air filters
Smoke prevention
United States—National air pollution control
administration

AIR pollution—*Continued*

Laws and legislation
See Pollution—Laws and legislation

Measurement
Air pollution surveillance systems. G. B. Morgan and others. bibliog il Science 170: 289-96 O 16 '70

Auto exhaust, pollution and weather patterns; adaptation of testimony before subcommittee on air and water pollution, March, 1970. V. J. Schaefer. Bul Atom Sci 26:31-3 O '70

Build your own air-pollution tester; wet impingement system. R. Day and J. Ortmann. il Pop Sci 197:97-9 O '70

5,000 join in air pollution survey; Project Help your environment carried out by Northeastern environmental council. V. A. Mohnen. il por Cons 25:10-15 Ag '70

Physiological effects
Air pollution and human health. L. B. Lave and E. P. Seskin. bibliog il Science 169:723-33 Ag 21 '70

Auto pollution: a threat to health? Todays Health 48:55 N '70

Donora, Pennsylvania; smog episode of October 1948. C. Bowen. Atlan 226:27-8+ N '70

Hazards of trace elements. R. H. Gilluly. il Sci N 97:560-1 Je 6 '70

Statistics
Air; EQ index. il Nat Wildlife 8:28-9 O '70; Same. Schol Teach Jr/Sr High pA4-5 O 5 '70

Study and teaching
Our eighth graders tackled air pollution. J. L. Brown il Todays Ed 59:60-1 F '70

Antarctic Regions
Antarctic meteorology. M. J. Rubin. il por Bul Atom Sci 26:48-54 D '70

Europe, Western
Sulfur: simulated long-range transport in the atmosphere. H. Reiquam. bibliog il Science 170:318-20 O 16 '70

Great Britain
British air problems. P. F. Brooks. Am City 85:24 Ap '70

AIR pollution and cancer. See Cancer—Causes

AIR raid shelters
See also
Atomic bomb shelters

AIR raids
See also
Cambodian-Vietnamese conflict—Aerial operations
Israeli-Arab war, 1967- —Aerial operations
Vietnamese war, 1957- —Aerial operations

AIR reduction company
Why they weren't the last to know; Airco chemicals & plastics div. employees Bsns W p 17-18 Mr 7 '70

AIR safety. See Aviation—Safety devices and measures

AIR sampling
You can sample the air around you. A. Hulstrunk. il Cons 25:48+ Ag '70

AIR-sea interaction. See Ocean-atmosphere interaction

AIR shippers association. See Cooperative associations

AIR ships. See Airships

AIR shows. See Aviation—Exhibitions

AIR shuttles. See Airlines—Shuttle service

AIR supported structures
Infinitely expandable future of air structures. M. Villecco. il Arch Forum 133:40-3 S '70
Rise of the bubble. il Time 96:58 D 21 '70

AIR taxi service
Travel notes; Airspur corp. R. Joseph. Esquire 73:42+ My '70
See also
Executive airlines, inc.
Golden eagle aviation

AIR terminals. See Terminals

AIR traffic control
ATC automation facing key test. P. J. Klass. il Aviation W 93:50-3 Jl 20 '70
Automation creeps in; national air space system. il Sci N 97:340 Ap 4 '70
Awake, dreamers; increase in midair collisions. R. L. Collins. Flying 87:24 N '70
Cost tests delay airspace system plans. D. C. Winston. il Aviation W 92:70 F 9 '70
FAA, traffic controllers gear for future relations. J. P. Woolsey. Aviation W 92:30-1 My 25 '70

Flow control facility eases center loss. C. E. Schneider. Aviation W 93:25 S 7 '70
How to end air collisions; Secant-B defensive piloting system. il Bsns W p 128+ Ap 11 '70
Life saver; corridors for high-speed aircraft. R. B. Parke. Flying 86:44 Ja '70
New data link may lessen communication workload. B. M. Elson. il Aviation W 93:44+ N 30 '70
Tame blue yonder. il Nations Bsns 58:76-8+ Mr '70
Taming radar weather clutter. H. L. McFann. il Electr World 83:44-5 Ja '70
Understaffing since about 1965; excerpts from the final report of the Air traffic controller career committee. U S News 68:26 Ap 13 '70
Will you lose your right to fly? F. A. Tinker. il Pop Mech 134:88-91+ O '70
See also
Airports—Traffic control
Artificial satellites—Air traffic control applications
Radar in aviation
Transponders

AIR traffic controllers (persons)
Air traffic still hampered despite controllers return. Aviation W 92:29 Ap 20 '70
FAA acts to improve controller program. J. P. Woolsey. Aviation W 92:19 F 16 '70
On top; lack of communication between controller and airborne pilot. R. L. Collins. Flying 86:104+ Je '70
Real issue in air slowdown; with excerpts from report of the Air traffic controller career committee. il U S News 68:24-6 Ap 13 '70
See also
Professional air traffic controllers organization
Strikes—United States—Air traffic controllers

Training
Wanted: black air traffic controllers. il Ebony 25:54-6+ Ap '70

AIR transport agreements. See Aviation—International aspects

AIR transport association of America
Increased budget for FAA urged in ATA testimony. K. Johnsen. Aviation W 93:17 Ag 31 '70
Trunks face $123 million loss. J. P. Woolsey. Aviation W 93:26 D 14 '70

AIR transportation, Military. See Transportation, Military

AIR travel
Air travel: how to get off the ground. Bsns W p 107-8 Je 13 '70
Jet-age scramble; Chicago's O'Hare. il Life 70:56-66 Ja 8 '71
Jumbo jets; how they're doing. il U S News 68:44 Mr 16 '70
New world of air travel. B. Kocivar. il Mlle 70:215-18 Mr '70
Tips for traveling by plane. E. Welke. Bet Hom & Gard 48:20 Ag '70
Travel in the '70s. K. Ludvigsen. Mech Illus 66:44-5 Ja '70
Travel poll results. Aviation W 93:39 S 28 '70
Winter air fares lower than ever. il Travel & Camera 33:20+ F '70
See also
Business travel
Private flying

Physiological aspects
See Aviation—Physiological aspects

Statistics
Growth in U.S. air passengers; table. Aviation W 93:49 S 14 '70
Increase/decrease in passenger boardings by U.S. carriers at selected international points; table. Aviation W 93:51 O 12 '70
1969 air passengers between the United States, other countries by flag of carrier; table. Aviation W 93:42-3 N 9 '70
1969 international air passengers at U.S. ports; table. Aviation W 93:39 N 23 '70

Taxation
Costlier to fly; new aircraft-use taxes. U S News 68:60 My 25 '70
Invisible tax. Newsweek 76:54+ Ag 10 '70
Supreme court in Montana voids state tax on airline passengers. Aviation W 92:34 Ja 26 '70
Tiptoeing through the tourist taxes. il Sat R 54:33-4+ Ja 2 '71

Canada
Water wilderness; seaplane journey up the untamed coastline. D. Butwin. il Sat R 53:45-6+ D 5 '70

AIR travel with children. See Travel with children

AIR West, inc.
Air West plans stock issue to assure its sale to Hughes. Aviation W 92:29 Mr 23 '70
Hughes purchase of Air West near completion; suit possible. Aviation W 92:27 Mr 30 '70
New owner strives to rebuild Air West. Aviation W 92:38 My 11 '70

AIRBOATS, Fishing. See Fishing—Implements and appliances

AIRBUSES. See Airplanes, Jet

AIRCO. See Air reduction company

AIRCRAFT carriers
Attack aircraft carrier; our forward defense posture; address, March 4, 1970. T. H. Moorer. Vital Speeches 36:392-4 Ap 15 '70
Flattops face a flight for survival. il Bsns W p90 Ap 11 '70
Waiting for Apollo 13; aboard the Iwo Jima. B. Kocivar. il Pop Sci 197:44-6+ Ag '70

AIRCRAFT industry and trade. See Airplane industry and trade

AIRCRAFT shows. See Aviation—Exhibitions

AIRDROP
Anti-pollution aid keyed to air drop. C. E. Schneider. il Aviation W 92:92-3+ My 25 '70

AIRFOILS
Advanced airfoils studied for transports. D. A. Brown. il Aviation W 92:55-7+ Je 22 '70
Wing; where the action is. P. Garrison. il Flying 88:44-8 Ja '71

AIRHART, Sharon
Country mouse, city mouse. por Redbook 135:10+ S '70

AIRLIFT, Military. See Transportation, Military

AIRLIFT International, inc.
Airlift plans strong air freight emphasis. H. D. Watkins. il Aviation W 93:34-6 Ag 31 '70
Airlift plea denied. Aviation W 93:33 N 16 '70

AIRLINE holding companies
Two carriers form holding units. Aviation W 93:27 Jl 6 '70

AIRLINE hostesses See Airlines—Hostesses

AIRLINE magazines. See Periodicals for airline passengers

AIRLINE maintenance. See Airplanes—Maintenance and repair

AIRLINE passenger head taxes. See Air travel —Taxation

AIRLINES
See also
International air transport association

Advertising
Eastern seeks to exploit stronger markets. R. S. Kahn. Aviation W 92:25-6 F 16 '70

Agreements
See Airlines—Cooperation

Automation
Airlines test automated seat selection. R. S. Kahn. il Aviation W 92:30 Mr 2 '70
Automated ticketing systems tested. R. S. Kahn. Aviation W 92:32-3 F 9 '70
Computer handles twelve operations for SAS. Aviation W 92:61 F 2 '70
See also
Airlines—Luggage handling
Airlines—Reservation systems
Computers—Airline applications

Baggage handling
See Airlines—Luggage handling

Beverage and food service
Airlines stress food service competition. H. D. Watkins. il Aviation W 93:30-1+ N 23 '70
L-1011 passes food service system test. N. S. Himmel. il Aviation W 92:48+ Ap 6 '70

Captains
See also
Yadven, A.

Communication systems
New data link may lessen communication workload. B. M. Elson. il Aviation W 93:44+ N 30 '70

Consolidations and mergers
American way; American airlines plan to absorb Trans-Caribbean airways. Newsweek 75:70 F 2 '70
American, Western in merger agreement. W. H. Gregory. il Aviation W 93:24-5 N 9 '70
Board grants tentative approval to Eastern-Caribair merger step. H. D. Watkins. Aviation W 93:30 N 16 '70

Britain creates a private airline; Caledonian/BUA. il Bsns W p34 Ja 9 '71
Delta, National Did CAB consider alternatives to Northeast merger. Aviation W 92:28 F 23 '70
Eastern to acquire Caribair. Aviation W 93:25 N 2 '70
Hawaii merger plan poses monopoly vs. subsidy issue; proposed merger of Hawaiian and Aloha airlines. R. G. O'Lone. Aviation W 92:32 Ja 26 '70
Mating season; American airlines to purchase Trans Caribbean. Time 95:65 F 2 '70
Northeast loses part of its dowry. Bsns W p16 Ja 9 '71
Northwest weighs merger ruling options. J. P. Woolsey. Aviation W 94:26 Ja 11 '71
Only mergers can bail out the airlines. Bsns W p37 Ja 9 '71
PSA merger voted by Air California. Aviation W 92:31 Ap 13 '70

Cooperation
Aeroflot Japan service reflects pooling. D. C. Winston. il Aviation W 92:26-7 Ap 13 '70
Swissair/AUA pact. Aviation W 93:38 S 28 '70
USSR-Japan pooling pact expected to set pattern. L. Doty. Aviation W 92:34 Ap 27 '70
Vienna waltz; Austrian airlines planning partnership with Swissair. Time 96:80+ O 12 '70

Cost of operation
Costs may slow airline growth. E. H. Kolcum. Aviation W 93:22-3 N 2 '70
Is there any way to run an airline? T. Alexander. Fortune 82:117+ S '70
U.S. trunks react to cost rise. W. H. Gregory. il Aviation W 92:24-8 Je 8 '70
See also
Airplanes, Jet—Cost of operation

Employees
See also
Air lines employees association, International
Airlines—Hostesses

Equipment and supplies
Airlines stress perfection to suppliers. il Aviation W 93:12-13 D 28 '70

Fares
Atlantic tariffs snag IATA talks R. G. O'Lone. Aviation W 93:25-6 O 12 '70
Bargain-hunting for air fares. Sunset 144:37-8 Ja '70
Board suspends Hawaii filings. H. D. Watkins. Aviation W 93:24-5 Jl 20 '70
By air to Tokyo, the choices. il Sunset 144:27 Ja '70
CAB examiner urges 11 per cent rate of return. L. Doty. Aviation W 93:24 N 30 '70
CAB girds for major fare investigation. Aviation W 92:35-6 Mr 16 '70
CAB orders new tariff filings. Aviation W 93:21 Ag 3 '70
Carrier jousting expected in new fare hike filings. H. D. Watkins. Aviation W 93:27-8 D 7 '70
Carriers seek fare-setting power. L. Doty. Aviation W 94:23-4 Ja 11 '71
Carriers weigh new fare bids; CAB blocks summer, 747 rises. H. D. Watkins. Aviation W 92:34 My 18 '70
Conflicting fare increases filed. Aviation W 92:34 My 11 '70
Consolidated manual of tariffs redesigned to ease computation. Aviation W 92:36 My 25 '70
Excursion fare will get IATA scrutiny. R. S. Kahn. Aviation W 93:30-1 Ag 10 '70
Fare increase filings continue as carriers await CAB action. Aviation W 93:28 N 23 '70
Hawaii fare filings may stall rate rise. Aviation W 93:29 Jl 6 '70
How cheaply can you fly? Bet Hom & Gard 48:19 Ja '70
IATA keys advance spade work to avoiding Honolulu stalemate. Aviation W 92:34 Je 8 '70
IATA to attack fare deadlock at Tehran. R. G. O'Lone. Aviation W 93:22-3 O 26 '70
Invisible tax. Newsweek 76:54+ Ag 10 '70
Legal clarification awaited in domestic fare tangle. H. D. Watkins. Aviation W 93:25-6 O 19 '70
Management record may sway fare case. H. D. Watkins. Aviation W 93:28-9 N 9 '70
Market would set fares under proposed bilateral. L. Doty. Aviation W 93:23-4 N 2 '70
Momentum builds for new fare increases. Aviation W 92:32-3 Ap 27 '70

AIRLINES—Fares—*Continued*

New limited fare filings expected. H. D. Watkins. Aviation W 93:29-30 O 5 '70

New triangle fares take in Hawaii. Sunset 144:32 F '70

Pacific, Asia, Australia fares set. R. G. O'Lone. Aviation W 93:24-5 O 19 '70

Seating, fare issues speeded by CAB in tariff investigation. Aviation W 93:25 N 30 '70

Survival is issue in clash over bulk fares. R. G O'Lone. il Aviation W 92:179+ Mr 9 '70

Three-part fare review planned. H. D. Watkins. Aviation W 92:29-31 F 9 '70

U.K. fare increase. Aviation W 92:26 F 16 '70

U.S. airlines to seek simpler IATA fares. H. D. Watkins. Aviation W 92:24-5 Je 15 '70

Weak traffic clouds fare impact. H. D. Watkins. Aviation W 93:22-3 N 30 '70

Who sets the plane fares? K. G. J. Pillai. il Nation 210:177-80 F 16 '70

Winter air fares: lower than ever. il Travel & Camera 33:20+ F '70

Anecdotes, facetiae, satire, etc.

Airline rate war. A. Buchwald. il Holiday 47: 88 F '70

Federal aid

See also
Local service airlines—Federal aid

Finance

Air carrier financing woes stall deliveries of finished transports. Aviation W 93:34 O 19 '70

Airline income, expense; tables. Aviation W 92:43 My 4; 93-37 Jl 6; 40 O 5 '70; 94:34 Ja 11 '71

Airlines tighten their seat belts. il por Newsweek 76:85 O 19 '70

CAB examiner urges 11 per cent rate of return. L. Doty. Aviation W 93:24 N 30 '70

Downdraft hits airline profits. il Bsns W p23 Ag 1 '70

Eastern places three-year cost of traffic delays at $137 million. K. J. Stein. il Aviation W 92:30-1 Ap 27 '70

First-quarter returns show mixed results. Aviation W 92:33 My 4 '70

Increases in airline operating revenues; tables. Aviation W 92:41 Ap 27 '70

MAC charter purchases decline. il Aviation W 93:23 Ag 17 '70

$100 million loss by U.S. airlines seen in 1970. Aviation W 93:24 N 2 '70

Paying for jumbo. il Time 96:65 Ag 31 '70

Transportation; with yardsticks of management performance. il Forbes 105:179-80 Ja 1 '70; 107:168-9 Ja 1 '71

Trunkline profit, loss; tables. Aviation W 92: 28 Ap 13; 36 My 25; 93:49 Ag 24; 30 D 7 '70

Trunks face $123 million loss. J. P. Woolsey. Aviation W 93:26 D 14 '70

U.S. airline increases in operating revenues, first six months, 1970 over 1969; table. Aviation W 93:39 S 21 '70

U.S. airline revenues & expenses; tables (cont) Aviation W 93:41 S 28 '70

U.S. scheduled airline operating revenues & expenses, 1969; tables. Aviation W 92:42-3 Ap 27 '70

Why airlines are in trouble. il U S News 69:24-6 N 9 '70

See also
Airlines—Cost of operation
Airlines—Non-scheduled operations—Finance
Airlines—Securities

Food service

See Airlines—Beverage and food service

Freight service

See Air freight service

Hostesses

American has a way with young women; stewardesses conduct charm courses in ghettos. V. Louviere. il Nations Bsns 58:19 Ja '70

FAA eases new attendant rule temporarily for eight airlines. Aviation W 92:36 My 4 '70

Let's travel: is there an airline in your future? il Mlle 70:122-3 Mr '70

Stewardesses help promote Pan Am 747s. R. S. Kahn. il Aviation W 94:30-1 Ja 11 '71

Hotel operations

Another airline turns innkeeper. Bsns W p50 Mr 28 '70

Insurance

Airline risk insurance rates rise prohibitively following bombings. Aviation W 92:234 Mr 9 '70

Airway war escalates; with editorial comment. il Bsns W p21-2, 134 S 12 '70

Hijacking hostage: insurance rates. il Bsns W p 39 S 19 '70

Jumbo insurance for the jumbo jets. il Bsns W p36 Ja 17 '70

Jumbo risk. Time 96:92+ S 21 '70

Relations of U.S. airlines altered. H. D. Watkins. Aviation W 93:23-4 S 28 '70

Who will pay for the burned-out 747? il Bsns W p64+ D 5 '70

International services

Asian airline prepares for world routes; Malaysia-Singapore airlines. C. Brownlow. il Aviation W 92:43+ Ap 6 '70

747 dominates planning for 1970 market. L. Doty. il Aviation W 92:147-9+ Mr 9 '70

European-Asiatic

Siberia to divert polar air traffic. D. C. Winston. il Aviation W 92:18-19 Ap 6 '70

Siberian route offers few navaids. L. Doty. il Aviation W 92:24-6 Ap 13 '70

Transatlantic

Pressures from U.K. increasing for Atlantic capacity restrictions. P. Woolsey. Aviation W 93:26 Ag 24 '70

Transatlantic capacity outpaces traffic. il Aviation W 93:74 O 26 '70

Transoceanic

Forty gateways for overseas flights; table. Bet Hom & Gard 48:112 O '70

Transpacific

American Pacific strategy evolving. W. H. Gregory. il Aviation W 93:26-30 N 30 '70

Booked for travel; Braniff's Hawaii service. D. Butwin. Sat R 53:46+ Ja 17 '70

By air to Tokyo, the choices. il Sunset 144:27 Ja '70

Increased competition, capacity challenge Pacific airlines. R. G. O'Lone. il Aviation W 93:72-3 O 26 '70

Pacific award sparked early response. W. H. Gregory. il Aviation W 93:40-1+ D 7 '70

Parting shots. W. Zinsser. il Life 68:63-6 Ja 23 '70

Load factor

See Airlines—Traffic

Luggage handling

Eastern strives to curtail baggage losses. H. D. Watkins. il Aviation W 93:28-9+ Ag 17 '70

Mail room conveyor system proposed for baggage handling. il Aviation W 92:34 F 23 '70

New airport shows the way; automated baggage handling system. il Bsns W p33 D 26 '70

Maintenance and repair

See Airplanes—Maintenance and repair

Management

Management record may sway fare case. H. D. Watkins. Aviation W 93:28-9 N 9 '70

Anecdotes, facetiae, satire, etc.

Complete instructions for running an airline. H. Sutton. il Sat R 53:48+ Ap 11 '70

Military use

Air America: anything goes. il Newsweek 75:37 Ap 6 '70

Non-scheduled operations

CAB plans charter rule changes. Aviation W 92:34 My 18 '70

CAB unit expands investigation of alleged illegal charter actions. Aviation W 93:29 Jl 6 '70

CAB wants the affinity back in flying. Bsns W p94+ Jl 25 '70

Congress enters airline charter dispute. J. P. Woolsey. Aviation W 93:24 Ag 17 '70

Dog fight over charter flights. il Bsns W p 128+ F 28 '70

Dogfight over landing rights; Belgian ban on U.S. charter flights to Brussels. il Bsns W p 114 My 9 '70

Groups fight change in charter flights. T. Schuchat. Har Yrs 10:4-5 D '70

If you are planning a charter flight. il U S News 68:60-2 Mr 9 '70

Little airlines that seek new skies; supplementals. il Bsns W p22 O 3 '70

AIRLINES—Non-scheduled operations—*Cont.*

Permanent certificate awards to Atlantic supplementals urged. H. D. Watkins. Aviation W 94:24-5 Ja 11 '71

Supplemental policy spurs clash. L. Doty. Aviation W 92:22-3 F 16 '70

Supplementals fear for existence; with table. J. P. Woolsey. Aviation W 92:31-2 My 4 '70

Survival is issue in clash over bulk fares. R. G. O'Lone. il Aviation W 92:179+ Mr 9 '70

Travel as a package deal; with report on Russian tour by M. Leatherbee. il Life 68: 42-9 Mr 20 '70

See also
Air America, inc.

Finance

Success that kills. Forbes 106:20-1 D 1 '70

Supplemental airline revenues and expenses; tables. Aviation W 92:47 Ap 27; 42 Je 8; 93:45 O 5 '70; 94:31 Ja 11 '71

Supplementals' earnings drop for first half. Aviation W 93:23 Ag 31 '70

Statistics

Comparison of North Atlantic charter activity, first six months of 1970 over 1969; table. Aviation W 93:45 O 5 70

Supplemental airline revenues and expenses; tables. Aviation W 92:47 Ap 27; 93:45 O 5 '70

Passenger service

Airline reliance on service indices varies. W. H. Gregory. il Aviation W 92:26-7 Je 15 '70

Airlines feel 747 impact on frequencies. Aviation W 92:31 Ap 27 '70

Airplane talk. W. F. Buckley, jr. Nat R 22: 584 Je 2 '70

Amenities increased by TWA in bid for 707 coach traffic. il Aviation W 93:26 N 2 '70

Continental's 747s to Hawaii nearly full. il Aviation W 93:27-8 Jl 13 '70

Crowds pose major 747 problem. R. S. Kahn. Aviation W 92:25-6 Je 29 '70

Major trunks start movie fees. Aviation W 92:33 My 4 '70

Passenger service fixes planned for 747. W. H. Gregory. Aviation W 93:24-5 Ag 3 '70

Who pays for missed airlines connections? Consumer Rep 34:620 N '69

See also
Periodicals for airline passengers

Passenger traffic

See Airlines—Traffic

Passengers

For jet setters only? profile of today's air travelers. G. Hendricks. Aviation W 93:11 O 19 '70

Pooled operations

See Airlines—Cooperation

Public relations

Stewardesses help promote Pan Am 747s. R. S. Kahn. il Aviation W 94:30-1 Ja 11 '71

See also
Periodicals for airline passengers

Rates

See Air freight service—Rates; Airlines —Fares

Regulations

See Aviation—Laws and regulations

Reservation systems

American testing new ticket device. Aviation W 93:64 Jl 13 '70

Automated ticketing systems tested. R. S. Kahn. Aviation W 92:32-3 F 9 '70

CAB tightens enforcement on oversales. L. Doty. il Aviation W 92:28 Je 29 '70

Common reservations systems studied. R. S. Kahn. Aviation W 93:39 D 7 '70

Computer helps deploy reservations staff. il Aviation W 93:38-9 Ag 3 '70

Europe plans reservations net for 1972. R. F. Coburn. Aviation W 92:63 Ja 26 '70

Reservations world purchased. Aviation W 93:32 D 21 '70

TWA reserves space with IBM. Bsns W p88-9 O 31 '70

Safety devices and measures

See Aviation—Safety devices and measures

Securities

Airline stocks regain some favor despite credit crisis. Aviation W 93:31-2 Ag 10 '70

Airlines. il Forbes 105:24-6+ Je 1 '70

CAB criticized by aide of Nader on airline ownership reporting. Aviation W 93:25 Ag 24 '70

Shuttle service

Eastern studies air-shuttle improvements. J. P. Woolsey. il Aviation W 92:39-41+ My 18 '70

Smoking problem

See Smoking on aircraft

Statistics

Airline traffic; tables. See occasional issues of Aviation week & space technology

Boeing 747 aircraft operations and cost data; table. Aviation W 93:37 D 21 '70

Boeing 747 aircraft operations and traffic data, first six months of 1970; table. Aviation W 93:32-3 Ag 24 '70

Comparison of North Atlantic charter activity, year 1969 over 1968; tables. Aviation W 92:55 Ap 6 '70

Four-engine turbojet/fan load factors; table. Aviation W 93:38 S 28 '70

Growth in North Atlantic traffic and service, year 1969 over 1968; tables. Aviation W 92:39 Mr 30 '70

Growth trends; U.S. airlines passenger traffic, passenger revenues; tables. Aviation W 92:157 Mr 9 '70

Mainland-Hawaii market participation; tables. Aviation W 92:46 My 11; 93:33 O 12; 30 N 9; 45 D 7; 34 D 14 '70; 94:27 Ja 11 '71

North Atlantic air passengers, load factors, first six months of 1970; tables. Aviation W 93:38-9 O 5 '70

North Atlantic air passengers, load factors, year 1969; tables. Aviation W 92:40-1 Mr 30 '70

Passenger boardings by U.S. carriers; table. Aviation W 93:35 O 12; 41 N 9 '70

Paying for jumbo. il Time 96:65 Ag 31 '70

Summary of U.S. airline Pacific operations; table. Aviation W 93:34 N 30 '70

Trunkline load factors; tables. Aviation W 92:28 Mr 16; 29 Ap 13; 30 My 18; 260 Je 22; 93:23 Jl 23; 21 Ag 17; 31 N 16; 33 D 7 '70; 94:27 Ja 4 '71

Trunkline on time performance; tables. Aviation W 92:27 Mr 30; 33 My 4; 27 Je 1; 93:30 Jl 6; 28 Jl 27; 30 S 7; 36+ O 19; 36 N 16; 39 D '70; 94:28 Ja 11 '71

Turbojet/turbofan aircraft 1969 operating factors, all services; tables. Aviation W 92:44-5 Mr 23 '70

Turbojet/turbofan aircraft 1969 traffic and load factors in scheduled service; tables. Aviation W 92:42-3 Mr 23 '70

Turboprop aircraft operations and traffic for year 1969; tables. Aviation W 92:56-7 Ap 6 '70

Turboprop load factors; table. Aviation W 93:39 N 2 '70

Two/three-engine turbojet/fan load factors; table. Aviation W 93:40 S 28 '70

U.S. airline mail and cargo carried, twelve months ending June 30, 1970; table. Aviation W 93:54 O 26 '70

U.S. airline operations and traffic, year 1969; tables. Aviation W 92:38-9 Mr 2 '70

U.S. airline scheduled service load factors; table. Aviation W 93:26 Ag 31 '70

U.S. airline scheduled service traffic growth, first six months 1970 over 1969; table. Aviation W 93:37 Ag 31 '70

U.S. domestic trunk traffic. il Aviation W 93: 23 Ag 24 '70

U.S.-North Atlantic passenger traffic; tables. Aviation W 92:37 Je 1; 40 Je 8; 93:45 Jl 13; 23 Ag 3; 34 S 21; 57 N 16; 30 D 14 '70

Taxation

Advance payment tax studied. Aviation W 92:28 Mr 30 '70

Airport/airways bill tax features draw domestic airline opposition. Aviation W 92:28 F 9 '70

See also
Air travel—Taxation

Terminals

See Terminals

Tickets

See also
Airlines—Reservation systems

Traffic

Airline curbs boost load factor. L. Doty. Aviation W 93:21-2 Ag 17 '70

Airline traffic slump extends into September. Aviation W 93:26 O 12 '70

American expects meager traffic growth. il Aviation W 93:28 D 21 '70

Atlantic traffic spurting toward record. R. S. Kahn. il Aviation W 92:31-2 My 18 '70

CAB studies load factor fares standard. Aviation W 93:30 D 14 '70

AIRLINES—Traffic—*Continued*

CAB unit favors load factor standards. H. D. Watkins. Aviation W 93:28-30 Jl 27 '70

Competition slows National traffic return. il Aviation W 93:35+ Ag 17 '70

Eastern seeks to exploit stronger markets. R. S. Kahn. Aviation W 92:25-6 F 16 '70

Economy muddies 1970 traffic outlook. W. H. Gregory. il Aviation W 92:159+ Mr 9 '70

Expo 70 sparks Pacific traffic. Aviation W 93:22-3 Ag 31 '70

Extended peak foreseen on Atlantic. R. S. Kahn. Aviation W 93:22-3 Ag 3 '70

Fiscal woes brake capacity gains. H. D. Watkins. Aviation W 92:33-4 My 11 '70

Florida, Caribbean traffic rises. R. S. Kahn. Aviation W 92:28-9 Ap 13 '70

Hawaii market tests airline policies. H. D. Watkins. il Aviation W 92:31-4 Ap 6 '70

Initial October traffic results extend slump. Aviation W 93:27 N 9 '70

Labor day traffic extends slump. Aviation W 93:25 S 14 '70

Local growth benefits Pacific Southwest. W. S. Hieronymus. il Aviation W 92:36-7 My 11 '70

May traffic disappoints major trunks. H. D. Watkins. Aviation W 92:31-3 Je 8 '70

Modest traffic upturn foreseen. H. D. Watkins. Aviation W 93:26-7 D 21 '70

747 draws high passenger loads. R. G. O'Lone. il Aviation W 92:27-9 My 18 '70

Three trunks join in capacity cut: American, Trans World and United. L. Doty. il Aviation W 93:22-3 S 7 '70

Traffic lag may spur new capacity cuts. Aviation W 93:27 D 14 '70

Traffic slump hits major trunks. J. P. Woolsey. Aviation W 93:25-6 Jl 27 '70

Trunk traffic rises 8.1 per cent during January. Aviation W 92:234 Mr 9 '70

Weak traffic clouds fare impact. H. D. Watkins. Aviation W 93:22-3 N 30 '70

Weather, absent controllers cut Easter holiday air travel. R. S. Kahn. Aviation W 92:35 Ap 6 '70

See also
Alaska airlines

Alaska

Asia, Southeastern

Asian airline prepares for world routes; Malaysia-Singapore airlines. C. Brownlow. il Aviation W 92:43+ Ap 6 '70

Singapore tourist drive keyed to airline. C. Brownlow. Aviation W 92:32 Ap 13 '70

Australia

Australian carriers pick advanced 727. R. G. O'Lone. Aviation W 93:29 D 14 '70

Austria

Austrian airlines to re-equip. il Aviation W 92:36 Ja 26 '70

Vienna waltz; Austrian airlines planning partnership with Swissair. Time 96:80+ O 12 '70

Bahama Islands

Bahamas airways schedules daily New York-Nassau service. Aviation W 93:32 Jl 6 '70

Bahamas airways suspends operations. Aviation W 93:34 O 19 '70

Chile

Chile expected to ask Cuba route. L. Doty. il Aviation W 93:26-7 D 7 '70

Czechoslovakia

Czech jet buy tied to Soviet pressure. D. E. Fink. il Aviation W 93:30-1 S 28 '70

Denmark

Pastor's hobby; Sterling airways. il pors Newsweek 76:69 S 21 '70

Europe

Europe plans reservations net for 1972. R. F. Coburn. Aviation W 92:63 Ja 26 '70

Europe, Eastern

All-salami airlines. il Time 95:90-1 My 4 '70

Fiji

Tourism development shapes Fiji airways' regional role. W. H. Gregory. il Aviation W 93:38-9+ D 21 '70

France

Air inter aims to lure short-haul traffic. R. F. Coburn. il Aviation W 92:33 F 23 '70

Sporting outing; Air France European tours. il Travel 134:16 N '70

Germany (Federal Republic)

Budget airline takes on Lufthansa; Atlantis. Bsns W p44 Je 6 '70

Lufthansa's cargo marketing emphasizes U.S.-German traffic. Aviation W 93:36 N 16 '70

Great Britain

See also
British European airways corporation
British overseas airways corporation

Routes

BOAC ordered to give certain routes to proposed new carrier. Aviation W 93:32 Ag 10 '70

BOAC route transfers fought. Aviation W 93:31 N 30 '70

Britain creates a private airline; Caledonian/BUA. il Bsns W p34 Ja 9 '71

Hawaii

Hawaii merger plan poses monopoly vs. subsidy issue; proposed merger of Hawaiian and Aloha airlines. R. G. O'Lone. Aviation W 92:32 Ja 26 '70

Hawaiian carriers urged to agree on plan for restricting schedules. il Aviation W 92:33 Je 29 '70

Iceland

Hippie carrier. il Time 96:61 Ag 17 '70

India

Indian airlines to order 737s to fly on high-density routes. Aviation W 92:36 Mr 16 '70

Iran

Iran air seeking East-West gateway role. E. H. Kolcum. il Aviation W 93:33-4 D 14 '70

Israel

El Al growth surges despite Arab threats. E. H. Kolcum. il Aviation W 92:34-5 Je 15 '70

Loyal to El Al. Newsweek 75:68 Je 29 '70

Italy

Italians, Lebanese seek to identify missile that hit Alitalia DC-8. E. H. Kolcum. Aviation W 93:20 Jl 6 '70

Japan

Crane that lays the golden eggs; Japan air lines. il Forbes 106:20-1 Ag 15 '70

JAL establishes Japan as air hub. L. Doty. il Aviation W 92:27+ Ap 20 '70

Japanese carriers study giant jets. Aviation W 93:32 S 28 '70

Japanese gardens on a jumbo jet. il House & Gard 138:94 Ag '70

Siberian route offers few navaids. L. Doty. il Aviation W 92:24-6 Ap 13 '70

New Zealand

Air New Zealand studies wide-body jets. B. Miller. il Aviation W 93:26-7 Jl 20 '70

Puerto Rico

Eastern to acquire Caribair. Aviation W 93:25 N 2 '70

Russia

Aeroflot Japan service reflects pooling. D. C. Winston. il Aviation W 92:26-7 Ap 13 '70

Dreadful first for Aeroflot. Time 96:42 O 26 '70

Flight to Trabzon; hijacking against Aeroflot. Newsweek 76:42 O 26 '70

New chief of Aeroflot sets efficiency drive. Aviation W 93:24 S 7 '70

Scandinavia

See also
Scandinavian airlines system

Switzerland

Swissair expects profits to continue despite pinch. R. F. Coburn. il Aviation W 93:57-8 Jl 20 '70

Vienna waltz; Austrian airlines planning partnership with Swissair. Time 96:80+ O 12 '70

United States

Adversity perils competitive goals. L. Doty. Aviation W 93:25-6 N 23 '70

Airline issues. Aviation W 93:11 D 7; 11 D 21 '70

Airlines. il Forbes 105:24-6+ Je 1 '70

Airlines are too bearish; interview, ed. by G. R. Rosen. S. D. Browne. por Duns 95:10-11+ Mr '70

Airlines are urged to study markets. Aviation W 93:28 O 12 '70

AIRLINES—United States—*Continued*

Matchmaking aloft. Time 97:72 Ja 18 '71
Three trunks join in capacity cut: American, Trans World and United. L. Doty. il Aviation W 93:22-3 S 7 '70
See also
Aeronautics, Commercial—United States
Air transport association of America
Collective bargaining—Airlines
Strikes—United States—Airlines
also names of airlines, e.g. Eastern airlines

Routes

Airline secret gets hit by flak; agreement to cut competing routes. il Bsns W p74 S 26 '70
American plans increases in Caribbean flights, seats. Aviation W 94:26-7 Ja 11 '71
Bruising battle ranges for Hawaii market. H. D. Watkins. Aviation W 92:34-6 Ap 13 '70
Competition slows National traffic return. il Aviation W 93:35+ Ag 17 '70
Five carriers awarded rights in CAB's Omaha case decision. Aviation W 93:37 Jl 20 '70
Hawaii market tests airline policies. H. D. Watkins. il Aviation W 92:31-4 Ap 6 '70
High cost of competition. Time 96:82 O 12 '70
See also
Local service airlines—Routes

Virgin Islands

Boats with wings: Antilles air boats, inc. il Mech Illus 66:106-7 D '70
AIRLINES, Supplemental. See Airlines—Non-scheduled operations
AIRPLANE accident investigation. See Aviation—Accident investigation
AIRPLANE batteries. See Storage batteries
AIRPLANE cabins

Airlines offering 747 coach lounges. Aviation W 93:33 N 16 '70
Cabin modifications proposed for 747. N. S. Himmel. il Aviation W 93:34-5+ Ag 24 '70
L-1011 offers lower deck innovations. il Aviation W 93:36-7 N 2 '70
Modular van studied to carry passengers in cargo aircraft. il Aviation W p92:30 F 16 '70
Pods for passengers; interchangeable capsules serving as departure lounge at the airport and passenger van in the aircraft. F. K. Coffee. il Mech Illus 66:68-9+ N '70
Profitability rise sought for 747. R. G. O'Lone. il Aviation W 92:24-6 Mr 16 '70
747 rear lounge opposed by TWA. Aviation W 92:33 Je 8 '70

Air conditioning

See Airplanes—Air conditioning

Decoration

See Airplane decoration

Pressurization

See Airplanes—Pressurization
AIRPLANE carriers. See Aircraft carriers
AIRPLANE crews

737 flight crew ruling could have broader applications. Aviation W 92:38 Ap 6 '70

Training

American seeks training flight reductions. J. P. Woolsey. il Aviation W 93:41+ Jl 13 '70
AIRPLANE decoration

Luxury marks Playboy enterprises DC-9. il Aviation W 92:42-3 Mr 16 '70
AIRPLANE engines

Horse power; Rolls-Royce, Garrett and Franklin. J. Fricker; R. Blodget; J. Gilbert. il Flying 86:82-6+ Mr '70
See also
Gas turbines, Aircraft
Helicopter engines
Jet airplane engines

Cooling

Hot-weather flying. A. Trammell. il Flying 87:76-8 Ag '70

Design

Details of new Tiara engine line shown; high-speed, low-weight piston engine. il Aviation W 92:45 Mr 2 '70
Lower vibration, noise expected from high-speed piston engines. E. J. Bulban. Aviation W 92:23-4 F 23 '70
Sound of the seventies? Continental Tiara engine. S. Wilkinson. il Flying 86:70-3 My '70

Exhaust

How the jets kicked the smoking habit. M. Schultz. il Pop Mech 134:104-5+ Jl '70
See also
Jet airplane engines—Exhaust

Fuel

See also
Gas turbines, Aircraft—Fuel

Lubrication

Check your oil? spectrometric oil analysis. R. Blodget. Flying 87:79-80 Jl '70

Manufacturing

Specialization marks engine consortiums. E. H. Kolcum. il Aviation W 93:69-70+ S 7 '70

Specifications

U.S. reciprocating engines; tables (cont) Aviation W 92:143-4 Mr 9 '70

Throttle

Rich, lean or just right? P. Garrison. Flying 87:82-3 Jl '70
AIRPLANE fares. See Airlines—Fares
AIRPLANE hangars. See Hangars
AIRPLANE hijacking

Act of patriotism; hijacking of Olympic airways' plane by Arab terrorists. il Time 96:19-20 Ag 3 '70
Aerial piracy: an international crime. D. Lawrence. U S News 69:116 S 21 '70
Airway war escalates; with editorial comment. il Bsns W p21-2, 184 S 12 '70
Arab guerrillas adopt air piracy as tactic. il Aviation W 93:33+ S 14 '70
Chaos in the sky; Palestinian guerrillas strike at the big jets; with report of earlier hijacking by L. Khaled. il Life 69:30-7 S 18 '70
Dilemma of the airlines. il Newsweek 75:33-4+ Mr 9 '70
Drama on the desert: the week of the hostages. il Time 96:18-20+ S 21 '70
Dreadful first for Aeroflot. Time 96:42 O 26 '70
Flight to Trabzon; hijacking against Aeroflot. il Newsweek 76:42 O 26 '70
Fly me to Pyongyang; Japan air lines 727. il Newsweek 75:40+ Ap 13 '70
Forcible diversion of civil aircraft in flight. UN Mo Chron 7:173-4 Ja '70
Frustrating case of TWA flight 741. il Bsns W p34+ O 10 '70
Grounding the hijackers. Cato. Nat R 22:936 S 8 '70
Higher appeal; TWA flight 486, Phoenix, Ariz. to Washington, D.C. il por Newsweek 75:32 Je 15 '70
Hijack policy reflects conservative view. H. J. Coleman. Aviation W 92:43+ Ap 13 '70
Hijack war; Palestinian terrorists hijack four airliners; with report by L. Jenkins. il Newsweek 76:20-8 S 21 '70
Hijacker evades detection system. Aviation W 92:27 F 23 '70
Hijacking impact swells airline problems. H. D. Watkins. Aviation W 93:28-9 S 21 '70
Hijacking of commercial aircraft; Security council calls for legal steps; with text of resolution. UN Mo Chron 7:7-8 O '70
Hostages for hijackers? Russian, Turkish and U.S. involvement. Newsweek 76:37 N 9 '70
I'd rather be hijacked; congressional statements. H. H. Vinnedge. il New Repub 163:17-19 N 28 '70
In Arab hands: thirty-eight U.S. hostages. il U S News 69:21 S 28 '70
Japanese 727 hijacking may prod Asians to stiffen air piracy laws. L. Doty. Aviation W 92:38 Ap 6 '70
Murder in the sky; Eastern airlines DC-9. il Newsweek 75:23 Mr 30 '70
Murder on the airlines. R. Hotz. Aviation W 92:9 Mr 23 '70
No one danced in the aisle; Olympic airways Boeing 727. il Newsweek 76:27 Ag 3 '70
$100 million skyjack; TWA flight 486. Phoenix, Ariz. to Washington, D.C. il por Time 95:25 Je 15 '70
Ordeal for the innocent; story of hijack victims; Arab hijackers. il U S News 69:20-1 S 21 '70
Pictures on board a hijacked plane. R. Buchanan. il por Life 68:30-1 Je 19 '70
President acts on ICAO resolution to deter aircraft hijacking; letter, October 13, 1970. R. M. Nixon. Dept State Bul 63:541 N 2 '70
Profile of a skyjacker; psychiatric study findings of D. Hubbard. il por Newsweek 76:69 Ag 24 '70
Relations of U.S. airlines altered. H. D. Watkins. Aviation W 93:23-4 S 28 '70

AIRPLANE hijacking—*Continued*

Representatives of thirteen nations end talks on aircraft hijacking; text of joint communique; December 19, 1969. Dept State Bul 62:31 Ja 12 '70

Rising terrorism in the airlanes; conference to consider measures to deter. il U S News 68:10 Mr 9 '70

Samurai skyjackers. il Time 95:30+ Ap 13 '70

Secretary-General's press conference; September 10, 1970. Thant. UN Mo Chron 7:30-9 O '70

Stopping skyjackers: drive to get a better U.S. system. il U S News 68:31-2 Je 15 '70

U.S. and the skyjackers: where power is vulnerable; act of Arab extremists. il Time 96:12-13 S 21 '70

U.S., Cuba cooperate closely on hijackers. Aviation W 93:28 N 23 '70

U.S. sees anti-hijacking support in Soviets' membership in ICAO. J. P. Woolsey. Aviation W 93:26 N 23 '70

Where are they now? 1953 incident involving Czech pilot M. J. Slovak. il pors Newsweek 76:12 O 26 '70

White House drive gains to unify international laws on air piracy; with editorial comment. L. Doty. Aviation W 93:9, 25 S 28 '70

Why not frisk? Nation 210:741 Je 22 '70

Caricatures and cartoons

Hijack! cartoons. J. Noonan. Cath World 212:211-12 Ja '71

Insurance

See Airlines—Insurance

Prevention

Actions to deal with the menace of air piracy; statements, with text of resolution and letter to ICAO. R. M. Nixon; C. W. Yost; C. F. Butler Dept State Bul 63:341-3 S 28 '70

Air guards to ride shotgun. il Sr Schol 97:9-10 S 28 '70

Airlines demand stiffer hijack penalties. Aviation W 93:32 Jl 6 '70

Airlines vs. hijackers. il Newsweek 76:76-8 O 26 '70

Anti-hijacking drive gains added impetus. L. Doty. Aviation W 93:27 O 19 '70

Anti-hijacking plans augmented. Aviation W 93:32 N 9 '70

Anti-hijacking proposals proliferate. L. Doty. il Aviation W 93:26-7 S 21 '70

Armed courier thwarts TWA hijack attempt. Aviation W 93:30 S 21 '70

As the war against skyjackers steps up. il U S News 69:15-16 D 28 '70

Cost of anti-hijacking measures to be borne mainly by airlines. J. P. Woolsey. Aviation W 93:29 N 9 '70

Crisis and aftermath. Nation 211:226 S 21 '70

Davis to lead hijacking prevention drive. J. P. Woolsey. Aviation W 93:26 S 28 '70

Eastern accelerates anti-hijack preboarding screening program. Aviation W 92:34 My 4 '70

Eastern spurs hijacking drive. Aviation W 93:27 N 23 '70

How science will foil the skyjackers. P. Wahl. il Pop Sci 197:58-60+ N '70

How the airlines hope to stop the hijackers. M. Schultz. il Pop Mech 133:83-5 My '70

How to end skyjacking; interview. C. C. Tillinghast, jr. il pors U S News 69:48-52 O 12 '70

How to stop air piracy. il Newsweek 76:28-9 S 21 '70

How to stop hijacking. Nat R 22:985-6 S 22 '70

IATA chief spurs anti-hijack program. E. H. Kolcum. il Aviation W 93:32-3 D 7 '70

IATA, official of Munich airport debate over anti-hijacking roles. Aviation W 93:29 N 16 '70

Military men riding as airliner guards. Aviation W 93:28 O 12 '70

Outlook: a sharp decline in hijackings; interview. B. O. Davis. por U S News 69:17 D 28 '70

President Nixon receives declaration by ICAO against aircraft hijacking; exchange of letters. R. M. Nixon; W. Binaghi. Dept State Bul 63:302-3 S 14 '70

Prevention of hijacking switches from passive to active measures. J. P. Woolsey. Aviation W 93:29-30 S 21 '70

Searching for weapons. Sci N 98:271 S 26 '70

Sky marshal program graduates first class. Aviation W 94:22 Ja 4 '71

Stiffer measures rejected in Nixon hijacking plans; with editorial comment. L. Doty. Aviation W 93:9, 30-1 O 5 '70

Strong anti-hijack treaty signed; may be implemented by mid-year. Aviation W 94:26 Ja 4 '71

Terror attacks on air travel: what can be done. il U S News 69:17-19 S 21 '70

Traveler finds his voice; proposals of ASTA. H. Sutton. Sat R 54:14 Ja 2 '71

United Nations calls for measures against aircraft hijacking; statement, December 12, 1969; with text of resolution. D. B. Fascell. Dept State Bul 62:69-71 Ja 19 '70

United States proposal on unlawful seizure of aircraft for blackmail purposes adopted by ICAO council; statement with texts of U.S. resolutions, October 1, 1970. J. A. Volpe. Dept State Bul 63:449-53 O 1 '70

Walking the plank at 30,000 feet. H. Sutton. il Sat R 54:30-2+ Ja 2 '71

What to do about the skyjackers? Time 96:25 S 21 '70

When armed guards ride your plane. il U S News 69:22-3 S 28 '70

White House expands hijack talks. L. Doty. Aviation W 93:28-9 N 16 '70

AIRPLANE industry and trade

Foreign accent. J. Fricker. See issues of Flying

See also

Airplanes—Manufacture

Helicopter industry and trade

Directories

Marketing directory section. Aviation W 93:23+ D 28 '70

Finance

Business aircraft sales slump worsens. C. E. Schneider. il Aviation W 92:18-19 Je 1 '70

General aviation deliveries, billings sag. C. E. Schneider. Aviation W 93:18 Jl 27 '70

Light aircraft in a tailspin. il Bsns W p30-1 Mr 21 '70

Troubled aircraft industry: is the worst over? il U S News 69:68-9 D 7 '70

International aspects

Special report: European joint projects. il Aviation W 93:37-9+ S 7 '70

Specialization marks engine consortiums. E. H. Kolcum. il Aviation W 93:69-70+ S 7 '70

Tight budgets spur U.S.-U.K. collaboration. C. Brownlow. il Aviation W 93:83+ S 7 '70

Statistics

U.S. business & utility aircraft shipments; tables. See occasional issues of Aviation week & space technology

Brazil

Brazil pushes five major projects. D. A. Brown. il Aviation W 94:62-3+ Ja 11 '71

Buying a brand-new aircraft industry. il Bsns W p46-7 Mr 14 '70

Czechoslovakia

Czech industry turns eastward. D. E. Fink. il Aviation W 93:46-7+ O 5 '70

Europe, Western

A-300B airbus picks up momentum. H. J. Coleman. il Aviation W 93:28-31 O 19 '70

Europe aims at advanced jets. il Aviation W 92:200 Mr 9 '70

Europe expects aircraft sales dip. R. F. Coburn. Aviation W 92:74+ My 25 '70

Special report: European joint projects. il Aviation W 93:37-9+ S 7 '70

France

Potential U.S. market for Mercure spurs facilities expansion plan. D. E. Fink. Aviation W 92:42+ Je 8 '70

Spanish-Libyan Mirage sale bolsters French industry. Aviation W 92:23-4 Ja 19 '70

Great Britain

Airbus battle flares at Farnborough. H. J. Coleman. il Aviation W 93:14-17 S 14 '70

British invade U.S. subcontract market. il Aviation W 93:92-3 S 7 '70

Foreign accent. J. Fricker. il Flying 86:100-1 Je '70

See also

Britten-Norman, ltd.

Handley Page aircraft, ltd.

Rolls-Royce, ltd.

Israel

Israelis begin major aircraft effort; Israel aircraft industries. E. H. Kolcum. Aviation W 92:53-4 Je 1 '70

AIRPLANE industry and trade—*Continued*

Japan

Japan seeks light aircraft sales. il Aviation W 92:64-6 Mr 30 '70
Japanese aircraft revival pushed. C. Brownlow. il Aviation W 92:65-7 Ja 26 '70
New variants of PS-1 considered. C. Brownlow. il Aviation W 92:52-3+ Mr 16 '70

Netherlands

Fokker F-28 transport marketing strategy based on small orders and varied models. H. J. Coleman. il Aviation W 92:94-5+ Ap 27 '70

Rumania

Rumania developing own designs. H. J. Coleman. il Aviation W 92:39-41 Je 29 '70

Switzerland

New piston versions of Porter planned; Pilatus. il Aviation W 92:89+ My 25 '70
Swiss aircraft industry declining. R. F. Coburn. Aviation W 92:51+ Je 29 '70

United States

Economy paces outlook for jets; business jet manufacturers. D. A. Brown. il Aviation W 92:185-7+ Mr 9 '70
Improvement in market foreseen by business aircraft companies. Aviation W 93:20 S 7 '70
Manufacturers foresee no sales growth. il Aviation W 93:16 D 28 '70
Mergers, markets shaping strategies for next decade. E. J. Bulban. il Aviation W 92:193-5+ Mr 9 '70
Mitsubishi made in the U.S. il Bsns W p43 Je 6 '70
1971 business flying projections decline. C. E. Schneider. Aviation W 93:22-3 D 21 '70
Optimism returning for business flying. Aviation W 93:14-16 S 28 '70
Withering aircraft industry. D. Cordtz. il Fortune 82:114-17+ S '70
See also
Collective bargaining—Airplane industry
Helicopter industry and trade—United States
also names of airplane manufacturing companies, e.g. Northrop corporation

AIRPLANE models

Competitions

World's biggest little airplane meet; Academy of model aeronautics' national competition. H. G. McEntee. il Pop Sci 197:108-9 Jl '70

Engines

Now: a 12.6-ounce Wankel engine. H. G. McEntee. il Pop Sci 197:12 D '70

Manufacture

New method used for SST models. R. G. O'Lone. il Aviation W 92:55-6 Ap 13 '70
AIRPLANE ownership. See Airplanes, Private
AIRPLANE parts

Manufacture

See also
Alliance ventures, inc.
AIRPLANE propellers
Back to basics. P. Garrison. Flying 86:70-2 F '70
End that bites. J. M. Lowery. il Flying 86:84-5 F '70
P-38 from Piper? B. Kocivar. il Pop Mech 133:87-9+ My '70
AIRPLANE racing
Foreign accent: Great Australian air race. J. Fricker. il Flying 86:30-1+ Mr '70
Ladies' day at the races: All women's international air race. M. Kvaka. il Flying 87:62-3 Ag '70
We fly an NPA proficiency race, and lose. P. Garrison. il Flying 86:42-4+ My '70
AIRPLANE seats. See Airplanes—Seats
AIRPLANE shelters. See Hangars
AIRPLANE taxi service. See Air taxi service
AIRPLANE tires. See Tires, Airplane
AIRPLANE transportation of animals. See Animals—Transportation
AIRPLANE travel. See Air travel
AIRPLANE wakes. See Atmospheric turbulence
AIRPLANE wings
Augmentor wing flight tests set. W. S. Hieronymus. il Aviation W 94:48+ Ja 4 '71
F-14A uses large titanium wing section. il Aviation W 93:51 Ag 17 '70

Wing pivot fitting for F-111F will have boron-epoxy doubler. Aviation W 93:17 D 7 '70
Wing: where the action is. P. Garrison. il Flying 88:44-8 Ja '71
See also
Airfoils
Flaps, Airplane

AIRPLANES
Back to basics. P. Garrison. il Flying 86:62-3 Ja; 70-2 F; 58-9 Ap '70
See also
Salvage (airplanes)
Seaplanes

Air conditioning

Environmental control system market sought. il Aviation W 92:62 F 2 '70

Anchorage

See Airplanes—Mooring

Cabins

See Airplane cabins

Certification

See Airplanes—Standards

Chartering

CAB to expand its investigations to East coast charter operators. Aviation W 93:39 Mr 30 '70
CAB unit hits affinity charter practices. J. P. Woolsey. Aviation W 92:38 F 2 '70; Reply. M. G. Manak. 92:66 Mr 2 '70
Germany plans to restrict U.S. affinity unit charters. Aviation W 92:23-4 F 16 '70
If you are planning a charter flight. il U S News 68:60-2 Mr 9 '70
Protests spur CAB to delay issue of eased military charter rules. D. C. Winston. Aviation W 92:24 F 16 '70
See also
Airlines—Non-scheduled operations

Collectors and collecting

Foreign accent; Shuttleworth collection. J. Fricker. il Flying 87:18-19 N '70
Resurrection of a flivver. R. Hegge. il Mech Illus 66:65 Ja '70
World war I aircraft fly again in Rhinebeck's rickety rendezvous. H. Arden. il por Nat Geog 138:578-87 O '70

Control

Pro's nest; nosewheel steering. T. H. Block. Flying 87:20 Ag '70
See also
Airplanes—Stability and stabilizers
Airplanes, Military—Control
Automatic pilot (airplanes)

Cooling

See Airplanes—Air conditioning

Cost of operation

Temporary cost saving measures could have long-term effect; corporate flight departments. Aviation W 93:74-5 S 21 '70

Decoration

See Airplane decoration

Design

Powerplant, airfoil research emphasized. il Aviation W 93:13-14 D 28 '70
See also
Airplane cabins
Airplanes, Freight—Design
Airplanes, Light—Design
Airplanes, Military—Design

Electronic equipment

Airlines consider new avionics concept. il Aviation W 92:66 Mr 16 '70
Altitude alerter production pushed. K. J. Stein. il Aviation W 93:52-3+ Jl 27 '70
Avionics combinations to cut user cost. K. J. Stein. il Aviation W 93:71-2 S 21 '70
New avionics products. See occasional issues of Aviation week & space technology
See also
Airplanes—Safety devices and measures
Automatic pilot (airplanes)
Computers—Aeronautic use
Navigation, Aerial—Aids and devices

Engines

See Airplane engines

Environmental control

See Airplanes—Air conditioning

AIRPLANES—*Continued*

Equipment
Product news (cont of) New products. See issues of Flying
See also
Airplanes, Freight—Equipment
Oxygen apparatus

Escape devices
Safe but stranded after a bomb scare in midair. il Life 69:48-9 O 2 '70
They'll fly ejection seats to safety. P. Wahl. il Pop Sci 196:60-1 Ap '70

Exhibitions
See Aviation—Exhibitions

Fastenings
See Fastenings

Fires and fire protection
Apollo flameproofing seen aiding aircraft. Aviation W 92:67 Mr 16 '70

Flaps
See Flaps, Airplane

History
See Aeronautics—History

Ice protection
Do it yourself. A. Trammell. Flying 86:42 Ja '70
How to handle icing. R. L. Collins; A. Trammell. Flying 87:65-8+ D '70

Inspection
Five minutes for safety. C. L. Cook. Flying 86:84-5 Ja '70
See also
Airplanes, Military—Inspection

Instrument boards
On the gauges. S. Wilkinson. Flying 87:32 D '70
See also
Airplanes, Supersonic—Instrument boards

Instrument flying
See Aviation—Instrument flying

Landing
ALPA committee scores FAA all-weather landing program. B. M. Elson. Aviation W 93:27 Jl 27 '70
Down with bounce drill. R. Blodget. il Flying 86:14-15 Ja '70
Follow me through; glide-path control. R. Blodget. il Flying 87:18-19 Ag; 24-5 S '70
Landing aids to triple under ten-year plan. P. J. Klass. Aviation W 92:29 Mr 2 '70
Microwave ILS concepts develop. P. J. Klass. Aviation W 92:119-20 Ap 27 '70
Microwave landing study complete. P. J. Klass. il Aviation W 93:48-9+ O 19 '70
Multiple-antenna landing system seen upgrading touchdown aid. Aviation W 92:58-9 Ap 20 '70
Pro's nest; IFR approaches. T. H. Block. Flying 87:10 N '70
Safer flying: the plans under way; instrument-landing systems. il U S News 69:36 N 30 '70
See also
Airplanes, Jet—Landing

Landing gear
Down and locked? C. Knight. il Flying 88:50-1 Ja '71
Fourth Musketeer; new outward-retracting wheels. R. C. Collins. il Flying 86:42-7 Mr '70
Wheel-less plane lands on a cushion of air. P. Wahl. il Pop Sci 196:122 Je '70

Leasing and renting
Jet-propelled bankers. il Forbes 106:19 Ag 15 '70

Maintenance and repair
Pan Am devises new maintenance control. L. Doty. il Aviation W 92:56-8 Mr 23 '70
Post-strike service provides challenges; National airlines maintenance program. H. D. Watkins. il Aviation W 93:37+ Ag 10 '70
See also
Airplanes, Used—Maintenance and repair

Manufacture
Machine research aims at shaving costs. E. J. Bulban. il Aviation W 92:232-9+ Je 22 '70
See also
Airplanes, Jet—Manufacture

Marketing
A-300B marketing team broadens effort. il Aviation W 93:45+ S 7 '70
Citation marketing plans unveiling. Aviation W 93:78 Ag 24 '70
Germans push for settlement of airbus marketing dispute. Aviation W 93:28 D 14 '70
Lockheed cautious on JetStars. D. A. Brown. Aviation W 93:88 N 16 '70
Marketing emphasized by Aerostar. E. J. Bulban. Aviation W 93:73 O 12 '70

Materials
See also
Airplanes, Light—Materials
Airplanes, Military—Materials

Mooring
Stakeout. A. Trammell. il Flying 86:18-19 Ap '70

Noise
NASA's quiet engine program focuses antinoise effort. il Aviation W 92:88-9 Je 22 '70
Why life near airports will get quieter. il Bsns W p44-5 F 7 '70
See also
Airports—Noise
Noise control

Passenger load
United move to five-abreast seats intensifies dispute in fare case. Aviation W 93:23 S 7 '70

Passenger service
See Airlines—Passenger service

Piloting
Airman's etiquette. T. H. Block. Flying 87:22-3 Jl '70
How to conquer crosswinds. R. Blodget. il Flying 87:61-4+ D '70
I learned about flying from that. See issues of Flying
Those terrible downwind turns. P. Garrison. Flying 86:58-9 Ap '70
See also
Aviation—Instrument flying
Meteorology, Aeronautic

Pressurization
Solid oxygen. A. Trammell. il Flying 87:78-9 Jl '70

Prices
New King air model has reduced price. Aviation W 93:77 O 12 '70
See also
Airplanes, Used—Prices

Propellers
See Airplane propellers

Protection against theft
Security alarm developed for parked aircraft. Aviation W 93:89 N 16 '70

Radar equipment
See also
Radar meteorology

Radio equipment
King KR-85 digital-tuned ADF. il Flying 86:15+ F '70

Safety devices and measures
Cessna 1971 models add safety features. Aviation W 93:77 O 12 '70
Electronic device will help pilots dodge midair collisions; EROS unit. R. L. Dilenschneider. il Pop Sci 196:24 My '70
How to end air collisions; Secant-B defensive piloting system. il Bsns W p 128+ Ap 11 '70
On top; Nader report on crashworthiness in light airplanes; with editorial comment. R. L. Collins. Flying 86:30-1, 36 Ap '70
Precision frequency device developed; collision avoidance system. Aviation W 92:21 Ap 6 '70
Small-plane CAS seems feasible. P. J. Klass. Aviation W 92:57-8 Ap 20 '70
See also
Airplanes—Escape devices
Airplanes—Ice protection
Altimeters
Oxygen apparatus

Seats
Hot war erupts over airline seats. Bsns W p88 O 31 '70
TWA seating plan suspended. Aviation W 92:29 Ja 19 '70
United move to five-abreast seats intensifies dispute in fare case. Aviation W 93:23 S 7 '70

AIRPLANES—*Continued*

Specifications

Leading international aircraft; tables (cont) Aviation W 92:116-20 Mr 9 '70
Leading turbine-powered business aircraft; tables (cont) Aviation W 2:130-1 Mr 9 '70
U.S. agricultural aircraft; tables (cont) Aviation W 92:124 Mr 9 '70
U.S. and Canadian STOL aircraft; tables (cont) Aviation W 92:124 Mr 9 '70
U.S. and Canadian VTOL aircraft; tables (cont) Aviation W 92:144 Mr 9 '70
U.S. business, personal and utility aircraft; tables (cont) Aviation W 92:132 Mr 9 '70
U.S. commercial transports; tables (cont) Aviation W 92:121 Mr 9 '70
U.S. military aircraft; tables (cont) Aviation W 92:101-2 Mr 9 '70
USSR military and civil aircraft; tables (cont) Aviation W 92:109 Mr 9 '70
See also
Airplanes—Standards

Speed

Wind, speed and range. D. Lowry. Flying 87:82-3 N '70
See also
Airplanes, Supersonic

Spinning

Spins. M. R. Bryan. Flying 86:56-7 Je '70

Stability and stabilizers

NASA studying vortex, slow flight areas; wingtip spoiler tests. R. G. O'Lone. il Aviation W 93:61+ S 21 '70
Stabilators. P. Garrison. Flying 86:62-3 Ja '70

Stalling

Why practice stalls? R. Blodget. il Flying 86:14-15+ Mr '70

Standards

FAA asks transport certification on all new ten passenger aircraft. C. E. Schneider. Aviation W 93:19 Jl 6 '70
Plan proposed to simplify exports; export certification. C. E. Schneider. il Aviation W 92:67-8 Mr 23 '70
See also
Airplanes, Jet—Standards
Airplanes, Military—Standards
Airplanes, Supersonic—Standards

Storage

See also
Hangars

Storm hazards

See Aviation—Storm hazards

Take-off

Thirty seconds over Toledo. R. C. Stanbery. Flying 87:80 Ag '70
Use clearance delivery, it's quicker; IFR departure clearance. W. Berkley. il Flying 88:81-2 Ja '71

Testing

See also
Airplanes, Military transport—Testing

Wings

See Airplane wings

AIRPLANES, Aerobatic
Aerobatic aircraft developed in France. il Aviation W 93:86-7 N 16 '70
Foreign accent; Victa Airtourer. J. Fricker. il Flying 86:26-7+ Ja '70
Fun-plane; Champion Citabria 7KCAB. A. Trammell. Flying 87:38-43 N '70
Great antique, the Great Lakes. J. Gilbert. il Flying 87:73-7+ Jl '70
Pilot report:
Saab MFI-15. J. Fricker. il Flying 87:78-82 D '70

AIRPLANES, Amphibious
Spectra, the ultimate amphibian? J. Holt. il Pop Sci 197:47 Ag '70
Water birds; Thurston teal and turboprop-goose. R. B. Weeghman and R. Blodget. il Flying 86:47-63 My '70

AIRPLANES, Business
Beech stagger wing; excerpt from Great planes. J. Gilbert. il Flying 87:68-9+ O '70
Foreign accent; Dassault and Hawker Siddeley minijet programs. J. Fricker. il Flying 86:90-1+ My '70
Hoover's aerobatics a key factor in Shrike sales increase. C. M. Plattner. il por Aviation W 92:40-4 Mr 2 '70
Merlins. A. Trammell. il Flying 87:78-81+ O '70
See also
Airplanes in business
Helicopters, Business

Cost of operation
See Airplanes—Cost of operation

Design

Aircraft growth tied to airport advances. E. J. Bulban. il Aviation W 93:55-7+ S 21 '70
Commodore jet tests to resume. il Aviation W 92:54-5 Je 15 '70
New era opening in aircraft design. C. E. Schneider. il Aviation W 92:249-50 Je 22 '70
Why does Cessna's jet go so slow? A. Trammell. il Flying 86:42-7 F '70

Marketing
See Airplanes—Marketing

Photographs

Merlin 4 designs details shown. Aviation W 93:72 O 12 '70

Specifications
See Airplanes—Specifications

Testing

Falcon F offers improved utility. C. E. Schneider. il Aviation W 93:64-6 N 9 '70
Falcon 10 completes initial flight tests. il Aviation 93:24 D 14 '70
Pilot report:
Cessna. R. L. Collins. il Flying 87:35-42 O '70
Interceptor 400. A. Trammell. il Flying 87:68-71 Ag '70
Learjet 24C. A. Trammell. il Flying 87:40-3 D '70
Pressurized Navajo. A. Trammell. il Flying 88:36-9 Ja '71
Sabreliner 60. A. Trammell. il Flying 86:66-72 Ap '70

AIRPLANES, Drone
LTV develops high-altitude recon drone. E. J. Bulban. il Aviation W 92:56-7+ F 2 '70
Remotely piloted aircraft studied. B. Miller. il Aviation W 92:14-15 Je 1 '70
Unmanned aircraft gain favor. B. Miller. il Aviation W 93:67-70+ N 16 '70
U.S. drones and target missiles; tables. Aviation W 92:111 Mr 9 '70
USAF widens unmanned aircraft effort. B. Miller. il Aviation W 93:46-7+ N 9 '70

AIRPLANES, Experimental
Amateur-built aircraft. D. M. Berk. il Consumer Bul 53:25-8 Ja '70
Experimental civilian aircraft; new field for NASA. Sci N 98:413 N 28 '70
Subsonic transport for 1980's. Sci N 98:478 D 26 '70
Variety of new research aircraft sought. il Aviation W 92:67-70 Je 22 '70

AIRPLANES, Freight

Design

Lockheed mass cargo system; suitable aircraft for plan studied. D. A. Brown. il Aviation W 92:32-4 Ja 19 '70

Equipment

Modular van studied to carry passengers in cargo aircraft. il Aviation W 92:30 F 16 '70

AIRPLANES, Hijacking of. See Airplane hijacking

AIRPLANES, Hypersonic. See Airplanes, Supersonic

AIRPLANES, Jet
Airbus is ready, but the airlines are not. il Bsns W p80-1 Jl 18 '70
American 747 records high load factors for first week. R. S. Kahn. Aviation W 92:26-8 Mr 16 '70
BOAC modifies Boeing 747s while its pilots boycott them. il Aviation W 93:26 Jl 13 '70
Can airways handle the giant jets? interview. J. H. Shaffer. il por U S News 69:38-42 Ag 10 '70
Germans face increasing M45H costs; Rolls-Royce/Snecma engine for the VFW 614. E. H. Kolcum. Aviation W 93:18 Ag 17 '70
Giant tri-jets are coming. B. Kocivar. il Pop Sci 197:50-2+ D '70
How the 747 came to fly; inaugural flight. il Bsns W p78-9 Ja 31 '70
Jumbo and the gremlins. il Time 95:65 F 2 '70
Jumbo beats the gremlins. il Time 96:68 Jl 13 '70
Jumbo jets: how they're doing. il U S News 68:44 Mr 16 '70
Jumbo jets: relief, or a new headache? Sr Schol 95:17 Ja 5 '70

AIRPLANES, Light—*Continued*
Materials
Resin in the sun; Windecker's plastic Eagle. A. Trammell. il Flying 86:36-41+ My '70

Prices
See Airplanes—Prices

Safety devices and measures
See Airplanes—Safety devices and measures

Specifications
See Airplanes—Specifications

Testing
Pilot report:
Aerostar 600. J. Gilbert. il Flying 87: 32-4 Ag '70
Beech's bigger Baron. A. Trammell. il Flying 86:48-54 Je '70
Bonanza F33A. R. L. Collins. il Flying 87: 34-9 D '70
Cessna Centurion. A. Trammell. il Flying 86:76-81+ Je '70
Cessna 150, 172 and Cardinal. R. L. Collins. il Flying 87:44-52 D '70
Cessna Super Skymaster. A. Trammell. il Flying 88:52-7+ Ja '71
Cherokee Arrow 200. S. Wilkinson. il Flying 86:48-52 F '70
New Cardinal. S. Wilkinson. il Flying 86:52-5+ Ja '70
New Lark. R. Blodget. il Flying 86:44-7 Ap '70
Six thousand miles by Cherokee 180E. J. Gilbert. il Flying 86:46-51+ Ja '70

AIRPLANES, Military
Early study of users aided F 5 program; supersonic fighter. W. S. Hieronymus. il Aviation W 92:46-7+ Mr 16 '70
Price, past experience with F-5 swung new international fighter. Aviation W 93:20 N 30 '70
See also
Airplanes, Drone
Airplanes, Restored
Airplanes, Vertical take-off and landing

Armaments
Spanish HA-200 weapons varied. il Aviation W 93:51 Jl 13 '70
See also
Guided missiles—Launching from airplanes

Control
Robot air force flutters its wings. il Bsns W p46 Ja 2 '71
Survivable controls gain emphasis. M. L. Yaffee. il Aviation W 92:40-3 F 2 '70
Tests of remotely piloted fighter likely. Aviation W 93:20-1 S 28 '70
To reduce risks and costs; remotely piloted vehicles. il Sci N 98:302 O 10 '70
Unmanned aircraft gain favor. B. Miller. il Aviation W 93:67-70+ N 16 '70

Cost
Cost, time doubts led to B-1 fund slash. D. C. Winston. Aviation W 93:20 Ag 10 '70

Design
B-1 design has forward fins. Aviation W 92: 53 My 4 '70
First A-4M flight tested; new avionics package lags. C. M. Plattner. il Aviation W 92: 105-7 Ap 27 '70
Hot new fighter for the navy. K. V. Brown. il Pop Mech 133:83-6+ Ja '70
LTV proposing modified F-8 for export. il Aviation W 92:85 Ap 6 '70
Milan production based on export market. il Aviation W 92:56-7 Mr 16 '70
MRCA moves into design phase; multi-role combat aircraft program. il Aviation W 93:37-9+ S 7 '70
Navy phasing A-7Es into operation. C. M. Plattner. il Aviation W 92:38-9+ F 16 '70

Electronic equipment
Battle intensifies for MRCA avionics. il Aviation W 93:77-8 S 7 '70
Competition for NRCA avionics stiffens. B. Miller. Aviation W 93:23 D 14 '70
F-15 avionics suppliers selection nears. P. J. Klass. Aviation W 92:22-3 Ja 19 '70
New gunsight concept evaluated; lead-computing optical gunsight. B. Miller. il Aviation W 93:40-1+ Ag 17 '70
USAF sets two-stage B-1 avionics system. P. J. Klass. Aviation W 92:23 Ja 26 '70

Inspection
Board seeks inspection method for F-111 operational aircraft. Aviation W 92:24 Ja 26 '70

Materials
F-14A uses large titanium wing section. il Aviation W 93:51 Ag 17 '70
Use of boron composite growing. il Aviation W 93:48-9 Ag 31 '70

Radar equipment
AWACS keyed to milestone plan. B. M. Elson. il Aviation W 93:65-6+ Ag 24 '70
Boeing wins AWACS award. il Aviation W 93:22 Jl 13 '70

Specifications
See Airplanes—Specifications

Standards
F-111 crash spurs tightening of standards. il Aviation W 92:59-61 Mr 23 '70
FAA spurns Nader unit request. C. E. Schneider. Aviation W 93:53-5 Ag 17 '70

Testing
Crash of F-14 delays testing by 4-6 weeks. il Aviation W 94:21-2 Ja 11 '71
F-111 is flexing its wings. il Bsns W p30 Ap 4 '70
Felled bird; the F-14. il Sci N 99:24 Ja 9 '71
Navy to quicken flight test pace. il Aviation W 93:69 O 12 '70

Wings
See Airplane wings

Europe, Western
Anglo-French Jaguar fighter enters production cycle. il Aviation W 93:54-5+ S 7 '70
German parliament asks MRCA cost data; engine change sought. Aviation W 92:19 F 16 '70
Germany's aerospace role to be determined in near future. E. H. Kolcum. il Aviation W 92:16-18 My 4 '70
Jaguar production starts with eighty ordered. il Aviation W 92:111-13 Ap 27 '70
MRCA consortium planning family of military aircraft. il Aviation W 93:13 S 14 '70
MRCA moves into design phase; multi-role combat aircraft program. il Aviation W 93:37-9+ S 7 '70
MRCA moves to prototype phase. Aviation W 93:15 Jl 20 '70
MRCA program officials rebut reports on problems of aircraft. Aviation W 92:21-2 F 23 '70
Take-off time for NATO's new fighter. Fortune 82:79-80 S '70

France
Atlantics perform major ASW tasks. D. E. Fink. il Aviation W 93:48-9+ Ag 10 '70
Milan production based on export market. il Aviation W 92:56-7 Mr 16 '70

Germany (Federal Republic)
Weapons shaped German MRCA choice. Aviation W 92:24 Je 1 '70

Great Britain
Harriers readied for NATO role. H. J. Coleman. il Aviation W 94:13-15 Ja 4 '71

Israel
Homemade jet for Israel; Super-Mirage. Time 96:21 N 9 '70
Israelis may refit Mirages with GE J79s. Aviation W 93:21 N 16 '70

Italy
Macchi sees wide market for MB.326K. R. F. Coburn. il Aviation W 93:69-70 S 14 '70

Netherlands
Dutch air force converts to NF-5. D. E. Fink. il Aviation W 93:46-7+ Ag 17 '70

Russia
USSR military and civil aircraft; tables (cont) Aviation W 92:109 Mr 9 '70

Sweden
Viggen recommended for air defense role. E. H. Kolcum. il Aviation W 93:53-4 D 21 '70

Switzerland
Swiss aircraft industry declining. R. F. Coburn. Aviation W 92:51+ Je 29 '70
Swiss delay on fighter clouds price. Aviation W 93:19 Ag 17 '70

AIRPLANES, Military—*Continued*
United States
Air force studies F-14 interceptor buy. il Aviation W 94:17-18 Ja 4 '71

America's deadly new bomber; B-1. H. M. Mason, jr. il Mech Illus 66:74-6+ O '70

AX flight evaluation set for mid-1972. C. Brownlow. il Aviation W 94:20-1 Ja 4 '71

Budget constraints, crash cloud F-111 production program future. il Aviation W 92:19 Ja 19 '70

Competitive prototype program planned for USAF AX aircraft. Aviation W 92:25 My 4 '70

F-15 deliveries tied to milestone concept. C. Brownlow. il Aviation W 93:20-1 S 14 '70

F-14 crash shakes Grumman. il Bsns W D 16 Ja 9 '71

Fighter pilot's fighter plane: F-15. K. Brown. il Pop Mech 134:73-7 D '70

Go ahead decision on new long-range bomber. il U S News 68:50 Je 15 '70

Major incentives offered for B-1. C. Brownlow. il Aviation W 92:12-13 Je 15 '70

Northrop fighter takes off again. il Bsns W p24 N 28 '70

One for the money: B-1 contract to North American Rockwell. Newsweek 75:83 Je 15 '70

Our new B-1 bomber; high, low, fast, and slow. K. Kocivar. il Pop Sci 197:86-7+ N '70

Partial modernization due for tactical air. il Aviation W 92:35-6 Mr 9 '70

Phantom Phantom jets. Nation 210:102 F 2 '70

Plane to help front-line GIs. il Bsns W p 113 Ap 25 '70

Senate report blasts procurement of F-111. D. C. Winston. il Aviation W 93:19-20 D 21 '70

Sharing the blackbird; use of YF-12A for research. J. Eberhart. il Sci N 97:204-5 F 21 '70

Shock waves of Lockheed's gamble. il Bsns W p 14-15 Ja 9 '71

TFX verdict; summary of report. Aviation W 94:7 Ja 4 '71

Thirty tons of deadly adaptability; the Phantom F-4. il Life 69:30-1 S 25 '70

AIRPLANES, Military transport
Advisory group suggests C-5A changes. Aviation W 92:259 Je 22 '70

Delivery stretch asked for C-5. Aviation W 92:20 F 16 '70

USAF readies C-5 squadron while continuing flight testing. Aviation W 93:69 O 12 '70

USAF reverting to original C-5A operational format. C. Brownlow. il Aviation W 93:15-16 Jl 6 '70

Testing
Air force/Lockheed C-5A undergoes tests at Edwards. il Aviation W 92:46-9 Mr 2 '70

C-5A exhibits agility despite size. D. A. Brown. il Aviation W 92:40-2+ Je 1 '70

AIRPLANES, Old
Collectors and collecting
See Airplanes—Collectors and collecting

AIRPLANES, Private
Hugh Hefner's jet black bunny in the sky. H. Ehrlich. il pors Look 34:62-5 Je 2 '70

Swift wings to bright horizons; photographs by E. Schweikardt; with account by J. Kirshenbaum and R. M. Mechen. Sports Illus 32:50-64 My 25 '70

Towns with wings; California communities for airplane owners. H. E. Jackson. il Travel 134:54-9 Ag '70

See also
Private flying

AIRPLANES, Research. See Airplanes, Experimental

AIRPLANES, Restored
Bird from Brooklyn; Brunner-Winkle Bird. J. Gilbert il Flying 86:48-54 Ap '70

Gulf Hawk; great antique. F. Tallman. il Flying 87:45-7+ Ag '70

World war two revisited; flying restored planes for the movie Battle of Britain. V. H. Bellamy. il por Flying 86:56-64 Mr '70

AIRPLANES, Short take-off and landing
Airport, terminal saving found for STOL. D. A. Brown. il Aviation W 93:28 Jl 20 '70

American STOL requests sent to thirteen manufacturers. D. A. Brown. Aviation W 93:22-3 Ag 17 '70

Another look at STOL mods. R. Blodget. il Flying 88:32-5+ Ja '71

Bertin studies turbofan STOL transport. il Aviation W 93:30 N 2 '70

Japan nears aerospace decisions; proposed Nihon YS-33 short-haul tri-jet STOL transport. C. Brownlow. il Aviation W 92:50-1 Mr 2 '70

Plane that makes airfields obsolete British-built Harrier. K. Brown. il Pop Mech 133:80-3+ Je '70

So you want to fly slow? Robertson/STOL Piper Cherokee. M. E. Dowd. il Pop Mech 135:96-7 Ja '71

Super Cub+short wing=Super Bipe STOL. J. Kotula. il por Pop Sci 196:64-7+ Ja '70

Users study joint STOL program. D. A. Brown. Aviation W 93:23-4 Jl 13 '70

Your STOL-bus is coming. B. Kocivar. il Pop Sci 196:86-8 My '70

Design
Arava design stresses simplicity. E. H. Kolcum. il Aviation W 92:58-9 Je 8 '70

Specifications
See Airplanes—Specifications

AIRPLANES, Supersonic
Airline chiefs affirm support of SST prototype program. Aviation W 93:19-20 D 14 '70

Big boomer. Nation 210:675 Je 8 '70

Big boondoggle. Nation 211:196-7 S 14 '70

Boeing, FAA divided on SST prototype. R. G. O'Lone. Aviation W 92:22 F 2 '70

Boomdoggle. M. A. Eriksen. New Repub 163:17-18 D 5 '70

Can airways handle the giant jets? interview. J. H. Shaffer. il por U S News 69:40-1 Ag 10 '70

Commercial service with Tu-144 as early as 1972 is Soviet goal. Aviation W 93:32 N 16 '70

Concorde's crucial year. R. Hotz. Aviation W 92:11 F 2 '70

Congress: score one for persistence; W. Proxmire's campaign against SST. il Time 96:13-14 D 14 '70

Facts on SST; address, October 2, 1970. B. Goldwater. Vital Speeches 37:40-4 N 1 '70

Fifteen top economists oppose SST. P. M. Boffey. Science 169:1292 S 25 '70

Fight for the SST. Newsweek 76:66+ Ag 17 '70

For Europe's Concorde, a make-or-break test. il U S News 69:46 S 7 '70

French, British agree on February for Concorde production decision. Aviation W 93:25 D 21 '70

Here comes superplane. il Am Heritage 21:114-15 Ap '70

House funds SST in close vote. Aviation W 92:26-7 Je 1 '70

Hypersonic transport study grows. R. G. O'Lone. il Aviation W 92:44-7+ Je 22 '70

I hold in my hand; noncompliance with Environmental quality act. Nation 211:292 O 5 '70

Is the SST really necessary? H. Sutton. il Sat R 53:14-17+ Ag 15 '70; Reply. R. L. Garwin. 53:17 S 5 '70

Is U.S. out of the supersonic race? il U S News 68:58 D 14 '70

New pterodactyl? Concorde. il Newsweek 76:102+ N 23 '70

Onward and upward; technical, environmental, and economic problems of supersonic air transportation. K. Hohenemser. il Environ 12:22-7 My '70

Panel votes SST $210 million. Aviation W 93:16-18 D 14 '70

Parting shots; back to the drawing board, birdmen! il Life 69:75-6 S 11 '70

Ready for metal cutting. il Sci N 97:501 My 23 '70

Scientists argue environmental effects. Aviation W 93:21 D 14 '70

Senate defeat sends SST funds to conference. Aviation W 93:24 D 7 '70

Shadow of a doubt on the Concorde. il Bsns W p40 F 21 '70

Showdown on the SST; will U.S. stay in the running? il U S News 69:44-6 S 7 '70

Single-class SST concept seen profitable. H. J. Coleman. il Aviation W 92:33-4 Mr 23 '70

SST. H. C. Wallich. Newsweek 76:79 S 21 '70

SST bailouts worry Boeing. Bsns W p74+ Mr 14 '70

SST: boon or boom-doggle? Time 95:64 Je 1 '70

SST: build, or bury? pro and con discussion. Sr Schol 97:16-17 D 7 '70

SST: commercial race or technology experiment? L. J. Carter. il Science 169:352-5 Jl 24 '70

SST filibuster delays funding for DOT. Aviation W 93:24 D 21 '70

AIRPLANES, Supersonic—*Continued*
SST hits the Senate barrier. il Newsweek 76:83-4 D 14 '70
SST: is it worth the price? il U S News 68:70 My 25 '70
SST officials strive to blunt opposition. R. G. O'Lone. Aviation W 93:16-17 Ag 10 '70
SST plans soar. il Sr Schol 95:13-15 O 13 '69
SST rejection. il Sci N 98:444-5 D 12 '70
SST: sitting duck for budget cutters. il Bsns W p58-9 Je 6 '70
SST talk. W. F. Buckley, jr. Nat R 23:50 Ja 12 '71
Superjet! il Forbes 105:23-4 Ap 15 '70
Supersonic shock wave. R. Hotz. Aviation W 93:11 D 14 '70; Discussion. 94:70 Ja 11 '71
Sweeping up studies. Sci N 98:61 Jl 25 '70
This month's feature: Congress and the supersonic transport. Cong Digest 49:289-310 D '70
To fly or not to fly? SST project. J. Eurnham. Nat R 22:666 Je 30 '70
Volpe rebuts critics of SST program. R. G. O'Lone. il Aviation W 92:28 Je 15 '70
What the SST means. J. Burnham. Nat R 22:194 F 24 '70; Discussion. 22:387+ Ap 21 '70
Will the SST pollute the stratosphere? Science 168:1562 Je 26 '70
Your first ride in an SST, sooner than you think. B. Kocivar. il Pop Sci 197:70-2+ Jl '70
See also
Airplanes, Military
Cost
SST backers debate future steps. Aviation W 94:14-15 Ja 11 '71
SST cost rise augurs battle in Congress. D. C. Winston. il Aviation W 92:20-1 My 18 '70
SST test, development shortcuts sought. Aviation W 92:24-5 F 9 '70
Terms tightened in SST contract. H. D. Watkins. Aviation W 93:14-15 Ag 10 '70
Design
Pan Am chief hits Concorde initial design. Aviation W 92:21 F 16 '70
Instrument boards
Instrument panel for Tu-144 shown. il Aviation W 93:34 D 7 '70
Models
See Airplane models
Standards
Delay in Concorde Mach 2 tests to slip certification only slightly. Aviation W 93:30 Jl 6 '70
Testing
Booms over Britain; Concorde. il Newsweek 76:103 S 21 '70
Concords SST enters Mach 2 development phases. D. E. Fink. il Aviation W 92:30-1+ Mr 16 '70
SST flight goals outlined. Aviation W 92:56 Ap 13 '70
AIRPLANES, Theft of
See also
Airplanes—Protection against theft
AIRPLANES, Training
Britain and Italy to compete in world trainer market. Aviation W 93:53 S 7 '70
French will lead Alphajet team. Aviation W 93:15 O 12 '70
AIRPLANES, Used
Planes, planes everywhere; airlines' surplus capacity. il Forbes 106:20-1 D 15 '70
Maintenance and repair
Boeing Wichita aims at surplus market. E. J. Bulban. il Aviation W 93:41+ S 14 '70
Marketing
Pan Am seeks Falcon use contracts. C. E. Schneider. Aviation W 94:52-3 Ja 4 '71
Prices
Used aircraft prices slide in Europe. R. F. Coburn. il Aviation W 92:41-2 Je 8 '70
Purchasing
Good buys in used planes. J. L. Scherer. il Mech Illus 66:55-7 Je '70

Testing
Summer sale:
Bonanza. il Flying 87:55 Jl '70
Cessna 120. S. Wilkinson. il Flying 87:48-52 Jl '70
Cessna 182. R. L. Collins. il Flying 87:44-7 Jl '70
Comanche. il Flying 87:54 Jl '70
Mooney 21. il Flying 87:56 Jl '70
Tri-Pacer. il Flying 87:53 Jl '70
Used-aircraft pilot report (title varies)
Aero Commander twins. R. L. Collins. il Flying 86:67-71 Ja '70
Beech Debonair. P. Garrison. il Flying 87:61-8 S '70
Cessna Cardinal. P. Garrison. il Flying 87:62-8 N '70
Economy six packer from Piper. A. Trammell. il Flying 87:32-6+ S '70
Luscombe Silvaire. S. Wilkinson. il Flying 88:65-8+ Ja '71
AIRPLANES, Vertical take-off and landing
Applications decision is key hurdle for V/STOL. il Aviation W 92:144-6+ Je 22 '70
British intercity V/STOL effort faces indefinite postponement. H. J. Coleman. Aviation W 92:18 F 16 '70
German evaluation group selects Do.231 for civil V/STOL need. Aviation W 93:19 Jl 27 '70
Goal of industry dispersal spurs fund bid for V/STOL research. il Aviation W 92:27 F 9 '70
Marines plan for Harrier introduction. W. S. Hieronymus. il Aviation W 93:55-6 S 14 '70
Need for leadership. R. Hotz. Aviation W 93:9 Jl 13 '70
Plane that makes airfields obsolete: British-built Harrier. K. Brown. il Pop Mech 133 80-3+ Je '70
V/STOL feasibility plan studied. D. A. Brown. Aviation W 92:22-3 Je 15 '70
VTOL aircraft designs shown at Hanover. il Aviation W 92:60-1 My 11 '70
Specifications
See Airplanes—Specifications
AIRPLANES in agriculture
Planting corn by airplane. B. Coffman. Farm J 94:52B Ap '70
U.S. agricultural aircraft; tables (cont) Aviation W 92:124 Mr 9 '70
History
Bax seat. G. Baxter. il Flying 87:114 Ag '70
AIRPLANES in business
Business flying's changing environment; symposium, with editorial comment. Aviation W 93:9, 40-3+ S 21 '70
Intercontinental business flying; symposium. il Aviation W 93:40-1+ D 14 '70
Recession spurs some firms to boost aircraft utilization. Aviation W 93:17 S 28 '70
See also
Airplanes, Business
History
Golden age of corporate flying. A. Trammell. il Flying 87:44-9 O '70
International aspects
See Aviation—International aspects
AIRPLANES in fire protection
Aircraft help battle fires in California. il Aviation W 93:22-3 O 5 '70
Bucket brigade with wings. il Bsns W p20 O 3 '70
AIRPLANES in fishing. See Airplanes in hunting and fishing
AIRPLANES in forest fire protection. See Forest fire patrol, Aerial
AIRPLANES in hunting and fishing
Angry men; plunder of Alaska's wildlife. B. East. il Outdoor Life 146:31-3+ D '70
Trolling from an airplane. B. Rankin. il Field & S 75:80 My '70
AIRPLANES in medical service
See also
Helicopters, Ambulance
AIRPLANES in moving pictures
World war two revisited; flying restored planes. V. H. Bellamy. il por Flying 86:56-64 Mr '70
AIRPLANES in police work
Use of helicopters, airplanes by police agencies increasing. il Aviation W 93:91+ S 21 '70
AIRPLANES in sports
See also
Helicopters in sports
AIRPORT and airway development act. See Aviation—Laws and regulations

AIRPORT buildings
Building types study. il Arch Rec 148:117-32 Ag '70
Decentralized terminal planned for Rome. R. F. Coburn. il Aviation W 92:35-6 F 16 '70
Fiberglass reinforced plastic forms have electric heat to cure concrete. il Arch Rec 147: 159 Je '70
Jumbo jet; airport problems. il U S News 68:11 Ja 26 '70
Lighting
Engineers develop lighting design from model tests. il Arch Rec 147:147-52 F '70
AIRPORT landing fees. See Airports—Finance
AIRPORT servicecenters, inc.
Ground equipment service chain planned by new firm. il Aviation W 92:35 Je 15 '70
AIRPORT theft
Thieves thriving at bustling Heathrow. Aviation W 92:32+ Mr 2 '70
AIRPORTS
Buildings
See Airport buildings
Design
Building types study. il Arch Rec 148:117-32 Ag '70
Equipment
American 707s get new cargo loaders. Aviation W 93:37 S 28 '70
Jumbo jet; airport problems. il U S News 68:11 Ja 26 '70
Mobile passenger stairway developed for giant jet use. il Aviation W 92:61 F 2 '70
Pods for passengers; interchangeable capsules serving as departure lounge at the airport and passenger cabin in the aircraft. F. K. Coffee. il Mech Illus 66:68-9+ N '70
See also
Airport servicecenters, inc.
Federal aid
Conferees compromise on five-year, $3-billion airport/airways bill. Aviation W 92:33 Ap 27 '70
House action delays airways fund fight. K. Johnsen. Aviation W 93:25 D 14 '70
Finance
Airport/airways bill tax features draw domestic airline opposition. Aviation W 92: 28 F 9 '70
Conferees agree on user tax plan. Aviation W 92:27 My 11 '70
Conferees compromise on five-year, $3-billion airport/airways bill. Aviation W 92:33 Ap 27 '70
User tax measure may get swift Senate unit action. Aviation W 92:26 Ja 26 '70
Users charged. R. B. Parke. Flying 87:40 Jl 13 '70
Laws and regulations
New Jersey court sets curfew for jets. C. E. Schneider. Aviation W 92:22-3 Je 8 '70
Luggage handling
See Airlines—Luggage handling
Marking
Follow me through; glide-path guidance with runway diamonds. R. Blodget. Flying 87:24-5 S '70
Noise
San Francisco sets airport noise limit. Aviation W 93:37 D 21 '70
Planning
Airports that bring the planes to the people. il Bsns W p98-100 F 14 '70
Denmark plans major air terminal. E. H. Kolcum. il Aviation W 92:35-6 F 9 '70
FAA to present ten-year facilities plans. Aviation W 92:24-5 Ja 19 '70
Forces for change in airport planning and design. il Arch Rec 148:60-1 Ag '70
Ocean airport proposed for California. N. S. Himmel. il Aviation W 93:33+ O 5 '70
Runways
Renovate runways before resurfacing; Long Beach, Calif. il Am City 85:74-5 Ag '70
Second try was slurry seal; Contra Costa County's airport. R. S. Latchaw. il Am City 85:68+ D '70
See also
Airports—Marking
Safety devices and measures
Safer flying: the plans under way; instrument-landing systems. il U S News 69:36 N 30 '70

Security measures
Airlines vs. hijackers. il Newsweek 76:76-8 O 26 '70
New bill would delay air cargo theft legislation for more study. D. C. Winston. Aviation W 92:32 Mr 23 '70
Pressure rising for tightened security. R. S. Kahn. il Aviation W 93:29-31 O 26 '70
Thirty-three gateways to have screening. Aviation W 93:24 N 30 '70
See also
Airplane hijacking—Prevention

Snow and ice removal
How to keep an airport open in winter; Springfield regional airport, Vt. D. Gurney. il Am City 85:56 S '70
New runway de-icer termed effective after LaGuardia test. R. S. Kahn. Aviation W 92:34 Mr 30 '70

Standards
Airports gird for U.S. certification. R. G. O'Lone. Aviation W 93:57-8 Ag 3 '70

Traffic
Air travel: how to get off the ground. Bsns W p 107-8 Je 13 '70
Tests of 747 wake accelerated. Aviation W 92:25-6 F 23 '70
Will you lose your right to fly? F. A. Tinker. il Pop Mech 134:88-91+ O '70

Traffic control
FAA issues separation standards for control of giant jet traffic. Aviation W 92:225+ Mr 9 '70
FAA to start area control with Atlanta. il Aviation W 92:32-3 My 25 '70
New York transfers smoothly to Metroplex traffic system. Aviation W 93:64 Jl 13 '70
On top; terminal-control-area rule. R. L. Collins. Flying 87:14-16+ O '70
Pilots blame FAA in jam of Washington air traffic. C. E. Schneider. Aviation W 93:21-2 Ag 31 '70
Traffic plan flops in Washington. J. P. Woolsey. Aviation W 93:20-1 Ag 31 '70

Transportation problems
Advanced airport transit system planned; Dallas/Ft Worth, Tex. regional airport. il Aviation W 93:54-5 Ag 3 '70
Travel in the '70s. K. Ludvigsen. Mech Illus 66:44-5 Ja '70
Australia
See also
Melbourne, Australia—Airports

California
Ocean airport proposed for California. N. S. Himmel. il Aviation W 93:33+ O 5 '70
Second try was slurry seal; Contra Costa County's airport. R. S. Latchaw. il Am City 85:68+ D '70
Towns with wings; communities for airplane owners. H. E. Jackson. il Travel 134:54-9 Ag '70
Use of California satellite airports grows. Aviation W 93:24-5 Ag 24 '70
See also
Los Angeles—Airports
San Francisco—Airports

Denmark
See also
Copenhagen—Airports

Florida
Everglades jetport threat remains despite promises from Washington. Audubon 72: 116 Ja '70
Everglades: pregnant with risks. H. Bloomfield. il Am For 76:24-7+ My '70
Fight for the Everglades. A. W. Smith. Nat Parks 44:2 Ja '70

Great Britain
See also
London—Airports
Hawaii
See also
Honolulu—Airports

Illinois
See also
Chicago—Airports
Ireland
Irishman with chutzpah. por Duns 96:75 N '70

Italy
See also
Rome (city)—Airports

AIRPORTS—*Continued*

Maine

How one city beat a cutback. il U S News 69:43-4 O 5 '70

Nevada

See also
Las Vegas, Nev.—Airports

New Jersey

New Jersey court sets curfew for jets; Morristown, N.J. municipal airport. C. E. Schneider. Aviation W 92:22-3 Je 8 '70

New York (state)

Air base now business airport; Stewart air force base. Aviation W 92:92 F 23 '70

Texas

Advanced airport transit system planned; Dallas/Ft Worth, Tex, regional airport. il Aviation W 93:54-5 Ag 3 '70
See also
Dallas—Airports
Houston, Tex.—Airports

United States

Can airways handle the giant jets? interview. J. H. Shaffer. il por U S News 69:38-40 Ag 10 '70
Forty gateways for overseas flights; table. Bet Hom & Gard 48:112 O '70
See also subhead Airports under names of cities, e.g. Bangor. Me.—Airports

Washington (state)

See also
Seattle—Airports

AIRPORTS, Floating
FLAIR, the way-out floating airport. P. Wahl. il Pop Sci 197:54-5+ Ag '70

AIRPORTS, Stealing from. See Airport thefts

AIRSHIPS
Unforgettable, unforgotten; Hindenburg. A. Waugh. Nat R 22:952+ S 8 '70

AIRSPACE (international law)
Hostages for hijackers? Russian, Turkish and U.S. involvement. Newsweek 76:37 N 9 '70
Long detour; Soviet-Turkish border incident. il Time 96:32 N 23 '70
Out of all proportion; U-8 affair. il Time 96:21-2+ N 9 '70
U-8 incident. il Newsweek 76:60 N 2 '70
U.S. requests release of aircraft and passengers by U.S.S.R. Dept State Bul 63:653-4 N 23 '70

AIRSPUR corporation
Travel notes. R. Joseph. Esquire 73:42+ My '70

AIRSTREAM, inc.
Home on the range; Airstream Wally Byam caravan. B. Gilbert. il Sports Illus 33:46-8+ Jl 6 '70

AIRWAYS
See also
Airlines—Great Britain—Routes

Traffic control

See Air traffic control

AIRWORTHINESS directives. See Aviation—Laws and regulations

AISHWARYA, crown princess of Nepal
Marriage of convenience. il por Time 95:29 Mr 9 '70 *
Nepal: come, let us marry. il pors Newsweek 75:46-47D Mr 16 '70 *
Nepal's right royal wedding. il por Life 68:34-5 Mr 13 '70 *

AITKEN, Jonathan
From John Bull to Uncle Sam: how to run an empire. il Am Heritage 21:44-5+ Ag '70

AIX-EN-PROVENCE
Provençal weekend. D. Butwin. il Sat R 53:44+ O 17 '70

AIX-EN-PROVENCE festival. See Music festivals—France

AKAI, Saburo
Cool cat and his red-hot company. il por Bsns W p46 Ap 25 '70 *

AKAI electric company. See Electronic apparatus industry and trade—Japan

AKOKAWE; musical comedy. See Musical comedies, revues, etc.—Criticisms, plots, etc.

AKRON, Ohio

City planning

Parking garage built to give downtown a lift. J Alkire. il Am City 85:65-7 Ag '70

AKRON, Ohio. public library
Akron gets beautiful new library in downtown area. il Library J 95:967+ Mr 15 '70

AKRON. University
Building takeover at the University of Akron; shots fired in Buchtel Hall. J. E. Milkereit. Sch & Soc 98:374-5 O '70
Dream for three; Chamber ballet and the Dance institute. D. Hering. il pors Dance Mag 44:72-6 Ap '70

AL-QADDAFI, Muammar. See Qaddafi, M.

ALABAMA
See also
Crenshaw County
Justice, Administration of—Alabama
Music festivals—Alabama

Education, Department of

Intellectual freedom: C. Robinson case. J. F. Krug and J. A. Harvey. Am Lib 1:533 Je '70
Move to drop Robinson case refused by federal court. Library J 95:1154 Mr 15 '70
NEA files suit against Alabama state education department; case of Mrs C. Robinson. Library J 95:713 F 15 '70

Politics and government

George does it again. Nat R 22:502-3 My 19 '70
Here comes that man again! V. Gold. Nat R 22:566 Je 2 '70
Primaries. Nation 210:709 Je 15 '70
Primaries. il Time 95:16-17 My 18 '70
Season openers: primaries. il Time 95:19 My 4 '70
Wallace and the shape of politics. S. Alsop. Newsweek 75:108 My 4 '70
Wallace country; gubernatorial primary candidates. il por Newsweek 75:30+ My 4 '70
Wallace on the move. por Newsweek 75:20-1 Mr 9 '70
Wallace rides again. R. M. Williams. New Repub 162:12-13 My 21 '70
Wallace's Waterloo? Alabama primary. il por Newsweek 75:42 My 18 '70

ALABAMA educational television network. See Television stations, Educational

ALABAMA 500 race. See Automobile racing

AL AKSA mosque. See Jerusalem—Holy places

ALAMPI, Phillip
Horses are a household word in New Jersey. il Parks & Rec 5:33-5 F '70

ALANINE
Alanine: key role in gluconeogenesis. P. Felig and others. bibliog il Science 167:1003-4 F 13 '70

ALANO, Roberto Morales-. See Morales-Alano, R.

AL AQSA mosque. See Jerusalem—Holy places

ALARMS
See also
Burglar alarms
Electric alarms
Fire alarms

ALASKA
Great land: boom or doom? il Time 96:44-7+ Jl 27 '70
Last frontier. S. Wright. il pors Am West 7:32-7 N '70
Special issue: Alaska il Nat Parks & Con Mag 44:2+ N '70
See also
Botany—Alaska
Camping—Alaska
Christmas—Alaska
Conservation of resources—Alaska
Earthquakes—Alaska
Ecology—Alaska
Environmental policy—Alaska
Eskimos
Fishing—Alaska
Forests and forestry—Alaska
Geology—Alaska
Hunting—Alaska
Kenai Peninsula
Land—Alaska
Land tenure—Alaska
Landscape protection—Alaska
Music festivals—Alaska
Nome
Petroleum—Alaska
Petroleum industry and trade—Alaska
Public lands—Alaska
Roads—Alaska
Wilderness areas—Alaska
Wildlife conservation—Alaska

Appropriations and expenditures

What do you do with $900,000,000? D. Wittner. il Life 68:38-42 Ap 10 '70

Climate

Water pollution in Alaska: present and future. F. B. Lotspeich; reply. C. E. Logsdon. Science 167:1316+ Mr 6 '70

ALASKA—*Continued*

Description and travel

Cruising to Alaska. il Sunset 144:85-6 Ap '70

Economic policy

Alaska: politicians and natives, money and oil. L. Lapham. il Harper 240:85-102 My '70
Great land: boom or doom? il Time 96:44-7+ Jl 27 '70

Maps

Alaska 1970. Nat Parks & Con Mag 44:18-19 N '70

Native races

See Indians of North America—Alaska

Parks and reserves

Keystone Canyon. J. E. Hoffman, jr. il Parks and Rec 5:29-31 D '70

ALASKA airlines
Alaska studies Soviet air ties. Aviation W 93: 21 N 2 '70
Flight of the Samovar. il Time 95:74 F 9 '70

ALASKA cedar. See Cedar

ALASKA festival of music. See Music festivals —Alaska

ALASKA fur seals. See Seals (animals)

ALASKA pipeline. See Petroleum—Pipelines

ALASKA railroad
Seward's folly again? il Forbes 106:17 Jl 1 '70

ALBA, María del Rosario Cayetana Stuart Fitz-James, 18, duquesa de
In Spain: the vital modern Duchess of Alba. il pors Vogue 156:178-83 O 1 '70 *

ALBACORE fishing
Action on the color front; new hotspot for longfins. H. Williams. il por Outdoor Life 146:72-5+ Ag '70

ALBANIA
See also
Foreign visitors in Albania

Foreign relations

Albania: the first few breezes of change. A. Tillier. il por Newsweek 76:47-8 S 7 '70

Politics and government

Emulating Mao. Time 95:30 F 23 '70

ALBANY, N.Y.

Air pollution

5,000 join in air pollution survey; Project Help your environment carried out by Northeastern environmental council. V. A. Mohnen. il por Cons 25:10-15 Ag '70

ALBATROSSES
Great albatrosses. W. L. N. Tickell. il Sci Am 223:84-93 bibliog(p 132) N '70
Haunted sands of Laysan. G. Laycock. il Audubon 72:42-9 Mr '70

ALBEDO, Planetary. See Earth—Radiation

ALBEE, A. L. and others
Ages, irradiation history, and chemical composition of lunar rocks from the Sea of Tranquillity. il Science 167:463-6 Ja 30 '70

ALBEE, Edward
Decade of engagement. il Sat R 53:19-20 Ja 24 '70

about

Demons also believe; parodying the eucharist. S. Terrien. Chr Cent 87:1481-3+ D 9 '70 *

ALBEE, George Wilson
Academic vs. professional psychology; excerpts from address. por Sch & Soc 98: 462 D '70

ALBERS, Josef
Josef Albers: prophet and presiding genius of American op art. S. Hunter. il pors Vogue 156:70-3+ O 15 '70 *

ALBERT I, prince of Monaco
Prince Albert's way of catching squid. S. Schlee. il por Natur Hist 79:20+ F '70 *

ALBERT, Carl
Democratic appraisal of Nixon's record so far: interview. il pors U S News 69:58-61 Ag 24 '70
Excerpt from debate, September 15, 1969. Cong Digest 49:14+ Ja '70

about

Coming upheaval in Congress. J. Fischer. Harper 241:21-2+ O '70; Reply with rejoinder. G. I. Coogan. 241:17 O '70 *
Congress gets ready to battle Nixon. il Bsns W p66-70 Ja 9 '71 *
End of an era in Congress. pors U S News 68:35 Je 1 '70 *
Most likely to succeed. por Newsweek 75:27 Je 1 '70 *

ALBERT, Eddie
Sad and sorry look at pollution; ed. by E. Crimmin. il Motor B 126:10-12 O '70

ALBERT, R. D. and Lindstrom, P, J.
Auroral-particle precipitation and trapping caused by electrostatic double layers in the ionosphere. bibliog il Science 170:1398-401 D 25 '70

ALBERT Victor, duke of Clarence and Avondale
Parting shots; Clarence the Ripper? P. O'Neil. il pors Life 69:85-8 N 13 '70 *
Who was Jack the Ripper? por Time 96:29 N 9 '70 *

ALBERT Schweitzer hospital. See Hospitals— Gabon

ALBERTA
See also
Calgary

ALBERTINI, Richard J. and DeMars, Robert
Diploid azaguanine-resistant mutants of cultured human fibroblasts. bibliog il Science 169:482-5 Jl 31 '70

ALBINO, Joseph. See Pearson, J. F. jt. auth.

ALBONE, Eric, and McCaull, Julian
Freighted with hazard. bibliog il Environ 12: 18-26+ D '70

ALBRECHT, Charles
Defusing a coronary, with gas. il pors Life 68:75-6 Ap 17 '70 *

ALBRIGHT, Horace Marden
Conservation hall of fame. il por Nat Wildlife 7:10-11 O '69
Interview with Horace Marden Albright. pors Parks & Rec 5:22-3+ D '70

about

Horace M. Albright: Audubon medalist, 1969. il por Audubon 72:31 Mr '70 *

ALBRIGHT, J. F. and others
Antigen competition: antigens compete for a cell occurring with limited frequency. bibliog il Science 167:196-8 Ja 9 '70

ALBRIGHT, Robert
On the death of my son; poem. Nation 212: 54 Ja 11 '71

ALBUFEIRA, Portugal
Color it paradise. J. Bryan, 3d. Nat R 22: 516 My 19 '70

ALBUQUERQUE, N.Mex.
Data transmission network speeds customer service. D. Mann. il Am City 85:98-9 F '70

Housing

City of adobe and light: La Luz. M. C. Spires. il Am Home 73:50-5 Mr '70

ALCATOR (alto campus torus) devices. See Plasma (ionized gases)

ALCATRAZ (island)
Alcatraz: the Indian uprising that worked. W. Hedgepeth. il Look 34:44-5 Je 2 '70
Day on Alcatraz with the Indians. K. Boyle. New Repub 162:10-11 Ja 17 '70
Indians offer $24 in glass beads for Alcatraz. il Sr Schol 96:20 My 18 '70
None but the brave; government tightens squeeze on the Rock. il Newsweek 76:38-9 Jl 6 '70
Parting shots. il Life 68:65-8 F 13 '70

ALCHEMY
Great moments in chemistry; tr. by R. E. Oesper. F. Szabadvary. il Chem 43:5-7 D '70

ALCINDOR, Lewis
It's more fun without Lew. C. Kirkpatrick. il Sports Illus 32:8-11 F 2 '70
Lew turns small change to big Bucks. T. Maule. il pors Sports Illus 32:20-2+ Mr 9 '70 *
Proud tower. il por Newsweek 76:92+ D 14 '70 *
Team it took to beat big Lew. il por Life 68: 58-9+ My 1 '70 *

ALCOA. See Aluminum company of America

ALCOHOL
Vinum omnia vincit. R. Maloney. Atlan 225: 114-16 F '70
See also
Liquor problem

Physiological effects

Alcohol and your brain. A. Q. Maisel. Read Digest 96:65-9 Je '70
Alcoholism: a new theory distilled. G. D. Everett. Chr Today 14:38 F 27 '70
Drinker's guide to safe holiday driving; interview. W. Keller. il por Todays Health 48:8+ D '70
Impairment of shock avoidance learning after long-term alcohol ingestion in mice. G. Freund. bibliog il Science 168:1599-601 Je 26 '70
Neurologist suggests tips for tipplers. Todays Health 48:64 S '70

ALCOHOL—Physiological effects—*Continued*
Pyrazole and induction of fatty liver by a single dose of ethanol. G. O. Bustos and others. bibliog il Science 168:1598-9 Je 26 '70
Reduced nicotinamide-adenine dinucleotide phosphate oxidase: activity enhanced by ethanol consumption. C. S Lieber and L. M. DeCarli. bibliog il Science 170:78-80 O 2 '70

See also
Alcoholism
Drinking and traffic accidents

ALCOHOL and youth
On the drinking habits of the very young. il Esquire 73:142-3 Mr '70
Study reveals drinking habits of teen-agers. Todays Health 48:72 N '70

ALCOHOL dehydrogenase. See Dehydrogenases

ALCOHOL education. See Temperance—Study and teaching

ALCOHOL in the body
Alcohol aversion in the rat: behavioral assessment of noxious drug effects. M. Nachman and others. bibliog il Science 168:1244-6 Je 5 '70
Alcohol oxidation in rats inhibited by pyrazole, oximes, and amides. D. Lester and G. D. Benson. bibliog il Science 169:282-4 Jl 17 '70

ALCOHOLIC drinks. See Liquors

ALCOHOLICS
Moral career of a bum; excerpt from You owe yourself a drunk. J. P. Spradley. il Trans-Action 7:16-29 My '70
Women alcoholics: what can be done to help them. Good H 170:157-9 F '70
See also
Church work with alcoholics

ALCOHOLISM
Alkaloids from catecholamines in adrenal tissue: possible role in alcoholism. G. Cohen and M. Collins. bibliog il Science 167:1749-51 Mr 27 '70
Behavioral problems; address, July 31, 1970. L. F. Presnall. Vital Speeches 37:79-83 N 15 '70
Big drinkers; urban scene. Newsweek 76:57 Jl 6 '70
Business fights the big hangover. Bsns W p 112 Mr 7 '70
On campus: drugs vs. drinking. Mlle 70:230 Mr '70
Rules of drunkenness; views in Drunken comportment. il Time 95:54 Je 8 '70
Try at treatment; legislation toward providing rehabilitative facilities and attitudes. Sci N 97:551 Je 6 '70
Vodka on the rocks. il Time 95:24 F 16 '70
Writer's vice. il Time 96:59 O 5 '70
See also
Alcohol and youth
Liquor problem

Research
Alcohol, amines, and alkaloids: a possible biochemical basis for alcohol addiction. V. E. Davis and M. J. Walsh. bibliog il Science 167:1005-7 F 13 '70; Discussion. 169:1104-6; 170:1113-15 S 11, D 4 '70
Blood concentrations of acetaldehyde and ethanol in chronic alcoholics. E. Majchrowicz and J. H. Mendelson. bibliog il Science 168:1100-2 My 29 '70

Study and teaching
See Temperance—Study and teaching

Therapy
Cop challenges the church. M. A. Dunlavey. il Chr Cent 87:759-60 Je 17 '70
Women alcoholics: what can be done to help them. Good H 170:157-9 F '70

ALCOHOLS
Disintegration of charged liquid jets: results with isopropyl alcohol. A. L. Huebner. il Science 168:118-19 Ap 3 '70

ALCOTT, Michael
(ed) See Besret, B. Boquen

ALCOVY RIVER
Wilderness or wasteland? the blights of channelization. B. B. Blackburn. il Liv Wildn 34:27-32 Spr '70

ALDAN, Daisy
I awake in these hills; He has entered midnight; poems. Poetry 116:147-8 Je '70

ALDEBURGH, England
Britten and the borough: on the winds of the North Sea. T. Heinitz. il Sat R 53:80+ Mr 14 '70

ALDEBURGH festival. See Music festivals—England

ALDEHYDES
Phenolic aldehydes: generation from fossil woods and carbonaceous sediments by oxidative degradation. R. F. Leo and E. S. Barghoorn. bibliog il Science 168:582-4 My 1 '70
Prebiotic synthesis of propiolaldehyde and nicotinamide. M. J. Dowler and others. bibliog il Science 169:1320-1 S 25 '70
See also
Acetaldehyde

ALDEN, John
John Alden. B. Robinson. il por Yachting 128:62-3+ O '70 *

ALDER
Fast forest of alders to shade your entry; white alder. il Sunset 144:136 Ja '70

ALDERFER, Clayton P.
Understanding laboratory education: an overview. bibliog il Mo Labor R 93:18-27 D '70

ALDERSON, Wendell
Some of my best friends are phonies. il Opera N 35:8-11 D 19 '70

ALDRETE, J. Antonio
Liver: outer limit of the state of the art. J. Bockel. il pors Sci N 97:202-3 F 21 '70

ALDRICH, George H.
Department supports ratification of genocide convention; statement, April 24, 1970. Dept State Bul 63:14-15 Jl 6 '70

ALDRICH, Richard S.
Development assistance to Latin America. Yale R 60:53-62 O '70

ALDRIDGE, Bill G.
Physics in the open-door college. il por Phys Today 23:46-51 Mr '70

ALDRIDGE, Ira, award. See Association for the study of Negro life and history

ALDRIDGE, John W.
Eudora Welty: metamorphosis of a southern lady writer. Sat R 53:21-3+ Ap 11 '70
Hemingway between triumph and disaster. por Sat R 53:23-6+ O 10 '70

about
New longings abroad in the land. B. DeMott. Sat R 53:24-6 Jl 4 '70 *

ALDRIN, Edwin E. 1930-
About the man on the moon. H. L. Masin. il pors Sr Schol 95:36 S 22 '69

about
How Apollo 11 changed three famous men. G. Farmer. pors Life 69:60 Jl 17 '70 *
See also
Space flight to the moon—Manned flights—Apollo 11 flight

ALDRIN
Aldrin: removal from lake water by flocculent bacteria. W. O. Leshniowsky and others. bibliog il Science 169:993-5 S 4 '70
Doctored grapes? J. R. Coyne, jr. il Nat R 22:88 Ja 27 '70

ALEKSEENKO, N. ÍU.
Directional hearing: effect of unilateral change of the sound duration. bibliog il Science 167:1009-10 F 13 '70

ALEKSEI, patriarch
Obituary
America 122:461 My 2 '70 *
Patriarch Alexei. Chr Cent 87:555 My 6 '70 *

ALEPPO pine. See Pine

ALESSANDRO, Victor
Native son. il pors Opera N 34:14-15 Ap 11 '70 *

ALESSIO, John
Johnny is in *agua* hot. A. Wright. il pors Sports Illus 33:50-2+ Ag 3 '70 *

ALEUTIAN ISLANDS
See also
Ecology—Aleutian Islands

ALEWIFE fishing
Alewives spell action. G. Heinold. il Outdoor Life 145:44+ Ap '70

ALEXANDER, Alberta
Try tea and see. il Org Gard & Farm 17:100-1 Ag '70

ALEXANDER, Christopher
Pattern language. R. Montgomery. il Arch Forum 132:52-9 Ja '70 *

ALEXANDER, Clifford L. 1933-
Alexander's plan. il Time 95:17 F 23 '70 *

ALEXANDER, Donald G.
Liveable cities. bibliog f Cur Hist 59:85-90+ Ag '70
New directions in urban financing. bibliog f Cur Hist 59:278-82+ N '70

ALEXANDER, Edgar
Obituary
America 122:inside cover F 7 '70. D. R. Campion

ALEXANDER, Floyce
Homage to Miguel Hernandez; poem. Nation 210:215 F 23 '70
ALEXANDER, Frank
Texas plane crash: nonviolent man's final act brings destruction and death. R. R. Winkelmann. Chr Cent 88:26+ Ja 6 '71 *
ALEXANDER, Genevieve
Bits of nature and hand-me-downs. il por Org Gard & Farm 17:53-6 O '70
ALEXANDER, Herbert E. and Meyers, H. B.
Financial landslide for the G.O.P. il Fortune 81:104-5+ Mr '70
ALEXANDER, Holmes
Dean of conservative columnists. J. Chamberlain. Nat R 22:742-3 Jl 14 '70 *
ALEXANDER, James
Computer geared to grow with a city. il Am City 85:84+ N '70
ALEXANDER, James, Jr
More phones, better service, less cost. il por Am City 85:137-8 O '70
ALEXANDER, Jean
Black literature for the culturally deprived curriculum. Engl J 591:229-33 D '70
ALEXANDER, John W.
Why am I at this school? Chr Today 14:12-13 S 11 '70
ALEXANDER, Lloyd
Identifications and identities. bibliog il por Wilson Lib Bul 45:144-8 O '70
No laughter in heaven; address, July 29, 1969. Horn Bk 46:11-19 F '70
ALEXANDER, M. See Focht, D. D. jt. auth.
ALEXANDER, Pamela
Making it; poem. Atlan 226:58 N '70
Prophet as the time of day; poem. Atlan 226:82 Jl '70
ALEXANDER, R. W.
Is this our daughter? story. Good H 170:110-11 Ap '70
ALEXANDER, Raymond Pace
Judge Alexander honored. il por Negro Hist Bul 33:98 Ap '70 *
TRB from Washington. New Repub 163:4 D 26 '70 *
ALEXANDER, Russ
1-2-3-4 on a mast; minimum space, multiband ham antenna. il Pop Electr 33:27-30 Ag '70
ALEXANDER, Shana
Feminine eye. See issues of McCalls
ALEXANDER, Tom
Hot new promise of thermonuclear power. il Fortune 81:94-7+ Je '70
Is there any way to run an airline? Fortune 82:117+ S '70
Psychologists are rediscovering the mind. il Fortune 82:108-11+ N '70
Some burning questions about combustion. il Fortune 81:130-1+ F '70
ALEXANDRE (hairdresser)
Alexandre the great. il por Newsweek 75:59 Je 8 '70 *
ALEXANDRIA, Va.

George Washington masonic museum
See Washington, G.—Museums, relics, etc.

Sanitary affairs
Big shredder eats a junked car a minute. B. W. Brown. il Am City 85:70-1 Jl '70
ALEXEENKO, N. Y. See Alekseenko, N. IU.
ALFALFA
Alfalfa that pays as well as corn. O. Bay. Farm J 94:M6 F '70
ALFALFA weevils
Special report on the alfalfa weevil. il Suc Farm 68:no3 46 F '70
Wasps help fight the alfalfa weevil. G. Reynolds. il Farm J 94:20-1+ S '70
AL FATAH (organization) See Fedayeen
ALFRED P. Sloan foundation
Foundations: taking stock after the tax reform bill. J. Walsh. Science 167:1598+ Mr 20 '70
ALFREY, Elsie V.
Horse-radish, the three-way plant. il Org Gard & Farm 17:76-7 Ja '70
ALFRINK, Bernardus Johannes, cardinal
Alfrink challenged. T Beeson. Chr Cent 87:1177 O 7 '70 *
ALFVÉN, Hannes
Divide and honor. pors Newsweek 76:100 N 9 '70 *
Magnetism to metabolism. Sci N 98:348 O 31 '70 *
Nobel laureates for 1970: Hannes Alfvén and Louis Neel. G. B. Lubkin. pors Phys Today 23:61-3 D '70 *
Nobel prize. A. J. Dessler. por Science 170:604-6 N 6 '70 *

Plasmas, magnets and sugars. il por Time 96:39 N 9 '70 *
—and Arrhenius, Gustaf
Mission to an asteroid. il Science 167:139-41; 170:1432 Ja 9, D 25 '70
ALGAE
Acetabularia chloroplast DNA: electron microscopic visualization. B. R. Green and H. Burton. bibliog il Science 168:981-2 My 22 '70
Bile pigment formation in plants. R. F. Troxler and others. bibliog il Science 167:192-3 Ja 9 '70
Biological nitrogen fixation in Lake Erie. D. L. Howard and others. bibliog il Science 169:61-2 Jl 3 '70
Evolution of photosynthesis. J. M. Olson. bibliog il Science 168:438-46 Ap 24 '70
Life in a snowbank. R. Gilluly. il Sci N 98:80-1 Jl 25 '70
Mosaic mutants: absence in a eucaryotic organism. A. Fjeld. bibliog il Science 168:843-4 My 15 '70
Seeks solution to growth of algae in lakes. Am City 85:30 My '70
Subsurface photosynthesis; chlorophyll c. il Sci N 98:58-9 Jl 25 '70
See also
Dinoflagellates
Euglena
Kelp
Lichens
Plankton
Red tide
Stoneworts

Conferences
Phylogeny and morphogenesis in the algae. J. F. Fredrick. Science 169:403-4 Jl 24 '70
ALGAE, Fossil
Phanerozoic stromatolites: noncompetitive ecologic restriction by grazing and burrowing animals. P. Garrett. bibliog il Science 169:171-3 Jl 10 '70
Stromatolites used to determine the time of nearest approach of earth and moon. M. R. Walter. bibliog Science 170:1331-2 D 18 '70
ALGARVE, Portugal
See also
Albufeira
ALGEBRA
See also
Diophantine analysis
ALGEO, Jack
How to feed a high-wheat finishing ration; interview. il Farm J 93:B8-9 O '69
ALGER, Fred
No way but up. A. Hershman. por Duns 95:89-90 F '70 *
ALGER, Horatio, Jr
Horatio Alger: failure. M. Cowley. il Horizon 12:62-5 Sum '70 *
ALGERIA
Algeria's second revolution. E. Behr. il Newsweek 76:32-5 Jl 20 '70
See also
Sahara Desert

Foreign relations
Fleeing leftists: why they pick Algeria. il por U S News 69:36 N 9 '70
Our other man in Algiers. S. De Gramont. il N Y Times Mag p30+ N 1 '70

History
Algeria, Israel and the Al Fatah. R. W. Fox. Commonweal 92:184-5 My 8 '70

Revolution, 1954-1962
Algerian peasant revolt; excerpts from Peasant revolts in twentieth century. E. R. Wolf. il Trans-Action 7:33-46 My '70
Revolt without revolution. R. W. Fox. Nation 211:154-6 Ag 31 '70
Wolves in the city, by P. Henissart. Review Newsweek il 76:112+ S 14 '70. G. Wolff
ALGOL. See Stars, Eclipsing binary
ALI, Muhammad. See Clay, C.
ALIANZA (Federal alliance of land grants) See Land tenure—United States
ALICE in Wonderland. See Carroll, L. pseud.
ALICE in Wonderland. See Characters in literature
ALICE in Wonderland; drama. See Gregory, A.
ALICE Tully Hall. See Lincoln Center for the performing arts, New York—Juilliard school
ALIEN labor
Caribbean: this side of paradise; aliens in the Virgin Islands. P. Nabokov. Nation 210:332-5 Mr 23 '70
Italians are coming; western workers in the USSR. Newsweek 76:81-2 D 21 '70
Virgin Islands: shame in the U.S. tropics. J. Star. il Look 34:17-21 Mr 10 '70

ALIENATION (social psychology)
Black veterans return. J. Fendrich and M.
Pearson. il Trans-Action 7:32-7 Mr '70
Blackness and madness. T. S. Szasz. Yale R
59:333-41 Mr '70
Drug abuse and social alienation; address,
1970. A. I. Malcolm. il Todays Ed 59:28-31
S '70
New reformation, by P. Goodman. Review
Sat R 53:43+ My 23 '70 H. S. Resnik
ALIENATION, Social. See Alienation (social
psychology)
ALIENS
See also
Alien labor
Citizenship
ALIENS, Deportation of. See Deportation
ALILUNAS, Leo J. and Chazanof, William
Enigma of Negro history. Clear House 45:
29-31 S '70; Same abr. Ed Digest 36:38-9 D
'70
ALINSKY, Saul David
Professional radical, 1970; interview, ed. by
M. K. Sanders. il Harper 240:35-42 Ja '70
about
Radical Saul Alinsky: prophet of power to
the people; Time essay. por Time 95:56-7
Mr 2 '70 *
ALITALIA (airline) See Airlines—Italy
ALJURE, Dumar
Private war of a guerrilla. R. L. Maullin. il
por Trans-Action 7:45-54 bibliog(p64) Mr
'70 *
ALKALOIDS
Alkaloid from fire ant venom: identification
and synthesis. J. G. MacConnell and others.
bibliog il Science 168:840-1 My 15 '70
See also
Colchicine

Physiological effects
Alkaloids from catecholamines in adrenal tis-
sue: possible role in alcoholism. G. Cohen
and M. Collins. bibliog il Scienne 167:1749-
51 Mr 27 '70
ALKANES. See Hydrocarbons
ALKEMA, Chester Jay
Experimenting with tempera. il Design 71:
26-30 mid-Wint '70
Exploring with melted wax crayon; excerpts
from The complete crayon book. il Design
71:4-7 Sum '70
Scrap materials. il Design 71:4-9 Fall '69
ALKENES. See Olefins
ALKIRE, James
Parking garage built to give downtown a
lift. il Am City 85:65-7 Ag '70
ALL about love and marriage; story. See Cave,
H.
ALL Africa conference of churches. See Re-
ligious conferences—Africa
ALL-America cities
All America cities 1969. T. Barry. il Look
34:60-4 Mr 10 '70
ALL-America football team. See Football
players
ALL around the town; drama. See Larson,
E.
ALL India congress on evangelism. See Reli-
gious conferences—India
ALL risk personal property insurance. See In-
surance—All risk policies
ALL season vehicle. See Crawler vehicles
ALL-Star baseball game
All-Star thing. il Time 96:33 Jl 27 '70
Boo-boo or baby for Bowie; selection of All-
Star team by the fans. W. Leggett. il por
Sports Illus 32:22-4+ Je 15 '70
ALL-star football game
One-night season; K.C. vs. College All-Stars.
J. Jares. il Sports Illus 33:8-11 Ag 10 '70
Owners and players fumble on in Philly; Super
bowl champs vs. College All-Stars. A.
Wright. il Sports Illus 33:46-7 Ag 3 '70
ALL-terrain vehicles. See Motor vehicles, Am-
phibious
ALL year schools. See School year
ALLAGASH WILDERNESS WATERWAY. See
Wilderness areas—Maine
ALLAN, J. R. See Schopf, T. J. M. jt. auth.
ALLAN, James
Strategy for fired executives. il Duns 96:44-5
S '70
ALLAN, Skip
Sails, spars, and rigging. il Motor B 126:
72-3 D '70; 127:60+ Ja '71
ALLARD, William Albert
Hutterites, plain people of the West. il Nat
Geog 138:98-125 Jl '70

ALLDREDGE, Melvin Wilson
New teeth for the lion? por Forbes 105:44 F
15 '70 *
ALLEGIANCE
Higher patriotism; ideas of the Founding
fathers. N. Cousins. Sat R 53:20 Jl 4 '70
See also
Naturalization
ALLEGIANCE, Oaths of. See Loyalty, Oaths of
ALLEGOOD, Wandell
Ah-chaf-ah-lie-ah spells bass. il Outdoor
Life 145:68-9+ Mr '70
ALLEGORY (art) See Symbolism in art
ALLEGRO, John Marco
Allegro troppo. Newsweek 76:66 Ag 31 '70 *
Jesus as mushroom. il Time 95:49 Je 8 '70 *
Marinating the mushroom. J. A. Fitzmyer.
America 123:206-7 S 26 '70 *
ALLELOMORPHISM
DNA synthesis during yeast sporulation:
genetic control of an early developmental
event. R. Roth and K. Lusnak. bibliog il
Science 168:493-4 Ap 24 '70
Gibbon fibrinopeptides: identification of a
glycine-serine allelism at position B-3. G. A.
Mross and others. bibliog il Science 170:
468-70 O 23 '70
ALLEN, Alan A. and others
Natural oil seepage at Coal Oil Point, Santa
Barbara, California. bibliog il Science 170:
974-7 N 27 '70
ALLEN, Dick
Pop epics. Poetry 117:115-17 N '70
Theory of the alternate universe; To the
S-F woman; Escape velocity; Poster poem;
poems. Poetry 115:219-23 Ja '70
ALLEN, Durward L.
Environmental pollution: an ecological per-
spective. Ed Digest 36:51-4 D '70
ALLEN, Dwight W.
Frenzy at U. Mass. por Time 96:34 D 21 '70 *
ALLEN, Elizabeth
Who wants to throw a cannonball? Writer
83:25-6+ O '70
ALLEN, Eric R. See Cadle, R. D. jt. auth.
ALLEN, Ethan
Ethan Allen, by C. A. Jellison. Review
Sat R 53:36 F 7 '70. S. N. Katz
ALLEN, George
You win! You're fired! A. Wright. por Sports
Illus 33:34-6+ S 7 '70 *
ALLEN, Gwenfread E.
Guadalcanal today. il Travel 133:60-6 Ap
'70
ALLEN, Hardy
Indianapolis 500 pit: no place for a green-
horn. il pors Ebony 25:112-14+ My '70 *
ALLEN, Hope E.
Fantasy or reality? Education in the inner
city. Clear House 44:356-9 F '70
ALLEN, Ivan, 1911-
Growing up liberal in Atlanta. il por N Y
Times Mag p4-5+ D 27 '70
ALLEN, James Browning
Excerpt from Senate debate, March 11, 1970.
Cong Digest 49:145+ My '70
ALLEN, James E.
How Catholics are making up their minds on
birth control. il Chr Cent 87:915-18 Jl 29 '70
ALLEN, James Edward, 1911-
Competence for all as the goal for secondary
education; excerpts from address. Ed Di-
gest 36:24-7 S '70
Education for survival; adaptation of ad-
dress, January 1970. il Am Ed 6:18-23 Mr
'70
International education year 1970; statement.
Sch & Soc 98:318 Sum '70
Kids our high schools forget; interview. por
Nations Bsns 58:70-2 Je '70
Right to read. Ed Digest 35:20-2 Mr '70
Right to read, target for the 70's; address,
September 23, 1969. Sch & Soc 98:82-4 F '70
We can end juvenile illiteracy. Read Digest
96:157-8+ Ap '70
about
Advice from the top. J. Lloyd. Sr Schol 95:
Schol Teach 2 O 13 '69 *
Allen affair. por Newsweek 75:17-18 Je 22
'70 *
Allen asks educator's views on U.S. center of
lifelong learning. Aging 183:14 Ja '70 *
Allen's dismissal clouds right-to-read pro-
gram. S. Wagner. Pub W 197:40 Je 22 '70 *
Commissioner Allen learns reading is FUN-
damental. J. Lloyd. il por Sr Schol 96:Schol
Teach 2 Ja 26 '70
Dissenter in the administration. Time 95:50
My 11 '70 *

ALLEN, Larry
Color TV by remote control. il Radio-Electr 42:45-9 Ja '71
Programmed automatic fine tuning. il Radio-Electr 41:57-61 F '70
Stereo multiplex FM in 1970 cars. il Radio-Electr 41:61+ Je '70

ALLEN, Leland C. and Kollman, P. A.
Theory of anomalous water. bibliog il Science 167:1443-54 Mr 13 '70

ALLEN, Lewis M.
Printing with the handpress; excerpts. il Pub W 198:58-60 Jl 20 '70

ALLEN, Linda
(ed) Look you like; questions and answers. See issues of Today's health

ALLEN, Lorin B.
Well supply is best for Vicksburg. il Am City 85:125+ My '70

ALLEN, Mickey
Indians don't cry. il Read Digest 97:111-14 N '70

ALLEN, Reginald
Artist life. D. J. Soria. por Hi Fi 20:secII 4-6+ My '70 *

ALLEN, Rex Whitaker
Future of the profession. Arch Rec 147:123-6 F '70

ALLEN, Richie
Bird in hand and a burning Busch. W. Leggett. il por Sports Illus 32:18-23 Mr 23 '70 *
Candles are burning low in Philly. W. Leggett. il por Sports Illus 32:40-1 Je 1 '70 *
Richie Allen: I'm my own man. L. J. Banks. il pors Ebony 25:88-90+ Jl '70 *

ALLEN, Robert Thomas
Leave my world alone. il Read Digest 96:195-8 Ap '70

ALLEN, Robert V.
(comp) Articles and other books received; Soviet Union. See issues of American historical review

ALLEN, Rodney F.
Their time is now. Schol Teach Jr/Sr High p 19+ D 7 '70

ALLEN, Sue
Chicago book show, a review. bibliog il Pub W 197:52+ My 4 '70

ALLEN, Susan T. See Svec, K. H. jt. auth.

ALLEN, Tom
Pork promoter no. 1. il por Farm J 93:H13+ O '69

ALLEN, Ward P.
Realizing the benefits of space technology; direct broadcast satellites; statement, May 11, 1970. Dept State Bul 63:95-9 Jl 20 '70
U.S. discusses work of U.N. Outer space committee; statement, September 1, 1970. Dept State Bul 63:398-402 O 5 '70

ALLEN, William
Point of order. il Newsweek 75:21-2 Ap 13 '70 *

ALLEN, William M.
Diagonal periodic relationship. bibliog il por Chem 43:22-4 Ap '70

ALLEN, Woody
Hassidic tales, with a guide to their interpretation by the noted scholar. New Yorker 46:31-2 Je 20 '70
A look at organized crime. New Yorker 46:24-5 Ag 15 '70

ALLENDE GOSSENS, Salvador
Sovereign right of revolution; interview, ed. by D. Lee. por Time 96:35 S 21 '70

about

Allende casts a shadow on business. por Bsns W p28 N 7 '70 *
Best way for Chile. Nation 211:228 S 21 '70 *
Center stage for Chile's Marxist president. il por Newsweek 76:52+ N 2 '70 *
Chile: a Marxist at the top? il por Newsweek 76:49 S 21 '70 *
Chile and the US. New Repub 163:9-10 N 7 '70 *
Chile starts chasing the capitalists. il por Time 97:68 Ja 4 '71 *
Chile: the expanding left. il pors Time 96:23-4+ O 19 '70 *
Chile: the making of a precedent. il por Time 96:34-5 S 21 '70 *
Chile turns to Marxism. T. M. Gannon. America 123:321-2 O 24 '70 *
Chile: victory and violence. il por Time 96:16 N 2 '70 *
Chileans have elected a revolution. N. Gall. il pors N Y Times Mag p26-7+ N 1 '70 *
Chile's new president declares attitude on religion. Chr Today 15:44 Ja 1 '71 *
Clearing the way. Newsweek 76:64 O 12 '70 *
Crucial decision. il por Time 96:24 S 7 '70 *
Expectations in Chile. W. R. Long. New Repub 163:8-9 N 28 '70 *

Fidel was glad. Nat R 22:982+ S 22 '70 *
Give up? J. Burnham. Nat R 22:1205 N 17 '70 *
Mandate for a Marxist. por Newsweek 76:58 S 14 '70 *
Marxist in first. il por Sr Schol 97:4 O 5 '70 *
Marxist regime? P. Zottele. Chr Cent 87:1429-30 N 25 '70 *
No miracle worker. Newsweek 76:57 N 16 '70 *
October revolution in Chile? S. Rodman. Nat R 22:1053-5 O 6 '70 *
Political avalanche occurs in Chile. J. S. Bradshaw. Chr Cent 87:163-4 S 30 '70 *
Projecting the common touch. Time 96:33-4 N 16 '70 *
Tightening the noose. Newsweek 77:30 Ja 4 '71 *

ALLENTOWN, Pa.
Stores
Hometown store takes to the road; Hess's. il Bsns W p118-20 Je 20 '70

ALLER, Lawrence H.
Planetary nebulae. See issues of Sky and telescope to July 1970

ALLERGIC bronchial asthma. See Asthma

ALLERGIC encephalomyelitis. See Encephalomyelitis

ALLERGY
Allergies, G. D. Barkin and J. P. McGovern. il Todays Ed 59:42-4 N '70
Answers to your questions plus cake and cookie recipes for allergy diets. R. H. Smithies. il Good H 170:180+ Mr '70
Christmas allergy. Newsweek 76:38 D 28 '70
Detergents: side effects of the washday miracles; pollution and allergy. N. Gruchow. Science 167:151 Ja 9 '70
How to cope with your allergy. A. S. Markovits. il Mech Illus 66:65-7 My '70
In vitro lymphocyte reactivity during depression of tuberculin hypersensitivity by 6-mercaptopurine. B. Zweiman and S. M. Phillips. il Science 169:284-5 Jl 17 '70
Mites and commercial extracts of house dust. G. W. Wharton. bibliog il Science 167:1382-3 Mr 6 '70
Tuberculin-active carbohydrate that induces inhibition of macrophage migration but not lymphocyte transformation. S. D. Chaparas and others. bibliog il Science 170:637-9 N 6 '70
See also
Food allergy
Shwartzman phenomenon

ALLEY, C. O. and others
Apollo 11 laser ranging retro-reflector: initial measurements from the McDonald observatory. bibliog il Science 167:368-70 Ja 23 '70
Laser ranging retro-reflector: continuing measurements and expected results. bibliog il Science 167:458-60 Ja 30 '70

ALLIANCE for labor action
ALA hard sell softens the South. il Bsns W p60+ F 21 '70

ALLIANCE for progress
Alliance rhetoric versus Latin American reality. A. F. Lowenthal. For Affairs 48:494-508 Ap '70
Beginning anew in Latin America; excerpt from address. E. M. Kennedy. Sat R 53:18-21 O 17 '70

ALLIANCE ventures, inc.
Control of plant for minority workers being transferred. Aviation W 93:61 N 9 '70

ALLIANCES
Collective security; address, June 15, 1970. L. L. Lemnitzer. Vital Speeches 36:669-71 Ag 15 '70
Entangling alliances. D. Fromkin. For Affairs 48:688-700 Jl '70
Needed: a single alliance to keep world peace. D. Lawrence. U S News 68:100 Je 22 '70
See also
International organizations, Regional
Nato

ALLIED bank international. See New York (city)—Banks

ALLIED chemical building. See New York (city)—Buildings

ALLIED supermarkets. See Supermarkets

ALLILUEVA, Svetlana. See Stalina, S. I.

ALLIN, Roger W.
Values! address. il Parks & Rec 5:20-3+ N '70

ALLIONE, Louis
Up in his balloon. il por Life 69:62-5 Ag 21 '70 *

ALLIS-Chalmers manufacturing company
Allis rejoins the power play. il Bsns W p40 F 28 '70
Merger of Whites eases grip on Allis. Bsns W p22-3 Ag 22 '70

ALLISON, Bobby
Allison act. S. Kelly. il pors Hot Rod 23:92-5 N '70 *
ALLISON, Donnie
Allison act. S. Kelly. il pors Hot Rod 23:92-5 N '70 *
ALLISON, Graham, and others
Limits to intervention. For Affairs 48:245-61 Ja '70
ALLISON, Jim, Jr
All-Republican Senate? Jim Allison's working on it. D. R. Maxey. il por Look 34:34-6+ O 20 '70 *
ALLISON, Truett, and Van Twyver, Henry
Evolution of sleep; with biographical sketches. il pors Natur Hist 79:8, 56-65 F '70
ALLISON and Busby (firm) See Publishers and publishing—Great Britain
ALLIUMS
Alliums for the garden. P. M. Synge. il Horticulture 49:26-7+ Ja '71
Beautiful onions. N. M. Shopis il Home Gard 57:52 O '70
ALLON, Yigal
Middle East: a secret rendezvous. il pors Time 96:26 N 23 '70 *
ALLONBY, Charles
Autumn leaves that blossom in the spring. il Org Gard & Farm 17:40-3 S '70
It hasn't been easy. il Am City 85:47-8 D '70
ALLOPURINOL
Allopurinol: alteration in pyrimidine metabolism in man. W. N. Kelley and T. D. Beardmore. bibliog il Science 169:388-90 Ji 24 '70
Orotidinuria induced by allopurinol. R. M. Fox and others. bibliog il Science 168:861-2 My 15 '70
ALLOTT, Gordon
Campus unrest; address, September 5, 1970. Vital Speeches 36:758-60 O 1 '70
ALLOWANCES, Duty free. See Duty free importation
ALLOWAY, Lawrence
Art. See issues of Nation
ALLOYS
Alloys beyond superalloys; dispersion-strengthened alloys. E. Gross. il Sci N 97:107-8 Ja 24 '70
Fiber composite alloys: preparation by controlled dissociation of metallic solid solutions. A. Fesolowich and others. bibliog il Science 167:1374-6 My 6 '70
Uses for an alloy with a memory; nitinol. il Chem 43:26 My '70
    See also
Samarium alloys
ALLPHIN, Willard
Stereo ain't dead. il Mod Phot 34:80-1+ Ap '70
—See Lees, A. jt. auth.
ALLSTATE enterprises stock fund. See Investment trusts
ALLUSIONS
Study of the allusions in Bradbury's Fahrenheit 451. P. Sisario. Engl J 59:201-5+ F '70
ALMEIDA, Antonio de
Uproar: Previn and afterwards. C. Cunningham. Hi Fi 20:secII 25+ Ap '70 *
ALMEIDA MOTTA, João Pedro de
Portuguese passion. H. Weinstock. Sat R 53:53 Ji 25 '70 *
ALMORA, India
Killer leopard of Danpur. J. Shepherd. il Sports Illus 32:18-19 Mr 2 '70
ALNUS rhombifolia. See Alder
ALOHA airlines. See Airlines—Hawaii
ALONSO, Nina
Crosby pond; poem. New Yorker 46:50 O 24 '70
ALOU, Felipe
To improve an Alou, age him. P. Carry. Sports Illus 33:48 Ag 17 '70 *
ALOU, Jesus
To improve an Alou, age him. P. Carry. Sports Illus 33:48 Ag 17 '70 *
ALOU, Matty
To improve an Alou, age him. P. Carry. Sports Illus 33:48 Ag 17 '70 *
ALPAR, Gitta
Top tenors, on L.P. A. Favia-Artsay. pors Hobbies 75:39 Je '70 *
ALPERN, David M.
Playing post office; letter to editor. por Newsweek 75:24 Ap 6 '70
ALPERT, D. and Bitzer, D. L.
Advances in computer-based education. bibliog il Science 167:1582-90 Mr 20 '70
ALPERT, Helen
Our military retirees point the way. il Har Yrs 10:6-11 Ag '70
Spruce yourself up for the holidays. Har Yrs 10:6-8+ D '70
Their community needs them. il pors Har Yrs 10:43-5+ Je '70

ALPERT, Hollis
But who wrote the movie? il Sat R 53:8-11 D 26 '70
SR goes to the movies. See issues of Saturday review
Visconti in Venice. il por Sat R 53:16-18 Ag 8; 20 D 19 '70
ALPHA autoradiography. See Autoradiography
ALPHA ray spectrometry. See Spectrum analysis
ALPHA systems, inc.
How to manage a professor. Bsns W p40 Ag 22 '70
ALPHA waves. See Brain waves
ALPHABET
Africa to zenith: a modern alphabet; children's book aimed at black Americans. il Time 96:60 D 7 '70
    See also
Lettering
ALPHABET museum, Tel Aviv
Doctor David Diringer and the Alphabet museum. I. Soifer. il por Pub W 198:48+ S 7 '70
ALPINE climbing. See Mountaineering
ALPINE COUNTY, Calif.
Gay mecca no. 1. il Time 96:12 N 2 '70
ALPINE ecology. See Mountain ecology
ALPREN, Morton
On meanings in relationships in curriculum and instruction. bibliog f Sch & Soc 98:100-2 F '70
ALPS
    See also
Avalanches
ALSATIAN cookery. See Cookery, French
ALSATIAN wines. See Wine
ALSBERG, Henry Garfield
Obituary
    Pub W 198:28 D 7 '70
ALSCHULER, Alfred S. jr
Building quality tennis courts. il Parks & Rec 5:27-8+ O '70
ALSOP, Joseph
Reading Soviet intentions. New Repub 163:17-19 O 3 '70
Russia's menacing new challenge in the Middle East. Read Digest 97:47-51 Ag '70
ALSOP, Stewart
[Column on public affairs] See issues of Newsweek
Integration: a tragic failure. Read Digest 96:93-4 My '70
    about
Machiavelli? speculations on the President's machinations. Nation 210:676 Je 8 '70 *
ALSTON, Elizabeth
Artichokes. il Look 34:66-7 Ap 7 '70
Picnic for Thanksgiving. il Look 34:82-3 N 17 '70
ALT, Ray
World record ram. il por Outdoor Life 146:68-71+ N '70
ALTAMIL corporation
Ex-owner didn't fit in. pors Bsns W p64+ F 14 '70
ALTAMONT raceway music festival. See Music festivals—California
ALTARS
Seventeenth century portable altar. il Hobbies 75:104-5 Mr '70
ALTBACH, Philip G.
Gandhi: in history as in life, a man of enormous complexity. Commonweal 92:16-17 Mr 13 '70
ALTER, Robert
Eliot, Lawrence & the Jews. Commentary 50:81-6 O '70
On Lea Goldberg & S. Y. Agnon. bibliog f Commentary 49:83-6 My '70
Shalit case. Commentary 50:55-61 Jl; 16 N '70
Zionism for the 70's. bibliog f Commentary 49:47-57 F; 12+ My '70
ALTERNATIVE press periodicals. See Counter culture literature
ALTHAUS, Keith
Poem: The terror of new sharp pencils, Toy soldiers; poems. Poetry 117:24-5 O '70
ALTIMETERS
Altitude alerter production pushed. K. J. Stein. il Aviation W 93:52-3+ Jl 27 '70
Product news; automatic encoding altimeter. il Flying 88:20+ Ja '71
ALTITUDE, Influence of
Physiology of high altitude. R. J. Hock. il Sci Am 222:52-8+ F '70
ALTITUDE flying. See Aviation—Altitude flying
ALTITUDE indicators. See Altimeters
ALTMAN, Nathan D.
Avanti still means forward. D. A. Jedlicka. il por Esquire 73:116-17+ Ap '70 *

ALTMAN, Robert
Creation in chaos. il por Time 96:62 Jl 13 '70 *
ALTMEYER, Robert
Is the army a welfare state? Nat R 22:300
Mr 24 '70
ALTOONA, Pa, public library
New Altoona library features color, space and
comfort. Library J 95:943 Mr 1 '70
ALTSHULER, Kenneth Z. and Rainer, J. D.
Observations on psychiatric services for the
deaf. bibliog Ment Hy 54:535-9 O '70
ALUM, Manuel
Manuel Alum, Kaufmann concert hall, NYC.
T. Borek. Dance Mag 45:74 Ja '71 *
ALUMINAUT (research submarine) See Sub-
marine research vehicles
ALUMINUM
    See also
Plants, Effect of aluminum on

                    Prices
Aluminum prices head for the roof. il Bsns W
p26 Ap 18 '70
ALUMINUM, Structural
Applied aluminum finishes: guidelines for
specifiers. W. W. Binger; R. C. Spooner; A.
H. Bushey. il Arch Rec 147:151-2 My '70
ALUMINUM automobile engines. See Auto-
mobile engines—Materials
ALUMINUM boats. See Boats—Materials
ALUMINUM company of America
Finance-minded boss for Alcoa. por Bsns W
p40 Je 27 '70
ALUMINUM finishing. See Metal finishing
ALUMINUM foil mulch. See Mulching
ALUMINUM industry and trade

                    Finance
Aluminum cutbacks reduce the glut. Bsns W
p45 O 17 '70

                    Australia
Emerging giant Down Under; Comalco ltd. il
Forbes 105:42-5 Je 15 '70

                United States
Aluminum eyes an auto market. Bsns W p88
Ap 18 '70
Aluminum predicts upward stability. Bsns W
p30 N 14 '70
    See also
Reynolds metals company
ALUMINUM polishes. See Polishing materials
ALUMINUM roofing. See Roofing
ALUMINUM wire. See Wire, Aluminum
ALUMNI. See College graduates
ALUMNI funds. See Colleges and universities
—Gifts, legacies, etc.
ALVARADO, Juan Velasco. See Velasco Alva-
rado, J.
ALVAREZ, Carlos
Gator aid. H. L. Masin. pors Sr Schol 97:
26-7 O 26 '70 *
ALVAREZ, Luis Echeverría. See Echeverría
Alvarez, L.
ALVAREZ, Luis W.
Exploring pyramids using cosmic rays. il
Chem 43:42-3 Jl '70 *
—and others
Search for hidden chambers in the pyramids:
adaptation of address, April 30, 1969. bib-
liog il Science 167:832-9 F 6 '70
Search for magnetic monopoles in the lunar
sample. bibliog il Science 167:701-3 Ja 30
'70
ALVAREZ, T. Ralph. See Boucek, R. J. jt.
auth.
ALVAREZ, Walter Clement
Looking at medicine. Look 34:8 Ag 11; 12-13
S 22; 42 D 15 '70
ALVES, Márcio Moreira
Brazil: a country where Christians are out-
laws. il Cath World 212:65-8 N '70
Christians, Marxists and dictatorship in Bra-
zil. Chr Cent 87:723-7 Je 10 '70
Kidnapped diplomats: Greek tragedy on a
Latin stage. Commonweal 92:311-14 Je 26
'70
ALVES, Rubem
Resurrection of Utopia. Chr Cent 87:347 Mr
25 '70 *
ALVIN Ailey American dance theater
Alvin Ailey American dance theater; Brook-
lyn academy of music. M. Marks. il Dance
Mag 44:79-81 F '70
Alvin Ailey American dance theatre; Brook-
lyn academy of music, NYC. J. Anderson.
Dance Mag 44:79-80 Je '70
Dance. N. Goldner. Nation 210:571-2 My 11
'70

ALVORD, Tom
Try a mini-farm at your camp. il Camp Mag
42:21 Je '70
ALWAN, Ameen
Blind Mexican; Banderillero: poems. New
Repub 162:21 Ja 31 '7J
ALWIN Nikolais dance company
Alwin Nikolais dance theatre with Carolyn
Carlson; City center theatre. D. Hering. il
Dance Mag 44:83-5 F '70
Choreography, music, costumes, sets, etc, etc.
by Alwin Nikolais. H. C. Schonberg. il por
N Y Times Mag p56-7+ D 6 '70
Nikolais dance theatre; New York city
center. M. Marks. Dance Mag 44:73 Jl '70
Space follies: the Alwin Nikolais dance the-
atre. il Vogue 155:192-3 F 1 '70
ALYEA, Brant
Another bad trade pays off. W. Leggett. por
Sports Illus 32:64+ My 11 '70
ALZA corporation
Alza's big promise. por Duns 97:53 Ja '71
AMABILE, George
Hadrian's villa: water, wind & stone; poem.
New Yorker 46:40 Mr 28 '70
AMABIS. J. M. and Cabral, Dulce
RNA and DNA puffs in polytene chromosomes
of rhynchosciara: inhibition by extirpation
of prothorax. bibliog il Science 169:692-4
Ag 14 '70
AMALGAMATED clothing workers of America
Is right of access coming? ACWA suit against
four Chicago newspapers. G. Cranberg.
Sat R 53:48-9+ Ag 8 '70
AMALGAMATED meat cutters and butcher
workmen of North America
Winners and losers: meat cutters strike
against IBP. il Forbes 105:30+ My 1 '70
AMALRIK, Andrei
Brave parasite. W. J. Parente. New Repub
163:26-7 N 7 '70 *
Involuntary journey. pors Newsweek 76:61
N 23 '70 *
Repression with flowers. Time 95:28 Je 1 '70 *
Russia's courageous dissenters. A. Alvarez.
Sat R 53:45-6 N 28 '70 *
Soviet dissenter: visit from the KGB. il por
Newsweek 75:43 Je 1 '70 *
Trial of a protester. America 123:482 D 5 '70 *
Voice silenced, a voice raised. Time 96:28+
N 23 '70 *
AMAN, George
September; poem. America 123:260 O 10 '70
AMANITIN. See Toxins and antitoxins
AMANTADINE hydrochloride
Amantadine-dopamine interaction; possible
mode of action in Parkinsonism. R. P.
Grelak and others. bibliog il Science 169:
203-4 Jl 10 '70
AMARAL, Anthony
Nevada's endangered pelicans. il Nat
Parks & Con Mag 44:23-7 Jl '70
AMARILLO, Tex.
Lights that match the elegance of a civic
center. T. Abrahamson. il Am City 85:128+
Ap '70
AMARYLLIS
Amaryllis, the giants of the indoor garden.
C. M. Fitch. il Home Gard 57:26-7 O '70
Spectacular amaryllis. R. M. Peters. il Hor-
ticulture 48:30-1+ D '70
    See also
Lycoris
AMATEUR astronomers. See Astronomers,
Amateur
AMATEUR athletic union of the United States
Victory over Germany but a loss to the AAU;
suspension of three of the U.S. team. P.
Putnam. Sports Illus 33:48 Jl 27 '70
AMATEUR bicycle league national cycling
championship. See Bicycle racing
AMATEUR chamber music players. See Musi-
cians, Amateur
AMATEUR moving pictures. See Moving pic-
tures, Amateur
AMATEUR musicians. See Musicians, Ama-
teur
AMATEUR photographers. See Photographers
AMATEUR photography. See Photography
AMATEUR radio operators. See Radio opera-
tors. Amateur
AMATEUR radio stations. See Radio stations,
Amateur—Equipment
AMATEUR sailors. See Seamen
AMATEUR scientists. See Scientists, Amateur
AMATEUR seamen. See Seamen
AMATEUR theatricals
    See also
Moving pictures, Amateur

AMATEURISM (sports)
Amateurs on the skids? future of winter Olympics. il por Newsweek 77:55-6 Ja 11 '71
Name is the name of the game; amateurism and Olympics. W. Johnson. il Sports Illus 32:12-17 Mr 9 '70
Olympics and modern philosophy; amateur status of Soviet skiers. A. Lunn. Nat R 22:840 Ag 11 '70

AMATI, Paolo
Chloramphenicol: effect on DNA synthesis during phage development in escherichia coli. bibliog il Science 168:1226-8 Je 5 '70

AMAX. See American metal climax, inc.

AMAYA, Mario
Canada: Jack Chambers. il Art in Am 58: 118-21 S '70
Canada's group of seven. il Art in Am 58: 122-5 My '70
Collectors: Mr and Mrs Jack W. Glenn. il por Art in Am 58:86-93 Mr '70

AMAZON RIVER
Amazing Amazonia. L. Hossack. il Travel 133:40-5+ Je '70
World's worst animals; excerpts from The Amazon. R. Furneaux. il Horizon 12:112-17 Wint '70

AMBASSADORS
Off the top shelf; new US ambassador to France. il por Newsweek 75:53 Mr 16 '70
See also
Annenberg, W. H.
Negro ambassadors
United States—Diplomatic and consular service

AMBASSADORS wives
Ambassador's wife. Trans-Action 7:8+ N '69

AMBERFISH fishing
Yellowtails by the ton. L. Miracle. il por Outdoor Life 145:60-3+ F '70

AMBERINA glass. See Glassware

AMBOINESE
Emergency landing. il Time 96:33 S 14 '70
Overnight stay. il por Newsweek 76:60 S 14 '70

AMBROSE, Myles J.
Narcotics; address, June 23, 1970. Vital Speeches 36:612-15 Ag 1 '70

AMBULANCE helicopters. See Helicopters, Ambulance

AMBULANCES
Ambulance hustlers; investigation into private ambulance company abuses in Chicago. il Newsweek 76:56 Jl 6 '70

AMCHITKA ISLAND
Resolution on impending test on Amchitka Island. Liv Wildn 33:33-4 Aut '69

AMEBAS
Amoebas biology and the public. il por Sci N 98:443-4 D 12 '70
Amoebic killers; naegleria gruberi. il Sci N 98:245 S 19 '70
Artificial life synthesis. Newsweek 76:79-80 N 23 '70
Making of an amoeba. Time 96:52 N 23 '70
Reassembly of living cells from dissociated components. K. W. Jeon and others. bibliog il Science 167:1626-7 Mr 20 '70
Reconstituted amoebas. Sci Am 222:57-8 My '70
Transformation of tetramitus amebae into flagellates. C. Fulton. bibliog il Science 167:1269-70 F 27 '70

AMEN, Carol
Church magazine market. Writer 83:27-8 D '70
Dieting till death. il Sci Digest 67:27-31 My '70
Hyacinths to feed the soul. Read Digest 96: 201-2 Mr '70

AMENDMENTS to the Constitution. See United States—Constitution—Amendments

AMERICA
See also
United States
     Antiquities
See also
Man, Prehistoric
Mayas
Paleo-Indians
     Discovery and exploration
Ancient landings in America; findings of C. H. Gordon. J Lear. il Sat R 53:18-19+ Jl 18 '70
Canaanite Columbus? the Metcalf stone. il por Newsweek 76:65 O 26 '70
First discovery of America. C. Ogburn, jr. il Horizon 12:92-9 Wint '70
Jews first American settlers? J. R. Greisch. Chr Today 15:46 N 6 '70
See also
Vikings

AMERICA (periodical)
Of many things: editorial changes. D. R. Campion. America 123:inside cover S 5 '70
See also
Campion award

AMERICA illustrated (periodical)
Ads that pierce the iron curtain; USIA magazine. Bsns W p30+ Jl 18 '70

AMERICAN academy of orthopedic surgeons
Medical sciences. Sci N 97:127 Ja 31 '70

AMERICAN addresses. See Speeches, addresses, etc.

AMERICAN-AFRO studies. See Afro-American studies

AMERICAN airlines, inc.
American begins flying own 747. Aviation W 93:30 Jl 20 '70
American expects meager traffic growth. il Aviation W 93:28 D 21 '70
American has a way with young women; stewardesses conduct charm courses in ghettos. V. Louviere. il Nations Bsns 58: 19 Ja '70
American plans increases in Caribbean flights, seats. Aviation W 94:26-7 Ja 11 '71
American seeks to develop Fiji market. Aviation W 93:40 D 21 '70
American seeks training flight reductions. J. P. Woolsey. il Aviation W 93:41+ Jl 13 '70
American 747 records high load factors for first week. R. S. Kahn. Aviation W 92:26-7 Mr 16 '70
American 707s get new cargo loaders. Aviation W 93:37 S 28 '70
American STOL requests sent to thirteen manufacturers. D. A. Brown. Aviation W 93:22-3 Ag 17 '70
American stresses basic role as carrier. L. Doty. Aviation W 93:33-4 O 12 '70
American testing new ticket device. Aviation W 93:64 Jl 13 '70
American, TWA report losses. il Aviation W 92:41 Mr 23 '70
American, Western in merger agreement. W. H. Gregory. il Aviation W 93:24-5 N 9 '70
American's Pacific strategy evolving. W. H. Gregory. il Aviation W 93:26-30 N 30 '70
Australian service approval nears. Aviation W 93:30 Jl 6 '70
Pan Am 1969 loss $25.2 million; American reports profit gain. il Aviation W 92:26 F 16 '70

AMERICAN antiquarian society, Worcester, Mass.
Furniture owned by the American antiquarian society. W. D. Garrett. il Antiques 97:402-7 Mr '70

AMERICAN architecture. See Architecture, American

AMERICAN art. See Art, American

AMERICAN artist (periodical)
Sterling McIlhany: the new editor. R. J. Riedinger. Am Artist 34:5 Ja '70
Student drawing competition. N. Kent. il Am Artist 34:38-44+ Je '70

AMERICAN artists. See Artists, American

AMERICAN association for the advancement of science
AAAS officers, committees, and representatives for 1970. Science 167:1154-7 F 20 '70
AAAS presidency: controversy flares over Seaborg candidacy. P. M. Boffey. Science 170:1177-80 D 11 '70
AAAS: Seaborg wins election; scientific freedom panel created. P. M. Boffey. Science 170:1283-5 D 18 '70
AAAS won't absorb Science service. P. M. Boffey. Science 170:418 O 23 '70
Defoliants, a closed case? Commonweal 93: 363 Ja 15 '71
Fallout over Seaborg. il por Time 97:49 Ja 4 '71
In-house politics at AAAS. por Sci N 98: 460-1 D 19 '70
Squabbling scientists. por Newsweek 76:118-19 D 14 '70
Time of torment for science. il por Sci N 99:5-6 Ja 2 '71
Young scientists and the AAAS. M. Lipkin, jr. Science 170:683 N 13 '70
     Meetings
Out of the grooves of academe; dissent at annual meetings. D. Grumbach. Commonweal 91:468-70 Ja 30 '70
     Meetings, 1969
AAAS council meeting, 1969. D. Wolfle. il Science 167:1151-3 F 20 '70
Introspection. Sci Am 222:42-4 F '70
1969 meeting of the AAAS: a brief appraisal. W. G. Berl. Science 167:1157-8 F 20 '70

AMERICAN association for the advancement of science—*Continued*

Meetings, 1970

AAAS annual meeting; program. il Science 170:874-97 N 20 '70
AAAS: conflict, confrontation, consideration. il Sci N 99:21-2 Ja 9 '71
Political science, 1970; effort by activists to take over meeting. il Newsweek 77:78 Ja 11 '71
Program notes, AAAS annual meeting. Science 170:1341 D 18 '70
Scientists' dilemma. Nation 212:68-9 Ja 18 '71

Committee on science in the promotion of human welfare

Promotion of human welfare; letter. W. Modell. Science 170:1254+ D 18 '70

AMERICAN association of evangelical students
Evangelical students: alive and well. R. L. Love. Chr Today 14:34 My 22 '70

AMERICAN association of homes for the aging
Senator Moss gets AAHA honor; urges stricter U.S. standards; Award for distinguished service to the aging. por Aging 182:9 D '69

AMERICAN association of junior colleges
Community services by community colleges; establishment of a National council on community services for community and junior colleges. Sch & Soc 98:17-18 Ja '70

AMERICAN association of neurological surgeons. See Harvey Cushing society

AMERICAN association of physics teachers
APS-AAPT meet in Chicago. M. S. Rothenberg. il Phys Today 23:53-5 Ja '70
Chicago meeting involved with society; with editorial comment. G. B. Lubkin. Phys Today 23:67+, 112 Mr '70
See also
Commission on college physics

AMERICAN association of retired persons
AARP, NRTA, hold biennial meetings; report big growth; late start plan continued by $251,880 grant. il Aging 190:12-13 Ag '70

AMERICAN association of school administrators
Money talks at AASA; annual meeting. Sr Schol 96:Schol Teach 2 Ap 6 '70

AMERICAN association of school librarians
AASL: a matter of pride. E. Geller. il Library J 95:2955, 2971-7 S 15 '70
Adrift in new directions; midwinter in Chicago. E. Geller. il Library J 95:1169-72 Mr 15 '70
Business as usual; 1970 ALA conference. P. Schuman. il Library J 95:2977-80 S 15 '70
Dix mix nix on 321.8; AASL affiliation with ALA and DAVI. E. Geller. Library J 95:193 Ja 15 '70
Executive malaise. E. Geller. Library J 95:711 F 15 '70
What stake in ALA? E. Geller. Library J 95:1143 Mr 15 '70

AMERICAN association of state colleges and universities
Responsible professors. T. H. Clancy. America 124:45 Ja 16 '71

AMERICAN association of university professors
Responsible professors. T. H. Clancy. America 124:45 Ja 16 '71

AMERICAN association of variable star observers
AAVSO holds its 59th fall meeting. Sky & Tel 40:364 D '70

AMERICAN astronomical society
American astronomers report; highlights of some papers. See occasional issues of Sky and telescope

AMERICAN athletes. See Athletes

AMERICAN authors. See Authors, American

AMERICAN avitron, inc.
Dynamic growth companies. il pors Nations Bsns 58:88-91 Ap '70

AMERICAN ballads. See Ballads, American

AMERICAN ballet company
American ballet co. in Early songs; Brooklyn academy of music, NYC. D. Hering. il Dance Mag 44:74 Je '70
Dance:
Choreographer E. Feld. N. Goldner. Nation 210:477-8 Ap 20 '70
Poem forgotten at Brooklyn academy of music. N. Goldner. Nation 211:505-6 N 16 '70
Feld in Brooklyn; premiere of Early songs. W. Terry. Sat R 53:44 My 2 '70
No strings. H. Saal. il Newsweek 75:84 Ap 13 '70

AMERICAN ballet theatre
American ballet theatre. W. Terry. il Sat R 53:35 Jl 18; 36 Ag 1 '70

American ballet theatre; Brooklyn academy of music. J. Anderson. il Dance Mag 44:26-7 F '70
American ballet theatre reaches the great divide. M. Marks and J. Anderson. il Dance Mag 44:28-35 S '70
Dance. J. Maskey. Hi Fi 20:MA10-11 O '70
Dance; eight new productions and six revivals presented at New York state theater. N. Goldner. Nation 211:58-60 Jl 20 '70
Dance; Lilac garden, Petrouchka and Fall River legend. J. Maskey. il Hi Fi 20:MA8-9 N '70
Dance me a river. H. Saal. il Newsweek 76:86 Jl 6 '70
1940-1970: an American ballet image. W. Terry. il Sat R 53:58-9+ Je 20 '70
Opening night 1940; a memoir. L. F. Rosen. il Dance Mag 44:34-7 D '70
Stars in search of a heaven. A. Rich. il Time 96:51 Jl 20 '70
Those were the days, my friends; interview, ed. by O. Maynard. D. Saddler. il pors Dance Mag 44:38-42 D '70
Three hits by Feld. W. Terry. il Sat R 53:58 N 21 '70
Through a glass, brightly. O. Maynard. il Dance Mag 44:48-63 Je '70

AMERICAN bankers association
Bankers' view: a slow upturn. il U S News 69:56-9 O 26 '70
How bankers view prospects for business. il U S News 68:58 Je 1 '70

AMERICAN Baptist convention. See Baptists in the United States

AMERICAN bar association
Bar association committee urges actions to aid elderly. Aging 184:26 F '70
Bar association forms law book marketing committee. Pub W 198:36 O 12 '70
Lawyers and student dissent. Sch & Soc 98:10-11 Ja '70
Role of the bar in selection of justices; excerpts from report. il U S News 68:84-7 Je 1 '70
Supreme court and the A.B.A. selecting Supreme court nominees. Time 96:43 Ag 10 '70

AMERICAN basketball association
Haywood affair. il por Time 97:44+ Ja 18 '71
Million-dollar war. il Newsweek 75:63-4 Ap 6 '70

AMERICAN bishop's conference. See National conference of Catholic bishops

AMERICAN bison. See Buffaloes

AMERICAN book publishers council
Debate on the peace resolution. il Pub W 197:39-40 Je 1 '70
International book fairs: how to attend them, how to avoid them. Pub W 197:30-2 My 4 '70
New hope for market research; report of meeting. il Pub W 197:27-9 My 25 '70
New survey shows paperback growth rate. il Pub W 197:78-9 Je 29 '70
1969 in review: book trade organizations. il Pub W 197:52-5 F 9 '70
See also
Association of American publishers (proposed)

Religious publishers group
Religious ghetto; summary of addresses. E. Borowitz; M. Boyd. pors Pub W 197:37-9 Je 1 '70
Religious publishers seek ways to meet a crisis. Pub W 197:34-6 Ap 20 '70
See also
Association of American publishers—Religious book publishing division

AMERICAN booksellers association
ABA announces plans for September regional meeting. Pub W 198:248-9 Ag 31 '70
ABA convention, June 7-10, 1970; program and list of exhibitors. Pub W 197:85-7 Je 8 '70
ABA convention opens with awards presentations. Pub W 197:42 Je 15 '70
ABA 1970; with summaries of addresses. il Pub W 197:56-72 Je 29 '70
1969 in review: book trade organizations. il Pub W 197:54 F 9 '70
San Francisco regional: bookselling in time of crisis. P. Elder. il Pub W 198:26-9 N 9; 30-2 N 23 '70
Trade winds; convention. C. Amory. Sat R 53:10-11 Je 27 '70
White House home library.. bibliog il Pub W 197:47-52 Mr 2 '70

AMERICAN broadcasting companies
ABC tries again for top TV spot. il Bsns W p28 My 16 '70
Age of Reasoner. Time 96:70 N 16 '70
No. 3, and trying harder; ABC's twelve new shows. R. Burgheim. il Time 96:79 O 5 '70

AMERICAN businessmen. See Businessmen
AMERICAN camping association
ACA board tackles critical issues. Camp Mag 42:31 N '70
ACA management study under way. A. Hilton. Camp Mag 42:6+ Je '70
Accounting to ACA members. E. F. Schmidt. por Camp Mag 42:4+ Ap '70
Changing of the guard. J. J. Kirk. por Camp Mag 42:4 Mr '70
Cross-country '71 conventions planned. il Camp Mag 42:6 S '70
Day in the life of a . . ; ACA office. E. F. Schmidt. por Camp Mag 42:4 S '70
Ecology comes to camp. J. J. Kirk. por Camp Mag 42:4 N '70
Lawsuit against ACA; with ACA interracial statement. E. F. Schmidt. Camp Mag 42:6-7+ My '70
Let's talk about a new ACA. N. E. Wieters. por Camp Mag 42:4 Ja '70
News of the month. See issues of Camping magazine
Program highlights of 1970 national convention in St Louis. il Camp Mag 42:7-8 F '70
St Louis convention announces seminars, special interest sessions, kindred groups. il Camp Mag 42:6-7 Ja '70
Slate chosen for ACA offices. il Camp Mag 42:6 N '70
Trying sixties a prelude to the 70's. F. M. Washburn. por Camp Mag 42:4 F '70
AMERICAN can company
Dent in American can. A. A. Butkus. il por Duns 95:38-41 Ap '70
AMERICAN cancer society
Life sciences. Sci N 97:344 Ap 4 '70
Smoking dogs; Tobacco institute tries to discount cancer studies. R. J. Bazell. il Science 170:515 O 30 '70
AMERICAN Catholicism. See Catholic church in the United States
AMERICAN Catholics. See Catholics in the United States
AMERICAN cement corporation
Butler sues former producer of Aerostar. Aviation W 94:66 Ja 11 '71
AMERICAN chambers of commerce. See Chambers of commerce
AMERICAN chemical society
Chemistry. Sci N 98:272 S 26 '70
Chemists formulate portable pensions. Bsns W p38 F 28 '70
AMERICAN children. See Children—United States
AMERICAN city (periodical)
American city awards bring added honors; Award of merit for leadership. il Am City 85:92+ Je '70
1969 merit award winners. il Am City 85:65-7 F '70
AMERICAN civil liberties union
A.C.L.U. dinner; fiftieth anniversary. New Yorker 46:34-5 D 19 '70
ACLU join Scanlan's in dispute with printer. Pub W 198:29 N 2 '70
Role of the mass media. Cur 114:44-6 Ja '70
AMERICAN coins. See Coins
AMERICAN college of surgeons
Medical sciences. Sci N 97:317 Mr 28 '70
Surgeons' latest on cancer, slipped discs; spring meeting. U S News 68:88 Ap 6 '70
AMERICAN college theatre festival. See Drama festivals
AMERICAN colonial history. See United States—History—Colonial period
AMERICAN cookery. See Cookery, American
AMERICAN council of Christian churches
ACCC struggles on despite McIntire's actions. Chr Cent 87:1556 D 30 '70
Will the real ACCC please stand up? Chr Today 15:27 D 4 '70
AMERICAN council on education
How top educators rate graduate schools now. U S News 70:70-1 Ja 11 '71
Politics and tax exemption; educators issue guidelines. Library J 95:2749 S 1 '70
Still no. 1; ACE's new report on graduate schools. il Newsweek 77:58 Ja 11 '71
Study of campus tensions. Sch & Soc 98:206 Ap '70
Tensions on the campus. S. M. Linowitz. por Sch & Soc 98:115-16 F '70
AMERICAN courier corporation
Post office gets a private rival. il Bsns W p22 N 28 '70
AMERICAN cyanamid company
Duel over Elizabeth Arden. il Bsns W p48 O 17 '70
AMERICAN dance symposium. See Dance conferences
AMERICAN designers. See Costume designers
AMERICAN documentation institute. See American society for information science

AMERICAN drama
See also
Theater—United States
AMERICAN eagles. See Eagles
AMERICAN economic assistance. See Economic assistance, American
AMERICAN economic association
Economists at bay; annual meeting. R. Lekachman. Duns 96:9 F '71
Unconventional becomes respectable. Bsns W p62 Ja 9 '71
AMERICAN education week
American education week. P. G. Pafiolis. Todays Ed 59:62 S '70
American education week: 1970. il Todays Ed 59:49 My '70
AMERICAN educational publishers institute
AAP emerges; newly federated organization meets in atmosphere charged by national issues; summaries of addresses. il Pub W 197:42-5 Je 1 '70
As student tempers rise, AEPI and NACS huddle on tactics. Pub W 197:37 Ap 20 '70
1969 in review; book trade organizations. il Pub W 197:52 F 9 '70
See also
Association of American publishers (proposed)
AMERICAN eiders. See Ducks, Wild
AMERICAN Enka corporation
Roarin' rockets! It's Brand-rex. il Bsns W p44 Jl 11 '70
AMERICAN express; story. See Feeley, C.
AMERICAN express company
Trick is managing money. il Bsns W p76-7+ Je 6 '70
AMERICAN farm bureau federation
Farm bureau celebrates 50th. Farm J 94:31 Ja '70
AMERICAN federation of government employees
American federation of government employees. M. H. Cimini. Mo Labor R 93:33-4 O '70
New era for federal workers; bigger unions, strike threats. il U S News 69:62-4 Ag 24 '70
Unfaithful servants. J. Ridgeway. Ramp Mag 9:9-10+ D '70
AMERICAN federation of labor and Congress of industrial organizations
AFL-CIO guideline; a 10 per cent pay boost in '70. Bsns W p 102 F 28 '70
AFL-CIO talks protectionism. il Bsns W p66 Mr 28 '70
Division in labor; issue of the Vietnamese war. Nation 210:707-8 Je 15 '70
Fire alarm; Executive council meeting. il Newsweek 75:59-60 Mr 2 '70
Labor starts to mend its divided house. il Bsns W p 17-18 O 31 '70
Labor's split political personality. J. Hill. Commonweal 92:382-3 Ag 7 '70; Reply with rejoinder. N Dolan. 93:54-5 O 9 '70
Many-sided Mr Meany. J. Corry. il por Harper 240:52-8 Mr '70
Men in line to succeed Meany. il Nations Bsns 58:68-70 My '70
Troubled times for unions? A size-up by top leaders. il U S News 69:80-1 Ag 17 '70
Unions open fire on Nixon over jobs, civil rights. il U S News 68:69-70 Mr 9 '70

Committee on political education
Labor and the new deal coalition. B. L. Masse. America 123:193 S 26 '70

Industrial union department
Changing attitude of U.S. labor unions toward world trade. W. C. Shelton. Mo Labor R 93:51-4 My '70

United farm workers organizing committee
And now, lettuce. D. Henninger. New Repub 163:9-11 O 10 '70
Bishops in the vineyard. L. T. King. Commonweal 92:214 My 15 '70
Bitter fruit in the vineyards. D. L. Hallett. il pors Nations Bsns 58:80-3 F '70
Black eagle wins; end of grape strike. il por Time 96:10-11 Ag 10 '70
Breakthrough agreement in Coachella Valley. Chr Cent 87:469 Ap 22 '70
Breakthrough in Coachella Valley. V. Salandini. America 122:470-1 My 2 '70; Reply. C. C. Crawford. 122:619 Je 13 '70
Chavez and the Teamsters. J. J. Berman and J. Hightower. Nation 211:427-31 N 2 '70
Contracts in the Coachella. Time 95:21 Ap 13 '70
Dow on the farm; court injunction by Bud Antle inc. against the UFWOC's picketing. New Repub 163:8 D 12 '70

AMERICAN federation of labor and Congress of industrial organizations—United farm workers organizing committee—*Continued*
Eagle over the lettuce fields. N. C. Mills. Commonweal 93:140-1 N 6 '70
From fruit bowl to salad bowl. Time 96:18 S 14 '70
Grape pickers win contract. America 122:400 Ap 18 '70
Harvest nears for Cesar Chavez. il Bsns W p62+ Je 27 '70
Labor, 1970. Nation 211:162 S 7 '70
Lessons of the grape strike. V. Salandini. America 123:285-7 O 17 '70
Rendering unto Cesar. R. L. Cleath. por Chr Today 14:32-3 Jl 3 '70
Tilting with the system; interview. ed. by B. Fitch. C. Chavez. il Chr Cent 87:204-7 F 18 '70
Victory for Cesar Chavez. il por Newsweek 76:56+ Ag 10 '70
Victory of César Chavez. W. F. Buckley, jr. Nat R 22:965 S 8 '70

AMERICAN federation of labor and Congress of industrial organizations and American library association

Joint committee on library services to labor groups
See American library association and American federation of labor and Congress of industrial organizations—Joint committee on library services to labor groups

AMERICAN federation of state, county and municipal employees
Longest strike; Maryland's Garrett County road workers. il Newsweek 76:81 N 30 '70

AMERICAN federation of teachers
AFT: action on the picket line; New Orleans convention. S. Holzman. il Sr Schol 95: Schol Teach 1-2 S 29 '69
American federation of teachers. R. W. Glass. Mo Labor R 93:34-6 O '70
Black history gaps revealed in AFT encyclopedia survey. Library J 95:4312 D 15 '70
Merger of NEA and AFT locals; Flint, Mich. Sch & Soc 98:15-16 Ja '70
Teachers open drive to sell unionism; classroom materials. U S News 68:88 My 18 '70
Toward real teacher power; a single, unified organization. il Sr Schol 95:Schol Teach 1 N 17 '69

AMERICAN fiction
Contemporary American novella: an existential approach. G. Steinley. Engl J 59:52-8 Ja '70
See also
Negro fiction
Western stories

AMERICAN film institute
Lost films from the National film collection. R. Koszarski. il Film Q 23:31-7 Wint '69

AMERICAN fisheries society
Century of fish conservation. H. Clepper. il Am For 76:16-19+ N '70

AMERICAN flag. See Flags—United States

AMERICAN folk art. See Folk art

AMERICAN folk music. See Folk music, American

AMERICAN folk songs. See Folk songs, American

AMERICAN football league
Fuel for the feud. il Time 96:41 O 12 '70

AMERICAN forces Vietnam radio-television network
How the G.I.'s in Viet Nam don't learn about the war. R. Hodierne. il por N Y Times Mag p28-9+ Ap 12 '70
Like it is; Robert Lawrence served with court martial charges. Nat R 22:74 Ja 27 '70

AMERICAN forestry association
AFA and the environmental crusade. C. A. Connaughton. Am For 76:7 My '70
AFA honored by Keep America beautiful. il Am For 76:5 F '70
Credit where credit is due; Man of the year distinguished service award. por Am For 76:6 My '70
Looking for areas of agreement on the forest conservation front. il Am For 76:36 Jl '70
Y'all come! To AFA's 95th annual meeting. il Am For 76:32-3 Ag '70

AMERICAN foundation on automation and employment
Automation house; interview. T. W. Kheel. New Yorker 46:30-2 Mr 14 '70

AMERICAN Friends service committee
Quaker appeal for peace; excerpt from Search for peace in the Middle East. Cur 121:59-64 S '70
Realpolitik is peace; excerpt from Search for peace in the Middle East. il Trans-Action 7: 20-3 Jl '70

AMERICAN furniture. See Furniture, American

AMERICAN geophysical union
Earth sciences. Sci N 97:434 My 2 '70

AMERICAN heart association
Fat debate. il Newsweek 76:98 N 23 '70
Medical sciences. Sci N 98:404 N 21 '70

AMERICAN hemerocallis society
Outstanding day-lilies. Home Gard 57:18 O '70

AMERICAN heritage dictionary of the English language. See English language—Dictionaries

AMERICAN heritage society awards
American heritage society awards: announcing the winners. Am Heritage 21:120 Ag '70
American heritage society awards; with nominees. il Am Heritage 21:3, 116 F '70

AMERICAN high school students. See High school students

AMERICAN historical association
Bare-knuckled historians. R. Radosh. Nation 210:108-10 F 2 '70
Out of the grooves of academe; dissent of annual meetings. D. Grumbach. Commonweal 91:468-9 Ja 30 '70
Radical chic in academe; annual meeting. Newsweek 77:58-9 Ja 11 '71
Revisionism: a new, angry look at the American past; Time essay. il Time 95:14-15 F 2 '70
Scholars and society; annual convention. New Repub 162:7-8 Ja 17 '70
Turning history upside down; annual convention. C. Solway. Sat R 53:13-15+ Je 20 '70

AMERICAN historical review (periodical)
Articles for the AHR: an editorial. Am Hist R 75:1577-80 O '70

AMERICAN home products corporation
American home; a reticent giant. il Bsns W p76-7+ Mr 21 '70

AMERICAN house decoration. See House decoration, American

AMERICAN humor. See Humor, American

AMERICAN idealism. See Idealism

AMERICAN Indian movement
Lutherans and American Indians: a confrontation. E. R. Trexler. Chr Cent 87: 1103-5 S 16 '70

AMERICAN institute for foreign study
Overseas study for teenagers. J. Robbins. il Parents Mag 45:50-1+ Jl '70

AMERICAN institute for foreign trade, Phoenix, Ariz. See Thunderbird graduate school of international management

AMERICAN institute of architects
A.I.A. revamps professional ethics, stresses ecology at uneasy Boston convention. il Arch Rec 148:35-7+ Ag '70
Buckminster Fuller gets A.I.A. gold medal, synergetic spin-offs keep coming. il por Arch Rec 147:41 F '70
Fourteen receive this country's highest architectural awards. il Arch Rec 147:40-1 Je '70
Future of the profession. R. W. Allen. il Arch Rec 147:123-6 F '70
Some random thoughts on and from the Boston convention. W. F. Wagner, jr. Arch Rec 148:9-10 Ag '70

Headquarters
A.I.A. national headquarters building by TAC. il Arch Rec 148:43-6 Ag '70

AMERICAN institute of biological sciences
Environmental sciences. Sci N 98:36 Jl 11 '70

AMERICAN institute of certified public accountants
End game; Accounting principles board kills off accounting gimmicks. Newsweek 76:84+ Jl 13 '70
New trouble for mergers. Time 96:68-9 Jl 13 '70
Profits without honor. Time 95:62 Mr 9 '70
Words, words, words. il Forbes 106:54-5 O 1 '70

AMERICAN institute of graphic arts fifty books exhibit. See Book exhibits

AMERICAN Institute of physics
Age of change; role of AIP. H. W. Koch. bibliog il por Phys Today 23:27-32 Ja '70
Information-program questions; letters. L. J. Creek; A. Herschman. Phys Today 23: 13+ D '70
Report on AIP; 1969. J. T. Scott. il Phys Today 23:43-7+ Je '70

AMERICAN insurance association
Rough ride and new roads ahead for auto insurers. il Bsns W p 118 Mr 28 '70

AMERICAN insurance group
Child of empire. il Forbes 105:40 Mr 15 '70

AMERICAN intellectuals. See Intellectuals

AMERICAN investments abroad. See Investments, Foreign

AMERICAN iris society
Golden anniversary salute to the American
iris society. il Home Gard 57:20-1 Je '70
AMERICAN Irish. See Irish Americans
AMERICAN language. See English language
AMERICAN legion
Aging Legion faces a new enemy; People's
army jamboree. il Life 69:28-31 S 11 '70
Confronting the Legion; plans for Portland
protest. Nation 211:101 Ag 17 '70
AMERICAN liberalism. See Liberalism
AMERICAN libraries (periodical)
Shower for a new baby; letters to the editor.
Am Lib 1:327-8 Ap '70
Simple and plain; letter to the editor. H.
Bliss. Am Lib 1:742-3 S '70
AMERICAN libraries abroad
See also
American library in Paris
AMERICAN library association
ALA award winners; 1970. il Am Lib 1:808-13
S '70
ALA awards. il Wilson Lib Bul 45:33 S '70
ALA awards, citations, and scholarships,
1971. Am Lib 1:978-82 N '70
ALA identity crisis: dilemma or delaying de-
vice? A. Curley. por Library J 95:2089-90
Je 1 '70
ALA 1970 election results. il Wilson Lib Bul
45:25 S '70
ALA nominating committee report, 1971. Am
Lib 1:958-9 N '70
ALA officers and awards. Library J 95:2957-8
S 15 '70
ALA seeks 1971 award nominees. Library J
95:4313+ D 15 '70
AV task force survey report; with reply by
J. Brown. C. W. Stone. Am Lib 1:40-5 Ja
'70
Awards and citations ALA. 1970. il Library
J 95:2636-7 Ag '70
Can't see and won't listen: ALA AV com-
mittee proposal for an office of audiovisual
services, not funded; letter to the editor.
R. L. Ducote. Am Lib 1:836-7 O '70
Confessions of a middle-of-the-road militant;
change in ALA. J. Eubanks. il Am Lib
1:437-9 My '70; Discussion. 1:739 S '70
Council nominee identifies himself; letter to
the editor. D. Cohen. Am Lib 1:113-F '70
Democratization of the association. Am Lib
1:366-70+ Ap '70
Editor's choice; Executive board in action.
G. R. Shields. Am Lib 1.1025 D '70
Editor's choice; sanctity: libraries, clients,
IRS, ALA. G. R. Shields. Am Lib 1:749-50
S '70
First splinter candidate files for ALA presi-
dent. Library J 95:1265-6 Ap 1 '70; Discus-
sion. 95:1263, 1782, 2035 Ap 1, My 15, Je 1
'70
Know your ALA program 68-69. Am Lib
1:72-8, 154-7+, 266-7+ Ja-Mr '70
Let your son shine in: giving younger ones a
chance in running ALA. E. M. Oboler. Am
Lib 1:747 S '70
Library response to a restive world; address,
July 3, 1970. L. M. Bradshaw. por Am Lib
1:688-90 Jl '70
Like Jack's magic beans: controversy at the
Detroit conference over IRS's inspection of
private reading habits. J. F. Krug and
J. A. Harvey. Am Lib 1:843-5 O '70
Litmus test of tyranny. T-men vs. librarians.
W. R. Eshelman. Wilson Lib Bul 45:5-7 S
'70
Lovebites & loobies: future of ALA. J. M.
Carter. il Library J 95:3885 N 15 '70
Merit and importance; ALA taking a stand
on political issues. J. Forman. Am Lib 1:
745-6 S '70
National press and television coverage: IRS
incident. J. F. Krug and J. A. Harvey. Am
Lib 1:1026-7 D '70
New ALA officers. il Library J 95:2595 Ag '70
New directions for ALA. Am Lib 1:238-41
Mr '70
1970 ALA election returns. il Am Lib 1:691-4
Jl '70
Of note: SRRT report; reprint. Am Lib 1:106
F '70
Plus ça change: twenties through the six-
ties. J. H. Shera. il por Library J 95:979-
86 Mr 15 '70; Reply. P. Schuman. 95:1781-2
My 15 '70
Reader interest in bombs checked by T-men;
with editorial comment. il Library J 95:2591,
2593 Ag '70
Richard Darling outlines presidential plat-
form. Library J 95:1537 Ap 15 '70
Richard Darling proposed as ALA president.
Library J 95:1144 Mr 15 '70

What's the difference? refusal of ALA to
take a stand on social or political issues;
letter to the editor. P. Bixler. Am Lib 1:
835 O '70
Where was ALA? how to make ALA more
responsible and responsive; letter to the
editor. D. Burgess. Library J 95:833 Mr
1 '70
See also
American association of school librarians

Meetings
Anecdotes, facetiae, satire, etc.
Loyalty begins at home; ALA midwinter
meeting in Daleyland. K. Nyren. Library
J 95:963 Mr 15 '70

Meetings, 1970
Activism gap; ALA midwinter 1970. J. Berry;
K. Nyren. il Library J 95:987-99 Mr 15 '70
Adrift in new directions; midwinter in Chi-
cago. E. Geller. il Library J 95:1169-72 Mr
15 '70
ALA conference guide. J. Berry. Library J
95:2093 Je 1 '70
ALA conference roundup. Library J 95:1695,
2074-5 My 1, Je 1 '70
ALA: exercise in self-examination. Pub W
198:24-7 Ag 17 '70
ALA 1970: notes & comments. W. R. Eshel-
man, A. Plotnik; R. Bartnofsky. il Wilson
Lib Bul 45:14+ S '70
Another opening another show; Detroit 1970;
symposium. il Am Lib 1:660-85+ Jl '70
Channels for change; midwinter in Chicago.
J. Berry. Library J 95:611 F 15 '70
Conference roundup; symposium. il Library
J 95:2613-37+ Ag '70
Detroit as drama; or, Is the process the only
payoff? R. B. Moses. Am Lib 1:841-2 O '70
Detroit conference placement center. il por
Am Lib 1:311 Ap '70
Editor's choice; issues offered for ALA De-
troit conference. G. R. Shields. Am Lib
1:431 My '70
Five percent amendments; petition process
for membership meetings and nominations.
J. Berry. Library J 95:2045 Je 1 '70
Free in Detroit! il Library J 95:2091-5 Je 1
'70
Highlights of annual conference, June 28-
July 4, 1970. il Am Lib 1:791-801 S '70
Midwinter 1970: the neo-establishment talk-
fest. il Am Lib 1:217-35 Mr '70
1970 ALA conference, Detroit, June 28-July
4; announcement. Am Lib 1:78-82 Ja '70
Sub-zero in Chicago; ALA's business meet-
ing. A. Plotnik and W. R. Eshelman. il
Wilson Lib Bul 44:687-92+ Mr '70
Tentative program of the 89th annual ALA
conference; with revised and late entries.
Am Lib 1:413, 466-81 My '70
Underground Detroit for SLA and ALA con-
ventioneers. H. Malone. il por Wilson Lib
Bul 44:931-9 My '70
Up against the wall; highlights of the Detroit
conference, June 27-July 3. E. Geiller. il Li-
brary J 95:2967-70 S 15 '70
What's on the menu for Detroit? il Am Lib
1:464-5 My '70

Meetings, 1971
ALA-Dallas ground rules: a tight little
schedule. Library J 95:4083-4 D 1 '70
Editor's choice; association policy at Los
Angeles midwinter meeting. G. R. Shields.
il Am Lib 1:943 N '70
Job placement service at ALA midwinter
reduced. Library J 95:4084 D 1 '70
1971 ALA midwinter meeting. Am Lib 1:1082-3
D '70
1971 midwinter meeting Los Angeles, January
18-23. Am Lib 1:804-5 N '70

Adult services division
Notable books of 1969 selected by ALA group.
Pub W 197:128-9 F 23 '70; Same. Am Lib
1:276-7 Mr '70; Library J 95:1270 Ap 1 '70,
Todays Ed 59:54-5 My '70
Notable nominations. Am Lib 1:91, 297-8,
714-15, 1088 Ja, Mr, Jl, D '70

Children's services division
Business as usual; 1970 ALA conference. P.
Schuman. il Library J 95:2977-80 S 15 '70
Notable children's books of 1969. il Am
Lib 1:384-7 Ap '70; Same. PTA Mag 64:
22-4 My '70; Library J 95:1894 My 15 '70;
Pub W 197:47-8 Je 1 '70

Committee on new directions
ACONDA summary. Am Lib 1:685 Jl '70
Action report. D. H. Clift. Am Lib 1:938-9 N
'70
ALA-Dallas ground rules: a tight little
schedule. Library J 95:4083-4 D 1 '70

AMERICAN library association—Committee on new directions—*Continued*
ALA: exercise in self-examination. Pub W 198:24-5 Ag 17 '70
ALA 1970: ACONDA tries its wings. W. R. Eshelman; A. Plotnik; R. Bartnofsky. il Wilson Lib Bul 45:21-3 S '70
ALA reaction; letter to the editor. R. H. Rosichan. Library J 95:3702 N 1 '70
ALA was the subject; ACONDA. J. Berry. il Library J 95:2613-22 Ag '70
Chapters and new directions; letters to the editor. Am Lib 1:521 Je '70
Dix mix nix on 321.8; AASL affiliation with ALA and DAVI. E. Geller. Library J 95: 193 Ja 15 '70
Dix on the Dix mix; letter to the editor. W. S. Dix. Library J 95:1139 Mr 15 '70
Enter ACONDA; summary of discussion of report at membership meeting in Detroit. G. R. Shields and others. il Am Lib 1: 671-84 Jl '70
Intellectual freedom: ALA midwinter. K. Nyren. il Library J 95:997-9 Mr 15 '70
Intellectual freedom: statement of ALA Intellectual freedom committee on Activities committee on new directions for ALA. J. F. Krug and J. A. Harvey. Am Lib 1:533-5 Je '70
Memo to members. Am Lib 1:451-4 My '70
Mixed bag debate. H. R. Galvin. Am Lib 1:745 S '70
On taking a stand; letter to the editor. P. Bixler. Am Lib 1:329-30 Ap '70
Status in the 80s; letter to the editor. G. F. Heise. Am Lib 1:522-4 Je '70
Up against the wall; ACONDA at annual meeting. E. Geller. Library J 95:2968-70 S 15 '70

Committee on organization
Closed COO-operation; letter to the editor. H. W. Tuttle. Library J 95:2201 Je 15 '70

Constitution
ALA constitution and bylaws. il Am Lib 1: 985-93 N '70
Amendments to the constitution and bylaws. Am Lib 1:1085-6 D '70

Constitution and bylaws committee
Constitution and bylaws; committee report. Am Lib 1:448-9 My '70

Council
ALA voting analysis reveals trend. Library J 95:2750+ S 1 '70
Chapters and new directions; letters to the editor. Am Lib 1:521 Je '70
Electing an ALA council. J. Berry. Library J 95:1683 My 1 '70
Midwinter membership meeting voted; council poll. Am Lib 1:869-70 O '70
Procedure at council; letter to the editor. T. L. Bonn. Am Lib 1:938 N '70
321.8 rides again; more reforms urged. Library J 95:1787-8 My 15 '70

Finance
ALA 1970: understanding money. W. R. Eshelman; A. Plotnik; R. Bartnofsky. il Wilson Lib Bul 45:19+ S '70
Tax-exempt status; an ALA report. R. McClarren. Am Lib 1:607 Je '70
Treasurer's report. il Am Lib 1:1074-80 D '70

Intellectual freedom committee
Intellectual freedom: ALA midwinter. N. Nyren. il Library J 95:997-9 Mr 15 '70
Intellectual freedom in Detroit. S. Havens. il Library J 95:2623-6 Ag '70
Intellectual freedom: statement of ALA Intellectual freedom committee on Activities committee on new directions for ALA. J. F. Krug and J. A. Harvey. Am Lib 1:533-5 Je '70

Library administration division
ALA investigating team slaps U. of Mo. wrist. Library J 95:4211 D 15 '70
Tenure investigation: library administration division's report concerning nonrenewal of contracts of five librarians, University of Missouri library. Am Lib 1:983-4 N '70

Library education division
Foreign library manpower raises basic new issues; LED institute. Library J 95:3722 N 1 '70

Library technology program
Memo to ALA/LTP; new media J. Berry. Library J 95:2857 S 15 '70

Membership
ALA: a professional or a library association. C. M. Weisenberg. Am Lib 1:1060-1 D '70
ALA voting analysis reveals trend; 1970 Council election. Library J 95:2750+ S 1 '70
Democracy and meetings: extension of Membership meeting, cancellation of YASD board meeting. M. A. Hanna. Am Lib 1: 746-7 S '70
Five percent amendments; petition process for membership meetings and nominations. J. Berry. Library J 95:2045 Je 1 '70
Membership dilemma. R. Sheridan. Am Lib 1:52-5 Ja '70
Midwinter membership meeting voted; council poll. Am Lib 1:869-70 O '70
1969 statistics on ALA membership. Am Lib 1:379 Ap '70
School librarian says goodbye; letter to the editor. Am Lib 1:524 Je '70

Notable books council
See American library association—Adult services division

Office for intellectual freedom
ALA testimony presented to Commission on obscenity and pornography; statement, May 4, 1970. J. F. Krug. Am Lib 1:653-5 Jl '70
See also
Freedom to read foundation

Office for recruitment
Youthful ALA recruitment director interviewed. M. Barber. il pors Wilson Lib Bul 44:917-19 My '70

Publishing department
See also
Choice (periodical)

Reference services division
Of note; reference and subscription books review committee. Am Lib 1:204 Mr '70

Social responsibilities of libraries round table
ALA reaction; letter to the editor. R. H. Rosichan. Library J 95:3702 N 1 '70
Free in Detroit! il Library J 95:2091-5 Je 1 '70
In search of soul; pre-conference institute. P. Schuman. il Library J 95:2632-4 Ag '70
Overdue: ALA and the black librarian; strategy for midwinter and beyond, excerpts from The black librarian in America, ed. by E. J. Josey. R. Wedgeworth. por Wilson Lib Bul 45:495-7 Ja '71
SRRT statements from candidates; letters to the editor. Am Lib 1:330 Ap '70
Status of women in libraries: task force meets in Detroit; SRRT. P. Schuman. Library J 95:2635 Ag '70
Task force on gay liberation meeting. Am Lib 1:1013 D '70
Touch of bramble, glimpse of beauty: In search of soul preconference institute of SRRT. H. H. Eason. Am Lib 1:1018 D '70

Young adult services division
Business as usual; 1970 ALA conference. P. Schuman. il Library J 95:2977-80 S 15 '70
Democracy and meetings: extension of Membership meeting, cancellation of YASD board meeting. M. A. Hanna. Am Lib 1:746-7 S '70
Twenty-two choice teen books announced by ALA. Library J 95:1894 My 15 '70
AMERICAN library association and American federation of labor and Congress of industrial organizations

Joint committee on library services to labor groups
Outrage! elimination of Newsletter; letter to the editor. A. K. Herling. Am Lib 1:934-5 N '70
AMERICAN library in Paris
American library in Paris: fifty years of service. L. E. Bone. il Am Lib 1:279-83 Mr '70; Correction. 1:526 Je '70
AMERICAN library trustee association
Library trustee role questioned at Chicago; summary of address. January 1970. J. Smith. Library J 95:839 Mr 1 '70
AMERICAN lions. See Pumas
AMERICAN literary anthology
Story excluded from ALA #3; NEA cancels fourth edition. Pub W 198:58 S 28 '70

AMERICAN literature
At halfway point; state literary maps. B. W. Fuson. bibliog f Engl J 59:87-98 Ja '70
Literature; grand opera vs the now sound. R. W. Hall. Engl J 59:1150-3 N '70
See also
American poetry
Ballads, American
Negro literature
Pastoral literature

Themes
See Literature—Themes

AMERICAN Lutheran church. See Lutheran church in the United States

AMERICAN management association
Management experts have troubles, too. il Bsns W p37-8 My 23 '70

AMERICAN medical association
Abortion, dues and malpractice. Sci N 98:8 Jl 4 '70
AMA: new directions; annual meeting. il Newsweek 76:60 Jl 6 '70
Debate over National health insurance. il Time 96:68 O 12 '70
Facing the health crisis. il Sci N 98:446 D 12 '70
Health care: AMA white paper offers traditional solutions. R. J. Bazell. Science 170: 1287-8 D 18 '70
Medical sciences. Sci N 98:14 Jl 4 '70
Schizophrenia at the A.M.A. Time 96:36 Jl 6 '70
TV's on-again romance with medicine. J. N. Bell. il Todays Health 48:24-9+ Mr '70
Where doctors fail. J. H. Knowles. il Sat R 53:21-3+ Ag 22 '70

AMERICAN merchant marine. See Merchant marine—United States

AMERICAN metal climax, inc.
Friendly takeover in the copperbelt; nationalization of Zambia's copper industry. il Bsns W p24+ Ag 22 '70

AMERICAN military assistance. See Military assistance, American

AMERICAN minorities. See Minorities

AMERICAN motors corporation
American motors' crucial year. Bsns W p 17 O 3 '70
Chapin's folly? A. A. Butkus. por Duns 95: 63-4 My '70

AMERICAN museum in Britain
Colonial cakes and cookies. il Am Home 73: 80+ Ap '70
Most entertaining museum in England. J. Egan. il Am Home 73:74-9+ Ap '70

AMERICAN museum of natural history, New York
Age of frightened men; exhibition in Hall of Mexico and Central America. D. Davis. il Newsweek 75:103 Je 1 '70

AMERICAN national cattlemen's association
What consumers really think of beef and beef producers; ANCA consumer education program. R. Stallbaumer, jr. il Farm J 94:B20 S '70

AMERICAN Negroes. See Negroes

AMERICAN novelists. See Novelists, American

AMERICAN occupation of Japan. See Japan—History—Allied occupation, 1945-1952

AMERICAN opera society
Good marks for Goldmark; concert version of The Queen of Sheba. I. Kolodin. Sat R 53: 47 Ap 11 '70
Music to my ears; concert version of La fille du régiment at Carnegie Hall. I. Kolodin. Sat R 53:63 F 28 '70
Musical events:
 Donizetti's La fille du régiment. W. Sargeant. New Yorker 46:110 F 21 '70
 Karl Goldmark's The Queen of Sheba. W. Sargeant. New Yorker 46:128-9 Ap 4 '70
Report:
 Goldmark's Queen of Sheba. J. W. Freeman. Opera N 34:24 My 16 '70
 La fille du régiment. S. Jenkins. Opera N 34:32 Mr 21 '70

AMERICAN optical corporation
Next-morning delivery by air is goal for American optical. il Aviation W 93:100-1 O 26 '70

AMERICAN ospreys. See Ospreys

AMERICAN painting. See Painting, American

AMERICAN petroleum institute
Petroleum industry's role in the preservation of the environment. F. N. Ikard. il Parks & Rec 5:18-21+ My '70

AMERICAN pewter. See Pewter

AMERICAN philosophical association
Radical chic in academe; annual meeting. Newsweek 77:58-9 Ja 11 '71

AMERICAN philosophy. See Philosophy

AMERICAN physical society
APS-AAPT meet in Chicago. M. S. Rothenberg. il Phys Today 23:53-5 Ja '70
Chicago meeting involved with society; with editorial comment. G. B. Lubkin. Phys Today 23:67+, 112 Mr '70
Ferment among the physicists. il Sci N 97: 452-3 My 9 '70
Physical sciences. Sci N 97:151, 457; 98:424 F 7, My 9, D 5 '70

AMERICAN poetry
Allen Ginsberg and the 60's. M. Dickstein. bibliog f Commentary 49:64+ Ja '70
In the verse patch. R. Wallace. Sat R 53:34-6 Ja 17 '70
Keys to ourselves. J. Kessler. pors Sat R 53: 34-6+ My 2 '70
Naked poetry; recent American poetry in open forms, ed. by S. Berg and R. Mezey. Review
 Poetry 116:35-9 Ap '70. H. Nemerov
Poetry wreck; address, December 8, 1969. K. Shapiro. il por Library J 95:632-5 F 15 '70
See also
Ballads, American
Haiku, American
Negro poetry
Poets, American

AMERICAN poets. See Poets, American

AMERICAN political science association
Behavioral sciences. Sci N 98:250 S 19 '70
Relevance and a new candidate; Caucus for a new political science. Sci N 98:245 S 19 '70

AMERICAN pork congress
Hogmen plan biggest meeting ever. J. Russell. Farm J 94:50F Mr '70
Pork industry goes first class. R. Wilmore. Farm J 94:H20 Ap '70

AMERICAN portraits. See Portraits, American

AMERICAN pottery. See Pottery, American

AMERICAN power boat association
APBA action report. J. D. Paris. See issues of Motor boating
Louisville power squadron wins Chapman award. il Motor B 125:46 Mr '70
More power to you. M. Crook. See issues of Yachting

AMERICAN prints. See Prints

AMERICAN program bureau. See Lectures and lecturing

AMERICAN psychiatric association
Correlating the Fifteen indices with hospital achievement awards. A. D. Pokorny. Ment Hy 54:575-6 O '70
Mental health; convention in San Francisco preoccupied with the psychic condition of the Nation. Time 95:14 My 25 '70

AMERICAN psychological association
APA information plan funded. C. Holden. Science 170:1385 D 25 '70
Behavioral sciences. Sci N 98:251 S 19 '70
NISP: noisy signal in psychology; proposed National information system for psychology. J. Loevinger. Trans-Action 7:10 My '70
Psychology: apprehension over a new communications system. P. M. Boffey. Science 167:1228-30 F 27 '70; Discussion. 168:194+, 1041 Ap 10, My 29 '70
Soma-environmental revolution, pornography, synergistic consciousness, sex with patients; 78th annual convention. E. C. Kennedy. il N Y Times Mag p52-3+ D 6 '70; Reply. E. Klemperer. p2 D 20 '70

AMERICAN public opinion. See Public opinion —United States

AMERICAN public works association
APWA honors public works men. il Am City 85:148 My '70

AMERICAN quartet. See Choral groups and societies

AMERICAN radium society
Medical sciences. Sci N 97:272 Mr 14 '70

AMERICAN Red cross. See Red cross—United States

AMERICAN reporters. See Reporters and reporting

AMERICAN revolution. See United States—History—Revolution

AMERICAN Revolution bicentennial commission. See United States—American Revolution bicentennial commission

AMERICAN royal live stock and horse show. See Livestock shows

AMERICAN salesmasters, ltd.
Dynamic growth companies: American salesmasters, ltd. il por Nations Bsns 58:68-71 Jl '70

AMERICANS—*Continued*

Anecdotes, facetiae, satire, etc.
All-American game. il Mlle 70:208-9 Ap '70
New American credo; comp. by S. Kanfer and
J. T. Elson. il Time 96:43 S 28 '70
AMERICANS abroad. See Americans in foreign
countries
AMERICANS for community cooperation in
other nations. See Accion international
AMERICANS in Australia
Americans are emigrating to Australia. H.
Gordon. il N Y Times Mag p75+ My 17 '70
AMERICANS in Belgium
Brussels: the multinationals move in. il
Bsns W p 138-9 D 19 '70
AMERICANS in California, Lower. See Ameri-
cans in Mexico
AMERICANS in Canada
Need to hate; draft dodgers and deserters. S.
Alsop. Newsweek 76:80 Jl 27 '70
They can't go home again; draft dodgers
and deserters in Canada. S. Alsop. News-
week 76:88 Jl 20 '70
AMERICANS in England
Executive abroad; the Donnells in London.
J. Ross-Skinner. il pors Duns 96:48-51 Ag
'70
London's American emigrés. il Newsweek 76:
44+ N 30 '70
U.S. journal: Grosvenor square; Protection and
welfare consul. C. Trillin. New Yorker 46:
108+ S 19 '70
Why U.S. executives become anglophiles. il
Bsns W p65 My 30 '70
AMERICANS in Ethiopia
Ordinary guy in Ethiopia; Lalmba associa-
tion. C. W. Hall. il por Read Digest 97:
157-8+ Jl '70
AMERICANS in Europe
American youth in Europe '70; symposium.
il Holiday 47:26-31 Je '70
William Carlos Williams and the old world.
H. Levin. Yale R 59:520-31 Je '70
See also
United States—Army—Forces in Europe
AMERICANS in foreign countries
Business has its own embassies; American
chambers of commerce for American busi-
nessmen overseas. J. L. Caldwell. il Nations
Bsns 58:86-7 My '70
Department warns of penalties for drug
violations abroad; announcement, March 31,
1970. Dept State Bul 62:549-51 Ap 27 '70
Dollars and cents of working abroad. il
Bsns W p88+ D 19 '70
Foreign military service by U.S. citizens;
Department statement, November 11, 1969.
Dept State Bul 61:635-6 D 29 '69
Latest American exodus. il Time 96:13-15 N
30 '70
Letter to a new expatriate; Time essay. H.
Grunwald. il Time 96:14-15 N 30 '70
Open season on drug smugglers. R. Chelmin-
ski. il Life 68:28-35 Je 26 '70
Sizing up a job offer overseas. Bsns W p 115-
16 D 19 '70
Working abroad is not all fun. il Bsns W
p65-7 Mr 21 '70
See also
United States—Armed forces—Forces in for-
eign countries

Employment
U.S. jobs overseas: fewer of them now. il
U S News 69:44 Jl 20 '70
Where the jobs are: Geneva, London, Paris,
Rome. N. A. Comer. Mlle 71:114-15+ Je
'70
AMERICANS in France
J'etais jeune fille au pair a Paris (I was a
mother's helper in Paris) S. Solberg. il
Seventeen 29:144-5+ F '70
AMERICANS in Germany
See also
United States—Army—Forces in Europe
United States—Army—Forces in Germany
AMERICANS in Istanbul. See Americans in
Turkey
AMERICANS in Italy
Mary Simons reports on Rome's latest con-
venience: Dial-a-strike. M. Simons. por
Look 34:14 F 24 '70
AMERICANS in Jordan
Sitting ducks; U.S. embassy staff in Amman.
il Newsweek 76:44 Jl 13 '70
AMERICANS in Laos
Laos: plain (and fancy) talk. Newsweek 75:
34+ Mr 23 '70
Lousing up Laos: analysis of President
Nixon's March 6 statement. J. Osborne.
New Repub 162:15-17 Mr 21 '70
What the U.S. is doing there. il Time 95:24
Mr 9 '70

AMERICANS in Latin America
Working to a Latin beat. J. Kruger. Mlle
70:128+ Ja '70
AMERICANS in London. See Americans in
England
AMERICANS in Lower California. See Ameri-
cans in Mexico
AMERICANS in Mexico
Baja experienced. P. Fusco. il Look 34:38-47
S 8 '70
AMERICANS in Paris. See Americans in France
AMERICANS in Peru
Few thorns among the roses; letter to Mrs
Nixon from North Americans for peace in
Southeast Asia movement. B. Thompson.
Chr Cent 87:1009 Ag 26 '70
AMERICANS in Rome. See Americans in Italy
AMERICANS in Russia
Lapel diplomacy; Moscow's reaction to anti-
Soviet demonstrations by U.S. Jews. Time
97:27 Ja 18 '71
AMERICANS in the Netherlands
Profiles; Netherlands. A. Bailey. New Yorker
46:34-40+ Ag 8; 32-8+ Ag 15 '70
AMERICANS in Turkey
Love affair: James Baldwin and Istanbul. C.
E. Adelsen. il pors Ebony 25:40-2+ Mr '70
AMERICANS in Vietnam
Hated Americans; anti-Americanism in South
Vietnam. il Newsweek 76:39+ Ag 17 '70
AMERICA's cup race. See Yacht racing
AMERICIUM
Radioactive scientist. Time 95:68 Mr 2 '70
AMES, Amyas
Silent spring of our symphonies. il Sat R
53:81-3 F 28 '70
AMES, B. Charles
Trappings vs. substance in industrial mar-
keting. il Harvard Bsns R 48:93-102 Jl '70
AMES, Bruce N. See Singer, C. E. jt. auth.
AMES, Morgan
First lady of the blues. por Hi Fi 20:86-7
O '70
Prime rock, a quality report from Crosby,
Stills, Nash and Young. il Hi Fi 20:secI 70-1
Jl '70
—and others
Lighter side. See issues of High fidelity
section I
AMES, Norma
In a mini-world of lichens. il Nat Wildlife
8:48-9 Ap '70
AMES, Suzanne
Breath of life. il Opera N 34:6-7 Mr 21 '70
AMES and Rollinson (firm)
Lettering with a golden touch. il Bsns W p93
Je 6 '70
AMES research center. See United States—Na-
tional aeronautics and space administration
—Ames research center
AMEY, Ronald L.
Barnacle glue. bibliog il por Chem 43:44-6 Jl
'70
AMFAC, inc.
Still swinging. il Forbes 106:22-3 D 15 '70
AMHERST college, Amherst, Mass.
Amherst college science center, Amherst,
Mass. il Arch Rec 147:112-13 Ja '70
Big scale science center on a small scale
campus. il Arch Rec 147:114-18 F '70
AMIAMA-TIÓ, Fernando
OAS General assembly. il pors Américas 22:
2-5 S '70
AMICHAI, Yehuda
Comment. N. Sullivan. Poetry 116:125 My
'70 *
AMIDES
See also
Polyamides
AMINES
Microelectrophoresis of biogenic amines on
hypothalamic thermosensitive cells. A. L.
Beckman and J. S. Eisenman. bibliog il
Science 170:334-6 O 16 '70
See also
Catecholamines
Naphthylamines
AMINO acids
Amateur scientist; experiments in generating
the constituents of living matter from in-
organic substances. C. Fromer. il Sci Am
222:130-4+ Ja '70
Amino acids in a meteorite. Sci N 98:429 D
5 '70
Amino acids in a meteorite. Sky & Tel 41:27
Ja '71
Bio-organic compounds and glassy micropar-
ticles in lunar fines and other materials.
S. W. Fox and others. bibliog il Science
167:767-70 Ja 30 '70
Catalytic activities of thermally prepared poly-
α-amino acids: effect of aging. D. L. Rohlfing. bibliog il Science 169:988-1000 S 4 '70

AMINO acids—*Continued*
Life out there. il por Newsweek 76:118 D 14 '70
Mars Viking mission given new impetus; amino acids in meteorite. R. G. O'Lone. Aviation W 93:21 D 7 '70
Matter of life; finding amino acids in meteorites. por Time 96:68-9 D 14 '70
Racemization of amino acids in sediments from Saanich Inlet, British Columbia. K. A. Kvenvolden and others. bibliog il Science 169:1079-82 S 11 '70
Shock synthesis of amino acids in simulated primitive environments. A. Bar-Nun and others. bibliog il Science 168:470-3 Ap 24 '70; Reply with rejoinder. H. R. Hulett. 170:1000-2 N 27 '70
Steps toward life; catalyst of genesis. il Time 95:52 My 11 '70
Structure and function of antibodies. G. M. Edelman. il Sci Am 223:34-42 bibliog(p 128) Ag '70
Synthesis of amino acids by the heating of formaldehyde and ammonia. S. W. Fox and C. R. Windsor. bibliog il Science 170:984-6 N 27 '70
See also
Alanine
Cysteine
Cystine
Dopa
Ethylamine
Feeding and feeding stuffs—Amino acid content
Glycine
Leucine
Peptides
Phenylalanine
Polyamides
Rhodanine
Threonine
Tryptophan
AMIS, Kingsley
Fraud in bed; excerpt from I want it now. Vogue 156:98 S 15 '70
—and Conquest, Robert
Short educational dictionary. N Y Times Mag p4+ Ja 10 '71
AMISH Mennonites. See Mennonites
AMISTAD (periodical)
Black studies in glass houses. R. Whittemore. New Repub 162:25-7 My 9 '70
Ship of rebels. il Newsweek 75:65 Ap 6 '70
AMMAN, Battle of. See Jordan—Civil war, 1970
AMMER, Dean S.
Side effects of planning. il Harvard Bsns R 48:32-4+ My '70
AMMON, Richard I. Jr
Practical way to teach spelling. Ed Digest 35:53-4 Mr '70
AMMONIA
Foresight can save your eyes; anhydrous ammonia. Suc Farm 69:22 Ja '71
AMMONS, A. R.
If anything will level with you water will; Conserving the magnitude of uselessness; Unifying principle; Spiel; Transaction; Cut the grass; Runoff; Pluralist; poems. Poetry 115:297-310 F '70
One more time; poem. Harper 241:134 O '70
September drift; Mountain talk; Here & now; Square; Admission; Cougar; Project; Reversal; Dominion; Countering; Working still; Then one; Play; poems. Poetry 117:7-19 O '70

about
New beginning. R. Howard. Nation 212:90+ Ja 18 '71 *
AMMUNITION
See also
Cartridges
AMMUNITION industries. See Munitions industries
AMNESIA
Amnesia produced by electroconvulsive shock or cycloheximide: conditions for recovery. D. Quartermain and others. bibliog il Science 169:683-6 Ag 14 '70
Retrograde amnesia: production of skeletal but not cardiac response gradient by electroconvulsive shock. B. Hine and R. M. Paolino. bibliog il Science 169:1224-6 S 18 '70
AMNESTY
See also
Political prisoners
AMNESTY international (organization)
Profiles. E. J. Kahn, jr. New Yorker 46:44-6+ Ag 22 '70
AMNIOTIC liquid
Checkup for the unborn. R. Gore. il Life 69:73-4+ S 18 '70
Lesch-Nyhan syndrome: preventive control by prenatal diagnosis. J. A. Boyle and others. bibliog il Science 169:688-9 Ag 14 '70; Correction. 170:1333 D 18 '70

Right to be well-born; use of amniocentesis. W. Cole. il Todays Health 49:42-4+ Ja '71
AMO, Anthony William
Anton Wilhelm Amo (Anthony William Amo) F. Wolf. Negro Hist Bul 33:78-9 Mr '70 *
AMOBARBITAL
Frequency-specific relation between hippocampal theta rhythm, behavior, and amobarbital action. J. A. Gray and G. G. Ball. bibliog il Science 168:1246-8 Je 5 '70
AMOEBAS. See Amebas
AMOEBIC meningoencephalitis. See Encephalitis
AMOR, Benjamin Mendoza y. See Mendoza y Amor, B.
AMORETTI, Giorgio
Don't make a move or he'll chute. il por Life 68:62-5 My 29 '70 *
AMOROSO LIMA, Alceu. See Lima, A. A.
AMOROUS Senator; story. See Fowler, G.
AMORPHOUS semiconductors. See Semiconductors
AMORY, Cleveland
After living with man, a dolphin may commit suicide. Holiday 47:16+ My '70
Israel in siege. Read Digest 96:147-8+ Ap '70
Trade winds. See issues of Saturday review
AMOS, William H.
Teeming life of a pond. il Nat Geog 138:274-98 Ag '70
AMOSKEAG mills. See Textile mills
AMOSOV, Nikolai Mikhailovich
1991; concerning Notes from the future. G. St George. il Look 34:54-8+ Jl 14 '70 *
AMPELOPSIS
Blueberry creeper grows anywhere. il Sunset 145:136 Ag '70
AMPEX corporation
Ampex record. T. J. Murray. Duns 95:60-1 Ap '70
Tangle in tapes. il Time 95:84 F 23 '70
AMPHETAMINES
Amphetamine: differentiation by d and l isomers of behavior involving brain norepinephrine or dopamine. K. M. Taylor and S. H. Snyder. bibliog il Science 168:1487-9 Je 19 '70
Pep pills for youngsters; treatment of hyperactive children in Omaha. il U S News 69:49 Jl 13 '70
Slowdown for pep pills; new restrictions. Newsweek 76:77 Ag 17 '70
"Speed" that kills, or worse. J. Black. il N Y Times Mag p 14-15+ Je 21 '70; Same abr. with title Tempting siren called "speed." Read Digest 97:153-7 O '70
Why speed kills. Newsweek 76:121 N 16 '70
AMPHIBIA
See also
Eye (amphibia)
Frogs
Salamanders
Toads
Tree frogs and tree toads

Orientation
See Orientation
AMPHIBIOUS airplanes. See Airplanes, Amphibious
AMPHIBIOUS motor vehicle camping. See Camping
AMPHIBOLES
See also
Hornblende
AMPHIPODS
See also
Beach fleas
AMPHITHEATERS
See also
Hollywood bowl
AMPHITRYON; drama. See Hacks, P.
AMPHITRYON; drama. See Molière, J. B. P.
AMPLIFIERS
Assemble a frequency equalizer; unity gain amplifier. G. Meyerle. il Pop Electr 33:51-9 O '70
Assembling a universal tiger; power amplifier. D. Meyer. il Pop Electr 33:31-5+ O '70
Build a RIAA/NAB preamplifier. N. P. Huffnagel. il Pop Electr 33:61-4 Ag '70
Build modular six-channel stereo mixer preamp. G. D. Hanchett. il Radio-Electr 41:36-9 O '70
Build the X10/X100 instrument sensitivity booster. J. Bongiorno. il Pop Electr 33:43-7 Jl '70
Cross-modulation and intermodulation in receiver R.F. amplifiers. J. Knepler. il Electr World 83:55-8 Mr '70

AMPLIFIERS—*Continued*

Easy to build, transistor headphone amplifier. G. C. Getleben. il Radio-Electr 41:38 Jl '70

FET & op-amp audio circuits. N. Doyle. il Radio-Electr 41:46-9 Jl '70

Four channel amplifier for multi-speaker systems. L. H. Garner. il Electr World 84:28-30 N '70

Harman-Kardon Citation Twelve. T. W. Barnes. il Radio-Electr 42:80+ Ja '71

Hi-fi product report:
  Dynaco SCA-80 integrated stereo amplifier. il Electr World 84:23 D '70
  McIntosh MC-3500 power amplifier. il Electr World 83:13-14 Ap '70

MOSFET utility preamp for test equipment. J. F. Sterner. il Electr World 84:62-3 Ag '70

New developments in monolithic op amps. R. C. Dobkin. il por Electr World 84:45-8 Jl '70

Peaked amplifier for single-signal C-W. I. Queen. il Radio-Electr 41:84-5 Ap '70

Simple new amplifying device is adapted to driving a pen recorder. J. B. Shackleford. il Sci Am 222:130-2+ My '70

Small-size hi-fi stereo amplifier. W. W. Schopp. il Electr World 85:34 Ja '71

Ten emitter-coupled oscillator circuits. F. Maynard. il Radio-Electr 41:33-5 My '70

Design

Designing solid-state stereo amplifiers (title varies) M. Horowitz. il Radio-Electr 41:38-40+ D '70; 42:61-3 Ja '71 (to be cont)

Testing

Hi-fi product report:
  Marantz model 16 power amplifier. il Electr World 83:6+ F '70

AMPUTEES

Rehabilitation

See also
Artificial limbs

AMRAM, David
Joe Frazier, singer and champ. Vogue 155:148+ My '70

AMSDEN, Saralee
Have you ever tried contracting for grades? Engl J 59:1279-82 D '70

AMSTERDAM, Anthony
Advocate for underdogs. por Time 95:67 My 25 '70 *

AMSTERDAM, Netherlands
Do your thing capital. il Newsweek 76:47 Ag 10 '70

Traffic control in a Dutch tunnel; Coen tunnel, Amsterdam. il Am City 85:106 F '70

Airports

Does Amsterdam have the best airport in the world? Schiphol, Amsterdam's international airport. N. Grace. Holiday 47:16+ Ap '70

Description

Amsterdam when the windows steam up. B. Anderson. il Sat R 53:40-1+ S 12 '70

She's got style: Amsterdam. M. Cantwell. il Mlle 71:113+ Je '70

Galleries and museums

News from Amsterdam. L. R. Borch. il Antiques 97:18+ Ja '70

Petronella Oortman doll house, Rijksmuseum, Amsterdam. S. A. Parvin. il Hobbies 74:148 F '70

Historic houses, etc.

House of Anne Frank. A. Fooner. Travel & Camera 33:16+ Je '70

Hotels, restaurants, etc.

Amsterdam's a surprising city even for those who don't surprise easily. A. Karlen. il Holiday 47:42-3+ Ja '70

Music

Report:
  Luigi Dallapiccola's Prigioniero. J. Mindszenthy. il Opera N 34:28 F 7 '70
  Suppé's Boccaccio. J. Mindszenthy. il Opera N 34:28 My 16 '70
  Walküre by Netherlands opera foundation. J. Mindszenthy. Opera N 34:34 Ap 18 '70

Riots

Busting the Dam. il Newsweek 76:42 S 7 '70

AMSTERDAM international airport. See Amsterdam, Netherlands—Airports

AMULETS
Love amulets. il Design 71:35 mid-Wint '70

AMUSEMENT parks
Antique carousel revived; Magic mountain, Calif. il Design 72:14-16 Wint '70

Disney world wakes sleepy Orlando. il Bsns W p42-4 N 14 '70

Labor peace of Disney world; Orlando, Fla. US News 70:43 Ja 4 '71

Log ride; Knott's berry farm in Buena park, Calif. il Parks & Rec 5:37 My '70

U.S. journal: Pinellas County, Florida; attractions. C. Trillin. New Yorker 46:52-6 Ja 2 '71

AMUSEMENTS
Late in October the haunted houses will open; northern California. il Sunset 145:47 O '70

See also
Camping—Activities
Circus
Games
Mathematical recreations
Night clubs
Puzzles
Sideshows

AMYGDALOID body
Amygdaloid nucleus: new afferent input from the vomeronasal organ. S. S. Winans and F. Scalia. bibliog il Science 170:330-2 O 16 '70

ANACONDA company
Colt diesel that led to disaster. il Bsns W p84+ Ja 9 '71

ANACOSTIA RIVER
Story of the Nachatank River. H. J. Randall. il Liv Wildn 34:21-3 Sum '70

ANAEMIA. See Anemia

ANAHEIM Angels (baseball) See Baseball clubs

ANAHEIM, Calif.
See also
Disneyland park

ANALGESICS
Excedrin's headache. New Repub 163:7 Ag 15 '70

What's the best way to kill pain? G. M. Knox. Bet Hom & Gard 48:22+ My '70
See also
Aspirin
Dextropropoxyphene
Morphine

ANALOGY
Analogies in chemistry. Chem 43:29 S; 27 N '70

Analogy: the scientist's trick for problem solving. R. Dreistadt. il Sci Digest 67:36-43 Ap '70

Want to invent something? Then try using analogy. R. Dreistadt. il Sci Digest 67:62-7 My '70

ANALYSIS, Conformational. See Conformational analysis

ANARCHISM and anarchists
Anarchism in revival. K. Widmer. Nation 211:501-3 N 16 '70

Desperate romantics. K. Crawford. Newsweek 76:46 S 14 '70

From far right to far left, and farther, with Karl Hess. J. Boyd. il pors N Y Times Mag p48-9+ D 6 '70

Power: the enshrined heresy. R. Sampson. Nation 212:14-20 Ja 4 '71
See also
Terrorism

ANARCHISTS. See Anarchism and anarchists

ANATOL, A. pseud. See Kuznefsov, A. P.

ANATOMICAL models
Plastic man for practice X rays. il Sci Digest 67:86-7 Je '70

ANATOMY
See also
Physiology

ANATOMY, Artistic
See also
Human figure in photography

ANATOMY, Comparative
See also
Jaws (animals)

ANAYA, Yosi
Traveling with Mlle. il Mlle 71:310-15 Ag '70

ANCESTRY. See Genealogy

ANCHOR rope reels. See Boats—Equipment

ANCHORAGE, Alaska

Galleries and museums

For an introduction to Alaska, try this Anchorage museum. il Sunset 144:74 My '70

ANCHORITES. See Hermits

ANCIENT history. See History, Ancient

ANCIENT sculpture. See Sculpture, Ancient

AND then she smiled; story. See Delman, D.

AND then there was love; story. See Coffer, H. L.

ANDALUSIA (historic house) See Pennsylvania—Historic houses, etc.

ANDALUSIA, Spain
Washington Irving's Andalusia. V. Condon.
il por Travel 134:52-6+ O '70

ANDELSON, Robert V.
Campus unrest; address, May 29, 1970. Vital
Speeches 36:619-21 Ag 1 '70

ANDEREGG, Chester
Last call for moose. il pors Outdoor Life
145:60-3+ Ja '70

ANDERS, Edward
Water on the moon? bibliog Science 169:1309-
10 S 25 '70
—See Lancet, M. S. jt. auth.

ANDERS, William A.
See also
Space flight to the moon—Manned flights—
Apollo 8 flight

ANDERSEN, Arthur, and company
Fat maverick stirs up the accounting pro-
fession. A. M. Louis. il Fortune 82:96-9+
D '70

ANDERSEN, Hans Christian
Tinderbox; dramatization. See Jones, D. C.

about
Monster in the imagination. il por Time 96:
60-1 O 19 '70 *

ANDERSON, A. T. jr, and others
Petrologic history of moon suggested by
petrography, mineralogy, and crystallography. bibliog il Science 167:587-90 Ja 30 '70

ANDERSON, Ann
Lifestyle. il por Am Home 73:10+ D '70

ANDERSON, Anne
Man your oars! il Yachting 129:102-3 Ja '71

ANDERSON, Barbara
Ordeal at San Francisco state college. il por
Library J 95:1275-80 Ap 1 '70

ANDERSON, Burton
Amsterdam when the windows steam up. il
Sat R 53:40-1+ S 12 '70

ANDERSON, D. Carl
Open-pian schools. Ed Digest 36:8-10 N '70

ANDERSON, D. Chris
Learning to be helpless. il por Sci Digest 68:
94-5 N '70 *

ANDERSON, D. M.
Dodder weevils in simultaneous association
with parasitic plants and their hosts. bibliog il Science 168:132-3 Ap 3 '70

ANDERSON, Dave
(ed) See Stram, H. Pro football's dazzling
new look

ANDERSON, David C.
Ambiguities of defeat. Cur 114:6-8 Ja '70

ANDERSON, Dewey
Giant sequoia, monarchs of the living. il Nat
Parks 44:14-18 Mr '70
Lake Tahoe: then & now. il Nat Parks &
Con Mag 44:4-11 Ap '70
Mineral King, a fresh look. il Nat Parks &
Con Mag 44:8-10 My '70

ANDERSON, Donald Jack
Greatest fishing secret ever. il Field & S 74:
62-5+ Ap '70
New look at the old deer camp. il Field &
S 74:72-3+ Mr '70

ANDERSON, Duwayne M. and others
Bentonite debris flows in northern Alaska.
bibliog Science 164:173-4; 167:1015 Ap 11.
F 13 '70

ANDERSON, Edward H.
Videotape recording. Todays Ed 59:40 Ja '70

ANDERSON, Fred
Growing pains of medical care. New Repub
162:15-18 Ja 17; 13-16 Ja 24; 17-19 F 7; 38
Mr 21 '70

ANDERSON, French
Genetic engineering. J. Rohler. Chr Today
14:50-1 Ap 10 '70 *

ANDERSON, Henry W.
Outdoor miniature village. S. A. Parvin.
il por Hobbies 75:144-5+ Jl '70 *

ANDERSON, Ian
Ian's be-in. il pors Life 68:79-80 My 8 '70 *

ANDERSON, Jack
Fleeting moments. il Nation 210:216-17 F 23
'70

ANDERSON, James P.
It's nice to be a pioneer. il pors Sch Arts
70:30-3 D '70

ANDERSON, Jean P.
Reading and writing can be fun for the underachiever! Engl J 59:1119-21+ N '70

ANDERSON, John Bayard
Excerpt from debate. April 15, 1970. Cong
Digest 49:188+ Je '70

ANDERSON, John D. and others
Martian mass and earth-moon mass ratio
coherent S-band tracking of Mariners 6 and
7. bibliog il Science 167:277-9 Ja 16 '70

ANDERSON, John F.
Who speaks for the concerns of library service? address, 1970. bibliog il Am Lib 1:
1062-8 D '70

ANDERSON, Jon
Rowing at dawn; Creative writing 307; It's
the beginning; so much for sentiment; poems. Poetry 116:141-6 Je '70

ANDERSON, Kenneth N.
After cyclamates: what's next on the FDA's
food target list? il Sci Digest 67:16-23 F '70
Complex causes of indigestion. Har Yrs
10:31-2+ Jl '70
Incredible balsa tree. il Sci Digest 68:70-4 N
'70
What to do if your car goes into the water. il
Pop Mech 134:92-5+ Ag '70

ANDERSON, Margaret C.
Exuberance and ecstasy. J. M. Edelstein. New
Repub 162:19-22 Je 13 '70 *

ANDERSON, Mary Lou
What if this Christmas you took time; poem.
PTA Mag 65:29 D '70

ANDERSON, Orson L.   See Schreiber, E.
jt. auth.

ANDERSON, Pat
Lifestyle. il por Am Home 73:10+ D '70

ANDERSON, Philip W.
How Josephson discovered his effect; adapta-
tion of address, September 1970. bibliog il por
Phys Today 23:23-5+ N '70

ANDERSON, Ralph A.
Using power line as accurate time standard.
il Electr World 83:46-7+ My '70

ANDERSON, Raymond Kemp
Barth on Tillich: neo-gnosticism? pors Chr
Cent 87:1477-81 D 9 '70

ANDERSON, Robert
Assault on American industry; address, July
10, 1970. Vital Speeches 36:655-8 Ag 15 '70

about
At North American more of the same. Bsns
W p37 F 28 '70

ANDERSON, Robert H. and Seibert, Rochelle
Community planning for preprimary education; with study-discussion program. bibliog il PTA Mag 64:8-10+, 34 My '70

ANDERSON, Robert Orville
Fastest draw in the oil game. il pors Bsns W
p62-5+ Ap 18 '70 *

ANDERSON, Robert Woodruff
Thoughts on playwriting. Writer 83:12-14+ S
'70

ANDERSON, Roland G.
Pyramid of electron configuration. il Chem
43:27 Je '70

ANDERSON, Thelma
Spring is a maple-sugar time. il Org Gard &
Farm 17:116-18 Mr '70

ANDERSON, Tom
Constitutional government under God; address, April 20, 1970. Vital Speeches 36:
459-66 My 15 '70

ANDERSON, Viola
Who's who in the hospital? il Todays Health
48:64-5 O '70

ANDERSON, Walter W.
How do buoys get there? il Yachting 127:
108-9+ Ja '70

ANDERSON, Mrs William
Flowers from beads. R. Wrenn. il pors Design
71:26-9 Spr '70 *

ANDERSON, William A.
Blind coach leads the way. D. P. Brewster.
il pors Har Yrs 10:38-41 Jl '70 *

ANDERSON, William Robert
Let's send SABMIS to sea now. Read Digest
96:102-6 F '70

ANDERSON, William W. and Bullis, H. R. jr
Search the shrimp beds by sub; with biographical sketches. il pors Sea Front 16:
112-19, 126-7 Mr '70

ANDERSON-IVANTZOVA, Elizaveta
In the shadow of Russian tradition; interview,
ed. by M. Horosko. por Dance Mag 45:36-7
Ja '71

ANDES mountains
Conquest of Huila. P. C. Ritterbush. il por
Américas 22:19-27 Ja '70

ANDRADE, Jorge Carrera. See Carrera Andrade, J.

ANDRADE, Joseph
Materials science & engineering, a modern
multidiscipline. il por Chem 43:13-15 Ap '70

ANDRE, Bob
Different world. il por Yachting 127:68-9+ F
'70

ANDRE, Carl
Holding the floor. D. Waldman. bibliog il
Art N 69:60-2+ O '70 *

ANDRE, Harry
Insulin murders. L. B. Taylor, jr. Todays
Health 48:50-3+ D '70 *

ANDREAE, Christopher
Boston, new directions. il Art in Am 58:102-3
My '70

ANDREI, abp
Soviet archbishop released from prison, reinstated by church. M. Bourdeaux. Chr Cent 87:674 My 27 '70 *

ANDRESEN, Ivar
Top tenors, on L.P. A. Favia-Artsay. pors Hobbies 75:36+ Je '70 *

ANDRESKI, Stanislav
Case for war. il por Time 95:46-7 Mr 9 '70 *

ANDRESON, Laura
Laura Andreson. B. Kester. il Craft Horiz 30:12-17 D '70 *

ANDRETTI, Mario
Money in his pocket, speed in his soul. K. Chapin. il por Sports Illus 32:38-40+ My 11 '70 *
Sebring of feet and feats. R. F. Jones. il Sports Illus 32:57 Mr 30 '70 *

ANDREW, Charles L.
Build dynamic diode tester. il Pop Electr 33:53+ Jl '70

ANDREWS, Danny
Clancy's gym is Danny's turf. H. Aronson. il pors Sports Illus 32:40-4 Mr 23 '70 *

ANDREWS, James F.
Circulation and weather of 1969. il Weatherwise 23:4-11+ F '70

ANDREWS, Jay D. See Hopkins, S. H. jt. auth.

ANDREWS, Julie
New life of Julie Andrews. G. Christy. il pors Good H 170:90-1+ My '70 *

ANDREWS, Lewis M.
Communes and the work crisis. Nation 211. 460-3 N 9 '70
—See Schlosberg, M. S. jt. auth.

ANDRON, Jon
Yachting interviews; ed. by B. Crabtree. il por Yachting 128:67+ Jl '70

ANDROS blue holes. See Ocean bottom

ANDROS ISLAND, Bahama Islands
Diving into the blue holes of the Bahamas. G. J. Benjamin. il Nat Geog 138:346-63 S '70

ANDRUS, Aileen
At home; story. Mlle 71:164-5 O '70

ANECDOTES
Truth, crushed to earth, just lies there; true, funny stories. G. Ace. Sat R 53:8 Je 20 '70
Where and when to use anecdotes. J. J. Green. Writers Digest 50:23-5 Mr '70
also subhead Anecdotes, facetiae, satire, etc. under various subjects, e.g. Conduct of life—Anecdotes, facetiae, satire, etc.

ANEMIA
Blood engineers; thalassemia. il Newsweek 75:98 My 18 '70
Discriminating disease; sickle cell anemia treated with solution of urea. il Time 96:41 D 21 '70
Healing the sickle cells. il Newsweek 76:77 D 14 '70
Heterozygous beta thalassemia: balanced globin synthesis in bone marrow cells. E. Schwartz. bibliog il Science 167:1513-14 Mr 13 '70
Pagophagia in the albino rat. S. C. Woods and R. S. Weisinger. bibliog il Science 169:1334-6 S 25 '70
Sickle cell anemia and malaria. il Chem 43:22 Je '70

ANEMONES, Sea. See Sea anemones

ANESTHESIOLOGISTS. See Anesthetists

ANESTHETICS
Nightmare anesthetic; ketamine. Newsweek 76:88+ S 28 '70
What's the best way to kill pain? G. M. Knox. Bet Hom & Gard 48:22+ My '70

ANESTHETISTS
How anesthesiologists save lives. W. S. Ross. il Read Digest 96:144-8+ Mr '70

ANGELES, Victoria de los
Two sopranos: a discovery and an old friend. P. G. Davis. pors Hi Fi 20:secI 79 Je '70 *

ANGELL, Alan
Christian democracy in Chile. bibliog f Cur Hist 58:79-84+ F '70

ANGELL, C. A. and Sare, E. J.
Vitreous water: identification and characterization. bibliog Science 168:280-1 Ap 10 '70

ANGELL, Roger
Floto letters. New Yorker 46:34-7 F 21 '70
Outgoing bag. New Yorker 46:32-4 O 3 '70
Sad Arthur; story. New Yorker 46:33-5 Mr 14 '70
Sporting scene (cont) New Yorker 46:110+ O 31 '70
Turtletaub and the foul distemper; story. New Yorker 46:26-9 My 30 '70

ANGELOU, Maya
I know why the caged bird sings; excerpts. il Harper 240:86-98 F '70

I know why the caged bird sings; former singer recalling childhood. il pors Ebony 25:62-4+ Ap '70
Nina Simone: high priestess of soul. il Redbook 136:77+ N '70

ANGELS (baseball) See Baseball clubs

ANGELS in art
Glory of the Lord shone round about them. il Time 96:28-33 D 28 '70

ANGER
Child in anger. H. G. Ginott. McCalls 97:32+ Mr '70
See also
Hostility (psychology)
Temper

ANGINO, E. E. and others
Arsenic in detergents: possible danger and pollution hazard. bibliog il Science 168:389-90, 1526; 170:870-2 Ap 17, Je 26, N 20 '70

ANGIOKERATOMA
Enzyme replacement in Fabry's disease, an inborn error of metabolism. C. A. Mapes and others. bibliog il Science 169:987-9 S 4 '70
Fabry's disease: alpha-galactosidase deficiency. J. A. Kint. bibliog il Science 167:1268-9 F 27 '70
Genetic inactivation of the α-galactosidase locus in carriers of Fabry's disease. G. Romeo and B. R. Migeon. bibliog il Science 170:180-1 O 9 '70

ANGKOR, Cambodia
Glories of Angkor. il Life 68:48-57 Je 5 '70
Mysterious Angkor, jungle city of the dead. L. S. De Camp. il Sci Digest 67:18-23 Ap '70

ANGLER fish
Anglerfish, the fisherman with a built-in lure. G. Heinold. il Sci Digest 67:20-4 Ja '70

ANGLERFISH. See Angler fish

ANGLEWORMS. See Earthworms

ANGLICAN chants. See Chants (Gregorian, plain, etc)

ANGLICAN church. See Church of England

ANGLICAN church in New Zealand. See Church of England in New Zealand

ANGLING. See Fishing

ANGLO-SAXON poetry
See also
Beowulf

ANGLUND, Joan Walsh
Slice of snow; poem. il Ladies Home J 87:106-7 O '70

ANGUILLA (island)
Anguilla sojourn; English language *haibun.* R. Spiess. il Travel 134:56-61 D '70

ANHYDROUS ammonia. See Ammonia

ANILINE dyes. See Coal tar colors

ANIMAL art. See Animals in art

ANIMAL behavior. See Animals—Habits and behavior

ANIMAL calling
Elk charge this bugle. H. Rate. il Field & S 75:54-5+ O '70
Pied Piper of Texas. H. Swiggett. il Nat Wildlife 8:34-5 F '70

ANIMAL communication
Chimp learns to talk, but not very well. il Sci Digest 68:31 S '70
Education of Sarah; teaching a chimpanzee to converse. il Time 96:51-2 S 21 '70
How they taught a chimp to talk. B. Ford. bibliog il Sci Digest 67:10-17 My '70
Language, name, and concept. J. Bronowski and U. Bellugi. bibliog il Science 168:669-73 My 8, '70; Reply with rejoinder. M. L. Linton. 169:328 Jl 24 '70
See also
Insect communication

ANIMAL experimentation
Emotionally induced increases in effective osmotic pressure and subsequent thirst. E. Deaux and J. W. Kakolewski. bibliog il Science 169:1226-8 S 18 '70
Future space bioscience; extrapolation of biomedical studies on animals to human astronauts. Space World G-7-79:40-1 Jl '70
Lack of coincidence between neural and behavioral manifestations of cortical spreading depression. T. J. Carew and others. bibliog il Science 169:1339-42 S 25 '70
Monkey see, monkey do, as Not George helps science study you. il Todays Health 48:18 O '70
More fuel for the pill controversy; use of beagles in testing. B. J. Culliton. Sci N 98:402 N 21 '70
See also
Laboratory animals
Maze tests
Vivisection

ANIMAL extinction. See Animals, Extinct

ANIMAL fats. See Oils and fats, Edible

ANIMAL intelligence
Chimp learns to talk, but not very well. il
Sci Digest 68:31 S '70
See also
Animal learning
Maze tests

ANIMAL introduction
Doctor Hibben's New Mexican ark; endangered African species in desert of New
Mexico. R. Gannon. il por Sci Digest 68:
23-9 O '70

ANIMAL language. See Animal communication

ANIMAL learning
Frequency-specific relation between hippo-
campal theta rhythm, behavior, and amo-
barbital action. J. A. Gray and G. G. Ball.
bibliog il Science 168:1246-8 Je 5 '70
Hormonal effects on ontogeny of swimming
ability in the rat: assessment of central
nervous system development. S. Schapiro
and others. bibliog il Science 168:147-51 Ap
3 '70
Intermodal equivalence of stimuli in apes. R.
K. Davenport and C. M. Rogers. bibliog il
Science 168:279-80 Ap 10 '70; Reply. N.
Geschwind. 168:1249 Je 5 '70
Learning in the autonomic nervous system.
L. V. DiCara. il Sci Am 222:30-9 bibliog (p
146) Ja '70
Olfactory stimuli and the pseudo-extinction
effect. E. A. Wasserman and D. D. Jen-
sen; reply with rejoinder. M. E. Deutsch.
Science 169:402 Jl 24 '70
Prolonged learning and split-brain cats. J. A.
Sechzer. bibliog il Science 169:889-92 Ag 28
'70
See also
Memory

ANIMAL locomotion
Crayfish swimming: alternating motor output and giant fiber activity. J. E. Schrameck. bibliog il Science 169:698-700 Ag 14
'70
How snakes move. C. Gans. il Sci Am 222:
82-6+ bibliog(p 152) Je '70
Limb movements in a monotreme (tachyglossus aculeatus): a cineradiographic analysis. F. A. Jenkins, jr. bibliog il Science
168:1473-5 Je 19 '70
Turbulence and swimming animals. il Sea
Front 16:374-6 N '70
See also
Insects—Flight

ANIMAL lore
Unnatural history. J. W. Krutch. il Audubon
72:36-40 N '70

ANIMAL medical centers. See Veterinary medicine

ANIMAL migration. See Animals—Migration

ANIMAL painting and illustration. See Animals
in art

ANIMAL populations
Cat's whiskers; system of identifying lions by
whisker patterns. Sci Am 223:94 S '70
Control of population; excerpt from The so-
cial contract. R. Ardrey. il Life 68:48-52+
F 20 '70
Environmental deterioration and declining
species. J. E. Forbes. il Cons 25:21-6 Ag
'70
Unexplained Australian plague; mouse erup-
tion. Sci N 97:290 Mr 21 '70
Violent way; excerpt from The social contract.
R. Ardrey. il Life 69:56B-56D+ S 11 '70
See also
Fish populations
Insect populations

Control

Control of population; excerpt from The social contract. R. Ardrey. il Life 68:48-52+
F 20 '70; Same abr. with title Nature and
the case for birth control. Read Digest 96:
116-20 Je '70
Great buffalo hunt? Shoot? Slaughter? Ari-
zona's surplus bison shoot at Raymond
ranch. B. Gilbert. il Sports Illus 33:36-8+
N 23 '70
Managing the Yellowstone elk. G. F. Cole. il
Nat Parks & Con Mag 44:20-2 S '70
Reporter at large; controlling the prairie dog
and protecting the black-footed ferret, in
South Dakota. F. McNulty. il New Yorker
46:40-2+ Je 13 '70
See also
Animals, Predatory—Control

ANIMAL repellents
Your kitchen is a garden center! G. Abraham. il Org Gard & Farm 17:41-3 F '70

ANIMAL sculpture
Hollowed-out animal sculpture; sculpting a
hippo. P. Rothenberg. il Ceram Mo 18:21-3
S '70

ANIMAL sociology. See Animals—Habits and
behavior

ANIMAL stories. See Animals—Stories

ANIMAL tagging
Polar bear at home in the Arctic wasteland.
il Sci Digest 67:58-61 Ap '70
They bag live polar bears. J. Rychetnik. il
Nat Wildlife 8:10-13 D '69

ANIMAL television programs. See Animals on
television programs

ANIMAL thefts
Computer fights dognappers. Am City 85:118
Mr '70

ANIMAL toys. See Toys

ANIMAL training. See Animals—Training

ANIMAL waste disposal. See Fertilizers and
manures—Handling

ANIMALS
See also
Abnormalities (animals)
Carnivora
Mammals
Odors of animals
Pets
Photography of animals
Teeth (animals)
Wildlife
Zoology
also names of animals, e.g. Bears

Anecdotes, facetiae, satire, etc.
Tomorrow's critters. C. E. Gillham. il Audubon 72:41-3 N '70

Capture
How to catch a hippopotamus; or an ele-
phant, or a zebra, or a buffalo. R. P. Cross-
ley. il Pop Mech 133:102-6+ Ja '70; Same.
Sci Digest 67:10-16 Mr '70
See also
International animal exchange, inc.

Diseases and pests
See also
Communicable diseases in animals
Deficiency diseases in animals
Veterinary medicine

Food and feeding
Bare zone between California shrub and
grassland communities: the role of animals.
B. Bartholomew. bibliog il Science 170:1210-
12 D 11 '70

Habits and behavior
Control of population; excerpt from The social contract. R. Ardrey. il Life 68:48-52+
F 20 '70; Same abr. with title Nature and
the case for birth control. Read Digest 96:
116-20 Je '70
Poaching on Tarzan's turf; hunting habits;
study findings of George B. Schaller and
Gordon R. Lowther. il Newsweek 76:54-5
Ag 17 '70
Sane community: a density problem? P. Leyhausen. il UNESCO Courier 23:26-32 Ag
'70
Should we ape the chimpanzee? D. Behr-
man. il UNESCO Courier 23:7-18 Ag '70
Social subordination, population density, and
mammalian evolution. J. J. Christian. bib-
liog Science 168:84-90 Ap 3 '70; Reply with
rejoinder. M. D. F. Udvardy. 170:344-6 O 16
'70
Talk with Konrad Lorenz; ed. by F. de
Towarnicki. K. Z. Lorenz. il por N Y
Times Mag p4-5+ Jl 5 '70
Violent way; excerpt from The social con-
tract. R. Ardrey. il Life 69:56B-56D+ S 11
'70
War is not in our genes. S. Carrighar. il
UNESCO Courier 23:40-5 Ag '70
Wondrous creatures of the night. J. George.
il Read Digest 96:182-8 Ja '70
Zoo stories: Bronx zoo, house of nocturnal
animals. New Yorker 45:29-30 F 14 '70
See also
Courtship of animals
Hibernation
Sexual behavior in animals
See also Birds—Habits and behavior, and
similar headings

Intelligence
See Animal intelligence

Jaws
See Jaws (animals)

Language
See Animal communication

Memory
See Memory

ANIMALS—*Continued*

Migration

Migration of the barren-ground caribou. J. P. Kelsall. il Natur Hist 79:98-106 Ag '70

What creatures, other than birds, migrate? Sci Digest 67:89-90 My '70

See also

Crustaceans—Migration

Lemmings

Orientation

See Orientation

Photographs

Dreams of a basset. Good H 171:206 D '70

Hooves that rock the cradle. J. Cooke. il Sports Illus 32:30-5 Mr 9 '70

They live here, too. K. Hillyard. Har Yrs 10:26-30 Jl '70

Wildlife at a big game pub; Rhodesia. il Am For 76:6-7 F '70

See also

Photography of animals

Protection

Remodeled deathtrap; escape ramp for bighorns from waterhole in Chocolate Mountains, Calif. M. Bowen. il Nat Parks 44:26 Ja '70

See also

Birds—Protection

Game protection

Sight

See Sight (animals)

Sleep habits

See Animals—Habits and behavior

Stories

Intruders. P. P. Sturges. il Liv Wildn 33:15-18 Aut '69

See also

Burros—Stories

Dogs—Stories

Training

Teaching animals with electronic language. C. J. Strickler. il Pop Mech 134:79-82+ D '70

See also

Birds—Training

Cats—Training

Transportation

Bucking up the Pakistanis; transporting black buck antelope from Texas back to West Pakistan. V. Kraft. il Sports Illus 32:62-3 Ap 27 '70

Dogs can fly too. R. Barlow il por Field & S 74:130-2+ Ja '70

Getting your dog there, and back again. J. R. Falk. il Field & S 74:222-4+ Ap '70

Treatment

Watching the animals; Des Moines slaughterhouse. R. Rhodes. il Harper 240:91-4 Mr '70

See also

Royal society for the prevention of cruelty to animals

Vivisection

ANIMALS, Abnormalities of. See Abnormalities (animals)

ANIMALS, Domestication of. See Domestication

ANIMALS, Effect of light on. See Light—Physiological effects

ANIMALS, Effect of ozone on. See Ozone—Physiological effects

ANIMALS, Extinct

When a race breathes no more; extinction of forty-seven species of U.S. wildlife. W. J. Hickel. il Sports Illus 33:70+ D 14 '70

Wiped out & unsung. A. Solem. il Nat Parks & Con Mag 44:7-8 Ag '70

See also

Dinosaurs

Mammoths

Mastodons

ANIMALS, Food habits of. See Animals—Food and feeding

ANIMALS, Germ free. See Germfree life

ANIMALS, Imaginary

Snouters, by H. Stümpke. Review

Environ 12:34-5 Je '70. K. Shea

ANIMALS, Infancy of

Monkeys are therapists; pathological behavior induced by isolation. J. Moriarty. il Sci N 98:100 Ag 1 '70

ANIMALS, Mechanical

See also

Birds, Mechanical

ANIMALS, Mythical

On the trail of bigfoot. G. H. Harrison. il Nat Wildlife 8:4-9 O '70

See also

Animal lore

ANIMALS, Predatory

See also

Carnivora

Coyotes

Wolves

Control

Mike Frome. M. Frome. Am For 76:48 My '70; Reply. T. J. Sullivan. 76:76-7 O '70

ANIMALS, Rare. See Rare animals

ANIMALS, Respiration of. See Respiration

ANIMALS, Training of. See Animals—Training

ANIMALS, Treatment of. See Animals—Treatment

ANIMALS and children. See Children and animals

ANIMALS as carriers of infection

Toxoplasma gondii in cats; fecal stages identified as coccidian oocysts. J. K. Frenkel and others. bibliog il Science 167:893-6 F 6 '70

ANIMALS in art

American bestiary. M. S. Haverstock. il Art in Am 58:38-71 Jl '70

Bennington poodle. L. F. Reals. il Hobbies 75:80 Je '70

Dogs that live forever; Osthaus paintings. K. Evans and G. Evans. il por Field & S 75:234-5+ Je '70

Jeweled beasts of royal hordes; animal style exhibition at Asia house. G. B. Washburn. il Art N 69:28-31 Mr '70

Portrait of Den-Den; J. Wyeth paints a pig. il por Newsweek 75:73 Ap 27 '70

Wildlife of Sinai. W. Ferguson. il Audubon 72:32-41 Mr '70

See also

Birds in art

ANIMALS in captivity. See Zoological gardens

ANIMALS in design. See Design, Decorative—Animal forms

ANIMALS in religion, folklore, etc.

Holy cats and sacred cows. J. O'Connell. il Sci Digest 67:57-61 My '70

ANIMALS in the Bible. See Bible—Natural history

ANIMALS on television programs

Let's call it like it is. C. E. Gillham. il Field & S 75:48-9+ N '70

Saturday morning TV is going ape. il Life 69:62-5 O 2 '70

ANIMATED display figures. See Models (display figures)

ANISFIELD-Wolf awards

SR's 1970 Anisfield-Wolf awards. N. Sofian. Sat R 53:23-4 Ap 11 '70

ANITA Caspary, Sister. See Caspary, A.

ANKLE fractures. See Fractures

ANN Rose M. Guga, Sister. See Guga, A. R. M.

ANNABEL'S (night club) See Night clubs—England

ANNAPOLIS naval academy. See United States naval academy, Annapolis

ANNE, princess of Great Britain

Accent on youth in a royal visit. il pors U S News 69:50-1 Jl 27 '70 *

Anne of the twenty years. H. Ehrlich. il pors Look 34:28-35 Jl 28 '70 *

Charles & Anne & David & Julie & Tricia; visit to the White House. pors Time 96:10-11 Jl 27 '70 *

Commoner's guide to conversation with Charles and Anne. il pors Life 69:64A-66 Jl 17 '70 *

Company from Britain. il por Time 96:11-12 Jl 20 '70 *

Lingering love of the royal; White House visit. H. Sidey. pors Life 69:4+ Jl 31 '70 *

People are talking about... por Vogue 156:82-3 Jl '70 *

Princess Anne: Britain's royal swinger. il pors Good H 171:44-6+ Jl '70 *

Very private world of Princess Anne. J. Merchant. por Seventeen 29:122-3+ Je '70 *

Young Windsors pay a call. il pors Newsweek 76:12-13B Jl 27 '70 *

ANNE Frank museum. See Amsterdam, Netherlands—Historic houses, etc.

ANNELIDS

Antitumor activity in mice of tentacles of two tropical sea annelids. F. L. Tabrah and others. bibliog il Science 170:181-3 O 9 '70

Curious bristle-worms; polychaeta. J. D. George. il Sea Front 16:291-9 S '70

See also

Nervous system—Annelids

ANNELL, Charles, and Helz, Armin
Emission spectrographic determination of trace elements in lunar samples. bibliog il Science 167:521-3 Ja 30 '70

ANNENBERG, Walter H.
Annenberg, by G. Fonzi. Review
  Bsns W il p8 Mr 21 '70. E. W. Barrett *
Fall and rise of Walter Annenberg. il por McCalls 97:72-9+ Je '70 *
Moe's boy Walter at the Court of St James's. A. J. Reichley. il pors Fortune 81:88-93+ Je '70 *
Squire of Grosvenor square. il por Time 95: 32 F 9 '70

ANNEXATIONS, Municipal. See Cities and towns—Growth

ANNIVERSARIES
  See also
Fourth of July
United States—Declaration of independence— Centennial celebrations, etc.

ANNUAL meetings, Stockholders. See Stockholders meetings

ANNUAL reports, Corporate. See Corporation reports

ANNUALS (plants)
Annuals and vegetables; new introductions for 1971. il Horticulture 49:18-21+ Ja '71
Annuals for bright summer color. il Home Gard 57:26-7 Ap '70
Which annuals for early planting? il Sunset 145:183 S '70

ANNUALS, College. See College annuals

ANNUITIES
Variable annuities: a good hedge against inflation? Bet Hom & Gard 48:16+ Ja '70
Variable annuities fight inflation. W. R. Hoffer. il Har Yrs 10:14-16 Jl '70
  See also
College professors and instructors—Pensions Insurance, Life

ANOMALOUS water. See Water

ANOREXIA. See Appetite

ANORTHOSITE
Lunar anorthosites. J. A. Wood and others. bibliog il Science 167:602-4 Ja 30 '70
Lunar anorthosites: rare-earth and other elemental abundances. H. Wakita and R. A. Schmitt. bibliog il Science 170:969-74 N 27 '70

ANOTHER day, another war; story. See Lepis, C. B.

ANOTHER mother for peace (organization)
Homework for peace. B. S. Smith. il Parents Mag 45:122 O '70

ANOTHER redskin bit the dust; drama. See Dias, E. J.

ANRIG, Gregory R.
Federal Right to read program; summary of address, May 12, 1970. Pub W 197:41-2 Je 1 '70
Washington report; make way for the students; excerpts from report, ed. by J. Lloyd. Sr Schol 95:Schol Teach 2 D 1 '69

ANSERMET, Ernest
Ernest Ansermet, his last recordings. R. S. Brown. por Hi Fi sec I 20:95 F '70

ANSOFF, H. Igor
B-school for entrepreneurs of change. il por Bsns W p82+ Ap 25 '70 *

ANSOFF, Igor. See Ansoff, H. I.

ANSON, Robert
Report from a captured correspondent. il por Time 96:18-19 S 7 '70
  about
And then there were seventeen. il por Newsweek 76:56 S 7 '70 *

ANSWERING service, Telephone. See Telephone —Answering service

ANT venom. See Venom

ANTARCTIC exploration
Developing the U.S. Antarctic research program; Operation Deep Freeze. T. O. Jones. por Bul Atom Sci 26:81-4 D '70
Emergence of Antarctica: the mythical land. L. M. Gould. il por Bul Atom Sci 26:5-10 D '70
Evolution of a venture in Antarctic science; Operation Tabarin and the British Antarctic survey. V. Fuchs. il por Bul Atom Sci 26:75-80 D '70
Science and logistics in Antarctica. G. de Q. Robin. il por Bul Atom Sci 26:90-3 D '70

ANTARCTIC REGIONS
Antarctica since the IGY; symposium. il Bul Atom Sci 26:2-104 D '70
Journey south to a cold summer; Lindblad winter trip to Antarctica. M. Hemingway. il por Sports Illus 33:44-8 N 2 '70
President Nixon announces review of U.S. policy for Antarctica. Dept State Bul 63: 572-3 N 9 '70

Soviet research in Antarctica. P. Senko and M. Ravich. il Sci N 98:185-6 Ag 22 '70
  See also
Air pollution—Antarctic Regions
Ecology—Antarctic Regions
Geology—Antarctic Regions
Ice—Polar Regions
Natural resources—Antarctic Regions
Paleobotany—Antarctic Regions
Paleontology—Antarctic Regions

Climate
Drilling through the ice cap: probing climate for a thousand centuries. C. C. Langway, jr. and B. L. Hansen. il por Bul Atom Sci 26:62-6 D '70

ANTARCTIC research. See Polar research

ANTARCTIC treaty, 1959
Antarctic treaty. P. C. Daniels. il pors Bul Atom Sci 26:11-15 D '70

ANTEATERS
Adopting an anteater; excerpt from Encounter with animals. G. Durrell. il McCalls 97: 52+ S '70
Limb movements in a monotreme (tachyglossus aculeatus): a cineradiographic analysis. F. A. Jenkins, jr. bibliog il Science 168: 1473-5 Je 19 '70

ANTELL, Mark. See McCaull, J. jt. auth.

ANTELOPE hunting
  See also
Pronghorn hunting

ANTELOPES
Bucking up the Pakistanis; transporting black buck antelope from Texas back to West Pakistan. V. Kraft. il Sports Illus 32:62-3 Ap 27 '70
  See also
Cookery—Game

ANTENNAE
Antennal receptors: reactions to female sex attractant in periplaneta americana. J. Boeckh and others. bibliog il Science 168:589 My 1 '70

ANTENNAS (electronics)
C.E.T. test. D. Glass. Electr World 83:74 F '70
Space structure tests planned; self-erecting flexible rib concept for large antennas in space. B. M. Elson. il Aviation W 94:47+ Ja 11 '71
  See also
Radar—Antenna and scanning mechanisms
Radio antennas
Radio telescopes
Television antennas

ANTHOLOGIES
Selfish art; anthology of opinions on anthologies and children's books. W. Cole. il por Pub W 197:89-91 F 23 '70

ANTHONY, David
Gift from a stranger; story. Good H 171:75-7 S '70

ANTHONY, Don
Libya; the role of sports in a developing country. il Parks & Rec 5:38-9 Ap '70

ANTHONY, Gordon
In homage to Frederick Ashton. il pors Dance Mag 44:64-9 Je '70

ANTHONY, James R.
Printed editions of Andre Campra's L'Europe galante. bibliog f il Mus Q 56:54-73 Ja '70

ANTHONY, Robert N.
What should cost mean? bibliog f il Harvard Bsns R 48:121-31 My '70

ANTHRACITE carving. See Carving (art industries)

ANTHROP, Donald F.
Environmental side effects of energy production. il Bul Atom Sci 26:39-41 O '70

ANTHROPOLOGY
Recent physical anthropology. W. W. Howells. bibliog f Ann Am Acad 389:116-26 My '70
  See also
Evolution
Man
Man—Migrations
Man, Prehistoric

History
History, anthropology, and mass movements. G. L. Mosse. bibliog f Am Hist R 75:447-52 D '69

ANTHROPOLOGY, Theological. See Man (theology)

ANTHROPOMETRY
  See also
Fingerprints

ANTI-BALLISTIC missile system. See Guided missiles—Defenses

ANTIBIOTIC contamination of food. See Food contamination

ANTIBIOTIC feed supplements
Could you stay in business without additives? R. Wilmore. Farm J 94:H28 O '70
Three pounds of steak, without antibiotics, if possible. il Org Gard & Farm 17:84-9 Mr '70

ANTIBIOTICS
Antagonism by DDT of the effect of valinomycin on a synthetic membrane. B. D. Hilton and R. D. O'Brien. bibliog il Science 168:841-3 My 15 '70; Reply. F. Matsumura. 169:1343 S 25 '70
Antimycoplasmal antibiotics and hybrid sterility in drosophila paulistorum. R. P. Kernaghan and L. Ehrman. bibliog il Science 169:63-4 Jl 3 '70
Combine antibiotics, boost gains. Suc Farm 68:no5 B16 Mr '70
FDA wins round in Panalba fight. N. Gruchow. Science 167:1710 Mr 27 '70
Hope for Paget's disease cure; mithramycin. A. J. Snider. Sci Digest 69:59 Ja '71
Out with combination drugs. Sci N 98:9 Jl 4 '70
Piggyback antibiotics: bad medicine. Consumer Rep 35:446-7 Jl '70
Potassium ion specific electrode with high selectivity for potassium over sodium. M. S. Frant and J. W. Ross, jr. bibliog il Science 167:987-8 F 13 '70
See also
Antimycin
Bacteria—Resistance and sensitivity
Carbenicillin
Chloramphenicol
Colicines
Gramicidin
Penicillin

ANTIBODIES. See Antigens and antibodies

ANTIBODIES, Fluorescent
Prolactin localization in the primate pituitary by immunofluorescence. D. C. Herbert and T. Hayashida. bibliog il Science 169:378-9 Jl 24 '70

ANTICOAGULANTS
New drug for blood clots: urokinase. il Newsweek 76:62 N 30 '70

ANTI-COMMUNIST measures. See Communism—Anti-Communist measures

ANTI-COMMUNIST measures in the United States. See Communism—United States—Anti-Communist measures

ANTI-COMMUNIST movements

Asia, Southeastern
Where reds begin to look like losers; report. C. S. Foltz, jr. il U S News 68:29 Ap 27 '70

Cambodia
Cambodian puzzle; Viet Cong and North Vietnamese embassies sacked. il por Newsweek 75:39 Mr 23 '70

Cuba
Bay of piglets. il Newsweek 75:41 My 4 '70

Indonesia
Berkeley mafia and the Indonesian massacre; with editorial comment. D. Ransom. il Ramp Mag 9:26-9+ O '70

Oman
After the party's over. A. de Borchgrave. il Newsweek 76:29 D 28 '70

ANTI-CRIME legislation. See Crime prevention

ANTIDEPRESSANTS
Norepinephrine turnover and metabolism in rat brain after long-term administration of imipramine. J. J. Schildkraut and others. bibliog il Science 168:867-9 My 15 '70

ANTI-DISCRIMINATION bill. See Discrimination in employment

ANTIDIURETIC hormone. See Vasopressin

ANTI-DUMPING. See Dumping (commercial policy)

ANTI-EARTHQUAKE buildings. See Earthquakes and building

ANTIFERROMAGNETISM. See Magnetism

ANTIFLU drug. See Amandatine hydrochloride

ANTIFREEZE solutions
Antileak antifreeze, good for small leaks. Consumer Rep 35:75 F '70
FTC ties a can to a Zerex ad. Bsns W p30+ D 5 '70
Hot battle over antifreeze; problems of producers. Bsns W p54+ Ag 15 '70
No leak antifreeze: Zerex. Consumer Bul 53:14 Ap; 23 Ag '70

ANTIFREEZE testers
Test your own antifreeze. il Consumer Bul 54:4+ Ja '71

ANTIGENS and antibodies
Antibody to nuclear material eluted from isolated spleen vessels in systemic lupus erythematosus. K. H. Svec and S. T. Allen. bibliog il Science 170:550-1 O 30 '70
Antigen competition: a paradox. R. H. Waterston. bibliog il Science 170:1108-10 D 4 '70
Antigen competition: antigens compete for a cell occurring with limited frequency. J. F. Albright and others. bibliog il Science 167:196-8 Ja 9 '70
Australia antigen: distribution during Cohn ethanol fractionation of human plasma. D. D. Schroeder and M. M. Mozen. bibliog il Science 168:1462-4 Je 19 '70
Cross-reactions between streptococcal M proteins and human transplantation antigens. A. A. Hirata and P. I. Terasaki. bibliog il Science 168:1095-6 My 29 '70
How your body keeps you well. R. Brecher and E. Brecher. Read Digest 96:89-93 F '70
Lymphocytic responses to streptococcal antigens in glomerulonephritic patients. J. B. Zabriskie and others. bibliog il Science 168:1105-8 My 29 '70
Mechanism of antibody diversity: germ line basis for variability. L. Hood and D. W. Talmage. bibliog il Science 168:325-34 Ap 17 '70
Microcytotoxicity test: detection in sarcoma patients of antibody cytotoxic to human sarcoma cells. W. C. Wood and D. L. Morton. bibliog il Science 170:1318-20 D 18 '70
Myxovirus antibody increases in human connective tissue disease. P. E. Phillips and C. L. Christian. bibliog il Science 168:982-4 My 22 '70
Radioresistance of cooperative function of carrier-specific lymphocytes in antihapten antibody responses. D. H. Katz and others. bibliog il Science 170:462-4 O 23 '70
Selective destruction of target cells by diphtheria toxin conjugated to antibody directed against antigens on the cells. F. L. Moolten and S. R. Cooperband. bibliog il Science 169:68-70 Jl 3 '70
Serum hepatitis antigen (SH): rapid detection by high voltage immunoelectroosmophoresis. A. M. Prince and K. Burke. bibliog il Science 169:593-5 Ag 7 '70
Soluble HL-A7 antigen: localization in the β-lipoprotein fraction of human serum. R. K. Charlton and C. M. Zmijewski. bibliog il Science 170:636-7 N 6 '70
Specificity of antigen recognition by human lymphocytes in vitro. D. C. Zoschke and F. H. Bach. bibliog il Science 170:1404-6 D 25 '70
Structure and function of antibodies. G. M. Edelman. il Sci Am 223:34-42 bibliog(p 128) Ag '70
Tests for Australian antigen answer a need; serum hepatitis. J. Bockel. il Sci N 97:584-5 Je 13 '70
Theory of self-nonself discrimination. P. Bretscher and M. Cohn. bibliog il Science 169:1042-9 S 11 '70
See also
Antiserum
Complements (immunity)

ANTI-INFLATION measures. See Inflation (finance)

ANTI-INTELLECTUALISM. See Intellectuals

ANTI-KNOCK gasoline. See Gasoline—Anti-knock and anti-knock mixtures

ANTI-LEWIS B factor. See Blood groups

ANTILLES air boats, inc. See Airlines—Virgin Islands

ANTIMALARIALS
Antimalarials: effects on in vivo and in vitro protein synthesis. K. A. Conklin and S. C. Chou. bibliog il Science 170:1213-14 D 11 '70
See also
Atabrine
Chloroquine

ANTIMONY
Antimony holdout has buyers in a bind. il Bsns W p 16 My 2 '70

ANTIMYCIN
Antimycin A: stimulation of cell division and protein synthesis in tetrahymena pyriformis. C. Elson and others. bibliog il Science 168:385-6 Ap 17 '70

ANTIN, David
Fifteen verbs for the astronauts; poem. Nation 210:92 Ja 26 '70
Lead kindly blight. il Art N 69:36-9+ N '70

ANTIN, Eleanor
Women without pathos. Art N 69:45 Ja '71

ANTI-OIL-pollution laws. See Water pollution—Laws and legislation

ANTIOXIDANTS
Bradykinin inhibition by butylated hydroxyanisole. L. P. Posati and M. J. Pallansch. il Science 168:121-2 Ap 3 '70
ANTI-PARTICLES. See Particles (nuclear physics)
ANTIPERSPIRANTS. See Deodorants
ANTIPHONARIES (music)
Responsories and prosa for St. Stephen's day at Salisbury. R. Steiner. bibliog f il Mus Q 56:162-82 Ap '70
ANTI-POLLUTION devices. See Automobile engines—Exhaust
ANTI-POLLUTION policy. See Environmental policy
ANTI-POLLUTION stocks. See Pollution control industries—Securities
ANTI-POVERTY program, 1969-. See Public welfare—United States
ANTIPROTONS. See Protons
ANTIQUE airplanes
    See Aeronautics—History

Collectors and collecting
    See Airplanes—Collectors and collecting
ANTIQUE automobile club of America
Hershey with nuts; annual eastern national fall meet. il Motor T 22:52-3+ Ap '70
ANTIQUE automobiles

Collectors and collecting
    See Automobiles—Collectors and collecting
ANTIQUE dealers
Cat street, Hong Kong. F. Robertson. il Holiday 47:44-5+ F '70
ANTIQUE dealers fair and exhibition, London. See Antiques—Exhibitions
ANTIQUE love story. See Gilliatt, P.
ANTIQUES
Antiques; questions & answers. L. A. Boger. See issues of House & garden incorporating Living for young homemakers
Bold way with antiques; home of the Eugene V. Kleins, Beverly Hills, Calif. L. Grundy. il House B 112:80-5 S '70
Clues and footnotes; ed. by W. D. Garrett (cont) il Antiques 97:36+ Ja; 212+ F '70
Living with antiques:
    George Eveleigh house, Charleston. F. R. Edmunds. il Antiques 97:579-83 Ap '70
    Old Lyme, Conn. W. T. Donoho. il Antiques 98:922-6 D '70
    Small château near Brussells. E. D. Flory. il Antiques 97:730-3 My '70
Philipsburg manor, Upper Mills at North Tarrytown, New York. J. T. Butler. il Antiques 97:864-71 Je '70
State department antiques. C. Cutler. il Art in Am 58:74-7 S '70
    See also
Chairs
Heirlooms

Bibliography
Books about antiques; ed. by R. Davidson. See issues of Antiques
Books reviewed. Hobbies 75:106-7+ Ag '70

Care
How to preserve fine furnishings. E. Kinard. House B 112:36+ Mr '70

Exhibitions
Calendar of shows. See issues of Antiques
English painter of light. E. P. Birk. Antiques 97:164 F '70
Scouting the antique market; Antique dealers' fair and exhibition, London. J. Friedberg. Travel & Camera 33:72-3 My '70

History
Clues and footnotes; ed. by W. D. Garrett. See issues of Antiques
ANTIQUING of furniture. See Furniture—Finishing
ANTIQUITIES. See Archeology
ANTI-SEMITISM
Anti-Zionism, anti-Semitism and the Christian mind. A. T. Davies. Chr Cent 87:987-9 Ag 19 '70; Discussion. 87:1228+ O 14 '70
Arson returns to Munich. M. L. Kahn. America 122:386-8 Ap 11 '70
Bad scene at Oberammergau. Chr Cent 87: 651 My 27 '70
Can anti-Semitism be measured? L. S. Dawidowicz. bibliog f Commentary 50:36-43 Jl '70; Discussion. 50:18+ N '70
Caught in the crossfire; Russia. R. Brackman. il Nat R 22:564-5+ Je 2 '70
Current passions: letter from Oberammergau. H. O. J. Brown. il Nat R 22:890 Ag 25 '70

Has bias locked up the room at the top? Bsns W p38-9 Ja 24 '70
Jews in the mind of France. R. Winegarten. Commentary 50:64-8 N '70
On the Jewish question in the Soviet Union. B. Tzion. il N Y Times Mag p24-5+ My 3 '70
Opinion of mankind; Jewish hijacking case. Nation 212:34 Ja 11 '71
Perennial outrage: anti-Semitism in the New Testament. R. E. Willis. Chr Cent 87:990-2 Ag 19 '70
Socialism of fools: the new left calls it anti-Zionism. S. M. Lipset. il N Y Times Mag p6-7+ Ja 3 '71
ANTI-SEMITISM in literature
Eliot, Lawrence & the Jews. R. Alter. Commentary 50:81-6 O '70
ANTISERUM
Antigen receptor molecules: inhibition by antiserum against kappa light chains. J. Lesley and R. W. Dutton. bibliog il Science 169:487-8 Jl 31 '70
ANTI-SLAVERY movement. See Slavery—United States
ANTI-SMOG devices. See Automobile engines—Exhaust
ANTI-SMOKING clinics. See Smoking
ANTI-STRIKE legislation. See Labor laws and legislation—United States
ANTITRUST division. See United States—Justice, Department of—Antitrust division
ANTITRUST legislation. See Trusts, Industrial—Law
ANTI-VIETNAM demonstrations. See Vietnamese war, 1957- —Protests, demonstrations, etc, against
ANTIVIRAL agents. See Viruses—Inactivation
ANTIVIRAL proteins. See Interferon
ANTIVIVISECTION. See Vivisection
ANTLER cribbage board. See Cribbage boards
ANTONIO, Juan
Brief biography. S. Goodman. il por Dance Mag 44:70-1 My '70
ANTONIONI, Michelangelo
Antonioni; interview, ed. by C. T. Samuels. il por Vogue 155:96-7+ Mr 15 '70
Let's talk about Zabriskie Point. il por Esquire 74:68-9+ Ag '70

            about
Films. S. Kauffmann. New Repub 162:20+ Mr 14 '70 *
Thalberg didn't look happy: or, With Antonioni at Zabriskie Point. B. Gindoff. il Film Q 24:3-6 Fall '70
ANTROBUS, Edmund
Traveler's choice. Travel 134:10 Ag '70
ANTS
Ant war; the imported fire ant. D. W. Coon and R. R. Fleet. bibliog il Environ 12:28-38 D '70
Attine fungus gardens contain yeasts. S. E. Craven and others. bibliog il Science 169: 184-6 Jl 10 '70
Biochemical basis of the fungus-attine ant symbiosis. M. M. Martin. bibliog il Science 169:16-20 Jl 3 '70
Fighting the fire ant; toxic side effects from Mirex. il Time 96:40 N 2 '70
Tiny warriors of Africa; the driver ant. il Life 68:60-5 Je 19 '70
Wonderful world of ants. E. G. Fanning. il Horticulture 48:28-9+ Mr '70
ANUSZKIEWICZ, Richard
Graphics '70. D. H. Karshan. il por Art in Am 58:56-9 Mr '70 *
ANXIETY
Attacks of anxiety. A. J. Snider. il Sci Digest 68:64-5 D '70
Teacher and the anxious child. J. E. Sieber and S. B. Crockenberg. Todays Ed 59:76-7 O '70
Way of handling anxiety. B. Spock and M. E. Bergen. Redbook 135:46+ My '70
What children worry about. R. M. Silberstein and C. Levine. il Parents Mag 45: 56-7+ My '70
    See also
Fear
Worry
ANZUS (Australia, New Zealand, United States) council. See Anzus council
ANZUS council
ANZUS council holds twentieth meeting at Washington; text of communique, September 26, 1970. Dept State Bul 63:446-8 O 19 '70
AOKI, Kikumaro, and Siegel, F. L.
Hyperphenylalaninemia: disaggregation of brain polyribosomes in young rats. bibliog il Science 168:129-30 Ap 3 '70

AORTA
Surgery
See Blood vessels—Surgery

APACHE Indians
Managing cash the tribal way; Jicarilla Apache tribe. il Bsns W p26 D 26 '70

APANTELES. See Parasites—Insects

APARTHEID. See South Africa—Race problems

APARTHEID; story. See Litvinov, I.

APARTMENT decoration. See Apartments

APARTMENT house incinerators. See Refuse incinerators

APARTMENT houses
Building types study; with introd. by E. K. Thompson. il Arch Rec 148:143-56 S '70
Chicago style: glass-house living at its loftiest; Lake point tower. J. L. O'Neill. il Am Home 73:48-55+ F '70
High-rise recreation; Arlington County, Va. L. Neeld. il Parks & Rec 5:50 My '70
Record apartments of the year. il Arch Rec 147:86-102 mid-My '70
See also
Row houses
Skyscrapers

Condominium plan ownership
Dollars and sense of condominiums. M. G. Huntoon, jr. il Am Home 73:54-5+ Ja '70
New way to afford a second home. D. Green. il Mech Illus 66:65-7+ F '70
Own a home, escape chores, save taxes: it's catching on. il U S News 69:88-9 D 7 '70
Well-built condominium; Heritage woods, Conn. J. H. Ingersoll. il House B 112:36 O '70

Cooperative ownership
See also
Apartment houses—Condominium plan ownership

Garden apartments
Much more than garden-type apartments; environmental apartments. il Bsns W p 146-7 Mr 14 '70

APARTMENT houses, Prefabricated
Boxes for lowrise; Boxes for highrise. il Arch Forum 132:52-5 Ap '70

APARTMENTS
Break with the past; duplex at the Dakota. R. Reif. il N Y Times Mag p72-3 S 20 '70
Chessy Rayner's apartment: in two small rooms I can pile up eighteen people for dinner. il McCalls 97:100-1 Ap '70
Chez Mlle: apt for a man. P. Bartlett. il Mlle 70:94-5 F '70
Colour at full cry in Mr and Mrs Steven Jacobson's N.Y. apartment. il Vogue 156:132-7 Ag 1 '70
Eleanor & Frank Perry: collaboration also sets the scene at home. S. Nirenberg. il pors House B 112:72-3+ Ag '70
Free-form future. B. Plumb. il N Y Times Mag p50-1 Mr 29 '70
No century gap here; Manhattan apartment. R. Reif. il N Y Times Mag p 104-5 Ap 5 '70
On the scene: away from home. il Seventeen 29:142-3+ My '70
Op-art-ment: the Paris apartment of M and Mme Francois Catroux. il Vogue 155:122-5 F 15 '70
Penthouse underground; basement apartment in Paris. N. Skurka. il N Y Times Mag p 100-1 N 22 '70
Personal stamp. il N Y Times Mag p48-9 Je 28 '70
Space games: the Paris apartment of Mme Raymonde Zehnacker. il Vogue 155:126-7 F 15 '70
Underdramatizing it; Aaron Donner's manhattan apartment. N. Skurka. il N Y Times Mag p 104-5 N 29 '70
Valentino's Roman roof-top. il por Vogue 155:148-53 Ap 15 '70

APARTMENTS, Remodeled
Apartment? it's really more of a compartment. il House B 112:130-3 My '70
Architect mixes landmark drama with a casual lifestyle. N. Craig. il House B 112:31-4 Jl '70
Cutups and cutouts; student apartment. B. Plum. il N Y Times Mag p70-1 Ja 25 '70
From warehouse to penthouse. il House B 112:96-8 Je '70
Her own look. il N Y Times Mag p50-1 Je 14 '70
Marvelous makeover. L. Grundy. il House B 112:78-81 Mr '70
New York apartment: sleek for the 70s. il Am Home 73:86-9 My '70

We did it: slum flat made into handsome apartment; ed. by S. Nirenberg. V. Hart. il por House B 112:3+ Jl '70

APATITE
See also
Hydroxapatite

APERITIF wines. See Wine

APERITIFS. See Liquors

APES
Intermodal equivalence of stimuli in apes. R. K. Davenport and C. M. Rogers. bibliog il Science 168::279-80 Ap 10 '70; Reply. N. Geschwind. 168:1249 Je 5 '70
See also
Chimpanzees
Gibbons

APES, Fossil
Gigantopithecus. E. L. Simons and P. C. Ettel. il Sci Am 222:76-85 bibliog(p 146) Ja '70
In the pongid line; gigantopithecus. il Sci N 97:193 F 21 '70

APGAR, Virginia
Liberated, all liberated. il pors Vogue 155:116 Je '70 •

APHASIA
Organization of language and the brain; adaptation of address, December 28, 1969. N. Geschwind. bibliog il Science 170:940-4 N 27 '70

APHASIA, Aural. See Word deafness

APHIDS. See Plant lice

APHORISMS and apothegms
Creating aphorisms. W. Lambdin. Todays Ed 59:25 Ap '70
Poor woman's almanac. B. Pfizer. See issues of Ladies' home journal

APHRODISIACS
Riding the sex wave; West Germany. Newsweek 75:108 Ap 20 '70

APHRODITE of Cnidus. See Sculpture, Greek

APICELLA, Anthony J. and Giampa, A. J.
General music in the schools. Ed Digest 35:52-3 Ja '70

APOCALYPSE at the Plaza; story. See Klein, N.

APOCALYPTICISM
Radical kingdom, by R. R. Ruether. Review Commonweal 92:462-4+ S 18 '70. G. Baum

APOGAMY
Apospory in sorghum bicolor (L.) Moench. W. W. Hanna and others. bibliog il Science 170:338-9 O 16 '70

APOLLO 8 flight. See Space flight to the moon—Manned flights—Apollo 8 flight

APOLLO 11 flight. See Space flight to the moon—Manned flights—Apollo 11 flight

APOLLO 12 flight. See Space flight to the moon—Manned flights—Apollo 12 flight

APOLLO 13 flight. See Space flight to the moon—Manned flights—Apollo 13 flight

APOLLO lunar module. See Space vehicles—Landing systems—Moon

APOLLO lunar surface experiments package. See Moon—Exploration—Equipment

APOLLO project. See Space flight to the moon

APOLLO telescope mount. See Artificial satellites—Astronomical applications

APOLOGETICS
Potential of apologetics. M. J. Erickson. Chr Today 14:6-8 Jl 17; 13-15 Jl 31 '70
See also
Witness bearing (Christianity)

APOSPORY. See Apogamy

APOSTAL, Robert A. and Halcrow, J. H.
Personality characteristics of mental health center patients classified by referral source. bibliog Ment Hy 54:295-7 Ap '70

APOTHEOSIS. See Deification

APPALACHIAN MOUNTAINS
See also
Blue Ridge Mountains

APPALACHIAN REGION
Appalachian pictures; excerpt from Appalachian wilderness. E. Abbey. il Audubon 72:4-13 S '70
Gray woman of Appalachia. H. S. Arnow. il Nation 211:684-7 D 28 '70
Lament for the Appalachian hills. H. M. Caudill. il Am For 76:8-11+ My '70; Discussion. 76:2 S; 3 O '70
Not so Beverly hillbillies. M. D. Daley. Commonweal 92:4-5 Mr 13 '70
Teen corps: soldiers with shovels. J. E. Roper. il por Read Digest 97:37-8+ D '70
See also
Arts and crafts—Appalachian Region
Public health—Appalachian Region

History
Progress reached our valley. H. S. Arnow. il Nation 211:71-7 Ag 3 '70

APPALACHIAN REGION—*Continued*
Recovery program, 1965-
Appalachian program: a mechanism for a national growth policy? L. J. Carter. Science 169:32-5 Jl 3 '70
Progress in Appalachia: a model for federal aid? il U S News 68:79-80 Mr 23 '70
See also
United States—Appalachian regional commission
APPALACHIAN regional commission. See United States—Appalachian regional commission
APPALACHIAN TRAIL
Mighty dream come true. A. Birch. il por Har Yrs 10:14-15 F '70
APPALACHIAN volunteers. See Volunteers in service to America
APPARENT velocity illusion. See Optical illusions
APPEASEMENT. See International relations
APPEL, Albert
Need is apparent for greater camp use. il Camp Mag 42:12+ N '70
APPEL, Alfred, jr
Tale of a tub for our time. A. Alvarez. Sat R 53:27-9+ Je 13 '70 *
APPEL, Fredric C.
Coming revolution in transportation. Read Digest 96:96-100 Ap '70
APPENDICITIS
Children and appendicitis. L. W. Sauer. il PTA Mag 64:29-30 Mr '70
APPENZELL, Switzerland
Swiss notes. N. S. Hazelton. Nat R 22:683 Je 30 '70
APPETITE
Dieting till death; anorexia nervosa. C. Amen. il Sci Digest 67:27-31 My '70
APPETITE, Abnormal. See Pica (pathology)
APPETIZERS
Filled pastry shell appetizers. Sunset 144:198 My '70
From the Danes, beef appetizers. il Sunset 144:193 My '70
Good companions, appetizer foods and apéritifs. il Sunset 145:114 S '70
Hors d'oeuvres from seven great chefs. H. McCully. il House B 112:130-1 N '70
Hors d'oeuvres galore. F. M. Crawford. il Am Home 73:80-1 N '70
APPLAUSE; musical comedy. See Musical comedies, revues, etc.—Criticisms, plots, etc.
APPLE juice
See also
Cider
APPLE RIVER
Last rump bump of summer. il Life 69:42-5 O 2 '70
APPLEBAUM, Janet
Finding a style. R. Hattersley. il Pop Phot 67:102-5 N '70
APPLEBY, Albert R.
Businessmen against the war (sic) S. Weissman. il Ramp Mag 9:34-6 D '70
Striped ties for peace. Newsweek 75:72 Mr 30 '70 *
APPLEGATE, Judith
What is art deco? il Art N 69:38-42+ D '70
APPLEGATE, Richard
New England's memorial forests. il Am For 76:12-15 Ja '70
APPLEMAN, Mark
Fault. dear Brutus... por Forbes 106:54-5 O 15 '70 *
APPLEMAN, Philip
Revision, poem. New Repub 162:21 F 21 '70
APPLES
And mankind got mom's apple pie! K. Kraft and P. Kraft. il Todays Health 48:60-3 O '70
Wild apples over Indianapolis. R. Rodale. il Org Gard & Farm 17:21-4 O '70
See also
Cookery—Fruit
APPLETON, Jon
Current chronicle. Mus Q 56:116-19 Ja '70
APPLIANCE repairmen. See Repairmen
APPLIANCE warranties. See Warranty
APPLICATIONS for positions
Do's and don'ts of executive resumes. C. R. Boll. il Duns 95:47-8 F '70
How to read a resumé. P. Meyer. Duns 96:49-50+ O '70
Strategy for fired executives. J. Allan. il Duns 96:44-5 S '70
See also
Employment interviewing
APPLICATIONS technology satellites. See Artificial satellites
APPLIED art. See Arts and crafts

APPLIED data research, inc.
Turning disaster into a sales pitch. il Bsns W p52 Mr 14 '70
Unbundled at ADR. A. A. Butkus. por Duns 95:62-3 My '70
APPLIED science. See Technology
APPORTIONMENT (election law)
Battle in the states over future power in Congress. il U S News 69:41-3 N 30 '70
Big shifts in political power: impact of 1970 census. il U S News 69:26-8 S 21 '70
How the census shapes the vote. il Bsns W p46-7 N 28 '70
APPRAISAL. See Real property—Valuation
APPRECIATION of art. See Art —Appreciation
APPRECIATION of literature. See Literature —Appreciation and interpretation
APPRECIATION of music. See Music—Appreciation
APPRENTICES
New training plan in Britain's construction industry. H. A. Perry. il Mo Labor R 93:27-31 F '70
APPROACHING Simone; drama. See Terry, M.
APPROVAL motive. See Child study
APRICOT trees
Apricots by the bucketful, from your own garden! B. Kenny. il Org Gard & Farm 17:50-3 D '70
APRICOTS
Apricots, nectarines and almonds. G. L. Slate. il Horticulture 48:42-3+ My '70
APRIL, Robert W. and Hume, D. N.
Environmental mercury: rapid determination in water at nanogram levels. il Science 170:849-50 N 20 '70
APRONS
Apron stays on by itself. il Sunset 145:89 D '70
APT, Charles
Charles Apt in Portugal. J. H. Michel. il por Am Artist 34:54-62 Ap '70 *
APTHEKER, Bettina
Berkeley's meddlesome regents. Nation 211:169-73 S 7 '70
APTHEKER, Herbert
Anti-slavery medallions in the Martin Jacobowitz collection. bibliog il Negro Hist Bul 33:114-21 My '70
APTITUDE tests
Knell for the numbers game? scholastic aptitude test. J. Cass. Sat R 53:57 F 21 '70
AQUACULTURE. See Fish culture
AQUANAUTS
Tektite: unique observations of men under stress. R. H. Gilluly. il Sci N 98:400-1 N 21 '70
AQUARIAN alphaphone. See Electrophysiology —Apparatus
AQUARIUMS
Aquarium opened at department's Cape Vincent fisheries research station. W. A. Pearce. il Cons 25:20 O '70
Behind the boom in tropical fish; home aquariums. F. Dickenson. il Read Digest 97:202-6+ N '70
New ocean science show at Hawaii's Sea life park. il Sunset 145:43-4 N '70
Put a tropical fish in your tank. il Changing T 23:35-7 D '69
Spiraling look into the sea; Boston's undersea museum. il Time 95:52-3 Mr 23 '70
AQUATIC birds. See Water birds
AQUATIC life. See Fresh water biology
AQUATIC plants
See also
Eelgrass
Wild rice
AQUATIC sports
Memo from '69; ed. by F. Rohr, jr. il Motor B 125:25-40 Ja '70
Red cross national aquatic and small-craft schools. Camp Mag 42:50-1 Mr '70
Water sports; ed. by F. Rohr, jr. See issues of Motor boating to April 1970
See also
Boats and boating
Motor boat racing
Sailing
Surf riding
Yachts and yachting

Equipment
Water sports equipment. il Motor B 127:216-17 Ja '71
AQUATIC weed control
Kills water weeds, sinks algae, too; Aquathol plus and Hydrothol. Farm J 94:30 Jl '70
AQUIFERS. See Water, Underground

AQUITAINE company of Canada, ltd. See
    Petroleum industry and trade—France
ARAB bread. See Bread
ARAB federation (proposed)
    All for one and one for all? il Newsweek
    76:58 N 23 '70
    Eglibdan? Sudeglib? or Libdangypt? il Time
    96:27 N 23 '70
ARAB-Israeli war, 1967-. See Israeli-Arab war,
    1967-
ARAB-Jewish relations. See Jewish-Arab re-
    lations
ARAB refugees. See Refugees, Arab
ARAB states
    Can Russia take over the Arab world? J.
    Law. il U S News 68:72-6 Je 8 '70
        See also
    Arab federation (proposed)
    Education—Arab states
    Egypt
    Guerrillas—Arab states
    Jewish-Arab relations
    Maghreb
            Defenses
    Bombs and blue-outs. il Time 95:26 Ja 26
    '70
            Foreign relations
    Arab world: torn by quarrels and controver-
    sies. J. N. Wallace. il U S News 69:16 Ag 3
    '70
    Strategy left by Nasser; blackmail the U.S.
    with Arab oil. M. Copeland. il Life 69:36-7
    O 9 '70
    Up in arms; Libya-Egypt-Sudan alliance. il
    Newsweek 75:53-4 Ja 26 '70
            Israeli occupation, 1967-
    Settling in along the border. M. Clark. il
    Time 97:35-6 Ja 4 '71
        See also
    Jordan—Israeli occupation, 1967-
            Nationalism
    Fedayeen: new factor in the Middle East. J.
    B. Sheerin; discussion. Cath World 211:4,
    32-3, 52, 148 Ap-My, Jl '70
            Politics
    After Nasser... what next for the Mid-
    dle East? il Newsweek 76:34-5 O 12 '70
    Arab radicalism: problems and prospects. G.
    Lenczowski. Cur Hist 60:32-7+ Ja '71
    Arab summit: poles apart. il Time 96:27-8
    O 5 '70
    Death of Nasser. Nation 211:322 O 12 '70
    Jordan's nine-day war. il Newsweek 76:36-7
    O 5 '70
    New leader and an uneasy truce. il por News-
    week 76:53-4 O 19 '70
    Political housekeeping. Time 96:26 N 30 '70
    With Nasser gone, new dangers in Mideast.
    J. Law. il por U S News 69:20-1 O 12 '70
            History
    Documentary project on Arab politics and
    diplomacy. Sch & Soc 98:200-1 Ap '70
ARAB terrorists. See Terrorism
ARABIA
        See also
    Oman
ARABS
        See also
    Arab states
    Jewish-Arab relations
    Palestinian Arabs
ARABS in Israel. See Palestinian Arabs
ARABS of Palestine. See Palestinian Arabs
ARACHNIDS
        See also
    Mites
    Spiders
ARAGON, Louis
    European literary scene. R. J. Clements.
    Sat R 53:29 Ap 4 '70
    Letter from Paris. Genêt. New Yorker 46:50-2
    Jl 11 '70 *
ARAGONITE
    Dredging money from the Bank; from Great
    Bahama Bank. C. Phinizy. il Sports Illus 33:
    22-5 Jl 6 '70
ARAMBURU, Pedro Eugenio
    Act of revenge. Time 95:39 Je 15 '70 *
ARAN ISLANDS
    Aran Islands. H. P. Koenig. il Travel 133:
    42-7+ Ap '70
ARANA OSORIO, Carlos Manuel
    Guatemala and the guerrillas. G. A. Geyer.
    New Repub 163:17-19 Jl 4 '70
    Guerrilla hunter. Newsweek 75:56 Mr 16 '70 *
    Real good relationship. J. C. Goulden. Nation
    210:646-8 Je 1 '70 *

Step to the right. il por Time 95:43 Mr 16
    '70 *
ARANTES DO NASCIMENTO, Edson
    Pelé and pals retire the cup. T. Maule. il por
    Sports Illus 32:24-5 Je 29 '70 *
    Something to cheer about. il por Time 96:32 Jl
    6 '70 *
ARARAT, MOUNT
    Ark search strikes snag. Chr Today 14:52 S
    11 '70
    In the wake of the ark. il Sci N 97:574-5
    Je 13 '70
    Old problem arises anew; age of wood sam-
    ples. Chr Today 14:34 Jl 31 '70
ARAUCANA chickens. See Poultry
ARAVAIPA and Parla Canyons primitive
    areas. See Wilderness areas—Arizona
ARBACIA. See Sea urchins
ARBASINO, Alberto
    Fantastic Tosi. il Vogue 156:384-7+ S 1 '70
    Gae Aulenti: new force in Italian design; tr.
    by A. Foulke. il Vogue 156:118-23+ Jl '70
ARBITRATION, Commercial
    Arbitrator's decision upheld by court; arbi-
    tration clauses in publishing agreements.
    H. F. Pilpel and K. P. Norwick. Pub W 198:
    16 N 30 '70
ARBITRATION, Industrial
    One answer to the strike wave? compulsory
    arbitration. U S News 68:85-6 Ap 20 '70
        See also
    Collective bargaining
    Industrial relations
    International chamber of commerce—Court of
    arbitration
            United States
    Compromise that makes everybody mad;
    Emergency public interest protection bill.
    Bsns W p28 Mr 14 '70
    Nixon's cure for crisis strikes in transporta-
    tion. U S News 68:16 Mr 9 '70
    Strike ban for rails, is trucking next? il U S
    News 68:53-4 Mr 16 '70
ARBITRATION, International
    Controlling local conflicts; address, April 29,
    1970. E. L. Richardson. Dept State Bul 62:
    628-31 My 18 '70
    U.S. accedes to convention on foreign arbi-
    tral awards; statement. September 30, 1970.
    R. D. Kearney. Dept State Bul 63:598 N 9
    '70
        See also
    International law
    Peace
ARBOR day
            Drama
    Hotel Oak. C. Boiko. Plays 29:47-52 Ap '70
ARBORETUMS
        See also
    Washington, D.C.—National arboretum
ARC lamps. See Electric lamps, Arc
ARC welders. See Welders
ARCADE manufacturing company
    Arcade manufacturing co. il Hobbies 75:
    98J-98K Ap '70
ARCATA national corporation
    Forced march. il Forbes 106:42 Ag 15 '70
ARCATA redwood company. See Arcata national
    corporation
ARCE, Lee
    Best antelope in seventy years. il por Outdoor
    Life 145:44-5+ Ja '70
ARCEO, Sergio Méndez, bp. See Méndez
    Arceo, S.
ARCH Ward stakes. See Horse racing
ARCHAEOLOGY. See Archeology
ARCHAEOPTERYX. See Birds, Fossil
ARCHDIOCESE of Boston. See Catholic church
    —Dioceses
ARCHDIOCESE of Los Angeles. See Catholic
    church—Dioceses
ARCHEOLOGICAL pillage. See Pillage
ARCHEOLOGICAL research. See Archeology—
    Methodology
ARCHEOLOGISTS
        See also
    Archeology as a profession
ARCHEOLOGISTS, Amateur. See Scientists,
    Amateur
ARCHEOLOGY
    Archaeology in outer space. R. L. Schuyler.
    Space World G-3-75:13 Mr '70
    Chemistry and archaeology; symposium. Chem
    43:5-33 bibliog(p47) Jl '70
        See also
    Anthropology
    Art, Primitive
    Cave drawings and paintings
    Excavations (archeology)
    Indians of South America—Antiquities

ARCHEOLOGY—*See also—Continued*
Man, Prehistoric
Mummies
Petroglyphs
Picture writing
Pyramids
Stone age

History

How studying the past became a science. il Chem 43:5-7 Jl '70

Methodology

Answering the question when? J. Zimmerman. il Chem 43:22-3+ Jl '70
Ceramics from an eighteenth-century wilderness fort; Fort Michilimackinac. J. J. Miller. 2d. il Antiques 97:888-92 Je '70
Cluster analysis and multidimensional scaling of archeological sites in northern Chile. D. L. True and R. G. Matson. bibliog il Science 169:1201-3 S 18 '70
Experiment with time. G. Bibby. il Horizon 12:96-101 Spr '70
Glow reveals pottery age; thermoluminescent dating. Sci Digest 67:62-4 Ja '70
Magnetometer evidence of a structure within the La Venta pyramid. F. Morrison and others. bibliog il Science 167:1488-90 Mr 13 '70
Obsidian hydration rate for the Klamath basin of California and Oregon. L. Johnson, jr; reply. C. W. Meighan. bibliog il Science 170:99-100 O 2 '70
Science of ancient artifacts. J. Zimmerman. il Chem 43:28-33 Jl '70
Search for hidden chambers in the pyramids; adaptation of address, April 30, 1969. L. W. Alvarez and others. bibliog il Science 167: 832-9 F 6 '70
See also
Radiocarbon dating

ARCHEOLOGY, Submarine
Mysterious ships of Lake Nemi. L. S. De Camp. il Sci Digest 67:68-72 Je '70
Project Santa Maria. Travel 134:9 S '70
Resurrecting the oldest known Greek ship. M. L. Katzev. il Nat Geog 137:840-57 Je '70

ARCHEOLOGY as a profession
Fascinating career in archaeology. C. Peet. il Sci Digest 68:42-6 Jl '70

ARCHER, Sellers G.
Our man on the moon. il pors Am For 76:8-11 Ja '70

ARCHERD, William Dale
Insulin murders. L. B. Taylor, jr. Todays Health 48:50-3+ D '70 *

ARCHERY
Information, please. G. H. Gillelan. il Outdoor Life 145:116+ F '70
See also
Fishing with bow and arrow
Hunting with bow and arrow

Competitions

Arrows across the border; worldwide archery contests. G. H. Gillelan. il Outdoor Life 146: 94+ Jl '70
Right start; youthful archers. G. H. Gillelan. il Outdoor Life 145:174+ Ap '70

Equipment

So, what else is new? G. H. Gillelan. il Outdoor Life 146:36+ O '70
Tackle care. G. H. Gillelan. il Outdoor Life 146:104+ Ag '70
See also
Bow and arrow

ARCHES, Triumphal and memorial
Arch; Washington memorial. New Yorker 46: 19-21 Ag 29 '70

ARCHIPENKO, Alexander
Inventive sculptor. D. Davis. il por Newsweek 76:70 Ag 3 '70 *

ARCHITECTS
Architect you can communicate with; interview. P. S. Du Pont, 4th. il por House & Gard 137:16+ Mr '70
Great yacht designers. B. Robinson. il por Yachting 127:54-5+ F; 66-7+ My; 128:62-3+ O '70
New architects. il Newsweek 75:59 My 4 '70
New developments in Japanese architecture; with introd. by M. F. Schmertz. il Arch Rec 148:109-28 S '70
New dimensions of architectural practice. W. F. Wagner, jr. Arch Rec 147:9-10 Ja '70
See also
American institute of architects
Architecture as a profession
Negro architects
also names of architects, e.g. **P.M.** Rudolph

Fees

Architects' fees: their place in library planning. J. Orne. il por Library J 95:4099-106 D 1 '70
Case against percentages. P. B. Farrell, jr. Arch Forum 133:72-3 Jl '70

Training

See Architectural education

ARCHITECTS contracts. See Building—Contracts and specifications
ARCHITECTURAL decoration. See Decoration and ornament, Architectural
ARCHITECTURAL designs. See Architecture —Designs and plans
ARCHITECTURAL education
Education in the 1970's: teaching for an altered reality. Arch Rec 148:128-33 O '70
Minorities in the profession. E. P. Berkeley. Arch Forum 132:56-9 Je '70
See also
Bauhaus
ARCHITECTURAL exhibitions. See Architecture—Exhibitions
ARCHITECTURAL firms
Clients in the 1970's: new realities, more management. B. F. Gordon. il Arch Rec 148:138-43 O '70
Practice in the 1970's: the response to change. W. B. Foxhall. il Arch Rec 148:154-61+ O '70
See also
Kaplan and McLaughlin, architects (firm)
Roth, Emery, and sons
ARCHITECTURAL lighting. See Lighting, Architectural and decorative
ARCHITECTURAL models
Parthenon made of paper. P. Zakroff. il Design 71:40-1 Sum '70
Throw away cathedral; model of Lincoln cathedral. il Design 71:32-4 mid-Wint '70
ARCHITECTURAL record (periodical)
Record interiors; selection of twelve designs. il Arch Rec 147:97-120 Ja '70
ARCHITECTURAL schools. See Architectural education
ARCHITECTURAL symbols. See Symbols
ARCHITECTURE
Architectural business. See issues of Architectural record
Architectural metaphysic of Louis Kahn. S. Braudy. il pors N Y Times Mag p72-3+ N 15 '70
Buildings in the news. See issues of Architectural record
Focus; monthly review of notable buildings. See issues of Architectural forum
Forum; monthly review of events and ideas. See issues of Architectural forum
See also
Air-supported structures
Apartment houses
Auditoriums
Bank buildings
Beach architecture
Church architecture
City halls
City planning
Clubhouses
College architecture
Columns (architecture)
Computers—Architectural use
Concrete construction
Domes
Exhibition buildings
Factories
Fountains
Hillside architecture
Industrial buildings
Laboratories—Architecture
Library architecture
Lobbies (architecture)
Museums—Architecture
Music pavilions
Office buildings
Orchestra shells
Orientation (architecture)
Recreation buildings
Remodeling (architecture)
School buildings
Theater buildings

Awards, prizes, etc.

Fourteen receive this country's highest architectural awards. il Arch Rec 147:40-1 Je '70
Record interiors; selection of twelve designs. il Arch Rec 147:97-120 Ja '70

Bibliography

Book reviews. Arch Rec 147:129-30 Ap '70
Books. See issues of Architectural forum

Competitions

Award winner at under $20,000. B. Plumb. il Am Home 73:64-6+ Ag '70

ARCHITECTURE—*Continued*

Conservation and restoration

Adaptive use of Charleston buildings in historic preservation. F. R. Edmunds. il Antiques 97:590-5 Ap '70

Bleak fate of the Yankee mills. il Life 69:58-61 S 4 '70

Bringing new life to old landmarks. il Changing T 25:33-4 Ja '71

New religious landmarks. G. Everett. Chr Today 14:35 Je 19 '70

Preservation and volunteers; reprint. Hobbies 75:76+ Je '70

Preservation history; reprint. C. B. Hosmer, jr. Hobbies 75:82 Jl '70

Proposal for Paterson. A. Chatfield-Taylor. il Arch Forum 132:72-7 Ja '70

Reawakening: from gloom to gleam at Sag Harbor. il House B 112:60-3 Jl '70

Rise and fall of an American architecture; Metropolitan museum of art exhibit; reprint. Hobbies 75:74+ Jl '70

Russia looks to its past. J. Dornberg. il Newsweek 76:52+ S 14 '70

Saving our landmarks. W. Von Eckardt. il Sat R 53:52-3 S 5 '70

Wrecker's dozen. D. G. McCullough. il Am Heritage 21:104-5 F '70

See also
Houses, Restored
Newport, R.I.—Historic houses, etc.

Designs and plans

Adventures in architectural services on the frontiers of change; with introd. by W. B. Foxhall. il Arch Rec 147:107-18 Mr '70

Design and process: four projects by the John Andrews office. R. Jensen. il Arch Rec 147:131-46 F '70

Hitler as architect. il Time 96:76 O 5 '70

Pattern language; contribution of C. Alexander's center for environmental structure to the science of design. R. Montgomery. il Arch Forum 132:52-9 Ja '70

Record interiors; selection of twelve designs. il Arch Rec 147:97-120 Ja '70

See also
Architecture, Domestic—Designs and plans

Economic aspects

Architecture in the 1970's: gearing performance to needs. W. F. Wagner, jr. Arch Rec 148:117 O '70

Exhibitions

Architecture; P. Soleri's exhibition at Corcoran gallery. F. Gutheim. Nation 210:446 Ap 13 '70

Humanizing the cities; display at the Museum of modern art, New York. W. Von Eckardt. il Sat R 53:72 N 7 '70

Our nineteenth-century architectural heritage; Rise of an American architecture, exhibition at the Metropolitan museum of art. S. B. Sherrill. il Antiques 97:784 Je '70

Le style Guimard; exhibition at the Museum of modern art. R. Reif. il N Y Times Mag p92-3 Mr 8 '70

To Moma, from Germany; lightweight architecture of F. Otto. N. R. Piene. il Art in Am 58:118-19 My '70

Philosophy

Chaos as architecture. F. Schulze. il Art in Am 58:88-96 Jl '70

Issues in architecture. See issues of Architectural record

Message as an architectural medium. H. C. Schulitz. il Arch Forum 132:44-9 My '70

New dimensions of architectural practice. W. F. Wagner, jr. Arch Rec 147:9-10 Ja '70

Social aspects

Architects design for a new client: the poor. J. Hale. il Arch Rec 148:144-7 O '70

Design for the 1970's: a new professional conscience. M. F. Schmertz. il Arch Rec 148:118-27 O '70

Future of the profession. R. W. Allen. il Arch Rec 147:123-6 F '70

Study of street life precedes town house design; Martin Luther King square. il Arch Rec 147:110-11 Mr '70

Urban design as part of the governmental process. J. Barnett. il Arch Rec 147:131-50 Ja '70

Specifications

See Building—Contracts and specifications

Study and teaching

Architectural boom in the visual arts. A. R. M. Guga. il Sch Arts 69:20-1 Ap '70

Architecture in high school. R. E. Timerson. il Design 71:14-16 Fall '69

Studio teaching is out of date. J. Barnett. Arch Rec 148:131-2 O '70

Visual perception and environmental design. B. Farmer. il Sch Arts 69:12-15 Ap '70

See also
Architectural education

Europe, Western

Europe's iron palaces span another century. il Life 69:71-5 D 4 '70

France

See also
Architecture, Domestic—France
Architecture, French

Germany (Federal Republic)

Pinwheel museum. il Arch Forum 132:60-3 Mr '70

India

See also
Taj Mahal

Japan

New developments in Japanese architecture; with introd. by M. F. Schmertz. il Arch Rec 148:109-28 S '70

New York (state)

See also
New York (city)—Architecture

Rhode Island

See also
Newport, R.I.—Architecture

Russia

Magnificence of Mother Russia; wooden buildings of Kizhi Island. D. Thomas. il Holiday 48:64-5 Jl '70

Spain

Stepped factory; Diestre plant near Zaragossa. il Arch Forum 132:72-5 Ap '70

United States

Architecture in the 1970's: gearing performance to meet the needs; symposium. il Arch Rec 148:117-61+ O '70

Buildings in the news. See issues of Architectural record

Four centuries of building; exhibition in U.S. pavilion at Expo '70. P. Blake. il Art in Am 58:70-3 Mr '70

See also
Architecture, American
Architecture, Domestic—United States
Skyscrapers
also subhead Architecture under names of cities, e.g. Newport, R.I.—Architecture

ARCHITECTURE, American

Architectural blight, and light. J. Jacobs. Art in Am 58:53+ N '70

Cesar Pelli, public architect. S. Moholy-Nagy. il por Arch Forum 132:42-7 Mr '70

Micajah Burnett and the buildings at Pleasant Hill. J. C. Thomas. il por Antiques 98:600-5 O '70

Mormon art and architecture. M. S. Young. il Art in Am 58:66-9 My '70

Rise and fall of an American architecture; Metropolitan museum of art exhibit; reprint. Hobbies 75:74+ Jl '70

Rise of an American architecture; exhibition at Metropolitan museum. W. McQuade. il Life 69:14 Ag 14 '70

Shaker meetinghouses of Moses Johnson. M. B. Péladeau. il Antiques 98:594-9 O '70

ARCHITECTURE, Buddhist

See also
Borobudur, Java

ARCHITECTURE, Domestic

Architect speaks his mind; interview. J. C. Walker. il por House & Gard 138:58+ O '70

Family home section. J. R. Cary. il Parents Mag 45:92-5 My '70

Interior patio idea; new style atriums. il Sunset 144:94-7 Mr '70

Mingling work and living; interview. M. Breuer. por House & Gard 137:12+ F '70

There's no accounting for houses; celebrities' homes. L. Lyons. House & Gard 138:28 Jl '70

See also
Apartments
Architecture, Modern
Bathrooms
Beach architecture
Building materials
Cabins
City houses
Concrete houses
Farmhouses
Guest houses

ARCHITECTURE, Domestic—*See also*—*Cont.*

Hillside architecture
House construction
House decoration
Houses, Prefabricated
Houses, Remodeled
Housing projects
Kitchens
Laundries
Pantries
Roofs
Row houses
Soundproofing
Vacation houses

Competitions
See Architecture—Competitions

Conservation and restoration
See Architecture—Conservation and restoration

Designs and plans
Architect you can communicate with; interview. P. S. Du Pont, 4th. il por House & Gard 137:16+ Mr '70
Best buys in new homes 1970. il Good H 170: 112-22+ F '70
Five distinctive houses. il Arch Rec 148:109-20 N '70
Five genuine 1970 houses. N. Seney. il Bet Hom & Gard 48:48-57 Ap '70
Four houses in the sun. il House B 112:37-59 Ja '70
How a talented architect stretched his building dollar. A. Stagg. il House & Gard 137: 110-15 Ap '70
How architect and owner create the personal house. il House & Gard 137:64-75 Ja '70
How space is shaped and what it expresses; interview. R. Whitton. por House & Gard 137:22+ Ap '70
Is there any hope for people who want their own home? il Bet Hom & Gard 48:35-43 Ag '70
P/M's 17th mother's conference home. J. R. Cary. il Parents Mag 46:74-7 Ja '71
Pretty and practical new house. J. R. Cary. il Parents Mag 45:112-13 N '70
Record houses of 1970. il Arch Rec 147:25-85 mid-My '70
Shingles: a portfolio of three houses. il House B 112:131-40 Ap '70
Tall roofs angling for the sun. il House B 112:76-8 My '70
Three architects speak their minds. B. Baldwin; W. W. Wurster; H. Gifford. pors House & Gard 137:12+ Je '70
Two sculptures in wood: beach houses that live in harmony with nature. M. Miller. il House B 112:30-6 Ag '70
Well-built house (cont of) Well-built well-kept house. J. H. Ingersoll. See issues of House beautiful

History
More perfect union. J. M. Gutman. Nation 210:250-2 Mr 2 '70

Arizona
Outrigger walls give this desert house a colorful sun-bounce patio. il Sunset 144:66-8 Ja '70

Bahama Islands
Temple to the sun in the Bahamas: a designer team creates a holiday sanctuary on a dune in Eleuthera. il House B 112:38-42 Ja '70

Block Island
Weekend house for entertaining; C. Owen's house. il House & Gard 138:82-5 D '70

Brazil
Exciting escape house; built by architect S. Bernardes. J. DeLong. il House B 112: 72-7 Je '70

California
Le champignon: unique tower is a practical weekend retreat. J. De Long. il House B 112:37-40 Ag '70
Concrete house for a rocky ridge in Palm Springs. il Arch Rec 148:116-17 N '70
Controlled geometry shapes house for a woodland site. il Arch Rec 147:127-30 F '70
Family sanctuary: in winter, a study in serenity. il House B 112:45-7 Ag '70
Gibbs house. Palos Verdes Peninsula, Calif. il Arch Rec 147:48-9 mid-My '70
Holloway's hideaway; Laguna Beach. J. DeLong and S. Nirenberg. il House B 112:42-7 Jl '70
House facing the High Sierras, John Rex residence North Forks. il Arch Rec 148:87-90 D '70

House in the forest, on ⅓ acre. B. Plumb. il Am Home 73:48-51 Jl '70
House of seven levels. J. DeLong. il House B 112:86-93 S '70
House on a seaside cliff. il House & Gard 137:90-1 Je '70
Joyous house of the Warners. il por Vogue 155:170-5 Je '70
Maison impossible. J. DeLong. il House B 112:82-5 F '70
Most beautiful view in the world; house in the Big Sur. J. Peter. il Look 34:70-3 Ap 21 '70
Naff house, Pajaro Dunes, Calif. il Arch Rec 147:30-1 mid-My '70
Old Victorian house in San Francisco begins its second life. il Sunset 144:78-9 F '70
Private residence, Marin County, Calif. il Arch Rec 147:70-1 mid-My '70
Studio house tucked in the woods. il Sunset 145:116 O '70
They bought a builder's house, then remodeled while it was still new. il Sunset 145:80-1 O '70
Three-family co-op in western ski country; octagonal ski house in Bear Valley. il Am Home 73:56-7 D '70
Towering like a tree; ski architecture. M. Spires. il Am Home 73:44-7 Ja '70
Very personal house and garden of the John Walkers: five stories of sunlight. il House & Gard 138:110-15 O '70

Canada
Private residence, Canada. il Arch Rec 147: 50-3 mid-My '70

Connecticut
Country living in the European manner. L. Grundy and S. Nirenberg. il House B 112: 58-9 Ag '70
Duke of Xanadu at home. R. Hughes. il por Time 96:82-3+ O 26 '70
Hillside house in Sherman. il Arch Rec 148: 112-13 N '70
Lifestyle; church converted to a house. il Am Home 73:10 O '70
McSpadden house Riverside, Conn. il Arch Rec 147:36-7 mid-My '70
Private residence, Cheshire, Conn. il Arch Rec 147:26-9 mid-My '70
Private residence, Conn. il Arch Rec 147:66-9 mid-My '70
White magic. il House & Gard 137:94-103 Ap '70

Delaware
Patterns; the house of Mr and Mrs Pierre S. du Pont IV. A. Stagg. il House & Gard 137:108-15 Mr '70

England
House with a view for the neighbors. il Mech Illus 66:67 N '70
Lookout house. il N Y Times Mag p54-5 Ag 16 '70

Finland
Finn swoop: the house of Mr and Mrs Yrjö Kukkapuro. il Vogue 155:130-3 Ap 15 '70

Florida
Concrete block house in Fort Lauderdale. il Arch Rec 148:110-11 N '70
How a talented architect stretched his building dollar. A. Stagg. il House & Gard 137: 110-15 Ap '70
New sense of living, 1971; home of Mr and Mrs Giora Novak. il pors Vogue 157:124-7 Ja 1 '71
Pole house in Sarasota. il Arch Rec 148:114-15 N '70
Steinsnyder house, Miami, Fla. il Arch Rec 147:32-5 mid-My '70

France
House that owes its life to its setting. S. G. Lewin. il House B 112:48-51 Ag '70
See also
Architecture, French

Greece, Modern
By the Aegean, the new and the old: an artist splashes color into a white house on ancient Patmos. E. Sverbeyeff. il House B 112:53-9 Ja '70

Haiti
Bonjour, M'sieu Peabody; designer's home. il por McCalls 97:88-93 Mr '70

Ireland
In Dublin, a two-for-one spectacular: home of architect Sam Stephenson. il House B 112:104-8 My '70

ARCHITECTURE, Domestic—*Continued*

Kentucky

Bennett house, Lexington, Ky. il Arch Rec 147:54-5 mid-My '70

Long Island, N.Y.

Barn reborn. il House & Gard 137:124-9 Mr '70

Basement special; B. Baldwin's home in East Hampton. il N Y Times Mag p 104-5 Ap 12 '70

Curry house, Montauk Point, N.Y. il Arch Rec 147:72-3 mid-My '70

Downtown takes a trip to the seashore: architect Harry Bates vacation beach houses. P. Knight. il Sports Illus 33:42-6 S 28 '70

House for two: great swooping arch; house designed for Mr and Mrs B. Geller. A. Stagg. il House & Gard 137:68-73+ F '70

House in a sunken garden. il House & Gard 137:86-9 Je '70

Joy of summer at home; Eric Mulvanys' house. il House & Gard 137:56-61 Je '70

Parabolic-arch house by Marcel Breuer and Herbert Beckhard. il Arch Rec 148:115-18 Jl '70

Shingle house in Huntington. il Arch Rec 148:118-20 N '70

Very private house; Amagansett, L.I. il House B 112:54-7 Ag '70

Young-family house with a future. il Good H 171:122-8+ S '70

Maryland

Hillside house. il N Y Times Mag p92-3 My 17 '70

Smernoff house, Montgomery County, Md. il Arch Rec 147:38-41 mid-My '70

Massachusetts

Clifftopper on the seacoast. B. Plumb. il Am Home 73:58-61 S '70

Cooper house, Orleans, Mass. il Arch Rec 147:62-5 mid-My '70

Grey house, Wellfleet, Mass. il Arch Rec 147:80-1 mid-My '70

Michigan

Second-home assets for a one-house family. V. D. Hahn. il pors Am Home 73:68-71 S '70

Minnesota

Flowing space that's sprayed on burlap. il Life 68:64-7 Mr 13 '70

New Mexico

American treasury of Southwest living; symposium. il Am Home 73:49-69+ Mr '70

Rebirth in the Southwest: an architect and his wife rescue an old adobe. J. De Long. il House B 112:43-9 Ja '70

New York (state)

Articulate house. il House B 112:41-4 Ag '70

Shelter in the woods. il Arch Forum 132:36-9 Mr '70

Three-generation compound; Breuer-designed home for Vera Neumann. il Am Home 73:72-3 S '70

Very personal garden and house of Mrs Quaintance Mason. il House & Gard 138:90-5 N '70

Winged weekend flight; Greenport. il House B 112:68-71 D '70

Worden house, Lake George, N.Y. il Arch Rec 147:56-9 mid-My '70

Yankee barn with a Gallic accent; home of Susan Mason, Cross River. R. Reif. il N Y Times Mag p46-7 Ag 9 '70

See also
Architecture, Domestic—Long Island

North Carolina

Private residence, western North Carolina. il Arch Rec 147:46-7 mid-My '70

Oregon

Island of space in a sea of trees; Eugene. J. Delong. il House B 112:74-9 D '70

Ugly duckling in Portland is done over inside and out. il Sunset 144:80-1 F '70

Pennsylvania

Benenson house, Hawley, Pa. il Arch Rec 147:82-5 mid-My '70

Puerto Rico

Yesterday, today in Spanish San Juan. J. Peter and E. Alston. il Look 34:56-9 Je 16 '70

Tennessee

Open house; open-plan interior in Memphis. B. Plumb. il N Y Times Mag p72-3 F 22 '70

Texas

Country space ten minutes from the city. F. Heard and J. DeLong. il House B 112:84-91 Mr '70

Great house for two or two hundred; C. D. Tandy house; with interview of architect. I. M. Pei. il House & Gard 138:114-23 N '70

Tunisia

Moon house; a vacation house of ideas in Tunisia; interview. G. Berthelot. il House & Gard 137:120-3 Mr '70

United States

Four centuries of American style. M. Spires. il Am Home 73:39-47 F '70

How architect and owner create the personal house. il House & Gard 137:64-75 Ja '70

Is there any hope for people who want their own home? il Bet Hom & Gard 48:35-43 Ag '70

More-for-your-money houses. N. Seney. il Bet Hom & Gard 48:36-7 Ja '70

Vermont

Haven in New England snows; ski house of the Neil Goodwin's. B. Plumb. il Am Home 73:52-5+ D '70

McCune house, Londonderry, Vt. il Arch Rec 147:74-5 mid-My '70

Package house full of surprises. D. McCluggage. il por Am Home 73:64-7+ Ap '70

Suspended from a hill. il Am Home 73:48-9+ Ja '70

Virgin Islands

From Vermont to St Croix: a New England couple escapes the winter at this poolside pavilion. il House B 112:50-2 Ja '70

Virginia

See also
Monticello (historic house)

Washington, D.C.

Space opened up for family living; Georgetown house. il House & Gard 138:102-7 S '70

Washington (state)

It's three houses in one, with the feeling of a country lodge. il Sunset 144:92-3 Je '70

Kirk house, Mercer Island, Wash. il Arch Rec 147:76-9 mid-My '70

Western states

See also
Western home awards

ARCHITECTURE, French
Le style Guimard; exhibition at the Museum of modern art. R. Reif. il N Y Times Mag p92-3 Mr 8 '70
See also
Architecture, Domestic—France

ARCHITECTURE, German
To Moma, from Germany; lightweight architecture of F. Otto. N. R. Piene. il Art in Am 58:118-19 My '70

ARCHITECTURE, Gothic
Senator Morrill's Gothic cottage at Strafford, Vermont. L. Wodehouse. il Antiques 98:237-41 Ag '70

ARCHITECTURE, Hillside. See Hillside architecture

ARCHITECTURE, Modern
Omnibuildings. W. Karp. il Horizon 12:48-55 Wint '70
See also
Bauhaus

ARCHITECTURE, Primitive
See also
Indians of North America—Dwellings

ARCHITECTURE, Pueblo. See Pueblo architecture

ARCHITECTURE, Russian
Russia looks to its past. J. Dornberg. il Newsweek 76:52+ S 14 '70

ARCHITECTURE, School. See School buildings

ARCHITECTURE and climate
From Vermont to St Croix: a New England couple escapes the winter at this poolside pavilion. il House B 112:50-2 Ja '70
Steinsnyder house, Miami, Fla. il Arch Rec 147:32-5 mid-My '70

ARCHITECTURE as a profession
Future of the profession. R. W. Allen. il Arch Rec 147:123-6 F '70

ARCHIVES
See also
Oral history

ARCINIEGAS, Germán
  Tannenbaum and Latin America; address,
    January 8, 1970. il por Américas 22:27-31
    Ap '70
  Word with Germán Arciniegas; interview, ed.
    by E. B. Labrada. por Américas 22:15-19
    Ag '70

ARCOLOGIES. See City planning

ARCTIC char fishing. See Char fishing

ARCTIC exploration
    See also
  Exploration, Aeronautic

ARCTIC REGIONS
  Murder in legal limbo; case of U.S. v. Esca-
    milla. il por Time 96:58 S 28 '70
    See also
  Alaska
  Antarctic Regions
  Ecology—Arctic regions
  Jenny Lind Island
  Northwest Passage
  Paleontology—Arctic Regions
  Transportation—Arctic Regions

ARCTIC research. See Polar research

ARCY, Jean d'
  Challenge to cooperation. il Sat R 53:24-5+
    O 24 '70

ARDEN, Elizabeth, sales corporation
  Duel over Elizabeth Arden. il Bsns W p48
    O 17 '70

ARDEN, Eugene
  King scholars at C. W. Post college. Todays
    Ed 59:72 S '70

ARDEN, Harvey
  World war I aircraft fly again in Rhine-
    beck's rickety rendezvous. il por Nat Geog
    138:578-87 O '70

ARDEN, John
  John Arden's Serjeant Musgrave's dance: a
    highly relevant play for young people. M. A.
    Hoke. Engl J 59:633-7 My '70 *
  Serjeant Musgrave's dance. Criticism
    Engl J 59:633-7 My '70 *

ARDEN-Mayfair, Inc. See Supermarkets

ARDMAN, Harvey. See Ardman, P. jt. auth.

ARDMAN, Perri, and Ardman, Harvey
  Every woman's guide to varicose veins.
    Ladies Home J 87:46+ My '70

ARDOIN, John
  Civic opera, hits and misses. il Hi Fi 20:secII
    26+ Mr '70

ARDREY, Dan
  Capital-hopper's guide. il Sat R 53:80-1+
    F 21 '70
  Obscure museums. Travel & Camera 33:18-
    20 N '70
  Smiling through Africa. il pors Esquire 73:
    94-6+ F '70
  Studious summers for young salts. Sat R 53:
    86-7 F 21 '70

ARDREY, Robert
  Control of population; excerpt from The so-
    cial contract. il Life 68:48-52+ F 20 '70;
    Same abr. with title Nature and the case for
    birth control. Read Digest 96:116-20 Je '70
  Trade winds; interview, ed. by C. Amory.
    Sat R 53:18+ N 7 '70
  Violent way; excerpt from The social con-
    tract. il Life 69:56B-56D+ S 11 '70; Same
    abr. with title Is man naturally violent?
    Read Digest 97:115-19 D '70

            about
  Out on a limb. il Time 96:59+ O 5 '70 *
  Scientific amateur expands his territory. R.
    Graves. por Life 69:1 S 11 '70 *

AREA navigation. See Navigation, Aerial

AREES, Edward A. and Mayer, Jean
  Monosodium glutamate-induced brain lesions:
    electron microscopic examination. bibliog il
    Science 170:549-50 O 30 '70

AREHART, Joan Lynn
  Baby on the way. il Parents Mag 46:48-9+
    Ja '71

ARENDT, Hannah
  Reflections. New Yorker 46:70+ S 12 '70

ARENSBERG, Walter Conrad
  Walter Arensberg and Marcel Duchamp. K.
    Kuh. Sat R 53:36-7+ S 5 '70 *

ARGENTINA
    See also
  Chaco
  Colleges and universities—Argentina
  Moving pictures—Argentina
  Patagonia
            Antiquities
  Secrets of the stones. B. Pastor. il Améri-
    cas 22:32-7 Ap '70

            Intellectual life
  New developments in Buenos Aires. E. L.
    Johnson. il Art in Am 58:150-2 N '70
  Profiles; autobiographical notes, ed. by N. T.
    Di Giovanni. J. L. Borges. New Yorker
    46:40-4+ S 19 '70

            Politics and government
  Argentina's new military government. D.
    C. Jordan. Cur Hist 58:85-90+ F '70
  Coup no. 8. il por Newsweek 75:38+ Je 22 '70
  Fall of a corporate planner. il Time 95:38 Je
    22 '70

ARGENTINE literature
  Profiles; autobiographical notes, ed. by N.
    T. Di Giovanni. J. L. Borges. New Yorker
    46:40-4+ S 19 '70

ARGENTINE poetry

            Translations into English
  Adam cast forth; One morning in 1649;
    Rose and Milton; tr. by R. Eberhart. J.
    L. Borges. Poetry 116:299-301 Ag '70
  After the Japanese; tr. by N. T. Di Giovanni.
    J. L. Borges. New Yorker 46:199 D 5 '70
  Israel; poem. tr. by N. T. Di Giovanni. New
    Yorker 45:34 F 7 '70

ARGINASE
  Friendly virus; injections of Shope papilloma
    virus to aid arginemia victims. Newsweek
    76:88 S 28 '70

ARGON
  Cosmic ray production of rare gas radio-
    activities and tritium in lunar material. R.
    W. Stoenner and others. bibliog il Science
    167:553-5 Ja 30 '70
  Tritium and argon radioactivities in lunar
    material. E. L. Fireman and others. bibliog
    il Science 167:566-8 Ja 30 '70

ARGONAUTA
    See also
  Paper nautilus

ARGOS
  Traditional enmity between Sparta and
    Argos: the birth and development of a
    myth. T. Kelly. bibliog f il Am Hist R
    75:971-1003 Ap '70

ARGUEDAS, Antonio
  Accusing hands. Time 95:35 F 23 '70 *

ARGUMENT
  Distant persuasion. il Time 96:27 S 7 '70

ARGUS research corporation
  Patient is in pain but he isn't dying. por
    Forbes 105:64-5 Je 1 '70

ARGYROPHILIC carcinoids. See Tumors

ARIADNE auf Naxos; opera. See Strauss, R.

ARIAS
    See also
  Phonograph records—Arias

ARID regions
  Urbanization in the arid lands; AAAS sym-
    posium, December 26-27, 1970. C. O. Hodge.
    il Science 170:655-6 N 6 '70
    See also
  Irrigation

ARIDOR, Yoram
  Reluctant Israelis; interview. Time 96:23 Ag
    10 '70

ARIELI, Yehoshua
  Reluctant Israelis; interview. Time 96:23 Ag
    10 '70

ARIOSTO, Lodovico
  Orlando furioso; dramatization. See Ronconi,
    L.

ARISTOCRACY
    See also
  Upper classes

ARISTOTLE
  Hi, mistress: a remembrance of a gentle
    guide. B. Brophy. Vogue 155:92-3+ F 15
    '70*

ARITHMETIC

            Study and teaching
  Nondecimal instruction revisited. D. E.
    Cruikshank and W. R. Arnold. Ed Digest
    35:44-5 F '70
    See also
  Mathematics—Study and teaching

ARITHMETIC, Mental
  Short cuts to the answers. W. Parkhurst. Sci
    Digest 68:94-5 D '70
  Try this shortcut; reprint. W. Parkhurst. Sci
    Digest 68:85 Jl '70

ARIZONA
    See also
  Architecture, Domestic—Arizona
  Fishing—Arizona
  Grand Canyon
  Havasu Canyon
  Hubbell trading post national historic site
  Hunting—Arizona
  Monument Valley
  Powell, Lake

ARIZONA—*Continued*

Description and travel

Into the Apache country: for the camping, the fishing, the Apaches. il Sunset 145: 26-8 Ag '70

Historic houses, sites, etc.

Ghost town that refused to die: Jerome, Ariz. N. Deak. il Todays Health 48:56-9 F '70

ARIZONA Desert botanical garden. See Botanical gardens

ARIZONA Indians. See Indians of North America

ARIZONA state university, Tempe

Devil's devil; Arizona state Sun Devils football team. il Newsweek 76:56 O 26 '70

ARIZONA. University, Tucson

Environmental research laboratory

Tilling the desert under plastic skies; integrated power-water-food system. il Bsns W p92+ My 9 '70

ARK, Noah's. See Noak's ark

ARKANSAS

See also
Buffalo River
Fishing—Arkansas
Hot Springs National Park
Justice, Administration of—Arkansas
Ouachita Mountains
Ozark Mountains
Prisons—Arkansas

Politics and government

Arkansas upset. il por Time 96:16 S 21 '70

ARKANSAS RIVER WATERWAY

Ocean comes to Oklahoma. C. Bakal. il Read Digest 97:121-4 N '70

Seaports for an inland empire. il U S News 68:90-2 My 25 '70

Taming a wild one. il Sr Schol 96:15 F 9 '70

Waterway that couldn't be done. il Bsns W p 124-5 S 12 '70

ARKIN, Alan

Making of Little murders. L. Cohen. il por Sat R 53:19-21 Ag 8 '70 *

Some are more Yossarian than others. il pors Time 95:66-8+ Je 15 '70 *

Yossarian in Connecticut. B. Farrell. il Life 69:50-2+ O 2 '70 *

ARLEN, Michael J.

Exiles; a memoir. New Yorker 46:45-8+ Ap 11; 41-50+ Ap 18 '70

about

Smart set. G. Mallet. Nation 210:666-8 Je 1 '70 *

Son of the Green hat. G. Wolff. il pors Newsweek 75:98+ My 11 '70 *

Under the green hat. il por Time 95:84+ Je 8 '70 *

ARLINGTON, Tex.

Stores

Forum 303: much more than just a place to shop. il Arch Rec 147:120-3 Mr '70

ARLINGTON, Va.

Establishment of Freedom's village in Arlington, Virginia. F. James. bibliog il Negro Hist Bul 33:90-3 Ap '70

National cemetery

Requiem for Arlington? il Newsweek 75:29 Je 8 '70

ARLINGTON COUNTY, Va.

All you see is the stream. H. S. Hulme, jr. il Am City 85:77-8 Mr '70

High-rise recreation. L. Neeld. il Parks & Rec 5:50 My '70

ARLINGTON National cemetery. See Arlington, Va.—National cemetery

ARMADILLOS

Armored force is on the march. E. Shrake. il Sports Illus 34:52-3 Ja 4 '71

ARMAGNAC, Alden P.

Gem diamonds created in lab. il Pop Sci 197:82-3+ S '70

NDT: will it mean flawless products for you? il Pop Sci 196:90-3+ Ja '70

Super flywheel to power zero-emission car. il Pop Sci 197:41-3+ Ag '70

Underwater satellites to tap offshore oil. il Pop Sci 197:60-1 D '70

ARMAMENT industries. See Munitions industries

ARMAMENTS

See also
Disarmament
Munitions
Tanks, Military
War

ARMBRISTER, Trevor

Coal-black shame of the UMW. Read Digest 97:135-40 O '70

ARMCHAIRS. See Chairs

ARMCO steel corporation

Spare hand who went beyond the dream of Leonardo da Vinci. B. C. Huselton. il Nations Bsns 58:50-1 Ja '70

Student designers tackle leisure area; Armco sponsored projects. Y. Fogel. il Parks & Rec 5:24-6 My '70

ARMED forces

See also subhead Armed forces under names of countries, e.g. United States—Armed forces

Appropriations and expenditures

History's greatest dead end; world spending. F. Blackaby. il Sat R 53:19-21+ Mr 14 '70

ARMED forces day and week

U.S. journal: Fort Dix, New Jersey in 1970; Governors Island, in 1959. C. Trillin. New Yorker 46:40-2+ Je 6 '70

ARMED robbery. See Robberies and assaults

ARMED services committee. See United States —Congress—House—Armed services, Committee on

ARMERDING, Carl Edwin

Fruitful year in the Old Testament field. Chr Today 14:3-6 F 13 '70

Old Testament as a whole. Chr Today 15:17-19 D 18 '70

—and Gasque, W. W.

Bible as a whole. Chr Today 15:18-21 N 6 '70

ARMOR plate

Armor used as airframe for helicopter. C. Brownlow. il Aviation W 93:65-8 O 12 '70

ARMOUR, Richard

Blurb me a blurb; poem. Pub W 197:41 Mr 16 '70

East is East but West is best. Sat R 53:4 O 3 '70

Humor to the rescue. il Parents Mag 45:48-9+ Jl '70

Reference books for writers. Writer 83:23-5 F '70

Small solution. Sat R 53:24 N 14 '70

To run a bookstore; poem. Pub W 198:47 S 7 '70

What can you be funny about? Writer 83:21-3 D '70

ARMS control. See Disarmament

ARMS control and disarmament agency. See United States—Arms control and disarmament agency

ARMS control legislation. See Firearms—Laws and regulations

ARMS sales. See Purchasing, Military

ARMS smuggling. See Smuggling

ARMSTRONG, Christopher, and others

William H. Armstrong. il por Horn Bk 46: 356-8 Ag '70

ARMSTRONG, Dwight Alan

Madison bombers. il pors Newsweek 76:28-9 S 14 '70 *

ARMSTRONG, James, bp

On responding to the crisis; interview, ed. by R. G. Kemper. Chr Cent 87:622-3 My 20 '70

People are doing...badly in Brazil. il por Chr Cent 88:14-16 Ja 6 '71

ARMSTRONG, Karleton Lewis

Madison bombers. il pors Newsweek 76:28-9 S 14 '70

ARMSTRONG, Louis

It's seventy for Satch. il pors Ebony 25: 80-2 S '70 *

Man who revolutionized jazz; symposium. il pors Sat R 53:13-19+ Jl 4 '70 *

ARMSTRONG, Marion

Movies (title varies) See occasional issues of Christian century

ARMSTRONG, Marjorie. See Armstrong, O. K. jt. auth.

ARMSTRONG, Neil A.

Commercial service with Tu-144 as early as 1972 is Soviet goal. Aviation W 93:32 N 16 '70 *

How Apollo 11 changed three famous men. G. Farmer. pors Life 69:60 Jl 17 '70 *

News from the world of space exploration. il Space World G-12-84:43 D '70 *

Where are they now? por Newsweek 76:8 Jl 27 '70 *

See also
Space flight to the moon—Manned flights—Apollo 11 flight

ARMSTRONG, O. K. and Armstrong, Marjorie

Are beef prices out of line? Read Digest 96: 130-2+ Ap '70

ARMSTRONG, Richard

Looming money revolution down South. il Fortune 81:66-9+ Je '70

ARMSTRONG, Robert L.
Student council: whither goest thou? Clear House 44:553-5 My '70

ARMSTRONG, William Howard
Newbery acceptance; address, June 30, 1970. il Horn Bk 46:352-5 Ag '70

about

Newbery and Caldecott winners for 1969 books. il por Pub W 197:125-6 F 23 '70 *
William H. Armstrong. C. Armstrong and others. il por Horn Bk 46:356-8 Ag '70 *

ARMSTRONG-JONES, Antony Charles Robert, 1st earl of Snowdon. See Snowdon, A. C. R. A.-J.

ARMSTRONG cork company
Theme of success; let the buyer have faith. J. H. Binns. il Nations Bsns 58:53-4 Ja '70

ARMY and air force exchange service. See United States—Armed forces—Post exchanges

ARMY bands. See Bands (music)

ARMY engineers. See United States—Army—Corps of engineers

ARMY life. See Military life

ARMY rejections. See Military service—Physical and mental fitness

ARMY security agency. See United States—Army security agency

ARMY wives. See Service mens wives

ARMYTAGE, Stephen Green-. See Green-Armytage, S.

ARMYTAGE, Walter Harry Green
Battles for the best: some educational aspects of the welfare-warfare state in England; excerpts from History and education. ed. by P. Nash. bibliog Sch & Soc 98: 229-37 Ap '70

ARMYWORM moths. See Moths

ARMYWORMS
Armyworms cause havoc. il Suc Farm 68:no3 W28 F '70
Toxic factor produced by a granulosis virus in armyworm larva: effect on apanteles militaris. H. K. Kaya. bibliog il Science 168:251-3 Ap 10 '70

ARNATT, Keith
Parting shots; an earth artist goes underground. il pors Life 69:62-3 Ag 14 '70 *

ARNDT, Rudolf G.
Changeable newt. il Cons 24:11-13+ Ag '69

ARNESON, Robert
Ceramics of Robert Arneson. D. Zack. il Craft Horiz 30:36-41+ Ja '70 *

ARNETT, Edward M.
Computer-based chemical information services; adaptation of address, April 1970. il Science 170:1370-6 D 25 '70

ARNETT, Keeton
Commercial compost-making at home. il pors Org Gard & Farm 17:44-8 Ap '70

ARNETT, Peter
Looking back on the war; ed. by M. Parker. il por Newsweek 76:72 Jl 20 '70

about

Spiking the loot. il por Newsweek 75:76 My 18 '70 *
Time to decompress. il pors Time 96:34 Ag 3 '70 *

ARNHEM, Battle of, 1944
Dawdling in the Dutch woods. H. Sutton. Sat R 53:40-1 D 19 '70

ARNING, Lee D.
Making brokers toe the mark. por Bsns W p84 Jl 18 '70 *

ARNO, Stephen F.
River of no return. il Nat Parks 44:18-23 Ja '70

ARNOLD, Danny
TV vs. movies; interview. ed. by N. Vogel. Writers Digest 50:42+ Ap '70

ARNOLD, Dean E.
Lake Erie, alive but changing. il Cons 25: 23-30+ D '70

ARNOLD, Edward
Interference from left field. il Pop Electr 32: 44-6 Mr '70

ARNOLD, Gordon D.
Vendor looks at low-bid buying. il por Am City 85:107+ Ap '70

ARNOLD, Rus
Answers by Arnold. See issues of Travel & camera
Freelance job idea: slide presentations. il Writers Digest 51:34-6+ Ja '71
How and where to sell photos and photo-illustrated articles. il Writers Digest 50: 24-6 Jl '70
Photographer's guide. Travel & Camera 33: 64+ Je; 58-60 O '70

Special Canada report. Travel & Camera 33: 64+ Je '70
Writer with a camera. por Writers Digest 50:46-8 S; 50+ N '70

ARNOLD, William R. See Cruikshank, D. E. jt. auth.

ARNOTT, H. J. and others
Retinal tapetum lucidum: a novel reflecting system in the eye of teleosts. bibliog il Science 169:478-80 Jl 31 '70

ARNOTT, Struther
Crystallography of DNA: difference synthesis supports Watson-Crick base pairing. bibliog il Science 167:1694-700 Mr 27 '70

ARNOW, Harriette (Simpson)
Gray woman of Appalachia. il Nation 211: 684-7 D 28 '70
Progress reached our valley. il Nation 211: 71-7 Ag 3 '70

ARNSTEIN, Helene S.
How babies learn to wait. il Parents Mag 45:39-41+ D '70
Telephonitis, the teen-age hangup. il Todays Health 48:40-1+ F '70

AROMATIC hydrocarbons. See Hydrocarbons

ARON, Raymond
There is no Raymond Aron cult: talk with a reasonable man; interview. ed. by M. Viorst. por N Y Times Mag p34-5+ Ap 19 '70

ARONE, John B.
Students in the Statehouse. Todays Ed 59:17 O '70

ARONOW, Don
From my ocean racers: a better boat for you; ed. by W. B. Hartley. il por Pop Sci 196:80-3 F '70

about

How can you beat two Don Aronows? T. Bottomley. il por Motor B 125:10-11+ F '70 *

ARONSON, Boris
Boris Aronson sketchbook. S. Jenkins. il por Opera N 35:21-3 Ja 2 '71 *

ARONSON, Harvey
Clancy's gym is Danny's turf. il pors Sports Illus 32:40-4 Mr 23 '70

ARONSON, Henry M.
For the defense. New Yorker 46:39-40 N 7 '70 *

ARONSON, Steven M. L.
Urbane trash. Poetry 116:40-2 Ap '70

ARP, Leon J.
Race to save an infant's life. il pors Life 69:36-9 Jl 24 '70 *

ARPINO, Gerald
Capricorn combine. A. Fatt. il pors Dance Mag 44:32-6 O '70 *

ARRABAL, Fernando
Arrabal, panic plays. T. Bishop. Vogue 155:32 Mr 15 '70 *
Demons also believe; parodying the eucharist. S. Terrien. Chr Cent 87:1481-3+ D 9 '70 *

ARRANGEMENT of flowers. See Flowers, Arrangement of

ARREST
How I faced my son's drug arrest. G. Astor, Look 34:87-8+ D 15 '70
Imprisoning the poor: untried prisoners in the Santa Rita rehabilitation center. D. G. Shockley. Chr Cent 87:1286 O 28 '70
Jail insurance; California organization created to get people out of jail. il Newsweek 77:61 Ja 11 '71
Trapped like rats; P. Laporte's suspected kidnap killers. il Newsweek 77:44+ Ja 11 '71
Your child under arrest? L. M. Brown. Bet Hom & Gard 48:20 My '70

See also

Bail
Fugitives from justice

ARRHENIUS, Gustaf, and others
Phase chemistry, structure, and radiation effects in lunar samples. il Science 167:659-61 Ja 30 '70
—See Alfvén, H. jt. auth.

ARRIGHI, Mel
Castro complex. Criticism
New Yorker 46:142-3 N 28 '70 *

ARROGANCE. See Pride and vanity

ARROWHEADS
Bowhunting's controversial new arrow; tranquilizer arrow. C. Conley. il Field & S 75:50-1+ O '70
New kind of bowhunting; hypodermic arrowheads. G. H. Gillelan. il Outdoor Life 145:132+ Je '70

ARROWSMITH, William
Toward universities of the public interest. Cur 118:46-51 My '70

ARROYO, Martina
 L'Italiana di Harlem. por Time 96:46 S 28
 '70 *
ARSENIC
 Arsenic in detergents: possible danger and
 pollution hazard. E. E. Angino and oth-
 ers. bibliog il Science 168:389-90 Ap 17 '70;
 Discussion. 168:1525-6; 170:870-2 Je 26, N
 20 '70
ARSENIC in detergents. See Detergents
ART
    See also
 Advertising art
 Artists
 The Arts
 Arts and crafts movement
 Assemblage (art)
 Children in art
 Childrens art
 Christian art and symbolism
 Composition (art)
 Computers in art
 Cubism
 Design
 Expressionism (art)
 Eye in art
 Fishing in art
 Frescoes
 Hunting in art
 Jesus Christ—Art
 Landscape painting
 Lithography
 Medicine and art
 Mural painting and decoration
 Nature in art
 Painting
 Pen drawing
 Performing arts
 Photography, Artistic
 Plastics as an art form
 Posters
 Prints
 Realism in art
 Sculpture
 Space flight in art
 Symbolism in art
 Vietnamese war, 1957- —Art

    Appreciation
 How an artist holds our attention: line, color
 & form: excerpt from The many ways of
 seeing. J. G. Moore. il Design 71:4-9 mid-
 Wint '70
 Intimations of mortality. N. Lynton. Art in
 Am 58:43 N '70
 Let them eat worms! R. Lynes. Art in Am
 58:21 S '70
 Readers' choice (cont) il por Art in Am 58:25
 Ja '70
    Awards
 Awards and honors. See issues of Design

    Bibliography
 Art books for Christmas. il Am Artist 34:
 25-8+ N '70
 Art books of 1970. L. Kirstein. Nation 211:
 695+ D 28 '70
 Art: pre-Columbian to pinstripe. G. H. Ham-
 ilton. il Sat R 53:41-3 N 28 '70
 Book review section. See issues of Design
 Book reviews. See issues of American artist
 Books. J. Jacobs. See issues of Art in America

    Collections
    See Art—Private collections

    Collectors and collecting
 Buying and a sense of history. Sat R 53:60-1
 Ja 31 '70
 How to collect primitive art. N. R. Piene.
 House & Gard 137:48-9+ Ja '70
 Nobody doesn't like Mr Sara Lee; collection
 of N. Cummings; with report by M. C.
 Wrenn. il pors Life 69:76-80 O 23 '70
 Why I collect art. J. A. Michener. il Read
 Digest 96:147-52 My '70
    See also
 Art—Private collections
 Art as an investment

    History
 Duty of the prince is magnificence. M.
 Bishop. il pors Horizon 12:54-79 Aut '70

    Competitions
 American artist's student drawing competition. N. Kent. il por Am Artist 34:38-44+
 Je '70
 1970 Scholastic awards. il Sr Schol 96:13 My
 18 '70
    See also
 Childrens art—Competitions

    Conservation and restoration
 R for aging art; Spain's Central institute of
 restoration of works of art and archaeology.
 N. López Pellón. il Américas 22:31-7 Ag '70

    Education
    See Art education

    Exhibitions
 African images, powers and presences; exhibition at Washington's National gallery
 of art. il Time 95:44-7 F 2 '70
 African sculpture exhibition at National
 gallery of art. Negro Hist Bul 33:99-100
 Ap '70
 Art. L. Alloway. Nation 211:573-4, 700-1; 212:
 61-2 N 30, D 28 '70, Ja 11 '71
 Art 1970: new blood. D. Davis. il Newsweek
 76:88-9 O 5 '70
 Art; Spaces, exhibition at the Museum of
 modern art. L. Alloway. Nation 210:222 F
 23 '70
 Art; Venice biennale. L. Alloway. Nation
 210:637-8 My 25 '70
 Art world (cont) H. Rosenberg. New Yorker
 45:62+ Ja 24; 46:82+ F 21; 90+ Mr 28;
 103-4+ My 9; 48-52 Jl 18; 149-54; O 10;
 136+ N 7 '70
 Art's poet laureate; L. Baskin on view at
 Washington's National collection of fine
 arts. D. Davis. il por Newsweek 75:86 Je 29
 '70
 Beknighted Malta; council of Europe's exhibition. M. Gendel. il Art N 69:44-7+ Sum
 '70
 Big Dada; retrospective of F. Picabia's
 works at the Guggenheim museum. D.
 Davis. il por Newsweek 76:81-2 S 28 '70
 Blithe deceivers; The reality of appearance
 exhibition. K. Kuh. il Sat R 53:38-9 Jl 25 '70
 Boston's centenary acquisitions. il Art in Am
 58:130 Ja '70
 Bulletin board. See issues of American
 artist
 Burning issues; U.S. at the Venice biennale.
 T. B. Hess. Art N 69:27 Sum '70
 Coming soon, art exhibits. See issues of De-
 sign
 Cubism from all sides; exhibition at the Los
 Angeles County museum of art. il por News-
 week 76:65-6 D 28 '70
 Current and coming. E. P. Birk. See issues
 of Antiques
 Exercises in taste. J. B. Myers. il Craft Horiz
 30:50-3 My '70
 Exhibition preview: retrospective for Georgia
 O'Keeffe; Whitney museum of American
 art. L. Goodrich. il Art in Am 58:80-5 S
 '70
 Ferndale's racing sculpture; Ferndale art fes-
 tival. il Sunset 144:43 My '70
 For the happy few, and gurus, too; Saenre-
 dam, tantric art, Monet exhibitions in Paris.
 M. Conil-Lacoste. il Art N 69:34-5 Mr '70
 Fun art; environmental art, tech art par-
 ticipatory art. T. Meehan. il Horizon 11:4-
 15 Aut '69
 Gerbil ex machina; Software exhibition at the
 Jewish museum, N.Y. T. B. Hess. Art N
 69:23 D '70
 Goings on about town. See issues of New
 Yorker
 Information please; show at New York's
 Museum of modern art. D. Davis. il News-
 week 76:47 Jl 20 '70
 Jesus artists; exhibition called Revival! at
 the Corcoran gallery, Washington, D.C.
 D. Davis. il Newsweek 76:97+ O 26 '70
 London: Vienna secession: from art nouveau
 to 1970 exhibition. J. Russell. Art N 69:54
 Ja '71
 Making the gallery scene. B. Wasserman. il
 Sch Arts 69:32-5 F; 36-9 Mr; 70:30-3 O '70
 Matisse; exhibition in Paris celebrates 100th
 birthday. il pors Life 69:30-43 Ag 28 '70
 Maturity and a touch of madness; German
 expressionist exhibition at the Marlbor-
 ough-Gerson gallery. K. Kuh. il Sat R 53:
 64-5 F 28 '70
 Medieval men; Style 1200 exhibition at the
 Met. il Newsweek 75:64-9 Mr 23 '70
 Midnight snack of Andy Warhol; Raid the
 icebox. T. W. Moore. il Chr Cent 87:396-7
 Ap 1 '70
 New York gallery notes. G. Glueck. See is-
 sues of Art in America
 On tour at the Elvehjem art center. il De-
 sign 72:4-8 Fall '70
 Return of the real; 22 realists on view at
 New York's Whitney. D. Davis. il News-
 week 75:105 F 23 '70
 Reviews and previews. See issues of Art
 news

ART—Exhibitions—*Continued*

Royal road to art; Gainsborough exhibition in the Queen's gallery at Buckingham palace. D. Davis. il Newsweek 75:109 Je 15 '70

Spaces, sensory overload; exhibition at Museum of modern art. B. Rose. Vogue 155:30 Mr 15 '70

Streamlined style: Art Deco exhibition at Finch college. D. Davis. il Newsweek 76:99 N 9 '70

Surprising displays; Brooklyn museum and other rare shows. C. J. McNaspy. America 122:598-9 My 30 '70

Sweet wind out of the dark; The year 1200 exhibition at the Met. il Time 95:62 F 23 '70

Three pens against the sword; against violence at the Metropolitan. D. Davis. il Newsweek 76:71 Ag 3 '70

Time for spaces; display at Manhattan's museum of contemporary crafts. il Time 95:43-4 F 2 '70

Venice; biennials. M. Gendel. Art N 69:63+ S '70

What is black art? exhibition at the Museum of fine arts, Boston. D. Davis. il Newsweek 75:89-90 Je 22 '70

Where and when to exhibit. See issues of Art news

See also
Architecture—Exhibitions
Art—Private collections
Arts and crafts—Exhibitions
Childrens art—Exhibitions
Drawings—Exhibitions
Exhibitions, Traveling
Folk art—Exhibitions
Metropolitan museum of art, New York
Museum of modern art, New York
Osaka, Japan—Worlds fair, 1970—Art
Pottery—Exhibitions
Prints—Exhibitions
Sculpture—Exhibitions
Whitney museum of American art, New York

Expertising

Information please; International foundation for art research. T. B. Hess. Art N 69:31 My '70

Lost masterpiece is found. il Newsweek 76:68-9 Jl 27 '70

Galleries and museums

Museum accessions. R. Davidson. See issues of Antiques

See also
Art—Exhibitions
California. University—Berkeley campus—Art museum
Museum store association
   also subhead Galleries and museums under names of cities, e.g. Washington, D.C.—Galleries and museums; *also* names of museums, e.g. Metropolitan museum of art

Architecture
See Museums—Architecture

History

Unity in diversity; excerpt from Masterpieces of fifty centuries. K. Clark. House & Gard 138:68-9+ D '70

Womens liberation, woman artists and art history; symposium, with editorial comment. il Art N 69:22-49+ bibliog(p70-1) Ja '71

See also
Art nouveau (movement)

International aspects

Universal language of children's art, and modernism; address, April 29, 1970. R. Motherwell. Am Scholar 40:24-7 Wint '70

Periodicals

See also
Art in America (periodical)
School arts (periodical)

Philosophy

African art; compositional vs. modal esthetics. E. Sellin. Yale R 59:215-27 D '69

Artist speaks: Robert Morris; interview, ed. by E. C. Goossen. R. Morris. il por Art in Am 58:104-11 My '70

Modern art. R. G. Beelke. il Todays Ed 59:36-9 Mr '70

Tradition and vitality. K. Nakamura. il Craft Horiz 30:10-11 My '70

Prices

Art under $500. N. R. Piene. il Art in Am 58:94-101 My '70

Excelsior! Van Gogh's Cypress. Time 95:50 Mr 9 '70

Highest ever; Velásquez's Juan De Pareja. il Time 96:77 D 7 '70

Wheeling and dealing; auction of contemporary American art. il Newsweek 76:89 N 30 '70

World's record Velásquez. il Life 69:39 D 11 '70

See also
Art as an investment

Private collections

Americans in Paris; Stein collection at the Museum of modern art. D. Davis. il por Newsweek 76:80-81B D 14 '70

Art; Stein collection exhibition. L. Alloway. Nation 212:61-2 Ja 11 '71

At home with art, the Lawrence Bloedel guesthouse. il Art in Am 58:80-5 My '70

At home with art: the villa of Count Giuseppe Panza di Biumo. T. Trini. il por Art in Am 58:102-9 S '70

Collectors: Dr and Mrs Irving Levitt. M. Esterow. il Art in Am 58:72-7 My '70

Collectors: Mr and Mrs Jack W. Glenn. M. Amaya. il por Art in Am 58:86-93 Mr '70

Cummings event in Washington. D. Cooper. il Art N 69:34-7+ Sum '70

Dubuffet at work; Musée de l'art brut. C. Cutler. il Art in Am 58:108-13 Jl '70

Early America's artless art; Garbisch collection. W. A. H. Birnie. il Read Digest 96:142-8 F '70

Exhibition preview; four Americans in Paris; the collections of G. Stein and her family. J. R. Mellow. il pors Art in Am 58:84-91 N '70

How I didn't get Mr Gulbenkian's art. J. Walker. il por Horizon 12:28-43 Sum '70

Howald's American line. K. Linville. il Art N 69:52-5 Sum '70

Introducing the National gallery of Switzerland; Oskar Reinhart collection bequeathed to the Swiss state. J. Russell. il Art N 69:50-1+ Ap '70

Iranian caviare to the general; the Mahboubian art. H. A. La Farge. il Art N 69:46-51 D '70

John D. Rockefeller, III Oriental collections. G. B. Washburn; P. Pal; P. C. Swann. il Art N 69:36-51 S '70

Joy of living with flowers and art; the very personal collection of Enid Haupt. il House & Gard 138:70-9 D '70

Lehman collection. R. Davidson. il Antiques 97:86+ Ja '70

Letter from Paris; theft of remaining Caillebotte collection of impressionist works. Genêt. New Yorker 46:85-6 Ag 22 '70

Lifestyle; young New York collectors. il Am Home 73:8+ F '70

Light of Asia; John D. Rockefeller III collection on display. D. Davis. il por Newsweek 76:97 O 26 '70

Nobody doesn't like Mr Sara Lee; collection of N. Cummings; with report by M. C. Wrenn. il pors Life 69:76-80 O 23 '70

Patrons and roped climbers; Stein collection. R. Hughes. il por Time 96:76-81 D 14 '70

See also
Art in the home
Barnes foundation, Merion, Pa.

Psychology

Aesthetic judgment in children. I. J. Child. Trans-Action 7:47-51 My '70

Art and the life of feeling. S. McIlhany. Am Artist 34:5 D '70

Autopolaroid; photographs, with interview. L. Samaras. Art in Am 58:66-83 N '70

Feeling and form. A. W. Saunders. il Sch Arts 70:34-6 O '70

What is a painting? M. Polanyi. il Am Scholar 39:655-69 Aut '70

Social aspects

See Art and society

Study and teaching

Art and the elementary teacher. R. M. Ebken. il Sch Arts 70:12-13 O '70

Art for the mentally retarded child. M. N. Steinhauser. il Sch Arts 69:30-1 Mr '70

Artist at work; a key to understanding. R. W. Neperud. Ed Digest 35:49-51 My '70

Clipboard. V. G. Timmons. See issues of School arts

Evaluation of children's picture making. E. Walton. il Sch Arts 70:6-7 N '70

Foot painting. il Design 71:22-4 Spr '70

Motivation. S. R. Rainey. il Sch Arts 70:8-9 Ja '71

Preparing to teach elementary art. J. A. Rubin. Ed Digest 35:38-41 Mr '70

ART—Study and teaching—*Continued*

Putting together an art lesson. J. W. Burgner. il Sch Arts 70:16-19 S '70

Seeing sound; art lesson for deaf students. J. W. Bell. il Sch Arts 70:26-9 S '70

Turned-on art; sound, motion, light make art classes relevant in Newton, Mass. A. Hurwitz. il Am Ed 6:14-17 Mr '70

See also
Art—Appreciation
Art education
Art teachers
Colleges and universities—Departments of the arts
Costume design—Study and teaching
Design—Study and teaching
Drawing—Study and teaching
Industrial arts—Study and teaching
Painting—Study and teaching

Materials

Cardboard carpentry. G. J. Brady. il Design 71:30-1 Fall '69

Creative uses of scrap materials. R. G. Lewie. il Sch Arts 69:11 F '70

Egg carton jewelry boxes. M. Beckton. il Design 71:40-1 mid-Wint '70

Rubber band & string prints; suggestions for classes of very young children. M. J. Acosta. il Design 71:22-3 Fall '69

Scrap materials; a source of motivation in art. C. J. Alkema. il Design 71:4-9 Fall '69

Seven kinds of sunburst. il Design 71:10-11+ Wint '69

Shoebox constructs instruct. D. L. Dubler. il Sch Arts 70:24-5 S '70

Sponge and starch painting. il Design 71:28-9 Sum '70

Treasures from a wood scrap bin. H. H. Foster. il Design 71:13 Fall '69

Weaving with weeds. V. R. Jackson. il Design 71:34-6 Wint '69

See also
Arts and crafts—Study and teaching—Materials
Sculpture—Study and teaching—Materials

Projects

Cylinder art. H. H. Foster. il Design 71:4-6 Wint '69

Fantastics on plastics. il Design 71:36-7 mid-Wint '70

Love amulets. il Design 71:35 mid-Wint '70

Scrap materials; a source of motivation in art. C. J. Alkema. il Design 71:4-9 Fall '69

Ten towns in New York; project for teenagers sponsored by New York state council on the arts. P. Smith. il Sch Arts 69:18-19 Ap '70

Textile designs with foam rubber. R. M. Koch. il Sch Arts 69:14-15 F '70

See also
Collage
Masks (for the face)
Mosaics
Mural painting and decoration
Paper work
Puppets and puppet plays

Technique

Artist speaks: Robert Morris; interview, ed. by E. C. Goossen. R. Morris. il por Art in Am 58:104-11 My '70

How an artist holds our attention: line, color & form; excerpt from The many ways of seeing. J. G. Moore. il Design 71:4-9 mid-Wint '70

Materials of art versus the art of materials (cont) H. Aach. il Craft Horiz 30:40-1+ Mr '70

Seeing eye, the thinking hand; excerpts from The many ways of seeing. J. G. Moore. il Design 71:4-9 Spr '70

See also
Sculpture—Technique

Themes

Art of evil; power in the blood. il Esquire 73:112-13 Mr '70

Art world: paintings of Klansmen at the Marlborough. H. Rosenberg. New Yorker 46:136+ N 7 '70

Early New England textile village in art. R. M. Candee. il Antiques 98:910-15 D '70

Money for money's sake. J. Lipman. il Art in Am 58:76-83 Ja '70

Portrait of a house. J. Larmoth. il House B 112:40-1 F '70

Thirty-year sculpture project; limewood triptych. M. B. Kane. il Am Artist 34:38-43+ Ja '70

See also
Fish in art
Flowers in art

Indians in art
Morocco in art
Negroes in art
Violence in art
West in art
Words in art

Therapeutic use

See Art therapy

Valuation

See also
Art sales

Africa

See also
Arts and crafts—Africa

Argentina

New developments in Buenos Aires. E. L. Johnson. il Art in Am 58:150-2 N '70

California

Century of art; Century of California painting exhibition. il Design 72:10-12 Wint '70

Southern California scene. B. Rose. Vogue 155:112 Ap 1 '70

England

See Art—Great Britain

Great Britain

Lord Eccles and art. T. Beeson. Chr Cent 87:1276 O 28 '70

See also
Art, British

Italy

See also
Art—Sicily

Japan

See also
Arts and crafts—Japan

Latin America

Art in Latin America. E. L. Johnson. il Art in Am 58:150-2 N '70

Netherlands

See also
Kröller-Müller museum

Sicily

Art of Sicily. K. Kuh. il Sat R 53:16-23 O 3 '70

Spain

Canvassing the Spanish galleries. P. Brooks. il Sat R 53:70-3 S 12 '70

R for aging art; Spain's Central institute of restoration of works of art and archaeology. N. López Pellón. il Américas 22:31-7 Ag '70

Switzerland

See also
National gallery of Switzerland, Winterthur

Taiwan

Puppets, painters, and players of Taiwan. il Travel & Camera 33:76-80 Mr '70

Taiwan; the country and its art. J. L. Cohen. il Travel & Camera 33:73-5 Mr '70

United States

See also
Art, American
Federal art project
Painting, American

ART, Abstract

Abstract painting now, refiners. B. Rose. Vogue 156:34 Jl '70

Do you remember Rudolf Bauer? exhibition at the Hutton gallery. L. Campbell. il Art N 69:56-7+ N '70

In the eye of the beholder; J. Levi. W. S. Wilson. il por Art N 68:52-3+ Mr '70

Making the gallery scene. B. Wasserman. il Sch Arts 69:36-9 Mr '70

New color painters; Lyrical abstraction exhibition at the Aldrich museum of contemporary art, Ridgefield, Conn. D. Davis. il Newsweek 75:34-6 My 4 '70

Squaring the circle and vice-versa. L. Campbell. il por Art N 68:38-41+ F '70

See also
Abstract expressionism

Study and teaching

Discovery of abstraction; introduction of seventh grade students to abstract art. G. Barfuss. il Sch Arts 69:30-1 Je '70

ART, African

African art; compositional vs. modal esthetics. E. Sellin. Yale R 59:215-27 D '69

African images, powers and presences; exhibition at Washington's National gallery of art. il Time 95:44-7 F 2 '70

ART, African—*Continued*
African sculpture exhibition at National gallery of art. Negro Hist Bul 33:99-100 Ap '70
See also
Arts and crafts—Africa

ART, American
American art at the Gibbes art gallery in Charleston. F. W. Bilodeau. il Antiques 98: 782-6 N '70
Art-makers of nineteenth-century America, by R. Lynes. Review
Atlan 226:134-7 N '70. J. Jacobs
Collectors: Dr and Mrs Irving Levitt. M. Esterow. il Art in Am 58:72-7 My '70
Editorial: Art in America yesterday and tomorrow. J. Lipman and A. Bower. Art in Am 58:54-5 Ja '70
Episodes from the sixties. H. Kramer. il Art in Am 58:56-61 Ja '70
Howald's American line. K. Linville. il Art N 69:52-5 Sum '70
Iceman cometh; symptoms of the seventies. J. Jacobs. il Art in Am 58:62-7 Ja '70
Mormons; contribution to American art. C. Carmer; M. S. Young. il Art in Am 58: 52-71 My '70
On and off the avenue; Shaker museum at Hancock, Mass. J. Malcolm. New Yorker 46:62-5 Ag 8 '70
Revival of the fittest; the nineteenth century. R. Lynes. por Art in Am 58:27 Mr '70
See also
Art, Negro (American)
Artists, American
Arts and crafts—United States
Painting, American
Whitney museum of American art, New York

Exhibitions
Coy women, purple upholstery, cosmic landscapes; exhibition of American 19th-century art. A. Goldin. il Art N 69:40-5+ My '70
High style; Metropolitan museum's exhibition of 19th century American art, architecture and decoration. il Time 95:82-3 My 25 '70
New color painters; Lyrical abstraction exhibition at the Aldrich museum of contemporary art, Ridgefield, Conn. D. Davis. il Newsweek 75:84-6 My 4 '70
19th century America at the Met. R. Phelps. il Life 68:10 Je 19 '70

ART, Asian
Light of Asia; John D. Rockefeller III collection on display. D. Davis. il por Newsweek 76:97 O 26 '70

ART, Austrian
Danube mannerists; exhibition of Danube school prints and drawings. B. A. Rifkin. il Art N 68:56-8+ F '70
London: Vienna secession: from art nouveau to 1970 exhibition. J. Russell. Art N 69:54 Ja '71

ART, British
Traveling ideas: Germany, England; new kind of international style. E. C. Baker. il Art N 69:38-40+ Sum '70
See also
Painting, British
Royal academy of arts, London

ART, Buddhist
Boston's oriental autumn; Zen masterpieces at the Museum of fine arts. J. M. Rosenfield. il Art N 69:42-5+ N '70
Face of Zen; show at Boston's Museum of fine arts. D. Davis. il Newsweek 76:88 N 30 '70
Sudden enlightenment; Zen art show at the Boston museum of fine arts. R. Hughes. il Time 96:76 D 14 '70

ART, Chinese
Puppets, painters, and players of Taiwan. il Travel & Camera 33:76-80 Mr '70
Taiwan; the country and its art. J. L. Cohen. il Travel & Camera 33:73-5 Mr '70

ART, Commercial
Art for everyone. S. McIlhany. Am Artist 34:5 O '70
Commercial arts. M. Glaser and J. Snyder. il Am Artist 34:9+ O; 14 N; 14-15 D '70
See also
Advertising art
Push pin studios, inc.

ART, Decorative. See Decoration and ornament; Design, Decorative

ART, Egyptian
Missed view; unshipped treasures of the Cairo museum due to U.S.-Egyptian relations. il Time 96:54-5+ Jl 20 '70

ART, English. See Art, British

ART, Eskimo. See Eskimos—Art

ART, Fantastic
Dream world of Odilon Redon. A. Werner. il Am Artist 34:40-5+ N '70
Mad world of Hieronymus Bosch; analysis of The garden of earthly delights. G. Highet. il Horizon 12:66-81, sup(folded reproduction) Spr '70
Oliver Grimley; pen draughtsman. H. C. Pitz. il pors Am Artist 34:28-34 Ja '70
See also
Fantasy in art

ART, French
Paris; the lettrist movement. C. Cutler. il Art in Am 58:116-19 Ja '70
Wrightsman rooms at the Metropolitan museum of art. J. Parker. il Antiques 97:102-8 Ja '70
See also
Painting, French

ART, German
Danube mannerists; exhibition of Danube school prints and drawings. B. A. Rifkin. il Art N 68:56-8+ F '70
Traveling ideas: Germany, England; new kind of international style. E. C. Baker. il Art N 69:38-40+ Sum '70
See also
Painting, German

ART, Graphic
See also
Graphic arts

ART, Greek
See also
Vases, Greek

ART, Influence of. See Art therapy

ART, Italian
See also
Florence—Art
Milan, Italy—Art

ART, Japanese
Boston's oriental autumn; the John Powers collection at the Fogg. J. M. Rosenfield. il Art N 69:42-5+ N '70
Orient express; Expo 70, Osaka, is a marriage of art and industry. E. C. Munro. il Art N 69:48-51+ Sum '70
See also
Art, Buddhist

ART, Latin American
Art of the Americas, ancient and Hispanic, by P. Kelemen. Review
Américas il 22:40-4 Ag '70. F. L. Phelps
Hemisphere art See issues of Américas
Saints and brothers; exhibit of Spanish arts in the Americas at the Smithsonian institute. R. E. Ahlborn. il Américas 22:6-13 S '70

ART, Medieval
Art; The year 1200 at the Metropolitan museum. L. Alloway. Nation 210:285-6 Mr 9 '70
Journey to the year 1200; exhibition at the Metropolitan museum of art. C. R. Baldwin. il Art N 69:30-5+ Ap '70
Medieval men; Style 1200 exhibition at the Met. il Newsweek 75:64-9 Mr 23 '70
Sweet wind out of the dark; The year 1200 exhibition at the Met. il Time 95:62 F 23 '70
1200 and all that; Metropolitan museum's exhibition. C. J. McNaspy. America 122:254-5 Mr 7 '70
See also
Christian art and symbolism
Metropolitan museum of art, New York—Cloisters

ART, Mexican
Mexico and the American artist. D. Gillen. il por Am Artist 34:32-9+ Ap '70
See also
Pottery, Mexican

ART, Modern
Art as act. D. Davis. Art in Am 58:31 Mr '70
Art; conceptual art. L. Alloway. Nation 211: 61-2 Jl 20 '70
Art; hard-to-exhibit forms of art. L. Alloway. Nation 210:92-3 Ja 26 '70
Art world; art and life. H. Rosenberg. New York 46:44-7 Ja 2 '71
Art world; de-aestheticization. H. Rosenberg. New Yorker 45:62+ Ja 24 '70
Art world; dilemmas of a new season. H. Rosenberg. New Yorker 46:149-54 O 10 '70
Art world; Whitney annual and the Bauhaus. H. Rosenberg. New Yorker 46:82+ F 21 '70
Artworks and packages, by H. Rosenberg. Review
Art N 69:47+ Mr '70. M. Mudrick
Checkup; interpretation of a medical checkup by a conceptual artist. D. Burgy. il pors Art in Am 58:108-11 Mr '70
Close look at optical art. S. McIlhany. il Am Artist 34:32-7 Je '70
Conceptual art as opera. A. Goldin and R. Kushner. il Art N 69:40-3 Ap '70

ART, Modern—*Continued*

Craftsman for today, dreamer for tomorrow; work of V. Vasarely. il Time 95:56-8 Je 22 '70

Culture collision. B. Rose. Vogue 156:98 O 1 '70

Dubuffet, the subversive smothered with love; working on *l'Hourloupe objects.* S. De Gramont. il por Horizon 12:88-105 Sum '70

Electronic wallpaper; N. J. Paik and his video synthesizer. D. Davis. il por Newsweek 76:54 Ag 24 '70

Episodes from the sixties. H. Kramer. il Art in Am 58:56-61 Ja '70

Exhibition preview: four Americans in Paris; the collections of G. Stein and her family. J. R. Mellow. il pors Art in Am 58:84-91 N '70

Fling, dribble and dip. il Life 68:62-6 F 27 '70

Fun art; environmental art, tech art, participatory art. T. Meehan. il Horizon 11:4-15 Aut '69

Hark, hark! The art at heaven's gate sings; exhibition at the Museum of contemporary crafts. il Esquire 73:140-5 My '70

How they do talk, those conceptualists. B. Schiff. New Repub 162:27-8 Ap 25 '70

Iceman cometh: symptoms of the seventies. J. Jacobs. il Art in Am 58:62-7 Ja '70

Letter from Paris; Salon des independants, now showing at the Grand palais. Genêt. New Yorker 46:130-2 Ap 18 '70

Millenniums of modern art; Brancusi's counterparts in African sculpture. il Life 68:62-6 Mr 20 '70

Mr Processionary at the conceptacle; Information show at Museum of modern art. D. Shapiro. il Art N 69:58-61 S '70

Modern art. R. G. Beelke. il Todays Ed 59:36-9 Mr '70

Nam June Paik: he composes pictures on TV. W. F. Wilson. il por Pop Phot 66:102+ F '70

Nowhere to sit down: chairs as art objects. R. Hughes. il por Time 96:62 N 9 '70

Perilous equilibrium; B. Riley's optical paintings. R. Hughes. il por Time 96:82-3 N 16 '70

Personal pop. D. Darro. il por Newsweek 75:98-9 Mr 9 '70

Poet of the personal. il por Time 95:50-1+ Mr 9 '70

Pop goes the easel. S. McIlhany. il Am Artist 34:46-51+ F '70

Portrait of the artist as a wet hen. il Esquire 73:134-9 Ap '70

Swimming pool art. il Life 69:76-80 O 9 '70

Where is the art? concept art. B. Goldsmith. il Harp Baz 103:144-7 My '70

See also
Abstract expressionism
Art déco
Assemblage (art)
Bauhaus
Cubism
Dadaism
Electric lamps in art
Environment (art)

Anecdotes, facetiae, satire, etc.

Plato on pop art. G. Wagner. Nat R 22:1066-7 O 6 '70

Exhibitions

Two happenings at Southern Illinois university; Unfired clay exhibition. E. Johnson; W. Fuhrmann. il Craft Horiz 30:36-41+ O '70

ART, Municipal
Urban street: provocative forum in Minneapolis. P. Wolf. il Art in Am 58:118-23 N '70

ART, Mythology in. See Mythology in art

ART, Negro (American)
Black art in America. B. Rose. il Art in Am 58:54-67 S '67

Focus on black artists: a project for schools and community; exhibition at Philadelphia civic center. R. J. Craig. il Sch Arts 70:30-3 N '70

Object: diversity. il Time 95:80-7 Ap 6 '70

What is black art? exhibition at the Museum of fine arts, Boston. D. Davis. il Newsweek 75:89-90 Je 22 '70

See also
Negroes in art

ART, Oriental
John D. Rockefeller, III Oriental collections. G. B. Washburn; P. Pal; P. C. Swann. il Art N 69:36-51 S '70

See also
Art, Buddhist
Art, Chinese
Art, Japanese

ART, Persian
Iranian caviare to the general; the Mahboubian art. H. A. La Farge. il Art N 69:46-51 D '70

ART, Polish
Royal academy Polonaise; 1,000 years of Polish art. J. Russell. il Art N 68:34-7 F '70

ART, Pre-Columbian
See also
Sculpture, Pre-Columbian

ART, Prehistoric. See Art, Primitive

ART, Primitive
Baton of Montgaudier; engraved art on the reindeer antler from stone age France. A. Marshack. il por(p8) Natur Hist 79:56-63 Mr '70

Dubuffet at work; Musée de l'art brut. C. Cutler. il Art in Am 58:108-13 Jl '70

How to collect primitive art. N. R. Piene. House & Gard 137:48-9+ Ja '70

Six villages near Salzburg. J. Lipman and M. Pálffy. il Art in Am 58:102-5 Jl '70

Symbols in the stone age; analysis of ice age art. il por Sci N 97:242 Mr 7 '70

See also
Cave drawings and paintings

ART, Religious. See Christian art and symbolism

ART, Russian
See also
Icons

ART, Scottish
See also
Painting, Scottish

ART, Spanish American. See Art, Latin American

ART and children. See Children and art

ART and industry
See also
Art, Commercial
Business in the arts award

ART and literature
Art and English; designing sets project. T. R. Pokorny. il Sch Arts 69:40 Je '70

ART and medicine. See Medicine and art

ART and music
Marin and music; with excerpts from Marin's writings. C. Gray. il Art in Am 58:72-81 Jl '70

ART and nature. See Nature (aesthetics)

ART and photography
Gallery; photographs; excerpts from Picasso's third dimension. G. Mili. Life 69:8-9 D 4 '70

Today's painters use the photographer's eye. M. Mann. il Pop Phot 66:29+ My '70
See also
Photography, Artistic

ART and politics
Between solitude and solidarity; Camus' writings. B. Murchland. Commonweal 93:91-5 O 23 '70

La jeune peinture, protest and politics. M. Gibson. il Art in Am 58:142-5 N '70

ART and psychoanalysis. See Psychoanalysis and art

ART and science
See also
Art and technology

ART and society
Arise you prisoners of art history; New art association's manifesto. T. B. Hess. Art N 69:35 N '70

Art and confrontation. Review
New Yorker 46:54+ Je 6 '70. H. Rosenberg

Art and social change. M. Roman. il Américas 22:12-20 F '70

Art as communication. V. J. Popolizio. il Sch Arts 70:8-9 D '70

Artist and the city. S. McIlhany. Am Artist 34:5 N '70

From class art to mass art. J. B. Hightower. Art in Am 58:25 S '70

Lord Eccles and art; British new minister for the arts. T. Beeson. Chr Cent 87:1276 O 28 '70
See also
Art—International aspects

ART and state
Federal support for the visual arts, by F. V. O'Connor. Review
New Repub 162:24-7 F 28 '70. B. Schiff
See also
State encouragement of science, literature and art

ART and technology
Art and technology; exhibition in U.S. pavilion at Expo '70. M. Tuchman. il Art in Am 58:78-9 Mr '70

Art as communication. V. J. Popolizio. il Sch Arts 70:8-9 D '70

Art; exhibition Explorations. L. Alloway. Nation 210:476-7 Ap 20 '70

ART and technology—*Continued*
Gerbil ex machina; Software exhibition at the Jewish museum. N.Y. T. B. Hess. Art N 69:23 D '70
Getting it together, ambitious; art and technology projects. B. Rose. Vogue 156:304 S 1 '70
Improbable marriage. D. Davis. il Newsweek 75:100-1 Ap 20 '70

ART appreciation. See Art—Appreciation

ART as a profession
Sexual art-politics. E. C. Baker. il Art N 69:47-8+ Ja '71

ART as an investment
Art as investment: the profits, risks. il U S News 68:90-2 Je 8 '70
Art for the sake of speculation. Bsns W p24-5 Jl 4 '70
Bull market in Western art. il Bsns W p92-3 Je 13 '70

Anecdotes, facetiae, satire, etc.
Financial perspicacity. S. E. Lee. Art in Am 58:14-15 Jl '70

ART auctions. See Art sales

ART collecting. See Art—Collectors and collecting

ART collectors. See Art—Collectors and collecting

ART colonies. See Artists colonies

ART competitions. See Art—Competitions

ART dealers
Boston, new directions; Parker street 470. C. Andreae. il Art in Am 58:102-3 My '70
By appointment only. il Time 96:56-9 Ag 3 '70
Eight gamblers on young artists; art dealers in New York. il Vogue 155:176-7 F 1 '70
First family of avant-garde art, Castelli clan; with report by D. Bourdon. il pors Life 68:70-4 My 1 '70
Living the élan of art life. B. Rose. Vogue 155:178-9+ F 1 '70
New dealing. E. H. Varian. il Art in Am 58: 68-73 Ja '70

ART déco
What is art deco? J. Applegate. il Art N 69:38-42+ D '70

ART deco exhibition. See Art—Exhibitions

ART education
Are we entertaining or educating? C. T. Schuch. il Sch Arts 69:24-6 Ap '70
Art and the slow learner. M. G. Emlen. il Sch Arts 69:10-12 Mr '70
Art as an answer. S. McIlhany. Am Artist 34:6 Ag; 5 S '70
Art education for the culturally different. D. L. Barclay. il Sch Arts 69:14-17 Mr '70
Build with youth for a better world. Z. L. Huffman. il Sch Arts 70:20-1 N '70
Camouflage in the classroom; the use of deception in teaching perception. R. Behrens. bibliog il Sch Arts 69:24-5 F '70
Gestalt and the visual arts. R. Behrens. il Design 71:10-12 mid-Wint '70
Seeing eye, the thinking hand; excerpts from The many ways of seeing. J. G. Moore. il Design 71:4-9 Spr '70
Where the fine arts can flourish. E. B. Epstein. il Todays Ed 59:52-4 O '70
You can't weld in a mini skirt; case for a unified arts course. W. G. Clark. il Sch Arts 70:22-5 O '70
See also
Art—Appreciation
Art—Study and teaching
Colleges and universities—Departments of the arts
Moving pictures in art education

ART emergency fund
Letter to editor. Art in Am 58:33 N '70

ART exhibitions. See Art—Exhibitions

ART exhibitions, Traveling. See Exhibitions, Traveling

ART exhibits, School. See School exhibits

ART festivals. See Art—Exhibitions

ART festivals, Children's. See Children's art—Exhibitions

ART forgeries. See Forgery of works of art

ART galleries, Commercial. See Art dealers

ART glass. See Glass, Ornamental

ART in America (periodical)
Letter to the editor from the Art magazine committee. Art in Am 58:17 S '70

ART in motion. See Kinetic art

ART in the home
Art today. P. Rumely. il Bet Hom & Gard 48:62-5+ Ap '70
Artful renter; time-testing art in your own living room. A. Ogden. House B 112:21-2 Ap '70

At home with art: Fred Mueller's penthouse. il Art in Am 58:82-7 Jl '70
At home with art: the Samuel Rautbord house. il Art in Am 58:92-7 Ja '70
Collectors: Mr and Mrs Jack W. Glenn. M. Amaya. il por Art in Am 58:86-93 Mr '70
For art's sake: N.Y. apartment of A. Glimcher. il N Y Times Mag p90-1 My 3 '70
From painters and sculptors: rooms and furniture that surprise and refresh. il House & Gard 138:64-9 Jl '70
Medium in his home: SoHo loft of P. Gee. J. Broudy. il por Look 34:30-1 Jl 14 '70
On and off the avenue; prints, reproductions, drawings, stained glass, tapestry. J. Malcolm. New Yorker 46:63-4+ Je 20 '70
One of life's great pleasures is living with the pictures you love. W. Baldwin. il House & Gard 138:18-20+ N '70
See also
Antiques
Art—Private collections

ART in the school
Ethnic art gallery. F. G. Gilmartin. il Sch Arts 69:8 F '70

ART institute, Chicago. See Chicago art institute

ART loans
Artful renter; time-testing art in your own living room. A. Ogden. House B 112:31-2 Ap '70
Missed view; unshipped treasures of the Cairo museum due to U.S.-Egyptian relations. il Time 96:54-5+ Jl 20 '70
Royal academy Polonaise; 1,000 years of Polish art. J. Russell. il Art N 68:34-7 F '70

ART materials. See Artists materials

ART metal work
Decorative panels with metal. P. Rothenberg. il Design 71:26-9 Fall '69
Jeweled beasts of royal hordes; animal style exhibition at Asia house. G. B. Washburn. il Art N 69:28-31 Mr '70
See also
Fretwork
Ironwork
Jewelry
Repoussé work

Exhibitions
All that glitters: Goldsmith '70. H. Drutt. il Craft Horiz 30:42-5+ Ag '70

ART nouveau (movement)
On and off the avenue; Hector Guimard exhibition at the Museum of modern art. J. Malcolm. New Yorker 46:89-92 My 2 '70
Visconti; house on Ischia. K. Radkai. il pors Vogue 156:182-9+ N 1 '70
See also
Art déco

ART objects
Art's new originals; multiples: machine-made art objects. J. Gruen. il Am Home 73:50+ Ap '70
See also
Art in the home
Display of antiques, art objects, etc.
Fans

Conservation and restoration
See Art—Conservation and restoration

ART objects, British
English decorative arts at the M. H. de Young memorial museum. D. G. Keith. il Antiques 97:712-17 My '70

ART objects, Reproductions of. See Reproductions of works of art

ART patronage
Artist as uneconomic man. R. Lynes. il Sat R 53:25-8+ F 28 '70
Merchants and masterpieces, by C. Tomkin. Review
Art in Am 58:27+ S '70. J. Jacobs
Public art and private gallery. J. Wines. il Art in Am 58:74-5 Ja '70

ART prices. See Art—Prices

ART project, Federal. See Federal art project

ART sales
Art at auction 1968-1969; excerpts. P. Wilson. il Antiques 97:398-401 Mr '70
Coming auctions. See issues of Art news
Highest ever; Velásquez's Juan De Pareja. il Time 96:77 D 7 '70
See also
Art—Prices
Parke-Bernet galleries, inc.

ART schools
Art school directory. Am Artist 34:17-40 Mr '70
Building for the arts. R. Montgomery. il Arch Forum 132:80-9 Ja '70
See also
San Francisco art institute

ART societies
See also names of art societies, associations, etc. e.g. Provincetown art association

ART strike. See Strikes—United States—Artists

ART students
University art student. S. McIlhany. il Am
Artist 34:52-8 Mr '70
ART studios. See Artists studios
ART teachers
Look at learning. S. McIlhany. Am Artist 34:5
Mr '70

Education
Saturday school for future teachers; University of Texas art department project. il Design 71:16-19 Sum '70

ART thefts
Letter from Paris; theft of remaining Cail-
lebotte collection of impressionist works.
Genêt. New Yorker 46:85-6 Ag 22 '70
ART therapy
Art and social change. M. Roman. il Américas
22:12-20 F '70
Crafting animals in wool. il Design 71:33-5
Sum '70
ART trade
Try some: they're homemade; crafts made
and sold by women. A. M. Cunningham. il
Mlle 70:184-5+ Mr '70
See also
Art dealers
Art sales
ART workers coalition
Ars gratia artis? AWC protest at MOMA. il
Newsweek 75:80 F 9 '70
Letter to the editor from the Art magazine
committee. Art in Am 58:17 S '70
Pickets on Parnassus. E. C. Baker. il Art
N 69:30-3+ S '70
ARTAUD, Antonin
Vocation for madness. S. De Gramont. pors
Horizon 12:48-55 Spr '70 *
ARTERIES
Neuromuscular contacts in intracranial arter-
ies of the cat. E. Nelson and M. Rennels.
bibliog il Science 167:301-2 Ja 16 '70

Surgery
See Blood vessels—Surgery
ARTERIOSCLEROSIS
Elevation of aortic proline hydroxylase;
a biochemical defect in experimental
arteriosclerosis. G. C. Fuller and R. O.
Langner. bibliog il Science 168:987-9 My 22
'70
Progress through fluid dynamics. B. J. Cul-
liton. il Sci N 97:415-16 Ap 25 '70
ARTHRITIS
Arthritis. Todays Ed 59:74-5 O '70
Copper bracelets are a put-on. M. Michael-
son. il Todays Health 48:27-9+ Je '70
Curious case of the copper band. G. Cant.
il Sports Illus 33:37-41 Ag 3 '70
Surgery that aids arthritis victims. il Bsns
W p 116+ Ap 25 '70
See also
Gout

Therapy
How to keep active in farming when arthritis
strikes. G. F. Thomson. Farm J 94:32D Ja
'70
ARTHUR, King (romances, etc)
Tennyson anyone? interpreting Idylls of the
king today. A. H. Leitch. Chr Today 15:
48-9 D 18 '70
ARTHUR, Jean
Very personal garden of Jean Arthur. il House
& Gard 138:70-3 Jl '70 *
ARTHUR, Phil
Build a Woofer guard. il Pop Electr 33:49-
52 Jl '70
ARTHUR, Thomas C.
Psalm at twenty-three. Chr Cent 87:1123 S
23 '70
ARTHUR, William B.
Whatever happened to mankind's dream of
peace? il Look 34:13-17 D 29 '70
ARTHUR Andersen and company. See Ander-
sen, Arthur, and company
ARTHUR Kill rehabilitation center. See Nar-
cotic addicts—Rehabilitation
ARTICHOKES
See also
Cookery—Vegetables
ARTICLES for periodicals. See Periodical ar-
ticles
ARTICULATION (speech) See Diction
ARTIFACTS, Indian. See Indians of North
America—Implements
ARTIFICIAL deformities. See Deformities
ARTIFICIAL diamonds. See Diamonds, Artifi-
cial
ARTIFICIAL fur. See Fur, Artificial
ARTIFICIAL gut. See Intestines, Artificial

ARTIFICIAL hearts. See Hearts, Artificial
ARTIFICIAL insemination
Can A.I. cut your breeding costs? O. Bay.
Farm J 94:32C Ja '70
New tools help A.I. work better. J. Russell.
il Farm J 93:H26-27 O '69
Osborndale ivanhoe lies a-mold'ring in the
grave. R. Eddy. Esquire 73:204 Ap '70
Registered beef breeders tell how they use
A.I. O. Bay. Farm J 93:38B O '69
You can learn, as I did, to breed your cows
with AI. B. Fowler. il Farm J 93:25-7+ N
'69
ARTIFICIAL insemination, Human
Babies in question. J. C. Hefley and M.
Hefley. il Todays Health 48:16-19+ Ag '70
ARTIFICIAL intelligence
Meet Shaky, first electronic person. B.
Darrach. il Life 69:58B-58D+ N 20 '70
ARTIFICIAL kidneys. See Kidneys, Artificial
ARTIFICIAL lakes. See Lakes, Artificial
ARTIFICIAL larynx. See Larynx, Artificial
ARTIFICIAL lawns. See Turf, Artificial
ARTIFICIAL light gardening
Build a light garden for winter salads. R. F.
Krause. il Org Gard & Farm 17:111-12 O
'70
Guide to gardening with artificial light. il
Good H 171:154-5 S '70
ARTIFICIAL limbs
Two lives of Carol Ross. L. David. por Good
H 170:65+ F '70
ARTIFICIAL marble. See Marble, Artificial
ARTIFICIAL pacemaker (heart) See Pace-
maker, Artificial (heart)
ARTIFICIAL reefs. See Reefs, Artificial
ARTIFICIAL respiration. See Respiration, Ar-
tificial
ARTIFICIAL satellites
Applications technology satellite program. il
Space World G-9-81:18-20 S '70
Apollo 16 to launch satellite. Aviation W 92:
23 Mr 30 '70
Man vs. machines in space: what the future
holds; technology applications program. il
U S News 68:78-9 My 11 '70
On future power from the sun. il Chem 43:25
Mr '70
Roster of space activity. R. N. Watts, jr.
Sky & Tel 39:81-2 F '70
Satellite report; tables. See issues of Space
world
Space applications launch talks expected soon
on draft pact. Aviation W 93:18 O 5 '70
Spin-off from space satellites. G. Gregory. il
UNESCO Courier 23:8-12 Mr '70
See also
Space stations

Agricultural use
ERTS could aid crop blight fight. Z. Strickland. Aviation W 93:50 D 21 '70

Air traffic control use
Air traffic control satellites. il Space World
G-6-78:48-9 Je '70
Competing concepts slow ATC satellites. il
Aviation W 92:212-14+ Mr 9 '70
Satellite air traffic control study planned.
Aviation W 92:25 Ja 26 '70
Satellites to steer by. L. Lessing. il Fortune
82:115-17+ Ag '70

Astronomical use
Another orbiting astronomical observatory.
R. N. Watts, jr. il Sky & Tel 40:349-50 D
'70
Apollo telescope mount. R. N. Watts, jr. il
Sky & Tel 40:202-5 O '70
Apollo telescope mount. il Space World G-3-
75:10-12 Mr '70
First X-ray astronomy satellite. R. N. Watts.
jr. il Sky & Tel 41:14-17 Ja '71
Intercosmos 1. B. Petrov. il Space World
G-3-75:30-1 Mr '70
Manned telescope. il Space World G-4-76:42-
3 Ap '70
Monitoring the sun's violence. D. E. Thomsen.
il Sci N 98:258-9 S 19 '70
OAO to produce four years' data. Z. Strick-
land. il Aviation W 93:69+ N 23 '70
OAO-II looks at larger universe. il Space
World G-5-77:4-8 My '70
Obtaining data on the sun by satellite; use of
ultraviolet spectrometer. il Chem 43:22-3 Ja
'70
OGO-5 observes huge comet cloud. il Space
World G-8-80:38-9 Ag '70
Picking up the pieces; OAO III. il Sci N 98:
427-8 D 5 '70

ARTIFICIAL satellites—Astronomical use—*Cont.*
Pioneer 6: measurement of transient Faraday rotation phenomena observed during solar occultation. G. S. Levy and others; reply. K. H. Schatten. il Science 168:395-6 Ap 17 '70
Ultraviolet astronomy: progress with the OAO. A. L. Hammond. Science 170:960-1 N 27 '70

Electronic equipment
See also
Antennas (electronics)

Launching from space
Small satellites for Apollo 16, 18 under construction. Aviation W 92:65 Je 8 '70

Meteorological use
Atmosphere explorer satellite. il Space World G-5-77:37 My; G-7-79:42 Jl; G-12-84:19 D '70
How new weather satellites will give you more reliable forecasts. W. Von Braun. il Pop Sci 197:61-3 N '70
Inefficiency hurts weather photo program; U.S.-USSR program. P. J. Klass. il Aviation W 93:78-9+ N 16 '70
Modification of Agena studied to triple payload of Nimbus. Aviation W 92:69 Ap 27 '70
New weather satellite planned; synchronous. P. J. Klass. il Aviation W 94:43+ Ja 4 '71
News from the world of space exploration; upper atmosphere layer temperature measurements. Space World G-10-82:43 O '70
Nimbus 4 launched successfully. il Space World G-7-79:4-7 Jl '70
Nimbus 4 to expand data on atmosphere. Aviation W 92:22 Ap 6 '70
Proposed space-weather experiment. il Space World H-1-85:42-3 Ja '71
Satellite observations of lightning. J. A. Vorpahl and others. bibliog il Science 169:860-2 Ag 28 '70
Tiros-M, new era in global weather prediction. il Space World G-9-81:4-10 S '70
Weather satellites' first decade marked by significant achievement. il Space World G-8-80:28-30 Ag '70
What's the weather report? I. Geller. il Duns 95:87-90 Mr '70

Military use
Data relay satellite sought for early warning network. Aviation W 92:21 Ja 19 '70
East-West race stays in orbit. il Bsns W p28-9 N 14 '70
Soviet satellite intercepts appear planned to deter orbital weapons. Aviation W 93:21 N 9 '70

Navigational use
News from the world of space exploration; studies and evaluation of 21-satellite system. Space World G-9-81:45 S '70
Satellite clusters studied for triservice navigation. B. Miller. Aviation W 92:20-1 F 2 '70
Satellites to steer by. L. Lessing. il Fortune 82:115-17+ Ag '70

Orbits
Hope for deep-dipping satellites. J. Eberhart. il Sci N 97:109-10 Ja 24 '70

Propulsion systems
See Space vehicles—Propulsion systems

Use in research
Earth resources satellites. Space World G-2-74:48-9 F '70
ERTS can do anything. il Sci Digest 67:37-8 Ja '70
Explorer dies; Explorer I. Time 95:57 Ap 13 '70
How can spacecraft systems function in the areas of conservation and environment? Space World G-8-80:32-3 Ag '70
Prospector takes to the sky; ERTS satellite. il Bsns W p 104 N 14 '70
Sensors pose earth satellite challenge. il Aviation W 92:124+ Je 22 '70
Unmanned efforts assuming greater role. il Aviation W 92:69+ Mr 9 '70
Where are they now? Explorer 1, 1958-1970. il Newsweek 75:12 Ap 13 '70
Workaday jobs earth satellites will do; earth-resource satellites. il Changing T 24:23-4 Jl '70

Use in tracking and trailing
Nimbus 3 elk tracking experiment. il Space World G-6-78:14-18 Je '70

ARTIFICIAL satellites, Chinese
China in space race: meaning to U.S. US News 68:79 My 11 '70

China joins the space age. il Sci N 97:427-8 My 2 '70
China orbits a satellite. Newsweek 75:42 My 4 '70
In the wake of Mao's moon. il Time 95:44+ My 11 '70

ARTIFICIAL satellites, European
French withhold ESRO satellite funds. D. E. Fink. il Aviation W 93:22-3 D 7 '70
Intercosmos 1. B. Petrov. il Space World G-3-75:30-1 Mr '70

ARTIFICIAL satellites, French
France to emphasize satcoms. Aviation W 92:24 My 25 '70
French succeed with launching PEOLE orbiter. Aviation W 93:21 D 21 '70

ARTIFICIAL satellites, German
AZUR: satellite landmark. T. Shoemaker. il Sci N 97:208 F 21 '70

ARTIFICIAL satellites, Japanese
In space at last; Ohsumi launch. S. Griffin. il Sci N 97:232 F 28 '70

ARTIFICIAL satellites, Russian
Case for candor; Soviet space tests of satellite killer. R. Hotz. Aviation W 93:9 N 30 '70
Soviet satellite intercepts appear planned to deter orbital weapons. Aviation W 93:21 N 9 '70
Soviets orbit eight navigation satellites. Aviation W 92:27 My 4 '70
Soviets resume multiple tests with satellite intercept vehicles. Aviation W 93:20 N 2 '70
Space scouts made in the USSR; Cosmos satellites. Space World G-7-79:26-7 Jl '70
USSR accelerates recon satellite pace. P. J. Klass. il Aviation W 92:72-4+ Ap 6 '70

ARTIFICIAL sweeteners. See Sugar substitutes
ARTIFICIAL teeth. See Teeth, Artificial
ARTIFICIAL turf. See Turf, Artificial
ARTILLERY ranges. See Bombing and gunnery ranges
ARTIST reporters. See Reporters and reporting
ARTISTIC ability. See Creation (literary, artistic, etc)
ARTISTIC photography. See Photography, Artistic

ARTISTS
Artist as uneconomic man. R. Lynes. il Sat R 53:25-8+ F 28 '70
See also
Art as a profession
Negro artists
Women as artists

Political activities
See also
Art workers coalition

ARTISTS, American
Artist's studio. N. Kent. il Am Artist 34:56-68 Ja '70
Seven startlers: the Pulsa people of Yale university. il Vogue 155:174-5+ F 1 '70
See also
Art workers coalition
Burgy, D.
Cowboy artists of America
Dine, J.
Flavin, D.
Golub, L.
Laliberté, N.
Liberman, A.
Mahoney, C. A.
O'Keeffe, G.
Oppenheim, D.
Painting, American
Pratt, R. L.
Russell, C. M.
Selig, M.
Warhol, A.
West, B.

ARTISTS, Canadian
Vancouver: scene and unscene; interview with artists, curators, dealers and critics; ed. by P. Selz. il Art in Am 58:122-6 Je '70
See also
Houston, J.
Painting, Canadian

ARTISTS, Dominican
See also
Colson, J.

ARTISTS, German
See also
Painting, German
Wunderlich, P.

ARTISTS, Greek
See also
Samaras, L.

ARTISTS, Hungarian
See also
Moholy-Nagy, L.

ARTISTS, Italian
   See also
Giacomelli, M.
Painting, Italian
ARTISTS, New Zealand
   See also
McIntyre, P.
ARTISTS, Norwegian
   See also
Munch, E.
ARTISTS, Spanish
   See also
Painting, Spanish
Sanchez, A.
ARTISTS colonies
Bohemia's last frontier; artists and galleries
  in SoHo. il Time 95:82 My 25 '70
Living big in a loft; SoHo artists association.
  il Life 68:61-5 Mr 27 '70
What is happening to our art colony? Prov-
  incetown, Mass. K. Kuh. Sat R 53:42-3 O
  31 '70
ARTISTS easels. See Easels
ARTISTS materials
Art mart. See issues of American artist
Artist speaks: Robert Morris; interview, ed.
  by E. C. Goossen. R. Morris. il por Art in
  Am 58:104-11 My '70
Clipboard. V. G. Timmons. See issues of
  School arts
Drawing with an unusual tool; razor blades.
  E. E. Niemann. il por Am Artist 34:46-52
  Ja '70
Materials of art versus the art of materials
  (cont) H. Aach. il Craft Horiz 30:40-1+
  Mr '70
New sources, new materials. il Art N 69:
  81 Sum; 78-9 S '70
Painting, drawing, and printmaking sup-
  ports. R. Massey. il Am Artist 34:22-6 S '70
Painting knives: variety and use. F. Taubes.
  il Am Artist 35:50-5+ Ja '71
Ralph Mayer's technical question & answer
  page. R. Mayer. See issues of American
  artist
Throw away cathedral; model of Lincoln
  cathedral. il Design 71:32-4 mid-Wint '70
What's new, where to buy it. See issues
  of Design
   See also
Paint brushes
Plastics as art material
ARTISTS strike. See Strikes—United States—
  Artists
ARTISTS studios
Artist's ideal studio. R. Massey. il Am Artist
  35:30-4 Ja '71
Artist's studio. N. Kent il Am Artist 34:56-68
  Ja '70
Living big in a loft. il Life 68:61-5 Mr 27 '70
Los Angeles artists' studios. B. A. Bengston.
  il Art in Am 58:100-9 N '70
Robert Indiana; interview, ed. by E. Sver-
  beyeff and S. Nirenberg. R. Indiana. il por
  House B 112:52-5+ F '70
Through the hole in the floor, a two-story-
  high family studio. il Sunset 144:94-5 F '70
Westbeth: artists in residence. E. P. Berkeley.
  il Arch Forum 133:44-9 O '70
The ARTS
Emphasis. B. Diamonstein. Harp Baz 103:
  184-5 Mr; 98-9+ Je '70
U.S. culture moves west. il U S News 67:62-7
  S 7 '70
   See also
Art

Finance
Business of culture; symposium. il Sat R 53:
  17-32+ F 28 '70
Has America turned its back on the arts?
  il Sr Schol 96:10-14 My 4 '70

Philosophy
Opinion: the art of living. E. Roditi. por Mile
  71:18+ O '70

Social aspects
See The Arts and society

Study and teaching
Anatomy of pretentiousness. R. Evett. Atlan
  227:75-9 Ja '71
Art subverts the curriculum. R. M. Gummere,
  jr. il Nation 211:368-71 O 19 '70
Artist as teacher. B. G. Morison. il Sat R 53:
  51-3+ D 19 '70
Black arts for black youth; community arts
  movement in the ghetto. D. D. Bushnell.
  il Sat R 53:43-6+ Jl 18 '70
Student center for the living arts; Dayton,
  Ohio. S. E. York. il Todays Ed 59:30-2 N '70
ARTS and crafts
Craft kit; Celluclay. il Consumer Bul 53:22
  Ja '70

Crafts for the uncrafty; yarn flowers, stained
  glass, foil antiquing, couching. M. B. Smith.
  il Bet Hom & Gard 48:88-91 Mr '70
Crafts today. N. Krevitsky. il Am Artist 35:
  16 Ja '71
Fun things to do for all ages. M. B. Smith.
  il Bet Hom & Gard 48:4+ Ag '70
   See also
Batik
Collage
Design, Decorative
Enamel and enameling
Folk art
Glass, Ornamental
Handicraft
Hooking
Ironwork
Jewelry
Leather work
Needlework
Paper work
Papier-mâché
Pewter
Plastics work
Tapestry
Weaving
World crafts council

Bibliography
Book review section. See issues of Design
Books. See issues of Craft horizons
New books. See issues of School arts
Resource materials. V. G. Timmons. See is-
  sues of School arts

Exhibitions
Art in other media; show at the Burpee art
  gallery, Rockford, Ill. il Craft Horiz 30:
  18-21 D '70
British designer craftsmen; exhibition at the
  Smithsonian institution, Washington. il
  Ceram Mo 18:26-7 '70
Calendar; where to show. See issues of Craft
  horizons
Enamels 70. il Ceram Mo 18:21-3 My '70
Exhibition '70: eleven states biennial of the
  Midwest. J. Floch and A. Efiand. il Craft
  Horiz 30:34-5+ O '70
Exhibitions. See issues of Craft horizons
Hobby from the sea: Driftwood show, Gray-
  land, Wash. H. Pearson. il Design 72:39-41
  Fall '70
Johnson collection at Cranbrook; Objects:
  USA. J. Ashbery. il Craft Horiz 30:34-9+
  Mr '70
Nut art in quake time; kookie California
  ceramics in Objects U.S.A. D. Jack. il Art N
  69:38-41+ Mr '70
Seeing things; Objects: USA: the Johnson
  collection of contemporary crafts. N. Git-
  telson. Harp Baz 103:23+ F '70

Study and teaching
Adrift with driftwood. E. Dean and J. Dean.
  il por Har Yrs 10:19-20 Jl '70
Travel and study directory; lists of schools
  and colleges in the U.S.A. and abroad. il
  Craft Horiz 30:28-41 My '70
   See also
California college of arts and crafts, Oakland,
  Calif.

Materials
Clipboard. V. G. Timmons. il Sch Arts 70:4
  Ja '71
What's your bag? create some kind of bag
  from discarded clothing. F. Marlow. il Sch
  Arts 69:24-5 Je '70

Africa
Travelogue (title varies) (cont) M. M. Patch.
  il Craft Horiz 20:30-5+ Ja '70

Appalachian Region
Lifestyle; Mountain artisans. il Am Home 73:
  10 S '70

California
Adrift with driftwood. E. Dean and J. Dean.
  il por Har Yrs 10:19-20 Jl '70

Caribbean Region
See it made in the Caribbean (plus Bermuda
  and the Bahamas) D. L. McFadden. il
  Travel 134:53-9 S '70

Europe, Western
See it made in Europe. D. L. McFadden.
  il Travel 133:54-9+ Ap '70

France
Fans of the Napoleonic era. E. Oldham. il
  Antiques 97:135-9 Ja '70

Guatemala
Handcraft in Yucatán and Guatemala. E.
  Benson. il Craft Horiz 30:48-9+ My '70

ARTS and crafts—*Continued*

Ireland

Ireland. il Craft Horiz 30:20-7 My '70

Japan

See it made-in Japan. D. L. McFadden. il Travel 133:51-5 Je '70

Peru

Off the track in Cuzco, Peru; store to help Indian craftsmen. il Sunset 144:72 Mr '70

United States

Crafts and nature. S. McIlhany. Am Artist 34:5 F '70

Functionalism in Shaker crafts. E. M. Dodd. il Antiques 98:588-93 O '70

Indian influence in city decorating; furnishing apartments in New Mexico. H. Brown. il Am Home 73:70-1+ Mr '70

Lifestyle: crafts of New Mexico. il Am Home 73:12+ Mr '70

Old ways may be tomorrow's new ways; Pennsylvania Dutch crafts. il Org Gard & Farm 17:30-3 D '70

Try some: they're homemade. A. M. Cunningham. il Mlle 70:184-5+ Mr '70

See also

Museum of contemporary crafts, New York

Yucatan

Handcraft in Yucatán and Guatemala. E. Benson. il Craft Horiz 30:48-9+ My '70

ARTS and crafts, Indian. See Indians of North America—Industries

ARTS and crafts movement

New craftsmen. il Newsweek 75:72+ F 16 '70

ARTS and crafts trade. See Art trade

ARTS and crafts workshops. See Workshops

The ARTS and industry

New mission for business. G. A. Spater. il Sat R 53:29-31 F 28 '70

The ARTS and society

Who are the culturally deprived? J. B. Hightower. Sat R 53:41-2 Jl 18 '70

The ARTS and state

Agnes De Mille speaks to Congress on the state of the arts; address, with excerpts from testimony, February 9, 1970. A. De Mille. por Dance Mag 44:34-5+ My '70

America's stake in the arts. R. L. Stevens. il Sat R 53:18-21 F 28 '70

Editorial; Governor Rockefeller's appeal for additional funds. W. Como. il Dance Mag 44:29 Mr '70

Government and the arts. N. Hanks. Sat R 53:32 F 28 '70

See also

United States—National foundation on the arts and the humanities

ARTS centers, Community. See Community arts centers

ARTS education. See The Arts—Study and teaching

ARTS workers coalition

Art; artists protests. L. Alloway. Nation 211: 381-2 O 19 '70

ARTSAY, Aida Favia-. See Favia-Artsay, A.

ARTSIMOVICH, Lev Andreevich

Controlled nuclear fusion: energy for the distant future. il por Bul Atom Sci 26:47-55 Je '70

Studying physics at Moscow state university: adaptation of address, April 18, 1969. il por Phys Today 23:34-40 Ja '70

ARTUSO, Alfred A. and others

Madison plan really swings. il Todays Ed 59:14-17 N '70

ARVILLE Garland murder trial. See Trials (murder)

ASAKAWA, Takako

Brief biography. S. Goodman. il pors Dance Mag 45:66-7 Ja '71 *

ASARCO. See American smelting and refining company

ASBELL, Bernard

Helping children to grow up smart. il Redbook 135:34+ Jl '70

I don't know why I'm calling, nobody can help me. Redbook 135:53+ Je '70

ASBESTOS

Cancer threat greater than cigarettes? asbestos fibers. F. G. Loyd. il Todays Health 48: 30-1+ Jl '70

ASBURY, Barbara. See Galvin, H. R. jt. auth.

ASBURY college, Wilmore, Ky.

Asbury revival blazes cross-country trail. J. Nelson and J. Rohler. Chr Today 14:46+ Mr 13 '70

Revival at Asbury. J. Nelson. Chr Today 14: 36-7 F 27 '70

ASBURY PARK, N. J.

Riots

Across the tracks. il Newsweek 76:21-2 Jl 20 '70

Trouble across the tracks. il Time 96:13 Jl 20 '70

ASCENSION of Jesus Christ. See Jesus Christ —Resurrection and ascension

ASCETICISM

Desert hermits. A. J. Toynbee. il Horizon 12: 22-7 Spr '70

ASCH, Rosalie Lang

Designing playground equipment. il Sch Arts 69:16-17 Ap '70

Masks: linkage between cultures. il Sch Arts 69:20-1 Je '70

ASCHAFFENBURG, E. Lysle

New Orleans' Pontchartrain. G. Cotler. il por Holiday 47:54-7 Je '70 *

ASCHER, Amalie Adler

Traditional gladiolus arrangements. il Horticulture 48:38-9 S '70

ASCORBIC acid. See Vitamins—Vitamin C

ASCOT races. See Horse racing

ASEXUAL reproduction. See Reproduction, Asexual

ASGILL, Sir Charles

Melancholy case. A. L. Damon. il por Am Heritage 21:18-19+ F '70 *

ASH, Roy L.

How the White House got its new management tools; interview. il pors Nations Bsns 58:44-6 Ag '70

about

Recipe for a new bureaucracy. il por Bsns W p 118+ N 21 '70 *

ASH, Volcanic. See Volcanic ash, tuff, etc.

ASH council. See United States—President's advisory council on executive organization

ASH trays

Throw away ash trays. il Design 71:17 Spr '70

ASHANTI (native race) See Ghana—Native races

ASHBERY, John

Bell: virtuosity without self-interest. il pors Art N 68:44-5+ F '70

Johnson collection at Cranbrook. il Craft Horiz 30:34-9+ Mr '70

Miro's bronze age. il Art N 69:34-6 My '70

Place for everything. il por Art N 69:32-3+ Mr '70

Summer; poem. Harper 240:41 Ja '70

about

Insights and oversights in the poetic vision. J. W. Hughes. Sat R 53:34 Ag 8 '70 *

Sortes Vergilianae. R. Howard. Poetry 117: 50-3 O '70 *

ASHBROOK, Joseph

Astronomical scrapbook. See issues of Sky and telescope

Findings from Mercury's transit. il Sky & Tel 40:20-4 Jl '70

ASHBROOK, William

Eleven-day wonder. il Opera N 35:24-5 D 5 '70

ASHBY, Neal

Are you sure you don't have diabetes? il Mech Illus 66:42-4+ D '70

ASHDOWN, Ian E.

Multi-tone: guitarist's tone control. il Electr World 85:68-9 Ja '71

ASHE, Arthur, 1943-

Center court at Wimbledon. il pors Travel & Camera 33:48-53 My '70

about

No to Arthur Ashe. S. Uys. New Repub 162: 17-18 F 14 '70 *

Sports hero. il pors Harp Baz 103:110-13 My '70 *

ASHE, James

Amplified zener. il Radio-Electr 41:41-2 Je '70

Sine-sweep generator for R.F./I.F. testing. il Electr World 85:72-5 Ja '71

—and Eisenberg, John

Solid-state V.O.M. il Electr World 83:74-5 Ja '70

ASHER, Thomas R.

Lawyer looks at libraries and censorship; address, 1970. por Library J 95:3247-9 O 1 '70

ASHKENAZY, Vladimir

Musician of the month. H. Kupferberg. il por Hi Fi 20:secII 7+ My '70 *

ASHLAND, Ore, Shakespeare festival. See Shakespeare festivals

ASHLAND college, Ashland, Ohio

After show biz, slow biz; Ashland Eagles, the Nation's no. 1 basketball team. P. Carry. il Sports Illus 31:34-7 D 15 '69

ASHLEY, Nova Trimble
Knitwit; poem. Good H 171:10 N '70
ASHMOLEAN museum. See Oxford, England—
Galleries and museums
ASHTON, Sir Frederick
Dance magazine award, 1969. il por Dance
Mag 44:28-9+ My '70 *
In homage to Frederick Ashton; with editorial
comment. G. Anthony. il pors Dance Mag
44:64-9 Je '70 *
In honor of Sir Frederick. W. Terry. por Sat
R 53:33 Jl 4 '70 *
ASHTON, Paul
Health security program; medicine in the
free enterprise system; address, September
9, 1970. Vital Speeches 37:100-2 D 1 '70
ASIA
Asia in the decade of the seventies; ad-
dress, February 28, 1970. U. A. Johnson.
Dept State Bul 62:381-7 Mr 23 '70; Same.
Vital Speeches 36:386-9 Ap 15 '70
Asia on the move; a first-hand report. C.
S. Foltz, jr. il U S News 69:66-9 Ag 3 '70
What future for Asia? W. W. Rostow. Read
Digest 97:109-11 D '70
See also
Folklore—Asia
Hunting—Asia
Mongolia
Paul VI, pope—Visit to Asia and the Pacific
Region
Recreation—Asia
United Nations—Economic commission for
Asia and the Far East
United States—Armed forces—Forces in Asia

Defenses
Beyond Agnew mission; a U.S. plan for pull-
ing back from Asia. il U S News 69:18-19
Ag 31 '70
Lowering the U.S. profile throughout Asia.
il Time 97:20+ Ja 18 '71
Passing the buck to Tokyo. A. Axelbank.
Nation 211:293-5 O 5 '70

Description and travel
Exotic Asia; symposium. il Holiday 47:30-
49+ F '70
Up the Pacific-Orient; memos from seven
businessmen. il Esquire 74:100-5 Ag '70

Economic policy
Address by the Secretary-General at the
Assembly for one Asia; April 11, 1970. Thant.
UN Mo Chron 7:46-51 My '70

Foreign relations
Address by the Secretary-General at the
Assembly for one Asia; April 11, 1970.
Thant. UN Mo Chron 7:46-51 My '70
Asia and the prospects for world order; ad-
dress, April 1970. J. S. Clark. bibliog f
Ann Am Acad 390:27-37 Jl '70

United States
See United States—Foreign relations—
Asia
History
Bibliography
Articles and other books received; comp. by
H. Conroy. See issues of American historical
review
Articles and other books received; comp. by
C. Hobbs. See issues of American historical
review
Maps
Asia. Sr Schol 95:21 S 22 '69; 97:15 S 21 '70
Politics
Asia; hustle on the left, bustle on the right.
Sr Schol 97:14 S 21 '70
China, Russia and the United States; a Brit-
ish view. R. Scott. For Affairs 48:334-43
Ja '70
What price Asianization? il Newsweek 75:30+
Je 8 '70
See also
Balance of power
Roads
See Roads—Asia
ASIA, CENTRAL
See also
Afghanistan
ASIA, SOUTHEASTERN
See also
Airlines—Asia, Southeastern
Anti-Communist movements—Asia, South-
eastern
Asia, Southern
Cambodia
Communism—Asia, Southeastern

Dams—Asia, Southeastern
Ecology—Asia, Southeastern
Indochina
Petroleum—Asia, Southeastern

Defenses
Any answers must involve all of southeast
Asia. K. T. Young. il Life 68:40-1 My 8 '70
Down Under; new problems as U.S. Britain
shift roles; with interview with K. Holy-
oake, ed. by C. S. Foltz, jr. il U S News
69:20-1 Ag 31 '70
Hidden crisis in Asia. E. O. Reischauer. Read
Digest 96:77-81 F '70
Nixon doctrine. F. Lewis. Atlan 226:6+ N '70
Price of pullout; Asians' message to Agnew.
il U S News 69:29-30 S 7 '70
U.S. supports decisions taken at meeting of
Asian ministers; Department statement re-
garding communique, May 18, 1970. Dept
State Bul 62:710 Je 8 '70
What a Communist victory in Laos would
mean. il U S News 68:21 Mr 23 '70
Where reds begin to look like losers; report.
C. S. Foltz, jr. il U S News 68:29 Ap 27 '70
See also
Southeast Asia treaty organization

Description and travel
Twelve eyes on Asia. A. Rothstein. il Travel
& Camera 33:62-7 O '70

Foreign relations
United States
See United States—Foreign relations—
Asia, Southeastern

Politics
Eye for the dragon, by D. Bloodworth.
Review
Bsns W il p 12-14 O 17 '70. R. de Paolo
New multipolar balance in East Asia; im-
plications for United States policy; ad-
dress, April 1970, with questions and an-
swers. A. D. Barnett. Ann Am Acad 390:
73-86 Jl '70
Southeast Asia, 1970; symposium. bibliog f
il Cur Hist 59:321-61 D '70
Under Secretary Johnson interviewed for
Voice of America; July 17, 1970. U. A.
Johnson. Dept State Bul 63:188-93 Ag 17 '70
What price Asianization? il Newsweek 75:30+
Je 8 '70
ASIA, SOUTHERN

Foreign relations
Presence in southern Asia of outside powers;
address, April 1970, with questions and answers. W. H. Wriggins. Ann Am Acad
390:48-62 Jl '70

United States
See United States—Foreign relations—
Asia, Southern
ASIA, SOUTHWESTERN

Description and travel
Crawling through Southwest Asia. F. Chu.
il pors Esquire 73:94-6+ F '70
ASIAN art. See Art, Asian
ASIAN astrologers. See Astrologers
ASIAN dancing. See Dancing, Asian
ASIAN development bank
Board of governors of the Asian development
bank holds annual meeting at Seoul; state-
ment, April 10, 1970. D. M. Kennedy. Dept
State Bul 62:579-82 My 4 '70
President recommends contribution to Asian
special fund; message, February 25, 1970.
R. M. Nixon. Dept State Bul 62:397-8 Mr 23
'70
ASIAN highway. See Roads—Asia
ASIAN literature

Study and teaching
Many rivers reaching the one sea; Asian
literature in the high school. E. B. Stam-
bolian. bibliog f Engl J 59:27-30 Ja '70
ASIATIC cholera. See Cholera
ASIATIC-European airline services. See
Airlines—International sevices—European-
Asiatic
ASIMOV, Isaac
Fourth revolution. il Sat R 53:17-20 O 24 '70
Isaac Asimov explains; questions and an-
swers. See issues of Science digest
Story machine; drama; reprint. Plays 29:25-
34 My '70
Sun vanishes. il Look 34:68-70+ Mr 10 '70
ASINOF, Eliot
Peace suicides. Seventeen 29:174+ Mr '70

ASPARAGINASE
L-Asparaginase-deficient mutants of yeast. G. E. Jones and R. K. Mortimer. bibliog il Science 167:181-2 Ja 9 '70
L-asparaginase-induced immunosuppression: effects on antibody-forming cells and serum titers. A. K. Chakrabarty and H. Friedman. bibliog il Science 167:869-70 F 6 '70
Glycine inhibition of asparaginase. W. L. Ryan and H. C. Sornson. bibliog il Science 167:1512-13 Mr 13 '70

ASPARAGUS
Ornamental asparagus ferns, they're elegant and tough. il Sunset 145:138-9 Ag '70
ASPARTYLPHENYLALANINE methyl ester. See Sugar substitutes
ASPATURIAN, Vernon V.
Soviet aims in east Europe. bibliog f Cur Hist 59:206-11+ O '70
ASPEN, Colo.
Explosion in a boom town. R. Rapoport. il Sports Illus 33:26-7 S 14 '70

Politics and government
Still wild; Hunter Thompson's campaign for sheriff. Nation 211:516 N 23 '70
ASPEN film conference. See Moving picture industry—United States
ASPEN international design conference. See International design conference
ASPEN music festival. See Music festivals—Colorado
ASPEN systems corporation of Pittsburgh
Consulting the computer. il por Time 95:68 My 4 '70
ASPHALT driveways. See Driveways
ASPHALT pavements. See Pavements, Asphalt
ASPHYXIA
Cerebral hemorrhage in relation to birth asphyxia. W. F. Windle. bibliog il Science 167: 1000-2 F 13 '70
See also
Respiration, Artificial
ASPIC
Cold elegance. C. Claiborne. il N Y Times Mag p68-9 My 24 '70
ASPINALL commission. See United States—Public land law review commission
ASPIRATION level
Potential of sociology as a liberating curriculum; excerpt from Social science in the schools; ed. by I. Morrissett. R. Perrucci. bibliog Sch & Soc 98:478-9+ D '70
ASPIRIN
Acetylsalicylic acid: no chromosome damage in human leukocytes. I. Mauer and others. bibliog il Science 196:198-201 Jl 10 '70
Aspirin: intestinal damage in rats. D. A. Brodie and others. bibliog il Science 170: 183-5 O 9 '70
Dangerous common drugs. A. J. Snider. il Sci Digest 68:41-2 O '70
ASPY, David N.
How did he get there? Ed Digest 35:49 Ap '70
ASSAD, Hafez
Golan offensive. Newsweek 75:40-2 F 16 '70 *
ASSASSINATION
War on violence. R. Drinnon. bibliog il Wilson Lib Bul 45:68-77 S '70; Reply. J. Jamieson. 45:236 N '70
See also
Kennedy, J. F.—Assassination
Kennedy, R. F.—Assassination
Lincoln, Abraham—Assassination
ASSATEAGUE ISLAND
Assateague off season. R. Engh and J. Engh. il Travel 134:58-61+ N '70
ASSAULT and battery
When you get mugged; give up, shut up, pay up. I. Mothner. il Look 34:66-8 Ag 25 '70
ASSEMBLAGE. See Collage
ASSEMBLAGE (art)
How to explain pictures to a dead hare; work of J. Beuys. U. Meyer. il Art N 68:54-7+ Ja '70
Mythmaker; V. Boghosian's work. il Time 95:54 F 9 '70
Toward simplicity. R. R. Hillis. il Design 72: 26-8 Fall '70
Traveling ideas: Germany, England; new kind of international style. E. C. Baker. il Art N 69:38-40+ Sum '70
ASSEMBLIES, School. See School assemblies
ASSEMBLY, Right of
Go fight city hall. Newsweek 75:89 Je 8 '70
See also
Free speech
ASSEMBLY line methods
See also
Automobile factories

ASSEMBLY plants, Automobile. See Automobile factories
ASSES and mules
God save the mule; effect of mechanization on pack mules. G. Hallam. il Am For 76:4-5+ Ag '70
Mule. T. H. Savory. il Sci Am 223:102-9 D '70
ASSESSMENT of public schools. See Education—Evaluation
ASSETS, Liquid. See Liquidity (economics)
ASSISTANCE in emergencies
Cost of involvement; people in Chicago bar fail to help Mrs Robert Boyce. Newsweek 75:59 F 9 '70
Subway samaritan; experiments conducted by Columbia students. il Time 95:44 Ja 19 '70
ASSISTANT teachers. See Teachers aides
ASSOCIATED church press (organization)
Associated church press honors thirteen publications. Chr Cent 87:527 Ap 29 '70
Toward a Christian press association. Chr Cent 87:716 Je 10 '70
ASSOCIATED colleges at Claremont. See Claremont colleges, Calif.
ASSOCIATED milk producers, inc.
Dairy power. N. Reeder and D. Braun. il Farm J 94:28 O '70
ASSOCIATED press
Times square news; sign around the Allied chemical tower. New Yorker 46:20-2 Ag 1 '70
ASSOCIATION (biology) See Symbiosis
ASSOCIATION for computing machinery
Computers; display at twenty-fifth annual conference. New Yorker 46:33-4 S 12 '70
ASSOCIATION for social economics
New forms and old goals of social reform. B. L. Masse. America 123:272 O 10 '70
ASSOCIATION for supervision and curriculum development
ASCD holds world conference on education. Sr Schol 96:Schol Teach 7 My 4 '70
ASCD seeks curriculum renewal; annual meeting. D. L. Burleson. Sr Schol 96:Schol Teach 1 Ap 27 '70
ASSOCIATION for the integration of management
AIM aims blacks at executive suites. il Bsns W p34 Je 20 '70
ASSOCIATION for the study of Negro life and history
54th anniversary convention in Birmingham. il Negro Hist Bul 32:12-13 D '69
Paul Robeson receives Ira Aldridge award from history association. Negro Hist Bul 33:128 My '70
ASSOCIATION for tropical biology
Adaptive aspects of insular evolution; report of meeting. R. W. Matthews and J. R. Matthews. Science 167:909-10 F 6 '70
ASSOCIATION of American dance companies
AADC adds an A for activist; report on fourth annual conference, June 4-7, 1970. M. Marks. Dance Mag 44:83+ Ag '70
ASSOCIATION of American publishers
AAP asks withdrawal of review copies ruling. Pub W 198:36-7 S 7 '70
AAP emerges; newly federated organization meets in atmosphere charged by national issues; summaries of addresses. il Pub W 197:36-45 Je 1 '70
AAP establishes Minority manpower office. Pub W 198:45-6 S 14 '70
AAP proposes alternative to negative option ban. S. Wagner. Pub W 198:33 N 9 '70
ABPC, AEPI consolidate at joint annual meeting; with editorial comment. Pub W 197:33, 38 My 25 '70
ABPC-AEPI merger plan should stimulate new ideas. C. B. Grannis. Pub W 197:44 Mr 30 '70
ABPC and AEPI announce details of merger proposal, for vote at joint meeting. il Pub W 197:53-4 Ap 27 '70
New acronym: AAP. W. R. Eshelman. Wilson Lib Bul 44:990 Je '70
New voice on the international scene. W. B. Wiley. il por Pub W 198:pt2 158-9 S 21 '70
U.S. public education faces new factors for change. il Pub W 199:27-9 Ja 4 '71

Religious book publishing division
RBPD hears tips on success in children's books. Pub W 198:19 D 14 '70
ASSOCIATION of American railroads
Countdown for America's railroads; ASTRO recommendations; address, September 22, 1970. T. M. Goodfellow. Vital Speeches 37: 56-8 N 1 '70

ASSOCIATION of American university presses
Scholarly publishing lives (sort of); AAUP annual meeting; excerpts from addresses, with editorial comment. Pub W 198:34-8, 53 Jl 27 '70
ASSOCIATION of American university presses annual book show. See Book exhibits
ASSOCIATION of Boston urban priests. See Priests—Associations, institutions, etc.
ASSOCIATION of college and research libraries
See also
Choice (periodical)
ASSOCIATION of executive recruiting consultants
Headhunters lop one of their own. il por Bsns W p28-9 F 14 '70
ASSOCIATION of investment brokers
Rank-and-file brokers' revolt. il Bsns W p90-1 Ja 31 '70
ASSOCIATION of museum stores. See Museum store association
ASSOCIATION of nations. See United Nations
ASSOCIATION of research libraries
ARL Chicago meeting spotlights key issues. Library J 95:2052-3 Je 1 '70
ASSOCIATIONS, institutions, etc.
Freelance opportunities with associations. M. A. DeVries. Writers Digest 50:28-30+ S '70
Of organizations and democracy. Trans-Action 7:10+ Mr '70
See also
Citizens associations
Trade and professional associations
ASSYRO-Babylonian astronomy. See Astronomy, Assyro-Babylonian
ASSYRO-Babylonian literature
See also
Gilgamesh
ASTEROIDS
Asteroid masses and densities. il Sky & Tel 40:139-40 S '70
Asteroid vesta: spectral reflectivity and compositional implications. T. B. McCord and others. bibliog il Science 168:1445-7 Je 19 '70
Asteroids, a space menace. il Sci Digest 68: 73 S '70
Diversity of asteroids. Sci Am 223:46+ Ag '70
Expedition to Eros. il Time 95:45 Ja 26 '70
Geographos swings past earth. F. Pilcher and L. J. Boss. il R Pop Astron 63:11-13 Ag '69
Man on an asteroid? il Chem 43:26-7 My '70
Mission to an asteroid. H. Alfvén and G. Arrhenius. il Science 167:139-41 Ja 9 '70; Discussion. 167:1758; 170:1431-2 Mr 27, D 25 '70
Observing the asteroids. F. Pilcher. il R Pop Astron 63:23 Ag '69
Story of a lost planet: 155 Scylla. J. Ashbrook. il por Sky & Tel 40:361-2 D '70
ASTERS
See also
Fleabanes
ASTHMA
Asthma, the demon that thrives on myths; interview, ed. by B. Scott. E. F. Ellis. pors Todays Health 48:42-3+ Je '70
Pharmacological differentiation of allergic and classically conditioned asthma in the guinea pig. D. R. Justesen and others. bibliog il Science 170:864-6 N 20 '70
What hope for asthmatics? il Changing T 24:33-5 Ja '70
Would you believe these children have asthma? Children's asthma research institute and hospital. il Sci Digest 69:43-5 Ja '71
ASTILBES
Astilbes. A. R. Buckley. il Horticulture 48:38-9 Jl '70
ASTIN, Alexander W.
Should college applicants be selected by lottery? Science 167:1075-6 F 20 '70
ASTOR, Gerald
Good guys wear war paint. il Look 34:56-61 D 1 '70
Heart transplants do work. il por Look 34: 43-4+ D 29 '70
How I faced my son's drug arrest. Look 34: 87-8+ D 15 '70
My hands are free again. il Look 34:49-50 Jl 14 '70
Pied Piper of the new children's crusade. il por Look 34:36-8 Ag 25 '70
Who is a Jew? il pors Look 34:32-4 Je 16 '70
World's toughest air force: it keeps Israel alive. il Look 34:17-23 Je 30 '70
Your friendly neighborhood betting shop. il Look 34:54-6 Jl 28 '70
(ed) See Gorkin, L. Here is the latest radical plan
ASTROLITE. See Explosives

ASTROLOGERS
Dukuns, bomohs and gurus. il Time 96:31 N 9 '70
ASTROLOGY
Astrology-Rx for boredom? E. Scheimann. il Har Yrs 10:17-18 S '70
Astrology: something to conjure with? il Sr Schol 97:8-9 N 2 '70
Beating the Dow with sun power and the zodiac. il Bsns W p84-5 Ja 17 '70
Eye on the sky. X. Pové. See issues of Harper's bazaar
Feminine eye. S. Alexander. por McCalls 97:6 Mr '70
Holiday travel horoscope. il Holiday 47:13 Ja '70
Horoscope. M. E. Crummere. See issues of Vogue
Horoscopes (cont) S. Leek. Ladies Home J 86:41-2 D '69; 87:42-3 Ja; 30 F; 32+ Mr '70
Horoscopes. M. Woodruff. See issues of McCall's
1970 traveler's zodiac. C. Pepper. il Travel 133:57-9+ Ja '70
Not in the stars; proscriptions against the broadcast by radio and television stations of astrology material. P. Nathan. Pub W 198:41 Ag 24 '70
Revised zodiac. il Time 96:44 N 23 '70
Squinting at the stars of sport; horoscope in forecasting sports. J. Bruce. il Sports Illus 32:52-4+ Ja 19 '70
What a priest sees in astrology. R. F. Capon. por Redbook 135:63+ Ag '70
Your zodiac love chart. il Ladies Home J 87:80-1 Ag '70

Anecdotes, facetiae, satire, etc.
Afternoon with an astrologer: a predictable visit. B. Stine. Sr Schol 97:42 O 26 '70
Better boating with the stars. S. Parenteau. il Motor B 127:82-3 Ja '71
ASTRONAUTICS. See Space flight
ASTRONAUTS
Astronauts are human too. W. B. Furlong. il Todays Health 49:16-20+ Ja '71
Astronaut's mind. J. Walsh. il Esquire 74:123-7+ S '70
How Apollo 11 changed three famous men. G. Farmer. pors Life 69:50 Jl 17 '70
Making of an ex-astronaut, by B. O'Leary. Review
    Sat R 53:31-2 My 16 '70. J. Lear
Marshaling the good guys; R. M. Nixon's interest in the astronauts. H. Sidey. il Life 69:2B Ag 21 '70
Rebellion among the astronauts; excerpt from The making of an ex-astronaut. B. O'Leary. il por Ladies Home J 87:143-6 Mr '70
Roads of earth and space; impressions of Soviet cosmonauts on U.S. tour. K. Feoktistov. il por Space World G-3-75:38-9 Mr '70
16th annual Mr Travel award: Apollo 11 crew il Travel 134:54-7 Jl '70
See also
Space flight
Women as astronauts
also names of astronauts, e.g. A. I. Bean

Clothing
News from the world of space exploration; fluidic controller for modulating spacesuit temperatures. il Space World G-3-75:49-50 Mr '70
Particle track identification: application of a new technique to Apollo helmets. R. L. Fleischer and others. bibliog il Science 170: 1189-91 D 11 '70
Space suits for Project Apollo. il Space World G-7-79:10-11 Jl '70

Health and hygiene
Accommodations for living in space studied by NASA. Z. Strickland. il Aviation W 92: 61-2+ My 4 '70
Blastoff bloodbank. M. C. Leeds. Todays Health 49:21 Ja '71
Isolating the astronauts; preflight quarantine. Sci N 98:285 O 3 '70
News from the world of space exploration; Apollo crew health program. Space World H-1-85:47-8 Ja '71
See also
Space flight—Physiological aspects

Training
Alan Shepard gets set for the moon. L. Wainwright. il pors Life 69:48-50B+ Jl 31 '70
Astronauts get added training due to Apollo 14 mission delays. Z. Strickland. Aviation W 93:82-3+ N 16 '70

ASTRONAUTS—Training—*Continued*
NASA astronauts take a dive. il Space World G-10-82:4-6 O '70
Science in space; notes of an ex-astronaut. B. O'Leary. il Nation 210:522-6 My 4 '70

ASTRONAUTS as businessmen
Spacemen find business can be adventure, too. il Nations Bsns 58:80-3 Ap '70

ASTRONAUTS families
Joyous triumph of Apollo 13. il Life 68:28-36 Ap 24 '70

ASTRONOMERS
See also
Burnham, S. W.
Halley, E.
Slipher, V. M.
Vogel, E.

ASTRONOMERS, Amateur
Amateur astronomers. See issues of Sky and telescope
Amateurs in action. See issues of Review of popular astronomy to August 1969
Gleanings for ATM's; ed by R. E. Cox. See issues of Sky and telescope

ASTRONOMICAL conferences
Highlights from the Sacramento convention. il Sky & Tel 40:278-81 N '70
Notes on the 36th meeting at Stellafane. il Sky & Tel 40:219-20 O '70
Planetarium educators conference. N. Sperling. il Sky & Tel 41:7-9 Ja '71
Riverside telescope meeting. il Sky & Tel 40:28-30 Jl '70

ASTRONOMICAL distances
Extragalactic distance scale. il Sky & Tel 39:93-4 F '70
Lunar laser reflector. J. E. Faller and E. J. Wampler. il Sci Am 222:38-50 Mr '70
Stromatolites used to determine the time of nearest approach of earth and moon. M. R. Walter. bibliog Science 170:1331-2 D 18 '70

ASTRONOMICAL instruments
Josephson detectors make astronomical observations. G. B. Lubkin. il Phys Today 23:55-6 Ap '70
See also
Radio telescope
Spectrograph
Spectroscope
Telescopes

ASTRONOMICAL league
Astronomical league convenes in Rochester. P. A. Valleli. il Sky & Tel 40:149-51 S '70

ASTRONOMICAL models
Globular-cluster stars. I. Iben, jr. il Sci Am 223:26-39 bibliog(p 136) Jl '70

ASTRONOMICAL museums
Restoration at Greenwich observatory. D. Howse. il Sky & Tel 40:4-9 Jl '70

ASTRONOMICAL observations. See Astronomy —Observations

ASTRONOMICAL observatories
Amateur scientist; ambitious observatory is built by father and son. J. Wikswo and J. Wikswo, jr. il Sci Am 222:114-18+ Ap '70
Big Bear solar observatory. H. Zirin. il Sky & Tel 39:215-19 Ap '70
Garvey ranch observatory. J. P. Little. il R Pop Astron 63:28-9 Ag '69
Ten-inch Newtonian with counterpoised canopy. E. K. Owen. il Sky & Tel 40:169-**74 S '70**

Location
Observing sites in California. il Sky & Tel 40:206-7 O '70

Chile
Image-tube observatories at Cerro Tololo. M. F. Walker. bibliog il por Sky & Tel 40:132-8 S '70

Great Britain
Restoration at Greenwich observatory. D. Howse. il Sky & Tel 40:4-9 Jl '70
Visits to Stonehenge and Herstmonceux. il Sky & Tel 40:198-200 O '70

Hawaii
Hawaiian eye; Mauna Kea observatory. il Time 96:46-7 Jl 6 '70
Mauna Kee observatory dedicated. il Sky & Tel 40:276-7 N '70

Russia
Planetary astronomer visits the Soviet Union. D. P. Cruikshank. il Sky & Tel 39:76-9 F '70

ASTRONOMICAL photography
Astro-photography. See issues of Review of popular astronomy to August 1969
Automatic photography of eclipsing variables. G. O. Rawstron. il Sky & Tel 39:397-9 Je '70
Celestial photography with fiber-optics image tubes. P. W. Hodge. il Sky & Tel 39:234-5 Ap '70

Combining camera lenses for solar photography. A. Boyko. il Sky & Tel 39:134-5 F '70
Eclipse photography with a new color film. C. W. Wyckoff and P. R. Leavitt. il Sky & Tel 40:72-3 Ag '70
Far-ultraviolet photography of Orion: interstellar dust. R. C. Henry and G. R. Carruthers. bibliog il Science 170:527-31 O 30 '70
Hints on planetary photography for amateurs. R. B. Minton. il Sky & Tel 40:56-9, 116-18 Jl-Ag '70
Shadow bands and the March solar eclipse. A. T. Young. il Sky & Tel 40:176-81 S '70 (to be cont)
Techniques tomorrow; photographing the 1970 total solar eclipse. B. Sherman. il Mod Phot 34:62+ O '70
When the moon hides the sun, be ready. D. B. Eisendrath. il Pop Phot 66:14+ Mr '70

Apparatus and supplies
Hints on eclipse instrumentation for photography. R. E. Cox. il Sky & Tel 39:124-6 F '70
Hypersensitizing films for astrophotography. J. M. Santos. il Sky & Tel 40:322-3 N '70

ASTRONOMICAL photometry. See Photometry, Astronomical

ASTRONOMICAL research
See also
Astrophysics

ASTRONOMICAL societies
Oriental astronomical association meets in Kyoto. T. Sato. il Sky & Tel 40:363 D '70
See also names of astronomical societies, e.g. Astronomical league

ASTRONOMICAL spectroscopy
Composition of Saturn's rings. il Sky & Tel 39:14 Ja '70; Correction. 39:80 F '70
Formaldehyde absorption coefficients in the vacuum ultraviolet (650 to 1850 angstroms) E. P. Gentieu and J. E. Mentall. bibliog il Science 169:681-3 Ag 14 '70
Lunar spectral reflectivity (0.30 to 2.50 microns) and implications for remote mineralogical analysis. T. B. McCord and T. V. Johnson. bibliog il Science 169:855-8 Ag 28 '70
Microwave detection of thioformaldehyde. D. R. Johnson and F. X. Powell. bibliog il Science 169:679-80 Ag 14 '70
New technique for meteor study. il Sky & Tel 40:353-4 D '70
Search for the $1_{10} \leftarrow 1_{11}$ transition of interstellar thioformaldehyde. N. J. Evans, 2d. and others. bibliog il Science 169:680-1 Ag 14 '70
See also
Comets—Spectra
Stars—Constitution
Stars—Spectra

ASTRONOMICAL test instruments. See Testing instruments

ASTRONOMY
Astronomy. J. Stokley. See fourth issue of each month of Science news
See also
Asteroids
Astrology
Astrophysics
Comets
Computers—Astronomical use
Constellations
Ephemerides
Galaxies
Lasers—Astronomical use
Magellanic clouds
Meteorites
Meteors
Milky way
Nebulae
Occultations
Planets
Quasars
Radio astronomy
Rockets—Astronomical use
Satellites
Sky
Solar system
Space astronomy
Stars
Universe

Bibliography
Books and the sky. See issues of Sky & telescope

Charts, diagrams, etc.
Evening sky map for [month] See issues of Review of popular astronomy to August 1969
Exploring the heavens with the Society's new map. Nat Geog 138:194-5, sup (folded map) Ag '70

ASTRONOMY—Charts, diagrams, etc.—*Cont.*
Sky reporter. J. P. Wiley, jr. See issues of Natural history
Southern stars. See issues of Sky & telescope
Stars for [the month] See issues of Sky & telescope

History

S. W. Burnham's Lick and Yerkes years. J. Ashbrook. il Sky & Tel 39:363-4 Je '70
Some mathematical curiosities embedded in the solar system. M. Gardner. il Sci Am 222:108-12 Ap '70

Observations

Forms in the sky; using analogy in astronomy. C. A. Whitney. il por Natur Hist 79: 26-31 Ja '70
Image-tube observations at Cerro Tololo. M. F. Walker. bibliog il por Sky & Tel 40: 132-8 S '70
See also
Stars—Observations

Periodicals

New journals. J. T. Scott. bibliog Phys Today 23:54-5 Ag '70

Study and teaching

Artificial stars in a teaching laboratory; Glasgow university. D. Clarke. il Sky & Tel 39:295-7 My '70

Tables, etc.

Events of 1971 in the Graphic time table. il Sky & Tel 41:33-5 Ja '71
ASTRONOMY, Assyro-Babylonian
Earliest recorded eclipse. Sky & Tel 41:26 Ja '71
ASTRONOMY, Spherical and practical
See also
Azimuth
ASTRONOMY missions board. See United States—National aeronautics and space administration—Astronomy missions board
ASTROPHOTOGRAPHY. See Astronomical photography
ASTROPHYSICS
Chandrasekhar on scientists and society. H. Chandra. por Bul Atom Sci 26:11-14 N '70
Forms in the sky; using analogy in astronomy. C. A. Whitney. il por Natur Hist 79: 26-31 Ja '70
Gravity waves may come from black holes. D. E. Thomsen. il Sci N 98:480-1 D 26 '70
See also
Magnetic fields (cosmic physics)
Stars—Evolution
Universe
ASWAN HIGH DAM
Osman the efficient. il por Time 96:69 Jl 13 '70
ASYLUM, Right of
Coast guard explains: return of Simonas Kudirka. W. F. Buckely, jr. Nat R 22:1421 D 29 '70
Disobeying orders. Chr Today 15:28 Ja 1 '71
How Simas was returned; would-be defector Simonas Kudirka. Time 96:11 D 28 '70
Nightmare off Gay Head; case of rejected Lithuanian sailor, Simonas Kudirka. il Newsweek 76:46+ D 14 '70
No sanctuary for Simonas; case of would-be Soviet defector, Simonas Kudirka. Time 96: 21-2 D 14 '70
Soviet sailor seeks U.S. haven, but loses; case of Simas Kudirka. il U S News 69:30 D 14 '70
ASYMMETRY. See Symmetry (biology)
AT home; story. See Andrus, A.
AT the Boar's head; opera. See Holst, G.
AT the stroke of midnight; story. See Warner, S. T.
ATABRINE
Fluorescent labeling of chromosomal DNA: superiority of quinacrine mustard to quinacrine. T. Caspersson and others. bibliog Science 170:762 N 13 '70
Quinacrine: mechanisms of antimalarial action. K. Van Dyke and others. bibliog il Science 169:492-3 Jl 31 '70
ATATÜRK, Kamâl
In search of youth: a biographical quest. B. K. Walker. Horn Bk 46:319-22 Je '70 *
ATCHESON, Richard
Distant sound of flutes. il Holiday 47:32-7+ F '70
God, gurus and Gay guerrillas. il Holiday 47: 52-5+ Mr '70
Majorca: where European girls are. il Holiday 47:64-5+ Ja '70
Notes from the jealous generation. il Holiday 47:28-31 Je '70
ATHANS, Sister Christine
Nun to head corporate ministry in Phoenix. M. H. Walling. Chr Cent 87:902 Jl 22 '70 *

ATHEISM
Can atheists be parents? case of John and Cynthia Burke of Newark, N.J. Time 96: 71 D 7 '70
God in exile, by C. Fabro. Review
Cath World 21:34-5 Ap '70. E. L. Donahue
ATHENAGORAS I, patriarch
Succession to Easter Orthodox patriarchy, a problem in Turkey. L. Hansen. Chr Cent 87:547 Ap 29 '70 *
ATHENS, Greece
Antiquities
Porch from which Paul preached? Chr Today 14:34 Jl 31 '70
Site of Socrates' trial; stoa of the Basileus. il Time 96:46 Jl 6 '70
ATHEROSCLEROSIS. See Arteriosclerosis
ATHERTON, Pauline
LEEP at Syracuse: School of library science. J. A. McCrossan. Am Lib 1:493-4 My '70 *
ATHLETES
Big jocks; American professionals of the past. il Esquire 73:124-9 Ap '70
Coming revolt of the athletes; J. Scott and college athletics. L. Shecter. il pors Look 34:43-7 Jl 28 '70
Jack Armstrong is dead. F. G. Loyd. Todays Health 48:47-8+ O '70
Sports heros; with comment by G. Guinness. il Harp Baz 103:101-29 My '70
Success is a journey. W. F. Russell. il pors Sports Illus 32:80-2+ Je 8 '70
Who's next? pictorial review of sports in 1970. il Sports Illus 33:44-69 D 21 '70
See also
Amateurism (sports)
Baseball players
Basketball players
Clothing and dress—Athletes
Football players
Sports hall of fame
Women as athletes
Ethics
See also
Baseball players—Ethics
Religion
See also
Sports—Religious aspects
ATHLETES wives
Exasperating art of living with big-time athlete. K. D. Fury. il Redbook 135:76-7+ My '70
ATHLETIC clubs
Charged Atoms; Brooklyn's mostly black Atoms track club for women. il Newsweek 76:42 Jl 20 '70
Clancy's gym is Danny's turf; sparring partner for big name fighters. H. Aronson. il pors Sports Illus 32:40-4 Mr 23 '70
ATHLETICS
See also
College athletics
Fencing
Football
Olympic games
Running
School athletics
Sports
Sportsmanship
Track athletics
Wrestling
ATHLETICS (baseball) See Baseball clubs
ATHOS, Anthony G.
Is the corporation next to fall? bibliog f il Harvard Bsns R 48:49-61 Ja '70
ATKIN, John
Traditional cruising boats. il por Motor B 125:94-5 Ja '70
ATKINS, Neil P.
What do they want? Ed Digest 35:19-21 My '70
ATKINSON, Brooks
Biscayne Bay. il Audubon 72:36-46+ S '70
Flagwaving. New Repub 162:13-14 F 14 '70
Many worlds of Joseph Wood Krutch. il por Sat R 53:17 Jl 25 '70
ATKINSON, Carroll
Introducing students to psychology. Sch & Soc 98:164-5 Mr '70
ATKINSON, P. W. and Gilby, A. R.
Autoxidation of insect lipids: inhibition on the cuticle of the American cockroach. bibliog Science 168:992 My 22 '70
ATKINSON, Robert E.
Gardener's almanac; ed. by E. Haraszty. il McCalls 97:70-1+ My; 44+ Je; 48+ Jl; 24+ Ag; 26+ S; 98:50+ O; 33+ N; 21+ D '70; 44 Ja '71
ATKINSON, Ti-Grace
Four of a kind, yet different. pors Newsweek 75:72-3 Mr 23 '70 *

ATLANTA
Metro forestry in Atlanta: tree power. A. R. Shirley. il Am For 76:8-11+ O '70

Banks

Atlanta banker with a social conscience: Citizens & Southern national bank. il por Bsns W p34+ Jl 25 '70

Crime

Ultimate hustle; guests robbed at home of G. Williams. Newsweek 76:31 N 9 '70

Description

Traveltips. Schol Teach Jr/Sr High p37-8 N 2 '70

Education

At once; desegregation protest. il Newsweek 75:15 Ja 26 '70
Year-round schooling: how it really works. J. Barnes. por Parents Mag 45:42 My '70

Elections

Shooting an elephant; 1969 mayoralty election. R. Cleghorn. Nation 210:358-61 Mr 30 '70

Employees

See also
Atlanta—Strikes

Institute of the black world

Think tank for black scholars. A. Poinsett. il por Ebony 25:46-8+ F '70

Monuments, statues, etc.

Peachtree center acquires new sculpture; work by C. O. Perry. il Design 72:38-9 Wint '70

Negroes

Growing up liberal in Atlanta. I. Allen, jr. il por N Y Times Mag p4-5+ D 27 '70

Politics and government

See also
Atlanta—Elections

Strikes

Siege of Atlanta; garbagemen's strike. Newsweek 75:61 Ap 6 '70
Strike troubles pile up for cities and states. il U S News 68:70 Ap 6 '70

ATLANTA ballet
Atlanta ballet in dance repertoire, 1970, Symphony hall, Atlanta. D. Hering. Dance Mag 44:95-8 My '70

ATLANTA Hawks (basketball team) See Basketball teams

ATLANTA public library
John Ferguson, outreach librarian. il pors Wilson Lib Bul 45:424-5 D '70
Obscenity and pornography statement further justified. J. F. Krug and J. A. Harvey. Am Lib 1:752 S '70
Of note: policy on investigations by IRS and other law enforcement agencies. Am Lib 1:729 S '70

ATLANTIC (periodical)
Atlantic makes waves. il Time 96:73-4 O 12 '70

ATLANTIC alliance. See NATO

ATLANTIC CITY
Dowager's decline. il Newsweek 75:86-7 Je 8 '70

Hotels, restaurants, etc.

Return of a $1 guest; sale of the Ambassador hotel. por Newsweek 76:89 N 16 '70

ATLANTIC college. See Schools—Wales

ATLANTIC community
Atlantic community; symposium. Cur Hist 58:257-303+ My '70

ATLANTIC community development group for Latin America
Company that nurtures Latin business. Bsns W p64+ Jl 11 '70

ATLANTIC continental shelf. See Continental shelf

ATLANTIC fleet weapons range. See Bombing and gunnery ranges

ATLANTIC OCEAN
Crustal plates in the central Atlantic. M. M. Ball and C. G. A. Harrison. bibliog il Science 167:1128-9 F 20 '70
Layered basic complex in oceanic crust, Romanche fracture, equatorial Atlantic Ocean. W. G. Melson and G. Thompson. bibliog il Science 168:817-20 My 15 '70
Probing the Atlantic's past. il Sci N 98:460 D 19 '70
See also
Baltic Sea
Gulf Stream
Jamaica Bay
North Sea

ATLANTIC salmon. See Salmon

ATLANTIS (airline) See Airlines—Germany (Federal Republic)

ATLAS, James
Death of Attila József; poem. Poetry 117:98-9 N '70
Lighting the lamps; poem. New Yorker 45:30 F 7 '70

ATLAS cedar. See Cedar

ATMOSPHERE
Stratospheric ozone with added water vapor: influence of high-altitude aircraft. H. Harrison. bibliog il Science 170:734-6 N 13 '70
See also
Fog
Meteorology
Sun—Atmosphere
Winds

ATMOSPHERE, Upper
Auroral-particle precipitation and trapping caused by electrostatic double layers in the ionosphere. R. D. Albert and P. J. Lindstrom. bibliog il Science 170:1398-401 D 25 '70
Upper atmosphere as seen from Antarctica. R. A. Helliwell. il por Bul Atom Sci 26:55-61 D '70
See also
Rockets—Meteorological use

ATMOSPHERE explorer satellite. See Artificial satellites—Meteorological use

ATMOSPHERE-ocean Interaction. See Ocean-atmosphere interaction

ATMOSPHERIC aerosols. See Aerosols

ATMOSPHERIC dust. See Dust

ATMOSPHERIC electricity
See also
Auroras
Thunderstorms

ATMOSPHERIC microorganisms. See Air microbiology

ATMOSPHERIC nucleation
Condensation nuclei: production of very large numbers in country air. V. J. Schaefer. bibliog Science 170:851-2 N 20 '70

ATMOSPHERIC oxygen. See Oxygen

ATMOSPHERIC pollution. See Air pollution

ATMOSPHERIC pressure
See also
Airplanes—Pressurization

ATMOSPHERIC research
Atmosphere: a clouded horizon. E. K. Peterson. il Environ 12:32-9 Ap '70; Reply with rejoinder. L. Van Valen. 12:39, 44-5 D '70
Atmospheric absorption anomalies in the ultraviolet near an altitude of fifty kilometers. A. J. Krueger; reply. J. F. Noxon. Science 168:1120-1 My 29 '70
Atmospheric photochemistry. R. D. Cadle and E. R. Allen. bibliog il Science 167:243-9 Ja 16 '70
Polar ice and the global climate machine. J. O. Fletcher. il por Bul Atom Sci 26:40-7 D '70
Supercivilized weather and sky show. H. Lansford. il Natur Hist 79:92-7+ bibliog (p 133) Ag '70
Tracers in the air. A. K. Blackadar and J. A. Dutton. Weatherwise 23:182-5 Ag '70
Wonder of the sky. J. A. Dutton. il por Weatherwise 23:109-11+ Je '70
See also
National center for atmospheric research
Polar research

ATMOSPHERIC temperature
See also
Flying saucers

ATMOSPHERIC turbulence
Clear air turbulence; a mystery may be unfolding. J. A. Dutton and H. A. Panofsky. bibliog il Science 167:937-44 F 13 '70; Reply. R. C. Wanta. 168:607 My 1 '70
Electronics goes CAT catching. W. Garrison. il Pop Electr 33:29-34 N '70
FAA vortex concern mounting. il Aviation W 92:31 My 25 '70
Fighting the CAT that threatens you from a clear blue sky. K. J. Scribner. il por Pop Sci 196:60-3 My '70
Lasers studied as turbulence detector. il Aviation W 93:86+ Jl 13 '70
Latest CAT incident increases concern. Aviation W 93:31 N 16 '70
Mobilizing a search for invisible signs in the sky. E. Gross. il Sci N 97:134-5 Ja 31 '70
NASA studying vortex, slow flight areas. R. G. O'Lone. il Aviation W 93:61+ S 21 '70
On top; wake turbulence. R. L. Collins. Flying 86:28-30 Je '70

ATMOSPHERIC turbulence—*Continued*
Search for ways to tame turbulence. il Bsns W
p 136 F 21 '70
Tests of 747 wake accelerated. Aviation W 92:
25-6 F 23 '70
Your traffic is a KB-50... L. A. Prosch. il
Flying 86:94+ Je '70

ATOMIC age
Modern man is obsolete; excerpts; reprint.
Sat R 53:16-18+ Ag 1 '70
Now we are all sons-of-bitches; birth of the
atomic age, July 16, 1945. W. L. Laurence.
il por Sci N 98:39-41 Jl 11 '70
Segrè and Heisenberg: genesis of the atomic
age. E. Segrè; W. Heisenberg. il por Bul
Atom Sci 26:32-9 N '70

ATOMIC blasting
A-blast for gas; Colorado controversy. Sr
Schol 95:20 S 29 '69
Hopes dim for a second canal. il Sci N 97:
363-5 Ap 11 '70
How I learned to live with radioactivity and
love it, in Colorado. S. Gascoyne. Common-
weal 92:7-9 Mr 13 '70
Plowshare at the crossroads. G. W. Johnson.
il por Bul Atom Sci 26:83-91 Je '70
Plowshare: struggling to live. il Sci N 97:89-
90 Ja 24 '70
Project Gasbuggy and catch-85. P. Metzger.
il N Y Times Mag p26-7+ F 22 '70
Underground nuclear testing. il Environ 11:
3-13+ Jl '69; Reply. J. T. Ramey. 11:34-5
S '69
U.S., U.S.S.R. hold talks at Moscow on peaceful uses of nuclear explosions, joint communique, February 20, 1970. Dept State
Bul 62:343-4 Mr 16 '70
Will nuclear blasts boost gas supplies? Project Rulison. il Bsns W p21-2 Ag 1 '70

ATOMIC bomb casualty commission
Hiroshima/Nagasaki: ABCC perseveres in
sensitive studies. P. M. Boffey. il Science
168:679-83 My 8 '70

ATOMIC bomb shelters
Entire town in one obsolete missile site;
Lawn, Tex. J. Zachry. il Am City 85:87
Jl '70
Remember bomb shelters? R. Bongartz. Es-
quire 73:130+ My '70
Whatever happened to the program for fall-
out shelters? il U S News 68:10 Mr 2 '70

ATOMIC bombs
Bombs or reactors? L. Fermi. por Bul Atom
Sci 26:28-9 Je '70
See also
Hydrogen bombs

Ethical aspects
See Atomic warfare—Ethical aspects

History
Atomic anniversary. il Time 96:10 Jl 20 '70
Manhattan project: a mighty thunder. il Sr
Schol 96:6-7 My 11 '70
Now we are all sons-of-bitches; birth of the
atomic age, July 16, 1945. W. L. Laurence.
il por Sci N 98:39-41 Jl 11 '70
Projection and recollection; symposium. il Bul
Atom Sci 26:7-34 Je '70
Trinity+twenty-five years; symposium. il Bul
Atom Sci 26:2-116 Je '70
Twenty five years ago two cities two bombs.
il Life 69:30-1 Jl 31 '70
Twenty-five years of the A-bomb, and how
it changed the world. il Sr Schol 96:3-8 My
11 '70

Physiological effects
See Radioactivity—Physiological effects

Testing
Poisonous mushrooms. il UNESCO Courier 23:
6-7 N '70

Testing, Detection of
Comprehensive test ban; report of SIPRI con-
ference. Environ 11:45 Jl '69
Rerun on Amchitka; cannikan test. il Sci
N 97:367-8 Ap 11 '70

Testing, Underground
Nuclear explosions and distant earthquakes;
a search for correlations. J. H. Healy and
P. A. Marshall. bibliog il Science 169:176-7
Jl 10 '70
Resolution on impending test on Amchitka
Island. Liv Wildn 33:33-4 Aut '69
Underground nuclear explosions and the con-
trol of earthquakes. C. Emiliani and others;
discussion. bibliog il Science 167:1011-14 F
13 '70
Underground nuclear testing. il Environ 11:
3-13+ Jl '69; Reply. J. T. Ramey. 11:34-5
S '69

ATOMIC clocks
Cesium-beam atomic clock. V. Philibert. il
Electr World 83:40-1+ Je '70

ATOMIC energy. See Atomic power

ATOMIC energy agency. See International
atomic energy agency

ATOMIC energy commission. See United
States—Atomic energy commission

ATOMIC fuels. See Nuclear fuels

ATOMIC industrial forum
Bridging the gap; address, February 5, 1970.
H. G. Slater. Vital Speeches 36:399-402
Ap 15 '70

ATOMIC industries. See Atomic power industry

ATOMIC medicine
Nuclear physics in medicine. G. L. Brown-
ell and R. J. Shalek. bibliog il pors Phys
Today 23:32-6+ Ag '70
See also
Radioisotopes—Medical use

ATOMIC nuclei
See also
Nuclear physics

Energy levels
See Energy levels (quantum mechanics)

Fission
See Nuclear fission

Fusion
See Nuclear fusion

ATOMIC orbitals
Exploring G and H orbitals by computer. G.
G. Schlessinger. il Chem 43:22-4 Mr '70

ATOMIC pacemaker. See Pacemaker, Artificial
(heart)

ATOMIC physics. See Nuclear physics

ATOMIC power
Power and fuel resources. R. W. Holcomb.
Cur Hist 58:330-6+ Je '70
See also
Nuclear fusion
Nuclear reactors
Underdeveloped areas—Atomic power

Economic aspects
Bombs or reactors? L. Fermi. por Bul Atom
Sci 26:28-9 Je '70
Fostering international cooperation in peace-
ful uses of atomic energy; statement,
November 28, 1969. W. B. Buffum. Dept
State Bul 61:637-40 D 29 '69
International challenge; adaptation of address,
August 10, 1970. G. T. Seaborg. Bul Atom Sci
26:5-7 N '70
Nuclear energy and the environment. A. M.
Weinberg. il por Bul Atom Sci 26:69-74 Je '70
See also
Atomic blasting
Atomic power industry
Atomic power plants

International aspects
In the wake of Mao's moon. il Time 95:44+
My 11 '70
International atom; symposium. il Bul Atom
Sci 26:35-68+ Je '70
See also
International atomic energy agency

Medical use
See Atomic medicine

Social aspects
Bottleneck for the nuclear genie. il Bsns W
p50 D 5 '70
Nuclear energy and the environment. A. M.
Weinberg. il por Bul Atom Sci 26:69-74
Je '70
See also
Atomic age

Canada
Light on heavy water. Sci N 98:58 Jl 25 '70

Europe, Western
Atomic energy in continental western Europe. J. Gueron. il por Bul Atom Sci 26:62-
8+ Je '70

Great Britain
Britain in the atomic age. R. E. Peierls. il
por Bul Atom Sci 26:40-6 Je '70

India
India contemplates the bomb. G. H. Quester.
Bul Atom Sci 26:13-16+ Ja '70
Progress in nuclear technology. S. K.
Ghaswala. il Sci N 97:444 My 2 '70

ATOMIC power—*Continued*

Japan

Japan and the NPT. S. Griffin. Sci N 97:184 F 14 '70

Japan and the nuclear age. R. Imai. il por Bul Atom Sci 26:35-9 Je '70

South Africa

Puzzle from South Africa. Sci N 98:135 Ag 15 '70

South Africa: how valid the claim for a uranium process? D. S. Greenberg. Science 169:563 Ag 7 '70

United States

See Atomic power

ATOMIC power industry

Energy for tomorrow; coordinated planning; address, September 22, 1970. W. E. Johnson. Vital Speeches 37:29-32 O 15 '70

Europe plots assault on a U.S. monopoly; reactor fuel market. Bsns W p30 Mr 14 '70

Nuclear controversy; address, November 16, 1970. S. R. Knapp. Vital Speeches 37:145-9 D 15 '70

Nuclear power: rise of an industry. E. Creutz. il por Bul Atom Sci 26:75-82 Je '70

See also

CNA nuclear leasing (firm)

Public relations

Bridging the gap; address, February 5, 1970. H. G. Slater. Vital Speeches 36:399-402 Ap 15 '70

Europe, Western

Westinghouse starts over, over there; Westinghouse electric nuclear energy systems Europe. Bsns W p34-5 D 5 '70

Westinghouse worries the French again. Fortune 82:45 D '70

ATOMIC power plants

Bottleneck for the nuclear genie. il Bsns W p50 D 5 '70

Can our rivers stand the heat? W. Langewiesche. Read Digest 96:76-80 Ap '70

Con Ed loses its nuclear punch. Bsns W p 19 Jl 4 '70

Energy for man and environmental protection. P. Sporn; discussion. Science 166:1459-60+; 167:1439 D 19 '69, Mr 13 '70

Glutton for punishment; GPU's Oyster Creek plant. il Forbes 105:34 F 15 '70

Heat waste; study of Turkey Point plant's effect on Biscayne Bay. B. Stearns. il Sea Front 16:154-63 My '70

New river; sixteen nuclear power plants on the Great Lakes. il Environ 12:36-40 Ja '70

Nuclear energy: benefits versus risks. W. H. Jordan. bibliog il por Phys Today 23:32-8 My '70; Discussion. 23:104 My; 9-11 Jl; 9+ S; 9+ N '70

Nuclear power and thermal pollution: Zion, Illinois. P. F. Gustafson. il Bul Atom Sci 26:17-23 Mr '70

Patient earth; excerpts. ed. by J. Harte and R. Socolow. il Phys Today 23:28-9 D '70

Pollution problems, resource policy, and the scientist. A. W. Eipper. bibliog Science 169:11-15 Jl 3 '70

Power generation: the next thirty years. R. W. Holcomb. Science 167:159-60 Ja 9 '70

Tempest in a nuclear teapot; thermal pollution. F. Graham, jr. il Audubon 72:12-19 Mr '70

See also

Nuclear reactors

Radioactive waste disposal

Accidents and injuries

Catch 24,400; or, Plutonium is my favorite element; fire at Rocky Flats plant. R. Rapoport. il Ramp Mag 8:16-21 My '70

Muckuppery along the Potomac. R. Bongartz. Esquire 73:70+ Je '70

Location

Atom as pollutant. il Newsweek 75:56-7 F 16 '70

Bananas in Vermont. R. M. Klein. il Natur Hist 79:10-12+ bibliog(p82) F; 10-12 Mr '70; Reply. S. E. Beall, jr. 79:8 My '70

Enlightenment strikes a utility. il Bsns W p 142+ Mr 28 '70

Nuclear power plant locations, 1970; map. Sr Schol 96:Schol Teach 4 My 11 '70

Statement of concern; possible effects of nuclear power plant on Chesapeake Bay. E. Radford and others. bibliog il Environ 11:18-27 S '69

Water and air; proposed plant at Shoreham, NY. H. G. Paster. il New Repub 163:24-6 O 31 '70

Regulation

Question of jurisdiction; federal vs. state control. il Sci N 97:406 Ap 25 '70

ATOMIC power plants (space vehicles)   See Space vehicles—Atomic power plants

ATOMIC radiation. See Radioactivity

ATOMIC research

Application and research; symposium. il Bul Atom Sci 26:69-98 Je '70

Open arms research: defroster for the cold war? pro and con discussion. Sr Schol 96:9-10 My 11 '70

See also

Accelerators (electrons, etc)

Hanford works, Richland, Wash.

Europe, Western

See also

European organization for nuclear research

Great Britain

See also

Great Britain—Atomic energy authority

India

India contemplates the bomb. G. H. Quester. Bul Atom Sci 26:13-16+ Ja '70

India's nuclear policy of three negatives. H. R. Vohra. il Bul Atom Sci 26:25-7 Ap '70

United States

See Atomic research

ATOMIC research laboratories

Los Alamos: focus of an age. A. K. Smith. il por Bul Atom Sci 26:15-20 Je '70

Los Alamos: from weapon shop to scientific laboratory. C. I. Mitchell. il Bul Atom Sci 26:24-7 N '70

See also

Brookhaven national laboratory

California. University—Lawrence radiation laboratories

ATOMIC storage batteries. See Storage batteries

ATOMIC submarines. See Submarine boats, Atomic powered

ATOMIC theory

Early views on forces between atoms. L. Holliday. il Sci Am 222:116-22 bibliog(p 148) My '70

ATOMIC warfare

Defenses

Amendment to U.S.-U.K. atomic energy agreement transmitted to the Congress, message, January 26, 1970. R. M. Nixon. Dept State Bul 62:361 Mr 16 '70

Arms race, escalation of total madness. P. Noel-Baker. il UNESCO Courier 23:4-5+ N '70

New nuclear strategy for America? il U S News 68:32-4 Ap 13 '70

See also

Civil defense

United States—Defenses

Ethical aspects

Arms race, escalation of total madness. P. Noel-Baker. il UNESCO Courier 23:4-5+ N '70

Conscience of a physicist. R. R. Wilson. il por Bul Atom Sci 26:30-4 Je '70

What hath man wrought! twenty-five years after; reprint. D. Lawrence. U S News 69:96+ Ag 17 '70

Psychological aspects

False God; excerpt from Boundaries: psychological man in revolution. R. J. Lifton. Atlan 226:104-6+ O '70

ATOMIC warfare, Prevention of. See War, Prevention of

ATOMIC warfare and society

Misconceptions concerning nuclear weapons. B. N. Cantrell. Chr Cent 87:1219-20 O 14 '70

ATOMIC waste. See Radioactive waste disposal

ATOMIC weapons

Great weapons heresy, by T. W. Wilson, jr. Review

Life 68:12 F 27 '70. R. E. Lapp

Military atom. H. A. Bethe; R. E. Lapp; D. H. Frisch. il Bul Atom Sci 26:99-115 Je '70

Nuclear weapons for U.N? W. W. Watson. Bul Atom Sci 26:48 Mr '70

Nuclear weapons over the Middle East? Israel's probable capacity for making and delivering a nuclear bomb. M. Lerner. Cur 121:57-9 S '70

Pax atomica. J. Burnham. Nat R 22:729 Jl 14 '70

ATOMIC weapons—*Continued*
Personal view of the arms race: address,
June 1969. H. F. York. Bul Atom Sci 26:
27-31 Mr '70
Worry about atomic bases. il U S News 68:
68 Mr 16 '70

Accidents
Muckuppery along the Potomac. R. Bongartz. Esquire 73:70+ Je '70
So far, so good. M. Leitenberg. bibliog il Environ 12:26-35 Jl '70

History
Nuclear weapons: past and present. R. E.
Lapp. por Bul Atom Sci 26:103-6 Je '70

International control
Arms race, escalation of total madness. P.
Noel-Baker. il UNESCO Courier 23:4-5+ N
'70
Federal Republic of Germany signs nuclear
nonproliferation treaty; statement, Novem-
ber 28, 1969. W. P. Rogers. Dept State Bul
61:545 D 15 '69
Geneva disarmament conference agrees on
text of treaty banning emplacement of
nuclear weapons on the seabed; statement,
September 1, 1970; with revised draft treaty.
J. F. Leonard. Dept State Bul 63:362-6 S
28 '70
India's nuclear policy of three negatives.
H. R. Vohra. il Bul Atom Sci 26:25-7
Ap '70
Japan and the NPT. S. Griffin. Sci N 97:184
F 14 '70
Japan is 94th nation to sign nuclear non-
proliferation treaty; exchange of remarks,
February 3, 1970. T. Shimado; W. P. Rogers.
Dept State Bul 62:228-9 Mr 2 '70
Notes on the proliferation non-treaty. L
Ponte. il Nat R 22:1340-3+ D 15 '70
Nuclear bombs for everybody: a new worry
at Helsinki. il U S News 69:61-3 D 14 '70
Nuclear China and U.S. arms policy. A. D.
Barnett. For Affairs 48:427-42 Ap '70
Nuclear proliferation and security. J. P. De
Gara. bibliog f il por Int Concil 578:5-69
My '70
Nuclear treaty ratified. America 122:290-1 Mr
21 '70
Open arms research: defroster for the cold
war? pro and con discussion. Sr Schol 96:
9-10 My 11 '70
Paris, Pretoria, Peking. . . proliferation? G.
H. Quester. Bul Atom Sci 26:12-16 O '70
President Nixon ratifies nuclear nonprolifera-
tion treaty; remarks, November 24, 1969.
R. M. Nixon; W. P. Rogers. Dept State
Bul 61:544-5 D 15 '69
Treaty on the nonproliferation of nuclear
weapons enters into force; remarks, March
5, 1970. W. P. Rogers; J. R. Stevenson; R.
M. Nixon. Dept State Bul 62:410-12 Mr 30
'70
United States and U.S.S.R. table revised draft
treaty banning emplacement of nuclear
weapons on the seabed; statement, April
23, 1970, with text of the revised draft
treaty. J. F. Leonard. Dept State Bul 62:
663-7 My 25 '70
U.S. discusses progress in arms control;
statement, November 17, 1969. C. W. Yost.
Dept State Bul 61:600-7 D 22 '69

ATOMIC weapons and disarmament
Against a common fate. S. Chase. il Bul
Atom Sci 26:9-10 My '70
Arms control: current prospects and prob-
lems. J. B. Wiesner. il Bul Atom Sci 26:
6-8+My '70
Disarmament problems. H. A. Bethe. por Bul
Atom Sci 26:99-102 Je '70
Issues of thermonuclear war termination; ex-
cerpts from War termination, issues and
concepts. H. Kahn. bibliog f il Ann Am
Acad 392:133-72 N '70
Misconceptions concerning nuclear weapons.
B. N. Cantrell. Chr Cent 87:1219-20 O 14
'70
Nixon and the arms race. New Repub 162:
9-10 Ap 18 '70
No time to slack off on arms control. H. L.
Davis. Phys Today 23:92 Jl '70
Nuclear proliferation and security. J. P. De
Gara. bibliog f il por Int Concil 578:5-69 My
'70
Personal view of the arms race; address,
June 1969. H. F. York. Bul Atom Sci 26:
27-31 Mr '70
President asks Senate approval of proto-
col 11 to Treaty for the prohibition of
nuclear weapons in Latin America; text of
message, and Secretary Rogers' report, with
additional protocol 11 and proposed U.S.
statement. R. M. Nixon; W. P. Rogers.
Dept State Bul 63:305-9 S 14 '70

Proposed unilateral disarmament step. E. Tel-
ler. Cur 119:63-4 Je '70
Scientist's role in arms control. B. T. Feld.
Bul Atom Sci 26:7-8+ Ja '70
Small bombs and big bombs. N. Cousins. Sat
R 53:22 Je 27 '70
Verification of nuclear arms limitations: an
analysis. H. Scoville, jr. Bul Atom Sci 26:
6-11 O '70
See also
Strategic arms limitation talks

ATOMIC weights
1969 table of atomic weights. E. Wichers and
H. S. Peiser. il Chem 43:38-41 Jl '70

ATOMIC wood. See Wood, Irradiated

ATOMISM
Early views on forces between atoms. L.
Holliday. il Sci Am 222:116-22 bibliog(p 148)
My '70

ATOMS
Atom revealed; University of Chicago
physicists photograph individual atoms. il
Newsweek 75:63 Je 1 '70
Building exotic atoms. D. E. Thomsen. il Sci
N 98:385-6 N 14 '70
Exotic atoms. Sci Am 223:45 N '70
Individual atoms photographed. A. Crewe. il
Sci N 97:524 My 30 '70
Photo of single atoms by electron microscope.
G. B. Lubkin. Phys Today 23:41-2 Ag '70
Visibility of single atoms. A. V. Crewe and
others. bibliog il Science 168:1338-40 Je 12
'70
Visible atoms. il Sci Am 223:48 Ag '70
See also
Atomic theory
Atomic weights
Nuclear physics
Nucleons
Quantum theory

ATOMS smashing apparatus. See Accelerators
(electrons, etc)

ATOMS track club. See Athletic clubs

ATRIUM houses. See Architecture, Domestic

ATROCITIES
See also
Cambodian-Vietnamese conflict—Atrocities

ATROCITIES of war. See World war, 1939-1945
—Atrocities

ATROPHIC rhinitis in swine. See Swine—Diseases and pests

ATROPINE
Double antidote. Sci N 98:137 Ag 15 '70

ATROPINESTERASE. See Esterases

ATTACHED houses. See Row houses

ATTAWAY, David, and Parker, P. L.
Sterols in recent marine sediments. bibliog il
Science 169:674-6 Ag 14 '70

ATTENTION
Attention and psychological change in the
young child. J. Kagan. bibliog il Science 170:
826-32 N 20 '70

ATTINE ants. See Ants

ATTITUDE change
Stability of attitudes in psychiatric attendants following training. M. K. Distefano,
jr. and M. W. Pryer. bibliog Ment Hy 54:
433-5 Jl '70

ATTITUDES
See also
Dogmatism
Moral attitudes
Political attitudes
Public opinion
Race attitudes
Students—Attitudes
Value (psychology)
Youth—Attitudes

ATTLEBORO, Mass.

Education
Creativity takes over; visual arts program.
L. Rich. il Am Ed 6:16-22 D '70

ATTORNEY and client
Love of client, or law? ABA criticisms of
W. Kunstler's selection of clients. Time
95:40 Je 29 '70

ATTORNEY General (United States) See
United States—Justice, Department of

ATTORNEYS. See Lawyers

ATTRACTING of birds. See Birds, Attracting of

ATTRIBUTES of God. See God—Attributes

ATTUCKS, Crispus
Boston massacre and Crispus Attucks. il
Negro Hist Bul 33:56-7 Mr '70 *

ATTUCKS, Crispus, memorial monument. See
Boston—Monuments, statues, etc.

ATTWOOD, William
Birth of the bikini. il Look 34:78+ My 19
'70
Cuba revisited: how to see Havana without
getting hijacked. il por Look 34:15-17 Ap
7 '70
(ed) See Norodom Sihanouk. From Peking:
Sihanouk talks to Americans
ATWATER, Marshall A.
Planetary albedo changes due to aerosols.
bibliog il Science 170:64-6 O 2 '70
ATWOOD, George
Favorite pioneer recording artists. J. Walsh.
il pors Hobbies 75:37-40+ Ap; 37-40 My
'70 *
ATWOOD, Harriet
Favorite pioneer recording artists. J. Walsh.
il pors Hobbies 75:37-40+ Ap; 37-40 My
'70 *
ATWOOD, Margaret
Descent; poem. New Yorker 46:50 Je 27 '70
Girl and horse, 1928; poem. Atlan 225:70 Ja
'70
Hesitations outside the door; poem. Poetry.
117:100-7 N '70
about
Comment. M. Van Duyn. Poetry 115:432-3 Mr
'70 *
AUBERT, Alvin
Spirit of freedom; poem. Negro Hist Bul 33:
125 My '70
AUBREY, James Thomas, 1918-
MGM is cutting more than film. il por Bsns
W p23 My 9 '70 *
AUBUCHON, Norbert
Could you learn to fly a chopper? il Pop Sci
196:52-3+ Ap '70
Crazy, tricky, wonderful sport of island hop-
ping. il Pop Sci 196:71-3+ Mr '70
One engine, one ocean and you! il Flying 87:
29-31+ N '70
AUCHINCLOSS, Kenneth
Early warning system for happenings in
nature. il N Y Times Mag p 129-32 Ap 12
'70
AUCHINCLOSS, Louis
Aristocracy is dead but society lives on. il
Holiday 47:50-1+ F '70
Days of wrath; story. Redbook 135:76-7 Je
'70
In search of innocence. il pors Am Heritage
21:28-33 Je '70
Never leave me, never leave me. il pors Am
Heritage 21:20-2+ F '70
AUCKLAND, New Zealand
Long day's journey into winter. D. Butwin.
il Sat R 53:34-5+ Ag 1 '70
AUCTIONEERS
Elegant auctioneers, by W. Towner. Review
Sat R 53:42-3 N 7 '70
See also
Auctions
AUCTIONS
Dreams for sale; MGM auction. K. Fleming.
il Newsweek 75:36-7 My 4 '70
First fiddles; two Stradivarius violins auc-
tioned at Sotheby's. il Newsweek 76:121
N 2 '70
Going, going, gone! C. Stratton. Farm J
94:52F Ap '70
How the hog auctions are doing. B. Coff-
man. Farm J 94:24 Je '70
Ignoble end of Elizabeth. G. Walter. il Life 69:
32-6 S 11 '70
Livestock auctions, weekly or oftener, in thir-
ty-nine northern California towns. il Sun-
set 145:56+ N '70
Memories on the block: MGM auctions. il Life
68:42-8+ My 22 '70
New way to buy a car. D. Demske. il Mech
Illus 66:64-6+ N '70
Of rags and iron roses; the Dorotheum,
Viennese pawn-shop-cum-auction house. il
Newsweek 76:96+ O 12 '70
Old wine at heady prices. il Bsns W p92
Je 6 '70
Parke-Bernet photographic auction, a $61,870
bonanza. J. Schneider. il Mod Phot 34:129-
30 My '70
Relics: Rock relics auction, proceeds for peace
candidates. New Yorker 46:40-1 O 24 '70
See also
Art sales
Book sales
Nation-wide auto auctions. ltd.
AUDEN, Wystan Hugh
Aliens; poem. New Yorkers 46:58 N 21 '70
Auden in the looking glass; excerpts from
Commonplace book. por Atlan 225:62-6 My
'70
Books (cont) New Yorker 46:133-8 Ap 4:
153-9 S 12 '70
(tr) See Lysohorsky, O. Poet: Room for all:
At the circus; Trees in courtyards

about
Aging Autolycus. D. Hoffman. Nation 210:
151-3 F 9 '70
Insights and oversights in the poetic vision.
J. W. Hughes. Sat R 53:33 Ag 8 '70 *
Lines in lieu of a review. D. Hine. Poetry
117:211-15 D '70 *
Maker of libretti. I. F. Stravinsky. Harper
240:113-14 Ap '70 *
Merton and Auden. T. Materer. pors Com-
monweal 91:577-80 F 27 '70; Reply with
rejoinder. M. G. Walsh. 92:51+ Mr 27 '70 *
Poet in praise of limestone. F. Kermode.
por Atlan 225:67-71 My '70 *
Poet of the age of anxiety. W. Schott. il pors
Life 68:52-3+ Ja 30 '70
Sabine farm near Kirchstetten. M. K. Spears.
Yale R 60:90-101 O '70 *
AUDET, Ronald A.
Frost at midnight: the other Coleridge. Engl
J 59:1080-5 N '70
AUDI (automobile) See Automobiles, Foreign
AUDIENCE participation. See Audiences
AUDIENCES
Kissinger, Kennedy and order; disruptive
tactics by audiences. W. F. Buckley, jr.
Nat R 22:532 My 19 '70

Anecdotes, facetiae, satire,
etc.
Welcome to the club; operagoers. A. Farkas.
Opera N 34:6-7 F 21 '70
AUDIENCES, Papal. See Papal audiences
AUDIO dealers
Push money=spiff=bribe. Consumer Rep 36:
24 Ja '71
AUDIO fairs
Four channel at Westbury; New York hi-fi
show. I. Berger. Sat R 53:57 O 31 '70
AUDIO generators. See Signal generators
AUDIO mixers. See Sound—Apparatus
AUDIO research. See Radio research
AUDIO transformers. See Radio transformers
AUDIO-visual aids
Audiovisual guide, comp. by M. Moore. Li-
brary J 95:1583-4+, 3973-5+ Ap 15, N 15 '70
A-V clinic; questions and answers. D. Molner.
School Teach Jr/Sr High p39 S 21; 34 O 5;
21 D 7 '70
AV products roundup. D. Molner. il School
Teach Sec Teach Sup p22-4 N 3 '69; 22-3
Ap 6 '70
A-V roundup. D. Molner. School Teach Jr/Sr
High p40-1 S 21; 31 N 2 '70
Educational media and independent study.
N. Linck. Ed Digest 35:29-31 Ap '70
Instructional technology: some implications
for teachers. il Todays Ed 59:33-40 N '70
Off the shelf and into the classroom; Balti-
more County mobile educational technology
unit. D. K. Jaffe. il Am Ed 6:13-16 Ag '70
Remote access audio-video information sys-
tem. D. M. Crossman. Ed Digest 36:47-50
D '70
Resource materials. V. G. Timmons. See is-
sues of School arts
Screenings: media mix (cont) Library J 95:
1925, 2992-3, 3615, 4330-1 My 15, S 15, O 15,
D 15 '70
Student sensitivity in media production; stu-
dent help in the instructional services cen-
ter. R. S. Rosenfeld. Clear House 44:382-4
F '70
Teacher goes to own aid; TV and film self-
evaluation. il Sr Schol 96:Schol Teach 1
F 2 '70
Technology and the urban arts. D. D. Bush-
nell. Sat R 53:44 Jl 18 '70
See also
Education market
Film strips
Instructional materials centers
Libraries and audio-visual materials
Literature—Study and teaching—Aids and
devices
Moving picture projectors
Pictures in education
Projectors
Teaching machines
Transparencies
Bibliography
American Indians: a bibliography of sources;
nonprint materials. J. N. Naumer. il Am
Lib 1:863-4 O '70

Indexes
Evaluation gap: a/v reviewing. with special
emphasis on filmstrips. J. French. bibliog il
Library J 95:1162-6+ Mr 15 '70

AUDIO-visual instruction
Audio-visual education in Ivory Coast. P. Thierry. il Sch & Soc 98:424-6 N '70
Audiovisuals in reading. R. A. McCracken. bibliog Library J 95:1907-8 My 15 '70
Individualized learning in the flexible school; elementary schools, Broward County, Fla. F. Hatfield and I. Gullette. Am Lib 1:169-70 F '70
Man's world: an electronic experience in the humanities. S. May. Engl J 59:413-15+ Mr '70
Mediated teaching: does it make a difference? G. Halverson. il Schol Teach Sec Teach Sup p 10-12+ N 3 '69
    See also
Educational media personnel
Libraries and audio-visual materials
Moving pictures in education
School excursions
Television in education
Video recorders and recording—Educational use
AUDIO-visual specialists. See Educational media personnel
AUDIO voltmeters. See Voltmeters
AUDITING
Effective corporate audit committee. R. K. Mautz and F. L. Neumann. bibliog f il Harvard Bsns R 48:57-65 N '70
    See also
Tax auditing
AUDITIONS. See Theatrical production and direction
AUDITORIUMS
Iowa's prairie auditorium; C. Y. Stevens auditorium, State university, Ames. R. Jensen. il Arch Rec 148:75-80 D '70
Juilliard school. il Arch Rec 147:121-30 Ja '70
AUDITORY perception. See Sound perception
AUDUBON, John James
Vespers thrust. il Audubon 72:40-1 My '70
AUDUBON medal
Horace M. Albright: Audubon medalist, 1969. il por Audubon 72:31 Mr '70
AUDUBON naturalist society of the Central Atlantic states
Conservationists turn on for children of the concrete. A. Dennis. il Nat Parks & Con Mag 44:4-9 Je '70
AUDUBON societies
    See also
National Audubon society
AUERBACH, Arnold M.
Joe Hill revisited; poem. Sat R 53:4 N 7 '70
AUERBACH, Oscar, and Spencer, S. M.
New hope for heavy smokers. Read Digest 96:129-31 F '70
AUGER, Eugene
Santa Claus, California. T. Tyler. por Time 96:12 D 28 '70 *
AUGMENTOR wing. See Airplane wings
AUGSBURGER, David
Augsburgers: saints in shoe leather. por Chr Today 14:44-5 S 11 '70 *
AUGSBURGER, Myron S.
Augsburgers: saints in shoe leather. por Chr Today 14:44-5 S 11 '70 *
AUGSPURGER, George L.
Direct vs reverberant sound for stereo speakers. il Electr World 84:40-1+ S '70
AUGSTEIN, Rudolf
Germany's leading publishers renounce church taxation. E. E. Turner. Chr Cent 87:1164-6 S 30 '70 *
AUGUSTA, Ga.

Education
Blind children learn to relate; Windsor Spring elementary school, Richmond County schools. E. Johnson and T. Merriweather. il Am Lib 1:168-9 F '70

Riots
Killings in Jackson and Augusta. America 122:577 My 30 '70
Senseless waste. il Newsweek 75:36+ My 25 '70
South: death in two cities. il Time 95:22+ My 25 '70
AUGUSTA national golf club course. See Golf courses
AUGUSTINE, Saint
Augustianism and theology, by H. de Lubac. Review
    Cath World 211:136-7 Je '70. M. J. Gallagher
AULENTI, Gae
Gae Aulenti: new force in Italian design; tr. by A. Foulke. A. Arbasino. il Vogue 156: 118-23+ Jl '70 *
AURAS
Experiments with Schlieren auras. D. L. Heiserman. il Sci Digest 69:75-8 Ja '71

AURELIO, Richard
New York's other mayor. il por Newsweek 76:65-6 Jl 27 '70 *
AURINTRICARBOXYLIC acid. See Carboxylic acids
AURIOL, Jacqueline (Douet)
I live to fly; condensation. il pors Read Digest 97:241-4+ O '70
AURORAS
August 16th lunar eclipse and aurora. il Sky & Tel 40:210-13 O '70
Auroral-particle precipitation and trapping caused by electrostatic double layers in the ionosphere. R. D. Albert and P. J. Lindstrom. bibliog il Science 170:1398-401 D 25 '70
Mid-October auroral display. il Sky & Tel 40:394-5 D '70
Notes on some recent auroras. il Sky & Tel 39:400-1 Je '70
AUSTER, Paul
(tr) See Dupin, J. Frugal path
AUSTIN, Glenn
Pediatrician says it is time we outgrow camp physical exams. Camp Mag 42:14 F '70
AUSTIN, Mrs Hewson
Ceramic stitchery. R. Wrenn. il pors Design 71:38-41 mid-Sum '70 *
AUSTIN, I. G. and Mott, N. F.
Metallic and nonmetallic behavior in transition metal oxides. bibliog il Science 168: 71-7 Ap 3 '70
AUSTIN, John Paul
Environmental renewal or oblivion: quo vadis? address, April 16, 1970. Vital Speeches 36:470-5 My 15 '70
AUSTIN, Neale W.
Survey of the teaching of Latin in secondary schools. Sch & Soc 98:252-4 Ap '70
—and Clark, J. L. D.
Survey of the teaching of French, Spanish, and German in secondary schools. Sch & Soc 98:250-2 Ap '70
AUSTRAL ISLANDS. See Tubuai Islands
AUSTRALIA
Australia as an Indo-Pacific power. H. G. Gelber. bibliog f Cur Hist 58:223-8+ Ap '70
Dulhunty, hard man of the Outback: the traveling showman. il pors Life 69:46-54 O 30 '70
South Australia, gateway to the great outback. H. Walker. il Nat Geog 137:441-81 Ap '70
    See also
Airlines—Australia
Aluminum industry and trade—Australia
Automobile racing—Australia
Botany—Australia
Cattle industry and trade—Australia
English language in Australia
Fisheries—Australia
Immigration and emigration—Australia
Investments, Foreign (in Australia)
Mines and mineral resources—Australia
Mining industry and finance—Australia
Murray River
Nickel industry and trade—Australia
Northern Territory
Papua-New Guinea (territory)
Publishers and publishing—Australia
Steel industry and trade—Australia
Sydney
Western Australia
Wildlife conservation—Australia

Antiquities
Ancient man in Kow swamp. L. Bickel. il Sci N 97:254-5 Mr 7 '70
Archaeology booms in Australia. L. Bickel. il Sci N 97:468 My 9 '70
Prehistory Down Under; engraved rocks of Koonalda cave. D. J. Mulvaney. il Natur Hist 79:44-51 Ap '70

Civilization
Letter from Europe. A. Burgess. Am Scholar 40:119-22 Wint '70

Description and travel
Outback. A. Linkletter. il por Travel & Camera 33:29-33+ N '70
Wide look at a continent. J. Clayton. il Travel & Camera 33:53-7 N '70

Economic conditions
Booming Australia: a nation coming of age. C. S. Foltz, jr. il U S News 69:69-71 Jl 20 '70

Foreign relations
Australia as an Indo-Pacific power. H. G. Gelber. bibliog f Cur Hist 58:233-8+ Ap '70

AUSTRALIA—*Continued*

Native races

Journey to Pulykara. R. A. Gould. il Natur Hist 79:56-67 bibliog(p 90) D '70

Newest frontier; Aborigines advancement league. D. Butwin. il Sat R 53:39-41 Ag 22 '70

Photographs

Down Under. J. A. Langley. Travel & Camera 33:24-8 N '70

Religious institutions and affairs

Two hundred years of Australia. L. Morris. Chr Today 14:10-12 Jl 3 '70

World around us (cont) Chr Cent 87:1364-6 N 11 '70

See also

Church of England in Australia

Social conditions

Newest frontier. D. Butwin. il Sat R 53:39-41 Ag 22 '70

AUSTRALIA, New Zealand, United States treaty council. See Anzus council

AUSTRALIA, Western. See Western Australia

AUSTRALIA antigen. See Antigens and antibodies

AUSTRALIAN economic assistance. See Economic assistance, Australian

AUSTRALIAN English. See English language in Australia

AUSTRIA

See also

Airlines—Austria

Hunting—Austria

Innsbruck

Political parties—Austria

Shopping and shoppers—Austria

History

Bibliography

Articles and other books received; comp. by A. H. Price. See issues of American historical review

Politics and government

See also

Political parties—Austria

Religious institutions and affairs

World around us. Chr Cent 87:1433 N 25 '70

AUSTRIAN art. See Art, Austrian

AUSTRIAN cookery. See Cookery, Austrian

AUSTRIAN painting. See Painting, Austrian

AUSTRIAN pastry. See Pastry

AUTHORITY

Autonomy vs. authority? W. H. Becker. il Chr Cent 87:1149-53 S 30 '70

If Hitler asked you to electrocute a stranger, would you? P. Meyer. il Esquire 73:72-3+ F '70

When is *an* authority *in* authority? E. Stevens. America 122:46 Ja 17 '70

Would you obey a Hitler? J. Reinert. il Sci Digest 67:34-9 My '70

AUTHORITY (religion)

See also

Bible—Inspiration

Popes—Infallibility

AUTHORS

Authors & editors. See issues of Publishers' weekly

From the land of me... to the land of you. W. F. Nolan. Writer 83:18-20 Je '70

Full-time freelance writer: who is he? M. Renz. il Writers Digest 50:24-6+ D '70

What is the writer's social responsibility? N. Cousins. il Writers Digest 50:30-1+ Ja '70

What it's like to free-lance. R. Lardner. il Sat R 54:47-9 Ja 9 '71

Writer in the year: 2001. F. Pohl. il Writers Digest 50:36-9 Ja '70

See also

Authorship

Children as authors

Copyright

Dramatists

Editors and editing

Librarians as authors

Literary agents

Literature

Novelists

Poets

Prisoners as authors

Women as authors

Health and hygiene

Doctor's doctors; S. Johnson. H. F. Ellis. New Yorker 46:114-16+ S 19 '70

AUTHORS, African

Better yesterdays, better tomorrows: the dilemma of African writers. M. Fairman. Chr Cent 87:699-700 Je 3 '70

See also

African literature

AUTHORS, American

Where have all the writers gone? To Iowa City, that's where. J. Hess. il Holiday 47:60-3+ Je '70

Writers: 1920-1970; with editorial comment. C. Canfield. il Writers Digest 50:16-17, 25-9+ Ja '70

Writer's vice; alcoholism. il Time 96:59 O 5 '70

See also

Adams, H.

Agee, J.

American literature

Bradbury, R.

Brooks, V.

Clark, E.

Clemens, S. L.

Dos Passos, J.

Fitzgerald, F. S. K.

Henry, B.

Irving, W.

Melville, H

Novelists, American

O'Connor, F.

Poe, E. A.

Puzo, M.

Sendak, M.

Vidal, G.

West, N.

Williams, W. C.

Wilson, E.

Wolfe, T.

Woolf, L. S.

AUTHORS, Argentine

See also

Borges, J. L.

AUTHORS, British. See Authors, English

AUTHORS, Colombian

See also

Arciniegas, G.

AUTHORS, Czech

See also

Kafka, F.

AUTHORS, Danish

See also

Andersen, H. C.

AUTHORS, English

See also

Bagnold, E.

Belloc, H.

Carroll, L. pseud.

Chesterton, G. K.

Christie, A.

Conrad, J.

Coward, N.

Dickens, C.

Forster, E. M.

Gibbon, E.

Greene, G.

Mitford, J.

Orwell, G. pseud.

Russell, B. R.

Sillitoe, A.

AUTHORS, French

Colette, Cocteau, and Proust. R. Phelps. il Mlle 72:124-5+ D '70

See also

Aragon, L.

Camus, A.

Charrière, H.

Cocteau, J.

Colette, S. G.

Malraux, A.

Mauriac, F.

Sade, D. A. F. de

Saint Exupéry, A. de

Simenon, G.

Voltaire, F. M. A. de

Weil, S.

AUTHORS, German

See also

Grass, G.

Hanfstaengl, E. F. S.

Hesse, H.

Unruh, F. von

AUTHORS, Irish

See also

Behan, B.

O'Connor, F.

AUTHORS, Italian

See also

Pavese, C.

AUTHORS, Japanese

See also

Mishima, Y. pseud.

AUTHORS, Jewish
See also
Malamud, B.
Weil, S.
Wiesel. E.

AUTHORS, Mexican
See also
Fernández de Lizardi, J. J.

AUTHORS, Russian
Russia's courageous dissenters. A. Alvarez.
por Sat R 53:27+ N 28 '70
See also
Amalrik, A.
Russian literature
Solzhenitsyn, A. I.

AUTHORS, Scottish
See also
Boswell, J.
Grahame, K.
Scott, W

AUTHORS, South African
See also
Gordimer, N.

AUTHORS, Spanish
See also
Menéndez Pidal, R.

AUTHORS, Swiss
See also
Walser, R.

AUTHORS agents. See Literary agents

AUTHORS and libraries. See Libraries and authors

AUTHORS and publishers
Adventures of a short story. G. Jennings.
Writer 83:20-2+ Ja '70
Endless steppe, for children only? excerpts
from address, April 8, 1970. E. Hautzig.
Horn Bk 46:461-8 O '70
Find publisher or perish. N. Brown. Pub W
198:32-4 O 5 '70
Forbidden subjects in slick fiction. M. J.
Gerber. Writers Digest 50:32-3 Ap '70
It's push, not pull. L. Conger. Writer 83:9-10
F '70
Market newsletter. See issues of Writer
New York market letter. H. B. Jacobs.
See issues of Writer's digest
Positive view of literary auctions. S.
Meredith. Pub W 198:27-8 O 26 '70
Publisher as the mad hatter, or, the writer
as Alice. M. Holroyd. Pub W 197:24-6
Mr 16 '70
Teen fiction markets. Writers Digest 50:
35+ Je '70
Trade winds; interview, ed. by C. Amory.
B. Cerf. Sat R 53:12+ D 12 '70
Vanity services: a consumer alert. C. B.
Grannis. Pub W 197:60 Mr 2 '70
Where to sell manuscripts. See issues of
Writer
Writer's market; late news! See issues of
Writer's digest
See also
Literary agents

Anecdotes, facetiae, satire, etc.
Acceptance of the month club. M. Bennett.
Pub W 198:22-3 D 7 '70

AUTHORS colonies
Foundation grants and fellowships for writers;
Yaddo and MacDowell writers colonies. D.
Dempsey. il Writers Digest 50:48-53+ Ja
'70

AUTHORS conferences
Bread loaf 1970: boot camp for writers. A.
Caruba. il Pub W 198:32-5 S 21 '70. Reply.
W. Sloane. 198:15-16 O 12 '70
Summer's special flora. A. Caruba. Pub W
197:18-19 My 11 '70
Which writers' conference should I attend?
D. Stuart. Writers Digest 50:20-2 My '70
Writers' conferences 1970. Writer 83:25-9+ My
'70
Writers' conferences 1970. Writers Digest 50:
22-3+ My '70

AUTHORS markets. See Authors and publishers
AUTHORSHIP
Anyone can not. L. Conger. Writer 83:7-8
S '70
Begetting of "The begatting"; how three
freelancers parlayed a book idea into a book
sale, movie option and Orson Welles record.
L. Haynes. il Writers Digest 50:30-1 Ag '70
Freelance opportunities with associations.
M. A. DeVries. Writers Digest 50:28-30+ S
'70
Full-time freelancer. O. Stewart. il por Writers Digest 50:23+ Ap '70
Help! The editors of Writer's digest answer your questions. See issues of Writer's digest
Hidden book; writing The after-dinner gardening book. R. W. Langer. Writer 83:24-6
Ag '70

How I do it. Writers Digest 51:9 Ja '71
Interest curve. J. Ball. Writer 83:9-12 Jl '70
It's never too late to get started. M. L.
Barr. Writers Digest 51:31 Ja '71
Learning by mail; writing courses. il Writers
Digest 50:31 S '70
Long voyage; writing about far-off places.
H. Innes. Writer 83:25 Mr '70
Odyssey of a friend; letters to W. F. Buckley, jr, 1955-1957. W. Chambers. bibliog f
Nat R 22:76-82 Ja 27 '70
Privacy and production. P. S. Curry. Writer
83:9-11+ Mr '70
Questions for writers. J. Williams. Writer 83:
18-20+ D '70
Second thoughts. A. Holland. See issues
of Writer's digest
See also
Advertising copy
Authors
Authors conferences
Biography
Childrens literature—Technique
Creative writing
Drama—Technique
Fiction—Authorship
Fiction—Technique
Literary research
Moving picture authorship
Plagiarism
Poetics
Poetry—Authorship
Short story
Style, Literary
Teachers—Publications
Technical writing
Television authorship

Bibliography
Basic reference books for writers. C.
Flowers. Writer 83:27-8+ O '70
Books for writers. Writers Digest 50:53 My;
50-1 Je; 44 Jl; 46 Ag '70
Writer's library. See issues of Writer

Collaboration
As-told-to article. J. Stocker. il Writers Digest 50:20-2 Ap '70
I'm a fiction ghost. J. Pearl. Writers Digest 50:30-2 Je '70
Presidential ghost story. C. Roberts. il
Newsweek 77:21-2 Ja 11 '71

Competitions
See Literature—Competitions

AUTISM
Growing pains. Todays Health 48:12-13 Mr '70
AUTOERYTHROCYTE sensitization. See
Autoimmune diseases
AUTOGIROS
Caution: gyrocopter. P. Garrison. il Flying
86:68-74 Mr '70
Fun vehicle that flies. V. W. Kondra and
others. il Mech Illus 66:60-1+ Mr '70
AUTOGRAPH collectors' club. See Universal
autograph collectors' club (international)
AUTOGRAPHS
Musicians' autographs. R. Eyer. il Hi Fi
20:secI 61-4 Ap '70
Penmanship that pays off; autograph market.
il por Bsns W p 116-17 Ap 18 '70
See also
Universal autograph collectors' club (international)
AUTOIMMUNE diseases
Stigmata: a matter of mind or miracle? autoerythrocyte sensitization. B. Hildenbrand.
il Todays Health 48:57-9+ Ag '70
See also
Encephalomyelitis
AUTOMATIC cameras. See Cameras
AUTOMATIC chokes. See Automobile engines
—Choke
AUTOMATIC control
See also
Feedback control systems
Inertial guidance systems
AUTOMATIC data processing. See Electronic
data processing
AUTOMATIC direction finders. See Airplanes—
Radio equipment
AUTOMATIC doors. See Doors, Mechanically
operated
AUTOMATIC elevators. See Elevators
AUTOMATIC geophysical stations. See Geophysical stations
AUTOMATIC indexing. See Computers—Indexing use
AUTOMATIC lenses. See Lenses, Photographic

AUTOMATIC pilot (airplanes)
Business jet micro autopilot developed. P. J. Klass. il Aviation W 93:67-9 N 9 '70
Product news; Bendix FCS-810 flight-control system. il Flying 87:30+ D '70
AUTOMATIC pilot (boats)
Automatic pilot for outboards. C. R. Meyers. il Pop Sci 197:80-1 Jl '70
Let a robot do your steering. E. A. Zadig. il Motor B 126:48-9+ Jl '70
Marine electronics; power & sail. il Motor B 125:99-101 My '70
AUTOMATIC projectors. See Projectors
AUTOMATIC sprinklers. See Fire sprinklers
AUTOMATIC transmission. See Automobiles—Transmission
AUTOMATIC turntable. See Phonograph—Record changers
AUTOMATIC vehicle monitoring. See Radio in traffic control
AUTOMATIC washing machines. See Washing machines
AUTOMATION
More spending to automate. il Bsns W p54-5 N 28 '70
See also
American foundation on automation and employment
College libraries—Automation
Computers—Industrial use
Libraries—Automation
Machinery, Automatic
School libraries—Automation

Social aspects
Pentagon of power; excerpts. L. Mumford. il Horizon 12:4-21 Aut '70
AUTOMATION house. See New York (city)—Galleries and museums
AUTOMATONS
Coming of the humanoids: android fiction. N. P. Hurley; reply. N. Rosa. Commonweal 91:494-5 Ja 30 '70
Home-made Otto-tron: the ideal pal. il pors Ebony 25:64-6+ Je '70
My machine loves me. B. Ford. il Sci Digest 68:43-8+ S '70
See also
Manipulators
AUTOMOBILE accessories. See Automobiles—Equipment
AUTOMOBILE accidents. See Traffic accidents
AUTOMOBILE alarms. See Automobiles—Electronic equipment
AUTOMOBILE assembly plants. See Automobile factories
AUTOMOBILE auctions. See Auctions
AUTOMOBILE batteries. See Storage batteries
AUTOMOBILE boat trailers
How to buy a used trailer. J. A. Emmett. il Outdoor Life 145:28+ F '70
Keel positioning guide. G. Hensley. il Motor B 126:58 D '70
Trailers. il Motor B 125:232-5 Ja '70
AUTOMOBILE bodies. See Automobiles—Bodies
AUTOMOBILE brakes. See Brakes, Automobile
AUTOMOBILE burglar alarms. See Automobiles—Protection against theft
AUTOMOBILE buying. See Automobiles—Purchasing
AUTOMOBILE camping. See Camping
AUTOMOBILE dealers
Dealers are still waiting. il Bsns W p 11-12 My 2 '70
Detroit's new models: black auto dealers. il Ebony 25:66-8+ F '70
GM dealers sing the slowdown blues. il Bsns W p30 O 24 '70
Son of the Catskills: J. Hamilton of the Delhi motor company, Delhi, N.Y. Harper 241:79-82 S '70
See also
Automobile salesmen
Nation-wide auto auctions, ltd.
National automobile dealers association
Volkswagen of America, inc.
AUTOMOBILE drivers
Solving mysteries for female motorists. V. Louviere. il Nations Bsns 58:14 Je '70
Telltale signs of the dangerous driver. il Good H 170:151 Je '70
See also
Automobile racing drivers
Drinking and traffic accidents

Psychology
Behind the auto mask. Time 96:63 O 26 '70
Men honk more. Sci Digest 67:69 Ap '70
AUTOMOBILE driving
Are you an unconscious driver? D. L. Gregg. il Bet Hom & Gard 48:114 N '70

Called for icing. B. Sanders. il Motor T 22:54+ D '70
Defensive driving: a strategy for staying alive. il Changing T 24:7-10 Jl '70
Driver syndrome miscellany. Sci Digest 67:27-9 Ap '70
Drivin' with Dan; questions and answers. D. Gurney. See issues of Popular mechanics
Getting a grip on things; holding the steering wheel. D. McCluggage. Am Home 73:34+ Ag '70
It's not too late to get set for winter driving. il Consumer Bul 53:35-6 Ja '70
Scrambled eggs; driving practice with Subaru 360 on miniature course. il Motor T 22:55 Je '70
Skillful driver:
If a bike cuts across your path. il Pop Sci 197:115 Jl '70
If a car blocks your lane. il Pop Sci 197:46 O '70
If a tractor blocks you. il Pop Sci 197:97 Ag '70
If other cars crash ahead of you. il Pop Sci 196:112 Ap '70
If the car behind you can't stop, il Pop Sci 196:44 F '70
If you meet a sleeping driver. il Pop Sci 196:22 Mr '70
If you must swerve on ice. il Pop Sci 197:126 N '70
If your brakes go out. il Pop Sci 197:26 S '70
If your car jumps. il Pop Sci 196:24 Je '70
If your car skids. il Pop Sci 197:12 D '70
If your tire blows out. il Pop Sci 196:132 Ja '70
If your trailer jackknifes. il Pop Sci 196:26 My '70
Slippery road, don't hit the brakes. D. McCluggage. il por Am Home 73:22+ Ja '70
So you think you are a safe driver, eh? Defensive driving course. A. Markovich. il Mech Illus 66:68-70+ F '70
To my daughter, on acquiring her first car. P. Gallico. Read Digest 97:100-2 Jl '70
Tom McCahill tells you how to drive and stay alive in winter. T. McCahill. il Mech Illus 66:62-4+ Ja '70
See also
Automobile signals
Automobile touring

Anecdotes, facetiae, satire, etc.
Never say drive! E. Bombeck. il Good H 170:26+ My '70

Competitions
Automotive awards. M. Spiegel. il Sr Schol 95:25-6 D 8 '69
Scholastic magazines automotive awards. il Sr Schol 97:45 S 28 '70

Fog hazards
Too fast in fog; twenty-nine car collision on New Jersey turnpike. E. D. Fales, jr. il Pop Mech 134:84-9+ S '70; Same abr. Read Digest 97:180-2+ O '70

Study and teaching
Driver-ed, learn while you play; game. il Consumer Bul 53:23 D '70
Driver education: are we getting our money's worth? M. Lamm. il Parents Mag 45:48-9+ Je '70
Leave the driving lessons to mother. D. McCluggage. il Am Home 73:64+ My '70
School for skids. E. Dahlquist. il por Motor T 22:101-2 Ap '70
Should you teach your teen-ager to drive? Bet Hom & Gard 48:70+ Ag '70
So you think you are a safe driver, eh? Defensive driving course. A. Markovich. il Mech Illus 66:68-70+ F '70

Italy
Sex and the Italian driver. J. Burgess. il Holiday 47:58-9+ Ja '70; Same abr. Read Digest 97:110-13 S '70
AUTOMOBILE driving and drinking. See Drinking and traffic accidents
AUTOMOBILE emblems. See Emblems
AUTOMOBILE engineering
New engineering; priorities for the 70's; address, January 14, 1970. E. N. Cole. Vital Speeches 36:236-40 F 1 '70
AUTOMOBILE engines
Armstrong+327 Chevy=572 horsepower. B. Lang. il Hot Rod 23:96-9 My '70
Big lift; long-slot rocker arms. B. Lang. il Hot Rod 23:106-7 N '70

AUTOMOBILE engines—Exhaust—*Continued*
Tune up and tune out air pollution. M.
Schultz. il Pop Mech 134:156-9 O '70
Two-way attack. Sci N 98:60-1 Jl 25 '70
U.S. seeks cleaner auto engines. N. Gruchow.
Science 169:569 Ag 7 '70
Who's kidding who? il Motor T 22:22-4 Je
'70
See also
Carbon monoxide

Fuel
Bottled heat; racing on propane. A. B. Shu-
man. il Motor T 22:50+ F '70
Convert to LP gas. J. Zmuda. il Pop Sci 197:
43-5 Jl '70
Driving with methane. E. Gross. il Sci N
97:73-4 Ja 17 '70
LP-gas cuts police car costs, improves per-
formance; Chandler, Ariz. W. T. Louthan.
il Am City 85:87-8 Je '70
Natural gas: one way to cut auto smog?
il U S News 68:61 Ja 19 '70
Pollution free autos: Detroit is ready to
move. il U S News 68:12 F 23 '70
Propane power! Should you switch to LP-
gas? F. A. Tinker. il Pop Mech 134:85-7+
O '70
See also
Gasoline

Fuel consumption
Fuel meet takes gas; Bakersfield fuel & gas
championships. J. Dianna. il Hot Rod 23:
100-1 Je '70
Performance tests, Detroit vs. Union oil.
B. Hartford. il Pop Mech 133:94-7 Ap '70
Tricks you can use to save gas; Shell mileage
marathon. J. P. Norbye. il Pop Sci 196:
108+ Ap '70

Fuel feeding
EFI: a squirt in the right direction. K.
Ludvigsen. il Motor T 22:60-3 N '70
Electronic fuel injection reduces air pollution.
F. W. Holder. il Electr World 84:48-9+ S
'70
Racing injection for VWs. J. Thawley. il
Hot Rod 23:104-5 My '70
Testing VW's electronic fuel-injection system.
F. W. Holder and R. D. Springs. il Electr
World 83:88-9 Ja '70
Timed fuel injection. B. Lang. il Hot Rod 23:
56-8 F '70

Heaters
Warm-up break-in; recirculatory device. J.
Dianna. il Hot Rod 23:72-3 D '70

Ignition
Bridging the gap. E. K. Von Delden. il Hot
Rod 23:92-5 F '70
Do it up right. Accel kit for a Corvette dis-
tributor. B. Lang. il Hot Rod 23:68-9 D '70
Psst. Hey, mister, wanna meet a nice tran-
sistor? capacitive discharge ignition sys-
tems. A. B. Shuman. il Motor T 22:76 S '70
Spark-a-plenty. J. Dianna. il Hot Rod 23:52 Je
'70
Tune up your car with a vom. L. E. Frenzel,
jr. il Radio-Electr 41:23-5 Ap '70
When will you have a waterproof ignition sys-
tem? M. Schultz. il Pop Mech 134:86-7 Ag '70
Wired in; distributor and spark plugs. B.
Lang. il Hot Rod 23:98-9 Je '70
See also
Spark plugs

Lubrication
See Automobiles—Lubrication

Maintenance and repair
Good car maintenance can help reduce air pol-
lution. il Good H 171:152 Ag '70
How to keep down the high cost of tune ups.
T. Tappett. il Mech Illus 66:86-8+ Ja '70
How to service PCV systems. P. Jones. il
Suc Farm 68:B12 S '70
It's electricity that makes your car go. il
Changing T 24:15-17 Ag '70
R for rough idle. T. Tappett. il Mech Illus
66:98-100+ Ag '70
Shop talk. J. Dianna. See issues of Hot rod
Tune up and tune out air pollution. M.
Schultz. il Pop Mech 134:156-9 O '70
Tune your car to cut pollution, now. E. F.
Lindsley. il Pop Sci 197:100-2+ Ag '70

Materials
Aluminum packs power for GM. Bsns W p76
Ag 1 '70

Mufflers
New: a catalytic converter that really cleans
up auto exhaust. J. P. Zmuda. il Pop Sci
197:47-9 D '70
On the inside track in the muffler race; catalytic mufflers for pollution control. il Bsns
W p 112+ My 2 '70

Whats' all the noise about straight-through
mufflers? M. Lamm. il Pop Mech 134:88-91+
D '70

Parts
See Automobile parts

Radiators
Aluminum eyes an auto market. Bsns W p88
Ap 18 '70

Repairing
See Automobile engines—Maintenance and
repair

Research
See Automobile research

Superchargers
Huff 'n puff and other stuff; adding a super-
charger to the Vega. S. Kelly. il Hot Rod
23:42-4 D '70
New boost for turbocharged cars. J. Sloniger.
il Pop Sci 196:50+ My '70
Turbocharge! H. MacInnes. il Hot Rod 23:58-
60 O '70

Testing
Auto race where cleanliness counts; Clean air
car race. il Bsns W p90+ Ag 15 '70
Clean air car race. Newsweek 76:97+ S 14 '70
Great clean air car race. W. Wyss. il Motor T
22:60-2+ D '70
Great race for cleaner air. il Chem 43:3 O '70
How to exhaust exhaust; clean-air car race.
Sci Am 223:44 N '70
May the cleanest car win; Clean air car race.
il Newsweek 76:62 Ag 31 '70
PS previews the great clean-air car race. E.
H. Arctander. il Pop Sci 197:50-2+ Ag '70
Put-ons for Ford of Cleveland; 351-C engine.
S. Kelly. il Hot Rod 23:48-50 Ag '70
Ready to race against smog; clean air race.
with report by R. Gore. il Life 69:44-6 S
4 '70
Valve train evaluator. J. Thawley. il Hot
Rod 23:94-6 O '70
Who really won the clean-air car race?
B. Hartford. il Pop Mech 134:40 N '70

Valves
Jr. stock head prepping. J. Dianna. il Hot
Rod 23:40-2 Mr '70
What this country needs is a good five-cent
three-valve head. J. McFarland. il Motor
T 22:82-3 Mr '70
AUTOMOBILE equipment. *See* Automobiles—
Equipment
AUTOMOBILE exhibitions. *See* Automobiles—
Exhibitions
AUTOMOBILE factories
See also
Automobile industry and trade
Ford motor company

Automation
GM's mini: the very model of automation;
Vega plant. il Bsns W p26 Ag 8 '70
Made in Ohio by robots; General motors'
unimates. R. Lund. il Pop Mech 134:81-3+
S '70

Employees
Blue-collar blues on the assembly line. J.
Gooding. il Fortune 82:68-71+ Jl '70
Showdown in Detroit. Newsweek 76:65+ Jl 20
'70
Violence in the factories. il Newsweek 75:66-
7 Je 29 '70
What it's like on the auto assembly line.
M. Weston. Newsweek 76:81 S 14 '70
See also
Strikes—United States—Automobile industry
and trade
AUTOMOBILE industry and trade

Advertising
Auto strike costs magazines a bundle. Bsns
W p27 S 26 '70
Away from the youth image. Time 95:77 F 9
'70

Employees
See Automobile factories—Employees

Finance
Automotive products; with yardsticks of
management performance. il Forbes 105:
191-3 Ja 1 '70; 107:160-3 Ja 1 '71
Rivals have thrived during the GM strike.
il Bsns W p23 N 14 '70
Wintry gloom deepens in Detroit. il Bsns W
p23 F 7 '70

AUTOMOBILE industry and trade—*Continued*

International aspects

Global reshuffle for the big three. il Bsns W p40+ S 19 '70

Industrial and commercial relations; western Europe and the Soviet Union; address, October 12, 1970. G. Agnelli. Vital Speeches 37:93-6 N 15 '70

Public relations

Rap 'n 'pinion. J. Wangers. por Motor T 22:12 Ap '70

Quality control

Can FTC put a governor on Detroit? proposed automobile quality control act. il Bsns W p31-2 F 28 '70

Securities

Auto stocks. C. Morgello. il por Newsweek 75:88 Mr 16 '70

Striking viewpoint. C. Morgello. il Newsweek 76:69 S 28 '70

Used cars

Rap 'n 'pinion. L. Baney. Motor T 22:12 Je '70

Slightly used bargains. il Time 95:77 F 9 '70

See also
Nation-wide auto auctions, ltd.

Wages and hours

Wages in motor vehicle and parts plants. G. L. Stelluto. il Mo Labor R 93:46-7 S '70

See also
Collective bargaining—Automobile industry

Brazil

Where Ford is hot on VW's heels. il Bsns W p44 My 16 '70

Europe, Western

Auto slump? Not in Europe. il U S News 68:43 Ja 26 '70

Import report. E. Seidler. See issues of Motor trend

Politics on wheels. Time 96:33 S 14 '70

U.S. trend in Europe: mix or match cars; General motors and Chrysler subsidiaries. il U S News 70:46 Ja 11 '71

France

Citroen's driver is told to walk. Bsns W p55-6 My 23 '70

Germany (Federal Republic)

Coup for Bonn? Daimler-Benz and the Russian truck factory deal. Newsweek 76:67 S 7 '70

Hottest thing on four wheels; BMW. il Bsns W p64 Mr 28 '70

Great Britain

Morgan comes back. Newsweek 75:64 Je 22 '70

Troubles in autos for Britain, too. U S News 69:66 D 14 '70

Why the Lotus is in high gear. il por Bsns W p41 F 7 '70

See also
British Leyland motor corporation
Rootes motors, ltd.

Italy

Daylighting hits Fiat production. Bsns W p35 N 14 '70

Illness of convenience. Newsweek 77:58 Ja 4 '71

Japan

Brake on Japan's auto boom. Fortune 82:75 Ag '70

Fast pace of Japanese cars; Toyota and Nissan roles in the U.S. il Bsns W p42+ Ag 8 '70

Japan: now no. 2 in autos, trucks and going for no. 1. il U S News 68:42-3 Je 1 '70

Japanese labor's silken tranquillity; conditions at Toyota. il Time 96:81-2 O 5 '70

Rap 'n 'pinion. H. Bradley. Motor T 22:14 N '70

Russia

Into the auto age, at last. il Time 96:28 S 21 '70

Is there a Ford in Russia's future? il Bsns W p41+ Ap 18 '70

Russia turns to wheels. D. Reed. il Read Digest 97:163-4+ S '70

Soviets stall in race for the auto age. il Bsns W p42-3 F 14 '70

Year of the auto. il Newsweek 75:83+ Ap 27 '70

United States

Advance look at '71 cars; smaller, cleaner-burning engines, new safety features. il U S News 68:30-3 My 4 '70

As they see it: interview. S. E. Knudsen. por Forbes 106:63-4 N 15 '70

Auto sales spurt; shortages coming? il U S News 69:52 Jl 20 '70

Autos: shifting down for the '70s. il Time 95:80-1 F 23 '70

Beleaguered Detroit fights back. il Newsweek 75:73-7 Ap 6 '70

Big three in Japan. il Newsweek 76:80-1 N 30 '70

Bugging Detroit; competition from imports. R. W. Dietsch. New Repub 162:10-11 Mr 7 '70

Dealers are still waiting. il Bsns W p 11-12 My 2 '70

Detroit: a new era. il Forbes 105:23-4 Je 15 '70

Detroit listening post. R. Lund. See issues of Popular mechanics

Detroit report. J. Dunne. See issues of Popular science monthly

Detroit slams the door on its 1970s. il Bsns W p 14 Ag 8 '70

Detroit tries a U-turn on warranties. il Bsns W p44-5+ Jl 25 '70

Electricity, turbine, steam or what? R. Gore. Life 69:46 S 4 '70

Exciting race in a ho-hum year; Chevrolet vs. Ford. il Bsns W p22 Ap 11 '70

Inside Detroit. See issues of Motor trend

Marking time. E. Dahlquist. Motor T 22:6 O '70

Minis meet the imports. il Bsns W p68-71 Ag 15 '70

Motor Trend interview: troubles in the years ahead. J. Beltz. pors Motor T 22:72+ D '70

New year puzzles Detroit. il Bsns W p 11-12 Ja 2 '71

Other bumps in the road. por Newsweek 76:82-3 S 14 '70

Outlook for auto sales now. il U S News 69:31 N 30 '70

There's a Ford in my past; interview, ed. by B. Beason. S. E. Knudsen. il pors Mech Illus 66:45-7+ F '70

What's happening to '70 car sales. il U S News 68:42-3 Ja 26 '70

See also
Automobile dealers
Collective bargaining—Automobile industry
Strikes—United States—Automobile industry and trade
United automobile, aerospace and agricultural implement workers of America
also names of automobile manufacturing companies, e.g. American motors corporation

AUTOMOBILE industry strikes. See Strikes—United States—Automobile industry and trade

AUTOMOBILE inspection. See Automobiles—Inspection

AUTOMOBILE insurance. See Insurance, Automobile

AUTOMOBILE insurance companies. See Insurance companies

AUTOMOBILE jacks. See Jacks

AUTOMOBILE laws and regulations
See also
Insurance, Automobile
Traffic violations

Russia

Pedestrian roulette. il Newsweek 76:102+ O 19 '70

AUTOMOBILE locks and keys

Double helping of protection; Kar-Lok. B. Lang. il Hot Rod 23:57 O '70

Mini-spool lockers. B. Lang. il Hot Rod 23:59 Mr '70

Stop thief! electric hood lock. E. Rickman. il Hot Rod 23:61 Ap '70

World's most thiefproof car lock. S. M. Gallager. il Pop Mech 133:38-9+ Ap '70

AUTOMOBILE mechanics (persons)

Indianapolis 500 pit: no place for a greenhorn. il pors Ebony 25:112-14+ My '70

Should mechanics have to have a license? M. Schultz. il Pop Mech 135:73-5 Ja '71

Tom McCahill sounds off on service. T. McCahill. il Mech Illus 66:43-5+ My '70

Training

Automotive awards. M. Spiegel. il Sr Schol 95:25-6 D 8 '69

Rap 'n 'pinion; proposed college level courses for racing mechanics. J. Holman. por Motor T 22:16 S '70

AUTOMOBILE models

Here comes the Spectre; race-car kit. H. G. McEntee. il Pop Sci 197:26 O '70

AUTOMOBILE racing—*Continued*
What's a nice Yankee like you doing in
    victory lane? 12th annual Daytona 500. A.
    B. Shuman. il Motor T 22:80-3+ Ap '70
When to finish was enough; Daytona races.
    E. Dahlquist. il Motor T 22:74-5+ Ap '70
When victory was just a broken engine away;
    Monterey Castrol Grand prix. C. Koch. il
    Motor T 22:32-4+ D '70
Wild Bill show; interview, ed. by J. Dianna.
    B. Shrewsberry. il pors Hot Rod 23:62-4
    O '70
Wild bunch; inaugural Professional drag-
    ster association funny car nationals. B.
    Lang. il Hot Rod 23:44-5 Mr '70
Winning with restrictions; Charlotte 500. S.
    Kelly. il por Hot Rod 23:74-6 D '70
Winternationals numbers ten. J. Dianna. il
    Hot Rod 23:28-31 Ap '70
World finals 1969; NRHA winternationals.
    J. Thawley. il Hot Rod 23:34-7 Ja '70
Yankee Pete and his reb getaway car; at
    Daytona 500. R. F. Jones. il por Sports Il-
    lus 32:16-17 Mr 2 '70

    See also
Automobile speed records
Automobiles, Racing
Midget automobile racing
Motor vehicle racing
Speedways

        Accidents and injuries
Flaming dash for life; Jacky Ickx at the
    Spanish Grand prix. il Life 68:46-7 My 8 '70
Petty amount of trouble; photographs. Hot
    Rod 23:102-3 S '70

        Caricatures and cartoons
Once upon a principality; 28th Monaco
    Grand prix. J. J. Sempé. il Sports Illus 32:
    32-7 My 4 '70

        Economic aspects
Auto racing: another pro football? il Forbes
    106:42-3 Jl 1 '70
Rap 'n' pinion. A. Granatelli. por Motor T 22:
    18 My '70
Rap 'n 'pinion. R. Petty. por Motor T 22:
    18 Mr '70
Rap 'n 'pinion; question of contracts. B. Mc-
    Crary. por Motor T 22:18 F '70
Rap 'n 'pinion; sports compared to govern-
    ment. L. Richter. por Motor T 22:16+ Ja
    '70

        History
Or more precisely, the legend of Barney Old-
    field. L. W. Steinwedel. il Motor T 23:38-
    40+ Ja '71

        Rules
NHRA's '70 rules and you. J. Dianna. il Hot
    Rod 23:88-9 Mr '70
NHRA's '71 rules changes. J. Hart. il Hot
    Rod 23:78-9 D '70
Racing rules. Pop Mech 133:S58-62 Ja '70;
    135:S17-18+ Ja '71

        Safety devices and measures
Racing's most frightening corners; ed. by
    G. S. Brown. J. Stewart. il por Sports
    Illus 33:38-49 O 12 '70

        Study and teaching
How I became a racing driver in three easy
    lessons. B. Hartford. il Pop Mech 135:86-
    90 Ja '71

        Terminology
Auto racing glossary. Pop Mech 133:S23+
    Ja '70

        Africa, East
East African safari. il Ebony 25:112-14+
    Mr '70

        Australia
Down-Under digs. R. Brock. il Hot Rod 23:
    114-16 Ap '70

        Europe, Western
Europe's fastest festivals. R. Deardorff. il
    Travel 133:60-5 Ja '70
Tour de France. il Motor T 22:88 Ja '70

        France
Power to the Porsches; Le Mans Grand prix.
    il Time 95:66 Je 29 '70

        New Zealand
South Pacific scene. W. G. A. Porter. il Hot
    Rod 23:94 S '70
AUTOMOBILE racing, Photography of. See
    Photography of sports
AUTOMOBILE racing drivers
Can-Am cars. il Pop Mech 133:S12 Ja '70

Can the Can-Am kings blitz the brick-
    yard? B. Hartford. il Pop Mech 133:90-
    3+ My '70
Championship. il Pop Mech 133:S4 Ja '70
Dandy Dick Landy; interview, ed. by J.
    Dianna. D. Landy. il pors Hot Rod 23:58-
    60 Ja '70
Drag racing. il Pop Mech 133:S28, S37 Ja '70
Formula A; and other formulas and classes.
    il Pop Mech 133:S24 Ja '70
Formula 1. il Pop Mech 133:S20 Ja '70
Funny girl. S. Kelly. il pors Hot Rod 23:68-70
    Mr '70
Hot rod's 1969 top ten. J. Dianna. il Hot
    Rod 23:90-1 F '70
Indy '70; preview of things to come, with
    handicapping guide and chart. L. Neham-
    kin. il Motor T 22:34-9+ My '70
Jackie Stewart; interview, ed. by E. Seid-
    ler. J. Stewart. il pors Motor T 22:60-2 Mr
    '70
Motor trend interview. E. Carlsson. pors
    Motor T 22:85-6+ F '70
Motor trend interview. P. M. Carlsson. por
    Motor T 23:70+ Ja '71
Motor trend interview; ed. by E. Dahlquist.
    D. Gurney. pors Motor T 22:90+ Ja '70
1971 auto racing guide. il Pop Mach 135:S3-
    4+ Ja '71
'70 racing preview symposium. il Motor T
    22:39-54+ Mr '70
Stock cars. il Pop Mech 133:S8 Ja '70
Super season wind-up; NHRA world finals.
    R. Guldahl, jr. and J. Dianna. il Hot Rod
    24:44-5 Ja '71
Trans-Am. il Pop Mech 133:S16 Ja '70
    See also
Borsch, W.
Hielscher, B.
McEwen, T.
McLaren, B.
Prudhomme, D.
Ronda, G.
Yarbrough, L. R.
AUTOMOBILE racing timers. See Timing
    devices
AUTOMOBILE radiators. See Automobile en-
    gines—Radiators
AUTOMOBILE radios. See Automobiles—Ra-
    dio equipment
AUTOMOBILE renting. See Automobiles—Leas-
    ing and renting
AUTOMOBILE research
Progress report on smogless motoring. J.
    Lear. Sat R 53:44-5 Ag 1 '70
Who's kidding who? il Motor T 22:22-4 Je
    '70
    See also
Automobiles, Experimental
AUTOMOBILE rides. See Automobile touring
AUTOMOBILE salesmen
How I made $193.85 selling cars. R. Rapoport.
    Atlan 225:75-8 Ja '70
AUTOMOBILE service stations
Exact-fare gas. il Newsweek 75:67 Mr 30 '70
Jarrell's junior stockers. J. Dianna. il Hot
    Rod 23:78-80 Ja '70
Quiet, calm Sunday afternoon. L. Laye. il
    Motor T 22:68-9 Mr '70
Tom McCahill sounds off on service. T.
    McCahill. il Mech Illus 66:43-5+ My '70
AUTOMOBILE shows. See Automobiles—Ex-
    hibitions
AUTOMOBILE signals
Hubcap gap; means of communication be-
    tween drivers. D. McCluggage. il Am Home
    73:50+ S '70
AUTOMOBILE speed alarms. See Automobiles
    —Electronic equipment
AUTOMOBILE speed records
Drag racing records. Pop Mech 133:S30 Ja '70
Indianapolis 500 pole winners. Pop Mech 133:
    S41 Ja '70
1971 auto racing guide. il Pop Mech 135:
    S3-4+ Ja '71
Outstanding land speed records. il Pop Mech
    133:S14-15 Ja '70
Winners of Indianapolis 500. Pop Mech 133:
    S6 Ja '70
Winners of major NASCAR races. Pop Mech
    133:S10 Ja '70
World speed records on land. Pop Mech
    133:S18 Ja '70
AUTOMOBILE speedways. See Speedways
AUTOMOBILE stealing. See Automobiles, Theft
    of
AUTOMOBILE styling. See Automobiles—De-
    sign
AUTOMOBILE thefts. See Automobiles, Theft
    of
AUTOMOBILE tires. See Tires, Automobile
AUTOMOBILE tools. See Tools

AUTOMOBILE tops. See Automobiles—Roofs

AUTOMOBILE touring
Park outing. il Bet Hom & Gard 48:43-5 Je '70
Tips on packing a car for travel. il Good H 171:147 Ag '70
  See also
Airstream, inc.

Canada
Across Canada in a motor home. J. Linkletter. il Pop Mech 133:122-5+ F '70

Europe, Western
Shunpike tour of Europe. N. D. Ford. bibliog il Har Yrs 10:6-13+ Ap '70

Great Britain
Driving. J. Dugdale. Travel & Camera 33:68-9 My '70

Japan
They said I was crazy to drive in Japan. R. P. Crossley. il Pop Mech 134:126-9+ O '70

Mexico
Mexico. N. D. Ford. il Har Yrs 10:14-21+ Je '70

New Mexico
Family vacation in New Mexico. J. Simpson. il Am Home 73:92+ Mr '70

Russia
Raz, dva, tri, and you're off! E. Sparn. il Sr Schol 95:18 N 17 '69

United States
10,000 miles in the new Gremlin. J. Davis. il Pop Sci 197:54-6 Jl '70
200 attractions along the interstates. E. Welke. il Bet Hom & Gard 48:129-33+ My '70

History
Motoring marvels of yesteryear. M. Holmes. il Todays Health 48:54-5+ Mr '70

AUTOMOBILE touring with children. See Travel with children

AUTOMOBILE towing. See Towing

AUTOMOBILE traffic. See City traffic

AUTOMOBILE trailer camps
Following the covered wagons on an asphalt trail. R. Bailey. Life 69:28-9 Ag 14 '70

AUTOMOBILE trailer hitches. See Automobiles—Equipment

AUTOMOBILE trailers
Caravans on the open road; with report by R. Bailey. il Life 69:20-9 Ag 14 '70
Hard-top tent camper rides dual-use trailer. M. Philips. il Pop Sci 196:88-91+ Ap '70
Holiday home on wheels. A. Eisenberg and H. Eisenberg. il Parents Mag 45:48-50+ Ag '70
Home on the range; Airstream Wally Byam caravan. B. Gilbert. il Sports Illus 33:46-8+ Jl 6 '70
How to match a trailer to your car. V. L. Oertle. il Pop Mech 134:71-2+ Jl '70
How to pamper a camper. D. L. Gregg. il Bet Hom & Gard 48:120+ Ap '70
New gypsies. Esquire 74:109-10 S '70
New space program for vacations; Cimarron II travel trailer. D. D. Vigren. il Pop Sci 196:82-3+ Mr '70
Penny-pinchin' hauler; race car trailer. J. Dianna. il Hot Rod 23:110-11 Ag '70
Pushbutton camping comfort; folding travel trailer. H. Shuldiner. il Pop Sci 196:84-5+ Mr '70
Recreation roundup. H. Shuldiner. il Pop Sci 196:22+ F '70
Trailing a tent-on-wheels through mid-America. E. H. Arctander. il Pop Sci 196:84-5+ Mr '70
  See also
Automobile boat trailers
Houseboats—Automobile trailer combination
Mobile homes

Leasing and renting
Camping mobility. R. Deardorff. il Travel 133:60-2 Mr '70

Lighting
Single-filament tail light converter. M. Beier. il Pop Electr 33:66 D '70

Safety devices and measures
Two trouble spots in camping vehicles: carbon monoxide poisoning and flash fires. Consumer Bul 53:22 S '70

AUTOMOBILE trips. See Automobile touring

AUTOMOBILE warranty. See Warranty

AUTOMOBILE washing.   See Automobiles—Cleaning

AUTOMOBILE waxes. See Waxes

AUTOMOBILE wheels.   See   Automobiles—Wheels

AUTOMOBILE wiring. See Automobiles—Electric wiring

AUTOMOBILE workers. See Automobile factories—Employees

AUTOMOBILE wrecking industry. See Automobiles—Wrecking

AUTOMOBILES
Advance look at Detroit's 1971 models. R. Huntington. il Consumer Bul 53:7-12 O '70
Almost a limousine; Toronado, Riviera, Thunderbird. J. Brokaw. il Motor T 22:67-71 D '70
American motors mounts its assault! M. Lamm. il Pop Mech 134:100-2+ O '70
America's GTs, symbol of our age. il Motor T 22:76-9+ Ap '70
Autos 1970. il Consumer Rep 35:196-245 Ap '70
Badge of performance; Javelin, Hornet and Matador. B. Sanders. il Motor T 22:34-6 S '70
Beware the quiet fish; Barracuda 340. S. Kelly. il Hot Rod 24:34-6 Ja '71
Big noise in Ford country. il Motor T 22:36-7+ O '70
Boss to like; Mustang. S. Kelly. il Hot Rod 23:38-40 Ja '70
Bridging the insurance gap; Olds comes up with an answer to rising supercar insurance rates. K. Ludvigsen. il Motor T 22:68-9+ F '70
Buick bunch. il Motor T 22:42-4 O '70
Camaro Rally sport. il Consumer Bul 53:27-8 S '70
Cars. D. L. Gregg. See issues of Better homes and gardens
Cars of the '70s. D. MacDonald. Mech Illus 66:42-3 Ja '70
Changes; Pontiac. il Motor T 22:48-50 O '70
Chargers of the Dodge brigade. A. B. Shuman. il Motor T 22:24-7+ D '70
Chrysler corp: it's add your own option year. B. Hartford. il Pop Mech 134:103-7+ O '70
Chrysler-Plymouth rapid transit system. J. Brokaw. il Motor T 22:66-7+ S '70
Compleat manufacturer; Chevrolet. il Motor T 22:76-7+ O '70
Conservative luxury: Pontiac Executive, Mercury Monterey and Chrysler Newport. B. Sanders. il Motor T 22:62-5+ F '70
Detroit '71: preview wrap-up. J. Brokaw. il Motor T 22:38-41+ Ag '70
Dodge material. J. Brokaw. il Motor T 22:48-51 S '70
Dodge material, factory remnants. A. B. Shuman. il Motor T 22:88-9 O '70
Easy-to-fix cars. R. Lund. il Pop Mech 133:83:5+ F '70
Establishment motor pool; AMC Ambassador, Plymouth Fury and Ford LTD. J. Brokaw. il Motor T 22:24-7 N '70
Firebirds I've known and loved. A. B. Shuman. il Motor T 22:96-7+ My '70
First color photographs of the '71 cars. J. Dunne. Pop Sci 197:74-5 Ag '70
First of the 1971 cars. il Mech Illus 66:49-52 S '70
Flock of Firebirds for 1970. B. Kilpatrick. il Pop Mech 133:50+ Mr '70
Full-sized, low priced cars: Galaxie, Impala, Fury, Catalina, Ambassador. il Consumer Rep 35:80-8 F '70
GM's sporty movers; family movers. B. Hartford. il Pop Mech 134:108-15+ O '70
How the 1971 cars really will be better. R. Lund. il Pop Mech 134:71-3+ Ag '70
How the '70 models stack up; performance comparisons. M. Spiegel. il Sr Schol 96:18 Ap 13 '70
How to fit your car to your person. T. Tappett. il Mech Illus 66:74-6+ Mr '70
It's a Maserrariac, white eyes; new Firebird. A. B. Shuman. il Motor T 22:48-9+ F '70
King of the hill; Lincoln Continental Mark III and Cadillac Eldorado. B. Sanders. il Motor T 22:78-80 Jl '70
Look's fifteenth annual new car preview: forecast '71. A. Rothenberg. il Look 34:64-73+ O 6 '70
Monte Carlo: Chevrolet's new luxury car. il Consumer Bul 53:25-7 S '70
Motor trend interview. P. Ustinov. il pors Motor T 22:98+ My '70
Motor trend's 1971 new car buyer's guide. il Motor T 22:28-35 O '70
Mustang makes it happen. B. Sanders. il Motor T 22:60-2+ S '70
News on wheels. M. Spiegel. il Sr Schol 96:20-1 Mr 23 '70

AUTOMOBILES—*Continued*

1970 Camaro, better for being late. M. Lamm. il Pop Mech 133:40+ Mr '70
1970 cars. il Changing T 23:25-32 D '69
1970 cars; intermediates. il Consumer Bul 53: 28-36 Jl '70
1970+ Firebird. J. R. Connor. il Mech Illus 66:137-8 Ap '70
1970 'Vette. E. Dahlquist. il Motor T 22:88-9 Mr '70
1971 cars. il Changing T 24:25-32 D '70
1971 cars! R. W. Irvin. il Mech Illus 66: 59-63+ O '70
1971: year of the car. M. Spiegel. il Sr Schol 97:32-3+ O 26 '70
Old fashioned bargain; intermediate size cars. B. Sanders. il Motor T 22:30-3+ My '70
Plymouth-Imperial. J. Brokaw. il Motor T 22: 94-5+ O '70
PM owners report:
  AMC Hornet. M. Lamm. il Pop Mech 134: 124-7 S '70
  American motors Rebel. M. Lamm. il Pop Mech 133:149-51 Ap '70
  Buick Riviera. M. Lamm. il Pop Mech 134:96-9 S '70
  Chevrolet Monte Carlo. M. Lamm. il Pop Mech 133:142-5 Ap '70
  Chevy Camaro, Pontiac Firebird. M. Lamm. il Pop Mech 134:83-7+ D '70
  Dodge Challenger. M. Lamm. il Pop Mech 133:96-9 Je '70
  Dodge Polara. M. Lamm. il Pop Mech 134:116-19+ Jl '70
  Ford Mustang. M. Lamm. il Pop Mech 133:128-31 My '70
  Ford Thunderbird. M. Lamm. il Pop Mech 134:116-19+ Ag '70
  Mercury Cougar. M. Lamm. il Pop Mech 134:106-9+ Jl '70
  Oldsmobile Toronado. M. Lamm. il Pop Mech 133:118-21 Je '70
  Plymouth Barracuda. M. Lamm. il Pop Mech 133:102-5 My '70
  Valiant and Duster. B. Hartford. il Pop Mech 133:90-3 Mr '70
Quattroporte decision; Maverick. il Motor T 22:63 S '70
Reasonable alternative. J. Brokaw. il Motor T 23:58-62 Ja '71
Return of the letter car: Chrysler 300H. il Motor T 22:28+ Ap '70
'70 Z/28: the gray deceiver; the Camaro. A. B. Shuman. il Motor T 22:32-3 Mr '70
'71 autos make their debut, and the accent is on variety. il U S News 69:40-2 S 21 '70
'71 cars: what Detroit isn't telling you yet. J. Dunne. il Pop Sci 196:50-1+ Je '70
'71 Ford, Lincoln-Mercury line-up. B. Hartford. il Pop Mech 134:116-19+ S '70
'71 new car preview. il Motor T 22:26-31+ Jl '70
Seventy-one performers. S. Kelly. il Hot Rod 23:32-9 O '70
Silent majority: the family sedan. B. Sanders. il Motor T 22:64-7+ Mr '70
Standard of excellence, revised; Cadillac. il Motor T 22:66-7 O '70
Tale of the tiger; 1970 GTO. J. McFarland. il Motor T 22:79-80+ Je '70
Three 1970 cars: Chevelle, Torino, Satellite. il Consumer Bul 53:7-13 Mr '70
Three 1970 full-size cars: Chevrolet Impala, Ford Galaxie, Plymouth Fury. il Consumer Bul 53:7-13 Ap '70
Trailering with the new cars. B. Behme. il Field & S 75:112-15 N '70
Truck and car news (cont of) What's new. P. B. Jones. See issues of Successful farming
Ultimate Grand Prix. il Motor T 22:62-3 Jl '70
Upward-bound rockets; Oldsmobiles. il Motor T 22:70-2 O '70
What's an 'S' doing on a Rolls-Royce? Stutz Blackhawk. J. Lamm. il Motor T 22:104+ Je '70
With dignity and muscle; Lincoln-Mercury. B. Sanders. il Motor T 22:40-4+ S '70
Without a taste of Geritol; Buick GC Stage I. B. Sanders. il Motor T 22:66-8 Ja '70
  See also
Jeep automobiles
Motor trucks
Sports cars
Station wagons

Accessories
See Automobiles—Equipment

Accidents
See Traffic accidents

Advertising
See Automobile industry and trade—Advertising

Air conditioning
Sensational new auto air conditioner: it cools without refrigerant. E. F. Lindsley. il Pop Sci 197:54-5 D '70
What to do to keep your car's cool. il Mech Illus 66:84-5+ Je '70

Batteries
See Storage batteries

Bearings
Smoother approach. B. Neumann. il Hot Rod 23:62-4 Je '70

Bodies
Basic body dimension (cont) il Consumer Rep 35:221-3 Ap '70
One-man auto body shop. M. Schultz. il Pop Mech 134:120-1 D '70
Rebirth of the roadsters; multitude of dune buggies and kits. J. Thawley. il Hot Rod 23:34-41 S '70

Brakes
See Brakes, Automobile

Camping equipment
Build this three-way Travelpod. C. R. Gretz. il Pop Mech 133:158-62+ F '70
  See also
Automobile trailers

Cams
Timing AM cams. B. Lang. il Hot Rod 23:96 N '70

Carburetors
See Carburetors

Care
See Automobiles—Maintenance and repair

Chassis
Chassis preppin'. J. Dianna. il Hot Rod 23: 104-6 Ap '70

Cleaning
How to keep a car's finish like new. D. L. Gregg. Bet Hom & Gard 48:8+ My '70
Let high-pressure water wash your car. R. S. Hedin. il Pop Sci 196:106-7 Mr '70

Clutches
Clutch blueprinting; by the numbers. J. Dianna. il Hot Rod 23:48-50 Jl '70
Fragmentary evidence. B. Lang. il Hot Rod 23:82-3 Ja '70
Nine-roller clutch. B. Lang. il Hot Rod 23: 124-5 Je '70

Collectors and collecting
Fun and profits in vintage cars. Bsns W p71 Ag 22 '70
Hershey with nuts; Antique automobile club of America annual eastern national fall meet. il Motor T 22:52-3+ Ap '70
Hispano Suiza. il Motor T 22:36-7 Mr '70
Replicars: the ultimate luxury. K. Prentiss. il Holiday 48:56-8 Jl '70
Where are they now? the Edsel lives. il Newsweek 76:22 O 12 '70
With thee, Bug, I plight my troth; Bugatti car. R. Campbell. il Sports Illus 33:62-4+ N 9 '70
  See also
Automobile museums
Automobiles, Racing—Collectors and collecting

Control
  See also
Automobiles—Speed control

Cost of operation
High cost of driving & what to do about it. il Changing T 24:35-8 S '70
What does it cost to own and use a car? Consumer Bul 53:35 Mr '70

Design
Auto repairs: the insurers vs. Detroit; with editorial comment. il Bsns W p44+, 132 My 9 '70
Automobile: studies in steel. W. L. Mitchell. il Sch Arts 69:33-4 Ap '70
Avanti still means forward. D. A. Jedlicka. il por Esquire 73:116-17+ Ap '70
Car of the year; product planners. il Motor T 22:39-41+ F '70
End to obsolescence? changes in the new models. il Time 95:83 My 18 '70
How the Gremlin lost its tail; interview. R. A. Teague. il Pop Mech 134:88-91+ Ag '70
Inside Detroit. See issues of Motor trend

AUTOMOBILES—Design—*Continued*
MI unveils the 1971 cars. R. W. Irvin. il Mech Illus 66:39-42+ Jl '70
Motor trend interview. E. Estes. por Motor T 22:64+ Jl '70
Mustangs that didn't make it. W. Wyss. il Motor T 23:64-8 Ja '71
Next ten years. K. Ludvigsen. il Motor T 22:62-5+ Ja '70
Rap 'n 'pinion; automobile designers. G. Bordinat. por Motor T 22:26 O '70
'71 cars; something new at last? R. Lund. il Pop Mech 133:71-4+ Je '70
Showtime; International automobile show in New York city. il Motor T 22:36-43 Ap '70
Specialty cars. Consumer Rep 35:219-20 Ap '70
This isn't your common everyday Vanden Plas Tourer; Ruger Tourer. M. Denny. il por Motor T 22:50-3+ D '70
Tom McCahill's color portfolio of the 1971 cars. T. McCahill. il Mech Illus 66:80-2+ N '70
See also
Automobiles—Bodies
Automobiles, Compact—Design
Automobiles—Safety devices and measures

Differential
See Automobiles—Transmission

Drive shafts
See Automobiles—Propeller shafts

Driving
See Automobile driving

Electric equipment
Engine saver; oil pressure safety switch. B. Lang. il Hot Rod 23:118 O '70
Improved four-way flasher. D. R. Hicke. il Pop Electr 33:80 Ag '70
It's electricity that makes your car go. il Changing T 24:15-17 Ag '70

Electric wiring
Wiring. J. Dianna. il Hot Rod 23:50-2 S '70

Electronic equipment
Blinker reminds you to gas up. R. F. Graf and G. J. Whalen. il Pop Sci 196:98+ Ap '70
Build! Lights-on reminder. R. M. Marston. il Radio-Electr 41:60-1 Ap '70
Build lights-on reminder. R. F. Zollweg. il Radio-Electr 41:66 My '70
Dash computer tells when to change oil. E. F. Lindsley. il Pop Sci 197:88 Ag '70
Fill 'er up! The blinker says so. R. F. Graf and G. J. Whalen. il Pop Sci 197:95+ My '70
How to troubleshoot some of those new-fangled gadgets. M. Schultz. il Pop Mech 133:146-9 My '70
Save yourself a ticket with this auto speed alarm. G. J. Whalen and R. F. Graf. il Pop Mech 133:132-3 Je '70
Solid-state tach & add-on speed alarm. R. M. Marston. il Radio-Electr 41:33-8 Ap '70
Stay-awake alarm. R. M. Marston. il Radio-Electr 41:52-4 S '70
See also
Computers—Automotive use

Emblems
See Emblems

Equipment
How to match a trailer to your car. V. L. Oertle. il Pop Mech 134:71-2+ Jl '70
Latest scoop; bolt-on hood scoop. E. Rickman. il Hot Rod 23:72 Ap '70
Lonely passion of Karl E. Smith; rear view mirror. T. Tyler. il por Time 96:16 Jl 20 '70
New hitches that take the worry out of trailering. A. J. Hand. il Pop Sci 196:118-20 Ap '70
Options: which are worth buying? (cont) Consumer Rep 35:205-8 Ap '70
Product trends. See issues of Motor trend
SEMA showtime. E. Rickman. il Hot Rod 23:126-7 Ap '70
Strictly for stocks; towing equipment. J. Dianna. il Hot Rod 23:95 S '70
Trailer-hitching guide puts you right on target. C. G. Hansen. il Pop Sci 196:95 Je '70
Vega put-ons. S. Kelly. il Hot Rod 23:86 D '70
What's new. See issues of Hot rod
When birds & beasts went motoring; radiator mascots and hood ornaments. M. Lamm. il Audubon 72:36-9 Ja '70
See also
Automobiles—Camping equipment
Automobiles—Electric equipment

Automobiles—Protection against theft
Automobiles—Safety devices and measures
Automobiles—Tape equipment
Odometers
Prestolite company

Exhaust
See Automobile engines—Exhaust

Exhibitions
Concours d'elegance; show of classic vintage cars, Hillsborough, Calif. B. Whittington. il Har Yrs 10:26-7 My '70
Detroit's bumps get harder; Chicago auto show. il Bsns W p32-3 F 28 '70
Hershey with nuts; Antique automobile club of America annual eastern national fall meet. il Motor T 22:52-3+ Ap '70
Paris: the fall collection. E. Dahlquist. il Motor T 22:82-4 Ja '70
Show & go. See issues of Hot rod
Showtime; International automobile show in New York city. il Motor T 22:36-43 Ap '70
Turin; renaissance & reformation. E. Seidler. il Motor T 22:78-80+ F '70
See also
Automobiles, Racing—Exhibitions

Fastenings
See Fastenings

Four wheel drive
Man's machine. B. Behme. il Field & S 75:146-9 O '70
See also
Station wagons—Four wheel drive

Fuel systems
See Automobile engines—Fuel feeding

Gearing
Dragster O.D. M. Schofield. il Hot Rod 23:94-5 Mr '70
Gearbox fix for plain Volks. J. Thawley. il Hot Rod 23:62-3 F '70
Latest in beetle *schticks*. J. McFarland. il Motor T 22:95 F '70
One more improvement; VW Hurst Saf-T trigger shifter. D. Evans. il Hot Rod 23:83 F '70
See also
Automobiles—Steering gear
Automobiles—Transmission

Handbooks, manuals, etc.
Here's a book all car owners should read. il Changing T 24:15-16 F '70

History
Well-preserved sexagenarian; 1910 Oldsmobile Limited. J. Lamm. il Motor T 22:90-1+ O '70
See also
Automobile museums

Anecdotes, facetiae, satire, etc.
Automobile, History of (1896-1984) H. Morgan. Sat R 53:6+ S 19 '70

Hoods
Glass bonnet. B. Lang. il Hot Rod 23:88 F '70

Ignition
See Automobile engines—Ignition

Inspection
How to make your own safety inspection. T. Tappett. il Mech Illus 66:108-10+ F '70

Insurance
See Insurance, Automobile

Leasing and renting
European cars, lease, rent or buy? Har Yrs 10:5 Ap '70
Executive in the hired car; with comments by businessmen. J. Perham. il Duns 96:40-1+ N '70
Fly and drive and explore! H. Bims. il Ebony 25:156-60+ Je '70
Slightly used bargains. il Time 95:77 F 9 '70

Locks
See Automobile locks and keys

Lubrication
Oil pump exercise. B. Lang. il Hot Rod 23:102 Ja '70
Panning for horsepower. J. Thawley. il Hot Rod 24:84-6 Ja '71
Pickups, pumps and pans. B. Lang. il Hot Rod 23:46-8 Mr '70

AUTOMOBILES—*Continued*

Maintenance and repair

Auto repairs a woman can make. il Good H 170:136 Ja '70
Auto repairs: the insurers vs. Detroit; with editorial comment. il Bsns W p44+, 132 My 9 '70
Automobile clinic; questions and answers. M. Schultz. See issues of Popular mechanics
Beat the high cost of body repairs. J. Davis. il Pop Sci 196:122+ My '70
Chemical tools for home car care. R. Day. il Pop Sci 197:120 N '70
Easy-to-fix cars. R. Lund. il Pop Mech 133: 83-5+ F '70
Fix-it-yourself approach; Ford's Pinto. il Time 96:57-8 Ag 17 '70
Frequency-of-repair records: 1964 to 1969. il Consumer Rep 35:228-33 Ap '70
How to know when your car has had it. D. L. Gregg. Bet Hom & Gard 48:4+ Jl '70
How to make your car last and last and last. T. Tappett. il Mech Illus 66:119-21+ O '70
How to set up a home diagnostic and tune-up center for your car. R. Day. il Pop Sci 196:151-6+ Ja '70
Is your car ready for a vacation trip? J. P. Norbye. il Pop Sci 196:81 My '70
It's not too late to get set for winter driving. il Consumer Bul 53:35-6 Ja '70
Maybe your car needs a tune-up. il Changing T 25:45-7 Ja '71
Motor trend interview; problems facing car owners. P. A. Hart. il pors Motor T 22:92+ Ap '70
New look at spring service. T. Tappett. il Mech Illus 66:96-8+ Ap '70
One-man auto body shop. M. Schultz. il Pop Mech 134:120-1 D '70
Saturday mechanic. M. Schultz. See issues of Popular mechanics
Say, Smokey; questions and answers. S. Yunick. See issues of Popular science monthly
Shop talk. J. Dianna. See issues of Hot rod
Smokey answers your eight most-asked auto questions. S. Yunick. il pors Pop Sci 196: 58-9+ F '70
Taking care of your car. See issues of Popular science monthly
Taking care of your car. il Pop Sci 196:40 F; 112 Mr '70
Ten-point inspection for carefree summer driving. M. Schultz. il Pop Mech 133:128-31 Je '70
Tune-up by tape. Travel 134:17 O '70
Where to take your car for service. D. L. Gregg. Bet Hom & Gard 48:128+ Mr '70
Will car servicing get better or worse? D. L. Gregg. Bet Hom & Gard 48:8+ O '70
See also
Automobile mechanics (persons)
Automobile service stations

Manufacture
See also
Automobile factories
Automobile industry and trade
Automobile parts

Materials
Glass bonnet. B. Lang. il Hot Rod 23:88 F '70

Noise
How to deal with squeaks and rattles. T. Tappett. il Mech Illus 66:90-2 My '70

Parking
See Automobile parking

Parts
See Automobile parts

Polishing
See Automobiles—Cleaning

Prices
Full-sized, low-priced cars. Consumer Rep 35: 216-19 Ap '70
GM and Ford cut fleet discounts. il Bsns W p30 Je 13 '70
GM starts up and hikes prices. Bsns W p22-3 N 28 '70
1970 cars. il Changing T 23:25-32 D '69
1971 cars: heading for the price you want. Bsns W p81 O 3 '70
Price surprise from GM's Vega. il Bsns W p23 S 12 '70
Strike gives Pinto a head start. il Bsns W p31-2 S 19 '70

Propeller shafts
How about a lid? low-investment drivetrain. A. B. Shuman. il Motor T 22:28-9 D '70

Protection against theft
Bettered mousetrap. C. Baker. il Hot Rod 23: 64-5 Jl '70
Here they are: results of the $25,000 anti-car-theft competition. E. A. Zadig. il por Pop Sci 196:72-3 Je '70
Well, shut my fuel! B. Lang. il Hot Rod 23:63 My '70
See also
Automobile locks and keys

Purchasing
Cost of living; helpful hints. B. Furness. Mc-Calls 97:18+ S '70
How to become a smiling used-car buyer. M. Lamm. il Pop Mech 133:85-9 Je '70
How to buy a new car. Consumer Rep 34: 401-4 D '69
How to buy your new Barracuda. il Motor T 22:30-1 D '70
How to buy your new Camaro. il Motor T 22:32-3 N '70
How to buy your new Montego. il Motor T 23: 30-1 Ja '71
Look before you vote! M. Spiegel. Sr Schol 95:20 N 10 '69
Money-saving guide to car buying. il Consumer Rep 35:198-200 Ap '70

Radio equipment
Consumers guide to cut-rate car radios. il Mech Illus 66:79 My '70
Short-wave converter. L. Lisle. il Radio-Electr 41:50-2 Mr '70
Stereo multiplex FM in 1970 cars. L. Allen. il Radio-Electr 41:61+ Je '70

Maintenance and repair
Ten solid-state car radio problems. H. L. Davidson. il Radio-Electr 41:57-9 Ap '70

Rating
Ratings of the 1970 U.S. cars. il Consumer Rep 35:212-20 Ap '70
Track-testing the '70 cars; Union 76 performance trial results. il Changing T 24:11-13 Ap '70

Rattles
See Automobiles—Noise

Repairing
See Automobiles—Maintenance and repair

Roofs
Caring for your convertible. G. Baron. il Mech Illus 66:112-13+ Ap '70

Safety devices and measures
All aboard the miracle bandwagon; questioning the effectiveness of the air bag restraint system. Motor T 22:8-9 Ag '70
Are crowded highways getting safer? il U S News 68:50-2 F 2 '70
Auto safety: we've come a long way, but there's still a long way to go. J. P. Norbye and J. Dunne. il Pop Sci 197:76-7 O '70
Bird that hoots if drivers doze. Bsns W p53 Jl 4 '70
Cars of the future, safety first. il U S News 68:34-6 Mr 30 '70
Cars will be safer, if this idea works; air bags. il Changing T 24:31-3 N '70
Digital drunk test. Newsweek 75:78 Je 1 '70
Drive to make autos safer: what the government wants. il U S News 69:35-6 Ag 31 '70
Drunk-driver detector. Am City 85:8 D '70
Faster road to a safer car. il Bsns W p23 O 31 '70
Great sack race. il Motor T 22:8-9+ Jl '70
How to buy a safe kiddie seat for your car. A. Laidlaw. il Mech Illus 66:66-7+ Mr '70
How to make your own safety inspection. T. Tappett. il Mech Illus 66:108-10+ F '70
New engineering; priorities for the 70's; address, January 14, 1970. E. N. Cole. Vital Speeches 36:236-40 F 1 '70
Pushbuttons v. drunks; physiological tester to judge a driver's condition. il Time 95:58 Je 1 '70
Safe at any speed? air bags and bumper-and-ramp system. il Newsweek 76:54 S 7 '70
Safety: a few new requirements. Consumer Rep 35:54 Ja '70

AUTOMOBILES—Safety devices and measures
—*Continued*

Safety: a progress report. il Consumer Rep 35:234-8 Ap '70

What's ahead in safer cars. U S News 68: 5 F 9 '70

See also
Automobiles—Testing
Safety belts

Scrapping
See Automobiles—Wrecking

Service stations
See Automobile service stations

Shock absorbers
Double-duty snubbers. J. Dianna. il Hot Rod 23:98-9 Jl '70

Shows
See Automobiles—Exhibitions

Skidding
School for skids. E. Dahlquist. il por Motor T 22:101-2 Ap '70

There's an easier way to stop, anti-skid systems. il Motor T 22:72-4 Jl '70

Things they don't teach in driver ed! M. Lamm. il Pop Mech 134:97-9+ N '70

See also
Pavements—Slipperiness

Social aspects
Motorcar vs. America. C. Ogburn, jr. il Am Heritage 21:104-10 Je '70

Real population explosion. J. R. Kasun. il America 123:112-14 S 5 '70

Specifications
Guide to mechanical specifications; tables. il Consumer Rep 35:224-7 Ap '70

Three Dodge cars tested: Challenger, Charger, and Dart. il Consumer Bul 53:36 F '70

Speed
See also
Automobile speed records

Speed control
Speed-control kit for your car. J. Copeland. il Pop Sci 197:134 O '70

Springs and suspension
Front end lowdown. B. Lang. il Hot Rod 23:106-9 O '70

What you can do about tired suspension. T. Tappett. il Mech Illus 66:76-8+ D '70

Starting
How to beat three wintertime starting problems. M. Schultz. il Pop Mech 134:138-41 D '70

Warm-up for break-in; recirculatory device. J. Dianna. il Hot Rod 23:72-3 D '70

Statistics
Real population explosion. J. R. Kasun. il America 123:112-14 S 5 '70

Steering gear
ABCs of front ends and steering. R. W. Temple. il Pop Mech 133:108-13+ Mr '70

Grab a wheel deal. E. Rickman. il Hot Rod 23:87 Mr '70

Power steering for jeeps. J. Thawley. il Hot Rod 23:108-9 Mr '70

Stopping
How to solve sudden stall. M. Schultz. il Pop Mech 134:148-51 S '70

How to stop stalling and learn to love your car. T. Tappett. il Mech Illus 66:98-100+ Je '70

Styling
See Automobiles—Design

Tape equipment
Remote speakers for car stereo. H. L. Davidson. il Radio-Electr 41:53 Ap '70

Stereo on wheels. L. Steckler. il Radio-Electr 41:33-5 Je '70

Tape players for automobiles. il Consumer Bul 53:19-24 Je '70

Trying to cross the country by cassette. I. Berger. Sat R 53:93-4 F 28 '70

Testing
Come back little Ethyl. A. B. Shuman. il Motor T 22:84-7 O '70

Hot rod road test:
  Earth mover; Chevelle Malibu SS454. S. Kelly. il Hot Rod 23:64-6 My '70
  Firebird: '70 model. S. Kelly. il Hot Rod 23:34-5 F '70
  Hornet SC/360. R. Guldahl, jr. il Hot Rod 23:36-9 D '70
  New entry: Duster. S. Kelly. il Hot Rod 23:60-1 Mr '70
  Oldsmobile W-machines. S. Kelly. il Hot Rod 23:102-3 Ap '70
  Small wonder; Camaro. S. Kelly. il Hot Rod 23:36-7 Mr '70
  Too much of a Rebel. S. Kelly. il Hot Rod 23:52-3 F '70
  Winged-foot street rod; Montego Cyclone. S. Kelly. il Hot Rod 23:40-1 Ap '70

How CU buys, tests and rates its cars. Consumer Rep 35:209-11 Ap '70

Intermediate cars: Chevrolet Chevelle, Buick Skylark, Plymouth Satellite, AMC Rebel, and Ford Torino. il Consumer Rep 35:46-53 Ja '70

Norbye-Dunne report:
  Detroit's economy cars are basic, but not so cheap. J. P. Norbye and J. Dunne. il Pop Sci 196:122-7 Ja '70
  Intermediate sixes. J. P. Norbye and J. Dunne. il Pop Sci 196:32+ Ap '70
  '70 personal cars. J. P. Norbye and J. Dunne. il Pop Sci 196:30+ F '70
  Supercars for the '70's are here. J. P. Norbye and J. Dunne. il Pop Sci 197:24+ Jl '70

PM road test:
  AMC's new Hornet. B. Kilpatrick. il Pop Mech 133:96-9+ F '70

Performance tests, Detroit vs. Union oil. B. Hartford. il Pop Mech 133:94-7 Ap '70

Road testing the 340, 440-6, and Hemi 'Cudas: isn't there an easier way to earn my Canadian club? A. B. Shuman. il Motor T 22:40-2 My '70

Specialty cars; Dodge Challenger, Plymouth 'Cuda, Mustang Boss, Chevrolet Monte Carlo. il Consumer Rep 35:294-9 My '70

Three Dodge cars tested: Challenger, Charger, and Dart. il Consumer Bul 53:31-6 F '70

Tom McCahill tests (title varies)
  Buick Riviera. T. McCahill. il Mech Illus 66:70-2+ Ap '70
  Buick's Riviera GS. T. McCahill. il Mech Illus 66:48-9+ N '70
  Ford Galaxie 500. T. McCahill. il Mech Illus 66:62-3 N '70
  Ford Torino. T. McCahill. il Mech Illus 66:147-9 Mr '70
  Plymouth Duster 340. T. McCahill. il Mech Illus 66:38+ F '70
  Plymouth's Sebring Plus. T. McCahill. il Mech Illus 66:71-3 O '70
  Pontiac GTO on the world's fastest track. T. McCahill. il Mech Illus 66:50-2+ Ja '70
  Pontiac's Grand Ville. T. McCahill. il Mech Illus 66:167-9 O '70
  Z28 Camaro. T. McCahill. il Mech Illus 66:52-3+ Jl '70

Torino road test; Car of the year candidates. il Motor T 22:34-8 F '70

See also
Automobiles—Rating
Automobiles, Foreign—Testing

Tires
See Tires, Automobile

Towing
See Towing

Traction
Now, Buick offers better traction on slippery roads. J. P. Norbye and J. Dunne. il Pop Sci 197:78 O '70

Trailers
See Automobile trailers

Transmission
Chevy/hemi trans swap. J. Dianna. il Hot Rod 23:40-1 My '70

Handy automatic; Hurst-a-matic shifter. J. Dianna. il Hot Rod 23:55 N '70

High-stall automatics; racing converters. B. Lang. il Hot Rod 23:120-1 O '70

How to fix your automatic transmission. M. Schultz. il Pop Mech 134:136-9+ Jl '70

How to troubleshoot a differential. M. Schultz. il Pop Mech 133:140-3 Ja '70

Key to the locker. S. Kelly. il Hot Rod 23:118-19 Je '70

Key West, automatically; new automatic transmission for the Renault 16 sedanwagon. B. Kilpatrick. Mech Illus 66:34+ My '70

AUTOMOBILES—Transmission—*Continued*
Low-drag automatic for pros. J. Dianna. il
  Hot Rod 24:46-8 Ja '71
Maybe you need an overdrive. C. J. Baker.
  il Pop Mech 135:130-3+ Ja '71
Putting the pow into Powerglide. J. Thawley.
  il Hot Rod 23:44-5 N '70
Smoke runs with a five-speed; Dick Loehr's
  pro stocker. S. Kelly. il Hot Rod 23:42-4
  S '70
Timely shift; Borg-Warner's new Super T-
  10. E. Rickman. il Hot Rod 23:62-3 Mr '70
Turbo terrific; valve-body metering plate and
  pan gasket. B. Lang. il Hot Rod 24:96 Ja '71
VW posi for a quarter; limited-slip differen-
  tial. J. Thawley. il por Hot Rod 23:110-12
  Ap '70
  See also
Automobiles—Gearing

Warranty
  See Warranty

Washing
  See Automobiles—Cleaning

Wheels
Ford's better idea: collapsing front wheels.
  il Consumer Rep 35:657-8 N '70
Seventy years of wheels! il Pop Mech 134:
  112-14 D '70
VW wheel adapters. E. Rickman. il Hot Rod
  23:92 Mr '70

Windows
Shutter bug; rear window louvers. E. Rickman. il Hot Rod 23:95 My '70

Windshield defrosters
Warming to wired windshields. il Bsns W
  p 154 Mr 28 '70

Windshield wipers
Put a speed control on your windshield
  wipers. R. F. Graf and G. J. Whalen. il
  Pop Mech 133:138-9 Ja '70

Windshields
Fog, ice, snow on auto glass. Sunset 144:40
  Ja '70

Wrecking
Better scrap comes in from the cold; cryo-
  genic process. il Bsns W p54 O 31 '70
Big shredder eats a junked car a minute;
  Alexandria, Va. B. W. Brown. il Am City
  85:70-1 Jl '70
Costly plague of junked cars. il Bsns W
  p61+ Ap 4 '70
Smokeless car salvage; Cedar Rapids area.
  Am City 85:27 N '70
AUTOMOBILES, Abandoned. See Automobiles
  —Wrecking
AUTOMOBILES, Care of. See Automobiles—
  Maintenance and repair
AUTOMOBILES, Compact
Advance look at '71 cars. il U S News 68:30-3
  My 4 '70
All the king's horses.   A. B. Shuman. il
  Motor T 22:86-8+ Ap '70
AMC Gremlin. il Consumer Rep 35:444-5 Jl
  '70
Autos: shifting down for the '70s; American
  motors first subcompact, the Gremlin. il
  Time 95:80-1 F 23 '70
Battle of the small cars: the imports fight
  back. il U S News 69:62-3 O 5 '70
Beleaguered Detroit fights back; sub-com-
  pacts. il Newsweek 75:73-7 Ap 6 '70
Chevy's top brass talks about Vega: starlet
  with a future; interview, ed. by J. Dunne.
  J. Z. DeLorean. il pors Pop Sci 197:56-7+
  S '70
Chrysler goes abroad for mini. il Bsns W p20
  Jl 4 '70
Chrysler tries without a mini. il Bsns W p58-
  9 S 5 '70
Clever cars,   these   Pintos;   interview. J.
  Naughton il pors Motor T 22:52-5+ S '70
Compact cars. il Consumer Rep 35:212-13 Ap
  '70
Compact cars: the latest entries. il U S News
  69:34 Ag 31 '70
Debut for subcompacts. il Time 96:92 S 21 '70
Detroit's first midget joins fight on foreign-
  ers. il Bsns W p23-4 F 14 '70
Detroit's minis: how much muscle? R. Lund.
  il Pop Mech 134:84-7+ Jl '70
Detroit's new mini-compacts. J. Dunne. il
  Pop Sci 196:52-3+ F '70
Eight exciting little cars that save you
  money, too. J. P. Norbye and J. Dunne.
  il Pop Sci 197:67-73 O '70

Fix-it-yourself approach; Ford's Pinto. il
  Time 96:57-8 Ag 17 '70
Ford's top brass talks about Pinto power;
  interview, ed. by J. Dunne. J. B. Naughton.
  il pors Pop Sci 197:54-5+ S '70
GM's John DeLorean: powerhouse behind
  the Vega. A. Rothenberg. il pors Look 34:
  54-7 Ag 25 '70
Gremlin, American motors' new car. il Con-
  sumer Bul 53:14-16 N '70
Gremlins will get you if you don't watch
  out! American motors' new subcompact.
  M. Lamm. il Pop Mech 133:106-9 Ap '70
Here come the minicars. il U S News 68:36-7
  F 16 '70
Hot stuff for Mavericks. S. Kelley. il Hot
  rod 23:90-2 Ja '70
How the Gremlin lost its tail; interview.
  R. A. Teague. il Pop Mech 134:88-91+
  Ag '70
Little cars; Datsun PL510, Chevrolet Vega,
  Toyota Corona, Ford Pinto, VW Super
  Beetle, AMC Gremlin. il Consumer Rep 36:
  8-17 Ja '71
Little ones are hotter than ever. il Bsns W
  p20-1 Ap 11 '70
McCall's tests the new mini cars. il McCalls
  98:94-5 O '70
Micro muscle; Vega and Pinto. il Motor T
  22:73-4 N '70
Minis are out to rule the road. M. Lamm;
  B. Hartford. il Pop Mech 134:112-15+ S '70
Minis meet the imports. il Bsns W p68-71 Ag
  15 '70
New American minicars, how they compare.
  il Changing T 24:21-3 Je '70
New Gremlin has power and style. J. Davis.
  il Pop Sci 196:65 Ap '70
1970 cars. il Consumer Bul 53:28-36 Jl '70
1970 Gremlin. E. Dahlquist. il Motor T 22:
  70-1+ Mr '70
1970 Gremlin; interview. R. A. Teague. por
  Motor T 22:72 Mr '70
Now: the U.S. minicars. il U S News 69:28-30
  Ag 17 '70
Nuts and bolts; Vega and the automatic car
  wash. New Repub 163:10-11 N 7 '70
Range war; Mustang. C. Kock. il Motor T 23:
  32-7 Ja '71
Rap 'n 'pinion; European interest in the
  Vega and Pinto. E. Seidler. por Motor T
  22:14 D '70
Second look at the Ford Cortina. Consumer
  Rep 35:5-6 Ja '70
'70 1/2 Sunbeam Avenger. J. Lowrey. il Mo-
  tor T 22:98+ Ap '70
Son of Road Runner; Project Duster. C.
  Koch. il Motor T 22:44-6+ Ag; 32-3 S '70
Son of Road Runner; Project Duster. J. Lamm.
  il Motor T 22:32-4 Jl '70
Three 1970 compact cars; Nornet 6, Nova 6,
  Valiant V-8. il Consumer Bul 53:28-34 Je '70
Three small voices in the wilderness: Mave-
  rick, Hornet, Duster. B. Sanders. il Motor
  T 22:44-7+ Ja '70
Vega: engineering. A. B. Shuman. il Motor
  T 22:36-7+ Ag '70
Vega, small-car star. S. Kelly. il Hot Rod
  23:36-9 N '70
Vega 2300. B. Sanders and J. Brokaw. il
  Motor T 22:30-5 Ag '70
Where are they now? what ever happened to
  Baby J? il Newsweek 75:16 Ap 6 '70
Working out the Gremlins. A. B. Shuman.
  il Motor T 22:67-8+ Ap '70
  See also
Automobiles, Foreign

Design
Engineering and driving Ford's horse of a
  different color; Pinto. B. Sanders. il Mo-
  tor T 22:59+ S '70
Enter the Vega. il Newsweek 76:66 Ag 17 '70
GM's mini: the very model of automation;
  Vega. il Bsns W p26 Ag 8 '70

Prices
  See Automobiles—Prices

Testing
Compact and sub compact cars; Toyota
  Corona Mark II, Plymouth Duster, AMC
  Hornet, Ford Maverick, Datsun PL510,
  Volkswagen sedan. il Consumer Rep 35:
  377-85 Je '70
Pinto: Ford's new mini-pony. M. Spiegel. il
  Sr Schol 97:44 S 28 '70
10,000 miles in the new Gremlin. J. Davis. il
  Pop Sci 197:54-6 Jl '70
Tom McCahill tests (title varies)
  AMC's new Gremlin. T. McCahill. il Mech
  Illus 66:58-60+ Jl '70
  Ford Pinto & the Chevy Vega 2300. il
  Mech Illus 66:57-62 S '70

AUTOMOBILES, Electric
Cars and air pollution. L. Fermi; discussion.
Bul Atom Sci 26:43-4 My '70
Cordless electric; Globe Union electric car.
il Motor T 22:59 D '70

AUTOMOBILES, Experimental
Cerv II: Corvette experimental (non) racing
vehicle. K. Ludvigsen. il Motor T 22:48-
50+ N '70
How about a lid? Boss 302. A. B. Shuman.
il Motor T 22:28-9 D '70
New: Minto's unique steamless steam car;
antipollution car. E. F. Lindsley. il Pop
Sci 197:51-3+ O '70
PS previews the great clean-air car race.
E. H. Arctander. il Pop Sci 197:50-2+ Ag
'70

AUTOMOBILES, Foreign
All hail the Audi. E. Dahlquist. il Motor T
22:84-5+ My '70
Audi's GT. il Motor T 22:66 D '70
Battle of the small cars: the imports fight
back. il U S News 69:62-3 O 5 '70
Capri. J. Lamm. il Motor T 22:30+ Ap '70
Capricious Citroën. J. Lamm. il Motor T 23:
28 Ja '71
Citroën DS-21: an automotive anomaly. il
Consumer Rep 35:177-81 Mr '70
Citroën SM: come drive the world's most un-
usual production car! J. P. Norbye. il Pop
Sci 197:64-5 S '70
Eleven year plan; Volvo. il Motor T 22:44+
My '70
For America only; mid-engine GT. K. Lud-
vigsen. il Motor T 22:44-6+ Ap '70
For mini-warfare, a bigger beetle. il Time
96:82+ O 5 '70
Import invasion hits high tide. A. Rothen-
berg. il Look 34:30-7+ Ap 7 '70
Import report. E. Seidler. See issues of Motor
trend
Imported sedans: Peugeot 504, Audi 100LS,
Saab 99E, BMW 2002. il Consumer Rep 35:
437-43 Jl '70
Is there a three-wheeler in your future?
Bond Bug. M. Lamm. il Pop Mech 135:106-9
Ja '71
Micro-cars. il Life 69:76-9 D 11 '70
Morgan comes back. Newsweek 75:64 Je 22
'70
Mouse of the rising sun: Subaru 1100 FF-1
Star. E. Dahlquist. il Motor T 22:84-5+ Ap
'70
1970 Volkswagens. J. R. Connor. il Mech
Illus 66:30+ Ja '70
Now, a plush British grand tourer; Triumph
Stag. D. Scott. il Pop Sci 197:16 Ag '70
Ominous Opel. il Motor T 22:83 D '70
PM owners report:
Datsun. B. Hartford. il Pop Mech 133:126-
9+ F '70
Mercedes-Benz. M. Lamm. il Pop Mech
135:100-3+ Ja '71
Safe at any speed: the Jensen FF. I. Ireland.
il Pop Mech 133:114-16 Je '70
Second best car in the world: Mercedes 300
SEL 3.5. E. Dahlquist il Motor T 22:22-4+
S '70
Some people think the Mercedes is the best
car in the world, but not BMW. E. Dahl-
quist. il Motor T 22:70-3 Ja '70
Special! Commuters: $1600 and under; Honda
600 and Fiat 850. C. Koch. il Motor T 22:
64+ N '70
Still no sayonara for the Subaru 360. Con-
sumer Rep 35:192 Ap '70
Super-Beetle? 1971 VW. M. Spiegel. il Sr
Schol 97:30 N 16 '70
Super Citroën. E. Seidler. il Motor T 22:80-2
My '70
Ultimate 2002: BMW. il Motor T 22:53 N '70
La vérité; Peugeot 504. A. B. Shuman. il
Motor T 22:74-6 F '70
VW scene: dyno building. J. Dianna. il Hot
Rod 23:96-8 Ja '70
What this country needs is a good $25,000
car. T. Hogg. Esquire 74:32+ Ag '70
Who's afraid of Vega, Pinto and Gremlin?
Not Toyota. S. Hattori. pors Motor T
22:65-6+ Ag '70
Not VW. S. Perkins. pors Motor T 22:65-
6+ Ag '70
Yankee captives vs. Toyota. C. Koch. il Mo-
tor T 22:38-41+ D '70
Your target for today: Volkswagen. A. B.
Shuman. il Motor T 23:22-7 Ja '71
See also
Sports cars

Collectors and collecting
See Automobiles—Collectors and collecting

Design
Front-wheel drive takes a new turn. J. P.
Norbye. il Pop Sci 196:96-100 Ja '70

Gearing
See Automobiles—Gearing

History
Eternal ghost; Rolls-Royce Silver Ghost. L.
W. Steinwedel. il Motor T 22:86-90+ Je '70

Marketing
Fast pace of Japanese cars. il Bsns W
p42+ Ag 8 '70
See also
Volkswagen of America, inc.

Testing
Compact and sub compact cars; Toyota
Corona Mark II, Datsun PL510, Volkswagen
sedan. il Consumer Rep 35:377-85 Je '70
Five sports cars; Datsun 24OZ,Opel GT, MGB
GT, Porsche 914, Triumph GT6. il Consumer
Rep 35:550-7 S '70
Hot rod road test:
Super Beetle. S. Kelly. il Hot Rod 24:
72-5 Ja '71
Motor trend's 1970 import car of the year;
Porsche 914-914/6. il Motor T 22:64-9+ Je '70
Norbye-Dunne report:
From Japan, little two-door sedans with
a low, low price. J. P. Norbye and J.
Dunne. il Pop Sci 197:32+ D '70
Small car Detroit doesn't make: four
doors, four seats, four cylinders. J. P.
Norbye and J. Dunne. il Pop Sci 197:
36+ N '70
These compact sedans are part-time
wagons. J. P. Norbye and J. Dunne.
il Pop Sci 197:32+ S '70
$3,000-$4,000 imported family cars. J.
P. Norbye and J. Dunne. il Pop Sci
197:24+ Ag '70
Old pro tries out the world's most advanced
car: Mercedes' experimental mid-engine
sports car. J. Fitch. il Pop Mech 133:88-
91 Ja '70
Test driving Colt and Cricket. M. Lamm.
il Pop Mech 135:32+ Ja '71
Test driving the new Renault 16 automatic.
B. Hartford. il Pop Mech 133:38+ Je '70
Tom McCahill tests (title varies)
Austin America. T. McCahill. il Mech
Illus 66:135-7 Ag '70
Colt & Cricket. T. McCahill. il Mech Illus
66:38-41+ D '70
Two great second cars: Renault 16 and
Simca 1204. T. McCahill. il Mech Ilus 66:
48-50+ Je '70

Transmission
See Automobiles—Transmission

Wheels
See Automobiles—Wheels

AUTOMOBILES, Military
See also
Motor trucks, Military

AUTOMOBILES, Municipal
Hand-me-downs cuts costs for city fleet; motor pool for one-year-old police cars. Milford, Conn. C. J. Hughes. il Am City 85:106
Je '70

AUTOMOBILES, Old

Collectors and collecting
See Automobiles—Collectors and collecting

AUTOMOBILES, Police

Cost of operation
LP-gas cuts police car costs, improves per-
formance; Chandler, Ariz. W. T. Louthan. il
Am City 85:87-8 Je '70

AUTOMOBILES, Racing
Back-motor digger. S. Kelly. il Hot Rod 23:
40-2 N '70
Big go Gatorsville. D. Evans. il Hot Rod 23:
44-6 My '70
Bill Jenkins' super toy. B. Lang. il Hot Rod
23:34-7 Jl '70
Bucks-up racer. il Hot Rod 23:52-4 Ja '70
Buggymaster of the roaring dunes; B. Meyers,
builder of the Manx. B. Yates. il por Sports
Illus 32:52-3 Je 29 '70
Can the Can-Am kings blitz the brickyard?
B. Hartford. il Pop Mech 133:90-3+ My '70
Chevy V-16 fueler. R. Guldahl, jr. il Hot
Rod 24:28-31 Ja '71
Come drive Mercedes' Wunderwagen, wow!
J. P. Norbye. il Pop Sci 196:86-7 F '70
Coming of age in Pomona; NHRA's winter-
nationals. A. B. Shuman. il Motor T 22:
48-51+ Ap '70
Day they dug up Babs. K. Prentiss. il
Holiday 47:62-3 F '70

AUTOMOBILES, Racing—*Continued*

Dayto, oops, naaaa. S. Kelly. il Hot Rod 23: 68-71 My '70

Dear Parnelli: well, about time. Henry Ford II. K. Chapin. il por Sports Illus 33: 69-70+ S 28 '70

Eight years later; Ferrari racing, interview. R. Hill. il pors Motor T 22:42-3+ N '70

Formula A; and other formulas and classes. il Pop Mech 133:S24+ Ja '70

Formula vee for fun. J. Thawley. il Hot Rod 23:30-4 Mr '70

Four cylinder, twin cam, sixteen valve American dream; Offenhauser engines. G. Borgeson. il pors Motor T 22:56-61+ My '70

Gurneyized Trans-Am MoPars. J. Thawley. il Hot Rod 23:66-8 Ap '70

Holman & Moody parts proliferation. A. B. Shuman. il Motor T 22:74-5 Ja '70

Indy '70; preview of things to come, with handicapping guide and chart. L. Nehamkin. il Motor T 22:34-9+ My '70

Jarrell's junior stockers. J. Dianna. il Hot Rod 23:78-80 Ja '70

Landy's dandy pro-stocker. J. Dianna. il Hot Rod 23:48-50 My '70

Lee Roy's secret weapon. B. Kilpatrick. il pors Pop Mech 133:86-8+ F '70

Mickey's monocoque funny. E. Rickman. il Hot Rod 23:34-6 Ap '70

Mid-engine for the marshes. A. B. Shuman. il Motor T 22:70-1+ N '70

Mr Bo-Weevil. B. Lang. il pors Hot Rod 23:48-50 D '70

New Olds tricks. J. Dianna. il Hot Rod 23: 102-4 Ag '70

No way to treat a mystique; Ferrari and Porsche at Daytona International R. F. Jones. il Sports Illus 32:20-3 F 9 '70

Pabst's blue ribbon; last Scarab ever built. il por Motor T 22:46-8 D '70

Pre-Indy snooping. E. Rickman. il Hot Rod 23:36-9 My '70

Project Jr. 'Vette. J. Dianna. il Hot Rod 24: 76-9 Ja '71

Roddin' at random. See issues of Hot rod

Scratch building a pro stocker. J. Dianna. il Hot Rod 23:80-5 N '70

Secrets of Grumpy Jenkins. A. B. Shuman. il Motor T 22:32-4+ Je '70

Serious funny business. D. Wadley. il pors Hot Rod 23:76-8 My '70

'70 racing preview; symposium. il Motor T 22: 39-54+ Mr '70

Solving the Riddler. J. Dianna. il Hot Rod 23:64-6 S '70

Sorting out drag racers. il Mech Illus 66: 64-5+ Ag '70

Sox & Martin's heads-up hemi. J. Diana. il Hot Rod 23:36-8 F '70

Thing of shapes to come; Plymouth's Super-Bird. A. B. Shuman. il Motor T 22:38-41 Ja '70

Uhlenhaut; Grand prix cars. L. W. Steinwedel. il por Motor T 22:54-6+ Ap '70

Vacuum cleaner car; Chaparral 2J. il Newsweek 76:49 Jl 27 '70

What's a nice Yankee like you doing in victory lane? 12th annual Daytona 500. A. B. Shuman. il Motor T 22:80-3+ Ap '70

When to finish was enough; Daytona races. E. Dahlquist. il Motor T 22:74-5+ Ap '70

Why the rest of you are losers; Johnny Lightning 500. J. Brokaw. il Motor T 23: 52-7+ Ja '71

Wild Willie. B. Lang. il pors Hot Rod 23:52-4 My '70

See also

Motor vehicles, Racing

Collectors and collecting

Man who collects Offenhausers; interview, ed. by J. McFarland. V. Conze. il por Motor T 22:48-50 Ja '70

Design

Box? Bar of soap? No, it's a car; Hall's Chaparral 2J. B. Yates. il por Sports Illus 33:16-17 Jl 20 '70

New concepts for fuelers. E. K. Von Delden. il Hot Rod 23:38-42 Ag '70

Equipment

Strictly for stocks. J. Dianna. See issues of Hot rod

Exhibitions

Art on four wheels; Louvre show of automotive design. il Life 68:70-3 My 22 '70

Maintenance and repair

Quiet, calm Sunday afternoon. L. Laye. il Motor T 22:68-9 Mr '70

See also

Automobile mechanics (persons)

Models

See Automobile models

Parts

See Automobile parts

Safety devices and measures

Fragmentary evidence; SEMA's new guidelines for dragster safety. B. Lang. Hot Rod 23:82-3 Ja '70

Trailers

See Automobile trailers

Transmission

See Automobiles—Transmission

AUTOMOBILES, Remodeled

Bettering the Boss. S. Kelly. il Hot Rod 23: 100 My '70

Formula vee for fun. J. Thawley. il Hot Rod 23:30-4 Mr '70

Hide the VW's sting. B. Lang. il Hot Rod 23:106 F '70

Hot stuff for Mavericks. S. Kelly. il Hot Rod 23:96-8 Ja '70

Landy's dandy pro-stocker. J. Dianna. il Hot Rod 23:48-50 My '70

Marvy mini muscle car; Maverick to a Mavi GT. J. Lamm. il Motor T 22:74 My '70

Monkeyin' around with some LT-1 parts. J. McFarland. il Motor T 22:68-70 My '70

Muscle for Mavericks. B. Lang. il Hot Rod 23:40-1 F '70

Project Duster· Chrysler 340 project engine. J. Dianna. il Hot Rod 23:48-50 Je '70

Schizo-wagen; Miller Havens bolt-on. E. Rickman. il Hot Rod 23:106-7 Jl '70

Serious funny business. D. Wadley. il pors Hot Rod 23:76-8 My '70

Sox & Martin's heads-up hemi. J. Diana. il Hot Rod 23:36-8 F '70

VW scene: dyno building. J. Dianna. il Hot Rod 23:96-8 Ja '70

AUTOMOBILES, Restored

1932 air-cooled Franklin. J. Lamm. il Motor T 22:36-8 Jl '70

AUTOMOBILES, Steam

Homebuilt steam car takes to the road! J. Zmuda. il Pop Mech 135:114-16+ Ja '71

Steam car may save us. A. Q. Mowbray. il Nation 210:207-11 F 23 '70

AUTOMOBILES, Theft of

Conference focuses on auto thefts. Am City 85:32 Ap '70

World's most thiefproof car lock. S. M. Gallager. il Pop Mech 133:38-9+ Ap '70

See also

Automobiles—Protection against theft

AUTOMOBILES, Toy

Hot pace in a big mini-race; great toy auto race between Mattel and Topper. R. H. Boyle. il Sports Illus 33:38-44 D 7 '70

Kiddie cars and tractors. il Consumer Rep 35:632-7 N '70

AUTOMOBILES, Used

After the great odometer raid; peddling resetting keys. Consumer Rep 35:579-80 O '70

How to become a smiling used-car buyer. M. Lamm. il Pop Mech 133:85-9+ Je '70

How to buy a used car. il Consumer Rep 34: 405-21 D '69

New way to buy a car. D. Demske. il Mech Illus 66:64-6+ N '70

See also

Automobile industry and trade—Used cars

Prices

How to get the most for your car at trade-in time. D. L. Gregg. Bet Hom & Gard 48:12+ S '70

Purchasing

How to buy a used sports car. B. Berger. il Mech Illus 66:50-1+ My '70

Special used car guide. il Motor T 22:38-44+ Je '70

AUTOMOTIVE engineering. See Automobile engineering

AUTOMOTIVE fuel. See Automobile engines—Fuel

AUTOMOTIVE fuels. See Motor fuels

AUTOMOTIVE industries

Finance

Automotive products; with yardsticks of management performance. il Forbes 105: 191-3 Ja 1 '70; 107:160-3 Ja 1 '71

AUTOMOTIVE research. See Automobile research

AUTOMOTIVE transportation. See Transportation, Automotive

AUTONOMIC nervous system. See Nervous system

AUTOPILOTS. See Automatic pilot (airplanes)

AUTORADIOGRAPHY
Nonphotographic alpha autoradiography and neutron-induced autoradiography. K. Becker and D. R. Johnson. bibliog il Science 167:1370-2 Mr 6 '70
Periphyton: autoradiography of zinc-65 adsorption. F. L. Rose and C. E. Cushing. bibliog il Science 168:576-7 My 1 '70
Postnatal muscle fiber assembly; localization of newly synthesized myofibrillar proteins. E. Morkin. bibliog il Science 167:1499-501 Mr 13 '70

AUTOTRANSFORMERS. See Electric transformers

AUTOXIDATION. See Oxidation

AUTUMN
Autumn's bare, bright beauty. J. Bishop. il Read Digest 97:128-30 O '70

Poetry
How many autumns? H. W. Gall. il Nat Wildlife 7:17 O '69

AUTUMN leaves. See Color of leaves

AVAKIAN, Aram
Independent. il por Newsweek 75:100+ Mr 16 '70 *

AVALANCHES
Cold is the grave; Val d'Isère disaster. il Newsweek 75:49 F 23 '70
From snowflake to avalanche. E. R. LaChapelle. il Natur Hist 79:30-8 F '70
Nature's deadly whim; disasters in Alpine Europe. il Time 95:28 Mr 9 '70
Sense of risk; snowslide at Swiss mountain of Reckinken. Newsweek 75:40+ Mr 9 '70
White death; studies by members of Switzerland's Federal institute for snow and avalanche research. il Time 95:34+ Mr 9 '70

AVALLONE, Michael
How I sold a series of paperback mystery novels. por Writers Digest 51:24-5+ Ja '71

AVANT-garde dancing. See Dancing

AVANT-garde theater. See Theater, Experimental

AVANTI motor corporation
Avanti still means forward. D. A. Jedlicka. il por Esquire 73:116-17+ Ap '70

AVCO corporation
Caught in the backlash. il Forbes 106:17-18 S 1 '70
Diversified and still waiting. il por Bsns W p78+ Ag 29 '70
Kendrick R. Wilson of Avco; making corporate marriages work; interview. K. R. Wilson, jr. por Nations Bsns 58:62-8 Ap '70

AVE Maria (periodical)
Ave atque vale. S. J. Adamo. America 122:377-8 Ap 4 '70
Now it's official; Ave Maria; phased out in favor of A.D. 1970. J. Deedy. Commonweal 91:522 F 13 '70

AVEDISIAN, Edward
Factory art vs. studio art. B. Rose. Vogue 155:68 Je '70 *

AVEDON, Richard
Shows we've seen; retrospective at the Minneapolis institute of arts. R. McCullough. Pop Phot 67:52+ N '70 *

AVEN, Samuel D. and Breazler, Eldon
Pass or fail credit for student teaching. Clear House 44:309 Ja '70

AVENA. See Oats

AVENA coleoptiles. See Coleoptiles

AVENS, Roberts
Manifesto for a theology of the present. Cath World 212:20-3 O '70

AVERAGES, Stock. See Stocks—Price indexes and averages

AVERETT, Walter
Amateur scientist. il Sci Am 223:116-21 D '70

AVERY, Milton
Art; exhibition at the Brooklyn museum. L. Alloway. Nation 210:349 Mr 23 '70 *
Quiet one. il por Time 95:58-9+ Mr 16 '70 *

AVIATION
Foreign accent. J. Fricker. See issues of Flying
See also
Air travel
Balloon ascensions
Gliding and soaring
Navigation, Aerial
Private flying
  also headings beginning Aeronautic; Aeronautics; Airplane; Airplanes

Accident investigation
Beech challenges safety board's findings in Air south 99 accident. Aviation W 93:67 D 14 '70

Colorado crash may spur new regulations. C. E. Schneider. Aviation W 93:23-4 O 12 '70
On top; public hearing on Cherokee/DC-9 collision. Flying 86:16-18 Ja '70

Accidents
Colorado crash may spur new regulations. C. E. Schneider. Aviation W 93:23-4 O 12 '70
Crash of F-14 delays testing by 4-6 weeks. il Aviation W 94:21-2 Ja 11 '71
Crew activities cited in crash at Bradford. Aviation W 92:36 Mr 16 '70
Days of stillness at Wichita state; football team's plane crash. W. Johnson. il Sports Illus 33:20-1 O 19 '70
F-111 crash finding blames pilot error. Aviation W 93:20 N 2 '70
Felled bird; the F-14. il Sci N 99:24 Ja 9 '71
Last flight of the Carib Queen. W. S. Bacon. il Pop Mech 134:94-101+ D '70
Mystery of 09303; Soviet aircraft on relief flight to Peru. il Time 96:21 Ag 3 '70
National safety board report:
Crews, ATC cited in mid-air crash. il Aviation W 92:57-63 Mr 2 '70
Navaid signals cited in crash of FH-227. Aviation W 92:91 My 25 '70
New JT9D inspections ordered in wake of Air France 747 blast. Aviation W 93:24-S 7 '70
Safety check. See issues of Flying
Two Lockheed C-5s damaged in mishaps. Aviation W 92:17 Je 1 '70
Weather accidents. R. L. Collins. Flying 86:88-90 Je '70
See also
Sabotage

Altitude flying
Second of May is safety day; FAA physiological training day for pilots. Flying 86:65-6 Mr '70

Bibliography
Books. See issues of Flying

Cost
See Airplanes—Cost of operation

Crimes
See Crimes aboard aircraft

Exhibitions
Avionics display boosts Hanover show. R. F. Coburn. il Aviation W 92:21-2 My 4 '70
Foreign accent: Farnborough show. J. Fricker. il Flying 88:16-19 Ja '71
Reading air show. il Flying 86:62-3 Je '70
Russia threatens Turin boycott. Aviation W 92:17 Je 15 '70
U.K. stressing collaborative efforts; air display at Farnborough. H. J. Coleman. il Aviation W 93:14-16 S 7 '70
U.S. plans to increase hard sell during Paris air show in 1971. Aviation W 92:22 F 23 '70
With a German accent; Hanover air show. J. Fricker. il Flying 87:66-7 Ag '70

Fog problem
Fog chasers. il Sci Digest 68:16-17 D '70
Ground fog? Where'd it come from? C. J. Grimm, 3d. il Flying 86:82-3 Ap '70

History
See Aeronautics—History

Ice problem
See Airplanes—Ice protection

Instrument flying
Cockpit confusion. J. R. Bonde. Flying 86:64 My '70
FAA answers all-weather critics. C. E. Schneider. Aviation W 93:58-9 Ag 10 '70
On top. R. L. Collins. Flying 86:14-16+ My '70

International aspects
Airlines, State dept. clash on policy. L. Doty. Aviation W 92:29-30 My 25 '70
Alaska studies soviet air ties. Aviation W 93:21 N 2 '70
Chile expected to ask Cuba route. L. Doty. il Aviation W 93:26-7 D 7 '70
Customs is primary operational problem. Aviation W 93:63 D 14 '70
Dogfight over landing rights; Belgian ban on U.S. charter flights to Brussels. il Bsns W p 114 My 9 '70
Germany plans to restrict U.S. affinity unit charters. Aviation W 92:23-4 F 16 '70
Great circle route affords access to European cities. Aviation W 93:62 D 14 '70
How the 747 came to fly and why Italy won't let it land. Bsns W p79 Ja 31 '70

AVIATION—International aspects—*Continued*
Joint efforts aid overseas business flights. Aviation W 93:86-7 S 21 '70
Latest airline attacks find U.S. lacking policy for firm response. Aviation W 92:25 Mr 2 '70
Market would set fares under proposed bilateral. L. Doty. Aviation W 93:23-4 N 2 '70
Micronesia award creates dilemma for administration. L. Doty. Aviation W 92:27-8 Je 1 '70
New international policy revealed. L. Doty. Aviation W 92:26-7 Ja 19 '70
New rules for airspace urged in Europe. R. F. Coburn. Aviation W 93:45-6 Jl 13 '70
Pan Am seeks Micronesian route support. L. Doty. Aviation W 93:24 Ag 31 '70
Pan Am 747 schedules rejected by Italy. L. Doty. Aviation W 92:36 F 2 '70
Policy, politics block Micronesia award. L. Doty. Aviation W 93:27 Jl 6 '70
President Nixon approves policy statement on international air transportation; statement, June 22, 1970, text of policy statement. R. M. Nixon. Dept State Bul 63:86-91 Jl 20 '70
Pressures from U.K. increasing for Atlantic capacity restrictions. P. Woolsey. Aviation W 93:26 Ag 24 '70
Russians alter bilateral approach; Bermuda-type agreement. L. Doty. Aviation W 93:26-7 Ag 10 '70
Soviets ask bilateral airworthiness talks. Aviation W 94:16-17 Ja 11 '71
Stiffer measures rejected in Nixon hijacking plans; with editorial comment. L. Doty. Aviation W 93:9, 30-1 O 5 '70
Strong anti-hijack treaty signed; may be implemented by mid-year. Aviation W 94:26 Ja 4 '71
Supplemental policy spurs clash. L. Doty. Aviation W 92:22-3 F 16 '70
Tests of 747 wake accelerated. Aviation W 92:25-6 F 23 '70
U.S. and Lebanon conclude air transport arrangement. Dept State Bul 63:315 S 14 '70
U.S. and Mexico amend and extend air transport agreement. Dept State Bul 63:206 Ag 17 '70
U.S. and the Netherlands amend air transport agreement; Department announcement, amendment to agreement; with exchange of notes. Dept State Bul 62:73-5 Ja 19 '70
U.S. Italy reach new bilateral agreement. L. Doty. il Aviation W 92:29-30 Je 8 '70
U.S. seeking multilateral treaties. L. Doty. Aviation W 92:30 Ja 26 '70
United States and Italy sign air transport agreement. Dept State Bul 63:122 Jl 27 '70
United States and Japan amend air transport agreement; Department announcement; with exchange of notes. Dept State Bul 61:573-4 D 15 '69
United States and Malaysia sign air transport agreement; Department announcement with text of agreement; February 2, 1970. Dept State Bul 62:266-70 Mr 2 '70
United States and Morocco sign air transport agreement; Department announcement with text of agreement. Dept State Bul 62:398-403 Mr 23 '70
United States and Thailand amend air transport agreement; Department announcement; with exchange of notes; March 3, 1970. Dept State Bul 62:535 Ap 20 '70
United States and the Congo sign air transport agreement. Dept State Bul 63:287 S 7 '70
USSR-Japan pooling pact expected to set pattern. L. Doty. Aviation W 92:34 Ap 27 '70
See also
Air freight service—International aspects
Airlines—International services
Airspace (international law)
International air transport association
International civil aviation organization

Laws and regulations
Airworthiness directives (cont) Flying 86:100 Ap '70
Business aviation facing changes in laws, regulations. D. A. Brown. il Aviation W 93:40-3 S 21 '70
Carriers seek fare-setting power. L. Doty. Aviation W 94:23-4 Ja 11 '71
Commuter airline rules stiffened. Aviation W 92:27 Je 29 '70
FAA to require defect reports. Aviation W 92:68 Mr 16 '70
New airport and airways act faces pressure for revision. D. C. Winston. Aviation W 93:43+ S 21 '70

Private cargo faces tangled legal thicket. Aviation W 93:140-1+ O 26 '70
Regulations to spur operations changes. C. E. Schneider. Aviation W 93:48-50 S 21 '70
Relations of U.S. airlines altered. H. D. Watkins. Aviation W 93:23-4 S 28 '70
White House drive gains to unify international laws on air piracy; with editorial comment. L. Doty. Aviation W 93:9, 25 S 28 '70
See also
Airports—Laws and regulations
Airports—Traffic control
United States—Federal aviation administration

Lightning hazards
Lightning and the new-generation aircraft. A. A. Few. Science 168:1011 My 22 '70
Lightning hazards to rockets. il Space World G-11-83:42-3 N '70

Meteorological aspects
See Meteorology, Aeronautic

Night flying
Right night approach. J. B. Gilstrap. Flying 87:105 S '70

Physiological aspects
Keeping healthy at 30,000 feet. S. Murata. il Todays Health 48:20-3+ My '70
Second of May is safety day; FAA physiological training day for pilots. Flying 86:65-6 Mr '70
Wacky biological clocks. A. J. Snider. Sci Digest 68:67 D '70

Psychological aspects
Flying fraidycats fight fear in the sky. K. V. Brown. il Todays Health 48:24-6+ Je '70

Safety devices and measures
Closely watched planes. il Time 95:26 Mr 9 '70
Dilemma of the airlines. il Newsweek 75:33-4+ Mr 9 '70
Follow me through; natural collision-avoidance system. R. Blodget. Flying 86:24+ Je '70
Safety check; fuel exhaustion. R. L. Collins. Flying 87:20+ S '70
Tame blue yonder. il Nations Bsns 58:76-8+ Mr '70
See also
Airplanes—Safety devices and measures
Oxygen apparatus
Parachuting
Proximity warning indicators
Radio beacons

Storm hazards
Safety check. R. L. Collins. Flying 86:22-3+ Je '70
Safety check; flameout. J. Gilbert. il Flying 86:32-3+ Ja '70
Storms and polluted air caused airline delays around New York. Aviation W 93:28 Ag 10 '70

Study and teaching
See Aeronautics—Study and teaching

Stunt flying
Aerobatics; survival school in the sky. F. Harvey. il pors Pop Sci 197:58-60 S '70
And we win the world aerobatics, too. il Flying 87:80 S '70
Foreign accent; sixth World aerobatic championships preview. J. Fricker. Flying 87:34-5 Jl '70
Hoover's aerobatics a key factor in Shrike sales increase. C. M. Plattner. il por Aviation W 92:40-4 Mr 2 '70
In-fright report. G. Baxter. il Flying 87:140 S '70
Look, ma, no hands. W. Johnson. il Sports Illus 33:106-10+ S 14 '70
Swiss team attracts new pilots. E. H. Kolcum. il Aviation W 93:46-7+ S 28 '70

Transatlantic flights
Captain. J. Gilbert. il por Flying 86:65-61 Ja '70
Varied navaids ease transatlantic flights. K. J. Stein. il Aviation W 93:52+ D 14 '70

Transcontinental flights
Six thousand miles by Cherokee 180E. J. Gilbert. il Flying 86:46-51+ Ja '70
U.S. journal; N.Y./L.A./N.Y; trip on the Boeing 747. C. Trillin. New Yorker 46:66+ Ap 4 '70

AVIATION—*Continued*

Transoceanic flights

Inertial aids fill primary overwater role. K. J. Stein. il Aviation W 93:56-7+ O 19 '70
Needs spur transoceanic flights; corporate operations. C. E. Schneider. il Aviation W 93:40-1+ D 14 '70

Winter flying

Cold-weather operation. J. Diblin. il Flying 86:86-7+ F '70
No way out. D. E. Miller. Flying 87:72 N '70

Bahama Islands

One engine, one ocean and you! N. Aubuchon. il Flying 87:29-31+ N '70

Europe

Planning eases European flight initiation. il Aviation W 93:46+ D 14 '70

United States

Aviation policy report submitted. L. Doty. Aviation W 93:16-17 O 26 '70
Initial civil aviation plan due September 1. K. Johnsen. il Aviation W 92:60+ Je 22 '70
Piper cub vs. the 747. B. Bernstein. il N Y Times Mag p34-5+ Mr 8 '70; Reply with rejoinder. K. Bailey and J. West. p34+ Mr 22 '70
See also
Airlines—United States

AVIATION, Electronics in. See Electronics in aviation

AVIATION associations
Aerospace calendar. See issues of Aviation week & space technology
Calendar. See issues of Flying
See also names of aviation associations, e.g. International air transport association

AVIATION clubs
Club scene. G. Thomas. Flying 86:112 F; 25 Mr '70

AVIATION education
See also
Aeronautics—Study and teaching
Air pilots—Training
Aviation schools

AVIATION exhibitions. See Aviation—Exhibitions

AVIATION records
Three world records for the BD-2. il Flying 86:52-3 Mr '70

AVIATION schools
Editorial; proposed Gill Robb Wilson memorial aeronautical science center at the Embry-Riddle aeronautical institute. R. B. Parke. por Flying 86:40 Mr '70
FAA studies approved flight school revisions. Aviation W 93:81 S 21 '70
Long weekend; total-immersion course. R. B. Weeghman. Flying 86:77-8 My '70
Pilot training franchises offered. E. J. Bulban. il Aviation W 93:56-8 N 2 '70

AVINERI, Shlomo
Israel and the new left. Trans-Action 7:79-83 Jl '70
Palestinians and Israel. bibliog f Commentary 49:31-44 Je; 50:10+ S; 32+ N; 24 D '70

AVIONICS. See Airplanes—Electronic equipment; Electronics in aviation

AVIONICS industry. See Electronic apparatus industry and trade

AVIONICS technicians. See Electronic technicians

AVIONS Marcel Dassault. See Airplane industry and trade—France

AVIŽIENIS, Algirdas
Star is born. Time 96:50 D 7 '70 *

AVNERY, Uri
Super-Jew and super-Arab. por Life 68:14 Mr 20 '70

AVOCADOS
See also
Cookery—Fruit

AVOIDANCE (psychology)
Impairment of shock avoidance learning after long-term alcohol ingestion in mice. G. Freund. bibliog il Science 168:1599-601 Je 26 '70
Prenatal and birth complications linked by schizophrenia research. J. Moriarty and L. Massett. il por Sci N 98:15-16 Jl 4 '70

AVON, Anthony Eden, 1st earl of
Can France and Britain help end the Vietnam war? address. il U S News 68:92+ Je 15 '70

AWA odori dancers. See Dancing, Japanese

AWAKE and sing; drama. See Odets, C.

AWAKENING of Granville; drama. See Nolan, P. T.

AWARD of merit for leadership. See American city (periodical)

AWARDS. See Rewards, prizes, etc.

AWARENESS house. See Narcotic addicts—Rehabilitation

AWE. See Wonder

AXELBANK, Albert
Passing the buck to Tokyo. Nation 211:293-5 O 5 '70
—and Nakamura, Koji
Three-power gamble. il Nation 211:678-81 D 28 '70

AXELROD, David. See Trilling, D. M. jt. auth.

AXELROD, Julius
How the Nobelists won. il pors Newsweek 76:83 O 26 '70 *
Neurobiology: on the research frontier. pors Sci N 98:331 O 24 '70 *
Nobel prize: three share 1970 award for medical research. S. Udenfriend. pors Science 170:422-3 O 23 '70 *

AXON, Gordon V.
Buying gems and jewelry. il Consumer Bul 53:4+ D '70

AXONAL transport. See Biological transport

AXOPLASMIC transport. See Biological transport

AXTHELM, Pete
City game; excerpt. il Harper 241:85-94 O '70
Sports. Vogue 156:58 S 15; 36 O 15; 76 N 15 '70

AYALA, G. F. and others
Penicillin as epileptogenic agent: its effect on an isolated neuron. bibliog il Science 167:1257-60 F 27 '70

AYALA, Mme Hector de
Space-age Moorish. il pors Vogue 155:198-201 Ap 1 '70 *

AYALA, Stephen C. and Lee, Dwayne
Saurian malaria: development of sporozoites in two species of phlebotomine sandflies. bibliog il Science 167:891-2 F 6 '70

AYLOR, Kay
Harlem teams on top. il Am Ed 6:32 My '70

AYRES, James E.
Death of Captain Cook: two views. il Antiques 97:724-7 My '70

AYRTON, Michael
Daedalus and I. il por Horizon 12:56-65 Spr '70

AZALEAS
Garden of azaleas. R. K. Patrick. il Horticulture 48:32-4 F '70
If you play it right, up to eleven months of azalea bloom. il Sunset 145:80-3 N '70

AZAROWICZ, Edward N.
Bug as garbage man. Time 96:36 D 21 '70 *

AZHAR university, Cairo. See Colleges and universities—Egypt

AZIMUTH
Sun is your compass. C. Miller. il Motor B 126:34-5+ Jl '70

AZIMUTH sundials. See Sundials

AZMITIA, Efrain C. Jr, and others
In vivo conversion of ^{3}H-L-tryptophan into ^{3}H-serotonin in brain areas of adrenalectomized rats. bibliog il Science 169:201-3 Jl 10 '70

AZORES
There's nothing gray about the Azores. V. Kelly. il Read Digest 97:146-52 S '70

AZTECS
Florentine codex. H. H. Harvey. il Natur Hist 79:42-51+ D '70
In an Aztec market. A. J. Sadulé il Américas 22:2-8 My '70

AZUR (artificial satellite) See Artificial satellites, German

B

B. Dalton bookseller. See Booksellers and bookselling—Nevada

B-1 (airplane) See Airplanes, Military—United States

BART (Bay area rapid transit) See San Francisco—Transit systems

BASF corporation. See Chemical industries—Germany (Federal Republic)

BBC. See British broadcasting corporation

BCC. See British council of churches

BCG (Bacillus Calmette) See Tuberculosis—Vaccines

BEA. See British European airways corporation

BEDC. See National black economic development conference

BEF. See Businessman's educational forum

BACTERIA—*Continued*

Resistance and sensitivity

Altered dihydrofolate reductase associated with drug-resistance transfer between rodent plasmodia. R. Ferone and others. bibliog il Science 167:1263-4 F 27 '70

Blunted weapons. K. P. Shea. bibliog il Environ 12:28-35+ Ja '70

Menace in moon soil? effect on bacteria. Time 95:47 Mr 30 '70

BACTERIA, Effect of antibiotics on. See Bacteria—Resistance and sensitivity

BACTERIA, Effect of heat on. See Heat—Physiological effects

BACTERIA, Fossil. See Micropaleontology

BACTERIA, Pathogenic

Sulfate-binding protein from salmonella typhimurium: physical properties. R. Langridge and others. bibliog il Science 169:59-61 Jl 3 '70

BACTERIA, Photosynthetic

Carbon dioxide-fixation in photosynthetic green sulfur bacteria. R. Sirevag and J. G. Omerod. bibliog il Science 169:186-8 Jl 10 '70

Evolution of photosynthesis. J. M. Olson. bibliog il Science 168:438-46 Ap 24 '70

BACTERIAL cells

Phage, colicins, and macroregulatory phenomena; Nobel lecture, December 12, 1969. S. E. Luria. bibliog Science 168:1166-70 Je 5 '70

BACTERIAL genetics. See Microbial genetics

BACTERIAL proteins

Microtubular spherulites: development and growth in solutions of bacteriochlorophyll protein. R. A. Olson. bibliog il Science 169:81-2 Jl 3 '70

See also
Tuberculin

BACTERIAL spores

Bacterial spore outgrowth: its regulation. J. N. Hansen and others. bibliog il Science 168:1291-8 Je 12 '70; Reply with rejoinder. H. D. Bolch. 170:372 N 20 '70

Ribosomes from spores of bacillus cereus T. F. M. Feinsod and H. A. Douthit. bibliog il Science 168:991 My 22 '70

BACTERIOCHLOROPHYLL protein. See Bacterial proteins

BACTERIOLOGICAL warfare. See Biological warfare

BACTERIOLOGY

See also
Bacteriolysis
Microbiology

BACTERIOLYSIS

Vibriolytic antibody-forming cells: a new application of the Pfeiffer phenomenon. R. F. McAlack and others. bibliog il Science 168:141-2 Ap 3 '70

See also
Bacteriophage
Lysozyme

BACTERIOPHAGE

Bacteriophage induced transfer RNA in escherichia coli. V. Daniel and others. bibliog il Science 167:1682-8 Mr 27 '70

Coevolution of escherichia coli and bacteriophages in chemostat culture. M. T. Horne. bibliog il Science 168:992-3 My 22 '70

Phage, colicins, and macroregulatory phenomena; Nobel lecture, December 12, 1969. S. E. Luria. bibliog Science 168:1166-70 Je 5 '70

Recognition of DNA in bacteria. S. E. Luria. il Sci Am 222:88-92+ bibliog(p 146) Ja '70

Spherical protein shell formation from an 11S subunit of bacteriophage f₂. P. O. Zelazo and R. H. Haschemeyer. bibliog il Science 168:1461-2 Je 19 '70

BADA, Jeffrey L. and others

Marine sediments: dating by the racemization of amino acids. bibliog il Science 170:730-2 N 13 '70

BADAL, James J.

Prisoner: 1337; occupation: conductor, Boston symphony orchestra. il pors Hi Fi 20:55-60 O '70

BADARACCO, Robert

Why not create a marsh? il Parks & Rec 5:29-30 Je '70

BADGLEY, John H.

American territorial presence in Asia; address, April 1970, with questions and answers. bibliog f Ann Am Acad 390:38-47 Jl '70

BADISCHE anilin und soda-fabrik. See Chemical industries—Germany (Federal Republic)

BAEDECKER, Philip A. and Wasson, J. T.

Gallium, germanium, indium, and iridium in lunar samples. bibliog il Science 167:503-5 Ja 30 '70

BAER, Betty

Yale & female. il Look 34:24-7 F 24 '70

BAEZ, Joan

Joan Baez and David Harris: we're just non-violent soldiers. W. Hedgepeth. il pors Look 34:58-61+ My 5 '70 *

Joan Baez: One day at a time. E. Sander. Sat R 53:61 Mr 28 '70 *

SAGGAGE. See Luggage

BAGNOLD, Enid

Enid Bagnold's autobiography. N. Houghton. por Sat R 53:30 S 26 '70 *

Enid Bagnold's autobiography: flashing. J. Stafford. Vogue 156:98 N 1 '70 *

BAGS

Sailor's bag, endlessly useful, easy to make. il Sunset 144:115-16 My '70

Small and tall canvas bags to help swimmers keep sorted out. il Sunset 145:88+ Jl '70

What's your bag? create some kind of bag from discarded clothing. F. Marlow. il Sch Arts 69:24-5 Je '70

See also
Handbags
Plastic bags

BAGUENA, Mariano

Flamenco in Spain. il Sat R 53:48+ S 12 '70

BAGUIO, Philippines

Bold move in Baguio. Time 96:59 Jl 27 '70

BAHAISM

Bahai in black Africa: a force to contend with. O. Okite. Chr Today 14:53 Mr 13 '70

BAHAMA ISLANDS

Bahamian cruise regatta; Out island regatta. George Town Great Exuma. P. Leslie. il Yachting 128:59+ N '70

Dredging money from the Bank; from Great Bahama Bank. C. Phinizy. il Sports Illus 33:22-5 Jl 6 '70

First time to the Bahamas. T. Kelly. il Yachting 128:56-7+ N '70

See also
Airlines—Bahama Islands
Andros Island
Architecture, Domestic—Bahama Islands
Aviation—Bahama Islands
Eleuthera Island
Gardens—Bahama Islands
Grand Bahama Island
Nassau
Paleontology—Bahama Islands
Tourist trade—Bahama Islands

Description and travel

In the Abacos. W. T. Stone. il Yachting 128:58+ N '70

Mailboat to Exuma. H. Reussille. il Travel 134:52-5 N '70

Politics and government

Mr Pindling; interview. L. O. Pindling. New Yorker 46:28-30 O 3 '70

BAHAMA ISLANDS Open tournament. See Golf—Tournaments

BAHAMAS airways. See Airlines—Bahama Islands

BAHAMAS 500 race. See Motor boat racing

BAHARIAN, Bedros

Needed: more housing for the elderly. il por Am City 85:91-2 Ap '70

BAHREIN

See also
United Nations—Bahrein

Antiquities

See also
Dilmun

BAIL

Boondocks jail the future; high bail for Negroes in Homer, La. N. C. Chriss. il Nation 211:495-6 N 16 '70

Using the system; New York state municipal bonds in payment. il por Time 96:13 Jl 20 '70

When is bail excessive? Black Panthers on trial in Manhattan. Time 95:42 F 9 '70

See also
Preventive detention

BAILEY, Anthony

Profiles; Netherlands. New Yorker 46:34-40+ Ag 8; 32-8+ Ag 15 '70

René Dubos. il por Horizon 12:56-61 Sum '70

BAILEY, Bob

Discovery: Bob Bailey. J. Dreyfuss. il Mod Phot 34:80-1+ My '70 *

BAILEY, C. Lloyd

Toward a better world for all children. por Parents Mag 45:30 Ag '70

BAILEY, Francis Lee

F. Lee Bailey, headhunter. P. Wilkes. il pors N Y Times Mag p34-5+ S 20 '70; Reply. G. H. Brown. p64 O 18 '70 *

BAILEY, Fred, Jr
Using futures. il Suc Farm 68:28-9+ Ja; no2
66-7+ F; no3 32-3+ F; no5 28-9 Mr '70
Using futures, earn storage or buy feed. il
Suc Farm 68:no2 66-7+ F '70
Using futures, how to sell on the market. il
Suc Farm 68:28-9+ Ja '70
BAILEY, Glenn W.
Conglomerate bucks a trend. por Bsns W p
110+ Jl 11 '70 *
BAILEY, Howald
Puccini's pot of gold. Opera N 34:16 Mr 7
'70
BAILEY, J. C. and others
Mineralogical and petrological investigations
of lunar samples. bibliog il Science 167:592-
4 Ja 30 '70
BAILEY, J. Martin
Ecumenism and communication. Chr Cent
87:241 F 25 '70
BAILEY, Jane H.
Farewell to the barleycorn inch. il Sci Digest
62:26-30 Ja '71
BAILEY, John
Test: rate yourself in savoir-faire! New
Yorker 46:38-9 Ap 18 '70
BAILEY, Peter
Black art's amazing fund-raiser. il pors
Ebony 25:70-2+ Je '70
Black courage in Klan country. il pors Ebony
25:136-41 Ap '70
From Jets to Mets to Knicks? il Ebony 25:
120-2+ Mr '70
BAILEY, Ronald
Following the covered wagons on an asphalt
trail. Life 69:28-9 Ag 14 '70
BAILEY, Ronald Beresford
Why black studies? il Ed Digest 35:46-8
My '70
BAILEY, Suzanne
Be kind to your babysitter; she may be my
daughter. il Parents Mag 45:44-5 Ag '70
BAILING out of airplanes. See Parachuting
BAILLIE, Stuart
San Jose librarians charge intimidation. Li-
brary J 95:613-14 F 15 '70 *
BAILOR, Shirley
Snow maidens; poem. Good H 171:140 D '70
BAILYN, Bernard
Political mimesis; a comment. Am Hist R 75:
361-3 D '69
BAIN, Helen
National foundation for the improvement of
education; interview. Todays Ed 59:24-5 N
'70
We must be reasoning activists; adaptation
of address. il pors Todays Ed 59:22-5 S '70
BAINBRIDGE, John
Garbo is 65; excerpts from Garbo. pors Look
34:48-50+ S 8 '70
BAIRD, Robert W.
Doctor Baird of East Harlem. W. F. Buck-
ley, jr. Nat R 22:100 Ja 27 '70
BAIT
Getting the bait's a ball. G. Elliott. il Out-
door Life 145:62-3+ My '70
See also
Earthworms
BAJA CALIFORNIA. See California, Lower
BAJA 1000 race. See Motor vehicle racing—
Mexico
BAKAL, Carl
Ocean comes to Oklahoma. il Read Digest 97:
121-4 N '70
BAKAN, David
Education; address, November 13, 1969. bib-
il Sci Am 222:88-92+ bibliog(p 146) Ja '70
BAKE, William A. Jr
Georgia granite; with biographical sketch. il
Natur Hist 79:4, 32-7 O '70
BAKED beans. See Cookery—Vegetables
BAKER, Adolph
Physics and antiphysics. il por Phys Today
23:34-40 Mr '70
BAKER, Clyde J.
Bettered mousetrap. il Hot Rod 23:64-5 Jl '70
Maybe you need an overdrive. il Pop Mech
135:130-3+ Ja '71
Pep up your car with cool air. il Pop Sci
196:50 Mr '70
BAKER, D. James, Jr
Models of oceanic circulation; with bio-
graphical sketch. il Sci Am 222:16, 114-21
Ja '70
BAKER, Dale B.
Communication or chaos? adaptation of ad-
dress, December 29, 1969. Science 169:739-
42 Ag 21 '70
BAKER, Dave
Professor plays jazz. il pors Ebony 25:104-
6+ My '70 *
BAKER, Elizabeth C.
Critic's choice: Serra. il Art N 68:26-7 F '70
Frank Stella; perspectives. il por Art N 69:
46-9+ My '70

Morris Louis: veiled illusions. il Art N 69:36-
9+ Ap '70
Pickets on Parnassus. il Art N 69:30-3+ S '70
Sexual art-politics. il Art N 69:47-8+ Ja '71
Traveling ideas: Germany, England. il Art N
69:38-40+ Sum '70
BAKER, Howard H. Jr
Excerpt from debate, Febuary 17, 1970. Cong
Digest 49:126 Ap '70
BAKER, James T.
Two cities of Thomas Merton. Cath World
211:151-5 Jl '70
BAKER, Janet
More than enough; interview, ed. by S.
Jenkins. por Opera N 34:28-9 Mr 7 '70

about

Best of Baker. D. Hamilton. Hi Fi 20:secI
86 Je '70 *
Passion and purity. por Time 96:68+ S 21
'70 *
BAKER, Kathy
Goblin dance; poem. il Horn Bk 46:509 O
'70
BAKER, Leonard
Our ailing medical schools. il Sat R 53:56-7
D 19 '70
BAKER, Lucinda
You promised; story. Ladies Home J 87:
98-9 O '70
BAKER, Norman
Life and death of the good ship Ra. il por
Sports Illus 32:66-8+ Ap 20 '70
BAKER, Orville
Compulsory English. Clear House 45:253-4
D '70
BAKER, Patricia
Bliss in a box of crayons. il Parents Mag
45:74 O '70
BAKER, Philip John Noel-. See Noel-Baker,
P. J.
BAKER, Richard G.
Pollen sequence from late quaternary sedi-
ments in Yellowstone Park. bibliog il Sci-
ence 168:1449-50 Je 19 '70
BAKER, Robert
How to handle violence. il por Time 95:40
Ja 26 '70
BAKER, Roger
Amateur scientist; ed. by C. L. Stong. il
Sci Am 222:143-5 Je '70
BAKER, Russell
Everything you always wanted to know about
football. Read Digest 97:59-60 O '70
Life's precious moments (winter division) il
Read Digest 97:35-6 D '70
BAKER, Vincent S.
Black Americans want in. Nat R 22:892-3 Ag
25 '70
BAKERS and bakeries
Kakes and kookies for kollege kids. J. Kuh.
por Ladies Home J 87:143 S '70
BAKER'S neighbor; drama. See Thane, A.
BAKERSFIELD, Calif.
Diesel engines cut sweeping costs. il Am
City 85:54 Jl '70
BAKERSFIELD fuel and gas championships.
See Automobile engines—Fuel consumption
BAKING
GH's new holiday baking cookbook. il Good
H 171:100-15 N '70
How to line your cake pans. J. Pépin. il
House B 112:90 D '70
See also
Bakers and bakeries
Bread
Coffee cake
Cookies
Dough
Flour
Food mixes
Pastry
Pie
Shortcake

Terminology

Glossary of baked-goods terms. Good H 170:
192 Mr '70
BAKKE, E. Wight
Reflections on the future of bargaining in
the public sector; excerpt from address,
May 1970. Mo Labor R 93:21-5 Jl '70
BAKOS, Gustav A.
Flare star in Messier 6. il Sky & Tel 40:214
O '70
BAKSHIAN, Aram, Jr
Bastille day revisited. Nat R 22:734-5+ Jl 14
'70
BALAGUER, Joaquin
Closer to chaos. Time 95:34 Ap 13 '70 *
Image-makers at work. Nat R 22:553 Je 2
'70 *
Keeping the lid on. il por Time 95:42 My
25 '70 *

BALAKRISHNAN, S.
Denitrification biologically. bibliog il Am City 85:56-8 D '70
BALANCE of nature. See Ecology
BALANCE of payments
Anger at dollar imperialists. Time 95:77-8 Je 22 '70
Britain's austerity lid is lifted, a bit. il Bsns W p 118 Ap 18 '70
Did Harold Wilson save the pound? J. E. Powell. il Nat R 22:306-8 Mr 24 '70
Dollar gets a new threat. il Bsns W p 18-19 My 2 '70
Dollar's future as Europe sees it; interview, ed. by A. Zanker. M. Iklé. il por U S News 68:66-70 Ap 13 '70
Everybody's money worries. P. Passell and L. Ross. il Trans-Action 7:30-2 My '70
Financial setting for 1970; address, February 25-27, 1970. F. A. Southard, jr. Vital Speeches 36:375-8 Ap 1 '70
International bookkeeping really counts. W. F. Butler. por Nations Bsns 58:54-5 Ag '70
Question of confidence. Newsweek 75:79+ F 23 '70
Taxes & related problems; address, December 1, 1970. W. Bennett. Vital Speeches 37:166-70 Ja 1 '71
Trade tide lifts the floating dollar; Canada. il Bsns W p51-2 O 17 '70
Weaker dollar: business drag. il U S News 69:71-3 Ag 10 '70
When plus is minus. Time 95:76 Mr 2 '70
BALANCE of power
America's balance of power. D. Lawrence. U S News 68:104 Ap 20 '70
Defense: Laird warns of Soviet technological threat. A. Hamilton. Science 167:1360 Mr 6 '70
New multipolar balance in East Asia: implications for United States policy; address, April 1970, with questions and answers. A. D. Barnett. Ann Am Acad 390:73-86 Jl '70
Soviet power cited to aid military budget; with editorial comment. D. C. Winston. il Aviation W 92:11, 23-4 My 4 '70
Suez is the front to watch. G. W. Ball. il N Y Times Mag p 10-11+ Je 28 '70
War and the balance of power; some Christian reflections; address, November 11, 1969. J. V. Schall. Vital Speeches 36:211-17 Ja 15 '70
Wood is getting dry. S. Alsop. Newsweek 76:108 O 5 '70
BALANCE of trade
United States international trade prospects; challenge of new world competitive forces; address, March 9, 1970. K. N. Davis, jr. Vital Speeches 36:390-2 Ap 15 '70
See also
Balance of payments
BALANCE sheets. See Financial statements
BALANCED diet. See Diet
BALANCHINE, George
Firebird: grand controversy; with interview, ed. by O. Maynard. il por Dance Mag 44:43-58 Ag '70
about
Dance; Suite no. 3. N. Goldner. Nation 211:701-2 D 28 '70 *
Fascinating rhythm. H. Saal. il Newsweek 75:85 F 16 '70 *
First flight of a bright new Firebird. il pors Life 69:32-7 Jl 31 '70 *
Hatching a new Firebird. H. Saal. por Newsweek 75:89 Je 8 '70 *
Manhattan, wry and sweet. il Time 95:73-4 F 16 '70 *
BALAZS, Eugene E.
High school journalism is dead! Dead! Dead! Engl J 59:1283-4 D '70
BALBINDER, Elias. See Callahan, R. 3d, jt. auth.
BALD eagles. See Eagles
BALDASSARI, Salvatore, abp
Visitor stopped at St Apollinare. E. Cochrane. Commonweal 92:452-3 S 18 '70 *
Witch hunting in Italy. J. Deedy. Commonweal 92:26 Mr 20 '70 *
BALDNESS
Why some women lose their hair. Good H 170:177 My '70
BALDRIDGE, Letitia
(ed) See Bruce, E. B. Peaceful pleasures of Christmas
BALDWIN, Benjamin
Three architects speak their minds. pors House & Gard 137:12+ Je '70
BALDWIN, Carl R.
Imago Clarkensis. T.V. il Art N 69:62-5+ N '70
Journey to the year 1200. il Art N 69:30-5+ Ap '70

BALDWIN, D. H, company
Money makes beautiful music at Baldwin. il Bsns W p58+ My 23 '70
BALDWIN, Frank
Korean solution for Vietnam? New Repub 163:19-21 Jl 18 '70
BALDWIN, George B.
Brain drain or overflow? bibliog f For Affairs 48:358-72 Ja '70
BALDWIN, Hanson Weightman
Russia's big red fleet. Read Digest 97:155-6+ N '70
Soft words vs. hard facts. Read Digest 96:84-8 Mr '70
BALDWIN, James
Love affair: James Baldwin and Istanbul. C. E. Adelsen. il pors Ebony 25:40-2+ Mr '70 *
BALDWIN, Joel
Disappearing beauty of the salt marsh; photographs. il Look 34:24-31 Ap 21 '70
BALDWIN, Nancy
Approach to making boxes. il Ceram Mo 18:18-21 N '70
BALDWIN, Ralph B.
Summary of arguments for a hot moon. bibliog Science 170:1297-300 D 18 '70
BALDWIN, Ruth E. See Cloninger, M. R. jt. auth.
BALDWIN, William
Beautiful floor. House & Gard 137:12-13+ Ap '70
Decorator speaks his mind. See issues of House & garden incorporating Living for young homemakers
How five rooms reflect five personalities. il House & Gard 138:104-9 O '70
BALEARIC ISLANDS
See also
Iviza (island)
BALFOUR, Michael
Wife is. . ; excerpts. il Read Digest 96:100-1 F '70
BALGOOYEN, Warren
Teaching the environment to 2,500 youngsters. C. Schweikert. il por Org Gard & Farm 17:83-5 Jl '70 *
BALI
Shorthand notes on Bali: posthouses on the jet circuit. D. Messinesi. il Vogue 156:92+ D '70
See also
Gardens—Bali
BALIN, Robert P.
[Electronics quiz] il Pop Electr 32:30+ Je; 33:44+ D '70; 34-32 Ja '71
BALINT, Nicholas G.
(comp) As others see us. See issues of Saturday review
(comp) Letters to the world's editors. See issues of Saturday review
BALL, Charles E.
Trenches vs. uprights for high moisture milo. Farm J 93:B25 N '69
BALL, Fred
Metal inlays in enameling. il Ceram Mo 18:14-16 Ap '70
Sgraffito with liquid enamels. il Ceram Mo 18:26-8 S '70
White-on-white enameling. il Ceram Mo 18:20-1+ O '70
BALL, G. G. See Gray, J. A. jt. auth.
BALL, George W.
Economic policy: who's in charge? por Newsweek 76:38-9 D 14 '70
Suez is the front to watch. il N Y Times Mag p 10-11+ Je 28 '70
BALL, J. A. and others
Search for an effect of the sun on the frequency of 18-centimeter radiation. bibliog il Science 167:1755-7 Mr 27 '70
BALL, John
Interest curve. Writer 83:9-12 Jl '70
BALL, Lee Lewis
Arrange a family frame-up. il Am Home 73:28+ Jl '70
BALL, M. M. and Harrison, C. G. A.
Crustal plates in the central Atlantic. bibliog il Science 167:1128-9 F 20 '70
BALL, Robert
Bernie Cornfield: the salesman who believed himself. il por Fortune 82:136-41+ S '70
Ostpolitik: the era of negotiation in Europe. il Fortune 82:68-71+ D '70
BALL parks. See Baseball fields; Stadiums
BALLADS
See also
Phonograph records—Songs
BALLADS, American
Pug-nosed Lil and The girl with the blue velvet band. A. Fife and A. Fife. il pors Am West 7:32-7 Mr '70
Spurs and saddlebags; ballads of the cowboy. A. Fife and A. Fife. il Am West 7:44-6 S '70

BALLANTINE, Bill
Circus: the second hundred years. il Holiday
47:50-1+ Ap '70
BALLENGEE, James M.
That abandoned quarry may be a water asset.
il Am City 85:69-71 F '70
BALLET
Dance. J. Maskey. il Hi Fi 20:secII 9+ Jl '70
Evening of a faun. F. Robinson. il pors
Opera N 34:26-9 F 21 '70
Presstime news. See issues of Dance maga-
zine
Reviews. See issues of Dance magazine
To be a dancer; V. Verdy and E. Villela talk
about the art. S. J. Cohen. il pors Opera N
34:26-9 Ap 18 '70
World of dance. W. Terry. See issues of
Saturday review
See also
Choreography
Metropolitan opera ballet
Moving pictures—Dance films
Television broadcasting—Dancing

Competitions
Judgment in Moscow; the first international
ballet competition. A. De Mille. Atlan 226:
107-8+ Ag '70

History
Comedy classic: Coppélia. W. Terry. il por
Sat R 53:51 Je 6 '70
Neglected masterpiece: La Sylphide. W. Ter-
ry. il Sat R 53:43 Ja 17 '70
Petrouchka: Diaghilev's 1911, Joffrey's 1970;
with sketches by A. N. Benois. O. May-
nard. il Dance Mag 44:47-61 F '70

Canada
Les Grands ballets canadiens, Salle Wilfried-
Pelletier, Montreal. M. Marks. il Dance
Mag 44:77-80 D '70

France
Letter from Paris; June season, international
attractions. Genêt. New Yorker 46:60 Je 27
'70
Letter from Paris; three ballets at the Opéra.
Genêt. New Yorker 46:123 Ap 4 '70

Germany (Federal Republic)
American in Germany: dancing for Cranko;
interview, ed. by O. Maynard. J. Reece. il
pors Dance Mag 44:34-7 Mr '70
Germany after the fall: ballet's revitalization.
G. Loney and N. M. Stoop. il Dance Mag
44:28-42 Ag '70

Great Britain
See also
Royal ballet, Great Britain

Guinea
Les ballets africains, New York city center,
NYC. N. Mason. Dance Mag 44:85-6 O '70

Mexico
See also
Ballet folklórico of Mexico

Russia
In the shadow of Russian tradition; inter-
view, ed. by M. Horosko. E. Anderson-
Ivantzova. por Dance Mag 45:36-7 Ja '71
See also
Bolshoi ballet

Sweden
Sons and mothers: Niklas Ek and Birgit Cull-
berg. G. Loney. il pors Dance Mag 44:32-7
Ap '70

United States
Ballet in Death Valley. il por Life 68:42-3 Ap
17 '70
BALLET companies
Across the Hudson: Festival 70 programs.
W. Terry. Sat R 53:19 My 9 '70
American in Germany: dancing for Cranko;
interview, ed. by O. Maynard. J. Reece. il
pors Dance Mag 44:34-7 Mr '70
Arthur Mitchell & the Dance theater of Har-
lem. O. Maynard. il pors Dance Mag 44:
52-64 Mr '70
Ballet West in Cinderella: Kingsbury hall,
Salt Lake city. J. Anderson. il Dance Mag
44:20+ Je '70
Ballet with soul; Dance theatre of Harlem at
Jacob's Pillow. il por Newsweek 76:64 Ag
31 '70
Béjart's XXth century. W. Terry. il por Sat
R 53:42 D 19; 36+ D 26 '70
Boston ballet company; Savoy theatre. S.
Smoliar. Dance Mag 44:81-2+ Ap '70
Chipping the stone; John Neumeier begins to
shape the Frankfurter opern ballett. N.
M. Stoop. il por Dance Mag 44:36-9 Ag '70

Contemporary ballet ensemble of New York,
Clark center, NYC. T. Borek. Dance Mag
44:74 D '70
Cranko's Munich deputy; Ed Dutton. G.
Loney. il pors Dance Mag 44:28-30 Ag '70
Dance repertory company; Oyster Bay theatre,
Long Island. N. Mason. Dance Mag 44:79 Jl
'70
Dance theatre of Harlem, classic. L. Joel.
Vogue 155:76 Je '70
From Profiteer to choreographer: Dieter Klos
of the Gelsenkirchen ballet. N. M. Stoop.
il pors Dance Mag 44:40-2 Ag '70
Garden state ballet; Orrie De Nooyer hall,
Hackensack, N. J. N. Mason. Dance Mag
44:22-3 Je '70
I work only for the young; M. Béjart and the
Ballet of the twentieth century. N. M.
Stoop. il pors Dance Mag 45:42-55 Ja '71
Kind of oneness, regional ballet and its festi-
vals. D. Hering. il Dance Mag 44:47-62 O
'70
Sweet smell of money; schizophrenic saga
of the Houston ballet. D. Hering. il Dance
Mag 44:72-8 My '70
With a little bit of luck; First chamber
dance co. of New York. J. Gale. il Dance
Mag 44:68-73 Mr '70
See also
American ballet company
American ballet theatre
Atlanta ballet
Boston ballet company
City center Joffrey ballet
Metropolitan opera ballet
National ballet
New York city ballet
Pennsylvania ballet company
Royal ballet, Great Britain
BALLET dancers. See Dancers
BALLET exercises. See Exercise
BALLET festivals. See Dance festivals
BALLET folklórico of Mexico
Ballet folklórico of Mexico, New York city
center, NYC. M. Marks. Dance Mag 45:73
Ja '71
World of dance; New York visit. W. Terry.
il Sat R 53:52 D 5 '70
**BALLET of the twentieth century (organiza-
tion) See Ballet companies**
BALLET production. See Dance production
BALLET schools. See Dance schools
BALLET theatre. See American ballet theatre
**BALLET West (dance company) See Ballet
companies**
BALLETS
Choreographies
See Choreography

Criticisms
Cinderella
Sat R il 53:58 N 7 '70
Confetti
Dance Mag 44:42 My '70
Consort
Sat R 53:58 N 21 '70
Coppélia
Dance Mag il 44:62-7 Jl '70
Sat R il 53:51 Je 6 '70
Dances at a gathering
Nation 210:189 F 16 '70
Dracula
Dance Mag il 44:46-9 Ja '70
Vogue 155:112 F 1 '70
Early songs
Newsweek il 75:84 Ap 13 '70
Sat R 53:44 My 2 '70
Fall River legend
Hi Fi 20:MA9 N '70
Firebird
Dance Mag 44:22 N '70
Dance Mag il 44:43-58 Ag '70
Hi Fi 20:MA10-11 S '70
Life il 69:32-7 Jl 31 '70
Newsweek 75:89 Je 8 '70
Giselle
New Yorker 46:57 Ja 2 '71
Time il 97:57 Ja 4 '71
Goldberg variations
Sat R 53:32 Ag 15 '70
In the night
Dance Mag il 44:28-9 Ap '70
Nation 210:189 F 16 '70
Newsweek il 75:96-7 F 9 '70
Sat R 53:49 F 21 '70
Lilac garden
Hi Fi il 20:MA8 N '70
Minotaur
Dance Mag il 44:62-7 Jl '70
Missa brevis
Dance Mag il 44:62-7 Jl '70
Mot solen
Dance Mag 44:62-5 N '70

BALLETS—Criticisms—*Continued*
Nutcracker
Dance Mag 44:92-3 F '70
Pain
Dance Mag il 44:42-8 Jl '70
Peloponnesian war
Dance Mag il 44:68-71 Ag '70
Petrouchka
Dance Mag il 44:36-8 My '70
Dance Mag il 44:47-61 F '70
Hi Fi 20:MA9 N '70
Nation 210:478 Ap 20 '70
Sat R 53:41 Ap 11 '70
Pineapple Poll
Dance Mag il 44:38-9+ My '70
New Yorker 46:107 Mr 7 '70
Newsweek 75:63-4 Mr 16 '70
Time il 95:69 Mr 16 '70
Poem forgotten
Nation 211:505-6 N 16 '70
Sat R 53:58 N 21 '70
Poème de l'extase
Dance Mag il 44:32-5 Ag '70
Reveries
Dance Mag il 44:28+ Ap '70
Sat R 53:58-9 Ja 31 '70
Ritual D
Dance Mag il 44:26-7 S '70
River
Newsweek 76:86 Jl 6 '70
Romeo and Juliet
Sat R 53:58 My 23 '70
Ropes of time
Dance Mag il 44:44-7 My '70
Hi Fi 20:MA11 S '70
Signals
Nation 211:604 D 7 '70
Solarwind
Dance Mag il (p40-1) 44:42 My '70
Still point
Nation 211:446 N 2 '70
New Yorker 46:139-40 O 10 '70
Suite no. 3
Nation 211:701-2 D 28 '70
Newsweek 76:117 D 14 '70
Swan lake
Nation 210:188-9 F 16 '70
Times past
Newsweek 76:102-3 Jl 13 '70
Valse fantaisie
Sat R 53:58 Ja 31 '70
Who cares?
Dance Mag il 44:26-8 Ap '70
Nation 210:252-3 Mr 2 '70
New Yorker 45:123 F 14 '70
Newsweek il 75:85 F 16 '70
Sat R il 53:41 Mr 7 '70
Time il 95:73-4 F 16 '70

Production and direction
See Dance production
Les BALLETS africains. See Ballet—Guinea
BALLIET, Richard F. See Schusterman, R. J. jt. auth.
BALLIETT, Whitney
Jazz (cont) New Yorker 46:78+ My 23 '70
Musical events (cont) New Yorker 46:66-9 Jl 25 '70
Our far-flung correspondents (cont) New Yorker 46:114-18+ Ap 25 '70
Our local correspondents. New Yorker 46:52-5 Je 27 '70
Profiles; R. Charles. por New Yorker 46:44-6+ Mr 28 '70
Profiles; B. Short. por New Yorker 46:28-35 D 26 '70
BALLINGER, Ronald B.
South Africa and the wind of change. Cur Hist 58:165-9+ Mr '70
BALLISTIC missile testing. See Guided missiles—Testing
BALLISTICS
Apollo 12 lunar module impact: laboratory simulation and possible downrange ballistic effects. H. F. Swift and others. bibliog il Science 169:851-4 Ag 28 '70
Un BALLO in maschera; opera. See Verdi, G.
BALLOON ascensions
Doomed flight of The free life. il Life 69:38-40 O 23 '70
Get along, little bubble. P. Garrison. il Flying 86:77-83+ F '70
Lift, liberty and the pursuit of happiness. H. Peterson. il Sports Illus 33:64-7+ O 19 '70
Up, up and away; The free life missing. il Newsweek 76:30 O 5 '70
BALLOON astronomy. See Balloons—Research use
BALLOONISTS
See also
Allione, L.

BALLOONS
Up in his balloon; L. Allione, montgolfier champ. il por Life 69:62-5 Ag 21 '70
See also
Balloon ascensions

Research use
Latest flight of Stratoscope 11; balloon-borne telescope. J. A. Ashbrook. il Sky & Tel 39:365-7 Je '70
BALLOONS, Meteorological
Adapting the ghost balloons. K. Frazier. il Sci N 97:393 Ap 18 '70
BALLOT
See also
Voting machines
BALLPARKS. See Baseball fields; Stadiums
BALLS
See also
Golf balls
BALLS (parties)
Bal Oriental in the middle of the Seine. il Vogue 155:62-9+ F 15 '70
In the grand manner; centennial ball of the Metropolitan museum of art. il Newsweek 75:70-3 Ap 27 '70
Spectacular decorating for a great party: the Metropolitan museum centennial ball. il House & Gard 138:60-3 Jl '70
BALSA
Balsa will cushion Mars lander system. il Space World G-8-80:34-6 Ag '70
Incredible balsa tree. K. Anderson. il Sci Digest 68:70-4 N '70
BALSAM fir
Ode to the balsam. L. C. White. il Am For 76:8-10 D '70
BALTAZAR, Eulalio R.
God in an evolving world; excerpt from God within process. por Cath World 211:103-6 Je '70
BALTIC SEA
Bad times for a multinational sea. H. J. Barnes. il Sci N 97:356 Ap 4 '70
Death in the deep; chemical warfare agents of World war II. Newsweek 76:33-4 Ag 24 '70
Stagnant sea. S. H. Fonselius. bibliog il Environ 12:2-11+ Jl '70
BALTIMORE
City planning
How Baltimore tamed the highway monster. J. Gooding. il Fortune 81:128-9+ F '70
Education
Reaching out to Danny; dropout prevention programs. R. H. Levine. il Am Ed 6:10-14 Jl '70
Gardens
Our garden in the city. B. Young. il Horticulture 48:24-5+ Je '70
Libraries
See also
Enoch Pratt free library, Baltimore
Politics and government
New wind blowing. P. J. McCaffrey. New Repub 163:10 O 24 '70
Riots
Effects of the Baltimore riots on psychiatric hospital admissions. G. D. Klee and K. Gorwitz. Ment Hy 54:447-9 Jl '70
Transit systems
How Baltimore tamed the highway monster. J. Gooding. il Fortune 81:128-9+ F '70
BALTIMORE civic opera company
Report:
Donizetti's Don Pasquale. F. C. Smith. il Opera N 34:32 Mr 28 '70
BALTIMORE Colts (football club) See Football clubs
BALTIMORE COUNTY, Md.
How to use contractors for snow removal. A. F. Jungers. il Am City 85:79-81 O '70
Mobile education technology; Board of education. D. Meryman. il Am Lib 1:162-4 F '70
Education
Off the shelf and into the classroom; Mobile educational technology unit. D. K. Jaffe. il Am Ed 6:13-16 Ag '70
BALTIMORE orioles. See Orioles
BALTIMORE Orioles (baseball) See Baseball clubs
BAMBOO
This bamboo row grows indoors. il Sunset 144:96 F '70

BAN, John R.
Twenty-five cardinal principles for the school principal. Clear House 44:441-5 Mr '70

BANANAS
See also
Cookery—Fruit

BANCROFT family
Bancroft coat-of-arms. H. K. Eilers. il Hobbies 74:158-9 F '70

BAND music
See also
Phonograph records—Band music

BANDAGES and bandaging
First aid; the arm sling. C. J. Potthoff. Todays Health 48:64-5 O '70

BANDARANAIKE, Sirimavo
Dry-eyed and flying high. por Time 95:35-6 Je 8 '70 *
Mrs B is back. Newsweek 75:41 Je 8 '70

BANDERMANN, L. W. See Singer, S. F. jt. auth.

BANDING, Bird. See Bird banding

BANDS (music)
Deep River ancient muster; fife-and-drum corps gathering. R. Ostling. il Time 96:14 Ag 3 '70
Don't get around much anymore; the rehearsal band. W. Conover. il Sat R 53:98-9 Mr 14 '70
Famous Civil war band lives again. A. Marquis. il Hobbies 75:48-9+ S '70
Jazz: New York notes. W. Balliett. New Yorker 46:78+ My 23 '70
Sy Oliver, bandleader; with discography. S. Dance. il pors Sat R 53:64-5+ My 16 '70
Walter Howard Loving, military band conductor; Philippine constabulary band. J. Davis. il Negro Hist Bul 33:127 My '70
See also
Prison bands
Rock 'n' roll groups

BANDS, Military. See Bands (music)

BANDSAWS. See Saws

BANDY, William
Squatters of Miffland; report. R. Rein. il por Time 96:19 N 9 '70 *

BANEY, Lou
Rap 'n 'pinion. Motor T 22:12 Je '70

BANFF springs hotel. See Hotels, taverns, etc.—Canada

BANFIELD, Edward Christie
Cities to live in; excerpts from The unheavenly city. Cur 119:44-9 Je '70

about
Rethinking cities. il Time 95:64+ Je 1 '70 *
Theory of the lower class: Edward Banfield, the maverick of urbanology. R. Todd. Atlan 226:51-5 S '70 *
Unheavenly city. G. B. Porter. por Newsweek 75:56 Mr 23 '70 *

BANG, Betsy G. See Kim, C. S. jt. auth.

BANGKOK

Description
Bangkok: a gourmet treat. K. Willenson. il Travel & Camera 33:86-7 Mr '70
Bangkok: where Anna met the King of Siam. G. Cotler. il Holiday 47:38-41+ F '70

BANGOR, Me.
How one city beat a cutback. il U S News 69:43-4 O 5 '70
Look before you leap into total-cost billing. L. E. Donnelly. il Am City 85:89+ F '70

Airports
City that came back; emergence of Bangor international airport. il Newsweek 75:58-9 F 9 '70

BANGOR International airport. See Airports —Maine

BANJO, Electronic. See Musical instruments, Electronic

BANK accounting. See Banks and banking— Accounting

BANK advertising
Bank finds a new way to give; merchandise giveaways in lieu of cash interest on new deposits. il Bsns W p32 Ap 4 '70
Giveaway binge. il Newsweek 76:62+ Jl 20 '70
Tuckabuckaway; free gifts. N. Gittelson. Harp Baz 103:46+ S '70
Wigs and blenders: banks' latest gifts. il U S News 69:60-1 Ag 3 '70

BANK buildings
Big bank in Little Rock; Worthen bank building. il Arch Rec 148:105-8 N '70
Bulwark in lower Manhattan; Manufacturers Hanover trust's new operations center. J. M. Dixon. il Arch Forum 132:62-7 Ja '70
First national bank of Chicago. il Arch Rec 148:137-40 S '70

Sculptural expression of tradition in San Francisco: Bank of America tower. il Arch Rec 148:126-32 Jl '70
Seattle's tall one. il Arch Rec 147:129-36 Je '70

BANK consolidations and mergers
Merging to fight U.S. bankers; Crédit Lyonnais and Commerzbank. Bsns W p41 O 24 '70

Great Britain
Merchant bank merger rocks tradition; Hill Samuel-Metropolitan merger. Bsns W p38 Jl 18 '70

BANK credit. See Credit

BANK credit cards. See Credit cards

BANK deposits

Interest
Banks get more room to scramble; boost in Regulation Q ceiling. Bsns W p29 Ja 24 '70
Fed cracks Q ceiling to help the banks. Bsns W p40+ Je 27 '70

BANK deposits, Foreign
Foreign bank accounts: the need for legislation; address. E. T. Rossides. Vital Speeches 36:526-30 Je 15 '70
Scandal of secret Swiss bank accounts. il Time 95:83-4 Mr 16 '70
Secret bank accounts; address, May 27, 1970. R. M. Morganthau. Vital Speeches 36:553-5 Jl 1 '70
Trying to unveil secret bank accounts; Patman bill. il Bsns W p98+ F 28 '70
Who's got a secret? Newsweek 75:72+ Mr 30 '70

BANK failures
Blowup in Basel; scandal of the Swiss affiliate of the United California bank. Newsweek 76:81 O 5 '70
Eatontown caper. il por Newsweek 76:46+ Ag 24 '70
$5-million that disappeared; How Eatontown took the shutdown. il Bsns W p 17-19 Ag 15 '70
Scandal in Basel. Time 96:86 O 5 '70

BANK holding companies
Banks need more freedom to compete. H. C. Wallich. Fortune 81:114-15+ Mr '70; Reply. J. L. Robertson. 82:66 N '70
Citibank's parent adopts a consultant; Cresap, McCormick & Paget, inc. Bsns W p 17 Ja 9 '71
See also
Marine midland banks, inc.
Western bancorporation

Laws and legislation
Banks that run businesses: limits under the new rules. U S News 69:55-6 D 21 '70
Battle over banking's limits. Bsns W p29 D 5 '70
Closer to limiting banks to banking. Bsns W p40 Ap 25 '70
Curbs for one-bank holding companies. U S News 69:62 S 28 '70
Fed to rule on bank growth. Bsns W p27 D 26 '70
One bank holding companies; bill before Congress; address, April 28, 1970. W. Patman. Vital Speeches 36:523-6 Je 15 '70
Senate banking bill loosens the reins. Bsns W p 16 Jl 11 '70

BANK loans. See Loans, Bank

BANK management
Case of the embattled banker. T. R. Piper. il Harvard Bsns R 48:144-6+ N '70

BANK mergers. See Bank consolidations and mergers

BANK of America national trust and savings association
Battle of the banks, California-style. il Bsns W p86-9 Ja 31 '70
From Dustbowl to Saigon: the "Peoples bank" builds an empire. M. Sweeney. il por Ramp Mag 9:24-5+ N '70
Striped ties for peace; A. R. Appleby questions Vietnam operations. Newsweek 75:72 Mr 30 '70
Unbreakable bank; attacks on West coast branches. il Newsweek 76:28+ N 9 '70

BANK of the Commonwealth. See Detroit— Banks

BANK protection. See Banks and banking— Protection

BANK rates. See Interest

BANK robberies. See Robberies and assaults

BANK street college of education, New York
Joint use of collections. E. Kulleseid and W. Gossage. il Am Lib 1:173-5 F '70

BANK strike

Ireland

See Strikes—Ireland

BANKAMERICARDS. See Credit cards

BANKERS

See also

American bankers association

BANKHEAD, Annie Mae

Her town. E. Keiffer. il pors Good H 171: 34+ S '70 *

BANKING as a profession

Career-minded? Look at banking. il Changing T 25:35-7 Ja '71

BANKING law

Foreign bank accounts: the need for legislation; address. E. T. Rossides. Vital Speeches 36:526-30 Je 15 '70

Scandal of secret Swiss bank accounts. il Time 95:83-4 Mr 16 '70

Secret bank accounts: bill before Congress; address, May 27, 1970. R. M. Morganthau. Vital Speeches 36:553-5 Jl 1 '70

Trying to unveil secret bank accounts; Patman bill. il Bsns W p98+ F 28 '70

Who's got a secret? Newsweek 75:72+ Mr 30 '70

See also

Bank holding companies—Laws and legislation

Banks and banking—Regulation

BANKRUPTCY

After Penn central, who next? il Newsweek 76:63+ Jl 6 '70

Biggest bankruptcy ever; Penn central's financial collapse. il Time 96:58+ Jl 6 '70

Du Pont card house. il por Newsweek 76: 110+ N 23 '70

How bankruptcy laws can help the little man. il Ebony 26:62-4+ D '70

Motsey's millions. Newsweek 76:80+ D 7 '70

New battles boil up over the trust fund; with editorial comment. Bsns W p20-1, 92 O 3 '70

What hope for the New Hope? il Bsns W p21 Jl 25 '70

See also

Business failures

Corporations—Reorganization

BANKS, Lacy J.

Black football players in the white South. il Ebony 26:131-2+ D '70

Black suicide. il Ebony 25:76-8+ My '70

Kansas City's top cop. il pors Ebony 25:35-8+ O '70

Military meets the Afro. il pors Ebony 25: 86-92 S '70

Richie Allen: I'm my own man. il pors Ebony 25:88-90+ Jl '70

Vet-rookie duo sparks Cincinnati machine. il pors Ebony 25:70-1+ S '70

BANKS, Louis

View through youthful eyes. il Fortune 81: 76-7+ Ap '70

BANKS, Coin

Bureau or chest bank. F. H. Griffith. il Hobbies 75:51-2 O '70

Ceramic world of Bonnie Staffel. R. D. Bonham. il por Ceram Mo 18:19-23 Mr '70

Old mechanical banks. F. H. Griffith. See issues of Hobbies

BANKS, Planted. See Gardens, Hillside

BANKS and banking

Fifty largest commercial banks outside the U.S. E. J. Tracy. il Fortune 82:148-50 Ag '70

See also

Agricultural credit

Banking as a profession

Credit

Credit unions

Development banks

Interest

Investment banking

Loans, Bank

Savings and loan associations

United States—Federal reserve board

Accounting

Finance; with yardsticks of management performance. il Forbes 105:140+ Ja 1 '70

When push came to shove for the bankers. il Fortune 81:309 My '70

Advertising

See Bank advertising

Automation

Automated banking, fastest draw in the West. R. Hazelleaf. il Pop Sci 197:46 S '70

Checking accounts

Get in the checkbook balancing act. T. Irwin. Am Home 73:78b Ag '70

Those no-charge checking accounts. il Changing T 24:16 D '70

See also

Checks

Anecdotes, facetiae, satire, etc.

My checkbook and me. E. Bombeck. Good H 170:64+ Mr '70

Consolidations and mergers

See Bank consolidations and mergers

Customer relations

Lorelei way to sell stock; Düsseldorf bank investors' club. il Bsns W p43 F 14 '70

Dividend reinvestment plans

Dividend for Citibank. R. Levy. Duns 97: 52-3 Ja '71

Finance

Finance; with yardsticks of management performance. il Forbes 107:173-5 Ja 1 '71

Foiled; bank refusal to supply performance figures. Forbes 106:7 N 1 '70

Year bankers made the best of it. il Bsns W p33 Ja 17 '70

Foreign business

Blowup in Basel; scandal of the Swiss affiliate of the United California bank. Newsweek 76:81 O 5 '70

California bank with a Swiss puzzle; United California bank. Bsns W p27-8 S 12 '70

Scandal in Basel. Time 96:86 O 5 '70

Holding companies

See Bank holding companies

Investments

American bankers hit a new market; financing Australian ventures of U.S. companies. Bsns W p42-3 My 30 '70

Laws

See Banking law

Management

See Bank management

Protection

Security is golden. il Time 97:71 Ja 4 '71

Regulation

Banks need more freedom to compete. H. C. Wallich. Fortune 81:114-15+ Mr '70; Reply. J. L. Robertson. 82:66 N '70

McLaren's hatchet swings at the banks. Bsns W p24 Ap 4 '70

Savings departments

See also

Savings deposits

Securities handling

Opportunity, thy name is pollution; legislation to let commercial banks underwrite water and sewage bonds. il Forbes 105:21-2 Mr 1 '70

Service

See also

Banks and banking—Dividend reinvestment plans

Brazil

Banco de Boston's end run to Belem. Bsns W p22 Ja 2 '71

California

Battle of the banks, California-style. il Bsns W p86-9 Ja 31 '70

See also

Bank of America national trust and savings association

Los Angeles—Banks

Europe, Western

Marriage of money; Crédit Lyonnais, and Commerzbank partnership. Time 96:106 O 26 '70

Merging to fight U.S. bankers; Crédit Lyonnais and Commerzbank. Bsns W p41 O 24 '70

Tomorrow's banking giants. G. J. Henry. Forbes 106:68-9 D 1 '70

Georgia

Irrepressible Mills B. Lane; Citizens and Southern bank. I. Ross. il por Read Digest 96:17+ F '70

See also

Atlanta—Banks

Germany (Federal Republic)

Lorelei way to sell stock. il Bsns W p43 F 14 '70

BANKS and banking—*Continued*

Great Britain

Capitalist strike against reds: Moscow Narodny bank in London. U S News 69:62 Jl 13 '70
See also
Bank consolidations and mergers—Great Britain

Illinois
See also
Chicago—Banks

Ireland

Lots of checks, but no balances; bank strike. il Bsns W p26 Ag 22 '70
Who needs 'em? il Forbes 106:36-7 S 1 '70

Japan

Japanese banks flex their muscles. il Bsns W p44-6 O 10 '70
Yen stops here; embezzlement at Fuji bank, Tokyo branch. Time 96:87 N 16 '70

Massachusetts
See also
Boston—Banks

Michigan
See also
Detroit—Banks

Pennsylvania
See also
Philadelphia—Banks

Switzerland

Scandal of secret Swiss bank accounts. il Time 95:83-4 Mr 16 '70
Trying to unveil secret bank accounts. il Bsns W p98+ F 28 '70
Who's got a secret? Newsweek 75:72+ Mr 30 '70

United States

Are those 11,400 banks really necessary? S. Rose. il Fortune 82:112-14+ N '70
Fifty largest commercial banks. il Fortune 81:204-5 My '70
Jet-propelled bankers. il Forbes 106:19 Ag 15 '70
Task ahead; address, May 14, 1970. J. L. Robertson. Vital Speeches 36:520-3 Je 15 '70
See also
American bankers association
Bank failures
Banking law
Custodianship accounts
Export-import bank of the United States of America
Savings banks
United States—Federal reserve board
also subhead Banks under names of cities, e.g. Boston—Banks

Utah

Bank with five apostles on its side; Zions Utah bancorporation. il Bsns W p 110+ Mr 14 '70

BANKS and banking, Cooperative
See also
Savings and loan associations

BANKS and banking, International
Banking's new ties. il Bsns W p 106 D 19 '70
Where the grass looks greenest. Bsns W p87 Ja 31 '70
Where the money talk is multilingual; White, Weld. il Bsns W p76-8 Ap 4 '70
Window on the world; Allied bank international. il Forbes 106:34-5 Ag 15 '70
See also
Eurodollar market
Export-import bank of the United States of America
International bank for reconstruction and development
Money—International aspects

BANKS and banking, Negro
Blacks build up their bank power. il Bsns W p92-4 D 5 '70
Green power for blacks; First independence national bank, Detroit. Newsweek 75:68+ Je 29 '70

BANKS for cooperatives. See United States—Farm credit administration

BANKSIA
It's bank control, traffic director, wildlife sanctuary. il Sunset 145:238 N '70

BANNEKER, Benjamin
Benjamin Banneker: he didn't fit the image. por Sr Schol 95:24 S 15 '69 *

BANNISTER, Roger
Where are they now? il pors Newsweek 75: 18 My 11 '70 *

BANTAM books, inc.
Something to crow about: Bantam's 25th year. il Pub W 197:30-5 Je 22 '70

BANTAMS. See Poultry

BANZHAF, John F. 3d
Banzhaf's bandits. Time 95:15-16 Mr 2 '70 *
Besieged crusader. por Bsns W p23 Ja 2 '71 *
Consumers' friend at school. por Bsns W p90 O 31 '70 *
Law professor behind ASH, SOUP, PUMP and CRASH. J. A. Page. il por N Y Times Mag p32-3+ Ag 23 '70; Reply. R. H. Quinn. p33 S 27 '70 *

BAPTIST foundation of America, inc.
Strange company. Chr Today 14:43 Ag 21 '70

BAPTIST world alliance
Baptist world congress dominated by Southern Baptists. F. Sharp. Chr Cent 87:1000-1 Ag 19 '70
World Baptists: touring Tokyo. J. L. Huffman. Chr Today 14:38-9 Ag 21 '70

BAPTISTE, Hansom Prentice, Jr
Pseudo-sacrosanct role of intelligence in education. Ed Digest 36:24-7 D '70

BAPTISTS
See also
Baptist world alliance

BAPTISTS in Rumania
Chance for Baptists in Communist Romania. D. B. Funderburk. Chr Cent 87:1466 D 2 '70

BAPTISTS in Russia
Russian Baptist leader imprisoned. M. Bourdeaux. Chr Cent 87:830 Jl 1 '70
Soviet Baptist sect suffering. America 122: 261 Mr 14 '70

BAPTISTS in the United States
American Baptists: a conservative mood; sixty-third annual meeting. J. Adams. Chr Today 14:36-7 Je 5 '70
Bickering Baptists; Southern Baptist convention's 125th anniversary meeting. il Time 95:54 Je 15 '70
Committed Baptists; group in Birmingham, Ala. Time 96:42 N 9 '70
First Baptist, Birmingham: a case study of old wineskins bursting. D. G. Shockley. Chr Cent 87:1462-3 D 2 '70
GARBC: debating Neo-evangelicalism. Chr Today 14:31 Jl 31 '70
Growing up a Baptist; Southern Baptists. M. Frady. Mlle 70:156+ Mr '70
Highlighting the American Baptist convention, 1970. G. W. Weber. Chr Cent 87:875-6 Jl 15 '70
Morality gap shootout; Southern Baptist convention. W. Henley. Chr Today 14:45 Ap 10 '70
Negro Baptists praise God and country. R. Chandler. Chr Today 15:42 O 9 '70
Precious in his sight; First Baptist church of Birmingham, Ala, and a black applicant. il Newsweek 76:69-70 Ag 10 '70
Reader not a censor, insists SBC aide. Chr Cent 87:1178 O 7 '70
Riders on the earth together; Southeastern Baptist seminary's conference. G. H. Shriver, jr Chr Cent 87:512-14 Ap 22 '70
Southern Baptist recall: Broadman too broad; 125th anniversary sessions of the Southern Baptist convention meeting. R. L. Love. Chr Today 14:32 Je 19 '70
Southern Baptists: institutional give and take. Chr Today 15:43 D 18 '70
Southern Baptists on the spot; decision to revise controversial new book; with editorial comment. Chr Today 14:21, 34 Jl 3 '70
Southern Baptists, Roman Catholics resume dialogue; meeting at St Joseph's abbey. R. Ryland. Chr Cent 87:461-2 Ap 15 '70
Southern Baptists: sect or denomination? G. H. Shriver, jr. Chr Cent 87:1093-4 S 16 '70; Reply with rejoinder. G. R. Payne. 87:1286 O 28 '70
Spare the Baptists; defection of two professors at the University of Richmond. Newsweek 75:75-6 Ap 20 '70
Verdict at First Baptist; black applicants denied membership in Birmingham, Ala. Newsweek 76:107-8 O 12 '70
We're really world Baptists; Southern Baptists. il Newsweek 76:52-3 Jl 20 '70
Whither Southern Baptists? Southern Baptists convention. Chr Today 14:3-5 Ap 24 '70
Yea, nay and amen; Southern Baptist convention's 125th anniversary meeting. il Newsweek 75:62 Je 15 '70

BAR-NUN, A. and others
Shock synthesis of amino acids in simulated primitive environments. bibliog il Science 168:470-3; 170:1001-2 Ap 24, N 27 '70

BARBADOS
Our home on Barbados; renting a house in the Caribbean. F. S. Friedman. il Travel & Camera 33:24+ Ja '70

Hotels, restaurants, etc.

Chicken a Caribbean treat; Caribbee hotel, Hastings. M. Woodward. il Travel 134:12 D '70

BARBECUE briquets. See Briquets (fuel)

BARBECUE carts. See Serving carts

BARBECUE cookery
Budget barbecue meats. il Bet Hom & Gard 48:17+ Jl '70
Doubling up on barbecued chicken. Sunset 144:179 Je '70
For a crowd: a whole lamb or a whole pig. il Sunset 145:68-70 Jl '70
Here is a barbecue meal that ten to twelve-year-olds can handle. il Sunset 145:58-9 Ag '70
How to light your fire. il Consumer Rep 35:410 Jl '70
Two smoke-cooking surprises. Sunset 145: 140 S '70

BARBECUE grills
Consumer's guide to outdoor grills. il Mech Illus 66:89 Je '70
Now: cookout fun indoors, anytime! electric countertop grill. W. C. Leckey. il Pop Mech 134:152-5 D '70
Vertical grills: attention, backyard chefs! il Consumer Bul 53:33 Ag '70

BARBEE, Margaret S. and others
Effect of work therapy on patients' responses to other hospital therapies. bibliog il Ment Hy 54:92-6 Ja '70

BARBER, Anthony
Filling Macleod's shoes. il pors Newsweek 76:30 Ag 3 '70 *
Heath's new neighbor. por Bsns W p30 Ag 1 '70 *
Letter from London. M. Panter-Downes. New Yorker 46:158+ N 14 '70 *

BARBER, Margaret
Youthful ALA recruitment director interviewed. il pors Wilson Lib Bul 44:917-19 My '70

BARBER, Noël
Brave land lost; the tragic fall of Tibet; excerpts from From the land of lost content. il por Read Digest 96:205-8+ F '70

BARBER, Red
My most unforgettable character. See issues of Reader's digest

BARBER, Theodore Xenophon
Questioning hypnosis. il por Time 96:54-5 Jl 13 '70

BARBER; story. See O'Connor, F.

BARBER chairs
Manufacture
See also
Takara company

BARBER poles
Ye olde barber pole; home workshop replicas. D. Shiner. il Design 71:10-12 mid-Sum '70

BARBERRIES
See also
Mahonias

BARBERS and barber shops
Hair. Newsweek 76:79 O 5 '70

BARBEY, Bruno
Loire Valley. il Travel & Camera 33:40-7 Ap '70

BARBIROLLI, Sir John
Barbirolli's last sessions. E. Greenfield. il Hi Fi 20:18+ N '70 *
Obituary
Hi Fi 20:MA32 O '70
Newsweek por 76:77 Ag 10 '70. H. Saal Opera N por 35:29 O 10 '70. G. Fitzgerald

BARBITURATES
See also
Amobarbital
Phenobarbital

BARBOUR, Arthur J.
Painting a watercolor in acrylic. il Am Artist 34:48-53+ Je '70
Watercolor page: with biographical sketch. il por Am Artist 34:66-7+ F '70

BARBOUR, Ian G.
Ecological ethic. il Chr Cent 87:1180-4 O 7 '70

BARBWIRE theater. See Theater—United States

BARCELONA
Description
Spain: fresh flashes. D. Messinesi. Vogue 156: 102+ O 1 '70

Galleries and museums
From Pablo, with love; early works to Picasso museum. Time 95:82 Mr 23 '70
Gift of the master; Picasso donates works to the Picasso museum. il por Newsweek 75:64 Mr 23 '70

Music
Report:
Montserrat Caballé in Bellini's Norma. F. G. Barker. il Opera N 34:32 Mr 14 '70

BARCELONA traction, light and power company, ltd.
Barcelona traction case; International court of justice judgment. UN Mo Chron 7:24 Mr '70

BARCLAY. Doris L.
Art education for the culturally different. il Sch Arts 69:14-17 Mr '70

BARD, Bernard
Case for parent participation in the schools. il Parents Mag 45:49-51+ Mr '70
Death of the report card. Ladies Home J 87: 160-1 O '70
New York city principals: on the razor's edge. il Sat R 53:58-9+ Ja 24 '70
Prescription for learning. il Parents Mag 45: 58-9+ S '70

BARDACH, John E. and Villars, Trudy
Three fleeing bullheads; with biographical sketches. il Natur Hist 79:2, 36-41 bibliog(p 133) Ag '70

BARDACKE, Frank
Super bowl. Ramp Mag 8:6 Mr '70

BARDIN, C. Wayne, and others
Pseudohermaphrodite rat: end organ insensitivity to testosterone. bibliog il Science 167:1136-7 F 20 '70

BARDS and bardism
See also
Troubadours

BARENBOIM, Daniel
Barenboim, Beethoven, and the thirty-two. I. Kolodin. Sat R 53:48-9 N 7 '70 *
Inside the outside family. il pors Time 96: 74 D 7 '70 *
Jackie and Danny and sometimes Pinky. J. Roddy. il pors Look 34:84-6 N 17 '70 *
People are talking about... pors Vogue 155: 94-5 F 15 '70 *

BARFUSS, Gerald
Discovery of abstraction. il Sch Arts 69:30-1 Je '70

BARGA, Italy
Opera off the beat; Opera Barga. P. Elvins. il Opera N 34:14-16 My 16 '70

BARGA opera festival. See Music festivals—Italy

BARGAIN sales
Christmas prices take the down escalator. il Bsns W p 14 D 26 '70
How to hunt for bargains. il Changing T 24:7-11 Ag '70; Same abr. with title Smart shopper's guide to bargains. Read Digest 97:112-14 D '70
Pallid showing at the white sales. il Bsns W p32 Ja 24 '70
Shopping the white sales. Good H 172:139-40 Ja '71
What to look for in January sales. Good H 170:132-3 Ja '70

Anecdotes, facetiae, satire, etc.
Supply and demand. A. Hayne. Look 34:92 D 15 '70

BARGHOORN, Elso S. and others
Micropaleontological study of lunar material. il Science 167:775 Ja 30 '70
—See Leo, R. F. jt. auth.

BARGHUSEN, Herbert R. and Hopson, J. A.
Dentary-squamosal joint and the origin of mammals. bibliog il Science 168:573-5 My 1 '70

BARHAM, Richard Harris
Books. E. Wilson. New Yorker 46:206+ N 21 '70 *

BARIL, Earl F. and others
DNA polymerase activities associated with smooth membranes and ribosomes from rat liver and hepatoma cytoplasm. bibliog il Science 169:87-9 Jl 3 '70

BARING, George Rowland Stanley, 3d earl of Cromer. See Cromer, G. R. S. B.

BARISH, Keith
Is the game up at Gramco? with editorial comment. J. Ross-Skinner and A. Hershman. il por Duns 96:3, 28-31+ S '70 *

BARIUM
Looking into swallowing problems; barium fudge for X-ray contrast media. J. Bockel. il Sci N 97:601 Je 20 '70

BARK beetles. See Beetles

BARKER, Andy
All hail Andy Barker. N. Cousins. Sat R 53:26 Ag 8 '70 *

BARKER, B. Devereux, 3d
Deep water racing. See issues of Yachting
Designs. See issues of Yachting

BARKER, C. Austin
Forces behind stock market ups and downs. por Nations Bsns 58:27 Je '70

BARKER, Colleen, and Medina, Johnnie
Nursery tale trio; drama. Plays 30:69-72 Ja '71

BARKER, Edwin S. and others
Mars: detection of atmospheric water vapor during the southern hemisphere spring and summer season. bibliog il Science 170:1308-10 D 18 '70

BARKER, I. K. See Stoltz, D. R. jt. auth.

BARKER, Jeffery L. and Carpenter, D. O.
Thermosensitivity of neurons in the sensori-motor cortex of the cat. bibliog il Science 169:597-8 Ag 7 '70

BARKIN, Al
Labor's split political personality. J. Hill. Commonweal 92:382-3 Ag 7 '70 *

BARKIN, Gilbert D. and McGovern, J. P.
Allergies. il Todays Ed 59:42-4 N '70

BARKLEY, Auther Gates
Higher appeal. il por Newsweek 75:32 Je 15 '70 *
$100 million skyjack. il por Time 95:25 Je 15 '70 *
Pictures on board a hijacked plane. R. Buchanan. il por Life 68:30-1 Je 19 '70 *

BARKLEY, Fred A.
Torn tissue becomes tradition. il Sch Arts 70:19 D '70

BARKLEY, Katherine, and Weissman, Steve
Eco-establishment. Ramp Mag 8:48-9+ My '70

BARKLEY, Richard L.
Respectable rioter. il por Time 96:14 Jl 27 '70 *

BARKS. See Sailing vessels

BARLEV, Haim
Israel's Bar-Lev: how to cope with the Arab armies; interview. ed. by M. Levin. il por Time 95:39 Ap 6 '70

BARLEY
Chromosomal aberrations induced in barley by LSD. M. P. Singh and others. bibliog il Science 169:491-2 Jl 31 '70
Gene for improved nutritional value in barley seed protein. L. Munck and others. bibliog il Science 168:985-7 My 22 '70
See also
Feeding and feeding stuffs—Barley

BARLEY yellow dwarf virus. See Viruses, Plant

BARLOW, Roger
Dogs can fly too. il por Field & S 74:130-2+ Ja '70

BARMAN, Alicerose, and Cohen, Lisa
Parent and child. N Y Times Mag p91+ N 8 '70

BARNACLES
Barnacle glue. R. L. Amey. bibliog il por Chem 43:44-6 Jl '70
Barnacle glue. J. Singer. il Sea Front 16:96-103 Mr '70
Barnacles as chemical manufacturers. il Chem 43:26 O '70
Goose barnacles. A. G. Melvin. il Hobbies 75:146 Mr '70
How is muscle turned on and off? G. Hoyle. il Sci Am 222:84-93 bibliog(p 130) Ap '70
New approaches to anti-fouling. il Motor B 125:178-9 My '70
Z disc ultrastructure in scutal depressor fibers of the barnacle. R. A. Leyton and W. C. Ullrick. bibliog il Science 168:127-8 Ap 3 '70

BARNARD, Charles N.
What True's new editorial image means to writers. Writers Digest 50:33 Mr '70

BARNARD, Christiaan Neethling
Clichés come true. A. T. Baker. il por Time 96:72+ Jl 20 '70 *
Curious split life of Dr Christiaan Barnard. C. B. Pepper. Vogue 156:124-5+ S 15 '70 *
Drive to be first. M. Clark. il pors Newsweek 75:72-3 Je 29 '70 *
One life. J. Lear. Sat R 53:46 My 23 '70 *

BARNARD, Scott
Brief biography. S. Goodman. il pors Dance Mag 44:60-1 D '70 *

BARNARD'S star. See Stars

BARNES, Albert Coombs, collection. See Barnes foundation, Merion, Pa.

BARNES, Clive
West End story. il Sat R 53:52+ S 12 '70

BARNES, David J.
Coral skeletons: an explanation of their growth and structure. bibliog il Science 170:1305-8 D 18 '70

BARNES, F. A.
Canyonlands by night. il Travel 134:64-6 Ag '70

BARNES, H. J.
Bad times for a multinational sea. il Sci N 97:356 Ap 4 '70
Compensation for camp victims. Sci N 97:604 Je 20 '70
Threat to salmon fishing. il Sci N 97:78 Ja 17 '70

BARNES, Ivan
Metamorphic waters from the Pacific tectonic belt of the West coast of the United States. bibliog il Science 168:973-5 My 22 '70

BARNES, Jarvis
Year-round schooling: how it really works. por Parents Mag 45:42 My '70

BARNES, Mary
R. D. Laing: in search of a new psychiatry. J. S. Gordon. il por Atlan 227:62-6 Ja '71 *

BARNES, Peter
All-volunteer army? il New Repub 162:19-23 My 9 '70
Farewell, free enterprise. New Repub 163:15-18 O 17 '70

BARNES foundation, Merion, Pa.
Fine arts; Barnes collection. C. J. McNaspy. America 122:510-11 My 9 '70

BARNET, Richard J.
Are we and Hanoi in the same war? Cur 116:3-9 Mr '70

BARNETT, A. Doak
New multipolar balance in East Asia: implications for United States policy; address, April 1970, with questions and answers. Ann Am Acad 390:73-86 Jl '70
Nuclear China and U.S. arms policy. For Affairs 48:427-42 Ap '70

BARNETT, Correlli
How nations take defeat. Horizon 12:4-11 Sum '70

BARNETT, F. J.
Compost convert in Australia. Org Gard & Farm 17:92+ F '70

BARNETT, John
LBJ state park. il Parks & Rec 5:32-4+ D '70

BARNETT, Jonathan
Studio teaching is out of date. Arch Rec 148:131-2 O '70
Urban design as part of the governmental process. il Arch Rec 147:131-50 Ja '70

BARNETT, Paul
Black continentals. il Negro Hist Bul 33:6-10 Ja '70

BARNETT, Stephen R.
Newspaper lobby. New Repub 163:11-12 Jl 18 '70
Press monopoly: Mr Agnew's oversights. Nation 210:72-5, 610+ Ja 26, My 25 '70

BARNEY, Lem
For the defense: Barney of the Lions; with report by B. Bruns. il pors Life 69:34-7 N 6 '70 *

BARNEY, LeRoy
When youngsters cheat. Parents Mag 45:49-51 My '70

BARNS and stables
Exit: all chores from the dairy barn; controlled-environment barn. D. Braun. il Farm J 93:32-3 N '69
Get the most from free stalls. il Suc Farm 68:64 O '70
His confinement barn can be open or closed. D. Malena. il Suc Farm 68:no5 B32 Mr '70
L-barn splits diner from beds. D. Seim. il Farm J 94:54S-54T F '70
Pony parlor. il Farm J 94:B26 F '70
Their barn is a real calf-saver. il Suc Farm 68:no3 D12 F '70
Top calf barn for 120-cow farm. il Suc Farm 68:L12 O; G14 N '70
Yankee original. Irish imprint; remodeling of Connecticut barn. il House B 112:80-3 Ja '70
See also
Cattle sheds
Milking parlors

Equipment
Dairy ideas California style. il Suc Farm 68:D10+ Ag '70
Easy dairy ideas to try. il Suc Farm 68:G6-7 My '70
Three free-stall barn ideas. il Suc Farm 68:D14-15 Ag '70

Floors
Nonslip dairy floors. Suc Farm 68:C10 Ag '70

Heating and ventilation
How much ventilation does your livestock need? Suc Farm 68:D24 O '70
They went to closed beef confinement. D. Malena. il Suc Farm 68:C4 Je '70

BARNUM, Phineas Taylor
Gallery: a leaf from P. T. Barnum's album. il por Life 68:8-9 Ap 17 '70 *

BARNUM and Bailey circus. See Circus

BARO, Gene
Caro. il por Vogue 155:208-11+ My '70
Plea for savouries. Vogue 155:138-9 F 15 '70
Soul food. Vogue 155:80+ Mr 1 '70

BAROMETERS
Make this handsome banjo barometer. W. C. Lammey. il Pop Mech 134:150-2 Jl '70

BARON, Charles
Starting a mental health association. Ment
Hy 54:247-50 Ap '70
BARON, Gerald
Caring for your convertible. il Mech Illus 66:
112-13+ Ap '70
BARON, Harry
Golf is not a fair game. il Esquire 73:142-9
Ap '70
BARON, Robert Alex
Let quiet be public policy; excerpt from
The tyranny of noise. Sat R 53:66-7 N 7
'70
Noise; adapted from The tyranny of noise.
Vogue 156:150-1+ N 1 '70
Quiet: what you can do to preserve it; ex-
cerpts from The tyranny of noise. House &
Gard 138:128-9 O '70
BARON Ochs (operatic character) See Charac-
ters in opera
BAROQUE music. See Music, Baroque
BARR, David
Tiny wolves of the water; with biographical
sketch. il por Natur Hist 79:3, 40-5 Je '70
BARR, Marc Lee
It's never too late to get started. Writers
Digest 51:31 Ja '71
BARR, Ruth L.
Embossing Arabic letters and numbers on new
raised-line polyethylene paper: an aid for
the blind. bibliog il Science 169:94-5 Jl 3 '70
BARRAN, David Haven
Briton wins top spot in the Shell empire.
por Bsns W p40 O 24 '70 *
BARRAULT, Jean Louis
Rabelais. Criticism
Nation 210:700-1 Je 8 '70 *
New Yorker 46:70 My 30 '70 *
Newsweek il 75:104 Je 1 '70 *
Sat R 53:12+ My 16 '70 *
BARRELS
Old reliable rainbarrel. G. F. Bush. il Org
Gard & Farm 17:82 S '70
BARRERA, Antonio Imbert. See Imbert Bar-
rera, A.
BARRET, Richard Carter
Little-known ceramic treasures from the Ben-
nington potteries. il Antiques 98:100-9 Jl '70
BARRETT, Barbara
Branch shop with new slant on togetherness.
il Pub W 197:55-6 Je 1 '70
BARRETT, Gerald V. and Franke, R. H.
Psychogenic death: a reappraisal. bibliog il
Science 167:304-6 Ja 16 '70
BARRETT, J. S.
Henry Poolman story. il pors Outdoor Life
145:68-71+ Ap '70
BARRETT, Larry
Percy Green vs. McDonnell aircraft. Nation
210:404-5 Ap 6 '70
Wounded GIs. Nation 210:51-3 Ja 19 '70
BARRETT, Peter
Extra season for grouse. il Field & S 75:
50-1+ S '70
Real Ted Trueblood. por Field & S 75:42-3+
D '70
Where the bluegill is king. il Field & S 75:
34-5+ D '70
BARRETT, Roger K.
Motives for witnessing. good or evil? Chr
Today 14:12-14 Jl 17 '70
BARRIE, Sir James Matthew, bart
J. M. Barrie, by J. Dunbar. Review
Sat R il 53:27-8 S 12 '70. P. Burton *
Little minister; dramatization. See Thane, A.
BARRIENTOS, Maria
Maria Barrientos. A. Favia-Artsay. por Hob-
bies 75:36+ Mr '70 *
BARRIGER, John Walker
As I see it; interview. por Forbes 106:38+
Ag 15 '70
BARRINS, Phyllis C.
Drug abuse: newest and most dangerous
challenge. Ed Digest 35:24-6 Ja '70
BARRON, John
KGB; condensation. il Read Digest 97:201-15+
Ag '70
Schooling of a Soviet spy; excerpts from
KGB. il por Read Digest 96:225-8+ Ap;
217-22+ My '70
BARRON, Karen D.
Books about antiques. Antiques 98:740+ N
'70
BARRON, Tilton
Clark's Goddard library: a mod solution. il
Library J 95:2412-13 Jl '70
BARRON'S (periodical)
Barron's pacification. J. Deedy. Common-
weal 92:210 My 15 '70
BARRUS, Gabby
How to keep bear out of your camp. Field &
S 74:68-9+ Ap '70
No license...no limit. il Field & S 75:46-7+
D '70
BARRY, Anne
Legal abortion mess. McCalls 98:30+ Ja '71

BARRY, Jack
Fifty ways from Sunday; poem. America
123:560 D 26 '70
Winter wind; poem. America 123:260 O 10 '70
BARRY, Joseph Amber
Most glamorous half mile in the world. il
Sat R 53:59-60+ S 12 '70
Paris on a sentimental note. il Sat R 53:64-5+
Mr 14 '70
BARRY, Les
Traveler's camera. See issues of Popular
photography
BARRY, Rick
Yes, Rick, there is a Virginia. P. Carry. pors
Sports Illus 33:16-17 Ag 24 '70 *
BARRY, Thomas
All America cities 1969. il Look 34:60-4 Mr 10
'70
Why there can't be another Woodstock.
Look 34:28+ Ag 25 '70
BARS and barrooms
Ale, cheese, onions and women; McSorley's
old ale house, Manhattan. J. R. Coyne, jr.
Nat R 22:997 S 22 '70
Best bartender in New York: Tony Tisi of
Wilby's. J. Corry. por Harper 241:47-51
Ag '70
Britannia rules the pubs. il Forbes 105:46-7
Mr 15 '70
Clydes bar, Washington, D.C. il Arch Rec
147:106-7 Ja '70
Dublin barfly's book of etiquette. C. O'Brien.
il Sat R 53:44-5+ S 12 '70
Elaine's. J. O'Reilly. il Holiday 47:69-70 Ap '70
Jack and Charlie's hideaway house: 21 club.
L. Lyons. il Holiday 47:77-9 Ja '70
London chop house, Detroit. M. Beltaire.
Holiday 47:78 F '70
McSorley's old ale house: oldest bar in New
York city. R. Burgheim. il Holiday 47:84-6
My '70
Pubs of London. B. Belford. Travel &
Camera 33:67 My '70

Automation
Computer that tends the bar; Electra-bar. il
Bsns W p46 S 26 '70
BARS for the home
Build this picture-bar. W. C. Leckey. il
Pop Mech 134:146-9 Ag '70
Handsome space-saving bar. H. Wicks. il
Pop Mech 134:160-3 S '70
BARSTOW, H. P.
Fifty kinds of food on a city lot. il por Org
Gard & Farm 17:38-41 Jl '70
BARTEL, Constance
Good-looking homemaker. See issues of
American home
BARTELL, Irma
Protesters with rakes. il Horticulture 48:18-
19 Ag '70
BARTELS, John
Bartels of New Jersey. por Time 97:12-13
Ja 11 '71 *
BARTELSMEYER, Ralph R.
Ecology and environment; address. Arch
Forum 132:48-9+ Je '70
BARTER
Douglas hams it up to sell seven DC-9s. il
Bsns W p60 Mr 28 '70
BARTH, Karl
Barth on Tillich: neo-gnosticism. R. K.
Anderson. pors Chr Cent 87:1477-81 D 9
'70 *
BARTH, Markus
Albert Speer and the miracle of forgiveness.
Chr Cent 87:1537-8 D 23 '70
BARTHEL, Joan
Here's Johnny! il pors Life 68:50-4 Ja 23 '70
How to merchandise an actor on TV. il por
N Y Times Mag p 14+ O 25 '70
Of fathers, sons and love. il pors Life 68:61-
2+ My 15 '70
BARTHELME, Donald
Adventure; story. Harp Baz 104:92-5 D '70
Brain damage; story. New Yorker 46:42-3 F
21 '70
Death of Edward Lear; story. New Yorker
46:21 Ja 2 '71
Film. New Yorker 46:31 S 26 '70
Nation of wheels. il New Yorker 46:36-9 Je 13
'70
Newsletter. New Yorker 46:23 Jl 11 '70
Phantom of the opera's friend; story. New
Yorker 45:26-7 F 7 '70
Porcupines at the university; story. New
Yorker 46:32-3 Ap 25 '70
Rise of capitalism. New Yorker 46:45-7 D
12 '70
Sentence; story. New Yorker 46:34-6 Mr 7 '70
The show. New Yorker 46:26-9 Ag 8 '70

about

Freaked out on Barthelme. R. Schickel. il
por N Y Times Mag p 14-15+ Ag 16 '70 *

BARTHELMES, Wes
Greening of Congress. Nation 211:552-5 N 30 '70
Pollution and the poor. Commonweal 91: 549-50 F 20 '70
Republican strategy, southern fried. Commonweal 91:420-1 Ja 16 '71

BARTHOLOMEW, Bruce
Bare zone between California shrub and grassland communities: the role of animals. bibliog il Science 170:1210-12 D 11 '70

BARTHOLOMEW, Cecilia
Only way to fly. Writer 83:15-18 Ap '70

BARTLETT, Dewey Follett
Governor is a businessman. N. A. Martin. por Duns 95:50-2+ Je '70 *

BARTLETT, Phyllis
Chez Mlle. See issues of Mademoiselle

BARTLETT, William Henry
Bartlett forgeries: Coke Smyth originals. R. Davidson. il Antiques 97:202+ F '70 *

BARTNOFSKY, Ruth
Results: WLB's cover contest for children. il Wilson Lib Bul 44:632-6 F '70

BARTÓK, Béla
Report: performance of Bluebeard's castle. S. L. Fogel. Opera N 34:32 Ja 31 '70
Bartók's Castle. J. W. Freeman. il por Opera N 35:6-7 O 31 '70 *
Bartók's extraordinary quartets. R. P. Morgan. por Hi Fi 20:58-61 S '70 *
Bela Bartok, Budapest and afterwards. G. Sandor. il por Hi Fi 20:MA13+ S '70 *
Bluebeard's castle. Criticism
Opera N 35:6-7 O 31 '70 *
Music to my ears; concert performance of Bluebeard's castle. I. Kolodin. Sat R 53: 35 D 19 '70 *
Music to my ears; concert performance of Bluebeard's castle by the Pittsburgh symphony. Sat R 53:58 F 14 '70 *

BARTON, Anthony
Continuum; reprint. bibliog il Library J 95: 4317-23 D 15 '70

BARTON, Derek Harold Richard
Principles of conformational analysis; Nobel prize lecture, December 13, 1969. bibliog il Science 169:539-44 Ag 7 '70

BARTON, Dorothea H.
New helps for the handicapped. il Har Yrs 10:37-41 S '70

BARTON, Linda-Lee
Face to face with a Maine lobsterman. por Seventeen 29:14 F '70

BARTOW, Fla.
Education
Experiment with joint committees; Polk education association. J. G. Bouch. Todays Ed 59:66 S '70

BARTZ, Fredrica K.
Immodest proposal. Engl J 59:43 Ja '70

BARWOOD, Aileen Vincent-. See Vincent-Barwood, A.

BARZANI, Mustapha
Kurdish truce. L. Jenkins. il por Newsweek 76:41 D 7 '70 *

BARZUN, Jacques
Berlioz a hundred years after. bibliog f il Mus Q 56:1-13 Ja '70
Loyalty and dissent: Catholic radicals today. America 122:684-5 Je 27 '70
Uncommon carrier of truth. Am Scholar 39: 556-7 Aut '70

BASAL readers. See Readers (books)

BASALT
Heating of basalts with a carbon dioxide laser. M. Blander and others. bibliog il Science 170:435-8 O 23 '70
Petrogenesis of lunar basalts and the internal constitution and origin of the moon. A. E. Ringwood and E. Essene. bibliog il Science 167:607-10 Ja 30 '70
Thermochemical remanent magnetization and thermal remanent magnetization: comparison in a basalt. K. Kellogg and others. bibliog il Science 170:628-30 N 6 '70
Water in the earth's mantle: melting curves of basalt-water and basalt-water-carbon dioxide. R. E. T. Hill and A. L. Boettcher. bibliog il Science 167:980-2 F 13 '70

BASCOM, Paul
Roxana's doll house. S. A. Parvin. il Hobbies 75:144-6+ Je '70 *

BASCOM, Roxana
Roxana's doll house. S. A. Parvin. il Hobbies 75:144-6+ Je '70 *

BASEBALL
Baseball and the national mythology. D. Halberstam. Harper 241:22-5 S '70
How about a new TV deal for baseball? R. Kahn. il Life 68:10 Mr 20 '70

Manager of a high minor; University of Southern California baseball team. P. Carry. il por Sports Illus 32:52+ Je 15 '70
See also
Batting (baseball)
Little leagues
World series (baseball)

Accidents and injuries
Return from the dark; excerpt from Seeing it through. T. Conigliaro. il pors Sports Illus 32:60-4+ Je 22; 34-8+ Je 29 '70

Bibliography
Hits and errors. Z. Sutherland. Sat R 53:38 Je 27 '70

History
Hairiest team of all: bearded House of David baseball team. J. Kirshenbaum. il Sports Illus 32:104-6+ Ap 13 '70
Only the ball was white, by R. W. Peterson. Review
Newsweek il 95:109-109A+ My 25 '70. P. D. Zimmerman

Study and teaching
To the tune of a hickory (well, ash) stick; Kansas City Royals baseball academy, Sarasota, Fla. W. Leggett. il por Sports Illus 34:50-1 Ja 4 '71

Japan
Foul ball in Japan; investigation into fixes, bribes and gambling. il Newsweek 75:99 Mr 30 '70

BASEBALL bats
Batter up! J. A. Lynch. il Am For 76:32-5+ N '70

BASEBALL clubs
Avenging Angel; A. Johnson and the California Angels. il por Newsweek 76:74-5 S 7 '70
Ball four, by J. Bouton, ed. by L. Schecter. Review
New Yorker 46:79 Jl 25 '70. R. Angell
Baseball parks, new attractions for tourists; with directory. A. R. Roalman. il Todays Health 48:42-5+ My '70
Big red machine; Cincinnati Reds. il por Time 96:35 Ag 24 '70
Bird in hand and a burning Busch; Cardinals of 1970. W. Leggett. il por Sports Illus 32: 18-23 Mr 23 '70
Birds hop for a lively bantam; manager of Baltimore Orioles. A. Wright. il por Sports Illus 32:74-6+ Ap 13 '70
Birds of a feather flock to Bob; owner of Washington Senators. R. Blount, jr. il por Sports Illus 33:26-8+ N 2 '70
Birth of the Brewers. Newsweek 75:131 Ap 20 '70
Bottom of the heap; Chicago White Sox. il Newsweek 76:68-9 Ag 10 '70
Candles are burning low in Philly. W. Leggett. il por Sports Illus 32:40-1 Je 1 '70
Chicago streaks for nice-guy Durocher. H. Peterson. Sports Illus 32:50 My 4 '70
Cincinnati's red machine. il Newsweek 76: 78-9 Ag 17 '70
Cincy cannonball; leader in National league West. W. Leggett. il Sports Illus 33:12-17 Jl 13 '70
Destructive force of Robby the robber. il pors Time 96:58 O 26 '70
Discord defied and deified; Robinsons, Frank and Brooks of Baltimore Orioles. M. Kram. il pors Sports Illus 33:26-8+ O 5 '70
Dreamy times for Mini-bombers; New York Yankees. P. Carry. il por Sports Illus 32:20-2+ Je 22 '70
Enter Senator Flood. Newsweek 76:71 N 16 '70
Good pitch but no no-hit; Rube Walker about Met pitchers. R. Blount, jr. Sports Illus 32:70 My 25 '70
Head fit for a triple crown; H. Killebrew of Minnesota Twins. P. Carry. il por Sports Illus 33:14-15 Ag 3 '70
How Durocher blew the pennant; Cubs loss to Mets. W. B. Furlong. por Look 34:55-6+ Mr 10 '70
How to score from first on a sacrifice; black leagues of the old days; ed. by J. Holway. J. Bell. il pors Am Heritage 21: 30-6 Ag '70
Hula, moolah and no blahs, the Hawaiian Islanders. R. F. Jones. Sports Illus 33:40-1 Ag 24 '70
In a changing cast, one guy still gives a hoot; Cardinal pitcher Gibson. W. Leggett. por Sports Illus 33:75-6 S 21 '70
In Montreal they love Le Grand Orange; Expos R. Staub. M. Mulvoy. il pors Sports Illus 33:38-9 Jl 6 '70

BASEBALL clubs—*Continued*

Inside baseball; anger over J. Bouton's Ball four. por Time 95:76-7 Je 15 '70

Leading man without a voice; T. Harper, Brewers leadoff batter. L. Keith. il por Sports Illus 33:44 S 7 '70

Lefty makes the Angels sing. R. Blount, jr. por Sports Illus 32:28-9 Je 8 '70

Little general; Cincinnati Reds. il por Time 95:69 My 11 '70

Little luck would be a relief; D. Knowles, Senators relief pitcher. D. Delliquanti. Sports Illus 33:92 S 14 '70

McLain: with love and hisses; prodigal Tiger pitcher returns. P. Carry. il por Sports Illus 33:42-3 Jl 13 '70

Mad Hatter's guests; major contenders for the National league's eastern division title. il Newsweek 76:79+ S 28 '70

Milwaukee is falling in love quietly this time; newly arrived Brewers, former Seattle Pilots. P. Carry. il Sports Illus 32:50-2 Ap 27 '70

My love/hate affair with baseball; excerpts from Ball four, ed. by L. Shecter. J. Bouton. il pors Look 34:82+ Je 2; 60-2+ Je 16 '70

No disgruntlements round here; Bucs in first place in National league East. R. Blount, jr. il por Sports Illus 33:18-21 Ag 10 '70

N.Y. Mets, 1970: trouble in paradise. L. Shecter. il Look 34:76+ Ap 21 '70

On, brave old Atlanta team! H. Peterson. Sports Illus 32:50+ My 18 '70

Out! Short to yellow to red; Oakland Athletics. R. Blount, jr. Sports Illus 32:58-9 Mr 30 '70

Pitcher in the wry; anger over J. Bouton's Ball four. P. Axthelm. il por Newsweek 75:59 Je 15 '70

Red menace from staid Cincy; talented rookies. W. Leggett. pors Sports Illus 32:24-7 Ap 20 '70

Renaissance in pinstripe; New York Yankees. il Newsweek 76:68-9 Jl 13 '70

Richie Allen: I'm my own man; Cardinals' pennant hope. L. J. Banks. il pors Ebony 25:88-90+ Jl '70

Sam of 1,000 ways; Cleveland Indians' left-handed pitcher. P. Jordan. Sports Illus 33:36-40 Ag 17 '70

Say it again, Rube! praising Met pitchers. W. Bingham. il Sports Illus 32:10-13 Je 1 '70

Season of the slugger; hitters winning against pitchers. Time 95:59 Je 8 '70

Seaver prepares to strike; Mets pitcher. B. Surface. il pors N Y Times Mag p36-7+ Ap 5 '70

Second, without any motion; Los Angeles Dodgers in second place in the National league West. W. Leggett. por Sports Illus 33:38-9 Ag 10 '70

Sportin' life; New York Mets. il Newsweek 75:63 Mr 23 '70

Sporting scene; pennant races and the World series. R. Angell. New Yorker 46:110+ O 31 '70

Tale of the derailed Metro; former manager of Kansas City Royals. R. Blount, jr. Sports Illus 32:43 Je 22 '70

Team that eats managers; Boston Red Sox. M. Mulvoy. il por Sports Illus 32:20-1 Mr 16 '70

Ted Williams; my year; American league manager of the year. J. Underwood. Sports Illus 32:50-3+ Ja 26 '70

That big Red machine has developed a few sputters; Cincinnati Reds in pennant race. W. Leggett. il Sports Illus 33:18-19 O 5 '70

They're playing those grinders again; three-way race for the championship of the National league's eastern division. W. Leggett. il Sports Illus 33:16-21 S 28 '70

This big man is the cool man; Pittsburgh Pirates in pennant race. R. Blount, jr. il por Sports Illus 33:16-18 O 5 '70

Three Birds who mainly stay; Baltimore's big three pitching staff. R. Blount, jr. il pors Sports Illus 33:30-2+ O 12 '70

To the tune of a hickory (well, ash) stick; Kansas City Royals baseball academy, Sarasota, Fla. W. Leggett. il por Sports Illus 34:50-1 Ja 4 '71

Tumultuous spring but a fine season ahead; baseball 1970. W. Leggett. il Sports Illus 32:48-60+ Ap 13 '70

Vet-rookie duo sparks Cincinnati machine; Perez, Simpson energize Reds' pennant drive. L. J. Banks. il pors Ebony 25:70-1+ S '70

Watch out! There are more en route; Baltimore Orioles' farm system. P. Carry. il Sports Illus 33:16-17 Ag 31 '70

Week. See occasional issues of Sports illustrated published during baseball season

What rain? New York Yankees vs Orioles. Newsweek 76:42 Jl 20 '70

Win the pennant, somebody. il Life 69:36-9 S 25 '70

Yanks are coming, or so they hope. P. Carry. il Sports Illus 32:67+ Ap 6 '70

See also
All-Star baseball game
World series (baseball)

Advertising

Selling the Senators; giveaways to promote games. il Newsweek 76:82 Jl 13 '70

Organization and administration

Curt Flood strikes out. Newsweek 76:62 Ag 24 '70

Curt Flood's complaint; antitrust suit over reserve clause. il por Newsweek 75:85 Je 1 '70

Fair or foul? il por Sr Schol 96:14+ F 16 '70

Found, an Abe Lincoln of baseball; C. Flood's court action for changing the reserve clause. por Ebony 25:110-11 Mr '70

Players go to bat against baseball; reserve system violation of civil rights. il por Bsns W p74+ F 28 '70

BASEBALL fans

Take me out of the ball game; rowdies get into the sports act. W. Bingham. il Sports Illus 32:22-3 Ap 27 '70

BASEBALL fields

Cloverleaf baseball complex Keegan field Yuma, Ariz. H. Hernandez. il Parks & Rec 5:42 My '70

BASEBALL fixes. See Bribery

BASEBALL managers

Caged, tamed and on a tear; manager L. Durocher of the Chicago Cubs. P. Carry. il Sports Illus 32:28-9 My 11 '70

Frank Robinson's cool assault on the black-manager barrier. L. Shecter. il por Look 34:82-4+ My 5 '70

See also
Baseball clubs
Williams, D.
Williams, T.

BASEBALL players

All-Star thing. il Time 96:33 Jl 27 '70

Annual baseball roundup: one hundred grand men. il Ebony 25:128-30+ Je '70

Another bad trade pays off; B. Alyea of the Minnesota Twins. W. Leggett. por Sports Illus 32:64+ My 11 '70

Ball four, by J. Bouton, ed. by L. Schecter. Review
New Yorker 46:79 Jl 25 '70. R. Angell

Baseball and the national mythology. D. Halberstam. Harper 241:22-5 S '70

Birds of a feather flock to Bob; owner of Washington Senators. R. Blount, jr. il por Sports Illus 33:26-8+ N 2 '70

Boo-boo or baby for Bowie; selection of All-Star team by the fans. W. Leggett. il por Sports Illus 32:22-4+ Je 15 '70

Bright glow of spring training; photographs by W. Iooss, jr. Sports Illus 32:24-9 Mr 2 '70

Cincinnati's red machine. il Newsweek 76:78-9 Ag 17 '70

Empty issue? Curt Flood's suit. Sports Illus 32:9 F 9 '70

Fair or foul? il por Sr Schol 96:14+ F 16 '70

Flying start for the big bad Birds; Baltimore Orioles vs Cincinnati Reds. W. Leggett. il Sports Illus 33:14-17 O 19 '70

Full series for a fleet pair; battle for the American league batting title. W. Leggett. il pors Sports Illus 33:18-21 Ag 24 '70

Good pitch but no no-hit; Rube Walker about Met pitchers. R. Blount, jr. Sports Illus 32:70+ My 25 '70

Hall of famer for sure, report on J. Bench by R. Bruns. il por Life 68:36-40 Je 5 '70

Heroes a la mode; World series through the years. H. L. Masin. il Sr Schol 97:19 O 12 '70

Hit records. H. L. Masin. il Sr Schol 97:26-7 S 28 '70

How to score from first on a sacrifice; black leagues of the old days; ed. by J. Holway. J. Bell. il pors Am Heritage 21:30-6 Ag '70

Is baseball really like that? views of J. Bouton. R. L. Tobin. il Sat R 53:43-4 Jl 11 '70

Jim Bouton's instant replay. J. Kaplan. Sports Illus 33:36 Ag 31 '70

Johnny Bench: supercatcher for the big red machine. W. B. Furlong. il por N Y Times Mag p8-9+ Ag 30 '70

Just for the record. H. L. Masin. il Sr Schol 96:26-7 My 18 '70

BASEBALL players—*Continued*

Knuckleballer; J. Bouton. New Yorker 46: 39-40 O 24 '70

Lots of stuff and no nonsense; A. Messersmith. R. Blount, jr. il por Sports Illus 32:22-4+ My 18 '70

Most likely to succeed; rookies. H. L. Masin. Sr Schol 96:17 Ap 6 '70

My love/hate affair with baseball; excerpts from Ball four, ed. by L. Shecter. J. Bouton. il pors Look 34:82+ Je 2; 60-2+ Je 16 '70

New tintype heroes; photographs. M. Kauffman. Sports Illus 33:26-35 Jl 6 '70

Only the ball was white, by R. W. Peterson. Review
Newsweek il 95:109-109A+ My 25 '70. P. D. Zimmerman

Players go to bat against baseball; reserve system violation of civil rights. il por Bsns W p74+ F 28 '70

R. Jackson, meet R. Jackson. H. Peterson. Sports Illus 32:56 Je 8 '70

Renaissance in pinstripe; New York Yankees. il Newsweek 76:68-9 Jl 13 '70

Return from the dark; excerpt from Seeing it through. T. Conigliaro. il pors Sports Illus 32:60-4+ Je 22; 34-8+ Je 29 '70

Say it again, Rube! praising Met pitchers. W. Bingham. il Sports Illus 32:10-13 Je 1 '70

Sportin' life; New York Mets. il Newsweek 75:63 Mr 23 '70

Sporting scene; pennant races and the World series. R. Angell. New Yorker 46:110+ O 31 '70

They're playing those grinders again; three-way race for the championship of the National league's eastern division. W. Leggett. il Sports Illus 33:16-21 S 28 '70

Tumultuous spring but a fine season ahead; baseball 1970. W. Leggett. il Sports Illus 32: 48-60+ Ap 13 '70

Watch out! There are more en route; Baltimore Orioles' farm system. P. Carry. il Sports Illus 33:16-17 Ag 31 '70

Yea, Mr Mays. R. Blount, jr. il pors Sports Illus 33:10-13 Jl 27 '70
See also names of baseball players, e.g. F. Robinson

Ethics

Denny McLain: ready for his comeback try; Detroit Tigers pitching star. W. Leggett. il pors Sports Illus 32:20-1 Je 29 '70

Downfall of a hero; D. McLain, pitcher of Detroit Tigers. M. Sharnik. il por Sports Illus 32:16-21 F 23 '70

Slap on the wrist; B. Kuhn's handling of the D. McLain affair. P. Axthelm. por Newsweek 75:48 Ap 13 '70

Recruiting
See Baseball scouting

Salaries, pensions, etc.

No-strike season; new contract. Newsweek 75:68 Je 8 '70

BASEBALL scouting

You can't beat the draft; the bird dogs spot the bright young players first. P. Jordan. il Sports Illus 33:50-2+ Jl 27 '70

BASEBALL teams. See Baseball clubs

BASEBALL umpires. See Umpires (sports)

BASEBALLS

Funny ball, funny bounces; theories about the lively ball. H. Weiskopf. il Sports Illus 33:20-2+ Jl 20 '70

BASEMENTS and cellars

Basic basement beautification. L. Netti. il Mech Illus 66:62-5+ Mr '70
See also
Dampness in buildings

BASERGA, Renato. See Serota, F. T. jt. auth.

BASES (chemistry)

Bronsted-Lowry acid-base theory, a brief survey. D. L. Morris. por Chem 43:18-19 Mr '70

BASES, Military. See Military bases

BASESCU, Sabert

(ed) Why so many women can't stand their own mothers; interviews. il Redbook 135: 78-9+ Je '70

BASHLINE, L. James

Presbyterian buck. il Field & S 75:172-3+ O '70

Straight-down fishing vs. the hot lake problem. il Field & S 74:56-7+ F '70

Truth about New Brunswick salmon. il Field & S 75:34-5+ Jl '70

BASILE, D. V.

Hydroxy-L-proline- and 2,2'-dipyridyl-induced phenovariations in the liverwort Nowellia curifolia. bibliog il Science 170: 1218-20 D 11 '70

BASKET flowers

Enchanting fragrance from a summer lily. B. Brinhart. il Home Gard 57:38 Jl '70

BASKETBALL

After show biz, slow biz; Ashland Eagles, the Nation's no. 1 basketball team. P. Carry. il Sports Illus 31:34-7 D 15 '69

Alcindor II? A. Gilmore playing his junior year for the Dolphins of Jacksonville university. il por Newsweek 75:76 F 9 '70

Barnburner in the old barn; Kentucky Wildcats vs Indiana Hoosiers. J. Jares. il Sports Illus 33:24-5 D 21 '70

Big Mac fills a tall order; J. McDaniels of Western Kentucky state college. W. F. Reed. Sports Illus 34:46 Ja 4 '71

Bonny year for Buffalo Bob; undefeated team reaching for NCAA title. W. F. Reed. il por Sports Illus 32:16-17 Ja 19 '70

City game; excerpt. P. Axthelm. il Harper 241:85-94 O '70

College basketball. il Sports Illus 33:32-46+ N 30; 108+ D 21 '70

Court magician; N.C.A.A. tournament. il por Time 95:48+ Mr 23 '70

Dealers roll to a title; Hawkeyes Big Ten championship. J. Jares. Sports Illus 32:47-8 Mr 9 '70

Even end to an eventful year; four college teams meet in College Park, Md. C. Kirkpatrick. il Sports Illus 32:26-8+ 23 '70

Ex-doughboy who can shoot with the best; R. Simpson of Michigan state. J. Jares. Sports Illus 32:44 Ja 19 '70

Forty-seven years a shot-freak; W. Hetzel. R. Blount, jr. il por Sports Illus 32:45-9 Ap 20 '70

Hello, drip, drip! Goodby, UCLA; recruiter B. Boyd at USC. J. Jares. il Sports Illus 31:55-6 D 15 '69

It's more fun without Lew; UCLA basketball players. C. Kirkpatrick. il Sports Illus 32:8-11 F 2 '70

Jes' li'l ol' country boys; Stephen F. Austin's Lumberjacks. P. Carry. Sports Illus 32:38 F 2 '70

Louisiana hot-shot. il por Time 95:57 F 16 '70

Odds on for the pro bowl. C. Kirkpatrick. Sports Illus 32:47-8 F 9 '70

One more war to go; South Carolina's fighting Gamecocks. C. Kirkpatrick. il Sports Illus 32:12-15 Mr 2 '70

Point and (sob) counterpoint; Mississippi college Choctaws. D. Russell. Sports Illus 32:42-3 Mr 2 '70

Power of prayer and a few sharp elbows; Ohio university's Bobcats. P. Carry. Sports Illus 32:40 F 16 '70

Rise of the bossy Ivies; basketball champions. J. Jares. il Sports Illus 32:16-17 F 16 '70

So some stars fell on Indiana; ABA's championship playoffs. P. Carry. il Sports Illus 32:16-17 Je 1 '70

Team it took to beat big Lew. il por Life 68:58-9+ My 1 '70

Texas triple threat; D. Jones, L. Johnson, A. Batro. il pors Ebony 25:49-51+ Jl '70

Time for the mighty scramble; UCLA favored to win NCAA basketball championship. J. Jares. il Sports Illus 32:22-7 Mr 16 '70

Toughest kid on anybody's block; J. Roche of University of South Carolina. C. Kirkpatrick. il por Sports Illus 34:20-2+ Ja 4 '71

Very nice place to visit; Utah universities. C. Kirkpatrick. il Sports Illus 33:55-6 D 14 '70

Week; college basketball. J. Jares. Sports Illus 33:56+ D 14 '70; 34:46+ Ja 4 '71

You gotta have heart; New York Knickerbockers against the Los Angeles Lakers. il Newsweek 75:93 My 18 '70
See also
American basketball association
National basketball association

Anecdotes, facetiae, satire, etc.

How to win at basketball: cheat. B. Cosby. il Look 34:65-7 Ja 27 '70

Refereeing
See Sports officiating

Rules

In praise of dunking. il Newsweek 76:73 D 21 '70

BASKETBALL coaches. See Coaches (athletics)

BASKETBALL players

All America basketball. W. J. McKean. il Look 34:53-4 Mr 24 '70

Basketball's double threat; Oscar Robertson and Lew Alcindor of the Milwaukee Bucks. P. Axthelm. Vogue 156:76 N 15 '70

BASS, Jack
White violence in Lamar. New Repub 162:10-12 Mr 28 '70

BASS, Sam
Sam Bass & the myth machine. H. H. Smith. por Am West 7:31-5 Ja '70 *

BASS
Florida bass invade California. B. Grant. il Field & S 74:46-7+ F '70
Sunfish family; and bass fishing. A. J. McClane. il Field & S 74:53-9+ Ap '70

BASS fishing
Ah-chaf-ah-lie-ah spells bass; lower Atchafalaya basin floodway. W. Allegood. il Outdoor Life 145:68-9+ Mr '70
Ancient lure that stripers can't resist. J. B. Robinson. il Field & S 74:60-1+ Ap '70
Bass from the bottom up. B. Brady. il por Outdoor Life 146:56-7+ N '70
Bass in the treetops. C. Elliott. il Outdoor Life 146:60-1+ S '70
British bass. D. Fletcher. il Sea Front 16:164-9 My '70
Camanche, hot new bass lake. L. Green. il Field & S 74:66-7+ Ap '70
Catch big bass right now. J. Brang. il pors Outdoor Life 145:92-3+ Ap '70
Clearwater and smallmouth. D. Pryce. il Field & S 75:24-5+ Jl '70
Fast bass in Puerto Rico; black bass. D. Ladd. il Field & S 75:154-5+ My '70
Fishing paradise in the Prairies. W. Davis. il Mech Illus 66:59+ Ja '70
Fly fishing for bass. A. J. McClane. il Field & S 75:62-5 Jl '70
Goggle-eyes'll get you; rock bass fishing in Miami County. B. Scifres. il por Outdoor Life 146:82-3+ O '70
Hot weather hot spot. H. F. Blaisdell. il Field & S 75:86-9+ Jl '70
How to catch more bass. J. Palmer. il Field & S 75:48-9+ Ag '70
How to think like a bass. J. Robinson and H. Carroll. il Field & S 75:56-7+ N '70
It's spring for smallmouths; New England bass. J. B. Robinson. il por Outdoor Life 145:54-5+ My '70
Jiggerpoling for lunkers. B. Phillips. il Outdoor Life 145:54-5+ Je '70
Largemouths are predictable; Clear Lake, Calif. J. Brooks. il Outdoor Life 145:76-8+ My '70
Lower the odds on lunker bass. S. Fagerstrom. il Field & S 74:78-9+ Mr '70
Maine's predictable Saco River stripers. P. McLain. il Field & S 75:72-3+ My '70
Most fishermen catch limits of bass in Ruby marshes. il Sunset 145:40 S '70
New hotspot for channel bass; and red-drum fishing. K. Osborne. il por Outdoor Life 145:70-3+ My '70
New Jersey's best bet for smallmouths. J. B. Robinson. il Field & S 74:198-201+ Ap '70
Nova Scotia's striped sea barse. G. Heinold. il pors Outdoor Life 146:62-4+ Jl '70
Now's a time for bass. R. Tinsley. il Outdoor Life 145:66-7+ F '70
Prospecting for Florida bass. G. Laycock. il Field & S 75:56-7+ My '70
Redwing black bass. B. Underwood. il por Outdoor Life 146:48-9+ Jl '70
Rocks on the brain. G. Heinold. il Outdoor Life 145:36+ F '70
Stripers in the desert; Lake Havasu and Colorado River. B. Grant. il Field & S 75:52-3+ My '70
Sunfish family; and bass fishing. A. J. McClane. il Field & S 74:53-9+ Ap '70
Too many bass. T. Janes. il Outdoor Life 145:60-1+ Je '70
What the experts taught me. P. Bauer. il por Outdoor Life 146:68-71+ Ag '70

BASSAE temple. See Temples—Greece, Ancient

BASSETT, Howard
Mighty dream come true. A. Birch. il por Har Yrs 10:14-15 F '70 *

BASSINGTHWAIGHTE, James B.
Blood flow and diffusion through mammalian organs. bibliog il Science 167:1347-53 Mr 6 '70

BASSIOUNI, M. Cherif
Palestinians: refugees or a people? il Cath World 211:257-62 S '70

BASTILLE
Bastille day revisited. A. Bakshian, jr. Nat R 22:734-5+ Jl 14 '70

BASTILLE day
Letter from Paris. Genêt. New Yorker 46:77-8 Jl 25 '70

BASTIN, J. A. and others
Infrared and thermal properties of lunar rock. bibliog il Science 167:728-30 Ja 30 '70

BATAVIA accelerator. See Accelerators (electrons, etc)

BATCHELDER, Clifton
Matter of money. Newsweek 75:44 My 11 '70 *

BATEMAN, Hester
Silver sugar tongs by Hester Bateman. L. F. Reals. il Hobbies 75:120+ Jl '70 *

BATES, Harry
He shrinks big buildings to size. P. Knight. por Sports Illus 33:46 S 28 '70 *

BATES, Marston
Jungle in the house; excerpts. il por Sci Digest 67:27-32 Je; 68:20-4 Jl; 34-8 Ag; 26-30 S; 30-3 O; 32-7 N '70

BATES, Scott
Fable of the way-out leaf; poem. New Repub 162:26 My 9 '70

BATH houses. See Bathhouses

BATH iron works corporation
Old shipyard moves in new ways. Bsns W p 148+ Mr 14 '70
Those were the days; mass-produced luxury yachts in July 1929. J. A. MacDonald. il por Yachting 127:50-2+ F '70

BATH preparations
Set your own beauty-farm routine; programs and products. S. Lindsay. il House B 112:44+ O '70

BATH rooms. See Bathrooms

BATHHOUSES
Build this poolhouse for less than $500; interview. ed. by H. Wicks. S. Corsak. il Pop Mech 133:124-7 Ap '70
Mrs Robert F. Kennedy: our pool house is the children's escape hatch. il House & Gard 138:32-7 Jl '70

BATHING. See Baths

BATHING suits
Birth of the bikini. W. Attwood. il Look 34:78+ My 19 '70
Down to the sea in style. il Time 95:58-62 Je 1 '70

BATHROOM fixtures
Turn your bath into a spa at home. il House B 112:60+ O '70
See also
Toilets

BATHROOM scales. See Scales (weighing instruments)

BATHROOMS
Bathroom revolution. D. X. Manners. il Am Home 73:124+ My '70
Beauty, bath and bedroom. il House & Gard 137:114-21 My '70
David Hicks was here. il Ladies Home J 87:30+ Ja '70
Easy ways to clean your bathroom. Redbook 134:68+ Ap '70
It began with the two-basin counter. il Sunset 144:78 Ja '70
Molded bathrooms complete in a package. H. Brown. il Am Home 73:100-2 My '70
New bathroom for old. L. Rubsamen. il Mech Illus 66:90-2 D '70
Room with a bath; D. Hicks-designed bathing parlors. N. Skurka. il N Y Times Mag p80-1 N 1 '70
Splash hit. il House B 112:109-15 My '70
Super bath-bedroom. il House & Gard 137:88-91 Ja '70

BATHS
Airborne ablutions; Japan's hot-bath cablecar system. il Newsweek 76:79 Jl 6 '70
Bath: new beauty retreat. S. Obre. il Ladies Home J 87:88-9 Mr '70
Bathing beautifully. il Redbook 134:88-9+ Ap '70
Introduction to the beauty bath. il Good H 170:122-3+ Mr '70
Your wonder under-water world. il Vogue 156:104-6 Ag 15 '70
See also
Bath preparations
Sun baths

BATHS, Finnish. See Sauna

BATHTUB racing. See Boat racing

BATHTUBS
These two tubs offer a view. il Sunset 144:122 Mr '70

BATIK
Batik. D. Persels. il Sch Arts 70:26-7 N '70
Chalk batik. E. B. Vollmar. il Sch Arts 70:28-9 Ja '71
Working in batik. E. N. Johnson. il Design 71:32-3 Spr '70

BATKI, John
Never touch a butterfly; story. New Yorker 46:42-5 My 9 '70
(tr) See József, A. Glasses; O Europe; On evening clouds; Fine summer evenings

BATON ROUGE, La.

Education
Baton Rouge desegregates. F. Guillory. America 122:650-2 Je 20 '70

BATS
Bat-guano cave environment. J. A. Harris.
 bibliog Science 169:1342-3 S 25 '70
Echo-ranging neurons in the inferior collicu-
 lus of bats. N. Suga. bibliog il Science 170:
 449-52 O 23 '70
Echolocation in bats; excerpts from The
 word of bats. A. Novick. il Natur Hist
 79:32-41 Mr '70
Fiction and fact about bats. R. Winter. il
 Sci Digest 67:31-5 Ap '70
Social organization in the bat myotis
 adversus. P. D. Dwyer. bibliog il Science
 168:1006-8 My 22 '70
BATS, Baseball. See Baseball bats
BATSHEVA dance company. See Dancing, Is-
 raeli
BATSON, E. Beatrice
John Bunyan and the contemporary student.
 Chr Today 14:11-13 S 11 '70
BATTELLE, Phyllis
Helen Meyner: my miracle pregnancy at forty-
 one. il por Ladies Home J 87:36+ F '70
BATTELLE memorial institute, Columbus, Ohio
Big lab that tackles the tough ones. J. F.
 Pearson. il Pop Mech 133:90-4+ F '70
Long-range prospects in book production. V.
 Strauss. il Pub W 198:28-31 D 14 '70
Why the AEC dropped Battelle; with edi-
 torial comment. il Bsns W p 110+, 124 N
 21 '70
BATTEN, James K.
You must be out of your mind to be out alone
 after dark in a neighborhood like this. il
 N Y Times Mag p22-3+ Mr 22 '70
BATTENFELD, Billie
Name of the game is incredible. il Motor B
 126:56-7+ S '70
BATTERIES for boats. See Storage batteries
BATTERS, Baseball. See Baseball players
BATTERY chargers. See Storage battery
 chargers
BATTERY charging. See Electric batteries—
 Charging
BATTING (baseball)
Batting trainer. J. Capotosto. il Mech Illus
 66:82-3+ My '70
BATTING records. See Sports records
BATTLE CREEK, Mich.
Bus happening in Battle Creek. il Am City
 85:52-3 D '70
BATTLE of Rocky Port; story. See McCarthy,
 M.
BATTLE of Shrivings; drama. See Shaffer, P.
BATTLE of the sexes. See Women and men
BAUDELAIRE, Charles Pierre
Baudelaire and music. E. Lockspeiser. Yale
 R 59:498-506 Je '70 *
BAUER, Benjamin
Speaker tests can be relevant to the listen-
 ing experience. il Hi Fi 20:secI 42-9 Je '70
BAUER, Erwin A.
Christmas trip to Texas. il pors Outdoor
 Life 146:34-7+ D '70
Games whitetails play. il Outdoor Life 145:66-
 9+ My '70
High on a horseback. il Outdoor Life 145:
 62-5+ Mr '70
Hoof it to heaven. il por Outdoor Life 145:
 80-3+ Ap '70
Hottest sport on ice. il por Nat Wildlife
 9:54-7 D '70
Hunting in Iran. il por Outdoor Life 145:58-
 61+ My; 146:44-7+ Jl '70
Start from the bottoms. il Outdoor Life 146:
 78-9+ S '70
—and East, Ben
Gravediggers. il Outdoor Life 146:29-31+ Jl
 '70
BAUER, John P.
Nouns and pronouns at Carver junior high.
 Engl J 59:970-1 O '70
BAUER, Parker
What the experts taught me. il por Outdoor
 Life 146:68-71+ Ag '70
BAUER, Roberto
Obituary
 Opera N por 34:13 F 7 '70. R. Bing
BAUER, Rudolf
Do you remember Rudolf Bauer? L. Camp-
 bell. il Art N 69:56-7+ N '70 *
BAUHAUS
Art world: Whitney annual. H. Rosenberg.
 New Yorker 46:82+ F 21 '70
Bauhaus. il Bet Hom & Gard 48:58-9 O '70
Cultural transplants. M. Jay. Commentary
 49:78+ Mr '70
Until April 26; the great Bauhaus show in
 Pasadena's new art museum. il Sunset 144:
 68 Ap '70
BAULING, Fay. See Neisser, E. G. jt. auth.

BAUM, Gregory
Future at Brussels. Cath World 212:137-40 D
 '70
Institutional hang-up. Commonweal 92:212-13
 My 15 '70
BAUMAN, John F.
Poverty in the urban ghetto. bibliog f Cur
 Hist 59:283-9+ N '70
BAUMANN, Elwood
London-Sydney marathon. il Motor T 22:90-3
 Mr '70
BAUMEISTER, Philip, and Pincus, Gerald
Optical interference coatings; with biogra-
 phical sketches. il Sci Am 223:10, 58-68+
 D '70
BAUMEL, Rachael Bail
Integrated trio goes south. il Hi Fi 20:secII
 26-7+ Jl '70
BAUNSGAARD, Hilmar
President Nixon holds talks with prime min-
 ister of Denmark. Dept State Bul 62:632
 My 18 '70
BAUX, Les
Les Baux and the pleasures of Provence. S.
 Spender. il Travel & Camera 33:36-9 Ap '70
BAVARIAN cream. See Desserts
BAVIER, Robert Newton, 1918-
From the cockpit. See issues of Yachting
What really goes on? il Yachting 128:50-1+
 S '70
BAVLEY, Fred
New horizons for disadvantaged youth. il
 Camp Mag 42:16+ F '70
BAWER, Bruce, and Hawkins, W. J.
Electronic tick-tack-toe in a cigarette box.
 il Pop Sci 197:78-9+ D '70
BAXENDELL, Joseph, 1815-1887
Field of Arcturus; mystery of T Bootis and
 other problematical stars. J. Ashbrook. il
 Sky & Tel 39:87-8 F '70 *
BAXT, George
Affair at Royalties; story. Redbook 135:159-81
 S '70
BAXTER, Gordon
Bax seat. Flying 86:150 Je; 87:114 Ag; 140
 S; 110 N; 110 D '70
BAXTER, Nancy Niblack
Voyage of a retired navy tug: an offbeat odys-
 sey. il Motor B 125:140-4+ Ap '70
BAXTER, Neal
Sow spreads in cow country. il Farm J 94:
 H12-13+ F '70
BAY area rapid transit. See San Francisco—
 Transit systems
BAY company. See Hudson's Bay company
BAY guardian (newspaper)
Raising hell on the Bay. il por Time 96:88+ N
 23 '70
BAY OF PIGS veteran association
Whatever happened to the Bay of Pigs
 veterans? il U S News 68:16 Mr 9 '70
BAYARD Cutting arboretum, Long Island,
 N.Y.
Bayard Cutting arboretum. O. M. Steward.
 il Horticulture 48:36-7 Jl '70
BAYER, Ann
Changing careers: five Americans begin again
 in their middle years. il Life 68:50-7 Je 12
 '70
BAYER, Charles H.
Confessions of an abortion counselor. Chr
 Cent 87:624-6 My 20 '70
BAYER, David L.
Urban Peru: political action as sellout. il
 por Trans-Action 7:36+ N '69
BAYERISCHE motoren werke. See Automobile
 industry and trade—Germany (Federal Re-
 public)
BAYH, Birch Evans, 1928-
Excerpt from Senate debate, March 11, 1970.
 Cong Digest 49:140+ My '70
        about
Bayh's last stand. por Newsweek 76:29 O 5
 '70 *
Birch Bayh isn't a household word, yet. R.
 Sherrill. il pors N Y Times Mag p28-9+ F
 15 '70 *
Crusader in spite of himself. il por Newsweek
 75:36 Ap 20 '70 *
BAYH amendment. See United States—Con-
 stitution—Amendments
BAYLIS, Douglas
Update your front yard. il Horticulture 48:
 38-41 My '70
BAYNE, Tom
(ed) See Heaton, M. Maurice Heaton's
 laminated panels
BAYONNE, N.J.
Old fashioned at twenty-seven; high school
 reunion. S. V. Roberts. il pors N Y Times
 Mag p45-7+ D 6 '70; Discussion. p43-4+
 Ja 10 '71

BAYREUTH

Description

More about Bayreuth: both Wagner and rococo parts. N. S. Hazelton. Nat R 22: 1259 D 1 '70

Hotels, restaurants, etc.

Bayreuth; even the *kartoffelknoede* is Wagnerian. P. Moor. il por Sat R 53:52-3+ Mr 14 '70

BAYREUTH festival

Bayreuth; even the kartoffelknoedel is Wagnerian. P. Moor. il por Sat R 53:52-3+ Mr 14 '70

Bayreuth touch; Wagner's Ring of the Nibelung, uncut. N. S. Hazelton. Nat R 22:1111 O 20 '70

More about Bayreuth: both Wagner and rococo parts. N. S. Hazelton. Nat R 22: 1259 D 1 '70

Report:

Wolfgang Wagner's production of Ring des Nibelungen. J. H. Sutcliffe. il Opera N 35:26 S 19 '70

Wolfgang is not Wieland. G. Movshon. il Hi Fi 20:MA24-6 O '70

BAYREUTH festspielhaus

Bayreuth touch. N. S. Hazelton. Nat R 22: 1111 O 20 '70

BAYS and gulfs

See also

Fjords

BAZELON, David T.

Highbrowland. M. Decter. Commentary 50: 69-71 Ag '70 *

BAZZANO, Gaetano, and others

Monosodium glutamate: feeding of large amounts in man and gerbils. bibliog il Science 169:1208-9 S 18 '70

BE nice to Mr Mitchell; story. See Crawford, C.

BEACH, David D.

Houseboats. il por Motor B 125:96-7 Ja '70

BEACH architecture

Cooper house, Orleans, Mass. il Arch Rec 147:62-5 mid-My '70

Curry house, Montauk Point, N.Y. il Arch Rec 147:72-3 mid-My '70

Downtown takes a trip to the seashore: architect Harry Bates vacation beach houses. P. Knight. il Sports Illus 33:42-6 S 28 '70

Dune house tailor-made for children. il House & Gard 137:80-3 Je '70

Four-use visitor center for national seashore; Point Reyes National Seashore, San Francisco. il Arch Rec 147:138-9 My '70

House on a sandy island. il House & Gard 137:92-5 Je '70

House on a seaside cliff; mid-Californian coast. il House & Gard 137:90-1 Je '70

Naff house, Pajaro Dunes, Calif. il Arch Rec 147:30-1 mid-My '70

Open to sun and spray. L. Hammel. il N Y Times Mag p74-5 Je 7 '70

Privacy on a peninsula. il Am Home 73:50-3 Je '70

Spare but rewarding plan for leisure. il House B 112:66-9 Ag '70

Temple to the sun in the Bahamas: a designer team creates a holiday sanctuary on a dune in Eleuthera. il House B 112: 38-42 Ja '70

Tranquillity on an island. il Am Home 73: 54-5 Je '70

Two sculptures in wood: beach houses that live in harmony with nature. M. Miller. il House B 112:30-6 Ag '70

With an atrium came a bonus: privacy plus. il House B 112:64-6 Jl '70

BEACH clothes. See Clothing and dress

BEACH erosion

Barrier beaches of eastern America. C. J. Schuberth. il Natur Hist 79:46-55 Je '70

Wandering sands. J. M. Roberts. il Américas 22:9-14 Ag '70

See also

Shore protection

BEACH fleas

Pheromone transport and reception in an amphipod. E. Dahl and others. il Science 170:739 N 13 '70

BEACH umbrellas. See Umbrellas

BEACHES

Big Sur storm. S. Abrams. il Natur Hist 79: 8-10+ Ag '70

In between storms, why not a winter's day at the beach? il Sunset 144:28-9 Ja '70

Open beaches: bill in Congress based on Texas law. R. C. Eckhardt. il Parks & Rec 5:21-3+ Ag '70

Protecting a natural beach. J. E. Wilson. il Cons 24:28-31 Ap '70

Sand for the people; Oregon decision on public use of beachland. Nation 210:196 F 23 '70

What price peace? polluted city beaches. il Newsweek 76:66 Jl 27 '70

See also

Shore protection

Singing sands

BEACONS

Build a blinking beacon to guide you home. J. G. Busse. il Pop Mech 134:130-1 Jl '70

See also

Radio beacons

BEADED flowers. See Flowers, Artificial

BEADLE, Muriel

Parent and child. N Y Times Mag p75+ Mr 22; 60+ S 20 '70

BEAGLES, Alice M.

Typewriters in libraries. bibliog por Library J 96:46-7 Ja 1 '71

BEAKS, Birds. See Bills (birds)

BEAL, Wanda

Fashions by Wanda Beal. J. Kuh. por Ladies Home J 87:54 Je '70 *

BEALER, Alex

Workshop: blacksmithing; excerpts from The art of blacksmithing. il Craft Horiz 30:42-5 O '70

BEALL, George

What's happening to Atlantic salmon? il Field & S 75:36-7+ Jl '70

BEALL, M. Leroy, Jr. See Nash, R. G. jt. auth.

BEALL Woods, Ill. See Forests, State

BEALS, Margaret

Margaret Beals: dance, poetry, music; the Cubiculo, NYC. N. Mason. Dance Mag 44:77 Je '70 *

BEAMS, Molecular. See Molecular beams

BEAN, Alan L.

Our man on the moon. S. G. Archer. il pors Am For 76:8-11 Ja '70

BEAN, Caroline Van Hook

Caroline Van Hook Bean; interview. New Yorker 46:34 Ap 18 '70

BEAN, Fern

Lady says ... Har Yrs 10:34-7 F '70

BEAN, Jerry L.

Mantis in action. il Org Gard & Farm 17:124-6 Mr '70

BEAN, Roy

Stories of the old West. E. Hough. Field & S 75:174+ Je '70 *

BEAN bags. See Beanbags

BEAN rust. See Rusts (botany)

BEAN salads. See Salads

BEANBAGS

Clown, tortoise, and Mr 5 by 5. il Sunset 145:96 D '70

Super bean bag; styrene pellets. il Sunset 145:50-1 Ag; 130 N '70

BEANE, Alpheus C.

Where are they now? R. Levy. pors Duns 95:40 Je '70 *

BEANS

Fall bush beans are best. L. Riotte. il Org Gard & Farm 17:90-1 Ag '70

Send your beans up a pole. S. R. Ogden. il por Org Gard & Farm 17:32-5 O '70

Two months from now, overwhelmed with beans. il Sunset 144:210+ Je '70

See also

Cookery—Vegetables

Soybeans

BEANY'S private eye; drama. See Miller, H. L.

BEAR hunting

Average deer hunt? Catskill Mountains. J. Walters. il por Outdoor Life 146:68-9+ O '70

Bear for the barbershop. D. D. Kerscher. il por Outdoor Life 145:60-1+ Mr '70

Bears and bear dogs. D. M. Newell. il Field & S 74:64-5+ F '70

Can you top this? ed. by E. E. Kurrus, jr. H. M. Oliver. il Outdoor Life 145:94-7+ Ap '70

Cyanide Creek affair. W. J. McRae. il por Outdoor Life 145:44-7+ Je '70

High-climb Kodiaks. D. Powell. il pors Outdoor Life 145:58-9+ F '70

I came for bear; black bear hunting in Quebec. G. McKenna. il Outdoor Life 145:50-3+ My '70

Nothing's wrong with Nanook; Alaskan polar bears. W. Page. il Field & S 74:46-7+ Ja '70

On the trail of the grizzly. S. Wright. il pors Am West 7:32-7 N '70

Perilous cruise for Alaskan brown bear; reprint. D. J. Singer. il Field & S 75: 200-4+ Je '70

$2,903.55 polar bear. P. Moon. il Audubon 72:149-52 N '70

Walkin' bear. E. E. Kurrus, jr. il pors Outdoor Life 146:46-9+ D '70

We hunted down a man-killer; grizzly. G. D. Gosling. il por Outdoor Life 146:45-7+ N '70

BEARD, Frank
Pro; Frank Beard on the golf tour; excerpts. pors Sports Illus 32:64-8+ My 18; 36-40+ My 25; 24-8 Je 1 '70
BEARD, James A.
How to take the nonsense out of cooking. H. Frankel. il pors Redbook 135:68-9+ O '70 *
James Beard's cooking classes. il pors House & Gard 137:117-20+ Ap '70 *
Kitchen secrets of five master cooks; with recipes. J. Wilson. il pors House & Gard 138:76-7+ Jl '70 *
Man who wears the no. 1 apron. il por Bsns W p99 Ap 4 '70 *
—and Aaron, Sam
How to eat better for less money; excerpt. il por Ladies Home J 87:98-103+ S '70
BEARDED irises. See Irises
BEARDMORE, Thomas D. See Kelley, W. N. jt. auth.
BEARDS
Sex and 5 o'clock shadow; research by a Cambridge university scientist on the rate of growth of the male's beard. il Time 95: 44-5 Je 15 '70
BEARDSLEY, Jene E.
How like a winter your illness has been; poem. Chr Cent 87:266 Mr 4 '70
BEARINGS (machinery)
See also
Automobiles—Bearings
BEARS
Bears in my hair. O. A. Fredrickson. il pors Outdoor Life 145:36-9+ Ja '70
Countdown for polar bears. E. Layne. il Am Heritage 21:117 Ap '70
Drunken bears of Hoosac Tunnel. K. Collins. il Outdoor Life 145:70-1 Mr '70
Happy pair of hairy sports; middleweight wrestling champion and a wrestling bear. F. Deford. il pors Sports Illus 32:52-6+ F 23 '70
Housebreaker. B. Bousfield. il Outdoor Life 146:50-3+ S '70
How to keep bear out of your camp. G. Barrus. Field & S 74:68-9+ Ap '70
Human injury inflicted by grizzly bears. S. Herrero. bibliog il Science 170:593-8 N 6 '70
Parting shots; two bears named Smokey. S. Mahoney. il Life 68:72-4 Ap 3 '70
Polar bear at home in the Arctic wasteland. il Sci Digest 67:58-61 Ap '70
Weaning grizzly bears. A. S. Leopold. il Natur Hist 79:94-101 Ja '70
What every camper should know about bear. R. L. Tucker. il Field & S 74:60-1+ Mr '70
White rulers of an icy realm; five countries study habits and take census of polar bears. il Life 68:82-6 My 8 '70
BEARS (football club) See Football clubs
BEASLEY, Bruce
Age of lucite dawns in Sacramento. E. Hotaling. il pors Art N 69:50-1+ My '70 *
BEASLEY, Joseph Diehl
Birth-control success story no. 1. A. Gordon. Read Digest 96:80-4 Ja '70
Will we say "it just happened," when the world overpopulates itself to extinction? J. Lelyveld. il por N Y Times Mag p30+ Jl 19 '70 *
BEASLEY, M. L. and Collins, R. L.
Water-degradable polymers for controlled release of herbicides and other agents. il Science 169:769-70 Ag 21 '70
BEASLEY, Michael
Leaving time; story. Atlan 225:88-92 My '70
BEATLES
Beatle roundup. il Newsweek 76:85 S 7 '70
Beatles decide to let it be, apart. il A. Goldman. il Life 68:38-9 Ap 24 '70
Beatles minus one. H. Saal. il por Newsweek 75:95 Ap 20 '70
Hello, goodbye, hello. il por Time 95:57 Ap 20 '70
New culture. R. Goldstein. Vogue 156:99+ Ag 1 '70 *
Spector of the Beatles. Time 95:64 My 18 '70
Swan songs. J. Morgenstern. Newsweek 75: 93-4 Je 8 '70
See also
Harrison, G.
BEATNIKS
See also
Hippies
BEATON, Cecil
Unconquerable Mae. pors Vogue 155:130-1 Je '70
about
Beaton's love affair with the rich and royal. M. Mann. il Pop Phot 67:29-30+ N '70 *
BEATRICE foods company
New rules. Forbes 106:17 Ag 1 '70

BEATTY, Jerome, jr
Funny stories. Esquire 74:44+ N '70
Trade winds. See issues of Saturday review to May 20, 1970
BEATTY, Warren
Warren Beatty; public image vs. private man. M. Davidson. il pors Good H 171:84-5+ Ag '70 *
BEATTY family
Beatty coat-of-arms. H. K. Eilers. il Hobbies 75:150-2 Je '70
BEAUCLAIR, Gotthard de
Gotthard de Beauclair; delight in design. il por Pub W 197:72-3 F 9 '70 *
BEAUFORT COUNTY, S.C.
See also
Hilton Head Island
BEAUMAN, Sally
Who's so liberated? Why? il Vogue 156:382-3+ S 1 '70
BEAUMONT, Francis, and Fletcher, John
Woman hater. Criticism
Commonweal 92:390 Ag 7 '70
BEAUMONT, Lee R.
Sacred cows in business education. Ed Digest 36:42-3 O '70
BEAUTIFUL soup; story. See Newlove, D.
BEAUTROW, P. A.
Tradition gave way to imagination. il Am City 85:87-9 Ag '70
BEAUTY, Personal
Air, fire, earth, water. il Seventeen 29:132-5 Mr '70
Be a summer beauty. il Good H 171:76-7 Jl '70
Beauty as personality. S. K. Majumdar. Vogue 156:123+ O 1 '70
Beauty bulletin. See issues of Vogue
Beauty checkout. See issues of Vogue
Beauty scene (title varies) P. Van Wagenen. See issues of Parents' magazine & better family living
Beauty scene; questions and answers. P. Van Wagenen. Parents Mag 45:23 Ja '70
Beauty scrapbook. Harp Baz 103:148-9 O '70
Body; a total experience. il Harp Baz 103:114-17 Ap '70
Cold enough for you? il Redbook 136:80-1+ N '70
Encounter on the F train. J. Brondfield. il Read Digest 97:119-20 N '70
Exciting is as exciting does. E. Sheppard. Harp Baz 103:163 O '70
Face America loves. B. Wysor. il Harp Baz 103:106-8 F '70
Fourteen ways to be beautiful; secrets of fourteen models. il McCalls 97:72-5 My '70
Good-bye 1960's, hello 1970! S. Harney. il Ladies Home J 87:68-9 Ja '70
Good-looking homemaker. C. Bartel. See issues of American Home
Good looks & good health. R. Warfield. See issues of House & garden incorporating Living for young homemakers
Haven't we seen you somewhere before? il Redbook 134:86-9+ F '70
International beauty bulletin. il Vogue 155: 70-6 Mr 15 '70
Listen! This will curl your hair. il McCalls 97:80-3 F '70
Look you like; questions and answers, ed. by L. Allen. See issues of Today's health
Lying about your age. K. Gordon. Harp Baz 103:228 Mr '70
Project: you; don't let tension destroy looks. Ladies Home J 87:121 S '70
Secret weapons of the beautiful people. Vogue 156:134-5+ O 1 '70
Serenity is a state of mind. il Harp Baz 104: 132-3 D '70
Stay young and beautiful. P. Van Wagenen. See issues of Parents' magazine & better family living
There's change in the air! il Seventeen 29: 96-7 Je '70
Tips on winter beauty. F. Henderson. Parents Mag 45:23 D '70
Twenty no-time-to-fuss beauty tips. il Good H 172:70-1 Ja '71
What's the beauty's secret? il Vogue 155:188-91 F 1 '70
Who stays young? ed. by S. Obre. Wilhelmina; G. Greene. il Ladies Home J 87:64-9+ F '70
You never looked prettier; makeover of forty-seven year old housewife. S. Obre. il pors Ladies Home J 87:96-7 S '70
See also
Baths
Cosmetics
Exercise
Grooming, Personal
Hairdressing
Hand
Make-up
Manicuring
Skin

BEAUTY, Personal—*Continued*

Equipment and supplies
Electric grooming gadgets. il Changing T 23: 39-40 D '69

BEAUTY contests
Teenage America: engagement in Fort Worth. K. Perutz. il Harper 240:96-102+ Mr '70; Discussion. 240:14+ Je '70
Where are they now? former Miss Americas. pors Newsweek 76:22 S 14 '70

BEAUTY operators
Bazaar's beauty Baedeker. Harp Baz 103:102 S '70
Co-heads; hair parlors set up just for male/female crops. il Mlle 71:90-1 Jl '70

BEAUTY preparations. See Cosmetics

BEAUTY queens. See Beauty contests

BEAUTY resorts. See Health resorts, watering places, etc.

BEAUTY shops
Metamorphosis. Great Neck, N.Y: beauty parlor and men's boutique. il Arch Rec 147: 115 Ja '70
See also
Beauty operators

BEAUVOIR, Simone de
On aging; excerpt from La vieillesse, tr. by J. Oringer and D. Kolodney. il Ramp Mag 9:19-24 S '70
Terrors of old age: interview. ed. by S. Saler. por Newsweek 75:54 F 9 '70

about
Letter from Paris; S. de Beauvoir's La vieillesse. Genêt. New Yorker 46:87-90 Mr 7 '70 *

BEAUX stratagem; drama. See Farquhar, G.

BEAVEN, Mary H.
Delete English courses from the curriculum. Engl J 59:900-2 S '70
Thoughts of a hippie sitter. Todays Ed 59: 61-2 N '70

BEAVER, Paul
Earth people's pop; In a wild sanctuary. E. Sander. pors Sat R 53:37 Ag 29 '70 *

BEAVERS
Old chiseltooth master craftsman of the woods. J. Swedberg and C. Scott. il Nat Wildlife 8:10-12 Ag '70

BECH swings? story. See Updike, J.

BECHTEL, Donald L.
Curriculum changes in the social studies. Clear House 44:364-7 F '70

BECHTEL, Louise (Seaman)
Timely response; address, November 1969. J. MacRae. Horn Bk 46:189-94 Ap '70 *

BECHTOLD, Jack
TC switch, for remote control. il Pop Electr 32:52-5 Ap '70

BECK, Albert W.
Refreshing change in the ARC swimming program. il Camp Mag 42:18-19 F '70
Self-evaluation. Sch Arts 70:38-9 S '70

BECK, Dave
Where are they now? pors Newsweek 75:16 F 23 '70 *

BECK, Evelyn Torton
(tr) See Singer. I. B. Mentor

BECK, Frances
Give yourself a treat. Har Yrs 10:18 Ap '70

BECK, Joan
Should parents teach preschoolers to read? il Todays Health 48:36+ My '70

BECK, John D.
Curious-yellow. il Am City 85:73-6 Mr '70

BECK, Ray
Cider squeezin'. il Org Gard & Farm 17:47-9 S '70

BECK, Robert E. and Schultz, J. S.
Hindered diffusion in microporous membranes with known pore geometry. bibliog il Science 170:1302-5 D 18 '70

BECK, Simone
—See Child, J. jt. auth.

about
Making of a masterpiece. P. Simon. il pors McCalls 98:84-5+ O '70 *
Up the years from cassoulet. B. Suyker. Atlan 226:110+ D '70 *

BECK industries, inc.
Wrong foot forward. pors Time 96:65 Jl 27 '70

BECKELHYMER, Hunter
Grams and damns. Chr Cent 87:267-8 Mr 4 '70

BECKER, Charles
Arrogance of virtue (in old New York) R. Starr. New Repub 163:19-21 D 26 '70 *

BECKER, Dorothy
Relax on Maine's inland waterways. il Travel 133:68-70 Je '70

BECKER, Gerald L. See Goldhammer, K. jt. auth.

BECKER, Howard S. and Horowitz, I. L.
Culture of civility. il Trans-Action 7:12-19 Ap '70

BECKER, Joseph J.
Permanent magnets; with biographical sketch. il Sci Am 223:10, 92-100 bibliog (p 140) D '70

BECKER, Klaus, and Johnson, D. R.
Nonphotographic alpha autoradiography and neutron-induced autoradiography. bibliog il Science 167:1370-2 Mr 6 '70

BECKER, Neil
How to fight those costly bacterial infections; interview. ed. by R. Wilmore. il Farm J 94:H10-12 Mr '70

BECKER, William H.
Autonomy vs. authority? il Chr Cent 87: 1149-53 S 30 '70

BECKET, James
Inquisition Greek style; excerpts from Barbarism in Greece. il Ramp Mag 8:44-8 Ap '70

BECKET, Marta
Ballet in Death Valley. il por Life 68:42-3 Ap 17 '70 *

BECKETT, John Reymond
Leisure-time headaches at Transamerica. il por Bsns W p40-1+ O 31 '70 *

BECKETT, Samuel
Smeraldina's billet doux; story. Vogue 156: 124-5 Ag 1 '70

about
Anguish and the comedy of Samuel Beckett. H. Kramer. Sat R 53:27-8+ O 3 '70 *
Letter from Paris; Beginning to end, selection from works performed by J. MacGowran. Genêt. New Yorker 46:120-1 My 16 '70 *
Off Broadway; Jack MacGowran in the works of Samuel Beckett. E. Oliver. New Yorker 46:142 N 28 '70 *
Paradox of Samuel Beckett. C. Hughes. por Cath World 211:26-8 Ap '70 *
Theater; Beginning to end, selection from works performed by J. MacGowran. il por Time 95:62+ My 11 '70 *
Theater; Jack MacGowran in the works of Samuel Beckett. H. Clurman. Nation 211:605-6 D 7 '70 *
Wipe your glosses on what you know. L. Grever. New Repub 163:23-4 Jl 11 '70 *

BECKLEY, Gilbert Lee
No. 11 off the boards. il por Time 95:16-17 Mr 2 '70 *

BECKMAN, Alexander L. and Eisenman, J. S.
Microelectrophoresis of biogenic amines on hypothalamic thermosensitive cells. bibliog il Science 170:334-6 O 16 '70

BECKMAN, R. O.
Stage setting for White House conference. il por Har Yrs 10:42-4 Jl '70

BECKTON, Monica
Egg carton jewelry boxes. il Design 71:40- mid-Wint '70

BECKWOURTH, James Pierson
Historied generation gap! P. W. Schmidtchen. il pors Hobbies 75:134+ S '70 *

BED; story. See Vivante, A.

BEDDING
Beautiful bed. il House & Gard 137:78-83 Ja '70
See also
Blankets
Mattresses
Quilts
Sheets

BEDE, James
Our supersecret, superquiet plane. K. V. Brown. il Pop Mech 133:94-7 Mr '70 *
Wizard of Cuyahoga. J. Gilbert. il pors Flying 86:48-52+ Mr '70 *

BEDFORD-Stuyvesant. See Brooklyn

BEDFORD-Stuyvesant restoration corporation, Brooklyn
Face to face with a resolute renovator; Bedford-Stuyvesant's Restore Superblock youth patrol. por Seventeen 29:62 Ap '70

BEDNARZ, Wilma
Cucumber tree mystery. il Am For 76:48-50 D '70

BEDQUILTS. See Quilts

BEDROOM furniture
Build this early American bedroom set. M. J. Johnson. il Pop Mech 134:146-9 Jl; 154-7+ Ag '70

BEDROOMS
Beautiful bedrooms. il Good H 170:128-36 Mr '70
Design for living; homemade hangout. P. Bartlett. il Mlle 71:332-3 Ag '70
Family room and an apartment for parents. il Bet Hom & Gard 48:62-3 My '70

BEDROOMS—*Continued*
Gloria the great's patchwork bedroom. il por Vogue 155:206-9+ F 1 '70
Groom a room with color. il Seventeen 29: 160-3 Mr '70
Master bedroom, bath, dressing room, and a study. il Bet Hom & Gard 48:54-5 My '70
Master bedroom off by itself. il Bet Hom & Gard 48:61 My '70
Most personal room of all: your bedroom. W. Baldwin. House & Gard 137:10-11 Je '70
Private parents' suite. il Bet Hom & Gard 48:56 My '70
Super bath-bedroom. il House & Gard 137: 88-91 Ja '70
See also
Childrens rooms
Guest rooms

BEDS
Beautiful bed. il House & Gard 137:78-83 Ja '70
Bedtime story; canopy beds for little girls. R. Reif. il N Y Times Mag p36-7 Jl 19 '70
Look what's happening in beds! F. K. Coffee. il Mech Illus 66:87-9+ O '70
Suddenly there are twin bunks. il Sunset 144: 127 My '70
Waves of Morpheus; water bed. il Time 96:42 S 7 '70
See also
Boats—Berths
Mattresses

BEDSPREADS. See Coverlets

BEDWETTING. See Urine—Incontinence

BEE-activated bio-analyzer. See Biological apparatus and supplies

BEE stings. See Insect bites and stings

BEE-tree hunting. See Bees

BEEBE, Lorraine
Should abortion laws be liberalized? interview, ed. by C. Remsberg and B. Remsberg. pors Good H 170:92-3+ Mr '70

BEECH

Diseases and pests

Department fights beech disease and decline; beech bark disease, an insect-fungus complex. W. H. Buzzard, jr. and J. H. Risley. il Cons 24:10-13 Je '70

BEECH aircraft corporation
Beech challenges safety board's findings in Air South 99 accident. Aviation W 93:67 D 14 '70
Beech makes its move. il Forbes 105:48 F 1 '70

BEECH bark disease. See Beech—Diseases and pests

BEECH-Nut life savers, inc. See Squibb Beech-nut, inc.

BEECHAM, Sir Thomas
Sir Thomas Beecham: concluding a nine-part discography. W. Botsford. por Am Rec G 36:258-65+ D '69

BEECHAM group, ltd.
Outfit that raises British eyebrows. il Bsns W p96-7+ N 7 '70

BEEF
Beef budget stretchers. L. Driggs. il Har Yrs 10:6-8 Mr '70
See also
Cookery—Meat

Marketing

See Meat—Marketing

Prices

See Meat—Prices

BEEF cattle. See Cattle, Beef

BEEF imports. See Import quotas

BEEF industry. See Meat industry and trade

BEELER, Joe
Cowboy artists of America. il Am Artist 34: 66-74+ Ap '70

BEELKE, Ralph G.
Modern art. il Todays Ed 59:36-9 Mr '70

BEER
And now, sweet beer. Time 96:72 S 28 '70
Beer hops old frontiers. il Bsns W p40-1 F 7 '70
See also
Brewing industries
Coors, Adolph, company
Rheingold corporation

Therapeutic use

Beer for the aged. il Time 95:53 Je 29 '70
R for a short beer; treating elderly mental patients. il Newsweek 75:72 My 25 '70

BEERSHEBA, Israel
Ancient Beersheba wins new town honor. Am City 85:75 Ap '70

BEES
Bee language. Cons 24:35 Je '70
Brood care in halictine bees. G. Knerer; reply. S. W. T. Batra and G. E. Bohart. bibliog Science 168:875 My 15 '70
Communication of direction by the honey bee. J. L. Gould and others. bibliog il Science 169:544-54 Ag 7 '70
Communication of direction by the honey bee. J. L. Gould and others. bibliog il Science 169:544-54 Ag 7 '70; Reply. F. G. Hill. 170: 578 N 6 '70
Death of the bees; use of carbaryl insecticide, Sevin, by vegetable canners in Minnesota. Sci N 98:349-50 O 31 '70
Defending the dance of the bees. T. C. Lucey. Sci N 98:150 Ag 15 '70
Hunting the bee tree. A. R. Chapman. il Am For 76:16-19 Ag '70
On with the dance; recruiting behavior of bees. Sci Am 223:60 O '70
What does the bee dance say? Sci Digest 68:48 N '70

BEESON, Jack
Beeson on camera; interview, ed. by Q. Eaton. por Opera N 34:13 Mr 21 '70
about
My heart's in the highlands. Criticism
Opera N 34:32 Ap 4 '70 *

BEESON, Trevor Randall
Introducing Trevor Beeson. Chr Cent 87:317 Mr 18 '70 *

BEETHOVEN, Ludwig van
Barenboim, Beethoven, and the thirty-two; F. Blumental plays the E-flat piano concerto. I. Kolodin. Sat R 53:48-9 N 7 '70 *
Beethoven: a bicentennial tribute. F. E. Gaebelein. Chr Today 15:7-8+ D 4 '70 *
Beethoven bookshelf. E. Forbes. por Sat R 53 :73 Ja 31 '70
Beethoven, by G. R. Marek. Review
Hi Fi 20:secII 29 Mr '70. R. C. Marsh *
Beethoven in retrospect: 1770-1970; symposium. il Sat R 53:59-68+ N 28 '70 *
Beethoven L. van. R. Evett. Atlan 225:103-5 Ja '70
Beethoven on records:
Chamber music. R. C. Marsh. il Hi Fi 20: secI 60-8+ My '70 *
Choral music. H. C. R. Landon. Hi Fi 20:secI 70-2+ F '70 *
Concertos. H. Goldsmith. il Hi Fi 20:secI 51-6+ Ag; 66-8 S '70 *
Fidelio and the songs. G. Movshon. il Hi Fi 20:secI 81-5+ Ja '70 *
Orchestral music. D. Hamilton. Hi Fi 20:secI 62-5+ Jl '70 *
Piano sonatas. H. Goldsmith. il Hi Fi 20: 63-6+ O '70 *
String quartets. R. P. Morganu. Hi Fi 20: secI 73-6+ Ap '70 *
Beethoven's conversation books. K. H. Köhler. il Hi Fi sec I 20:56-63 Ja '70
Beethoven's ears. il por Time 96:44 Ag 10 '70 *
Beethoven's Missa solemnis. R. Thibodeau. por Commonweal 93:328-9 D 25 '70 *
Beethoven's Vienna: beuschel, backhendl, and a birthday. G. Marek. il Sat R 53:50-1+ Mr 14 '70 *
Bernstein's Beethoven Nine. M. N. Kanny. Am Rec G 36:964 Ag '70 *
Best buys in Beethoven records. il Changing T 24:37-8 D '70 *
Claudio Arrau: virtuosity of the mind and the spirit. R. Kennedy. Am Rec G 37:25 S '70 *
Costs of creativity. Chr Cent 87:1471 D 9 '70 *
Do we overestimate Beethoven? J. Meyerowitz. Hi Fi sec I 20:77-80 Ja '70
Fidelio. Criticism
New Yorker 46:55-6 D 26 '70 *
Opera N il 35:17-20+ Ja 2 '71 *
Sat R 54:16 Ja 2 '71 *
Great mogul Beethoven: genius got in the way. A. Burgess. Vogue 155:132-3 Mr 15 '70 *
Happy bicentennial. W. F. Buckley. jr. Nat R 22:1314 D 1 '70 *
Happy birthday Mr Beethoven. W. F. Rickenbacker. Nat R 22:1120+ O 20 '70 *
Hegel, Beethoven, Wordsworth: 1770-1970. H. Gross. Am Scholar 40:142-56 Wint '70 *
Heiligenstadt testament. il Hi Fi sec I 20:57 Ja '70
Joke for Beethoven. C. J. McNaspy. America 122:166-7+ F 14 '70 *
Late Beethoven and Schoenberg by Erich Leinsdorf: first-rate. M. Kanny. Am Rec G 36:488-9 Mr '70 *
Lively arts: special albums for 200th anniversary. R. Hemming. il Sr Schol 97:22-3 D 7 '70
Man who set music free. H. C. Schonberg. por Read Digest 96:110-15 Je '70 *
Master's voice; conversation notebooks. il por Time 95:73 F 16 '70 *

BEETHOVEN, Ludwig van—*Continued*
Music to my ears; concert performance of
  Fidelio. I. Kolodin. Sat R 53:55 Ja 31 '70
Music to my ears; Fuch-Balsam recital of
  sonatas. I. Kolodin. Sat R 53:47 Ap 11 '70 *
Music to my ears; program by G. Szell and
  C. Curzon in Philharmonic Hall. I. Kolodin.
  Sat R 53:28 Ap 25 '70 *
On Beethoven's piano sonatas. I. Stravinsky.
  Harper 240:34+ My '70 *
One of the great Ninths. M. N. Kanny. Am
  Rec G 36:651-2 My '70 *
Probity and wisdom: Barenboim's Beethoven.
  M. N. Kanny. Am Rec G 36:350 Ja '70 *
Recordings; live performances by L. Bern-
  stein and P. Badura-Skoda in Vienna. M.
  Mayer. Esquire 74:24+ S '70 *
Recordings. M. Mayer. Esquire 73:14+ Mr '70 *
Report: Leonard Bernstein's Fidelio. S. Jen-
  kins. Opera N 34:32 F 28 '70 *
Schnabel: coherence, conviction. Am Rec G
  37:20+ S '70 *
Stokowski's splendid one-disc phase 4 Ninth.
  H. Goldsmith. Hi Fi 20:secI 74 Ag '70 *
Travel, with Beethoven on the side. I. Kolo-
  din. Sat R 53:44-5 Ap 11 '70 *
200-candlepower. il Time 96:43 D 28 '70 *
Where were you the night of November 20,
  1805? G. R. Marek. il Opera N 35:24-6 Ja
  2 '71 *

Bibliography
Beethoven literature and how it grew; comp.
  by R. Breuer, with comments by I. Kolodin.
  Sat R 53:64-6 N 28 '70

BEETLES
Cereal leaf beetle continues to spread. L. D.
  Rawson. il Suc Farm 68:B6 Ja '70
Elm bark derived feeding stimulants for the
  smaller European elm bark beetle. R. W.
  Doskotch and others. bibliog il Science
  167:380-2 Ja 23 '70
Nature's toy train, the railroad worm. D. L.
  Tiemann. il pors Nat Geog 138:56-67 Jl '70
Pheromone response in pine bark beetles: in-
  fluence of host volatiles. G. B. Pitman; re-
  ply. W. D. Bedard. bibliog il Science 167:
  1638-9 Mr 20 '70
Sex attractant of the grass grub beetle. R.
  F. Henzell and M. D. Lowe. bibliog il
  Science 168:1005-6 My 22 '70
Sex pheromones: abolition of specificity in
  hybrid bark beetles. G. N. Lanier. bibliog
  il Science 169:71-2 Jl 3 '70
  See also
Flour beetles
Weevils

BEGGAR on horseback; drama. See Kauf-
  man, G. S. and Connelly, M.
BEGINNING of grief; story. See Woiwode, L.
BEGINNING to end; (dramatic reading) See
  Dramatic readings
BEGONIAS
Beauty that loves the shade! tuberous be-
  gonias. B. Brinhart. il Home Gard 57:28
  Ja '70
Constant bloom with begonias. A. Stanley.
  il Org Gard & Farm 17:104 S '70
BEHAN, Brendan
Borstal boy; dramatization. See McMahon, F.
  about
Brendan Behan: the ignominy of success. S.
  Callery. por Commonweal 93:87-91 O 23
  '70 *
BEHAVIOR. See Manners and customs
BEHAVIOR (psychology)
Agonistics: rituals of conflict. H. L. Nie-
  burg. bibliog f Ann Am Acad 391:56-73 S
  '70
Blackness and madness. T. S. Szasz. Yale
  R 59:333-41 Mr '70
Catch the child being: social reinforcement
  technique. D. G. Tinsley and J. P. Ora.
  il Todays Ed 59:24-5 Ja '70
Fresh way of understanding yourself; excerpt
  from Chatelaine. M. Landsberg. Read Di-
  gest 97:219-22+ O '70
Human zoo, by D. Morris. Review
  Natur Hist il 79:104-6 Ja '70. R. Fox
Nobody ever learned anything from violence,
  except how to duck. C. Holland. Mlle 72:
  177+ N '70
Psychodynamics of racism. J. Daniels. Chr
  Today 15:12+ O 9 '70
Violent way; excerpt from The social contract.
  R. Ardrey. il Life 69:56B-56D+ S 11 '70;
  Same abr. with title Is man naturally vio-
  lent? Read Digest 97:115-19 D '70
  See also
Electronic behavior control
Group relations training
Motivation (psychology)
BEHAVIOR, Group. See Group (sociology)

BEHAVIOR of animals. See Animals—Habits
  and behavior
BEHAVIORAL research laboratories
Where private firm runs public school. il U S
  News 69:41 O 12 '70
BEHAVIORAL sciences
Behavioral sciences. See issues of Science
  news
  See also
Center for advanced study in the behavioral
  sciences, Stanford, Calif.

Conferences
Human behavior and its control, AAAS sym-
  posium, December 30, 1970. W. A. Hunt. il
  Science 169:901-2 Ag 28 '70
BEHAVIORISM
Walden two: three? Many more? R. Todd.
  il por N Y Times Mag p24-5+ Mr 15 '70
BEHIND-the-lens meters. See Exposure meters
BEHME, Bob
All terrain vehicles in the 70's. il Field & S
  75:44-7+ Ag '70 *
Vehicles. por Field & S 75:104-5 Ag; 108-12
  S; 146-9 O; 112-15 N; 80-2 D '70
BEHREND, Erika R. and others
Interference and forgetting in bird and fish.
  bibliog il Science 167:389-90 Ja 23 '70
BEHRENDT, David
Away with tradition. il Am Ed 6:18-22 Ja '70
BEHRENS, Richard
Alkaline glaze. Ceram Mo 18:26+ O '70
Chromium, the swinging glaze colorant.
  Ceram Mo 17:33 D '69
Cobalt blues at cone 9. il Ceram Mo 18:31 My
  '70
Dust glazing. il Ceram Mo 18:19 F '70
Frits for the art potter. Ceram Mo 18:32-3
  Mr '70
Glazes from Barnard slip. Ceram Mo 18:33 S
  '70
Handcrafted ceramic buttons. il Ceram Mo
  18:28-9 Ja '70
Volcanic ash bodies and glazes. il Ceram Mo
  18:28 D '70
Yellow glazes. Ceram Mo 18:31 N '70
BEHRENS, Roy
Camouflage in the classroom. bibliog il Sch
  Arts 69:24-5 F '70
Gestalt and the visual arts. il Design 71:10-12
  mid-Wint '70
BEHRMAN, Daniel
Hunting clues to an ancient supercontinent.
  il UNESCO Courier 23:28-32 Jl '70
Understanding man's aggressiveness. il
  UNESCO Courier 23:4-18+ Ag '70
BEHRMAN, Stanley J.
Face architecture. S. Morini. il Vogue 156:
  101 Ag 15 '70 *
BEHUNIN, Homer
Primeval palms. il por Time 96:46-7 S 7 '70 *
BEIDLEMAN, Richard G.
George Engelmann, botanical gatekeeper of
  the West. il Horticulture 48:42-3+ Ap '70
BEIER, Marvin
Single-filament tail light converter. il Pop
  Electr 33:66 D '70
BEIRUT university. See American university
  of Beirut
BEISSWENGER, Paul J. and Spiro, R. G.
Human glomerular basement membrane:
  chemical alteration in diabetes mellitus.
  bibliog il Science 168:596-8 My 1 '70
BEISWENGER, John
Electronic combination ignition lock. il Pop
  Electr 33:40-2 Jl '70
BÉJART, Maurice
Béjart's XXth century. W. Terry. il por Sat
  R 53:42 D 19; 36+ D 26 '70 *
I work only for the young. N. M. Stoop. il pors
  Dance Mag 45:42-55 Ja '71 *
BEKAERT (firm) See Belgium—Industries
BELAFONTE, Harry
Harry and Lena off the cuff! il pors Ebony
  25:128-9 Mr '70 *
BELAK, Edmund R. Jr
Finger Lakes turnover trout. il Cons 24:14-15
  Ag '69
BELANGER, Jerome
Our homestead just grew like crabgrass! il
  Org Gard & Farm 17:96-9 N '70
BEL canto. See Singing
BELDING, Melvin E. and others
Peroxidase-mediated virucidal systems. bib-
  liog il Science 167:195-6 Ja 9 '70
BELFAST
Two sides of a troubled Belfast street. L.
  Lamont. il Time 96:26 Jl 20 '70

Riots
Ulster's unending feud. il Time 96-25 Jl 20 '70
BELFORD, Barbara
Mexico to Persia. Travel & Camera 33:23-
  4+ F '70

BEL GEDDES, Norman. See Geddes, N. B.
BELGIAN castles. See Castles
BELGIAN CONGO. See Congo (Democratic Republic)
BELGIAN cookery. See Cookery, Belgian
BELGIAN endive. See Chicory
BELGIUM
    See also
Americans in Belgium
Ballet—Belgium
Bruges
Canals—Belgium
Investments, Foreign (in Belgium)
Mining industry and finance—Belgium

        History
      Bibliography
Articles and other books received; comp. by P. H. Laurent. See issues of American historical review

       Industries
Wire maker bets on a U.S. market; Bekaert. Bsns W p49 F 28 '70

    Religious institutions and affairs
    See also
Bruges, Belgium—Religious institutions and affairs
BELIEF and doubt
    See also
Credulity
Skepticism
BELIEF in God. See Faith
BELIZE
Revolution in Belize. T. C. Wright. America 122:219-20 F 28 '70
BELL, Anthony
Print exporting. Pub W 198:pt2 184-5 S 21 '70
BELL, Arthur
Screen. Commonweal 92:318 Je 26 '70
BELL, Barbara
Scotland's monster lake. il Travel 133:60-2 Je '70
BELL, James
How to score from first on a sacrifice; ed. by J. Holway. il pors Am Heritage 21:30-6 Ag '70
BELL, Janice Wightman
Seeing sound. il Sch Arts 70:26-9 S '70
BELL, Joseph N.
America's oldest debt: justice for the Indians. il Good H 172:78-9+ Ja '71
Could Danish smut laws work here? il Todays Health 48:24-9+ N '70
Fond farewell to back-to-school night. Todays Health 48:16-17+ S '70
Hotline for troubled teen-agers. il Read Digest 97:41-6 N '70
Let my dad go home. Good H 170:65+ Je '70
TV's on-again romance with medicine. il Todays Health 48:24-9+ Mr '70
(ed) See Linkletter, A. We must declare war on drugs
BELL, L. Nelson
Layman and his faith. See issues of Christianity today
BELL, Leland
Bell: virtuosity without self-interest. J. Ashberry. il pors Art N 68:44-5+ F '70 *
BELL, Léonie
Old fashioned roses for fall bloom. il Home Gard 57:58-9 Ap '70
BELL, Louise Price
Cactus as food. Horticulture 48:8+ F '70
BELL, Marvin
Put back the dark: In the home; Lovesong; Service for two; Daily grind; Homage to Alfred Stieglitz; Music of the spheres; poems. Poetry 115:415-21 Mr '70
       about
Singing to spite this hunger. H. Taylor. Nation 210:122-4 F 2 '70
BELL, Terrel Howard
On being educated in 1991: address, September 26, 1970. Vital Speeches 37:88-90 N 15 '70
BELL, Thomas P.
He whistles while he works. W. F. Reed. il pors Sports Illus 33:22-7 Ag 10 '70 *
BELL, Vic
[Electronics quiz] Pop Electr 32:32 F '70
BELL and Howell company
Another victim. il Forbes 105:22-3 F 15 '70
BELL telephone laboratories
Bell labs scaling down. Sci N 97:525 My 30 '70
BELL telephone system
AT&T foresees increasing use of satellites in integrated system. K. Johnsen. Aviation W 93:21 O 26 '70
Ma Bell takes her lumps. M. T. Bloom. Read Digest 96:206-10 Ap '70

BELLAMY, Vivian H.
World war two revisited. il por Flying 86:56-64 Mr '70
BELLER, Irv
Latin America's unemployment problem. bibliog il Mo Labor R 93:3-10 N '70
BELLER, William S.
Coastal areas and seashores. bibliog f Cur Hist 59:100-4+ Ag '70
BELLES, L. L.
Arcade manufacturing co. il Hobbies 75:98J-98K+ Ap '70
BELLEVUE, Neb.
Children as hostages? question of aid to impacted districts. Time 95:23 Ap 13 '70
BELLFLOWERS. See Campanulas
BELLINI, Vincenzo
Druids of Gaul. O. S. Rachleff. il Opera N 34:8-12 Ap 4 '70 *
Long line; classical melody carries romantic drama. J. W. Freeman. il Opera N 34:24-5 Ap 4 '70 *
Music to my ears: Cossotto in Norma. I. Kolodin. Sat R 53:58 O 24 '70 *
Norma. Criticism
    Hi Fi il 20:secII 10-12+ My '70 *
    New Yorker 46:143-4 Mr 14 '70 *
    Newsweek 75:63 Mr 16 '70 *
    Opera N il 34:17-20 Ap 4 '70 *
    Opera N il 34:24-5 Ap 4 '70*
    Opera N il 35:14-15, 19-22 D 19 '70 *
    Sat R 53:28 Mr 21 '70 *
    Sat R 53:58 O 24 '70 *
    Time il 95:69 Mr 16 '70 *
Rumble of Etna, the lilt of Bellini. R. Jacobson. il Sat R 53:70+ Mr 14 '70 *
Star vehicle. S. Jenkins. Opera N 35:14-15 D 19 '70 *
BELLINO, Robert
Perspectives of military and civilian retirement. bibliog Ment Hy 54:580-3 O '70
BELLOC, Hilaire
Belloc, ed. by H. van Thal. Review
    New Repub 163:30 N 7 '70 *
Hilaire Belloc, Edwardian radical. J. P. McCarthy. America 123:66-9 Ag 8 '70 *
His own worst critic. G. Wills. Nat R 22:1218+ N 17 '70 *
BELLOW, Saul
Mr Bellow considers his planet. J. Howard. il pors Life 68:57-8+ Ap 3 '70 *
Saul Bellow and the dogmas of possibility. B. DeMott. por Sat R 53:25-8+ F 7 '70
Saul Bellow: seer with a civil heart. por Time 95:81-2+ F 9 '70
BELLS
On collecting ornate bells. L. P. Hammond. il(p 1) Hobbies 75:117 N '70
BELLUGI, Ursula. See Bronowski, J. jt. auth.
BELMONT stakes. See Horse racing
BELOIT, Wis.
       Education
School designed for kids; Beloit-Turner middle school. J. Cass. il Sat R 53:65-7+ Mr 21 '70
BELOUS, Robert
Kenai. il Field & S 75:28-31+ Jl '70
Unsolved problems of Alaska's North Slope. il Nat Parks & Con Mag 44:16-17+ N '70
Walk above the woods. il Nat Wildlife 8:50-4 Ap '70
BELT, Forest H.
Color TV for 1970. il Electr World 83:48-50+ F: 50-2+ Mr '70
Radio & television news. See issues of Electronics world
RCA's solid-state color chassis CTC 40. il Electr World 83:48-50+ My '70
Television: twenty years from now. il Electr World 83:25-9 Ja '70
BELTAIRE, Mark
London chop house. Holiday 47:78 F '70
BELTRAN, Enrique
Forestry and the public domain; address (cont) il Am For 76:36-7+ Ja '70
BELTS
Focus on the waist. il Good H 171:208 D '70
Nitty gritty bang bang; bullet belt. il Time 97:48 Ja 4 '71
BELTS, Safety. See Safety belts
BELTZ, George, and Kohn, D. A.
Independent study in five Missouri high schools. Clear House 44:334-7 F '70
BELTZ, John
Motor Trend interview. pors Motor T 22:72+ D '70
BEN, Philip
Pompidou's France. New Repub 162:8-9 F 28 '70
BEN-DAK, Joseph D.
China in the Arab world. bibliog f il Cur Hist 59:147-52+ S '70

BEN ELIEZER, Israel
In praise of the Baal Shem Tov, tr. by D.
Ben-Amos and J. R. Mintz. Review
Commentary 50:88-90 S '70. A. A. Cohen *
BEN-GURION, David
Lion's last roll call; remarks, ed. by M.
Levin. por Time 95:20-1 Je 1 '70
BEN SALAH, Ahmed
L' affaire Ben Salah. il por Newsweek 75:45+
My 4 '70 *
Peasants revenge. Newsweek 75:46 Je 8 '70 *
BEN Taub general, Houston. See Houston. Tex.
—Hospitals
BENCH, Johnny
Bench strength. H. L. Masin. por Sr Schol
96:26-7 Ap 27 '70 *
Hall of famer for sure; with report by B.
Bruns. il por Life 68:36-40 Je 5 '70 *
Johnny Bench: supercatcher for the big red
machine. W. B. Furlong. il por N Y Times
Mag p8-9+ Ag 30 '70 *
Little general. il por Time 95:69 My 11 '70 *
BENCH-tables. See Tables
BENCH vises. See Vises
BENCHES
Benches you'll want to build for your deck.
il Pop Mech 134:170-1 S '70
Planter bench; at Chemical bank Home gar-
den of ideas. il Home Gard 57:32 Ag '70
Under the bench is the sail locker. il Sunset
145:115 O '70
See also
Work benches
BENCHLEY, Peter
Coaching: the new in sport. il Travel &
Camera 33:40-5+ F '70
Five in spots for the midnight chic. il N Y
Times Mag p25-7+ N 8 '70
Hard times in Manhattan. il N Y Times Mag
p8-9+ S 6 '70
Life's tempo on Nantucket. il Nat Geog 137:
810-39 Je '70
Long, glamorous summer in Southampton.
il Holiday 47:48-51+ Je '70
Tall ships of Mystic. il Travel & Camera
33:26-31 Jl '70
BENCHLEY, Robert Charles
Robert Benchley, by B. Rosmond. Review
Atlan 225:113-15+ Ap '70. L. Kronenber-
ger *
Newsweek por 75:94+ Mr 30 '70. P. D.
Zimmerman *
BENDER, Marylin
Why your clothes cost so much. il McCalls
97:94-5+ My '70
BENDINER, Robert
Great expectations, a quarter of a century
later. il N Y Times Mag p36-7+ Ap 26 '70
BENDIX, Dorothy
(ed) When is a social issue a library issue?
bibliog il Wilson Lib Bul 45:42-85 S '70
BENDOW, Burton
Film critics. Nation 211:344+ O 12 '70
BENEDICT, Robert
Teen corps: soldiers with shovels. J. E. Roper.
il por Read Digest 97:37-8+ D '70 *
BENEDIKT, Michael
Comment. Poetry 115:422-5 Mr '70
On earth; Wonders of the arm; poems. Poetry
115:411-14 Mr '70
BENEFIT performances
See also
Opera—Benefit performances
Performing arts—Benefit performances
BENFIELD, William, Jr
Church uniting, slowly. por Time 95:48 Mr 2
'70 *
BENGAL, West. See West Bengal
BENGALI poetry
Translations into English
For my forty-eighth winter; Two birds;
B. Bose. Poetry 116:285-6 Ag '70
BENGLIS, Lynda
Social conditions can change. Art N 69:43 Ja
'71
BENGSTON, Billy Al
Los Angeles artists' studios. il Art in Am 58:
100-9 N '70
BENIRSCHKE, Kurt. See Wurster, D. H. jt.
auth.
BENJAMIN, Curtis G.
Book publishing's hidden bonanza. il Sat R
53:19-21+ Ap 18 '70
U.S.S.R. book production facts, fancies, and
fallacies. Pub W 198:25-6 N 2 '70
BENJAMIN, Fred
Fred Benjamin dance company; Clark center,
NYC. T. Borek. Dance Mag 44:88 Ag '70 *
Fred Benjamin dance company: the Cubiculo.
J. Armstrong. Dance Mag 44:90 Mr '70 *

BENJAMIN, George J.
Diving into the blue holes of the Bahamas.
il Nat Geog 138:346-63 S '70
BENJAMIN, Joel
New repertory dance theatre; 92nd st. Y. J.
Anderson. Dance Mag 44:85-6 Ap '70 *
BENKOVIC, Fred
Famous Civil war band lives again. A. Mar-
quis. il Hobbies 75:48-9+ S '70 *
BENN, Anthony Wedgwood
British labor calls for new synthesis. B. L.
Masse. America 123:309 O 24 '70 *
BENNET-CLARK, H. C. and Ewing, A. W.
Love song of the fruit fly; with biographical
sketches. il Sci Am 223:15, 84-90+ Jl '70
BENNETT, Alan
Forty years on. Criticism
Nation 211:190 S 7 '70 *
BENNETT, Hank
Short-wave listening. See issues of Popular
electronics to August 1970
BENNETT, John Coleman
Great controversy in the churches; address,
April 12, 1970. Chr Cent 87:659-63 My 27
'70
about
Benisons on Bennett. R. M. Brown. por Chr
Cent 87:663-4 My 27 '70 *
Of many things. D. R. Campion. America
122:inside cover My 30 '70 *
BENNETT, John R.
Unbundled at ADR. A. A. Butkus. por
Duns 95:62-3 My '70 *
BENNETT, José Rolz-. See Rolz-Bennett, J.
BENNETT, Leon
Insect flight: life and rate of change of in-
cidence. bibliog il Science 167:177-9 Ja 9 '70
BENNETT, Lerone, jr
Liberation. por Ebony 25:36-8+ Ag '70
Making of black America. il Ebony 25:70-2+
Ag; 46-8+ O; 26:70-2+ D '70
Road not taken. il Ebony 25:70-2+ Ag '70
BENNETT, Margaret, pseud.
Acceptance of the month club. Pub W 198:
22-3 D 7 '70
BENNETT, Margret
Vegetables in the rose garden. il Org Gard
& Farm 17:50-1 S '70
BENNETT, Michael
Michael Bennett's Coco. N. Russell. il pors
Dance Mag 44:72-8 F '70
BENNETT, Michael Alan
Theme of responsibility in Miller's A can-
ticle for Leibowitz. Engl J 59:484-9 Ap '70
BENNETT, Ralph Kinney
Brotherhood of the bomb. Read Digest 97:102-
6 D '70
Detectives in smocks. Read Digest 96:201-2+
Ja '70
Henry Jackson: a statesman of uncommon
quality. por Read Digest 97:110-15 Jl '70
BENNETT, Robert A.
NCTE councilletter. Engl J 59:421-2 Mr '70
BENNETT, Sid
Courage of Sid Bennett. J. E. Roper. por
Read Digest 96:199-201 Ap '70 *
BENNETT, Wallace Foster
Taxes & related problems; address. December
1, 1970. Vital Speeches 37:166-70 Ja 1 '71
BENNINGTON college, Bennington, Vt.
At Bennington the boys are the coeds. T.
Meehan; discussion. N Y Times Mag p4+
Ja 25 '70
BENNINGTON pottery. See Pottery, American
BENNINGTON ware. See Pottery, American
BENNION, John W.
School superintendent as philosopher. Sch &
Soc 98:25-7 Ja '70
BENNY, Jack
Five happy moments. il por Esquire 74:138 D
'70
BENOIS, Alexandre
Petrouchka: Diaghilev's 1911. Joffrey's 1970.
O. Maynard. il Dance Mag 44:47-61 F '70
BENREY, Ronald M.
Flasher beacon for your boat or car. il Pop
Sci 197:86-7+ Ag '70
Light of the future, from semiconductors. il
Pop Sci 197:76-9+ D '70
'71 TVs, color 'em natural. il Pop Sci 197:74-
5+ N '70
BENSALEM college. See Fordham university
BENSCHOTER, C. A. and others
Apollo 11: exposure of lower animals to lunar
material. il Science 169:470-2 Jl 31 '70
BENSKY, Lawrence
(tr) See Le Vaillant, Y. Opus Dei: Spain on
the cross
BENSON, Charles
On ditching Israel. Nat R 22:1206-10; 23:14+
N 17 '70, Ja 12 '71
Strategic alternative? Nat R 22:1206-10 N 17
'70

BENSON, Elaine
Handcraft in Yucatán and Guatemala. il Craft Horiz 30:48-9+ My '70
BENSON, George Charles Sumner
Academic world and military education; address, March 7, 1970. Vital Speeches 36:542-4 Je 15 '70
BENSON, Gordon D. See Lester, D. jt. auth.
BENSON, Richard
Corrosion at sea. il Sea Front 16:172-81 My '70
BENSON Needham Univas (firm) See Advertising agencies
BENTHAM, Jeremy
Defense of usury. M. Friedman. Newsweek 75:79 Ap 6 '70 *
BENTHEM, Roelof Jan
Concrete cage; excerpts from Urbanization and the countryside. il UNESCO Courier 23: 54-60 Ag '70
BENTHOS
Benthic life in the fjords of Norway. M. Berrill. il Natur Hist 79:53-9 N '70
BENTINCK, Catherine A. and others
Social adequacy of state mental hospital patients. bibliog Ment Hy 54:421-4 Jl '70
BENTLEY, David R. and Hoy, R. R.
Postembryonic development of adult motor patterns in crickets: a neural analysis. bibliog il Science 170:1409-11 D 25 '70
BENTLEY, Helen Delich
American press; address, February, 20, 1970. Vital Speeches 36:329-32 Mr 15 '70
Merchant marine; address, May 12, 1970. Vital Speeches 36:569-72 Jl 1 '70

about
Lady tells it like it is. H. J. Sievers. America 123:5 Jl 11 '70 *
BENTLEY, Joseph
Later novels of Huxley. Yale R 59:507-19 Je '70
BENTON, Robert. See Newman, D. jt. auth.
BENTON, Sally
Wife of Man talk. Mlle 70:44 F '70
BENTON, Thomas Hart
Old man and the river. R. F. Jones. il pors Sports Illus 33:28-34 Ag 10 '70 *
BENTON, William
Success didn't spoil Bill Benton. H. Brucker. por Sat R 53:35-6 F 28 '70 *
BENTON HARBOR, Mich.
Hairiest team of all: bearded House of David baseball team. J. Kirshenbaum. il Sports Illus 32:104-6+ Ap 13 '70
BENTONITE
Bentonite debris flows in northern Alaska. D. M. Anderson and others; reply with rejoinder. D. B. Prior and C. Ho. bibliog il Science 167:1014-15 F 13 '70
BENTSEN, Bill
One-design develops. il Yachting 128:70-1+ N '70
BENTSEN, Lloyd, 1921–
Can a rich guy lose in Texas. W. W. Hamilton, jr. Nation 211:274-7 S 28 '70 *
Democratic primary, G.O.P. gain. il pors Time 95:37 My 11 '70 *
Hot after Yarborough. R. Dugger. New Repub 162:11-12 Ap 18 '70 *
BENTZ, Thomas Orrin
Lent went; poem. Chr Cent 87:469 Ap 22 '70
BENVENUTI, Nino
Night Carlos made a no-no out of Ni-no. W. Wynn. il pors Sports Illus 33:80-2 N 16 '70 *
Ulterior motive for Umag. D. J. Hamblin. il por Sports Illus 32:14-15 Je 1 '70 *
BENZEDRINE. See Amphetamines
BENZOFLAVONE. See Flavones
BEOWULF
Our Germanic epic. G. Johnston. Poetry 115: 274-6 Ja '70
Supplement for teaching Beowulf. J. Milosh. Engl J 59:646-54 My '70
BEQUIA (island)
Beautiful barkeep of Bequia. P. Coffin. il pors Look 34:56-61 D 15 '70
My island of life. K. Westfall. il por Redbook 135:26+ Ag '70
Whalers of Bequia. T. W. Burgess. il Nat R 22:629 Je 16 '70
BERCZELLER, Richard
Paternity. New Yorker 46:34-41 Je 27 '70
BEREAVEMENT
How we face sorrow and grief. J. Brothers. Good H 172:32+ Ja '71
Psychology of death; concerning report by Columbia researchers. il Newsweek 76:103-4 S 14 '70
When faced with grief. M. Wylie. Read Digest 97:103-5 N '70
BEREGOVOI, Georgii
Cosmonautics: a look at the future. Space World G-6-78:30-1 Je '70

BERELSON, Bernard
National family-planning programs: where we stand; excerpts from address. Science 169:931 S 4 '70
BERENICE; drama. See Racine, J. B.
BERENSON, Marisa
Marisa Berenson takes the lotus position. por Vogue 156:104-5 Jl '70 *
BERENSON, Ruth
American nineteenth century. il Nat R 22: 636-7 Je 16 '70
Plight of realism today. il Nat R 22:474-5 My 5 '70
BERENSTAIN, Janice. See Berenstain, S. jt. auth.
BERENSTAIN, Stanley, and Berenstain, Janice
It's all in the family. il Good H 171:96-9 O '70; 172:30-1 Ja '71
BERENYI, Ivan
Computers in eastern Europe; with biographical sketch. il Sci Am 223:15, 102-8 O '70
BERG, Alban
Lulu. Criticism
Mus Q il 56:349-66 Jl '70 *
Some rhythmic and metric techniques in Alban Berg's Lulu. D. Jarman. bibliog f il Mus Q 56:349-66 Jl '70 *
BERG, David W.
Independent study: transfusion for anemic English programs. Engl J 59:254-8 F '70
Option plan: learning is student-centered. Clear House 45:107-11 O '70
BERG, Gene
VW posi for a quarter. J. Thawley. il por Hot Rod 23:110-12 Ap '70 *
BERG, Otto E. and McDonnell, J. A. M.
Filamentary crystal growth associated with impact craters from hypervelocity microparticles. il Science 168:820-2 My 15 '70
BERG, Paul
Twentieth century masks. il Sch Arts 69:18-19 F '70
BERG, Roland H.
Face-lifts for men. il pors Look 34:80-2+ D 1 '70
Trans-sexuals: male or female? il Look 34: 28-31 Ja 27 '70
We have a chance to beat leukemia now. il Look 34:26-8+ My 5 '70
(ed) See Gwinup, G. The one sensible way to diet
(ed) See Tyler, E. T. Pill is safe
BERG, Stephen
Comment. Poetry 116:260-4 Jl '70
Kiss; Unnamed shapes; The dead; Directions for being Jesus; As the days pass and darken; Nick's photograph of Jeff, me, and Arlene; Soul; Heartache; poems. Poetry 115:375-84 Mr '70
Times; poem. Poetry 117:79 N '70
BERGEN, Candice
Miss Bergen protests, but not too much; with account. by M. Paley. il pors Life 69:40-4 Jl 24 '70 *
Princess who belched. pors Time 96:83-4 N 2 '70
BERGEN, Norway

Description
900 years of Bergen: song of Norway. il Sat R 53:59 Mr 14 '70
BERGER, Allen
Questions asked about speed reading. Clear House 44:272-8 Ja '70
So you want to know more about reading? bibliog il por Wilson Lib Bul 45:254-69 N '70
BERGER, Bob
How to buy a used sports car. il Mech Illus 66:50-1+ My '70
How to photograph your home. il Mech Illus 66:112-13 N '70
New mirror lenses: short in size but long on reach. il Pop Mech 134:136-7 Ag '70
BERGER, Hans
Discoverer of the brain wave. J. L. O'Leary. Science 168:562-3 My 1 '70 *
BERGER, Ivan
Adventures with a musical erector set. il por Sat R 53:40-1 D 26 '70
Consumer electronic show: observations and reservations about four-channel. il Sat R 53:51 Jl 25 '70
Doing the four-channel two-step. Sat R 53: 51+ Je 27 '70
Dolby and four channel: two interim reports. Sat R 53:73 Ap 25 '70
Filming Paris without the Eiffel tower. il Pop Phot 66:82-3+ Je '70
Four-channel at Westbury. Sat R 53:57 O 31 '70
Hi-fi convenience revolution. Sat R 53:57-8 S 26 '70
Philosophy, fidelity, and sonic pleasure. Sat R 53:69 Mr 28 '70

BERGER, Ivan—*Continued*
Seeing machines for movie makers. il Pop Phot 66:98-100+ Ap '70
Sound all around: the new multi-directional speakers. il Pop Sci 196:86-8 Mr '70
Trying to cross the country by cassette. Sat R 53:93-4 F 28 '70
Video tape: this year won't quite be next year. Sat R 53:78+ Ja 31 '70

BERGER, Jon, and Lovberg, R. H.
Earth strain measurements with a laser interferometer. bibliog il Science 170:296-303 O 16 '70

BERGER, Michael L.
Middletown: 1970. Clear House 45:89-91 O '70

BERGER, Thomas
Son and hair; story. il Esquire 73:69-71 F '70

BERGER, Wolfgang H. and Parker, F. L.
Diversity of planktonic foraminifera in deep-sea sediments. bibliog il Science 168:1345-7 Je 12 '70

BERGERY, Bettina
Bright is the colour of the new-love hair. il Vogue 156:115-17 O 1 '70
Joie de vivre. il Vogue 155:130-3 Ap 1 '70

BERGES, Ruth
Composer as a man of letters: Hector Berlioz. il pors Am Rec G 36:612-22 My '70
Napoleon of opera. por Opera N 34:6-7 Ap 18 '70

BERGHE, Herman van den
Nuclear sexing in a population of Congolese metropolitan newborns. bibliog il Science 169:1318-20 S 25 '70

BERGMAN, Ingmar
Current cinema. P. Gilliatt. New Yorker 46: 103-4+ Je 13 '70 *
Rags of time: Ingmar Bergman's Wild strawberries. H. R. Greenberg. Am Imago 27: 66-82 Spr '70 *
Silence of God: creative response to the films of Ingmar Bergman, by A. Gibson. Review Cath World 211:43-4 Ap '70. R. Steele. *

BERGMAN, Ingrid
Ingrid Bergman speaks out; interview, ed. by D. Lurie. il por Ladies Home J 87:141-2 O '70

BERGQUIST, Laura
France's Madame Pompidou: first lady with pizzaz. il pors Look 34:40-7 Ja 27 '70

BERIfA, Lavrentii Pavlovich
Death of Stalin, the menace of Beria. N. S. Khrushchev. il pors Life 69:54-58+ D 11 '70 *
Khrushchev: showdown in the Kremlin. il por Time 96:38+ D 14 '70 *

BERING land bridge
First discovery of America. C. Ogburn, jr. il Horizon 12:92-9 Wint '70

BERINGIANS. See Paleo-Indians

BERIO, Luciano
Berio, blueprint; Carnegie Hall performance of This means that. Vogue 155:58 Ag 15 '70 *
Music to my ears. I. Kolodin. Sat R 53:40 Mr 7 '70 *
Music to my ears: performance of Sinfonia. I. Kolodin. Sat R 53:58-9 O 24 '70 *
Musical events: production of This means that. W. Sargeant. New Yorker 46:80 F 28 '70
Opera. Criticism
Hi Fi il por 20:MA12-13+ N '70 *
Sat R 53:8 Ag 29 '70 *

BERK, Donald M.
Amateur-built aircraft. il Consumer Bul 53: 25-8 Ja '70

BERK, Richard A. See Rosi, P. H. jt. auth.

BERKELEY, Busby
Busby and Ruby. il por Newsweek 76:63 Ag 3 '70 *
Busby Berkeley and his gorgeous girls. il por Vogue 155:202-3 My '70 *

BERKELEY, Calif.
Sleeping giant stirs: mayor's plans for vigilantes. il Newsweek 75:76 Mr 16 '70

Education
How school busing works in one town. G. Samuels. il N Y Times Mag p38-9+ S 27 '70

Parks and playgrounds
No one plays in no man's land; boycott of People's park. R. Rapoport. il Sports Illus 32:20-1 Je 15 '70
State of insurrection & rebellion. T. H. Watkins. il Am West 7:42-7 Ja '70

Police
State of insurrection & rebellion. T. H. Watkins. il Am West 7:42-7 Ja '70

Police department
They shoot hippies, don't they? with introd. by T. Hayden, and interview with R. Charles. F. Browning. il Ramp Mag 9:14-23 N '70

Riots
It's still there, but maybe not much longer. J. R. Coyne, jr. Nat R 22:305 Mr 24 '70
Postscript to People's park; indictments of Alameda County sheriff's deputies for misusing their authority in Berkeley. Time 95: 15-16 F 16 '70
Trashing Telegraph ave. il Newsweek 76:61-2 S 7 '70

Stores
Trashing Telegraph ave. il Newsweek 76:61-2 S 7 '70

BERKELEY campus. See California. University—Berkeley campus

BERKELEY plantation. See Virginia—Historic houses, etc.

BERKLEY, George E.
On being called doctor. Ed Digest 36:32-4 D '70

BERKOFF, Charles E.
Synthetic juvenile hormone and "synthetic juvenile hormone" bibliog Science 168:1607 Je 26 '70

BERKOVITZ, Robert
Four-channel stereo, the new surround sound. il Electr World 83:39-41+ F '70
New trends in sight and sound systems. il Pop Sci 197:68-9+ N '70

BERKOWITZ, Kenneth. See Carder, B. jt. auth.

BERKOWITZ, Roger M. and Lee, K. C.
Picture tour of the Toledo museum. il Design 71:4-9 mid-Sum '70

BERKSHIRE HILLS
Home to the enduring Berkshires. C. McCarry. il Nat Geog 138:196-221 Ag '70

BERKSHIRE theatre festival. See Theater—United States

BERKSON, Bill
New Gustons. il por Art N 69:44-7+ O '70

BERL, Kathe
Combining enamels and plastics (cont) il Ceram Mo 18:23+ F '70

BERL, Walter G.
Brief guide to the 1970 AAAS annual meeting. Science 170:874 N 20 '70

BERLAND, Theodore
Dental care. il Todays Ed 59:59+ My '70
Silencing invisible pollution. il Todays Health 48:16-18+ Jl '70

BERLE, Adolf Augustus, 1895-
School relationships; address, July 8, 1970. Vital Speeches 36:715-17 S 15 '70

BERLIN, Doris A.
Mental health in and out of public health. bibliog Ment Hy 54:288-94 Ap '70

BERLIN, Newton H.
Water your garden from below. il Org Gard & Farm 17:127 Mr '70

BERLIN, Richard D.
Specificities of transport systems and enzymes. bibliog il Science 168:1539-45 Je 26 '70

BERLIN

Description
City divided. D. Butwin. il Sat R 53:41+ Jl 11 '70
Music-lover's guide to Berlin. J. H. Sutcliffe. il Opera N 34:6-13 F 28 '70

Intellectual life
Memory's defense: the real life of Vladimir Nabokov's Berlin. R. C. Williams. Yale R 60:241-50 D '70

BERLIN (East Berlin)

Music
Porgy comes to Germany. P. Moor. Hi Fi 20:secII 28-9 Ag '70
Report:
Alan Bush's Joe Hill. J. H. Sutcliffe. il Opera N 35:30 D 5 '70
Porgy and Bess at East Berlin's Komische oper. J. H. Sutcliffe. il Opera N 34:33-4 Mr 14 '70
Production by East Berlin's Staatsoper. J. H. Sutcliffe. il Opera N 34:30-1 F 14 '70
Productions of Lortzing's Zar und Zimmermann and Weber's Freischütz at East Berlin Staatsoper. J. H. Sutcliffe. il Opera N 35:30-2 N 21 '70
Ravel's Heure espagnole and Puccini's Gianni Schicchi. J. H. Sutcliffe. il Opera N 35:33 D 12 '70

BERLIN (West Berlin)

Industries
Berlin diary, 1970. G. R. Rosen. il Duns 96: 65+ S '70

BERLIN (West Berlin)—*Continued*

Music

Behind the scenes. P. Moor. Hi Fi 20:secI 22 Mr '70
Report:
Alan Bush's Joe Hill. J. H. Sutcliffe. il Opera N 35:30 D 5 '70
La forza del destino at West Berlin's Deutsche oper. J. H. Sutcliffe. Opera N 34:30 Mr 28 '70
Something called six days of music. P. Moor. Hi Fi 20:secII 27 Je '70

Protests, demonstrations, etc.

Letter from Berlin; reaction to the American invasion of Cambodia. J. Wechsberg. New Yorker 46:69-72 Je 27 '70

BERLIN, N.H.
ABE and the twentieth century pioneers; adult basic education classes. D. Lamoureux. il Todays Ed 59:60-1 Ja '70

BERLIN, Battle of, 1945
Fall of Berlin. il Newsweek 75:41-2 My 4 '70

BERLIN free university. See Colleges and universities—Germany (Federal Republic)

BERLIN question, 1945-
Berlin; four-power talks. D. Cook. Atlan 227: 6+ Ja '71
Big issue. Newsweek 75:42 F 23 '70
Conceding a point; four-power talks. il Newsweek 75:45 Ap 6 '70
Europe: a symbolic act of atonement; Big four meeting. il por Time 96:25 D 21 '70
What now for Berlin? America 123:194-5 S 26 '70

BERLINER, Martha D. and Reca, M. E.
Release of protoplasts in the yeast phase of histoplasma capsulatum without added enzyme. bibliog il Science 167:1255-7 F 27 '70

BERLINRUT, Peter
On the passage of time. Commentary 50:44-54 Jl '70

BERLIOZ, Hector
Anna Pashley, one of the exciting events of the year. P. L. Miller. Am Rec G 37:16-17 S '70 *
Berlioz a hundred years after. J. Barzun. bibliog f il Mus Q 56:1-13 Ja '70 *
Berlioz from the Tabernacle; Grande messe des morts. R. Lawrence. il Sat R 53:60 Mr 28 '70 *
Berlioz' Les Troyens, conquered at last. D. Hamilton. il Hi Fi 20:secI 65-7 Ag '70 *
Berlioz's Les Troyens: recording. I. Kolodin. il por Sat R 53:43-4 Jl 25 '70 *
Burst of Berlioz; recordings. R. Lawrence. il Sat R 53:66+ Ap 25 '70 *
Composer as a man of letters. R. Berges. il pors Am Rec G 36:612-22 My '70 *
Grand passions and grander talent, in a grandly romantic time. B. McCabe. Commonweal 92:119-20 Ap 17 '70 *
Memoirs of Hector Berlioz, by D. Cairns. Review
Am Rec G 36:768-9 My '70. R. Berges *
New Troyens, in print and in sound. T. Heinitz. Sat R 53:76 Ap 25 '70 *
Not two flutes, you scoundrels! Two piccolos! Two piccolos! Oh, what brutes! F. V. Grunfeld. il pors Horizon 12:102-11 Aut '70 *
Postscript: a souvenir of Janet Baker's Dido at Covent Garden. P. L. Miller. Am Rec G 36:941 Ag '70 *
Recordings; live performance of Les Troyens at Covent Garden. M. Mayer. Esquire 74:28+ S '70 *
Symphoniste fantastique. M. Curtiss. Nation 210:88+ Ja 26 '70
Les Troyens. E. Greenfield. il Am Rec G 36:936-41 Ag '70 *

BERLITZ, Charles Frambach
Zulu made simple. Horizon 12:120 Sum '70

BERMAN, Claire
Parent and child. il N Y Times Mag p92+ S 27 '70

BERMAN, Edgar
Hormones in the White House. pors Time 96: 13 Ag 10 '70 *

BERMAN, Jeffrey A.
Birth of a black business. Harvard Bsns R 48:4-6+ S '70

BERMAN, Jerry J. and Hightower, Jim
Chavez and the Teamsters. Nation 211:427-31 N 2 '70

BERMAN, Merrill I. See Tuft, L. H. jt. auth.

BERMAN, Sanford
African magazines for American libraries. il por Library J 95:1289-93 Ap 1 '70

BERMUDA
See also
Gardens—Bermuda
Paleontology—Bermuda

Description and travel
Teachers who know their onions vacation in Bermuda. E. Logan. il Schol Teach Sec Teach Sup p28-9 F 2 '70

BERMUDA agreement. See Aviation—International aspects

BERMUDA ocean race. See Yacht racing

BERMÚDEZ, José Y.
(tr) See González de Ledo, L. Senor Augusto

BERNARD, Claude
Why don't you practice medicine the way other doctors do? R. Dunlop. il por Todays Health 48:34-5+ Jl '70; Same with title Claude Bernard, father of experimental medicine. Sci Digest 68:79-84 D '70 *

BERNARD, Thomas A.
My I.Q. is 20/20. il Todays Ed 59:31 Mr '70

BERNARDS, Solomon S.
Judaic studies in college and seminary classrooms. Chr Cent 87:993-4 Ag 19 '70

BERNAYS, Anne
What are you supposed to do if you like children? por Atlan 225:107-9 Mr '70; Same. Cur 117:38-43 Ap '70

BERNE, Eric
Sex games people play; excerpt from Sex in human loving. il Ladies Home J 87:80+ O '70

BERNHARD, Lucian
Matchless art of Lucian Bernhard. R. Foster. il Am Artist 34:54-9+ D '70 *

BERNHEIMER, Martin
Contempo '70; Boulez at Ojai. il Hi Fi 20: secII 22-3 Ag '70

BERNS, Michael W. and Rounds, D. E.
Cell surgery by laser; with biographical sketches. il Sci Am 222:10, 98-103+ bibliog (p 126) F '70

—and others
Enzyme inactivation with ultraviolet laser energy (2650 angstroms) bibliog il Science 169:1215-17 S 18 '70

BERNSTEIN, Burton
Piper cub vs. the 747. il N Y Times Mag p34-5+ Mr 8; 36 Mr 22 '70

BERNSTEIN, Felicia (Montealegre)
That party at Lenny's. il pors Time 95:80+ Je 15 '70 *

BERNSTEIN, Jane Alix
Overdue. por Wilson Lib Bul 44:1065 Je '70

BERNSTEIN, Jeremy
Reporter at large. il New Yorker 46:44-6 My 2; 46-8+ My 9 '70

BERNSTEIN, Leonard
Aaron Copland, an intimate sketch. il por Hi Fi 20:53-5 N '70
about
First video-cassette recording: Bernstein leads Verdi's Requiem. E. Greenfield. il por Hi Fi 20:secI 22+ Je '70 *
Letter from Paris; L. Bernstein's conducting of Mahler's Third symphony. Genêt. New Yorker 46:142-4 Mr 21 '70 *
Music to my ears; Bernstein's Fidelio. I. Kolodin. Sat R 53:55 Ja 31 '70
Music to my ears; Stravinsky's Les noces. I. Kolodin. Sat R 53:24 O 17 '70 *
Musical events; two opening programs of Philharmonic. W. Sargeant. New Yorker 46:137-8 O 3 '70
Recordings; live performance of Fidelio at the Vienna staatsoper. M. Mayer. Esquire 74:24+ S '70 *
That party at Lenny's; T. Wolfe's article in New York magazine. il pors Time 95:80+ Je 15 '70 *
Upper East side story. il por Time 95:14 Ja 26 '70

BERNSTEIN, Peter L.
Inflation: the wrong medicine. Nation 210: 168-71 F 16 '70

BERNSTEIN, Robert L.
Publisher looks at publishing. Ed Digest 36: 40-3 D '70

BERNSTEIN, Stephen, and Herzberg, Joseph
Small group experience with psychiatric aides. bibliog Ment Hy 54:113-17 Ja '70

BERNSTEIN, Victor H.
Earth, love it or leave it. Redbook 135:97+ My '70

BERRIDGE, H. R.
Environment action: a hometown approach. il Org Gard & Farm 17:27-9 Je '70
Way with wild transplants. il Org Gard & Farm 17:100-1 Ja '70

BERRIES
See also
Fruit culture
also names of berries, e.g. Blueberries

BERRIGAN, Daniel
How to make a difference. Commonweal 92: 384-6 Ag 7 '70; Same abr. Cur 122:25-7 O '70
Life at the edge. Chr Cent 87:787-90 Je 24 '70

BERRIGAN, Daniel—*Continued*
New man: the compleat soldier. il Sat R 53: 31-4+ F 14 '70
Notes from the underground; interview. New Yorker 46:20-3 Jl 25 '70
Notes from the underground; or, I was a fugitive from the F.B.I. por Commonweal 92:263-5 My 29 '70
Passion of Dietrich Bonhoeffer; poem. Sat R 53:17-22 My 30 '70

about
Christmas card from the FBI; statement. W. Stringfellow and A. Towne. Commonweal 93:364 Ja 15 '71 *
Daniel Berrigan winds the spring tighter. J. Finn. Commonweal 92:145-8 Ap 24 '70 *
Of many things. D. R. Campion. America 123: inside cover Ag 22 '70; Discussion. 123:133, 162 S 12-19 '70
Personal history. I. Evans. por Sat R 53:28+ Ap 11 '70 *
Priest who stayed out in the cold. P. Nobile. il por N Y Times Mag p8-9+ Je 28 '70 *
Profiles. F. Du Plessix. pors New Yorker 46: 44-6+ Mr 14 '70 *
Sayings of chairman Jesus. R. Drinnon. Nation 210:534-6 My 4 '70 *
Taking Fr Berrigan seriously. Commonweal 92:379-80 Ag 7 '70 *
Taking of Father Dan. il por Newsweek 76: 37 Ag 24 '70 *
Temptations a revolutionary encounters; excerpts from No bars to manhood. Time 95: 65 My 4 '70 *
Toward martyrdom. il por Time 96:48 Ag 24 '70 *
Trial of the Catonsville nine. Criticism Nat R 22:1173 N 3 '70 *

BERRIGAN, Philip
Bulls and Berrigans. por Newsweek 75:106 My 4 '70 *
How to make a difference. D. Berrigan. Commonweal 92:384-6 Ag 7 '70 *
Profiles. F. Du Plessix. pors New Yorker 46: 44-6+ Mr 14 '70 *

BERRIGAN brothers
Berrigans in prison. K. L. Woodward. Commonweal 92:428-30 S 4 '70 *
Berrigans; jail for the Christian conscience. il pors Time 95:65-6 My 4 '70 *
Berrigans: radical activism personified. G. C. Zahn. pors Cath World 212:125-30 D '70
Berrigan's suit. J. Deedy. Commonweal 93: 210 N 27 '70 *
Forty-eight hours with the Berrigans. B. Fitch. il por Chr Cent 87:643-6 My 20 '70 *
Hoover and the Berrigans; East Coast conspiracy to save lives organization. America 123:509 D 12 '70
Inmate manuscripts. R. H. Smith. Pub W 198:29 D 7 '70
J. Edgar, Dan and Phil. J. Deedy. Commonweal 93:290 D 18 '70
Plots and conspiracies. New Repub 163:7 D 12 '70
Resistance priests. por Newsweek 76:94 Ag 17 '70 *

BERRILL, Michael
Benthic life in the fjords of Norway; with biographical sketch. il Natur Hist 79:8, 53-9 N '70

BERRY, Betty, and Traiger, Lynn
Bonjour, M Durand-Ruel. il por Art N 69: 44-7+ Ap '70

BERRY, Leonard J.
Skiing the snows of yesteryear. il Esquire 74:154-9 N '70

BERRY, R. Stephen
Perspectives on polluted air, 1970. il Bul Atom Sci 26:2+ Ap '70

BERRY, Sidney B. 1926-
Case study of an army star. L. H. Lapham. il pors Life 69:54-6+ S 25 '70 *

BERRY, Wendell
September 2; poem. Poetry 116:77 My '70
To the unseeable animal; poem. Mlle 71: 116 S '70

about
Comment. R. B. Shaw. Poetry 117:112-13 N '70 *

BERRY, William A.
William A. Berry; illustrator/painter. S. E. Meyer. il Am Artist 34:80-5 Mr '70 *

BERRY bearing plants
Shrubs that sport berries. G. Taloumis. il Home Gard 58:28-9+ Ja '71
See also
Hawthorns

BERRYHILL, Robert
600 meters per day. il Am City 85:107-8 S '70

BERRYMAN, John
Antithesis; poem. New Repub 163:17 Jl 25 '70
Death ballad. New Yorker 46:28 Jl 25 '70
Down & back; poem. Am Scholar 39:614-15 Aut '70
Five addresses to the Lord; poem. Sat R 53:23 S 26 '70; Excerpt. Commonweal 92:461 S 18 '70
Prayer for the self; poem. Harper 241:94 O '70
Soviet Union; poem. Nation 211:409 O 26 '70
Two poems: The hell poem; Olympus. Atlan 226:96-7 N '70

about
Full count. C. Molesworth. Nation 210:217-19 F 23 '70 *
Love, art and money. H. Carruth. Nation 211:437-8 N 2 '70; Reply with rejoinder. J. Berryman. 211:546 N 30 '70 *

BERSANI, Leo
Narrative murder. Yale R 59:376-90 Mr '70

BERTHELOT, Gaston
Moon house; a vacation house of ideas in Tunisia; interview. il House & Gard 137: 120-3 Mr '70

BERTHS on boats. See Boats—Berths

BERTLES, John F. and others
Hemoglobin interaction: modification of solid phase composition in the sickling phenomenon. bibliog il Science 169:375-7 Jl 24 '70

BERTMAN, Bernard, and Sandiford, D. J.
Second sound in solid helium; with biographical sketches. il Sci Am 222:10, 92-101 My '70

BERTOLINO, James
Comment. R. Magowan. Poetry 116:196-7 Je '70 *

BERTON, Lee
How to beat inflation with ostrich eggs and popsicle sticks. Esquire 73:78+ My '70

BERTRAM, Richard
Legend in their own time. F. T. Moss. il Yachting 129:88-90+ Ja '71 *

BERUBE, Allan
Making peace with man and nature. Cur 117: 3-10 Ap '70

BERUBE, Maurice R.
Benign neglect for education too. Commonweal 92:52-3 Mr 27 '70
Right to college. Commonweal 92:81-4 Ap 3 '70

BERYLLIUM
Beryllium, one of the metals that takes Apollo to the moon. il Space World G-8-80:14-22 Ag '70

BESRET, Bernard
Boquen; interview, ed. by M. Alcott. por Cath World 212:143-5 D '70

BEST, Georgie
Gorgeous Georgie. il por Time 95:76 My 18 '70 *

BEST, Nelson E. jr
Pariah reborn; poem. Nat Parks & Con Mag 44:26 Je '70
River and the path; poem. Nat Parks 44:22 F '70

BEST and company. See New York (city)—Stores

BEST sellers
Best sellers. See issues of Publishers' weekly
Hardcover best sellers of 1969 in the U.S. book trade. A. P. Hackett. il Pub W 197: 40-3 F 9 '70
Paperback best sellers of the year 1969. il Pub W 197:44-7 F 9 '70

BESTER, Alfred
Italian Italy. il Holiday 48:36-7+ Jl '70

BETA-CAROTENE. See Carotene

BETA glucuronidase. See Enzymes

BETA Persei. See Stars, Eclipsing binary

BETA rays
Second-class currents in beta decay? G. B. Lubkin. il Phys Today 23:17+ S '70

BETA thalassemia. See Anemia

BETEL
Senescence in detached betel leaves: role of the petiole. S. D. Mishra and B. K. Gaur. bibliog il Science 167:387-8 Ja 23 '70

BETHANY fellowship, Bloomington, Minn. See Missionary societies

BETHE, Hans Albrecht
Disarmament problems. por Bul Atom Sci 26: 99-102 Je '70

BETHEA, Tom
Ulterior motive for Umag. D. J. Hamblin. il por Sports Illus 32:14-15 Je 1 '70 *

BETHEL rock festival. See Music festivals—New York (state)

BETHELL, Nicholas
Solzhenitsyn can still write, he just can't publish. il N Y Times Mag p36-7+ Ap 12 '70

BETHGE, Ebernard
  Aftermath of Flossenburg: Bonhoeffer, 1945–1970; interview, ed. by H. E. Wright. por Chr Cent 87:656-9 My 27 '70
BETHLEHEM
  Bethlehem bids for normalcy; Christmas celebration. D. Baker. Chr Today 15:40 Ja 1 '71
BETHLEHEM steel corporation
  Bethlehem builds a price ceiling. Bsns W p27 F 14 '70
  Bethlehem steel's new price gambit. Bsns W p21 My 9 '70
BETSY Ross; drama. See Roberts, H. M.
BETTELHEIM, Bruno
  Dialogue with mothers. See issues of Ladies' home journal
  Knitting: its role in the life of Dr Bruno Bettelheim. N Y Times Mag p21+ F 8 '70
  New way to raise kids; interview, ed. by J. Whitbread. il por Look 34:64+ F 24 '70
  Perils of overexposing youth to college. Ed Digest 35:35-8 Ap '70
  Sex, virginity, money; interview, ed. by A. Talmey. Vogue 156:94-5+ Ag 1 '70
    about
  In defense of the wild things. M. A. Taylor. il Horn Bk 46:642-6 D '70 *
BETTER business bureaus
  Better business? Newsweek 75:60 Mr 2 '70
BETTING. See Gambling
BETTS, Austin Wortham
  Case for research; address, July 27, 1970. Vital Speeches 36:720-3 S 15 '70
BETTS, Leonidas
  Unfathomably mysterious. bibliog f Engl J 59:44-7+ Ja '70
BEUYS, Joseph
  How to explain pictures to a dead hare. U. Meyer. il Art N 68:54-7+ Ja '70
BEVAN, William
  Introducing William Bevan. B. Glass. Science 170:21 O 2 '70 *
BEVERAGE industry
    See also
  Soft drinks industry
BEVERAGE trays. See Trays
BEVERAGES
  Boating man's drink book. il Motor B 126:60-4 Jl '70
  Drinking woman's beauty brew. Harp Baz 103:154 O '70
  Elevation of soda pop. il por Time 96:51 O 19 '70
  For calorie counters: diet drinks. House & Gard 137:100 Ja '70
  Fruit syrups convert into instant tall summer coolers. il Sunset 145:118 Ag '70
  Green summer; vegetable drinks. il Harp Baz 103:92-3 Je '70
  Lunchtime drinks. House & Gard 137:130+ Mr '70
  Refreshers. il Bet Hom & Gard 48:64-5 Ag '70
  Summer sipping essentials; with recipes. M. Solaro. il Todays Health 48:50-2 Ag '70
  Super summer slimmers; with recipes. il Seventeen 29:138-9+ Je '70
  Things mother never taught you: cooling it with summer drinks. il Ladies Home J 87:92 Ag '70
  Toast to safer driving. M. Solaro. il Todays Health 48:60-3 D '70
    See also
  Cider
  Liquors
  Punch (beverage)
  Tea
  Wassail
  Wine
    Advertising
  Out-of towner; Dr Pepper. il Newsweek 76:72+ S 28 '70
BEVERIDGE, James J.
  Hunting gear for the Rockies. il Field & S 75:50-1+ N '70
BEVERLY HILLS, Calif.
    Police department
  Cop-in; J. P. Kimble case. Newsweek 75:26 Ap 13 '70
  Cop-out; liberal chief dumped. por Newsweek 75:34-5 Ap 6 '70
    Stores
  Shop-prowling in Beverly Hills. il Sunset 145:52-3 Ag '70
BEVINEAU, William A.
  Humanity; poem. Negro Hist Bul 33:83 Mr '70
BEWITCHMENT. See Magic
BEWLEY, Thomas A. and Li, C. H.
  Primary structures of human pituitary growth hormone and sheep pituitary lactogenic hormone compared. bibliog il Science 168:1361-2 Je 12 '70

BEYLE, Marie Henri
  Travel as a passport to freedom. A. Alvarez. il Sat R 54:17-18 Ja 2 '71 *
BEZZANT, Robert G.
  How to make an outfall in San Francisco Bay mud. il Am City 85:83-5 My '70
BHATTACHARYYA, Pinakilal, and others
  Colicin-tolerant mutants of escherichia coli: resistance of membranes to colicin El. bibliog il Science 168:998-1000 My 22 '70
BHAVE, Vinoba
  Where are they now? il pors Newsweek 75:10 Ja 26 '70
BHUTTO, Zulfikar Ali
  Step in the right direction. Time 96:29-30 D 21 '70 *
  Two-man sweep. il pors Newsweek 76:44 D 21 '70 *
BIAFRA
  Note:
  For material after January 15, 1970. See heading Nigeria
  Biafra, by C. O. Ojukwu. Review
    Sat R 53:32-3 Ja 31 '70. C. Miller
  Epitaph for Biafra. V. Bourjaily. il N Y Times Mag p32-3+ Ja 25 '70
  U.S. welcomes Nigerian statement on daylight relief flights to Biafra. Dept State Bul 61:635 D 29 '69
BIANCHI, Eugene C.
  Free ministry. Commonweal 91:450-3, 566-7 Ja 23, F 20 '70
  John XXIII, Vatican II, and American Catholicism. Ann Am Acad 387:30-40 Ja '70
BIBB, William R. See Thompson, T. J. jt. auth.
BIBBY, Geoffrey
  Experiment with time. il Horizon 12:96-101 Spr '70
  Looking for Dilmun; excerpts. il Horizon 11:54-9 Aut '69
BIBLE
  Most expensive bit of printing in the world; Gutenberg Bible. P. W. Schmidtchen. il Hobbies 75:134-6+ Jl '70
    See also
  Lectionaries
  Sex in the Bible
    Antiquities
    See also
  Noah's ark
    Bibliography
  Bible as a whole. C. E. Armerding and W. W. Gasque. Chr Today 15:18-21 N 6 '70
  1970 books on the Bible. D Stanley. America 123:436-8+ N 21 '70
  Spring Bibles and related books. il Pub W 197:51-3 Mr 9 '70
    Biography
    See also
  Women in the Bible
    Commentaries
  New Catholic commentary on Holy Scripture, ed. by R. C. Fuller and others. Review
    Cath World 211:93-4 My '70. N. J. McEleney
    Criticism, interpretation, etc.
  Healing narratives in Mark. D. M. Slusser. Chr Cent 87:597-9 My 13 '70
  What do evangelicals believe about the Bible? K. Runia. Chr Today 15:3-6 D 4; 8-10 D 18 '70
  Whither Southern Baptists? Southern Baptist convention. Chr Today 14:3-5 Ap 24 '70
    See also
  Bible—Commentaries
    Distribution
    See Bible—Publication and distribution
    Food
  New discovery in the quest of the historical Jesus; the primacy of food in the Gospel. G. H. Clark. il Chr Today 15:12-13 Ja 15 '71
    Homiletical use
  Missing: one knife; reprint from October 10, 1960. L. N. Bell. Chr Today 14:34-5 Ag 21 '70
    Inspiration
  Inspiration of Scripture. J. L. Kelso. Chr Today 14:6-9 Je 5 '70
    See also
  Revelation
    Interpretation
    See Bible—Criticism, interpretation, etc.
    Natural history
  Rediscovery: Parson Jonathan Fisher. A. Winchester. il Art in Am 58:92-9 N '70

BIBLE—*Continued*

Publication and distribution

Behind the iron curtain: Bibles. J. J. Van Capelleveen. Chr Today 15:53-4 N 20 '70

Study

See Bible study

Translations

See Bible—Versions

Versions

Catholics replace Douay with New American Bible. Pub W 198:37 S 7 '70
Checklist of new and standard Bibles. il Good H 171:159 D '70
Crucial issue in Bible translation. B. L. Goddard. Chr Today 14:12-13 Jl 3 '70
Designing and producing the New English Bible. il Pub W 197:74+ Mr 9 '70
New American Bible. Chr Today 15:29 O 23 '70
New American Bible. R. Clifford. America 123:435-6 N 21 '70
New Bible for Catholics; New American Bible. il Time 96:58+ O 12 '70
New English Bible. F. F. Bruce. Chr Today 14:8-11 Ja 30 '70
New English Bible. Review
America 122:455 Ap 25 '70. C. J. McNaspy Sat R il 53:46+ F 28 '70. I. Asimov
New English Bible: a comparison. J. A. Sanders. il Chr Cent 87:326-8 Mr 18 '70
New English Bible: back to beginnings. Time 95:56 Mr 23 '70
New English Bible: on its way to best-seller lists. U S News 68:34-5 Ap 6 '70
Readable Bible: New English Bible. Newsweek 75:113-14 Mr 23 '70
Translating the Bible; New English Bible compared with other translations. D. Daiches. Commentary 49:59-68 My '70
You've come a long way, Bible! P. C. Rule. il America 123:433-4 N 21 '70
See also
Bible—Old Testament—Versions

Women

See Women in the Bible

Old Testament

Old Testament times, by R. K. Harrison. Review
Chr Today 15:22-3 N 6 '70. G. L. Archer, jr

Bibliography

Fruitful year in the Old Testament field. C. E. Armerding. Chr Today 14:3-6 F 13 '70
Old Testament as a whole. C. E. Armerding. Chr Today 15:17-19 D 18 '70

Versions

Masterly job on Job; excerpts from King James and New English Bible versions. Time 95:57 Mr 23 '70
New English Bible Old Testament. C. H. Gordon. Chr Today 14:6-8 Mr 27 '70

Genesis

Genesis and ecology: does subdue mean plunder? D. E. Gowan. il Chr Cent 87:1188-91 O 7 '70

Job

Masterly job on Job; excerpts from King James and New English Bible versions. Time 95:57 Mr 23 '70

Jonah

Prophet Jonah: the story of an intrapsychic process. J. More. Am Imago 27:3-11 Spr '70

New Testament

Perennial outrage: anti-Semitism in the New Testament. Chr Cent 87:990-2 Ag 19 '70

Bibliography

Some new directions in New Testament study. R. P. Martin. Chr Today 14:10-13 F 13 '70

Gospels

Gospels and the Oberammergau passion play. Sister Louis-Gabriel. il Cath World 211:13-17 Ap '70
Understanding Scripture. G. C. Berkouwer. Chr Today 14:40 My 22 '70
See also
Jesus Christ—Teaching

Mark

Christ of St Mark. V. P. McCorry. America 122:inside back cover Je 27 '70
Healing narratives in Mark. D. M. Slusser. Chr Cent 87:597-9 My 13 '70

BIBLE study

That priceless hour. L. N. Bell. Chr Today 14:31-2 My 8 '70

BIBLER, R. Alan

COGs vs chaos. bibliog il Am City 85:94+ S '70

BIBLIOGRAPHY

See also subhead Bibliography under various subjects, e.g. Bible—Bibliography

BIBLIOGRAPHY, National

Cuba

National bibliographer in exile: Fermin Peraza Sarausa of Cuba, 1907-1969. I. Zimmerman. il pors Wilson Lib Bul 44:1060-3 Je '70

BIBLIOTHERAPY

See also
Libraries, Hospital

BICENTENNIAL of the Republic. See United States—Declaration of independence—Centennial celebrations, etc.

BICH, Bruno

French challenge. il Motor B 126:44-5+ Ag '70

BICH, Marcel, baron

Challenger from France. il por Bsns W p36-7 Ag 15 '70 *
Gallic challenger. il por Newsweek 76:68 Ag 10 '70 *

BICHON frise. See Dogs

BICKEL, Alexander M.

Desegregation: where do we go from here? New Repub 162:20-2 F 7; 28-30 Mr 21 '70; Same abr. with title Education or integration? Cur 118:31-6 My '70
Judging the Chicago trial. bibliog f Commentary 51:31-40 Ja '71
Revolution of unreason. New Repub 163:18-21 O 17 '70
Tolerance of violence on the campus. New Repub 162:15-17 Je 13 '70

about

Conservative activist. por Time 96:40 Ag 17 '70 *

BICKERDYKE, Mary Ann (Ball)

Nurse who outranked the general. R. Dunlop. il Todays Health 48:56-7+ My '70 *

BICKERS, Jack

Grow-out feeder contracts. il Farm J 93:12 O '69
New kind of order buyer. Farm J 93:B23 N '69
No-tillage corn and soybeans. il Farm J 94:34-7+ My '70

BICKNELL, Mary

Earthworm farm in your backyard? il Har Yrs 10:17-18+ Ag '70

BICKNELL, Stan

Permafrost, Alaska's cold, cold ground. il Sci Digest 68:60-5 O '70

BICYCLE industry and trade

U.S. lags in the bike race. il Bsns W p42 S 19 '70
What kind of bike d'ya ride? il Forbes 106:60 D 1 '70

BICYCLE racing

Fast Eddy; Tour de France. il Newsweek 76:49 Jl 27 '70
King of the road; E. Merckx in the Tour de France. il por Time 96:35-6 Ag 24 '70
Merrily they rolled along; Amateur bicycle league's national championships. J. Bruce. il Sports Illus 33:24-5 Ag 31 '70
See also
Motorcycle racing

BICYCLE routes. See Cycling

BICYCLE trips. See Cycling trips

BICYCLES

Bicycle built for none. Sci Am 222:58 My '70
Build this Tom Thumb mini-bike. G. Schatzlein. il Pop Mech 133:168-71 Ja '70
Converting your bike into an exerciser. il Consumer Rep 35:193-4 Ap '70
How to power a bicycle with a car battery. R. Pannanen. il por Pop Sci 197:79+ O '70
Stability of the bicycle. D. E. H. Jones. bibliog il pors Phys Today 23:34-40 Ap '70
Unridable bicycle. il Time 95:78 Je 8 '70
See also
Cycling

BICYCLING. See Cycling

BIDDING, Competitive. See Municipal contracts

BIDDLE, John

Sailing films for the hot stove league. T. Gibbs. il por Motor B 126:11 N '70 *

BIEBER, Cleora F.

Weed for all gardens. il Org Gard & Farm 17:60-1 F '70

BIEDERMAN, Charles Joseph

Structurist for a new age. il por Time 95:46-7+ Ja 26 '70

BIEL, Heinz H.
  Stock analysis. See issues of Forbes
BIENNALE, Venice. See Art—Exhibitions
BIERING, Mary Francis
  New multi-purpose camp offers ideas you
  can use. il Camp Mag 42:8-9 S '70
BIERL, Barbara A. and others
  Potent sex attraction of the gypsy moth: its
  isolation, identification, and synthesis. bib-
  liog il Science 170:87-9 O 2 '70
BIERMANN, Wolf
  Dragon slayer. por Time 97:28+ Ja 18 '71 *
BIG BEAR solar observatory. See Astronomical
  observatories
BIG Bog wilderness. See Wilderness areas—Min-
  nesota
BIG business
  See also
  Corporations—Size
  Industries, Size of
BIG Red Riding Hood; drama. See Cable, H.
BIG SUR, Calif.
  Big Sur cycle. B. Thomas. il Travel 134:40-3
  N '70
  Big Sur storm. S. Abrams. il Natur Hist 79:
  8-10+ Ag '70
  Most beautiful view in the world; house in
  the Big Sur. J. Peter. il Look 34:70-3 Ap
  21 '70
BIG THICKET
  Big Texas Thicket. C. Pirtle. il Travel 134:
  28-33 S '70
BIG trees. See Sequoia, Giant
BIGELOW, Martha Mitchell
  Public opinion and the passage of the Mis-
  sissippi black codes. bibliog Negro Hist
  Bul 33:11-16 Ja '70
BIGELOW, Ronald C. See Leslie, L. L. jt.
  auth.
BIGGERS, John D. See Graves, C. N. jt. auth.
BIGGS, Ken
  Ken Biggs: color magic. il Pop Phot 66:82-5 Ap
  '70 *
BIGGS, Ronald Arthur
  Residuals for a robber. il por Newsweek 75:63
  My 4 '70 *
BIGGS, W. Gale, and Waite, P. J.
  Can TV really detect tornadoes? bibliog il
  Weatherwise 23:120-5 Je '70
BIGHORNS. See Mountain sheep
BIKE routes. See Cycling
BIKE ways. See Cycling
BIKINI
  Twenty-three nuclear explosions later. J.
  Cameron. il N Y Times Mag p24-5+ Mr 1
  '70
BIKINIS. See Bathing suits
BILATERAL air agreements. See Aviation—
  International aspects
BILE pigments
  Bile pigment formation in plants. R. F.
  Troxler and others. bibliog il Science 167:
  192-3 Ja 9 '70
  Substrate-induced conjugation of bilirubin in
  genetically deficient newborn rats. M. M.
  Thaler. bibliog il Science 170:555-6 O 30 '70
  Transfer of bilirubin uridine diphosphate-
  glucuronyltransferase to enzyme-deficient
  rats. H. E. Rugstad and others. bibliog il
  Science 170:553-5 O 30 '70
BILGE pumps. See Boats—Equipment
BILINGUAL instruction
  Bilingually advantaged. J. R. Gates. il To-
  days Ed 59:38-40+ D '70
  Experiments in bilingual education. Sch &
  Soc 98:19 Ja '70
  Necessity for bilingual education. A. Rod-
  riguez. bibliog il por Wilson Lib Bul 44:
  724-30 Mr '70
  Reading resources and Project LEER. M. D.
  Shepard. bibliog il por Wilson Lib Bul 44:
  743-50 Mr '70
  What will it be? Reading or machismo and
  soul? E. O. Vail. Clear House 45:92-6 O '70
    Bibliography
  Bilingual education: a special report from
  CAL/ERIC. A. M. Malkoc and A. H. Rob-
  erts. Engl J 59:721-9+ My '70
BILINS. See Bile pigments
BILIRUBIN. See Bile pigments
BILIRUBIN uridine diphosphate-glucuronyl-
  transferase. See Transferases
BILL (anatomy) See Bills (birds)
BILL collecting. See Collecting of accounts
BILL Henley's new horizon; story. See Chac-
  here, L.
BILL of rights (United States) See United
  States—Constitution—Bill of rights

BILLARD, Jules B.
  Panama, link between oceans and conti-
  nents. il Nat Geog 137:402-40 Mr '70
  Revolution in American agriculture. il Nat
  Geog 137:147-85 F '70; Same abr. with title
  Farming's fantastic new look. Read Digest
  96:216-18+ Je '70
BILLBOARDS
  Billboards with choice targets. il Bsns W
  p 122 Ap 11 '70
  Blight blossoms on the American highway;
  with report by J. Neary. il Life 69:26-34
  Jl 24 '70
  Cracking the highway trust; proposal to
  broaden use of Federal highway trust fund.
  il por Time 95:59 Je 15 '70
  Message as an architectural medium. H. C.
  Schultz. il Arch Forum 132:44-9 My '70
BILLERA, I. John
  Motivating the millionaires. il por Time 95:
  68+ Je 8 '70 *
BILLIARD tables
  Fun for the family: a bumper-pool table you
  can build. J. Capotosto. il Pop Mech 133:
  146-9+ Ja '70
BILLIARDS
  Big jamboree at Johnston City. Ill. J. Mor-
  gan. il Atlan 225:64-7 Ap '70

    Caricatures and cartoons
  Pool. A. Roth. il Sports Illus 33:46-51 D 14
  '70
BILLING
  Bugs in billing: problems for customers and
  business. il U S News 69:74-5 Ag 24 '70
  Data transmission network speeds customer
  service; electric and water utilities; Al-
  buquerque, N.Mex. D. Mann. il Am City
  85:98-9 F '70
  How to cope with computer billing. J. Pink-
  ham. Bet Hom & Gard 48:114+ Mr '70
  News item: man bites Ford; lawsuit over
  errors in computer billing. Consumer Rep
  35:132-3 Mr '70
  Speed up water billing, simply; Eastern
  municipal water district. Hemet, Calif. il
  Am City 85:62-3 N '70
  Why we went to computerized billing; Padu-
  cah, Ky. B. Gibbons. il por Am City 85:67+
  Ja '70
    See also
  Charge accounts (retail trade)
BILLINGS, Bruce Hadley
  Taiwan: U.S. tries one-man experiment in
  postaid assistance. J. Walsh. por Science
  170:835-9 N 20 '70 *
BILLINGS, William
  Musical tanner. A. M. Lingg. il Opera N 34:
  26-8 F 14 '70 *
BILLINGS, Zilpha W.
  Self-selection classroom. il Todays Ed 59:14-
  16 O '70
  My daughter loves school, can she be learn-
  ing anything? D. Divoky. il Redbook 136:
  71+ N '70 *
BILLINGS, Mont. public library
  Five-story bonanza for Billings. S. Hake. il
  Library J 95:620+ F 15 '70
BILLINGSLEY, Orzell
  Incorporation: a new tactic for saving black
  areas. C. C. Douglas. il pors Ebony 25:100-
  2+ Ag '70 *
BILLIONAIRES. See Millionaires
BILLS, Agnes
  Professionalism begins with student teaching.
  bibliog f Clear House 45:156-60 N '70
BILLS (birds)
  Bird beaks designed for use. il Nat Wildlife
  8:23 Ap '70
BILLS, Private
  Growing rich on the alien. T. D. Williams. il
  Nation 211:614-17 D 14 '70
BILLY Noname; musical comedy. See Musical
  comedies, revues, etc.—Criticisms, plots,
  etc.
BILODEAU, Francis W.
  American art at the Gibbes art gallery in
  Charleston. il Antiques 98:782-6 N '70
BILOXI, Miss.
  Senior activity program survives hurricane
  Camille in Biloxi, Miss. il Aging 190:6-7 Ag
  '70
BILSKI, Catherine
  Exciting new products. See issues of Popular
  mechanics
  Publications worth writing for. Pop Mech 134:
  69 O; 55 N '70
BILTMORE forest school. See Forestry schools
  and education
BIMETALLISM
  See also
  Silver as money
BIMINI; story. See Hemingway, E.

BIMS, Hamilton
Felicia Weathers: dauntless diva. il pors Ebony 25:52-6+ My '70
Fly and drive and explore! il Ebony 25:156-60+ Je '70

BINAGHI, Walter
President Nixon receives declaration by ICAO against aircraft hijacking; letter, July 16, 1970. Dept State Bul 63:302-3 S 14 '70

BINARY stars. See Stars, Double

BINDER, Herman A.
Their community needs them. H. Alpert. il Har Yrs 10:43-5+ Je '70 *

BINDING (books) See Bookbinding

BINFORD, Tom
Rap 'n' pinion. por Motor T 22:14 Ag '70

BING, Rudolf
Man in box 13. M. Mayer. il por Opera N 35:6-10 S 19 '70 *
Met looks for a new boss. H. Saal. il por Newsweek 75:108+ My 18 '70 *
Sponsors' salute. il por Opera N 35:26-7 D 5 '70 *

BING Crosby national pro-amateur championship. See Golf—Tournaments

BINGAMAN, John W.
Winter on Glacier Point. il Nat Parks 44:11-13 F '70

BINGER, Carl
Living high on wit, wisdom, and love. Sat R 53:12-14+ Jl 25 '70

BINGHAM, Marshall
Life begins at forty-two. il por Am City 85:111 Jl '70

BINGHAM, Sallie
Growing up an Episcopalian. Mlle 70:158+ Mr '70
Mourning; story. Mlle 71:179 My '70

BINGHAM, Walter
Ghost patrol of golf. il Sports Illus 32:36-40 Mr 9 '70
Golf. Sports Illus 32:60+ Mr 23 '70
No one could trump the Aces. il Sports Illus 33:18-21 Jl 6 '70
Real scrap was for 60th place. il Sports Illus 33:26-7 D 21 '70
Say it again, Rube! il Sports Illus 32:10-13 Je 1 '70
Sudden death at Forest Hills. il por Sports Illus 33:26-7 S 21 '70
Take me out of the ball game. il Sports Illus 32:22-3 Ap 27 '70
Tennis. Sports Illus 32:61-2+ Ap 6; 50-1 Jl 13 '70
Track & field (title varies) il Sports Illus 33:60+ N 2 '70
Welcome back, Mister Hogan. il pors Sports Illus 32:18-21 My 18 '70

BINGHAM, Warren
Dissent and reaction: vigilante activity at NBS labs in Boulder. P. M. Boffey. por Science 169:163-4 Jl 10 '70 *

BINH, Nguyen-thi-, Mme. See Nguyen-thi-Binh, Mme

BINKLEY, Kenneth M.
Checkpoint. See issues of Flying to April 1970

BINNS, James Hazlett
Theme of success: let the buyer have faith. il pors Nations Bsns 58:53-4 Ja '70

BINOCULAR vision. See Sight

BINOCULARS. See Field glasses

BINSTOCK, Louis
What's your maturity quotient? excerpts from Power of maturity. Read Digest 96:122-3 Mr '70

BINZEN, Bill
Gallery: photographs. il Life 68:6-9 F 13 '70
Photographer's West Indies. il Travel & Camera 33:55-9 Ja '70

BIO-ANALYZER. See Biological apparatus and supplies

BIOASSAY. See Biological assay

BIOASTRONAUTICS. See Space flight—Physiological aspects

BIOCHEMICAL differentiation. See Differentiation (biology)

BIOCHEMICAL reactions. See Chemical reactions

BIOCHEMISTRY
Free radicals in biological systems. W. A. Pryor. il Sci Am 223:70-6+ bibliog(p 128) Ag '70
Life sciences. See occasional issues of Science news

Research on sugar nucleotides brings honor to Argentinian biochemist. E. Cabib. por Science 170:608-9 N 6 '70
    See also
American society of biological chemists
Bioenergetics
Biosynthesis
Enzymes
Metabolism
Molecular biology
Neurochemistry

Conferences
History of biochemistry and molecular biology. J. T. Edsall. Science 170:349-51 O 16 '70

BIOELECTRICAL impedance. See Impedance (electricity)

BIOELECTRICITY. See Electrophysiology

BIOENERGETIC analysis. See Group relations training

BIOENERGETICS
Energy cycle of the biosphere. G. M. Woodwell. il Sci Am 223:64-74 bibliog (p262) S '70

BIOENGINEERING. See Biomedical engineering

BIOGENESIS. See Life (biology)—Origin

BIOGRAPHICAL dictionaries
Who's who for everyman: business of selling vanity. G. Cranberg. Sat R 53:65-6+ My 9 '70; Reply with rejoinder. P. C. Krouse. 45 Jl 11 '70
    See also
Dictionary of scientific biography

BIOGRAPHY
Fine Hart of biography. S. Maloff. Commonweal 91:513-15 F 6 '70
Lively lady was a secret scholar; Lady A. Fraser, author of Mary queen of Scots R. B. Stolley. il pors Life 68:42-4+ F 20 '70

Bibliography
Biography (cont) M. Adelman, jr. America 122:479-80; 123:466-8 My 2, N 28 '70
Biography bookshelf. il Schol Teach Sec Teach Sup p8-9 My 4 '70

BIOLOGICAL and chemical weapons. See Chemical and biological weapons

BIOLOGICAL apparatus and supplies
Mighty anti-pollution weapon: the honeybee; use of bee-activated bio-analyzer. A. Hamilton. il pors Sci Digest 68:9-14 O '70

BIOLOGICAL assay
Absorption of proteins and peptides in the far ultraviolet. A. H. Woods and P. R. O'Bar. bibliog il Science 167:179-81 Ja 9 '70
Immunoassay of plasma low-density lipoproteins. R. S. Lees. bibliog il Science 169:493-5 Jl 31 '70
Immunoglobulin production: method for quantitatively detecting variant myeloma cells. P. Coffino and others. bibliog il Science 167:186-8 Ja 9 '70
Insulin levels in primates by immunoassay. G. V. and O. B. Crofford. bibliog il Science 169:1312-13 S 25 '70
Radioreceptor assay of adrenocorticotropic hormone: new approach to assay of polypeptide hormones in plasma. R. J. Lefkowitz and others. bibliog il Science 170:633-5 N 6 '70
Solid-phase radioimmunoassay of protein biosynthesis. H. C. Sox, jr. and B. Mohit. bibliog il Science 168:1467-8 Je 19 '70

BIOLOGICAL balance. See Ecology

BIOLOGICAL clocks. See Biology—Periodicity

BIOLOGICAL control of insects. See Insect control—Biological control

BIOLOGICAL physics
New basic laws: physicists in biology. il Sci N 98:430-1 D 5 '70
    See also
Biophysical society

BIOLOGICAL research
Amoebas, biology and the public. il por Sci N 98:443-4 D 12 '70
Biologists look ahead; formation of Council for biology in human affairs. Nation 210:229-30 Mr 2 '70
Biology of the way-out. J. Eastman. Natur Hist 79:24-9 My '70
On the life sciences; address, March 5, 1970. J. Mayer. Vital Speeches 36:402-7 Ap 15 '70
    See also
Association for tropical biology
Ecological research
Embryology, Experimental
Federation of American societies for experimental biology

BIOLOGICAL research—See also—*Continued*
Genetic research
Germfree life
Institute of human biology
International biological program
International laboratory of genetics and biology
Plankton research

Federal aid
Life sciences: whistling in the dark for another $250 million. R. J. Bazell. Science 170:1285-7 D 18 '70

BIOLOGICAL societies
See also
American institute of biological sciences

BIOLOGICAL transport
Amino acid transport in hepatoma cell cultures during tyrosine aminotransferase induction. E. L. Krawitt and others. bibliog il Science 169:294-6 Jl 17 '70
Fluid transport: concentration of the intercellular compartment. B. J. Wall and others. bibliog il Science 167:1497-8 Mr 13 '70
Insulin-stimulated glucose uptake by subcellular particles from adipose tissue cells. D. B. Martin and J. R. Carter, jr. bibliog il Science 167:873-4 F 6 '70
Metabolic dependence of fast axoplasmic transport in nerve. S. Ochs and N. Ranish. bibliog il Science 167:878-9 F 6 '70
Moving molecules across membranes. B. J. Culliton. il Sci N 98:42-3 Jl 11 '70
Rapid axonal transport of sulfated mucopolysaccharide proteins. J. S. Elam and others. bibliog il Science 170:458-60 O 23 '70
Specifications of transport systems and enzymes. R. D. Berlin. bibliog il Science 168:1539-45 Je 26 '70
Water transport in the cloaca of lizards: active or passive? D. E. Murrish and K. Schmidt-Nielsen. bibliog il Science 170:324-6 O 16 '70
See also
Blood-brain barrier

BIOLOGICAL warfare
Biological weapons race; international cooperation; address, August 5, 1970. J. Lederberg. Vital Speeches 36:740-3 O 1 '70
See also
Chemical and biological weapons

BIOLOGISTS
See also
Conservation as a profession
Lysenko, T. D.

BIOLOGY
Life sciences. See occasional issues of Science news
See also
Adaptation (biology)
Biological research
Cell division (biology)
Cryobiology
Ecology
Environment
Enzymes
Evolution
Fresh water biology
Heredity
Homology (biology)
Institute of human biology
Life (biology)
Marine biology
Microbiology
Molecular biology
Mutation (biology)
Neurobiology
Phylogeny
Polymorphism (biology)
Regeneration (biology)
Space biology
Species
Variation (biology)

Field work
Biological field work; proposed guidelines. N. G. Hairston. Science 169:8 Jl 3 '70

Periodicity
Acetylcholine concentrations in rat brain: diurnal oscillation. I. Hanin and others. bibliog il Science 170:341-2 O 16 '70
Circadian rhythm of brain self-stimulation behavior. M. Terman and J. S. Terman. bibliog il Science 168:1242-4 Je 5 '70
Circadian rhythms in human heart homograft. I. A. Kraft and others. bibliog il Science 169:694-6 Ag 14 '70
Clock of the malaria parasite. F. Hawking. il Sci Am 222:123-31 Je '70
Diurnal variation of spontaneous uterine activity in nonpregnant primates (macaca mulatta) G. M. Harbert, jr. and others. bibliog il Science 170:82-5 O 2 '70

Erythropoiesis in the dog: the periodic nature of the steady state. A. Morley and F. Stohlman, jr; reply. A. S. Iberall. Science 168:152 Ap 3 '70
Extraoptic celestial orientation in the southern cricket frog acris gryllus. D. H. Taylor and D. E. Ferguson. bibliog il Science 168:390-2 Ap 17 '70
Extraretinal light perception: entrainment of the biological clock controlling lizard locomotor activity. H. Underwood and M. Menaker. bibliog il Science 170:190-3 O 9 '70
Fungal endogenous rhythms expressed by spiral figures. J. A. Bourret and others; reply with rejoinder. B. M. Swenney. Science 169:1229 S 18 '70
Harderian gland: influence on pineal hydroxyindole-O-methyltransferase activity in neonatal rats. L. Wetterberg and others. bibliog il Science 170:194-6 O 9 '70
Indole metabolism in the pineal gland: a circadian rhythm in N-acetyltransferase. D. C. Klein and J. L. Weller. bibliog il Science 169:1093-5 S 11 '70
Jet time syndrome. P. J. C. Friedlander. il Sci Digest 67:10-15 Je '70
Many clocks of man; 24-hour rhythm. J. D. Palmer. il Natur Hist 79:52-9 Ap '70
Neuroendocrine control of ecdysis in silkmoths. J. W. Truman and L. M. Riddiford. bibliog il Science 167:1624-6 Mr 20 '70
Persisting circadian rhythm of cell division in a photosynthetic mutant of euglena. R. M. Jarrett and L. N. Edmunds, jr. bibliog il Science 167:1730-3 Mr 27 '70
When two hearts beat as two. Sci Am 223:60 O '70
See also
Photoperiodism

Study and teaching
Survey of the teaching of biology in secondary schools. W. Kastrinos. Sch & Soc 98:241-2 Ap '70
See also
Nature study

BIOMARINE industries
How a little fish hooked a big one; Biomarine's closed-cycle underwater breathing system. il Bsns W p88+ F 28 '70

BIOMECHANICS. See Human engineering

BIOMEDICAL engineering
Biomedical engineering. R. F. Rushmer and L. L. Huntsman. il Science 167:840-4 F 6 '70
Gathering of specialists; tackling the problems of artificial organs. B. J. Culliton. il pors Sci N 97:347-9 Ap 4 '70

BIOMEDICAL research. See Medical research

BIOMOLECULES. See Molecules—Models

BIOPHYSICAL society
Biophysics. Sci N 91:260 Mr 14 '70

BIOPHYSICS. See Biological physics

BIORHYTHM. See Biology—Periodicity

BIOSATELLITE program
Future space bioscience; extrapolation of biomedical studies on animals to human astronauts. Space World G-7-79:40-1 Jl '70

BIOSYNTHESIS
Adenosine 3',5'-monophosphate adrenocorticotropic hormone, and adrenocortical cytosol protein synthesis. M. F. Grower and E. D. Bransome, jr. bibliog il Science 168:483-5 Ap 24 '70
Amateur scientist; experiments in generating the constituents of living matter from inorganic substances. C. Fromer. il Sci Am 222:130-4+ Ja '70
Antimalarials: effects on in vivo and in vitro protein synthesis. K. A. Conklin and S. C. Chou. bibliog il Science 170:1213-14 D 11 '70
Catecholamine biosynthesis in brains of rats treated with morphine. D. H. Clouet and M. Ratner. bibliog il Science 168:854-6 My 15 '70
Gene at last. il por Sci N 97:547 Je 6 '70
Gene makers; first artificial synthesis of a gene. il por Newsweek 75:91 Je 15 '70
Making a gene. Sci Am 223:49-50 Jl '70
Partial reversion in yeast: genetic evidence for a new type of bifunctional protein. B. Dorfman and others. bibliog il Science 168:1482-4 Je 19 '70
Prebiotic synthesis of propiolaldehyde and nicotinamide. M. J. Dowler and others. bibliog il Science 169:1320-1 S 25 '70
Secrets of the cell; first artificial synthesis of a gene. il por Time 95:43-4 Je 15 '70
Shock synthesis of amino acids in simulated primitive environments. A. Bar-Nun and others. bibliog il Science 168:470-3 Ap 24 '70; Reply with rejoinder. H. R. Hulett. 170:1000-2 N 27 '70

BIOSYNTHESIS—*Continued*
Solid-phase radioimmunoassay of protein bio-synthesis. H. C. Sox, jr. and B. Mohit. bibliog il Science 168:1467-8 Je 19 '70
Steps toward life; catalyst of genesis. il Time 95:52 My 11 '70
Synthesis of amino acids by the heating of formaldehyde and ammonia. S. W. Fox and C. R. Windsor. bibliog il Science 170:984-6 N 27 '70
Vesicular and synaptoplasmic synthesis of acetylcholine. A. K. Ritchie and A. M. Goldberg. bibliog il Science 169:489-90 Jl 31 '70
BIPHENYL compounds. See Diphenyl compounds
BIRCH, Alison Wyrley
Community where drug addicts grow up. il PTA Mag 65:2-5 N '70; Same abr. with title Where addicts become adults. Read Digest 97:92-6 D '70
Mighty dream come true. il por Har Yrs 10:14-15 F '70
BIRCH, John, society. See John Birch society
BIRCH, Martin
Persuasive scents in moth sex life; with biographical sketch. il Natur Hist 79:6, 34-9+ bibliog(p88) N '70
BIRCH
New Hampshire's eleven birches. H. R. Russell. il Nat Parks 44:23-6 Mr '70
BIRCKNER, Wolfgang. See Birkner, W.
BIRD, Caroline
What today's couples want that their parents didn't. Ladies Home J 87:70+ Je '70
BIRD, Joan
Using the system. il por Time 96:13 Jl 20 '70 *
BIRD, John Malcolm
Building mountain ranges: a plate tectonics model. K. Frazier. il pors Sci N 98:143-5 Ag 15 '70 *
BIRD, Lewis Penhall, and Reilly, C. T.
Sex education and the church; excerpt from A time to love. Chr Today 14:10-13 Je 5 '70
BIRD; story. See Goldreich, G.
BIRD attracting. See Birds, Attracting of
BIRD banding
Banding and wildlife management. il Cons 24:38 F '70
BIRD calling
Fine art of turkey calling. L. Dietz. il Field & S 75:54-5+ N '70
Strange way to fool pheasant. J. Palmer. il Field & S 75:48-9+ S '70
Want bird close-ups? Call them with tape. G. Perkins and C. Perkins. il Pop Phot 67:74-5+ Jl '70
BIRD calls. See Birds—Song
BIRD dogs
Do you know your bird dogs? quiz. D. Du Bois. Outdoor Life 145:78-80+ F '70
Dogs. D. M. Duffey. See issues of Outdoor life
Employment for Fred; retrieving golf balls. R. Rau. il Field & S 75:100-2 Jl '70
See also
Field trials (dogs)
Pointers (dogs)
Setters

Anecdotes, facetiae, satire, etc.
Dog for all seasons. P. McManus. il Field & S 75:50-1+ Ag '70

Training
See Dogs—Training
BIRD feeders. See Feeders (birds)
BIRD flight. See Birds—Flight
BIRD gardens
North side shelterbelt for our birds. N. W. Bubel. il Org Gard & Farm 17:86-8+ N '70
What to plant for the birds. E. M. Woodford. il Horticulture 49:38+ Ja '71
BIRD houses (in zoos) See Zoological gardens—Buildings
BIRD migration. See Birds—Migration
BIRD-of-paradise-flowers
Success with the bird-of-paradise. il Home Gard 57:26-8 D '70
BIRD photography. See Photography of birds
BIRD populations
Control
Pigeon control by chemosterilization: population model from laboratory results. J. Sturtevant. bibliog il Science 170:322-4 O 16 '70
Strictly for the birds: corn kernels treated with Ornitrol. Newsweek 75:61 Mr 9 '70
BIRD protection. See Birds—Protection
BIRD refuges. See Bird sanctuaries
BIRD sanctuaries
See also
Laysan (island)

England
Gulls of Walney Island. B. R. MacRoberts and M. H. MacRoberts. il pors(p8) Natur Hist 79:64-9 Mr '70
How I adopted Nijinsky, my son the swan; Peter Scott's Wildfowl trust, Slimbridge, England. G. Cant. il Sports Illus 32:58-9 Ap 6 '70

Illinois
Winter haven; ice-free area on Arbor Lake west of Chicago. il Parks & Rec 5:39+ My '70

North Carolina
Mother Goose lives on; Lockhart Gaddy's wild goose refuge. E. Simpson. il pors Am For 76:44-8 O '70

Pennsylvania
Wings over Hawk Mountain. D. S. Heintzelman. il Nat Wildlife 8:22-7 Ag '70

Utah
Birds have two great stopover places around Great Salt Lake. il Sunset 144:84-5 My '70
BIRD shooting. See Shooting
BIRD songs. See Birds—Song
BIRD study
Notes and comment; bird watching on Block Island. New Yorker 46:27-8 Ag 22 '70
See also
Photography of birds

Anecdotes, facetiae, satire, etc.
Bird is a verb. M. Cheney. il Audubon 72:42-3 Ja '70
BIRD watching. See Bird study
BIRDHOUSES (in zoos) See Zoological gardens—Buildings
BIRDS
Garden clowns: tufted titmouse. Carolina chickadee and white-breasted nuthatch. M. D. Hodgins. il Horticulture 48:34-5 S '70
See also
Ear (birds)
Ornithology
Parasites—Birds
Rare birds
State birds
Water birds
also names of birds, e.g. Eagles

Anatomy
See also
Bills (birds)

Anecdotes, facetiae, satire, etc.
Tomorrow's critters. C. E. Gillham. il Audubon 72:41-3 N '70

Banding
See Bird banding

Color sense
See Color sense

Ecology
Teacher tips: new bird ranges and environment. J. A. Weeks. bibliog il Cons 24:30 Je '70

Egg laying
See Oviposition
Eyes
See Eye (birds)

Flight
Formation flight of birds. P. B. S. Lissaman and C. A. Shollenberger. il Science 168:1003-5 My 22 '70

Food and feeding
Winter vegetarians. H. Borland. il Audubon 72:inside cover Ja '70
See also
Bird gardens
Feeders (birds)

Geographical distribution
New bird ranges and environment. W. B. Sabin. il Cons 24:22-9 Je '70

Habits and behavior
Innocent in birdland. L. Rosten. il Sat R 53:14-15 S 5 '70
Luck of Prince Philip: excerpts from Wildlife crisis. Prince Philip. il por Look 34:29-33 O 20 '70
See also
Estivation

Memory
See Memory

BIRDS—*Continued*

Migration
Fall bird migration. P. M. Kelsey. il Cons 24:
31 Ag '69
Great gabble over Iowa lakes. D. Levin. il
Sports Illus 32:40-3 My 18 '70
Weekend pilot; Audubon updated. F. K.
Smith. Flying 86:122 Mr '70
See also
Orientation

Orientation
See Orientation

Photographs
Feathers in your Christmas tree. Nat Wildlife
9:41-3 D '70
Nature's jewels. Am For 76:24-5 Jl '70

Protection
Bird in the hand. il Natur Hist 79:76-9 Ja '70
Luck of Prince Philip; excerpts from Wildlife
crisis. Prince Philip. il por Look 34:29-33
O 20 '70
So long, duck. V. B. Moore. il Read Digest
96:124-8 Ap '70
See also
Bird sanctuaries
Birds of prey—Protection
Game birds—Protection
International council for bird preservation

Sanctuaries
See Bird sanctuaries

Sleep
See Sleep (birds)

Song
Hunting with a tape recorder. C. Perkins and
G. Perkins. il por Field & S 74:86-7 Ap '70
Ontogeny of bird song. F. Nottebohm. bib-
liog il Science 167:950-6 F 13 '70; Reply
with rejoinder. R. E. Lemon. 170:1333-5 D
18 '70
Song of a bird. N. Smith. il Nat Wildlife 8:34
Je '70
Vocal imitation and individual recognition of
finch calls. P. C. Mundinger. bibliog il Sci-
ence 168:480-2 Ap 24 '70

Study
See Bird study

Training
Bird who came to dinner. D. A. Caccia. il
Org Gard & Farm 17:50-1 Jl '70
Training school for birds. W. Hartley and E.
Hartley. il Sci Digest 69:32-6 Ja '71

Africa
See also
Flamingos

Australia
See also
Kookaburras

Denmark
See also
Storks

Hawaii
Hawaiian Islands of birds. G. Laycock. il
Audubon 72:44-61 Ja '70

Islands of the Pacific
See also
Albatrosses

Japan
See also
Japanese long-tailed fowls

Nevada
Nevada's endangered pelicans. A. Amaral. il
Nat Parks & Con Mag 44:23-7 Jl '70

New York (state)
New bird ranges and environment. W. B.
Sabin. il Cons 24:22-9 Je '70

BIRDS, Attracting of
Fill your yard with songbirds. il Changing T
24:15-16 Ap '70
Perches are for the birds. B. Miles. Home
Gard 57:50 Mr '70
Ways to attract birds to your garden. M. D.
Hodgins. il Home Gard 57:26-32 N '70
See also
Bird gardens

BIRDS, Fossil
Archaeopteryx: notice of a new specimen. J.
H. Ostrom. bibliog il Science 170:537-8 O 30
'70
Giving a big bird a lift; pteranodon. il Time
95:51 Mr 16 '70
**How birds began to fly; archaeopteryx. il
Time 96:50 D 7 '70**

Pteranodon: first of the hot-blooded flappers. M. Priestley. il Sci Digest 68:86-7 S
'70
See also
Penguins, Fossil

BIRDS, Injurious and beneficial
How I protect my harvest from the birds.
M. L. Coonse. Home Gard 57:74 Ja '70
See also
Scarecrows

BIRDS, Mechanical
Eternal nightingale. G. Martin. il Hobbies 75:
98M-98N Ag '70

BIRDS, Rare. See Rare birds

BIRDS, Rescue of. See Birds—Protection

BIRDS eggs
See also
Egg shells

BIRDS in art
Eagle: spacecraft of the pre-scientific age. J.
P. De Souza. il UNESCO Courier 23:23-7
Je '70
**Lansdowne, a portfolio; excerpts from Birds
of the eastern forest. J. F. Lansdowne.
Audubon 72:56-65 N '70**
National wildlife visits Arthur Singer. D. Kirk-
patrick. il pors Nat Wildlife 8:58-63 D '69

BIRDS in religion, folklore, etc.
Eagle: spacecraft of the pre-scientific age.
J. P. De Souza. il UNESCO Courier 23:
23-7 Je '70

BIRDS of prey
See also
Condors
Eagles
Predation (zoology)

Protection
Don't shoot! All hawks, owls, eagles and vul-
tures are protected by law; drawings. H.
W. Trimm. Cons 24:17 Je '70

BIRDWHISTELL, Ray
Way we speak body language. F. Davis. il
por N Y Times Mag p8-9+ My 31 '70 *

BIRENDRA, crown prince of Nepal
Marriage of convenience. il por Time 95:29
Mr 9 '70 *
Nepal: come, let us marry. il pors Newsweek
75:46-47D Mr 16 '70 *
Nepal's right royal wedding. il por Life 68:
34-5 Mr 13 '70 *

BIRGI, Muharrem Nuri
H.E. the Ambassador M. Nuri Birgi: the
fragile, funny arts. N. Lyon. Vogue 155:
117 Mr 1 '70 *

BIRK, Eileen P.
Books about antiques. Antiques 98:272, 568+
Ag, O '70
Current and coming. See issues of Antiques

BIRKEBAK, Richard C. and others
Thermal radiation properties and thermal conductivity of lunar material. il Science 167:
724-6 Ja 30 '70

BIRKNER, David
Winter walk on the Washington coast. il Nat
Parks 44:23-4 F '70

BIRKNER, Wolfgang
Glories of the hunt. il Time 95:54-5+ Ap 20
'70 *

BIRMINGHAM, John Leonard Wilson, bp of.
See Wilson, J. L.

BIRMINGHAM, Stephen
Fall and rise of Walter Annenberg. il por
McCalls 97:72-9+ Je '70
Pinehurst for golf, Southern Pines for horses.
il Holiday 47:30-5+ Ap '70
Talk industry. il Holiday 47:60-1+ F '70

BIRMINGHAM, Ala.

Cemeteries
Terry funeral. America 122:30 Ja 17 '70

Churches
Alabama church refuses membership to black
mother and daughter. Chr Cent 87:1178 O
7 '70
First Baptist, Birmingham: a case study of
old wineskins bursting. D. G. Shockly. Chr
Cent 87:1462-3 D 2 '70
Precious in his sight; First Baptist church and
a black applicant. il Newsweek 76:69-70 Ag
10 '70
Verdict at First Baptist; black applicants denied membership. Newsweek 76:107-8 O 12
'70

Religious institutions and affairs
Committed Baptists. Time 96:42 N 9 '70

BIRMINGHAM small arms company. See Motorcycle industry and trade

BIRNBAUM, Eugene A.
Books & ideas. Fortune 81:175-6 Ap '70

BIRNBAUM, Hugh
Basic guide to exposure. il Travel & Camera
33:77-9 My '70
BIRNEY, Earle
Canadian chronicle. P. D. Scott. Poetry 115:
353-4 F '70 *
BIRNIE, William A. H.
Early America's artless art. il Read Digest
96:142-8 F '70
New look in stamp collecting. il Read Digest
97:174-9 O '70
BIRRELL, George, and others
How to build and operate an inexpensive
polarograph. bibliog il pors Chem 43:26-9 Mr
'70
BIRSTEIN, Ann
Going to the movies. Vogue 155:210-11+ Mr
1 '70
Movies. See occasional issues of Vogue
BIRTH. See Childbirth
BIRTH control
Birth control after 1984; adaptation of ad-
dress, May 6, 1970. C. Djerassi. bibliog il
Science 169:941-51 S 4 '70
Birth control in America, by D. M. Kennedy.
Review
Commonweal 92:299-300 Je 12 '70. W. L.
O'Neill
Birth-control success story no. 1. A. Gordon.
Read Digest 96:80-4 Ja '70
Control of population; excerpt from The so-
cial contract. R. Ardrey. il Life 68:48-52+
F 20 '70; Same abr. with title Nature and
the case for birth control. Read Digest 96:
116-20 Je '70
Ecology: the new religion? R. L. Schueler.
America 122:292-5 Mr 21 '70
Family planning and the poor. W. M. Hern.
New Repub 163:17-19 N 14 '70
Family planning or population control? J.
Reston. Read Digest 97:163-4 D '70
Integrated incentives for fertility control. L.
W. Kangas. bibliog il Science 169:1278-83 S
25 '70; Discussion. 170:1256+ D 18 '70
Laws to limit family size. L. Lader. Parents
Mag 45:58-61 O '70
Licensing: for cars and babies. B. M. Rus-
sett. Bul Atom Sci 26:15-19 N '70
Make love, not babies; childlessness; views
of the Nathaniel Freedlands. M. Kasindorf.
il Newsweek 75:111 Je 15 '70
Man's decline as a species. A. H. Drummond,
jr. bibliog il Sci Digest 68:26-31 Jl '70
Miss Stephanie Mills vs. motherhood. A. Wolff.
il por Look 34:58-9 Ap 21 '70
More babies needed, not fewer; interview, ed.
by L. Kent. J. Jacobs. Vogue 156:86-7 Ag 15
'70
National family-planning programs: where we
stand; excerpts from address.. B. Berelson.
Science 169:931 S 4 '70
New feminism: potent force in birth-control
policy. L. J. Carter. Science 167:1234-6 F
27 '70
No more unwanted children. il UNESCO
Courier 23:24-7+ F '70
One man's answer to overpopulation; vasec-
tomy. il pors Life 68:42-7 Mr 6 '70
Opinion: the case for compulsory birth con-
trol. E. Chasteen. por Mlle 70:142+ Ja '70
Parenthood: right or privilege? G. Hardin.
Science 169:427 Jl 31 '70; Discussion. 170:
257-9+ O 16 '70
Perfect contraceptive population. L. Bumpass.
and C. F. Westoff. bibliog il Science 169:
1177-82 S 18 '70
Population control, sterilization, and ignor-
ance; results of Cornell university survey.
T. Eisner and others. Science 167:337 Ja 23
'70; Discussion. 168:62 Ap 3 '70
Population growth. H. C. Wallich. News-
week 75:70 Je 29; 76:60 Ag 10 '70
Population strategy. A. W. Smith. Nat Parks
44:2 F '70
Rhythm method doubted. il Sci Digest 67:73
My '70
Smaller families: a national imperative. G.
J. Hecht. por Parents Mag 45:24+ Jl '70
United States population policy, origins and
development; address, August 21, 1970. P. P.
Claxton, jr. Dept State Bul 63:317-26 S 21
'70
Will we say "it just happened." when the
world overpopulates itself to extinction?
Louisiana family planning program. J.
Lelyveld. il por N Y Times Mag p24-5+
Jl 19 '70
ZPG; new movement challenges the U.S. to
stop growing. il Life 68:32-7 Ap 17 '70
See also
Abortion
Contraceptives
Malthusianism

History
Faces from the past; M. Sanger. R. M. Ketchum. il por Am Heritage 21:52-3 Je '70

Laws and legislation
Population package; Family planning ser-
vices and Population research act of 1970. il
Time 96:36 D 21 '70

Periodicals
True precautions; True to life. published by
Atlanta's Emory university. Newsweek 76:
55 O 26 '70

Religious aspects
Abortion: holy innocents? Chr Today 14:39
My 8 '70
Birth control and Jewish law, by D. M. Feld-
man. Review
Chr Cent 87:632-3 My 20 '70. J. M.
Gustafson
Commentary 50:64-7 Ag '70. I. Greenberg
Birth control wars. J. Deedy. Commonweal 92:
2 Mr 13 '70; Reply. A. C. Francia. 92:102
-3 Ap 3 '70
Contraception and abortion: American Catho-
lic responses. D. Callahan. bibliog f Ann
Am Acad 387:109-17 Ja '70
Ex-F.A.O. head charges contradiction in
Pope's policies on birth control. Chr Cent
87:135 F 4 '70
Failure of the rhythm method. il Good H
170:10+ F '70
How Catholics are making up their minds on
birth control. J. E. Allen. il Chr Cent 87:915-
18 Jl 29 '70
Plea for reconciliation; break between the
Archbishop of Washington and his priests.
America 122:446 Ap 25 '70; Reply with re-
joinder. J. C. Ford. 122:571 My 30 '70
Vitiating Humanae vitae; Catholic renewal
movements leaflet. T. Beeson. Chr Cent
87:1032-3 S 2 '70
Will a miracle child be born this year? P. S.
Buck. il Ladies Home J 87:63+ D '70

Great Britain
Casanova controversy. il por Time 97:27 Ja 11
'71
Lesson from Casanova; birth-control pamphlets prepared by Britain's Health education
council. il Newsweek 77:59 Ja 11 '71
Tax-supported sterilization wins in London
despite Catholic drive. Chr Cent 87:591
My 13 '70
Vitiating Humanae vitae; Catholic renewal
movements leaflet. T. Beeson. Chr Cent
87:1032-3 S 2 '70

India
Population trends in an Indian village. C. E.
Taylor. il Sci Am 223:106-112+ Jl '70

Latin America
Toward a third world theology; reaction to
Humanae vitae. America 122:90 Ja 31 '70

Mexico
Mexico ambivalent on birth control. F. U.
Ross. il Chr Cent 87:1428-9 N 25 '70

Peru
Birth control wars. J. Deedy. Commonweal
92:2 Mr 13 '70; Reply. A. C. Francia. 92:
102-3 Ap 3 '70
CFM and the pill. J. Deedy. Commonweal 91:
442 Ja 23 '70

Underdeveloped areas
See Underdeveloped areas—Birth control

United States
See Birth control
BIRTH defects. See Deformities
BIRTH order
Does birth sequence affect intelligence? il
Good H 170:148-9 Je '70
Oldest, youngest child: which is
best off? B. Bettelheim. Ladies Home J 87:
12+ My '70
BIRTH rate
Proliferation of the species. Natur Hist 79:
50-1 Ja '70
See also
Birth control
Population, Increase of

India
See also
Birth control—India

Japan
Japan: a crowded nation wants to boost its
birthrate. P. M. Boffey. Science 167:960-2
F 13 '70; Reply. A. R. Sweezy. 169:97 Jl 3 '70

BIRTH rate—*Continued*

United States

Deceptive birth rates. P. R. Ehrlich and J. P. Holdren. Sat R 53:58 O 3 '70

Man and his environment; adaptation of address, March 19, 1970. A. J. Coale. Science 170:132-6 O 9 '70

Population heads for a zero growth rate; with editorial comment. il Bsns W p 102-4, 118 O 24 '70

BIRTHDAY parties. See Entertaining

BISBEE, Charles
How to be a tough nice guy. il Nations Bsns 58:79 Je '70

BISCAY, BAY OF
Age of the Bay of Biscay: evidence from seismic profiles and bottom samples. E. J. W. Jones and J. I. Ewing; reply. N. D. Watkins and A. Richardson. bibliog Science 167: 209 Ja 9 '70

BISCAYNE BAY
Biscayne Bay: the endless fight to save it; with photographs by J. A. Kern. B. Atkinson. Audubon 72:36-46+ S '70

Heat waste; study of Turkey Point plant's effect on Biscayne Bay. B. Stearns. il Sea Front 16:164-63 My '70

Power play over pollution. il Bsns W p28-9 Mr 21 '70

BISCAYNE NATIONAL MONUMENT
Biscayne Bay: the endless fight to save it; with photographs by J. A. Kern. B. Atkinson. Audubon 72:36-46+ S '70

BISCHOFF, James L. and others
Composition of interstitial waters of marine sediments: temperature of squeezing effect. bibliog il Science 167:1245-6 F 27 '70

BISCUIT mixes. See Food mixes

BISHKO, C. J.
(comp) Articles and other books received; Spain and Portugal. See issues of American historical review

BISHOFF, Louella M.
Revolutions and revelations in games people play. il Hobbies 74:152-3 Ja; 150-1+ F '70

BISHOP, Beata
At home with the barons and earls. il Sat R 53:46-7+ S 12 '70

BISHOP, George D. See Myers, D. G. jt. auth.

BISHOP, Jim
Autumn's bare, bright beauty. il Read Digest 97:128-30 O '70
Summer snapshot. il Read Digest 97:77-8 Jl '70
Winter is . . . il Read Digest 96:132-3 Ja '70

BISHOP, John A.
Redox reactions and the acid-base properties of solvents. bibliog il Chem 43:18 Ja '70

BISHOP, Jordan
Liturgy as subversive activity. Commonweal 93:324-7 D 25 '70
Schools, si; education, no. Commonweal 93: 17-20 O 2 '70

BISHOP, Joseph W. Jr
Quality of military justice. il N Y Times Mag p32-8+ F 22; 39-40 Ap 12 '70

BISHOP, Lee R.
Slide rule as a frequency calculator. Electr World 83:53 My '70

BISHOP, Lloyd K.
Bureaucracy and educational change. bibliog Clear House 44:305-9 Ja '70

BISHOP, Morris
Duty of the prince is magnificence. il pors Horizon 1:54-79 Aut '70
Father Boetti, or Sheik Mansour. il Horizon 12:44-5 Sum '70
Have buckler, will swash. por Horizon 11:76-7 Aut '69
Montaigne's soul mate. por Horizon 12:102-3 Spr '70

BISHOP, Robert L.
Television. New Repub 162:23-5 Mr 28 '70

BISHOP, Thomas
Ionesco on Olympus. por Sat R 53:21-3+ My 16 '70
Theatre. Vogue 155:32 Mr 15 '70

BISHOPS
Making of bishops; Church of England appointments. T. Beeson. Chr Cent 87:1405-6 N 25 '70
Ten year term for the bishop. J. P. Leary. il Cath World 212:194-6 Ja '71
See also
Episcopacy
National conference of Catholic bishops
Pastoral letters

BISON, American. See Buffaloes

BISON in design. See Design, Decorative—Animal forms

BISQUE doll heads. See Doll heads

BISQUE-headed dolls. See Dolls

BISQUES. See Soups

BISSET, Jacqueline
It's a drag to be pretty. il pors Life 68:60-3 F 13 '70

BITMAN, Joel, and others
DDT-induced inhibition of avian shell gland carbonic anhydrase: a mechanism for thin eggshells. bibliog il Science 168: 594-6 My 1 '70

BITTLE, Camilla R.
Magic words; story. Good H 170:82-3 Je '70

BITZER, D. L. See Alpert, D. jt. auth.

BIVALVES. See Mollusks

BIXLER, Frances M.
What is a good high school newspaper? Engl J 59:119-21 Ja '70

BIZET, Georges
Carmen. Criticism
Sat R 53:44 Ag 8 '70 *
Naked Carmen laid bare. C. L. Osborne. Hi Fi 20:120 S '70 *
Real Carmen. P. G. Davis. Hi Fi 20:83-4 N '70 *

BJORKMAN, Ake V.
Plastics needn't be a problem. Am City 85: 148+ S '70

BLACK, Barbara
Cloisters. il Horticulture 49:34-5 Ja '71
Food plants America gave the world. il Horticulture 48:24-7+ Jl '70

BLACK, Betty Jo
Controversy over the pill. B. Surface. il por Good H 170:64-5+ Ja '70

BLACK, John D.
Opinion. Mlle 71:33+ My '70

BLACK, Jonathan
"Speed" that kills, or worse. il N Y Times Mag p 14-15+ Je 21 '70; Same abr. with title Tempting siren called "speed." Read Digest 97:153-7 O '70

BLACK, Shirley (Temple) See Temple, S.

BLACK Americans. See Negroes

BLACK and Decker manufacturing company
Where the British deputy shows the way. il Bsns W p78-9 N 28 '70

BLACK and white films. See Photography—Films

BLACK and white transparencies. See Transparencies

BLACK bass fishing. See Bass fishing

BLACK bear hunting. See Bear hunting

BLACK bears. See Bears

BLACK buck antelopes. See Antelopes

BLACK Buffaloes (infantry) See United States—Army—Infantry

BLACK capitalism
Beginnings of black capitalism. il Time 95:95-6 Ap 6 '70
Birth of a black business. J. A. Berman. Harvard Bsns R 48:4-6+ S '70
Black capitalism, by T. L. Cross. Review
Fortune il 82:197-8 Ag '70, C. E. Silberman
Black capitalism: a study in frustration. il Newsweek 76:70-2 S 28 '70
Black capitalism now: success or failure? il U S News 69:38-41 N 23 '70
Economic integration and the progress of the Negro community. A. F. Brimmer. il por Ebony 25:118-21 Ag '70
Mortgage banking: blacks share the action. il Ebony 25:80-2+ Jl '70
Report from Detroit. A. Scott. il Fortune 81: 71-2 F '70
Testing black capitalism. B. L. Masse. America 123:491-2 D 5 '70
Uphill road to black capitalism. C. L. Frankel. Nations Bsns 58:60-2+ D '70

BLACK cod. See Sablefish

BLACK code. See Negroes—Civil rights—History

BLACK congress on evangelism. See Religious conferences

BLACK consciousness. See Negroes—Nationalism

BLACK economic development conference. See National black economic development conference

BLACK economic union. See Cooperative associations

BLACK educational services, inc.
Black capitalism gets a boost in Chicago. il Pub W 197:51-2 Je 22 '70

BLACK-eyed peas. See Cowpeas

BLACK-footed ferrets. See Ferrets

BLACK Hawks (hockey team) See Hockey teams

BLACK HILLS, S.D.
See also
Crazy Horse (Sioux Indian)—Statues, portraits, etc.

BLACK lice. See Plant lice

BLACK magic. See Witchcraft

BLACK maple. See Maple

BLACK markets
Pilgrim's progress: adjustment to home life by an American exchanged prisoner of war from Hong Kong in 1943. E. Hahn. New Yorker 46:28-30 Ag 15 '70

BLACK masonry. See Freemasons. Negro

BLACK MESA country. See Cimarron County, Okla.

BLACK militants. See Negro militants

BLACK Mountain review. See Poetry—Periodicals

BLACK music. See Negro music

BLACK Muslims
Case of Harry X; court rules free. il Newsweek 76:48 Jl 27 '70
Cattle poisoners. Newsweek 75:24+ Mr 30 '70
Elijah Muhammad: prophet and architect of the separate nation of Islam. H. J. Massaquoi. il pors Ebony 25:78-80+ Ag '70
Muslims in Alabama. il Time 95:12 F 2 '70
Whatever happened to the Black Muslims? Negroes building farm empire. il U S News 69:33-4 S 21 '70

BLACK nationalism. See Negroes—Nationalism

BLACK Panther party
And now Yale. il Time 95:59 My 4 '70
And then there were none. Time 95:28 Ap 27 '70
Assault on the courts; trials of Chicago seven and Black Panthers. Nat R 22:189-90 F 24 '70
Behind the turmoil at Yale; black power and the courts. il U S News 68:41-2 My 11 '70
Black Panthers and their white hero-worshipers. J. Fischer. Harper 241:18+ Ag '70; Discussion. 241:6+ O '70
Black Panthers and white radicals; notes from New Haven. P. Starr. Commonweal 92:294-7 Je 12 '70
Black Panthers: the hard edge of confrontation; report, and interview with E. Cleaver, ed. by G. Parks. il Life 68:18-27 F 6 '70
Caged Panthers. Time 95:47 Mr 16 '70
Conspiracy trial; thirteen New York Black Panthers. il Newsweek 76:26 N 9 '70
Controversial verdict; inquest on killings, Chicago. Newsweek 75:23 F 2 '70
Dick Gregory on campus. W. F. Buckley, jr. Nat R 22:1420 D 29 '70
Dispute over raid; police, Panthers clash in Chicago. il Sr Schol 95:3-4 Ja 12 '70
Double agent: thirteen Harlem Black Panthers on trial. Newsweek 76:33-4 N 23 '70
Eighth conspirator is a prisoner of war; excerpt from The trial. T. Hayden. il por Ramp Mag 9:45-50 Jl '70
Electric circus; pretrial hearing of the Panthers charged with conspiring to bomb public places in New York. il Time 95:14-15 F 16 '70
Enforcer; the Rackley case; McLucas trial; testimony of George Sams. Newsweek 76:32-3 Ag 17 '70
Feds' war on the Panthers. Nation 210:229 Mr 2 '70
Fred Hampton's apartment. R. Stern. Nation 210:325-6 Mr 23 '70
Free Huey. por Newsweek 75:30 Je 15 '70
Have a Panther to lunch. W. F. Buckley. jr. Nat R 22:168 F 10 '70
Heavy baggage; raid on the Panther headquarters. Nation 211:37 Jl 20 '70
Here and now for Bobby Seale; tr. by J. Oringer. J. Genet. Ramp Mag 8:30-1 Je '70
Ice him; A. Rackley case. Newsweek 76:25 Ag 3 '70
Is it too late for you to be pals with a Black Panther? il Esquire 74:141-7 N '70
Jungle justice for the Panthers. America 122:573 My 30 '70
Justice cops out: the Chicago police shoot-in; report of the January 1970 grand jury. N. Lewin. New Repub 162:14-18 Je 6 '70
Murtagh's formula. il Newsweek 75:22-3 Mr 9 '70
New Haven: the missing context. A. R. Dolan. Nat R 22:502 My 19 '70
New Haven under siege; rally in support of eight Black Panthers. P. Goldberger. Sr Schol 96:18 My 18 '70
Order in the court; New York trial. il Newsweek 75:27 F 16 '70
Our own man in Algiers; with statement by E. Cleaver. S. De Gramont. il N Y Times Mag p30-1+ N 1 '70
Panther and bulldog. il por Newsweek 75:52+ My 4 '70
Panthers against the wall. D. A. Schanche. il por Atlan 225:55-61 My '70

Panthers and pigs. Chr Today 14:25 Ja 16 '70
Panthers and preachers. Chr Today 14:32 Ja 16 '70
Panthers and the law. il Newsweek 75:26-30 F 23 '70
Panthers go to Temple. R. Rosen and S. Madden. Commonweal 93:6-7 O 2 '70
Panthers in court. New Yorker 46:30 F 21 '70
Panthers on trial. il Time 95:25+ My 11 '70
Perspective on the Panthers. T. Milstein. bibliog f Commentary 50:35-43 S '70; Discussion. 50:23 S '70; 51:10+ Ja '71
Philadelphia boomerang; police panic over Panthers. J. Higgins. il Nation 211:332-6 O 12 '70
Philadelphia's guerrilla war. il Newsweek 76:30-1 S 14 '70
Picking up the gun, by E. Anthony. Review Cath World 211:135-6 Je '70. B. N. Odell Nation 210:313-14 Mr 16 '70. G. Marine New Repub 162:30-1 Ap 4 '70. C. Hightower Sat R il 53:38-40 F 28 '70. M. Charyn
Politics of repression; symposium. W. H. Ferry. Cur 115:33-45 F '70
Questions remain; police raid on apartment in Chicago. Time 95:26 My 25 '70
Rapping with the Panthers in white suburbia. G. E. Stearn. il N Y Times Mag p28-9+ Mr 8 '70
Rising clamor for black separatism; Revolutionary people's constitutional convention in Philadelphia. il U S News 69:82-3 S 21 '70
Rumbling in Babylon: Panthers host a parley. T. W. Moore. Chr Cent 87:1296-300 O 28 '70
Second thoughts; case of the Chicago seven. Newsweek 75:46 My 18 '70
Seize the time, by B. Seale. Review Newsweek 75:104+ Je 15 '70. R. A. Sokolov
Slap on the wrist; Illinois dropping charges of attempted murder against the seven Panthers. Newsweek 75:41 My 25 '70
That party at Lenny's. il pors Time 95:80+ Je 15 '70
Those Black Panthers. J. C. Haughey. America 122:43-5 Ja 17 '70
Trial in New Haven; A. Rackley case. il Newsweek 76:20-1 Jl 27 '70
Trial itself put on trial; Yale student strike and rally. America 122:487 My 9 '70
Union seminary directors veto request for Black Panther bail. Chr Cent 87:470 Ap 22 '70
Upper East side story. il por Time 95:14 Ja 26 '70
Verdict in New Haven; trial of Lonnie McLucas. il Newsweek 76:34-5 S 14 '70
Voir dire; selecting a jury for the Panther 21 trial. New Yorker 46:38-9 O 10 '70
When is bail excessive? Time 95:42 F 9 '70
When the Panther came to Yale. R. Brustein. il N Y Times Mag p7-9+ Je 21 '70; Reply with rejoinder. K. Keniston. p2+ Jl 12 '70
Who killed Alex Rackley? il por Newsweek 75:22 Mr 30 '70
Year of harassment. R. Cover. il Nation 210:110-13 F 2 '70

BLACK power
Black consciousness and the black church: a historical-theological interpretation. J. H. Cone. bibliog f Ann Am Acad 387:49-55 Ja '70
Black power as an urban ideology. H. C. Relyea. Ed Digest 35:46-9 F '70
Black power comes to Greene County. il Fortune 81:70-5 Je '70
Black revolutionary power. J. Boggs. il por Ebony 25:152-5 Ag '70
Black theology and black liberation; address. J. H. Cone. il Chr Cent 87:1084-8 S 16 '70
Learn baby learn; address, May 24, 1970. M. T. Bowie. Vital Speeches 36:604-6 Jl 15 '70
Political gospel. F. Herzog. il Chr Cent 87: 1380-3 N 18 '70
White liberals and black power in Negro education, 1865-1915. J. M. McPherson. bibliog f il Am Hist R 75:1357-86 Je '70

BLACK racism. See Racism

BLACK rodeos. See Rodeos

BLACK SEA
Black Sea: recent sedimentary history. D. A. Ross and others. bibliog il Science 170:163-5 O 9 '70
Carbon-13 in Black Sea waters and implications for the origin of hydrogen sulfide. W. G. Deuser. bibliog il Science 168:1575-7 Je 26 '70

BLACK studies. See Afro-American studies

BLACK tailed deer hunting. See Deer hunting

BLACK theology. See Negroes—Religion

BLACK walnut trees. See Walnut trees

BLACK watch farms, inc.
Tax shelter caves in on city farmers. J. Carlson. il Farm J 94:18-19+ N '70

BLACK world (periodical)
Digest of rage. il por Time 96:89 S 21 '70

BLACKABY, Frank
History's greatest dead end. il Sat R 53:19-21+ Mr 14 '70

BLACKADAR, Alfred K. and Dutton, J. A.
Tracers in the air. Weatherwise 23:182-5 Ag '70
—See Dutton, J. A. jt. auth.

BLACKBALLING. See Blacklisting

BLACKBOARDS
Bear and his friends, blackboards all. il Sunset 145:86 D '70

BLACKBODY radiation
Does the microwave background have a hump in its spectrum? G. B. Lubkin. bibliog Phys Today 23:56 Jl '70

BLACKBURN, Benjamin Bentley, 1927-
Excerpt from address, April 22, 1970. Cong Digest 49:215+ Ag '70
Wilderness or wasteland? il Liv Wildn 34. 27-32 Spr '70

BLACKBURN, Clark W.
Time to strengthen family ties. por Parents Mag 45:30 D '70

BLACKBURN, Dan
Shriver on the road. New Repub 163:9 Jl 11 '70
Youth on the Hill: up against the marble wall. Nation 210:719-21 Je 15 '70

BLACKBURN, Morris
Morris Blackburn back on nature's trail. H. C. Pitz. il por Am Artist 34:20-4+ N '70 *

BLACKBURN, Paul
Poem for the manufacturers. Nation 212:92 Ja 18 '71

BLACKBURN, Robin
Rebirth of the revolution. il Nation 211:582-7 D 7 '70

BLACKFISH fishing. See Tautog fishing

BLACKLISTING
Firing and hiring of Fredy Jones; anti-union practices of textile companies in North Carolina. R. Scott New Repub 163:12-15 Jl 25 '70
Looking for trouble; court rules on army blacklist of potential U.S. civilians. Newsweek 75:35-6 My 4 '70
Nothing to worry about; House committee on internal security list of guest speakers at colleges. Nation 211:580 D 7 '70
Radicals and Mr Ciardi. N. Cousins. Sat R 53:24 D 12 '70
Spying on civilians; monitoring of political and social protest activities of civilians by army intelligence. Time 95:17-18 Mr 9 '70
Study of TV violence: seven top researchers blackballed from panel. P. M. Boffey and J. Walsh. Science 168:949-52 My 22 '70
See also
Boycott

BLACKLISTING of scientists
HEW blacklists: new security procedures officially adopted. P. M. Boffey. Science 170:142-4 O 9 '70
HEW: blacklists scrapped in new security procedures. B. Nelson. Science 167:154-6 Ja 9 '70
HEW's security. B. Nelson. Trans-Action 7:5-6 Ja '70

BLACKLOCK, Don
Putting reed switches to work. il Electr World 84:38-42 Ag '70

BLACKMON, Rosemary
Why women panic about age. Vogue 155:98-9+ F 15 '70

BLACKMUN, Harry Andrew
Blackmun: his views on the issues; statements to the Senate judiciary committee. por U S News 68:48 My 18 '70

about
Blackmun nomination, turning point for High court? il por U S News 68:22+ Ap 27 '70 *
Blackmun's baptism. il Time 96:68-9 O 5 '70 *
Man for all reasons. il por Newsweek 75: 29 Ap 27 '70 *
Nixon makes a winning choice. il por Time 95:19-21 Ap 27 '70 *
Repairing the damage. Time 95:17 My 18 '70 *
Star witness. il por Newsweek 75:41+ My 11 '70 *
Supreme court restoration. Chr Cent 87:653 My 27 '70 *

Third man. il por Newsweek 75:28-9 Ap 27 '70 *
Will he (yawn) make it? Nat R 22:446 My 5 '70 *

BLACKOUTS (electric power)   See Electric power failures

BLACKSMITHING
Contemporary blacksmith; 1970. R. Pearson. il Craft Horiz 30:22-7 D '70
Workshop: blacksmithing; excerpts from The art of blacksmithing. A. Bealer. il Craft Horiz 30:42-5 O '70

BLACKWELL, Elizabeth
Elizabeth Blackwell: first woman doctor. por Sr Schol 96:18 Mr 2 '70 *
Founding mothers. il pors Vogue 155:112-13 Je '70 *

BLACKWOOD, Linda
Castle-hopping in Spain, on $5 a day! il Schol Teach Sec Teach Sup p 12-13 Mr 9 '70
Hey! I'm learning too! il Schol Teach Sec Teach Sup p6-8 N 3 '69
Travel tips. Schol Teach Sec Teach Sup p30 N 3 '69

BLADDER cancer. See Cancer

BLADDER tumors. See Tumors

BLADENSBURG, Md.

Education
Teachers help interview prospective teachers. D. I. Zatz. Todays Ed 59:47 F '70

BLADES, Saw. See Saws

BLAINE, Graham B. jr
American family change-up. il Vogue 155:87+ Je '70

BLAINE, Ruth
English comes alive. il Am Ed 6:26-8 Je '70

BLAIR, Eric. See Orwell, G. pseud.

BLAIR, I. M. See Edgington, J. A. jt. auth.

BLAIR, James C.
Controversial computers. il Duns 96:37 N '70

BLAIR, John R. and Snyder, Ruby
Automated library system: Project LEEDS. il Am Lib 1:172-3 F '70

BLAIR, Jonathan S.
Keeping house in a Cappadocian cave. il Nat Geog 138:126-46 Jl '70

BLAIR, William D. jr
Communication: the weak link in our foreign relations? address, October 16, 1970. Dept State Bul 63:580-6 N 9 '70; Same. Vital Speeches 37:109-13 D 1 '70

BLAIR, William L.
Survival radio for Apollo. il Electr World 84: 38-40+ N '70

BLAIR and company
See also
Capital management corporation

BLAIRE, Philip
Syncro slide adds sound to your slide show. il Radio-Electr 41:73-4 Ap '70

BLAIS, Marie Claire
Manuscripts of Pauline Archange; story, tr. by D. Coltman. il Harp Baz 103:222-5 Mr '70

BLAISDELL, Harold F.
Hot weather hot spot. il Field & S 75:86-9+ Jl '70
How fishermen fool fish and vice versa. il Field & S 75:76-7+ Je '70

BLAKE, Eugene Carson
God in the global village. Ladies Home J 86: 133 D '69
Seven questions about COCU; excerpts from statement by W.C.C.'s General secretary. Chr Cent 87:242-3 F 25 '70

about
Blake on human rights. Chr Cent 87:588 My 13 '70 *

BLAKE, Fay M.
Faculty status: where it's at. Am Lib 1: 767-8 S '70
Status search. Library J 95:2096 Je 1 '70
—See Josey, E. J. jt. auth.

BLAKE, George
Springing of George Blake, by S. Bourke. Review
New Repub 163:28-30 S 5 '70. A. Campbell *

BLAKE, James
Letters from James Blake; southern con, American author. Esquire 74:76-9+ Ag '70

BLAKE, Peter
Four centuries of building. il Art in Am 58: 70-3 Mr '70

BLAKE, Robert. See Thorp, R. jt. auth.

BLAKE, Wendon
Painting watercolors in acrylic; excerpts from Acrylic watercolor painting. il Am Artist 34:36-41+ D '70

BLAKE, William
Blake and a tradition. J. McGann. Poetry 117:45-9 O '70 *

BLAKELY, W. Paul
Parable of poetry and pedagogy. Engl J 59:
945-6 O '70
BLAKEMORE, W. B.
Beyond sectarianism. Chr Cent 87:237 F 25
'70
BLAKESLEA trispora. See Fungi
BLAKESLEE, Alton L.
Today's health news. See issues of Today's
health
BLANCHARD, Duncan C. and Syzdek, Law-
rence
Mechanism for the water-to-air transfer and
concentration of bacteria. bibliog il Science
170:626-8 N 6 '70
BLANCHARD, Leslie
Color digest. il pors Harp Baz 104:121 Ja '71
Les BLANCS; drama. See Hansberry, L.
BLAND, Joellen
Oliver Twist; dramatization of novel by C.
Dickens. Plays 30:54, 85-96 N '70
Prince and the pauper; dramatization of a
story by M. Twain. Plays 30:85-96 O '70
BLANDA, George
George Blanda is alive and kicking. il por
Time 96:74 N 23 '70 *
Kick in time. il Newsweek 76:114 N 23 '70 *
Let George do it, and he does. T. Maule.
il por Sports Illus 33:30-2+ N 23 '70 *
Tale of two quarterbacks; with report by
B. Bruns. il pors Life 69:44-7 D 4 '70 *
BLANDAU, Richard J. See Gaddum, P. jt.
auth.
BLANDER, Milton, and others
Heating of basalts with a carbon dioxide
laser. bibliog il Science 170:435-8 O 23 '70
BLANDFORD, Athina (Livanos) Onassis
Spencer-Churchill, marchioness of
Jackie's fabulous Greek; excerpts from Those
fabulous Greeks. D. Lilly. pors Look 34:36+
Je 30 '70 *
BLANK, Blanche D.
School is not a state. Nation 210:690-2 Je
8 '70
BLANK, Joseph P.
Earthquake! The horror that hit Peru. il
Read Digest 97:77-83 O '70
Face to face with hurricane Camille. il Read
Digest 96:62-7 Mr '70
Gifts of Gregory Menn. Read Digest 97:108-12
Ag '70
Long return of Warrant officer Meade. il por
Read Digest 97:73-7 D '70
Rescue on the Freeway. il Read Digest
96:73-7 My '70
Tom Morgan's two-way gift. por Read Digest
96:71-5 Ap '70
You can make it, baby; condensation. il por
Read Digest 96:219-23+ Ja '70
BLANKETS
Blankets. il Consumer Rep 35:590-3 O '70
New kind of blanket. il Consumer Bul 53:23
Ja '70
See also
Electric blankets, coverlets, etc.
BLASBERG, Robert
Reform art for a reform era. il Craft Horiz
30:24-7 O '70
BLASCHKA, Rudolph
Glass flowers. F. Kaltenbach. il por Horti-
culture 48:36-7 F '70 *
BLASER, Robin
Comment. R. Magowan. Poetry 116:197-8 Je
'70 *
BLASS, Bill
Mr Charm; interview. Vogue 156:146 N 15 '70
BLAST cleaning. See Sand blast
BLAST waves. See Shock waves
BLASTING
Fire in the hole! excerpts from Western min-
ing. O. E. Young, jr. bibliog il Am West 7:
15-19 Jl '70
BLASTING, Atomic. See Atomic blasting
BLATCHFORD, Joseph H.
Peace corps: making it in the seventies. For
Affairs 49:122-35 O '70; Same abr. with ti-
tle Present status of the Peace corps. Cur
124:37-44 D '70
about
Can business aid the Peace corps? il por
Bsns W p 124 Ap 11 '70 *
Fresh spark plug for the Peace corps.
B. Clark. Read Digest 96:20-1+ My '70 *
Reports: Washington. E. B. Drew. Atlan 226:
10+ Jl '70 *
BLATNIK, John A.
Excerpt from debate. July 31, 1970. Cong
Digest 49:238+ O '70
BLAUKOPF, Kurt
Behind the scenes. Hi Fi sec I 20:22+ Ja '70;
25 F '70
BLAUSHILD, David
Man who woke up Cleveland. por Bsns W
p72 Ap 11 '70 *

BLAVATSKY, Helene Petrovna (Hahn-Hahn)
Mysterious Madame Blavatsky K. Vonne-
gut, jr. il por McCalls 97:66-7+ Mr '70 *
BLAZEK, Douglas
Pathological graffiti; poem. Nation 212:88 Ja
18 '71
What we once knew; Usage of a life; Fishing
in a city; poems. Poetry 116:152-6 Je '70
BLEACHES. See Bleaching materials
BLEACHING
Tie-and-bleach is an easy switch on tie-and-
dye. il Sunset 145:90+ Ag '70
BLEACHING (photography) See Photogra-
phy—Retouching
BLEACHING materials
Short course in chlorine bleach. il Good H
171:177 Jl '70
BLEDSOE, Theodore R.
Radiation phobia. Nat R 22:361 Ap 7 '70
BLEEDING. See Hemorrhage
BLEGEN, Judith
Virtuoso; interview, ed. by R. Zachary. por
Opera N 35:11 Ja 2 '71
BLEGVAD, Erik
Art of being Denmark; with drawings. il
Holiday 47:44-7 Ja '70
BLEICKEN, Gerhard David
Tale of two signatures. Forbes 105:17 Mr 15
'70 *
BLENDERS, Electric. See Household appli-
ances, Electric
BLENDINGER, Jack
Student attitudes toward teacher activism. il
Clear House 44:268-71 Ja '70
BLESSITT, Arthur O.
Blessitt is the cross-bearer. J. R. Greisch.
Chr Today 14:31 Jl 17 '70 *
Rally round the cross. A. Eggebroten. il Chr
Today 14:42-3 Ag 21 '70 *
BLIGHTED areas. See Slums
BLIND
Blindisms. Trans-Action 7:8 S '70
First miracle worker: Samuel Gridley Howe.
L. Lader. il Todays Health 48:42-3+ S '70
What? Laugh at a blind boy? Butterflies are
free, suggested by the life of H. Krents. T.
Prideaux. il pors Life 68:57-8 F 6 '70
See also
School libraries—Services to the blind
Sculpture—Exhibitions for the blind
Sports for the blind

Printing and writing
systems
Embossing Arabic letters and numbers on new
raised-line polyethylene paper: an aid for
the blind. R. L. Barr. bibliog il Science 169:
94-5 Jl 3 '70
BLIND, Apparatus for the
Electronic sight for the blind. Sci Digest
68:77 N '70
BLIND, Books for the
To see and to touch: Twin vision Braille
publishing company, Tarzana, Calif. W. A.
Horn. il Am Ed 6:35-6 Ag '70
BLIND, Gardens for the
Beauty is not in the eyes of these beholders.
M. McEachern. il Todays Health 48:79-80
N '70
BLIND, Nature trails for the. See Trails
BLIND characters in opera. See Characters
in opera
BLIND dating. See Dating
BLINDNESS
See also
Blind
BLINDS, Duck. See Duck blinds
BLISH, James
Tale that wags the god. il Am Lib 1:1029-33
D '70
BLISS, L. C.
Biologist explains: why we must plan now
to protect the Arctic. il Bul Atom Sci 26:
34-8 O '70
BLISS and Laughlin industries, inc
We're not a steel company. R. Levy. por
Duns 95:51-2+ F '70
BLIZZARDS. See Snowstorms
BLOATING
Make milk, not bloat; pasturing alfalfa. Farm
J 94:D9 Je '70
BLOCH'S book shop and publishing company.
See Booksellers and bookselling—New York
(state)
BLOCK, H. and R, inc.
Paper empire? il Forbes 106:19-20 N 15 '70
BLOCK, Jean Libman
Doctor was an adventuress. il Todays Health
48:20-1+ Ag '70

BLOCK, Jean Libman—*Continued*
Girl who found a face. il Good H 170:30+ Ap
'70; Same abr. Read Digest 97:49-53 Jl '70
How I got into the movies. Good H 171:52+ Ag
'70
My family is dying! Read Digest 96:171-2+
Ap '70
My husband the cook. il Good H 171:42+ O
'70
Wild wig wave. Read Digest 96:103-5 Ja '70

BLOCK, Libbie
This town needs a doctor; novel. Good H
170:90-3 Ap; 88-9 My; 88-9 Je '70

BLOCK, S. and others
Polymorphism in benzene, naphthalene, and
anthracene at high pressure. bibliog il Science 169:586-7 Ag 7 '70

BLOCK, Thomas H.
Pro's nest. Flying 87:22-3 Jl; 20 Ag; 10 N;
94-5 D '70
Up-tight pilot. il Flying 87:76-7+ S '70

BLOCK, Victor
Growing menace of VD. Parents Mag 45:86-
7+ N '70
Holiday on a farm. il Parents Mag 45:42-3+
Je '70
Two-year college comes of age. il Parents
Mag 45:52-4 D '70

BLOCK books
Before Gutenberg: the block-book. P. Standard. il Pub W 198:58+ S 14 '70

BLOCK groups. See Citizens associations

BLOCK ISLAND
Notes and comment: bird watching. New
Yorker 46:27-8 Ag 22 '70
See also
Architecture, Domestic—Block Island

BLOCK printing
Easy way to block-print Christmas cards
using paint. il Sunset 145:80 D '70
Produce prints; supermarket produce tray
prints. B. Tisinger. il Sch Arts 70:22-3
S '70

BLOCKER, Clyde E.
Dissent and the college student in revolt. bibliog Sch & Soc 98:20-3 Ja '70

BLOCKS (engine) See Automobile engines

BLODGET, Robert
Follow me through. See issues of Flying

BLOEDEL, Lawrence
At home with art: the Lawrence Bloedel
guesthouse. il Art in Am 58:80-5 My '70 *

BLOESCH, Donald G.
True and false ecumenism. Chr Today 14:3-5
Jl 17 '70

BLOMBERG, Ronnie
Sports. R. Kahn. Esquire 74:58+ S '70 *

BLOND hair. See Hair

BLOOD, Thomas
Have buckler, will swash. M. Bishop. por
Horizon 11:76-7 Aut '69

BLOOD
Yes, you're a blue blood. A. S. Freese. il To-
days Health 48:46-8+ Ag '70
See also
Erythropoiesis

Analysis and chemistry
Australia antigen: distribution during Cohn
ethanol fractionation of human plasma. D. D.
Schroeder and M. M. Mozen. bibliog il Science 168:1462-4 Je 19 '70
Automatic analysis of blood cells. M. Ingram
and K. Preston, jr. il Sci Am 223:72-82 bib-
liog(p 132) N '70
Tests for Australian antigen answer a need;
serum hepatitis. J. Bockel. il Sci N 97:584-5
Je 13 '70

Circulation
Recovery of neuronal function after pro-
longed cerebral ischemia. K. A. Hossmann
and K. Sato. bibliog il Science 168:375-6
Ap 17 '70; Reply with rejoinder. D. Silver-
man. 170:1000 N 27 '70
Shear degradation of fibrinogen in the circu-
lation. S. E. Charm and B. L. Wong. bib-
liog il Science 170:466-8 O 23 '70
See also
Blood-brain barrier
Blood flow
Pulse

Circulation, Disorders of
Divining rod for blood; measuring blood
flow directly. Newsweek 75:72 My 25 '70
See also
Hypertension

Coagulation
Coagulation inhibitor elicited by thrombin. E.
Marciniak. bibliog il Science 170:452-3 O 23
'70
See also
Anticoagulants
Fibrinogen

Corpuscles and platelets
See also
Leukocytes
Lymphocytes

Dialysis
See Kidneys, Artificial

Diseases
Immunoglobulin M heavy chain disease: in-
tracellular origin of the mu chain fragment.
J. Buxbaum and others. bibliog il Science
169:770-3 Ag 21 '70
See also
Anemia
Autoimmune diseases
Leukemia

Flow
See Blood flow

Formation
See also
Marrow

Parasites
In competition for bird life: parasites. W. B.
Stone and R. D. Manwell. il Cons 24:14-17
F '70
See also
Hemoglobin

Pigments

Plasma
See also
Blood donors
Blood substitutes

Pressure
See Blood pressure

Proteins
Adam and ape. Sci Am 222:46 F '70
Circulating immunoglobulin M: increased
concentrations in endemic and sporadic
goiter. S. C. Werner and others. bibliog il
Science 170:1201-2 D 11 '70
Heritable fragile site on chromosome 16:
probable localization of haptoglobin locus
in man. R. E. Magenis and others. bibliog
il Science 170:85-7 O 2 '70
Immunoassay of plasma low-density lipoproteins. R. S. Lees. bibliog il Science 169:
493-1 Jl 31 '70
Immunoglobin structure: amino terminal sequences of kappa chains from genetically
similar mice (BALB/c) L. E. Hood and
others. bibliog il Science 170:1207-10 D 11
'70
Immunoglobulin M heavy chain disease: intracellular origin of the mu chain fragment.
J. Buxbaum and others. bibliog il Science
169:770-3 Ag 21 '70
Immunoglobulin production: method for quantitatively detecting variant myeloma cells.
P. Coffino and others. bibliog il Science 167:
186-8 Ja 9 '70
Macroglobulin structure: variable sequence of
light and heavy chains. H. Köhler and others. bibliog il Science 169:56-9 Jl 3 '70
Structure and function of antibodies. G. M.
Edelman. il Sci Am 223:34-42 bibliog(p 128)
Ag '70
Ultrastructure of secretory and high-polymer
serum immunoglobulin A of human and
rabbit origin. S. E. Svehag and B. Bloth.
bibliog il Science 168:847-9 My 15 '70
See also
Cytochromes
Fibrinogen

Serum
See Serum

Storage
Plasticizers from plastic devices: extraction,
metabolism, and accumulation by biological
systems. R. J. Jaeger and R. J. Rubin. bibliog il Science 170:460-2 O 23 '70

Testing
Hemagglutination assay for antigen and
antibody associated with viral hepatitis.
G. N. Vyas and N. R. Shulman. bibliog il
Science 170:332-3 O 16 '70
Rapid screening test for detecting hepatitis-
associated antigen. C. A. Saravis and oth-
ers. bibliog il Science 169:298-9 Jl 17 '70
Testing for HAA antigen. Sci N 98:367 N 7
'70

BLOOD—*Continued*

Transfusion

Sweating blood; risking serum hepatitis from blood transfusions. il Time 96:57 O 19 '70

Velocity

See Blood flow

Viscosity

Shear dependence of effective cell volume as a determinant of blood viscosity. S. Chien. bibliog il Science 168:977-9 My 22 '70

BLOOD, Artificial. See Blood substitutes

BLOOD banks

Policing the plasma plants. il Time 96:43 Ag 17 '70

See also
Blood donors

BLOOD-brain barrier

New insight into the brain's defenses. W. Cole. il Todays Health 48:50-3 Mr '70

BLOOD donors

Blood by the bucket. New Repub 163:7-8 S 26 '70

Blood money; man with the anti-Lewis B factor. por Newsweek 76:77 Ag 17 '70

Policing the plasma plants. il Time 96:43 Ag 17 '70

Protecting the donors. Sci N 98:113-14 Ag 8 '70

Sweating blood; risking serum hepatitis from blood transfusions. il Time 96:57 O 19 '70

BLOOD flow

Blood flow and diffusion through mammalian organs. J. B. Bassingthwaighte. bibliog il Science 167:1347-53 Mr 6 '70

Measurement

Blood velocity measurements in intact subjects. O. C. Morse and J. R. Singer. bibliog il Science 170:440-1 O 23 '70

Divining rod for blood; measuring blood flow directly. Newsweek 75:72 My 25 '70

BLOOD groups

Blood money; man with the anti-Lewis B factor. por Newsweek 76:77 Ag 17 '70

Homozygous Hb J Tongariki: evidence for only one alpha chain structural locus in Melanesians. R. K. Abramson and others. bibliog il Science 169:194-6 Jl 10 '70

BLOOD pressure

Train yourself to stay well; visceral learning. M. Pines. il McCalls 97:48+ Je '70

See also
Hypertension

BLOOD pump. See Hearts, Artificial

BLOOD red roses; musical comedy. See Musical comedies, revues, etc.—Criticisms, plots, etc.

BLOOD sacrifice. See Sacrifice, Human

BLOOD substitutes

Man-made blood; fluorocarbon-polyol mixtures. il Newsweek 76:100 N 2 '70

BLOOD vessels

See also
Cardiovascular system

Catheterization

See Catheterization

Surgery

Auto crashes and the heart; cases of injury to the aorta. il Time 96:36 Jl 27 '70

Defusing a coronary, with gas. il pors Life 68:75-6 Ap 17 '70

New lease on life for heart sufferers; direct vein-bypass procedure. L. Galton. il Read Digest 97:98-102 S '70

BLOOM, Arthur D. See Choi, K. W. jt. auth.

BLOOM, Joel

My goals for camping; statements from presidential candidates. il por Camp Mag 42:7 N '70

BLOOM, Justin L. See Seaborg, G. T. jt. auth.

BLOOM, Murray Teigh

Fairly sad story of a Wall Street broker. il pors N Y Times Mag p 12-13+ Je 14 '70

How to read a stock market letter. il N Y Times Mag p48-9+ N 15; 144 D 6 '70

Ma Bell takes her lumps. Read Digest 96: 206-10 Ap '70

Time to clean up our probate courts. Read Digest 96:112-15 Ja '70

BLOOM, Sherman

Spontaneous rhythmic contraction of separated heart muscle cells. bibliog il Science 167:1727-9 Mr 27 '70

BLOOM, Stephen E.

Trisomy-3,4 and triploidy (3A-ZZZW) in chick embryos: autosomal and sex chromosomal nondisjunction in meiosis. bibliog il Science 170:457-8 O 23 '70

BLOOMFIELD, Howard V.

The beautiful and the dammed. il Am For 76:12-15+ S '70

Everglades: pregnant with risks. il Am For 76:24-7+ My '70

BLOOMFIELD, Joseph

Test yourself: what do you know about reading? il por Wilson Lib Bul 45:242-5 N '70

BLOOMFIELD, N.J.

Floodlighting adds beauty, usefulness; project to draw attention to classic municipal building. S. Friedman. il Am City 85:122 Mr '70

Description

Look and learn via city tours. il Am City 85:144 My '70

BLOOMFIELD HILLS, Mich.

Gardens

In Bloomfield Hills, Michigan: a garden of fountains and flowers; Cranbrook house park and gardens. G. G. Dibble. il Home Gard 57:42-3 Ag '70

BLOOMINGTON, Ill.

Police

Protection tax wins voter yes. il Am City 85:100+ Ag '70

BLOOMQUIST, Lillian. See Petter, M. jt. auth.

BLOOMSBURY group

Rediscovery: the Bloomsbury painters. M. Holroyd. il Art in Am 58:116-23 Jl '70

BLOTH, B. See Svehag, S. E. jt. auth.

BLOUNT, Nathan S.

Summary of investigations relating to the English language arts in secondary education: 1969. bibliog Engl J 59:677-90 My '70

—and Searles, J. R.

(eds) Teaching materials. See issues of English journal

BLOUNT, Roy, jr

Baseball (cont) Sports Illus 32:58-9 Mr 30; 70 My 25; 43 Je 22; 46 Je 29 '70

Baseball's week. Sports Illus 33:87 S 28 '70

Birds of a feather flock to Bob. il por Sports Illus 33:26-8+ N 2 '70

Calvin and the kiddie corps. il Sports Illus 33:26-8+ N 16 '70

Forty-seven years a shot-freak. il por Sports Illus 32:45-9 Ap 20 '70

Impatience of Mrs Job. il pors Sports Illus 33:24-9 Ag 24 '70

Lefty makes the Angels sing. por Sports Illus 32:28-9 Je 8 '70

Lots of stuff and no nonsense. il por Sports Illus 32:22-4+ My 18 '70

No disgruntlements round here. il por Sports Illus 33:18-21 Ag 10 '70

Spicy day at Penn. il por Sports Illus 32:58-9 Mr 9 '70

This big man is the cool man. il por Sports Illus 33:16-18 O 5 '70

Three Birds who mainly stay. il pors Sports Illus 33:30-2+ O 12 '70

Week. Sports Illus 32:70+ My 25; 41-2 Je 1; 60-2 Je 15; 43-4+ Je 22; 46-7 Je 29; 33: 39-41 Jl 6; 92-3 S 7 '70

BLOUNT, Winton Malcolm

Overhauling the mails; interview. il por U S News 68:46-51 My 4 '70

about

Strike that stunned the country. il pors Time 95:10-16 Mr 30 '70 *

BLOWERS, Snow. See Snow blowers, throwers, etc.

BLOY, Léon

Battle of Wagner. C. Matz. pors Opera N 34: 6-7 Ja 31 '70

BLUE bell, inc.

Clothing maker flies own cargo. D. A. Brown. il Aviation W 93:136-7+ O 26 '70

What recession? il Forbes 105:26-7 Je 15 '70

BLUE collar workers. See Labor and laboring classes

BLUE daisies

Old standby revisited. il Sunset 144:234-5 Mr '70

BLUE geese. See Geese, Wild

BLUE-green algae. See Algae

BLUE laws. See Sunday legislation

BLUE marguerites. See Blue daisies

BLUE RIDGE MOUNTAINS

Flying visit; Beech Mountains. S. Wilkinson. Flying 87:109 Ag '70

BLUE whales. See Whales

BLUEBEARD'S castle; opera. See Bartók, B.

BLUEBERRIES
Doing with fresh blueberries. Sunset 145: 118 Jl '70
Our traveling blueberries. R. B. Fair. il Org Gard & Farm 17:34-6 Ag '70
BLUEBERRY creeper. See Ampelopsis
BLUEBIRDS
Farmers: key to bluebird survival? R. Van Vorse. il Farm J 94:50V Mr '70
Our state bird, the bluebird. il Cons 24:35 Je '70
BLUECHER, Heinrich
Obituary
Nat R 23:24-5 Ja 12 '71. P. P. Witonski
BLUEFIN tuna fishing. See Tuna fishing
BLUEFISH fishing
Carolina blues. K. Osborne. il pors Outdoor Life 146:70-1+ O '70
BLUEGILL fishing. See Sunfish fishing
BLUEGRASS music. See Folk music, American
BLUEMEL, Elinor
Summer white house. il por Am West 7:24-5 S '70
BLUEPRINTS
See also
Copyright—Blueprints
BLUES. See Depression, Mental
BLUES (songs, etc)
Blues for Janis. por Time 96:54 O 19 '70
See also
Phonograph records—Blues (songs, etc)
BLUESTONE, Irving
UAW fills a slot in its GM lineup. por Bsns W p25 Je 6 '70 *
BLUHDORN, Charles G.
Hollywood is not Fort Knox, I can guarantee you that. il por Life 68:44-5 F 27 '70
BLUM, Albert A.
Union prospects and programs for the 1970's. bibliog f Mo Labor R 93:36-9 Mr '70
BLUM, John Morton
That kind of a liberal: Franklin D. Roosevelt after twenty-five years. Yale R 60:14-23 O '70
BLUM, Sam
Group therapy: a special report. il Redbook 134:102-3+ Mr '70
Liza. il por Redbook 134:66-7+ F '70
Marijuana clouds the generation gap. il N Y Times Mag p28-9+ Ag 23 '70
Why so many young women steal from stores. il Redbook 135:72-3+ O '70
Why we let go when we drink. Redbook 135:96+ My '70
—See Krich, A. jt. auth.
BLUMBERG, Donald
Ex-patient as change agent. Ment Hy 54:159-60 Ja '70
BLUMBERG, Stanley A. See Owens, G. jt. auth.
BLUMENFELD, Erwin
He put the nude on the Coca Cola chair. J. Deschin. il Pop Phot 66:22+ Mr '70 *
BLUMENTAL, Felicja
Music to my ears; performance of Beethoven's E-flat piano concerto. I. Kolodin. Sat R 53:48-9 N 7 '70 *
BLUMENTHAL, Richard D.
Ins and outs. J. Osborne. New Repub 162: 11-12 My 9 '70 *
BLUMENTHAL, W. Michael
World of preferences. For Affairs 48:549-60 Ap '70
BLUMRICH, Josef F.
Design. Science 168:1551-4 Je 26 '70
BLUNDERS
My I.Q. is 20/20. T. L. Bernard. il Todays Ed 59:31 Mr '70
BLUTCHER, Laurence
$2 misunderstanding. A. Cooper. Newsweek 76:45 Ag 3 '70 *
BLY, Donald D.
Gel permeation chromatography. bibliog il Science 168:527-33 My 1 '70
BLY, Robert
Anarchists fainting; poem. Harper 240:118 Ap '70
Owning homes; poem. Nation 211:411 O 26 '70
BLYTH, Marion D.
Case for irrelevance. Engl J 59:380-3+ Mr '70
BLYTH, Myrna
Two; story. Redbook 134:100-1 Mr '70
BOA constrictors
Unexpected twist. V. M. Grinager. il pors Outdoor Life 145:22-3 Ja '70
BOARD games. See Games
BOARD of governors of the Federal reserve system. See United States—Federal reserve board
BOARDS of directors. See Corporations—Directors

BOARDS of education. See School boards
BOAT berths. See Boats—Berths
BOAT building. See Boatbuilding
BOAT buying. See Boats—Purchasing
BOAT camping. See Camping
BOAT clubs
Port Elco rendezvous; Port Elco club. G. F. Hammond. il Motor B 126:46+ N '70
Steam lives! Puget Sound live steamers. E. Crimmin. il Motor B 126:48-9+ S '70
BOAT co-ownership. See Partnership
BOAT engines. See Marine engines
BOAT handling. See Boats and boating
BOAT hoists. See Boats—Equipment
BOAT industry. See Boatbuilding
BOAT insurance. See Insurance, Marine
BOAT lifts. See Boats—Equipment
BOAT locks and keys
Electronic combination ignition lock. J. Beiswenger. il Pop Electr 33:40-2 Jl '70
BOAT models. See Ship and boat models
BOAT ownership
See also
Boats—Purchasing
BOAT propellers. See Propellers
BOAT racing
Bathtub racing circuit. E. Crimmin. il Motor B 126:50+ Ag '70
Tacking through the rapids; white water dinghy race. J. A. McVie. il Motor B 126:51 Ag '70
Who won what? comp. by R. Ianuzzi. Motor B 125:26+ F '70
See also
Hydroplane racing
Kayak racing
Motor boat racing
Rowing
Sailboat racing
Yacht racing
BOAT repairing. See Boats—Maintenance and repair
BOAT shows. See Boats—Exhibitions
BOAT toilets. See Boats—Toilet facilities
BOAT tools. See Tools
BOAT trailers. See Automobile boat trailers
BOAT varnishing. See Varnish and varnishing
BOATBUILDING
Arrivederci Italia. T. Bottomley. il Motor B 125:74-6+ My '70
Boating business. W. Robberson. See issues of Yachting
Build a glass-bottom boat. il Mech Illus 66:92+ Mr '70
Build this pontoon fun raft. H. Wicks. il Pop Mech 133:138-41 Mr '70
Build this turtle boat for the fun of it! H. Kelly. il Pop Mech 134:143-5+ Jl '70
Cartop johnboat. S. Clements. il Mech Illus 66:110-12+ Mr '70
Nick Marchetti's spaghetti boats. A. Zidock, jr. il pors Motor B 125:14+ Ap '70
One man's career: J. McQueen. il por Yachting 127:80-1+ Ja '70
Unsinkable uniboat. H. Kelly. il Mech Illus 66:81-2+ Mr '70
Ways of the Orient; with photographs. F. Jacobs. Motor B 126:42-7 S '70
Where have the seams gone? revolution in techniques, 1945-1970. J. Smith. il Yachting 127:74-5+ Ja '70
You can build a spillproof canoe. G. Daniels. il Pop Mech 133:176-81 Ap '70
See also
Hulls (naval architecture)
Shipbuilding
Yacht building

Anecdotes, facetiae, satire, etc.
Tin boats of Scrog Lake. D. R. Van Volkenburg. il Motor B 126:52-5+ D '70
BOATING clothes. See Clothing and dress—Sports clothes
BOATING for women. See Women in boating
BOATING industry
Facts and the figures. P. M. Wilson. Yachting 129:62+ Ja '70
Information sources & manufacturers of boatkeeping supplies. Motor B 125:69 Ap '70
BOATING industry association
Flotation tests. A. W. Limburg. il Motor B 125:172-5 Ap '70

BOATING organizations
  Checklist of sources; a roundup of boating organizations, information, literature, and schools. T. Bottomley. Motor B 125:134-8 Ja '70
  General organizations and special interest organizations. T. Bottomley. Motor B 127:163-5 Ja '71
BOATING picnics. See Picnics
BOATING schools. See Boats and boating—Study and teaching
BOATS

Batteries
See Storage batteries

Berths
Below decks. il Motor B 127:144-7 Ja '71

Cabins
Below decks. il Motor B 127:144-7 Ja '71

Camping equipment
This camper doesn't miss the boat. G. Reiger. il Pop Mech 133:124-5 Mr '70

Care
See Boats—Maintenance and repair

Chartering
See Boats—Leasing and renting

Corrosion
See Corrosion and anticorrosives

Design
Design details in fiberglass. B. Cobb, jr. il Yachting 127:80-2 Ap '70
Design showcase. il Motor B 125:156-63 Ja '70
Designs. B. D. Barker. 3d. See issues of Yachting
You and your boat; ideas of twelve top designers. il Motor B 125:93-117 Ja '70
  See also
Boats—Cabins

Displacement
See Displacement (ships)

Electric equipment
How it works, dockside power. C. Miller. il Motor B 125:228+ Mr '70
New electric anti-fouling system. C. Miller. il Motor B 125:63 Ap '70
Wiring for electronics. C. Miller. bibliog il Motor B 125:94+ Je '70

Electronic equipment
Boating instruments you can build from kits. S. M. Gallager. il Pop Mech 134:126-9 Jl '70
Choosing electronics for the small boat. B. McKeown. il Mech Illus 66:72-4+ Ja '70
Electronics. il Motor B 125:226-31+ Ja '70; 127:150-3+ Ja '71
For cruisers: all-in-all electronic command center. il Pop Sci 196:48 My '70
Marine electronics, 1970 style. J. West. il Yachting 127:71-3+ Ap; 60-2 My; 128:68-70 Jl; 60-2+ Ag '70
Marine electronics; power and sail, ed. by C. Miller. See issues of Motor boating

Equipment
Anchor rope reel. G. P. Manning. il Motor B 125:140-1 Je '70
Big dipper bilge pumps. W. Robberson and E. Robberson. il Yachting 127:222 F '70
Boat lifts for one man, plus helpers. il Sunset 145:72 Ag '70
Build this cockpit galley. P. Perrett. il Pop Mech 134:162-3 Ag '70
Cabin talk. M. Wiley. See issues of Yachting
Compleat powerboat, the ultimate auxiliary. il Motor B 127:150-1 Ja '71
Equip your new boat. il Motor B 127:148-9+ Ja '71
Equipment. il Motor B 125:236-41+ Ja '70; 127:254-8+ Ja '71
Gadgets and gilhickies. J. Smith. See issues of Yachting
Getting the galley ready. R. L. Williamson. il Motor B 125:76-7 Ap '70
It's new. See issues of Yachting
New & novel for 71. il Motor B 126:46-51 D '70
New for the boatman. il Mech Illus 66:90-1 Mr '70
New gear for 1970. F. M. Paulson. il Field & S 74:116-18+ F '70
Rigging up for amphibious adventure. F. M. Paulson. il Field & S 74:168-73+ Mr '70
Seen at the boat show, and worth noting. C. Miller. il Motor B 125:62-4 Ap '70
Wall mounted memo pad. G. Manning. il Motor B 125:180-1 My '70
Waterfront news. See issues of Yachting

What's new. See issues of Motor boating
Yachting's boat show. il Yachting 129:121-2+ Ja '71
Yachting's boat show in print. il Yachting 127:127-37+ Ja; 211-12+ F; 220+ Mr '70
  See also
Canoes—Equipment
Sailboats—Equipment

Exhibitions
Antique boat of the year; sixth annual Antique boat show, Clayton, N.Y. T. Bottomley. il Motor B 126:47+ N '70
Boat-show calendar. Outdoor Life 145:84 Ja '70
Boat show calendar. Yachting 127:126 Ja; 218 F '70; 129:119+ Ja '71
Boat show time again. G. F. Hammond. Motor B 126:34 O '70
Boats: sixtieth National boat show. New Yorker 45:24-5 F 7 '70
Everything that floats but money; New York's annual boat show. il Bsns W p34-5 Ja 31 '70

Finance
Money matters. il Motor B 127:152-3 Ja '71

Fires and fire protection
Fire! Fire! The cry that strikes terror. E. A. Zadig. il Motor B 125:10-12+ Je '70

Hulls
See Hulls (naval architecture)

Launching
  See also
Yachts—Launching

Leasing and renting
Boating vacations abroad. P. Reavis. il Motor B 125:62-3+ My '70
Which boat is best? G. F. Hammond. il Motor B 126:41+ D '70

Maintenance and repair
After haul-out; saving hours of fitting-out chores next spring. W. Robberson. Yachting 128:60+ O '70
Boatkeeper. See issues of Motor boating
How to hold maintenance to a minimum. B. McKeown. il Mech Illus 66:71+ F '70
Keep it clean. il Motor B 125:66-7 Ap '70
Maintenance with new products. W. Robberson. Yachting 127:70+ Ap '70
Ten quick checks to improve your boat's performance. L. M. Pierce. il Pop Sci 196:76-7 Je '70
Those new miracle cures for ailing wooden boats. G. Daniels. il Pop Sci 196:102-3+ My '70

Bibliography
Sources of maintenance information. E. Horan. Yachting 127:70+ Ap '70

Materials
Build a glass-bottom boat. il Mech Illus 66:92+ Mr '70
Care and repair of wood boats. J. Gardner. il Field & S 75:124-8 N '70
Classic boats in fiberglass. B. Cobb, jr. il Yachting 129:100-1+ Ja '71
Design details in fiberglass. B. Cobb, jr. il Yachting 127:80-2 Ap '70
Fiberglass age. B. Cobb, jr. il Yachting 127:76-8 Ja '70
Flotation tests. A. W. Limburg. il Motor B 125:172-5 Ap '70
How to judge a fiberglass boat. J. A. Emmett. il Outdoor Life 145:38+ Ap '70
Kelley's one-piece plastic boat. R. S. Fairchild. il Pop Sci 196:79 Je '70
Look what's happening to aluminum boats. A. J. Hand. il Pop Sci 196:124+ Ap '70
New approach to ferro-cement. T. Bottomley. il Motor B 126:21+ S '70
Reconstructing fiberglass. T. Cobb. il Yachting 128:154 N '70
  See also
Sailboats—Materials
Yachts—Materials

Prices
How much does boating really cost? B. McKeown. il Mech Illus 66:49+ My '70

Propellers
See Propellers

Protection against theft
Burglarproof your boat. B. McKeown. il Mech Illus 66:60+ Ap '70
Intrusion alarm for your boat. B. Kasha. il Motor B 126:80 D '70
  See also
Boat locks and keys

BOATS and boating—*Continued*
Periodicals
See also
Powerboat (periodical)

Safety devices and measures
Boat owner's safety log; U.S. coast guard stations maintaining a continuous listening watch on the International distress and calling frequency. R. Humphrey. Motor B 125:142-3+ Ja '70
Do you know the three R's? D. Du Bois. Outdoor Life 145:74-5 Ja '70
Helping hand; Ohio's South shore CC. A. Mastics. il Yachting 129:110+ Ja '71
Helping hand; USCG safety center. A. Hemenway. il Yachting 129:110+ Ja '71
New devices that help when your boat's in distress. J. Roe. il Pop Sci 196:78-9 Je '70
See also
Lightning protection

Statistics
Facts and figures: increases in boating since 1945. P. M. Wilson. Yachting 127:79+ Ja '70

Study and teaching
Check list of sources; a roundup of boating organizations, information, literature, and schools. T. Bottomley. Motor B 125:140-1 Ja '70
Schools. Motor B 127:167-8+ Ja '71
See also
Rowing—Study and teaching
Sailing—Study and teaching

BOB and Ray (comedians)
Bob and Ray. New Yorker 46:36-8 O 31 '70
Boys in the attic. H. Hewes. Sat R 53:19 O 10 '70 *
Funny gentlemen. J. Kroll. pors Newsweek 76:87 O 5 '70 *
Kidders of the cliché. T. E. Kalem. Time 96:72 O 19 '70 *
Theatre; Bob and Ray—the two and only. B. Gill. New Yorker 46:66 O 3 '70 *

BOB Jones university, Greenville, S.C.
BJU and the IRS. Chr Today 15:22 Ja 15 '71
Bob Jones: no to IRS? loss of tax-exempt status. Chr Today 15:39 Ja 1 '71

BOBCAT hunting
My no. 1 game; hunting on Garden Peninsula. E. Harger. il por Outdoor Life 146:94-5+ O '70

BOBCATS
Call me bob. C. Elliott. il Outdoor Life 145:26 Mr '70
Little lions. C. A. DeViney. il Am For 76:4+ My '70
Sam and Eloise bobcat; letter. W. H. Carr. il Am For 76:40-1 S '70

BOBER, Arie
Middle East and the intellectuals. Commentary 50:5+ O '70
about
Matzpen and its sponsors. C. Gershman. Commentary 50:52-3 Ag '70; Discussion. 50:5+ O; 14 D '70 *

BOBRICK, Sam. See Clark, R. jt. auth.

BOBROW, Michael L.
Planning the hospital for a changing system of health service. Arch Rec 148:95-7 D '70

BOBWHITES. See Quails

BOCCARDO, James
Troika of torts. il por Time 96:68 D 7 '70 *

BOCCE. See Bowling

BOCK, Claudio Walter F.
Birth control for economic development? Science 168:607-8 My 1 '70

BOCK, Eve Chybová
Legacy of John Amos Comenius. il Chr Today 15:11-14 N 6 '70

BOCK, Frederick
Mistaken cats; poem. Poetry 116:22-3 Ap '70

BOCK, James
Ponte Vecchio for St Louis. B. Thorne. il Arch Forum 132:60-1 Ja '70 *

BOCK, Joanne
Grand Pa Wiener, painter of many worlds. il Antiques 98:266-9 Ag '70

BOCK, Louis
Folk pottery of Guatemala. il Ceram Mo 18:12-15 F '70

BOCK, Wayne D.
Hyalinea baltica and the plio-pleistocene boundary in the Caribbean Sea. bibliog il Science 170:847-8 N 20 '70

BOCKOVEN, J. Sanbourne
Community mental health: a new search for social orientation. Ment Hy 54:172-9 Ja '70

BOCKRATH, Roger
Murderers ordered him to take their pictures. R. Graves. pors Life 69:2A Ag 21 '70 *

BOCONÓ fault. See Faults (geology)

BODE, Carl
Duplex; poem. Am Scholar 39:294 Spr '70
School; poem. New Repub 162:33 Mr 21 '70
Sonnet: the seer. Sat R 53:26 My 16 '70

BODE, Fred A. Jr
Geranium man. N. C. Gray. il por Am Home 73:22-3 Jl '70 *

BODEGA Y QUADRA, Juan Francisco de la
Quadra's and Vancouver's island. M. B. McGuire. il por Américas 22:2-8 Jl '70 *

BODGER, Joan
Dirty word smokescreen. N. Ladof. il por Library J 95:2424-6 Jl '70 *
Joan Bodger vindicated by ALA investigation. por Library J 95:3221 O 1 '70 *
Proceedings and findings; Library bill of rights; ALA report. E. Castagna and others. bibliog Am Lib 1:694-704 Jl '70 *

BODIES; story. See Oates, J. C.

BODMER, Walter F. and Cavalli-Sforza, L. L.
Intelligence and race; with biographical sketches. il Sci Am 223:15, 19-29 bibliog (p 144) O '70

BODY, Human
See also
Physiology

Anecdotes, facetiae, satire, etc.
People and products; a useful decalogue; address, October 6, 1969. M. Leeds. Vital Speeches 36:303-6 Mr 1 '70

BODY fluids
See also
Biological transport

BODY image
Who's beautiful to whom, and why? B. Ford. il Sci Digest 69:9-15 Ja '71

BODY language. See Communication, Nonverbal

BODY temperature. See Temperature, Animal and human

BODY types. See Man—Constitution

BODY weight. See Weight (physiology)

BOE, Thelma
Pork promoter no. 1. T. Allen. il por Farm J 93:H13+ O '69 *

BOECKH, Jürgen, and others
Antennal receptors: reactions to female sex attractant in periplaneta americana. bibliog il Science 168:589 My 1 '70

BOEING company
Aerospace industry hits some bumpy air. il Newsweek 75:62-4 Mr 2 '70
Appalachia in Seattle? il Newsweek 76:56 Ag 17 '70
Boeing considers wide-body 727 version. R. G. O'Lone. il Aviation W 93:36-7 Jl 20 '70
Boeing cutbacks shake economy of Seattle area. R. G. O'Lone. il Aviation W 92:14-17 Je 29 '70
Boeing earnings drop sharply; other first quarter results mixed. Aviation W 92:26-7 My 4 '70
Boeing forms committee to seek new markets, ways to diversify. Aviation W 93:24 N 23 '70
Boeing sales soar, but not for long. il Bsns W p26 N 21 '70
Boeing sees cost rise in SST slowdown. Aviation W 93:18-19 D 14 '70
Boeing Wichita aims at surplus market. E. J. Bulban. il Aviation W 93:41+ S 14 '70
Boeing wins AWACS award. il Aviation W 93:22 Jl 13 '70
Boeing's future changes to cloudy; 747 sales disappointing. il Bsns W p 124-5+ Mr 28 '70
Boeing's quarterly earnings, sales up. Aviation W 93:16 N 2 '70
Deliveries fall, Boeing profits slump in year. Aviation W 92:230-1 Mr 9 '70
Helicopter bread line. J. C. Goulden. Nation 212:50-2 Ja 11 '71
Latest 737 planned for use abroad. R. G. O'Lone. Aviation W 92:81+ Ap 6 '70
Lift for Boeing; flying radar station contract. il Newsweek 76:65 Jl 20 '70
Long-term prospects for 747 held favorable by Boeing officer. Aviation W 92:28 Mr 30 '70
NASA picks Boeing for Kennedy support. Aviation W 93:23 N 30 '70
New method used for SST models. R. G. O'Lone. il Aviation W 92:55-6 Ap 13 '70
Profitability rise sought for 747. R. G. O'Lone. il Aviation W 92:24-6 Mr 16 '70
Schools, housing feel Boeing pinch; with editorial comment. R. G. O'Lone. il Aviation W 93:9, 44-6 Jl '70

BOEING company—*Continued*
Seattle under siege: the troubles of a company town. K. Prager. il Time 97:28-9 Ja 4 '71
747 flap track improvement discussed by Boeing, airlines. R. G. O'Lone. Aviation W 93:30 N 9 '70
SST bailouts worry Boeing. Bsns W p74+ Mr 14 '70
Striving to maintain Drew Pearson's standards. W. F. Buckley, jr. Nat R 23:50-1 Ja 12 '71
Terms tightened in SST contract. H. D. Watkins. Aviation W 93:14-15 Ag 10 '70
BOEING 747. See Airplanes, Jet
BOEKI Daigaku. See Business education—Japan
BOELENS, Wim L.
Democratic movement in Dutch Catholicism. Cath World 211:112-15 Je '70
BOER, Charles
Comment. D. Zaiss. Poetry 116:54-6 Ap '70 *
BOERCKER, Fred D. and others
Employment status of recent recipients of the doctorate. bibliog il Science 168:930-9 My 22 '70
BOERMA, Addeke H.
World agricultural plan; with biographical sketch. il Sci Am 223:12, 54-63+ bibliog(p 128) Ag '70
BOESMAN and Lena; drama. See Fugard, A.
BOETH, Richard
Assault on privacy. il Newsweek 76:15-17+ Jl 27 '70; Same abr. with title Is privacy dying? Read Digest 97:93-7 O '70
BOETSCH, Jacques
Monday of Mikis Theodorakis; reprint. il pors Sat R 53:14-15+ My 9 '70
BOETTCHER, A. L. See Hill. R. E. T. jt. auth.
BOETTI, Giovanni Battista
Father Boetti, or Sheik Mansour. M. Bishop. il Horizon 12:44-5 Sum '70 *
BOETTINGER, Henry M.
Technology in the manager's future; adaptation of address, June 1970. bibliog f il Harvard Bsns R 48:4-6+ N '70
BOGAN, Louise
Louise Bogan, 1897-1970. J. Ciardi. il por Sat R 53:20+ F 21 '70 *
Obituary
New Yorker 45:132 F 14 '70 *
BOGARDE, Dirk
Visconti in Venice. H. Alpert. il por Sat R 53:16-18 Ag 8 '70; Reply with rejoinder. L. Visconti. 53:20 D 19 '70 *
BOGEN, Robert W. See Sutherland, F. jt. auth.
BOGER, Louise Ade
Antiques; questions & answers. See issues of House & garden incorporating Living for young homemakers
BOGGS, Dane R. See Chervenick, P. A. jt. auth.
BOGGS, Hale
Excerpt from debate, April 16. 1970. Cong Digest 49:181+ Je '70
BOGGS, James
Black revolutionary power. il por Ebony 25: 152-5 Ag '70
BOGHOSIAN, Varujan
Mythmaker. il Time 95:54 F 9 '70
BOGOTA, Colombia
Galleries and museums
Colombian gem; Gold museum. H. Ruffin. il Américas 22:13-17 Mr '70
BOGS
Teen girls' battle of the bogs. Sr Schol 95:16 N 3 '69
La BOHÈME; opera. See Puccini, G.
BOHEMIANISM
See also
Hippies
BÖHM, Karl
Music to my ears; performance of Elektra. I. Kolodin. Sat R 53:46 D 12 '70 *
BOHM, Mary Frances
Butchart gardens. il Horticulture 48:38-9┐ Ag '70
Cincinnati nature center. il Horticulture 48:26-7+ My '70
BOHMANN, John
Six days in April: life and hard times of a Masters rookie. C. Kirkpatrick. il pors Sports Illus 32:50-4+ Ap 6 '70 *
BOHN, James
Oikos. il Harp Baz 103:192+ O '70
BOHNEN, Michael
Unruly giant. D. E. Prosser. il por Opera N 34:24-5 Ja 31 '70
BOHUSLAN, Sweden
Bohuslan, Sweden's answer to the Riviera. N. Stewart. il Travel 134:44-9+ Ag '70

BOIKO, Claire
Destination: Christmas! drama. Plays 30: 43-52, 96 D '70
Hotel Oak; drama. Plays 29:47-52 Ap '70
Joe White and the seven lizards; drama. Plays 29:1-12 My '70
Mobius strip; drama. Plays 30:13-22, 66 O '70
One hundred words; drama. Plays 29:45-8 My '70
Pepe and the cornfield bandit; dramatization of a fable of Old Mexico. Plays 30: 47-52 O '70
Petticoat revolution; drama. Plays 29:21-9 Ap '70
BOILER plants
See also
Steam power plants
BOILERMAKERS
See also
Babcock and Wilcox, ltd.
BOILING points
Amateur scientist; how to make an isoteniscope: an apparatus for measuring the boiling point of fluids. W. Averett. il Sci Am 223:116-21 D '70
BOISE Cascade corporation
Field of knowledge fetches $21-million. il Bsns W p 19-20 Ag 8 '70
Thousands play where Boise Cascade works. V. Louviere. il Nations Bsns 58:17 O '70
Will quality tell? il Forbes 106:51-2 Jl 15 '70
BOITO, Arrigo
Mefistofele. Criticism
New Yorker 46:105 S 19 '70 *
BOJAXHIU, Agnes Gonxha. See Teresa, Mother
BOK, Derek Curtis
President for Harvard. por Time 97:46 Ja 18 '71 *
—and Dunlop, J. T.
How trade union policy is made; excerpt from Labor and the American community. Mo Labor R 93:17-20 F '70
BOKASSA, Jean Bedel
President's daughter. il por Newsweek 76:33 D 7 '70 *
BÖKÖNYI, Sándor
Animal remains from Lepenski vir. bibliog il Science 167:1702-4 Mr 27 '70
BOLACK, Thomas Felix
Modern Johnny Appleseed. V. Kraft. il por Sports Illus 33:78-9+ N 30 '70 *
BOLAND, Edward P.
Excerpt from debate, May 27, 1970. Cong Digest 49:296+ D '70
BOLAND, John. See Moore, R. H. jr. jt. auth.
BOLDT, George Hugo
Anarchy in Tacoma; case of the Seattle Seven. por Time 96:46 D 28 '70 *
BOLES, Paul Darcy
Brother whistler; story. Seventeen 29:124-5 Je '70
I thought you were a unicorn; story. Seventeen 29:168-9 Ap '70
Summer candles; story. Ladies Home J 87: 72-3 Ag '70
BOLIN, Bert
Carbon cycle; with biographical sketch. il Sci Am 223:33+, 124-32 bibliog(p263-4) S '70
BOLIVIA
See also
Charcas
Guerrillas—Bolivia
Petroleum industry and trade—Bolivia
Political prisoners—Bolivia
Potosí
Politics and government
Bolivia: friend or foe? S. Rodman. Nat R 22:1211+ N 17 '70
Coup time again. Sr Schol 95:16 O 13 '69
Latin America: the shrinking middle. il Time 96:22-3 O 19 '70
Mandate acted upon. M. Arias. Chr Cent 87: 188-90 F 11 '70
Now you see a leftist, now you don't. H. Estenssoro B. Commonweal 93:316-18 D 25 '70
Revolution: back and forth. M. Arias. Chr Cent 87:1394-7 N 18 '70
Revolving presidency. il por Newsweek 76: 60+ O 19 '70
World around us. M. Arias. il Chr Cent 87: 1295-6 O 28 '70
Religious institutions and affairs
World around us. Chr Cent 87:308-9 Mr 11 '70
BOLKER, Henry I. and Brenner, H. S.
Polymeric structure of spruce lignin. bibliog il Science 170:173-6 O 9 '70

BOLL, Carl R.
Do's and don'ts of executive resumes. il Duns 95:47-8 F '70

BOLLING, Richard
Lindsay for president. il Look 34:73-5+ My 5 '70

BOLOGNA, Italy
Description
Italian Italy. A. Bester. il Holiday 48:36-7+ Jl '70

BOLOTOWSKY, Ilya
Squaring the circle and vice-versa. L. Campbell. il por Art N 68:38-41+ F '70 *

BOLSHEVISM. See Communism—Russia

BOLSHOI ballet
No Bolshoi. Newsweek 76:67-8 D 21 '70
Young Bolshoi in Spain. C. Irizarry. il Dance Mag 44:63-7 O '70

BOLT, Robert
Vivat! Vivat Regina. *Criticism*
New Yorker 46:160-1 N 14 '70 *

BOLTIN, Lee
Ancient Mexico and Central America; photographs; with biographical sketch. Natur Hist 79:4, 30-5 bibliog(p79) My '70

BOLTON, Robert H.
Brazilian torture: specifically new, specifically terrible. Chr Cent 87:387-8 Ap 1 '70

BOLTS and nuts
Guide to nuts & bolts. R. J. De Cristoforo. il Mech Illus 66:106-7+ N '70
Solve holding problems with a threadless nut. B. W. Ervin. il Pop Mech 134:181 O '70

BOMB detectors. See Detectors

BOMB shelters. See Atomic bomb shelters

BOMB squad, New York city. See New York (city)—Police

BOMB threats. See Threats

BOMBARDIER, ltd.
Snow job? il Forbes 105:35 F 1 '70

BOMBAY
Bombay: wealth, shantytowns, speakeasies. D. Moraes. il N Y Times Mag p34-5+ O 11 '70

BOMBE. See Desserts

BOMBECK, Erma
Up the wall (cont) Good H 170:16+ Ja; 64+ Mr; 26+ My; 171:28+ Jl; 62+ S; 34+ N '70; 172:48+ Ja '71
about
Up the wall with Erma. il por Time 95:42 Ap 13 '70 *

BOMBER command (British) See Great Britain—Royal air force—Bomber command

BOMBERS (airplanes) See Airplanes, Military

BOMBING and gunnery ranges
Navy vs. Culebra; the Atlantic fleet weapons range. G. Walter. il Life 68:47 Ap 10 '70

BOMBING planes. See Airplanes, Military

BOMBINGS, Racial. See Terrorism

BOMBINGS, Terrorist. See Terrorism

BON dancing. See Dancing, Japanese

BONAFEDE, Dom
Commissar of credibility. Nation 210:392-6 Ap 6 '70

BONAPARTE, Yvonne
Inspiration; poem. Negro Hist Bul 33:106 Ap '70

BONATTI, Enrico, and Tazieff, Haroun
Exposed guyot from the Afar Rift, Ethiopia. bibliog il Science 168:1087-9 My 29 '70
—See Gomberg, D. N. jt. auth.

BONAVENA, Oscar
Two down, one to go. il pors Time 96:48 D 21 '70 *
Weary butterfly. il pors Newsweek 76:68+ D 21 '70 *

BONBARD, Leo
Buddy is everybody's buddy. C. Phinizy. il pors Sports Illus 33:30-2+ D 7 '70

BONCI, Alessandro
Top tenors, on L.P. A. Favia-Artsay. pors Hobbies 75:35 Je '70 *

BOND, Edward
Saved. *Criticism*
America 124:47-8 Ja 16 '71 *
Nation 211:508 N 16 '70 *
New Yorker 46:133-5 N 7 '70 *
Newsweek il 76:88 N 9 '70 *
Time 96:48 N 9 '70 *
Vogue. il por 157:86 Ja 1 '71 *

BOND, Edward Lupton, 1913-
Developing responsible promotion; consumer information policies; address, October 15, 1970. Vital Speeches 37:124-8 D 1 '70

BOND, Horace Julian. See Bond, J.

BOND, Julian
Other voices, other strategies; interview. ed. by W. Terry. il pors Time 95:23-4+ Ap 6 '70
What now? address, July 2, 1970. Am Lib 1: 847-8 O '70

BONDE, James R.
Cockpit confusion. Flying 86:64 My '70

BONDED fabrics. See Textile fabrics, Laminated

BONDI, Inge
Drooping tulip heralds new business. J. Deschin. il Pop Phot 67:32+ Ag '70 *

BONDS, Ozell, Jr
Case for independent black trade unions. il por Ebony 25:142-4 Ag '70

BONDS
Aid for the markets. H. Wallich. Newsweek 75:84 Je 8 '70
Banks share in fight against pollution: earth bonds. V. Louviere. Nations Bsns 58:19 D '70
Better buy bonds, long-term bonds; interview. J. S. Nye. Forbes 105:52-3 F 15 '70
Bond market: a patch of blue. il Bsns W p 15-16 Jl 11 '70
Bonds: a market for everyman or a passing fancy? il Forbes 106:17-18 Jl 15 '70
Bonds: lure for savings; interview. S. Homer. por U S News 70:31-2 Ja 4 '71
Bonds: up sharply, but still some bargains for buyers. il U S News 69:77 D 14 '70
Dip in interest rates: what it means to borrowers. il U S News 69:65-7 Jl 27 '70
Eurobonds get caught in the squeeze. il Bsns W p74-5 Jl 18 '70
Long and short of five-year bonds. A. Hershman. Duns 95:47-9 Mr '70
Market in bonds. C. Morgello. il Newsweek 75:86 Mr 23 '70
Polluton foes find a friend at the bank. Bsns W p 19-20 Jl 4 '70
Small saver needs a better deal. Changing T 24:45-7 My '70
Solid switch to long-term debt. il Bsns W p22-3 N 7 '70
Why buy bonds? C. Rolo. Bet Hom & Gard 48:32+ D '70
Why investors rush for bonds. il Bsns W p 110 F 14 '70
See also
Municipal bonds
Saving and savings
State bonds
Taxation of bonds, securities, etc.

Marketing
Tips on buying & selling stocks & bonds. il Changing T 24:35-8 F '70

Rating
Men who make treasurers tremble; A. C. Esokait of Moody's and H. R. Fraser of S&P's. pors Forbes 106:19-20 S 1 '70

Taxation
See Taxation of bonds, securities, etc.

BONDS, Convertible
Low-risk risk? with table. Forbes 106:16 Jl 1 '70
Personal business. Bsns W p 107 S 26 '70
Will the sun shine again on convertibles? il Bsns W p 104 S 26 '70

BONDS, Earth. See Bonds

BONDS, Government
Big cash-ins of savings bonds. U S News 68:94-5 Ap 6 '70
Bonus for holders of U.S. savings bonds. U S News 69:75-6 Ag 24 '70
Higher rate on savings bonds, but disappointment for many. il U S News 68:92-4 F 16 '70
Lending money to Uncle Sam. G. Town. Har Yrs 10:21+ Jl '70
Savings bonds turn political. por Bsns W p41 My 23 '70
See also
State bonds

BONDS, Municipal. See Municipal bonds

BONDS, Revenue
Opportunity, thy name is pollution; legislation to let commercial banks underwrite water and sewage bonds. il Forbes 105:21-2 Mr 1 '70

BONDS, State. See State bonds

BONDURANT, Bob
Car of the year; cars panel. por Motor T 23:63 Ja '71 *

BONE, Larry Earl
American library in Paris: fifty years of service. il Am Lib 1:279-83 Mr '70
—and Hartz, F. R.
Taking the full ride. bibliog il pors Library J 95:3244-6 O 1 '70

BONE marrow. See Marrow

BONE resorption. See Bones—Diseases

BONE surgery. See Orthopedia

BONEFISH fishing
Bonefish for everybody. G. Heinold. il Outdoor Life 145:12+ Ja '70

BONERS. See Blunders

BONES
　　See also
Cartilage

　　　　　Diseases
Endotoxin: stimulation of bone resorption in tissue culture. E. Hausmann and others. bibliog il Science 168:862-4 My 15 '70
Let's wipe out osteoporosis. G. Town. Har Yrs 10:32-3 O '70
Repairing brittle bones; calcium infusions for osteoporosis. B. J. Culliton. il Sci N 97:562-3 Je 6 '70
Strengthening brittle bones; remedy for osteoporosis. il Time 96:43-4 Ag 17 '70
　　See also
Osteogenesis imperfecta
Paget's disease
Rickets

BONEWITS, Isaac
Bachelor of magic. il por Newsweek 75:78 Je 22 '70 *

BONFANTE, Jordan
Three are each other's only close friends. il pors Life 69:49-52+ S 18 '70
(ed) See Hussein. Isolation of a king

BONGARTZ, Roy
It's called earth art, and boulderdash. il N Y Times Mag p 16-17+ F 1 '70
It's not called Hells Canyon for nothing. il Holiday 47:52-3+ My '70
Muckuppery along the Potomac. Esquire 73:70+ Je '70
Remember bomb shelters? Esquire 73:130+ My '70
Three meanies. il Esquire 74:107-14+ Ag '70
Wayne Cochran lets the sunshine in and vice versa. pors Esquire 73:108-10+ Ap '70
Who am I? The Indian sickness. Nation 210:496-8 Ap 27 '70

BONGIORNO, James
Build the add-on squarer. il Pop Electr 32:51-3+ My '70
Build the X10/X100 instrument sensitivity booster. il Pop Electr 33:43-7 Jl '70
Lab-quality pulse generator. il Radio-Electr 41:37-41+ F '70

BONHAM, Roger D.
Ceramic world of Bonnie Staffel. il por Ceram Mo 18:19-23 Mr '70
Liturgical enamels of Charles Bartley Jeffery. il por Ceram Mo 18:14-17 D '70
Paper core pottery. il Ceram Mo 18:14-17 My '70
Robert Engle, the man behind the faces; Robert Engle demonstrates throwing off the hump. il pors Ceram Mo 18:12-15 Ja '70
Tom Shafer demonstrates building a jar. il pors Ceram Mo 17:14-18 D '69

BONHOEFFER, Dietrich
Aftermath of Flossenburg: Bonhoeffer, 1945-1970; interview, ed. by H. E. Wright. E. Bethge. por Chr Cent 87·656-9 My 27 '70 *
Dietrich Bonhoeffer. Chr Today 14:34 Ap 10 '70 *
Dietrich Bonhoeffer, by E. Bethge. Review
Chr Cent 87:822-5 Jl 1 '70. C. Green *
Chr Today 15:17 D 4 '70. K. Hamilton *
Commonweal 93:27-8 O 2 '70. M. Marty *
New Repub 163:24+ S 19 '70. A. Wilder *
Sat R 53:17-22 My 30 '70. D. Berrigan *

BONI, Ada
Italian regional cooking; excerpts. il Ladies Home J 87:122-3+ My '70

BONI, John
Weakest link. Sat R 53:4 Jl 25 '70

BONILLA, Antulio Parrilla-. See Parrilla-Bonilla, A.

BONING of fishes. See Fish as food

BONINSEGNA, Celestina
Historical records. A. Favia-Artsay. pors Hobbies 74:36 F '70 *

BONITO fishing
Where little tuna hit the beach; Cape Hatteras, N.C. J. B. Robinson. il Field & S 75:64-5+ My '70

BONITOS (boats) See Sailboats

BONN, Myrtle
Reading pays. il Am Ed 6:26 O '70

BONN
　　　　　Music
Stockhausen versus Beethoven. P. Moor. Hi Fi 20:secII 27 Mr '70

BONNEFOUS, Jean Pierre
New Apollo? O. Maynard. il pors Dance Mag 45:38-41 Ja '71 *

BONNER, Harry
California's most fabulous fishing grounds. il Field & S 75:50-1+ D '70

BONNEVILLE national speed trials. See Automobile racing

BONSAI. See Trees, Dwarf

BONSE, Ulrich. See Hart, M. jt. auth.

BONUS system
Slump puts Santa on a diet. il Bsns W p37-8 D 19 '70

BONYNGE, Richard
Pinnacle; interview, ed. by F. Rizzo. pors Opera N 34:14-16 Ap 4 '70

　　　　　about
Giselle, all of it for the first time on records. C. J. Luten. por Am Rec G 36:868-9 Jl '70 *
Musical events: Gluck's Orfeo ed Euridice. W. Sargeant. New Yorker 46:134+ O 3 '70 *

BOOBY traps, Military. See Mines, Military

BOOHER, Edward E.
U.S. publishing's new look in newly developing countries; interview. il por Pub W 197:26-9 Ap 6 '70

BOOJUM trees. See Cirios

BOOK advertising. See Books—Advertising

BOOK auctions. See Book sales

BOOK awards, National. See National book awards

BOOK binding. See Bookbinding

BOOK cases. See Bookcases

BOOK catalogs. See Catalogs, Library

BOOK censorship. See Censorship

BOOK clubs
FTC challenges negative option mail sale. S. Wagner. Pub W 197:33-4 My 25 '70
International book clubs: a new way of getting books cheaply across many borders. H. R. Lottman. il Pub W 198:pt2 164-9 S 21 '70

BOOK collecting
Clarence Holte's search into the black past. il pors Ebony 25:94-6+ Ap '70
84, Charing Cross road; condensation. H. Hanff. il Read Digest 97:221-4+ D '70
　　See also
Libraries, Private

BOOK covers
Very quiet show has gems of '20s style design; Cover '70 exhibition. M. R. Kraner. bibliog il Pub W 198:62-6 N 16 '70

BOOK design
Cookbooks delight mind, eye, and palate. il Pub W 197:56-7 Mr 23 '70
Designer fuses elements in books with strong text and pictures. M. R. Kraner. il por Pub W 198:60-3 Jl 27 '70
Designing and producing the New English Bible. il Pub W 197:74+ Mr 9 '70
FullerAgelFiore: visual-verbal treatment for I seem to be a verb. M. R. Kraner. il Pub W 198:42-3 O 19 '70
Getting it all together in The rainbow box. M. R. Kraner. il Pub W 198:46-7 O 26 '70
Gotthard de Beauclair: delight in design. il por Pub W 197:72-3 F 9 '70
Interesting design may mean back to fundamentals, two University press designers tell AIGA clinic. Pub W 197:45-6 Mr 16 '70
New World's creative director builds a '70s image and sales, too; interview, ed. by M. R. Kraner. M. Charles. il por Pub W 198:48-50 D 28 '70
Peter Max, the ubiquitous designer and his book publishing debut. M. R. Kraner. il por Pub W 197:70-1 Ap 27 '70
Very quiet show has gems of '20s style design; Cover '70 exhibition. M. R. Kraner. bibliog il Pub W 198:62-6 N 16 '70
Virginia Lee Burton's dynamic sense of design. L. Kingman. il Horn Bk 46:449-60, 593-602 O-D '70

BOOK ends and bookracks
Two bookrests and study aids. il Consumer Bul 53:27-8 F '70

BOOK exhibits
AIGA fifty books show. P. Darras. il bibliog Pub W 197:28+ My 18 '70
Chicago book show, a review. S. Allen. bibliog il Pub W 197:52+ My 4 '70
Multiple tie-in: book and exhibit; Israel: the reality. il Pub W 197:38-9 Ja 12 '70
New titles, services shown at Irish bookmen's exhibit. Pub W 197:19-20 My 18 '70
Publishing at Radcliffe; Work in print exhibition. il Pub W 197:40-1 Je 15 '70
Southern and Midwestern book choices announced. Pub W 197:67-8 Mr 2 '70

BOOKBINDING
Mini-giant of the bindery industry. il Ebony 25:128-30+ My '70
Stronger books, possible savings; Hellerbond method. L. Shatzkin. il Pub W 198:66-8 N 16 '70

Materials
Modern museum's soft book for Oldenburg's soft sculptures. il Pub W 198:52 N 9 '70

BOOKCASES
Best decoration in the world is a roomful of books. W. Baldwin. House & Gard 138:6-7+ D '70
Black iron & red wood. il Mech Illus 66:110 Ap '70

BOOKCHIN, Murray
Toward an ecological solution. il Ramp Mag 8:6-8+ My '70

BOOKLETS. See Pamphlets

BOOKMOBILES
Denver, Colorado: El Número cinco; summer bookmobile. F. A. Bucy. il Wilson Lib Bul 44:765-6 Mr '70
San Joaquin Valley, California: la Biblioteca ambulante. M. B. Reynolds. Wilson Lib Bul 44:767 Mr '70

BOOKRACKS. See Book ends and bookracks

BOOKS
See also
Block books
Copyright

Advertising
Christmas headlines a la Brentano. il Pub W 198:267 Ag 31 '70
Fall highspots, October—December. il Pub W 198:207-35 Ag 31 '70
Making good guy ads work; Chinook book-shop. J. Noyes. il Pub W 197:147-9 Je 8 '70
Publisher and bookseller get together on advertising. Pub W 198:32 O 26 '70
Publishing scene; using sales to create advertising. D. Dempsey. Sat R 53:33 My 9 '70
September books; promotional calendar. il Pub W 197:88-107 Je 8 '70
Spring highspots, February through May. il Pub W 197:199-231 Ja 26 '70
Summer books; June through August. il Pub W 197:29-52 Ap 27 '70

See also
Book week
Booksellers and bookselling—Publicity
Publishers' publicity association
Review copies of books

Anecdotes, facetiae, satire, etc.
Letter to an unknown (and likely to remain so) author. Pub W 198:44 O 26 '70

Classification
See Classification

Collectors and collecting
See Book collecting

Exhibitions
See Book exhibits

Indexes
Terms of reference. F. Littler. Sat R 53:24 N 14 '70

Marketing
Long-range prospects in book production. V. Strauss. il Pub W 198:28-31 D 14 '70

Out of print books
Out of print. M. Holroyd. Am Scholar 39:310+ Spr '70

Photographic reproduction and projection
See also
Microforms

Prices
See also
Books—Reprints

Reprints
New nostalgia: many happy returns. B. Klaw. il Am Heritage 21:34-9 Je '70
Profiles: G. Mardersteig, printer of Officina Badoni and Stamperia Valdonega editions in Verona, Italy. W. Sargeant. por New Yorker 46:32-6+ Jl 11 '70
Reprint hassle: airing in Detroit. Library J 95:2601-2 Ag '70
Reprint wish-fulfillment; letter to the editor. S. Crane. Library J 95:3701 N 1 '70

Bibliography
Books to come. il Library J 96:111-12+ Ja 1 '71

Reprints, Unauthorized
See Copyright—Unauthorized reprints

BOOKS. Filmed. See Film adaptations
BOOKS, Illustration of. See Illustration of books and periodicals
BOOKS abroad prize. See Literary prizes
BOOKS and reading
Books. M. Muggeridge. See issues of Esquire
Books in the field. bibliog il por Wilson Lib Bul 44:616-31 F '70
Bookshelf. P. Goldberger. Sr Schol 96:17 F 16 '70
Case for irrelevance. M. D. Blyth. Engl J 59:380-3+ Mr '70
Neglected books; a symposium. Am Scholar 39:318+ Spr '70
Peripatetic reviewer. E. Weeks. See issues of Atlantic

See also
Biography
Book selection
Books as gifts
Childrens literature
Childrens reading
High school students—Reading
Illustrated books
Immoral literature and pictures
International book year, 1972
Libraries
Libraries, Private
Libraries and readers
Literary criticism
Literature
National book committee
Picture books
Recreation—Literature
Religious literature
Right to read program
Young adults reading

Best books
Best books for young adults, 1968-1969. Todays Ed 59:16-17 Ap '70
Book review; ed. by J. Serebnick and others. See issues of Library journal
Books; critics' choices for Christmas (cont) Commonweal 93:254-61 D 4 '70
Critic's choice of 1970; comp. by G. Wolff. il Newsweek 76:94-6 D 21 '70
Fall book roundup. V. S. Kearney. America 123:461-2+ N 28 '70
Notable books of 1969 selected by ALA group. Pub W 197:128-9 F 23 '70; Same. Am Lib 1:276-7 Mr '70; Library J 95:1270 Ap 1 '70; Todays Ed 59:54-5 My '70
Notable nominations. Am Lib 1:91, 297-8, 714-15, 1088 Ja, Mr, Jl, D '70
Recent and, alas, neglected. Commonweal 93:108-9 O 23 '70
Six on the isle. L. Conger. Writer 83:8-10 Ja '70
Year's best books. Time 97:76 Ja 4 '71

See also
Book selection
Childrens literature

Bibliography
Books. See issues of Business week
Books to come; ed. by J. P. Donathan. Library J 95:527-88, 2322-77, 3313-14+ F 1, Je 15, O 1 '70
Choice books for the special season. Sat R 53:30+ N 28 '70
Deck the shelves; for $3.95 and up. il Time 96:92-4+ D 14 '70
Emphasis. B. Diamonstein. Harp Baz 103:184-5 Mr; 98-9+ Je; 102 O '70
Fall highspots, October—December. il Pub W 198:207-35 Ag 31 '70
International highspots, October 1970-April 1971. il Pub W 198:pt2 98-134+ S 21 '70
New books; for your house and garden. J. Herbert. House & Gard 137:60+ Ap '70
New fall books. P. C. Rule. America 123:236-7+ O 3 '70
New Yorker lists at this season some books by its contributors published during the year (cont) New Yorker 46:180-1 N 28 '70; Same. 46:92-3 D 19 '70
Note/book. America 123:24, 47, 74, 102, 130, 158, 185, 217, 244, 271, 303, 332, 385, 414 Jl 11-N 14 '70
October-December previews. il Pub W 197:108-27 Je 8 '70
Portfolio of summer reading. R. Lekachman. Duns 96:9 Ag '70
Readers miscellany; a sampling of books for special interests. J. Fletcher. Library J 95:498-9, 907, 1372-3, 1729-30, 2157, 2446-7 F 1, Mr 1, Ap 1, My 1, Je 1, Jl '70
Reviewer's choice. M. Maddocks. il Life 68:10 F 6; 12 Je 5; 69:6-7 Ag 7; 16-17 O 23; 10 D 4 '70

BOOKS and reading—Bibliography—*Continued*
Short reviews: books. P. Adams. See issues of Atlantic
Spring book roundup. America 122:473-81 My 2 '70
Spring highspots, February through May. il Pub W 197:199-231 Ja 26 '70
Spring previews 1971. January through June. il Pub W 198:236-46 Ag 31 '70
Summer books; June through August. il Pub W 197:29-52 Ap 27 '70
Summer previews, June through September. Pub W 197:232-40 Ja 26 '70
This week. See issues of Christian century
Weekly record. See issues of Publishers' weekly
White House home library. bibliog il Pub W 197:47-52 Mr 2 '70

Study and teaching
See Literature—Study and teaching

United States
See Books and reading

BOOKS as gifts
Art books for Christmas. il Am Artist 34:25-8+ N '70
Beautiful books for Christmas people. il Harp Baz 104:122-3 D '70
Pile them under the tree. Chr Cent 87:1516-18 D 16 '70
'Tis the season for list making. S. Powell. Bsns W p6 D 12 '70
See also
Books and reading—Best books

BOOKS for children. See Childrens literature
BOOKS for the sick
See also
Libraries, Hospital
BOOKS in print (publication)
Books in print 1969: an analysis of errors. N. Cambier and others. il Am Lib 1:901-2 O '70
BOOKSELLERS and bookselling
Who really cares about the retail bookstore? C. B. Grannis. Pub W 197:25 My 11 '70
See also
Books—Advertising
Books—Marketing
Canvassing
College bookstores
Publishers and publishing

Art literature
See also
Museum store association

Childrens literature
Feedback on children's books; highlights of panel discussion, June 8, 1970. il Pub W 197:56-9+ Je 29 '70
Report from England; London's Children's book centre. Z. Sutherland. Sat R 53:28 Jl 25 '70

Drama
Selling drama and film books in Manhattan; Drama book shop and Gotham book mart. M. B. Tarshish. il Pub W 197:44-6 My 25 '70

Greeting cards
Pointers on selling personalized greetings. Pub W 198:55-6 S 14 '70

Immoral literature and pictures
New York porno shops booming on borrowed time. M. O'Hanlon. il Pub W 198:45-6 D 28 '70

Insurance
Developing a balanced insurance program. H. D. Greene, 3d. Pub W 198:35-6 D 7; 25 D 14 '70

International aspects
International book clubs: a new way of getting books cheaply across many borders. H. R. Lottman. il Pub W 198:pt2 164-9 S 21 '70

Jewish literature
Jewish bookstore-publisher: tradition, innovation; Bloch's book shop and publishing company. M. B. Tarshish. il Pub W 198:45-6 S 7 '70

Occult literature
Brentano's new boutique. il Pub W 198:55-6 Jl 20 '70
Shop venture into unknown; Gnostica bookstore, Minneapolis. C. L. Weschcke. il Pub W 197:71-3 Mr 9 '70

Paperback books
About children's paperbacks, the bookseller cries "I want more!" il Pub W 198:41 Jl 20 20 '70

Publicity
Store advertising and publicity; highlights of panel discussion, June 9, 1970. il Pub W 197:64-5 Je 29 '70

Religious literature
Morehouse-Barlow bookstore reaches a wide constituency. Pub W 198:68-9 S 28 '70
New generation Christian bookstore; Logos bookstore, Ann Arbor. J. Carlson. il por Pub W 198:28-9 N 30 '70
Religious books for the general bookstore; highlights of panel discussion, June 9, 1970. il Pub W 197:62-3 Je 29 '70
See also
Christian booksellers association

Secondhand books
Ex libris; Lowdermilk's in Washington to make way for subway terminal. il Time 95:19 F 23 '70

Stock
Canadian alternative to inventory proposals. il Pub W 198:55 S 14 '70
Continuing discussion of inventory controls. G. R. Smith. Pub W 198:38-9 Ag 10 '70
Organizing book inventory the A&A way. J. Huenefeld. Pub W 197:90-1 Je 29 '70
RAP-TAG and EDP: happy marriage? P. Welsh. Pub W 198:46 S 21 '70
Record keeping alone isn't inventory control. L. Shatzkin. Pub W 198:41-2 Ag 3 '70
Tag answers booksellers' ordering/inventory plea. il Pub W 197:29 My 11 '70

Technical literature
Getting technical about books at K&B. il Pub W 198:59-60 N 16 '70

Textbooks
Barnes & Noble's revitalization program. Pub W 198:69-70 S 28 '70
Opman's rebuttal. G. R. Smith. Pub W 197:26-7 My 18 '70

California
ABA announces plans for September regional meeting. Pub W 198:248-9 Ag 31 '70
Ecology book store story; Berkeley, Calif. R. D. Shoop. il Org Gard & Farm 17:70-2 N '70

Canada
See also
Canadian booksellers association

Colorado
Making good guy ads work; Chinook bookshop. J. Noyes. il Pub W 197:147-9 Je 8 '70

England
Blend of traditional and modern; Heffers bookstore in Cambridge. il Pub W 198:43-5 O 26 '70
84, Charing Cross road; condensation. H. Hanff. il Read Digest 97:221-4+ D '70
Report from England; London's Children's book centre. Z. Sutherland. Sat R 53:28 Jl 25 '70

Finland
Finnish bookstore: opulence, realism and sharply contemporary design. il Pub W 197:76-7 F 2 '70

Great Britain
Chicago and Aviemore: a contrast. G. R. Smith. il Pub W 198:43-4 O 12 '70
See also
Booksellers and bookselling—England

Illinois
Getting technical about books at K&B. il Pub W 198:59-60 N 16 '70
Kroch's & Brentano's engaged in major store revitalization. il Pub W 197:258-60 Ja 26 '70
Remodeling adds freshness to K&B; remodeled main store, Chicago. il Pub W 198:44-6 N 9 '70

Massachusetts
Bookshop is thirty miles at sea; Mitchell's book corner, Nantucket. il Pub W 198:39-40 Ag 24 '70

Michigan
New generation Christian bookstore; Logos bookstore, Ann Arbor. J. Carlson. il por Pub W 198:28-9 N 30 '70

Minnesota
Shop ventures into unknown; Gnostica bookstore, Minneapolis. C. L. Weschcke. il Pub W 197:71-3 Mr 9 '70

BOOKSELLERS and bookselling—*Continued*

Missouri
Money loses in bookbuyer's battle. il Pub W
198:26 D 14 '70

Nevada
Strip's bookseller; B. Dalton. il Pub W 198:
39-40 O 19 '70

New York (state)
Barnes & Noble's revitalization program. Pub
W 198:69-70 S 28 '70
Books enter a third world at F.A.O. Schwarz.
il Pub W 197:71-2 Mr 2 '70
Brentano's new boutique. il Pub W 198:55-6
Jl 20 '70
Christmas headlines a la Brentano. il Pub W
198:267 Ag 31 '70
G. Schirmer's sells books. M. B. Tarshish. il
Pub W 197:143-4 F 23 '70
Jewish bookstore-publisher: tradition, inno-
vation; Bloch's book shop and publishing
company. M. B. Tarshish. il Pub W 198:45-6
S 7 '70
Laurel: haven for photo book buffs; Laurel
book center, in New York city. J. Deschin.
il Pop Phot 66:28+ Je '70
La librería, New York, is center for Latin cul-
ture. il por Pub W 197:67-8 Ja 19 '70
Morehouse-Barlow bookstore reaches a wide
constituency. Pub W 198:68-9 S 28 '70
New York porno shops booming on bor-
rowed time. M. O'Hanlon. il Pub W 198:45-
6 D 28 '70
Odyssey of an art book dealer in New York;
Wittenborn's of New York. M. B. Tarshish.
il por Pub W 198:43-4 Jl 6 '70
Personal bookshop succeeds in shopping center area; Paperbacks, etc. Smithtown. E.
Oliver. Pub W 197:48-9 Ap 20 '70
Seaport bookshop lures readers downtown
in New York. il Pub W 198:29-30 N 23 '70
Selling drama and film books in Manhattan; Drama book shop and Gotham book
mart. M. B. Tarshish. il Pub W 197:44-6
My 25 '70

North Carolina
Branch shop with new slant on together-
ness; Intimate bookshop, Chapel Hill, N.C.
B. Barrett. il Pub W 197:55-6 Je 1 '70

Ohio
Night Higbee's put out the red carpet. il por
Pub W 197:40-1 Mr 16 '70

United States
Book-of-the-day club; how Ladies and gentle-
men, Easy Aces has been faring. G. Ace.
Sat R 53:6 O 31; 8 D 19 '70
Booksellers for peace announce fall plans. Pub
W 198:51 O 5 '70
Chicago and Aviemore: a contrast. G. R.
Smith. il Pub W 198:43-4 O 12 '70
Direct sales of books in America; excerpts
from address. G. R. Smith. Pub W 197:
51-4 Je 15 '70; Reply. H. M. Levin. 198:
15-18 Ag 10 '70
Look at mass marketing in the 1970s. D.
Yellen. Pub W 198:31-2 Ag 24 '70
Opinionated man. G. R. Smith. See occa-
sional issues of Publishers' weekly
Profits up as booksellers look to paper;
Bookshop openings show evidence of new
growth. Pub W 197:69-71 F 9 '70
Retailing. See issues of Publishers' weekly
See also
American booksellers association
Christian booksellers association
College bookstores
Women's national book association

Washington, D.C.
Ex libris; Lowdermilk's in Washington to
make way for subway terminal. il Time 95:
19 F 23 '70
Lowdermilk bookshop is victim of progress.
Pub W 197:54-5 Mr 23 '70

BOOKSHELVES. See Bookcases

BOOKSTORES. See Booksellers and bookselling; College bookstores

BOORSTIN, Daniel J.
American century; myth vs. reality; inter-
view. il por U S News 69:64-7 O 19 '70
Case of hypochondria. por Newsweek 76:27-9
Jl 6 '70; Same abr. with title Is America
really sick? Read Digest 97:92-4 S '70

BOOT and shoe industry. See Shoes—Trade and
manufacture

BOOTH, Gary M. and Metcalf, R. L.
Phenylthioacetate: a useful substrate for the
histochemical and colorimetric detection of
cholinesterase. bibliog il Science 170:455-7 O
23 '70

BOOTH, Martha
Memo to English teachers re: individualized
reading. Engl J 59:1276-8 D '70

BOOTH, Philip
Lines from an orchard once surveyed by
Thoreau; poem. Harper 241:75 Ag '70

BOOTLEGGING of commodities. See Black
markets

BOOTS and shoes. See Shoes

BOOZ, Charles S. Jr
America's cup: hanging by a thread? il
Motor B 126:46+ Ag '70

BOOZ, Rose M. and Cobb, Tony
It can be done. il Yachting 128:55-7 O '70

BOQUEN monastery. See Monasteries

BORCH, Fred J.
GE puzzle. A. A. Butkus. il por Duns 96:34-
8+ Jl '70 *

BORCHERDING, J. W. See Everett, G. M.
jt. auth.

BORCHERDING, James R.
Dairy management (cont of) What's new.
See issues of Successful farming

BORDEAUX
Music
Report:
European premiere of The plough and
the stars. D. Stevens. Opera N 34:27-8
My 16 '70

BORDELLOS. See Prostitution

BORDINAT, Gene
Rap 'n 'pinion. por Motor T 22:26 O '70

BORENSTEIN, E. Lorenz
Jazz. il Travel & Camera 33:32-5+ S '70

BORES (persons)
Doing their tiresome thing; Time essay. D.
Auchincloss. il Time 96:31 Jl 13 '70
Who blew the U.S. nose count? F. Deford. il
Sports Illus 33:72-3+ D 21 '70

BORETZ, Allen. See Murray, J. jt. auth.

BORGENICHT, Evelyn
(ed) Time out for TV. See issues of PTA
magazine
—See Davidson, M. jt. auth.

BORGES, Jorge Luis
Adam cast forth; One morning in 1649; Rose
and Milton; poems, tr. by R. Eberhart.
Poetry 116:299-301 Ag '70
After the Japanese; poem, tr. by N. Di
Giovanni. New Yorker 46:199 D 5 '70
Challenge; story, tr. by N. T. Di Giovanni
and the author. New Yorker 46:32-3 My
23 '70
Doctor Brodie's report; story, tr. by the au-
thor and N. T. Di Giovanni. Atlan 227:67-70
Ja '71
Ibn Hakkan al-Bokhari, dead in his labyrinth;
story, tr. by N. T. Di Giovanni and the
author. New Yorker 46:34-8 Ap 25 '70
Israel; poem, tr. by N. T. Di Giovanni. New
Yorker 45:34 F 7 '70
Man on the threshold; story, tr. by the author
and N. T. Di Giovanni. New Yorker 46:39-
41 Ap 4 '70
Meeting; story, tr. by N. T. Di Giovanni
and the author. New Yorker 46:30-3 Ag
8 '70
Profiles; autobiographical notes, ed. by N. T.
Di Giovanni. New Yorker 46:40-4+ S 19
'70
Reader; poem, tr. by N. T. Di Giovanni.
Harper 241:6 D '70
—and Casares, A. B.
Evening with Ramón Bonavena; story, tr.
by N. T. Di Giovanni and the authors. New
Yorker 46:38-41 D 19 '70
Immortals; story, tr. by the authors and N.
T. Di Giovanni. New Yorker 45:34-5 F 14 '70

about
At home in his mind. R. Christ. Nation
211:86-8 Ag 3 '70 *
Books. G. Steiner. New Yorker 46:109-10+ Je
20 '70 *
Dagger of deliverance. E. Warner. por Time
96:80 N 30 '70 *
Fantasist of the intellect. J. Finn. New Repub
163:28+ D 5 '70 *
People are talking about... por Vogue 155:
160-1 Mr 1 '70 *

BORGESE, Elisabeth (Mann)
Prospects for peace in the oceans. il Sat R
53:15-22 S 26 '70

BORGESON, Griffith
Engines of Ing. Ferrari. il por Motor T 22:
34-7+ N '70
Four cylinder, twin cam, sixteen valve American dream. il pors Motor T 22:56-61+ My
'70

BORGSTROM, Georg A.
Dual challenge of health and hunger: a global
crisis; reprint. il Bul Atom Sci 26:42-6 O
'70

BORLAND, Hal
Flowers of the fifty. Audubon 72:18-27 Jl '70
Plains, a boy, a summer day; excerpt from
Country editor's boy. il Audubon 72:42-7
My '70; Same. Read Digest 97:37-41 Ag
'70
Quiet in the night. il Audubon 72:26-7 N '70
Snowstorm. il Audubon 72:4-13 Ja '70
BORLAND, Tracy
Modern art around you; photographs. Farm
J 94:44-5 Mr '70
BORLAUG, Norman Ernest
Nobel for greening. il por Newsweek 76:50-1
N 2 '70 *
Nobel peace prize: developer of high-yield
wheat receives award. L. R. Brown. por
Science 170:518-19 O 30 '70 *
Peace and the green revolution. il por Sci N
98:347 O 31 '70 *
Sowing a green revolution. por Time 96:42
N 2 '70 *
Wheat breeder who won the Peace prize;
with editorial comment. C. P. Streeter. il
pors Farm J 94:16-17+, 46 D '70 *
Wheat whiz wins. por Sr Schol 97:8 N 16
'70 *
BORMAN, Frank
Colonel Borman reports on trip on behalf of
prisoners of war; transcript of news confer-
ence, September 2, 1970. Dept State Bul
63:344-6 S 28 '70
U.S. prisoners of war in southeast Asia; ad-
dress, September 22, 1970. Dept State Bul
63:405-8 O 12 '70; Same. Vital Speeches 37:
24-6 O 15 '70
about
Colonel Borman undertakes mission relating
to prisoners of war; statement, August 7,
1970. R. M. Nixon. Dept State Bul 63:276
S 7 '70 *
See also
Space flight to the moon—Manned flights—
Apollo 8 flight
BORMANN, F. Herbert, and Likens, G. E.
Nutrient cycles of an ecosystem; with bio-
graphical sketches.. il Sci Am 223:15, 92-101
O '70
BORN, Max
Obituary
Phys Today por 23:97+ Mr '70. M. G.
Mayer *
BORNE, Mortimer
Chromatic wood sculpture of Mortimer
Borne; interview. il Natur Hist 79:28-33+
N '70
BORNELH, Giraut de. See Giraut de Bornelh
BORNEMEIER, Walter Carl
Rx for the family-doctor shortage. Read Digest
97:103-7 Jl '70
Revolution in medical care; address, June
24, 1970. Vital Speeches 36:632-4 Ag 1 '70
BORNEO
See also
Investments, Foreign (in Borneo)
BOROBUDUR, Java
Borobudur. A. J. Toynbee. il Horizon 12:16-25
Wint '70
BORODIN, Aleksandr Porfir'evich
Borodin Second symphony: five views. M. N.
Kanny. por Am Rec G 36:420-1 F '70 *
BOROSON, Warren
Parent and child. il N Y Times Mag p87+
D 13 '70
BOROUGH of Manhattan community college.
See New York (city) City university of New
York—Borough of Manhattan community
college
BOROWITZ, Eugene B.
Jewish theology faces the 1970's. bibliog f
Ann Am Acad 387:22-9 Ja '70
Religious ghetto: summary of addresses. pors
Pub W 197:38 Je 1 '70
BORRELLI, Mario
Naples' Father Borrelli to leave priesthood.
Chr Cent 87:1344 N 11 '70 *
BORROWING of money. See Credit
BORSCH, William
Wild Willie. B. Lang. il pors Hot Rod 23:
52-4 My '70 *
BORST, Lyle B.
Megalithic plan underlying Canterbury
cathedral. bibliog Science 163:567-70; 166:
774; 167:333 F 7, N 7 '69. Ja 23 '70
BORST, Robert D.
Space-saver hutch built in a closet. il Pop
Mech 134:102-4 Ag '70
BORSTAL boy; drama. See McMahon, F.
BORTON, Terry
What's left when schools' forgotten? il Sat
R 53:69-71+ Ap 18 '70
BORUS, Michael E.
Using unemployment insurance wage reports
as a data source. Mo Labor R 93:66-7 Jl
'70

BOS, Megchelina Shore-. See Shore-Bos, M.
BOSC, Robert
Charles de Gaulle: they remember him well.
por America 123:563-4 D 26 '70
BOSCH, Hieronymus
Mad world of Hieronymus Bosch. G. Highet.
il Horizon 12:66-81, sup(folded reproduction)
Spr '70 *
BOSE, Buddhadeva
For my forty-eighth winter; Two birds;
poems. Poetry 116:285-6 Ag '70
BOSE, Keith
Fired at 49. I. Taves. il pors Look 34:44-7+
D 1 '70 *
BOSERUP, Anders
Politics of protracted conflict. il Trans-Action
7:22-31 bibliog(p64) Mr '70
BOSHINSKI, Blanche
Kids rule for writing. Writers Digest 50:31-2
Jl '70
BOSLEY, Harold A.
Quiet storm in the churches. Chr Cent 87:
1449-52 D 2 '70
BOSOM exercise. See Exercise
BOSS, Benjamin
Star cataloguer. il por Sky & Tel 40:351 D
'70 *
BOSS, Lewis J.
Notes on 1969 solar and lunar eclipses. il R
Pop Astron 63:10-11 Ag '69
—See Pilcher, F. jt. auth.
BOSSEN, David A.
Portrait of a promising young venture. il
por Forbes 105:35 Je 15 '70 *
BOSTELMANN, Carl John
Remembering names of American rivers;
poem. il Am For 76:40-1 Ap '70
BOSTON

Architecture
Boston granite. il Arch Forum 132:64-9 Je '70

Art
Boston. J. Koethe. Art N 69:18+ My; 30+ O
'70; 12+ Ja '71
See also
National center of Afro-American artists

Banks
Banco de Boston's end run to Belem. Bsns W
p22 Ja 2 '71
It takes more than a banker to run a bank;
State street bank & trust co. il por Bsns W
p38-40 N 7 '70

City hall
Boston's open center: City hall plaza. J. M.
Dixon. il Arch Forum 132:24-31 Je '70

City planning
Back Bay's sedate square. il Arch Forum
133:60-3 O '70
Innovative lighting dramatizes garage design.
J. F. Mulhern and W. R. McGrath. il Am
City 85:114+ Ja '70

Climate
Boston's heaviest snowstorm of record. C. H.
Pierce. il Weatherwise 22:230-5 D '69

Clubs
Social history of the greater Boston clubs,
by A. W. Williams. Review
Newsweek il 76:116+ O 19 '70. K. Auchincloss

Education
Come to the Store-front learning center. T.
Mofford and J. Mofford. il Schol Teach Sec
Teach Sup p 13-15 F 2 '70
In Roxbury, way out of a fortress. J. Kozol.
Ed Digest 35:12-15 My '70

Galleries and museums
Boston, new directions; Parker street 470.
C. Andreae. il Art in Am 58:102-3 My '70
See also
Boston children's museum
Boston museum of fine arts
Boston museum of science

History
Why Massachusetts loves the Kennedys. F.
Russell. il Nat R 22:836-9 Ag 11 '70

Hospitals
Boston city hospital. il Arch Rec 147:119-24
My '70
Doctor in the TV set; MGH system for
telediagnosis. il Life 69:77-9 N 27 '70
Five patients; excerpt. M. Crichton. Ladies
Home J 87:34+ Jl '70

BOSTON—*Continued*

Housing

Beggars' war; controversy over off-campus housing in Boston area. il Newsweek 76:72 S 7 '70

Boston housing forecasts a national crisis. J. Willy. America 122:556-9 My 23 '70

Lighting

Back to gas lights; Bay Village area. il Am City 85:130 Ap '70

Monuments, statues, etc.

Crispus Attucks; address at dedication of monument, 1888. J. Fiske. il Negro Hist Bul 33:58-68 Mr '70

Music

Behind the scenes. M. Steinberg. il Hi Fi 20: secl 15-16 Jl '70

Report:
Good soldier Schweik. H. Neville. Opera N 34:24-5 Je 13 '70
See also
Boston symphony orchestra
Opera company of Boston

Police

Staying alive; violence by the Tactical patrol force; letter. J. A. Stillman. New Repub 162:30-1 My 30 '70

Politics and government

Breeze that whispered Louise. Nat R 22:1038 O 6 '70

Why Massachusetts loves the Kennedys. F. Russell. il Nat R 22:836-9 Ag 11 '70

Social settlements

Ellis memorial & Eldredge house, inc. il Antiques 98:554 O '70

Water supply

Boston worries over radioactive water. Am City 85:26 Ag '70

BOSTON archdiocese. See Catholic church—Dioceses

BOSTON ballet company
Boston ballet company; Savoy theatre. Boston. S. Smoliar. Dance Mag 44:22 Je '70
Boston ballet company with University chorale of Boston college; Alice Tully Hall, NYC. M. Marks. Dance Mag 44:93 My '70
Comedy classic; Coppélia. W. Terry. il por Sat R 53:51 Je 6 '70
Notes from Boston. M. Marks. il Dance Mag 44:62-7 Jl '70

BOSTON bluefish fishing. See Pollack fishing

BOSTON Bruins (hockey team) See Hockey teams

BOSTON children's museum
Children's museum whets kids' curiosity. A. Rosenthal. il Todays Health 48:45-8 Jl '70

BOSTON colleges and universities. See Colleges and universities—Massachusetts

BOSTON marathon. See Running

BOSTON massacre, 1770
Boston massacre and Crispus Attucks. il Negro Hist Bul 33:56-7 Mr '70

BOSTON museum of fine arts
Back Bay centennial. il Newsweek 75:105-6 F 23 '70
Boston museum runs 360-degree show to save historic Back Bay area. L. Drukker. il Pop Phot 66:60 Ap '70
Boston's centenary acquisitions. il Art in Am 58:130 Ja '70
Boston's centennial coup, with paintings. Life 68:36-43+ F 13 '70
Centennial in Boston. E. P. Birk. Antiques 97:168+ F '70
Smuggled treasure; question of how museum acquired portrait of Eleonora Gonzaga. Time 97:56 Ja 18 '71

BOSTON museum of science
Point of view. Science 170:145 O 9 '70; Discussion. 170:1358-9 D 25 '70

BOSTON Patriots (football club) See Football clubs

BOSTON Red Sox (baseball) See Baseball clubs

BOSTON symphony orchestra
Bird with inward fire: M. T. Thomas. il por Time 96:57 S 14 '70
Gentlemen, more dolce please! by H. E. Dickson. Review
Am Rec G il 36:380-2+ Ja '70. G. S. Fox
Kid from Boston: M. T. Thomas. H. Saal. por Newsweek 75:86 Ap 13 '70
Musical events:
Concert in Philharmonic Hall conducted by M. T. Thomas. W. Sargeant. New Yorker 46:89-90 Ap 11 '70

Musical events; concert in Philharmonic Hall. W. Sargeant. New Yorker 46:162-3 O 24 '70
With Michael Tilson Thomas, the show really goes on! interview, ed. by R. Hemming. M. T. Thomas. il pors Sr Schol 97:22-4 O 26 '70

History

Prisoner: 1337; occupation: conductor, Boston symphony orchestra. J. J. Badal. il pors Hi Fi 20:55-60 O '70

BOSTON undersea museum. See Aquariums

BOSTON university
First hurrah; new president, J. R. Silber. por Newsweek 77:32 Ja 4 '71

BOSTONIANS
Who are the HUB men? sports, politics and tradition in Boston. F. Deford. il Sports Illus 33:54-6+ Jl 13 '70

BOSWELL, James
Doctor's doctors; S. Johnson. H. F. Ellis. New Yorker 46:114-16+ S 19 '70 *
Wonder to behold. G. Wolff. il por Newsweek 76:115B-115C+ N 16 '70 *

BOTANICAL exploration
George Engelmann, botanical gatekeeper of the West. R. G. Beidleman. il Horticulture 48:42-3+ Ap '70

BOTANICAL gardens
Twenty acres of desert discovery; Desert botanical garden, Arizona. il Sunset 144:33 Ja '70
See also
Bayard Cutting arboretum, Long Island, N.Y.
Brooklyn botanic garden

BOTANICAL libraries
First conference, horticultural and botanical libraries. Horticulture 48:46-7 Mr '70
See also
Horticultural libraries

BOTANICAL research
Sense of time. A. W. Galston. Yale R 59: 448-54 Mr '70
Some plants found to thrive in moon soil. il Aviation W 92:58 My 4 '70

BOTANY
See also
Cell division (botany)
Chromosomes (botany)
Coleoptiles
Fertilization of plants
Fresh water flora
Lichens
Mutation (botany)
Mycology
Plants
Pollen
Variation (botany)

Ecology

See also
Forest ecology

History

Food plants America gave the world. B. Black. il Horticulture 48:24-7+ Jl '70

Nomenclature

See also
Plant names, Popular

Physiology

See also
Chloroplasts
Fruit-bud development
Growth (plants)
Plants—Respiration
Plants—Transpiration

Study and teaching

Children's gardens in New York city schools: an educational report dated 1897. A. Schatz and V. Schatz. il Org Gard & Farm 17:67-9 N '70

Teacher tips: pollination. J. A. Weeks. il Cons 24:32 Ap '70

Alaska

Plants of the Far North. M. Williams. il Horticulture 48:28-30+ Jl '70

Australia

Flora of Australia. il Am For 76:36-9 F '70

California

Bare zone between California shrub and grassland communities: the role of animals. B. Bartholomew. bibliog il Science 170: 1210-12 D 11 '70

BOTANY, Economic
See also
Plants, Edible
Weeds

BOTANY, Medical
Discoveries in the mailbox. E. Gibbons. Org
Gard & Farm 17:82-4 My '70
Hawthorn berry for the heart. J. I. Rodale.
il Org Gard & Farm 17:112-15 F; 128-30
Mr; 106-9 Ap; 91-2+ My; 100-1 Je; 77-9
Jl; 98-9 Ag '70
Home grown health aids. Home Gard 57:27
Ja '70
What we have forgotten about pot, a pharma-
cologist's history: cannabis sativa. S. H.
Snyder. il N Y Times Mag p26-7+ D 13 '70
See also
Hallucination and illusion producing plants
BOTETOURT COUNTY, Va.

Historic houses, etc.
Botetourt County, Virginia, begins its third
century. F. M. Lewis. il Antiques 97:456+
Ap '70
BOTSCHUIVER, Theo
Inflate and float. il Life 68:76-9 Ap 10 '70 *
BOTSFORD, Ward
Best Sacre on records today. il Am Rec G 37:
10-11+ S '70
In the grand manner. por Am Rec G 36:
690-1 My '70
Irreplaceable artifacts from musical ages past.
Am Rec G 36:339-40 Ja '70
Martha. il Am Rec G 36:872-4 Jl '70
Der Rosenkavalier. il Am Rec G 36:396-401
F '70
Sir Thomas Beecham: concluding a nine-part
discography. por Am Rec G 36:258-65+ D
'69
BOTSTEIN, Leon
Experimental president. por Newsweek 76:
40 Ag 3 '70 *
Student as president. por Time 96:32+ Jl 13
'70 *
BOTSWANA

Economic conditions
Road to independence. P. Webb. il por News-
week 76:46 O 26 '70 *
BOTTEL, Helen
Helping your teens to handle sex. Read
Digest 96:140-2 Mr '70
BOTTLE industry. See Glass container industry
BOTTLED water. See Water, Bottled
BOTTLES
Mere alcohol doesn't thrill them at all; col-
lecting ceramic bottles of booze. P. Knight.
il por Sports Illus 33:76-7 N 30 '70
Pop bottles: explosives in the market basket?
il Consumer Rep 35:158-60 Mr '70
See also
Glass container industry
BOTTO, Louis
They shoot dirty movies don't they? il Look
34:56+ N 3 '70
BOTTOM fishing. See Fishing
BOTTOMLEY, Thomas R.
Antique boat of the year. il Motor B 126:47+
N '70
Arrivederci Italia. il Motor B 125:74-6+ My
'70
Check list of sources. Motor B 125:134-41
Ja '70
Electro compass. il Motor B 126:28+ O '70
New approach to ferro-cement. il Motor B
126:21+ S '70
Outboards victorious. il Motor B 126:47-9+
Ag '70
Speed on the water. il Motor B 125:61-4+
F '70
BOUCEK, Robert J. and Alvarez, T. R.
5-Hydroxytryptamine: a cytospecific growth
stimulator of cultured fibroblasts. bibliog
il Science 167:898-9 F 6 '70
BOUCH, James G.
Experiment with joint committees. Todays
Ed 59:66 S '70
BOUCHER, Gene
With Gene Boucher after the opera: herbs
and bonsai. E. McDonald. il por House B
112:167-8 F '70 *
BOUDIN, André, and Deutsch, Sarah
Geochronology: recent development in the
lutetium-176/hafnium-176 dating method.
bibliog il Science 168:1219-20 Je 5 '70
BOUDIN, Eugène Louis
Misnomer. J. Jacobs. Art in Am 58:139+ Ja '70
BOUDIN, Kathy
House on 11th street. il pors Newsweek 75:29-
30 Mr 23 '70 *
House on 11th street. il Time 95:10 Mr 23
'70 *
Two girls from no. 18. J. Neary. il pors Life
68:26-9 Mr 27 '70 *
BOUL' Mich; story. See De Gramont, S.

BOULANGER, Nadia
[Photograph] B. Brandt. Harp Baz 103:138-9
F '70
BOULAT, Pierre
Scouting both sides of an angry border. R.
Graves. pors Life 68:3 Je 12 '70 *
BOULDEN, James B. and Buffa, E. S.
Corporate models: on-line, real-time systems.
il Harvard Bsns R 48:65-83 Jl '70
BOULDER, Colo.

Sanitary affairs
Municipal collection and disposal costs less
in Colorado cities of 10,000 or more. R. G.
Westdyke. il Am City 85:16 Jl '70
BOULDER, Colo, public library
Hurdles, problems, rewards: a total system
concept work. A. Mathews. il Am Lib 1:
151-3 F '70
BOULDING, Kenneth E.
Ecology & environment; excerpts from Social
science in the schools. ed. by I. Morrissett
and W. S. Stevens, jr. il Trans-Action 7:
38-44 Mr '70
Look at national priorities. il Cur Hist 59:
65-72+ Ag '70
Scientific revelation. il Bul Atom Sci 26:13-
18 S '70
BOULEZ, Pierre
Everybody's talking about Pierre Boulez;
interview, ed. by R. Hemming. por Sr
Schol 95:23 D 8 '69

about
Pelléas by Debussy, Maeterlinck, and Boulez.
R. Jacobson. Sat R 53:45 D 26 '70 *
BOULTON, Laura (Crayton)
Urge to dance; ed. by G. Loney. il Dance
Mag 44:48-57 My '70
BOULWARE, Lemuel R.
Helping shareowners help themselves; ad-
dress, November 7, 1970. Vital Speeches 37:
155-60 D 15 '70
BOULWARISM in collective bargaining. See
Collective bargaining
BOUMEDIENNE, Houari
Living question mark. il por Newsweek 76:33
Jl 20 '70 *
BOUNDARIES
See also subhead Boundaries under names
of countries, states, etc. e.g. Mexico—Boun-
daries
BOUNDARIES of love; story. See Schiller,
M.
BOUNDARY waters canoe area. See Wilderness
areas—Minnesota
BOUNTY (ship)
Historied generation gap! P. W. Schmidtchen.
il pors Hobbies 75:134+ S '70
BOUQUET, Dominic
Enough life to support new fruit. G. Shearer.
il por Org Gard & Farm 17:52-3 S '70 *
BOUQUETS
Spur-of-the-moment bouquets. il House &
Gard 138:52-5 D '70
BOURASSA, Robert
No to separatism. Time 95:47 My 11 '70 *
While Canada waited. M. M. Dorcy. America
122:525-6 My 16 '70 *
BOURBON whiskey. See Whiskey
BOURGEOISIE. See Middle classes
BOURJAILY, Vance
Epitaph for Biafra. il N Y Times Mag p32-
3+ Ja 25 '70
Middle age meets the kid ghetto. il pors
N Y Times Mag p46-7+ N 29 '70
BOURKE, George
From tip to top in Florida. See issues of
Travel
BOURRET, J. A. and others
Fungal endogenous rhythms expressed by
spiral figures. bibliog Science 166:763-4; 169:
1229 N 7 '69, S 18 '70
BOUSFIELD, Bill
Housebreaker. il Outdoor Life 146:50-3+ S '70
BOUTET, Nicholas Noël
Nicholas Boutet: master craftsman. C. G.
Worman. il Hobbies 75:158-9 Mr '70 *
BOUTHOUL, Gaston
Who's afraid of war? F. Ungeheuer. Harper
241:28-31 D '70 *
BOUTILIER, Joy
Joy Boutilier dance company; Henry st.
settlement playhouse, NYC. N. Mason.
Dance Mag 44:81 Jl '70 *
BOUTIQUES. See Specialty stores
BOUTON, James Alan. See Bouton, Jim
BOUTON, Jim
My love/hate affair with baseball; excerpts
from Ball four. ed. by L. Shecter. il pors
Look 34:82+ Je 2; 60-2+ Je 16 '70

BOUTON, Jim—*Continued*

about

Books. R. Angell. New Yorker 46:79 Jl 25
'70 *
Inside baseball. por Time 95:76-7 Je 15 '70 *
Is baseball really like that? R. L. Tobin.
il Sat R 53:43-4 Jl 11 '70 *
Jim Bouton's instant replay. J. Kaplan. Sports
Illus 33:36 Ag 31 '70 *
Knuckleballer. New Yorker 46:39-40 O 24 '70 *
Pitcher in the wry. P. Axthelm. il por News-
week 75:59 Je 15 '70 *
Sports. R. Kahn. Esquire 74:14+ D '70 *
Trade winds. C. Amory. Sat R 53:10-11 Ag
1 '70 *

BOUTWELL, Jane
Matter of national concern. il Opera N 34:
6-13 Je 13 '70
(ed) See Sparemblek, M. Prime mover

BOUTWELL, William D.
Happenings in education. See issues of PTA
magazine

BOUVERIE, Jacob, 2d earl of Radnor. See Radnor, J. B.

BOVASSO, Julie
Gloria and Esperanza. Criticism
New Yorker 45:57 F 14 '70 *

BOVÉ, John L. and Siebenberg, Stanley
Airborne lead and carbon monoxide at 45th
street, New York city. il Science 167:986-7
F 13 '70

BOW and arrow
Is your gear O.K? G. H. Gillelan. il Outdoor
Life 146:28+ N '70

BOW fishing. See Fishing with bow and arrow

BOW hunting. See Hunting with bow and arrow

BOWATERS wilderness areas. See Wilderness
areas—Tennessee

BOWDEN, James H.
Wife of Bath in meditation; poem. Chr Cent
87:596 My 13 '70
You can take Salem out of the country, but—.
Chr Cent 87:1562-3 D 30 '70

BOWDEN, Mary
Different track. il House B 112:34 N; 20 D '70

BOWDEN, Norris
$45,000 life of Norris Bowden. il pors Bsns
W p 124-6+ Mr 21 '70 *

BOWDOIN college, Brunswick, Me.
Bowdoin eliminates college board test requirements. Sch & Soc 98:271-2 Sum '70

BOWEN, Catherine (Drinker)
We've never asked a woman before. por
Atlan 225:82-6 Mr '70

BOWEN, Croswell
Donora, Pennsylvania. Atlan 226:27-8+ N '70

BOWEN, Ezra
Break a leg? not likely. Am Home 73:36+ Ja
'70

BOWEN, Jack L.
Air-dielectric trimmers. por Electr World
83:37-41 Ap '70

BOWEN, John
Eastern gold rush. il Travel 133:48-53 My '70

BOWEN, Mary
Remodeled deathtrap. il Nat Parks 44:26 Ja
'70
Teacher's guide to good discipline. il Parents
Mag 45:50-2 Je '70

BOWEN, William
Books & ideas. Fortune 81:198-9 F '70

BOWER, Anthony
Paris burgeoning? il Art in Am 58:112-13
S '70

BOWER, Libbie B. and Elam, Barbara
Developing an inner city mental health association. Ment Hy 54:215-20 Ap '70

BOWERING, George
Comment. W. Heyen. Poetry 115:429 Mr '70 *

BOWERMAN, Bill
Freshman and the great guru. P. Putnam. il
pors Sports Illus 32:28-31 Je 15 '70 *

BOWERS, Faubion
Behind the mask. il Opera N 34:8-12 Ap 18
'70
How to light the stage. il Opera N 34:26-9
Ap 4 '70
Sexes: getting it all together. il Sat R 54:16-
19 Ja 9 '71
Twenty-five years ago: how Japan won
the war. il pors N Y Times Mag p5-7+ Ag
30; 136-7 S 13 '70
(ed) See Sills, B. Bubbles

BOWERS, H. Paxton. See Burke, J. G. jt. auth.

BOWERS, Lucille. See Bowers, W. F. jt. auth.

BOWERS, Raymond. See Brooks, H. jt. auth.

BOWERS, Warner F.
Movable garden, indoors and out. il Org
Gard & Farm 17:44-6 S '70
—and Bowers, Lucille
Putting the garden to bed for the winter. il
Org Gard & Farm 17:25-7 O '70

BOWERY. See New York (city)

BOWES, Al, and Kendall, Jack
Porcupine predicament. il Outdoor Life 145:
64-5 My '70

BOWFISHING. See Fishing with bow and arrow

BOWIE, Maceo T.
Learn baby learn; address, May 24, 1970.
Vital Speeches 36:604-6 Jl 15 '70

BOWIE, S. H. U. See Simpson, P. R. jt. auth.

BOWKER, R. R, company
See also
Books in print (publication)
Carey-Thomas award

BOWL football games. See Football

BOWLES, Jerry G.
Brian O'Doherty whispers in ogham. il por
Art N 69:34-5+ S '70

BOWLEY, Clinton J. and others
Sunglint patterns: unusual dark patches. bib-
liog Science 165:1360-2; 167:1757 S 26 '69,
Mr 27 '70

BOWLINE knot. See Knots and splices

BOWLING
Bocce at home. il Sunset 145:66-7 Jl '70
Ladies of the lanes. J. L. O'Neill. il Am Home
73:34+ S '70
Seniors strike for fun. M. Nagel. il Har
Yrs 10:40-1 Ja '70

BOWMAN, Barbara H. and others
Cystic fibrosis: characterization of the inhibitor to ciliary action in oyster gills. bibliog il Science 167:871-3 F 6 '70

BOWMAN, David, and Rousseau, R. W.
Major ecumenical proposal. America 122:70-2
Ja 24 '70

BOWMAN, Jean G.
What's cooking? Org Gard & Farm 17:114-16
Ja '70

BOWMAN, M. Bruce
Drawing. il Sch Arts 70:8-9 N '70
Zodiac designs. il Design 71:7 Wint '69

BOWMAN, Robert L. See Ito, Y. jt. auth.

BOWMAN, Robert M.
Decay: blessing in disguise. America 123:114-17
S 5 '70

BOWNE and company
Public after 194 years. il Forbes 105:40 Mr 1
'70

BOWRING, Dave
(ed) See Lohre, D. Silver bullet for me

BOWSER, Hallowell
Eggomaniacs. il Sat R 53:20 Jl 18 '70
Gentle gendarmes. Sat R 53:22 Mr 28 '70
Thinking with your blood. Sat R 53:26 S 19
'70

BOX huckleberries
Gaylussacia brachycera. H. Smith and D.
Smith. il Horticulture 48:26-7 N '70

BOX lunches. See Lunches

BOX tricks. See Tricks

BOXERS
Of boxers and boxing. il Ebony 25:164-5 O
'70
Salute to Joe; Joe Louis day. C. Higgins. il
pors Ebony 25:158-62 O '70
See also names of boxers, e.g. C. Clay

BOXES, cases etc.
Approach to making boxes. N. Baldwin. il
Ceram Mo 18:18-21 N '70
Box display. J. F. Warwick. il Sch Arts 70:
32-3 S '70
Cigar box art; opera-related subjects. il
Opera N 34:14-15 Mr 14 '70
Decorative cheeseboxes. W. Catlin. il Design
71:38-9 Sum '70
See also
Chests
Key cases, holders, etc.
Mailboxes

BOXING
Bring on Ali; Frazier vs. Ellis. il por News-
week 75:94 Mr 2 '70
Chancey games in Ohio; Dean Chance enter-
prises. M. Cope. il por Sports Illus 32:26-8+
Mr 30 '70
Chip off the old redwood; California's R.
Lunny, the top U.S. Olympic hope. S.
Treadwell. il por Sports Illus 33:44-5 Ag 10
'70
Clancy's gym is Danny's turf: sparring part-
ner for big name fighters. H. Aronson. il
pors Sports Illus 32:40-4 Mr 23 '70
Fathers and sons: Cerdan vs Paduano. il
pors Newsweek 75:93 My 25 '70
For Mexico (and the world) R. Olivares vs
C. Castillo. P. Putnam. il pors Sports Illus
32:18-19 Ap 27 '70
Free at last? Ellis-Frazier fight. il por Time
95:51+ Mr 2 '70
He moves like silk, hits like a ton; Muhammad Ali. M. Kram. il pors Sports Illus 33:
16-19 O 26 '70

BOXING—*Continued*
Hooked and smoked out; Joe Frazier-Jimmy Ellis fight. il Sports Illus 32:22-3 F 23 '70
In this corner, the official heavyweight champ. P. Wood. il pors N Y Times Mag p52-3+ N 15 '70
Muddle, then a zinger; Muhammad Ali-Oscar Bonavena fight. M. Kram. il Sports Illus 33:26-7 D 14 '70
Mystery in pursuit of a legend; son of French boxer, M. Cerdan. M. Kram. il pors Sports Illus 32:38-40+ Ap 13 '70
Night Carlos made a no-no out of Ni-no; C. Monzón-N. Benvenuti fight. W. Wynn. il pors Sports Illus 33:80-2 N 16 '70
No longer a legend, but not all hoax; M. Cerdan's American debut. M. Kram. Sports Illus 32:82+ My 25 '70
Número uno; Weiland vs. Urtain. il por Time 95:60 Ap 20 '70
Of boxers and boxing. il Ebony 25:164-5 O '70
One round of boxing was more than enough; Frazier-Foster fight. P. Putnam. il pors Sports Illus 33:20-1 N 30 '70
Petit Marcel and la grande mystique. pors Time 95:74 My 25 '70
Power broker; J. Frazier-Bob Foster fight. Newsweek 76:92 N 30 '70
Return of an exiled champ. P. Axthelm. il pors Newsweek 76:56-60+ N 9 '70
Return of the ringmaster; C. Clay vs. J. Quarry. il pors Time 96:35 N 9 '70
Salute the grand old flag-raiser George F; aspiring heavyweight's ideal opponent. M. Kane. por Sports Illus 33:56-7 Ag 17 '70
Shadow and substance; Rocky Marciano vs Cassius Clay. Sports Illus 32:6 F 2 '70
Sham battle; Rocky Marciano-Muhammad Ali computerized fight. il Newsweek 75:50 F 2 '70
Show biz is out, boxing is in; Frazier vs. Ellis. M. Kram. il Sports Illus 32:14-15 F 16 '70
Smashing return of the old Ali; J. Quarry vs. Muhammad Ali. M. Kram. il pors Sports Illus 33:18-19 N 2 '70
Son of King Kong; Noell's ark ape show. il Newsweek 76:23-4 Jl 20 '70
Two down, one to go; Clay-Bonavena fight. il por Time 96:48 D 21 '70
Ulterior motive for Umag; Benvenuti-Bethea world middle weight championship fight in Yugoslavia. D. J. Hamblin. il por Sports Illus 32:14-15 Je 1 '70
Viva Mantequilla. M. Crawford. il pors Ebony 25:58-60+ Mr '70
Watching the man in the mirror. G. Plimpton. il por Sports Illus 33:80-3+ N 23 '70
Weary butterfly; Muhammad Ali and O. Bonavena. il pors Newsweek 76:68+ D 21 '70

BOXING fans. See Sports fans
BOY friend; musical comedy. See Musical comedies, revues, etc.—Criticisms, plots, etc.
BOY in a red tie; story. See Montagne, R.
BOY scouts
Brave, clean and relevant. Newsweek 75:53-4 Mr 9 '70
Digging the Stoners; black and Puerto Rican Stoners of south Brooklyn. il Time 96:11-12 N 30 '70
Motivated to be better; youth-serving agencies. A. E. Iverson. il Todays Ed 59:34-5 Mr '70
See also
Cub scouts
Explorer scouts
Exploring, a new path to a better America. J. G. Hubbell. Read Digest 97:131-4 O '70
BOY who laughed; story. See Litvinov, I.
BOYCOTT
And now, lettuce. D. Henninger. New Repub 163:9-11 O 10 '70
Breakthrough in Coachella Valley. V. Salandini. America 122:470-1 My 2 '70; Reply. C. C. Crawford. 122:619 Je 13 '70
Eagle over the lettuce fields. N. C. Mills. Commonweal 93:140-1 N 6 '70
Huelga! The boycott that worked. R. B. Taylor. Nation 211:167-9 S 7 '70
Lessons of the grape strike. V. Salandini. America 123:285-7 O 17 '70
Positive spending; moratorium on buying by anti-war groups. New Repub 162:12 My 30 '70
Tilting with the system; interview, ed by B. Fitch. C. Chavez. il Chr Cent 87:204-7 F 18 '70
Whatever happened to the grape strike and boycott? il por U S News 68:58 Ap 6 '70

BOYD, Andrew
Hard times in Ulster. Nation 210:422-3 Ap 13 '70
Paisley in Parliament. Nation 210:549-50 My 11 '70
BOYD, Bob
Hello, drip, drip! Goodby, UCLA. J. Jares. il Sports Illus 31:55-6 D 15 '69
BOYD, Catherine
Girl who wouldn't be missed; story. Redbook 134:169-91 Mr '70
BOYD, George N.
Movies (title varies) Chr Cent 87:944-5, 1160+ Ag 5, S 30 '70
Movies and the sexual revolution; should the ratings be revised? Chr Cent 87:1124-5 S 23 '70
BOYD, James
From far right to far left, and farther, with Karl Hess. il pors N Y Times Mag p48-9+ D 6 '70
I gave Thurmond 100 per cent loyalty and now I give Mr Nixon 100 per cent. il pors N Y Times Mag p 12-13+ F 1 '70
Nixon's southern strategy; it's all in the charts. il pors N Y Times Mag p25+ My 17 '70
BOYD, Joe Dan
Where the past lives again. il Farm J 94:50B-50C My '70
BOYD, Malcolm
Religious ghetto; summary of addresses. pors Pub W 197:38-9 Je 1 '70
BOYD, Mary Maxine
Parks for all seasons, and for all people. il Parks & Rec 5:22-3+ My '70
BOYD, Richard W. and Murphy, J. T.
Changes in the House; a prediction. New Repub 163:12-14 O 24 '70
BOYD, Robin
Glimpse of the future. il Arch Forum 132:32-5 Mr '70
BOYD, Waldo T.
Build a transcipitor. il Pop Electr 32:31-5+ Je '70
BOYDSTON, Grover
Now it's Neurotics anonymous. por Time 95:58 Mr 2 '70 *
BOYLAN, Brian Richard
(ed) See Rovinsky, J. J. How chronic health problems affect pregnancy
BOYLE, Irma
Babies after sixty-five? interview, ed. by K. F. Westfall. il Har Yrs 10:34-7 Ap '70
BOYLE, J. A. and others
Lesch-Nyhan syndrome; preventive control by prenatal diagnosis. bibliog il Science 169:688-9 Ag 14 '70
BOYLE, James Ambrose
Official report on the Kennedy case; with excerpts from testimony by E. M. Kennedy. il por U S News 68:56-60 My 11 '70
about
County judge in national limelight. U S News 68:77 My 11 '70 *
Judge's harsh verdict on Teddy Kennedy; with excerpts from transcript. il por Newsweek 75:47-8+ My 11 '70 *
BOYLE, Kay
Day on Alcatraz with the Indians. New Repub 162:10-11 Ja 17 '70
about
I poems and You poems. R. W. French. Nation 210:695-6+ Je 8 '70 *
BOYLE, Magdalene
My tussle with tees. il Har Yrs 10:17-18 Jl '70
BOYLE, Peter
Reluctant hero of the hardhats. M. Durham. il pors Life 69:69-70 O 16 '70 *
BOYLE, Robert H.
Big cat on the prowl. il pors Sports Illus 32:14-17 F 9 '70
Fishing (cont) Sports Illus 32:54-5 My 18 '70
Happiness boys at the track. il Sports Illus 33:20-1 O 12 '70
Hot pace in a big mini-race. il Sports Illus 33:38-44 D 7 '70
My struggle to help the President. il Sports Illus 32:32-4 F 16 '70
Oral Roberts; small but oh, my! il Sports Illus 33:64-5 N 30 '70
Panacea for a salty Yankee. il por Sports Illus 32:28-30+ Ap 20 '70
Poison roams our coastal seas. il Sports Illus 33:70-4+ O 26 '70
TV wins on points. il Sports Illus 33:14-17 N 2 '70

BOYLE, Tony. See Boyle. W. A.

BOYLE, William Anthony
Boyle takes the oath; Senate labor subcommittee hearing. por Newsweek 75:72 Mr 30 '70 *
Jock's legacy. Newsweek 75:80+ Mr 16 '70 *
New questions for mine workers' head. U S News 68:78 Mr 23 '70 *
Vindication for Jock Yablonski. Time 95:25 Mr 16 '70 *
Yablonski's legacy. Newsweek 75:35-6 F 23 '70 *
BOYLE'S law. See Gases
BOYNTON, Dori Watson
Norman Laliberté: painter, graphic artist & craftsman. il Am Artist 34:52-9 F '70
BOYNTON, Robert M. and Whitten, D. N.
Visual adaptation in monkey cones: recordings of late receptor potentials. bibliog il Science 170:1423-6 D 25 '70
BOYS
How to get along with boys. D. A. Sugarman and R. Hochstein. il Seventeen 29:134-5+ F '70
Little boys romantic. A. J. Snider. il Sci Digest 68:43 O '70
Plus fours. L. Norris. Atlan 225:120-2+ Je '70
Pooky Peckinpaugh's Christmas list; excerpt from Miss Pooky Peckinpaugh. K. Thompson. Harp Baz 104:86-7 D '70
Tom Sawyer boyhood, 1970 style. P. Powell. il pors Life 69:50-7 O 9 '70
Young living; questions and answers. A. Wood. See issues of Seventeen
See also
Adolescence
Little leagues
Negro youth
Runaway boys and girls
BOYS as cooks. See Cookery by children
BOYS clubs
See also
Boy scouts
BOYS rooms. See Childrens rooms
BOYS schools. See Private schools
BOYS shoes. See Shoes
BOYSENBERRIES
See also
Cookery—Fruit
BOYUM, Joy Gould, and Scott, Adrienne
Film: a share in the great tradition. il Schol Teach Jr/Sr High p24-5 N 2 '70
BOZE, Nancy S.
Ethnic literature. Clear House 44:527-30 My '70
BOZZACCHI, Giuseppina
Comedy classic. W. Terry. il por Sat R 53:51 Je 6 '70 *
BRA. See Brassieres
BRABYN, Howard
Year of the whale. il UNESCO Courier 23:65-8 Ag '70
BRACE, C. Loring
Origin of man. il Natur Hist 79:46-9 Ja '70
BRACE, William F. and Byerlee, J. D.
California earthquakes: why only shallow focus? bibliog il Science 168:1573-5 Je 26 '70
BRACELETS
Copper bracelets are a put-on. M. Michaelson. il Todays Health 48:27-9+ Je '70
Copper bracelets for arthritis: fraud or cure? Good H 171:181 O '70
Curious case of the copper band. G. Cant. il Sports Illus 33:37-41 Ag 3 '70
Green wrist mania; copper bracelet fad. il Time 96:56 Jl 6 '70
BRACKEN, Peg
Not with a bang but a hiccup. Sat R 53:3 D 26 '70
Peg Bracken: an exclusive interview; ed. by F. Cameron. il por Writers Digest 50:24-6 My '70
BRACKET fungi shelves. See Shelves
BRACKISH-water clams. See Clams
BRACKMAN, Jacob
Films. See issues of Esquire
BRACKMAN, Roman
Caught in the crossfire. il Nat R 22:564-5+ Je 2 '70
BRADBURN, Norman M.
Selecting the questions to be asked in surveys. Mo Labor R 93:27-9 Ja '70
BRADBURY, Ray
Martian chronicles: sea provocative study. J. Grimsley. Engl J 59:1239-42 D '70 *
Study of the allusions in Bradbury's Fahrenheit 451. P. Sisario. Engl J 59:201-5+ F '70 *
BRADBURY, Will
Genius on the prowl. il pors Life 69:57-60+ O 30 '70
Sexual inadequacy: what can be done. il pors Life 68:42-6 My 1 '70; Same abr. Read Digest 97:63-6 Ag '70

BRADERMAN, Eugene M.
International copyright: a world view; address, February 16, 1970. Dept State Bul 62:486-93 Ap 13 '70
Washington diplomatic conference approves Patent cooperation treaty; remarks, May 25, 1970. Dept State Bul 63:43-4 Jl 13 '70
BRADFORD, Ernle
Battle of the Nile; excerpts from Mediterranean: portrait of a sea. il pors Horizon 12:84-95 Aut '70
Faeroes, isles of maybe. il Nat Geog 138:410-42 S '70
BRADFORD, Phil
Investment analysis. M. S. Rothenberg. por Phys Today 23:27-8 My '70 *
BRADLEY, Arnold L.
Superintendent and negotiations. Clear House 44:278 Ja '70
BRADLEY, Harry
Rap 'n 'pinion. por Motor T 22:14 N '70
BRADLEY, Jack
(ed) Trumpet fanfare; discussion. il Sat R 53:19+ Jl 4 '70
BRADLEY, Kathryn H. See Schulman, J. D. jt. auth.
BRADLEY, Michael E.
Outer seven at ten. Cur Hist 58:264-8 My '70
Prospects for Soviet agriculture. bibliog f Cur Hist 59:226-31+ O '70
BRADLEY, Sam
God for me; poem. Chr Cent 87:992 Ag 19 '70
Summer's ruby-throat; poem. Commonweal 92:170 My 1 '70
BRADSHAW, George
Boats: the life you take with you. Vogue 155:246+ My '70
BRADSHAW, Hank
Arizona land of built-in fishing. il Field & S 74:37-9+ Ja '70
Fold and trail fish house. il Outdoor Life 146:12-12A N '70
Late great grouse hunting. il Field & S 74:48-9+ Ja '70
Out in Hemingway country. il pors Field & S 75:70-1+ Je '70
Ozark crappie jamboree. il Field & S 74:70-1+ Ap '70
Rainbows through the ice. il Field & S 75:104-7+ D '70
BRADSHAW, Lillian (Moore)
Library response to a restive world; address, July 3, 1970. por Am Lib 1:688-90 Jl '70
BRADSHAW, Terry
I wanted to go with a loser. G. Ronberg. por(cover) Sports Illus 32:25 F 9 '70 *
Trials of a rookie. il pors Newsweek 76:58-60+ O 5 '70 *
BRADY, Bruce H.
Bass from the bottom up. il por Outdoor Life 146:56-7+ N '70
BRADY, Gary J.
Cardboard carpentry. il Design 71:30-1 Fall '69
BRADY, Raymond
Irish way. il Duns 96:74+ N '70
Wall Street beat. See issues of Dun's
BRADY, St Elmo
St Elmo Brady: the lengthened shadow. S. P. Massie. il Chem 43:7 N '70 *
BRADYKININ
Bradykinin inhibition by butylated hydroxyanisole. L. P. Posati and M. J. Pallansch. il Science 168:121-2 Ap 3 '70
BRAHM, Walter
Connecticut state librarian: bypass city libraries? summary of annual report. Library J 96:15-16+ Ja 1 '71
BRAHMS, Johannes
Extraordinary clarity, Gary Graffman's Paganini variations. M. N. Kanny. Am Rec G 36:354-5 Ja '70 *
From the Arturo Toscanini society: memorable Strauss. C. J. Luten. il Am Rec G 36:330-1 Ja '70 *
Outstanding release in every respect. M. N. Kanny. Am Rec G 36:966 Ag '70 *
Records:
Rinaldo, Schicksalslied. Opera N 34:35 F 28 '70 *
Russian Angels in America. S. Fleming. il Hi Fi 20:secI 71-2 My '70 *
Solid gold in Cleveland. M. Kanny. il Am Rec G 36:884-5 Jl '70 *
BRAIDING
Braid-it-yourself beach hat. il Sunset 144:122+ My '70
BRAIDWOOD, Robert John. See Çambel, H. jt. auth.

BRAIN
Brain lesions in an infant rhesus monkey treated with monosodium glutamate. J. W. Olney and L. G. Sharpe; discussion. Science 167:1016-17 F 13 '70
Don't use the kitchen-sink approach to enrichment; adaptation of address. D. Krech. il Todays Ed 59:30-2+ O '70
Superior colliculus: single unit responses to stimulation of visual cortex in the cat. J. T. McIlwain and H. L. Fields. bibliog il Science 170:1426-8 D 25 '70

See also
Amygdaloid body
Brain waves
Hypothalamus
Intellect
Memory
Meninges
Pituitary body
Sleep

Analysis and chemistry
Acetylcholine concentrations in rat brain: diurnal oscillation. I. Hanin and others. bibliog il Science 170:341-2 O 16 '70
Can chemicals stimulate learning capacity? L. Ernst. Ed Digest 35:32-3 My '70
Clues from a chemical; PCPA's effects on serotonin. L. Campbell. il Sci N 98:287-9 O 3 '70
L-Dihydroxyphenylalanine: effect on S-adenosylmethionine in brain. R. J. Wurtman and others. bibliog il Science 169:395-7 Jl 24 '70
L-Dopa: effect on concentrations of dopamine, norepinephrine, and serotonin in brains of mice. G. M. Everett and J. W. Borcherding. il Science 168:849 My 15 '70
L-Dopa-induced release of cerebral monoamines. K. Y. Ng and others. bibliog il Science 170:76-7 O 2 '70
Drinking and eating elicited by cortical spreading depression. J. P. Huston and J. Bures. bibliog il Science 169:702-4 Ag 14 '70
In vivo conversion of ^{3}H-L-tryptophan into ^{3}H-serotonin in brain areas of adrenalectomized rats. E. C. Azmitia, jr. and others. bibliog il Science 169:201-3 Jl 10 '70
Intracranial self-stimulation and wakefulness: effect of manipulating ambient brain catecholamines. S. K. Roll. bibliog il Science 168:1370-2 Je 12 '70
Lack of coincidence between neural and behavioral manifestations of cortical spreading depression. T. J. Carew and others. bibliog il Science 169:1339-42 S 25 '70
Mind research: the promise and the peril; protein synthesis in the brain. F. Warshofsky. Read Digest 96:119-23 Ap '70
Norepinephrine metabolism in brainstem of spontaneously hypertensive rats. Y. Yamori and others. bibliog il Science 170:544-6 O 30 '70
Parkinson's disease: activity of L-dopa decarboxylase in discrete brain regions. K. Lloyd and O. Hornykiewicz. bibliog il Science 170:1212-13 D 11 '70
Serotonin-containing neurons in brain: depression of firing by monoamine oxidase inhibitors. G. K. Aghajanian and others. bibliog il Science 169:1100-2 S 11 '70
Tolerance to morphine-induced increases in [^{14}C]catecholamine synthesis in mouse brain. C. B. Smith and others. bibliog il Science 170:1106-8 D 4 '70
Turnover of the brain specific protein, S-100. T. J. Cicero and B. W. Moore. bibliog il Science 169:1333-4 S 25 '70

Diseases
Transmissible mink encephalopathy: experimental transmission to the squirrel monkey. R. J. Eckroade and others. bibliog il Science 169:1088-90 S 11 '70
Violence is predictable; episodic dyscontrol syndrome. A. Rosenthal. il Todays Health 48:56-7+ N '70
See also
Aphasia
Hydrocephalus
Leukodystrophy
Parkinson's disease

Localization of functions
Epileptic focus location: spectral analysis method. W. Gersch and G. V. Goddard. bibliog il Science 169:701-2 Ag 14 '70
Functional organization of the brain. A. R. Luria. il Sci Am 222:66-72+ bibliog(p 146) Mr '70
Neural symbolic activity: a psychophysical measure. N. Weisstein. bibliog il Science 168:1489-91 Je 19 '70; Reply with rejoinder. R. Sekuler and R. Armstrong. 170:1226-8 D 11 '70

Organization of language and the brain; adaptation of address, December 28, 1969. N. Geschwind. bibliog il Science 170:940-4 N 27 '70
Thermosensitivity of neurons in the sensorimotor cortex of the cat. J. L. Barker and D. O. Carpenter. bibliog il Science 169:597-8 Ag 7 '70
Visual discrimination of movement: midbrain or forebrain? C. R. Hamilton and J. S. Lund. bibliog il Science 170:1428-30 D 25 '70

See also
Electronic behavior control
Split brain

Surgery
Mechanics of medicine; radiosurgery. A. S. Freese. il Pop Mech 135:93-4 Ja '71
See also
Split brain

Weight
Brain evolution: new light on old principles. H. J. Jerison. bibliog il Science 170:1224-5 D 11 '70
Brain weight increases resulting from environmental enrichment; a directional dominance in mice. N. D. Henderson. bibliog il Science 169:776-8 Ag 21 '70

BRAIN-blood barrier. See Blood-brain barrier
BRAIN damage
Chemistry of violence. F. C. Klein. Sci Digest 68:8-12 D '70
Monosodium glutamate-induced brain lesions: electron microscopic examination. E. A. Arees and J. Mayer. bibliog il Science 170:549-50 O 30 '70
Prenatal and birth complications linked by schizophrenia research. J. Moriarty and L. Massett. il por Sci N 98:15-16 Jl 4 '70
Recovery of neuronal function after prolonged cerebral ischemia. K. A. Hossmann and K. Sato. bibliog il Science 168:375-6 Ap 17 '70; Reply with rejoinder. D. Silverman. 170:1000 N 27 '70

BRAIN damage; story. See Barthelme, D.
BRAIN damaged children
Words for a deaf daughter, by P. West Review
Commentary 51:106-7 Ja '71. J. Kaplan
Newsweek il 76:76 Ag 31 '70. R. A. Gross
Time il 96:60+ S 7 '70. R. Z. Sheppard

Education
Tom Morgan's two-way gift: patterning program. J. P. Blank. por Read Digest 96:71-5 Ap '70
BRAIN drain
Brain drain at Negro colleges. A. Poinsett. il Ebony 25:74-6+ O '70
Brain drain changes its direction. il Bsns W p56 O 10 '70
Brain drain: fewer scientists enter U.S. more seek to leave. T. P. Southwick. Science 169:565-6 Ag 7 '70
Brain drain in the Philippines: a case study. A. Muriel. Bul Atom Sci 26:38-9 S '70
Brain drain or overflow? G. B. Baldwin. bibliog f For Affairs 48:358-72 Ja '70
Foreign scientists in the United States. H. G. Grubel. il Bul Atom Sci 26:9-12 Ap '70
How to cope with the brain drain. America 122:176 F 21 '70
International talent migration and the foreign student. J. C. Shearer. bibliog f Mo Labor R 93:55-9 My '70

History
Brain drain: an age-old problem. S. Dedijer. il Bul Atom Sci 26:9-11 Mr '70
BRAIN hemorrhage. See Cerebral hemorrhage
BRAIN lesions. See Brain damage
BRAIN research. See Brain
BRAIN rhythm. See Brain waves
BRAIN stimulation. See Electronic behavior control
BRAIN waves
Brain waves. D. M. Rorvik. il Look 34:88+ O 6 '70
Learning to be hypnotized. P. Boyle. Sci Digest 68:71 D '70
Monkey see, monkey do, as Not George helps science study you. il Todays Health 48:18 O '70
Think by radio? tests on chimp's brain. Sr Schol 97:4-5 O 12 '70
Turning on with alpha waves. il Life 69:60-1 Ag 21 '70
BRAINERD, Walter
One man's answer to overpopulation. il pors Life 68:42-7 Mr 6 '70 *

BRAINERD, Minn.
U.S. journal: fifth annual Paul Bunyan snow-mobile derby. C. Trillin. New Yorker 45:68-71+ Ja 24 '70
BRAKEMEN. See Railroads—Employees
BRAKES
Instant-stop break for power tools. il Mech Illus 66:136-7 O '70
BRAKES, Automobile
Bolt-on binders; disc brake installation. J. Dianna. il Hot Rod 23:46-8 Ja '70
Brake-down. B. Lang. il Hot Rod 23:32-3 Ap '70
Four-wheel antilock brakes give you sure stops on glare ice. J. Dunne. il Pop Sci 197:82-3+ N '70
How to do a complete brake job. M. Schultz. il Pop Mech 133:170-3 Ap '70
How to do a complete brake system checkout. M. Schultz. il Pop Mech 133:184-7+ Mr '70
There's an easier way to stop. anti-skid systems. il Motor T 22:72-4 Jl '70

Maintenance and repair
Car-brake problems? Check these points. il Good H 170:175 My '70
How to do a complete disc brake job. M. Schultz. il Pop Mech 134:138-41 Ag '70
BRAKHAGE, Stan
Stan Brakhage, the courage of perception. A. Sainer. Vogue 156:298 S 1 '70 *
BRALL, Carlyn. See Groner, A. jt. auth.
BRALY, Malcolm
Prison games and other escapes. il Sports Illus 33:48-55 Ag 10 '70
BRAMER, George R.
Truth and harmony as rhetorical goals; adaptation of address, November, 1969. bibliog f Engl J 59:826-33 S '70
BRANAN, Karen
Citizen power. il Am Ed 6:14-17 Ap '70
Cocoon kids encounter city crises. il Schol Teach Sec Teach Sup p 12-13 My 4 '70
New duds for the old duchess. il Schol Teach Sec Teach Sup p8-9+ F 2 '70
Touching teachers. il Schol Teach Jr/Sr High p20-2 S 21 '70
Westledge, an exciting new concept in education. il Parents Mag 45:64-5+ F '70
When teachers do their thing, it's called DS or is it? il Schol Teach Jr/Sr High p 10-12+ O 5 '70
—and Murphy, M. K.
Answering the black's Who am I? Schol Teach Sec Teach Sup p4-6+ Ja 5 '70
Controversy in the classroom. il Parents Mag 45:37-9+ Je '70
BRANCH Brook park. See Newark. N.J.—Parks and playgrounds
BRANCH factories, Foreign
Will the multinationals lose a loophole? possible repeal of section 807 of U.S. tariff code. il Bsns W p28 My 2 '70
BRANCHES in house decoration. See Fruits, vegetables, etc. in decoration
BRANCUSI, Constantin
Millenniums of modern art. il Life 68:62-6 Mr 20 '70 *
BRAND, Sister Helena
Structure signals in The hunchback in the park. Engl J 59:195-200 F '70
BRAND, Max, pseud. See Faust. F.
BRAND, Stewart
Brand new earth; the Whole earth catalog. il por Newsweek 75:60 Je 8 '70 *
Whole earth catalog. il Pub W 197:20-1 My 11 '70 *
Whole Whole earth catalog. E. McClanahan and G. Norman. Esquire 74:95-6+ Jl '70 *
BRAND name goods. See Branded merchandise
BRAND names. See Trade marks and trade names
BRAND-rex division. See American Enka corporation
BRANDED merchandise
Consumer goods; with yardsticks of management performance. il Forbes 105:116+ Ja 1 '70; 107:148+ Ja 1 '71
BRANDEIS university, Waltham, Mass.
Bitterness at Brandeis; reactions to letter by M. Meyers. il por Newsweek 76:54-5 N 9 '70
BRANDIES, Monica
Fred Jenkins' incredible organic gardens. il Org Gard & Farm 17:49-51 Ap '70
BRANDO, Marion
Star time? A. Knight. Sat R 53:56 N 21 '70 *
BRANDON, Henry
Nixon after the honeymoon. il Sat R 53:16-18 Ja 24 '70
Reports: Washington. Atlan 225:4+ Mr '70
State of affairs. See issues of Saturday review

BRANDRETH, Dale A. and Johnson, R. E.
Composition differences at surfaces detected by adsorption and desorption of radiotracers. il Science 169:864 Ag 28 '70
BRANDT, Bill
[Photograph] Harp Baz 103:138-41 F '70

about
Bill Brandt: a haunting combination of strange and familiar. J. Szarkowski. il Mod Phot 34:84-9 O '70 *
BRANDT, Nat, and Brandt, Y. K.
Words are not just for talking. il Redbook 134:59+ F '70
BRANDT, Robert W. See Waters, W. E. jt. auth.
BRANDT, Willy
Another Berlin wall. Newsweek 75:52-3 Ja 26 '70
Don't pull the GI's out of Europe; interview, ed. by J. R. Moskin. por Look 34:82+ Ap 21 '70
No wanderer. por Time 95:27 Ja 26 '70
President Nixon and Chancellor Brandt hold talks at Washington; exchange of greetings and toasts, April 10, 1970. Dept State Bul 62:573-7 My 4 '70
Talk with Willy Brandt; excerpts from interview, ed. by B. van Voorst and J. Moskau. por Newsweek 76:33 Ag 10 '70

about
Back on the track. Newsweek 76:50 N 23 '70 *
Divided Germans talk at last. il pors U S News 68:37 Mr 30 '70 *
End of an era: the German summit. il por Newsweek 75:39 Mr 30 '70 *
Europe: a symbolic act of atonement. il por Time 96:25 D 21 '70 *
Germany: the rocky road to recognition. Time 96:22 Ag 3 '70 *
Man of the year: Willy Brandt. il pors Time 97:6-7+ Ja 4 '71 *
Real issues in Nixon-Brandt talks. il por U S News 68:80 Ap 20 '70 *
Stalin-Hitler pact, 1970 model? W. S. Schlamm. Nat R 22:946-7 S 8 '70 *
Technical mistake. il por Newsweek 75:61 My 11 '70 *
Triumph for Brandt. por Time 95:15 Ap 20 '70 *
Two Germanys face to face. il pors Time 95:18 Mr 23 '70 *
West Germany looks to the East. il por Time 95:37-8+ Mr 16 '70 *
Willy and Willi. Newsweek 75:35 Mr 2 '70 *
Willy Brandt turns East. N. Muhlen. Nat R 22:676-7 Je 30 '70 *
Willy's woes. il por Newsweek 76:43-4 Jl 27 '70 *
BRANDT, Yanna Kroyt. See Brandt, N. jt. auth.
BRANDWEIN, Paul F.
Needed: an environmental bill of rights. il Am For 76:28-33 Ap; 36-8 My '70
BRANDYWINE CREEK
Coaching: the new in sport. P. Benchley. il Travel & Camera 33:40-5+ F '70
Let's sing Auld lang syne for the upper Brandywine. L. B. Leopold. il Natur Hist 79:4-6+ Je '70
BRANG, James
Catch big bass right now. il pors Outdoor Life 145:92-3+ Ap '70
BRANIFF international airways
Acker named Braniff president; will prepare airline for sale. Aviation W 93:31 S 7 '70
Braniff readies 747 Hawaiian service. E. J. Bulban. il Aviation W 93:34-5 D 21 '70
IAM sees Braniff cutback keyed to sale. Aviation W 93:28 Jl 6 '70
South American market on threshold of growth. E. J. Bulban. il Aviation W 93:67-9 O 26 '70
BRANLEY, Franklin
Conceptions of the universe. Natur Hist 79:30+ bibliog(p90) D '70
BRANN, Henry Walter
Freud as philosopher. bibliog Am Imago 27:122-39 Sum '70
BRANSCOMB, Lewis M.
Branscomb talks of NBS after his first year; interview, ed. by J. B. Phelps. por Phys Today 23:73-5 S '70
BRANSOME, Edwin D. Jr. See Grower, M. F. jt. auth.
BRANTON, Daniel. See Davy, J. G. jt. auth.
BRASILIA, Brazil
Brasilia: city in the wilderness. il Time 95:36 My 18 '70
BRASS work
Brass, the metal that works with you. W. E. Burton. il Pop Sci 197:92-4+ D '70
BRASSAVOLA nodosa. See Orchids

BRASSIERES
Ban the bra. G. Plaut. il Look 34:54-7 F 24 '70

BRAUD, William G.
Extinction in goldfish: facilitation by intra-cranial injection of RNA from brains of extinguished donors. bibliog il Science 168:1234-6 Je 5 '70

BRAUDY, Susan
Architectural metaphysic of Louis Kahn. il pors N Y Times Mag p72-3+ N 15 '70
It's happening in Sun Valley. Am Home 73:50-3+ Ja '70

BRAUER, Donald G.
Placing a dollar sign on urban parks. il Parks & Rec 5:14-16 N '70

BRAUN, Eva
Long long days with the Fuhrer; excerpts from Inside the Third reich. A. Speer. il pors Life 68:58-58B+ Ap 24 '70 *

BRAUN, Saul
From 1-A to 4-F and all points in between. il N Y Times Mag p34-5+ N 29 '70
Sendak raises the shade on childhood. il por N Y Times Mag p34-5+ Je 7 '70

BRAUNTHAL, Gerard
West German foreign policy in ferment. Cur Hist 58:292-7 My '70

BRAUTIGAN, Richard
Lost chapters of Trout fishing in America; story. Esquire 74:152-3 O '70
Pacific radio fire; story. Mlle 71:105 Jl '70
Sand castles; story. Mlle 71:104-5 Jl '70
1692 cotton mather newsreel; story. Mlle 71:104 Jl '70
Winter rug; story. Vogue 156:98 Ag 1 '70

about
Comment. L. Warsh. Poetry 115:444-6 Mr '70 *
Gentle poet of the young. J. Stickney. il pors Life 69:49-52+ Ag 14 '70 *

BRAVERMAN, Miriam
Songmy: the human imperative. il por Library J 95:211-13 Ja 15 '70

BRAVERY. See Courage

BRAY, J. R.
Solar activity index: validity supported by oxygen isotope dating. bibliog il Science 168:571-2 My 1 '70

BRAY, William Gilmer
Excerpts from series of reports on pollution, May 19, 1970. Cong Digest 49:208+ Ag '70

BRAYBROOKE, Neville
Gandhi's spiritual classic. por Chr Cent 87:423 Ap 8 '70
Note on Kenneth Grahame. il Horn Bk 46:504-7 O '70
Poets at Bethlehem. il Cath World 212:140-2 D '70

BRAZELTON, T. Berry
Case for sibling rivalry. il Redbook 135:76-7+ O '70
What makes a good father. il Redbook 135:74-5+ Je '70

BRAZIL
See also
Amazon River
Architecture, Domestic—Brazil
Automobile industry and trade—Brazil
Banks and banking—Brazil
Brasilia
Coffee industry and trade—Brazil
Elections—Brazil
Forests and forestry—Brazil
Guerrillas—Brazil
Hotels, taverns, etc.—Brazil
Law—Brazil
Mato Grosso
Medicine—Brazil
Moving pictures—Brazil
Prisons—Brazil
Recreation—Brazil
Rio de Janeiro
Roads—Brazil
Roosevelt River
Secret societies—Brazil
Slavery—Brazil
Vocational education—Brazil
Zoology—Brazil

Description and travel
Brazilian duo; Belo Horizonte and Ouro Preto. B. F. Carruthers. il Travel 134:46-9+ D '70

Economic conditions
Highway to save the stricken Northeast; Trans-Amazon highway. il Bsns W p34-5 N 14 '70
See also
São Paulo (city) Brazil—Economic conditions

Foreign opinion
Torture in Brazil. R. Della Cava. Commonweal 92:129+ Ap 24 '70; Discussion. 92:307+, 378-9+ Je 26, Ag 7 '70

History
Brazil's revolution six years later. A. A. Lima. il America 122:646-9 Je 20 '70

Industries
See also
Airplane industry and trade—Brazil

Intellectual life
Recife school of Brazil. J. C. Torchia-Estrada. Américas 22:41-2 F '70

Monetary policy
Miracle of the crawling peg. il Bsns W p52-3 F 21 '70

Native races
See Indians of South America—Brazil

Politics and government
Affluent cage; Operation Cage unleashed. Newsweek 76:56+ N 23 '70
Atrocities charged: Brazil loses Lutheran assembly. Chr Today 14:36 Jl 3 '70
Brazilian torture: specifically new, specifically terrible. R. H. Bolton. Chr Cent 87:387-8 Ap 1 '70; Discussion. 87:727-8 Je 10 '70
Brazil's military regime. H. J. Rosenbaum. Cur Hist 58:73-8+ F '70
Brazil's revolution six years later. A. A. Lima. il America 122:646-9 Je 20 '70
Letter to Pope Paul; with reference to police torture. I. Illich. Commonweal 92:428-9 S 4 '70; Reply. J. J. Kaufmann. 93:55 O 9 '70
People are doing . . . badly in Brazil. J. Armstrong. il Chr Cent 88:14-16 Ja 6 '71
Politics by Torquemada. Nation 211:546 N 30 '70
Raising the ransom price; G. E. Bucher kidnaped by urban guerrillas in Rio. por Time 96:27 D 21 '70
Repression in Brazil: protest vs. protocol. T. Quigley. Commonweal 93:366 Ja 15 '71 Je 26 '70
Torture in Brazil. R. Della Cava. Commonweal 92:129+ Ap 24 '70; Discussion. 92:307+, 378-9+, 451+ Je 26, Ag 7, S 18 '70
See also
Elections—Brazil

Religious institutions and affairs
World around us. Chr Cent 87:1494 D 9 '70
World around us. J. Del Nero. Chr Cent 87:1001 Ag 19 '70
See also
Church and state in Brazil
Lutheran church in Brazil
Pentecostal churches in Brazil
Protestants in Brazil

Social conditions
Christians, Marxists and dictatorship in Brazil. M. M. Alves. Chr Cent 87:723-7 Je 10 '70

Social history
See also
Slavery—Brazil

BRAZILIAN cookery. See Cookery, Brazilian

BREA, LA. See La Brea, Los Angeles

BREAD
ABCs of baked beans. il Am Home 73:62 F '70
ABC's of tea breads. il Am Home 73:86 S '70
Baking better bread. Sci Digest 69:37-8 Ja '71
Being a cautionary tale for women hell-bent on baking bread. A. Chamberlin. McCalls 97:38+ S '70
Bread winners; salt-rising and sour dough. J. Hewitt. il N Y Times Mag p88 My 3 '70
Christmas breads and puddings. il Ladies Home J 87:84-8 D '70
Christmas recipes; sampler of Norwegian recipes. il Parents Mag 45:58-61+ D '70
Christmas scene-stealer; stollen. C. Claiborne. il N Y Times Mag p 126 D 6 '70
Cornbread with cheese and chiles. il Sunset 145:145 O '70
Fast and fancy fruit breads. il Bet Hom & Gard 48:91-2 O '70
Fragrant loaf for the Easter breakfast table. il Sunset 144:154+ Mr '70
Fresno's super sandwich; peda bread. il Sunset 144:102-3 Ap '70
Fruit and nut breads. il Sunset 145:158-9 N '70
Have you tried a nut bread? il Sunset 144:124-5 F '70

BREAD—*Continued*

Heat's on bread; nutrition debate. Sr Schol 97:7 N 16 '70

Help yourself to a breadstick. il Sunset 145: 153 O '70

It's baked in a two-pound coffee can. il Sunset 144:162 Je '70

Making your own onion buns. il Sunset 145: 163 S '70

Organic food success story: flourless bread. M. Franz. il Org Gard & Farm 17:88-90 F '70

Perfect yeast bread. S. Whittier. il Good H 170:128 F '70

This bread is traditional Jewish hallah. il Sunset 144:168-9 Ap '70

This is Arab peasant bread. il Sunset 144: 138-9 Je '70

Ummm-mm! Just smell that fresh bread! with recipe. il Changing T 25:18 Ja '71

Versatile refrigerated rolls. N. Benson. il Bet Hom & Gard 48:102 My '70

See also
Coffee cake
Dough
Flour

BREAD, Frozen
See also
Dough, Frozen

BREAD loaf writers' conference. See Authors conferences

BREAKFAST foods. See Cereal foods

BREAKFASTS

All about breakfast. R. H. Smithies. il Good H 171:166+ O '70

Better breakfast ideas (cont) il Bet Hom & Gard 48:102-3 F; 116 Ap; 100 O '70

Bountiful breakfasts; excerpts. S. DeBaun. il Ladies Home J 87:88-90 Je '70

Breakfast with Godfrey. il Time 95:72 Mr 16 '70

What you really should eat for breakfast. il Changing T 24:11-13 D '70

See also
Brunches

BREAST

Surgery

Breast-cancer debate; mastectomy study. Newsweek 76:121 N 16 '70

BREAST cancer. See Cancer

BREAST feeding

Advice from a nursing mother . P. Feinstein. Redbook 136:12-13+ N '70

Happy mother's guide to successful nursing. il Parents Mag 45:52-3+ F '70

When mothers need mothering. D. Raphael. il N Y Times Mag p67+ F 8 '70

BREAST milk. See Milk, Human

BREASTED, Mary

Grant v. Lee. il por Time 96:52-3 Ag 31 '70 *

BREATH, Shortness of. See Emphysema

BREATHING apparatus. See Respiratory apparatus

BREAZIER, Eldon. See Aven, S. D. jt. auth.

BRECCIA

Apollo 11 lunar science conference; papers, with editorial comment. bibliog il Science 167:447, 449-784 Ja 30 '70; Correction. 167: 1759 Mr 27 '70

BRECHER, Edward M. See Brecher, R. jt. auth.

BRECHER, Ruth, and Brecher, E. M.

How your body keeps you well. Read Digest 96:89-93 F '70

BRECHT, Bertolt

Good woman of Setzuan. Criticism
Nation 211:542 N 23 '70 *
New Repub 163:20 N 28 '70 *
New Yorker 46:141 N 14 '70 *
Newsweek 76:74 N 16 '70 *

BRECKMAN, Jack

How to end air collisions. il Bsns W p 128+ Ap 11 '70 *

BREDBERG, Göran, and others

Scanning electron microscopy of the organ of corti. bibliog il Science 170:861-3 N 20 '70

BREECH-loading rifles. See Rifles

BREEDING
See also
Cattle breeding
Horse breeding
Inbreeding
Plant breeding
Swine breeding

BREEDLOVE, Craig

Speed king without a kingdom. J. Kirshenbaum. il pors Sports Illus 32:64-8+ Ap 27 '70 *

BREEDLOVE, J. R. Jr, and Trammell, G. T.

Molecular microscopy: fundamental limitations. bibliog il Science 170:1310-13 D 18 '70

BREER, Robert

Onward and upward with the arts. C. Tomkins. New Yorker 46:84+ O 3 '70 *

BREGENZ festival. See Music festivals— Austria

BREINER, Leon

Murder trial of Dr Ossian Sweet; reprint. T. J. Fleming. il pors Ebony 25:106-8+ O '70 *

BREITBARD, Bob

Not so silent minority. M. Mulvoy. il por Sports Illus 34:54-5 Ja 4 '71 *

BREJCHA, Vernon

Throw the lid first. il Ceram Mo 18:18-19 My '70

BREL, Jacques

Alive and well. pors Time 95:64-5 My 18 '70 *

BREMER, John

High school with no walls. H. S. Resnik. Ed Digest 35:16-19 Mr '70 *

Parkway experiment. il por Time 95:55 Mr 23 '70

BRENBERGER, Richard W.

Finding your forest. il Am For 76:44-5 F '70

BRENGELMAN, Fred

Generative phonology and the teaching of spelling. Engl J 59:1113-18 N '70

BRENNAN, John

Jimmy Breathless goes to college. Nat R 22: 258 Mr 10 '70

BRENNAN, Ray

Investigative reporter: Ray Brennan; interview, ed. by C. Remsberg and B. Remsberg. il por Writers Digest 50:20-3+ F '70

BRENNER, Helen S. See Bolker, H. l. jt. auth.

BRENNER, Joseph

Free clinic for street people; medical care without a hassle. il por N Y Times Mag p30-1+ O 11; 114-15 N 8 '70

BRENNINKMEYER, C. and A, company

Brenninkmeyer: the secrecy is woven in. il Bsns W p68+ My 9 '70

BRENTANO's bookstores (New York) See Booksellers and bookselling—New York (state)

BRENTON, Myron

Parent and child. N Y Times Mag p72+ O 25 '70

BRESLER, Robert J.

War-making machinery. il Nation 211:105-9 Ag 17 '70

BRESLIN, Jimmy

Jimmy Breslin. pors Vogue 155:194-5 F 1 '70

BRESLOW, Doris G. and Dempsey, Vincent

Local association of the month. Todays Ed 59:56-7 F '70

BRESNAHAN, James F.

Rahner's Christian ethics. il America 123:351-4 O 31 '70

BRESSON. Henri Cartier-. See Cartier-Bresson. H.

BRETH, Fred E.

Four new ones from Europe. il Farm J 94: D8-9+ D '70

BRETHREN, Church of the. See Church of the Brethren

BRETONNE, Nicolas Edme Restif de la. See Restif de la Bretonne, N. E.

BRETSCHER, Peter, and Cohn, Melvin

Theory of self-nonself discrimination. bibliog il Science 169:1042-9 S 11 '70

BREUER, Gusti

Those were the days. il Opera N 34:6-11 My 16 '70

BREUER, Marcel

Mingling work and living; interview. por House & Gard 137:12+ F '70

BREUER, Robert

Strauss to Schuh: letter from the last years. Sat R 53:95-6 F 28 '70

BREUGHEL, Peeter. See Brueghel, P.

BREUVERY, Emmanuel Saguez de

E. de Breuvery, third world's servant (1903-1970) F. K. Drolet. il America 122:128-30 F 7 '70

BREVOORT, Harry

Cecropia. il Am For 76:46-7 D '70

BREWER, Albert Preston

George does it again. Nat R 22:502-3 My 19 '70 *

Here comes that man again! V. Gold. Nat R 22:566 Je 2 '70 *

How George did it. il por Time 95:16 Je 15 '70 *

Wallace country. il por Newsweek 75:35 My 4 '70 *

BREWER, Carl

Reluctant dragon torments the Red Wings. G. Ronberg. il por Sports Illus 32:46-7 Ja 26 '70

BREWER, Richard

Death by the plow; with biographical sketch. il Natur Hist 79:2, 28-35+ bibliog(p 133) Ag '70

BREWERS (baseball) See Baseball clubs

BREWING industries
Britannia rules the pubs. il Forbes 105:46-7
Mr 15 '70
See also
Beer
Coors, Adolph, company
Hamm, Theodore, brewing company
Rheingold corporation
Schlitz, Joseph, brewing company

Securities
Beer stocks stay frothy. il Bsns W p79-80
F 7 '70
BREWSTER, Dorothy P.
Blind coach leads the way. il pors Har Yrs
10:38-41 Jl '70
BREWSTER, John W.
Doc ex. bibliog il por Wilson Lib Bul 44:
941+ My '70
BREWSTER, Kingman, 1919-
If not reason, what? address, December 29,
1969. Vital Speeches 36:346-9 Mr 15 '70;
Same. Am Scholar 39:243-52 Spr '70; Ex-
cerpts. Science 168:423 Ap 24 '70
Politics of academia. Sch & Soc 98:211-14
Ap '70
Toward the voluntary university; excerpts
from address. Cur 117:19-21 Ap '70
Vote of confidence. Newsweek 76:75-6 O 12
'70
about
How Brewster does it at Yale. il por News-
week 75:68-9 Je 15 '70 *
Panther and bulldog. il por Newsweek 75:
52+ My 4 '70 *
Who's irresponsible? New Repub 162:10 My
9 '70 *
Yale proves dissent doesn't have to turn out
that way. J. K. Jessup. il por Life 68:38-
40 My 15 '70 *
BREZHNEV, Leonid Il'ich
Lenin; address, April 21, 1970. Vital Speeches
36:482-98 Je 1 '70
about
Birthday for Lenin and a boost for Brezhnev.
il por Time 95:30+ Ap 27 '70 *
Brezhnev tops the list. il por Newsweek 75:
38+ Ap 27 '70 *
Drift and delay. Newsweek 76:38+ Jl 27
'70 *
B for Russia. il por Time 95:29-30 F 23 '70 *
Soviet Union: leadership at the crossroads.
il pors Time 95:33-6 My 4 '70 *
Stalin-Hitler pact, 1970 model? W. S. Schlamm.
Nat R 22:946-7 S 8 '70 *
Troubles and tremors. il por Newsweek 75:
33+ Ap 13 '70 *
BRIAND, Paul L. jr
America, the violent; address, July 8, 1970.
Vital Speeches 36:674-9 S 1 '70
BRIANE, Mireille
Ballet comes to Binghamton. L. Chiavaroli.
il pors Dance Mag 44:28-32 Je '70 *
BRIANSKY, Oleg
Ballet comes to Binghamton. L. Chiavaroli.
il pors Dance Mag 44:28-32 Je '70 *
BRIBERY
Foul ball in Japan; investigation into fixes,
bribes and gambling. il Newsweek 75:99 Mr
30 '70
BRICK, Donald B.
Computerized fire alarm. il Am City 85:32
Ag '70 *
BRICKLIN, Mal
Scrambled eggs. il Motor T 22:55 Je '70 *
BRICKMAKING
How to resurrect bricks from ashes; Tech
process. il Bsns W p48 Ag 1 '70
BRICKMAN, William W.
Books for educators (cont) Sch & Soc 98:
309-17 Sum '70
Ethical values, education, and the morality
crisis. Sch & Soc 98:456-7 D '70
Jan Amos Comenius (1592-1670) cosmopolitan
citizen and ecumenical educator. bibliog
Sch & Soc 98:436-9 N '70
BRICKNER, Balfour
Vietnam and the Jewish community. Chr
Cent 87:531-4 Ap 29 '70
BRIDGE (game)
Best play was not the answer. C. Goren. il
Sports Illus 32:52-3 Ap 20 '70
Bland bid brings a spicy score. C. Goren.
Sports Illus 33:40-1 Jl 27 '70
Bridge. A. Truscott. See issues of New York
times magazine
Case of bucking the system; World cham-
pionship bridge competition, Stockholm.
C. Goren. il Sports Illus 33:70-1 D 7 '70
Goren's Christmas quiz (cont) C. Goren. il
Sports Illus 33:78-80+ D 21 '70
Hand of the man who invented contract. C.
Goren. il Sports Illus 33:47 Ag 10 '70

They call it precision for good reason. C.
Goren. il Sports Illus 32:57 My 18 '70
This king was truly the monarch. C. Goren.
il Sports Illus 32:60-1 Je 8 '70
Time for excellence. C. Goren. il Sports Illus
32:50 F 23 '70
Whale of a hand and a player, too. C. Goren.
il por Sports Illus 33:104 S 14 '70
BRIDGE, Flying. See Navigating bridge
BRIDGE construction
Bridge replaced in halves to avoid closing
river crossing; Girard avenue bridge over
Schuykill River, Philadelphia. il Am City
85:28 Je '70
We did it; ed. by C. L. Miller. R. G. Young.
il House B 112:57-8+ Ap '70
BRIDGE players
Mathe, moxie and stamina turned the trick.
C. Goren. il Sports Illus 33:62-4 D 14 '70
No one could trump the Aces; America's
first victory in sixteen years. W. Bingham.
il Sports Illus 33:18-21 Jl 6 '70
Spotting the winners. C. Goren. il Sports
Illus 33:80 O 12 '70
This king was truly the monarch. C. Goren.
il Sports Illus 32:60-1 Je 8 '70
This tigress burned very bright; S. Young.
C. Goren. il Sports Illus 33:73-4 N 16 '70
Time for excellence. C. Goren. il Sports Illus
32:50 F 23 '70
BRIDGE tournaments
Case of bucking the system; World cham-
pionship bridge competition, Stockholm.
C. Goren. il Sports Illus 33:70-1 D 7 '70
Dallas aces. il Newsweek 75:75 Mr 2 '70
Handful of Aces; favored to win world title.
W. Johnson. il por Sports Illus 32:68-72+
Mr 23 '70
Mathe, moxie and stamina turned the trick.
C. Goren. il Sports Illus 33:62-4 D 14 '70
No one could trump the Aces; America's
first victory in sixteen years. W. Bingham.
il Sports Illus 33:-18-21 Jl 6 '70
Sky-high stakes on London bridge; Omar
Sharif's circus and the English experts.
V. Mollo. il Sports Illus 32:18-19 Ja 26 '70
BRIDGEPORT, Conn.

Education
Magic of puppetry; project in Bridgeport,
Conn. inner-city schools. J. S. Zeliff. il
Parents Mag 45:46-7+ Jl '70

Libraries
See also
Bridgeport, Conn, public library
BRIDGEPORT, Conn, public library
Bridgeport's audiovisual story hours.   J. A.
McCrossan. Am Lib 1:493 My '70
BRIDGEPORT, Ill. See Chicago
BRIDGES, Beau
Beau Bridges starts a new family. il pors
Ebony 25:96-8+ O '70 *
Of fathers, sons and love. J. Barthel. il pors
Life 68:61-2+ My 15 '70 *
BRIDGES, Juli
Beau Bridges starts a new family. il pors
Ebony 25:96-8+ O '70 *
BRIDGES, Lloyd
Of fathers, sons and love. J. Barthel. il pors
Life 68:61-2+ My 15 '70 *
BRIDGES

Construction
See Bridge construction

Maintenance and repair
Admixture increases freeze-thaw durability
of concrete; Midland, Mich. il Am City 85:
34 My '70

Turkey
Mile of steel for the Bosporus. il Bsns W
p49 Ja 17 '70
BRIDGES, Concrete
Need a bridge in a hurry? Montgomery Coun-
ty, Ala. il Am City 85:119-20 S '70
BRIDGES, Remodeled
Ponte Vecchio for St Louis. B. Thorne. il
Arch Forum 132:60-1 Ja '70
BRIDGES, Wooden
See also
Covered bridges
BRIDSTON, Keith
From "-ty" to "-tics". Chr Cent 87:435 Ap
15 '70 *
BRIDSTON, Paul Joseph
What the senator didn't disclose. W. Lam-
bert. pors Life 69:26-9 Ag 28 '70 *
BRIEGER, Gottfried, and Butterworth, F. M.
Drosophila melanoglaster; identity of male
lipid in reproductive system. bibliog Science
167:1262 F 27 '70
BRIEN, Alan
What it's really like to be a man. Mlle 71:57+
Jl '70

BRIER, Arnold M. and others
Inflammation and herpes simplex virus: release of a chemotaxis-generating factor from infected cells. bibliog il Science 170: 1104-6 D 4 '70
BRIER, Herbert S.
Amateur radio. See issues of Popular electronics to August 1970
Amateur radio equipment 1970-1971. il Pop Electr 33:51-3+ Ag '70
BRIGANDS and robbers
Jesse James legend. P. Strickler. il pors Life 68:72 Je 12 '70
See also
Outlaws
BRIGGS, Jean L.
Kapluna daughter: living with Eskimos; excerpt from Women in the field, ed. by P. Golde. il por Trans-Action 7:12-24 Je '70
BRIGGS, Shirley A.
Remembering Rachel Carson. il por Am For 76:8-11 Jl '70
BRIGGS, Thomas H.
Reflections of a humanist. Ed Digest 35:34-7 Ja '70
BRIGHAM, Besmilr
Angel; poem. Harp Baz 103:157 Ag '70
BRIGHAM, Robert
Down to the sea in cement. il Life 69:70-3 S 11 '70
BRIGHAM Young university, Provo, Utah
Are we bandwagoneers? reasons against changing to LC at Brigham Young university library. M. E. Lamson; reply. S. W. Hilyard. Am Lib 1:111 F '70; Rejoinder. 1: 530 Je '70
Other side of the Y; attitude toward Negroes of the Church of Jesus Christ of Latter-day saints. W. F. Reed. il Sports Illus 32:38-9 Ja 26 '70
U.S. journal. C. Trillin. New Yorker 46:120+ Mr 21 '70
BRIGHT, James R.
Evaluating signals of technological change. bibliog f il Harvard Bsns R 48:62-70 Ja '70
BRIGHT promise; story. See Duncan, L.
BRIGHT shores; story. See Litvinov, I.
BRIGHTMAN, Robert
Sky's the limit with this 200-power telescope. il Pop Mech 134:166-73+ D '70; 135: 152-7 Ja '71
BRIGHTON pavilion. See Palaces
BRIGHTOWER; drama. See Schary, D.
BRILL, Earl. See Radomski, J. L. jt. auth.
BRILLIANT, Alan
Five pamphlets. Poetry 116:125-9 My '70
BRILLOUIN, Léon
Obituary
Phys Today por 23:125+ Ja '70. L. H. Thomas
BRIMMER, Andrew Felton
Economic integration and the progress of the Negro community. il por Ebony 25:118-21 Ag '70
BRIN, Irene
Irene Brin. por Harp Baz 103:74-5 Jl '70 *
BRINDLEY, Pat
Delights of water gardening. il Horticulture 48:20-2+ Ag '70
England's cottage gardens. il Home Gard 57:16-17+ Ag '70
Gardens of Shakespeare's town. il Home Gard 57:26-9 Mr '70
BRINHART, Betty
Enchanting fragrance from a summer lily. il Home Gard 57:38 Jl '70
Queen of the perennials, the oriental poppy. il Org Gard & Farm 17:66-8 Mr '70
Rhododendrons for every garden. il Org Gard & Farm 17:82-4 Ap '70
Tigridias. il Horticulture 48:20-1 Jl '70
BRINKMAN, Gervase
Correctional libraries and LSCA title IV-A. bibliog Am Lib 1:380-3 Ap '70
BRINNIN, John Malcolm
Roethke plain; poem. Atlan 225:58-60 Mr '70
Saul, afterward, riding east; poem. New.Yorker 46:36 F 28 '70
BRINTON, Mrs Willard C.
Brinton at 95. H. Keppler. il por Mod Phot 34: 66-7 Ag '70 *
BRION, Helen H.
School nurse to the rescue. il Todays Ed 59:26-7 N '70
BRIQUETS (fuel)
Barbecue briquets. il Consumer Rep 35:409-11 Jl '70; Discussion. 35:704 N '70
BRISSENDEN, Robert W. and Lennard, H. L.
Organization of mental health services and its effect on the treatment career of the patient. bibliog Ment Hy 54:416-20 Jl '70
BRISTER, Bob
New range for record heads. il pors Field & S 75:42-3+ O '70

BRISTLECONE pine. See Pine
BRISTLEWORMS. See Annelids
BRISTOL, James
Draft repeal; interview. New Yorker 46:34-6 Mr 21 '70
BRISTOL-Myers company
Billion-dollar bet. il Forbes 105:13-14 Ja 15 '70
Excedrin's headache. New Repub 163:7 Ag 15 '70
BRITISH
British, by A. Glyn. Review
Bsns W p8 D 19 '70. S. Shepard
Sat R 53:37-8 N 7 '70. A. Kendrick
No connection with real Britons. Q. Crewe. Vogue 155:62 Ap 15 '70
See also
English
Welsh
BRITISH Antarctic survey. See Antarctic exploration
BRITISH art objects. See Art objects, British
BRITISH broadcasting corporation
Cracked lens? BBC-Indian dispute over TV documentary series, Reflections in a lens. Sr Schol 97:5 O 5 '70
BRITISH COLUMBIA
British Columbia; growing pains. H. McLeod. Chr Cent 88:48-9 Ja 13 '71
See also
Georgia, Strait of
Jervis Inlet
Vancouver
Vancouver Island

Description and travel
From Prince George or from Kamloops, two routes into the Yellowhead country. il Sunset 144:44-6 My '70
Showstoppers of British Columbia; Victoria, Vancouver. D. Messinesi. Vogue 156:36 Jl '70
Water wilderness; seaplane journey up the untamed coastline. D. Butwin. il Sat R 53:45-6+ D 5 '70
BRITISH Commonwealth. See Commonwealth of nations
BRITISH communications satellites. See Communications satellites, British
BRITISH council of churches
British churchmen react to racism. Chr Cent 87:591 My 13 '70
Important victory; support for WCC's program to combat racism. T. Beeson. Chr Cent 87:1341-2 N 11 '70
Oh! Peterborough! Chr Cent 87:985 Ag 19 '70
Without prophetic fire; fighting racism in Africa. T. Beeson. Chr Cent 87:1244 O 21 '70
BRITISH dramatists. See Dramatists, English
BRITISH empire. See Commonwealth of nations
BRITISH European airways corporation
BEA unit will use 707-123Bs prior to widebodied purchase. Aviation W 93:29 D 7 '70
BRITISH HONDURAS
Offbeat Caribbean; British Honduras. D. Teague. il Yachting 127:56-7+ Mr '70
See also
Belize
Fishing—British Honduras

Antiquities
See Indians of Central America—Antiquities—British Honduras
BRITISH in Africa
African dream, by B. Gardner. Review
Sat R 53:26-7 Ag 1 '70. C. Miller
BRITISH Labor party. See Labor party (Great Britain)
BRITISH Leyland motor corporation
Car Maker's dented dream. il Bsns W p32-3 Ja 9 '71
BRITISH military assistance. See Military assistance, British
BRITISH money. See Money—Great Britain
BRITISH museum
Miss Love and Aphrodite. il Newsweek 76: 79 N 23 '70
BRITISH national theatre. See Theater—Great Britain
BRITISH national union of teachers. See Teachers unions
BRITISH Open golf tournament. See Golf—Tournaments
BRITISH overseas airways corporation
BOAC gears support facilities for 747. J. P. Woolsey. il Aviation W 93:50-1 S 14 '70
BOAC modifies Boeing 747s while its pilots boycott them. il Aviation W 93:26 Jl '70
BOAC ordered to give certain routes to proposed new carrier. Aviation W 93:32 Ag 10 '70

BRITISH overseas airways corporation—*Cont.*
BOAC pilots reject wage offer; other unions ask larger raises. Aviation W 94:28 Ja 11 '71
BOAC route transfers fought. Aviation W 93:31 N 30 '70
On returning to America. W. F. Buckley, jr. Nat R 22:1231 N 17 '70
Why BOAC's jumbos are white elephants. il Bsns W p38-9 Jl 18 '70
BRITISH painting. *See* Painting, British
BRITISH parliamentary papers. *See* Government publications
BRITISH petroleum company
Eric Drake of BP; making a splash in the U.S. market; interview. E. Drake. il pors Nations Bsns 58:62-7 Jl '70
BRITISH poetry
Both sides of the water. R. B. Shaw. Poetry 117:108-12 N '70
BRITISH royal ballet. *See* Royal ballet, Great Britain
BRITISH VIRGIN ISLANDS
Off-beat British Virgin islands. D. Marley. il Harp Baz 104:56+ D '70
Updating the British Virgin Islands. G. Cary. Yachting 128:61+ N '70
BRITISH Woolworth. *See* Woolworth, F. W. and company, ltd.
BRITTANY
Brittany is all sorts of things. P. L. Buckley. Nat R 22:209+ F 24 '70
BRITTEN, Benjamin
Another turn. G. Martin. il Opera N 34:6-7 Mr 7 '70 *
Benjamin Britten: twenty-five years of opera. G. Martin. Yale R 60:24-44 O '70 *
Britten and the borough; on the winds of the North Sea. T. Heinitz. il Sat R 53:80+ Mr 14 '70 *
Peter Grimes. Criticism
Sat R 53:57 Je 20 '70 *
Phoenix at Snape, festival of Britten. T. Heinitz. Sat R 53:55 Jl 25 '70 *
Turn of the screw. Criticism
Commonweal 92:317-18 Je 26 '70 *
New Yorker 46:144-5 Mr 15 '70 *
Opera N il 34:6-7 Mr 7 '70 *
Sat R 53:28 Mr 21 '70 *
BRITTEN, Roy J. and Kohne, D. E.
Repeated segments of DNA; with biographical sketches. il Sci Am 222:12, 24-31 bibliog(p 130) Ap '70
BRITTEN-Norman, ltd.
Underdog is flying high. il Bsns W p72+ Ja 17 '70
BROADCAST corn planting. *See* Corn—Seeding
BROADCAST music, inc.
Keeping score. Time 96:28 Ag 17 '70
BROADWAY, New York (theater district) *See* New York (city)—Theater
BROADWAY-Hale stores, inc.
More real than apparent. il por Forbes 105:48 Mr 15 '70
BROCHER, Tobias
Play schools for parents. il Time 97:55 Ja 11 '71 *
BROCHURES. *See* Pamphlets
BROCK, Alice
Eating at Alice's restaurant; excerpts from Alice's restaurant cookbook. il pors McCalls 97:92-3+ F '70
BROCK, Antony
Battle against illiteracy: a Unesco survey. Sch & Soc 98:181+ Mr '70
BROCK, Donald
Children's books capture college market. Pub W 197:41-2 Ap 6 '70 *
BROCK, Paul
Mystery of the singing sands. il Sci Digest 68:63-7 Ag '70
Seadog signals; or, Who do you recommend for admiral's woman? Motor B 125:132-5 Je '70
BROCK, Peggy Ann
(ed) See Williams, T. H. Exclusive interview with T. Harry Williams
BROCK, Terry
Gargoyle. S. J. Adamo. America 122:537-8 My 16 '70 *
BROCK, Thomas D. and Darland, G. K.
Limits of microbial existence: temperature and pH. bibliog il Science 169:1316-18 S 25 '70
BROCK, William Emerson, 1930-
Tennessee's William Brock. il por Time 96: 18-19 N 16 '70 *
BROCKETT, E. D.
Poker game where talk was the payoff. il por Nations Bsns 58:82-3 Ja '70
BRO-DART industries
Bro-dart sues CBS and Holt, demands sale of Saunders. Pub W 197:57 Mr 2 '70

BRODER, David S.
Critique on Constitution experiments. Cur 123:24-6 N '70
BRODERICK, Dorothy M.
Conspiracy against youth. por Library J 95: 214-15 Ja 15 '70
BRODIE, David A. and others
Aspirin: intestinal damage in rats. bibliog il Science 170:183-5 O 9 '70
BRODINE, Virginia. See Risebrough, R. jt. auth.
BRODSKY-Gould productions, inc.
Elliott Gould as the entrepreneur. M. Mayer. il pors Fortune 82:108-11+ O '70
BRODY, Jane E.
VD is on the rise again. Read Digest 97:181- 2+ N '70
BRODY, Michael James, 1948-
Manchild caper. il por Newsweek 75:21-2 F 2 '70
World is one big put-on. il por Time 95:13 F 2 '70
BROECKER, Wallace S.
Man's oxygen reserves. bibliog Science 168: 1537-8 Je 26 '70; Same with title Enough air. il Environ 12:26-31 S '70
BROGAN, Colm
Letter from London (cont) Nat R 22:148-9 F 10 '70
Voyage autour de ma chambre. Nat R 22:897 Ag 25 '70
BROGAN, Sir Denis William
How it looks from the colonies. See issues of Esquire to May 1970
How often he was right: some parting thoughts on de Gaulle. New Repub 163: 19-20 D 5 '70
BROIDA, H. P. and others
Is ozone trapped in the solid carbon dioxide polar cap of Mars? bibliog Science 170:1402 D 25 '70
BROILERS, Electric. *See* Household appliances, Electric
BROKAW, Dennis
Chaparral; photographs. Audubon 72:5-12 N '70
BROKAW, Jim
Great insurance debate. il Motor T 22:72-4+ Ag; 30-1+ S; 38-40+ O '70
BROKEN ARROW, Okla.
Upgraded signs give positive identity. B. Secrest. il Am City 85:108+ Ap '70
BROKEN bones. *See* Fractures
BROKEN homes
See also
Children of divorced parents
BROKERS
Bear market for brokers. il Time 95:91 Je 15 '70
Blood in the Street; NYSE and Amex plans to merge service functions. il Newsweek 75:76+ Je 15 '70
Brokers scramble to repair the damage. il Bsns W p 116-18 Je 6 '70
Busted brokers bounce back. il Time 97:59-60 Ja 11 '71
De-greening of Wall Street; cost reductions. Time 97:68-9 Ja 4 '71
Do broker exams make the grade? il Bsns W p54 D 26 '70
Fairly sad story of a Wall Street broker. M. T. Bloom. il pors N Y Times Mag p 12-13+ Je 14 '70
Gambling game that Wall Street plays; with editorial comment. il Bsns W p58-61+, 102 O 31 '70
Going public. Newsweek 75:68+ F 9 '70
If your broker fails, a new insurance plan. il U S News 68:101-2 Ap 13 '70
Leading broker calls for new rules to aid investors; excerpts from address, September 15, 1970. D. T. Regan. pors U S News 69:61-2 S 28 '70
Looking for more money; trading on the exchange and Wall Street. il Time 95:82+ Mr 30 '70
Making brokers toe the mark. por Bsns W p84 Jl 18 '70
Market: time for a new broom; reform proposals. il Newsweek 76:71-3+ N 30 '70
Nightmare's end? Newsweek 76:51+ D 28 '70
Picking a broker who won't do you wrong. il Changing T 24:39-41 D '70
Regulation of investments; interview. H. H. Budge. il pors U S News 69:52-6 S 7 '70
Rising attack on stock exchange insiders. il Time 96:58-9 Ag 10 '70
Rising fourth market. por Time 96:110 O 26 '70
Stripping secrecy from the big board; with editorial comment. il Bsns W p70-2, 94 N 28 '70
To catch a thief: results of finger-printing of employees. Newsweek 75:77-8 F 16 '70

BROKERS—*Continued*
Turmoil in securities industry: meaning for investors. il U S News 69:35-7 N 23 '70
Victims: lock, stock and over the barrel. il Newsweek 76:76 N 30 '70
Wall Street:
When brokers go broke. C. Morgello. il Newsweek 75:76 Ap 6 '70
Wall Street: a group is born. C. Morgello. il Newsweek 75:82 Ap 20 '70
When relations with your broker break down. Bsns W p91-2 O 31 '70
When the broker goes broke. Time 96:78+ O 12 '70
Winds of scandal on Wall Street. il Newsweek 76:87-8+ O 12 '70
Woes of Wall Street. Newsweek 76:107-8 N 23 '70

See also
Association of investment brokers
Bache and company
Donaldson, Lufkin and Jenrette, inc.
Dreyfus corporation
Du Pont, F. I. Glore Forgan and company
Goodbody and company
Halle and Stieglitz (firm)
Merrill Lynch, Pierce, Fenner and Smith, inc.
Odd lots securities, ltd.
Oppenheimer fund, inc.
Salomon brothers and Hutzler (firm)
Weiss, Peck and Greer (firm)

Commissions
Big board tries a new price plan. il Bsns W p36 F 21 '70
Brokerage fees: how big a raise? il U S News 69:61 N 9 '70
Changing the rules; negotiated rates. C. Morgello. il Newsweek 76:80 O 26 '70
Compromised compromise. Forbes 105:22 Mr 1 '70
Higher brokerage fees for investors? U S News 69:55-6 Jl 13 '70
Higher commissions? H. C. Wallich. Newsweek 75:77 Mr 30 '70
Higher fees for brokers; effect on investors' planning. il U S News 68:79-80 Mr 2 '70
Manny Cohen looks at the market; interview, ed. by G. R. Rosen. M. Cohen. por Duns 95:10-12+ Ap '70
Merrill Lynch still wants small investors. il Bsns W p90-4 Ap 4 '70
New campaign to repave Wall Street. il Time 96:73-4 N 30 '70
New expenses for investors in stocks; cost of transactions. il U S News 68:79 Ap 20 '70
New stockbroker commissions, how they work. il Changing T 24:4 Je '70
Rank-and-file brokers' revolt. il Bsns W p90-1 Ja 31 '70
Snubbing the small investor; proposed new commission plan of the NYSE. Duns 95:124 Mr '70
Tax aid urged for stockbrokers. U S News 69:67 S 21 '70

Consolidations and mergers
Thundering Herd to the rescue; Merrill Lynch, Pierce, Fenner & Smith take over Goodbody's business. il Newsweek 76:73 N 9 '70

Finance
Herd still thunders profitably. Bsns W p21 O 31 '70

Insurance
Billion for peace of mind; bills to Congress. il Time 95:71 Je 29 '70
Brokers' aim: self-insurance. Bsns W p 122 Ap 25 '70
Capital mess on Wall Street. C. J. Loomis. il Fortune 82:141+ Jl '70
Holding the bag. Newsweek 76:72 S 21 '70
New battles boil up over the trust fund; with editorial comment. Bsns W p20-1, 92 O 3 '70
New protection for investors when brokers go under. il U S News 70:37-8 Ja 4 '71
Protection for Wall Street's clients. Bsns W p 116 My 2 '70
Protection fund in a cross fire; securities industry vs. Senator Muskie. Bsns W p20 S 5 '70
Restoring confidence; House passes legislation establishing a Securities investors protection corp. C. Morgello. il Newsweek 76:88 D 14 '70
BROKOWSKI, William W.
Composition strategy that worked. Engl J 59:984-6 O '70
BROMAN Betty L.
Let children talk. Ed Digest 35:30-1 Mr '70

BROMBERG, Conrad
Transfers. Criticism
Nation 210:157-8 F 9 '70
New Yorker 45:56+ Ja 31 '70
BROMILEY, Geoffrey W.
Wide choice in church history and theology. Chr Today 14:6-8+ F 13 '70
BROMINE
See also
Perbromates
BROMLEY, Albert W.
Fisheries story at Cape Vincent. il Cons 24: 16-17 Ag '69
BROMLEY, David Allan
Haggerty, McElroy, Bromley stress relevance. T. Johnides. por Phys Today 23:62 D '70 *
BROMMER, Gerald F.
Prints without cutting. il Sch Arts 70:10-11 D '70
BROMODEOXYURIDINE
New light on malignancy; BUdR. Newsweek 75:73 Je 29 '70
BROMWICH, David L.
Lysergic Götterdämmerung. Commentary 50: 55-9 D '70
BRONDFIELD, Jerome
Encounter on the F train. il Read Digest 97:119-20 N '70
BRONER, E. M.
Traveler and his telling; story. Commentary 50:69-73 S '70
BRONFENBRENNER, Urie
Somebody, let it, please God, be somebody. por Time 96:37 D 28 '70

about
Beyond doctor Spock. P. Steinfels. Commonweal 93:342 Ja 8 '71 *
Do businessmen make poor parents? Bsns W p20 D 26 '70 *
Ivan v. Johnny. il Time 95:54+ Ap 27 '70 *
BRONG, Gerald R. and Pasternak, E. F.
N-I-H syndrome. il pors Library J 95:3877-8 N 15 '70
BRONIKOWSKI, Ray J.
Vacuums, the pursuit of practically nothing. il Sci Digest 67:52-6 Mr '70
BRONOWSKI, Jacob
High-minded and light-hearted. Nation 210: 166 F 16 '70
—and Bellugi, Ursula
Language, name, and concept. bibliog Science 168:669-73; 169:328 My 8, Jl 24 '70
BRONSON, William
Eskimo. il Am West 7:34-47 Jl '70
Great beer can bust. il Audubon 72:146-7 N '70
BRONX, N.Y.
Horrors of heroin; Hunts Point scene. R. Severo. Read Digest 96:72-5 Ja '70

City planning
Weiner and Gran: a brilliant design for the Bronx. il Arch Rec 148:129-36 S '70

Crime
Railroads' new worry: looters. il U S News 69:20-1 Jl 27 '70

Housing
Kibbutz in the Bronx; Co-op city. il Newsweek 76:90+ O 5 '70

Social conditions
Last stop on the D train: in the land of the new racists. L. Kriegel. Am Scholar 39:272-88 Spr '70
BRONX children's psychiatric hospital.   See Children—Hospitals, Psychiatric
BRONX zoo. See New York zoological park
BRONZE sculpture. See Metal sculpture
BRONZES
Rockefeller bronzes: the Indian tradition. P. Pal. il Art N 69:48-9+ S '70
BROOK gardens. See Water gardens
BROOK trout. See Trout
BROOK trout fishing. See Trout fishing
BROOKE, David S. See Parsons, C. S. jt. auth.
BROOKE, Edward William
Excerpt from debate, December 18, 1969. Cong Digest 49:92+ Mr '70
Our ultimate goal is individual freedom. por Ebony 25:160-3 Ag '70

about
Up from silence. il por Time 95:14-15 Mr 23 '70 *
BROOKER, Robert
Strategy that saved Montgomery Ward; interview, ed. by J. McDonald. il por Fortune 81:168-71+ My '70

BROOKHAVEN national laboratory
Medical research center
Fallout and Marshallese; report. il Bul Atom
Sci 26:45 Mr '70
BROOKHISER, Richard
Story of the posting of the theses. Nat R
22:196-8 F 24 '70
BROOKLYN
Michael Semak: a photographer involved
with life's human drama; photographing
the people of Bedford-Stuyvesant. M.
Edelson. il Pop Phot 67:98-101+ N '70

Elections
See New York (city)—Elections

Historic houses, etc.
Watchtower on Brooklyn Heights. il Arch
Forum 132:40-1 Mr '70

Music
See also
Brooklyn academy of music

Sanitary affairs
Lunch at ten-thirty; service by Seventh
avenue neighbors association to sanitation-
men of District 30. New Yorker 46:20-2 Ag
15 '70

Theater
Love a duck; production of Tarot, at the
Chelsea theater center. J. Kroll. Newsweek
76:61 D 28 '70
Over the river; Chelsea theater center. J.
Kroll. il Newsweek 76:88 N 9 '70

Urban renewal
See also
Bedford-Stuyvesant corporation
BROOKLYN academy of music
Academy. New Yorker 46:44 N 14 '70
Report:
Abu Hassan, by Carl Maria von Weber.
H. E. Phillips. Opera N 34:23 Je 13 '70
BROOKLYN botanic garden
Old juniper: a bonsai, newest acquisition.
New Yorker 46:37-9 N 7 '70
Teaching the environment to 2,500 young-
sters; Teatown Lake reservation in Ossin-
ing, N.Y. C. Schweikert. il por Org Gard
& Farm 17:83-5 Jl '70
BROOKLYN CENTER, Minn.
Plan before you plow. H. Davis. il Am City
85:30 Ja '70
BROOKLYN public library
Can this marriage be saved? materials
selection policy. D. Bass; discussion. Li-
brary J 94:4321-2; 95:429 D 1 '69, F 1 '70

Branches
Life is short, death is sure; Coney Island
branch; excerpt from annual report. S.
Schickler. il Am Lib 1:35-8 Ja '70
BROOKS, Bryce
Leaving the drug world behind. R. Mos-
kowitz. il Am Ed 6:3-6 Ja '70; Same. Ed
Digest 35:5-7 My '70
BROOKS, Charles W.
Z: politics on film. Commentary 49:26+ My
'70
BROOKS, Christopher
Haunted houses of Staten Island. il Travel
134:50-2+ S '70
BROOKS, David B.
Uncivil servants. D. Sanford. New Repub
162:13-14 My 16 '70 *
Unfaithful servants. J. Ridgeway. Ramp Mag
9:9-10+ D '70 *
BROOKS, Harvey, and Bowers, Raymond
Assessment of technology; with biographical
sketches. il Sci Am 222:10, 13-21 F '70
BROOKS, James W.
Wildlife in Alaska. il Nat Parks & Con
Mag 44:28-30 N '70
BROOKS, Joe
Fishing. See issues of Outdoor life
Fishing in New Zealand (cont) il pors Out-
door Life 145:56-7+ Ja '70
Spincaster's way. il pors Outdoor Life 146:
96-8+ O '70
BROOKS, John
Clean break with the past. il Am Heritage
21:4-7+ Ag '70
Our far-flung correspondents. New Yorker
46:182-4+ N 21 '70
BROOKS, Mary M.
Parent and child. il N Y Times Mag p97+
Ap 5 '70
BROOKS, P. F.
British streams are getting cleaner, slowly.
il Am City 85:78+ Jl '70

BROOKS, Patricia
Canvassing the Spanish galleries. il Sat R
53:70-3 S 12 '70
Travel tips for Expo year in Japan. House
& Gard 137:60+ Mr '70
BROOKS, Patricia K.
Report from Japan. il Art in Am 58:122-4 Mr
'70
BROOKS Paul
When kids write their congressman. America
122:341-2 Mr 28 '70
BROOKS, Paul, 1909-
Oklawaha: the sweetest water-lane in the
world. il Audubon 72:34-6+ Jl '70
BROOKS, Peter
Critical university. Mlle 70:104-5+ Ja '70
BROOKS, Robert R. R.
People versus food; excerpt from address.
Sat R 53:10-14+ S 5 '70
BROOKS, Van Wyck
Men of letters. A. Trachtenberg. Nation 211:
117-20 Ag 17 '70 *
Van Wyck Brooks-Lewis Mumford letters.
ed. by R. E. Spiller. Review
New Repub 163:21-2+ S 19 '70. H. Kra-
mer *
Newsweek pors 76:82+ S 7 '70. R. A.
Gross *
Sat R 53:48-9 Ag 22 '70. D. Littlejohn *
BROOKS RANGE wilderness area. See Wilder-
ness areas—Alaska
BROOMSTICK beauty; drama. See Miller,
H. L.
BROONZY, Bill
Big Bill reconsidered. P. Welding. il por Sat
R 53:62-3 F 14 '70 *
BROPHY, Brigid
Hi, mistress. Vogue 155:92-3+ F 15 '70
about
He-she with linguistic leprosy. A. Alvarez.
por Sat R 53:25-7+ Ja 24 '70
BROSE, Friedrich K.
Layoff in California. il por Library J 95:3741-
4 N 1 '70
BROSNAC, Andre
Build a photographic wash tester. il Pop
Electr 32:65-6 My '70
BROTH. See Soups
BROTHELS. See Prostitution
BROTHER whistler; story. See Boles, P. D.
BROTHERHOOD; drama. See Ward, D. T.
BROTHERHOOD of man

Bibliography
Books for brotherhood. il Commonweal 91:
583-6 F 27 '70
BROTHERHOOD of railway and airline clerks,
inc.
Court vetoes antistrike tactic. Bsns W p78+
N 7 '70
BROTHERHOODS
Equal rights for brothers. E. Glynn. America
123:64-5 Ag 8 '70; Discussion. 123:105 S 5
'70
BROTHERS, Joyce
How to appeal to women. por Mech Illus 66:
35-7+ Ag '70
On being a woman. See issues of Good house-
keeping
BROTHERS and sisters. See Siblings
BROUGHTON, T. Alan
Hathaway; poem. Liv Wildn 33:26 Wint '69
BROUGHTON, T. Robert S.
(comp) Articles and other books received;
ancient. See issues of American historical
review
BROUN, Heywood Hale
Man of letters. il por Newsweek 75:82 Ja
26 '70
BROW, Robert
Cake; story. Chr Today 14:12-13 Ag 21 '70
BROWARD COUNTY, Fla.
Education
Individualized learning in the flexible school;
elementary schools. F. Hatfield and L
Gullette. Am Lib 1:169-70 F '70
BROWER, Brock
Agnew on the warpath. il pors Life 69:26-31
O 16 '70
Don't get Agnew wrong. il pors Life 68:64-6+
My 8 '70
about
Glorious fun with an honorable profession.
R. Graves. por Life 69:1 O 16 '70 *
BROWER, Michael, and Little, Doyle
White help for black business. Harvard Bsns
R 48:4-6+ My '70
BROWER, Robert
Sensitivity training aids our staff develop-
ment program. por Camp Mag 42:14+ N
'70

BROWN, A. M. See Walker, J. L. jr. jt auth.

BROWN, Allison W. jr
New legal weapon for blacks: Trans-Action
7:4-5 Je '70

BROWN, Barry
Starting at the top. H. V. Fondiller. il por
Pop Phot 67:117-18 Ag '70 *

BROWN, Bernard B.
Powerboat race to Bermuda. il Yachting 127:
69-71 My '70

BROWN, Brendan F.
Constitutional relation of church and state;
address, January 26, 1970. Vital Speeches
36:359-62 Ap 1 '70
Crime of abortion; address, April 9, 1970. Vital Speeches 36:549-53 Jl 1 '70

BROWN, Byron W.
Big shredder eats a junked car a minute. il
Am City 85:70-1 Jl '70

BROWN, Carolyn
Dance magazine award, 1969. il por Dance
Mag 44:30-1 My '70 *

BROWN, Christy
Miracle. S. K. Oberbeck. por Newsweek 75:
98+ Je 8 '70 *
Wakes and confessions. por Time 95:99-100
Je 15 '70 *

BROWN, Clarence J.
Excerpt from address, September 10, 1970.
Cong Digest 49:298+ D '70

BROWN, Courtney C.
Remodeling management structures. por Nations Bsns 58:46 N '70

BROWN, David A.
Problems of success. Aviation W 93:9 S 21
'70 *

BROWN, Dennis A.
For fall planting: the little gems of spring-
time. il Home Gard 57:32-5+ O '70
Shaded garden. il Home Gard 57:20-7 Jl '70

BROWN, Dorothy Foster
Button collecting. See issues of Hobbies

BROWN, Francis
Book power. R. A. Sokolov. il pors Newsweek 76:114-114A N 2 '70 *

BROWN, Fred
Army to be saved. il por Time 97:55 Ja 4 '71 *
Breaking ranks. J. D. Douglas. Chr Today
15:58 N 6 '70 *
Crisis for Salvationists. Chr Cent 87:1114 S
23 '70 *
Salvation army officer ousted in dispute over
book. Chr Cent 87:1312 N 4 '70 *
Salvation by censorship? T. Beeson. Chr Cent
87:812 Jl 1 '70 *

BROWN, G. Malcolm, and others
Petrographic, mineralogic, and X-ray fluorescence analysis of lunar igneous-type rocks
and spherules. bibliog il Science 167:599-
601 Ja 30 '70

BROWN, Garry
Excerpt from debate, September 17, 1969. Cong
Digest 49:30 Ja '70

BROWN, George Alfred
Levantine laugh-in. por Time 95:26 F 2 '70

BROWN, George Bosworth. See Stöhrer, G. jt.
auth.

BROWN, George Edward, 1920–
Great Tunney-Brown fight. D. Neff. il por
Time 95:15 Je 15 '70

* BROWN, George Hay
New South as census shows it; excerpts from
address, October 23, 1970. U S News 69:54
N 2 '70

BROWN, George Mackay
Eye of the hurricane: story. Atlan 225:71-4
Mr '70
Time to keep; story. Mlle 70:164-5 Mr '70
Wireless set; story. Atlan 225:89-91 Ja '70

BROWN, Gwilym S.
Tennis. il Sports Illus 33:50+ S 7; 94-6 S 14
'70
Week (college football) Sports Illus 33:52-4
N 2 '70
What will he think of next? il pors Sports
Illus 32:38-42+ My 4 '70
(ed) See Stewart, J. Racing's most frighten-
ing corners

BROWN, H. Douglas
Gems and minerals. See issues of Hobbies

BROWN, H. Rap
Losers on U.S. 1. il pors Newsweek 75:28 Mr
23 '70
Rap Brown: on FBI's most wanted list. il por
U S News 68:110-11 My 18 '70 *

BROWN, Harold O. J.
Current passions. il Nat R 22:890 Ag 25 '70
Evolution, revolution, or victory. Chr Today
14:4-6 Ap 10 '70
Oberammergau: is it anti-Semitic? Chr To-
day 14:24 Je 19 '70
Post-and pre-Christianity. Chr Today 14:3-5
S 25 '70

BROWN, Harrison
Human materials production as a process in
the biosphere; with biographical sketch. il
Sci Am 223:38, 194-8+ bibliog(p266) S '70

BROWN, Helen Gurley
Helen Gurley Brown only wants to help. N.
Ephron. por Esquire 73:74-5+ F '70 *
You are the more cupcakeable for being
a Cosmopolitan girl. W. F. Buckley, jr. Nat
R 22:999-1000 S 22 '70 *

BROWN, J. P. S.
Authors & editors. A. P. Hackett. por Pub
W 197:39-40 Mr 2 '70 *

BROWN, James I.
Look's twenty-day course in quick reading.
Look 34:71+ Ja 27; 62+ F 10 '70; Same. abr.
with title You can read faster. Read Digest
96:169-70+ My '70

BROWN, James Wilson
Personal viewpoint. Am Lib 1:44-5 Ja '70

BROWN, Jimmy
Jim Brown comes to Mississippi. C. Gillespie.
Nation 211:236-9 S 21 '70 *

BROWN, Joe. See Brown, J. P. S.

BROWN, John, 1800-1859
To purge this land with blood, by S. B.
Oates. Review
Newsweek il por 76:80+ Jl 6 '70. R. A.
Gross *

BROWN, John Anthony
Position paper on dormitory intervisitation;
statement. Sch & Soc 98:379-81 O '70

BROWN, John Carter
Square peg in a square hole. R. Lynes. il
pors Art in Am 58:80-5 Mr '70 *

BROWN, Joseph
Jazz variation; poem. America 122:472 My 2
'70

BROWN, Joseph A.
Note to a priest; poem. Cath World 212:176
Ja '71

BROWN, Julie L.
Our eighth graders tackled air pollution. il
Todays Ed 59:60-1 F '70

BROWN, Kevin V.
Fighter pilot's fighter plane. il Pop Mech
134:73-7 D '70
Flying fraidycats fight fear in the sky. il To-
days Health 48:24-6+ Je '70
Hot new fighter for the navy. il Pop Mech
133:83-6+ Ja '70
How you can own and fly your own whirly-
bird. il Pop Sci 197:40-2+ Jl '70
Men are full of weak points. il Todays
Health 48:64-6 N '70
Our supersecret, superquiet plane. il Pop
Mech 133:94-7 Mr '70
Plane that makes airfields obsolete, il Pop
Mech 133:80-3+ Je '70
When your eyes flunk the 20-20 test. il Todays
Health 48:22-5+ Ag '70

BROWN, Lester R.
Human food production as a process in the
biosphere; with biographical sketch. il Sci
Am 223:38, 160-70 bibliog(p265) S '70

BROWN, Louis M.
Family legal matters. Bet Hom & Gard 48:
26+ Ap; 20 My; 30 Je; 28+ O; 6 N; 18 D '70
Illness and injury: the legal steps you must
know about. Bet Hom & Gard 48:30 Je '70

BROWN, Margery Finn
Farewell disaster, hello bliss; story. McCalls
98:66-7 Ja '71
In the forests of Riga the beasts are very
wild indeed; story. McCalls 97:56-7 Jl '70

BROWN, Michael E.
Condemnation and persecution of hippies.
bibliog por Trans-Action 6:33-46 S '69; Excerpts. Cur 112:9-13 N '69; Trans-Action
7:72 Ja '70

BROWN, Newell
Find publisher or perish. Pub W 198:32-4
O 5 '70

BROWN, Norman B. and Huff, W. H.
Price indexes for 1970: Serial services. il Library J 95:2428-9 Jl '70

BROWN, Oscar, 1926–
Moral the merrier. il por Time 95:63 Mr 30
'70 *

BROWN, Pete
Brown is beautiful. il por Newsweek 75:58
F 16 '70 *

BROWN, Phillip King
Men sell confessions too! Writers Digest 50:
26-8+ Ag '70

BROWN, Rap. See Brown, H. R.

BROWN, Rex V.
Do managers find decision theory useful? il
Harvard Bsns R 48:78-89 My '70

BROWN, Richard Maxwell
Page 48; an escape from paranoia. Am West
7:48 Ja '70

BROWN, Robert McAfee
Benisons on Bennett. por Chr Cent 87:663-4 My 27 '70
Discoveries and dangers. por Chr Cent 87: 40-5 Ja 14 '70
Mayday for America. Commonweal 92:266-8 My 29 '70
Open letter to Spiro T. Agnew. Chr Cent 87:1213-17 O 14 '70

BROWN, Robert S.
Steel city skydiver aids troubled teens. il pors Ebony 25:72-4+ Jl '70 *

BROWN, Roscoe C. Jr
NYU institute of Afro-American affairs. por Sch & Soc 98:146-7 Mr '70 *

BROWN, Rosellen
Surviving; poem. Atlan 226:61 Jl '70

BROWN, Rosemary
Opus posthumous. il por Newsweek 77:90 Ja 11 '71 *
Rosemary's babies. I. Kolodin. por Sat R 53: 53 O 31 '70 *
Voices of silence. il por Time 96:68 Jl 6 '70 *

BROWN, Royal S.
Alexander Schneider's Christmas present. il por Hi Fi 20:secII 24-5 Mr '70 *
Ernest Ansermet, his last recordings. por Hi Fi sec I 20:95 F '70
Shostakovich's banned Babi Yar symphony in the original version. il por Hi Fi 20:secI 77-8 Je '70

BROWN, Rustie
There's an undeniable link between skating and dancing! il Dance Mag 44:34-7 Ja '70

BROWN, Sam
What strategy for peace leadership. Cur 122:21-5 O '70

BROWN, Sonny
Prison records. por Time 96:64+ N 2 '70 *

BROWN, Spencer
At the ground-breaking. . ; poem. il Wilson Lib Bul 45:451 Ja '71

BROWN, Stewart A.
Camp objectives must be specific if they are to be meaningful. il Camp Mag 42:15-16 N '70

BROWN, Terry
Emigrants' guide for women. il Am West 7: 12-17+ S '70

BROWN, Thomas H.
River of Doubt. il pors Américas 22:15-23 O '70

BROWN bread. See Bread

BROWN trout fishing. See Trout fishing

BROWNE, Le Lieu
Caste and class in the Chaco. Nation 211: 239-42 S 21 '70

BROWNE, Merle Lynn
Trade winds. C. Amory. Sat R 53:6 Jl 25 '70 *

BROWNE, Richard
Ram for the records; ed. by B. Hartford. il por Outdoor Life 146:72-5+ O '70

BROWNE, Roberts S.
Separation. por Ebony 25:46-8+ Ag '70

BROWNE, Secor D.
Airline issues. Aviation W 93:11 D 7 '70
Airlines are too bearish; interview, ed by G. R. Rosen. por Duns 95:10-11+ Mr '70
Airlines tighten their seat belts. il por Newsweek 76:85 O 19 '70 *
Browne seeks broadened role for CAB. L. Doty. Aviation W 93:32-3 S 14 '70 *

BROWNE, Tom
Vixen and the boy. il Nat Parks & Con Mag 44:22-3 Je '70

BROWNELL, Gordon L. and Shalek, R. J.
Nuclear physics in medicine. bibliog il pors Phys Today 23:32-6+ Ag '70

BROWNFELD, Allan C.
Irrelevance of American politics. Yale R 60: 1-13 O '70

BROWNING, Elizabeth (Barrett)
Books. W. H. Auden. New Yorker 46:153-9 S 12 '70 *

BROWNING, Frank
From rumble to revolution: the Young Lords. il Ramp Mag 9:19-25 O '70
They shoot hippies, don't they? Ramp Mag 9:14-23 N '70

BROWNING, Harley L.
Life expectancy and life cycles. Cur 114:55-62 Ja '70

BROWNING, Robert
Books. W. H. Auden. New Yorker 46:153-9 S 12 '70 *

BROWNJOHN, Alan
Comment. R. B. Shaw. Poetry 117:108-9 N '70 *

BROWNMILLER, Susan
Con Ed's Charles Luce: all power (sometimes) to the people. il pors N Y Times Mag p34-5+ Ap 12 '70
Sisterhood is powerful. il N Y Times Mag p26-7+ Mr 15 '70; Same abr. Cur 117:28-38 Ap '70
Women re women. Mlle 70:184+ F '70

BROWNSTEIN, Michael
Trumpets are coming; Strolling with the adults; poems. Poetry 116:149-51 Je '70

BROWNSTONES (houses) See New York (city) —Architecture

BROWNVILLE, Neb.
Ghost town on the river: excerpts from The world and the parish. ed. by W. M. Curtin. W. Cather. il por Am Heritage 21:68-72 O '70

BROY, Anthony
Modern industry. il Duns 96:79-80+ S '70

BROZEN, Yale
Toward an ultimate solution. il Sat R 53: 30-1+ My 23 '70

BRUBAKER, Charles William
Building types study. il Arch Rec 148:121-7 N '70

BRUBECK, Dave
Alaska's fifteenth festival. J. D. Car. Hi Fi 20:MA26+ S '70 *

BRUCAN, Silviu
Task of saving the seas cannot be delayed. il Sat R 53:20 S 26 '70

BRUCE, David K. E.
[Plenary sessions] on Vietnam held at Paris. See issues of Department of state bulletin, August 6, 1970–
about
Bruce's debut. Newsweek 76:43 Ag 17 '70 *
New man in Paris. por Time 96:8-9 Jl 13 '70 *
New team takes up the quest for peace. pors U S News 69:38 Ag 3 '70 *
Oenologist's dilemma. Time 96:28 S 28 '70 *
Tough test for a real pro. il por Newsweek 76:22 Jl 13 '70 *

BRUCE, Evangeline (Bell)
Peaceful pleasures of Christmas; interview, ed. by L. Baldridge. Harp Baz 104:142-3 D '70
about
Rooms they love to live in. il por House & Gard 138:34-9 Ag '70 *

BRUCE, F. F.
New English Bible. Chr Today 14:8-11 Ja 30 '70

BRUCE, Jeannette
Aikido. Sports Illus 33:6´-6+ O 26 '70
Merrily they rolled along. il Sports Illus 33: 24-5 Ag 31 '70
Squinting at the stars of sport. il Sports Illus 32:52-4+ Ja 19 '70

BRUCKER, Herbert
Can printed news save a free society? Sat R 53:52-4+ O 10 '70
Conscience for the press. Sat R 53:59-61 My 9 '70

BRUDER, Joerg
Yachting interviews. E. Horan. il por Yachting 127:61+ F '70 *

BRUDNOY, David
Delectations. Nat R 22:737 Jl 14 '70
Dirty little war. Nat R 22:453 My 5 '70
Free them now! Nat R 22:1404 D 29 '70
Hayakawa at Northeastern. Nat R 22:202 F 24 '70
Japan's campus turmoil. Nat R 22:147 F 10 '70
Losing it at the movies. Nat R 22:1309-11 D 1 '70
Television. Nat R 22:1009+ S 22 '70

BRUEGHEL, Peeter, the elder
Tower of Babel; paintings. UNESCO Courier 23:35-8 Ag '70

BRUELL, Jan H. and others
Inheritance of a cardiac arterial asymmetry in mice. bibliog il Science 167:199-200 Ja 9 '70

BRUGES, Belgium
Galleries and museums
Pleasures spiritual and temporal; Hôpital Saint-Jean. N. S. Hazelton. Nat R 22:572 Je 2 '70
Religious institutions and affairs
Pleasures spiritual and temporal. N. S. Hazelton. Nat R 22:572 Je 2 '70

BRUGMANN, Bruce
Raising hell on the Bay. il por Time 96:88+ N 23 '70 *

BRUNCHES
Come to brunch and bring the kids; with recipes. il Parents Mag 45:72-5+ Mr '70
Elegant brunch; after the prom or before graduation; with recipes. il Bet Hom & Gard 48:46+ Je '70
Sunday brunch. il Bet Hom & Gard 48:29 N '70

BRUNDAGE, Avery
Amateurs on the skids? il por Newsweek 77:55-6 Ja 11 '71 *

BRUNEAU CANYON, Idaho. See Canyons

BRUNER, Jan, and Kennedy, Donald
Habituation: occurrence at a neuromuscular junction. bibliog il Science 169:92-4 Jl 3 '70
BRUNER, Jerome Seymour
Skill of relevance or the relevance of skills. il Sat R 53:66-8+ Ap 18 '70

about

Jerome Bruner maintains: infants are smarter than anybody thinks. M. Pines. il pors N Y Times Mag p32-3+ N 29 '70 *
BRÜNING, Heinrich
From the past: Kerensky & Brüning. P. Steinfels. Commonweal 92:310 Je 26 '70 *
BRUNING, Walter F.
Short cuts to a trimmer garden. il Home Gard 57:18-19+ Ag '70
BRUNNER, Richard F.
Core-memory sense amplifiers. il Electr World 84:53-4 Jl '70
Differential comparators. il Electr World 84: 37 Jl '70
BRUNO, Brother. See Laverdiere, B.
BRUNS, Renee
Diploma hunting with a camera. il Pop Phot 66:110-13+ Je '70
Look what photography's doing to greeting cards. il Pop Phot 67:96-7+ O '70
BRUNSWICK corporation
Brunswick cuts trouble adrift. il Bsns W p 16-17 O 3 '70
BRUSH
See also
Chaparral
BRUSH fires
Ordeal by fire storm. il Time 96:18 O 12 '70
BRUSHES
See also
Paint brushes
BRUSSELS
Description
Brussels for a day. J. Bryan, 3d. il Holiday 47:50-1+ Ja '70
Music
Report:
Tristan und Isolde. L. Mueller. Opera N 35:34 D 12 '70
BRUSTEIN, Robert
Honest, intelligible radical politics. New Repub 163:15-17 S 26 '70; Same. Cur 123:20-3 N '70
Revolution as theatre. New Repub 162:13-17 Mr 14; 30-1 Ap 25 '70; Same. Cur 118:3-8 My '70
When the Panther came to Yale. il N Y Times Mag p7-9+ Je 21; 34-5 Jl 12 '70
BRY, Ed
May day in North Dakota. il Audubon 72: 57-64 Mr '70
BRYAN, George T. and Ertürk, Erdogan
Production of mouse urinary bladder carcinomas by sodium cyclamate. bibliog il Science 167:996-8 F 13 '70
—and others
Production of urinary bladder carcinomas in mice by sodium saccharin. bibliog il Science 168:1238-40 Je 5 '70
BRYAN, J. 3d
Brussels for a day. Holiday 47:50-1+ Ja '70
Color it paradise. Nat R 22:516 My 19 '70
Colosseum: world's bloodiest acre. il Read Digest 96:234-6+ Je '70
Who needs computers? Horizon 12:46-7 Spr '70
BRYAN, Marcus R.
Back to basics. Flying 86:56-7 Je '70
BRYAN, Robert
Ceramics of Beatrice Wood. il por Craft Horiz 30:28-33 Mr '70
BRYAN, William J. 1926-
My Sony, the doctor (William J. Bryan jr. M.D.) D. Slavitt. il Esquire 74:164-5+ O '70 *
BRYAN-Chamorro treaty. See Nicaragua Canal (proposed)
BRYANT, Barbara Everitt
Rockets and restaurants in motor city. il por Library J 95:2085-8 Je 1 '70
BRYANT, David
Sowing the wind. Chr Today 14:13-15 Je 5 '70
BRYANT, William Cullen
Autumn woods: poem. Nat Wildlife 8:54 O '70
BRYCE CANYON NATIONAL PARK
Creating an effective interpretive program. D. W. Halloran. il Nat Parks 44:10-13 Mr '70
BRYNNER, Roc
Opium; dramatization of J. Cocteau's journal. Criticism
Nation 211:414 O 26 '70 *
BRYOPHYTES
See also
Liverworts

BRYOZOA
Phylum ectoprocta, order cheilostomata: microprobe analysis of calcium, magnesium, strontium, and phosphorus in skeletons. T. J. M. Schopf and J. R. Allan. bibliog il Science 169:280-2 Jl 17 '70
BRZEZINSKI, Zbigniew
America and Europe. bibliog f For Affairs 49:11-30 O '70
Emerging technetronic era; excerpts from Between two ages. Cur 124:56-64 D '70
Revolution it is not? Cur 118:21-2 My '70
Russia's bureaucracy, loaded with incompetents; interview. il pors U S News 68:71-2 Ap 20 '70
Technetronic America; excerpts from Between two ages. Newsweek 76:36 Jl 20 '70
BUBBLE chambers
Bubble chambers are ready to study neutrinos. Phys Today 23:61+ Ja '70
BUBBLES
Plastic bubbles and how to blow them. A. V. Grosse. bibliog il pors Chem 43:24-7 N; 25-7 D '70
Science's answer to violence: bubbles. il pors Sci Digest 67:74-7 Ap '70
BUBEL, Nancy W.
Boy plus zucchini equals good eating and pocket money. il Org Gard & Farm 17:90-3 Ap '70
Gourmet gardeners like 'em small! il pors Org Gard & Farm 17:120-2 Mr '70
North side shelterbelt for our birds. il Org Gard & Farm 17:86-8+ N '70
BUBER, Martin
Martin Buber on Jesus: a Jewish reading. D. J. Moore. il America 122:630-3 Je 13 '70 *
BUCER, Martin. See Butzer, M.
BUCHA, V. and others
Geomagnetic intensity: changes during the past 3000 years in the western hemisphere. bibliog il Science 168:111-14 Ap 3 '70
BUCHANAN, Henry A.
Stream. Good H 171:176 N '70
BUCHANAN, Mary Elizabeth (Torrance)
Obituary
Parents Mag por 45:12 My '70. G. J. Hecht *
BUCHANAN, Pat
Ghost hunt. por Newsweek 75:26 Je 8 '70 *
BUCHANAN, Roger
Pictures on board a hijacked plane. il por Life 68:30-1 Je 19 '70
BUCHANAN, S. and Cruddace, R. G.
How rockets work. il Space World H-1-85: 13-22+ Ja '71
BUCHANAN, William
Nineteenth-century Scottish painting. il Antiques 98:394-9 S '70
BUCHANAN, William J.
Making of a champion. il Read Digest 96:106-12 Mr '70
BUCHER, Giovanni Enrico
Raising the ransom price. por Time 96:27 D 21 '70 *
BUCHER, J. Frank
Fast and easy: bar-plant trees and vines. il Org Gard & Farm 17:80-1 N '70
BUCHER, Julia D.
She who hesitates. il por Redbook 136:29+ N '70
BUCHER, Lloyd Mark
Matter of accountability, by T. Armbrister. Review
Bsns W por p8 Ag 15 '70. D. Fausch *
Pueblo variously remembered. W. A. McWhirter. por Life 69:8 Ag 21 '70 *
Pueblo's story. il por Newsweek 76:110+ S 14 '70 *
Trade winds. C. Amory. Sat R 53:13 Ag 8 '70 *
Where are they now? por Newsweek 75:16 Je 8 '70 *
BUCHSBAUM, Walter H.
Automatic vehicle monitoring. il Electr World 83:42-4+ Je '70
New test signal for color TV. il Electr World 84:37 Ag '70
BUCHTEL college. See Akron. University
BUCHWALD, Art
Airline rate war. il Holiday 47:88 F '70
Washington householder speaks his mind; interview. por House & Gard 138:26+ Ag '70

about

Sheep on the runway. Criticism
America 122:256-7 Mr 28 '70 *
Commonweal 92:143-5 Ap 24 '70 *
Nation 210:220 F '70 *
New Yorker 45:70+ F 7 '70
Newsweek 75:102 F 16 '70 *
Sat R 53:22 F 21 '70 *
Time il 95:65-6 F 16 '70 *
BUCK, Carlton C.
Ministering to alcoholics. Chr Today 14:29 Jl 17 '70 *

BUCK, Pearl (Sydenstricker)
Rose Kennedy; excerpt from The Kennedy women. il pors Good H 170:68-71+ Je '70
Two in love; story. Good H 171:60-1 D '70
Will a miracle child be born this year? il Ladies Home J 87:63+ D '70

BUCKINGHAM palace art exhibitions. See Art —Exhibitions

BUCKLEY, A. R.
Astilbes. il Horticulture 48:38-9 Jl '70

BUCKLEY, Emerson
What a conductor does. il por Opera N 34:26-9 Mr 28 '70

BUCKLEY, Fergus Reid
Delectations (cont) Nat R 22:1166 N 3 '70
Father was as much a figure of awe as of fun. il pors Life 69:42-4 D 18 '70
Letter from Madrid (cont) Nat R 22:943-4 S 8 '70
Revolt of Enoch Peters; reprint of 1960 article. il Nat R 22:886-9 Ag 25 '70

BUCKLEY, Jack
Behind the scenes. Hi Fi 20:21+ N '70

BUCKLEY, James L.
Conservative upset in the making in liberal New York? il pors U S News 69:30-1 Ag 31 '70 *
False front campaign funds: how they work. por U S News 70:57 Ja 11 '71 *
Hi, there! Your next senator. J. L. Kilpatrick. il Nat R 22:1154-8 N 3 '70 *
How Buckley won New York. il por Newsweek 76:37-8+ N 16 '70 *
New York's James Buckley. il por Time 96:18-19 N 16 '70 *
Nixon and the New York election. W. F. Buckley, jr. Nat R 22:805 Jl 28 '70 *
Onward and upward. Nat R 22:827-8 Ag 11 '70 *
Other Buckley. il pors Time 96:12-13 Ag 24 '70 *
Senator Buckley. W. F. Buckley, jr. Nat R 22:1314-15 D 1 '70 *
Something new is added. J. Burnham. Nat R 22:1198-9 N 17 '70 *

BUCKLEY, Marylou
Charioteer at Delphi; poem. America 122:131 F 7 '70

BUCKLEY, Priscilla L.
African safari. il Harp Baz 103:118+ S '70
Delectations (cont) Nat R 22:209+, 1059 F 24, O 6 '70
Notes on a fifteenth anniversary. Nat R 22:1260+ D 1 '70
Theater. Nat R 22:370-1, 905-6 Ap 7, Ag 25 '70
They also serve. Nat R 22:786-7+ Jl 28 '70

BUCKLEY, Tom
Oh! Copenhagen! il N Y Times Mag p32-4+ F 8 '70
Ottinger: study of a quiet candidate. pors N Y Times Mag p40-1+ O 25 '70
Student moves into the 14th C.D. il pors N Y Times Mag p 10-11+ Je 21 '70
Tennessee Williams survives. il por Atlan 226:98-106+ N '70
Testing of Pierre Trudeau. il pors N Y Times Mag p50-1+ D 6 '70
Whitney Young: black leader or "Oreo cookie"? il pors N Y Times Mag p32-3+ S 20; 64 O 18 '70
With the National geographic on its endless, cloudless voyage. il N Y Times Mag p 10-11+ S 6 '70

BUCKLEY, William Frank, 1881-1958
Father was as much a figure of awe as of fun. F. R. Buckley. il pors Life 69:42-4 D 18 '70 *

BUCKLEY, William Frank, 1881-1958, family
Buckleys: extraordinary family. il Newsweek 76:38 N 16 '70
Buckleys of Great Elm; with photographs by A. Eisenstaedt, and editorial comment. B. Dunn. il pors Life 69:1, 34-41+ D 18 '70
First family of conservatism. L. C. Dubois. pors N Y Times Mag p 10-11+ Ag 9 '70

BUCKLEY, William Frank, 1925-
In the beginning . . . Nat R 22:1263-5 D 1 '70
Notes & asides. See issues of National review
On the right. See issues of National review
Why we need a black president in 1980. Look 34:59 Ja 13 '70
You are the more cupcakeable for being a Cosmopolitan girl. Nat R 22:999-1000 S 22 '70

about

William Buckley problem: case of nonsupport. B. DeMott. por Sat R 53:29-31+ Ag 8 '70 *
Words that slay, wisdom that mends. W. Herberg. Nat R 22:738 Jl 14 '70 *

BUCKS (basketball team) See Basketball teams

BUCKWALTER, Len
Build the original radio. il Mech Illus 66:74-5+ D '70
Careers in aviation electronics. il Radio-Electr 41:48-50 Je '70
Five worst jobs. il Mech Illus 66:84-6+ O '70
Here come the video photographs! il Mech Illus 66:45-7+ D '70
How to buy a soldering iron. il Mech Illus 66:86-8+ Je '70
How to get those blacked-out games on your TV. il Pop Mech 134:100-3+ N '70
Latest turn-ons: police & firemen! il Mech Illus 66:61-3+ Ag '70
Liquid crystals, light wonder of the world. il Mech Illus 66:57-9+ Mr '70
Pick and play your own TV shows. il Pop Mech 133:130-3 F '70

BUCY, Frances A.
Denver, Colorado: El Número cinco. il Wilson Lib Bul 44:765-6 Mr '70

BUCY, Myrtis
Gift wrapped in blue sky. Har Yrs 10:14 D '70

BUDBERG, Moura (Zakrevskaia) baroness
Astonishing history of Moura Budberg. K. Tynan. il por Vogue 156:162-3+ O 1 '70 *

BUDD, Julie
Awake and sing. il pors Time 96:41 Jl 27 '70 *

BUDD, Penelope Rowland
Gardener reflects on Maine in May. il Home Gard 57:20-1 My '70

BUDD company
Budd tries to get out of its rail cars. il Bsns W p 16-17 My 2 '70

BUDDHA and Buddhism
See also
Buddhists
Soka Gakkai (sect)
Zen Buddhism

BUDDHISM and Christianity. See Christianity and other religions

BUDDHIST art. See Art, Buddhist

BUDDHISTS
Seoul brothers; world conference of the leaders of Buddhism. il Newsweek 76:59 O 26 '70
Victory for the Buddhists; return to political life in South Vietnam. il Time 96:22 S 14 '70

BUDGE, Hamer Harold
As they see it; interview. por Forbes 105:48 Ap 15 '70
Regulation of investments; interview. il pors U S News 69:52-6 S 7 '70

BUDGET

France

See also
France—Armed forces—Appropriations and expenditures

Great Britain

Britain's austerity lid is lifted, a bit. il Bsns W p 118 Ap 18 '70
U.K. defense budget $5.4 billion for 1970. Aviation W 92:24 F 23 '70

Israel

Economic tightrope. il Newsweek 75:80-2 F 16 '70

United States

Back to the chopping block. Time 95:11-12 Ja 26 '70
Birth of a budget. J. Osborne. New Repub 162:15-17 F 14 '70
Budget for fiscal 1971. America 122:149 F 14 '70
Budget of the United States government, fiscal year 1971; excerpts. R. M. Nixon. il Dept State Bul 62:234-40 Mr 2 '70
Budget with a bite. il Newsweek 75:65-7 F 9 '70
Can Congress live within Nixon's budget? with editorial comment. il Bsns W p28-9, 108 F 7 '70
Coming budget: more thrust, yes; much more, no. il Fortune 82:22 D '70
Deficit clouds the new budget year. Bsns W p 14 Jl 4 '70
Dollars and cents and politics. il por Newsweek 75:19-20 F 9 '70
Fiscal 1970 budget delay generates cost problems. Aviation W 92:45+ F 16 '70
Full employment budget: here's what it means. U S News 69:17 N 30 '70
Nation's co-signer; possible federal surplus. H. C. Wallich. Newsweek 75:88 My 11 '70
Necessary discipline. Fortune 81:79-80 Mr '70
1972-75 budgets. D. Wolfle. Science 168:69 Ap 3 '70
Nixon already grappling with 1972 budget. Bsns W p31 Ag 22 '70
Nixon budget: from surplus to a deficit. il U S News 68:66-7 Ja 1 '70
Nixon budget: science funding remains tight. P. M. Boffey and others. il Science 167:845-8 F 6 '70

BUDGET—United States—*Continued*

Nixon transition budget. R. Hotz. Aviation W 92:11 Mr 2 '70

Nixon's budget shakes up the priorities. il Bsns W p90+ F 14 '70

Nixon's budget: thin slices for new goals. il Time 95:8-9 F 9 '70

Nixon's first budget: over the 200-billion mark. il U S News 68:46-9 F 9 '70

Nixon's temptation to shift policy. il Time 96:86 N 16 '70

Pin the blame on the donkey. Bsns W p29 Ap 25 '70

Politics of Mr Nixon's economics. Life 68:28 F 13 '70

Research and education in danger. il Sci N 97:57-9 Ja 17 '70

Road to a 200-billion budget. il U S News 68:64-5 F 16 '70

Robert Mayo: calling signals on history's biggest budget. il por U S News 68:10 Ja 19 '70

Runaway federal deficits: a warning from Wilbur Mills; excerpts from address, October 21, 1970. W. D. Mills. il por U S News 69:68-9 N 9 '70

Shifting priorities in Nixon's first budget. il Sci N 97:143-50 F 7 '70

Special report: fiscal 1971 budget; symposium. il Aviation W 92:16-28 F 9 '70

Surplus that isn't. il Newsweek 75:79 Ap 20 '70

Surplus to generate more capital. il Bsns W p 104+ Mr 14 '70

Taxes & related problems; address, December 1, 1970. W. Bennett. Vital Speeches 37:166-70 Ja 1 '71

There is a threat of losing control. il Bsns W p 100-1 O 17 '70

What hangs in balance on budgets? A. G. Matamoros. por Nations Bsns 58:82-3 Jl '70

White House nightmare: spending that can't be cut. il U S News 68:85-6 Mr 9 '70

Why President Nixon can't balance his budgets. il U S News 69:77-9 Jl 20 '70

Writing on the wall. New Repub 162:11-12 F 14 '70

See also
Taxation—United States
United States—Appropriations and expenditures
United States—Budget, Bureau of the

BUDGET, Business

New budgets cut a swath in costs. il Bsns W p43-4 D 19 '70

Zero-base budgeting. P. A. Pyhrr. il Harvard Bsns R 48:111-21 N '70

BUDGET, Household

Are you for the budget, or is the budget for you? V. Cadden. Redbook 134:97+ Mr '70

Family money management; ed. by P. Lindberg. See issues of Better homes and gardens

How much money do you need? C. Coiro. il Har Yrs 10:48-50 Ja '70

How to handle a family financial crisis. S. Porter. Ladies Home J 87:52+ N '70

How to make a family budget. il Good H 170:156 Je '70

In some places living costs less; guideline budgets of the Bureau of labor statistics. il Changing T 24:23-5 Ag '70

Inflation and family budgets. America 122:35 Ja 17 '70

Is your family's spending out of line? Bureau of labor statistics guidelines. il Changing T 24:6-10 Ap '70

One family's spending: the first ten years. il Changing T 24:25-30 Ja '70

To combat inflation: what you can do. R. O'Brien. il Read Digest 97:78-81 N '70

Anecdotes, facetiae, satire, etc.

My checkbook and me. E. Bombeck. Good H 170:64+ Mr '70

BUDGET, Personal

Being a lily. S. T. Warner. New Yorker 46:155-9 O 10 '70

How to budget. C. V. Neal. il Todays Ed 59:48-9 S '70

See also
Finance, Personal
Saving and savings

BUDGET bureau (United States) See United States—Budget, Bureau of the

BUDGETS, Library. See Libraries—Finance

BUDNIK, Dan

Rodeo blues. Travel & Camera 33:78+ Jl '70

BUECHE, Arthur M.

Into the barn, and a lofty future. il pors Nations Bsns 58:74-5 Ja '70

BUECHLER, James

Stone soup; dramatization of a Russian folk tale. Plays 30:67-70 O '70

BUECHNER, Thomas S.

Norman Rockwell revisited. il Life 69:16 N 13 '70

Norman Rockwell's America; excerpts from Norman Rockwell: artist and illustrator. il por Good H 171:74-82 D '70

BUEGEL, Kenneth F.

Build IC volume expander. il Radio-Electr 41:36-9 Mr '70

New IC multiplex detector. il Radio-Electr 41:33-5 Mr '70

"Radar" burglar stopper. il Radio-Electr 41:36-40 Je; 44-5 Jl '70

Ultimate, R-E's new FM stereo tuner. il Radio-Electr 41:36-40+ My '70

BUEHLER, Sandra K.

Slum storefront library serves San Francisco poor. il Library J 95:1798 My 15 '70 ●

BUELL, Albert H.

Gloxinias for brilliant color. il Home Gard 57:48-9+ N '70

BUENOS AIRES

Music

Change in Buenos Aires; modernization of Teatro Colón. B. F. Carruthers. il Opera N 34:20-1 My 16 '70

Report: productions at the Teatro Colon. G. Knepler. il Opera N 34:31-2 F 7 '70

BUENOS AIRES. University. See Colleges and universities—Argentina

BUFFA, Elwood S. See Boulden, J. B. jt. auth.

BUFFALO Bill. See Cody. W. F.

BUFFALO, N.Y.

Housing

Buffalo waterfront development, Buffalo. il Arch Rec 148:96-100 N '70

Libraries

See also
Buffalo and Erie County, N.Y. public library

BUFFALO and Erie County, N.Y. public library

Prisoners, patients, and public libraries. D. C. Rittenhouse. il por Wilson Lib Bul 45:490-3 Ja '71

BUFFALO campus, State university of New York. See New York (state). State university—Buffalo campus

BUFFALO grass

Why we like buffalo grass. C. M. Foley. Org Gard & Farm 17:64 F '70

BUFFALO hunting

Ride for life in a buffalo herd; excerpt from autobiography. O. C. Marsh. il Am Heritage 21:46-7+ Je '70

BUFFALO in design. See Design, Decorative—Animal forms

BUFFALO RIVER

Old man and the river. R. F. Jones. il pors Sports Illus 33:28-34 Ag 10 '70

BUFFALO Sabres (hockey team) See Hockey teams

BUFFALOES

Buffalo roundup for ecology's sake. il Sci Digest 68:86-9 D '70

Great buffalo hunt? Shoot? Slaughter? Arizona's surplus bison shoot at Raymond ranch. B. Gilbert. il Sports Illus 33:36-8+ N 23 '70

Where are they now? il Newsweek 75:16 Ap 27 '70

See also
Water buffaloes

BUFFER solutions

Interference in the Lowry method for protein determination. J. D. Gregory and S. W. Sajdera. Science 169:97-8 Jl 3 '70; Reply. L. V. Turner and K. L. Manchester. 170:649 N 6 '70

BUFFET meals

Festive holiday buffets: with recipes and menu. F. M. Crawford. il Am Home 73:58-60+ D '70

Five special buffets. H. McCully. il House B 112:90-1+ Je '70

For New Year's day a make-ahead buffet. R. Molter il Parents Mag 46:56-9+ Ja '71

Freeze-ahead holiday buffet. il McCalls 98:70-1+ D '70

Holiday buffet for everyone in the family. R. H. Smithies. il Good H 171:144+ D '70

Sumptuous summer buffet. J. Uetz. il Am Home 73:62-3+ Ag '70

Three salads at once, in one summer buffet. il Sunset 144:140-1 Je '70

BUFFUM, William Burnside

Fostering international cooperation in peaceful uses of atomic energy; statement, November 28, 1969. Dept State Bul 61:637-40 D 29 '69

Sharing the practical benefits of new technology in the peaceful uses of outer space; statement, December 10, 1969. Dept State Bul 62:63-7 Ja 19 '70

BUFFUM, William Burnside—*Continued*

U.N. reaffirms objectives for reunification of Korea; statement, November 11, 1969. Dept State Bul 61:609-10 D 22 '69

U.N. Security council adopts new measures concerning Namibia; statement July 29, 1970. Dept State Bul 63:284-6 S 7 '70

United Nations force in Cyprus extended through December 1970; statement, June 9, 1970. Dept State Bul 63:20-1 Jl 6 '70

U.S. abstains on Security council resolution on South Africa; statement, July 23, 1970. Dept State Bul 63:203-5 Ag 17 '70

U.S. abstains on U.N. resolution on Lebanese complaint against Israel; statement, September 5, 1970. Dept State Bul 63:402-3 O 5 '70

U.S. vetoes Security council resolution on Southern Rhodesia; supports compromise resolution; statement, March 13, 1970. Dept State Bul 62:503-4 Ap 13 '70

BUFO marinus. See Toads

BUG repellants. See Insect baits and repellants

BUGG, Charles E. and Thewalt, Ulf

Crystal structure of serotonin picrate, a donor-acceptor complex. bibliog il Science 170:852-4 N 20 '70

BUGG, Ralph T.

Should Johnny (or Johnnie) play ball? il Todays Health 48:56-8+ S '70

—and Scott, H. G.

I cured myself with wool ... Todays Health 48:56-7 Je '70

BUGLES

Clay bugles. J. Goldman. il Ceram Mo 18: 27-9 Je '70

BUGS, Artificial. See Fishing lures, flies, etc.

BUHL, David. See Snyder, L. E. jt. auth.

BUHLER, Kathryn C.

Silver tureens in the Campbell museum collection; excerpts from the catalogue. il Antiques 97:904-9 Je '70

BÜHRLE, Dieter

Fines wound a gun maker. Bsns W p35 D 5 '70 *

BUILDING

Architectural business. See issues of Architectural record

See also
Architecture
Building sites
Concrete construction
House construction

Contracts and specifications

Guardrails against legal pitfalls in design and construction. Arch Rec 147:67-8 Mr '70

Cost

Architectural economics: the concept of total cost. R. D. Steyert. il Arch Rec 148:81-2 O '70

Building costs. W. H. Edgerton. See issues of Architectural record

Construction versus inflation. R. F. Young. il Arch Rec 147:69 Ja; 61 F; 85 Ap '70

Cost knowledge: tool for budget, program and design. B. Perkins. Arch Rec 147:83-4 Je '70

Evaluating hidden cost factors. B. Perkins. Arch Rec 148:60-1 Jl '70

High cost of construction: what hope in the 1970's? W. F. Wagner, jr. Arch Rec 148: 9-10 O '70

Isn't the best way to cut costs to cut time. W. F. Wagner, jr. Arch Rec 147:9 Je '70

Economic aspects

Clients in the 1970's: new realities, more management. B. F. Gordon. il Arch Rec 148:138-43 O '70

Employees

See Building workers

Estimates

Cost knowledge: tool for budget, program and design. B. Perkins. Arch Rec 147:83-4 Je '70

Guidelines for early planning estimates. B. Perkins. il Arch Rec 147:81-2 Ap '70

Some common errors in cost control programs. B. Perkins. Arch Rec 147:61-2 Ja '70

Finance

See also
Housing finance
Mortgages

Specifications

See Building—Contracts and specifications

Standards

Hazards and hurdles in developing standards: a case history. il Arch Rec 147:147-50 My '70

Statistics

F. W. Dodge construction outlook: 1971. G. A. Christie. il Arch Rec 148:67-70 N '70

BUILDING, Adobe

Adobe look and how it got that way. M. C. Spires. il Am Home 73:24+ Mr '70

Decorating in the adobe mood; Santa Fe home of Mrs Lois Field. il Am Home 73: 64-5 Mr '70

House just for you. V. Jaxon. il Har Yrs 10: 14-16 Ag '70

Rebirth in the Southwest: an architect and his wife rescue an old adobe. J. De Long. il House B 112:43-9 Ja '70

Strength and beauty of Santa Fe style; adobe home of Mrs Sallie Wagner. il Am Home 73:60-3 Mr '70

BUILDING, Iron and steel

Europe's iron palaces span another century. il Life 69:71-5 D 4 '70

New York's doomed palaces of iron. il Life 69: 56-61 Ag 14 '70

BUILDING and earthquakes. See Earthquakes and building

BUILDING and loan associations. See Savings and loan associations

BUILDING consultants, Library. See Library consultants

BUILDING costs. See Building—Cost

BUILDING estimates. See Building—Estimates

BUILDING fittings

Building components. See issues of Architectural record

Product reports. See issues of Architectural record

Twenty great home fix-up ideas. il Mech Illus 66:83-93 F '70

BUILDING industry

Architect vs. the builder: does it have to be that way? W. F. Wagner, jr. Arch Rec 147:9 F '70

As housing slump ends, how big a boom ahead. il U S News 69:24-5 Ag 3 '70

Current trends in construction. R. M. Young. See issues of Architectural record to June 1970

Economy, ecology, and zero population growth. J. E. Carlson. Arch Rec 148:59-60 Ag '70

Great housing crisis. il Newsweek 75:69+ Je 22 '70

Home building is ripe for a boom. il Changing T 24:26-30 Ag '70

Homebuilders think more constructively; hearings of the Joint economic committee. Bsns W p 16 Jl 25 '70

Housing enters the era of the superbuilder. il Bsns W p50-3 D 26 '70

Is the crisis a catastrophe? il Forbes 107: 76-9 Ja 1 '71

Man-hour requirements decline in hospital construction. M. F. Riche. il Mo Labor R 93:48 N '70

Mobile homes move into the breach. L. A. Mayer. il Fortune 81:126-30+ Mr '70

New government and industry partnership for building more housing. D. Pellish. il Arch Forum 133:58-61 Jl '70

New model in housing; interview, ed. by G. R. Rosen. H. Finger. por Duns 95:10-11+ Je '70

Regions in perspective. J. E. Carlson. il Arch Rec 148:85 S; 93 O '70

Revolution in housing. il Nations Bsns 58: 88:91 My '70

Trying to rebuild an ailing industry. il Bsns W p28 Je 6 '70

What's ahead in housing: builders tell their troubles. il U S News 68:57-8 F 2 '70

See also
Collective bargaining—Building industry
Dillingham corporation
Houses, Prefabricated
Kaufman and Broad building company
Skyline corporation
Stirling homex corporation
Strikes—United States—Building industry
Walter, Jim, corporation

Employees

Jobs for Negroes: battle goes on. U S News 68:83 Ja 26 '70

Philadelphia plan survives test. America 122: 325 Mr 28 '70

Spotlight on firms in the ups and downs business. il Nations Bsns 58:101 N '70

BUILDING industry—Employees—*Continued*
This month's feature: Congress & minority employment policy; controversy over the Philadelphia plan. Cong Digest 49:67-96 Mr '70
Unions open fire on Nixon over jobs, civil rights. il U S News 68:69-70 Mr 9 '70
See also
Building workers

Exhibitions
New industry looks at itself; Industrialized building exposition and congress. Bsns W p88+ N 14 '70

Finance
F. W. Dodge 1970 construction outlook: mid-year update. G. A. Christie. il Arch Rec 148:59-60 Jl '70
Where is the money coming from? R. M. Young. Arch Rec 147:71 My; 93 Je '70

Securities
Housing stocks raise the roof. il Bsns W p92 O 24 '70
There's nothing like a dream; Stirling Homex. il Forbes 105:26-7 My 1 '70
Time to take shelter? C. Morgello. il por Newsweek 75:70 Je 22 '70
Too early to bet on the mod squad? builders of modular housing. il Bsns W p 132+ Mr 28 '70

Statistics
Spotlight on firms in the ups and downs business. il Nations Bsns 58:101 N '70

Wages and hours
Building trades versus the people; with editorial comment. G. Burck. il Fortune 82: 67-8, 94-7+ O '70
Compensation in the construction industry. A. Strasser. Mo Labor R 93:64-5 My '70
Construction pay push is raising the roof; with editorial comment. il Bsns W p74+, 140 Ap 18 '70
Construction versus inflation: labor's role. Arch Rec 147:61 F '70
Gaining ground on wage costs. Bsns W p 114+ Je 13 '70

Germany (Federal Republic)
Communist builders rake in the D-marks. il Bsns W p33 S 12 '70

Great Britain
New training plan in Britain's construction industry. H. A. Perry. il Mo Labor R 93:27-31 F '70

BUILDING laws and regulations
Cleaner water hurts the builders; building ban for water pollution control. Bsns W p28-9 Je 6 '70
See also
United States—National council for development standards (proposed)
Zoning law
BUILDING lots. See Building sites
BUILDING machinery industry and trade
See also
Clark equipment company
BUILDING materials
Aluminum house. il Mech Illus 66:12+ My '70
Building components. See issues of Architectural record
Construction vs. inflation: materials. R. M. Young. il Arch Rec 147:85 Ap '70
Fiberglass reinforced plastic forms have electric heat to cure concrete. il Arch Rec 147: 159 Je '70
Ideas to build on. J. H. Ingersoll. See issues of House beautiful
Lightweight components. il Arch Forum 132: 58-61 Ap '70
New building materials for 1970: build color and pattern into the house. il House & Gard 137:76-7 Ja '70
Patios, paths & garden walls. il Changing T 24:19-21 Ag '70
Product reports. See issues of Architectural record
See also
Aggregates (building materials)
Aluminum, Structural
Building, Adobe
Concrete blocks
Lumber
Metals in building
Plastics in building
Roofing
Vermiculite
Wood

Testing
See also
Fire testing

BUILDING materials industry

Finance
Building materials; with yardsticks of management performance. il Forbes 105:157 Ja 1 '70; 107:73-4 Ja 1 '71

Securities
Wall Street beat. R. Brady. Duns 97:67 Ja '71

BUILDING research
Architect vs. the builder: does it have to be that way? W. F. Wagner, jr. Arch Rec 147:9 F '70
See also
United States—National council for development standards (proposed)
BUILDING sites
Controlled geometry shapes house for a woodland site. il Arch Rec 147:127-30 F '70
How the geologist can help your city; geological mapping of hillside areas, Los Angeles. C. A. Richards. il Am City 85:34-6 Je '70
Private residence, Canada. il Arch Rec 147: 50-3 mid-My '70
Shelter in the woods. il Arch Forum 132:36-9 Mr '70
Smernoff house, Montgomery County, Md. il Arch Rec 147:38-41 mid-My '70
Space for your addition. il Bet Hom & Gard 48:118+ My '70
See also
Hillside architecture
Housing projects—Site planning
BUILDING stones
See also
Granite
BUILDING trades. See Building industry
BUILDING trades unions
Black Monday's Sunday allies. il Ramp Mag 8:34-8 Ja '70
Building trades versus the people; with editorial comment. G. Burck. il Fortune 82: 67-8, 94-7+ O '70
Integration drive fails to overcome. il Bsns W p48+ Je 6 '70
Outreach program; address, January 12, 1970. G. Meany. Vital Speeches 36:230-4 F 1 '70
Rebuilding the building trades. Fortune 81:66 Ap '70
Veto power? il Forbes 105:158+ Ja 1 '70
BUILDING workers
Around city hall. A. Logan. New Yorker 46: 104-8 Je 6 '70
Building unions under U.S. pressure. U S News 68:89-90 F 23 '70
Compensation in the construction industry. A. Strasser. Mo Labor R 93:64-5 My '70
Hard hats; demonstrations around Wall Street and city hall. il Newsweek 75:34-5 My 25 '70
Hard hats: the rampaging patriots. F. J. Cook il Nation 210:712-19 Je 15 '70
Joe Kelly has reached his boiling point; why the construction workers holler. U.S.A. all the way! R. Rogin. il pors N Y Times Mag p 12-14+ Je 28 '70
My hard hat problem, and yours. T. Williams. il Esquire 74:138-44 O '70
Workers' Woodstock; flag-waving pro-Nixon demonstrators in lower Manhattan. il Time 95:12 Je 1 '70

Training
New training plan in Britain's construction industry. H. A. Perry. il Mo Labor R 93:27-31 F '70
Nonapprentice sources of training in construction. H. G. Foster. bibliog il Mo Labor R 93:21-6 F '70
BUILDINGS
Focus; monthly review of notable buildings. See issues of Architectural forum
Forum; monthly review of events and ideas. See issues of Architectural forum
See also
Bank buildings
Factories
Industrial buildings
Skyscrapers
Theater buildings
also subhead Buildings under names of cities, e.g. Vancouver, British Columbia—Buildings

Equipment
See Building fittings

Photographs
Pictures that might help us think about ways to make architecture. il Arch Rec 148:134-7 O '70

BUILDINGS, Abandoned
In the inner cities: acres of abandoned buildings. il U S News 68:54-6 Ja 26 '70
When landlords walk away. il Time 95:88+ Mr 16 '70
Wildfire of abandonment. il Bsns W p57+ Ap 4 '70

BUILDINGS, Prefabricated
See also
Apartment houses, Prefabricated
Houses, Prefabricated

BUILDINGS, Remodeled
Life begins at forty-two; converting old library structure into municipal administration building; Montrose, Colo. M. Bingham. il por Am City 85:111 Jl '70
See also
Houses, Remodeled

BUILDINGS, Restoration of. See Architecture—Conservation and restoration

BUILDINGS, Round
Circular prestressing cuts slab thicknesses and costs in a circular tower. il Arch Rec 147:157-8 Je '70

BUILT in furniture. See Furniture, Built in

BUIST, Eleanor
Bibliographic sputnik? steps toward cataloging at source in the U.S.S.R. bibliog il por Wilson Lib Bul 44:1033-9 Je '70

BUJOLD, Geneviève
Kitten purring Beethoven. il por Time 95:90+ Mr 30 '70 *

BULBS
Bulbs from our West. M. G. Schmidt. il Horticulture 48:14-17 N '70
For fall planting: the little gems of springtime. D. A. Brown. il Home Gard 57:32-5+ O '70
Plan bulb combinations now. B. Miles. il Horticulture 48:22-5+ My '70
Put them in special pots, then bring them indoors. il Sunset 144:74-5 F '70
Some uncommon bulbs. B. Miles. il Horticulture 48:22-5+ N '70
Spring begins now; plant hardy bulbs in autumn. E. McDonald. il House B 112:126-31+ O '70
Success with bulbous plants. K. S. Taylor. il Horticulture 48:36-7+ O '70
Summer-flowering bulbs. A. J. Hebert. il Horticulture 48:50-3 Mr '70
There's still time to plant spring bulb color in your garden. il Sunset 145:242 N '70
See also
Crocuses
Forcing (plants)
Gladiolus
Tulips

BULBS, Light. See Electric lamps

BULEKOV, V. See Shvarev, V. jt. auth.

BULGAKOV, Valentin F.
Tolstoy in the last year of his life; excerpts, tr. by A. Dunnigan. por Harp Baz 104:58-61 Ja '71

BULGARIA
Politics and government
What's going on now behind the Iron curtain. R. A. Haeger. il U S News 69:89 N 9 '70

Religious institutions and affairs
Ecumenism in Sofia and Bucharest. J. R. Nelson. Chr Cent 87:437-9 Ap 15 '70

BULL fights. See Bullfights

BULL nettle. See Tread-softly

BULLATY, Sonja, and Lomeo, Angelo
Snowstorm; photographs. il Audubon 72:4-13 Ja '70

BULLET belts. See Belts

BULLETIN of the atomic scientists
Twenty-five years later. E. Rabinowitch. il por Bul Atom Sci 26:4-6+ Je '70

BULLETINS
Mass communication: church bulletins. C. Melaro. Sat R 53:9-10 D 19 '70

BULLETS
Brush rifle: shooting through brush. J. O'Connor. il Outdoor Life 146:80-1+ S '70
Law, order, dum-dums. J. Deedy. Commonweal 92:2 Mr 13 '70
Newest antiriot weapon: bullets of wood. il U S News 69:36 Jl 20 '70
Vietnamization on Main Street: the dumdum bullet. R. Wells. il Nation 211:38-41 Jl 20 '70
See also
Cartridges

BULLFIGHTERS
I'll dress you in gold. F. R. Buckley. Nat R 22:943-4 S 8 '70
See also
Ordóñez, C.

BULLFIGHTS
I'll dress you in gold. F. R. Buckley. Nat R 22:943-4 S 8 '70
Sun also sets; hero of Hemingway novel. S. Adams. il Sports Illus 32:56-60+ Je 29 '70

BULLHEADS
Three fleeing bullheads. J. Bardach and T. Villars. il Natur Hist 79:36-41 bibliog (p 133) Ag '70

BULLINS, Ed
Pig pen. Criticism
Nation 210:668 Je 1 '70 *
New Yorker 46:72-3 My 30 '70 *

BULLIS, Harvey Raymond, 1924-. See Anderson. W. W. jt. auth.

BULLIS, Jerald
Invocation, an elegy. Yale R 60:257-8 D '70

BULLOCK, Barbara
Wynn Bullock. il Mod Phot 34:84-9+ My '70

BULLOCK, Wynn
Wynn Bullock: in the midst of life we are in death. M. Mann. il Pop Phot 67:92-3+ Jl '70 *
Wynn Bullock: tracing the roots of man in nature. B. Bullock; J. N. Ueismann. il Mod Phot 34:84-9+ My '70 *

BULLS
Bull of the year: V-61. il Life 69:75 O 23 '70
Don't be misled when buying a bull. D. Malena. il Suc Farm 68:D18 Ap '70
Dud stud; case of Fabian, in Austria. Newsweek 75:92-3 Mr 23 '70
Know your bull costs. Suc Farm 68:L8 O '70
Osborndale Ivanhoe lies a-mold'ring in the grave. R. Eddy. Esquire 73:204 Ap '70
They breed meat-type bulls. J. Davis. il Suc Farm 68:no5 D4 Mr '70
Tips on selecting a bull. Suc Farm 68:61 O '70

BULLYING. See Children—Management and training

BULTHUIS, G. Thomas
Building a new library for a new college. A. Caruba. por Pub W 198:29-30 O 26 '70 *

BUMBLE BEE, Ariz. See Abandoned towns

BUMMER; story. See Aguallo, T.

BUMPASS, Donald E.
Video tape recorders. Clear House 44:562-4 My '70

BUMPASS, Larry, and Westoff, C. F.
Perfect contraceptive population. bibliog il Science 169:1177-82 S 18 '70

BUMPERS, Dale
Arkansas upset. il por Time 96:16 S 21 '70 *

BUNCHE, Ralph Johnson
Talk with Ralph Bunche; interview. Holiday 47:27 Ap '70

BUNDY, McGeorge
Charting the complexities; remarks to advisory panel of the Committee on science and astronautics. por Sat R 53:56-7+ Ap 4 '70
Fresh prescription for disengagement in Vietnam; excerpt. pors Newsweek 75:31-2 My 25 '70
What is learning? address, August 3, 1970. Vital Speeches 36:710-13 S 15 '70

about
Bold investing. P. A. Samuelson. Newsweek 75:82 My 4 '70 *

BUNDY, Rex
Stoves for the homesteader. il Am West 7:38-9 N '70

BUNKER, Don L.
Why should anyone study chemistry? il por Chem 43:16-17 S '70

BUNKER, Ellsworth
Ambassador Bunker discusses Viet-Nam on Meet the press; transcript of interview, May 10, 1970. Dept State Bul 62:686-91 Je 1 '70

about
New team takes up the quest for peace. pors U S News 69:38 Ag 3 '70 *

BUNKER-Ramo corporation
Squeeze play yields a computer. il Bsns W p49 N 21 '70

BUNKS. See Beds

BUNTING, John Richard, 1925-
Doctor Galbraith? Or Dr Friedman? interview. pors Forbes 106:44+ D 15 '70

about
Fast on his feet in Philadelphia. il por Bsns W p76+ F 14 '70 *
Man who cut the prime. por Time 96:73 S 28 '70 *

BUÑUEL, Luis
Bunuel on pilgrimage. A. Michelson. Commonweal 92:63-5 Mr 27 '70 *
Demons also believe; parodying the eucharist. S. Terrien. Chr Cent 87:1481-3+ D 9 '70 *

BUONO da mangiare; story. See Hastings, A.

BURGLARPROOFING of boats. See Boats—
Protection against theft
BURGLARY and burglars
First floor rear at the jungle's edge; apart-
ment on the edge of Spanish Harlem
burgled twice in two weeks. B. Farrell.
Life 68:18B Ja 23 '70
How burglars break in. Mech Illus 66:68-9
Jl '70
BURGLARY protection
Burglarproofing your home. il Mech Illus 66:
68-74+ Jl '70
Burglars will get you, if you don't watch out.
J. Galub. Am Home 73:108+ S '70
Cool way to turn off burglars; device to
turn room lights on and off. il Mech
Illus 66:96-8+ My '70
Safeguard your home while vacationing. il
Good H 171:142 Jl '70
Security men thrive on the wages of fear. il
Bsns W p 112-14 Je 20 '70
To catch a thief. il Newsweek 76:59-60 Jl 27 '70
See also
Burglar alarms
BURGMEIER, Frank
Power equipment. il Horticulture 48:38 Mr
'70
BURGNER, Jack W.
Elementary filmmaking. il Sch Arts 69:20-
3 F '70
Putting together an art lesson. il Sch Arts
70:16-19 S '70
BURGOS trial. See Trials—Spain
BURGY, Donald
Checkup. il pors Art in Am 58:108-11 Mr '70
BURIAL
See also
Funeral rites and ceremonies
Indians of North America—Mortuary customs
BURK, Dean
Apricot pit bit. por Sci N 98:55-6 Jl 25 '70 *
BURKE, Alexander J. jr
New beginning: a raid on the inarticulate.
Engl J 59:99-104+ Ja '70
BURKE, Diane. See Burke, J. jt. auth.
BURKE, J. Herbert
Excerpt from debate, April 15, 1970. Cong
Digest 49:189+ Je '70
BURKE, John, and Burke, Diane
In the matter of the adoption of E. Chr
Cent 88:36 Ja 13 '71
BURKE, John Gordon, and Bowers, H. P.
Institutional censorship. il pors Library J
95:468-9 F 1 '70
BURKE, Kathleen. See Prince, A. M. jt. auth.
BURKE, Kenneth
Two poems of abandonment. New Repub
162:27 My 30 '70
BURKE, Kenyon C.
Trip to Israel. il por Negro Hist Bul 33:94-6
Ap '70
BURKE, Molly
Beautiful barkeep of Bequia. P. Coffin. il pors
Look 34:56-61 D 15 '70 *
BURKE, R. E. and others
Catch property in single mammalian motor
units. bibliog il Science 168:122-4 Ap 3 '70
BURKE, Tom
Dennis Hopper saves the movies. por Esquire
74:138-41+ S '70
Princess Leda's castle in the air. il Esquire
73:104-11+ Mr '70
Sweeter options of John D. MacArthur and
Truman Capote. il pors Esquire 74:210-14+
D '70
BURKHART, Roger
Miracle tool for prospectors. il Sci Digest
67:45-8+ F '70
BURLAGE, John D.
Little boy learns to hear. il Parents Mag 45:
82-5 N '70
BURLESQUE. See Vaudeville
BURLIN, Paul
Paul Burlin's last paintings. J. Schuyler. il
por Art N 69:28-9+ D '70 *
BURLINGAME, A. L. and others
Lunar organic compounds: search and cha-
racterization. bibliog il Science 167:751-2
Ja 30 '70
BURLINGTON, Vt.

Education
My daughter loves school, can she be learn-
ing anything? Flynn school. D. Divoky. il
Redbook 136:71+ N '70
BURLINGTON industries, Inc.
Treading your way to the top. E. R. Calla-
way. il Nations Bsns 58:62-3 Ja '70
BURMA

Description and travel
Closed door to Burma is beginning to open.
il Sunset 145:33-4+ O '70

Politics and government
Burma: the obscure domino. R. Butwell. bib-
liog f il Cur Hist 59:339-44+ D '70
Reports: Burma. S. Seagrave. Atlan 225:32+
Ap '70
Revolution on the Burma trail? V. P. Nan-
da. il Commonweal 91:530-1 F 13 '70
Voice from the jungle; U Nu plotting his
comeback. il por Time 96:31-2 D 7 '70
Which is the Burma road, Ne Win or U Nu?
H. D. S. Greenway. il pors N Y Times Mag
p34-5+ My 3 '70
BURMAN, Ben Lucien
India's incredible snake charmers. il Read
Digest 97:49-50+ O '70
BURN, Harry Thomas
Man whose vote gave women the vote. W.
Cahn. por Look 34:60+ Ag 25 '70 *
BURNERS, Electric. See Electric stoves
BURNETT, Carol
To make music in the heart; interview. ed.
by G. Christy. il por Good H 171:68-9+ D
'70
BURNETT, Frances (Hodgson)
Real Little Lord Fauntleroy. T. McCarthy. il
pors Am Heritage 21:50-5+ F '70 *
BURNETT, Dame Ivy Compton-. See Comp-
ton-Burnett, I.
BURNETT, Joe R.
Changing the social order: the role of school-
ing. Ed Digest 35:5-8 Mr '70
BURNETT, Micajah
Micajah Burnett and the buildings at Pleas-
ant Hill. J. C. Thomas. il por Antiques 98:
600-5 O '70 *
BURNETT, Vivian
Real Little Lord Fauntleroy. T. McCarthy.
il pors Am Heritage 21:50-5+ F '70 *
BURNHAM, Charles W. See Lindsley, D. H.
jt. auth.
BURNHAM, Donald Clemens
Still picking and choosing. il por Forbes 105:
38-9 Mr 15 '70 *
BURNHAM, James
(ed) After liberalism, what? Nat R 22:1263-
89 D 1 '70
Notes on authority, morality, power. Nat R
22:1283-91 D 1 '70
Protracted conflict (cont of) Third world war.
See issues of National review
BURNHAM, Sherburne Wesley
How S. W. Burnham became an astronomer.
J. Ashbrook. por Sky & Tel 39:225 Ap '70 *
S. W. Burnham's Lick and Yerkes years. J.
Ashbrook. il Sky & Tel 39:363-4 Je '70 *
BURNHAM, Sophy
Women's lib: the idea you can't ignore. il
Redbook 135:78-9+ S '70
BURNING the couch; story. See Woiwode, L.
BURNS, Arthur Frank
Arthur Burns: the stage has been set for a
recovery; address, December 7, 1970. por
U S News 69:64-8 D 21 '70; Same with title
Basis for lasting prosperity. Vital Speeches
37:162-6 Ja 1 '71
Control of government expenditures; address,
December 2, 1969. Vital Speeches 36:194-7
Ja 15 '70
Quotations from Chairman Burns. Time 95:
52 Je 1 '70
Word on dips in the monetary rates; excerpts
from statement, March 18, 1970. U S News
68:65-6 Mr 30 '70
about
Burns and guidelines. M. Friedman. News-
week 75:86 Je 15 '70 *
Burns changes the mood at the Fed. il por
U S News 68:44 Je 1 '70 *
Burns takes over a Fed under fire; with
editorial comment. il por Bsns W p31-2,
120 Ja 31 '70
Fencing match. il por Newsweek 75:71-2 F
16 '70 *
How fast should money grow? pors Bsns W
p59-60 Ag 8 '70 *
Let's make a deal. il Newsweek 76:78+ D 21
'70 *
Little trauma at the Fed. M. Seeger. Esquire
74:36+ S '70 *
New chairman at the Fed. M. Friedman.
Newsweek 75:68 F 2 '70
One man, one vote. por Forbes 105:24-5 Mr 1
'70 *
BURNS, Eileen
(ed) See DiGiuseppe, E. Two young singers
have proved standouts at the Met
BURNS, Haywood
Can a black man get a fair trial in this country? il N Y Times Mag p5+ Jl 12; 21+ S
27 '70; Same abr. with title Race and fair
trial. Cur 121:12-19 S '70

BURNS, James MacGregor
F.D.R: the last journey; excerpts from Roosevelt: the soldier of freedom. il pors Am Heritage 21:8-11+ Ag '70
FDR: the untold story of his last year. il por Sat R 53:12-15+ Ap 11 '70
BURNS, Julie
(ed) See Miller, H. There are so many idiots among my fans that I wonder who the hell I'm writing for
BURNS, Martin
Patio-door plant rack. il Org Gard & Farm 17:73 N '70
BURNS, Roger G. and Newton, R. E.
Precision controlled flames fight air pollution. il Am City 85:98+ My '70
BURNS and scalds
Burned child, seared parent. Time 96:41 Jl 6 '70
First aid; chemical injuries. C. J. Potthoff. Todays Health 48:74 D '70
Riku Ruopsa's trial by fire. A. Rankin. il Read Digest 97:69-73 N '70
BURNS park. See Denver—Parks and playgrounds
BURNSVILLE, Minn.
Suburban fire-police integration a must. S. R. Dornfeld. il Am City 85:78 F '70
BURPEE, W. Atlee, company
Burpee, maker of five million gardens a year. il Home Gard 57:46-7+ D '70
BURR, Aaron
Duel that changed our history. T. Fleming. il Read Digest 97:190-5 Ag '70 *
BURR, Gray
Comment. D. Zaiss. Poetry 116:56-7 Ap '70 *
BURR, Raymond
My Naitauba. il pors Travel & Camera 33: 46-9 Ja '70
BURR, Robert N.
Recent developments in Latin American history. Ann Am Acad 388:133-44 Mr '70
BURRILL, B. D.
Sailmaker to the twelves. il por Yachting 128:56-7+ S '70
BURROS
Stories
Amorous Senator: the scandalous life of a lopeared burro; excerpt from Timber line. G. Fowler. il Am West 7:28-31 Mr '70
BURROUGH, Loretta
This time forever; story. Good H 171:82-3 Ag '70
BURROUGHS, Ben
Syndicated poet: Ben Burroughs. C. J. Milazzo. por Writers Digest 50:27+ O '70 *
BURROUGHS, John
Hot tips for using glue guns. il Pop Mech 134:188-91 S '70
Install a circuit for a 230-v. arc welder. il Pop Mech 133:178-81 F '70
Ornamental scrollwork you can do at home. il Pop Mech 133:192-5 Mr '70
Tools and tricks the pros use with copper tubing. il Pop Mech 135:164-7 Ja '71
BURROUGHS, John, 1837-1921
John Burroughs, New York's early defender of the environment. P. D. Westbrook. il pors Cons 25:30-2 Ag '70 *
BURROUGHS corporation
Avionics offers prime target for air cargo expansion. Aviation W 93:122-3 O 26 '70
Burroughs: the great puller-together. il Forbes 107:24 Ja 1 '70
Low-key debut from Burroughs. Bsns W p33 O 10 '70
BURROWS, Jack
Ringo. Am West 7:17-21 Ja '70
BURROWS, Larry
Expo '70; photographs. Life 68:37-43 Mr 27 '70
Glories of Angkor; photographs. il Life 68: 48-57 Je 5 '70
Tragic aftermath in Pakistan; photographs. Life 69:26-35 D 4 '70
BURROWS, Stuart
Full force; interview. ed. by S. Von Buchau. por Opera N 35:19 O 10 '70
BURRUS, Donald R.
Look at the next five years. por Nations Bsns 58:73-4 S '70
BURT, Leo Frederick
Madison bombers. il pors Newsweek 76:28-9 S 14 '70 *
BURT, Samuel M.
Education and industry can make a great team! Todays Ed 59:34-6 D '70
BURTCHAELL, James T.
Purpose of church. Commonweal 92:437-41 S 4 '70
BURTON, Courtney
Courtney Burton named to Foundation board. W. H. Thomasson. il por Parks & Rec 9: 59+ S '70 *

BURTON, E. Milby
Charleston furniture. il Antiques 97:910-14 Je '70
Charleston silver. il Antiques 97:915-17 Je '70
BURTON, Hugh. See Green, B. R. jt. auth.
BURTON, Richard
Last game Richard Burton lost. pors Vogue 157:102-5 Ja 1 '71
about
How do I love thee? Let me count the ways. J. Roddy. il pors Look 34:28-30 Je 16 '70 *
BURTON, Robert, 1577-1640
Anatomy of melancholy. A. Burgess. il por Horizon 12:48-53 Aut '70 *
BURTON, Virginia Lee
Virginia Lee Burton's dynamic sense of design. L. Kingman. il Horn Bk 46:449-60, 593-602 O-D '70 *
BURTON, Walter E.
Add motion to your photo slides. il Pop Mech 133:164-7+ Ap '70
Brass, the metal that works with you. il Pop Sci 197:92-4+ D '70
Handy homemade shop tools. il Pop Mech 133:184-5 F '70
How to machine a boring-bar holder with extra talents. il Pop Sci 196:127 My '70
How to make and use an angle post. il Pop Mech 133:176-9 Ja '70
Spoonholder rack for your favorite lamp. il Pop Mech 135:160-1 Ja '71
Twelve great lathe tricks. il Pop Mech 134: 178-81+ Jl '70
BUS stop shelters. See Shelters
BUSCH, August A. 1899-
Bird in hand and a burning Busch. W. Leggett. il por Sports Illus 32:18-23 Mr 23 '70 *
BUSCH, Fred
Basals are not for reading. Ed Digest 36: 16-19 D '70
BUSCH gardens. See Tampa, Fla.—Parks and playgrounds
BUSH, Buford
Vietnam: recreational leadership training. il Parks & Rec 5:40-2+ Ap '70
BUSH, George F.
Lampreys in the Lakes; with biographical sketch. il Sea Front 16:142-7, 191 My '70
Old reliable rainbarrel. il Org Gard & Farm 17:82 S '70
BUSH, Joseph Kerr, 1944?-1969
Bulletins from bad guy land; excerpts from letters. por Time 95:12 Mr 23 '70
BUSH, Monroe
Pines together; poems. Am For 76:41 F '70
Reading about resources. See issues of American forests
BUSH, Vannevar
Pieces of the action. P. H. Abelson. Science 170:265 O 16 '70 *
BUSH; story. See Ranck, H.
BUSH beans. See Beans
BUSHA, Virginia
Poetry in the classroom: "Ex-basketball player." Engl J 59:643-5 My '70
BUSHMAN, John H.
Power of language: can the student survive without it? Engl J 59:1091-5 N '70
BUSHNELL, Don D.
Black arts for black youth. il Sat R 53:43-6+ Jl 18 '70
BUSHNELL, Louise
What's happened to Eve? address, September 10, 1970. Vital Speeches 36:749-52 O 1 '70
BUSINESS
If I were twenty-one today; address, April 20, 1970. W. W. Keeler. Vital Speeches 36: 539-42 Je 15 '70
See also
Advertising
Chambers of commerce
Christmas business
Corporations
Credit
Efficiency, Industrial
Electronics in business
Entrepreneurs
Finance
Financial statements
Free enterprise
Ideas in business
Location in business and industry
Profit
Retail trade
Salesmen and salesmanship
Stock exchange
Bibliography
Books to come. Library J 95:3842+ N 1 '70
Books to come; ed. by J. Donathan. Library J 95:943-7, 2572-5 Mr 1, Jl 1 '70
Business books of 1969; comp. by J. B. Woy. il por Library J 95:863-6 Mr 1 '70

BUSINESS—Bibliography—*Continued*
Scientific, technical, business and medical highspots; international list. Pub W 198: pt2 146-56 S 21 '70
Some business highspots; April-September. il Pub W 197:50-8 Ap 13; 198:41-8 N 16 '70

Foreign expansion

Britannia rules the pubs. il Forbes 105:46-7 Mr 15 '70
Europe faces the technology gap. W. Goldstein. Yale R 59:161-78 D '69
Global corporation is here to stay. D. C. King. il America 123:229-31 O 3 '70; Reply. P. Matthews. 123:363-4 N 7 '70
Irish eyes are smiling at American business. il Nations Bsns 58:28-31 Je '70
Small company enters the European market. J. K. Sweeney. Harvard Bsns R 48:126-32 S '70
See also
Corporations—Foreign subsidiaries

International aspects

Fortune multinational report. Fortune 82:75-7 Ag; 79-81 S; 47-9 O; 47-9 N; 45-7 D '70
International business. See issues of Dun's
New responsibilities of business; address, June 9, 1970. D. Seymour. Vital Speeches 36:679-82 S 1 '70

Periodicals

See also
Harvard business review
Institutional investor (periodical)

Political aspects

What businessmen think of President Nixon; a Time-Louis Harris poll. il Time 95:80-2 My 18 '70

Psychology

Corporate guerrilla chief. il pors Bsns W p 102+ Mr 28 '70
Up the organization, by R. Townsend. Review Sat R 53:30-1 Ap 4 '70. W. Benton

Public relations

Corporation becomes a target. il Time 95:94+ My 11 '70
Crushing cost of consumerism; comments of members of the Presidents' panel. G. R. Rosen. il Duns 95:36-7 Ap '70
Helping shareowners help themselves; address, November 7, 1970. L. R. Boulware. Vital Speeches 37:155-60 D 15 '70
It's face-to-face with dissidents. il Bsns W p94+ My 2 '70
Learning the hard way. L. L. L. Golden. il Sat R 53:114 Mr 14 '70
Now the head man's on TV. R. Levy. il Duns 95:59-61 My '70
See also
Business and the press
Corporate image

Small business

See Small business

Social aspects

Accountability: Campaign to make General motors more responsibility. J. Featherstone New Repub 162:9-10 F 28 '70
Anatomy of activism for executives. S. A. Culbert and J. M. Elden. il Harvard Bsns R 48:131-42 N '70
Burn, bank, burn. il Forbes 105:59-70 My 15 '70
Business fights pollution, and the Nation profits. il Nations Bsns 58:29-30 F '70
Business taxation and the poor; liberalized depreciation rules. America 122:385 Ap 11 '70
Coming triumph over indifference; address, May 14, 1970. G. Symonds. Vital Speeches 36:555-9 Jl 1 '70
Commotion at GM; campaign to make General motors responsible. L. J. Carter. New Repub 162:8-9 Je 6 '70
Corporate giant stresses individuals; ITT executive association. V. Louviere. Nations Bsns 58:18 S '70
Corporation becomes a target. il Time 95:94+ My 11 '70
Executive as social activist. il Time 96:62-8 Jl 20 '70
GM makes criticism a family affair; forms five-man public policy committee. Bsns W p 19 S 5 '70
How businessmen pitched in to save a city; Newark, N.J. il pors Nations Bsns 58:44-8 D '70
How social responsibility fits the game of business. J. McDonald. il Fortune 82:104-6+ D '70

If I were twenty-one today; address, April 20, 1970. W. W. Keeler. Vital Speeches 36: 539-42 Je 15 '70
Is business meeting the challenge of urban affairs? J. Cohn. il Harvard Bsns R 48:68-82 Mr '70
Is the corporation dead? address, September 22, 1970. D. W. Lufkin. Vital Speeches 37: 90-3 N 15 '70
Is the corporation next to fall? A. G. Athos. bibliog f il Harvard Bsns R 48:49-61 Ja '70
Leadership; address, May 23, 1970. R. F. Delaney. Vital Speeches 36:621-2 Ag 1 '70
Lending a hand with social ills; Stanford volunteers and Committee for corporate responsibility. il Bsns W p 106+ Mr 7 '70
Loss of zeal. Newsweek 75:83 Mr 23 '70
New look at urban priorities; corporate cooperation; address, December 3, 1969. E. Goldston. Vital Speeches 36:282-6 F 15 '70
New responsibilities of business; the international market; address, June 9, 1970. D. Seymour. Vital Speeches 36:679-82 S 1 '70
Packaging social science for profit. il Bsns W p50+ My 2 '70
Politics by other means; corporate responsibility. H. Henderson. Nation 211:617-21 D 14 '70
Politics of pollution; why are the corporations cooperating? M. Harrington. Commonweal 92:111-14 Ap 17 '70
Practical way to get involved; urban fellows program. il Bsns W p80 N 28 '70
Profit alone is not enough; interview, ed. by L. L. L. Golden. J. M. Roche. Sat R 53:55 Ag 8 '70
Rebels in grey flannel suits. Forbes 106:46 S 15 '70
Shifting social structure. L. L. L. Golden. Sat R 53:66-7 Ja 17 '70
Social responsibility of business is to increase its profits. M. Friedman. il N Y Times Mag p32-3+ S 13 '70; Discussion. p 14+ O 4; 90 O 25 '70; America 123:226 O 3 '70
Social responsibility of business is to increase its profits. M. Friedman. il N Y Times Mag p32-3+ S 13 '70; Discussion. p 14+ O 4 '70; America 123:226 O 3 '70
Stinging the corporations. G. I. Maeroff. Nation 210:753-6 Je 22 '70
Taking stock; Campaign GM. il Newsweek 75:109 Ap 27 '70
Top priority: renovating our ideology. G. C. Lodge. bibliog f Harvard Bsns R 48:43-55 S '70
Toward a wider constituency; resolutions by Campaign G.M. il Time 95:54+ Je 1 '70
Whose business is business? student drive to persuade major corporations to become more socially responsible. R. W. Dietsch. New Repub 162:13-14 Ap 25 '70
Why an outmoded ideology thwarts the new business conscience. G. C. Lodge. por Fortune 82:106-7+ O '70; Same abr. with title Top priority: renovating our ideology. bibliog f Harvard Bsns R 48:43-55 S '70
Why we need new businessmen. C. Kaufmann. Look 34:76+ Ja 13 '70
Young people, the establishment, and the quality of life; excerpt from The human environment and business. H. Ford, 2d. Read Digest 97:139-42 Jl '70
See also
Accion international
Business and race problems
Council on economic priorities
National alliance of businessmen

Anecdotes, facetiae, satire, etc.

What happened when Refractory & brake ran afoul of the U.S. godwit lobby; a fantasy. W. Zinsser. il Life 68:42-3 Ap 24 '70

Terminology

New businessman's lexicon. Time 96:78 O 12 '70

BUSINESS, Retirement from. See Retirement
BUSINESS administration. See Business management and organization
BUSINESS airplanes. See Airplanes, Business
BUSINESS and alcoholism. See Alcoholism
BUSINESS and education
College moves off campus to teach. il U S News 69:46-7 Ag 17 '70
Considerations for administrators when big business moves into education. R. Gilkey. Clear House 45:191-2 N '70
Corporate executive and educational change proposals. J. W. Schaller. Ed Digest 35: 30-1 Ja '70

BUSINESS and education—*Continued*
Education and industry can make a great team! S. M. Burt. Todays Ed 59:34-6 D '70
Education and industry: troubled partnership. E. Carlson. il Sat R 53:45-7+ Ag 15 '70
Education must relate to a way of life. Ed Digest 36:8-11 O '70
Exchange of understanding: Business-education day. il Nations Bsns 58:20 Mr '70
Industry-sponsored school programs. Todays Health 48:70 F '70
Leisure & education; with yardsticks of management performance. il Forbes 105:201 Ja 1 '70; 107:176-8 Ja 1 '71
  See also
Business education
College students and business
Education market
Performance contracts (education)
BUSINESS and golf. See Golf and business
BUSINESS and government. See Industry and state
BUSINESS and professional women
Guerrilla guide for working women. R. Townsend. McCalls 97:68-9+ S '70
  See also
Secretaries
Woman—Occupations
  also Women as executives; Women as scientists; etc.
BUSINESS and race problems
Birth of a black business. J. A. Berman. Harvard Bsns R 48:4-6+ S '70
Is business pulling out of the ghetto? Bsns W p23 Mr 7 '70
Race relations is their business. S. Friedman. il N Y Times Mag p44+ O 25 '70
White help for black business. M. Brower and D. Little. Harvard Bsns R 48:4-6+ My '70
  See also
National alliance of businessmen
BUSINESS and religion
Christian stake in dollar power. Chr Today 14:22 Je 19 '70
Church and office bridge a gap; Church & industry institute's internship program. Bsns W p52 S 26 '70
Rock, business, and Trinity church. New Yorker 46:20-1 Jl 18 '70
Skyhooks: reprint from May-June 1955 issue. O. A. Ohmann. bibliog f Harvard Bsns R 48:4-6+ Ja '70
BUSINESS and state. See Industry and state
BUSINESS and the arts. See The Arts and industry
BUSINESS and the community. See Business —Social aspects
BUSINESS and the environmental movement. See Industry and the environmental movement
BUSINESS and the press
Playing the patsy. L. L. L. Golden. Sat R 53:62-3 Je 13 '70
BUSINESS arbitration. See Arbitration, Commercial
BUSINESS as a profession. See Businessmen
BUSINESS budget. See Budget, Business
BUSINESS charts
  See also
Stocks—Price indexes and averages
BUSINESS clothes. See Clothing and dress
BUSINESS committee for the arts (BCA) See Business in the arts award
BUSINESS communication. See Communication in management
BUSINESS conditions
Budding hopes for an upturn. il Bsns W p 18-19 Ag 1 '70
Business and finance. See issues of Newsweek
Business outlook. See issues of Business week
Business plays it cautious. il Bsns W p26 F 14 '70
Business roundup. S. S. Parker and others. See issues of Fortune
Can we have a bust? I. T. Ellis. por Nations Bsns 58:84-5 Mr '70
Cities where business is best. il U S News 68: 58:61 Ap 13; 69:40-3 S 14 '70
Dividends from the drop. il Time 95:66 Je 8 '70
Fighting recession. P. A. Samuelson. Newsweek 75:75 Je 22 '70
First faint notes of optimism. il Bsns W p 14 Jl 25 '70
How bankers view prospects for business. il U S News 68:58 Je 1 '70
How's business? latest nationwide survey. il U S News 69:20+ D 14 '70
Latest on business trends. il U S News 68:13-14 Mr 30 '70

Plus & minus; business activity of the week. See issues of U.S. news & World report
Prices: what to expect now; leading economists interviewed on price and wage outlook. il U S News 68:17-19 Ap 13 '70
Signs of slowdown; latest trends in business. il U S News 68:19-20 Ja 19 '70
Still, the mood is confident. il Bsns W p27-8 Ja 31 '70
Too much of a good thing; last half of the sixties. il Forbes 105:31-3 Ja 1 '70
Trend of American business. See issues of U.S. news & World report
Twelve industries moving ahead in the midst of a downturn. il U S News 68:62-3 Ap 27 '70
War gloom and market jitters. il por Bsns W p 19-20 My 9 '70
What business can count on from Washington. il U S News 69:42-3 N 16 '70
  See also
Business cycles
Business depression
Business failures
Business forecasting
Economic conditions
Inflation (finance)
  also subhead Economic conditions under names of countries, states, etc. e.g. United States—Economic conditions
BUSINESS conferences
Top idea men trade ideas. il Bsns W p32-3 Ja 31 '70
BUSINESS consolidations and mergers
Acquisitions and mergers. Aviation W 92:70 Ja 26; 53 Ap 20; 93:88-9 Jl 13 '70
Behind the breakup in big business mergers. il U S News 69:44-6 Jl 27 '70
Changes in U.S. merger policy? U S News 69:57 N 30 '70
Clashing head on over merger rules. Bsns W p 19 Jl 25 '70
Contingent payouts cut acquisition risks. W. R. Reum and T. A. Steele. 3d. bibliog f il Harvard Bsns R 48:83-91 Mr '70
End game; Accounting principles board kills off accounting gimmicks. Newsweek 76:84+ Jl 13 '70
Master plan for merger negotiations. G. E. MacDougal and F. V. Malek. il Harvard Bsns R 48:71-82 Ja '70
Merger of Whites eases grip on Allis. Bsns W p22-3 Ag 22 '70
Merging up, divesting down. Fortune 81:202 Je '70
New trouble for mergers. Time 96:68-9 Jl 13 '70
New type plays the acquisition game. il Bsns W p22-3 D 5 '70
Plan to integrate your acquisitions. R. A. Howell. il Harvard Bsns R 48:66-76 N '70
Psychologist diagnoses merger failures. H. Levinson. bibliog f Harvard Bsns R 48:139-47 Mr '70
Shooting for the big time, and making it. J. A. Ryder. il Nations Bsns 58:102-3 Ja '70
Some hard new rules for the merger game; proposed accounting changes. il Bsns W p50+ Ap 11 '70
Warning: never pick up a stranger. il Bsns W p29 Ap 18 '70
What price safety? Universal oil products' merger with Calumet & Hecla. il Forbes 105:45 Mr 15 '70
  See also
Bank consolidations and mergers
Corporations—Divestiture
Diversification in industry
  also subhead Consolidations and mergers under various subjects, e.g. Food industry and trade—Consolidations and mergers

Accounting

CPAs finally agree on a merger rule. Bsns W p23 Jl 4 '70
Words, words, words. il Forbes 106:54-5 O 1 '70

Europe, Western

Europe's love affair with bigness. P. Siekman. il Fortune 81:94-9+ Mr '70

France

Reshaping of Saint-Gobain. il Bsns W p47 Ja 31 '70

Great Britain

Rivals sidetrack a big London merger; Metropolitan estate & property corp. Bsns W p26 Jl 25 '70
BUSINESS consultants
Citibank's parent adopts a consultant; Cresap, McCormick & Paget, inc. Bsns W p 17 Ja 9 '71
Lean times bring out the fat-cutters; cost-reduction consultants. il Bsns W p56+ Ap 18 '70

BUSINESS consultants—*Continued*
Packaging social science for profit. il Bsns W p50+ My 2 '70
See also
Alpha systems, inc.
Public relations consultants

BUSINESS cooperation
Problem of the new chief executive. S. R. Stuart. il Duns 95:24-6 Ja '70

BUSINESS costs. See Cost

BUSINESS council
Blue ribbon business council. G. R. Rosen. il Duns 95:37-41 Ja '70
Impact of Cambodia: a business size-up. U S News 68:44 My 18 '70
Nixon's salesmen stick to their story; Business council meeting. il Bsns W p26-7 My 16 '70

BUSINESS cycles
Business cycle is back again. il Bsns W p47-8 Ja 2 '71
Cycle riders take a new turn. il Bsns W p66-7 O 3 '70
Postwar price cycles: a new chronology; excerpt from address, September 1970. G. H. Moore. il Mo Labor R 93:11-17 D '70
See also
Business depression

BUSINESS decision making. See Decision making

BUSINESS depression
Borderline case of recession? il Time 95:60-1 Mr 9 '70
Business finally calls it a recession. il Bsns W p76-8 My 30 '70
Doctor, it hurts; 1970 recession. Nat R 23:22 Ja 12 '71
Economy: crisis of confidence. il Time 95:39-42+ Je 1 '70
Hard times, 1970: an oral history of the recession. S. Terkel. il N Y Times Mag p 10-11+ D 20 '70
Hard times '70: facts, figures and. . . Newsweek 75:74 My 25 '70
How business is meeting the squeeze. il U S News 68:32-4 Mr 9 '70
How deep a slump coming? what top economists say. il U S News 68:24-7 Mr 2 '70
How recession can kill. Newsweek 76:62 N 30 '70
How the slump looks to three experts. M. Friedman; P. A. Samuelson; H. Wallich. pors Newsweek 75:78-9 My 25 '70
Is the Nation wallowing in recession? B. L. Masse. America 122:575 My 30 '70
1970: the year of the hangover. il Time 96:52-6 D 28 '70
Nixon's new worries about recession. il Time 95:81-2 Mr 30 '70
Nixon's recession? Time 97:70 Ja 18 '71
Recession, please go away! D. Lawrence. U S News 68:84 Mr 30 '70
Recessions. H. C. Wallich. Newsweek 75:91 Ap 20 '70
Signals off; prediction of next U.S. financial crash by A. Upgren. il Newsweek 75:80-1 My 18 '70
Struggle to cope with recession. Time 95:79-80 F 16 '70
Topsy-turvy ups and downs. il Newsweek 75:23-4 Je 1 '70
Under way: a drive to head off recession. il U S News 68:34-5 F 23 '70
We must stand firm against inflation. M. Friedman. Read Digest 96:202-4+ Je '70
Whatever it's called, it's a slump. il Newsweek 75:79-80 Mr 16 '70
When is it a recession? il Bsns W p 108+ Ap 18 '70
See also
Business conditions

BUSINESS depression, 1929-1939
Dreams deferred, promises betrayed. M. Dubofsky. Nation 210:438-40 Ap 13 '70
Hard times; by S. Terkel. Review
Cath World 211:278 S '70. R. J. Meister
Commonweal il 92:319-21 Je 26 '70. S. Maloff
Life il 68:17 Ap 17 '70. H. Clurman
Nation 210:376+ Mr 30 '70. N. Algren
New Yorker 46:152+ My 16 '70. L. E. Sissman
Hard times remembered; excerpts from Hard times. S. Terkel. il Am Heritage 21:36-45 Ap '70
Migrant mother: 1936. P. Taylor. il Am West 7:41-5 My '70
Physics in the great depression. C. Weiner. bibliog il Phys Today 23:31-6+ O '70
Shattered dream, by G. Smith. Review
America 123:300-1 O 17 '70. R. J. Meister
When times were really hard; excerpt from Hard times: an oral history of the great depression. S. Terkel. il Atlan 225:73-9+ Ap '70

BUSINESS districts
City malls: fresh life for downtown. il U S News 70:52-4 Ja 11 '71
Comeback starts for big-city downtowns. il U S News 69:17-20 Ag 3 '70
Downtown is looking up. W. McQuade. il Fortune 81:132-6+ F '70
Downtown Richmond makes it. il Am City 85:140-1 Je '70
Fifth avenue turns into a mall. il Bsns W p22 Jl 18 '70
Future of the central city. A. Ganz. il Am City 85:57-9 Ag '70
Giving the piazzas back to the people. il Bsns W p 126 Je 27 '70
How to plan for the urban spirit; Los Angeles. A. C. Martin. il Am City 85:82+ F '70
It hasn't been easy; Miami, Okla. serpentine downtown. C. Allonby. il Am City 85:47-8 D '70
Mall adjusted. P. Bulter. Sat R 53:4+ Je 20 '70
Mall that communications built; Coos Bay, Ore. C. E. Mahanay. il Am City 85:76+ O '70
Minneapolis businessmen bring new life to downtown area. il Parks & Rec 5:33 My '70
People, yes; cars, no. W. Von Eckardt. Sat R 53:62-3 O 3 '70
Should automobiles be banned from urban centers? pro and con discussion. il Sr Schol 96:12-13 Mr 2 '71
See also
Industrial districts
Shopping centers
Lighting
Lighting on the mall; Pittsburgh. il Am City 85:116 Ja '70

BUSINESS education
B-school for entrepreneurs of change; Vanderbilt's Graduate school of management. il por Bsns W p82+ Ap 25 '70
Budget cutters worry B-schools. Bsns W p 15 D 26 '70
MBA itch is mostly myth. Bsns W p30 S 26 '70
New business student. il Newsweek 76:76 O 12 '70
Revitalized curriculum for business education. R. F. Schuck. Clear House 45:32-6 S '70
Sacred cows in business education. L. R. Beaumont. Ed Digest 36:42-3 O '70
Should executives go back to school? management programs criticized. A. A. Butkus. il Duns 96:36-8 S '70
See also
Carnegie-Mellon university, Pittsburgh—Graduate school of industrial administration
Cornell university, Ithaca, N.Y.—Graduate school of business and public administration
Harvard university—Graduate school of business administration
Stanford university, Stanford, Calif.—Graduate school of business
Thunderbird graduate school of international management, Phoenix, Ariz.
Japan
B-school where language comes first; Institute for international studies, known as Boeki Daigaku. il Bsns W p44+ Mr 21 '70

BUSINESS enterprises, New
Plan to utilize West coast aerospace unemployed proposed; regional investment promotion corporations to encourage establishment of new businesses. Aviation W 93:61 N 30 '70
Students flunk at new ideas; Globus, inc, offer. V. Louviere. Nations Bsns 58:14 Jl '70

BUSINESS ethics
Can an executive afford a conscience? excerpt from The executive conscience. A. Z. Carr. bibliog f il Harvard Bsns R 48:58-64 Jl '70

BUSINESS executives move for Vietnam peace
Businessmen against the war (sic) S. Weissman. il Ramp Mag 9:32-7 D '70

BUSINESS expansion. See Industrial expansion

BUSINESS expenses. See Expense accounts (business)

BUSINESS failures
Business counts the casualties. il Bsns W p26-7 F 7 '70
Business failures. R. Wyant. See issues of Dun's
Tales of three losers. il pors Time 96:64-5 Jl 27 '70
See also
Bank failures
Bankruptcy

BUSINESS flying. See Airplanes in business

BUSINESS forecasting
Accentuating the positive. il Nations Bsns 58:34-8 Ap '70

As top economists forecast business; Conference board's annual forum. il U S News 70:56-63 Ja 4 '71

As White House sees business. il U S News 68:51 F 9 '70

Business: a look ahead. See issues of Nation's business

Business: a turn to optimism. U S News 69: 15 Jl 27 '70

Business in 1970-71: official forecast. il U S News 69:16 Ag 31 '70

Business outlook as Europe sees it. il U S News 70:34-5 Ja 11 '71

Business outlook at midyear. il U S News 69: 15-17 Jl 13 '70

Businessmen's expectations. il Duns 95:121 Mr; 105 Je; 96:99 S; 76 D '70

Economic outlook now; excerpts from testimoney before a joint House-Senate committee. il U S News 69:54-8 Ag 3 '70

First look at '71: a slow climb back; price rises by Time's Board of economists. il Time 96:76-7 O 12 '70

Green light for a business speedup; views of top executives. il Nations Bsns 58:27-32 Ja '70

Has business turned the corner? what leading economists say. il U S News 69:13-15 S 7 '70

In your region: the business prospects. il U S News 70:12-15 Ja 4 '70

Look ahead into 1971 by top advisers to business. il U S News 69:36-7 S 28 '70

Next turn in business; how experts size up the prospects. il U S News 68:11-13 My 4 '70

'71: will it bring recovery? il U S News 70: 8-10 Ja 4 '71

Trend of American business. See issues of U.S. news & World report

Worst is over; poll of top executives. il Nations Bsns 58:28-31 Jl '70

See also
Forecasts (economics)
Stocks—Price forecasting

BUSINESS games. See Management games

BUSINESS hours
See also
Hours of labor
Libraries—Hours of opening
Store hours

BUSINESS in the arts award
Esquire-BCA fourth annual business in the arts awards; with editorial comment. Esquire 74:6+, 30-1 Jl '70

BUSINESS insurance. See Insurance, Business

BUSINESS intelligence
See also
Spies, Industrial

BUSINESS liquidation. See Liquidation

BUSINESS literature
Specialized investment services: reference materials for the public library. R. S. Burgess. il por Library J 95:867-9 Mr 1 '70

BUSINESS location. See Location in business and industry

BUSINESS machine industry. See Office equipment industry

BUSINESS machines corporation, International. See International business machines corporation

BUSINESS management and organization
Accuracy of long-range planning. R. F. Vancil. il Harvard Bsns R 48:98-101 S '70

Beyond Theory Y. J. J. Morse and J. W. Lorsch. bibliog f il Harvard Bsns R 48: 61-8 My '70

Business says it can handle bigness. il Bsns W p 108-10+ O 17 '70

Deadwood in the executive suite. G. Berkwitt. il Duns 95:35-7 Mr '70

Do you need a new bright hand? A. Uris. il Nations Bsns 58:72-4+ Jl '70

Emerging EDP pattern. C. W. Hofer. bibliog il Harvard Bsns R 48:16-18+ Mr '70

Executive trends. J. Costello. See issues of Nation's business

How to lock out the Mafia. C. Grutzner. bibliog f il Harvard Bsns R 48:45-58 Mr '70

Management by whose objectives? H. Levinson. bibliog f Harvard Bsns R 48:125-34 Jl '70

Management evolution in the quantitative world. R. F. Vandell. il Harvard Bsns R 48:83-92 Ja '70

Matrix management: a tough game to play. J. Perham. il Duns 96:31-4 Ag '70

Measuring management: 1969. il Forbes 105:43 Ja 1 '70

Measuring management: 1970. il Forbes 107: 70 Ja 1 '71

New myths of management. G. Berkwitt. Duns 96:25-7+ S '70

Plan to integrate your acquisitions. R. A. Howell. il Harvard Bsns R 48:66-76 N '70

Remodeling management structures. C. C. **Brown. por Nations Bsns 58:46 N '70**

Rise of the corporate planner; adaptation of address, May 1970. G. A. Steiner. il Harvard Bsns R 48:133-9 S '70

Shoe-leather executive. G. Berkwitt. il Duns 96:33-5 N '70

Side effects of planning. D. S. Ammer. il Harvard Bsns R 48:32-4+ My '70

Technology, management & society, by P. F. Drucker. Review
Bsns W p8+ Ap 25 '70. C. L. Walton, jr.

Theory and practice of planning. R. J. Mockler. bibliog Harvard Bsns R 48:148-50+ Mr '70

Up the organization, by R. Townsend. Review
Fortune il 81:303+ My '70. A. Miller
New Yorker 46:161-2+ Ap 18 '70. L. E. Sissman
Sat R 53:30-1 Ap 4 '70. W. Benton

Up the organization: excerpts. R Townsend. il Harper 240:73-90 Mr '70

Up the organization man. W. A. McWhirter. il pors Life 68:61-2+ Ap 17 '70

When the cards don't go your way. il Forbes 107:23-8 Ja 1 '71

Year of the corporate ax. il Newsweek 76:61-2 Jl 20 '70

See also
Airlines—Management
American management association
Bank management
Bonus system
Budget, Business
Business consultants
Business cooperation
Business records
Computers—Business use
Corporations
Credit managers
Decision making
Diversification in industry
Executive ability
Executives
Harvard university—Graduate school of business administration
Industrial expansion
Industrial management and organization
International institute for the management of technology (proposed)
Inventories
Marketing
Personnel management
Work measurement

Case studies
Problems in review. il Harvard Bsns R 48: 4-6+ Mr; 150-2+ My; 140-2+ S; 144-6+ N '70

Programmed case: the misfired missive; Dashman case. A. M. Hodgson and W. R. Dill. bibliog Harvard Bsns R 48:140-2+ S; 105-10 N '70

Employee participation
Motivating people with meaningful work. W. J. Roche and N. L. MacKinnon. bibliog il Harvard Bsns R 48:97-110 My '70

Japan
How to negotiate in Japan. H. F. Van Zandt. bibliog f il Harvard Bsns R 48:45-56 N '70

BUSINESS organization. See Business management and organization

BUSINESS recession. See Business depression

BUSINESS records
Why it's harder to run a business. il U S News 69:29-31 Jl 20 '70

BUSINESS research
See also
Market research

BUSINESS risks. See Risk

BUSINESS schools. See Business education

BUSINESS statistics
Figures of the week. See issues of Business week

See also
Business forecasting

BUSINESS success. See Success

BUSINESS travel
Job travel isn't glamorous for him, or her. C. B. Howes. il Todays Health 48:27-9+ S '70
What a husband's business trips do to a marriage. L. Tornabene. Ladies Home J 87:75-6+ My '70
Working jet set. il Nations Bsns 58:50-1 S '70
See also
Airplanes in business

BUSINESS trips. See Business travel

BUSINESS women. See Business and professional women

BUSINESSMAN'S educational forum
Businessmen against the war (sic) S. Weissman. il Ramp Mag 9:32-7 D '70
Pinstripes for peace. Newsweek 75:85B-86+ My 11 '70

BUSINESSMAN'S educational fund. See Businessman's educational forum

BUSINESSMEN
Brother, you can spare the time. V. R. Moseman. il Nations Bsns 58:84-5 F '70
Businessmen in the news. See issues of Fortune
Do businessmen make poor parents? Bsns W p20 D 26 '70
Expense-account splurge in Japan. U S News 68:86-7 Mr 9 '70
Faces behind the figures. See issues of Forbes
In voting on great Americans, business gets the business. D. L. Lewis. il Nations Bsns 58:88-9 Mr '70
Job travel isn't glamorous for him, or her. C. B. Howes. il Todays Health 48:27-9+ S '70
Money men. See issues of Forbes
When businessmen sparked a revolution. il Nations Bsns 58:52-7 Jl '70
Why we need new businessmen. C. Kaufmann. Look 34:76+ Ja 13 '70
See also
Astronauts as businessmen
Capitalists and financiers
Corporations—Directors
Executives
National alliance of businessmen
Negro businessmen

Health and hygiene
Executive health; the dangers of a stroke. Bsns W p 119 S 12 '70
Why are they running, stretching, starving? W. McQuade. il Fortune 82:132-5+ Ag '70
Why executives flame out. D. Joy. il Nations Bsns 58:50-2 Je '70
See also
Executives—Health programs

Religious life
See also
Christian businessmen's committee international

BUSINESSMEN as public officers. See Public officers

BUSINESSMENS committee international, Christian. See Christian businessmen's committee international

BUSONI, Ferruccio
Busoni's Doktor Faust; recording. R. Jacobson. il por Sat R 53:44-5 Jl 25 '70 *
Doktor Faust. P. L. Miller. il Am Rec G 36:864-5+ Jl '70 *
Prophetic Doktor Faust. D. Hamilton. il Hi Fi 20:sec1 69-70 Jl '70 *
Recorded legacy of Ferruccio Busoni. D. Hamilton. por Hi Fi sec I 20:77-8 F '70 *

BUSSE, James G.
Build a blinking beacon to guide you home. il Pop Mech 134:130-1 Jl '70
Build a cryptolock. il Pop Electr 34:42-4+ Ja '71
Patio control brings lights up s-l-o-w-l-y. il Pop Sci 197:123-4 O '70

BUSTOS, Gonzalo Orchard, and others
Pyrazole and induction of fatty liver by a single dose of ethanol. bibliog il Science 168:1598-9 Je 26 '70

BUSWELL, Christa H.
Reading and the aged. bibliog il por Wilson Lib Bul 45:467-8+ Ja '71

BUTANE
See also
Liquified petroleum gas

BUTCHART gardens. See Gardens—Canada

BUTCHER, Russell D.
Let's stop mining in our national parks and wilderness areas. il Am For 76:28-31+ S '70

BUTENHOFF, Wallace
Don't get me wrong; ed. by L. Levitt. por Time 95:21 My 25 '70

BUTKUS, Alvin A.
GE puzzle. il por Duns 96:34-8+ Jl '70

about
Odyssey of Alvin Butkus. Duns 96:3 Jl '70 *

BUTKUS, Dick
Nobody thinks I can talk. R. F. Jones. por Sports Illus 33:64-9 S 21 '70 *

BUTLER, Charles F.
Text of U.S. letter to president of the council of the ICAO; September 11, 1970. Dept State Bul 63:343 S 28 '70

BUTLER, E. E. and Petersen, L. J.
Sexual reproduction in geotrichum candidum. bibliog il Science 169:481-2 Jl 31 '70

BUTLER, Henry F.
Polish premieres at Butler U. Hi Fi sec II 20:28+ Ja '70

BUTLER, J. George
Toward postal reorganization. il Chr Cent 87:104-8 Ja 28 '70

BUTLER, Jacqueline S.
Student council, elementary style. il Todays Ed 59:58-9 S '70

BUTLER, James K. Jr
Public relations specialist in pork; interview, ed. by J. D. Boyd. Farm J 94:H14+ Mr '70

BUTLER, Joseph T.
Philipsburg manor, Upper Mills at North Tarrytown, New York. il Antiques 97:864-71 Je '70

BUTLER, Josephine D.
Morgan follows through. S. Moorefield. il Am Ed 6:31-3 Ja '70 *

BUTLER, Michael
Like father, unlike son. il por Forbes 105:56 Je 1 '70 *

BUTLER, Patrick
Ages of heroes. Sat R 53:4 Jl 11 '70
Mall adjusted. Sat R 53:4+ Je 20 '70

BUTLER, Robert N.
Recycling rigid life patterns. Cur 114:62-4 Ja '70

BUTLER, William F.
International bookkeeping really counts. por Nations Bsns 58:54-5 Ag '70

BUTLER, William R.
Campus and the student, 1970; address, May 4, 1970. Vital Speeches 36:566-9 Jl 1 '70

BUTLER aviation international, inc.
Aerostar story: the machine, and the man. J. Gilbert; P. Garrison. il Flying 87:30-7 Ag '70
Butler sues former producer of Aerostar. Aviation W 94:66 Ja 11 '71
Marketing emphasized by Aerostar. E. J. Bulban. Aviation W 93:73 O 12 '70

BUTLER university, Indianapolis
Polish premieres at Butler U. H. F. Butler. Hi Fi sec II 20:28+ Ja '70

BUTLER'S tray. See Trays

BUTRICO, Frank A.
Solid wastes and land pollution. Cur Hist 59: 13-17 Jl '70

BUTTERCRUNCH lettuce. See Lettuce

BUTTERFIELD, Fox
When the crunch comes, can Taiwan hold together? il N Y Times Mag p14-15+ Ja 18 '70

BUTTERFISH. See Sablefish

BUTTERFLIES
Butterflies, yes! fate of harmless or beneficial insects. A. W. Smith. Nat Parks 44:2 Mr '70
Cardiac glycosides and distastefulness: some observations on the palatability spectrum of butterflies. S. S. Duffey. bibliog il Science 169:78-9 Jl 3 '70
Heart poisons and the monarch. M. Rothschild and B. Ford. il Natur Hist 79:36-7 Ap '70
Migrating monarchs. Sci Digest 67:30 Ap '70

BUTTERFLIES are free; drama. See Gershe, L.

BUTTERWORTH, Frank M. See Brieger, G. jt. auth.

BUTTONS
Bass Rock; Dalrymple family livery button. D. F. Brown. il Hobbies 75:128-9 D '70
Button collecting. D. F. Brown. See issues of Hobbies
Handcrafted ceramic buttons. R. Behrens. il Ceram Mo 18:28-9 Ja '70
See also
Campaign buttons, etc.

BUTWELL, Richard
Burma: the obscure domino. bibliog f il Cur Hist 59:339-44+ D '70
Philippines under Marcos. bibliog f Cur Hist 58:196-201+ Ap '70

BUTWIN, David W.
Booked for travel. See issues of Saturday review
Finns and Finlandia. il Sat R 53:54+ Mr 14 '70
Yankee go home and other friendly salutations. il Sat R 54:28-9+ Ja 2 '71

BUTYLATED hydroxyanisole. See Antioxidants

BUTYRALDOXIME
Alcohol aversion in the rat: behavioral assessment of noxious drug effects. M. Nachman and others. bibliog il Science 168:1244-6 Je 5 '70

BUTZER, Martin
Melanchthon and Bucer, ed. by W. Pauck. Review
Chr Cent 87:273 Mr 4 '70. W. H. Lazareth *

BUXBAUM, Joel, and others
Immunoglobulin M heavy chain disease: intracellular origin of the mu chain fragment. bibliog il Science 169:770-3 Ag 21 '70

BUXTON, E. Brewster
Tropical disturbance Eline, 1898. il por Weatherwise 23:222-3+ O '70

BUYERS
Professional buyers spend cautiously. il Bsns W p22-3 Je 6 '70

BUYING. See Purchasing, Household; Shopping and shoppers

BUYING, Industrial. See Purchasing, Industrial

BUYING clubs. See Purchasing, Cooperative

BUYING motives. See Market research

BUZZARD, William H. jr, and Risley, J. H.
Department fights beech disease and decline. il Cons 24:10-13 Je '70

BYARD, Herbert
Sternhold and Hopkins puzzle. Mus Q 56:221-9 Ap '70

BYCHOWSKI, Gustav
Potential of psychoanalytic biography: Zeligs on Chambers and Hiss. bibliog f Am Imago 26:233-41 Fall '69

BYE, Richard E.
Bye lines. Library J 96:49 Ja 1 '71

BYERLEE, James D. See Brace, W. F. jt. auth.

BYERS, Mrs Mellon
Rooms they love to live in. il por House & Gard 138:44-7 Ag '70 *

BYHAM, William C.
Assessment centers for spotting future managers. il Harvard Bsns R 48:150-60+ Jl '70

BYKOFSKY, Stuart D.
What the writer should know about tape recorders. il Writers Digest 50:31-3+ O '70

BYLINSKY, Gene
Computers little helpers create a brawling business. il Fortune 81:84-7+ Je '70
Limited war on water pollution. il Fortune 81:103-7+ F '70
Long, littered path to clean air and water. il Fortune 82:112-15+ O '70

BYRAM, E. T. and others
X-ray survey of Centaurus A. bibliog il Science 169:366-8 Jl 24 '70

BYRAM, Ephraim Niles
Ephraim Byram, versatile nineteenth-century craftsman. J. M. Perkins il por Antiques 97:746-7 My '70 *

BYRD, Harry Flood, 1914-
Flight of the Byrd. Time 95:19-20 Mr 30 '70 *
One in, one out. Newsweek 75:21-2 Mr 30 '70 *

BYRD, Jeryl
My year of crisis. il por Redbook 135:12+ O '70

BYRD, Robert Carlyle
West Virginia Byrd. P. R. Wieck. New Repub 163:11-13 D 12 '70 *

BYRD family
Byrds of Virginia, by A. Hatch. Review
Sat R 53:35-6 F 7 '70. W. Sullivan

BYRNE, Katharine
Repentant dropouts. il America 122:522-4 My 16 '70

BYRNE, Robert
Mail animal. Sat R 53:4-5 Ag 8 '70

BYRNES, George
Predict & win. il Motor B 126:60-1+ Ag '70

BYRNES, John W.
Excerpt from debate, April 15, 1970. Cong Digest 49:178+ Je '70

BYRON, George Gordon Noël Byron, 6th baron
Uninhibited Byron, by B. Grebanier. Review
Sat R 53:32 O 17 '70. H. C. Webster *

BYRON, William J.
Vision of American religious life. America 123:14-15 Jl 11 '70

BYWATER, Hector Charles
Japan strikes; 1941. W. H. Honan. il por Am Heritage 22:12-15+ D '70 *

C

C-5A (airplane) See Airplanes, Military transport

CAA. See College art association of America

CAB. See United States—Civil aeronautics board

CAI (computer-assisted instruction) See Computers—Educational use

CAM (computer aided manufacturing) See Computers—Industrial use

CAREL (Central Atlantic regional educational laboratory) project. See Dancing—Study and teaching

CAT (clear air turbulence) See Atmospheric turbulence

CATV system
Asleep at the switch of the wired city. F. W. Friendly. Sat R 53:58-60 O 10 '70; Same abr. with title Today's short supply of air time. Cur 124:28-33 D '70
Battle stations. R. L. Shayon. Sat R 53:56 Ja 31 '70
Big changes in TV, phones: upheaval in communications. il U S News 69:50-2 Jl 13 '70
Bonus for CATV subscribers: cable FM. E. A. Lacy. il Pop Electr 34:60-2 Ja '71
Cable television: birth of a new giant? il Changing T 24:19-23 N '70
CATV is coming to your town. W. G. Salm. il Pop Sci 196:88-9+ Je '70
CATV+NCPL=VRS: Video reference service over a community TV system at Natrona County public library. K. E. Dowlin. il pors Library J 95:2768-70 S 1 '70
Hitches in the cable: television in New York. S. W. Dean, jr. il Nation 211:41-5 Jl 20 '70
New FCC tune elates cable-TV. Bsns W p38 My 23 '70
Pap from a different spoon? R. L. Bishop. New Repub 162:23-5 Mr 28 '70; Discussion. 162:29-30 Je 13 '70
Television: twenty years from now. F. H. Belt. il Electr World 83:25-9 Ja '70
To wire a nation. Time 95:66+ Je 1 '70
Troubles of television, and a coming revolution. il U S News 69:58-60 D 21 '70
What educational media specialists ought to know about CATV. Ed Digest 35:48-51 Ja '70
Wired nation. R. L. Smith. il Nation 210: 582-606 My 18 '70

Securities
Legal narcotic? C. Rolo. por Forbes 106:54-5 S 1 '70

CATV system and copyright. See Copyright—Broadcasting rights

C. and A. Brenninkmeyer company. See Brenninkmeyer, C. and A, company

CB radio. See Citizens radio service

CBS. See Columbia broadcasting system, inc.

CBW research. See Chemical and biological weapons

CC. See Common cause (political organization)

CCCNY. See Council of churches of the city of New York

CCEI. See Colorado committee for environmental information

CCIR. See International radio consultative committee

CCN. See Christian council of Nigeria

CCP. See Commission on college physics

CDC. See Control data corporation

CEA. See United States—Council of economic advisers

CED. See Committee for economic development

CEDAC (computerized energy distribution and automated control system) See Computers—Automotive use

CEQ. See United States—Council on environmental quality

CERN (Conseil européen pour la recherche nucléaire) See European organization for nuclear research

CHIF. See Connecticut housing investment fund

CIA. See United States—Central intelligence agency

CICOP (Catholic Inter-American cooperation program) See Religious conferences

CIDOC. See Center of intercultural documentation

CIECC (Inter-American council for education, science, and culture) See Inter-American council for education, science, and culture

CIF. See Construction industry foundation

CLA. See California library association

CMSW. See Conference of major superiors of women's institutions of the United States of America

CNA financial corporation
CNA: there's leverage in leasing. A. Hershman. por Duns 95:42-4 My '70

CNA nuclear leasing (firm)
  CNA: there's leverage in leasing. por Duns 95:42-4 My '70
CNES (Centre national d'études spatiales) See France—National center for space studies
COCU. See Consultation on church union
CODAF. See United States-Mexico commission for border development and friendship
COG (councils of government) See Municipal government
COM. See Concerned officers movement
COM (computer output microfilming) See Computers—Input-output equipment
COO. See American library association—Committee on organization
COS. See Central opera service
COSMEP. See Committee of small magazine editors and publishers
CPB. See Corporation for public broadcasting
CPC. See Christian preaching conference
CPC (Christian peace conference) See Peace conferences
CPC international, Inc.
  CPC: momentum from a foreign affiliate. il Bsns W p64-5+ D 19 '70
CPTA (chlorophenylthio-triethylamine hydrochloride) See Ethylamine
CREI. See Capitol radio engineering institute
CRS. See Catholic relief services
CRT. See Cathode ray tubes
CSD. See American library association— Childrens services division
CTC (Christian training center) See World Christian training center
CU. See Consumers union of United States
C. V. STARR and company. See Starr, C. V. and company
CAB drivers. See Taxicab drivers
CABALA
  See also
  Sabbathaians
CABALLÉ, Montserrat
  Musical events; recital in Philharmonic Hall. New Yorker 46:171-2 D 5 '70
CABANAC, M. and Duclaux, R.
  Obesity; absence of satiety aversion to sucrose. bibliog il Science 168:496-7 Ap 24 '70
CABANAS. See Bathhouses
CABBAGES
  Starting cabbages in a bread box. J. R. Coggins. il Org Gard & Farm 17:54-5 F '70
CABEZA PRIETA game range.   See Game preserves
CABEZA PRIETA wilderness area (proposed) See Wilderness areas—Arizona
CABIB, Enrico
  Research on sugar nucleotides brings honor to Argentinian biochemist. por Science 170:608-9 N 6 '70
CABIN cruisers. See Cruisers (pleasure boats)
CABINET (Great Britain); Cabinet (Spain); etc. See Great Britain—Cabinet; Spain—Cabinet; etc.
CABINET (newspaper)   See Milford, N.H.—Newspapers
CABINET officers
  Phone calls that didn't get through. H. Sidey. Life 68:4 My 29 '70

Children
  Hello, dad. . . il Newsweek 75:33-4 Je 1 '70

Dismissal
  Casting-out of Wally Hickel. H. Sidey. il Life 69:6 D 4 '70
  Rocky road to oblivion. M. McGrory. America 123:508 D 12 '70
CABINET officers, Resignation of
  Few resignations might help: Time essay. il Time 95:16 Je 1 '70
CABINET work
  New twists on building fine furniture: a marble-topped table. F. L. Greenwald. il Pop Sci 196:110+ My '70
  See also
  Woodworking
CABINETMAKERS
  Dunlap cabinetmakers. C. S. Parsons and D. S. Brooke. il Antiques 98:224-31 Ag '70
  Indiana cabinetmakers and allied craftsmen, 1815-1860. A. Whallon. il Antiques 98:118-25 Jl '70
  Lyell, Slover, Taylor, Phyfe, et al. E. L. Frelinghuysen. il Antiques 97:119-20 Ja '70
  See also
  Lannuier. C. H.
CABINETS (furniture)
  Backyard barbeque pantry. R. Capotosto. il Mech Illus 66:90-1 Jl '70

Cabinet for your guns. il Pop Mech 133:154-8 Ja '70
Chairside sewing cabinet. W. C. Leckey. il Pop Mech 133:172-4 F '70
Laundry hideaway. J. Capotosto. il Mech Illus 66:114-15 O '70
Projection unit supports projector, stores everything. il Sunset 145:114+ N '70
Space-saver hutch built in a closet. R. D. Borst. il Pop Mech 134:102-4 Ag '70
  See also
  Kitchen cabinets
CABINS
  Kentucky cabin playhouses. il House & Gard 137:76-7 Je '70
  New look at the old deer camp. D. J. Anderson. il Field & S 74:72-3+ Mr '70
  Weekend place in Idaho, a big open deck and almost half a house. il Sunset 145:60-1 Ag '70
CABINS, Boat. See Boats—Cabins
CABLE, Harold
  Big Red Riding Hood; drama. Plays 29:11-21 Mr '70
  Way, way down South; drama. Plays 30:14-24 N '70
CABLE television. See CATV system
CABLES
  See also
  Electric cables
CABLEWAYS
  Airborne ablutions; Japan's hot-bath cable-car system. il Newsweek 76:79 Jl 6 '70
  Higher rider; technical manager of Sandia Peak tramway. il Mech Illus 66:82-3 Ag '70
  Next stop mountaintop; New Mexico's Sandia Peak tramway. il Travel 134:56-7 N '70
  Sky-lift: a great way to move up in the world. W. Langewiesche. il Read Digest 97:170-2+ N '70
CABORO BASSA project. See Hydroelectric plants
CABOT, Louis Wellington
  Cabot's transfusion. A. A. Butkus. por Duns 95:63-4 Je '70 *
CABOT, Paul Codman
  It isn't over yet; interview. por Forbes 105:80 Je 15 '70
CABOT, Cabot and Forbes (firm)
  Looking like new; industrial parks. il Nations Bsns 58:93-4+ O '70
CABOT corporation
  Cabot's transfusion. A. A. Butkus. por Duns 95:63-4 Je '70
CABRAL, Amilcar
  Our army is our whole people; excerpts from remarks; ed. by R. Levine. il por Newsweek 75:38-9 Mr 9 '70
CABRAL, Dulce. See Amabis, J. M. jt. auth.
CACCIA, David A.
  Bird, who came to dinner. il Org Gard & Farm 17:50-1 Jl '70
CACCINI, Giulio
  Vocal ornamentation in Caccini's Nuove musiche. H. W. Hitchcock. bibliog f il Mus Q 56:389-404 Jl '70 *
CACTUS
  Cactus as food. L. P. Bell. Horticulture 48:8+ F '70
  Cactus you can eat; leaf cactus. R. J. Wyndham. il Org Gard & Farm 17:102 Jl '70
  Home greenhouse. J. A. Eaton. Home Gard 57:14-15 Je '70
  Mini desert on a table. K. Adler. il Home Gard 57:28-9 O '70
  Your garden indoors. F. S. David. il Home Gard 57:55 Jl '70
CADBURY Schweppes, ltd.
  Cadbury's new Schweppervescence. il Forbes 106:62-3 O 15 '70
CADDEN, Vivian
  Are you for the budget, or is the budget for you? Redbook 134:97+ Mr '70
  Credit-ability gap: a wise woman's guide to buying without cash. Redbook 135:58+ S '70
  Half the money and twice the cheer. il Redbook 136:42+ D '70
  Truth that saves money in the supermarket. Redbook 135:30+ Jl '70
CADE, John Frederick Joseph
  Help for the manic-depressive. por Time 95:46 Ap 20 '70 *
CADEAUX, Ralph
  U.S. journal: Grosvenor square. C. Trillin. New Yorker 46:108+ S 19 '70 *
CADIEUX, Charles L.
  Exploring Lake Powell. il Yachting 128:72-3+ N '70
CADLE, Richard D. and Allen, E. R.
  Atmospheric photochemistry. bibliog il Science 167:243-9 Ja 16 '70

CADMIUM poisoning
Cadmium toxicity decreased by dietary ascorbic acid supplements. M. R. S. Fox and B. E. Fry, jr. bibliog il Science 169:989-91 S 4 '70
CADWALADER, George
Transatlantic by Cal-20. il Yachting 127:60-1+ Ap; 56-8+ My '70
CADY, Jack
I take care of things; story. Yale R 59:242-8 D '69
CAEN, Herb
Herb Caen: his power is awesome. G. Sales. il Holiday 47:76-7+ Mr '70 *
CAESAREAN section. See Cesarean section
CAETANO, Marcello
Salazar's legacy survives in Portugal. W. E. Greening. Chr Cent 87:708-9 Je 3 '70 *
Thaw in Portugal. D. L. Wheeler. For Affairs 48:769-81 Jl '70 *
CAFFEINE
Caffeine: grounds for concern? Consumer Rep 36:34 Ja '71
Monosodium glutamate; under suspicion as a mutagen. Consumer Bul 53:16-19 Mr '70
CAFFI, Andrea
What is society? L. Abel. bibliog f Commentary 50:45-55 S '70 *
CAGE, John
Seated one day at the I-Ching; plexigrams. J. Russell. il por Art N 68:52-3+ Ja '70
Two metamorphosis night. W. F. Rickenbacker. Nat R 22:690-1 Je 30 '70 *
CAGE; drama. See Cluchey, R.
CAGES
His rabbit hutch lifts open. il Sunset 144: 141 Ap '70
CAGNONI, Romano
Last days of Biafra; photographs. Life 68: 20-7 Ja 23 '70
CAHALAN, T. L.
Two showy lobelias. Horticulture 48:52-3 My '70
CAHAN, Abraham
Becoming American. I. Howe. Commentary 49:88-90 Mr '70 *
CAHILL, John Patrick
Fathers and sons. il pors Newsweek 75:24+ F 9 '70
CAHILL, William Thomas
Guide for Nixon in '72; New Jersey's '69 election. il pors U S News 68:32-3 Ja 19 '70
CAHN, Edgar S.
(ed) Our shameful failure with America's Indians; excerpts from Our brother's keeper: the Indian in white America. Read Digest 96:104-9 Ap '70
CAHN, Robert
But why, George? E. N. Layne. il por Am Heritage 21:113 Je '70 *
CAHN, William
Man whose vote gave women the vote. por Look 34:60+ Ag 25 '70
CAIDIN, Martin
Hottest job in the world. il Pop Mech 133: 89-92+ Ap '70
CAIN, Edward R.
Stars and stripes forever. Commonweal 92: 61-2 Mr 27 '70
CAIN, Elna
Household toys. il Design 71:30-3 mid-Sum '70
CAIN, Emily
Mother tiger; story. Redbook 135:76-7 S '70
Prelude to joy. Redbook 136:81+ D '70
CAIN, Seymour
Yishuv and Diaspora: a study of history. Chr Cent 87:668-71 My 27 '70
CAINES, Robert
That mess on the Prestile. F. Graham, jr. il Am Heritage 21:106-12 F '70; Discussion. 21:94-5 Ag '70 *
CAIRNS, Bill
Labrador's trophy trout country. il Travel & Camera 33:50-3 Je '70
CAIRO
Cairo's war: now you see it, now you don't. D. Holden. il N Y Times Mag p32-3+ My 24 '70
Description
Cairo journal. J. Colebrook. Commentary 50: 45-55 O '70
Galleries and museums
Fabulous treasures of Cairo's museums. il UNESCO Courier 23:18-19 Ap '70
History
Cairo: 1,000 years of history inscribed in stone. A. R. Zaky. il UNESCO Courier 23:10-16 Ap '70
CAIRO, Ill.
Madness in Cairo. Newsweek 76:52 N 9 '70

Negroes
Flying black medics. il Ebony 25:81-4+ Je '70
Guerrilla war in Cairo. Nation 211:516 N 23 '70
Race war: close-up of beleaguered Cairo, Illinois. il U S News 69:42-5 D 21 '70
Reports: Cairo, Illinois. S. Darst. Atlan 225: 16+ Mr '70
CAJUN country. See Louisiana
CAJUNS. See Acadians in Louisiana
CAKE
Apricot brandy pound cake. il Sunset 145: 130 D '70
Cakes: present-tense Victoriana. M. Happel. il Ladies Home J 86:96-7+ D '69
Connoisseurs' cakes. C. Claiborne. il N Y Times Mag p52 Ag 9 '70
Golden miniatures; fruitcakes you bake in a soup can. E. W. Manning. il Farm J 94:42 N '70
Good projects for a youthful cook. Each is a one-bowl cake. il Sunset 145:167 N '70
Holiday cakes. H. McCully. il House B 112: 86-7+ D '70
Home-baked cakes. il Good H 170:119-21+ Mr '70
Jelly-roll call. M. Happel. il Ladies Home J 87:76-7+ F '70
Nutcakes: sweet temptations; recipes. J. Retz. il Am Home 73:90-1+ O '70
Seed cakes with tea or coffee. Sunset 144:110 Ja '70
Serve it warm and upside down. il Sunset 145:150 S '70
Two delicious dessert recipes from Rome. il Sunset 144:150 F '70
Two experiments with pound cake. il Sunset 144:209 Mr '70
See also
Baking
Cheesecake
Coffee cake
Shortcake
CAKE; story. See Brow. R.
CAKE, Frozen. See Food, Frozen
CAKE mixes. See Food mixes
CALABRIA, Italy
See also
Sila, La
CALAM, John
New books. See issues of Saturday review
CALAMITIES. See Disasters
CALCIFEROL. See Vitamins—Vitamin D
CALCIFICATION
Microarchitecture and deposition of gastropod nacre. S. W. Wise, jr. bibliog il Science 167:1486-8 Mr 13 '70
Silicon: a possible factor in bone calcification. E. M. Carlisle. bibliog il Science 167:279-80 Ja 16 '70
See also
Calcium in the body
CALCITE
High-magnesian calcite: leaching of magnesium in the deep sea. D. N. Gomberg and E. Bonatti. bibliog il Science 168:1451-3 Je 19 '70
CALCITONIN
Calcitonin. H. Rasmussen and M. M. Pechet. il Sci Am 223:42-50 O '70
CALCIUM
See also
Plants, Effect of calcium on
CALCIUM carbonate
See also
Aragonite
Calcite
CALCIUM compounds
See also
Hydroxyapatite
CALCIUM in the body
Cell communication, calcium ion, and cyclic adenosine monophosphate. H. Rasmussen. bibliog il Science 170:404-12 O 23 '70
How an eggshell is made. T. G. Taylor. il Sci Am 222:88-95 bibliog(p 146) Mr '70
Repairing brittle bones; calcium infusions for osteoporosis. B. J. Culliton. il Sci N 97: 562-3 Je 6 '70
Strengthening brittle bones. il Time 96:43-4 Ag 17 '70
See also
Calcium metabolism
CALCIUM metabolism
p,p'-DDT: effect on calcium metabolism and concentration of estradiol in the blood. D. B. Peakall. bibliog il Science 168:592-4 My 1 '70

CALCIUM oxalate
Calcium oxalate: crystallographic analysis in solid aggregates in urinary sediments. F. Catalina and L. Cifuentes. bibliog il Science 169:183-4 Jl 10 '70
CALCULATING charts. See Charts, Calculating
CALCULATING devices
Price calculators help to find cost per ounce. il Consumer Bul 53:34-5 Mr '70
  See also
Adding machines
Slide rule
CALCULATING machines, Electronic
Calculator to fit the pocket. il Bsns W p28-9 Ap 18 '70
Carry this calculator in your pocket. A. Fisher. il Pop Sci 197:59 Ag '70
CALCUTTA
India's second city firmly in red hands. il U S News 68:72 Mr 2 '70
Oh, Calcutta! il Newsweek 75:60-1 Ap 6 '70
Profiles. V. Mehta. New Yorker 46:47-52+ Mr 21 '70

Relief work
See India—Relief work

Riots
Where death looked down. Time 95:39 Mr 30 '70

Social conditions
Indian revolutionaries with a Chinese accent; the Naxalites. D. Moraes. il N Y Times Mag p30-1+ N 8 '70
CALDECOTT medal
Caldecott award acceptance; address, June 30, 1970. W. Steig. Horn Bk 46:359-60 Ag '70
Newbery and Caldecott winners announced. Pub W 197:66 F 2 '70
Newbery and Caldecott winners for 1969 books. il por Pub W 197:125-6 F 23 '70
Newbery-Caldecott and Ingalls awards. il Wilson Lib Bul 44:692 Mr '70
Newbery-Caldecott-Wilder awards. il Library J 95:1173 Mr 15 '70
Newbery/Caldecott/Wilder winners. Pub W 198:27 Ag 17 '70
Rocky! disqualification of 1969 winner by W. Steig because of poor taste of one of illustrations; discussion. Am Lib 1:525 Je '70
CALDER, Alexander
Graphics '70: Alexander Calder. D. H. Karshan. il por Art in Am 58:48-51 My '70 *
CALDER, Peter Ritchie, baron Ritchie-Calder. See Ritchie-Calder, P. R. C.
CALDERA, Rafael
President Nixon meets with President Caldera of Venezuela; exchange of greetings, toasts and address to Congress, June 2-5, 1970. Dept State Bul 62:793-9 Je 29 '70
Venezuelan president visits Washington, OAS headquarters. il por Américas 22:43 Jl '70 *
CALDERAS. See Craters
CALDERONE, Mary (Steichen)
It's really the men who need liberating. por Life 69:24 S 4 '70

about
Siecus-swayed librarians sought by concerned parents. Library J 95:3585 O 15 '70 *
CALDWELL, Bettye M.
Helping children to grow up smart. B. Asbell. il Redbook 135:34+ Jl '70 *
CALDWELL, Dean
Conquest of El Capitan. il pors Time 96:12 N 30 '70 *
CALDWELL, Earl
Appeal for credibility. Newsweek 75:74 My 11 '70 *
End to fishing. Time 96:46 N 30 '70 *
How much privilege? il por Newsweek 75:77-8 Ap 13 '70 *
Journalist's privilege. il por Newsweek 76:87 N 30 '70 *
Limit on subpoena of notes of reporters and authors. H. F. Pilpel and K. P. Norwick. Pub W 197:33-4 My 4 '70 *
CALDWELL, Jay S. and Shnayer, S. W.
Truth about readiness. il Library J 95:1909-10 My 15 '70
CALDWELL, Joe
Beware of the Hawks. F. Deford. il por Sports Illus 32:22-7 Ap 13 '70 *
CALDWELL, Louis O.
Focus for pastoral counseling. Chr Today 15:34-5 O 23 '70
CALDWELL, Lynton K.
Authority and responsibility for environmental administration. Ann Am Acad 389:107-15 My '70

CALDWELL, Philip
Truck is now. T. J. Murray. il por Duns 95:42+ Ja '70
CALENDAR clocks. See Clocks
CALENDAR trick. See Mathematical recreations
CALENDARS
Christmas shopper. D. Lawson. il Craft Horiz 30:8 D '70
Feminist yearbook; publication of The liberated woman's appointment calendar and survival handbook 1971. il Newsweek 76:114+ N 16 '70
Writer with a camera. R. Arnold. por Writers Digest 50:46-8 S '70
CALF barns. See Barns and stables
CALF feeding contracts. See Contracts, Agricultural
CALF pens
They can handle 228 calves at one time. il Suc Farm 68:no4 E2-3 Mr '70
CALGARY, Alberta
Calgary stampede; drawings by Paul Hogarth; with account by E. Whitehead. il Sports Illus 33:34-9 Jl 13 '70
CALGARY stampede. See Rodeos
CALHOUN, John
Calhoun's horrible mousery. S. Alsop. Newsweek 76:96 Ag 17 '70 *
CALHOUN, John Caldwell
John C. Calhoun: voice of the South. por Sr Schol 95:12 N 10 '69 *
CALHOUN, Mary
Focusing the picture book. il Writer 83:20-3 Jl '70
CALIBRATION
How to calibrate your granular applicator. L. D. Rawson. il Suc Farm 68:D12 Ap '70
Using power line as accurate time standard; for calibrating scopes. R. A. Anderson. il Electr World 83:46-7+ My '70
CALIBRATORS
Build a gated 100-kHz calibrator. F. H. Tooker. il Pop Electr 33:53-9 S '70
Build a time base calibrator. R. J. Valentine. il Pop Electr 34:33-5+ Ja '71
500/50-kHz frequency standard. N. Johnson. il Pop Electr 32:63-4+ My '70
CALIENTE race track. See Race tracks
CALIFANO, Joseph Anthony, 1931-
Return of pocketbook politics. H. Sidey. Life 68:4 Ap 3 '70 *
CALIFORNIA
California evil. C. Karpel. il Esquire 73:99-100 Mr '70
Waiting for the big bump. il Newsweek 76:58 S 28 '70
  See also
Agriculture—California
Airports—California
Alpine County
Architecture, Domestic—California
Art—California
Arts and crafts—California
Banks and banking—California
Booksellers and bookselling—California
Botany—California
Camps—California
Colleges and universities, State—California
Conservation of resources—California
Contra Costa County, Calif.
Death Valley
Devils Postpile National Monument
Diablo Range
Education—California
Environmental policy—California
Festivals—California
Fishing—California
Gardening—California
Gardens—California
Geology—California
Hunting—California
Justice, Administration of—California
Landscape protection—California
Legislation—California
Marin County
Morro Bay
Music festivals—California
Orange County
Prisons—California
Public welfare—California
Recreation areas—California
Redwood National Park
Riverside County
Roads—California
San Francisco Bay
Santa Catalina Island
Santa Clara County
School libraries—California
Sierra Nevada
Skis and skiing—California
Squaw Valley
Tahoe, Lake

CALIFORNIA—See also—*Continued*
Trials—California
Unemployment—California
Vigilance committees—California
Water supply—California
Wilderness areas—California
Wildlife conservation—California
Yosemite National Park

Antiquities
See Indians of North America—Antiquities—California

Capitol
Central plant heats and cools California's capitol. il Arch Rec 147:167-70 Ja '70

Climate
Deuterium content of snow cores from Sierra Nevada area. I. Friedman and G. I. Smith. bibliog il Science 169:467-70 Jl 31 '70

Description and travel
Bay area flea markets. il Sunset 145:3-4 Jl '70
California, even more so. Vogue 156:36 Ag 15 '70
Forgotten wilds: the teeming marshes and lagoons along California's urban coast. il Sunset 144:46-8+ Ap '70
Hiking in to the McCabe lakes. il Sunset 144:68+ Je '70
Mariposa to the valley. il Sunset 144:39 Ap '70
Where do San Franciscans play? K. Lamott. il Holiday 47:62-3+ Mr '70

Education, Department of
Retiring Rafferty. il por Newsweek 76:71-3 N 16 '70

Highways, Division of
How to keep the snow-plows moving. H. C. Ammon. il Am City 85:36 F '70

Historic houses, etc.
See also
Colfax highway association

History
See also
Vigilance committees—California

Industries
Executive life, California style. T. J. Murray. il Duns 95:48-50+ My '70
See also
Agriculture—California

Land tenure
See Land tenure—United States

Parks and reserves
Don't fight, negotiate! East Bay regional park district. F. J. Monteagle. il Parks & Rec 9:38-9+ S '70
Great wounds at Malakoff, and the softening of wind and water and time. il Sunset 145:40-1 O '70
Miwok mortars and petroglyphs; Indian Grinding Rock State Historical Monument. il Sunset 145:64 N '70
Recreation for forty million people. W. P. Mott, jr. il Arch Rec 147:132-3 My '70
When winter's over, but before the summer crowds, a great time to visit Coloma; Marshall gold discovery state historical park. il Sunset 144:62-3 My '70

Photographs
California trip; excerpt. D. Stock. il Pop Phot 67:74-7 Ag '70

Politics and government
California: Jess Unruh, Populist. P. Kerby. Nation 211:393-6 O 26 '70
California's club movement: the palsy of the CDC. F. Carney. Nation 210:526-30 My 4 '70
Center shifts right; J. Unruh campaign. J. R. Coyne, jr. Nat R 22:1159-60 N 3 '70
Challenging Rafferty; California campaign. il Time 96:58 N 2 '70
Democratic straw; voter-registration statistics. M. E. Leary. Nation 211:388-9 O 26 '70
Enough of Reagan? G. Lubenow. New Repub 162:14-15 F 14 '70
Enter Ron Dellums: radical; with interview, ed. by E. Glynn. America 123:483-7 D 5 '70
Hottest candidate in either party. P. O'Neil. il pors Life 69:26-9 O 30 '70
In California: big names on the political battlefield. il U S News 69:74-5 S 21 '70
Primaries. Nation 210:709 Je 15 '70

Remarkable Mr Riles. M. E. Leary. New Repub 163:12 D 19 '70
Reports: California. M. E. Leary. Atlan 226: 20+ Ag '70; Discussion. 226:40 N '70
Ronald Reagan is giving 'em heck. S. V. Roberts. il por N Y Times Mag p42-3+ O 25 '70
Simon says: Senate and gubernatorial candidates. Newsweek 75:34 Je 1 '70
Test case in California; 13th congressional district candidates. W. Seifert. New Repub 163:8-9 O 31 '70
Unseen foe: N. Simon vs. H. Salvatori. pors Forbes 106:22 Ag 15 '70
Why a sixty-three-year-old tycoon worth $100-million wants to run for the Senate; N. Simon. S. V. Roberts. il pors N Y Times Mag p 10-12+ My 31 '70

Race problems
U.S. journal: Los Angeles Indian population. C. Trillin. New Yorker 46:92+ Ap 18 '70

Recreation
See Recreation—United States

Religious institutions and affairs
See also
San Diego County, Calif.—Religious institutions and affairs

Social conditions
Disfranchise the old. D. J. Stewart. New Repub 163:20-2 Ag 22 '70

State library commission
L.A. library union opposes commission: new director for LAPL. Library J 95:112 Ja 15 '70

Suffrage
See Suffrage—United States

CALIFORNIA, GULF OF
Craziest cruise afloat; with Arizona gringos in a Mexican shrimp boat. W. H. Porter. il Motor B 126:46-7+ O '70
See also
Fishing—California, Gulf of

CALIFORNIA, LOWER
Down Baja by private plane. il Sunset 145: 8 N '70
See also
Fishing—California, Lower

Description
Baja experienced. P. Fusco. il Look 34:38-47 S 8 '70

CALIFORNIA big trees. See Sequoia, Giant
CALIFORNIA college of arts and crafts, Oakland, Calif.
Oakland's CCAC. R. Montgomery. il Arch Forum 132:86-9 Ja '70
CALIFORNIA computer products, inc.
CalComp's love-hate. T. J. Murray. Duns 96: 50 D '70
CALIFORNIA Democratic council. See Political clubs and associations
CALIFORNIA earthquakes. See Earthquakes —United States
CALIFORNIA fire, 1970. See Brush fires
CALIFORNIA 500. See Automobile racing
CALIFORNIA grape pickers strike. See Strikes —United States—Farm labor
CALIFORNIA highway patrol. See Police, State
CALIFORNIA Indians. See Indians of North America
CALIFORNIA institute of technology, Pasadena
See also
Jet propulsion laboratory
CALIFORNIA library association
Bag lunches, champagne: California LA's 72nd. W. R. Eshelman. il Wilson Lib Bul 45:347+ D '70
California complex; conference. J. Berry. Library J 95:105 Ja 15 '70
California librarians debate new association. Library J 95:4085 D 1 '70
California model. J. Berry. Library J 95: 4081 D 1 '70
December in San Francisco; annual convention. G. R. Shields. Am Lib 1:108 F '70
New directions; excerpts from report, ed. by G. R. Shields. P. Ackerman and others. Am Lib 1:1021-2 D '70
CALIFORNIA library commission. See California—State library commission
CALIFORNIA nursery, Fremont, Calif. See Nurseries (horticulture)
CALIFORNIA relays. See Running

CALIFORNIA. San Fernando Valley state college. Northbridge
L.A.'s Scottsboro boys case. S. H. Harris. Commonweal 91:548-9 F 20 '70
Partial rectification; black student leaders released from jail. J. Deedy. Commonweal 92:258 My 29 '70

CALIFORNIA. State college, San Francisco
Overheated campuses of the Bay area. H. Wilner. il Holiday 47:72-3+ Mr '70

Art department
Campus photo boom! photographs by ten students; with introd. by J. Scully. Mod Phot 34:54-63 S '70

Library
Ordeal at San Francisco state college. B. Anderson. il por Library J 95:1275-80 Ap 1 '70

CALIFORNIA. State college, San Jose
San Jose librarians charge intimidation; director Dr S. Baillie. Library J 95:613-14 F 15 '70
Tenure controversy: rejected San Jose engineer is wed to a red. P. M. Boffey. por Science 170:420-2 O 23 '70

CALIFORNIA state polytechnic college, San Luis Obispo
This soufflé always falls; Cal Poly the best small-college team. H. Weiskopf. Sports Illus 32:49-50+ F 16 '70

CALIFORNIA teachers association
Striking proposition; Los Angeles city school system. il Time 95:54 Ap 27 '70

CALIFORNIA. University
Berkeley's meddlesome regents. B. Aptheker. Nation 211:169-73 S 7 '70
California: university on trial. il Newsweek 76:83-91+ N 23 '70
Governor v. the university. D. Neff. il por Time 95:69-70+ Mr 30 '70
Higher-cost education. Newsweek 75:68 Mr 2 '70
Jocks 1, war 0; athletes protest United States Southeast Asia policy. J. Scott. il Ramp Mag 9:15-18 Ag '70
University of California: political and financial woes. P. M. Boffey. Science 169: 1058+ S 11 '70

Berkeley campus
Berkeley mafia and the Indonesian massacre; with editorial comment. D. Ransom. il Ramp Mag 9:26-9+ O '70
Berkeley scene: change is the norm. il Newsweek 76:86-90 N 23 '70
Campus politics: decentralization is pattern at Berkeley, Stanford. J. Walsh. Science 168:1187-90 Je 5 '70
Center of action; Berkeley student center. R. Montgomery. il Arch Forum 132:64-71 Ap '70
Current chronicle; Monteverdi's L'incoronazione di poppea, Cavalli's Erismena and Mozart's Idomeneo. W. C. Holmes. il Mus Q 56:478-84 Jl '70
No one plays in no man's land; boycott of People's park. R. Rapoport. il Sports Illus 32:20-1 Je 15 '70
On not becoming revolutionary; excerpt from Ready for the rain. R. Gozzi, jr. il Nation 211:492-4 N 16 '70
Overheated campuses of the Bay area. H. Wilner. il Holiday 47:72-3+ Mr '70
Radicalizing of a guest teacher at Berkeley. J. Holt. il N Y Times Mag p30-1+ F 22 '70; Discussion. p6+ Mr 15 '70
Still no. 1; ACE's new report on graduate schools. il Newsweek 77:58 Ja 11 '71
We can do the impossible. R. Rodale. il Org Gard & Farm 17:23-6 Je '70
Where are the Savios of yesteryear? W. Greene. il N Y Times Mag p6-9+ Jl 12 '70

Art museum
New museum for now; Berkeley's new University art museum. P. Selz. il Art in Am 58:158-9 N '70
New museum in Berkeley is itself a work of concrete sculpture. il Sunset 145:34-5 N '70
Provocative museum. il Time 96:82 N 16 '70

Lawrence hall of science
Research Olympus for science teaching. C. Weiss. il Sci N 97:581-3 Je 13 '70

Hastings college of law, San Francisco
Where you have to be retired to be hired. C. Stevenson. Read Digest 96:21-4+ Je '70

La Jolla campus
Gulp: there goes UCal La Jolla. J. Hart. Nat R 22:1046+ O 6 '70

Lawrence radiation laboratories
Gofman and Tamplin: harassment charges against AEC, Livermore. P. M. Boffey. pors Science 169:838-43 Ag 28 '70
Science and politics: free speech controversy at Lawrence laboratory. P. M. Boffey. Science 169:743-5 Ag 21 '70

Libraries
See also
California. University—San Diego campus—Libraries

Los Angeles campus
Chancellor in a crossfire. il por Time 95:63 My 18 '70
Davis affair. il por Newsweek 75:78 Je 22 '70
Hardly the last word; case of A. Davis. por Time 95:45 Je 29 '70
Indeed do it! demonstrations following J. Rubin's speech at UCLA. W. F. Buckley, jr. Nat R 22:533 My 19 '70
UCLA; simple, awesomely simple. C. Kirkpatrick. Sports Illus 33:39-43 N 30 '70

Riverside campus
Staying alive; letter. W. Garling. New Repub 162:29-30 My 30 '70

San Diego campus
City vs. campus violence; city police on the campus. W. J. McGill. il por Am City 85: 78+ N '70

Libraries
Sensation in San Diego. il Library J 95: 4145 D 1 '70

Santa Barbara campus
Commencement at Isla Vista; disorders. Nation 210:772 Je 29 '70
Isla Vista war; campus violence in a class by itself. W. Griffith. il N Y Times Mag p 10-11+ Ag 30 '70; Discussion. p 16 S 20 '70
New campus stepchildren; Isla Vista community development. G. H. Wierzynski. il Time 97:72 Ja 4 '71
Powerless students. D. Nevin. il McCalls 97:44-5+ Jl '70
Why they burned the bank. R. Flacks and M. Mankoff. Nation 210:337-40 Mr 23 '70

Santa Cruz campus
Old idea flowers anew at Santa Cruz; with report by B. Villet. il Life 68:52-60+ My 8 '70
Organic classrooms are here! M. C. Goldman. il Org Gard & Farm 17:66-8 S '70
Organic revolution goes to college. M. C. Goldman. il Org Gard & Farm 17:56-61 Ja '70

CALIFORNIA wines. See Wine
CALIFORNIA Zephyr (train) See Railroads—Trains

CALIFORNIANS
Disfranchise the old. D. J. Stewart. New Repub 163:20-2 Ag 22 '70
How seven families lead the good life. il Am Home 73:8+ Jl '70
Special season of the young; some beautiful girls. il Life 69:46-53 Jl 10 '70

CALISHER, Hortense
Women re women. Mlle 70:188-9+ F '70

CALKINS, Verna
Exercise break. Writer 83:28-9 F '70

CALL for action. See Urban coalition (organization)

CALLAHAN, Daniel
Christopher Dawson. Commonweal 92:284 Je 12 '70
Contraception and abortion: American Catholic responses. bibliog f Ann Am Acad 387: 109-17 Ja '70
Paging the unbandaged. America 123:143 S 12 '70
about
Morality of abortion. K. L. Woodward. por Newsweek 75:64-5 Je 8 '70 *

CALLAHAN, Harry
Gallery; photographs. Life 68:6-9 Mr 27 '70

CALLAHAN, Michael A.
Confrontation in cinema city. America 122: 392-4 Ap 11 '70

CALLAHAN, Robert, 3d, and Balbinder, Elias
Tryptophan operon: structural gene mutation creating a "promoter" and leading to 5-methyltryptophan dependence. bibliog il Science 168:1586-9 Je 26 '70

CALLAHAN, William S. See Friedman, H. A. jt. auth.

CALLAS, Maria
Callas and Tebaldi, yesterday and today. G. Movshon. il pors Hi Fi sec I 20:89-90 Ja '70
Jackie's fabulous Greek; excerpts from Those fabulous Greeks. D. Lilly. pors Look 34:43-6 Je 30 '70 *
Records. Opera N 34:35 F 7 '70
CALLAWAY, Ely R.
Threading your way to the top. il por Nations Bsns 58:62-3 Ja '70
CALLEJÓN DE HUAYLAS. See Huaylas, Callejón de
CALLENBACH, Ernest
Comparative anatomy of folk-myth films; Robin Hood and Antonio das Mortes. il Film Q 23:42-7 Wint '69
CALLERY, Sean
Brendan Behan: the ignominy of success. por Commonweal 93:87-91 O 23 '70
CALLEY, William Laws, jr
Confessions of Lieutenant Calley; interview, ed. by J. Sack. Esquire 74:113-19+ N '70

about

Calley at My Lai. il Newsweek 76:52-3 D 14 '70 *
Calley's confessions. por Time 96:15 O 12 '70 *
Calley's defense. il Newsweek 76:25-6 D 21 '70 *
Command influence. il Newsweek 75:28 F 2 '70
How I broke the Mylai 4 story. S. M. Hersh. il por Sat R 53:46-9 Jl 11 '70 *
Journalist sues Viking, Esquire, over Calley story. Pub W 198:30 O 19 '70 *
Lieutenant Calley at bay. il por Time 96:14-15 D 21 '70 *
My Lai: the case against Calley. il por Time 96:18 D 14 '70 *
They make me feel important. por Newsweek 76:19 D 28 '70 *
Way to get rich; contract with Esquire magazine and Viking press. il Newsweek 76:78-80 N 16 '70 *
CALLEY trial. See Courts martial and courts of inquiry
CALLIGRAPHY
Calligraphy in the curriculum. P. Vandervoort, 2d. il Sch Arts 70:34-6 D '70
Donald Jackson: calligrapher & illuminator. F. Johnson. il por Am Artist 34:17-23+ My '70
Recollections of the Lyceum & Chautauqua circuits. by I. Briggs and R. F. DaBoll. Review
    Am Artist il 34:56-8 Ag '70. F. Johnson
    See also
    Ames and Rollinson (firm)
CALLISON, Charles H.
National outlook. See issues of Audubon
CALLOT, Jacques
Masques and massacres. H. Zerner. il Art N 68:59-61+ F '70 *
CALLS of birds. See Birds—Song
CALORIES, Food. See Diet; Food values
CALORIMETRY conference
Calorimetry. G. C. Sinke. Science 167:1526 Mr 13 '70
CALUMET and Hecla-Universal oil products merger. See Business consolidations and mergers
CALVERT, James Francis
New broom at navy. il por Time 95:50 My 11 '70 *
CALVES
Let's raise a baby calf! R. J. Holliday. il Org Gard & Farm 17:62-5 Je '70
Raise your own calves in corn country? il Suc Farm 68:D16 N '70

Care

Calf-raising ideas from a top dairyman. J. R. Borcherding. il Suc Farm 69:B12 Ja '71
Growing calves is his specialty. J. Fetterolf. il Suc Farm 68:D20 O '70
Latest calf raising tips from an AG college. D. Hillman. Suc Farm 68:no4 E4 Mr '70
Raising dairy calves inside or out. il Suc Farm 68:G4 S '70
Try these calf-saving ideas. il Suc Farm 68:no4 E6 Mr '70
You learn fast with a thousand calves. O. Bay. il Farm J 93:26B-27+ O '69

Feeding

Low-cost veal from grain. T. R. Capener. il Farm J 94:54P+ F '70
CALVIN, John
John Calvin: theologian and evangelist. C. G. Fry. Chr Today 15:3-6 O 23 '70 *
CALVING. See Cows
CALVINO, Italo
Smog; story; excerpt from The watcher & other stories. Harp Baz 103:138-9 O '70

CALYCANTHUS. See Sweet scented shrub
CAMARA, Helder Pessôa, abp
Archbishop Câmara: our Nobel candidate, too. Chr Cent 87:717 Je 10 '70 *
Collision in Latin America. por Time 95:44 F 9 '70
Encounter in Recife. B. Tyson. il pors Chr Cent 87:720-2 Je 10 '70 *
Violence of a peacemaker, by J. De Broucker. Review
    Commonweal 93:228-9 N 27 '70. T. Quigley
CAMARANO, Chris
Letter from Camp Venceremos. il Ramp Mag 9:6+ Ag '70
CAMARGUE, France
Gauloises men. D. Butwin. il Sat R 53:42-4 O 10 '70
CAMARGUE ponies. See Ponies
CAMBEL, Ali B.
Impact of energy demands. bibliog il Phys Today 23:38-43+ D '70
CAMBEL, Halet, and Braidwood, R. J.
Early farming village in Turkey; with biographical sketches. il Sci Am 222:25, 51-6 Mr '70
CAMBIER, Nora, and others
Books in print 1969; an analysis of errors. il Am Lib 1:901-2 O '70
CAMBODIA
Through Indian country. K. Buckley. il Newsweek 75:29-30 Ap 13 '70
    See also
    Angkor
    Anti-Communist movements—Cambodia
    Communism—Cambodia
    Economic assistance in Cambodia
    Flags—Cambodia
    Guerrillas—Cambodia
    Missions—Cambodia
    Pnompenh
    Political prisoners—Cambodia
    United States—Foreign relations—Cambodia

Antiquities

    See also
    Angkor

Armed forces

No place is safe any more; report from the war zone. K. M. Chrysler. il U S News 69:10-11 Jl 6 '70
Where victories are in short supply. J. N. Wallace. il U S News 68:17 My 11 '70

Army

Instant army. F. Sully. il Newsweek 76:29 Jl 27 '70
Ordeal in Cambodia; odds on survival now. K. M. Chrysler. il U S News 69:18-19 Jl 13 '70
Under siege. D. Cameron. il Newsweek 76:27 Ag 24 '70

Defenses

Cam Ranh II. il Newsweek 76:51 Jl 6 '70

Foreign relations

But will the ARVN withdraw? il Newsweek 75:47+ Je 1 '70
Lon Nol reads no newspapers and never uses a telephone. H. Kamm. il pors N Y Times Mag p28-9+ D 13 '70
What Cambodia wants from U.S; interview, ed. by C. S. Foltz, jr. Lon Nol. il por U S News 68:30-1 Ap 13 '70

United States

    See United States—Foreign relations—Cambodia

Industries

    See also
    Rubber industry and trade

Politics and government

And what about Laos & Cambodia? il Sr Schol 96:11-13 Ap 13 '70
At stake in Cambodia. America 122:384 Ap 11 '70
Birth of a republic. Time 96:40 O 19 '70
Cambodia in the balance; report from the scene. il U S News 68:28-30 Ap 13 '70
Cambodia: runaway coup d'etat. M. Osborne. Nation 210:678-80 Je 8 '70
Cambodia: struggle for survival. il Time 96:22 Jl 13 '70
Cambodia's neutrality. America 122:405 Ap 18 '70
Changing Cambodia. D. P. Chandler. bibliog f Cur Hist 59:333-8+ D '70
Coup in Cambodia; how Sihanouk lost out; with eyewitness account by C. S. Foltz, jr. il por U S News 68:18-20 Mr 30 '70
Dear Prince; since you went away... A. J. Langguth. il N Y Times Mag p4-5+ Ag 2 '70

CAMBODIA—Politics and government—*Cont.*
From Vietnam to Indochina; Sihanouk falls. il por Newsweek 75:31-2 Mr 30 '70
Indochina: the calm before the storm? il Newsweek 75:36-7 Ap 6 '70
Letter from Indo-China. R. Shaplen. New Yorker 46:57-70+ Jl 11 '70
Lon Nol and Sihanouk speak out. il pors Time 96:27 S 28 '70
Lon Nol reads no newspapers and never uses a telephone. H. Kamm. il pors N Y Times Mag p28-9+ D 13 '70
Mounting uneasiness in southeast Asia. il Time 95:36-7 Ap 6 '70
Prince falls in Asia and U.S. troubles rise. il pors Life 68:30-1 Ap 3 '70
Reports: Cambodia. H. D. S Greenway. Atlan 226:32+ Jl '70
Road to Phnom Penh: Cambodia takes up the gun. B. Garrett. il Ramp Mag 9:32-5+ Ag '70
Ten days or ten years. Time 95:27-8 My 18 '70

Riots
Cambodian puzzle; Viet Cong and North Vietnamese embassies sacked. il por Newsweek 75:39 Mr 23 '70
Upsetting the balance; outbursts of anti-Communist violence. il Time 95:26 Mr 23 '70

CAMBODIAN-Vietnamese conflict
After U.S. leaves Cambodia. J. N. Wallace. il U S News 68:29-30 Je 1 '70
Any answers must involve all of southeast Asia. K. T. Young. il Life 68:40-1 My 8 '70
Between the lines; report from Phnom-Penh. R. Anson. il Time 95:79 My 4 '70
But will the ARVN withdraw? il Newsweek 75:47+ Je 1 '70
Cam Ranh II. il Newsweek 76:51 Jl 6 '70
Cambodia: a reporter's diary. A. de Borchgrave. il Newsweek 75:38-9 Je 15 '70
Cambodia asks U.S. aid. il Sr Schol 96:6-7 My 4 '70
Cambodia: caught in a cross fire; with report by K. Buckley. il Newsweek 75:22-5 My 4 '70
Cambodia: Communists on the rampage. il Time 95:28+ My 4 '70
Cambodia: odds on a red take-over U S News 69:14-15 Jl 20 '70
Cambodia: on verge of collapse? J. N. Wallace. il U S News 68:15-16 My 4 '70
Cambodia: the perils of moving in; with report by J. Saar. il Life 68:36-9 My 8 '70
Cambodian confusion. Commonweal 92:107-8 Ap 17 '70
Cambodian crisis. W. F. Buckley, jr. Nat R 22:585 Je 2 '70
Cambodia's lost patrimony; Angkor Wat seized by the North Vietnamese. il Newsweek 75:24+ Je 22 '70
Cambodia's minimiracle: can it last? il U S News 69:53 Ag 24 '70
Everybody's foe in Cambodia: the monsoons. il U S News 68:23 Je 8 '70
Future of Cambodia. Norodom Sihanouk. For Affairs 49:1-10 O '70
Holding out. M. Parker. il Newsweek 76: 50 S 7 '70
How sad to be a Cambodian; situation in Phnom Penh. A. de Borchgrave. il Newsweek 75:48 Je 29 '70
Indochina: more and more fighters. il Time 95:28-9 Je 15 '70
Indochina: the rising tide of war. il Time 95: 33-4 Je 22 '70
Indochina's crumbling frontiers. il Time 95: 24+ Ap 20 '70
Letter from Indo-China. R. Shaplen. New Yorker 46:130+ My 9; 125-8+ My 16; 57-70+ Jl 11; 118-20+ D 19 '70
New crunch for the U.S. in Indochina. il Time 95:14-15 My 4 '70
New dangers in Cambodia. il Time 95:23-4 Je 29 '70
No place is safe any more: report from the war zone. K. M. Chrysler. il U S News 69:10-11 Jl 6 '70
Ordeal in Cambodia: odds on survival now. K. M. Chrysler. il U S News 69:18-19 Jl 13 '70
Reports: Cambodia. H. D. S. Greenway. Atlan 226:32+ Jl '70
Road to Phnom Penh: Cambodia takes up the gun. B. Garrett. il Ramp Mag 9:32-5+ Ag '70
Sanitizing the sanctuaries. il Time 95:16-18 My 11 '70
Slicing the parrot's beak; Vietnam border incidents. il Newsweek 75:50 Ap 20 '70
Smashing red sanctuaries: the gains so far. il U S News 68:31-2 My 25 '70
So far, so good. Nat R 22:545 Je 2 '70

Turnabout in Cambodia. il por Newsweek 76: 57 O 12 '70
View from Saigon: Thieu speaks out; interview, ed. by O. Elliott. Nguyen-van-Thieu. por Newsweek 75:26-7 My 11 '70
War in Cambodia: ending or just beginning? il U S News 68:46-7 Je 22 '70
When Cambodia becomes South Vietnam's war—. W. S. Merick; J. N. Wallace. il U S News 68:21-3 Je 8 '70
See also
Vietnam (Republic)—Army—Forces in Cambodia

Aerial operations
Bombs away; growing U.S. involvement. il Newsweek 76:39 Ag 17 '70
Boom-boom Lon Nol. il Newsweek 76:46 N 9 '70

American participation
After Cambodia: the fight to save face. J. J. Stone. Commonweal 92:381-2 Ag 7 '70
Ambassador Bunker discusses Viet-Nam on Meet the press; transcript of interview, May 10, 1970. E. Bunker. Dept State Bul 62:686-91 Je 1 '70
And so we leave Cambodia... il Newsweek 76:16-22 Jl 13 '70
As two correspondents see it. A. de Borchgrave; M. Parker. il Newsweek 76:23-4+ Jl 13 '70
As U.S. leaves Cambodia: success or failure? il U S News 69:9 Jl 6 '70
Balance sheet on Cambodia; the Cambodia operation; interview. R. Thompson. il por U S News 68:31-2 Je 1 '70
Cambodia. N. Cousins. Sat R 53:24+ My 16 '70; Correction. 53:15 My 30 '70
Cambodia and Israel. Chr Today 14:21-2 My 22 '70
Cambodia: E-mines-3. Nat R 22:600 Je 16 '70
Cambodia: Nixon's trap. F. Schurmann. il Nation 210:651-6 Je 1 '70
Cambodia: now it's Operation Buy Time. il Time 95:28-34 My 25 '70
Cambodia plus two months: a military appraisal. W. C. Moore. il por U S News 69:31-2 S 7 '70
Cambodia: the wreck we left behind; with report by J. Saar. il Life 69:23-30 Jl 10 '70
Cambodia to doomsday. New Repub 162:9-10 My 9 '70
Cambodia: toward war by proxy. il Time 95: 21-2+ Je 1 '70
Cambodia: We're cache counters. il Newsweek 75:43-5 My 25 '70
Cambodian catch. Nation 210:546 My 11 '70
Cambodian report; with excerpts from television report by R. M. Nixon. il Newsweek 75:29-30 Je 15 '70
Cambodian venture: an assessment. il Time 96:16-17 Jl 6 '70
China; American involvement in Indochina. H. Yu. Chr Cent 87:798 Je 24 '70
Cold-blooded aggression. Commonweal 92:211-13 My 15 '70
Collision with Congress? il Newsweek 75:35-6 My 18 '70
Congress, Vietnam, Mideast: the President's appraisal; excerpts from radio and TV interview, July 1, 1970. R. M. Nixon. il por U S News 69:20-2 Jl 13 '70
Conversation with the President; transcript of radio and TV interview, July 1, 1970. R. M. Nixon. Dept State Bul 63:101-13 Jl 27 '70; Same abr. with title Congress, Vietnam, Mideast: the President's appraisal; excerpts from radio and TV interview, July 1, 1970. il por U S News 69:20-2 Jl 13 '70
Cooper-Church amendment: is it constitutional? C. D. Williams. Nat R 22:731-3 Jl 14 '70; Reply with rejoinder. J. Lotterman. 22:1031+ O 6 '70
Danger of the Cambodian expansion; interview, ed. by R. W. McManus. E. O. Reischauer. Cur 120:17-21 Ag '70
Dear senator... New Repub 162:6 Je 6 '70
Duel over the power to make war. il por Newsweek 75:29-31 My 25 '70
Feet on the flypaper. R. Hotz. Aviation W 92:13 My 11 '70
Fighting in Cambodia: the real meaning: reports from Saigon and Pnompenh. W. S. Merick; J. N. Wallace. il U S News 68:37-9 My 18 '70
French expert's view: China, the real winner in Cambodia. P. Devilers. Look 34:64 Ag 25 '70
From Peking: Sihanouk talks to Americans; questions and answers, ed. by W. Attwood. Norodom Sihanouk. Look 34:102+ O 20 '70
Getting the boys home; McGovern-Hatfield amendment. New Repub 162:5-6 My 30 '70
GI's into Cambodia: Americans react. il U S News 68:18-19 My 11 '70

CAMBODIAN-Vietnamese conflict—American participation—*Continued*

Graduation exercise; Vietnamization for the ARVN. Nation 210:643-4 Je 1 '70

Hanoi has suffered a crippling blow. W. C. Moore. por U S News 68:46-7 Je 22 '70

Hello, dad. .; views of children of U.S. Cabinet officers. il Newsweek 75:33-4 Je 1 '70

How Nixon decided to invade Cambodia. D. R. Maxey. il Look 34:22-5 Ag 11 '70

In search of an elusive foe. il Time 95:24+ My 18 '70

Into another slough. Nation 211:194 S 14 '70

Letter from Paris. Genêt. New Yorker 46: 117 My 16 '70

Letter from Washington. R. H. Rovere. New Yorker 46:146+ My 16: 114-16 Je 13 '70

Machiavelli? speculations on the President's machinations. Nation 210:676 Je 8 '70

Manhood game. N. Cousins. Sat R 53:14 My 30 '70

Mr Nixon's gamble; Chairman Mao's breakthrough. H. J. Morgenthau; R. H. Yoakum. New Repub 162:15-18 My 23 '70

My war, my way. New Repub 162:5-6 Je 13 '70

New burdens of war; raising the stakes in Indochina. il Time 95:10-15 My 11 '70

Nixon's gamble: operation total victory? il Newsweek 75:22-6+ My 11 '70

Notes and comment; Administration's motives. New Yorker 46:21-2 My 30 '70

Notes and comment; Credibility gap. New Yorker 46:17-18 Jl 18 '70

Notes and comment; critical week in US. il New Yorker 46:31-5 My 16 '70; Excerpt. Forbes 105:17-18 Je 15 '70

Notes and comment; Nixon's decision to invade. New Yorker 46:31-3 My 9 '70

Now is the time for all good men to come to the aid of their President. Nat R 22: 500-1 My 19 '70

On the President's yellow pad. S. Alsop. Newsweek 75:106 Je 1 '70

Open options in southeast Asia. Cato. Nat R 22:505 My 19 '70

Operation successful; outcome uncertain. il Newsweek 75:49+ My 18 '70

President; explains his decision on IndoChina; address, April 30, 1970. R. M. Nixon. il U S News 68:22-4 My 11 '70; Same with title Cambodia: a difficult decision. Vital Speeches 36:450-2 My 15 '70; Same abr. with title Cambodia strike: defensive action for peace. Dept State Bul 62:617-21 My 18 '70

President needs our help because we need his. M. Ways. Fortune 81:57-8 Je '70; Same with title Helping the President help us. Cur 120:9-13 Ag '70; Discussion. Fortune 82: 83-4 Ag '70

President Nixon, Cambodia and new chances for peace. J. G. Hubbell. il Read Digest 97:54-63 Jl '70

President Nixon's news conference of May 8, 1970. R. M. Nixon. Dept State Bul 62:641-5 My 25 '70

President Nixon's white paper on Cambodia; text, June 30, 1970. R. M. Nixon. il U S News 69:81-6 Jl 13 '70; Same with title Report on the conclusion of the Cambodian operation. Dept State Bul 63:65-75 Jl 20 '70

President reports on the war in Cambodia; address, June 3, 1970. R. M. Nixon. il por U S News 68:77-9 Je 15 '70; Same with title Cambodian sanctuary operation: an interim report. Dept State Bul 62:761-4 Je 22 '70

President's war powers: what Senate finally voted; Cooper-Church amendment. il U S News 69:29 Jl 13 '70

Profile in courage; Nixon's decision to send troops. K. Crawford. Newsweek 75:54 My 11 '70

Quickly out or deeper in? il Sr Schol 96:17 My 18 '70

Rent-a-troop. Nation 211:164-5 S 7 '70

Return to confrontation; sending U.S. combat troops into Cambodia. il Time 95:22+ My 18 '70

Richard Nixon's ten days; decision on Cambodia. il por Newsweek 75:36+ My 18 '70

Road to madness. J. Osborne. New Repub 162:11-13 My 16 '70

Sanctuaries and temples: misery in Cambodia Chr Cent 87:780 Je 24 '70

Secretary Rogers discusses Cambodia action in interview for television; transcript of program, May 4, 1970. W. P. Rogers. Dept State Bul 62:646-50 My 25 '70

Secretary Rogers interviewed on Face the Nation; transcript of program, June 7, 1970. W. Rogers. Dept State Bul 62:785-92 Je 29 '70

Secretary Roger's news conference of May 13, 1970. W. P. Rogers. Dept State Bul 62: 673-80 Je 1 '70

Secretary Rogers' news conference of June 25, 1970. W. P. Rogers. Dept State Bul 63:28-30 Jl 13 '70

Shaking down the crisis. H. Sidey. il Life 68:4 My 22 '70

Shock to foes, and friends: American invasion of Cambodia. il Newsweek 75:57-8 My 18 '70

Staying alive until 1973. New Repub 162: 1+ My 16 '70

Textbook exodus. Time 96:24 Jl 6 '70

Timing of the gamble; Nixon's decision to attack the Communist sanctuaries in Cambodia. S. Alsop. Newsweek 75:112 My 11 '70

U.N. notified of defense measures taken by U.S. South Viet-Nam forces; text of letter, May 5, 1970. C. W. Yost. Dept State Bul 62:652 My 25 '70

Under Secretary Richardson interviewed on issues and answers; transcript of program, May 10, 1970. E. L. Richardson. Dept State Bul 62:681-6 Je 1 '70

U.S. notifies U.N. of withdrawal from Cambodian territory; text of letter, July 1, 1970. C. W. Yost. Dept State Bul 63:77 Jl 20 '70

United States military actions in Cambodia: questions of international law; address, May 28, 1970. J. R. Stevenson. Dept State Bul 62:765-70 Je 22 '70

United States moves into Cambodia. America 122:517 My 16 '70

War: keynote for Democrats in '70? address, May 9, 1970. L. F. O'Brien. por U S News 68:97-9 My 25 '70

War policy splits Congress. il Sr Schol 97:2-3 S 21 '70

War: toward the deadline and beyond. il Time 95:21 Je 8 '70

Weight of Cambodia on a delicate policy; with editorial comment. il Bsns W p 18-19, 132 My 9 '70

What can concerned churchmen do about the war in Indochina? J. Armstrong; G. McGovern; M. Hatfield. Chr Cent 87:622-3 My 20 '70

What happened? Nation 210:579-80 My 18 '70

Why Cambodia? J. Osborne. New Repub 163:7-9 Jl 11 '70

Winding up the Cambodian hard sell. il Time 96:6-8 Jl 13 '70

Anecdotes, facetiae, satire, etc.

Mr Dooley in peace and war. P. Steinfels. Commonweal 92:262 My 29 '70

Protests, demonstrations, etc, against

At war with war. il Time 95:6-12 My 18 '70

Briefcase brigade; New York lawyers pleading for peace in southeast Asia. Time 95: 12-13 Je 1 '70

Business students catch the campus fever. il Bsns W p22-3 My 16 '70

Cambodia protest: the real meaning. Nat R 22:548 Je 2 '70

Campus confronts the capital; cabinet officers and presidential aides listen to protests. H. Sidey. Life 68:4 Je 12 '70

Days of dissent. R. Chandler. Chr Today 14: 42 Je 5 '70

Dissent spreads to Nobelists, industrial scientists. P. M. Boffey. Science 168:1325 Je 12 '70

If Cambodia falls to reds: why Nixon acted. il U S News 68:15-17 My 11 '70

Inevitable American tragedy; Kent state killings. il Sci N 97:451-2 My 9 '70

Jocks 1, war 0; California university athletes protest. J. Scott. il Ramp Mag 9:15-18 Ag '70

Kent and Cambodia. Commonweal 92:235-6 My 22 '70

Kent state: four deaths at noon. il Life 68: 30-5 My 15 '70

Letter from Berlin. J. Wechsberg. New Yorker 46:69-72 Je 27 '70

May day. il Newsweek 75:32-3 My 11 '70

New protesters. W. F. Buckley, jr. Nat R 22:697 Je 30 '70

Notes and comment; excerpts from address, May 1970. J. V. Lindsay. New Yorker 46:33 My 16 '70

Notes and comment; young people. New Yorker 46:34-5 My 16 '70

On looking back at Cambodia; reprint. P. Worsthorne. Nat R 22:825 Ag 11 '70

Power to what people? K. Crawford. Newsweek 75:41 My 25 '70

Princeton commitment: a race against mace. J. Shepherd. il Look 34:12+ Je 16 '70

Rebellion of the campus. il Newsweek 75:28-30 My 18 '70

TRB from Washington; march on Washington, May 10. New Repub 162:4 My 23 '70

CAMBODIAN - Vietnamese conflict—American participation—Protests, demonstrations, etc, against—*Continued*

Two gatherings: National coalition for a responsible congress; New York city bar association. New Yorker 46:22-4 My 30 '70

War rallies: pro and con. il U S News 68: 89 Je 1 '70

Weekend everyone went to school. N. Cousins. Sat R 53:33 My 23 '70

Atrocities

Crucial test; massacres of Vietnamese civilians. F. Sully; P. Brinkley-Rogers. il Newsweek 75:37-8 Ap 27 '70

New horror in Indochina; Cambodian pogrom against country's Vietnamese minority. il Time 95:36+ Ap 27 '70

Night of death at Takeo. R. Anson and T. D. Allman. il Time 95:41 Ap 27 '70

Campaigns and battles

Battle in a forgotten war; Prey Totung. Time 97:36+ Ja 4 '71

Under siege; Kompong Thom. D. Cameron. il Newsweek 76:27 Ag 24 '70

Economic aspects

Impact of Cambodia: a business size-up; Business council views. U S News 68:44 My 18 '70

Evacuation of civilians

Exodus on the Mekong. J. Willwerth. il Time 95:33 My 25 '70

Legal aspects

United States military actions in Cambodia: questions of international law; address, May 28, 1970. J. R. Stevenson. Dept State Bul 62:765-70 Je 22 '70

Personal narratives

Talking with Cambodians. J. R. Thomson. Nat R 22:788+ Jl 28 '70

War correspondents

And then there were seventeen. il por Newsweek 76:56 S 7 '70

Beyond the checkpoint; newsmen listed as dead or missing. il pors Newsweek 75:65 Je 15 '70

Confusion in Cambodia; perils for newsmen reporting from Indochina. Newsweek 75: 65 My 25 '70

Forty days; release of Elizabeth Pond, Richard Dudman and Mike Morrow. il Newsweek 75:55 Je 29 '70

Missing in Cambodia. il Time 95:57 My 25 '70

Report from a captured correspondent. R. Anson. il por Time 96:18-19 S 7 '70

Spooky trips through silent, empty landscapes. R. Graves. Life 68:3 My 8 '70

Three come back; release of three American correspondents. il Time 95:60 Je 29 '70

Time to decompress; reporters H. Faas and P. Arnett leaving Indochina. il pors Time 96:34 Ag 3 '70

Twenty-three captured, one dead. il por Time 95:80 Je 15 '70

CAMBRIDGE, Mass.

Architecture

Closure and appropriate scale for a street in Cambridge; new office building. il Arch Rec 148:119-21 Jl '70

Protests, demonstrations, etc.

Street people push Cambridge up against the wall. P. A. Farrell. il Pub W 198:49-51 O 5 '70

Public health

Free clinic for street people; medical care without a hassle. J. Brenner. il por N Y Times Mag p30-1+ O 11 '70; Discussion. p 114-16 N 8 '70

Riots

Dirty little war: April. D. Brudnoy. Nat R 22:453 My 5 '70

Social conditions

Dagger in the heart of town: Mass. planners and Cambridge workers. G. Fellman and others. il Trans-Action 7:38-47 S '70

Stores

Bright glass prism on Brattle street; Benjamin Thompson's Design research building. il Arch Rec 147:105-12 My '70

CAMBRIDGE, Md.
Losers on U.S. 1; bombers and the Brown case. il pors Newsweek 75:28 Mr 23 '70

CAMBRIDGEPORT medical clinic. See Health clinics

CAMDEN, N.J.

Galleries and museums

Silver tureens in the Campbell museum collection; excerpts from the catalogue. K. C. Buhler. il Antiques 97:904-9 Je '70

CAMELLIAS
Camellias, as the judge sees them. H. E. Dryden. il Horticulture 48:22-4+ F '70

Camellias for Christmas. H. E. Dryden. Horticulture 48:24+ D '70

More fun with camellias. W. A. Wheeler, jr. il Horticulture 49:32-3+ Ja '71

CAMEOS
American presidents in glass sulphides. T. H. Marsh. il Hobbies 75:102+ Jl '70

CAMERA batteries. See Electric batteries

CAMERA buying. See Cameras—Purchasing; Moving picture cameras—Purchasing

CAMERA cases
Turn that camera carton into a fancy fitted case. il Pop Mech 133:168 Ap '70

CAMERA industry. See Photographic apparatus industry and trade

CAMERA lenses. See Lenses, Photographic

CAMERA magazines. See Cameras—Loading

CAMERA shutters
Inside focal-plane shutters. N. Goldberg. il Pop Phot 67:88-91+ Jl '70

Inside front shutters. N. Goldberg. il Pop Phot 66:98-100+ Je '70

Control

For photographers: a nifty $50 radio control. P. Wahl. il Pop Sci 197:59 D '70

Remote camera shutter release. A. A. Mangieri. il Pop Electr 33:65-8 Jl '70

CAMERA stores. See Photographic apparatus industry and trade

CAMERA supports
At last! The perfect gun stock? home-made telephoto lens mount. il Mod Phot 34: 116-17+ Ag '70

Gunstock support for photo sharpshooters. R. Scott. il Pop Sci 197:110 S '70

New use for you, ol' bean bag. C. W. Kennedy. il Pop Phot 66:38+ Mr '70

Readers' report. il Mod Phot 34:86-7 Ag '70

Two gunstock bounts for telephoto shooting. S. M. Gallager. il Pop Mech 134:132-4 Ag '70

CAMERA tripods
Keppler on the SLR. H. Keppler. il Mod Phot 33:32+ D '69

Look what this tripod can do! E. H. Ortner. il Pop Sci 197:59 D '70

35's forgotten accessory. L. Drukker. il Pop Phot 67:82-3+ S '70

CAMERAS
Annual guide to forty-seven top cameras. il Mod Phot 33:85-132 D '69

Antique camera sampler, comp. by E. S. Lothrop, jr. and H. Zucker. il Pop Phot 67:94-7 N '70

Basic camera; the box with a hole in it. D. Vestal. il Travel & Camera 33:77-81 F '70

Behind the scenes. See issues of Modern photography

Biggest little camera in the world. B. Murphy. il Pop Mech 133:106-9+ My '70

Binoculars with a photographic memory; Nicnon. P. Wahl. il Pop Sci 197:63 O '70

Camera news. See issues of Travel & camera

Casual cameras do their thing. N. Goldberg. il Pop Phot 67:64+ O '70

Disposable cameras? Instamatic 44. il Forbes 105:23 Mr 1 '70

Feininger; let the subject dictate format when you choose a camera. A. Feininger. il Mod Phot 34:58+ Je '70

Finally grown, Simon/Wide makes it. Simon. il Pop Phot 66:60+ My '70

First look. See issues of Popular photography

How to avoid second guessing about second bodies. N. Rothschild. il Pop Phot 67:78-81 S '70

Lab report. See issues of Popular photography

New instamatic X cameras. N. Rothschild. il Pop Phot 67:46+ O '70

Now it's Instamatic X; drop-in-cartridge cameras. il Consumer Bul 54:38-40 Ja '71

Our camera on the moon; Apollo lunar surface close-up camera. N. Rothschild. il Pop Phot 66:100 F '70

Readers report. il Mod Phot 34:86-7 Ag; 104-5+ O '70

Shutter's an earful and he's got a nose for pictures; Mick-A-Matic and Simplex Snapper cameras. H. Keppler. il Mod Phot 34: 18 F '70

CAMERAS—*Continued*

Still cameras. il Consumer Rep 34:277-88 D '69

That Simon/wide, and how it grew; self-made camera to take wide-field pictures. il Pop Phot 66:58+ Ap '70

35mm cameras. il Consumer Rep 35:666-75 N '70

Unique new view camera tilts like a rocking chair; Sinar-p. B. Schwalberg. il Pop Phot 67:110-11+ D '70

View from Kramer; perfect view camera. A. Kramer. il Mod Phot 34:56+ Je '70

View from Kramer; view cameras. A. Kramer. Mod Phot 34:34+ Ag '70

Whole generation has never known the view camera. A. Rothstein. Travel & Camera 33:14 My '70

Why I take lousy pictures with great cameras; lack of automatic controls. W. Hanson. il Pop Phot 67:108-9 Ag '70

Wider than wide and super-sharp: the Hologon with its 15-mm lens. L. Drukker. il Pop Phot 66:74-6+ Ap '70

Wild equipment I have known. S. Nathan. il Pop Phot 67:62+ S '70

See also
Eastman Kodak company
Mirrors for cameras
Moving picture cameras
Polaroid Land cameras
Single-lens reflex cameras
Television cameras
View finders

Care
See Cameras—Maintenance and repair

Collectors and collecting
Camera collector. J. Schneider. See issues of Modern photography
What's so great about antique cameras? N. Goldberg. il Pop Phot 66:56+ Je '70

Control
See Camera shutters—Control

Design
Are they building cameras upside down? N. Rothschild. il Pop Phot 66:55-7+ F '70
Better way to swing & tilt; Sinar-p view camera. L. Mannheim. il Mod Phot 34:86+ S '70
Your camera's built-in margin for error. N. Goldberg. il Pop Phot 67:69-71+ S '70

History
Take a Kodak with you; G. Eastman's collection. C. Davidson. il Am Heritage 21:48-51 Je '80
Those wonderful wish book cameras. K. Poli. il Pop Phot 66:66-7+ Ap '70

Loading
How to flatten your film for sharper pictures. H. Maersk-Moller. il Mod Phot 34:78-9+ Ap '70
Is the film plane in your camera doing its job? B. Sherman. il Mod Phot 34:80-1+ F '70
Take a number from 1 to 100; magazines for the Hasselblad 500C and 500EL. S. Nathan. il Pop Phot 67:68+ D '70

Maintenance and repair
How to succeed as an occasional photographer. W. Hanson. il Pop Phot 67:78-9+ O '70
Personalize your camera. N. Goldberg. il Pop Phot 67:62+ Jl '70
Simple camera checks for good summer shooting. P. Geraci. il Pop Mech 133:124-7 Je '70
Which camera? And other stoppers. N. Goldberg. il Pop Phot 67:58+ Ag '70
Your enemy, the sun. N. Rothschild. il Pop Phot 67:67-9+ Ag '70

Prices
Budget cameras. il Mech Illus 66:73 Mr '70

Purchasing
Caution! Cost-cutting corners ahead. N. Goldberg. il Pop Phot 67:79-81+ D '70
Check, then buy! E. C. Scully. il Mod Phot 33:46-7+ D '69
Feininger; camera selection. A. Feininger. Mod Phot 34:51-2+ Jl '70
For the child who has everything: give your kid a camera! L. Barry. il Pop Phot 67:106-7 D '70
How to choose a camera. il Consumer Bul 53:21-6 My '70
Which camera? And other stoppers. N. Goldberg. il Pop Phot 67:58+ Ag '70

Testing
How to predict camera failure. N. Goldberg. il Pop Phot 66:48+ Mr '70
Modern tests. See issues of Modern photography
Test reports. See issues of Travel & camera
Testing? Watch for these pitfalls. N. Goldberg. il Pop Phot 67:62+ D '70

CAMERAS, Used
How to tell a good used camera from a bad one. J. Hard. il Mech Illus 66:110-13+ O '70
View from Kramer; used view camera. A. Kramer. Mod Phot 34:62+ My '70

CAMERAS on space vehicles. See Space vehicles—Equipment

CAMERATA chorale. See Choral groups and societies

CAMERMAN, Arthur, and Camerman, Norman
Diphenylhydantoin and diazepam: molecular structure similarities and steric basis of anticonvulsant activity. bibliog il Science 168:1457-8 Je 19 '70

CAMERMAN, Norman. See Camerman, A. jt. auth.

CAMERON, Duncan F.
Museums for moderns. il UNESCO Courier 23:22-6+ O '70

CAMERON, Eleanor
Art of Elizabeth Enright (cont) Horn Bk 46:26-30 F '70

CAMERON, Eugene N.
Opaque minerals in lunar samples. bibliog il Science 167:623-5 Ja 30 '70

CAMERON, Frank
(ed) See Bracken, P. Peg Bracken: an exclusive interview

CAMERON, James
Twenty-three nuclear explosions later. il N Y Times Mag p24-5+ Mr 1 '70

CAMERON, Juan
Armed forces' reluctant retrenchment. il Fortune 82:68-73+ N '70
Gold enters a not-so-gilded age. il Fortune 81:98-101+ Ap '70
Richard Nixon's very personal White House. il por Fortune 82:56-9+ Jl '70

CAMERON, Roderick A.
Five who care. il Look 34:38 Ap 21 '70

CAMERON, Sheila M.
First woman chancellor named by Anglican diocese. Chr Cent 87:72 Ja 21 '70

CAMEROON REPUBLIC
See also
Church and state in the Cameroon Republic

CAMIN, Joseph H. See Moss, W. W. jt. auth.

CAMINO real: drama. See Williams, T.

CAMMAROSANO, Joseph R.
Our current inflation. America 122:369-72 Ap 4 '70

CAMP, Charles L.
Song of man. il Am West 7:18-23 S '70

CAMP accidents. See Accidents

CAMP activities. See Camping—Activities

CAMP administration. See Camps—Administration

CAMP children
Campers make more friends; dining room seating plan. H. W. Thwing. il Camp Mag 42:16-18 Je '70

Photographs
Instant camp evaluation. M. Hartwig. Camp Mag 42:12-13 My '70

Transportation
Day camp busing. M. Melamed. il Camp Mag 42:17-18 My '70
Transportation guide for camp directors. M. Melamed. il Camp Mag 42:18+ Mr '70

CAMP clothes. See Clothing and dress—Children

CAMP cookery
Big hot sandwiches in camp. il Sunset 144:188 Ap '70
Camp chef. C. B. Colby. See issues of Outdoor life
Camping cookery; with recipes. J. H. Winchester. il Travel 134:64-6 Jl '70
Campsite specials. E. W. Manning. il Farm J 94:38 Jl '70
Food outlook for 1970. il Camp Mag 42:14 Ap '70
Forget the cook's parade unless—. G. W. Lankton. Camp Mag 42:22-4 N '70
Good planning plus imagination equals happy eating. L. Crockett. il Camp Mag 42:25 Ja '70
How to use convenience foods at camp. W. Weir. il Camp Mag 42:44-5 Mr '70
How to use easy desserts in camp menus. H. Cashman. Camp Mag 42:22-4 My '70

CAMP cookery—*Continued*
Low calorie foods for campers. W. Davis. il Mech Illus 66:34+ Jl '70
Systematic menu planning. V. W. Riches. Camp Mag 42:12-13 F '70
Tasty make-ahead camp meals. Sunset 145: 126-7 Jl '70

CAMP counselors
Camp director's role in staff orientation. C. B. Rotman. il Camp Mag 42:11+ Ap '70
Counselor hair styles. S. Van Matre. Camp Mag 42:15-16 My '70
How to choose only successful camp counselors. H. G. Dimock. il por Camp Mag 42: 8-10 Ap '70
How to plan your pre-camp and in-camp staff training. E. Klein. Camp Mag 42:15 Je '70
Sensitivity training aids our staff development program. R. Brower. por Camp Mag 42:14+ N '70
Training project aids black youth. K. Fraser. il Camp Mag 42:27 Ja '70

Recruiting
How you can conduct better staff interviews; excerpts from Interviewing techniques for the non-personnel executive. Camp Mag 42: 22-3+ Ja '70

CAMP discipline
Pot, pills and people; Camp JCA, California. M. Schlesinger. Camp Mag 42:10-11+ Mr '70

CAMP equipment. See Camping—Outfits, supplies, etc.

CAMP fire girls
Adventure: Camp fire girls style. G. Harper. il Parks & Rec 9:35-6+ S '70
Indians don't cry. M. Allen. il Read Digest 97:111-14 N '70

CAMP Lejeune. See Military training camps

CAMP libraries
Library goes to camp; Lindberg school district, St Louis County, Mo. M. Petter and L. Bloomquist. Am Lib 1:166-8 F '70

CAMP management. See Camps—Administration

CAMP sites, facilities, etc.
Camping '70; symposium. il Pop Mech 133: S1+ My '70
Farm campsites for extra income. J. M. Crider. Farm J 94:43 O '70
Keep on top of maintenance with this monthly calendar; excerpts from Maintenance for camps and other outdoor recreation facilities. A. A. Nathans. Camp Mag 42:11-13 S '70
Marks of a good campground. C. B. Colby. il Outdoor Life 145:20+ Ap '70
New multi-purpose camp offers ideas you can use: Rancho del Chaparral, near Cuba, N.Mex. M. F. Biering. il Camp Mag 42:8-9 S '70
Newest thing under the sun: condominium campsites. F. K. Coffee. il Mech Illus 66:42-4 Ag '70
Organized group conference camp in Oregon woods. il Arch Rec 147:136-7 My '70
See also
Kampgrounds of America, inc.

CAMP stoves
Trail stove shields canned heat from wind. N. Fallon. il Pop Sci 196:104 Je '70

CAMPAIGN buttons, etc.
Pin-backs. D. F. Brown. il Hobbies 75:127-8+ Je '70

CAMPAIGN chests. See Chests

CAMPAIGN funds
Antiwar group raises $250,000. A. L. Hammond. Science 170:514 O 30 '70
Both parties start campaign with a search for cash. U S News 68:32-3 Mr 2 '70
Buying my time. New Repub 163:7 O 24 '70
Campaign costs. J. McLaughlin. America 122:482 My 2 '70
Cheaper campaigns? bill to limit spending. Newsweek 75:94 Ap 27 '70
False front campaign funds: how they work. por U S News 70:57 Ja 11 '71
Financial landslide for the G.O.P. H. E. Alexander and H. B. Meyers. il Fortune 81:104-5+ Mr '70
High cost of democracy; election spending for Senate, House and governor races in four states. il Time 96:11-12 N 23 '70
Letter from Washington; limiting money for television and radio time. R. H. Rovere. New Yorker 46:134-5 O 24 '70
Money influence in elections, and afterwards. D. Lawrence. U S News 69:100 N 9 '70
Nixon 1, Senate 0; bill to limit campaign spending on TV and radio. Time 96:25 D 7 '70
Political campaigns; 1968 elections. Trans-Action 7:8+ Mr '70

Politics and money. Commonweal 92:331-2 Jl 10 '70
Rich GOP gets richer. Bsns W p 100 O 10 '70
Short change for the opposition; Democratic fund raising. il Bsns W p31 F 14 '70
Smoke-screen veto. Nation 211:388 O 26 '70
Time for candidates; Pastore bill vetoed. New Repub 163:10 D 5 '70
Veto sustained; bill to limit spending on TV and radio. il Newsweek 76:21-2 D 7 '70
What wins elections today? Sr Schol 97:15-17 O 12 '70

CAMPAIGN issues
Crime & the liberal audience. J. Q. Wilson. Commentary 51:71-8 Ja '71
Forgotten issue; war in Vietnam. K. Crawford. Newsweek 76:38 N 2 '70
GOP and God; priest influences Catholics on abortion issue in California. L. T. King. Commonweal 93:37-8 O 9 '70
Issues that lost, men who won. il Time 96:16-23 N 16 '70
Law and order politics; President Nixon's approach. H. Sidey. Life 69:4 O 30 '70
Nixon turns a campaign into a crusade; rising rate of terrorism and crime. il Bsns W p29 O 24 '70
Now the game plan's target is '72. il Bsns W p 16 N 7 '70
Peace and pollution. P. Burnham. Nat R 22: 1392 D 29 '70
Political mood: right on. il Newsweek 76:32-3 O 19 '70
Politics of fear. Commonweal 93:163-4 N 13 '70
Politics of prejudice; Republican party strategy. Nation 211:260-1 S 28 '70
Rate your candidate; key environmental issues; with editorial comment. M. Frome. Field & S 75:6, 60-5+ S '70
Real majority, by R. M. Scammon and B. J. Wattenberg. Review Atlan 226:69-73 D '70. M. Janeway
Voices of the people; environmental cause. M. Frome. Field & S 75:30+ N '70
Voting our pocketbooks. R. W. Dietsch. Nation 211:358-60 O 19 '70
Wood is getting dry. S. Alsop. Newsweek 76: 108 O 5 '70

CAMPAIGN management
Image-makers beware; Great Britain and United States. A. Cooke. Nat R 22:1103-4 O 20 '70

CAMPAIGN organizers. See Campaign management

CAMPAIGN volunteers. See Political campaigns

CAMPAIGNS, Advertising. See Advertising campaigns

CAMPAIGNS, Money raising. See Fund raising

CAMPAIGNS, Political. See Political campaigns

CAMPAIGNS, Presidential. See Presidential campaigns

CAMPANER, Peter
How to make a wobbler minnow lure. il Pop Mech 133:152-4 Ap '70

CAMPANULAS
Italian bellflower: it's a trailer. il Sunset 144:216 Je '70

CAMPARI family
Little red bottles. S. Spitzer. il Holiday 48: 38-9 Jl '70

CAMPARI-Milano company. See Liquor industry and trade—Italy

CAMPBELL, Beatrice Stella (Tanner) See Campbell, Mrs Patrick

CAMPBELL, D. B. and others
Radar interferometric observations of Venus at 70-centimeter wavelength. bibliog il Science 170:1090-2 D 4 '70

CAMPBELL, F. W. See Maffei, L. jt. auth.

CAMPBELL, Fred
Artist with wood. D. Shiner. il por Design 72:24-5 Fall '70 *

CAMPBELL, Glen
Glen Campbell: the all-American country boy; interview, ed. by L. Dowty. il pors Good H 170:42+ F '70
My good times and bad. por Ladies Home J 87:62-3+ F '70
about
Never gonna be a country boy again. T. Smothers. il pors Look 34:70-4 F 24 '70 *

CAMPBELL, J. Phil, 1917-
Credit and the farm of the future; address, March 17, 1970. Vital Speeches 36:431-4 My 1 '70

CAMPBELL, James S.
Usefulness of commission studies of collective violence. bibliog f Ann Am Acad 391:168-76 S '70

CAMPBELL, John Coert
Arab-Israeli conflict: an American policy. For Affairs 49:51-69 O '70

CAMPBELL, John Franklin
Rumblings along the Red Sea: the Eritrean question. il For Affairs 48:537-48 Ap '70
What is to be done? Gigantism in Washington. For Affairs 49:81-99 O '70
CAMPBELL, John Wood, 1910-
I list in numbers. T. Sturgeon. Nat R 22: 266 Mr 10 '70 *
CAMPBELL, Josie P.
Deceit and violence: motifs in The narrative of Arthur Gordon Pym. Engl J 59: 206-12 F '70
CAMPBELL, Jule
Sporting look. il Sports Illus 33:42-3 Jl 27 '70
CAMPBELL, Lawrence
Do you remember Rudolf Bauer? il Art N 69:56-7+ N '70
Great-circle route. il por Art N 69:52-7+ Ap '70
Squaring the circle and vice-versa. il por Art N 68:38-41+ F '70
CAMPBELL, Louise Cooper
Charles Abrams, 1901-1970. por Arch Forum 132:62-3 Ap '70
CAMPBELL, Meg
Final answer; story. Redbook 136:66-7 N '70
CAMPBELL, Oren
U.S. journal: Nampa, Idaho. C. Trillin. New Yorker 46:104+ O 31 '70 *
CAMPBELL, Patrick
How to live the sweet life in the south of France. il Holiday 47:52-3+ Je '70
CAMPBELL, Mrs Patrick
Truth about Pygmalion, by R. Huggett. Review
Newsweek 76:90A O 26 '70. R. A. Sokolov *
CAMPBELL, Roald F. and Layton, D. H.
Growing expectations for American education. Ed Digest 35:1-4 Ja '70
CAMPBELL, Robert
With thee, Bug, I plight my troth. il Sports Illus 33:62-4+ N 9 '70
CAMPBELL, Robert D.
Records. Chr Cent 87:1355-6 N 11 '70
CAMPBELL-PURDIE, Wendy
This woman fights the Sahara with trees. J. Graham. il pors Sci Digest 69:20-3 Ja '71 *
CAMPBELL museum collection. See Camden, N.J.—Galleries and museums
CAMPBELL soup company
FTC refuses to stiffen Campbell's soup order. Consumer Rep 35:456 Ag '70
In the service of soup: a great collection. E. Gaines. il Antiques 97:109-18 Ja '70
CAMPERS. See Camp children
CAMPERS (trailers) See Automobile trailers
CAMPERS and coaches, Truck
Across Canada in a motor home. J. Linkletter. il Pop Mech 133:122-5+ F '70
Build this pickup camper. R. Wovries. il Mech Illus 66:74-8 F '70
Camper van with more room in the rear. J. Copeland. il Pop Sci 197:65 N '70
Caravans on the open road; with report by R. Bailey. il Life 69:20-9 Ag 14 '70
Foldout camper; Notow aluminum camper. C. Conley. il Field & S 75:167 O '70
For your wagon, build this pop-up camper. J. R. Fund. il Pop Sci 196:64-6+ Je '70
Home that travels. M. Dorn. il Har Yrs 10: 18 F '70
Made for each other: chassis and motor home. J. Davis. il Pop Sci 197:48 O '70
Posh pad for family safari; Glastron motor home. C. R. Meyer. il Pop Sci 196:80-1+ Mr '70
South of the border in a truck camper. E. H. Ortner. il Pop Sci 196:82-3+ Mr '70
Super motor home. il Mech Illus 66:93 D '70
Two mountain weeks in a Minihome. A. Lees. il Pop Sci 196:80-1+ Mr '70
Why Winnebago is number one. J. M. Liston. il Pop Mech 133:120-5+ My '70
You can build this motor home for under $3900. J. M. Liston. il Pop Mech 135:136-9+ Ja '71

Leasing and renting
Get a flying start on your camping vacation; Fly-in/camp-out program. H. Shuldiner. il Pop Sci 196:82-3 My '70
Homes for rent, on wheels. il Bsns W p50 F 14 '70
If you try out a camper by renting. Sunset 144:145 My '70

Maintenance and repair
Now's the time for camper clean-up. Sunset 145:39 D '70

Safety devices and measures
Inside a camper box. il Consumer Rep 35:495 Ag '70

Testing
MI tests:
Astro Twin camper. W. T. McKeown. il Mech Illus 66:100-1+ My '70
PM tests:
Dodge Corey Cruiser. B. Kilpatrick. il Pop Mech 133:104-5+ Mr '70

Toilet facilities
Johns for campers. B. McKeown. il Mech Illus 66:102-3+ My '70

CAMPING
Automobile in the wilderness; reprint of December, 1904 article. W. A. Babson. il Field & S 75:216-19+ Je '70
Camp wild for best fishing. A. W. Prince. il pors Field & S 75:58-9+ My '70
Camping. C. B. Colby. See issues of Outdoor life
Camping, now try it on two wheels. J. Davis. il Pop Sci 196:90-1 Je '70
Camping '70; symposium. il Pop Mech 133: 81+ My '70
Camping with a snowmobile. B. McKeown. il Mech Illus 66:32-3+ D '70
Camping with an ATV? C. B. Colby. il Outdoor Life 146:12+ S '70
Case for the sandtini. J. Fredericks. il Field & S 74:76-7+ Mr '70
Don't knock park camping. T. H. Taylor and L. Taylor. il Nat Wildlife 8:46-7 O '70
For the wilderness traveler; You can take it with you! il Liv Wildn 34:38-9 Spr '70
Let your 9-11's enjoy wilderness camping, too; Camp Sequoyah for boys, N.C. P. J. Garrison. il Camp Mag 42:13+ N '70
Memorable camps. T. Trueblood. il Field & S 74:40+ Mr '70
On-the-go camping. W. Mitchell. See issues of Popular mechanics
Smooth way to boat-camp. B. McKeown. il Mech Illus 66:83+ Mr '70
Take your winter vacation on a snowmobile. C. R. Meyer. il por Pop Sci 196:40-3 Ja '70
Under one tent! E. Bombeck. il Good H 171:28+ Jl '70
Walden III. F. Powledge. il Esquire 73:100-3+ Je '70
What's a good camper? C. B. Colby. il Outdoor Life 146:20+ Ag '70
See also
Camp cookery
Camp sites, facilities, etc.
Outdoor life
Wilderness survival

Activities
Informal theater: camp activity for everybody. J. B. Kase. il Camp Mag 42:16-17+ Mr '70
Joy of discovery through camping; address. D. Pelegrino. Camp Mag 42:14 Mr '70
More tested ideas to spark your camp program. Camp Mag 42:12+ Je '70
Try a mini-farm at your camp. T. Alvord. il Camp Mag 42:21 Je '70

Bibliography
Books in review. See issues of Camping magazine
Current reading. Camp Mag 42:28 S; 26 N '70

Economic aspects
See Camps—Finance

Educational aspects
Camp can be much more than just fun and games. M. Tener. il Camp Mag 42:14 Ja '70
Checkpoints for fighting the drug menace in camp; education program at Camp Narrin, Mich. S. C. Huck and P. A. Denomme. Camp Mag 42:19+ S '70
How to develop a good Indian lore program; Camp Sequoyah, N.C. M. Miller. il Camp Mag 42:12-13 Ap '70
Learning in camp: the fourth force in total education; excerpts from address. M. Penn. il Camp Mag 42:13-14 Je '70
Organized camp: a laboratory for learning; 12-month school year and organized camping. J. J. Kirk. por Camp Mag 42:4 Je '70. Reply. L. V. Baldwin. 42:30 S '70
Preparing groups for weekend camp programs. S. J. Makoff il Camp Mag 42:46-7 Mr '70
Three phase program starts leader training at eight years old; Van Buren youth camp, Mich. K. V. Washburn, jr. il Camp Mag 42:20+ F '70

Health aspects
Fats of life; camp for overweight boys. H. L. Masin. il Sr Schol 95:22 Ja 12 '70
Helpful hints from a camp nurse. E. Means. il Camp Mag 42:20+ Ap '70
Pediatrician says it is time we outgrow camp physical exams. G. Austin. Camp Mag 42:14 F '70; Discussion. 42:34 N '70

CAMPING—*Continued*

Outfits, supplies, etc.

Back packing for pleasure, think light! S. Wojcik. il Cons 24:48+ Je '70

Camping, good family fun. Suc Farm 68:56 Ap '70

Camping out of your pocket. B. McKeown. il Mech Illus 66:58-60 Je '70

Gifts for campers. C. B. Colby. il Outdoor Life 146:16+ D '70

Hot tips for cold days; camping out in subzero weather. V. Kraft. il por Sports Illus 32:48-9 Ja 26 '70

More new camping gear. C. B. Colby. il Outdoor Life 145:10+ Je '70

New gear for the '70's. C. B. Colby. il Outdoor Life 145:12+ My '70

'70 camping equipment. il Pop Mech 133:S20 My '70

Smooth way to boat-camp. B. McKeown. il Mech Illus 66:83+ Mr '70

What's new (title varies) See issues of Camping magazine

What's new, improved, practical, for your camp (cont) il Camp Mag 42:32-3 Ja '70

Your 1970 buying guide. Camp Mag 42:20+ Mr '70

See also
Automobiles—Camping equipment
Boats—Camping equipment
Camp cookery
Camp stoves
Rope
Sleeping bags

Leasing and renting

Rental route to low-cost camping. B. McKeown. il Mech Illus 66:54-6+ Ap '70

See also
Camping magazine

Periodicals

Safety devices and measures

Air sleeping bags before using. Camp Mag 42:25 Je '70

Check the kids' summer camp for safety. il Changing T 24:29-31 My '70

Fourteen camp accidents which could have been avoided. Camp Mag 42:16+ Ja '70

How to wreck a national park; overcrowding; Grand Teton National Park. C. S. Wren. il Look 34:77-8+ Je 16 '70

Nature's nuisances. C. B. Colby. il Outdoor Life 145:16+ F '70

New buddy plan aids waterfront safety. A. L. Lent. il Camp Mag 42:14+ My '70

Songs and music

Singing camp is a happy camp; Northwest Camp Cherith, Wash. A. Short. il Camp Mag 42:11 Je '70

Study and teaching

Camp director reports on Midwest training center. R. Telleen. il Camp Mag 42:20 Je '70

How to plan your pre-camp and in-camp staff training. E. Klein. Camp Mag 42:15 Je '70

Sensitivity training aids our staff development program. R. Brower. por Camp Mag 42:14+ N '70

Alaska

Wilderness adventure in Alaska. B. Thomas. il Travel 133:34-9+ Je '70

Canada

Camping in western Canada. C. B Colby. il Outdoor Life 146:14-16+ O '70

High on a horseback. E. A. Bauer. il Outdoor Life 145:62-5+ Mr '70

Pushbutton camping comfort; folding travel trailer. H. Shuldiner. il Pop Sci 196:84-5+ Mr '70

Colorado

How to start your family camping. E. Welke il Bet Hom & Gard 48:141-6 Mr '70

Europe, Western

Camping out is in for Americans seeing Europe. H. F. Schell. il Todays Health 48:44-7+ Mr '70

See also
Camping—Italy

Hawaii

Why wait for Hawaii? il Sunset 144:46-55 Ja '70

Italy

Camping mobility. R. Deardorff. il Travel 133:60-2 F '70

Mexico

South of the border in a truck camper. E. H. Ortner. il Pop Sci 196:82-3+ Mr '70

Minnesota

Camp wild for best fishing. A. W. Prince. il pors Field & S 75:58-9+ My '70

United States

Are campers slobs? B. Hackett. il Am For 76:36-9+ Ap '70

Camping out with all the conveniences. il Sports Illus 32:32-7 Je 1 '70

Hoof it to heaven; backpacking. E. A. Bauer. il por Outdoor Life 145:80-3+ Ap '70

How and where to camp. C. B. Colby. Outdoor Life 145:37-40 Mr '70

How to go boat camping. J. A. Emmett. il Outdoor Life 145:30+ Mr '70

Mississippi camping. H. Fowler and C. Fowler. il Motor B 125:65-7+ F '70

Off-season campers beat the vacation rush. il Bet Hom & Gard 48:8+ F '70

We hit the RV trail! symposium. il Pop Sci 196:78-85+ Mr '70

Winter adventure: desert camping. il Bet Hom & Gard 48:25-6 D '70

See also
American camping association
Kampgrounds of America, inc.

CAMPING, Cost of. See Camps—Finance

CAMPING, Value of
Camp objectives must be specific if they are to be meaningful; YMCA Camp Tockwogh, Del. S. A. Brown. il Camp Mag 42: 15-16 N '70

Camping needs revival of the fundamental ethic; excerpts from address. G. A. Harrison. por Camp Mag 42:8-10 Je '70

Challenge: children and youth in the 70's. J. H. Douglass. Camp Mag 42:12 Ja '70

Factors to consider in stimulating and motivating campers; address. H. L. Haskell. il Camp Mag 42:12-13 Mr '70

How to make camping significant in the 1970's. G. Konopka por Camp Mag 42:8-11 Ja '70

Joy of discovery through camping; address. D. Pelegrino. Camp Mag 42:14 Mr '70

Learning in camp: the fourth force in total education; excerpts from address. M. Penn. il Camp Mag 42:13-14 Je '70

My goals for camping; statements from presidential candidates. J. Bloom; N. Wieters. il por Camp Mag 42:7 N '70

Today's children and tomorrow's world? K. Kester. Camp Mag 42:20-1 S '70

Values of camping. A. F. Luehrs. por Camp Mag 42:4 My '70

CAMPING magazine
Howard Galloway begins 25th year as Camping magazine editor-publisher; letters to the editor. Camp Mag 42:34 Ja '70

CAMPING outfits. See Camping—Outfits, supplies, etc.

CAMPION, Donald R. See Kelly, J. R. jt. auth.

CAMPION award
Of many things. D. R. Campion. America 122:inside cover My 9 '70

CAMPO, Sofia del
Latin festival on L.P. A. Favia-Artsay. pors Hobbies 75:36 S '70 *

CAMPOS, Joseph J. and others
Cardiac responses on the visual cliff in prelocomotor human infants. bibliog il Science 170:196-7 O 9 '70

CAMPRA, André
Printed editions of André Campra's L'Europe galante. J. R. Anthony. bibliog f il Mus Q 56:54-73 Ja '70 *

CAMPS
Camps for every kind of kid. S. V. Estep. il Parents Mag 45:66-8 My '70

Preparing groups for weekend camp programs. S. J. Makoff. il Camp Mag 42:46-7 Mr '70

See also
American camping association
Camp sites, facilities, etc.
Camping—Outfits, supplies, etc.

Activities
See Camping—Activities

Administration

Camp director's role in staff orientation. C. B. Rotman. il Camp Mag 42:11+ Ap '70

Camp should be a benevolent dictatorship. A. Sharenow. por Camp Mag 42:16 Ap '70

Camping needs revival of the fundamental ethic; excerpts from address. G. A. Harrison. por Camp Mag 42:8-10 Je '70

Careful design results in attractive, functional camp office; Camp Greylock, Becket, Mass. il Camp Mag 42:10 S '70

Factors to consider in stimulating and motivating campers; address. H. L. Haskell. il Camp Mag 42:12-13 Mr '70

CAMPS—Administration—*Continued*

Four views on camping as a profession; symposium. Camp Mag 42:10-11+ F '70

Good property maintenance needs a good property manager. W. Worley. Camp Mag 42:22+ F '70

How to choose only successful camp counselors. H. G. Dimock. il por Camp Mag 42: 8-10 Ap '70

Transportation guide for camp directors. M. Melamed. il Camp Mag 42:18+ Mr '70

Counselors
See Camp counselors

Desegregation

Lawsuit against ACA; with ACA inter-racial statement. E. F. Schmidt. Camp Mag 42: 6-7+ My '70

Seven step program helps to integrate camp. M. Liener. il Camp Mag 42:14-15 S '70

Dining halls

Campers make more friends; seating plan. H. W. Thwing. il Camp Mag 42:16-18 Je '70

Finance

Cost of camping. H. Galloway. il Camp Mag 42:8-11 My '70

Public relations

Forty promotion techniques to aid camp public relations. Camp Mag 42:11 Ja '70

Standards

Check the kid's summer camp for safety. il Changing T 24:29-31 My '70

California

Pot, pills and people; camp JCA. M. Schlesinger. Camp Mag 42:10-11+ Mr '70

Colorado

And what do you do in the winter? Sanborn western camps. R. Sanborn. il Camp Mag 42:8-10 N '70

Delaware

Camp objectives must be specific if they are to be meaningful. S. A. Brown. il Camp Mag 42:15-16 N '70

Maryland

Country camp for day and overnight use; Milldale camps of the Jewish community center, Baltimore. il Arch Rec 147:134 My '70

Massachusetts

Careful design results in attractive, functional camp office; Camp Greylock, Becket. il Camp Mag 42:10 S '70

New horizons for disadvantaged youth; Kidde Kamp. F. Bavley. il Camp Mag 42:16+ F '70

Michigan

Checkpoints for fighting the drug menace in camp; education program at Camp Narrin. S. C. Huck and P. A. Denomme. Camp Mag 42:19+ S '70

Three phase program starts leader training at eight years old; Van Buren youth camp. K. V. Washburn, jr. il Camp Mag 42:20+ F '70

Missouri

Library goes to camp; Lindberg school district, St Louis County. M. Petter and L Bloomquist. Am Lib 1:166-8 F '70

New Jersey

Day camp international style; Project World Wide, Woodbridge, N.J. A. Staflin. il Parents Mag 45:46-7+ Ap '70

Need is apparent for greater camp use; the Appel farm. A. Appel. il Camp Mag 42: 12+ N '70

New Mexico

New multi-purpose camp offers ideas you can use; Rancho del Chaparral, near Cuba. M. F. Biering. il Camp Mag 42:8-9 S '70

New York (state)

Fats of life; camp for overweight boys. H. L. Masin. il Sr Schol 95:22 Ja 12 '70

North Carolina

How to develop a good Indian lore program; Camp Sequoyah. M. Miller. il Camp Mag 42: 12-13 Ap '70

Let your 9-11's enjoy wilderness camping, too; Camp Sequoyah for boys. P. J. Garrison. il Camp Mag 42:13+ N '70

Ohio

Day camp develops year-round operation; Red Raider camps. R. F. Smith. il Camp Mag 42:10-11 N '70

Oregon

Organized group conference camp in Oregon woods. il Arch Rec 147:136-7 My '70

Vermont

Extending camp season offers three benefits; Teela-Wooket camps. A. Hayden. il Camp Mag 42:11-12 N '70

Washington (state)

Singing camp is a happy camp; Northwest Camp Cherith. A. Short. il Camp Mag 42:11 Je '70

CAMPS for the handicapped
See also
Camps for the socially handicapped

CAMPS for the socially handicapped
New horizons for disadvantaged youth; Kidde Kamp, Mass. F. Bavley. il Camp Mag 42:16+ F '70

CAMPUS CITY, Chicago. See Illinois. University—Chicago campus

CAMPUS crusade for Christ (organization)
Spiritual bomb at Dallas; EXPLO '72. Chr Today 15:43 Ja 1 '71

CAMPUS life. See Student life

CAMPUS ombudsman. See Ombudsman (education)

CAMPUS planning
Campus of many spaces; Rissho university, Tokyo. il Arch Forum 132:34-9 My '70
Designs for the campus; building types study. il Arch Rec 147:101-18 F '70
Skidmore college. il Arch Rec 147:91-102 Mr '70
Two more for Columbus. il Arch Forum 132: 22-31 Mr '70
See also
College architecture

CAMPUS police. See Colleges and universities—Security measures

CAMPUS recruiting programs. See Recruiting of employees

CAMS
See also
Automobiles—Cams

CAMUS, Albert
Albert Camus. M. A. Sperber; J. L. Stamm; H. Slochower. bibliog f Am Imago 26:269-94 Fall '69
Albert Camus and Christianity, by J. Onimus. Review
Cath World 211:277 S '70. P. J. Cunningham *
Between solitude and solidarity. B. Murchland. Commonweal 93:91-5 O 23 '70 *

CAN company, American. See American can company

CAN openers, Electric. See Household appliances, Electric

CANADA
See also
Agricultural administration—Canada
Air travel—Canada
Americans in Canada
Architecture, Domestic—Canada
Atomic power—Canada
Automobile touring—Canada
Ballet—Canada
British Columbia
Camping—Canada
Children—Canada
Church union—Canada
Coal mines and mining—Canada
Conservation of resources—Canada
Cruising—Canada
Drug laws and legislation—Canada
Environmental movement—Canada
Eskimos
Fisheries—Canada
Fishing—Canada
Geology—Canada
Hotels, taverns, etc.—Canada
Hunting—Canada
Immigration and emigration—Canada
Investments, Foreign (in Canada)
Jervis Inlet
Library schools and education—Canada
Maritime Provinces
Metropolitan government—Canada
Money—Canada
National parks and reserves—Canada
Negroes in Canada
Nuns' Island
Paleontology—Canada
Petroleum—Canada
Phonograph record industry—Canada

CANADY, Robert Lynn. See Seyfarth, J. T. jt. auth.

CANAL cruising. See Cruising

CANALS

See also
Panama Canal
Suez Canal

Belgium

Ever see a canal on wheels? Charleroi to Brussels. il Sci Digest 67:84-5 Ja '70

Central America

Diggers beat nukes, by default. il Sci N 98:445 D 12 '70
Hopes dim for a second canal. il Sci N 97:363-5 Ap 11 '70
Which route for the Isthmian canal? A. S. Reyner. bibliog f il Cur Hist 58:102-6+ F '70
See also
Nicaraguan canal (proposed)

Florida

See also
Cross Florida Barge Canal

Ireland

Canals of Ireland. M. Connelly. il Holiday 48:48-53 Jl '70

Ohio

Frank N. Wilcox: a review of his last book. N. Kent. il Am Artist 34:30-1+ Ap '70

Washington (state)

Other side of the locks; Lake Washington Ship Canal; ed. by E. Crimmin. il Motor B 126:54-5+ Jl '70

CANARY ISLANDS

See also
Gardening—Canary Islands
Lanzarote
Tenerife

CANCER

Bladder cancer induction by aromatic amines: role of N-hydroxy metabolites. J. L. Radomski and E. Brill. bibliog il Science 167:992-3 F 13 '70
Breast cancer; ed. by H. M. Hobbs. A. King. Redbook 135:22+ S '70
Cancer; symposium. il UNESCO Courier 23: 4-32 My '70
My year of crisis; breast cancer. J. Byrd. il por Redbook 135:12+ O '70
New hope for heavy smokers. O. Auerbach and S. M. Spencer. Read Digest 96:129-31 F '70
Production of mouse urinary bladder carcinomas by sodium cyclamate. G. T. Bryan and E. Erturk. bibliog il Science 167:996-8 F 13 '70
Struggle for life itself; ed. by M. Mesinger. M. Piazza. pors McCalls 97:88-9+ F '70
You'd never know I had skin cancer. R. Stavely. por Har Yrs 10:44-5 S '70
See also
Leukemia
Sarcoma
Tumors

Causes

Air pollution and lung cancer. R. E. Waller. il UNESCO Courier 23:30-2 My '70
Botanical detective story; high-tannin foods associated with gullet cancer. il Sci Digest 68:84-6 O '70
Cancer threat greater than cigarettes? asbestos fibers. F. G. Loyd. il Todays Health 48:30-1+ Jl '70
Cause of cancer. il por Environ 12:22-5 Je '70
Charges on the cell membrane. Sci N 97:312-13 Mr 28 '70
Cigarettes and cancer. G. Godber. il UNESCO Courier 23:10-13 My '70
Lymphomas in mice: failure of induction after a graft-versus-host reaction. G. B. Rossi and C. Friend. bibliog il Science 167:1383-5 Mr 6 '70
New clues in the virus-cancer mystery. C. R. Goodheart and B. Goodheart. il Todays Health 48:32-5 Je '70
Radiation: the invisible casualties. J. W. Gofman and A. R. Tamplin. bibliog il Environ 12:12-19+ Ap '70
See also
Cancer research

Diagnosis

Detecting breast-cancer; mammography. Newsweek 75:51 Je 8 '70

Prevention and control

False notion: cancer=incurable. E. C. Easson. il UNESCO Courier 23:23-6 My '70
See also
American cancer society

Therapy

Avoid the surgery all women fear; mastectomy. O. Cope. Vogue 156:82-3+ O 15 '70
Cancer attitudes count. A. J. Snider. Sci Digest 68:65 D '70
Cancer: battle report; immunotherapy. M. Clark. il Newsweek 75:55-6 Ap 6 '70
Immunotherapy of cancer: an experimental model in syngeneic guinea pigs. B. S. Kronman and others. bibliog il Science 168:257-9 Ap 10 '70
I've learned to live with cancer; radiotherapy. Seventeen 29:138-9+ My '70
Pion cancer therapy: positron activity as an indicator of depth-dose. M. C. Taylor and others. bibliog il Science 169:377-8 Jl 24 '70
Using the cancer cures we have now; ed. by W. S. Ross. A. I. Holleb. por Todays Health 48:48-9+ Ap '70
See also
American radium society
Laetrile
Leukemia—Therapy

CANCER cells

Acetylcholine sensitivity and distribution on mouse neuroblastoma cells. A. J. Harris and M. J. Dennis. bibliog il Science 167: 1253-5 F 27 '71
Cancer and electrical voltage. il Chem 43:24 Je '70
Cell surface coatings and membrane potentials of malignant and nonmalignant cells. L. Hause and others. bibliog il Science 169: 601-3 Ag 7 '70
Malignant messenger; findings of H. Rubin. J. Lear. Sat R 53:48 Mr 21 '70
Overgrown cells; overgrowth stimulating factor discovered by Harry Rubin. il Newsweek 75:93 Mr 16 '70
Overgrowth stimulating factor released from rous sarcoma cells. H. Rubin. bibliog il Science 167:1271-2 F 27 '70
Plasmalemmal and subsurface complexes in human leukemic cells: membrane bonding by zipperlike junctions. F. T. Sanel and A. A. Serpick. bibliog il Science 168:1458-60 Je 19 '70
Probing the secret of the cell. N. Odartchenko. il UNESCO Courier 23:17-22 My '70

CANCER in plants. See Tumors, Plant

CANCER inhibiting substances

Antitumor activity in mice of tentacles of two tropical sea annelids. F. L. Tabrah and others. bibliog il Science 170:181-3 O 9 '70
Dimethylbenzanthracene tumorigenesis and aryl hydrocarbon hydroxylase in mouse skin: inhibition by 7,8-benzoflavone. H. V. Gelboin and others. bibliog il Science 170: 169-71 O 9 '70
Hydroxyurea: suppression of two-stage carcinogenesis in mouse skin. P. C. Chan and others. bibliog il Science 168:130-2 Ap 3 '70
New leukemia breakthrough; cystosine arabinoside. Sci Digest 67:56 Ja '70
Polyinosinic-polycytidylic acid inhibits chemically induced tumorigenesis in mouse skin. H. V. Gelboin and H. B. Levy. bibliog il Science 167:205-7 Ja 9 '70
Tumorigenesis in mouse skin: inhibition by synthetic inhibitors of proteases. W. Troll and others. bibliog il Science 169:1211-13 S 18 '70
See also
Asparaginase
Bromodeoxyuridine
Methotrexate

CANCER producing substances

After cyclamates: what's next on the FDA's food target list? K. N. Anderson. il Sci Digest 67:16-23 F '70
Contraceptives and dysplasia: higher rate for pill choosers. E. Stern and others. bibliog il Science 169:497-8 Jl 31 '70
Danger of cancer in food; controversy over repeal of the Delaney clause. J. Carper. Sat R 53:47-9+ S 5 '70
Growth in vitro of cells from hyperplastic nodules of liver induced by 2-fluorenylacetamide or aflatoxin B₁. M. Slifkin and others. bibliog il Science 167:285-7 Ja 16 '70
Mutagens and carcinogens; letter. G. P. Redei. Science 170:1038-9 D 4 '70
Oncogenic purine derivatives; evidence for a possible proximate oncogen. G. Stöhrer and G. B. Brown. bibliog il Science 167:1622-4 Mr 20 '70
Vertical grills: attention, backyard chefs! il Consumer Bul 53:33 Ag '70
See also
Fluorenylacetamide
Naphthylamines

CANCER research
Assessing the state of cancer research. B. J. Culliton. il Sci N 99:12-13 Ja 2 '71
Cancer: battle report. M. Clark. il Newsweek 75:55-6 Ap 6 '70
Cancer research: Senate consultants likely to push for planned assault. R. J. Bazell. Science 170:304-5 O 16 '70
Cancer viruses in primates. R. Kinard. bibliog Science 169:828-31 Ag 28 '70
Conquest of cancer: proposed National cancer authority. il Sci N 98:459 D 19 '70
Expanding on a classic view; role of cell membranes in cancer. B. J. Culliton. il Sci N 97:509-10 My 23 '70
Finding a cancer clue; RNA-dependent DNA polymerase. Time 96:41 D 21 '70
Growth in vitro of cells from hyperplastic nodules of liver induced by 2-fluorenylacetamide or aflatoxin B₁. M. Slifkin and others. bibliog il Science 167:285-7 Ja 16 '70
Last gasp for cigarettes? smoking dogs research. S. M. Spencer. Read Digest 96:92-5 Ap '70
Malignant messenger; findings of H. Rubin. J. Lear. Sat R 53:48 Mr 21 '70
Mathematics of cancer; steady-state theory. Sci N 98:270 S 26 '70
Matter of priorities. Commonweal 91:524 F 13 '70
New light on malignancy; BUdR. Newsweek 75:73 Je 29 '70
Overgrown cells; overgrowth stimulating factor discovered by Harry Rubin. il Newsweek 75:93 Mr 16 '70
Overgrowth stimulating factor released from rous sarcoma cells. H. Rubin. bibliog il Science 167:1271-2 F 27 '70
Probing the secret of the cell. N. Odartchenko. il UNESCO Courier 23:17-22 My '70
Production of urinary bladder carcinomas in mice by sodium saccharin. G. T. Bryan and others. bibliog il Science 168:1238-40 Je 5 '70; Reply. L. P. Brower. 170:553 O 30 '70
Seeking cancer cures. il Newsweek 76:48 Ag 31 '70
Smoking and cancer in dogs. Time 95:48 F 16 '70
Smoking beagles. il Newsweek 75:86 F 16 '70
Teminism marches on; RNA-dependent DNA polymerase. Sci N 98:432 D 5 '70
Teminism on the go. il Sci N 98:243-4 S 19 '70
Triumph for a heretic. il Newsweek 76:56-7 Jl 20 '70
Tumors in smoking dogs. Sci N 97:169 F 14 '70
Upsetting dogma. il Time 96:57 Jl 20 '70
Whole virus from a human tumor. il Sci N 97:611-12 Je 27 '70
CANCER tests. See Cancer—Diagnosis
CANDEE, Richard M.
Early New England textile village in art. il Antiques 98:910-15 D '70
CANDID photography. See Photography— Portraits
CANDIDA. See Yeasts
CANDIDA; drama. See Shaw, G. B.
CANDIDATES, Political
Antiwar congressional candidates, 1970 (title varies) New Repub 162:7-9 My 30; 7 Je 6; 7 Je 13; 163:10-13 Jl 4; 9 Ag 1; 14-16 O 24 '70
Bella; B. Abzug, congressional candidate from New York city's 19th district. il por Newsweek 76:28-9 O 5 '70
Black candidates: which party? il Sr Schol 97:13 O 12 '70
Blacker than thou; contestants to District of Columbia's first non-voting delegate to Congress. E. E. Plowman. Chr Today 15:27 Ja 15 '71
Bossism bogy. il por Time 95:22-3 Ap 13 '70
Candidates by any name. Time 95:18-19 Mr 9 '70
Candidates: T. Sorensen for the Democratic nomination to the Senate; H. Samuels for governor. New Yorker 46:27-30 Je 20 '70
Carswell's campaign. por Newsweek 75:21 Je 29 '70
Clean feeling of achievement; New Democratic coalition congressional candidates. New Repub 162:29-11 Mr 14 '70
Clergy as politicians. Chr Cent 87:1175 O 7 '70
Collars in the ring; clerical candidates. il Newsweek 75:105 My 4 '70
Coming leadership fight; Senate GOP leadership. Cato. Nat R 22:777 Jl 28 '70
Countdown to November; New York state gubernatorial candidates. Nat R 22:393 Ap 21 '70

Fight for the Senate. il Newsweek 76:19-20 Jl 20 '70
First hurrah? U.S. Senate seat from New York. Nat R 22:601 Je 16 '70
Goldberg variation; New York state candidates. il por Newsweek 75:22-3 Ap 13 '70
Heirs to disaster; Newark's mayoralty race. il Newsweek 75:63+ My 25 '70
How the races look in the homestretch. il Newsweek 76:26-7 N 2 '70
How they're rated in the tight races; congressional candidates' past performance through the eyes of ACA, ADA and COPE. il Nations Bsns 58:104-5 O '70
Hunt for voters; 1970 elections. il Sr Schol 97:7-12 O 12 '70
If you can't beat 'em ..; R. H. Carswell candidacy. il por Newsweek 75:29 My 4 '70
Joe Duffey's race. P. R. Wieck. New Repub 163:9-10 Ag 15 '70
Letter from Washington. Cato. Nat R 22:1150 N 3 '70
Mediator: A. Young of Atlanta's fifth congressional district. por Time 96:17 O 5 '70
Mr Goldberg runs for office. New Yorker 46:27-9 Je 13 '70
New Adlai. il por Newsweek 76:38+ O 12 '70
New household word: G. Harrold Carswell, candidate for Florida's Republican senatorial nomination. il por Time 95:19-20 My 4 '70
Nixon and the New York election; one of the contestants J. L. Buckley. W. F. Buckley, jr. Nat R 22:805 Jl 28 '70
Of many things; Campion award. D. R. Campion. America 122:inside cover My 9 '70
Of many things; Fr Drinan's candidacy. D. R. Campion. America 122:inside cover Mr 21 '70; Discussion. 122:599 Je 6 '70
Off-year: see how they run. il Newsweek 76:36-9 S 21 '70
Patrician and the pol; R. Taft-J. A. Rhodes debate, Cincinnati. pors Newsweek 75:30 My 4 '70
Political gains by Negroes. il U S News 69:40-1 Jl 13 '70
Political races to watch in this year's campaign. pors U S News 68:57-9 Mr 30 '70
President's candidates. il Time 96:11-12 Jl 27 '70
Priest candidates and the U.S. Congress. America 123:422 N 21 '70; Reply. J. P. Boland. 123:504 D 12 '70
Rate your candidate; key environmental issues; with editorial comment. M. Frome. Field & S 75:6, 60-5+ S '70
Real George: L. Romney's bid for the Republican Senate nomination from Michigan. por Newsweek 75:21 Mr 9 '70
Red herring; senatorial candidates, Ohio. il por Newsweek 76:29 O 26 '70
Republican assault on the Senate. il Time 96:18-22+ O 26 '70
Republicans and hard hats; New York senatorial race. Nat R 22:989 S 22 '70
Rites of spring; political scene in New York and California. Time 95:19 Mr 30 '70
Rock of ages. il por Newsweek 76:43-4 O 19 '70
Running against Teddy. il pors Newsweek 76:21-2 Ag 24 '70
Running uphill; Democratic candidates for U.S. Senate seat from New York. il por Newsweek 75:19-20 Je 22 '70
Selling of the candidates 1970. il Newsweek 76:34-8+ O 19 '70
'70 political trends in the South. il U S News 69:37-40 O 12 '70
Struggle for the statehouses. il Time 96:8-9 N 2 '70
Student campaign to get peace elected. C. Leinster. il Life 68:45-6 Je 5 '70
Studio to stump; broadcast personalities as candidates. il Newsweek 76:122 N 2 '70
Vermont Democrats: Hoff's campaign. P. R. Wieck. New Repub 163:11-13 O 3 '70
View from the Rockies; Wyoming; Colorado; New Mexico. P. R. Wieck. New Repub 163: 12-13 Ag 1 '70
We're all peace candidates now. Nation 211:36 Jl 20 '70
When the war issue was raised-. il U S News 68:22-3 Je 15 '70
Who won, who lost? peace and new priorities candidates. New Repub 163:8 N 21 '70
Wing and a prayer; Tennessee gubernatorial candidates. pors Bsns W p96 Mr 14 '70
See also
Political campaigns
Presidential candidates
Vice-presidential candidates

CANDIDATES, Political—*Continued*

Health

Glory road leads to exhaustion. H. Johnson. il Todays Health 48:34-7+ N '70

Chile

October revolution in Chile? S. Rodman. Nat R 22:1053-5 O 6 '70

Egypt

Candidates to fill Cairo's leadership vacuum. Time 96:23 O 12 '70
Death of Nasser; presidential contenders. il Newsweek 76:33-4 O 12 '70

Great Britain

Doffing the cloth cap; British parliamentary candidates. il Time 95:31-2 Je 15 '70
Odd men out; Great Britain. il por Newsweek 75:36+ Je 22 '70

CANDIED citrus peel. See Confectionery

CANDLAND, Shelby V.
How the paniolo came. il Américas 22:7-9 Ja '70

CANDLE holders. See Candlesticks

CANDLES *
Deannie's candles. J. Kuh. Ladies Home J 87:19 My '70
Decorations highlight the beauty of candle power; Christmas candles. V. D. Hahn. il Am Home 73:38-9+ D '70
Glow of candles: for warmth, romance. A. Kolb. House B 112:28-9 D '70
Out, out, brief candle! il Forbes 105:50-1 Mr 1 '70

CANDLESTICKS
Fabric candles. D. Meier. il Design 71:36-7 Sum '70
Handcrafted wood block candleholders. il Sunset 145:98-9 Jl '70
Holiday candle stand. E. Waltner and W. Waltner. il Pop Mech 134:182-3 N '70

CANDY
Child's play candies; with recipes. J. Uetz. il Am Home 73:62+ D '70
Give sweet thoughts for Christmas; with recipes. il Farm J 93:40-1 D '69
Little chocolate mint truffles. il Sunset 145: 152 D '70
Oh, what a beautiful box of candy! il Farm J 94:62-3 My '70
Successful candy every time. E. W. Manning. il Farm J 94:46-8 O '70
See also
Confectionery

CANDY industry and trade
See also
Cadbury Schweppes, ltd.

CANE, Melville
Poems; Eloquent April; Time enough for that. Am Scholar 39:270-1 Spr '70
Robert Frost: an intermittent intimacy; excerpt from Eloquent April. Am Scholar 40: 158+ Wint '70

CANFIELD, Cass
Writers: 1920-1970. il Writers Digest 50:25-9+ Ja '70

CANFIELD, G. L.
Ex-owner didn't fit in. pors Bsns W p64+ F 14 '70 *

CANFIELD, Helen S.
Peter Parley; address. October 9, 1969. bibliog il Horn Bk 46:135-41, 274-82, 412-18 Ap-Ag '70

CANFIELD, James
High cost of non-teaching assignments. Clear House 44:296-9 Ja '70

CANGEMI, Joseph P.
Variety of American-type schools abroad. Clear House 45:174-6 N '70

CANN, John R. and Goad, W. B.
Bimodal sedimenting zones due to ligand-mediated interactions. bibliog il Science 170: 441-5 O 23 '70

CANNABIS. See Marijuana

CANNAS
Colorful cannas. H. Nix. Horticulture 48:34-5 Je '70

CANNED food
See also
Cookery—Canned food
Meat, Canned

CANNED food industry
See also
Del Monte corporation
Green giant company
Libby, McNeill and Libby (firm)

CANNED hams. See Meat, Canned

CANNELLONI. See Cookery, Italian

CANNERIES
Death of the bees; use of carbaryl insecticide, Sevin, by vegetable canners in Minnesota. Sci N 98:349-50 O 31 '70

CANNES international film festival
Happy in Cannes. I. Shaw. Harper 241:26+ S '70
Revolution on the Riviera; International film festival, Cannes. il Time 95:98 My 25 '70

CANNIBALISM
Cannibalistic revenge in Jalé warfare. K. F. Koch. il por Natur Hist 79:40-51 F '70

CANNIBALISM (insects)
Flour beetles: responses to extracts of their own pupae. M. F. Ryan and others. bibliog il Science 170:178-80 O 9 '70

CANNING and preserving
Canning the late-summer harvest; recipes for relishes. J. Uetz. il Am Home 73:90-2+ S '70
Into your pantry this summer: canned jars of brandied fruit. il Sunset 144:158-9 Je '70
Worth preserving. H. McCully. il House B 112:112-13+ S '70
See also
Jelly, jam, etc.
Pickles and relishes

CANNIZZARO, Stanislao
Chemists' involvement in society. R. Ferreira. il pors Chem 43:12-13 D '70 *

CANNON, Dyan
Dyan Cannon booms. S. Gordon. il pors Look 34:72-4 Jl 14 '70 *

CANNON, John
Cannon fire in a bright new arena. K. Chapin. Sports Illus 33:35 Ag 24 '70 *

CANNON, M. Hamlin
Morrisite war. bibliog il Am West 7:4-9+ N '70

CANNON, Philip Jan
Lunar landslides. il Sky & Tel 40:215-18 O '70

CANNON, Poppy
Poppy Cannon's meal-a-day menus. See issues of Ladies' home journal

CANNON, William B.
Are we faced with a new aristocracy? Cur 124:22-6 D '70

CANNON group, Inc.
Kids at Cannon. il pors Time 96:60 Ag 31 '70

CANOE building. See Boat building

CANOE paddles
How to make a better canoe paddle. J. M. Jeffers. il Pop Sci 197:83+ Ag '70

CANOE racing
Sporting scene. J. McPhee. New Yorker 46: 126+ Mr 21 '70
See also
Kayak racing

CANOE trips
If Mr Thoreau calls, tell him I've left the country; rowing up the Concord and Merrimack Rivers. R. Mungo. il Atlan 225:72-82+ My '70
It's canoeing time on the Russian; Sonoma County's Russian River. il Sunset 144:3-4 Ap '70
Making the family or group canoe trip. J. W. Kelly. il Cons 24:48+ Ap '70
Northwest Passage. B. Skovbo. il Natur Hist 79:56-65 Je '70
Wilderness besieged, the canoe country of Minnesota. S. F. Olson. il Audubon 72:28-33 Jl '70

CANOES

Equipment

Redwood canoe goes sailing. F. McGuckin and J. Payne. il Pop Sci 197:80-2 Ag '70

CANOES and canoeing
Fast-water boating. J. A. Emmett. il Outdoor Life 146:30+ Ag '70
How to unswamp a canoe. D. I. Williams. il Outdoor Life 146:66-7 Jl '70
Look at the glass canoe. F. M. Paulson. il Field & S 75:124-30 S '70
Sportsmen's canoes. P. Pulling. il Field & S 75:82 O '70
Three-way redwood canoe. F. McGuckin and J. Payne. il Pop Sci 197:89-91 Jl '70
What's new in canoes. B. McKeown. il Mech Illus 66:64+ S '70

CANON law
Priests, politics and canon law. America 123: 110 S 5 '70
Rome's opportunity; the revised Code of canon law. Commonweal 92:133 Ap 24 '70
See also
Marriage (canon law)
Marriage—Annulment (canon law)

CANONIZATION
Again, the forty martyrs. T. Beeson. Chr Cent 87:1373 N 18 '70
Anglicanizing the canonization breach. J. D. Douglas. Chr Today 15:44 O 23 '70

CANONIZATION—*Continued*
Canterbury and canonization. Chr Cent 87: 782 Je 24 '70; Reply. J. Satterthwaite. 87: 1045 S 2 '70
Forty more saints. P. Hebblethwaite. America 123:399-400 N 14 '70
Martyrs' blood today; Protestant and Catholic anger at proposed canonization of the forty martyrs. C. Northcott. Chr Cent 87: 134 F 4 '70
CANOPY beds. See Beds
CANS

Manufacture
See also
American can company
Continental can company
CANT, Gilbert
Curious case of the copper band. il Sports Illus 33:37-41 Ag 3 '70
Nature. Sports Illus 32:58-9 Ap 6 '70
CANTALOUPES. See Melons
CANTATAS
Joke for Beethoven. C. J. McNaspy. America 122:166-7+ F 14 '70
See also
Phonograph records—Cantatas
CANTERBURY, Arthur Michael Ramsey, abp of. See Ramsey, A. M.
CANTERBURY, William Laud, abp of. See Laud, W.
CANTERBURY cathedral. See Cathedrals— England
CANTERBURY pilgrimage. See Pilgrims and pilgrimages
CANTON, China
Canton under communism, by E. Vogel. Review Nation 210:506-8 Ap 27 '70. R. M. Pfeffer
Tremble! Intensely tremble! excerpts from The dragon wakes. C. Hibbert. il por Horizon 12:114-19 Sum '70
CANTON, Ohio
Blow your leaves and bale them. F. Elaass. il Am City 85:38 O '70
More than just a building. L. C. Dubs. il Am City 85:119+ Je '70
CANTORS, Jewish
Cantors in Curaçao; American conference of cantors, Curaçao. il Newsweek 76:102 Jl 13 '70
CANTRELL, Burton Neal
Misconceptions concerning nuclear weapons. Chr Cent 87:1219-20 O 14 '70
CANTRELL, Clyde H. See Punke, H. H. jt. auth.
CANTWELL, Mary
Eat. See issues of Mademoiselle
Journey. il Mlle 71:184-5+ S '70
CANTWELL, Robert
Booktalk. Sports Illus 32:8 Ap 13 '70
Real McCoy. por Sports Illus 32:52-6+ Je 1 '70
CANVASSING
Britannica rues a wave of zeal. Bsns W p34-5 N 21 '70
FTC order against Crowell-Collier upheld. Pub W 197:43 Je 15 '70
FTC renews attack on door-to-door-book-selling. Pub W 198:50-1 Jl 27 '70
Proposes cooling-off period for door-to-door sales. S. Wagner. Pub W 198:32 O 19 '70
CANVASSING, Political. See Political campaigns
CANYONS
Down, down into Idaho's Bruneau. il Sunset 145:56 O '70
See also
Grand Canyon
Hells Canyon
CAPACITANCE meters. See Electric meters
CAPACITIVE discharge ignition. See Automobile engines—Ignition
CAPE BRETON ISLAND

Historic houses, etc.
Louisbourg, the forgotten fortress. J. Lunn. il Antiques 97:872-9 Je '70
CAPE COD
Island consciousness. B. B. Chamberlain. il Natur Hist 79:114-15+ Ag '70
Some fancy capework. H. Sutton. il Sat R 53:38+ S 5 '70
To the tip of Cape Cod. B. Schill and B. Schill. il Yachting 128:56-8 Ag '70
CAPE HATTERAS NATIONAL SEASHORE RECREATION AREA
Dune country. B. Schill and B. Schill. il Yachting 127:72-3 F '70
CAPE hunting dogs. See Wild dogs
CAPE KENNEDY. See Kennedy, Cape
CAPE marigolds
Cape marigold. W. Radcliffe. Horticulture 48:8 Ap '70

This ground cover is quick, it's good-looking, and it's ready to be discovered; African daisy, osteospermum. il Sunset 145:221 O '70
CAPE VINCENT, N.Y.
Fisheries story at Cape Vincent. A. W. Bromley. il Cons 24:16-17 Ag '69
CAPE VINCENT Great Lakes fisheries research station. See New York (state)—Conservation department
CAPELL, Frank A.
New Jersey: the state of Mafia; attempt to discredit F. B. Lacey. F. J. Cook. il Nation 210:561-3+ My 11 '70 *
CAPEN, Barbara M.
Planning the perennial garden. il Horticulture 48:20-1+ N '70
CAPENER, Ted R.
Low-cost veal from grain. il Farm J 94: 54P+ F '70
CAPERS, Donna
Higher country. R. D. Campbell. Chr Cent 87: 1355-6 N 11 '70 *
CAPERS, Hedge
Higher country. R. D. Campbell. Chr Cent 87:1355-6 N 11 '70 *
CAPILLARITY
See also
Surface tension
CAPITAL
Bottomless pit of capital demand. il Bsns W p 158-60+ O 17 '70
See also
Free enterprise
Liquidity (economics)
Small business—Finance
CAPITAL, Venture
Has the bear market killed venture capital? il Forbes 105:28-30+ Je 15 '70
He feeds capital to the computers; Data science ventures. por Bsns W p28 Ag 29 '70
Improving on the general; Data science ventures, inc. por Forbes 105:78+ Ap 15 '70
Money is there. pors Forbes 106:45-6 D 1 '70
Singer: a new way to make money? A. Hershman. por Duns 95:22-3+ Ja '70
Smart money draws a crowd. il Bsns W p92-5 F 28 '70
Take-charge guy in venture capital. pors Bsns W p72 O 24 '70
Venture capital, corporation style. il Forbes 106:41-2 Ag 1 '70
Venture capitalist with a solid intuition. il por Bsns W p 102-3 My 30 '70
What do you do with $81 million por Forbes 160:42+ Jl 15 '70
CAPITAL area modern dance council, inc, Saratoga. See Dance schools
CAPITAL cities broadcasting corporation
Another exclusive; acquisition of the San Juan star. Newsweek 76:90 Jl 13 '70
CAPITAL gains tax. See Income tax—Capital gains tax
CAPITAL investments
Business keeps its planning buoyant. il Bsns W p25 Mr 14 '70
Business spenders keep a steady pace; with editorial comment. il Bsns W p20-1, 114 N 7 '70
Capacity burden. il Fortune 81:20 Je '70
Capital investment paradox: boom-time outlays, recession-time overcapacity. il Fortune 82:20 D '70
Capital spending is the key. R. Lekachman. por Duns 95:9 Mr '70
500 biggest corporations by capital expenditures; with directory. Forbes 105:111-12+ My 15 '70
Last prop gives way. il Fortune 81:15-16 Mr '70
More spending to automate. il Bsns W p54-5 N 28 '70
New ways to get more. Time 95:66-7 F 2 '70
Pursestrings are drawn tighter. Bsns W p24-5 Jl 18 '70
Spenders shrug off the danger signs. il Bsns W p 13-14 My 2 '70
Spring tonic. Newsweek 75:86 Mr 23 '70
Weighing risk in capacity expansion. J. R. Virts and R. W. Garrett. il Harvard Bsns R 48:132-41 My '70
We're still cutting back; comments of members of the Dun's presidents' panel. G. R. Rosen. il Duns 96:27-30 Ag '70
See also
Art as an investment
Industrial expansion
Investment tax credit
CAPITAL management corporation
Investing with tax dollars. il Bsns W p66+ Ja 17 '70
CAPITAL market. See Money market
CAPITAL punishment
Clemency in Arkansas. por Time 97:50 Ja 11 '71
Death row; a new kind of suspense. il Newsweek 77:23-4+ Ja 11 '71

CAPITAL punishment—*Continued*
Delay on the death penalty; case of W. Maxwell. il por Time 95:60 Je 15 '70
Matter of life or death. Nations Bsns 58:28 N '70
Primitive relic: death sentence. E. Gertz. Nation 212:48-50 Ja 11 '71
See also
Hanging
CAPITAL spending. See Capital investments
CAPITALISM
Man who would make everybody richer; Kelsonian theory. il por Time 95:72-3 Je 29 '70
Myths the liberals live by. P. McGouldrick. il Nat R 22:151-3+ F 10 '70
See also
Black capitalism
Free enterprise
CAPITALISM and communism. See Communism and democracy
CAPITALISTS and financiers
Mysterious Mr Michael. A. A. Butkus. il por Duns 96:29-32 N '70
CAPITAN, El (mountain) See Yosemite Valley
CAPITOL industries, inc.
Capitol industries is off on another spin. il Bsns W p 146-7 Ap 25 '70
See also
Capitol records, inc.
CAPITOL radio engineering institute
Engineering level opportunities for you. A. W. Burawa. il Pop Electr 32:76-80 F '70
CAPITOL records, inc.
Capitol records alters airfreight usage. Aviation W 93:106 O 26 '70
How Capitol records plays the market. Bsns W p 147 Ap 25 '70
CAPITOL REEF NATIONAL MONUMENT
Capitol Reef: extended monument. D. S. Follows. il Nat Parks & Con Mag 44:4-9 Jl '70
CAPITOLS
See also subhead Capitol under names of countries, states, etc. e.g. Minnesota—Capitol
CAPITULATIONS, Military
How hostilities have ended; peace treaties and alternatives. Q. Wright. bibliog f Ann Am Acad 392:51-61 N '70
War termination and conflict theory: value premises, theories, and policies. B. A. Carroll. bibliog f Ann Am Acad 392:14-29 N '70
CAPLAN, S. Roy. See Weinstein, J. N. jt. auth.
CAPLEY, G. W.
Pastime returns to the coast. il Yachting 127:54-5+ My '70
CAPLIN, Morris D.
Invaluable resource: the school volunteer. bibliog Clear House 45:10-14 S '70
CAPLIN, Mortimer M.
Five ears in the Zeckendorf labyrinth. il pors Bsns W p98-9+ Ap 25 '70 *
No privacy for 1040. Time 95:19 Ap 27 '70 *
CAPOBIANCO, Tito
Whence a production? interview. ed. by F. Rizzo. il pors Opera N 34:26-9 Mr 21 '70
CAPON, Robert Farrar
Let us exalt earth, not heaven. Redbook 136:62-3+ D '70
Priest's wise and witty view of sex without guilt. por Redbook 135:73+ My '70
Steps in the right direction. il Sports Illus 33:46-8+ Ag 31 '70; Same abr. Read Digest 97:124-6 D '70
What a priest sees in astrology. por Redbook 135:63+ Ag '70
CAPONI, Donna
Hanging in for women's lib; B. Gilbert. il por Sports Illus 33:49 Jl 13 '70 *
CAPOTE, Truman
Sweeter options of John D. MacArthur and Truman Capote. T. Burke. il pors Esquire 74:258+ D '70 *
CAPOTOSTO, John
Batting trainer. il Mech Illus 66:82-3+ My '70
Central vacuum cleaning system. il Mech Illus 66:132-4 O '70
Colorful storage cubes. il Mech Illus 66:80+ D '70
Drive-thru snowmobile shelter. il Mech Illus 66:108-10 N '70
Electric control for garage doors. il Mech Illus 66:114-15 N '70
Fun for the family: bumper-pool table you can build. il Pop Mech 133:146-9+ Je '70
Hideaway office. il Mech Illus 66:102+ S '70
Laundry hideaway. il Mech Illus 66:114-15 O '70
Ping table. il Mech Illus 66:108-9 Ag '70

Put the squeeze on trash. il Mech Illus 66:101+ Je '70
Stow-away home show center. il Mech Illus 66:116-18 Ap '70
—and Connor, J. R.
Study-storage wall. il Mech Illus 66:91-3 N '70
CAPOTOSTO, Rosario
Blow it up big. il Pop Mech 134:155-7 N '70
For nightime beauty, illuminate! il Mech Illus 66:90-2+ Je '70
How to turn a wood vase that holds water. il Pop Sci 196:179-81 Ja '70
Laminate a lawn-chair frame. il Pop Sci 196:79-83+ Ap '70
Put life in any room with a rock-garden waterfall. il Pop Mech 134:148-51 D '70
CAPP, Al
Advice to Princeton alumni; excerpts from address, 1970. il Nat R 22:994-6+ S 22 '70

about
Al Capp at bay. W. F. Buckley, jr. Nat R 22:1124 O 20 '70 *
Cappital punishment. R. Woodley. il Esquire 74:160-1+ N '70 *
Missionary to the campus. il por Newsweek 75:79 Je 22 '70 *
CAPPADOCIA
Keeping house in a Cappadocian cave. J. S. Blair. il Nat Geog 138:126-46 Jl '70
CAPRI
Capri: Italy's enchanted rock. C. Mitchell. il Nat Geog 137:794-809 Je '70
CAPSULES
Biochemical microcapsules. Sci N 97:389 Ap 18 '70
CAPTIVE nations week
Time to remember. Nat R 22:774-5 Jl 28 '70
CAR, James D.
Alaska's fifteenth festival. Hi Fi 20:MA26+ S '70
CAR games; story. See Conroy, F.
CAR operating costs. See Automobiles—Cost of operation
CAR radios. See Automobiles—Radio equipment
CAR stereo tapes. See Automobiles—Tape equipment
CARAMEL
You make a mess, or you make magic. il Sunset 144:158-9 F '70
CARAMOOR festivals. See Music festivals—New York (state)
CARAS, Roger
Source of the thunder; excerpt. il Audubon 72:82-4+ N '70
CARAVELLE (restaurant) See New York (city) —Hotels, restaurants, etc.
CARAVELLO, Ed
They shared a victory over heroin. B. Davidson. il pors Good H 171:102-3+ O '70 *
CARBACHOL
Lateral hypothalmic control of killing: evidence for a cholinoceptive mechanism. D. E. Smith and others. bibliog il Science 167:900-1 F 6 '70
CARBARYL. See Insecticides
CARBENICILLIN
Penicillin and patents; combating pseudomonas. Sci N 98:164 Ag 22 '70
CARBIDE tools. See Cutting tools
CARBIDES
See also
Titanium carbide
Tungsten carbide
CARBO, Bernie
Red menace from staid Cincy. W. Leggett. pors Sports Illus 32:24-7 Ap 20 '70 *
CARBOHYDRATE metabolism
Alanine: key role in gluconeogenesis. P. Felig and others. bibliog il Science 167:1003-4 F 13 '70
CARBOHYDRATES in the body
See also
Carbohydrate metabolism
CARBON
Carbon cycle. B. Bolin. il Sci Am 223:124-32 bibliog(p263-4) S '70
Concentration and isotopic composition of carbon and sulfur in Apollo 11 lunar samples. I. R. Kaplan and J. W. Smith. bibliog il Science 167:541-3 Ja 30 '70
News; glass-like carbon for rocket nozzles. il Space World G-4-76:48-9 Ap '70
Pyrolysis-hydrogen flame ionization detection of organic carbon in a lunar sample. R. D. Johnson and C. C. Davis. bibliog il Science 167:759-60 Ja 30 '70
Total carbon and nitrogen abundances in lunar samples. C. B. Moore and others. bibliog il Science 167:495-7 Ja 30 '70

CARBON—*Continued*

Isotopes

Carbon isotope fractionation in the Fischer-Tropsch synthesis and in meteorites. M. S. Lancet and E. Anders. bibliog il Science 170:980-2 N 27 '70

Carbon-13 in Black Sea waters and implications for the origin of hydrogen sulfide. W. G. Deuser. bibliog il Science 168:1575-7 Je 26 '70

CARBON compounds

Apollo 11 lunar science conference: organic chemistry; symposium. bibliog il Science 167:751-80 Ja 30 '70
See also
Fluorocarbons
Hydrocarbons

CARBON dioxide

Atmosphere: a clouded horizon. E. K. Peterson. il Environ 12:32-9 Ap '70; Reply with rejoinder. L. Van Valen. 12:39, 44-5 D '70

Carbon cycle. B. Bolin. il Sci Am 223:124-32 bibliog(p263-4) S '70

Water in the earth's mantle: melting curves of basalt-water and basalt-water-carbon dioxide. R. E. T. Hill and A. L. Boettcher. bibliog il Science 167:980-2 F 13 '70

Physiological effects

Unified account of the variable effects of carbon dioxide on nerve cells. J. L. Walker, jr. and A. M. Brown. bibliog il Science 167:1502-4 Mr 13 '70

CARBON monoxide

Annals of medicine: a woman with a headache. B. Roueché. New Yorker 45:60-8 Ja 31 '70

Auto pollution: a threat to health. Todays Health 48:55 N '70

Chemical reactivity of atmospheric carbon monoxide. Chem 43:22 N '70

How carbon monoxide affects your driving. W. S. Bacon. il Pop Sci 196:72-5+ Ja '70

Invisible killer. il Time 95:58 Ja 26 '70

Medical sciences; International conference on biological effects of carbon monoxide. Sci N 97:96 Ja 24 '70

No consensus on CO research. Sci N 97:59 Ja 17 '70

Ocean: a natural source of carbon monoxide. J. W. Swinnerton and others. bibliog il Science 167:984-6 F 13 '70

CARBON tetrachloride

Use caution with carbon tet. R. G. Hildreth. Sci Digest 68:48 D '70

CARBONADOS. See Diamonds, Industrial

CARBONATED beverages. See Beverages

CARBONATES
See also
Lithium carbonate

CARBONDALE, Ill.

More than a dozen things HEW is doing in the Midwestern town. il U S News 69:32-3 D 7 '70

CARBONIC anhydrase. See Enzymes

CARBONIUM compounds

Stable carbonium ions in solution. G. A. Olah. bibliog il Science 168:1298-311 Je 12 '70

CARBORUNDUM company

Trying a two-pronged strategy. il Bsns W p69+ D 19 '70

CARBOXYLIC acids

Aurintricarboxylic acid and initiation factors of wheat embryo. A. Marcus and others. bibliog il Science 167:1735-6 Mr 27 '70

CARBURETORS

Carter's little liver pills; Thermo-Quad. J. Thawley. il Hot Rod 23:52 Ap '70

Deuce of a carb. J. Thawley. il Hot Rod 23:67 D '70

How much carburetor do you need? R. Huntington. il Pop Mech 134:144-7+ N '70

Openings for everyone. S. Kelly. il Hot Rod 23:34-9 Je '70

Strictly for stocks; accelerator pump. J. Dianna. il Hot Rod 23:110 O '70

Way-out Webers; bolt-on for Beetles. il Hot Rod 24:90-2 Ja '71

CARCINOGENIC substances. See Cancer producing substances

CARCINOIDS. See Tumors

CARD catalogs (for libraries) See Catalogs, Library

CARD tables. See Tables

CARDENOLIDES

Heart poisons and the monarch. M. Rothschild and B. Ford. il Natur Hist 79:36-7 Ap '70
See also
Cardiac glycosides

CARDER, Brooks, and Berkowitz, Kenneth

Rats' preference for earned in comparison with free food. il Science 67:1273-4 F 27 '70

CARDIAC diseases. See Heart—Diseases

CARDIAC glycosides

Cardiac glycosides and distastefulness: some observations on the palatability spectrum of butterflies. S. S. Duffey. bibliog il Science 169:78-9 Jl 3 '70

CARDIAC muscle. See Heart—Muscle

CARDIAC neuroses. See Neuroses

CARDIAC pacers. See Pacemaker, Artificial (heart)

CARDINALS

Burden of age. Commonweal 93:291-2 D 18 '70

Burdens of age; papal decree on retirement and papal election voting. Newsweek 76:47 D 7 '70

Of many things; age limit on cardinals. D. R. Campion. America 123:inside cover D 12 '70

CARDINET, George H. jr

Trail riding. il Parks & Rec 5:43-4 F '70

CARDIOVASCULAR strokes. See Heart—Diseases

CARDIOVASCULAR system

Diseases

Vascular lesions: possible pathogenetic basis of the generalized Shwartzman reaction. E. Gaynor and others. bibliog il Science 170:986-8 N 27 '70

CARDIOVASCULAR system (insects)

Nervous control of the heart during thoracic temperature regulation in a sphinx moth. B. Heinrich. bibliog il Science 169:606-7 Ag 7 '70

CARDON, Charlotte M.

Steward observatory's new 90-inch reflector. il R Pop Astron 63:7-9 Ag '69

CARDOZO, Arlene

Redbook reader Mrs Richard Cardozo: a guest at her own table. il por Redbook 134:104-8+ Ap '70 *

CARDOZO, Benjamin Nathan

Notes and comment. New Yorker 46:33 Ap 4 '70 *

CARDS

Jokers are trumps. D. Powills. il Hobbies 75:152-3 O '70

Playing cards. D. Powills. See issues of Hobbies
See also
Bridge (game)
Standard packaging corporation—Stancraft products division
Tarot

Collectors and collecting

Searching for a hobby? reprint. D. Powills. Hobbies 75:141+ Jl '70

History

Playing cards & their diverse effects on man. J. Paulsen. il Hobbies 75:150-1 Ap; 150-1 My '70

Playing cards of Spain. D. Powills. il Hobbies 75:150-2 Mr '70

Story of the pasteboards. D. Powills. Hobbies 75:148-9 Je '70

CARDS, Catalog. See Catalog cards

CARDS, Greeting. See Greeting cards

CAREER literature. See Vocational literature

CAREER switching. See Occupational mobility

CAREERS. See Occupations; Professions

CAREERS for women. See Woman—Employment; Woman—Occupations

CARETTA caretta. See Turtles

CAREW, Thomas J. and others

Lack of coincidence between neural and behavioral manifestations of cortical spreading depression. bibliog il Science 169:1339-42 S 25 '70

CAREW, Topper

Interview with Topper Carew; ed. by W. Roberts. il Sat R 53:46-8 Jl 18 '70

CAREY, James W. and Quirk, J. J.

Mythos of the electronic revolution. Am Scholar 39:219-41, 395-424 Spr-Sum '70

CAREY-Thomas award

Knopf wins Carey-Thomas publishing award. Pub W 197:129 Je 8 '70

CAREY transportation, inc.

Pan Am-Carey pact approved; bus service to Kennedy airport. Aviation W 92:34 Ja 19 '70

CARGAS, Harry J.

Death comes to a Nobel prize winner. il America 123:234-6 O 3 '70

Death is alone; excerpt from Death and hope. il Cath World 210-369-72 Mr '70

TV violence and sports. America 122:610-11 Je 6 '70

CARGO airlines. See Air freight service

CARGO ships. See Freight vessels

CARIBAIR. See Airlines—Puerto Rico

CARIBBEAN-Atlantic airlines, inc. See Airlines
—Puerto Rico
CARIBBEAN REGION
Beautiful, seething Caribbean; symposium. il
Look 34:17-28 Mr 10 '70
Islands of the Caribbean. H. Mitchell. bib-
liog f Cur Hist 58:107-10+ F '70
Photographer's West Indies. B. Binzen. il
Travel & Camera 33:55-9 Ja '70
See also
Arts and crafts—Caribbean Region
Cruising—Caribbean Region
Geology—Caribbean Region
Nutrition problems—Caribbean Region
Swan Islands
Tourist trade—Caribbean Region
Yachts and yachting—Caribbean Region

Description and travel
Caribbean island-hopping. M. Z. Lenci.
Travel & Camera 33:72-5 Ja '70
Crazy, tricky, wonderful sport of island hop-
ping. N. Aubuchon. il Pop Sci 196:71-3+
Mr '70
Great ports of call. F. Rohr, jr. il Travel &
Camera 33:50-4+ Ja '70
Grooving in the Caribbean. L. Gage. il pors
Esquire 73:95+ F '70
Two kids and a cat. P. Smyth. il Motor B
126:58-60+ N '70
Welcome to the Caribbean. L. A. Copersino.
il Home Gard 75:56-7 Ja '70
Where to cop out in the Caribbean. B. Gil-
lam. Mlle 71:138-9+ My '70

Negroes
Black militancy in balmy waters. il Newsweek 75:40 My 4 '70

Politics
Turmoil in the Caribbean. il Newsweek 75:39-
40 My 4 '70

Riots
"Tourism is whorism" il Time 96:24+ Ag 3 '70

Social conditions
"Tourism is whorism" il Time 96:24+ Ag
3 '70
CARIBBEAN SEA
Depth-finding by eye-ball; water's depth is
color coded. E. S. Maloney. Motor B 126:
29-30 N '70
CARIBOU
Migration of the barren-ground caribou. J.
P. Kelsall. il Natur Hist 79:98-106 Ag '70
CARIBOU hunting
Don't shoot the first caribou. G. G. Sikes. il
Outdoor Life 146:58-9+ N '70
CARICATURES and cartoons
Cartoonist Q's. J. Markow. See issues of
Writer's digest
Credit. J. Noonan. Cath World 211:128-9 Je
'70
Going for the jugular; political cartoons of
W. W. Sanders. il por Newsweek 76:55 S
28 '70
Jules Feiffer. J. Feiffer. New Repub 162:19
My 23; 163:22 N 7; 21 D 5 '70
Power of the great outdoors; character of
Mark Trail, teaching conservation practices.
E. B. Dodd. il Am For 76:14-15 O '70
Watch for these birds; editors. R. Jenkins.
il Writers Digest 50:52-3 Je '70
See also
Comics (books, strips, etc)
also subhead Caricatures and cartoons
under various subjects, e.g. Pollution
—Caricatures and cartoons
CARIES, Dental. See Dental caries
CARINGELLA, Charles
Build a three-channel time receiver. il Pop
Electr 33:33-5+ D '70
CARL, David L.
Project mobilization. Clear House 44:519-22
My '70
CARLAN, Charles
Small cities can use big machines. il Am
City 85:117+ Ap '70
CARLETON, R. Milton
Should you grow your own vegetables? il
Home Gard 57:34-42 F '70
CARLETON, William G.
Excerpt from article in Yale review, October
1968. Cong Digest 49:149+ My '70
Government's historical role in conservation.
Cur Hist 58:321-7+ Je '70
CARLETON college, Northfield, Minn.
Silent generation meets the class of 1970. M.
Gartner. il Sat R 53:52-3+ Ag 15 '70
CARLIN, Jerome E.
Store front lawyers in San Francisco. il
Trans-Action 7:64-74 Ap '70
CARLIN, Robert E.
Return of the Rockford. il Flying 87:52-7 N '70

CARLISLE, Edith M.
Silicon; a possible factor in bone calcifica-
tion. bibliog il Science 167:279-80 Ja 16 '70
CARLISLE, G. R.
What are heated soybeans worth? il Farm J
94:H18 Mr '70
CARLISLE, Norman
How to speed up your reactions. il Mech
Illus 66:60-1+ Ja '70
They handle the hot stuff. il Pop Mech 133:
106-9+ F '70
CARLISLE, Thomas John
Job's wife; poem. Sat R 53:22 Jl 4 '70
Vacancy; poem. Chr Cent 87:111 Ja 28 '70
CARLISLE Indian industrial school, Carlisle,
Pa.
Great white father's little red Indian school.
D. T. Chapman. il Am Heritage 22:48-53+
D '70
CARLOS, Walter
Moog is more than a vogue. C. S. Wren. il
por Look 34:24+ Ap 7 '70 *
CARLSEN, G. Robert
Interest rate is rising. Engl J 59:655-9 My '70
CARLSEN, Karen L.
Is it time to move the rhubarb? il Org
Gard & Farm 17:100-1 Ap '70
CARLSON, Edward Elmer
Loner who lost. pors Time 97:69 Ja 4 '71 *
New boss at United; into the black? il por
Newsweek 77:50 Ja 4 '71 *
CARLSON, Elliot
Education and industry; troubled partner-
ship. il Sat R 53:45-7+ Ag 15 '70
CARLSON, Jack J.
Kaiser's black gold. T. J. Murray. por Duns
96:66-7 Jl '70 *
CARLSON, James
New generation Christian bookstore. il por
Pub W 198:28-9 N 30 '70
CARLSON, James E.
Economy, ecology, and zero population
growth. Arch Rec 148:59-60 Ag '70
Regions in perspective. il Arch Rec 148:85 S;
93 O '70
CARLSON, Leland H.
(comp) Articles and other books received;
British Commonwealth and Ireland. See is-
sues of American historical review
CARLSON, Peter S.
Induction and isolation of auxotrophic mu-
tants in somatic cell cultures of nicotiana
tabacum. bibliog il Science 168:487-9 Ap 24
'70
CARLSON, Ruth Kearney
Asian folktales; lively, recent editions. bib-
liog il por Wilson Lib Bul 45:372-83 D '70
CARLSON, Toby N. See Prospero, J. M. jt.
auth.
CARLSON, William S.
Ice survey by the U.S. coast guard. bibliog il
Science 168:396-7 Ap 17 '70
CARLSSON, Erik
Motor trend interview. pors Motor T 22:85-6+
F '70
CARLSSON, Pat (Moss)
Motor trend interview. por Motor T 23:70+
Ja '70
CARLTON, Lillian E.
Elegy written in the recreation room. Horn
Bk 46:64-5 F '70
CARLYLE LAKE, Ill. See Lakes, Artificial
CARMEN; opera. Bizet, G.
CARMER, Carl
Panorama of Mormon life; with paintings
by C. C. A. Christensen. il Art in Am 58:
52-65 My '70
CARMODY, John T.
Rahner's spiritual theology. America 123:345-
7 O 31 '70
CARMODY, Thomas J
Transistor base-emitter junctions for voltage
regulation. il Electr World 84:90 S '70
CARMOY, Guy de
France and the Atlantic community. Cur Hist
58:269-75 My '70
CARNATION company
Uncontented Carnation. il Forbes 106:44-5 Jl 1
'70
CARNEGIE, Andrew
Andrew Carnegie, by J. F. Wall. Review
Bsns W p8 O 10 '70. R. Craib *
Sat R 53:34-5 N 21 '70. M. R. Konvitz *
Mister Carnegie's library; a librarian's
memories of her librarian mother in Moberly,
Mo. C. E. Werkley. il por Am Heritage 21:
65-8 F '70 *
Rich man's burden, and how Andrew Car-
negie unloaded it; excerpts from Andrew
Carnegie. J. F. Wall. il pors Am Heritage
21:58-67+ O '70 *

CARNEGIE, Andrew—*Continued*
What Princeton really needed; excerpt from Andrew Carnegie. J. F. Wall. il pors Am Heritage 21:91-2 Je '70 *
You can take a boy out of Dunfermline. . ; excerpts from Andrew Carnegie. J. F. Wall. il por Horizon 12:80-3 Aut '70 *

CARNEGIE commission on higher education
Blueprint for reform of medical education. il Sci N 98:363-4 N 7 '70
Calling Dr. reform. Newsweek 76:70 N 9 '70
Calls for flexibility. Sat R 53:58-9 D 19 '70
Colleges open to all: Carnegie commission proposal. U S News 68:26 Mr 16 '70
Higher education's financial crisis. R. H. Smith. Pub W 198:20 D 14 '70
Less college for more people. Time 96:60 D 7 '70
Medical education: Carnegie panel urges expansion, acceleration. J. Walsh. Science 170:713-14 N 13 '70
New plan: college degree in three years. il U S News 69:64 D 7 '70
New role for community colleges. il Sat R 53: 54-5 Jl 18 '70
Open the doors: report on community colleges. il Newsweek 76:77 Jl 6 '70
Toward equal access to college. Sat R 53:73 Ap 18 '70

CARNEGIE hero fund commission
U.S. journal: Long Island; H. Eyman, hero investigator on Adrian Hoek-John Hughes case. C. Trillin. New Yorker 46:32-6+ Jl 18 '70

CARNEGIE libraries. See Libraries—United States

CARNEGIE-Mellon university, Pittsburgh
Doctor of arts degree. H. G. Stever. Science 170:587 N 6 '70

Graduate school of industrial administration
Making a B-school more relevant. il Bsns W p58-60 D 5 '70

CARNEIRO, Robert L.
Theory of the origin of the state. bibliog Science 169:733-8; 170:931 Ag 21, N 27 '70

CARNER, JoAnne (Gunderson)
Hard day's week for a new lady pro. P. Ryan. il por Sports Illus 32:44-5 F 23 '70 *

CARNEY, Francis
California's club movement. Nation 210:526-30 Mr 4 '70

CARNEY, M. K.
Economics of the Black manifesto. por Chr Cent 87:171-4 F 11 '70

CARNEY, Richard P.
When Richard Carney buys goldfish. por Forbes 106:33-4 Ag 1 '70 *

CARNIVAL
Bacchanal in Bavaria: Fasching. P. Moore. il Sat R 53:62+ S 12 '70

CARNIVAL; story. See Walker, T.

CARNIVALS (circus) See Sideshows

CARNIVORA
Poaching on Tarzan's turf; hunting habits; study findings of George B. Schaller and Gordon R. Lowther. il Newsweek 76:54-5 Ag 17 '70

CARNOW, Bertram W.
Pollution invites disease. il Sat R 53:38-40+ Jl 4 '70

CARNOY, Judith Milgrom
Kaiser: you pay your money and you take your chances. il Ramp Mag 9:26-31 N '70

CARO, Anthony
Caro. G. Baro. il pors Vogue 155:208-11+ My '70 *
Closing the gaps. J. Russell. il Art N 69:37-9 Mr '70 *

CAROL sing; story. See Updike, J.

CAROLINA Cougars (basketball team) See Basketball teams

CAROLINE ISLANDS
See also
Palau (islands)
PulUwat (island)

CAROTENE
Safe from the sun; beta-carotene treatments. Newsweek 75:76-7 Je 22 '70

CAROTENOIDS
See also
Lycopene

CAROUSELS. See Merry-go-rounds

CARP fishing
Big fish in town. R. Gilsvik. il por Outdoor Life 145:72-3+ Je '70
Carp for the bow. G. H. Gillelan. il por Outdoor Life 145:146+ My '70
Roll call for carp. J. Stabile. il Outdoor Life 146:42-3+ Jl '70

CARPENTER, Charlotte
Magic we almost missed. il Farm J 94:44 Ja '70

CARPENTER, David O. See Barker, J. L. jt. auth.

CARPENTER, Elizabeth
Gooey dish of loyalty pudding. P. Benchley. il Life 68:14 Ja 30 '70
Silent majority. il McCalls 97:40-1+ Jl '70

CARPENTER, Richard A.
How Congress focuses on the environment. Sat R 53:43 Ag 1 '70
Information for decisions in environmental policy. il Science 168:1316-22 Je 12 '70

CARPENTER, Scott
Ingenious tools work for you beneath the sea. il por Pop Sci 196:56-7 Je '70
Scuba diving for fun. il por Pop Sci 196:51+ F '70
Undersea colonies: how soon? interview. pors U S News 68:39-40 Mr 30 '70

CARPENTERS
See also
Cabinetmakers

CARPENTERS; drama. See Tesich, S.

CARPENTRAS, France
Pope's Jews. por Time 96:49 Ag 24 '70

CARPENTRY
See also
Cabinet work
Joints (carpentry)
Woodworking

CARPER, Jean
Case of the yellow killer. Todays Health 48:53-4+ S '70
Cirrhosis: a growing threat to life. Todays Health 48:26-7+ F '70
Danger of cancer in food. il Sat R 53:47-9+ S 5 '70
Secretary Finch is not alarmed. Nation 210: 262-5 Mr 9 '70
Truth in life insurance. il Nation 212:45-8 Ja 11 '71

CARPET cleaning. See Rugs and carpets—Care

CARPETS. See Rugs and carpets

CARR, Albert Z.
Can an executive afford a conscience? excerpt from The executive conscience. bibliog f il Harvard Bsns R 48:58-64 Jl '70

CARR, Archie
Green sea turtles in peril. il Nat Parks & Con Mag 44:19-24 Ap '70

CARR, William G.
New ideas in an ancient land. il Todays Ed 59:28-9 N '70

CARR, William Henry
Sam and Eloise bobcat; letter. il Am For 76: 40-1 S '70

CARRELL, H. L. and others
Fluorocitrate inhibition of aconitase: relative configuration of inhibitory isomer by X-ray crystallography. bibliog il Science 170:1412-14 D 25 '70

CARRERA ANDRADE, Jorge
Decade of my poetry. il por Américas 22:9-13 Jl '70

CARRIAGES
See also
Coaches and coaching

CARRICK, Robert W.
They have to come to Pete. il por Yachting 127:52+ Je '70
Twelve-meter story. il Yachting 128:50-2+ Ag '70
Where do old Cup boats go? il Yachting 128: 60-1+ S '70

CARRIERS
Transportation needs a drastic overhaul; with editorial comment. il Bsns W p68-9+, 116 N 14 '70
Transportation; with yardsticks of management performance. il Forbes 105:179-80 Ja 1 '70; 107:168-9 Ja 1 '71
See also
Forwarding companies
Transportation

CARRIERS (animals)
Getting your dog there, and back again. J. R. Falk. il Field & S 74:222-4+ Ap '70

CARRIERS of infection
Case of the disappearing cook; Typhoid Mary Mallon. M. Sufrin. il pors Am Heritage 21: 37-43 Ag '70
See also
Animals as carriers of infection
Flies as carriers of infection

CARRIGHAR, Sally
War is not in our genes. il UNESCO Courier 23:40-5 Ag '70

CARRILLO, Julián
Carrillo from CRI, an important release on several counts. P. L. Miller. Am Rec G 36:274 D '69

CARRINGTON, Elsie R. and Jacobs, Evelyn
How the fetus is nourished. Redbook 134:24+
F '70

CARROLL, Berenice A.
War termination and conflict theory; value
premises, theories, and policies. bibliog f
Ann Am Acad 392:14-29 N '70

CARROLL, Diahann
Tale of two Julias; interview, ed. by Mrs
M. W. Evers. il pors Ladies Home J 87:
60+ My '70

about

Changes. R. L. Shayon. Sat R 53:46 Ap 18
'70 *

CARROLL, Gena
Dream for three. D. Hering. il pors Dance
Mag 44:72-6 Ap '70 *

CARROLL, George A.
Spar telescope of Lockheed solar observatory.
il Sky & Tel 40:10-13 Jl '70

CARROLL, Hanson. See Robinson, J. B. jt.
auth.

CARROLL, Irwin R.
Monolithic multipliers. il por Electr World
84:49-51 Jl '70

CARROLL, James
Campus ministry as imagination. il Cath World
212:88-91 N '70
Dear companions; poem. Cath World 212:34
O '70
Hard prayer; poem. Cath World 212:64 N '70
I am a man of the past; poem. Cath World
212:188 Ja '71

CARROLL, John S.
Reveille out West. New Repub 162:12-13 Mr
7 '70

CARROLL, Lewis, pseud.
Alice in Wonderland; dramatization. See
Gregory, A.

about

Alice for adolescents. M. A. D'Ambrosio.
Engl J 59:1074-5+ N '70 *

CARROLL, Ronald L.
Calculating strip-line impedance. il Electr
World 84:31 S '70
Semiconductor injection lasers. il Electr
World 83:45-7 Mr '70
Simple linear laboratory-quality ohmmeter. il
Electr World 83:60 My '70

CARROLL, Wallace
Murder of English; adaptation of address. Ed
Digest 36:29-31 O '70

CARRUTH, Eleanor
Kaufman & Broad's private housing boom.
il Fortune 82:119 Jl '70

CARRUTH, Hayden
Baler; poem. Nation 211:478 N 9 '70

CARRUTHERS, Ben F.
Brazilian duo. il Travel 134:46-9+ D '70
Change in Buenos Aires. il Opera N 34:20-1
My 16 '70
Historic route through Ethiopia. il Travel
133:38-41+ Ap '70

CARRUTHERS, George R. See Henry, R. C.
jt. auth.

CARRY, Peter
Baseball (cont) il Sports Illus 32:67+ Ap 6;
50-2 Ap 27; 52+ Je 15; 33:42-3 Jl 13; 47 Jl 20;
48 Ag 17 '70
Basketball. il Sports Illus 33:50-1 Jl 20 '70
Basketball's week (title varies) See issues of
Sports illustrated published during basket-
ball season
Caged, tamed and on a tear. il Sports Illus
32:28-9 My 11 '70
Dreamy times for Mini-bombers. il por Sports
Illus 32:20-2+ Je 22 '70
Head fit for a triple crown. il por Sports
Illus 33:14-15 Ag 3 '70
If you want Tom, easy does it. il pors Sports
Illus 32:28-31 Jl '70
Lacrosse. Sports Illus 32:62-3 My 4; 78 My
25 '70
Mellow wine in a new bottle. il pors Sports
Illus 33:16-19 D 7 '70
Pro basketball. il por Sports Illus 32:55+ Ap
20; 33:66-7 N 2; 68-9 D 14 '70
So some stars fell on Indiana. il Sports Illus
32:16-17 Je 1 '70
Stars earn their stripes. il por Sports Illus
33:22-3 N 30 '70
Surface case of bugs in the rugs. il Sports
Illus 33:40-2+ S 14 '70
These unknown JCs are tomorrow's BMOCs.
Sports Illus 32:40 F 23 '70
Watch out! There are more en route. il
Sports Illus 33:16-17 Ag 31 '70
We have a slight delay in show time. il por
Sports Illus 33:28-9 O 26 '70
Week. Sports Illus 33:43-5 Jl 13; 47 Jl 20; 39-
41 Ag 10; 48-9 Ag 17; 44+ S 7 '70
Yes, Rick, there is a Virginia. pors Sports
Illus 33:16-17 Ag 24 '70

CARS (automobiles) See Automobiles
CARSON, Christopher
King of the mountain men. por Sr Schol 95:
11 O 13 '69 *

CARSON, Clarice
Best foot forward; interview. ed. by R.
Zachary. por Opera N 34:14 F 14 '70

CARSON, Hampton L.
Chromosome tracers of the origin of species.
bibliog il Science 168:1414-18 Je 19 '70

CARSON, Johnny
Here's Johnny! J. Barthel. il pors Life 68:50-4
Ja 23 '70

CARSON, Kit. See Carson, Christopher

CARSON, Neke
Art of evil. il Esquire 73:112-13 Mr '70 *

CARSON, Rachel
Remembering Rachel Carson. S. A. Briggs. il
por Am For 76:8-11 Jl '70 *
Silent spring: the genesis and the storm; excerpts from Since silent spring. F. Graham,
jr. il por Audubon 72:70-2+ Ja '70

CARSON-Newman college, Jeffrey City, Tenn.
Tale of two schools: playing with moral fire?
E. Plowman and R. Stephens. Chr Today
15:42 D 4 '70

CARSWELL, George Harrold
Carswell: I have an open mind; letter to
Senate judiciary committee. por U S News
68:18 F 16 '70

about

After the Carswell defeat, Nixon's new
strategy. il pors U S News 68:19-21 Ap 20
'70 *
Anatomy of a victory. Nation 210:450 Ap 20
'70 *
Annals of politics. R. E. Harris. New Yorker
46:60-4+ D 5; 53-8+ D 12 '70 *
Approaching the bench. Time 95:11 F 9 '70
Bitter trial of G. Harrold Carswell. il por
Time 95:12-13 Ap 20 '70 *
Carswell file. il por Newsweek 75:29 Mr 16
'70 *
Carswell, ideology & the Supreme court. P.
Steinfels. Commonweal 91:504 F 6 '70
Carswell in trouble. por Time 95:10 Ap 6
'70 *
Carswell nomination: new direction for High
court. il por U S News 68:18-19 F 2 '70 *
Carswell on the stand. il por Newsweek 75:
22-4 F 9 '70
Carswell postscript. N. Cousins. Sat R 53:27
Ap 25 '70 *
Carswell rejected. Sr Schol 96:15 Ap 27 '70 *
Carswell vs. Cramer: Senate fight with na-
tional overtones. pors U S News 69:34-5 S 7
'70 *
Carswell's campaign. por Newsweek 75:21 Je
29 '70 *
Carswell's deed. Newsweek 75:24 F 23 '70 *
Carswell's fiasco. il pors Newsweek 76:39 S
21 '70 *
Counting out Carswell. il por Newsweek 75:
26-7 Ap 6 '70 *
Four crucial nays: why they did it. il Time
95:10-11 Ap 20 '70 *
G for George. Nation 210:99-100 F 2 '70 *
Haynsworth to Carswell. New Repub 162:7-
8 Ja 31 '70 *
Here comes the judge. il por Newsweek 75:19
F 2 '70 *
If you cant' beat em . . . il por Newsweek 75:29
My 4 '70 *
Judge and his past. por Sr Schol 96:13 F 9
'70 *
Judge Carswell's bruises; Senate debate.
Newsweek 75:21 Mr 30 '70 *
Judge Carswell's mediocrity. Nat R 22:429
Ap 21 '70 *
Letter from Washington. R. H. Rovere. New
Yorker 46:138+ Ap 18 '70 *
Mediocrity factor. il por Time 95:15 Mr 2 '70
Moment of truth; Senate reactions to Nixon-
Saxbe exchange. Newsweek 75:20-1 Ap 13
'70 *
New household word. il por Time 95:19-20
My 4 '70 *
Nixon crisis: advice but no consent. il pors
Newsweek 75:35-40 Ap 20 '70 *
No to Carswell. New Repub 162:7-8 F 28 '70 *
Not so simple issue. Time 95:18-19 Ap 13
'70 *
Once more, with feeling. por Time 95:8-9 F 2
'70
Oops! Wrong again! Chr Cent 87:131 F 4 '70
Pity the South. Nation 210:355-6 Mr 30 '70 *
Politics of Carswell. S. Alsop. Newsweek
75:132 Ap 20 '70 *
Seat for mediocrity? Time 95:18-19 Mr 30
'70 *
Seventh crisis of Richard Nixon. il pors
Time 95:8-15 Ap 20 '70 *
Verdict on the Florida judge. il por Time
96:16-17 S 21 '70 *
When senators quizzed Carswell. por U S
News 68:9 F 9 '70

CARSWELL, George Harrold, family
Carswells of Tallahassee. Newsweek 75:22-3 F 9 '70
CARTELS (industry) See Trusts, Industrial
CARTER, Edward William
More real than apparent. il por Forbes 105: 48 Mr 15 '70 *
CARTER, Elliott, 1908-
Carter's virtuoso concerto. D. Hamilton. il por Hi Fi 20:secI 22 My '70 *
Early Carter expertly performed. R. P. Morgan. Hi Fi sec I 20:84 F '70 *
Music to my ears; Concerto for orchestra as conducted by Leonard Bernstein. R. Jacobson. Sat R 53:50 F 21 '70 *
Quartets by Carter. I. Kolodin. Sat R 53:28 My 2 '70 *
Very different impression of Elliott Carter. D. W. Moore. Am Rec G 36:498 Mr '70 *
CARTER, James L. and MacGregor, I. D.
Mineralogy, petrology, and surface features of lunar samples 10062,35, 10067,9, 10069,30, and 10085,16. il Science 167:661-3 Ja 30 '70
CARTER, James R. Jr. See Martin, D. B. jt. auth.
CARTER, John Mitchell
Viewpoint. Library J 95:135, 1001, 1817, 2431, 2889, 3885 Ja 15, Mr 15, My 15, Jl, S 15, N 15 '70
CARTER, Leon J. 3d
Continuum (son-to-mother) poem. Negro Hist Bul 33:147 O '70
CARTER, Luther J.
Commotion at GM. New Repub 162:8-9 Je 6 '70
CARTER, Manfred A.
Black fullback; poem. Chr Cent 87:69 Ja 21 '70
Black; poem. Chr Cent 87:1117 S 23 '70
Burning city; poem. Chr Cent 87:1315 N 4 '70
CARTER, Margaret
Don't love me, don't leave me; story. Ladies Home J 87:137-44 Ap '70
CARTER, Mary
Pack trip in the High Sierras. il Holiday 47: 62-5+ My '70
CARTER, N. L. and others
Deformation of silicates from the Sea of Tranquillity. il Science 167:666-9 Ja 30 '70
CARTER, Robert
Visit with Cape Codders; excerpt from Carter's coast of New England; ed. by D. Ford. il Yachting 128:59+ Ag '70
CARTER, Virginia M.
Nevada's desert waterfowl. il Nat Parks & Con Mag 44:18-21 Je '70
CARTHEW, Anthony
Rebel in Armagh jail, the hater in the pulpit. il pors N Y Times Mag p 12-13+ Ag 9 '70
CARTIER, John O.
Chug up a laker. il Outdoor Life 145:58-9+ Mr '70
Grouse on the upbeat. il Outdoor Life 146:70-1+ S '70
Hotspot for trophy whitetails. il por Outdoor Life 146:66-7+ N '70
Ice-out lakers. il Outdoor Life 145:72-5+ Ap '70
CARTIER-BRESSON, Henri
Henri Cartier-Bresson's Japan; photographs. il Travel & Camera 33:36-43 Mr '70

about

Photographing people. J. Hughes. il Travel & Camera 33:90-2 Mr '70 *
CARTIER, Inc.
Cartier changes with the trend. il por Bsns W p 116 F 14 '70
CARTILAGE
Dentin matrix transformation: rapid induction of alkaline phosphatase and cartilage. C. B. Huggins and M. R. Urist. bibliog il Science 167:896-8 F 6 '70
CARTOGRAPHY
Atlas shrugged: Russians tinker with their maps in 1967 World atlas. il Newsweek 75: 35 F 2 '70
Fra Mauro, he inspired Columbus and the Apollo astronauts. il Space World G-9-81: 22 S '70
See also
Computers—Cartographic use
CARTONS, Milk. See Milk containers
CARTOONISTS
See also
Capp, A.
Goldberg, R.
Lurie, R.
Nast, T.
Sanders, W. W.
CARTOONS. See Caricatures and cartoons
CARTOP boats. See Boats and boating
CARTRIDGE, Phonograph. See Phonograph—Pickup

CARTRIDGE projectors. See Projectors
CARTRIDGE television. See Video recorders and recording
CARTRIDGES
Alas, the poor .25 calibers! J. O'Connor. il Outdoor Life 145:88+ F '70
Another look at the .270. J. O'Connor. il Outdoor Life 146:98+ Jl '70
Best for mule deer? W. Page. il Field & S 75:88-9+ O '70
5mm Magnum: hot new cartridge with a rifle to match. P. Wahl. il Pop Sci 197:68-9 Jl '70
Remington .25/06 and 5 mm. Magnum. J. O'Connor. il Outdoor Life 145:160+ Ap '70
Thunder and lightning. W. Page. il Field & S 75:68-71+ Jl '70
CARTRIDGES, Stereo. See Phonograph—Stereophonic pickup
CARTS
See also
Serving carts
CARTWHEELS; story. See Fineman, M.
CARTWRIGHT, Rufus
Ask Rufus; questions and answers. See issues of Mechanix illustrated
CARTY, Rico
Beeg hoppy fella. il por Time 95:66-7 Je 29 '70 *
God's better batter. il por Newsweek 75:93-4 My 25 '70 *
CARUBA, Alan
Bread loaf 1970; boot camp for writers. il Pub W 198:32-5 S 21 '70
Building a new library for a new college. por Pub W 198:29-30 O 26 '70
Marshall McLuhan lives on Sesame street. il Pub W 197:28-31 Ap 20 '70
Peter Rabbit is alive and well, despite his age. il Pub W 198:82-5 Jl 13 '70
Small publishers' company: co-op in the age of conglomerates. il Pub W 198:30 1 Ag 24 '70
Summer's special flora. Pub W 197:18-19 My 11 '70
CARUBELLI, R. and Griffin, M. J.
Neuraminidase activity in HeLa cells: effect of hydrocortisone. bibliog il Science 170: 1110-12 D 4 '70
CARVALHO, Joaquim de Montezuma de
Menéndez Pidal. il pors Américas 22:2-6 Ja '70
CARVER, Bob
Spray ballet; photographs. Motor B 125:12-13 Ap '70
CARVER, George Washington
George Washington Carver story. S. P. Massie. il pors Chem 43:18-21 S '70 *
CARVING (art industries)
Coal-black art. il pors Ebony 25:92-4+ Mr '70
Internal carving: little-known art; plastics craft. A. Westerfield and H. Wicks. il Pop Mech 135:150-1 Ja '71
See also
Scrimshaw
Soap sculpture
Wood carving
CARVING (meat, etc)
Carving the holiday turkey. il Bet Hom & Gard 48:11 D '70
How to cook and carve a goose. il Sunset 145: 188 N '70
CARY, Bob
Judge of Disappointment Mountain. il por Outdoor Life 146:32-5+ Jl '70
CARY, Ginny
Updating the British Virgin Islands. Yachting 128:61+ N '70
CARY, Jane Randolph
Family home section. il Parents Mag 45:95-8 Mr; 92-5 My '70
What's new for children. See occasional issues of Parents' magazine & better family living
CARY, William Lucius
Where are they now? il pors Newsweek 76: 10 N 30 '70 *
CARYA illinoensis. See Pecan trees
CASALS, Marta (Montanez)
Pablo Casals: the meaning of love; excerpts from Joys and sorrows. P. Casals. il pors McCalls 97:70-3+ Ap '70
CASALS, Pablo
Age and youth. McCalls 97:142 Ap '70
Pablo Casals: the meaning of love; excerpts from Joys and sorrows. il pors McCalls 97: 70-3+ Ap '70

about

Casals collected and recollected. il pors Life 68:78-81 Ap 17 '70 *
Music to my ears; Salud Casals at Philharmonic Hall. I. Kolodin. Sat R 53:28 My 2 '70 *
Musical events; Salud Casals at the Philharmonic Hall. W. Sargeant. New Yorker 46:127 Ap 25 '70 *

CASTING (fishing)
Across the river and under the trees. A. J. McClane. il Field & S 75:100-3 Ag '70
Spincaster's way. J. Brooks. il pors Outdoor Life 146:96-8+ O '70
See also
Fly casting

CASTING (sculpture)
Sand cast your own sculpture. N. Djerassi. il Har Yrs 10:34-6 My '70
See also
Plaster casts

CASTING reels. See Fishing tackle

CASTLE, Wendell
Wharton Esherick 1887-1970. il pors Craft Horiz 30:10-11+ Ag '70

CASTLES
Another tramp abroad; Neckar region, West Germany. D. Butwin. il Sat R 53:40-1 Je 27 '70
Castle detour in Switzerland: Werdenberg. il Sunset 144:43 Je '70
Castle-hopping in Spain, on $5 a day! L. Blackwood. il Schol Teach Sec Teach Sup p 12-13 Mr 9 '70
Chateaux of the Loire. H. P. Koenig. il Travel & Camera 33:68-71 Ap '70
Living with antiques; a small château near Brussels. E. D. Flory. il Antiques 97:730-3 My '70

CASTLETON-ON-HUDSON, N.Y.
What happened to the attempts to clean up the majestic, the polluted Hudson? W. Greene. il N Y Times Mag p28-9+ My 3 '70

CASTORO, Rosemarie
Artists transgress all boundaries. il Art N 69:45 Ja '71

CASTORS, Pickle. See Pickle dishes

CASTRATION
How to avoid problems when castrating. J. G. Clark. Farm J 94:B32 F '70

CASTRATION of criminals and defectives
Legal castration; West German law. il Newsweek 75:87-8 F 23 '70

CASTRO, Emilio
Emilio Castro named editor at large. Chr Cent 87:717 Je 10 '70 *

CASTRO, Fidel
Castro's failures, in his own words; excerpts from address, July 26, 1970. U S News 69:43 Ag 10 '70

about
Castro as Oedipus Rex. R. R. Fagen. Trans-Action 7:56-7 Mr '70 *
Castro comes to the surface. il pors Life 68:40-1 Ap 17 '70 *
Castro on the contradictions in Cuba; excerpt from Guerrillas in power; with introd. by D. Horowitz. K. S. Karol. il Ramp Mag 9:43-8 D '70 *
Castro's time running out? il U S News 68:48-50 Mr 9 '70 *
Charisma or democratization? K. S. Karol. Cur 124:52-5 D '70 *
Cuba revisited: how to see Havana without getting hijacked. W. Attwood. il por Look 34:15-17 Ap 7 '70 *
Cuba's recent setbacks. E. Gonzalez. Cur 124:45-52 D '70 *
Impossible importation. Nation 211:100 Ag 17 '70 *

CASTRO complex; drama. See Arrighi, M.

CASTS
See also
Plaster casts

CASUALTIES. See Israeli-Arab war, 1967—Casualties; Vietnamese war, 1957—Casualties

CASUALTY insurance. See Insurance, Casualty

CAT street. See Hong Kong—Streets

CATALINA, Fernando, and Cifuentes, Luis
Calcium oxalate: crystallographic analysis in solid aggregates in urinary sediments. bibliog il Science 169:183-4 Jl 10 '70

CATALINA ISLAND. See Santa Catalina Island

CATALOG cards
Cataloging-in-publication gains new backing; role of LC. Library J 95:3718+ N 1 '70
LC card game; letters to the editor. Am Lib 1:650-2 Jl '70
LC card service facing more delays. Library J 95:613 F 15 '70
Standardization in commercial children's cataloging: a comparative study of 100-odd titles. F. E. DeHart. il por Library J 95:744-9 F 15 '70
Typewriters in libraries; a short history of mechanization. A. M. Beagles. bibliog por Library J 96:46-7 Ja 1 '71

CATALOG codes. See Cataloging

CATALOGING
Bibliographic sputnik? steps toward cataloging at source in the U.S.S.R. E. Buist. bibliog il por Wilson Lib Bul 44:1033-9 Je '70
Cataloging-in-publication gains new backing; role of LC. Library J 95:3718+ N 1 '70
Cataloging in source raises new interest; meeting at ALA-Detroit. Library J 95:2598+ Ag '70
Plan presented for cataloging-in-publication. Pub W 198:35 O 5 '70
Publishers to discuss cataloging within books. Pub W 198:45 S 14 '70
Top priority for cataloging-in-source. J. L. Wheeler; discussion. Library J 95:608 F 15 '70
See also
Catalogs, Library
Subject headings

CATALOGING, Computerized. See Libraries—Automation

CATALOGS
See also
Periodicals—Catalogs
Phonograph records—Catalogs
Stars—Catalogs

CATALOGS, Library
Spreading state library riches for peanuts: Micro-automated catalog system. O. P. Gillock, jr. il Wilson Lib Bul 45:354-5+ D '70
Yale catalog study yields rich data. Library J 95:3720 N 1 '70

CATALOGS, Mail order
Brand new earth; the Whole earth catalog. il por Newsweek 75:60 Je 8 '70
Help! Take me out! Let me go! Johnson Smith catalogue of jokes and novelties. W. Zinsser. il Life 69:12 Jl 24 '70
Like, wow, Montgomery Ward! il Bsns W p47-8 Mr 28 '70
One of photography's best sellers, and it's only a catalog. N. Goldberg. il Pop Phot 67:76-7+ Jl '70
1652 pages of the American dream; the Sears, Roebuck catalog. F. Powledge. il Esquire 74:190-3+ D '70
Treasure guides for workshoppers. M. Philips. il Pop Sci 196:128-31+ Ja '70
Whole earth catalog. il Pub W 197:20-1 My 11 '70
Whole Whole earth catalog. E. McClanahan and G. Norman. Esquire 74:95-6+ Jl '70

CATALOGS, Publishers
Bookstore and the salesman. G. R. Smith. Pub W 197:49-50 Ja 12 '70

CATALOGS, Seed and plant
How to read a rose catalog. il Home Gard 57:26-7 F '70
Seed time and the catalogs. J. S. Raynor. Horticulture 48:40+ D '70

CATALYSIS
Catalytic activities of thermally prepared poly-α-amino acids: effect of aging. D. L. Rohlfing. bibliog il Science 169:998-1000 S 4 '70
Note on enzymic catalysis. il Chem 43:27 S '70

CATALYST (organization)
Go-go mother. N. Gittelson. Harp Baz 103:25+ Ap '70

CATALYSTS
Palladium: preparation and catalytic properties of particles of uniform size. J. Turkevich and G. Kim. bibliog il Science 169:873-9 Ag 28 '70

CATAMARANS
Cat that flies. il Life 68:28-31 F 6 '70
Flat-top Cat comes in a kit. G. Daniels. il Pop Sci 197:57 Jl '70
Multihulls. il por Motor B 125:108-9 Ja '70
Two kids and a cat. P. Smyth. il Motor B 126:58-60+ N '70

CATANIA, Sicily
In Etna's shadow; photographs of Bellini's birthplace. Opera N 35:12-13 D 19 '70
Rumble of Etna, the lilt of Bellini. R. Jacobson. il Sat R 53:70+ Mr 14 '70

CATARACTS (eye defect)
Cataracts produced in rats by yogurt. C. P. Richter and J. R. Duke. bibliog il Science 168:1372-4 Je 12 '70
Testing the vision of cataract patients by means of laser-generated interference fringes. D. G. Green. bibliog il Science 168:1240-2 Je 5 '70

CATASTROPHES. See Disasters

CATCHERS, Baseball. See Baseball players

CATECHETICS
Catechetics, R.I.P. G. Moran. Commonweal 93:299-302 D 18 '70

Bibliography
Catechetics 1970. America 123:39-43 Jl 25 '70

CATECHISMS
See also
Catholic church—Catechisms

CATECHOLAMINES
Adenyl cyclase of cultured mammalian cells: activation by catecholamines. M. H. Makman. bibliog il Science 170:1421-3 D 25 '70
Tolerance to morphine-induced increases in [^{14}C]catecholamine synthesis in mouse brain. C. B. Smith and others. bibliog il Science 170:1106-8 D 4 '70
See also
Dopamine
Norepinephrine

CATERERS and catering
Airlines stress food service competition. H. D. Watkins. il Aviation W 93:30-1+ N 23 '70
Bazaar's bazar; catering services. il Harp Baz 104:136-7 D '70
Hors d'oeuvres business. J. Kuh. Ladies Home J 87:68 Ap '70
Parties without panic: professional party-helpers. M. Siple. House B 112:76+ N '70

CATERPILLAR tractor company
Can Cat move the world? N. A. Martin. il Duns 95:34-7+ My '70
Caterpillar's global image. Duns 96:33-4 D '70

CATERPILLAR tractors. See Crawler vehicles

CATERPILLARS
Cecropia. H. Brevoort. il Am For 76:46-7 D '70
Saddled prominent. J. H. Risley. il Cons 24:29-30 Ag '69
See also
Armyworms

CATFISH fishing
Spree of cats. D. Pryce. il pors Outdoor Life 146:64-5+ Ag '70

CATFISHES
Watch out for walking catfish. il Sunset 144:60 Ap '70

CATHARSIS
Catharsis, linguistics & all that. J. Thompson. bibliog f Commentary 50:65-73 O '70

CATHEDRALS
Models
See Architectural models

England
Canterbury pilgrims today. R. Wickerd and F. Wickerd. il Travel 134:34-9+ D '70
Megalithic plan underlying Canterbury cathedral. L. B. Borst; discussion. bibliog Science 164:769-70; 166:772-4; 167:333 My 16, N 7 '69, Ja 23 '70

Italy
Doors of Orvieto. il Time 96:56-7 Ag 31 '70
Milan offers its visitors a 14th century walk in the sky. il Sunset 145:30+ N '70

CATHER, Willa Sibert
Ghost town on the river; excerpts from The world and the parish, ed. by W. M. Curtin. il por Am Heritage 21:68-72 O '70

about
Dark dimension of Willa Cather's My Antonia. L. Feger. Engl J 59:774-9 S '70 *

CATHERINE II, empress of Russia
Domestic policies of Peter III and his overthrow. M. Raeff. bibliog f Am Hist R 75:1289-310 Je '70 *

CATHETERIZATION
Radio-frequency thrombosis of vascular malformations with a transvascular magnetic catheter. J. A. Taren and T. O. Gabrielsen. bibliog il Science 168:138-41 Ap 3 '70

CATHETERS
Radio-frequency thrombosis of vascular malformations with a transvascular magnetic catheter. J. A. Taren and T. O. Gabrielsen. bibliog il Science 168:138-41 Ap 3 '70

CATHEY, Henry M.
Recent discoveries in seed germination. il Horticulture 48:36-7+ My '70

CATHODE ray tube composition. See Phototypesetting

CATHODE ray tubes
Digital scan used in flat TV display. B. Miller. il Aviation W 92:53-5 Mr 2 '70

CATHOLIC adult education. See Adult education

CATHOLIC book week. See Book week

CATHOLIC church
Brussels declaration. il Time 96:44-5 S 28 '70
Brussels hosts the theologians; Concilium congress on The future of the church. R. A. McCormick and others. il America 123:232-4 O 3 '70
Church as a family. R. E. Meagher America 122:37-9 Ja 17 '70

Church in the year 2000; Commonweal paper; symposium; discussion. Commonweal 91:287+, 443+ N 28 '69, Ja 23 '70
Church torn between dogma and dissent; with report by J. Cogley. il pors Life 68:22-31 Mr 20 '70
Crisis of faith, by F. Sontag. Review
America 123:270 O 10 '70. R. W. Lambeck
Future at Brussels; Concilium congress on the future of the church. G. Baum. Cath World 212:137-40 D '70
Of many things; true Christian pluralism. D. R. Campion. America 122:inside cover Mr 7 '70
Political congress. il Newsweek 76:62-3 S 28 '70
Religion in tomorrow's world; interview, ed. by A. Kucherov. J. Wright. il por U S News 69:56-61 Ag 31 '70
Roman Catholic church, by J. L. McKenzie. Review
Cath World 210:224-6 F '70. K. P. Coyle
Six Catholics to extinction. P. R. Gastonguay. Cath World 212:189-93 Ja '71
Theologo '70. J. Horgan. Commonweal 93:39 O 9 '70
Theology sprouts at Brussels; world congress on The future of the church. T. Beeson. Chr Cent 87:1145-6 S 30 '70
Timeless Christian, by E. Von Kuehnelt-Leddihn. Review
Nat R 22:901-2 Ag 25 '70. F. D. Wilhelmser
While theologians talked; congress on The future of the church. J. J. van Capelleveen. Chr Today 15:50 O 9 '70
See also
Canon law
Canonization
Church renewal—Catholic church
Confession
Councils and synods
Ecclesiastical courts
Ecumenical movement
Excommunication
Laity—Catholic church
Lent
Liturgical movement—Catholic church
Martyrs
Mass
Opus Dei (secular institute)
Papacy
Pastoral letters
Priests
Reformation
Religious orders
Saints
Vatican council, 1869-1870
Vatican council, 2d
Vatican council, 3d (proposed)
Women and the church

Authority
See Church—Authority

Bibliography
Loyalty and dissent: some books to the point. America 122:686-8 Je 27 '70

Bulletins
See Bulletins

Catechisms
Catechetics debate: 1970. America 123:35 Jl 25 '70

Clergy
Clergy redistributed; Congregation for the clergy congress. America 122:621 Je 13 '70
See also
Priests
Vocation in religion

Dioceses
Boston priests at grips with the diaspora; Association of Boston urban priests. T. D. Corrigan. Cath World 212:35-6 O '70
Quiet revolt; archdiocese of Los Angeles. K. LaMott. por Horizon 12:68-72 Wint '70
Sharing the wealth; the archdiocese of New York. Commonweal 92:180 My 8 '70
State of a diocese; Victoria, British Columbia. D. J. Roche. America 122:366-7 Ap 4 '70

Discipline
See also
Excommunication
Marriage (canon law)
Obedience (canon law)

Education
Call it sabotage! R. V. Staudacher. America 122:72-5 Ja 24 '70
Catholic schools and religious education. M. O'Neill. America 122:338-41 Mr 28 '70; Discussion. 122:485, 599 My 9, Je 6 '70

CATHOLIC church—Education—*Continued*

De-schooling the teaching orders. I. Illich. por America 124:12-14 Ja 9 '71
Religious education for all: finding the means. M. O'Neill. il America 122:626-30 Je 13 '70
See also
Catholic colleges and universities
Catholic schools
Center of intercultural documentation
Theological seminaries, Catholic

Eucharist

Bread and life. V. P. McCorry. America 123:76-inside back cover Ag 8 '70
Christian cultus. V. P. McCorry. America 122:inside back cover My 30 '70

Finance

Ecclesiastics and lucre. T. Beeson. Chr Cent 87:884 Jl 22 '70
Matter of principal; National association of laymen criticizes management of diocesan finances. Newsweek 76:101-2 N 30 '70
Sharing the wealth; the archdiocese of New York. Commonweal 92:180 My 8 '70
Who wants Catholic schools? J. M. Swomley, jr. Nation 211:627-9 D 14 '70

Government

Catholic church professionals. J. H. Fichter. bibliog f Ann Am Acad 387:77-85 Ja '70
Catholic concerns: celibacy, due process. Chr Today 14:32-3 Ja 30 '70
Concern about collegiality. Chr Cent 87:909 Jl 29 '70
Due process in the church; speedy redress of grievances. America 122:30 Ja 17 '70
John XXIII, Vatican II, and American Catholicism. E. C. Bianchi. Ann Am Acad 387:30-40 Ja '70
Priests' union: talking tougher. Chr Today 14:38+ Ap 24 '70
Suenens calls for a new deal. J. A. O'Brien. Chr Cent 87:818-21 Jl 1 '70
See also
Papacy

History

Great confrontations: Leo X and Luther. L. B. Smith. il pors Horizon 12:90-5 Spr '70

Infallibility

See also
Popes—Infallibility

Liturgy and ritual

Danger, liturgy at work. T. Beeson. Chr Cent 87:1528-9 D 23 '70
Federation of diocesan liturgical commissions. J. L. Cunningham. America 123:97-8 Ag 22 '70
Here lies community: R.I.P. J. Hitchcock. America 122:578-81 My 30 '70; Discussion. 122:639; 123:49, 287-90 Je 20, Ag 8, O 17 '70
Is there any hope for liturgy? G. S. Sloyan. Commonweal 92:56-60 Mr 27 '70; Discussion. 92:155+ My 1 '70
Liturgical reform, again? J. Gallen. America 124:20-2 Ja 9 '71
Liturgy as subversive activity. J. Bishop. Commonweal 93:324-7 D 25 '70
Liturgy, the celebration of life. M. Krebs. America 123:147-9 S 12 '70
Marrying the liturgy. R. Haughton. Cath World 210:197-8 F '70
Where the new liturgy limps. L. R. Ward. Commonweal 92:404-5 Ag 21 '70
See also
Antiphonaries (music)
Divine office
International committee on English in the liturgy
Lectionaries
Liturgical movement—Catholic church
Mass

Missions

Biafra minus missionaries. A. Jaffe. il Newsweek 75:86+ Ap 13 '70
Exiled from Nigeria. D. King. America 122:245 Mr 7 '70
Missions for today. C. J. McNaspy. America 122:416-18 Ap 18 '70; Discussion. 122:544, 661 My 23, Je 27 '70
Profiles: Missionaries of charity, Calcutta. V. Mehta. New Yorker 46:97-8+ Mr 21 '70
Where have all the missionaries gone? J. Rohler. Chr Today 14:51 Mr 13 '70

Mozarabic rite

Antiphons, responsories and other chants of the Mozarabic rite, by C. W. Brockett, jr.
Review
Mus Q 56:125-30 Ja '70. D. M. Randel

Music

See Church music

Negroes

Black first. Time 96:30 S 7 '70

Relations

Jews

Jewish leaders laud Vatican document. Chr Cent 87:39 Ja 14 '70
Pope's Jews. por Time 96:49 Ag 24 '70

Protestant churches

Lutheran-Catholic accord. Chr Cent 87:1440 D 2 '70
On disowning an expert; H. J. McSorley's dismissal. America 123:537 D 19 '70
Southern Baptists, Roman Catholics resume dialogue; meeting at St Joseph's abbey. R. Ryland. Chr Cent 87:461-2 Ap 15 '70
Will Catholics recognize Protestant ministries? il Time 95:76 My 25 '70

Relations (diplomatic)

United Nations

United Nations and the Holy See. J. A. Lucal. il America 123:315-17 O 24 '70

United States

Ambassador Lodge reports on visit to the Vatican; transcript of news conference, August 6, 1970. H. C. Lodge. Dept State Bul 63:277-8 S 7 '70
Henry Cabot Lodge goes to the Vatican. Chr Today 14:22 Jl 3 '70
Lodge to the Vatican. Chr. Cent 87:779 Je 24 '70
New emissary to the Pope. por Time 96:46 Jl 13 '70
President's man at the Vatican. America 122:640 Je 20 '70

Yugoslavia

Rome and Yugoslavia: relations restored. Chr Cent 87:1033 S 2 '70
Tito & the Pope. M. M. Mestrovic. Commonweal 93:36-7 O 9 '70

Renewal

Trying to be co-responsible: interview, ed. by J. T. Ryan. T. Roberts. il por Cath World 211:22-5 Ap '70

Rites and ceremonies

See also
Sacraments

Societies

See also
Knights of Columbus
Pax Romana

CATHOLIC church and communism

Working group 7; Catholics and Communists in Hong Kong. N. Hunter. Commonweal 93:60-1 O 16 '70

CATHOLIC church and international relations. See Church and international relations

CATHOLIC church and politics. See Church and politics

CATHOLIC church and psychiatry. See Psychiatry and religion

CATHOLIC church and race problems. See Church and race problems

CATHOLIC church and social problems. See Church and social problems

CATHOLIC church and war. See War and religion

CATHOLIC church in Africa
Report from East Africa; bishops of five East Africa countries meet. C. De Souza. il America 123:117-18 S 5 '70

CATHOLIC church in Asia
Two worlds of Catholicism. Time 96:67 D 14 '70

CATHOLIC church in Australia
Two worlds of Catholicism. Time 96:67 D 14 '70

CATHOLIC church in Bolivia
See also
Church and state in Bolivia

CATHOLIC church in Brazil
Another crime of passion. America 122:260 Mr 14 '70
Church in Brazil. il Newsweek 76:94-5 Ag 17 '70
Priest tells of torture. Chr Today 15:50+ O 9 '70
See also
Church and state in Brazil

CATHOLIC church in Canada
State of a diocese; Victoria, British Columbia. D. J. Roche. America 122:366-7 Ap 4 '70

CATHOLIC church in Colombia
Banned Colombian Catholic journal folds; La hora. Chr Cent 87:527 Ap 29 '70

CATHOLIC church in Czechoslovakia
Peace priests surface again. America 122: 572 My 30 '70
CATHOLIC church in England
Step toward reunion; Anglican and Catholic scholars meet. il Newsweek 75:60 Ja 26 '70
CATHOLIC church in France
Defections from priesthood mount in France. Chr Cent 87:935 Ag 5 '70
CATHOLIC church in Great Britain
Good start; national conference of Roman Catholic priests in England and Wales. T. Beeson. Chr Cent 87:780 Je 24 '70
CATHOLIC church in Hong Kong
Working group 7; Catholics and Communists in Hong Kong. N. Hunter. Commonweal 93:60-1 O 16 '70
CATHOLIC church in Hungary
New mood in Hungary. K. Huszar. il Newsweek 76:67 Ag 31 '70
See also
Church and state in Hungary
CATHOLIC church in Italy
Isolotto: test case for Italian Catholicism. J. J. Carey. Chr Cent 87:336+ Mr 18 '70
View from Rome: a complex religious situation. N. Pittienger. Chr Cent 87:1360-2 N 11 '70
Visitor stopped at St Apollinare; the controversial Archbishop of Ravenna. E. Cochrane. Commonweal 92:452-3 S 18 '70
Witch hunting in Italy; case of the Archbishop of Ravenna. J. Deedy. Commonweal 92:26 Mr 20 '70
See also
Church and state in Italy
CATHOLIC church in Latin America
CICOP 1970: prelude to conscientization. T. M. Gannon. il America 122:214-18 F 28 '70; Discussion. 122:285, 320 Mr 21-28 '70
Church and colonialism: the betrayal of the third world, by H. Camara. Review
Commonweal 91:462-3 Ja 23 '70. J. A. Page
Church in Latin America. T. G. Sanders. For Affairs 48:285-99 Ja '70
Collision in Latin America. por Time 95:44 F 9 '70
Latin America's revolutionary churches. E. Castro. Chr Cent 87:1081-2 S 16 '70
Latin America: the church militant. N. Gall. bibliog f Commentary 49:25-37 Ap '70
Medellin guidelines. M. J. Drinkwater. America 22:2258 Mr 14 '70
Medellin guidelines: Latin American episcopal conference statement. V. T. Mallon. America 122;92-6 Ja 31 '70
New rebels: clerics in Latin America. J. Benham. il U S News 69:92-5 D 14 '70
Pentecostal breakthrough. J. L. Klaiber. il America 122:99-102 Ja 31 '70
Toward a third world theology; reaction to Humanae vitae. America 122:90 Ja 31 '70
See also
Church and state in Latin America
CATHOLIC church in Mexico
Closed society of the Chamulas. K. O'Connor. il Cath World 211:58-62 My '70
CATHOLIC church in Nigeria
Biafra minus missionaries. A. Jaffe. il Newsweek 75:36+ Ap 13 '70
CATHOLIC church in Paraguay
Paraguay ends church relief. America 122:61 Ja 24 '70
See also
Church and state in Paraguay
CATHOLIC church in Poland
Muted celebration. Chr Cent 88:3 Ja 6 '71
Poland's mini-revolution. Chr Today 15:21-2 Ja 15 '71
CATHOLIC church in Rhodesia
See also
Church and state in Rhodesia
CATHOLIC church in South America. See Catholic church in Latin America
CATHOLIC church in Spain
Judgment on the Burgos trial. T. M. Gannon. America 124:23-4 Ja 9 '71
Opus Dei: Spain on the cross; tr. by L. Bensky. Y. Le Vaillant. il Ramp Mag 8: 14+ F '70
Spanish resistance grows bolder. A. Power. Commonweal 92:332-5 Jl 10 '70
See also
Church and state in Spain
CATHOLIC church in Tanzania
Tanzania's seminar study year 1969. C. De Souza. America 122:300-2 Mr 21 '70
CATHOLIC church in the Netherlands
Alfrink challenged; married priests who preside at the eucharist. T. Beeson. Chr Cent 87:1177 O 7 '70
Cardinal Suenens: a plea for dialogue; interview, ed. by H. Fesquet. L. Suenens. por Cath World 211:216-20 Ag '70

Democratic movement in Dutch Catholicism. W. L. Boelens. Cath World 211:112-15 Je '70
Dutch hierarchy accused of reneging on celibacy issue. Chr Cent 87:1147-8 S 30 '70
Holy pragmatism in Holland. T. Beeson. Chr Cent 87:932 Ag 5 '70
In Dutch with Rome: celibacy and schism. F. Franck. Commonweal 91:502-3 F 6 '70
Letter from Holland; Dutch pastoral council. J. C. Haughey. America 122:450-2 Ap 25 '70
Linen on the authority line: Pope Paul's letter on the celibacy issue. Chr Cent 87: 132 F 4 '70
More trouble in Holland. il por Time 97:61 Ja 18 '71
New challenge to celibacy rule for priests; the Dutch pastoral council vote. U S News 68:12 Ja 26 '70
Of many things: the Dutch pastoral council. D. R. Campion. America 122:inside cover Ja 31 '70
Pontificate of lost opportunities. F. Franck. Commonweal 92:30-1 Mr 20 '70
Schism with Rome? il Newsweek 75:79 F 9 '70
Uncoupling celibacy; Dutch pastoral council V. T. G. Fuechtman. America 122:102+ Ja 31 '70
CATHOLIC church in the Philippines
Papal visit sets stage for Philippine revolution. N. Ramientos. Chr Today 15:41 Ja 1 '71
Peripatetic Pope: Philippine peregrinations. J. Novotney. il Chr Today 15:38 D 18 '70
To find itself: a young nation's mission. H. de la Costa. America 123:542-4 D 19 '70
CATHOLIC church in the United States
Bishops' spring meeting; shared responsibility; with editorial comment. E. Glynn. America 122:491, 496 My 9 '70
Change of the guard; new spiritual head of American Catholics. il por Time 96:61 S 21 '70
Christian unity, the U.S. scene. J. C. Haughey. il America 123:261-3 O 10 '70; Reply. B. F. Law. 123:389 N 14 '70
Due process in the church; speedy redress of grievances. America 122:30 Ja 17 '70
Future is for priests; address, October 16, 1969. J. J. Egan. il Cath World 210:262-5 Mr '70
Here lies community: Deo gratias! E. C. Kennedy. America 123:85-9 Ag 22 '70; Discussion. 123:287-90 O 17 '70
History of the Catholic church in the United States, by T. T. McAvoy. Review
Commonweal 93:307-8 D 18 '70. J. P. Dolan
John XXIII, Vatican II, and American Catholicism. E. C. Bianchi. Ann Am Acad 387:30-40 Ja '70
Night the peace bus left New Harley. R. H. Robbins. il Cath World 210:256-61 Mr '70
Old-time dialogue; Msgr. Uylenbroeck's talk with laymen in major Catholic centers. Commonweal 92:355-7 Jl 24 '70; Discussion. 92:427+ S 4 '70
Passing the hat; retirement of Cardinal Cushing. il pors Newsweek 76:82 S 21 '70
Radical Catholic; address. C. O. Rice. il por Cath World 211:156-60 Jl '70
Renewal: Tennessee model. T. M. Gannon. America 122:152-5+ F 14 '70
Yes, but; suggested National pastoral council. Commonweal 92:4 Mr 13 '70
See also
Catholics in the United States
Church union—United States
Knights of Columbus
National pastoral council (proposed)
CATHOLIC church in Venezuela
Caldera's caldron. J. Deedy. Commonweal 93: 162 N 13 '70
CATHOLIC church in Vietnam
Cross and the Bo-tree, by P. Gheddo. Review
Commonweal 92:467-9 S 18 '70. T. Fox
CATHOLIC church in Yugoslavia
See also
Church and state in Yugoslavia
CATHOLIC college professors and instructors. See College professors and instructors
CATHOLIC colleges and universities
America's directory of colleges, 1970. America 123:374-6 N 7 '70
College deans discern the times; meeting of Jesuit college deans. W. J. Parente. America 123:176-7 S 19 '70
Diocese and Catholic higher education. A. F. Horrigan. il America 122:342-4 Mr 28 '70
From backwater to mainstream, by A. M. Greeley. Review
Sat R 53:83-4 My 16 '70. R. Hassenger

CATHOLIC colleges and universities—*Cont.*
Rome replies (act II); the Congregation for Catholic education. N. G. McCluskey. il America 122:330-4 Mr 28 '70
See also
Fordham university
Mercy college, Dobbs Ferry, N.Y.
Notre Dame college of Staten Island
Notre Dame, Ind. University
St. Vincent archabbey and college, Latrobe, Pa.

Federal aid
Catholic colleges on trail: Tilton V. Finch, II, C. M. Whelan. America 122:122-4 F 7 '70
Catholic colleges pass the test; Tilton v. Finch. C. M. Whelan. America 122:368 Ap 4 '70

Finance
Alma mater: color it in red; Carnegie commission on higher education report. America 123:533 D 19 '70

CATHOLIC dissenters. See Dissenters. Religious
CATHOLIC education. See Catholic church—Education
CATHOLIC fiction. See Catholic literature
CATHOLIC inter-American cooperation program. See Religious conferences
CATHOLIC junior colleges
Catholic junior colleges; directory. America 122:back cover Je 27 '70
CATHOLIC lay teachers unions. See Teachers unions
CATHOLIC laymen. See Laity—Catholic church
CATHOLIC library association
New directions for the Catholic library association; a conference report. E. Corry. Wilson Lib Bul 44:912+ My '70
CATHOLIC literature
Vital tradition, by G. Kellogg. Review America 124:52-3 Ja 16 '71. F. L. Kunkel

Bibliography
Lenten reading suggestions. America 122:163-6 F 14 '70
Religion (cont) E. S. Stanton. America 122:472-4; 123:469-70 My 2, N 28 '70
CATHOLIC newspapers. See Catholic press
CATHOLIC Pentecostals. See Pentecostal churches
CATHOLIC periodicals. See Catholic press
CATHOLIC press
Ave atque vale; beginning of A.D. 1970. S. J. Adamo. America 122:377-8 Ap 4 '70
Bishops' poll, the results of their attitudes toward diocesan newspapers. S. J. Adamo; reply. J. A. Gelin. America 122:115 F 7 '70
Catholic press: has the wake started? G. E. Sherry. America 123:91-3 Ag 22 '70; Discussion. 123:133, 189, 247 S 12, 26, O 10 '70
Dispirit of St Louis. S. J. Adamo; discussion. America 121:603; 122:29 D 20 '69, Ja 17 '70
Exceptions; National Catholic register takeover by Twin circle publishing company. S. J. Adamo. America 123:500 D 5 '70
Gargoyle; T. Brock and Pittsburgh Catholic. S. J. Adamo. America 122:537-8 My 16 '70
Lively wake; the National Catholic register. S. J. Adamo. America 123:245-6 O 3 '70
Lyons goes full circle. Chr Today 14:47 S 11 '70
Mini mags. S. J. Adamo. America 122:482-3 My 2 '70
Miracle in Maine; Church world. S. J. Adamo. America 122:283-4 Mr 14 '70
Mixed bag; newsweeklies advisory boards. S. J. Adamo. America 122:415 N 14 '70
Now it's official. J. Deedy. Commonweal 91:522 F 13 '70
Press. S. J. Adamo. See issues of America
Press scene; good-bye to Interchange, and the Messengers. J. Deedy. Commonweal 92:130 Ap 24 '70
Right moves; the case of the takeover of the National register by Twin circle. Commonweal 92:404 Ag 21 '70
Signs of hope; growth of ecumenism. S. J. Adamo. America 122:200 F 21 '70
Substandard; Catholic substandard and times. S. J. Adamo. America 122:112-13 Ja 31 '70
Whispering; Chicago voice. S. J. Adamo. America 122:617-18 Je 6 '70
Zodiac failure; cessation of AD 70. S. J. Adamo. America 123:75-6 Ag 8 '70
See also names of Catholic periodicals, e.g. Herder correspondence (periodical)
CATHOLIC press association
Catholic press: has the wake started? G. E. Sherry. America 123:91-3 Ag 22 '70; Discussion. 123:133, 247 S 12, O 10 '70

Toward a Christian press association. Chr Cent 87:716 Je 10 '70
CATHOLIC-Protestant marriages. See Marriages, Mixed
CATHOLIC relief services
CRS in Paraguay. J. Deedy. Commonweal 93:34 O 9 '70
Rumania and Peru and CRS. America 122:664 Je 27 '70
CATHOLIC school and public school relations. See Educational cooperation
CATHOLIC schools
Agents for Christian community; the Catholic school. C. A. Koob. il America 122:335-7 Mr 28 '70
Catholic schools. N. G. McCluskey; reply. J. H. Bolin. America 122:143 F 14 '70
Catholic schools and religious education. M. O'Neill. America 122:338-41 Mr 28 '70; Discussion. 122:485, 599 My 9, Je 6 '70
Catholic schools seek data, help. Sr Schol 96:Schol Teach 1 Ap 6 '70
Giving Americans a choice; alternatives to public education. M. O'Neill. America 122:66-70 Ja 24 '70; Reply. R. E. Brady. 122:360 Ap 4 '70
Jesuit high school. R. A. Schroth. Commonweal 91:472-5 Ja 30 '70
President as cheerleader for parochial schools. Chr Cent 87:319 Mr 18 '70
Q. Are parochial schools, the answer? A. Well, er uhh . . . G. Grant. Commonweal 92:85-7 Ap 3 '70
Religious education for all: finding the means. M. O'Neill. il America 122:626-30 Je 13 '70
S.O.S. for Catholic schools, by C. Koob and R. Shaw. Review
Cath World 212:215 Ja '71. B. Downey
Volunteer teacher program; Archdiocese of New York. America 123:534 D 19 '70
Where is the Catholic school system heading? C. A. Koob. America 123:169-71 S 19 '70; Reply. V. T. Mallon. 123:475 D 5 '70
See also
Education and state
Jesuits—Education

Desegregation
Catholic school integration suit; dual school system in Opelousas, La. America 123:50 Ag 8 '70
Catholic segregation; it's almost 1954; Opelousas, La. J. A. Cozzi. Commonweal 93:317 D 25 '70
Church schools in the South. America 122:121 F 7 '70
I teach in a racist school. P. Flinn. America 123:201-3 S 26 '70; Discussion. 123:305, 389 O 24, N 14 '70
Louisiana desegregation, and Catholic schools. F. Guillory. il America 123:119-21 S 5 '70
Sister speaks up. Commonweal 91:524 F 13 '70

Federal aid
Are parochial schools imperiled? J. M. Swomley, jr. Chr Cent 88:40-3 Ja 13 '71
Catholic school crisis: is public aid the answer? R. Chandler. Chr Today 15:26-7 Ja 14 '71
Constitutional relation of church and state; address, January 26, 1970. B. F. Brown. Vital Speeches 36:359-62 Ap 1 '70
Should parochial schools get public funds? J. N. Miller. Read Digest 96:113-16 F '70

Finance
Boston story; study of schools of the Boston archdiocese. J. Deedy. Commonweal 92:178 My 8 '70
Catholic bishops pledge recommitment to parochial schools. Chr Cent 88:38 Ja 13 '71
Catholic school crisis: is public aid the answer? R. Chandler. Chr Today 15:26-7 Ja 15 '71
Catholic schools go forward. Sr Schol 96:Schol Teach 1-2 My 4 '70
Crisis of confidence. il Newsweek 75:75-6 F 2 '70
Who wants Catholic schools? J. M. Swomley, jr. Nation 211:627-9 D 14 '70
CATHOLIC students' mission crusade
Signs of the times; phasing out of the organization. Commonweal 92:474 S 25 '70
CATHOLIC substandard and times (newspaper) See Catholic press
CATHOLIC teachers. See Teachers
CATHOLIC thought. See Religious thought
CATHOLICS
Can Catholics learn anything from evangelical Protestants? P. W. Witte. Cath World 212:85-7 N '70; Same. Chr Today 15:12-14 D 18 '70
Six Catholics to extinction. P. R. Gastonguay. Cath World 212:189-93 Ja '71

CATHOLICS in Europe
Kirche and Chiesa: what European Catholics think. Time 97:66+ Ja 11 '71
CATHOLICS in Great Britain
Tools of the papacy. J. Deedy. Commonweal 91:604 Mr 6 '70
CATHOLICS in Northern Ireland
Bloody Ulster: an Irishman's lament. B. Moore. il Atlan 226:58-62 S '70
Rebel in Armagh jail, the hater in the pulpit. A. Carthew. il pors N Y Times Mag p 12-13 Ag 9 '70
CATHOLICS in the United States
Growing up a Catholic. B. Guinan. Mlle 70: 157+ Mr '70
Memories of a (latter-day) Catholic girlhood. K. Mulherin. Commonweal 91:610-19 Mr 6 '70; Discussion. 92:77+ Ap 3 '70
CATIONS
Enzymes activated by monovalent cations. C. H. Suelter. bibliog il Science 168:789-95 My 15 '70
CATLEDGE, Turner
Forty years on the Times. S. W. Little. Sat R 54:50 Ja 9 '71 *
CATLIN, Wynelle
Decorative cheeseboxes. il Design 71:38-9 Sum '70
CATO, pseud.
Letter from Washington. Nat R 22:352, 399, 505, 555, 665, 777, 830, 884, 936, 992, 1044, 1150, 1258, 1336, 1391 Ap 7-21, My 19-Je 2, 30, Jl 28-O 6, N 3, D 1-29 '70
CATOOSA, Okla.
Ocean comes to Oklahoma. C. Bakal. il Read Digest 97:121-4 N '70
CATS
Evoked response and behavior in cats. R. A. Hall and others. bibliog il Science 170:998-1000 N 27 '70
Hypersexuality and behavioral changes in cats caused by administration of p-chlorophenyl-alanine. J. Ferguson and others. bibliog il Science 168:499-501 Ap 24 '70
Number coding in association cortex of the cat. R. F. Thompson and others. bibliog il Science 168:271-3 Ap 10 '70
Quandary of cats; antivivisectionist lobbying aids passage of new law in California. il Newsweek 76:103 D 7 '70
Room 8: a venture in immortality. M. Cole. il PTA Mag 64:6-7 Ap '70
Superior colliculus: single unit responses to stimulation of visual cortex in the cat. J. T. McIlwain and H. L. Fields. bibliog il Science 170:1426-8 D 25 '70
Visual experience modifies distribution of horizontally and vertically oriented receptive fields in cats. H. V. B. Hirsch and D. N. Spinelli. bibliog il Science 168:869-71 My 15 '70

Food and feeding
Right food for your pet. il Good H 171:187 O '70
Truth about pet foods. L. Coe. il Pop Mech 134:123-5+ O '70

Training
Watchdog cats! R. D. Goban. Har Yrs 10:32 Ja '70
CATS, Photography of. See Photography of animals
CATS as carriers of infection. See Animals as carriers of infection
CATTELL, David T.
Dissent and stability in the Soviet Union. Cur Hist 59:220-5+ O '70
CATTELL, Everett L.
Grim alternatives in Christian higher education. Chr Today 14:3-5 Jl 3 '70
CATTLE
See also
Bulls
Calves
Pastures

Breeding
See Cattle breeding

Care
Beef cow problems: what to do. D. Malena. il Suc Farm 68:56 O '70
How to get a better return on your treatments. J. G. Clark. Farm J 93:B22 O '69
How to stay away from drug-residue problems. J. G. Clark. Farm J 94:B28 O '70

Confinement methods
Beef confinement. D. Malena and R. Krumme. il Suc Farm 68:41-5 My '70
Open-front confinement for beef feeding. W. Kester. Farm J 94:B10-11 My '70

Semi-confinement for cows looks good. M. Vance. Suc Farm 68:C7 Ag '70
See also
Cattle sheds

Culling
See Cows—Culling

Diseases and pests
See also
Cattle, Beef—Preconditioning
Cows—Diseases and pests

Feeding
Farmer feeder charts his future. D. Seim. Farm J 94:B7 My '70
Faster gains inside, winter and summer. Farm J 94:B31 F '70
Forage is their specialty. il Suc Farm 68:B10-11 Ja '70
Glad I feed indoors; open-sided shelters. D. Seim. il Farm J 93:B28-29+ N '69
Growing feeder cattle, a new opportunity. Suc Farm 68:B7 Je '70
He made his grass go four times further. il Suc Farm 68:G4 Ap '70
How to feed a high-wheat finishing ration; interview. J. Algeo. il Farm J 93:B8-9 O '69
Is beef feeding for your farm? Suc Farm 68: B9 S '70
Long-distance ration mixing; computer used by feedlots. il Farm J 94:B13 Mr '70
Making it go as you grow; farmer-feeders. D. Seim. il Farm J 94:B10-11+ Ag '70
News from the beef-feeding industry. See issues of Farm journal
Should you boost protein with high-energy rations? B. Coffman. Farm J 94:B16 My '70
Stretched-out silage harvest. D. O'Brien. il Farm J 94:B8-9 My '70
Their feedlot goal: 3 lbs. of grain per day. J. Davis. il Suc Farm 68:D14 O '70
This tenant is a top-notch cattle feeder. D. Malena. il Suc Farm 68:32-3 Ag '70
Three pounds of steak, without antibiotics, if possible. il Org Gard & Farm 17:84-9 Mr '70
Try before you buy; new programs, equipment and ideas. D. Seim. il Farm J 93:B38 N '69
You can feed for better carcasses. D. Malena. il Suc Farm 68:D12 O '70
See also
Calves—Feeding
Cattle—Confinement methods
Cows—Feeding
Feeding and feeding stuffs
Feedlots
Grazing

Performance records and registration
See also
Cattle, Beef—Performance records and registration

Prices
Market analysis. See issues of Farm journal
Pricecast. See issues of Farm journal
Why the price shakes? beef cattle. il Farm J 93:B23 O '69
CATTLE, Beef
Beef management (cont of) What's new. D. Malena. See issues of Successful farming
Here are more new beef breeds. D. Malena. il Suc Farm 68:37 My '70
How they're making beef cows pay. T. McCartney. il Suc Farm 68:A4-5 N '70
Successful beef management. il Suc Farm 68:no3 D4-6+ F; no5 D1-5 Mr; D11 S; D1-3+ O '70
What makes an ideal steer? Suc Farm 68: B5 Ag '70

Care
See Cattle—Care

Feeding
See Cattle—Feeding

Marketing
Beef marketing. Farm J 94:31 Je '70
Better way to sell Holstein beef. J. D. Ritchie. il Farm J 93:B16-17 O '69
Market action shifts to the feedlot. W. Kester. il Farm J 94:B8-9 O '70
More trading muscle for the cattle feeder. W. Kester. il Farm J 94:B8-9+ N '70
New ways to sell beef. D. Malena. il Suc Farm 63:no3 D6 F '70
Will Mexico dry up feeder exports? C. Ball. il Farm J 93:B12 O '69
See also
Cattle marketing information service, inc.
Feedlots

CATTLE, Beef—*Continued*

Performance records and registration

His weaning weights: up 158 lbs. D. Malena. il Suc Farm 68:34-5 Ap '70

Preconditioning

P-C feeders gain ground in Dakotas. W. Kester. il Farm J 94:B6-7+ Mr '70

Prices

See Cattle—Prices

Weight

See Cattle, Weight and measurements of

CATTLE, Weight and measurements of

How big is big enough? beef cattle. il Farm J 94:B16 Ag '70

Pick bulls and feeders that will produce more meat. R. Long. il Suc Farm 68:no5 D2-3 Mr '70

CATTLE barns. See Barns and stables

CATTLE breeding

Crossbreeding: an answer to the cowman's squeeze. il Farm J 94:50-1+ F '70

Dairy breeding checkups pay off. Suc Farm 68:no3 G14 F '70

F₁ heifers. C. E. Ball. il Farm J 94:39+ Mr '70

Faster gainers with quality carcasses, too; crossbreeding. D. Seim. il Farm J 94:B17 S '70

How the exotics are shaking up the beef business. J. A. Rohlf. il Farm J 94:20-3 N '70

How your cows might handle calves from those big European breeds. il Farm J 94:32D O '70

Let figures do the talking. il Farm J 93:36I N '69

Sell 60 lbs. more calf per cow; breed heifers a month early. O. Bay. il Farm J 62F Mr '70

This ranch breeds the kind of calves that feeders order by 'phone. C. E. Ball. il Farm J 94:B14-15+ O '70

You can't get sentimental about cattle. il Suc Farm 68:B12 My '70

See also
Artificial insemination
Bulls
Cows—Testing

CATTLE corrals

Handling plan that makes the cattle do the work. il Suc Farm 68:D12 S '70

CATTLE-Fax. See Cattle marketing information service, inc.

CATTLE feed. See Feeding and feeding stuffs

CATTLE feedlots. See Feedlots

CATTLE handling

Handling tips when you treat your own. J. G. Clark. il Farm J 94:B22-3 Ag '70

Ideas for easier cattle handling. il Suc Farm 68:no3 D10 F '70

Low cost cattle handling: B. Helderman, Missouri. il Suc Farm 68:D22 O '70

New cattle-handling ideas; photographs. Suc Farm 68:G6 N '70

See also
Cattle corrals

CATTLE industry and trade

Are we heading for a shorter beef supply? J. A. Rohlf. il Farm J 94:37 Ja '70

Beef extra. See issues of Farm journal

Beef up cow-calf profits; Missouri. B. Coffman. Farm J 94:A11 Ja '70

Case for cows in the Corn Belt. Farm J 94:35 Ja '70

Fall feeder market: get set for the toughest bargaining ever. W. Kester. il Farm J 94:B8-9+ S '70

Raise their own feedlot replacements; farmer-feeders cow herds. D. Seim. il Farm J 94:B10-11+ N '70

Tax shelter caves in on city farmers; Black watch farms, inc. J. Carlson. il Farm J 94:18-19+ N '70

What's ahead for the seventies? il Farm J 94:B9 F '70

Why a western cowman chose the Corn Belt. R. Sanders. il Suc Farm 68:28-9 My '70

See also
Meat industry and trade

History

Crackers and cattle kings; cattle trade in Florida. V. C. Rummel. il Américas 22:36-41 S '70

International aspects

Canadian looks south at U.S. feeders, markets. J. D. Ritchie. Farm J 93:B31 N '69

Australia

Big beef from Down Under. il Bsns W p35 N 21 '70

Mexico

Will Mexico dry up feeder exports? C. Ball. il Farm J 93:B12 O '69

CATTLE marketing information service, inc.

Cattle-fax: new help for smarter marketing. il Suc Farm 68:no3 D8 F '70

Faster draw on cattle prices; Cattle-Fax service. il Bsns W p 110+ Ap 11 '70

CATTLE ponies. See Ponies

CATTLE preconditioning. See Cattle, Beef—Preconditioning

CATTLE sheds

Glad I feed indoors; open-sided shelters. D. Seim. il Farm J 93:B28-29+ N '69

How much shelter do feedlots really need? il Suc Farm 69:35-9 Ja '71

How much shelter for your cattle. Suc Farm 68:60 O '70

Shelter may be your answer to higher feed grain prices. Farm J 94:B23 O '70

CATTLEMEN

See also
American national cattlemen's association
Cowboys

CAUCUS

Power in the House; caucus for military money bills proposed. J. Smith. New Repub 162:10 My 30 '70

CAUCUS for a new political science. See American political science association

CAUDILL, Harry Monroe

Lament for the Appalachian hills. il Am For 76:8-11+ My; 2 S '70

CAUDILL, Rebecca

Child and his books. il PTA Mag 64:28-9 F '70

CAULFIELD, Patricia

Oklawaha unspoiled; photographs. Audubon 72:37-40 Jl '70

Touch and see. il Nat Wildlife 7:18-19 O '69

La CAUSE du peuple (newspaper) See Newspapers—France

CAUSES of war. See War, Causes of

CAUSTIC soda industry. See Chemical industries

CAVA, Ralph Della. See Della Cava, R.

CAVAGNARO, David

Meadow morning; photographs. Audubon 72:28-35 N '70

CAVALIERS (basketball team) See Basketball teams

CAVALLERIA rusticana; opera. See Mascagni, P.

CAVALLI-SFORZA, Luigi Luca. See Bodmer, W. F. jt. auth.

CAVANAGH, Denis

Reforming the abortion laws: a doctor looks at the case. il America 122:406-11 Ap 18 '70

CAVANAGH, Jerome Patrick

From the mayor's chair; interview. pors Sr Schol 96:10 Mr 2 '70

CAVANAUGH, Arthur

Leaving home; story. Redbook 135:131-53 Jl '70

Place setting. Writer 84:16-18+ Ja '71

CAVE, Hugh

All about love and marriage; story. Good H 170:70-1 My '70

Small-town girl; story. Good H 172:60-1 Ja '71

Two very special people; story. Good H 170:96-7 Ap '70

CAVE drawings and paintings

Feminine eye; visit to Lascaux cave. S. Alexander. McCalls 97:6 S '70

Prehistory Down Under; engraved rocks of Koonalda cave. D. J. Mulvaney. il Natur Hist 79:44-51 Ap '70

CAVE dwellers

Keeping house in a Cappadocian cave. J. S. Blair. il Nat Geog 138:126-46 Jl '70

CAVE fauna and flora

Bat-guano cave environment. J. A. Harris. bibliog Science 169:1342-3 S 25 '70

Life in the underground world. N. Sullivan. il Nat Wildlife 8:21-4 O '70

CAVELL, Marcia

Visions of a new religion. il Sat R 53:12-14+ D 19 '70

CAVENDER, Kenneth
(tr) See Molière, J. B. P. Dom Juan

CAVERLY, Joseph

Golden Gate park centennial. il por Parks & Rec 5:24-6+ O '70

CAVES

Down, down, down; Pennsylvania's deepest cave. N. W. Davis. il Nat Wildlife 7:34-7 O '69

Exploring the world within. B. Gilbert. il Read Digest 96:177-8+ F '70

CAVES—*Continued*
Fantastic Caverns. G. Gideon. il Travel 133: 50 F '70
How good are you as a speleologist? quiz. J. Daugherty and M. Daugherty. il Sci Digest 68:74-5+ Jl '70
Idaho's mile-long tube of lava. Sunset 144:60 Je '70

CAVETT, Dick
On student protest, TV censorship, blacks on TV; interview. ed. R. Hemming. por Sr Schol 95:20+ O 20 '69

about
Can praise ruin Dick Cavett? il pors Newsweek 76:105-6 O 5 '70 *
Cavett off camera; with report and editorial comment by B. Darrach. il pors Life 69:3. 36-42 O 30 '70 *
Dick Cavett: the brightest boy on the block. J. Egan. il pors Good H 171:44-5+ N '70 *
First for Cavett. il pors Time 96:74 O 26 '70 *
Late-night talker who knows how to listen. J. Leonard. por Life 68:10 F 13 '70
—See Frost, D. jt. auth.

CAVIAR
Light, fresh, slightly salty, it's red caviar. il Sunset 145:156 S '70

CAVITATION
Propeller-pox; your wheels could die of it. E. A. Zadig. il Motor B 125:172-4 My '70
Supersaturation of gases in water: absence of cavitation on decompression from high pressures. E. A. Hemmingsen. bibliog il Science 167:1493-4 Mr 13 '70

CAYMAN ISLANDS
Discover the Cayman Islands. H. Turcotte. il Travel 134:44-9+ Jl '70

ÇAYÖNÜ excavations. See Turkey—Antiquities

CAYUGA LAKE
Patient earth; excerpts. ed. by J. Harte and R. Socolow. il Phys Today 23:28-9 D '70
Pollution problems, resource policy, and the scientist. A. W. Eipper. bibliog Science 169:11-15 Jl 3 '70

CEAUSESCU, Nicolae
President Nixon meets with President Ceausescu of Romania; exchange of greetings and toasts, October 26, 1970. Dept State Bul 63:648-50 N 23 '70

about
Communist comes to talk business. il por Bsns W p28 O 31 '70 *

CECERE, James G.
Form of lithography. il Sch Arts 70:28-9 D '70

CECIL, Lamar
Creation of nobles in Prussia, 1871-1918. bibliog f il Am Hist R 75:757-95 F '70

CEDAR
Loners of Alaska. A. S. Harris. il por Am For 76:20-3+ My '70
Painful lessons of the cedars of Lebanon. L. Thomas. il por Nat Wildlife 8:50-5 D '69
This is weeping atlas cedar. il Sunset 145:248 N '70

CEDERBERG, Elford Alfred
Excerpt from debate, September 17, 1969. Cong Digest 49:28 Ja '70

CEDERGREN, Harry R.
Subdrains can protect streets from seepage. il Am City 85:99-100 O '70

CEILINGS
To top off a beautiful room, you need the right ceiling. W. Baldwin. House & Gard 138:12-13 Ag '70

CELANESE corporation of America
Operation redeployment. Forbes 106:18 Ag 15 '70

CELEBRATIONS
Special madness; Brazil celebrates 1970 World cup victory. il Newsweek 76:55 Jl 6 '70
See also
Centennials
United States—Declaration of independence—Centennial celebrations, etc.

CELEBRITIES
Before the colors fade (cont) il Am Heritage 21:28-9+ F; 92-6 Ap '70
Big jocks; American professionals of the past. il Esquire 73:124-9 Ap '70
Celebrity spotlight. E. N. Mintz. See issues of Travel
Day I was proudest of my child; symposium. ed. by D. Robinson. il Good H 170:70-3+ Ja '70

Doing their tiresome thing; Time essay. D. Auchincloss. il Time 96:31 Jl 13 '70
Dreams that never fade; boyhood aspirations of prominent men. J. H. Pollack. il Nations Bsns 58:48-51 Ag '70
From hair to eternity. il Esquire 74:74-5 Ag '70
Marriages that beat the odds: eight famous couples tell how they've stayed happily married. M. Davidson. il Good H 171:72-5 Jl '70
Men & women who shaped the '60's. il Sr Schol 95:9-11 S 22 '69
New faces of 1970; the Chicago seven and their engagements. il Newsweek 75:33-4 Ap 6 '70
Parting shots; how these familiar faces would have looked 100 years ago. il por Life 68: 66A-68 Je 19 '70
Scene/seen. L. Lerman. il Mlle 71:165-9 S; 186-8 O '70
Suzy. L. Hershey. il por Ladies Home J 87: 80-1+ S '70
There's no accounting for houses. L. Lyons. House & Gard 138:28 Jl '70
What famous people like to drink. House & Gard 138:89 Jl '70
Where famous people go. B. Gillam. Mlle 71: 154-6 Je '70
See also
Great men
Negro celebrities
Women, Famous

Anecdotes, facetiae, satire, etc.
A few to admire. L. Rosten. Look 34:16 Mr 24 '70
Heroes and antiheroes. Chr Cent 87:127 Ja 28 '70

CELERIAC
Celery root, good cook's salad discovery. il Sunset 145:159 O '70

CELERY
Put celery in your garden. E. L. Onstott. il Org Gard & Farm 17:35-7 F '70

CELERY root. See Celeriac

CELESTIAL photography. See Astronomical photography

CELIBACY
Cardinal Suenens: a plea for dialogue; interview. ed. by H. Fesquet. L. Suenens. por Cath World 211:216-20 Ag '70
Catholic concerns: celibacy, due process. Chr Today 14:32-3 Ja 30 '70
Celibacy and clericalism. T. W. Guzie. Cath World 211:120-4 Je '70
Celibacy, jewel or crown of thorns? Time 95:52-3 F 23 '70
Celibacy: tightening the ratchet; with editorial comment. Chr Today 14:26, 39 F 27 '70
Celibacy vows: mandate or mistake? Chr Today 14:44 Mr 13 '70
Dutch hierarchy accused of reneging on celibacy issue. Chr Cent 87:1147-8 S 30 '70
In Dutch with Rome. F. Franck. Commonweal 91:502-3 F 6 '70
Linen on the authority line; Pope Paul's letter. Chr Cent 87:132 F 4 '70
New challenge to celibacy rule for priests; the Dutch pastoral council vote. U S News 68:12 Ja 26 '70
Of many things; Pope Paul's views on priestly celibacy. D. R. Campion. America 122:inside cover F 14 '70
Papacy and celibacy. Cur Cent 87:1113 S 23 '70
Pope, Cardinal Danielou attack foes of mandatory celibacy. Chr Cent 87:199 F 18 '70
Reflections on priesthood and marriage. G. Grudzen; discussion. Cath World 210:244-5; 211:4 Mr-Ap '70
Triumph of realism on Maundy Thursday. Chr Cent 87:412 Ap 8 '70
Uncoupling celibacy; Dutch pastoral council V. T. G. Fuechtmann. America 122:102+ Ja 31 '70
Waiting game; Vatican warfare against dissenting priests. Chr Cent 87:261 Mr 4 '70
Wright's writ; Roman Catholic priests invited to renew ordination promises. il por Newsweek 75:88-9 F 23 '70
See also
Virginity

CELL division (biology)
Mitochondrial RNA synthesis during mitosis. H. Fan and S. Penman. bibliog il Science 168:135-8 Ap 3 '70
Persisting circadian rhythm of cell division in a photosynthetic mutant of euglena. R. M. Jarrett and L. N. Edmunds, jr. bibliog il Science 167:1730-3 Mr 27 '70
Trisomy-3,4 and triploidy (3A-ZZZW) in chick embryos; autosomal and sex chromosomal nondisjunction in meiosis. S. E. Bloom. bibliog il Science 170:457-8 O 23 '70

CELL division (botany)
Chromosome pairing: effect of colchicine on an isochromosome. C. J. Driscoll and N. L. Darvey. bibliog il Science 169:290-1 Jl 17 '70
Chromosome pairing within genomes in maize-tripsacum hybrids. J. R. Harlan and others. bibliog il Science 167:1247-8 F 27 '70
Colcemid sensitivity of fission yeast and the isolation of colcemid-resistant mutants. S. Lederberg and G. Stetten. bibliog il Science 168:485-7 Ap 24 '70
CELL membranes. See Membranes (biology)
CELLARS. See Basements and cellars
CELLER, Emanuel
Excerpts from debate, September 11 and 17, 1969. Cong Digest 49:12+, 29 Ja '70

about
Celler is tempted to call for a law. Bsns W p35 Ja 17 '70
CELLINI, Benvenuto
Living in a renaissance time. P. W. Schmidt-chen. il por Hobbies 75:134-6+ Mr '70 *
CELLISTS
See also
Du Pré, J.
Warburg, G.
CELLO music
See also
Phonograph records—Cello music
CELLO playing
See also
Ensemble playing
CELLOPHANE tape. See Adhesive tape
CELLS
Birefringent filamentous organelle in BHK-21 cells and its possible role in cell spreading and motility. R. D. Goldman and E. A. C. Follett. bibliog il Science 169:286-8 Jl 17 '70
Differentiation of immature mucous cells into parietal, argyrophil, and chief cells in stomach grafts. M. Matsuyama and H. Su-zuki. bibliog il Science 169:385-7 Jl 24 '70
Divergent biological effects of adenosine and dibutyryl adenosine 3',5'-monophosphate on the isolated fat cell. S. S. Solomon and others. bibliog il Science 169:387-8 Jl 24 '70
Neuraminidase activity in HeLa cells: effect of hydrocortisone. R. Carubelli and M. J. Griffin. bibliog il Science 170:1110-12 D 4 '70
Reassembly of living cells from dissociated components. K. W. Jeon and others. bibliog il Science 167:1626-7 Mr 20 '70
Reconstituted amoebas. Sci Am 222:57-8 My '70
Why fat kids stay fat; study findings. Newsweek 76:82-3 O 19 '70
See also
Bacterial cells
Cancer cells
Centrosomes
Chromatin
Cytology
Differentiation (biology)
Embryology
Fibroblasts
Genes
Golgi apparatus
Macrophages
Membranes (biology)
Nerve cells
Rod and cone cells
Tumor cells
Conferences
Control of form in cells. B. Satir. Science 167:307-9 Ja 16 '70

Culture
See Tissues—Culture

Inclusions
See also
Mitochondria
Protoplasts
CELLS, Effect of radiation on. See Radiation—Physiological effects
CELLULAR differentiation. See Differentiation (biology)
CELLULAR therapy
Man who turned sheep into gold; Doctor Niehans. W. S. Ross. il por Todays Health 48:26-9+ O '70
CEMENT
See also
Concrete
CEMENT industry and trade
Cement climbs out of a rut. il Bsns W p76 N 28 '70
CEMENT sculpture. See Sculpture
CEMENT yachts. See Yachts—Materials

CEMENTS, Adhesive
Glues for household repairs. il Consumer Bul 53:28 O '70
Household cements. il Consumer Bul 53:31-2 My; 16-17 Jl '70
CEMETERIES
Grave situation; inaptly or ineptly named burial grounds. Chr Cent 87:1027 Ag 26 '70
Integration in death; burial of Private Bill Terry. Chr Cent 87:37 Ja 14 '70
See also
National cemeteries—United States
CENDRARS, Miriam
Miriam Cendrars: curry, powder with power. N. Lyon. Vogue 155:123 F 1 '70
La CENERENTOLA; opera. See Rossini, G.
CENOZOIC period. See Geology, Stratigraphic—Cenozoic; Paleontology—Cenozoic
CENSORSHIP
Communications control, ed. by J. Phelan. Review
Cath World 212:165-6 D '70. H. T. Walshak
Conscience for the press: an American newspaper council? H. Brucker. Sat R 53:59-61 My 9 '70
'Lasciuious vngodly love'. P. Michelson. Nation 210:245-7 Mr 2 '70
Self-help law book cleared in N.Y. court; concerning How to avoid probate. Library J 95:842 Mr 1 '70
Who are the real censors? selection of English classes. R. T. LaConte. Ed Digest 36:44-6 O '70
See also
Freedom of the press
Government and the press
Immoral literature and pictures
Information, Freedom of
Intellectual liberty
Israeli-Arab war, 1967- —Censorship
Libraries—Censorship
Moving picture censorship
Obscenity (law)
Postal censorship
School libraries—Censorship
Television broadcasting—Censorship

Europe, Eastern
Writers' block. il pors Newsweek 75:38+ Mr 2 '70
France
European scene: French censorship. H. R. Lottman. Pub W 198:36 S 21 '70
Great Britain
Decline of pornography. W. F. Buckley, jr. Nat R 22:325 Mr 24 '70
Russia
Involuntary journey; M. Rostropovich letter of criticism. pors Newsweek 76:61 N 23 '70
Solzhenitsyn; a candle in the wind. por Time 95:25 Mr 23 '70
CENSORSHIP of mail. See Postal censorship
CENSUS
Great head count. il Time 95:33 Mr 23 '70
See also
United States—Census
CENSUS of agriculture. See Farm census—United States
CENTAUR (booster) See Space vehicles—Propulsion systems
CENTENARIANS
218 biographees listed by SSA in two new volumes of America's centenarians. il Aging 187:6-7 My '70
CENTENNIALS
Centennial observance of Charles Dickens death. J. Walsh. il pors Hobbies 75:48-50+ Je '70
Dickens ferment. H. R. Mayes. Sat R 53:14+ Ap 4 '70
Million dollar bus trip; Tacoma centennial bus caravan. il Am City 85:108 F '70
See also
United States—Declaration of independence—Centennial celebrations, etc.
CENTER for advanced study in the behavioral sciences, Stanford, Calif.
Behavioral sciences; the view at the Center for advanced study. J. Walsh. il Science 169:654-8 Ag 14 '70
CENTER for media study (proposed)
Violence study assesses media; report by study group of the National commission on the causes and prevention of violence. America 122:87 Ja 31 '70
CENTER for short-lived phenomena. See Smithsonian institution—Center for short-lived phenomena

CENTER for the study of democratic institutions, Santa Barbara, Calif.
Prospects for peace in the oceans; summary of the Pacem in Maribus convocation. E. M. Borgese. il Sat R 53:15-22 S 26 '70

CENTER of intercultural documentation
Ivan Illich and CIDOC as theater. S. Bliss. Chr Cent 87:1463-6 D 2 '70
Profiles; I. Illich. por New Yorker 46:40-4+ Ap 25 '70

CENTER opera company, Minneapolis
Center opera goes way out; premiere performance of Oedipus and The sphinx. J. Gerstel. il Hi Fi sec II 20:26-7 F '70
How to sing a nightmare: Werner Egk's 17 days and 4 minutes and Harrison Birtwistle's Punch and Judy. J. Gerstel. il Hi Fi 20:secII 24+ Ag '70
Really with it. R. D. Daniels. il Opera N 34: 24-7 Mr 7 '70
Report:
Harrison Birtwistle's Punch and Judy in Minneapolis. P. Gainsley. Opera N 34:32 Mr 21 '70
Production of two original works. P. Gainsley. il Opera N 34:30-1 Ja 24 '70
The wanderer: a ballad of now, by Paul and Martha Boesing. P. Gainsley. Opera N 34:31 Ap 18 '70

CENTERPIECES. See Table decoration
CENTERS for the performing arts
See also
Community arts centers
Lincoln Center for the performing arts, New York

CENTO. See Central treaty organization
CENTRAL AMERICA
See also
British Honduras
Canals—Central America

Description and travel
Down that Pan American highway. E. A. Jahn. il Travel 133:30-5 Ja '70 (to be cont)

Economic policy
See also
Central American program of economic integration

Foreign relations
Costa Rica and her neighbors. D. B. Heath. Cur Hist 58:95-101+ F '70

CENTRAL AMERICAN common market. See Central American program of economic integration
CENTRAL AMERICAN program of economic integration
Common market with little in common. il Bsns W p53 F 21 '70
CENTRAL AMERICAN sculpture. See Sculpture, Central American
CENTRAL and southern Florida flood control district
River-eater; destruction of the Kissimmee. P. Matthiessen. il Audubon 72:52-3 Mr '70
CENTRAL CITY festival. See Music festivals —Colorado
CENTRAL EUROPE
See also
Transylvania
CENTRAL flow control facility. See United States—Federal aviation administration
CENTRAL heating. See Heating from central stations
CENTRAL intelligence agency. See United States—Central intelligence agency
CENTRAL opera service
Report:
C.O.S. in Santa Fe. J. Rockwell. Opera N 35:28 O 10 '70
CENTRAL park. See New York (city)—Parks and playgrounds
CENTRAL park zoo. See New York (city)— Parks and playgrounds
CENTRAL railroad company of New Jersey
Jersey central's life after death. il Bsns W p72-3 D 12 '70
CENTRAL treaty organization
CENTO council of ministers meets at Washington; statement, with text of communique, May 15, 1970. W. P. Rogers. Dept State Bul 62:711-12 Je 8 '70
CENTRAL vacuum cleaning systems. See Vacuum cleaning
CENTRALIZATION in government. See Decentralization in government
CENTRE national d'études spatiales. See France—National center for space studies

CENTRIFUGATION
Equilibrium density-gradient procedure for selection of synchronous cells from asynchronous cultures. T. O. Sitz and others. bibliog il Science 168:1231-2 Je 5 '70; Reply with rejoinder. E. C. Anderson. 170:97 O 2 '70
Separation of plant particles; report of meeting. C. A. Price. Science 168:282-3 Ap 10 '70
CENTRIFUGES
Studying the effects of gravity. E. Driscoll. il Sci N 98:77-9 Jl 25 '70
Test crews study spinning effects of space station. il Space World G-11-83:22-3 N '70
Test supports ability of crews to work in artificial gravity. Aviation W 94:47 Ja 4 '71
CENTRIOLES. See Centrosomes
CENTROSOMES
Electron probe X-ray microanalysis of a normal centriole. P. W. Schafer and J. A. Chandler. bibliog il Science 170:1204-5 D 11 '70
CENTS. See Coins
CENTURY plants. See Agaves
CEPHALOCARIDA. See Crustaceans
CEPHALOPODS
See also
Paper nautilus
CERAMI, Charles A.
Will the dollar be devalued via the back doors? il Nations Bsns 58:98-100 N '70
CERAMIC buttons. See Buttons
CERAMIC flute. See Flute
CERAMIC frits. See Frits
CERAMIC materials
Tinyvision; electronics experiment. il Time 95:52 My 18 '70
CERAMIC sculpture
Ancient Mexico and Central America; photographs. L. Boltin. Natur Hist 79:30-5 bibliog(p79) My '70
Hollowed-out animal sculpture; sculpting a hippo. P. Rothenberg. il Ceram Mo 18:21-3 S '70
Ken Shores. R. Griffin. il Craft Horiz 30:26-9 Ag '70
Our sungods. C. Heiple. il Sch Arts 69:22-3 Ap '70
People pots. P. Landman. il Sch Arts 69:36-7 Je '70
Pinch pot owls. R. Goettsch. il Ceram Mo 18:24-5 Ja '70
Quarter century of American ceramic art. J. Lovoos. il Am Artist 34:20-5 F '70
CERAMIC tile mosaics. See Mosaics
CERAMICS. See Pottery
CERCARIA
Swimmer's itch. G. F. Levy and J. W. Folstad. bibliog il Environ 11:14-16+ D '69
CERDAN, Marcel, 1916-1949
Fathers and sons. il pors Newsweek 75:93 My 25 '70 *
CERDAN, Marcel, 1944?-
Fathers and sons. il pors Newsweek 75:93 My 25 '70 *
Gimmick for boxing: Caucasian charisma. J. Flaherty. pors Life 68:12 Je 12 '70 *
Mystery in pursuit of a legend. M. Kram. il pors Sports Illus 32:38-40+ Ap 13 '70 *
No longer a legend, but not all hoax. M. Kram. Sports Illus 32:82+ My 25 '70 *
Petit Marcel and la grande mystique. pors Time 95:74 My 25 '70 *
CEREAL foods
Breakfast of chumps? Time 96:65 Ag 3 '70
Breakfast of what? views of R. B. Choate, jr. Newsweek 76:57-8 Ag 3 '70
Breakfasts, the meal you shouldn't skip. F. J. Stare. Ladies Home J 87:122+ N '70
Cereal critic aids his targets. il Bsns W p59 O 3 '70
Cereal tempest; views of Robert B. Choate, jr. Sr Schol 97:5-6 S 14 '70
Chemical breakfast; controversy over fortified cereals. D. Sanford. New Repub 163: 12-15 Ag 22 '70
Gadfly buzzes around the table. il por Bsns W p 116 S 26 '70
Not by cereal alone. Time 96:57 Ag 17 '70
Package of trouble for cereal makers. il Bsns W p24 Ag 1 '70
Storm in the cereal bowl. J. Cross. Nation 211:133 Ag 31 '70
Tempest in a cornflakes bowl. Sci N 98:134 Ag 15 '70
What's behind those breakfast-cereal headlines? il Good H 171:215-16 N '70
What's for breakfast? Moss subcommittee debate. il U S News 69:45 Ag 17 '70

CEREAL foods—*Continued*
Willing suspension of disbelief. Chr Cent 87:
951 Ag 5 '70
See also
Cookery—Cereals
CEREAL leaf beetles. See Beetles
CEREALS. See Grain
CEREBRAL hemorrhage
Cerebral hemorrhage in relation to birth asphyxia. W. F. Windle. bibliog il Science 167:1000-2 F 13 '70
CEREBRAL palsied children
I have the chance to try. C. Finnell. Todays Ed 59:74-5 N '70
CEREBROSIDES
Tubules of globoid leukodystrophy: a right-handed helix. E. J. Yunis and R. E. Lee. bibliog il Science 169:64-6 Jl 3 '70
CEREBROSPINAL fluid
See also
Blood-brain barrier
CERENKOV radiation. See Radiation
CERF, Bennett
John O'Hara; excerpts from eulogy. Pub W 197:21-3 Je 22 '70
Trade winds; interview, ed. by C. Amory. Sat R 53:12+ D 12 '70
CERRO corporation
Fortune's wheel; new president. por Newsweek 75:74 Je 22 '70
CERRO TOLOLO inter-American observatory. See Astronomical observatories—Chile
CERTIFICATION of airplanes. See Airplanes—Standards
CERTIFICATION of airports. See Airports—Standards
CERVANTES, Alfonson Juan
Federal revenue sharing and the cities; address, October 13, 1970. Vital Speeches 37: 83-8 N 15 '70
about
Mayor, the Mob and the lawyer. D. Walsh. il pors Life 68:24-31 My 29 '70 *
CERVANTES SAAVEDRA, Miguel de
La Mancha. F. V. Grunfeld. il Horizon 11:40-7 Aut '69
CERVIX
Diseases
Contraceptives and dysplasia: higher rate for pill choosers. E. Stern and others. bibliog il Science 169:497-8 Jl 31 '70
More about the pill: UCLA findings on frequency of cervical dysplasia. Newsweek 76: 78+ O 12 '70
CESAREAN section
Facts and fallacies about cesarean births. G. Goldreich. il Parents Mag 45:52-3+ My '70
CESSNA aircraft company
Cessna sees sales gain with new models. E. J. Bulban. il Aviation W 93:65-7 D 14 '70
Pilot training franchises offered. E. J. Bulban. il Aviation W 93:56-8 N 2 '70
Why does Cessna's jet go so slow? A. Trammell. il Flying 86:42-7 F '70
CEYLON
See also
Sigiriya
Description and travel
Ceylon; a larger-than-life travel poster. G. Cotler. il Holiday 47:40-3+ Ap '70
Game preserves, beach resorts, temples, jungle: Ceylon is a discovery. il Sunset 144:58+ F '70
Gems and wildlife in Ceylon. S. Wiedel. Travel & Camera 33:60 N '70
Serene satisfactions of a visit to Ceylon. B. Taper. il Travel & Camera 33:34-43+ N '70
Politics and government
Dry-eyed and flying high. por Time 95:35-6 Je 8 '70
CÉZANNE, Paul
Powerhouse; National gallery buys painting entitled The artist's father. il Newsweek 76:102 O 12 '70 *
Trophy of tenacity. il por Time 96:64 O 12 '70 *
CHABAN-DELMAS, Jacques Pierre Michel
Political chicken. il por Newsweek 76:50 S 21 '70 *
Politics Bordelaise. il pors Time 96:29 S 28 '70 *
CHACE, Marian
In memoriam. por Dance Mag 44:90 S '70 *
CHACHERE, Lee
Bill Henley's new horizon; story. Har Yrs 10:39-40 Mr '70
CHACO
Caste and class in the Chaco. L. L. Browne. Nation 211:239-42 S 21 '70

CHAD
Beau Geste war in heart of Africa. il U S News 68:46-7 Ja 19 '70
Last Beau Geste. il Time 95:32 F 16 '70
Unknown war; Moslem guerrillas, Christian government. J. White and M. Mueller. Commonweal 92:476-7 S 25 '70
CHAFFEE, John, jr. and Wagner, Patricia
Teachers do make a difference. il Am Ed 6:23-5 My '70
CHAFFIN, Lavor K.
How to raise reading scores. il Am Ed 6: 12-15 D '70
CHAGAS' disease. See Trypanosomiasis
CHAIKIN, Joseph
After innocence, what? il Time 95:63 Je 1 '70 *
CHAIN gear
Get longer life from roller chains. Suc Farm 68:no4 C2 Mr '70
CHAIN hotels. See Hotels, taverns, etc.
CHAIN letters
To break the chain. Chr Cent 87:1051 S 2 '70
Weakest link. J. Boni. Sat R 53:4 Jl 25 '70
CHAIN saws. See Saws
CHAIN stores
See also
Broadway-Hale stores, inc.
Federated department stores, inc.
Fisher foods, inc.
Grant, W. T. company
Grocery trade
Jewel companies, inc.
Kresge, S. S. company
National speed centers
Supermarkets
Woolworth, F. W. and company, ltd.
CHAIRS
Bravissimo! great new Italian chairs. il Redbook 134:117-21 Mr '70
Chairs by Lannuier at New York's city hall. M. M. Craigmyle. il Antiques 97:258-9 F '70
Chez Mlle: squashies. P. Bartlett. il Mlle 70: 98-9 Mr '70
Colonial-style sweetheart chair. il Pop Mech 133:178-9 Mr '70
Could you bend up a chair from foamboard? L. Walker. il Pop Sci 196:106-9 F '70
Early American furniture; excerpts. J. T. Kirk. il Antiques 98:428-31 S '70
Flip-over ladder-chair. W. C. Lecky. il Pop Mech 133:175-6 F '70
Foam furniture rises like bread. il Pop Sci 196:25 Je '70
How to build a captain's chair of Danish design. F. A. Taggart. il Pop Sci 196:133-7+ Ja '70
Nowhere to sit down; chairs as art objects. R. Hughes. il por Time 96:62 N 9 '70
Sculpture-chairs for the now generation. A. Lees. il Pop Sci 197:76-7+ Ag '70
Sitting easy. V. D. Hahn. il Am Home 73: 56-9+ Fall '70
Smart new chairs from old. D. Shiner. il Design 72:32-3 Fall '70
Twelve chairs. il Good H 171:104-9 Ag '70
Twelve very comfortable chairs. C. Garner. il Bet Hom & Gard 48:40+ S '70
CHAISE longues
Roll-around patio sun-lounge. il Sunset 145: 83 Ag '70
Les CHAISES; drama. See Ionesco, E.
CHAIX, Richard
Achieving effective collaboration in the design of fountains. il Arch Rec 148:105-8 D '70
CHAKRABARTY, Asit K. and Friedman, Herman
L-Asparaginase-induced immunosuppression: effects on antibody-forming cells and serum titers. bibliog il Science 167:869-70 F 6 '70
CHALCEDONY
Chalcedony bomb. H. D. Brown. il Hobbies 75:156 D '70
CHALET ski club. See Sports clubs
CHALIDZE, Valerii
Human rights committee; interview. Newsweek 76:57 D 21 '70
CHALK, O. Roy
Chalk on a shoestring. por Forbes 106:47-8 Ag 15 '70 *
End of the line. por Time 95:20+ My 4 '70 *
CHALL, Jeanne S.
Chall revisited. P. Groff. bibliog por Library J 95:1904-6+ My 15 '70 *
CHALLENGE; story. See Borges, J. L.
CHALMERS, Edwin Laurence, 1923-
Where will dedicated anarchists focus attention? interview. por U S News 69:20-2 S 7 '70

CHAMAECYPARIS. See False cypress
CHAMBER dance company of New York. See Ballet companies
CHAMBER music
Alexander Schneider's Christmas present; Christmas string seminar. R. S. Brown. il por Hi Fi 20:secII 24-5 Mr '70
See also
Ensemble playing
Phonograph records—Chamber music
CHAMBER opera society of Baltimore
Chamber opera society: young and promising. A. C. Rackemann; F. Rackemann. Hi Fi sec il 20:27 Ja '70
CHAMBERLAIN, Barbara Blau
Island consciousness. il Natur Hist 79:114-15+ Ag '70
CHAMBERLAIN, Clinton J.
Profitable concession. il Parks & Rec 5:29-30+ Mr '70
CHAMBERLAIN, Gary M.
Week of group therapy for a region. il Am City 85:105-6+ O '70
CHAMBERLAIN, Lewis
Martin Luther; poem. Chr Today 14:4 Ap 24 '70
CHAMBERLAIN, Richard
Kildare as Hamlet. il por Time 96:70 N 16 '70 *
CHAMBERLAIN, Wilt
They'll know my name again; interview, ed. by B. Bruns. por Life 68:50 Mr 13 '70
about
Long way with West, all the way with Wilt? il pors Life 68:46-9 Mr 13 '70 *
CHAMBERLIN, Anne
Being a cautionary tale for women hell-bent on baking bread. McCalls 97:38+ S '70
CHAMBERS, Gurney
Michael John Demiashkevich: the way of an essentialist. bibliog f Sch & Soc 98:108-10 F '70
CHAMBERS, Jack
Canada: Jack Chambers. M. Amaya. il Art in Am 58:118-21 S '70 *
CHAMBERS, Whittaker
Odyssey of a friend; letters to W. F. Buckley, jr. 1954-1961. bibliog f Nat R 22:22-32, 76-82, 132-7+ Ja 13, Ja 27, F 10 '70
about
Dedicated madness. D. Cort. Nation 210; 185-6 F 16 '70 *
History hit us. R. A. Gross. il por Newsweek 75:77+ F 2 '70
Odyssey of a friend, by W. F. Buckley, jr. Review
Commentary 49:85-8 Je '70. A. Weinstein *
Odyssey was ended. L. Berg. Harper 241: 98-101 Jl '70 *
Potential of psychoanalytic biography: Zeligs on Chambers and Hiss. G. Bychowski. bibliog f Am Imago 26:233-41 Fall '70 *
Revisionist view. J. K. Galbraith. New Repub 162:17-19 Mr 28 '70 *
Words from the center of sorrow. por Time 95:67+ Mr 9 '70 *
CHAMBERS of commerce
Business has its own embassies; American chambers of commerce for American businessmen overseas. J. L. Caldwell. il Nations Bsns 58:86-7 My '70
See also
International chamber of commerce
CHAMOIS hunting
Wiedmannsdank! hunting red deer and chamois in Austria. W. Page. il Field & S 74: 80-3+ Ap '70
CHAMPAGNE
Champagne. il Consumer Rep 34:638-42 N '69
Drinking champagne & brandy, by Y. Carter. Review
Consumer Bul il 53:4+ Ja '70
Uses and misuses of champagne. il Esquire 74:138-9 N '70
CHAMPAIGN, Ill.
Education
Local associations of the month. J. Pittman and C. Thomasson. Todays Ed 59:80 O '70
CHAMULA Indians. See Indians of Mexico
CHAN, Elaine
Sea and me. il por Seventeen 29:154-5+ Ap '70
CHAN, Eva Lee, and others
Cell interaction in an immune response in vitro: requirement for theta-carrying cells. bibliog il Science 170:1215-17 D 11 '70
CHAN, Po-chuen, and others
Hydroxyurea: suppression of two-stage carcinogenesis in mouse skin. bibliog il Science 168:130-2 Ap 3 '70

CHANAUD, Robert C.
Aerodynamic whistles; with biographical sketch. il Sci Am 22:16, 40-6 bibliog(p 146) Ja '70
CHANCE, Britton, jr
Intrepid 1970: the designer's view. il Yachting 129:94-6+ Ja '71
about
Bright new Chance at the cup. H. D. Whall. il por Sports Illus 33:28-31 Jl 13 '70 *
Leave it to Chance. il por Time 96:75 S 21 '70 *
CHANCE, Dean
Chancey games in Ohio. M. Cope. il por Sports Illus 32:26-8+ Mr 30 '70 *
CHANCE
Logic of chance. W. Parkhurst. Sci Digest 68:87-8 Ag '70
Rules of chaos; excerpts. S. Vizinczey. il McCalls 97:76-7+ My; 32+ Je '70
See also
Probabilities
CHANDIGARH, India
Jinxed jewel. il Time 95:33 F 9 '70
CHANDLER, David
Louisiana still jumps for mobster Marcello. il pors Life 68:30-7 Ap 10 '70
CHANDLER, David P.
Changing Cambodia. bibliog f Cur Hist 59: 333-8+ D '70
CHANDLER, E. Russell
Crucial issues in the Mideast. Chr Today 14:14-15 F 27 '70
CHANDLER, Edna W.
So you're not a politician! Har Yrs 10:13-14 O '70
CHANDLER, Edna Walker
Different kind of Christmas tree. il Am For 76:32-4 D '70
CHANDLER, John A. See Schafer, P. W. jt. auth.
CHANDLER, Marvin
Challenge of consumerism. Duns 95:112 Ap '70 *
CHANDLER, Ariz.
Air force aids city in disaster prevention. il Am City 85:58 Mr '70
LP-gas cuts police car costs, improves performance. W. T. Louthan. il Am City 85: 87-8 Je '70
CHANDRA, G. S. Sharat
Drowning; poem. Nation 211:570 N 30 '70
CHANDRA, Helen
Chandrasekhar on scientists and society. por Bul Atom Sci 26:11-14 N '70
CHANDRASEKHAR, Subrahmanyan
Chandrasekhar on scientists and society. H. Chandra. por Bul Atom Sci 26:11-14 N '70 *
CHANELES, Sol, and Snyder, Jerome
Santa makes a change; story. Parents Mag 45:46-9 D '70
CHANEY, Ed
Too much for the Columbia River salmon. il Nat Wildlife 8:18-21 Ap '70
CHANG, Thomas M. S.
Biochemical microcapsules. Sci N 97:389 Ap 18 '70 *
CHANGE
See also
Educational innovations
Social change
Technological change
CHANGE, Educational. See Educational innovations
CHANGE of fashion; story. See Wiser, W.
CHANGE of life in women. See Menopause
CHANGE of sex
Trans-sexuals: male or female? R. H. Berg. il Look 34:28-31 Ja 27 '70
CHANGING times (periodical)
Find out how your investments are really doing; new Changing times computer service. il Changing T 24:47-9 Mr '70
CHANNEL bass fishing. See Bass fishing
CHANNELS (hydraulic engineering)
Crisis on our rivers. J. N. Miller and R. Simmons. il Read Digest 97:78-83 D '70
Ditches are quicker; channelization, the Soil conservation service program. W. Humphrey. il por Life 69:58-61 Ag 7 '70
Gravediggers; channelization program of the CSC. E. A. Bauer and B. East. il Outdoor Life 146:29-31+ Jl '70
CHANOCK, R. M.
Control of acute mycoplasmal and viral respiratory tract disease. bibliog il Science 169:248-56 Jl 17 '70
CHANTILLY, France
Sporting scene; Prix du jockey club, and Prix de Diane. F. Feldkamp. New Yorker 46:62+ Je 6 '70

CHANTS (Gregorian, plain, etc)
  Performance of the Old Hall descant settings.
    A. B. Scott. bibliog f il Mus Q 56:14-26 Ja
    '70
  Responsories and prosa for St Stephen's day
    at Salisbury. R. Steiner. bibliog f il Mus Q
    56:162-82 Ap '70
CHAO, E. C. T. and others
  Petrology of unshocked crystalline rocks and
    shock effects in lunar rocks and minerals.
    bibliog il Science 167:644-7 Ja 30 '70
CHAPARAS, Sotiros D. and others
  Tuberculin-active carbohydrate that induces
    inhibition of macrophage migration but not
    lymphocyte transformation. bibliog il Sci-
    ence 170:637-9 N 6 '70
CHAPARRAL
  Chaparral. S. F. Kircher. il Audubon 72:4-15
    N '70
CHAPARRAL 2J. See Automobiles, Racing
CHAPEL attendance. See Church attendance
CHAPIN, Kim
  Money in his pocket, speed in his soul. il
    por Sports Illus 32:38-40+ My 11 '70
  Motor sports (cont) Sports Illus 32:63+ Je
    15; 33:69-70+ S 28; 62-3 O 19 '70
CHAPIN, Roy Dikeman, 1915-
  Chapin's folly? A. A. Butkus. por Duns 95:
    63-4 My '70 *
CHAPLAINS, College. See Colleges and univer-
    sities—Religious life
CHAPLAINS, Congressional. See United States
    —Congress—Chaplains
CHAPLAINS, Military
  Antiwar spirit seen hurting chaplaincy re-
    cruitment. Chr Cent 87:1034 S 2 '70
  Military chaplaincy, by G. C. Zahn. Review
    Cath World 211:40-2 Ap '70. G. MacEoin
    Commonweal 92:70-1 Mr 27 '70. M. Siegel
  Onward Christian soldiers: dehumanization
    and the military chaplain. R. E. Klitgaard.
    il Chr Cent 87:1377-80 N 18 '70; Discussion.
    87:1569; 88:20 D 30 '70, Ja 6 '71
CHAPLAINS, Police
  God squads. il Newsweek 76:63 S 28 '70
CHAPMAN, A. R.
  Hunting the bee tree. il Am For 76:16-19
    Ag '70
CHAPMAN, Colin
  Why the Lotus is in high gear. il por Bsns
    W p41 F 7 '70 *
CHAPMAN, Daniel
  Will Mia's sister make it? il pors Look 34:
    48-53 S 22 '70
CHAPMAN, Daniel T.
  Great white father's little red Indian school.
    il Am Heritage 22:48-53+ D '70
CHAPMAN, Mrs John D.
  American family on the move: the Chapmans.
    il por Vogue 155:86-7 Je '70 *
CHAPMAN, John Jay
  Only true defiance. C. McWilliams. Nation
    210:442-4 Ap 13 '70 *
CHAPMAN, Leonard F. 1913-
  After troop withdrawal; address, June 23,
    1970. Vital Speeches 36:628-31 Ag 1 '70
CHAPMAN, Sydney
  Obituary
    Phys Today 23:83 S '70. J. A. Van Allen
CHAPMAN, Victoria
  Plus and a minus. il Sr Schol 95:19 N 17 '69
CHAPPELL, John. See Veeh, H. H. jt. auth.
CHAPPELL, Warren
  Chappell's printing history is issued; his
    work in the book arts exhibited. il Pub W
    198:50-1 N 9 '70 *
CHAPPELL, William Venroe, 1922-
  Crime; address, March 30, 1970. Vital Speeches
    36:423-5 My 1 '70
CHAPPELL, Winston and others
  Experiment in integration. Ed Digest 35:38-41
    Ja '70
CHAR fishing
  Greenland salmon. M. Sosin. il Field & S
    75:54-5+ My '70
  This is adventure; char and trout fishing.
    R. Cochran. il pors Outdoor Life 146:36-9+
    Jl '70
  Wilderness adventure in Alaska; Dolly Var-
    den trout fishing. B. Thomas. il Travel
    133:34-9+ Je '70
CHARACEAE. See Stoneworts
CHARACTER
    See also
  Personality
  Temperament
CHARACTER analysis
  Those telltale executive gestures. J. Ross-
    Skinner. il Duns 95:66-7 Mr '70
    See also
  Character tests
  Palmistry
CHARACTER education. See Moral education

CHARACTER reading. See Character analysis;
    Graphology
CHARACTER sketches
  My most unforgettable character. R. Barber.
    See issues of Reader's digest
CHARACTER tests
  What's your maturity quotient? excerpts from
    Power of maturity. L. Binstock. Read Di-
    gest 96:122-3 Mr '70
    See also
  Personality tests

        Anecdotes, facetiae, satire, etc.
  Kool-keeping kwiz. C. Kohler. Pop Electr
    32:63-4 Je '70
CHARACTERIZATION
  Behavioral objectives in the English class-
    room: a model; Shane as example of unit
    on characterization analysis. L. Dieter.
    Engl J 59:1259-62+ D '70
  Characterization. W. Harrison. Writer 83:21-
    3+ Je '70
  Characters in Wanderland. M. Dutton. Writer
    83:22-4 O '70
  Getting to know them. N. Lofts. Writer 83:
    9-10+ N '70
  Give your characters free rein. G. Roark.
    Writer 83:13-15 Jl '70
  Heroes and villains in stories for children
    and teenagers; excerpts from Writing for
    children and teenagers. L. Wyndham. il
    Writers Digest 50:32-3+ N '70
  Long, long trail. R. F. Delderfield. Writer
    84:9-12 Ja '71
  Novelist as village idiot. U. Zilinsky. Writer
    83:24-6 D '70
CHARACTERIZATION (acting) See Acting
CHARACTERS in literature
  Ages of heroes. P. Butler. Sat R 53:4 Jl 11 '70
  Art of Herman Melville: the author of Pi-
    erre. R. J. Nelson. Yale R 59:197-214 D '69
  Everything is a character. G. Cuomo. Writer
    83:15-16+ F '70
  Looking backwards, and ahead, with Alice. N.
    Hentoff. il Wilson Lib Bul 45:169-71 O '70
  Portis' True grit: adventure story or ent-
    wicklungsroman? R. B. Shuman. Engl J
    59:367-70 Mr '70
  Real Little Lord Fauntleroy. T. McCarthy. il
    pors Am Heritage 21:50-5+ F '70
  Uncommon man. L. Gemello and W. E.
    Wilde. Engl J 59:1266-9 D '70
    See also
  Characterization
  Don Juan
  Women in literature
CHARACTERS in opera
  Curious girl; Puccini's girl, Minnie. R. Mohr.
    Opera N 34:24-5 Mr 14 '70
  Disadvantaged youth. J. Ferris. Opera N 34:13
    Mr 14 '70
  How to say it: a pronunciation guide for the
    Metropolitan opera's 1970-71 broadcasts.
    Opera N 35:28-9 D 12 '70
  Letter from Lerchenau; facetious letter from
    Baron Ochs to a kinsman, May 27, 1746.
    F. Rizzo. Opera N 34:16 F 28 '70
  Sight and insight; blind characters in opera.
    S. Zisselman. Opera N 34:6-7 F 14 '70
CHARCAS, Bolivia
  Potosí and Charcas. R. P. Romecín. il Amé-
    ricas 22:2-7 Mr '70
CHARCOAL briquets. See Briquets (fuel)
CHARCOAL drawing
  Drawing with erasers. M. Acosta. il Design
    71:27 Sum '70
CHARDIN, Pierre Teilhard de. See Teilhard
    de Chardin, P.
CHARDKOFF, Richard B.
  Cuna revolt. il Américas 22:14-21 Jl '70
  Fort San Lorenzo. il Américas 22:2-8 F '70
CHARGE accounts (retail trade)
  Bugs in billing: problems for customers and
    business. il U S News 69:74-5 Ag 24 '70
  Credit-ability gap: a wise woman's guide to
    buying without cash. V. Cadden. Redbook
    135:58+ S '70
  Warning! Double-check those charge ac-
    counts. il Changing T 24:7-10 O '70
CHARGE-coupled devices. See Semiconductors
CHARGE-mosaic membranes. See Membranes
    (technology)
CHARGERS, Battery. See Storage battery
    chargers
CHARISMATA. See Gifts, Spiritual
CHARITABLE societies
    See also
  Charities

CHARITIES
Power of a woman at Christmas. il Ladies Home J 87:46 D '70
Rich man's burden, and how Andrew Carnegie unloaded it; excerpts from Andrew Carnegie. J. F. Wall. il pors Am Heritage 21:58-67+ O '70
See also
Community chests
Corporations—Charitable contributions
Foundations, Charitable and educational
Fund raising
Giving

CHARITY
Soup, soap, and salvation. Chr Today 15:24 D 4 '70

CHARITY; story. See Nissenson, H.

CHARLEROI-BRUSSELS CANAL. See Canals—Belgium

CHARLES V, emperor of the Holy Roman empire
Charles V, by O. von Habsburg. Review Nat R 22:848-9 Ag 11 '70. E. M. von Kuehnelt-Leddihn *

CHARLES V, the Wise, king of France
Duty of the prince is magnificence. M. Bishop. il pors Horizon 12:54-79 Aut '70

CHARLES, prince of Wales
Accent on youth in a royal visit. il pors U S News 69:50-1 Jl 27 '70 *
Charles & Anne & David & Julie & Tricia; visit to the White House. pors Time 96:10-11 Jl 27 '70 *
Commoner's guide to conversation with Charles and Anne. il pors Life 69:64A-66 Jl 17 '70 *
Lingering love of the royal; White House visit. H. Sidey. pors Life 69:4 Jl 31 '70 *
Young Windsors pay a call. il pors Newsweek 76:12-13B Jl 27 '70 *

CHARLES, J.
Using silicon transistors as zeners. il Electr World 83:86 Ja '70

CHARLES, Milton
New World's creative director builds a '70s image and sales, too; interview, ed. by M. R. Kraner. il por Pub W 198:48-50 D 28 '70

CHARLES, Ray
Profiles. W. Balliett. por New Yorker 46:44-6+ Mr 28 '70 *

CHARLES, Ron
They shoot hippies, don't they? interview, ed. by F. Browning. Ramp Mag 9:21-3 N '70

CHARLES Evans Hughes awards. See National conference of Christians and Jews

CHARLESON, Jack
Sans stove. il por Motor B 125:68-9+ Je; 126:58+ Jl '70

CHARLESTON, S. C.
Special Charleston issue; symposium. il Antiques 97:538-95 Ap '70

Architecture
Architectural trends in Charleston. A. Simons. il Antiques 97:545-55 Ap '70

Churches
Mortuary art in Charleston churches. C. V. Hershey. il Antiques 98:800-7 N '70

City planning
Endangered Charleston. R. Kirk. Nat R 22:628 Je 16 '70

Description
Charms of Charleston. J. G. Smith. il Travel & Camera 33:28-33+ F '70
Step by step through Charleston. R. Deardorff. il Travel 133:32-7 Ap '70
Walk through Charleston. J. G. Smith. il Travel & Camera 33:69-70 F '70

Galleries and museums
American art at the Gibbes art gallery in Charleston. F. W. Bilodeau. il Antiques 98:782-6 N '70

Historic houses, etc.
Architectural trends in Charleston. A. Simons. il Antiques 97:545-55 Ap '70
George Eveleigh house home of Mr and Mrs Huger Sinkler. F. R. Edmunds. il Antiques 97:579-81 Ap '70
Josiah Smith house, home of Mr and Mrs Thomas R. Bennett. F. R. Edmunds. il Antiques 97:582-3 Ap '70
Seven great Charleston houses. W. H. J. Thomas il Antiques 97:556-70 Ap '70

History
Gallantry under fire. D. Vestal. il Travel & Camera 33:34-9 F '70
History of Charleston, 1670-1860. G. C. Rogers, jr. Antiques 97:540-1 Ap '70

Maps
Town plan of Charleston. R. Wright. Antiques 97:542-4 Ap '70

Public buildings
Public buildings of Charleston. B S. Ravenel. il Antiques 97:584-9 Ap '70

CHARLESTON furniture. See Furniture, American

CHARLESTON silver. See Silverware

CHARLESWORTH, James C.
(ed) New American posture toward Asia. bibliog f Ann Am Acad 390:1-113 Jl '70

CHARLEY'S aunt; drama. See Thomas, B.

CHARLIER, Patricia S. See Charlier, R. H. jt. auth.

CHARLIER, Roger Henri, and Charlier, P. S.
Matthew Fontaine Maury, Cyrus Field and the physical geography of the sea. il pors Sea Front 16:272-81 S '70

CHARLOT, Jean
Jean Charlot. S. Baciu. il por Américas 22:22-9 Jl '70 *

CHARLOTTE, N.C.

Education
Busing quandary. il Newsweek 76:63 Ag 24 '70
Southern city, troubled, angry, divided. il U S News 68:29-32 Mr 16 '70

Parks and playgrounds
Scout power builds a park in one day. il Am City 85:99+ Je '70

CHARLTON, Ronald K. and Zmijewski, C. M.
Soluble HL-A7 antigen: localization in the β-lipoprotein fraction of human serum. bibliog il Science 170:636-7 N 6 '70

CHARM, Stanley E. and Wong, B. L.
Shear degradation of fibrinogen in the circulation. bibliog il Science 170:466-8 O 23 '70

CHARM, Walter B.
Microfossil and the sea floor. il Sea Front 16:71-6 Mr '70

CHARM. See Personality

CHARMS
See also
Amulets

CHARRETTE committees. See Citizens associations

CHARRIÈRE, Henri
Authors & editors. D. N. Mount. il por Pub W 198:19-21 D 28 '70 *
Banality of evil. D. Littlejohn. New Repub 163:23-4 O 3 '70 *
Butterflies are free. S. K. Oberbeck. il por Newsweek 76:81-2 S 7 '70 *
Fabulous escapes of Papillon. il pors Life 69:46-52+ N 13 '70 *
Pinning down a butterfly. il por Newsweek 75:50 Mr 16 '70 *
Travels with Papi. por Time 96:90+ S 14 '70 *

CHARTER airlines. See Airlines—Non-scheduled operations

CHARTER company
Land, money or oil. Forbes 106:53 N 1 '70
What the senator didn't disclose; J. Tydings hasn't met the standards he has set. W. Lambert. pors Life 69:26-9 Ag 28 '70

CHARTER of the United Nations. See United Nations—Charter

CHARTERING of airplanes. See Airplanes—Chartering

CHARTERING of yachts. See Yachts—Chartering

CHARTIER, Myron R.
Christian sensitivity. Chr Today 14:9-10 Jl 3 '70

CHARTS, Calculating
Easy way to determine reflex enclosure dimensions. E. G. Lescault. il Pop Electr 33:64 D '70
Nomogram aids voltage-drop calculations. J. E. McAlister. il Electr World 84:46 D '70
Nomograms for resonant-circuit Q. D. W. Moffat. il Electr World 83:30-1 My '70
Voltage regulator design nomograms. C. W. Young. il Electr World 84:32-3 Ag '70

CHARTS, Nautical. See Nautical charts

CHARTS, Stock. See Stocks—Price indexes and averages

CHASAN, Daniel Jack
On this side, nothing but virgin wilderness; on that side, nothing but virgin wilderness; down the middle, the Trans Alaska pipeline. Esquire 73:129+ Je '70

CHEMICAL and biological weapons
Behind the Nixon policy for chemical and biological warfare; excerpts from testimony before the Senate committee on foreign relations, April 30, 1969. M. S. Meselson. Bul Atom Sci 26:23-4+ Ja '70
CBW: interagency conflicts stall administration action. S. Z. Goldhaber. Science 169: 454-6 Jl 31 '70
Chemical and biological defense policies and programs; statement, November 25, 1969; with text of 1925 Geneva protocol and U K draft convention. R. M. Nixon. Dept State Bul 61:541-3 D 15 '69
Chemical and biological methods of warfare; statement, December 10, 1969; with text of resolutions. J. F. Leonard. Dept State Bul 62:95-9 Ja 26 '70
Chemical and biological weapons. M. S. Meselson. il Sci Am 222:15-25 My '70
Closing the CBW loophole. Sci N 97:194+ F 21 '70
Control of chemical and biological weapons; statement, August 27, 1970. J. F. Leonard. Dept State Bul 63:330-6 S 21 '70
Geneva protocol on gases and bacteriological warfare resubmitted to the Senate; President Nixon's message and Secretary Rogers' report. R. M. Nixon; W. P. Rogers. Dept State Bul 63:273-5 S 7 '70
Germs and toxins. Commonweal 91:523-4 F 13 '70
Horror of bacteriological and chemical weaponry. il UNESCO Courier 23:15-17+ N '70
Same old gas. J. Deedy. Commonweal 93:58 O 16 '70
U.S. rejects germ war. Sr Schol 95:4-5 Ja 12 '70
U.S. renounces use of toxins as a method of warfare; White House announcement, February 14, 1970. Dept State Bul 62:226-7 Mr 2 '70
U.S. supports inclusion of toxins in biological warfare convention; statement, April 20, 1970. J. F. Leonard. Dept State Bul 62:731 Je 8 '70
United States explains position on chemical and biological weapons; statement, with text of a U.S. working paper, March 17, 1970. J. F. Leonard. Dept State Bul 62: 552-7 Ap 27 '70
  See also
Gases, Asphyxiating and poisonous
Tear gas
    Accidents
Muckuppery along the Potomac. R. Bongartz. Esquire 73:70+ Je '70
CHEMICAL apparatus and supplies
Amateur scientist; how to make an isoteniscope: an apparatus for measuring the boiling point of fluids. W. Averett. il Sci Am 223:116-21 D '70
Hofmann apparatus and leak rate of gases. J. Harshman and G. Melville. il pors Chem 43:26 Je '70
Measurement of fast biochemical reactions, flow and relaxation methods. A. N. Schechter. bibliog il Science 170:273-80 O 16 '70
CHEMICAL bonds
Chemical bond and solid-state physics; adaptation of address. March 1969. J. C. Phillips. bibliog il por Phys Today 23:23-30 F '70
Electron-repulsion theory: application to aliphatic and aromatic hydrocarbons. S. Zuffanti. bibliog il por Chem 43:8-13 My '70
Hydrogen bonding in hydrochloric acid solutions. S. C. Lee and R. Kaplow. bibliog il Science 169:477-8 Jl 31 '70
Ionic bonding in solids. J. E House, jr. bibliog il por Chem 43:18-22 F '70
Polywater: possibility of p-electron delocalization. R. P. Messmer. bibliog Science 168: 479-80 Ap 24 '70
Proposed new structure for polywater. il Chem 43:22 My '70
Structural aspects of interatomic charge-transfer bonding; Nobel prize lecture, June 9, 1970. O. Hassel. bibliog il Science 170: 497-502 O 30 '70
Symmetric hydrogen bonds give form to anomalous water. il Sci N 97:287 Mr 21 '70
  See also
Molecular orbitals
CHEMICAL burns. See Burns and scalds
CHEMICAL elements
Diagonal periodic relationship. W. M. Allen. bibliog il por Chem 43:22-4 Ap '70
From Mendeleev to Mendelevium and beyond; evolution of the periodic table. G. T. Seaborg. il por Chem 43:6-9+ Ja '70
How well do you know the elements? quiz. Sci Digest 68:25+ N '70

Mineral cycles. E. S. Deevey, jr. il Sci Am 223:148-68 bibliog(p264-5) S '70
Theodore William Richards and the periodic table; adaptation of address, December 29, 1969. J. B. Conant. bibliog Science 168:425-8 Ap 24 '70
  See also
Actinide elements
Atomic weights
Earths, Rare
    Atomic no. 105
Element 105. il Chem 43:20 Je '70
Element 105: Flerov reiterates Dubna priority claim. G. B. Lubkin. Phys Today 23:18 N '70
Element 105 synthesized and named hahnium by Berkeley researchers. R. W. Holcomb. Science 168:810 My 15 '70
Elemental discovery; chemical element may be named hahnium. Time 95:52 My 11 '70
Enter no. 105. il Newsweek 75:109-10 My 11 '70
Next in the transactinides. Sci N 97:430 My 2 '70
Upward and Hahnward. Sci Am 222:48-9 Je '70
    Atomic no. 113
Predicted properties of elements 113 and 114. O. L. Keller, jr. bibliog il por Chem 43: 8-11 N '70
CHEMICAL equations
Redox reactions and the acid-base properties of solvents. J. A. Bishop. bibliog il Chem 43: 18 Ja '70
CHEMICAL formulas. See Chemistry—Notation
CHEMICAL geology. See Geochemistry
CHEMICAL industries
Grim pursuit of quicksilver; tightening of leaks by chlor-alkali producers. il Bsns W p42+ Jl 18 '70
  See also
American cyanamid company
Chemical plants
Dow chemical company
Du Pont de Nemours, E. I. and company
Fertilizer industry and trade
Imperial chemical industries, ltd.
Lubrizol corporation
Monsanto company
Rohm and Haas company
Shell chemical company
Union carbide corporation

    Agricultural operations
Chemical companies take to the land. Bsns W p30+ N 21 '70

    Finance
Chemicals feel the profit sting. Bsns W p45 O 17 '70
Chemicals; with yardsticks of management performance. il Forbes 105:85-7+ Ja 1 '70; 107:88+ Ja 1 '71
Mixed results for the majors. il Bsns W p38+ Ap 25 '70

    Germany (Federal Republic)
BASF backs off from a beachhead; proposed South Carolina plant il Bsns W p29-30 Ap 11 '70
BASF gets a bid from Georgia. Bsns W p31 Ap 25 '70
BASF trips on synthetic fibers. por Bsns W p24 D 26 '70
Battle of Beaufort; conservation collides with the jobless. A. Simon. New Repub 162:11-15 My 23 '70
Chemical giants wince at a profit pinch. il Bsns W p34+ S 26 '70
Hoechst: tomorrow the world? J. Ross-Skinner. por Duns 95:71-2+ Je '70
Introduction to the setting and characters of the tragical farce or farcical tragedy of Victoria Bluffs, S.C; BASF corp. in New York city to open plant. A. Ternes. il Natur Hist 79:8-10+ Ap '70
Shrimp boats are a-comin'; protests to BSAF plant. il Am For 76:26-7 Jl '70
View from Hilton Head; Badische anilin und soda-fabrik. M. Frady. il Harper 240:103-12 My '70
    Italy
More state control; case of Montecatini Edison. Time 96:92 N 2 '70
More state control over Montedison. Bsns W p28-9 O 31 '70
CHEMICAL information services. See Science —Information services
CHEMICAL plants
Jackpot is a chemical plant; PASA's Argentine petrochemical plant. il Bsns W p48 F 28 '70

CHEMICAL plants—*Continued*

Location

BASF backs off from a beachhead; proposed South Carolina plant. il Bsns W p29-30 Ap 11 '70

BASF gets a bid from Georgia. Bsns W p31 Ap 25 '70

Battle of Beaufort; conservation collides with the jobless. A. Simon. New Repub 162:11-15 My 23 '70

Fight at Hilton Head; BASF project. il Newsweek 75:71-2+ Ap 13 '70

Fight for Hilton Head Island; proposed site of BASF plant. H. Drane. il Am For 76:12-15+ My '70

Introduction to the setting and characters of the tragical farce or farcical tragedy of Victoria Bluffs, S.C; BASF corp. in New York city to open plant. A. Ternes. il Natur Hist 79:8-10+ Ap '70

Shrimp boats are a-comin'; protests to BSAF plant. il Am For 76:26-7 Jl '70

Troubled little island; proposed site of American subsidiary of BASF. il Time 95:55+ Ja 26 '70

View from Hilton Head; Badische anilin und soda-fabrik. M. Frady. il Harper 240:103-12 My '70

CHEMICAL reactions

Bimodal sedimenting zones due to ligand-mediated interactions. J. R. Cann and W. B. Goad. bibliog il Science 170:441-5 O 23 '70

Measurement of fast biochemical reactions; flow and relaxation methods. A. N. Schechter. bibliog il Science 170:273-80 O 16 '70

Orbital rendezvous. Sci Am 223:46 Ag '70

Orbital symmetry control of chemical reactions. R. Hoffmann and R. B. Woodward. bibliog il Science 167:825-31 F 6 '70

Substitution reactions in metal complexes. J. E. House, jr. bibliog il por Chem 43:11-14 Je '70

See also
Chemical equations

Velocity
See Chemical reactions

CHEMICAL research

No doubt about suffering; crisis in organic chemistry. Sci N 97:476-7 My 16 '70

See also
Gordon research conferences

CHEMICAL societies
See also
American chemical society

CHEMICAL tillage. See Tillage

CHEMICAL tools. See Tools

CHEMICAL warfare

Memo to the chemists; importance of supporting Senate ratification of the Geneva protocol of 1925. Nation 211:166 S 7 '70

Pains over U.S. gas policy: won't ban tear gas or herbicides. Sr Schol 95:5 Ja 12 '70

See also
Chemical and biological weapons

CHEMICAL workers
See also
International federation of chemical and general workers' unions

CHEMICALS
See also
Agricultural chemicals
Plasticizers

Manufacture
See also
Chemical industries

Prices

Where price rises cheer an industry. il Bsns W p30 D 5 '70

Transportation

Dangerous route to Houston. il Bsns W p26 My 9 '70

CHEMISTRY

Chemistry. See occasional issues of Science news

See also
Alchemy
Biochemistry
Chemical elements
Chemical equations
Gases
Geochemistry
Hydrolysis
Photochemistry
Photographic chemistry
Poisons
Radicals (chemistry)
Stereochemistry

Experiments

Lab bench. See issues of Chemistry

History

Great moments in chemistry; tr. by R. E. Oesper (cont) F. Szabadvary il Chem 43:5-7 D '70

Theodore William Richards and the periodic table; adaptation of address, December 29, 1969. J. B. Conant. bibliog Science 168:425-8 Ap 24 '70

Information services
See Science—Information services

Notation

Fixed valence and molecular formula verification. E. Garfield and others. bibliog il Chem 43:13-15 O '70

Proposed structural shorthand for organic chemistry. G. W. Evans. il Chem 43:18-19 My '70

Study and teaching

Survey of the teaching of chemistry in secondary schools F. J. Fornoff. Sch & Soc 98:242-3 Ap '70

CHEMISTRY, Analytic

Lab bench. See issues of Chemistry
See also
Chromatographic analysis
Polarograph and polarography
Proteins—Analysis
Separation (chemistry)
Spectrophotometry

Quantitative
See also
Volumetric analysis

CHEMISTRY, Organic

Apollo 11 lunar science conference: organic chemistry: symposium. bibliog il Science 167:751-80 Ja 30 '70

Singlet molecular oxygen from superoxide anion and sensitized fluorescence of organic molecules. A. U. Khan. bibliog il Science 168:476-7 Ap 24 '70

See also
Biosynthesis
Enzymes

Notation
See Chemistry—Notation

CHEMISTRY, Physical and theoretical
See also
Atomic weights
Compressibility
Molecular association
Phases (chemistry)
Radiochemistry
Solution (chemistry)

CHEMISTRY, Technical
See also
Coal tar colors

CHEMISTRY as a profession

Why should anyone study chemistry? D. L. Bunker. il por Chem 43:16-17 S '70

CHEMISTRY in literature

Chemistry in language and literature. E. G. De France. por Chem 43:16-17 Ap '70

CHEMISTS

Chemists' involvement in society. R. Ferreira. bibliog il pors Chem 43:16-17 O; 12-13 D '70

See also
American society of biological chemists

CHEMOSTERILIZATION. See Sterilization, Sexual

CHEMOSURGERY

Help is on the way. il Vogue 156:172 N 1 '70

CHEMOTAXIS. See Chemotropism

CHEMOTHERAPY

Transfer of interferon-producing macrophages: new approach to viral chemotherapy. L. A. Glasgow. bibliog il Science 170:854-6 N 20 '70

CHEMOTROPISM

Inflammation and herpes simplex virus: release of a chemotaxis-generating factor from infected cells. A. M. Brier and others. bibliog il Science 170:1104-6 D 4 '70

CHEN, Di, and Tufte, O. N.

Optical memories, now and in the future. pors Electr World 84:56-60 O '70

CHEN, Tina

Tina Chen, China doll. por Vogue 156:20 Ag 1 '70 *

CHEN, Tseh-an, and Granados, R. R.

Plant-pathogenic mycoplasma like organism: maintenance in vitro and transmission to zea mays L. bibliog il Science 167:1633-6 Mr 20 '70

CHENEY, Frances Neel
  Current reference books. See issues of Wilson
    library bulletin
CHENEY, Margaret
  Bird is a verb. il Audubon 72:42-3 Ja '70
CHENG, Roger J.
  Water drop freezing: ejection of microdrop-
    lets. bibliog il Science 170:1395-6 D 25 '70
CHENNAULT, Anna
  Air America: flying the U.S. into Laos. P.
    D. Scott. por Ramp Mag 8:39-42+ F '70
CHENNAULT, Claire Lee
  Air America: flying the U.S. into Laos. P.
    D. Scott. por Ramp Mag 8:39-42+ F '70 *
CHENOWETH, J. Ray
  Mystery of rockhounding. il Har Yrs 10:34-6
    Je '70
CHERINGTON, Paul W.
  Transportation mess: some practical solu-
    tions; interview. por Forbes 107:170+ Ja 1
    '71
  Transportation turnaround? interview, ed. by
    G. R. Rosen. por Duns 96:14-16+ Jl '70
CHERMAYEFF, Ivan
  Images of America. il Art in Am 58:60-1 Mr
    '70
            about
  Sign. D. Davis. il por Newsweek 77:89 Ja 11
    '71 *
CHERNE, Leo
  Struggle for survival; address, February 18,
    1970. Vital Speeches 36:407-11 Ap 15 '70
CHERNOV, Viktor Mikhailovich
  Lenin: a contemporary portrait; reprint from
    March 15, 1924 issue. For Affairs 48:471-7 Ap
    '70
CHEROKEE Indians
  Theft of a nation: apologies to the
    Cherokees. P. Collier. il por Ramp Mag
    9:35-45 S '70
CHERRY, Jim
  NEA expels school superintendent. Sch & Soc
    98:14-15 Ja '70
CHERRYSTONE juniper. See Juniper
CHERVENICK, Paul A. and Boggs, D. R.
  Bone marrow colonies: stimulation in vitro
    by supernatant from incubated human
    blood cells. bibliog il Science 169:691-2 Ag
    14 '70
CHERWONY, Walter. See Orth, H. R. jt. auth.
CHESAPEAKE appreciation day. See Regattas
CHESAPEAKE BAY
  Chesapeake Bay fights for its life. il Bsns
    W p40-1+ Mr 7 '70
  Statement of concern: possible effects of nu-
    clear power plant. E. Radford and others.
    bibliog il Environ 11:18-27 S '69
    See also
  Tangier Island
CHESEBRO, Ann
  We did it; ed. by E. Kinard. il House B 112:
    52+ My '70
CHESHER, Richard H.
  Destruction of Pacific corals by the sea star
    acanthaster planci. bibliog Science 165:280-
    3; 1275 Jl 18 '69. F 27 '70
CHESHIRE, Maxine
  Liberated, all liberated. il pors Vogue 155:
    122-3 Je '70 *
  That Cheshire cat. S. B. Conroy. il pors
    Ladies Home J 87:80-1+ Mr '70 *
CHESS
  Chess corner. A. Horowitz. See issues of
    Saturday review
  Cognitive model of problem-solving in chess.
    M. J. Scurrah and D. A. Wagner. il Science
    169:209-11 Jl 10 '70
  Enigma tries a new role; R. Fischer as a
    spirited team player. L. Evans. Sports Illus
    33:85-7 O 12 '70
  Is Boris good enough? Fischer-Spassky match
    at the Yugoslav tournament. il News-
    week 75:130-1 Ap 20 '70
  Rest of the world sort of strikes back; great-
    est match in the history of chess. L. Evans.
    Sports Illus 32:62-3 Ap 20 '70
CHESS sets
  Chess for Christmas. il Sunset 145:74-5 D '70
CHESSMEN
  Enchanted chessmen. F. V. Grunfeld. il Hori-
    zon 12:100-3 Wint '70
CHEST banks. See Banks, Coin
CHESTATEE regional library, Gainesville, Ga.
  Chestatee, Georgia: library and regional HQ.
    il Library J 95:4139 D 1 '70
CHESTER COUNTY, Pa.
  Coaching: the new in sport. P. Benchley. il
    Travel & Camera 33:40-5+ F '70
      Historic houses, etc.
  Wyeth country. M. Evans. il Am Home 73:
    74-82+ O '70

CHESTERFIELD, Philip Dormer Stanhope, 4th
    earl of
  Ill conduct and manners of students on their
    travels abroad. Sch & Soc 98:33+ Ja '70
CHESTERTON, Gilbert Keith
  GBS/GKC, by W. B. Furlong. Review
    America 123:101-2 Ag 22 '70. W. T. Noon *
  G. K. Chesterton, ed. by W. H. Auden. Re-
    view
    Commonweal 93:151-2 N 6 '70. G. Wills *
  Shaw and Chesterton, by W. B. Furlong.
    Review
    Cath World 212:157-8 D '70. K. M. Res-
    taino *
CHESTNUT trees
  Connecticut revives the chestnut. C. T. Hub-
    bard. il Am For 76:26-8 D '70
CHESTS
  Beautiful budget chest. J. Capotosto. il Mech
    Illus 66:74-5+ My '70
  Campaign chest. il Mech Illus 66:114+ Mr '70
  How to build a mini-chest in Spanish style.
    R. J. De Cristoforo. il Pop Sci 197:83-5+
    D '70
  Kindling and storage box. il Mech Illus 66:80-
    1 My '70
  You can create period styling with stock
    moldings. R. Wortham. il Pop Mech 133:
    166-8 Je '70
CHESTS, Community. See Community chests
CHEVALIER, Jean
  American color know-how transplanted to
    France. Pub W 198:pt2 186-7 S 21 '70
CHEVROLET motor company. See General
    motors corporation—Chevrolet division
CHEVRON oil company
  Big balloon caper; controversial ad. News-
    week 75:80+ Ap 27 '70
  Chevron indicted; toughest federal action
    against a polluter. Time 95:41 My 18 '70
  Crude on troubled waters. il Newsweek 75:77-
    8 Ap 6 '70
CHEW, Geoffrey F.
  Hadron bootstrap: triumph or frustration?
    bibliog il Phys Today 23:23-8 O '70
CHEWING tobacco. See Tobacco
CHEYENNE frontier days (festival) See
    Rodeos
CHEYENNE rodeo. See Rodeos
CHEZ Vito (restaurant) See New York (city)
    —Hotels, restaurants, etc.
CHI, Cheng
  Fortune smiles on this cookie. A. Verschoth. il
    por Sports Illus 32:48+ Je 22 '70 *
  Iron girl. il por Newsweek 75:80 Je 22 '70 *
  Records are falling to a China doll. il pors
    Life 69:34-5 Jl 10 '70 *
  Taiwan flash. il por Time 96:33 Jl 20 '70 *
CHIANG Ching. See Mao, T. T. Mme
CHIANG, Ching-kuo
  Shot at Chiang. il por Time 95:53 My 4 '70 *
  U.S. and Taiwan: new issues for old allies.
    il por US News 68:52 My 4 '70 *
  Vice Premier Chiang of China visits the
    United States. Dept State Bul 62:622 My
    18 '70 *
CHIANG, Kai-shek
  If Asia were clay in the hands of the West:
    the Stilwell mission to China, 1942-44; ex-
    cerpts from Stilwell. B. W. Tuchman. il
    pors Atlan 226:68-84 S '70 *
CHIAPPETTA, Jerry
  Fantastic island for whitetail. il por Field &
    S 75:38-9+ N '70
  McCormick tract. il por Field & S 75:76-7+
    My '70
CHIAVAROLI, Linda
  Ballet comes to Binghamton. il pors Dance
    Mag 44:28-32 Je '70
CHICAGO
  On the south side; Bridgeport. il por News-
    week 76:35-6 Jl 13 '70
        Airports
  CAB urges further Midway use. Aviation
    W 93:41 Ag 10 '70
  Chicago, CAB at odds over Midway. H. D.
    Watkins. Aviation W 92:53+ Ap 27 '70
  Fine mixup over Midway. il Bsns W p57-8+
    Ap 25 '70
  Jet-age scramble. il Life 70:56-66 Ja 8 '71
        Architecture
  Chicago style: glass-house living at its loft-
    iest; Lake point tower. J. L. O'Neill. il
    Am Home 73:48-55+ F '70
  First national bank of Chicago. il Arch Rec
    148:137-40 S '70
  Reaching for the skies; proposed skyscraper
    by Sears. Time 96:62 Ag 10 '70
  Soaring skylines: Chicago's new entry; the
    Sears tower. il U S News 69:65 Ag 10 '70

CHICAGO—Architecture—*Continued*
Strength and cohesiveness for a crowded block in Chicago; new fifteen story building. il Arch Rec 148:122-5 Jl '70
Thirty-story slab of ingenuity: Time-Life building. J. M. Dixon. il Arch Forum 133: 20-7 S '70
See also
Skyscrapers

Art
Chicago (cont) Art N 69:22 Mr '70
Chicago. R. Wagner. Art N 69:28+ O '70; 10+ Ja '71

Banks
Banker who tells it like it is; First national bank of Chicago. il por Bsns W p76-8 Je 20 '70

Bookstores
See Booksellers and bookselling—Illinois

Buildings
Bright new light on a sex symbol; Playboy building's xenon arc lamp. il Bsns W p22 Jl 4 '70
High society; John Hancock building. il Time 97:48 Ja 4 '71
Tall one; John Hancock center. J. M. Dixon. il Arch Forum 133:36-45 Jl '70
View from the 92nd floor; John Hancock center. il Newsweek 75:47 F 2 '70

City planning
Practical way to get involved; urban fellows program. il Bsns W p80 N 28 '70

Crime
Walk and talk; killing of James Severin and Anthony Rizzato. il pors Newsweek 76:23+ Ag 3 '70

Description
City of the big shoulders. T. Willis. il Opera N 35:8-12 O 31 '70

Education
English comes alive; program, conducted by Northwestern university's curriculum center in English. R. Blaine. il Am Ed 6:26-8 Je '70
McAndrew case: Britain at the Chicago bar; incident of 1927. H. K. Hutton and C. Galgoci. Sch & Soc 98:112-15 F '70
Magnet school; Disney experiment in elementary education. il Newsweek 76:75 O 12 '70
Moms are a must; Chicago's child-parent education centers. L. Wille. il Am Ed 6: 24-9 Ap '70
Project Wingspread; space-age education. J. Sternberg. il Schol Teach Sec Teach Sup p6-8 D 1 '69; Same abr. Ed Digest 35:16-17 Ap '70

Fire, October 1871
When the Midwest burned. D. A. Haines and E. L. Kuehnast. bibliog il Weatherwise 23:112-19 Je '70

Galleries and museums
See also
Chicago art institute
Museum of science and industry

Harbor
Exposed mooring; dockage bribes and the Chicago park district. il Newsweek 75:58 Je 22 '70

Haymarket square riot, 1886
Four score and six years ago; Wobblies, Weatherman and Haymarket square. R. W. Gibbons. Commonweal 92:285 Je 12 '70
Genteel backlash: Chicago 1886; excerpts from Nineteenth century cities. R. Sennett. il Trans-Action 7:41-50 Ja '70

History
Chicago: growth of a metropolis, by H. M. Mayer and R. C. Wade. Review
New Repub 162:28-9 F 21 '70. H. N. Jacobsen

Hotels, restaurants, etc.
Dining in/out with Esquire; Chez Paul. Esquire 73:35 My '70
Summer party ideas from a country restaurant; Farmer's Daughter in Orland Park, Ill. il House & Gard 138:92-3 Ag '70

Housing
Breakthrough for Chicago buyers; aid through the Contract buyers league. America 122:662 Je 27 '70

Chicago blacks fight a race tax. il Bsns W p78-9 Ja 24 '70
Curse of contract buying; evictions. C. C. Douglas. il Ebony 25:43-6+ Je '70
Jesuits and the contract buyers league. R. F. Smith. Chr Cent 87:246+ F 25 '70
Vertical ghetto; Cabrini-Green. il Newsweek 76:76 S 7 '70

John Hancock center
See Chicago—Buildings

Labor and laboring classes
Slave shops; day-labor agencies. il Newsweek 75:53 Mr 9 '70

Libraries
See also
Chicago public library

Monuments, statues, etc.
Four score and six years ago; Wobblies, Weathermen and Haymarket square. R. W. Gibbons. Commonweal 92:285 Je 12 '70
Rally round the Picasso, boys! E. Hotaling. il Art N 68:46-7+ Ja '70

Music
Behind the scenes. R. C. Marsh. il Hi Fi 20:secI 14 Jl '70
City of the big shoulders. T. Willis. il Opera N 35:8-12 O 31 '70
Report:
Concert-form operas. J. Stedman and G. Mc Elroy. il Opera N 35:23 S 5 '70
See also
Chicago symphony orchestra
Lyric opera of Chicago
Ravinia festival

Negroes
Breakthrough for Chicago buyers; aid through the Contract buyers league. America 122:662 Je 27 '70
Chicago blacks fight a race tax. il Bsns W p78-9 Ja 24 '70
Chicago: turning against the gangs. il por Time 96:13 Jl 27 '70
Courage of Sid Bennett. J. E. Roper. por Read Digest 96:199-201 Ap '70
Jesuits and the contract buyers league. R. F. Smith. Chr Cent 87:246+ F 25 '70
You can make it, baby! condensation. J. P. Blank. il por Read Digest 96:219-23+ Ja '70

Newspapers
Is right of access coming? ACWA suit against four Chicago newspapers. G. Cranberg. Sat R 53:48-9+ Ag 8 '70
See also
Chicago daily news

Parades
Who loves a parade? clearing parade litter. il Am City 85:38 Ag '70

Police
Ambushes in Chicago. Time 96:13 Ag 24 '70
Chicago: truth and Elrod. Time 96:17 Je 22 '70
Controversial verdict; inquest on Black Panther killings. Newsweek 75:23 F 2 '70
Dilemma of the black cop. R. Hall. il pors Life 69:60-60B+ S 18 '70
Heavy baggage; raid on the Panther headquarters. Nation 211:37 Jl 20 '70
Justice cops out; report of the January 1970 grand jury. N. Lewin. New Repub 162:14-18 Je 6 '70
Questions remain; police raid on Black Panther apartment. Time 95:26 My 25 '70
Slap on the wrist; Illinois dropping charges of attempted murder against the seven Panthers. Newsweek 75:41 My 25 '70
Walk and talk; killing of James Severin and Anthony Rizzato. il pors Newsweek 76:23+ Ag 3 '70

Politics and government
Take heart from the heartland. A. M. Greeley. New Repub 163:16-19 D 12 '70; Reply. T. Kelly. 163:9-11 D 26 '70

Poor
Uptown: poor whites in Chicago, by T. Gitlin and N. Hollander. Review
Nation 211:280-1 S 28 '70. S. Terkel

Religious institutions and affairs
Chicago's black churchmen: how their new executive sees their role. M. Stone. Chr Cent 87:578-80 My 6 '70
Needed: a new vision of the kingdom; North Side cooperative ministry in Chicago. Chr Cent 87:239-40 F 25 '70
See also
Moody Bible institute, Chicago

CHICAGO—*Continued*

Riots

Behind the Chicago conspiracy trial; with editorial comment. P. Glusman. il Ramp Mag 8:7+, 39-47 Ja '70
Courage of Sid Bennett. J. E. Roper. por Read Digest 96:199-201 Ap '70
Rock scene in Chicago's Grant Park. il Time 96:12 Ag 10 '70
Siege of Chicago: opinions of police action at convention. Trans-Action 7:12 Mr '70
Trial; excerpts. T. Hayden. il Ramp Mag 9:10-11+ Jl '70
Who killed Woodstock? Mayor Daley's pot festival. Grant park. il Newsweek 76:19 Ag 10 '70
See also
Chicago—Haymarket square riot, 1886

Sanitary affairs

Transporting wastes to build soils. J. Olds. il Org Gard & Farm 17:43-7 D '70

Social conditions

Social worker: survival expert in urban slums; Woodlawn, Chicago. R. Gosswiller. il Todays Health 48:59-62 S '70
See also
Chicago—Labor and laboring classes
Chicago—Poor
Institute for Jesuit community organizers, Chicago

Stockyards

Farewell to Hog Alley. Newsweek 76:67-8 Jl 20 '70
Gone with the atrocious wind. J. Morgenstern. Newsweek 76:21 N 23 '70
Market action shifts to the feedlot. W. Kester. il Farm J 94:B8-9 O '70

Streets

Traction salt spreader serves high-accident areas. il Am City 85:44 O '70

Strikes

Truck drivers' long dispute: costly blow to business. il U S News 68:51-2 Je 15 '70

Theater

Mecca for blackness; Affro-arts theater. il Ebony 25:96-8+ My '70

Traffic courts

Best traffic court in the Nation; Chicago. R. Schiller. Read Digest 96:219-20+ Ap '70

Transit systems

Automated bus system. il Am City 85:130+ S '70

Water and sewers department

Computer analyzes a hydraulic colossus. S. J. Rand. il Am City 85:102+ Je '70

Water supply

Big numbers tell Chicago's water story. Am City 85::50 S '70

Worlds Columbian exposition, 1893

Great Chicago piano war. P. Hume and R. Hume. il pors Am Heritage 21:16-21 O '70

CHICAGO and North Western railway
Can Heineman peddle a deadhead? proposed sale of Chicago & North Western railway to employees. por Bsns W p 19 O 3 '70
Gandy dancers' line; North Western employees transportation co. to acquire railroad. Time 96:79 O 19 '70
Railroad, anyone? Forbes 106::30 O 1 '70
Ties that bind; employee-ownership plan. Newsweek 75:68 Ap 6 '70
CHICAGO art institute
American silver at the Art institute of Chicago. D. A. Hanks. il Antiques 98:418-22 S '70
CHICAGO Bears (football club) See Football clubs
CHICAGO Black Hawks (hockey team) See Hockey teams
CHICAGO book clinic annual exhibit. See Book exhibits
CHICAGO Bulls. See Basketball teams
CHICAGO conspiracy trial. See Trials (conspiracy)
CHICAGO convention, 1968. See National conventions, Democratic
CHICAGO Cubs (baseball) See Baseball clubs
CHICAGO daily news
Horizontal in Washington. por Time 96:42 Ag 17 '70
CHICAGO fifteen trial. See Trials (conspiracy)
CHICAGO lyric opera. See Lyric opera of Chicago

CHICAGO, Milwaukee, St Paul and Pacific railroad company
Trouble rides the Milwaukee. il Bsns W p28-9 My 16 '70
CHICAGO park district
Exposed mooring; dockage bribes. il Newsweek 75:58 Je 22 '70
CHICAGO public library

Branches

Woodlawn: a photographic essay; with photos taken by Negro children under the direction of S. Rush. M. A. Fitzharris. il Am Lib 1:892-5 O '70
CHICAGO seven trial. See Trials (conspiracy)
CHICAGO symphony orchestra
Carlo Maria Giulini, in Chicago, a splendid diversity of excellences. M. Kanny. il Am Rec G 37:80-2+ O '70
Concerto by Levy, Solti, and Wild; the comic art of Tito Gobbi; concert performances of three operas. I. Kolodin. Sat R 53:35 D 19 '70
Musical events: all-Mahler program under G. Solti. W. Sergeant. New Yorker 45:56-7 Ja 17 '70
Musical events; concerts in Carnegie Hall, conducted by G. Solti. W. Sargeant. New Yorker 46:135 D 19 '70
See also
Ravinia festival
CHICAGO. University
Disciplinary procedures at the University of Chicago. Sch & Soc 98:204+ Ap '70
Small school Talent Search. Sch & Soc 98:72 F '70
University and the modern condition; excerpt from Point of view: talks on education. E. H. Levi. Science 170:1263 D 18 '70
CHICAGO university press
Direct sales: a different view. H. M. Levin. Pub W 198:15-18 Ag 10 '70
CHICAGO voice (newspaper) See Catholic press
CHICAGO White Sox (baseball) See Baseball clubs
CHICANOS. See Mexican Americans
CHICKEN as food. See Cookery—Poultry
CHICKEN curry. See Curry
CHICKEN fights. See Cock fighting
CHICKENS. See Poultry
CHICKERING, Lisa. See Porterfield, J. jt. auth.
CHICORY
Aristocrat of the winter crops; Belgian endive. J. J. Meeker. il pors Org Gard & Farm 17:34-8 S '70
This weed is chicory. il Sunset 145:146 Ag '70
CHIDESTER, Ann
Memory tree; story. Good H 170:72-3 Je '70
CHIEF justices. See Judges
CHIEF of naval operations. See United States —Navy department—Chief of naval operations
CHIEFS (football club) See Football clubs
CHIEFS of staff. See United States—Joint chiefs of staff
CHIEN, Shu
Shear dependence of effective cell volume as a determinant of blood viscosity. bibliog il Science 168:977-9 My 22 '70
CHILD, Irvin L.
Aesthetic judgment in children. Trans-Action 7:47-51 My '70
CHILD, Julia
—and Beck, Simone
Mastering the art of French cooking, volume two; excerpts. il McCalls 98:86-91+ O; 107-14 N '70 (to be cont)

about

How to take the nonsense out of cooking. H. Frankel. il pors Redbook 135:68-9+ O '70 *
Julia's moon walk with French bread. G. Greene. il por Life 69:8 O 23 '70 *
Kitchen secrets of five master cooks; with recipes. J. Wilson. il pors House & Gard 138:74-5+ Jl '70 *
Making of a masterpiece. P. Simon. il pors McCalls 98:84-5+ O '70 *
Up the years from cassoulet. B. Suyker. Atlan 226:110+ D '70 *
CHILD abuse
No language but a cry. R. D'Ambrosio. Good H 171:64-7+ Ag '70
CHILD accidents. See Accidents
CHILD art. See Childrens art
CHILD care centers. See Day nurseries

CHILD caring agencies. See Child welfare

CHILD guidance clinics
Help found: team care for disturbed children. C. V. Morrison and D. N. Morrison. il Todays Health 48:34-6+ Mr '70

CHILD health. See Children—Care and hygiene

CHILD marriage
Is incest really dull? Time 96:40-2 Ag 24 '70

CHILD obesity. See Corpulence

CHILD photography. See Photography of children

CHILD psychiatry
Ethical considerations in the involuntary commitment of children and in psychological testing as a part of legal procedures. K. Tooley. Ment Hy 54:484-9 O '70
How psychotherapists deal with their children; discussion, ed. by H. Ginott. Vogue 155: 90-1+ Mr 15 '70
Myths about childhood homosexuality. W. J. Gadpaille. Todays Health 49:45-7+ Ja '71
See also
Child guidance clinics
Children—Hospitals, Psychiatric
Mentally ill children

CHILD psychology. See Child study

CHILD psychotherapy. See Psychotherapy

CHILD study
Attention and psychological change in the young child. J. Kagan. bibliog il Science 170: 826-32 N 20 '70
Bliss in a box of crayons. P. Baker. il Parents Mag 45:74 O '70
Chimps instead of Spock. il Time 96:51 N 30 '70
Crucial years for learning; findings of Harvard's pre-school project. C. Lang. il Parents Mag 45:62-3+ S '70
How babies learn to wait; findings of the Infant development research project. H. S. Arnstein. il Parents Mag 45:39-41+ D '70
Kids who crave approval. C. Lang. il N Y Times Mag p66+ O 18 '70
Middle years of childhood; pre-teen years. J. M. Hoag. il Parents Mag 45:56-7+ O '70
Of time and the child. D. Elkind. il N Y Times Mag p90+ O 11 '70
Profiles: E. H. Erikson. R. Coles. por New Yorker 46:51-4+ N 7; 59-60+ N 14 '70
Psychologists are rediscovering the mind. T. Alexander. il Fortune 82:108-11+ N '70
Stages of man; theory of E. Erikson. il por Time 96:51-2 N 30 '70
What children worry about. R. M. Silberstein and C. Levine. il Parents Mag 45:56-7+ My '70
See also
Birth order
Child guidance clinics
Children—Language
Play
Bibliography
On the vagaries of child-care books. S. Olofson. il Am Lib 1:1036-44 D'70

CHILD suicide. See Suicide

CHILD-to-child tutoring program. See Tutors and tutoring

CHILD welfare
Study of child welfare in ten nations. Sch & Soc 98:19 Ja '70
See also
Adoption
Children—Care and hygiene
Children—Institutional care
Day nurseries
Detention homes
Foster grandparent program
United Nations children's fund

United States
Allowances for our children; George McGovern's plan. America 122:116 F 7 '70
Beyond Doctor Spock. P. Steinfels. Commonweal 93:342 Ja 8 '71
Child advocacy and ecological planning. W. W. Lewis. Ment Hy 54:475-83 O '70
Dilemma of child care. R. B. Miller. America 122:125-8 F 7 '70
Economic status of families headed by women; AFDC program. R. L. Stein. il Mo Labor R 93:3-10 D '70
See also
Day nurseries
White House conference on children and youth, 1970

CHILD welfare workers. See Social workers

CHILDBIRTH
Birth by appointment; induced labor. il Newsweek 76:85 Jl 20 '70
How to give birth to a daughter. R. Eldridge. il Redbook 135:80-1+ My '70

Miracle of the beginning: a child is born; pictures and text by the baby's father. S. Kalkstein. il Good H 172:62-5 Ja '71
New man in the delivery room: the father. S. Olds and L. Witt. il Todays Health 48: 52-6 O '70
Until the doctor comes; instruction booklet issued to New York schools. Newsweek 75: 56 F 9 '70
What it costs now to have a baby. S. Porter. il Ladies Home J 87:32-3 Jl '70
Will a miracle child be born this year? P. S. Buck. il Ladies Home J 87:63+ D '70
See also
Cesarean section
Obstetrics

Anecdotes, facetiae, satire, etc.
Reaping fatherhood's rewards, at 50. W. Stanton. il McCalls 97:50 Je '70

CHILDERS, David
Prepare now for big watermelons. il Org Gard & Farm 17:94-6 D '70

CHILDERS, Joanne
Lines on revisiting an old home, now, a funeral parlor: poem. Commonweal 91:458 Ja 23 '70

CHILDHOOD. See Children

CHILDHOOD schizophrenia. See Schizophrenia

CHILDLESSNESS. See Birth control; Sterility

CHILDREN
Children of Christmas. J. M. Flagler. il Look 34:50-5 D 29 '70
Middle years of childhood; pre-teen years. J. M. Hoag. il Parents Mag 45:56-7+ O '70
See also
Adoption
Birth order
Cabinet officers—Children
Cookery by children
Education of children
Family
Family, Size of
Family life
Fathers
Mothers
Moving pictures and children
Museums—Work with children
Negro children
Parents
Play
Preschool children
Problem children
Siblings
Socially handicapped children
Television broadcasting and children
Travel with children
Aggressiveness
See Aggressiveness (psychology)
Anxiety
See Anxiety
Care and hygiene
Growing pains; questions and answers. See issues of Today's health
Parents and children in seventeenth-century France. by D. Hunt. Review
N Y Times Mag p99-100+ Mr 15 '70. R. Kramer
Show me a sick child and I'll show you a very tired mother. G. Hickman. il Redbook 134: 75+ Ap '70
Your child's health. L. W. Sauer. See issues of PTA magazine
See also
Baby sitters
Child welfare
Children—Management and training
Children—Preparation for medical and dental care
Convalescence
Infants—Care and hygiene
Pediatrics
Caricatures and cartoons
Small wonders. R. Marcus. See issues of Good housekeeping
Charities, protection, etc.
See Child welfare
Clothing and dress
See Clothing and dress—Children
Day care
See Day nurseries
Dental service
See Dental service
Development
See Children—Growth and development

CHILDREN—*Continued*

Diseases

Cystinosis: selective induction of vacuolation in fibroblasts by L-cysteine-D-penicillamine disulfide. J. D. Schulman and K. H. Bradley. bibliog il Science 169:595-7 Ag 7 '70

Human cystinosis: intracellular deposition of cystine. K. Hummeler and others. bibliog il Science 168:859-60 My 15 '70

Pediatrician's guide to colds, grippe, flu; excerpts from When your child is ill. S. Karelitz Ladies Home J 87:36+ Ja '70

Say it with a stomachache. S. Olds. il Todays Health 48:41-3+ N '70

Tumors in children. L. W. Sauer. PTA Mag 65:27-8 N '70

Your child's health. L. W. Sauer. See issues of PTA magazine

See also
Children—Care and hygiene
Pediatrics
also names of childrens diseases, e.g. Measles

Education

See Education of children

Etiquette

See Etiquette for children and youth

Growth and development

Boy with imagination plus. E. Hunter. il Parents Mag 45:42-3+ D '70

Can children get smarter? with study-discussion program, by M. M. Conant. E. S. Schaefer. bibliog il PTA Mag 65:10-12+, 35 S '70

Child advocacy and ecological planning. W. W. Lewis. Ment Hy 54:475-83 O '70

Child's-eye view of the world. S. Sherman. il Parents Mag 45:50 Ja '70

If you're worried about your child's growth. S. Podair. il Parents Mag 45:70-1+ N '70

Intellectual development of children from interracial matings. L. Willerman and others. bibliog il Science 170:1329-31 D 18 '70

Origin of personality. A. Thomas and others. il Sci Am 223:102-9 bibliog(p 128) Ag '70

Signs of emotional adjustment and disturbance. B. Spock. Redbook 135:22+ Je '70

Vitamins for young minds; with study-discussion program, by R. Strang. F. J. Estvan. bibliog il PTA Mag 64:6-8, 35 Ja '70

See also
Adolescence
Child study
Children—Care and hygiene
Infants—Growth and development

Hairdressing

See Hairdressing

Health

See Children—Care and hygiene

Hospitals, Psychiatric

Great house for children copes with the urban scene; Bronx children's psychiatric hospital. il Arch Rec 147:162-3 Ja '70

Hospitalizing the young: is it for their own good? H. H. Weiss and E. F. Pizer. bibliog Ment Hy 54:498-502 O '70

Imprisonment

Rescue of Donald and Richard; boys saved from an adult prison. W. Hartley and E. Hartley. il Good H 171:12+ Jl '70

Institutional care

Ethical considerations in the involuntary commitment of children and in psychological testing as a part of legal procedures. K. Tooley. Ment Hy 54:484-9 O '70

No language but a cry. R. D'Ambrosio. Good H 171:64-7+ Ag '70

Language

Don't use the kitchen-sink approach to enrichment; adaptation of address. D. Krech. il Todays Ed 59:30-2+ O '70

Getting ready to read; with study-discussion program, by M. M. Conant. E. L. Cohen. bibliog il PTA Mag 65:18-20, 32 N '70

How to talk to a baby; excerpt from Penny candy. J. Kerr. il Read Digest 97:104-6 O '70

How well does your preschooler speak? E. D. Freud and M. Weiser. il Parents Mag 46: 40-1+ Ja '71

Language, name, and concept. J. Bronowski and U. Bellugi. bibliog Science 168:669-73 My 8 '70; Reply with rejoinder. M. L. Linton. 169:328 Jl 24 '70

Tots in the tower of babble. W. Cole. il Todays Health 48:54-5+ D '70

Words are not just for talking. N. Brandt and Y. Brandt. il Redbook 134:59+ F '70

Law

Children as tax shelters. Forbes 106:71 N 1 '70

Put investments in a child's name? Uniform gifts to minors act. il Changing T 24:31-2 F '70

See also
Adoption
Illegitimacy
Juvenile courts
Parent and child (law)

Management and training

Are you raising a perfectionist? M. Krebs and R. Krebs. il Todays Health 48:39-41 Ag '70

Babies after sixty-five? interview. ed. by K. F. Westfall. I. Boyle. il Har Yrs 10:34-7 Ap '70

Bringing up the next generation; Moravian communal rearing of children. Trans-Action 7:10 Jl '70

Coming of age at sea. J. A. Heilman. il Yachting 127:97+ Ja '70

Family clinic; ed. by P. B. Katz. See issues of Parents' magazine & better family living

Giving children the gifts of faith and courage. R. F. Kennedy. por Ladies Home J 86:60 D '69

Growing pains; questions and answers. See issues of Today's health

How I won the war against littering. E. Sotiriou. il Parents Mag 45:68-9+ O '70

How psychotherapists deal with their children; discussion. ed. by H. Ginott. Vogue 155:90-1+ Mr 15 '70

How to be a successful parent. D. E. Hamachek. il Parents Mag 45:35-7+ Ag '70

How to settle children's squabbles. M. R. Weisbord. il Parents Mag 45:38-9+ Ja '70

How to talk to your children. J. Fincher. il McCalls 98:16+ Ja '71

Meddling grandmothers. B. Bettelheim. Ladies Home J 87:26+ S '70

Mother, let me do it myself! il Changing T 23:47-8 D '69

New way to raise kids; interview; ed. by J. Whitbread. B. Bettelheim. il por Look 34: 64+ F 24 '70

Rearing rads, rebs, & regulars; with study-discussion program J. Katz. bibliog il PTA Mag 64:8-10, 33 Ap '70

Some solutions to the boredom of child care. B. Spock. Redbook 136:46+ N '70

Taking the child's emotional temperature; with study-discussion program. D. Graves. bibliog il PTA Mag 64:5-7, 35 F '70

Temper, temper, temper, temper, temper! children's tantrums. A. E. Trieschman. il N Y Times Mag p99+ Ap 12 '70

They called my son a bully. il Good H 171:12+ N '70

Uncovering your child's masked messages. W. Kempler. il Todays Health 48:54-5+ Ap '70

Way of handling anxiety. B. Spock and M. E. Bergen. Redbook 135:46+ My '70

What do you want to be when you grow up? N. E. Scofield. il Parents Mag 45:40-1+ Je '70

What faith can do; child's faith in himself; with study-discussion program, by M. M. Conant. D. Gordon. bibliog il PTA Mag 65: 6-8, 34 D '70

When to put your foot down; with study-discussion program, by E. Harris and D. Harris. D. Grace. bibliog il PTA Mag 64:2-4, 34 My '70

See also
Camp discipline
Child study
Discipline
Moral education
Parent-child relationship
Quarrels

Bibliography

Books for parents; comp. by P. Pinson. See issues of Parents' magazine & better family living

On the vagaries of child-care books. S. Olofson. il Am Lib 1:1036-44 D '70

Nutrition

Children, food, and sex; questions and answers. D. Reuben. McCalls 97:38+ Ag '70

Coping with a picky eater. Sci Digest 68:78-9 N '70

Development means giving children a chance. Chr Cent 87:259 Mr 4 '70

CHILDREN—Nutrition—Continued

Eat! Says fat little Johnny's mother. C. B. Hicks. il Todays Health 48:48-60+ F '70
Fat child is father of the man. B. W. Wyden. il N Y Times Mag p89-90+ S 13 '70; Same abr. with title Overweight? A fresh look at the problem. Read Digest 97:129-32 D '70
Hunger and the preschool child; FAO's dairy scheme. R. L. Tobin. il Sat R 53:18 Jl 11 '70
Malnourished bodies, malnourished minds; with study-discussion program. L. V. Wilder. bibliog il PTA Mag 64:10-12+, 33 Mr '70
See also
Lunches
School lunches

Photographs

Child's playground of verses. G. Gladstone. Life 69:56-9 Jl 24 '70

Political attitudes
See Political attitudes

Preparation for medical and dental care

Home visits ease youngsters' hospital fears. A. Rosenthal. il Todays Health 48:54-5 Ag '70

Psychiatry
See Child psychiatry

Psychology
See Child study

Punishment
See Children—Management and training

Religion

Enclave; Episcopal baptism at the age of twelve in Quaker community of Whittier, Calif. M. F. K. Fisher. New Yorker 46:48-50 D 12 '70
Must babies wear religious tags; matching religions in adoption. A. Lake. il Good H 171:78-9+ N '70
What not to tell your child about religion. T. Howard. il Redbook 135:67+ Je '70
See also
Religious education

Sayings

What is a brother? excerpts. L. P. McGrath and J. Scobey. il Good H 170:74-5 F '70

Social and economic status
See also
Socially handicapped children

Speech
See Children—Language

Suicide
See Suicide

Surgery

Infant hernias. Sci Digest 67:55 Ap '70
See also
Children—Preparation for medical and dental care

Training
See Children—Management and training

Canada

Making of a hockey slave: from the cradle to the NHL. L. Shecter. il Look 34:70-4 F 10 '70

France

Parents and children in seventeenth-century France, by D Hunt. Review
N Y Times Mag p99-100+ Mr 15 '70. R. Kramer

Russia

Ivan v. Johnny. il Time 95:54-5 Ap 27 '70
Two worlds of childhood, by U. Bronfenbrenner and J. C. Condry, jr. Review
Commonweal 92:392-3 Ag 7 '70. S. Callahan
Science 169:1190-2 S 18 '70. H. K. Geiger

United States

Ivan v. Johnny. il Time 95:54-5 Ap 27 '70
Two worlds of childhood, by U. Bronfenbrenner and J. C. Condry, jr. Review
Commonweal 92:392-3 Ag 7 '70. C. Callahan
Science 169:1190-2 S 18 '70. H. K. Geiger
See also
Negro children

Vietnam (Republic)
See also
Vietnamese, war, 1957- —Children

CHILDREN, Adopted

Beau Bridges starts a new family. il pors Ebony 25:96-8+ O '70
Who am I? Where did I come from? girl's search for real mother. J. T. Freeman. il Ladies Home J 87:74+ Mr '70
CHILDREN, Arrest of. See Arrest
CHILDREN, Backward. See Slow learning children
CHILDREN, Blind. See Blind
CHILDREN, Cost of raising. See Domestic finance
CHILDREN, Deaf. See Deaf
CHILDREN, Deformed. See Deformities
CHILDREN, Delinquent. See Juvenile delinquency
CHILDREN, Education of. See Education of children
CHILDREN, Exceptional
See also
   Children, Gifted
   Children, Handicapped
   Minimal brain dysfunction
   Problem children
CHILDREN, First-born
First baby in the house. G. Youcha. il Parents Mag 45:62-3+ O '70
First-born, fortune's favorite? W. Boroson. il N Y Times Mag p87+ D 13 '70
CHILDREN, Gifted
Some bright children can't read; with study-discussion program, by E. Harris and D. Harris. J. L. Laffey. bibliog il PTA Mag 65:9-11+, 34-5 O '70
See also
High school students, Mentally superior

Education

Better schooling for bright youngsters. T. Irwin. il Parents Mag 45:40-1+ Ja '70
Why are we afraid of these children? Mirman school for academically gifted children, Los Angeles. J. Fincher. il McCalls 97:41+ Ag '70
CHILDREN, Handicapped
Epilogue to a dream: boy with incurable bone disease, osteogenesis imperfecta. G. Geisman. Redbook 134:89+ Mr '70
Laura's bastille of silence. P. Steinfels. Commonweal 93:270 D 11 '70
See also
Cerebral palsied children
Deaf

Education

Art and the special child. J. A. Parker. il Sch Arts 69:32-3 Mr '70
Breakthrough in early education of handicapped children. il Am Ed 6:34-5 Ja '70
Coinstruction of normal and handicapped children. il Sch & Soc 98:463 D '70
Girl who found a face. J. L. Block. il Good H 170:30+ Ap '70; Same abr. Read Digest 97:49-53 Jl '70
Madison plan really swings; placing of handicapped children in regular classrooms. A. A. Artuso and others. il Todays Ed 59:14-17 N '70
New outlook for education of handicapped children. E. W. Martin. il Am Ed 6:7-10 Ap '70
See also
Brain damaged children—Education
CHILDREN, Hard of hearing. See Deaf
CHILDREN, Hyperactive. See Hyperkinesis
CHILDREN, Illegitimate. See Illegitimacy
CHILDREN, Photography of. See Photography of children
CHILDREN, Preschool. See Preschool children
CHILDREN, Problem. See Problem children
CHILDREN, Professional
See also
Children as models
CHILDREN, Psychotic. See Mentally ill children
CHILDREN, Runaway. See Runaway boys and girls
CHILDREN, Sick. See Sick children
CHILDREN and animals
Boys and dogs together. T. Trueblood. il Field & S 75:28+ Je '70
CHILDREN and art
Aesthetic judgment in children. I. J. Child. Trans-Action 7:47-51 My '70
See also
Childrens museums
CHILDREN and death
Answer at nightfall. A. Gordon. il Read Digest 97:143-5 S '70
Helping children cope with sorrow. M. C. Martin. Parents Mag 45:42-3+ Ag '70

CHILDRENS fantasies
Prospect street moon. T. J. Cottle. Sat R 53: 21-4+ F 14 '70
CHILDRENS fears. See Fear
CHILDRENS fishing. See Fishing
CHILDRENS furniture. See Furniture. Childrens
CHILDRENS games. See Games
CHILDRENS gardens
Giant corn, giant pumpkins, giant sunflowers. il Sunset 144:220-1 My '70
How two boys in Pasadena grow jungly plants with long names. il Sunset 144:122-3 Ja '70
Victory gardens for vegetable-hating kids. K. Kraft and P. Kraft. il Todays Health 48:58-62 My '70
Washington's youth gardens. il Parks & Rec 5:47-8+ Je '70
Youngest gardener was five, the oldest sixteen; winners of Sunset garden contest. il Sunset 144:218-19 Ap '70
See also
School gardens
Competitions
Protesters with rakes; Cleveland children's garden fair. I. Bartell. il Horticulture 48: 18-19 Ag '70
CHILDRENS homes. See Homes, Institutional
CHILDRENS librarians
Closed circuit children's books. E. J. Gaines. Library J 95:1455 Ap 15 '70; Reply. P. D. Beard. 95:2739 S 1 '70
Commitment and conscience in children's services. M. Jehu. por Wilson Lib Bul 45:168 O '70
CHILDRENS libraries. See Libraries, Childrens
CHILDRENS lies. See Lying
CHILDRENS literature
Children's books: a Canadian's view of the current American scene; address, November 14, 1969. S. Egoff. Horn Bk 46:142-50 Ap '70
Children's literature as a scholarly resource: the need for a national plan. J. Fraser; reply. B. B. Pennington. Library J 95:960 Mr 15 '70
Children's literature for today's world; where will it lead? symposium, ed. by M. J. Durham. bibliog il Wilson Lib Bul 45:142-68 O '70
Closed circuit children's books. E. J. Gaines. Library J 95:1455 Ap 15 '70; Reply P. D. Beard. 95:2739 S 1 '70
Coming to terms with criticism; address, June 19, 1969. P. Heins. Horn Bk 46:370-5 Ag '70
Fade far away, dissolve, and quite forget. L. Russ. Pub W 197:37 Ja 12 '70
Fantasy and self-discovery. R. Helson. il Horn Bk 46:121-34 Ap '70
In house and out house; authenticity and the black experience in children's books; with discussion. B. Tate. il por Library J 95:3581, 3595-8 O 15 '70
Kinds of books we give children: whose nonsense? J. Lester. il por Pub W 197:86-8 F 23 '70
Little Miss Muffet fights back; NOW (National organization for women) bibliography of children's books showing females in nonstereotyped roles. Library J 95:3947+ N 15 '70
Looking beyond his own block; selecting books of interest to both black and white children. V. Walter and N. Schimmel. bibliog il Wilson Lib Bul 45:163-7 O '70
No laughter in heaven; address, July 29, 1969. L. Alexander. Horn Bk 46:11-19 F '70
On children's literature: a runcible symposium. B. J. Lifton. il Horn Bk 46:255-63 Je '70
Peter Parley; address, October 9, 1969. H. S. Canfield. bibliog il Horn Bk 46:135-41, 274-82 Ap-Je '70 (to be cont)
Scratching the surface of nosepower; scents applied to the printed page. il Pub W 198: 42-3 Ag 24 '70
Selfish art; anthology of opinions on anthologies and children's books. W. Cole. il por Pub W 197:89-91 F 23 '70
Standardization in commercial children's cataloging; a comparative study of 100-odd titles. F. E. DeHart. il por Library J 95: 744-9 F 15 '70
34th man; Jewish culture in children's fiction. L. Daniels. bibliog il por Library J 95:738-43 F 15 '70
Through a feminist eye; childrens books. Library J 95:4309+ D 15 '70

Timely response; address, November 1969. J. MacRae. Horn Bk 46:189-94 Ap '70; Reply. P. Heines. 46:253 Je '70
See also
Book week
Booksellers and bookselling—Childrens literature
Children's book council
Childrens poems (by children)
Childrens reading
Childrens stories
Fairy tales
Horn book magazine
Newbery medal
Picture books for children
Publishers and publishing—Childrens literature
Scientific literature for children
Series, Book

Awards and prizes
Report from England; the Farjeon award. Z. Sutherland. Sat R 53:52 Ag 22 '70

Bibliography
Best books for spring 1970; ed. by L. N. Gerhardt and others. il Library J 95:1911-13 My 15 '70
Best books of the year 1970; selected by the SLJ book review editors. L. N. Gerhardt and others. il Library J 95:4324-8 D 15 '70
Book review; ed. by L. N. Gerhardt and others. See second issue of each month of Library journal
Booklist (title varies) P. Heins and others. See issues of Horn book magazine
Books for boys and girls. H. Wilson. See issues of Parents' magazine & better family living
Books for children (title varies) R. Gagliardo. See issues of PTA magazine to June 1970
Books for young people. Z. Sutherland. See issues of Saturday review
Books to come; ed. by S. T. Halbreich. Library J 95:1221-47, 3659-96 Mr 15, O 15 '70
Children's books. See issues of Publishers' weekly
Children's books at Christmastime. E. Sheehan. America 123:494-9 D 5 '70
Children's books for fall. il Pub W 198:89-121 Jl 13 '70
Children's books for spring. Z. Sutherland. Sat R 53:41-7+ My 9 '70
Children's books for spring; with editorial comment. il Pub W 197:92-124, 132 F 23 '70
Children's books to remember (cont) Pub W 197:35 Mr 30; 74-5 Je 20; 198:57 S 28 '70
Children's paperbacks (cont) Library J 95: 265-8, 1979-81, 2997-8+ Ja 15, My 15, S 15 '70
Christmas books for children. J. Stafford. New Yorker 46:200+ D 5 '70
Fanfare 1970; the Horn book's honor list; books of 1969. Horn Bk 46:496-7 O '70
For the young; dreams and memories. il Time 96:68+ D 21 '70
From the Christmas crop, books to give children. PTA Mag 65:30-2 D '70
Leafing beneath the Christmas tree. Z. Sutherland. il Sat R 53:31-2 D 19 '70
Little house syndrome vs. Mike Mulligan and Mary Anne; juvenile books on ecology, conservation, and pollution. K. M. Heylman. il por Library J 95:1562-8 Ap 15 '70
1969 children's books of international interest. Todays Ed 59:2+ N '70
Notable children's books of 1969. il Am Lib 1:384-7 Ap '70; Same. PTA Mag 64:22-4 My '70; Library J 95:1894 My 15 '70; Pub W 197: 47-8 Je 1 '70
Selected list of children's books (cont) E. M. Graves. il Commonweal 92:245-8+; 93: 198-207 My 22, N 20 '70

Book reviews
See Book reviews

Criticism
See Literary criticism

Illustrations
See Illustration of books and periodicals

Study and teaching
Children's literature: books for teaching it. R. Weber. Wilson Lib Bul 45:172-9 O '70

Technique
Art of Elizabeth Enright (cont) E. Cameron. Horn Bk 46:26-30 F '70
Coffee break book and other lies. J. Yolen. Writer 83:21-2 N '70

CHILDRENS literature—Technique—*Continued*
Double image: language as the perimeter of culture; address, 1969. E. Konigsburg. il por Library J 95:731-4 F 15 '70
Kids rule for writing. B. Boshinski. Writers Digest 50:31-2 Jl '70
Writing for children. I. Hunt. Writer 83:17-20 Mr '70

Themes
Bitter-coated sugar pills; children's literature. P. Fox. Sat R 53:34 S 19 '70

Denmark
Small countries, big projects. Z. Sutherland. Sat R 53:66 O 24 '70

Great Britain
Mrs Trimmer, guardian of education. J. St John. il por Horn Bk 46:20-5 F '70

Italy
Puppet's progress; Pinocchio. M. Bacon. il Atlan 225:88-90+ Ap '70

Russia
Confessions of an old story-teller; tr. by L. G. Leighton. K. I. Chukovskii. Horn Bk 46:577-91 D '70 (to be cont)

Sweden
Small countries, big projects. Z. Sutherland. Sat R 53:66 O 24 '70

CHILDRENS literature, Influence of
Identification and identities. L. Alexander. bibliog il por Wilson Lib Bul 45:144-8 O '70
Looking backwards, and ahead, with Alice. N. Hentoff. il Wilson Lib Bul 45:169-71 O '70

CHILDRENS manners. See Etiquette for children and youth

CHILDRENS museums
World for children. il Newsweek 75:93+ F 23 '70
See also
Boston children's museum

CHILDRENS parties
Christmas is for children too. R. F. Pomeroy. il Redbook 136:73-4 D '70

CHILDRENS periodicals (by children)
See also
Kids (periodical)

CHILDRENS phonograph records. See Phonograph records—Childrens records

CHILDRENS plays
Informal theater: camp activity for everybody. J. B. Kase. il Camp Mag 42:16-17+ Mr '70

CHILDRENS poems (by children)
Ah, poets; K. Koch's project. il por Time 96:26-7 D 28 '70
Horn book league. See issues of Horn book magazine
Junior McCall's club. See issues of McCall's
Juvenile bards; how K. Koch turned children on. il por Newsweek 75:54 Ap 6 '70
New new poets in old old America. A. Adoff. por Pub W 198:86-8 Jl 13 '70
On a sailboat of sinking water; Koch on new methods of teaching children to write poetry. B. Farrell. il por Life 68:4 My 15 '70
On Christmas day no more current events; poems by schoolchildren. K. Koch. il N Y Times Mag p5-7 D 20 '70
Poems by Japanese children; excerpts from There are two lives; ed. by R. Lewis and tr. by H. Kimura. Mlle 72:166-7 N '70
Wishes, lies & dreams; excerpts. ed. by K. Koch. il Harp Baz 104:140-1 D '70

CHILDRENS poems (for children)
See also
Nursery rhymes

CHILDRENS poetry
Confessions of an old story-teller; tr. by L. G. Leighton. K. I. Chukovskii. Horn Bk 46:577-91 D '70 (to be cont)
See also
Childrens poems (by children)

CHILDRENS poetry (for children)
Someone could win a polar bear; Rules; Lesson. J. Ciardi. il Sat R 53:14 My 23 '70

CHILDRENS quarrels. See Quarrels

CHILDRENS reading
Child and his books. R. Caudill. il PTA Mag 64:28-9 F '70
Children and books. P. Heins. Horn Bk 46:119 Ap '70
Commissioner Allen learns reading is FUN-damental; RIF program. J. Lloyd. il Sr Schol 96: Schol Teach 2 Ja 26 '70
Different library, different school! City and country school library. M. B. Piel. il Pub W 198:78-81 Jl 13 '70
Long view. T. Taylor. Sat R 53:44 F 21 '70

Reading guidance effects on children; project in an elementary school in rural Florida. J. A. McCrossan. Am Lib 1:88 Ja '70
Reading is FUN-damental; interview, ed. by G. D. Fischer. M. C. McNamara. il pors Todays Ed 59:20-3 F '70
Voices from the past; excerpts from November 16, 1929 issue of The Saturday review of literature, ed. by Z. Sutherland. Sat R 53:36 Ja 24 '70
See also
Childrens literature
Right to read program

CHILDRENS religion. See Children—Religion

CHILDRENS responsibility. See Responsibility

CHILDRENS rooms
Boys' room has poster walls, upper and lower berths. il Sunset 145:101 O '70
Children's rooms: color them happy. il Farm J 94:48 Ja '70
For Buffy and Jody, two very special rooms. R. Fitzgerald. il por House B 112:37-41 D '70
Great ideas for children's rooms. J. R. Cary. il Parents Mag 45:100-3 S '70

CHILDRENS safety seats. See Automobiles—Safety devices and measures

CHILDRENS seat belts. See Safety belts

CHILDRENS services division, American library association. See American library association—Childrens services division

CHILDRENS shoes. See Shoes

CHILDRENS songs
See also
Camping—Songs and music

CHILDRENS sports. See Sports for children

CHILDRENS squabbles. See Quarrels

CHILDRENS stories
Santa makes a change. S. Chaneles and J. Snyder. Parents Mag 45:46-9 D '70
Unfinished story. See issues of Today's education
Velveteen rabbit. M. Williams. il McCalls 97:84-5 Ap '70

Technique
See Childrens literature—Technique

CHILDRENS theater. See Theater, Childrens

CHILDRENS thefts. See Shoplifting

CHILDRESS, Bob
Man who moved a mountain, by R. C. Davids. Review
Farm J 94:28B N '70. L. Palmer *

CHILDS, Charles Wendal
Assignment to neglect. il Life 68:28 My 22 '70
Black studies at Cornell: the troubled path to understanding. il Life 68:56-60+ Ap 17 '70

about
Exploring a campus in transition. R. Graves. il pors Life 68:3 Ap 17 '70 *

CHILDS, James, and Eskridge, John
Make your VTVM a megger too. il Pop Electr 33:50 Ag '70

CHILDS, Sister Maryanna
Confrontation in Derry, 575 A.D; poem. Cath World 211:267 S '70

CHILDS, Rita Jean
[Dont] report, react! Engl J 59:981-2 O '70

CHILD'S play; drama. See Marasco, R.

CHILE
See also
Airlines—Chile
Astronomical observatories—Chile
Candidates, Political—Chile
Communism—Chile
Elections—Chile
Government ownership—Chile
Investments, Foreign (in Chile)
National parks and reserves—Chile
Political campaigns—Chile
Political parties—Chile
United States—Foreign relations—Chile

Antiquities
See Indians of South America—Antiquities—Chile

Economic conditions
Allende casts a shadow on business. por Bsns W p28 N 7 '70
Chile: the expanding left; from Christian democrats to anarchic urban terrorists. il pors Time 96:23-4+ O 19 '70

Economic policy
Tightening the noose. Newsweek 77:30 Ja 4 '71

Expropriation policy
Chile starts chasing the capitalists. il pors Time 97:68 Ja 4 '71

CHILE—*Continued*

Foreign relations

Fretful neighbors. Time 96:29 O 19 '70

United States

See United States—Foreign relations—Chile

Industries

See also

Copper industry and trade—Chile

Politics and government

Center stage for Chile's Marxist president. il por Newsweek 76:52+ N 2 '70

Chile: another Cuba? il U S News 69:33-4 S 21 '70

Chile: victory and violence. il por Time 96: 16 N 2 '70

Chileans have elected a revolution. N. Gall. il pors N Y Times Mag p26-7+ N 1 '70

Christian democracy in Chile. A. Angell. bibliog f Cur Hist 58:79-84+ F '70

Clearing the way. Newsweek 76:64 O 12 '70

Commune called Paradise; V. Toro and his band of revolutionaries. il por Time 95:30 Je 1 '70

Confrontation in Chile. E. von Kuehnelt-Leddihn. Nat R 22:515 My 19 '70

Deck is stacked; or, It's tough to be red in Chile. Trans-Action 7:11-12 F '70

Expectations in Chile. W. R. Long. New Repub 163:8-9 N 28 '70

Give up? J. Burnham. Nat R 22:1205 N 17 '70

Marxist regime? P. Zottele. Chr Cent 87: 1429-30 N 25 '70

No miracle worker. Newsweek 76:57 N 16 '70

Political avalanche occurs in Chile. J. S. Bradshaw. Chr Cent 87:1163-4 S 30 '70

Politics of protest; sit-in movement in Maryland. Trans-Action 7:11 F '70

Projecting the common touch. Time 96:33-4 N 16 '70

Violent ordeals of democracy. Chr Cent 87: 1307 N 4 '70

With Chile run by a Marxist, what U.S. can expect. il U S News 69:20-1 N 9 '70

See also

Communism—Chile

Elections—Chile

Political parties—Chile

Religious institutions and affairs

Chile's new president declares attitude on religion. Chr Today 15:44 Ja 1 '71

CHILEAN folk art. See Folk art

CHILEANS

Tightening the noose. Newsweek 77:30 Ja 4 '71

CHILES, Lawton

Dent in a hard hat. New Repub 163:10 N 14 '70 •

CHILL factor. See Winds

CHILLAG, Dana. See Mendelson, J. jt. auth.

CHIMERAS (biology) See Mosaics (biology)

CHIMES

How to tune in on the breeze; wind chimes. il House B 112:12 Ag '70

Wind chimes. S. Gallaway and J. Gallaway. il Ceram Mo 18:20-2 Ap '70

CHIMNEY cleaning

Check your chimney for winter. Changing T 24:16 N '70

CHIMPANZEES

Chimp discovers its self. il Sci Digest 67:67 Ap '70

Chimps instead of Spock. il Time 96:51 N 30 '70

Education of Sarah. il Time 96:51-2 S 21 '70

How they taught a chimp to talk. B. Ford. bibliog il Sci Digest 67:10-17 My '70

Language, name, and concept. J. Bronowski and U. Bellugi. bibliog Science 168:669-73 My 8 '70; Reply with rejoinder. M. L. Linton. 169:328 Jl 24 '70

Should we ape the chimpanzee? D. Behrman. il UNESCO Courier 23:7-18 Ag '70

Son of King Kong: Noell's ark ape show il Newsweek 76:23-4 Jl 20 '70

Think by radio? tests on chimp's brain. Sr Schol 97:4-5 O 12 '70

CHIMPANZEES on television programs. See Animals on television programs

CHIMSKY, Jean

1970 poetry contest. Writers Digest 50:36-7+ O '70

CHINA

See also

Education—China

Mongolia

Opium trade—China

Paleontology—China

Peking

Prisoners of war in China

Taiwan

United States—Foreign relations—China

Armed forces

History

If Asia were clay in the hands of the West: the Stilwell mission to China, 1942-44; excerpts from Stilwell. B. W. Tuchman. il pors Atlan 226:68-84 S '70

Foreign relations

United States

See United States—Foreign relations—China

History

T'ang. E. Hahn. il Horizon 11:88-103 Aut '69

1900-

For God, for China and for Yale: the open door in action. J. Israel. bibliog f Am Hist R 75:796-807 F '70

Making of a myth by P. A. Varg. Review Am Hist R 75:1393-6 Je '70. T. J. McCormick

Yankee among the war lords; excerpts from Utmost try. B. W. Tuchman. il pors Am Heritage 21:22-31+ O '70

CHINA (People's Republic)

Army's man. por Time 96:26 Ag 24 '70

Does China matter much? S. Alsop. Newsweek 75:84 Ja 26 '70

Mainland China, 1970; symposium. bibliog f il Cur Hist 59:129-69+ S '70

See also

Canton

Communism—China (People's Republic)

Communist party (China [People's Republic])

Concentration camps—China (People's Republic)

Education—China (People's Republic)

Environmental policy—China (People's Republic)

Prison camps—China (People's Republic)

Space research—China (People's Republic)

Trials—China (People's Republic)

United Nations—China (People's Republic)

Armed forces

Chinese factionalism and Sino-Soviet relations. U. Ra'anan. Cur Hist 59:134-41 S '70

Power of the Chinese military. R. L. Powell. bibliog f Cur Hist 59:129-33+ S '70

Bibliography

What worries Chairman Mao. O. E. Clubb. Sat R 53:32-4 Ap 25 '70

Commerce

Bargains from Mao; Communist stores in Hong Kong. il Newsweek 76:60 Ag 31 '70

So long at the fair; four principles for dealings with Japanese firms. il Newsweek 75: 82 Je 8 '70

Defenses

Nuclear China and U.S. arms policy. A. D. Barnett. For Affairs 48:427-42 Ap '70

Diplomatic and consular service

Lights go on again. il por Time 96:20+ S 7 '70

Economic conditions

Big changes inside red China. il U S News 68:52-5 Je 22 '70

China; themes of self-reliance. H. Yu. Chr Cent 87:678 My 27 '70

New look into Mao's China. J. Myrdal. il Look 34:19-26 F 10 '70

Plight of the people in red China. P. K. T. Sih. Cath World 212:200-2 Ja '71

What life is like in one little corner of China; interview, ed. by K. Chrysler. il U S News 68:54-5 Je 22 '70

See also

Communism—China (People's Republic)

Economic policy

China; Maoist economic development. H. Yu. Chr Cent 87:926 Jl 29 '70

China's economy; experiments in Maoism. J. S. Prybyla. bibliog f Cur Hist 59:159-64+ S '70

See also

Communism—China (People's Republic)

CHINA (People's Republic)—*Continued*

Economic relations

China and Japan: different beds, different dreams. W. LaFeber. Cur Hist 59:142-6+ S '70

China in the Arab world. J. D. Ben-Dak. bibliog f il Cur Hist 59:147-52+ S '70

Foreign relations

And now Rome; diplomatic ties with Communist China. America 123:422-3 N 21 '70

Back in the arena. il Time 95:27-8 Je 1 '70

China courts the barbarians. il Newsweek 76:51-2 N 16 '70

China; new open posture in international relations. H. Yu. Chr Cent 87:1434 N 25 '70

Fourth dimension; U.S. China, Russia to talk. il Newsweek 75:55 Ja 26 '70

French expert's view: China, the real winner in Cambodia. P. Devillers. Look 34:64 Ag 25 '70

Pros and cons of recognition. Time 96:43 N 16 '70

Social whirl. Newsweek 76:43 Jl 27 '70

See also

China (People's Republic)—Diplomatic and consular service

Arab states

China in the Arab world. J. D. Ben-Dak. bibliog f il Cur Hist 59:147-52+ S '70

Asia, Southeastern

China and the United States: collision course? O. E. Clubb. bibliog f Cur Hist 59:153-8+ S '70

New devil figure. Newsweek 75:58+ Ap 20 '70

Thaw in U.S.-Chinese relations? O. E. Clubb. Cur 117:56-61 Ap '70

Canada

See Canada—Foreign relations—China (People's Republic)

Japan

China and Japan: different beds, different dreams. W. LaFeber. Cur Hist 59:142-6+ S '70

Passing the buck to Tokyo. A. Axelbank. Nation 211:293-5 O 5 '70

Three-power gamble: Japan, China, USA. A. Axelbank and K. Nakamura. il Nation 211:678-81 D 28 '70

Russia

See Russia—Foreign relations—China (People's Republic)

United States

See United States—Foreign relations—China (People's Republic)

History

What makes Mao a Maoist. S. R. Schram. il N Y Times Mag p36-7+ Mr 8 '70

Politics and government

Big changes inside red China. il U S News 68:52-5 Je 22 '70

China. H. Yu. See issues of Christian century

China: period of suspense. L. La Dany. For Affairs 48:701-11 Jl '70

Eyes right. il Newsweek 77:28 Ja 4 '71

Plight of the people in red China. P. K. T. Sih. Cath World 212:200-2 Ja '71

See also

Communism—China (People's Republic)

Communist party (China [People's Republic])

Population

Chinese peoples. I. B. Taeuber. il Natur Hist 79:52-6 Ja '70

Religious institutions and affairs

Marxist ABCs. Chr Today 14:39 Ja 16 '70

See also

Christians in China

Church and state in China (People's Republic)

Social conditions

China. H. Yu. Chr Cent 87:126 Ja 28 '70

New look into Mao's China. J. Myrdal. il Look 34:19-26 F 10 '70

See also

Communism—China (People's Republic)

CHINA (porcelain) See Pottery

CHINATOWN, New York city. See New York (city)—Chinatown

CHINATOWN, San Francisco. See San Francisco—Chinatown

CHINCHAR, Michael

Where are they now? il pors Newsweek 75:12 Mr 2 '70 *

CHINESE

Chinese peoples. I. B. Taeuber. il Natur Hist 79:52-6 Ja '70

CHINESE; drama. See Schisgal, M.

CHINESE AMERICANS

See also

New York (city)—Chinatown

San Francisco—Chinatown

CHINESE art. See Art, Chinese

CHINESE artificial satellites. See Artificial satellites, Chinese

CHINESE cookery. See Cookery, Chinese

CHINESE economic assistance. See Economic assistance, Chinese

CHINESE furniture. See Furniture, Chinese

CHINESE gooseberries. See Yangtaos

CHINESE in the United States

See also

New York (city)—Chinatown

San Francisco—Chinatown

CHINESE-Japanese war, 1931-1932

Shanghai crisis of 1932: the basis of British policy. C. Thorne. bibliog f Am Hist R 75:1616-39 O '70

CHINESE-Japanese war, 1937-1945

Japan strikes: 1937; excerpts from Utmost try. B. W. Tuchman. il pors Am Heritage 22:4-11+ D '70

CHINESE language

Study and teaching

Ph.D. program in Chinese studies. il Sch & Soc 98:396-8 N '70

CHINESE New Year. See New Year

CHINESE pottery. See Pottery, Chinese

CHINESE space vehicles. See Space vehicles, Chinese

CHINESE technical assistance. See Technical assistance, Chinese

CHINESE villages. See Villages

CHINLE boarding school. See Indians of North America—Education

CHINOOK bookshop, Colorado Springs. See Booksellers and bookselling—Colorado

CHINOOK salmon fishing. See Salmon fishing

CHINTZ

Chintz cools it. il House B 112:68-71 Je '70

Origins of chintz. R. Davidson. il Antiques 98:242-5 Ag '70

CHIP off the old; story. See Ross, I.

CHIPPENDALE furniture. See Furniture, English

CHISHOLM, James

Home-made Otto-tron: the ideal pal. il pors Ebony 25:64-6+ Je '70 *

CHISHOLM, Shirley A.

Number one method. Nation 210:69-70 Ja 26 '70

Visiting feminine eye. por McCalls 97:6 Ag '70

about

First black woman in the U.S. House of Representatives. Negro Hist Bul 33:128 My '70 *

CHISUM, James

Behind the bad behavior. il Am Ed 6:32-4 Ag '70

CHIVALRY

See also

Romances

CHLOR-ALKALI industry. See Chemical industries

CHLORAMPHENICOL

Chloramphenicol: effect on DNA synthesis during phage development in escherichia coli. P. Amati. bibliog il Science 168:1226-8 Je 5 '70

Peculiar success of Chloromycetin. il Consumer Rep 35:616-19 O '70

5S RNA synthesized by escherichia coli in presence of chloramphenicol: different 5'-terminal sequences. B. G. Forget and B. Jordan. bibliog il Science 167:382-4 Ja 23 '70

CHLORDANE

Oxychlordane, animal metabolite of chlordane: isolation and synthesis. B. Schwemmer and others. bibliog il Science 169:1087 S 11 '70

CHLORIDES

See also

Manganese chlorides

CHLORINATION of water. See Water purification

CHLORINE bleach. See Bleaching materials

CHLORINE compounds

Pollution by organic chemicals. P. H. Abelson. Science 170:495 O 30 '70

CHLORMADINONE
Abortion without surgery? Time 95:39-40 F 9 '70
CHLOROMYCETIN. See Chloramphenicol
CHLOROPHENYLALANINE. See Phenylalanine
CHLOROPHYLL
Chlorophyll derivatives in middle eocene sediments. D. L. Dilcher and others. bibliog il Science 168:1447-9 Je 19 '70
Spectra of backscattered light from the sea obtained from aircraft as a measure of chlorophyll concentration. G. L. Clarke and others. bibliog il Science 167:1119-21 F 20 '70
Subsurface photosynthesis; Chlorophyll c. il Sci N 98:58-9 Jl 25 '70
See also
Chloroplasts
Porphyrins
CHLOROPLASTS
Genetic activity of mitochondria and chloroplasts. U. W. Goodenough and R. P. Levine. il Sci Am 223:22-9 N '70
CHLOROQUINE
Plasmodium falciparum in owl monkeys: drug resistance and chloroquine binding capacity. C. D. Fitch. bibliog il Science 169:289-90 Jl 17 '70
CHLORPROMAZINE
Reticular stimulation and chlorpromazine: an animal model for schizophrenic overarousal. C. Kornetsky and M. Eliasson; reply with rejoinder. M. I. Phillips and P. B. Bradley. Science 168:1122-3 My 29 '70
CHOATE, Robert B. Jr
Breakfast of what? il por Newsweek 76:57-8 Ag 3 '70 *
Cereal critic aids his targets. il Bsns W p59 O 3 '70 *
Cereal tempest. Sr Schol 97:5-6 S 14 '70 *
Gadfly buzzes around the table. il por Bsns W p 116 S 26 '70
Package of trouble for cereal makers. il Bsns W p24 Ag 1 '70 *
Willing suspension of disbelief. Chr Cent 87: 951 Ag 5 '70 *
CHOATE school, Wallingford, Conn. See Private schools
CHOCOLATE
See also
Cookery—Chocolate
Hershey foods corporation
CHOCOLATE truffles. See Candy
CHOI, Kyoo W. and Bloom, A. D.
Biochemically marked lymphocytoid lines: establishment of Lesch-Nyhan cells. bibliog il Science 170:89-90 O 2 '70
CHOICE (periodical)
Professional developments reviewed: Choice as a selection tool. J. O. Lehman. bibliog Wilson Lib Bul 44:957-61 My '70
CHOICE of occupation. See Occupations
CHOIRS
Matter of identification; singers in a photograph of the Victor male chorus. J. Walsh. il Hobbies 75:37-41+ Jl '70
Musical events; performance of Netherlands chamber choir at Hunter college. W. Sargeant. New Yorker 46:82-3 F 28 '70
See also
Phonograph records—Choral music
Westminster choir
CHOKE, Automobile. See Automobile engines—Choke
CHOKERS. See Necklaces
CHOKES, Shotgun. See Shotguns
CHOKING
Choking on food, what to do. Good H 171:159 S '70
Killer that comes to dinner. H. E. Dark. il Todays Health 48:9-10+ Ap '70
CHOLERA
Bracing for El Tor. il Time 96:22+ S 14 '70
Deadly epidemic. il Sr Schol 97:4-5 S 21 '70
Potent pandemic; Threat in the Middle East. il Time 96:59 Ag 31 '70
Scourge of the East. il Newsweek 76:77-8 S 7 '70
Southward to Guinea. il Sci N 98:216 S 12 '70
CHOLERA, Hog. See Hog cholera
CHOLESTEROL
Do animal fats cause heart attacks? D. Braun. il Farm J 93:24-5+ O '69
Fact and fiction about cholesterol. J. D. Wassersug. il Sci Digest 68:18-21 D '70
Genetic variation of cholesterol ester content in mouse adrenals. C. H. Doering and others. bibliog il Science 170:1220-2 D 11 '70
CHOLINE
See also
Acetylcholine
Hemicholinium

CHOLINESTERASE
Phenylthioacetate: a useful substrate for the histochemical and colorimetric detection of cholinesterase. G. M. Booth and R. L. Metcalf. bibliog il Science 170:455-7 O 23 '70
CHOMSKY, Noam
After pinkville what? Cur 115:18-30 F '70

about

Position of Noam Chomsky. L. Abel; discussion. Commentary 48:9-10+ Ag; 12+ O; 4+ D '69; 49:4+ Mr '70 *
Schlesinger vs. Chomsky. A. Schlesinger, jr. Commentary 49:14+ Je '70 *
CHONA, Harbans S.
Doc ex revisited: does it answer the needs? bibliog por Wilson Lib Bul 45:513-15 Ja '71
CHOPIN, Frédéric François
Alfred Cortot, poet with a soul. W. Botsford. Am Rec G 36:340 Ja '70 *
Chopin and Sand: in the wake of that Majorcan winter. R. McMullen. il Sat R 53:78-9+ Mr 14 '70 *
Chopin by Ivan Moravec, perverse, and yet fascinating. L. Gerber. Am Rec G 36:424 F '70 *
Dinu Lipatti: more to be venerated than criticized. L. Gerber. Am Rec G 36:566 Ap '70 *
Garrick Ohlsson: art of playing Chopin; interview. G. Ohlsson. New Yorker 46:16-18 Ja 2 '71 *
CHOPIN, Kate (O'Flaherty)
St Louis woman. S. K. Oberbeck. por Newsweek 75:102B+ F 23 '70 *
CHOPIN international piano competition. See Music—Competitions
CHOPPING blocks
See also
Cutting boards
CHOPS. See Cookery—Meat
CHORAL groups and societies
Premier-American quartet. J. Walsh. il Hobbies 74:38+ F; 75:38-40+ Mr '70
Recordings; Camerata chorale. M. Mayer. Esquire 73:88+ Ap '70
CHORAL music
See also
Phonograph records—Choral music
CHORAL singing
See also
Choral groups and societies

Instruction and study

Vocal music teacher, pianoless. J. M. Simpson. Clear House 44:271 Ja '70
CHORALES
How J. S. Bach composed four-part chorales. R. L. Marshall. bibliog f il Mus Q 56: 198-220 Ap '70
CHOREOGRAPHY
Choreographers theatre. J. Lahr. il Dance Mag 44:46-51 Mr '70
Firebird: grand controversy; with interview, ed. by O. Maynard. G. Balanchine. il por Dance Mag 44:43-58 Ag '70; Discussion. 44:22 N '70
Rudi van Dantzig's The ropes of time. J. Percival. il Dance Mag 44:44-7 My '70
Sokolow odyssey continued. J. Gale. il pors Dance Mag 44:42-6 F '70
CHOREOGRAPHY conferences. See Dance conferences
CHOTEAU, Mont.

Water supply

Matter of opinion: microcosm. A. B. Guthrie, jr. Am West 7:48 Jl '70; Same with title Day Choteau went dry. il Audubon 72:153 N '70
CHOTINER, Murray M.
Chotiner's comeback. il por Newsweek 75: 21-2 Je 22 '70 *
White House hard hats. E. B. Drew. il por Atlan 226:51-7 O '70 *
CHOU, En-lai
Lights go on again; plans for trip abroad. il por Time 96:20+ S 7 '70 *
CHOU, S. C. See Conklin, K. A. jt. auth.
CHOU, Wen-chung
Sound world of Chou Wen-chung. A. Frankenstein. Hi Fi 20:secI 84 Jl '70 *
Very special: the music of Chou Wen-chung. A. Cohn. por Am Rec G 36:886 Jl '70 *
CHOW, Tsaihwa J. and Earl, J. L.
Lead aerosols in the atmosphere: increasing concentrations. bibliog il Science 169:577-80 Ag 7 '70

CHOW sam see. See Cookery, Chinese

CHOWDER
ABCs of clam chowder. il Am Home 73:112
My '70
Chilled seafood soup that you don't have to
cook. il Sunset 145:116 Jl '70
CHRISM. See Sacraments
CHRISS, Nicholas C.
Boondocks jail the future. il Nation 211:495-
6 N 16 '70
Can a black be acquitted? Nation 211:690-1
D 28 '70
CHRIST. See Jesus Christ
CHRIST, Jacob, and Goldstein, Shirley
Four techniques in dealing with psychotic
disorders in the outpatient clinic. Ment Hy
54:105-8 Ja '70
CHRIST-JANER, Arland Frederick
New president of college board. Sch & Soc
98:272-4 Sum '70 *
CHRISTENING of ships. See Ships—Launch-
ing
CHRISTENSEN, Carl Christian Anton
Panorama of Mormon life. C. Carmer. il Art
in Am 58:52-65 My '70 *
CHRISTENSEN, Francis
Upon first looking into Christensen's Rhe-
toric. A. Solkov. Engl J 59:834-6 S '70 *
CHRISTENSON, Reo M.
Dealing with pornography. Cur 123:31-8 N
'70
Don't blame the system! Chr Cent 87:784-7
Je 24 '70
CHRISTIAN, Charles L. See Phillips, P. E. jt.
auth.
CHRISTIAN, John J.
Social subordination, population density, and
mammalian evolution. bibliog Science 168:
84-90; 170:345-6 Ap 3, O 16 '70
CHRISTIAN art and symbolism
Imago Clarkensis, T.V; critique of K. Clark's
views on early British monastic art. C. R.
Baldwin. il Art N 69:62-5+ N '70
Liturgical enamels of Charles Bartley Jeffery.
R. D. Bonham. il por Ceram Mo 18:14-17 D
'70
Rumania's open churches. P. Blake. il Time
96:48-53 Ag 10 '70
See also
Altars
Angels in art
Church architecture
Cross and crosses
Icons
Jesus Christ—Art
Mary, Virgin—Art
CHRISTIAN associates (organization) See
Pennsylvania—Religious institutions and af-
fairs
CHRISTIAN booksellers association
Christian booksellers forge ahead in research
and sales. Pub W 198:43-4 S 14 '70
CHRISTIAN businessmen's committee interna-
tional
Business evangelism. Chr Today 15:47-8 N 6
'70
CHRISTIAN century (periodical)
Emilio Castro named editor at large. Chr
Cent 87:717 Je 10 '70
Farewell to anglophobia; merger of New
Christian and The Christian century. Chr
Cent 87:684 Je 3 '70
Journalism for oikoumene; New Christian will
merge with the Christian century. Chr Cent
87:315-16 Mr 18 '70
Letters to the editor; use of obscenity with
editorial comment. Chr Cent 87:575-6 My 6
'70
News editorship established. por Chr Cent 87:
684 Je 3 '70
Profile of you; findings from questionnaires.
Chr Cent 87:652 My 27 '70
Ralph D. Abernathy; editor at large. Chr
Cent 87:749 Je 17 '70
CHRISTIAN church, Disciples of Christ
Evangelism and heresy. Chr Today 14:26 F 27
'70
Names
See Churches—Names
CHRISTIAN civilization. See Civilization, Chris-
tian
CHRISTIAN colleges. See Church colleges
CHRISTIAN communication. See Communica-
tion (theology)
CHRISTIAN council of Nigeria
War-torn Nigeria on the mend; church aid.
A. Millard. Chr Cent 87:1300 O 28 '70
CHRISTIAN democrats (Chile) See Political
parties—Chile
CHRISTIAN doctrine. See Theology
CHRISTIAN education. See Religious educa-
tion
CHRISTIAN endeavor union. See World's
Christian endeavor union

CHRISTIAN ethics
Better than looking on. J. E. Mulligan.
America 122:468-9 My 2 '70; Discussion.
123:69-70 Ag 8 '70
Changeless. L. N. Bell. Chr Today 14:22-3
Ja 16 '70
Church and poverty. L. N. Bell. Chr Today
14:27 Mr 27 '70
Church as moral decision-maker, by J. M.
Gustafson. Review
America 123:380 N 7 '70. F. X. Winters
Days for searing scrutiny. C. F. H. Henry.
Chr Today 15:41-2 N 6 '70
Eternal yes. L. N. Bell. Chr Today 14:22-3 F
13 '70
Force: a Christian option? Chr Today 14:20
Ja 30 '70
Life of service; excerpt from The new man
for our time. E. Trueblood. Chr Today 14:
3-5 Ja 30 '70
Optimist; scientific reverence for truth. L.
Morris. Chr Today 15:45-6 D 4 '70
Poison in the cup. L. N. Bell. Chr Today 14:
38-9 S 11 '70
Puritan's ought and Paul's ought. R. Haugh-
ton. Cath World 211:53-4 My '70
Rahner's Christian ethics. J. F. Bresnahan.
il America 123:351-4 O 31 '70
Resurrection of Utopia. Chr Cent 87:347 Mr
25 '70
Word. V. P. McCorry. See issues of America
See also
Church and social problems
Love (theology)
Sin
CHRISTIAN existentialism. See Christianity
and existentialism
CHRISTIAN fellowship. See Fellowship of the
Spirit
CHRISTIAN healing. See Faith cure
CHRISTIAN humanism. See Humanism
CHRISTIAN intellectuals. See Christians—In-
tellectual life
CHRISTIAN leadership
Evangelicals and the black revolution; ex-
cerpts from address. T. Skinner. Chr Today
14:10-12+ Ap 10 '70
Generation without fathers. H. Nouwen. Com-
monweal 92:287-94 Je 12 '70; Reply. J. L.
Kater, jr. 92:403+ Ag 21 '70
What moves men as stewards? W. J. Wern-
ing. Chr Today 14:11-13 Ap 24 '70
CHRISTIAN life
As for you. L. N. Bell. Chr Today 14:18-19
Jl 13 '70
Aspects of a theology of play. J. V. Schall.
il Cath World 212:69-73 N '70
Back to the woods. R. Haughton. Cath World
211:101-2 Je '70
Bridges to the past. R. Haughton. il Cath
World 212:175-6 Ja '71
Let God speak. R. Haughton. Cath World
211:197-8 Ag '70
Life of service; excerpt from The new man
for our time. E. Trueblood. Chr Today 14:
3-5 Ja 30 '70
Living in hope: future perspectives in Chris-
tian thought, by L Boros. Review
Cath World 211:281-2 S '70. P. J. Fleming
Reflections in retrospect. F. E. Gaebelein.
Chr Today 14:9-12 Jl 31 '70
Religious life in low profile. K. McDonnell. il
America 123:16-20 Jl 11 '70
Respectable or Christian? R. Haughton. Cath
World 211:245-6 S '70
Victory through surrender. L. N. Bell. Chr
Today 15:23-4 Ja 15 '71
Word and the videotape; address. D. E. John-
son. Chr Today 14:8-11 S 25 '70
See also
Asceticism
Faith
Fellowship of the Spirit
Holiness
Prayer
Stewardship, Christian
CHRISTIAN literature
African challenge; Christian literature. O.
Okite. Chr Today 14:36 My 22 '70
CHRISTIAN love. See Love (theology)
CHRISTIAN missions. See Missions
CHRISTIAN names. See Names, Personal
CHRISTIAN pacifism. See Pacifism
CHRISTIAN peace conference, Prague. See
Peace conferences
CHRISTIAN preaching conference
Preaching in the 1970's. D. Durken. America
122:587-9 My 30 '70
CHRISTIAN reformed church. See Reformed
churches
CHRISTIAN sociology. See Sociology, Christian
CHRISTIAN stewardship. See Stewardship,
Christian

CHRISTIAN witness. See Witness bearing (Christianity)

CHRISTIANITY
Aftermath of Flossenburg: Bonhoeffer, 1945-1970; interview, ed. by H. E. Wright. E. Bethge. por Chr Cent 87:666-9 My 27 '70
Christianity: the true humanism. W. S. Reid. Chr Today 14:9-11 Je 19 '70
Counterfeit Christianity. Chr Today 14:28 Ap 24 '70
Crisis of the church. H. Lindsell. Chr Today 14:4-6 S 11 '70
Here lies community: Deo gratias! E. C. Kennedy. America 123:85-9 Ag 22 '70; Discussion. 123:287-90 O 17 '70
McLuhan on religion. Chr Today 14:34 F 13 '70
Myth of the Judeo-Christian tradition; excerpts. A. A. Cohen; discussion. Commentary 49:4+ Ja; 14+ Mr '70
Permanent mission. V. P. McCorry. America 123:28 inside back cover Jl 11 '70
Power of Pentecost: we need it now more than ever. W. R. Miller. Chr Cent 87:592-4 My 13 '70
Purpose of church. J. Burtchaell. Commonweal 92:437-41 S 4 '70
Religion of joy. V. P. McCorry. America 123: 530 D 12 '70
Slowly does it; the Messiah has come. V. P. McCorry. America 123:132-3 S 5 '70
See also
Apocalypticism
Catholic church
Christian ethics
Christian life
Church
Civilization, Christian
God
Jesus Christ
Jesus Christ—Teachings
Modernism
Paul, Saint—Teachings
Religion
Religion and science
Theology

Anecdotes, facetiae, satire, etc.
Convert. L. Woodrum. Chr Today 14:17 Je 5 '70

Evidences
See Apologetics

CHRISTIANITY, Primitive. See Church history—Primitive and early church

CHRISTIANITY and communication. See Communication (theology)

CHRISTIANITY and existentialism
Is the new theology self-defeating? M. D. Hunnex. Chr Today 15:9-12 Ja 15 '71

CHRISTIANITY and law. See Religion and law

CHRISTIANITY and other religions
Another gospel. L. N. Bell. Chr Today 14: 29-30 F 27 '70
Bible misuse. Chr Today 14:35 F 27 '70
Christian kibbutz: blossoming like a rose? D. Baker. Chr Today 14:37 Ap 24 '70
Convocation presses toward a new theology of Israel. A. L. Eckardt. Chr Cent 87:1521-2 D 16 '70
Delegates of four faiths hold Beirut dialogue. L. H. Dean. Chr Today 14:42-3 Ap 24 '70
Eastern religions; a new interest and influence. W. L. King. Ann Am Acad 387:66-76 Ja '70
Israeli munitions and the Jewishness of Jesus. Chr Cent 87:164-5 F 11 '70; Discussion. 87:397-8 Ap 1 '70
Must Christians be anti-Semitic? M. Zeik. Commonweal 91:557-8 F 20 '70
Oberammergau: is it anti-Semitic? with editorial comment. H. O. J. Brown. Chr Today 14:22, 24 Je 19 '70
People Israel lives. E. L. Fackenheim. bibliog f por Chr Cent 87:563-8 My 6 '70; Reply. R. L. Rubenstein. 87:921-3 Jl 29 '70
Perennial outrage: anti-Semitism in the New Testament. R. E. Willis. Chr Cent 87:990-2 Ag 19 '70
Peril and promise of wider ecumenism; Ajaltoun meeting. Chr Cent 87:524-5 Ap 29 '70
Protestant hangups with the counter-culture. R. L. Johnson. Chr Cent 87:1318-20 N 4 '70
Shall we evangelize the Jews? Chr Today 14: 33-4 Mr 13 '70
Some reflections on the Jewish-Christian dialogue in the light of the six-day war. M. Vogel. bibliog f Ann Am Acad 387:96-108 Ja '70
Unknown war; Moslem guerrillas, Christian government. J. White and M. Mueller. Commonweal 92:476-7 S 25 '70
Zen Buddhism and western alienation from nature. W. R. Hoyt. Chr Cent 87:1194-6 O 7 '70

CHRISTIANITY and politics. See Church and politics

CHRISTIANITY and psychiatry. See Psychiatry and religion

CHRISTIANITY and science. See Religion and science

CHRISTIANITY and social problems. See Church and social problems

CHRISTIANITY and the world. See Church and the world

CHRISTIANITY and war. See War and religion

CHRISTIANITY in literature
Between earth and heaven; Shakespeare, Dostoevsky, and the meaning of Christian tragedy. by R. L. Cox. Review
Commonweal 91:588-9 F 27 '70. S. Teselle

CHRISTIANITY today (periodical)
Statement of purpose. Chr Today 15:30-1 O 9 '70

CHRISTIANS
Ancient word for modern churches. M. M. Shideler. Chr Cent 87:1509-13 D 16 '70
Another gospel. L. N. Bell. Chr Today 14:29-30 F 27 '70
Christian sensitivity. M. R. Chartier. Chr Today 14:9-10 Jl 3 '70
Dawn of reality. R. Haughton. Cath World 212:117-18 D '70
Mark of the Christian; excerpt. F. A. Schaeffer. Chr Today 14:7-8+ S 11 '70
Post-and pre-Christianity. H. O. J. Brown. Chr Today 14:3-5 S 25 '70
Refugees! L. N. Bell. Chr Today 15:24-5 O 23 '70

Intellectual life
Mirror of these ten years. J. Ellul. por Chr Cent 87:200-4 F 18 '70

Persecution
See Persecution

CHRISTIANS and Jews. See Christianity and other religions

CHRISTIANS in Africa
Africans and Christianity. America 122:600 Je 6 '70
Antibiotic Christ. E. G. Dalbey, jr. Chr Cent 87:695-8 Je 3 '70
Big gains for Christian faiths in black Africa. il U S News 69:50-2 D 28 '70

CHRISTIANS in Asia
See also
Eastern Asia Christian conference

CHRISTIANS in China
Christianity lives on in China. M. T. Paan. Chr Today 14:3-5 F 27 '70

CHRISTIANS in Czechoslovakia
Church in a Marxist society. by J. M. Lochman. Review
Commonweal 93:157-8 N 6 '70. C. C. West

CHRISTIANS in Finland
Communists can be Christian; Christians, Communist in Finland. W. S. Salisbury. Chr Cent 87:1519-20 D 16 '70

CHRISTIANS in the Philippines
Christianity and nationalism. L. Morris. Chr Today 14:50-1 Ag 21 '70

CHRISTIANS in Sudan
Christianity in the Sudan: facing Arab colonialism? Chr Today 15:44-5 D 18 '70

CHRISTIANSEN, Andrew
Issues of war and peace. America 122:302-3 Mr 21 '70

CHRISTIANSON, Gale Edward
Test-tube backlash. Commonweal 93:9-13 O 2 '70

CHRISTIE, Agatha
Moonstones and mousetraps. H. R. Mayes. Sat R 53:4+ O 17 '70 *

CHRISTIE, George A.
F. W. Dodge 1970 construction outlook: midyear update. il Arch Rec 148:59-60 Jl '70

CHRISTIE, Sherry
Not with a bang: hair. il por Mlle 70:252-3 Ap '70

CHRISTINE Athans, Sister. See Athans, C.

CHRISTMAN, Kenneth
Photographic serigraphy. il Sch Arts 70:16-18 D '70

CHRISTMAS
Camellias for Christmas. H. E. Dryden. Horticulture 48:24+ D '70
Children of Christmas. J. M. Flagler. il Look 34:50-5 D 29 '70
Christmas! J. Mills. il Read Digest 97:69-72 D '70
Christmas at my father's house; excerpt from My father's house. P. B. Kunhardt, jr. il McCalls 98:44-5+ D '70
Christmas doesn't just happen. J. Ciabattari. il por Redbook 136:22+ D '70
Christmas is a glorious gift to be shared. D. Hardie. House & Gard 138:22+ D '70
Christmas issue. il Redbook 136:61-81+ D '70
Christmas seal. P. B. Price. PTA Mag 65:17 D '70

CHRISTMAS—_Continued_

Christmas: the cosmic light show. J. B. Shepherd. il Cath World 212:123-4 D '70

Glowing season; symposium. il Am Home 73: 37-51 D '70

Holidays are happiness. il Har Yrs 10:26-31 D '70

In affirming the celebrative, we are saying yes! P. E. Kaylor. Mlle 72:80-1+ D '70

Magic room. S. M. Jones. Good H 171:83+ D '70

Make it the merriest Christmas! E. D. Craster and M. B. Smith. il Bet Hom & Gard 48:42-67+ D '70

More than holly: holiness. L. N. Bell. Chr Today 15:23-4 D 18 '70

One must be very careful of Christmas. E. McCarthy. McCalls 98:4 D '70

Peaceful pleasures of Christmas; interview, ed. by L. Baldridge. E. Bruce. Harp Baz 104:142-3 D '70

Remembrance of Christmas. M. C. Smith. il House B 112:56-7 D '70

Six with the true spirit of Christmas. M. Gough. House B 112:60-1 D '70

Someday: a real Christmas; reprint from December 23, 1955 issue. D. Lawrence. U S News 69:68 D 28 '70

Tinsel and tissue; an assortment of seasonable oddments. il Changing T 24:14-15 D '70

Vanishing Christmas person. E. Sheppard. il Harp Baz 104:106-7 D '70

What people are doing. . . House & Gard 138:39 D '70

Why we gave up kidnapping. T. McHale. il McCalls 98:40+ D '70

See also
Christmas eve
Jesus Christ—Nativity

Alaska

Christmas at sixty below. P. S. Coyne. Nat R 22:1405 D 29 '70

Israel

Bethlehem bids for normalcy. D. Baker. Chr Today 15:40 Ja 1 '71

CHRISTMAS bonuses. See Bonus system

CHRISTMAS books. Childrens. See Childrens literature

CHRISTMAS breads. See Bread

CHRISTMAS buffet. See Buffet meals

CHRISTMAS business

Christmas consumer as Scrooge. Time 96:54-5 D 28 '70

Christmas prices take the down escalator. il Bsns W p 14 D 26 '70

Death of tinsel. Newsweek 77:51 Ja 4 '71

Good year for Christmas trade. il U S News 69:16-18 D 21 '70

Gyps that thrive at Christmas. il Changing T 23:12 D '69

Hallelujah chorus was missing. il Bsns W p 13 Ja 2 '71

It's Christmas or never for the big stores. il Bsns W p25 D 5 '70

Shoppers signal a so-so Christmas. il U S News 69:50-2 N 2 '70

CHRISTMAS cake. See Cake

CHRISTMAS candles. See Candles

CHRISTMAS candy. See Candy

CHRISTMAS cards

Easy way to block-print Christmas cards using paint. il Sunset 145:80 D '70

How to package Christmas. R. Lynes. Art in Am 58:39 N '70

In faint praise of Christmas cards; Time essay. P. Herrera. il Time 96:33 D 21 '70

Trim a tree with light. J. T. Dreyfuss. il Mod Phot 33:182-3 D '69

When Christmas cards can help others. il Good H 171:186 O '70

CHRISTMAS carol; drama. See Hackett, W.

CHRISTMAS carols
See also
Phonograph records—Christmas music

CHRISTMAS comes to Hamelin; drama. See Mills, G. E.

CHRISTMAS cookery

Christmas baking. il Ebony 26:168+ D '70

Christmas is for children too. R. F. Pomeroy. il Redbook 136:69-70 D '70

Christmas riches. il Ladies Home J 86:94-5+ D '69

Cooking ahead for Christmas. il McCalls 98: 66-75+ N '70

Festive holiday buffets: with recipes and menu. F. M. Crawford. il Am Home 73: 58-60+ D '70

House & garden Christmas present cookbook. L. J. Reich. il House & Gard 138: 88+ D '70

How to take the hectic out of holiday cooking. D. Eby. Bet Hom & Gard 48:68-74 D '70

Roll on, O Yuletide! with recipes. N. S. Hazelton. Nat R 22:1408+ D 29 '70

Twelve days of Christmas cookbook. il Redbook 136:114-22 D '70
See also
Christmas dinners
Christmas meals

CHRISTMAS cookies. See Cookies

CHRISTMAS cribs

Crèches: symbols of peace. il Good H 171: 32-3 D '70

Cutout crèche, our gift to you. J. Stith. il Bet Hom & Gard 48:56-7 D '70

Simple crèche to treasure. il Am Home 73: 50-1 D '70

Slab construction over a newspaper core; chèche figures. J. E. Kozlowski. il Ceram Mo 18:18-20 D '70

Wall crèche you'll cherish. il Farm J 94:25 D '70

CHRISTMAS decorations

Christmas is his best crop; G. Wright of Laurens County, Ga. il Farm J 94:22-3+ D '70

Christmas snowflakes in the window. il Sunset 145:52-5 D '70

Christmas trees by the dozen. il Ladies Home J 87:58+ D '70

Deck the halls and. . . Bob Perkins's floral decorations. N. Skurka. il N Y Times Mag p42-3 D 20 '70

Harmonious hangings. il Bet Hom & Gard 48:62-5+ D '70

Holiday decorating ideas. M. Kraft. il Good H 171:86-91 D '70

Holidays are happiness. il Har Yrs 10:26-31 D '70

Let your children deck the tree. A. Wiglama. il House B 112:62-7 D '70

Merry makings from paper. il Good H 171: 118-19+ D '70

Papier-mâché animals for an animal tree. il Sunset 145:62-3 D '70

Put your heart into these handmades. il Farm J 93:46-7 D '69

Sparkling decorations of light. il House & Gard 138:60-7 D '70

Turn bits of colorful yarn and felt into these delightful tree trimmings and our giant (two-foot) Christmas stocking. V. P. Guild. il Good H 171:124-5+ D '70

'Twas the night before Christmas. il Ladies Home J 86:79-85+ D '69

Wax wonders. il Bet Hom & Gard 48:48-9+ D '70
See also
Christmas projects
Christmas tree lights
Christmas trees

CHRISTMAS decorations, Outdoor

Build PM's sequence Santa electric greeting card. W. C. Leckey. il Pop Mech 134:172-5+ N '70

Nation's capital turns on for Christmas. il Am City 85:72+ D '70

Way-out welcomes. il Bet Hom & Gard 48: 44-5 D '70

Why not think big: a wall of chicken wire supports the giant arrow, a door wreath, a grand swag tree. il Sunset 145:70-1 D '70

CHRISTMAS dinners

Gather together for a festive feast; with recipes. il Farm J 93:38-9+ D '69

Holiday birds. House B 112:96-8 D '70

CHRISTMAS eve

It says here . . . A. B. Heath. Nat R 22:1395-6 D 29 '70

CHRISTMAS gifts

Best buy gifts, 1969. il Consumer Rep 34: 662-3 N '69

Best buy gifts 1970. il Consumer Rep 35:688-90 N '70

Books and records to give for Christmas. J. Herbert. House & Gard 138:30-2 D '70

Boutique of gifts to sew. E. D. Craster. il Bet Hom & Gard 48:60-3+ N '70

Christmas from the kitchen; gifts to make from kitchen equipment. il Ladies Home J 87:38 D '70

Christmas game that everyone can play: rerouting presents. N. Gittelson. Harp Baz 104:22+ D '70

Christmas shopping guide; suggestions for artist friends. il Am Artist 34:22-4 D '70

Decorating newsletter; how to resolve the couples gift dilemma. Am Home 73:24-5 D '70

CHRISTMAS gifts—*Continued*
Easy do's that produce great Christmas gifts. D. L. Brightbill. il Am Home 73:70-5+ N '70
Gift boutique; Christmas treasures for giving. il House B 112:42-53 D '70
Gifts that last forever, love of the outdoors. T. Trueblood. il Field & S 75:14-15+ D '70
Great house gifts. il House & Gard 138:99 D '70
Half the money and twice the cheer. V. Cadden. il Redbook 136:42+ D '70
Make the gifts they'll really love from our fabulous forty-two. il Good H 171:124-8+ N '70
More gift ideas for people interested in natural gardening. il Sunset 145:177 D '70
Museum finds. il McCalls 98:38 D '70
Museums; great places to buy offbeat gifts. il Changing T 24:13-15 N '70
121 Christmas present ideas. Vogue 156:162-3+ N 15 '70
Plan to give; hope to get. L. Lerman. Mlle 72:164-5+ N '70
Redbook's guide to Christmas gifts with more love than money. il Redbook 136:90-8+ D '70
Twenty-five newsy gifts, sure to please. il Good H 171:120-3 D '70
What does an ecologically defensive gardener really want for Christmas? il Sunset 145:66-7 D '70
Zip gifts. il Bet Hom & Gard 48:60-1+ D '70
See also
Books as gifts
Christmas projects
Christmas shopping
Food as gifts
Plants as gifts
Wrapping of packages

Anecdotes, facetiae, satire, etc.
Gift-buying guide. Chr Cent 87:1499 D 9 '70
I declare; an Englishwoman's Christmas list. G. Perint. Harp Baz 104:144 D '70
Letters of thanks; excerpts. M. Kempadoo. il Ladies Home J 86:58 D '69

CHRISTMAS gifts for children
How did you know what I wanted, mom? S. D. Stutz. il Parents Mag 45:50-1+ D '70
On and off the avenue (cont) New Yorker 46:137-40+ D 12 '70
This year's Christmas toys. Changing T 24:6 D '70

CHRISTMAS gifts for men
Beauty & the bath. S. Lindsay. il House B 112:42+ N '70
Getting high on hardware. il Esquire 74:196-203 D '70
Gifts for fishermen. V. Evanoff. Motor B 126:21 D '70
Has a beard appeared near you? il Sunset 145:72-3 D '70
His & hers; gifts to make. N. O'Leary. il Ladies Home J 87:104-5+ N '70
Holiday gifts for men only: cosmetics. il Ladies Home J 87:36 D '70
Mlle's Christmas male bag. il Mlle 72:98-105 D '70
On and off the avenue (cont) New Yorker 46:101-11 D 19 '70
100 great gifts for guys. Harp Baz 104:97-9 D '70

CHRISTMAS gifts for the aged
Santa's bag is choosing; gifts for nursing-home patients. M. Thurber. il Todays Health 48:40-1 D '70

CHRISTMAS gifts for the home
From home base. M. K. Spencer. Am Home 73:28 D '70
Gifts in now materials: stainless steel and plastic. il McCalls 98:82-5 N '70
Gifts to build. il Bet Hom & Gard 48:12-13 D '70
Gifts you could never give before. M. Davidson. il Ladies Home J 86:48+ D '69
Great house gifts. il House & Gard 138:139-41 N '70
How to find the perfect Christmas present for everyone on your list. il House & Gard 138:100-13 N '70
On and off the avenue (cont) New Yorker 46:147-52+ N 28 '70
Short guide to Christmas composure. N. Schramm. House B 112:22+ N '70

CHRISTMAS gifts for women
Baubles, bangles and beads for Christmas. Bsns W p81 D 12 '70
Bazaar's Christmas scrapbook. il Harp Baz 104:100-5 D '70
His & hers; gifts to make. N. O'Leary. il Ladies Home J 87:104-5+ N '70
On and off the avenue (cont) New Yorker 46:141-2+ N 21 '70

CHRISTMAS greens
Jubilate herbis. N. Farber. Horn Bk 46:592 D '70
Tales the trees could tell. G. Nicholson. il Am For 76:12-15 D '70
See also
Christmas trees
Holly
Mistletoe

CHRISTMAS literature
See also
Christmas poetry

CHRISTMAS literature, Childrens. See Childrens literature

CHRISTMAS meals
Christmas eve supper. il Farm J 94:24 D '70
Christmas party cookbook. il Good H 171:92-117 D '70
Ladies' home journal Handbook of holiday cuisine; excerpts. M. Happel and E. Harrington. il Ladies Home J 87:80-8+ D '70
Make-ahead suppers, each family size, choose one to serve on Christmas Eve. il Sunset 145:126-7 D '70
Make it a Christmas picnic: Puerto Rico; with recipes. E. Alston. il Look 34:60-2 D 29 '70
See also
Christmas dinners

CHRISTMAS music
See also
Phonograph records—Christmas music

CHRISTMAS parties. See Childrens parties; Entertaining

CHRISTMAS plants. See House plants

CHRISTMAS plays
Texts
Case of the silent caroler. H. L. Miller. Plays 30:1-12 D '70
Christmas carol; dramatization of story by C. Dickens. W. Hackett. Plays 30:83-95 D '70
Christmas comes to Hamelin. G. E. Mills. Plays 30:53-60, 96 D '70
Destination: Christmas! C. Boiko. Plays 30:43-52, 96 D '70
Littlest elf. F. B. Watts. Plays 30:76-7, 96 D '70
Second shepherd's play. F. E. Head. Plays 30:37-42 D '70
Standing up for Santa. A. Fisher. Plays 30:66-8 D '70

CHRISTMAS poetry
And the word was made flesh. A. Craig. Chr Today 15:4 D 4 '70
Christmas: eve and morn. P. G. Jackson. Chr Today 15:18 D 18 '70
Christmas poems; comp. by T. J. O'Connell. America 123:560-1 D 26 '70
On Christmas eve; poem. P. Havard. il Farm J 93:37 D '69
Poets at Bethlehem. N. Braybrooke. il Cath World 212:140-2 D '70
Rest on the flight into Egypt; poem, tr. by M. W. Hess. R. M. Rilke. Cath World 212:118 D '70
Shout for Christmas. A. Kenseth. Chr Cent 87:1548 D 23 '70
This Christmas night. M. Wilson. Good H 171:186 D '70

CHRISTMAS presents. See Christmas gifts

CHRISTMAS projects
Christmas is for children too. R. F. Pomeroy. il Redbook 136:66-74 D '70
Ecological Christmas. il Nat Parks & Con Mag 44:25 D '70
Fifty-five happy ideas for holiday making and giving. il Am Home 73:43-50 D '70
Gifts the children make. il Bet Hom & Gard 48:50-1 D '70

CHRISTMAS shopping
How to avoid pre-Christmas panic (next year) K. D. Fury. Redbook 136:83+ D '70
Shopping excursion into the gold country. il Sunset 145:28-9 D '70

CHRISTMAS stockings. See Christmas decorations

CHRISTMAS stories
Gifted child. M. Cousins. Ladies Home J 86:32 D '69

CHRISTMAS stories, Childrens. See Childrens stories

CHRISTMAS string seminar. See Chamber music

CHRISTMAS table decoration. See Table decoration

CHRISTMAS toys. See Toys

CHRISTMAS tree lights
Build your own dancing light display. D. Rimmer and R. F. Graf. il Pop Mech 134:144-6 D '70

CHRISTMAS tree ornaments. See Christmas decorations

CHRISTMAS trees
Christmas allergy. Newsweek 76:38 D 28 '70
Christmas tree. D. S. Manks. Horticulture 48:25+ D '70
Different kind of Christmas tree; redwood. E. W. Chandler. il Am For 76:32-4 D '70
Glorious tree. il House & Gard 138:40-7 D '70
How to buy a Christmas tree. il Consumer Rep 34:623 N '69
How to make our cookie Christmas tree. M. Ying and S. Whittier. Good H 171:10 D '70
How to make our five-foot paper tree. P. C. Ficarotta. il Good H 171:10+ D '70
How to select a Christmas tree. Good H 171:158 D '70
Keep your Christmas tree fresh and fireproof. Farm J 94:36 D '70
Living Christmas tree. House & Gard 138:98 D '70
Tree: Rockefeller Center. New Yorker 46:32-4 D 19 '70
Trees of yuletide. R. B. Kirkpatrick. il Nat Wildlife 9:12-16 D '70
Trees to treasure. il Bet Hom & Gard 48:52-3+ D '70
CHRISTMAS window displays. See Show windows
CHRISTMAS wrappings. See Wrapping of packages
CHRISTMAS wreaths
Christmas is his best crop; G. Wright of Laurens County, Ga. il Farm J 94:22-3+ D '70
Making Christmas wreaths. J. Kuh. por Ladies Home J 86:143 D '69
CHRISTOLOGY. See Jesus Christ
CHRISTOPHE, Henri, king of Haiti
Great Haitian epic. G. de Zéndegui. il pors Américas 22:2-11 Je '70 *
CHRISTOPHER, William F.
Marketing planning that gets things done. il Harvard Bsns R 48:56-64 S '70
CHRISTOPHERSEN, R. G.
You can drive your own well. il Pop Mech 133:188-91+ Ap '70
CHRISTY, George
In the pink in Mexico. Mlle 70:126-7+ Ja '70
New life of Julie Andrews. il pors Good H 170:90-1+ My '70
(ed) See Burnett, C. To make music in the heart
CHROMAN, Eleanor
Potter's workshop. il Ceram Mo 18:20 My '70
CHROMATIN
Satellite DNA in constitutive heterochromatin of the guinea pig. J. J. Yunis and W. G. Yasmineh. bibliog il Science 168:263-5 Ap 10 '70
CHROMATOGRAPHIC analysis
Countercurrent chromatography: liquid-liquid partition chromatography without solid support. Y. Ito and R. L. Bowman. bibliog il Science 167:281-3 Ja 16 '70
Droplet countercurrent chromatography. T. Tanimura and others. il Science 169:54-6 Ji 3 '70
Gas chromatography: medical diagnostic aid. M. W. Ruchelman. bibliog il por Chem 43:14-19 D '70
Gel permeation chromatography. D. D. Bly. bibliog il Science 168:527-33 My 1 '70
Lab bench; identifying artificial color on oranges. Chem 43:29-30 F '70
Plasminogen: purification from human plasma by affinity chromatography. D. G. Deutsch and E. T. Mertz. bibliog il Science 170:1095-6 D 4 '70
Separating lanthanides by ion exchange chromatography. L. W. McKeen. bibliog il por Chem 43:28-31 My '70
CHROMIUM glaze colorant. See Glazes and glazing
CHROMOSOMES
Acetylsalicylic acid: no chromosome damage in human leukocytes. I. Mauer and others. bibliog il Science 169:198-201 Jl 10 '70
Aedes aegypti: origin of a new chromosome from a double translocation heterozygote. P. T. McDonald and K. S. Rai. bibliog il Science 168:1229-30 Je 5 '70
Cause of cancer. il por Environ 12:22-5 Je '70
Chromosomal abnormalities in the human population: estimation of rates based on New Haven newborn study. H. A. Lubs and F. H. Ruddle. bibliog il Science 169:495-7 Jl 31 '70
Chromosomal localization of mouse satellite DNA. M. L. Pardue and J. G. Gall. bibliog il Science 168:1356-8 Je 12 '70
Chromosome number variation in a stick insect didymuria violescens (leach) E. Craddock. bibliog il Science 167:1380-2 Mr 6 '70
Chromosome tracers of the origin of species. H. L. Carson. bibliog il Science 168:1414-18 Je 19 '70

Congenital criminals? Johns Hopkins project. Newsweek 75:98-9 My 18 '70
Cytogenetic studies with cyclamate and related compounds. D. R. Stoltz and others. il Science 167:1501-2 Mr 13 '70
Heritable fragile site on chromosome 16: probable localization of haptoglobin locus in man. R. E. Magenis and others. bibliog il Science 170:85-7 O 2 '70
Indian muntjac, muntiacus muntjak: a deer with a low diploid chromosome number. D. H. Wurster and K. Benirschke. bibliog il Science 168:1364-6 Je 12 '70
Isolation and zonal fractionation of metaphase chromosomes from human diploid cells. E. L. Schneider and N. P. Salzman. bibliog il Science 167:1141-3 F 20 '70
Late DNA replication in male mouse meiotic chromosomes. N. Odartchenko and M. Paviillard. bibliog il Science 167:1133-4 F 20 '70
Nuclear sexing in a population of Congolese metropolitan newborns. H. van den Berghe. bibliog il Science 169:1318-20 S 25 '70
Polyploidy in the common tree toad hyla versicolor Le Conte. A. O. Wasserman. bibliog il Science 167:385-6 Ja 23 '70
Puffing and histone acetylation in polytene chromosomes. U. Clever and E. G. Ellgaard. bibliog il Science 169:373-4 Jl 24 '70
Pursuit of Y. Newsweek 76:70 Ag 24 '70
RNA and DNA puffs in polytene chromosomes of rhynchosciara: inhibition by extirpation of prothorax. J. M. Amabis and D. Cabral. bibliog il Science 169:692-4 Ag 14 '70
Trisomy-3,4 and triploidy (3A-ZZZW) in chick embryos: autosomal and sex chromosomal nondisjunction in meiosis. S. E. Bloom. bibliog il Science 170:457-8 O 23 '70
See also
Chromatin

CHROMOSOMES (botany)
Chromosomal aberrations induced in barley by LSD. M. P. Singh and others. bibliog il Science 169:491-2 Jl 31 '70
Chromosomal drift, a new phenomenon in plants. W. H. Lewis. bibliog il Science 168:1115-16 My 29 '70

Pairing
See Cell division (botany)
CHROMOSPHERE. See Sun—Atmosphere
CHRONICLE, San Francisco. See San Francisco chronicle
CHRYSANTHEMUMS
Autumn magic; ed. by E. Haraszty. R. E. Atkinson. il McCalls 98:38+ N '70
Grow florist-size mums. A. L. Thon. il Home Gard 57:18-19+ Ap '70
CHRYSLER corporation
Chrysler: a whole new ball game. Forbes 106:25 S 15 '70
Chrysler goes abroad for mini. il Bsns W p20 Jl 4 '70
Chrysler rides out the bumps. il Time 96:90+ N 2 '70
Chrysler tries without a mini. il Bsns W p58-9 S 5 '70
Chrysler's private hard times. A. M. Louis. il por Fortune 81:102-5+ Ap '70
Compleat company. M. Crook. il Yachting 127:64-6+ Ap '70
Skidding Chrysler switches drivers. il por Bsns W p30-1 Ja 17 '70
See also
Rootes motors, ltd.
CHRYSLER marine engine division. See Chrysler corporation
CHRYSOSTOMOS, bp
Greek orthodoxy: the junta defied. T. Cosmades. Chr Today 14:38-9 Ja 16 '70
CHU, Franklin
Crawling through Southwest Asia. il pors Esquire 73:94-6+ F '70
CHU, Hung-ti
Education in mainland China. Cur Hist 59:165-9+ S '70
CHUCK hunting. See Woodchuck hunting
CHUKAR shooting. See Partridge shooting
CHUKOVSKII, Kornei Ivanovich
Confessions of an old story-teller; tr. by L. G. Leighton. Horn Bk 46:577-91 D '70 (to be cont)
CHUNG, S. H. See Pomeranz, B. jt. auth.
CHURCH, Frank
Foreign policy; address, December 3, 1970. Vital Speeches 37:170-3 Ja 1 '71
Gunboat diplomacy & colonialist economics. Trans-Action 7:25-32 Je '70
Latin America; address, April 10, 1970. Vital Speeches 36:418-23 My 1 '70
Toward a new Latin American policy; excerpts from address. Cur 117:49-55 Ap '70

CHURCH, Frank—*Continued*

about

Senate: unloving acts. por Time 95:9-10 Je 1 '70 *

CHURCH

Church to come; adaptation of address, April 9, 1970. D. H. C. Read. America 122:550-4 My 23 '70

Sins of the church. G. C. Berkouwer. Chr Today 15:58-9 N 20 '70

What kind of church do we want? J. J. Drag. Chr Today 14:29-30 Ja 30 '70

See also
Christianity
Mission of the church
Women and the church

Authority

Church confronts loyalty and dissent; symposium. America 122:668-85 Je 27 '70

Figgis, Constance, and the Divines of Paris; excerpts from address, December 30, 1966. F. Oakley. bibliog f Am Hist R 75:368-86 D '69

If you could make one change in the church, what would it be? symposium. Commonweal 92:159-66 My 1 '70; Reply. D. Grumbach. 92:325-6 Je 26 '70

Politics, impolitics and unpolitics; Échanges et dialogue. Chr Cent 87:525 Ap 29 '70

Rome replies (act II); the Congregation for Catholic education. N. G. McCluskey. il America 122:330-4 Mr 28 '70

Storm on the Holy See. J. Horgan. il Sat R 53:19-21+ Mr 28 '70

Structures, authority and all that. L. M. Orsy. America 122:221 F 28 '70

See also
Popes—Primacy

Mission

See Mission of the church

Purpose

See Mission of the church

CHURCH, Negro. See Negroes—Religion

CHURCH and education
See also
Catholic schools
Church schools
Private schools and religion
Religious education

CHURCH and international relations
See also
Catholic church—Relations (diplomatic)—United Nations

CHURCH and politics

Betrayals of purpose. Chr Today 14:22-3 Ja 30 '70

GOP and God; priest influences Catholics on abortion issue in California. L. T. King. Commonweal 93:37-8 O 9 '70

Great controversy in the church; address, April 12, 1970. J. C. Bennett. Chr Cent 87:659-63 My 27 '70

Politics and church. L. M. Orsy. America 122:303-4 Mr 21 '70

Respect for law, respect for persons. J. B. Sheerin. Cath World 211:50-1 My '70

CHURCH and race problems

Alabama church refuses membership to black mother and daughter. Chr Cent 87:1178 O 7 '70

Black concerns in the White House; black Baptist ministers at White House. Chr Today 14:46+ Ap 10 '70

Blacks and COCU: a new honesty. C. Rogers. Chr Cent 87:1554 D 30 '70

Changes in the black ghetto: Cleveland; white and black Unitarians form separate units. J. G. Mearns. il pors Sat R 53:13-14+ Ag 1 '70

Church must change or die. Mrs F. Marker. il Redbook 136:70+ N '70

Clash over urban ministry styles; dismissal of P. Lawson. Chr Cent 87:1507 D 16 '70

Clergy involvement in civil rights. J. K. Hadden. bibliog f Ann Am Acad 387:118-27 Ja '70

Cordial welcome, if you're white. Chr Today 14:28 F 27 '70

Evangelicals and the black revolution; excerpts from address. T. Skinner. Chr Today 14:10-12+ Ap 10 '70

Ian Smith's Rhodesia: only the churches stand in the way; with editorial comment. O. W. Okite. Chr Today 14:26, 44 Je 5 '70

Kansas City Methodists: horse of a different color; missions to the Black Panthers. J. S. Tinney. Chr Today 14:41 Ap 24 '70

Methodism under siege; General conference. D. Kucharsky. Chr Today 14:36-7 My 8 '70

Methodists vow new priorities; with editorial comment. D. Kucharsky. Chr Today 14:22, 31-2 My 22 '70

Political gospel. F. Herzog. il Chr Cent 87:1380-3 N 18 '70

Precious in his sight; First Baptist church of Birmingham, Ala, and a black applicant. il Newsweek 76:69-70 Ag 10 '70

Verdict at First Baptist: black applicants denied membership in Birmingham, Ala. Newsweek 76:107-8 O 12 '70

White ethnics and black empowerment. C. Rogers. Chr Cent 87:1372 N 18 '70; Reply. I. M. Levine. 88:46 Ja 13 '71

Work of depolarization; U.S. Catholic conference statement. Commonweal 93:3-4 O 2 '70

See also
Catholic schools—Desegregation
Interreligious foundation for community organization
National Catholic conference for interracial justice

CHURCH and race problems in Rhodesia

Bleak future for black Rhodesians. O. Eby. Chr Cent 87:899-901 Jl 22 '70

CHURCH and race problems in South Africa

Guns for God; WCC's gift to African liberation movements. Time 96:74 O 5 '70

South African Christians: apartheid and Elections. O. W. Okite. Chr Today 14:32-3 Ja 16 '70

CHURCH and social problems

Attraction of Adventism. D. Kucharsky. Chr Today 14:35 Ja 30 '70

Bishops and the hellish circle; NCCB's campaign for human development. Chr Cent 87:1245 O 21 '70

Bombs or Bibles? Get ready for revolution! V. C. Grounds. Chr Today 15:4-6 Ja 15 '71

Breaking the circle of poverty; U.S. bishops organize. T. M. Gannon. America 123:394-5 N 14 '70

Case for sexual restraint. Chr Today 14:31-2 Mr 13 '70

Christian as a visitor. Chr Today 14:23 Mr 27 '70

Church and poverty. L. N. Bell. Chr Today 14:27 Mr 27 '70

Church and the poor. V. P. McCorry. America 123:387-8 N 7 '70

Church in the marketplace; Smith-Haven ministries. A. W. Godfrey. Cath World 212:83-4 N '70

Evangelical responsibility in a secularized world. K. Runia. Chr Today 14:11-14 Je 19 '70

Evangelism as social therapy. Chr Today 14:28-9 Ag 21 '70

Fire and Blackstone, by J. R. Fry. Review Commonweal 92:67-8 Mr 27 '70. S. Terkel

Gift for the neighborhood; church to do urban developing of their own. il Time 95:77 My 11 '70

Great transition. Chr Today 14:20-1 Mr 27 '70

Harlem, rebellion and resurrection. W. Stringfellow. Chr Cent 87:1345-8 N 11 '70

How clergymen view hippiedom. H. M. Hacker. il Chr Cent 87:887-91 Jl 22 '70

If you could make one change in the church, what would it be? symposium. Commonweal 92:159-66 My 1 '70; Reply. D. Grumbach. 92:325-6 Je 26 '70

Lording it over the church; Puerto Rican group called the Young Lords. il Chr Today 14:31 Ja 30 '70

Middle America: theologically formed. C. P. Lutz. Chr Cent 87:323-5 Mr 18 '70; Discussion. 87:640 My 20 '70

More about relevance. L. N. Bell. Chr Today 14:35-6 Mr 13 '70

MUST: missionary thrust or bust? R. Hull, jr. Chr Cent 87:665-7 My 27 '70; Reply. N. F. Fisher. 87:1291-4 O 28 '70

Protestant clergy: new forms of ministry, new forms of training. R. H. Luecke. bibliog f Ann Am Acad 387:86-95 Ja '70

Rich churches and poor people. W. W. Grant. Chr Today 14:11-12 F 27 '70

Store-front churches in the inner city; helping recently arrived migrants adapt to urban living. L. S. Sata and others. bibliog Ment Hy 54:256-60 Ap '70

Time for action! L. N. Bell. Chr Today 14:18-19 Je 19 '70

Winds of promise; what critical youth wants. C. F. H. Henry. Chr Today 14:29-30 Je 5 '70

World around us. See issues of Christian century

See also
Association for social economics
Birth control—Religious aspects
Christian ethics
Church and politics
Church and race problems
Church work
Social action
Sociology, Christian

CHURCH and social problems—*Continued*

Latin America

Church in Latin America. T. G. Sanders. For
Affairs 48:285-99 Ja '70
Latin America: the church militant. N. Gall.
bibliog f Commentary 49:25-37 Ap '70
New rebels: clerics in Latin America. J. Benham. il U S News 69:92-5 D 14 '70

CHURCH and state
Caesar as God. J. V. Schall. Commonweal
91:505-10 F 6 '70; Discussion. 91:526, 571+ F
13, 27 '70
Compulsory chapel at U.S. academies. America 122:176 F 21 '70; Reply. D. H. Vaught.
122:544 My 23 '70
See also
Government, Resistance to
Religious liberty

Germany (Federal Republic)
See also
Church tax—Germany (Federal Republic)

CHURCH and state in Bolivia
Bolivian regime moves against the church.
Chr Cent 87:851-2 Jl 8 '70

CHURCH and state in Brazil
Brazil: a country where Christians are outlaws. M. M. Alves. il Cath World 212:65-8
N '70
Brazil and the Pope. Commonweal 92:284 Je
12 '70
Brazil: order vs. disorder; Archbishop Costa's talk to army cadets. America 123:536-7
D 19 '70
Christians, Marxists and dictatorship in
Brazil. M. M. Alves. Chr Cent 87:723-7 Je
10 '70
Embattled Brazil. J. Deedy. Commonweal 93:
162 N 13 '70
Torture in Brazil. R. Della Cava. Commonweal 92:129+ Ap 24 '70; Discussion. 92:451+
S 18 '70
See also
Catholic church in Brazil

CHURCH and state in China (People's Republic)
China; Article 88 of China's constitution. H.
Yu. Chr Cent 87:1302 O 28 '70

CHURCH and state in Czechoslovakia
See also
Catholic church in Czechoslovakia

CHURCH and state in Great Britain
Antidisestablishmentarianism. J. D. Douglas.
Chr Today 15:32 Ja 15 '71
See also
Church of England

CHURCH and state in Hungary
Hungarian Catholics gain concession from
Communists. Chr Cent 87:1058 S 9 '70
See also
Catholic church in Hungary

CHURCH and state in Israel
Who is a Jew? synagogue and state in Israel.
M. Zeik. Commonweal 92:114-17 Ap 17 '70

CHURCH and state in Italy
Church-state embroilment. America 122:259
Mr 14 '70

CHURCH and state in Latin America
Priests in politics. Sr Schol 97:20-1 O 19 '70
See also
Catholic church in Latin America

CHURCH and state in Lesotho
Oppression in Southern Africa. O. W. Okite.
Chr Today 14:32 Jl 17 '70

CHURCH and state in Paraguay
Bishops and the dictator. America 122:604-
5 Je 6 '70
Christ in Paraguay? Chr Cent 87:68 Ja 21 '70
CRS in Paraguay. J. Deedy. Commonweal 93:
34 O 9 '70
Paraguay ends church relief. America 122:61
Ja 24 '70

CHURCH and state in Poland
Polish politics; struggle over Oder-Neisse
dioceses. il pors Newsweek 75:110+ Mr 16
'70
See also
Catholic church in Poland

CHURCH and state in Portugal
Portugal's religious freedom bill criticized by
Catholic bishops. Chr Cent 88:8 Ja 6 '71

CHURCH and state in Rhodesia
Church vs. state in Rhodesia; Protestant
and the Land tenure act. America 122:
516 My 16 '70
Confrontation in Rhodesia; united Christian
front opposing the government. America
122:381 Ap 11 '70
Crisis of conscience. por Time 95:58 Ap 13
'70
Dilemma in Rhodesia; bishops and the Land
tenure act. America 123:79-80 Ag 22 '70
Proud church in Rhodesia. America 122:448
Ap 25 '70

Rhodesian bishops: no apartheid; new Land
tenure act. F. Sekyewa. Commonweal 92:
308-9 Je 26 '70
Rhodesian bishops take a stand. America 123:
134 S 12 '70
Rhodesia's bishops speak out. P. Crane.
America 122:412 Ap 18 '70

CHURCH and state in South Africa
Ramsey's return, or back at the palace. J.
D. Douglas. Chr Today 15:41-2 Ja 1 '71

CHURCH and state in Spain
Eight Basque priests released in Spain. Chr
Cent 87:934 Ag 5 '70
Showdown ahead for Spain. W. E. Greening. il America 123:487-9 D 5 '70; Discussion. 124:2 Ja 9; 29 Ja 16 '71
See also
Catholic church in Spain

CHURCH and state in the Cameroon Republic
Church and state in Cameroon. J. Derrick.
il por America 124:18-20 Ja 9 '71

CHURCH and state in Turkey
Turkey beset by mosque-state woes. T. Cosmades. Chr Cent 87:93 Ja 21 '70

CHURCH and state in Yugoslavia
Tito & the Pope. M. M. Mestrovic. Commonweal 93:36-7 O 9 '70

CHURCH and the world
Christians and revolution. J. H. Nederhood.
Chr Today 15:7-9 Ja 1 '71
Civil war in the church. J. B. Sheerin. Cath
World 210:194-5 F '70
Ecological disaster and the church. J. B.
Cobb, jr. il Chr Cent 87:1185-7 O 7 '70
Evolution, revolution, or victory. H. O. J.
Brown. Chr Today 14:4-6 Ap 10 '70
Gospel of the dynamic middle. G. M. Docherty. Chr Cent 87:863-6 Jl 15 '70
Messianic core; the left tradition in church
and society. R. Ruether. il Commonweal
91:423-5 Ja 16 '70; Reply. A. M. Farrell.
91:499 F 6 '70
More about relevance. L. N. Bell. Chr Today
14:35-6 Mr 13 '70
Quiet storm in the churches. H. A. Bosley.
Chr Cent 87:1449-52 D 2 '70
Radical secularity and radical grace. J. M.
Lochman. por Chr Cent 87:911-14 Jl 29 '70
Religious life in low profile. K. McDonnell.
il America 123:16-20 Jl 11 '70
Sticking point: religious tutelage. R. J. Westley. America 123:172-5 S 19 '70
Who is polarizing the church? C. P. Hinerman. Chr Today 15:8-10 N 6 '70
Why churches are worried. il U S News 68:
42-6 Mr 23 '70
Word and the videotape; address. D. E. Johnson. Chr Today 14:8-11 S 12 '70

CHURCH architecture
Church for the revised Catholic liturgy;
Church of St Thomas Aquinas, Indianapolis.
il Arch Rec 147:119-22 F '70
Church under a great tent; St Paul's Lutheran
church in Sarasota, Fla. V. Lundy. il Arch
Forum 133:76-81 Jl '70
Design for belonging. W. Von Eckardt. il Sat
R 53:68-9 D 5 '70

CHURCH art. See Christian art and symbolism

CHURCH attendance
Case of the wholly secular chapel. D. M.
Kelley. Chr Cent 87:1166-9 S 30 '70
Compulsory chapel at U.S. academies. America 122:176 F 21 '70; Reply. D. H. Vaught.
122:544 My 23 '70
Nice guys finish last; study by G. W. Comstock. Time 97:61 Ja 18 '71
Ready, aim, pray! L. Pfeffer. Commonweal
93:274-6 D 11 '70
Summer-slump solutions. Chr Cent 87:1003
Ag 19 '70
Warning: may be beneficial to your health.
Chr Today 15:27 Ja 1 '71

Anecdotes, facetiae, satire, etc.
Seek ye first... Chr Cent 87:519 Ap 22 '70

CHURCH bulletins. See Bulletins

CHURCH colleges
Changing partnerships in Christian higher
education. D. L. McKenna. Chr Today
14:5-7 Ag 21 '70
Church colleges are peculiar institutions.
G. M. Schurr. Chr Cent 87:1154-7 S 30 '70
College consumers; rocking the boat. J. Rohler. Chr Today 14:36-7 Ja 30 '70
Evaluating Christian colleges. Chr Today
14:23 Mr 27 '70
Getting a fresh start. A. H. Leitch. Chr Today 14:39 Je 19 '70
Idea of a Christian college. A. F. Holmes.
Chr Today 14:6-8 Jl 31 '70
Plight of the Christian liberal-arts college.
S. R. Obitts. Chr Today 14:8-10 Ap 24 '70
See also
Bob Jones university, Greenville, S.C.

CHURCH colleges—*Continued*
Federal aid
Grim alternatives in Christian higher education. E. L. Cattell. Chr Today 14:3-5 Jl 3 '70
Finance
Wanted: donors for Christian colleges. Chr Today 14:23 Je 19 '70
CHURCH conferences. See Religious conferences
CHURCH cooperation. See Religious cooperation
CHURCH councils. See Councils and synods
CHURCH decoration and ornament
   See also
Altars
CHURCH discipline
   See also
Excommunication
CHURCH finance
Budget squeeze in churches. America 123: 51 Ag 8 '70
Coming confrontation on the church's war investments. S. C. Rose. Chr Cent 87: 1209-11 O 14 '70
Concealing the crunch; National council of churches' annual review. Chr Cent 87:1440 D 2 '70; Reply. F. Coates. 88:19 Ja 6 '71
Less spending on church buildings. America 122:602 Je 6 '70
New statistics confirm downturn. D. Kucharsky. Chr Today 14:40 F 27 '70
New-style attack on the denominational budget. L. E. Schaller; discussion. Chr Cent 87:84, 116 Ja 21-28 '70
Now's the time to give. Chr Today 14:19 S 25 '70
Physicians, heal yourselves; churches and universities, social implications of their investments. B. H. Smith. America 123: 282-5 O 17 '70
   See also
Catholic church—Finance
Church property
Church tax
CHURCH going. See Church attendance
CHURCH government
Church politics, by K. R. Bridston. Review Commonweal 92:150-1 Ap 24 '70. R. A. Schroth
From "-ty" to "-tics"; need for open acknowledgement of church politics. Chr Cent 87:435 Ap 15 '70
   See also
Catholic church—Government
CHURCH history
   See also
Catholic church—History
International association for the study of history of religions
Religious thought
Reformation
United States—Church history
Bibliography
Wide choice in church history and theology. G. W. Bromiley. Chr Today 14:6-8+ F 13 '70
Primitive and early church
Hegelian dialectic in theology. J. N. Jonsson. Chr Today 14:14-16+ S 11 '70
CHURCH leadership. See Christian leadership
CHURCH membership
Bye-bye Babylon. D. H. Gill. Chr Today 15: 17-18+ N 20 '70
New statistics confirm downturn. D. Kucharsky. Chr Today 14:40 F 27 '70
CHURCH music
All nite soul: ceremony in St Peter's Lutheran church. New Yorker 46:38-9 O 31 '70
Liturgical music for today. C. J. McNaspy. America 123:401-4 N 14 '70; Discussion. 123: 504 D 12 '70
Music in honor of St Thomas of Canterbury; with list of hymns. D. Stevens. bibliog f il Mus Q 56:311-48 Jl '70
Musical events; Washington square Methodist church program; Music for earth, peace, and soul. W. Sargeant. New Yorker 46:123-4 My 16 '70
New church music. D. E. Kucharsky. il Chr Today 14:35-6 Mr 27 '70
Only the organ. T. Beeson. Chr Cent 87:1056 S 9 '70
Rock, business, and Trinity church. New Yorker 46:20-1 Jl 18 '70
Shape of church music in the '70s. C. F. Schalk. Chr Cent 87:1445-9 D 2 '70

Silent organs, empty churches. J. G. Dwyer. il Cath World 211:29-31 Ap '70
   See also
Chants (Gregorian, plain, etc)
Choirs
Chorales
Hymns
Mass (music)
Oratorios
Phonograph records—Choral music
Phonograph records—Church music
Responses (music)
CHURCH of Abyssinia. See Ethiopic church
CHURCH of Christ in the Congo (Democratic Republic)
New Congo superchurch. O. W. Okite. Chr Today 14:37-8 Jl 3 '70
CHURCH of Christ uniting (proposed) See Consultation on church union
CHURCH of Christian liberty. See Sects
CHURCH of England
Anglicans get new synod. J. D. Douglas. Chr Today 15:38 D 4 '70
First woman chancellor named by Anglican diocese. Chr Cent 87:72 Ja 21 '70
History's dubious legacy; relationship with English state. T. Beeson. Chr Cent 87:1506-7 D 16 '70
Looking Romewards; secessionist drums. J. D. Douglas. Chr Today 14:38 Ja 16 '70
No revolution in sight. T. Beeson. Chr Cent 87:1310 N 4 '70
Step toward reunion; Anglican and Catholic scholars meet. il Newsweek 75:60 Ja 26 '70
   See also
Church union—Great Britain
Clergy
   See also
Bishops
CHURCH of England in Australia
Questions of truth; archbishop's refusal to pray with the Pope. por Newsweek 76:59 O 26 '70
CHURCH of England in New Zealand
General synod: no revolution. R. M. O'Grady. Chr Cent 87:741-2 Je 10 '70
CHURCH of Ethiopia. See Ethiopic church
CHURCH of Jesus Christ of Latter-day saints. See Mormons and Mormonism
CHURCH of Pakistan
Four bodies merge to form Church of Pakistan. Chr Cent 87:1443 D 2 '70
CHURCH of Scotland
Chaos at the kirk: pills, but no miracles? General assembly. J. D. Douglas. Chr Today 14:34-5 Je 19 '70
Church of Scotland General assembly. C. A. Smith. Chr Cent 87:924-5 Jl 29 '70
Scotland; plan of union, Church of Scotland with the Congregational church. I. Logan. Chr Cent 87:852-3 Jl 8 '70
CHURCH of the Brethren
Brethren board supports eight draft resisters. Chr Cent 87:414 Ap 8 '70
Brethren find cause to celebrate hope. R. N. Miller. Chr Cent 87:976-8 Ag 12 '70
CHURCH polity. See Church government
CHURCH property
Chances for schism: a legal green light. A. L. Scanlan. America 122:150-2 F 14 '70
Rich churches and poor people. W. W. Grant. Chr Today 14:11-12 F 27 '70
Seceding churches win property; with editorial comment. Chr Today 14:26-7, 36 F 13 '70
Taxation
Benevolent neutrality; Supreme court ruling. Newsweek 75:77 My 18 '70
Churches await impact of tax reform. D. E. Kucharsky. Chr Today 14:31 Ja 16 '70
High court weighs church tax exemptions. Chr Today 14:31 Ja 16 '70
No genuine nexus, Supreme court decision. Chr Today 14:27-8 Je 5 '70
No tax on religion. Time 95:44 My 18 '70
Should houses of worship be taxed? il Good H 171:12+ Ag '70
Should we tax church wealth? K. G. Gross. il Look 34:25-7 My 19 '70
Supreme court reaffirms church tax exemption. Chr Cent 87:621 My 20 '70
Supreme court upholds church tax exemptions. Chr Today 14:32 My 22 '70
Tax churches? What Supreme court says. U S News 68:105 My 18 '70
Walz case; Supreme court's decision in church tax exemptions. C. M. Whelan. America 122:518-19 My 16 '70
CHURCH registers. See Registers of births, etc.

CHURCH-related colleges. See Church colleges
CHURCH related schools. See Catholic schools;
Church schools
CHURCH renewal
Awakening ahead? Chr Today 14:17 S 25 '70
Conserve and progress. G. C. Berkouwer.
Chr Today 14:45-6 F 27 '70
Going underground; new British organiza-
tion called ONE. T. Beeson. Chr Cent 87:
717 Je 10 '70
Great controversy in the church; address,
April 12, 1970. J. C. Bennett. Chr Cent 87:
659-63 My 27 '70
Humanism and the churches. Chr Today 14:
32-3 Ap 10 '70
Of many things. D. R. Campion. America
122:inside cover My 30 '70
Polarization within the churches. A. B.
Haines. Chr Cent 87:1039-41 S 2 '70
Prophets and guardians, by M. Trevor
Review
Commonweal 91:589-90 F 27 '70. D.
O'Brien
Student's open letter to God. D. R. Knighton.
Chr Today 14:16 Je 5 '70
Winds of promise; what critical youth wants.
C. F. H. Henry. Chr Today 14:29-30 Je 5 '70
See also
Mission of the church

Catholic church
Catechetics. R. I. P. G. Moran. Commonweal
93:299-302 D 18 '70
Change and decay: Roman style. D. F. Wells.
Chr Today 14:6-8 S 25 '70
Church confronts loyalty and dissent; sym-
posium. America 122:668-85 Je 27 '70
Day after aggiornamento. B. J. Nauer. il
America 124:36-40 Ja 16 '71
Democratic movement in Dutch Catholicism.
W. L. Boelens. Cath World 211:112-15 Je '70
Faith in focus; play or battle. L. M. Orsy.
America 122:162 F 14 '70
How dare the preacher preach? J. Torrens.
il Cath World 211:251-5 S '70
If you could make one change in the church,
what would it be? symposium. Common-
weal 92:159-66 My 1 '70; Reply. D. Grum-
bach. 92:325-6 Je 26 '70
Lessons from history and elsewhere. J. L. Mc-
Kenzie. por Chr Cent 87:839-42 Jl 8 '70
Myths, meaning and Vatican III. A. M.
Greeley. America 123:538-42 D 19 '70; Re-
ply. W. L. Dolan. 124:29 Ja 16 '71
Of many things: Christian revolution. D. R.
Campion. America 122:inside cover F 21 '70
Of many things; the notion of public accoun-
tability. D. R. Campion. America 122:inside
cover Ap 4 '70
Psychiatrist reflects on the changing church.
T. L. Doyle. America 122:240-3 Mr 7 '70
Religion: seekers and settlers. J. C. Haughey.
America 124:8 Ja 9 '71
State of a diocese; Victoria, British Columbia.
D. J. Roche. America 122:366-7 Ap 4 '70
Tensions in a church alive. J. B. Sheerin.
Cath World 212:115-16 D '70
See also
Mission of the church
CHURCH schools
Creed and color in the school crisis. Chr
Today 14:32-3 Mr 27 '70
See also
Catholic schools
Education and state

Federal aid
Blaine repeal begins. America 122:172 F 21
'70
Formulas for state and federal aid; non-
public schools. America 122:328 Mr 28 '70
Freedom and financing; address, April 17,
1970. G. R. La Noue. Vital Speeches 36:563-
6 Jl 1 '70
Jewish agency criticizes Rockefeller stand
on parochial aid issue. Chr Cent 87:167
F 11 '70
New trend: state money for private schools.
il U S News 68:34-6 My 4 '70
Nonpublic schools and American children.
America 123:481 D 5 '70

Finance
Parochaid: more support, more lawsuits. Sr
Schol 96:Schol Teach 1 My 11 '70
CHURCH services
Dionysus in Boston; H. Cox's Easter serv-
ice. il por Newsweek 75:77+ My 11 '70
See also
Church music
Worship
CHURCH silver. See Silverware

CHURCH statistics
See also
Church membership
CHURCH supplies
Peddlers of paraphernalia. Chr Cent 87:1203
O 7 '70
CHURCH surveys. See Religious surveys
CHURCH tax
See also
Church property—Taxation

Germany (Federal Republic)
Germany's leading publishers renounce church
taxation. E. E. Turner. Chr Cent 87:1164-6
S 30 '70
CHURCH union
Opposition to Presbyterian union mounts in
South. A. Matthews. Chr Today 15:45-6
N 20 '70
See also
Church renewal
Consultation on church union
Ecumenical movement
Episcopacy and church union

Canada
Canadian church-to-be assumes visibility. G.
Lane. Chr Cent 87:369+ Mr 25 '70
Evangelical consolidation in Canadian denom-
inations. L. K. Tarr. Chr Today 14:24 S 25
'70
Trouble in church union. J. R. Mutchmor.
Chr Cent 87:1492+ D 9 '70
United to oppose union; proposed merger
of the United, Anglican, and Disciple de-
nominations. L. K. Tarr. Chr Today 15:44
Ja 1 '71
See also
United church of Canada

Great Britain
Again, the forty martyrs. T. Beeson. Chr
Cent 87:1373 N 18 '70
Building a better bridge. J. D. Douglas. Chr
Today 15:57-8 O 9 '70
Free church union in '72? T. Beeson. Chr Cent
87:1441-2 D 2 '70
New English merger plan. J. D. Douglas.
il Chr Today 14:37 Jl 31 '70
Unity: where are we in Britain? K. Slack.
Chr Cent 87:1281-3 O 28 '70

India
Some Methodists reject union; new church
of North India inaugurated. J. V.
Koilpillai. Chr Cent 87:1397-8 N 18 '70

United States
Christian unity, the U.S. scene. J. C. Haugh-
ey. il America 123:261-3 O 10 '70; Reply. B.
F. Law. 123:389 N 14 '70
Orthodox and reformed Presbyterians delay
union. Chr Today 14:46 Ag 21 '70
Unity: above ground and below. M. Hands-
picker and W. D. Wagoner. Chr Cent 87:
419-22 Ap 8 '70
CHURCH vestments
Peddlers of paraphernalia. Chr Cent 87:1203
O 7 '70
CHURCH women united
Church women united honor Margaret Chase
Smith. Chr Cent 87:559 My 6 '70
CHURCH work
How many ways your church can help you!
il Changing T 24:45-6 Ap '70
Stepping ahead with your church. B. Furst;
D. Nichols; R. E. Holman. il por Har Yrs
10:6-11 My '70
See also
Church and social problems
Pastoral theology
CHURCH work with alcoholics
Ministering to alcoholics. C. C. Buck. Chr
Today 14:29 Jl 17 '70
CHURCH work with the aged
I was sick and you visited me. R. E. Holman.
il por Har Yrs 10:11 My '70
CHURCH work with the deaf. See Church
work with the handicapped
CHURCH work with the handicapped
Breaking the sound barrier; ministry to the
deaf. A. Eggebroten. Chr Today 15:42 O
23 '70
CHURCH work with youth
Church in the marketplace; Smith-haven
ministries. A. W. Godfrey. Cath World 212:
83-4 N '70
CHURCH world (newspaper) See Catholic press
CHURCHES
Better use of church buildings. P. Nettle-
ton. Chr Today 14:36 Ag 21 '70
See also
Church architecture
also subhead Churches under names of
cities, e.g. New York (city)—Churches

CHURCHES—*Continued*

Membership
See Church membership

Names

And now the Presbyterians; church names of the Presbyterian church. Chr Cent 87:647 My 20 '70
Disciples get into the act; church names of Disciples of Christ. Chr Cent 87:551 Ap 29 '70
Shivers at Naked Creek. Chr Cent 87:679 My 27 '70
Time to move on: post script and finis to our church directory; Baptist churches. Chr Cent 87:903 Jl 22 '70
What's in a name? names of Lutheran churches. Chr Cent 87:431 Ap 8 '70

Ethiopia

Searching out medieval churches in Ethiopia's wilds. G. Gerster. il Nat Geog 138:856-84 D '70

Rumania

Rumania's open churches. P. Blake. il Time 96:48-53 Ag 10 '70

United States

Plantations and parish churches of the Carolina low county. il Antiques 97:571-5 Ap '70
See also subhead Churches under names of cities, New York (city)—Churches
CHURCHES, Shaker
Shaker meetinghouses of Moses Johnson. M. B. Péladeau. il Antiques 98:594-9 O '70
CHURCHES of Christ
Rainbow over Abilene; Abilene Christian college lectures. R. Durham. Chr Today 14:31 Mr 27 '70
CHURCHILL, Allen
Trade winds. C. Amory. Sat R 53:5 Ag 29 '70 *
CHURCHILL, Mary P.
Hooray for Thanksgiving; drama. Plays 30:67-8 N '70
CIABATTARI, Jane
Christmas doesn't just happen. il por Redbook 136:22+ D '70
CIARDI, John
Emeritus addresses the school; poem. New Yorker 46:32 Je 13 '70
Good cause; Fool too fast; Nice place for the kids; Hereafter; Kranzfeldt; poems. il Sat R 53:41 Mr 28 '70
Manner of speaking. See occasional issues of Saturday review
Manner of speaking; defense against accusation by HISC of being a radical. Sat R 53:12+ N 7 '70
Someone could win a polar bear; Rules; Lesson; poems. il Sat R 53:14 My 23 '70

about

Radicals and Mr Ciardi. N. Cousins. Sat R 53:24 D 12 '70 *
CICADAS
Seventeen-year locust, a report for 1971. R. G. Coleman. il Horticulture 49:24 Ja '71
Seventeen year locust: a troublemaker on the march. B. C. Kilvert. il Home Gard 57:24-5 Je '70
Seventeen year locust to invade eastern U. S. C. E. Sommers. Suc Farm 68:37 Je '70
Why the cricket chirps. il Time 96:39 Ag 24 '70
CICARELLI, James S. See Landers, C. E. jt. auth.
CICERO, Marcus Tullius
Cicero on growing older. A. E. Everett. Har Yrs 10:25 S '70 *
CICERO, Theodore J. and Moore, B. W.
Turnover of the brain specific protein, S-100. bibliog il Science 169:1333-4 S 25 '70
CIDER
Cider squeezin'. R. Beck. il Org Gard & Farm 17:47-9 S '70
CIENFUEGOS naval base. See Navy yards and naval stations
CIFUENTES, Luis. See Catalina, F. jt. auth.
CIGAR boxes. See Boxes, cases, etc.
CIGAR smoking. See Smoking
CIGARETTE-making machines
What? Pot? Not Laredo. il Forbes 106:48 N 1 '70
CIGARETTE paper
Cancer and cigarette paper. il Sci Digest 67:18 My '70
CIGARETTE smoke
Cigarette smoke: the effect of residue on mitochondrial structure. J. R. Kennedy and A. M. Elliott. bibliog il Science 168:1097-8 My 29 '70
CIGARETTE smoking. See Smoking

CIGARETTE smoking and youth. See Smoking and youth
CIGARETTES
Lively corpse. il Forbes 106:57-8 S 15 '70
Ten ways to a safer cigarette. A. J. Snider. Sci Digest 69:56 Ja '71

Advertising

Annals of advertising; ban on television and radio commericals. T. Whiteside. New Yorker 46:42-8+ D 19 '70
Bright spark for cigarette makers. il Bsns W p64-5 D 26 '70
Last drag; ban on broadcast advertising. il Newsweek 77:65 Ja 4 '71
Long affair; the networks. Nation 212:69 Ja 18 '71
Snuffing out commercials. Newsweek 75:69 Mr 16 '70
To beat the ban. Time 97:60 Ja 11 '71
TV and cigarettes. Sr Schol 95:18-20 S 29 '69
What happens when the Marlboro man leaves. il Time 96:96 N 23 '70
Where the cigarette men go after the TV ban. il Bsns W p64-5+ N 21 '70
You can take Salem out of the country, but—. J. H. Bowden. Chr Cent 87:1562-3 D 30 '70
CILIA and ciliary motion
Cystic fibrosis: characterization of the inhibitor to ciliary action in oyster gills. B. H. Bowman and others. bibliog il Science 167:871-3 F 6 '70
See also
Flagella
CIMARRON COUNTY, Okla.
Good day at Black Mesa; with paintings. G. M. Sutton. Audubon 72:58-67 Jl '70
CINCINNATI

Description

Kultur on the Ohio. D. Butwin. il Sat R 53:50-2 N 14 '70

Music

Verdian Otello at the Cincinnati zoo opera. I. Kolodin. Sat R 53:44 Ag 8 '70
Zoo opera going strong. H. S. Humphreys. il Hi Fi 20:MA22-3 O '70
Zoo story. il Opera N 34:14-16 Je 13 '70
See also
Cincinnatti symphony orchestra

Sanitary affairs

Graduated weirs speed infiltration tests. A. D. Caster. il Am City 85:22 Mr '70

Water department

Metal coatings cut tank maintenance. il Am City 85:22 O '70
CINCINNATI milacron. See Cincinnati milling machine company
CINCINNATI milling machine company
Kicking the doldrums at Cincinnati milacron. A. T. Demaree. il Fortune 82:72-7+ D '70
CINCINNATI nature center. See Nature centers
CINCINNATI Reds (baseball) See Baseball clubs
CINCINNATI symphony orchestra
Cincinnati kid. H. Saal. il por Newsweek 76:124-5 O 19 '70
CINCINNATI, University
Growth of Raymond Walters branch college; first off-campus college. il Sch & Soc 98:206-7 Ap '70
CINDERELLA; ballet. See Ballets—Criticisms
CINDERELLA and friends; drama. See Cheatham, V. R.
CINEMA. See Moving pictures
CINEMATHÈQUE francaise, Paris. See Moving picture film collections
CINNAMATES
Self-inhibitor of bean rust uredospores: methyl 3,4-dimethoxycinnamate. V. Macko and others. bibliog Science 170:539-40 O 30 '70
CIPNIC, Dennis J.
How to deal with editors like a pro. il Pop Phot 67:71-3+ O '70
This little free lance stayed home. il Pop Phot 66:71-3+ My '70
CIPRIANO, Anthony
Portrait head in clay. D. Preiss. il por Am Artist 34:30-5+ F '70
CIPRIANO, Kathleen
Hors d'oeuvres business. J. Kuh. Ladies Home J 87:68 Ap '70 *
CIRCADIAN rhythms. See Biology—Periodicity
CIRCLES
Cylinder art. H. H. Foster. il Design 71:4-6 Wint '69
CIRCO dell' Arte. See Circus
CIRCULAR buildings. See Buildings, Round
CIRCULAR saws. See Saws
CIRCULAR stairs. See Stairways

CIRCULATION departments In libraries. See
Libraries—Circulation, loans, etc.
CIRCULATORY system (insects) See Cardio-
vascular system (insects)
CIRCUMCISION
Case against circumcision. Time 96:58 O 19
'70
Circumcision v. circumspection. Sci Am 223:
45 N '70
CIRCUS
Circo dell' Arte, canon of tricks. J. Gruen.
Vogue 155:114 Ap 1 '70
Circus: the second hundred years; Ringling
bros. and Barnum & Bailey circus. B. Bal-
lantine. il Holiday 47:50-1+ Ap '70
Colossal centennial; Ringling bros and
Barnum & Bailey. A. Keneas. il Newsweek
75:98 Ap 6 '70
Enclave; Great London circus in Whittier,
Calif. M. F. K. Fisher. New Yorker 46:
175-6+ N 14 '70
Funniest college on earth; college of clowns
at winter quarters of Ringling brothers,
Barnum & Bailey circus. W. Zinsser. il
Life 68:62-6 F 20 '70
Greatest show on earth. P. Schrag. Sat R 53:27
Ap 25 '70
Greatest showman on earth; Ringling bros.
and Barnum & Bailey circus. il por Time
95:74+ My 4 '70
CIRCUS, Amateur
These kids don't have to run away to join
the circus; Sailor circus troupe. A. Rosen-
thal. il Todays Health 48:42-7 F '70
CIRCUS performers
See also
Children as circus performers
Clowns
CIRIOS
It's a boojum! J. W. Krutch. il por Nat Wild-
life 8:36-7 Je '70
CIRRHOSIS of the liver. See Liver—Diseases
CISLER, Lucinda
Abortion reform: the new tokenism; excerpt
from Notes (from the second year) radical
feminism (May 1970) Ramp Mag 9:19-21 Ag
'70
CITIES and towns
City as a threatened ecosystem. S. F. Wil-
liams. Arch Forum 133:48-9+ S '70
Metropolis and the transformation of re-
sources. R. L. Meier. il Bul Atom Sci 26:
2-5+ My '70
World cities of the future; AAAS syposium,
December 26-30, 1970. B. Gross. il Science
170:657 N 6 '70
See also
Business districts
City and town life
City traffic
Education, Urban
Ekistics
Housing
Neighborhoods
Parks
Playgrounds
Plazas
Slums
Sociology, Urban
Trees in cities
Urbanization
also headings beginning City, Community,
Municipal, Street, Urban

Consolidation
Consolidated community works better; con-
solidation of Leakesville, Spray and Draper,
plus and the Meadow Greens sanitary dis-
trict, N.C. A. W. Stewart. il Am City 85:
79-80 Mr '70
Defenses
See also
Civil defense
Finance
See Municipal finance
Growth
Does the smaller city have a future? il Chang-
ing T 24:25-8 Je '70
Economy of cities, by J. Jacobs. Review
Nation 210:117-19 F 2 '70. S. Zoll
Explosion in a boom town; Aspen, Colo.
R. Rapoport. il Sports Illus 33:26-7 S 14 '70
Future of the central city. A. Ganz. il Am
City 85:57-9 Ag '70
Incorporation: a new tactic for saving black
areas. C. C. Douglas. il pors Ebony 25:
100-2+ Ag '70
Indianapolis consolidates with surrounding
Marion County. J. F. Zimmerman. Am City
85:76 Ja '70
Liveable cities. D. G. Alexander. bibliog f Cur
Hist 59:85-90+ Ag '70

Tomorrow's cities: go up, spread out or start
over? il Changing T 24:19-22 Ap '70
See also
Metropolitan areas
Suburbs
Names
See Names, Geographical
Planning
See City planning
Religious life
See City churches
Sports
See Sports—United States
Transportation
See Urban transportation
Zone system
See Zoning
Australia
See also
New cities and towns
Europe
See also
New cities and towns
Europe, Western
Pragmaesthetics. J. E. Curtis. il Parks &
Rec 5:15-17+ Jl '70
These are the cities they like. il Holiday 47:
40-3 Je '70
Where the jobs are: Geneva, London, Paris,
Rome. N. A. Comer. Mlle 71:114-15 Je '70
Germany (Federal Republic)
See also
New cities and towns
Israel
See also
New cities and towns
Netherlands
Profiles. A. Bailey. New Yorker 46:32-8+ Ag
15 '70
United States
Are American cities obsolete? address,
August 10, 1970. S. C. Jackson. Vital
Speeches 36:706-10 S 15 '70
Conspiracy against American cities. J. V.
Lindsay. il Redbook 135:78-9+ O '70
Economy of cities, by J. Jacobs. Review
Trans-Action 7:84-7 Ap '70. G. Sternlieb
In the inner cities: acres of abandoned build-
ings. il U S News 68:54-6 Ja 26 '70
More wildlife for urban America. J. J.
Shomon. il Cons 24:2-7 F '70
New look at urban priorities: corporate co-
operation: address, December 3, 1969. E.
Goldston. Vital Speeches 36:282-6 F 15 '70
New shape of America; symposium, with
editorial comment by R. Graves. il Life
70:1-13+ Ja 8 '71
Nine happy places. il Esquire 74:146-53 D '70
Nixon's plans for future of U.S. cities and
small towns. il U S News 69:30-2 Jl 6 '70
Our cities, are they really doomed? il Sr Schol
96:2-12 F 16 '70
Photography and the city. J. Fraser. Yale R
59:228-41 D '69
Rethinking cities. il Time 95:64+ Je 1 '70
Unheavenly city, by E. C. Banfield. Review
Commonweal 92:466 S 18 '70. R. Beinart
Fortune 81:197-8 Je '70. I. Kristol
Urban America; symposium. bibliog f Cur
Hist 59:257-99+ N '70
See also
Abandoned towns
All-America cities
Metropolitan areas
New cities and towns
Urban renewal
History
Historical roots of our urban crisis. J. F.
Richardson. Cur Hist 59:257-61+ N '70
Vietnam (Republic)
Urban trend. il Time 96:35-6 Ag 31 '70
CITIES and towns, Ruined, extinct, etc.
Portobelo. G. de Zéndegui. il Américas 22:20-
30 Ag '70
See also
Portobelo
Teotihuacán, Mexico
Tikal, Guatemala
CITIZENS against Tydings (organization) See
Pressure groups
CITIZENS and Southern national bank of At-
lanta. See Atlanta—Banks

CITIZENS and Southern national bank of Georgia. See Banks and banking—Georgia

CITIZENS associations
Block power; revival of block groups. il Newsweek 75:47-8 F 2 '70
Cities; York's charrette. il Time 95:40 My 11 '70
What is charrette planning for schools? W. D. Boutwell. PTA Mag 65:30-1 O '70
See also
Crime prevention—Citizen participation
National citizens committee for broadcasting

CITIZENS committee for broadcasting. See National citizens committee for broadcasting

CITIZENS committees. See Citizens associations

CITIZENS councils. See Citizens associations

CITIZENS for a quieter city, inc.
Silencing invisible pollution. T. Berland. il Todays Health 48:16-18+ Jl '70

CITIZEN'S mortgage. See Investment trusts

CITIZENS obligations. See Citizenship

CITIZENS radio service
CB! For better? Or worse? O. P. Ferrell. Pop Electr 33:7 O '70
EMCBT organized for mobile CB-ers. Electr World 84:11 Jl '70
See also
REACT (organization)

Equipment
CB troubleshooter's casebook; comp. by A. J. Mueller. See issues of Radio-electronics
Fix CB fast (cont) A. J. Mueller. Radio-Electr 41:78 Mr '70
Novel CB tone-call system. D. E. Fahenstock. il Radio-Electr 41:92 F '70
See also
Radio telephone

CITIZENS' scholarship foundation of America, inc.
Citizen power; mobilize for scholarships. J. Leedom. il Am Ed 6:21 Jl '70

CITIZENSHIP
Binationals; dual nationality. Newsweek 76:107-107A N 2 '70
Man without a country; case of T. G. Jolley. Newsweek 75:29 Mr 30 '70
Toward participatory citizenship; proposal for a national citizens lobby; excerpt from Natural enemies? A. Klein. Cur 121:3-11 S '70
Who is a Jew? B. Shalit case. G. Astor. il pors Look 34:32-4 Je 16 '70
Who is a Jew? il por Time 95:50-1 F 2 '70
Who is a Jew? Israeli high court ruling on nationality. il por Newsweek 75:70 F 2 '70
See also
Common cause (political organization)
Naturalization
Patriotism

CITIZENSHIP, Education for
Educating future citizens of the international community; address, February 11, 1970. M. Collins. bibliog f Dept State Bul 62:230-3 Mr 2 '70
See also
Education and democracy

CITIZENSHIP recognition day
Protection of all U.S. citizens reaffirmed by President Nixon; remarks, September 17, 1970. R. M. Nixon. Dept State Bul 63:410-12 O 12 '70

CITRATES
See also
Fluorocitrates

CITROEN (automobile) See Automobiles, Foreign

CITROEN (firm) See Automobile industry and trade—France

CITRON, Harvey
Doing it the hard way. il por Esquire 73:104-7 F '70

CITRUS fruit industry
When the frost is on the orange; Florida crop. il Bsns W p34-5 Ja 24 '70

CITY and country
Country mouse, city mouse. S. Airhart. por Redbook 135:10+ S '70
See also
City and town life
Country life

CITY and country school. See New York (city) —Education

CITY and town life
Big city syndrome. D. Behrman. UNESCO Courier 23:20+ Ag '70

Experience of living in cities; adaptation of address, September 2, 1969. S. Milgram. bibliog il Science 167:1461-8 Mr 13 '70
How to live in the city and stay sane. L. Lerman. Mlle 70:250-1+ Ap '70
Is Main Street still there? P. Schrag. il Sat R 53:20-5 Ja 17 '70
People pollution; excerpt from The doomsday book. G. R. Taylor. il Ladies Home J 87:74+ O '70
Quality of urban life, by H. J. Schmandt and W. Bloomberg jr. Review
Trans-Action 7:58-9 Je '70. N. E. Long
See also
City and country

Study and teaching
Cocoon kids encounter city crises; course at West Hartford's Conard high school. K. Branan. il Schol Teach Sec Teach Sup p 12-13 My 4 '70

CITY beaches. See Beaches

CITY bonds. See Municipal bonds

CITY center Joffrey ballet
City center Joffrey ballet, New York city center. M. Marks. Dance Mag 45:70 Ja '71
City center Joffrey ballet, New York city center, NYC. M. Marks. Dance Mag 44:72-4 D '70
Cranked up. H. Saal. il Newsweek 75:63-4 Mr 16 '70
Dance; Joffrey's Pineapple Poll. J. Maskey. il Hi Fi 20:secII 9+ My '70
Dance. N. Goldner. Nation 210:346-7 Mr 23 '70
Dance; Petrouchka. N. Goldner. Nation 210:478 Ap 20 '70
Dance; presentation of The still point. N. Goldner. Nation 211:446 N 2 '70
Friend Petrouchka; New productions, and repertoire. D. Hering and T. Borek. il Dance Mag 44:36-43+ My '70
How the Joffrey ballet got that way. J. Gale. il Dance Mag 44:37-41 O '70
Joffrey: pro and con. W. Terry. il Sat R 53:47-8 Mr 28 '70
Musical events; performance of Confetti. W. Sargeant. New Yorker 46:129 Ap 4 '70
Musical events; performance of Pineapple Poll. W. Sargeant. New Yorker 46:107 Mr 7 '70
Musical events; revival of The still point. W. Sargeant. New Yorker 46:139-40 O 10 '70
Petrouchka returns. W. Terry. il Sat R 53:41 Ap 11 '70
Plaster bonbons. il Time 95:69 Mr 16 '70
Review in the raw. D. Hering. il Dance Mag 44:74-5 Ja '70
Verve, nerve and fervor. J. T. Elson. il Time 96:73+ N 16 '70

CITY churches
Christ and cosmopolis. C. G. Fry. Chr Today 14:3-6 Je 5 '70

CITY consultants. See Government consultants, Municipal

CITY employees associations. See Employees associations

CITY foresters. See Foresters

CITY gardens
City gardeners beat pollution and inflation. M. Franz. il Org Gard & Farm 17:26-33 Ag '70
Our garden in the city. B. Young. il Horticulture 48:24-5+ Je '70
Tiny garden that leads four lives. E. McDonald. il House B 112:72-3 D '70
See also
Roof gardens

CITY government. See Municipal government

CITY growth. See Cities and towns—Growth

CITY halls
City hall for Santa Rosa, Calif. il Arch Rec 147:102-3 Ja '70
New city hall, old site; Janesville, Wis. K. A. Samek. il Am City 85:90+ My '70
Working city hall; Oneida, N.Y. il Am City 85:73 Ja '70

CITY houses
Barglow house, Chicago, Ill. il Arch Rec 147:60-1 mid-My '70
Dash of theatre for an old carriage house; Jerry Herman's home in New York. il House B 112:122-5 My '70
Jerry Orbach; interview, ed. by M. Sutphen. J. Orbach. il pors House B 112:64-7 F '70
Many-level living; San Francisco. il House & Gard 137:70-1 Ja '70
Power of thinking thin. B. Plumb. il Am Home 73:68-71 O '70
Private residence, New York city. il Arch Rec 147:42-5 mid-My '70

CITY houses—*Continued*
Space opened up for family living; George-town house. il House & Gard 138:102-7 S '70
Surprising Victorian; renovated townhouse in Brooklyn. il Arch Forum 133:36-9 S '70
CITY improvement. See Municipal improvement
CITY life. See City and town life
CITY magazines. See Periodicals—United States
CITY managers
Urban administration, a new ball game. L. P. Cookingham. il por Am City 85:63-6 Ja '70
CITY parks. See Parks
CITY planners
See also
Doxiadis, C. A.
Ponte, V. de P.
CITY planning
Arcologist; Arcosanti, Soleri's pioneer city in the Arizona desert. D. Davis. il por Newsweek 75:78-9 Mr 2 '70
Arcology; an answer for the years ahead. il Parks & Rec 5:41+ My '70
Arcology of Paolo Soleri. S. Moholy-Nagy. il Arch Forum 132:70-5 My '70
Consultant game. Newsweek 76:46 Ag 3 '70
Designer in the desert. W. Karp. il por Horizon 12:30-9 Aut '70
Economy of cities, by J. Jacobs. Review Nation 210:117-19 F 2 '70. S. Zoll
Future by design? address, March 17, 1970. R. G. Howes. Cath World 211:221-5 Ag '70
How planning saves $$$$$. W. D. Fromm. Am City 85:80+ Ag '70
How to get off-street parking. bibliog il Am City 85:91-3+ Ja '70
Making cities better places to live. il por(cover) Bsns W p36-9 Ag 22 '70
Paolo Soleri thinks very big; supercities or arcologies. S. D. Kohn. il por N Y Times Mag p26-7+ Jl 26 '70; Reply. J. Lobell. p30+ Ag 23 '70
Parking garage exteriors. il Am City 85:105-7 Ja '70
People, yes; cars, no. W. Von Eckardt. Sat R 53:62-3 O 3 '70
Portable garage. il Am City 85:108+ Ja '70
Study and research=new concept and techniques; integrated communities: apartments, offices and the shopping center. il Arch Rec 147:130-2 Mr '70
Ten ways to make your city more attractive. W. H. Whyte. House & Gard 138:100-1 S '70
Towns with wings; California communities for airplane owners. H. E. Jackson. il Travel 134:54-9 Ag '70
Urban focus 1970: people! il Am City 85:116+ F '70
We can build space age cities now. J. W. Hudson. il Nat Wildlife 8:4-9 Ag '70
Will they ever finish Bruckner boulevard? by A. L. Huxtable. Review
Art in Am 58:59+ N '70. J. Jacobs
See also
Business districts
Cities and towns
Housing
Rural planning
Streets
Suburbs
Traffic engineering
Urban renewal
also subhead City planning under names of cities, e.g. Houston, Tex.—City planning

Bibliography
Creative urbanists. W. Von Eckardt. il Sat R 53:48-9 Ag 1 '70

Study and teaching
Needed: more urban affairs courses. H. H. Newlin. Am City 85:154-5+ S '70

Zone system
See Zoning
CITY sales tax. See Sales tax
CITY streets. See Streets
CITY traffic
Cars and cities on a collision course. A. T. Demaree. il Fortune 81:124-8+ F '70
Should automobiles be banned from urban centers? pro and con discussion. il Sr Schol 96:12-13 Mr 2 '70
Staving off auto paralysis. il Bsns W p54-6+ F 28 '70
See also
Pedestrians
also subhead Street traffic under names of cities, e.g. Wichita, Kan.—Street traffic
CITY transportation. See Urban transportation

CITY trees. See Trees in cities
CITY university of New York. See New York (city). City university
CIVIC centers. See Municipal centers
CIVIL aeronautics board. See United States—Civil aeronautics board
CIVIL death
See also
Prisoners—Legal status, laws, etc.
CIVIL defense
Air force aids city in disaster prevention; Chandler, Ariz. il Am City 85:58 Mr '70
Civilian sanctuary and target avoidance policy in thermonuclear war. E. O. Stillman. Ann Am Acad 392:116-32 N '70
See also
Air defenses
Atomic bomb shelters
CIVIL disobedience. See Government, Resistance to
CIVIL engineering
See also
Dams
CIVIL engineers
Global earth-shapers in complex competition. W. McQuade. il Fortune 81:78-81+ Ap '70
CIVIL liberties. See Civil rights
CIVIL liberties union, American. See American civil liberties union
CIVIL liberty. See Liberty
CIVIL rights
Blake on human rights. Chr Cent 87:588 My 13 '70
See also
Assembly, Right of
Citizenship
Due process of law
Free speech
Information, Freedom of
Liberty
Privacy, Right of
United Nations—Commission on human rights
Woman—Equal rights
also subhead Civil rights under various subjects, e.g. Soldiers—Civil rights

France
Repression in France; new anti-destroyer law. J. Deedy. Commonweal 92:282 Je 12 '70

Latin America
Freedom equals liberation. J. L. Klaiber. il America 122:606-9 Je 6 '70
Twelve countries sign American convention on human rights; the pact of San José. il Americas 22:44-5 Ja '70

Mexico
Mexican students in jail. America 122:88 Ja 31 '70

Northern Ireland
Church leaders on Ulster strife. America 122:663 Je 27 '70
Impasse in Ulster. Chr Cent 87:1309-10 N 4 '70
Ireland's quest for peace. America 122:464 My 2 '70
Reform comes to Ulster. America 122:32 Ja 17 '70
Riots in Ulster. il Sr Schol 95:29-30 S 22 '69
Ulster revisited. C. R. Hughes. il America 122:413-15 Ap 18 '70

Rhodesia
Blunt words for Rhodesia; United Methodist Bishop A. T. Muzarewa banned from tribal areas. America 123:106 S 5 '70

Russia
In quest of justice, ed. by A. Brumberg. Review
Commentary 50:100-5 D '70. M. Friedberg
Peculiarism: East and West. Nation 210:452-3 Ap 20 '70

United States
Compliance gap. Time 96:18 O 19 '70
Hoover's conspiracy; letter to the editor. D. Kirk and others. Commonweal 93:291+ D 18 '70
Infrastructure of repression. Nation 210:482-3 Ap 27 '70
It's a crime. R. W. Dietsch. New Repub 162:9-10 Je 13 '70
Mitchell's answer to critics: look at the facts. por U S News 68:17 F 16 '70
New rulings on public assembly, free speech; U.S. Supreme court decisions. U S News 68:95 Je 8 '70
Notes and comment; dangerous precedents of Chicago seven trial. New Yorker 46:29-30 Mr 7 '70
On tracking down dissent. N. Hentoff. Cur 121:37-41 S '70
Price of dependency, by R. M. O'Neil. Review
Nation 210:796-7 Je 29 '70. P. Chevigny

CIVIL rights—United States—*Continued*
Public safety and private rights. il Time 96:30+ Jl 27 '70
Question of repression. W. Goodman. Commentary 50:23-8 Ag '70; Discussion. 50:16+ N '70
Quiet voice: business suit; Mitchell's program for repression. Nation 210:451-2 Ap 20 '70
Something is wrong; address, November 23, 1969. F. M. Freeman. Vital Speeches 36: 364-7 Ap 1 '70
See also
Freedom of the press
Negroes—Civil rights
United States—Commission on civil rights
United States—Constitution—Bill of rights
CIVIL rights act of 1964
Bus to integration bogs down; with editorial comment and report on Civil rights act of 1964 by L. Panetta. il Life 68:22-32 Mr 13 '70
CIVIL rights commission. See United States —Commission on civil rights
CIVIL rights demonstrations
Anger, outrage, frustration; protest march through rural Georgia to Atlanta. il Newsweek 75:24-5 Je 1 '70
Black revival in the South; march against repression from Perry to Atlanta, Ga. il Time 95:10-12 Je 1 '70
Politics of protest; sit-in movement in Maryland. Trans-Action 7:11 F '70
Year 10 A.G: after Greensboro. Commonweal 91:547-8 F 20 '70
CIVIL rights organizations
See also
National welfare rights organization
Southern Christian leadership conference

Russia
Human rights committee; interview. V. Chalidze. Newsweek 76:57 D 21 '70
Solzhenitsyn's day; joins a committee for human rights. il Newsweek 76:52+ D 21 '70
CIVIL rights workers
Murder in Mississippi; condensation of Attack on terror. D. Whitehead. il Read Digest 97:191-6+ S '70
CIVIL service
See also
Bureaucracy

United States
Civil service career? L. David. il Mech Illus 66:65-7+ S '70
Nixon vs. the veteran bureaucrats. Bsns W p31 Ag 1 '70
See also
Government employees
National civil service league
CIVIL service league. See National civil service league
CIVILIAN defense. See Civil defense
CIVILIAN-military relations. See United States —Armed forces—Relations with civilians
CIVILIAN morale. See Morale, National
CIVILIZATION
Boundaries, by R. J. Lifton. Review
Nation 211:470-2 N 9 '70. A. Lahr
Critique of violence, by A. Caffi. Review
Commentary 50:45-55 S '70
70's; symposium. il Look 34:17-36+ Ja 13 '70
So who needs liberation? R. Dickinson. Chr Cent 88:43-6 Ja 13 '71
Vertical is to live, horizontal is to die. R. B. Fuller; reply. J. Barzun. Am Scholar 39: 514 Sum '70
See also
Anthropology
Atomic age
Culture
Ethics
History
Man—Migrations
Manners and customs
Renaissance
Social change
Technology and civilization
War and civilization
also subhead Civilization under names of countries, e.g. United States—Civilization

History
Evolution of man and society, by C. D. Darlington. Review
Sat R 53:46-8 Ag 22 '70. J. Platt
Our ecological crisis. C. Quigley. Cur Hist 59:1-12 Jl '70
See also
Europe, Western—Civilization—History

CIVILIZATION, Ancient
See also
Mayas
CIVILIZATION, Christian
Christocentric world history. R. Ruether. por Commonweal 93:251-3 D 4 '70
Cultural understanding. R. Kirk. Nat R 22: 363 Ap 7 '70
Nymphs and shepherds. P. Hebblethwaite. Cath World 211:55-7 My '70
CIVILIZATION, Modern. See Civilization
CIVILIZATION and science. See Science and civilization
CIVILIZATION and technology. See Technology and civilization
CLAIBORNE, Craig
Food. See issues of New York times magazine
Kitchen primer; excerpts. il Ladies Home J 87:78-9+ F '70
about
How to take the nonsense out of cooking. H. Frankel. il pors Redbook 135:68-9+ O '70 *
Kitchen secrets of five master cooks; with recipes. J. Wilson. il pors House & Gard 138:82-3+ Jl '70 *
Out of the restaurants. por Time 96:52 D 21 '70 *
CLAIBORNE, Sybil
Great western civilization caper; story. Esquire 74:106 Ag '70
CLAIMS
Settling a personal injury claim yourself. L. M. Brown. Bet Hom & Gard 48:28+ O '70
CLAIRVOYANCE
Astrology, horoscopes. M. Woodruff. McCalls 97:22+ My '70
CLAM chowder. See Chowder
CLAMAN, Henry N. See Levine, M. A. jt. auth.
CLAMBAKES
Shellfish barbecue the way it's done on Puget Sound. il Sunset 144:108-10 My '70
CLAMPS
Using a radial-arm as a routing clamp. W. G. Waggoner. il Pop Sci 197:109 D '70
CLAMS
Geoduck hunting. J. W. Phillips. il Sea Front 16:246-50 Jl '70
Ocean paradise; pismo clams. B. Grant. il Field & S 74:55-7+ Mr '70
Rangia cuneata on the East coast: thousand mile range extension, or resurgence? S. H. Hopkins and J. D. Andrews. bibliog il Science 167:868 F 6 '70
See also
Cookery—Shellfish
CLANCY, Roger
Mullet madness. il Sea Front 16:49-50 Ja '70
CLANCY, Thomas H.
Are martyrs relevant? America 123:320 O 24 '70
Public pulse: elections, 1970. America 123:393 N 14 '70
Responsible professors. America 124:45 Ja 16 '71
Washington front. America 123:166 S 19 '70
(ed) See Mikulski, B. Ethnic American
about
Of many things. D. R. Campion. America 123: inside cover S 5 '70 *
CLANTON, Gordon
Records. Chr Cent 88:25-6 Ja 6 '71
CLAPHAM, T. W.
Tunneling solves tough sewer-construction problem. il Am City 85:105+ F '70
CLAPP, Earle Hart
Obituary
Am For 76:11 S '70. J. B. Craig
CLAPP, James
Five passionate feminists. il pors McCalls 97:55+ Jl '70
CLAPP, Verner W.
Public libraries and the network idea; address, April 26, 1968. il Library J 95:121-4 Ja 15 '70
CLAPPER, Louis S.
Crackdown on water polluters. il Nat Wildlife 8:14-17 F '70
Land between the lakes. il Nat Wildlife 8:38-41 Je '70
Washington report. See issues of National wildlife
CLAPPER rails. See Rails (birds)
CLAREMONT colleges, Calif.
Science labs in a garden. il Arch Forum 132: 30-3 My '70
CLARION music society, Inc.
Musical events; Monteverdi's Vespro della Beata Vergine, in Alice Tully Hall. W. Sargeant. New Yorker 46:150+ Ap 18 '70
Report; production of Medea in Corinto in Lincoln Center's new Alice Tully Hall. F. Merkling. Opera N 34:32 Ja 24 '70

CLARK, Art
He makes mechanical feeding work; interview. ed by P. B. Jones. il Suc Farm 68: no3 26-7 F '70
CLARK, Blair
Westmoreland appraised; questions and answers. Harper 241:96-101 N '70
CLARK, Blake
Fresh spark plug for the Peace corps. Read Digest 96:20-1+ My '70
Nine steps to a longer life. Read Digest 97: 84-7 O '70
CLARK, Cynthia
Freelance house-sitting. J. Kuh. por Ladies Home J 87:132 Mr '70 *
CLARK, D. Neil
I dry and store. il por Farm J 93:A4-31 D '69
CLARK, Dennis
On the heavy weather race; interview. ed. by E. Horan. il por Yachting 128:82+ Jl '70
Passion of protracted conflict. il Trans-Action 7:15-21 (bibliog(p64) Mr '70
CLARK, Earl
Mt Rainier, the live time bomb in Seattle's back yard. il Sci Digest 68:45-8+ Ag '70
CLARK, Eleanor
Cataract of motion. C. Bedient. Nation 211: 21-2 Jl 6 '70
CLARK, Evans
Obituary
    Nation 211:197-8 S 14 '70
CLARK, Fred C. Jr
All about displacement cruisers. il Motor B 126:38-41+ S '70
Baltic Baedeker. il Motor B 125:60-1+ My '70
Inflatable boats. il Yachting 127:84-5+ Ap '70
CLARK, Gerald
Canada's P.M. is not a simple swinger nor a radical reformer. il por N Y Times Mag p26-7+ Ja 25 '70
Day the Montreal police went on strike. il Read Digest 96:107-12 F '70
CLARK, Geraldine
Bureaucracy commitment? por Library J 95:209-10 Ja 15 '70
CLARK, Gordon H.
New discovery in the quest of the historical Jesus. il Chr Today 15:12-13 Ja 15 '71
CLARK, H. C. Bennet-. See Bennet-Clark, H. C.
CLARK, Hank
Portable sink makes hot water. il Pop Mech 133:159 Ja '70
CLARK, Howard R.
Rollaway projection stand for slides or movies. il Pop Mech 134:152-4 N '70
CLARK, James Gardner, Jr
Where are they now? il pors Newsweek 76: 16 S 21 '70 *
CLARK, James H. and Gorski, Jack
Ontogeny of the estrogen receptor during early uterine development. bibliog il Science 169:76-8 Jl 3 '70
CLARK, Jim, 1941?-
Honeymoon adventure. il Field & S 74:62-3+ Mr '70
CLARK, John L. D. See Austin, N. W. jt. auth.
CLARK, John R.
Mathematical education: yesterday and today; interview. Todays Ed 59:50-1 D '70
CLARK, Joseph G.
Feedlot health. See issues of Farm Journal
CLARK, Joseph S.
Asia and the prospects for world order; address, April 1970. bibliog f Ann Am Acad 390:27-37 Jl '70
CLARK, Kenneth Bancroft
Governance of universities in the cities of man. Am Scholar 39:566+ Aut '70

about
Washington mess. por Newsweek 76:70 O 5 '70 *
CLARK, Kenneth McKenzie Clark, baron
Unity in diversity; excerpt from Masterpieces of fifty centuries. House & Gard 138: 68-9+ D '70

about
Clark's tour. Time 95:53 Mr 9 '70 *
Imago Clarkensis. T. V. C. R. Baldwin. il Art N 69:62-5+ N '70 *
CLARK, Mark Wayne
Five happy moments. por Esquire 74:136 D '70
CLARK, Petula
And the Pet goes on. por Time 95:59 F 23 '70 *
CLARK, Ramsey
Criminal justice in times of turbulence; excerpts from Crime in America. Sat R 53: 21-4+ S 19 '70

Death of privacy. por McCalls 97:66-7+ F '70
Justice in a torn nation; interview. ed. R. Sherrill. Nation 211:587-91 D 7 '70
Law and moral leadership. Nation 210:783-5 Je 29 '70
On violence, peace and the rule of law. For Affairs 49:31-9 O '70
School integration and the American character. il Parents Mag 46:37-9+ Ja '71
Trade winds; interview. ed. by C. Amory. Sat R 53:12-13 D 5 '70

about
Bulldog vs. jellyfish. Newsweek 76:23+ N 30 '70 *
Justice, by R. Harris. Review
    Life il por 68:16 Mr 13 '70. W. Sheed *
Too prominent to be relevant. por Time 95: 42 F 9 '70
TRB from Washington. New Repub 163:4 N 28 '70 *
CLARK, Ron, and Bobrick, Sam
Norman, is that you? Criticism
    Nation 210:285 Mr 9 '70
    New Yorker 46:77-8 F 28 '70
    Time 95:69 Mr 2 '70 *
CLARK, Ross L.
Toronto's metro, it works! il Am City 85: 75-8 S '70
CLARK, Steve
American eider. il Sea Front 16:302-8 S '70
CLARK, Sydney
Britain's stately homes. il Travel 133:42-7+ My '70
CLARK, Tom
Comment. L. Warsh. Poetry 115:441-3 Mr '70 *
CLARK, Walter Van Tilburg
Failure of speech in The ox-bow incident. D. E. Houghton. Engl J 59:1245-51 D '70 *
CLARK, William G.
You can't weld in a mini skirt. il Sch Arts 70:22-5 O '70
CLARK COUNTY, Nev.
Electrolytic treatment permits three-way effluent reuse. il Am City 85:22 D '70
CLARK equipment company
George Spatta of Clark equipment co; interview. G. Spatta. il Nations Bsns 58:34-6+ Ja '70
CLARK university, Worcester, Mass.

Libraries
Clark's Goddard library: a mod solution. T. Barron. il Library J 95:2412-13 Jl '70
Fixed-function library; Goddard library. B. Connolly. il por Wilson Lib Bul 44:858-60 Ap '70
CLARKE, Arthur Charles
Beyond Babel; adaptation of address, December 1969. il UNESCO Courier 23:32-7 Mr '70

about
Homer in 2001; comparisons between the Odyssey and 2001: a space odyssey. P. Drake. Engl J 59:1270-1 D '70 *
CLARKE, Charles V.
Reduce park maintenance costs. Am City 85:132+ O '70
CLARKE, David
Artificial stars in a teaching laboratory. il Sky & Tel 39:295-7 My '70
CLARKE, Donald M.
Recordings. New Repub 163:27-9 D 12 '70
CLARKE, George L. and others
Spectra of backscattered light from the sea obtained from aircraft as a measure of chlorophyll concentration. bibliog il Science 167:1119-21 F 20 '70
CLARKE, Jeremiah
Jeremiah Clarke's trumpet tunes: another view of origins.. T. F. Taylor. bibliog il Mus Q 56:455-62 Jl '70 *
CLARKE, John
Glade walker; poem. New Yorker 45:38 Ja 31 '70
CLARKE, Thomas E.
On Americanizing Karl Rahner. America 123: 337-9 O 31 '70
Step forward at Mundelein. il America 123: 198-200 S 26 '70
CLARKE, William J. and others
Strontium-90: effects of chronic ingestion on farrowing performance of miniature swine. bibliog il Science 169:598-600 Ag 7 '70
CLARKSON, Frank E. and others
Family size and sex-role stereotypes. bibliog Science 167:390-2 Ja 23 '70
CLARKSON, Helen S.
Categorical imperative option; poem. Chr Today 15:6 Ja 1 '71

CLARY, Doris H.
Music and dance for the disadvantaged. Ed Digest 35:50-2 Ap '70

CLARY, John J.
Converting England. T. J. Murray. Duns 97: 53-4 Ja '71 *

CLASS (game) See Games

CLASS actions. See Actions and defenses

CLASS discussions. See Discussion method (education)

CLASS distinction. See Leisure class; Social classes

CLASS reunions. See High school graduates

CLASS struggle. See Social conflict

CLASS trips. See School excursions

CLASSEN, J.
Halley's comet in 1682. il Sky & Tel 39:102 F '70

CLASSICAL literature
What's relevant in classical literature? address, November 1969. S. Hickman. Engl J 59:375-9 Mr '70

CLASSIFICATION
Are we bandwagoneers? reasons against changing to LC at Brigham Young university library. M. E. Lamson; reply. S. W. Hilyard. Am Lib 1:111 F '70; Rejoinder. 1: 530 Je '70
Shelf classification, or else. A. C. Foskett. il por Library J 95:2771-3 S 1 '70

CLASSIFICATION of insects. See Insects—Classification

CLASSIFICATION of movies. See Moving pictures—Classification

CLASSIFICATION of sciences

Conferences

Theory and practice of classification in diverse disciplines. T. J. Crovello. Science 169:505 Jl 31 '70

CLASSIFIED defense information. See Defense information, Classified

CLASSIFIED documents. See Security classification (government documents)

CLASSROOM gardens. See School gardens

CLASSROOM management
Catch the child being; social reinforcement technique. D. G. Tinsley and J. P. Ora. il Todays Ed 59:24-5 Ja '70
Chance for identity, integrity, and independence. V. B. Hatch. Ed Digest 35:9-12 Ja '70
High school teachers' discipline problems. Sch & Soc 98:393-4 N '70
Let children talk. B. L. Broman. Ed Digest 35:30-1 Mr '70
Teaching freshman English in middle earth. P. Hezel. Engl J 59:387-92 Mr '70

CLASSROOMS
Come to the Store-front learning center. T. Mofford and J. Mofford. il Schol Teach Sec Teach Sup p 13-15 F 2 '70
Roomful of one-room schoolhouses; truncated octahedrons. il Life 69:32-3 N 6 '70

CLATHRATE hydrates. See Hydrates

CLAUSEN, Alden Winship
Changing perspectives; address, September 8, 1970. Vital Speeches 36:746-9 O 1 '70
Is our financial mechanism adequate for the 70s? address, April 2, 1970. Vital Speeches 36:428-31 My 1 '70

CLAVERTON manor. See American museum in Britain

CLAWSON, Marion
State parks; vital to the times. Parks & Rec 5:35-6+ D '70

CLAXTON, Philander P. Jr
United States population policy, origins and development; address, August 21, 1970. Dept State Bul 63:317-26 S 21 '70

CLAY, Cassius
Clay vs. Marciano; the super fight. il pors Life 68:42-3 Ja 30 '70
I'm sorry, but I'm through fighting now. il por Esquire 73:120-2+ My '70

about

Ali's army. il por Life 69:28-30 D 18 '70 *
Fight: fans' opinions. New Yorker 46:16-17 D 26 '70 *
He moves like silk, hits like a ton. M. Kram. il pors Sports Illus 33:16-19 O 26 '70 *
No more boasting, just the fight. il pors Life 69:44-9 O 23 '70 *
Promoters spar for Ali's next bout. Bsns W p21 D 12 '70 *
Return of an exiled champ. P. Axthelm. il pors Newsweek 76:56-60+ N 9 '70 *
Return of the ringmaster. il pors Time 96:35 N 9 '70 *
Return to the ring. il por Newsweek 76:123-4 S 14 '70 *

Smashing return of the old Ali. M. Kram. il pors Sports Illus 33:18-19 N 2 '70 *
Two down, one to go. il pors Time 96:48 D 21 '70 *
Watching the man in the mirror. G. Plimpton. il por Sports Illus 33:80-3+ N 23 '70 *
Weary butterfly. il pors Newsweek 76:68+ D 21 '70
Welcome back, Ali! M. Kane. il pors Sports Illus 33:20-3 S 14 '70 *

CLAY, Rena
Hub of the instructional program. il Am Lib 1:170-2 F '70

CLAY, William L.
Excerpt from debate, September 15, 1969. Cong Digest 49:17+ Ja '70

CLAY
Casting with native red clays. R. Halsted. il Ceram Mo 18:24-6 N '70
Clay colloids. W. H. Slabaugh. il por Chem 43:8-12 Ap '70; Correction. 43:31 O '70
Digging for clay. J. Schloemer. il pors Ceram Mo 18:24-5 My '70

CLAY cloisonné. See Cloisonné

CLAY industries

Wages and hours

Wages in structural clay products manufacturing. J. C. Bush. il Mo Labor R 93: 38-9 D '70

CLAY modeling. See Modeling

CLAY sculpture. See Ceramic sculpture

CLAYTON, William H.
Release of the chronic psychiatric patient. bibliog Ment Hy 54:407-10 Jl '70

CLAYTON COUNTY libraries. See Flint River regional library, Griffin, Ga.

CLAYTONIA. See Spring beauties

CLEAGE, Albert B. Jr
Wyatt T. Walker takes issues with Cleage's black nationalism. Chr Cent 87:471 Ap 22 '70 *

CLEAN air race. See Automobile engines—Testing

CLEAN-up campaigns. See Cleaning of cities, towns, etc.

CLEANERS, Drain. See Drain cleaners

CLEANING
Clothing-care labels that last. B. Furness. McCalls 98:46+ O '70
See also
House cleaning
Kitchen utensils—Care
Rugs and carpets—Care
Sewer cleaning
Street cleaning
Ultrasonic cleaning
Vacuum cleaning
also subhead Cleaning under various subjects, e.g. Water pipes—Cleaning

CLEANING and dyeing industry

Wages and hours

Employment in laundry, drycleaning, and valet services; with charts. E. W. Abramson. il Mo Labor R 93:43-7 N '70

CLEANING compositions
Cleaners and polishes for aluminum and two rust removers for metal. il Consumer Bul 53:31-2 Ag '70
Hand cleaners. il Consumer Rep 35:594-5 O '70
Instant cleaning. Redbook 135:43+ Jl '70
Keep it clean. il Motor B 125:66-7 Ap '70
Know the differences in toilet-bowl cleaners. E. Taylor. Good H 172:112 Ja '71
Mixing household cleaners; dangerous results. il Consumer Bul 53:20 S '70
Oven cleaners. il Consumer Rep 35:423-5 Jl '70
Window cleaners. il Consumer Bul 53:38-40 S '70
See also
Detergents
Polishing materials

CLEANING machinery and appliances
See also
Tennant, G. H. company

CLEANING of cities, towns, etc.
Project Pride, Detroit's fifty-five-block party. il Am City 85:30 Ag '70
See also
Street cleaning

CLEANING of fishes. See Fish as food

CLEANLINESS
Dirty linen; myth of German cleanliness. il Time 95:30+ My 18 '70

CLEANSING creams. See Cosmetics

CLEAR, Delbert K.
Decentralization; issues and comments. bibliog Clear House 44:259-67 Ja '70; Same. Ed Digest 35:8-11 My '70

CLEAR-air turbulence. See Atmospheric turbulence

CLEARWATER (sloop) See Sloops

CLEARWATER RIVER
Last log drive. A. Tussing. il Am For 76: 16-19 Jl '70

CLEATH, Robert L.
Hope in the midst of horror. Chr Today 14: 3-5 Mr 27 '70

CLEAVE, Maureen
Hip Baroness Wootton of Abinger. il por N Y Times Mag p4+ My 10 '70

CLEAVER, Bill
Authors & editors. L. Russ. por Pub W 197: 47-8 Ja 19 '70

CLEAVER, Eldridge
Cleaver speaks. il pors N Y Times Mag p31+ N 1 '70
Eldridge Cleaver in Algiers. a visit with Papa Rage; interview. ed. by G. Parks. il pors Life 68:20-3 F 6 '70
   about
Panthers against the wall. D. A. Schanche. il por Atlan 225:55-61 My '70 *

CLEAVER, Vera
Authors & editors. L. Russ. por Pub W 197: 47-8 Ja 19 '70

CLEBSCH, Edward E. C.
Campus teach-in on the environmental crisis; 1970. Liv Wildn 34:10-12 Spr '70

CLEGHORN, Reese
High noon for Tex Ritter. il pors N Y Times Mag p 10-11+ Jl 12 '70
Segregation academies: the old South tries again. il Sat R 53:76-7+ My 16 '70
Segregation by tax exemption. Nation 210: 785-6 Je 29 '70
Shooting an elephant. Nation 210:358-61 Mr 30 '70
View from Maddox country. Nation 210:486-90 Ap 27 '70
When readers become suspect. Cur 121:42-6 S '70

CLEMENS, Cyril
Mark Twain & Harry S Truman. Hobbies 74: 141+ Ja '70
Mark Twain and Richard M. Nixon. Hobbies 75:142-3 N '70
Personal glimpses of the presidents. Hobbies 75:142-3 Jl '70

CLEMENS, Samuel Langhorne
Huckleberry Finn as tragedy. H. P. Simonson. Yale R 59:532-48 Je '70
Mark Twain & Harry S Truman. C. Clemens. Hobbies 74:141+ Ja '70
Prince and the pauper; dramatization. See Bland, J.
   about
Mark Twain and Richard M. Nixon. C. Clemens. Hobbies 75:142-3 N '70 *
Mark Twain, by M. Geismar. Review
   New Repub 163:21-4 N 28 '70. J. Seelye *
   Time por 96:80+ N 30 '70. J. Skow *

CLEMENS, Walter C. Jr
Ecology of weaponry. il Bul Atom Sci 26: 27-31 S '70; Same with title Dynamics of the arms race. Cur 123:57-63 N '70

CLEMENT, Stanley L.
Is the teaching profession gaining or losing? Clear House 44:556-8 My '70

CLEMENTS, John A. and others
Pulmonary surfactant and evolution of the lungs. bibliog il Science 169:603-4 Ag 7 '70

CLEMENTS, Mary Jane
Good start in school. il Parents Mag 45: 38-9 Ag 11 '70

CLEMENTS, Robert J.
Bill of rights for wronged translators. Sat R 53:30-2 Je 20 '70
European literary scene. See issues of Saturday review

CLEMENTS, Sid
Cartop johnboat. il Mech Illus 66:110-12+ Mr '70

CLEMONS, Loretta Anne
Blue-eyed blackness; poem. Negro Hist Bul 33:17 Ja '70

CLEPPER, Henry
Century of fish conservation. il Am For 76: 16-19+ N '70

CLERGY
Challenge of the ministry. D. Hillis. Chr Today 15:25 D 18 '70
Exodus from the pastorate. Chr Today 14:34-5 Ap 10 '70
Exodus of Protestant ministers? J. C. Haughey. America 122:243-4 Mr 7 '70
Minister and the marketing orientation. Chr Today 14:31-2 F 27 '70
Protestant clergy: new forms of ministry. new forms of training. R. H. Luecke. bibliog f Ann Am Acad 387:86-95 Ja '70

Team ministry. J. G. Corazzini. Cath World 212:206-8 Ja '71
Theological education 1970; symposium. Chr Cent 87:472-80+ Ap 22 '70
   See also
Chaplains, Military
Negro clergy
Parishes
Pastoral theology
Preaching
Sermons
Women as ministers

Costume
   See also
Church vestments

Education
Coventry's pilot program; further training for the clergy. T. Beeson. Chr Cent 87:1113 S 23 '70
Protestant clergy: new forms of ministry. new forms of training. R. H. Luecke. bibliog f Ann Am Acad 387:86-95 Ja '70
Some basic assumptions for continuing education. C. H. Reid. Chr Cent 87:472-4 Ap 22 '70
   See also
Clergy economic education foundation

Political activities
Activist cleric. D. Rabinowitz. Commentary 50:81-3 S '70; Reply with rejoinder. B. Woodward. 50:26+ D '70
As clergymen enter politics: the new trend. il por U S News 69:19-21 Ag 10 '70
Campus minister: rebel or reconciler? C. S. Evans. Chr Today 14:3-5 My 8 '70
Clergy as politicians. Chr Cent 87:1175 O 7 '70
Clergy score poorly in great election game. Chr Today 15:35 D 4 '70
Clergymen-candidates: many called, but few chosen. il U S News 69:20-1 N 16 '70
Clerical candidates. il Time 95:22 Je 8 '70
Collars in the ring. il Newsweek 75:105 My 4 '70
Political fever; see clergy run. Chr Today 14: 49-50 Ap 15 '70
Why they ran us out of Jenkintown. M. Moore and T. W. Moore. il pors Look 34: 98 O 20 '70

Salaries, allowances, etc.
Clergy discount: boon or bane? Chr Today 14:27 Ja 16 '70

CLERGY and laymen concerned about Vietnam. See Vietnamese war, 1957- —Protests, demonstrations. etc. against

CLERGY and race problems. See Church and race problems

CLERGY economic education foundation
Clergymen are given down-to-earth insight. V. Louviere. Nations Bsns 58:19 Ap '70

CLERICAL workers. See Office workers

CLERKS (retail trade)
Wanted: someone to watch the store. il Bsns W p52+ S 19 '70

CLESS, Elizabeth L.
Modest proposal for the educating of women. Am Scholar 38:618-27; 39:520 Aut '69, Sum '70

CLEVELAND, J. M.
Plutonium, the lively element (cont) bibliog il por Chem 43:10-13 Ja '70

CLEVELAND, James Colgate
Excerpt from debate, September 15, 1969. Cong Digest 49:28+ Ja '70

CLEVELAND, Richard S.
Japanese porcelains in American and Canadian collections. il Antiques 98:927-31 D '70

CLEVELAND
Churches
Changes in the black ghetto: Cleveland; white and black Unitarians form separate units. J. G. Mearns. il pors Sat R 53:13-14+ Ag 1 '70

Housing
Cleveland housing puts HUD to the test. il Bsns W p28 Jl 18 '70

Lighting
Cleveland regains lighting fame. il Am City 85:138 S '70

Music
   See also
Cleveland orchestra

Negroes
Cleveland housing puts HUD to the test. il Bsns p28 Jl 18 '70
Oh, that Ahmed. Poor, poor Ahmed. They're going to fry his black, skinny ass. D. Pearce. il Esquire 73:123-35+ Mr '70

CLEVELAND—Negroes—*Continued*
Survey of employer attitudes toward training the disadvantaged; excerpt from Training programs of private industry in the Greater Cleveland area. J. L. Iacobelli. il Mo Labor R 93:51-5 Je '70

Police
Support for the badge; community response on assaults on police. Time 96:19 O 12 '70

Police department
Black and blue in Cleveland. T. Sheridan. il Nation 211:48-50 Jl 20 '70
Cop out; resignation of W. Ellenburg. Newsweek 75:33+ F 16 '70

Politics and government
Close-up of a city in distress: the story of Cleveland. il pors U S News 69:43-4 Ag 17 '70
Fiasco in Cleveland. por Time 95:15 F 16 '70
Stokes' general takes his leave. pors Bsns W p62 Ag 8 '70
Troubles that face Carl Stokes. il por Bsns W p44+ D 19 '70

Riots
Oh, that Ahmed. Poor, poor Ahmed. They're going to fry his black, skinny ass. D. Pearce. il Esquire 73:128-35+ Mr '70

Social conditions
See also
Cleveland—Negroes
CLEVELAND Cavaliers (basketball team) See Basketball teams
CLEVELAND children's garden fair. See Childrens gardens—Competitions
CLEVELAND Cliffs iron company
Cliffs iron frees itself. Bsns W p 112 Je 6 '70
Ransom of Cleveland Cliffs. il Forbes 106: 32 Jl 15 '70
CLEVELAND Indians (baseball) See Baseball clubs
CLEVELAND orchestra
Musical events; performance of Bruckner's Eighth symphony, L. Lane, conducting. W. Sargeant. New Yorker 46:108 Mr 7 '70
Profiles. J. Wechsberg. New Yorker 46:38-42+ My 30 '70
Szell memorial concert; tribute by the orchestra in Severance Hall. B. Murray. Hi Fi 20:MA14 O '70
CLEVELAND symphony orchestra. See Cleveland orchestra
CLEVELAND trust company
McLaren's hatchet swings at the banks. Bsns W p24 Ap 4 '70
When a bank holds the purse strings. Bsns W p54 Jl 25 '70
CLEVELAND zoo. See Zoological gardens
CLEVER, Ulrich, and Ellgaard, E. G.
Puffing and histone acetylation in polytene chromosomes. bibliog il Science 169:373-4 Jl 24 '70
CLIBURN, Van
Youth week in the concert halls. I. Kolodin. Sat R 53:56 My 23 '70 *
CLICHÉ; story. See Steers, N. A.
CLICHÉS. See English language—Terms and phrases
CLIFF, Edward P.
Clearing the air. J. B. Craif. Am For 76:11 D '70 *
CLIFFORD, Clark McAdams
Fresh prescriptions for disengagement in Vietnam; excerpt. pors Newsweek 75:31-2 My 25 '70
Set a date in Vietnam. Stick to it. Get out. il pors Life 68:34-8 My 22 '70
CLIFFORD, John
Accent on youth. il Sat R 53:53-9 Ja 31 '70
CLIFFORD, Richard
New American Bible. America 123:435-6 N 21 '70
CLIFFORD, William
Aperitif. il Holiday 47:64-5+ F '70
Holiday drinks. House B 112:88+ D '70
Liebfraumilch. House B 112:62+ My '70
Trapping the truffle, jugging the hare. il Sat R 53:66+ S 12 '70
Well-favored wines of Alsace. House B 112: 102-4 F '70
Wine-tasting party. il House B 112:48+ Ap '70
CLIFFORD, William (United Nations official)
United Nations and the prevention of crime. UN Mo Chron 7:65-70 My '70
CLIFTON, H. Edward, and others
Tektite 1, man-in-the sea project: marine science program. bibliog il Science 168:659-63 My 8 '70

CLIMACTERIC
See also
Menopause
CLIMATE
Coming: ice-free Arctic? Sci Digest 67:39 Ja '70
How man endangers the climate. G. J. F. MacDonald. Cur 114:17-24 Ja '70
Ice cores: clues to past climates. L. Purrett. il Sci N 98:369-70 N 7 '70
Man-made climatic changes. H. E. Landsberg. bibliog il Science 170:1265-74 D 18 '70
Sea-air explanation; causes of cooler weather. Sci N 98:412 N 28 '70
See also
Antarctic Regions—Climate
Paleoclimatology
Plants, Effect of climate on
Weather
also subhead Climate under names of continents, countries, cities, etc. e.g. Boston —Climate

History
Polar ice and the global climate machine. J. O. Fletcher. il por Bul Atom Sci 26:40-7 D '70
CLIMATE and architecture. See Architecture and climate
CLIMATE and health. See Weather—Mental and physiological effects
CLIMATE simulators. See Environmental simulators
CLIMBING plants
Indoor vines. M. E. Ross. il Horticulture 49: 29-30+ Ja '71
See also
Ampelopsis
Gourds
CLINE, Victor Bailey
How violence affects children. il por Life 68: 57-8 Ja 30 '70
CLINICAL tests. See Diagnosis
CLINICAL thermometers. See Thermometers, Clinical
CLINICS
See also
Health clinics
Psychiatric clinics
Reading clinics
CLOACA (zoology)
Water transport in the cloaca of lizards: active or passive? D. E. Murrish and K. Schmidt-Nielsen. bibliog il Science 170:324-6 O 16 '70
CLOCK and watch makers
Civilization's debt to the watchmaker. O. R. Hagans. il Hobbies 75:124+ My; 124+ Je '70
See also
Switzerland—Industries
CLOCK and watch museum, Germany. See Museums
CLOCK at 8:16; story. See Lanham, E.
CLOCK industry
See also
Switzerland—Industries
CLOCK radios. See Radio receivers
CLOCKS
Clock that tells the tides. L. A. Harlow and H. R. Pfister. il Pop Sci 196:136-7+ F '70
Clocks worth watching. M. Kraft. il Good H 171:116-21 N '70
Different track. M. Bowden. il House B 112: 20 D '70
Minute striking & calendar clock. O. R. Hagans. il Hobbies 75:125-6 Ap '70
Of time and taste: European clocks in the Bliss collection. J .S. Johnson. il Antiques 97:90-5 Ja '70
See also
Atomic clocks

Collectors and collecting
Unusual clocks in the collection of Clyde N. Fahrney. O. R. Hagans. il Hobbies 74:126-7+ F; 75:125-7 Mr '70

History
Eternal nightingale. G. Martin. il Hobbies 75:98M-98N Ag '70
Origins of feedback control; water clock. O. Mayr. il Sci Am 223:110-13 O '70
Unusual French skeleton clock. O. R. Hagans. il Hobbies 74:126-7+ Ja '70

Photographs
Simon Nathan says try clocking. Pop Phot 67:82-3 Jl '70
CLOCKS, Electric
Early American wall clock. il Pop Mech 134: 176-7+ N '70
Old clocks in bold new housings. il Sunset 145:97 O '70

CLOCKS, Electronic
Assemble the Popular electronics digivista (title varies). C. G. Kay and D. Meyer. il Pop Electr 33:25-32 D '70; 34:71-4 Ja '71
Build multipurpose IC digital clock. L. Walker. il Radio-Electr 41:46-51 Ag; 97+ S '70
Digital clock update. L. G. Riddle. il Radio-Electr 41:54-5+ Ag '70
24-hour digital clock. D. L. Steinbach. il Electr World 84:41-5+ N '70

CLOISONNÉ
Clay cloisonné. P. Rothenberg. il Ceram Mo 18:22-3 O '70
Liturgical enamels of Charles Bartley Jeffery. R. D. Bonham. il por Ceram Mo 18:14-17 D '70

CLOISTERS (museum) See Metropolitan museum of Art, New York—Cloisters

CLONINGER, Marion R. and Baldwin, R. E.
Aspartylphenylalanine methyl ester: a low-calorie sweetener. bibliog il Science 170:81-2 O 2 '70

CLOR, Harry M.
Intellectual freedom: are you a moralist, a libertarian, or a Clorist? J. F. Krug and J. A. Harvey. Am Lib 1:433-4 My '70 *

CLOSE, Charles
Presenting Charles Close. C. Nemser. il pors Art in Am 58:98-101 Ja '70

CLOSE, Marjorie
Marjorie Close. San Francisco realist. F. Whitaker. il por Am Artist 34:20-6+ Ja '70

CLOSE-up lenses. See Lenses, Photographic

CLOSE-up photography. See Photography, Close-up

CLOSED circuit television. See Television, Closed circuit

CLOSETS
Child's wardrobe: a housekeeper you can build. R. Capotosto. il Pop Sci 197:128 O '70
For a less noisy furnace this coming winter; furnace closet. il Sunset 145:107-8 S '70
See also
Storage in the home

CLOTH, Photography on. See Photography on glass, metal, pottery, etc.

CLOTHES dryers
Combination washer and dryer; Skinny mini. il Consumer Rep 36:5-7 Ja '71
Portable clothes dryers. il Consumer Rep 35:599-601 O '70
Washers & dryers: an up-to-the-minute report. J. R. Cary. il Parents Mag 45:95-8 Mr '70

CLOTHES washing machines. See Washing machines

CLOTHING, Protective
See also
Clothing, Waterproof
Pressure suits

CLOTHING, Waterproof
Foul weather gear. M. E. Slate. il Motor B 125:111+ Mr '70
Foul weather gear is beautiful. il Yachting 127:72-6+ My '70

CLOTHING and dress
Battle of the hemline. il Newsweek 75:70-34+ Mr 16 '70; Same abr. with title Hullabaloo over hemlines. Read Digest 96:70-3 Je '70
Big costume party. E. Sheppard. Harp Baz 103:204-5 S '70
Claude and the long look. pors Time 95:44 Mr 9 '70
Clothes that tell a story. il Life 69:38-41 Jl 17 '70
Command decisions in favor of pants. il Bsns W p20 O 31 '70
Crafty about fashion. N. Comer. il Mlle 70:186-7 Mr '70
Designers and the midi beauty. il Harp Baz 103:242-55 S '70
Fashion: does the midi look spell E-d-s-e-l? il Forbes 106:28-30+ S 15 '70
Fashion leaders? styles. A. M. Schiro. il N Y Times Mag p 104-5 N 15 '70
Fashion planning; or, How to make your fashion dollars go further. il Good H 171:100-1+ Jl '70
Fashions by Wanda Beal. J. Kuh. por Ladies Home J 87:54 Je '70
For goodness snakes, the serpents have come. il Time 95:48 Mr 16 '70
French line. il Time 95:58 F 9 '70
Funnies take a swing at fashion. G. Plaut. il Look 34:100-2+ My 19 '70
Hem and the haw. il Newsweek 76:80-1 O 5 '70
Hems down, business up? il Sr Schol 96:15-16 Ap 6 '70
I cured myself with wool . . . R. Bugg and H. G. Scott. Todays Health 48:56-7 Je '70
It's knickers sans droop. il Life 69:80-3 N 27 '70

Let the sun shine in; treated cotton-polyester. il Life 68:52-3 My 22 '70
Line of most resistance; midi or longuette. il Time 95:42+ Mr 23 '70
Long way out. il Time 96:80 O 26 '70
Making the midi move. Harp Baz 103:120 Je '70
Midi muscles in. il Life 69:22-9 Ag 21 '70
Midi without fear. T. Owett. il Ladies Home J 87:74-5 Ag '70
Mini-midi-maxi madness. N. Lobsenz. il Good H 171:61+ Ag '70
Nixon ladies and their summer dresses. il Life 68:42-5 My 8 '70
Onward and downward with hemlines: the midi look. il Life 68:38-45 Mr 13 '70
Out on a limb with the midi. il por Time 96:76-81 S 14 '70
Pantsuits rescue garment makers. il Bsns W p54 Ja 2 '71
Parting shots; the midi that wouldn't die. il Life 69:73-6 O 30 '70
Signs of quality in clothing. il Good H 170:209 Mr '70
Skirt skirmishes; mini-midi battle. il Newsweek 75:90 My 18 '70
Stuck with the midi and pushing hard. il Bsns W p 106-8 O 10 '70
To what lengths? il Newsweek 75:93 F 23 '70
West Virginia's super sewing bee; turning patchwork designs into fashions. il Life 69:58-62 Jl 31 '70
See also
Brassieres
Costume
Costume design
Dress accessories
Eskimos—Costume and adornment
Fashion
Fur
Indians of North America—Costume and adornment
Sewing
Shawls
Shoes
Trousers

Athletes
Athlete as peacock. il Time 97:44-7 Ja 4 '71

Care
Ways to make clothes last longer. il Changing T 24:29-30 O '70
What you should know about the new rainwear. il Good H 170:192 Ap '70

Children
Choosing children's camp clothes. il Good H 171:124 Jl '70
Slipover shift for a young girl painter. il Sunset 144:148 Ap '70

Cleaning
See Cleaning

History
King's new clothes. J. H. Plumb. il Horizon 12:12-13 Sum '70

Materials
Ringing success; garments of aluminum rings from pop-top cans. il Time 96:84 S 21 '70

Men
His bazaar. C. Kriebel. See issues of Harper's bazaar
Male plumage; with editorial comment. il por Life 69:3, 42-9 S 25 '70
Men's shops are gaudy, not rich. il Bsns W p20-1 N 28 '70
Three stylish jockeys. il Life 68:60-3 F 6 '70
See also
Fur coats, wraps, etc.
Grooming, Personal
Raincoats
Shirts
Underwear

Prices
How to save money; in the clothing store. R. O'Brien. Read Digest 96:65-8 Ap '70
Why your clothes cost so much. M. Bender. il McCalls 97:94-5+ My '70

Size
Why your clothes don't fit. B. Furness. McCalls 98:6+ D '70

Sports clothes
All in the jeans. il Time 97:35 Ja 11 '71
Clothing. il Motor B 127:234-5 Ja '71
Hunting gear for the Rockies. J. J. Beveridge. il Field & S 75:50-1 N '70
Most astounding look for the links since Oddjob graced the greens; golf clothes. il Esquire 73:151-5 Ap '70
Things to wear at sundance, kid. J. Campbell. il Sports Illus 33:42-3 Jl 27 '70

CLOTHING and dress—*Continued*

Students

Adolescent dress: understanding the issues. M. E. Roach. Ed Digest 35:39-41 F '70
Dress codes in disarray. il Sr Schol 95:Schol Teach 1-2 O 20 '69
Dress codes: we forget our own advice. M. J. Weinberger. Clear House 44:471-3 Ap '70
Which would you pick up? Guess again; findings of University of Dayton study. il Life 68:61-2 Mr 13 '70

CLOTHING expenditures. See Clothing and dress—Prices

CLOTHING industry
Fashion firms use airfreight for essential fast delivery. Aviation W 93:120-1 O 26 '70
Skirt skirmishes; mini-midi battle. il Newsweek 75:90 My 18 '70
    See also
Blue bell, inc.

Finance

Dressmakers are hemmed in. il Bsns W p20-1 Jl 11 '70

United States

Fashion: does the midi look spell E-d-s-e-l? il Forbes 106:28-30+ S 15 '70
Men's shops are gaudy, not rich. il Bsns W p20-1 N 28 '70
    See also
Aileen, inc.
Strauss, Levi, and company
Villager industries, inc.

CLOTHING prices. See Clothing and dress—Prices

CLOTURE rule. See United States—Congress—Senate—Rules and practice

CLOUD, Preston
Lunar science and planetary history. Science 169:1159 S 18 '70
Russian roulette? Science 167:1323 Mr 6 '70
—and Gibor, Aharon
Oxygen cycle; with biographical sketches. il Sci Am 223:33, 110-18+ bibliog(p263) S '70
—and others
Micromorphology and surface characteristics of lunar dust and breccia. bibliog il Science 167:766-8 Ja 30 '70

CLOUD, Stanley
Cover story; Russia expels. il por Newsweek 75:60-1 Je 22 '70 *

CLOUD physics
    See also
Atmospheric nucleation

CLOUD seeding. See Rain making; Weather control

CLOUDS
Life in the clouds; theories of B. C. Parker. Newsweek 76:57 O 5 '70
Life in the sky. B. C. Parker. il Natur Hist 79:54-9 O '70
    See also
Fog

CLOUDS, Magellanic. See Magellanic clouds

CLOUET, Doris H. and Ratner, Milton
Catecholamine biosynthesis in brains of rats treated with morphine. bibliog il Science 168:854-6 My 15 '70

CLOUGH, Roy L. jr
Build this electronic banjo. il Pop Mech 134:175-7+ O '70

CLOUSE, Bonnidell
Psychosocial origins of stability in the Christian faith. Chr Today 14:12-14 S 25 '70

CLOUSER, K. Danner
Abortion, classification and competing rights. Chr Cent 87:626-8 My 20 '70

CLOVERLEAF Colt. See Revolvers

CLOWNS
Funniest college on earth; college of clowns at winter quarters of Ringling brothers. Barnum & Bailey circus. W. Zinsser. il Life 68:62-6 F 20 '70

CLUB houses. See Clubhouses

CLUB Méditerranée. See Vacation villages

CLUB-plan vacation homes. See Vacation villages

CLUBB, O. Edmund
China and the United States: collision course? bibliog f Cur Hist 59:153-8+ S '70
Thaw in U.S.-Chinese relations? Cur 117:56-61 Ap '70

CLUBHOUSES
Golf and tennis club on Long Island Sound; Montauk golf and racquet club. il Arch Rec 147:144-6 My '70
Princeton's glass pavilion; Prospect faculty center. M. Villecco. il Arch Forum 132:60-3 Je '70

CLUBS
Patients helping patients; friendship club at Boulder mental health center. D. Hawxhurst and H. Walzer. bibliog Ment Hy 54:370-3 Jl '70
Psychiatric social clubs come of age. S. Grob. bibliog Ment Hy 54:129-36 Ja '70
    See also
Agricultural societies
Boat clubs
Childrens clubs
College clubs and societies
Cookery clubs
Discotheques, etc.
Fishing clubs
Metropolitan opera club
Negroes—Clubs, societies, etc.
Political clubs and associations
Swimming clubs
Travel clubs
Womens clubs and societies

CLUBS (weapons)
Indian and Eskimo clubs. C. Miles. il Hobbies 75:154-6 O; 154-6 N '70

CLUBS, Negro. See Negroes—Clubs, societies, etc.

CLUCHEY, Rick
Cage. Criticism
    New Yorker 46:50 Je 27 '70 *
Special report; Barbwire theater. P. Goldberger. il por Sr Schol 95:8-9 N 3 '69 *

CLURMAN, Harold
Film festival. Nation 211:315-17, 347-9 O 5, 12 '70
Theatre. See issues of Nation

CLUSTER housing. See Housing projects—Site planning

CLUTCH size (biology) See Fertility

CLUTCHES (machinery)
New overrunning clutch has no moving parts. il Pop Sci 196:58 Je '70

CLUTCHES, Automobiles. See Automobiles—Clutches

CLYDES bar, Washington, D.C. See Bars and barrooms

CLYNE, J. V.
The establishment; address, December 2, 1969. Vital Speeches 36:209-11 Ja 15 '70

CNIDOSCOLUS texanus. See Tread-softly

COACHES (athletics)
Another nightmare for the year ahead. D. Jenkins. il Sports Illus 33:46-8 S 14 '70
Big-time college football is on the skids. S. Padwe. il Look 34:66-9 S 22 '70
Cousy makes the Royals run; coach of Cincinnati Royals. W. Leggett. il por Sports Illus 32:14-17 Ja 26 '70
Doc and George bloom late; released from bullpen coaching duties. R. Blount, jr. Sports Illus 32:46 Je 29 '70
Impatience of Mrs Job. R. Blount, jr. il pors Sports Illus 33:24-9 Ag 24 '70
Love-in at the Utah natatorium; swimming coach D. Reddish. W. F. Reed. il Sports Illus 32:50+ Mr 16 '70
Pick up your purse, coach, and let's go; coaching girls' basketball team. G. V. Packard. il Sports Illus 33:88-90+ N 30 '70
Quakers pull a swift one on the Charles; T. Nash new crew coach at Penn. H. D. Whall. il por Sports Illus 32:74+ My 11 '70
Two gods too many; Ohio state, Texas and Notre Dame battle for national title. D. Jenkins. il Sports Illus 33:14-17 N 9 '70
Winningest coach takes his lumps; J. Paterno of Penn State. J. Newcombe. il por Life 69:44-6 O 9 '70
    See also
Bowerman, B.
Dedeaux, R.
Fitch, B.
Kush, F.
Schaeffler, W.
Wooden, J.

COACHES (music) See Singing teachers

COACHES All-America football game. See Football

COACHES and coaching
Coaching: the new in sport. P. Benchley. il Travel & Camera 33:40-5+ F '70

COACHING. See Coaches and coaching

COAGULATION of blood. See Blood—Coagulation

COAGULATION of sewage. See Sewage disposal—Coagulation

COAKLEY, William Leo
Lesson in wildness; poem. Nation 210:248 Mr 2 '70

COAL
        Combustion
    See Combustion

COAL—*Continued*

Prices

TVA: coal gets cheaper, or else. il Bsns W
  p52 N 21 '70
COAL briquets. See Briquets (fuel)
COAL carving. See Carving (art industries)
COAL industry

United States

Big coal crisis burns itself out. il Bsns W
  p74-5 D 5 '70
Coal's hollow prosperity. il Newsweek 77:51+
  Ja 4 '71
Why coal users are turning gray. il Bsns W
  p27 Ap 18 '70
Yablonski's unfinished business. R. Nader. il
  Nation 210:70-2 Ja 26 '70
  See also
  Peabody coal company
COAL miners
Consol no. 9: a decent burial; victims and
  dependents of the Farmington, W.Va. 1968
  disaster. il Time 96:21 D 14 '70
Life and death underground; Clay County
  Poor people's association holds mock trial
  on inadequate enforcement of the Federal
  coal mine health and safety act of 1969.
  R. Cassidy. New Repub 163:13-14 D 12 '70
  See also
  United mine workers of America
COAL mines and mining
  See also
  Coal supply

Accidents and explosions

Consol no. 9: a decent burial; victims and
  dependents of the Farmington, W. Va. 1968
  disaster. il Time 96:21 D 14 '70
Merry Christmas! explosion near Hyden, Ky.
  Nation 212:70-1 Ja 18 '71
  See also
  Coal mines and mining—Safety devices and
  measures

Safety devices and measures

Coal's hollow prosperity. il Newsweek 77:51+
  Ja 4 '71
Confusion in the coalfields. W. Sinclair. New
  Repub 163:17-18 Jl 18 '70
Death by runaround. S. Cupps. il Nation 211:
  146-8 Ag 31 '70
Down to the mine in space suits. il Bsns W
  p83-4 D 12 '70
Getting something done; Federal coal mine
  health and safety act. E. McCarthy. por
  McCalls 97:28 Ap '70
Life and death underground; Clay County
  Poor people's association holds mock
  trial on inadequate enforcement of the
  Federal coal mine health and safety act
  of 1969. R. Cassidy. New Repub 163:13-14
  D 12 '70
New mine safety law. Sr Schol 96:16-17 F 2
  '70
Reform that hasn't stopped disaster. il Bsns
  W p20 Ja 9 '71
Slowness in response. Sci N 97:575 Je 13 '70
Will tough laws stifle coal mining? Federal
  coal mine health & safety act. il Bsns W
  p31 My 16 '70

Stripping operations

Lament for the Appalachian hills. H. M.
  Caudill. il Am For 76:8-11+ My '70; Dis-
  cussion. 76:2 S; 3 O '70
Strip-mine reformer. por Bsns W p74 Ja 9 '71

British Columbia

See Coal mines and mining—Canada

Canada

Kaiser's black gold. T. J. Murray. Duns 96:
  66-7 Jl '70
Mining coal for hungry steel mills; Kaiser resources complex in British Columbia. il
  Bsns W p 114+ Je 27 '70

United States

See also
Coal industry—United States
COAL research
Clean power from coal. A. M. Squires. bib-
  liog il Science 169:821-8 S 28 '70
Tapping coal to get oil and gas. Bsns W
  p52+ O 17 '70
COAL supply
Big coal crisis burns itself out. il Bsns W
  p74-5 D 5 '70
Scramble for coal. Fortune 82:79 S '70
COAL tar colors
Mauve not improved. il Chem 43:5 My '70

COALE, Ansley J.
Man and his environment; adaptation of ad-
  dress, March 19, 1970. Science 170:132-6
  O 9 '70
COALINGA, Calif.

Transit systems

Mini-bus proves a giant for inter-city service.
  G. H. Marcussen. il Am City 85:128 Mr '70
COALITION against the SST (organization)
  See Pressure groups
COAST changes
  See also
  Beach erosion
COAST guard. See United States—Coast guard
COAST guard academy, United States. See
  United States coast guard academy, New
  London, Conn.
COASTAL Caribbean, inc.
Fire one; taking limestone from Lake Okee-
  chobee. W. F. Buckley, jr. Nat R 22:1367 D
  15 '70
COASTAL engineering. See Shore protection
COASTAL marshes. See Salt marshes
COASTAL states gas producing company
Gold from junk wells. il Fortune 81:248 My
  '70
COASTAL waters. See Territorial waters
COASTS
  See also
  Estuaries
  Pacific coast
  Seashore

United States

Battle for America's crowded coastlines. il
  U S News 69:44-7 Ag 10 '70
CO-AUTHORSHIP. See Authorship—Collab-
  oration
COAXIAL connectors. See Electric connectors
COBALT
Cobalt blues at cone 9. R. Behrens. il Cer-
  am Mo 18:31 My '70
COBALT alloys
Permanent magnets. J. J. Becker. il Sci Am
  223:92-100 bibliog(p 140) D '70
COBB, Boughton, jr
Classic boats in fiberglass. il Yachting 129:
  100-1+ Ja '71
Design details in fiberglass. il Yachting 127:
  80-2 Ap '70
Fiberglass age. il Yachting 127:76-8 Ja '70
COBB, Carl M.
Solving the doctor shortage. il Sat R 53:24-
  6+ Ag 22 '70
COBB, John B. Jr
Ecological disaster and the church. il Chr
  Cent 87:1185-7 O 7 '70
COBB, Tony
Reconstructing fiberglass. il Yachting 128:
  154 N '70
  —See Booz, R. M. jt. auth.
COBRAS
Cobra, India's good snake. H. Miller. il Nat
  Geog 138:392-409 S '70
COBURN, James
James Coburns: we live in a house of travel
  treasures. il pors House & Gard 138:42-7
  Jl '70 *
COBURN, Judith
Off the pill? Ramp Mag 8:46-9 Je '70
COCA COLA company
Candor that refreshes. il Time 96:59 Ag 10
  '70
Coke's formula: keep the image fresh. il
  Bsns W p66-7+ Ap 25 '70
Coke's migrants get a new deal. il Bsns W
  p 109-10 N 14 '70
Environmental renewal or oblivion; quo
  vadis? address, April 16, 1970. J. P. Austin.
  Vital Speeches 36:470-5 My 15 '70
Just a little pregnant? Forbes 106:36 Jl 15 '70
Letting the genie out of the bottle. C. W.
  Adams. il Nations Bsns 58:64-5 Ja '70
$100 misunderstanding; alleged deception in
  promotional game. Newsweek 76:70 Jl 20 '70
Prize snafu in the Coke game. Bsns W p32
  Jl 18 '70
Real thing; ecology teaching aid. il Time 96:
  46 D 14 '70
Things go wrong for Coca-Cola; FTC moves
  on Big name bingo contest. Consumer Rep
  35:578 O '70
COCAINESTERASE. See Esterases
COCCIDIOSIS
1,3-bis(p-chlorobenzylideneamino)quanidine
  hydrochloride (robenzidene): new poultry
  anticoccidial agent. S. Kantor and others.
  bibliog il Science 168:373-4 Ap 17 '70
COCHLEA. See Labyrinth (ear)

COCHRAN, Rod
This is adventure. il pors Outdoor Life 146:
36-9+ Jl '70
Troll for early trout. il Field & S 74:52-3+
F '70
COCHRAN, Wayne
Wayne Cochran lets the sunshine in and vice
versa. R. Bongartz. pors Esquire 73:108-10+
Ap '70 *
COCHRANE, Eric
Visitor stopped at St Apollinare. Commonweal
92:452-3 S 18 '70
COCK fighting
Bloody nights on the lone prairie; chicken-
fighting. D. Russell. il Sports Illus 32:48-51
Mr 23 '70
COCKBURN, Alexander
What it's like in Belfast. il Ramp Mag 9:8+
O '70
COCKBURN, Claud
Triumph for the clan O'Brien. il por Sports
Illus 33:14-15 Jl 6 '70
COCKER, Joe
Sound of superscapegoat. A. Goldman. pors
Life 68:13 Je 19 '70 *
Which one is Joe? il por Time 95:67 Ap 13 '70 *
COCKFIGHTING. See Cock fighting
COCKLEBURS
Floral inducing extract from xanthium. H. K.
Hodson and K. C. Hamner. bibliog il Sci-
ence 167:384-5 Ja 23 '70
COCKROACHES
Antennal receptors: reactions to female sex
attractant in periplaneta americana. J.
Boeckh and others. bibliog il Science 168:
589 My 1 '70
Autoxidation of insect lipids: inhibition on
the cuticle of the American cockroach. P.
W. Atkinson and A. R. Gilby. bibliog Sci-
ence 168:992 My 22 '70
Energy transduction: inhibition of cockroach
feeding by naphthoquinone. D. M. Norris
and others. bibliog il Science 170:754-5
N 13 '70
Fluid transport: concentration of the inter-
cellular compartment. B. J. Wall and oth-
ers. bibliog il Science 167:1497-8 Mr 13 '70
COCKTAIL cafes. See Bars and barrooms
COCKTAILS
Cocktail mixes. il Consumer Rep 35:539-43 S
'70
Lunchtime drinks. House & Gard 137:130+ Mr
'70
New ways to greet the cocktail hour. E.
Kinard. House B 112:140-10 O '70
Premixed cocktails. il Consumer Rep 35:103-8
F '70
Thirsty sportsman's choice. il Esquire 74:104-
5 Jl '70
COCO; musical comedy. See Musical comedies,
revues, etc.—Criticisms, plots, etc.
COCOA
Prices
Cocoa futures leave a bitter taste. Bsns W
p32 S 26 '70
COCONUT
See also
Cookery—Coconut
COCOPAH Indians. See Indians of North Amer-
ica
COCTEAU, Jean
Opium; dramatization. See Brynner, R.
about
Angels and artifacts. M. Duffy. il por Time
96:77 S 28 '70 *
Cocteau: a biography, by F. Steegmuller. Re-
view
America 123:545 D 19 '70. H. Peisson *
Colette, Cocteau, and Proust. R. Phelps. il
Mlle 72:124-5+ D '70 *
Image of Cocteau. F. Brown. Nation 211:379
O 19 '70 *
CO-CURRICULAR activities. See Student ac-
tivities
COD, CAPE. See Cape Cod
COD fishing
Fishing the deep freeze. T. Kerasote. il por
Outdoor Life 146:38-41+ D '70
CODDING, George A. jr
Tentative obituary. Nation 211:307 O 5 '70
CODDINGTON, Dean C. and Milliken, J. G.
Future of federal contract research centers.
bibliog f il Harvard Bsns R 48:103-16 Mr '70
CODFISH fishing
See also
Pollack fishing
CODY, William Frederick
Cody, kings. & coronets. D. Russell. il pors
Am West 7:4-10+ Jl '70 *
COE, Charles
One simple decision. Nat R 22:950+ S 8 '70

COE, Lee
Truth about pet foods. il Pop Mech 134:123-
5+ O '70
CO-ED dormitories. See Dormitories
COEDUCATION
At Bennington the boys are the coeds. T.
Meehan; discussion. N Y Times Mag p4+
Ja 25 '70
Coeducation as a world trend. R. Greenough.
Sch & Soc 98:31-2 Ja '70
Girls at Yale. P. Goldberger. il Todays Ed
59:50-1 O '70
Greening of the fighting Irish. J. Kirshen-
baum. il Sports Illus 33:76-8+ D 14 '70
Here come the girls; new trend among boys'
prep schools. Newsweek 75:70 My 25 '70
Yale & female; Meanwhile . . . back at Vas-
sar. B. Baer; W. J. McKean. il Look 34:
24-8+ F 24 '70
COELENTERATES
See also
Corals
Sea anemones
Sea pens
Sponges
COEXISTENCE. See World politics, 1945-
COEXISTENCE policy. See United States—
Foreign relations—Russia
COFFEE, Frank K.
Are you ready for a new career? il Mech
Illus 66:60-2+ D '70
Family fun amphibians. il Mech Illus 66:46-
8+ Jl '70
How to keep burglars out. il Mech Illus 66:
70-2+ Jl '70
Newest thing under the sun: condominium
campsites. il Mech Illus 66:42-4 Ag '70
There's money in your attic! il Mech Illus
66:92-4+ O '70
Things to do now to cut your 1970 taxes.
il Mech Illus 66:50-2+ N '70
COFFEE
Instant coffees. il Consumer Rep 36:32-5 Ja
'71
See also
Caffeine
Prices
Iced coffee chills a pact on prices. il Bsns W
p44 F 14 '70
U.S. battles Brazil to a coffee break. il
Bsns W p 15-16 Ag 8 '70
COFFEE cake
Good idea. or two: mincemeat coffeecake,
lemon loaves. J. Hewitt. N Y Times Mag
p96 N 8 '70
COFFEE cups. See Cups
COFFEE industry and trade
See also
International coffee council
Brazil
Bitter brew for the economy. il Bsns W p27
Jl 25 '70
Iced coffee chills a pact on prices; Brazilian
freeze. il Bsns W p44 F 14 '70
U.S. battles Brazil to a coffee break. il
Bsns W p 15-16 Ag 8 '70
COFFEE parties. See Entertaining
COFFEE pots, percolators, etc.
Electric coffee-makers. Consumer Rep 34:
98-106 D '69
COFFEE rust. See Rusts (botany)
COFFEE table books. See Picture books
COFFEE tables. See Tables
COFFEE trees
Diseases and pests
Coffee nerves in Brazil. il Time 96:46 O 19 '70
See also
Rusts (botany)
COFFER, Helene Lewis
And then there was love; story. Good H 170:
66-7 F '70
Love song; story. Good H 171:84-5 O '70
COFFEY, J. I.
Soviet ABM and arms control. il Bul Atom
Sci 26:39-43 Ja '70
COFFEY, Raymond R.
Teach-in on the environment. Nation 210:390-
2 Ap 6 '70
COFFEY, Samuel J.
Planning facilities for an educational pro-
gram. Clear House 45:169-72 N '70
COFFIN, David L.
Profitable problems. A. A. Butkus. por Duns
96:60 O '70 *
COFFIN, LaVerne W.
Writing song lyrics. Engl J 59:954-5 O '70
COFFIN, Patricia
Beautiful barkeep of Bequia. il pors Look
34:56-61 D 15 '70

COFFIN, William Sloane, 1924-
Conspiracy charges dropped against Coffin. Goodman. Chr Cent 87:655 My 27 '70 *
COFFINO, Philip and others
Immunoglobulin production: method for quantitatively detecting variant myeloma cells. bibliog il Science 167:186-8 Ja 9 '70
COFFINS
Man's best friend, R.I.P; pet casket. il Chr Cent 87:1303 O 28 '70
COGAR corporation
Billboards with choice targets. il Bsns W p 122 Ap 11 '70
COGGESHALL, Roger G.
Propagation of hybrid rhododendrons. il Horticulture 48:30-1+ My '70
COGGINS, C. W. jr, and others
Lycopene accumulation induced by 2-(4-chlorophenylthio)-triethylamine hydrochloride. bibliog Science 168:1589-90 Je 26 '70
COGGINS, Dessie-Ellen
Bulk freezing saves time, money and effort. il Org Gard & Farm 17:110-12 N '70
Five steps to creativity. il Parents Mag 45: 52-3+ Mr '70
COGGINS, Jack Roland
Dry-farming free-use land. il Org Gard & Farm 17:54-6 S '70
Starting cabbages in a bread box. il Org Gard & Farm 17:54-5 F '70
Watermelons at your back door! il Org Gard & Farm 17:74-5 Ap '70
Why I plant the whole potato. il Org Gard & Farm 17:58-9 Mr '70
COGLEY, John
Paul, poor fellow, has no friends. Life 68:30-1 Mr 20 '70

about

He studied the Pope, she followed a friend. R. Graves. il por Life 68:3 Mr 20 '70 *
COHELEACH, Guy
Killer! painting. il Audubon 72:40-1 Ja '70
Unknown owl; painting. Audubon 72:56-7 Jl '70
Vespers thrush; painting. il Audubon 72:40-1 My '70

about

National wildlife visits Guy Coheleach. R. B. Kirkpatrick. il pors Nat Wildlife 8:41-3 O '70 *
COHEN, Abraham
Screenings: 8mm (cont) Library J 95:228, 762, 1183, 1924-5 Ja 15, F 15, Mr 15, My 15 '70
COHEN, Abraham, 1913-
Sports hall of fame. il por Parks & Rec 5:28-9 Ap '70
COHEN, Alvin J. and Hassan, Farkhonda
Iron in synthetic quartz: heat and radiation induced changes. bibliog il Science 167:176-7 Ja 9 '70
COHEN, Arthur Allen
Myth of the Judeo-Christian tradition; excerpts. Commentary 48:73-7 N '69; 49:6+ Ja '70
COHEN, Audrey
Self-made college. il por Time 96:53-4 Jl 6 '70 *
COHEN, Bessie
Return of $1 guest. por Newsweek 76:89 N 16 '70 *
COHEN, Daniel
Enigma of the lost Etruscans. il Sci Digest 68:10-16 S '70
Mystery of the Nazca lines. il Sci Digest 67: 46-8+ My '70
Those mysterious woolly mammoths. il Sci Digest 67:44-8+ Ja '70
COHEN, Edwin Samuel
Can income tax forms ever be simplified? excerpts from address, March 18, 1970. por U S News 68:76-7 Ap 6 '70
COHEN, Eleanor L.
Getting ready to read. il PTA Mag 65:18-20 bibliog(p32) N '70
COHEN, Gerald, and Collins, Michael
Alkaloids from catecholamines in adrenal tissues: possible role in alcoholism. bibliog il Science 167:1749-51 Mr 27 '70
COHEN, Isidore M.
Man who came to dinner. Newsweek 75:74 Je 8 '70 *
COHEN, Jerome Alan
China policy. Atlan 227:12+ Ja '71
COHEN, Joan Lebold
Taiwan; the country and its art. il Travel & Camera 33:73-5 Mr '70
COHEN, Larry
America as film, film as America. il Art in Am 58:68-73 S '70
Making of Little murders. il por Sat R 53: 19-21 Ag 8 '70

about

Nature of the crime. Criticism New Yorker 46:62+ Ap 4 '70 *

COHEN, Lauren W.
Romeo and Juliet: living is being relevant. Engl J 59:1263-5+ D '70
COHEN, Lisa. See Barman, A. jt. auth.
COHEN, Manuel Frederick
Manny Cohen looks at the market; interview, ed. by G. R. Rosen. por Duns 95:10-12+ Ap '70
COHEN, Martin
Extravagant tour that's everything, except expensive. Redbook 134:71-2+ Mr '70
COHEN, Philip P.
Biochemical differentiation during amphibian metamorphosis. bibliog il Science 168:533-43 My 1 '70
COHEN, Richard
Public aid to nonpublic schools in 1969. Sch & Soc 98:300-1 Sum '70
COHEN, Robert M. See Ray, E. jt. auth.
COHEN, Selma Jeanne
To be a dancer. il pors Opera N 34:26-9 Ap 18 '70
COHEN, Stanley, and others
Estrogenic induction of ornithine decarboxylase in vivo and vitro. bibliog il Science 170:336-8 O 16 '70
COHESION
    See also
Adhesion
COHN, Arthur
Elie Siegmeister: a record of more than ordinary importance. por Am Rec G 36:520-1 Mr '70
First recordings of works by Leon Kirchner and Henry Weinberg, a celebration of newness. il Am Rec G 36:552-3 Ap '70
First recordings: Sessions and Lees. Am Rec G 36:298+ D '69
Playing and conducting that simply could not be bettered. pors Am Rec G 37:148-51 N '70
Virtuosic crackerjack. il por Am Rec G 36: 656-7 My '70
COHN, Cal K. and others
Reduced catechol-O-methyltransferase activity in red blood cells of women with primary affective disorder. bibliog il Science 170:1323-4 D 18 '70
COHN, Jules
Is business meeting the challenge of urban affairs? il Harvard Bsns R 48:68-82 Mr '70
COHN, Melvin. See Bretscher, P. jt. auth.
COHO salmon. See Salmon
COIL springs. See Springs (mechanism)
COIN banks. See Banks, Coin
COINAGE of words. See Words, New
COINS
Cents of 1793. C. French. il Hobbies 75:132 Mr '70
Coin quiz. C. F. French. See issues of Hobbies
Coming: a new batch of silver dollars; Eisenhower dollars. il U S News 69:55 D 21 '70
Silver coins: sell 'em or save 'em? il Changing T 24:36 My '70
Unlucky threes. C. F. French. il Hobbies 75: 132 D '70
Whatever happened to silver coins and certificates? il U S News 68:14 F 16 '70
Whatever happened to the Eisenhower dollar? il U S News 69:43 N 23 '70
    See also
Silver as money
COIRO, Cynthia
Dentists put teeth in research. Har Yrs 10: 48-9 Je '70
How did you sleep last night? il Har Yrs 10:22-5 Ag '70
How much money do you need? il Har Yrs 10:48-50 Ja '70
Keep your feet walking. il Har Yrs 10:48-50 Mr '70
Magic of exercise. bibliog il Har Yrs 10:14-18 My '70
Senior power breaks the barriers. il Har Yrs 10:6-12 O '70
COIT, Lew G.
It's a good time to buy stocks; interview. il Changing T 24:35-40 Ap '70
COKE, Van Deren
Toys of Tecomatepec. il Américas 22:36-41 Mr '70
COKE industry and trade
Coke squeeze pinches steel. il Bsns W p46 Mr 14 '70
Kaiser's black gold. T. J. Murray. Duns 96: 66-7 Jl '70
Mining coal for hungry steel mills; Kaiser resources complex in British Columbia. il Bsns W p 114+ Je 27 '70
COLA beverages. See Beverages
COLAS, Alain
Another ocean, another record. il por Yachting 127:74+ F '70

COLBERT, Lester Lum
Where are they now? R. Levy. pors Duns 95: 41-2 Je '70 *

COLBY, Carroll B.
Camp chef. See issues of Outdoor life
Camping. See issues of Outdoor life
Unexpected twist. V. M. Grinager. il pors Outdoor Life 145:22-3 Ja '70

COLCHICINE
Chromosome pairing: effect of colchicine on an isochromosome. C. J. Driscoll and N. L. Darvey. bibliog il Science 169:290-1 Jl 17 '70

COLD
See also
Cryobiology

Physiological effects
Ragged edge of life; chill factor. J. B. Scott. il Field & S 75:48-9 D '70
Wind chill factor. B. Kevern. il Sci Digest 68:56-9 D '70

Therapeutic use
Engineers apply skills to medical devices; heat transfer projects. il Todays Health 48:13 Ag '70
Hippocrates vindicated; effects of cold on bleeding. Time 97:60 Ja 4 '71

COLD (disease)
Case of vitamin C. por Sci N 98:477 D 26 '70
Living with a runny nose; interview. D. A. J. Tyrrell. il Sci Digest 68:56-60 S '70
New research in seeking to prevent the common cold. il Good H 170:192 Mr '70
Pediatrician's guide to colds, grippe, flu; excerpts from When your child is ill. S. Karelitz. Ladies Home J 87:36+ Ja '70
Think twice about that sore throat. G. M. Knox. Bet Hom & Gard 48:16+ N '70
Vitamin C, anyone? theories of L. Pauling. por Newsweek 76:63-4 N 30 '70

COLD drinks. See Beverages

COLD frames
Cold frame salads; buttercrunch. K. McReynolds. il Org Gard & Farm 17:86 F '70
My movable three-in-one cold frame. O. E. Henderson. il Org Gard & Farm 17:58 Jl '70

COLD soups. See Soups

COLD storage
See also
Food preservation and preservatives

COLD war. See World politics; World politics, 1945-

COLD war (United States and Russia) See United States—Foreign relations—Russia

COLD weather
Jacques frost; Europe's recent winter weather. il Time 97:27-8 Ja 18 '71

COLD weather photography. See Photography—Cold weather conditions

COLDS. See Cold (disease)

COLDWELL, Banker and company
Head start; growing into a national company. il Forbes 106:46 O 1 '70

COLE, Edward N.
New engineering; address, January 14, 1970. Vital Speeches 36:236-40 F 1 '70

COLE, Glen F.
Managing the Yellowstone elk. il Nat Parks & Con Mag 44:20-2 S '70

COLE, K. C.
Prague, two years after. il N Y Times Mag p7-9+ Ag 16 '70

COLE, Kathleen
Illiteracy, abettor of poverty. Focus 20:12 Ja '70

COLE, Larry
Street kids; excerpt. Harp Baz 10:168 N '70

COLE, Martin
Room 8: a venture in immortality. il PTA Mag 64:6-7 Ap '70

COLE, Mary Howland
Chinatown's library. il por Wilson Lib Bul 45:482-4 Ja '71

COLE, Richard C.
Runabouts and utility boats. il por Motor B 125:98-9 Ja '70

COLE, Vicki Lynne
Bring-us-together girl. il por Newsweek 75: 16 Je 1 '70 *

COLE, William
New insight into the brain's defenses. il Todays Health 48:50-3 Mr '70
Right to be well-born. il Todays Health 49: 42-4+ Ja '71
Selfish art. il por Pub W 197:89-91 F 23 '70
Tots in the tower of babble. il Todays Health 48:54-5+ D '70
(ed) See Serrato. J. C. Let's give foreign doctors a fair shake

COLE, William (journalist)
Televised *Samizdat*. por Newsweek 76:43 Ag 10 '70 *

COLEBROOK, Joan
Cairo journal. Commentary 50:45-55 O '70
Our far-flung correspondents. New Yorker 46: 70+ S 5 '70

COLEMAN, A. D.
Roy DeCarava: thru black eyes. il Pop Phot 66:68-71+ Ap '70
Russians are here! il Pop Phot 66:88-91+ Je '70

COLEMAN, James Samuel
Teachers do make a difference; current status of research on pupil achievement. J. Chaffee, jr. and P. Wagner. il Am Ed 6:23-5 My '70 *

COLEMAN, John A.
Lords of the rock. America 122:465-7 My 2 '70

COLEMAN, Lonnie
Place for Polly. Criticism
New Yorker 46:95 Ap 25 '70 *

COLEMAN, Michael
Brief biography. S. Goodman. pors Dance Mag 44:72-3 Ag '70 *

COLEMAN, Robert G.
Seventeen-year locust, a report for 1971. il Horticulture 49:24 Ja '71

COLEOPTILES
Dextranase activity in coleoptiles of avena. A. N. J. Heyn. bibliog il Science 167:874-5 F 6 '70

COLERIDGE, Samuel Taylor
Frost at midnight: the other Coleridge. R. A. Audet. Engl J 59:1080-5 N '70 *
Rime of the ancient mariner: the agony of thirst. M. J. Lupton. bibliog f Am Imago 27:140-59 Sum '70 *

COLES, Robert
Doctor and newcomers to the ghetto; excerpt from Children of crisis. Am Scholar 40:66-80 Wint '70
Fashionable kind of slander. Atlan 226:53-5 N '70
Lord of the ghettos. il Commonweal 93:167-74 N 13 '70
Profiles: E. H. Erikson. por New Yorker 46:51-4+ N 7; 59-60+ N 14 '70
(ed) Teaching morality: a parent's most difficult challenge; interviews. Redbook 136: 82+ D '70

COLETTE, Sidonie Gabrielle
Colette, Cocteau, and Proust. R. Phelps. il Mlle 72:124-5+ D '70 *
Undying fascination of Colette. R. Phelps. il pors McCalls 97:12+ S '70 *

COLETTE; drama. See Jones, E.

COLFAX highway association
Historic district gets saved from both progress and neglect. il Sunset 145:52+ N '70

COLGATE, Richard M.
Colgate's gift establishes Morgan horse breeding farm. il por Parks & Rec 5:30-2 F '70 *

COLGATE, Steve
12-meter gear, 1970 style. il Yachting 129: 92-3 Ja '71

COLIC
Colic: a new approach to a common problem. R. C. Grady. il Parents Mag 45:42-3+ Jl '70

COLICINES
Colicin-tolerant mutants of escherichia coli: resistance of membranes to colicin El. P. Bhattacharyya and others. bibliog il Science 168:998-1000 My 22 '70
Phage, colicins, and macroregulatory phenomena; Nobel lecture, December 12, 1969. S. E. Luria. bibliog Science 168:1166-70 Je 5 '70

COLIFORM bacteria. See Colon bacilli

COLLAGE
Am I in art or English? use of collage for communication. J. Gates. Engl J 59:988-9 O '70
Golda Lewis: from collage to compage. G. Lewis. il Craft Horiz 30:52-3 Ag '70
Junk prints. L. J. Miller. il Design 72:17-19 Fall '70
Monster in the imagination: fantasy doodles, collages and paper cutouts, by H. C. Andersen. il por Time 96:60-1 O 19 '70
Occurrence: Z. David's pictures with paper matches. New Yorker 46:31 Ag 22 '70
Paper as a personal medium. H. S. Paston. il Design 72:29 Wint '70
Place for everything. J. Ashbery. il por Art N 69:32-3+ Mr '70
Strong currents; R. Rauschenberg show at the Pasadena art museum. D. Davis. il por Newsweek 76:69B Jl 27 '70

COLLAGEN
Collagen: mobile water content of frozen fibers. R. E. Dehl. bibliog il Science 170: 738-9 N 13 '70
Collagen molecules: distribution of alpha chains. J. G. Nold and others. bibliog il Science 170:1096-8 D 4 '70

COLLAGENASE
Collagenase; report of meeting. I. Mandl. Science 169:1234-6+ S 18 '70

COLLECT calls; story. See Adler, R.

COLLECTING. See Collectors and collecting

COLLECTING of accounts
Business piles up for bill collectors. il Bsns W p25 S 12 '70

COLLECTIVE bargaining
AFL-CIO guideline: a 10 per cent pay boost in '70. Bsns W p 102 F 28 '70

Another year of crisis bargaining. il U S News 70:41-2 Ja 4 '71

Art of bluffing in labor negotiations. D. Lawrence. U S News 68:96 Mr 16 '70

Cost of living inflates union wage demands. il Bsns W p84-5 F 7 '70

Freedom to strike is in the public interest. T. Kennedy. bibliog f il Harvard Bsns R 48:45-57 Jl '70; Same abr. with title Should we abolish all strikes? Cur 121:32-6 S '70

Getting harder to talk tough. Bsns W p42 F 21 '70

How to win at the bargaining table. W. Wingo. il Nations Bsns 58:38-42 F '70

New pattern for bargaining; coordinated bargaining by unions. Bsns W p51 S 5 '70

No quiet on labor front. il Newsweek 75:65-6 Ap 13 '70

Profiles; T. W. Kheel. F. C. Shapiro. New Yorker 46:36-44+ Ag 1 '70

Steel bargaining tops '71's calendar. Bsns W p72-3 Ja 9 '71

Student bargaining. J. Harrison. New Repub 163:10-11 N 21 '70; Discussion. 163:31-2 D 12 '70

Union and industry leaders look ahead, and see trouble. il U S News 68:61-2 Je 1 '70

Union bargaining goals in the 1970's. R. A. Oswald. bibliog f Mo Labor R 93:40-2 Mr '70

U.S. can't afford what labor wants; with editorial comment. il Bsns W p 104-8, 134 Ap 11 '70

Wages of inflation. il Newsweek 75:70-1 F 16 '70

Who cares about the public interest? compulsory arbitration. D. Lawrence. U S News 69:80 D 21 '70

Worker participation in Swedish enterprise; excerpt from Worker participation in the enterprise: the Swedish experience. R. B. Peterson. Mo Labor R 93:48-50 Ap '70

See also
Industrial relations
Trade agreements

Agricultural machinery industry
Farm equipment talks bog down. Bsns W p70-1 O 3 '70

Air pilots
Added benefits sought by pilots. L. Doty. Aviation W 93:22-3 Ag 24 '70

BOAC pilots reject wage offer; other unions ask larger raises. Aviation W 94:28 Ja 11 '71

Airlines
Emergency boards in the airline industry, 1936-69; Railway labor act's emergency dispute procedures. M. H. Cimini. il Mo Labor R 93:57-65 Jl '70

Airplane industry
Agreement reached in airline strike. U S News 68:64 Je 1 '70

Automobile industry
After the offer: collision course in Detroit. il Bsns W p13-14 S 5 '70

As auto makers brace for a strike. il U S News 68:80-2 My 11 '70

Auto talks fail to melt the ice. Bsns W p43-4 O 17 '70

Auto talks take the direct route; with editorial comment. il Bsns W p 17, 100 Jl 25 '70

Auto workers' demands for 1970. il U S News 69:59-60 Jl 20 '70

Back to the big table. il Bsns W p24-5 O 10 '70

Before the auto strike can be ended—. il U S News 69:82-3 O 5 '70

Big stakes in the auto talks. il Time 96:53-4 S 7 '70

Both sides talk tough in Detroit: some of the issues. Bsns W p 16-17 Ag 22 '70

Collision course in Detroit. il Time 96:82 S 14 '70

Costly end to a costly strike. il Newsweek 76:101-2 N 23 '70

Deadline for auto strike: where both sides stand. il U S News 69:63-4 S 14 '70

Detroit girds for war. America 123:54-5 Ag 8 '70

Drawing the line for auto talks. Bsns W p69 Je 27 '70

GM and Ford take positions for July 15 wage talks. il U S News 69:65-6 Jl 6 '70

Heading for the strike nobody wants. il por Newsweek 76:79-80+ S 14 '70

Higher wages in a poor year? U S News 68:78 Mr 23 '70

On the long, rocky road to an auto contract. Bsns W p60 Ag 1 '70

Record wage hike for auto workers: Reuther's strategy. il U S News 68:81-2 Ap 27 '70

Strike outlook for the rest of 1970. il U S News 69:101-3 S 21 '70

Talks grind down toward the deadline. Bsns W p22-3 S 12 '70

UAW and companies state their cases. il U S News 69:52-3 Ag 3 '70

UAW rehearses some tough bargaining talk. il Bsns W p 124+ Ap 25 '70

Why Reuther faces toughest bargaining test. il por U S News 68:63-4 My 4 '70

History
One strike and you're out; interview. L. G. Seaton. pors Motor T 22:26-8+ S '70

Book Industries and trade
Harper & Row employees to seek arbitration. Pub W 197:38-9 Mr 30 '70

Building industry
Black Monday's Sunday allies. il Ramp Mag 8:34-8 Ja '70

Broader roof over building talks. Bsns W p80+ Jl 11 '70

Construction management & union; address, October 7, 1970. J. E. Healy, 2d. il Vital Speeches 37:113-16 D 1 '70

Labor peace of Disney world; Orlando, Fla. U S News 70:43 Ja 4 '71

Electric industries
GE strike didn't kill Boulwarism. Bsns W p32 O 24 '70

General electric settlement; pattern for the future? il U S News 68:67-8 F 9 '70

Government employees
When cities collide with the unions; with editorial comment. il Bsns W p24-7+, 56 2 '71

Farm labor
Bishops in the vineyard. L. T. King. Commonweal 92:214 My 15 '70

Chavez: one battle ends, another begins. U S News 69:49-51 Ag 10 '70

Grape fight spreads to other crops. L. M. Palmer. Farm J 94:22 S '70

Farmers
Potato growers protest with fire. il Bsns W p29-30 Ap 4 '70

Government employees
Changing policies in public employee labor relations; with table. J. P. Goldberg. bibliog f Mo Labor R 93:5-14 Jl '70

Crucial tests for hands off policy in strikes. il U S News 68:71-3 Ap 13 '70

Impasse, grievance, and arbitration in federal collective bargaining. R. W. Glass. il Mo Labor R9 3:55-7 Ap '70

Mailmen flout Trudeau's limit. Bsns W p 116 S 12 '70

Postal workers test federal procedures. U S News 69:84 O 5 '70

Reflections on the future of bargaining in the public sector; excerpt from address, May 1970. E. W. Bakke. Mo Labor R 93:21-5 Jl '70

Revolt of public workers. il Newsweek 75:78A-78B My 4 '70

Ways to bargain with public workers; proposal by the Twentieth century fund. U S News 68:83 Ap 28 '70

Hospital employees
Plan to resolve impasses in hospital bargaining. T. W. Kheel and L. B. Kaden. Mo Labor R 93:45-8 Ap '70

Maritime workers
Dock workers set tough goals. Bsns W p69 N 28 '70

Municipal employees
Mayors skeptical about arbitration. U S News 68:51-2 Je 29 '70

Pay boosts for public-service workers. U S News 69:88-9 S 28 '70

COLLECTIVE bargaining—*Continued*

Petroleum industry

Job hazards hit the bargaining table. Bsns W p88 D 12 '70

Railroads

Double trouble for railroads. U S News 69: 87-8 S 28 '70

For Congress: a lonesome whistle? long fight over firemen. U S News 69:60-1 Jl 20 '70

Hard bargaining around the bend. Bsns W p25 N 14 '70

How rail threat was postponed. U S News 69:84 O 5 '70

Once again: threat of nationwide rail strike. il U S News 69:37-8 N 23 '70

Pressure builds for a rail strike. Bsns W p53+ D 5 '70

Rail fight goes another round; with editorial comment. il Bsns W p41-2 D 19 '70

Throttling down the rail crisis. Bsns W p78 Jl 18 '70

Why the railroad disputes still go on and on. U S News 69:46 D 21 '70

Steel industry

New pattern for basic steel? Bsns W p78 N 7 '70

Steelworkers unveil contract demands. U S News 69:66-7 N 30 '70

Anecdotes, facetiae, satire, etc.

Revolt of Enoch Peters; reprint of 1960 article. il Nat R 22:886-9 Ag 25 '70

Teachers

Achieving a meeting of minds. R. Perry. Todays Ed 59:34-5 F '70

Collective bargaining vs. collective gaining. R. Wynn. Ed Digest 36:13-16 S '70

Impact of school decentralization on collective bargaining. M. H. Moskow and K. McLennan. Mo Labor R 93:51-3 Ap '70

Is the teaching profession gaining or losing? S. L. Clement. Clear House 44:556-8 My '70

NEA prepares for the 1970's. H. F. Cohany. Mo Labor R 93:30-1 S '70

Teacher militancy and collective negotiations. L. S. Vander Werf; S. M. Elkin; J. W. Maguire. bibliog Sch & Soc 98:171-7 Mr '70

Teachers' strike ends in lost ground; East St Louis, Ill. U S News 69:71 D 7 '70

Today chancery, tomorrow Albany; settling with lay teahers. P. Tracy. Commonweal 91:574-5 F 27 '70

Trucking industry

As truckers moved toward deadline. U S News 68:71 Ap 6 '70

Industry pact wins teamster approval. U S News 68:64 Je 1 '70

Teamsters, truckers: wide gap on wages. U S News 68:56 Ja 19 '70

Trucking pact: a pattern for big raises in other industries? U S News 69:60 Jl 13 '70

Trucks highball toward a crisis. il Bsns W p22-3 Ap 4 '70

COLLECTIVE bargaining, industry wide

Too much democracy in bargaining. B. L. Masse. America 122:462 My 2 '70

Way to fence in construction pay; bill for area-wide bargaining. Bsns W p53 D 5 '70

COLLECTIVE farms

Russia

Rural Russia today. M. K. Whyte. il Trans-Action 7:26-32 Ja '70

COLLECTIVE labor agreements. See Trade agreements

COLLECTIVE security. See International security

COLLECTIVE settlements

Art of group scrounging. R. Gustaitis. Holiday 47:55+ Mr '70

Bringing up the next generation; Moravian communal rearing of children. Trans-Action 7:10 Jl '70

Communes: a challenge to all of us. M. Mead. Redbook 135:51-2 Ag '70

Communes and nurseries: are they as good for children as they are helpful to mothers? B. Spock. Redbook 135:28+ O '70

Communes and the work crisis. L. M. Andrews. Nation 211:460-3 N 9 '70

Has monogamy failed? H. A. Otto. Sat R 53:23-5+ Ap 25 '70

Living together in California. M. Zane. il Nation 211:360-3 O 19 '70

New designs for family living. M. Mead. Redbook 135:22+ O '70

New Mexico: no mecca for hippies. S. F. Wheeler. Chr Cent 87:828-30 Jl 1 '70

New way to raise kids; interview, ed. by J. Whitbread, B. Bettelheim. il por Look 34: 64+ F 24 '70

On the edge of disaster; rural communes. R. Hoffmann. Mlle 70:222-3+ Ap '70

Open land: getting back to the communal garden. S. Davidson. il Harper 240:91-100+ Je '70; Reply with rejoinder. 241:6+ Ag '70

Walden two; three? Many more?; Twin Oakes commune, Va. R. Todd. il por N Y Times Mag p24-5+ Mr 15 '70

Wow, like let's really try to win; C. Oliver's life at a commune. B. Newnham. il pors Sports Illus 33:50-4 O 12 '70

Your global alternative: communes, experiments, jails and hidey-holes. H. Gardner. il Esquire 74:106-9 S '70

See also
Shakers
Synanon city, Calif.

Israel

Growing up in a kibbutz. L. Verin. il Parents Mag 45:56-8+ Ap '70

Our life on a border kibbutz. C. Abrams and A. Abrams. il pors Nat Geog 138:364-91 S '70

COLLECTORS and collecting

Collectors' notes; ed. by E. Gaines. See issues of Antiques

There's money in your attic! F. K. Coffee. il Mech Illus 66:92-4+ O '70

See also
Autographs
Book collecting
Bottles
Display of antiques, art objects, etc.
Dolls
Miniature objects
also subhead Collectors and collecting under various subjects, e.g. Rocks—Collectors and collecting

COLLEGE, Choice of

College & careers. D. Klein. See issues of Seventeen

COLLEGE administration. See Colleges and universities—Administration

COLLEGE administrators. See College officials

COLLEGE admission. See Colleges and universities—Entrance requirements

COLLEGE All-Star game. See All-Star football game

COLLEGE alumni. See College graduates

COLLEGE and school drama

Big adventures; new works at the University of California at Davis and Boston university. H. Hewes. Sat R 53:16 Mr 21 '70

Report:
  Stanley Silverman's Elephant steps at Hunter college. J. W. Freeman. Opera N 34:23 Je 13 '70

War and pieces; student unrest becomes creative theater. C. Matheson and others. il Todays Ed 59:20-3 Mr '70

COLLEGE and school journalism

Innocent bystander; Harvard's Halcyon. L. E. Sissman. Atlan 227:26-8 Ja '71

Libel and private college newspapers. J. S. Corcoran. bibliog Sch & Soc 98:354-6 O '70

Paper tiger, with teeth. J. Marks. Mlle 71: 226-7+ Ag '70

Should high schools give student editors a free hand? pro and con discussion. Sr Schol 96:8-9 F 2 '70

Student newspapers should be free, accurate, and fair. Sch & Soc 98:327 O '70

Teaching writing; Teachers and writers collaborative newsletter and Foxfire. J. Featherstone. New Repub 163:11-14 Jl 11 '70

Their time is now; three books on the high school underground press. R. F. Allen. Schol Teach Jr/Sr High p19+ D 7 '70

Too bad; excerpts from high school underground newspapers. il Esquire 73:61-2 F '70

What does student writing tell us? R. G. Holland. il Todays Ed 59:37-8+ My '70

What is a good high school newspaper? F. M. Bixler. Engl J 59:119-21 Ja '70

COLLEGE and the community. See Colleges and universities—Public relations

COLLEGE annuals

Kidspeak; University of Connecticut's yearbook, Nutmeg. W. F. Buckley, jr. Nat R 22:1178 N 3 '70

COLLEGE aptitude tests. See Aptitude tests

COLLEGE architecture

Academic village; State university college at Purchase, N.Y. J. Dixon. il Arch Forum 133:34-41 N '70

Amherst college science center, Amherst, Mass. il Arch Rec 147:112-13 Ja '70

Architectural analogy; St Vincent science center. R. Jensen. il Arch Rec 147:125-30 My '70

COLLEGE architecture—*Continued*

Big scale science center on a small scale campus. il Arch Rec 147:114-18 F '70

Building types study. il Arch Rec 147:143 Je '70

Campus: architecture's show place. il Time 96:76-82 S 21 '70

Campus of many spaces; Rissho university, Tokyo. il Arch Forum 132:34-9 My '70

Campus within a campus; Academic complex and art center at the University of Wisconsin in Madison. P. Blake. il Arch Forum 133:42-7 N '70

Center of action; Berkeley student center. R. Montgomery. il Arch Forum 132:64-71 Ap '70

Designs for the campus; building types study. il Arch Rec 147:101-18 F '70

Mathematics at Yale: new mathematics building. E. P. Berkeley. il Arch Forum 133:62-5 Jl '70; Discussion. 133:64-6 O '70

New galaxies at Chicago circle. J. Dixon. il Arch Forum 133:24-33 N '70

Retreat for executives: Oxford center for management studies. il Arch Forum 132:40-3 My '70

Science building; contemporary yet sedate, for an old southern college. il Arch Rec 147:110-11 F '70

Science labs in a garden; Claremont, Calif. il Arch Forum 132:30-3 My '70

Skidmore college. il Arch Rec 147:91-102 Mr '70

Two parts into one whole; Fine Hall and Jadwin Hall, Princeton. il Arch Forum 133:52-7 Jl '70

See also
Dormitories
Gymnasiums

COLLEGE art association of America
Art association tremors have familiar ring. Library J 95:2860 S 15 '70
Art librarians desert ALA and SLA for CAA. Library J 95:1265 Ap 1 '70

See also
New art association

COLLEGE at Old Westbury. See New York (state). State university—College at Old Westbury

COLLEGE athletes. See Athletes

COLLEGE athletics
Dissident varsity. S. Murdock. Nation 210:305-8 Mr 16 '70

See also
Basketball
Football
Gymnasiums
Lacrosse
Rowing
Track athletics

COLLEGE attendance. See Colleges and universities—Attendance

COLLEGE bookstores
Are college bookstores contributing to unrest? Pub W 198:37-8 N 2 '70
Boarded-up bookstore window. C. B. Grannis. Pub W 198:48 S 14 '70
Children's books capture college market. Pub W 197:41-2 Ap 6 '70
College bookstores and their customers: service or non-service. P. A. Farrell. il Pub W 198:18-19 N 30 '70
College stores feel the impact of tomorrow; excerpts from address. K. White. Pub W 197:45-6 My 4 '70
Earnings/patronage refund: worst Harvard coop year. Pub W 198:27 D 14 '70
Good riddance, 1970; duck, 1971. G. R. Smith. Pub W 199:41-2 Ja 4 '71
Revolution in campus bookselling: second look. I. Sanderson. Pub W 198:138-40 Jl 13 '70
Service industry which doesn't like to serve. R. H. Smith. Pub W 197:42 Ap 20 '70
Spaciousness key to Memphis state store. R. Hoffman. il Pub W 198:58-9 Jl 27 '70
Street people push Cambridge up against the wall. P. A. Farrell. il Pub W 198:49-51 O 5 '70
Student strikes and book sales; the Dartmouth experience. P. Johnson, jr. Pub W 198:265-6 Ag 31 '70

See also
Booksellers and bookselling—Textbooks
National association of college stores

COLLEGE buildings. See College architecture

COLLEGE clubs and societies
Negro-Caucasian club: a history; the American students' first-inter-racial organization. O. C. Johnson. il Negro Hist Bul 33:35-41 F '70

COLLEGE commencements. See Commencements

COLLEGE credits. See Grading and marking (students)

COLLEGE deans
Legal speedster: R. R. Davenport, dean of Duquesne university law school S. W. Morris. il pors Ebony 26:48-50+ D '70

COLLEGE degrees. See Degrees, Academic

COLLEGE discipline
Crackdown on campus. il Newsweek 76:96+ D 7 '70
Disciplinary procedures at the University of Chicago. Sch & Soc 98:204+ Ap '70
What student rights in education? excerpt from Academic freedom and academic anarchy. S. Hook. Cur 117:21-7 Ap '70

COLLEGE dormitories. See Dormitories

COLLEGE drama. See College and school drama

COLLEGE education
College is a family affair. il pors Ebony 25:50-2+ Mr '70
Crisis in American higher education; address, February 7, 1970. E. A. Walker. Vital Speeches 36:362-4 Ap 1 '70
Decade of change in southern higher education. Sch & Soc 98:434-5 N '70
Educational opportunity: Great Britain. R. Haughton. Cath World 212:7-8 O '70
Helping the needy go to college; the President's plan; text of message to Congress, March 19, 1970. R. M. Nixon. il por U S News 68:51-4 Mr 30 '70; Same. Am Ed 6:28-31 My '70
Let's break the go-to-college lockstep. E. K. Faltermayer. il Fortune 82:98-103+ N '70
Resource allocation in higher education. J. A. Kershaw and A. M. Mood. Mo Labor R 93:46-8 Mr '70
Right to college. M. R. Berube. Commonweal 92:81-4 Ap 3 '70
Toward a pluralistic university? Sch & Soc 98:395 N '70
Toward the voluntary university; excerpts from address. K. Brewster, jr. Cur 117:19-21 Ap '70
What's going on in schools & colleges. See issues of Changing times

See also
Coeducation
Colleges and universities—Attendance
Colleges and universities—Curriculum
Educational acceleration
Humanities
Liberal education
Professional education

Aims and objectives

Aims of university reform. Sch & Soc 98:32-3 Ja '70

Are universities babysitters or what? M. Novak. Cur 117:16-18 Ap '70

Battle for earth; the supreme challenge to modern education; address, August 1, 1970. H. J. Zitko. Vital Speeches 36:692-6 S 1 '70

Campus unrest: the erosion of excellence; address, May 29, 1970. R. V. Andelson. Vital Speeches 36:619-21 Ag 1 '70

Challenges facing urban universities; adaptation of address, December 12, 1968. H. C. Syrett. Sch & Soc 98:89-91 F '70

Do students want education? M. Novak. Commonweal 92:10-13 Mr 13 '70; Reply. M. Raffini. 92:107 Ap 17 '70

Educated man in the age of Aquarius; address, June 7, 1970. R. White. Vital Speeches 36:638-9 Ag 1 '70

Enforced conformity; the big lie; address, June 9, 1970. N. M. Pusey. Vital Speeches 36:588-92 Jl 15 '70

Freedom and order on the campus; adaptation of address, January 12, 1970. S. E. Stumpf. Sch & Soc 98:401-3 N '70

Governance of universities in the cities of man; democratization of American higher education. K. B. Clark. Am Scholar 39:566+ Aut '70

Higher education as viewed by college and university presidents. R. L. Osmunson. bibliog Sch & Soc 98:367-70 O '70

How relevant are your courses? D. Klein. Seventeen 29:64+ Ap '70

Mess in higher education: faculty responsibility; address, October 17, 1969. S. J. Tonsor. Vital Speeches 36:250-3 F 1 '70

New reformation notes of a neolithic conservative, by P. Goodman. Review
Commonweal 93:152-5 N 6 '70. J. B. Gordon

On being educated in 1991; address, September 26, 1970. T. H. Bell. Vital Speeches 37:88-90 N 15 '70

COLLEGE education—Aims and objectives—
Continued
Preface to the catalogue of Curmudgeon college. J. Fischer. Harper 240:18+ Je '70; Same abr. with title Cheers for old Curmudgeon! Read Digest 97:188-90 S '70; Discussion. Harper 241:8-9 Ag '70
Proposal for combating campus revolution. E. B. Weisse. Sch & Soc 98:404-5 N '70
Purpose and function of the university. V. R. Potter and others. bibliog Science 167: 1590-3 Mr 20 '70; Reply. W. Stephenson. 168: 1041 My 29 '70
Reason as a basis for educational change. Sch & Soc 98:459-60 D '70
Revitalizing the college. Sch & Soc 98:7-10 Ja '70
Toward universities of the public interest. W. Arrowsmith. Cur 113:46-51 My '70
Value imperative. W. R. Barnhart. Chr Today 14:5 Jl 31 '70
What business is a university in? I. Kristol. il N Y Times Mag p30-1+ Mr 22 '70; Same abr. with title Toward universities for education. Cur 118:51-6 My '70; Reply with rejoinder. M. B. Goldstein. N Y Times Mag p 16+ Ap 19 '70

Anecdotes, facetiae, satire, etc.
Leo Rosten's handy-dandy plan to save our colleges. L. Rosten. Look 34:76+ D 15 '70

History
Universities and students, then and now. il Sch & Soc 98:6-7 Ja '70

COLLEGE education, Cost of
College costs: $5,000 a year a likely figure. il Bsns W p 121 Je 6 '70
College fees: it pays to plan ahead. Bsns W p65 Ag 8 '70
Getting into college: chances now. il U S News 68:28-30 Mr 23 '70
Rising cost of going to college. il U S News 68:32-3 F 9 '70

COLLEGE education, Experimental
College moves off campus to teach. il U S News 69:46-7 Ag 17 '70
For tomorrow's students, multiple choices. Fortune 82:147-8+ N '70
Free-form reforms on campus. il Time 97:46+ Ja 18 '71

COLLEGE education, Value of
Evils of occupational upgrading. J. W. Dykstra. Sch & Soc 98:98-100 F '70

COLLEGE education and state
Public support for private colleges. Sch & Soc 98:376-7 O '70

COLLEGE enrollment. See Colleges and universities—Attendance; Junior colleges—Attendance

COLLEGE entrance examination board
Bowdoin eliminates college board test requirements. Sch & Soc 98:271-2 Sum '70
New president of college board. Sch & Soc 98:272-4 Sum '70
Panel urges SAT overhaul. Sr Schol 96: Schol Teach 1-2 Ap 27 '70

Scholastic aptitude test
C for college boards. Time 96:49-50 N 16 '70
Calls for flexibility. Sat R 53:58 D 19 '70

COLLEGE entrance requirements. See Colleges and universities—Entrance requirements

COLLEGE football. See Football

COLLEGE football players. See Football players

COLLEGE for human services. See New York (city)—Education

COLLEGE freshmen. See College students

COLLEGE graduates
Advice to Princeton alumni; excerpts from address, 1970. A. Capp. il Nat R 22:994-6+ S 22 '70
New business student. il Newsweek 76:76 O 12 '70
Opportunities for community college graduates. Sch & Soc 98:396 N '70
Voices of Harvard '70. R. Todd. il N Y Times Mag p26-9+ Je 7 '70; Discussion. p56 Je 28 '70
Youth goals and national goals; address, June 7, 1970. M. Collins. Dept State Bul 62:804-7 Je 29 '70
See also
Colleges and universities—Graduate work

Employment
B.A.+M.A.+Ph.D=O? Sat R 53:77 Mr 21 '70
Bear market in sheepskins. Time 95:84 Mr 30 '70

Doctoral glut. il Newsweek 75:114 Mr 16 '70
Fewer jobs for the class of '70. il U S News 68:38-41 Mr 9 '70
Jobless graduates: a chronic condition? il U S News 69:75 Jl 27 '70
Most black college grads still want jobs where the money is. il Ebony 25:42-44A+ My '70
Once and future five-year gap; the Harvard class of '64. il Esquire 74:117-18 S '70
When grads go looking for jobs. il U S News 69:31 D 21 '70

COLLEGE graduates, Negro
Most black college grads still want jobs where the money is. il Ebony 25:42-44A+ My '70
Voices of Fisk '70. C. E. Lincoln and C. E. Lincoln. il N Y Times Mag p30-1+ Je 7 '70

COLLEGE grounds
See also
Campus planning

COLLEGE housing. See College students—Housing

COLLEGE investments. See Colleges and universities—Investments

COLLEGE journalism. See College and school journalism

COLLEGE librarians
Faculty status: where it's at. F. M. Blake. Am Lib 1:767-8 S '70
Layoff in California; San Diego state college library. F. K. Brose. il por Library J 95:3741-4 N 1 '70
Librarian and the scholar; eternal enemies; address, February 20, 1970. R. H. Logsdon. il por Library J 95:2871-4 S 15 '70
Sour grapes: easy answer to question of faculty status; letter to the editor. K. M. Cottam. Library J 95:2202 Je 15 '70
Status of California state college librarians; ALA report. Am Lib 1:57-9 Ja '70
Status search: California state college librarians. F. Blake. Library J 95:2096 Je 1 '70

Salaries
Graves of academe. Wilson Lib Bul 45:122 O '70; Reply. H. D. Gordon. 45:360-1 D '70

Tenure
ALA investigating team slaps U. of Mo. wrist. Library J 95:4211 D 15 '70
Tenure investigation: library administration division's report concerning nonrenewal of contracts of five librarians, University of Missouri library. Am Lib 1:983-4 N '70

COLLEGE libraries
Academic library building in 1970. J. Orne. il Library J 95:4107-12 D 1 '70
Are academic libraries too noisy? J. A. McCrossan. Am Lib 1:396 Ap '70
Building a new library for a new college; Ramapo college. A. Caruba. por Pub W 198: 29-30 O 26 '70
Educating the academic librarian. E. J. Josey and F. M. Blake. bibliog il pors Library J 95:125-30 Ja 15 '70
Librarian and the scholar; eternal enemies; address, February 20, 1970. R. H. Logsdon. il por Library J 95:2871-4 S 15 '70
Student unrest and the library. M. B. Cassata. bibliog il por Wilson Lib Bul 45:78-85 S '70
Undergrad library role questioned in Detroit. Library J 95:2594 Ag '70
Undergraduate library. J. Orne. il por Library J 95:2230-3 Je 15 '70

Acquisitions
Librarian vs. publisher; Drexel institute of technology, Philadelphia. J. Kesselman. il por Library J 95:4221-4 D 15 '70

Administration
See College library administration

Architecture
See Library architecture

Automation
How to computerize your serials and periodicals when you don't know how; experience of University of Alaska library. M. Matthews and S. Sherman. pors Wilson Lib Bul 44:861-4 Ap '70
LEEP at Syracuse: School of library science. J. A. McCrossan. Am Lib 1:493-4 My '70

Circulation, loans, etc.
Student-faculty common loan policy at Stevens institute. J. A. McCrossan. Am Lib 1:396-7 Ap '70

COLLEGE libraries—*Continued*

Federal aid

Federal aid to college libraries. Sch & Soc 98:399 N '70
HEA 11: quo vadis? G. Krettek and E. D. Cooke. Wilson Lib Bul 44:1080-1 Je '70

Instruction in use

See Libraries—Instruction in use

Standards

Faculty status: where it's at. F. M. Blake. Am Lib 1:767-8 S '70
Sour grapes: easy answer to question of faculty status; letter to the editor. K. M. Cottam. Library J 95:2202 Je 15 '70
Status of California state college librarians; ALA report. Am Lib 1:57-9 Ja '70
Status search: California state college librarians. F. Blake. Library J 95:2096 Je 1 '70

COLLEGE libraries and audio-visual materials. See Libraries and audio-visual materials
COLLEGE libraries and publishers
Librarian vs. publisher; Drexel institute of technology, Philadelphia. J. Kesselman. il por Library J 95:4221-4 D 15 '70
COLLEGE libraries and research. See Libraries and research
COLLEGE libraries and state
See also
College libraries—Federal aid
COLLEGE library administration
Invisible librarian; excerpt from The black librarian in America, ed. by E. J. Josey. E. Mapp. il por Library J 95:3745-7 N 1 '70
See also
College librarians—Tenure
COLLEGE library architecture. See Library architecture
COLLEGE library catalogs. See Catalogs, Library
COLLEGE life. See Student life
COLLEGE museums
See also
California. University—Berkeley campus—Art museum
Wisconsin. University—Elvehjem art center
COLLEGE newspapers. See College and school journalism
COLLEGE of cardinals. See Cardinals
COLLEGE of Southern Utah. See Utah. Southern Utah state college, Cedar City
COLLEGE officials
Administrators for community colleges. Sch & Soc 98:209-10 Ap '70
Sexism on the campus: women's rights in teaching and administrative positions. P. Woodring. Sat R 53:80+ My 16 '70
See also
College presidents
Ombudsman (education)
COLLEGE operas, revues, etc.
Current chronicle; Monteverdi's L'incoronazione di poppea, Cavalli's Erismena and Mozart's Idomeneo at University of California, Berkeley. W. C. Holmes. il Mus Q 56:478-84 Jl '70
Report:
Butterfly widow, by Isang Yun, at Northwestern university's Opera workshop. G. McElroy. Opera N 34:31 Ap 18 '70
Così fan tutte at Hofstra university. S. Gould. il Opera N 34:32-3 Mr 28 '70
Hans Werner Henze's The miracle theater at Marymount Manhattan college. H. E. Phillips. Opera N 34:31 Mr 21 '70
Luigi Cherubini's Medea at Hartt college of music. W. D. Miranda. Opera N 34:31 Ap 18 '70
Masked ball at Indiana university opera theatre. C. P. Speaks. Opera N 34:33 Mr 28 '70
Puccini's Gianni Schicchi and Martinu's Comedy on the bridge, at the University of Michigan. J. Carr. Opera N 35:23 O 10 '70
Das Rheingold, in English, at the University of Illinois. S. Jenkins. Opera N 35:31 Ja 2 '71
Robert Ashley's That morning thing at Mills college. J. Rockwell. Opera N 34:33 Ja 31 '70
University of Hartford's Hartt college production of Prokofiev's Duenna. W. D. Miranda. il Opera N 35:23 S 5 '70
COLLEGE orchestras. See Orchestras
COLLEGE periodicals. See College and school journalism
COLLEGE presidents
Another campus crisis: finding a president. il Newsweek 76:68-70 Ag 31 '70
New generation of college presidents. il Time 95:65 F 9 '70

Survey of college presidents: what will happen on campus this fall. Ladies Home J 87:79+ S '70
Wanted: superman for college president. il Bsns W p58-9 S 19 '70
Why college presidents are quitting. il U S News 69:30-2 Ag 3 '70
See also
Botstein, L.
Johnson, H. W.
Wharton, C. R. jr
COLLEGE professors and instructors
Absentee college professor; imbalance between consulting jobs and teaching. Parks & Rec 5:9 Jl '70
Mess in higher education; faculty responsibility; address, October 17, 1969. S. J. Tonsor. Vital Speeches 36:250-3 F 1 '70
Problems ahead for the lay theologian. R. Van Allen. il Cath World 212:37-9 O '70
Radicalized professor: a portrait. D. Rabinowitz. Commentary 50:62-4 Jl '70; Discussion. 50:18+ S '70
Teachers' role in campus revolt. il U S News 68:36-8 Je 15 '70
Where you have to be retired to be hired. C. Stevenson. Read Digest 96:21-4+ Je '70
Will teacher be the new drop-out? A. Beichman; reply. F. E. Crossland. N Y Times Mag p 21+ Ja 25 '70
See also
Academic freedom
American association of university professors
Colleges and universities—Administration
Strikes—United States—College professors and instructors
Teachers and students
Theologians
University centers for rational alternatives
Women as college professors and instructors

Anecdotes, facetiae, satire, etc.

Academic protocol: from the G. Swinger manual. D. S. Greenberg. Science 170:47 O 2 '70

Employment

See College professors and instructors—Supply and demand

Pensions

Threatened faculty pensions; TIAA-CREF regulation problem. D. Wolfle. Science 167:823 F 6 '70; Reply. W. B. Harman, jr. 168:522 My 1 '70

Political activities

Halloween special: hobgoblins and witches. il Sat R 53:72 N 21 '70
Kraus' vindication. J. Deedy. Commonweal 91:466 Ja 30 '70
Lions 6, Christians 0; anti-war and election campaign activities. Sat R 53:86-7 Je 20 '70
Not guilty, but . . ; case of J. Froines. G. Johnson. New Repub 163:9-10 Jl 25 '70
On being an unfashionable professor. J. P. Roche. il por N Y Times Mag p30-1+ O 18 '70; Discussion. p 22+ N 8 '70
Price of campus peace. Life 68:38 My 29 '70
Tax exemption and political activities. Sch & Soc 98:328+ O '70
Too dangerous to teach: J. Froines and Irving Wainer. G. Johnson. New Repub 163:18-19 S 5 '70; Reply. C. T. Duncan. 163:31 O 3 '70
What business is a university in? I. Kristol. il N Y Times Mag p30-1+ Mr 22 '70; Same abr. with title Toward universities for education. Cur 118:51-6 My '70; Reply with rejoinder. M. B. Goldstein. N Y Times Mag p 16+ Ap 19 '70

Promotion

Academic gamesmanship, by P. L. van den Berghe. Review
Sat R 53:60-1 D 19 '70. P. Woodring

Qualifications

Questions of value. E. R. Rowe. Sch & Soc 98:349-51 O '70

Rating

When college students grade the faculty; University of Illinois. T. Dillman. Todays Ed 59:62+ F '70

Salaries, allowances, etc.

Faculty salaries: 1969-70 year may have ended an era for academe. J. Walsh. il Science 170:306-8 O 16 '70

Selection and appointment

See also
College professors and instructors—Qualifications

Statistics

Selected characteristics of college faculty members. W. V. Grant. il Am Ed 6:33 N '70

COLLEGE professors and instructors—*Cont.*

Supply and demand

Academic recession; lack of job openings. C.
  E. Landers and J. S. Cicarelli. New Repub
  162:14-16 My 9 '70
Brain drain at Negro colleges. A. Poinsett. il
  Ebony 25:74-6+ O '70
Doctoral glut. il Newsweek 75:114 Mr 16 '70
Hard times on campus. A. Wolfe. il Nation
  210:623-7 My 25 '70
Too many doctors. Time 95:45+ Je 29 '70

Tenure

Halloween special: hobgoblins and witches.
  il Sat R 53:72 N 21 '70
Tenure controversy: rejected San Jose engi-
  neer is wed to a red. P. M. Boffey. por
  Science 170:420-2 O 23 '70
COLLEGE radio stations. See Radio stations
COLLEGE recruiting of police. See Police—
  Recruiting
COLLEGE sports. See College athletics
COLLEGE STATION, Tex.
  Street signs should be seen. il Am City 85:116
  Jl '70
COLLEGE student activities.   See Student
  activities
COLLEGE student opinion. See Student opinion
COLLEGE students
Academic freedom and responsibility. Sch &
  Soc 98:138-41 Mr '70
Campus counterrevolution? Nat R 22:549-
  50 Je 2 '70
Dissent and the college student in revolt.
  C. E. Blocker. bibliog Sch & Soc 98:20-3
  Ja '70
Freshmen in 1970; interview. F. A. Hargadon.
  New Yorker 46:42-4 D 12 '70
Generation not for barricades. J. Didion.
  Life 68:26 Je 5 '70
Graduation day for '70; with excerpts from
  commencement addresses. il Life 68:20-9
  Je 19 '70
Guest editors advise; college freshmen. J.
  Harayda. Mlle 71:206 O '70
Lawyers and student dissent. Sch & Soc
  98:10-11 Ja '70
New campus mood: from rage to reform.
  il Time 96:38+ N 30 '70
One semester of Daniel Zuckerman. D. Zuck-
  erman. Esquire 74:114-16+ S '70
Real root of student disorder? S. I. Haya-
  kawa. Read Digest 97:167-8 N '70
Revised contract for college students. J. F.
  Ohles. Sch & Soc 98:23-4 Ja '70
Straight talk; views of A. Heard and J.
  Cheek. Newsweek 76:40-1 Ag 3 '70
Student syndrome; views of Alexander Heard
  and James Cheek. K. Crawford. Newsweek
  76:28 Ag 10 '70
Student unrest: sources and consequences; ex-
  cerpts from address, October 21, 1969. L.
  Eisenberg. bibliog Science 167:1688-92 Mr 27
  '70
Two perceptions. il Time 95:59-60 My 4 '70
War was two years ago; Harvard after twen-
  ty years. R. Maloney. Atlan 225:61-3 Mr '70
  See also
Coeducation
College athletics
College clubs and societies
College graduates
Colleges and universities—Administration—
  Student participation
Foreign students in the United States
Foreign study
Negro students
Self government in education
Student demonstrations
Student life
Student militants
Student movement
Teachers and students
Young Americans for freedom (organiza-
  tion)

Adjustment

Have we overlooked the obvious? campus
  population increase as cause of student un-
  rest. D. Lawrence. U S News 69:96 O 5 '70
Quit teaching students; and help them to
  learn. A. Q. Lynch. Todays Ed 59:58-9
  N '70
School grades and group therapy. S. Tenen-
  baum. Ment Hy 54:525-9 O '70
Students and the university: the vacuum. M.
  Novak. Chr Cent 87:413 Ap 8 '70
Undergraduates' anxieties. Sch & Soc 98:204
  Ap '70

Aid

  See Negro students—Aid; Student aid;
  Student loans

Anecdotes, facetiae, satire, etc.

Strategies for a real academic revolution;
  adaptation of address, September 1969. W.
  B. Graves. il Todays Ed 59:26-7 S '70

Attitudes

See Students—Attitudes

Civil rights

See Students—Civil rights

Demonstrations

See Student demonstrations

Discipline

See College discipline

Employment

Jobless rates and students who work. B. L.
  Masse. America 123:385-7 N 7 '70

Federal aid

See Student aid

Grading

See Grading and marking (students)

Health and hygiene

Abortion: the academic angle. Mlle 72:145
  D '70
Dogmatism, religiosity and mental health in
  college students. H. G. Richek and others.
  Ment Hy 54:572-4 O '70

Housing

Beggars' war; controversy over off-campus
  housing in Boston area. il Newsweek 76:
  72 S 7 '70
Collegetown, Phase I, Sacramento state college, Sacramento, Calif. il Arch Rec 147:
  98-9 mid-My '70
  See also
Dormitories

Mental hygiene

See College students—Health and hygiene

Political activities

After Cambodia and Kent: academe enters
  congressional politics. L. J. Carter. Science
  168:955-6 My 22 '70
After Kent. Nation 210:610-11 My 25 '70
After Kent state: the first hundred days. P.
  Schrag. il Sat R 53:12-15+ Ag 29 '70
Aggressive moderates. il Time 95:81 Je 1 '70
American student politics. S. Warnecke. Yale
  R 60:185-98 D '70
Anatomy of activism for executives. S. A.
  Culbert and J. M. Elden. il Harvard Bsns
  R 48:131-42 N '70
Campus and the campaigns. Nations Bsns
  58:24 O '70
Campus and the student, 1970; address. May
  4, 1970. W. R. Butler. Vital Speeches 36:566-9
  Jl 1 '70
Campus politics: decentralization is pattern
  at Berkeley, Stanford. J. Walsh. Science 168:
  1187-90 Je 5 '70
Campus politics; guidelines from the Ameri-
  can council on education. New Repub 163:
  10 Ag 1 '70
Candidates take second look at campus
  troublemakers. il U S News 69:29-30 S 28 '70
Cease-fire on campus. il Newsweek 76:79 O
  19 '70
Does college radicalization stick? R. Kirk. Nat
  R 22:1058 O 6 '70
Faded crusade. il Newsweek 76:31 N 2 '70
How goes the second children's crusade? or-
  ganizing M.N.C. student power. il Time 96:
  14-15 Jl 20 '70
Lions 6, Christians 0; anti-war and elec-
  tion campaign activities. Sat R 53:86-7 Je
  20 '70
Mlle's campus reports. Mlle 71:208-9+ Ag '70
New right. il Newsweek 76:24-5 D 7 '70
New student crusade: working in the system.
  il Time 95:19-20 My 25 '70
Opinion: politicizing the university. J. Rud-
  man. por Mlle 71:92+ Ag '70
Our far-flung correspondents; Dartmouth '70
  and the war. N. Perrin. New Yorker 46:53-8
  Jl 18 '70
Pied Piper of the new children's crusade:
  A. Lowenstein. G. Astor. il por Look 34:36-8
  Ag 25 '70
Political campus. Nat R 22:605+ Je 16 '70
Politicizing colleges: the Princeton plan; ad-
  dress, June 15, 1970. K. Spalding. Vital
  Speeches 36:622-5 Ag 1 '70
Princeton commitment: a race against mace.
  J. Shepherd. il Look 34:12+ Je 16 '70
Report card on the President; A. Heard's
  report. M. McGrory. America 123:53 Ag 8
  '70

COLLEGE students—Political activities—*Cont.*

Revolution at home and abroad; parallels between Germany and U.S; address, September 8 and 9, 1970. K. I. Falk. Vital Speeches 37:58-61 N 1 '70

Revolution on American campuses; an analysis. P. J. Weber. il Cath World 210:248-52 Mr '70

Rules for political action; Stanford university. Sch & Soc 98:461 D '70

Student and faculty problems; student demands for political equality. Sch & Soc 98: 264-5 Sum '70

Student bargaining. J. Harrison. New Repub 163:10-11 N 21 '70; Discussion. 163:31-2 D 12 '70

Student campaign to get peace elected. C. Leinster. il Life 68:45-6 Je 5 '70

Student campaigners; do they turn on or put off the voters? il Sr Schol 97:14 O 12 '70

Student moves into the 14th C. D. T. Buckley. il pors N Y Times Mag p 10-11+ Je 21 '70

Student strikes and book sales; the Dartmouth experience. P. Johnson, jr. Pub W 198:265-6 Ag 31 '70

Student-student polarization plagues U.S. campuses. S. Z. Goldhaber. Science 169:38 Jl 3 '70

Student vote; prohibitive intervention by election boards. E. Jannson. New Repub 163:11-12 S 19 '70

Students' record as campaigners. il U S News 69:28 N 16 '70

Students who came to dinner. T. E. Quigley. Commonweal 91:470-1 Ja 30 '70

Talking back. New Repub 163:7-8 O 10 '70

Tax exemption and political activities. Sch & Soc 98:328+ O '70

Taxes v. student politics. il Time 96:32 Ag 3 '70

Third avenue opens to protesting students. il Sci N 97:475-6 My 16 '70

Time out for students; Princeton plan. New Repub 163:7 O 17 '70

Tragedy at Kent state. T. Gallagher. il Good H 171:82-3+ O '70

Universities in ferment. il Newsweek 75:66-8+ Je 15 '70

Will Dr Heard be heard? the attitudes and concerns of college youth. America 123:55 Ag 8 '70

Working from within; Princeton movement for a new Congress. il Newsweek 75:69-70 My 25 '70

Year of the cop-out; Princeton plan. il Time 96:10 N 2 '70

Youth and foreign policy. S. J. Kelman. For Affairs 48:414-26 Ap '70

Youth wants to know; student delegations on mission to Washington. il Newsweek 75:33 My 25 '70

Youthful volunteers; working for peace candidates in the November elections. Time 96: 12 Jl 27 '70

See also
Student movement
Students for a democratic society (organization)
Vietnamese war, 1957- —Protests, demonstrations, etc. against

Race attitudes
See Race attitudes

Religion
Asbury revival blazes cross-country trail. J. Nelson and J. Rohler. Chr Today 14:46+ Mr 13 '70

Dogmatism, religiosity and mental health in college students. H. G. Richek and others. Ment Hy 54:572-4 O '70

Florida Easter week: student "Exkursions". A. Taft. Chr Today 14:40 Ap 24 '70

John Bunyan and the contemporary student. E. H. Batson. Chr Today 14:11-13 S 11 '70

Radicalizing liturgy; experiment in exposure education. J. D. Groppe. Cath World 212: 30-4 O '70

Revival of ritual on campus. J. W. Goetz. il Cath World 212:24-8+ O '70

Sowing the wind; a special report from Kent state university. D. Bryant. Chr Today 14: 13-15 Je 5 '70

Visions of a new religion. M. Cavell. il Sat R 53:12-14+ D 19 '70

Why am I at this school? J. W. Alexander. Chr Today 14:12-13 S 11 '70

See also
Colleges and universities—Religious life

Selection
See Student selection

Sexual behavior
Co-ed dorms, an intimate revolution in campus life; Oberlin college, Ohio, with report by K. Thorsen. il Life 69:32-41 N 20 '70

How college students feel about love, sex and marriage. M. Peters and W. Peters. il Good H 170:84-5+ Je '70

Psychosocial analysis of sex-policing on campus; address, December 7, 1965. J. P. Fell. Sch & Soc 98:351-4 O '70

Volunteer service
See Volunteer service

COLLEGE students, Married

Housing
See College students—Housing

COLLEGE students, Negro. See Negro students

COLLEGE students, Women
College women 1970: a whole new can of worms. J. Marks. Mlle 70:258+ F '70

See also
Coeducation
Education of women
Law students, Women

COLLEGE students and business
Business and the radicals: the students, how wide is the gap? with comments of members of the presidents' panel. G. R. Rosen. il Duns 95:47+ Je '70

Campus and the corporation; address, December 5, 1969. G. Symonds. Vital Speeches 36: 378-83 Ap 1 '70

Generating goodwill toward the young; E. L. Winter. V. Louviere. il por Nations Bsns 58:13 Ag '70

How students see you now. W. Wingo. il Nations Bsns 58:54-8 My '70

Open line to the students. il Bsns W p 122 Je 27 '70

Students flunk at new ideas; Globus, inc, offer. V. Louviere. Nations Bsns 58:14 Jl '70

View through youthful eyes. L. Banks. il Fortune 81:76-7+ Ap '70

See also
Negro students and business

COLLEGE students and environmental problems. See Environmental movement

COLLEGE students and the pollution issue. See Environmental movement

COLLEGE students and war
Face down: climax to the hardship tour; undergraduate veterans of the Vietnamese war. W. G. Pelfrey. New Repub 163:13-14 Jl 18 '70

War and the students; campus antiwar sentiment. Time 96:53 Jl 6 '70

COLLEGE teachers. See College professors and instructors

COLLEGE textbooks. See Textbooks

COLLEGE theatricals. See College and school drama

COLLEGE verse
Undergraduate poems; comp. by J. Moffitt. America 122:444-5 Ap 5 '70

COLLEGE work-study program. See Education, Cooperative

COLLEGE yearbooks. See College annuals

COLLEGES, Small. See Small colleges

COLLEGES and business. See Business and education

COLLEGES and universities
Critical university. P. Brooks. Mlle 70:104-5+ Ja '70

Five crises of the university; address, February 1970. J. A. Perkins. il UNESCO Courier 23:28-32 Je '70

If not reason, what? address, December 29, 1969. K. Brewster, jr. Vital Speeches 36: 346-9 Mr 15 '70

Uneasy return to campus. il Time 96:65 S 21 '70

See also
Academic freedom
Catholic colleges and universities
Church colleges
College education
College students
Education of women
Free universities
International university (proposed)
Law schools
Liberal education
Student movement
Summer schools
Vocational education
also types of colleges, e.g. Medical colleges

COLLEGES and universities—Entrance re-
quirements—*Continued*
Steps to take if not accepted by a college.
Good H 170:190-1 Mr '70
These colleges have room. il Changing T 24:
37-40 My '70
   See also
College entrance examination board
Student selection

Federal aid
Campus computers: federal budget cuts hit
university centers. M. W. Oberie; reply. P.
Armer and others. Science 167:1198-9 F 27 '70
Higher education: administration silent on
institutional aid. L. J. Carter. Science
170:832-3 N 20 '70
Right to college. M. R. Berube. Common-
weal 92:81-4 Ap 3 '70
Science funds: NSF survey probes effects of
shifts in federal aid. D. S. Greenberg. il
Science 170:609-10+ N 6 '70
Who benefits from higher education sub-
sidies. W. L. Hansen. il Mo Labor R 93:43-6
Mr '70
   See also
Church colleges—Federal aid
Negro colleges and universities—Federal aid

Finance
Academic finance: British system smoothly
functions in 50th year; University grants
committee. D. S. Greenberg. Science 169:
658-60 Ag 14 '70
Better management in higher education: ad-
dress, July 25, 1970. S. Umbeck. Vital
Speeches 37:102-5 D 1 '70
College budgets feel the violence. Bsns W p23
My 16 '70
College depression. Time 96:73 D 14 '70
Colleges feel the money pinch. il U S News
68:35-6 Je 22 '70
Coming: a financial backlash against colleges?
excerpts from address, June 19, 1970. R. A.
Freeman. por U S News 68:72-3 Je 29 '70
Crisis in American higher education; address,
February 7, 1970. E. A. Walker. Vital
Speeches 36:362-4 Ap 1 '70
Financial crisis on the campus. il Bsns W
p56-7+ My 30 '70
Great depression; report of the Carnegie com-
mission on higher education. Newsweek
76:78 D 14 '70
Higher-cost education; education fee for
California undergraduates. Newsweek 75:
68 Mr 2 '70
How colleges cope with the red ink. il Bsns
W p56-7+ N 21 '70
Money crisis for colleges: why. il U S News
69:49-52 O 19 '70
Public support for private colleges. Sch & Soc
98:376-7 O '70
Subsidies for the well-to-do: the case of
California. Trans-Action 7:4+ S '70
Talk-in at the Times; conference of eleven
presidents. Nat R 22:774 Jl 28 '70
Tax exemption and political activities. Sch &
Soc 98:328+ O '70
Taxes v. student politics. il Time 96:32 Ag
3 '70
To meet college crisis: cuts in faculties,
courses, students. il U S News 69:54-5 D 14
'70
   See also
Catholic colleges and universities—Finance
Church colleges—Finance
College education, Cost of
Colleges and universities—Gifts, legacies, etc.
Colleges and universities—Investments

Gifts, legacies, etc.
Businessmen sour on college support. Na-
tions Bsns 58:22 S '70
Funds for higher education. Sch & Soc 98:19+
Ja '70
Plea to alumni not to forsake their colleges.
D. Lawrence. U S News 70:84 Ja 11 '71
Spurning a giver; John D. Rockefeller, 3d's
offer to Massachusetts colleges. por Time
96:35 D 21 '70
Voluntary support of higher education. Sch &
Soc 98:332+ O '70

Graduate work
Effect of the draft on graduate physics edu-
cation. W. E. Meyerhof. il Science 168:918-
19 My 22 '70
How top educators rate graduate schools now;
American council on education ratings. U S
News 70:70-1 Ja 11 '71
No place for blue-collars. D. M. Gray. Com-
monweal 93:13-14, 79 O 2, 16 '70
Still no. 1; ACE's new report on graduate
schools. il Newsweek 77:58 Ja 11 '71

Investments
Better idea for endowments. il Bsns W p44 D
26 '70
Bold investing; 1969 Barker report. Managing
educational endowments. P. A. Samuelson.
Newsweek 75:82 My 4 '70
Managing higher educational endowments.
Sch & Soc 98:377-8 O '70
Market teaches colleges a lesson. il Bsns W
p62+ Je 20 '70
Physicians, heal yourselves; churches and
universities, social implications of their in-
vestments. B. H. Smith. America 123:282-5
O 17 '70

Laws and legislation
Constitution on campus. il por Time 95:64+
Mr 23 '70
Keeping it cool on the campus. R. M. Hall,
jr. New Repub 162:11-12 Ap 4 '70; Discus-
sion. 162:27-9 My 16 '70

Political control
College, politics, and society. Sch & Soc 98:
330 O '70
Politicized university. Sch & Soc 98:331 O '70

Public relations
Academic-labor alliance formally established.
D. Shapley. Science 170:614 N 6 '70
Challenges facing urban universities; adapta-
tion of address, December 12, 1968. H. C.
Syrett. Sch & Soc 98:89-91 F '70
Intellectuals start wooing trade unions. B.
L. Masse. America 124:33 Ja 16 '71
Labor-campus link: union heads, academic
leaders discuss alliance. D. Shapley. Sci-
ence 170:516+ O 30 '70
Toward universities of the public interest.
W. Arrowsmith. Cur 118:46-51 My '70
University and society. M. Levitt. bibliog Sch
& Soc 98:342-6 O '70

Religious life
Academic freedom in evangelical perspective.
Chr Today 14:20-1 Jl 3 '70
Campus minister: rebel or reconciler? C. S.
Evans. Chr Today 14:3-5 My 8 '70
Campus ministry as imagination. J. Carroll.
il Cath World 212:88-91 N '70
Christian teachers: making crucial contribu-
tions. R. L. Cleath. Chr Today 14:50 S 11
'70
Church, the university and social policy, by
K. Underwood and others. Review
Chr Cent 87:506-7+ Ap 22 '70. F. T.
Trotter
Commonweal 91:484+ Ja 30 '70. J. Walsh
Sticking point: religious tutelage. R. J.
Westley. America 123:172-5 S 19 '70
   See also
Campus crusade for Christ (organization)
College students—Religion
University Christian movement

Research
Academic research: OST aide sees no shift
in financial situation. D. S. Greenberg.
Science 170:952-4 N 27 '70
Case for research; government & university;
address, July 27, 1970. A. W. Betts. Vital
Speeches 36:720-3 S 15 '70
Chained campuses. S. Solomon. New Repub
163:12-13 S 19 '70
College war labs wear camouflage. il Bsns W
p36+ O ? '70
Colleges in action. See issues of Science digest
Congress requires relevance for DOD re-
search; with editorial comment. G. B. Lub-
kin. il Phys Today 23:63-5, 112 F '70
Controversy at MIT; reply. R. M. Byers.
Aviation W 92:66 Mr 2 '70
Declassified; Columbia and Stanford. Sci Am
222:58-9 Mr '70
Laird seeks industry aid to defeat Mansfield
amendment. A. Hamilton. Science 167:1599
Mr 20 '70
Military research network. M. Klare. Nation
211:327-32 O 12 '70
M.I.T: March 4 revisited amid political
turmoil. A. Hamilton. il Science 167:1475-
6 Mr 13 '70
Section 203 compounds research-funding
squeeze. J. B. Phelps. Phys Today 23:61-4
My '70
Troubled times for academic science. P. H.
Abelson. Science 168:525 My 1 '70
Two-way benefits of defense research; letter.
F. R. Eirich. Science 167:1198 F 27 '70
A vote for Mansfield; letter. J. Orear. il Phys
Today 23:9+ My '70

COLLEGES and universities—*Continued*

Security measures
City vs. campus violence; city police on the campus. W. J. McGill. il por **Am City** 85:78+ N '70
Policing the campus. il **Time** 95:44 My 25 '70
Ready for the worst. il **Newsweek** 76:42+ S 21 '70

Social life
See Student life

Statistics
See also
Colleges and universities—Attendance

Student recruiting
Lone recruiter. il por **Newsweek** 76:61-2 O 26 '70
See also
Talent Search programs (education)

Taxation
Tax-exempt; guidelines from the American council on education for Princeton plan participators. **Sat R** 53:55 Ag 15 '70

Teaching
Project to improve college teaching. **Sch & Soc** 98:134 Mr '70
See also
Junior colleges—Teaching

Africa, East
Letter from Africa: higher education in East Africa. K. S. Forland. il **Bul Atom Sci** 26:42-5 Ap '70

Argentina
Physics and politics in Latin America; a personal experience; University of Buenos Aires. L. M. Falicov. **Bul Atom Sci** 26:8-10+ N '70

Arizona
See also
Arizona state university, Tempe

California
Master plan: higher education for the millions. il **Newsweek** 76:84-5 N 23 '70
Status search: state college librarians. F. Blake. **Library J** 95:2096 Je 1 '70
See also
California. University
Claremont colleges
Mills college, Oakland
Stanford university
Whittier college, Whittier

Colombia
Physics and politics in Latin America; a personal experience. L. M. Falicov. **Bul Atom Sci** 26:8-10+ N '70

Connecticut
See also
Connecticut. University, Storrs
Trinity college, Hartford
Wesleyan university, Middletown
Yale university

Czechoslovakia
Purging the university. il **Newsweek** 76:65 Jl 13 '70

Egypt
Al-Azhar the resplendent. il **UNESCO Courier** 23:17 Ap '70

England
See also
Oxford. University

Florida
See also
Florida. University

France
France: the enemy within. E. Behr. il **Newsweek** 75:42-4 Je 8 '70
The summit: three great schools. S. Saler. **Newsweek** 75:43 Je 8 '70
Vincennes: academic self-service. C. Dreyfus. il **Mlle** 71:150-1+ Je '70

Georgia
See also
Georgia, University, Athens

Germany (Democratic Republic)
550th birthday of the University of Rostock. W. W. Brickman. **Sch & Soc** 98:304-6 Sum '70

Germany (Federal Republic)
Aims of university reform. **Sch & Soc** 98: 32-3 Ja '70

Professors strike back; West Berlin's Free university. **Time** 95:55 Ja 26 '70
Tübingen revisited. G. O'Collins. **America** 122: 275-6 Mr 14 '70
See also
Theological seminaries—Germany (Federal Republic)

Great Britain
Academic finance: British system smoothly functions in 50th year; University grants committee. D. S. Greenberg. **Science** 169: 658-60 Ag 14 '70
See also
Colleges and universities—Scotland

Illinois
See also
Chicago. University
Illinois. University
Northwestern university, Evanston
Rockford college, Rockford

Indiana
See also
Earlham college, Richmond
Notre Dame, Ind. University

Iowa
See also
Iowa. University, Iowa City
Parsons college, Fairfield

Japan
Campus of many spaces; Rissho university, Tokyo. il **Arch Forum** 132:34-9 My '70
Japan II; university turmoil is reflected in research. P. M. Boffey. il **Science** 167:147-50+ Ja 9 '70

Kansas
See also
Kansas state university, Manhattan
Kansas state university of agriculture and applied science, Manhattan
Kansas. University, Lawrence

Kentucky
See also
Asbury college, Wilmore

Lebanon
See also
American university of Beirut

Maine
See also
Bowdoin college, Brunswick

Maryland
See also
Maryland. University, College Park

Massachusetts
Beggars' war; controversy over off-campus housing in Boston area. il **Newsweek** 76: 72 S 7 '70
See also
Amherst college, Amherst
Brandeis university, Waltham
Clark university, Worcester
Hampshire college
Harvard university
Massachusetts institute of technology, Cambridge
Massachusetts. University, Amherst
Radcliffe college, Cambridge

Michigan
See also
Michigan state university, East Lansing
Michigan. University, Ann Arbor

Minnesota
See also
Carleton college, Northfield
Minnesota. University, Minneapolis

Mississippi
See also
Jackson state college, Jackson
Mississippi college, Clinton
Mississippi state university, State college
Mississippi. University

Missouri
See also
Lindenwood college, St Charles
Missouri. University, Columbia

Nebraska
See also
John Fitzgerald Kennedy college, Wahoo

New Hampshire
See also
Dartmouth college, Hanover
Franconia college, Franconia
New Hampshire. University, Durham

COLLEGES and universities—*Continued*

New Jersey
See also
Princeton university
Ramapo college, Mahwah
Rutgers university, New Brunswick

New York (state)
See also
Columbia university
Cornell university, Ithaca
Fordham university
New York (state). State university
New York university
Sarah Lawrence college, Bronxville
Skidmore college, Saratoga Springs
Syracuse university, Syracuse
Vassar college, Poughkeepsie
Yeshiva university

North Dakota
See also
North Dakota. University, Grand Forks

Ohio
See also
Akron. University
Cincinnati. University
Kenyon college, Gambier
Oberlin college, Oberlin
Ohio. Kent state university
Ohio state university, Columbus

Oklahoma
See also
Oklahoma. University, Norman
Oral Roberts university, Tulsa

Oregon
See also
Oregon. State university, Portland

Pennsylvania
See also
Carnegie-Mellon university, Pittsburgh
Duquesne university, Pittsburgh
Lafayette college, Easton
Lehigh university, Bethlehem
St Vincent archabbey and college, Latrobe

Puerto Rico
See also
Puerto Rico. University

Russia
Studying physics at Moscow state university;
adaptation of address, April 18, 1969. L.
A. Artsimoviech. il por Phys Today 23:34-
40 Ja '70

Scotland
Artificial stars in a teaching laboratory. D.
Clarke. il Sky & Tel 39:295-7 My '70
Student dorms on a Scottish coast; St An-
drews university. J. Stirling; C. Jencks. il
Arch Forum 133:50-7 S '70

South Africa
South Africa: university system follows apartheid pattern; government enforces limits on
academic dissenters. D. S. Greenberg. il
Science 169:260-4+ Jl 17 '70

South Carolina
See also
Bob Jones university, Greenville
South Carolina. State college, Orangeburg

Southern states
See also
Negro colleges and universities

Tennessee
See also
Carson-Newman college, Jeffrey City
Fisk university, Nashville
Vanderbilt university, Nashville

Texas
See also
Abilene Christian college, Abilene
North Texas state university, Denton
Southern Methodist university, Dallas
Texas technological university, Lubbock
Texas. University

United States
Campus '69; address, November 14, 1969. W. L.
Reilly. Vital Speeches 36:270-2 F 15 '70
Changes coming in American colleges; inter-
view. S. B. Gould. il por U S News 68:78-
82 Je 8 '70
Colleges in action. See issues of Science
digest
Let's keep our dual system; private and
public; address, March 3, 1970. R. C. Tyson.
Vital Speeches 36:414-16 Ap 15 '70

New American university; the sleep of rea-
son; address, January 22, 1970. P. B. Kur-
land. Vital Speches 36:314-17 Mr 1 '70
New campus mood: from rage to reform.
il Time 96:38+ N 30 '70
Old main in jeopardy. Chr Cent 87:1143 S 30
'70
Tensions on the campus. S. M. Linowitz. por
Sch & Soc 98:115-16 F '70
Threat of impatience; excerpts from address,
December 29, 1969. K. Brewster, jr. Science
168:423 Ap 24 '70
Trustee of the culture; excerpt from ad-
dress. A. MacLeish. Sat R 53:18-19 D 19
'70
Universities in ferment. il Newsweek 75:66-8+
Je 15 '70
What's going on in schools & colleges. See
issues of Changing times
Will teacher be the new drop-out? A. Beich-
man; reply. F. E. Crossland. N Y Times
Mag p21+ Ja 25 '70
See also
Church colleges
Junior colleges
Medical colleges
Negro colleges and universities
Small colleges

Utah
Very nice place to visit; Utah universities.
C. Kirkpatrick. il Sports Illus 33:55-6 D 14
'70
See also
Brigham Young university, Provo
Utah. University, Salt Lake City

Virginia
South to spring. D. Butwin. il Sat R 53:53-4+
My 23 '70
See also
Hollins college, Hollins College, Va.

Washington, D.C.
See also
Gallaudet college
George Washington university
Washington, D.C. Federal city college

Washington (state)
See also
Washington (state). University, Seattle

Wisconsin
See also
Wisconsin. University

COLLEGES and universities. Experimental
Bensalem. I. Taves. il Look 34:28-32 My 19 '70
Experimental colleges. Esquire 74:111-12+ S
'70
Nobody hassles us, everybody listens. B. Vil-
let. Life 68:60+ My 8 '70
See also
California. University—Santa Cruz campus
Franconia college, Franconia, N.H.
Free universities
Hampshire college
New York (state). State university—College
at Old Westbury

COLLEGES and universities, Municipal
See also
New York (city). City university

COLLEGES and universities, State
Colleges of the forgotten Americans, by A.
Dunham. Review
Sat R 53:62-3 Ja 24 '70. P. Woodring
State universities: report terms desegrega-
tion largely token. B. Nelson; discussion.
Science 166:167; 167:123-4 O 10 '69, Ja 9 '70
See also
National association of state universities and
land grant colleges
also names of state colleges and uni-
versities, e.g. Florida. University

California
Is freedom academic? California state col-
leges; address, December 12, 1969. G. S.
Dumke. Vital Speeches 36:272-6 F 15 '70
Status of California state college librarians;
ALA report. Am Lib 1:57-9 Ja '70
See also
California. State college, San Francisco
California. State college, San Jose

Utah
See also
Utah. Southern state college, Cedar City

COLLEGES and universities, Traveling
Travel: the going things; World campus
afloat. S. Cuneo. il Mlle 71:102 S '70

COLLEGES for women
See also
Finch college, New York
Hollins college, Hollins College, Va.
Lindenwood college, St Charles, Mo.

COLLEMBOLA. See Springtails

COLLIER, James Lincoln
How to support your husband's ego. Read Digest 96:108-11 Ja '70
Time to give divorced men a break. Read Digest 96:64-8 F; 39-41 My '70

COLLIER, Peter
Red man's burden. il Ramp Mag 8:26-38 F '70; Same abr. Cur 119:22-6 Je '70
Theft of a nation: apologies to the Cherokees. il por Ramp Mag 9:35-45 S '70
(ed) See Ehrlich, P. Ecological destruction is a condition of American life

COLLINS, Bud
Tennis (cont) Sports Illus 32:49 Ja 19 '70

COLLINS, David R.
I'd rather do it myself; drama. Plays 29:35-46 Mr '70

COLLINS, Judy
Take the lilies and the lace; excerpt from The Judy Collins songbook. il pors McCalls 97:66-7+ Ap '70

COLLINS, Kenalene
Drunken bears of Hoosac Tunnel. il Outdoo Life 145:70-1 Mr '70

COLLINS, Kreigh
Up north or down east. il Motor B 126:52-3+ O '70

COLLINS, Michael. See Cohen, G. jt. auth.

COLLINS, Michael, 1930-
Communicating about foreign policy; address, February 21, 1970. Dept State Bul 62:393-6 Mr 23 '70
Communicating with today's youth; address, May 11, 1970. Dept State Bul 62:694-6 Je 1 '70
Educating future citizens of the international community; address, February 11, 1970. bibliog f Dept State Bul 62:230-3 Mr 2 '70
Mr Collins becomes assistant secretary for public affairs; remarks at swearing-in ceremony. Dept State Bul 62:142-3 F 2 '70
National foreign policy conference for editors and broadcasters; remarks, January 15, 1970. Dept State Bul 62:113-16+ F 2 '70
Preparing youth for a world of unprecedented complexity; excerpt from address, March 7, 1970. Dept State Bul 62:425-6 Mr 30 '70
Youth goals and national goals; address, June 7, 1970. Dept State Bul 62:804-7 Je 29 '70

about

How Apollo 11 changed three famous men. G. Farmer. pors Life 69:50 Jl 17 '70 *
See also
Space flight to the moon—Manned flights—Apollo 11 flight

COLLINS, Morton
He feeds capital to the computers; Data science ventures. por Bsns W p28 Ag 29 '70 *
Improving on the general. por Forbes 105:78+ Ap 15 '70 *

COLLINS, Richard L.
On top. See issues of Flying
Safety check. Flying 86:22-3+ Je; 87:20+ S; 10 O; 14+ D '70

COLLINS, Robert L.
Unilateral inhibition of sound-induced convulsions in mice. bibliog il Science 167:1010-11 F 13 '70

COLLINS, Russell Lewis. See Beasley, M. L. jt. auth.

COLLINS, Sheila D.
Women and the church: poor psychology, worse theology. Chr Cent 87:1557-9 D 30 '70

COLLINS, Thomas
Inquiring about retiring; questions and answers. See issues of Harvest years

COLLINS radio company
Battle for survival. il Forbes 106:48 D 1 '70
Collins turns to computers for aid. Bsns W p20 Mr 7 '70

COLLISION avoidance systems. See Airplanes—Safety devices and measures

COLLISION warning instruments. See Proximity warning indicators

COLLISIONS, Automobile. See Traffic accidents

COLLODI, Carlo, pseud. See Lorenzini, C.

COLLOIDS
Clay colloids. W. H. Slabaugh. il por Chem 43:8-12 Ap '70; Correction. 43:31 O '70
Polywater: a hydrosol? S. L. Kurtin and others. bibliog il Science 167:1720-2 Mr 27 '70
See also
Aerosols
Electrophoresis

COLLOQUY (periodical)
Churches and money. Chr Today 14:27-8 Ap 24 '70

COLMER, William Meyers
Excerpt from debate, July 30, 1970. Cong Digest 49:236+ O '70
Excerpt from debate, September 16, 1969. Cong Digest 49:11+ Ja '70

COLODNE, Carl
You can't lynch my soul; poem. Negro Hist Bul 33:105 Ap '70

COLOGNE, Germany

Music

Report:
Production of Boris Godunov. H. Koegler. Opera N 35:34 N 21 '70
Sándor Szokolay's Hamlet. H. Koegler. Opera N 34:34 Mr 21 '70

COLOMBIA
Biggest little man in Colombia. S. Seegers and K. Seegers. por Read Digest 96:159-64 Ja '70
See also
Andes mountains
Colleges and universities—Colombia
Elections—Colombia
Guerrillas—Colombia
Saint Andrews Island

Antiquities

See Indians of South America—Antiquities—Colombia

Description and travel

Colombia, from Amazon to Spanish Main. L. McIntyre. il Nat Geog 138:234-73 Ag '70
Conquest of Huila. P. C. Rittersbush. il por Américas 22:19-27 Ja '70
Vacation in Colombia. M. F. Taft. il Américas 22:36-9 O '70

Politics and government

Colombia's close call. S. Rodman. Nat R 22:511+ My 19 '70
El columpio; 1970 presidential election. Nation 210:548-9 My 11 '70
Patterns of conflict in Colombia, by J. L. Payne. Review
Trans-Action 7:88-90 Ap '70. R. H. Dix

Religious institutions and affairs

See also
Catholic church in Colombia

COLOMBO, Emilio
No. 33. Time 96:18 Ag 17 '70 *

COLOMBO, Joseph
Italian power. il Newsweek 75:22 Je 22 '70 *

COLON bacilli
Coliform aerosols emitted by sewage treatment plants. A. P. Adams and J. C. Spendlove. bibliog il Science 169:1218-20 S 18 '70

COLONIAL furniture. See Furniture, American

COLONIAL history (United States). See United States—History—Colonial period

COLONIAL life and customs
See also
Old Sturbridge village, Sturbridge, Mass.

COLONIAL Penn group, inc.
Insurer of oldsters. J. Poindexter. Duns 96:51 D '70

COLONIAL sugar refining company, ltd. See Sugar—Manufacture and refining

COLONIES
See also
Imperialism
United Nations—Special committee on the situation with regard to the implementation of the declaration on the granting of independence to colonial countries and peoples
United Nations—Trusteeship council
also subhead Colonies under names of countries, e.g. United States—Colonies

COLONIES, Artists. See Artists colonies

COLONIZATION
See also
Imperialism

COLONNESE, Louis
Unanswered questions about a tragedy; excerpts from interview. Commonweal 92:456-7 S 18 '70

COLOR
Color as system. L. Finkelstein. il Craft Horiz 30:42-3+ Mr '70
True color and artificial light; molecular arc lamp. il Chem 43:20-1 D '70
See also
Photochromic substances

Psychology

Color: a clue to your character. M. Kohler. il Seventeen 29:158-9 Mr '70

COLOR adaptation. See Eye—Accommodation

COLOR bar generators. See Testing instruments

COLOR blindness
Contradiction in terms; color-blind painters. Sci Am 222:48 Ap '70
Exactly what is color blindness? Sci Digest 67:81-2 Ap '70
How much do you know about color blindness? quiz. Sci Digest 69:15+ Ja '71

COLOR film processing. See Photography—Developing and developers

COLOR films. See Photography—Films

COLOR in furniture. See Color in house decoration

COLOR in gardens. See Gardens—Color

COLOR in house decoration
All out for color. il Am Home 73:64-7 O '70
Art of mastering the mix. il House B 112:91-123 O '70
Blondes & silvers. il House & Gard 137:78-85 F '70
Color power; use of bold colors in a rented apartment. il N Y Times Mag p78-9 My 24 '70
Color splurge. il Am Home 73:59-62 O '70
Color to the rescue. V. D. Hahn. il Am Home 73:14+ O '70
Colour at full cry in Mr and Mrs Steven Jacobson's N.Y. apartment. il Vogue 156:132-7 Ag 1 '70
Cost-cutting supergraphics. V. D. Hahn. il Am Home 73:63 O '70
Decorating zest; lacquer colors and lacquer looks. il House & Gard 137:102-7 Mr '70
Decorators talk color. House B 112:122-3 Ap '70
Deep color, bold art in the apartment of Charles Evans il House & Gard 137:46-9 F '70
Fabric color impact; Celanese house showcase. il House B 112:35-41 Jl '70
Fabric sets the color scheme. il Good H 170:140-7+ Ap '70
Great flower show of color. il House B 112:89-121 Ap '70
Green: color it cool. N. Mandelbaum. il Ladies Home J 87:76-7 Jl '70
Groom a room with color. il Seventeen 29:160-3 Mr '70
Hothouse colors and beautiful contrasts at the Virgil Sherrills. House & Gard 137:54-9 F '70
House & garden colors 1971. il House & Gard 138:90-7 S '70
How to stretch your decorating dollars. il House & Gard 137:72-87 Ap '70
New bath coloring-book. R. Warfield. House & Gard 138:28+ S '70
New look of color; lacquered, patterned, silvered. il House & Gard 137:92-101 Mr '70
Personal approach to color; nine women tell why they have chosen the colors they live with. il House & Gard 138:71-89 S '70
Power of color. W. Baldwin. House & Gard 137:10-12 Mr '70
Pulsating color in new fluorescent plastics. il House & Gard 138:98-9 S '70
Start with white. il House B 112:70-3 S '70
Super things for the house in super pinks. il House & Gard 138:112-15 S '70
Tips on selecting the right color when decorating. il Good H 170:159 F '70
Twenty-five very smart rooms. P. Rumely. il Bet Hom & Gard 48:44-57+ Ag '70

COLOR key process. See Photography—Printing processes

COLOR matching
Products of a psychedelic age; new instruments for color control in industry. il Bsns W p82 Ag 1 '70

COLOR measurement
See also
Color matching

COLOR negative films. See Photography—Films

COLOR of leaves
New England's fall fantasia. M. Perry. il Home Gard 57:24-7 S '70
What part of the photosynthesis process causes leaves to change colors in the fall. Sci Digest 68:88-9 O '70

COLOR of man
Black, white and colored; excerpt from Jungle in the house. M. Bates. il Sci Digest 68:26-30 S '70

COLOR organ
Color organs & strobe lights enhance music. F. W. Holder. il Electr World 85:42-4+ Ja '71
High-power color organ. R. A. Hertzler. il Electr World 84:78-80 S '70
Mosaicon. New Yorker 46:32 S 12 '70
Psychedelia 1. D. Lancaster. il Pop Electr 31:27-35+ S '69; Correction. 32:13 F '70

COLOR photography
Color adds a new information dimension to make the barely seen and unseen visible. B. Sherman. il Mod Phot 34:38-9 Ag '70

Color and camera: Marti Felbinger. il Pop Phot 66:84-7 My '70
Color clinic. D. B. Eisendrath. See Issues of Popular photography to May 1970
Color image builder; Dennis Rizzuto. il Pop Phot 66:77-81 Ap '70
Do you see in color? J. Scully. il Mod Phot 34:76-81+ O '70
Ed Scully on color. E. Scully. See issues of Modern photography
Ken Biggs: color magic. il Pop Phot 66:82-5 Ap '70
Photography; images in color. E. Keller. il Chem 43:8-11 D '70

Competitions
See Photography—Competitions

COLOR photography printing. See Photography—Printing processes

COLOR print projectors. See Projectors

COLOR printing
American color know-how transplanted to France. J. Chevalier. Pub W 198:pt2 186-7 S 21 '70
Shoot powdered ink for color printing. S. V. Jones. Sci Digest 68:78 D '70

COLOR sense
Amateur scientist; the color vision of pigeons is tested in a Skinner box. J. S. Moran. il Sci Am 223:124-9 O '70
Trichromatic mechanisms in single cortical neurons. P. Gouras. bibliog il Science 168:489-92 Ap 24 '70
See also
Color blindness

COLOR slides. See Transparencies

COLOR television. See Television, Color

COLOR television cameras. See Television cameras

COLOR television receivers. See Television receivers, Color

COLOR vision. See Color sense

COLORADANS
Catch Colorado; people who shape the state. il Vogue 156:114-27 N 15 '70

COLORADO
See also
Booksellers and bookselling—Colorado
Camps—Colorado
Fishing—Colorado
Gardens—Colorado
Public health—Colorado
Skis and skiing—Colorado
Vigilance committees—Colorado

Description and travel
Colorado, a gigantic plaything. M. R. Henry. Vogue 156:78+ N 15 '70
Opera, melodrama in Colorado; Central City and Cripple Creek. Sunset 145:46 Jl '70

Social life and customs
Catch Colorado; people who shape the state. il Vogue 156:114-27 N 15 '70

COLORADO committee for environmental information
Colorado committee. Environ 12:15 My '70
Colorado environmentalists; scientists battle AEC and army. B. Nelson. Science 168:1324+ Je 12 '70

COLORADO earthquakes. See Earthquakes—United States

COLORADO library association
Librarian as subversive: Colorado LA conference. W. R. Eshelman. Wilson Lib Bul 45:230+ N '70

COLORADO RIVER
Canyonlands by night; Moab, Utah boat ride. F. A. Barnes. il Travel 134:64-6 Ag '70
Hoover Dam hangover; through the canyons and rapids. A. Schafer. il Motor B 127:62+ Ja '71
Sixteenth annual Colorado River cruise. J. Joseph. il Motor B 125:68-71 My '70
See also
Grand Canyon
Havasu Lake
Powell, Lake

COLORADOANS. See Coloradans

COLORED light. See Light, Colored

COLORING matter in food
Lab bench; identifying artificial color on oranges. Chem 43:29-30 F '70

COLORS. See Color

COLOSSEUM, Rome
Colosseum: world's bloodiest acre. J. Bryan, 3d. il Read Digest 96:234-6+ Je '70

COLQUITT, Betsy
Poor heart; poem. Chr Cent 87:416 Ap 8 '70

COLSON, Frank A.
Workshop; kiln building with space age materials. il Craft Horiz 30:46-8 Ag '70

COLSON, Jaime
Master draftsman. R. Squirru. il **Américas** 22:31-5 Ja '70 *

COLT, Jon
Build a D.C. transformer. il Pop Electr 32: 35+ Mr '70

COLT industries, inc.
Colt diesel that led to disaster. il Bsns W p84+ Ja 9 '71

COLT revolvers. See Revolvers

COLTER, James R.
Local association of the month. Todays Ed 59:64 N '70

COLTMAN, Derek
(tr) See Blais, M. C. Manuscripts of Pauline Archange

COLTS (football club) See Football clubs

COLUM, Padraic
Another world from mine. New Yorker 46:46-9 O 10 '70

COLUMBIA, Md.
City made to human measure. il Life 70:76-83 Ja 8 '71
Columbia, gem of America's new towns. J. L. O'Neill. il Am Home 73:95+ My '70
Jim Rouse's satellite city. J. Peter. il por Look 34:55-7 F 10 '70
New unity in the new city; shared religious facilities. America 123:370 N 7 '70

COLUMBIA broadcasting system, inc.
Atrocity story; replay of stabbing incident in Vietnam. il Newsweek 75:67 Je 1 '70
Blowup; CBS substantiates Vietnamese atrocity incident. R. L. Shayon. Sat R 53:16 Je 6 '70
CBS' fast draw on home TV tapes. il Bsns W p50+ Mr 28 '70
CBS will enter proprietary resident school field. Pub W 198:33 N 9 '70
Dann v. Klein: the best game in town. pors Time 95:98+ My 25 '70
Delayed replay. il Time 95:66 Je 1 '70
How CBS copes with TV pressures. il Bsns W p58-61+ Jl 4 '70
How Mike Dann keeps his job at CBS. il pors Bsns W p78+ My 2 '70
Nielsen to newspeak: CBS seeks an image. il Ramp Mag 9:46-8+ N '70
Overhaul at CBS. Time 95:77 Mr 2 '70
Prime time to leave. por Newsweek 76:59 Jl 6 '70

COLUMBIA Eagle hijacking. See Ship hijacking

COLUMBIA-Presbyterian medical center. See New York (city)—Columbia-Presbyterian medical center

COLUMBIA records, inc.
Supersonic boom. por Time 96:72-3 S 28 '70

COLUMBIA RIVER
Death by degrees for salmon; thermal pollution special studies at Bonneville. M. Davenport. Field & S 74:76-7 Ap '70
Too much for the Columbia River salmon. E. Chaney. il Nat Wildlife 8:18-21 Ap '70
See also
Willapa Bay

COLUMBIA university
Bill McGill takes over Columbia's hot campus. K. Lamott. il por N Y Times Mag p26-7+ Ag 23 '70
Columbia gets its man. por Time 95:40 F 16 '70
Eric Brown; anti-war demonstration. New Yorker 46:30-1 Ap 25 '70
History-of-physics laboratory. S. Devons and L. Hartmann. il pors Phys Today 23:44-9 F '70
Homecoming; return of W. J. McGill. por Newsweek 75:69 F 16 '70

School of law
Healer for Columbia. por Time 95:45 Ap 20 '70

School of library service
Columbia L.S. students bus to D.C. condemn war. il Library J 95:2207 Je 15 '70

COLUMBIAN exposition of 1893. See Chicago—Worlds Columbian exposition, 1893

COLUMBUS, Christopher

Drama
Ghost from Genoa; reprint from October 1955 issue. E. J. Dias. Plays 30:53-60, 77 O '70

COLUMBUS, Ind.

Public schools
Two more for Columbus. il Arch Forum 132: 22-31 Mr '70

COLUMELLA, Lucius Junius Moderatus
Journey down a Roman road. A. S. Taormina. il Cons 24:5-7 Ag '69 *

COLUMNISTS. See Journalists; Women as journalists

COLUMNS (architecture)
Water-filled columns keep building frames cool in fires. A. Fisher. il Pop Sci 196:63 My '70

COLUMNS (newspapers) See Newspapers—Sections, columns, etc.

COLUMNS (periodicals) See Periodicals—Sections, columns, etc.

COLVILLE, William
Have narrow rows been oversold? interview, ed. by C. E. Sommers. il pors Suc Farm 68: 30-1+ S '70

COLVIN, Bruce
Art of the medieval blacksmith. il Craft Horiz 30:24-7+ Mr '70

COLVIS, L. L.
Think you're big enough to bargain with a packer? Farm J 94:H7+ My '70

COMA
Unconsciousness. C. J. Potthoff. Todays Health 48:64 Ag '70

COMALCO ltd. See Aluminum industry and trade—Australia

COMBINATION locks. See Locks and keys

COMBINES. See Harvesting machinery

COMBUSTION
Clean power from coal. A. M. Squires. bibliog il Science 169:821-8 Ag 28 '70

COME back to me; story. See Ernst, P.

COMEDIANS
Great comedians as theologians. F. T. Trotter. Chr Cent 87:101-2 Ja 28 '70
U.S. journal; west Forty-fourth street; showcase for comedians of limited talent at the Improvisation. C. Trillin. New Yorker 46: 148+ O 17 '70
See also
Cavett, D.
Dangerfield, R.
Gardner, D.
Keaton, B.
Smothers brothers

COMÉDIE française
Comédie française in a Molière festival. City center theater. D. Hering. il Dance Mag 44:88-91 Ap '70
Health; interview with troupe members. New Yorker 46:31-2 Mr 7 '70
House of Molière; visit to New York. H. Saal. il Newsweek 75:103 F 16 '70
Theatre; Molière festival at City center. New Yorker 45:57-8+ F 14; 46:60+ F 21 '70
Theater; production of Dom Juan in New York. New Repub 162:18 F 28 '70

COMEDY
What's so funny? comedienne J. Rivers sizes up our sense of humor. T. Thompson. il pors Life 70:69-70+ Ja 8 '71
See also
Comedians
Humor
Television broadcasting—Humor

COMENIUS, Johann Amos
Legacy of John Amos Comenius. E. C. Bock. il Chr Today 15:11-14 N 6 '70 *
Tercentenary of Camenius' death: education for world peace. W. W. Brickman; J. D. Pope; L. Kurdybacha. bibliog il Sch & Soc 98:436-46 N '70 *

COMER, Nancy Axelrad
Crafty about fashion. il Mlle 70:186-7 Mr '70
Hokahe! il Mlle 71:158-9+ O '70
Magazine jobs U.S.A. Mlle 71:160+ S '70
Where the jobs are: Geneva, London, Paris, Rome. Mlle 71:114-15 Je '70
Women are discriminated against [but they deserve it] Mlle 70:248-9+ F '70

COMETS
All-Japanese comet: 1970m. Sky & Tel 40: 352 D '70
Another bright comet; comet 1969i. Sky & Tel 39:83 F '70
Another sungrazing comet; comet White-Ortiz-Bolelli. il Sky & Tel 40:15-16 Jl '70
Comet Bennett's fine show. il Sky & Tel 39: 330-3 My '70
Comet in ultraviolet; Tago-Sato-Kosaka. il Sci N 97:241 Mr 7 '70
Comet 1969g observed around the world. il Sky & Tel 39:262-6 Ap '70
Comet 1970a appears. Sky & Tel 39:160 Mr '70
Comet spotting; Tago-Sato-Kosaka. il Newsweek 75:57 F 9 '70
Comet Tago-Sato-Kosaka, 1969g. il Sky & Tel 39:196-8 Mr '70
Encke's comet is back. Sky & Tel 40:259 N '70
Great comet of 1970; comet Bennett. il Sky & Tel 39:351-6 Je '70

COMETS—*Continued*
New comet Abe 1970g. Sky & Tel 40:140 S '70
New comet in early morning sky; comet
Fujikawa. il R Pop Astron 63:13 Ag '69
    See also
Halley's comet

Photographs
Photos of comet 1969g from Cerro Tololo. Sky
& Tel 39:228-31 Ap '70

Spectra
Spectra of comet Tago-Sato-Kosaka. F. Dossin. il Sky & Tel 39:152-3 Mr '70

COMFORTERS. See Quilts

COMIC literature. See Humor

COMIC strips. See Comics (books, strips, etc)

COMICS (books, strips, etc)
Comic realities. il Newsweek 76:98-99B N 23
'70
Dirigible; comic strip. G. Viertel. Harp Baz
104:62-5 Ja '71
Friday Foster. New Yorker 46:33-4 Mr 21 '70

COMINS, Jeremy
Embossing without a press. il Sch Arts 70:
26-7 D '70

COMMAGER, Henry Steele
America's heritage of bigness. Sat R 53:10-12
Jl 4 '70
Choosing Supreme court judges. New Repub
162:13-16 My 2 '70
Conversations with historians; excerpts from
Interpreting American history, ed. by J. A.
Garraty. il por Am Heritage 21:58-60 F '70
Has the small college a future? il Sat R 53:
62-4+ F 21 '70
Is freedom dying in America? il por Look
34:16-21 Jl 14 '70

COMMANDAY, Robert
Floyd's Of mice and men. il Hi Fi 20:secII
28-9 Ap '70

COMMANDOS. See Guerrillas

COMMEMORATIVE medals. See Medals

COMMEMORATIVE stamps. See Postage stamps

COMMENCEMENT addresses. See Baccalaureate addresses

COMMENCEMENTS
Commencement and counter-commencement.
il Time 95:46+ Je 15 '70
Commencement theme, 1970: reconciliation.
America 122:644 Je 20 '70
Commencement time: bitter protests to the
end. il U S News 68:33-4 Je 22 '70
Dear diary. W. F. Buckley, jr. Nat R 22:
748 Jl 14 '70
Educational opportunity: Great Britain. R.
Haughton. Cath World 212:7-8 O '70
Graduation day at Kent state. il Newsweek
75:20-1 Je 22 '70
Graduation day for '70; with excerpts from
commencement addresses. il Life 68:20-9
Je 19 '70
Happy (?) graduation. Chr Today 14:22 My
22 '70

COMMENSALISM. See Symbiosis

COMMERCE
Changing perspectives; world trade and finance; address, September 8, 1970. A. W.
Clausen. Vital Speeches 36:746-9 O 1 '70
Economic report of the President and the annual report of the Council of economic advisers; excerpts. R. M. Nixon. il Dept State
Bul 62:240-53 Mr 2 '70
Improving the trading opportunities of the
developing countries through generalized
preferences; statement, March 31, 1970. E.
M. Cronk. Dept State Bul 62:612-15 My 11
'7i
    See also
Balance of payments
Business conditions
Communist countries—Commerce
Competition, International
Dumping (commercial policy)
Free enterprise
Free trade and protection
Import quotas
Investments, Foreign
Raw materials
Suez Canal
Tariff—United States
World trade week
    also headings beginning Commercial; *also*
    subhead Commerce under names of countries, e.g. United States—Commerce

COMMERCE department (United States) See
United States—Commerce, Department of

COMMERCIAL arbitration. See Arbitration,
Commercial

COMMERCIAL art. See Art, Commercial

COMMERCIAL banks. See Banks and banking

COMMERCIAL finance companies. See Finance
companies

COMMERCIAL law
    See also
Trusts, Industrial—Law
Warranty

COMMERCIAL paper. See Negotiable instruments

COMMERCIAL products
Consumer goods; with yardsticks of management performance. il Forbes 105:116+ Ja 1
70:107:148+ Ja 1 '71
Disposables. il House B 112:92-3+ Mr '70
    See also
Commodity exchanges
Products, New
Quality of products
Raw materials

Anecdotes, facetiae, satire, etc.
People and products; a useful decalogue;
address, October 6, 1969. M. Leeds. Vital
Speeches 36:303-6 Mr 1 '70

Endorsements
    See Advertising—Testimonials

COMMERCIAL travelers. See Salesman and
salesmanship

COMMERCIAL treaties and agreements. See
United States—Commercial treaties and
agreements

COMMERCIALS. See Television advertising

COMMERS, Mary C.
Operation English freedom. Engl J 59:674-6
My '70

COMMISSION on college physics
What our left hand has been doing. J. M.
Fowler and R. West. bibliog il pors Phys
Today 23:24-9+ Mr '70

COMMISSION on faith and order. See World
council of churches

COMMISSION on law and public affairs. See
National Jewish commission on law and
public affairs

COMMISSIONER of education. See United
States—Education, Office of

COMMISSIONS, Independent regulatory. See
Independent regulatory commissions

COMMISSIONS of inquiry
Credit due; Catholic churchmen on presidential and national commissions. Commonweal
93:138 N 6 '70
Crime, violence, and social disorder. AAAS
symposium, December 29-30, 1970. J. Coates
and A. Sagalyn. Science 170:1120-1 D 4
'70
Knowledge for what? presidential commissions. Nation 211:132 Ag 31 '70
Something is out of commission. T. H.
Clancy. America 123:166 S 19 '70

Anecdotes, facetiae, satire, etc.
Commission on commissions. V. Gold. Nat R
22:1038 O 6 '70

COMMISSIONS of the United Nations. See
name of commission as subhead under
United Nations. e.g. United Nations—Commission for social development

COMMISSIONS of the United States government. See name of commission as subhead under United States, e.g. United
States—Commission on narcotic drugs

COMMITTEE for a sane nuclear policy. See
National committee for a sane nuclear policy

COMMITTEE for development planning of the
United Nations. See United Nations—Committee for development planning

COMMITTEE for economic development
High level call for guidelines. Time 96:86
D 7 '70
Making Congress more effective. R. L. Tobin.
Sat R 53:22 O 31 '70
Metropolitan government gets a boost. Bsns
W p71 F 21 '70
Poverty: a losing war; report on urban
poverty. il Newsweek 76:117 N 23 '70

COMMITTEE for environmental information
Space available; excerpts from testimony before the Joint congressional committee on
atomic energy, January 29, 1970. M. Peterson. bibliog il Environ 12:2-9 Mr '70

COMMITTEE for environmental Information,
Colorado. See Colorado committee for environmental information

COMMITTEE for human rights, Russia. See
Civil rights organizations—Russia

COMMITTEE of small magazine editors and
publishers
Life among the littles; report of annual
meeting. J. Wilentz. il Pub W 198:25-7 Ag 3
'70

COMMITTEE of twenty-four. See United Nations—Special committee on the situation with regard to the implementation of the declaration on the granting of independence to colonial countries and peoples

COMMITTEE on challenges of modern society. See NATO—Committee on challenges of modern society

COMMITTEE on new directions. See American library association—Committee on new directions

COMMITTEE on organization. See American library association—Committee on organization

COMMITTEE on political education. See American federation of labor and Congress of industrial organizations—Committee on political education

COMMITTEE on science in the promotion of human welfare. See American association for the advancement of science—Committee on science in the promotion of human welfare

COMMITTEE on the challenges of modern society. See NATO—Committee on the challenges of modern society

COMMITTEE on the peaceful uses of outer space. See United Nations—Committee on the peaceful uses of outer space

COMMITTEES, Congressional. See United States—Congress—Committees

COMMODITIES. See Commercial products

COMMODITY exchanges
Blight that sows panic. il Newsweek 76:51 Ag 31 '70
Futures traders try the West. il Bsns W p30 O 10 '70
Grain futures hit the sky. il Bsns W p22 Ag 22 '70
How blight affected corn futures last year. F. Bailey, jr. Suc Farm 69:D6-7 Ja '71
Market's lonely man; caller at the New York coffee and sugar exchange. R. Levy. il Duns 96:60 O '70
Speculators whet their appetites. il Bsns W p 19 Jl 11 '70
Using futures, earn storage or buy feed. F. Bailey, jr. il Suc Farm 68:no2 66.7+ F '70
Using futures, how to sell on the market. F. Bailey, jr. il Suc Farm 68:28-9+ Ja '70
Using futures, marketing clues from the market. F. Bailey, jr. il Suc Farm 68:no5 28-9 Mr '70
Using futures, you can speculate. F. Bailey, jr. il Suc Farm 68:no3 32-3+ F '70
When the frost is on the orange; orange juice futures. il Bsns W p34-5 Ja 24 '70
See also
Grain trade

Japan
Hill of beans leads to a scandal. Bsns W p29 O 31 '70

COMMON carriers. See Carriers

COMMON cause (political organization)
Cause célèbre. il pors Time 97:16 Ja 18 '71
CC: citizens' lobby in the public interest. H. J. Sievers. America 123:109 S 5 '70
Common cause; a new citizens' lobby; address, September 11, 1970. J. W. Gardner. Cur 123:3-8 N '70
Gardner builds a citizens' lobby. il Bsns W p25 O 31 '70
Gardner's cause. il por Newsweek 76:23-4 D 7 '70

COMMON market in Central America. See Central American program of economic integration

COMMON market in western Europe. See European economic community

COMMON stocks. See Stocks

COMMONER, Barry
Beyond the teach-in. il por Sat R 53:50-2+ Ap 4 '70
Soil & fresh water: damaged global fabric. il Environ 12:4-11 Ap '70
Super technology, will it end the good life? por Field & S 75:59+ Je '70

about
Clash of gloomy prophets. por Time 97:56 Ja 11 '71 *
Paul Revere of ecology. por Time 95:58 F 2 '70

COMMONWEALTH of nations
From John Bull to Uncle Sam: how to run an empire. J. Aitken. il Am Heritage 21· 44-5+ Ag '70
Imperial sunset: Britain's liberal empire, 1897-1921, by M. Beloff. Review
Sat R 53:36-7 Mr 21 '70. C. Miller

COMMONWEALTH united corporation
Can Commonwealth united make it? il Bsns W p 114+ Mr 7 '70

COMMUNAL living. See Collective settlements

COMMUNAL settlements. See Collective settlements

COMMUNES. See Collective settlements

COMMUNICABLE diseases
Plague year for killer diseases? il U S News 69:48 S 7 '70
See also
Animals as carriers of infection
Carriers of infection
Virus diseases
also names of communicable diseases, e.g. Cholera

COMMUNICABLE diseases in animals
Mammalian ecology and epidemiology of zoonoses. I. Muul. bibliog Science 170:1275-9 D 18 '70
Transmissible mink encephalopathy: experimental transmission to the squirrel monkey. R. J. Eckroade and others. bibliog il Science 169:1088-90 S 11 '70

COMMUNICATION
Biocybernetics of the dynamic communication of emotions and qualities; AAAS symposium, December 29, 1970. M. Clynes. Science 170:764-5 N 13 '70
Communications as a discipline. J. McLaughlin. America 122:140 F 7 '70
Communications; ed. by R. L. Tobin. See Communications issues of Saturday review
Getting to know each other better. R. L. Tobin. Sat R 53:20 Mr 7 '70
See also
Cybernetics
Information, Freedom of
Interlibrary communication
Language and languages
Mass media
Public relations

International aspects
Mexican wonders; International symposium on the media of communication. C. J. McNaspy. America 123:529-30 D 12 '70
Modern communications. C. T. Vetter, jr. Vital Speeches 36:505-12 Je 1 '70
See also
Hot line (Washington-Peking) (proposed)

COMMUNICATION (theology)
Bye-bye Babylon. D. H. Gill. Chr Today 15:17-18+ N 20 '70
Christian communications; revival of rhetoric? D. E. Kucharsky. Chr Today 14:52 Ap 10 '70
Ecumenism and communication; cooperation among denominational journals. J. M. Bailey. Chr Cent 87:241 F 25 '70
Pastor, what was that you said? J. T. Young. Chr Today 15:26-7 N 20 '70
Sacramental humanism. P. Verghese. Chr Cent 87:1116-20 S 23 '70; Reply. J. N. D. Kelly. 87:1489 D 9 '70
Ten year term for the bishop. J. P. Leary. il Cath World 212:194-6 Ja '71
Training for a time of change. R. L. Howe. Chr Cent 87:477-80 Ap 22 '70
See also
Mass media in religion

COMMUNICATION, Animal. See Animal communication

COMMUNICATION, Interlibrary. See Interlibrary communication

COMMUNICATION, Nonverbal
Body language, by J. Fast. Review
Newsweek il 75:87+ Je 22 '70
Body language, what it reveals about you. B. Ford. il Sci Digest 68:16-21 Ag '70
Bodyspeak: the way you move. il Vogue 156:389-90+ S 1 '70
Human potential: the revolution in feeling. il Time 96:54-8 N 9 '70
Non-verbal communication and the teacher. C. W. Garner. bibliog Sch & Soc 98:363-4 O '70
Parting shots; what are the politicians really saying? Body language tells you. il Life 69: 82-4 O 9 '70
Those telltale executive gestures. J. Ross-Skinner. il Duns 95:66-7 Mr '70
Way we speak body language; kinesics. F. Davis. il por N Y Times Mag p8-9+ My 31 '70
See also
Gesture

COMMUNICATION and traffic
See also
Airlines—Communication systems
International telephone and telegraph corporation
Telecommunication

COMMUNICATION in education
Does humanity grow in your classroom? English composition and literature. F. T. Wilhelms. Schol Teach Jr/Sr High p34-5 S 21 '70

Internal communications. F. C. Mayer. Clear House 44:290-5 Ja '70

Media revolution: its educational implications. R. Pratte. Clear House 45:207-11 D '70

Non-verbal communication and the teacher. C. W. Garner. bibliog Sch & Soc 98:363-4 O '70

COMMUNICATION in government
Decisions in the White House. H. J. Sievers. America 122:263 Mr 14 '70

Nixon in a crisis of leadership. H. Sidey. il por Life 68:28-9 My 15 '70

Phone calls that didn't get through. H. Sidey. Life 68:4 My 29 '70

Who speaks for the United States? contradictory policy statements. il por Newsweek 76:31-2 Jl 27 '70

COMMUNICATION in management
Communicate through your supervisors. L. I. Gelfand. Harvard Bsns R 48:101-4 N '70

Effective communication; address, July 1970. W. Wiesman. Vital Speeches 36:723-5 S 15 '70

If they just don't seem to get your message. il Changing T 24:39-40 Je '70

Intelligence in industry: the uses and abuses of experts; excerpts from Organizational intelligence. H. L. Wilensky. bibliog f Ann Am Acad 388:46-58 Mr '70

Keeping in touch during a walkout. V. Louviere. Nations Bsns 58:18 S '70

Problem of the new chief executive. S. R. Stuart. il Duns 95:24-6 Ja '70

COMMUNICATION in science
Communication in the physical and the social sciences. W. D. Garvey and others. il Science 170:1166-73 D 11 '70

Communication or chaos? adaptation of address, December 29, 1969. D. B. Baker. Science 169:739-42 Ag 21 '70

See also
Science—Information services

COMMUNICATION theory. See Information theory

COMMUNICATIONS, Military
See also
Communications satellites—Military use
United States—Navy—Communication systems

COMMUNICATIONS, Police. See Police communication systems

COMMUNICATIONS, Privileged. See Confidential communications

COMMUNICATIONS media study group tour. See Travel study courses

COMMUNICATIONS network, NASA. See United States—National aeronautics and space administration—Communications network

COMMUNICATIONS research
TV vs. print; study findings of H. Krugman. Newsweek 76:122-3 N 2 '70

COMMUNICATIONS research machines, inc.
Field of knowledge fetches $21-million. il Bsns W p 19-20 Ag 8 '70

COMMUNICATIONS satellite corporation
AT&T and Comsat wire a satellite deal. Bsns W p49 O 17 '70

Battle opens for ground stations. Aviation W 92:30 My 4 '70

Comsat industries? Forbes 105:20-1 Mr 15 '70

Comsat loses some thrust. Bsns W p38-9 F 28 '70

85,000-circuit satcom forecast. K. Johnsen. Aviation W 93:14-15 S 21 '70

FCC tunes in on Comsat again. Bsns W p30-1 Je 20 '70

Insured for space. il Newsweek 75:64 Ja 26 '70

Intelsat on ice? B. Maddox. New Repub 162: 10-11 My 16 '70

Satcom policy spurs immediate response. K. Johnsen. Aviation W 92:67 F 9 '70

Troubles pile up for first business in space. il U S News 68:64-5 My 18 '70

TV eyes birds; new satellite system? Sr Schol 95:15 N 10 '69

COMMUNICATIONS satellites
Added starter files for satcom permit; International board of trade of Los Angeles and Western telecommunications. il Aviation W 93:17 N 30 '70

Applications technology satellite program. il Space World G-9-81:18-20 S '70

AT&T and Comsat wire a satellite deal. Bsns W p49 O 17 '70

AT&T, Comsat system to use two satellites. P. J. Klass. Aviation W 93:20-1 O 26 '70

Beyond Babel; adaptation of address, December 1969. A. C. Clarke. il UNESCO Courier 23:32-7 Mr '70

Can satellites replace the bike? Western union's plans for a domestic communications satellite system. il Bsns W p20 Ag 15 '70

Communications satellite program; message to the Congress, February 26, 1970. R. M. Nixon. Dept State Bul 62:534 Ap 20 '70

Communications satellites. P. H. Abelson. Science 170:813 N 20 '70

Communications satellites. il Space World G-12-84:24-9 D '70

Domestic communications satellites: FCC still looking at the options. R. J. Samuelson. Science 168:1190+ Je 5 '70

Early hybrid aerosat effort sought. P. J. Klass. Aviation W 93:14-15 Ag 24 '70

85,000-circuit satcom forecast. K. Johnsen. Aviation W 93:14-15 S 21 '70

FCC increases frequency bands available for domestic satcoms. K. Johnsen. Aviation W 93:23-4 O 5 '70

FCC notified by five firms of domestic satcom plans. K. Johnsen. Aviation W 93:18 Ag 24 '70

FCC throws open domestic satcom field. K. Johnsen. Aviation W 92:19 Mr 30 '70

Hughes plans domestic TV satellites. K. Johnsen. Aviation W 94:16 Ja 4 '71

More satcom plans announced; broadcasters postpone decision. Aviation W 93:18 Ag 31 '70

NATO communications satellite. il Space World G-7-79:14-15 Jl '70

Open skies; domestic policy. Newsweek 75: 74 F 2 '70

Outlook for direct TV satellite is mixed. il Aviation W 92:139+ Je 22 '70

Plum in the sky. il Sci N 98:160 Ag 22 '70

Post office to participate in domestic Satcom case. K. Johnsen. Aviation W 93:51 D 21 '70

Private L-band aerosat system proposed. P. J. Klass. Aviation W 94:19 Ja 11 '71

Realizing the benefits of space technology: direct broadcast satellites; statement, May 11, 1970. W. P. Allen. Dept State Bul 63:95-9 Jl 20 '70

Satcom policy spurs immediate response. K. Johnsen. Aviation W 92:67 F 9 '70

Satellite with a private beam. S. V. Jones. Sci Digest 68:67 N '70

Spin-off from space satellites. G. Gregory. il UNESCO Courier 23:8-10 Mr '70

Talks set on proposals for aerosat. P. J. Klass. il Aviation W 93:47-9 Ag 3 '70

Transmission delays and echoes in satellite communications. R. G. Gould. il Electr World 84:34-6+ Ag '70

TV eyes birds; new satellite system? Sr Schol 95:15 N 10 '69

U.S. domestic satellite costs cited in study. il Aviation W 92:64-5 Mr 16 '70

VHF aerosat backed in Europe. Aviation W 93:31 S 7 '70

World's first TV broadcast satellite. W. Von Braun. il Pop Sci 196:64-6 My '70

See also
Communications satellite corporation
International telecommunications satellite consortium

Economic aspects
Competition for domestic satellites; Nixon's new guidelines. Bsns W p98 Ja 31 '70

Educational use
Education beyond the horizon. L. P. Grayson. bibliog Science 170:1376-82 D 25 '70

U.S. and India join in project for instructional TV via satellite; text of letter; December 11, 1969. S. Sen; C. W. Yost. Dept State Bul 62:44-5 Ja 12 '70

Ground stations
Battle opens for ground stations. Aviation W 92:30 My 4 '70

International aspects
Controversy grows on frequency for use on aeronautical satellite; with editorial comment. P. J. Klass. Aviation W 92:9, 34 Je 29 '70

Discord over aero-sat increasing. P. J. Klass. Aviation W 92:51-3+ My 18 '70

NATO satcom nears operational status. D. E. Fink. Aviation W 92:20-1 Je 1 '70

President Nixon, King Hassan open communications satellite service; exchange of remarks, January 7, 1970. R. M. Nixon; Hassan II. Dept State Bul 62:129 F 2 '70

COMMUNICATIONS satellites—International aspects—*Continued*

Toward the global village; with editorial comment. I. Asimov; S. Mickelson; J. d'Arcy. il Sat R 53:17-26 O 24 '70

U.S. group to help plan for 1971 space telecommunications meeting; Department announcement, May 4, 1970. Dept State Bul 62:714-15 Je 8 '70

Military use

New DOD satcoms nearing launch. P. J. Klass. il Aviation W 94:40-1+ Ja 11 '71

Testing

Intelsat 4 passes vacuum testing. il Space World G-7-79:16-17 Jl '70

COMMUNICATIONS satellites, British

Skynet A: Britain's first communications satellite. il Space World G-5-77:34-6 My '70

COMMUNICATIONS satellites, Canadian

Canadian satcom builders spark debate. Aviation W 93:17 Jl 13 '70

Competition tightens on Canadian satcom. Aviation W 93:20 Jl 27 '70

COMMUNICATIONS satellites, Italian

Italian industry to fund satcom; Sirio satellite. Aviation W 92:79 Ap 6 '70

COMMUNISM

Empire and revolution, by D. Horowitz. Review

　Ramp Mag 8:60+ F '70. T. Gitlin

Humanism and terror, by M. Merleau-Ponty. Review

　Commonweal 93:225-6 N 27 '70. D. Howard

Lenin; address, April 21, 1970. L. I. Brezhnev. Vital Speeches 36:482-98 Je 1 '70

Many faces of communism; symposium. il Sr Schol 95:4-17 N 17 '69

Marxism in the twentieth century, by R. Garaudy. Review

　America 123:301-2 O 17 '70. Q. Lauer

Nature of communism in the emergent world. B. P. Kiernan. Yale R 59:321-32 Mr '70

See also

Collective settlements

Communist countries

Communist parties

Socialism

Anti-Communist measures

Carl McIntire's victory; in this sign conquer; with editorial comment. W. Willoughby. il Chr Today 14:25, 35 Ap 24 '70

See also

United States—Foreign relations—Anti-Communist measures

History

Growth & division of communism. il Sr Schol 95:6-10 N 17 '69

Lenin (1870-1970) N. D. Roodkowsky. por Cath World 211:107-11 Je '70

Asia, Southeastern

What a Communist victory in Laos would mean. il U S News 68:21 Mr 23 '70

See also

Anti-Communist movements—Asia, Southeastern

Cambodia

Cambodia in the balance; report from the scene. il U S News 68:28-30 Ap 13 '70

Cambodia: the wreck we left behind; with report by J. Saar. il Life 69:23-30 Jl 10 '70

Cambodian civil war; Khmer rouge activities. O. Schell. New Repub 162:12-14 Je 6 '70

Coup in Cambodia; how Sihanouk lost out; with eyewitness account by C. S. Foltz, jr. il por U S News 68:18-20 Mr 30 '70

Test in Cambodia. Nat R 22:392 Ap 21 '70

Chile

Chile going. H. C. Wallich. Newsweek 76:99 N 2 '70

How Communists took power in Chile. il U S News 69:33-5 D 21 '70

See also

Communist party (Chile)

China (People's Republic)

China: the siege of the ants; celebrating 21st anniversary of Communist victory. il Time 96:36-44 N 16 '70

Is Chinese communism godless? N. Hunter. il Cath World 212:197-9 Ja '71

Mao ethic and environmental quality. L. A. Orleans and R. P. Suttmeier. bibliog Science 170:1173-6 D 11 '70

What makes Mao a Maoist. S. R. Schram. il N Y Times Mag p36-7+ Mr 8 '70

Cuba

Cuba revisited after ten years of Castro. Viator. For Affairs 48:312-21 Ja '70

Inside Cuba; workers and revolution; excerpt from Revolutionary politics and the Cuban working class. M. Zeitlin. il Ramp Mag 8: 10-11+ Mr '70

Letter from Camp Verceremos. C. Camarano. il Ramp Mag 9:6+ Ag '70

Europe, Eastern

Communists: ironic reversal; Ordeal of A. Dubček and Stalin's return. pors Time 96: 30-1 Jl 6 '70

Dissent cannot be shot down or arrested. P. Young. il pors Life 68:61+ My 1 '70

France

See also

Communist party (France)

Germany (Democratic Republic)

Report on the other Germany. B. van Voorst. il por Newsweek 76:50-2 D 21 '70

Hungary

Hungary today. J. Wechsberg. il Sat R 53:21-3+ N 28 '70

See also

Communist party (Hungary)

Indonesia

See also

Anti-Communist movements—Indonesia

Communist party (Indonesia)

Italy

Low-profile Communists; results of Communist rule in Emilia-Romagna. il Time 97:34-5 Ja 4 '71

See also

Communist party (Italy)

Laos

All-out war menaces Laos. S. W. Sanders. il U S News 68:13 F 23 '70

In the President's words; what U.S. is doing in Laos; statement, March 6, 1970. R. M. Nixon. por U S News 68:86-8 Mr 16 '70; Same with title Scope of the U.S. involvement in Laos. Dept State Bul 62:405-9 Mr 30 '70

Laosization. Nat R 22:294-5 Mr 24 '70

What reds are up to in Laos. il U S News 68:35-6 Mr 16 '70

Mediterranean Region

Russians in the Mediterranean. E. von Kuehnelt-Leddihn. Nat R 22:891 Ag 25 '70

Poland

Barriers to change; interview, ed. by B. van Voorst. J. Szczepanski. Newsweek 77:23-4 Ja 4 '71

Communism under the Poles. W. F. Buckley, jr. Nat R 22:696 Je 30 '70

See also

Communist party (Poland)

Russia

Can Lenin's communism survive? Russia at crossroads. il pors U S News 68:66-70 Ap 20 '70

History lesson; letter. M. Salvadori. Nat R 22:721 Jl 14 '70

Lenin; Address, April 21, 1970. L. I. Brezhnev. Vital Speeches 36:482-98 Je 1 '70

Leninism; any number can play. por Newsweek 75:39 Ap 27 '70

Red fascism: the merger of Nazi Germany and Soviet Russia in the American image of totalitarianism, 1930's-1950's. L. K. Adler and T. G. Paterson. bibliog f Am Hist R 75:1046-64 Ap '70; Discussion. 75:2155-64 D '70

See also

Communist party (Russia)

United States

Crusade for morality; address, June 10, 1970. M. Rountree. Vital Speeches 36:597-602 Jl 15 '70

Odyssey of a friend; letters to W. F. Buckley, jr. 1954-1955. W. Chambers. bibliog f Nat R 22:22-32 Ja 13 '70

Odyssey of a friend; letters to W. F. Buckley jr. 1955-1957. W. Chambers. bibliog f Nat R 22:76-82 Ja 27 '70

See also

Rosenberg, Julius and Ethel, case

COMMUNISM—United States—*Continued*

Anti-Communist measures

Chinese spaceship: conception of H. S. Tsien, scientist deported in 1955. J. Lear. Sat R 53:62 My 16 '70

Our years of fear. T. I. Emerson. il Sat R 53:29-31+ Ja 17 '70

See also

John Birch society

United States—Subversive activities control board

Vietnam (Republic)

Chau affair. il por Newsweek 75:45 Mr 2 '70

How to make a martyr. il por Time 95:25 Mr 9 '70

Anti-Communist measures

See also

Vietnamese war, 1957-

COMMUNISM and democracy

Church in a Marxist society, by J. M. Lochman. Review

Commonweal 93:157-8 N 6 '70. C. C. West

Many faces of communism. il Sr Schol 95:4-6 N 17 '69

COMMUNISM and education

Cuba's schools, ten years later. M. Leiner. il Sat R 53:59-61+ O 17 '70

COMMUNISM and religion

Carl McIntire's victory: in this sign conquer; with editorial comment. W. Willoughby. il Chr Today 14:25, 35 Ap 24 '70

Christ to a marxist. J. Deedy. Commonweal 91:522 F 13 '70

Christian faith and the Marxist criticism of religion, by H. Gollwitzer. Review

America 123:214-15 S 26 '70. Q. Lauer

Conversations with Marxists. H. B. Kuhn. Chr Today 14:39 Jl 31 '70

Dialogue agenda. M. Shelly. Chr Cent 87:1262 O 21 '70

Is Chinese communism godless? N. Hunter. il Cath World 212:197-9 Ja '71

Urgency of Marxist-Christian dialogue. Review

Cath World 212:97-8 N '70. J. Conway

See also

Church and state in Yugoslavia

COMMUNISM and the Catholic church. See Catholic church and communism

COMMUNIST countries

Aspects of life under communism; symposium. il Sr Schol 95:18-20+ N 17 '69

Communism in turmoil: how red are its faces? il Sr Schol 95:11-17 N 17 '69

See also

China (People's Republic)

Europe, Eastern

Tourist trade—Communist countries

Commerce

Back of all the talk about doing business with the reds. il U S News 69:77-8 D 21 '70

Coexistence and commerce, by S. Pisar. Review

Sat R 53:29-31+ S 19 '70. D. Schoenbrun

East-West trade: wielding a tender sword. il por Time 96:88+ N 16 '70

Industrial and commercial relations; address, October 12, 1970. G. Agnelli. Vital Speeches 37:93-6 N 15 '70

COMMUNIST countries and the West. See World politics, 1945-

COMMUNIST parties

Worldgram: from the capitals of the world. U S News 69:45-6 O 5 '70

Purges

See also

Communist party (China [People's Republic])—Purges

Communist party (Czechoslovakia)—Purges

Communist party (Russia)—Purges

COMMUNIST party (Chile)

Chilean background. W. F. Buckley, jr. Nat R 22:1179 N 3 '70

COMMUNIST party (China [People's Republic])

Madame Mao's concerto. il Newsweek 75:46 Je 8 '70

Stamp of approval; forthcoming meeting of the National people's congress. Newsweek 76:52 S 21 '70

Purges

Mao makes the trials run on time. R. Hughes. il N Y Times Mag p22-3+ Ag 23 '70; Reply with rejoinder. A. S. Whiting. p41+ N 15 '70

COMMUNIST party (Czechoslovakia)

Fighting the tide. il por Newsweek 75:44 F 9 '70

Ordeal of A. Dubček. por Time 96:30 Jl 6 '70

Purges

Confession, by A. London. Review

Nation 211:598-600 D 7 '70. C. L. Markmann

Purge in Prague. il por Time 95:28+ F 9 '70

COMMUNIST party (France)

L'affaire Garaudy. il Newsweek 75:42+ F 23 '70

Clampdown in the West. il por Time 95:24+ F 23 '70

Dissent of Roger Garaudy. R. Salloch. New Repub 162:17-19 Mr 7 '70

Excommunication of Roger Garaudy. A. Woodrow. Commonweal 92:28-30 Mr 20 '70

Letter from Paris; intellectual rebellion sparked by R. Garaudy. Genêt. New Yorker 46:92-3 F 21 '70

Prelude to revolution: France in May 1968, by D. Singer. Review

Nation 211:213-14+ S 14 '70. C. Oglesby

COMMUNIST party (Hungary)

Brezhnev's blessing; tenth party congress. il Time 96:37 D 7 '70

COMMUNIST party (India)

Indian revolutionaries with a Chinese accent; the Naxalites. D. Moraes. il N Y Times Mag p30-1+ N 8 '70

On the march; land grab by Naxalites. il Time 96:23-4 Ag 24 '70

COMMUNIST party (Indonesia)

Communist collapse in Indonesia, by A. C. Brackman. Review

Sat R 53:39+ My 2 '70. J. M. Allison

COMMUNIST party (Italy)

Foreign report: Italy's happy Communists. C. Sterling. Harper 240:24+ F '70

Now, a red belt spread across Italy? il U S News 68:94 Je 22 '70

COMMUNIST party (Poland)

How's your ostpolitik? J. Burnham. Nat R 23:26 Ja 12 '71

Poland erupts, Gomulka steps out. il por Newsweek 76:21-2+ D 28 '70

Poland's new regime: gifts and promises. il por Time 97:33-4 Ja 4 '71

Polish unpleasantness. Nat R 23:20 Ja 12 '71

Rough road ahead for Polish leaders. il por U S News 70:64 Ja 4 '71

With Gomulka gone a new generation takes over. il pors Newsweek 77:22 Ja 4 '71

COMMUNIST party (Russia)

Are things really improving in the USSR? T. Szamuely. il Nat R 22:250-7 Mr 10 '70

Drift and delay. Newsweek 76:38+ Jl 27 '70

Indecision at the top. Time 96:18+ Jl 27 '70

Kremlin leaders: men with a very large number of crackpot ideas; excerpts from testimony. R. Conquest. il U S News 68: 57 F 9 '70

Stalin's successors. R. Conquest. For Affairs 48:509-24 Ap '70

Who is Mr X? S. Alsop. Newsweek 77:68 Ja 4 '71

See also

Russia—Politics and government

Political bureau

Failure of communications; impending shake-ups. il Newsweek 75:58 Ap 20 '70

That puzzling Politburo plague. il Time 95: 23-4 Ap 20 '70

Troubles and tremors; scuffling in the Politburo. il por Newsweek 75:33+ Ap 13 '70

Purges

Contribution of Robert Conquest. G. Niemeyer. Nat R 22:315-16 Mr 24 '70

COMMUNIST party (United States)

Enigmatic Angela. il pors Time 96:28 O 26 '70

COMMUNIST strategy

From Vietnam to Indochina. il por Newsweek 75:31-4+ Mr 30 '70

Russians in the Mediterranean. E. von Kuehnelt-Leddihn. Nat R 22:891 Ag 25 '70; Reply. I. C. Kidd. jr. 22:1192 N 17 '70

Russia's foreign triumphs. H. Trewhitt; A. de Borchgrave; J. Axelbank. il Newsweek 76:42-4 S 28 '70

COMMUNISTIC settlements. See Collective settlements

COMMUNISTS

See also

Communist parties

COMMUNITARIAN movement. See Collective settlements

COMMUNITIES (ecology) See Ecology

COMMUNITY and business. See Business—Social aspects

COMMUNITY and the college. See Colleges and universities—Public relations

COMMUNITY and the school. See School and the community

COMMUNITY antenna television system. See CATV system

COMMUNITY arts centers
Black arts for black youth; community arts movement in the ghetto. D. D. Bushnell. il Sat R 53:43-6+ Jl 18 '70
　　See also
Washington, D.C.—Community centers

COMMUNITY centers
1,800-member Florida center plans retirees housing project. il Aging 191:19 S '70
　　See also
Recreation centers
Senior centers
　　also subhead Community centers under names of cities, e.g. Minneapolis—Community centers

COMMUNITY chests
Ignorant philanthropists. B. Dinerman. Nation 210:369-72 Mr 30 '70

COMMUNITY college graduates. See College graduates

COMMUNITY colleges. See Junior colleges

COMMUNITY control of schools. See School management and organization

COMMUNITY councils. See Citizens associations

COMMUNITY development

Ireland

Commissar is a priest; plans of J. McDyer for Glencolumbkille. J. Roddy. il pors Look 34:56-8 Mr 24 '70

Latin America

Community development conference held; first Inter-American conference. Américas 22:45 O '70
　　See also
Accion international

Peru

Rural Peru: peasants as activists. W. F. Whyte. il por Trans-Action 7:37-47 N '69
Urban Peru: political action as sellout: case study of Ica. D. L. Bayer. il por Trans-Action 7:36+ N '69

United States

Architects design for a new client: the poor. J. Hale. il Arch Rec 148:144-7 O '70
Catfish empire; activities of J. L. McCown in Hancock County, Ga. Newsweek 76:48+ O 19 '70
Model cities, model for failure. D. Stoloff. Arch Forum 132:78-9+ Ja '70
Model cities workshop discusses planning programs for elderly. il Aging 184:4-6 F '70
Seattle's Model cities program develops services for elderly. Aging 184:7-8 F '70
Urban Vietnamization; on developing self-reliant black and brown communities; address, November 21, 1969. B. Holman. Vital Speeches 36:246-50 F 1 '70
　　See also
New York (state)—Urban development corporation

COMMUNITY development corporations
Atlanta banker with a social conscience: Citizens & Southern national bank. il por Bsns W p34+ Jl 25 '70

COMMUNITY education
Community education, best hope for society. W. F. Totten. bibliog il Sch & Soc 98: 410-13 N '70
Seventies; restructuring the educational system; address, November 24, 1970. M. A. Rapp. Vital Speeches 37:173-7 Ja 1 '71
Student goal centered learning program. K. L. Foster. Clear House 45:212-15 D '70

COMMUNITY health centers. See Health centers

COMMUNITY life
　　See also
Church and social problems
Citizens associations
Neighborhoods
Social education

COMMUNITY mental health centers. See Mental health centers

COMMUNITY mental health service. See Mental health service

COMMUNITY news service
Covering the minorities. il Time 96:31-2 Ag 10 '70

COMMUNITY organization
Changes in the black ghetto: East Palo Alto. W. Stegner. Sat R 53:12+ Ag 1 '70
Getting into the act. W. Von Eckardt. il Sat R 53:43-4 Jl 4 '70
Professional radical, 1970; interview, ed. by M. K. Sanders. S. Alinsky. il Harper 240: 35-42 Ja '70

Waking up people power; Institute for Jesuit community organizers, Chicago. T. M. Gannon and J. R. Hacala. America 123:520-1 D 12 '70

COMMUNITY planning. See City planning

COMMUNITY power
Getting into the act. W. Von Eckardt. il Sat R 53:43-4 Jl 4 '70
　　See also
Community organization

COMMUNITY recreation. See Recreation

COMMUNITY schools
Leonard Covello and the community school. F. Cordasco. bibliog f por Sch & Soc 98:298-9 Sum '70

COMMUNITY service
Brother, you can spare the time. V. R. Moseman. il Nations Bsns 58:84-5 F '70
Community action (title varies) (cont) il Sunset 144:107-8, 134 Mr; 124+ Ap; 145:24 Ag; 35+ S; 86-7 O; 52+ N '70
Is business meeting the challenge of urban affairs? J. Cohn. il Harvard Bsns R 48:68-82 Mr '70
Once upon a time: a fable of student power. N. Postman. il N Y Times Mag p 10-11 Je 14 '70
Their community needs them. H. Alpert. il Har Yrs 10:43-5+ Je '70
Women you'd like to know. il Farm J 94:60-1 My '70
　　See also
Volunteer service

COMMUNITY shopping centers. See Shopping centers

COMMUNITY swimming pools. See Swimming pools

COMMUTER airlines. See Local service airlines

COMMUTERS
Impact of commuters on the Mexican-American border area. A.-S. Ericson. bibliog f il Mo Labor R 93:18-27 Ag '70

COMMUTING
　　See also
Railroads—Commuter service

COMPACT cars. See Automobiles, Compact

COMPACTORS. See Refuse and refuse disposal—Apparatus

COMPANIES. See Corporations

COMPANION crops
Growing Jerusalem artichokes with corn. D. Criner. il Org Gard & Farm 17:90-2 Mr '70

The COMPANY. See Los Angeles—Theater

COMPANY; musical comedy. See Musical comedies, revues, etc.—Criticisms, plots, etc.

COMPANY airplanes. See Airplanes, Business

COMPANY economists. See Economists

COMPANY flags. See Corporations—Flags, insignia, etc.

COMPANY presidents (in business) See Executives

COMPARATIVE education. See Education, Comparative

COMPARATIVE religion. See Religions

COMPARATORS
Differential comparators. R. F. Brunner. il Electr World 84:37 Jl '70

COMPARISON shopping. See Shopping and shoppers

COMPASS
Compass for your boat. E. S. Maloney. il Motor B 126:22+ D '70
Electro compass. T. Bottomley. il Motor B 126:28+ O '70
How it works: the yacht compass. C. Miller. il Motor B 125:16 Je '70
Quick cures for compass error. J. Martenhoff. il Pop Sci 196:148-9 Ja '70
Your best friend, the compass. S. T. Simonsen. il Yachting 127:72-4+ Je '70
　　See also
Orienteering (sport)

COMPASSION. See Sympathy

COMPENSATION (law)
　　See also
Damages
Insurance, Workmens compensation

COMPENSATION of non-combatants. See World war, 1939-1945—Compensation of non-combatants

COMPETITION, International
Japan's drive to outstrip U.S. il U S News 68:26-8 Ap 6 '70
Making Ricardo's prophecy come true. Bsns W p61-2 D 19 '70
　　See also
Free trade and protection

COMPETITION, Unfair
　　See also
Dumping (commercial policy)

COMPETITIONS
How to blow a tractor engine and $1000 in 30 seconds flat; Tractor pulling contest. D. K. O'Brien. il Farm J 94:18-19+ Ag '70
16th annual tobacco spit-off. P. Range. il Time 96:13 Ag 17 '70
Sporting scene; Scotland's Highland gatherings and games. A. Reid. New Yorker 46: 60-70 Ag 29 '70
Uhh, Janet, Janet.., is that you? U.S. Pillow-fighting championship. il Sports Illus 33: 18-19 Ag 3 '70
    See also
Advertising—Prize contests
    also subhead Competitions under various subjects. e.g. Photography—Competitions

COMPETITIVE bidding. See Municipal contracts

COMPETITIVE sports. See Sports

COMPLAINTS
Action lines: nagging complaints are sweet music to them. il Mech Illus 66:45-7+ Ag '70
Fine art of complaining; excerpt from The action approach. G. Weinberg. Read Digest 97:81-4 S '70
Nothing works anymore. D. Sanford. il New Repub 162:21-4 F 14 '70

COMPLEMENTS (immunity)
Genetically controlled total deficiency of the fourth component of complement in the guinea pig. L. Ellman and others. bibliog il Science 170:74-5 O 2 '70
Immune virolysis: effect of antibody and complement on C-type RNA virus. S. Oroszlan and R. V. Gilden. bibliog il Science 168:1478-80 Je 19 '70

COMPLEXES (psychology)
Camus' The fall: the Icarus complex. M. A. Sperber. Am Imago 26:269-80 Fall '69
    See also
Oedipus complex

COMPLEXION. See Skin

COMPOSERS
    See also
Women as musicians

COMPOSERS, American
    See also
Abrams, R.
Bacharach, B.
Billings, W.
Cage, J.
Copland, A.
Dlugoszewski, L.
Gottschalk, L. M.
Krenek, E.
Marks, J.
Sessions, R.

COMPOSERS, Austrian
    See also
Mahler, G.
Mozart, J. C. W. A.

COMPOSERS, Czech
    See also
Dvořák, A.

COMPOSERS, English
    See also
Britten, B.

COMPOSERS, French
    See also
Adam, A. C.
Berlioz, H.
Campra, A.
Debussy, C.
Jolivet, A.

COMPOSERS, German
Does his music speak for our age? interview. ed. by R. Hemming. H. W. Henze. il por Sr Schol 96:15-17 My 4 '70
    See also
Beethoven, L. van
Flotow, F. von
Händel, G. F.
Hindemith, P.
Mendelssohn, F.
Reger, M.
Schumann, R. A.
Schütz, H.
Strauss, R.
Wagner, R.

COMPOSERS, Hungarian
    See also
Bartók, B.
Kodály, Z.

COMPOSERS, Italian
Italy's ottocento: notes from the musical underground. B. Friedland. bibliog f il Mus Q 56:27-53 Ja '70
    See also
Berio, L.
Busoni, F.
Corelli, A.
Giordano, U.
Lolli, A.
Mercadante, S.

Respighi, O.
Spontini, G.
Verdi, G.
Vivaldi, A.
Zandonai, R.

COMPOSERS, Polish
    See also
Chopin, F. F.
Penderecki, K.

COMPOSERS, Russian
    See also
Shostakovich, D. D.
Skriabin, A. N.
Tchaikovsky, P. I.

COMPOSERS string quartet. See String quartets

COMPOSITE materials
Advanced composite materials. T. M. Cornsweet. il Science 168:433-8 Ap 24 '70
New space-age materials. G. Gregory. il UNESCO Courier 23:24-6 Mr '70
Wide use of composites expected. W. S. Hieronymus. il Aviation W 92:29-35 Je 22 '70

COMPOSITE photography. See Photomontage

COMPOSITION (art)
Isolation of a single aspect of nature. R. Henkes. il Design 71:20-1 Sum '70

COMPOSITION (music)
Beeson on camera; interview. ed. by Q. Eaton. J. Beeson. por Opera N 34:13 Mr 21 '70
Debussy's dream House: libretto based on E. A. Poe's The fall of the house of Usher. E. Lockspeiser. il pors Opera N 34:8-12 Mr 21 '70
Eleven-day wonder; Donizetti's Don Pasquale. W. Ashbrook. il Opera N 35:24-5 D 5 '70
Händel's Tamerlano: the creation of an opera. J. M. Knapp. bibliog f il Mus Q 56: 405-30 Jl '70
How to write a rock 'n' roll song. L. Hutchinson. il Sr Schol 97:24 D 14 '70
Long, long road; Plough and the stars. E. Siegmeister. il por Opera N 34:26-9 Mr 14 '70
Questions about music. by R. Sessions. Review
    New Yorker 46:57 Ja 2 '71. W. Sargeant
Songs of a people; folk music in opera. N. Payne. il Opera N 34:8-12 F 21 '70
Words without song; excerpt from address. N. Rorem. Am Rec G 36:468-9+ Mr '70
    See also
Musical forgeries and mystifications

COMPOSITION (photography)
Discovery; ideas of George A. Peterson. J. Dreyfuss. il Mod Phot 34:84-5+ Mr '70
Feininger. A. Feininger. il Mod Phot 34:46+ My '70
Uptight or far out. il Mod Phot 34:90-3 Je '70
    See also
Photography—Still life

COMPOSITION (rhetoric) See Rhetoric

COMPOSITION, English. See English language —Composition

COMPOST
Autumn leaves that blossom in the spring. C. Allonby. il Org Gard & Farm 17:40-3 S '70
Commercial compost-making at home. K. Arnet. il pors Org Gard & Farm 17:44-8 Ap '70
Compost convert in Australia. F. J. Barnett. Org Gard & Farm 17:92+ F '70
Composting octogenarian. V. L. Rinelli. il por Org Gard & Farm 17:54-5 My '70
George Washington's composting experiment. A. Schatz and V. Schatz. il Org Gard & Farm 17:86-7 Jl '70
My mountain of leaves. B. Gilford. il Org Gard & Farm 17:54-6 N '70
Prime step in fourteen-day composting. E. Van Wicklen. il Org Gard & Farm 17:40-1 D '70
Put your garbage to work. M. Franz. il Org Gard & Farm 17:52-7 Mr '70
Return garden wastes to the soil. il Home Gard 57:45 Jl '70
Years we began using garbage. R. C. Adams. Org Gard & Farm 17:67 Ja '70
    See also
Fertilizers and manures
Organic gardening
Refuse as fertilizer

Preservation and storage
Compost bins versus pollution. M. Franz. il Org Gard & Farm 17:38-43 Ap '70
Compost box. il Mech Illus 66:100-1 Ap '70
His earthworms work for him. P. Delfeld. il Org Gard & Farm 17:71-2+ Ag '70
Our movable compost bin. B. Wahlfeldt. il por Org Gard & Farm 17:110 Mr '70

COMPOST grinders and grinding
Compost shredder. il Home Gard 57:53 Ag '70
COMPOST shredders. See Compost grinders and grinding
COMPREHENSION
See also
Reading comprehension
COMPREHENSIVE drug abuse prevention and control act of 1970. See Drug laws and legislation
COMPRESSED air
Squeezing power out of thin air. il Bsns W p76 Ag 1 '70
COMPRESSIBILITY
Compressibilities of lunar crystalline rock, microbreccia, and fines to 40 kilobars. D. R. Stephens and E. M. Lilley. bibliog il Science 167:731-2 Ja 30 '70
Sound velocity and compressibility for lunar rocks 17 and 46 and for glass spheres from the lunar soil. E. Schreiber and others. bibliog il Science 167:732-4 Ja 30 '70
COMPSTON, William, and others
Rubidium-strontium chronology and chemistry of lunar material. bibliog il Science 167:474-6 Ja 30 '70
COMPTON, Gail W.
Argonaut octopus: rare find from the sea. il Sci Digest 68:32-4 Jl '70
What is the world's deadliest animal? il Sci Digest 68:24-8 Ag '70
—See Zeiller, W. jt. auth.
COMPTON, Neil
Television. Commentary 48:18-21 Jl '69; 49: 12+ Ja; 18+ Ap '70
COMPTON-BURNETT, Dame Ivy
Talking to Dame Ivy; interview, ed. by K. Dick. por Harp Baz 103:170-3+ My '70
COMPUCOMP corporation
CompuComp reduces its computer services. Pub W 198:41 D 7 '70
COMPULSORY arbitration. See Arbitration, Industrial
COMPULSORY military service. See Military service, Compulsory
COMPUTER-assisted instruction. See Computers—Educational use
COMPUTER-based service companies
Computer software companies: how many are houses of cards? il Forbes 105:40-2 F 15 '70
See also
CompuComp corporation
Data processing service centers
University computing company
COMPUTER billing. See Billing
COMPUTER circuits. See Computers—Circuits
COMPUTER communications, inc.
Dynamic growth companies. il Nations Bsns 58:44-8 Je '70
COMPUTER equipment industry
See also
Memorex corporation
COMPUTER flight planning. See Computers—Aeronautic use
COMPUTER graphics
Computer display systems. G. A. Michael. bibliog il por Phys Today 23:30-6 Jl '70
Computer displays. I. E. Sutherland. il Sci Am 222:56-60+ bibliog(p 152) Je '70
Computer potentials for the graphic designer; excerpts from Graphic design for the computer age. E. A. Hamilton. il Pub W 198: 40+ Ag 10 '70
Games computers play. S. Shatavsky. il Pop Sci 197:44 O '70
Graphic computer terminals. D. L. Heiserman. il Electr World 84:34-6+ O; 35-7+ N '70
COMPUTER industry
Computers little helpers create a brawling business. G. Bylinsky. il Fortune 81:84-7+ Je '70
Computers: out of the slump. il Newsweek 76: 78-80 N 9 '70
Everybody in. il Forbes 106:20-1 Ag 15 '70
GE and Honeywell test their match. il Bsns W p30-1 My 30 '70
Honeywell and GE team up as no. 2. Bsns W p44 My 23 '70
Independents twist the elephant's tail. Bsns W p 16-17 Ja 2 '71
Wearing out the insulation. il Time 95:83 Ap 20 '70
World boom in computers, and a challenge to U.S. il U S News 68:78-81 Mr 9 '70
See also
Bunker-Ramo corporation
Burroughs corporation
Collins radio company
Computer machinery corporation
Control data corporation
Electronic associates, inc.

Honeywell, inc.
International business machines corporation
Iomec, inc.
Magnetic head corporation
National cash register company
RCA corporation
Scientific control corporation
Texas instruments, inc.
Viatron computer systems corporation
Xerox corporation

Consolidations and mergers
Honeywell tries to make its merger work; acquisition of GE's computer division. il Bsns W p92-3+ S 26 '70

Customer relations
Talking back to IBM; Britain's IBM computer users association. J. Ross-Skinner. Duns 97:52 Ja '71

Exhibitions
Computers; display at twenty-fifth annual conference of the Association for computing machinery. New Yorker 46:33-4 S 12 '70

Finance
Information processing; with yardsticks of management performance. il Forbes 105:92-4 Ja 1 '70; 107:81-2+ Ja 1 '71

Securities
Blame IBM. R. Brady. il por Duns 95:109-10 Mr '70

Europe, Eastern
Computers in eastern Europe. I. Berenyi. il Sci Am 223:102-8 O '70

Europe, Western
New allies enter the computer wars; Control data joins in setting up International data. Bsns W p34 N 21 '70
Rivals are nipping at IBM's heels. Bsns W p48-9 Ja 17 '70

Japan
Japanese computers: closing the gap. N. A. Martin. il Duns 96:75+ O '70
COMPUTER machinery corporation
Small company enters the European market. J. K. Sweeney. Harvard Bsns R 48:126-32 S '70
COMPUTER match-making. See Computers—Social use
COMPUTER output microfilming. See Computers—Input-output equipment
COMPUTER processing. See Electronic data processing
COMPUTER programming. See Programming (computers)
COMPUTER software. See Programming (computers)
COMPUTER technicians. See Electronic technicians
COMPUTER technology, inc.
Management fee prompts a row. Bsns W p68 F 14 '70
COMPUTER voting systems. See Voting machines
COMPUTER workers
You are an interfacer of black boxes. R. Todd. il Atlan 25:64-70 Mr '70
COMPUTERIZED fire alarm. See Fire alarms
COMPUTERIZED typesetting. See Computers—Printing use
COMPUTERS
Behold the computer revolution. P. T. White. il por Nat Geog 138:593-633 N '70
Computers can be fun. il Sci Digest 68:47-8 D '70
Computers in eastern Europe. I. Berenyi. il Sci Am 223:102-8 O '70
Creative computers. W. Cross. il Sci Digest 68:9-15 Ag '70
Problem solver, problem maker. il Bsns W p 184-5+ O 17 '70
Quiet stir of thought, or, What the computer cannot do; adaptation of address, May 1969. J. H. Shera; reply. K. W. Jaffe. Library J 95:101-2 Ja 15 '70
Record-keeping in the space age; address, June 9, 1970. R. P. Henderson. Vital Speeches 36:585-8 Jl 15 '70
Supercomputers join the lineup. Bsns W p65 N 14 '70
World boom in computers, and a challenge to U.S. il U S News 68:78-81 Mr 9 '70
See also
Computer industry
Electronic data processing
Memory devices (computers)
Programming (computers)
Telephone—Data transmission systems

COMPUTERS—*Continued*

Aeronautics use

ATC automation facing key test. P. J. Klass. il Aviation W 93:50-3 Jl 20 '70

Automatic altitude reporting. R. L. Collins. il Flying 87:80+ Jl '70

Computer tests jet engine fuel controls. K. J. Stein. Aviation W 93:44-5 Ag 17 '70

Concepts for pilots range studied; electronic air combat maneuvering range. B. Miller. il Aviation W 93:42-4 S 28 '70

Course-line computer: who needs it? R. L. Collins. Flying 87:38-40+ Ag '70

Instant flight plan. R. B. Weeghman. Flying 86:43-5 Je '70

New airborne computer concepts evolve. il Aviation W 92:213+ Je 22 '70

Phone unit prints computer flight plans. B. M. Elson. il Aviation W 93:59-60+ D 14 '70

SST digital flight control evolves. il Aviation W 92:66+ My 25 '70

See also
Airlines—Communication systems

Agricultural use

His cattle feeding is computerized. D. Malena. il Suc Farm 68:A4 O '70

Instant answers to farming questions. J. Carlson. il Farm J 94:62H Mr '70

Long-distance ration mixing. il Farm J 94:B13 Mr '70

New way to test payoff potential before you invest. G. Reynolds. Farm J 94:39 O '70

Space-age cattle feeders; computer record-keeping for feedlots. W. Kester. il Farm J 94:B22 F '70

Air freight service use

Industry watches two pioneering freight data systems. K. J. Stein. il Aviation W 93:144-6 O 26 '70

Air traffic control use

See Computers—Aeronautic use

Airline use

Computer helps deploy reservations staff. il Aviation W 93:38-9 Ag 3 '70

Eastern's Center speeds response time. K. J. Stein. il Aviation W 92:35-7 Je 1 '70

Where airlines must pioneer. il Bsns W p86-8+ Mr 7 '70

See also
Airlines—Reservation systems

Anecdotes, facetiae, satire, etc.

How to stop worrying and love the computer. Newsweek 76:18 Jl 27 '70

Archeological use

Computer helps scholars re-create an Egyptian temple. R. W. Smith. il pors Nat Geog 138:634-55 N '70

Architectural use

Computer firm programs structural design analysis. il Arch Forum 133:52-3 O '70

Computerized cost estimating is ready now, almost. B. Perkins. Arch Rec 147:65-6 F '70

Information retrieval for design and specification. Arch Rec 147:65-6 My '70

Practice in the 1970's: the response to change. W. B. Foxhall. il Arch Rec 148:157-9 O '70

Semantics of architecture machines. N. Negroponte and L. B. Groisser. il Arch Forum 133:38-41 O '70

Art use

New talent: the computer. S. VanDerBeek. il por Art in Am 58:86;91 Ja '70

Astronomical use

Automated optical astronomy. F. C. Livingstone. il Sci N 97:273 Mr 14 '70

Automotive use

Now! A computer for your car; CEDAC. D. Demske. il Mech Illus 66:32+ F '70

Banking use

Financial paper: variations on themes of McLuhan. G. T. Dunne. bibliog f Harvard Bsns R 48:90-6 My '70

Biological use

Automatic analysis of blood cells. M. Ingram and K. Preston, jr. il Sci Am 223:72-82 bibliog(p 132) N '70

See also
Computers—Medical use

Business use

At last: real computer power for decision makers. C. H. Jones. bibliog f il Harvard Bsns R 48:75-89 S '70

Cash drawers that talk computer. il Bsns W p66-7 Ag 29 '70

Census data: tailored to suit you. Nations Bsns 58:52 Ag '70

Corporate models: better marketing plans. P. Kotler. bibliog f il Harvard Bsns R 48:135-49+ Jl '70

Corporate models: on-line, real-time systems. J. B. Boulden and E. S. Buffa. il Harvard Bsns R 48:65-83 Jl '70

Detour to 1984; credit bureau files. A. R. Miller. Nation 210:648-51 Je 1 '70

Find out how your investments are really doing; new Changing times computer service. il Changing T 24:47-9 Mr '70

GE will share a wealth of data; management analysis and projection system. il Bsns W p88+ My 9 '70

How a tiny store keeps the books; Nassau liquors in Princeton, N.J. il por Bsns W p80-1 Ja 9 '71

Management evolution in the quantitative world. R. F. Vandell. il Harvard Bsns R 48:83-92 Ja '70

Savings for you and the government. Nations Bsns 58:20 Ja '70

Weighing risk in capacity expansion. J. R. Virts and R. W. Garrett. il Harvard Bsns R 48:132-41 My '70

See also
Billing
Computers—Tax use
Information systems, Management

Cartographic use

Computer-aided chart making evaluated. C. E. Schneider. il Aviation W 92:69+ My 11 '70

Cataloging use

See Libraries—Automation

Chemical use

Chemistry by computer. A. C. Wahl. il Sci Am 222:54-8+ bibliog(p 130) Ap '70

Exploring G and H orbitals by computer. G. G. Schlessinger. il Chem 43:22-4 Mr '70

Revolution in crystallography. W. C. Hamilton. bibliog il Science 169:138-41 Jl 10 '70

Circuits

Chips are down. Sci Am 223:44-5 N '70

Core-memory sense amplifiers. R. F. Brunner. il Electr World 84:53-4 Jl '70

Easy-to-build computer logic circuits. M. Mandl. il Radio-Electr 41:44-8 My '70

Future evolution of the computer; adaptation of address, October 1969. R. Landauer. bibliog il por Phys Today 23:22-8 Jl '70

IC experimenter's corner:
Build a shift register. D. Lancaster. il Pop Electr 32:43-7 My '70

Logic design course. J. Williams. Radio-Electr 41:88 N '70

Power dissipation in information processing. R. W. Keyes. bibliog il Science 168:796-801 My 15 '70

R-E's logic laboratory. D. Korman. il Radio-Electr 41:33-7 D '70; 42:52-4+ Ja '71

Squeeze play yields a computer. il Bsns W p49 N 21 '70

College library use

See College libraries—Automation

Control use

Computer that does just enough; GRI's 909. il Bsns W p78+ Ag 22 '70

GE tries harder on process controls. Bsns W p52 O 17 '70

See also
Machine tools—Control

Design

Future evolution of the computer; adaptation of address, October 1969. R. Landauer. bibliog il por Phys Today 23:22-8 Jl '70

This system starts with integration. il Bsns W p27 S 12 '70

Digital computers

Digital computers in physics research; symposium. bibliog il Phys Today 23:22-8+ Jl '70

Economic use

IBM gauges the climate. Time 95:67-8 Ja 26 '70

COMPUTERS—*Continued*

Educational use

Advances in computer-based education. D. Alpert and D. L. Bitzer. bibliog il Science 167:1582-90 Mr 20 '70; Reply with rejoinder. 168:1397-8+ Je 19 '70

City and school system share a computer; Danbury, Conn. J. P. Edwards. il Am City 85:105+ Ap '70

Computer harvests migrant records. M. P. Pfeil. il Am Ed 6:6-9 N '70

Computer in education. B. P. Hansen. Clear House 45:195-200 D '70

Computers and adaptive education. H. E. Mitzel. il Am Ed 6:23-6 D '70

Computers in physics instruction. G. Schwarz and others; reply. D. L. Shirer. il Phys Today 23:15+ Ap '70

High marks in the teaching business; Westinghouse learning's Project PLAN. il Bsns W p32+ My 2 '70

New campus hero; the computer. H. Manchester. il PTA Mag 64:2-4 F '70; Same abr. Read Digest 96:33-4+ Mr '70

Probing Project PLAN (Program for learning in accordance with needs) in California. L. A. Gutkind. il Schol Teach Jr/Sr High p20-3 O 5 '70

Realistic look at the flexible schedule. R. R. Gard. Clear House 44:425-9 Mr '70

Student, teacher, and machine. il Sch & Soc 98:4-6 Ja '70

Will the computer kill education? B. L. Hicks. Ed Digest 36:10-12 S '70

See also
Teaching machines

Anecdotes, facetiae, satire, etc.

Great electron-pedantic project. C. Kohler. il Pop Electr 32:48-52 F '70

School talk. E. Bombeck. il Good H 171:62+ S '70

Employment use

Job banks: system covers forty-two cities. U S News 69:76 Jl 27 '70

Meet the electronic talent scout. il Nations Bsns 58:74-6 N '70

Engineering use

Computer-designed asphalt pavement; experiment near San Diego, Calif. J. F. Shook. il Am City 85:68+ F '70

Errors

How to cope with computer billing. J. Pinkham. Bet Hom & Gard 48:114+ Mr '70

News item: man bites Ford; lawsuit over errors in computer billing. Consumer Rep 35:132-3 Mr '70

Sticky ticket wicket. Time 95:16 Mr 2 '70

Geological use

Fit between Africa and Antarctica: a continental drift reconstruction. R. S. Dietz and W. P. Sproll. bibliog il Science 167:1612-14 Mr 20 '70

Government use

Business bridges a government gap; Federal assistance information reporting. V. Louviere. Nations Bsns 58:17 O '70

I spy, you spy. E. Marshall. New Repub 163:15-16 O 3 '70

Plugging in the pols; proposed congressional computer system. Forbes 106:18-19 O 1 '70

Privacy, security, and a free America; address, September 15, 1970. F. Horton. Vital Speeches 37:44-7 N 1 '70

Profit from 1970 census data. A. R. Eckler. il Harvard Bsns R 48:4-6+ Jl '70

Highway engineering use

See Computers—Engineering use

Income tax use

See Computers—Tax use

Indexing use

Automatic text analysis. G. Salton. bibliog il Science 168:335-43 Ap 17 '70

Industrial use

Automated fabrication could cut costs; CAM system. Aviation W 92:247-8 Je 22 '70

Instrumentation goes modern. I. Geller. il Duns 95:75-6+ Ap '70

Manpower implications of computer control in manufacturing. A. S. Herman. il Mo Labor R 93:3-8 O '70

Manufacturing by the numbers: a total systems concept of manufacturing; address, September 16, 1970. H. E. Markley. Vital Speeches 37:143-5 D 15 '70

Poseidon checkout computerized. B. M. Elson. il Aviation W 92:48-9+ F 16 '70

See also
Computers—Control use
Machine tools—Control

Input-output equipment

Computers that talk. F. W. Holder. il Electr World 84:38-9+ D '70

Race for microfilm. il Bsns W p53-4 My 9 '70

Investment use

Computer aids stock transfer. Bsns W p85 Je 20 '70

Financial paper: variations on themes of McLuhan. G. T. Dunne. bibliog f Harvard Bsns R 48:90-6 My '70

One big push-button market for all? C. Morgello. il Newsweek 76:74-5 N 30 '70

Laws and regulations

Computer and the law. S. H. Lieberstein. il Duns 95:58-60 Mr '70

Leasing and renting

See also
United States leasing international, inc.

Legal use

Consulting the computer. il por Time 95:68 My 4 '70

Medical use

Drug effect prediction by computer. E. E. Gloye and R. J. Marcus. il Science 169:89-91 Jl 3 '70

Will computers take over? J. Frye. Electr World 83:50-2 Je '70

Meteorological use

Computing the link between sea and air; studying ocean's effects on climate. K. Frazier. il Sci N 97:533-5 My 30 '70

Watchdog for floods; New England system. il Sci N 97:60-1 Ja 17 '70

Military use

Why air force wants computers in the sky. il U S News 70:51 Ja 11 '71

See also
Vietnamese war, 1957- —Equipment and supplies

Miniaturization

Instrumentation goes modern. I. Geller. il Duns 95:75-6+ Ap '70

Space-age electronics and pocket computers. G. Gregory. UNESCO Courier 23:29-30 Mr '70

Municipal use

City and school system share a computer; Danbury, Conn. J. P. Edwards. il Am City 85:105+ Ap '70

Computer analyzes a hydraulic colossus; Chicago's water department. S. J. Rand. il Am City 85:102+ Je '70

Computer geared to grow with a city; Tempe, Ariz. J. Alexander. il Am City 85:84+ N '70

Computer improves refuse collection. Am City 85:32 My '70

Computerized municipal information system; Sunnyvale, Calif. J. Gordon. il Am City 85:96-7+ Je '70

Data transmission network speeds customer service; electric and water utilities; Albuquerque, N.Mex. D. Mann. il Am City 85:98-9 F '70

In-service training enhances a computer system; Fort Worth, Tex. H. D. McMahan. il Am City 85:126+ S '70

Inventory your streets for better management; Waco, Tex. C. H. Hoge and J. E. Lykes, jr. il Am City 85:98+ Mr '70

Make information systems work for you; Wichita Falls, Tex. G. G. Fox. il Am City 85:108+ Mr '70

New cash control and data collection system; Ramapo, N.Y. A. Palermo. il por Parks & Rec 5:32-3 Mr '70

600 meters per day; Ontario, Ohio. R. Berryhill. il Am City 85:107-8 S '70

Tiny E-cell monitors your equipment; Los Angeles. il Am City 85:22 Jl '70

Why we went to computerized billing; Paducah, Ky. B. Gibbons. il por Am City 85:67+ Ja '70

See also
Computers—Traffic control use

Philatelic use

Computer and philately. H. Herst, jr. Hobbies 75:131+ Mr '70

CONCERTOS
See also
Phonograph records—Concertos
CONCERTS
Happenings of the Beethoven year. Sat R 53:68 N 28 '70
Szell memorial concert; tribute by the Cleveland orchestra in Severance Hall. B. Murray. Hi Fi 20:MA14 O '70
Tureck & Fox play Bach; Glen Cove, N.Y. J. Hiemenz. il Hi Fi 20:MA16-17 S '70
See also
Dance concerts
Museum concerts
CONCESSIONS (food, etc)
Service through concessions. W. Frederickson, jr. il Parks & Rec 9:40-2+ S '70
CONCHOLOGY. See Shells (conchology)
CONCIERGES. See Doorkeepers
CONCILIAR theory. See Church—Authority
CONCILIUM (periodical)
Concilium to be continued. America 122:288 Mr 21 '70
CONCILIUM congress on The future of the church. See Religious conferences
CONCORD, Calif
Make a pleasing entrance; city signs. D. R. Convis and G. F. A. Trump. il Am City 85:134 Ap '70
CONCORD festival. See Music festivals—California
CONCORD hotel. See Hotels, taverns, etc.—United States
CONCORD RIVER
If Mr Thoreau calls, tell him I've left the country. R. Mungo. il Atlan 225:72-82+ My '70
CONCORDE airliner. See Airplanes, Supersonic
CONCORDE supersonic transport. See Airplanes, Supersonic
CONCORDIA theological seminary, St Louis
Discord at Concordia. Newsweek 77:41 Ja 4 '71
Heresy at Concordia? A matter of interpretation. Chr Today 14:40 My 21 '70
CONCOURS d'elegance. See Automobiles—Exhibitions
CONCRETE

Expansion and contraction
Now: a concrete that doesn't need joints. R. Day. il Pop Sci 197:84-5 Jl '70
CONCRETE, Ornamental
See also
Garden ornaments
CONCRETE blocks
Building block that needs no mortar; Wedge blocks. il Pop Sci 197:102 S '70
CONCRETE construction
Circular prestressing cuts slab thicknesses and costs in a circular tower. il Arch Rec 147:157-8 Je '70
Concrete panels. il Arch Forum 132:56-7 Ap '70
That magnificent mud: reinforced concrete. W. McQuade. il Fortune 82:88-95 D '70
Thinnest circular concrete plate spans 130 ft to roof a gymnasium. il Arch Rec 147:160-1 Je '70
CONCRETE garden ornaments. See Garden ornaments
CONCRETE houses
Inexpensive concrete house. il Mech Illus 66:117 N '70
New house for under $5,000; precast concrete. S. V. Jones. il Sci Digest 67:71 Mr '70
CONCRETE pavements. See Pavements, Concrete
CONCRETE work
Good old concrete is something else today. N. Seney. il Bet Hom & Gard 48:74-81 Mr '70
CONCRETIONS
See also
Geodes
CONDEE, Ralph Waterbury
Milton's dialogue with the epic: Paradise regained and the tradition. Yale R 59:357-75 Mr '70
CONDENSATION
Orientation order of dipole molecules in the surface of embryonic droplets. F. F. Abraham. bibliog il Science 168:833-5 My 15 '70
See also
Atmospheric nucleation
CONDENSATION control in buildings. See Dampness in buildings
CONDIMENTS
See also
Saffron
CONDITIONED responses
Conditioned vocalizations as a technique for determining visual acuity thresholds in sea lions. R. J. Schusterman and R. F. Balliet. bibliog il Science 169:498-501 Jl 31 '70

Extinction in goldfish facilitation by intracranial injection of RNA from brains of extinguished donors. W. G. Braud. bibliog il Science 168:1234-6 Je 5 '70
Problems and pitfalls of establishing an Operant conditioning-token economy program. J. Montgomery and R. D. McBurney. Ment Hy 54:382-7 Jl '70
Reinforcement of competing behavior during extinction. H. Leitenberg and others. bibliog il Science 169:301-3 Jl 17 '70
See also
Operant conditioning
Reinforcement (psychology)
CONDOMINIUM campsites. See Camp sites, facilities, etc.
CONDOMINIUM plan ownership. See Apartment houses—Condominium plan ownership
CONDOMS. See Contraceptives
CONDON, Vesta
Washington Irving's Andalusia. il por Travel 134:52-6+ O '70
CONDORS
Source of the thunder: excerpt. R. Caras. il Audubon 72:82-4+ N '70
CONDUCT of life
Celebrate celebrate! Dance to the music of the universe; symposium. Mlle 72:73-81+ D '70
Hang-ups that haunt us. N. V. Peale. Read Digest 96:133-6 Je '70
Keeping going; excerpt. P. La Farge. il McCalls 98:49+ Ja '71
Living high on wit, wisdom, and love. C. Binger. Sat R 53:12-14+ Jl 25 '70
Magic we almost missed. C. Carpenter. il Farm J 94:44 Ja '70
Radical suburb and expansive man; excerpt from The radical suburb. J. B. Orr and F. P. Nichelson. Cur 122:3-10 O '70
Recycling rigid life patterns. R. N. Butler. Cur 114:62-4 Ja '70
Solving problems in living: the citizen's viewpoint. W. B. Eddy and others. bibliog il Ment Hy 54:64-72 Ja '70
Taming of individuals and the state. N. Cousins .Sat R 53:26 Ja 17 '70
Vision of the human revolution. W. Hedgepeth. il Look 34:60-7 Ja 13 '70
Who's using overkill? P. S. Hurley. America 122:181-2 F 21 '70
See also
Charity
Christian life
Contentment
Courage
Duty
Faith
Forgiveness
Friendship
Honesty
Human relations
Joy
Leisure
Loneliness
Love
New Years resolutions
Patriotism
Popularity
Pride and vanity
Self control
Success
Work
Worth
Youth—Conduct of life

Anecdotes, faceiae, satire, etc.
In praise of reticence: Time essay. M. Maddocks. il Time 96:50 N 23 '70
CONDUCT unbecoming; drama. See England, B.
CONDUCTING (music)
Madman; interview. ed. by M. J. Matz. C. Franci. por Opera N 34:17 My 16 '70
New exercise for a longer life. L. I. Gordon. il Vogue 156:152-3+ N 1 '70
What a conductor does. E. Buckley. il por Opera N 34:26-9 Mr 28 '70
Why I didn't become a heart specialist. J. Mester. por Hi Fi 20:31 O '70
With Michael Tilson Thomas, the show really does go on! interview. ed. by R. Hemming. M. T. Thomas. il pors Sr Schol 97:22-4 O 26 '70
See also
Conductors (music)
CONDUCTIVITY. See Electric conductivity
CONDUCTIVITY gages. See Gages
CONDUCTORS (music)
Bravissimo! il Vogue 155:180-3 Ap 1 '70
Conductor's world, by D. Wooldridge. Review New Yorker 46:106-7 S 19 '70. W. Sargeant
How to say it: a pronunciation guide for the Metropolitan opera's 1970-71 broadcasts. Opera N 35:28-9 D 12 '70

CONDUCTORS (music)—*Continued*
Musical events; symphony conductors. W. Sargeant. New Yorker 46:178+ D 12 '70
See also
Barenboim, D.
Bernstein, L.
Bonynge, R.
Dixon, D.
Dohnanyi, C. von
Fleisher, L.
Gilbert, D.
Horenstein, J.
Klemperer, O.
Maazel, L.
Mehta, Z.
Ozawa, S.
Solti, G.
Szell, G.
Thomas, M. T.
CONE, Fairfax Mastick
Saying it plainly. Sat R 53:67 Ja 17 '70
When advertising talks to everyone. Sat R 53:56-7+ O 10 '70
CONE, James H.
Black consciousness and the black church: a historical-theological interpretation. bibliog f Ann Am Acad 387:49-55 Ja '70
Black theology and black liberation; address. il Chr Cent 87:1084-8 S 16 '70
Black theology: we were not created for humiliation. Ladies Home J 86:132 D '69
Toward a black theology. il por Ebony 25: 113-16 Ag '70
CONE cells. See Rod and cone cells
CONE dwellers. See Cave dwellers
CONE mills corporation
Educating the city slicker. Forbes 105:22-3 Je 1 '70
CONFECTIONERY
Citrus peel for the holidays. il Sunset 145: 212 N '70
See also
Candy
CONFEDERATE memorial of Stone Mountain. See Stone Mountain memorial
CONFEDERATE STATES of America
Their tattered flag, by F. E. Vandiver. Review Sat R 53:32-3 Mr 28 '70. E. M. Thomas
CONFERENCE of governors. See Governors conference. 1970
CONFERENCE of major superiors of men's institutes
Vision of American religious life. W. J. Byron America 123:14-15 Jl 11 '70; Discussion. 123: 63-4 Ag 8 '70
CONFERENCE of major superiors of women's institutions of the United States of America
CMSW takes a sharp new turn. J. C. Haughey. America 123:208 S 26 '70; Discussion. 123:389, 417 N 14-21 '70
CONFERENCE of non-aligned nations, Lusaka, 1970. See International conferences
CONFERENCE of non-nuclear-weapon states. See United Nations conference of non-nuclear-weapon states
CONFERENCE of the committee on disarmament. See United Nations—Committee on disarmament
CONFERENCE on human survival. See United Nations conference on human survival
CONFERENCE on justice in America. See Congressional conference on justice in America
CONFERENCE on the peaceful uses of atomic energy. See International conference on the peaceful uses of atomic energy. 4th Geneva. 1971
CONFERENCE on the standardization of geographical names. See United Nations conference on the standardization of geographical names
CONFERENCES
Coming events. See issues of Parks & recreation
Conventions: when & where. See issues of American city
See also
Authors conferences
Business conferences
Inter-American conferences
International conferences
Library conferences
Medical conferences
Press conferences
Religious conferences
CONFERENCES on science and world affairs. See Pugwash conference on science and world affairs
CONFESSION
Can we renew the Sacrament of penance? D. F. Gomez. il Cath World 211:67-70 My '70
Reform of penance. C. Kiesling. il America 122:652+ Je 20 '70

CONFESSION story. See Short story
CONFETTI; ballet. See Ballets—Criticisms
CONFIDENTIAL communications
See also
Privacy, Right of

Taxation

Mr 1040: row over access to tax records by C. Mollenhoff. il por Newsweek 75:34-5 Ap 27 '70
Security leak at the 1040 level. por Bsns W p32+ Ap 18 '70
CONFINEMENT feeding of swine. See Swine—Confinement methods
CONFLICT (psychology)
Fixation produced by conflict. E. B. Karsh. bibliog il Science 168:873-5 My 15 '70
Make conflict work for you; excerpts from Organizational behaviour. J. Kelly. bibliog f il Harvard Bsns R 48:103-13 Jl '70
CONFLICT, Social. See Social conflict
CONFLICT of generations. See Generation gap
CONFLICT of interests (public office)
Dowdy's comedown. por Newsweek 75:24-5 Ap 13 '70
Nixon: with a little help for his friends. B. Fitch. il pors Ramp Mag 8:58-62+ Mr '70
What the senator didn't disclose; J. Tydings hasn't met the standards he has set. W. Lambert. pors Life 69:26-9 Ag 28 '70
CONFORMATIONAL analysis
Conformational analysis; or, How some molecules wiggle. J. B. Dence. bibliog il por Chem 43:6-10 Je '70
Diphenylhydantoin and diazepam: molecluar structure similarities and steric basis of anticonvulsant activity. A. Camerman and N. Camerman. bibliog il Science 168:1457-8 Je 19 '70
Principles of conformational analysis; Nobel prize lecture, December 13, 1969. D. H. R. Barton. bibliog il Science 169:539-44 Ag 7 '70
Shapes of organic molecules. J. B. Lambert. il Sci Am 222:58-66+ bibliog(p 146) Ja '70
Solution conformation of valinomycinpotassuim ion complex. M. Ohnishi and D. W. Urry. bibliog il Science 168:1091-2 My 29 '70
CONFORMITY
Declaration of independence. E. Sheppard. il Harp Baz 103:106-7 Jl '70
See also
Dissenters
CONGENITAL malformations. See Deformities
CONGER, Clement Ellis
Clement Conger: diplomatic treasure hunter. M. Evans. por Am Home 73:50+ N '70 *
CONGER, Lesley
Off the cuff. See issues of Writer
CONGLOMERATE corporations
As they see it; interview, ed. by James Cook. R. Little. pors Forbes 106:38-41 D 15 '70
Conglomerates will come back; interviews. J. D. Wright; F. J. Nunlist; J. J. Ling. pors Forbes 107:110-12 Ja 1 '71
John Lobb's orphan asylum; interview. J. Lobb. por Forbes 106:24-5 Jl 1 '70
See also
Amfac, inc.
Avco corporation
Celanese corporation of America
Dolly Madison industries, inc.
Government investigations—Conglomerate corporations
International telephone and telegraph corporation
Kidde, Walter, and company
Ling-Temco-Vought, inc.
Litton industries, inc.
Michigan general corporation
National industries, inc.
Signal companies, inc.
Simon Norton, inc.
Textron, inc.
Transamerica corporation
TRW, inc.
White consolidated industries, inc.

Finance

Multicompanies; with yardsticks of management performance. il Forbes 105:96+ Ja 1 '70; 107:105-7 Ja 1 '71

Securities

Bear market in conglomerates. il Bsns W p63 My 9 '70

Yugoslavia

Socialist conglomerate builds up steam; Energoinvest. il Bsns W p 118+ F 14 '71
CONGO (capital Kinshasa) See Congo (Democratic Republic)

CONGO (Democratic Republic)
 See also
Public health—Congo (Democratic Republic)

Politics and government

Heart specialist. Time 96:31 Jl 6 '70
Something to celebrate; tenth anniversary.
 il por Newsweek 76:50+ Jl 13 '70
Taming of the Congo. R. W. Howe. New Republic 163:15-16 Ag 1 '70

Religious institutions and affairs

 See also
Church of Christ in the Congo (Democratic
 Republic)
CONGO (Democratic Republic)-United States
 air agreement. See Aviation—International
 aspects
CONGREGATION for Catholic education
Rome replies (act II) N. G. McCluskey. il
 America 122:330-4 Mr 28 '70
CONGREGATIONAL church in Scotland
Scotland; plan of union. Church of Scotland
 with the Congregational church. I. Logan.
 Chr Cent 87:852-3 Jl 8 '70
CONGRESS (United States) See United States
 —Congress
CONGRESS of African people
It's nation time! A. Poinsett. il Ebony 26:98-
 100+ D '70
CONGRESS of the international association
 for the history of religions. See International association for the study of history of
 religions
CONGRESS of Vienna. See Vienna, Congress of,
 1814-1815
CONGRESSIONAL aides. See Public officers
CONGRESSIONAL campaigns. See Political
 campaigns
CONGRESSIONAL candidates. See Candidates,
 Political
CONGRESSIONAL committees. See United
 States—Congress—Committees
CONGRESSIONAL conference on justice in America
Law and order 1970; with comment by R.
 Clark. R. L. Smith. il Nation 210:774-85
 Je 29 '70
Whose crime is it? J. B. Sheerin. Cath World
 212:3-4 O '70
CONGRESSIONAL cup race. See Yacht racing
CONGRESSIONAL elections. See Elections—
 United States
CONGRESSIONAL library. See United States
 —Library of Congress
CONGRESSIONAL procedure. See United States
 —Congress—Rules and practice
CONGRESSIONAL reorganization. See United
 States—Congress—Reorganization
CONGRESSMEN
Advice to a new congressman. B. B. Conable, jr. il Nations Bsns 58:32-6 D '70
Congress's nine old men. il Newsweek 75:
 20-1 F 2 '70
Eckhardt of Texas: the Democratic hard core.
 E. M. Yoder, jr. il Harper 240:28+ Je '70
Lame-duck life; defeated members. Newsweek 76:53-4 D 14 '70
Military congressman. Time 95:67 My 25 '70
New breed of in-House expert; legislative
 technicians. il Bsns W p53 My 30 '70
 See also
Conflict of interests (public office)
Members of Congress for peace through law
United States—Congress

Ethics
 See Political ethics

Health

How to stay healthy; interview. R. J. Pearson. il por U S News 68:60-3 Ap 6 '70

Religion

Ninety-second Congress: a religious census.
 il Chr Today 15:33-4 D 4 '70

Salaries, allowances, etc.

In ten years on Capitol hill: staff up 67 per
 cent, expenses 156 per cent. il U S News
 69:55 S 28 '70

Term

Parting shots: the distinguished gentlemen
 from yesterday. il Life 68:81-4 Ap 10 '70
Why not four years for both the president
 and Congress? D. Lawrence. U S News 68:
 76 F 2 '70
CONGRESSMEN, Letters to. See Lobbying
CONGRESSWOMEN
Women candidates: the voters' verdict. il U S
 News 69:30 N 16 '70
 See also
Chisholm, S.

CONIFERS
How to control mouse damage in conifers;
 meadow mice. J. W. Caslick and W. R.
 Eadie. il Cons 24:48-9 Ag '69
 See also
Cypress
Evergreens
Larch
CONIGLIARO, Tony
Seeing it through; excerpts. il pors Sports
 Illus 32:60-4+ Je 22; 34-8+ Je 29 '70
CONIL-LACOSTE, Michel
For the happy few, and gurus, too. il Art N
 69:34-5 Mr '70
Paestum. il UNESCO Courier 23:4-9 Ap '70
Paris. See issues of Art news
CONJUGATION, Metabolic. See Metabolism
CONKLIN, K. A. and Chou, S. C.
Antimalarials: effects on in vivo and in vitro
 protein synthesis. bibliog il Science 170:
 1213-14 D 11 '70
CONLEY, Clare
Mountains of home. il Field & S 75:66-7+ Je
 '70
What makes chukar run? il Field & S
 74:54-5+ F '70
CONLIN, Joseph R.
Case of the very American militants. il Am
 West 7:4-10+ Mr '70
CONLY, Robert Leslie
Luxembourg, the quiet fortress. il Nat Geog
 138:68-97 Jl '70
CONNALLY, John Bowden, 1917–
Battles that Connally will face. il por Bsns
 W p36-7 D 19 '70 *
Connally appointment. Nation 211:676 D 28
 '70 *
Connally-Kennedy shift: its meaning. il por
 U S News 69:11 D 28 '70 *
Here come the rangers. Nat R 22:1384-5 D
 29 '70 *
John Connally's other careers. il pors Newsweek 76:14-15 D 28 '70 *
Matter of sides. por Time 96:14-15 Jl 27 '70 *
Mr Nixon enlists a Texas Democrat. il por
 Newsweek 76:13-15 D 28 '70 *
New Texan on the Potomac. il por Time 96:
 9 D 28 '70 *
President Nixon takes a Democrat. il por
 Time 96:8-10 D 28 '70 *
This appointment signifies something fundamental; excerpts from news briefing, December 14, 1970. R. M. Nixon. U S News 69:
 10 D 28 '70 *
CONNECTICUT
 See also
Architecture, Domestic—Connecticut
Conservation of resources—Connecticut
Fishing—Connecticut
Music festivals—Connecticut
Trials—Connecticut

Antiquities

 See Indians of North America—Antiquities—Connecticut

Historic houses, etc.

Hatheway house, and its garden. U. Toomey.
 il Horticulture 48:26-7+ S '70
Living with antiques; Old Lyme. W. T.
 Donoho. il Antiques 98:922-6 D '70
 See also
Norwalk, Conn.—Historic houses, etc.

Parks and reserves

Day the sea ran out of flounder; Hammonassett state park. S. W. Hitchcock. por(p4)
 Natur Hist 79:28-31+ Mr '70

Politics and government

Connecticut: signs an era is ending. il U S
 News 69:32 Ag 31 '70
Duffey campaign. Nation 211:133 Ag 31 '70
Joe Duffey's race. P. R. Wieck. New Republic 163:9-10 Ag 15 '70
New old politics; democratic senatorial primary. il por Newsweek 76:29 Ag 31 '70
CONNECTICUT housing investment fund
New way to integrate the suburbs. il Bsns
 W p 168+ Mr 28 '70
CONNECTICUT opera association
Report:
 Aida. W. D. Miranda. il Opera N 35:31
 D 12 '70
 Carmen and Barber of Seville. Opera N
 34:30 Ap 11 '70
 Salome. W. D. Miranda. il Opera N 34:
 32-3 Ja 31 '70
CONNECTICUT parole board. See Parole
CONNECTICUT RIVER
Calefaction of a river. D. Merriman. il Sci
 Am 222:42-52 My '70
The Connecticut: priorities in conflict. E. P.
 Berkeley. il Arch Forum 133:28-35 S '70

CONNECTICUT state library, Hartford
  Connecticut state librarian; bypass city libraries? summary of annual report. W. Brahm. Library J 96:15-16+ Ja 1 '71
CONNECTICUT. University, Storrs
  Kidspeak. W. F. Buckley, jr. Nat R 22:1178 N 3 '70
CONNECTIVE tissues
  See also
  Fibroblasts
      Diseases
  Myxovirus antibody increases in human connective tissue disease. P. E. Phillips and C. L. Christian. bibliog il Science 168: 982-4 My 22 '70
  See also
  Lupus erythematosus
CONNECTORS
  See also
  Electric connectors
CONNELL, Elizabeth B.
  Pill in perspective. Read Digest 97:118-22 O '70
CONNELL, Evan S. jr
  Beginnings. Writer 83:9-11 S '70
CONNELLAN, Leo
  Watching Jim Shoulders; poem. Nation 210: 158 F 9 '70
CONNELLY, Charles
  Morocco. il Travel & Camera 33:38-47+ S '70
CONNELLY, Dolly
  Healthiest new town in America. il Am Home 74:39+ Ja '70
  Wilderness family that helped save the swans. il por Life 68:56 Ap 10 '70
CONNELLY, Marc
  Before the colors fade: Green pastures recalled; interview, ed. by J. L. Phillips. il pors Am Heritage 21:28-9+ F '70 *
  Canals of Ireland. il Holiday 48:48-53 Jl '70
  —See Kaufman, G. S. jt. auth.
CONNER, John W.
  Book marks. See issues of English journal
CONNER, Wilkie
  How one writer sold a book review column idea. Writers Digest 50:18 F '70
CONNER, William W.
  Bring your first aid up-to-date. il Pop Mech 133:S18 My '70
CONNERY, Donald S.
  June in England. il Travel & Camera 33:26-37+ My '70
CONNERY, John R.
  Law and conscience. il America 122:178-81 F 21 '70
CONNOLLY, Brendan
  Fixed-function library. il por Wilson Lib Bul 44:858-60 Ap '70
CONNOR, J. Robert. See Capotosto, J. jt. auth.
CONNOR, Jean
  Museum designs exhibition for children. il Sch Arts 69:28-9 Je '70
CONNORS, Joy
  They're on their way. il Am Ed 6:23-5 Je '70
CONNORS, Mike
  Mannix: where the action is; interview, ed. by P. Hudson. il pors Sr Schol 97:40 O 26 '70
CONOCO. See Continental oil company
CONOVER, Willis
  Don't get around much anymore. il Sat R 53:98-9 My 14 '70
CONQUEST, Robert
  American psychodrama called "Everyone hates us." N Y Times Mag p28-9+ My 10 '70
  Discontent in Russia: threat to the Kremlin? interview. por U S News 69:58-9 D 28 '70
  Kremlin leaders: men with a very large number of crackpot ideas; excerpts from testimony. il U S News 68:57 F 9 '69
  Stalin's successors. For Affairs 48:509-24 Ap '70
  —See Amis, K. jt. auth.
      about
  Contribution of Robert Conquest. G. Niemeyer. Nat R 22:315-16 Mr 24 '70 *
CONRAD, Donald B.
  Learning on the Q/T. Clear House 44:534-7 My '70
CONRAD, Joseph
  Lord Jim: big deal. D. R. Silkowski. Engl J 59:780-1 S '70 *
  My father, by B. Conrad. Review
    New Repub 163:19-20 D 19 '70. A. Mizener *
CONROY, Frank
  Car games; story. New Yorker 45:27-9 Ja 17 '70
  Manson wins! A fantasy. il Harper 241:53-9 N '70
  Mysterious case of R; story. New Yorker 46:23-4 Ag 29 '70

      about
  Short visits with five writers and one friend. B. Midwood. il pors Esquire 74:150-3 N '70 *
CONROY, Hilary
  (comp) Articles and other books received; East Asia. See issues of American historical review
CONROY, Sarah Booth
  That Cheshire cat. il pors Ladies Home J 87: 80-1+ Mr '70
CONSCIENTIOUS objectors
  CO riddle; case of Elliott A. Welsh, 2d. and the Supreme court ruling. Newsweek 75: 19 Je 29 '70
  C.O.'s private battle. il por Time 96:35 N 23 '70
  Conscientious objection: Supreme court reaffirms 1965 ruling. New Repub 163:10 Jl 18 '70
  Conscription, conscience and the Court. Chr Cent 87:908-9 Jl 29 '70
  Defective justice; Willard Gaylin's study of Vietnam war resisters. J. Lear. Sat R 53:47 Ap 18 '70
  Defining conscientious objectors; Supreme court decision. Chr Today 14:21 Jl 17 '70
  Draft board weighs the question of sincerity; case of M. Edgell. M. Mok. il pors Life 69: 16D-23 Jl 24 '70
  Greatest victory; conscientious objector status. Chr Cent 87:99 Ja 28 '70
  How Court ruling changes draft. il U S News 68:17-19 Je 29 '70
  Judge Wyzanski and selective conscientious objection. J. A. Rohr. America 122:182-5 F 21 '70; Reply. P. J. Henriot. 122:319 Mr 28 '70
  Law and conscience. J. R. Connery. il America 122:178-81 F 21 '70
  Man who beat the army; case of H. Tobias. B. Donovan. New Repub 162:17-19 Ja 31 '70
  Our far-flung correspondents; Dartmouth '70 and the war. N. Perrin. New Yorker 46:53-8 Jl 18 '70
  Reinterpreting the draft law. Chr Today 14:31 Jl 3 '70
  Right pew, wrong church; case of P. W. Goguen. J. Keelan. il Commonweal 92:359-64 Jl 24 '70
  Selective conscientious objection: progress report. P. J. Riga. il Cath World 211:161-5 Jl '70
  Selective objectors and the Court. America 123:6 Jl 11 '70
  Who must serve; beliefs and the draft. il Sr Schol 97:6-7 S 14 '70
  Who's sincere? Supreme court ruling: Selective service director's guidelines. por Time 95:40 Je 29 '70
CONSCIOUSNESS
  Fact is: we like to be drugged. J. C. Oates. McCalls 97:69 Je '70
  Marcuse's eroticized man: a new synthesis of action-contemplation. R. Hindery. por Chr Cent 87:136-8 F 4 '70
CONSCIOUSNESS-expanding drugs. See Hallucinogenic drugs
CONSCRIPTION. See Military service, Compulsory
CONSCRIPTION, Military. See Military service, Compulsory
CONSEIL européen pour la recherche nucléaire. See European organization for nuclear research
CONSERVATION as a profession
  Conservation careers for women. A. LaBastille. il por Cons 24:31-4 Je '70
  Welcome back to school from the old professor. M. Frome. Field & S 75:34-5 S '70
CONSERVATION associations
  Conservationists at the barricades. J. Main. il Fortune 81:144-7+ F '70
  Politics of ecology. H. Wheeler. il Sat R 53:51-2+ Mr 7 '70
  Private interests and public lands. R. S. Gilmour. Cur Hist 59:36-42+ Jl '70
  See also
  American fisheries society
  American forestry association
  Audubon naturalist society of the Central Atlantic states
  Environmental associations, committees, etc.
  National Audubon society
  National wildlife federation
  Sierra club
CONSERVATION education. See Conservation of resources—Study and teaching; Environmental education
CONSERVATION education center. See National parks and conservation association

CONSERVATION law. See Conservation of resources—Legal aspects

CONSERVATION library center. See Denver public library—Conservation library center

CONSERVATION movement. See Environmental movement

CONSERVATION of photographs. See Photographs—Conservation and restoration

CONSERVATION of resources

Am I a faithful steward? J. Strohm. il Nat Wildlife 8:2-9 D '69

American heritage society awards; with nominees. il Am Heritage 21:3, 116 F '70

American land; symposium, ed. by D. G. McCullough (cont) il Am Heritage 21:97-115+ F: 97-117 Ap '70; discussion. 21:117-18 F '70

American land; symposium, ed. by A. Wolff. il Am Heritage 21:93-113 Je; 97-120+ Ag; 94-113 O '70

Congressional reports. Nat Parks & Con Mag 44:34 My '70

Conservation. M. Frome. See issues of Field & stream

Conservation and the economy. W. F. Rickenbacker. Nat R 22:242 Mr 10 '70

Conservation battles won. G. Silk. il Life 69:28-40 Jl 4 '70

Conservation: high priority. Nat R 22:70+ Ja 27 '70

Country doctor looks at conservation and health; cooperation between agencies in West Virginia. D. Hale. il pors Am For 76:16-18+ Ja '70

Dam outrage: the story of the army engineers. E. B. Drew. il Atlan 225:51-62 Ap '70

Death row. See issues of Audubon

Earthmanship. D. Lambert. Nat Parks 44: 15-16 Ja '70

EQ critical list. See issues of National wildlife

Garden-club ladies. il Time 95:13 Je 1 '70

Helium: costs jeopardize future of government conservation program. P. M. Boffey. Science 167:1593-6 Mr 20 '70

Look at national priorities. K. E. Boulding. il Cur Hist 59:65-72+ Ag '70

National outlook. C. H. Callison. See issues of Audubon

National parks association; report of the president and general counsel, May 22, 1970. A. W. Smith. Nat Parks & Con Mag 44: 17-20 My '70

National resource revenue sharing. W. W. Porter, 2d. il por Am For 76:24-7+ Ja '70

Needed: a rebirth of community. il Newsweek 75:47 Ja 26 '70

News & commentary. See issues of National parks magazine

1970 National EQ index. il Nat Wildlife 8:25-40 O '70; Same. Schol Teach Jr/Sr High pA1-16 O 5 '70

Perspective. J. H. Plumb. Sat R 53:25 Mr 7 '70

Place for snakes as well as naked lovers. G. B. Leonard. il Look 34:80-5 Ja 13 '70

Problems in the environmental decade; testimony before House conservation and natural resources subcommittee. A. W. Smith. Nat Parks & Con Mag 44:25-7 Ap '70

Quality of life; a proposed program for global action by the UN; address, April 21, 1970. R. N. Gardner. Vital Speeches 36:466-70 My 15 '70

Spirit of the seventies. A. H. Seed, jr. il por Am For 76:12-15+ Ap '70

State of the Union between man and nature. R. M. Nixon. por Field & S 75:56-7+ Je '70

Trees on the back lot; need for the conservation of genetic information. G. Marine. Nat Parks & Con Mag 44:4-6 Ag '70

Ultimately, it's the consumer. B. Cowan. Nat Parks & Con Mag 44:24 Je '70

Urban conservation; adaptation of address. D. F. Rettie. Parks & Rec 9:33-4+ S '70

Washington report. L. S. Clapper. See issues of National wildlife

Weeds, bugs, Americans. J. Fowles. il Sports Illus 33:84-8+ D 21 '70

See also
Environmental defense fund, inc.
Environmental movement
Forest conservation
Landscape protection
Natural resources
Nature conservancy (organization)
Raw materials
Reclamation of land
Shore protection
United States—Interior, Department of
Watersheds
Wilderness areas
Wildlife conservation

History

Ecology before Columbus. T. Grieder. il Américas 22:21-8 My '70

George Bird Grinnell: grandfather of conservation. M. Frome. Field & S 75:52+ Je '70

Government's historical role in conservation. W. G. Carleton. Cur Hist 58:321-7+ Je '70

Mike Frome. M. Frome. por Am For 76:3+ Mr '70

Rise of American esthetic conservation; Muir, Mather, & Udall. D. H. Strong. il pors Nat Parks 44:4-9 F '70

Legal aspects

Lawsuits defend natural areas. Liv Wildn 34:58-9 Spr '70

Needed: an environmental bill of rights. P. F. Brandwein. il Am For 76:28-33 Ap; 36-8 My '70

Page forty-eight; a taint from technocracy. L. W. Douglas. Am West 7:48 Mr '70

Summary of New York state's new environmental conservation law. Cons 24:6-7 Je '70

See also
Wildlife conservation—Laws and legislation

Study and teaching

Adventure: Camp fire girls style. G. Harper. il Parks & Rec 9:34-6+ S '70

Dynamics of the Rogers conservation education center. J. A. Weeks. il Cons 25:7-9 D '70

Ecology; new cause, new career. M. A. Guitar. il Mlle 70:190-3+ Ap '70

Regional approach to conservation education; Project RACE. J. E. Passer. il Cons 24:8-9 Je '70

Success story: Youth development and conservation corps, state of Washington. D. H. Reynaud. il Parks & Rec 5:28-9 Jl '70

Yes, we are teaching Johnny conservation. G. H. Harrison. il Nat Wildlife 8:42-7 Ap '70

Alaska

Alaskan wilderness: going, going, gone? C. Hunter. il Nat Parks & Con Mag 44:11-15 N '70

Alaska's economic resources & environmental quality. G. W. Rogers. Nat Parks & Con Mag 44:8-10 N '70

Great land: boom or doom? il Time 96:44-7+ Jl 27 '70

Report from Alaska. R. B. Weeden. il Liv Wildn 34:50-1 Spr '70

California

Bay that refused to die. F. Hutchinson. il Am For 76:24-7+ Ap '70

Canada

Canada in the '70's, make or break. D. H. Pimlott. por Field & S 75:61+ Je '70

Connecticut

Teen girls' battle of the bogs. Sr Schol 95: 16 N 3 '69

Europe, Western

For a cleaner Europe; Nature conservation year. J. Lambert. il Sci N 97:280 Mr 14 '70

Florida

Fight for the Everglades. A. W. Smith. Nat Parks 44:2 Ja '70

Israel

Nature preservation in Israel. D. J. Elazar. il Liv Wildn 34:24-9 Sum '70

Japan

Grappling with crowding. S. Griffin. il Sci N 97:396 Ap 18 '70

Maine

Dilemma of Machiasport. F. Graham, jr. il Audubon 72:106-11 Jl '70

Genesis revised. J. B. Craig. Am For 76:7 Jl '70

Maine to regulate commercial development. R. D. Butcher. Liv Wildn 34:54-5 Sum '70

New Jersey

Environment action: a hometown approach; Citizens for conservation, Bernards Township, N.J. H. R. Berridge. il Org Gard & Farm 17:27-9 Je '70

New York (state)

Protecting a natural beach. J. E. Wilson. il Cons 24:28-31 Ap '70

Summary of New York state's new environmental conservation law. Cons 24:6-7 Je '70

See also
New York (state)—Environmental conservation, Department of

CONSERVATION of resources—*Continued*

Oregon

French Pete for people; Willamette national forest, Ore. A. Netboy. il Am For 76:16-18+ My '70

Tennessee

Poison in Tennessee; vole eradication. M. Frome. Field & S 74:30+ Ja '70

Vermont

Green Mountain profile. Liv Wildn 34:60 Spr '70

Wales

How green was my valley; protests against flooding of valleys. il Newsweek 75:48 Ap 6 '70

CONSERVATION of wildlife. See Wildlife conservation

CONSERVATION of works of art. See Art—Conservation and restoration

CONSERVATION officers
    See also
New York (state)—Conservation department —Employees

CONSERVATIONIST (periodical)
Conservationist costs and awards. Cons 24:1 Ag '69

CONSERVATISM
Conservative is the way to sound; with report on R. Reagan by P. O'Neil and views of the average voter. il Life 69:24-32 O 30 '70
Did you ever see a dream walking? ed. by W. F. Buckley, jr. Review
    Nat R 22:573+ Je 2 '70 D. Brudnoy
Letter from Washington; conservatism of R. A. Taft compared to Nixon administration. R. H. Rovere. New Yorker 46:72+ Jl 18 '70
New right. il Newsweek 76:24-5 D 7 '70
South of John C. Calhoun; spokesman for southern conservatism. il por Time 96:46 N 30 '70
Wallace Stevens in the tropics; a conservative protest. J. Pinkerton. Yale R 60:215-27 D '70
What about Ehrlichman? departure of conservatives from the administration. Cato. Nat R 22:830 Ag 11 '70
Where conservatives can't lose; Texas. W. Murchison, jr. Nat R 22:1164 N 3 '70
    See also
Liberalism
Right and left (political science)
Young Americans for freedom (organization)

Bibliography

Conservative consensus. P. P. Witonski. Nat R 22:1304-7 D 1 '70

CONSERVATIVE party (Great Britain)
Now or never for Tory Heath? il por U S News 68:36 Je 1 '70
Three conservative musketeers: E. Powell, A. Douglas-Home, Q. Hogg. C. Brogan. Nat R 22:148-9 F 10 '70
Tory, Tory, hallelujah. il pors Newsweek 75: 30+ Je 29 '70

CONSOLIDATED Edison company of New York
Con Ed and the good life: a question of power. il Newsweek 76:76+ Jl 13 '70
Con Ed loses its nuclear punch. Bsns W p 19 Jl 4 '70
Con Ed's Charles Luce: all power (sometimes) to the people. S. Brownmiller. il pors N Y Times Mag p34-5+ Ap 12 '70
Early warning; summer cutbacks. Newsweek 75:67 Mr 30 '70
Fish and power plants; Storm King Mountain pumped-storage project. A. C. Jensen; reply with rejoinder. L. W. Mantell. Cons 24:42-3 Ap '70
Meters: Victor Lombardo, reader on his rounds. New Yorker 45:21-4 Ja 17 '70
Playing games with nature. Commonweal 92:427-8 S 4 '70. Reply. S. A. Mallard. 92: 490 S 25 '70
Rehabilitation of Con Edison. Nation 210:435 Ap 27 '70
Sweating it out with borrowed kilowatts. il Bsns W p22-3 Ag 1 '70

CONSOLIDATED foods corporation
Rehash at Consolidated. pors Newsweek 75: 64+ Ja 26 '70

CONSOLIDATED freightways, inc.
Trucker takes to the sea and air. il por Bsns W p44-5+ O 3 '70

CONSOLIDATED schools
Design for regenerating a city; human resources center in Pontiac, Mich. W. W. Chase. il Am Ed 6:8-13 Mr '70

CONSOLIDATION coal company
Outsmarting themselves. Forbes 106:80 O 15 '70
Returning beauty to the land; Friendship park in eastern Ohio. Nations Bsns 58:19 Ja '70

CONSOLIDATIONS, Business. See Business consolidations and mergers

CON SON prison. See Prisons—Vietnam (Republic)

CONSORT; ballet. See Ballets—Criticisms

CONSORTIUM of publishers for employment. See COPE program

CONSPIRACY
Another death plot? plots to kill J.F.K. at the Nov. 2, 1963, army-air force game in Chicago. por Time 95:17 Ap 20 '70
Conspiracy in Ireland; arms smuggling. S. Cronin. Commonweal 93:188-90 N 20 '70
Hoover and the Berrigans; East Coast conspiracy to save lives organization. America 123:509 D 12 '70
J. Edgar, Dan and Phil. J. Deedy. Commonweal 93:290 D 18 '70
Now the U.S. takes on the Chicago twelve; indictments. il Newsweek 75:19-20 Ap 13 '70
    See also
Trials (conspiracy)

CONSTABLE, Rosalind
Vanishing Indian. Art in Am 58:45 Ja '70

CONSTANT voltage transformers. See Electric transformers

CONSTANTS. See Units

CONSTELLATIONS
Barnard's star: the search for other solar systems; stars and planets and the constellation Ophiuchus. P. Van De Kamp. il Natur Hist 79:38-43 Ap '70
Magnetic dwarf in Draco. il Time 96:45 S 14 '70
    See also
Stars

CONSTITUTION (frigate)
Memorandum to Oliver Wendell Holmes. C. B. Mitchell. il Am Heritage 21:23-7+ F '70

CONSTITUTION (United States) See United States—Constitution

CONSTITUTIONAL amendments. See United States—Constitution—Amendments

CONSTITUTIONAL conventions
    See also
United States—Constitutional convention (proposed)
United States—Constitutional convention, 1787

CONSTITUTIONAL law
Figgis, Constance, and the Divines of Paris; excerpts from address, December 30, 1966. F. Oakley. bibliog f Am Hist R 75:368-86 D '69
    See also
Due process of law

CONSTITUTIONS, State
New bill of rights for Illinois. Nation 211: 421-2 N 2 '70

CONSTRICTORS (snakes) See Boa constrictors

CONSTRUCTION, Concrete. See Concrete construction

CONSTRUCTION contracts. See Building—Contracts and specifications

CONSTRUCTION industry. See Building industry

CONSTRUCTION industry foundation
Architect vs. the builder: does it have to be that way? W. F. Wagner, jr. Arch Rec 147:9 F '70

CONSTRUCTION materials. See Building materials

CONSTRUCTION workers. See Building workers

CONSULAR service. See United States—Diplomatic and consular service

CONSULTANTS
    See also
Government consultants, Municipal
Library consultants
Psychiatric consultants
Public relations consultants
Tax consultants

CONSULTATION, Psychiatric. See Psychiatric consultation

CONSULTATION on church union
Blacks and COCU: a new honesty. C. Rogers. Chr Cent 87:1554 D 30 '70
Church of Christ uniting. America 122:362 Ap 4 '70
Church uniting, slowly. por Time 95:48 Mr 2 '70
COCU: a critique. H. Lindsell. Chr Today 15: 3-5 O 9; 8-10+ O 23 '70; Discussion. 15:21-2 N 20 '70
COCU alternatives. Chr Today 15:26-7 D 18 '70

CONSULTATION on church union—*Continued*

COCU 1970: a symposium; with editorial comment. Chr Cent 87:227, 231-43 F 25 '70

COCU plan of union: is this the house I can live in? with editorial comment. R. Chandler. il Chr Today 14:31, 40-1 Mr 13 '70

Consultation on church union. America 122:232 Mr 7 '70

Embracing COCU. il Chr Today 14:44 Ap 10 '70

Episcopacy and church unity, today and to-morrow. America 122:601 Je 6 '70

Nuts and bolts of union vote. Chr Today 14:44-5 Ap 10 '70

Paradox of contemporary Christendom. Chr Today 14:20 Jl 17 '70

Plan of union: the nose on COCU's face; with editorial comment. R. Chandler. Chr Today 14:22, 30 Mr 27 '70

Presbyterian lay group opposes COCU. Chr Today 15:41-2 D 4 '70

Quiet victory in St Louis. A. Geyer. il Chr Cent 87:349-50 Mr 25 '70

Selling COCU to 24 million. R. Chandler. Chr Today 14:43-4 Ap 10 '70

Toward a single church; Church of Christ uniting. il Newsweek 75:52 Mr 2 '70

Whither unity? A case study; Church of Christ uniting and Bethany Park Christian church, Lawrence, Kan. T. Miller. Chr Cent 87:891-3 Jl 22 '70; Discussion. 87:1423-4, 1457-9 N 25-D 2 '70

Anecdotes, facetiae, satire, etc.

Leftovers from St Louis. Chr Cent 87:380 Ap 1 '70

CONSUMER affairs, Department of (proposed)
See United States—Consumer affairs, Department of (proposed)

CONSUMER behavior. See Consumers

CONSUMER class actions. See Actions and defenses

CONSUMER complaints. See Complaints

CONSUMER credit

Consumer credit. il Consumer Rep 34:388-92 D '69

Hard facts about easy credit. il Changing T 24:27-30 N '70

How smart a borrower are you? Bet Hom & Gard 48:8+ Ja '70

When you must borrow money. S. Margolius. Todays Ed 59:68-70 O '70

See also
Credit cards
Loans, Personal

Laws and legislation

How the truth-in-lending law works. Good H 170:194 My '70

Some lies about truth-in-lending. Consumer Rep 35:72-3 F '70

Staying one-up on credit rates. J. S. Wilson. Bet Hom & Gard 48:8+ N '70

CONSUMER credit legislation. See Consumer credit—Laws and legislation

CONSUMER education

Buying guide issues. 1969-70. il Consumer Rep 34:1-448 D '69; 35:1-439 D '70

How other women save money in stores; symposium, ed. by B. M. Grant. il Redbook 136:68-9+ N '70

Suggested guidelines for consumer education. Review
New Repub 163:26 D 12 '70. D. Sanford

Why not collect labels? value of collecting food and textile labels. Consumer Bul 53: 15-16 S '70

See also
Consumer protection

CONSUMER electronics show. See Electronic apparatus and appliances—Exhibitions

CONSUMER frauds. See Fraud

CONSUMER goods. See Commercial products

CONSUMER price index. See Price indexes

CONSUMER protection

Action lines: nagging complaints are sweet music to them. il Mech Illus 66:45-7+ Ag '70

Banzhaf's bandits. Time 95:15-16 Mr 2 '70

Concerned consumer. J. S. Wilson. Bet Hom & Gard 48:4+ Mr; 46+ Ap; 12 My; 36 S; 8+ N '70

Concerned consumer. Bet Hom & Gard 48: 30 D '70

Consumer protection; address. November 23, 1969. H. Frazier. Vital Speeches 36:265-70 F 15 '70

Consumerism: what is it? Consumer Bul 53: 21-3 Ag '70

Consumerism: where the buyers stands. Bsns W p 131 Ap 25 '70

Consumer's friend at school; J. F. Banzhaf's advocate groups. por Bsns W p90 O 31 '70

Cost of living. B. Furness. See issues of McCall's

Crushing cost of consumerism; comments of members of the Presidents' panel. G. R. Rosen. il Duns 95:36-7 Ap '70

Developing responsible promotion; consumer information policies; address, October 15, 1970. E. L. Bond, jr. Vital Speeches 37:124-8 D 1 '70

FTC gets tough. por Time 96:80 O 19 '70

Got a gripe? Here's where to complain; names and addresses of agencies and organizations. il Changing T 24:31-4 Mr '70

Imported radio showdown. J. Darr. Radio-Electr 41:26+ Ap '70

Irate consumer; annual Consumer assembly. il por Newsweek 75:63 Ja 26 '70

It's a racket! consumer gyps and how to spot them. il Sr Schol 96:11-12 Ja 26 '70

Law professor behind ASH, SOUP, PUMP and CRASH; J. Banzhaf. J. A. Page. il por N Y Times Mag p32-3+ Ag 23 '70; Reply. R. H. Quinn. p33 S 27 '70

Let the buyer be aware; untested new products. A. R. Roalman. il Todays Health 48:66-7+ Mr '70

Nader's biggest raid; summer projects. il por Newsweek 75:67-8 Je 29 '70

Nader's raiders; consumer crusade against major corporations. America 122:491 My 9 '70

Nader's raiders on the FDA; science and scientists misused. P. M. Boffey. Science 168:349-52 Ap 17 '70

Nader's raiders strike again. il por Time 95: 88 Mr 30 '70

New consumerism: let the buyer be aware. Sr Schol 97:14-18 S 28 '70

New incentive to produce a better product? pork. R. Wilmore. Farm J 94:H20 My '70

Nothing works anymore. D. Sanford. il New Repub 162:21-4 F 14 '70

Smell it, then sell it; supermarket dating of products. New Repub 162:8-9 Ap 25 '70

Storm in the cereal bowl. J. Cross. Nation 211:133 Ag 31 '70

Thrust of consumerism. Nation 210:324 Mr 23 '70

Two legal reforms to protect shoppers' rights. il Changing T 24:23-4 Ap '70

Virginia Knauer: what she tells the President about consumers. il por Nations Bsns 58: 34-8 Jl '70

See also
Consumers union of United States
Labels—Laws and legislation
Underwriters' laboratories, inc.
Unit pricing
United States—Consumer affairs, Department of (proposed)
United States—National commission on product safety
United States—President's committee on consumer interests

Laws and legislation

Consumer power grows in Congress. Bsns W p20 Jl 11 '70

Defending consumers; proposed Independent consumer agency act. S. Lazarus. New Repub 163:10 S 26 '70

Docket; notes on government actions taken to enforce consumer protection laws. See issues of Consumer reports

Learning the hard way. L. L. L. Golden. il Sat R 53:114 Mr 14 '70

Let there be lumens; FTC regulation on life ratings. Newsweek 76:58-9 Ag 3 '70

Magna carta? bill emerging in Congress. Newsweek 75:81+ My 18 '70

Multimillion-dollar floodgate; Eckhardt-Tydings bill. il Forbes 105:28-9 My 1 '70

New consumerism. J. E. Kenney. America 122:270-2 Mr 14 '70

New York leads the consumer crusade. il Bsns W p50-3 Ja 31 '70

Rosenthal's lament; bill defeated. New Repub 163:8 D 12 '70

Rush to protect consumers. il U S News 68: 44-7 F 2 '70

U.S.'s toughest customer; R. Nader & raiders. Read Digest 96:76-80 Mr '70

See also
National consumer law center
Packaging—Laws and legislation

Japan

Britannica rues a wave of zeal. Bsns W p34-5 N 21 '70

CONSUMER reports (periodical)
Catalogue of caveats. il Time 96:38 Ag 24 '70
CONSUMERS
Consumerism and trade. H. C. Wallich. Newsweek 76:61 Ag 31 '70
Don't sell the buyer short; interview. J. A. Howard. por Nations Bsns 58:34-5 Ag '70
Selling to the hottest market ever. il Bsns W p 124-6+ O 17 '70
Speaker for the house. C. Montgomery. See issues of Good housekeeping
Take in a new partner, the consumer. W. G. Kaye. il Nations Bsns 58:54-7 F '70
Ultimately, it's the consumer. B. Cowan. Nat Parks & Con Mag 44:24 Je '70
Women and the myth of consumerism. E. Willis. il Ramp Mag 8:13-16 Je '70
See also
Consumer education
Consumer protection
CONSUMERS union, inc.
Will the real CU please stand up? Consumer Rep 35:508-9 S '70
CONSUMERS union of United States
CU files suits against Seagram and Hamm. Consumer Rep 35:6 Ja '70
CU wins injunction against Hamm. Consumer Rep 35:508 S '70
Members choose six for CU board. Consumer Rep 35:580 O '70
Members elect seven to CU board. il Consumer Rep 34:624 N '69
Re: a case of caveat emptor; Allied radio shack. Consumer Rep 35:662-3 N '70
VA releases more hearing-aid data. Consumer Rep 35:8 Ja '70
See also
Consumer reports (periodical)
CONSUMPTION (economics)
Abundance isn't the full answer; Consumer buying indicators findings. B. L. Masse. America 122:289 Mr 21 '70
Consumer goods are leading the recovery. il Fortune 82:20 S '70
Counting the pennies, and dollars. il Bsns W p24-5 My 30 '70
Man and his environment; adaptation of address, March 19, 1970. A. J. Coale. Science 170:132-6 O 9 '70
Nonbuying mood. Time 95:76 Je 22 '70
Playing it tight; decline in luxury spending. il Newsweek 75:81 Ap 20 '70
Poverty of affluence. R. Lekachman. Commentary 49:39-44 Mr '70; Reply with rejoinder. B. Shalcovitch. 50:10+ Jl '70
Why people aren't spending. il U S News 69:38-40 S 28 '70
CONTACT lenses
About those contact lenses. G. M. Knox. Bet Hom & Gard 48:24+ My '70
Contact lenses, what the doctors now say. Read Digest 97:155-6+ S '70
New look at contacts. Ladies Home J 87:16 Ap '70
CONTAGIOUS diseases. See Communicable diseases
CONTAINER corporation of America
See also
Marcor. inc.
CONTAINER gardening. See Gardening
CONTAINERIZATION (freight)
Airlines push containers, but purchase program lags. J. P. Woolsey. il Aviation W 93:80-2+ O 26 '70
Dramatic change in course for shipping. il Nations Bsns 56:77-80 My '70
End run around U.S. ports; Canadian national rys. integrated container service. il Bsns W p54+ Ap 25 '70
Japanese set sail for New York. il Bsns W p32-3 D 26 '70
CONTAINERS
Taking the lid off a new food can; plastic cans. Bsns W p46+ Ap 4 '70
Will returnables make a comeback? Bsns W p25-6 O 31 '70
See also
Bottles
Milk containers
CONTAINERS, Pressurized. See Pressure packaging
CONTAINERS for shipping
See also
Containerization (freight)
CONTAMINATION from the moon. See Earth —Contamination
CONTAMINATION of food. See Food contamination
CONTAMINATION of the earth. See Earth— Contamination
CONTEE, Clarence G.
Ethiopia and the Pan-African movement. 1945-1963. il por Negro Hist Bul 33:122-5 My '70
CONTEMPLATION. See Meditation

CONTEMPLATIVE orders
Contemplative life and the sociologist. M. Rowe. Chr Cent 87:1412-16 N 25 '70; Discussion. 88:20 Ja 6 '71
Dignity of person includes contemplatives. J. C. Haughey. America 123:404-5 N 14 '70; Discussion. 123:475 D 5 '70
CONTEMPORARY ballet ensemble of New York, See Ballet companies
CONTEMPORARY music. See Music
CONTEMPORARY music, International. See International society for contemporary music
CONTEMPORARY rooms. See Period rooms
CONTEMPT of court
Anarchy in Tacoma; case of the Seattle Seven. por Time 96:46 D 28 '70
Gag rule: ominous trend. D. Meade. Cur Cent 87:589-90 My 13 '70
How to control the court. il Time 95:31 Mr 9 '70
Judicial process on trial; vulnerability proved by trial of Chicago seven. il Newsweek 75:25-6+ Mr 2 '70
Murtagh's formula. il Newsweek 75:22-3 Mr 9 '70
New ruling; order in the court means what it says; Supreme court ruling. il U S News 68:63 Ap 13 '70
Order in the courtroom. Time 95:51 Ap 13 '70
Point of order: Supreme court's ruling in the Allen case. il Newsweek 75:21-2 Ap 13 '70
Split verdict: who won? Chicago seven. il Sr Schol 96:13-14 Mr 9 '70
What ever happened to order in the court? Sr Schol 97:15-16 D 14 '70
What provoked the most-severe contempt citations on record. por U S News 68:6-7 Mr 2 '70
CONTENTMENT
Secret of contentment. Chr Today 15:33 O 9 '70
Les CONTES d'Hoffmann; opera. See Offenbach J.
CONTESTS. See Competitions
CONTI, Franco, and Tasaki, Ichiji
Changes in extrinsic fluorescence in squid axons during voltage-clamp. bibliog il Science 169:1322-4 S 25 '70
CONTINENTAL airlines
Continental plans 747 Hawaiian service. Aviation W 92:36 F 2 '70
Continental's 747s to Hawaii nearly full. il Aviation W 93:27-8 Jl 13 '70
Sears big user of Continental 747 to Hawaii. il Aviation W 93:134 O 26 '70
Use of California satellite airports grows. Aviation W 93:24-5 Ag 24 '70
CONTINENTAL can company
Continental can braces for a clash. Fortune 82:81 S '70
Opening the lid on a Pandora's box. il Bsns W p38+ Ap 11 '70
CONTINENTAL copper and steel industries, inc.
Is there method. . ? il Forbes 106:19 D 1 '70
CONTINENTAL drift
Afar triangle. R. Tazieff. il Sci Am 222:32-40 bibliog(p 126) F '70
Antarctic geology and Gondwanaland. C. Craddock. il Bul Atom Sci 26:33-9 D '70
Birth of an ocean; Afar triangle. il Time 95:68 Mr 2 '70
Bones on Coalsack Bluff; a story of drifting continents. J. Lear. il Sat R 53:46-51 F 7 '70
Breakup of Pangaea. R. S. Dietz and J. C. Holden. il Sci Am 223:30-41 bibliog(p 144) O '70
Continental drift and the diversity of species. Sci N 98:396 N 21 '70
Farewell to Atlantis. il Newsweek 76:101 S 28 '70
Fit between Africa and Antarctica: a continental drift reconstruction. R. S. Dietz and W. P. Sproll. bibliog il Science 167:1612-14 Mr 20 '70
Hunting clues to an ancient supercontinent. D. Behrman. il UNESCO Courier 23:28-32 Jl '70
Jigsaw of the primeval world; Glomar Challenger's findings. il Life 68:60-3 Ja 30 '70
Paleomagnetism and Gondwanaland. M. W. McElhinny and G. R. Luck. bibliog il Science 168:830-2 My 15 '70
Piecing together the past; Uralides. il Sci N 98:285 O 3 '70
Sahara grooves; this area once located at the South Pole. Sr Schol 96:15 My 11 '70
South united; computer reconstruction of Gondwanaland. K. Frazier. il Sci N 97:229 F 28 '70
Triassic tetrapods from Antarctica; evidence for continental drift. D. H. Elliot and others. bibliog il Science 169:1197-201 S 18 '70

CONTINENTAL oil company
Continental oil's symbol success. V. Louviere. il Nations Bsns 58:21 N '70
CONTINENTAL shelf
Suspended matter in surface waters of the Atlantic continental margin from Cape Cod to the Florida Keys. F. T. Manheim and others. bibliog il Science 167:371-6 Ja 23 '70
Who owns the shelf? Time 96:70-1 S 14 '70
CONTINENTS
See also
Continental drift
CONTINUATION schools. See Evening and continuation schools
CONTINUOUS sessions. See School year
CONTOS, Catherine
Greedy amateur. il Hi Fi sec II 20:13-15 F '70
CONTOUR farming
He crops hills safely. W. Waltner and E. Waltner. il Suc Farm 68:A8 N '70
CONTRA COSTA COUNTY, Calif.
Tour de force in water-plant design. S. R. Komatsu and R. W. Johnston. il Am City 85:60-2 Ag '70
CONTRACEPTION. See Birth control
CONTRACEPTIVES
Amber light for the pill; Nelson subcommittee hearings. il Newsweek 75:48-9 F 2 '70
Anti-pregnancy treatment: when doctors use it. Good H 170:167 F '69
Biological and medical aspects of contraception, by B. Duffy and J. Wallace. Review
Cath World 211:280 S '70. P. R. Gaston-guay
Birth control after 1984; adaptation of address, May 6, 1970. C. Djerassi. bibliog il Science 169:941-51 S 4 '70
Confusion on the pill; Nelson hearings. M. Mintz. New Repub 162:10-11 Ja 31 '70
Contraceptive technology: advances needed in fundamental research. L. J. Carter. Science 168:805-7+ My 15 '70
Contraceptives and dysplasia: higher rate for pill choosers. E. Stern and others. bibliog il Science 169:497-8 Jl 31 '70
Controversy over the pill. B. Surface. il por Good H 170:64-5+ Ja '70
Crackdown; FDA withdraws C-Quens and Provest. Newsweek 76:100 N 2 '70
Enough to move FDA; relation of estrogen to bloodclotting. Sci N 97:430-1 My 2 '70
FDA: efficiency drive stumbles over the issue of drug efficiency; effects of Demulen. T. P. Southwick. Science 169:1188-9 S 18 '70; Reply. D. C. Goldberg. 170:491 O 30 '70
FDA goes to the consumer. Sci N 97:266 Mr 14 '70
FDA writes another warning. Sci N 97:599 Je 20 '70
Final warning? revised pamphlet with birth-control pills. Newsweek 75:76 Je 22 '70
Improved birth control devices that could replace the pill. Good H 172:129 Ja '71
Improving mechanical birth control methods; intrauterine devices. B. J. Culliton. il Sci N 98:121-3 Ag 8 '70
Is the pill safe? Sr Schol 96:15 Mr 16 '70
Male contraceptive: a better pill? L. Witt. il Todays Health 48:16-19+ Je '70
Minipill in limbo. Sci N 97:93 Ja 24 '70
More about the pill; UCLA findings. Newsweek 76:78+ O 12 '70
More fuel for the pill controversy; use of beagles in testing. B. J. Culliton. Sci N 98:402 N 21 '70
New doubts about the pill. il Life 68:28-9 F 27 '70
New use recommendations for birth control pills. Good H 171:153 Ag '70
Off the pill? J. Coburn. Ramp Mag 8:46-9 Je '70
Other side of the pill. Newsweek 75:45-6 Mr 9 '70
Perils of the pill; Senate hearings. il Newsweek 75:21 Ja 26 '70
Pill and your skin. Vogue 155:216+ My '70
Pill caution. Time 95:46 Ap 20 '70
Pill: do its benefits outweigh its hazards? Consumer Rep 35:314-19 My '70
Pill: how much warning is enough? Consumer Rep 35:329 Je '70
Pill in perspective. E. B. Connell. Read Digest 97:118-22 O '70
Pill is hard to follow. Bsns W p80 Ja 31 '70
Pill: is it safe? U S News 68:10 Ja 26 '70
Pill is safe; ed. by R. H. Berg. E. T. Tyler. il Look 34:65-6 Je 30 '70
Pill on trial. pors Time 95:60+ Ja 26 '70
Pill trial. por Time 95:32+ Mr 9 '70
Plain talk about the pill. il Newsweek 75:93 Mr 16 '70
Poll on the pill. il Newsweek 75:52-3 F 9 '70

Prognosis for the development of new chemical birth-control agents; adaptation of address. October 22, 1969. C. Djerassi; discussion. Science 166:1575-6; 167:1315-16 D 26 '69, Mr 6 '70
Recalling a pill; chlormadinone. Time 95:39 F 9 '70
Trouble with the IUD. Newsweek 75:73 My 25 '70
What kids still don't know about sex. T. Fleming and A. Fleming. il Look 34:59-60+ Jl 28 '70; Same abr. Read Digest 97:153-6 D '70
What you should know about the pill; text of AMA pamphlet. Todays Health 48:9-10 S '70
Who should take the pill? excerpt from Two children by choice. I. Rossman. Parents Mag 45:54-7+ F '70
Why I'll give my daughter the pill. P. H. Wade. il por Redbook 135:30+ Je '70
Why there is growing concern about the safety of the pill. il Good H 170:129-31 Ja '70

Advertising
Fear of the pill aids an industry; mass-media advertising. Bsns W p89 Mr 21 '70
Proselytizers for prophylactics; Population services, inc. promotes condoms. il Time 96:97+ D 7 '70

CONTRACT plan (education)
Contract for grades. E. F. Dash. bibliog il Clear House 45:231-5 D '70
Have you ever tried contracting for grades? S. Amsden. Engl J 59:1279-82 D '70

CONTRACTORS
Horrors of home repair; unskilled and inaccessible craftsmen. W. A. McWhirter. il Life 68:58-60+ Je 5 '70

CONTRACTS
Lack of signed writing nullifies agreement. H. F. Pilpel and K. P. Norwick. Pub W 198:30-1 O 26 '70
See also
Building—Contracts and specifications
Labor contracts
Municipal contracts

CONTRACTS, Agricultural
Bypass marketing altogether with forward contracting; hogs. B. W. Ebbing. Farm J 94:H7+ Ag '70
Contract details can cost you; hog contracting. G. Grimes. Farm J 94:H15 N '70
Feeder pig contract that keeps everyone happy. D. Seim. Farm J 93:H28 O '69
Grow-out feeder contracts. J. Bickers. il Farm J 93:12 O '69
There's strength in numbers; feeders join forces to buy cattle directly from producers. il Farm J 94:B42 F '70
Two dairy farm agreements and how they work. il Suc Farm 68:G8-9 My '70
Will packers control more livestock production? interview. C. B. Cox. Farm J 94:M1 F '70

CONTRACTS, Government
Aerospace dominates defense contractors. Aviation W 93:18 N 23 '70
Aerospace tries to pick up the pieces. il Bsns W p48-50+ D 12 '70
Army missile becomes a target; Shillelagh vs. Huges-built TOW missile. Bsns W p 130-1 Mr 28 '70
ATS award switch broadens controversy. D. C. Winston. Aviation W 93:22-3 S 14 '70
Bailing out Lockheed. Newsweek 77:66 Ja 11 '71
Cheers and tears. Nation 210:740 Je 22 '70
Contractors claw at the money door. Bsns W p 14 Ja 2 '71
Cost overruns bring on the SEC. il Bsns W p31 Je 6 '70
Cost tests delay airspace system plans. D. C. Winston. il Aviation W 92:70 F 9 '70
Defense department lists leading 100 contractors for fiscal 1970; table. Aviation W 93:58-61 N 30 '70
Defense's fly before you buy policy; recommendations of the Fitzhugh report. il por Newsweek 76:53-4 Ag 10 '70
Discrimination: women charge universities, colleges with bias. N. Gruchow. Science 168:559-61 My 1 '70
Education complex. il por Newsweek 76:72-3 S 7 '70
Even thinner menu for contractors. il Bsns W p30-1 Je 27 '70
F-15 avionics suppliers selection nears. P. J. Klass. Aviation W 92:22-3 Ja 19 '70
Failure free warranty idea lauded, wider use desired. P. J. Klass. Aviation W 92:57-8 F 9 '70
Fairchild Hiller gets a recount. Bsns W p 18 Jl 11 '70

CONTRACTS, Government—*Continued*
Fiscal 1970 budget delay generates cost problems. Aviation W 92:45+ F 16 '70
Fuel for the fires on defense profits. il Bsns W p30 Ap 11 '70
Future of federal contract research centers. D. C. Coddington and J. G. Milliken. bibliog f il Harvard Bsns R 48:103-16 Mr '70; Reply. 48:28+ Jl '70
GAO attacks NASA's Saturn 5 incentives W. J. Normyle. Aviation W 92:25-6 Ap 6 '70
GAO reports affects contractor relations. W. J. Normyle. Aviation W 93:18-19 Jl 13 '70
Independent research due closer scrutiny. P. J. Klass. Aviation W 92:21-2 Mr 16 '70
Lean times loom for suppliers. il por Bsns W p 115:16 F 28 '70
Lift for Boeing: flying radar station contract. il Newsweek 76:65 Jl 20 '70
Lockheed plans litigation, rejects fixed C-5A loss. C. Brownlow. Aviation W 94:17-18 Ja 11 '71
Lockheed scandal; C-5A cost overrun affair. J. G. Phillips. New Repub 163:19-23 Ag 1 '70
Lockheed's lament. il Time 95:82 My 18 '70
Loser's victory helps contractors. Bsns W p74 O 3 '70
Major DOD procurements at war with reality. H. B. Drake. il Harvard Bsns R 48:119-40 Ja '70
Major incentives offered for B-1. C. Brownlow. il Aviation W 92:12-13 Je 15 '70
Military spending; impact on business; interview. D. Packard. il por U S News 69: 44-8 Ag 3 '70
Modern times; navy destroyers contract to Litton industries. Newsweek 76:75-6 Jl 6 '70
Moon program's business brain trust; Apollo executive group. E. Clark. il pors Nations Bsns 58:32-4+ My '70
Myth of war profiteering. G. E. Berkley; reply. V. Perlo. New Repub 162:23-5 F 7 '70
NASA asks quick shuttle replies. W. J. Normyle. Aviation W 92:16-17 F 23 '70
NASA to scrutinize ATS award in Apollo accident-type review. Aviation W 93:19 Jl 20 '70
No shortcuts; excerpts from address. J. G. Merrell. Aviation W 92:13 Ap 6 '70
100 top NASA contractors listed according to net value of direct awards July 1, 1969—December 31, 1969; table. Aviation W 93:58-9 Jl 6 '70
One more chance bomber; B-1 contract. Fortune 82:27 Jl '70
Packard: defense on a diet; interview. ed. by A. A. Butkus. D. Packard. por Duns 96: 10-14 Ag '70
Peace bonanza that went bust; cutbacks of military programs. il Bsns W p66-8 S 5 '70
Pentagon cuts: the worst is yet to come; interview. R. C. Moot. il por Bsns W p94+ S 12 '70
Pentagon juggles its contractors. il Bsns W p82 N 14 '70
Pentagon's new rules on tools. Bsns W p 116+ F 28 '70
Philco-Ford gets satellite award. Aviation W 93:22 Ag 10 '70
Poverty pocket; lack of funds to fill order for C5A planes. New Repub 162:7-8 Mr 28 '70
Procedures controversy persists in ATS development competition. Aviation W 93:20 Jl 27 '70
Retreat from gold-plated contracts. il Bsns W p96-7 Jl 11 '70
Return of the destroyer; contract for construction of multipurpose destroyers. il Sci N 98:7-8 Jl 4 '70
Roots of the C-5 agony. Bsns W p 15 Ja 9 '71
Safeguard prize goes for a bargain. il Bsns W p31 Ap 4 '70
Shuttle group readies proposal requests. il Aviation W 92:17-18 Ja 19 '70
Small contract with lots of clout: air force sponsored International fighter. il Bsns W p 19 Mr 7 '70
SST backers debate future steps. Aviation W 94:14-15 Ja 11 '71
Status of major U.S. European defense. aerospace programs. Aviation W 92:14-18 Mr 9 '70
Struggle over a destroyer contract. Bsns W p31-2 Je 27 '70
Swipe at R&D overhead. il Bsns W p50 Mr 14 '70
Terms tightened in SST contract. H. D. Watkins. Aviation W 93:14-15 Ag 10 '70
Turbo train faces price increases. Aviation W 93:49 S 28 '70

When Mars is a milk run; space shuttle program. il Bsns W p95-6 Ap 11 '70
See also
Government investigations—Government contracts
Military-industrial complex
United States—Commission on government procurement
United States—Labor, Department of—Federal contract compliance, Office of

Accounting
Accounting board naming nears. Aviation W 93:19-20 Ag 24 '70
Accounting fight flares. por Bsns W p68 Ja 24 '70
Industry faces uphill fight on cost accounting rules. K. Johnsen. Aviation W 92:19-20 Ja 26 '70
Senate approves bill to establish uniform cost accounting practice. K. Johnsen. Aviation W 93:17 Jl 20 '70
Senate group split on proposal to establish standard accounting. K. Johnsen. Aviation W 92:24 Ap 6 '70
Standards or straitjacket? congressional demands for a uniform accounting system. C. A. Dana. Aviation W 93:9 Ag 17 '70

Renegotiation
See also
United States—Renegotiation board

Subcontracting
Subcontract competition for B-1 beginning. il Aviation W 93:59+ S 14 '70
Subcontractors lash out at the system. Bsns W p96+ O 31 '70

CONTRACTS, Land. See Land contracts
CONTRACTS, Municipal. See Municipal contracts
CONTRERAS, Gloria
Gloria Contreras dance company; 92nd street Y, NYC. M. Marks. Dance Mag 44:75 Je '70
CONTRIBUTIONS; drama. See Shine, T.
CONTROL circuits. See Electronic control
CONTROL data corporation
Control data divides the power. il Bsns W p34 Ap 25 '70
CONTROL of production. See Production control
CONTROLLED fires. See Forest fires—Controlled fires
CONTROLLED fusion. See Nuclear fusion
CONTROLLED-release preparations. See Delayed-action preparations
CONVALESCENCE
How ya gonna keep them down? care of bedridden children. M. M. Brooks. il N Y Times Mag p97+ Ap 5 '70
CONVALESCENT homes. See Nursing homes
CONVENIENCE foods. See Food—Ready-to-cook food
CONVENTIONS
Conventions: when & where. See issues of American city
CONVENTIONS (treaties) See Treaties
CONVENTS and nunneries
Nuns' story; exploitation of Keralan nuns in Europe. il Newsweek 76:53 S 7 '70
Scandal in the convents; Indian girls in European convents. America 123:135 S 12 '70
Trafficking in nuns? Indian novices from Kerala in European convents. il Time 96:30 S 7 '70
See also
Contemplative orders
CONVERSATION
See also
Gossip

Anecdotes, facetiae, satire, etc.
Well-tempered dinner guest: results of competition on dinner-table conversation starters with uncommunicative partners. N. S. Hazelton. Nat R 22:157 F 10 '70
CONVERSATION corners. See Living rooms
CONVERSATION radio programs. See Radio broadcasting—Conversation programs
CONVERSATION television programs. See Television broadcasting—Conversation programs
CONVERSE, Philip E. and Schuman, Howard
Silent majorities and the Vietnam war; with biographical sketches. il Sci Am 222:12, 17-25 Je '70
CONVERSION
See also
Evangelistic work
CONVERTERS. See Electric current converters
CONVERTIBLE bonds. See Bonds, Convertible
CONVICT ships. See Prison ships

CONVICTS. See Prisoners
CONVULSIONS
Brain adenosine triphosphate: decreased concentration precedes convulsions. A. P. Sanders and others. bibliog il Science 169:206-8 Jl 10 '70; Reply with rejoinder. R. C. Collins and others. 170:1430-1 D 25 '70
Unilateral inhibition of sound-induced convulsions in mice. R. L. Collins. bibliog il Science 167:1010-11 F 13 '70
See also
Epilepsy
CONWAY, Frances G.
Dictation: the last few minutes. Engl J 59:983+ O '70
CONWAY, Gordon, and others
DDT on balance. bibliog il Environ 11:3-5 S '69
CONWAY, John Horton
Fantastic combinations of John Conway's new solitaire game. life. M. Gardner. il Sci Am 223:120-3 O '70 *
CONWAY, Mimi, and Knapp, Dan
Day in the life of the Chairman. il por Esquire 73:120-3+ Ap '70
CONWAY, Pat
Private and public interests, keep tennis courts open year-round. il Parks & Rec 5: 34-5+ Mr '70
CONWELL, Esther M.
Negative differential conductivity. bibliog il por Phys Today 23:35-41 Je '70
CONZE, Vincent
Man who collects Offenhausers; interview, ed. by J. McFarland. il por Motor T 22:48-50 Ja '70
COOGAN, David, and Kaplan, H. K.
Moving the hard to move. Ment Hy 54:520-4 O '70
COOK, Ann, and Mack, Herbert
British primary school. Ed Digest 35:36-8 F '70
COOK, Charles Leroy
Five minutes for safety. Flying 86:84-5 Ja '70
COOK, Chauncey William Wallace
Decision that built managers. il por Nations Bsns 58:76-7 Ja '70
Food for Americans: prices, safety, new products; interview. il pors U S News 68:74-8 Je 1 '70
COOK, Delbert J.
He brought a stream back to life. R. Tunley. il por Read Digest 97:19-22+ Jl '70 *
COOK, Don
Berlin. Atlan 227:6+ Ja '71
Reports. Atlan 225:14+ Ja '70
Reports: Europe. Atlan 226:22-3+ Jl '70
COOK, Fred J.
Big gamble on gambling. il Nation 211:9-13 Jl 6 '70
Hard-hats: the rampaging patriots. il Nation 210:712-19 Je 15 '70
Jackals at J.F.K. il N Y Times Mag p30-1+ Ap 12 '70
John Jay: college for cops. il Nation 211: 555-8 N 30 '70
New Jersey: the state of Mafia. il Nation 210:560-3+ My 11 '70
People v. the mob; or, Who rules New Jersey? il N Y Times Mag p9-11+ F 1 '70
When you just give money to the poor. il N Y Times Mag p23+ My 3 '70
COOK, George Smith
Gallantry under fire. D. Vestal. il Travel & Camera 33:34-9 F '70 *
COOK, James
Death of Captain Cook: two views. J. E. Ayres. il Antiques 97:724-7 My '70 *
In the wake of Captain Cook. J. Guzzwell. il Yachting 128:50-1+ D '70; 129:98-9+ Ja '71 *
COOK, Marlow Webster
Excerpt from address, March 9, 1970. Cong Digest 49:148+ My '70
COOK, Robert C.
View from dead men's shoulders. il Nat Parks 44:10 F '70
COOK books. See Cookbooks
COOK coffee company. See Cook united, inc.
COOK ISLANDS
Captain's paradise. J. P. Gabriel. il Travel 134:60-1 Ag '70
COOK united, inc.
Diversification chokes growth. il Bsns W p52-3 Ja 2 '71
COOKBOOKS
From Carolina kitchen: Charleston receipts. N. Wood. Travel & Camera 33:68 F '70
Making of a masterpiece; J. Child's and S. Beck's Mastering the art of French cooking, volume two. P. Simon. il pors McCalls 98:84-5+ O '70

Mastering the art of French cooking, by J. Child and S. Beck. Review
Life il 69:8 O 23 '70. G. Greene
Newsweek il 76:94+ N 9 '70. R. A. Sokolov
Mythological travels, by D. Spoerri. Review
Vogue 156:300 S 1 '70. J. Gruen
Publishers report all-time best-selling cookbooks. Pub W 197:51-2 Mr 23 '70
Supper of the lamb, by R. F. Capon. Review
Writer 84:7-8 Ja '71. L. Conger

Bibliography
Chefs de tout: a cookbook quartet. M. Duffy. il Time 96:100+ D 7 '70
Cookbooks 1970. House B 112:70+ N '70
Cream of the cookbook crop. F. M. Crawford. Am Home 73:26 D '70
Fall cookbooks preview. il Pub W 198:36-42 S 14 '70
Spring-summer cookbooks. il Pub W 197:35-44 Mr 23 '70
COOKE, Alistair
Image-makers beware. Nat R 22:1103-4 O 20 '70
COOKE, Bernard
If you could make one change in the church, what would it be? Commonweal 92:163-4 My 1 '70
COOKE, Eileen D. See Krettek, G. jt. auth.
COOKE, Jerry
Hooves that rock the cradle. il Sports Illus 32:30-5 Mr 9 '70
COOKE, Terence James, cardinal
Out to lunch; reply. J. D. McGowan. Commonweal 91:438-9 Ja 16 '70
COOKERY
ABC's of family meal planning. C. Brock. il Parents Mag 45:72-3+ F '70
Betsy McCall cookbook. S. Robinson and M. Eckley. il McCalls 97:48-56 Ag '70
Busy woman's speedy gourmet cookbook. il McCalls 98:56-9 Ja '71
Camp chef. C. B. Colby. See issues of Outdoor Life
Chef. See issues of Better homes and gardens
Classic meals that really please a man; with menus. il Good H 170:94-109 F '70
Cooking lesson. J. Jaffry. See issues of American home
Cooking tips; from James Beard's kitchen. House & Gard 137:123+ Ap '70
Cooking with fewer calories; with menus. il Good H 170:124-39 Ap '70
Date with a dish. See issues of Ebony
Eat. M. Cantwell. See issues of Mademoiselle
Eat better, pay less, excerpts from three cookbooks. J. Beard; D. Lucas: M. Field; ed. by M. Happel. il Ladies Home J 87: 98-103+ S '70
Eating at Alice's restaurant; excerpts from Alice's restaurant cookbook. A. Brock. il pors McCalls 97:92-3+ F '70
Entrées: cool & collected. M. Happel. il Ladies Home J 87:86-7+ Ag '70
Fast and fancy saucy main dishes. il Bet Hom & Gard 48:75-6 Ag '70
Food. C. Claiborne. See issues of New York times magazine
Food gazette. M. McKendry. il Vogue 156: 43 Jl; 47+ Ag 1; 311 S 1; 107 O 1; 111 N 1; 105 D '70; 157:43 Ja 1 '71
Food in vogue. N. Lyon. See issues of Vogue to April 1, 1970
Food men like. D. Eby. il Bet Hom & Gard 48:64-71+ F '70
Food questions you ask; with answers. See issues of American home to October 1970
From our kitchen; with recipes (title varies) L. Driggs. See issues of Harvest years
Grains revisited. il Ladies Home J 87:74+ Ja '70
Great do-ahead dishes for all occasions. il Good H 170:92-107 My '70
Hearty main dishes. il Parents Mag 45:92-5+ O '70
How to stretch your food budget; with recipes. il Parents Mag 45:72-5+ My '70
How to take the nonsense out of cooking: Julia Child, James Beard and Craig Claiborne at home (with recipes) H. Frankel. il pors Redbook 135:68-9+ O '70
James Beard's cooking classes; with recipes. il pors House & Gard 137:117-20+ Ap '70
Journal cookbook of the month. See issues of Ladies' home journal
Kitchen primer; excerpts. C. Claiborne. il Ladies Home J 87:78-9+ F '70
Kitchen secrets of five master cooks; with recipes. J. Wilson. il pors House & Gard 138:74-86+ Jl '70
Mistakes many cooks make, and how to avoid them. D. Eby. il Bet Hom & Gard 48:70-81 Ap '70

COOKERY—*Continued*

Mrs Leavitt lends a hand; demonstrating how to use government-issue commodities. J. E. Roper. por Read Digest 96:132-4 F '70

[Month] menus; with recipes. See issues of Sunset

[Monthly column on cookery] G. Maddox. See issues of Today's health to June 1970

Nobody ever tells you these things; questions and answers. H. McCully. See issues of House beautiful

On the spear? meatballs, liver and bacon, or oysters. il Sunset 144:183-4 Mr '70

100 ways to feed your family better, for less. R. H. Smithies. il Good H 170:141-4 My '70

Pennysaver cookbook; excerpts. D. Morris and I. Morris. il Ladies Home J 87:96-7+ Mr '70

Plea for savouries. G. Baro. Vogue 155:138-9 F 15 '70

Profits from the kitchen; with recipes. E. W. Manning. il Farm J 94:78-9 Ap '70

Quick summer cooking. il Good H 170:90-105 Je '70

Redbook reader Mrs Richard Cardozo: a guest at her own table. il por Redbook 134:104-8+ Ap '70

Redbook's timesaver cookbook. il Redbook 135:106-16 My '70

Skillet meals for two. il Redbook 135:100-1+ Jl '70

Sunset's kitchen cabinet. See issues of Sunset

Twice as much good eating from your food dollar starting with beef; chicken; bologna; ground beef; tuna and ham. il Bet Hom & Gard 48:56-68+ Ja '70

Two-burner cooking; with recipes. F. M. Crawford. il Am Home 73:64+ Je '70

You can tackle any dish, it's all in knowing how. C. Brock. il Parents Mag 45:62-3+ Ap '7

See also
Appetizers
Aspic
Baking
Bread
Breakfasts
Buffet meals
Candy
Casserole cookery
Caterers and catering
Christmas cookery
Christmas dinners
Christmas meals
Clambakes
Confectionery
Cookbooks
Cookies
Curry
Custards
Desserts
Diet
Dinners and dining
Entertaining
Fondues
Food mixes
Frying
Glazing (food)
Ice cream, ices, etc.
Jelly, jam, etc.
Lunches
Meals
Menus
Meringue
Olives
Pastry
Pickles and relishes
Pie
Pressure cookery
Puddings
Salads
Sandwiches
Sauces
Soufflés
Soups
Spices
Tarts
Television broadcasting—Cookery programs
Thanksgiving dinners
Thermometers, Cooking
Wedding meals

Bibliography
See Cookbooks—Bibliography

Competitions
Look: two top cooks! teen winners in 1970 Pillsbury bake-off; with recipes. il Seventeen 29:144 Je '70

Winning recipes men love; Favorite man's favorite recipe contest. D. Eby and J. McCloskey. il Bet Hom & Gard 48:68-78 N '70

Measurements
Do you know your cooking arithmetic? Parents Mag 45:106 O '70

Study and teaching
Cooking lesson; all-male session at the Helen Worth cooking school. New Yorker 46:36-7 Mr 21 '70

Cooking tips from Le Cordon Bleu. House & Gard 138:125+ S '70

Dione and her cooking kids; with recipes. E. Alston. il pors Look 34:50-2 Ag 11 '70

House & garden visits two cooking classes at Le Cordon Bleu in Paris. il House & Gard 138:117-18+ S '70

Redbook guide to the basic steps of food preparation (cont) il Redbook 134:94-102 F '70

Terminology
See also
Baking—Terminology

Canned food
Gourmet afloat:
Artful meals from cans. E. Slepian. il Motor B 126:132-3 Jl '70

Cereals
What's cooking?
Inflation, grains and hippies. F. Nusz. il Org Gard & Farm 17:110-11+ Ap '70

Cheese
Cheese main dishes. il Bet Hom & Gard 48:99-100 My '70
See also
Cheesecake

Chocolate
Luscious chocolate desserts. il Bet Hom & Gard 48:88 O '70

Coconut
Tropical fruit with sticky rice. il Sunset 144:170 Ap '70

Eggs
Expert egg. il Ladies Home J 87:124-5+ My '70

How can you beat an egg? equipment for mixing and cooking eggs. il McCalls 97:106-7 Mr '70

Perfect hard-cooked eggs. S. Whittier. il Good H 172:108 Ja '71

They're dressed-up deviled eggs. il Sunset 145:138-9 Jl '70

Fish
Baked stuffed red snapper. J. Jaffry. il Am Home 73:76-7 S '70

Brazilian way with fish. il Sunset 144:200 Mr '70

Complete fish & seafood cookbook. il Good H 170:106-18 Mr '70

Cook's discovery: Greenland turbot. Sunset 144:204 Mr '70

Danish salmon, delicious, colorful. Sunset 145:122 Ag '70

Fish story you can cook; with recipes. il McCalls 97:86-95+ Ap '70

Fisherman's luck in your own backyard. L. Witt. il Todays Health 48:49-52 Jl '70

Lingcod has much to recommend it. Sunset 145:154 O '70

Prize catch of fish recipes. il Redbook 134:128-9+ Mr '70

Sablefish, smoked or simmered. Sunset 145:128 Jl '70

Salmon mousse in aspic. J. Jaffry. il Am Home 73:110-11 My '70

Salmon surprises. C. B. Colby. il Outdoor Life 146:22 N '70

Sesame trout. C. B. Colby. il Outdoor Life 145:22 My '70

Sushi: Japanese box lunch; with recipes. E. Alston. il Look 34:46-7 F 10 '70

Swimming sweet and sour trout. il Sunset 144:160 F '70

See also
Caviar
Chowder
Cookery—Shellfish
Fish as food

Fruit
All dated up; date souffle and date pie. J. Hewitt. il N Y Times Mag p40 My 31 '70

And mankind got mom's apple pie! K. Kraft and P. Kraft. il Todays Health 48:60-3 O '70

Banana desserts. il Bet Hom & Gard 48:111 Ap '70

Cooking with mandarins. il Sunset 144:178+ Mr '70

Creative cranberry cookbook. L. Driggs. il Har Yrs 10:35-40 N '70

Danes are fond of applecake. il Sunset 145:133 D '70

COOKERY—Fruit—*Continued*

Danes, the Italians, and the Germans all use poached apple rings or slices. il Sunset 145:221+ N '70

Dessert surprise: it's avocado. il Sunset 144: 203 Mr '70

Fast and fancy fruit desserts. il Bet Hom & Gard 48:71-2 Jl '70

Fast and fancy pear desserts. il Bet Hom & Gard 48:89-90 S '70

Fresh fruit dessert bonanza. M. Crawford. il Am Home 73:58-9+ Jl '70

Fresh fruits of summer. D. Eby and P. Pollock. il Bet Hom & Gard 48:62-3 Ag '70

Fresh ideas with summer fruit. il Good H 171:86-99 Jl '70

Fresh! the fruits of the season. H. McCully. il House B 112:70-2+ Jl '70

Fresh try with peaches. il Sunset 145:125 Ag '70

Little red berry that brightens your table: cranberry. E. W. Manning. il Farm J 93:51 N '69

Mouth-watering ways to fix all those apples. E. W. Manning. il Farm J 93:44-5+ O '69

Oh boysenberry. il Sunset 144:78-9 Je '70

Pineapple is here. il Ladies Home J 87:102-3+ Ap '70

Pink grapefruit; with recipes. E. Alston. il Look 34:36-7 Ja 27 '70

Pretty pickle; fruit-stuffed citrus. J. Hewitt. il N Y Times Mag p82+ F 15 '70

Strawberry caper; with recipes. il Seventeen 29:164-5+ My '70

Strawberry time. il Ebony 25:146+ My '70

These are delicious poached pears. il Sunset 145:174 O '70

This is the month to try mangoes. il Sunset 144:147-8 Je '70

What's cooking?

　Pantry full of crab apple recipes. J. G. Bowman. Org Gard & Farm 17:114-16 Ja '70

Work wonders with raisins. il Ladies Home J 87:120+ N '70

See also
Blueberries
Canning and preserving

Game

Antelope kabob. C. B. Colby. il Outdoor Life 146:20 D '70

Barbecued duck anonymous. H. G. Tapply. il Field & S 74:64 Ja '70

Big-game heart. C. B. Colby. il Outdoor Life 146:19 S '70

Dining on pheasant in Montreal. M. Woodward. il Travel 133:25 Je '70

If he brings home venison. Sunset 145:208 N '70

Mastering the art of Himalayan cooking; snow leopard. G. Jonas. Esquire 73:20+ Je '70

Quick quail. C. B. Colby. il Outdoor Life 145: 16 Je '70

Rabbit fry. C. B. Colby. il Outdoor Life 146: 32 O '70

Ringneck recipes. C. B. Colby. Outdoor Life 145:22 F '70

Roast-duck dinner. C. B. Colby. Outdoor Life 146:16 Jl '70

To make a squirrel stew. O. B. Eustis. il Field & S 75:66-7+ S '70

Tradition with a twist; casseroles of rabbit and pheasant. J. Hewitt. il N Y Times Mag p96 N 22 '70

Trapping the truffle, jugging the hare. W. Clifford. il Sat R 53:66+ S 12 '70

Venison: from the freezer to the table. P. M. Kelsey and J. Tanck. il Cons 24:48-9 F '70

Ways for wapiti; elk meat. C. B Colby. il Outdoor Life 145:21 Ja '70

Wild game birds. il Bet Hom & Gard 48: 26+ O '70

Leftovers

Art of réchauffé. M. Happel. il Ladies Home J 87:92-3+ Mr '70

Good ideas for using and storing holiday-food leftovers. il Good H 171:162 D '70

Things mother never taught you. il Ladies Home J 87:74 S '70

Liquors

Le Calvados. V. Ernoult and J. Pépin. House B 112:114+ S '70

Christmas presents made with great spirits. House & Gard 138:102-4 D '70

Meat

Advance planning; lamb and dill casserole. C. Claiborne. il N Y Times Mag p80 Mr 22 '70

Autumn picnic with cold terrine, a glorious French meat loaf. il Sunset 145:78-9 O '70

Beef from our kitchen; with recipes. il Har Yrs 10:9-12 My '70

Burgers and buns: but different! il Bet Hom & Gard 48:64-5 Jl '70

Cabbage leaves with meat inside. il Sunset 145:122 S '70

Centuries-old art of meat pickling. il Sunset 145:138-9 O '70

Cold elegance; daube of beef. C. Claiborne. il N Y Times Mag p68-9 My 24 '70

Cooking in clay; with recipes. J. Vetz. il Am Home 73:84+ Mr '70

Cooking with cool: meatballs with a Swedish accent. il Seventeen 29:142 Je '70

Crown roast of pork. J. Jaffry. il Am Home 73:60-1 F '70

Don't murder the hamburger. H. McCully. il House B 112:72-3+ Ja '70

Eat: Italian veal birds. M. Cantwell. il Mlle 70:100+ Mr '70

Fast and fancy beef roasts. il Bet Hom & Gard 48:83-4 F '70

Fast and fancy sausage main dishes. il Bet Hom & Gard 48:91-2 N '70

Fast & fancy ways with chops. il Bet Hom & Gard 48:89-90 Ap '70

For the steak man. il Bet Hom & Gard 48: 68-71+ F '70

Great lamb stickup; with recipes. H. McCully. il House B 112:128-9+ Ap '70

Ground beef: shape now, bake later. Sunset 145:210 N '70

Ground beef, when time is short. Sunset 144: 186-7 My '70

Hearty-main-dish dinners for two. il Sunset 145:121 Ag '70

Hot dog and hamburger cookbook. il Redbook 135:119-26 O '70

How to pick a tender, juicy steak. il Changing T 24:20 Jl '70

How to roast a pig. Bet Hom & Gard 48:21 Je '70

How to save money on meats. il Redbook 134:92-3+ Ap '70

Jellied Swedish meat loaf. il Sunset 145:122 Jl '70

Kidney classics and a kidney secret. Sunset 144:199 Ap '70

Last-minute main dishes. Farm J 93:54 N '69

Loaf with a secret; ham in rye. J. Hewitt. il N Y Times Mag p41 Ag 2 '70

Making the most of lamb. J. Hewitt. il N Y Times Mag p66 Ja 10 '71

Meat comes in in a crisp and tasty overcoat. il Sunset 144:90-1 Ja '70

Meats that get better the longer they cook: braisable beef, pork, veal, lamb. D. Eby and N. Benson. il Bet Hom & Gard 48:92-100+ Mr '70

Mother Hazelton's friendly tips. N. S. Hazelton. Nat R 22:90 Ja 27 '70

New heights for beef: fillet of beef in aspic. C. Claiborne. il N Y Times Mag p88-90 O 18 '70

One big roast cooked two ways. Sunset 144: 169 Je '70

Outdoor rotisserie roasts. il Bet Hom & Gard 48:33+ My '70

Pan steaks from a roast. il Sunset 144:168-9 My '70

Pecan stuffed ham, roast sirloin tip, two roasted capons. il Am Home 73:82-7+ N '70

Perfect pairing; pork chops with sauce charcuterie. C. Claiborne. il N Y Times Mag p54 F 1 '70

Pork: the price is right. M. Happel. il Ladies Home J 87:72-3+ Ja '70

Prime recipes with beef. H. McCully and J. Pépin. il House B 112:138-9+ O '70

Pure Greek: baked lamb shanks. C. Claiborne. il N Y Times Mag p75 O 4 '70

Quickly, with quality; rack of lamb dinner. C. Claiborne. il N Y Times Mag p82-3 O 25 '70

Roast leg of lamb; roast lamb boulangère. J. Jaffry. il Am Home 73:94-5 Ap '70

Roll out the roast. il Parents Mag 45:54-8 Ja '70

Sausage suppers. il Sunset 145:179-80 N '70

Shanks; of lamb, veal, ham, beef. Sunset 144: 134+ F '70

Special on meat. il Good H 170:78-95 Ja '70

Summer special: potato sausage and jellied meat loaf. J. Hewitt. il N Y Times Mag p52 Je 28 '70

Things mother never taught you: about braising. il Ladies Home J 87:112 O '70

Thrifty meat shopping with Betty Furness. il McCalls 97:96-7+ F '70

Tripe twice. C. Claiborne. il N Y Times Mag p72 F 8 '70

When money's no object; saffron beef; chicken with saffron cream sauce. C. Claiborne. il N Y Times Mag p36 Ja 3 '71

COOKERY—Meat—*Continued*

Winter pears with pork chops. il Sunset 144: 174 Ap '70

See also
Barbecue cookery
Cookery—Game
Hash
Stew

Milk

Milk and milk products. il Good H 171:158+ N '70

Mushrooms

Forest mushrooms from Japan. il Sunset 145: 186+ O '70

Mustard

Touch of hot mustard; with recipes. E. Alston. il Look 34:86-7 Ap 21 '70

Nuts

Nuts: how to crack, blanch, and chop them. il Bet Hom & Gard 48:82 N '70
Things mother never taught you: meatless meals. il Ladies Home J 87:100 Mr '70

Organic food

Eat for health in your home. J. Kinderlehrer. il por Org Gard & Farm 17:76-8 D '70

Poultry

And next day's leftover dinner will be simply duck soup. il Sunset 145:84-5 O '70
Chicken is champ. C. Claiborne. il N Y Times Mag p53 Ag 23 '70
Chicken plus. C. Claiborne. il N Y Times Mag p42 Jl 12 '70
Conversation makers; chicken in pineapples. J. Hewitt. il N Y Times Mag p46 Jl 19 '70
Eat: chicken in a pot. M. Cantwell. Mlle 71: 74+ O '70
Farm woman is champion chicken cook; with recipe. Farm J 94:39 Ag '70
Hit the clay with the hammer, and there's the Beggar's chicken. il Sunset 145:62-3 S '70
Holiday birds. House B 112:96-8 D '70
How to cook and carve a goose. il Sunset 145:188 N '70
How to roast the holiday turkey. il Bet Hom & Gard 48:81 N '70
Moroccan affair; chicken with pickled lemons. C. Clairborne. il N Y Times Mag p70 F 22 '70
Poached bird in hand. House B 112:152+ My '70
Questions you ask about turkey. il Parents Mag 45:106+ N '70
Susan, our beginning cook, learns how to roast chicken and turkey. il Good H 171: 142 N '70
Turkey, classic to convenient. il Bet Hom & Gard 48:84-5 N '70
Turkey talk; corn bread stuffing. C. Claiborne. il N Y Times Mag p 108 N 15 '70
Turkey with the dressing outside. Sunset 145:163-4 N '70
You start with turkey breasts. il Sunset 145:142-3 O '70

See also
Barbecue cookery
Cookery—Game

Rice

Remember the rice diet? il McCalls 97:32+ Ap '70
Tropical fruit with sticky rice. il Sunset 144: 170 Ap '70

Sea food

Complete fish & seafood cookbook. il Good H 170:106-18 Mr '70
Holiday-makers; seafood crepes. C. Claiborne. il N Y Times Mag p36 D 20 '70
Hot-weather stew. C. Claiborne. il N Y Time Mag p72 My 10 '70

See also
Cookery—Shellfish

Shellfish

Anything goes, with shrimp. C. Claiborne. il N Y Times Mag p 102 N 29 '70
Coquilles Saint Jacques. J. Jaffry. il Am Home 74:64-5 Ja '71
Crayfish. il Sunset 144:88-91 Je '70
Creole capers; shrimp creole. C. Claiborne. il N Y Times Mag p44 Je 14 '70
Curry favorite; shrimp Madras. C. Clairborne. il N Y Times Mag p84 Mr 8 '70
Delicacies from the sea. il Ebony 25:108+ F '70
Dip a crawdad. C. B. Colby. il Outdoor Life 145:30 Ap '70
How to cook shrimp. S. Whittier. il Good H 170:134 My '70

How to eat a crab. C. Claiborne. il N Y Times Mag p64 Ag 30 '70
Magnificent mussel. S. V. Thompson. il Holiday 47:56-7+ Ja '70
New shell game: coquiles Saint-Jacques. H. McCully. il House B 112:150-1 My '70
Oysters on a bed of noodles. il Sunset 144:112 Ja '70
Patriots' snack: lobster roll. C. Claiborne. il N Y Times Mag p44 Je 21 '70
Shrimp and rice, good companions. Sunset 145:196 N '70
What every good cook should know about oysters, mussels and clams. il Redbook 135:94-5+ O '70

See also
Clambakes

Vegetables

ABC's of baked beans. il Am Home 73:62 F '70
America's best vegetable recipes; review, with recipes. il Farm J 94:72-3+ Mr '70
Artichokes. E. Alston. il Look 34:66-7 Ap 7 '70
Best potatobakes. il Bet Hom & Gard 48: 89 N '70
Chiles for stew or party dip. Sunset 144:190 Ap '70
Crunchy outside, creamy inside: potato puff balls. il Sunset 144:127 F '70
First course is the show stopper, a vegetable surprise. il Sunset 145:202+ N '70
Fresh is beautiful. il McCalls 97:96-102+ My '70
From Mexico it's jicama. il Sunset 144:202 Ap '70
Garden speedway; the superfresh Belgian food of the Baron René Boël. N. Lyon Vogue 156:432 S 1 '70
Great vegetables. A. D. Hawkes. il House & Gard 137:87-9+ F '70
Green grow the tomatoes. E. Alston. il Look 34:40-1 Jl 28 '70
Mastering the art of French cooking, volume two; excerpts. J. Child and S. Beck. il McCalls 98:107-14 N '70
More winning ways with vegetables. B. B. Smith. Todays Health 48:62-3 My '70
Now's the time to stuff a red bell pepper. il Sunset 145:160 O '70
Potato pan-flips. il Seventeen 29:172-3+ Mr '70
Showing off with artichokes; with recipes. il Sunset 144:98-101 Mr '70
Slow-cooked onions are mellow, limp, delicious. il Sunset 145:173 N '70
Sweet potatoes and yams. il Bet Hom & Gard 48:97 O '70
Things mother never taught you: meatless meals. il Ladies Home J 87:100 Mr '70
Vegetables simmered in marinade. il Sunset 144:172-3 My '70
Versatile squash. il Ebony 25:168+ O '70
Vote for beans. L. Witt. il Todays Health 48:60-3 N '70
What's cooking?
Black beans, from garden to soup bowl. P. E. Mahan. Org Gard & Farm 17:99 D '70
Bravo for beans. C. Fessenden. il Org Gard & Farm 17:132-3+ Mr '70
Let's enjoy our soybeans. J. W. Holm. il pors Org Gard & Farm 17:114-16 N '70
Saltless sauerkraut, our seven-day marvel. B. T. Hunter. il Org Gard & Farm 17: 116-18+ F '70
Sprouts are special. G. Lefever. il Org Gard & Farm 17:90-3 Je '70
Strong taste of spring. M. C. Goldman. il Org Gard & Farm 17:98-103 My '70
What's leafy, green, and to the rescue? spinach cookery. J. Savoy. il Todays Health 48:50-2 S '70
Work wonders with vegetables and stuffings. il Ladies Home J 87:104 S '70
Zucchini, great in combinations. Sunset 145: 138-9 S '70

See also
Canning and preserving

Wine

Gourmet afloat:
Cooking with wine. E. Slepian. Motor B 126:108-10 Ag '70

COOKERY, American

American classic recipes. D. Eby. il Bet Hom & Gard 48:72-81 O '70
Authors & editors; V. M. Grosvenor's ideas on southern cooking. D. N. Mount. por Pub W 197:49-50 Je 29 '70
Colonial cakes and cookies. il Am Home 73: 80+ Ap '70
Cross-country cook's tour. C. Brock. il Parents Mag 45:58-61+ Jl '70

COOKERY, American—*Continued*
Eat: menu for an American meal. M. Cant-
well. Mlle 70:76 Ap '70
Four festive dinners. il Ebony 25:166+ Ap '70
From a Carolina kitchen: Charleston receipts.
N. Wood. Travel & Camera 33:68 F '70
Good Maine life of the Blakely Babcocks;
with recipes. E. Alston. il Look 34:44-7 O
6 '70
Indian savor, Southwest tang; with recipes.
F. M. Crawford. il Am Home 73:72+ Mr '70
Soul food. G. Baro. Vogue 155:80+ Mr 1 '70
Soul food. V. M. Grosvenor. il McCalls 97:
72-5 S '70
Soul food! il Good H 171:110-12+ Jl '70

COOKERY, Austrian
Austria. Good H 171:109-10 S '70
Kitzbühel confections. F. M. Crawford. il Am
Home 73:78-80+ Ja '70
Strawberry ice cream crêpes. il Sunset 144:
215 My '70

COOKERY, Basque
Boardinghouse reach Basque style; with
recipes. E. Alston. il Look 34:98-9 My 19 '70

COOKERY, Belgian
Garden speedway: the superfresh Belgian
food of the Baron René Boël. N. Lyon.
Vogue 156:432 S 1 '70

COOKERY, Brazilian
Brazilian way with fish. il Sunset 144:200 Mr
'70
Brazil's fay-zhwa-da, it's a zesty mix of
beans and meats: feijoada. il Sunset 144:
118-20+ F '70

COOKERY, Chinese
All *wok* and no play; D. Kaye as a cook. S.
F. Kaye. il pors Vogue 156:168-9+ D '70
Chinese way with lettuce. C. Claiborne. il
N Y Times Mag p72 Je 7 '70
Chow sam see, fried tree threads. il Sunset
145:134+ S '70
Encyclopedia of Chinese food and cooking, by
W. W. Chang and others. Review
Atlan 227:98-9 Ja '71. C. Chiang
How to make Chinese chicken salad. il Sun-
set 145:206 N '70
Inside each mandarin pancake flavors as-
semble. il Sunset 144:158-60 Mr '70
It's easy to make won ton, all you need are
the skins. il Sunset 144:194+ My '70
Roast duck from a Chinese kitchen. Sunset
144:180 Ap '70
Spicy side of Danny Kaye. il pors Look 34:
36-8 Mr 10 '70
Swimming sweet and sour trout. il Sunset
144:160 F '70
Szechuan way: shrimp and chicken. C. Clai-
borne. il N Y Times Mag p89+ S 27 '70
What's cooking?
Let's enjoy our soybeans. J. W. Holm.
il pors Org Gard & Farm 17:114-16 N
'70

COOKERY, Danish
Anything but ordinary, beef in hash, patties.
il Sunset 145:116+ D '70
Danes are fond of applecake. il Sunset 145:133
D '70
Danish salmon, delicious, colorful. Sunset
145:122 Ag '70

COOKERY, English
England. Good H 171:111-12 S '70

COOKERY, European
Seven-country tour of great home cooking.
il Good H 171:100-14 S '70
Trapping the truffle, jugging the hare. W.
Clifford. il Sat R 53:66+ S 12 '70

COOKERY, Finnish
It's billowy and it's delicious; Finnish pancake. il Sunset 145:155 S '70

COOKERY, Foreign. See Cookery, International

COOKERY, French
Almond tart, quickly made; gateau pithiviers.
il Sunset 144:206 Mr '70
Autumn picnic with cold terrine, a glorious
French meat loaf. il Sunset 145:78-9 O '70
Cook as communicator; recipes of Jacques
Manière. N. Lyon. Vogue 156:197+ N 1 '70
La cuisine; excerpts. R. Oliver. il por Ladies
Home J 86:92-3+ D '69
Fabulous finale; French dessert. J. Pépin. il
House B 112:128-9+ N '70
Favorite holiday soups and desserts; excerpts
from Mastering the art of French cooking,
by J. Child and S. Beck. il McCalls 98:58-
61+ D '70
Flourishes with food; coq au vin; a casserole
to crow about. il McCalls 97:46+ Mr '70
France. Good H 171:107 S '70
French menu cookbook; excerpts. R. Olney.
il Ladies Home J 87:88-9+ Ag '70
French provincial lamb ragout. il Sunset 144:
144 F '70
Hooray, you're a gourmet! il Seventeen 29:
182-5+ Ap '70

House & garden visits two cooking classes
at Le Cordon Bleu in Paris. il House &
Gard 138:117-18+ S '70
Making of a masterpiece; J. Child's and S.
Beck's Mastering the art of French cook-
ing. volume two. P. Simon. il pors Mc-
Calls 98:84-5+ O '70
Mastering the art of French cooking, by J.
Child and S. Beck. Review
Life il 69:8 O 23 '70. G. Greene
Newsweek il 76:94+ N 9 '70. R. A. Soko-
lov
Mastering the art of French cooking, volume
two; excerpts. J. Child and S. Beck. il
McCalls 98:86-91+ O; 107-14 N '70 (to be
cont)
Pâté maison. J. Jaffry. il Am Home 73:64+ D
'70
Peerless pairing; pots de creme and floren-
tines. C. Claiborne. il N Y Times Mag
p90+ Ap 26 '70
Puff paste. J. Jaffry. il Am Home 73:82-3+
Mr '70
Put everything in and wait: backeoffe, Alsa-
tian casserole. il Sunset 144:142 F '70
Quiche Lorraine, elegant and easy. il McCalls
97:106+ Ap '70
Quintessence of quiche. M. Happel. il Ladies
Home J 87:116-17+ N '70
Sautéed trout with mushrooms. F. M. Craw-
ford. il Am Home 73:62-3 Ja '70
Stews from France. il Ladies Home J 87:74-5+
F '70

COOKERY, German
Germany. Good H 171:112-13 S '70

COOKERY, Greek
Greek classic; spanakopitta and crab meat
wrapped in phyllo. C. Claiborne. il N Y
Times Mag p44 Mr 29 '70
Lamb chops and leeks with a lemon sauce.
il Sunset 144:182 My '70
Moussaka the Athenian way. il Sunset 145:
116 Ag '70
This Greek meal arrives in a boat-shaped bun.
il Sunset 145:112+ D '70

COOKERY, Hawaiian
Interlude on an unspoiled island; wild vege-
tables for a wild luau. E. Gibbons. Org
Gard & Farm 17:88-91 Jl '70
Treasures of the Hawaiian Islands. il Good H
171:130 Jl '70

COOKERY, Himalayan
Mastering the art of Himalayan cooking. G.
Jonas. Esquire 73:20+ Je '70

COOKERY, Hungarian
Romance of Hungarian cooking. il Good H
170:184 My '70

COOKERY, Indian
Indian savor, Southwest tang; with recipes. F.
M. Crawford. il Am Home 73:72+ Mr '70

COOKERY, Indian (East Indian)
Bazaar of Indian dishes. il Good H 172:120
Ja '71
Jevayala chala; with recipes. il House B
112:130+ Ap '70
Miriam Cendrars: curry, powder with power.
N. Lyon. Vogue 155:123 F 1 '70

COOKERY, International
Comtesse Armand de La Rochefoucauld:
champagne thrift. N. Lyon. Vogue 155:161
My '70
Dramatic foreign specialties. il Bet Hom &
Gard 48:10 Ag '70
Food gazette. M. McKendry. il Vogue 156:105
D '70
International chef. M. Woodward. See issues
of Travel
Personality lunch in kitchens around the
world. il House & Gard 137:131+ Mr '70
Super ski food. F. M. Crawford. il Am Home
73:63-4+ Ja '70
Viva Mexican cooking! il Good H 170:210
Mr '70

COOKERY, Irish
Glory be! what blessings here; with recipes.
il McCalls 97:94-101+ Mr '70

COOKERY, Italian
Art of Venetian cooking. il McCalls 97:92-9+
S '70
Eat; Italian veal birds. M. Cantwell. Mlle 70:
100+ Mr '70
Eat; pasta. M. Cantwell. Mlle 71:100+ S '70
Ham and pasta in rolls. il Sunset 144:200 Ap
'70
How to prepare perfect pasta. S. Whittier.
il Good H 170:118 Je '70
Italian cheese for Easter. il Sunset 144:199
Mr '70
Italian regional cooking; excerpts. A. Boni.
il Ladies Home J 87:122-3+ My '70
Italian table. W. Root. il Holiday 48:30-1+
Jl '70
Italy. Good H 171:113-14 S '70

COOKERY, Italian—*Continued*
Now there's a quick way to make *manicotti*. il Sunset 144:180 My '70
Pasta, e basta. B. Montresor. Vogue 155:208-9+ Mr 1 '70
Pesto. il Sunset 145:56-7 Ag '70
Pleasures of pasta. H. McCully. il House B 112:98-100+ F '70
Saltimbocca American style. il McCalls 97:42 S '70
Vitello tonnato. J. Jaffry. il Am Home 73:70-1 Je '70
Who ever heard of round lasagne? il Sunset 144:160+ Ap '70
See also
Macaroni

COOKERY, Jamaican
Jamaican dining with a flair. M. Woodward. il Travel 135:14 Ja '71

COOKERY, Japanese
Hot pot and hibachi. F. M. Crawford. il Am Home 73:76-9 F '70
It's polite to slurp in Japan. B. Rich. il Seventeen 29:30 Mr '70
Sushi; Japanese box lunch; with recipes. E. Alston. il Look 34:46-7 F 10 '70
Two ways to go, and either way you get a great sukiyaki. il Sunset 144:76-7 F '70
Yakitori is simply broiled chicken. il Sunset 144:177 Ap '70

COOKERY, Latin American
Sauce of the Americas; guacamole. il Sunset 144:92-3 My '70

COOKERY, Lebanese
From Lebanon, a chewy soup. il Sunset 144:189 My '70
Lamb and yogurt, okra and cucumbers, olives and artichokes? il Sunset 145:224+ N '70

COOKERY, Marine
Boil-in-a-bag is the new easy answer to cooking afloat. il Sunset 145:104-5 Jl '70
Gourmet afloat:
Artful meals from cans. E. Slepian. il Motor B 126:132-3 Jl '70
Boil a bag or so. E. Gibbs. Motor B 126:102-4 S '70
Cooking with wine. E. Slepian. Motor B 126:108-10 Ag '70
Stew. E. Slepian. il Motor B 125:60+ Je '70

COOKERY, Mexican
Adding a yodel to the enchilada. C. Claiborne. il N Y Times Mag p 109 S 13 '70
Enchiladas with barbecued foods. Sunset 144:180-1 Je '70
Perk up your palate with a Mexican dish. il Ebony 25:136+ Mr '70
Sopas de Mexico. il Sunset 145:76-7 S '70
Steak tacos with guacamole. il Sunset 144:182 Ap '70
Sweet snack from Mexico: sopapillas. il Sunset 144:186 My '70
Viva Mexican cooking! il Good H 170:210 Mr '70

COOKERY, Middle Eastern
Taste surprise, fried falafil. il Sunset 144:148 F '70
See also
Cookery, Lebanese

COOKERY, Moroccan
Breaking the fast in Morocco; soup *harira*. M. Woodward. il Travel 133:74 My '70
Moroccan affair; chicken with pickled lemons. C. Claiborne. il N Y Times Mag p70 F 22 '70
Moroccan picnic in the U.S.A. M. McKendry. il Vogue 156:43 Jl '70

COOKERY, North African
Chicken, lamb, vegetables, wheat, and a hot, hot sauce: couscous. il Sunset 144:128 F '70

COOKERY, Norwegian
Christmas recipes. il Parents Mag 45:58-61+ D '70
In the Viking spirit. F. M. Crawford. il Am Home 73:76-7+ Ja '70
Norse treat: krum kake. J. Hewitt. il N Y Times Mag p 107 Mr 15 '70

COOKERY, Oriental
Ginger sauce for cracked crab. il Sunset 144:165 F '70
Good cook's discovery: oriental foods. il Sunset 144:96-7 Je '70
Oriental switch, savory custards. Sunset 145:110-11 Ag '70
See also
Cookery, Chinese

COOKERY Ornamental
Fairy tale castle. il Ladies Home J 86:98+ D '69

COOKERY, Outdoor
Fisherman's luck in your own backyard: outdoor fish cookery. L. Witt. il Todays Health 48:49-52 Jl '70
Making the most of lunch breaks. T. Trueblood. il Field & S 75:22+ Ag '70

New character for a cookout classic: beef. il Am Home 73:64+ Jl '70
Open-fire feasts. C. B. Colby. il Outdoor Life 146:24 Ag '70
Turnabout cookout; with recipes. il Bet Hom & Gard 48:40+ Je '70
See also
Barbecue cookery
Camp cookery
Clambakes
Outdoor meals

Equipment and supplies
Cooking and eating outdoors; with recipes, menus and equipment. L. S. Pappas. il House & Gard 137:97+ Je '70

Safety devices and measures
Tips for your home and family. Todays Health 48:77-8 My '70

COOKERY, Pakistani
Where for dinner tonight? il Sunset 145:130+ S '70

COOKERY, Portuguese
Double custard from Portugal. il Sunset 144:176 Mr '70

COOKERY, Pressure. See Pressure cookery

COOKERY, Puerto Rican
Make it a Christmas picnic; with recipes. E. Alston. il Look 34:60-2 D 29 '70
Yesterday today in Spanish San Juan; with recipes. J. Peter and E. Alston. il Look 34:58-9 Je 16 '70

COOKERY, Russian
Food gazette; eating Russian. M. McKendry. il Vogue 156:107 O 1 '70
Pirog and piroshki. il Sunset 144:162-4 My '70
Whole-meal soup, Russian *selianka*. Sunset 145:140 D '70

COOKERY, Scandinavian
See also
Cookery, Danish
Cookery, Norwegian
Cookery, Swedish

COOKERY, Southern. See Cookery, American

COOKERY, Spanish
Spain. Good H 171:110-11 S '70
Variation on a Spanish classic; paella. C. Claiborne. il N Y Times Mag p42 S 6 '70
Versatile paella. il McCalls 98:12 Ja '71

COOKERY, Swedish
Cooking with cool: meatballs with a Swedish accent. il Seventeen 29:142 Je '70
Mrs Lennart Hernod: the Swedish splurge. N. Lyon. 155:121 Ap 1 '70
Sweden. Good H 171:108-9 S '70

COOKERY, Swiss
Raclette, pickles, potatoes and wine. F. M. Crawford. il Am Home 73:64+ Ja '70

COOKERY, Turkish
H.E. the Ambassador M. Nuri Birgi: the fragile, funny arts. N. Lyon. Vogue 155:117 Mr 1 '70
Turks have a different and delicious way with eggplant. il Sunset 145:150 D '70

COOKERY by children
Child's play candies; with recipes. J. Uetz. il Am Home 73:62+ Jl '70
Dinner is ready, and I fixed it all by myself! il Sunset 144:158-9 Ap '70
Dione and her cooking kids; with recipes. E. Alston. il pors Look 34:50-2 Ag 11 '70
Good projects for a youthful cook. Each is a one-bowl cake. il Sunset 145:167 N '70
Here is a barbecue meal that ten to twelve-year-olds can handle. il Sunset 145:58-9 Ag '70
Recipes from a young cook. D. Franey. House B 112:44 F '70
Susan, our beginning cook. S. Whittier. See issues of Good housekeeping
You and your children's diet. B. Newman. il Good H 171:133-5 Ag '70

COOKERY by men
All *wok* and no play; D. Kaye as a cook. S. F. Kaye. il pors Vogue 156:168-9+ D '70
Chefs of the West. See issues of Sunset
Eat. A. Milner. Mlle 71:20+ Jl '70
How one man tackled his grocery bill: comparison in time and money between convenience foods and cooking from scratch. E. J. Dapron, jr. il Bet Hom & Gard 48:26-7+ Jl '70
My husband the cook. J. L. Block. il Good H 171:42+ O '70
Stagfest; when the boys are on their own; with recipes. il Bet Hom & Gard 48:41+ Je '70
When you leave the dinner to dad; your recipes for main dishes to freeze. il Parents Mag 45:64-5+ Ag '70

COOKERY clubs
If you want to start a gourmet-cooking club. Good H 170:135 Ja '70
COOKERY contests. See Cookery—Competitions
COOKERY programs. See Television broadcasting—Cookery programs
COOKIE trees. See Christmas trees
COOKIES
Back to the rolling pin. J. Hewitt. il N Y Times Mag p 100+ Ap 12 '70
Cooky pears for a pear tree, animals for an animal tree. il Sunset 145:60-1 D '70
Diamond crisps are flaky, buttery. il Sunset 144:115 Ja '70
Entertaining cookies. Redbook 134:146-7 Ap '70
Fast and fancy holiday cookies. il Bet Hom & Gard 48:79-80 D '70
Girl scout cookies taste of success. Bsns W p24-5 F 7 '70
Great spicy cookie. S. Sarvis. il Farm J 94:44-5 N '70
Lemon hearts and lemon rounds. il Sunset 144:157 F '70
Lunch-box cookies. il Bet Hom & Gard 48:99 O '70
Storybook cookies. Z. Coulson. il Good H 171:126-7+ D '70
Two crisp almond cookies. Sunset 144:200 My '70
What is she taste-testing? It's a cinnamon pinwheel. il Sunset 145:140 O '70
Winter's treats: Veronica's Christmas cookies. J. Hewitt. il N Y Times Mag p89-90 D 13 '70
COOKING. See Cookery
COOKING books. See Cookbooks
COOKING clubs. See Cookery clubs
COOKING schools. See Cookery—Study and teaching
COOKING thermometers. See Thermometers, Cooking
COOKING utensils. See Kitchen utensils
COOKING utensils, Electric. See Household appliances, Electric
COOKINGHAM, L. P.
Urban administration, a new ball game. il por Am City 85:63-6 Ja '70
COOKS
See also
Felio, H. G.
Stockli, A.
COOLEY, Denton Arthur
Texas tornado vs. Dr Wonderful. T. Thompson. il pors Life 68:62B-62D+ Ap 10 '70 *
COOLEY, Marion S.
Jewelry making for teens: a new direction. il Sch Arts 69:12-13 F '70
COOLEY'S anemia. See Anemia
COOLING
See also
Air conditioning from central stations
Airplane engines—Cooling
Automobile engines—Cooling
Heat transmission
COOMES, William
Assembling a camera shutter speed meter. il Pop Electr 33:73-7+ S '70
COON, Donald W. and Fleet, R. R.
Ant war. bibliog il Environ 12:28-38 D '70
COON hounds. See Hounds
COON hunting. See Raccoon hunting
COONEY, Joan Ganz
Sesame street. PTA Mag 64:25-6 Mr '70
about
Liberated, all liberated. il pors Vogue 155:118-19 Je '70 *
COONS, Edgar E. See Smith, N. S; Ungerleider, L. G. jt. auths.
CO-OP city. See Bronx, N.Y.—Housing
COOPER, David
Unshackled education. Clear House 45:22-5 S '70
COOPER, Douglas
Cubism from all sides; exhibition at the Los Angeles County museum of art. il por Newsweek 76:65-6 D 28 '70 *
Cummings event in Washington. il Art N 69:34-7+ Sum '70
COOPER, G. P.
Response of olfactory bulb neurons to X-rays as a function of nasal oxygen concentration. bibliog il Science 167:1726-7 Mr 27 '70
COOPER, Gloria (Vanderbilt) See Vanderbilt, G.
COOPER, Henry S. F. Jr.
Letter from the space center. New Yorker 46:80+ Ap 4 '70

COOPER, James Fenimore
Otsego Hall in Cooperstown, 1796-1799; excerpts from The legends and traditions of a northern county. il Antiques 98:180+ Ag '70
COOPER, Jane
Comment. M. Van Duyn. Poetry 115:434-6 Mr '70 *
COOPER, John Sherman
Senate: unloving acts. por Time 95:9-10 Je 1 '70 *
COOPER, Kenneth H.
Key to fitness at any age: the new aerobics; condensation. il Read Digest 96:213-30 Mr '70
COOPER, Lorraine S.
Random thoughts on moving to Washington from a senator's wife. House & Gard 138:24 Ag '70
COOPER, Martin
Beethoven in retrospect: England. Sat R 53:60+ N 28 '70
COOPER, Richard T.
Town turns on its children. Nation 211:517-19 N 23 '70
COOPER, Wilhelmina. See Wilhelmina (model)
COOPERATION
See also
Business cooperation
Collective settlements
Educational cooperation
International cooperation
Interracial cooperation
Library cooperation
Religious cooperation
COOPERATIVE associations
Co-ops face two-year tax fight. C. W. Gifford. Farm J 94:50L Mr '70
Farrowing co-ops coming on strong. J. Russell. il Farm J 94:H9+ O '70
Jim Brown comes to Mississippi; Black economic union helps residents of Marshall County. C. Gillespie. Nation 211:236-9 S 21 '70
New way to get feeder pigs: feeder pig co-op. J. Russell. il Farm J 93:H10-11+ O '69
Poor people's co-ops. J. De Muth. il America 123:489-90 D 5 '70
Shippers associations gaining. Aviation W 93:131+ O 26 '70
See also
Associated milk producers, inc.
Credit unions
Southern consumers cooperatives
Whole earth cooperative
COOPERATIVE buying. See Purchasing, Cooperative
COOPERATIVE education. See Education, Cooperative
COOPERATIVE international program for teacher education
New overseas study programs for future teachers. Sch & Soc 98:210+ Ap '70
COOPERATIVE living establishments. See Collective settlements
COOPERATIVE nursery schools. See Nursery schools
COOPERATIVE purchasing. See Purchasing, Cooperative
COOPERBAND, Sidney R. See Moolten, F. L. jt. auth.
COOPERMAN, Stanley
Comment. R. Magowan. Poetry 116:194-6 Je '70 *
COOPERSTOWN, N. Y.
Historic houses, etc.
Otsego Hall in Cooperstown, 1796-1799; excerpts from The legends and traditions of a northern county. J. F. Cooper. il Antiques 98:180+ Ag '70
COORDINATED bargaining. See Collective bargaining
COORDINATES
Natural coordinates for electrons in solids. J. Zak. bibliog il por Phys Today 23:51-4 F '70
COORDINATING committee of Black churchmen, Chicago. See National committee of Black churchmen
COORDINATING council of literary magazines
Culture trough. C. Johnson. Nation 211:150-2+ Ag 31 '70
COORS, Adolph, company
Brewery that breaks all the rules. il Bsns W p60-1+ Ag 22 '70
COOS BAY, Ore.
Mall that communications built. C. E. Mahanay. il Am City 85:76+ O '70
Student for a day; Michigan ave. school. E. Moffitt. Schol Teach Jr/Sr High p 10-11 D 7 '70

COOTE family
Coote coat-of-arms. H. K. Eilers. il Hobbies 75:118 Ag '70

CO-OWNERSHIP. See Partnership

COPE, Myron
Chancey games in Ohio. il por Sports Illus 32:26-8+ Mr 30 '70
(ed) See Hawkins, A. How intangible can you get
(ed) See Hawkins, A. Loose and fun-loving off the field

COPE, Oliver
Avoid the surgery all women fear. Vogue 156:82-3+ O 15 '70

COPE. See American federation of labor and Congress of industrial organizations—Committee on political education

COPE program
COPE: does it have a future? il Pub W 197:53-5 Je 22 '70
COPE inaugurates program, installs director, teacher. Pub W 197:57 Mr 2 '70

COPELAND, Lammot du Pont, Jr
Du Pont card house. il por Newsweek 76:110+ N 23 '70 *
Motsey's millions. Newsweek 76:80+ D 7 '70 *

COPELAND, Lila
Children: the drawings of Lila Copeland; interview, ed. by J. H. Michel. il por Am Artist 34:23-34+ D '70

COPELAND, Miles
Strategy left by Nasser: blackmail the U.S. with Arab oil. il Life 69:36-7 O 9 '70

about
CIA on the Nile. A. Campbell. New Repub 162:25-6 My 23 '70 *
Talky American. D. Stewart. Nation 210:759-60 Je 22 '70 *

COPENHAGEN

Airports
Denmark plans major air terminal. E. H. Kolcum. il Aviation W 92:35-6 F 9 '70

COPENHAGEN festival. See Music festivals—Denmark

COPEPODS
Wax esters in marine copepods. R. F. Lee and others. bibliog il Science 167:1510-11 Mr 13 '70

COPLAND, Aaron
Aaron Copland photo album; ed. by D. Hamilton. il pors Hi Fi 20:56-63 N '70 *

about
Aaron Copland, an intimate sketch. L. Bernstein. il por Hi Fi 20:53-5 N '70 *
Artist life. D. J. Soria. por Hi Fi 20:MA4-5+ N '70 *
Kid from Brooklyn. Newsweek 76:139 N 23 '70 *
Recordings of Copland's music. D. Hamilton. Hi Fi 20:64-6+ N '70 *

COPLEY, William Nelson
Hang-up on humor. il por Time 95:65 Je 29 '70 *

COPP, M. Philip
Where are all the twelves? il Motor B 126:62-4+ Ag '70

COPPELIA; ballet. See Ballets—Criticisms

COPPENS, P. and others
Electron population parameters from least-squares refinement of X-ray diffraction data. bibliog il Science 167:1126-8 F 20 '70

COPPER
See also
Feeding and feeding stuffs—Copper content

Prices
Getting handle on the copper market. Bsns W p24 Mr 7 '70
Hard times for copper-rich lands. il Bsns W p35 D 5 '70
Squeeze on two-tier copper. Bsns W p30 My 30 '70
U.S. copper cuts the pressure; two-tier pricing system. il Forbes 106:32-3 D 15 '70

COPPER, Weathering of. See Weathering

COPPER bracelets. See Bracelets

COPPER coins. See Coins

COPPER industry and trade
Dark cloud with a copper lining. il Forbes 105:26-8+ Mr 1 '70
Heavy, heavy. il Forbes 106:21 S 1 '70
See also
Anaconda company
Government investigations—Copper industry
Kennecott copper corporation

Chile
Why the copper men are getting edgy. il Bsns W p38-9 Ap 4 '70

United States
Copper men see red over pollution. il Bsns W p31 Je 13 '70
See also
Inspiration consolidated copper company

Zambia
Friendly takeover in the copperbelt. il Bsns W p24+ Ag 22 '70
Zambia. S. Meisler. Atlan 226:32+ S '70

COPPER jewelry. See Jewelry

COPPER mines and mining
See also
Kennecott copper corporation

Chile
See also
Continental copper and steel industries, inc.

Indonesia
See also
Copper mines and mining—West Irian

Peru
Social reform jolts the mine owners. il Bsns W p26 Ag 29 '70

West Irian
Copper entices Freeport sulphur. il Bsns W p29 N 28 '70
Freeport first? il Forbes 105:34-5 My 1 '70

COPPER repoussé. See Repoussé work

COPPER rods. See Rods, Copper

COPPER tubes. See Tubes, Copper

COPTIC church
See also
Ethiopic church

COPY, Advertising. See Advertising copy

COPY writers, Advertising. See Advertising copy writers

COPY writing. See Advertising copy

COPYING processes
Giant rival for the top copier cat. il Bsns W p33-4 Ap 25 '70
How to copy a video display; computer terminal invented by Photophysics. Bsns W p30 Ag 29 '70
Xerox's new anti-IBM machine. Bsns W p42+ My 23 '70
See also
Photography—Copying
Rank Xerox, ltd.
Transparencies—Copying
Xerox corporation

COPYRIGHT
Hands across the curtain; Russia's international agreement with Doubleday. Newsweek 76:90 N 16 '70
International copyright: a world view; address, February 16, 1970. E. M. Braderman. Dept State Bul 62:486-93 Ap 13 '70
Step toward cooperation in U.S.-U.S.S.R. publishing. Pub W 198:49 N 16 '70
What rights should you sell? Writers Digest 50:27 Jl '70

Blueprints
Let's clear up laws on copyright of plans. J. W. Giles. Arch Rec 148:39-40 D '70

Broadcasting rights
Cassette lesson. P. Nathan. Pub W 198:64 Jl 27 '70
Who sets the boundaries of creativity? revision bill and CATV. R. H. Smith. Pub W 198:30 Ag 17 '70

Duration
Copyright renewal rights of illegitimates cited a recurring problem. Pub W 197:34 My 7 '70

Renewal
See Copyright—Duration

Television rights
See Copyright—Broadcasting rights

Unauthorized reprints
Reprinter see, reprinter do; letter to the editor. G. G. Cremonesi. Am Lib 1:646 Jl '70

United States
Book's copyright upheld in serialization case. Pub W 197:39 Mr 30 '70
Congress expected to renew copyrights one more year. S. Wagner. Pub W 198:32 O 26 '70
Congress extends copyrights for one more year. Pub W 198:36 D 28 '70
Copyright revision dead for this year. S. Wagner. Pub W 198:36 S 7 '70
Copyright revision recedes further into the future. Pub W 198:27-8 D 7 '70

COPYRIGHT—United States—*Continued*
Justice Douglas-Evergreen case. Writers Digest 50:44+ Je '70
1969 in review. Pub W 197:51-2 F 9 '70
OE's new copyright policy. M. W. Bachrach. Am Ed 6:28-9 Ag '70
Rights and permissions. P. Nathan. See issues of Publishers' weekly
Senate schedules markup of copyright revision bill. S. Wagner. Pub W 198:49-50 Jl 27 '70
Status of copyright revision. Pub W 197:44-5 Je 1 '70; Discussion. 198:19-21 Ag 3; 197-9 Ag 31 '70

COPYRIGHT and television. See Copyright—Broadcasting rights

COPYRIGHT infringement
How photocopying pollutes sci-tech publishing; excerpts from address. January 13, 1970. W. M. Passano. il por Pub W 197:63-4 F 2 '70
Suit asks photocopying royalties. J. Walsh. Science 169:959 S 4 '70

CORAL dunes state park. See Utah—Parks and reserves

CORAL GABLES, Fla, public library
Coral Gables library keeps Spanish flavor. il Library J 95:446+ F 1 '70

CORAL reefs and islands
Destruction of Pacific corals by the sea star acanthaster planci. R. H. Chesher; discussion. bibliog Science 165:645; 167:209, 1274-5 Ag 15 '69; Ja 9, F 27 '70
Question of regeneration. il Sci N 97:525 My 30 '70
Starfish eaters; painted shrimp attacking crown-of-thorns. il Time 95:73 My 25 '70
Starfish threaten Pacific reefs; Acanthaster planci. J. A. Sugar. il Nat Geog 137:340-53 Mr '70
Unseen glories of the reef; Palau Islands. il Life 69:50-7 O 23 '70

CORALS
Coral skeletons: an explanation of their growth and structure. D. J. Barnes. bibliog il Science 170:1305-8 D 18 '70
Scleractinian coral exoskeletons: surface microarchitecture and attachment scar patterns. S. W. Wise. jr. bibliog il Science 169:978-80 S 4 '70

CORAZZINI, John G.
Team ministry. Cath World 212:206-8 Ja '71

CORBETT, J. Ralph
No strings. H. Saal. il Newsweek 75:84 Ap 13 '70 *

CORBIN, David R.
Practical expanded scale milliohmmeter. il Pop Electr 33:77-80 O '70

CORCORAN, John S.
Libel and private college newspapers. bibliog Sch & Soc 98:354-6 O '70

CORCORAN gallery of art, Washington, D. C.
Jesus artists: exhibition called Revival! D. Davis. il Newsweek 76:97+ O 26 '70

CORCOS, Chrystal
Illustrations of Murray Tinkelman. il por Am Artist 34:20-5+ O '70

CORDAGE
See also
Knots and splices

CORDASCO, Francesco
Leonard Covello and the community school. bibliog f por Sch & Soc 98:298-9 Sum '70

CORDAY, Betty
Opening the door to safer transplants. il Sci N 97:295-7 Mr 21 '70

CORDEIRO, Newton Velloso
Pantanal: 400,000 sq. km. of swampland in the Mato Grosso. il UNESCO Courier 23:14-15 Je '70

CORDELL, Arthur J. See Tanzer, M. jt. auth.

CORDIALS. See Liqueurs

CORDLESS lamps. See Lamps

CORDLESS shavers. See Razors

CORDON Bleu cooking school, Paris. See Cookery—Study and teaching

CORDS, Electric. See Electric cords

CORDTZ, Dan
Coming shake-up in telecommunications. il Fortune 81:68-71+ Ap '70
They're holding feet to the fire at Jersey standard. il Fortune 82:78-83+ Jl '70
Withering aircraft industry. il Fortune 82:114-17+ S '70

CORE drilling. See Drilling and boring (ice)

CORELLI, Arcangelo
Some Corelli attributions assessed; tr. by L. Wallach. H. J. Marx. bibliog f il Mus Q 56:88-98 Ja '70 *

CORELLI, Franco
Champion tenor defends his title. W. H. Honan. il pors N Y Times Mag p28-9+ F 8 '70; Same abr. Read Digest 96:83-7 My '70 *
Records. Opera N 34:35 F 7 '70

CORIGLIANO, John
Virtuosic crackerjack. A. Cohn. il por Am Rec G 36:656-7 My '70 *
Women's lib Carmen; The naked Carmen. il pors Time 96:28 Ag 17 '70 *

CORIOLIS force
Isaac Asimov explains; what is the Coriolis effect? I. Asimov. Sci Digest 69:82-3 Ja '71

CORLISS, Richard
Film chronicle (title varies) Nat R 22:41-3, 163-4, 369-70, 521+, 798+, 959-60, 1361-2 Ja 13, F 10, Ap 7, My 19, Jl 28, S 8, D 15 '70
Screen. Commonweal 91:620-1; 92:14-15, 118-19, 191-2, 368-9 Mr 6-13, Ap 17, My 8, Jl 24 '70

CORLISS, William R. See Mead, R. L. jt. auth.

CORMAN, Cid
(tr) See Jaccottet, P. Grapes and figs; I would like only to remove; Who will help me? None can come this far; I lifted up my eyes; And I now utterly in the celestial cascade

about
They lick the platter clean. R. J. Griffin. Nation 211:53 Jl 20 '70 *

CORN, Ira G. Jr
Handful of Aces. W. Johnson. il por Sports Illus 32:68-72+ Mr 23 '70 *

CORN
Alcohol dehydrogenase in maize: genetic basis for isozymes. J. G. Scandalios; discussion. Science 167:1519 Mr 13 '70
Alcohol dehydrogenase in maize: genetic basis for multiple isozymes. D. Schwartz; discussion. Science 167:1519 Mr 13 '70
Alcohol dehydrogenase in maize: genetic control of enzyme activity. Y. Efron. bibliog il Science 170:751-3 N 13 '70
Are corn yields leveling off? both sides of the story. R. Krumme; L. D. Rawson. il Suc Farm 68:8-9 Ja '70
Corn club that tries new ideas. D. Seim. Farm J 94:44 My '70
Corn research worth watching; effect of light on yield. Suc Farm 68:C12 Je '70
Growing Jerusalem artichokes with corn. D. Criner. il Org Gard & Farm 17:90-2 Mr '70
How your corn grows. C. E. Sommers. il Suc Farm 68:no3 28-9+ F '70
Maize leaf elongation: continuous measurements and close dependence on plant water status. T. C. Hsiao and others. bibliog il Science 168:590-1 My 1 '70
What causes unfilled corn ear tips? Suc Farm 68:no2 B4 F '70
See also
Feeding and feeding stuffs—Corn

Breeding
Look what they're doing with corn. R. D. Wennblom. il Farm J 94:46-7+ Mr '70

Cultivation
Corn: are you growing it the way you did in '61? B. Coffman. Farm J 94:50 My '70
Figure your profit from irrigated corn. Suc Farm 68:C2 Ag '70
Five-star high profit corn growing system. C. E. Sommers. il Suc Farm 68:25-7+ Ja '70
Have narrow rows been oversold? interviews ed. by C. E. Sommers. D. Duvick; W. Colville. il pors Suc Farm 68:28-31+ S '70
He fine-tunes his corn growing. Suc Farm 68:24-5 My '70
How the yield champs grow the rest of their corn. R. Sanders. il Suc Farm 69:28-9 Ja '71
How to make the most of weather. C. E. Sommers. il Suc Farm 68:30-1+ My '70
Is row farming outdated? J. C. Herman. il Suc Farm 69:A1 Ja '71
New measure of corn maturity; Growing degree days. B. Coffman. il Farm J 94:A1-3 F '70
No-till corn depends on herbicides. il Suc Farm 68:no3 W20 F '70
Replace nitrogen lost during rains. Suc Farm 68:A4 My '70
When and how much to feed corn. C. Sommers. il Suc Farm 68:36-7+ Ap '70
Your nine big corn decisions. R. Krumme and others. il Suc Farm 68:21-31 N '70

Diseases and pests
As a killer disease hits a major crop—. il U S News 69:60 O 26 '70
Blight that sows panic. il Newsweek 76:51 Ag 31 '70
Blighted corn; threat to cornbelt states. il Time 96:63-4 Ag 31 '70
Corn blight. Sci Am 223:54+ O '70
Corn blight threatens crop. N. Gruchow. Science 169:961 S 4 '70
Corn blight: what about next year? R. D. Wennblom. il Farm J 94:26 N '70

CORN—Diseases and pests—*Continued*
ERTS could aid crop blight fight. Z. Strickland. Aviation W 93:50 D 21 '70
Farm programs and the blight. Suc Farm 68:7 O '70
Grain futures hit the sky. il Bsns W p22 Ag 22 '70
How bad is the corn blight? R. D. Wennblom. il Farm J 94:21-3 O '70
How blight affected corn future last year. F. Bailey, jr. Suc Farm 69:D6-7 Ja '71
In the wake of a corn blight... il U S News 69:62 Ag 31 '70
Iowa corn insect control recommendations. H. Gunderson. Suc Farm 68:no3 W4 F '70
Money is not enough; southern corn blight R. Rodale. il Org Gard & Farm 17:23-6 D '70
See also
Corn rootworms
Yellows (plant disease)

Drying
New look at corn drying. P. B. Jones. il Suc Farm 68:34-5 S '70
New ways to handle corn so it keeps. G. W. Wormley. il Farm J 93:26-26A+ O '69

Harvesting
How these farmers harvest and sell corn. R. Sanders and R. Krumme. il Suc Farm 68:25-9 Je '70
How to handle combine problems. P. B. Jones. il Suc Farm 68:32-3 Je '70
How to harvest cornstalk silage. P. B. Jones. il Suc Farm 68:36-7 O '70
How to harvest your Indian corn. Sunset 145:259 N '70

Hybrids
Choosing the right hybrid. R. Krumme and others. il Suc Farm 68:28 N '70
Chromosome pairing within genomes in maize-tripsacum hybrids. J. R. Harlan and others. bibliog il Science 167:1247-8 F 27 '70
High-lysine corn: boon for hogmen? J. Russell. il Farm J 94:H12-13+ S '70
Multiple-ear corn coming. C. E. Sommers. il Suc Farm 68:B20 N '70
Which corn leaves work the hardest? interview, ed. by B. Coffman. J. Eastin. il Farm J 94:38A-38B Mr '70

Marketing
How these farmers harvest and sell corn. R. Sanders and R. Krumme. il Suc Farm 68:25-9 Je '70
I haul corn to the elevator; I dry and store. J. Sterling; D. N. Clark. il pors Farm J 93:A4-31 D '69

Moisture content
He's sold on high-moisture corn and silage. J. Davis. il Suc Farm 68:D18 O '70
Holding wet corn shortens its storage life. B. Coffman. Farm J 93:38D O '69

Planting
See Corn—Seeding

Seeding
Aerial-planted corn, here are results. C. E. Sommers. il Suc Farm 68:no4 D28 Mr '70
Broadcast corn has potential. il Suc Farm 68:no4 44 Mr '70
Corn in 12" rows outyields aerial-seeded by 37 bu. il Farm J 94:32E Ja '70
Faster ways to plant corn. G. L. Earle. il Suc Farm 68:no4 32-5 Mr '70
No-tillage corn saves time, cuts costs. il Farm J 94:62D Mr '70
Once-over or wide-path planting? P. Jones and G. Earle. il Suc Farm 69:32-3 Je '71
Plant corn early for highest yields. Suc Farm 68:48 Ap '70
Plant it shallow! D. Seim. Farm J 94:52P Ap '70
Planting corn by airplane. B. Coffman. Farm J 94:52B Ap '70
They plant corn in plastic envelopes. il Suc Farm 69:A4 Ja '71
Try this system for seed corn. il Suc Farm 68:61 Ap '70

Storage
Holding wet corn shortens its storage life. B. Coffman. Farm J 93:38D O '69
How long can you store shelled corn? T. B. McCartney. il Suc Farm 68:D18 N '70
Where will you put all that corn? B. Coffman and D. Seim. il Farm J 94:16-17+ Ag '70

Yield
See Crop yields
CORN, Frozen. See Vegetables, Frozen

CORN, Sweet
Cold-country corn; growing sweet corn in Vermont. S. R. Ogden. il pors Org Gard & Farm 17:36-9 Mr '70
CORN blight. See Corn—Diseases and pests
CORN breeding. See Corn—Breeding
CORN cribs. See Granaries
CORN earworm moths. See Moths
CORN handling. See Grain handling
CORN planting. See Corn—Seeding
CORN products company. See CPC international, inc.
CORN rootworms
Can use milo to fight rootworms. il Suc Farm 68:45 Je '70
Corn rootworm. D. Seim. Farm J 94:54F+ F '70
Keep a lookout for corn rootworms. il Suc Farm 68:no4 D20 Mr '70
What you need to know about the rootworm. il Suc Farm 68:no3 W26 F '70
What's the resistance problem all about? il Suc Farm 68:no4 D18 Mr '70
Where the corn rootworms are. Suc Farm 69:B20 Ja '71
CORN silage. See Silage
CORN stunt diseases. See Yellows (plant disease)
CORN trade. See Grain trade
CORNBREAD. See Bread
CORNELL, Joseph
Art; exhibition at the Metropolitan museum of art. L. Alloway. Nation 211:700-1 D 28 '70 *
CORNELL aeronautical laboratory, Inc.
Court blocks sale of Cornell lab. Aviation W 92:228 Mr 9 '70
CORNELL chamber orchestra. See Orchestras
CORNELL university, Ithaca, N.Y.
Black studies at Cornell: the troubled path to understanding. C. Childs. il Life 68:56-60+ Ap 17 '70

Graduate school of business and public administration
Cornell's cultural shock treatment; course on issues in the environment. il Bsns W p 104-5 Ja 31 '70
CORNERBACKS. See Football players
CORNFELD, Bernard
Fighting back: Bernard Cornfeld states his case; interview, ed. by O. Moore. por Newsweek 76:69 Jl 6 '70
Many woes of Bernie Cornfeld. J. Ross-Skinner. il por Duns 95:32-6 Ja '70

about
Bernie Cornfeld: the salesman who believed himself. R. Ball. il por Fortune 82:136-41+ S '70 *
Can all the King's men put I.O.S. together again? il Time 95:90-1 My 25 '70 *
Comedown for Cornfeld. por Time 95:88 My 4 '70 *
Cornfeld dumped. Time 96:71 Jl 13 '70 *
Cornfeld's comeback. Newsweek 76:48+ Ag 24 '70 *
Cornfeld's new bid for a comeback. por Bsns W p 19-20 Ag 1 '70 *
Crisis for Cornfeld; mutual funds. il por Newsweek 75:81 My 18 '70 *
Farewell to Cornfeld. il por Time 95:84-6 My 18 '70 *
Lavish hand with too little control. por Bsns W p 117 My 16 '70 *
Picking up from Bernie. Newsweek 75:86 My 25 '70 *
CORNING glass center, Corning, N.Y.
Model of glass factory of yesteryear. il Hobbies 75:98 Je '70
Pressed glass addition to Corning museum. il Hobbies 75:80+ My '70
Remnants of a fourth century glass factory; fragments uncovered in northwestern Israel. il Hobbies 75:82 Je '70
CORNING museum of glass. See Corning glass center, Corning, N.Y.
CORNSTALK silage. See Silage
CORNSWEET, Tobey M.
Advanced composite materials. il Science 168:433-8 Ap 24 '70
CORNUELLE, Herbert Cumming
Outsider, but no stranger. por Bsns W p 102 O 10 '70 *
CORONA, Solar. See Sun—Corona
CORONADO, Calif.
Grand old lady of Coronado: Hotel Del Coronado. N. C. Gray. il Am Home 73:30+ S '70
CORONARY artery disease. See Arteriosclerosis

CORONATIONS
See also
Nana Opoku Ware, 2d
CORPORATE acquisitions. See Business consolidations and mergers
CORPORATE budget. See Budget, Business
CORPORATE economists. See Economists
CORPORATE giving. See Corporations—Charitable contributions
CORPORATE image
Coke's formula: keep the image fresh. il Bsns W p66-7+ Ap 25 '70
Does the corporate image really change? G. Berkwitt. il Duns 95:19-21 Ja '70
Search for corporate identity. W. McQuade. il Fortune 82:140-1 D '70
CORPORATE income tax. See Corporations—Taxation
CORPORATE liquidation. See Liquidation
CORPORATE planning. See Business management and organization
CORPORATE reorganizations. See Corporations—Reorganization
CORPORATE responsibility. See Responsibility
CORPORATE state
Reflections: new generation in relation to the corporate state and the new consciousness. C. A. Reich. New Yorker 46:42-6+ S 26 '70
CORPORATION for public broadcasting
Buying an image on public TV. Z. B. Grant. New Repub 163:13 N 14 '70
Critics of television; address, January 15, 1970. J. W. Macy, jr. Vital Speeches 36: 286-8 F 15 '70
Potted plants, padded banks: Banks and the poor. Sedulius. New Repub 163:27-8 N 28 '70
TV's fourth network comes into its own. il U S News 69:45-6 O 12 '70
CORPORATION law
See also
Corporations—Reorganization
CORPORATION management. See Business management and organization
CORPORATION reports
Annual reports: do they keep the natives happy? Forbes 105:238 My 15 '70
Annual reports sound a muted note. il Bsns W p80+ Ap 4 '70
As I see it; interview. S. Davidson. il por Forbes 105:40+ Ap 1 '70
Broad view accompanies an annual report. V. Louviere. il Nations Bsns 58:13 Je '70
How to keep from being taken. il Forbes 105:222-6+ My 15 '70
What to look for in an annual report. il Changing T 23:23-4 D '69

Anecdotes, facetiae, satire, etc.
Wry report on annual reports. il Duns 95: 32-3 My '70
CORPORATIONS
American corporation, by R. J. Barber. Review
Bsns W il p6 Mr 7 '70. A. A. Berle
New Repub 162:39-40 My 9 '70. E. S. Herman
Dynamic growth companies. il Nations Bsns 58:48-53 F; 64-7 Mr; 88-91 Ap; 44-8 Je; 68-71 Jl; 76-9 S; 36-8 O; 72-3+ D '70
Economic sovereignties. A. S. Miller. Nation 210:538-40 My 4 '70
Five dimensions of American business; with directories. il Forbes 105:74-6+ My 15 '70
Giants of '29 revisited. il Fortune 81:258 My '70
Great moments and great men of American business; symposium, ed. by S. G. Slappey. Nations Bsns 58:47 Ja '70
How the 500 fared. Time 95:86 My 18 '70
Oldest companies. Fortune 81:316 My '70
Ten best-managed companies. il Duns 96:23-35 D '70
Top ten. il Forbes 105:34-9 Ja 1 '70
See also
Bonds
Business consolidations and mergers
Executives
Farm corporations
Investments
Limited partnership
Negro companies
Public utilities
Stockholders
Accounting
Accounting and the SEC; interview. J. J. Needham. por Duns 96:10-11+ O '70
As I see it; interview. S. Davidson. il por Forbes 105:40+ Ap 1 '70
Big bath; the write-off game. Newsweek 76: 54+ Jl 27 '70
Clashing head on over merger rules. Bsns W p 19 Jl 25 '70

It's time to call the auditors to account. Fortune 82:98 Ag '70
It's up to the SEC. G. R. Rosen. Duns 95:64+ Je '70
Profits without honor. Time 95:62 Mr 9 '70
There's another way to do it; British accountants. il Forbes 105:231-2+ My 15 '70
Underneath the balance sheets; foreign profits. il Bsns W p80+ D 19 '70
See also
Business consolidations and mergers—Accounting

Cash position
See Corporations—Finance

Charitable contributions
Countercurrents; stockholders vote against contributing to institutions devoted to the general welfare. L. L. L. Golden. Sat R 53:60 D 12 '70
Doing what has to be done; gifts programs and their administrators. L. L. L. Golden. il Sat R 53:79-80 F 14 '70
See also
Foundations, Charitable and educational

Directories
500 biggest corporations by assets. Forbes 105:99-100+ My 15 '70
500 biggest corporations by capital expenditures. Forbes 105:111-12+ My 15 '70
500 biggest corporations by market value. Forbes 105:87-8+ My 15 '70
500 biggest corporations by profits. Forbes 105:123-4+ My 15 '70
500 biggest corporations by revenues. Forbes 105:75-6+ My 15 '70
Fortune directory; of the Second 500 largest industrial corporations, with introd. by E. J. Tracy. il Fortune 81:98-125 Je '70
Fortune directory; 200 largest industrials outside the U.S. J. Cameron. il Fortune 82: 142-7+ Ag '70
Fortune directory; with introd. by E. Carruth. il Fortune 81:182-218 My '70
Roster of the country's biggest corporations. Forbes 105:136-75 My 15 '70
Where to find a company; tables. Forbes 105: 227-33 Ja 1 '70
Who's where in American industry; tables. Forbes 107:31-4+ Ja 1 '71

Directors
Board under fire. il Newsweek 76:58-60 Ag 31 '70
Is the board of directors obsolete? Duns 96: 72 Ag '70
Now the head man's on TV. R. Levy. il Duns 95:59-61 My '70
Why outside directors need to direct. il Bsns W p76-8 Jl 4 '70

Divestiture
Age of un-merger. A. Hershman. il Duns 95: 30-3 Je '70
Signal pulls out of gas stations. Bsns W p 17-18 S 5 '70
Why they turn to divestiture. il Bsns W p86-7 Ag 15 '70

Finance
Big losers on the big board. Forbes 106:26-7 Ag 1 '70
Brighter profit trend. il U S News 69:21 Ag 3 '70
Corporate funds: trying time for treasurers. il Fortune 82:24 N '70
Corporate scramble for capital. il Fortune 81: 27 Mr '70
Corporate sleuths on Wall Street. J. C. Perham. il Duns 95:29-31+ Ap '70
Costs bulge and margins shrink. il Bsns W p22-3 F 7 '70
Earnings gainers; fifty-four against the trend; with table. Forbes 106:42 D 15 '70
Earnings picture. C. Morgello. il Newsweek 75:65 Je 29 '70
Examples of what has happened to well-known issues. U S News 68:32 Mr 23 '70
Feeding the bears. Time 95:90 My 4 '70
Good news, and a caution. Newsweek 76: 93 N 2 '70
Hard road back to profitability. G. Burck. il Fortune 82:101-3+ Ag '70
Here's word on profits for fourth quarter. il U S News 68:50 F 9 '70
Missing dimension; research and development outlays; with directory. Forbes 105: 200+ My 15 '70
Money hunt. il Fortune 81:52+ My '70
More giants join the profit decline. il Bsns W p 12-13 My 2 '70
New fashions in financing. il Bsns W p21-2 F 7 '70
Pluses in productivity and profits. Fortune 82:19 S '70

CORPORATIONS—Finance—*Continued*
Profit forecast: a jarring note of optimism; with editorial comment. il Bsns W p 14-15, 132 Mr 7 '70
Profit lag: worst over? with table of company earnings. U S News 69:36 N 2 '70
Profit-seekers. por Duns 95:42-4 My '70
Profits: a fruit of productivity. R. Williams. por Nations Bsns 58:101 O '70
Profits falloff loses speed. il Bsns W p59 Ag 1 '70
Profits show a dash of improvement. il Bsns W p 18-19 O 31 '70
Profits: still down. il U S News 68:76 My 4 '70
Pursestrings are drawn tighter. Bsns W p24-5 Jl 18 '70
Put policy first in DCF analysis. P. Welter. bibliog f il Harvard Bsns R 48:141-8 Ja '70
R&D spending shoots for a 7 per cent gain. il Bsns W p 102+ My 23 '70
Report on American industry. il Forbes 105:43-9+ Ja 1 '70; 107:31-4+ Ja 1 '71
Rugged first quarter for earnings. Bsns W p24 Ap 18 '70
Second-quarter profits look fair. il Bsns W p23 Jl 18 '70
Slowdown hits earnings again. il Bsns W p29-30 Ja 24 '70
Slump puts Santa on a diet. il Bsns W p37-8 D 19 '70
Story of big companies in a year of squeeze; earnings of the top manufacturing companies. il U S News 68:42 Ap 6 '70
Third quarter looks underweight. Bsns W p44 O 17 '70
Tight money's painful payoff; cash squeeze. il Bsns W p28-9 Je 20 '70
Who's raking in the money; Europe's most profitable companies. Bsns W p56 O 17 '70
Why the big traders worry industry. il Bsns W p52-7+ Jl 25 '70
See also
Auditing
Budget, Business
Capital investments
Corporations—Accounting
Corporations—Valuation
Dividends
Profit
Small business—Finance
Stock purchase options

Statistics
Corporate cash; table. Forbes 105:47 Je 15 '70
Debt-free companies; table. Forbes 106:79 S 15 '70
Far poles of leverage; table. Fortune 81:222 My '70
500 biggest corporations by assets; with directory. Forbes 105:99-100+ My 15 '70
500 biggest corporations by profits; with directory. Forbes 105:123-4+ My 15 '70
500 biggest corporations by revenues; with directory. Forbes 105:75-6+ My 15 '70
Who's where in growth; tables. Forbes 105:53-8 Ja 1 '70
Who's where in profitability; tables. Forbes 105:44-9 Ja 1 '70; 107:40-2+ Ja 1 '71

Flags, insignia, etc.
O, say, can you see the company flag? R. Levy. il Duns 95:50-3 Mr '70

Foreign business
Prepare your company for inflation. B. A. Lietaer. il Harvard Bsns R 48:113-25 S '70

Foreign expansion
See Business—Foreign expansion

Foreign subsidiaries
Europe's cutback: made in U.S.A. J. Ross-Skinner. il Duns 96:57-8+ D '70
Foreign branches defy the slump. Bsns W p45-6 Je 20 '70
GE turns cool to a state partner; Italian affiliate Cogenel's cut back of holdings in Asgen. Bsns W p23 O 3 '70
Hand across the sea; Du Pont international. il Forbes 106:60+ S 15 '70
Knowhow jumps the language barrier. il Bsns W p 120-2 D 19 '70
Managing risks in foreign exchange. B. A. Lietaer. il Harvard Bsns R 48:127-38 Mr '70
What U.S. companies are doing abroad. See issues of U.S. news & World report
See also
Branch factories, Foreign

Location
See Location in business and industry

Names
Does the corporate image really change? G. Berkwitt. il Duns 95:19-21 Ja '70

Presidents
See Executives

Public relations
See Business—Public relations

Real estate operations
Corporate land rush of 1970. il Bsns W p72-7 Ag 29 '70
Signal: land is big money. T. J. Murray. por Duns 96:58-60 Jl '70

Reorganization
Five years in the Zeckendorf labyrinth. il pors Bsns W p98-9+ Ap 25 '70
Oilman Mecom taps the Chapter 10 field. por Bsns W p24 D 5 '70

Size
Attack on the big boys. il Bsns W p78+ O 17 '70
Bigness versus profitability. F. R. Wittnebert. il Harvard Bsns R 48:158-60+ Ja '70
Europe's love affair with bigness. P. Siekman. il Fortune 81:94-9+ Mr '70
Is corporate bigness getting you down? Bsns W p 153 O 17 '70
Numbers; or, Most giants are happy giants. il Forbes 105:176+ My 15 '70
TRB from Washington: stuck with bigness. New Repub 162:4 My 30 '70
Watch that waistline! il Forbes 105:214+ My 15 '70

Social aspects
See Business—Social aspects

Taxation
Backboning; proposed penalties for exceeding guideposts for reasonable wage increases. H. C. Wallich. Newsweek 76:90 D 14 '70
Billion-dollar subsidy; tax subsidy of Domestic international sales corporations. T. Stanton. Nation 211:463-4 N 9 '70
Bundle from America; Britain's Plessy co. acquisition of alloys. por Time 96:60-1 Ag 10 '70
Business taxation and the poor; liberalized depreciation rules. America 122:385 Ap 11 '70
Finding ways to beat the tax bite. il Bsns W p 107+ D 19 '70
Rise in local taxes; growing worry for business. il U S News 69:63-5 N 23 '70
Shot in the arm for our exports; DISC plan. Nations Bsns 58:99 O '70
Taming interstate taxes; income tax out-of-state businesses. Bsns W p54-6 My 2 '70

Valuation
500 biggest corporations by market value; with directory. Forbes 105:87-8+ My 15 '70
How stocks are valued. P. Lindberg. Bet Hom & Gard 48:4+ N '70
Who's where in the stock market; tables. Forbes 105:63-6+ Ja 1 '70; 107:51-3+ Ja 1 '71

CORPORATIONS, Foreign

United States
Invasion from abroad. N. A. Martin. il Duns 95:38-41 Mr '70

CORPORATIONS, International
Global corporation is here to stay. D. C. King. il America 123:229-31 O 3 '70; Reply. P. Matthews. 123:363-4 N 7 '70
Hoechst: tomorrow the world? J. Ross-Skinner. por Duns 95:71-2+ Je '70
Law firms go multinational. il Bsns W p36-8 Jl 11 '70
Price to the host country. M. Tanzer and A. J. Cordell. Nation 211:17-20 Jl 6 '70
Rougher road for multinationals; with editorial comment. il Bsns W p57-62+, 146 D 19 '70
See also
Black and Decker manufacturing company
Deltec international, ltd.
Nestlé company

CORPORATIONS, Law. See Law partnership

CORPORATIONS, Nonprofit
See also
Environmental action, inc.
Rand corporation
Science service, inc.

CORPORATIONS and education. See Business and education

CORPS of engineers. See United States—Army —Corps of engineers

CORPS of military police. See United States—Army—Corps of military police

CORPULENCE
Energetics; excerpts. G. Gwinup. il House B 112:50+ O '70

CORPULENCE—*Continued*
Fat child is father of the man. B. W. Wyden. il N Y Times Mag p89-90+ S 13 '70; Same abr. with title Overweight? A fresh look at the problem. Read Digest 97:129-32 D '70; Discussion. N Y Times Mag p42+ O 11, 111 N 1 '70
Fats of life; camp for overweight boys. H. L. Masin. il Sr Schol 95:22 Ja 12 '70
Few words of advice to discouraged dieters. H. Eustis. Redbook 134:96+ Mr '70
Forever thin; excerpts. T. I. Rubin. il Ladies Home J 87:69+ Ja; 60+ Mr; 94+ My '70
Hard facts about fat. Sci Digest 67:70 Mr '70
Help is on the way; water retention, massage, taping. Vogue 156:176-7 N 1 '70
Obesity: absence of satiety aversion to sucrose. M. Cabanac and R. Duclaux. bibliog il Science 168:496-7 Ap 24 '70
Simple secrets of losing weight. J. Mayer. Read Digest 96:136-9 Ja '70
Survival of the fattest. Mech Illus 66:12 Jl '70
What a wonderful beauty idea; reducing cellulite infiltrations. Harp Baz 104:22 Ja '71
Why fat kids stay fat; study findings. Newsweek 76:82-3 O 19 '70
See also
Weight (physiology)
Weight watchers, inc.
CORPUS CHRISTI, Tex.

Libraries
Corpus Christi, Texas; services for the disadvantaged. J. A. Murphey, jr. Wilson Lib Bul 44:763-5 Mr '70
CORPUS instrumentation. See World publishing company
CORRALS, Cattle. See Cattle corrals
CORRAND, Samuel
Why I prefer headphones. Hi Fi sec I 20:59 F '70
CORRECTION tape, Typewriter. See Typewriter supplies
CORRELATION (education)
Creative writing with a movie camera. G. F. Heinz. il Schol Teach Sec Teach Sup p20-1 N 3 '69
Experiment in integration. W. Chappell and others. Ed Digest 35:38-41 Ja '70
CORRELATION (statistics)
Neutron scattering verifies dynamic scaling. G. B. Lubkin. bibliog il Phys Today 23:59+ F '70
Psychogenic death: a reappraisal. G. V. Barrett and R. H. Franke. bibliog il Science 167:304-6 Ja 16 '70
CORRESPONDENCE schools and courses
Can you learn electronics by home study? L. E. Frenzel, jr. il Electr World 84:34-6 S '70
Engineering level opportunities for you. A. W. Burawa. il Pop Electr 32:76-80 F '70
Learning by mail; writing courses. il Writers Digest 50:31 S '70
Learning the new fun thing. L. David. il Mech Illus 66:58-60+ F '70
See also
Famous writers school
CORRESPONDENTS, Foreign. See Foreign correspondents
CORRESPONDENTS association, United Nations. See United Nations correspondents association
CORRIGAN, Dorothy D.
Quality of community life. Am Lib 1:1081-2 D '70
CORRIGAN, Thomas D.
Another last hurrah. Commonweal 93:5 O 2 '70
Boston priests at grips with the diaspora. Cath World 212:35-6 O '70
CORROSION and anticorrosives
Cleaners and polishes for aluminum and two rust removers for metal. il Consumer Bul 53:31-2 Ag '70
Corrosion at sea. R. Benson. il Sea Front 16:172-81 My '70
Help your boat fight corrosion. C. Miller. il Motor B 126:66-70+ O '70
Is galvanic corrosion following you? C. F. Kelley. il Yachting 128:69+ Ag '70
Saga of the rust-resistant ash truck; Detroit. J. B. Garvie. il Am City 85:88+ O '70
CORRY, Emmett
New directions for the Catholic library association; a conference report. Wilson Lib Bul 44:912+ My '70
CORRY, John
Best bartender in New York. por Harper 241: 47-51 Ag '70
Man called Perry Horse. il por Harper 241: 81-4 O '70

Many-sided Mr Meany. il por Harper 240:52-8 Mr '70
Politics of style. il Harper 241:60-4 N '70
Son of the Catskills. Harper 241:79-82 S '70
Television. Harper 241:42+ D '70
Washington, sex, and power. il Harper 241: 63-8 Jl '70
CORS, Paul B.
State libraries and intellectual freedom; ed. by J. F. Krug and J. A. Harvey. Am Lib 1:944-5 N '70
CORSA, Helen Storm
Dreams in Troilus and Criseyde. bibliog f Am Imago 27:52-65 Spr '70
CORSAK, Sven
Build this poolhouse for less than $500; interview, ed. by H. Wicks. Pop Mech 133: 124-7 Ap '70
CORSICA
See also
Elections—Corsica

Description and travel
Special travel correspondent: Corsica. H. Sutton. Holiday 47:14+ Ja '70
CORSO, Gregory
Spontaneous requiem; poem. il Ramp Mag 8:23-5 Mr '70
CORSON, Hazel W.
Wanted: a house to haunt; drama. Plays 30: 78-82 O '70
CORT, David
Dedicated madness. Nation 210:185-6 F 16 '70
CORT, John C.
Evolution of a Catholic worker. Commonweal 93:343-6 Ja 8 '71
CORTI, Organ of. See Labyrinth (ear)
CORTIS, Antonio
Latin festival on L.P. A. Favia-Artsay. pors Hobbies 75:36+ S '70 *
CORTISONE
Bone marrow and spleen: dissociation of immunologic properties by cortisone. M. A. Levine and H. N. Claman. bibliog il Science 167:1515-17 Mr 13 '70
See also
Hydrocortisone
CORTNEY, Philip
Gold, the dollar and the American economy; address, July 11, 1970. Vital Speeches 36: 725-9 S 15 '70
CORTRIGHT, Edgar M.
Time to stand; excerpts from address. Aviation W 93:9 N 2 '70
CORVETTE (sports car) See Sports cars
CORYNEUM canker of cypress. See Cypress—Diseases and pests
COSA nostra. See Mafia
COSBY, Bill
How to win at basketball; cheat. il Look 34:65-7 Ja 27 '70

about
Bill Cosby: the man, his work, his world. M. Davison. il pors Good H 170:86-9+ Mr '70 *
COSELL, Howard
Cosell: milder but does he satisfy? J. Leonard. il por Life 69:24 N 13 '70 *
Don and Howard show. pors Time 96:59 D 14 '70 *
COSGRAVE, Mary Silva
Outlook tower. See issues of Horn book
COSINDAS, Marie
Gallery; photographs. Life 69:8-11 N 27 '70
COSMETIC creams. See Cosmetics
COSMETIC industry and trade
See also
Arden, Elizabeth, sales corporation
Johnson products company, inc.
Perfume industry and trade
Rubinstein, Helena, inc.
Vanda cosmetics company
COSMETIC surgery. See Surgery, Plastic
COSMETICS
Beauty bag: the going things. Mlle 70:228 Mr '70
Beauty checkout. See issues of Vogue
Beauty mask face lift. C. Bartel. il Am Home 73:14-15 S '70
Beauty power of moisture. il Vogue 156:74-5+ O 15 '70
Black cosmetics. il Time 95:47 Je 29 '70
Black: makeup for the black girl. il Mlle 70:206-7 F '70
Cleansing creams and lotions. il Consumer Rep 35:76-9 F '70
Cosmetics, trick or treat. Har Yrs 10:12 D '70
Does Lasting beauty make beauty last? Consumer Rep 35:580 O '70
Getting down to earth: herb, fruit and vegetable cosmetics. il Mlle 72:114-15+ D '70

COSMETICS—*Continued*
How GH investigates beauty products. il Good H 170:6 My '70
Monteil's pedestal still full of air; Super-clean face wash. il Consumer Rep 35:399 Jl '70
Protect your skin from the unfriendly air. C. Bartel. il Am Home 74:14 Ja '71
Set your own beauty-farm routine; programs and products. S. Lindsay. il House B 112:44+ O '70
Still going strong. il Mlle 70:272-3 F '70
Sun worship. il Todays Health 48:36-9 Je '70
Sunburn's menace to the skin. il Consumer Bul 53:4+ Ag '70
Sweet smell of success; natural cosmetics. il Time 97:66 Ja 18 '71
What good do suntan lotions do? il Changing T 24:11-12 Jl '70
What's new in cosmetics? Har Yrs 10:9 D '70
  See also
Beauty, Personal
Deodorants
Make-up
Toilet preparations

COSMETICS for men
Digging the sun scene. C. Kriebel. Harp Baz 103:48-9 Jl '70
Grooming American men is big business. il Bsns W p90-1+ F 21 '70
Holiday gifts for men only. il Ladies Home J 87:36 D '70
Spruce yourself up for the holidays. H. Alpert. Har Yrs 10:6-8+ D '70
Tons and tons of toiletries. il Esquire 73:156-7 Ap '70

COSMETICS for Negroes. See Cosmetics

COSMETOLOGISTS. See Beauty operators

COSMIC physics
Swedish iconoclast recognized after many years of rejection and obscurity. A. J. Dessler. por Science 170:604-6 N 6 '70
  See also
Astrophysics
Magnetic fields (cosmic physics)

COSMIC rays
Apollo 14 will probe light flashes. Aviation W 92:51-2 Je 15 '70
Light in an astronaut's eye; Cerenkov radiation or cosmic-ray effects? il Sci N 97:523-4 My 30 '70
Particle track identification: application of a new technique to Apollo helmets. R. L. Fleischer and others. bibliog il Science 170:1189-91 D 11 '70

    Measurement
Exploring pyramids using cosmic rays. il Chem 43:42-3 Jl '70
Search for hidden chambers in the pyramids; adaptation of address, April 30, 1969. L. W. Alvarez and others. bibliog il Science 167:832-9 F 6 '70

COSMOGONY
  See also
Universe

COSMOLOGY
Case for a hierarchical cosmology. G. De Vaucouleurs. bibliog il Science 167:1203-13 F 27 '70
Cosmology: a search for two numbers. A. R. Sandage. bibliog il por Phys Today 23:34-41 F '70
Origin of galaxies. M. J. Rees and J. Silk. il Sci Am 222:26-35 bibliog (p 152) Je '70
Soviet work suggests mixmaster singularity at origin. G. B. Lubkin. pors Phys Today 23:59-60+ Mr '70
Supporting evidence for the theory of the steady state. D. E. Thomsen. il Sci N 97:464-5 My 9 '70
  See also
Universe

COSMOPOLITAN (periodical)
Helen Gurley Brown only wants to help. N. Ephron. por Esquire 73:74-5+ F '70
You are the more cupcakeable for being a Cosmopolitan girl. W. F. Buckley, jr. Nat R 22:999-1000 S 22 '70

COSMOS satellites. See Artificial satellites, Russian

COSSOTTO, Fiorenza
Cossotto in Norma. I. Kolodin. Sat R 53:58 O 24 '70 *
New sounds for the new Met season. I. Kolodin. Sat R 53:47 O 3 '70 *

COST
What should cost mean? R. N. Anthony. bibliog f il Harvard Bsns R 48:121-31 My '70
  See also
Labor cost
  also subhead Cost under various subjects, e.g. Airplanes, Jet—Cost

COST accounting
What should cost mean? R. N. Anthony. bibliog f il Harvard Bsns R 48:121-31 My '70

COST calculators. See Calculating devices

COST control
Cost reduction: panic from the word go. G. J. Berkwitt. il Duns 95:43-5 Je '70
Some common errors in cost control programs. B. Perkins Arch Rec 147:61-2 Ja '70
Year of the corporate ax. il Newsweek 76:61-2 Jl 20 '70

COST of airline operation. See Airlines—Cost of operations

COST of automobile operation. See Automobiles—Cost of operation

COST of college education. See College education, Cost of

COST of food. See Food—Prices

COST of living
Working abroad is not all fun. il Bsns W p65-7 Mr 21 '70
  See also
Budget, Household
Domestic finance
Rent

    Portugal
Blue heaven for greenbacks. R. Joseph. il Esquire 74:206-9+ D '70

    Puerto Rico
Americano retires to Puerto Rico. M. Polhemus. il por Har Yrs 10:6-11+ S '70

    United States
Best places to retire; symposium. il Har Yrs 10:35-8 Mr '70
Family budgets keep on rising; Department of labor report. U S News 70:42 Ja 4 '71
Finally, some real slowing of inflation. il U S News 69:29 O 5 '70
How living costs vary in thirty-nine places. il U S News 68:22 F 2 '70
How to stretch your inflated money. L. David. Read Digest 96:61-3 F '70
Indexes of comparative living costs from urban retired couple intermediate budget, spring 1967. il Har Yrs 10:27 Mr '70
Inflation over? not if you're buying. il U S News 68:40-1 Ap 6 '70
Prices (cont of) Consumer prices; tables; Wholesale prices; tables. See issues of Monthly labor review
Retired couple's bare living cost $2,777; moderate $3,940. Aging 182:13 D '69
What states offer the most for you in climate, housing, cost-of-living, services? Har Yrs 10:30-4 Mr '70
Where inflation takes its toll: the soaring cost of services. il U S News 68:30-1 Ja 19 '70
Why you can't live on your husband's salary. S. Porter. il Ladies Home J 87:40+ Ja '70
  See also
Food—Prices
Price indexes
Prices—United States

COST of living wage adjustments. See Wages—Cost of living adjustments

COST of medical services. See Medical service, Cost of

COSTA, Horacio de la
To find itself: a young nation's mission. il America 123:542-4 D 19 '70

COSTA, José Pedro, abp
Brazil: order vs. disorder. America 123:536-7 D 19 '70 *

COSTA, Simeon
How to be a tough old bird. Har Yrs 10:46-7 Je '70

COSTA BRAVA. See Spain

COSTA-GAVRAS
Current cinema (cont) P. Kael. New Yorker 46:172+ D 12 '70

COSTA RICA
  See also
Fishing—Costa Rica

    Description and travel
Catch that view from a volcano top. L. Barry. il Pop Phot 67:40+ Ag '70

    Politics and government
Costa Rica and her neighbors. D. B. Heath. Cur Hist 58:95-101+ F '70
Don Pepe's return. il por Time 95:33 F 16 '70

COSTA SMERALDA. See Sardinia

COSTELLO, John
Executive trends. See issues of Nation's business

COSTELLO, Paul
To Fran; poem. Nation 211:61 Jl 20 '70

COSTES, N. C. and others
Apollo 11 soil mechanics investigation. bibliog il Science 167:739-41 Ja 30 '70

COSTIKYAN, Edward N.
Cities can work. il Sat R 53:19-21+ Ap 4 '70

COSTUME
Adornment: for gods, for love, for war; excerpt from Le geste et la parole. A. Leroi-Gourhan. Vogue 156:151+ D '70
Bull, the rooster, the giraffe, the raccoon, the who's-it, Halloween comes in a walking paper bag. il Sunset 145:88-9 O '70
Nowadays, witches don't have to burn! il Consumer Bul 53:27 O '70
    See also
Fashion

Italy
Naked-tummy look. il Newsweek 76:38 S 7 '70

Mexico
    See also
Indians of Mexico—Costume and adornment

New Guinea
Spectacular highlanders of New Guinea, South Pacific; photographs. Vogue 156:146-57 D '70

COSTUME, Eskimo. See Eskimos—Costume and adornment

COSTUME, Indian. See Indians of North America—Costume and adornment

COSTUME, Theatrical
Fantastic Tosi. A. Arbasino. il Vogue 156:384-7+ S 1 '70
When is a costume? costumes for opera. J. Varona. il por Opera N 34:26-9 F 28 '70
    See also
Wolff-Fording company

COSTUME balls. See Balls (parties)

COSTUME design
Look of the damned; Valentino's line. il Newsweek 75:72 F 2 '70
Midi's compensations. il Time 95:50 Je 8 '70
Out on a limb with the midi. il por Time 96:76-81 S 14 '70
Rich little poor look; mountain artisans of Appalachia. il Newsweek 75:92 My 11 '70
    See also
Costume, Theatrical

Competitions
On campus: samples of winning entries: a wardrobe for a moon maiden. il Mlle 70:60 F '70

Study and teaching
Textile designs; teaching methods in fashion design. A. Newton and R. Hillestad. il Design 72:9-11 Fall '70

COSTUME designers
All men are not created equal, but if you think that deters designers, well, regardez. il Esquire 74:109-16 Jl '70
Bold beauty from a land at war; Israel's young fashion designers. il Life 68:40-7 Je 19 '70
Designers and the midi beauty. il Harp Baz 103:242-55 S '70
Punch, oui; power, non. il Time 96:46 Ag 3 '70
When is a costume? costumes for opera. J. Varona. il por Opera N 34:26-9 F 28 '70
    See also
Duskin, A.
Mellinger, F.
St Laurent, Y. M.
Scott, K.
Tosi, P.

COSTUME jewelry. See Jewelry

COTE, Henry B.
Double monoprints? il Sch Arts 70:38-9 Ja '71

COTLER, Gordon
Bangkok: where Anna met the King of Siam. il Holiday 47:38-41+ F '70
Biggest, best run and roughest rodeo in U.S. il Holiday 48:54-5+ Jl '70
Ceylon; a larger-than-life travel poster. il Holiday 47:40-3+ Ap '70
New Orleans' Pontchartrain. il por Holiday 47:54-7 Je '70
Preservation Hall. il Holiday 47:54-5+ My '70
Using 1957-59 as a base, try stealing home. New Yorker 46:36-7 My 16 '70

COTONEASTERS
Evergreen cotoneasters; rockspray. R. Weinberg. il Horticulture 48:32-3+ O '70

COTTAGE cheese
McCall's diet of the month: Cottage cheese. il McCalls 97:42+ Je '70

COTTAM, Clarence
Cows on Padre Island. il Nat Parks & Con Mag 44:27 S '70

COTTAM, Keith M.
Dues problem. Am Lib 1:574-5 Je '70

COTTER, James F.
Does poetry have an audience? America 122:187-8 F 21 '70
How to read black, in poetry. America 123:264-5 O 10 '70

COTTLE, Thomas J.
Prospect street moon. Sat R 53:21-4+ F 14 '70
Social class, college, and a dream deferred. il Sat R 53:60-1+ Ja 24 '70

COTTON, Steve
Earth day, what happened. il Audubon 72:112-15 Jl '70

COTTON
Hybrids
Faculative gymnosperm from an interspecific cotton hybrid. V. G. Meyer. bibliog il Science 168:886-8 Ag 28 '70

COTTON fabrics
What you should know about the new cottons. il Good H 170:154 My '70

COTTON industry and trade
United States and Poland conclude new cotton textile agreement; Department announcement; with exchange of notes. Dept State Bul 62:561-3 Ag 27 '70

COTTON knits. See Knit goods

COTTON trade
    See also
International cotton advisory committee

COTTONTAIL hunting. See Rabbit hunting

COTTONTAILS. See Rabbits

COUCH, Edward
Buster Couch: the button man. J. Dianna. il pors Hot Rod 24:50-2 Ja '71 *

COUCH, Thomas
Super flash. il Pop Electr 32:48-50+ My '70

COUCHES. See Sofas

COUGAR hunting. See Puma hunting

COUGARS. See Pumas

COULEE DAM. See Grand Coulee power and reclamation project

COULOMB functions
Coulomb energies in nuclei; report of meeting. A. A. Jaffe and others. Science 169:505-6 Jl 31 '70

COULTER, Charles L. and Greaves, M. L.
Cyclic cytidine 2',3'-phosphate: molecular structure. bibliog il Science 169:1097-8 S 11 '70

COULTER, Tim
Coffeehouse. S. Alsop. il Newsweek 75:116 Mr 16 '70 *

COUNCIL of churches, Canadian. See Canadian council of churches

COUNCIL of churches of the city of New York
Ambiguity of awards; Family of man award refused by C. Chavez. Chr Cent 87:1308 N 4 '70

COUNCIL of economic advisers. See United States—Council of economic advisers

COUNCIL of Europe
For a cleaner Europe; Nature conservation year. J. Lambert. il Sci N 97:280 Mr 14 '70

COUNCIL of Europe biennial. See Art—Exhibitions

COUNCIL of social advisers (proposed) See United States—Council of social advisers (proposed)

COUNCIL of the laity
Old-time dialogue; Msgr. Uylenbroeck's talk with laymen in major Catholic centers. Commonweal 92:355-7 Jl 24 '70; Discussion. 92:427+ S 4 '70

COUNCIL on economic priorities
Investors' guide to social concern. Bsns W p85 Je 20 '70
Report on paper. Time 96:41 D 28 '70
Stick and carrot; study of pollution control in the paper and pulp industry. Nation 212:4 Ja 4 '71

COUNCIL on environmental quality. See United States—Council on environmental quality

COUNCIL on international education exchange
New overseas study programs for future teachers. Sch & Soc 98:210+ Ap '70

COUNCIL on religion and international affairs
CRIA and the moral crisis. Chr Cent 87:132-3 F 4 '70

COUNCILS and synods
Council over Pope? Towards a provisional ecclesiology, by F. Oakley. Review Commonweal 91:490-2 Ja 30 '70. R. P. McBrien
Local church councils: under metamorphosis. R. Chandler. Chr Today 14:33-4 Ja 30 '70
    See also
Vatican council. 2d
Vatican council. 3d (proposed)
Vatican council. 1869-1870

COUNCILS of government. See Municipal government

COUNSELING
Young living; questions and answers. A. Wood. See issues of Seventeen
See also
Educational guidance
Genetic counseling
Pastoral counseling
Personnel service in education
Telephone in counseling
Vocational guidance
COUNSELING service, School. See Personnel service in education
COUNSELORS
See also
Camp counselors
Mental health counselors
Student counselors
COUNSILMAN, James E.
As easy as taking a stroll; ed. by C. Phinizy. il por Sports Illus 33:38-43 Jl 20 '70
COUNTER culture
Counter-culture and its apologists; with editorial comment. R. A. Nisbet; R. Starr; D. L. Bromwich. bibliog f Commentary 50: 5-6, 40-59 D '70
Das hip Kapital; a critique of the youth economy. C. Karpel. il Esquire 74:184-8+ D '70
Making of a counter culture; excerpts. T. Roszak. Horizon 12:20-1 Spr '70
Middle age meets the kid ghetto. V. Bourjaily. il N Y Times Mag p46-7+ N 29 '70
Up the country; revolution in southern Vermont. A. Nopkind. Ramp Mag 9:8-9 D '70
Visions of a new religion. M. Cavell. il Sat R 53:12-14+ D 19 '70

Anecdotes, facetiae, satire, etc.

Great speckled Post. il Esquire 74:215-23 D '70
COUNTER culture literature
Publications of the counter culture. J. R. Douglas. il por Wilson Lib Bul 45:364-71 D '70
COUNTERCURRENT chromatography. See Chromatographic analysis
COUNTERFEIT money. See Counterfeits and counterfeiting
COUNTERFEITS and counterfeiting
Telltale signs of counterfeit money. il Good H 171:150 Ag '70
See also
Forgery of works of art
COUNTERS (electrons, ions, etc)
Build $40 X-ray detector. R. K. Stoms and E. Kuerze. il Radio-Electr 42:36-9+ Ja '71
Scintillation radiological survey meters. J. G. Ello. il Electr World 83:39-43 Ja '70
COUNTERS, Kitchen. See Kitchen furniture
COUNTING boards. See Abacus
COUNTING cells. See Nerve cells
COUNTING machines and devices
Add-subtract MOS IC decimal counter. D. E. Lancaster. il Electr World 83:45-8+ Je '70
Assemble a digital measurements lab; 20-MHz frequency counter module. D. Meyer. il Pop Electr 33:51-3+ N '70
Build numeric glow tube DCU. D. Lancaster. il Pop Electr 32:33-5+ F '70
Digital instruments; counting and decoding circuits. D. L. Steinbach. il Electr World 84:47-50+ Ag; 50-2+ S '70
Introduction to electronic counters. D. L. Steinbach. il Electr World 85:35-8+ Ja '71
Make your own seven segment readout. D. C. Kroop. il Pop Electr 33:68-70 Ag '70
Numitron readout; simplified seven-segment display in one tube. V. Wood. il Pop Electr 32:73-5 Mr '70
Predetermining decimal counter. D. E. Lancaster. il Electr World 83:34-6+ My '70
COUNTRIES. See Nations
COUNTRY clubs
Country clubs for farmers. C. E. Ball. il Farm J 94:18-19+ Jl '70
Rich way to make a getaway: Tres Vidas country club, Acapulco. E. Shrake. il por Sports Illus 33:26-33 Ag 31 '70
COUNTRY estates
See also
Plantations

England

At home with the barons and earls. B. Bishop. il Sat R 53:46-7+ S 12 '70

Italy

At home with art: the villa of Count Giuseppe Panza di Biumo. T. Trini. il por Art in Am 58:102-9 S '70
Renaissance reborn; villa dei Vescovi. V. Lawford. il pors Vogue 156:152-7+ S 15 '70
COUNTRY houses
See also
Architecture, Domestic

COUNTRY life
Back to the woods. R. Haughton. Cath World 211:101-2 Je '70
Cornelius Ryan; interview. ed. by G. Henle. C. Ryan. il pors House B 112:56-9+ F '70
Environment of time. R. Haughton. Cath World 211:149-50 Jl '70
Living the good life, by H. Nearing and S. Nearing. Review
Harper 241:120-2 N '70. J. Thompson
New Repub 163:26-8 S 5 '70. M. Jezer
New ideas for homesteading. R. Rodale. il Org Gard & Farm 17:31-5 Mr '70
Okay, Thoreau, we know you're in there. A. R. Dodd. Sat R 53:55-6+ Je 13 '70
Plains, a boy, a summer day; excerpt from Country editor's boy. H. Borland. il Read Digest 97:37-41 Ag '70
Prophets of the good life; the Nearings of Vermont and Maine. Newsweek 76:100+ S 14 '70
See also
City and country
Farm life
Part time farming
Ranch life
Recreation, Rural
Village life
COUNTRY music. See Folk music, American
COUNTRY people: drama. See Gorky, M.
COUNTRY planning. See Rural planning
COUNTRY town life. See Village life
COUNTRY towns. See Cities and towns
COUNTY agents
County agents focus on the '70s. Farm J 93: 36D N '69
COUNTY fairs. See Agricultural exhibitions
COUNTY officers
See also
Sheriffs
COUPERIN, François
Grandeur of Couperin. P. H. Lang. Hi Fi 20: sec I 86 Mr '70 *
COUPLINGS
See also
Universal joints (mechanics)
COURAGE
We and our unwanted experiences. B. W. Overstreet. PTA Mag 65:21 O '70
You're braver than you think. M. B. Johnstone. Read Digest 97:177-8 N '70
COURSES of study
Curriculum: the non-life. W. J. Fitzpatrick. Clear House 44:333 F '70
Flow chart approach to curriculum study. R. C. Kolz and J. O'Dell. il Clear House 45:72-5 O '70
Fond farewell to back-to-school night. J. N. Bell. Todays Health 48:16-17+ S '70
Laissez-faire curriculum in the democratic school; address, November, 1969. A. P. Lehner. Engl J 59:803-10 S '70
Learning on the Q/T; quantity and time in curriculum strategies. D. B. Conrad. Clear House 44:534-7 My '70
On meanings in relationships in curriculum and instruction. M. Alpren. bibliog f Sch & Soc 98:100-2 F '70
Skill of relevance or the relevance of skills; curriculum reform. J. Bruner. il Sat R 53:66-8+ Ap 18 '70
See also
Afro-American studies
Association for supervision and curriculum development
Colleges and universities—Curriculum
High schools—Curriculum
Schedules, School
Vocational education
COURT, Margaret (Smith) See Smith, Margaret
COURT, Contempt of. See Contempt of court
COURT martial. See Courts martial and courts of inquiry
COURT of justice, international. See International court of justice, The Hague
COURT procedure. See Procedure (law)
COURT reporting (by newspapers) See Newspaper court reporting
COURT stenographers
Capitalist stenographers; Mary Jo Kopechne inquest transcript for publication. por Time 95:68 My 4 '70
COURTESY
Pleasant, friendly sound of good manners. R. Graves. Life 68:2A Je 19 '70
See also
Etiquette
COURTLY love
See also
Troubadours
COURTNEY, K. Diane, and others
Teratogenic evaluation of 2,4,5-T. bibliog il Science 168:864-6 My 15 '70

COURTNEY, Richard
NEA; as close as your phone. Todays Ed 59:
46-7 Ap '70
COURTS
See also
Contempt of court
Criminal procedure
Domestic relations courts
Judges
Jury
Justice, Administration of
Juvenile courts
Traffic courts

New York (state)
Women as property; criticisms of the Family
court system. V. Tomasson. New Repub
163:15-18 S 19 '70
See also
New York (city)—Courts

Ohio
Kent state gag; report of the Ohio special
grand jury. D. Sanford. New Repub 163:
14-17 N 7 '70

United States
Action to help clear logjam in courts. il U S
News 70:65 Ja 11 '71
American law, by J. P. Frank. Review
Sat R 53:34-5 Mr 21 '70. M. Mayer
Fortresses of the law; courtroom security.
Nation 211:612 D 14 '70
Interview with Chief Justice Warren E.
Burger. W. E. Burger. il pors U S News
69:32-6+ D 14 '70; Discussion. 70:66-9 Ja 11
'71
Justice in violent times. S. Mosk. Nation
211:431-4 N 2 '70
Only radical reform can save the courts.
J. Main. il Fortune 82:110-14+ Ag '70;
Same abr. Read Digest 97:106-10 N '70
U.S. court system under fire. il Sr Schol 97:
7-10 D 14 '70
What's wrong with the courts; the Chief
Justice speaks out; address, August 10,
1970. W. E. Burger. il por U S News
69:68-71 Ag 24 '70; Same abr. with title
Chief Justice Warren E. Burger speaks
out. Read Digest 97:108-9 N '70
See also
Courts martial and courts of inquiry
Justice, Administration of—United States
United States—Supreme court
also subhead Courts under names of
cities, e. g. San Rafael, Calif.—Courts
COURTS, International
See also
International court of justice, The Hague
COURTS, Military. See Courts martial and
courts of inquiry
COURTS, Municipal
Getting busted in New York; night court
is easily the greatest show in town. P.
Tracy. Commonweal 93:371-2 Ja 15 '71
COURTS martial and courts of inquiry
Calley at My Lai. il Newsweek 76:52-3 D 14
'70
Calley goes on trial. il por Newsweek 76:
16-17 N 30 '70
Calley's defense. il Newsweek 76:25-6 D 21 '70
Captain MacDonald's ordeal. il pors Time
97:50+ Ja 11 '71
Case of Lieutenant Duffy. Nation 210:419-20
Ap 13 '70
Counsel for the G.I. defense. Time 96:44-5
O 19 '70
Court-martial jurisdiction; rape case of I.
Relford. Nation 212:69-70 Ja 18 '71
Court-martial: the trial of one GI for mur-
der; case of L. McDowell. il por Newsweek
76:21 Ag 31 '70
For the defense: new office in Saigon to
furnish free civilian defense for service-
men facing courts-martial. New Yorker 46:
39-40 N 7 '70
Grass & the brass. D. Sanford. New Repub
162:11-12 Ap 25 '70
How the war is fought? My Lai massacre
trial. il por Newsweek 76:18-20 D 28 '70
Lieutenant Calley at bay. il por Time 96:14-15
D 21 '70
Mere gook rule; case of J. B. Duffy. il por
Newsweek 75:30 Ap 13 '70
Military justice is to justice as military music
is to music, by R. Sherrill. Review
Newsweek 75:103+ My 11 '70. G. Wolff
Mitchell case. il por Newsweek 76:30-1 O
26 '70
My Lai massacre, the prosecution rests. D.
C. Martin. New Repub 163:13 N 7 '70
My Lai: the case against Calley. il por Time
96:18 D 14 '70
My Lai trials begin. Time 96:11-12 N 2
'70

One not guilty for My Lai; case of D. Mitch-
ell. il por Time 96:10 N 30 '70
Ordeal of L/Cpl. Johnson; rape case. R.
Oliver. Nation 211:141-6 Ag 31 '70
Priest's progress; antiwar newsletter OM
promoting disloyalty. il por Time 95:78+
My 11 '70
Prosecution rests; My Lai trial. Newsweek
76:37-8 N 2 '70
U.S. military justice on trial. il Newsweek
76:18-20+ Ag 31 '70
Unlawful concert: an account of the Presidio
mutiny case, by F. Gardner. Review
Nation 210:628-30 My 25 '70. E. F. Sher-
man
See also
Military law
COURTS of domestic relations. See Domestic
relations courts
COURTS of inquiry. See Courts martial and
courts of inquiry
COURTSHIP
See also
Dating
COURTSHIP of animals
Elk drama in autumn; wild elk in the rut.
W. J. McRae. il Outdoor Life 146:40-1 Jl '70
COURTSHIP of insects
Love song of the fruit fly. H. C. Bennet-
Clark and A. W. Ewing. il Sci Am 223:84-
90+ Jl '70
COUSINS, Margaret
Gifted child; story. Ladies Home J 86:32 D
'69
COUSINS, Norman
Hiroshima. il Look 34:38-45 Ag 11 '70
New York's fight against pollution. il Sat R
53:53-4+ Mr 7 '70
What is the writer's social responsibility? il
Writers Digest 50:30-1+ Ja '70
about
Cartoonist Q's. J. Markow. Writers Digest
50:38-9 Jl '70 *
COUSINS, Peter
Christian teacher. Chr Today 15:16-18 O 9
'70
COUSTEAU, Jacques Yves
Dying oceans. il por Time 96:64 S 28 '70 *
COUSY, Bob
Cousy makes the Royals run. W. Leggett.
il por Sports Illus 32:14-17 Ja 26 '70
COVELLO, Leonard
Leonard Covello and the community school.
F. Cordasco. bibliog f por Sch & Soc 98:
298-9 Sum '70 *
COVENT Garden market. See London—Mar-
kets
COVENT Garden opera company. See Royal
opera, Great Britain
COVER, Robert
Year of harassment. il Nation 210:110-13 F 2
'70
COVER plants
Grand bank and ground covers. il Sunset 145:
146-7 Jl '70
See also
Moss pink
COVERED bridges
Bridgeport bridge's day, September 19. il
Sunset 145:35+ S '70
COVERLETS
Bedspreads. il Good H 171:168 Ag '70
Hand-woven coverlets in the Art institute of
Chicago. M. Davison. il Antiques 97:734-40
My '70
See also
Quilts
COW testing. See Cows—Testing
COWAN, Bruce
Ultimately, it's the consumer. Nat Parks &
Con Mag 44:24 Je '70
COWAN, Edward
Canada in search of itself. Nation 210:142-5
F 9 '70
COWAN, John
Travel. Vogue 156:36 O 15 '70
COWAN, Paul
Leftward odyssey. R. A. Gross. il por News-
week 75:108 Mr 16 '70 *
COWAN, Thaddeus M.
Megalithic rings: their design construction.
bibliog il Science 168:321-5 Ap 17 '70
COWARD, Sir Noel
Hay fever. Criticism
Nation 211:572 N 30 '70 *
New Yorker 46:103 N 21 '70 *
Newsweek il 76:137 N 23 '70 *
Private lives. Criticism
America 122:54 Ja 17 '70
Sir Noel and his friends. New Yorker 46:30 F
21 '70 *
Working theater. J. Richardson. Commentary
50:50-2 Ag '70 *

COWBOY artists of America
Cowboy artists of America. J. Beeler. il Am Artist 34:66-74+ Ap '70
COWBOY ballads. See Ballads, American
COWBOYS
Authors & editors. A. P. Hackett. por Pub W 197:39-40 Mr 2 '70
How the paniolo came. S. V. Candland. il Américas 22:7-9 Ja '70
Memories of Big Country. D. Jackson. il Life 68:40-8+ Ap 3 '70
Right on, cowboy! Okmulgee rodeo. il Ebony 25:115-18+ O '70
  See also
Cowboy artists of America
Rodeos

    Caricatures and cartoons
West of Our way; cartoonist's view of the cowman's life. F. Egan; W. H. Hutchinson. il Am West 7:18-25 My '70
COWBOYS (football club) See Football clubs
COWGILL, Ursula M.
People of York: 1538-1812; with biographical sketch. il Sci Am 222:16, 104-10+ Ja '70
COWLES, Gardner
Inside Look. il por Newsweek 76:73-4 S 14 '70 *
COWLES communications, inc.
Between friends; deal with the New York times. il Newsweek 76:69 N 9 '70
Cowles of the Times. Time 96:41 N 9 '70
Times acquiring substantial Cowles properties. Pub W 198:34 N 9 '70
COWLEY, Malcolm
Double life, half told. Atlan 226:105-6+ D '70
Horatio Alger: failure. il Horizon 12:62-5 Sum '70
COWLEY, Robert
Man who drew Pooh. il McCalls 97:12+ Ag '70
COWNE, Leslie J.
Case studies of volunteer programs in mental health. Ment Hy 54:337-46 Jl '70
COWPEAS
Black-eyed peas, the good luck vegetable. L. Riotte. il Org Gard & Farm 17:73-4 Ja '70
COWRIES
Fascination of the cowries. A. G. Melvin. il Hobbies 75:146-7 S '70
More about cowries. A. G. Melvin. il Hobbies 75:146 O '70
COWS
Guernseys I have loved. C. E. Werkley. Esquire 74:40+ O '70
How your cows might handle calves from those big European breeds. il Farm J 94:32D O '70
  See also
Cattle
Dairying

    Anecdotes, facetiae, satire, etc.
Cows are out! G. Logsdon. Farm J 93:36 N '69

    Breeding
See Cattle breeding

    Culling
What does dairy culling cost? Suc Farm 68: no3 G12 F '70

    Diseases and pests
Dairy problems: what to do. J. R. Borcherding. il Suc Farm 68:52-3 O '70
Watch for urea toxicity, nitrite poisoning. L. A. Baker. Farm J 94:D14 D '70
  See also
Worms, Intestinal and parasitic

    Feeding
Complete ration in a cube. G. Lorang. il Farm J 94:57 F '70
Eight-times-a-day feeding pays off. J. R. Borcherding. il Suc Farm 68:A6-7 Ja '70
L-barn splits diner from beds. D. Seim. il Farm J 94:54S-54T F '70
Least-cost feeds can be a myth; questions and answers. L. A. Baker. Farm J 93:D20 D '69

    Milk records
See Cows—Testing

    Testing
New ideas in production testing. J. R. Borcherding. il Suc Farm 68:no5 10 Mr '70
COX, Albert H. jr
U.S. economic policy; address, May 25, 1970. Vital Speeches 36:559-61 Jl 1 '70
COX, Charles K.
Fighting for bold ideas. il por Nations Bsns 58:86-7 Ja '70

COX, Clifton B.
Will packers control more livestock production? interview. Farm J 94:M1 F '70
COX, Donald (Black Panther)
Upper East side story. il por Time 95:14 Ja 26 '70
COX, Edward Finch
Tricia and Eddie. pors Newsweek 77:18 Ja 4 '71 *
COX, Harvey
Coming generation of clergy. Ladies Home J 86:130-1 D '69
Conspiracy against the Black Panthers? Cur 115:42-4 F '70
Experimenting with a simpler life style; interview. ed. by C. Fager. Chr Cent 88: 9-13 Ja 6 '71
If you could make one change in the church, what would it be? Commonweal 92:160 My 1 '70
Tired images transcended. Chr Cent 87:384-6 Ap 1 '70
    about
Dionysus in Boston. il por Newsweek 75:77+ My 11 '70 *
COX, James J.
Allow time for daydreams in the world of childhood. il Todays Health 48:48-9+ Je '70
COX, James L.
DDT residues in marine phytoplankton: increase from 1955 to 1969. bibliog il Science 170:71-3 O 2 '70
COX, Jeff
Anyone can homestead on two acres. il Org Gard & Farm 17:81-2+ O '70
Likely farms, unlikely places. il Org Gard & Farm 17:62-3+ D '70
Nowhere store that's going places. Org Gard & Farm 17:57-9 Ag '70
They go to court to protect the environment. Org Gard & Farm 17:78-81 S '70
COX, Kenneth Allen
Kenneth Cox. Nation 210:710 Je 15 '70 *
COX, Margaret M. and Moore, J. W.
Perbromate problem. bibliog il pors Chem 43:15-19 Je '70
COX, Robert E.
(ed) Gleanings for ATM's. See issues of Sky and telescope
COX, William Drought
What will he think of next? G. S. Brown. il pors Sports Illus 32:38-42+ My 4 '70 *
COYNE, John R. jr
Ale, cheese, onions and women. Nat R 22: 997 S 22 '70
Center shifts right. Nat R 22:1159-60 N 3 '70
Doctored grapes? il Nat R 22:88 Ja 27 '70
End of the multiversity. Nat R 22:560-1+ Je 2 '70
It's still there, but maybe not much longer. Nat R 22:305 Mr 24 '70
Kunstler constituency. Nat R 22:467 My 5 '70
COYNE, Patricia S.
Christmas at sixty below. Nat R 22:1405 D 29 '70
COYOTE hunting
Gray ghost. L. J. Marlatt. il Outdoor Life 146:58-9+ S '70
COYOTES
Owooo . . . . G. Helgeland. il Nat Wildlife 9:52-3 D '70
COZUMEL ISLAND
Enjoying the best of Cozumel. N. Sureck. Travel & Camera 33:58-9 N '70
Return to Cozumel. N. Sureck. il Travel & Camera 33:10+ N '70
CRAB apples
Wonderful world of crabapples. P. E. Keenan. il Horticulture 48:26-9+ O '70
  See also
Cookery—Fruit
CRAB grass
  See also
Pangola grass
CRAB nebula. See Nebulae
CRABAPPLES. See Crab apples
CRABBE, John K.
Those infernal electives. Engl J 59:990-3+ O '70
CRABS
Attack autotomy; a defense against predators. M. H. Robinson and others. bibliog il Science 169:300-1 Jl 17 '70
Crabs that change color overnight; fiddler crab. il Chem 43:27 Ap '70
Molting in land crabs: stimulation by leg removal. D. M. Skinner and D. E. Graham. bibliog il Science 169:383-5 Jl 24 '70
Story of Sally lightfoot: scarlet rock crabs. il Nat Wildlife 8:42-3 F '70
World of Sally lightfoot; photographs. L. Line. Audubon 72:52-5 Jl '70
  See also
Cookery—Shellfish
King crabs

CRABTREE, Bruce
Fjord-hopping by trawler-yacht through Princess Louisa inlet. il Yachting 127:54-5+ Mr '70
From Anchorage to Acapulco: the next boat. il Yachting 129:70-1+ Ja '71
CRABTREE, Donald E.
Flaking stone with wooden implements. bibliog il Science 169:146-53 Jl 10 '70

about

How to make stone age tools. il por Sci Digest 67:20-1 My '70 *
CRADDOCK, Campbell
Antarctic geology and Gondwanaland. il por Bul Atom Sci 26:33-9 D '70
CRADDOCK, Elysse
Chromosome number variation in a stick insect didymuria violescens (leach) bibliog il Science 167:1380-2 Mr 6 '70
CRADEN, Michael D. and Skelton, P. C.
Zoo-a-go-go. il Parks & Rec 5:25+ Ap '70
CRADLE of forestry in America. See National forests
CRAFT goods trade. See Art trade
CRAFT shops. See Art trade
CRAFTS, Edward C.
Dilemma of the Forest service. il Am For 76:8-9+ Je '70
Islands in time. il Am For 76:16-19+ D '70
Saga of a law. il Am For 76:12-19+ Je; 28-35 Jl '70
Will pollution win the public lands? address. il por Am For 76:28-31+ Ja '70
CRAFTS. See Arts and crafts; Handicraft
CRAFTSMANSHIP
Ephraim Byram, versatile nineteenth-century craftsman. J. M. Perkins. il por Antiques 97:746-7 My '70
Skills of the hands and senses, refined by time. il Fortune 81:106-13 Mr '70
CRAFTSMEN. See Labor and laboring classes
CRAGUN, Richard
Dame Margot and her new cavalier. W. Terry. il pors Sat R 53:62+ F 28 '70 *
CRAIG, Allan
And the word was made flesh; poem. Chr Today 15:4 D 4 '70
CRAIG, Anna C. See Freeman, W. J. jt. auth.
CRAIG, James B.
One third of the nation's land. il Am For 76:8-11+ Ag '70
They call it pocket wilderness. il Am For 76:22-5+ O '70
—See Hathaway, C. jt. auth.
CRAIG, Marjorie
Miss Craig's face-saving exercises; excerpt. il McCalls 97:78-83 S '70
Miss Craig's post-holiday shape-up exercises; excerpt from Miss Craig's twenty-one day shape-up program for men and women. il McCalls 98:40 Ja '71
CRAIG, Randall J.
Focus on black artists: a project for schools and community. il Sch Arts 70:30-3 N '70
CRAIG, W. S.
Not a question of size. il Environ 12:2-5 Je '70
CRAIGHEAD, Frank, Jr. See Craighead, J. jt. auth.
CRAIGHEAD, John, and Craighead, Frank, Jr
White-water adventure on wild rivers of Idaho. il pors Nat Geog 127:212-39 F '70
CRAIGHEAD-Jackson house. See Knoxville, Tenn.—Historic houses, etc.
CRAIGMYLE, Mary Martin
Chairs by Lannuier at New York's city hall. il Antiques 97:258-9 F '70
CRAIK, Kenneth H.
Environmental dispositions of environmental decision-makers. bibliog f Ann Am Acad 389:87-94 My '70
CRAMER, Chris H.
Viscosity of the Atlantic Ocean bottom. bibliog il Science 167:1123-4 F 20 '70
CRAMER, William Cato
Carswell vs. Cramer: Senate fight with national overtones. pors U S News 69:34-5 S 7 '70 *
Carswell's fiasco. il pors Newsweek 76:39 S 21 '70 *
If you can't beat em . . . il por Newsweek 75:29 My 4 '70 *
Verdict on the Florida judge. il por Time 96:16-17 S 21 '70 *
CRANBERG, Gilbert
Is right of access coming? Sat R 53:48-9+ Ag 8 '70
Who's who for everyman. Sat R 53:65-6+ My 9; 45 Jl 11 '70

CRANBERRIES
Varied uses for cranberries. Good H 171:170 N '70
See also
Cookery—Fruit
CRANBROOK gardens. See Bloomfield Hills, Mich.—Gardens
CRANE, Arnold
Arnold Crane; photographic materials collector extraordinary. R. F. McCullough. il por Pop Phot 66:96-7+ Ap '70 *
CRANE, H. Richard
Employment problem in perspective. por Phys Today 23:26-7 Ap '70
CRANE, Hart
Lost at sea. A. Trachtenberg. Nation 210:183-5 F 16 '70 *
Voyager, by J. Unterecker. Review
Poetry 116:256-9 Jl '70. J. Atlas *
CRANE, Paul A.
Crisis in Lesotho. il America 122:212-13, 562 F 28, My 23 '70
Rhodesia's bishops speak out. America 122:412 Ap 18 '70
CRANE, Stephen
Trilogy of irony; analysis of War is kind. E. E. Miller. Engl J 59:59-62 Ja '70
CRANE, William H.
Kimbanguist church and the search for authentic Catholicity. Chr Cent 87:691-5 Je 3 '70
CRANE company
All's fair in love & war; federal court ruling on American standard-Crane battle for WABCO. il Forbes 105:26-7 Ap 15 '70
CRANES (birds)
No gamebird like it; sandhill crane. B. W. Dalrymple. il Outdoor Life 145:56-9+ Je '70
Tale of whoopers and bottles and the throwaway economy. Audubon 72:103 Jl '70
Whooping promise. J. Phillips. il Sat R 53:59 O 3 '70
CRANFORD, W. H.
DDT-less mosquito control. il Am City 85:109+ Je '70
CRANIOLOGY
See also
Man, Prehistoric
CRANK calls. See Telephone calls
CRANKO, John
Monologues with meeting places: John Cranko, Marcia Haydee, ed. by N. M. Stoop. Dance Mag 44:35 Ag '70

about

American in Germany: dancing for Cranko; interview, ed. by O. Maynard. J. Reece. il pors Dance Mag 44:34-7 Mr '70 *
Pineapple Poll. Criticism
Newsweek il 75:63-4 Mr 16 '70 *
CRANKSHAW, Edward
What is Russia up to? Cur 121:52-4 S '70
CRANSTON, Alan
Expanded legislative reference service. por Library J 95:2221-2 Je 15 '70
Laos: next step in the Big Muddy. Nation 210:363-6 Mr 30 '70
CRANSTON, R.I.
Bridge at generation gap; EPIC project. M. E. Wade. il Am Ed 6:28-30 O '70
CRAPE myrtle
Crape myrtle; the shrub that laughs at drought. M. J. Rozell. il Org Gard & Farm 17:84-5 N '70
CRAPPIE fishing
How to have great fishing with the family. S. Marking. il Field & S 74:68-9+ F '70
Ozark crappie jamboree. H. Bradshaw. il Field & S 74:70-1+ Ap '70
CRARY, A. P.
Long look ahead. il por Bul Atom Sci 26:100-4 D '70
CRASH diets. See Diet
CRASSULA. See Jade plants
CRATER LAKE NATIONAL PARK
Crater Lake. H. D. Brown. il Hobbies 75:117 Ag '70
CRATERS
Caldera collapse in the Galápagos Islands, 1968. T. Simkin and K. A. Howard. bibliog il Science 169:429-37 Jl 31 '70
Travel to the moon, in your car. R. M. Walsh. il Pop Sci 196:84-5 My '70
CRATERS, Moon. See Moon—Surface
CRATERS OF THE MOON NATIONAL MONUMENT
America's moonscape. E. K. Leonardson. il Travel 133:56-9 Je '70
CRAVEN, Stephen E. and others
Attine fungus gardens contain yeasts. bibliog il Science 169:184-6 Jl 10 '70
CRAWFORD, Blaine. See Faux, E. J. jt. auth.

CRAWFORD, Constance
  Be nice to Mr Mitchell; story. McCalls 98:
    64-5 N '70
CRAWFORD, Don
  On the boards. por Dance Mag 44:27 Ag '70 *
CRAWFORD, Frances M.
  Hospitable Newport. il Am Home 73:60-1 Ag
    '70
CRAWFORD, Kenneth
  Swan song; last column before retirement.
    por Newsweek 76:20 D 28 '70
  Washington. See issues of Newsweek

about

  Salute to a valedictorian. por Newsweek 76:
    3 D 28 '70 *
CRAWFORD, Marc
  Viva Mantequilla. il pors Ebony 25:58-60+ Mr
    '70
CRAWFORD, Robert W.
  One more time! V. Kendrick. il por Parks
    & Rec 5:26-8 Je '70 *
CRAWFORD, W. L.
  Do-it-yourself solves some problems of rapid
    growth. il Am City 85:90+ S '70
CRAWL and creep therapy. See Brain dam-
  aged children—Education
CRAWLER vehicles
  Four-track crawler with hoverpads. D. Scott.
    il por Pop Sci 196:58-9+ My '70
  Meet the ASV; all season vehicle. F. C.
    Kilburn. il Mech Illus 66:74-5 N '70
  Rivet: the acrobatic tractor. D. Scott. il
    Pop Sci 197:83 O '70
  Snow eagle: first of the fast ATVs. J. Joseph.
    il Pop Mech 133:108-11 Ja '70
CRAYFISH
  Crayfish swimming: alternating motor output
    and giant fiber activity. J. E. Schrameck.
    bibliog il Science 169:698-700 Ag 14 '70
  See also
  Cookery—Shellfish
CRAYFISH fishing
  Crayfish. il Sunset 144:88-91 Je '70
CRAYON painting. See Encaustic painting
CRAZY Horse (Sioux Indian)

Statues, portraits, etc.

  How to carve a mountain. J. M. Liston.
    il por Pop Mech 133:76-9+ Je '70
  Man and his mountain; carving a statue of
    Chief Crazy Horse out of a solid granite
    mountain, the South Dakota Black Hills. il
    por Design 71:22-3 mid-Wint '70
CRAZY Willie and the choco-bars; story. See
  Prescott, K.
CREAL, Margaret
  Family life and early sorrows; story. Ladies
    Home J 87:38 Je '70
CREAM puffs. See Pastry
CREAMS, Shaving. See Shaving soap and cream
CREAMS for the face. See Cosmetics
CREASON, Frank, and Schilson, D. L.
  Cooperative center promotes development in
    the social studies. Clear House 44:411-14
    Mr '70
CREATION
  Test tubes and scripture. F. Stockwell. Chr
    Cent 87:528-31 Ap 29 '70
CREATION (literary, artistic, etc)
  Art and the special child. J. A. Parker. il
    Sch Arts 69:32-3 Mr '70
  Intimations of mortality. N. Lynton. Art in
    Am 58:43 N '70
  Six in the arts and how they live. House B
    112:51 F '70
  Teaching of creativity. H. H. Rempel. il De-
    sign 71:20 mid-Wint '70
  See also
  Creative writing
CREATIVE ability
  Dewey, Dixon, and the future of creativity.
    M. Nystrand and S. Zeiser. Engl J 59:1138-
    40 N '70
  Test your creativity. J. E. Gibson. Sci Di-
    gest 68:23-4+ S '70
CREATIVE arts festival. See Festivals—Ohio
CREATIVE education
  Creativity takes over; Attleboro, Mass, visual
    arts program. L. Rich. il Am Ed 6:16-22
    D '70
  Does humanity grow in your classroom? En-
    glish composition and literature. F. E. Wil-
    helms. Schol Teach Jr/Sr High p34-5 S 21
    '70
  Five steps to creativity. D.-E. Coggins. il
    Parents Mag 45:52-3+ Mr '70
  Karton kooks; creativity through art, Spring
    Branch independent school district, Hous-
    ton, Tex. J. Smith. il Sch Arts 69:10-11 Je
    '70
  Talent runs free at the Twin Cities in-
    stitute. C. Watson. il Am Ed 6:3-6 O
    '70
  See also
Education. Experimental

CREATIVE imagination. See Imagination
CREATIVE photography
  Egg comes first. J. Dreyfuss. il Mod Phot 34:
    96-9 Ja '70
CREATIVE teaching. See Creative education
CREATIVE writing
  What does student writing tell us? R. G. Hol-
    land. Todays Ed 59:37-8+ My '70

Competitions
  See Literature—Competitions

Study and teaching

  Another idea: teaching creative writing un-
    der government grants. B. S. Everett.
    Writers Digest 50:30+ O '70
  Audience-directed writing: magazines and
    personae. H. Rank. Engl J 59:405-8 Mr '70
  How a diary encouraged creative writing. N.
    K. Stroh. Ed Digest 35:54-5 Ja '70
  Students writing that sells. W. Swearingen.
    Todays Ed 59:31 F '70
  Teaching writing; Teachers and writers col-
    laborative newsletter and Foxfire. J. Feath-
    erstone. New Repub 163:11-14 Jl 11 '70
  Theory of the curriculum in composition:
    goals and writing assignments. R. L. Lar-
    son. Engl J 59:393-404+ Mr '70
  Writing workshop: what is it? B. Strout.
    Engl J 59:1128-30 N '70
CRÈCHES. See Christmas cribs
CREDIT
  Bottomless pit of capital demand. il Bsns
    W p 158-60+ O 17 '70
  Credit; cartoons. J. Noonan. Cath World 211:
    128-9 Je '70
  Line-of-credit: a plan to borrow. il Suc Farm
    68:43 S '70
  Money markets and interest rates: an in-
    flationary environment; address, April 29,
    1970. T. C. Gaines. Vital Speeches 36:536-9
    Je 15 '70
  Need a loan? First check these interest rates.
    il Good H 171:190 O '70
  On paper, things look a bit looser. il Bsns W
    p33 F 28 '70
  Reviving confidence in the financial mar-
    kets. il Fortune 82:20+ Ag '70
  Spur of credit. C. Morgello. il Newsweek 76:82
    O 5 '70
  Tight money's painful payoff; cash squeeze. il
    Bsns W p28-9 Je 20 '70
  See also
  Agricultural credit
  Charge accounts (retail trade)
  Collecting of accounts
  Consumer credit
  Credit unions
  Debtor and creditor
  Farm finance
  Finance—United States
  Finance companies
  Government lending
  Loans
  Loans, Bank
  Loans, Foreign
  Loans, Personal
  Negotiable instruments
  United States—Federal reserve board

Information services
  See Credit bureaus
CREDIT associations. See Credit unions
CREDIT bureaus
  Detour to 1984. A. R. Miller. Nation 210:
    648-51 Je 1 '70
CREDIT cards
  Can 50 million Americans be wrong? N. Git-
    telson. Harp Baz 104:16+ Ja '71
  Charge-a-tax; service for holders of Bank-
    Americard or MasterCharge card. il Time 95:
    70 Ja 26 '70
  Charge-account bankers: the new merchants.
    il Consumer Rep 36:49-54 Ja '71
  Credit cards: boon to beef sales? O. Bay. il
    Farm J 93:B10-11+ N '69
  Credit cards: easy come, easy go? il Sr Schol
    96:15-16 Mr 23 '70
  From Dustbowl to Saigon: the "Peoples
    bank" builds an empire; BankAmericard.
    M. Sweeney. il por Ramp Mag 9:42-3 N '70
  Hazards of unsolicited credit cards. B.
    Furness. il McCalls 97:58+ My '70
  Hidden costs of credit cards; bank credit
    cards. M. S. Schlosberg and L. M. An-
    drews. Nation 210:240-2 Mr 2 '70
  Learning to live with the credit card. F. Pow-
    ledge. Esquire 74:210-17+ N '70
  Little gift from your friendly banker. P.
    O'Neil. il Life 68:48-50A Mr 27 '70
  Now, safeguards for credit-card holders. il
    U S News 69:64 N 9 '70
  Saying charge it to tax collector. U S News
    68:91-2 Ja 26 '70

CREDIT cards—*Continued*
Those charge anything anywhere credit cards. il Changing T 24:6-10 Mr '70
  See also
American express company
ITO commercial credit card, inc.
CREDIT managers
Rise of the credit manager. T. J. Murray. il Duns 96:48-9+ N '70
CREDIT reporting agencies. See Credit bureaus
CREDIT system. See Grading and marking (students)
CREDIT unions
Big share of safety for credit unions. il Bsns W p26 S 5 '70
Uses of credit associations; highlights of panel discussion. Pub W 198:43-4 Jl 27 '70
CREDULITY

    Anecdotes, facetiae, satire, etc.
Day in the life: believer of all he reads and hears. Nat R 22:933 S 8 '70
CREELEY, Robert
Comment. J. McGann. Poetry 117:200-3 D '70 *
Comment. G. Sorrentino. Poetry 116:112-14 My '70 *
CRÉMIEUX, Robert Ezechiel
Pope's Jews. por Time 96:49 Ag 24 '70 *
CRENSHAW COUNTY, Ala.
U.S. journal: Luverne, Ala. G. T. Miller's plan to help despite trouble with the Klan. C. Trillin. New Yorker 46:53-8 Ag 29 '70
CREPES. See Griddle cakes
CRESAP, McCormick and Paget, inc. See Business consultants
CRESSEY, Donald Ray
Organized crime. New Repub 163:12-13 Jl 18 '70
CRETACEOUS period. See Paleontology—Cretaceous
CRETINISM
Cretinism in rats: enduring behavioral deficit induced by tricyanoaminopropene. J. W. Davenport. bibliog il Science 167:1007-9 F 13 '70
CREUTZ, Edward C.
Creutz sees a gradual increase in NSF support of applied science; interview. por Phys Today 23:61-3 N '70
Nuclear power: rise of an industry. il por Bul Atom Sci 26:75-82 Je '70
CREWE, Albert V.
—and others
Visibility of single atoms. bibliog il Science 168:1338-40 Je 12 '70

    about
Individual atoms photographed. il Sci N 97:524 My 30 '70 *
CREWE, Quentin
He spoke to me. He won't do that again. Vogue 156:148 Ag 1 '70
London. Vogue 155:106+ Mr 1; 62 Ap 15 '70
Natural phenomenon of N.Y. taxi drivers. Vogue 155:24 Mr 15 '70
New York restaurants. Vogue 155:154+ My '70
Paris restaurants. Vogue 156:38 O 15 '70
Rome restaurants. Vogue 156:276+ S 1 '70
CREWEL work
One stitch led to another; crewelwork designs in an eighteenth-century Connecticut farmhouse. R. Reif. il N Y Times Mag p66-7 Mr 1 '70
CREWMEN. See Seamen
CRIB deaths. See Infant mortality
CRIBBAGE boards
Antler cribbage board. R. Drayna. il Outdoor Life 145:199 Mr '70
CRICHTON, J. Michael
Five patients; excerpt. Ladies Home J 87:34+ Jl '70
High cost of cure: excerpt from Five patients. Atlan 225:49-57 Mr '70
People are talking about... por Vogue 156:100-1 S 15 '70 *
CRICHTON, Michael. See Crichton, J. M.
CRICK, Francis Harry Compton
DNA: test of structure? Science 167:1694 Mr 27 '70
CRICKET (game)
Letter from London; trouble over opposed visit of the white South African team. M. Panter-Downes. New Yorker 46:77-8 My 30 '70
Not quite cricket; British controversy over the South African team. il Newsweek 75:65-6 My 18 '70
Rite of summer. T. S. Matthews. Am Scholar 39:463-7 Sum '70; Reply. J. E. Gale. 39:732 Aut '70

CRICKET frogs. See Frogs
CRICKETS
Postembryonic development of adult motor patterns in crickets: a neural analysis. D. R. Bentley and R. R. Hoy. bibliog il Science 170:1409-11 D 25 '70
Why the cricket chirps. il Time 96:39 Ag 24 '70
CRIME and criminals
Bad names; descendants of infamous people. il Esquire 74:73-7 Jl '70
Congenital criminals? Johns Hopkins project. Newsweek 75:98-9 My 18 '70
  See also
Assassination
Bribery
Burglary and burglars
Capital punishment
Castration of criminals and defectives
Conspiracy
Crime prevention
Detectives
Embezzlement
Fugitives from justice
Insane, Criminal and dangerous
Justice, Administration of
Juvenile delinquency
Kidnapping
Loan sharks
Mafia
Murder
Negroes—Crime
Outlaws
Parole
Prisoners
Prisons
Punishment
Robberies and assaults
Self defense
Shoplifting
Treason
  also headings beginning Criminal

    Economic aspects
Crime costs to taxpayers are soaring: no end in sight. il U S News 69:18-19 D 28 '70
Crime expense now up to 51 billions a year. il U S News 69:30-4 O 26 '70

    International aspects
  See also
United Nations congress on the prevention of crime and the treatment of offenders

    California
  See also
Justice, Administration of—California

    Florida
Letters from James Blake: southern con. American author. J. Blake. Esquire 74:76-9+ Ag '70

    France
Tempting the devil; gang of bank robbers. Time 96:28 N 30 '70
  See also
Embezzlement

    Great Britain
Parting shots; Clarence the Ripper? P. O'Neil. il pors Life 69:85-8 N 13 '70
Who was Jack the Ripper? por Time 96:29 N 9 '70
  See also
Gangs
London—Crime

    Italy
Arrangement; the Casati case in Italy. il por Newsweek 76:52 S 21 '70

    Latin America
  See also
Kidnapping

    Louisiana
  See also
Mafia

    New Jersey
Murder New Jersey style; Judy Kavanaugh case. C. S. Wren and M. English. il Look 34:43-7 Mr 10 '70
People v. the mob: or, Who rules New Jersey? F. J. Cook. il N Y Times Mag p9-11 F 1 '70
  See also
Mafia

    Southern states
Muckraker's progress. Time 96:73 O 26 '70

    United States
Attorney General Mitchell: the tide is turning against crime; interview. J. N. Mitchell. il pors Nations Bsns 58:32-4+ Je '70
Crime in America, by R. Clark. Review
Life 69:20 N 13 '70. R. Sherrill
Sat R 53:35-7 N 28 '70. F. T. P. Plimpton

CRIME and criminals—United States—*Cont.*
Crime: some call it dissent; address, March 30, 1970. W. V. Chappell, jr. Vital Speeches 36:423-5 My 1 '70
Crime still rising, but pace is slower. il U S News 69:48 Ag 24 '70
Future cities: armed forts? il U S News 69: 39 S 21 '70
Justice; a bad week for the good guys. il pors Time 96:6-9 Ag 17 '70
Justice in a torn nation; interview, ed. R. Sherrill. R. Clark. Nation 211:587-91 D 7 '70
Little big man who laughs at the law; M. Lansky. N. Gage. il pors Atlan 226:62-9 Jl '70
More aid for cities in war against crime. il U S News 68:36-8 F 23 '70
Only the people as a whole can cure crime. D. Lawrence. U S News 68:92 Mr 9 '70
Organized crime: is it America's other government? il Sr Schol 96:5-9 Ap 6 '70
Shocking success story of public enemy no. 1; M. Lansky. W. Schulz. por Read Digest 96:54-9 My '70
What the police can, and cannot do about crime. il Time 96:34-6+ Jl 13 '70
Why streets are not safe; special report on crime. il U S News 68:15-21 Mr 16 '70
See also
Bronx, N.Y.—Crime
Gambling
Mafia
Negroes—Crime
Police—United States
Prisons—United States
Racketeering
United States—Federal bureau of investigation
Vigilance committees
also subhead Crime under names of cities, e.g. Atlanta—Crime

History
Professional criminals of America, by T. Byrnes. Review
Am Heritage il 21:37-9 Je '70. B. Klaw

Uruguay
See also
Kidnapping
CRIME and insanity. See Insane, Criminal and dangerous
CRIME and the press
How to handle violence. il por Time 95:40 Ja 26 '70
See also
Newspaper court reporting
CRIME as a campaign issue. See Campaign issues
CRIME control laws and legislation. See Crime prevention
CRIME in literature
See also
Detective and mystery stories
CRIME novels. See Detective and mystery stories
CRIME prevention
Anomaly of crime prevention; preventive detention clause and the no-knock provision. America 123:54 Ag 8 '70
Anticrime pace in Congress: much talk, little action. il U S News 69:22-4 Jl 27 '70
Citizens' war on crime; spreading across U.S. il U S News 68:55-8 Mr 23 '70; Same abr. with title America's citizen crime fighters. Read Digest 96:225-6+ Je '70
Crime-control act for capital: a model for the Nation? il U S News 69:59 Ag 3 '70
Crime fight progress: a police-GE product. V. Louviere. il Nations Bsns 58:19 Ap '70
Curbing crime; a policeman speaks out; interview. J. J. Harrington. Read Digest 97: 202+ D '70
Don't be a crime target. F. Robinson. Read Digest 97:107-10 O '70
Easy marks; protecting the taxi driver. il Time 96:84 S 21 '70
Ends and means; District of Columbia crime-control bill. Newsweek 76:21-2 Jl 27 '70
Fanatics at play; T. Wicker's opposition to the omnibus anticrime bill. W. F. Buckley, jr. Nat R 22:272 Mr 10 '70
How to outwit gun thieves. G. X. Sand. Field & S 75:54-5+ D '70
How to stop rise in crime; interview. L. Jaworski. il por U S News 69:40-3 Jl 20 '70
It's a crime. R. W. Dietsch. New Repub 162: 9-10 Je 13 '70
Lawlessness and disorder. Nation 210:770-1 Je 29 '70
Leader in drive to cut crime. por U S News 68:12 F 2 '70
More aid for cities in war against crime. il U S News 68:36-8 F 23 '70

Public safety and private rights. il Time 96: 30+ Jl 27 '70
Response to fear; D.C. crime bill. il por Time 96:10 Ag 3 '70
S.30: the seeds of repression; District of Columbia crime bill, with editorial comment. H. Schwartz. Nation 211:67, 70-1 Ag 3 '70
Soft-headed on crime; Organized crime control act of 1970. New Repub 163:5-6 O 24 '70
Some here-and-now steps to cut crime. E. K. Faltermayer. il Fortune 82:94-9+ Jl '70
Trading law for order; crime and drug control legislation. R. C. Eckhardt. Nation 211:687-90 D 28 '70
TRB from Washington; Organized crime control act of 1970. New Repub 163:4 O 17 '70
Tydings of no joy. A. Campbell. New Repub 162:10 Je 27 '70
United Nations and the prevention of crime. W. Clifford. UN Mo Chron 7:65-70 My '70
What Congress is doing about crime. il Nations Bsns 58:42-5 Ja '70
See also
Juvenile delinquency—Prevention
Police
United States—Justice. Department of—Law enforcement assistance administration

Citizen participation
Organized citizens vs. organized crime. il Nations Bsns 58:31-4 N '70

Study and teaching
See Criminological education
CRIME prevention exhibit. See Exhibitions. Traveling
CRIMEA conference, Yalta, Russia, 1945
FDR: the untold story of his last year; Yalta conference. J. M. Burns. il por Sat R 53:12-15+ Ap 11 '70
CRIMES. War. See War crimes
CRIMES aboard aircraft
Dilemma of the airlines. il Newsweek 75:33-4+ Mr 9 '70
ICAO actions may reduce aircraft civil violence threat. Aviation W 93:24 Jl 13 '70
See also
Airplane hijacking
CRIMES against humanity
Safety of diplomats and other people. N. Cousins. Sat R 53:26 Ap 25 '70
CRIMES and crimes; drama. See Strindberg, A.
CRIMINAL investigation
Investigative reporter: Ray Brennan; interview, ed. by C. Remsberg and B. Remsberg. il por Writers Digest 50:20-3+ F '70
Mystery of the unknown getaway car. Consumer Rep 35:73-4 F '70
See also
Electronics in criminal investigation, espionage, etc.
Television in criminal investigation
CRIMINAL justice, Administration of. See Justice, Administration of
CRIMINAL justice studies. See Criminological education
CRIMINAL law
Mitchell tests the Constitution. J. R. Lundy. Nation 210:205-7 F 23 '70
See also
Accomplices
Contempt of court
Crimes against humanity
Criminal procedure
Obscenity (law)
CRIMINAL procedure
Criminal justice in times of turbulence; excerpt from Crime in America. R. Clark. Sat R 53:21-4+ S 19 '70
High cost of criminal laws. America 123: 310-11 O 24 '70
Logjam in our courts; with editorial comment. D. Wittner. il Life 69:2A, 18-25 Ag 7 '70
More justice to come? G. L. Hallworth. America 122:390-1 Ap 11 '70
Nixon's plea: stop making heroes out of criminals; excerpts from remarks, August 3, 1970. R. M. Nixon. il por U S News 69: 70 Ag 17 '70
Trading law for order; dangerous offender category. R. C. Eckhardt. Nation 211:687-90 D 28 '70
What's needed to speed up justice; interview. E. B. Williams. il pors U S News 69:94-8 S 21 '70
See also
Arrest
Bail
Congressional conference on justice in America
Courts martial and courts of inquiry
Jury
Pleas (criminal procedure)
Preventive detention

CRIMINAL procedure—*Continued*

Study and teaching
See Criminological education
CRIMINALS. See Crime and criminals
CRIMINALS; drama. See Triana, J.
CRIMINOLOGICAL education
Criminal justice studies: a quietly emerging field. N. Gruchow. Science 167:1474 Mr 13 '70
CRIMINOLOGICAL laboratories
See also
United States—Federal bureau of investigation—Crime laboratory
CRIMINOLOGY. See Crime and criminals
CRIMMIN, Eileen
Bathtub racing circuit. il Motor B 126:50+ Ag '70
Closed course racing. il Motor B 126:54-9+ Ag '70
Gourmet ashore. il Motor B 125:61+ Je '70
Samoa. il Motor B 126:55-7+ N '70
Steam lives! il Motor B 126:48-9+ S '70
CRIMP, Douglas
Georgia is a state of mind. il Art N 69: 48-51+ O '70
CRINER, David
Growing Jerusalem artichokes with corn. il Org Gard & Farm 17:90-2 Mr '70
CRINKLEY, Richmond
Theater (cont) Nat R 22:319, 745, 851-2, 1308-9; 23:45-6 Mr 24, Jl 14, Ag 11, D 1 '70, Ja 12 '71
CRISIS; story. See Plagemann, B.
CRISPUS Attucks memorial monument. See Boston—Monuments, statues, etc.
CRISS-crossing; drama. See Magdalany. P.
CRISTOFANO, S. M.
One-man refuse collection crews. Am City 85: 86-8 Ap '70
CRISTOL, Allan H.
We need sheltered workshops for former mental patients. Ment Hy 54:444-6 Jl '70
CRITCHLOW, James
Bear & the dragon at war over science. Commonweal 91:572-3 F 27 '70
Episode in the life of Solzhenitsyn. por Commonweal 93:278-80 D 11 '70
CRITICAL flicker-fusion threshold. See Flicker phenomena
CRITICAL point
Neutron scattering verifies dynamic scaling. G. B. Lubkin. bibliog il Phys Today 23:59+ F '70
CRITICAL thinking. See Thought and thinking
CRITICISM
Critics on the critics; Harris survey, critics and criticism in the mass media. R. L. Shayon. Sat R 53:52-3 Mr 21 '70
See also
Educational criticism
Literary criticism
Moving picture criticism
CRITICISM, Personal. See Self evaluation
CRITICS
Apostle to the gentiles; drama critic. J. Lahr. F. Hirsch. Nation 211:600-1 D 7 '70
Confusion of realms, by R. Gilman. Review Commentary 49:61-4 Mr '70. G. Vidal
Critic prepares; work conference on dance criticism. S. J. Cohen. il Dance Mag 44: 24 F '70
Critics on the critics; Harris survey critics and criticism in the mass media. R. L. Shayon. Sat R 53:52-3 Mr 21 '70
Cruel, cruel critics; movie critics. S. Koch. il Sat R 53:12-14+ D 26 '70
Film critics; Lewis Jacobs and Andrew Sarris. B. Bendow. Nation 211:344+ O 12 '70
Learning to look, the Connecticut college American dance festival critics conference. E. W. Jacobs. il Dance Mag 44:24+ O '70
See also
Book reviewers and reviewing
Ebert, R.
Kael P.
Krutch, J. W.
Literary criticism
Music critics
Poetry—History and criticism
CRITTENDEN, George
Unspoiled pike of Washahigan Lake. il Field & S 75:60-1+ My '70
CRITTENDEN, Jordon
Impostor; story. Harp Baz 103:214-17 S '70
CRITTENDEN, L. B. and others
Susceptibility to an avian leukosis-sarcoma virus: close association with an erythrocyte isoantigen. bibliog il Science 169:1324-5 S 25 '70
CROCE, Arlene
Moiseyev and us. Atlan 26:128-30+ N '70

CROCHETING
Crochet it white and bright. il Redbook 134: 84-5+ F '70
Crocheting craze has them hooked. il Bsns W p35 Ja 31 '70
Striking fashions to crochet & weave. il Good H 171:110-12+ Ag '70
CROCKENBERG, Susan Belden. See Sieber, J. E. jt. auth.
CROCKER, John F. S. and Vernier, R. L.
Fetal kidney in organ culture: abnormalities of development induced by decreased amounts of potassium. bibliog il Science 169:485-7 Jl 31 '70
CROCKETT, George William, 1909-
Black thoughts of Judge Crockett. J. H. Dygert. Esquire 74:120+ D '70 *
Judge in a city of fear. il por Time 95:60 Ap 6 '70 *
CROCKETT, James Underwood
In your greenhouse. See issues of Horticulture
CROCKETT, Lela
Good planning plus imagination equals happy eating. il Camp Mag 42:25 Ja '70
CROCUSES
Crocus in now for early color. il Sunset 145: 216 O '70
Crocuses. M. M. Graff. il Horticulture 48: 18-21 O '70
CROFFORD, Oscar B. See Mann, G. V. jt. auth.
CROGHAN, Leo M.
Farewell to the tribunal. il America 123:227-9 O 3 '70
CROLEY, Victor A.
Annual hibiscus, as easy to grow as zinnias! il Org Gard & Farm 17:59 Jl '70
CROMER, George Rowland Stanley Baring, 3d earl of
Classy choice. il por Newsweek 76:55-6 N 23 '70 *
CRONEBERGER, Robert B. and Welbourne, J. C. Jr
Triumph & tragedy: a play in two acts. il pors Library J 95:1705-8 My 1 '70
CRONIN, Sister Maureen
Non-military dimensions of NATO. America 123:89-90 Ag 22 '70
CRONIN, Sean
Conspiracy in Ireland. Commonweal 93:188-90 N 20 '70
CRONK, Edwin M.
Improving the trading opportunities of the developing countries through generalized preferences; statement, March 31, 1970. Dept State Bul 62:612-15 My 11 '70
CRONKITE, Walter, 1916-
What does Walter Cronkite really think? interview, ed. by O. Fallaci. il pors Look 34: 57-62 N 17 '70
What it's like to broadcast news; excerpt from address. por Sat R 53:53-5 D 12 '70

about

Memoirs from beyond the tomb; L. Johnson-W. Cronkite TV interviews. R. Kuttner. Commonweal 91:606-7 Mr 6 '70 *
Newsman in the middle. P. Hudson. por Sr Schol 96:20 Ap 27 '70 *
CRONYN, Willard M.
Interstellar scattering of pulsar radiation and its effect on the spectrum of NP0532. bibliog il Science 168:1453-5 Je 19 '70
CROOK, Mel
Compleat company. il Yachting 127:64-6+ Ap '70
More power to you. See issues of Yachting

about

Mel Crook recipient of sixteenth annual Ole Evinrude award. il por Yachting 127:47 Mr '70 *
CROP estimating. See Agricultural forecasts
CROP forecasts. See Agricultural forecasts
CROP reporting service. See Agricultural forecasts
CROP reports. See Agriculture—Statistics
CROP yields
Extra light boosts soybean yields 25 per cent. Farm. J 94:28D N '70
Light could be limiting your corn yields. C. E. Sommers. il Suc Farm 68:no5 24-5+ Mr '70
Make those harvest checks. C. E. Sommers. il Suc Farm 68:32-3 O '70
See also
Soil productivity rating

CRUCIFIXION of Christ. See Jesus Christ—Crucifixion

CRUDDACE, R. G. See Buchanan, S. jt. auth.

CRUDE oil. See Petroleum

CRUELTY, Theater of. See Theater, Experimental

CRUELTY to animals. See Animals—Treatment

CRUET stands
Continental pewter epergnes, cruet stands, and sugar bowls. R. M. Vetter. il Antiques 98:88-93 Jl '70

CRUICKSHANK, Alexander M.
Gordon research conferences; 1970 program. Science 167:1390-402+ Mr 6 '70

CRUIKSHANK, Dale P.
Planetary astronomer visits the Soviet Union. il Sky & Tel 39:76-9 F '70

CRUIKSHANK, Douglas E. and Arnold, W. R.
Nondecimal instruction revisited. Ed Digest 35:44-5 F '70

CRUISERS (pleasure boats)
Accommodations for the cruising boat. P. L. Rhodes. il por Motor B 125:128-33 Mr '70
All about displacement cruisers. F. C. Clark, jr. il Motor B 126:38-41+ S '70
Basic power cruisers. D. Martin. il por Motor B 125:112-13 Ja '70
Cabin rises to the occasion on new sailing cruiser. H. Luckett. il Pop Sci 197:59 Ag '70
Carvel day cruiser; hot runabout with a foc 'sle. J. Roe. il Pop Sci 196:74-5 Je '70
Cruisers. il Motor B 125:182-91+ Ja '70
Cruisers and houseboats '71; what's new for the new year? T. Gibbs. il Motor B 126:54-60+ O '70
Displacement cruisers. C. Wittholz. il por Motor B 125:116-17 Ja '70
Inland cruising; Texas lakes. D. Wood. il por Yachting 127:82-3+ My '70
Motorsailers. P. L. Rhodes. il por Motor B 125:114-15 Ja '70
Offshore cruisers, power & sail. F. MacLear. il por Motor B 125:110-11 Ja '70
Pastime returns to the coast. G. W. Capley. il Yachting 127:54-5+ My '70
Traditional cruising boats. J. Atkin. il por Motor B 125:94-5 Ja '70

Design
From Anchorage to Acapulco: the next boat. B. Crabtree. il Yachting 129:70-1+ Ja '71

Equipment
Customizing stock cruisers. G. Manning. il Motor B 125:56-9+ Ap '70

CRUISERS, Fishing. See Fishing boats

CRUISES. See Cruising

CRUISING
Alaska south. il Yachting 127:110-11+ Ja '70
Armchair cruising; symposium. il Yachting 127:54-66+ Mr '70
At sea with the Union Jacks; aboard the Oriana. H. Sutton. il Sat R 53:43-5 F 7 '70
By outboard to Georgian Bay. Hiro; T. Yamashiro; P. Yamashiro. il Motor B 125:112-17 Mr '70
California's-eye view of the ICW. H. M. Rizer. il Motor B 125:72-3+ My '70
Choosing a vacation waterway; ed. by F. M. Paulson. il Field & S 75:122-7 My '70
Cove hopping Havasu. M. Rizer. il Motor B 126:48-9+ N '70
Craziest cruise afloat; with Arizona gringos in a Mexican shrimp boat. W. H. Porter. il Motor B 126:46-7+ O '70
Cruises, cruisers and cruising; symposium. il Motor B 125:91-139+ Mr '70
Cruising is where you find it; making the most of Lake Michigan. R. M. Withrow. il Yachting 128:58-9+ Jl '70
Cruising to Alaska. il Sunset 144:85-6 Ap '70
80,000 miles by outboard. R. Marston. il Yachting 127:67+ Ap '70
Exploring Lake Powell. C. L. Cadieux. il Yachting 128:72-3+ N '70
First time south. T. Kelly. il Yachting 128:66-7+ O '70
Florida for the boatman in 1970. E. S. Maloney. il Motor B 126:52-4 N '70
Four new ways to skin the cruising cat. J. G. Mearns; J. Seville. Motor B 125:126-7 Mr '70
Inland cruising; Texas lakes. D. Wood. il por Yachting 127:82-3+ My '70
Journey south to a cold summer; Lindblad winter trip to Antarctica. M. Hemingway. il por Sports Illus 33:44-8 N 2 '70
Kansas to Ketchikan. R. H. Frederickson. il Yachting 128:56-7+ D '70
Kicking the habit on the high seas; Santa Paula's stop-smoking cruise. Bsns W p31 S 26 '70

Kicking the habit; report on Santa Paula's stop-smoking cruise. B. McCabe. il Time 96:64 D 14 '70
Leisurely cruising, Donzi style. W. J. Schieffelin, 3rd. il Yachting 127:58-9+ F '70
Malawi: portrait of a lake. G. Ross. il Travel 134:34-9+ N '70
Northland memory. C. Mitchell. il Yachting 129:66-9+ Ja '71
Party cruise; Los Angeles to Guadalupe Island. C. Pepper. il Travel 135:58-61 Ja '71
Relax on Maine's inland waterways. D. Becker. il Travel 133:68-70 Je '70
Rift in the curtain; the Dalmatian coast. C. Mitchell. il Yachting 128:50-2+ Jl; 53-5+ Ag '70
Southern yachting: special report. il Yachting 128:53-67+ N '70
To the tip of Cape Cod. B. Schill and B. Schill. il Yachting 128:56-8 Ag '70
Travel notes:
Cruise on the Arcadia from Vancouver to Alaska. R. Joseph. Esquire 74:52+ O '70
Cruising along western Europe's inland waterways. R. Joseph. Esquire 74:62+ O '70
Two exotic, off-beat winter vacations. C. Landau; E. Crimmin. il Motor B 126:55-7+ N '70
Up north or down east. K. Collins. il Motor B 126:52-3+ O '70
Voyage of a retired navy tug: an offbeat odyssey. N. N. Baxter. il Motor B 125:140-4+ Ap '70
See also
River trips
Voyages

Anecdotes, facetiae, satire, etc.
101 hints for cruising guests. M. E. Slate. il Motor B 125:123+ Mr '70

Canada
Fjord-hopping by trawler-yacht through Princess Louisa Inlet. B. Crabtree. il Yachting 127:54-5+ Mr '70

Caribbean Region
Houseboats among the Virgins. G. F. Hammond. il Motor B 126:38-41+ D '70
In the wake of Columbus: Windjammer cruises. S. Hart. il Travel 134:28-33+ O '70
Offbeat Caribbean: Haiti. J. Laird. il Yachting 127:58-9+ Mr; 57-9+ Ap '70

Papua-New Guinea (territory)
Heart of New Guinea. C. Heacock. il Yachting 127:64-6+ Mr '70

Scandinavia
Baltic Baedeker. F. C. Clark, jr. il Motor B 125:60-1+ My '70

Scotland
Scotland's monster lake. B. Bell. il Travel 133:60-2 Je '70

CRUISING houseboats. See Houseboats

CRUISING with children. See Travel with children

CRUMLEY, Francis V.
Rescue missions broaden ministries. D. Kucharsky. Chr Today 14:41-3 F 13 '70 •

CRUMMERE, Maria Elise
Horoscope. See Issues of Vogue

CRUMPLER, Jane
Living with uncertainty: the families who wait back home. il pors Time 96:18-19 D 7 '70

CRUSH, Marion
Overdue. por. Wilson Lib Bul 45:180-1 O '70

CRUSO, Thalassa
Gardener speaks her mind; interview. House & Gard 138:24+ O '70

CRUSTACEANS
Reproductive system of hutchinsoniella macracantha. A. Y. Hessler and others. bibliog il Science 168:1464 Je 19 '70
See also
Barnacles
Beach fleas
Copepods
Crabs
Crayfish
Nervous system—Crustaceans

Migration
Migration of the spiny lobster. W. F. Herrnkind. il Natur Hist 79:36-43 bibliog(p79) My '70

CRUSTACEANS, Fossil
Isopod from the Pennsylvanian of Illinois; Hesslerella shermani. F. R. Schram. bibliog il Science 169:854-5 Ag 28 '70
CRUTCHFIELD, Doug
Thanks to Doug Crutchfield Fru Nilsen can dance again. il Ebony 25:86-91 Ap '70 *
CRUZ, Victor Hernandez
Comment. N. Sullivan. Poetry 116:120-5 My '70 *
CRUZ-ROMO, Gilda
Latin expression. R. Zachary. il por Opera N 35:32-3 D 19 '70 *
CRY for us all; musical comedy. See Musical comedies, revues, etc.—Criticisms, plots, etc.
CRYDERMAN, Jim
Equestrian husbandry courses. Parks & Rec 5:42 F '70
CRYING
See also
Infants—Crying
CRYOBIOLOGY
Cryobiology: the freezing of biological systems. P. Mazur. bibliog il Science 168:939-49 My 22 '70
CRYOGENICS. See Low temperatures
CRYPTOGAMS
See also
Lichens
CRYPTOGRAPHY
Cryptic computers. Sci Am 222:52 Ja '70
Literate Incas; written language hidden in geometric designs, tocapus. il Time 96:49 Ag 17 '70
CRYSTAL cave; story. See Stewart, M.
CRYSTAL lenses. See Lenses, Photographic
CRYSTAL oscillators. See Oscillators, Crystal
CRYSTAL receivers. See Radio receivers
CRYSTALLIZATION
Crystallization of some lunar mafic magmas and generation of rhyolitic liquid. I. Kushiro and others. bibliog il Science 167:610-12 Ja 30 '70
Long-chain polymer crystals. A. Keller. bibliog il por Phys Today 23:42-50 My '70
CRYSTALLOGRAPHY
Chemical bond and solid-state physics; adaptation of address, March 1969. J. C. Phillips. bibliog il por Phys Today 23:23-30 F '70
Ionic bonding in solids. J. E. House, jr. bibliog il por Chem 43:18-22 F '70
Photographing the lead tree reaction. W. C. Ritz. bibliog il por Chem 43:28-9 S '70
Structural aspects of interatomic charge-transfer bonding; Nobel prize lecture, June 9, 1970. O. Hassel. bibliog il Science 170:497-502 O 30 '70
Superconductivity in layered structure organometallic crystals. F. R. Gamble and others. bibliog il Science 168:568-70 My 1 '70
Xenon hexafluoride: structure of a cubic phase at —80°C. R. D. Burbank and G. R. Jones. bibliog il Science 168:248-50 Ap 10 '70
See also
Crystallization
International union of crystallography
Liquid crystals
Polymorphism
X ray studies
Crystallography of DNA: difference synthesis supports Watson-Crick base pairing. S. Arnott. bibliog il Science 167:1694-700 Mr 27 '70
Diffraction and Mössbauer studies of minerals from lunar soils and rocks. P. Gay and others. bibliog il Science 167:626-8 Ja 30 '70
Fluorocitrate inhibition of aconitase: relative configuration of inhibitory isomer by X-ray crystallography. H. L. Carrell and others. bbliog il Science 170:1412-14 D 25 '70
Interferometry with X rays. M. Hart and U. Bonse. bibliog il pors Phys Today 23:26-31 Ag '70
Pyroxferroite: stability and X-ray crystallography of synthetic Ca$_{0.15}$ Fe$_{0.85}$ SiO$_3$ pyroxenoid. D. H. Lindsley and C. W. Burnham. bibliog il Science 168:364-7 Ap 17 '70
Revolution in crystallography. W. C. Hamilton. bibliog il Science 169:133-41 Jl 10 '70
CRYSTALS
Why do crystals form and why always in a certain shape? I. Asimov. Sci Digest 67:68-9 Ja '70
See also
Domain structure
Liquid crystals
Metal crystals
Conferences
Aspen conference on quantum crystals. N. R. Werthamer. Science 167:912-13 F 6 '70

CUADRA, Juan Francisco de la Bodega y.
See Bodega y Quadra, J. F. de la
CUADRA, Pablo Antonio
Hand and the head. il Américas 22:27-9 S '70
CUB scouts
Stories
Long live the lion. B. Rohde. Redbook 135:68-9 Je '70
CUBA
Cuba revisited after ten years of Castro. Viator. For Affairs 48:312-21 Ja '70
Cuba today; after eleven years of red rule. il U S News 68:48-9 Mr 9 '70
Lowdown from our man in Havana; author's experiences during Batista's reign of terror. G. Greene. Vogue 155:94-5+ Ap 15 '70
Today's Cuba and U.S. policy. W. Jeffries. Chr Cent 87:560-3 My 6 '70
See also
Bibliography, National—Cuba
Communism—Cuba
Education—Cuba
Negroes in Cuba
Science—Cuba
United Nations—Cuba
Defenses
Another test for U.S: threat of a Russian sub base in Cuba; submarine base at Cienfuegos. il U S News 69:22-3 O 12 '70
Economic conditions
Castro's failures, in his own words; excerpts from address, July 26, 1970. F. Castro. U S News 69:43 Ag 10 '70
Cuba revisited: how to see Havana without getting hijacked. W. Attwood. il por Look 34:15-17 Ap 7 '70
How Cuba has fared under its red ruler. il U S News 69:35-6 S 21 '70
Inside Cuba: workers and revolution; excerpt from Revolutionary politics and the Cuban working class. M. Zeitlin. il Ramp Mag 8:10-11+ Mr '70
Sugar si, prosperity no; Castro's big headache. il U S News 69:50-1 Jl 20 '70
Uptight about Cuba. E. Lamb. Nation 210:613-14 My 25 '70
See also
Communism—Cuba
Economic policy
Cuba's recent setbacks. E. Gonzalez. Cur 124:45-52 D '70
See also
Agricultural administration—Cuba
Foreign opinion
Letter from Camp Venceremos. C. Camarano. il Ramp Mag 9:6+ Ag '70
Foreign relations
Russia
See Russia—Foreign relations—Cuba
Politics and government
Castro on the contradictions in Cuba; excerpt from Guerrillas in power; with introd. by D. Horowitz. K. S. Karol. il Ramp Mag 9:43-8 D '70
Castro's time running out? il U S News 68:48-50 Mr 9 '70
Charisma or democratization? K. S. Karol. Cur 124:52-5 D '70
See also
Communism—Cuba
Social conditions
Cuba revisited: how to see Havana without getting hijacked. W. Attwood. il por Look 34:15-17 Ap 7 '70
See also
Communism—Cuba
CUBAN crisis, 1962
Irrationality and the Cuban missile crisis. Trans-Action 7:9 Ja '70
K. K. and K. Nat R 22:1386+ D 29 '70
Khrushchev: averting the apocalypse; gleanings from Khrushchev's memory. il por Time 96:31 D 21 '70
CUBAN refugees. See Refugees, Cuban
CUBANS in the United States
Bicultural Americans with a Hispanic tradition. A. D. Trejo. Wilson Lib Bul 44:722-3 Mr '70
See also
Refugees, Cuban
CUBISM
Cubism from all sides; exhibition at the Los Angeles County museum of art. il por Newsweek 76:65-6 D 28 '70

CUBS (baseball) See Baseball clubs

CUCKOOS
See also
Road-runners (birds)

CUCUMBERS
Put your melons in new ground. S. Fenell. il
Org Gard & Farm 17:72-3 Ap '70
We grow burpless cucumbers. M. J. Rozell.
il Org Gard & Farm 17:73 Je '70
What cucumbers are is adaptable. il Sunset
145:108 Ag '70

CUDDIHY, Michael
Friends; poem. Commonweal 93:302 D 18 '70
Night poem. Commonweal 91:556 F 20 '70

CUELLAR, Mike
Three Birds who mainly stay; Baltimore's
big three pitching staff. R. Blount, jr. il
pors Sports Illus 33:30-2+ O 12 '70 *

CUERNAVACA center. See Center of intercultural documentation

CUFF, Sergeant, pseud. See Winterich, J. T.

CULBERT, Samuel A. and Elden, J. M.
Anatomy of activism for executives. il Harvard Bsns R 48:131-42 N '70

CULEBRA ISLAND
AQAG to protest U.S. navy's test bombing
in Caribbean. Chr Cent 88:7 Ja 6 '71
Story of Culebra. Nation 211:133-4 Ag 31 '70

CULHANE, John
Report card on Sesame street. il N Y Times
Mag p34-5+ My 24 '70
Yachtsmen of Seawanhaka are different from
you and me. il N Y Times Mag p30-1+ S 13
'70

CULLBERG, Birgit
Sons and mothers: Niklas Ek and Birgit Cullberg. G. Loney. il pors Dance Mag 44:32-7
Ap '70 *

CULLERS, Benjamin. See Fink, N. W. jt.
auth.

CULLERS, Robert L. and others
Gadolinium: distribution between aqueous and
silicate phases. bibliog il Science 169:580-3
Ag 7 '70

CULLIGAN, Matthew Joseph
Culligan at Curtis. S. W. Little. il Sat R 53:
81-2 F 14 '70 *

CULLINAN, Elizabeth
Nora's friends; story. New Yorker 46:26-32
Ag 29 '70

CULLING. See Cows—Culling

CULSHAW, John
Porgy showed the way to the Ring. por Hi
Fi 20:secI 20 Ag '70

CULTIVATION of corn. See Corn—Cultivation

CULTIVATION of soybeans. See Soybeans—
Cultivation

CULTIVATION of wheat. See Wheat—Cultivation

CULTIVATORS
Hitches that speed up spring tillage. il Farm
J 94:42-3 Mr '70
New triple-threat tillage tool. B. Coffman. il
il Farm J 94:41 O '70

CULTS
See also
House of David

CULTS, Negro
See also
Black Muslims

CULTURAL centers
See also
Community arts centers
John F. Kennedy center for the performing
arts, Washington, D.C.

CULTURAL evolution. See Social change

CULTURAL exchanges. See Exchange of persons programs

CULTURAL lag. See Social change

CULTURAL migration. See Man—Migrations

CULTURAL property, Protection of (International law)
UNESCO committee drafts convention to protect cultural property; statement, April 13,
1970. M. B. Feldman. Dept State Bul 63:
22-4 Jl 6 '70

CULTURAL revolution. See Social revolution

CULTURALLY deprived children. See Socially
handicapped children

CULTURE
Play and ritual. C. J. McNaspy. America 122:
426-8 Ap 18 '70
Talk with Konrad Lorenz; ed. by F. de Towarnicki. K. Z. Lorenz. il por N Y Times
Mag p4-5+ Jl 5 '70
We no longer know how to bring our children into the world we have built; interview, ed. by C. Dreyfus. C. Lévi-Strauss.
por Mlle 71:236-7+ Ag '70
See also
Civilization
History
Indians of North America—Culture
Popular culture

CULTURE, American. See United States—Civilization; United States—Intellectual life;
United States—Popular culture

CULTURE, British. See Great Britain—Popular culture

CULTURE, Canadian. See Canada—Civilization

CULTURE, Russian. See Russia—Intellectual
life

CULTURE and war. See War and civilization

CUMBERLAND ISLAND
Georgia Sea island that slumbers like a
time capsule. B. Fancher. il Holiday 47:
56-9+ My '70
Interlude on an unspoiled island; wild vegetables for a wild luau. E. Gibbons. Org
Gard & Farm 17:88-91 Jl '70
Love-out on an island. E. Gibbons. il Org
Gard & Farm 17:82-4 Je '70

CUMBERLAND RIVER
River to run free; Big South Fork. E. N.
Layne. il Am Heritage 21:112 Je '70

CUMBERLEGE, Marcus
Comment. N. Sullivan. Poetry 116:122-3 My
'70 *

CUMMING, John R.
Beast of burden or playboy? Which role for
the student teachers' college supervisors.
bibliog Clear House 44:437-40 Mr '70

CUMMING, Umont O.
Chat with America's leading industrial spy.
J. Perham. Duns 96:32 O '70 *

CUMMINGS, Edward Estlin
Comment. R. B. Shaw. Poetry 115:278-80 Ja '70

CUMMINGS, Frederick
Tannahill taste. il Art N 69:32-3+ My '70

CUMMINGS, Nathan
Nobody doesn't like Mr Sara Lee; with report by M. C. Wrenn. il pors Life 69:76-80
O 23 '70 *
Rehash at Consolidated. pors Newsweek 75:
64+ Ja 26 '70

CUMMINGS, Nathan, collection. See Art—Private collections

CUMMINGS, Samuel
Merchant of menace. E. Shrake. il Sports
Illus 32:80-4+ Mr 11 '70 *

CUNA Indians. See Indians of Central America

CUNARD, Nancy
Promising race. G. Wolff. il por Newsweek
76:102+ O 5 '70 *

CUNARD steamship company
New bearings. por Forbes 106:31-2 Ag 15 '70

CUNNEEN, Sally
If you could make one change in the church,
what would it be? Commonweal 92:164
My 1 '70
Priest vs. Pastore. Chr Cent 87:1067-8 S 9 '70

CUNNINGHAM, Ann Marie
Try some; they're homemade. il Mlle 70:184-
5+ Mr '70
View from the masthead. il Mlle 71:161-3 S
'70

CUNNINGHAM, Carl
Uproar: Previn and afterwards. Hi Fi 20:secII
25+ Ap '70

CUNNINGHAM, Chet
How to turn newspaper items into article
checks! il Writers Digest 50:20-1 S '70

CUNNINGHAM, Constance
Scientific challenge; poem. Good H 171:166 S
'70

CUNNINGHAM, Eloise
Yesterday & tomorrow at Expo '70. il Hi Fi
20:MA22-3 N '70

CUNNINGHAM, Glenn
Excerpt from letter, February 26, 1970. Cong
Digest 49:210+ Ag '70

CUNNINGHAM, Imogen
Gallery: photographs. il Life 68:8-9 My 1 '70

CUNNINGHAM, James
James Cunningham & dancers; Judson memorial church, NYC. J. Anderson. Dance
Mag 44:73 Jl '70 *
James Cunningham and dancers. the Cubiculo.
J. Armstrong. Dance Mag 44:79 Ap '70 *

CUNNINGHAM, John T.
To walk a different way. il Parks & Rec 5:26-
8+ Ja '70

CUNNINGHAM, Joseph L.
Federation of diocesan liturgical commissions. America 123:97-8 Ag 22 '70

CUNNINGHAM, Katharine S.
Dance at St Paul's school. il Dance Mag
44:24-5 Je '70

CUNNINGHAM, Luvern L.
Community involvement in change. Ed Digest
35:1-4 Ap '70
Hey, man, you our principal? Ed Digest 35:
5-8 F '70

CUNNINGHAM, Merce
Fleeting moments. J. Anderson. il Nation 210:
216-17 F 23 '70 *
Merce in antic mood. W. Terry. il por Sat R
53:40 Ja 24 '70

CUNNINGHAM, Merce, dance company. See
Merce Cunningham dance company
CUNNINGHAM, Murry K. and others
From psychiatric hospital to nursing home.
Ment Hy 54:109-12 Ja '70
CUNNINGHAM, William P. and Scott, D. W.
Magruder Corridor controversy. Liv Wildn
33:36-9 Aut '69
CUOMO, George
Everything is a character. Writer 83:15-16+ F
'70
CUP of gold
Cup of gold vine. W. Radcliffe. Horticul-
ture 48:44 D '70
CUPBOARDS
See also
Kitchen cabinets
CUPID'S golden key ring; drama. See Miller,
H. L.
CUPPS, Stephen
Agnew and the Pastore bill. il Chr Cent 87:
77-9 Ja 21 '70
Death by runaround. il Nation 211:146-8 Ag
31 '70
CUPRESSUS. See Cypress
CUPS
Coffee, tea, and other cups; exhibition at the
Museum of contemporary crafts, New York.
il Ceram Mo 18:24-5 D '70
Constant cup; exhibition at the Museum of
contemporary crafts, New York. D. Law-
son. il Craft Horiz 30:54-7+ D '70
CURAÇAO (island)
How now, Curaçao? H. Sutton. Holiday 47:
8+ Je '70
CURATOLA, Tony
Tugboat test. R. Hattersley. il Pop Phot
66:116-19 Je '70 *
CURED salmon. See Fishery products—Preser-
vation
CURLEY, Arthur
ALA identity crisis: dilemma or delaying de-
vice? por Library J 95:2089-90 Je 1 '70
CURRAN, Grace Bilin
Social sermon in stone. il Design 71:18-20
Fall '69
CURRENCY question
Germany 1923: when inflation overshot the
mark. il Sr Schol 96:8-9 Ja 26 '70
Will the dollar be devalued via the back
door? C. A. Cerami. il Nations Bsns 58:
98-100 N '70
CURRENT, William R.
Pueblos of the four corners; photographs.
Arch Forum 133:44-7 S '70
CURRENT events
Forum; monthly review of events and ideas.
See issues of Architectural forum
In and out of the news. P. Kunhardt. Life
68:3 My 22 '70
Month in review. See issues of Current history
News & views. J. Deedy. See issues of Com-
monweal
1969 contemporary affairs test. Sr Schol 95:
35-6 S 15 '69
Odyssey of a friend: letters to W. F. Buck-
ley, jr, 1955-1957. W. Chambers. bibliog Nat
R 22:76-82 Ja 27 '70
Parting shots. See issues of Life
People and events. See issues of Senior
scholastic
Press section; notes and comment on the
news. See issues of Reader's digest
Scholastic scrapbook; a selection of items
from our past issues. Sr Schol 97:3-19 O 19
'70
CURRENT RIVER
Missouri's river of springs. J. P. Jackson. il
Travel 133:48-53 Ap '70
CURRENTS, Ocean. See Ocean currents
CURREY, John D. See Klein, L. jt. auth.
CURRICULUM. See Colleges and universities
—Curriculum; Courses of study; High
schools—Curriculum
CURRICULUM development, Association for.
See Association for supervision and cur-
riculum development
CURRICULUM planning
Bridge at generation gap: EPIC project. M.
E. Wade. il Am Ed 6:28-30 O '70
Skill of relevance or the relevance of skills;
curriculum reform. J. Bruner. il Sat R 53:
66-8+ Ap 18 '70
Their own week: pupils planning their own
curriculum. J. M. Brown and D. Emberlin.
Todays Ed 59:12 My '70
CURRIE, Elliott, and Skolnick, J. H.
Critical note on conceptions of collective be-
havior. bbiliog f Ann Am Acad 391:34-45 S
'70
CURRY, Peggy (Simson)
Privacy and production. Writer 83:9-11+
Mr '70
Regional poetry. Writer 83:21-3 Ag '70

CURRY
Conversation makers; lamb curry baked in
coconuts. J. Hewitt. il N Y Times Mag p46
Jl 19 '70
Curry favorite; shrimp Madras. C. Claiborne.
il N Y Times Mag p84 Mr 8 '70
Touch of India, chicken curry. il McCalls
98:42 O '70
CURTAIN and drapery fixtures
For men: the nuts and bolts of drapery rods.
R. Day. il Pop Sci 197:100-1 S '70
How to install: pushbutton draperies. W. C.
Leckey. il Pop Mech 134:163-5 D '70
CURTAINS and draperies
Decorating with sheets. C. Houck. Parents
Mag 45:16 Mr '70
How to make a window beautiful. W. Bald-
win. House & Gard 137:8-9 F '70
How to sew cafe curtains, Austrian shades,
Roman shades, and swags. il Bet Hom &
Gard 48:110+ My '70
How to sew lined draperies. il Bet Hom & Gard
48:92+ Ap '70
Institute answers your questions about drap-
eries. il Good H 171:136 S '70
Shopping for curtains? Try the easy-care
sheers. il Good H 170:172 Je '70
Windows: the dressing game. N. Mandel-
baum. il Ladies Home J 87:90-5 S '70
CURTIN, William M.
(ed) See Cather, W. S. Ghost town on the
river
CURTIS, Joseph E.
Pragmaesthetics. il Parks & Rec 5:15-17+ Jl
'70
CURTIS, Mike
I'm a football player, not a worker. S.
Myslenski. il por Sports Illus 33:10-11 Ag
10 '70 *
CURTIS, Paul
Where the geese beckon. il Field & S 75:52-3+
S '70
CURTIS, Philip C.
Ghosts at noon. il Time 96:76-7 O 5 '70 *
CURTIS, Will C.
Garden in the woods. J. A. Lynch. il Am For
76:20-3+ Mr '70 *
CURTIS, William
West's hottest deer hunting. il Field & S 75:
44-5+ N '70
CURTIS cup. See Golf
CURTIS publishing company
Curtis-Culligan story, by M. T. Culligan. Re-
view
Sat R il 53:81-2 F 14 '70. S. W. Little
Decline and fall, by O. Friedrich. Review
Sat R 53:61-2 Je 13 '70. S. W. Little
Good guys and publishers. C. Welles. Nation
211:217-18+ S 14 '70
See also
Saturday evening post
CURTISS, Mina
Symphoniste fantastique. Nation 210:88+ Ja 26
'70
CURZAN, Myron P.
Voting for president. New Repub 162:14-16 Ap
18 '70
CURZON, Clifford
Music to my ears; all-Beethoven program in
Philharmonic Hall. I. Kolodin. Sat R 53:28
Ap 25 '70 *
Musical events; all-Beethoven program in Phil-
harmonic Hall. W. Sargeant. New Yorker
46:150 Ap 18 '70 *
CURZON, George Nathaniel, 1st marquis Cur-
zon of Kedleston. See Curzon of Kedles-
ton, G. N. C.
CURZON of Kedleston, George Nathaniel Cur-
zon, 1st marquis
Superior person, by K. Rose. Review
Sat R il por 53:36-8 Mr 14 '70. C. Miller *
CUSCUNA, Michael
Month's jazz. Am Rec G 36:995 Ag '70
—See Summerlin, E. jt. auth.
CUSHEN, Arthur
First person DX'ing. il pors Pop Electr 32:
74-5 F '70
CUSHING, Alexander Cochrane
What goes up must ski down. A. Wright. il
por Sports Illus 32:28-31 F 9 '70
CUSHING, C. E. See Rose, R. L. jt. auth.
CUSHING, Harvey society. See Harvey Cush-
ing society
CUSHING, Richard James, cardinal
Another last hurrah. T. D. Corrigan. Com-
monweal 93:5 O 2 '70; Reply. J. G. Bogan.
93:267+ D 11 '70 *
Big man in a long red robe. il pors Time 96:64
N 16 '70 *

CUSHING, Richard James, cardinal—*Continued*
Change of the guard. il por Time 96:61 S 21 '70 *
Obituary
Chr Cent 87:1374 N 18 '70. J. Finn
Nat R 22:1203 N 17 '70. W. F. Buckley, jr.
Newsweek il por 76:123 N 16 '70 *
Of many things. D. R. Campion. America 123: inside cover N 14 '70 *
Passing the hat. il pors Newsweek 76:82 S 21 '70 *

CUSHING, Tom
Grin and bare it! adaptation. See McGuire, K.

CUSHIONS
Super bean bag; styrene pellets. il Sunset 145: 50-1 Ag; 130 N '70
See also
Pillows

CUSTARDS
Cheese custard for brunch. il Sunset 145:155 D '70
La crème de la crème; French custard molds. M. Happel. il Ladies Home J 87:120-1+ My '70
Double custard from Portugal. il Sunset 144: 176 Mr '70
Floating island; creamy custard desserts; with recipes. E. Alston. il Look 34:64-5 S 22 '70
Oriental switch, savory custards. Sunset 145: 110-11 Ag '70

CUSTER, George Armstrong
Haunting new vision of the Little Big Horn. il Am Heritage 21:101-3 Je '70 *

CUSTODIAN accounts. See Custodianship accounts

CUSTODIANSHIP accounts
Children as tax shelters. Forbes 106:71 N 1 '70
Put investments in a child's name? il Changing T 24:31-2 F '70

CUSTODY; story. See Hobson, L. Z.

CUSTOM spraying and dusting. See Spraying and dusting

CUSTOMER relations
See also
Banks and banking—Customer relations
Computer industry—Customer relations

CUSTOMS service
Let's raise more hell; demand of reasonable return in comfort and service for our money. S. Alsop. Newsweek 75:100 Mr 9 '70

CUSTOMS. See Manners and customs

CUSTOMS college. See United States—Customs, Bureau of—National training center

CUSTOMS service

Great Britain
Taking a trip abroad this summer? means test for tourists. D. Sanford. New Repub 162:10-11 Je 13 '70

United States
Booming traffic in drugs: the government's dilemma. il U S News 69:40-1 D 7 '70
Customs college. il Travel 134:64-7 D '70
Narcotics; address, June 23, 1970. M. J. Ambrose. Vital Speeches 36:612-15 Ag 1 '70

CUSTOMS service and tourists
Customs inspectors miss a lot, but don't count on it. J. Lee and B. Lee. il Holiday 47:36-7+ Ap '70
Formalities, for those who go foreign. J. Hart. Yachting 127:246-7 My '70
Some Russian customs to be avoided. N. Simon. il Pop Phot 66:32+ F '70
Taking a trip abroad this summer? means test for tourists. D. Sanford. New Repub 162:10-11 Je 13 '70
Vacationing in jail. il Sr Schol 96:19 My 18 '70
War on drugs; its meaning to tourists. il U S News 69:68 S 7 '70

CUTICLE (insects)
Autoxidation of insect lipids: inhibition on the cuticle of the American cockroach. P. W. Atkinson and A. R. Gilby. bibliog Science 168:992 My 22 '70

CUTLER, Carol
Dubuffet at work. il Art in Am 58:108-13 Jl '70
Paris: the lettrist movement. il Art in Am 58: 116-19 Ja '70
Paris: the new surrealists. il Art in Am 58:129-32 Mr '70
State department antiques. il Art in Am 58: 74-7 S '70

CUTLER, Horace G.
Growth inhibitor from young expanding tobacco leaves. bibliog Science 170:856-7 N 20 '70

CUTOUT work. See Paper work

CUTTING boards
Block party. il McCalls 98:72-3+ Ja '71

CUTTING costs. See Cost control

CUTTING machines
See also
Pantographs

CUTTING tools
Big edge on tool costs; titanium carbide. coating. il Bsns W p98 Jl 25 '70
Primer on plug cutters. R. J. De Cristoforo. il Mech Illus 66:98-9 N '70

CUTTINGS, Plant. See Plant propagation

CUYAHOGA FALLS, Ohio
Soil studies help create music. il Am City 85:64 My '70

CUYAHOGA HEIGHTS, Ohio
Utopia in suburbia. Bsns W p39 S 5 '70

CYBERNETICS
Cybernetics in city hall; adaptation of address, 1968. E. S. Savas. bibliog il Science 168:1066-71 My 29 '70; Discussion. 169:1155 S 18 '70
See also
Information theory

CYBIS porcelain figurines. See Figurines

CYCLADES (islands)
Isles of Greece: the Cyclades. S. Wiedel. il Travel & Camera 33:36-41+ O '70
See also
Naxos (island)

CYCLAMATES. See Sugar substitutes

CYCLAMEN
Cyclamen species. J. Thibodeau. il Horticulture 48:24-5 Ag '70
Florists' cyclamen are just the plants for fall-to-spring color. il Sunset 145:218 O '70

CYCLES, Business. See Business cycles

CYCLING
Big race; fastest, cheapest way to get to work in Washington, D.C. E. N. Layne. il Am Heritage 21:119 Ag '70
Bike to work: Sixtieth street and Fifth avenue to Battery park. New Yorker 46:28-9 S 26 '70
Ride on! New York bike-in. il Newsweek 76: 102 S 28 '70
Wheeling their way. il Time 96:42-3 Jl 27 '70
See also
Bicycle racing

Anecdotes, facetiae, satire, etc.
Day the bicycles came. O. W. Freeman. il Har Yrs 10:19-20 Ag '70

CYCLING trips
Big Sur cycle. B. Thomas. il Travel 134:40-3 N '70

CYCLISTS
See also
Merckx, E.

CYLINDER locks. See Locks and keys

CYLINDERS (engines, etc)
Is your head screwed on right? E. Slepian. il Motor B 126:23+ Jl '70
See also
Automobile engines—Cylinders

CYCLONES
Beshi . . . beshi; with report by M. Parker. il Newsweek 76:32-3 D 7 '70
Blast of a killer typhoon. il Sr Schol 97:3 D 14 '70
East Pakistan: the politics of catastrophe. il Time 96:28+ D 7 '70
East Pakistan: the wave. D. Moraes. il N Y Times Mag P26-7+ Ja 10 '71
Night of terror. P. Parshall. Chr Today 15: 40-1 D 18 '70
Pakistan calamity: fate, wrath or providence? J. C. Haughey. America 123:479 D 5 '70
Pakistan: when the demon struck. il Time 96:16+ N 30 '70
Pakistani tragedy; with report and interviews. M. Parker. il Newsweek 76:34-6 N 30 '70
Portrait of a deadly pinwheel; storm ravages East Pakistan. il Life 69:41-2 N 27 '70
Tragic aftermath in Pakistan. il Life 69: 26-35 D 4 '70
Walk through a deathly quiet countryside. H. Ellithorpe. il por Life 69:5 D 4 '70

CYPRESS
Monterey cypress. J. W. Wilson. Horticulture 48:40-1 Jl '70

Diseases and pests
Monterey cypress, a fatal fungus disease is spreading in California; coryneum canker. il Sunset 145:253 N '70

CYPRINODONTIDAE. See Killifishes

CYPRUS
Approaching flashpoint. il Time 95:29 F 16 '70
No cheers. Newsweek 75:42+ Ap 6 '70
Under the threat of guns. il Time 95:37 Mr 30 '70
See also
United Nations—Armed forces—Forces in Cyprus

CYPRUS mines corporation
Cyprus plans ahead. T. J. Murray. Duns 96: 59-60 S '70

CYST nematodes. See Nematodes

CYSTATHIONASE. See Enzymes

CYSTEINE
Cystinosis: selective induction of vacuolation in fibroblasts by L-cysteine-D-penicillamine disulfide. J. D. Schulman and K. H. Bradley. bibliog il Science 169:595-7 Ag 7 '70

CYSTIC fibrosis
Beta glucuronidase activity in skin components of children with cystic fibrosis. G. E. Gibbs and G. D. Griffin. bibliog il Science 167:993-4 F 13 '70
Cystic fibrosis. L. W. Sauer. PTA Mag 65: 27 D '70
Cystic fibrosis: characterization of the inhibitor to ciliary action in oyster gills. B. H. Bowman and others. bibliog il Science 167: 871-3 F 6 '70

CYSTINE
Absence of cystathionase in human fetal liver: is cystine essential? J. A. Sturman and others. bibliog il Science 169:74-6 Jl 3 '70
Human cystinosis: intracellular deposition of cystine. K. Hummeler and others. bibliog il Science 168:859-60 My 15 '70

CYSTINOSIS. See Children—Diseases

CYTIDINE phosphates
Cyclic cytidine 2',3'-phosphate; molecular structure. C. L. Coulter and M. L. Greaves. bibliog il Science 169:1097-8 S 11 '70

CYTOCHROMES
Double nuclear magnetic resonance observation of electron exchange between ferri- and ferrocytochrome c. R. K. Gupta and A. G. Redfield. bibliog il Science 169:1204-6 S 18 '70
Phosphorylation coupled to the transfer of electrons from glutathione to cytochrome c. A. A. Painter and F. E. Hunter, jr. bibliog il Science 170:552-3 O 30 '70

CYTOGENETICS. See Chromosomes

CYTOKININS. See Kinins

CYTOLOGY

Methodology

Bulk isolation in nonaqueous media of nuclei from lyophilized cells. W. M. Kirsch and others. bibliog il Science 168:1592-5 Je 26 '70
Cytoplasmic extraction: polyribosomes and heterogeneous ribonucleoproteins without associated DNA. D. Fromson and M. Nemer. bibliog il Science 168:266-7 Ap 10 '70
Inside-out red cell membrane vesicles: preparation and purification. T. L. Steck and others. bibliog il Science 168:255-7 Ap 10 '70
Isoantigenic variants: isolation from human diploid cells in culture. R. Adman and D. A. Pious. bibliog il Science 168:370-2 Ap 17 '70
Quantitation of strain BALB/c mouse peritoneal cells. E. Shelton and others. bibliog il Science 168:1232-4 Je 5 '70
See also
Centrifugation

CYTOPLASM
See also
Mitochondria

CZECH poetry

Translations into English

Poet; Room for all; At the circus; Trees in courtyards; tr. by I. Levatin and W. H. Auden. O. Lysohorsky. Poetry 116:273-8 Ag '70

CZECH pottery. See Pottery, Czech

CZECHOSLOVAKIA
See also
Airlines—Czechoslovakia
Colleges and universities—Czechoslovakia
Ecology—Czechoslovakia
Education and state in Czechoslovakia
Morale, National—Czechoslovakia
Moving picture industry—Czechoslovakia
Opava
Opera—Czechoslovakia
Performing arts—Czechoslovakia
Prague
Public officers—Czechoslovakia
Russia—Foreign relations—Czechoslovakia
Skis and skiing—Czechoslovakia
Trials—Czechoslovakia

Economic conditions

Bitterest winter. Time 95:31 F 9 '70

Industries

See also
Airplane industry and trade—Czechoslovakia

Intellectual life

Prague's whispering gallery. M. Kustow. il N Y Times Mag p34-5+ S 13 '70

Occupation, 1968-

Czechoslovaks: between hope and fear. F. Ungeheuer. il Harper 241:71-7 Ag '70
Intervention, by I. D. Levine. Review
Sat R 53:34+ F 7 '70. A. Dallin
Prague: nothing is forever. D. North. il Nation 211:102-5 Ag 17 '70
Requiem for Czechoslovakia. G. Feifer. Read Digest 97:83-8 N '70

Protests, demonstrations, etc, against

Lessons from the Czech ordeal; guidelines for nonviolent opposition. J. Power. il Chr Cent 87:1011-13 Ag 26 '70
Tear gas in Prague. Sr Schol 95:28-9 S 22 '69

Politics and government

Approaching total eclipse. il por Time 95:39-40 Ap 6 '70

Religious institutions and affairs

New threats to Czech churches. America 122: 402 Ap 18 '70
See also
Catholic church in Czechoslovakia
Christians in Czechoslovakia

Social conditions

Silent observance. Time 96:34 Ag 31 '70

Treaties

Russia

See Russia—Treaties—Czechoslovakia

CZECHS
Where they are now; liberal reform leaders. il Newsweek 76:34-5 Ag 24 '70

D

DAP I (dipetidyl aminopeptidase) See Enzymes

DATO. See Discover America travel organization

DCU (decade counting unit) See Counting machines and devices

DDT (insecticide)
Antagonism by DDT of the effect of valinomycin on a synthetic membrane. B. D. Hilton and R. D. O'Brien. bibliog il Science 168:841-3 My 15 '70; Reply. F. Matsumura. 169:1343 S 25 '70
Attack on DDT (cont) Time 95:59 Je 15 '70
DDT: friend or enemy? R. C. Di Iorio. Horticulture 48:22-3 Je '70
DDT-induced inhibition of avian shell gland carbonic anhydrase: a mechanism for thin eggshells. J. Bitman and others. bibliog il Science 168:594-6 My 1 '70
DDT makers force delay in USDA ban. Nat Parks 44:28 Mr '70
DDT on balance. G. Conway and others. bibliog il Environ 11:3-5 S '69
DDT phaseout proposed by HEW Secretary Finch. Nat Parks 44:27 Ja '70
DDT story. E. Keller. il Chem 43:8-12 F '70; Reply. P. Cammer. 43:37-8 Ap '70
Diminishing sources. il Sci N 97:613 Je 27 '70
Induced photolysis of DDT. L. L. Miller and R. S. Narang. bibliog il Science 169:368-70 Jl 24 '70
p,p'-DDT: effect on calcium metabolism and concentration of estradiol in the blood. D. B. Peakall. bibliog il Science 168:592-4 My 1 '70
Systems studies of DDT transport. H. L. Harrison and others. bibliog il Science 170:503-8 O 30 '70

Injurious effects

Danger! pesticides at work. W. B. Furlong. il Good H 170:82-3+ Mr '70
Death comes to the peregrine falcon. D. R. Zimmerman. il N Y Times Mag p8-9+ Ag 9 '70; Discussion. p73 Ag 30 '70
Notes and comment: ospreys in danger. New Yorker 46:19 Ag 15 '70
Reports: pesticides. F. Graham jr. Atlan 226:22+ S '70; Discussion. 226:36+ N '70
Silent spring: the genesis and the storm; excerpts from Since silent spring. F. Graham, jr. il por Audubon 72:70-2+ Ja '70

Residues

Biological magnification of DDT. P. M. Kelsey. Cons 24:31 Ag '69
DDT in mother's milk. C. F. Wurster. Sat R 53:58-9 My 2 '70

DDT (insecticide)—Residues—*Continued*
DDT metabolism: oxidation of the metabolite 2,2-bis(p-chlorophenyl)ethanol by alcohol dehydrogenase. J. E. Suggs and others. Science 168:582 My 1 '70
DDT metabolites and analogs: ring fission by hydrogenomonas. D. D. Focht and M. Alexander. bibliog il Science 170:91-2 O 2 '70
DDT residues in marine phytoplankton: increase from 1955 to 1969. J. L. Cox. bibliog il Science 170:71-3 O 2 '70
DDT testing of lake fishes continues. A. Woldt and J. E. Gavagan. il Cons 25:28-9 Ag '70
Earth, air, water. J. Frost. bibliog il Environ 11:14-29+ Jl '69
First results: DDT residues. Cons 24:38 F '70
Poison roams our coastal seas. R. H. Boyle. il Sports Illus 33:70-4+ O 26 '70

DDVP (insecticide) See Insecticides

D. H. Baldwin company. See Baldwin, D. H, company

DISC (Domestic international sales corporations) See Export trade—Federal aid

DLP. See United States—Education, Office of —Libraries and educational technology, Bureau of—Library programs, Division of

DMI. See Dolly Madison industries, inc.

DNA
Acetabularia chloroplast DNA: electron microscopic visualization. B. R. Green and H. Burton. bibliog il Science 168:981-2 My 22 '70
Brain enhancement in tadpoles: increased DNA concentration after somatotrophin or prolactin. R. K. Hunt and M. Jacobson. bibliog il Science 170:342-4 O 16 '70
Chloramphenicol: effect on DNA synthesis during phage development in escherichia coli. P. Amati. bibliog il Science 168:1226-8 Je 5 '70
Chromosomal localization of mouse satellite DNA. M. L. Pardue and J. G. Gall. bibliog il Science 168:1356-8 Je 12 '70
Cytoplasmic extraction: polyribosomes and heterogeneous ribonucleoproteins without associated DNA. D. Fromson and M. Nemer. bibliog il Science 168:266-7 Ap 10 '70
Defect in DNA synthesis in skin of patients with xeroderma pigmentosum demonstrated in vivo. J. H. Epstein and others. bibliog il Science 168:1477-8 Je 19 '70
DNA-membrane complex: macromolecular content and stimulation of enzymatic activity by polyadenylic acid. W. Firshein and R. G. Gillmor. bibliog il Science 169:66-8 Jl 3 '70
DNA synthesis during yeast sporulation: genetic control of an early developmental event. A. Roth and K. Lusnak. bibliog il Science 168:493-4 Ap 24 '70
DNA synthesis in the anterior pituitary of the male rat: effect of castration and photoperiod. W. C. Hymer and others. bibliog il Science 167:1629-31 Mr 20 '70
Encapsidation of free host DNA by simian virus 40: a simian virus 40 pseudo-virus. D. M. Trilling and D. Axelrod. bibliog il Science 168:268-70 Ap 10 '70
Fluorescent labeling of chromosomal DNA: superiority of quinacrine mustard to quinacrine. T. Caspersson and others. bibliog Science 170:762 N 13 '70
Fourier analysis and the structure of DNA. J. Donohue; discussion. bibliog il Science 167:1693-702 Mr 27 '70
Idiosyncrasies of DNA structure; Nobel lecture, December 12, 1969. A. D. Hershey. bibliog il Science 168:1425-7 Je 19 '70
Late DNA replication in male mouse meiotic chromosomes. N. Odartchenko and M. Pavillard. bibliog il Science 167:1133-4 F 20 '70
Pathways through networks of branched DNA. O. Smithies. il Science 169:882-3 Ag 28 '70
Polyinosinic acid . polycytidylic acid: inhibition of DNA synthesis stimulated by isoproterenol. F. T. Serota and R. Baserga. bibliog il Science 167:1379-80 Mr 6 '70
Recognition of DNA in bacteria. S. E. Luria. il Sci Am 222:88-92+ bibliog(p 146) Ja '70
Repeated segments of DNA. R. J. Britten and D. E. Kohne. il Sci Am 222:24-31 bibliog(p 130) Ap '70
Replicating DNA: structure of colicin factor E1. J. Inselburg and M. Fuke. bibliog il Science 169:590-2 Ag 7 '70
Satellite DNA in constitutive heterochromatin of the guinea pig. J. J. Yunis and W. G. Yasmineh. bibliog il Science 168:263-5 Ap 10 '70
Sunlight ultraviolet and bacterial DNA base ratios. C. E. Singer and B. N. Ames. bibliog il Science 170:822-6 N 20 '70

Triumph for a heretic. il Newsweek 76:56-7 Jl 20 '70
Trouble on the DNA front. bibliog il Chem 43:24-5 O '70
Two way street for genetics; RNA-to-DNA inversion. Sci N 98:54 Jl 25 '70
Undogmatic dogma; transfer from RNA to DNA. Sci Am 223:44 N '70
Upsetting dogma. il por Time 96:57 Jl 20 '70
DNA polymerase. See Polymerase
DOT. See United States—Transportation, Department of
DPRC (Defense program review committee) See United States—National security council
DSRV (deep submergence rescue vehicle) See Submarine boats
DA, Popovi
Indian values. il por Liv Wildn 34:25-6 Spr '70
DABBS, James McBride
He made you feel like somebody. D. W. Shriver, jr. Chr Cent 87:866-9 Jl 15 '70 *
DACEY, Norman F.
Self-help law book cleared in N.Y. court. Library J 95:842 Mr 1 '70 *
DACOSTA, Vernon
Batter up: world series quiz. Har Yrs 10: 18 O '70
DACTYLOSCOPY. See Fingerprints
DADAISM
Remember Dada: Man Ray at eighty. S. De Gramont. il pors N Y Times Mag p6-7+ S 6 '70
DADDARIO, Emilio Quincy
Daddario: scientific community's friend on the Hill is leaving. D. S. Greenberg. por Science 169:1291-3 S 25 '70; Reply. F. A. Long. 170:1254 D 18 '70 *
Future of a subcommittee. Sci N 97:289-90 Mr 21 '70 *
Our top priority; address, June 2, 1970. W. B. Johnson. Vital Speeches 36:618-19 Ag 1 '70 *
Predicting the consequences of technology. J. Lear. por Sat R 53:44-6 Mr 28 '70 *
DADOLLE, Susanne
(ed) See Pompidou, C. Madame Pompidou
DAFFODILS. See Narcissus
DAFFODILS, Peruvian. See Basket flowers
DAGUERREOTYPES
New lease on life for daguerreotypes; Enyeart process. J. Deschin. il por Pop Phot 67:42+ N '70
DAHEIM, David C.
War of Klitticlamma County. il Opera N 34: 8-11 Ja 24 '70
DAHL, Erik, and others
Pheromone transport and reception in an amphipod. il Science 170:739 N 13 '70
DAHLIAS
It's dahlia time! Home Gard 57:13 S '70
DAHLQUIST, Eric
Marking time. See Issues of Motor trend
DAHLSTROM, Max, and Merriam, John
Last chance for the White Clouds. il Nat Parks & Con Mag 44:9-13 Ag '70
DAHOOD, Thomas S.
Modeling in clay. il Design 71:13 Sum '70
DAHRENDORF, Ralf
German Ostpolitik; address, April 22, 1970. Vital Speeches 36:517-20 Je 15 '70
DAICHES, David
Translating the Bible. Commentary 49:59-68 My '70
DAIFUKU, Hiroshi
Art and monuments of Java. il UNESCO Courier 23:22-7 Jl '70
DAILY news, Chicago. See Chicago daily news
DAILY news, New York
President's editorialist: R. Maury. por Time 96:45 Ag 31 '70
DAIMLER-Benz, ag. See Automobile industry and trade—Germany (Federal Republic)
DAIRY barns. See Barns and stables
DAIRY cooperative associations. See Dairymen's associations
DAIRY farm management
Compare your profits with these farms. Suc Farm 68:A4 S '70
He uses cost-cutting ideas. J. Albino and T. McCartney. il Suc Farm 68:D24 N '70
His dairying changes pay off. J. R. Borcherding. il Suc Farm 68:G4 N '70
Management ideas from a top dairy herd. J. R. Borcherding. il Suc Farm 69:26-7 Ja '71
Shuffle system: small step towards a big herd. R. Garrett. il Farm J 94:54I F '70
Steers make a dairy flexible. D. Braun. il Farm J 94:10-11 D '70
Successful dairy management. il Suc Farm 68:no4 E2-4+ Mr; G1-4+ My; D9-10+ Ag '70

DALY, Mary
If you could make one change in the church, what would it be? Commonweal 92:161-2 My 1 '70
Problem of hope. Commonweal 92:314-17 Je 26 '70

DAMAGES
He's insured, sock it to him! il Forbes 105:63-4+ Ap 15 '70
Jet noise, fumes trial could set precedent. Aviation W 92:44-6 My 11 '70
No teaching, no tuition: N.Y.U. sued. Time 96:66 O 26 '70
Settling a personal injury claim yourself. L. M. Brown. Bet Hom & Gard 48:28+ O '70
Softening crime's impact. Nations Bsns 58: 24 Ja '70
Troika of torts. il por Time 96:68 D 7 '70
See also
Liability (law)

D'AMATO, Anthony A.
Environmental degradation and legal action. Bul Atom Sci 26:24-6 Mr '70

D'AMBOISE, Jacques
Extraordinary anniversary. S. Goodman. il pors Dance Mag 44:28-31 N '70 *

D'AMBROSIO, Michael A.
Alice for adolescents. Engl J 59:1074-5+ N '70

D'AMBROSIO, Richard
No language but a cry. Good H 171:64-7+ Ag '70

DAMICO, James
Trial of A. Lincoln. Criticism
Nation 210:733-4 Je 15 '70 *

DAMON, Allan L.
Melancholy case. il por Am Heritage 21:18-19+ F '70

DAMPNESS in buildings
Take the sweat out of condensation problems. S. J. Howard. il Pop Mech 134:164-6 Ag '70
Wet basements: what can be done. il Good H 171:158 S '70

DAMS
BOR recommends against Salem church dam. Nat Parks & Con Mag 44:28 Jl '70
Dam outrage: the story of the army engineers. E. B. Drew. il Atlan 225:51-62 Ap '70
Death row; Gillham dam project on the Cossatot River. W. Jack, Jr. il Audubon 72: 139 S '70
Fabridam. M. E. Fay. il Parks & Rec 5:34-5+ Ag '70
Global earth-shapers in complex competition. W. McQuade. il Fortune 81:78-81+ Ap '70
Inflatable, fabric dam helps form new recreation areas. il Arch Forum 132:97 My '70
Last great dam. B. Norton. il Audubon 72: 12-27 Ja '70
North Cascades Dam raises international controversy; raising Ross Dam. R. D. Butcher. Liv Wildn 34:54 Sum '70
Potomac River dams; testimony and excerpts from remarks of other witnesses at Senate hearings. A. W. Smith. il Nat Parks & Con Mag 44:23-6 S '70
Requiem for a small town; Sopris, Colo. on the bank of the Purgatoire River. N. Wood. il Am Heritage 22:62-7 D '70
Too much for the Columbia River salmon. E. Chaney. il Nat Wildlife 8:18-21 Ap '70
See also
Hoover Dam

Asia, Southeastern
Ecologists in the Mekong; proposed Pa Mong and Stung Treng Dams. New Repub 162:6-7 Mr 28 '70

Egypt
See also
Aswan High Dam

Mozambique
Digging in; controversy over the Cabora Bassa project. il Newsweek 76:60 N 16 '70

DAMSEL flies. See Dragonflies

DANA, Charles A.
Standards or straitjacket? Aviation W 93:9 Ag 17 '70

DANA, Robert
Woman on the mall; poem. New Yorker 46: 177 N 21 '70

DANA, Thomas F.
Acanthaster: a rarity in the past? bibliog Science 169:894 Ag 28 '70

DANAKIL
Afar triangle. H. Tazieff. il Sci Am 222:32-40 bibliog(p 126) F '70
Birth of an ocean; Afar triangle. il Time 95: 68 Mr 2 '70

DANAKIL (native race) See Ethiopia—Native races

DANBURY, Conn.
City and school system share a computer. J. P. Edwards. il Am City 85:105+ Ap '70

DANCE, Stanley
Empress still reigns. por Sat R 53:41+ Ag 29 '70
Louis Armstrong, American original. il pors Sat R 53:13-14 Jl 4 '70
Recordings reports: jazz LPs. See issues of Saturday review
Sy Oliver, bandleader. il pors Sat R 53:64-5+ My 16 '70

DANCE accompanists. See Pianists

DANCE companies
Across the Hudson; Festival 70 programs of Garden state ballet and Repertory dancers of New Jersey. W. Terry. Sat R 53:19 My 9 '70
Eleo Pomare dance company; Brooklyn academy of music. T. Borek. Dance Mag 44:73-4 Jl '70
Ethel Winter dance company; 92nd street Y. J. Anderson. Dance Mag 44:79 Ja '70
Eugene James dance company, Kaufmann concert hall, NYC. N. Mason. Dance Mag 45:72 Ja '71
Fred Benjamin dance company, Clark center, NYC. T. Borek. Dance Mag 45:72 Ja '71
Group motion; Higgins hall theater; move to Philadelphia. M. Marks. Dance Mag 44:87-8 Ap '70
Jose Limon dance company; Fashion institute of technology. J. Armstrong Dance Mag 44:93 F '70
Movements black: Dance repertory theatre, inc, the Cubiculo, NYC. L. Pastore. Dance Mag 45:71 Ja '71
New England dance theatre; Lucy Wheelock auditorium, Boston. S. Smoliar. Dance Mag 44:89+ F '70
Paul Sanasardo dance co. Louis Falco & co. of featured dancers; New York city center. J. Anderson. Dance Mag 44:78 Jl '70
Repertory dance theatre of Utah, Loeb drama center, Harvard U. S. Smoliar. Dance Mag 44:76 D '70
Repertory dancers of New Jersey; Orrie De Nooyer hall, Hackensack, NJ. M. Marks. Dance Mag 44:23+ Je '70
When summoned; production by the Repertory dance theatre. W. Terry. il Sat R 53:48 O 17 '70
See also
Alvin Ailey American dance theater
Alwin Nikolais dance company
Association of American dance companies
Los Angeles dance theatre
Martha Graham and dance company
Merce Cunningham dance company
Moiseyev dance company
Murray Louis dance company
Paul Taylor dance company

Finance
Tax reform act. I. Fisher. Dance Mag 41:6 D '70; 45:83 Ja '71

DANCE concerts
Anatomical soul Emanu-el midtown Y, NYC. L. Pastore. Dance Mag 44:81 Ag '70
Ballet soiree; Fashion institute of technology, NYC. M. Marks. Dance Mag 44: 75 Je '70
ChoreoConcerts, the New school, NYC. N. Mason. Dance Mag 45:74-6 Ja '71
ChoreoConcerts workshop; St Peter's church gym, NYC. J. Armstrong. Dance Mag 44: 89 My '70
Choreo-concerts workshop spring series; St Peter's church gymnasium, NYC. J. Anderson. Dance Mag 44:75-6 Jl '70
Choreography by Batya Zamir; Emanu-El midtown Y. J. Anderson. Dance Mag 44: 94 F '70
Choreography by Lar Lubovitch; 92nd street Y. D. Hering. il Dance Mag 44:86-7 F '70
Church street dance company; the Cubiculo, NYC. J. Anderson. Dance Mag 44:76 Je '70
Cliff Keuter and Gus Solomons, jr; the Cubiculo. J. Armstrong. Dance Mag 44:82-3 Ja '70
Cliff Keuter dance company, the Cubiculo, NYC. T. Borek. Dance Mag 44:75-6 D '70
Clyde Morgan & Carla Maxwell, the Cubiculo, NYC. L. Pastore. Dance Mag 44:76 D '70
Contemporary dance concert; Henry street settlement playhouse. M. Marks. Dance Mag 44:80-1 Ap '70

DANCE concerts—*Continued*
  Cubiculo year. D. Hering. il Dance Mag 44:
    80+ O '70
  Dance artists of Japan; 92nd street Y, NYC.
    T. Borek. Dance Mag 44:75 Je '70
  Deborah Brandt and Cecily Dell; the Cu-
    biculo. NYC. N. Mason. Dance Mag 44:81
    Ag '70
  Environments II; Judson memorial church,
    NYC. J. Anderson. Dance Mag 44:81 Jl '70
  Evening of Barbara Roan things, the Cubi-
    culo, NYC. L. Pastore. Dance Mag 45:72
    Ja '71
  Frances Alenikoff; the Cubiculo. T. Borek.
    Dance Mag 44:77 Ja '70
  Jan Van Dyke and Robert Streicher, the
    Cubiculo, NYC. L. Pastore. Dance Mag 45:
    76 Ja '71
  Joel Harrison and Susan Matheke, the
    Cubiculo, NYC. M. Marks. Dance Mag 45:
    73 Ja '71
  Kaleidoscope; Fordham university, NYC. M.
    Marks. Dance Mag 44:81 Jl '70
  Keith Lee, evening of firsts; Clark center for
    the performing arts. T. Borek. Dance Mag
    44:88-9 F '70
  Lonny Joseph Gordon and Barbara Gardner,
    the Cubiculo, NYC. N. Mason. Dance Mag
    44:77 D '70
  Lucas Hoving dance company, Rod Rodgers
    dance company; New York city center. T.
    Borek. Dance Mag 44:77-8 Jl '70
  Marian Sarach/Charles Creegan; Judson me-
    morial church, NYC. N. Mason. Dance
    Mag 44:88 My '70
  Mary Anthony dance theatre, Fashion insti-
    tute of technology, NYC. D. Hering. Dance
    Mag 44:76-7 D '70
  Meredith Monk's Juice; theatre cantata for
    three places. D. Hering. il Dance Mag 44:
    34-7 F '70
  New choreographers' concert, Clark center,
    NYC. T. Borek. Dance Mag 44:82-3 Je
    '70
  New dance group studio presents; Riverside
    church, NYC. T. Borek. Dance Mag 44:
    79-80 Jl '70
  1970 dance concert School of performing arts,
    NYC. M. Marks. Dance Mag 44:79 Ag '70
  Paul Plumadore and Carol Turoff; the Cubi-
    culo, NYC. E. Jacob. il Dance Mag 44:
    81-2 Jl '70
  Paul Sanasardo dance co, Louis Falco &
    co. of featured dancers; New York city
    center. J. Anderson. Dance Mag 44:78 Jl '70
  Phoebe Neville, Micki Goodman, Philip Hip-
    well; the Cubiculo. J. Armstrong. Dance
    Mag 44:93-4 My '70
  Raw recital by Meredith Monk & Don Pres-
    ton; Whitney museum, NYC. J. Ander-
    son. Dance Mag 44:83 Je '70
  Robert Streicher and Peggy Cicierska, the
    Cubiculo, NYC. N. Mason. Dance Mag 44:
    78+ S '70
  Rosalind Pierson, Robert Christopher and
    Marvin Gordon's ballet concepts; the Cu-
    biculo, NYC. M. Marks. Dance Mag 44:80
    Je '70
  Three new works by Bertram Ross and
    Martha Graham's El Penitente; Kaufman
    concert hall, N.Y.C. E. Jacob. Dance Mag
    44:81 Ag '70
  Toby Armour, Becky Arnold, Phoebe Neville;
    the Cubiculo. J. Armstrong. Dance Mag 44:
    94 F '70
  Toby Armour, Gey Delanghe and Sheila
    Sobel; the Cubiculo, NYC. L. Pastore.
    Dance Mag 44:82:+ Ag '70
  Wendy Papakonstantis, Michael Henry,
    Laura Veldhuis; the Cubiculo, NYC. T.
    Borek. Dance Mag 44:20+ My '70

DANCE conferences
  Bella; American dance symposium. W. Terry.
    por Sat R 53:22 S 12 '70
  Convention carousel: a pictorial statement on
    dance teacher organizations' summer con-
    ventions. N. M. Stoop. il Dance Mag 44:
    66-71 N '70
  Convention time! Dance teacher organiza-
    tions. N. M. Stoop. il Dance Mag 44:91 S:
    91+ O '70
  Critic prepares; work conference on dance
    criticism. S. J. Cohen il Dance Mag 44:24
    F '70
  Learning to look, the Connecticut college
    American dance festival critics conference.
    E. W. Jacobs. il Dance Mag 44:24+ O '70
  Theme was variations; choreography confer-
    ences. R. A. Thom. il Dance Mag 44:36-41
    N '70

DANCE critics. See Critics
DANCE critic's conference. See Dance conferences

DANCE festivals
  Across the Hudson: Festival 70 programs of
    Garden state ballet and Repertory dancers
    of New Jersey. W. Terry. Sat R 53:19 My 9
    '70
  Black dance; events in Wichita, Lee and New
    York. W. Terry. il Sat R 53:26+ S 26 '70
  Calendar of international summer dance
    events (cont) Dance Mag 44:60+ My '70
  Contrasts, good and bad; Jacob's Pillow.
    W. Terry. il Sat R 53:18 Ag 29 '70
  Ecstasy: body and being; New York dance
    festival. W. Terry. il por Sat R 53:45 O 10
    '70
  Festival four: gala performance, Northeast
    regional ballet festival, Toronto. D. Her-
    ing. il Dance Mag 44:75-7 S '70
  Festival one gala performance Southwestern
    regional ballet festival Little Rock, Arkan-
    sas; April 11, 1970. D. Hering. il Dance Mag
    44:72-3 Je '70
  Festival three: gala performance, Pacific re-
    gional ballet festival, Fresno, Calif. D. Her-
    ing. il Dance Mag 44:74+ S '70
  Festival two: gala performance, Southeastern
    regional ballet festival; Nashville, Tenn.
    April 25, 1970. D. Hering. il Dance Mag
    44:70-1 Jl '70
  Kind of oneness, regional ballet and its festi-
    vals. D. Hering. il Dance Mag 44:47-62 O
    '70
  Merce in antic mood; M. Cunningham & co.
    at the Festival of dance, Brooklyn aca-
    demy. W. Terry. il por Sat R 53:40 Ja 24
    '70
  New York dance festival, Delacorte theatre,
    NYC. L. Pastore. Dance Mag 44:74-7 N '70
  Remember: Jacob's Pillow was a stone. T.
    Shawn. il pors Dance Mag 44:49-61 Jl '70
  Stars over the Berkshires; Jacob's Pillow
    dance festival. W. Terry. il Sat R 53:38
    Jl 11 '70
  Trio of festivals; Saratoga performing arts
    center; Connecticut college American dance
    festival; and Jacob's pillow dance festival.
    W. Terry. il Sat R 53:32 Ag 15 '70

DANCE films. See Moving pictures—Dance films
DANCE institute, Akron. See Dance schools
DANCE institutes and workshops
  Dance theater workshop; Manhattan school
    of music. D. Haring. Dance Mag 44:78 Ja
    '70
  Dance theatre workshop; Manhattan school
    of music, NYC. J. Anderson. Dance Mag
    44:76 Je '70

DANCE magazine
  Dance magazine awards 1969. il pors Dance
    Mag 44:27-33+ My '70
  Dance magazine awards: recognition of a
    world community; with addresses, May 25,
    1970. il Dance Mag 44:59-67 Ag '70
  Editorial; changes in Dance magazine. J.
    Gordon. il por Dance Mag 44:27 Ja '70

DANCE of death; drama. See Strindberg, A.
DANCE production
  And tomorrow? What did the Martha Gra-
    ham dance company, without Miss Graham,
    tell us about her art and its future? D.
    Hering. il Dance Mag 44:24-9 D '70
  Supering with the Royal ballet. S. W. McDer-
    mott. il Dance Mag 44:62-9 Ap '70

DANCE repertory company, Long Island. See
  Ballet companies
DANCE schools
  Ballet comes to Binghamton; Roberson ballet
    school. L. Chiavaroli. il pors Dance Mag
    44:28-32 Je '70
  Dream for three; Chamber ballet and the
    Dance institute. D. Hering. il pors Dance
    Mag 44:72-6 Ap '70
  Main Street on Broadway; Don Farnworth's
    dance school. N. M. Stoop. il pors Dance
    Mag 44:30-3 Jl '70
  Saratoga school of modern dance: chapter one
    in a dream come true. S. S. Mack. il Dance
    Mag 44:40-1 Jl '70

DANCE teachers
  Convention carousel: a pictorial statement on
    dance teacher organizations' summer con-
    ventions. N. M. Stoop. il Dance Mag 44:
    66-71 N '70
  Convention time! N. M. Stoop. il Dance Mag
    44:91 S: 91+ O '70

DANCE theater of Harlem. See Ballet compa-
  nies
DANCE theater workshop. See Dance insti-
  tutions and workshops
DANCER, Stanley
  Stanley's most happy Jug. W. F. Reed, jr.
    il por Sports Illus 33:60+ O 5 '70 ●

DANCERS
Big leap; defections of Russian dancers. il por Newsweek 76:86 S 21 '70
Brief biography. S. Goodman. See issues of Dance magazine
Dancer prepares, by J. Penrod and J. G. Plastino. Review
  Dance Mag 44:22+ Ap '70. O. Maynard
Feast of Robbins and some other birds. L. Lerman. il por Mlle 70:176-8 Mr '70
From Russia with love: Alexander Filipov. N. M. Stoop. il pors Dance Mag 44:30-3 D '70
From tadpoles to... D. Hering. il Dance Mag 44:76-9 Mr '70
Presstime news. See issues of Dance magazine
Tribute to 1969 and a salute to the 1970's! il Dance Mag 44:38-45 Ja '70
  See also
Negro dancers
  also names of dancers, e.g. S. Barnard
DANCES at a gathering; ballet. See Ballets—Criticisms
DANCING
Carousel; photo essay on dance around the world (title varies) il Dance Mag 44:28-33 F; 38-45 Mr; 38-43 Ap; 58-69 My; 33-9 Je; 34-9 Jl; 41-3 S; 43-59 D '70
Dance marathons; look back in horror. H. Stern. il Dance Mag 44:68-71 F '70
Dancing: a dramatic exercise in beauty. il Harp Baz 103:106-7 Ap '70
Lamentations and cheers; performance of the Peloponnesian war. by D. Nagrin. W. Terry. il pors Sat R 53:57 F 14 '70
Opera today! il Dance Mag 44:70-3 S '70
Opinion: on dance. D. Jowitt. por Mlle 72: 58+ N '70
Presstime news. See issues of Dance magazine
Reviews. See issues of Dance magazine
World of dance. W. Terry. See issues of Saturday review
  See also
Choreography
Eurythmics
Moving pictures—Dance films
Television broadcasting—Dancing

Competitions
  See also
Ballet—Competitions

Study and teaching
Dance at St Paul's school; Concord, N.H. K. S. Cunningham. il Dance Mag 44:24-5 Je '70
Teaching the classroom teacher to teach dance; CAREL project. N. W. Prevots. il Dance Mag 45:28-9+ Ja '71
DANCING, African
African dance company of Ghana; New York city center. T. Borek. Dance Mag 44:80 Ja '70
Arthur Hall Afro-American dance co; Brooklyn academy of music. T. Borek. Dance Mag 44:73 Jl '70
Charles Moore and Daniel Barrajanos. Clark center for the performing arts, NYC. L. Pastore. Dance Mag 45:79-80 Ja '71
DANCING, Asian
Asha Devi, the Cubiculo, NYC. M. Marks. Dance Mag 44:78 S '70
DANCING, Haitian
Jean-Leon Destine and his Afro-Haitian dance company, 92nd street Y, NYC. M. Marks. Dance Mag 44:81 Ag '70
DANCING, Indian (East Indian)
Dances from India, Kaufmann concert hall, NYC. L. Pastore. Dance Mag 45:76 Ja '71
Indra-Nila; the Cubiculo, NYC. N. Mason. Dance Mag 44:77 Jl '70
Matteo and the Indo-American dance co; Kaufman 92nd St. Y. T. Borek. Dance Mag 44:22 Ja '70
Musical events; Hindu Kerala Kalamandalum Kathakali dance company at Hunter college. W. Sargeant. New Yorker 46:172-3 D 5 '70
Ritha Devi in Dances of India, Julia Richmond auditorium, NYC. J. Anderson. Dance Mag 44:80-1 Ag '70
Sachi Devi Mallegowda & Malini Srirama, the Cubiculo, NYC. N. Mason. Dance Mag 45:77 Ja '71
Sukanya; New York university education theatre. M. Marks. Dance Mag 44:88 Mr '70
Vija Vetra in an evening of Indian dance, music, & poetry; the Cubiculo. T. Borek. Dance Mag 44:84 Ap '70
DANCING, Israeli
Dance; Batsheva dance company performance at City center. New York. N. Goldner. Nation 211:701-2 D 28 '70

DANCING, Japanese
Bon dancing this summer in Hawaii. il Sunset 145:44 Jl '70
Let your camera follow the dance. the Awa odori Japanese dance. W. Lane il Travel 133:79 Ja '70
DANCING, Jewish
Light, lively and Yiddish, Belasco theatre. NYC. N. Mason. Dance Mag 45:76 Ja '71
DANCING, Marathon. See Dancing
DANCING, Mexican
  See also
Ballet folklórico of Mexico
DANCING, Russian
  See also
Moiseyev dance company
DANCING, Spanish
  See also
Flamenco
Molina, J.
DANCING, Thai
Phakavali dancers; Hunter college assembly hall, NYC. L. Pastore. Dance Mag 44:92 My '70
DANCING, Yiddish. See Dancing, Jewish
DANCING in religion, folklore, etc.
Urge to dance; primitive dancing rituals. ed. by G. Loney. L. Boulton. il Dance Mag 44:48-57 My '70
DANCING in television. See Television broadcasting—Dancing
DANDRUFF
Help is on the way. Vogue 156:174 N 1 '70
What to do about dandruff. il Good H 171: 182-3 O '70
DANE, John, 3d
Some great Dane from Tulane. H. D. Whall. il por Sports Illus 33:20-1 N 9 '70 *
Yachting interviews. ed. by E. Horan. il pors Yachting 127:68-9+ Je '70
D'ANGELO, Edward
Philosophers as critical thinking consultants. Sch & Soc 98:166 Mr '70
DANGERFIELD, Rodney
Thirty-year loser is a winner. A. Goldman. por Life 69:3 Ag 28 '70 *
DANGEROUS goods, Transportation of. See Hazardous substances—Transportation
DANGEROUS occupations and trades. See Occupations, Hazardous
DANGEROUS toys. See Toys, Hazardous
DANHOF, Clarence H.
Transferring technology by transferring people. il Mo Labor R 93:62-3 My '70
DANIEL, Arthur
Sampling with seniors. R. Levy. por Duns 96: 50-1 D '70 *
DANIEL, Evelyn. See Wasserman, P. jt. auth.
DANIEL, James
Giving unwed schoolgirl mothers a second chance. il PTA Mag 64:8-10+ Je '70; Same abr. with title Case of the pregnant schoolgirl. Read Digest 97:169-73 S '70
DANIEL, Margaret (Truman)
White House pets; excerpts. il Ladies Home J 87:110-12 Ja '70
DANIEL, Oliver
Caper by Mauricio Kagel. il Sat R 53:68 Ja 31 '70
Fruits of industry, or what AR hath wrought. Sat R 53:47-8 D 26 '70
Holes in the cheese, cantos from the cantons. Sat R 54:58-9 O 31 '70
DANIEL, V. and others
Bacteriophage induced transfer RNA in escherichia coli. bibliog il Science 167:1682-8 Mr 27 '70
DANIEL Yankelovich, inc. See Yankelovich, Daniel, inc.
DANIELLI, James F.
Amoebas, biology and the public. il por Sci N 98:443-4 D 12 '70 *
DANIELS, Alice
School's role in emotional health. il PTA Mag 64:16-18+ bibliog(p34) Ap '70
DANIELS, Bill
Stars earn their stripes. P. Carry. il por Sports Illus 33:22-3 N 30 '70 *
DANIELS, Boston
Kansas City's top cop. L. J. Banks. il pors Ebony 25:35-8+ O '70 *
DANIELS, George E.
Flat-top Cat comes in a kit. il Pop Sci 197:57 Jl '70
Look what you can do with a swivel-blade sabre saw. il Pop Mech 134:184-6+ O '70
Reach for your staple gun. il Pop Sci 196: 114+ F '70
Those new miracle cures for ailing wooden boats. il Pop Sci 196:102-3+ My '70
You can build a spillproof canoe. il Pop Mech 133:176-81 Ap '70
DANIELS, Guy
Basilisk; poem. Sat R 53:8 O 10 '70

DANIELS, Joseph
Psychodynamics of racism. Chr Today 15:12+
O 9 '70
Psychopathology of racism. Chr Today 15:7-8
Ja 15 '71
DANIELS, Leona
34th man. bibliog il por Library J 95:738-43
F 15 '70
DANIELS, Lyn K.
New equation: Nature center, community involvement. il Am For 76:20-3+ N '70
DANIELS, M. E.
Sailing on a bedsheet. il Mech Illus 66:122-4
Mr '70
DANIELS, Mel
Indiana has a hot new poet. P. Carry. il por
Sports Illus 32:55+ Ap 20 '70 *
DANIELS, Paul Clement
Antarctic treaty. il pors Bul Atom Sci 26:
11-15 D '70
DANIELS, Robert D.
Ebb and flow. il Opera N 35:30-1 D 19 '70
Really with it. il Opera N 34:24-7 Mr 7 '70
DANIELS, Stephen
Variable-rate repeating strobe light you can
build. il Pop Sci 196:130-1 My '70
DANISH cookery. See Cookery, Danish
DANKO, Michael E. Jr
Banker's stocks. R. Brady. por Duns 96:92-
3 S '70 *
DANN, Michael Harold
Dann v. Klein: the best game in town. pors
Time 95:98+ My 25 '70 *
How Mike Dann keeps his job at CBS. il pors
Bsns W p78+ My 2 '70 *
Mr Dann of Sesame street. Time 96:48 Jl 6
'70 *
Prime time to leave. por Newsweek 76:59 Jl 6
'70 *
DANPUR. See Almora, India
D'ANTONIO, Lawrence E. and others
Malaria resistance: artificial induction with
a partially purified plasmodial fraction. bibliog il Science 168:1117-18 My 29 '70
DANTZIG, Rudi van
Rudi van Dantzig's The ropes of time. J.
Percival. il Dance Mag 44:44-7 My '70 *
DANZIG, Martin E.
Education of the community mental health
assistant: dovetailing theory with practice. Ment Hy 54:357-63 Jl '70
DAPHNES
Some questions for daphne growers. il Sunset 144:248 Mr '70
DAPRON, Elmer J. Jr
How one man tackled his grocery bill. il Bet
Hom & Gard 48:26-7+ Jl '70
D'ARAZIEN, Steve
Blue water boondoggle. il Nation 211:498-500
N 16 '70
DAR ES SALAAM, Tanzania
Dar. E. Hahn. New Yorker 46:25-9 Jl 18 '70
DARK, Harris Edward
Killer that comes to dinner. il Todays Health
48:9-10+ Ap '70
Seeing it like it was. il Todays Health 48:
30-3 O '70
DARK glasses. See Sun glasses
DARKROOM equipment. See Photography—
Processing—Apparatus and supplies
DARKROOM technique in photography. See
Photography—Processing
DARKROOM timers. See Photography—Processing—Apparatus and supplies
DARKROOMS. See Photography—Studios and
darkrooms
DARLAND, Gary K. and others
Thermophilic, acidophilic mycoplasma isolated
from a coal refuse pile. bibliog il Science
170:1416-18 D 25 '70
—See Brock, T. D. jt. auth.
DARLING, Richard J.
Be your own Mr Fixit. il Har Yrs 10:28-9
My '70
DARLING, Richard L.
When is a social issue a school library issue?
Wilson Lib Bul 45:63 S '70

about

First splinter candidate files for ALA president. Library J 95:1265-6 Ap 1 '70; Discussion. 95:1263, 1782, 2035 Ap 1, My 15, Je 1
'70 *
Richard Darling proposed as ALA president.
Library J 95:1144 Mr 15 '70 *
DARLINGTON, Cyril Dean
Origins of agriculture; with biographical
sketch. il Natur Hist 79:46-57 My '70
DARR, Ann
Before dawn; Love is; poems. New Repub
162:26 F 14 '70

DARR, Jack
Home appliance electronics. il Radio-Electr
41:26 D '70
In the shop, with Jack. See issues of Radio-electronics
Service clinic; questions and answers. See
issues of Radio-electronics
DARRACH, Brad
Easy rider runs wild in the Andes. il pors
Life 68:48-50+ Je 19 '70
Meet Shaky, first electronic person. il Life
69:58B-58D+ N 20 '70
Tragedy of backchat and bons mots. por Life
69:17 O 16 '70
Unexpected meeting with a former slave;
Dick Cavett off camera. il pors Life 69:3,
38-42 O 30 '70
DARRAS, Penny
AIGA fifty books show. bibliog il Pub W 197:
28+ My 18 '70
DARRELL, Robert Donaldson
Percy Grainger posy. por Hi Fi 20:secI 86 Ag
'70
Recharting the muddied waters of Swan lake.
il Hi Fi 20:secI 79-81 Ap '70
Tape deck. See issues of High fidelity section I
DARROW, Clarence Seward
Murder trial of Dr Ossian Sweet; reprint. T.
J. Fleming. il pors Ebony 25:106-8+ O '70 *
DARST, Stephen
Reports: Cairo, Illinois. Atlan 225:16+ Mr
'70
DART, Justin Whitlock
Can Dart take on Avon; T. J. Murray. por
Duns 97:57-8+ Ja '71 *
DARTMOUTH college, Hanover, N.H.
Our far-flung correspondents; seniors and the
war. N. Perrin. New Yorker 46:53-8 Jl 18 '70
Student strikes and book sales: the Dartmouth experience. P. Johnson, jr. Pub W
198:265-6 Ag 31 '70
Teaching president. il por Newsweek 75:75
F 2 '70
DARVEY, N. L. See Driscoll, C. J. jt. auth.
DARVICK, Herman M.
Autograph collectors' club celebrates 5th year.
Hobbies 75:140-1+ D '70
DARVON. See Dextropropoxyphene
DARWIN, Charles Robert
Father of ecology. P. W. Schmidtchen. il pors
Hobbies 75:134-6+ Je '70 *
DASH, Edward F.
Contract for grades. bibliog il Clear House 45:
231-5 D '70
DASHMAN case. See Business management and
organization—Case studies
DASSAULT, Marcel, company. See Airplane
industry and trade—France
DATA banks. See Information storage and retrieval systems
DATA processing service centers
Data transmission network speeds customer
service; electric and water utilities; Albuquerque, N.Mex. D. Mann. il Am City 85:
98-9 F '70
Overseas punchline that pays off. il Bsns W
p40 Ja 2 '71
DATA processing workers. See Computer
workers
DATA storage and retrieval systems. See Information storage and retrieval systems
DATA transmission systems
FCC lets everyone in on data action. Bsns W
p30 Jl 18 '70
Instant information: coming battle for a 10-billion market. il U S News 69:62-4 D 28
'70
See also
Facsimile transmission
Telephone—Data transmission systems
DATES (fruit)
See also
Cookery—Fruit
DATING
Blind-dating. S. Rice. Seventeen 29:158-9+
Ap '70
In my opinion; who needs a real relationship?
J. Marynard. por Seventeen 29:232 F '70
On the scene: alone together. il Seventeen 29:
136-7 F '70
Talking it over with Gay Head; questions
and answers. Gay Head. See issues of
Senior scholastic
When dating starts. J. Brothers. Good H 171:
42+ Ag '70
DATING by computers. See Computers—Social
use
DATSUN (automobile) See Automobiles, Foreign
DATTA, Prasanta. See Feldberg, R. S. jt. auth.
DAUBE of beef. See Cookery—Meat
DAUGHERTY, Bob
Burning issue. Ed Digest 35:35 F '70

DAUGHERTY, John, and Daugherty, Molly
Quiz. See issues of Science digest
DAUGHERTY, Molly. See Daugherty, J. jt. auth.
DAUGHTERS and mothers. See Parent-child relationship
D'AULAIRE, Emily. See D'Aulaire, O. jt. auth.
D'AULAIRE, Ola, and D'Aulaire, Emily
Lesson of the lemmings. il Read Digest 97: 167-9+ Ag '70
DAUMIER, Honoré
Crayon dipped in acid. il Design 71:32-3 Fall '69
DAUPHIN, Manitoba
Only game in town; hockey. W. Johnson. il Sports Illus 32:54-6+ F 16 '70
DAUSSET, Jean. See Rapaport, F. T. jt. auth.
DAVENPORT, Guy
Apocalypse next exit. Nat R 22:1302-4 D 1 '70
DAVENPORT, John, 1904–
Come squeeze or bust, in Ho-Jo we trust. il por Fortune 81:176-9+ My '70
Fork in the road. Fortune 81:82 Mr '70
Industry starts the big cleanup. il Fortune 81:114-17+ F '70
U.S., the law, and Chief Justice Burger. il por Fortune 82:146-50+ S '70
DAVENPORT, John W.
Cretinism in rats: enduring behavioral deficit induced by tricyanoaminopropene. bibliog il Science 167:1007-9 F 13 '70
DAVENPORT, Marcia
Congenital builder's itch. House & Gard 137:56+ My '70
DAVENPORT, Marge
Death by degrees for salmon. Field & S 74: 76-7 Ap '70
DAVENPORT, Richard K. and Rogers, C. M.
Intermodal equivalence of stimuli in apes. bibliog il Science 168:279-80 Ap 10 '70
DAVENPORT, Ronald R.
Legal speedster. S. W. Morris. il pors Ebony 26:48-50+ D '70 *
DAVENPORT, Stephen, Jr
Comeback of the oyster. il N Y Times Mag p22-4+ D 20 '70
DAVENPORT, la.

Parks and playgrounds
Private and public interests, keep tennis courts open year-round; racquets club. P. Conway. il Parks & Rec 5:34-5+ Mr '70
DAVENPORT, la, public library
Dash in Davenport. il Library J 95:4137 D 1 '70
DAVID, Edward E. Jr
David sworn in as top science aide. D. S. Greenberg. Science 169:1185 S 18 '70 *
Federal science: differences of opinion in the highest councils. P. M. Boffey. Science 170: 1383-4 D 25 '70 *
New man for Nixon. por Sci N 98:158 Ag 22 '70
New science adviser. pors Newsweek 76:63 Ag 31 '70 *
Nixon's science adviser: genesis, progress of a surprising appointment. D. S. Greenberg. Science 170:417-19 O 23 '70 *
Science adviser: Dubridge retires, David nominated as successor. J. Walsh. pors Science 169:843-4 Ag 28 '70 *
DAVID, F. S.
Your garden indoors. See issues of Home garden & flower grower
DAVID, Henry P.
Mental health and social action programs for children and youth in international perspective. bibliog Ment Hy 54:503-9 O '70
DAVID, Lester
Civil service career? il Mech Illus 66:65-7+ S '70
Ethel: bravest of the Kennedys; excerpt from Ethel: the story of Mrs Robert F. Kennedy. il pors Good H 171:92-5+ N '70
How to choose a lawyer. Mech Illus 66:65-7+ Jl '70
How to keep your family fiscally fit. il Mech Illus 66:29-31+ D '70
How to manage time-payment buying. Mech Illus 66:39-41 Mr '70
How to save 20 per cent with your own buying club. il Mech Illus 66:41-3+ Je '70
How to stretch your inflated money. Read Digest 96:61-3 F '70
Learning, the new fun thing. il Mech Illus 66:58-60+ F '70
Miracle babies. il Ladies Home J 87:85+ Ap '70
Two lives of Carol Ross. por Good H 170: 65+ F '70
Vocations of the '70s. Mech Illus 66:40-1 Ja '70
Worst of the medical swindlers: the arthritis quacks. Read Digest 96:98-102 Ja '70

DAVID, Saul
Secrets of the Hollywood establishment. il por Esquire 74:64-5+ Ag '70
DAVID, Wilfred D.
Eye care. il Todays Ed 59:40-1 Mr '70
DAVID, Zorro
Occurence. New Yorker 46:31 Ag 22 '70 *
DAVID McKay company. See McKay, David company
DAVIDE Campari-Milano company. See Liquor industry and trade—Italy
DAVIDHAZY, Andrew
How I broke the reality barrier. il Pop Phot 67:74-7 O '70
DAVIDSON, Bill
They shared a victory over heroin. il pors Good H 171:102-3+ O '70
Two-paycheck family. il Good H 170:86-7+ My '70
DAVIDSON, Bruce
At home in East Harlem; interview, ed. by M. R. Weiss. il Sat R 53:54-5 S 19 '70
Light and color of a lovely city; photographs. Holiday 47:42-7 Mr '70
DAVIDSON, Carla
Take a Kodak with you. il Am Heritage 21: 48-51 Je '70
DAVIDSON, Henry A.
Law and the mentally ill. Ment Hy 54:180-5 Ja '70
DAVIDSON, Homer L.
Horizontal efficiency coil checker. il Radio-Electr 41:67-8 My '70
Remote speakers for car stereo. il Radio-Electr 41:53 Ap '70
Ten solid-state car radio problems. il Radio-Electr 41:57-9 Ap '70
DAVIDSON, Jack L.
Responsibility; address, June 11, 1970. Vital Speeches 36:631-2 Ag 1 '70
DAVIDSON, L. A.
Cost and other considerations; poem. Cath World 212:8 O '70
Moment of summer; poem. Horn Bk 46:363 Ag '70
DAVIDSON, Linn
How to resurface your deck with vinyl. il Pop Mech 133:182-4+ Ja '70
DAVIDSON, Marcelle, and Borgenicht, Evelyn
Television environment. PTA Mag 64:31-2 My '70
DAVIDSON, Margaret
America on the move. il Ladies Home J 87: 46+ Ag '70
DAVIDSON, Muriel
Bill Cosby: the man, his work, his world. il pors Good H 170:86-9+ Mr '70
Bright new world of Mary Tyler Moore. il pors Good H 172:58-9+ Ja '71
How nice drugs killed my sister. il Good H 171:96-7+ S '70
Marriages that beat the odds. il Good H 171: 72-5 Jl '70
Warren Beatty: public image vs. private man. il pors Good H 171:84-5+ Ag '70
DAVIDSON, Ronald G. and others
Genetic polymorphisms of human mitochondrial glutamic oxaloacetic transaminase. bibliog il Science 169:391-2 Jl 24 '70
DAVIDSON, Ruth
(ed) Books about antiques. See issues of Antiques
Louis XIII cabinet at Toledo. il Antiques 97: 893-5 Je '70
Museum accessions. See issues of Antiques
Origins of chintz. il Antiques 98:242-5 Ag '70
DAVIDSON, Sara
Bernadette Devlin: an Irish revolutionary in Irish America. il por Harper 240:78-87 Ja '70
Girls on the bandwagon. McCalls 97:42-3+ Ag '70
Open land: getting back to the communal garden. il Harper 240:91-100+ Je; 241:8 Ag '70
To treat a disturbed person, treat his family. il por N Y Times Mag p 10-11+ Ag 16 '70
Tom and Nancy Seaver. il pors McCalls 97: 65-7+ My '70
DAVIDSON, Sidney
As I see it; interview. il por Forbes 105:40+ Ap 1 '70
DAVIE, Donald
Cold spring in Essex; poem. Harper 240:116 F '70
DAVIES, Alan T.
Anti-Zionism, anti-Semitism and the Christian mind. Chr Cent 87:987-9 Ag 19 '70
DAVIES, Don
Come out from under the ivy. il Am Ed 6:28-31 Mr '70
Teacher numbers game. Am Ed 6:7-8 O '70
DAVIS, Adelle
Adelle Davis and the new nutrition; interview, ed. by J. Poppy. pors Look 34:62+ D 15 '70

DAVIS, Al
Best worst man in football. P. Axthelm.
Vogue 156:36 O 15 '70 *
DAVIS, Angela
Her revolutionary voice cries damnation on
the system; excerpts from film interview,
June 27, 1970. il por Life 69:26-7 S 11 '70

about

Angela Davis and the Regents. W. F. Buck-
ley, jr. Nat R 22:748-9 Jl 14 '70 *
Angela Davis case. il pors Newsweek 76:18-
22+ O 26 '70 *
Angela's return. il Time 97:27 Ja 4 '71 *
Davis affair. il por Newsweek 75:78 Je 22
'70 *
Enigmatic Angela. il pors Time 96:28 O 26
'70 *
FBI foils flight. por Sr Schol 97:4 N 9 '70 *
Fugitive. il por Time 96:14 Ag 31 '70 *
Girl who has everything. Nat R 22:1144 N 3
'70 *
Hardly the last word. por Time 95:45 Je 29
'70 *
Path of Angela Davis. il pors Life 69:20D-27
S 11 '70 *
Professor's guns. il por Time 96:13 Ag 24
'70 *
Soledad brother: the prison letters of George
Jackson. D. N. Mount. Pub W 198:19-21
O 26 '70 *
Soledad story. il por Newsweek 76:21 Ag 24
'70 *
Whither Angela Davis? Chr Today 14:22 Jl 17
'70 *
DAVIS, Benjamin Oliver, 1912-
Outlook: a sharp decline in hijackings; inter-
view. por U S News 69:17 D 28 '70

about

Close-up of a city in distress: the story of
Cleveland. il pors U S News 69:43-4 Ag 17
'70 *
Exit the general. Newsweek 76:21 Ag 10 '70 *
Stokes' general takes his leave. pors Bsns W
p62 Ag 8 '70 *
DAVIS, Bernard D.
Prospects for genetic intervention in man;
adaptation of address, December 1969. bib-
liog Science 170:1279-83 D 18 '70
DAVIS, Bertha
Teaching strategies for the slow-learning so-
cial studies student. Ed Digest 35:43-5 Ap
'70
DAVIS, Catherine C. See Johnson, R. D. jt.
auth.
DAVIS, Chester C.
Case of the invisible billionaire. il pors News-
week 76:75-6+ D 21 '70 *
DAVIS, Christopher
Oh! Hillard Elkins! por Esquire 74:135-7+
N '70
DAVIS, Chuck
Chuck Davis dance company; the Cubiculo,
NYC. N. Mason. Dance Mag 44:80 Jl '70 *
DAVIS, Clare
Build this charming curio cabinet. il Pop
Mech 134:172-4 O '70
DAVIS, Clive
Supersonic boom. por Time 96:72-3 S 28 '70 *
DAVIS, Danny K.
Sister debates a brother on that black man-
white woman thing; interview. ed. by K.
Mehlinger. il pors Ebony 25:130-3 Ag '70
DAVIS, Don
Is omnidirectionality desirable in a loudspeak-
er? il Electr World 84:44-5+ Ag '70
—and Palmquist, Don
Equalizing the sound system to match the
room. il Electr World 83:34-6 Ja '70
DAVIS, Douglas M.
Art as act. Art in Am 58:31 Mr '70
DAVIS, Elise Miller
Simple shortcut that will set you free. Read
Digest 96:165-6+ Ap '70
DAVIS, Flora
Way we speak body language. il por N Y
Times Mag p8-9+ My 31 '70
DAVIS, Fred
San Francisco's mystique. il Trans-Action 7:
75-80 Ap '70
DAVIS, Harold L.
Introducing our new look. Phys Today 23:92
S '70
DAVIS, Hugh J.
Pill on trial. pors Time 95:60+ Ja 26 '70
DAVIS, Ivan
Davis, protean pianist. I. Kolodin. Sat R
53:71 Ja 31 '70
DAVIS, Jefferson
First integrated jury impaneled in the United
States, May, 1867. il Negro Hist Bul 33:
134 O '70 *
Their tattered flags, by F. E. Vandiver. Re-
view
Sat R 53:32-3 Mr 28 '70. E. M. Thomas *

DAVIS, Jim
Testing Moto Guzzi's newest V-twin. il Pop
Sci 196:94-5 Ja '70
DAVIS, John Warren
NAACP legal defense and educational fund
has achieved fantastic record in major
breakthroughs in securing constitutional
rights for Negroes. por Negro Hist Bul 33:
135-6 O '70
DAVIS, John William
Davis to succeed Daddario in committee
chairmanship. C. Holden. por Science 170:
1284 D 18 '70 *
John Davis likely to succeed Daddario. J. B.
Phelps. por Phys Today 23:73+ S '70 *
DAVIS, Joseph Hilliard
New light on Joseph H. Davis, left hand
painter. N. F. Little. il Antiques 98:754-7
N '70 *
DAVIS, Julia
Walter Howard Loving, military band con-
ductor. il Negro Hist Bul 33:127 My '70
DAVIS, Karen
Ability is ageless. il Har Yrs 10:46-7 My '70
DAVIS, Kathleen
Exploring the great outdoors. il Parents Mag
45:62-3+ Mr '70
How well do you know your children? il Par-
ents Mag 45:39-41+ Jl '70
DAVIS, Kenneth Newton, 1926-
United States international trade prospects;
address, March 9, 1970. Vital Speeches 36:390-
2 Ap 15 '70

about

Free-for-all over protection. por Bsns W p20
My 2 '70 *
Protectionist push. Newsweek 76:66-7 Jl 6 '70 *
DAVIS, Kenneth P.
Wilderness and forests tomorrow. Cur Hist
59:91-4+ Ag '70
DAVIS, Mike
After the fire is over. il por Mech Illus 66:39-
41+ Ag '70
DAVIS, Miles
Miles of music. H. Saal. il por Newsweek 75:
99-100 Mr 23 '70 *
DAVIS, Nevin W.
Down, down, down; Pennsylvania's deepest
cave. il Nat Wildlife 7:34-7 O '69
DAVIS, Paul H.
Educator's view: six crucial changes colleges
need. il Nations Bsns 58:60+ My '70
DAVIS, Peter G.
Behind the scenes. il Hi Fi sec I 20:20 Ja '70
Opera on film: pitfalls aplenty. il Hi Fi 20:
MA12-13 O '70
Real Carmen. Hi Fi 20:83-4 N '70
Repeat performance. See issues of High fi-
delity section I
Requiem of consolation. Hi Fi 20:secI 94 Ap
'70
Return of Magda Olivero. Hi Fi 20:secI 77-8
Mr '70
Switzerland, another musical tour through
the cantons. Hi Fi 20:92 S '70
Tchaikovsky's musical novel. il Hi Fi 20:87-
8 O '70
Two sopranos: a discovery and an old friend.
pors Hi Fi 20:secI 79 Je '70
World's most complete record store? il Hi Fi
20:62-3 S '70
DAVIS, Ronald L.
Sopranos and six-guns. il Am West 7:10-17+
N '70
DAVIS, Ruth Danielson
Watercolor textiles. L. Rienks. il pors Design
71:16-18 mid-Sum '70 *
DAVIS, Starkey D. and others
Teratogenicity of vitamin B₆ deficiency: om-
phalocele, skeletal and neural defects, and
splenic hypoplasia. bibliog il Science 169:
1329-30 S 25 '70
DAVIS, Sue
McGraw-Hill picketed by women in publish-
ing. Pub W 198:35 Jl 6 '70 *
DAVIS, Virginia E. and Walsh, M. J.
Alcohol, amines and alkaloids: a possible bio-
chemical basis for alcohol addiction. bib-
liog il Science 167:1005-7; 169:1105-6; 170:
1114-15 F 13, S 11, D 4 '70
DAVIS, Wayne H.
More or less people. il New Repub 162:19-21
Je 20 '70
DAVIS, William
Trade winds; interview. ed. by C. Amory.
Sat R 53:16 N 28 '70
DAVIS, William J.
Motoneuron morphology and synaptic con-
tacts: determination by intracellular dye in-
jection. bibliog il Science 168:1358-60 Je 12
'70
DAVIS, William J. (priest)
Prelate and the prisoners. il Commonweal
91:527-9 F 13 '70

DAVIS, William M.
Slurry seal proves itself. il Am City 85: 120+ S '70
DAVIS, Wynn
Crazy way to catch lakers. il por Outdoor Life 146:78-9+ Ag '70
How to fillet fish. il Mech Illus 66:54-5 Jl '70
Outdoors with Wynn Davis. See issues of Mechanix illustrated
DAVISON, Bruce
Bruce Davison: hope for the future; interview, ed. by E. Miller. il por Seventeen 29: 166-7+ Ap '70
DAVISON, Frederic Ellis
Third black general ends eighteen-month tour as brigade commander in Vietnam. Negro Hist Bul 33:49 F '70 *
DAVISON, Jean
Getting started in crossword puzzles. il Writers Digest 50:31-3 My '70
DAVISON, Mildred
Hand-woven coverlets in the Art institute of Chicago. il Antiques 97:734-40 My '70
DAVISON, Peter
New sounds, new silences. Atlan 227:96-8 Ja '71
DAVISSON, Farrell
Oil threatens Acadia. il Nat Parks & Con Mag 44:4-7 D '70
DAVY, J. Gordon, and Branton, Daniel
Subliming ice surfaces: freeze-etch electron microscopy. bibliog il Science 168:1216-18 Je 5 '70
DAWE, Albert R. and others
Summer hibernation induced by cryogenically preserved blood trigger. il Science 168:497-8 Ap 24 '70
DAWIDOWICZ, Lucy S.
Can anti-Semitism be measured? bibliog f Commentary 50:36-43 Jl; 26 N '70
DAWLEY, Joseph
Dawley re-asserts realism. R. Kolbe. il Am Artist 34:69-76 Mr '70 *
DAWSON, Christopher Henry
In memoriam. C. J. McNaspy. America 122: 634 Je 13 '70 *
Obituary
Chr Cent 87:719 Je 10 '70 *
Commonweal 92:284 Je 12 '70. D. Callahan *
DAWSON, G. D. and others
Dorsal root potentials produced by stimulation of fine afferents. bibliog il Science 167:1385-7 Mr 6 '70
DAWSON, Glyn, and Stein, A. O.
Lactosyl ceramidosis: catabolic enzyme defect of glycosphingolipid metabolism. bibliog il Science 170:556-8 O 30 '70
DAWSON, Len
Route of the super Chiefs. il por Time 95: 35 Ja 26 '70
Wham, bam, Stram! T. Maule. il pors Sports Illus 32:10-15 Ja 19 '70
DAY, Brad
Strange end of Shamrock IV. il Yachting 128: 59+ S '70
DAY, Dorothy
Father church and the motherhood of God. D. Grumbach. Commonweal 93:268-9 D 11 '70 *
DAY, Eleanor
Caged passion; poem. Good H 171:11 S '70
DAY, Mary Elizabeth
Selling recreation. il por Parks & Rec 5:27-8+ My '70
DAY, Richard
ABCs of water heaters. il Mech Illus 66:102-4 Ag '70
Chemical tools for home car care. il Pop Sci 197:120 N '70
Facts on fence. il Mech Illus 66:93-5+ My '70
For men: the nuts and bolts of drapery rods. il Pop Sci 197:100-1 S '70
Hot tips on your car's cooling system. il Pop Sci 197:94-6+ Jl '70
How to set up a home diagnostic and tune-up center for your car. il Pop Sci 196:151-6+ Ja '70
Maybe you can afford a second home. il Mech Illus 66:50-2+ Ap '70
New ways to get money for home improvements. il Mech Illus 66:100-1+ N '70
Now: a concrete that doesn't need joints. il Pop Sci 197:84-5+ Jl '70
Plastic piping makes you an instant plumber. il Pop Mech 134:172-5+ S '70
Seven ways to prepare your house for winter. il Mech Illus 66:95-7 O '70
Your own wheel/tire upkeep center. il Pop Sci 197:104+ D '70
—and Ortmann, Jon
Build your own air-pollution tester. il Pop Sci 197:97-9 O '70
DAY, Robin
Troubled reflections of a TV journalist. Read Digest 97:131-2+ N '70

DAY, Thomas
Fakery of guitar masses. il Cath World 211: 270-2 S '70
DAY before heartbreak; story. See Gadzikowski, C.
DAY camp children. See Camp children
DAY camps. See Camps
DAY care centers. See Day nurseries
DAY care for children. See Day nurseries
DAY in fun city; story. See Morgan, J.
DAY-labor agencies. See Employment agencies
DAY lilies
Controlling day-lily pests. Home Gard 57:12 My '70
Day-lilies. M. Price. il Home Gard 57:28-9+ Jl '70
18th century day lilies at Williamsburg. V. Blankenship. il Home Gard 57:62-3 F '70
Evergreen daylilies. R. P. Merry. Horticulture 48:26-7 Ag '70
Outstanding day-lilies. Home Gard 57:18 O '70
Outstanding daylilies. A. Viette. il Horticulture 48:34-5 My '70
DAY nurseries
Big business tangles with day care problems. il Life 69:42-7 Jl 31 '70
Business booms for day-care franchises. Sr Schol 96:Schol Teach 2 F 9 '70
Business takes care of the kiddies. il Bsns W p50-1 O 31 '70
Child care: a franchise business. PTA Mag 64:14 Mr '70
Communes and nurseries: are they as good for children as they are helpful to mothers? B. Spock. Redbook 135:28+ O '70
Day-care business. A. Lake. il McCalls 98: 60-1+ N '70
Day care: it's a lot more than child's play. il Bsns W p 110+ Mr 21 '70
Day care services: our best investment for the future; new legislation. J. H. Reid. por Parents Mag 45:12+ Ap '70
Day care: the boom begins. il Newsweek 76: 92-5+ D 7 '70
Facts about starting a day-care center. il Good H 171:156 S '70
If mother works, who will take care of the kids? il Changing T 24:13-15 Mr '70
Kentucky fried children; day care problem. J. Featherstone. New Repub 163:12-16 S 5 '70
New developments in day care. M. A. Wessel. il Parents Mag 45:76-7+ N '70
What day care means to the children, the parents, the teachers, the community, the President. P. Lynden. il N Y Times Mag p30-1+ F 15 '70; Reply with rejoinder. L. Gates. p60+ Mr 15 '70
Women you'd like to know; day care center for children of migrant laborers. il Farm J 94:60-1 My '70
DAY of absence; drama. See Ward, D. T.
DAY of judgment. See Judgment day
DAY of prayer
President designates Day of prayer for American prisoners of war. proclamation; May 6, 1970. R. M. Nixon. Dept State Bul 62:653 My 25 '70
DAYAN, Moshe
Demanding position. Newsweek 76:58+ N 23 '70 *
I deal with the realities. M. Elkins. por Newsweek 76:42 D 21 '70 *
Inching toward the table. por Time 96:30+ D 14 '70 *
Israel's Dayan: also seeking a solution. por U S News 69:39 D 21 '70 *
Middle East on the Potomac. il pors Newsweek 76:41-2 D 21 '70 *
Moshe the mild. il por Time 96:25 N 30 '70 *
DAYCO corporation
Now you see it. Forbes 105:45 Ja 15 '70
DAYDREAMS
Allow time for daydreams in the world of childhood. J. J. Cox. il Todays Health 48: 48-9+ Je '70
DAYDREAMS; story. See Gerber, M. J.
DAYHOFF, Margaret Oakley. See McLaughlin, P. J. jt. auth.
DAYLIE, Holmes
Chicago: turning against the gangs. il por Time 96:13 Jl 27 '70 *
DAYLIGHT saving
Never resetting the clock. Nations Bsns 58:18 Jl '70
DAYLILIES. See Day lilies
DAYS of wrath; story. See Auchincloss. L.
DAYTON, P. G. See McNay, J. L. jt. auth.

DAYTON, Ohio
Education
Student center for the living arts. S. E. York.
il Todays Ed 59:30-2 N '70
Police department
Dayton's mod cops. il por Newsweek 76:51-2
N 9 '70
Water supply
Repair stays strong. Am City 85:50 S '70
DAYTON Hudson foundation. See Foundations,
Charitable and educational
DAYTONA BEACH, Fla.
Industry's hidden dividends. il Nations Bsns
58:80+ O '70
DAYTONA 500. See Automobile racing
DAYTONA 200. See Motorcycle racing
DEACON; story. See Updike, J.
DEACONS
Survey results spur formation of Italian dia-
conate order. Chr Cent 87:1555 D 30 '70
DEAD SEA
Sea of chemicals. M. Sherwood. il por Chem
43:34-6 Jl '70
DEADMAN, pseud.
Staged sixties; excerpts. il Ramparts 8:43-51
F '70
DEAF
Little boy learns to hear. J. D. Burlage.
il Parents Mag 45:82-5 N '70
Reaching the deaf: report of an in-hospital
group. R. E. Geller. Ment Hy 54:388-92 Jl
'70
Words for a deaf daughter, by P. West. Re-
view
Commentary 51:106-7 Ja '71. J. Kaplan
Newsweek il 76:76 Ag 31 '70. R. A. Gross
Time il 96:60+ S 7 '70. R. Z. Sheppard
Education
My daughter hears with her eyes; John Tracy
clinic. M. Levine. il por Redbook 134:10+
Ap '70
Seeing sound; art lesson for deaf students.
J. W. Bell. il Sch Arts 70:26-9 S '70
They hear the sound of silence; rehabilitation
of deaf children. S. Moffat. il N Y Times
Mag p97+ N 29 '70
See also
Gallaudet college. Washington, D.C.
Rehabilitation
Observations on psychiatric services for the
deaf. K. Z. Altshuler and J. D. Rainer.
bibliog Ment Hy 54:535-9 O '70
DEAF, Apparatus for the
See also
Hearing aids
DEAF-mutes
Blind justice and a deaf-mute. Time 97:51
Ja 11 '71
DEAFNESS
See also
Deaf
Ear
Hearing
Noise—Physiological effects
DEAK, Niklas
Ghost town that refused to die. il Todays
Health 48:56-9 F '70
DEAKIN, James
1972? il pors Esquire 73:55-9+ F '70
DEALERS, Art. See Art dealers
DEALERS, Automobile. See Automobile dealers
DEAN, Dizzy
Another shadow. il por Time 95:58 Mr 9 '70 *
DEAN, Edith, and Dean, Jim
Adrift with driftwood. il por Har Yrs 10:19-20
Jl '70
DEAN, Geoffrey
Multiple sclerosis problem: with biographical
sketch. il Sci Am 223:15, 40-6 bibliog(p 136)
Jl '70
DEAN, George M.
California state horsemen's association. Parks
& Rec 5:39 F '70
DEAN, Jay Hanna. See Dean, D.
DEAN, Jerome Herman. See Dean, D.
DEAN, Jim. See Dean, E. jt. auth.
DEAN, Sidney W. Jr
Hitches in the cable: television in New York.
il Nation 211:41-5 Jl 20 '70
DEAN, William D.
International mortality lottery. Chr Cent 87:
449-50 Ap 15 '70
DEANS, Law school. See College deans
DE ANZA planetarium. See Planetariums
DEAR Janet Rosenberg, dear Mr Kooning;
drama. See Eveling, S.

DEARBORN, Mich.
See also
Henry Ford museum and Greenfield Village
Police department
Police dummy sells safety. J. B. O'Reilly. il
Am City 85:26 Je '70
DEARDORFF, Robert
Camping mobility. il Travel 133:60-2 F '70
Europe's fastest festivals. il Travel 133:60-5
Ja '70
Redbook's guide to honeymoons and other
vacations. il Redbook 136:35-42 N '70
Step by step through Charleston. il Travel
133:32-7 Ap '70
Step by step through Richmond. il Travel
134:42-7+ S '70
Step by step through St Augustine. il Travel
134:40-5 D '70
DEAS, Alston
Charleston ornamental ironwork. il Antiques
97:748-51 My '70
DEAS, Walter
Venomous octopus; with biographical
sketch. il Sea Front 16:357-9, 382 N '70
DEATH
Death is alone; excerpt from Death and hope.
H. J. Cargas. il Cath World 210:269-72
Mr '70
Hope in the midst of horror. R. L. Cleath.
Chr Today 14:3-5 Mr 27 '70
Need for a theology of death. F. Minton. Chr
Cent 87:352-5 Mr 25 '70; Discussion. 87:767-8
Je 17 '70
Problems in the meaning of death; AAAS
symposium, December 29, 1970. L. R. Kass.
il Science 170:1235-6 D 11 '70
See also
Bereavement
Children and death
Euthanasia
Funeral rites and ceremonies
Future life
Suicide
Causes
Casualties of our time. A. B. Ford. bibliog
il Science 167:256-63 Ja 16 '70
Psychology
Dying with dignity. D. Wolfle. Science 168:
1403 Je 19 '70; Discussion. 169:717 Ag 21 '70
How America lives with death. K. L. Wood-
ward. il Newsweek 75:81-2+ Ap 6 '70
DEATH (biology)
Score card for death. A. J. Snider. Sci Di-
gest 68:58 Ag '70
DEATH, Fear of. See Fear
DEATH and children. See Children and death
DEATH of Edward Lear: story. See Barthelme,
D.
DEATH penalty. See Capital punishment
DEATH rate. See Mortality
DEATH row prisoners. See Prisoners
DEATH VALLEY
Ballet in Death Valley. il por Life 68:42-3 Ap
17 '70
DEAUX, Edward, and Kakolewski, J. W.
Emotionally induced increases in effective
osmotic pressure and subsequent thirst. bib-
liog il Science 169:1226-8 S 18 '70
DEBAKEY, Michael Ellis
Texas tornado vs. Dr Wonderful. T. Thomp-
son. il pors Life 68:62B-64D+ Ap 10 '70 *
DEBATES and debating
See also
Forums (discussion and debate)
DEBAUN, Jack R. and others
Reactivity in vivo of the carcinogen N-
hydroxy-2-acetylaminofluorene: increase by
sulfate ion. bibliog il Science 167:184-6 Ja
9 '70
DEBAUN, Stephen
Bountiful breakfasts; excerpts. il Ladies
Home J 87:88-90 Je '70
DE BEERS consolidated mines, ltd.
Bear market in diamonds. il Bsns W p55
My 23 '70
Diamonds: the grit behind the glitter. il
Forbes 105:20-2+ F 1 '70
Everything's coming up diamonds. G. Young.
il Pop Mech 133:116-19+ Mr '70; Same.
Sci Digest 68:68-73 O '70
DEBLASSIE, Richard R.
Counseling practicum on the verge of bank-
ruptcy? Clear House 45:161-3 N '70
DE BOLT, William Walter
Good Friday eclipse; poem. Chr Cent 87:357
Mr 25 '70
Jumper; poem. Chr Cent 87:526 Ap 29 '70
Modern Pharisee talks to himself; poem.
Chr Cent 87:628 My 20 '70

DEBRAY, Jules Régis
Debray's release. il por Newsweek 77:29-30
Ja 4 '71 *
DEBRAY, Régis. See Debray, J. R.
DEBRÉ, Michel
Debré vs. the brass. Newsweek 75:35-6 Ap 13
'70 *
DEBT
Worry grows: paying personal debts. il U S
News 68:66-8 Je 22 '70
See also
Bankruptcy
Collecting of accounts
Debtor and creditor
DEBTOR and creditor
Artful dodgers; ploys used to defer bill pay-
ments. Newsweek 76:113-14 N 16 '70
DEBTS, Public
United States
Higher ceiling for national debt? U S News
68:60 Je 8 '70
DEBUSSY, Claude
Boulez' Debussy, lucid and illuminating. D.
Hamilton. Hi Fi sec I 20:98 Ja '70
Debussy's dream House. E. Lockspeiser. il
pors Opera N 34:8-12 Mr 21 '70 *
On DGG, an exquisite Debussy recital. L.
Gerber. Am Rec G 36:826 Je '70 *
Pelléas by Debussy, Maeterlinck, and Boulez.
R. Jacobson. Sat R 53:45 D 26 '70 *
Pelléas et Mélisande. Criticism
New Yorker 46:107 Mr 28 '70 *
New Yorker 46:153-4 Ap 18 '70 *
New Yorker 46:143-4 O 31 '70
Sat R 53:65 F 14 '70 *
Sat R 53:48 Ap 4 '70 *
Piano music of Mozart and Debussy. H.
Goldsmith. il Hi Fi 20:secI 81-3 Ap '70 *
DECAMP, Dot
Smith/Jones. Library J 95:3451 O 15 '70
DE CAMP, L. Sprague
Evolution: still on trial after 100 years. il Sci
Digest 67:17-21 Mr '70
Mysterious Angkor, jungle city of the dead. il
Sci Digest 67:18-23 Ap '70
Mysterious ships of Lake Nemi. il Sci Di-
gest 67:68-72 Je '70
Solving the mystery of the Street of the
dead. il Sci Digest 68:28-33 D '70
Tower of mystery. il Sci Digest 68:15 O '70
DECARBOXYLASE
Estrogenic induction of ornithine decarboxy-
lase in vivo and vitro. S. Cohen and oth-
ers. bibliog il Science 170:336-8 O 16 '70
L-Glutamic acid decarboxylase: a new type in
glial cells and human brain gliomas. B.
Haber and others. bibliog il Science 168:598-
9 My 1 '70
DECARLI, Leonore M. See Lieber, C. S. jt.
auth.
DECAY, Dental. See Dental caries
DECAY of wood. See Wood—Decay
DECCA navigator company, ltd.
Decca navigation pioneer retires. Aviation W
93:33 N 16 '70
DECENTRALIZATION in government
British labor calls for new synthesis; A. W.
Benn's conclusions. B. L. Masse. America
123:309 O 24 '70
Can the Nixon administration be doing some-
thing right? the new regional system. J.
Fischer. Harper 241:22-4+ N '70
Resurgence of state power. il Bsns W p 102+
O 17 '70
DECENTRALIZATION in school administration.
See School management and organization
DECHAR, Peter
Peter Dechar. D. H. Karshan. il por Art in
Am 58:31-4 Jl '70 *
DECIMAL counters. See Counting machines
and devices
DECISION alternative ration evaluation. See
Decision making
DECISION making
Assessment of multiattribute preferences. R.
L. Keeney. bibliog il Science 168:1491-2 Je
19 '70
At last: real computer power for decision
makers. C. H. Jones. bibliog f il Harvard
Bsns R 48:75-89 S '70
Corporate models: on-line, real-time systems.
J. B. Boulden and E. S. Buffa. il Harvard
Bsns R 48:65-83 Jl '70
Do managers find decision theory useful? R.
V. Brown. il Harvard Bsns R 48:78-89 My '70
Facing up to decisions. J. Brothers. por Good
H 170:44+ Ap '70
Focus on leadership in group decision mak-
ing. M. L. Marshall. Clear House 45:41-4
S '70
Let DARE make your solid-waste decisions;
decision alternative ration evaluation. A.
J Klee. il Am City 85:100-3 F '70

Power and politics in organizational life. A.
Zaleznik. il Harvard Bsns R 48:47-60 My '70
RSVP cycles, by L. Halprin. Review
Arch Forum 133:78 N '70. G. Clay
Technology in the manager's future; adapta-
tion of address, June 1970. H. M. Boettinger.
bibliog f il Harvard Bsns R 48:4-6+ N '70
See also
Management games
DECISION making (political science)
Henry's wonderful machine; the Kissinger
policy process. J. Osborne. New Repub 162:
11-13 Ja 31 '70
President Nixon, Cambodia and new chances
for peace. J. G. Hubbell. il Read Digest
97:54-63 Jl '70
DECKER, Howard F.
Five dozen ideas for teaching the newspaper
unit. Engl J 59:268-72 F '70
DECKER, William
Rodeo. il Travel & Camera 33:42-51 Jl '70
DECKS
How to resurface your deck with vinyl. L.
Davidson. il Pop Mech 133:182-4+ Ja '70
DECKS (outdoor rooms) See Outdoor rooms
DECLARATION of human rights. See Universal
declaration of human rights
DECLARATION of independence. See United
States—Declaration of independence
DÉCO art. See Art déco
DE COFF, Linda
Five young beauties & how they get that
way. il pors Mlle 72:135-41 N '70 *
DECORATION and ornament
Broomstick people. il Design 71:12-13 Wint '69
Easy-to-make holiday decorations. il Parents
Mag 45:116 O '70
Inflammatory art: nineteenth-century fire-en-
gine panels. il Am Heritage 21:40-5 Je '70
Putting on a room; People paper. il Time
96:62 O 5 '70
See also
Art déco
Christmas decorations
Decoupage
Design, Decorative
Enamel and enameling
Frescoes
Fretwork
Graffito decoration
House decoration
Mosaics
Paper work
Pottery—Decoration
Shellwork
Tapestry
Tinware
Wall hangings
DECORATION and ornament, Architectural
Design for living. A. G. Wolter. il por Design
71:29 Wint '69
Making an impression in Mexico. P. Thomas
and F. J. Thomas. il Américas 22:30-5 S
'70
Message as an architectural medium. H. C.
Schultz. il Arch Forum 132:44-9 My '70
Pragmaesthetics; urban decor in Europe. J.
E. Curtis. il Parks & Rec 5:15-17+ Jl '70
See also
Ironwork
Mural painting and decoration
Mural painting and decoration. Exterior
DECORATION and ornament, Personal
Instant-hairdo accessories. il Good H 171:
98-9 N '70
Long, straight hair goes to the ball. il
McCalls 98:54-5 D '70
DECORATION day. See Memorial day
DECORATIONS, Christmas. See Christmas dec-
orations
DECORATIONS of honor
Tarnished medals. Newsweek 76:65 N 2 '70
DECORATIVE arts. See Decoration and orna-
ment
DECORATIVE design. See Design, Decorative
DECORATIVE lighting. See Lighting, Archi-
tectural and decorative
DECOUPAGE
Decoupage: the art of cut and paste. V. Mc-
Alister. il Har Yrs 10:38-9 Ap '70
DE CRISTOFORO, R. J.
Choosing & using saber-saw blades. il Mech
Illus 66:90-2+ S '70
Facts on files. il Mech Illus 66:94-6 Ag '70
Guide to nuts & bolts. il Mech Illus 66:106-
7+ N '70
How to cut square holes. il Mech Illus 66:
116-17+ O '70
How to sharpen tools. il Mech Illus 66:93-5
Ap '70
Primer on plug cutters. il Mech Illus 66:98-9
N '70
Snips story. il Mech Illus 66:70-1+ D '70
—See Fiechter, P. E. jt. auth.
DECROW, Karen
Opinion. Mlle 70:34+ F '70

DEFENSE program review committee. See United States—National security council

DEFENSES, Air. See Air defenses

DEFERRARI, Teresa M.
Religion and the social sciences. il Cath World 212:209-10 Ja '71

DEFERRED payment plan. See Instalment plan

DEFICIENCY diseases
Mystery of vitamins. Newsweek 76:69 **Ag** 24 '70
See also
Calcium in the body

DEFICIENCY diseases in animals
New nutritional disease for hogs; selenium-vitamin E deficiency. J. Russell. Farm J 93:36F N '69

DEFICIT spending. See Government spending policy

DEFOLIATION
Agent Orange affair; suspending use in Viet Nam. il Time 96:39-40 N 2 '70
Blight that failed; herbicide operations in Vietnam. il Newsweek 77:79 Ja 11 '71
Defoliants, a closed case? AAAS study. Commonweal 93:363 Ja 15 '71
Ecological effects of the war in Vietnam. G. H. Orians and E. W. Pfeiffer. bibliog il Science 168:544-54 My 1 '70; Discussion. 169:6, 1030 Jl 3, S 11 '70
Ecology of war. Sci Am 223:48-9 Jl '70
Let's hear it for pollution. il it's in Asia; Senate debate. H. H. Vinnedge. New Repub 163.14-15 O 17 '70
Operation Wasteland; South Viet Nam. il Time 95:70-3 My 25 '70
Ravaged soil of Vietnam. J. B. Kelley. il Cath World 211:71-3 My '70
Reporter at large; aerial spraying of trees in Vietnam. T. Whiteside. New Yorker 45:32-8+ F 7; 46:124-9 Mr 14; 64-6+ Jl 4 '70
United States experts report on defoliation in Cambodia. Dept State Bul 61:635 D 29 '69

DEFORD, Frank
Beware of the Hawks. il por Sports Illus 32:22-7 Ap 13 '70
East is Knicks but west is West. il Sports Illus 32:30-2+ My 11 '70
Happy pair of hairy sports. il pors Sports Illus 32:52-6+ F 23 '70
In for two plus the title. il Sports Illus 32:14-17 My 18 '70
Knicks drive in high. il Sports Illus 32:12-17 Ap 27 '70
Loop has gone hoops-a-daisy. il Sports Illus 32:18-19 F 9 '70
Merger, madness and Maravich. il por Sports Illus 32:23-30+ Ap 6 '70
Pro basketball (cont) Sports Illus 32:40+ F 2 '70
Roller derby. il Sports Illus 33:56+ O 5 '70
Run it up the flagpole, Johnny. il por Sports Illus 33:74-6+ S 28 '70
TV talk. Sports Illus 33:9 O 5; 9 O 26; 13 D 14 '70
Who are the HUB men. il Sports Illus 33:54-6+ Jl 13 '70
Who blew the U.S. nose count? il Sports Illus 33:72-3+ D 21 '70

DEFORMATION (mechanics)
See also
Rheology

DEFORMATION of rocks. See Rocks—Deformation

DEFORMITIES
Girl who found a face. J. L. Block. il Good H 170:30+ Ap '70; Same abr. Read Digest 97:49-53 Jl '70
Price of a trip? possibility of chromosome damage to germ cells by LSD. Time 95:43 F 23 '70
Right not to be born; refusal to grant therapeutic abortion in case of rubella baby. M. K. Sanders. il Harper 240:92-9 Ap '70
Thalidomide sequel; compensation by German manufacturers to parents of all thalidomide-deformed children. il Time 95:39 F 9 '70
What's your trademark? occupational markings. S. P. Gerber. il Mech Illus 66:72-3+ F '70

DE FRANCE, Ellen Gerard
Chemistry in language and literature. por Chem 43:16-17 Ap '70

DEFREES, Sister Madeline
Pegasus and six blind Indians. Engl J 59:928-37 O '70

DE GARA, John P.
Nuclear proliferation and security. bibliog f il por Int Concil 578:5-69 My '70

DE GAULLE, Charles. See Gaulle, C. de

DEGENS, Egon T. and Ross, D. A.
Red Sea hot brines; with biographical sketches. il Sci Am 222:12, 32-42 Ap '70
—and others
Fossil membranes and cell wall fragments from a 7000-year-old Black Sea sediment. bibliog il Science 168:1207-8 Je 5 '70

DE GEREZ, Toni
Three times lonely; address, October 1968. il Horn Bk 46:66-73 F '70

DEGLER, Carl N.
Slavery in Brazil and the United States: an essay in comparative history; address, April 1969. bibliog f Am Hist R 75:1004-28 Ap '70

DEGOLYER, Everette Lee
Mr De, by L. Tinkle. Review
Sat R por 53:32-3 D 12 '70. R. Girdler *

DE GRAMONT, Nancy
Snow storm; poem. Mlle 72:140 D '70

DE GRAMONT, Sanche
Académie française; excerpt from The French: portrait of a people. Horizon 11:48-51 Aut '69
Boul' Mich; story. il Harper 241:106-8 O '70
Dubuffet, the subversive smothered with love. il por Horizon 12:88-105 Sum '70
How one pleasant, scholarly young man from Brazil became a kidnapping, gun-toting, bombing revolutionary. il pors N Y Times Mag p43-5+ N 15 '70
How to train an American wife. Vogue 155:132-3+ Je '70
Our other man in Algiers. il N Y Times Mag p30+ N 1 '70
Remember Dada: Man Ray at eighty. il pors N Y Times Mag p6-7+ S 6 '70
Vocation for madness. pors Horizon 12:48-55 Spr '70

DEGREES, Academic
Austerity at New York: degree dropping. Chr Today 14:52 Ap 10 '70
Degree reform by degrees; doctor of ministry. F. T. Trotter. Chr Cent 87:861 Jl 15 '70
Degrees by examination, external degree program in New York state. Sat R 53:64-5 O 17 '70
D.min: First or second theological degree? L. H. DeWolf. Chr Cent 87:1211 O 14 '70; Discussion. 87:1388 N 18 '70
Doctor of arts degree. H. G. Stever. Science 170:587 N 6 '70
Doctoral glut. il Newsweek 75:114 Mr 16 '70
On being called doctor. G. E. Berkley. Ed Digest 36:32-4 D '70
Ph.D. holders in private industry. M. F. Crowley il Mo Labor R 93:65-6 Ag '70
Too many doctors. Time 95:45+ Je 29 '70
See also
Diplomas, Fraudulent

DEGREES, Honorary
Gaudeamus igitur. Nat R 22:659 Je 30 '70
Kudos (cont) il Time 95:47-8 Je 8; 49 Je 15; 49-50 Je 22 '70

DEGRELLE, Léon
Last of the Quislings. il por Newsweek 75:46+ F 23 '70 *

DE GROOT, Roy Andries
Movable feast (cont) Esquire 73:36+ Je; 74:98+ N '70
Random harvest of Albert Stockli. il por Esquire 74:150-1+ O '70
Weekend of incredible gluttony. il Esquire 73:135-9+ My '70
Wine-lover's tour of the Loire. il House B 112:74-5+ Jl '70
Wine-lover's tour of the Rhône. il House B 112:80-2 Ag '70

DEHAAN, Thurston
Presenting Thurston DeHaan, organic gardener. F. Hilliker. il pors Org Gard & Farm 17:28-31 O '70 *

DEHART, Florence E.
Generating a spirit of inquiry. bibliog Am Lib 1:602-5 Je '70
Standardization in commercial children's cataloging. il por Library J 95:744-9 F 15 '70

DEHL, R. E.
Collagen: mobile water content of frozen fibers. bibliog il Science 170:738-9 N 13 '70

DEHUMIDIFIERS
Consumer's guide to dehumidifiers. il Mech Illus 66:75 Jl '70

DEHYDROGENASES
Alcohol dehydrogenase in maize: genetic basis for isozymes. J. G. Scandalios; discussion. Science 167:1519 Mr 13 '70
Alcohol dehydrogenase in maize: genetic basis for multiple isozymes. D. Schwartz; discussion. Science 167:1519 Mr 13 '70
Alcohol dehydrogenase in maize: genetic control of enzyme activity. Y. Efron. bibliog il Science 170:751-3 N 13 '70

DEHYDROGENASES—*Continued*
DDT metabolism; oxidation of the metabolite 2,2-bis(p-chlorophenyl)ethanol by alcohol dehydrogenase. J. E. Suggs and others. Science 168:582 My 1 '70
Horseshoe crab lactate dehydrogenases; evidence for dimeric structure. R. K. Selander and S. Y. Yang. bibliog il Science 169:179:81 Jl 10 '70
Horseshoe crab lactate dehydrogenase; tissue distribution and molecular weight. E. J. Massaro. bibliog il Science 167:994-6 F 13 '70
Lactate dehydrogenase isozymes; further kinetic studies at high enzyme concentration. T. Wuntch and others. bibliog il Science 169:480-1 Jl 31 '70
Physiological concentrations of lactate dehydrogenases and substrate inhibition. J. Everse and others. bibliog il Science 168:1236-8 Je 5 '70
Quartet in amino acids; structure of lactate dehydrogenase. Sci Am 222:48 Je '70
DE-ICERS. See Airplanes—Ice protection
DEIFICATION
Deification of Mao. H. Welch. il por Sat R 53:25+ S 19 '70
DEINHARDT, Friedrich, and others
ST-feline fibrosarcoma virus; induction of tumors in Marmoset monkeys. bibliog il Science 167:881 F 6 '70
DEJEAN, Maurice
KGB; condensation. J. Barron. il Read Digest 97:201-15+ Ag '70 *
DE JERSEY, Katherine
Not in the stars. P. Nathan. Pub W 198:41 Ag 24 '70 *
DEKNATEL, John H.
High performance powerboats. il por Motor B 125:100-1 Ja '70
DE KOONING, Elaine, and Drexler, Rosalyn
Dialogue. il Art N 69:40-1+ Ja '71
DELACORTE, George Thomas
Trade winds; interview, ed. by C. Amory. Sat R 53:14 O 31 '70
DELACORTE, Valerie
Trade winds; interview, ed. by C. Amory. Sat R 53:14 O 31 '70
DELACROIX, Eugène
Delacroix in Africa. R. McMullen. il por Horizon 11:60-75 Aut '69
DELANEY, Barbara Snow
Shakers today. il Antiques 98:618-22 O '70
DELANEY, James J.
Congressman who fights for safe food. M. C. Goldman. Org Gard & Farm 17:66-70 My '70
DELANEY, Robert F.
Leadership; address, May 23, 1970. Vital Speeches 36:621-2 Ag 1 '70
DELANEY clause. See Food laws and legislation
DELAUNAY-TERK, Sonia
[Photograph] B. Brandt. Harp Baz 103:140-1 F '70
DELAWARE
See also
Architecture, Domestic—Delaware
Brandywine Creek
Camps—Delaware
Chesapeake Bay
DELAWARE RIVER
Dirty flows the Delaware. G. Alexander. il Newsweek 76:68-73 N 2 '70
DELAY devices
Build a Woofer guard. P. Arthur. il Pop Electr 33:49-52 Jl '70
DELAYED-action preparations
Water-degradable polymers for controlled release of herbicides and other agents. M. L. Beasley and R. L. Collins. Science 169:769-70 Ag 21 '70
DELBANCO, Nicholas
In from the islands out from the town; story. Esquire 73:120-2 Je '70
DELBRÜCK, Max
Physicist's renewed look at biology; twenty years later. bibliog Science 168:1312-15 Je 12 '70
DELDERFIELD, Ronald Frederick
Authors & editors. B. A. Bannon. por Pub W 197:29-30 Ja 12 '70
Long, long trail. Writer 84:9-12 Ja '71
DELFELD, Paula
His earthworms work for him. il Org Gard & Farm 17:71-2+ Ag '70
DELGADO, José Manuel Rodriguez
Brain researcher José Delgado asks: what kind of humans would we like to construct? M. Scarf. il pors N Y Times Mag p46-7+ N 15 '70; Discussion. p21+ D 13 '70 *
Shock for Paddy. il por Newsweek 76:88 S 28 '70 *
DELINQUENT children. See Juvenile delinquency

DELINQUENT girls. See Girls, Delinquent
DELINQUENTS. See Juvenile delinquency
DELIUS, Frederick
Koanga. Criticism
Time il 97:56 Ja 4 '71 *
Koanga. F. Stevenson. il Opera N 35:34-5 D 19 '70 *
Road to Samarkand, by G. Jahoda. Review
Am Rec G por 36:712-13+ My '70. J. Coveney
DELIVERY of goods
See also
United parcel service
DELLA CAVA, Ralph
Torture in Brazil. Commonweal 92:129+, 398-9 Ap 24, Ag 7 '70
DELLA FEMINA, Jerry
It's a tough life. il por Time 95:78 Je 22 '70 *
Trade winds. C. Amory. Sat R 53:4 Jl 4 '70 *
DELLINGER, David
Dove militant. B. Wasserstein. New Repub 163:28-9 Ag 22 '70 *
DELLIQUANTI, Don
Baseball. Sports Illus 33:92-3 S 14 '70
DELLUMS, Ronald V.
Enter Ron Dellums: radical; with interview, ed. by E. Glynn. America 123:483-7 D 5 '70
DELMAN, David
And then she smiled; story. Ladies Home J 87:60-1 Jl '70
DELMAS, Jacques Pierre Michel Chaban-. See Chaban-Delmas, J. P. M.
DEL MONTE, Maurice
Dutchman in a box. il pors Life 69:71-2 N 20 '70 *
DEL MONTE corporation
Pain of plenty. il Forbes 106:54 D 15 '70
DE LONE, Richard H. and De Lone, S. T.
John Dewey is alive and well in New England. il Sat R 53:69-71+ N 21 '70
DE LONE, Susan T. See De Lone, R. H. jt. auth.
DE LONG, James
Le champignon. il House B 112:37-40 Ag '70
DELOREAN, John Zachary
Chevy's top brass talks about Vega; starlet with a future; interview, ed. by J. Dunne. il pors Pop Sci 197:56-7+ S '70

about

GM's John DeLorean: powerhouse behind the Vega. A. Rothenberg. il pors Look 34:54-7 Ag 25 '70
New kind of wheel at GM. B. Yates. il pors Sports Illus 31:39-42+ D 15 '69
DELORENZO, Tony
Motor trend interview. pors Motor T 22:78+ N '70
DELORIA, Vine, Jr
This country was a lot better off when the Indians were running it. il por N Y Times Mag p32-3+ Mr 8 '70
DELPHINIUMS
Cool, blue summer. R. E. Atkinson and E. Haraszty. il McCalls 97:24+ Ag '70
Delphiniums for towering spikes. D. E. Stebbins. il Home Gard 57:28-9 My '70
DELSEMME, A. H. and Wenger, A.
Superdense water ice. bibliog Science 167:44-5; 170:654 Ja 2; N 6 '70
DELTA air lines
Delta expects to top airline growth rate. Aviation W 92:29 F 23 '70
Delta planning stresses quiet innovation. J. P. Woolsey. il Aviation W 92:30-1+ Mr 30 '70
Delta starts 747 service. Aviation W 93:26-7 N 2 '70
Delta's profit rises 14 per cent in fiscal 1970. Aviation W 93:36 O 5 '70
Delta's profits, revenues rise. Aviation W 93:39 Ag 3 '70
It all began with the boll weevil. C. H. Dolson. il Nations Bsns 58:667 Ja '70
Optimism marks Delta forecasts. J. P. Woolsey. il Aviation W 92:27-9 Mr 23 '70
DELTA booster. See Space vehicles—Propulsion systems
DELTA Queen (steamship) See Steamships and steamboats
DELTEC international, ltd.
Partnership for multinational growth. Fortune 82:195 Ag '70
Where angels fear to tread. il Forbes 105:38 Ap 1 '70
DE LUCIA, Fernando
Top tenors, on L.P. A. Favia-Artsay. pors Hobbies 75:35 Je '70 *
DELWICHE, C. C.
Nitrogen cycle; with biographical sketch. il Sci Am 223:38, 136-46 bibliog(p264) S '70
DEMARCO, Norman
Film invasion. Clear House 46:61-4 S '70

DEMAREE, Allan T.
Age of anxiety at AT&T. il Fortune 81:156-9+ My '70
Cars and cities on a collision course. il Fortune 81:124-8+ F '70
G.E.'s costly ventures into the future. il Fortune 82:88-93+ O '70
Kicking the doldrums at Cincinnati milacron. il Fortune 82:72-7+ D '70

DEMAREST, David P. Jr
Slang and profanity; their uses in English composition. Clear House 45:76-80 O '70

DEMARS, Robert. See Albertini, R. J. jt. auth.

DEMECOLCINE
Colcemid sensitivity of fission yeast and the isolation of colcemid-resistant mutants. S. Lederberg and G. Stetten. bibliog il Science 168:485-7 Ap 24 '70

DE MÉDICIS, Rinaldo
Cubic FeS, a metastable iron sulfide. bibliog il Science 170:1191-2 D 11 '70

DEMETROPOULOS, Charles
Watercolor page; with biographical sketch. il Am Artist 34:44-5+ Ja '70

DEMIASHKEVICH, Michael John
Michael John Demiashkevich: the way of an essentialist. G. Chambers. bibliog f Sch & Soc 98:108-10 F '70 *

DE MILLE, Agnes
Agnes De Mille speaks to Congress on the state of the arts; address, with excerpts from testimony, February 9, 1970. por Dance Mag 44:34-5+ My '70
Judgment in Moscow. Atlan 226:107-8+ Ag '70

DEMOCRACY
Are we faced with a new aristocracy? W. B. Cannon. Cur 124:22-6 D '70
"—If democracy survives" Am City 85:12 Jl '70
Is constitutional democracy doomed? W. D. Phelan, jr. Cur 116:40-6 Mr '70
Manner of speaking; defense against accusation by HISC of being a radical. J. Ciardi. Sat R 53:12+ N 7 '70
Radical Saul Alinsky: prophet of power to the people; Time essay. por Time 95:56-7 Mr 2 '70
Urban civilization & its discontents; theories of the Founding fathers. I. Kristol. Commentary 50:29-35 Jl '70; Discussion. 50:4, 40+ N '70; 51:23-6 Ja '71
Violent ordeals of democracy; Canada and Chile. Chr Cent 87:1307 N 4 '70
See also
Communism and democracy
Liberalism
Town meeting

DEMOCRATIC clubs. See Political clubs and associations

DEMOCRATIC convention. See National convention, Democratic

DEMOCRATIC party
About democracy; new rules of the McGovern commission. New Repub 162:9-10 F 7 '70
Bossism bogy. il por Time 95:22-3 Ap 13 '70
Clean feeling of achievement; New Democratic coalition congressional candidates. New Repub 162:9-11 Mr 14 '70
Coming upheaval in Congress. J. Fischer. Harper 241:21-2+ O '70
Dark horse. por Newsweek 75:30-1 Mr 2 '70
Democratic cheer. K. Crawford. Newsweek 76:57 D 14 '70
Democratic doldrums. Nat R 22:770+ Jl 28 '70
Democratic malady. S. Alsop. Newsweek 75:96 Mr 2 '70
Democratic unity. New Repub 163:8-9 N 21 '70
Democratic year? K. Crawford. Newsweek 75:26 Ap 13 '70
Democrats' biggest gain. il U S News 69:26-7 N 16 '70
Democrats: defensive politics. il Time 96:11 S 28 '70
Democrats: divided and dispirited. il Time 95:12+ F 16 '70
Democrats' new strategy for a comeback this year. il por U S News 68:40-1 Mr 23 '70
Democrats on the mend. M. McGrory. America 122:207 F 28 '70
Democrats: spooked by abstractions. R. Sherrill. il Nation 211:295-302 O 5 '70
Democrats: waiting for lefty. Nat R 22:186+ F 24 '70
Ed Muskie, and the pack. il por Newsweek 76:33-5+ N 16 '70
For Democrats: a way out of their differences? summary of statements. H. H. Humphrey. il por U S News 68:17 F 23 '70
Form sheet on the dark horses. L. Gapay. Nation 211:202-6 S 14 '70

Galbraith purge; referendum '70. K. Crawford. Newsweek 75:29 F 9 '70
Give youth a voice. Sr Schol 95:15-16 O 13 '69
Goldberg variation; New York state candidates. il por Newsweek 75:22-3 Ap 13 '70
Governors: a Democratic blitz. il Newsweek 76:44+ N 16 '70
Great purge. W. F. Buckley, jr. Nat R 22:169 F 10 '70
How Democrats hope to make the most of '71. il U S News 70:20-2 Ja 4 '71
Humphrey's imperative. K. Crawford. Newsweek 76:25 Ag 24 '70
Incompetent opposition; lack of leadership vs. Vietnamese war. Nation 210:580 My 18 '70
Is a two-party South really here at last? il U S News 68:26-8 F 9 '70
Leaderless majority; seniority in the House. L. Gapay. Nation 210:134-6 F 9 '70
Lindsay for president; need to replace McCormack. R. Bolling. il Look 34:73-5+ My 5 '70
Loyal opposition; Democratic policy council adopts program for the '70s. K. Crawford. Newsweek 75:36 F 23 '70
Loyal opposition; TV time. por Newsweek 76:73 Jl 20 '70
Lucky Democrats; 1970 elections. C. McWilliams. Nation 211:485-7 N 16 '70
Mission impossible? il por Newsweek 75:35-6 Mr 16 '70
1972? J. Deakin. il pors Esquire 73:55-9+ F '70
Nixon's loyal opposition. Nation 210:34-5 Ja 19 '70
Now is the time; fund-raising gala at Miami Beach. Newsweek 75:23-4 F 16 '70
Politics of resentment. M. Novak. Commonweal 92:481-3 S 25 '70; Same. Cur 123:13-18 N '70
Radical strategy: don't form a fourth party; form a new first party. M. Harrington. il N Y Times Mag p28-9+ S 13 '70
Real majority, by R. M. Scammon and B. J. Wattenberg. Review
Atlan 226:69-73 D '70. M. Janeway
New Repub 163:26-7 O 24 '70. L. Ross
Reluctant chief; L. O'Brien. por Bsns W p56+ F 21 '70
Return of the pro. por Time 95:16 Mr 2 '70
Southern strategy. Newsweek 76:31-2 N 23 '70
Strategy for Democrats; excerpts from The real majority. R. M. Scammon and B. J. Wattenberg. New Repub 163:17-21 Ag 15 '70; Same abr. with title Strategy for the outs. Cur 122:14-20 O '70; Reply with rejoinder. P. F. Rousselot and R. E. Vickery, jr. New Repub 163:30-1 S 26 '70
Television politics; loyal opposition scramble for equal time. K. Crawford. Newsweek 76:24 Jl 20 '70
Time to listen. K. Crawford. Newsweek 75:28 Je 29 '70
Top Democrat talks about party's debt; interview. H. H. Humphrey. por U S News 68:32-3 Mr 2 '70
West Virginia Byrd; replacing Edward M. Kennedy as majority whip? P. R. Wieck. New Repub 163:11-13 D 12 '70
What happened to the new politics? New Democratic coalition. P. R. Wieck. New Repub 162:12-13 F 28 '70
Who but Ted? S. Alsop. Newsweek 75:100 Ap 13 '70
Who needs the Democrats? J. K. Galbraith. il Harper 241:43-53+ Jl '70
Who needs the liberals? views of John Kenneth Galbraith and Samuel Lubell. P. Kemble. Commentary 50:57-64 O '70
Who vs. Nixon in '72? il U S News 69:37-9 N 16 '70
Winning in November is not enough. J. K. Galbraith. New Repub 162:13-14 Je 13 '70; Reply. G. Allott. 163:31-4 Ag 15 '70
Winning with(out) students; the victory of J. D. Duffey in the Connecticut Democratic primary. America 123:107 S 5 '70
See also
National conventions, Democratic

DEMOGRAPHY
Demography and human ecology; some apparent trends. L. F. Schnore. bibliog f il Ann Am Acad 390:120-8 Jl '70
Demography of primitive populations. N. McArthur. bibliog Science 167:1097-101 F 20 '70
Feedbacks in economic and demographic transition: adaptation of address, June 1969. H. Frederiksen; reply. W. B. Greenough, 3d. Science 167:237 Ja 16 '70
See also subhead Population under names of continents, countries, e.g. Europe—Population

DEMONOLOGY
 See also
 Devil
 Satanism
 Witchcraft
DEMONSTRATION cities program. See Urban
 renewal
DEMONSTRATIONS. See Protests, demonstra-
 tions, etc.
DEMONSTRATIONS against Israeli-Arab war.
 See Israeli-Arab war, 1967- —Protests, dem-
 onstrations, etc. against
DEMONSTRATIONS against Vietnamese war.
 See Vietnamese war, 1957- —Protests,
 demonstrations, etc. against
DEMOS, John
 Underlying themes in the witchcraft of sev-
 enteenth-century New England; address,
 April 1967. bibliog f Am Hist R 75:1311-26
 Je '70
DEMOTT, Benjamin
 In and out of Women's lib. por Atlan 225:
 110-12+ Mr '70
 More life school and James Dickey. il por
 Sat R 53:25-6+ Mr 28 '70
 New longings abroad in the land. Sat R
 53:23-6 Jl 4 '70
 Stone men to the contrary, the time to argue
 is now. por Life 68:28B Ap 17 '70
DEMPSEY, David
 Environment bookshelf. Sat R 53:61 Mr 7
 '70
 Foundation grants and fellowships for
 writers. il Writers Digest 50:48-53+ Ja;
 48-9 F '70
 Libraries and the inner city. il Sat R 53:
 22-3 Ap 18 '70
 Mead and her message. il por(p 1) N Y Times
 Mag p23+ Ap 26 '70; Same abr. with title
 Provocative, prophetic Margaret Mead. Read
 Digest 97:127-31 Ag '70
 Sorry, there is no perfect golf swing. il N Y
 Times Mag p 10-11+ Jl 26 '70
DEMPSEY, Hugh
 Thin red line in the Canadian West. il Am
 West 7:24-30 Ja '70
DEMPSEY, Michael Ryan, bp
 Breaking the circle of poverty. T. M. Gan-
 non. America 123:394-5 N 14 '70 *
DEMPSEY, Tom
 Kick in time. il Newsweek 76:114 N 23 '70 *
DEMPSEY, Vincent. See Breslow, D. G. jt.
 auth.
DEMPSTER, G. R.
 History in houses; Craighead-Jackson house.
 il Antiques 98:110-14 Jl '70
DEMSCH, Berthold
 Games teachers shouldn't play with prin-
 cipals. Clear House 45:86-8 O '70
DEMSKE, Dick
 Career in selling for you? il Mech Illus 66:
 45-7+ N '70
 Franchise fever strikes again. il Mech Illus
 66:50-2+ F '70
 New way to buy a car. il Mech Illus 66:
 64-6+ N '70
 Now! A computer for your car. il Mech
 Illus 66:32+ F '70
DEMULEN. See Contraceptives
DEMUTH, Jerry
 Movie (cont) Chr Cent 87:1454-5 D 2 '70
 Poor people's co-ops. il America 123:489-90 D
 5 '70
 Public school turnovers in the South. il
 America 123:377-9 N 7 '70
DENBY, David
 Dirty movies: hard-core and soft. Atlan 226:
 99-102 Ag '70
 Movies. See issues of Atlantic, January
 1970-
DENBY, Robert V.
 Inservice education for secondary English
 teachers: so little time... so much to
 learn! Engl J 59:594-602 Ap '70
 Literary analysis in secondary English class-
 es. Engl J 59:438-48 Mr '70
 —See Harvey, R. C. jt. auth.
DENCE, Joseph B.
 Conformational analysis; or, How some mole-
 cules wiggle. bibliog il por Chem 43:6-10
 Je '70
DENDRITES. See Nerve cells
DE NEEVE, Bernardine
 Scholtens: two artist-weavers from the
 Netherlands. il pors Craft Horiz 30:24-9 Ja
 '70
DENEVAN, William M.
 Aboriginal drained-field cultivation in the
 Americas. bibliog il Science 169:647-54 Ag 14
 '70
DENGLER, Harry W.
 Hollies for the holidays. il Am For 76:20-3 D
 '70

DENHOLTZ, Elaine G.
 Give them a performance. Todays Ed 59:55
 O '70
DENISON, George
 Legal weapon the Mafia fears most. Read
 Digest 96:81-5 Je '70
 Put the mail-order smut merchants out of
 business! Read Digest 96:209-10+ My '70
DENISON mines, ltd
 Steve Roman's waiting game. por Forbes
 106:28-9 O 1 '70
DENITRIFICATION of sewage. See Sewage
 disposal—Nitrogen removal
DENMARK
 See also
 Aged—Denmark
 Airlines—Denmark
 Childrens literature—Denmark
 Libraries—Denmark
 Music festivals—Denmark
 Publishers and publishing—Denmark
 Regional planning—Denmark

 Antiquities
 Bog bodies of Denmark. il Chem 43:2 Jl '70
 Experiment with time. G. Bibby. il Horizon
 12:96-101 Spr '70

 Colonies
  See also
 Faroe Islands

 Description and travel
 Art of being Denmark; with drawings. E.
 Blegvad. il Holiday 47:44-7 Ja '70

 Moral conditions
 Could Danish smut laws work here? J. N.
 Bell. il Todays Health 48:24-9+ N '70
 Oh! Copenhagen! T. Buckley. il N Y Times
 Mag p32-4+ F 8 '70
 When pornography curbs are lifted—. A. Zan-
 ker. il U S News 69:68-9 O 19 '70

 Social conditions
 Street people of Denmark. D. Smith. Nation
 211:559-61 N 30 '70
DENMARK and the United States
 President Nixon holds talks with prime min-
 ister of Denmark. H. Baunsgaard; R. M.
 Nixon. Dept State Bul 62:632 My 18 '70
DENNIS, Alice
 Conservationists turn on for children of the
 concrete. il Nat Parks & Con Mag 44:4-9 Je
 '70
DENNIS, David W.
 Excerpt from debate. September 15, 1969. Cong
 Digest 49:26 Ja '70
DENNIS, Everette E. See Woloshin, A. A. jt.
 auth.
DENNIS, Johnnie T.
 Down on farm grew nation's no. 1 teacher.
 il por Sr Schol 96:Schol Teach 1-2 My 18
 '70 *
 Teacher of the year 1970. W. J. McKean. il
 pors Look 34:50-2+ Je 2 '70 *
DENNIS, Michael J. See Harris, A. J. jt. auth.
DENNY, Matthew
 This isn't your common everyday Vanden
 Plas Tourer. il por Motor T 22:50-3+ D '70
DENOMINATIONAL budgets. See Church fi-
 nance
DENOMINATIONAL colleges. See Church col-
 leges
DENOMINATIONALISM. See Sects
DENOMINATIONS, Religious. See Sects
DENOMME, Philip A. See Huck, S. C. jt. auth.
DENSEN-GERBER, Judianne
 Liberated, all liberated. il pors Vogue 155:
 117 Je '70 *
DENSITY gradient centrifugation. See Centri-
 fugation
DENSON, E. P.
 Hunting abroad? Know this law. il Outdoor
 Life 146:66+ D '70
DENT, Harry
 I gave Thurmond 100 per cent loyalty and now
 I give Mr Nixon 100 per cent. J. Boyd. il
 pors N Y Times Mag p 12-13+ F 1 '70

 about
 Sham or surrender? J. Osborne. New Repub
 162:15-17 Mr 7 '70 *
 White House hard hats. E. B. Drew. il por
 Atlan 226:51-7 O '70 *
DENT, John H.
 Protectionism versus free trade; address,
 September 29, 1970. Vital Speeches 37:47-9
 N 1 '70
DENTAL caries
 Prevention
 Chemical to fight tooth decay. J. Bockel. il
 Sci N 97:536-7 My 30 '70
 How tooth decay may soon be ended. il
 Good H 171:139-41 Jl '70

DENTAL decay. See Dental caries
DENTAL enamel. See Teeth
DENTAL hygiene. See Teeth—Care and hygiene
DENTAL insurance. See Insurance, Dental
DENTAL research
Dentists put teeth in research. C. Coiro. Har Yrs 10:48-9 Je '70
DENTAL service
Needed: a national dental health plan for children. W. G. Magnuson. por Parents Mag 45:44 F '70
DENTISTRY
Dentistry and its victims. by P. Revere. D.D.S. Review
Newsweek il 77:59-60 Ja 11 '71
See also
Dental research
Dental service
Orthodontics
Ultrasonic waves—Dental use
DENTON, George H. and Porter, S. C.
Neoglaciation; with biographical sketches. il Sci Am 222:12. 100-10 Je '70
DENVER

Architecture

Currigan Hall: a concept of simplicity for a building of complexity; exhibition hall. il Arch Rec 148:81-6 D '70

Description

Denver: the old roaring capital of the mountain West. V. McHugh. il Holiday 47:50-1+ My '70

Education

Denver doesn't quit on problem students. Z. Von Ende. il Am Ed 6:18-22 Je '70
Experience is their textbook; East high school. il Life 68:32-7 My 29 '70
Manpower training goes to college; Manpower development and training act skills center. G P Million il Am Ed 6:23-5 N '70
Manual high school: cutting class can get you to college. il pors Ebony 25:68-70+ My '70

Libraries

See also
Denver public library

Parks and playgrounds

Art in the park; Burns park. il Am City 85: 76-7 F '70
DENVER public library
Denver, Colorado: El Número cinco; summer bookmobile. F. A. Bucy. il Wilson Lib Bul 44:765-6 Mr '70

Conservation library center

Can man survive? B. J. Rule. il Library J 95:1448-9 Ap 15 '70
DEODORANTS
Choosing a deodorant-antiperspirant. il Consumer Bul 53:15-17 O '70
New sprays; feminine hygiene sprays. il Vogue 156:102-3+ Ag 15 '70
Sweat is almost obsolete. N. H. Mermelstein. Todays Health 48:40-1+ Je '70
DEOXYRIBONUCLEIC acid. See DNA
DEPALMA, Samuel
Overcoming the crisis of confidence: the U.S. view of the United Nations; address, May 23, 1970. Dept State Bul 62:747-52 Je 15 '70
United Nations budget estimates for 1971; statement, October 21, 1970. Dept State Bul 63:701-9 D 7 '70
United Nations in 1970's; address, October 11, 1970 Dept State Bul 63:574-9 N 9 '70
United Nations in the coming decade; address, September 25, 1970. Dept State Bul 63:454-8 O 19 '70
DE PAOLA, D.
Curse of the metered line; poem. Sat R 53:10 S 12 '70
DEPARTMENT of environmental conservation. See New York (state)—Environmental conservation, Department of
DEPARTMENT of housing and urban development. See United States—Housing and urban development, Department of
DEPARTMENT stores
Shutdowns stalk big-city stores. il Bsns W p28 O 10 '70
To ease the decorating trauma, the hand-holding store. House B 112:65-6 O '70
See also
Buyers
Federated department stores, inc.
Retail trade
Shopping centers
also subhead Stores under names of cities, e.g. New York (city)—Stores

Employees

Retailing. H. Wilinsky. il Seventeen 29:130-1+ F '70

Security measures

See Retail trade—Security measures
DEPAULA, Frankie
Gimmick for boxing: Caucasian charisma. J. Flaherty. pors Life 68:12 Je 12 '70 *
Harder they fall. P. Axthelm. il pors Newsweek 75:67-8 Je 8 '70 *
DEPERTUIS, C. Wesley.
Body build and heart attacks. A. J. Snider. il Sci Digest 69:57 Ja '71 *
DEPORTATION
Prisoner: 1337; occupation: conductor, Boston symphony orchestra. J. J. Badal. il pors Hi Fi 20:55-60 O '70
U.S. asks departure of two members of Cuban mission to the U.N; Department announcement. Dept State Bul 63:483-4 O 26 '70
DEPRECIATION
Try negative cash. E. H. Palmer. Am City 85:46 S '70
What's your machinery worth? il Suc Farm 68:84 Ap '70
See also
Investment tax credit
DEPRESSION, Business. See Business depression
DEPRESSION, Mental
After baby blues, why? il Sci Digest 67:65 F '70
How to beat the blues. Bet Hom & Gard 48: 116-17+ F '70
Reduced catechol-O-methyltransferase activity in red blood cells of women with primary affective disorder. C. K. Cohn and others. bibliog il Science 170:1323-4 D 18 '70
Separation and depression; AAAS symposium, December 27-28, 1970. J. P. Scott and F. C. Senay. il Science 170:1233-4 D 11 '70
DEPRIT, André, and others
Lunar ephemeris: Delaunay's theory revisited. bibliog il Science 168:1569-70 Je 26 '70
DEPTH indicators
Marine electronics; power & sail. il Motor B 125:97-9 My '70
DEPTH of field. See Photography—Focusing
DEPTH sounders. See Depth indicators
DE PUGH, Robert Bolivar
DePugh and the Minutemen: wonderland of the mind. W. Turner. pors Ramp Mag 8: 10+ Je '70 *
DE-QUILLING a dog. See Dogs—Care
DE RAGEOT, Roger H.
Journey into the tropics. il Américas 22:36-42 Jl '70
DER HOVANESSIAN, Diana
Mist; poem. Good H 172:171 Ja '71
DERIAGIN, Boris Vladimirovich
Superdense water; with biographical sketch. il Sci Am 223:10, 52-64+ bibliog (p 132) N '70

about

Deryagin and the Russians. por Sci N 98: 286 O 3 '70 *
Doubters and Deryagin. por Sci N 98:6 Jl 4 '70 *
DERMATOGLYPHICS
Hearts and palms. il Newsweek 76:103 S 14 '70
Kiss that tells; lip prints aid criminal identification. il Newsweek 76:76 O 19 '70
DEROCHE, Edward F.
Methods, materials, and the culturally disadvantaged. bibliog Clear House 44:420-4 Mr '70
DE ROO, Remi Joseph, bp
State of a diocese. D. J. Roche. America 122: 366-7 Ap 4 '70 *
DERR, Richard L.
Meeting community demands for decentralization of control. Sch & Soc 98:362 O '70
DERRICK, Jonathan
Church and state in Cameroon. il por America 124:18-20 Ja 9 '71
DERSHOWITZ, Alan M.
Terrorism & preventive detention: the case of Israel. bibliog f Commentary 50:67-78 D '70
DERVISHES
Tales of the dervishes, by I. Shah. Review
Nation 210:503-4 Ap 27 '70. J. Kritzeck
DE SAINTE COLOMBE, Paul
Pen-and-pencil therapy. il Time 96:51 S 21 '70
DESAIX, Pierre
Fine art of model testing. il Motor B 127: 134-5 Ja '71
They have to come to Pete. R. W. Carrick. il por Yachting 127:52+ Je '70
DESCH, Robert P.
Masks; poem. Chr Cent 87:268 Mr 4 '70
My Lai; poem. Chr Cent 87:134 F 4 '70

DESCHIN, Jacob
Sam Gottscho: nonagenarian flower power. il
Pop Phot 67:80-3+ O '70
Viewpoint. See issues of Popular photography
DESEGREGATION. See Catholic schools—Desegregation; Public schools—Desegregation
DESEGREGATION of camps. See Camps—Desegregation
DESERT botanical garden, Arizona. See Botanical gardens
DESERT juniper. See Juniper
DESERT regatta. See Regattas
DESERT vegetation
See also
Cactus
Cirios
DESERTED towns. See Abandoned towns
DESERTION, Military. See United States—Armed forces—Desertions
DESERTS
Desert wilderness. F. R. Fosberg. il Liv
Wildn 34:17-24 Spr '70
See also
Danakil
Oases
Sahara Desert
DE SICA, Vittorio
Vittorio De Sica's Roma; interview, ed. by
P. Dragadze. il por Travel & Camera 33:
26-34 Ap '70
DESIGN
Design. J. F. Blumrich. Science 168:1551-4
Je 26 '70
Design in the environment: sculpture, churches and buildings. il Sch Arts 69:27-32 Ap
'70
See also
International design conference
Textile design

Study and teaching
Decorative drawings. L. J. Miller. il Design
72:30-1 Wint '70
Designing playground equipment. R. L. Asch
il Sch Arts 69:16-17 Ap '70
Moveable abstractions. F. J. Kraft. il Design 71:25 Spr '70
Think three; using repetitive shapes K. K
Agee. il Design 72:22-3 Fall '70
3-D ink designs. G. J. Myers il Design 72:
36-8 Fall '70
Zodiac designs. M. B. Bowman. il Design 71:7
Wint '69
See also
Costume design—Study and teaching
DESIGN, Decorative
English decorative arts at the M. H. de Young
memorial museum. D. G. Keith. il Antiques
97:712-17 My '70
See also
Circles
Decoupage
Drawing
Graffito decoration
Lettering
Pottery—Decoration
Textile design
Textile fabrics

Animal forms
Reappearing American. D. F. Brown. il Hobbies 74:128-9 Ja '70

Plant forms
Summer zest; nature's touch for the house
and garden. il House & Gard 137:78-9 Je '70

Study and teaching
See Design—Study and teaching
DESIGN, Environmental. See Environmental
engineering (buildings)
DESIGN, Industrial
Restless genius of Norman Bel Geddes. A. J.
Pulos. il por Arch Forum 133:46-51 Jl '70
Student designers tackle leisure area; Armco
sponsored projects. Y. Fogel. il Parks &
Rec 5:24-6 My '70
See also
Human engineering
Systems engineering
DESIGN in photography. See Composition (photography)
DESIGN of automobiles. See Automobiles—Design
DESIGNERS
Gae Aulenti: new force in Italian design;
tr. by A. Foulke. A. Arbasino. il Vogue
156:118-23+ Jl '70
James Trittipo, designer for television. J. Lovoos. il por Am Artist 34:30-5+ O '70
See also
Costume designers
Furniture designers
Geddes, N. B.
Haight, P.
Lax, M.
Neumann, V.

DESIGNS, Architectural.   See Architecture—
Designs and plans
DESILLE family
DeSille coat-of-arms. H. K. Eilers. il Hobbies 75:148-9+ Ap '70 *
DESK-closets. See Studies (rooms)
DESKS
Hideaway office. J. Capotosto. il Mech Illus
66:102+ S '70
It's easy to make this desk. E. E. Hickman.
il Pop Sci 196:140 Ja '70
Projects to keep your workshop humming;
home study desk. P. Smith. il Pop Mech
134:192-3 O '70
Saddle-seat homework desk. il Pop Mech 133:
170-1 Mr '70
DESMARAIS, Paul G.
Montreal's shy wizard of finance. por Bsns W
p 130+ My 16 '70 *
DES MOINES

Finance
We renovated stores and print-shop operations. K. G. Ibson. il Am City 85:116+ Mr '70
DESMOSTEROL
Desmosterol as the major sterol in L-cell
mouse fibroblasts grown in sterol-free culture medium. G. H. Rothblat and others.
bibliog il Science 169:880-2 Ag 28 '70
DESOTO, Jewel
Ink blowing. il Design 72:24-5 Wint '70
DE SOUZA, Carlito
Report from East Africa. il America 123:117-
18 S 5 '70
Tanzania's seminar study year 1969. America
122:300-2 Mr 21 '70
DE SOUZA, José Patrocinio
Eagle: spacecraft of the pre-scientific age.
il UNESCO Courier 23:23-7 Je '70
DESPAIR
See also
Hope
DESROSIERS, Toussaint
Haitian voodoo. il Américas 22:35-9 F '70
DESSAUER, John P.
Psychic wages; new trends in personnel management. Pub W 198:27-9 D 28 '70
DESSERT wine. See Wine
DESSERTS
Bang-up finish: peach bombe. il McCalls 97:
57 Ag '70
Delectable desserts with cottage cheese. il Farm
J 94:47 Ja '70
Dessert is cheese with fruit or jelly. il Sunset 145:171 O '70
Desserts from Parents' magazine's new cookbook library. il Parents Mag 45:88 Ja '70
Desserts from private collections. il Redbook 134:130-2+ Mr '70
Fabulous finale; French dessert. J. Pépin. il
House B 112:128-9+ N '70
Favorite holiday soups and desserts; excerpts from Mastering the art of French
cooking, by J. Child and S. Beck. il McCalls 98:58-61+ D '70
Flaming desserts; flaming fruit sauces. il Bet
Hom & Gard 48:68-9 Ag '70
Flavorsome four: brandy Alexander pie; soufle roll; pots de creme; cheesecake. C.
Claiborne. il N Y Times Mag p20-1 D 27 '70
Great holiday desserts. il Redbook 136:108-13
D '70
Happy endings to family meals. C. Brock. il
Parents Mag 45:77-80+ S '70
Just desserts: with recipes. N. S. Hazelton.
Nat R 22:468 My 5 '70
Memorable desserts. il Am Home 73:88+ N
'70
Meringue with tang: lime torte, currant cakes,
raisin pie. J. Hewitt. il N Y Times Mag p97-
8 O 11 '70
Milk desserts on a dime. il Ladies Home J
87:94-5+ Mr '70
Mont Blanc: a gourmet delight made easy. il
McCalls 97:52 F '70
Party centerpieces that are really good
enough to eat! M. Ying. il Good H 171:70-3+
D '70
Peerless pairing: pots de creme and florentines. C. Claiborne. il N Y Times Mag
p90+ Ap 26 '70
Snowy soufflé to serve with berries. il Sunset
144:167 Je '70
Spectacular ice cream bombes. J. Jaffry. il
Am Home 73:72-3 Ag '70
Splendid fare; excerpts. A. Stockli. il Ladies
Home J 87:114-15 N '70
Star quality; chocolate Bavarian cream. C.
Claiborne. il N Y Times Mag p21 Jl 5 '70
Two delicious dessert recipes from Rome.
il Sunset 144:150 F '70
Two switches on zabaglione. il Sunset 144:
144 Je '70
When a light dessert is welcome. il Sunset
144:146 F '70

DESSERTS—*Continued*
Work wonders with dessert toppings; recipes.
il Ladies Home J 87:82+ Jl '70
See also
Cheesecake
Cookery—Fruit
Cookies
Custards
Ice cream, ices, etc.
Meringue
Pastry
Pie
Puddings
Tarts

DESSLER, A. J.
Swedish iconoclast recognized after many years of rejection and obscurity. por Science 170:604-6 N 6 '70

DESTINATION: Christmas! drama. See Boiko, C.

DESTINY. See Fate and fatalism

DESTROYERS. See Warships

DETECTION of guided missiles. See Guided missiles—Detection

DETECTIVE and mystery plays
Swiss chalet mystery. J. Murray. Plays 29:23-34 Mr '70
Ten-year-old detective; drama. L. Olfson. Plays 29:57-61 My '70

DETECTIVE and mystery stories
Death of a bloodsport. A. Shaffer. Harp Baz 104:122-3 N '70
Two lady writers make a killing. il Bsns W p48 My 9 '70
See also
Mystery writers of America, inc.
Television broadcasting—Crime programs

Authorship
Hard-bitten old pro who wrote Cotton. R. Chelminski. il pors Life 69:60-1 Ag 28 '70
How I sold a series of paperback mystery novels. M. Avallone. por Writers Digest 51:24-5+ Ja '71
Moonstones and mousetraps. H. R. Mayes. Sat R 53:4+ O 17 '70

Bibliography
Criminal record. J. T. Winterich and H. Frankel. See last issue of each month of Saturday review
Mystery, detective and suspense. M. K. Grant. See first issue of each month of Library journal

Technique
Case history of a first novel: writing The hand of Solange; with editorial comment by L. P. Ashmead. M. Rippon. Writer 83:12-16 Mr '70
Suspense in fiction. E. Ogilvie. Writer 83:11-14 Ja '70
Verisimilitude in the crime story. A. F. Nussbaum. Writer 84:13-15+ Ja '71
Writing a mystery. P. Moyes. Writer 83:11-14 Ap '70

DETECTIVES
Why real-life detective stories so often end with a rubber stamp. P. Wilkes. il N Y Times Mag p32-3+ Ap 19 '70

DETECTORS
Automatic sentry to warn of pollution. Bsns W p40 My 9 '70
Bomb sniffer. Time 95:47-8 Mr 30 '70
Computers v. pollution; fully automated air-pollution-warning system consisting of electric sniffers. il Time 95:84+ My 11 '70
See also
Counters (electrons, ions, etc)
Metal detectors

DETECTORS, Infrared
Army tests nocturnal HueyCobra. P. J. Klass. il Aviation W 93:57-9 O 5 '70
Fighting the CAT that threatens you from a clear blue sky. K. J. Scribner. il por Pop Sci 196:60-3 My '70
Infrared fire control tests start. B. Miller. il Aviation W 92:53-5 My 11 '70
Target sensor tested for Mirage 3. B. Miller. il Aviation W 93:48-50 N 2 '70
Thermography: coloring with heat. il Time 96:46-8 Ag 17 '70

DETENTION homes
Children in trouble: a national scandal; condensation. H. James. il Read Digest 96:257-62+ Je '70
Trying to bend young men away from crime; Robert F. Kennedy youth center. il Fortune 82:98-9 Jl '70

DETERGENT pollution of rivers, lakes, etc.
Arsenic in detergents: possible danger and pollution hazard. E. E. Angino and others. bibliog il Science 168:389-90 Ap 17 '70; Discussion. 168:1525-6; 170:870-2 Je 26. N 20 '70

Detergents: side effects of the washday miracles. N. Gruchow. Science 167:151 Ja 9 '70
Godfrey hangs out a new pollution line. il por Bsns W p38-9 F 21 '70
Warning: the green slime is here. S. D. Kohn. il N Y Times Mag p26-7+ Mr 22 '70
Washday blues. Sr Schol 96:15-16 Ja 26 '70

DETERGENTS
Action on enzyme detergents the FTC promises, the FDA does not. Consumer Bul 53:29 O '70
Arsenic and detergents. Chem 43:7 My '70
Arsenic question. Consumer Rep 35:530 S '70
Dead lakes: another washday miracle; phosphates. il Consumer Rep 35:528-31 S '70
Detergent dilemma. Good H 172:74-5+ Ja '71
Detergents and phosphates. il Nat Parks & Con Mag 44:28 Je '70
Enzyme detergents: effective and safe? il Consumer Bul 53:27-30 Ap '70
Enzymes in detergents. il Chem 43:25-6 F '70
Enzymes in hot water il Time 95:86 F 16 '70
Excessive emotion about detergents. P. H. Abelson. Science 169:1033 S 11 '70; Discussion. 170:1153-4 D 11 '70
Great detergent controversy. B. Furness. McCalls 98:20+ N '70
How much phosphate in your wash? chart. Audubon 72:152 N '70
Laundry detergents; phosphates containing arsenic. Consumer Bul 53:27 Je '70
NTA in for phosphates. Sci N 97:408 Ap 25 '70
NTA; possible substitute for phosphates in detergents. S. S. Epstein. bibliog il Environ 12:2-11 S '70
Phosphate stand-in goes down the drain. Bsns W p 17 D 26 '70
Phosphates, putrefaction, and the detergent dilemma. il Audubon 72:108 My '70
Potential substitute for phosphates in detergents. Chem 43:41-2 Jl '70
Race to clean up without pollutants. Bsns W p21-2 Ag 29 '70
Safe detergents, which ones, if any? il Org Gard & Farm 17:58-61 Je '70
Softer soap? recommendations to phase out phosphates. il Newsweek 76:52-3 Ag 24 '70
Solution becomes a problem; dangerous substitute for phosphates. il Sci N 98:475 D 26 '70
Suffolk bans detergents. Time 96:41 N 23 '70

Advertising
Godfrey hangs out a new pollution line. il por Bsns W p38-9 F 21 '70

DETJE, Frederick W.
Reform, revolution and food. il Sci N 98:86 Jl 25 '70

DETLEFSEN, Ellen Gay, and Schuman, Patricia
Overdue. il Wilson Lib Bul 44:962+ My '70

DETROIT
See also
Bloomfield Hills, Mich.

Banks
Fed ruling that shook Detroit; Bank of the Commonwealth's bid to open Nassau branch and to form an Edge act corporation. il Bsns W p25-6 Ap 11 '70
Green power for blacks; First independence national bank. Newsweek 75:68+ Je 29 '70
Parson's downfall; Bank of the commonwealth. Newsweek 76:51 Ag 24 '70

City planning
Visionary zeal in Detroit. Time 96:52 O 19 '70

Description
Detroit in 1970. il Library J 95:2097 Je 1 '70
Underground Detriot for SLA and ALA conventioneers. H. Malone. il por Wilson Lib Bul 44:931-9 My '70

Education
Commitment to achievement: Detroit's neighborhood educational project. F. T. Murdoch. il Am Lib 1:758-61 S '70

Education, Board of
Where did everyone go to? W. Grant. New Repub 163:20 S 5 '70

Galleries and museums
See also
Detroit institute of arts

Hotels, restaurants, etc.
London chop house. M. Beltaire. Holiday 47:78 F '70
Rockets and restaurants in motor city. B. E. Bryant. il por Library J 95:2085-8 Je 1 '70

DEVLIN, Polly
Factory for living in. il por Vogue 155:194-7+ Mr 1 '70
Women re women. Mlle 70:190-1+ F '70

DEVLIN, Wende
Beat poems of a beat mother. il Good H 170:80 Ap '70

DE VOLPI, Alexander
Expectations from SALT. il Bul Atom Sci 26:6-8+ Ap '70
MIRV, Gorgon Medusa of the nuclear age. Bul Atom Sci 26:35-8+ Ja '70

DEVONIAN period. See Paleontology—Devonian

DEVONS, Samuel, and Hartmann, Lillian
History-of-physics laboratory. il pors Phys Today 23:44-9 F '70

DE VRIES, John
Noah's ark. S. A. Parvin. il por Hobbies 75: 158 O '70 *

DE VRIES, Mary Ann
Freelance opportunities with associations. Writers Digest 50:28-30+ S '70

DEVRIES, Ted, and Tovatt, Anthony
This world of English. See issues of English journal

DEWEY, Christopher
Kids at Cannon. il pors Time 96:60 Ag 31 '70 *

DEWEY, John
Religion and American experience. R. J. Roth. il America 124:43-4 Ja 16 '71 *

DEWEY, John F.
Building mountain ranges: a plate tectonics model. K. Frazier. il pors Sci N 98:143-5 Ag 15 '70 *

DEWITT, Bryce S.
Quantum mechanics and reality. bibliog il Phys Today 23:30-5 S '70

DEWITT, Robert Lionne, bp
Episcopal bishop under attack. T. W. Moore. Chr Cent 87:1363-4 N 11 '70

DEWOLF, L. Harold
D.min: first or second theological degree? Chr Cent 87:1211 O 14 '70

DEXAMETHASONE
Tyrosine transaminase induction by dexamethasone in a new rat liver cell line. L. E. Gerschenson and others. bibliog il Science 170:859-61 N 20 '70

DEXTER, Anella, and Dexter, Laurence
Wilderness potential of Padre Island. il Nat Parks & Con Mag 44:14-19 Ag '70

DEXTER, Laurence. See Dexter, A. jt. auth.

DEXTER corporation
Profitable problems. A. A. Butkus. por Duns 96:60 O '70

DEXTROPROPOXYPHENE
Darvon termed no better than aspirin. Consumer Rep 35:629-30 N '70
Pain-killers and toxicity; Darvon. Sci Digest 67:74 My '70
Painful choice; Darvon. Newsweek 76:48 Ag 31 '70

DEYOUNG, Russell
How millions were tied to the cord of the future. il por Nations Bsns 58:80-1 Ja '70

DE YOUNG memorial museum. See M. H. De Young memorial museum, San Francisco

D'HARNONCOURT, René
Exercises in taste. J. B. Myers. il Craft Horiz 30:50-3 My '70; Reply. M. Omer. 30:9 Ag '70

DI, Tran-ba-. See Tran-ba-Di

DIABETES
Are you sure you don't have diabetes? N. Ashby. il Mech Illus 66:42-4+ D '70
Battle over a study; risks of oral hypoglycemic agents. Sci N 97:596 Je 20 '70
Debate over diabetes. Time 96:41 D 21 '70
How safe and effective are oral drugs for diabetes? Good H 172:123-4 Ja '71
Human glomerular basement membrane: chemical alteration in diabetes mellitus. P. J. Beisswenger and R. G. Spiro. bibliog il Science 168:596-8 My 1 '70
Learning to lead not-so-normal lives. A. Rosenthal. il Todays Health 48:56-7+ Ap '70
More on tolbutamide. Newsweek 76:90 D 21 '70
Problem with drugs; harmful effects of tolbutamide. Sci N 97:526-7 My 30 '70

DIABETES research
Meet the mystromys albicaudatus. il Sci Digest 68:65-6 Jl '70

DIABETICS diet. See Diet in disease

DIABLO RANGE
Varied landscapes of the Mount Hamilton Range. il Sunset 144:3 Je '70

DIADEMA. See Sea urchins

DIAGHILEV, Sergei Pavlovich
Diaghilev and the Ballets russes, by B. Kochno. Review
New Yorker 46:86-7 Ag 22 '70. Genet *

DIAGNOSIS
Diagnostic overkill and management of psychiatric problems. C. E. Goshen. Ment Hy 54:306-9 Ap '70
Doctor in the TV set; MGH system for telediagnosis. il Life 69:77-9 N 27 '70
Gas chromatography: medical diagnostic aid. M. W. Ruchelman. bibliog il por Chem 43:14-19 D '70
See also
Medicine—Practice
also subhead Diagnoses under names of diseases, e.g. Cancer—Diagnosis

DIAGNOSIS, Radioscopic
Looking into swallowing problems; barium fudge for X-ray contrast media. J. Bockel. il Sci N 97:601 Je 20 '70

DIAGNOSTICIAN; story. See Vivante, A.

DIALECT, Negro. See Negro-English dialects

DIALECTS
See also
English language—Dialects

DIALOGUE
Using dialogue in the outdoor article. T. Wendelburg. Writer 84:27-9 Ja '71
Writing dialogue. N. B. Gerson. Writer 83:15-17 Ag '70

DIALYSIS
Charge-mosaic membranes: dialytic separation of electrolytes from nonelectrolytes and amino acids. J. N. Weinstein and S. R. Caplan. bibliog il Science 169:296-8 Jl 17 '70
See also
Kidneys, Artificial

DIAMOND, Edwin
Drug scene in East Egg. il N Y Times Mag p28-9+ My 17; 57 Je 28 '70
Unveiling a 1970 model: the Lunar Rover. il N Y Times Mag p34-5+ Ap 5 '70

DIAMOND, Henry L.
Department of environmental conservation activated on July 1st at Albany ceremony; excerpts from address, ed. by J. E. Gavagan. il pors Cons 25:4-5 Ag '70
Interview with the new commissioner. pors Cons 24:3-5 Je '70

about

Governor creates Department of environmental conservation; Office of parks and recreation set up in new law; with editorial comment. N. A. Rockefeller. por Cons 24:1-3 Je '70 *

DIAMOND, James J.
Paging the unbandaged. D. Callahan. America 123:143 S 12 '70 *

DIAMOND, Milton
Intromission pattern and species vaginal code in relation to induction of pseudopregnancy. bibliog il Science 169:995-7 S 4 '70

DIAMOND, Neil
Tin pan tailor. W. Bender. il por Time 97:46-7 Ja 11 '71 *

DIAMOND, Robert S.
Self-portrait of the chief executive. il Fortune 81:181+ My '70
Shaken faith in Nixon; Fortune 500-Yankelovich survey. il Fortune 81:60-2 Je '70

DIAMOND cutting
Kindest cut of all; polished diamonds from Israel. il Time 96:62 Ag 17 '70

DIAMOND dealers club, Inc (New York)
Diamonds: the grit behind the glitter. il Forbes 105:20-2+ F 1 '70

DIAMOND HEAD
To the top of Diamond Head. il Sunset 144: 55 My '70

DIAMOND mines and mining
Diamond stampede; West Transvaal. il Newsweek 76:107 N 23 '70
See also
De Beers consolidated mines. ltd.

DIAMOND mines and mining, Submarine
Everything's coming up diamonds. G. Young. il Pop Mech 133:116-19+ Mr '70; Same. Sci Digest 68:68-73 O '70

DIAMOND trade. See Diamonds

DIAMONDBACKS. See Rattlesnakes

DIAMONDS
Diamonds: the grit behind the glitter. il Forbes 105:20-2+ F 1 '70
How to buy a diamond. J. McCarthy. il Read Digest 96:188-90+ My '70
Stone for Janet: Zale corporation's Light of peace. il Newsweek 75:69+ Ja 26 '70
What it takes to make a diamond sparkle. Good H 172:128 Ja '71
See also
Diamond cutting

DIAMONDS, Artificial
Gem diamonds created in lab. A. P. Armagnac. il Pop Sci 197:82-3+ S '70
Why the fake diamond market glitters. il Bsns W p 116-17 F 14 '70

DIAMONDS, Industrial
Sintered diamond: a synthetic carbonado. H. T. Hall. il Science 169:868-9 Ag 28 '70
DIAMONDS in submerged lands. See Diamond mines and mining, Submarine
DIAMONSTEIN, Barbaralee
Emphasis (cont) Harp Baz 103:200-3+ N '69; 184-5 Mr; 98-9+ Je; 112-13+ Ag; 102-3 O '70
100 women in touch with our time. il Harp Baz 104:104-10 Ja '71
DIANNA, John
Landy's dandy pro-stocker. il Hot Rod 23:48-50 My '70
Mr Bardahl. il pors Hot Rod 23:64-6 F '70
Project Duster. il Hot Rod 23:48-50 Je '70
Shop talk. See issues of Hot rod
Strictly for stocks. See issues of Hot rod
DIAPAUSE. See Insects—Development
DIAPERS, Infants
Great diaper rash: disposable diaper business. il Forbes 106:24-6+ D 15 '70
DIARRHEA
Globe-trotter's peril; traveler's diarrhea. Sci Am 222:64 Mr '70
DIAS, Earl J.
Another redskin bit the dust; drama. Plays 30:1-12 O '70
Ghost from Genoa; drama. reprint from October 1955 issue. Plays 30:53-60, 77 O '70
DIAZ ORDAZ, Gustavo
President Nixon and President Diaz Ordaz of Mexico, meet at Puerto Vallarta; remarks, and toasts, August 20-21, 1970. Dept State Bul 63:289-95 S 14 '70
President Nixon honors President Diaz Ordaz of Mexico at a state dinner in California; exchange of greetings and remarks, September 3, 1970. Dept State Bul 63:347-8, 352-5 S 28 '70
DIAZEPAM
Diphenylhydantoin and diazepam: molecular structure similarities and steric basis of anticonvulsant activity. A. Camerman and N. Camerman. bibliog il Science 168:1457-8 Je 19 '70
DIBBLE, Gladys Gage
In Bloomfield Hills, Michigan: a garden of fountains and flowers. il Home Gard 57:42-3 Ag '70
DIBBLE, Henry, pseud.
(ed) See Goodell, C. E. After ten years
DIBBLE, J. B.
Ducks are predictable. il Field & S 75:44-5+ S '70
DIBLIN, Joe
Cold-weather operation. il Flying 86:86-7+ F '70
DIBONA, Charles
For draft: change in command. il por U S News 68:9 F 9 '70
New recruit. por Time 95:12-13 F 9 '70
DI BONAVENTURA, Sara (Roosevelt)
Bringing up people. E. L. Gross. il pors Vogue 155:88-91+ Je '70 *
DIBUTYRYL cyclic adenosine monophosphate. See Adenosine monophosphate
DICARA, Leo V.
Learning in the autonomic nervous system: with biographical sketch. il Sci Am 222:16, 30-9 bibliog(p 146) Ja '70
DICE
Electronic dice. R. W. Fox. il Electr World 83:34-5+ F '70
DICK, Bernard F.
We/they: the new campus dialogue. il Nat R 22:562-3+ Je 2 '70
DICK, Kay
(ed) See Compton-Burnett, I. Talking to Dame Ivy
DICKENS, Charles
Christmas carol; dramatization. See Hackett, W.
Oliver Twist; dramatization. See Bland, J.

about

Centennial observance of Charles Dickens death. J. Walsh. il pors Hobbies 75:48-50+ Je '70 *
Charles Dickens (1812-1870) H. Levin. Am Scholar 39:670-6 Aut '70 *
Dickens a century later. J. Torrens. America 122:609-10 Je 6 '70 *
Dickens ferment; forthcoming centennial celebrations in England. H. R. Mayes. Sat R 53:14+ Ap 4 '70 *
Letter from London. M. Panter-Downes. New Yorker 46:75-6 Jl 25 '70 *
World of Charles Dickens, by A. Wilson. Review
    Life il por 69:8-9 S 4 '70. J. Fowles *
    Nation 211:540-1 N 23 '70. H. Yglesias *
    Time por 96:59 D 28 '70. C. Porterfield *
Bibliography
One thing and another. J. K. Hutchens. il Sat R 53:30 D 19 '70

DICKENSON, Fred
Behind the boom in tropical fish. il Read Digest 97:202-6+ N '70
DICKER, John J.
To fill the freezer, plant for the insects and yourself. il por Org Gard & Farm 17:69-71 Mr '70
DICKERMAN, Ernest M.
National park wilderness reviews (lost in the wilderness) il Liv Wildn 34:40-9 Spr '70
DICKEY, James
Everyone's notion of a poet. por Time 95:92 Ap 20 '70
Exchanges; poem. Atlan 226:63-7 S '70
Haunting the maneuvers; poem. Harper 240:95 Ja '70
Poet tries to make a kind of order; excerpt from Self-interviews, ed. by J. Reiss and B. Reiss. Mlle 71:142-3+ S '70
P.P.A. authors' press conference; excerpts. il pors Pub W 197:27-9 Mr 23 '70
Process of writing a novel; excerpts from address, March 1970. Writer 83:12-13 Je '70
Two days in September: story. excerpt from Deliverance. Atlan 225:78-108 F '70

about

More life school and James Dickey. B. DeMott. il por Sat R 53:25-6+ Mr 28 '70 *
More of Superpoet. J. Yardley. New Repub 163:26-7 D 5 '70 *
Resurrection for a little while. R. Howard. Nation 210:341-2 Mr 23 '70 *
DICKEY, R. P.
In my time; poem. Nation 212:62 Ja 11 '71
Wise son maketh a glad father; poem. Sat R 53:65 Mr 28 '70
DICKIE, Murray
Scotsman; interview, ed. by B. Fischer-Williams. por Opera N 35:16 Ja 2 '71
DICKINSON, Eleanor Creekmore
Art-gallery revival has drawing power. J. V. Lawing, jr. il Chr Today 15:38 O 23 '70 *
DICKINSON, Emily
Emily Dickinson's If you were coming in the fall: an explication. L. J. Richmond. Engl J 59:771-3 S '70 *
DICKINSON, Peter A.
Time for rewards. il Har Yrs 10:19-24 S; 19-23 O; 42-50 N; 38-47 D '70
DICKINSON, Richard
So who needs liberation? Chr Cent 88:43-6 Ja 13 '71
DICKSON, Frank A.
Idea a day. Writers Digest 50:26-7 Je; 11-12+ Ag '70
DICKSON, Paul
Singing to silent America. il Nation 210:211-13 F 23 '70
DICKSTEIN, Morris
Allen Ginsberg and the 60's. bibliog f Commentary 49:64+ Ja '70
DICTAPHONE corporation
Walter Finke of Dictaphone corp; interview. W. Finke. pors Nations Bsns 58:46-7+ Mr '70
DICTATING machines
    See also
Dictaphone corporation
DICTATORSHIP
Reflections: the megamachine; excerpts from The pentagon of power. L. Mumford. New Yorker 46:55-8+ O 24 '70
    See also
Fascism
DICTION
Take notice of the words ... S. Hughes. il por Opera N 34:8-13 F 14 '70
DICTIONARIES
    See also
Encyclopedias
    also subhead Dictionaries under names of languages, e.g. English language—Dictionaries
DICTIONARY of scientific biography
Authors & Editors. B. A. Bannon. por Pub W 197:23-4 Ap 13 '70
DIDION, Joan
Generation not for barricades. Life 68:26 Je 5 '70
Nine bike movies in seven vroom! Days. il Life 68:4 My 8 '70
1950 was more than twenty years ago. Life 68:20B Ja 30 '70
On the last frontier with VX and GB. il Life 68:22 F 20 '70
Piece of work for now and doomsday. il Life 68:20 Mr 13 '70
Scrapbook of a pink palace in the sand. il Life 68:26B Ap 24 '70
Ten long minutes in Punchbowl. il Life 68:26D Ap 10 '70
DIEFFENBACHIAS
Trigger-happy dieffenbachia. W. Radcliffe. il Horticulture 48:31 Jl '70

DIFFRACTION gratings
  See also
Moiré method
DIFFUSION
Hindered diffusion in microporous membranes
  with known pore geometry. R. E. Beck and
  J. S. Schultz. bibliog il Science 170:1302-5
  D 18 '70
  See also
Biological transport
DIGAN, Parig
Lectionary: a brand-new thing. America 123:
  291-2 O 17 '70
DIGESTION
  See also
Enzymes
DIGESTIVE system
  See also
Intestines

          Diseases
Complex causes of indigestion. K. Anderson.
  Har Yrs 10:31-2+ Jl '70
DIGGING machinery. See Excavating machinery
DIGHTMAN, Cameron R.
Fees and mental health services: attitudes
  of the professional. bibliog Ment Hy 54:
  401-6 Jl '70
DI GIOVANNI, Norman Thomas
  (tr) See Borges, J. L. After the Japanese
  (tr) See Borges, J. L. Challenge
  (tr) See Borges, J. L. Doctor Brodie's report
  (tr) See Borges, J. L. Ibn Hakkan al-Bok-
    hari, dead in his labyrinth
  (tr) See Borges, J. L. Israel
  (tr) See Borges, J. L. Man on the threshold
  (tr) See Borges, J. L. Meeting
  (ed) See Borges, J. L. Profiles
  (tr) See Borges, J. L. Reader
  (tr) See Borges, J. L. and Casares, A. B.
    Evening with Ramón Bonavena
  (tr) See Borges J. L. and Casares, A. B. Im-
    mortals
DIG-IT (Dramatic interpretation of the ghetto
  through improvisational theatre) See Theater, Negro
DIGISYNTONE. See Musical instruments, Elec-
  tronic
DIGITAL circuits. See Transistor circuits
DIGITAL computers. See Computers—Digital
  computers
DIGITAL counters. See Counting machines and
  devices
DIGITAL flight control. See Computers—
  Aeronautic use
DIGITAL readout tubes. See Electron tubes
DIGIUSEPPE, Enrico
Two young singers have proved standouts at
  the Met; interview, ed. by E. Burns. por
  Opera N 34:15 F 14 '70
DIHYDROFOLATE reductases. See Reductases
DIHYDROXYPHENYLALANINE. See Dopa
DI IORIO, Robert C.
DDT: friend or enemy? Horticulture 48:22-3
  Je '70
DILATION, Pupillary. See Pupil (eye)
DILCHER, David L. and others
Chlorophyll derivatives in middle eocene
  sediments. bibliog il Science 168:1447-9 Je
  19 '70
DILEMMA
Quantum mechanics and reality; dilemma of
  indeterminism. B. S. DeWitt. bibliog il Phys
  Today 23:30-5 S '70
DILENSCHNEIDER, Bob
Inflatables are here. il Mech Illus 66:44-5 Jl
  '70
DILL, William R. See Hodgson, A. M. jt. auth.
DILLARD, Hardy Cross
Judge Dillard; interview. New Yorker 46:27-8
  Mr 28 '70
DILLER, Phyllis
Phyllis Diller: the plant lady? E. McDonald.
  il pors House B 112:202-3 Ap '70 *
DILLINGER, Joseph R.
Shoveling out the work of a lifetime. C.
  Leinster. il por Life 69:38-42 S 18 '70 *
DILLINGHAM corporation
Dredging money from the Bank; from Great
  Bahama Bank. C. Phinizy. il Sports Illus
  32:22-5 Jl 6 '70
Outsider, but no stranger. por Bsns W p 102
  O 10 '70
DILLMAN, Terry
When college students grade the faculty.
  Todays Ed 59:62+ F '70
DILLON, C. Douglas. See Dillon, D.
DILLON, Douglas
Readers' choice. il por Art in Am 58:25 Ja '70
          about
President. New Yorker 46:35-6 Ap 4 '70 *

DILLON, Gordon W.
Library is more than a collection of books.
  Horticulture 49:36+ Ja '71
DILLON, Merton L.
White faces and black studies. Commonweal
  91:476-9 Ja 30 '70
DILLON, Richard H.
Black knight of the Zayante. por Am West
  7:20-1 Jl '70
DILLON, Thomas
Thomas Dillon: chemist & revolutionary. J.
  A. Schufle. il por Chem 43:18-21 Ap '70 *
DILMUN
Looking for Dilmun; excerpts. G. Bibby. il
  Horizon 11:54-9 Aut '69
DIMETHOXYCINNAMATE. See Cinnamates
DIMETHYLPOLYSILOXANE. See Silicones
DIMETHYLPROPYNYLBENZAMIDES. See
  Herbicides
DIMOCK, George
Crime and punishment in the Odyssey. Yale
  R 60:199-214 D '70
DIMOCK, Hedley G.
How to choose only successful camp coun-
  selors. il por Camp Mag 42:8-10 Ap '70
DIMORPHOTHECA. See Cape marigolds
DINE, Jim
Art; exhibition at the Whitney museum. L.
  Alloway. Nation 210:350 Mr 23 '70 *
Jim Dine's life-in-progress; exhibition at the
  Whitney museum. D. Shapiro. il Art N 69:
  42-6 Mr '70 *
Personal pop. D. Darro. il pop Newsweek 75:
  98-9 Mr 9 '70 *
Poet of the personal. il por Time 95:50-1+
  Mr 9 '70*
DINERMAN, Beatrice
Ignorant philanthropists. Nation 210:369-72
  Mr 30 '70
DINERS' club, inc.
Story behind Diners club symbol. Changing
  T 25:32 Ja '71
DINGELL, John David, 1926-
Saving the little wild places. il Nat Wildlife
  8:10-11 Ap '70
          about
Son of gangbusters. R. Starnes. Field & S 74:
  8+ Mr '70 *
DINGHIES. See Boats and boating
DINGHY racing. See Boat racing
DINING. See Dinners and dining
DINING halls
  See also
Camps—Dining halls
DINING rooms
Bright little dining space. il Bet Hom &
  Gard 48:64 My '70
Dining: new furniture, new approaches. P.
  Rumely. il Bet Hom & Gard 48:68-73 Mr '70
Dining room that goes all day long. il Bet
  Hom & Gard 48:74-5 My '70
DINNERS and dining
Choosing wines for dinner parties; excerpts
  from How to eat better for less money. S.
  Aaron. House & Gard 137:86+ F '70
Dining out in America, how old ways are
  changing. il U S News 68:92-4 Ap 20 '70
Easy, economical one-dish dinners. il Good H
  171:106-21 O '70
Eat: cold weather dinner. M. Cantwell. Mlle
  70:25+ Ja '70
Father's day specials; with recipes. il Parents
  Mag 45:54-6+ Je '70
Frankly fancy; food well worth the effort;
  with recipes. M. Kamman. il Farm J 94:84-
  5 F '70
Main dishes for dieters. il Redbook 135:96-7+
  Ag '70
Pecan stuffed ham, roast sirloin tip, two
  roasted capons; with recipes and menus. il
  Am Home 73:82-7+ N '70
Ten great family dinners for under $3 with
  recipes. F. M. Crawford. il Am Home 73:
  104-6+ My '70
This Easter dinner really is a picnic, Italian
  style with easy Easter pizza. il Sunset
  144:82-3 Mr '70
Twenty-eight easy summer dinners. il Red-
  book 135:102-6+ Je '70
Two weeks of delicious dinners designed to
  help you lose weight; with menus and reci-
  pes. R. H. Smithies. il Good H 170:147-50 Ja
  '70
  See also
Caterers and catering
Christmas dinners
Food, Frozen
Outdoor meals
Thanksgiving dinners

DINNERWARE. See Tableware

DINOFLAGELLATES
Gibberellic acid: a growth factor in the unicellular alga gymnodinium breve. Z. Paster and B. C. Abbott. bibliog il Science 169:600-1 Ag 7 '70

DINOSAURS
Carbon-13 and oxygen-18 in dinosaur, crocodile, and bird eggshells indicate environmental conditions. R. E. Folinsbee and others. bibliog il Science 168:1353-6 Je 12 '70
Where did all the dinosaurs go? I. Asimov. Sci Digest 67:79-80 Je '70

DIOCESAN colleges. See Catholic colleges and universities

DIOCESAN newspapers. See Catholic press

DIOCESES
See also
Catholic church—Dioceses

DIODE testers. See Testing instruments

DIODES
Amplified zener. J. Ashe. il Radio-Electr 41:41-2 Je '70
Amplified zener. C. J. Ulrick. il Electr World 84:42+ S '70
Light-emitting diodes. F. M. Mims, 3d. il Pop Electr 33:35+ N '70
Light of the future, from semiconductors. R. M. Benrey. il Pop Sci 197:76-9+ D '70
Semiconductor injection lasers. R. L. Carroll. il Electr World 83:45-7 Mr '70
Solid-state technology invades microwave frequencies. il Aviation W 92:204-5+ Je 22 '70
Using silicon transistors as zeners. J. Charles. il Electr World 83:36 Ja '70

DIOPHANTINE analysis
Diophantine analysis and the problem of Fermat's legendary last theorem. M. Gardner. il Sci Am 223:117-19 Jl '70

DIOSPYROS. See Persimmons

DIPHENYL compounds
Department of amplification; contamination caused by polychlorinated biphenyls, or PCBs. T. Whiteside. New Yorker 46:91-5 Je 20 '70
First DDT, now PCB. Sci N 98:332 O 24 '70
More letters in the wind: polychlorinated biphenyls. R. Risebrough and V. Brodine. bibliog il Environ 12:16-27 Ja '70
Polychlorinated biphenyl: interaction with duck hepatitis virus. M. Friend and D. O. Trainer. bibliog il Science 170:1314-16 D 18 '70

DIPHENYLHYDANTOIN
Diphenylhydantoin and diazepam: molecular structure similarities and steric basis of anticonvulsant activity. A. Camerman and N. Camerman. bibliog il Science 168:1457-8 Je 19 '70

DIPHOSPHOGLYCERIC acid. See Glyceric acid

DIPHTHERIA
Plague year for killer diseases? il U S News 69:48 S 7 '70

DIPLOMACY
See also
International relations
United States—Diplomatic and consular service

DIPLOMAS, Fraudulent
Rev. Dr, I presume? Chr Cent 87:279 Mr 4 '70

DIPLOMATIC and consular service
See also subhead Diplomatic and consular service under names of countries, e.g. United States—Diplomatic and consular service

DIPLOMATIC privileges and immunities
See also
United Nations—Privileges and immunities

DIPLOMATS
See also
Negro diplomats
United States—Foreign service

DIPLOMATS, Kidnapping of. See Kidnapping

DIPTERA
RNA and DNA puffs in polytene chromosomes of rhynchosciara: inhibition by extirpation of prothorax. J. M. Amabis and D. Cabral. bibliog il Science 169:692-4 Ag 14 '70

DIRAC, P. A. M.
Can equations of motion be used in high-energy physics? por Phys Today 23:29-31 Ap '70

DIRECT broadcast satellites working group. See United Nations—Committee on the peaceful uses of outer space

DIRECT election of presidents. See Presidents —United States—Election

DIRECT energy conversion
See also
Solar batteries
Thermionic emission

DIRECT mail advertising. See Advertising, Direct mail

DIRECT selling. See Canvassing

DIRECTION, Operatic. See Operatic production and direction

DIRECTION, Sense of. See Orientation

DIRECTION finding apparatus
See also
Radio beacons

DIRECTORS, Corporation. See Corporations—Directors

DIRECTORS, Moving picture. See Moving picture directors

DIRIGIBLE; comic strip. See Viertel, G.

DIRIGIBLES. See Airships

DIRINGER, David
Doctor David Diringer and the Alphabet museum. I. Soifer. il por Pub W 198:48+ S 7 '70 *

DIRKSEN, Everett McKinley
Dirksen: portrait of a public man, by N. MacNeil. Review
   Time 97:80 Ja 18 '71. L. Morrow *
Dirksen's ghost. G. W. Johnson. New Repub 162:14-15 Mr 7 '70 *
Dirksen's ghost. New Repub 163:8 Jl 25 '70 *

DIRTIEST show in town; drama. See Eyen, T.

DISABILITY
Casualties of our time. A. B. Ford. bibliog il Science 167:256-63 Ja 16 '70

DISABILITY insurance. See Insurance, Disability

DISADVANTAGED children. See Socially handicapped children

DISARMAMENT
Arms traffic and third world conflicts. G. Kemp. bibliog il por Int Concil 577:5-80 Mr '70
U.S. discusses problem of control of conventional arms; statement, text of U.S. working paper, August 13, 1970. J. F. Leonard. Dept State Bul 63:310-15 S 14 '70
Vietnam & Armageddon: peace, war & the Christian conscience, by R. F. Drinan. Review
   Commonweal 93:30-1 O 2 '70. J. Forest
We can reverse the arms race: a 10-point plan. H. F. York. il Life 69:40-1 D 11 '70
When and how to use SALT. J. J. Stone. For Affairs 48:262-73 Ja '70
See also
Atomic weapons and disarmament
Peace
Strategic arms limitation talks
United Nations—Committee on disarmament
United States—Defenses
War

DISARMAMENT agency. See United States—Arms control and disarmament agency

DISASTER relief
Politics of rescue; Peru and Rumania. il Time 95:40 Je 22 '70
See also
Civil defense

DISASTER relief service. See Red cross—Disaster relief service

DISASTERS
Parting shots; apocalyptic visions for our fragile little planet. il Life 69:63-6 S 4 '70
Reports: environmental disaster, acts of nature and man; symposium. il Bul Atom Sci 26:17-41 O '70
See also
Avalanches
Brush fires
Cyclones
Fires
Hurricanes
Shipwrecks

DISC brakes. See Brakes, Automobile

DISC jockeys
See also
Radio broadcasting—Music

DISCH, Tom
Turkish holiday; In a time of plague; poems. Poetry 117:154-5 D '70

DISCIPLES of Christ. See Christian church, Disciples of Christ

DISCIPLINE
Generation of tyrants. H. Van Horne. il Good H 170:102-3+ Mr '70
How to say no without guilt. B. Bettelheim. Ladies Home J 87:18+ Ag '70
Routines of life. R. Haughton. Cath World 212:63-4 N '70
Teacher's guide to good discipline; six classroom techniques that also work at home. M. Bowen. il Parents Mag 45:50-2 Je '70
When to put your foot down; with study-discussion program, by E. Harris and D. Harris. D. Grace. bibliog il PTA Mag 64:2-4, 34 My '70
See also
Camp discipline
Children—Management and training
College discipline
School discipline

DISCIPLINE, Library. See Library adminis-
tration
DISCIPLINE, Military
GI's in combat: how far does just following
orders go? il Sr Schol 95:9-10 Ja 5 '70
You can't just hand out orders; experience of
a company commander in Vietnam. J. Saar.
il pors Life 69:30-7 O 23 '70
DISCOTHEQUES, etc.
Her gift to the Greeks: a touch of soul. il
pors Ebony 25:134-6+ O '70
DISCOUNT
Discount-rate cut: how much impact? U S
News 69:66 N 23 '70
DISCOUNT houses (retail trade)
Discounting: a food chain reaction. il Bsns
W p44-6 S 26 '70
Grocery bills; effect of discount pricing in
Washington, D.C. D. Sanford. New Repub
163:12-14 O 17 '70
More discount sales for shoppers. il U S
News 69:14-15 Ag 31 '70
See also
Kresge, S. S, company
DISCOUNTS, Clerical. See Clergy—Salaries,
allowances, etc.
DISCOVER America travel organization
Grand prize: a free vacation. Bsns W p92 Mr
21 '70
100 perfect vacations. il Travel & Camera 33:
53-64 Jl '70
100 vacations in fifty states. M. Gough.
House B 112:42+ Je '70
DISCOVERIES in geography
See also
Antarctic exploration
DISCRIMINATION
Experiments in intergroup discrimination. H.
Tajfel. il Sci Am 223:96-102 bibliog(p 132)
N '70
See also
Anti-Semitism
Minorities
United Nations—Sub-commission on preven-
tion of discrimination and protection of
minorities
DISCRIMINATION (psychology)
Visual discrimination of movement: midbrain
or forebrain? C. R. Hamilton and J. S.
Lund. bibliog il Science 170:1428-30 D 25
'70
DISCRIMINATION, Racial. See Race discrim-
ination
DISCRIMINATION in education
Integrated, but unequal; report by civil rights
groups. Time 97:27 Ja 4 '71
New step against discrimination in educa-
tion. Sch & Soc 98:12 Ja '70
DISCRIMINATION in employment
Black Monday's Sunday allies. il Ramp Mag
8:34-8 Ja '70
Down to fundamentals: question of WMUU's
license renewal. R. L. Shayon. Sat R 53:
36-7 O 31 '70
Job discrimination, and what women can do
about it. A. S. Rossi. por Atlan 225:99-102
Mr '70
Minority hiring under new attack. il por Bsns
W p 110 Je 13 '70
Nixon bias suits get a political tag. Bsns W
p 21 D 26 '70
Percy Green vs. McDonnell aircraft. L. Bar-
rett. Nation 210:404-5 Ap 6 '70
Philadelphia problem. Time 96:61-2 Ag 17 '70
Report on the status of women. S. McBee.
McCalls 97:128 S '70
Teeth for job discrimination; enforcement
provisions of Title VII strengthened. Amer-
ica 123:108 S 5 '70
See also
Association for the integration of manage-
ment
Blacklisting
Equal pay for equal work
Negroes—Employment
United States—Equal employment opportuni-
ty commission
Woman—Employment
Woman—Equal rights
DISCRIMINATION in housing
Applied education; attempt by Rutgers uni-
versity Law school to reform the enforce-
ment of fair housing laws in New Jersey.
Newsweek 75:109 Ap 27 '70
Color zoning white. il Time 96:51 S 7 '70
Cracking the suburbs. R. W. Dietsch. New
Repub 163:8 S 5 '70
Do most Americans secretly want segrega-
tion? A. A. Ribicoff. por Look 34:13 S 8 '70
Genteel violence. N. S. Marcere. Good H 170:
89+ Ap '70
Lefrak goes to the ghetto; target of Justice
dept. il por Bsns W p28 Ag 15 '70
Moral dilemma of zoning. D. K. Shipler. il
Nation 211:80-3 Ag 3 '70

Zoning; the new battleground; excerpts. C.
Funnyé. Arch Forum 132:62-5 My '70
See also
Housing—Desegregation
Negroes—Housing
DISCRIMINATION in sports. See Segregation
in sports
DISCUS, pseud.
Music in the round. See issues of Harper's
magazine
DISCUSSION
Discussion effects on racial attitudes. D. G.
Myers and G. D. Bishop. bibliog il Science
169:778-9 Ag 21 '70
See also
Conversation
DISCUSSION groups. See Forums (discussion
and debate)
DISCUSSION method (education)
Books behind bars; American institute of dis-
cussion program at El Reno federal reform-
atory, Okla. il Am Ed 6:28-9 D '70
Controversy in the classroom. K. Branan
and M. K. Murphy. il Parents Mag 45:37-
9+ Je '70
No more teachers' dirty looks; classroom-
meeting techniques. L. A. Gutkind. il Schol
Teach Jr/Sr High p20-1+ N 2 '70
Turning on bright underachievers; Wellesley
senior high school, Mass. W. J. Freeman
and A. C. Craig. Todays Ed 59:52-3 F '70
Youth in rebellion, why? interview. W.
Glasser. il por U S News 68:42-6 Ap 27 '70
DISEASE, Diet in. See Diet in disease
DISEASE carriers. See Carriers of infection
DISEASES
Defunct diseases. Time 96:54-5 S 28 '70
See also
Autoimmune diseases
Communicable diseases
Deficiency diseases
Iatrogenic diseases
also subhead Diseases under parts of
the body, e.g. Digestive system—Diseases

Causes and theories of causation
See also
Traumatism

History
Natural history of disease; excerpt from
Jungle in the house. M. Bates. il Sci Digest
68:32-7 N '70
DISEASES, Hereditary. See Heredity of disease
DISEASES, Iatrogenic. See Iatrogenic diseases
DISEASES, Industrial

Prevention
See Industrial safety
DISEASES, Mental. See Mental illness
DISEASES, Prehistoric. See Paleopathology
DISEASES, Psychosomatic. See Medicine, Psy-
chosomatic
DISEASES of famous persons
George III and the mad business, by I. Mac-
alpine and R. Hunter. Review
Nation 211:220-1 S 14 '70. M. Byrd
Newsweek 76:67-8 Ag 3 '70. R. A. Gross
See also
Porphyria
DISH towels. See Towels
DISHES. See Pottery
DISHON, Colleen
Fireproofing our children. il Todays Health
49:38-41+ Ja '71
DISHONESTY. See Honesty
DISHWASHING and drying machines
$40 dishwasher with possibilities. il Con-
sumer Rep 35:4 Ja '70
Portable dishwashers. il Consumer Rep 34:
71-4 D '69
DISINTEGRATION of James Cherry; drama.
See Wanshel, J.
DISK memories. See Memory devices (com-
puters)
DISK plows. See Plows
DISK-throwing game. See Frisbee (game)
DISMAL SWAMP
Dismal delight. B. Thomas. il Travel 133:
48-51+ Ja '70
DISMISSAL of teachers. See Teachers—Dis-
missal
DISNEY, Dorothy Cameron
(ed) Can this marriage be saved? See issues
of Ladies' home journal
DISNEY, Walt
Walt Disney's psychedelic Fantasia. W. Zins-
ser. il Life 68:15 Ap 3 '70 *
DISNEY, Walt, productions
Disney on parade. il Newsweek 76:79 O 5 '70

DISNEY world. See Amusement parks
DISNEYLAND park, Anaheim, Calif.
New wonder in Disneyland; strike. il News-
week 76:68 S 21 '70
DISOBEDIENCE. See Obedience
DISPENSATIONS (canon law)
Immaculate Heart rebels. por Time 95:49-50
F 16 '70
DISPERSION strengthening
Alloys beyond superalloys. E. Gross. il Sci N
97:107-8 Ja 24 '70
DISPLACEMENTS (ships)
All about displacement cruisers. F. C. Clark,
jr. il Motor B 126:38-41+ S '70
Fine art of model testing. P. DeSaix. il Mo-
tor B 127:134-5 Ja '71
DISPLAY animations. See Models (display fig-
ures)
DISPLAY figures. See Models (display figures)
DISPLAY of antiques, art objects, etc.
Art in an old red barn. il House & Gard 137:
84-5 Je '70
Artful offices; investment management firm.
il Arch Forum 132:48-51 Mr '70
At home with art: the Lawrence Bloedel
guesthouse. il Art in Am 58:80-5 My '70
Collectors' finds in the summer house of Dr
and Mrs John Converse. il House & Gard
137:40-5 F '70
How to place and light sculpture. N. R. Piene.
House & Gard 137:18+ F '70
Pistol in the parlor; imaginative arrange-
ments of old letters, jewelry, and photos.
E. Mooberry. il por Har Yrs 10:13+ Mr '70
DISPLAY of merchandise
See also
Showrooms
DISPLAY offices. See Showrooms
DISPLAY systems, Information. See Informa-
tion display systems
DISPLAYS, Library. See Library exhibits
DISPLAYS, Window. See Show windows
DISPOSABLE diapers. See Diapers, Infants
DISPOSABLE products. See Commercial pro-
ducts
DISPOSAL of hazardous substances. See Haz-
ardous substances—Disposal in the ocean
DISPOSAL of poisonous gases. See Gases, As-
phyxiating and poisonous—Disposal in the
ocean
DISPOSAL of refuse. See Refuse and refuse
disposal
DISPOSAL of trade waste. See Trade waste
disposal
DISPUTES, International. See Arbitration, In-
ternational
DISSENT, Freedom of. See Free speech
DISSENT, Right of. See Free speech
DISSENTERS
Berrigans: radical activism personified. G. C.
Zahn. pors Cath World 212:125-30 D '70
Can Kremlin keep lid on dissenters? il U S
News 69:44 N 30 '70
Coffeehouse; Fort Dix antiwar coffeehouse.
S. Alsop. Newsweek 75:116 Mr 16 '70
Cold night in Flint. P. Tracy. Commonweal
91:447-50 Ja 23 '70
Culture and counterculture in U.S. politics.
G. W. Schwartzkopf. il America 123:396-8
N 14 '70; Reply. J. W. Evans. 123:531 D 19
'70
Decline of radicalism, by D. J. Boorstin. Re-
view
Fortune 81:191-2 Mr '70. I. Kristol
Different drummers: men and women who
changed the step of American history. See
issues of Senior scholastic to March 2, 1970
Discontent in Russia: threat to the Kremlin?
interview. R. Conquest. por U S News 69:
58-9 D 28 '70
Dissent and stability in the Soviet Union.
D. T. Cattell. Cur Hist 59:220-5+ O '70
Enough of government by street carnival! ex-
cerpt from address, October 30, 1969. S. T.
Agnew. Read Digest 96:85-8 F '70
History behind the headlines: echoes from the
past: anti-war protests. Sr Schol 95:15 N 3
'69
Manner of speaking; defense against accusa-
tion by HISC of being a radical. J. Ciardi.
Sat R 53:12+ N 7 '70
Notes from the underground; interview. D.
Berrigan. New Yorker 46:20-3 Jl 25 '70
Odyssey from liberal to radical. R. A. Mc-
Kenzie. Chr Cent 87:362-3 Mr 25 '70
On tracking down dissent. N. Hentoff. Cur
121:37-41 S '70
Protesters in the U.S.S.R. S. L. Levitsky.
America 122:613 Je 6 '70
Protesters, police, and politicians. J. Unruh.
Sat R 53:31+ F 21 '70
Reports: Washington: dissenters within. E.
B. Drew. Atlan 225:4+ Ja '70

Revolution: what Douglas foresees. por U S
News 68:17 F 16 '70
Russia: conformity and dissent. T. Szamuely.
Nat R 22:36-7 Ja 13 '70
Violent protest: a debased language; Time
essay. Time 95:15 My 18 '70
See also
Protests, demonstrations, etc.
DISSENTERS, Religious
Church confronts loyalty and dissent; sym-
posium. America 122:668-85 Je 27 '70
Church torn between dogma and dissent; with
report by J. Cogley. il pors Life 68:22-31
68:22-31 Mr 20 '70
Diary of a dissenting priest. P. Mayer. Com-
monweal 92:78-9 Ap 3 '70
Divine disobedience, by F. Du Plessix Gray.
Review
Cath World 212:98-9 N '70. C. J. Morgan
Chr Cent 87:1097-9 S 16 '70. J. Smith
Commonweal 92:298-9 Je 12 '70. A. A.
Cohen
New Repub 162:27-9 Je 27 '70. S. Maloff
Sat R il 53:23+ Je 13 '70. D. Schoenbrun
Vogue 156:42 Ag 1 '70. E. Hardwick
Priests and nuns: going their way. il Time
95:51-5+ F 23 '70
Radical kingdom, by R. R. Ruether. Review
Cath World 212:152-3 D '70. G. Grudzen
Religion: seekers and settlers. J. C. Haughey.
America 124:8 Ja 9 '71

History
Radical kingdom, by R. R. Ruether. Review
Commonweal 92:462-4+ S 18 '70. G. Baum
DISTANCES, Astronomical. See Astronomical
distances
DISTEFANO, M. K. Jr, and Pryer, M. W.
Stability of attitudes in psychiatric atten-
dants following training. bibliog Ment Hy
54:433-5 Jl '70
DISTILLERIES
Fighting the Scotch tide; Scotland's finest
malt whiskies. il Time 95:72 Je 8 '70
Scotch malt whiskey. J. McPhee. il Holiday
47:66-7+ Ja '70
DISTILLERS company, ltd. See Liquor indus-
try and trade—Great Britain
DISTILLING industries. See Liquor industry
and trade
DISTINGUISHED service award. See American
forestry association
DISTRIBUTION of food. See Food—Market-
ing
DISTRIBUTION of population. See Population,
Distribution of
DISTRIBUTION stations. See Warehouses
DISTRIBUTOR points.   See Automobile en-
gines—Ignition
DISTRICT 50, UMW. See United mine workers
of America—District 50
DISTRICT of Columbia. See Washington, D.C.
DISULFRAM
Intracranial self-stimulation and wakeful-
ness: effect of manipulating ambient brain
catecholamines. S. K. Roll. bibliog il Sci-
ence 168:1370-2 Je 12 '70
DITTES, James E. and Powers, C. W.
Reason for being at Union and Yale. Chr Cent
87:494-501 Ap 22 '70
DIURETICS and diuresis
See also
Spironolactone
DIVERS. See Diving, Submarine
DIVERSIFICATION in industry
Beyond the frontiers; new fields for adver-
tising agencies. il Time 96:54-5 S 7 '70
Big change in small loans. il Bsns W p48+ Je
13 '70
Money makes beautiful music at Baldwin.
il Bsns W p58+ My 23 '70
Rohr breaks out. T. J. Murray. il por Duns
95:62-3 Je '70
Where the cigarette men go after the TV
ban. il Bsns W p64-5+ N 21 '70
DIVERSIFIED technologies, Inc.
Singer: a new way to make money? A. Hersh-
man. pors Duns 95:22-3+ Ja '70
DIVESTITURE by corporations. See Corpora-
tions—Divestiture
DIVIDENDS
Dividends lose their stock appeal. il Bsns W
p 16 Mr 7 '70
Plow back dividends and make them grow.
Changing T 24:34 Ag '70
Precarious payouts? table. Forbes 106:38 S
1 '70
See also
Banks and banking—Dividend reinvestment
plans
DIVINATION
See also
Astrology

DIVINE office
Renewal and priestly prayer. M. Semple.
America 122:419-20+ Ap 18 '70; Discussion.
122:544 My 23 '70
DIVING, Submarine
See also
Archeology, Submarine
Diving apparatus
Diving suits
Ocean bottom
Skin diving

Physiological effects
Cold and the diver. J. P. Kowal. il Sea Front
16:42-7 Ja '70
DIVING apparatus
Coming: the safe 1000-foot dive. J. F. Pear-
son. il Pop Mech 133:114-17+ My '70

Fires and fire protection
Fire and the diver. il Sea Front 16:148-50
My '70
DIVING platforms, boards, etc.
You don't have to have a diving board to
have interesting diving. il Sunset 145:58-61
Jl '70
DIVING suits
Cold and the diver. J. P. Kowal. il Sea
Front 16:42-7 Ja '70
Down to the sea in style. il Time 95:58-62
Je 1 '70
DIVING test chambers. See Simulators
DIVINITY of Christ. See Jesus Christ—Divinity
DIVINITY schools. See Theological seminaries
DIVOKY, Diane
My daughter loves school, can she be learn-
ing anything? il Redbook 136:71+ N '70
Project ASPIRE: help for hopeless kids. il
Schol Teach Sec Teach Sup p20-2 F 2 '70
Young ideas in an old state. il Sat R 53:62+
Ap 18 '70
DIVORCE
Divorced after twenty years of marriage. il
Good H 171:56+ O '70
Twenty-year fracture; long-term marriages.
K. Donelson and I. Donelson. Har Yrs 10:
19-21+ F '70
See also
Children of divorced parents
Domestic relations courts
Marriage

Great Britain
Marriage breakdown; findings of Putting asunder report. Chr Cent 87:1528 D 23 '70

Italy
Church-state embroilment. America 122:259
Mr 14 '70
Divorce on the docket. il Time 96:35 D 14 '70
Making it legitimate. Newsweek 76:56 O 19
'70
Reports: Italy. I. R. Levine. Atlan 225:32 Ap
'70

Mexico
Demise of the quickie divorce. Time 96:96
N 16 '70
Divorce Mexican style; end of the quickie? il
Newsweek 76:43 Ag 24 '70

Morocco
"I divorce thee". L. Rosen. il Trans-Action
7:34-7 Je '70

New York (state)
Now the poor can get divorced, too. G.
Lichtenstein. il pors N Y Times Mag p30-1+
Ap 26 '70
United States
Disgrace of our divorce laws. E. M. Wylie.
il Good H 170:98-9+ Ap '70
Time to give divorced men a break. J. L.
Collier. Read Digest 96:64-8 F '70; Discus-
sion. 96:39-41 My '70
DIVORCE (canon law)
See also
Marriage—Annulment (canon law)
DIVORCEES
Women as property; criticisms of the Family
court system. V. Tomasson. New Repub
163:15-18 S 19 '70
DIXIE 500 race. See Automobile racing
DIXON. Dean
Dean Dixon. K. Kristoffersen. por Hi Fi 20:
secII 18-19 Ag '70 *
Dixon. il por Newsweek 76:62 Ag 3 '70 *
Music to my ears; first appearance on the
Philharmonic podium. I. Kolodin. Sat R
53:46 D 12 '70 *.
DIXON, John
Personal growth in the classroom: Dartmouth,
Dixon, and humanistic psychology. T. D.
Klein. bibliog f Engl J 59:235-43 F '70 *

DJAKARTA. See Jakarta, Indonesia
DJERASSI, Carl
Birth control after 1984; adaptation of ad-
dress, May 6, 1970. bibliog il Science 169:
941-51 S 4 '70
Prognosis for the development of new
chemical birth-control agents; adaptation
of address. October 22, 1969. bibliog Science
166:468-73; 167:1315-16 O 24 '69, Mr 6 '70
DJERASSI, Norma
Sand cast your own sculpture. il Har Yrs
10:34-6 My '70
DJERMAKOYE, I. S.
United Nations and decolonization. UN Mo
Chron 7:37-45 Mr '70
DJILAS, Milovan
Dissent cannot be shot down or arrested. P.
Young. il pors Life 68:61+ My 1 '70 *
DLUGOSZEWSKI, Lucia
Lucia Dlugoszewski, surfacing. J. Gruen.
Vogue 156:100 O 1 '70 *
DNIESTER RIVER
Dnester River; tr. by N. Precoda. P. Boga-
tenkov. Environ 12:36-7 N '70
DO-cao-Tri
Patton of the Parrot's Beak. por Time
95:35 Je 8 '70 *
Saigon's man in Cambodia: road to glory.
il por Newsweek 75:36 Je 8 '70
DO-it-yourself repairing. See Mechanics, House-
hold
DO-it-yourself work
See also
Plastics work
DOAK, E. Dale
Evaluating levels of thinking. Sch & Soc
98:177-8 Mr '70
DOAK, Wesley
Just dirt: a whole lot of it. Library J 95:2631
Ag '70
DOBBS, J. S.
Exhibiting reptiles. il Parks & Rec 5:23+
O '70
DOBKIN, Robert C.
New developments in monolithic op amps.
il por Electr World 84:45-8 Jl '70
DOBSON, Joan L.
Whoever heard of James Fenimore Cooper?
Engl J 59:1135-7+ N '70
DOBYNS, Stephen
Finding the direction; Ways of keys: Pass-
ing the word: Counterparts: poems. Poetry
115:319-23 F '70
DOCHERTY, George M.
Gospel of the dynamic middle. Chr Cent 87:
863-6 Jl 15 '70
DOCK strikes, Great Britain. See Strikes—
Great Britain
DOCKING of houseboats. See Houseboats—
Handling
DOCKS
See also
Marinas
Terminals
DOCKSTADER, Frederick J.
Folk arts, cross-country. il Art in Am 58:
74-7 Mr '70
DOCTOR Beeber; story. See Singer I. B.
DOCTOR Brodie's report; story. See Borges,
J. L.
DR Fish; drama. See Schisgal, M.
DOCTOR of arts degree. See Degrees, Aca-
demic
DOCTOR of ministry. See Degrees, Academic
DR Pepper company
Out-of-towner. il Newsweek 76:72+ S 28 '70
DR Seuss, pseud. See Geisel, T. S.
DOCTORATES. See Degrees, Academic
DOCTORS. See Physicians
DOCTORS assistants. See Medical workers
DOCTORS of philosophy. See Degrees, Aca-
demic
DOCTORS of the church
At last, two women doctors. America 122:
204 F 28 '70; Discussion. 122:318-19 Mr 28
'70
First women doctors of the church pro-
claimed by Pope Paul. Chr Cent 87:1246
O 21 '70
DOCUMENTARY films. See Moving pictures—
Documentary films
DOCUMENTARY phonograph records. See
Phonograph records—Documentary records
DOCUMENTARY photography. See Photogra-
phy, Documentary
DOCUMENTARY television programs. See Tele-
vision broadcasting—Documentary programs
DOCUMENTATION
See also
American society for information science
DOCUMENTS
See also
Government publications

DOCUMENTS expediting project. See United States—Library of Congress—Documents expediting project

DOCUMENTS office (United States) See United States—Superintendent of documents

DODD, Allen R.
Okay, Thoreau, we know you're in there. Sat R 53:55-6+ Je 13 '70

DODD, Edward Benton
Power of the great outdoors. il Am For 76: 14-15 O '70

DODD, Eugene Merrick
Functionalism in Shaker crafts. il Antiques 98:588-93 O '70

DODDER weevils. See Weevils

DODECAHEDRONS. See Polyhedrons

DODEMAN, Jacques
Intracom started as Int'l communications club. por Pub W 198:18 D 14 '70 *

DODGE, Robert O.
Michigan. il Parks & Rec 5:37-9+ D '70

DODGERS (baseball) See Baseball clubs

DODGSON, Charles Lutwidge. See Carroll, L. pseud.

DODSON, Charles H.
Magnetic tape: handle with care. il Pop Electr 32:85-7+ F '70

DODSON, Dan W.
Changes affecting human interaction. Ed Digest 36:34-8 O '70

DOELL, Richard R. and others
Magnetic studies of lunar samples. bibliog il Science 167:695-7 Ja 30 '70
—See Dalrymple, G. B. jt. auth.

DOEMEL, Nancy J.
Vocabulary for slow learners. Engl J 59:78-80 Ja '70

DOERING, Charles H. and others
Genetic variation of cholesterol ester content in mouse adrenals. bibliog il Science 170: 1220-2 D 11 '70

DOERING, David
Needed: a new vision of the kingdom. il Chr Cent 87:239-40 F 25 '70

DOG boots. See Shoes. Animal

DOG burials. See Indians of North America—Mortuary customs

DOG carriers. See Carriers (animals)

DOG grooming
Dog grooming. J. Kuh. por Ladies Home J 87:118 Ag '70

DOG houses. See Kennels

DOG pounds. See Pounds

DOG racing
Happy hounds on a coon race. il Travel 134: 57-61 O '70
Making of a champion: World championship sled dog race. W. J. Buchanan. il Read Digest 96:106-12 Mr '70

Anecdotes, facetiae, satire, etc.
Sam Spade goes to the dogs. P. Putnam. il Sports Illus 33:52-4+ Jl 20 '70

DOG tails. See Tails

DOG training. See Dogs—Training

DOGMATISM
Dogmatism, religiosity and mental health in college students. H. G. Richek and others. Ment Hy 54:572-4 O '70

DOGNAPPING. See Animal thefts

DOGS
Along came Joe. J. Susann. il por Ladies Home J 87:74+ Ap '70
Consumer's guide to buying a dog. Mech Illus 66:118 O '70
Dirty dogs; dung-eating. D. M. Duffey. il Outdoor Life 145:199-200+ Ap '70
Do cities really need dogs? il Time 96:35 Jl 20 '70
Dogs. D. M. Duffey. See issues of Outdoor life
Fitting a pup into the family. D. M. Lidster. il Bet Hom & Gard 48:126+ N '70
How much better is purebred than a mutt? J. Hunt. il McCalls 97:30+ Jl '70
Mini, midi, and maxi styles in dogs. J. Hunt. McCalls 98:39+ Ja '71
Mixed-up genes & pure-bred dogs; ten things to check when you buy a pup. D. Lipton. il Sci Digest 68:41-6 D '70
Mop comes back; Bichon frise. il Life 69: 36-7 Jl 10 '70
Pampered pooches. A. S. Flaumenhaft. il por Har Yrs 10:14-15 S '70
Panting in dogs: unidirectional air flow over evaporative surfaces. K. Schmidt-Nielsen and others. bibliog il Science 169:1102-4 S 11 '70
See also
Hounds
Hunting dogs
Watchdogs

Care
ABC's of dog care. D. M. Duffey. il Outdoor Life 146:108-10+ Jl '70
Bloody merry and other problems. G. B. Evans. Field & S 75:142+ N '70
Happiness is a clean puppy; excerpt from How to do almost anything. B. Bacharach. il McCalls 98:16+ N '70
Porcupine predicament. A. Bowes and J. Kendall. il Outdoor Life 145:64-5 My '70
Tooth care for your dog. D. M. Lidster. il Bet Hom & Gard 48:120+ My '70
When your dog has puppies. D. M. Lidster. il Bet Home & Gard 48:20+ Mr '70

Food and feeding
New facts on dog nutrition. D. M. Lidster. il Bet Hom & Gard 48:4+ Ap '70
Right food for your pet. il Good H 171:186-7 O '70
Truth about pet foods. L. Coe. il Pop Mech 134:123-5+ O '70
What to feed the family dog. il Changing T 24:43-4 Ag '70

Grooming
See Dog grooming

Kennels
See Kennels

Laws and legislation
New York: a city going to the dogs? C. Berman. il N Y Times Mag p92+ S 27 '70

Names
Anecdotes, facetiae, satire, etc.
What ever happened to Fido? Sat R 53:6 Jl 11 '70

Photographs
See Animals—Photographs

Purchasing
If a puppy is on your Christmas list. Good H 171:160 D '70
What price a hunting dog? D. M. Duffey. il Outdoor Life 146:148+ S '70

Stories
Dog who came in from the cold. W. Iversen. il Read Digest 97:127-30 S '70

Tails
See Tails

Training
Easy money raising dogs? D. M. Duffey. il Outdoor Life 145:110+ Ja '70
English spoken here; teach any dog to understand. H. G. Tapply. il Field & S 74:70 F '70
How to start a coonhound. D. M. Duffey. il por Outdoor Life 145:158-9+ My '70
Little lightning hits a dog; training with an electric collar. B. Warner. il Field & S 74:168-70+ F '70
Solving the delivery problem; training of a retriever. D. M. Duffey. il Outdoor Life 146: 132+ N '70
That gunshyness bugaboo. D. M. Duffey. il Outdoor Life 145:136+ F '70
Training roundup. D. M. Duffey. il Outdoor Life 146:130+ Ag '70
Two ways to train. L. Mueller. il Field & S 74:216-17+ Mr '70
White dog; excerpts. R. Gary. il por Life 69:58-58B O 9 '70

Transportation
See Animals—Transportation

DOGS, Photography of. See Photography of animals

DOGS, Stealing of. See Animal thefts

DOGS, Tattooing of. See Tattooing

DOGS, Wild. See Wild dogs

DOGS and children. See Children and animals

DOGS as laboratory animals. See Laboratory animals

DOGS in art. See Animals in art

DOGWOOD
Flowering dogwood. D. Wyman. il Horticulture 48:44-5 My '70

DOHERTY, John Stephen
Patio furniture you can build. il Mech Illus 66:128-31 Mr '70

DOHNANYI, Christoph von
D is for Dohnanyi. P. Gorner. por Opera N 35:24 O 31 '70 *

DOHNER, V. Alton
Drugs are not the problem. Ed Digest 36:25-8 N '70

DOHRN, Bernardine
Explosive words and deeds. il por Time 96:18 O 19 '70 *

DOIG, Ivan
Article research sources. Writers Digest 50:
41-2 Ja '70
DOLAN, Anthony R.
On campus and off (cont) Nat R 22:208 F 24 '70
DOLBY noise reduction unit. See Magnetic
recorders and recording—Equipment
DOLE, Robert J.
New and hungry chairman. por Time 97:13-14
Ja 18 '71 *
Nixon's champion. por Time 96:18 Jl 6 '70 *
One-upmanship. il Newsweek 76:37 Jl 6 '70 *
TRB from Washington; Sontay rescue mis-
sion. New Repub 163:4 D 12 '70
Will Dole do it? Nat R 22:1391 D 29 '70 *
DOLL clothes
Girls' & boys' costumes for dolls, pre-Civil
war. C. H. Fawcett. il Hobbies 74:48-9
Ja '70
Pre-Civil war doll costumes. C. H. Fawcett.
il Hobbies 75:48-9 Mr '70
DOLL heads
Many heads of Armand Marseille; bisque
doll heads. M. L. Morris. il Hobbies 75:
48-9+ N '70
DOLL houses
Business by accident; Matt and Jim White
of Pompano Beach, Fla. S. A. Parvin. il
Hobbies 75:142-3+ S '70
Dollhouses, yesterday and today. il Bet Hom
& Gard 48:54-5+ D '70
For the rolling seventies a doll-house-trailer.
il Sunset 145:56-7 D '70
Hobby becomes professional; Miniature con-
struction company, North White Plains,
N.Y. S. A. Parvin. il Hobbies 75:158 N '70
Petronella Oortman doll house, Rijksmuseum,
Amsterdam. S. A. Parvin. il Hobbies 74:148
F '70
Roxana's doll house. S. A. Parvin. il Hobbies
75:144-6+ Je '70
When the doll house is a houseboat, even
young boys get interested. il Sunset 144:
104-5 Mr '70
See also
Rooms, Miniature
DOLLAR gap. See Balance of payments
DOLLS
Debate in the doll house. T. J. Rakstis. il
Todays Health 48:28-31+ D '70
Dollology. C. H. Fawcett. See issues of Hob-
bies
Dolls of Tomoyo Kobayashi. T. Kobayashi
and L. Kobayashi. il Hobbies 75:48-9+ My
'70
Dolls that commemorate royalty; Empress
Eugenie of France & Carlotta & Maximilian
of Mexico. C. H. Fawcett. il Hobbies 75:
48-9+ Ap '70
Inter-tribal doll museum is one-of-a-kind. il
Hobbies 74:44 F '70
Many heads of Armand Marseille; bisque doll
heads. M. L. Morris. il Hobbies 75:48-9+
N '70
Mary Kennedy's glorified rag dolls; Mother
Goose at the Arkansas state college. C. H.
Fawcett. il Hobbies 75:41+ Je '70
My dolls' Christmases. M. D. Elliott. il Hob-
bies 75:48+ D '70
Tribal dolls of South Africa. J. Kressly. il
Negro Hist Bul 32:20-1 D '69

Collectors and collecting
What's in a name? C. H. Fawcett. il Hobbies
74:48-9 F '70

Exhibitions
Doll topics; reprint of October 1930. il Hob-
bies 75:41 Ag '70
DOLL'S house 1970; drama. See Luce, C. B.
DOLLY Madison Industries, Inc.
Unscrambling a conglomerate. por Bsns W
p 118+ Je 13 '70
DOLLY Varden trout fishing. See Char fishing
DOLMATCH, Theodore B.
Who will be accountable for accountability?
address, June 1970. por Library J 95:3955-7
N 15 '70
DOLPHINS (football club) See Football clubs
DOLPHINS (mammals)
After living with man, a dolphin may com-
mit suicide. C. Amory. Holiday 47:16+
My '70
Squeeze play; dolphin adaptation to increasing
water pressure. Sci Am 222:64 Mr '70
DOLSON, Charles H.
It all began with the boll weevil. il por
Nations Bsns 58:66-7 Ja '70
DOM Juan; drama. See Molière, J. B. P.
DOMAIN structure
Magnetic-bubble memories. il Electr World
84:48 O '70
Strange world of magnetic bubbles. A.
Fisher. il Pop Sci 196:65-7 F '70

DOMES
Art for everyday living: survival dome; oxy-
gen utility dome. D. Holmes. il Art in Am
58:78-9 S '70
Dome home. B. Berger. il Mech Illus 66:100+
O '70
New sense of living, 1971; home of Mr and
Mrs Giora Novak. il pors Vogue 157:124-7
Ja 1 '71
See also
Air-supported structures
Geodesic domes
DOMESTIC affairs council. See United States
—Domestic affairs council
DOMESTIC animals
See also
Asses and mules
Dogs
Domestication
Goats
Livestock
Poultry
                    Names
See also
Dogs—Names
DOMESTIC architecture. See Architecture,
Domestic
DOMESTIC economic assistance. See Economic
assistance, Domestic
DOMESTIC finance
Are you a smart money-manager? Take this
test. il Changing T 24:46-7 Je '70
Could most wives take over the family fi-
nances? P. Lindberg. il Bet Hom & Gard
48:14+ F '70
Dollars-and-cents basics for newlyweds. il
Changing T 24:6 Je '70
Family money management; ed. by P. Lind-
berg. See issues of Better homes and gar-
dens
Guide for stretching your buying dollar. il
Good H 170:168 F '70
How families fight inflation. il U S News 68:
66-9 F 16 '70
How to avoid debt problems. il Good H 171:
146 Jl '70
How to head off today's soaring costs. Bet
Hom & Gard 48:6+ Ja '70
How to hold down today's soaring costs.
Bet Hom & Gard 48:6+ F '70
How to keep your family fiscally fit. L. David.
il Mech Illus 66:29-31+ D '70
How to manage family finances. il Suc Farm
68:45 S '70
How to save money on appliances and fur-
nishings. R. O'Brien. Read Digest 97:95-7
S '70
Proven & practical ways to handle money,
better. il Changing T 24:25-9 Jl '70
Sidestepping the money gap; with report
by R. Woodbury. il Life 68:20-7 F 13 '70
Sixty-two ways to beat the high cost of liv-
ing. il Changing T 24:6-10 My '70; Same
abr. with title Forty-one ways to beat the
high cost of living. Read Digest 97:42-6
Ag '70
Spending your money; questions and answers.
S. Porter. See issues of Ladies' home jour-
nal
What a second income really means. P. Lind-
berg. il Bet Home & Gard 48:49+ Mr '70
What it costs now to have a baby. S. Porter.
il Ladies Home J 87:32-3 Jl '70
See also
Budget, Household
Budget, Personal
Debt
Purchasing, Household
Saving and savings

Anecdotes, facetiae, satire, etc.
Using 1957-59 as a base, try stealing home.
G. Cotler. New Yorker 46:36-7 My 16 '70
DOMESTIC international sales corporations.
See Export trade—Federal aid
DOMESTIC peace corps. See Volunteers in ser-
vice to America
DOMESTIC relations
See also
Family
Marriage
Quarrels
Wives
DOMESTIC relations courts
Women as property; criticisms of the Family
court system. V. Tomasson. New Repub
163:15-18 S 19 '70
DOMESTICATION
Animal remains from Lepenski vir. S.
Bökönyi. bibliog il Science 167:1702-4 Mr
27 '70
Potato. D. Ugent. bibliog il Science 170:1161-
6 D 11 '70
DOMINGO, Placido
Making love to the public. W. Bender. pors
Time 96:36 O 26 '70 *

DOMINICAN REPUBLIC
See also
Morale, National—Dominican Republic
Politics and government
Closer to chaos. Time 95:34 Ap 13 '70
Image-makers at work; J. Balaguer re-elected. Nat R 22:553 Je 2 '70
So Balaguer won. G. A. Geyer. New Repub 162:13-14 My 30 '70
See also
Elections—Dominican Republic
DOMINIONS, British. See Commonwealth of nations
DOMINO, Antoine
Where are they now? pors Newsweek 76:24 O 19 '70 *
DOMMEN, Arthur J.
Future of North Vietnam. Cur Hist 58: 229-32+ Ap '70
Laos in the second Indochina war. Cur Hist 59:326-32+ D '70
DON Carlo; opera. See Verdi, G.
DON Juan
European literary scene. R. J. Clements. Sat R 53:27 Jl 4 '70 *
DON Pasquale; opera. See Donizetti, G.
DON QUIXOTE (literary character) See Cervantes Saavedra, M. de
DON Rodrigo; opera. See Ginastera, A.
DONAHUE, Francis
International student: his six roles. Clear House 45:51-5 S '70
DONAHUE, John F.
Federated breaks the fund mold. por Bsns W p98+ Jl 11 '70 *
DONAHUGH, Robert H.
Best laid plan: OLDP, ALSO, and JSHP. Am Lib 1:973-7 N '70
DONALD, William Spooner
Will someone please hiccup my pat? Horizon 11:120 Aut '69
DONALDSON, J. L.
Innovation programs in sex education. il PTA Mag 64:26-8 biblio(p35-6) Ja '70; Same abr. Ed Digest 35:46-8 Ap '70
DONALDSON, Peter J.
He wanted to be Senator McLaughlin, S.J. America 123:428-32 N 21 '70
DONALDSON, R.
It's raining pictures! R. Donaldson's photography of raindrops. il Pop Phot 67:81-3 Ag '70 *
DONALDSON, William
As they see it; interview. por Forbes 105:46 Ap 15 '70
DONALDSON, Lufkin and Jenrette, inc.
Wall Street is shy about buying itself. il Bsns W p 116 Ap 18 '70
DONATHAN, Judith Putnam
(comp) Adult paperbacks. Library J 95:268-97, 1981-2001, 3002-4+ Ja 15, My 15, S 15 '70
(ed) Books to come (cont) Library J 95: 527-88, 919-35+, 2322-77, 2552-75, 2833+, 3313-14+ F 1, Mr 1, Je 15-Jl, S 1, O 1 '70
DONCEEL, Joseph
Rahner's argument for God. America 123: 340-2 O 31 '70
DONELSON, Irene
I remember . . . Santa and the snowbound bear. il Har Yrs 10:32-3 D '70
—See Donelson, K. jt. auth.
DONELSON, Kenneth, and Donelson, Irene
Tips for testators. il Har Yrs 10:39-42 Ag '70
Twenty-year fracture. Har Yrs 10:19-21+ F '70
DONES, Ray
Novel ultra-low-frequency woofer enclosure. il Electr World 83:43-5 My '70
DONIS, Miles
Ego trip; story. Redbook 134:94-5 Mr '70
DONIZETTI, Gaetano
Don Pasquale. Criticism
Opera N il 35:17-20, 24-5 D 5 '70 *
Eleven-day wonder. W. Ashbrook. il Opera N 35:24-5 D 5 '70 *
Lucia di Lammermoor. Criticism
New Yorker 46:80+ F 28 '70 *
Music to my ears; concert version of La fille du régiment at Carnegie Hall. I. Kolodin. Sat R 53:63 F 28 '70 *
Report:
La fille du régiment. S. Jenkins. Opera N 34:32 Mr 21 '70 *
Roberto Devereux. A. Sperber. il Am Rec G 36:660-3 My '70 *
Roberto Devereux. Criticism
New Yorker 46:161 O 24 '70 *
Newsweek il 76:99 O 26 '70 *
Sat R 53:41+ O 31 '70 *
Two (and a half) cheers for Anna Bolena. H. Weinstock. Sat R 53:39 D 26 '70 *
DONLAN, Dan M.
White trap: a motif. Engl J 59:943-4 O '70

DONNE, John
First poet in the world, in some things. P. W. Schmidtchen. il pors Hobbies 75:134-6 N '70 *
John Donne, by R. C. Bald. Review
Newsweek por 75:103+ Ap 27 '70. G. Wolff *
DONNELL, Elisworth
Executive abroad. J. Ross-Skinner. il pors Duns 96:48-51 Ag '70 *
DONNELLY, Leroy E.
Look before you leap into total-cost billing. il Am City 85:89+ F '70
DONNELLY. Russell
Saving of a river. il por Outdoor Life 145: 65-7+ Ap '70
DONNER party
"Always on the stretch": a western voyage; American family retraces the steps of the Donner party. R. Rhodes. il Harper 241:79-84+ N '70
DONOFRIO, Anthony F.
Child psychotherapy, help or hindrance? biblio Ment Hy 54:510-15 O '70
DONOHO, William T.
Living with antiques. il Antiques 98:922-6 D '70
DONOHUE, Jerry
Fourier series and difference maps as lack of structure proof: DNA is an example. biblio Science 167:1700-2 Mr 27 '70
DONOHUE, Sylvia S.
Education for survival: conservation comes first. por Parents Mag 45:18 Je '70
DONORA, Pa.
Donora, Pennsylvania. C. Bowen. Atlan 226: 27-8+ N '70
DONOVAN, Brian
Man who beat the army. New Repub 162:17-19 Ja 31 '70
DONOVAN, David L. See Wilbur, T. P. jt. auth.
DONOVAN, John
Observations about Children's book week. il Pub W 198:30-2 N 9 '70
DONOVAN, William Joseph
Donovan of OSS, by C. Ford. Review
Atlan 225:142-4 Mr '70. E. Weeks *
Newsweek por 75:102D+ F 23 '70. S. K. Oberbeck *
Our German wehrmacht is being stopped by a shadow; excerpts from Donovan of OSS. C. Ford. il por Am Heritage 21:56-7+ F '70 *
DON'T bother me, I can't cope; revue. See Musical comedies, revues, etc.—Criticisms, plots, etc.
DON'T look now; story. See Du Maurier. D.
DON'T love me, don't leave me; story. See Carter. M.
DONWAY, Roger
Wrath of the doves. Nat R 22:568-70 Je 2 '70
DOODLES (sketches)
Monster in the imagination; fantasy doodles, collages and paper cutouts by H. C. Andersen. il por Time 96:60-1 O 19 '70
DOOR locks. See Locks and keys
DOOR to door selling. See Canvassing
DOORKEEPERS
Vanishing concierge. il Newsweek 76:80-1 Ag 17 '70
DOORS
Accordion door for the shower. il Sunset 145: 133 O '70
Open-and-shut case for great doors. W. Baldwin. House & Gard 138:12-13+ S '70
See also
Garage doors
DOORS, Mechanically operated
Automatic doors aid efficiency, safety and security. il Arch Rec 48:109 D '70
DOORS, Sliding
Install a sliding glass door. il Mech Illus 66:82-4 S '70
Open the wall and let the outdoors in. H. Wicks. il Pop Mech 134:116-18 O '70
Sliding doors that let in the light. D. Huff. il Pop Sci 197:93 S '70
DOPA
L-Dihydroxyphenylalanine: effect on S-adenosylmethionine in brain. R. J. Wurtman and others. biblio il Science 169:395-7 Jl 24 '70
L-Dopa and its side effects. Sci Digest 68: 42 S '70
L-Dopa: effect of concentrations of dopamine, norepinephrine, and serotonin in brains of mice. G. M. Everett and J. W. Borcherding. il Science 168:849 My 15 '70
L-Dopa has set me free. F. Miller. Read Digest 97:115-19 Ag '70
L-Dopa-induced release of cerebral monoamines. K. Y. Ng and others. biblio il Science 170:76-7 O 2 '70
L-Dopa: limited approval. Newsweek 75:91 Je 15 '70
My hands are free again. G. Astor. il Look 34:49-50 Jl 14 '70

DOPA—*Continued*
Parkinson's disease: activity of L-dopa decarboxylase in discrete brain regions. K. Lloyd and O. Hornykiewicz. bibliog il Science 170: 1212-13 D 11 '70
Relief from Parkinson's; L-dopa approved by FDA subject to safeguards. Time 95:56 Je 15 '70

DOPAMINE
Amantadine-dopamine interaction: possible mode of action in Parkinsonism. R. P. Grelak and others. bibliog il Science 169:203-4 Jl 10 '70
Amphetamine: differentiation by d and l isomers of behavior involving brain norepinephrine or dopamine. K. M. Taylor and S. H. Snyder. bibliog il Science 168:1487-9 Je 19 '70

DOPE smuggling. See Smuggling

DOPING in sports
Happiness boys at the track; administering undetectable tranquilizer to horses. R. H. Boyle. il Sports Illus 33:20-1 O 12 '70
High-ho, high-ho, it's off to lift we go; nine medalists disqualified. H. Weiskopf. il Sports Illus 33:63-4+ S 28 '70
High-school sports flunk the saliva test. T. Irwin. Todays Health 48:44-6+ O '70
Tranquillity; horses being doped with tranquilizers. Sports Illus 33:15-16 N 16 '70

DOPPLER effect
Doppler: new heart of electronic navigation. C. Miller. il Motor B 126:76-8 S '70
Doppler shift measurements of nuclear lifetimes. J. R. MacDonald. bibliog il Science 167:1339-47 Mr 6 '70

DORCY, Michael M.
While Canada waited. America 122:525-6 My 16 '70

DORFMAN, Ben-Zion, and others
Partial reversion in yeast: genetic evidence for a new type of bifunctional protein. bibliog il Science 168:1482-4 Je 19 '70

DORIA, Giulia
Very special Tosca. F. Stevenson. Opera N 35:24-6 D 12 '70 *

DORIDEN. See Glutethimide

DORMAN, Sonya
Elegy for Bella, Sarah, Rosie and all the others. Sat R 53:37 Mr 28 '70
No, madame, I won't take anything from the garden when I move; poem. Sat R 53:48 D 12 '70

DORMANN, Henry O.
Presidential caper. il Time 95:21-2 Ap 13 '70 *

DORMITORIES
Co-ed dorms, an intimate revolution in campus life; Oberlin college, Ohio, with report by K. Thorsen. il Life 69:32-41 N 20 '70
Expressionist forms on a budget; new residence hall at the University of New Hampshire. il Arch Rec 148:101-4 N '70
Large campus residential complex designed to achieve a small-scaled residential character; State university college at New Paltz. il Arch Rec 147:106-9 F '70
Position paper on dormitory intervisitation; statement. J. A. Brown. Sch & Soc 98:379-81 O '70
Student dorms on a Scottish coast; St. Andrews university. J. Stirling; C. Jencks. il Arch Forum 133:50-7 S '70
When college dorms go coed. M. W. Lear. Read Digest 96:27-8+ F '70

DORN, Mallory
Home that travels. il Har Yrs 10:18 F '70

DORNBERG, John
In the Soviet isolation ward. il por Newsweek 76:25-6 D 28 '70

about
Expelled. por Newsweek 76:3 N 2 '70 *

DORNÉS, John
Parting shots. il por Life 68:66A-68 Je 19 '70

DORNFELD, Stevens R.
Suburban fire-police integration a must. il Am City 85:78 F '70

DORSEY, Edna J.
Flowers that run. il Design 71:10-12 Fall '69

DORSEY, Harold B.
Patient is in pain but he isn't dying. por Forbes 105:64-5 Je 1 '70 *

DORSEY, Jimmy
Brothers Dorsey. R. Gehman. il por Sat R 53:52-3+ Ja 17 '70

DORSEY, Tommy
Brothers Dorsey. R. Gehman. il por Sat R 53:52-3+ Ja 17 '70

DORSEY, William H. jr
Middle East balance? But Russia's gain. New Repub 163:12-13 Ag 15 '70

DORTMUND, Germany
Music
Report: production of M. D. Levy's Mourning becomes Electra. H. Koegler. Opera N 34:35 Ja 24 '70

DORY, John P. and Lord, R. J.
Does TF really work? bibliog f Harvard Bsns R 48:16-18+ N '70

DOSKOTCH, Raymond W. and others
Elm bark derived feeding stimulants for the smaller European elm bark beetle. bibliog il Science 167:380-2 Ja 23 '70

DOS PASSOS, John
Dos Passos: last of the big four. J. Chamberlain. Nat R 22:1100-1 O 20 '70 *
Obituary
Newsweek por 76:117-117A+ O 12 '70. R. A. Sokolov
Pub W 198:36-7 O 12 '70
Time por 96:12 O 12 '70

DOSSIN, François
Spectra of comet Tago-Sato-Kosaka. il Sky & Tel 39:152-3 Mr '70

DOT generators. See Testing instruments

DOTT, R. H. jr. See Medaris, L. G. jr, jt. auth.

DOTY, Roy
Wordless workship. See issues of Popular science monthly

DOUBELL, Ralph
Bubbles and bounces. P. Putnam. il por Sports Illus 32:10-13 Ja 26 '70
Ralph the rapscallion. il por Time 95:65 F 23 '70 *

DOUBLE stars. See Stars, Double

DOUBLE taxation. See Taxation, Double

DOUBLEDAY and company
Book-of-the-day club; how Ladies and gentlemen, Easy Aces has been faring. G. Ace. Sat R 53:6 O 31; 8 D 19 '70
Hands across the curtain; Russia's international agreement with Doubleday. Newsweek 76:90 N 16 '70
Step toward cooperation in U.S.-U.S.S.R. publishing. Pub W 198:49 N 16 '70

DOUBT, RIVER OF. See Roosevelt River

DOUGH
From our simple yeast dough, pizza, buns, rolls, swirls. il Sunset 145:174+ N '70
What's cooking?
Make your own leavening. B. T. Hunter. Org Gard & Farm 17:98-101 Jl '70

DOUGH, Frozen
Frozen bread dough: good but slow. Consumer Rep 35:269-70 My '70

DOUGHERTY, Richard M.
Is work simplification alive and well someplace? Am Lib 1:969-71 N '70

DOUGHNUTS
Downright delicious raised doughnuts. il Farm J 94:80 Ap '70

DOUGLAS, Carlyle C.
Curse of contract buying. il Ebony 25:43-6+ Je '70
Diogenes, put down your lamp! il pors Ebony 25:72-4+ Ap '70
Incorporation: a new tactic for saving black areas. il pors Ebony 25:100-2+ Ag '70

DOUGLAS, Gilean
Autumn mural; poem. Horn Bk 46:468 O '70

DOUGLAS, J. A. V. and others
Mineralogy and deformation in some lunar samples. bibliog il Science 167:594-7 Ja 30 '70

DOUGLAS, John R.
Publications of the counter culture. il por Wilson Lib Bul 45:364-71 D '70

DOUGLAS, Kirk
Kirk Douglas at large. R. Ebert. il por Esquire 73:88-93 F '70 *

DOUGLAS, Lewis Williams
Page forty-eight. Am West 7:48 Mr '70

DOUGLAS, Mary
Myth of primitive religion. bibliog il Commonweal 93:41-4 O 9 '70

DOUGLAS, Paul Howard
End to concealment. New Repub 162:22-4 Ap 25 '70

about
Where are they now? il Newsweek 76:21 N 16 '70 *

DOUGLAS, Stephen A.
Creeping self-reliance in Malaysia. Cur Hist 59:345-50+ D '70

DOUGLAS, William Orville
Bill Douglas has never stopped fighting the bullies of Yakima. M. Viorst. il pors N Y Times Mag p8-9+ Je 14 '70 *
Crude plot: crude plotters; impeachment move. Nation 210:483-4 Ap 27 '70 *
Douglas case. Time 95:78 My 11 '70 *

DOUGLAS, William Orville—*Continued*
Douglas Dossier. il por Newsweek 75:29-30+ Ap 27 '70 *
Impeach Douglas? K. Crawford. Newsweek 75:37 My 4 '70 *
Impeach Douglas? il por Time 95:21-2 Ap 27 '70 *
Impeaching Justice Douglas? with excerpts from address by G. R. Ford, April 15, 1970. il por U S News 68:25-6, 67-71 Ap 27 '70 *
Justice Douglas and the Supreme court. America 122:464 My 2 '70 *
Justice Douglas-Evergreen case. Writers Digest 50:44+ Je '70 *
Let's get Douglas. New Repub 162:9 My 2 '70 *
Mr Douglas' revolution. Nat R 22:481 My 5 '70 *
Open letter to: Norman Cousins, and others, from the editors of National review concerning Points of rebellion. Nat R 22:293-4 Mr 24 '70 *
Reston replies. Nat R 22:446+ My 5 '70 *
Revolution, rant and Justice Douglas. D. Seligman. por Life 68:4 My 1 '70 *
Revolution: what Douglas foresees. por U S News 68:17 F 16 '70 *
Where Douglas impeachment case stands now. U S News 69:91 D 14 '70 *
Wit and wisdom of Justice Douglas. Nat R 22:191 F 24 '70 *
DOUGLAS aircraft company. See McDonnell Douglas corporation
DOUGLAS cup race. See Yacht racing
DOUGLAS fir
Douglas fir. J. W. Wilson. il Horticulture 48:44-5+ F '70
DOUGLAS-HAMILTON, Helen (Hamilton) countess of Selkirk. See Selkirk, H. H. D.-H.
DOUGLAS-HOME, Sir Alexander Frederick
Three conservative musketeers C. Brogan. Nat R 22:148-9 F 10 '70
DOUGLASS, Frederick, home. See Washington, D.C.—Historic houses, etc.
DOUGLASS, Joseph H.
Challenge: children and youth in the 70s. Camp Mag 42:12 Ja '70
DOUGLASS, Suzanne
Collectors: poem. Good H 171:10 N '70
Water, water everywhere; poem. Good H 171:10 O '70
DOUŠA, Tomas, and others
[8-Arginine]-vasopressinoic acid: an inhibitor of rabbit kidney adenyl cyclase. bibliog il Science 167:1134-5 F 20 '70
DOUST, Dudley
Golf. Sports Illus 33:60+ O 26 '70
DOUTHIT, H. A. See Feinsod, F. M. jt. auth.
DOUVILLE, Judith A.
Determining the molar volume: a safe method. por Chem 43:25 Ja '70
DOVE shooting. See Mourning dove shooting
DOW, Orrin B.
Orrin B. Dow, public librarian. il por Wilson Lib Bul 45:200-1 O '70 *
DOW chemical company
Can corporations be tried for war crimes? G. Wald. Cur 120:56-63 Ag '70
Dow down. il Forbes 106:42-3+ N 15 '70
Dow on the farm; court injunction by Bud Antle inc. against the UFWOC's picketing. New Repub 163:8 D 12 '70
Jury's decision on war protestors. U S News 68:16 F 23 '70
DOW-Jones averages. See Stocks—Price indexes and averages
DOW Jones news service
Who now, Dow Jones? W. J. Slattery. Esquire 74:236-7 O '70
DOW Jones Open. See Golf—Tournaments
DOWBOR, Ladislas
How one pleasant, scholarly young man from Brazil became a kidnapping, gun-toting, bombing revolutionary. S. De Gramont il pors N Y Times Mag p43-5+ N 15 '70; Discussion. p22+ D 6; 79+ D 13 '70 *
DOWD, Merle E.
So you want to fly slow? il Pop Mech 135:96-7 Ja '71
DOWDEN, Anne Ophelia
Flowers of the fifty; paintings. Audubon 72:21-7 Jl '70
DOWDY, John
Excerpt from debate, September 11, 1969. Cong Digest 49:20+ Ja '70

about

Dowdy's comedown. por Newsweek 75:24-5 13 '70
DOWELL, Anthony
Pas de deux par excellence. O. Maynard. il pors Dance Mag 44:50-61 Ap '70 *

DOWELS
Primer on plug cutters. R. J. De Cristoforo. il Mech Ilius 66:98-9 N '70
DOWER, Michael
We've always wanted to be cops; with report by G. Moore. il pors Life 69:32-7 N 13 '70
DOWER, Michael, Jr
We've always wanted to be cops; with report by G. Moore. il pors Life 69:32-7 N 13 '70 *
DOWLER, Michael J. and others
Prebiotic synthesis of propiolaldehyde and nicotinamide. bibliog il Science 169:1320-1 S 25 '70
DOWLIN, C. Edwin. See Shubert, J. F. jt. auth.
DOWLIN, Kenneth E.
CATV+NCPL=VRS. il pors Library J 95:2768-70 S 1 '70
DOWNES, Mollie Panter-. See Panter-Downes, M.
DOWNES, Rackstraw
Watercolorist for all seasons. il Art N 69:54-7+ My '70
DOWNEY, Hugh
Ordinary guy in Ethiopia. C. W. Hall. il por Read Digest 97:157-8+ Jl '70 *
DOWNEY, Robert
Downey's Pound. New Yorker 46:30-2 F 28 '70 *
DOWNING, Gertrude L.
Student-teacher laboratory prepares a school for de facto desegregation. Clear House 45:37-40 S '70
DOWNTOWN areas. See Business districts
DOWST, Loring
What's the new American light whiskey going to taste like? il Holiday 47:44-5+ Ap '70
DOWTY, Leonhard
Bits and pieces; poem. Good H 170:140 Je '70
Dream to grow on; story. Good H 171:66-7 D '70
How do I love thee? poem. Good H 170:216 F '70
New Orleans. il Travel & Camera 33:26-31 S '70
Pilgrims' progress; story. Good H 171:90-1 N '70
Yes, my darling daughter; poem. Good H 172:154 Ja '71
(ed) See Campbell, G. Glen Campbell: the all-American country boy
DOXIADIS, Constantinos Apostolos
Ekistics, the science of human settlements. bibliog il Science 170:393-404 O 23 '70
Visionary zeal in Detroit. Time 96:52 O 19 '70 *
DOYLE, Sir Arthur Conan
Doctor did it. B. Scott. il Todays Health 48:57-9+ O '70 *
DOYLE, James Edward
Constitution on campus. il por Time 95:64+ Mr 23 '70 *
DOYLE, Norman
FET & op-amp audio circuits. il Radio-Electr 41:46-9 Jl '70
DOYLE, Thomas L.
Psychiatrist reflects on the changing Church. America 122:240-3 Mr 7 '70
DOZIER, Thomas
London particular. Travel & Camera 33:46-7 My '70
DRABIK, Alex
Where are they now? il pors Newsweek 75:12 Mr 2 '70 *
DRACULA; ballet. See Ballets—Criticisms
DRACULA: Sabbat; drama. See Katz, L.
DRAFT, Military. See Military service, Compulsory
DRAFT counseling. See Military service, Compulsory
DRAFT lottery. See Military service, Compulsory
DRAFT resisters. See Military service, Compulsory—Draft resisters
DRAFTING instruments. See Drawing instruments
DRAG, John J.
What kind of church do we want? Chr Today 14:29-30 Ja 30 '70
DRAG racing. See Automobile racing; Motor vehicle racing
DRAGADZE, Peter
(ed) See De Sica, V. Vittorio De Sica's Roma
DRAGON lady; story. See Kaplan, J.
DRAGON with the squeaky roar; drama. See Martens, A. C.
DRAGONFLIES
Symbiosis between euglena and damselfly nymphs is seasonal. R. L. Willey and others. bibliog il Science 170:80-1 O 2 '70

DRAGSTERS. See Automobiles, Racing

DRAIN cleaners
Drain cleaners. il Consumer Rep 35:481-4 Ag '70

DRAIN tiles
What's new for tiling. Suc Farm 68:49 Ag '70

DRAINAGE
Aboriginal drained-field cultivation in the Americas. W. M. Denevan. bibliog il Science 169:647-54 Ag 14 '70
He does his own tiling. il Suc Farm 68:B8 S '70
How should your garden flow? il Sunset 145:196+ O '70
Now's the time for hillside people to check their garden drainage. il Sunset 145:122-3 N '70
Solving drainage woes. il Home Gard 57:39 O '70
See also
Marshes
Mine drainage
Roads—Drainage
Storm sewers
Streets—Drainage

DRAINAGE tile. See Drain tiles

DRAKE, Bill
Rock and roll Muzak. il por Newsweek 75:85 Mr 9 '70 *

DRAKE, Eric
Eric Drake of BP; making a splash in the U.S. market; interview. il pors Nations Bsns 58:62-7 Jl '70

DRAKE, Guy
Country cads. pors Newsweek 75:84-6 Ap 13 '70 *

DRAKE, Hudson B.
Major DOD procurements at war with reality. il Harvard Bsns R 48:119-40 Ja '70

DRAKE, Phyllis
Homer in 2001. Engl J 59:1270-1 D '70

DRAKE, Robert
Don't they look natural? Chr Cent 87:1416+ N 25 '70
Legitimate pleasures of literature. Chr Cent 87:1253-5 O 21 '70

DRAMA
See also
College and school drama
Negro drama
Pageants
Television broadcasting—Drama

History
Dissolves by gaslight: antecedents to the motion picture in nineteenth-century melodrama. J. L. Fell. bibliog il Film Q 23:22-34 Spr '70

Study and teaching
See also
Yale university—School of drama

Technique
Before the colors fade: Green pastures recalled; interview, ed. by J. L. Phillips. il pors Am Heritage 21:28-9+ F '70
How to write a play M. Monigle. Writers Digest 50:40 Ja '70
Thoughts on playwriting. R. Anderson. Writer 83:12-14+ S '70

Themes
Innocence restaged. J. Richardson. Commentary 49:20+ Mr '70
Paradox of Samuel Beckett. C. Hughes. por Cath World 211:26-8 Ap '70

DRAMA book shop, New York. See Booksellers and bookselling—New York (state)

DRAMA critics. See Critics

DRAMA critics circle. See New York drama critics circle

DRAMA festivals
Capital risks: second American college theatre festival, Washington, D.C. H. Hewes. Sat R 53:16 My 30 '70
Summer repertory schedule, 1970. H. Hewes. Sat R 53:8 Je 27 '70
See also
Shakespeare festivals

Canada
Theatre; Shaw festival, Niagara-on-the-Lake, Ontario. J. Novick. Nation 211:189-90 S 7 '70

DRAMAS
Doll's house 1970. C. B. Luce. il pors Life 69:54-6+ O 16 '70
Lekythos; text. A. Holland. Mlle 72:178-9+ N '70
See also
Booksellers and bookselling—Drama

also subhead Drama under various subjects, e.g. Franklin, B.—Drama

Criticisms, plots, etc.
Going on about town. See issues of New Yorker
Life theater review. T. Prideaux. See issues of Life
Off Broadway. E. Oliver. See issues of New Yorker
Stage. G. Weales. Commonweal 92:193-4 My 8 '70
Theater (cont) Nat R 22:745, 851-2, 1173-4; 23:45-6 Jl 14, Ag 11, N 3 '70, Ja 12 '71
Theatre. H. Clurman. See issues of Nation
Theater. R. Crinkley. Nat R 22:319, 745, 851-2, 1308-9; 23:45-6 Mr 24, Jl 14, Ag 11, D 1 '70, Ja 12 '71
Theatre. B. Gill. See issues of New Yorker 162:25+ F 14; 20+ Ap 25 '70
Theater. H. Hewes. See issues of Saturday review
Theater. S. Kauffmann. See occasional issues of New republic
Theater. T. Lewis. See occasional issues of America to August 22, 1970
See also
New York (city)—Theater
Paris—Theater

Single works
See name of author for full entry
Alice in Wonderland. A. Gregory
Amphitryon. P. Hacks
Amphitryon. J. B. P. Molière
Approaching Simone. M. Terry
At the Boar's head. G. Holst
Awake and sing! C. Odets
Battle of Shrivings. P. Shaffer
Beaux' stratagem. G. Farquhar
Beggar on horseback. G. S. Kaufman and M. Connelly
Bérénice. J. B. Racine
Les blancs. L. Hansberry
Boesman and Lena. A. Fugard
Borstal boy. F. McMahon
Brightower. D. Schary
Brotherhood. D. T. Ward
Butterflies are free. L. Gershe
Cage. R. Cluchey
Camino real. T. Williams
Candida. G. B. Shaw
Carpenters. S. Tesich
Castro complex. M. Arrighi
Les chaises. E. Ionesco
Charley's aunt. B. Thomas
Child's play. R. Marasco
Chinese. M. Schisgal
Colette. E. Jones
Conduct unbecoming. B. England
Contributions. T. Shine
Country people. M. Gorky
Crimes and crimes. A. Strindberg
Criminals. J. Triana
Criss-crossing. P. Magdalany
Dance of death. A. Strindberg
Day of absence. D. T. Ward
Dear Janet Rosenberg, dear Mr Kooning. S. Eveling
Devil's disciple. G. B. Shaw
Dirtiest show in town. T. Eyen
Disintegration of James Cherry. J. Wanshel
Dr Fish. M. Schisgal
Dom Juan. J. B. P. Molière
Dracula: Sabbat. L. Katz
Dream on Monkey Mountain. D. Walcott
Effect of the gamma rays on man-in-the-moon marigolds. P. Zindel
Engagement baby. S. Shapiro
Enter a free man. T. Stoppard
Les femmes savantes. J. B. P. Molière
Five on the black hand side. C. L. Russell
Five star saint. E. A. Molloy
Forensic and the navigators. S. Shepard
Forty years on. A. Bennett
Gingerbread lady. N. Simon
Gloria and Esperanza. J. Bovasso
Good woman of Setzuan. B. Brecht
Grin and bare it! K. McGuire
Guerrillas. R. Hochhuth
Happiness cage. D. J. Reardon
Happy birthday, Wanda June. K. Vonnegut, jr
Harangues. J. A. Walker
Harvey. M. C. Chase
Hay fever. N. Coward
Hedda Gabler. H. Ibsen
Home. D. Storey
Inquest. D. Freed
Jakey fat boy. S. Eveling
La jeune fille à marier. E. Ionesco
La lacune. E. Ionesco
Landscape. H. Pinter
Last of the red hot lovers. N. Simon
Lemon sky. L. Wilson

DRAMAS—Criticisms, plots, etc.—Single works
—*Continued*
Life and times of Sigmund Freud. R. Wilson
Line of least existence. R. Drexler
Lovecraft's follies. J. E. Schevill
Madwoman of Chaillot. J. Giraudoux
Le malade imaginaire. J. B. P. Molière
La Marie Vison. S. Terayama
Memory bank. M. Duberman
Murderous angels. C. C. O'Brien
Nature of the crime. L. Cohen
Night Thoreau spent in jail. J. Lawrence and R. E. Lee
Nobody hears a broken drum. J. Miller
Les nonnes. See Nuns, below
Norman, is that you? R. Clark and S. Bobrick
Nuns. E. Manet
Oedipus. A. Sloan
One night stands of a noisy passenger. S. Winters
Operation Sidewinder. S. Shepard
Opium. R. Brynner
Orlando furioso. L. Ronconi
Our town. T. N. Wilder
Passing through from exotic places. R. Ribman
Persians. Aeschylus
Philanthropist. C. Hampton
Pig pen. E. Bullins
Place for Polly. L. Coleman
Place without doors. M. Duras
Play by Aleksandr Solzhenitsyn A. I. Solzhenitsyn
Playboy of the western world. J. M. Synge
Postcards. J. Prideaux
Prince of Peasantmania. F. Gagliano
Private lives. N. Coward
Pygmalion. G. B. Shaw
Rabelais. J. L. Barrault
Recruiting officer. G. Farquhar
Revenger's tragedy. C. Tourneur
The rivals. R. B. B. Sheridan
Room service. J. Murray and A. Boretz
Saved. E. Bond
School for scandal. R. B. B. Sheridan
Serjeant Musgrave's dance. J. Arden
Serpent. J.-C. Van Itallie
Sheep on the runway. A. Buchwald
Silence. H. Pinter
Slave ship. L. Jones
Sleuth. A. Shaffer
Son of man and the family. T. Taylor and A. Hall
Steambath. B. J. Friedman
Story theatre. P. Sills
Sunday dinner. J. C. Oates
Terminal. S. Yankowitz
This sporting life. D. Storey
Three sisters. A. P. Chekhov
Time of your life. W. Saroyan
Transfers. C. Bromberg
Trelawny of the Wells. A. W. Pinero
Trial of A. Lincoln. J. Damico
Trial of the Catonsville nine. D. Berrigan
Triumph of death. E. Ionesco
Trojan women. Euripides
Unseen hand. S. Shepard
Vivat! Vivat! Regina R. Bolt
Watercolor. P. Magdalany
What the butler saw. J. Orton
White House murder case. J. Feiffer
Wilson in the promise land. R. Van Zandt
Woman hater. F. Beaumont and J. Fletcher
Yard of sun. C. Fry
DRAMATIC criticism
See also
Dramas—Criticisms, plots, etc.
Moving picture criticism
DRAMATIC critics. See Critics
DRAMATIC education. See Acting—Study and teaching
DRAMATIC festivals. See Drama festivals
DRAMATIC form. See Drama—Technique
DRAMATIC play. See Childrens plays
DRAMATIC production. See Theatrical production and direction
DRAMATIC readings
Jack MacGowran in the works of Samuel Beckett. Criticism
    Nation 211:605-6 D 7 '70
    New Repub 163:20 D 12 '70
    New Yorker 46:142 N 28 '70
    Time il por 96:48 N 30 '70
Letter from Paris; beginning to end, selection from works of S. Beckett, performed by J. MacGowran. Genêt. New Yorker 46: 120-1 My 16 '70
Theater; beginning to end, selection from works of S. Beckett, performed by J. MacGowran. il por Time 95:62+ My 11 '70
DRAMATICS for children. See Childrens plays
DRAMATISTS
But who wrote the movie? H. Alpert. il Sat R 53:8-11 D 26 '70

DRAMATISTS, American
    See also
Albee, E.
Kelly, G. E.
Sherwood, R. E.
Simon, N.
Weiss, J.
Williams, T.
DRAMATISTS, English
Looking back without anger; whatever became of the angry young men? C. Sigal. il Commonweal 92:186-8 My 8 '70
    See also
Arden, J.
Fry, C.
DRAMATISTS, French
    See also
Molière, J. B. P.
DRAMATISTS, Greek
    See also
Sophocles
DRAMATISTS, Irish
    See also
Shaw, G. B.
DRAMATISTS, Italian
    See also
Pirandello, L.
DRAMATISTS, Spanish
    See also
Arrabal, F.
DRAMATIZATION by children. See Childrens plays
DRAMATIZATION in education
    See also
Role playing
DRAMATIZATION of history
Role playing: effective technique in the teaching of history. W. Dumas. Clear House 44:468-70 Ap '70
    See also
Sound and light programs
DRANE, Hank
Fight for Hilton Head Island. il Am For 76: 12-15+ My '70
DRAPEAU, Jean
Montreal's continuing festival. il Travel & Camera 33:40-1 Je '70

                    about
Run it up the flagpole, Johnny. F. Deford. il por Sports Illus 33:74-6+ S 28 '70 *
DRAPER, Imogene H.
Slum child. Clear House 45:48-50 S '70
DRAPER, Keith
Twelve New Zealand trout flies. il Field & S 74:84-7+ Mr '70
DRAPERIES. See Curtains and draperies
DRAPERY rods. See Curtain and drapery fixtures
DRAVO corporation
Tortoise tries to play the hare. il Bsns W p98+ F 21 '70
DRAWING
Drawing with an unusual tool; razor blades. E. E. Niemann. il por Am Artist 34:46-52 Ja '70
John Gundelfinger draws from life; excerpt from On-the-spot drawing. N. Meglin. il Am Artist 35:56-62 Ja '71
Lets ramble with a scramble; grotesque faces and masks. J. S. Lorr. il Design 72:20-1 Wint '70
Sketching a personal diary. M. Haller. il Am Artist 34:40-4+ Ap '70
Sketching from life; work of Robert Weaver. S. E. Meyer. il Am Artist 34:62-7+ My '70
Spontaneous drawings of Robert L. Pratt. J. Jellico. il por Am Artist 34:44-9 Ag '70
    See also
Charcoal drawing
Drawings
Figure drawing
Illustration of books and periodicals
Landscape drawing
Pastel drawing
Pen drawing
Scratchboard drawing
Silhouettes
                Competitions
    See Art—Competitions

                Study and teaching
Drawing; rugged log as subject matter. M. B. Bowman. il Sch Arts 70:8-9 N '70
Lesson in spot illustration. L. J. Miller. il Design 71:14-15 mid-Wint '70
Navajo children draw. C. Gross. il Sch Arts 70:14-15 N '70
Time to draw the line. S. McIlhany. Am Artist 34:5 Je '70
Wire drawings. M. Acosta. il Design 71:37 Wint '69

DRAWING, Childrens. See Childrens art

DRAWING instruments
Pen that floats puts zip in drafting; Xynetics 1000. il Bsns W p50 Ja 24 '70
See also
Pantographs

DRAWINGS
On and off the avenue; originals. J. Malcolm. New Yorker 46:72+ Je 20 '70
See also
Doodles (sketches)
Graffiti

Exhibitions
Demon drawings; J. Pollock's Psychoanalytic drawings at the Whitney museum. D. Davis. il Newsweek 76:104 N 2 '70
Design for evil; the Hitler-Speer exhibition at New York cultural center. D. Davis. il Newsweek 76:82 S 28 '70
Oxford line; selection of Italian drawings belonging to the Ashmolean museum, on exhibition at the Wildenstein gallery. J. Russell. il Art N 69:34-6+ O '70
Venetian virtuoso; G. Tiepolo drawings at Harvard's Fogg museum. D. Davis. por Newsweek 75:56 Mr 30 '70

DRAYTON Hall (historic house) See South Carolina—Historic houses, etc.

DREAM on Monkey Mountain; drama. See Walcott, D.

DREAM to grow on; story. See Dowty, L.

DREAMS
ESP in the dream laboratory. B. Ford. il Sci Digest 67:10-18 Ja '70
Freud's dreams revisited. L. Shengold. Am Imago 26:242-50 Fall '69
See also
Sleep

DREAMS in literature
Dreams in Troilus and Criseyde. H. S. Corsa. bibliog f Am Imago 27:52-65 Spr '70

DREDGING
Dredging money from the Bank; from Great Bahama Bank. C. Phinizy. il Sports illus 33:22-5 Jl 6 '70
Way to save the Great Lakes? proposed law for containment areas for dredgings. il U S News 68:72 Ap 27 '70

DREDGING machinery
Pumping money out of the sea; manned underwater dredge. il Bsns W p54-5 Jl 11 '70

DREISER, Theodore
Two Dreisers, by E. Moers. Review
Commentary 49:80+ Ja '70. A. Edelstein

DREISTADT, Roy
Analogy: the scientist's trick for problem solving. il Sci Digest 67:36-43 Ap '70
Want to invent something? Then try using analogy. il Sci Digest 67:62-7 My '70

DRESDEN
Air raids
Dresden rebuilt. il Time 95:32-3 F 23 '70

City planning
Dresden rebuilt. il Time 95:32-3 F 23 '70

Reconstruction
See Dresden—City planning

DRESS. See Clothing and dress

DRESS accessories
Doing their thing; preview at the Crazy horse saloon. il Newsweek 76:69 Ag 3 '70
See also
Belts

DRESSEL, Fred B.
Student teaching the public school's responsibility. Sch & Soc 98:163-4 Mr '70

DRESSING of game. See Game, Dressing of

DRESSING rooms
Husband-and-wife elbow room. il Sunset 145:96 S '70

DRESSMAKING
How to custom fit pants. C. Houck. il Parents Mag 45:24 S '70
See also
Sewing

DREW, Althea Jompen, pseud.
Women vs women. Mlle 70:185+ F '70

DREW, Elizabeth Brenner
Dam outrage: the story of the army engineers. il Atlan 225:51-62 Ap '70
Reports: Washington (cont) Atlan 225:4+ Ja; 4+ My; 4+ Je; 226:6+ Jl; 4+ Ag '70
White House hard hats. il por Atlan 226:51-7 O '70

DREXEL, Firestone (firm)
House for Firestone. Newsweek 76:90 D 14 '70

DREXEL, Harriman, Ripley, inc.
See also
Drexel, Firestone (firm)

DREXEL institute of technology, Philadelphia
Libraries
Librarian vs. publisher. J. Kesselman. il por Library J 95:4221-4 D 15 '70

DREXHAGE, Karl H.
Monomolecular layers and light; with biographical sketch. il Sci Am 222:26, 108-19 Mr '70

DREXLER, Rosalyn
Life art review. il Life 69:10 O 30 '70
Line of least existence. Criticism
Newsweek 75:95 F 9 '70
What I did November 15, 1969. Esquire 73:86+ My '70
—See De Kooning, E. jt. auth.

DREYFUS, Catherine
Skiing on the French frontier. il Mlle 72:191+ N '70
Vincennes: academic self-service. il Mlle 71:150-1+ Je '70
(ed) See Lévi-Strauss, C. We no longer know how to bring our children into the world we have built

DREYFUS corporation
Change and turmoil on Wall Street. il por Time 96:52-7 Ag 24 '70

DRIED flowers. See Flowers, Dried

DRIESSEN, Joachim
Everything but orgies; Deutsche sex partei. Newsweek 75:43 Mr 9 '70 *

DRIFT, Oceanic. See Ocean currents

DRIFTERS; story. See Michener, J. A.

DRIFTING of continents. See Continental drift

DRIFTWOOD
Adrift with driftwood. E. Dean and J. Dean. il por Har Yrs 10:19-20 Jl '70
Hobby from the sea. H. Pearson. il Design 72:39-41 Fall '70
Indians' way to finish driftwood. il Sunset 144:144 Ap '70

DRIGGS, Louise
Bland diets that sing! il Har Yrs 10:45-50 O '70
From our kitchen (title varies) See issues of Harvest years

DRILLING and boring (earth and rocks)
Tap only the best water in your well; selective sampling of aquifers, Santa Clara, Calif. R. R. Mortenson. il Am City 85:49-51 D '70
See also
Underwater drilling

DRILLING and boring (ice)
Drilling through the ice cap: probing climate for a thousand centuries. C. C. Langway, jr. and B. L. Hansen. il pors Bul Atom Sci 26:62-6 D '70

DRILLING and boring (woodwork)
How to cut square holes. R. J. De Cristoforo. il Mech Illus 66:116-17+ O '70

DRILLING and boring machinery
Drill with the locked-in memory. R. J. De Cristoforo. il Pop Sci 197:81 Jl '70
Good, inexpensive double-insulated drill; Rockwell 70. il Consumer Rep 35:330 Je '70
Guide to twist drills. il Mech Illus 66:88-9+ Jl '70
How to make a guide for accurate cross-drilling. R. Kouhoupt. il Pop Sci 197:91 D '70
How to pick the drill to fit the tap. R. Brightman. il Pop Mech 135:170-1 Ja '71
Low-priced ¼-inch electric drills. il Consumer Bul 54:20-3 Ja '71
Tapping crooked holes? try this gidget. R. A. Cox. il Pop Mech 133:170 Je '70

DRILLS (machinery) See Drilling and boring machinery

DRIMMER, Melvin
Teaching black history in America: what are the problems; address, December 28, 1969. Negro Hist Bul 33:32-4 F '70

DRINAN, Robert Frederick
Priest, law school dean, candidate for Congress; interview, ed. by C. E. Fager. por Chr Cent 87:1069-72 S 9 '70
State of the abortion question. Commonweal 92:108-9, 303 Ap 17, Je 12 '70
To have a voice and vote; letter to editor. America 122:599 Je 6 '70

about
As clergymen enter politics: the new trend. il por U S News 69:19-21 Ag 10 '70 *
Drinan's bid. Commonweal 93:114 O 30 '70 *
Father runs for Congress. W. Kennedy. il pors Look 34:18-22 S 22 '70 *
Is there a priest in the house? Chr Today 15:25 D 4 '70 *
Let us pray. W. F. Buckley, jr. Nat R 22:1073 O 6 '70 *

DRINAN, Robert Frederick—about—*Cont.*
New politics and old. il por Time 96:12 S 28 '70 *
Of many things. D. R. Campion. America 122:inside cover Mr 21 '70 *
Reverend father congressman. T. M. Gannon. America 123:424-8 N 21 '70; Discussion. 123: 531 D 19 '70 *

DRINK question. See Alcoholism; Liquor problem

DRINKING and traffic accidents
Agnew, alcohol, automobiles, and assessment. R. S. Morison. Science 169:819 Ag 28 '70; Reply with rejoinder. G. W. Packowski. 170:1156 D 11 '70
Crackdown on drunk drivers: a nationwide campaign. il U S News 69:24-5 Jl 6 '70
Drinker's guide to safe holiday driving; interview. W. Keller. il por Todays Health 48:8+ D '70
Is the social drinker really the worst killer on the road? il Bet Hom & Gard 48:58-9 F '70

DRINKING and youth. See Alcohol and youth

DRINKING fountains
Add a cold-water bubbler to your kitchen. B. Halley. il Pop Mech 134:166-7 Jl '70

DRINKING vessels
Goblets. M. Shacter. il por Ceram Mo 18: 17-19 Ap '70
Mettlach masterpieces; rare steins. J. Schwartz and E. Schwartz. il(p 1) Hobbies 75:64+ D '70
Some trick Greek vases. J. V. Noble. il Ceram Mo 18:18-23 Ja '70

DRINKING water
Tap flap; federal survey. Newsweek 76:62-3 Ag 31 '70
Troubled water; water from faucets. Time 96:40 Ag 31 '70
See also
Water, Bottled

Standards
America's drinking water is . . . is not safe; with editorial comment. H. J. Graeser. il pors Am City 85:8, 77-9+ Je '70
How safe is the Nation's drinking water? with list of U.S. cities with sub-standard drinking water systems. S. Lindsay. Sat R 53:54-5 My 2 '70

DRINKS. See Beverages; Liquors

DRINNON, Richard
War on violence. bibliog il Wilson Lib Bul 45:68-77 S '70

DRIOGRAPHY. See Printing, Offset

DRISCOLL, C. J. and Darvey, N. L.
Chromosome pairing: effect of colchicine on an isochromosome. bibliog il Science 169: 290-1 Jl 17 '70

DRIVE-in and curb services
See also
McDonald's corporation

DRIVER ants. See Ants

DRIVER'S seat; story. See Spark, M.

DRIVES (money raising) See Fund raising

DRIVESHAFTS.   See Automobiles—Propeller shafts

DRIVEWAYS
How to make a blacktop drive look like new. H. Wicks. il Pop Mech 134:178-9 S '70

DRIVING
See also
Coaches and coaching

DRIVING, Automobile. See Automobile driving

DROLET, Francis K.
E. de Breuvery, third world's servant (1903-1970) il America 122:128-30 F 7 '70

DRONE airplanes. See Airplanes, Drone

DROPOUTS
Athletes score with youngsters; Owens-Corning fiberglas corporation's Drop-in program. V. Louviere. il Nations Bsns 58:22 N '70
Breaking the diploma barrier; J. L. Smith's program in Kansas City, Mo. il por Time 96:49 S 7 '70
Employment of high school graduates and dropouts; with tables and charts. H. Hayghe. Mo Labor R 93:35-42 Ag '70
Reaching out to Danny; Baltimore dropout prevention programs. R. H. Levine. il Am Ed 6:10-14 Jl '70
Return of the dropouts; Florida ocean science institute. B. Robinson. il Motor B 126: 44-5 D '70
Second chance for dropouts. E. Rice. Sch & Soc 98:423-4 N '70
Thoughts of a dropout, ed. by M. Franklin. Todays Ed 59:15 F '70
White rites versus Indian rights; dropouts among Canadian Indians. A. D. Fisher. bibliog il por Trans-Action 7:29-33 N '69

DROPS
Orientation order of dipole molecules in the surface of embryonic droplets. F. F. Abraham. bibliog il Science 168:833-5 My 15 '70
Splash of a waterdrop at terminal velocity. C. K. Mutchler and L. M. Hansen. bibliog il Science 169:1311-12 S 25 '70
Water drop freezing: ejection of microdroplets. R. J. Cheng. bibliog il Science 170: 1395-6 D 25 '70

DROSOPHILA
Antimycoplasmal antibiotics and hybrid sterility in drosophila paulistorum. R. P. Kernaghan and L. Ehrman. bibliog il Science 169:63-4 Jl 3 '70
Chromosome tracers of the origin of species. H. L. Carson. bibliog il Science 168:1414-18 Je 19 '70
Drosophila melanogaster: identity of male lipid in reproductive system. G. Brieger and F. M. Butterworth. bibliog Science 167:1262 F 27 '70
Genetic load. C. Wills. il Sci Am 222:98-107 bibliog(p 146) Mr '70
Localization of 5S RNA genes on drosophila chromosomes by RNA-DNA hybridization. D. E. Wimber and D. M. Steffensen. bibliog il Science 170:639-41 N 6 '70
Love song of the fruit fly. H. C. Bennet-Clark and A. W. Ewing. il Sci Am 223:84-90+ Jl '70
Sex ratio in drosophila pseudoobscura: spermiogenic failure. D. Policansky and J. Ellison. bibliog il Science 169:888-9 Ag 28 '70
Simulation of the mating advantage in mating of rare drosophila males. L. Ehrman. bibliog il Science 167:905-6 F 6 '70
Temperature-sensitive mutations in drosophila melanogaster; adaptation of address, August 1969. D. T. Suzuki. bibliog il Science 170:695-706 N 13 '70

DROUGHT resistance of plants. See Plants—Drought resistance

DROWNING
Emergency whistle on Block Island. F. Miller. il Read Digest 96:121-6 Je '70

DRUG abuse
Broader attack on drug abuse, to dry up the flow of drugs. il U S News 68:38 Mr 23 '70
Drug abuse is your headache, too; excerpts from Drug abuse as a business problem. C. Kurtis. il Nations Bsns 58:38+ N '70
Drug abuse: newest and most dangerous challenge. P. C. Barrins. Ed Digest 34:24-6 Ja '70
Drug culture: use of stimulants, sedatives and tranquilizers by office workers. Bsns W p83-4 Ag 15 '70
Drug threat in business. Nation 211:484 N 16 '70
Drugs in decline? Chr Today 15:54 N 6 '70
Drugs: ten years to doomsday? H. Sutton. il Sat R 53:18-21+ N 14 '70
Drugs: we are just plain ignorant. J. R. Moskin. Look 34:108+ O 6 '70
Fact is: we like to be drugged. J. C. Oates. McCalls 97:69 Je '70
Furor over drugs; physicians vs. the Attorney General. il Newsweek 75:65+ Mr 30 '70
Hazards implicit in prescribing psychoactive drugs. H. L. Lennard and others. bibliog Science 169:438-41 Jl 31 '70; Discussion. 170:928-30 N 27 '70
How nice drugs killed my sister. M. Davidson. il Good H 171:96-7+ S '70
How to thwart the law on Rx drugs; Asthmador. Consumer Rep 35:192-3 Ap '70
Rising problem of drugs on the job. il Time 95:70 Je 29 '70
Unselling drugs; antidrug education and advertising. D. Sanford. New Repub 162:15-16 F 28 '70
We must fight the epidemic of drug abuse! A. Linkletter. Read Digest 96:56-60 F '70
What you can do about the drug problem. S. Grafton. il Parents Mag 45:72-5+ N '70
See also
Marijuana
Narcotics and youth

Conferences
Chronic non-psychiatric hazards of drugs of abuse. S. S. Epstein and J. Lederberg. Science 168:507+ Ap 24 '70
To youth, with love; White House conference on the drug problem. R. L. Shayon. Sat R 53:57 N 21 '70

DRUG abuse prevention and control act of 1970. See Drug laws and legislation

DRUG addicts. See Narcotic addicts

DRUG and hospital employees union (local 1199)
Labor, 1970. Nation 211:162 S 7 '70
Union with soul. A. H. Raskin. il N Y Times Mag p24-5+ Mr 22 '70

DRURY, Robert E.
  Interaction of plant hormones. bibliog Science 164:564-5; 168:877 My 2 '69, My 15 '70
DRUTT, Helen
  All that glitters: Goldsmith '70. il Craft Horiz 30:42-5+ Ag '70
DRY flies. See Fishing lures, flies, etc.
DRYDEN, Harold E.
  Camellias, as the judge sees them. il Horticulture 48:22-4+ F '70
  Camellias for Christmas. Horticulture 48:24+ D '70
DRYERS. See Clothes dryers
DRYFOOS, John M.
  Rally or no, it's not too late to short the frauds. il por Forbes 105:55+ Je 15 '70
DRYFOOS, Robert J. jr
  Two tactics for ethnic survival: Eskimo & Indian. il Trans-Action 7:51-4 Ja '70
DRYING
      See also
  Photography—Drying (films and prints)
DRYING (crops)
      See also
  Corn—Drying
  Grain—Drying
DRYING apparatus
      See also
  Clothes dryers
DRYLOTS. See Feedlots
DUAL nationality. See Citizenship
DUAL pricing. See Unit pricing
DUBAL, David
  Assimilating the artistic past, Ignaz Moscheles. por Am Rec G 37:90-1 O '70
DUBAY, William H.
  Fragile marriage of an ex-priest. il por McCalls 97:70-1+ S '70
DUBČEK, Alexander
  Alexander Dubcek's all too human face. Time 95:29 My 18 '70 *
  Approaching total eclipse. il por Time 95:39-40 Ap 6 '70 *
  Long fall. il por Newwseek 75:40 Je 22 '70 *
  Ordeal of A. Dubček. por Time 96:30 Jl 6 '70 *
  Purge in Prague. il por Time 95:28+ F 9 '70
  Requiem for Czechoslovakia. G. Feifer. Read Digest 97:83-8 N '70 *
DUBČEK, Anna
  Anna's agony. por Time 96:21 Jl 13 '70 *
DUBERMAN, Martin
  Memory bank. Criticism
      Nation 210:124 F 2 '70
      New Yorker 45:58 Ja 24 '70
DUBLER, Dorothea L.
  Shoebox constructs instruct. il Sch Arts 70:24-5 S '70
DUBLIN
  Letter from Dublin. J. Kramer. New Yorker 46:56-65 Jl 25 '70

Social life and customs
  Dublin barfly's book of etiquette. C. O'Brien. il Sat R 53:44-5+ S 12 '70
DUBLIN zoo. See Zoological gardens
DU BOIS, Donald
  Do you know the three R's? Outdoor Life 145:74-5 Ja '70
  Do you know your bird dogs? quiz. Outdoor Life 145:78-80+ F '70
DUBOIS, Graham. See Dubois, H. G.
DUBOIS, H. Graham
  Road to Valley Forge; drama. Plays 29:11-18 F '70
  St Patrick saves the day; drama. Plays 29:53-62 Mr '70
DUBOIS, L. Clayton
  First family of conservatism. pors N Y Times Mag p 10-11+ Ag 9 '70
DU BOIS, William Edward Burghardt
  Contributions of W. E. B. Du Bois to the New York Globe, and the New York Freeman, 1883-1885. bibliog Negro Hist Bul 33:47-8 F '70 *
DUBOS, Rene Jules
  Despairing optimist. Am Scholar 40:16-20 Wint '70
  Five who care. il Look 34:34 Ap 21 '70
  Genius of the place; with biographical sketch. il por Am For 76:16-19+ S '70
  Human landscape. Bul Atom Sci 26:31-7 Mr '70
  Mere survival is not enough for man. por Life 69:2 Jl 24 '70; Same abr. with title Why survival is not enough. Read Digest 97:111-12 O '70

  On controlling technology; excerpt from Reason awake. Cur 119:36-7 Je '70
  Tax on noise? A tax on congestion? interview. il pors Forbes 106:64+ S 15 '70

                    about
  René Dubos. A. Bailey. il por Horizon 12:56-61 Sum '70 *
DUBOSE, Carolyn P.
  Champion of welfare rights. il por Ebony 25:31-4+ Ap '70
  Chappie James; a new role for an old warrior. il pors Ebony 25:152-4+ O '70
DUBRIDGE, Lee Alvin
  Clearing the air: we can end pollution; interview, ed. by P. Lisagor. il PTA Mag 64:14-16 F '70
  DuBridge discusses science budget, support and organization; interview. por Phys Today 23:47-9 Ag '70
  How to control pollution; interview. il por U S News 68:48-52 Ja 19 '70
  Knowledge and the humane society. Science 169:331 Jl 24 '70

                    about
  DuBridge and his critics. P. M. Boffey; J. Walsh. Science 169:356-7 Jl 24 '70 *
  DuBridge's exit. Time 96:48 Ag 31 '70 *
  New man for Nixon. por Sci N 98:158 Ag 22 '70
  New science adviser. pors Newsweek 76:63 Ag 31 '70 *
  Rising debate on science policy. il por Sci N 98:57-8 Jl 25 '70 *
  Science adviser: Dubridge retires, David nominated as successor. J. Walsh. pors Science 169:843-4 Ag 28 '70 *
DUBROVNIK, Yugoslavia
  Rift in the curtain. C. Mitchell. il Yachting 128:50-2+ Jl '70
DUBS, L. C.
  More than just a building. il Am City 85:119+ Je '70
DUBUC, J. P. and McGinnis, R. C.
  Somatic association in avena sativa L. bibliog il Science 167:999-1000 F 13 '70
DUBUFFET, Jean
  Dubuffet at work. C. Cutler. il Art in Am 58:108-13 Jl '70 *
  Dubuffet, the subversive smothered with love. S. De Gramont. il por Horizon 12:88-105 Sum '70 *
DUCH, Ursule
  Sculptures in paper. il pors Design 71:22-4 Wint '69 *
DUCHAMP, Gaston. See Villon, J. pseud.
DUCHAMP, Marcel
  Art as words as art. L. Alloway. Nation 211:188-9 S 7 '70 *
  Walter Arensberg and Marcel Duchamp. K. Kuh. Sat R 53:36-7+ S 5 '70 *
DUCHARME, Edward R.
  Close reading and teaching. Engl J 59:938-42 O '70
DUCK as food. See Cookery—Poultry
DUCK blinds
  Goose hunting from underwater. P. McLain. il Field & S 75:40-3+ N '70
  Kentucky stump blind. M. Hodgson. il Field & S 75:56 D '70
DUCK hepatitis virus. See Hepatitis viruses
DUCK shooting
  Citified ducks satisfy. J. B. Robinson. il Outdoor Life 146:52-5+ N '70
  Doing the duck crawl; grand tour for mallards. J. J. Platt. il pors Outdoor Life 146:42-3+ D '70
  Ducks are predictable. J. B. Dibble. il Field & S 75:44-5+ S '70
  Pavlov's ducks fly to a last supper; Meadow view wildlife preserve. R. F. Jones. Sports Illus 32:46 Ja 19 '70
  Take me to your pichiguilas. N. Riley. il Outdoor Life 145:64-5+ F '70
  Whistlers like it mean. J. B. Robinson. il Outdoor Life 146:84-7+ O '70
      See also
  Fowling
DUCKLES, Robert. See Opton, E. M. jr. jt. auth.
DUCKS
  Why ducks don't swim faster. Chem 43:5 Je '70
DUCKS, Wild
  American eider. S. Clark. il Sea Front 16:302-8 S '70
  Limit the duck hunters? J. T. Shields. il Outdoor Life 146:47-9+ S '70
  North American ducks. J. Van Wormer. il Nat Wildlife 7:23-8 O '69
      See also
  Cookery—Game
  Duck shooting

DUCLAUX, R. See Cabanac, M. jt. auth.

DUDAR, Helen
Women's lib: the war on sexism. il News-week 75:71-4+ Mr 23 '70

DUDE ranches. See Ranch life

DUDEVANT, Amantine Lucile Aurore (Dupin)
See Sand, G. pseud.

DUE process of law
(Over)due process of law. Sr Schol 97:11-14 D 14 '70
See also
Congressional conference on justice in America
Jury

DUERR, Joseph
State $ for schools. Commonweal 92:243-5 My 22 '70

DUFAULT, Peter Kane
Leaving a station, Sunday, Feb. 1, 1970; poem. New Yorker 46:44 Ap 18 '70

DUFFET, John
Annapolis frostbiting. il Motor B 126:43-5 N '70
Plumbing maintenance. il Motor B 125:78 Ap '70
Stopping topside leaks. il Motor B 125:80 Ap '70

DUFFEY, Dave
South to Arkansas. il Motor B 126:52-3+ S '70

DUFFEY, David Michael
Dogs. See issues of Outdoor life
What generation gap? il por Outdoor Life 145:58-9+ Ja '70

DUFFEY, Joseph Daniel
Duffey campaign. Nation 211:133 Ag 31 '70 *
Joe Duffey's race. P. R. Wieck. New Repub 163:9-10 Ag 15 '70
New old politics. il por Newsweek 76:29 Ag 31 '70 *
Winning with(out) students. America 123:107 S 5 '70 *

DUFFEY, Richard F.
Tyranny of time; poem. Chr Cent 87:725 Je 10 '70

DUFFEY, S. S.
Cardiac glycosides and distastefulness; some observations on the palatability spectrum of butterflies. bibliog il Science 169:78-9 Jl 3 '70

DUFFIELD, John W.
Planting in Pag. il Am For 76:22-4+ F '70

DUFFIELD, Robert B.
Reflections on national laboratories; adden-dum. Bul Atom Sci 26:15-16 F '70

DUFFUS, Robert L.
Our flag is still there; reprint. il Read Digest 97:114-16 S '70

DUFFY, James B.
Case of Lieutenant Duffy. Nation 210:419-20 Ap 13 '70 *
Mere gook rule. il por Newsweek 75:30 Ap 13 '70 *

DUFRANE, Gerard, pseud.
Administering our state library agencies. Am Lib 1:23-6 Ja '70

DUGAN, Willis E. and McDonough, P. J.
Counseling services. il PTA Mag 64:16-18 bibliog(p35) My '70

DUGDALE, John
Driving. Travel & Camera 33:68-9 My '70

DUGGER, Ronnie
Hot after Yarborough. New Repub 162:11-12 Ap 18 '70

DUGUID, Sandra
Christ-hymn. Chr Today 15:6 Ja 15 '71

DUHÉ, Camille
How to shape up your husband. il Vogue 155:160-1+ Je '70

DUITZ, Murray
Move in for close-ups! il Pop Phot 66:94+ Mr '70

DUKAS, Paul
Record the musical world has been waiting for. L. Gerber. Am Rec G 36:327 Je '70 *

DUKE, James R. See Richter, C. P. jt. auth.

DUKE, Michael B. and others
Lunar soil: size distribution and mineralog-ical constituents. il Science 167:648-50 Ja 30 '70

DUKE, Vernon
Lerner and Duke revisited. I. Kolodin. Sat R 53:101 Mr 14 '70 *
Popular records. D. Watt. New Yorker 46:163-4+ O 24 '70 *

DUKE, William Meng
Whittaker: too far too fast? T. J. Murray. il por Duns 95:28-31+ F '70 *

DULAC, Margarita Walker
Werner Groshans: painter of realism & fan-tasy. il por Am Artist 34:54-60+ Je '70

DULHUNTY, Larry
Dulhunty, hard man of the Outback. il pors Life 69:46-54 O 30 '70 *

DULLES, Avery
Loyalty and dissent: after Vatican II. Ameri-ca 122:672-3 Je 27 '70
about
Seeking the word. W. F. Dewan. Cath World 211:42-3 Ap '70 *

DULLES international airport. See Wash-ington, D.C.—Airports

DULUTH, Minn.
Fresh look at graders, flexible heavy-weights. il Am City 85:44 O '70
Music
Report:
Production of Faust. P. Gainsley. Opera N 35:27 O 31 '70

DUMAS, Wayne
Role playing: effective technique in the teach-ing of history. Clear House 44:468-70 Ap '70

DU MAURIER, Daphne
Don't look now; story. Ladies Home J 87:70-1 D '70

DUMDUM bullets. See Bullets

DUMKE, Glenn S.
Is freedom academic? address, December 12, 1969. Vital Speeches 36:272-6 F 15 '70

DUMMIES. See Anatomical models

DUMPING (commercial policy)
Dumping: an old ban imposed anew. il News-week 76:73 O 5 '70

DUNAS, William
William Dunas in Job; Judson memorial church. T. Borek. Dance Mag 44:87-8 Mr '70 *

DUNBAR, Ernest
Music is where the money is. il Look 34:13-17 Ag 25 '70
Trouble: the high school radicals. il Look 34:70+ Mr 24 '70

DUNBAR, Roxanne
Four of a kind, yet different. pors News-week 75:73 Mr 23 '70 *

DUNCAN, Andrew
Year with the Queen; excerpts from The Queen's year. il por Look 34:34-40+ My 5; 43-6+ My 19 '70

DUNCAN, Bob
Fish story on film. il Pop Phot 67:110-13 Jl '70
Ups and downs of camera movements. il Pop Phot 67:110-11+ S '70

DUNCAN, C. J.
Changing market for serious books. Pub W 198:pt2 188-90 S 21 '70

DUNCAN, David Douglas
Gallery; photograph; excerpt from War with-out heroes. Life 69:4-5 D 18 '70
about
Duncan's Viet Nam. il Time 96:88 N 23 '70 *

DUNCAN, Jeff
Jeff Duncan and company, Brooklyn acad-emy of music, NYC. P. Richmond. Dance Mag 44:80 D '70 *

DUNCAN, Lois
Bright promise; story. Good H 170:90-1 Mr '70
From this day forward; story. Good H 170:116-17 Ap '70
Writing the teenage adventure novel. il Writ-ers Digest 50:33-5 Je '70

DUNCAN, Patricia D.
Trees on the rim; photographs. Am For 76:12-15 Jl '70

DUNCAN, Robert
Comment. G. Sorrentino. Poetry 116:114-17 My '70 *

DUNCAN, S. Blackwell
Wolf. il Nat Parks & Con Mag 44:23-4 O '70

DUNCAN, Sandy
Futures, great. pors Vogue 156:90-1 Jl '70 *

DUNCAN, Vera
Learn to know your Schlegelmilch ware. il Hobbies 75:69+ S '70

DUNE buggies. See Motor vehicles

DUNES, Sand. See Sand dunes

DUNHAM, David W.
Favorable grazing occultations, September-December, 1969. il R Pop Astron 63:25-6 Ag '69
Occultation highlights (cont) il Sky & Tel 40:184; 41:64 S '70, Ja '71

DUNISVELD, Johannus
Solo mission. F. Sully. Newsweek 77:65-6 Ja 4 '71 *

DUNLAP, John
Dunlap cabinetmakers. C. S. Parsons and D. S. Brooke. il Antiques 98:224-31 Ag '70 *

DUNLAP, Samuel
Dunlap cabinetmakers. C. S. Parsons and D. S. Brooke. il Antiques 98:224-31 Ag '70 *

DUNLAP furniture. See Furniture, American
DUNLAVEY, M. A.
Cop challenges the church. il Chr Cent 87:
759-60 Je 17 '70
DUNLOP, D. J.
Hematite: intrinsic and defect ferromagne-
tism. bibliog il Science 169:858-60 Ag 28 '70
DUNLOP, John T. See Bok, D. C. jt. auth.
DUNLOP, Richard
Abraham Jacobi; the children's physician.
il Todays Health 48:58-9+ Ap '70
History comes alive along the road to Ore-
gon. il Todays Health 48:44-9+ S '70
Nurse who outranked the general. il Todays
Health 48:56-7+ My '70
Why don't you practice medicine the way
other doctors do? il por Todays Health 48:
34-5+ Jl '70; Same with title Claude Ber-
nard, father of experimental medicine. Sci
Digest 68:79-84 D '70
DUNN, Betty
Buckleys of Great Elm. il pors Life 69:34-41
D 18 '70
DUNN, Charleta J. and Kowitz, G. T.
Teacher perceptions of correlates of acad-
emic achievement. bibliog f Sch & Soc
98:370-2 O '70
DUNN, David
Try giving yourself away; condensation.
Read Digest 97:98-100 Ag '70
DUNN, Diana R.
(ed) Message. . . and the reaction. il Parks &
Rec 5:22-5 Mr '70
Motorized recreation vehicles. il Parks & Rec
5:10-14+ Jl '70
DUNN, Max
Root art. il Design 71:14-16 Spr '70
DUNN, Oscar James
Remarks; reprint. por Negro Hist Bul 33:18
Ja '70
DUNN, Stephen
Teacher answering young radicals; poem. New
Repub 162:21 Mr 14 '70
DUNNE, B. B.
Transverse wave instability in a solid ex-
plosive. bibliog il Science 167:1124-6 F 20
'70
DUNNE, Gerald T.
Financial paper: variations on themes of
McLuhan. bibliog f Harvard Bsns R 48:90
My '70
DUNNE, Jim
Detroit report. See issues of Popular science
monthly
DUNNIGAN, Ann
(tr) See Bulgakov, V. F. Tolstoy in the last
year of his life
DUN'S (periodical)
Change of face. Duns 95:3 Ja '70
Whither Man on the move? Duns 96:3 Ag '70
DUNTZE, Wolfgang, and others
Saccharomyces cerevisiae: a diffusible sex
factor. bibliog il Science 168:1472-3 Je 19 '70
DUPIN, Jacques
Frugal path; poem, tr. by P. Auster. Poet-
ry 116:279 Ag '70
DU PIN GOUVERNET, Henriette Lucie (Dil-
lon) marquise de la Tour. See La Tour du
Pin Gouvernet, H. L. D. de
DU PLESSIX, Francine
Profiles; D. Berrigan and P. Berrigan. pors
New Yorker 46:44-6+ Mr 14 '70
Profiles. por New Yorker 46:40-4+ Ap 25 '70
Television. Vogue 156:56 S 15 '70

about
Liberated, all liberated. il pors Vogue 155:115
Je '70 *
DUPLESSY, Jean Claude, and others
Differential isotopic fractionation in benthic
foraminifera and paleotemperatures reas-
sessed. bibliog il Science 168:250-1 Ap 10 '70
DUPLEX apartments. See Apartments
DUPLICATING equipment. See Copying pro-
cesses
DUPLICATORS. See Copying processes
DUPONT, F. I, Glore Forgan and company
Hand from Dallas; aid from H. R. Perot. il
por Newsweek 76:85-6 D 7 '70
Perot zeroes in on F. I. duPont. por Bsns W
p39-40 D 19 '70
What ties Perot to Wall Street. il por
Bsns W p78 D 5 '70
DU PONT, Henry Francis, Winterthur museum.
See Henry Francis du Pont Winterthur mu-
seum
DU PONT, Pierre S. 4th
Architect you can communicate with; inter-
view. il por House & Gard 137:16+ Mr '70

DU PONT DE NEMOURS, E. I, and company
Du Pont formula: hear out the young. il Na-
tions Bsns 58:19 Mr '70
Du Pont writes off a refinery plan. Bsns W
p33 S 19 '70
Encourage the seeker, and find nylon. S.
Lenher. il Nations Bsns 58:68+ Ja '70
Hand across the sea; Du Pont international.
il Forbes 106:60+ S 15 '70
Lighting a fire under the sleeping giant. il
por Bsns W p40-1 S 12 '70
DU PRE, Jacqueline
Inside the outside family. il pors Time 96:
74 D 7 '70
Jackie and Danny and sometimes Pinky. J.
Roddy. il pors Look 34:84-6 N 17 '70 *
People are talking about. . . pors Vogue 155:
94-5 F 15 '70
DUPREE, A. Hunter
New policy for the government-university part-
nership. Science 169:131 Jl 10 '70
New rationale for science. Sat R 53:55-9 F 7
'70

about
Nixon administration accused of downgrad-
ing science. P. M. Boffey. Science 169:265
Jl 17 '70 *
DUPREE, Louis, and others
Ghar-i-Mordeh Gusfand (Cave of the dead
sheep): a new Mousterian locality in north
Afghanistan. bibliog il Science 167:1610-12
Mr 20 '70
DUQUESNE university, Pittsburgh, Pa.

School of law
Legal speedster: R. R. Davenport, dean. S.
W. Morris. il pors Ebony 26:48-50+ D '70
DURABLE press fabrics. See Textile fabrics,
Wrinkle resistant
DURABLE press household linen. See Linen,
Household
DURAND-RUEL, Paul
Bonjour M. Durand-Ruel. B. Berry and L.
Traiger. il por Art N 69:44-7+ Ap '70
DURAS, Marguerite
Place without doors. Criticism
Nation 212:61 Ja 11 '71 *
New Yorker 46:42 Ja 2 '71 *
Newsweek 77:80 Ja 11 '71 *
Sat R 54:8 Ja 9 '71 *
Time 96:63 D 14 '70 *
DURATION of life. See Longevity
DURBIN, Virginia
Country herb garden. il Horticulture 48:18-
21+ S '70
DURGIN, Don
TV: the worst of times or the best of times?
address, November 17, 1970. Vital Speeches
37:186-90 Ja 1 '71
DURHAM, Hugh
Odds on for the pro bowl. C. Kirkpatrick.
Sports Illus 32:47-8 F 9 '70 *
DURHAM, Mae J.
(ed) Children's literature for today's world;
where will it lead? bibliog il Wilson Lib Bul
45:142-68 O '70
DURHAM, N.C.

Sanitary affairs
Detroit and Durham honored for litter pre-
vention. Am City 85:46 Mr '70
DURICK, Joseph Aloysius, bp
Renewal: Tennessee model. T. M. Gannon.
America 122:152-5+ F 14 '70 *
DURK, David B.
Durk's gospel. il por Time 96:42-3 Jl 13 '70 *
Why don't you guys become cops? R. Daley.
il por Life 68:38A-38B+ Mr 20 '70 *
DURKEN, Daniel
Preaching in the 1970's. America 122:587-9
My 30 '70
DURKIN, Dolores
Reading readiness. Ed Digest 35:36-9 My '70
DUROCHER, Leo
Caged, tamed and on a tear. P. Carry. il
Sports Illus 32:28-9 My 11 '70 *
Chicago streaks for nice-guy Durocher. H.
Peterson. Sports Illus 32:50 My 4 '70 *
How Durocher blew the pennant. W. B. Fur-
long. por Look 34:55-6+ Mr 10 '70 *
DURRELL, Gerald Malcolm
Adopting an anteater; excerpt from Encoun-
ter with animals. il McCalls 97:52+ S '70
DURRELL, Lawrence
Rain rain go to Spain; poem. Harp Baz 103:
274 S '70

about
Durrell and the homunculi. A. Burgess. por
Sat R 53:29-31+ Mr 21 '70 *
DURSBAN. See Insecticides
DURSO, Joseph
Joan Whitney Payson. il por Vogue 155:92-
3+ Je '70

DUSKIN, Alvin
Protests and profits. por Newsweek 75:72-3 F 2 '70

DÜSSELDORF, Germany

Music

Report: production of Luigi Dallapiccola's Ulysses. H. Koegler. Opera N 34:34 F 28 '70

DUST
Radon-222 in the North Atlantic trade winds; its relationship to dust transport from Africa. J. M. Prospero and T. N. Carlson. bibliog il Science 167:974-7 F 13 '70

DUST, interstellar. See Matter, Interstellar

DUST allergy. See Allergy

DUTCH
Profiles; Netherlands. A. Bailey. New Yorker 46:34-40+ Ag 8; 32-8+ Ag 15 '70

DUTCH elm disease. See Elm—Diseases and pests

DUTCH GUIANA. See Surinam

DUTCH Reformed church in South Africa. See Reformed church in South Africa

DUTSCHKE, Rudi
You can't go home again; expulsion order from Britain. il pors Newsweek 76:47 S 28 '70 *

DUTTON, Ed
Cranko's Munich deputy: Ed Dutton. G. Loney. il pors Dance Mag 44:28-30 Ag '70 *

DUTTON, John A.
Wonder of the sky. il por Weatherwise 23:109-11+ Je '70

—and Blackadar, A. K.
Energy is energy. Weatherwise 23:231-4+ O '70

—and Panofsky, H. A.
Clear air turbulence: a mystery may be unfolding. bibliog il Science 167:937-44 F 13 '70

—See Blackadar, A. K. jt. auth.

DUTTON, Mary
Characters in Wanderland. Writer 83:22-4 O '70

DUTTON, Richard H.
Design and construction of regulated power supplies. il Electr World 83:30-3+ F '70

DUTTON, Richard W. See Lesley, J. jt. auth.

DUTY
Puritan's ought and Paul's ought. R. Haughton. Cath World 211:53-4 My '70

DUTY free importation
Unesco's free flow agreement. Sch & Soc 98:461 D '70

DUVALIER, François
Comedians revere the Doctor. J. A. Moreau. Nation 211:621-4 D 14 '70 *

DUVICK, Donald
Have narrow rows been oversold? interview, ed. by C. E. Sommers. il pors Suc Farm 68:29+ S '70

DVOŘÁK, Antonin
Dvorak's Requiem by Kertesz. G. L. Mayer. Sat R 53:59 S 26 '70 *
Incomparable art of Emanuel Feuermann. D. W. Moore. Am Rec G 37:12-13 S '70 *
Requiem of consolation. P. G. Davis. Hi Fi 20:secI 94 Ap '70 *

DWARF fruit trees. See Fruit trees, Dwarf

DWARF stars. See Stars, Dwarf

DWARF trees. See Trees, Dwarf

DWARFS
Giants and midgets. A. J. Snider. il Sci Digest 69:62-6 Ja '71

DWELLINGS. See Indians of North America—Dwellings

DWIGGINS, William Addison
Dwiggins marionettes, by D. Abbe. Review Pub W il 198:44+ Ag 3 '70. P. Standard *

DWORKIN, Martin S.
Whose Oscar? il Cath World 212:40-2 O '70

DWOSKIN, Robert P.
Constitutional rights of public librarians. bibliog por Library J 95:2417-21 Jl '70

DWYER, J. Gerald
Silent organs, empty churches. il Cath World 211:29-31 Ap '70

DWYER, James J.
It pays us to keep the old house. Har Yrs 10:22-3 Jl '70

DWYER, P. D.
Social organization in the bat myotis adversus. bibliog il Science 168:1006-8 My 22 '70

DYAL, Palmer, and others
Apollo 12 magnetometer: measurement of a steady magnetic field on the surface of the moon. bibliog il Science 169:762-4 Ag 21 '70

DYCH, William V.
(ed) See Rahner, K. Karl Rahner, an interview

DYERSVILLE, Ia.
Dilemma; new hospital that has everything except doctors. L. Wainwright. il Life 68:48-50+ My 29 '70

DYES and dyeing
Creativity of ancient man. E. Keller and J. Zimmerman. il Chem 43:20 Jl '70
Exciting crafts with dye. M. B. Smith. il Bet Hom & Gard 48:64-7+ S '70
Little guide to tie-dyeing. il Redbook 135:80-1+ Je '70
Profit hint: always say dye; tie-dyeing craze. il Bsns W p71 Ja 24 '70
Psychedelic tie-dye look. il por Time 95:36-9 Ja 26 '70
See also
Bleaching
Coal tar colors
Coloring matter in food
Hair—Dyeing and bleaching

DYGERT, James H.
Black thoughts of Judge Crockett. Esquire 74:120+ D '70

DYKE, William
Bombings, campus disorder; interview. il por U S News 69:74-9 O 5 '70

DYKSTRA, John W.
Demise of accountability; with editorial comment. Chr Today 14:14-16, 33 Ap 10 '70
Evils of occupational upgrading. Sch & Soc 98:98-100 F '70

DYLAN, Bob
Bob Dylan and the poetry of salvation. S. Goldberg. il pors Sat R 53:43-6+ My 30 '70 *
Bob Dylan, poet laureate of folk rock. J. Reddy. por Read Digest 96:249-50+ Je '70 *
Doctor Bob sums up; LP album entitled Self portrait. por Time 95:61 Je 22 '70 *
Dylan. P. Nelson. pors Sr. Schol 97:22-3+ D 14 '70 *
Rock, etc. E. Willis. New Yorker 46:181-2+ D 12 '70 *
Up from the basement; new album of records. C. E. Fager. Chr Cent 87:301-2 Mr 11 '70 *

DYNAMICS
Bicycle built for none. Sci Am 222:58 My '70
Stability of the bicycle. D. E. H. Jones. bibliog il pors Phys Today 23:34-40 Ap '70
Unridable bicycle. il Time 95:78 Je 8 '70

DYNAMITE
Dynamite is easy to buy, and to use. il Life 68:32-3 Mr 27 '70

DYNODES. See Photoelectric multipliers

DYSON, Freeman John
Future of physics; adaptation of address, March 1970. bibliog il Phys Today 23:23-6+ S '70
Reflections. New Yorker 46:44-6+ F 21 '70

DYSON, William H. and others
Cytokinin activity of ureidopurine derivatives related to a modified nucleoside found in transfer RNA. bibliog il Science 170:328-30 O 16 '70

DYSPLASIA of the cervix. See Cervix—Diseases

DYSTROPHY, Muscular
Ribonuclease-inhibitor system abnormality in dystrophic mouse skeletal muscle. B. W. Little and W. L. Meyer. bibliog il Science 170:747-9 N 13 '70

E

EACC. See Eastern Asia Christian conference

EADI (electronic attitude director indicator) See Aeronautic instruments—Display systems

EAI. See Electronic associates, inc.

EAT. See Experiments in art and technology

EBV (Epstein-Barr virus) See Herpesvirus

ECLA. See United Nations—Economic commission for Latin America

ECM (electronic countermeasures) See Electronics—Military use

ECOSOC. See United Nations—Economic and social council

EDF. See Environmental defense fund, inc.

EDP. See Electronic data processing

EDS. See Electronic data systems corporation

EEC. See European economic community

EEG. See Electroencephalography

EFI (electronic fuel injection) See Automobile engines—Fuel feeding

EFTA. See European free trade association

EG&G, inc.
Glamour stock that lost its glimmer. il Bsns W p 106-7 Ja 31 '70

E.I. Du Pont de Nemours and company. See
Du Pont De Nemours, E. I, and company
EJA. See Executive jet aviation, inc.
ELDO. See European launcher development organization
EMCBT (emergency monitoring citizens band team) See Radio communication—Emergency use
EPA. See United States—Environmental protection agency
ERIC. See Eric
EROS (eliminate range O system) See Airplanes—Safety devices and measures
ERTS (earth resources technology satellite) See Artificial satellites—Use in research
ESB (electrical stimulation of the brain) See Electronic behavior control
ESC. See European space conference
ESEA (elementary and secondary education act of 1965) See Education—Federal aid
ESP. See Extrasensory perception
ESRO. See European space research organization
ESSA. See United States—Environmental science services administration
ETV stations. See Television stations, Educational
EVR (electronic video recording) See Video recorders and recording
EADIE, W. R. See Caslick, J. W. jt. auth.
EADS bridge. See St Louis—Bridges
EAGLE, Diane
Gray; poem. Am Scholar 39:468-9 Sum '70
EAGLE glass and manufacturing company
Eagle glass and manufacturing company. A. G. Peterson. il Hobbies 75:112-13 Ap; 82-3 My '70
EAGLE in art. See Birds in art
EAGLES
Eagle: spacecraft of the pre-scientific age. J. P. De Souza. il UNESCO Courier 23:23-7 Je '70
Eagle to the sky, by F. Hamerstrom. Review
Sci Digest il 68:92-3 O '70. R. F. Dempewolff
Is the bald eagle doomed? G. Ott. il Nat Wildlife 8:4-9 Ap '70
EAGLETON, Thomas Francis
U.S. journal: Missouri. C. Trillin. New Yorker 46:108+ My 16 '70 *
EAKER, Ira Clarence
Some concerns about national security; address, June 5, 1970. Vital Speeches 36:701-4 S 1 '70
EAKINS, Thomas
Odd American. R. Moynihan. il Art N 69:50-3 Ja '71 *
Shows we've seen; traveling exhibit of Photographic works. R. F. McCullough. Pop Phot 67:57+ D '70 *
Thomas Eakins, American realist; at the Whitney museum of American art. S. B. Sherrill. il Antiques 98:480 O '70 *
EAMES, Charles
Poetry of ideas: the films of Charles Eames; with filmography. P. Schrader. il por Film Q 23:2-19 Spr '70 *
EAR
See also
Hearing
Labyrinth (ear)
Surgery
New hope for hearing; eardrum homografts. il Time 96:99 O 26 '70
EAR (birds)
Short-latency labyrinthine input to the vestibular nuclei in the pigeon. V. J. Wilson and R. M. Wylie. bibliog il Science 168:124-7 Ap 3 '70
EARDRUM. See Tympanic membrane
EARL, John L. See Chow, T. J. jt. auth.
EARLE, Anitra
Center for contemporary music. il Hi Fi 20:MA24-5 S '70
EARLE M. Jorgensen company. See Jorgensen, Earle M. company
EARLES, Mary L.
One wondrous year. il Read Digest 96:86-9 Ap '70
EARLEY, Elizabeth M. See Volpe, E. P. jt. auth.
EARLHAM college, Richmond, Ind.
Integrated library instruction. J. R. Kennedy, jr. il por Library J 95:1450-3 Ap 15 '70
EARLY, Tracy
New look at Vatican I. il Chr Cent 87:815-18 Jl 1 '70
Tourist's guide to New York churches. Chr Cent 87:1017-18 Ag 26 '70
EARLY songs; ballet. See Ballets—Criticisms
EARNINGS, Corporate. See Corporations—Finance

EARP, Wyatt
Wyatt Earp syndrome. C. L. Sonnichsen. il Am West 7:26-8+ My '70 *
EARPHONES
Join the revolution in stereo headphones. R. S. Lanier. il Pop Sci 197:76-7+ N '70
New concepts in headphones; symposium. il Hi Fi sec I 20:56-63 F '70
EARTH

Contamination

Puzzle of toxicity; effect of lunar soil on earth bacteria. Sci N 97:243 Mr 7 '70

Internal structure

Earth sciences; International symposium on mechanical properties and processes of the mantle. Sci N 98:38 Jl 11 '70
From the how to the why; Upper mantle project. Sci N 98:9 Jl 4 '70
Low-velocity zone of the earth's mantle: incipient melting caused by water. I. B. Lambert and P. J. Wyllie. bibliog il Science 169:764-6 Ag 21 '70
Phase change instability in the mantle. G. Schubert and others. bibliog il Science 169:1075-7 S 11 '70
Unfathomed forces driving earth's plates. K. Frazier. il Sci N 98:74-6 Jl 25 '70

Mantle
See Earth—Internal structure

Maps
See World maps

Photographs from space
Sunglint patterns: unusual dark patches. C. J. Bowley and others; reply with rejoinder. E. P. McClain and A. E. Strong. bibliog Science 167:1757 Mr 27 '70
We're fishing from outer space. G. Lee. il por Nat Wildlife 8:36-41 F '70

Radiation
Planetary albedo changes due to aerosols. M. A. Atwater. bibliog il Science 170:64-6 O 2 '70

Rotation
See also
Coriolis force

Surface
See also
Earth tides
Faults (geology)
EARTH, Effect of man on. See Man—Influence on nature
EARTH art. See Environment (art)
EARTH bonds. See Bonds
EARTH day. See Environmental movement—Earth day, April 22, 1970
EARTH movements
See also
Earth tides
Mine subsidences
Seismographs
Seismology
EARTH moving machinery. See Excavating machinery
EARTH resources satellites. See Artificial satellites—Use in research
EARTH satellite corporation
Remotely-sensed data use spurred. P. J. Klass. il Aviation W 93:44-5 D 21 '70
EARTH satellites (artificial) See Artificial satellites
EARTH sciences
Earth sciences. See issues of Science news
Inner and outer space. D. S. Cheever; T. Owen; D. L. Roberts. il Bul Atom Sci 26:22-34 F '70
See also
Climate
Geochemistry
Meteorology
Oceanography
EARTH tides
Earth tides. Chem 43:23 Je '70
Earth tides, global heat flow, and tectonics. H. R. Shaw. bibliog il Science 168:1084-7 My 29 '70
Tracking the moving earth. Sci N 97:170-1 F 14 '70
Transcontinental tidal gravity profile across the United States. J. T. Kuo and others. bibliog il Science 168:968-71 My 22 '70; Reply with rejoinder. D. A. Rigassi. 170:1002-3 N 27 '70
EARTHENWARE. See Pottery
EARTHQUAKE prediction
Tilt warning on quake. Sci N 99:8 Ja 2 '71
Warnings from the wells. Sci N 98:302 O 10 '70

EARTHQUAKES
How man endangers the climate. G. J. F. MacDonald. Cur 114:17-24 Ja '70
Nuclear explosions and distant earthquakes: a search for correlations. J. H. Healy and P. A. Marshall. bibliog il Science 169:176-7 Jl 10 '70
See also
Seismology
Tidal waves

Measurement
See Seismometry

Prediction
See Earthquake prediction

Research
Earthquake and avalanche; Peruvian disaster. il Sci N 98:94-5 Ag 1 '70
Study of the San Andreas fault: something very interesting is going on deep beneath the earth's surface. S. D. Smith. il N Y Times Mag p 16-17+ Ja 18 '70
Taming of earthquakes. il Time 96:46 S 7 '70
Underground nuclear explosions and the control of earthquakes. C. Emiliani and others; discussion. bibliog il Science 167:1011-14 F 13 '70

Alaska
Living on the edge. il Sci N 98:199-200 S 5 '70

Italy
Rise and fall. il Newsweek 75:53-4 Mr 16 '70
What's up in Pozzuoli? il Time 95:51 Mr 16 '70

Peru
Death by glacier; Yungay, Peru mudflow. Sci Am 223:46 Ag '70
Earthquake and avalanche. il Sci N 98:94-5 Ag 1 '70
Earthquake! The horror that hit Peru. J. P. Blank. il Read Digest 97:77-83 O '70
Infernal thunder over Peru. il Time 95:26-8 Je 15 '70
... May 31, 1970. F. L. Phelps. il Américas 22 21-6 S '70
OAS countries, employees rush to earthquake-stricken Peru. il Américas 22:44 Jl '70
Peru earthquake: a special study. il Bul Atom Sci 26:17-19 O '70
Peru: the aftermath. Time 95:40 Je 22 '70
Twentieth-century Pompeii. P. Kramer. il Newsweek 75:48 Je 15 '70

Turkey
Wiped off the map; Gediz. il Newsweek 75: 36 Ap 13 '70

United States
California earthquakes: why only shallow focus? W. F. Brace and J. D. Byerlee. bibliog il Science 168:1573-5 Je 26 '70
Montana's astounding earthquake area. B. Thomas. il Travel 133:40-5 F '70
Seismicity of Colorado: consistency of recent earthquakes with those of historical record. R. B. Simon; reply with rejoinder. E. Karp. bibliog Science 167:1518-19 Mr 13 '70
Waiting for the big bump; California. il Newsweek 76:58 S 28 '70

EARTHQUAKES and building
Technology; isolation system. il Arch Forum 132:48-9 Ap '70

EARTHS, Rare
Rare earth elements in returned lunar samples. L. A. Haskin and others. bibliog il Science 167:487-90 Ja 30 '70
Separating lanthanides by ion exchange chromatography. L. W. McKeen. bibliog il por Chem 43:28-31 My '70
See also
Gadolinium earths
Promethium

EARTHWORK
See also
Dams
Filling (earthwork)
Tamping machines

EARTHWORMS
Earthworm farm in your backyard? M. Bicknell. il Har Yrs 10:17-18+ Ag '70
Structure of the giant fibers of earthworms. B. Mulloney. bibliog il Science 168:994-6 My 22 '70

EASELS
Build your own easel. J. E. Kollas. il Design 72:13 Wint '70

EASLEY, S. C.
See-through tanks save money. il Am City 85:81 Mr '70

EASON, Helga H.
Miami, Florida. il Wilson Lib Bul 44:760-3 Mr '70

EASSON, Eric C.
False notion: cancer=incurable. il UNESCO Courier 23:23-6 My '70

EAST, Ben
Angry men. il Outdoor Life 146:31-3+ D '70 (to be cont)
Is it TAPS for wild Alaska? il Outdoor Life 145:43-5+ My '70
No. 1 endangered species: you! il Outdoor Life 145:32-4+ Ap '70
— See Bauer, E. A. jt. auth.

EAST
See also
Asia
Middle East

EAST AFRICA

Description and travel
Camera safaris: the civilized way. L. Barry. il Pop Phot 67:54+ Jl '70

EAST AFRICAN library association
East African conference: sharp conflicts emerge Library J 95:3864 N 15 '70

EAST AFRICAN safari auto rally. See Automobile racing—Africa, East

EAST ASIA Christian conference. See Eastern Asia Christian conference

EAST GERMAN refugees. See Refugees, German

EAST GERMANY. See Germany (Democratic Republic)

EAST Ghor irrigation project. See Irrigation— Jordan

EAST high school, Denver. See Denver—Education

EAST INDIANS
Reporter at large; Indian journal. V. Mehta. New Yorker 46:94+ Ap 11 '70

EAST PACIFIC rise. See Ocean bottom

EAST PAKISTAN. See Pakistan

EAST PALO ALTO. See Palo Alto, Calif.

EAST-West relations. See International relations

EAST-West trade. See Communist countries— Commerce

EASTAUGH, Cyril, bp
Oh! Peterborough! Chr Cent 87:985 Ag 19 '70 *

EASTER
Easter joy. V. P. McCorry. America 122:357-8 Mr 28 '70
Facing another Easter. America 122:329 Mr 28 '70
Worthy is the lamb that was slain; excerpts from The coming faith. C. Marney. Chr Cent 87:348 Mr 25 '70
See also
Jesus Christ—Resurrection and ascension

Anecdotes, facetiae, satire, etc.
Dark counsel at Easter. L. Woodrum. Chr Today 14:10 Mr 27 '70

Drama
Father's Easter hat. M. Hark and N. McQueen Plays 29:53-60 Ap '70
Rabbits who changed their minds. H. L. Miller. Plays 29:75-9 Mr '70

EASTER business. See Retail trade

EASTER eggs
See-into Easter egg; homemade sugar window eggs. il Sunset 144:80-1 Mr '70
You write on the egg with wax, then you dye it. il Sunset 144:141-2 Mr '70

EASTER music
See also
Phonograph records—Easter music

EASTER services. See Church services

EASTERN airlines
Anti-hijacking plans augmented. Aviation W 93:32 N 9 '70
Carriers seek alternatives to turbojet fuel dumping. H. D. Watkins. Aviation W 93:27-8 N 2 '70
Clean-air pilot. Time 96:40 N 2 '70
Eastern accelerates anti-hijack preboarding screening program. Aviation W 92:34 My 4 '70
Eastern places three-year cost of traffic delays at $137 million. K. J. Stein. il Aviation W 92:30-1 Ap 27 '70
Eastern seeks to exploit stronger markets. R. S. Kahn. Aviation W 92:25-6 F 16 '70
Eastern spurs hijacking drive. Aviation W 93:27 N 23 '70
Eastern starts pilot recruiting program. H. D. Watkins. Aviation W 93:32-3 Ag 3 '70
Eastern strives to curtail baggage losses. H. D. Watkins. il Aviation W 93:28-9+ Ag 17 '70
Eastern studies air-shuttle improvements. J. P. Woolsey. il Aviation W 92:39-41+ My 18 '70
Eastern to acquire Caribair. AviationW 93:25 N 2 '70

EASTERN airlines—*Continued*
Eastern's Center speeds response time. K. J. Stein. il Aviation W 92:35-7 Je 1 '70
Get a flying start on your camping vacation; Fly-in/camp-out program. H. Shuldiner. il Pop Sci 196:82-3 My '70
Out of the clouds? il Forbes 106:58 O 15 '70
EASTERN ASIA Christian conference
Toward an Asian theology. C. F. H. Henry. Chr Today 15:36-7 Ja 1 '71
EASTERN EUROPE. See Europe, Eastern
EASTERN GERMANY. See Germany (Democratic Republic)
EASTERN Orthodox church in the United States. See Orthodox Eastern church in the United States
EASTERN religions. See Religions
EASTERNERS
Out West, we trust one another. B. Goldwater. por Life 69:4 O 9 '70
EASTIN, John
Which corn leaves work the hardest? interview, ed. by B. Coffman. il Farm J 94:38A-38B Mr '70
EASTLACK, Joseph O. Jr, and McDonald, P. R.
CEO's role in corporate growth. il Harvard Bsns R 48:150-2+ My '70
EASTLAND, James Oliver
Excerpt from debate, February 9, 1970. Cong Digest 49:108+ Ap '70
EASTMAN, George
Take a Kodak with you. C. Davidson. il Am Heritage 21:48-51 Je '70 *
You press the button and we do the rest. F. S. Welsh. il pors Nations Bsns 58:70-1 Ja '70
EASTMAN, John
Biology of the way-out; with biographical sketch. Natur Hist 79:4, 24-9 My '70
Powwow; with biographical sketch. il Natur Hist 79:6,24+ N '70
EASTMAN Kodak company
Eastman employees focus on investments. V. Louviere. Nations Bsns 58:22 N '70
Emmy for an annual meeting? live question and answer telecast. V. Louviere. il Nations Bsns 58:14 Jl '70
Kodak and Polaroid; an end to peaceful coexistence. P. Siekman. il Fortune 82:82-7+ N '70
Kodak's instant cameraman. A. A. Butkus. por Duns 96:60+ S '70
Kodak's self-portrait; TV broadcast. Newsweek 75:88 My 11 '70
Take a Kodak with you; G. Eastman's collection. C. Davidson. il Am Heritage 21:48-51 Je '70
EASTON, Me.
That mess on the Prestile; pollution of stream running across Maine-New Brunswick border. F. Graham, jr. il Am Heritage 21:106-12 F '70; Discussion. 21:94-5 Ag '70
EASY chairs. See Chairs
EATING
See also
Appetite
Diet
Food
EATING, Psychology of
Forget the cook's parade unless—. G. W. Lankton. Camp Mag 42:22-4 N '70

Anecdotes, facetiae, satire, etc.
Soufflé for scientists; we are what we eat. Time 95:47-8 Mr 9 '70
EATING habits. See Food habits
EATON, Jerome A.
Home greenhouse. See issues of Home garden & flower grower
EATONTOWN, N.J.
Eatontown caper. il por Newsweek 76:46+ Ag 24 '70
$5-million that disappeared; How Eatontown took the shutdown. il Bsns W p 17-19 Ag 15 '70
EAU de vie. See Liquors
EBADI, Manuchair S. and others
Adenosine 3',5'-monophosphate in rat pineal gland: increase induced by light. bibliog il Science 170:188-90 O 9 '70
EBAN, Abba Solomon
Speaker; interview. New Yorker 46:45-8 N 14 '70
about
Visitors from Israel. Time 96:14 S 21 '70 *
Viva Eban. W. F. Buckley, jr. Nat R 22:1124-5 O 20 '70 *
EBAN, Suzy
Ismailia childhood. New Yorker 46:174-6+ D 5 '70

EBBING, Bernard W.
Bypass marketing altogether with forward contracting. Farm J 94:H7+ Ag '70
EBEL, Fred
Ham & the lady psychologist. Pop Electr 33:60-1+ S '70
EBEL, Robert L.
Case for true-false test items. Ed Digest 36:47-50 O '70
EBERHARDT, Dave
Berrigans in prison. K. L. Woodward. Commonweal 92:428-30 S 4 '70 *
Berrigans: jail for the Christian conscience. il pors Time 95:65-6 My 4 '70 *
Bulls and Berrigans. por Newsweek 75:106 My 4 '70 *
EBERHARDT, Lee
In-between irises. il Horticulture 48:30-1+ F '70
EBERHARDT, P. and others
Trapped solar wind noble gases, Kr^{81}/Kr exposure ages and K/Ar ages in Apollo 11 lunar material bibliog il Science 167:558-60 Ja 30 '70
EBERHART, Richard
As if you had never been; poem. New Yorker 46:38 O 3 '70
Comment. Poetry 115:345 F '70
Despair; poem. New Yorker 45:35 F 14 '70
Homage to the north; poem. New Yorker 46:54 D 12 '70
Suicide note; poem. New Yorker 46:36 Mr 28 '70
United 555; Time passes; poems. Poetry 117:39-40 O '70
Will; poem. Sat R 53:73 Mr 28 '70
(tr) See Borges, J. L. Adam cast forth; One morning in 1649; Rose and Milton
EBERT, Roger
Kirk Douglas at large. il por Esquire 73:88-93 F '70
Saturday at Lee . . . ing Marvin's. por Esquire 74:143-9+ N '70
about
Populist at the movies. por Time 95:59+ Mr 30 '70 *
EBKEN, Ruth M.
Art and the elementary teacher. il Sch Arts 70:12-13 O '70
EBONY fashion fair. See Fashion shows
ECCLES, David McAdam Eccles, 1st viscount
Lord Eccles and art. T. Beeson. Chr Cent 87:1276 O 28 '70 *
ECCLES, Marriner S.
Eccles: don't blame the Fed; interview, ed. by T. J. Murray. por Duns 96:10-12+ S '70
ECCLESIASTICAL architecture. See Church architecture
ECCLESIASTICAL courts
Farewell to the tribunal. L. M. Croghan. il America 123:227-9 O 3 '70
ECCLESIASTICAL law
See also
Canon law
ECCLESIATICAL music. See Church music
ECCLESIASTICAL supplies. See Church supplies
ECCLESIASTICAL vestments. See Church vestments
ECDYSIS. See Molting
ECHEVERRÍA ALVAREZ, Luis
Digging out. Time 96:42 D 14 '70 *
New leader in Mexico; meaning to U.S. il U S News 69:74 Jl 13 '70 *
Upward and onward. il por Time 96:27 Jl 13 '70 *
What made Luis run? il por Newsweek 76:44-5 Jl 13 '70 *
ECHEWA, T. Obinkaram
Name your son Tunku? America 122:185-7 F 21 '70
ECHIDNA. See Anteaters
ECHINODERMS
See also
Embryology—Echinoderms
Sea urchins
ECHO viruses
Rhodanine: a selective inhibitor of the multiplication of echovirus 12. H. J. Eggers and others. bibliog il Science 167:294-7 Ja 16 '70
ECHOLOCATION (physiology)
Echo-ranging neurons in the inferior colliculus of bats. N. Suga. bibliog il Science 170:449-52 O 23 '70
Echolocation in bats; excerpts from The world of bats. A. Novick. il Natur Hist 79:32-41 Mr '70
ECK, Marcel
Truth about lying; excerpt from Lies and truth. il N Y Times Mag p87+ Ap 26 '70

ECKERMAN, Carol O. See Rheingold, H. L. jt. auth.

ECKES, A. E.
Quebec joinder. il Am For 76:6-7+ Ap '70

ECKHARDT, Robert Christian
Open beaches. il Parks & Rec 5:21-3+ Ag '70
Trading law for order. Nation 211:687-90 D 28 '70

        about

Eckhardt of Texas. E. M. Yoder, jr. Harper 240:28+ Je '70 *

ECKLER, A. Ross
Profit from 1970 census data. il Harvard Bsns R 48:4-6+ Jl '70

ECKRICH, Catherine
I, Simon of Cyrene (si-ree-ne) poem. Cath World 211:25 Ap '70
Oh, you who also ride; poem. Cath World 211:155 Jl '70

ECKROADE, Robert J. and others
Transmissible mink encephalopathy: experimental transmission to the squirrel monkey. bibliog il Science 169:1088-90 S 11 '70

ECKSTEIN, George G.
Hochhuth's coup d'état (U.S.) Nation 211:124-6 Ag 17 '70

ECKSTEIN, Gustav
Female animal. McCalls 97:20 Ag '70

ECLIPSES
   See also
Occultations

ECLIPSES, Lunar
August 16th lunar eclipse and aurora. il Sky & Tel 40:210-13 O '70
Next month's lunar eclipse. il Sky & Tel 41:55-6 Ja '71
Notes on 1969 solar and lunar eclipses. L. J. Boss. il R Pop Astron 63:10-11 Ag '69
Partial lunar eclipse observed. il Sky & Tel 39:267 Ap '70

ECLIPSES, Photography of. See Astronomical photography

ECLIPSES, Solar
Accommodating sun. D. E. Thomsen. il Sci N 97:227 F 28 '70
Alcan total eclipse of July 10, 1972. C. H. Smiley. il Sky & Tel 41:10-13 Ja '71
Apparent research success. il Sci N 97:268 Mr 14 '70
Big blackout coming! A. Ewing. il Read Digest 96:41-2+ Mr '70
Blotting out the sun. il Sr Schol 96:16 Mr 2 '70
Darkness at noon. il Newsweek 75:59+ Mr 9 '70
Earliest recorded eclipse. Sky & Tel 41:26 Ja '71
Eclipse phenomena at the edge of totality. Sky & Tel 40:90-1 Ag '70
Ecliptic vibrations; view from Nantucket. J. S. Kunen. Esquire 74:72+ Jl '70
Enjoying the umbra. il Time 95:10 Mr 16 '70
Feminine eye. S. Alexander. McCalls 97:8 My '70
First eclipse reports. il Sky & Tel 39:211-14+ Ap '70
From above: solar eclipse, 7 March 1970. F. C. Parmenter. il Weatherwise 23:98-100 Ap '70
High altitude observatory's 1970 eclipse expedition. R. A. Kopp. il Sky & Tel 39:359-62 Je '70
March eclipse rocket program at Wallops Island. C. A. Accardo. il Sky & Tel 39:344-9 Je '70
More March 7th eclipse results. il Sky & Tel 40:77-80 Ag '70
1970 eclipse, an on-site account. il Chem 43:6-7 My '70
Notes on 1969 solar and lunar eclipses. L. J. Boss. il R Pop Astron 63:10-11 Ag '69
Observing a solar eclipse in the space age. il Space World G-6-78:4-13 Je '70
One way to peek at an eclipse. il Todays Health 48:4 Mr '70
Partial-eclipse observations on March 7th. il Sky & Tel 39:324-8 My '70
Partial phases of the March eclipse. il Sky & Tel 39:88-9 F '70
Recording shadow bands at the March eclipse. E. M. Paulton. il por Sky & Tel 39:132-3 F '70
Scientists' eclipse goals. L. J. Robinson. il Sky & Tel 39:167-71 Mr '70
Shadow bands and the March solar eclipse. A. T. Young. il Sky & Tel 40:176-81, 242-4 S-O '70
Sky spectacular. il Time 95:39 Mr 9 '70
Solar eclipse: nature's super spectacular. D. H. Menzel and J. M. Pasachoff. il Nat Geog 138:222-33 Ag '70
Space systems yield eclipse data. il Aviation W 92:16-18 Mr 16 '70
Sun vanishes. I. Asimov. il Look 34:68-70+ Mr 10 '70
Sun will darken March 7. T. D. Nicholson; L. B. Nadeau. il Natur Hist 79:26-8+ F '70
Total eclipse along the eastern seaboard. il Sky & Tel 39:285-9 My '70
When the day becomes dark. il U S News 68:14 Mr 9 '70
With the eclipse expeditions in Mexico. R. Little and L. J. Robinson. il Sky & Tel 39:280-4 My '70

       Photographs

Colorful total eclipse. Sky & Tel 39:308-9 My '70
Eclipse no one saw. Life 68:32-3 Mr 20 '70

ECLIPSING binaries. See Stars, Eclipsing binary

ECLOV, Shirley
Details, details! Writer 84:19-21 Ja '71

ECOLOGICAL models
Model man. il por Time 95:70 My 25 '70
Systems studies of DDT transport. H. L. Harrison and others. bibliog il Science 170:503-8 O 30 '70

ECOLOGICAL movement. See Environmental movement

ECOLOGICAL research
Ecology: the biome approach. R. Gilluly. il Sci N 98:204-5 S 5 '70
Effects of pollution on the structure and physiology of ecosystems. G. M. Woodwell. bibliog il Science 168:429-33 Ap 24 '70
Life studies flow from live volcanoes. R. H. Gilluly. il Sci N 97:411-13 Ap 25 '70
   See also
International biological program

ECOLOGY
Biosphere: symposium. il Sci Am 223:44-74+ bibliog(p262-6) S '70
Co-evolutionary race. P. R. Ehrlich and J. P. Holdren. Sat R 53:66 D 5 '70
Dawn for the age of ecology. il Newsweek 75:35-6 Ja 26 '70
Dominance and the niche in ecological systems. S. J. McNaughton and L. L. Wolf. bibliog il Science 167:131-9 Ja 9 '70; Reply with rejoinder. H. H. Shugart, jr. 170:1335 D 18 '70
Ecologist at bay. G. J. C. Smith. Sat R 54:68-9 Ja 2 '71
Ecology: a cause becomes a mass movement; with editorial comment, and report by J. Pekkanen. il Life 68:3, 22-30 Ja 30 '70
Ecology: the new religion? R. L. Schueler. America 122:292-5 Mr 21 '70
Fighting to save the earth from man. il Time 95:56-7+ F 2 '70; Same abr. with title Last chance for mother earth. Read Digest 96:63-7 My '70
Future of the future, by J. McHale Review Bul Atom Sci 26:44 Mr '70. R. Frisch
Genius of the place. R. J. Dubos. il por Am For 76:16-19+ S '70
Have you thanked a green plant today? way plants help to improve our environment. R. Rodale. il Org Gard & Farm 17:27-30 My '70
Island earth. M. Mead. por Natur Hist 79:22+ Ja '70
Our new awareness of the great web. W. Bowen. Fortune 81:198-9 F '70
Rhetoric of ecology. Life 68:36 Mr 6 '70
To trouble a star: the cost of intervention in nature. G. Hardin. Bul Atom Sci 26:17-20 Ja '70; Same abr. with title Ecology versus economics. Cur 116:34-9 Mr '70
Urban ecology today; AAAS symposium, December 30, 1970. F. Stearns. il Science 170:1006-7 N 27 '70
   See also
Birds—Ecology
Environment
Food chain (ecology)
Forest ecology
Fresh water ecology
Human ecology
Marine ecology
Mountain ecology
Paleoecology
Religion and ecology
Seashore ecology
Snow ecology
Zoology—Ecology

    Anecdotes, facetiae, satire, etc.

Notes and comment; printed material as compost. New Yorker 46:33 Mr 21 '70

    Caricatures and cartoons

Ecology, why must you torture me? J. Noonan. il Cath World 211:82-3 My '70
Oikos. J. Bohn. il Harp Baz 103:192+ O '70

ECOLOGY—*Continued*

Study and teaching

Ecology & environment; excerpts from Social science in the schools, ed. by I. Morrissett and W. W. Stevens, jr. il Trans-Action 7:38-44 Mr '70

Ecology and the child; S.F.-Oakland Bay area. H. Olkowski. il Org Gard & Farm 17:57-61 N '70

Ecology comes to camp; grant to ACA by Lilly endowment, inc. J. J. Kirk. por Camp Mag 42:4 N '70

Real thing; ecology teaching aid. il Time 96:46 D 14 '70

World under a dome; elements of a woodland environment transplanted indoors. F. Hoke. il Am For 76:12-14+ Mr '70

Alaska

Alaskan oil dilemma: ecology or prosperity? R. Gannon. bibliog il Sci Digest 68:14-19 Jl '70

Biologist explains: why we must plan now to protect the Arctic. L. C. Bliss. il Bul Atom Sci 26:34-8 O '70

Long pipe; Trans-Alaska pipeline system. R. Moxness. bibliog il Environ 12:12-23+ S '70

Our last great wilderness; oil and the ecological balance of Alaska's North Slope. W. Sullivan. il Am Heritage 21:98-117 Ag '70

Aleutian Islands

Aleutian ecosystem; AAAS symposium, December 26-27, 1970. W. S. Laughlin. il Science 169:1107-8 S 11 '70

Antarctic Regions

Survey of Antarctic biology: life below freezing. G. A. Llano. il por Bul Atom Sci 26:67-74 D '70

Arctic Regions

Concern for the Arctic environment. W. Kornberg. il Sci N 97:486-8 My 16 '70
See also
Ecology—Canada

Asia, Southeastern

Ecologists in the Mekong. New Repub 162:6-7 Mr 28 '70

Canada

Canada's Arctic in the age of ecology. T. Lloyd. il For Afffairs 48:726-40 Jl '70

Czechoslovakia

Familiar story; ecological alarm over proposed Šabina plant. D. N. Leff. il Environ 12:11-13 My '70

Florida

Cloudy Sunshine state; flirting with ecological disaster. il Time 95:48+ Ap 13 '70

Latin America

Ecology before Columbus. T. Grieder. il Américas 22:21-8 My '70

Vietnam

Blight that failed; herbicide operations in Vietnam. il Newsweek 77:79 Ja 11 '71

Defoliants, a closed case? AAAS study. Commonweal 93:363 Ja 15 '71

Ecological effects of the war in Vietnam. G. H. Orians and E. W. Pfeiffer. bibliog il Science 168:544-54 My 1 '70; Discussion. 169:6, 1030 Jl 3, S 11 '70

Ecology of war. Sci Am 223:48-9 Jl '70

Herbicides in Vietnam; AAAS study runs into a military roadblock. P. M. Boffey. Science 170:42-5 O 2 '70; Discussion. 170:1034+ D 4 '70

Let's hear it for pollution, if it's in Asia; Senate debate. H. H. Vinnedge. New Repub 163:14-15 O 17 '70

Operation Wasteland; South Viet Nam. il Time 95:70-3 My 25 '70

Ravaged soil of Vietnam. J. B. Kelley. il Cath World 211:71-3 My '70

Reporter at large; defoliation. T. Whiteside. New Yorker 45:32-8+ F 7; 46:124-9 Mr 14; 64-6+ Jl 4 '70

Vietnam refoliation; letter. J. A. Duke and J. T. McGinnis. Science 170:807 N 20 '70

ECOLOGY action (organization) See Environmental associations, committees, etc.

ECOLOGY begins at home; story. See Shapiro, T.

ECOLOGY book store, Berkeley, Calif. See Booksellers and bookselling— California

ECONOMETRIC models. See Economic models

ECONOMIC and social council

Meetings, 1970

Holds forty-ninth session. UN Mo Chron 7:70-8 Ag '70

ECONOMIC and social council of the United Nations. See United Nations—Economic and social council

ECONOMIC assistance

Foreign aid; global development; address, February 20, 1970. R. S. McNamara. Vital Speeches 36:338-41 Mr 15 '70
See also
International bank for reconstruction and development

ECONOMIC assistance, American

Annual report on foreign assistance program transmitted to Congress; letter, March 4, 1970. R. M. Nixon. Dept State Bul 62:499-500 Ap 13 '70

Budget of the United States government, fiscal year 1971; excerpts. R. M. Nixon. il Dept State Bul 62:234-40 Mr 2 '70

End to patchwork. il Time 96:9-10 S 28 '70

Foreign aid: reorganization should further abet research. J. Walsh. Science 169:1184-6+ S 18 '70

Foreign assistance act of 1969 signed into law; statement, December 31, 1969. R. M. Nixon. Dept State Bul 62:86 Ja 26 '70

Foreign assistance for the 'seventies message to Congress, September 15, 1970. R. M. Nixon. Dept State Bul 63:369-78 O 5 '70

Human solidarity; letter to editor. B. Evans. Commonweal 92:279 My 29 '70

Jumping into a pool; foreign aid. por Time 95:16 Mr 23 '70

New king of foreign aid: what White House proposes. il U S News 69:56-7 S 28 '70

Nixon and the new, new, new look of aid. Chr Cent 87:1144 S 30 '70

Opening to the future. P. Phelps. America 122:258 Mr 14 '70

Opening to the future; economic nationalism in Latin America. G. Plaza. il America 122:96-9 Ja 31 '70

Peterson report: making development truly international. Américas 22:45 My '70

Process of development; address, January 21, 1970. I. R. Hedges. Vital Speeches 36:290-5 Mr 1 '70

Secretary Rogers urges support for foreign assistance program; statement, September 12, 1970. W. P. Rogers. Dept State Bul 63:356-60 S 28 '70

Secretary stresses importance of funding foreign assistance program; statement, November 24, 1969. W. P. Rogers. Dept State Bul 61:593-5 D 22 '69

Task force report. Commonweal 92:77-8 Ap 3 '70

Underdeveloped countries: foreign aid; UN Second development decade; address, July 14, 1970. C. W. Yost. Vital Speeches 36:647-52 Ag 15 '70

U.S. foreign assistance in the 1970's a new approach, statement, March 8, 1970, with text of the report. R. M. Nixon. il Dept State Bul 62:447-67 Ap 6 '70

Washout; Peterson report. New Repub 162:11 Mr 21 '70

Will Congress buy a revamped aid plan? il Bsns W p31-2 Mr 14 '70

Work of peace. Commonweal 91:443-4 Ja 23 '70
See also
Food relief
Inter-American social development institute
United States—Agency for international development

ECONOMIC assistance, Australian

Churchmen and foreign aid. America 122:260 Mr 14 '70

ECONOMIC assistance, Canadian

Foreign aid turns to research. F. Poland. il Sci N 97:332 Mr 28 '70

ECONOMIC assistance, Chinese

China; aid projects in Africa. H. Yu. Chr Cent 87:1570 D 30 '70

ECONOMIC assistance, Communist
See also
Economic assistance, Russian

ECONOMIC assistance, Domestic

Betrayal of the poor. M. Harrington. Atlan 225:71-4 Ja '70

Federal revenue sharing and the cities; address, October 13, 1970. A. J. Cervantes. Vital Speeches 37:83-8 N 15 '70

Nixon's fight against hunger. il U S News 68:24-6 Ja 19 '70
See also
Community development—United States
Food relief—United States
Negative income tax
Volunteers in service to America

ECONOMIC theory. See Economics

ECONOMICS
Bleak outlook. P. A. Samuelson, Newsweek 75:64 Mr 2 '70
Does economics deserve a Nobel prize? M. Hudson. Commonweal 93:296-8 D 18 '70
Economics in the news (cont) il Sr Schol 95:17 S 15 '69; 96:19 Mr 2; 97:8-9 S 14; 14-18 S 28; 7 O 5; 12 O 26; 15 N 9; 9-13 N 16 '70
Friedmanism. n. doctrine of most audacious U.S. economist. M. Viorst. il por N Y Times Mag p22-3+ Ja 25 '70
Louis Kelso: nut or Newton? R. G. Sherrill. Nation 210:234-7 Mr 2 '70
Man and economics, by R. A. Mundell. Review Fortune 81:175-6 Ap '70. E. A. Birnbaum
Man who would make everybody richer; Kelsonian theory. il por Time 95:72-3 Je 29 '70
Paying for the good life; views of E. J. Mishan. L. Malkin. Commentary 50:95-7 S '70; Reply with rejoinder. E. J. Mishan. 50:8+ D '70
See also
American economic association
Capital
Capitalism
Consumption (economics)
Economic development
Efficiency, Industrial
Free enterprise
Leisure class
Liquidity (economics)
Money
Production
Prosperity

Mathematical models
See Economic models

Philosophy
Laissez-faire in a closed biosphere. Chr Cent 87:1403 N 25 '70

Study and teaching
Economic literacy of elementary school pupils. R. B. McKenzie. Ed Digest 36:41-3 N '70
See also
Clergy economic education foundation

Terminology
Glossary of economic terms. Sr Schol 96:18-19 Ja 26 '70

ECONOMICS and politics
Campaigners test their economic weapons. il Bsns W p 15 My 2 '70
Economics and elections. Nat R 22:1250 D 1 '70
Election economics. P. A. Samuelson. Newsweek 76:75 O 26 '70
Voters' impact. C. Morgello. il Newsweek 76: 94 N 16 '70

ECONOMICS literature
See also
Business literature

ECONOMISTS
Corporate economists carve a new domain. il Bsns W p74-5 N 28 '70
First look at '71: a slow climb back; price rise by by Time's Board of economists. il Time 96:76-7 O 12 '70
How deep a slump coming? what top economists say. il U S News 68:24-7 Mr 2 '70
More than Marxist. M. J. Ulmer. New Repub 163:13-14 D 26 '70
Prices: what to expect now; leading economists interviewed on price and wage outlook. il U S News 68:17-19 Ap 13 '70
See also
American economic association
Keynes, J. M. K.

ECONOMY runs. See Automobile engines—Fuel consumption

ECOS (organization)
ECOS. Liv Wildn 34:14 Spr '70

ECOSYSTEMS. See Ecology

ECTOPROCTA. See Bryozoa

ECUADOR
See also
Indians of South America—Ecuador
Petroleum industry and trade—Ecuador
San Antonio de Pichincha

Politics and government
Change in the script. il por Time 96:32 Jl 6 '70
Supreme leader; President Velasco's coup. por Newsweek 76:47 Jl 6 '70

ECUMENICAL council, 2d. See Vatican council 2d

ECUMENICAL movement
Agenda for a new generation; steps taken at Texas conference of churches. J. C. Evans. Chr Cent 87:382-3 Ap 1 '70
Anglican/Episcopal/Catholic union. America 122:549 My 23 '70
Church to come; adaptation of address, April 9, 1970. D. H. C. Read. America 122:550-4 My 23 '70
Coming soon: an ecumenical overhaul. D. Kucharsky. Chr Today 14:44+ F 13 '70
Ecumenism gets a new directory: Directory for the application of the decisions of Vatican council II concerning ecumenical matters. America 122:620 Je 13 '70
Faces of ecumenism. America 122:64 Ja 24 '70
Is ecumenism dead? J. R. Kelly. America 123: 258-9 O 10 '70
Major ecumenical proposal: NCC studies the feasibility of a general ecumenical council. D. Bowman and R. W. Rousseau. America 122:70-2 Ja 24 '70
Middle East trends toward ecumenism. G. Fitch; reply. J. R. Butler. Chr Cent 87:212 F 18 '70
Needed: new modes for internationalizing theological education. V. B. Rigdon and J. E. Will. Chr Cent 87:501-5 Ap 22 '70
Options for conciliarism; recommendations of the National council of churches. Chr Cent 87:747 Je 17 '70
Plague on three houses. J. R. Nelson. Chr Cent 87:232-3 F 25 '70
Process and power; the lineaments of valid ecumenical unification. S. C. Rose. Chr Cent 87:233-4 F 25 '70
Quest for Christian unity: 1971. America 124: 34 Ja 16 '71
Roman legions. C. F. H. Henry. Chr Today 14:29-30 Jl 3 '70
Signs of hope; growth of ecumenism. S. J. Adamo. America 122:200 F 21 '70
Step toward reunion; Anglican and Catholic scholars meet in England. il Newsweek 75:60 Ja 26 '70
Trends to intercommunion. C. J. Armbruster; discussion. America 121:575; 122:29 D 15 '69. Ja 17 '70
True and false ecumenism. D. G. Bloesch. Chr Today 14:3-5 Jl 17 '70
Unity: above ground and below. M. Handspicker and W. D. Wagoner. Chr Cent 87: 419-22 Ap 8 '70
Why should we care about ecumenical activity? C. J. Eichhorst. Chr Cent 87:1559-62 D 30 '70
See also
Religious cooperation
World council of churches

EDDY, Roger
Osborndale Ivanhoe lies a-mold'ring in the grave. Esquire 73:204 Ap '70

EDDY, William B. and others
Solving problems in living: the citizen's viewpoint. bibliog il Ment Hy 54:64-72 Ja '70

EDEL, Leon
Personal history. il por Sat R 53:34-5 Ap 11 '70

EDELMAN, Gerald Maurice
Structure and function of antibodies; with biographical sketch. il Sci Am 223:12, 34-42 bibliog (p 128) Ag '70

EDELSON, Edward
Rubella. Todays Ed 59:42-3 S '70
(ed) See Hreshchyshyn, M. M. Expectant mother
(ed) See Mikuta, J. J. Uterine tumors

EDELSON, Michael
Our man in Prague; new auto-focus system winner of Interkamera technical prize. il por Pop Phot 67:78-80 Ag '70

EDELSTEIN, J. M.
Fitting farewell. New Repub 162:26-8 Ap 4 '70

EDEN, Anthony, 1st earl of Avon. See Avon, A. E.

EDEN, N.C.
Consolidated community works better. A. W. Stewart. il Am City 85:79-80 Mr '70

EDGELL, Mark Allen
Draft board weighs the question of sincerity. M. Mok. il pors Life 69:16D-23 Jl 24 '70 *

EDGERTON, Robert B.
Rules of drunkenness. il Time 95:54 Je 8 '70 *

EDGERTON, William H.
Building costs. See issues of Architectural record

EDGINGTON, J. A. and Blair, I. M.
Luminescence and thermoluminescence induced by bombardment with protons of 159 million electron volts. bibliog il Science 167:715-17 Ja 30 '70

EDIBLE greens. See Greens, Edible

EDIBLE oils and fats. See Oils and fats, Edible

EDIBLE plants. See Plants, Edible

EDINBURGH

Description

Traveler's choice. E. Antrobus. Travel 134: 10 Ag '70

Music

Report:
Presentation of five Czech operas by the Prague national theater. F. Stevenson. il Opera N 35:28-9 O 31 '70

EDINBURGH festival of music and drama. See International festival of music and drama, Edinburgh

EDISON, Thomas Alva

His diary reveals an unsuspected Mr Edison. il por Am Heritage 22:68-74 D '70

about

Question of semantics; invention of radio. F. Shunaman. il por Pop Electr 33:27-30 O '70 *

Thomas Edison: pioneer of applied chemistry. B. M. Vanderbilt. il pors Chem 43:8-12 S '70 *

EDISON effect. See Thermionic emission

EDITING. See Editors and editing

EDITING amateur moving pictures. See Moving pictures, Amateur—Editing

EDITING moving pictures. See Moving pictures—Editing

EDITIONS stock. See Publishers and publishing—France

EDITORIALS

Act of usurpation; New Yorker editorial on Cambodia. Time 95:57+ My 25 '70

EDITORS and editing

As-told-to article. J. Stocker. il Writers Digest 50:20-2 Ap '70

Be good editors by being good publishers; excerpts from address, September 18, 1970. M. Jeanneret. il Pub W 198:24-6 O 18 '70

Editing doesn't stop with the manuscript. R. H. Smith. Pub W 197:38 My 4 '70

Editor and society; highlights from panel discussions. Pub W 198:44-6 Jl 27 '70

Journal editor's job; excerpts from address. M. Rosenblum. Pub W 198:47 Jl 27 '70

New Field & stream editors. il Field & S 75: 16+ Je '70

U.S. journal: Nampa, Idaho; O. Campbell, negative and controversial editor of the Idaho free press. C. Trillin. New Yorker 46:104+ O 31 '70

Anecdotes, facetiae, satire, etc.

Watch for these birds. R. Jenkins. il Writers Digest 50:52-3 Je '70

EDMISTON, Susan

Portrait of Anaïs Nin. por Mlle 71:134-5+ O '70

EDMONDS, Helen Grey

Establishing a framework for youth participation in the international community; statement, October 2, 1970. Dept State Bul 63: 588-96 N 9 '70

EDMONDSON, W. T.

Phosphorus, nitrogen and algae in Lake Washington after diversion of sewage. bibliog il Science 169:690-1 Ag 14 '70

EDMUND scientific company

One of photography's best sellers, and it's only a catalog. N. Goldberg. il Pop Phot 67: 76-7+ Jl '70

EDMUNDS, Frances R.

Adaptive use of Charleton buildings in historic preservation. il Antiques 97:590-5 Ap '70

Living with antiques in Charleston. il Antiques 97:579-83 Ap '70

EDMUNDS, Leland N. jr. See Jarrett, R. M. jt. auth.

EDSON, Lee

$C_{21} H_{22} N O_5$: a primer for parents and children. il N Y Times Mag p92-3+ My 24 '70

EDSON, Russell

Short visits with five writers and one friend. B. Midwood. il pors Esquire 74:150-3 N '70 *

EDUCATION

Radical school reform, ed. by B. Gross and R. Gross. Review
Commentary bibliog f 49:45-58 Je '70. S. McCracken; Discussion. 50:4+ Ag '70

Some thoughts on education by a thoughtful architect. S. P. Harkness. Arch Rec 148:10 D '70

See also
Agricultural education
Audio-visual instruction
Business and education

Business education
Coeducation
College education
Communication in education
Communications satellites—Educational use
Community education
Correspondence schools and courses
Educational sociology
Education of women
Foreign study
Illiteracy
Institute of international education
International education
Knowledge
Learning, Psychology of
Libraries
Memory
Motivation (education)
Nature study
Right to read program
Role playing
Self culture
Special classes and special schools
Teachers
Teaching
Textbooks
Volunteer workers in education
also headings beginning Educational; School; *also* subhead Education under various subjects, e.g. Negroes—Education; *also* Medical education; Vocational education; and similar headings

Aims and objectives

Christian teacher. P. Cousins. Chr Today 15: 16-18 O 9 '70

Crisis of confidence, and beyond. J. Cass. Sat R 53:61-2 S 19 '70

Education and the loss of self-esteem. C. A. Tesconi, jr. bibliog f Sch & Soc 98:102-6 F '70

Education for the 70's. W. C. Young. Clear House 44:387-90 Mr '70

Education; the future of human relations; address, November 13, 1969. D. Bakan. bibliog f Vital Speeches 36:219-24 Ja 15 '70

Letter to a teacher, by the schoolboys of Barbiana. Review
New Repub 163:25-6 Jl 18 '70. W. O'Neil

Making of a radical teacher. J. Fulcher. Engl J 59:384-6 Mr '70

Negativism and the hand that feeds us. J. M. Hansen. Clear House 45:204-6 D '70

On the irrelevance of relevance. P. H. Wagschal. Ed Digest 35:22-3 Ja '70

Preparing youth for a world of unprecedented complexity; excerpt from address, March 7, 1970. M. Collins. Dept State Bul 62:425-6 Mr 30 '70

Renaissance '70. K. D. Jenkins. bibliog f Clear House 44:338-42 F '70

Small piece of sky. P. B. Price. PTA Mag 64: 11 My '70

Space supremacy and the schools. W. W. Brickman. Sch & Soc 98:329 O '70

Teaching the young to love. J. R. Frymier. Ed Digest 35:9-12 F '70

Theory of the curriculum in composition: goals and writing assignments. R. L. Larson. Engl J 59:393-404+ Mr '70

What do they want? is school losing its meaning for students? N. P. Atkins. Ed Digest 35:19-21 My '70

What I want for my children. N. Hentoff. il Parents Mag 45:52-3+ S '70

Who needs schools? need for independent schools. J. H. Fischer. il Sat R 53:78-9+ S 19 '70

Why we need new schooling. J. Holt. Look 34:52 Ja 13 '70
See also
College education—Aims and objectives
Educational sociology

Anecdotes, facetiae, satire, etc.

It's time to tear down the old hotel. R. D. Wack. Clear House 44:504-5 Ap '70

Bibliography

Book reviews. See issues of Clearing house

Books for educators; U.S. and foreign. W. W. Brickman. Sch & Soc 98:309-17 Sum '70

New books. See issues of Saturday review

New educational materials. See issues of Education digest

Outstanding education books of 1968-69. Todays Ed 59:60-3 Mr '70

Curricula

See Courses of study

Economic aspects

Cost, and price, of education. G. C. Keller. Nation 210:242-4 Mr 2 '70

EDUCATION—Economic aspects—*Continued*
Go back to school, but in the right state. Trans-Action 7:12 F '70
See also
Colleges and universities—Finance

Evaluation

Evaluation: one state's approach. T. A. Olson and L. Marvin. Am Ed 6:33 My '70
Guidelines for school evaluation. J. Dal Santo. bibliog f Clear House 45:181-5 N '70
National assessment: a history and sociology; excerpt from New models for American education; ed. by J. Guthrie. R. W. Tyler. bibliog Sch & Soc 98:471-7 D '70
Program auditor: new breed on the education scene. W. S. Kruger. Am Ed 6:36 Mr '70
See also
National assessment of educational progress
Performance contracts (education)

Experimental methods

See Education, Experimental

Federal aid

Acceptable compromise: health and education bill. New Repub 162:11 Mr 14 '70
Aid for the rich; impacted aid. il Newsweek 75:55 F 9 '70
Another idea: teaching creative writing under government grants. Writers Digest 50:30+ O '70
Battle over a veto. Sr Schol 96:14 F 16 '70
Better way to spend the education dollar. il U S News 68:46 Mr 16 '70
Children as hostages? question of aid to impacted districts. Time 95:23 Ap 13 '70
Comparability. R. L. Fairley. Am Ed 6:20 O '70
Congress wins education appropriation battle. S. Wagner. Pub W 198:247 Ag 31 '70
Delayed impact: President Nixon's message on education reform. Newsweek 75:113-14 Mr 16 '70
Education: a show of power over funds for innovation; ESEA money. R. Karp. Science 167:1709-11 Mr 27 '70
Education funds and Title I of ESEA. C. B. Grannis. Pub W 197:42 Ja 12 '70
Education reform stirs. Nat R 22:412 Ap 21 '70
Education vouchers. P. A. Janssen. Am Ed 6:9-11 D '70
Education vouchers. C. Jencks. New Repub 163:19-21 Jl 4 '70
Elementary and secondary education amendments of 1969. J. S. Frohlicher. Am Ed 6:7-9 Jl '70
Federal funds. See issues of American education
Follow-up: bill to continue Elementary and secondary education act (ESEA) W. D. Boutwell. PTA Mag 64:11 Je '70
Funds for school aid, a veto and then... il U S News 68:4 F 9 '70
Impacted aid. W. D. Boutwell. PTA Mag 64:13 Mr '70
Impacted ghetto. D. Blackburn. Nation 210:517 My 4 '70
Inflation showdown over school funds. il U S News 68:6 F 2 '70
Jencks tuition voucher plan. America 122:644-5 Je 20 '70
Latest in Congress on mixed schools. U S News 68:88 Ap 20 '70
Let's fence this sacred cow; aid to federally impacted areas. K. O. Gilmore. Read Digest 97:76-80 S '70
More than defense. Sci N 97:146-7 F 7 '70
NEA charges Pres. Nixon reneged on campaign pledge to nation's teachers. Sch & Soc 98:199 Ap '70
Nixon reviews mandatory education funds. Library J 95:3583 O 15 '70
No magic in vouchers. Nation 210:773 Je 29 '70
Pay-as-you-go schooling; voucher plan. il Newsweek 76:49 Ag 10 '70
Poor education: Urban education task force report. New Repub 162:9-10 Mr 21 '70
Questions hang over U.S. education programs. S. Wagner. Pub W 197:55-6 Mr 9 '70
School message: learn to teach. il Time 95:11 Mr 16 '70
Schools make front-page news. W. D. Boutwell. PTA Mag 64:29-30 My '70
Senate subcommittee begins on education legislation. S. Wagner. Pub W 197:36-7 My 25 '70
U.S. school programs headed for three-year extensions. S. Wagner. Pub W 197:38 Mr 30 '70
USOE to investigate misuse of Title I funds. Sr Schol 95:Schol Teach 1-2 Ja 12 '70
Vindication in Congress. R. H. Smith. Pub W 198:39 S 7 '70
Voucher plan; NEA position. Todays Ed 59:80 N '70

Washington report:
Education lobby. J. Lloyd. Sr Schol 95:School Teach 7 D 8 '69
Education wins in the House. J. Lloyd. Sr Schol 95:Schol Teach 2+ S 22 '69
Washington retreating on education. J. Lloyd. Sr Schol 95:Schol Teach 2 N 10 '69
Where can one obtain information about the various federally aided programs in education? W. D. Boutwell. PTA Mag 65:32 O '70
White House plan for education: changes, cutbacks. il U S News 68:44-6 Ja 26 '70
See also
Catholic colleges and universities—Federal aid
Catholic schools—Federal aid
Church schools—Federal aid
College libraries—Federal aid
Colleges and universities—Federal aid
Libraries—Federal aid
Libraries, Institution—Federal aid
Private schools—Federal aid
Project Head start
Right to read program
School libraries—Federal aid
School libraries and state
Student aid
Student loans
Vocational education—Federal aid

Finance

See School finance

History

1970 as a centennial year in the history of education. F. Parker. Sch & Soc 98:110-12 F '70
See also
Education—United States—History

International aspects

Tercentenary of Comenius' death: education for world peace. W. W. Brickman; J. D. Pope; L. Kurdybacha. bibliog il Sch & Soc 98:436-46 N '70
See also
International education

International cooperation

See also
Students, Interchange of

Laws

See School laws and legislation

Objectives

See Education—Aims and objectives

Organization by years

Learning and maturation in middle school age youth. H. Thornburg. bibliog Clear House 45:150-5 N '70
Middle school as one psychologist sees it. W. W. Wattenberg. Ed Digest 35:26-9 Mr '70
Middle school muddle. J. Elkind. Clear House 44:400 Mr '70
Middle school v. junior high school. R. L. Hamm. Clear House 44:267 Ja '70
School designed for kids; Beloit-Turner middle school, Wis. J. Cass. il Sat R 53:65-7+ Mr 21 '70
What about the middle school? M. T. Wilson; S. H. Popper. Ed Digest 35:16-18 Ja '70

Philosophy

Michael John Demiashkevich: the way of an essentialist. G. Chambers. bibliog f Sch & Soc 98:108-10 F '70
What we owe children, by C. Gattegno. Review
New Repub 163:23-5 S 5 '70. P. Caws
William James and the octopus of higher education. J. Lindeman. por Sch & Soc 98:365-7 O '70
Youth in rebellion, why? interview. W. Glasser. il por U S News 68:42-6 Ap 27 '70
See also
Progressive education

Research

See Educational research

Statistics

Magnitude of the American educational establishment, 1960-1970. Sat R 53:67 S 19 '70
Statistic of the month. See issues of American education
Statistical look at education in the United States. W. V. Grant. il Am Ed 6:13-15 O '70
See also
Colleges and universities—Attendance
Junior colleges—Attendance
School attendance

EDUCATION—*Continued*

Study and teaching
See also
Teachers—Education

Africa, East
See also
Colleges and universities—Africa, East

Alaska
See also
Ketchikan, Alaska—Education

Arab states
Educational programs in Arab states. Sch &
Soc 98:306 Sum '70
Plight of the Palestine refugee schools. il
UNESCO Courier 23:15-17 O '70

Argentina
See also
Colleges and universities—Argentina

Arkansas
See also
Little Rock, Ark.—Education
Texarkana, Ark. and Tex.—Education

Brazil
See also
Vocational education—Brazil

California
California's evolution war: should Genesis get
equal time? R. Larsen. Chr Cent 87:251-3 F
25 '70
Juan's right to read; Whisman regional read-
ing/learning clinic. L. Goodman. il Am Ed
6:3-6 Jl '70
Probing Project PLAN (Program for learn-
ing in accordance with needs) L. A. Gut-
kind. il School Teach Jr/Sr High p20-3 O
5 '70
See also
Berkeley, Calif.—Education
California—Education, Department of
Colleges and universities—California
Los Angeles—Education
Sacramento, Calif.—Education
Santa Monica, Calif.—Education
South Lake Tahoe, Calif.—Education

China
History
Modern educational development in free China
since 1898. W. C. Lee. bibliog Sch & Soc
98:416-21 N '70

China (People's Republic)
China; education revolution. H. Yu. Chr Cent
87:1170 S 30 '70
China; experiments in education. H. Yu.
Chr Cent 87:1026 Ag 26 '70
Education in mainland China. H. T. Chu.
Cur Hist 59:165-9+ S '70

Colombia
See also
Colleges and universities—Colombia

Colorado
See also
Denver—Education

Connecticut
See also
Bridgeport, Conn.—Education
West Hartford, Conn.—Education

Cuba
Cuba's schools, ten years later. M. Leiner.
il Sat R 53:59-61+ O 17 '70
Schools, si; education, no. J. Bishop. Commonweal 93:17-20 O 2 '70

District of Columbia
See also
Washington, D.C.—Education

Egypt
See also
Colleges and universities—Egypt

England
See Education—Great Britain

Florida
Reading guidance effects on children; project
in an elementary school. J. A. McCrossan.
Am Lib 1:88 Ja '70
See also
Bartow, Fla.—Education
Broward County, Fla.—Education
Manatee County, Fla.—Education

France
See also
Colleges and universities—France

Georgia
PECE corps: career exploration. M. K.
Murphy. il School Teach Jr/Sr High p24-5
S 21 '70
SUCCESS in early counseling; Cobb County
Project SUCCESS for elementary school
students. M. K. Murphy. il Am Ed 6:3-7
Mr '70
See also
Augusta, Ga.—Education

Germany (Federal Republic)
West Germany: educational reform is the
major domestic issue. D. S. Greenberg. Science 167:1108-10 F 20 '70

Great Britain
British primary school. A. Cook and H. Mack.
Ed Digest 35:36-8 F '70
Little bit of chaos: use of the British infant
school. Open classroom approach in the
U.S. B. Gross and R. Gross. il Sat R 53:71-
3+ My 16 '70
Philosophy underlying the British primary
school: excerpts from Teaching in the Brit-
ish primary school. E. Moodhouse. Sch &
Soc 98:35-40+ Ja '70
Teaching English in the United Kingdom: a
comparative study, by J. Squire and R.
Applebee. Review
Engl J 59:291-5 F '70. S. Judy
See also
Public schools (endowed)—England

History
Battles for the best: some educational aspects of the welfare-warfare state in England; excerpts from History and education, ed. by P. Nash. W. H. G. Armytage.
bibliog Sch & Soc 98:229-37 Ap '70

Illinois
Evaluation: one state's approach. T. A. Ol-
son and L. Marvin. Am Ed 6:33 My '70
See also
Chicago—Education

India
Second chance for dropouts. E. Rice. Sch &
Soc 98:423-4 N '70

Indiana
See also
Gary, Ind.—Education
Indianapolis—Education

Iran
New idea in an ancient land; national
campaign against illiteracy. W. G. Carr.
il Todays Ed 59:28-9 N '70

Israel
Israel: research and education booming in
a nation at war. D. S. Greenberg. il Science 168:446-51 Ap 24 '70

Ivory Coast
Audio-visual education in Ivory Coast. P.
Thierry. il Sch & Soc 98:424-6 N '70

Japan
See also
Colleges and universities—Japan

Kansas
See also
Lawrence, Kan.—Education

Kentucky
Why must Lincoln die? experimental school
being killed. J. Star. il Look 34:64-8 Ag 11
'70

Latin America
Education revolution in Latin America. M.
Soler Roca. il UNESCO Courier 23:24-31
N '70
Revolution and education in Latin America.
I. Illich; M. Leiner; F. Hausssman. il Sat
R 53:56-63+ O 17 '70
Schools, si; education, no. J. Bishop. Com-
conweal 93:17-20 O 2 '70

Louisiana
Louisiana desegregation, and Catholic
schools. F. Guillory. il America 123:119-21
S 5 '70

Maryland
High school students and the campaign; elections '70. il Sr Schol 19:15 O 26 '70

Massachusetts
See also
Attleboro, Mass.—Education
Boston—Education

EDUCATION—*Continued*

Michigan

School defeat in Michigan; Proposal C. America 123:390 N 14 '70
See also
Detroit—Education

Minnesota

Learning and liking it; Lincoln elementary school in Staples. C. Watson. il Am Ed 6: 18:22 My '70
See also
Minneapolis—Education

Mississippi

Court rules out tax exemption for Mississippi's segregated academies. Chr Cent 87:103 Ja 28 '70
Crisis in Southern schools; interview. J. B. Williams. il por(p39) U S News 68:41 F 16 '70
Desegregation blocks cited in NEA Mississippi report. Library J 95:1537+ Ap 15 '70; Reply. E. T. McDonald. 95:2949 S 15 '70
Instant schools; segregationists open private, all-white schools. il Newsweek 75:59 Ja 26 '70
Integration in Mississippi. America 122:91 Ja 31 '70
School desegregation problems: are federal courts educators? address. January 3, 1970. J. B. Williams. Vital Speeches 36:306-9 Mr 1 '70
Talent lies hidden in the Delta. J. H. Mulligan. il Am Ed 6:13-16 My '70
See also
Piney Woods country life school
Yazoo City, Miss.—Education

Missouri

Independent study in five Missouri high schools. G. Beltz and D. A. Kohn Clear House 44:334-7 F '70
See also
St Louis County, Mo.—Education

Nevada

See also
Las Vegas, Nev.—Education

New England

John Dewey is alive and well in New England; free schools. R. H. De Lone and S. T. De Lone. il Sat R 53:69-71+ N 21 '70

New Hampshire

Ready, set, go! School readiness project. D. K. Jaffe. il Am Ed 6:9-12 Ag '70
Wide open for learning; Project SOLVE; schools without walls. R. C. Wing and P. H. Mack. il Am Ed 6:13-15 N '70

New Jersey

See also
Union County, N.J.—Education

New York (state)

See also
Rochester, N.Y.—Education

North Carolina

See also
Lexington, N.C.—Education

North Dakota

They'll never stop learning; excitement in North Dakota. A. Silberman. Read Digest 97:209-10+ Jl '70

Ohio

Little help from my friends; tutoring in Gambier elementary schools by students from Kenyon college. D. R. Maxey. il Look 34:22-4 Je 16 '70
See also
Dayton, Ohio—Education

Oregon

Student for a day; Michigan ave. school. Coos Bay. E. Moffitt. Schol Teach Jr/Sr High p 10-11 D 7 '70
See also
Milwaukie, Ore.—Education
Portland, Ore.—Education
Springfield, Ore.—Education

Pennsylvania

Social class, college, and a dream deferred; College and career night at Woodrow Wilson high school, Bristol Township, Pa. T. J. Cottle. il Sat R 53:60-1+ Ja 24 '70
See also
Abington, Pa.—Education
Mount Lebanon, Pa.—Education

Peru

See also
Indians of South America—Education

Polynesia

Teacher's guide to Polynesia. M. Mann. il Schol Teach Sec Teach Sup p 16-17+ Mr 9 '70

Puerto Rico

They put other associations to shame! Puerto Rico teachers association welfare services. il Todays Ed 59:57-9 O '70
See also
Puerto Rico. University

Rhode Island

125 years of service to Rhode Island; Rhode Island education association. S. J. Kapstein. Todays Ed 59:69 S '70

Russia

See also
Colleges and universities—Russia

History

Education, key to social transformation; V. Lenin's views. V. Stoletov. il UNESCO Courier 23:12-15 Jl '70
Lenin and cultural rights of minorities. L. A. Posti. il UNESCO Courier 23:16-21 Jl '70

Somalia

Somalia's new education system. Sch & Soc 98:465+ D '70

South Africa

See also
Colleges and universities—South Africa

South America

See Education—Latin America

South Carolina

See also
Greenville, S.C.—Education

Southern states

Against the malingerers. il Time 96:12 Jl 20 '70
Back to segregation, by order of the courts. J. J. Kilpatrick. il Nat R 22:611-26 Je 16 '70
Bad side of integration. il Time 96:32 Jl 13 '70
Black leader's idea for South's schools; interview. R. Innis. il por U S News 68:30-1 Mr 2 '70
Church schools in the South. America 122:121 F 7 '70
Crisis in Southern schools; six governors speak out; with interviews. il U S News 68: 38-44 F 16 '70
Desegregation: how much further? il Time 96:55-6 O 26 '70
Desegregation 1970; government moves against recalcitrant southern school districts. Newsweek 76:67-8 Jl 27 '70
Desegregation: the South is different. P. M. Rilling. New Repub 162:17-19 My 16 '70
Desegregation: the South's tense truce. il Time 96:39-40 S 14 '70
Do it; Justice department and Internal revenue service move against segregated schools. Newsweek 76:21 Jl 20 '70
Governors against the law; southern governors attempt to block desegregation. il Time 95:9-10 F 2 '70
How desegregation is working. J. B. Cumming, jr. il Newsweek 76:105-7 D 21 '70
Integrated, but unequal; report by civil rights groups. Time 97:27 Ja 4 '71
Mixmasters. il por Time 96:20 Jl 6 '70
Nearing normal. Newsweek 76:80 S 21 '70
New resistance to mixed schools. U S News 68:6-7 F 2 '70
Nixon watch: chicken, southern fried. J. Osborne. New Repub 162:13-14 F 21 '70
Official policy now on South's schools. il U S News 68:33 Ap 20 '70
Peaceful and orderly. il Newsweek 76:121 S 14 '70
Public school turnovers in the South. J. Demuth. il America 123:377-9 N 7 '70
School desegregation: the final breakthrough? what is happening in the South. il U S News 69:15-16 S 14 '70
Second thoughts? il Newsweek 76:26+ O 26 '70
Segregation academies: the old South tries again. R. Cleghorn. il Sat R 53:76-7+ My 16 '70
TRB from Washington: evasion of desegregation. New Repub 163:6 Jl 18 '70
Tide turning for the South? il U S News 68:29 Mr 2 '70
Unquiet schools; segregation disputes. New Repub 163:8 O 3 '70
See also
Negroes—Education
Public schools—Desegregation

EDUCATION—*Continued*

Taiwan

Modern educational development in free China since 1898. W. C. Lee. bibliog Sch & Soc 98:416-21 N '70

Tennessee

See also
Memphis, Tenn.—Education

Texas

See also
Dallas—Education
San Antonio, Tex.—Education
Texarkana, Ark. and Tex.—Education

United States

Annual report on education. W. D. Boutwell. PTA Mag 64:21-2 F '70
Are your sensitivities trained? R. Kirk. Nat R 22:1352 D 15 '70
Better way to spend the education dollar. il U S News 68:46 Mr 16 '70
Crisis in the classroom, by C. E. Silberman. Review
  America 123:407-9 N 14 '70. R. E. Forbes
  Life 69:12 O 30 '70. B. DeMott
  Look 34:16 D 1 '70. P. S. Prescott
  Newsweek 76:62+ O 26 '70. J. K. Footlick
  PTA Mag 65:15 N '70. P. B. Price
  Sat R 53:66-8 O 17 '70. F. G. Jennings
Delayed impact: President Nixon's message on education reform. Newsweek 75:113-14 Mr 16 '70
Education in America. P. Woodring and others. See issues of Saturday review
Educational developments in 1969. W. W. Brickman. Sch & Soc 98:8-9 Ja '70
Educational obsolescence. B. Glass. Science 170:1041 D 4 '70
Education's budget may be lean but it can still buy reforms. Sr Schol 96:Schol Teach 1-2 Ap 13 '70
Growing expectations for American education. R. F. Campbell and D. H. Layton. Ed Digest 35:1-4 Ja '70
Happenings in education. W. D. Boutwell. See issues of PTA magazine
Is America really sick? D. J. Boorstin. Read Digest 97:92-4 S '70
Joyless, mindless schools; comparing schools in England and United States. il Time 96: 57-8 N 2 '70
Middletown: 1970. M. L. Berger. Clear House 45:89-91 O '70
Murder in the schoolroom; excerpts from Crisis in the classroom. C. E. Silberman. il Atlan 225:82-94+ Je; 226:83-97 Jl; 85-9+ Ag '70; Discussion. 226:10+ O '70
Negativism and the hand that feeds us. J. M. Hansen. Clear House 45:204-6 D '70
New school year. Sr Schol 95:Schol Teach 1-2 O 13 '69
News and trends. See issues of Today's education
On seeing through the academic looking glass. W. Goldstein. Clear House 45:131-4 N '70
Prospects for the future of American education; excerpts from Foundations of American education. W. B. Ragan and G. Henderson. bibliog Sch & Soc 98:183-9 Mr '70
Public views its schools; survey sponsored by CFK, ltd. Sat R 53:64 O 17 '70
Retrospect and prospect. P. Woodring. Sat R 53:66 S 19 '70
School integration and the American character. R. Clark. il Parents Mag 46:37-9+ Ja '71
School message: learn to teach. il Time 95: 11 Mr 16 '70
Schools in the 1990's; predictions of K. A. Ryan. il por Sch & Soc 98:454+ D '70
Schools make news. See issues of Saturday review
Sensitivity and sensuality. R. Kirk. Nat R 23:36 Ja 12 '71
The seventies: a time for giant steps; excerpts from Curricula for the seventies. J. L. Frost and G. T. Rowland. Ed Digest 35:1-4 F '70
Seventies; restructuring the educational system; address, November 24, 1970. M. A. Rapp. Vital Speeches 37:173-7 Ja 1 '71
Teacher numbers game. D. Davies. Am Ed 6:7-8 O '70
Troubles pile up as schools open. il U S News 69:17-18 S 14 '70
William James and the octopus of higher education. J. Lindeman. por Sch & Soc 98:365-7 O '70
With education in Washington. **See issues** of Education digest

Women in league for better education. C. Aaron. Am Ed 6:32-3 Mr '70
See also
Adult education
American education week
American federation of teachers
Colleges and universities—United States
Community schools
Education—Southern states
Education—Statistics
Education and democracy
Education and state
Education of women—United States
Educational innovations
Equilization, Educational
Indians of North America—Education
Junior colleges
Labor and laboring classes—Education
National education association
Negroes—Education
Private schools
Public schools—United States
Right to read program
Rural schools—United States
School laws and legislation—United States
Schools—United States
United States. Education, Office of
Vocational education
  also subhead Education under names of cities, e.g. Denver—Education

History

Public schools: the myth of the melting pot; excerpt from Cobweb attitudes: essays in American education and culture. C. Greer. Ed Digest 35:1-4 Mr '70
Twentieth century books influencing American education. R. L. McCaul. Ed Digest 36:28-31 S '70

Utah

See also
Salt Lake City—Education

Vermont

Project ASPIRE: help for hopeless kids; Burlington high school program. D. Divoky. il Schol Teach Sec Teach Sup p20-2 F 2 '70
Young ideas in an old state; ASPIRE program; BEAM and Shaker Mountain schools in Burlington. D. Divoky. il Sat R 53:62+ Ap 18 '70
See also
Burlington, Vt.—Education

Virginia

Southern governor dramatizes the push for school integration; Governor Holton of Virginia. il por U S News 69:52 S 14 '70
See also
Colleges and universities—Virginia
Norfolk, Va.—Education
Prince Edward County, Va.—Education
Richmond, Va.—Education

Wisconsin

Away with tradition. D. Behrendt. il Am Ed 6:18-22 Ja '70
Something different in in-service education: Educational telephone network workshop. G. Hartung and R. Gelman. il Todays Ed 59:24-5 My '70
See also
Beloit, Wis.—Education
Milwaukee—Education

EDUCATION, Adult. See Adult education

EDUCATION, Agricultural. See Agricultural education

EDUCATION, Art. See Art education

EDUCATION, Boards of. See School boards

EDUCATION, Business. See Business education

EDUCATION, College. See College education

EDUCATION, Commissioner of. See United States—Education, Office of

EDUCATION, Comparative
Joyless, mindless schools; comparing schools in England and United States. il Time 96: 57-8 N 2 '70
Parallels of Negro and women's education. B. W. Newell. Sch & Soc 98:357-9 O '70
Two worlds of childhood: U.S. and U.S.S.R. by U. Bronfenbrenner. Review
  Sat R 53:74-5 Ap 18 '70. J. H. Fischer

EDUCATION, Consumer. See Consumer education

EDUCATION, Cooperative
All in a day's work-study. il Am Ed 6:12-14 Ja '70
Education and industry: troubled partnership. E. Carlson. il Sat R 53:45-7+ Ag 15 '70
For tomorrow's students, multiple choices. Fortune 82:147-8+ N '70

EDUCATION, Cooperative—*Continued*
On the house; work-school program for drop-outs: Rochester jobs inc. F. Trippett. il Look 34:66-8 D 29 '70
Support for collegiate cooperative education program. Sch & Soc 98:398 N '70
Westledge, an exciting new concept in education; indoor-outdoor, work study program. K. Branan. il Parents Mag 45:64-5+ F '70
EDUCATION, Cost of. See Education—Economic aspects
EDUCATION, Criminological. See Criminological education
EDUCATION, Elementary
Adapting British school reforms to U.S. needs. Sch & Soc 98:16-17 Ja '70
After years of climb: a drop in grade-school enrollment. il U S News 69:18 S 14 '70
British primary school. A. Clark and H. Mack. Ed Digest 35:36-8 F '70
Education à la carte. R. E. Migneault. Todays Ed 59:59 D '70
Little bit of chaos: use of the British infant school Open classroom approach in the U.S. B. Gross and R. Gross. il Sat R 53:71-3+ My 16 '70
Murder in the schoolroom; informal education; excerpts from Crisis in the classroom. C. E. Silberman. il Atlan 226:83-97 Jl '70
Self-selection classroom. Z. E. Billings. il Todays Ed 59:14-16 O '70
SUCCESS in early counseling; Cobb County, Ga, Project SUCCESS for elementary school students. M. K. Murphy. il Am Ed 6:3-7 Mr '70
Teaching the young to love. J. R. Frymier. Ed Digest 35:9-12 F '70
They'll never stop learning; excitement in North Dakota. A. Silberman. Read Digest 97:209-10+ Jl '70
We love you, Mr Tarbox; Rockford, Ill.'s Teacher development center and demonstration school. il Life 68:76-9 Ap 24 '70
Who needs schools? need for independent schools. J. H. Fischer. il Sat R 53:78-9+ S 19 '70
See also
Education of children
Montessori method of education
Readiness for school
School children
Schools, Experimental
EDUCATION, Evaluation of. See Education—Evaluation
EDUCATION, Experimental
Away with tradition; multiunit schools in Wisconsin. D. Behrendt. il Am Ed 6:18-22 Ja '70
Beyond the classroom: life experiences in the field. G. L. Williams. Clear House 45:81-5 O '70
Bold new directions for U.S. high schools. A. Silberman. Read Digest 97:87-91 Ag '70
Children who hate school. N. Hentoff. il Parents Mag 45:60-1+ F '70
City is our classroom; Philadelphia's Parkway program. C. H. Harrison. il Schol Teach Sec Teach Sup p 12-13 D 1 '69
Education without schools. M. O'Neill. Ed Digest 36:1-4 N '70
Experience is their textbook: East high school in Denver. il Life 68:32-7 My 29 '70
Experiment in democracy: the guided-choice curriculum; adaptation of address, June 1970. E. Hendryson. PTA Mag 65:22-4 N '70
Jencks's education plan: sure to backfire; national education voucher plan. C. Rogers. Chr Cent 87:1176 O 7 '70; Discussion. 87:1460 D 2 '70
Little bit of chaos: use of the British infant school Open classroom approach in the U.S. B. Gross and R. Gross. il Sat R 53:71-3+ My 16 '70
Murder in the schoolroom; informal education; excerpts from Crisis in the classroom. C. E. Silberman. il Atlan 226:83-97 Jl; 85-9+ Ag '70
Open-plan schools. D. C. Anderson. Ed Digest 36:8-10 N '70
PTA opposes OEO voucher system. PTA Mag 65:30-1 N '70
Probing Project PLAN (Program for learning in accordance with needs) in California. L. A. Gutkind il Schol Teach Jr/Sr High p20-3 O 5 '70
Project ASPIRE: help for hopeless kids. D. Divoky. il Schol Teach Sec Teach Sup p20-2 F 2 '70
Self-selection classroom. Z. W. Billings. il Todays Ed 59:14-16 O '70
Summerhill in Ithaca: East Hill elementary school. N Y il Newsweek. 75:65 F 23 '70
They'll never stop learning; excitement in North Dakota. A. Silberman. Read Digest 97:209-10+ Jl '70

We love you, Mr Tarbox; Rockford, Ill.'s Teacher development center and demonstration school. il Life 68:76-9 Ap 24 '70
When teachers do their thing, it's called DS or is it? differentiated staffing. K. Branan. il Schol Teach Jr/Sr High p 10-12+ O 5 '70
Wide open for learning; Project SOLVE; schools without walls in New Hampshire. R. C. Wing and P. H. Mack. il Am Ed 6:13-15 N '70
Young ideas in an old state; ASPIRE program; BEAM and Shaker Mountain schools in Burlington, Vt. D. Divoky. il Sat R 53:62+ Ap 18 '70
See also
College education, Experimental
Educational innovations
Goddard college, Plainsfield, Vt.
Philadelphia—Education
Progressive education
Schools, Experimental
EDUCATION, Higher. See College education; Colleges and universities
EDUCATION, Individual. See Individual instruction
EDUCATION, International. See International education
EDUCATION, Liberal. See Liberal education
EDUCATION, Medical. See Medical education
EDUCATION, Military. See Military education
EDUCATION, Moral. See Moral education
EDUCATION, Nautical. See Nautical education
EDUCATION, Office of. See United States—Education, Office of
EDUCATION, Preschool. See Preschool children—Education
EDUCATION, Primary. See Education, Elementary
EDUCATION, Professional. See Professional education
EDUCATION, Progressive. See Progressive education
EDUCATION, Religious. See Religious education
EDUCATION, Secondary
Competance for all as the goal for secondary education; excerpts from address. J. E. Allen, jr. Ed Digest 36:24-7 S '70
High school 1980, ed. by A. C. Eurich. Review
Engl J 59:1164-70 N '70. G. H. Henry
Murder in the schoolroom; excerpts from Crisis in the classroom. C. E. Silberman. il Atlan 226:85-9+ Ag '70
Secondary school as a residual agency. J. R. Dettre. bibliog f Clear House 44:515-18 My '70
Social class, college, and a dream deferred; College and career night at Woodrow Wilson high school, Bristol Township, Pa. T. J. Cottle. il Sat R 53:60-1+ Ja 24 '70
Who needs schools? need for independent schools. J. H. Fischer. il Sat R 53:78-9+ S 19 '70
See also
High schools
Junior high schools
Private schools
EDUCATION, Social. See Social education
EDUCATION, State departments of
See also
Alabama—Education, Department of
EDUCATION, Technical. See Technical education
EDUCATION, Theological. See Theological education
EDUCATION, Urban
Leonard Covello and the community school. F. Cordasco. bibliog f por Sch & Soc 98:298-9 Sum '70
Nature of urban education. E. Kruszynski. Sch & Soc 98:166-8+ Mr '70
New teacher education program for inner-city schools. Sch & Soc 98:268 Sum '70
EDUCATION, Vocational. See Vocational education
EDUCATION and business. See Business and education
EDUCATION and communism. See Communism and education
EDUCATION and democracy
Establishing a framework for youth participation in the international community; statement, October 2, 1970. H. G. Edmonds. Dept State Bul 63:588-96 N 9 '70
EDUCATION and economic problems. See School and social and economic problems
EDUCATION and industry. See Business and education
EDUCATION and social problems. See School and social and economic problems
EDUCATION and society. See Educational sociology

EDUCATION and sociology. See Educational sociology

EDUCATION and state
Blaine, Bundy and balderdash. America 122: 34-5 Ja 17 '70
Education complex. il por Newsweek 76:72-3 S 7 '70
New York state aid to private higher education. Sch & Soc 98:13 Ja '70
Public aid to nonpublic schools in 1969. R. Cohen. Sch & Soc 98:300-1 Sum '70
State $ for schools; state salary supplements to teachers. J. Duerr. Commonweal 92:243-5 My 22 '70
States face suits over financing. Sr Schol 96:Schol Teach 1-2 Mr 23 '70
Survey of nonpublic school assistance. Sch & Soc 98:301-2 Sum '70
Teacher opinion poll: public funds for private schools? il Todays Ed 59:41 N '70
Whose responsibility are education costs? W. Boutwell. PTA Mag 64:10 Ja '70
See also
College education and state
Education—Federal aid
United States—Education. Office of

EDUCATION and state in Czechoslovakia
Purging the university. il Newsweek 76:65 Jl 13 '70

EDUCATION and state in France
How to feed revolution. il Newsweek 75:44 Mr 23 '70

EDUCATION and travel. See Student travel

EDUCATION associations. See Educational associations

EDUCATION commission of the states
See also
National assessment of educational progress

EDUCATION for citizenship. See Citizenship, Education for

EDUCATION market
Breaking the jam-up in ed biz. H. S. Resnik. Vogue 156:302 S 1 '70
Education and industry: troubled partnership. E. Carlson. il Sat R 53:45-7+ Ag 15 '70

EDUCATION of adults. See Adult education

EDUCATION of children
As the twig is bent the tree's inclined. L. Kraft. il Nation 210:181-3 F 16 '70
Child-care gap; Urie Bronfenbrenner's studies of U.S. and Russian systems. il Newsweek 75:108 Ap 20 '70
Concern for the next generation; US vs. USSR. D. Wolfle. Science 167:1441 Mr 13 '70
How smart do you want your child to be? J. V. Tunney. McCalls 98:62+ O '70
Jensen vs. Lewontin; a comment. E. Rabinowitch. Bul Atom Sci 26:25-6 My '70
Thinking is child's play. by E. Sharp. Review New Yorker 46:166-8+ Ap 11 '70. R. Coles
Two worlds of childhood: U.S. and U.S.S.R. by U. Bronfenbrenner. Review Sat R 53:74-5 Ap 18 '70. J. H. Fischer
See also
Camping—Educational aspects
Childrens literature
Childrens museums
Childrens reading
Education, Experimental
Moral education
Nature study
Psychology, Educational
Readiness for school
Sex instruction
Teachers

EDUCATION of Indian children. See Indians of North America—Education

EDUCATION of librarians. See Library schools and education

EDUCATION of Negroes. See Negroes—Education

EDUCATION of prisoners
How to rape, pillage, and plunder your way through college. Esquire 74:112 S '70

EDUCATION of the aged. See Aged—Education

EDUCATION of women
College is a family affair. il pors Ebony 25: 50-2+ Mr '70
Modest proposal for the educating of women. E. L. Cless; reply with rejoinder. V. Schuck and P. P. A. Smith. Am Scholar 39:514+ Sum '70
Mother goes back to school. M. L. Moore. il Parents Mag 45:44-5+ Ap '70
Parallels of Negro and women's education. B. W. Newell. Sch & Soc 98:357-9 O '70
Repentant dropouts; academic comeback of the mature woman. K. Byrne. il America 122:522-4 My 16 '70
Trends in educational attainment. Sch & Soc 98:32 Ja '70
See also
Coeducation

EDUCATION week. See American education week

EDUCATIONAL acceleration
New plan: college degree in three years. il U S News 69:64 D 7 '70

EDUCATIONAL achievements. See Student achievements

EDUCATIONAL administration. See School management and organization

EDUCATIONAL associations
Local association of the month:
Champaign and Urbana, Ill. education associations. J. Pittman and C. Thomasson. Todays Ed 59:80 O '70
Classroom teachers of Dallas. J. L. Howard. Todays Ed 59:41 D '70
Education association of Norfolk. R. R. Richards. Todays Ed 59:39 My '70
Experiment with joint committees; Polk education association, Bartow, Fla. J. G. Bouch. Todays Ed 59:66 S '70
From weak and fragmented to strong and unified. F. L. Sheahan, jr. Todays Ed 59:53 Ap '70
Milwaukee teachers' education association. J. R. Colter. Todays Ed 59:64 N '70
Scarsdale teachers institute. D. G. Breslow and V. Dempsey. Todays Ed 59:56-7 F '70
Wichita project: a progress report. L. Streiff. Todays Ed 59:14+ Mr '70
125 years of service to Rhode Island; Rhode Island education association. S. J. Kapstein. Todays Ed 59:69 S '70
Professional negotiation. R. Perry; K. L. Law; R. Van Delinder, jr. and R. H. St Germain. Todays Ed 59:33-40 F '70
They put other associations to shame! Puerto Rico teachers association welfare services. il Todays Ed 59:57-9 O '70
See also
American association of school administrators
Association for supervision and curriculum development
Michigan education association
National council of teachers of English
Ohio education association

EDUCATIONAL broadcasting corporation
NET+WNDT=EBC. Newsweek 76:89-90 Jl 13 '70

EDUCATIONAL change. See Educational innovations

EDUCATIONAL conferences
Can library and education groups meet jointly? report. M. V. Gaver. Wilson Lib Bul 44:921-2 My '70
Dates of the month. See issues of Education digest
Exeter conference: role of children's fiction in education. P. Heins. Horn Bk 46:447 O '70
Letter from Lagos; conferences of West African universities. J. B. Schuyler. il America 123:204-6 S 26 '70
Professional calendar (cont) Todays Ed 59:8+ Ja; 16 My; 10 S '70
School records: invasion of privacy? Russell Sage foundation guidelines. I. McMahan. il Parents Mag 45:64-5+ S '70; Same abr. Ed Digest 36:5-7 D '70

EDUCATIONAL cooperation
Break with tradition: parochial and public schools combine resources to serve their pupils. J. Hincken. Clear House 44:315-16 Ja '70
Hitching up the small schools districts; shared services. F. L. Heesacker. il Am Ed 6:18-21 Ap '70
Project Wingspread: space-age education; Chicago project. J. Sternberg. il Schol Teach Sec Teach Sup p6-8 D 1 '69; Same abr. Ed Digest 35:16-17 Ap '70
See also
Theological seminaries—Cooperation

EDUCATIONAL criticism
Crisis in the classroom, by C. E. Silberman. Review
Newsweek 76:62+ O 26 '70. J. K. Footlick
Sat R 53:66-8 O 17 '70. F. G. Jennings
What the kids think. il Newsweek 76:80 S 21 '70

EDUCATIONAL discrimination. See Discrimination in education

EDUCATIONAL endowments. See Endowments

EDUCATIONAL equalization. See Equalization, Educational

EDUCATIONAL exchanges
International student and faculty exchange. 1968-69. D. L. Guyer. il Sch & Soc 98:178-81 Mr '70
Report on educational and cultural exchange program sent to Congress. R. M. Nixon. Dept State Bul 63:120 Jl 27 '70

EDUCATIONAL exchanges—*Continued*
Union carbide's Marshall plan. V. Louviere.
il Nations Bsns 58:14 Je '70
See also
Foreign students in the United States
Students, Interchange of
EDUCATIONAL experiments. See Education,
Experimental
EDUCATIONAL films. See Moving pictures—
Documentary films; Moving pictures in
education
EDUCATIONAL foundations. See Foundations,
Charitable and educational
EDUCATIONAL games. See Games
EDUCATIONAL guidance
Counseling services, with study-discussion
program, by C. S. Smallenburg and H. S.
Smallenburg. W. E. Dugan and P. J. Mc-
Donough. bibliog il PTA Mag 64:16-18, 34-
5 My '70
Guidance at an early age. J. G. Shane and
H. G. Shane. Ed Digest 35:21-3 F '70
Trends in elementary school counseling. G.
T. Kowitz. Ed Digest 35:24-7 F '70
See also
College students—Adjustment
Personnel service in education
School children—Adjustment
Vocational guidance
EDUCATIONAL innovations
Bridge at generation gap; EPIC project. M. E.
Wade. il Am Ed 6:28-30 O '70
Bureaucracy and educational change. L. K.
Bishop. bibliog Clear House 44:305-9 Ja '70
Discipline in the innovative school. J. F.
McCaffery and D. S. Turner. Clear House
44:491-6 Ap '70; Same abr. Ed Digest 36:
16-19 O '70
Education: a show of power over funds for
innovation; ESEA money. R. Karp. Sci-
ence 167:1709-11 Mr 27 '70
Innovation and change in education. W. W.
Brickman. Sch & Soc 98:202-3 Ap '70
Innovation mirage; a culture based on
change; address, September 9, 1970. J. A.
Howard. Vital Speeches 36:743-6 O 1 '70 √
Instructional technology: some implications
for teachers. il Todays Ed 59:33-40 N '70
Investment in innovation, by P. Woodring.
Review
Sat R 53:62-3 D 19 '70. F. M. Hechinger
Reach, touch, and teach, by T. Borton. Re-
view
Sat R 53:82 S 19 '70. R. E. Samples
School reorganization and the process of edu-
cational change; adaptation of address, June
29, 1967. R. I. Miller. bibliog Sch & Soc 98:
346-9 O '70
What's ahead for our schools? M. Smith. il
Parents Mag 45:49-51+ S '70
What's left when school's forgotten? process
approach to curriculum development. T.
Borton. il Sat R 53:69-71+ Ap 18 '70
Year of the active learner. T. J. O'Connell.
America 124:9 Ja 9 '71
See also
Education, Experimental
EDUCATIONAL laws and legislation. See
School laws and legislation
EDUCATIONAL leadership. See Leadership
EDUCATIONAL literature
See also
Publishers and publishing—Educational lit-
erature
EDUCATIONAL materials. See Teaching—Aids
and devices
EDUCATIONAL materials centers. See In-
structional materials centers
EDUCATIONAL media personnel
Bye, bye blackboard; new audio-visual job
opportunities. K. Grove. il Mlle 72:186-7+
N '70
EDUCATIONAL media selection centers. See
Instructional materials centers
EDUCATIONAL organization. See School man-
agement and organization
EDUCATIONAL parks. See Consolidated
schools
EDUCATIONAL planning
See also
Curriculum planning
Educational innovations
EDUCATIONAL psychology. See Psychology,
Educational
EDUCATIONAL records. See School reports
and records
EDUCATIONAL research
Does research in linguistics have practical
applications? address, November 1969. R.
C. O'Donnell. Engl J 59:410-12+ Mr '70
Labs and centers aim at educational im-
provement. il Am Ed 6:35-6 My '70
Policy framework for educational research.
H. D. Gideonse. bibliog il Science 170:1054-
9 D 4 '70

Research clues; questions and answers. See
issues of Today's education
Summary of investigations relating to the
English language arts in secondary education: 1969. N. S. Blount. bibliog Engl J 59:
677-90 My '70
See also
United States—National institute of education (proposed)

Federal aid
Program for regional educational research.
Sch & Soc 98:398 N '70
EDUCATIONAL resource centers. See Instruc-
tional materials centers
EDUCATIONAL resources information center.
See ERIC
EDUCATIONAL segregation. See Segregation
in education
EDUCATIONAL sociology
Agents for Christian community; the Catholic
school. C. A. Koob. il America 122:335-7
Mr 28 '70
Changes affecting human interaction. D. W.
Dodson. Ed Digest 36:34-8 O '70
Changing the social order: the role of school-
ing. J. R. Burnett. Ed Digest 35:5-8 Mr '70
Education in a changing society. R. C. Lons-
dale. Ed Digest 36:6-9 S '70
Imperatives in education. R. Thompson. Clear
House 44:323-9 F '70
Linear teacher and the non-linear McLuhan.
H. R. Smith. bibliog Clear House 45:126-8
O '70
See also
Education—Aims and objectives
School and social and economic problems
Socially handicapped—Education
Socially handicapped children—Education
EDUCATIONAL statistics. See Education—
Statistics
EDUCATIONAL study tours. See Travel study
courses
EDUCATIONAL surveys
See also
National assessment of educational progress
EDUCATIONAL television. See Television in
education
EDUCATIONAL television stations. See Tele-
vision stations, Educational
EDUCATIONAL testing service
What's the IQ of the IQ test? P. Pine. Ed
Digest 35:13-16 F '70
EDUCATIONAL tests and measurements
Case for true-false test items. R. L. Ebel.
Ed Digest 36:47-50 O '70
Results count, not methods. Sr Schol 95:Schol
Teach 2 D 8 '69
See also
College entrance examination board—Schola-
stic aptitude test
Grading and marking (students)
Intelligence tests
Students—Rating

Anecdotes, facetiae, satire, etc.
Test: rate yourself in savoir-faire! J. Bailey.
New Yorker 46:38-9 Ap 18 '70
EDUCATIONAL toys. See Toys
EDUCATIONAL workshops
Poetry is alive and well: a workshop blue-
print. P. B. Janeczko and R. Skapura.
Engl J 59:1131-4 N '70
Young professionals put it all together; sum-
mer program sponsored by the Institute
for the study of health and society. P.
Pine. il Am Ed 6:16-19 N '70
EDUCATORS
See also
College presidents
College professors and instructors
Teachers

EDWARDS, Charles Cornell
Charting a new role for embattled FDA.
B. J. Culliton. il pors Sci N 97:180-3 F
14 '70 *
Direct actionist polices food, drugs. por U S
News 69:50 Ag 17 '70 *
New broom at FDA. Sci N 97:120-1 Ja 31 '70
EDWARDS, Diane D. and Edwards, J. S.
Fetal movement: development and time
course. bibliog Science 169:95-7 Jl 3 '70
EDWARDS, Doc
Doc and George bloom late. R. Blount, jr.
Sports Illus 32:46 Je 29 '70 *
EDWARDS, Elizabeth
Dedicated teacher is the teaching profession's
greatest enemy. Todays Ed 59:53-4 N '70
EDWARDS, John P.
City and school system share a computer. il
Am City 85:105+ Ap '70
EDWARDS, Joseph S. See Edwards, D. D. jt.
auth.

EDWARDS, Mike W.
  Shenandoah, 1 long to hear you. il Nat Geog 137:554-88 Ap '70
  Through Ozark hills and hollows. il Nat Geog 138:656-89 N '70
EDWARDS, R. G. and Fowler, R. E.
  Human embryos in the laboratory; with biographical sketches. il Sci Am 223:10, 44-54 bibliog(p 140) D '70
EDWARDS, Rita Yokoi
  Ceramist's odyssey of clay: Japan. il Craft Horiz 30:14-15 My '70
EDWARDS, Sherman
  Sherman Edwards: the high school history teacher who turned the revolution into a musical; interview. il por Sr Schol 96:20-1 Mr 2 '70
      about
  1776: the idea that would not let go. J. Reddy. il por Read Digest 96:199-200+ F '70 °
EDWARDS, Miss.
      Community centers
  Civil rights conference center in Mississippi endangered. Chr Cent 87:525-6 Ap 29 '70; Discussion. 87:704-5 Je 3 '70
EELGRASS
  Life without oxygen. il Chem 43:25 F '70
EELLS, George
  What ever became of the common scolds? il Look 34:90+ N 3 '70
EELS
  Hotel for moray eels. il Sci Digest 67:90-1 Ap '70
EFF, Johannes
  Mile walk in the mock sins of the white man; poem. Nat R 22:1295 D 1 '70
  Ode to a dead union suit; poem. Nat R 22:835 Ag 11 '70
EFFECT of gamma rays on man-in-the moon marigolds; drama. See Zindel. P.
EFFELSBERG telescope. See Radio telescopes
EFFERSON, Aloise B.
  To a black girl holding a rose; poem. Negro Hist Bul 33:17 Ja '70
EFFICIENCY
  America the inefficient. il Time 95:72-8+ Mr 23 '70; Same abr. Read Digest 97:122-6 Jl '70
EFFICIENCY, Administrative
  Can the Nixon administration be doing something right? the new regional system. J. Fischer. Harper 241:22-4+ N '70
    See also
  United States—Advisory council on management improvement
EFFICIENCY, Agricultural. See Farm management
EFFICIENCY, Industrial
  Throw the rascal out! assault on business inefficiency. por Time 95:78 Mr 23 '70
    See also
  Executive ability
  Labor productivity
  Work measurement
EFLAND, Arthur. See Floch, J. jt. auth.
EFRON, Edith
  Television as a teacher. Ed Digest 35:13-15 Ja '70
EFRON, Yoel
  Alcohol dehydrogenase in maize: genetic control of enzyme activity. bibliog il Science 170:751-3 N 13 '70
EGAN, Ferol
  West of Out our way. il Am West 7:18-25 My '70
EGAN, James
  Dick Cavett: the brightest boy on the block. il pors Good H 171:44-5+ N '70
  Most entertaining museum in England. il Am Home 73:74-9+ Ap '70
EGAN, John J.
  Future is for priests; address. October 16. 1969. il Cath World 210:262-5 My '70
  If you could make one change in the church, what would it be? Commonweal 92:159 My 1 '70
EGBERT, Marion
  Music is what's happening. il Parks & Rec 5:22-4+ Je '70
EGBERT, Sherwood Harry
  Avanti still means forward. D. A. Jedlicka. il por Esquire 73:116-17+ Ap '70 °
EGEBERG, Roger Olaf
  Country's no. 1 health problem; interview. il pors U S News 68:68-73 F 23 '70
  Fluoridation for all: a national priority. por Todays Health 48:30-1+ Je '70
      about
  Egeberg says health plan in works. J. Walsh. Science 169:1295 S 25 '70 °
  Exit Egeberg; and Farmer. pors Time 96:15 D 14 '70 °

EGG (biology) See Embryology
EGG and the eye (gallery-restaurant) See Los Angeles—Hotels, restaurants, etc.
EGG cookers, Electric. See Household appliances, Electric
EGG laying (birds) See Oviposition
EGG shells
  Carbon-13 and oxygen-18 in dinosaur, crocodile, and bird eggshells indicate environmental conditions. R. E. Folinsbee and others. bibliog il Science 168:1353-6 Je 12 '70
  DDT-induced inhibition of avian shell gland carbonic anhydrase: a mechanism for thin eggshells. J. Bitman and others. bibliog il Science 168:594-6 My 1 '70
  How an eggshell is made. T. G. Taylor. il Sci Am 222:88-95 bibliog(p 146) Mr '70
  Marvelous eggshell. Chem 43:22 D '70
  Pesticides and the reproduction of birds. D. B. Peakall. il Sci Am 222:72-8 bibliog(p 130) Ap '70
EGGER, Hermann
  About azimuth sundials. il Sky & Tel 40:94-5 Ag '70
EGGERS, Hans J. and others
  Rhodanine: a selective inhibitor of the multiplication of echovirus 12. bibliog il Science 167:294-7 Ja 16 '70
EGGS
  Easter eggs every day; pastel-tinted eggs from Araucana chickens. M. Wilbur. il Org Gard & Farm 17:76-9 Ap '70
    See also
  Cookery—Eggs
  Easter eggs
  Egg shells
  Embryology
  Fishes—Eggs
  Poultry
EGGSHELLS. See Egg shells
EGO trip; story. See Donis, M.
EGOFF, Sheila
  Children's books: a Canadian's view of the current American scene; address, November 14, 1969. Horn Bk 46:142-50 Ap '70
EGYPT
    See also
  Arab federation (proposed)
  Cairo
  Candidates, Political—Egypt
  Colleges and universities—Egypt
  Foreign visitors in Egypt
  Ismailia
  Libraries—Egypt
  Morale, National—Egypt
  Public opinion—Egypt
  Red Sea
  Russians in Egypt
  Sinai (peninsula)
  Suez Canal
      Antiquities
  Egyptian prehistory: some new concepts. F. Wendorf and others. bibliog il Science 169:1161-71 S 18 '70
    See also
  Pyramids
  Temples—Egypt
      Civilization
  American innocent in the Middle East. M. Frady. il Harper 241:55-8+ O '70 (to be cont)
      Defenses
  Crucial test for old friends. il Time 96:20-1 S 14 '70
  Into the breach? New Repub 163:5-6 S 19 '70
  Moscow-on-the-Nile. Time 95:31+ Je 22 '70
  New missile sites threat to Israeli air supremacy. Aviation W 93:20 Ag 24 '70
  Of mosques and MIG's; Moscow's growing military role in Egypt. il Time 95:19-20 Je 1 '70
  Pattern of Soviet-UAR buildup of missiles at Suez emerges. Aviation W 93:21 S 28 '70
  Red star over the Nile. A. de Borchgrave. il Newsweek 75:38-42 Je 1 '70
  Relief for Egypt, anxiety for Israel. il Time 95:43-4 My 11 '70
  Russians fly defense missions for Egypt in Middle East conflict. Aviation W 92:27 My 4 '70
  Saboteurs of peace. il Newsweek 76:30 S 21 '70
  Shoring up Sadat. il Time 96:45 D 7 '70
  Soviets accelerating Mideast drive; with editorial comment. E. H. Kolcum. il Aviation W 92:9, 14-18 My 18 '70
  Soviets deploy new Suez defenses. il Aviation W 93:14-16 Jl 13 '70
  Why peace in Mideast hangs by a thread. il U S News 69:40-3 D 28 '70
  Why U.S. is worried about Mideast build-up. il U S News 69:44 O 26 '70

EGYPT—*Continued*

Economic conditions

What Nasser did. G. G. Stevens. Atlan 227: 45-7 Ja '71
Where Egypt stands. H. Smith. il Atlan 227: 39-45 Ja '71

Foreign relations

Way Egyptians see Israel, Uncle Sam, the SAM's. E. R. F. Sheehan. il N Y Times Mag p28-9+ S 20 '70

Israel

Mideast stories: the existence of Israel. J. Burnham. Nat R 22:1045 O 6 '70

United States

See United States—Foreign relations—Egypt

History

1952-

Cairo journal. J. Colebrook. Commentary 50: 45-55 O '70

Politics and government

Death of Nasser. il pors Newsweek 76:31-5 O 12 '70
Egypt's course now: in Nasser footsteps; with report by J. Law. il por U S News 69:41-2 O 19 '70
Nasser era. Chr Cent 87:1207 O 14 '70
Nasser's legacy: hope and instability. il pors Time 96:20-6+ O 12 '70
New leader and an uneasy truce. il por Newsweek 76:53-4 O 19 '70
Sadat takes over in Egypt. Sr Schol 97:3-4 N 2 '70
Strategy left by Nasser; blackmail the U.S. with Arab oil. M. Copeland. il Life 69:36-7 O 9 '70
Succession and stalemate. por Time 96:39 O 26 '70
Swift succession. il por Time 96:32+ O 19 '70
Where Egypt stands. H. Smith. il Atlan 227: 39-45 Ja '71
Who runs Egypt? E. R. F. Sheehan. il N Y Times Mag p30-1+ N 29 '70; Reply. F. Busi. p2 D 27 '70

EGYPTIAN poetry

Translations into English

Papyrus Harris 500; tr. by J. L. Foster. Poetry 116:304-12 Ag '70

EGYPTIAN rugs. See Rugs and carpets, Oriental

EHMANN, William D. and Morgan, J. W.
Oxygen, silicon, and aluminum in lunar samples by 14 MeV neutron activation. bibliog il Science 167:528-30 Ja 30 '70

EHRICKE, Krafft
Absolute necessity of space exploitation. Space World G-6-78:38-9 Je '70
Toward a three-dimensional civilization; interview. il pors Space World G-12-84: 4-11 D '70

EHRLICH, Anne H. See Ehrlich, P. R. jt. auth.

EHRLICH, Ava
On campus: is there an answer? A look at October 15. Mlle 70:130 Ja '70

EHRLICH, Henry
Anne of the twenty years. il pors Look 34:28-35 Jl 28 '70
David Frost; TV's intercontinental man. il pors Look 34:64-8 Mr 24 '70
Ladies save the lakes. il Look 34:60-1 Ap 21 '70
They hardly ever make passes at Glenda Jackson. il pors Look 34:36-41 D 29 '70
(ed) See Zanuck, D. F. Zanuck: last of the red hot star-makers

EHRLICH, Paul R.
Are there too many of us? il McCalls 97: 46-7+ Jl '70
Ecological destruction is a condition of American life; interview, ed. by P. Collier. il Mlle 70:188-9+ Ap '70
Man is the endangered species; interview. por Nat Wildlife 8:38-9 Ap '70
People pollution. il Audubon 72:4-9 My '70
Population overgrowth, the fertile curse. por Field & S 75:58+ Je '70
We're standing on the edge of the earth. Nat Wildlife 8:16-17 O '70
—and Ehrlich, A. H.
Food-from-the-sea myth. Sat R 53:53-5+ Ap 4 '70
—and Holdren, J. P.
Co-evolutionary race. Sat R 53:66 D 5 '70
Deceptive birth rates. Sat R 53:58 O 3 '70
Dodging the crisis. Sat R 53:73 N 7 '70
Hidden effects of overpopulation. Sat R 53: 52 Ag 1 '70

People problem. Sat R 53:42-3 Jl 4 '70
Why do people move? Sat R 53:51 S 5 '70
—and Raven, P. H.
Differentiation of populations. bibliog Science 165:1228-32; 167:1637 S 19 '69, Mr 20 '70

about

Ecology's angry lobbyist. D. M. Rorvik. il por Look 34:42-4 Ap 21 '70 *

EHRLICH, Sam
Gallery; photographs. Life 69:12-15 N 13 '70

EHRLICHMAN, John D.
Closing the performance gap. il pors Newsweek 75:16-17 Je 22 '70 *
How Nixon's White House works. il pors Time 95:15-20 Je 8 '70 *
Middle American who edits ideas for Nixon. R. B. Semple, jr. il pors N Y Times Mag p32-3+ Ap 12 '70 *
Rearranging furniture. J. Osborne. New Repub 163:8-9 Jl 4 '70 *
What about Ehrlichman? Cato. Nat R 22:830 Ag 11 '70 *

EHRMAN, Lee
Simulation of the mating advantage in mating of rare drosophila males. bibliog il Science 167:905-6 F 6 '70
—See Kernaghan, R. P. jt. auth.

EHRMANN, Herbert Brutus
Obituary
Nation 211:37 Jl 20 '70. R. L. Lurie

EHRMANN, Max
Desiderata; poem; reprint. Read Digest 97: 137 S '70

EIBER, Rick
Seen with a designer's eye; photographs. Pop Phot 67:92-3 O '70 *

EICH, Günter
Changed landscape; Clearings in the woods; poems, tr. by T. Savory. Poetry 116:362-3 Ag '70

EICHELBERGER, Clark M.
Call to leadership. Sat R 53:21+ Je 27 '70
Treading water. Sat R 53:24 S 26 '70

EICHHORN, Douglas
November 22, 1969; poem. Nation 210:350 Mr 23 '70

EICHHORN, Mary M. and Reinecke, R. D.
Vision information center: a user-oriented data base. bibliog il Science 169:29-31 Jl 3 '70

EICHHORST, Calvin J.
Why should we care about ecumenical activity? Chr Cent 87:1559-62 D 30 '70

EIDER ducks. See Ducks, Wild

EIDETIC imagery
Memory marvel; Stromeyer-Psotka findings. Newsweek 75:92 Mr 23 '70
Photographic memory. Sci Am 222:62+ Mr '70
Seeing is remembering. Sci Digest 67:23 My '70
Who needs computers, with mathematical prodigies like these? J. Bryan. 3d. Horizon 12:46-7 Spr '70

EIGHTEEN hundred and seventies
Looking back at the '70s. Sr Schol 95:6 D 8 '69

EIGHTEEN hundred and seventy-six
Centennial: American life in 1876, by W. P. Randel. Review
Atlan 225:95-8 Ja '70. L. Kronenberger

EIGHTEEN-nation committee on disarmament. See United Nations—Committee on disarmament

EIGHTEEN-year-old vote. See Suffrage—United States

EIGHTEENTH century
Fare backward, traveler: a refreshing sojourn in the eighteenth century. R. Joseph. il Esquire 74:130-5 S '70
See also
Enlightenment

EIKENBERRY, Peter
Student moves into the 14th C.D. T. Buckley. il pors N Y Times Mag p 10-11+ Je 21 '70 *

EILENBERGER, Robert F.
Carved clay compartment with hinged doors. il Ceram Mo 18:24-7 Ap '70
Creating facade forms. il Ceram Mo 17:30-2 D '69
Free form jars with lids. il Ceram Mo 18:26-9 F '70
Sectioned plates. il Ceram Mo 18:28-9 N '70

EILERS, Hazel Kraft
At the sign of the crest. See issues of Hobbies

EIMON, Pan Dodd
City tells its story. See issues of American city

EINSTEIN, Albert
Origin or relativity. por Time 95:45 Ja 26 '70

EINSTEIN theory. See Relativity (physics)

EINSTEIN'S theory of gravity. See Gravitation

EIPPER, Alfred W.
Pollution problems, resource policy, and the scientist. bibliog Science 169:11-15 Jl 3 '70
EISDORFER, Carl
Society stupid in attitude toward aging, expert asserts. Aging 182:8 D '69
—and others
Improvement of learning in the aged by modification of autonomic nervous system activity. bibliog il Science 170:1327-9 D 18 '70
EISELE, Albert A.
New Humphrey. New Repub 163:18-19 S 19 '70
EISELE, Donn Fulton
NASA veterans get new U.S. jobs. Aviation W 92:23 Je 1 '70 *
EISELEY, Loren
Cosmic prison; excerpts from The invisible pyramid. il Horizon 12:96-101 Aut '70
Last magician; excerpts from The invisible pyramid. Nat Parks & Con Mag 44:4-5 O '70
Star dragon; excerpt from The invisible pyramid. il Natur Hist 79:18+ Je '70
EISELEY, Richard
Smart shops and safaris. il Travel 134:60-1 S '70
EISENBERG, Arlene, and Eisenberg, Howard
Holiday home on wheels. il Parents Mag 45: 48-50+ Ag '70
Justice denied. Parents Mag 45:48-51 Ap '70
EISENBERG, Howard. See Eisenberg, A. jt. auth.
EISENBERG, John. See Ashe, J. jt. auth.
EISENBERG, Leon
Student unrest: sources and consequences; excerpts from address, October 21, 1969. bibliog Science 167:1688-92 Mr 27 '70
EISENBERG, Norman
Seven records (and one tape) to judge your headphones by. Hi Fi sec I 20:62-3 F '70
—See Long, R. jt. auth.
EISENBUD, Merril
Environmental protection in the city of New York. bibliog il Science 170:706-12 N 13 '70
EISENDRATH, Craig
Sweden: antidotes to welfare. Nation 211: 390-2 O 26 '70
EISENDRATH, David B. Jr
Color clinic. See issues of Popular photography to May 1970
EISENHOWER, David
Ike's grandson hits the '70 trail for Republicans. il por U S News 69:107 O 19 '70 *
EISENHOWER, Dwight David
Ike: an artist in iron. R. Rhodes. por Harper 241:70-7 Jl '70; Same abr. Read Digest 97:121-6 S '70 *
My memories of Ike. M. D. Eisenhower. por Read Digest 96:69-74 F '70 *
Notes of a soldier. K. Crawford. por Newsweek 75:106+ My 25 '70 *
Supreme commander as organization man. R. Steel. por Sat R 53:23-5+ Je 20 '70 *
EISENHOWER, Dwight David, 2d. See Eisenhower. D.
EISENHOWER, Julie (Nixon)
Nixon ladies and their summer dresses. il Life 68:45 My 8 '70 *
President's daughters. pors Vogue 155:98-9 Je '70 *
EISENHOWER, Mamie Geneva (Doud)
My memories of Ike. por Read Digest 96: 69-74 F '70
EISENHOWER dollar. See Coins
EISENMAN, Joseph S. See Beckman, A. L. jt. th.
EISENSTAEDT, Alfred
Alfred Eisenstaedt's Martha's Vineyard; photographs. Travel & Camera 33:17-25 S '70
Buckleys of Great Elm; photographs. il pors Life 69:34-41+ D 18 '70
Gallery; photographs. il Life 68:8-9 Mr 6; 6-9 Je 19 '70
about
In focus. il por Travel & Camera 33:4 S '70 *
EISENSTEIN, Elizabeth L.
Advent of printing in current historical literature: notes and comments on an elusive transformation. bibliog f Am Hist R 75:727-43 F '70
EISENSTEIN, Sergei Mikhailovich
Griffith's Russian fans. R. Sklar. Nation 211: 249-50 S 21 '70 *
Sergei Eisenstein and Upton Sinclair, ed. by H. M. Geduld and R. Gottesman. Review Newsweek il por 76:74 Ag 10 '70. G. Wolff *
EISNER, Thomas, and others
Population control, sterilization, and ignorance. Science 167:377 Ja 23 '70
EJECTION devices (airplanes) See Airplanes— Escape devices

EK, Niklas
Sons and mothers: Niklas Ek and Birgit Cullberg. G. Loney. il pors Dance Mag 44: 32-7 Ap '70 *
EKISTICS
Ekistics, the science of human settlements. C. A. Doxiadis. bibliog il Science 170:393-404 O 23 '70
EKLUND, Sigvard
International atom. il pors Bul Atom Sci 26:56-61 Je '70
EKLUTNA (village) See Indians of North America—Villages
EKTACOLOR print films. See Photography— Films
EL AL Israel airlines. See Airlines—Israel
EL KADDOUMI, Farouk. See Abu Lotuf
EL-ZOGHBY, Gamal. See Zoghby, G.
ELAM, Barbara. See Bower, L. B. jt. auth.
ELAM, John S. and others
Rapid axonal transport of sulfated mucopolysaccharide proteins. bibliog il Science 170:458-60 O 23 '70
ELAPSED-time indicators. See Timing devices
ELASTIC waves
Elastic wave velocities of lunar samples at high pressures and their geophysical implications. H. Kanamori and others. bibliog il Science 167:726-8 Ja 30 '70
ELASTICITY
See also
Compressibility
ELAZAR, Daniel J.
Nature preservation in Israel. il Liv Wildn 34:24-9 Sum '70
ELBA (island)
Elba. S. K. Oberbeck. il Travel & Camera 33:50-2+ N '70
ELBERG, S. S. See Warfel, A. H. jt. auth.
EL CAPITAN climb. See Mountaineering
ELDEN, James M. See Culbert, S. A. jt. auth.
ELDER, Frederick
Different 2001; excerpts from address. Cath World 211:63-6 My '70
ELDER, Paul
San Francisco regional: bookselling in time of crisis. il Pub W 198:26-9 N 9; 30-2 N 23 '70
ELDER, Richard W.
Free as a bird. il Parks & Rec 5:33 Ja '70
ELDREDGE, Linda
What do we do with our lives? letter. por Time 95:23 My 11 '70
ELDRIDGE, Richard
How to give birth to a daughter. il Redbook 135:80-1+ My '70
ELECTION districts
See also
Apportionment (election law)
ELECTION expenses. See Campaign funds
ELECTION forecasts. See Political forecasts
ELECTION laws
See also
Voters, Registration of
Voting, Absent

United States
Age of Aquarius; Senate amendment to enfranchise eighteen-year olds. Newsweek 75:30-1 Mr 23 '70
Extending the franchise. il Time 95:14 Mr 23 '70
History in an hour; 18 year old vote provision added to renewed Voting rights act of 1965. Time 95:13-14 Je 29 '70
Keep it brief; extension of the Voting rights act. New Repub 162:8 Je 20 '70
More federal rules on voting rights. il U S News 68:43 Je 29 '70
Now that Congress has O.K.'d the vote for eighteen-year-olds—liberalization of residence restrictions. il U S News 68:42-3 Je 29 '70
Presidential pragmatics; Voting rights act. Commonweal 92:332 Jl 10 '70 *
Young at heart; bill to enfranchise 18-year-olds. il Newsweek 75:19 Je 29 '70
Youth is served; Senate votes to lower voting age. K. Crawford. Newsweek 75:29 Mr 30 '70
See also
Suffrage—United States
ELECTIONEERING. See Political campaigns
ELECTIONS
See also
Campaign management
Political campaigns
Voting
Voting, Absent

Corrupt practices
Time to knock out the vote thieves! L. B. Nichols. Read Digest 97:120-4 Ag '70

ELECTIONS—*Continued*

Brazil

Too large a victory. Nation 211:613 D 14 '70

Chile

Best way for Chile. Nation 211:228 S 21 '70
Chile: a Marxist at the top? il por Newsweek 76:49 S 21 '70
Chile: the making of a precedent. il por Time 96:34-5 S 21 '70
Crucial decision. il por Time 96:24 S 7 '70
Difficult choices. Time 96:26 S 14 '70
Fidel was glad; S. Allende winner. Nat R 22:982+ S 22 '70
Mandate for a Marxist. Newsweek 76:58 S 14 '70
Marxist in first. il por Sr Schol 97:4 O 5 '70
    See also
Political campaigns—Chile

Colombia

Lapse of memory. Time 95:48 My 4 '70

Corsica

Corsican caper. Time 95:33 F 16 '70

Dominican Republic

Keeping the lid on. il por Time 95:42 My 25 '70

France

Comeuppance; Bordeaux by-election. Newsweek 76:46 O 5 '70
Letter from Paris; J.-J. Servan-Schreiber winner of by-election for Nancy deputy. Genêt. New Yorker 46:50 Jl 11 '70
Making of a deputy; by-election in Nancy. il por Newsweek 76:48-9 Jl 6 '70
Politics Bordelaise; by-election to elect a deputy to the French National assembly. il pors Time 96:29 S 28 '70

Germany (Federal Republic)

German switch-off. il Sr Schol 95:18-19 O 20 '69
Message from Ulbricht; three state elections. il Time 95:31 Je 29 '70

Great Britain

Bonaparte and the Iron Duke; Wilson's defeat. Nat R 22:718 Jl 14 '70
Chairman Wilson; general election. A. Howard. New Repub 162:12-13 My 30 '70
Harold Wilson: poll-axed. A. Lejeune. Nat R 22:730 Jl 14 '70
Letter from London. M. Panter-Downes. New Yorker 46:61-2 Jl 4 '70
Now or never for Tory Heath? il por U S News 68:36 Je 1 '70
Saying no to Labour. Nation 211:4 Jl 6 '70
Tory, Tory, hallelujah. il por Newsweek 75:30+ Je 29 '70
Unexpected triumph. il pors Time 95:16-18+ Je 29 '70
    See also
Public opinion polls

Guatemala

Guerrilla hunter. Newsweek 75:56 Mr 16 '70
Step to the right. il por Time 95:43 Mr 16 '70

Italy

Breathing spell; regional elections. il Newsweek 75:42+ Je 22 '70
Now, a red belt spread across Italy? il U S News 68:95 Je 22 '70

Kenya

Election year politics in Kenya. J. E. Hakes. bibliog f Cur Hist 58:154-9+ Mr '70
Reports: Kenya. S. Meisler. Atlan 225:26+ Mr '70

Mexico

What made Luis run? il por Newsweek 76:44-5 Jl 13 '70

Northern Ireland

Big fella wins; Bannside by-election. por Newsweek 75:61 Ap 27 '70
Paisley's progress. J. D. Douglas. Chr Today 14:40 My 8 '70

Pakistan

Step in the right direction. Time 96:29-30 D 21 '70
Two-man sweep. il pors Newsweek 76:44 D 21 '70

South Africa

Moral issue for South Africa; churchmen's statement. America 122:120-1 F 7 '70

Sweden

Still in the saddle. Newsweek 76:46 O 5 '70
Together again. il por Time 96:32 O 5 '70

United States

After all that fuss, U.S. voters ignored the slogans. H. Sidey. il Life 69:38-9 N 13 '70
After the election: who's in. Sr Schol 97:5-6 D 7 '70
And now, looking toward 1972. il Time 96:15-16 N 16 '70
Black victories. New Repub 163:10 D 5 '70
Do the people know how to judge Congress? D. Lawrence. U S News 69:96 O 26 '70
Economics and elections. Nat R 22:1250 D 1 '70
Election impact. il U S News 69:15-23+ N 16 '70
Election '70: the Democrats shape up. il Newsweek 76:30-8+ N 16 '70
Emerging purgatory. Commonweal 93:187-8 N 20 '70
Faking of a president, 1970. New Repub 163:7-9 N 14 '70
Fight for control of Congress. il U S News 68:28-30 Je 22 '70
Fight or switch? 1970 election results and the President's tactics. Nation 211:514 N 23 '70
From here to '72; symposium. Commonweal 93:214-21 N 27 '70
Headhunts and bellyaches; modern midterm election. Chr Cent 87:1371 N 18 '70
In quest of the new majority. M. S. Evans. Nat R 22:1161-3+ N 3 '70
Letter from Washington. R. H. Rovere. New Yorker 46:187-90+ N 14 '70
Love that pap! R. M. Nixon's view of results. J. Osborne. New Repub 163:14-15 N 28 '70
Lucky Democrats; 1970 elections. C. McWilliams. Nation 211:485-7 N 16 '70
Meaning of the '70 results: an expert's analysis; interview. J. Kraft. il por U S News 69:28-9 N 23 '70
Midterm votes: past patterns. il U S News 69:30-1 N 2 '70
New mood in Congress; eyes fixed on next November 3. America 122:90-1 Ja 31 '70
1970 election special. il Sr Schol 97:7-18 O 12 '70
Nixon's strategy for '72; 1970 election results. il U S News 69:21-4 N 23 '70
No reforms now. Sr Schol 97:4-5 N 9 '70
Normal mix-up. K. Crawford. Newsweek 76:48 N 16 '70
Off year: how America voted. il Newsweek 76:36 N 16 '70
Public pulse: elections, 1970. T. H. Clancy. America 123:393 N 14 '70
Real majority, by R. M. Scammon and B. J. Wattenberg. Review
    Nation 211:336-9 O 12 '70. J. Newfield
    Newsweek 76:33-4 S 14 '70. D. M. Alpern
Size-up by leaders in their own words; interviews with high officials and candidates. il U S News 69:31-6+ N 16 '70
Sorting out a mixed bag. Sr Schol 97:3-4 D 7 '70
Sweet and sour. Sr Schol 95:14+ D 1 '69
Symbolic races. Nat R 22:1199 N 17 '70
Toward a new system for choosing a president; basic voting reforms. il U S News 68:26-9 My 11 '70
TRB from Washington. New Repub 162:6 Mr 7 '70
TRB from Washington: Nixon's midterm try. New Repub 163:4 O 24 '70
Turn on the off year. Today Ed 59:63 S '70
Union-backed candidates: how they fared. il U S News 69:63-5 N 16 '70
    See also
Campaign issues
Candidates, Political
Presidential campaigns
Presidents—United States—Election
Primaries
Public opinion polls
Senators—Election
Suffrage—United States
Voting
    also subhead Politics and government under names of states, e.g. New York (state)—Politics and government
    also subhead Elections under names of cities, e.g. New York (city)—Elections

Vietnam (Republic)

Buddhists return; Senate elections. Newsweek 76:49 S 14 '70

ELECTIVE system in education
Those infernal electives. J. K. Crabbe. Engl J 59:990-3+ O '70

ELECTORAL college
ABC's of Senate's big debate on electing presidents. U S News 69:114-15 S 21 '70
Bad idea whose time has come; direct election of the President. I. Kristol and P. Weaver; discussion. N Y Times Mag p4+ D 21 '69; 101-2 F 8 '70
Filibuster in the works? Cato. Nat R 22:992 S 22 '70

ELECTORAL college—*Continued*
Hardy college spirit; Senate debate. Newsweek 76:42 S 21 '70
How not to elect a president: Time essay; Bayh amendment. Time 95:26-7 My 4 '70
Let's keep the electoral college: bulwark of our two-party system. R. C. Moe. il Nat R 22:356-9+ Ap 7 '70
Necessity not to change. il Time 96:16 O 12 '70
This month's feature: the question of U.S. electoral reform. Cong Digest 49:1-32 Ja '70
Urban votes. J. W. Wides and D. W. Stotlar. New Repub 162:9 Je 27 '70
Voting for president; direct election vs. the Federal system plan. M. P. Curzan. New Repub 162:14-16 Ap 18 '70
Wallace in '72. New Repub 162:7 Je 20 '70

ELECTRIC accidents. See Electricity, Injuries from

ELECTRIC alarms
Build the two-tone Waverly alarm. D. Lancaster. il Pop Electr 32:29-31 F '70; Correction. 32:104 Ap '70
Install-it-yourself electronic fire-theft alarm. S. M. Gallagher. il Pop Mech 134:160-1+ N '70
Panic button. P. Franson. il Electr World 83:41+ My '70
See also
Burglar alarms
Fire alarms

ELECTRIC apparatus and appliances, Domestic. See Household appliances, Electric

ELECTRIC apparatus Industry
Matsushita knows how to do it. N. A. Martin. il Duns 95:62-4+ F '70
Matsushita misreads the market. Fortune 82:47 N '70
See also
General electric company
I-T-E imperial corporation

Advertising
Whirlpool tunes in the consumer; Care-a-van, musical show. Nations Bsns 58:20 Ja '70

ELECTRIC autolite company. See Prestolite company

ELECTRIC automobiles. See Automobiles, Electric

ELECTRIC barbecue grills. See Barbecue grills

ELECTRIC batteries
Batteries come first! J. Forney. il Mod Phot 34:74-7+ S '70
New batteries for sportsmen. A. D. Livingston. il Field & S 75:26-7+ Jl '70
See also
Storage batteries

Charging
Recharge your nicads in ninety sec. E. Farber. Mod Phot 34:40+ Ag '70
Super speed charger: does it work? J Forney. il Mod Phot 34:54-5 Ja '70

ELECTRIC blankets, coverlets, etc.
Electric blankets: the importance of proper use and care. D. Quentzel. il Good H 171:204 D '70

ELECTRIC blenders. See Household appliances, Electric

ELECTRIC broilers. See Household appliances, Electric

ELECTRIC cables
See also
Electric lines

Installation
Sneaky tool snakes cable through your wall. J. Hand. il Pop Sci 197:85 Ag '70

ELECTRIC capacitors
Build an electrolytic restorer. G. J. Plamondon. il Pop Electr 33:46-50 O '70
Chip capacitors for IC's. D. L. Heiserman. il Electr World 84:40-2+ D '70
Choose-&-use capacitor guide. R. R. Marsh. il Radio-Electr 41:23-5 F '70
Variable capacitors; symposium. il Electr World 83:37-59 Ap '70
What do you know about capacitors? quiz. R. P. Balin. il Pop Electr 34:32 Ja '71

ELECTRIC circuits
Install a circuit for a 230-v. arc welder. J. Burroughs. il Pop Mech 133:178-81 F '70

ELECTRIC clocks. See Clocks, Electric

ELECTRIC clothes dryers. See Clothes dryers

ELECTRIC conductivity
Negative differential conductivity. E. M. Conwell. bibliog il pors Phys Today 23:35-41 Je '70
See also
Superconductivity
Tunneling (physics)

ELECTRIC conductors
See also
Microwave wiring
Semiconductors

ELECTRIC connectors
Care and handling of coaxial connectors the quick, foolproof way. W. I. Orr. il Pop Electr 33:47-9 Ag '70

ELECTRIC control
See also
Garage doors—Electric control

ELECTRIC cords
Extension wiring systems. il Consumer Rep 35:476-9 Ag '70

ELECTRIC current converters
Build a D.C. transformer; high voltage converter for non-semiconductors. J. Colt. il Pop Electr 32:35+ Mr '70
1C 12- to 6-V converter. E. A. Sack. il Electr World 83:68-9 Ja '70
See also
Klystrons

ELECTRIC current limiters
Electronic overload protection. J. L. Keith. il Pop Electr 32:54-6 Mr '70

ELECTRIC discharges
Miniature whirlwinds produced in the laboratory by high-voltage electrical discharges. R. T. Ryan and B. Vonnegut. bibliog il Science 168:1349-51 Je 12 '70

ELECTRIC discharges through gases
See also
Plasma (ionized gases)
Vacuum

ELECTRIC drills. See Drilling and boring machinery

ELECTRIC drills, Portable. See Drilling and boring machinery

ELECTRIC egg cookers. See Household appliances, Electric

ELECTRIC elevators. See Elevators

ELECTRIC engineering
See also
Electric power production
Institute of electrical and electronics engineers

ELECTRIC equipment
See also
Audio-visual aids

ELECTRIC equipment Industry
See also
Reliance electric company

Finance
Electronics and electrical products; with yardsticks of management performance. il Forbes 105:185-6+ Ja 1 '70

ELECTRIC fans
Twenty-inch portable and window-mounted fans. il Consumer Bul 53:7-11 Ag '70

ELECTRIC flashlights. See Flashlights, Electric

ELECTRIC generators
Build your own emergency generator. il Suc Farm 68:no2 56 F '70
Generators get in fighting trim. Bsns W p45-6 S '70
See also
Isotopic power generators

ELECTRIC hair setters. See Hair curlers

ELECTRIC household appliances. See Household appliances, Electric

ELECTRIC Industries
See also
Collective bargaining—Electric industries
Electric utilities
Emerson electric company
General electric company
Schoonmaker, A. G. company
Western electric company
Westinghouse electric corporation

ELECTRIC irons
News in steam irons. Bet Hom & Gard 48:101 O '70

ELECTRIC lamp Industry and trade
No glamour, just growth. il Forbes 106:40+ D 1 '70

ELECTRIC lamps
Before you turn on the light. il Redbook 136:88-9+ N '70
Different track; funshaped lamps. M. Bowden. il House B 112:34+ N '70
Leading lights. il House B 112:80-1 F '70
Let there be lumens; FTC regulation on life ratings. Newsweek 76:58-9 Ag 3 '70
Light in great shape. il House & Gard 137:66-7 F '70
Longer light bulb life? il Mech Illus 66:20 Je '70
Tan your way through winter. L. Hilts. il Todays Health 48:37-9 D '70

ELECTRIC lamps, Arc
Bright new light on a sex symbol; Playboy building's xenon arc lamp. il Bsns W p22 Jl 4 '70
True color and artificial light; molecular arc lamp. il Chem 43:20-1 D '70

ELECTRIC lamps, Flashing
Build a flashing distress signal. il Mech Illus 66:78 Ag '70
Flasher beacon for your boat or car. R. M. Benrey. il Pop Sci 197:86-7+ Ag '70
Super flash. T. Couch. il Pop Electr 32:48-50+ My '70

ELECTRIC lamps, Photoflash
Flashcube that fires itself. S. M. Gallager. il Pop Mech 134:68 Ag '70
Magicube: flash that works without batteries. J. Holt. il Pop Sci 197:67 S '70
New self-firing flashcubes never miss. S. M. Gallager. il Pop Mech 134:14 S '70
Will battery-free cubes rock camera world? H. Keppler. il Mod Phot 34:98+ O '70
You'll wonder where the batteries went! Magicube. W. F. Wilson. il Pop Phot 67:46+ O '70
See also
Photography, Flashlight

ELECTRIC lamps in art
Dan Flavin: fiat lux. W. S. Wilson. il por Art N 68:48-51 Ja '70

ELECTRIC lanterns
Build your own blackout light. W. G. Salm. il Pop Mech 134:158-9+ N '70

ELECTRIC light bulbs. See Electric lamps

ELECTRIC lighting
Illumination in the home. R. Wey. il Consumer Bul 53:34-6 S '70
See also
Christmas decorations, Outdoor
Light projection
Lighting, Architectural and decorative
Stage lighting

Control
Patio control brings lights up s-l-o-w-l-y. J. G. Busse. il Pop Sci 197:123-4 O '70

ELECTRIC lines

Poles
150-foot poles for a Texas-size lighting project. il Am City 85:118 O '70

Underground lines
Poles down, wires all underground; Carmel Knolls. Calif. il Sunset 144:124+ Ap '70
Underground power transmission. P. H. Rose. bibliog il Science 170:267-73 O 16 '70

ELECTRIC meters
Handy tune-up meter for your car; kit-builders' report. S. M. Gallager. il Pop Mech 133:148 Mr '70
IC capacitance meter. H. A. Wittlinger. il Electr World 84:44-7+ S '70
Know your meter. L. A. Harlow. il Radio-Electr 41:60-4 Jl '70
Melsey SN-2 wave/dip meter. il Electr World 83:74-5 Ap '70
See also
Meter reading
Ohmmeters
Voltmeters
Voltohmmeters

ELECTRIC mixers. See Household appliances, Electric

ELECTRIC motor trucks. See Motor trucks, Electric

ELECTRIC motors
See also
Outboard motors
Reliance electric company

Control
Feedback module for motor control. R. F. Schwabenlender. il Electr World 83:66 Ap '70
Photocell motor control demonstrator. B. Koval. il Pop Electr 32:46-8 Je '70
SCR controls for small motors. L. Fleming. il Electr World 83:36+ Je '70
Speed control for large d.c. motors. L. Fleming. il Electr World 85:78 Ja '71

ELECTRIC motors, Induction
Pen that floats puts zip in drafting; Xynetica 1000. il Bsns W p50 Ja 24 '70

ELECTRIC motors, Synchronous
Constant-speed motors for tape recorders; hysteresis synchronous motor. A. Williams. il Radio-Electr 41:49 O '70

ELECTRIC mowers. See Lawn mowers

ELECTRIC noise
Suppressing electrical noise. C. Miller. Motor B 126:94+ Jl '70
See also
Television receivers—Noise

ELECTRIC ovens
See also
Electric stoves

ELECTRIC plants
Environmental side effects of energy production. D. F. Anthrop. il Bul Atom Sci 26:39-41 O '70
Finding a place to put the heat; effects on the ecology of bodies of water. R. H. Gilluly. il Sci N 98:98-9 Ag 1 '70
Power generation: the next thirty years. R. W. Holcomb. Science 167:159-60 Ja 9 '70
Thermionic topping: a stopgap power source. E. Gross. il Sci N 97:490-1 My 16 '70
See also
Atomic power plants
Electric power
Electric utilities
Hydroelectric plants

Fuel
Clean power from coal. A. M. Squires. bibliog il Science 169:821-8 Ag 28 '70
Coal woes blacken utilities' outlook. il Bsns W p 18 Jl 4 '70
Crisis that looks permanent; fuel shortage. il Bsns W p 14-15 O 3 '70
Face-to-face with the power crisis. il Bsns W p52 Jl 11 '70

Interconnection
Reserve power for the East; direct current converter station at Eel River. il Bsns W p92 O 10 '70
Sweating it out with borrowed kilowatts. il Bsns W p22-3 Ag 1 '70

Location
Familiar story; ecological alarm over proposed Sabina plant. D. N. Leff. il Environ 12:11-13 My '70
Thermal pollution in the marine environment. A. C. Jensen. il Cons 25:8-13 O '70

ELECTRIC plants, Emergency
Safeguard your city with standby power. L. J. Mages. il Am City 85:73 N '70

ELECTRIC potential. See Potential, Electric

ELECTRIC power
Con Ed and the good life: a question of power. il Newsweek 76:76+ Jl 13 '70
Costs versus benefits of increased electric power. P. H. Abelson. Science 170:1159 D 11 '70
Crisis in power; with editorial comment by R. Graves. il Life 69:3, 26F-35 D 11 '70
Environment dilemma. il Nations Bsns 58:50-1+ N '70
Heat, smog, power crisis: where, and why. il U S News 69:14-16 Ag 10 '70
Isn't there enough power to go around? U S News 69:52 O 5 '70
More electric power: how on earth do we get it? D. B. Mansfield. Look 34:51+ D 1 '70
Warning: low voltage; federal report on power reserves. il Newsweek 75:123 My 18 '70
See also
Electric plants
Electric utilities
Hydroelectric power
Tennessee Valley authority
also subhead Electric power under names of cities, e.g. New York (city)—Electric power

Transmission
See Electric transmission

United States
See Electric power

ELECTRIC power distribution
See also
Electric lines
Electric plants—Interconnection

ELECTRIC power failures
Build your own blackout light. W. G. Salm. il Pop Mech 134:158-9+ N '70
Danger of more power blackouts. il U S News 68:48-50 Ap 20 '70
Power on a knife's edge. Sci N 97:550 Je 6 '70
Power shortage gets emergency treatment. Bsns W p32 My 16 '70
Utilities sweat over the summer. Bsns W p30 Je 6 '70

ELECTRIC power industry. See Electric utilities

ELECTRIC power plants. See Electric plants

ELECTRIC power pooling. See Electric plants—Interconnection

ELECTRIC power production
Fast breeder reactors. G. T. Seaborg and J. L. Bloom. il Sci Am 223:13-21 N '70
Impact of energy demands. A. B. Cambel. bibliog il Phys Today 23:38-43+ D '70
New space-age power sources. G. Gregory. il UNESCO Courier 23:27-8 Mr '70
New ways to more power with less pollution. L. Lessing. il Fortune 82:78-81+ N '70

ELECTRIC power production—*Continued*
Space available; excerpts from testimony before the Joint congressional committee on atomic energy, January 29, 1970. M. Peterson. bibliog il Environ 12:2-9 Mr '70
ELECTRIC ranges. See Electric stoves
ELECTRIC razors. See Razors
ELECTRIC refrigerators.   See Refrigerators, Electric
ELECTRIC relays
    See also
Relays, Time limit
ELECTRIC resistance
Nomograms for resonant-circuit Q. D. W. Moffat. il Electr World 83:30-1 My '70
    See also
Impedance (electricity)
Reactance (electricity)
ELECTRIC resistors
Super substitution box. R. Tenny. il Pop Electr 33:79-81 Jl '70
ELECTRIC rocket engines. See Rocket engines
ELECTRIC saws. See Saws
ELECTRIC scissors. See Scissors and shears
ELECTRIC serving carts. See Serving carts
ELECTRIC shavers. See Razors
ELECTRIC shock
Amnesia produced by electroconvulsive shock or cycloheximide: conditions for recovery. D. Quartermain and others. bibliog il Science 169:683-6 Ag 14 '70
Retrograde amnesia: production of skeletal but not cardiac response gradient by electroconvulsive shock. B. Hine and R. M. Paolino. bibliog il Science 169:1224-6 S 18 '70
    See also
Electricity, Injuries from
ELECTRIC signs
Times square news: sign around the Allied chemical tower, written by the Associated press. New Yorker 46:20-2 Ag 1 '70
Transit signs to tell it like it is; Bay area rapid transit system. il Am City 85:102 N '70
ELECTRIC soldering iron. See Soldering apparatus
ELECTRIC stoves
Cooking with glass. M. K. Spencer. il Am Home 74:66+ Ja '71
Corning counterange. il Consumer Rep 35:697 N '70
Electric ranges. Consumer Rep 34:93-7 D '69
Hot plates. il Consumer Rep 34:664-6 N '69
Ranges with self-cleaning ovens. il Consumer Rep 35:691-700 N '70
Thirty inch electric ranges with self-cleaning ovens. il Consumer Bul 53:7-13 N '70
ELECTRIC switches
Putting reed switches to work. D. Blacklock. il Electr World 84:38-42 Ag '70
Safety switch for mini-bikes; mercury switch. il Radio-Electr 41:92 O '70
ELECTRIC toasters
Electric toasters. il Consumer Rep 34:643-8 N '69
ELECTRIC tools
How to tune in on RPMs. P. E. Fiechter and R. J. De Cristoforo. il Pop Sci 196: 104-5 F '70

Brakes

See Brakes

Safety devices and measures

New safety rules for stationary power tools. R. Doty. il Pop Sci 197:100-1 O '70
ELECTRIC tools, Portable
Power tools. T. R. Haskett. il Radio-Electr 41:54-8 N '70
Rotary electric hobby tools. il Consumer Bul 53:4+ F '70
    See also
Black and Decker manufacturing company
ELECTRIC tractors. See Tractors
ELECTRIC transformers
Build the autotransformer package; variable ac voltage. J. R. Squires. il Radio-Electr 41:42-4 S '70
Ferroresonant transformer improves color TV. N. Ferency. il Electr World 83:46-7 F '70
    See also
Radio transformers
ELECTRIC transmission
Superconducting power transmission; adaptation of address. D. P. Snowden. bibliog Phys Today 23:42-3 D '70
    See also
Electric lines
Electric power

ELECTRIC utilities
Danger of more power blackouts. il U S News 68:48-50 Ap 20 '70
Economic impact of electric vehicles: a scenario. B. C. Netschert. il Bul Atom Sci 26: 29-35 My '70
Energy crisis: environmental issue exacerbates power supply problem. P. M. Boffey. Science 163:1554-9 Je 26 '70
Face-to-face with the power crisis. il Bsns W p52 Jl 11 '70
Power-short winter? interview. C. F. Luce. il por U S News 69:38-42 N 9 '70
To keep the light burning. il Forbes 106:22-6+ Jl 15 '70
Utilities sweat over the summer. Bsns W p30 Je 6 '70
    See also
Consolidated Edison company of New York
Florida power and light company
General public utilities corporation
Potomac electric power company of Washington, D.C.
Southern California Edison company

Finance

Making money work; Potomac electric power. S. Meisenberg. il Har Yrs 10:48-9 S '70

Public relations

Enlightenment strikes a utility. il Bsns W p 142+ Mr 28 '70

Regulation

    See also
United States—Federal power commission

Securities

Making money work; investing in electric utility companies. S. Meisenberg. il Har Yrs 10:41+ N '70
ELECTRIC vaporizers. See Vaporizers
ELECTRIC vehicles
Economic impact of electric vehicles: a scenario. B. C. Netschert. il Bul Atom Sci 26: 29-35 My '70
    See also
Automobiles, Electric
Motor buses, Electric
ELECTRIC voltage. See Voltage
ELECTRIC washing machines. See Washing machines
ELECTRIC waves
    See also
Electromagnetic waves
Electrooptics
Microwaves
ELECTRIC welders. See Welders
ELECTRIC wire and wiring
Shocking potential of grounding wires. il Consumer Rep 35:660 N '70
Wire that slices the cost of copper: sandwich of aluminum and copper. il Bsns W p49+ My 16 '70
    See also
Automobiles—Electric wiring
Boats—Electric equipment
Electric cables
Electric cords
ELECTRIC workers
    See also
Strikes—United States—Electric workers
ELECTRIC workers slowdown, Great Britain. See Strikes—Great Britain
ELECTRICAL stimulation of the brain. See Electronic behavior control
ELECTRICITY
    See also
Impedance (electricity)
Magnetism
Ohm's law
    also headings beginning Electric, Electro

History

Revolution in electrical technology, 1870-1900; AAAS symposium, December 27, 1970. O. Mayr. il Science 170:1339-40 D 18 '70

Social aspects

Mythos of the electronic revolution. J. W. Carey and J. J. Quirk. Am Scholar 39:219-41, 395-424 Spr-Sum '70
ELECTRICITY, Injuries from
First aid. C. J. Potthoff. Todays Health 48: 74 My '70
Protecting infants from electrical dangers. S. Murata. il Todays Health 48:70 Je '70
Strange effect of lightning on the body. Chem 43:23-4 My '70
ELECTRICITY, Static
Burning out your circuits without really trying. E. J. Queen. il Pop Electr 32:71 My '70

ELECTRICITY on boats. See Boats—Electric equipment
ELECTROCHEMICAL analysis
See also
Polarograph and polarography
ELECTROCONVULSIVE shock. See Electric shock
ELECTRODES
Potassium-adenosine triphosphate complex: formation constant measured with ion-selective electrodes. G. A. Rechnitz and M. S. Mohan. bibliog il Science 168:1460 Je 19 '70
Potassium ion specific electrode with high selectivity for potassium over sodium. M. S. Frant and J. W. Ross, jr. bibliog il Science 167:987-8 F 13 '70
ELECTROENCEPHALOGRAPHY
Cortical unit activity in desynchronized sleep. R. W. McCarley and J. A. Hobson bibliog il Science 167:901-3 F 6 '70
Discoverer of the brain wave. J. L. O'Leary. Science 168:562-3 My 1 '70
Facilitation of spindle-burst sleep by conditioning of electroencephalographic activity while awake. M. B. Sterman and others. bibliog il Science 167:1146-8 F 20 '70
ELECTROLYSIS
See also
Sewage disposal—Electrolytic treatment
ELECTROLYTIC treatment of trade wastes. See Trade waste disposal
ELECTROMAGNETIC spectrum. See Spectrum
ELECTROMAGNETIC theory
See also
Blackbody radiation
ELECTROMAGNETIC waves
Attenuation of an earth-space path measured in the wavelength range of 8 to 14 micrometers. R. W. Wilson. il Science 168:1456-7 Je 19 '70
Electromagnetics of the sea; report of NATO conference, June 1970. J. A. Wait. Science 170:1124+ D 4 '70
ELECTROMAGNETISM
See also
Faraday effect
ELECTRON beams. See Electrons—Beams
ELECTRON-bombardment ion engine. See Rocket engines
ELECTRON microprobe. See Electron probe microanalyzer
ELECTRON microscope and microscopy
Acetabularia chloroplast DNA: electron microscopic visualization. B. R. Green and H. Burton. bibliog il Science 168:981-2 My 22 '70
Atom revealed; University of Chicago physicists photograph individual atoms. il Newsweek 75:63 Je 1 '70
Electron microscope. il Chem 43:27-8 F '70
High-voltage transmission electron microscopy study of lunar surface material. S. V. Radcliffe and others. bibliog il Science 167:638-40 Ja 30 '70
Image-formation technique for scanning electron microscopy and electron probe microanalysis. K. F. J. Heinrich and others. bibliog il Science 167:1129-31 F 20 '70
Individual atoms photographed. A. Crewe. il Sci N 97:524 My 30 '70
Invisible world in 3-D. C. P. Gilmore. il Pop Sci 196:62-4+ Ap '70
Macrophage membranes viewed through a scanning electron microscope. A. H. Warfel and S. E. Elberg. bibliog il Science 170:446-7 O 23 '70
Photo of single atoms by electron microscope. G. B. Lubkin. Phys Today 23:41-2 Ag '70
Scanning electron microscopy of developing plant organs. R. H. Falk and others. bibliog il Science 168:1471-2 Je 19 '70
Scanning electron microscopy of fresh leaves of pinguicula. Y. Heslop-Harrison. bibliog il Science 167:172-4 Ja 9 '70
Scanning electron microscopy of the organ of Corti. G. Bredberg and others. bibliog il Science 170:861-3 N 20 '70
Scleractinian coral exoskeletons: surface microarchitecture and attachment scar patterns. S. W. Wise, jr. bibliog il Science 169:978-80 S 4 '70
Subliming ice surfaces: freeze-etch electron microscopy. J. G. Davy and D. Branton. bibliog il Science 168:1216-18 Je 5 '70
Visible atoms. il Sci Am 223:48 Ag '70
Visibility of single atoms. A. V. Crewe and others. bibliog il Science 168:1338-40 Je 12 '70
Visualization of bacterial genes in action. O. L. Miller, jr. and others. bibliog il Science 169:392-5 Jl 24 '70

Conferences
High-voltage electron microscopy. H. S. Bennett and others. Science 168:506-7 Ap 24 '70

ELECTRON multipliers. See Photoelectric multipliers
ELECTRON optics
Optoelectronics ,a growing field. L. Garner. il Pop Electr 32:79-80 My '70
See also
Image intensifiers
Television camera tubes
ELECTRON probe microanalyzer
Electron-microprobe analyses of phases in lunar samples. N. G. Ware and J. F. Lovering. bibliog il Science 167:517-20 Ja 30 '70
Electron microprobe analysis of lunar samples. I. Adler and others. il Science 167:590-2 Ja 30 '70
Electron probe X-ray microanalysis of a normal centriole. P. W. Schafer and J. A. Chandler. bibliog il Science 170:1204-5 D 11 '70
Image-formation technique for scanning electron microscopy and electron probe microanalysis. K. F. J. Heinrich and others. bibliog il Science 167:1129-31 F 20 '70
ELECTRON tubes
Digital instruments you can build; low-cost digital readouts. D. L. Steinbach. il Electr World 84:28-31+ Jl '70
Tube behind the army's SCR-268 radar; Eimac 100-TL. H. A. Zahl. il Electr World 83:37-9+ Je '70
ELECTRONIC alarms. See Electric alarms
ELECTRONIC apparatus and appliances
Build with IC's; electronic umpire. E. L. Miller. il Radio-Electr 41:46-7 D '70
Equipment report. J. Darr. See issues of Radio-electronics
New avionics products. See occasional issues of Aviation week & space technology
New products. See issues of Radio-electronics
New products & literature. See issues of Electronics world
Product gallery. See issues of Popular electronics
Technical topics. R. F. Scott. il Radio-Electr 41:59-61 My; 67-9 S '70
To the constructor; obtaining parts. R. F. Scott. Radio-Electr 41:6+ N '70
See also
Blind, Apparatus for the
Calculating machines. Electronic
Electron probe microanalyzer
Electronic control
Electronic instruments
Microwave wiring
Telescopes—Equipment
also subhead Electronic equipment under various subjects, e.g. Airplanes—Electronic equipment

Exhibitions
Big country: Consumer electronics show, at the Americana and Hilton hotels. New Yorker 46:21-2 Jl 11 '70
Sales sound a sweeter note; Consumer electronics show in New York. il Bsns W p24 Jl 4 '70

Maintenance and repair
C.E.T. test; measurements. D. Glass. Electr World 84:62 S '70
Service clinic; questions and answers. J. Darr. See issues of Radio-electronics
Technotes. See issues of Radio-electronics

Power supply
Build solid state power supplies. M. Mandl. il Radio-Electr 41:49-51 D '70
Build: Zener power box. I. Queen. il Radio-Electr 41:78-9 Jl '70
Design and construction of regulated power supplies. R. H. Dutton. il Electr World 83:30-3+ F '70
Stable one-IC reference supply. H. A. Wittlinger. il Electr World 84:70 Jl '70
Universal regulated power supply. R. A. Walton. il Electr World 84:60-1 Ag '70

Testing
EW lab tested. See issues of Electronics world
ELECTRONIC apparatus industry and trade
See also
Computer industry

Finance
Electronics and electrical products; with yardsticks of management performance. il Forbes 105:165-6+ Ja 1 '70
Electronics; with yardsticks of management performance. il Forbes 107:136+ Ja 1 '71

Great Britain
Britain's avionics industry expands export efforts to ease slowdown. Aviation W 92:216-17 Mr 9 '70

ELECTRONIC apparatus industry and trade—
Great Britain—*Continued*
U.K. electronics makers ask review of co-
operation policy. Aviation W 92:59 My 11
'70
See also
Electronic apparatus industry and trade—
Scotland

Italy

Italians try hand in a tough market; Socie-
tá generale semiconduttori. Bsns W p 106
F 14 '70

Japan

Cool cat and his red-hot company; Akai
electric. il por Bsns W p46 Ap 25 '70
See also
Computer industry—Japan

Mexico

Latins turn north to one of their own;
Majestic group. il Bsns W p49 Mr 21 '70

Scotland

Scotland's bonnie boom in electronics. il Bsns
W p26-7 Jl 4 '70

Taiwan

Counterattack base for U.S. companies. il
Bsns W p38 Jl 11 '70

United States

Avionics: new growth on the ground. L. Rich.
il Duns 95:79-80+ Je '70
Avionics offers prime target for air cargo
expansion. Aviation W 93:122-6 O 26 '70
Electronics geography quiz. T. Haskett. Pop
Electr 32:42+ Ap '70
Navcom newcomers; Bertea electronics, Dy-
nair, General aviation electronics and Edo-
Aire. R. Blodget. Flying 86:55-7 Ap '70
Rising electronics market expected. Aviation
W 93:85 S 14 '70
Troubled industry with a promising future. il
U S News 68:76-8 My 25 '70
See also
Collins radio company
EG&G, inc.
Energy conversion devices, inc.
Fairchild camera and instrument corporation
General instrument corporation
Hewlett Packard company
Milgo electronic corporation
Motorola, inc.
RCA corporation
Sylvania electric products, inc.
Tally corporation
Technitrol, inc.
Telex corporation
Texas instruments, inc.
Transitron electronic corporation
Varadyne, inc.
Varian associates

ELECTRONIC associates, inc.
Rest in peace. il Forbes 105:39 Ja 15 '70

ELECTRONIC attitude director indicator. See
Aeronautic instruments—Display systems

ELECTRONIC behavior control
Behavioral measure of homosynaptic and
heterosynaptic temporal summation in the
self-stimulation system of rats. L. G. Ungerleider and E. E. Coons. bibliog il Science 169:785-7 Ag 21 '70
Behavioral measurement of neural poststimulation excitability cycle: pain cells
in the brain of the rat. R. S. Kestenbaum. bibliog il Science 167:393-6 Ja 23 '70
Brain researcher José Delgado asks: what
kind of humans would we like to construct?
M. Scarf. il pors N Y Times Mag p46-7+ N
15 '70; Discussion. p21+ D 13 '70
Circadian rhythm of brain self-stimulation
behavior. M. Terman and J. S. Terman.
bibliog il Science 168:1242-4 Je 5 '70
Frequency-specific relation between hippocampal theta rhythm, behavior, and amobarbital action. J. A. Gray and G. G. Ball.
bibliog il Science 168:1246-8 Je 5 '70
Neural readout from memory during generalization. E. R. John and others; discussion.
bibliog il Science 169:303-5 Jl 17 '70
Reticular stimulation and chlorpromazine: an
animal model for schizophrenic overarousal.
C. Kornetsky and M. Eliasson; reply with
rejoinder. M. I. Phillips and P. B. Bradley.
Science 168:1122-3 My 29 '70
Shock for Paddy; stimoceiver. il por Newsweek 76:88 S 28 '70
Temporal summation and refractoriness in
hypothalamic reward neurons as measured
by self-stimulation behavior. N. S. Smith
and E. E. Coons. bibliog il Science 169:782-5
Ag 21 '70

ELECTRONIC brains. See Artificial intelligence

ELECTRONIC circuits
Noteworthy circuits. il Radio-Electr 41:85
F '70
Quiz on AC circuit theory. R. P. Balin. il
Pop Electr 33:44+ D '70
Technical topics (cont) R. F. Scott. il Radio-
Electr 41:42-3 F; 59-61 My; 67-9 S '70
Vector-circuit matching quiz. R. P. Balin.
il Pop Electr 32:30+ Je '70
See also
Computers—Circuits
Printed circuits
Radio circuits
Telephone circuits
Television circuits
Transistor circuits

Design

Designing LC tuned circuits. A. H. Seidman.
il por Electr World 83:54-6 Ap '70

Manufacture

Film carrier may cut microcircuit cost. il
Aviation W 93:48-9 D 21 '70

ELECTRONIC circuits, integrated
Bipolar semiconductor IC memories. J. J.
Rienzo and E. F. Tarbox. il pors Electr
World 84:44-5 O '70
Digital instruments. D. L. Steinbach. il Electr
World 84:50-2+ S '70
Experimenters, thirty IC circuits you can use.
R. M. Marston. il Radio-Electr 41:62-3+ F
'70
GE is unreeling new circuits. il Bsns W p22+
D 12 '70
Hybrid technology regains IC spotlight. L.
Stern. il Electr World 83:42-5+ F '70
IC experimenter's corner:
Build a shift register. D. Lancaster. il
Pop Electr 32:43-7 My '70
Build a signal injector. D. Lancaster. il
Pop Electr 32:43-5 Je '70
Build the 100-kHz standard. D. Lancaster.
il Pop Electr 32:56-8+ Ap '70
Build the two-tone Waverly alarm. D.
Lancaster. il Pop Electr 32:29-31 F '70
Input trigger source for digital circuits.
D. Lancaster. il Pop Electr 32:51-3 Mr
'70
IC memories, growth and future. D. Mrazek.
il Electr World 83:25-9+ Mr; 34-6+ Ap '70
Integrated circuit that is catching up; MOS
devices. il Bsns W p 134+ Ap 25 '70
Large-scale integration in electronics. F. G.
Heath. il Sci Am 222:22-31 F '70
Linear integrated circuits; symposium. il
Electr World 84:35-54 Jl '70
MOSFET semiconductor IC memories. R. N.
Noyce. il por Electr World 84:46-8 O '70
New IC multiplex detector. K. F. Buegel. il
Radio-Electr 41:33-5 Mr '70
One IC replaces entire I.F. strip; new FM
tuner. L. Steckler. il Radio-Electr 41:59-61
N '70
Thirty new IC circuits you can use. R. M.
Marston. il Radio-Electr 41:22+ Ag; 37-40+
N '70
See also
Computers—Circuits
Television circuits

Manufacture

Three masks make a circuit; new Bell laboratories process. Sci Am 222:46 Ap '70

ELECTRONIC clocks. See Clocks, Electronic

ELECTRONIC compass. See Compass

ELECTRONIC components. See Electronic apparatus and appliances

ELECTRONIC control
Newest control device is ceramic. L. Garner.
il Pop Electr 32:86-7+ Ap '70
TC switch, for remote control. J. Bechtold.
il Pop Electr 32:52-5 Ap '70
See also
Camera shutters—Control
Electric motors—Control
Telescopes—Equipment
Transistors—Control uses

ELECTRONIC counters. See Counting machines
and devices

ELECTRONIC data processing
Emerging EDP pattern. C. W. Hofer. bibliog
il Harvard Bsns R 48:16-18+ Mr '70
Problem solver, problem maker. il Bsns W
p 184-5+ O 17 '70
See also
Artificial intelligence
Computers
Data processing service centers
Data transmission systems
Information systems, Management
Telephone—Data transmission systems

ELECTRONIC data processing—*Continued*

Legal aspects
See Computers—Laws and regulations

Security measures
Computer: a target. J. Perham. il Duns 97:
34-6 Ja '71
Crime in industry: using the computer to
steal; address, September 9, 1970. H. S.
Gellman. Vital Speeches 37:152-5 D 15 '70
Cryptic computers. Sci Am 222:52 Ja '70

Study and teaching
Computer science for high school students.
il Sch & Soc 98:6 Ja '70
ELECTRONIC data processing workers. See
Computer workers
ELECTRONIC data systems corporation
Perils of Perot. por Time 95:88-9 My 4 '70
Perot's plunge. Newsweek 75:73 My 4 '70
ELECTRONIC dice. See Dice
ELECTRONIC digital computers. See Com-
puters—Digital computers
ELECTRONIC flash meters. See Exposure—
Meters
ELECTRONIC flash photography. See Photog-
raphy, Flashlight
ELECTRONIC games
Electronic checker game. il Pop Mech 134:
176-9+ N '70
Electronic football lets you play like the pros.
R. F. Graf and G. J. Whalen. il Pop Mech
134:146-50+ O '70
Electronic tick-tack-toe in a cigarette box. B.
Bawer and W. J. Hawkins. il Pop Sci 197:
78-9+ D '70
Penniac $150 game computer. R. R. Yost. il
Radio-Electr 41:44-8+ Ap '70
ELECTRONIC instruments
Assemble a digital measurements lab (title
varies) D. Meyer. il Pop Electr 33:51-3+
N '70; 34:63-7+ Ja '71
See also
Testing instruments
ELECTRONIC locks. See Locks and keys
ELECTRONIC medical apparatus. See Medical
electronics
ELECTRONIC mixers. See Sound—Apparatus
ELECTRONIC music. See Music, Electronic
ELECTRONIC music synthesizer. See Musical
instruments, Electronic
ELECTRONIC musical instruments. See Musical
instruments, Electronic
ELECTRONIC organ. See Organ
ELECTRONIC ovens
Facts about microwave ovens. Good H 171:
184 O '70
Microwave ovens, revolution in cooking. D. R.
McConnell. il Electr World 84:25-9+ Ag '70
Microwave rage. M. Davidson. il Ladies
Home J 87:28+ F '70

Radiation hazards
Microwave ovens, revolution in cooking. D.
R. McConnell. il Electr World 84:37-9+
S '70
Out of the frying pan. T. Aaronson. bibliog
il Environ 12:26-31 Je '70
ELECTRONIC parts. See Electronic apparatus
and appliances
ELECTRONIC photoflash units. See Photog-
raphy—Electronic equipment
ELECTRONIC service associations
What price independence? J. Frye. Electr
World 83:56-7 F '70
See also
National electronic associations
ELECTRONIC service shops
Divide up for efficiency; layout suggestions.
J. Darr. Radio-Electr 41:24 My '70
Service American and the independent. J.
Frye. Electr World 84:51-2 N '70
ELECTRONIC stethoscope. See Stethoscope,
Electric
ELECTRONIC technicians
Careers in aviation electronics. L. Buck-
walter. il Radio-Electr 41:48-50 Je '70
Careers in electronics, blueprint to your fu-
ture; computer maintenance. G. C. Garmus.
il Radio-Electr 41:52-4 N '70
Careers in electronics, blueprint to your fu-
ture; licensing and other means of achieving
recognition. L. E. Frenzel, jr. il Radio-
Electr 41:65-7 D '70
Technician training; Magnovox program. il
Radio-Electr 41:26 Je '70
Technicians in scientific electronics. D. L.
Heiserman. il Pop Electr 32:83-5 Ap '70
Vocation profile: marine electronics servic-
ing. R. Patton. il Electr World 84:23-5+ N
'70
See also
Capitol radio engineering institute
National electronic associations
Television servicemen

ELECTRONIC test instruments. See Testing
instruments
ELECTRONIC thermometers. See Thermom-
eters, Clinical; Thermometers and ther-
mometry
ELECTRONIC tick-tack-toe. See Electronic
games
ELECTRONIC timers. See Timing devices
ELECTRONIC video recording. See Video
recorders and recording
ELECTRONIC vote counters. See Voting ma-
chines
ELECTRONIC warfare. See Electronics—Mil-
itary applications
ELECTRONIC watches. See Watches, Electric
ELECTRONICS
Recent developments in electronics. See is-
sues of Electronics world
See also
Cathode ray tubes
Electron tubes
Medical electronics
Microelectronics
Oscillators, Crystal
Semiconductors
Transistors

Anecdotes, facetiae, satire, etc.
Kool-keeping kwiz. C. Kohler. Pop Electr
32:63-4 Je '70

Bibliography
Books (cont of) Book reviews. See issues of
Electronics world
Electronics library. See issues of Popular
electronics
New books. See issues of Radio-electronics

Military use
Military concentrating on reliability, cost. il
Aviation W 93:15 D 28 '70
New roles grow for electro-optics. B. Miller.
il Aviation W 92:155-8+ Je 22 '70
Pentagon plays electronic war games. il Bsns
W p76-7 Ja 31 '70
Strong ECM market found abroad. B. Miller.
Aviation W 93:62-3+ O 19 '70
World air defense market grows; automated
command/control systems. B. Miller. il
Aviation W 94:38-42 Ja 4 '71
See also
Vietnamese war, 1957- —Equipment and sup-
plies

Periodicals
See also
Electronics world (periodical)
Popular electronics (periodical)

Social aspects
Mythos of the electronic revolution. J. W.
Carey and J. J. Quirk. Am Scholar 39:219-
41, 395-424 Spr-Sum '70

Study and teaching
Electronics self-study course. K. J. Englert.
il Pop Electr 33:45-8 D '70

Terminology
Glossary. Motor B 125:106-7 My '70
ELECTRONICS as a profession
Careers in aviation electronics. L. Buck-
walter. il Radio-Electr 41:48-50 Je '70
Careers in electronics, blueprint to your fu-
ture. il Radio-Electr 41:45-6 S; 68-9+ O; 52-4
N; 65-7 D '70
Opportunity mirror; questions and answers.
D. L. Heiserman. See issues of Popular
electronics
See also
Electronic technicians
ELECTRONICS in aeronautics. See Electronics
in aviation
ELECTRONICS in agriculture
Farm uses for solid-state electronics. Suc
Farm 68:no4 C14 Mr '70
ELECTRONICS in aviation
Avionics: new growth on the ground. L. Rich.
il Duns 95:79-80+ Je '70
FAA plans $2.5 billion avionics growth. P. J.
Klass. il Aviation W 92:203+ Mr 9 '70
ELECTRONICS in business
Sharpen your image with electronic gear.
Bsns W p 121 Ap 18 '70
ELECTRONICS in criminal investigation, es-
pionage, etc.
Build Security I; scrambler system. J. Pina.
il Pop Electr 32:27-33 My '70
Cops hit the jackpot; Law enforcement as-
sistance administration grants for com-
puter and video tape systems. J. C.
Goulden. il Nation 211:520-33 N 23 '70
Defamation by wire tap; release of trans-
cript of recorded New Jersey Mafia con-
versations. Nation 210:66-7 Ja 26 '70

ELECTRONICS in criminal investigation, espionage, etc.—*Continued*
Mafia and the law; release of FBI transcripts of recorded conversations of the New Jersey Mafia. Commonweal 91:444 Ja 23 '70
Night scopes add extra insight to police work; Newton, Mass. W. F. Quinn. Am City 85:16 O '70
Wanted: electronic detectives. M. Schultz. il Pop Mech 135:110-13 Ja '71
See also
Wire tapping

ELECTRONICS in geophysics
Electronics & meteorites. L. G. Lawrence. bibliog il Electr World 84:23-6+ Jl '70

ELECTRONICS in medicine. See Medical electronics

ELECTRONICS in meteorology
Electronics goes CAT catching. W. Garrison. il Pop Electr 33:29-34 N '70

ELECTRONICS in navigation
Marine electronics, 1970 style. J. West. il Yachting 127:60-2 My; 128:68-70 Jl; 60-2+ Ag '70

ELECTRONICS in parapsychology
Electronics and parapsychology. L. G. Lawrence. bibliog il Electr World 83:27-9 Ap '70

ELECTRONICS in photography
Electronics in photography. J. R. Free. il Radio-Electr 41:33-4 F '70
See also
Photography—Electronic equipment

ELECTRONICS in pollution control
Electronics, the white knight? J. Frye. Electr World 84:55-6 Jl '70

ELECTRONICS in traffic control
Solving the traffic nightmare with electronics. A. Hamilton. il Sci Digest 69:46-8+ Ja '71

ELECTRONICS industry and trade. See Electronic apparatus industry and trade

ELECTRONICS research center. See United States—National aeronautics and space administration—Electronics research center

ELECTRONICS world (periodical)
Code-breaking for subscribers. Electr World 84:77 O '70

ELECTRONS
Electron-repulsion theory: application to aliphatic and aromatic hydrocarbons. S. Zuffanti. bibliog il por Chem 43:8-13 My '70
Natural coordinates for electrons in solids. J. Zak. bibliog il por Phys Today 23:51-4 F '70
Pyramid of electron configuration. R. G. Anderson. il Chem 43:27 Je '70
See also
Beta rays
Electron optics
Mesons
Molecular orbitals
Plasma (ionized gases)
Quantum electrodynamics

Beams
New polarized-electron source; letter. R. J. Krisciokaitis. Phys Today 23:15+ F '70
New solid-state devices evolve; electron beam semiconductors. B. M. Elson. il Aviation W 93:51+ D 7 '70

Emission
See also
Thermionic emission

Scattering
Some three-body atomic systems; adaptation of address, February 3, 1969. J. W. McGowan. bibliog il Science 167:1083-92 F 20 '70

ELECTRO-optical memories. See Memory devices (computers)

ELECTROOPTICS
New roles grow for electro-optics. B. Miller. il Aviation W 92:155-8+ Je 22 '70
No need for blinds; Varad dipolar electro-optic structure. S. V. Jones. il Sci Digest 68:59 O '70

ELECTROPHORESIS
Microelectrophoresis of biogenic amines on hypothalamic thermosensitive cells. A. L. Beckman and J. S. Eisenman. bibliog il Science 170:334-6 O 16 '70
Serum hepatitis antigen (SH): rapid detection by high voltage immunoelectroosmophoresis. A. M. Prince and K. Burke. bibliog il Science 169:593-5 Ag 7 '70
Threonine deaminase: a novel activitiy stain on polyacrylamide gels. R. S. Feldberg and P. Datta. bibliog il Science 170:1414-16 D 25 '70

ELECTROPHYSIOLOGY
Adenohypophysial transmembrane potentials: polarity reversal by elevated external potassium ion concentration. J. V. Milligan and J. Kraicer. bibliog il Science 167:182-4 Ja 9 '70

Auditory frequency-following response: neural or artifact? J. T. Marsh and others. il Science 169:1222-3 S 18 '70
Catch property in single mammalian motor units. R. E. Burke and others. bibliog il Science 168:122-4 Ap 3 '70
Cell surface coatings and membrane potentials of malignant and nonmalignant cells. L. Hause and others. bibliog il Science 169:601-3 Ag 7 '70
Changes of simple and complex spike activity of cerebellar Purkinje cells with sleep and waking. N. I. Mano. bibliog il Science 170:1325-7 D 18 '70
Cochlear nerve fiber discharge patterns: relationship to the cochlear microphonic. R. R. Pfeiffer and C. E. Molnar. bibliog il Science 167:1614-16 Mr 20 '70
Dorsal root potentials produced by stimulation of fine afferents. G. D. Dawson and others. bibliog il Science 167:1385-7 Mr 6 '70
Electrical coupling: low resistance junctions between mitotic and interphase fibroblasts in tissue culture. P. O'Lague and others. bibliog il Science 170:464-6 O 23 '70
Electricity & physiology. W. Garrison. il Pop Electr 34:27-31 Ja '71
Electrophysiological evidence for binocular disparity detectors in human visual system. A. Fiorentini and L. Maffei. bibliog il Science 169:208-9 Jl 10 '70
How is muscle turned on and off? G. Hoyle. il Sci Am 222:84-93 bibliog(p 130) Ap '70
Human auditory evoked potentials: possible brain stem components detected on the scalp. D. L. Jewett and others. bibliog il Science 167:1517-18 Mr 13 '70
Neural events and the psychophysical law. S. S. Stevens. bibliog il Science 170:1043-50 D 4 '70
Neurophysiological localization of the vertical and horizontal visual coordinates in man. L. Maffei and F. W. Campbell. bibliog il Science 167:386-7 Ja 23 '70
Number coding in association cortex of the cat. R. F. Thompson and others. bibliog il Science 168:271-3 Ap 10 '70
Predicting measures of motor performance from multiple cortical spike trains. D. R. Humphrey and others. bibliog il Science 170:758-62 N 13 '70
Proteins in excitable membranes. D. Nachmansohn. bibliog il Science 168:1059-66 My 29 '70; Discussion 170:1228-9, 1332-3 D 11-18 '70
Serotonin-containing neurons in brain: depression of firing by monoamine oxidase inhibitors. G. K. Aghajanian and others. bibliog il Science 169:1100-2 S 11 '70
Slow synaptic excitation in sympathetic ganglion cells: evidence for synaptic inactivation of potassium conductance. F. F. Weight and J. Votava. bibliog il Science 170:755-8 N 13 '70
Somatovisceral pathway: rapidly conducting fibers in the spinal cord. H. L. Fields and D. L. Winter. bibliog il Science 167:1729-30 Mr 27 '70
Superior colliculus: single unit responses to stimulation of visual cortex in the cat. J. T. McIlwain and H. L. Fields. bibliog il Science 170:1426-8 D 25 '70
Synaptic potentials recorded in cell cultures of nerve and muscle. G. D. Fischbach. bibliog il Science 169:1331-3 S 25 '70
Visual receptor potential: modification by injected current in the limulus lateral eye. V. J. Wulff and C. Mendez. bibliog il Science 168:1351-3 Je 12 '70
See also
Brain waves
Electroencephalography

Apparatus
Turning on with alpha waves; Aquarian alphaphone. il Life 69:60-1 Ag 21 '70

ELECTROPLATING
Self-powered gun for electroplating. P. Wahl. il Pop Sci 197:84 Ag '70

ELECTROSTATIC air filters. See Air filters

ELEGANCE. See Fashion

ELEKTRA; opera. See Strauss, R.

ELEMENTARY and secondary education act of 1965. See Education—Federal aid

ELEMENTARY education. See Education, Elementary

ELEMENTARY particles. See Particles (nuclear physics)

ELEMENTARY school buildings. See School buildings

ELEMENTARY school children. See School children

ELEMENTARY school counseling. See Educational guidance

ELEMENTARY school dropouts. See Dropouts
ELEMENTS, Chemical. See Chemical elements
ELEO Pomare dance company. See Dance
  companies
ELEPHANT hunting
  Elephants on the Zambezi. J. O'Connor. il por
    Outdoor Life 145:33-5+ Ja '70
ELEPHANTS
  Birth of elephant twins. il Sci Digest 69:24-5
    Ja '71
ELEPHANTS, Fossil
  See also
    Mammoths
    Mastodons
ELEUTHERA ISLAND
  Current and choice. D. Butwin. il Sat R 53:
    55-6 Mr 28 '70
ELEVATED sidewalks. See Sidewalks, Elevated
ELEVATORS
  Optimizing space requirements for elevators.
    W. W. Swartz. il Arch Rec 147:133-6 Mr '70
  Tandem elevators save space, improve ser-
    vice. il Arch Forum 133:50-1 O '70
  See also
    Otis elevator company
ELFENBEIN, Josef A.
  Puss-in-boots; dramatization of a fairy tale.
    Plays 29:67-73 F '70
ELGAR, Sir Edward William, 1st bart
  Sir Edward Elgar, a portrait. J. Diether. por
    Am Rec G 36:766-7 My '70 *
EL GORESEY, Ahmed. See Goresey, A.
ELI Lilly and company. See Lilly, Eli, and
  company
ELIAS, Nicholas
  Greece, three years after. il N Y Times Mag
    p30-1+ My 3 '70
ELIASSON, Mona. See Kornetsky, C. jt. auth.
ELIAV, Arie
  Lion's roar. por Time 95:26-7 Ja 26 '70
ELIOT, Charles William
  Americans not everyone knows. C. W. Fergu-
    son. por PTA Mag 64:12-14+ Ap '70 *
ELIOT, Lang
  Chartering in the Mediterranean. il Motor B
    125:63+ My '70
ELIOT, Thomas Stearns
  Antique drum, by T. Howard. Review
    Nat R 22:34 Ja 14 '70. R. Kirk
  Eliot, Lawrence & the Jews. R. Alter. Com-
    mentary 50:81-6 O '70 *
  T.S. Eliot & Ezra Pound: collaborators in
    letters. D. Gallup. pors Atlan 225:48-62
    Ja '70
ELISCU, Edward
  Washington synthetics; poem. Nation 211:118
    Ag 17 '70
ELISEEV, Aleksei
  Economic efficiency of space flight. por Space
    World G-10-82:17-19 O '70
ELISOFON, Eliot
  Borobudur; photographs. il Horizon 12:16-19
    Wint '70
ELIZABETH, princess of Toro
  Princess goes to work. J. A. Segal. il pors
    Look 34:48-50 Je 30 '70 *
ELIZABETH Arden sales corporation. See Ar-
  den, Elizabeth, sales corporation
ELIZALDE, Fernando de
  UFO; story. Américas 22:38-9 Ag '70
ELK
  Elk drama in autumn; wild elk in the rut.
    W. J. McRae. il Outdoor Life 146:40-1 Jl '70
  Managing the Yellowstone elk. G. F. Cole.
    il Nat Parks & Con Mag 44:20-2 S '70
  Mike Frome; endangered tule elk. M. Frome.
    Am For 76:3 My '70; Discussion. 76:7 S;
    77-9 O '70
  Tule elk preserve proposed. Nat Parks & Con
    Mag 44:31 My '70
ELK hunting
  Elk charge this bugle. H. Rate. il Field & S
    75:54-5+ O '70
  How to get started on elk. J. R. Olt. il Field
    & S 75:38-9+ Ag '70
  Hunt we'll remember. R. Merchant. il Out-
    door Life 146:72-3+ S '70
ELKHOLY, Hussein
  Shopping for a time-sharing service. bib-
    liog il por Phys Today 23:40-4 Jl '70
ELKIN, Herbert
  $3.50 enlarging-time meter. il Radio-Electr
    41:35-6 F '70
ELKIN, Sol M.
  Another look at collective negotiations for
    professionals. Sch & Soc 98:173-5 Mr '70
ELKIN, Stanley
  Memory expert; story. Esquire 73:152-4 My
    '70

ELKIND, David
  Erik Erikson's eight ages of man. il N Y
    Times Mag p25-7+ Ap 5 '70
  Exploitation and the generational conflict.
    Ment Hy 54:490-7 O '70
  Freud, Jung and the collective unconscious.
    il pors N Y Times Mag p23-5+ O 4 '70
  Parent and child. il N Y Times Mag p90+
    O 11 '70
ELKIND, Joel
  Middle school muddle. Clear House 44:400
    Mr '70
ELKINS, Hillard
  Oh! Hillard Elkins! C. Davis. por Esquire 74:
    135-7+ N '70 *
ELKINS, Michael
  I deal with the realities. por Newsweek 76:42
    D 21 '70
ELLEN, Sister Mary. See Mary Ellen, Sister
ELLEN Murphy, Sister. See Murphy, E.
ELLENBURG, William P.
  Cop out. Newsweek 75:33+ F 16 '70 *
  Fiasco in Cleveland. por Time 95:15 F 16 '70 *
ELLENSBURG, Wash.
  Wood poles with a modern appeal. E. H.
    Knight. Am City 85:142 My '70
ELLER, Vernard
  Sex power and the revolution. il Chr Cent
    87:291-3. 1567-8 Mr 11, D 30 '70
ELLERY, William
  I am going off the stage of life; excerpt from
    Sibley's Harvard graduates. C. K. Ship-
    ton. por Am Heritage 21:2 Ag '70 *
ELLGAARD, Erik G. See Clever, U. jt. auth.
ELLINGHAUS, William M.
  New voice at New York telephone. il por
    Bsns W p60-2+ S 5 '70 *
  Ringing in the new. por Newsweek 76:70-1
    S 7 '70 *
ELLINGSON, Careth
  Children with no alternative. Sat R 53:61 N
    21 '70
ELLINGSON, Marnie
  I wonder if I have an inner value I don't
    know about; story. Redbook 134:90-1 Mr
    '70
  Storm; story. Ladies Home J 87:60-1 F '70
ELLINGTON, Duke
  Dance me a river. H. Saal. il Newsweek
    76:86 Jl 6 '70 *
  Our local correspondents. W. Balliett. New
    Yorker 46:52-5 Je 27 '70 *
ELLINWOOD, Lynne
  In-depth market report: the lucrative con-
    fessions. Writers Digest 51:28-30+ Ja '71
ELLIOT, David H. and others
  Triassic tetrapods from Antarctica: evidence
    for continental drift. bibliog il Science 169:
    1197-201 S 18 '70
ELLIOT, Elisabeth
  No disappointment in Jesus? Chr Today 15:
    11-12 D 18 '70
ELLIOTT, Alfred M. See Kennedy, J. R. jt.
  auth.
ELLIOTT, Bob. See Bob and Ray (comedians)
ELLIOTT, Charles
  Bass in the treetops. il Outdoor Life 146:60-
    1+ S '70
  Do you really want to be a turkey shooter?
    il por Outdoor Life 145:72-5+ Mr '70
  Getting the bait's a ball. il Outdoor Life 145:
    62-3+ My '70
  High in the velvet. il por Outdoor Life 146:
    60-3+ Ag '70
ELLIOTT, Charles (priest)
  Rich country, poor country. America 123:
    455-7 N 28 '70
ELLIOTT, George Paul
  Femina sapiens. story. Esquire 73:126-7 Mr
    '70
  Never nothing. il Harper 241:83-90+ S '70
          about
  Recurrences. X. J. Kennedy. Nation 210:378-80
    Mr 30 '70 *
ELLIOTT, Margaret Drake
  My dolls, Christmases. il Hobbies 75:48+
    D '70
ELLIOTT, Marion
  Yuma County schools fine arts festival il
    Sch Arts 69:28-30 F '70
ELLIOTT, Osborn
  (ed) See Nguyen-van-Thieu. View from
    Saigon: Thieu speaks out
ELLIOTT, Robert
  Narcotics: a crucial area of secondary school
    responsibility. Ed Digest 36:44-7 S '70
ELLIOTT, Virginia A.
  Suburbia reaches out. Engl J 59:660-4+ My '70
ELLIS, Charles D.
  Let's solve the endowment crisis. bibliog f
    il Harvard Bsns R 48:92-102 Mr '70

ELLIS, Don D.
My toughest patrol. il pors Outdoor Life 146:
62-5+ D '70
ELLIS, Elliot F.
Asthma, the demon that thrives on myths;
interview, ed. by B. Scott. pors Todays
Health 48:42-3+ Je '70
ELLIS, H. F.
Doctor's doctors. New Yorker 46:114-16+ S
19 '70
ELLIS, Harlan Reed
HEW: blacklists scrapped in new security
procedures. B. Nelson. Science 167:154-6
Ja 9 '70
ELLIS, Helene
Detroit market letter. il Writers Digest 50:34-
5 D '70
ELLIS, Ira T.
Can we have a bust? por Nations Bsns 58:
84-5 Mr '70
ELLIS, Jimmy
Bring on Ali. il por Newsweek 75:94 Mr 2
'70 *
Free at last? il por Time 95:51+ Mr 2 '70 *
Show biz is out, boxing is in. M. Kram.
il Sports Illus 32:14-15 F 16 '70 *
ELLIS, W. Geiger. See Meade, R. A. jt. auth.
ELLIS, William S.
Lebanon, little Bible land in the crossfire of
history. il Nat Geog 137:240-75 F '70
ELLIS ISLAND
NEGRO: creating our own GNP. il News-
week 76:71 S 28 '70
ELLIS memorial settlement house. See Boston
—Social settlements
ELLISON, Jayne
Medical writing. il Writers Digest 50:34-5 N
'70
ELLISON, John. See Policansky, D. jt. auth.
ELLISON, Ralph
Indivisible man; interview, ed. by J. A. Mc-
Pherson. por Atlan 226:45-60 D '70
What America would be like without blacks.
il Time 95:54-5 Ap 6 '70

about

Black fiction: a second look. C. Mason. pors
Life 68:18 My 8 '70
ELLISTON, Valerie
Two who deserved each other; story. Red-
book 134:76-7 Ap '70
ELLITHORPE, Hal
Walk through a deathly quiet countryside.
il por Life 69:5 D 4 '70
ELLMAN, Leonard, and others
Genetically controlled total deficiency of the
fourth component of complement in the
guinea pig. bibliog il Science 170:74-5 O 2 '70
ELLO, J. G.
Scintillation radiological survey meters. il
Electr World 83:39-43 Ja '70
ELLSWORTH, Robert Fred
Technology and international relations, 1970
and beyond; address, October 6, 1970. Dept
State Bul 63:641-7 N 23 '70
ELLUL, Jacques
Grand illusion. R. A. Nisbet. Commentary 50:
40-4 Ag '70
Mirror of these ten years. por Chr Cent
87:200-4 F 18 '70
ELM
Diseases and pests
Ally to protect elms? il Cons 24:21 F '70
Is there a cure for Dutch elm disease? Good
H 170:135 Ja '70
ELMAN, Philip
Regulatory process; address, August 11, 1970.
Vital Speeches 36:764-8 O 1 '70
ELMAN, Richard M.
If you were on welfare. il Sat R 53:27-9+ My
23 '70
ELON, Amos
Israelis believe war is inevitable. il Life 68:
46-48B+ F 6 '70
EL PASO, Texas
Description
Traveler's choice. M. Vandenburgh. Travel
133:22 Ap '70
ELROD, Richard
Chicago: truth and Elrod. Time 95:17 Je 22
'70 *
ELSON, Charles, and others
Antimycin A: stimulation of cell division and
protein synthesis in tetrahymena pyrifor-
mis. bibliog il Science 168:385-6 Ap 17 '70
ELSON, John T.
Bourbon: America's brandy. Travel & Camera
33:14+ F '70
Little wines from the soul of France. il
Travel & Camera 33:48-9+ Ap '70
Scotch: the Highlands' gift to all the world.
il Travel & Camera 33:59-60+ My '70
White spirits. Travel & Camera 33:12+ S '70
—See Kanfer, S. jt. comp.

ELSTEIN, Herman, and Hartz, F. R.
Professional developments reviewed: 1969
standards for school media programs. pors
Wilson Lib Bul 44:865-6 Ap '70
ELTRA corporation
See also
Prestolite company
ELVEHJEM art center. See Wisconsin. Uni-
versity—Elvehjem art center
ELVINS, Peter
Opera off the beat. il Opera N 34:14-16 My 16
'70
ELYRIA, Ohio, public library
Administration experiment tried in Elyria,
Ohio. Library J 95:1430 Ap 15 '70
EMANCIPATION of women. See Woman—Equal
rights
EMANCIPATION proclamation
Abraham Lincoln's hardest decision. T. Flem-
ing. por Read Digest 96:94-9 F '70
EMANS, Elaine V.
Day lilies; poem. Good H 170:242 Mr '70
Finder; poem. Farm J 93:44 N '69
Happy New Year; poem. Good H 170:110 Ja
'70
EMBARGO
Franco-Greek Mirage negotiations hinge on
embargo policy of U.S. Aviation W 92:18
23 '70
French embargo on arms undefined. D. E.
Fink. il Aviation W 93:55 N 2 '70
EMBASSIES (buildings)
Fall and rise of Walter Annenberg; Winfield
house, London. S. Birmingham. il por Mc-
Calls 97:72-9+ Je '70
Sitting ducks; U.S. embassy staff in Amman.
il Newsweek 76:44 Jl 13 '70
EMBASSIES (United States) See United States
—Diplomatic and consular service
EMBELLISHMENT (music)
Ornament and structure; excerpt from Bar-
oque ornamentation in France, Italy and
Germany, F. Neumann. bibliog f il Mus Q
56:153-61 Ap '70
EMBELLISHMENT (vocal music)
Mozart with a flourish. C. Mackerras. il
Opera N 34:24-5 Ap 11 '70
Vocal ornamentation in Caccini's Nuove
musiche. H. W. Hitchcock. bibliog f il Mus
Q 56:389-404 Jl '70
EMBEZZLEMENT
Eatontown caper; National bank. il por News-
week 76:46+ Ag 24 '70
$5-million that disappeared; How Eatontown
took the shutdown. il Bsns W p 17-19 Ag
15 '70
Hill of beans leads to a scandal. Bsns W
p29 O 31 '70
$2,000,000 grudge; case of M. Ermacora. il por
Time 96:30 O 5 '70
EMBLEMS
Symbolizing recreation; Bloomfield Hills
recreation department, Mich. E. Wichert.
il Parks & Rec 5:52 Ap '70
'20s gleam in auto emblems; simulated vitre-
ous enamel. il Bsns W p80+ Ag 22 '70
EMBLEMS, State
See also
State birds
State flowers
EMBOSSED prints. See Prints
EMBROIDERY
Betsy McCall, my embroidery book. S. Robin-
son. il McCalls 98:62-5 D '70
Ceramic stitchery; clay birds on stitched
backdrops. R. Wrenn. il pors Design 71:38-
41 mid-Sum '70
How poppies bloom, with needle, canvas, and
yarn. E. Haraszty. il McCalls 97:49-51+
Jl '70
Stitch a bit of greenery. il Good H 170:122+
My '70
See also
Crewel work
Needlework
Table mats, tiles, etc.
EMBROIDERY workers
Manly art of embroidery. E. Gaines. il An-
tiques 98:446-7 S '70
EMBRY-Riddle aeronautical institute. See Avi-
ation schools
EMBRYOLOGY
See also
Amniotic liquid
Differentiation (biology)
Embryology, Experimental
Fetus
Metamorphosis
Placenta
Reproduction

Echinoderms
Egg machine. P. T. Lindstrom il por Natur
Hist 79:52-5 F '70

EMBRYOLOGY—*Continued*

Fishes

See also
Fishes—Eggs

Mammals

Carbon dioxide fixation by mouse embryos prior to implantation. C. N. Graves and J. D. Biggers. bibliog il Science 167:1506-8 Mr 13 '70

EMBRYOLOGY, Experimental
Human embryos in the laboratory. R. G. Edwards and R. E. Fowler. il Sci Am 223:44-54 bibliog(p 140) D '70

Moral and religious aspects

Playing God. il Newsweek 76:120 N 23 '70

EMERGENCIES. See First aid in illness and injury

EMERGENCIES, Assistance in. See Assistance in emergencies

EMERGENCY blackout lanterns. See Electric lanterns

EMERGENCY communication systems
See also
Radio communication—Emergency use

EMERGENCY electric plants. See Electric plants, Emergency

EMERGENCY legislation

Canada

See War and emergency legislation—Canada

EMERGENCY powers. See Presidents—United States—Powers and duties

EMERSON, Paul
Build your own portable water tester. il Pop Sci 197:127-8+ S '70

EMERSON, Suzanne U. and others
Bacterial flagella: polarity of elongation. bibliog il Science 169:190-2 Jl 10 '70

EMERSON electric company
Be prepared. il Forbes 106:24-5 N 1 '70
Emerson's new disarmament policy. il por Bsns W p 110+ Ja 24 '70

EMIGRATION. See Immigration and emigration

EMIGRATION and immigration law. See Immigration and emigration law

ÉMIGRÉS
Indiana family leaves the U.S. for keeps; Argast family moves to Canada. il Life 69:42-7 Jl 17 '70

EMILIA-ROMAGNA
Low-profile Communists; results of Communist rule. il Time 97:34-5 Ja 4 '71

EMILIANI, Cesare
Interglacial high sea levels and the control of Greenland ice by the precession of the equinoxes. bibliog Science 166:1503-4; 168:1606 D 19 '69, Je 26 '70
Pleistocene paleotemperatures. bibliog il Science 168:822-5 My 15 '70

EMINENT domain (international law)
How to counter expropriation. W. R. Hoskins. bibliog f Harvard Bsns R 48:102-12 S '70

EMINENT men. See Great men

EMISSION spectroscopy. See Spectrum analysis

EMLEN, Mary Gay
Art and the slow learner. il Sch Arts 69:10-12 Mr '70

EMLEN, Stephen Thompson
Celestial rotation: its importance in the development of migratory orientation. bibliog il Science 170:1198-201 D 11 '70

EMMET, Christopher
Missing element in the debate. Nat R 22:678-9+ Je 30 '70

EMMETT, J. A.
Boating. See issues of Outdoor Life
New boats and motors. il Outdoor Life 145:66-70+ Ja '70

EMOTIONALLY disturbed children. See Mentally ill children; Problem children

EMOTIONS
See also
Anger
Anxiety
Fear
Jealousy
Laughter
Love
Melancholy
Moods
Photography of emotions
Psychoanalysis
Temper
Worry

EMOTIONS in art. See Art—Psychology

EMPHYSEMA
New surgery for emphysema. Sci Digest 67:63 F '70

Diagnosis

New test may cut emphysema toll. il Bsns W p88+ S 12 '70

EMPIRICISM
Ernst Mach: the unconscious motives of an empiricist. L. S. Feuer. bibliog Am Imago 27:12-40 Spr '70

EMPLOYEE absenteeism. See Absenteeism

EMPLOYEE benefits. See Non-wage payments

EMPLOYEE counseling
Goodwill ambassador. J. Kuh. por Ladies Home J 87:117 F '70

EMPLOYEE incentives. See Incentives in industry

EMPLOYEE-management relations in government. See Collective bargaining—Government employees

EMPLOYEE morale
See also
Incentives in industry

EMPLOYEE ownership
Ties that bind; employee-ownership plan for railroad. Newsweek 75:68 Ap 6 '70

EMPLOYEE stock ownership. See Employees as stockholders

EMPLOYEE vacation. See Vacations, Employee

EMPLOYEES
See also
Labor turnover
Personnel management
Supervisors
also subhead Employees under various subjects, e.g. Building industry—Employees; *also* classes of employees, e.g. School employees

Clothing and dress

See Clothing and dress

Dismissal

See also
Executives—Dismissal
Layoff systems

Qualifications

Evils of occupational upgrading. J. W. Dykstra. Sch & Soc 98:98-100 F '70
Overeducation. D. Wolfle. Science 168:319 Ap 17 '70
Would Horatio Alger need a degree? J. W. Kuhn. il Sat R 53:54-5+ D 19 '70

Rating

Performance appraisal; managers beware. P. H. Thompson and G. W. Dalton. Harvard Bsns R 48:149-57 Ja '70

Relocation

Making it easier to make a move: TI home transfer service corp. V. Louviere. il Nations Bsns 58:13 Jl '70
See also
Executives—Relocation

Training

Helping the hard-core adjust to the world of work. L. Nadler. il Harvard Bsns R 48:117-26 Mr '70
Tangling with the manpower tangle. il Nations Bsns 58:64-6+ F '70
When language is a barrier: General foam's language classes. il Bsns W p 104+ F 28 '70
See also
Apprentices
Building workers—Training
Hard-core unemployed—Training
Opportunities industrialization centers, inc.

EMPLOYEES, Training of. See Employees—Training

EMPLOYEES, Transfer of
When an auto plant closes up; Ford's Dallas plant. il Bsns W p24-5 F 14 '70

EMPLOYEES as stockholders
Workers cool to lures of ownership; Renault and Volkswagen experiment. B. L. Masse. America 122:233 Mr 7 '70
See also
Employee ownership
Profit sharing

EMPLOYEES associations
Militant civil servants in New York city. F. F. Piven. il por Trans-Action 7:24-8+ N '69

EMPLOYEES representation in management
Campus revolt from an industrial relations perspective. F. H. Harbison. Mo Labor R 93:33-6 Mr '70

EMPLOYER-employee relations See Industrial relations; Personnel management

EMPLOYERS liability
See also
Insurance, Workmens compensation

EMPLOYMENT
Labor and the economy in 1969. R. W. Fisher. bibliog il Mo Labor R 93:30-43 Ja '70
See also
Age and employment
Part time employment
Student employment
Unemployment
also subhead Employment under various subjects, e.g. Youth—Employment

Stability
See Employment stabilization

Statistics
Employment and unemployment. household data; tables. See issues of Monthly labor review
Help wanted: what survey shows; Labor department report. U S News 69:52 Ag 10 '70
Women at work; symposium. bibliog f il Mo Labor R 93:3-44 Je '70
Work experience of the population; with tables. V. C. Perrella. il Mo Labor R 93:54-61 F '70
See also
Unemployment—Statistics

EMPLOYMENT agencies
Employment agencies that find $8,000-$15,000 jobs. il Changing T 24:40-2 Ag '70
Slave shops; day-labor agencies in Chicago. il Newsweek 75:53 Mr 9 '70
See also
Everything for everybody, inc.
Mature Temps, inc.
United States—Employment service

EMPLOYMENT contracts. See Labor contracts

EMPLOYMENT discrimination. See Discrimination in employment

EMPLOYMENT interviewing
Don't lose that job before you get it. il Changing T 24:17-18 My '70
How you can conduct better staff interviews; excerpts from Interviewing techniques for the non-personnel executive. Camp Mag 42:22-3+ Ja '70
See also
Video recorders and recording—Business use

EMPLOYMENT of the aged. See Age and employment

EMPLOYMENT stabilization
Stabilizing the economy; a proposal for full employment without inflation. M. J. Ulmer. il New Repub 162:13-16 Ja 31 '70; Reply. J. R. Kesselman. 163:24 Jl 25 '70; Rejoinder. 163:31-2 S 26 '70

EMPLOYMENT systems. See Recruiting of employees

EMPTY-handed man; story. See Wiser, W.

ENAMEL and enameling
Brush-on enamel designs. P. Rothenberg. il Ceram Mo 18:16-17 Ja '70
Combining enamels and plastics (cont) K. Berl. il Ceram Mo 18:23+ F '70
Enamel inlays in wood. P. Rothenberg. il Ceram Mo 18:32-3 Je '70
Enamels 70. il Ceram Mo 18:21-3 My '70
Gem making for the enamelist. L. S. Taylor. il Ceram Mo 17:27-9 D '69
Metal inlays in enameling. F. Ball. il Ceram Mo 18:14-16 Ap '70
Sgraffito with liquid enamels. F. Ball. il Ceram Mo 18:26-8 S '70
'20s gleam in auto emblems; simulated vitreous enamel. il Bsns W p80+ Ag 22 '70
White-on-white enameling. F. Ball. il Ceram Mo 18:20-1+ O '70
See also
Cloisonné

ENAMELS. See Enamel and enameling

ENCAPSULATION. See Capsules

ENCAUSTIC painting
Exploring with melted wax crayon; excerpts from The complete crayon book. C. Alkema. il Design 71:4-7 Sum '70

ENCEPHALITIS
Amoebic killers; amoebic meningoencephalitis. il Sci N 98:245 S 19 '70

ENCEPHALOMYELITIS
Experimental allergic encephalomyelitis: synthesis of disease-inducing site of the basic protein. E. H. Eylar and others. bibliog il Science 168:1220-3 Je 5 '70

ENCEPHALOPATHY. See Brain—Diseases

ENCHILADAS. See Cookery, Mexican

ENCKE'S comet. See Comets

ENCLOSURES, Loudspeaker. See Loud speaking apparatus—Cabinets

ENCOUNTER center. See Narcotic addicts—Rehabilitation

ENCOUNTER groups. See Group relations training

ENCYCLICALS
Vatican and mixed marriages; matrimonia mixta. R. W. Rousseau. Cur Cent 87:963-4+ Ag 12 '70

ENCYCLOPAEDIA Britannica, inc.
Libraries in miniature: a new era begins. J. Tebbel. il Sat R 54:41 Ja 9 '71
See also
Library resources, inc.

ENCYCLOPEDIA, Americana
Librarians help write Encyclopedia Americana. Library J 95:1432 Ap 15 '70

ENCYCLOPEDIA Britannica (Japan), ltd. See Publishers and publishing—Japan

ENCYCLOPEDIA salesmen. See Canvassing

ENCYCLOPEDIAS
Black history gaps revealed in AFT encyclopedia survey. Library J 95:4312 D 15 '70
See also
Music—Dictionaries and encyclopedias

ENDANGERED species conservation act. See Wildlife conservation—Laws and legislation

ENDEMIC goiter. See Goiter

ENDICOTT, Frank S.
Women's gains. Newsweek 77:70 Ja 11 '71 *

ENDIVE, Belgian. See Chicory

ENDOCRINOLOGY
See also
Pineal body

ENDORSEMENTS in advertising. See Advertising—Testimonials

ENDOTOXINS. See Toxins and antitoxins

ENDOWMENTS
Investments
Let's solve the endowment crisis; with summary of Ford foundation report. C. D. Ellis. bibliog f il Harvard Bsns R 48:92-102 Mr '70

ENDRESEN, Bergthor F.
Dynamic growth companies. il pors Nations Bsns 58:88-91 Ap '70 *

ENEMY of the people; drama. See Nolan, P. T.

ENERGOINVEST. See Conglomerate corporations—Yugoslavia

ENERGY. See Force and energy

ENERGY budget (geophysics)
Energy cycle of the earth. A. H. Oort. il Sci Am 223:54-63 bibliog(p262) S '70
See also
Bioenergetics
Hydrologic cycle

ENERGY conversion devices, inc.
Great hopes from Ovshinsky's little switches grow. L. Lessing. il por Fortune 81:110-14+ Ap '70

ENERGY levels (quantum mechanics)
Bonds and bands in semiconductors. J. C. Phillips. bibliog il Science 169:1035-42 S 11 '70; Reply with rejoinder. L. Pauling. 170:1432 D 25 '70
Doppler shift measurements of nuclear lifetimes. J. R. MacDonald. bibliog il Science 167:1339-47 Mr 6 '70
Inversion of excited states of transition-metal complexes. G. A. Crosby and others. bibliog il Science 170:1195-6 D 11 '70

ENERGY resources. See Power resources

L'ENFANT theatre. See Washington, D.C.—Theater

ENFIELD, Conn.
Lighting
Don't just add lights. C. S. Kissinger. il Am City 85:120 O '70

ENFORCEMENT of law. See Law enforcement

ENGAGEMENT baby; drama. See Shapiro, S.

ENGEL, A. E. J. and Engel, C. G.
Lunar rocks compositions and some interpretations. bibliog il Science 167:527-8 Ja 30 '70

ENGEL, A. S.
Dealing with pornography. Cur 123:38-43 N '70

ENGEL, Celeste G. See Engel, A. E. J. jt. auth.

ENGEL, Edgar L.
Postpartum care; ed. by D. Z. Meilach. Redbook 135:14+ Ag '70

ENGEL, Herbert M.
School prayer issue: a perverse paradox. il Cath World 211:125-7 Je '70

ENGEL, Mort
Fall lay-up; interview, ed. by E. L. Slepian. Motor B 126:10-12 S '70

ENGEL, W. King, and Meltzer, Herbert
Histochemical abnormalities of skeletal muscle in patients with acute psychoses. bibliog il Science 168:273-6 Ap 10 '70

ENGELHARD, Charles
Nijinsky's last dance. il por Newsweek 76: 73-4 O 19 '70 *
ENGELHARDT, W. von, and others
Shock metamorphism in lunar samples. bibliog il Science 167:669-70 Ja 30 '70
ENGELMANN, George
George Engelmann, botanical gatekeeper of the West. R. G. Beidleman. il Horticulture 48:42-3+ Ap '70 *
ENGGASS, Peter M.
Spain. bibliog il Focus 20:1-12 My '70
ENGH, Jeri
Case for year-round schools. Redbook 134:84+ Ap '70
Help for troubled girls. il Parents Mag 45: 66-8+ Mr '70
—See Engh, R. jt. auth.
ENGH, Keith
Cruelest trick-or-treat hoax. il pors Good H 171:12+ O '70
ENGH, Rohn, and Engh, Jeri
Assateague off season. il Travel 134:58-61+ N '70
ENGINE lifts. See Hoisting machinery
ENGINE models
Mini steam engine made with simple hand tools. A. Sprague. il Pop Mech 134:154-5+ Jl '70
ENGINEERING
Engineering sciences. See occasional issues of Science news
See also
Automobile engineering
Biomedical engineering
Environmental engineering
Petroleum engineering
Technology
Study and teaching
Education for innovation; address, December 29, 1969. M. Tribus. Vital Speeches 36:279-82 F 15 '70
ENGINEERING, Hydraulic. See Hydraulic engineering
ENGINEERING colleges
See also names of engineering colleges, e.g. Massachusetts institute of technology, Cambridge
ENGINEERING education
See also
Engineering—Study and teaching
ENGINEERING offices. See Offices
ENGINEERING research
See also
Highway research
ENGINEERING societies
See also
National academy of engineering
ENGINEERS
Ph.D. holders in private industry. M. F. Crowley. il Mo Labor R 93:65-6 Ag '70
See also
Civil engineers
Supply and demand
Cuts threaten industry capabilities. Aviation W 93:12-14 Ag 31 '70
Down and out along route 128. B. Rice. il N Y Times Mag p28-9+ N 1 '70; Discussion. p48+ N 22 '70
Engineering jobs. Sci N 97:480 My 16 '70
Projected requirements for technicians in 1980. M. F. Crowley. bibliog f il Mo Labor R 93:13-17 My '70
ENGINES
See also
Airplane engines
Automobile engines
Diesel engines
Flywheels
Gas and oil engines
Marine engines
Motorcycle engines
Rocket engines
ENGLAND, Barry
Conduct unbecoming. Criticism
America 124:47 Ja 16 '71 *
Nation 211:444 N 2 '70 *
New Repub 163:20+ N 7 '70 *
New Yorker 46:129 O 24 '70 *
Newsweek 76:86 O 26 '70 *
Sat R 53:12 O 31 '70 *
Time il 96:93-4 O 26 '70 *
ENGLAND, Ralph W. Jr
Police in our changing cities. bibliog f Cur Hist 59:273-7+ N '70
ENGLAND
Calendar for June events. il Travel & Camera 33:70-1 My '70
See also
Aldeburgh
Americans in England
Architecture, Domestic—England

Booksellers and bookselling—England
Cathedrals—England
Country estates—England
Gardens—England
London
Music festivals—England
Selborne
Theater—Great Britain
Walney Island
Water pollution—England
York
Description and travel
Antique drum, by T. Howard. Review
Nat R 22:34 Ja 13 '70. Re. Kirk
Canterbury pilgrims today. R. Wickerd and F. Wickerd. il Travel 134:34-9+ D '70
June in England; with photographs by S. Bullaty and A. Lomeo. il Travel & Camera 33:26-37+ My '70
Divorce
See Divorce—Great Britain
Economic conditions
See Great Britain—Economic conditions
Education
See Education—Great Britain
Galleries and museums
See also
Oxford, England—Galleries and museums
Historic houses, etc.
At home with the barons and earls. B. Bishop. il Sat R 53:46-7+ S 12 '70
Firle Place, Sussex. C. Musgrave. il Antiques 97:261-6 F '70
History
See Great Britain—History
Religious institutions and affairs
Religion in the doldrums. J. D. Douglas. Chr Today 14:59-60 Ap 10 '70
World around us (cont) Chr Cent 87:59-60, 460; Ja 14, Ap 15 '70
See also
Catholic church in England
Church of England
Social life and customs
Englishman's castle is his home. Q. Crewe. Vogue 155:106+ Mr 1 '70
See also
Theater—Great Britain
Victorian period
Vital statistics
See Great Britain—Vital statistics
World war, 1939-1945
See World war, 1939-1945—Great Britain
ENGLAND, Church of. See Church of England
ENGLAND and the United States
See also
Americans in England
United States—Foreign opinion—British
ENGLE, John D. Jr
Definition; poem. Chr Cent 87:1446 D 2 '70
ENGLE, Paul
Are we losing our pioneer spirit? il Nat Wildlife 9:5-11 D '70
ENGLE, Robert
Robert Engle, the man behind the faces; Robert Engle demonstrates throwing off the hump. R. D. Bonham. il pors Ceram Mo 18:12-15 Ja '70
ENGLEBARDT, Stanley L.
If your child has acne. Parents Mag 45:64-5+ O '70
Sailing vacation for new salts. il Todays Health 48:36-9+ Jl '70
ENGLEBERT, Victor
The Danakil; nomads of Ethiopia's wasteland. il Nat Geog 137:186-211 F '70
ENGLEHORN, Shirley
Fine till the nerves go ding. M. Mulvoy. il por Sports Illus 32:48+ Je 29 '70 *
ENGLERT, Kenneth J.
Electronics self-study course. il Pop Electr 33:45-8 D '70
ENGLERTH, William M.
Gunite gives me new life. il Am City 85:101-2 Jl '70
ENGLISH, Helen W.
Rock poetry, relevance, and revelation. bibliog Eng J 59:1122-7 N '70
ENGLISH, Margaret. See Wren, C. S. jt. auth.
ENGLISH
He spoke to me. He won't do that again. Q. Crewe. Vogue 156:148 Ag 1 '70
ENGLISH composition. See English language—Composition

ENGLISH cookery. See Cookery, English

ENGLISH daisies
Wild daisy and English daisy. il Sunset 144: 248-9 My '70

ENGLISH departments, College. See Colleges and universities—Departments of English

ENGLISH dictionaries. See English language—Dictionaries

ENGLISH drama
See also
London—Theater

ENGLISH fiction
European literary scene. R. J. Clements. Sat R 53:31 D 12 '70

ENGLISH furniture. See Furniture, English

ENGLISH grammar. See English language—Grammar

ENGLISH history. See Great Britain—History

ENGLISH in Africa. See British in Africa

ENGLISH language
American traditions of language use; their relevance today. M. G. Crowell. bibliog f Engl J 59:109-15 Ja '70
American usage: the consensus, by R. H. Copperud. Review
Atlan 226:108-10+ S '70. L. Kronenberger
Murder of English; adaptation of address. W. Carroll. Ed Digest 36:28-31 O '70
See also
Slang
Vocabulary

Composition
Am I in art or English? use of collage for communication. J. Gates. Engl J 59:988-9 O '70
Art of writing evaluative comments on student themes. D. G. Kehl. Engl J 59:972-80 O '70
Cabinet and the tool box; report writing; address, March 19, 1970. E. Miller. Vital Speeches 36:475-8 My 15 '70
Composition strategy that worked; correspondence with other students. W. W. Brokowski. Engl J 59:984-6 O '70
Compulsory English. O. Baker. Clear House 45:253-4 D '70
Dictation: the last few minutes. F. G. Conway. Engl J 59:983+ O '70
In the beginning; beginning school meaningfully. J. Kabatznick. Engl J 59:956-9 O '70
Myth and method. C. Logan. Engl J 59:548-50+ Ap '70
Nouns and pronouns at Carver junior high. J. P. Bauer. Engl J 59:970-1 O '70
One teaching experience. B. W. Overstreet. PTA Mag 64:21 Ap '70
Paragraph development in the modern age of rhetoric. R. A. Meade and W. G. Ellis. bibliog f il Engl J 59:219-26 F '70
Search for structures in the teaching of composition. S. Judy. Engl J 59:213-18+ F '70
Slang and profanity: their uses in English composition. D. P. Demarest, jr. Clear House 45:76-80 O '70
Student compositions: a schoolwide policy for all written work. T. W. Hipple. Clear House 44:523-6 My '70
Teaching writing in the junior high school. V. P. Redd. Engl J 59:540-7 Ap '70
Upon first looking into Christensen's Rhetoric. A. Solkov. Engl J 59:834-6 S '70
Visible voice: an approach to writing. L. Hamalian. Engl J 59:227-30 F '70
Writing for nobody. E. M. White. Ed Digest 35:32-3 Mr '70
See also
Creative writing
Rhetoric
Style, Literary

Creative activities
See also
College and school journalism

Courses of study
Abolish English! A. Franza. Engl J 59:798-9 S '70
Delete English courses from the curriculum. M. H. Beaven. Engl J 59:800-2 S '70
On defiling the sanctity of English. K. C. Halloran. Engl J 59:566-8 Ap '70
Option plan: learning is student-centered. D. W. Berg. Clear House 45:107-11 O '70
Those infernal electives. J. K. Crabbe. Engl J 59:990-3+ O '70

Dialects
Dialects and democracy; need for a dialectology unit. D. M. Griffin. Engl J 59:551-8 Ap '70
Strain of Strine. Time 96:60 Ag 24 '70
See also
Negro-English dialects

Dictionaries
American heritage dictionary of the English language, by W. Morris. Review
Consumer Bul il 53:14+ Ja '70
Nat R 22:92-3 Ja 27 '70. G. Davenport
Dictionaries old and new. B. Evans. il Todays Ed 59:24-7 F '70; Same abr. Ed Digest 35: 32-4 Ap '70; Discussion. Todays Ed 59:52-3 Mr '70
Dictionary as a tool in vocabulary development programs. W. Morris. Engl J 59:669-71 My '70
Gentlemen's guide to linguistic etiquette; American heritage dictionary of the English language. P. E. Kilburn. Ed Digest 36:52-3 N '70
Noah Webster's dictionary. W. Zinsser. il Life 69:16-17 S 25 '70
Selling of a dictionary; American heritage dictionary. il Time 95:96 My 11 '70
Usage, precise and otherwise; American heritage dictionary of the English language. R. Lynes. Harper 240:32+ Ap '70

Etymology
Down Glantwife: the uses of etymology. C. Laird. Engl J 59:1106-12 N '70
World of words. G. Mosler. Good H 170:185 My '70

Grammar
Refresher in English grammar. J. H. Middendorf. Writers Digest 50:36-7 Jl '70
See also
English language—Usage

Anecdotes, facetiae, satire, etc.
Fable for young grammarians. F. Wolfe. Engl J 59:569+ Ap '70

Idioms and provincialisms
See also
English language—Usage

Mood
In praise of the subjunctive. R. L. Tobin. Sat R 53:45-6 Ag 8 '70

Pronunciation
Concept of oracy. A. Wilkinson. Engl J 59:71-7 Ja '70

Anecdotes, facetiae, satire, etc.
Trade winds; Mispronunciation derby. C. Amory. Sat R 53:12-13 Ag 15 '70

Semantics
Politics and the name game; Time essay. M. Ways. il por Time 96:14-15 N 2 '70
Taxonomy of words: a study in meaning. F. W. Schufletowski. bibliog f Clear House 44:474-8 Ap '70

Study and teaching
ABE and the twentieth century pioneers; Adult basic education classes in Berlin, N.H. D. Lamoureux. il Todays Ed 59:60-1 Ja '70
Applied institutional linguistics in the classroom. C. James. bibliog il Engl J 59:1096-105 N '70
Bi-dialectalism: the linguistics of white supremacy. J. Sledd; reply. J. C. Maxwell. Engl J 59:1158-9 N '70
Black English. O. Mellan. New Repub 163: 15-17 N 28 '70
Case of the illogical ghoti; English for foreigners. J. F. Mocine. il Todays Ed 59:71-2 O '70
Changing face of English: one school's new program; basic skills tests instead of required courses. J. Risken. Engl J 59:524-7 Ap '70
Coming on center; address. J. P. Moffett. Engl J 59:528-33 Ap '70
Concept of oracy. A. Wilkinson. Engl J 59:71-7 Ja '70
Creative writing with a movie camera. G. F. Heinz. il Schol Teach Sec Teach Sup p20-1 N 3 '69
Dialects and democracy; need for a dialectology unit. D. M. Griffin. Engl J 59:551-8 Ap '70
Discovery through rock; with discography. B. Scoppa. il Schol Teach Jr/Sr High p 14-15 O 5 '70
Does humanity grow in your classroom? F. T. Wilhelms. Schol Teach Jr/Sr High p34-5 S 21 '70
English comes alive; program, conducted by Northwestern university's curriculum center in English. R. Blaine. il Am Ed 6:26-8 Je '70
Fostering practical communication skills. B. D. Stanford. Engl J 59:967-9 O '70
Generating a spirit of inquiry. F. DeHart. bibliog Am Lib 1:602-5 Je '70

ENGLISH language—Study and teaching—*Cont.*
imPALLA: a new approach to secondary
school language arts. W. M. Gordon and
others. il Engl J 59:534-9 Ap '70
It's a small world; address, November 1969.
R. S. Soffer. Engl J 59:416-20 Mr '70
Linguistic imagination. J. E. Miller, jr. Engl J
59:477-83+ Ap '70
Linguistics in the high school? V. L. Hig-
gins. Engl J 59:559-65+ Ap '70
Monkey on the bicycle: behavioral objectives
and the teaching of English; address, No-
vember, 1969. H. P. Guth. Engl J 59:785-92
S '70
New beginning; a raid on the inarticulate.
A. J. Burke, jr. Engl J 59:99-104+ Ja '70
New designs in English. E. R. Fagan. bib-
liog f Clear House 44:347-53 F '70
New duds for the old duchess. K. Branan. il
Schol Teach Sec Teach Sup p8-9+ F 2 '70
Nongrading electing, and phasing; basics of
revolution for relevance. D. F. Weise. Engl
J 59:122-30 Ja '70
Of behaviors, objectives, and English. A. C.
Purves. il Engl J 59:793-7 S '70
Power of language: can the student survive
without it? J. H. Bushman. Engl J 59:
1091-5 N '70
Preparing a curriculum guide. R. Reeves
and D. Knappenberger. bibliog Engl J 59:
520-3+ Ap '70
Priority projects for the teaching of English:
1970. B. O'Donnell. Engl J 59:868-74 S '70
Should ghettoese be accepted? W. Raspberry.
Todays Ed 59:30-1+ Ap '70
Slum child. I. H. Draper. Clear House 45:48-
50 S '70
Summary of investigations relating to the
English language arts in secondary educa-
tion: 1969. N. S. Blount. bibliog Engl J
59:677-90 My '70
Survey of the teaching of English in sec-
ondary schools. F. I. Godshalk. Sch & Soc
98:249-50 Ap '70
Teaching Americanese to Japanese teachers.
il Sch & Soc 98:464-5 D '70
Teaching English in the junior college; find-
ings from a national study. M. F. Shugrue.
Ed Digest 36:51-4 O '70
Teaching English in the United Kingdom:
a comparative study, by J. Squire and R.
Applebee. Review
Engl J 59:291-5 F '70. S. Judy
Tell me what you had in mind; daily con-
ferences with individual students. L. Mc-
Callister. Engl J 59:231-4 F '70
Ten commendments for teachers of English.
W. J. Reynolds. Engl J 59:672-3 My '70
This world of English. T. DeVries and A.
Tovatt. See issues of English journal
To preserve humanness: language and litera-
ture in the '70s and beyond. J. E. Miller,
jr. Engl J 59:1154-6 N '70
Try a quest. D. Wright. Engl J 59:131-3+ Ja '70
U.S. office of education: report on research
projects. D. V. Gunderson. Engl J 59:304-
7 F '70
Which ways now in the '70s? A. H. Grommon.
Engl J 59:692-6 My '70
With pride and alarm. M. Webster. Engl J
59:1285-8 D '70
    See also
Colleges and universities—Departments of
English
English language—Composition
English language—Courses of study
English literature—Study and teaching
Journalism—Study and teaching
National council of teachers of English
Spelling—Study and teaching

Aids and devices
Teaching materials; ed. by N. S. Blount and
J. R. Searles. See issues of English journal
    See also
Moving pictures in education

Bibliography
More sources of free and inexpensive ma-
terial. J. R. Searles. Engl J 59:846-53 S '70
Professional publications; ed. by D. Petitt.
See issues of English journal
Reference shelf for curriculum planning. Engl
J 59:1177-85, 1306-12, N-D '70
The scene; ed. by E. Farrell and L. Ruth.
Engl J 59:709-20 My '70

Subjunctive
    See English language—Mood

Terms and phrases
In my opinion; catch phrases don't com-
municate. J. Kaplan. por Seventeen 29:270
Ap '70
    See also
Jargon
Words

Anecdotes, facetiae, satire, etc.
Dictionary for the disenchanted. B. Rosen-
berg. il Harper 241:93-5 N '70
Short educational dictionary. K. Amis and
R. Conquest. N Y Times Mag p4+ Ja 10 '71

Usage
Taxonomy of words: a study in meaning. F.
W. Schufletowski. bibliog f Clear House
44:474-8 Ap '70

ENGLISH language in Australia
Strain of Strine. Time 96:60 Ag 24 '70

ENGLISH language in Great Britain
Turn of the tide. H. R. Mayes. Sat R 53:6+
N 14 '70

ENGLISH literature
    See also
Childrens literature—Great Britain
English fiction

Study and teaching
Case for irrelevance. M. D. Blyth. Engl J
59:380-3+ Mr '70
I do as I do, not as you say: using litera-
ture research in the classroom. D. R. Gal-
lo. bibliog Engl J 59:509-16 Ap '70
Is summer reading itself an old adage? D.
B. Lockerbie. Engl J 59:573-6 Ap '70
Literature and the now generation. V. R.
Mollenkott. Todays Ed 59:64-7 O '70
Who are the real censors? R. T. LaConte.
Ed Digest 36:44-6 O '70
    See also
Colleges and universities—Departments of
English
English language—Study and teaching

Aids and devices
Teaching freshman English in middle earth.
P. Hezel. Engl J 59:387-92 Mr '70

Bibliography
Literary analysis in secondary English
classes. R. V. Denby. Engl J 59:438-48 Mr
'70

Themes
    See Literature—Themes

ENGLISH money. See Money—Great Britain
ENGLISH national theatre. See Theater—
    Great Britain
ENGLISH painting. See Painting, British
ENGLISH pottery. See Pottery, English
ENGLISH setters. See Setters
ENGLISH silver. See Silverware
ENGLISH teachers
Making of a radical teacher. J. Fulcher.
Engl J 59:384-6 Mr '70
ENGRAVING
    See also
Callot, J.
Lithography
Monotypes
ENGRAVINGS
    See also
Prints
ENGRAVINGS, Rock. See Petroglyphs
ENLARGERS, Photographic. See Photography
    —Enlargers and enlarging
ENLARGING (photography) See Photography—
    Enlargers and enlarging
ENLARGING exposure meters. See Exposure
    meters
ENLIGHTENMENT
Enlightenment. P. Gay. il Horizon 12:40-5 Spr
    '70
Politics of authenticity: radical individualism
and the emergence of modern society, by M.
Berman. Review
    Nation 212:23-5 Ja 4 '71. E. Chill
ENNIS, Jean
Obituary
    Pub W 198:35 O 26 '70
ENOCH Pratt free library, Baltimore
Pratt's switching yard; letter to the editor.
E. Castagna. Library J 95:2742 S 1 '70
ENOS, Sondra Forsyth
Wisconsin dance idea: 1917-1970. il Dance
Mag 44:24-7+ N '70
ENRICHED bread. See Bread
ENRICHED food. See Food, Enriched
ENRIGHT, Elizabeth
Art of Elizabeth Enright (cont) E. Cameron.
Horn Bk 46:26-30 F '70 '
ENRIGHT, J. T.
Distortions of apparent velocity: a new op-
tical illusion. bibliog il Science 168:464-7
Ap 24 '70
    about
Strange Enright illusion. D. L. Heiserman.
il Sci Digest 68:15-17 N '70 *

ENRIGHT, Marlene
Go native, we did! il Org Gard & Farm 17: 80-1 Ja '70

ENROLLMENT, College. See Colleges and universities—Attendance

ENROLLMENT, School. See School attendance

ENSEMBLE playing
Three men on a hobby; remarks, ed. by I. Kolodin. I. Stern; E. Istomin; L. Rose. il pors Sat R 53:47-9 O 31 '70

ENSENADA race. See Yacht racing

ENSILAGE. See Silage

ENTER a free man; drama. See Stoppard. T.

ENTERPRISE, Free. See Free enterprise

ENTERPRISE fund. See Investment trusts

ENTERTAINERS
Dulhunty, hard man of the Outback: the traveling showman. il pors Life 69:46-54 O 30 '70
Teddy bears; two housewives who entertain children. J. Kuh. il Ladies Home J 87:145 O '70
See also
Beatles
Comedians
Geishas
Negro entertainers
Snake charmers
also names of entertainers, e.g. T. Lewis

ENTERTAINING
Beat the high cost of party giving. Bet Hom & Gard 48:42 Je '70
Chez mlle: men's parties; with recipes. P. Bartlett. Mlle 71:70-1 O '70
Coffee party. il Sunset 144:64-5 Ja '70
Come to the party; with menus and recipes. il Redbook 136:93-6+ N '70
Four personal views. S. Nirenberg. il House B 112:86-9+ N '70
Holiday parties. il McCalls 98:79 D '70
How to handle the holidays. Bet Hom & Gard 48:124 N '70
Ladies' day; with recipes. il Bet Hom & Gard 48:57+ Je '70
Ladies' home journal open house; with recipes. il Ladies Home J 87:87-97+ O '70
Men's parties. il Mlle 71:170-5 O '70
Menus and recipes from Washington parties. il House & Gard 138:83+ Ag '70
Mrs Hazelton throws a bash; fifteenth birthday of National review. il pors Nat R 22: 1296-301 D 1 '70
Notes for the hostess (title varies) See issues of House & garden incorporating Living for young homemakers
Official Washington: ideas for entertaining. il House & Gard 138:76-81 Ag '70
Party and picnic ideas you never thought of. il Bet Hom & Gard 48:50+ Je '70
Secrets of a great party giver; with recipes. M. Williams. il por House & Gard 138:127-30+ N '70
Summer party ideas from a country restaurant. il House & Gard 138:92-3 Ag '70
Three gatherings; fund raising parties in Manhattan. New Yorker 45:31-3 F 14 '70
Toast to the host. E. Sheppard. Harp Baz 104:162-3 N '70
Two great ways to give a good party; excerpt from A word to the wives. D. Rodgers and M. Rodgers. pors House & Gard 138: 88-9+ N '70
What makes a party great? M. Gough. House B 112:90-1+ N '70
What people are doing. House & Gard 138: 81-7 N '70
Wine-tasting party. W. Clifford. il House B 112:48+ Ap '70
Wine tasting party. il Bet Hom & Gard 48:28 Ap '70
See also
Balls (parties)
Breakfasts
Buffet meals
Caterers and catering
Childrens parties
Christmas meals
Dinners and dining
Games
Government entertaining
Guests
Lawn parties
Luncheons
Menus
Table setting
Wedding meals

ENTERTAINMENT industry
See also
Strikes—United States—Entertainment industry

ENTRANCE drives. See Driveways

ENTRANCE requirements, College. See Colleges and universities—Entrance requirements

ENTREPRENEURS
Potentates, by B. B. Seligman. Review
Atlan 227:92-5 Ja '71. L. Kronenberger
See also
Cox, W. D.

ENUNCIATION. See Diction

ENVIRONMENT
Biosphere; symposium. il Sci Am 223:44-74+ bibliog(p262-6) S '70
Charting the complexities; remarks to advisory panel of the Committee on science and astronautics. M. Bundy. por Sat R 53:56-7+ Ap 4 '70
Cleaning humanity's nest; symposium, with editorial comment by N. Cousins. il Sat R 53:47-54+ Mr 7 '70
Earth watch; comp. by S. Lindsay. Sat R 53:60 Mr 7; 58 Ap 4; 60-1 My 2; 66-7 Je 6; 46-7 Jl 4; 50-1 Ag 1; 54-5 S 5; 60-1 O 3; 70-1 N 7; 64-5 D 5 '70; 54:70-1 Ja 2 '71
Ecological destruction is a condition of American life; interview, ed. by P. Collier. P. Ehrlich. il Mlle 70:188-9+ Ap '70
Environment. See issues of Time
Environment: a national mission for the seventies; symposium, and statements by R. M. Nixon and E. S. Muskie. il pors Fortune 81:98-148+ F '70; Discussion. 81: 91-3 F; 51+ Ap '70
Environment and the quality of life. N. Cousins. See issues of Saturday review, March 7. 1970-
Environment for man, ed. by W. R. Ewald, jr. Review
Trans-Action 7:67-9 Ja '70. H. Winthrop
Environmental crisis; symposium. il Chr Cent 87:1180-92+ O 7 '70
Environmental sciences. See issues of Science news
Environmental side effects of energy production. D. F. Anthrop. il Bul Atom Sci 26:39-41 O '70
Five who care. R. Dubos. il Look 34:34 Ap 21 '70
Functioning at the new scale; coming soon, superscale. W. F. Wagner, jr. Arch Rec 148:9 D '70
Harmony with the life around us; adaptation of address. A. M. Lindbergh. il por Good H 171:62-3+ Jl '70
How I got radicalized: the making of an agitator for zero. J. Fischer. Harper 240: 18+ Ap '70
Issue of the year: the environment. il Time 97:21-2 Ja 4 '71
Last magician; excerpts from The invisible pyramid. L. Eiseley. Nat Parks & Con Mag 44:4-5 O '70
Mere survival is not enough for man. R. Dubos. por Life 69:2 Jl 24 '70; Same abr. with title Why survival is not enough. Read Digest 97:111-12 O '70
Of concern now. Bet Hom & Gard 48:28+ Ag '70
Politics of the environment; conference organized by the Institute for the study of health and society. G. Marine. Nation 210:82-4 Ja 26 '70
Possibilities of transformation: a report on the state of mankind: 1970. F. K. Kelly. Sat R 53:17-19+ Mr 7 '70
Ravaged environment. il Newsweek 75:30-40+ Ja 26 '70
Society and its physical environment; symposium, ed. by S. Z. Klausner. bibliog f il Ann Am Acad 389:1-115 My '70
Symposium on the shape of tomorrow. F. S. Forsberg. Field & S 75:55 Je '70
Week's watch. il Time 95:40+ Mr 23; 96:51 N 9 '70
Youth to the rescue? G. A. Nelson. Cur 114: 24-6 Ja '70
See also
Adaptation (biology)
Ecology
Man—Influence of environment
Man—Influence on nature
Nature
Pollution
United Nations conference on the human environment

Bibliography
Books about your house and garden. J. Herbert. House & Gard 138:68+ N '70
Environment book roundup. C. Lawson. Sat R 53:68 My 2 '70
Environment bookshelf. D. Dempsey. Sat R 53:61 Mr 7 '70
Little house syndrome vs. Mike Mulligan and Mary Anne; juvenile books on ecology, conservation, and pollution. K. M. Heyiman. il por Library J 95:1562-8 Ap 15 '70
Our world, and welcome to it! G. H. Siehl. il por Library J 95:1443-7 Ap 15 '70
Suggested readings on the environment. J. Hansen. Cur Hist 58:360+; 59:43-5+ Je-Jl '70

ENVIRONMENT—Bibliography—*Continued*
Survival: now or never. il Schol Teach Jr/Sr
High p28-30+ O 5 '70

Conferences

Solutions to environmental problems; AAAS
symposium, December 28, 1970. D. L.
Jameson. il Science 170:1118-19 D 4 '70
U.S. and Japan hold meetings on environ-
mental problems; text of joint communique.
Dept State Bul 63:670-1 N 30 '70

Economic aspects

Who owns the environment?   P. Schrag.
Sat R 53:63-9+ Jl 4 '70

Laws and legislation

Environment in the courtroom. J. L. Sax. il
Sat R 53:55-7 O 3 '70
Environmental law: courts demand DDT action, block pipeline road. L. J. Carter. Science 168:1322-4 Je 12 '70
Environmental lawyer urges: plead the Ninth
amendment! E. R. Roberts. il Natur Hist
79:18-19+ Ag '70

Poetry

Elements; Ingredients of expedience; Sing
me no country airs; Declaration of dependence; Instant archive; Maptrap. H. Gibson. il por Nat Wildlife 9:18-19 D '70

Study and teaching

Barriers fall. B. Kohl and others. il Environ
12:40-3 N '70
Beauty and the Beatles; or, Why can't
Johnny see? W. F. Wagner, jr. Arch Rec
147:9 Ap '70
Education for survival: conservation comes
first. S. S. Donohue. por Parents Mag 45:
18 Je '70
How physicists can contribute. M. L. Gold-
berger. il Phys Today 23:26-3+ D '70
Organic classrooms are here! M. C. Goldman.
il Org Gard & Farm 17:66-72 S '70
Sweden's youth says *nej* to pollution. M.
Michaelson. il Todays Health 49:22-5+ Ja
'71
Teaching the environment to 2,500 young-
sters; Teatown Lake reservation in Os-
sining, N.Y.   C. Schweikert. il por Org
Gard & Farm 17:83-5 Jl '70
    See also
Environmental education
Nature study

Terminology

Environmental glossary. R. F. Kunz. Sat R
54:67 Ja 2 '71

ENVIRONMENT (art)
Art; exhibition Explorations. L. Alloway.
Nation 210:476-7 Ap 20 '70
Art; Magic theater exhibition at Automation
house. L. Alloway. Nation 210:414 Ap 6 '70
Artist under stress; earth artist D. Oppen-
heim. D. Davis. il Newsweek 75:119 My 25
'70
Back to nature; ecological art of P. Hutch-
inson and D. Oppenheim. il pors Time 95:
62-3+ Je 29 '70
Clay unfired. E. Johnson; W. Fuhrmann. il
Craft Horiz 30:36-9 O '70
Designed for contemplation; Museum of con-
temporary crafts. G. Zoghby. il Craft Horiz
30:12-19+ Mr '70
Haus-rucker-co, live! il Craft Horiz 30:30-3
Ag '70
Improbable marriage; art and technology ex-
hibitions. D. Davis. il Newsweek 75:100-1
Ap 20 '70
It's called earth art, and boulderdash. R. Bon-
gartz. il N Y Times Mag p 16-17+ F 1 '70
Lead kindly blight; Oakland museum's Pol-
lution show. D. Antin. il Art N 69:36-9+
N '70
Letter to a nature lover. K. Kuh. Sat R 53:
50-1 Ap 25 '70
Parting shots; an earth artist goes under-
ground. il pors Life 69:62-3 Ag 14 '70
Sound enclosed land area, Milano, Italy;
work by D. Oppenheim. J. Gruen. Vogue
156:38 Ag 15 '70
Spaces, sensory overload; exhibition at
Museum of modern art. B. Rose. Vogue
155:30 Mr 15 '70

ENVIRONMENT and pesticides. See Pesticides
and the environment

ENVIRONMENT and state. See Environmental policy

ENVIRONMENTAL action groups. See Environmental associations, committees, etc.

ENVIRONMENTAL action, Inc.
Post-moratorium. New Repub 162:9 My 2 '70

ENVIRONMENTAL apartments.   See Apartment houses—Garden apartments

ENVIRONMENTAL associations, committees,
etc.
Better earth; report on Ecology action group,
Berkeley, Calif. S. V. Roberts. il N Y Times
Mag p8-9+ Mr 29 '70
Ecology: new cause, new career. M. A. Guitar.
il Mlle 70:190-3+ Ap '70
Editorial: Field & stream. C. Conley. Field
& S 75:6 Jl '70
Environmental action group; first report.
Field & S 75:8 S '70
New environmental conservation tool; en-
vironmental conservation councils. C. C.
Morrison, jr. il Cons 25:10-13 D '70
New: Field & stream environmental action
group. Field & S 75:14 Je '70
Seventeen's environment volunteer directory.
Seventeen 29:14+ Je '70
You can join up to combat the threats. Sun-
set 145:35-6 Ag '70

ENVIRONMENTAL conservation, Department
of.   See New York (state)—Environmental
conservation, Department of

ENVIRONMENTAL defense fund, Inc.
They go to court to protect the environ-
ment. J. Cox. Org Gard & Farm 17:78-81
S '70

ENVIRONMENTAL education
Careers doing something for the environ-
ment. il Changing T 24:35-8 Jl '70
College presidents and environmental educa-
tion. F. Farner. il Parks & Rec 5:31-3+ Ag
'70
Concept of environmental education. Ed Di-
gest 35:9-11 Mr '70
Continuing education for world affairs;
earth survival centers; address, October
15, 1970. A. J. Lewis. bibliog Vital Speeches
37:116-21 D 1 '70
Education for E-day and beyond. bibliog Sr
Schol 96:Schol Teach 7 Ap 6 '70
Education for survival; adaptation of address,
January 1970. J. E. Allen, jr. il Am Ed 6:18-
23 Mr '70
Environmental education. il Am Ed 6:21-5 O
'70
Environmental education; National environ-
mental education development program. il
Parks & Rec 5:42 Je '70
How should we treat environment? F. K.
Hare. bibliog Science 167:352-5 Ja 23 '70;
Reply. B. Lieberman. 168:316 Ap 17 '70
New courses on the environment. il G. Keller.
Seventeen 29:36+ My '70
Washington report; student testifies on en-
vironment act. J. Lloyd. Sr Schol 96:Schol
Teach 2 My 4 '70
What schools can do about pollution: sym-
posium. il Todays Ed 59:14-29 D '70
Whither conservation education? E. McAl-
lister. Clear House 45:103 O '70
    See also
Group for environmental education

ENVIRONMENTAL engineering
Technological imperative, social implications
of professional technology. D. B. Hertz.
bibliog f Ann Am Acad 389:95-106 My '70
Tilling the desert under plastic skies; in-
tegrated power-water-food system. il Bsns
W p92+ My 9 '70
    See also
Committee for environmental information
Life support systems (space environment)
Life support systems (submarine environ-
ment)

ENVIRONMENTAL engineering (buildings)
Artist and the city. S. McIlhany. Am Artist
34:5 N '70
Pleasantness made to order; portfolio. Fortune 81:137-43 F '70

ENVIRONMENTAL financing authority (proposed)   See United States—Environmental
financing authority (proposed)

ENVIRONMENTAL health
International research: its role in environmental biology. J. Higginson. bibliog Science 170:935-9 N 27 '70
Minor metals of the geochemical environment, health and disease; AAAS symposium, December 30, 1970. H. L. Cannon
and H. C. Hopps. Science 170:1232 D 11 '70
Pollution invites disease. B. W. Carnow. il
Sat R 53:38-40+ Jl 4 '70

ENVIRONMENTAL movement
AFA and the environmental crusade. C. A.
Connaughton. Am For 76:7 My '70
After Earth day. D. Wolfle. Science 168:657
My 8 '70
After the teach-in. Sci N 97:341-2 Ap 4 '70
American institutions and ecological ideals;
adaptation of address, December 29, 1969.
L. Marx. bibliog Science 170:945-52 N 27 '70
Better life. B. Plumb. il Am Home 74:40-2
Ja '71
Beyond a strategy of conservation. S.
Paradise. Cur 119:27-31 Je '70

ENVIRONMENTAL movement—Earth day,
April 22, 1970—*Continued*
Reflections on Earth day. N. Podhoretz.
Commentary 49:26+ Je '70; Discussion. 50:
10+ Ag '70
Souvenir of Earth day. il Life 68:38 My 1 '70
Special message to youth. R. S. Kilborne.
por Cons 24:2 Ap '70
Teach-in to save the earth. G. Nelson. Read
Digest 96:110-12 Ap '70
Two players in the E-day action. il pors
Bsns W p30 Ap 25 '70
Where were you on Earth day? G. Logsdon.
il Farm J 94:17+ Je '70

International aspects

Environmental concern is global. W. E.
Towell. Am For 76:32-3+ Je '70; Reply.
l. R. Martin. 76:75-6 O '70
Williamstown study of critical environmental problems; summary. il Bul Atom Sci
26:24-30 O '70

Marches, rallies, etc.

March: protest against the International automobile show. New Yorker 46:37 Ap 18 '70

Teach-ins

Beyond the teach-in. B. Commoner. il por
Sat R 53:50-2+ Ap 4 '70
Campus teach-in on the environmental cris-
is: 1970. E. E. C. Clebsch. Liv Wildn 34:
10-12 Spr '70
Earth day happenings, April 22; environmental gatherings on campuses. Sat R 53:
51 Ap 4 '70
Eco-Gemini: two for the teach-in. L. P. Ger-
lach. il Natur Hist 79:70-6 My '70
Enthusiasm mounts for teach-in; Environ-
mental teach-in; with editorial comment.
Nat Parks 44:18, 26 F '70
Environmental teach-in. D. Hayes. il Liv
Wildn 34:12-13 Spr '70
Environmental teach-in: a new round of
student activism? L. J. Carter. Science 167:
269 Ja 16 '70
Environmental teach-in; University of Mich-
igan meeting links concerns about pollu-
tion and upside-down society. L. J. Carter.
Science 167:1594-5 Mr 20 '70
Mike Frome. M. Frome. Am For 76:3+ Jl '70
National teach-in on the crisis of the en-
vironment; the library role. G. Nelson. Am
Lib 1:140-1 F '70
Reflections on youth and the teach-in. M.
Frome. Field & S 74:46+ Ap '70
Students call it dirty business; environmental
debate. il Bsns W p29-30 Mr 21 '70
Students mobilize for eco-action. A. San-
som. Parks & Rec 5:49+ Ap '70
Teach-in on the environment; program at
University of Michigan. R. R. Coffey. Na-
tion 210:390-2 Ap 6 '70
Teach-in to save the earth. G. Nelson. Read
Digest 96:110-12 Ap '70
Welcome teach-in. Cons 24:1 Ap '70

Canada

Pollution rebels go to the public; pollution
probe's campaign. il Bsns W p68 Ag 8 '70

Japan

Buddha v. pollution. il Time 96:40 D 28 '70

Sweden

Sweden's youth says *nej* to pollution. M.
Michaelson. il Todays Health 49:22-5+ Ja
'71

ENVIRONMENTAL policy
America . . . the beautiful? il Parks & Rec 5:
18-21 Mr '70
America's polluted environment; symposium.
bibliog Cur Hist 59:1-54 Jl '70
Antipollution program. il Sci N 97:147 F 7 '70
Authority and responsibility for environ-
mental administration. L. K. Caldwell. Ann
Am Acad 389:107-15 My '70
Cleanup campaign; Nixon sets targets; sum-
mary of message to Congress July 9, 1970.
il U S News 69:54 Jl 20 '70
Clearing the waters; special message to Con-
gress. Sci N 97:168 F 14 '70
Conservation caretaker; Environmental policy
act of 1969. por Time 95:46 F 9 '70
Country doctor looks at conservation and
health; cooperation between agencies in
West Virginia. D. Hale. il pors Am For 76:
16-18+ Ja '70
Cross-purposes in the environmental crusade.
M. Frome. Field & S 75:42+ My '70
Dollars and doubts. Sci N 97:122-3 Ja 31 '70
Ecological destruction is a condition of Ameri-
can life; interview ed. by P. Collier. P.
Ehrlich. il Mlle 70:188-9+ Ap '70
Ecology: a cause becomes a mass movement;
with editorial comment, and report by J.
Pekkanen. il Life 68:3, 22-30 Ja 30 '70

Ecology and environment; address. R. R.
Bartelsmeyer. Arch Forum 132:48-9+ Je
'70
Emerging legal strategies: judicial interven-
tion. J. L. Sax. bibliog f Ann Am Acad 389:
71-6 My '70
Environment; reform and recovery. Parks
& Rec 5:21 F '70
Environmental dispositions of environmental
decision-makers. K. H. Craik. bibliog f Ann
Am Acad 389:87-94 My '70
Environmental issue. R. Lekachman. Duns
95:7 My '70
Environmental problems and legislative re-
sponses. J. C. Oppenheimer and L. A.
Miller. il Ann Am Acad 389:77-86 My '70
Faster than a speeding bullet, more powerful
than a locomotive. W. F. Wagner, jr. Arch
Rec 147:9 Mr '70
Five who care. G. Nelson. il Look 34:32-3 Ap
21 '70
Foundation for human survival; address,
August 26, 1970. C. L. Hogan. Vital Speeches
36:755-8 O 1 '70
From pollution abatement to quality control.
E. S. Muskie. Cur 117:10-13 Ap '70
How do we get from here to there? T. H.
White. il Life 68:36-40+ Je 26 '70
How much, how soon for anti-pollution? R.
H. Gilluly. New Repub 162:7-8 Ja 24 '70
Idea whose time has come. M. McGrory.
America 122:89 Ja 31 '70
In two generations this nation will self-de-
struct: the environmental job; address,
April 15, 1970. F. Smith. Vital Speeches 36:
425-8 My 1 '70
Information for decisions in environmental
policy. R. A. Carpenter. il Science 168:1316-
22 Je 12 '70
Issue of the year: the environment. il Time
97:21-2 Ja 4 '71
Keeper of the conscience: President Nixon.
Sci Am 222:44 Ap '70
Latest moves on pollution control. il U S
News 68:5 F 2 '70
Laurance S. Rockefeller. Y. Fogel. il pors
Parks & Rec 5:14-17+ Mr '70
Legal redress of environmental disruption. J.
L. Sax. Arch Forum 132:50-1 My '70
Leisurely war on filth. New Repub 162:9-10
F 21 '70
Lip-service on ecology. J. Deedy. Common-
weal 93:314 D 25 '70
Memento mori to the earth. il Time 95:16-18
My 4 '70
Message . . . and the reaction; symposium, ed.
by D. R. Dunn. il Parks & Rec 5:22-5 Mr '70
Mr Herter becomes special assistant for en-
vironmental affairs; Department announce-
ment; with remarks by W. P. Rogers and
C. A. Herter. Dept State Bul 62:212-14 F 23
'70
National environmental policy act; text. Cur
Hist 59:46-7+ Jl '70
Needed: an environmental bill of rights. P. F.
Brandwein. il Am For 76:28-33 Ap; 36-
8 My '70
New environmental agencies; proposals. Sci
N 97:576 Je 13 '70
New politics of the environment. Chr Cent
87:36 Ja 14 '70
Nixon offers environmental program. L. J.
Carter. Science 167:1105 F 20 '70
Nixon starts the cleanup. Time 95:39+ F 23
'70
Now or never. J. B. Craig. Am For 76:11 F
'70
Options for a cleaner America; symposium.
bibliog f il Cur Hist 59:65-104+ Ag '70
Our environmental crisis. R. Reagan. il Na-
tions Bsns 58:24-8 F '70
Para-real estate: the handing out of re-
sources. J. Ridgeway. il Ramp Mag 8:28-33
My '70
Performance gap again. Commonweal 91:419-
20 Ja 16 '70
Politicians know an issue. il Newsweek 75:
33-4 Ja 26 '70
Politics of pollution; why are the corporations
cooperating? M. Harrington. Commonweal
92:111-14 Ap 17 '70
Politicians. Nat R 22:190 F 24 '70
Pollution and the poor. W. Barthelmes. Com-
monweal 91:549-50 F 20 '70; Discussion.
92:3+, 107+ Mr 13, Ap 17 '70
Pollution: everyone's in on the act. il Bsns
W p 116+ Ja 24 '70
Presidential specifics on the environment. Nat
Parks 44:27 Mr '70
President's environmental crusade and the
public lands. M. Frome. Field & S 74:36+ F
'70
Question of priorities: President Nixon's mes-
sage to Congress. Nation 210:194-5 F 23 '70
Rate your candidate; key environmental is-
sues; with editorial comment. M. Frome.
Field & S 75:6, 60-5+ S '70

ENVIRONMENTAL policy—*Continued*
Rebuttal; R. M. Nixon's proposals; E. E. Muskie's counterproposals. por Newsweek 75:18 F 2 '70
Reluctance and parsimony. Sci N 97:502 My 23 '70
Rescuing the environment: the President's program; excerpt from a message to Congress, February 10, 1970. R. M. Nixon. U S News 68:93-7 F 23 '70; Cur Hist 58:362-4 Je '70
Rhetoric of ecology. Life 68:36 Mr 6 '70
Saving the world, literally, becomes a national issue: a roundup of events. il Arch Rec 147:36 F '70
Somebody fouled up; symposium. il New Repub 163-13-29 O 31 '70
State of the planet address; State of the Union address. J. B. Sheerin. Cath World 210:242-3 Mr '70
This month's feature: Congress & federal pollution controls. Cong Digest 49:193-224 Ag '70
To my friends in the affluent society, greetings. J. K. Galbraith. por Life 68:20 Mr 27 '70
Up with the countryside. Farm J 94:98 Mr '70
See also
Conservation of resources
Environment—Laws and legislation
Human ecology
Man—Influence on nature
Pollution—Control
Pollution—Laws and legislation
United States—Council on environmental quality
United States—Environmental protection agency
Water pollution—Control

International aspects

For global initiative; what the UN can do. R. N. Gardner. Sat R 53:41+ Jl 4 '70
Our far-flung correspondents; world's first interdisciplinary conference on environmental pollution in Tokyo. F. C. Shapiro. New Yorker 46:93-4+ My 23 '70
Politics of earthmanship. A. T. Feraru. Nat Parks & Con Mag 44:19 S '70
To prevent a world wasteland; a proposal. G. F. Kennan. For Affairs 48:401-13 Ap '70

Alaska

Earth as seen from Alaska; Hickel in Earth day observances. P. Ryan. il Sports Illus 32:26-8+ My 4 '70

California

Reveille out West; anti-pollution issue in California. J. S. Carroll. New Repub 162:12-13 Mr 7 '70

China (People's Republic)

Mao ethic and environmental quality. L. A. Orleans and R. P. Suttmeier. bibliog Science 170:1173-6 D 11 '70

Florida

Victory in the Everglades. J. George. Read Digest 97:73-7 Ag '70

Maine

Payrolls and pickerel in Maine; imposition of strongest state anti-pollution controls in the U.S. il Time 95:52 F 16 '70
Setting the pace: Maine cracks down on the polluters. il Newsweek 75:22 F 16 '70

New York (state)

Department of environmental conservation activated on July 1st at Albany ceremony; excerpts from address, ed. by J. E. Gavagan. H. L. Diamond. il pors Cons 25:4-5 Ag '70
Governor appoints six citizen experts to new State environmental board. J. E. Gavagan. il Cons 25:2-3+ Ag '70
Governor creates Department of environmental conservation; Office of parks and recreation set up in new law; with editorial comment. N. A. Rockefeller. Cons 24:1-3 Je '70
Governor tells of plans for environment to legislature; message; with editorial comment. N. A. Rockefeller. por Cons 24:1, 12-13 F '70
New environmental conservation tool; environmental conservation councils. C. C. Morrison, jr. il Cons 25:10-13 D '70 (to be cont)

Vermont

Lessons from Vermont; lowering antipollution standards when competing for industry. Time 96:50 N 9 '70

ENVIRONMENTAL policy as a campaign issue. See Campaign issues
ENVIRONMENTAL pollution. See Pollution

ENVIRONMENTAL protection administration (proposed) See United States—Environmental protection administration (proposed)
ENVIRONMENTAL protection administration, New York. See New York (city)—Environmental protection administration
ENVIRONMENTAL protection agency. See United States—Environmental protection agency
ENVIRONMENTAL quality control. See Pollution—Control
ENVIRONMENTAL quality council. See United States—Council on environmental quality
ENVIRONMENTAL research laboratory. See Arizona. University, Tucson—Environmental research laboratory
ENVIRONMENTAL science services administration. See United States—Environmental science services administration
ENVIRONMENTAL simulators
World's climate in one lab; Biotron. il Sci Digest 68:70-1 D '70
ENVIRONMENTAL studies
Education vs pollution. il Sr Schol 96:Schol Teach 1 F 16 '70
Environmental dispositions of environmental decision-makers. K. H. Craik. bibliog f Ann Am Acad 389:87-94 My '70
How should we treat environment? F. K. Hare. bibliog Science 167:352-5 Ja 23 '70
ENVIRONMENTAL teach-ins. See Environmental movement—Teach-ins
ENVY
Envy: a theory of social behavior, by H. Schoeck. Review
  Cath World 211:228 Ag '70. G. Baum
  See also
Jealousy
ENYEART, James L.
New lease on life for daguerreotypes. J. Deschin. il por Pop Phot 67:42+ N '70 *
ENZYME detergents. See Detergents
ENZYME inhibitors. See Enzymes—Inactivation
ENZYME laundry products
Institute report on enzymes in the laundry; questions and answers. il Good H 170:142+ Ja '70
ENZYMES
Absence of cystathionase in human fetal liver: is cystine essential? J. A. Sturman and others. bibliog il Science 169:74-6 Jl 3 '70
Adenyl cyclase of cultured mammalian cells: activation by catecholamines. M. H. Makman. bibliog il Science 170:1421-3 D 25 '70
Age of the enzyme. J. Lentz. il Todays Health 48:32-3+ Ap '70
Beta glucuronidase activity in skin components of children with cystic fibrosis. G. E. Gibbs and G. D. Griffin. bibliog il Science 167:993-4 F 13 '70
Enzyme tailors; theories of D. E. Koshland. Newsweek 76:61 Jl 6 '70
Enzymes activated by monovalent cations. C. H. Suelter. bibliog il Science 168:789-95 My 15 '70
Explaining nature's catalysts; Koshland's theory. Time 96:46 Jl 6 '70
Hormone-sensitive adenyl cyclase: cytochemical localization in rat liver. L. Reik and others. bibliog il Science 168:382-4 Ap 17 '70
Intestinal enzymes: indicators of proliferation and differentiation in the jejunum. R. Fortin-Magana and others. bibliog il Science 167:1627-8 Mr 20 '70
News from the world of space exploration; use of DAP I to find the primary structure of many proteins. Space World H-1-85:49-50 Ja '71
Orbital rendezvous. Sci Am 223:46 Ag '70
Pulmonary hemorrhage in hamsters after exposure to proteolytic enzymes of bacillus subtilis. I. P. Goldring and others. bibliog il Science 170:73-4 O 2 '70
Self-assembly. Sci Am 222:45-6 F '70
Starting with the simple; inorganic model of nitrogenase. il Sci N 98:217-18 S 12 '70
Steroid hormones: effects on adenyl cyclase activity and adenosine 3',5'-monophosphate in target tissues. M. G. Rosenfeld and B. W. O'Malley. bibliog il Science 168:253-5 Ap 10 '70
Threonine deaminase: a novel activity stain on polyacrylamide gels. R. S. Feldberg and P. Datta. bibliog il Science 170:1414-16 D 25 '70
Trouble on the DNA front. bibliog il Chem 43:24-5 O '70
  See also
Acetylcholinesterase
Arginase
Asparaginase
Cholinesterase
Collagenase
Decarboxylase
Dehydrogenases

ENZYMES—See also—*Continued*
Esterases
Galactosidases
Hydrolases
Hydroxylases
Kinases
Lysozyme
Melatonin
Neuraminidase
Nucleases
Peroxidases
Plasminogen
Polymerase
Reductases
Ribonucleases
Synthetases
Thrombin
Transaminases
Transferases

Conferences

Enzyme regulation in mammalian tissues. G. Weber. Science 167:1018-20   F 13 '70

Inactivation

[8-Arginine]-vasopressionoic acid: an inhibitor of rabbit kidney adenyl cyclase. T. Dousa and others. bibliog il Science 167:1134-5 F 20 '70
DDT-induced inhibition of avian shell gland carbonic anhydrase: a mechanism for thin eggshells. J. Bitman and others. bibliog il Science 168:594-6 My 1 '70
Dimethylbenzanthracene tumorigenesis and aryl hydrocarbon hydroxylase in mouse skin: inhibition by 7,8-benzoflavone. H. V. Gelboin and others. bibliog il Science 170: 169-71 O 9 '70
Enzyme inactivation with ultraviolet laser energy (2650 angstroms) M. W. Berns and others. bibliog il Science 169:1215-17 S 18 '70
Fluorocitrate inhibition of aconitase: relative configuration of inhibitory isomer by X-ray crystallography. H. L. Carrell and others. bibliog il Science 170:1412-14 D 25 '70
Inhibition of phosphofructokinase by quinone methide and α-methylene lactone tumor inhibitors. R. L. Hanson and others. bibliog il Science 168:378-80 Ap 17 '70
Physiological concentrations of lactate dehydrogenases and substrate inhibition. J. Everse and others. bibliog il Science 168: 1236-8 Je 5 '70
Serotonin-containing neurons in brain: depression of firing by monoamine oxidase inhibitors. G. K. Aghajanian and others. bibliog il Science 169:1100-2 S 11 '70
Specific inhibition of nuclear RNA polymerase II by α-amanitin. T. J. Lindell and others. bibliog il Science 170:447-9 O 23 '70
Tumorigenesis in mouse skin: inhibition by synthetic inhibitors of proteases. W. Troll and others. bibliog il Science 169:1211-13 S 18 '70

Specificity

Enzyme specificity as a factor in regulation of fatty acid chain length in escherichia coli. M. D. Greenspan and others. bibliog il Science 170:1203-4 D 11 '70
Specificities of transport systems and enzymes. R. D. Berlin. bibliog il Science 168:1539-45 Je 26 '70

ENZYMES, Plant
Dextranase activity in coleoptiles of avena. A. N. J. Heyn. bibliog il Science 167:874-5 F 6 '70

ENZYMES in detergents. See Detergents

EOCENE period. See Paleobotany—Eocene

EPEL, David
Death of the oceans; address, March 13, 1970. Vital Speeches 36:411-14 Ap 15 '70

EPERGNES
Continental pewter epergnes, cruet stands, and sugar bowls. R. M. Vetter. il Antiques 98:88-93 Jl '70
Victorian flower stands. H. Wakefield. il Antiques 98:232-6 Ag '70

EPHEMERIDES
Lunar ephemeris: Delaunay's theory revisited. A. Deprit and others. bibliog il Science 168:1569-70 Je 26 '70

EPHRON, Nora
Helen Gurley Brown only wants to help. por Esquire 73:74-5+ F '70

EPIDEMICS
See also
Cholera
Diphtheria
Influenza

EPILEPSY
Epileptic focus location: spectral analysis method. W. Gersch and G. V. Goddard. bibliog il Science 169:701-2 Ag 14 '70
Neuroglia: gliosis and focal epilepsy. D. A. Pollen and M. C. Trachtenberg. bibliog Science 167:1252-3 F 27 '70

Penicillin as epileptogenic agent: its effect on an isolated neuron. G. F. Ayala and others. bibliog il Science 167:1257-60 F 27 '70

EPISCOPACY
Episcopacy and church unity, today and tomorrow. America 122:601 Je 6 '70

EPISCOPACY and church union
COCU: a critique; with editorial comment. H. Lindsell. Chr Today 15:8-10+, 28 O 23 '70

EPISCOPAL church. See Protestant Episcopal church

EPLEY, Richard. See Stringer, W. C. jt. auth.

EPOXY adhesives
Household cements. il Consumer Bul 53:16-17 Jl '70

EPP, Robert
U.S.-Japanese treaty crisis. bibliog f Cur Hist 58:202-8+ Ap '70

EPSTEIN, Al
Pool that comes in a kit. il Mech Illus 66:80+ Jl '70

EPSTEIN, Edward B.
Where the fine arts can flourish. il Todays Ed 59:52-4 O '70

EPSTEIN, Emanuel. See LaHaye, P. A. jt. auth.

EPSTEIN, Eugene V.
Enough of Stiffelio. Opera N 34:16 F 14 '70

EPSTEIN, Jason
Judging the Chicago trial. A. M. Bickel. bibliog f Commentary 51:31-40 Ja '71 *

EPSTEIN, John H. and others
Defect in DNA synthesis in skin of patients with xeroderma pigmentosum demonstrated in vivo. bibliog il Science 168:1477-8 Je 19 '70

EPSTEIN, Joseph
Homo/hetero: the struggle for sexual identity. il Harper 241:37-44+ S; 18+ N '70

EPSTEIN, Joseph, 1918-
Rate of decomposition of GB in seawater. bibliog il Science 170:1396-8 D 25 '70

EPSTEIN, Samuel, and Taylor, H. P. Jr
$^{18}O/^{16}O$, $^{30}Si/^{28}Si$, D/H, and $^{13}C/^{12}C$ studies of lunar rocks and minerals. bibliog il Science 167:533-5 Ja 30 '70
—and others
Antarctic ice sheet: stable isotope anlyses of Byrd station cores and interhemispheric climatic implications. bibliog il Science 168:1570-2 Je 26 '70

EPSTEIN, Samuel S.
Family likeness. il Environ 12:16-25 Jl '70
NTA. bibliog il Environ 12:2-11 S '70
—and others
Mutagenicity of trimethylphosphate in mice. bibliog il Science 168:584-6 My 1 '70

EPSTEIN-Barr virus. See Herpesvirus

EQUAL pay for equal work
Prejudice; women's wages. P. A. Samuelson. Newsweek 75:90 Mr 23 '70
Reducing discrimination: role of the Equal pay act. R. D. Moran. bibliog f Mo Labor R 93:30-4 Je '70

EQUAL rights for women. See Woman—Equal rights

EQUAL time rule (television) See Television laws and regulations

EQUALITY
What presidents once said about racial equality. D. Lawrence. U S News 68:76 F 9 '70
See also
Democracy
Individualism

EQUALITY in education. See Equalization, Educational

EQUALIZATION, Educational
Comparability. R. L. Fairley. Am Ed 6:20 O '70
End of the impossible dream. P. Schrag. il Sat R 53:68-70+ S 19 '70
Equal education and the law. H. Shanks. Am Scholar 39:255-69 Spr '70
How relevant is equality? R. L. Holloway. Ed Digest 35:19-21 Ja '70
Jefferson and his aristocracy of talent proposal. C. C. Lammers. Ed Digest 35:45-7 Ja '70
No place for blue-collars. D. M. Gray. Commonweal 93:13-14, 79 O 2, 16 '70
Our nation's schools: desegregation is not enough. G. D. Fischer. por Parents Mag 45:16 S '70
Race, class, and the limits of schooling. D. L. Kirp. Ed Digest 36:12-15 O '70

EQUATION of motion
Can equations of motion be used in high-energy physics? P. A. M. Dirac. por Phys Today 23:29-31 Ap '70

EQUATIONS, Chemical. See Chemical equations

EQUATIONS, Differential
See also
Equation of motion

EQUATORIAL Indians. See Indians of South America—Ecuador

EQUILIBRIUM (physiology)
See also
Labyrinth (ear)
EQUIPMENT, Industrial. See Industrial equipment
EQUIPMENT, Municipal. See Municipal equipment
EQUIPMENT industries
See also
Machine tool industry and trade
EQUIPMENT renting. See Lease and rental services
EQUITY
See also
Justice
ERASMUS, Desiderius
Erasmus, by G. Faludy. Review
Nation 212:93-4 Ja 18 '71. R. W. French
ERDMAN, Jean
Jean Erdman theater of dance; Brooklyn academy of music. N. Mason. il por Dance Mag 44:78-9 Jl '70 *
On with the dance at NYU: Jean Erdman seeks roots of style. J. Meredith. il por Dance Mag 44:44-9 Ap '70 *
ERDMAN, Paul
Blowup in Basel. Newsweek 76:81 O 5 '70 *
EREN, Nuri
U.N. veteran: interview. New Yorker 45:30-1 F 14 '70
United Nations and the common man. Sat R 53:18-21 O 31 '70
EREWHON trading company
Nowhere store that's going places. J. Cox. Org Gard & Farm 17:57-9 Ag '70
ERIC
ASIS takes over ERIC/CLIS and names new director. Library J 95:614+ F 15 '70
ERICKSON, Donald A.
Failure in Navaho schooling. il Parents Mag 45:66-8+ S '70
Nonpublic schools and educational reform. Ed Digest 35:1-4 My '70
ERICKSON, Millard J.
Potential of apologetics. Chr Today 14:6-8 Jl 17; 13-15 Jl 31 '70
ERICSON, David B. and Wollin, Goesta
Pleistocene climates in the Atlantic and Pacific Oceans: a comparison based on deep-sea sediments. bibliog il Science 167: 1483-5 Mr 13 '70
ERIE, LAKE
Aldrin: removal from lake water by flocculent bacteria. W. O. Leshniowsky and others. bibliog il Science 169:993-5 S 4 '70
Biological nitrogen fixation in Lake Erie. D. L. Howard and others. bibliog il Science 169:61-2 Jl 3 '70
Dying Lake Erie. Cons 24:37 F '70
IJC submits report on pollution of the lower Great Lakes; Department announcement; with excerpts from IJC report. Dept State Bul 62:807-9 Je 29 '70
Lake Erie, alive but changing. D. E. Arnold. il Cons 25:23-30+ D '70
Teacher tips: Lake Erie: alive but changing; with glossary. J. A. Weeks. Cons 25:31+ D '70
ERIE, Pa.
Water supply
Rubber keeps water in and debris out; Sigsbee reservoir. S. J. Prazer. il Am City 85:79-80 S '70
ERIGERON. See Fleabanes
ERIKSEN, Mary Ann
Boomdoggle. New Repub 163:17-18 D 5 '70
ERIKSON, Erik Homburger
Erikson speaks out; interview. il pors Newsweek 76:85-9 D 21 '70
about
Erik Erikson: the quest for identity. il por Newsweek 76:84-9 D 21 '70 *
Erik Erikson's eight ages of man. D. Elkind. il N Y Times Mag p25-7+ Ap 5 '70 *
Erik H. Erikson, by R. Coles. Review
Life 69:24 N 27 '70. W. Schott
Profiles. R. Coles. por New Yorker 46:51-4+ N 7; 59-60+ N 14 '70 *
Stages of man. il por Time 96:51-2 N 30 '70 *
ERITREA. See Ethiopia
ERMACORA, Marcel
$2,000,000 grudge. il por Time 96:30 O 5 '70 *
ERNANI; opera. See Verdi, G.
ERNOULT, Victor, and Pépin, Jacques
Le Calvados. House B 112:114+ S '70
ERNST, Leonard
Can chemicals stimulate learning capacity? Ed Digest 35:32-3 My '70
ERNST, Paul
Come back to me; story. Good H 170:79-81 Mr '70

EROS (asteroid) See Asteroids
EROSION
See also
Beach erosion
EROSION prevention and control
See also
Contour farming
EROTIC graffiti. See Graffiti
EROTIC literature
See also
Immoral literature and pictures
Sex in literature
ERRINGTON, Paul Lester
Of wilderness and wolves; excerpts. il Liv Wildn 33:3-7 Aut '69
ERROL, N.H. See Berlin, N.H.
ERRORS, Theory of
See also
Least squares
ERTEGUN, Mica
Mica+Chessy=MAC II. il pors McCalls 97: 96-101 Ap '70 *
ERTÜRK, Erdogan. See Bryan, G. T. jt. auth.
ERVIN, Samuel James, 1896-
Excerpt from address, September 25, 1969. Cong Digest 49:79+ Mr '70
about
Response to fear. il por Time 96:10 Ag 3 '70 *
Senator Ervin thinks the Constitution should be taken like mountain whisky, undiluted and untaxed. J. Herbers. il pors N Y Times Mag p50-1+ N 15 '70 *
ERWIN, Frank Craig, 1920-
Emperor of U.T. pors Time 96:54 Ag 10 '70 *
ERWITT, Elliott
Gallery; photographs. il Life 68:8-11 My 15 '70
about
Elliott Erwitt at the Smithsonian. S. Callahan. il por Life 68:12 My 15 '70 *
ERYTHROCYTES
Substrate stabilization; genetically controlled reciprocal relationship of two human enzymes. M. L. Greene and others. bibliog il Science 167:887-9 F 6 '70
See also
Erythropoiesis
ERYTHROPOIESIS
Erythropoiesis in the dog: the periodic nature of the steady state. A. Morley and F. Stohlman, jr; reply. A. S. Iberall. Science 168:152 Ap 3 '70
ESALEN Institute, Calif.
Esalen: three-day session at Hotel Diplomat. New Yorker 46:27-8 My 2 '70
Human potential: the revolution in feeling. il Time 96:54-8 N 9 '70
You don't have a body; you are your body; excerpt from Please touch. J. Howard. Mlle 71:153+ My '70
ESCALATOR clause (wages) See Wages—Cost of living adjustments
ESCAMILLA, Mario
Murder in legal limbo. il por Time 96:58 S 28 '70 *
ESCAPE devices (airplanes) See Airplanes——Escape devices
ESCAPE devices (space vehicles) See Space vehicles—Escape devices
ESCAPES
Fabulous escapes of Papillon. il pors Life 69:46-52+ N 13 '70
Leary's latest trip. por Newsweek 76:33 S 28 '70
Springing of George Blake, by S. Bourke. Review
New Repub 163:28-30 S 5 '70. A. Campbell
ESCHENBACH, Christoph
Christoph Eschenbach; interview, ed. by R. Hemming. por Sr Schol 96:16 F 9 '70
ESCHERICHIA coli
Bacteriophage induced transfer RNA in escherichia coli. V. Daniel and others. bibliog il Science 167:1682-8 Mr 27 '70
Chloramphenicol: effect on DNA synthesis during phage development in escherichia coli. P. Amati. bibliog il Science 168:1226-8 Je 5 '70
Coevolution of escherichia coli and bacteriophages in chemostat culture. M. T. Horne. bibliog il Science 168:992-3 My 22 '70
Colicin-tolerant mutants of escherichia coli: resistance of membranes to colicin El. P. Bhattacharyya and others. bibliog il Science 168:998-1000 My 22 '70
Cyclic adenosine monophosphate in bacteria. I. Pastan and R. Perlman. bibliog il Science 169:339-40 Jl 24 '70
Enzyme specificity as a factor in regulation of fatty acid chain length in escherichia coli. M. D. Greenspan and others. bibliog il Science 170:1203-4 D 11 '70

ESCHERICHIA coli—*Continued*
Fitness of an escherichia coli mutator gene. T. C. Gibson and others. bibliog il Science 169:686-8 Ag 14 '70
Globe-trotter's peril; traveler's diarrhea. Sci Am 222:64 Mr '70
Ribonuclease V of escherichia coli: susceptibility of heated ribosomal RNA and stability of R17 phage RNA. M. Kuwano and others. bibliog il Science 168:1225-6 Je 5 '70
5S RNA synthesized by escherichia coli in presence of chloramphenicol: different 5'-terminal sequences. B. G. Forget and B. Jordan. bibliog il Science 167:382-4 Ja 23 '70
See also
Colicines

ESHERICK, Wharton
Wharton Esherick 1887-1970. S. Maloof; W. Castle. il pors Craft Horiz 30:10-17 Ag '70 *

ESHLEMAN, Edwin D. and Walker, R. S.
Reforming itself; the issue   Congress won't face. America 122:124-5 F 7 '70

ESKIMO clubs. See Clubs (weapons)

ESKIMOS
Alaskan natives, time of crisis. J. Pender. il Nat Parks & Con Mag 44:23-7 N '70
Eskimos, nomads of the North. il Sr Schol 96:11-13 My 11 '70
Netsilik Eskimo, by A. Balikci. Review
Harper 241:122-3 N '70. J. Thompson
Two tactics for ethnic survival; Eskimo & Indian. R. J. Dryfoos, jr. il Trans-Action 7: 51-4 Ja '70

Art
Artists of the frozen North. T. Holloway. il por Design 72:4-8 Wint '70

Costume and adornment
Indian and Eskimo tools and clothing. C. Miles. il Hobbies 75:142-3+ Mr; 142-3 Ap '70

Health and hygiene
Walrus is good for the teeth. il Sci Digest 67: 22-3 Mr '70

Implements
Indian & Eskimo drills. C. Miles. il Hobbies 74:142-5 F '70
Indian and Eskimo tools and clothing. C. Miles. il Hobbies 75:142-3+ Mr; 142-3 Ap '70

Photographs
Eskimo. W. Bronson. il Am West 7:34-47 Jl '70

Social life and customs
Eskimo. W. Bronson. il Am West 7:34-47 Jl '70

ESKRIDGE, John. See Childs, J. jt. auth.
Kapluna daughter: living with Eskimos; excerpt from Women in the field, ed. by P. Golde. J. L. Briggs. il por Trans-Action 7: 12-24 Je '70

ESLICK, W. G.
Electronic flash tester. il Radio-Electr 41:66 My '70

ESOKAIT, Albert C.
Men who make treasurers tremble. pors Forbes 106:19-20 S 1 '70 *

ESPALIERS. See Fruit trees, Training of; Plants, Training of

ESPESETH, Robert D.
Hog farm becomes activities center. il Parks & Rec 5:38-9 O '70

ESPINOSA DE LOS MONTEROS M, A. and others
Insulin release from isolated human fetal pancreatic islets. bibliog il Science 168:1111-12 My 29 '70

ESPIONAGE
Enemy within; CIA report on Communist spies operating inside the government of South Vietnam. il Newsweek 76:65 N 2 '70
Who spies, and why? il Sr Schol 96:4-9 F 9 '70
See also
Secret service
Spies

ESPIONAGE, Industrial. See Spies, Industrial

ESPOSITO, Phil
Newcomer at the net. il por Time 95:58 Mr 9 '70 *

ESPOSITO, Tony
Newcomer at the net. il por Time 95:58 Mr 9 '70 *

ESPY, Hilda Cole. See Williams, L. jt. auth.

ESPY, James Pollard
Espy-Redfield dispute. D. M. Ludlum. pors Weatherwise 22:224-9+ D '69

ESPY, Robert Hamilton Edwin
Major ecumenical proposal. D. Bowman and R. W. Rousseau. America 122:70-2 Ja 24 '70

ESQUIRE (periodical)
Esquire presents the winners of its first International college film festival; with editorial comment. il Esquire 74:6, 155 Ag '70
Journalist sues Viking, Esquire, over Calley story. Pub W 198:30 O 19 '70
Smiling through the apocalypse. A. Gingrich. Esquire 73:12 Mr '70
Smiling through the apocalypse. ed. by H. Hayes. Review
Commentary 49:98+ My '70. E. Grossman
See also
Business in the arts award

ESSENCE (periodical)
Black venture. il Time 95:79-80 My 4 '70
Meaningful images. il Newsweek 75:74 My 11 '70

ESSENE, E. See Ringwood, A. E. jt. auth.

ESSEX, Martin
Getting through to the establishment. Ed Digest 35:42-4 Ja '70

ESSEX international, inc.
Jilter jilted. Forbes 105:58 Mr 1 '70

ESTATE planning
Estate plans: girding for a shake-up. Bsns W p97 S 19 '70
Wife insurance: how it fits your estate plan. Bsns W p95 O 24 '70

ESTATES, Decedents
See also
Executors and administrators

ESTENSSORO B., Hugo
Now you see a leftist, now you don't. Commonweal 93:316-18 D 25 '70

ESTEP, Sarah Virginia
Camps for every kind of kid. il Parents Mag 45:66-8 My '70

ESTERASES
Atropinesterase and cocainesterase of rabbit serum: localization of the enzyme activity in isozymes. C. Stormont and Y. Suzuki. bibliog il Science 167:200-2 Ja 9 '70
See also
Cholinesterase

ESTEROW, Milton
Collectors: Dr and Mrs Irving Levitt. il Art in Am 58:72-7 My '70

ESTERS
Wax esters in marine copepods. R. F. Lee and others. bibliog il Science 167:1510-11 Mr 13 '70

ESTES, Elliott
Motor trend interview. por Motor T 22:64+ Jl '70

ESTES, John E. and Golomb, Berl
Oil spills: method for measuring their extent on the sea surface. bibliog il Science 169: 676-8 Ag 14 '70

ESTIMATES
See also
Building—Estimates

ESTIVATION
Regulation of oxygen consumption and body temperature during torpor in a hummingbird, eulampis jugularis. F. R. Hainsworth and L. L. Wolf. bibliog il Science 168:368-9 Ap 17 '70

ESTORIL, Portugal
Blue heaven for greenbacks. R. Joseph. il Esquire 74:206-9+ D '70

ESTRADA, J. C. Torchia-. See Torchia-Estrada, J. C.

ESTRANGEMENT; story. See Walker, T.

ESTROGENS
Enough to move FDA; relation of estrogen to bloodclotting. Sci N 97:430-1 My 2 '70
Estrogenic induction of ornithine decarboxylase in vivo and vitro. S. Cohen and others. bibliog il Science 170:336-8 O 16 '70
Ontogeny of the estrogen receptor during early uterine development. J. H. Clark and J. Gorski. bibliog il Science 169:76-8 Jl 3 '70

ESTUARIES
Galveston Bay: test case of an estuary in crisis. L. J. Carter. il Science 167:1102-8 F 20 '70
Rangia cuneata on the East coast: thousand mile range extension. or resurgence? S. H. Hopkins and J. D. Andrews. bibliog il Science 167:868 F 6 '70

ESTUARY models. See Hydraulic models

ESTVAN, Frank J.
Vitamins for young minds. il PTA Mag 64: 6-8, bibliog(p35) Ja '70

ÉTAGÈRE. See Stands (furniture)

ETCHELLS, Skip
One-design sailboats. il por Motor B 125:102-3 Ja '70

ETERNAL life. See Immortality

ETERNAL life of Kerry Magill; story. See Littke, L. J.

ETHERS
Dissolving salt in benzene. il Chem 43:24 My '70

ETHICAL education. See Moral education

ETHICS
Freudian psychology and ethical doctrine. M. B. Zweig. bibliog f Am Imago 27:90-106 Spr '70
Let's have the courage of our doubts. R. K. Price, jr. Read Digest 97:219-20 Jl '70
New morality and the religious communities. J. T. Laney. bibliog f Ann Am Acad 387:14-21 Ja '70
  See also
Advertising ethics
Business ethics
Christian ethics
Conduct of life
Courage
Forgiveness
Good and evil
Honesty
Journalistic ethics
Justice
Labor ethics
Liberty
Literary ethics
Love
Marriage
Medical ethics
Moral attitudes
Moral conditions
Moral education
Obedience
Political ethics
School superintendents and principals, Professional ethics for
Self realization
Sexual ethics
Social ethics
Teachers, Professional ethics for
Television broadcasting—Moral aspects
Worth

ETHICS and law. See Law and ethics

ETHICS and science. See Science and ethics

ETHICS committee, House. See United States—Congress—House—Standards of official conduct, Committee on

ETHICS committee, Senate. See United States—Congress—Senate—Standards and conduct, Select committee on

ETHIOPIA
  See also
Americans in Ethiopia
Churches—Ethiopia
Danakil
Geology—Ethiopia
National parks and reserves—Ethiopia

Antiquities
Lalibela's ancient churches saved by a new preservative. il Sci Digest 68:84-5 Ag '70

Description and travel
Historic route through Ethiopia. B. F. Carruthers. il Travel 133:38-41+ Ap '70

Economic conditions
Long way to go. Newsweek 76:57+ N 16 '70

Foreign relations
Ethiopia: storm signals flashing for a U.S. friend. il por U S News 68:46-8 F 23 '70
Rumblings along the Red Sea: the Eritrean question. J. F. Campbell. For Affairs 48:537-48 Ap '70
  See also
Italo-Ethiopian war, 1935-1936

Native races
The Danakil: nomads of Ethiopia's wasteland. V. Englebert. il Nat Geog 137:186-211 F '70

Politics and government
Ethiopia: storm signals flashing for a U.S. friend. il por U S News 68:46-8 F 23 '70
Rumblings along the Red Sea: the Eritrean question. J. F. Campbell. il For Affairs 48:537-48 Ap '70

ETHIOPIAN orthodox church. See Ethiopic church

ETHIOPIC church
Ethiopian church: obstacle to progress. O. W. Okite. Chr Today 14:50 Ap 10 '70

ETHNIC dances. See Dancing in religion, folk-lore, etc.

ETHNIC enterprizes (firm)
Woman power; plant hiring only welfare mothers. il Ebony 26:89-91+ D '70

ETHNIC minorities. See Minorities

ETHNOGRAPHIC films. See Moving pictures—Ethnological films

ETHNOLOGICAL films. See Moving pictures—Ethnological films

ETHNOLOGICAL museums and collections
  See also
Indians of North America—Museums

ETHNOLOGY
Not by white might nor by black power. W. H. Hodges. Chr Today 15:5-10 O 9 '70
  See also
Anthropology
Civilization
Culture
Man—Migrations
Navigation, Primitive
Racial differences

Haiti
Haitian voodoo. T. Desrosiers. il Américas 22:35-9 F '70

ETHNOPSYCHOLOGY
Ethnic consciousness I. T. H. Clancy. America 124:10 Ja 9 '71
  See also
Negroes—Psychology
Social psychology

ETHOLOGY. See Animals—Habits and behavior

ETHRIDGE, John
Gettin' the lead out. il Motor T 22:48-50 My '70

ETHYL corporation
Is lead really good for us? il Forbes 106:26-7 S 15 '70
Leaden role. Bsns W p56 F 21 '70

ETHYLAMINE
Lycopene accumulation induced by 2-(4-chlorophenylthio)-triethylamine hydrochloride. C. W. Coggins, jr. and others. bibliog Science 168:1589-90 Je 26 '70

ETIQUETTE
How to cope with social disasters; excerpt from How to talk with practically anybody about practically anything. B. Walters. il por McCalls 98:74-5+ O '70
How to eat hard-to-handle food. il Good H 170:174 My '70
Monthly column. A. Vanderbilt. See issues of Ladies' home journal
Welcome but warning. E. Klein. Harp Baz 103:84-5 Ag '70
Who needs etiquette? M. Seligson. il Life 68:12 Mr 6 '70
  See also
Courtesy
Manners and customs

ETIQUETTE for children and youth
How important are good manners? M. B. Hoover. il Parents Mag 45:60-1+ Mr '70

ETON college. See Public schools (endowed)—England

ETRUSCANS
Enigma of the lost Etruscans. D. Cohen. il Sci Digest 68:10-16 S '70

ETTEL, Peter C. See Simons, E. L. jt. auth.

ETTER, Dave
Approaching 40; poem. Nation 210:798 Je 29 '70

ETYMOLOGY. See English language—Etymology

ETZIONI, Amitai
Fact-crazy, theory-shy? Science 170:391 O 23 '70
Indicators of the capacities for societal guidance. bibliog f il Ann Am Acad 388:25-34 Mr '70
Mr Nixon's voluntarism. il Commonweal 91:426-30 Ja 16 '70
Swing to the right? Trans-Action 7:12+ S '70; Same abr. Cur 122:11-14 O '70
Wrong top priority. Science 168:921; 169:532 My 22, Ag 7 '70

EUBANK, Wayne C.
Ghost billy of Heart Mountain. il por Outdoor Life 145:48-51+ Mr '70

EUBANKS, Jackie
Confessions of a middle-of-the-road militant. il Am Lib 1:437-9 My '70

EUCALYPTUS
New book for the eucalyptus people. il Sunset 144:222 Ap '70

EUCHARIST. See Catholic church—Eucharist; Lords Supper

EUGENICS
What controls for genetic engineering? J. Lederberg. Cur 121:48-51 S '70
  See also
Birth control
Heredity

EUGLENA
Persisting circadian rhythm of cell division in a photosynthetic mutant of euglena. R. M. Jarrett and L. N. Edmunds, jr. bibliog il Science 167:1730-3 Mr 27 '70
Symbiosis between euglena and damselfly nymphs is seasonal. R. L. Willey and others. bibliog il Science 170:80-1 O 2 '70

EULER, Ulf S. von
How the Nobelists won. il pors Newsweek 76:83 O 26 '70 *
Neurobiology: on the research frontier. pors Sci N 98:331 O 24 '70 *
Nobel prize: three share 1970 award for medical research. S. Udenfriend. pors Science 170:422-3 O 23 '70 *

EUPHORBIACEAE. See Tread-softly

EURAILPASS. See Railroads—Europe, Western

EUREKA, Calif.
Old houses are reminders of Eureka's lumbering past. il Sunset 145:59+ O '70

EUREKA SPRINGS, Ark.
A.J.C. protests federal funding of Gerald L. K. Smith project. Chr Cent 87:38 Ja 14 '70

EURIPIDES
Trojan women. Criticism
Dance Mag 45:76 Ja '71 *

EUROBONDS. See Bonds

EURODOLLAR market
Eurodollars, what are they? G. J. Henry. Forbes 105:81 Mr 1 '70
Money-machine magic of Eurodollars. il Bsns W p 114-15+ F 21 '70

EUROPA (ship) See Ocean liners

EUROPE
See also
Airlines—Europe
Americans in Europe
Aviation—Europe
Catholics in Europe
Foreign students in Europe
Golf courses—Europe
Immigration and emigration—Europe
Jews in Europe
Music—Europe
Music festivals—Europe
Pollution—Europe
Sports—Europe

Defenses
Proposed European security conference; excerpts from Prague communiqué and Brussels declaration. Cur Hist 58:305+ My '70

Description and travel
Europe on a musical scale; symposium. il Sat R 53:49-54+ Mr 14 '70
See also
Automobile touring—Europe

Foreign relations
See also
International security
United States
See United States—Foreign relations—Europe

History
Bibliography
Articles and other books received; comp. by R. E. Lindgren. See issues of American historical review
See also
15th century
Renaissance

20th century—Bibliography
Trends in historical writing about modern western Europe in the last five years. B. F. Hyslop. bibliog f Ann Am Acad 387:141-76 Ja '70

Maps
Europe. Sr Schol 95:16 S 22 '69; 97:9 S 21 '70

Politics
See also
European federation
International security

Population
Recent research in European historical demography. F. F. Mendels. bibliog f Am Hist R 75:1065-73 Ap '70

Religious institutions and affairs
See also
Reformation

Union (proposed)
See European federation

EUROPE, EASTERN
See also
Airlines—Europe, Eastern
Censorship—Europe, Eastern
Communism—Europe, Eastern
Labor and laboring classes—Europe, Eastern
Skis and skiing—Europe, Eastern
Youth—Europe, Eastern

Defenses
See also
Warsaw pact, 1955

Foreign relations
Germany (Federal Republic)
See Germany (Federal Republic)—Foreign relations—Europe, Eastern

History
Bibliography
Articles and other books received; comp. by C. Morley. See issues of American historical review

Industries
See also
Computer industry—Europe, Eastern

Treaties
See also
Warsaw pact, 1955

Union (proposed)
See European federation

EUROPE, WESTERN
Gathering of Europe's playgrounds. B. Gillam. il Mlle 70:259-64+ F '70
See also
Aerospace industries—Europe, Western
Air freight service—Europe, Western
Air pollution—Europe, Western
Airplane industry and trade—Europe, Western
Airplanes, Military—Europe, Western
Architecture—Europe, Western
Arts and crafts—Europe, Western
Atomic power—Europe, Western
Automobile industry and trade—Europe, Western
Automobile racing—Europe, Western
Banks and banking—Europe, Western
Business consolidations and mergers—Europe, Western
Camping—Europe, Western
Cities and towns—Europe, Western
Conservation of resources—Europe, Western
Evangelistic work—Europe, Western
Hotels, taverns, etc.—Europe, Western
Hunting—Europe, Western
Insurance, Health—Europe, Western
Labor and laboring classes—Europe, Western
Newspapers—Europe, Western
Night clubs—Europe, Western
Public opinion—Europe, Western
Publishers and publishing—Europe, Western
Railroads—Europe, Western
Restaurants—Europe, Western
Socialism—Europe, Western
Space research—Europe, Western
Student demonstrations—Europe, Western
Tourist trade—Europe, Western
Trade unions—Europe, Western
Trusts, Industrial—Europe, Western
Wages—Europe, Western

Armed forces
See also
United States—Armed forces—Forces in Europe

Civilization
History
Civilisation, by K. Clark. Review
Harper 241:100-2 S '70. H. Clurman
See also
European free trade association

Commerce
See also
European free trade association

Defenses
If U.S. pulls back from Europe. il U S News 68:78-9 Mr 16 '70
See also
Nato

Description and travel
Europe indoors; symposium. il Sat R 53:39-49+ S 12 '70
Fare backward, traveler: a refreshing sojourn in the eighteenth century. R. Joseph. il Esquire 74:130-5 S '70
Let's travel: student news, great flying. il Mlle 70:146-8+ F '70
Obscure museums. D. Ardrey. Travel & Camera 33:18-20 N '70
Sketching a personal diary. M. Haller. il Am Artist 34:40-4+ Ap '70
See also
Automobile touring—Europe, Western
Tourist trade—Europe, Western

Economic conditions
See also
Europe, Western—Industries
Unemployment—Europe, Western

Economic integration
Bold view of a transformed Europe by 1980; interview, ed. by A. de Borchgrave. F. M. Malfatti. por Newsweek 76:51 Ag 17 '70

EUROPE, WESTERN—Economic integration—
Continued
Boundaries of Europe. B. M. Russett. il
America 122:554-5 My 23 '70

Economic policy
See also
European economic community

Economic union
See European economic community

Foreign relations
Atlantic community; symposium. Cur Hist 58:
257-303+ My '70

United States
See United States—Foreign relations—
Europe, Western

History
Historiography
Trends in historical writing about modern
western Europe in the last five years. B. F.
Hyslop. bibliog f Ann Am Acad 387:141-76 Ja
'70

Industries
Europe's cutback; made in U.S.A. J.
Ross-Skinner. il Duns 96:57-8+ D '70
See also
Atomic power industry—Europe, Western
Computer industry—Europe, Western
Gas industry—Europe, Western

Politics
See also
European federation

Social life and customs
Europe indoors; symposium. il Sat R 53:39-
49+ S 12 '70

Union (proposed)
See European federation
EUROPE, WESTERN and the United States.
See Europe and the United States
EUROPE and the United States
Letter from Europe. A. Burgess. Am Scholar
39:502-4 Sum '70
See also
Americans in Europe
United States—Foreign opinion—European
EUROPEAN artificial satellites. See Artificial
satellites, European
EUROPEAN-Asiatic airline services. See Air-
lines—International services—European-Asi-
atic
EUROPEAN automobiles. See Automobiles,
Foreign
EUROPEAN center for nuclear research.
See European organization for nuclear
research
EUROPEAN common market. See European
economic community
EUROPEAN cookery. See Cookery, European
EUROPEAN economic community
Bank stock potentials. G. J. Henry. Forbes
106:56 S 1 '70
Bold view of a transformed Europe by 1980;
interview, ed. by A. de Borchgrave. F. M.
Malfatti. por Newsweek 76:51 Ag 17 '70
Britain in Europe at last? L. B. Tennyson.
Cur Hist 58:276-80 My '70
Clearing the decks; meeting of the Council of
ministers. Newsweek 75:49+ F 23 '70
Common market's reluctant applicant. Bsns
W p29 N 7 '70
Do the British want to join Europe? A.
Howard. New Repub 162:8-9 Ja 24 '70
EEC rule, but no test yet. Bsns W p 132+
D 19 '70
Europe: a rival or an also-ran. il Time 96:16-
17 Jl 13 '70
Fish and flag and Britain's future. il News-
week 76:73-4 Jl 13 '70
Milestone for the European community. P. H.
Laurent. Cur Hist 58:257-63 My '70
New sign points to monetary union; Eu-
ropean monetary units. Bsns W p28 N 28
'70
Pulling the cork; wine issue. il Newsweek
75:80-1 My 4 '70
Will Harold rat? European common market
applicant. Time 95:28-9 Mr 9 '70
EUROPEAN federation
Boundaries of Europe. B. M. Russett. il
America 122:554-5 My 23 '70
East and West: what if the twain meet?
A. de Borchgrave. il Newsweek 75:45-6 Mr
30 '70
Europe: getting it more together. Sr Schol
97:8 S 21 '70
What chance for a United States of Europe?
interview. J. Monnet. por Read Digest
97:158-62 O '70
EUROPEAN free trade association
Outer seven at ten. M. E. Bradley. Cur Hist
58:264-8 My '70

EUROPEAN Institute of science and technology.
See International institute for the manage-
ment of technology (proposed)
EUROPEAN launcher development organization
Europe shifts goals in funding squeeze. R.
F. Coburn. il Aviation W 92:89+ Mr 9 '70
Europeans moving to combine space launch,
research units. Aviation W 92:88+ Ap 27 '70
EUROPEAN literature
European literary scene. R. J. Clements. See
issues of Saturday review
EUROPEAN organization for nuclear research
CERN: rumors but no decision on site. D. S.
Greenberg. Science 167:1231 F 27 '70
CERN's new accelerator: Germans insist on
a site in Germany. D. S. Greenberg. Science
167:358-9 Ja 23 '70
Internationalism and world politics among
CERN scientists; the European elite panel
study. D. Lerner and A. H. Teich. il Bul
Atom Sci 26:4-10 F '70
Pooling brains to study the atom; Soviet-
CERN. il Bsns W p56-7 Ag 22 '70
Uncertainty at CERN; accelerator plans. Sci
N 98:94 Ag 1 '70
EUROPEAN space conference
British reject post-Apollo participation. D. E.
Fink. Aviation W 93:19 N 9 '70
Europe tries to patch space cooperation. D.
E. Fink. Aviation W 93:25-6 N 16 '70
European meeting moves to unify space pro-
grams. D. E. Fink. Aviation W 93:20-1
Ag 3 '70
Europeans push unified space agency. Avia-
tion W 93:17-18 N 2 '70
Europeans seek approval to join post-Apollo
work. D. C. Fink. Aviation W 93:20 Jl 13
'70
U.S. and European space conference officials
meet at Washington; joint statement. Dept
State Bul 63:389 O 5 '70
EUROPEAN space research organization
Europeans moving to combine space launch,
research units. Aviation W 92:88+ Ap 27 '70
French withhold ESRO satellite funds. D.
E. Fink. il Aviation W 93:22-3 D 7 '70
EUROPEAN union. See European federation
EUROPEAN war, 1914-1918

Prisoners and prisons
Prisoner: 1337; occupation: conductor, Boston symphony orchestra. J. J. Badal. il
pors Hi Fi 20:55-60 O '70

Russia
See also
Russia—History—Revolution, 1917-1921

United States
World war I and the liberal pacifist in the
United States. C. Chatfield. bibliog f Am
Hist R 75:1920-37 D '70
EUROPEAN war, 1939-1945. See World war,
1939-1945
EUROPEAN youth hostels. See Youth hostels
EURYTHMICS
N.Y. eurythmic group, Kaufman concert hall,
NYC. N. Mason. Dance Mag 44:74 N '70
EUSKADI. See Basque provinces
EUSTIS, Helen
Few words of advice to discouraged dieters.
Redbook 134:96+ Mr '70
EUSTIS, O. B.
To make a squirrel stew. il Field & S 75:66-
7+ S '70
EUTHANASIA
Euthanasia in England: a growing storm.
America 122:463 My 2 '70
EUTROPHICATION. See Water pollution
EVACUATION of civilians. See Cambodian-
Vietnamese conflict—Evacuation of civilians
EVALUATION (education) See Education—
Evaluation
EVAN, Frances
Diary of a face-life. McCalls 97:56+ Ap '70
EVANGELICAL church
Evangelicals and the American revolution. R.
V. Pierard. Chr Today 15:46-7 N 6 '70
See also
North American Christian convention
EVANGELICAL church in Canada
Canadian evangelism conference: a first. C. De
Mestral. Chr Cent 87:1301 O 28 '70
Will saints go marching out? D. Kucharsky.
Chr Today 14:27-9 S 25 '70
EVANGELICAL church in Germany
West Germany; partners though divided. F.
Lupsen. Chr Cent 87:1001-2 Ag 19 '70
EVANGELICAL church in Spain
Beleaguered Protestants; Spanish Evangeli-
cal church's general assembly. T. S. Goslin.
Chr Cent 87:949-50 Ag 5 '70
EVANGELICAL church of North America. See
Evangelical church

EVANGELICAL covenant church of America
Covenant church: smooth sailing? annual meeting. Chr Today 14:35 Jl 17 '70
Evangelical covenant church convenes. J. Lambert. Chr Cent 87:925 Jl 29 '70

EVANGELICALISM
Can Catholics learn anything from evangelical Protestants? P. W. Witte. Cath World 212:85-7 N '70; Same. Chr Today 15:12-14 D 18 '70
Catholic looks at evangelical Protestantism. K. McDonnell. Commonweal 92:408-13 Ag 21 '70; Discussion. 92:470, 491; 93-31 S 18-O 2 '70
Charting a course. C. F. H. Henry. Chr Today 14:28 Jl 31 '70
Evangelical Christianity's appeal. Chr Today 14:28 Ap 24 '70
Evangelical responsibility in a secularized world. K. Runia. Chr Today 14:11-14 Je 19 '70
Fundamentalism and American identity. E. R. Sandeen. Ann Am Acad 387:56-65 Ja '70
New life for the old-time religion. il U S News 69:84-7 O 19 '70
Revival at Asbury. J. Nelson. Chr Today 14:36-7 F 27 '70
Time to meet the evangelicals? .R E. Branson; discussion. Chr Cent 87:115-16 Ja 28 '70
What do evangelicals believe about the Bible? K. Runia. Chr Today 15:3-6 D 4; 8-10 D 18 '70
Where evangelism booms; Latin America. il U S News 69:86-7 O 19 '70

Bibliography
Choice evangelical books. Chr Today 14:21 F 13 '70

EVANGELISTIC work
Awakening ahead? Chr Today 14:17 S 25 '70
Billy Graham in Big Orange country. R. L. Love. il por Chr Today 14:33-4 Je 19 '70
Christ and cosmopolis. C. G. Fry. Chr Today 14:3-6 Je 5 '70
Evangelical pathbreaking. C. F. H. Henry. Chr Today 14:34-5 My 8 '70
Evangelical underground. C. F. Henry. Chr Today 14:41-2 Ap 10 '70
Evangelism as social therapy. Chr Today 14:28-9 Ag 21 '70
Incarnational evangelism. J. W. Haughton. Chr Today 14:10-12 Ag 21 '70
John Calvin: theologian and evangelist. C. G. Fry. Chr Today 15:3-6 O 23 '70
Key '73: new resources for evangelism. D. Kucharsky. Chr Today 14:34 Je 19 '70
Motives for witnessing, good or evil? R. K. Barrett. Chr Today 14:12-14 Jl 17 '70
Negro evangelical association moves toward activism. A. D. Orme. Chr Today 14:37 Ap 24 '70
New strides in the ghetto; World Christian training center. R. Klein. il por Chr Today 14:46-7 S 11 '70
Objections to evangelism. L. Morris. Chr Today 14:58-9 Mr 13 '70
Preaching and the power; B. Graham's crusades. il pors Newsweek 76:50-5 Jl 20 '70
Reaching the unchurched. Chr Today 14:43 F 13 '70
Seminar 70; gathering of more than 300 evangelical leaders. R. L. Love. Chr Today 14:36-7 Ap 24 '70
Shall we evangelize the Jews? Chr Today 14: 33-4 Mr 13 '70
Showers of blessing. Baton Rouge crusade. A. Matthews. il Chr Today 15:48-9 N 20 '70
Street Christians: Jesus as the ultimate trip. il Time 96:31-2 Ag 3 '70
Toward a theology of evangelism. D. G. Miller. Chr Today 14:5-8+ My 8; 9-12 My 22 '70
Unlocking evangelistic potential; Key '73 project. D. Kucharsky. por Chr Today 15:43-4 Ja 1 '71
What is the evangel? address. S. H. Moffett. Chr Today 14:3-6 Mr 13 '70
See also
American scientific affiliation
Campus crusade for Christ (organization)
Communication (theology)
Missions
National association of evangelicals
Revivals
Salvation army

Africa
African challenge: Christian literature. O. Okite. Chr Today 14:36 My 22 '70

Africa, East
Evangelism in Africa: not in a vacuum. O. Okite. Chr Today 14:34 Ja 30 '70

Europe, Western
Euro 70 crusade: never, so many; with editorial comment. D. Foster. il por Chr Today 14:24, 38 My 8 '70

Graham Dortmund crusade: a continent responds; some resist. Chr Today 14:34 Ap 24 '70

India
Evangelization crisis in India: a missionary's view. R. H. Lesser. il Cath World 211:166-71 Jl '70
Logos afloat; Operation Mobilization evangelistic crusades. T. Cosmades. Chr Today 15: 54-5 N 6 '70

Philippines
Manila crusade: bold new program. N. Ramientos. Chr Today 14:37 Je 19 '70

EVANOFF, Vlad
Fishing tackle, what you need for various species. Motor B 125:130+ Ap '70
Gifts for fishermen. Motor B 126:21 D '70
How was fishing last year? il Motor B 125: 22+ F '70
Sailfishing in southern waters. il Motor B 126:16+ N '70

EVANS, Anne S. and Goldberg, M. F.
Catholic seminarians in a secular institution. bibliog Ment Hy 54:599-64 O '70

EVANS, Barry R.
Canine Hilton. il Am City 85:125-6 Ap '70

EVANS, Bergen
Dictionaries old and new. il Todays Ed 59: 24-7 F '70; Same abr. Ed Digest 35:32-4 Ap '70

EVANS, Bill
Bill Evans alone. B. Korall. il por Sat R 53: 46-7 Jl 25 '70 *
When summoned. H. Terry. il Sat R 53:48 O 17 '70 *

EVANS, C. Stephen
Campus minister; rebel or reconciler? Chr Today 14:3-5 My 8 '70

EVANS, Charles J.
Black studies in Illinois. Negro Hist Bul 33: 43-4 F '70

EVANS, Cicely Louise
Eva's husband; story, excerpt from Nemesis wife. Redbook 136:145-67 N '70

EVANS, David
Lone recruiter. il por Newsweek 76:61-2 O 26 '70 *

EVANS, Don
Big go Gatorsville. il Hot Rod 23:44-6 My '70

EVANS, Frederick Henry
Evans: what price platinum prints? J. Deschin. il por Pop Phot 67:24+ Jl '70 *

EVANS, Gary W.
Proposed structural shorthand for organic chemistry. il Chem 43:18-19 My '70

EVANS, George Bird
Bloody merry and other problems. Field & S 75:142+ N '70
—See Evans, K. jt. auth.

EVANS, Glen
Those magnificent magazines in the flying machines. il Writers Digest 50:28-30+ Jl '70

EVANS, Howard T. Jr
Lunar troilite: crystallography. bibliog il Science 167:621-3 Ja 30 '70

EVANS, Illtud
Personal history. por Sat R 53:28+ Ap 11 '70

EVANS, Jane
I. Miller's new line; new president. por Newsweek 75:74-5 Je 22 '70 *

EVANS, John C.
White trees sit; poem. Horn Bk 46:641 D '70

EVANS, Kay, and Evans, G. B.
Dogs that live forever. il por Field & S 75:234-5+ Je '70

EVANS, Larry
Chess. Sports Illus 32:62-3 Ap 20; 33:85-7 O 12 '70

EVANS, Llewellyn Johnson
Crisis of transition; excerpts from address. Aviation W 92:9 F 16 '70

EVANS, Luther
Miami-Nassau race. Yachting 128:42 D '70

EVANS, M. Stanton
In quest of the new majority. Nat R 22:1161-3+ N 3 '70

EVANS, Margaret
Study hall: the villain. Clear House 44:372 F '70

EVANS, Mary
Clement Conger: diplomatic treasure hunter. por Am Home 73:50+ N '70
Painted country tinware. il Am Home 73:100-2+ S '70
Romantic Newport. il Am Home 73:51-4 Ag '70
Southwest Indian. il Am Home 73:76+ Mr '70
Wyeth country. il Am Home 73:74-82+ O '70
—See Hahn, V. D. jt. auth.

EVANS, N. J. 2d, and others
Search for the 1_{10}←1_{11} transition of interstellar thioformaldehyde. bibliog il Science 169: 680-1 Ag 14 '70

EVANS, Walker
Gallery; photographs. Life 69:6-9 Ag 14 '70
EVANSTON, Ill.
Education
I didn't know it felt that way; project. Understanding discrimination. L. S. Wilson. il PTA Mag 64:20-2 Je '70
Streets
Make pavements skid resistant. F. X. Schwartz. il Am City 85:121+ My '70
EVANSVILLE, Ind, public library
Northside residents achieve success in Evansville. il Library J 95:844 Mr 1 '70
EVAPORATION
See also
Sublimation
EVA'S husband; story. See Evans, C. L.
EVE of the wedding; story. See Trueblood, H. P.
EVELING, Stanley
Dear Janet Rosenberg, dear Mr Kooning. Criticism
Nation 210:510 Ap 27 '70 *
Sat R 53:16+ Ap 25 '70 *
Time il 95:51 Ap 20 '70 *
Jakey fat boy. Criticism
Nation 210:510 Ap 27 '70 *
Time 95:51 Ap 20 '70 *
EVENING and continuation schools
Nature and function of continuation education. D. R. Reed. Ed Digest 35:52-4 F '70
See also
Adult education
EVENING with Ramó Bonavena; story. See Borges, J. L. and Casares, A. B.
EVEREST, MOUNT
Reporter at large; trekking expedition to base. J. Bernstein. New Yorker 46:46-8+ My 9 '70
EVERETT, Alfred E.
Cicero on growing older. Har Yrs 10:25 S '70
EVERETT, Betty Steele
Another idea: teaching creative writing under government grants. Writers Digest 50: 30+ O '70
EVERETT, G. M. and Borchering, J. W.
L-Dopa: effect on concentrations of dopamine, norepinephrine, and serotonin in brains of mice. il Science 168:849 My 15 '70
EVERETT, Marietta
Upside-down world of Marietta. il pors Ebony 25:124-7 Je '70 *
EVERGLADES
Everglades. B. Schill and B. Schill. il Yachting 128:54-5 N '70
Everglades jetport threat remains despite promises from Washington. Audubon 72:116 Ja '70
Fight for the Everglades. A. W. Smith. Nat Parks 44:2 Ja '70
The 'Glades by houseboat. B. Hutchinson. il Yachting 128:64-5+ D '70
EVERGLADES NATIONAL PARK
Bitter struggle for a national park. J. G. Mitchell. il Am Heritage 21:97-109 Ap '70
Everglades: pregnant with risks. H. Bloomfield. il Am For 76:24-7+ My '70
In retrospect: the Everglades, the jetport, and the future. J. Browder. Audubon 72: 116-17 Mr '70
NPA at work. il Nat Parks & Con Mag 44: 28-30 Je '70
Outboard the untamed Everglades. F. M. Paulson. il Field & S 75:152-4+ O '70
Reprieve for Everglades Park. Liv Wildn 34: 61-2 Spr '70
EVERGREEN, Colo.
Nevergreen; resistance to 1976 Olympics. il Newsweek 76:94 D 14 '70
EVERGREEN review (periodical)
Justice Douglas-Evergreen case. Writers Digest 50:44+ Je '70
EVERGREENS
Evergreen review. L. J. Milne and M. Milne. il pors Natur Hist 79:80-91 Ja '70
Evergreens for wildlife. N. Smith. il Nat Wildlife 8:27 D '69
Needle-leaved evergreens for many purposes. A. R. Ireys. il Horticulture 48:36-9+ Ap '70
See also
Christmas trees
also names of evergreen trees and shrubs, e.g. Cypress
Diseases and pests
See also
Cypress—Diseases and pests
EVERS, Charles
Black, sassy and still tryin' to be independent. G. Goodman. il pors Look 34:22-6 Jl 14 '70 *
Fayette's mayor one year later. il por Bsns W p79 Jl 4 '70 *
Return of the boll weevil. J. M. Carter. Library J 95:1817 My 15 '70 *
Tiny leap forward. il por Newsweek 76:36+ Jl 13 '70 *

EVERS, James Charles. See Evers, C.
EVERS, Mrs Medgar W.
(ed) See Carroll, D. Tale of two Julias
EVERSE, Johannes, and others
Physiological concentrations of lactate dehydrogenases and substrate inhibition. bibliog il Science 168:1236-8 Je 5 '70
EVERSON museum. See Syracuse, N.Y.—Galleries and museums
EVERYTHING for everybody, inc.
Something for everyone. il Newsweek 76: 82-3+ D 7 '70
EVERYTHING is going to be all right; story. See Low, J.
EVETT, Robert
Anatomy of pretentiousness. Atlan 227:75-9+ Ja '71
Music (cont) Atlan 225:103-5 Ja; 134+ Mr; 122+ My; 226:117-18+ S '70
Music (cont) New Repub 162:27-9 F 28; 40-2 My 9; 163:24-6 Ag 15 '70
EVIDENCE (law)
See also
Evidence, Hearsay
Wire tapping
EVIDENCE, Expert
See also
Medical jurisprudence
EVIDENCE, Hearsay
New 5-to-4 majority; Supreme court ruling. Time 96:47 D 28 '70
Notes and comment; Supreme court decision in Dutton vs. Evans case. New Yorker 46: 15-16 Ja 2 '71
EVIL. See Good and evil
EVINRUDE boating foundation
Mel Crook recipient of sixteenth annual Ole Evinrude award. il por Yachting 127:47 Mr '70
EVOLUTION
Adam and ape. Sci Am 222:46 F '70
Adaptive aspects of insular evolution: report of meeting. R. W. Matthews and J. R. Matthews. Science 167:909-10 F 6 '70
Brain evolution: new light on old principles. H. J. Jerison. bibliog il Science 170:1224-5 D 11 '70
Cosmic prison; excerpts from The invisible pyramid. L. Eiseley. il Horizon 12:96-101 Aut '70
Eukaryotes versus prokaryotes: an estimate of evolutionary distance. P. J. McLaughlin and M. O. Dayhoff. bibliog il Science 168: 1469-71 Je 19 '70
Evolution of man and society, by C. D. Darlington. Review
Sat R 53:46-8 Ag 22 '70. J. Platt
Generation and maintenance of gradients in taxonomic diversity. F. G. Stehli and others; discussion. Science 166:1656-8; 168:1248-9 D 26 '69, Je 5 '70
See also
Life (biology)
Man—Origin and antiquity
Natural selection
Phylogeny
Plants—Evolution
Religion and science
Species
Stars—Evolution
Tennessee evolution controversy
Anecdotes, facetiae, satire, etc.
Tomorrow's critters. C. E. Gillham. il Audubon 72:41-3 N '70
Laws and legislation
California's evolution war: should Genesis get equal time? R. Larsen. Chr Cent 87:251-3 F 25 '70; Reply. H. O. J. Brown. 87:639 My 20 '70
Monkey war resumes; California controversy. Sci Am 222:55 My '70
See also
Tennessee evolution controversy
EVOLUTION, Social. See Social change
EVRY, Allen
Scratchboard: a versatile graphic medium. il Sch Arts 70:18-19 N '70
EVTUSHENKO, Evgenii Aleksandrovich
Under the skin of Statue of Liberty; tr. by A. C. Todd, jr. il por N Y Times Mag p34+ F 15 '70
EWING, Ann
Big blackout coming! il Read Digest 96:41-2+ Mr '70
EWING, Robert A.
Presenting Mike Selig. il por Art in Am 58: 86-7 My '70
EXAMINATIONS
See also
College entrance examination board

EXCAVATING machinery
Super scooper saves your back; ed. by H.
Wicks. S. Corsak. il Pop Mech 133:166-8 My
'70
See also
Dredging machinery
Graders (excavating machinery)
EXCAVATIONS (archeology)
Drying out a discovery; flooding of Marmes
man site. il Sci N 97:91-2 Ja 24 '70
Research and discovery at Louisbourg. J.
Fortier. il Antiques 97:380-7 Je '70
See also
Athens, Greece—Antiquities
Dilmun
Paestum
Turkey—Antiquities
EXCHANGE (barter) See Barter
EXCHANGE, Foreign. See Foreign exchange
EXCHANGE of persons programs
No Bolshoi. Newsweek 76:67-8 D 21 '70
See also
Educational exchanges
EXCHANGE students. See Students, Inter-
change of
EXCHANGES, Commodity. See Commodity ex-
changes
EXCHANGES, Educational. See Educational
exchanges
EXCHEQUER (Great Britain) See Great Brit-
ain—Exchequer
EXCITED states. See Energy levels (quantum
mechanics)
EXCLUSIVE agencies
See also
Franchise system
EXCOMMUNICATION
In-communication of Martin Luther. Chr
Cent 87:101 Ja 28 '70
Priests and nuns: going their way. il Time
95:51-5 F 23 '70
EXCURSIONS, School. See School excursions
EXECUTIONS and executioners
See also
Capital punishment
Hanging
EXECUTIVE ability
Are you an innovator or operator. C. A. Cerami.
il Nations Bsns 58:54-7 Je '70
Assessment centers for spotting future man-
agers. W. C. Byham. il Harvard Bsns R 48:
150-60+ Jl '70
Intuitive payoff; testing executives ability to
foresee the future and make decisions. Time
97:64 Ja 11 '71
EXECUTIVE agreements
See also
United States—Foreign relations—Executive
agreements
EXECUTIVE airlines, inc.
Air taxi asks CAB for route protection. Avia-
tion W 93:31 N 16 '70
EXECUTIVE departments

United States
See United States—Executive departments
EXECUTIVE jet aviation, inc.
Bizarre case of executive jet. il pors Bsns
W p80-2+ O 24 '70
Penn central: Pandora's box. il por News-
week 76:74+ N 9 '70
Planes of Penn central. G. Owens and S. A.
Blumberg. Nation 211:404 O 26 '70
Senate report bares links of railroad, Exec-
utive jet. J. P. Woolsey. Aviation W 94:28
Ja 4 '71
EXECUTIVE office of the president. See United
States—Executive office of the president
EXECUTIVE power
See also
Presidents—United States—Power and duties
EXECUTIVE stock options. See Stock pur-
chase options
EXECUTIVES
Agony of executive failure. Time 95:90 Ap 13
'70
Can an executive afford a conscience? excerpt
from The executive conscience. A. Z. Carr.
bibliog f il Harvard Bsns R 48:58-64 Jl '70
Can executives be remade? G. J. Berkwitt. il
Duns 96:31-3 Jl '70
Case of the lost executive. J. M. Seidenfeld.
il Nations Bsns 58:68-9+ Mr '70
CEO's role in corporate growth. J. O. Eastlack,
jr. and P. R. McDonald. il Harvard Bsns R
48:150-2+ My '70
Executive as social activist. il Time 96:62-8
Jl 20 '70
Executive life, California style. T. J. Murray.
il Duns 95:48-50+ My '70
Executives in ferment. G. J. Berkwitt. il Duns
97:23-5 Ja '71

For executives, fun city can be a hardship. il
Bsns W p64-9 F 7 '70
Great moments and great men of American
business; symposium. ed. by S. G. Slappey.
Nations Bsns 58:47 Ja '70
Lesson of leadership. See issues of Nation's
business
Man on the move (cont as) Spotlight. See
issues of Dun's
Management psychologists have landed. S.
Klaw. il Fortune 81:106-9+ Ap '70
New company president: ten steps to failure.
R. C. Wilson. il Nations Bsns 58:66-70
D '70
Pinning down your job in writing. Bsns W
p69 Ag 1 '70
Portrait of a man who has it made; typical
chief international officer of an American
corporation. Bsns W p33 S 12 '70
Pot-smoking young executives. S. Margetts.
il Duns 95:42-3 F '70
Power and politics in organizational life. A.
Zaleznik. il Harvard Bsns R 48:47-60 My '70
Problem of the new chief executive. S. R.
Stuart. Duns 95:24-6 Ja '70
Second thoughts on the office of the presi-
dent. il Bsns W p42-3 O 3 '70
Self-portrait of the chief executive; the For-
tune 500-Yankelovich survey. R. S. Dia-
mond. il Fortune 81:181+ My '70
Shoe-leather executive. G. Berkwitt. il Duns
96:33-5 N '70
Spotlight (cont of) Man on the move. See is-
sues of Dun's
Status symbols are changing, too. J. Smith.
il Duns 95:52-4+ My '70
What's coming in executive taxes; interview,
ed. by G. R. Rosen. B. Grund. il por Duns
95:56-7+ Mr '70
Why bosses should fire themselves. F. C.
Foy. por Forbes 105:93-4 Ap 15 '70
See also
Association for the integration of manage-
ment
Business management and organization
Corporations—Directors
Credit managers
Jews as executives
Leadership
Negro executives
United States—President's commission on
personnel interchange (proposed)
Women as executives

Applications for positions
See Applications for positions

Caricatures and cartoons
Corporate aviary. P. Hilton. il Nations Bsns
58:32-6 F '70

Compensation
See Executies—Salaries, allowances, etc.

Dismissal
Deadwood in the executive suite. G. Berkwitt.
il Duns 95:35-7 Mr '70
Hard times in high places. Newsweek 76:97-8
O 19 '70
Outplacing the dehired. Time 96:83 S 14 '70
Strategy for fired executives. J. Allan. il
Duns 96:44-5 S '70
White collars are a little wilted. Bsns W p15-
16 S 5 '70
Year of the executive axing. A. M. Louis. il
Fortune 82:142-6+ S '70

Health and hygiene
See Businessmen—Health and hygiene

Health programs
Can companies reduce heart attacks? J.
Smith. il Duns 95:51-2+ Ap '70

Investment activities
Apartment houses: new home for executive
cash. A. Hershman. il Duns 96:43-7 D '70

Qualifications
Company officers in striped pants? V. Lou-
viere. Nations Bsns 58:20 Ap '70
How to be a tough nice guy. C. Bisbee. il Na-
tions Bsns 58:79 Je '70
How to make executives behave. il Nations
Bsns 58:72-4 Ap '70
If he's hard to get along with, hire him. E. G.
Shuster. il Nations Bsns 58:66-8 Ag '70
Making of a company president. H. O.
Golightly. il Nations Bsns 58:78-9 N '70

Recreation
Anglers of industry. R. Levy. il Duns 96:40-3
S '70

Recruiting
Fast switch in semiconductors; from Signe-
tics to Intersil, inc. il por Bsns W p16 S 5
'70

EXECUTIVES—Recruiting—*Continued*
Outplacing the dehired. Time 96:83 S 14 '70
    See also
Association of executive recruiting consultants

Relocation
Executive abroad; the Donnells in London. J. Ross-Skinner. il pors Duns 96:48-51 Ag '70
Is management mobility obsolete. J. Perham. il Duns 96:46-8 Jl '70
U.S. unlocks door on executive visas. Bsns W p30+ Ap 11 '70

Retirement
See Retirement

Salaries, allowances, etc.
Better than cash: new ways to pay executives. il U S News 69:31-2 Ag 24 '70
Bosses take a cut in pay increases. Bsns W p49 O 17 '70
Compensation: unmasking phantom stock. Bsns W p95 O 10 '70
Confusing payday for men at the top. il Bsns W p80-1 O 10 '70
Cost/benefit analysis of executive compensation. G. W. Hettenhouse. bibliog f il Harvard Bsns R 48:114-24 Jl '70
Executive pay, a time of dramatic change; excerpt from Sixth annual management compensation study. R. E. Sibson. il Nations Bsns 58:89-93+ N '70
Hidden jokers in the new tax deck; Tax reform act of 1969. A. M. Louis. il Fortune 82:100-2+ Jl '70
How the top men fared in 1969. il Bsns W p59-63+ Je 13 '70
Look twice at restricted stock! J. Perham. il Duns 96:36-8 D '70
More income for most bosses. Bsns W p44 Mr 28 '70
Now they're swapping options. Duns 96:45 O '70
Phantom stock: better than options? J. C. Perham. il Duns 96:32-5+ S '70

Selection and appointment
How to read a resumé. P. Meyer. Duns 96: 49-50+ O '70

Sports
See Executives—Recreation

Supply and demand
Job hunters face grimmer prospects. il Bsns W p 19-20 D 12 '70
MBA itch is mostly myth. Bsns W p30 S 26 '70
More managers join the jobless. Bsns W p33-4 My 23 '70
RIF is a drag on the job market; reduction in forces. Bsns W p37 F 21 '70
White collars are a little wilted. Bsns W p 15-16 S 5 '70
Year of the executive axing. A. M. Louis. il Fortune 82:142-5+ S '70

Training
Adult education for the businessman. Bsns W p73 S 5 '70
Budget cutters worry B-schools. Bsns W p 15 D 26 '70
Retreat for executives; Oxford center for management studies. il Arch Forum 132:40-3 My '70
Should executives go back to school? management programs criticized. A. A. Butkus. il Duns 96:36-8 S '70
Way to the top. J. L. Dotson, jr. il Newsweek 75:80 Ap 27 '70
    See also
Group relations training

EXECUTIVES as public officers. See Public officers

EXECUTIVES as stockholders
    See also
Executives—Salaries, allowances, etc.

EXECUTIVES wives
Mrs Success; excerpt. L. Wyse. il Ladies Home J 87:50+ O; 58+ N '70
Up the executive ladder. E. M. Wylie. il Good H 171:78-9+ S '70
Your business is her business. A. Uris. il Nations Bsns 58:72-4+ My '70

EXECUTORS and administrators
If you're asked to be an executor. il Changing T 24:37-9 O '70

EXEMPTION from taxation. See Taxation, Exemption from

EXERCISE
About front: the tone to take; bosom exercises. il Vogue 155:60 Ap 1 '70
Beauty routines to keep you sexually alive. il Harp Baz 104:82-3 Ja '71

Biking to better breathing. il Sci Digest 67: 63-4 F '70
Body: a total experience. il Harp Baz 103:114-17 Ap '70
Dancing: a dramatic exercise in beauty. il Harp Baz 103:106-7 Ap '70
Easy thirty-day shape-up to keep you fit· with menus. J. La Lanne. il pors Mech Illus 66: 44-7+ Je '70
Exercise break. V. Calkins. Writer 83:28-9 F '70
Exercise program for the office. G. M. Knox. il Bet Hom & Gard 48:24 F '70
Exercise saved my life. M. Holmgren. por Har Yrs 10:16-17 My '70
Exercise, yes, but do it right! il Changing T 24:45-7 Ag '70
Exercises for an aching back: golf star Doug Sanders and his wife demonstrate. il Ladies Home J 87:52 Jl '70
Fit by five; headstart to make your child. J. A. Segal. il Look 34:76-7+ Ap 7 '70
How to have a good figure for life. A. Fabry. il Parents Mag 45:52-4 Jl '70
Key to fitness at any age; the new aerobics; condensation. K. H. Cooper. il Read Digest 96:213-30 Mr '70
Legsercises. il Vogue 156:78-81+ O 15 '70
Magic of exercise. C. Coiro. bibliog il Har Yrs 10:14-18 My '70
Miss Craig's face-saving exercises; excerpt. M. Craig. il McCalls 97:78-83 S '70
Miss Craig's post-holiday shape-up exercises; excerpt from Miss Craig's twenty-one day shape-up program for men and women. M. Craig. il McCalls 98:40 Ja '71
Moving toward a good mood; exercises by N. Kounovsky. il House & Gard 137:140-1 My '70
New cut of the throat; nexercises. il Vogue 156:126-9 Ag 1 '70
New exercise for a longer life; conducting music. L. I. Gordon. il Vogue 156:152-3+ N 1 '70
Pants fit now. J. Robbins. il Todays Health 49:58-9+ Ja '71
Pink is a second skin. il McCalls 97:78-9 Ap '70
Plan exercises that make you work. il House B 112:56-8 O '70
Redbook's choice: nine easy body-shaping exercises. il Redbook 134:108-16 Mr '70
Steps in the right direction: fitness in woodsplitting, walking and running. R. F. Capon. il Sports Illus 33:46-8+ Ag 31 '70; Same abr. Read Digest 97:124-6 D '70
Stretch is the name of the fitness game; M. Kahn's body rhythms. C. Bartel. il Am Home 73:14+ Ap '70
Trim-up time. il Seventeen 29:44 Ap '70
Tuned-up body; Gala fitness, N.Y. il Mlle 71:174-5 My '70
What a wonderful beauty idea; reducing cellulite infiltrations. Harp Baz 104:22 Ja '71
Why are they running, stretching, starving? W. McQuade. il Fortune 82:132-5+ Ag '70
Winter shape-up exercises. il Redbook 136: 82-3 N '70
    See also
Gymnastics
Isometric exercise

Anecdotes, facetiae, satire, etc.
Mü: breath control exercises in your automobile, while you are stuck in traffic. C. Tomkins. New Yorker 46:53 D 5 '70

EXERCISE, Yoga. See Yoga

EXERCISING equipment
Converting your bike into an exerciser. il Consumer Rep 35:193-4 Ap '70
Exercise equipment: jogging machines and exercise bikes. il Consumer Bul 53:13-19 F '70
How effective are those no work exercise devices? il Good H 171:145-7 Ag '70
It's all in your mind. Head of operations: the thinking-woman's exercise plan. il Harp Baz 103:80 Je '70
Off the fat of the land. il Newsweek 75:86+ Ap 20 '70
V-bar: open and closed all day. il Vogue 157:26 Ja 1 '71

EXHAUST fans. See Ventilators

EXHAUST gases. See Carbon monoxide

EXHAUST systems
    See also
Automobile engines—Exhaust

EXHIBITION buildings
Currigan Hall: a concept of simplicity for a building of complexity; exhibition hall, Denver. il Arch Rec 148:81-6 D '70
    See also
Pavilions

EXHIBITIONS
World travel calendar, 1971; comp. by F. Shemanski. Sat R 54:37-8+ Ja 2 '71
  See also
Audio fairs
Fairs
Garden exhibits
  also subhead Exhibitions under names of cities, e.g. Montreal—Exhibitions; *also* under various subjects, e.g. Pottery—Exhibitions
EXHIBITIONS, Traveling
California horizons; the touring exhibition Horizons: a century of California landscape painting. C. N. Stallone. il Art in Am 58:124-5 N '70
Mobile exhibit takes the police story to the people; Mobile crime prevention exhibit, Kansas City, Mo. J. R. Perry. il Am City 85:46 Ja '70
Seeing things; Objects: USA: the Johnson collection of contemporary crafts. N. Gittelson. Harp Baz 103:23+ F '70
Zoo-a-go-go: Toledo traveling zoo. M. D. Craden and P. C. Skelton. il Parks & Rec 5:25+ Ap '70
EXHIBITS
  See also
Library exhibits
EX-IM bank. See Export-import bank of the United States of America
EXISTENTIALISM
Need for loving strife; existential communication. A. Deeken. Cath World 211:74-7 My '70
  See also
Existentialist psychology
EXISTENTIALISM and Christianity. See Christianity and existentialism
EXISTENTIALIST psychology
Madness as an existential solution to an existential situation. W. F. Lynch. pors Commonweal 92:484-5 S 25 '70
Yes begins with a no; theories of R. May. il por Time 95:66+ Je 22 '70
EX-NUNS, priests, etc.
Free ministry. E. C. Bianchi. Commonweal 91:450-3 Ja 23 '70; Reply with rejoinder. P. J. Murnion. 91:566-7 F 20 '70
Nun's search for freedom drives her from the convent. M. Fay. il pors Life 68:26-7 Mr 20 '70
Priests and nuns; going their way. il Time 95:51-5+ F 23 '70
  See also
Marriage of priests
EXOCET missiles. See Guided missiles—Launching from ships
EXODUS house. See Narcotic addicts—Rehabilitation
EXOSKELETON. See Skeleton (invertebrates)
EXPANDING universe. See Universe
EXPANSION, House. See Houses, Remodeled
EXPANSION of industry. See Industrial expansion
EXPENDITURES, Family. See Domestic finance
EXPENDITURES, Personal. See Budget, Personal
EXPENDITURES, State. See State finance
EXPENSE accounts (business)
Expense-account splurge in Japan. U S News 68:86-7 Mr 9 '70
EXPERIENCE
We and our unwanted experiences. B. W. Overstreet. PTA Mag 65:21 O '70
  See also
Empiricism
EXPERIENCE (religion)
Mysticism in the laboratory; account of a visit to the Foundation for mind research. il por Time 96:72+ O 5 '70
Religion and American experience. R. J. Roth. il America 124:43-4 Ja 16 '71
EXPERIMENT stations, Agricultural. See Agricultural experiment stations
EXPERIMENTAL airplanes. See Airplanes, Experimental
EXPERIMENTAL art. See Art, Modern
EXPERIMENTAL automobiles; Experimental education; etc. See Automobiles, Experimental; Education, Experimental; etc.
EXPERIMENTATION on man. See Medical research—Experimentation on man
EXPERIMENTS, Field. See Field experiments (agriculture)
EXPERIMENTS in art and technology, Inc.
Getting it together, ambitious; art and technology projects. B. Rose. Vogue 156:304 S 1 '70
Onward and upward with the arts; EAT and the Pepsi pavilion at Expo '70. C. Tomkins. New Yorker 46:83-4+ O 3 '70

EXPERTISING in art. See Art—Expertising
EXPERTS. See Specialists
EXPLORATION, Aeronautic
Doomed flight of the Eagle. il Life 68:63-4 Ap 3 '70
EXPLORATIONS
  See also
Antarctic exploration
Latin America—Discovery and exploration
EXPLORER (satellite) See Artificial satellites—Use in research
EXPLORER scouts. See Boy scouts—Explorer scouts
EXPLORERS, English
  See also
Thesiger, W. P.
EXPLORERS, Swedish
Doomed flight of the Eagle. il Life 68:63-4 Ap 3 '70
EXPLOSIONS
Refinery blast that rocked Humble; Linden, N.J. il Bsns W p 17-18 D 12 '70
  See also
Coal mines and mining—Accidents and explosions
New York (city)—Explosions
Osaka, Japan—Explosions
Rochester, N.Y.—Explosions
Shock waves
EXPLOSIVES
Explosive with more bang; Astrolite. il Bsns W p58 My 9 '70
Highs from an explosive; intoxication from eating C-4. il Sci N 98:32 Jl 11 '70
Transverse wave instability in a solid explosive. B. B. Dunne. bibliog il Science 167:1124-6 F 20 '70
  See also
Dynamite
Mines, Military

Laws and legislation
To stop terror bombings; new laws White House asks. il U S News 68:20+ Ap 6 '70

Transportation
Mutiny by ruse; hijacking of S.S. Columbia Eagle. il Time 95:17 Mr 30 '70
EXPO 70. See Osaka, Japan—Worlds fair, 1970
EXPORT and import controls. See Foreign trade regulation
EXPORT controls
Administration of the Export administration act of 1969; executive order. R. M. Nixon. Dept State Bul 63:121-2 Jl 27 '70
EXPORT-import bank of the United States of America
Ex-im bank helps Yugoslavs buy DC-9s. L. Doty. Aviation W 92:28 Mr 16 '70
Ex-im's new boss fuels the trade race. il por Bsns W p48+ Mr 7 '70
Loan approval delay caused U.S. to lose fighter order. E. H. Kolcum. Aviation W 92:20 Ap 13 '70
Salesman runs a bank; H. Kearns and the Export-import bank of the United States. il por Nations Bsns 58:77-9 Jl '70
EXPORT-import bank of Washington. See Export-import bank of the United States of America
EXPORT trade
Buy American, please. il Forbes 105:36+ F 1 '70
Increases in shipping weights of total U.S. exports and imports; table. Aviation W 93:79 O 26 '70
Shipping weights of U.S. exports and imports by air, year 1969; table. Aviation W 93:42 O 26 '70
  See also subhead Commerce under names of countries, e.g. United States—Commerce

Federal aid
Billion-dollar subsidy; tax subsidy of Domestic international sales corporations. T. Stanton. Nation 211:463-4 N 9 '70
Shot in the arm for our exports; DISC plan. Nations Bsns 58:99 O '70
EXPOS (baseball) See Baseball clubs
EXPOSURE (photography) See Photography—Exposure
EXPOSURE meters
Building a printing exposure lightmeter. A. A. Mangieri. il Pop Electr 33:60-1+ O '70
Built-in light meters, eyes that see what you can't. P. Geraci. il Pop Mech 135:118-21 Ja '71
Electronic photoflash meter. W. W. Schopp. il Electr World 83:62-3 Je '70
Flash meters: do you really need them? il Mod Phot 34:94-5+ Ja '70
Keppler on the SLR; through-lens metering systems. Mod Phot 34:14+ Jl '70

EXPOSURE meters—*Continued*
Make your own electronic enlarging meter. R. S. Hedin. il Pop Mech 135:124-7 Ja '71
1970 exposure meter guide. il Mod Phot 34: 78-9 Jl '70
Phototronics; flash exposure meters. E. Farber. Mod Phot 34:40+ Ap; 53+ My '70
$3.50 enlarging-time meter. H. Elkin. il Radio-Electr 41:35-6 F '70
Why built-in meters should be sealed. N. Goldberg. il Pop Phot 66:56+ My '70
Wolfman on printing; Fixomet enlarging exposure meter. A. Wolfman. il Mod Phot 34:70+ O '70

Testing
Modern tests. il Mod Phot 34:106+ Ja '70
Sensorex & Sensomat have unique meters. il Mod Phot 33:106+ Ja '70

EX-PRESIDENTS of the United States. See Presidents—United States
L'EXPRESS (periodical) See Periodicals— France
EXPRESS companies
See also
REA express, inc.
EXPRESS highways
Motorcar vs. America. C. Ogburn, jr. il Am Heritage 21:104-10 Je '70
200 attractions along the interstates. E. Welke. il Bet Hom & Gard 48:129-33+ My '70

Federal aid
See Roads—Federal aid

California
Freeways in and around L.A. are a big plant-testing laboratory. il Sunset 144:226-8+ Mr '70
Helicopters undergo new tests as traffic units; California highway patrol. il Am City 85:58 Ap '70

Great Britain
Motorways in London, by J. M. Thomson. Review
Arch Forum 133:74 O '70. S. Woods

Massachusetts
Dagger in the heart of town: Mass. planners and Cambridge workers; proposed eight-lane freeway. G. Fellman and others. il Trans-Action 7:38-47 S '70

Pennsylvania
Spector of an unbuilt road; decay of Pittsburgh neighborhood along I-79 planned route. il Bsns W p 104+ My 2 '70

EXPRESSION
See also
Communication, Nonverbal
EXPRESSIONISM (art)
Letter from Paris; exhibition at the Musée national d'art moderne. Genêt. New Yorker 46:70-1 Ag 8 '70
Maturity and a touch of madness; German expressionist exhibition at the Marlborough-Gerson gallery. K. Kuh. il Sat R 53:64-5 F 28 '70
See also
Abstract expressionism
EXPROPRIATION. See Eminent domain (international law)
EXPULSION. See Deportation
EXTENSION cords. See Electric cords
EXTENSION education
Extension's big push; better nutrition for low-income families. J. Gillies. Farm J 94:74 F '70
See also
County agents
EXTERIOR mural painting and decoration. See Mural painting and decoration, Exterior
EXTERNAL degrees. See Degrees, Academic
EXTERRITORIAL jurisdiction. See Exterritoriality
EXTERRITORIALITY
Extraterritoriality in Canadian-United States relations; address, September 2, 1970. J. R. Stevenson. Dept State Bul 63:425-30 O 12 '70
EXTINCT animals. See Animals, Extinct
EXTINCTION of animals. See Animals, Extinct
EXTINCTION of conditioned responses. See Conditioned responses
EXTINCTION of man. See Man—Survival
EXTORTION
See also
Trials (extortion)
EXTRACTION of teeth. See Teeth—Extraction
EXTRACURRICULAR activities. See Student activities

EXTRAS (ballet) See Dance production
EXTRASENSORY perception
Automated ESP. Sci Digest 67:44 F '70
ESP in the dream laboratory. B. Ford. il Sci Digest 67:10-18 Ja '70
Scientist looks at ESP; visit with J. Pratt of University of Virginia. S. McBee. McCalls 97:50+ Mr '70
See also
Clairvoyance
EXTRATERRESTRIAL life. See Life on other planets
EXTRATERRITORIALITY. See Exterritoriality
EXTRAVAGANCE
See also
Luxury
Prosperity
EXTREMISM. See Right and left (political science)
EXTRUSION process
New process for making wire; continuous hydrostatic extrusion. J. Holt. il Pop Sci 197:81 S '70
EXUMA CAYS. See Bahama Islands
EXURBIA. See Suburbs
EYE
See also
Flicker phenomena
Pupil (eye)
Retina
Sight

Accommodation and refraction
Eye-phi and you. W. Hanson. il Pop Phot 66: 60-1+ Mr '70
Lens; a most imperfect eye. N. Goldberg. il Pop Phot 66:66-7+ Mr '70
Neural symbolic activity: a psychophysical measure. N. Weisstein. bibliog il Science 168:1489-91 Je 19 '70; Reply with rejoinder. R. Sekuler and R. Armstrong. 170:1226-8 D 11 '70
Retinoscopy and eye size. M. Glickstein and M. Millodot. bibliog il Science 168:605-6 My 1 '70
Visual adaptation in monkey cones: recordings of late receptor potentials. R. M. Boynton and D. N. Whitten. bibliog il Science 170:1423-6 D 25 '70

Care and hygiene
Eye care. W. D. David. il Todays Ed 59:40-1 Mr '70
Use your eyes for better retirement. J. R. Gregg. il por Har Yrs 10:14-18 Ja '70

Diseases and defects
Distorted world of the partially blind. il Sci Digest 68:59-61 N '70
Upside-down world of Marietta. il pors Ebony 25:124-7 Je '70
When your eyes flunk the 20-20 test. K. V. Brown. il Todays Health 48:22-5+ Ag '70
See also
Cataracts (eye defect)
Color blindness
Eyeglasses

Examination
Eye-mapping saves vision. il Sci Digest 67: 71-2 My '70

Photographs
Eyes have it! il Pop Phot 66:71-9 Mr '70
Getting 1:1 with an eyeball. E. Meyers. il Pop Phot 66:62-3+ Mr '70
Red eye, TV eye, and other eyes I have shot. A. Francekevich. il Pop Phot 66:68-70 Mr '70

Protection
See also
Eyeglasses

Surgery
New surgery saves eyes from blindness. A. J. Snider. Sci Digest 68:41 O '70
EYE (amphibia)
Cones of living amphibian eye: selective staining. A. M. Laties and P. A. Liebman. bibliog il Science 168:1475-7 Je 19 '70
Dendritic-tree anatomy codes form-vision physiology in tadpole retina. B. Pomeranz and S. H. Chung. bibliog il Science 170:983-4 N 27 '70
EYE (animals)
See also
Sight (animals)
EYE (birds)
Centrifugal effects in the avian retina. F. A. Miles. bibliog il Science 170:992-5 N 27 '70
EYE (fishes)
Aerial vision: unique adaptation in an intertidal fish. J. B. Graham and R. H. Rosenblatt. bibliog il Science 168:586-8 My 1 '70
Retinal tapetum lucidum: a novel reflecting system in the eye of teleosts. H. J. Arnott and others. bibliog il Science 169:478-80 Jl 31 '70

EYE (insects)
　See also
　Sight (insects)
EYE in art
　Open eye. K. Kuh. il Sat R 53:52-3 Mr 28 '70
EYE make-up. See Make-up
EYE of the hurricane; story. See Brown, G. M.
EYEGLASSES
　Do your specs and viewfinder get along? N.
　　Goldberg. il Pop Phot 66:48+ F '70
　Glasses: looking great. L. Obre. il Ladies
　　Home J 87:84-5 Ag '70
　Making glasses fit your job. J. Runninger.
　　il Pop Sci 197:96+ Ag '70
　3-D (?) TV viewer. il Consumer Bul 53:26
　　Je '70
　VIP health: a need for sharp vision. Bsns
　　W p73 Jl 4 '70
　You need safety glasses. A. S. Markovits.
　　Mech Illus 66:22 F '70
　　See also
　American optical corporation
　Contact lenses
　Lenses
　Sun glasses
EYELASHES, Artificial
　Eyes worth looking into. il Mlle 70:182-3 Mr
　　'70
EYEN, Tom
　Dirtiest show in town. Criticism
　　Time il 96:63 Jl 13 '70 *
EYER, Ronald
　Musicians' autographs. il Hi Fi 20:secI 61-4
　　Ap '70
EYLAR, E. H. and others
　Experimental allergic encephalomyelitis: syn-
　　thesis of disease-inducing site of the basic
　　protein. bibliog il Science 168:1220-3 Je 5
　　'70
EYMAN, Herbert
　U.S. journal: Long Island; hero investigator
　　on Adrian Hoek-John Hughes case. C. Tril-
　　lin. New Yorker 46:32-6+ Jl 18 '70 *
EYTON, J. Ronald
　North Dakota observatory and weather sta-
　　tion. il Sky & Tel 40:201 O '70
EZEKIEL, Herbert M.
　Density-modulus relationship in graphite
　　fibers made from acrylic yarns. bibliog il
　　Science 169:178-9 Jl 10 '70

F

FAA. See United States—Federal aviation ad-
　　ministration
FAO. See Food and agricultural organization
　　of the United Nations
FASEB. See Federation of American societies
　　for experimental biology
FASH (Fraternal association of steel haulers)
　　See International brotherhood of teamsters,
　　chauffeurs, warehousemen and helpers of
　　America
FBI. See United States—Federal bureau of in-
　　vestigation
FCC. See United States—Federal communica-
　　tions commission
FDA. See United States—Food and drug ad-
　　ministration
FEBC. See Far East broadcasting company
FFA. See Future farmers of America
FHLBB. See United States—Federal home loan
　　bank board
FIGC. See Federal insurance guaranty corpora-
　　tion (proposed)
FLIR (forward-looking infrared) sensors. See
　　Detectors, Infrared
FLQ. See Front for the liberation of Quebec
FM. See Radio frequency modulation
FM radio stations. See Radio stations, Fre-
　　quency modulation
FNMA. See Federal national mortgage asso-
　　ciation
FPC. See Fish protein concentrate; United
　　States—Federal power commission
FSAA. See Family service association of Amer-
　　ica
FTC. See United States—Federal trade com-
　　mission
FTRF. See Freedom to read foundation
FAAS, Horst
　Time to decompress. il pors Time 96:34 Ag 3
　　'70
FABER, John
　Gibraltar. il Travel 133:28-33 Je '70

FABER, M. D.
　Self-destruction in Oedipus Rex. bibliog Am
　　Imago 27:41-51 Spr '70
FABIAN, Monroe H.
　Joseph Wright's portrait of Frederick
　　Muhlenberg. il Antiques 97:256-7 F '70
FABIO, Rose Marie
　Hi, mom, what's for lunch? See issues of
　　Parents' magazine & better family living
FABRIC wall coverings. See Wall coverings
FABRICIUS, Frank H. and others
　Early holocene oöids in modern littoral sands
　　reworked from a coastal terrace, southern
　　Tunisia. bibliog il Science 169:757-60 Ag 21
　　'70
FABRICS. See Textile fabrics
FABRIDAMS. See Dams
FABRY, Anni
　How to have a good figure for life. il Parents
　　Mag 45:52-4 Jl '70
FABRY, Joseph, and Knight, Max
　On the raising of ostriches for little fun and
　　less profit. il Am West 7:22-6 Jl '70
FABRY'S disease. See Angiokeratoma
FACE exercises. See Exercise
FACE doodles. See Make-up
FACE lifting. See Surgery, Plastic
FACE peeling, Chemical. See Chemosurgery
FACES, Stone. See Rock profiles
FACIAL deformities. See Deformities
FACIAL paralysis. See Paralysis
FACIAL treatments. See Beauty, Personal
FACIALS. See Skin—Care and hygiene
FACIANE, Sister Lucy
　This mayor is Sister. Am City 85:51 D '70 *
FACING the forests; story. See Yehoshua, A.
　　B.
FACKENHEIM, Emil L.
　People Israel lives. bibliog f por Chr Cent 87:
　　563-8 My 6 '70
FACKRE, Gabriel
　Futurists and visionaries; hope's partners.
　　Chr Cent 87:1060-3 S 9 '70
FACSIMILE transmission
　Dividends from the postal strike, business
　　for facsimile and mailing services. Bsns
　　W p36+ Ap 25 '70
　Moving images a Japanese way; Visual sci-
　　ences' Remotecopier machine. il Bsns W
　　p30 Ag 29 '70
FACSIMILES of rare books. See Book rarities—
　　Facsimiles
FACTORIES
　Bleak fate of the Yankee mills. il Life 69:58-
　　61 S 4 '70
　Stepped factory; Diestre plant near Zaragos-
　　sa, Spain. il Arch Forum 132:72-5 Ap '70
　Westinghouse electric corporation nuclear
　　turbine plant, Charlotte, N.C. il Arch Rec
　　147:108-9 Ja '70
　　See also
　Textile mills
Equipment
　　See also
　Industrial equipment
Foreign branches
　　See Branch factories, Foreign
Location
　　See Location in business and industry
Shutdowns
　Vacation bonus, minus paycheck. Bsns W p26
　　Jl 18 '70
FACTORIES, Automatic. See Machinery, Au-
　　tomatic
FACTORY laws and legislation
　　See also
　Hours of labor
FACTORY management
　　See also
　Supervisors
FACTORY models
　Model of glass factory of yesteryear; Jay
　　Overmeyer model, Corning, N.Y, museum
　　of glass. il Hobbies 75:98 Je '70
FACTORY produced houses. See Houses, Pre-
　　fabricated
FACTORY wages. See Wages—United States
FACULTY clubhouses. See Clubhouses
FACULTY meetings. See Teachers meetings
FADER, Carroll G.
　Sea Ed. il Todays Ed 59:30-1 D '70
FADIMAN, William
　Hollywood: shivering in the sun. New Re-
　　pub 162:17-19 Je 27 '70

FADOS
Fado in Portugal. M. Howe. il Sat R 53:49+
S 12 '70
FADS
Creepy-boppers; monster-mania. il Newsweek
76:103-4 D 14 '70
Lions and lambs. E. Sheppard. Harp Baz 103:
192 Mr '70
Nostalgia. il Newsweek 76:34-8 D 28 '70
Radical chic is dead. S. Alsop. Newsweek
76:120 D 14 '70
FAEROE ISLANDS. See Faroe Islands
FAGAN, Edward R.
New designs in English. bibliog f Clear
House 44:347-53 F '70
FAGER, Charles E.
Movies (title varies) (cont) Chr Cent 87:87,
607, 702+, 733-4, 1022, 1227-8, 1386 Ja 21,
My 13, Je 3-10, Ag 26, O 14 N 18 '70
Records (title varies) (cont) Chr Cent 87:54+,
301-2. 999, 1566-7 Ja 14. Mr 11, Ag 19, D 30
'70
(ed) See Cox, H. Experimenting with a sim-
pler life style
(ed) See Drinan, R. Priest, law school dean,
candidate for Congress
(ed) See Stone, I. F. With atheists like him,
who needs believers?
FAGERSTROM, Stan
Lower the odds on lunker bass. il Field & S
74:78-9+ Mr '70
FAGLEY, Richard M.
Earth day and after. Chr Cent 87:440-2 Ap 15
'70
FAHRNEY, Clyde N.
Unusual clocks in the collection of Clyde N.
Fahrney. O. R. Hagans. il Hobbies 74:126-
7+ F; 75:125-7 Mr '70
FAILURE (psychology)
How nations take defeat. C. Barnett. Hori-
zon 12:4-11 Sum '70
FAILURE to assist in emergencies. See As-
sistance in emergencies
FAIN, James
Moods of the North Rim: Grand Canyon
National Park. il Nat Parks & Con Mag
44:4-7 My '70
FAIR, Ruth B.
Our traveling blueberries. il Org Gard & Farm
17:34-6 Ag '70
FAIRBANKS, Morse and company. See Colt in-
dustries, inc.
FAIRCHILD, John Burr
Out on a limb with the midi. il por Time
96:76-81 S 14 '70 *
**FAIRCHILD camera and instrument corpora-
tion**
Fairchild thinks the worst is over. Bsns W
p 18 Ag 8 '70
Fairchild undergoes reorganization. Aviation
W 93:85+ S 14 '70
Industry invades the reservation. il Bsns W
p72-3 Ap 4 '70
FAIRCHILD Hiller corporation
Fairchild Hiller gets a recount. Bsns W p 18
Jl 11 '70
**FAIRCHILD tropical garden, Coconut Grove,
Fla.**
Florida's favorite, the Fairchild tropical gar-
den. M. Perry. il Home Gard 58:46-8 Ja '71
FAIRFAX, John
How I rowed across the Atlantic and found
Florida. il Esquire 73:111-15+ Ap '70
FAIRFIELD, Calif.
Try photogrammetrisizing. J. L. Shilts. il por
Am City 85:66-7 D '70
FAIRHURST, Janet P.
Visit an early Dutch manor. il Home Gard
57:42+ My '70
FAIRIES
Isaac Asimov explains: origins of the little
people. I. Asimov. Sci Digest 68:90-1 S '70
FAIRLEY, Richard L.
Comparability. Am Ed 6:20 O '70
FAIRLIE, Henry
Middle class. il McCalls 97:42-3+ Jl '70
Minority report on U.S. violence. Cur 114:36-
40 Ja '70
FAIRMAN, Marion
Better yesterdays, better tomorrows: the
dilemma of African writers. Chr Cent 87:
699-700 Je 3 '70
FAIRMOUNT HEIGHTS, Md.
See also
High John library
FAIRNESS doctrine (television) See Television
laws and regulations
FAIRS
Country fair, great idea for a city backyard.
il Bet Hom & Gard 48:48-9 Je '70
Medieval faire; children's festival in Jackson
County, Ore. S. A. Nelson. il Parks & Rec
5:30-1 Jl '70
To put your town on the map. F. L. Koltun.
Read Digest 97:31-2+ S '70
See also
Audio fairs

FAIRY plays
Cinderella and friends. V. R. Cheatham.
Plays 30:78-82 D '70
Fairy ring. F. B. Watts. Plays 29:80-5 Mr '70
Golden goose; dramatization of Grimm's
fairy tales. R. V. Holmes. Plays 29:71-82,
96 Ap '70
If you meet a leprechaun. J. Feather. Plays
29:72-4, 85 Mr '70
Tinderbox; dramatization of a fairy tale by
H. C. Andersen. D. C. Jones. Plays 30:61-
5, 75 D '70
FAIRY ring; drama. See Watts, F. B.
FAIRY tales
In defense of the wild things. M. A. Taylor.
il Horn Bk 46:642-6 D '70
Peacock princess; a button story. D. F.
Brown. il Hobbies 75:127-8 Ap '70

Anecdotes, facetiae, satire, etc.

Just for laughs: the gingerbread house caper.
W. Stanton. Look 34:60 S 8 '70
FAISAL, king of Saudi Arabia. See Feisal
FAITH
Christian point; rebirth of God in our culture.
V. P McCorry. America 122:378 Ap 4 '70
Faith. E. Glynn. America 124:49 Ja 16 '71
First sign. V. P. McCorry. America 124:56
Ja 16 '71
God in an evolving world; excerpt from God
within process. E. R. Baltazar. por Cath
World 211:103-6 Je '70; Discussion. 211:244
S '70
I believe in God's unholy church. L. M. Oray.
America 122:189 F 21 '70
Is there a substitute for God? D. R. Klein.
Read Digest 96:51-5 Mr '70
Layman and his faith. L. N. Bell. See issues
of Christianity today
Model of faith: the centurion in the Gospel
of Luke. Chr Today 14:18 Jl 31 '70
Psychosocial origins of stability in the Chris-
tian faith. B. Clouse. Chr Today 14:12-14
S 25 '70
See also
Hope
FAITH and order movement. See World coun-
cil of churches
FAITH cure
Miracle woman: K. Kuhlman. il por Time 96:
62+ S 14 '70
FAKE fur. See Fur, Artificial
FALAFIL. See Cookery, Middle Eastern
FALANGISTS. See Fascism—Spain
FALCONBRIDGE nickel mines, ltd.
Falconbridge tries to be a bigger no. 2. il
Bsns W p42-3 N 28 '70
FALCONER, Raymond E.
Air pollution and the temperature inversion.
il Cons 25:21-7 O '70
FALCONS
Death comes to the peregrine falcon. D. R.
Zimmerman. il N Y Times Mag p8-9+ Ag 9
'70; Discussion. p73 Ag 30 '70
FALES, Dan
Aquanaut makes diving easy. il Pop Mech
134:152-4 S '70
FALES, Edward D. jr
Face in the Mustang window. il Pop Mech
134:88-94+ Jl '70; Same abr. with title Car
in the river. Read Digest 97:82-6 Ag '70
He earns $30,000 a year behind the wheel.
il pors Pop Mech 133:79-82+ My '70
Storm they still don't believe. il Pop Mech
134:90-5+ S '70
Too fast in fog. il Pop Mech 134:84-9+ S
'70; Same abr. Read Digest 97:180-2+ O '70
What every young mother should know about
auto safety; excerpt from Mothers and chil-
dren in cars. il Redbook 135:91+ S '70
FALES, Martha Gandy
Early American official silver; excerpts from
Early American silver for the cautious
collector. il Antiques 97:96-9 Ja '70
FALICOV, L. M.
Physics and politics in Latin America; a
personal experience. Bul Atom Sci 26:
8-10+ N '70
FALK, John R.
Getting your dog there, and back again. il
Field & S 74:222-4+ Ap '70
Pointer or setter. il Field & S 75:184-6+ O
'70
FALK, Karl I.
Revolution at home and abroad; address,
September 8 and 9, 1970. Vital Speeches 37:
58-61 N 1 '70
FALK, Richard A.
War crimes and individual responsibilty: a
legal memorandum. Trans-Action 7:33-40 Ja
'70
War crimes: the circle of responsibility. Na-
tion 210:77-82 Ja 26 '70

FALK, Richard H. and others
Scanning electron microscopy of developing plant organs. bibliog il Science 168:1471-2 Je 19 '70

FALL. See Autumn

FALL; story. See Pritchett, V. S.

FALL meals. See Meals

FALL RIVER legend; ballet. See Ballets—Criticisms

FALL vacations. See Vacations

FALLACI, Oriana
(ed) See Abu Lotuf. Hidden leader of the Arab guerrillas
(ed) See Cronkite, W. What does Walter Cronkite really think?
(ed) See Habash, G. Leader of the fedayeen: we want a war like the Vietnam war

FALLEN Sparrows (prison bands) See Prison bands

FALLER, James E. and Wampler, E. J.
Lunar laser reflector; with biographical sketches. il Sci Am 222:25; 38-50 Mr '70

FALLOUT shelters See Atomic bomb shelters

FALSE cypress
This coiffure? It's Oriental; golden thread cypress. il Sunset 144:139 Ja '70

FALSE eyelashes. See Eyelashes, Artificial

FALSE faces. See Masks (for the face)

FALSE pregnancy. See Pregnancy in animals

FALSEHOOD. See Lying

FALTER, Mary Elizabeth
Notes of a happy housekeeper. See issues of House & garden incorporating Living for young homemakers

FALTERMAYER, Edmund K.
Let's break the go-to-college lockstep. il Fortune 82:98-103+ N '70
Some here-and-now steps to cut crime. il Fortune 82:94-9+ Jl '70

FAMBROUGH, Douglas M.
Acetylcholine sensitivity of muscle fiber membranes: mechanism of regulation by motoneurons. bibliog il Science 168:372-3 Ap 17 '70

FAME
See also
Celebrities

FAMILY
American family: future uncertain; with comment by U. Bronfenbrenner. il Time 96:34-9 D 28 '70
Brutality of modern families. R. Sennett. il Trans-Action 7:29-37 S '70
Can the family survive? M. Mead. Redbook 135:52+ S '70
What happened to the family? N. W. Ackerman. Ment Hy 54:459-63 Jl '70
See also
Birth order
Children
Divorce
Fathers
Foster parents
Home
Marriage
Mothers
Parents
Widows

Italy

Italian family is a commune. A. Menen. il N Y Times Mag p22-3+ Mr 1 '70

FAMILY, Size of
Case for small families. E. J. Lieberman. il N Y Times Mag p86+ Mr 8 '70
Case for small family. Sci Digest 68:53-4 D '70
Cheaper by the duo? T. J. Rakstis. il Todays Health 48:46-7+ My '70
Failure of the rhythm method. il Good H 170:10+ F '70
Family size and sex-role stereotypes. F. E. Clarkson and others. bibliog Science 167:390-2 Ja 23 '70
Two children by choice; excerpts. I. Rossman. Parents Mag 45:58-9+ My '70

FAMILY assistance plan. See Public welfare—United States

FAMILY budget. See Budget, Household

FAMILY camping. See Camping

FAMILY care for mental patients. See Mentally ill—Home care

FAMILY corporations
Dynamic growth companies: Koch industries, inc. il Nations Bsns 58:48-53 F '70
See also
Brenninkmeyer, C. and A. company

FAMILY courts. See Domestic relations courts

FAMILY crisis intervention unit. See New York (city)—Police

FAMILY doctors. See Physicians

FAMILY farm operating agreements. See Father-son farm operating agreements

FAMILY farms organic growers' association. See Agricultural societies

FAMILY finance. See Domestic finance

FAMILY group therapy. See Family psychotherapy

FAMILY history. See Genealogy

FAMILY income. See Income

FAMILY life
American family change-up. G. B. Blaine, jr. il Vogue 155:87+ Je '70
American family: future uncertain; with comment by U. Bronfenbrenner. il Time 96:34-9 D 28 '70
Family life and sex education. bibliog Ment Hy 54:591-2 O '70
Humor to the rescue. R. Armour. il Parents Mag 45:48-9+ Jl '70
New designs for family living. M. Mead. Redbook 135:22+ O '70
On being an American boating parent. P. W. Dale. il Motor B 125:200-5 Ap '70
What shall we tell our children? M. Mead. Redbook 135:35+ Je '70
See also
Home
Music in the home

Anecdotes, facetiae, satire, etc.

Life's precious moments (winter division) R. Baker. il Read Digest 97:35-6 D '70
Man next door. B. Hillis. See issues of Better homes and gardens

Caricatures and cartoons

It's all in the family. S. Berenstain and J. Berenstain. il Good H 171:96-9 O '70; 172:30-1 Ja '71

FAMILY life and early sorrows; story. See Creal, M.

FAMILY limitation. See Birth control

FAMILY names. See Names, Personal

FAMILY of man award. See Council of churches of the city of New York

FAMILY planning. See Birth control

FAMILY psychotherapy
To treat a disturbed person, treat his family. S. Davidson. il por N Y Times Mag p 10-11+ Ag 16 '70

FAMILY quarrels. See Quarrels

FAMILY reunions
Family reunion. il Bet Hom & Gard 48:38-9+ Je '70

FAMILY rooms. See Living rooms

FAMILY service association of America
Time to strengthen family ties. C. W. Blackburn. por Parents Mag 45:30 D '70

FAMILY size. See Family, Size of

FAMILY therapy. See Family psychotherapy

FAMILY vacations. See Vacations

FAMILY weekly (periodical) See Newspapers—Magazine sections

FAMINES
See also
Food supply

FAMOUS men. See Great men

FAMOUS sayings. See Quotations

FAMOUS women. See Women, Famous

FAMOUS writers school
Let us now appraise famous writers. J. Mitford. il Atlan 226:45-54 Jl '70; Discussion. 226:40-4+ S '70
Queen of muckrakers. il por Time 96:52 Jl 20 '70

FAN, Hung, and Penman, Sheldon
Mitochondrial RNA synthesis during mitosis. bibliog il Science 168:135-8 Ap 3 '70

FAN belts, Automobile. See Automobile engines—Cooling

FANCHER, Betsy
Georgia Sea Island that slumbers like a time capsule. il Holiday 47:56-9+ My '70

La FANCIULLA del West; opera. See Puccini, G.

FANDEL, John
Crocuses; poem. Cath World 211:31 Ap '70
Elegy. Cath World 212:208 Ja '71
Letter; poem. Commonweal 93:158 N 6 '70
Little resignation. poem. Cath World 211:111 Je '70
Pilgrimage of the dew; poem. Commonweal 92:364 Jl 24 '70
Three views; poem. Commonweal 92:60 Mr 27 '70

FANNIE Mae. See Federal national mortgage association

FANNING, Eleanor G.
Wonderful world of ants. il Horticulture
48:28-9+ Mr '70
FANNING, James
Gardener's notes. See issues of House &
garden incorporating Living for young
homemakers
FANS
Fans of the Napoleonic era. E. Oldham. il
Antiques 97:135-9 Ja '70
FANS, Automobile. See Automobile engines—
Cooling
FANS, Baseball. See Baseball fans
FANS, Electric. See Electric fans
FANS, Ventilating. See Ventilators
FANTASIES, Literary
Looking backwards, and ahead, with Alice.
N. Hentoff. il Wilson Lib Bul 45:169-71 O
'70
FANTASTIC art. See Art, Fantastic
FANTASTIC CAVERNS, Missouri. See Caves
FANTASY
Fantasy and self-discovery. R. Helson. il
Horn Bk 46:121-34 Ap '70
See also
Childrens fantasies
Daydreams
Fairy tales
FANTASY in art
Peace in Middle Earth; paintings, with re-
port by D. Kolodney. il Ramp Mag 9:
35-8 O '70
FANTEL, Hans H.
All-in-one music centers: your best bet in
hi-fi? il Pop Mech 134:130-3 D '70
Cassette tape systems: now they're hi-fi.
il Pop Sci 197:70-3+ N '70
How to pick a phono pickup. il Pop Mech 133:
144-7+ Mr '70
Music from a waffle iron. il Opera N 34:17-19
Je 13 '70
Torture tracks for your hi-fi system: il Pop
Mech 133:132-4+ Ja '70
What's watt in choosing a hi-fi? il Pop
Mech 134:143-5+ O '70
FANTINI, Mario D.
Institutional reform. Todays Ed 59:43-4+ Ap
'70
Urban school reform: educational agenda for
tomorrow's America. Cur Hist 59:267-72+
N '70
FAR EAST
See also
Asia
Asia, Southeastern
Pacific countries
United Nations—Economic commission for
Asia and the Far East
Description and travel
Orient. S. Karnow. il Travel & Camera 33:
44-59 Mr '70
See also
Industries
Textile industry—Far East
FAR EAST broadcasting company
Bamboo missionary broadcaster. J. Kimber-
ley. il Pop Electr 32:61+ F '70
FAR right. See Right and left (political sci-
ence)
FARADAY, Michael
Michael Faraday; an informal sketch. R. E.
Oesper. pors Chem 43:16-17 Mr '70 •
FARADAY effect
Pioneer 6: measurement of transient Faraday
rotation phenomena observed during solar
occultation. G. S. Levy and others; reply.
K. H. Schatten. il Science 168:395-6 Ap 17
'70
FARADAY rotation. See Faraday effect
FARB, Judith
Romania. il Travel & Camera 33:46-52+ D
'70
FARB, Peter
New parks that aren't. il Audubon 72:28-35
Ja '70
FARBER, Barry
Hypocrisy, southern style. Sat R 53:4 Ap 25
'70
FARBER, Ed
Phototronics. See issues of Modern photo-
graphy
FARBER, Norma
Jubilate herbis. Horn Bk 46:592 D '70
Sloth moseying toward the manger; poem.
America 123:561 D 26 '70
Stitch in time; poem. Commonweal 92:367 Jl
24 '70
FARBER, Paul R.
Your first darkroom. Travel & Camera 33:
68-70+ Jl '70

FARBER, Stephen
End of the road? il Film Q 23:3-16 Wint '69
(ed) See Peckinpah, S. Peckinpah's return
FARBWERKE Hoechst a.g. See Chemical indus-
tries—Germany (Federal Republic)
FAREWELL disaster, hello bliss; story. See
Brown, M. F.
FARJEON award. See Childrens literature—
Awards and prizes
FARKAS, Andrew
Welcome to the club. Opera N 34:6-7 F 21 '70
FARKAS, L. L.
Careers in electronics, blueprint to your fu-
ture. il Radio-Electr 41:45-6 S; 68-9+ O
'70
FARM animals. See Livestock
FARM buildings
See also
Barns and stables
Calf pens
Cattle sheds
Granaries
Silos
Swine farrowing crates and pens
Swine houses
FARM bureau federation. See American farm
bureau federation
FARM bureaus. See American farm bureau
federation
FARM census
United States
What the census means to you. il Farm J 94:
62 Ja '70
FARM corporations
Incorporate? They did, for three different
reasons. R. Sanders. il Suc Farm 68:26-7 Ag
'70
Partnership or corporation? Tips from an
expert. il Suc Farm 68:G4 My '70
Tax shelter caves in on city farmers; Black
watch farms, inc. J. Carlson. il Farm J
94:18-19+ N '70
Two dairy farm agreements and how they
work. il Suc Farm 68:G8-9 My '70
When to incorporate your farm. R. N.
Weigle. Suc Farm 68:no2 B6 F '70
FARM credit administration. See United States
—Farm credit administration
FARM drainage. See Drainage
FARM equipment
Home-made and handy; photographs. See
issues of Farm journal
FARM finance
Farm credit; with editorial comment. R.
Krumme. il Suc Farm 68:22, 39-45 S '70
How do you feel about 1970? J. Carlson. Farm
J 94:27 F '70
How farmers would change PCAs and land
banks. C. W. Gifford. il Farm J 93:28+ D
'69
FARM forestry. See Woodlots
FARM houses. See Farmhouses
FARM income. See Agriculture—Economic as-
pects
FARM journal
Expert help to remodel your home. il Farm J
93:61 N '69
FARM kitchens. See Kitchens
FARM labor
Agribusiness in California. A. V. Krebs,
jr. Commonweal 93:45-7 O 9 '70
Beyond peace at Delano. America 123:80 Ag
22 '70
Farm help; add it when needed. R. Sanders.
Suc Farm 69:23 Ja '71
Feeders seek answers to hired help problem.
Farm J 93:B44 N '69
If you hire help, consider incentive plans.
R. Sanders. il Suc Farm 68:no3 25 F '70
See also
American federation of labor and Congress
of industrial organizations—United farm
workers organizing committee
Collective bargaining—Farm labor
Migrant labor
Part time employment
Strikes—United States—Farm labor
Health and hygiene
Nerve gas in the orchards; pesticide poison-
ing. R. B. Taylor. Nation 210:751-3 Je 22
'70
Wages and hours
Salary records help keep farm labor. Suc
Farm 68:A6 O '70
FARM land. See Land
FARM life
Letters from farm women. See issues of
Farm journal
Rural Russia today. M. K. Whyte. il Trans-
Action 7:26-32 Ja '70

FARM life—*Continued*
Smile: a memoir. E. Mueller. Mlle 72:96-7+
D '70
Unforgettable moments on the farm. L.
Campbell. Farm J 94:88 Ap '70
See also
Country life
Farm women
Ranch life

Anecdotes, facetiae, satire, etc.
Winter leaves me cold. J. Ritchie. Farm J
94:M12 F '70
FARM machinery. See Agricultural machinery
FARM management
Cropping strategy from eight top livestock
setups. J. R. Borcherding. il Suc Farm 68:
37-41 N '70
How big is big enough R. Sanders. il Suc
Farm 68:29-31 O '70
How to manage. R. Krumme. il Suc Farm
68:25-7 S '70
Instant answers to farm questions: talking
computer. J. Carlson. il Farm J 94:62H Mr
'70
More profit, not more acres. D. Seim. il Farm
J 94:M10 F '70
More than luck in making top farm income.
M. Hood. Suc Farm 69:D4 Ja '71
Points to consider when planning ahead. D.
Hanson. Suc Farm 68:30 Ap '70
Teamwork speeds up planting. Farm J 94:52H
Ap '70
See also
Crop yields
Dairy farm management
Farm corporations
Farm records
Father-son farm operating agreements
Swine farm management

Study and teaching
New breed of hired man: management
trainee. J. Russell. il Farm J 94:H8-9+ N
'70
FARM mechanization
Migrant workers. M. Friedman. Newsweek
76:60 Jl 27 '70
FARM museums. See Agricultural museums
FARM offices. See Offices
FARM operating agreements. See Father-son
farm operating agreements
FARM ownership
Credit and the farm of the future: family
owned or corporation; address, March 17,
1970. J. P. Campbell. Vital Speeches 36:
431-3 My 1 '70
How to be a smart farm buyer. R. Krumme.
Suc Farm 68:no5 A16 Mr '70
FARM partnership
Double shots of management know-how. il
Suc Farm 68:G2-4 My '70
Partnership or corporation? Tips from an ex-
pert. il Suc Farm 68:G4 My '70
Two farmers: one operation: Dick and Bob
Klosterman in Richland County, N.D. D.
Seim. il Farm J 93:18-19+ D '69
Two-man farms, a way to grow. il Farm J
94:16-17 S '70
FARM policy. See Agricultural administration
—United States
FARM prices. See Farm produce—Prices
FARM produce
Marketing
Dollar exports set a record. W. E. Swegle.
il Suc Farm 69:30-1 Ja '71
Export fight: can we win it? C. W. Gifford.
Farm J 94:A24 F '70
Let the customer harvest your crop. J. D.
Boyd. il Farm J 94:54K F '70
Marketing management. R. Sanders. See
issues of Successful farming
Russian farmer's big joke on Communism.
S. Ostrander and L. Schroeder. Farm J 93:
30A O '69
See also subhead Marketing under names
of farm produce. e.g. Corn—Marketing

Prices
Break for housewives, not for farmers. il
Fortune 82:24 S '70
See also subhead Prices under names of
farm produce, e.g. Potatoes—Prices

Storage
Fresh produce fresh? il Sunset 145:108-9 Jl
'70
See also
Vegetables—Storage

Transportation
Airlines losing ground in strawberry market.
Aviation W 93:112 O 26 '70

FARM records
File it easy, find it fast. il Farm J 94:A14
F '70
Progress, how to make and measure it. il
Suc Farm 68:A2 O '70
What your banker expects from you. R.
Krumme. Suc Farm 68:B1 N '70
FARM shops. See Workshops
FARM subsidies. See Agricultural administra-
tion—United States
FARM tenancy
This tenant is a top-notch cattle feeder. D.
Malena. il Suc Farm 68:32-3 Ag '70
FARM tractors. See Tractors
FARM trucks. See Motor trucks in agriculture
FARM vacations. See Vacations
FARM women
How farm women share the good-will spirit
the year round. il Farm J 93:42-3 D '69
I'm a farm wife transplant. L. Kurt. Farm J
94:89 Ap '70
Letters from farm women. See issues of
Farm journal
FARM woodlands. See Woodlots
FARM workshops. See Workshops
FARMER, Betsy
Visual perception and environmental design.
il Sch Arts 69:12-15 Ap '70
FARMER, Charles J.
Wyoming's first Rocky Mountain goat hunt.
il Field & S 75:56-7+ O '70
FARMER, Gene
How Apollo 11 changed three famous men.
pors Life 69:50 Jl 17 '70
Jones project: preparation of reminiscences
of N. Khrushchev for publication. R. Graves.
il pors Life 69:3 N 27 '70
FARMER, James
Exit Egeberg; and Farmer. pors Time 96:15
D 14 '70 *
FARMER-hunter relations
Deteriorating rancher-sportsman relations. H.
Rate. il Field & S 75:20+ S; 12+ O '70
How to keep free public hunting. B. E. Bur-
gin. il Cons 25:6-7 O '70
FARMERS
One man, one tractor. 1000 acres of corn and
soybeans. D. Seim. il Farm J 93:30-1+ N
'69
What city people think of farmers. Farm J
94:M4-5 F '70
See also
Agriculture
Collective bargaining—Farmers
Farmer-hunter relations

Public relations
See Agriculture—Public relations
FARMERS associations. See Agricultural so-
cieties
FARMERS cooperative associations. See Coop-
erative associations
FARMERS test plots. See Field experiments
(agriculture)
FARMERS wives. See Farm women
FARMHOUSES
Good ideas for the farmhouse core. R. Mar-
tens. il Farm J 93:46-8+ O '69
FARMHOUSES, Remodeled. See Houses, Re-
modeled
FARMING. See Agriculture
FARMING, Part time. See Part time farming
FARMING, Tax loss. See Agriculture—Eco-
nomic aspects
FARMINGDALE, N.Y, public library
Carl Gorton pays fine, quits library board.
Library J 95:2864+ S 15 '70
Intellectual freedom. J. F. Krug. Am Lib 1:
118 F '70
Orrin B. Dow, public librarian. il por Wilson
Lib Bul 45:200-1 O '70
Social responsibility survives budget cuts. il
Library J 95:1269 Ap 1 '70
FARMINGTON, W. Va. mine disaster. See
Coal mines and mining—Accidents and ex-
plosions
FARMS
See also
Agriculture
Dairy farms
Farm ownership
Swine farms
FARMS, Incorporated. See Farm corporations
FARMS, Large
5000 acre farms in the Corn Belt? L. R. Kyle.
il Suc Farm 68:30-1 Ag '70
It costs less to farm big. D. Hanson. il
Suc Farm 68:no5 17 Mr '70

FARMS, Model
Amishville U.S.A; tourist farm near Berne, Ind. B. Thomas. il Travel 134:46-51 O '70
Farm that makes fun pay; Upland Hills, recreation farm. G. Logsdon. il Farm J 94:M2-3 F '70

FARMS, Organic
More farms for organic food. M. C. Goldman. il Org Gard & Farm 17:68-73 D '70

FARNBOROUGH air show. See Aviation—Exhibitions

FARNER, Frank
College presidents and environmental education. il Parks & Rec 5:31-3+ Ag '70

FARNSWORTH, Albert H.
UN looks at earthman's world. Nat Parks & Con Mag 44:10 Jl '70

FARNSWORTH, Dana L.
Sex mores and sex morals. il PTA Mag 64:2-5 bibliog(p34) Ap '70

FARNWORTH, Don
Main Street on Broadway. N. M. Stoop. il pors Dance Mag 44:30-3 Jl '70 *

FAROE ISLANDS
Faeroes, isles of maybe. E. Bradford. il Nat Geog 138:410-42 S '70

FAROESE poetry

Translations into English
Company of the blind; So deep, so deep; tr. by G. Johnston. C. Matras. Poetry 116:330-2 Ag '70
White night; Stones; tr. by G Johnston. K. Hoydal. Poetry 116:333-4 Ag '70

FARQUHAR, George
Beaux' stratagem. Criticism
Nation 210:189-90 F 16 '70 *
Newsweek 75:56-7 F 2 '70
Time il 95:52 F 2 '70
Recruiting officer. Criticism
Nation 210:220 F 23 '70 *

FARR, Francis Bartow
Fairly sad story of a Wall Street broker. M. T. Bloom. il pors N Y Times Mag p 12-13+ Je 14 '70 *

FARRELL, Barry
Applause for Bacall. il pors Life 68:54A-54D Ap 3 '70
Column. See issues of Life
Indigestible dinner with Professor M. il Life 68:24B Mr 6 '70
On a sailboat of sinking water. il por Life 68:4 My 15 '70
Repression in the mirror. Life 68:22B Ap 3 '70
Yossarian in Connecticut. il pors Life 69:50-2+ O 2 '70

FARRELL, Ed, and Ruth, Leo
(eds) The scene (cont) Engl J 59:285-90, 709-20 F, My '70

FARRELL, Paul B. jr
Case against percentages. Arch Forum 133:72-3 Jl '70

FARRELL, Suzanne
New York's own comes home. W. Como. por Dance Mag 45:56-8 Ja '71 *
World of dance. W. Terry. Sat R 53:36+ D 26 '70 *

FARRIS, Nancy Pierson
Roses in the vegetable garden. il Org Gard & Farm 17:46-8 My '70

FARROW, Tisa
Juliet to a rebellious Romeo; interview. ed. by E. Miller. il pors Seventeen 29:136-7+ Je '70

about
Will Mia's sister make it? D. Chapman. il pors Look 34:48-5 S 22 '70 *

FASCELL, Dante Bruno
United Nations calls for measures against aircraft hijacking; statement, December 12, 1969. Dept State Bul 62:69-70 Ja 19 '70

FASCHING. See Carnival

FASCISM
See also
National socialism

Italy
Fascist modernization in Italy: traditional or revolutionary? R. Sarti. bibliog f Am Hist R 75:1029-45 Ap '70

Spain
Return of the ultras? Falangists pro-Franco demonstrations. il por Time 96:18-19 D 28 '70
Turning a page. il por Newsweek 76:26-7 D 28 '70

United States
Can it happen here? Is it already happening? P. Green. il N Y Times Mag p30-1+ S 20 '70; Discussion. p37 O 11; 12+ O 18 '70; Nation 211:290 O 5 '70
Philosophy of a corner linebacker. J. McMurtry. Nation 212:83-4 Ja 18 '71

FASHION
Best dressed women for 1970. il Ebony 25:163-4+ My '70
Fashion 1970. G. Guinness. Harp Baz 104:76-7 D '70
Goodbye, little girl. E. Sheppard. Harp Baz 103:134-5 Ap '70
What is chic, what is fashion? G. Guinness. Harp Baz 103:152-3 Ap '70
See also
Clothing and dress
Costume
Costume design
Dress accessories
Fads
Hairdressing

Anecdotes, facetiae, satire, etc.
Of miniskirts and pantyhose. J. Robbins. il Read Digest 96:81-3 Mr '70

History
See also
Clothing and dress—History

FASHION designers. See Costume designers

FASHION industry. See Clothing industry

FASHION shows
Finale for fashion? R. Gerneich fashion show. il por Time 95:39 Ja 26 '70
Liberated look; Ebony fashion fair's 1970 Paris collection. il Ebony 25:175-6+ O '70

FASI, Frank
Frank Fasi fights fiercely. Time 95:44+ F 23 '70 *

FASOLO, Ugo
Pigeons; poem. tr. by E. Pound. Atlan 226:94 N '70

FASSNACHT, Robert
Bomb kills physicist, damages equipment. G. B. Lubkin. il Phys Today 23:73-4 O '70 *

FAST breeder reactors. See Nuclear reactors

FASTENINGS
Improved fastener devices sought. W. S. Hieronymus. il Aviation W 92:54-5 Mr 23 '70
Panel put-ons; Dzus fasteners. B. Lang. il Hot Rod 23:48-9 Ap '70
Special wood fasteners make the job easier. P. McCafferty. il Pop Sci 197:96-7 D '70

FASTENINGS (machinery)
See also
Bolts and nuts

FASTING
Another look at abstinence. Chr Today 15:28+ N 6 '70
See also
Starvation

FAT
See also
Corpulence

FAT cells. See Cells

FAT content of foods. See Food—Fat content

FAT girl; story. See Gill, B.

FATAH. See Fedayeen

FATALISM. See Fate and fatalism

FATE and fatalism
Pakistan calamity: fate, wrath or providence? J. C. Haughey. America 123:479 D 5 '70

FATEH. See Fedayeen

FATHER Buh Buh Boo; story. See Sweat, J.

FATHER-son farm operating agreements
He's a tenant to his sons. R. Sanders. il Suc Farm 68:B24-5 Ja '70

FATHER-son relationship. See Parent-child relationship

FATHERHOOD, Education of. See Parent education

FATHERHOOD of God. See God

FATHERS
Daddy takes over; with photographs by Szasz. M. B. Karter. Good H 170:112-15 Ap '70
New man in the delivery room: the father. S. Olds and L. Witt. il Todays Health 48:52-6 O '70
Of fathers: heavenly, and not-so. Chr Today 14:25 Je 5 '70
What makes a good father. T. B. Brazelton. il Redbook 135:74-5+ Je '70
See also
Parent education

FATHERS day
Father's day specials; with recipes. il Parents Mag 45:54-6+ Je '70

FATHERS day gifts. See Gifts

FATHER'S Easter hat; drama. See Hark, M. and McQueen, N.

FATHERS of the church
See also
Augustine, Saint

FATIGUE
Chronic fatigue: what you can do about feeling tired. il Good H 171:165-7 N '70
What you can do about teen-age fatigue. J. D. Wassersug. il Sci Digest 67:25-8 Ja '70

FATS. See Oils and fats. Edible

FATT, Amelia
Impressions of Kay Mazzo. il pors Dance Mag 44:64 Ja '70

FATTOROSI, L. J.
Satire V from the scourge of vacuity; Retraction; poems. Nat R 22:570 Je 2 '70; Correction. 22:801 Jl 28 '70

FATTY acids. See Acids. Fatty

FATTY liver. See Liver—Diseases

FAUBOURG St Honoré. See Paris—Streets

FAUCETS. See Plumbing

FAULCONER, Estelle
Who says it's unethical? il Todays Ed 59:62-3 Ja '70

FAULK, Odie B.
Law & the land. Am West 7:14-16+ Ja '70

FAULKNER, Darwin
Tips on working as a technical writer. Writers Digest 50:23 Ag '70

FAULKNER, Douglas
Lesson from the hidden sea; photographs. Audubon 72:49-56 S '70

about

Douglas Faulkner: his beautiful sea and its creatures. M. Edelson. il Pop Phot 67:87-91 O '70 *

FAULKNER, William
Faulkner country. C. Hesse and S. Hesse. il Travel 134:68-70 D '70 *
Must the novelist crusade? E. Welty. il Writers Digest 50:32-5+ F '70 *
Postmaster: letter in 1924, charging him with neglect of duties as postmaster. M. Webster. New Yorker 46:50 N 21 '70 *
Syntactic and lexical problems in reading Faulkner. L. S. Golub. Engl J 59:490-6 Ap '70 **

FAULTS (geology)
Afar triangle. H. Tazieff. il Sci Am 222:32-40 bibliog (p 126) F '70
Boconó fault, Venezuelan Andes; evidence of postglacial movement. C. Schubert and R. S. Sifontes. bibliog il Science 170:66-9 O 2 '70
California earthquakes: why only shallow focus? W. F. Brace and J. D. Byerlee. bibliog il Science 168:1573-5 Je 26 '70
Central North Atlantic plate motions over the last 40 million years. J. D. Phillips and B. P. Luyendyk. bibliog il Science 170:727-9 N 13 '70
Study of the San Andreas fault: something very interesting is going on deep beneath the earth's surface. S. D. Smith. il N Y Times Mag p 16-17+ Ja 18 '70
Where the fault lies; San Andreas fault. Sci Am 223:41 D '70

FAUST, Frederick
Max Brand. by R. Easton. Review
    Sat R 53:30-1 Mr 28 '70. W. Decker *

FAUST; opera. See Gounod. C. F.

FAUSTER, Carl U.
Libbey commemorative revival of Amberina, 1917. il Hobbies 75:98J-98L Mr '70

FAUX, Eugene J. and Crawford, Blaine
Deaths in a youth program. Ment Hy 54:569-71 O '70

FAVIA-ARTSAY, Aida
Historical records. See issues of Hobbies

FAVORITE man's favorite recipe contest. See Cookery—Competitions

FAWCETT, Clara Hallard
Dollology. See issues of Hobbies

FAY, Harold
Beauty is where he finds it. R. Hattersley. il Pop Phot 67:98-101 S '70

FAY, Martha
Nun's search for freedom drives her from the convent. il pors Life 68:26-7 Mr 20 '70

FAY, Michael E.
Fabridam. il Parks & Rec 5:34-5+ Ag '70

FAY, Stephen
Era of dummies and darkies. il Commonweal 93:125-8 O 30 '70

FAYER, Ronald
Sarcocystis: development in cultured avian and mammalian cells. bibliog il Science 168:1104-5 My 29 '70

FAYETTE, Miss.
Black, sassy and still tryin' to be independent. G. Goodman. il pors Look 34:22-6 Jl 14 '70
Fayette's mayor one year later. il por Bsns W p79 Jl 4 '70
Tiny leap forward. il por Newsweek 76:36+ Jl 13 '70

FAYETTEVILLE, N.C.
Black courage in Klan country: building of a successful cleaning business. P. Bailey. il pors Ebony 25:136-41 Ap '70

FAZIO, Carl
Fantastic Fazios of foodland. il por Bsns W p 146+ F 21 '70 *

FEAR
Children's political fears. A. J. Snider. Sci Digest 68:63 D '70
Place for a happening; fear of dying. C. Heimsath. America 123:149-50 S 12 '70
School phobia and the fear of death. W. Tietz. bibliog Ment Hy 54:565-8 O '70
    See also
Anxiety
Courage
Nervousness
Phobias
Stage fright
Terrorism
Worry

FEATHER, Jean
If you meet a leprechaun; drama. Plays 29:72-4, 85 Mr '70
Poor man's clever daughter; drama. Plays 29:62-6 My '70
Quick-witted Jack; dramatization of a Scandinavian folk tale. Plays 30:57-64 Ja '71

FEATHERS

Stockpiling

See Stockpiling

FEATHERSTONE, Joseph
Accountability. New Repub 162:9-10 F 28 '70
Kentucky fried children. New Repub 163:12-16 S 5 '70
Teaching writing. New Repub 163:11-14 Jl 11 '70

FEATHERSTONE, Ralph
Losers on U.S. 1. il pors Newsweek 75:28 Mr 23 '70 *

FEATHERWORK
Ken Shores. R. Griffin. il Craft Horiz 30:26-9 Ag '70

FEBRUARY
February's frankness. Chr Today 14:27 F 27 '70

FEBRUARY revolution, 1848. See France—History—February revolution. 1848

FEDAYEEN
Algeria, Israel and the Al Fatah. R. W. Fox. Commonweal 92:184-5 My 8 '70; Discussion. 92:331+, 475+; 93:83+ Jl 10, S 25, O 23 '70
American innocent in the Middle East; Jordan. M. Frady. Harper 241:104-6+ N '70
Battle of Amman. J. Stork. Ramp Mag 9:14+ D '70
Birth of an Arab Soviet. L. Jenkins. il Newsweek 76:36 S 28 '70
Commandos: peace is their greatest fear. il Newsweek 76:27-8 S 21 '70
Death in distant places; sabotage of Swiss and Austrian planes. il Time 95:19 Mr 2 '70
Democratic solution for the Israeli-Palestinian problem: PDF view. N. Hawatmeh. Trans-Action 7:67 Jl '70
Doctor Habbash's strong medicine; Popular front for the liberation of Palestine. por Newsweek 76:28 S 21 '70
Fatah on the future of Palestine. Trans-Action 7:80-1 Jl '70
Fedayeen: Israel's fanatic foe. D. Reed. il Read Digest 97:168-73 O '70
Fedayeen: new factor in the Middle East. J. B. Sheerin; discussion. Cath World 211:432-3, 52, 148 Ap-My, Jl '70
Fire and steel for Palestine. J. M. Mecklin. il Fortune 82:84-9+ Jl '70
Hidden leader of the Arab guerrillas; interview, ed. by O. Fallaci. Abu Lotuf. il Look 34:24-6 Je 30 '70
Hussein's costly victory. il por Newsweek 76:35 O 5 '70
If it happens here, it will happen there. il Time 95:35 My 25 '70
Israel and the new left. S. Avineri. Trans-Action 7:79-83 Jl '70
Jordan's nine-day war. il Newsweek 76:36-7 O 5 '70
Leader of the fedayeen: we want a war like the Vietnam war; interview, ed. by O. Fallaci. G. Habash. il por Life 68:32-4 Je 12 '70
Liberation or genocide? PDF and Fatah positions. Y. Harkabi. il Trans-Action 7:62-7+ Jl '70
Palestine commandos: who wields the power. il U S News 69:25 S 21 '70
Palestinian resistance movement. J. B. Wolf. bibliog f Cur Hist 60:26-31+ Ja '71
Rebellious Palestinians. por Time 96:22 Ag 10 '70

FEDAYEEN—*Continued*
 Violent men of Amman. E. Pace. il N Y Times
  Mag p8–9+ Jl 19 '70
 War on the long breath. il Time 95:32-7 Mr
  30 '70
 Winter of discontent. L. Jenkins. il News-
  week 76:43 D 21 '70
  See also
 Guerrillas—Arab states
FEDDE, George A.
 Plated-wire magnetic film memories. por
  Electr World 84:53-5 O '70
FEDERAL agencies. See United States—Ex-
 ecutive departments
FEDERAL aid
  See also
 Art and state
 Government lending
 Subsidies
  also subhead Federal aid under vari-
  ous subjects e.g. Research—Federal aid
FEDERAL and municipal relations
 Federal-city relations in the 1960's. V. M.
  Goetcheus. bibliog f Cur Hist 59:262-6+
  N '70
 Mayors sound storm warning for Nixon. U S
  News 68:46 Je 29 '70
 More aid for cities in war against crime. il
  U S News 68:36-8 F 23 '70
 On the brink of bankruptcy. il Time 97:
  13-14 Ja 11 '71
 Worried cities look to Washington. il Bsns
  W p39 My 23 '70
FEDERAL and state relations
 We are embarked on a great new mission of
  reform; address. July 27, 1970. E. L. Rich-
  ardson. por U S News 69:57-9 Ag 17 '70
  See also
 Decentralization in government
 State finance—Federal aid
FEDERAL art project
 Memoirs of a WPA painter; excerpt from
  The new deal art project. ed. by F. V.
  O'Connor; with paintings. E. Laning. il por
  Am Heritage 21:38-57+ O '70
FEDERAL boards, bureaus, commissions, etc. of
 United States government. See names of
 boards, bureaus, etc. under United States,
 e.g. United States—Federal power commis-
 sion
FEDERAL city college. See Washington, D.C.
 Federal city college
FEDERAL coal mine health and safety act.
 See Coal mines and mining—Safety devices
 and measures
FEDERAL contract compliance, Office of. See
 United States—Labor, Department of—Fed-
 eral contract compliance, Office of
FEDERAL courts. See Courts—United States
FEDERAL crop reporting board. See United
 States—Agriculture, Department of
FEDERAL debt (United States) See Debts,
 Public—United States
FEDERAL documents. See Government pub-
 lications
FEDERAL employees. See Government em-
 ployees
FEDERAL expenditures. See United States—
 Appropriations and expenditures
FEDERAL government
 Federal government; the gnomes of Washing-
  ton; address, July 14, 1970. B. Goldwater.
  Vital Speeches 36:642-7 Ag 15 '70
 New federalism. H. Brandon. Sat R 53:14 F
  14 '70
  See also
 Decentralization in government
 Democracy
 Intergovernmental tax relations
 United States—Politics and government
FEDERAL insurance guaranty corporation (pro-
 posed)
 This month's feature: Congress & casualty
  insurance regulation. Cong Digest 49:33-64
  F '70
FEDERAL laboratories. See Laboratories,
 Government
FEDERAL land banks
 Money management; St Paul district bank's
  Co-farm loan program. R. Krumme. il Suc
  Farm 68:21 Je '70
FEDERAL lands. See Public lands—United
 States
FEDERAL medicine. See Medical service, State
FEDERAL national mortgage association
 Wall Street's favorite girl. il Time 96:90+
  D 7 '70
FEDERAL questionnaires. See Questionnaires
FEDERAL revenue sharing with states. See
 Intergovernmental tax relations
FEDERAL-state fiscal relations. See Intergov-
 ernmental fiscal relations

FEDERAL-state school lunch program. See
 School lunches
FEDERAL-state tax relations. See Intergov-
 ernmental tax relations
FEDERAL urban renewal programs. See Ur-
 ban renewal
FEDERALISM. See Federal government
FEDERATED department stores, inc.
 Federated's one-to-one commitment. Duns
  96:34 D '70
FEDERATED investors, inc. See Investment
 trusts
FEDERATION of American societies for ex-
 perimental biology
 Breaking up a giant. Sci N 97:429 My 2 '70
FEDERATION of diocesan liturgical commis-
 sions. See Catholic church—Liturgy and
 ritual
FEDERATION of Europe. See European fed-
 eration
FEDOROV, Evgenii Konstantinovich
 Antarctica: experimental proving ground for
  peaceful coexistence and international col-
  laboration. il por Bul Atom Sci 26:22-8 D
  '70
FEDOROV, Ye. K. See Fedorov, E. K.
FEE, Rodney J.
 Hog management (cont of) What's new. See
  issues of Successful farming
FEED grain plan. See Agricultural administra-
 tion
FEED grinders and grinding
 Feed center in a hayloft. il Suc Farm 68:
  G12 N '70
FEED mills (machinery) See Feed grinders and
 grinding
FEED supplements, Antibiotic. See Antibiotic
 feed supplements
FEEDBACK control systems
 Origins of feedback control; water clock, the
  thermostat and mechanisms for controll-
  ing windmills. O. Mayr. il Sci Am 223:110-
  18 O '70
FEEDER pig contracts. See Contracts, Agricul-
 tural
FEEDERS (birds)
 Bird feeding stations. J. Troy. il Ceram Mo
  18:13-15 Mr '70
 Ways to attract birds to your garden. M. D.
  Hodgins. il Home Gard 57:26-32 N '70
 What it attracts is a crowd. il Sunset 144:203
  F '70
FEEDERS, Poultry. See Poultry feeders
FEEDING and feeding stuffs
 Cropping strategy from eight top livestock
  setups. J. R. Borcherding. il Suc Farm 68:
  37-41 N '70
 Quick way to find feed bargains: by-product
  feeds. il Farm J 94:D6-7+ Je '70
 Test your forages and feed grains now. D.
  Rawson. Suc Farm 68:no3 G8 F '70
  See also
 Antibiotic feed supplements
 Cows—Feeding
 Feed grinders and grinding
 Forage plants
 Ralston Purina company
 Silage
 Sorghum
 Swine—Feeding

Amino acid content
 Other grains perform as well as corn. A. H.
  Jensen. Farm J 94:H18-19 N '70

Barley
 High-moisture barley. G. Lorang. Farm J
  94:B17 Ap '70

Copper content
 Copper improves hog gains, feed efficiency. J.
  Russell. Farm J 93:36B N '69

Corn
 Hogmen try high-lysine corn. B. Eftink. il
  Suc Farm 69:B8 Ja '71
 How that blighted corn is feeding. Farm J
  94:19 D '70
 Is ground corn the best feed? Suc Farm 68:
  A8 Ag '70
 More support for whole shelled corn. Farm J
  93:B27 N '69

Fiber content
 5 per cent roughage performs best in feeding
  trials. Farm J 93:B34 N '69

Grain
 New grain for livestock; triticale. C. P.
  Streeter. il Farm J 94:54L+ F '70
 New grain-processing methods. W. Kester.
  il Farm J 94:B10-11+ S '70

Manure
 Convert manure back into feed? N. Reeder.
  il Farm J 93:36K N '69

FEEDING and feeding stuffs—*Continued*

Medicated feed

How to avoid trouble with medicated hog feeds. R. Wilmore. Farm J 94:24E Ag '70
See also
Antibiotic feed supplements

Soybeans

Should you feed your own soybeans? hog nutrition. A. Oppedal. il Farm J 94:H10-11+ N '70
What are heated soybeans worth? hog rations. G. R. Carlisle. il Farm J 94:H18 Mr '70
What cooked soybeans are worth as feed. Suc Farm 62:no2 B 10 F '70

Testing

How to read feed test results. il Suc Farm 68:D8 O '70
Testing feed can save you money. il Suc Farm 68:D2-3 O '70

Wheat

How to feed a high-wheat finishing ration; interview. J. Algeo. il Farm J 93:B8-9 O '69
Wheat, your best feed buy now? C. E. Ball. Farm J 94:24C Ag '70
You can feed wheat. W. G. Luce. il Farm J 93:H16 N '69

FEEDING stations for birds. See Feeders (birds)

FEEDLOTS

Beef, eastern style; Greystone manor farms feedlot, Lancaster County, Pa. J. D. Ritchie. il Farm J 93:B20-21 N '69
Build a bruise-less feedlot. O. Bay. il Farm J 94:B20 Mr '70
Check this feeder's money-saving shortcuts. il Suc Farm 68:no2 58 F '70
Double-shift feedlot. G. Lorang. Farm J 94: B21 O '70
Farmer-feeders fight back; adapting commercial feedlot ideas and techniques. D. Seim. il Farm J 94:B36-37 F '70
Feedlot expansion in one jump. J. Hamilton. il Farm J 94:B12-13+ F '70
Feedlot with twenty acres under roof. il Farm J 94:B14 Ag '70
First feedlot financed by a foundation; LaJara feedlot financed by Ford foundation. O. Bay. il Farm J 93:B14 N '69
Grass feed steers? No more! shift to drylot. H. Simons. il Farm J 94:B11 O '70
He makes mechanical feeding work; interview, ed. by P. B. Jones. A. Clark. il Suc Farm 68:no3 26-7 F '70
He's a defensive feedlot operator. W. Messerly. Suc Farm 68:D22 N '70
How does this feeding operation look to you? il Suc Farm 68:no2 B14 F '70
How much shelter do feedlots really need? il Suc Farm 69:35-9 Ja '71
Ideas to improve your feedlot. il Suc Farm 69:B22 Ja '71
Low-cost feedlot: Edwin Aman, South Dakota. W. Waltner. il Suc Farm 68:D16-17 O '70
Low-cost feedlots: C. F. Cavanaugh, Iowa. J. Davis. il Suc Farm 68:D14 S '70
Low-cost feedlots: Dale Wyse, Ohio. J. Davis. il Suc Farm 68:D20 S '70
Low-cost feedlots: Kesslers & Mahnkens, Missouri. E. Stout. il Suc Farm 68:D16 S '70
New kind of order buyer; Vann-Roach cattle co. J. Bickers. Farm J 93:B23 N '69
New money to build feedlots. O. Bay. il Farm J 94:B10-11+ F '70
News from the beef-feeding industry. See issues of Farm journal
Pollution control system; feedlot runoff. W. Kester. il Farm J 94:B7+ N '70
Small feedlot pays if you're good enough. G. Lorang. il Farm J 94:B18 Mr '70
Space-age cattle feeders; computer record-keeping for feedlots. W. Kester. il Farm J 94:B22 F '70
Storm clouds over the big feedlots. W. Kester. il Farm J 94:B6-7 Ag '70
There's strength in numbers; feeders join forces to buy cattle directly from producers. il Farm J 94:B42 F '70
30,000-head feedlot in Michigan? J. D. Ritchie. il Farm J 94:B8-9+ Mr '70
We need more custom feedlots in the Northwest; interview, ed. by G. Lorang. L. Miller. il por Farm J 94:B40 F '70

FEELEY, Constance
American express; story. New Yorker 46:50-8 N 14 '70

FEES, Architects. See Architects—Fees

FEES, Tuition. See Colleges and universities —Finance

FEET. See Foot

FEGER, Lois
Dark dimension of Willa Cather's My Antonia. Engl J 59:774-9 S '70

FEICK, Ray E.
Developing a home study policy. Todays Ed 59:21 S '70

FEIFER, George
Requiem for Czechoslovakia. Read Digest 97:83-8 N '70

FEIFFER, Jules
Jules Feiffer. New Repub 162:19 My 23; 163:22 N 7; 21 D 5 '70
about
White House murder case. Criticism
Commonweal 92:143-5 Ap 24 '70 *
Nation 210:285 Mr 9 '70 *
New Yorker 46:78-9 F 28 '70 *
Newsweek il 75:78 Mr 2 '70 *
Sat R 53:12 Mr 7 '70 *
Time il 95:69 Mr 2 '70 *

FEIGEN gallery. See New York (city)—Galleries and museums

FEIGNED diseases. See Malingering

FEIN, Leonard J.
Limits of liberalism. il Sat R 53:83-5+ Je 20 '70

FEIN, Rashi
Case for national health insurance. il Sat R 53:27-9+ Ag 22 '70

FEINBERG, Gerald
Particles that go faster than light; with biographical sketch. il Sci Am 222:10, 68-73+ bibliog(p 126) F '70

FEINBERG, Mortimer R. and Tarrant, J. J.
How to make executives behave. il Nations Bsns 58:72-4 Ap '70

FEININGER, Andreas
Feininger. See issues of Modern photography

FEINMAN, Alvin
This tree; poem. Harper 241:16 O '70

FEINSOD, Fred M. and Douthit, H. A.
Ribosomes from spores of bacillus cereus T. bibliog il Science 168:991 My 22 '70

FEINSTEIN, Phylis
Advice from a nursing mother. Redbook 136:12-13+ N '70
—See Fish, S. A. jt. auth.

FEISAL, king of Saudi Arabia
Grand conspiracy; interview, ed. by A. de Borchgrave. King Faisal. por Newsweek 76:43 D 21 '70

FEIST, Gene. See Sloan, A. pseud.

FELBINGER, Marti
Color and camera; Marti Felbinger. il Pop Phot 66:84-7 My '70 *

FELD, Bernard T.
Scientist's role in arms control. Bul Atom Sci 26:7-8+ Ja '70
Sorry history of arms control. il Bul Atom Sci 26:22-6 S '70

FELD, Eliot
All this and dancing too. W. Terry. il por Sat R 53:48 Ap 25 '70 *
Dance. N. Goldner. Nation 210:477-8 Ap 20 '70 *
Three hits by Feld. W. Terry. il Sat R 53: 58 N 21 '70 *
Two Eliot Felds? D. Hering. il pors Dance Mag 45:59-65 Ja '71 *

FELD, Irvin
Greatest showman on earth. il por Time 95: 74+ My 4 '70 *

FELDBERG, Ross S. and Datta, P.
Threonine deaminase; a novel activity stain on polyacrylamide gels. bibliog il Science 170:1414-16 D 25 '70

FELDKAMP, Fred
Sporting scene. New Yorker 46:62+ Je 6 '70

FELDMAN, Irving
Warriors and the idiots; poem. Harper 240:51 Ap '70

FELDMAN, Leonard
Custom-tailored stereo. il Hi Fi 20:secI 42-7 Jl '70
Wire your backyard for stereo. il Hi Fi 20: secI 54-9 Je '70

FELDMAN, Mark B.
UNESCO committee drafts convention to protect cultural property; statement, April 13, 1970. Dept State Bul 63:22-4 Jl 6 '70

FELDMAN, Marvin J.
Zeroing-in on a program of zero rejects. Ed Digest 36:20-3 S '70

FELDMAN, Ruth
Small Christian; poem. Commonweal 92:297 Je 12 '70
(tr) See Pavese, C. Untitled
(tr) See Piccolo, L. Days

FELDSPAR
Cathodoluminescence properties of lunar rocks. R. F. Sippel and A. B. Spencer. bibliog il Science 167:677-9 Ja 30 '70
Crystallography of some lunar plagioclases. D. B. Stewart and others. bibliog il Science 167:634-5 Ja 30 '70
  See also
  Anorthosite

FELICIA amelloides. See Blue daisies

FELIG, Philip, and Lynch, Vincent
Starvation in human pregnancy: hypoglycemia, hypoinsulinemia, and hyperketonemia. bibliog il Science 170:990-2 N 27 '70
—and others
Alanine: key role in gluconeogenesis. bibliog il Science 167:1003-4 F 13 '70

FELIO, Harry Gordon
Papa Bonheur; chef at Grand hotel Oloffson, Haiti. P. O'Higgins. il McCalls 97:24+ Mr '70 *

FELKNOR, Bruce L.
Dreams and nightmares in the future for books; summary of address, October 6, 1970. ed. by D. B. Sutherland. Pub W 198: 26-7 N 2 '70

FELL, John L.
Dissolves by gaslight. bibliog il Film Q 23: 22-34 Spr '70

FELL, Joseph P.
Psychosocial analysis of sex-policing on campus; address, December 7, 1965. Sch & Soc 98:351-4 O '70

FELLINI, Federico
Federico Fellini on Satyricon; tr. by S. Morini. il por Vogue 155:168-71+ Mr 1 '70
Fellini's formula. il por Esquire 74:62-3+ Ag '70

      about
Current cinema. P. Kael. New Yorker 46: 134+ Mr 14 '70 *
Federico Fellini. D. Herman. bibliog il Am Imago 26:251-68 Fall '69 *
Fellini: he shoots dreams on film. B. Rollin. il pors Look 34:48-53 Mr 10 '70 *
Rome, B.C, A.F. il por Time 95:76-9+ Mr 16 '70 *
Whose Satyricon, Petronius's or Fellini's? G. Highet. bibliog f il por Horizon 12:42-7 Aut '70 *
Working with Fellini. B. Langman. il Mlle 70:74-5+ Ja '70

FELLMAN, Gordon, and others
Dagger in the heart of town: Mass. planners and Cambridge workers. il Trans-Action 7: 38-47 S '70

FELLOWSHIP of the Spirit
Fellowship of the Holy Spirit. H. A. Snyder. Chr Today 15:4-7 N 6 '70

FELLOWSHIPS. See Scholarships and fellowships

FELTRINELLI, Giangiacomo
Feltrinelli: there is no more personal a publisher. H. R. Lottman. pors Pub W 197: 60-2 F 2 '70 *
Trade winds. C. Amory. Sat R 53:4 Jl 4 '70 *

FELTRINELLI, Giangiacomo, editore. See Publishers and publishing—Italy

FEMINA, Jerry Della. See Della Femina, J.

FEMINA sapiens; story. See Elliott, G. P.

FEMINISM. See Woman—Equal rights; Womens liberation movement

Les FEMMES savantes; drama. See Molière, J. B. P.

FENCES
Facts on fence. R. Day. il Mech Illus 66: 93-5+ My '70
Pivoting fence for the pool. il Sunset 145: 122 O '70
Privacy screens that get admiring glances. il Pop Mech 134:158-9 Ag '70
Stylish fences serve a double purpose. il Home Gard 57:42 Je '70
They gained off-street parking, an entry patio. il Sunset 145:101 S '70
  See also
  Snow fences

FENCING
Face to face with the girl behind the sword. por Seventeen 29:86 My '70

FENDRICH, James, and Pearson, Michael
Black veterans return. il Trans-Action 7:32-7 Mr '70

FENDRICK, Louis R.
Conservation officer's job. il Cons 24:8-10 Ag '69
New York's snow patrol. il Cons 25:21-2 D '70

FENELL, Stella
Put your melons in new ground. il Org Gard & Farm 17:72-3 Ap '70

FENNELL, Perry C. Jr
New set of heroes. C. Lewis. il Am Ed 6:23 Ja '70 *

FENNIMORE, Flora
Developing the adolescent's self concept with literature. bibliog f Engl J 59:1272-5+ D '70

FENSTER, Leo
"Revolutionary" establishment. il Nation 211: 13-17 Jl 6 '70

FENTON, Tom
(ed) See Robbins, P. Antics

FENWICK, Daman Carlisle
How to ruin a beautiful retirement. il Har Yrs 10:22-4 Ap '70

FENWICK, Sara Innis
Getting along with reading teachers. bibliog il por Wilson Lib Bul 45:273-7 N '70

FEOKTISTOV, Konstantin
Roads of earth and space. il por Space World G-3-75:38-9 Mr '70

FERARU, Anne T.
Politics of earthmanship. Nat Parks & Con Mag 44:19 S '70

FERBER, Ellen
What makes humans human? il Am Ed 6:8-12 My '70

FEREBEE, Thomas W.
Where are they now? il pors Newsweek 76:10 Ag 10 '70 *

FERENCY, Neil
Ferroresonant transformer improves color TV. il Electr World 83:46-7 F '70

FERGUSON, C. Clyde, Jr
Relief and rehabilitation in Nigeria; statement, January 21, 1970. Dept State Bul 62:186-8 F 16 '70

FERGUSON, Denzel E. See Taylor, D. H. jt. auth.

FERGUSON, Eleanor A. See Humphry, J. A. jt. auth.

FERGUSON, George
Motor sports. il por Sports Illus 33:50+ N 9 '70

FERGUSON, Henrietta
Her gift to the Greeks: a touch of soul. il pors Ebony 25:134-6+ O '70 *

FERGUSON, James, 1913-
Military viewpoint; excerpts from address. Aviation W 92:11 Ja 19 '70

FERGUSON, James, and others
Hypersexuality and behavioral changes in cats caused by administration of p-chlorophenylalanine. bibliog il Science 168:499-501 Ap 24 '70

FERGUSON, John
John Ferguson, outreach librarian. il pors Wilson Lib Bul 45:424-5 D '70 *

FERGUSON, Walter
Wildlife of Sinai. il Audubon 72:32-41 Mr '70

FERGUSON, Wanda
Nasturtiums, cukes and tomatoes. il Org Gard & Farm 17:50-1 Mr '70
Perennials for cover-up jobs. il Org Gard & Farm 17:90-1 S '70
Something wonderful happened. Org Gard & Farm 17:78-9 Ja '70
Trouble with a steep bank. il Org Gard & Farm 17:76-7 F '70

FERIS, Charles
Tornado at Kent. Washington. on 12 December 1969. il Weatherwise 23:75-7+ Ap '70

FERLINGHETTI, Lawrence
Daredevil poetics: Ferlinghetti's definition of a poet. E. Kent. Engl J 59:1243-4+ D '70 *

FERM, Deane William
Latest scoop on Swedish sex. il Chr Cent 87: 45-8 Ja 14 '70

FERMI, Enrico
Enrico Fermi: physicist; excerpt. E. Segrè. il por Bul Atom Sci 26:32+ N '70 *

FERMI, Laura
Bombs or reactors? por Bul Atom Sci 26:28-9 Je '70

FERNANDEZ, Marta
La librería. New York. is center for Latin culture. il por Pub W 197:67-8 Ja 19 '70

FERNANDEZ DE LIZARDI, José Joaquín
Periquillo Sarniento. G. R. Pérez. il Américas 22:29-34 My '70 *

FERNÁNDEZ-MORÁN, H. and others
Mössbauer effect and high-voltage electron microscopy of pyroxenes in type B samples. bibliog il Science 167:686-8 Ja 30 '70

FERNANDINA ISLAND. See Galápagos Islands

FERNS
Five (or more) fingers of fern. il Sunset 144: 201 Je '70
Staghorn ferns. D. G. Huttleston. il Horticulture 48:26-7+ Je '70
Your garden indoors. F. S. David. il Home Gard 57:54 Ap '70
  See also
  Tree ferns

FERNSWORTH, Lawrence
Any port in a showdown. il Nation 211:489-91 N 16 '70

FERON, James
Time stands still in an Israeli-occupied town. il N Y Times Mag p30-3+ My 17 '70

FERONE, Robert, and others
Altered dihydrofolate reductase associated with drug-resistance transfer between rodent plasmodia. bibliog il Science 167:1263-4 F 27 '70
FERRARI, Enzo
Engines of Ing. Ferrari. G. Borgeson. il por Motor T 22:34-7+ N '70 *
FERRARI (sports car) See Sports cars
FERRÉ, Luis Alberto
Puerto Rico tries to cure sugar's ills. il Bsns W p61+ O 10 '70 *
FERREIRA, Ricardo
Chemists' involvement in society. bibliog il pors Chem 43:16-17 O; 12-13 D '70
FERRELL, Oliver P.
Direct & current. Pop Electr 33:7-8 S; 7 O; 7 N; 7 D '70; 34:7 Ja '71
FERRELL, Robert H.
Conversations with historians; excerpts from Interpreting American history, ed. by J. A. Garraty. il por Am Heritage 21:60-2 F '70
FERRELL, Tom
If the silent majority could talk, what would it say? pors Esquire 73:146-51+ My '70
FERREN, William P.
How rotten can you get? Motor B 126:66-9+ O '70
FERRER, José Figueres. See Figueres Ferrer, J.
FERRETS
Reporter at large; controlling the prairie dog and protecting the black-footed ferret, in South Dakota. F. McNulty. New Yorker 46: 40-2+ Je 13 '70
FERRI, Jim
Rhine; photographs. Travel & Camera 33: 20-4 O '70
FERRICYTOCHROME. See Cytochromes
FERRIES
Commuters, ahoy! ferry system in San Francisco. il Newsweek 76:83-4 O 12 '70
Great way to explore Sydney Harbour is by ferry. il Sunset 144:39+ Mr '70
New ferry from San Francisco to Sausalito. il Sunset 145:55 O '70
See also
Shipwrecks
FERRIS, John
Disadvantaged youth. Opera N 34:13 Mr 14 '70
Ironing. Sat R 53:12+ N 21 '70
Jug jug jug jug tu-whit tu-whoo; Sat R 53:4 Jl 11 '70
Memory of Grover A. Whalen restores my faith in the art of Wetzel the tailor. Sat R 53:4 Mr 7 '70
Press conference. Sat R 53:4 S 5 '70
FERRISS, Abbott L.
Social and personality correlates of outdoor recreation. bibliog f il Ann Am Acad 389:46-55 My '70
FERRITES (magnetic materials)
Ferrite-core memories. R. A. Hill. il por Electr World 84:49-52 O '70
FERRO-cement boats. See Boats—Materials
FERROCENE. See Organometallic compounds
FERROMAGNETISM. See Magnetism
FERRY, W. H.
Is a police state emerging? excerpts from address, Oct. 10, 1969. Cur 115:33-6 F '70
FERTILITY
Clutch size in birds: outcome of opposing predator and prey adaptations. R. E. Ricklefs. bibliog il Science 168:599-600 My 1 '70; Reply with rejoinder. J. Ghiselin. 170:649-51 N 6 '70
Nest parasitism, productivity, and clutch size in purple martins. W. W. Moss and J. H. Camin. bibliog il Science 168:1000-3 My 22 '70; Discussion. 170:1112 D 4 '70
FERTILITY, Human
See also
Conception
FERTILITY control. See Birth control
FERTILITY drugs
Fertility. il Newsweek 75:45 Mr 9 '70
FERTILITY of soils. See Soil fertility
FERTILIZATION (biology)
See also
Spermatozoa
FERTILIZATION (in vitro)
Fertility; test-tube baby experiment in England. il Newsweek 75:45 Mr 9 '70
Human embryos in the laboratory. R. G. Edwards and R. E. Fowler. il Sci Am 223: 44-54 bibliog(p 140) D '70
Test-tube babies: how soon? D. R. Zimmerman. Ladies Home J 87:32+ S '70
FERTILIZATION, Artificial. See Artificial insemination, Human
FERTILIZATION of plants
Pollination, vital link in plant life. E. C. Ogden. il Cons 24:21-7+ Ap '70
Teacher tips: pollination. J. A. Weeks. il Cons 24:32 Ap '70

FERTILIZER handling. See Fertilizers and manures—Handling
FERTILIZER industry and trade
Fertilizer makers make sales grow. il Bsns W p21-2 Jl 11 '70
How fertilizer dealers plan to win your order. B. Coffman. Farm J 94:54E F '70
One man's poison. il Forbes 105:56 Ap 1 '70
FERTILIZER spreaders
Faster ways to fertilize. C. E. Sommers. il Suc Farm 68:no4 28-9 Mr '70
Power loads the fertilizer fast. il Farm J 94: 48-9 F '70
FERTILIZERS and manures
Corn comes out, fertilizer goes on; fall farming. R. D. Wennblom. il Farm J 93:40 O '69
Fall fertilization adds flexibility. Suc Farm 68:46 S '70
Fertilizers and eutrophication. W. L. Meachem. Home Gard 57:44-5 S '70
Fertilizing lawns. il Consumer Bul 53:36 Ag '70
For better spring plants, fertilize this fall. Home Gard 57:44-5 S '70
How to fertilize growing crops organically during the summer. J. S. Park. Org Gard & Farm 17:42-3 Jl '70
More on eutrophication. F. R. Rickson. Home Gard 58:20+ Ja '71
Pollution, your problem, too; fertilizer and erosion. R. Sanders. il Suc Farm 68:14-15 N '70
Pollution, your problem, too; manure pollution control. R. Sanders. il Suc Farm 68: 34-5 O '70
Weed for all gardens. C. F. Bieber. il Org Gard & Farm 17:60-1 F '70
See also
Compost
Feeding and feeding stuffs—Manure
Lawns
Mulching
Sewage as fertilizer
Sewage irrigation

Handling
Animal polluters. il Time 96:51 S 14 '70
Feedlot pollution control. W. Kester. Farm J 94:B7 Ap '70
Foresight can save your eyes; anhydrous ammonia. Suc Farm 69:22 Ja '71
Manure handling costs. Farm J 94:B17 N '70
Manure mounds. W. Kester. il Farm J 94:B10 O '70
Oxidation ditches can eliminate odors, manure handling and pollution. J. Russell. Farm J 94:H10+ Ag '70
Pollution control system; feedlot runoff. W. Kester. il Farm J 94:B7+ N '70
Pollution, your problem, too; manure pollution control. R. Sanders. il Suc Farm 68:34-5 O '70
Sewage plant designed for livestock wastes. B. Lovelidge. il Farm J 94:54B-54C F '70
Tips for fertilizer handling. il Suc Farm 68: D14 Ap '70

Spreaders
See Fertilizer spreaders
FESCUE
Fescue tops corn profits. D. Dailey. il Suc Farm 68:no4 42 Mr '70
FESOLOWICH, A. and others
Fiber composite alloys; preparation by controlled dissociation of metallic solid solutions. bibliog il Science 167:1374-6 Mr 6 '70
FESQUET, H.
(ed) See Suenens, L. Cardinal Suenens: a plea for dialogue
FESSENDEN, Clara L.
What's cooking? il Org Gard & Farm 17:132-3+ Mr '70
FESTIVALS
World travel calendar, 1971; comp. by F. Shemanski. Sat R 54:37-8+ Ja 2 '71
See also
Dance festivals
Drama festivals
Indians of North America—Rites and ceremonies
International festival of music and drama, Edinburgh
Moving picture festivals
Music festivals
Shakespeare festivals

California
Cult of history; Renaissance pleasure faire. il Newsweek 76:102-3 S 28 '70
Dog-sledding, snowshoeing, and gunny-sack hopping. il Sunset 144:38-9 F '70
Lifestyle; Renaissance pleasure faires. il Am Home 73:12 S '70

England
Calendar for June events. il Travel & Camera 33:70-1 My '70

FESTIVALS—*Continued*

France

Letter from Paris; special entertainments during Grande semaine de Paris. Genêt. New Yorker 46:59-61 Je 27 '70

Letter from Paris; summer festival drama and music offerings. Genêt. New Yorker 46:69-70 Ag 8 '70

Germany (Federal Republic)

Bacchanal in Bavaria; Oktoberfest. P. Moor. il Sat R 53:62+ S 12 '70

Munich in October. F. Spelman. il Travel & Camera 33:30-5 O '70

Oktoberfest, mit chaser; Munich. H. Kenner. il Nat R 22:35+ Ja 13 '70

Hawaii

Bon dancing this summer in Hawaii. il Sunset 145:44 Jl '70

India

Cobra, India's good snake. H. Miller. il Nat Geog 138:392-409 S '70

Italy

Report:
 Productions at Spoleto. W. Weaver. Opera N 35:25 S 19 '70

Mexico

Day of the mules. il Américas 22:40-3 Je '70

Missouri

Seeing it like it was; folk festivals. H. E. Dark. il Todays Health 48:30-3 O '70

New Guinea

Presenting: the very recent past; Hagen show. M. Mead. il N Y Times Mag p28-9+ Mr 15 '70

New York (state)

Notes of a young radical; arts festival at Columbia university to benefit political prisoners. G. H. C. Knox. il Sat R 53:48-51+ Ag 15 '70

Thunder on the Finger Lakes; Grape festival at Naples. D. Butwin. il Sat R 53:53-4 N 7 '70

Yes; festival on the Central park mall called The people, yes! New Yorker 46:42-3 O 24 '70

Ohio

Festival king: Ohio. B. Thomas. il Travel 133:36-41 Ja '70

Happenings at Kent state: fifth annual Creative arts festival. A. Rich. il Hi Fi 20: secII 27+ My '70

Spain

Profiles; Valencia's spring and summer *ferias.* K. Tynan. il New Yorker 46:33-8+ Jl 25 '70

Switzerland

October's Swiss wine festivals. il Sunset 145: 8 O '70

United States

Summer music festivals '70 (title varies) Hi Fi 20:secII 22-4 Ap '70

Utah

Snowy high jinks coming in Utah. il Sunset 144:45-6 F '70

Wyoming

See also
Rodeos

FETROS, John G.
 Library research: using what we have. bibliog il Am Lib 1:360-4 Ap '70

FETUS
 Checkup for the unborn; withdrawing the amniotic fluid. R. Gore. il Life 69:73-4+ S 18 '70

Fetal movement: development and time course. D. D. Edwards and J. S. Edwards. bibliog il Science 169:95-7 Jl 3 '70

Fetuses for sale? London clinic accused of selling fetuses for research. il Newsweek 75:86 Je 1 '70

Insulin release from isolated human fetal pancreatic islets. A. Espinosa de los Monteros M. and others. bibliog il Science 168: 1111-12 My 29 '70

Live fetuses for sale. America 122:600 Je 6 '70

Right to be well-born; fetology. W. Cole. il Todays Health 49:42-4+ Ja '71

FETUS, Effect of drugs on the
 Pregnancies after chemotherapy of trophoblastic neoplasms. D. H. Van Thiel and others. bibliog il Science 169:1326-7 S 25 '70

FETUS, Effect of radiation on the
 Strontium-90: effects of chronic ingestion on farrowing performance of miniature swine. W. J. Clarke and others. bibliog il Science 169:598-600 Ag 7 '70

FETUS, Effect of viruses on the
 Fetal response to viral infection: interferon production in sheep. J. C. Overall, jr. and L. A. Glasgow. bibliog il Science 167: 1139-41 F 20 '70

FEUER, Lewis S.
 Ernst Mach: the unconscious motives of an empiricist. bibliog Am Imago 27:12-40 Spr '70

about

Inevitable American tragedy. il Sci N 97: 451-2 My 9 '70 *

FEUERMANN, Emanuel
 Feuermann mementos. H. Goldsmith. Hi Fi 20:secI 112 Ap '70 *

FEUERSINGER, Harry R.
 More tips from a puzzle specialist. Writers Digest 50:33 My '70

FEVER
 Fever and fever thermometers. il Changing T 24:16 My '70
 See also
 Lassa fever

FEVER thermometers. See Thermometers-Clinical

FEW, A. A.
 Lightning and the new-generation aircraft. Science 168:1011 My 22 '70

FEW days of summer; story. See Kjelgaard, B.

FEYDY, Anne
 Parlor feminist; story. Redbook 135:72-3 Jl '70

FIAT (automobile) See Automobiles, Foreign

FIAT company. See Automobile industry and trade—Italy

FIBBING. See Lying

FIBERGLASS boats. See Boats—Materials

FIBERGLASS canoes. See Canoes and canoeing

FIBERGLASS sailboats. See Sailboats—Materials

FIBERS
 Density-modulus relationship in graphite fibers made from acrylic yarns. H. M. Ezekiel. bibliog il Science 169:178-9 Jl 10 '70

Heavy betting on a light fiber; graphite. Bsns W p33 Ja 31 '70

Not yet for the birds; graphite fibers. Sci N 97:597 Je 20 '70
 See also
 Metal fibers
 Textile fibers, Synthetic

FIBRINOGEN
 Shear degradation of fibrinogen in the circulation. S. E. Charm and B. L. Wong. bibliog il Science 170:466-8 O 23 '70

FIBRINOPEPTIDES. See Peptides

FIBROBLASTS
 Cystinosis: selective induction of vacuolation in fibroblasts by L-cysteine-D-penicillamine disulfide. J. D. Schulman and K. H. Bradley. bibliog il Science 169:595-7 Ag 7 '70

Dentin matrix transformation: rapid induction of alkaline phosphatase and cartilage. C. B. Huggins and M. R. Urist. bibliog il Science 167:896-8 F 6 '70

Desmosterol as the major sterol in L-cell mouse fibroblasts grown in sterol-free culture medium. G. H. Rothblat and others. bibliog il Science 169:880-2 Ag 28 '70

Diploid azaguanine-resistant mutants of cultured human fibroblasts. R. J. Albertini and R. DeMars. bibliog il Science 169:482-5 Jl 31 '70

Electrical coupling: low resistance junctions between mitotic and interphase fibroblasts in tissue culture. P. O'Lague and others. il Science 170:464-6 O 23 '70

5-Hydroxytryptamine: a cytospecific growth stimulator of cultured fibroblasts. R. J. Boucek and T. R. Alvarez. bibliog il Science 167:898-9 F 6 '70

FIBROID tumors. See Tumors

FIBROSARCOMA virus. See Tumor viruses

FICHTER, Joseph H.
 Catholic church professionals. bibliog f Ann Am Acad 387:77-85 Ja '70

Holy Father church. Commonweal 92:216-18 My 15 '70

about

Jesuit high school. R. A. Schroth. Commonweal 91:472-5 Ja 30 '70

FICK, Alvin S.
 Ferdinand, the friendly bull moose. il Cons 25:2-3 D '70

What you can do about the environment. il Cons 25:489+ D '70

FICKER, Bill
 America's cup. il por Newsweek 76:60-3 S 21 '70 *

Intrepid indeed. por Time 96:39 Ag 3 '70 *

FICKLING, Skip
 And then there was Sidney Greenstreet. . ? Writer 83:14-16 N '70

FIELDS, Paul R. and others
Isotopic abundances of actinide elements in lunar material. bibliog il Science 167:499-501 Ja 30 '70

FIESTAS. See Festivals

FIFE, Alta. See Fife. A. E. jt. auth.

FIFE, Austin E. and Fife, Alta
Pug-nosed Lil and The girl with the blue velvet band. il pors Am West 7:32-7 Mr '70
Spurs and saddlebags. il Am West 7:44-6 S '70

FIFE and drum corps. See Bands (music)

FIFTEENTH amendment to the Constitution. See United States—Constitution—Amendments

FIFTH avenue. See New York (city)—Streets

FIFTH committee of the General assembly. See United Nations—Administrative and budgetary committee

FIFTY books of the year exhibit. See Book exhibits

FIG wasps. See Wasps

FIGGIS, John Neville
Figgis, Constance and the Divines of Paris; excerpts from address, December 30, 1966. F. Oakley. bibliog f Am Hist R 75:368-86 D '69 *

FIGHT between a white boy and a black boy in the dusk of a fall afternoon in Omaha, Nebraska; story. See Morris, W.

FIGHTING (psychology)
Can fighting make a good marriage better? G. Krupp. il Redbook 134:62-3+ F '70
See also
Aggressiveness (psychology)

FIGHTING, Hand-to-hand
See also
Karate

FIGS
Figs, right from your own tree! L. Riotte. il Org Gard & Farm 17:31-3 My '70

FIGUERES FERRER, José
Don Pepe's return. il por Time 95:33 F 16 '70 *

FIGURE drawing
Modeling in clay; helping students learn the initial study of the human figure. T. S. Dahood. il Design 71:13 Sum '70
See also
Human figure in art

FIGURE skating. See Skating

FIGURES of speech
Watch your figure. J. Stewart. Writer 83:24-7 Ap '70

FIGURINES
English earthenware figures in the Lake collection of the Everson museum. il Antiques 98:410-17 S '70
Porcelains for world figures; Cybis art porcelain studio, Trenton, N.J. P. Roberts. il Design 72:26-8 Wint '70

FIJI
Fijis; new island fling on the South Pacific swing. M. R. Henry. il Vogue 157:28 Ja 1 '71
Five hundred lime-green islands. J. Griffin. il Sat R 53:43-4+ O 24 '70
See also
Hotels, taverns, etc.—Fiji
Investments, Foreign (in Fiji)
Naitamba (island)
Suva
Tourist trade—Fiji
United Nations—Fiji

FIJI airways. See Airlines—Fiji

FILBERT, John W. See Graham, J. L. jt. auth.

FILES, Police. See Police records

FILES and filing (documents, etc)
This filing system works. R. W. Menning and L. L. Statler. Suc Farm 68:no3 A6 F '70

FILES and rasps
Facts on files. R. J. De Cristoforo. il Mech Illus 66:94-6 Ag '70

FILIBUSTERING in legislation. See United States—Congress—Senate—Rules and practice

FILION, Herve
Marlu has a bit of trouble. W. F. Reed. il por Sports Illus 33:22-3 Ag 24 '70 *

FILIP, Ota
Writers' block. il pors Newsweek 75:38+ Mr 2 '70 *

FILIPINOS in the United States navy. See United States—Navy—Foreign enlistments

FILIPOV, Alexander
From Russia with love. N. M. Stoop. il pors Dance Mag 44:30-3 D '70 *

FILLERS (in periodicals) See Periodical fillers

FILLETS, Fish. See Fish fillets

FILLING (earthwork)
Big loader offsets burning ban; Marshfield, Mass. E. Williams. il Am City 85:60-1 D '70
Double the life of your landfill; Millville, N.J. W. E. Shaw. il Am City 85:64 Je '70

How to doctor a quarry for landfill; Montgomery County, Pa. J. A. McHenry. il Am City 85:38 D '70
Monster; super compactor, Savannah, Ga. H. W. Jenkins. il Am City 85:146 S '70
Solution to garbage disposal with park land as the bonus; sanitary landfill. M. Villecco. il Arch Forum 133:60-2 N '70

FILLING stations. See Automobile service stations

FILLMORE, Charles
Heaven on earth. R. Rhodes. il Harper 240:116-22 My '70 *

FILLMORE, Myrtle
Heaven on earth. R. Rhodes. il Harper 240:116-22 My '70 *

FILLOUX, Jean
Deep-sea tides 1250 kilometers off Baja California. bibliog il Science 169:862-4 Ag 28 '70

FILM adaptations
Film: a share in the great tradition. J. G. Boyum and A. Scott. il Schol Teach Jr/Sr High p24-5 N 2 '70
I see everything twice: an examination of Catch-22. C. Thegze. il Film Q 24:7-17 Fall '70
Musical Scrooge: bah! Humbug! G. Shalit. il Look 34:28-32 D 15 '70
Rights and permissions. P. Nathan. See issues of Publishers' weekly

FILM critics. See Critics

FILM festival, Cannes. See Cannes international film festival

FILM festivals. See Moving picture festivals

FILM magazines. See Cameras—Loading

FILM strips
Countdown 3-2-1-0-we're off! P. E. Schwing. il Sch Arts 70:34 N '70
Do-it-yourself film kit. il Consumer Bul 53:35 Ag '70
Evaluation gap: a/v reviewing. J. French. bibliog il Library J 95:1162-6+ Mr 15 '70
Film clips for film study? letter to the editor. R. E. Sutton. Library J 95:3939-40 N 15 '70
Screenings: filmstrips. D. Lembo. See occasional issues of Library journal

FILMS
New polychroic film gives you amazing color effects. A. J. Hand. il Pop Sci 196:60-1 Je '70
Surface films compacted by moving water: demarcation lines reveal film edges. C. W. McCutchen. bibliog il Science 170:61-4 O 2 '70
See also
Photography—Films
Thin films

FILMS, Metallic
Solar control film; metallized reflective film. il Space World G-5-77:9-11 My '70

FILMS from books. See Film adaptations

FILMSTRIPS. See Film strips

FILOGAMO, Martin J.
New angle on accountability. Todays Ed 59:53 My '70

FILTER plants
Curious-yellow; pre-treatment with potassium permanganate; Pittsburgh. J. D. Beck. il Am City 85:73-6 Mr '70
Zeta-potential plus people potential; Longueuil, Quebec. D. Lamoureux. il por Am City 85:93-4+ F '70

FILTERS, Light. See Light filters

FILTERS and filtration
See also
Air filters
Filter plants
Water purification

FILTH in food. See Food contamination

FINAL answer; story. See Campbell, M.

FINANCE
See also
Banks and banking
Business conditions
Capital
Church finance
Commerce
Credit
Depreciation
Domestic finance
Farm finance
Housing finance
Inflation (finance)
Interest
Investment trusts
Investments
Loans
Money
Municipal finance
Negotiable instruments
Speculation
Stocks
also subhead Finance under various subjects e.g. Corporations—Finance

FINANCE—*Continued*

Study and teaching

Acid test; course in applied security analysis and investment management at Wisconsin university. il Newsweek 77:55 Ja 4 '71

Brazil

See also
Banks and banking—Brazil

Canada

Ottawa unpegs its dollar and waits. il Bsns W p32+ Je 6 '70
See also
Inflation (finance)
Money—Canada

Finland

See also
Inflation (finance)

Germany

See also
Money—Germany

Germany (Federal Republic)

See also
Inflation (finance)

Great Britain

See also
Banks and banking—Great Britain
Budget—Great Britain
Great Britain—Exchequer

Italy

See also
Money—Italy

Japan

See also
Japan—Economic conditions
Stock exchange—Tokyo

United States

As bankers see it: a slow rise in '71. il U S News 69:80-3 D 14 '70
What's ahead for business; interview. G. A. Freeman, jr. por U S News 68:38-41 Je 29 '70
See also
Bonds, Government
Budget—United States
Debts, Public—United States
Inflation (finance)
State finance
Stock exchange—New York (city)
Taxation—United States
United States—Appropriations and expenditures
United States—Budget, Bureau of the
United States—Commission on financial institutions (proposed)
United States—Economic conditions
United States—Environmental financing authority (proposed)
United States—Federal reserve board
United States—Monetary policy
Wall Street
also subhead Finance under names of cities, e.g. New York (city)—Finance

FINANCE, international

American business and international investment flows; address, December 11, 1969. N. Samuels. Dept State Bul 62:33-8 Ja 12 '70
Economic report of the President and the annual report of the Council of economic advisers; excerpts. R. M. Nixon. il Dept State Bul 62:240-53 Mr 2 '70
International finance. P. A. Samuelson. Newsweek 76:84 O 5 '70
See also
Balance of payments
Banks and banking, International
Eurodollar market
Foreign exchange
International bank for reconstruction and development
International monetary fund
Investments, Foreign
Loans, Foreign
Money—International aspects
Special drawing rights

FINANCE, Personal

Make 1971 your bench-mark year. il Changing T 25:6-10 Ja '71
Next, the financial supermarket. il U S News 68:100-1 My 18 '70
Spending your money; questions and answers. S. Porter. See issues of Ladies' home journal
Your personal finances. il Todays Ed 59: 68-70 O; 49-52 N; 46-8 D '70
See also
Consumer credit
Estate planning

Bibliography

Oracles of disaster. Newsweek 77:55+ Ja 4 '71

FINANCE, School. See School finance

FINANCE companies

Big change in small loans. Bsns W p48+ Je 13 '70
See also
GAC corporation

FINANCIAL institutions

Changing the rules; exchange membership. C. Morgello. il Newsweek 76:80 O 26 '70
Finance; with yardsticks of management performance. il Forbes 105:140+ Ja 1 '70; 107: 173-5 Ja 1 '71
Next, the financial supermarket. il U S News 68:100-1 My 18 '70
See also
Finance companies
Insurance companies
Investment trusts
Savings and loan associations
United States—Commission on financial institutions (proposed)

Investments

Where are the buyers? C. Morgello. il Newsweek 76:84 N 9 '70
Why the big traders worry industry. il Bsns W p52-7+ Jl 25 '70

FINANCIAL public relations. See Investor relations programs

FINANCIAL ratios

Ratios of manufacturing; with table (cont) Duns 96:70-3 N '70

FINANCIAL statements

Make your net worth grow. il Suc Farm 68:44 S '70
Watch the balance sheet. C. Morgello. il Newsweek 75:70 Ap 13 '70
See also
Corporation reports
Farm records

FINANCIERS. See Capitalists and financiers

FINCH, Robert Hutchison

Aches and pains of Robert Finch. Nation 210:644 Je 1 '70 *
Exit Dr Yolles. il por Newsweek 75:91-2 Je 15 '70 *
Finch: besieged and beleaguered; protesters occupy his office. il U S News 68:89 My 25 '70 *
Finch: first casualty of the Nixon Cabinet. il por Time 95:12-13 Je 15 '70 *
Finch steps down, to the White House. il por Newsweek 75:24-5 Je 15 '70 *
Finch's try for vindication. Time 95:13 Je 22 '70 *
Good soldier Finch. por Newsweek 75:30+ Je 1 '70 *
Health, education, and welfare of Robert Finch. S. McBee. il pors McCalls 97:58-9+ Jl '70 *
High-powered boss in a hot seat. I. Ross. por Read Digest 96:117-21 Mr '70 *
Integrating friends. J. Osborne. New Repub 162:12-14 Ap 18 '70 *
Nixon's liberal. Nation 210:739-40 Je 22 '70 *
On the beach with an old friend. H. Sidey. pors Life 68:2 Je 26 '70 *
Real Robert Finch stands up. R. Sherrill. il pors N Y Times Mag p6-7+ Jl 5 '70 *
Rescue of Bob Finch. J. Newcombe. il pors Life 68:32-3 Je 19 '70 *
Saving Bob Finch. J. Osborne. New Repub 162:9-10 Je 20 '70 *
Secretary Finch; how much is his influence waning? il por U S News 68:17 Mr 9 '70 *
Secretary Finch is not alarmed. J. Carper. Nation 210:262-5 Mr 9 '70 *
Sickness at HEW. por Time 95:56 Je 15 '70 *
Step in the right direction. M. McGrory. America 122:643 Je 20 '70 *

FINCH college, New York

Let 'em eat coquilles Saint-Jacques. T. Meehan. il N Y Times Mag p6-7+ D 27 '70

Museum of art

Streamlined style; Art Deco exhibition. D. Davis. il Newsweek 76:99 N 9 '70

FINCHER, Jack

How to talk to your children. il McCalls 98: 16+ Ja '71
Why are we afraid of these children? il McCalls 97:41+ Ag '70

FINCHES

Vocal imitation and individual recognition of finch calls. P. C. Mundinger. bibliog il Science 168:480-2 Ap 24 '70
See also
Indigo buntings

FINCK, Elliott
Root art. M. Dunn. il Design 71:14-16 Spr '70 *
FIND (friendless, isolated, needy, or disabled) project. See National council on the aging
FINDERS, View. See View finders
FINDLEY, Rowe
Old Salem: morning star of Moravian faith. il Nat Geog 138:818-37 D '70
FINE, David Sylvan
Madison bombers. il pors Newsweek 76:28-9 S 14 '70 *
FINEBERG, S. E. and Merimee, T. J.
Proinsulin: metabolic effects in the human forearm. bibliog il Science 167:998-9 F 13 '70
FINEMAN, Morton
Cartwheels; story. Ladies Home J 87:106-7 My '70
FINES, Library. See Libraries—Fines
FINGER, Harold B.
New model in housing; interview, ed. by G. R. Rosen. por Duns 95:10-11+ Je '70
FINGER, Seymour M.
Declaration on the twenty-fifth anniversary of the United Nations; statements, October 9 and 22, 1970. Dept State Bul 63:631-3 N 16 '70
Implementation of declaration on decolonization; statement, October 12, 1970. Dept State Bul 63:635 N 16 '70
U.S. abstains on U.N. resolution on Portuguese territories; statement, November 14, 1969. Dept State Bul 61:641-2 D 29 '69
U.S. discusses preparations for World youth assembly; statement, June 2, 1970. Dept State Bul 62:782-3 Je 22 '70
U.S. suggests fresh approach to study of decolonization; statement, April 1, 1970. Dept State Bul 62:557-60 Ap 27 '70
FINGER LAKES
Finger Lakes turnover trout. E. R. Belak, jr. il Cons 24:14-15 Ag '69
Thunder on the Finger Lakes. D. Butwin. il Sat R 53:53-4+ N 7 '70
See also
Cayuga Lake
FINGERLAP joints. See Joints (carpentry)
FINGERPRINTS
How good are you as a dactyloscopist? quiz. J. Daugherty and M. Daugherty. il Sci Digest 68:76-7+ O '70
See also
Dermatoglyphics
FINISHING, Textile. See Textile finishing
FINISHING materials
Cans; liquid finishes. il Bet Hom & Gard 48:46-7+ Ja '70
Testing
See also
Fire testing
FINK, Newton W. and Cullers, Benjamin
Student unrest. bibliog Clear House 44:415-19 Mr '70
FINK, Ronn
Overdue. por Wilson Lib Bul 45:308-9 N '70
FINKE, Walter
Walter Finke of Dictaphone corp; interview. pors Nations Bsns 58:46-7+ Mr '70
FINKELMAN, Robert B.
Magnetic particles extracted from manganese nodules; suggested origin from stony and iron meteorites. bibliog il Science 167:982-4 F 13 '70
FINKELSTEIN, Louis
Color as system. il Craft Horiz 30:42-3+ Mr '70
FINKLE, Dave
Discussions. See issues of Senior Scholastic
FINLAND
See also
Architecture, Domestic—Finland
Booksellers and bookselling—Finland
Finns
Helsinki
Description and travel
Finns and Finlandia; Hämeenlinna and Tampere. D. Butwin. il Sat R 53:54+ Mr 14 '70
Flight check to Finland. D. Messinesi. Vogue 155:60 Ap 15 '70
Winter fun in Finland. P. Patricoff. il Travel 133:52-6 Ja '70
Economic policy
Finland's formula for deflating inflation; interview. K. Waris. il por Nations Bsns 58:36-8 Ag '70
Foreign relations
Man on a tightrope; Moscow and Washington visits of U. K. Kekkonen. Newsweek 76:28 Ag 3 '70

Russia
See Russia—Foreign relations—Finland

United States
See United States—Foreign relations—Finland

Religious institutions and affairs
See also
Christians in Finland

Social life and customs
Finnish delight: fun, people, saunas. S. Morini. il Vogue 155:126-9+ Ap 15 '70
FINLEY, Charles O.
Should seals wear spats? Newsweek 75:87 Je 29 '70 *
FINLEY, James W.
White like me. il por Newsweek 75:76 Je 22 '70 *
FINLEY, Lawrence, and Mucha, Ronald
How to calculate refuse collection and disposal costs. Am City 85:88+ S '70
FINN, James
Daniel Berrigan winds the spring tighter. Commonweal 92:145-8 Ap 24 '70
Francois Mauriac. Commonweal 93:320-2+ D 25 '70
about
James Finn: editor at large. Chr Cent 87:317 Mr 18 '70 *
FINNEGAN, Barbara C.
Analysis of O'Connor's First confession. Engl J 59:48-51 Ja '70
FINNELL, Carolyn
I have the chance to try. Todays Ed 59:74-5 N '70
FINNEY, Albert
Musical Scrooge: bay! Humbug! G. Shalit. il pors Look 34:28-32 D '70
FINNISH baths. See Sauna
FINNISH cookery. See Cookery, Finnish
FINNS
Finnish delight: fun, people, saunas. S. Morini. il Vogue 155:126-9+ Ap 15 '70
FIONA; story. See Morris, W.
FIORDS. See Fjords
FIORENTINI, Adriana, and Maffei, Lamberto
Electrophysiological evidence for binocular disparity detectors in human visual system. bibliog il Science 169:208-9 Jl 10 '70
FIORI, Pamela
Boom town in the Bahamas. il Holiday 47:56-9 F '70
Undiscovered Italy. il Holiday 48:40-1+ Jl '70
FIR
White fir. D. Wyman. il Horticulture 48:44-5 S '70
See also
Balsam fir
Douglas fir
FIRE alarms
Computerized fire alarm; Dr Brick's system. il Am City 85:32 Ag '70
Sensitive burglar and fire alarm. F. H. Tooker. il Electr World 83:58-9 Je '70
FIRE ant venom. See Venom
FIRE ants. See Ants
FIRE apparatus
Hall of flame; museum at Kenosha, Wis. H. E. Smith. il Har Yrs 10:19 Ja '70
See also
Pumps
FIRE apparatus, Motor. See Fire engines
FIRE arms. See Firearms
FIRE control (aerial gunnery)
New gunsight concept evaluated; lead-computing optical gunsight. B. Miller. il Aviation W 93:40-1+ Ag 17 '70
FIRE departments
Public works fire wranglers; Scottsdale, Ariz. L. B. Witzeman and M. G. Stragier. il Am City 85:108+ My '70
See also
Firemen
Communications systems
Fire-police communications; St Joseph, Mo. B. H. Jones. il Am City 85:91+ Jl '70
FIRE engines
Fuel tank filters give fire engines more pep; Spokane, Wash. il Am City 85:48 N '70
Special-duty fire fighting; Lansing, Michigan's mini-fighter. il Am City 85:68 Ag '70
Yellow fire truck no longer curious; West Covina, Calif. C. I. Brandt. il Am City 85:26 Je '70

FIRE engines—*Continued*

History

Inflammatory art: nineteenth-century fire-engine panels. il Am Heritage 21:40-5 Je '70

FIRE escapes, Portable
Oriental way out! Safetydan escape cables. il Mech Illus 66:34 S '70

FIRE extinction
See also
Fire engines
Fire sprinklers

FIRE extinguishers
Fire extinguishers. Consumer Rep 34:144-7 D '69

FIRE fighting. See Fire protection

FIRE hydrants. See Hydrants

FIRE ISLAND
Barrier beaches of Eastern America. C. J. Schuberth. il Natur Hist 79:46-55 Je '70

FIRE losses. See Fires

FIRE-police officers. See Public safety officers

FIRE prevention. See Fire protection

FIRE protection
Don't let a mirror set your house on fire! il Consumer Bul 53:35 N '70
Fire protection guide on hazardous materials; Fire protection handbook. Consumer Bul 53:33 S '70
Preventing child burns. I. N. Holloway. il PTA Mag 64:14-15 Je '70
Science takes on a burning question; Office of fire research. Bsns W p42+ Ag 15 '70
See also
Airplanes in fire protection
Fire departments
Fire resisting materials
Fire sprinklers
Fire testing
Firemen
Fireproofing of textiles
Hydrants
Underwriters' laboratories, inc.

FIRE pumps. See Pumps

FIRE resisting materials
Apollo flameproofing seen aiding aircraft; Fluorel. Aviation W 92:67 Mr 16 '70
See also
Paint, Fire resisting

FIRE resisting textile fabrics. See Textile fabrics, Fire resisting

FIRE sprinklers
Cut fire protection costs; automatic sprinkler system; Fresno, Calif. il Am City 85:92+ Mr '70

FIRE testing
Full-scale fires used to test interior finishes. il Arch Rec 148:135-8 N '70

FIRE trucks. See Fire engines

FIREARMS
Getting the range. J. O'Connor. See issues of Outdoor life
Shooting. J. O'Connor. See issues of Outdoor life
Shooting; ed. by W. Page. See issues of Field & stream
See also
Pistols
Revolvers
Rifles
Shotguns

Laws and regulations

America as a gun culture; excerpt from American violence, ed. by R. Hofstadter and M. Wallace. il Am Heritage 21:4-11+ O '70
Cooling it. New Repub 162:11 My 30 '70
Crawfisher; H. Humphrey. Nation 211:387-8 O 26 '70
Defying the gun lobby. Nation 211:262 S 28 '70
Gun law enfeeblement; reply. J. M. Snyder. America 122:35 Ja 31 '70
Son of gangbusters; Treasury's anti-gun film. R. Starnes. Field & S 74:8+ Mr '70
Teacher opinion poll; gun control legislation. Todays Ed 59:11 Ja '70

Sights

How to sight-in a rifle. R. Schuessler. il Pop Mech 134:132-3+ S '70
How tough are scopes? W. Page. il Field & S 75:80-3 N '70
Keep both eyes on the birdie! Normark singlepoint. G. Reiger. il Pop Mech 134:44 S '70
Reticle in the scope. J. O'Connor. il Outdoor Life 145:152+ Ag '70
Some dope on iron sights. J. O'Connor. il Outdoor Life 146:100+ O '70

FIREARMS, Theft of
How to outwit gun thieves. G. X. Sand. Field & S 75:54-5+ D '70

FIREARMS industry and trade
Merchant of menace; S. Cummings. E. Shrake. il Sports Illus 32:80-4+ My 11 '70
Nicholas Boutet: master craftsman. C. G. Worman. il Hobbies 75:158-9 Mr '70

Korea (Republic)

Will the M-16 be made in Korea? il Bsns W p 116 O 24 '70

FIREBIRD; ballet. See Ballets—Criticisms

FIREMAN, Edward L. and others
Tritium and argon radioactivities in lunar material. bibliog il Science 167:566-8 Ja 30 '70

FIREMEN
Fireman Smith; Dennis E. Smith of New York fire department, a student of Irish poetry. New Yorker 46:18-19 Ag 29 '70

Training

Regional fire-training center for small cities; Inglewood, Calif. D. W. Ayres. Am City 85: 58 S '70

FIREMEN, Railroad. See Railroads—Employees

FIREPLACES
Easy way to add a fireplace. L. Netti. il Mech Illus 66:122-3+ O '70
Good cheer of a glowing fireplace. il Good H 170:100-5 Ja '70
How to install a prefab fireplace. il Bet Hom & Gard 48:28+ Mr '70
New fireplaces that solve problems. D. Huff. il Pop Sci 197:90-1+ S '70
See also
Stoves, Franklin

FIREPROOF construction
See also
Fire testing

FIREPROOFING of textiles
Fireproofing our children. C. Dishon. il Todays Health 49:38-41+ Ja '71

FIRES
After the fire is over. M. Davis. il por Mech Illus 66:39-41+ Ag '70
Disaster in a dance hall shatters a small French town. il Life 69:40-2 N 13 '70
Fire damage; aftermath of fire at Rocky Flats plutonium plant, with AEC statement. E. A. Martell and others. il Environ 12:14-21 My '70
'Twas the night before Christmas ..; White House fire, 1929. R. D. Heinl, jr. il por Am Heritage 22:105-9 D '70
Unusual silence; Saint-Laurent-du-Pont fire. il Time 96:34 N 16 '70
See also
Brush fires
Fire protection
Forest fires
Mine fires
Textile fabrics, Flammable

France

See Fires

FIRESTER, Joan. See Firester, L. jt. auth.

FIRESTER, Lee, and Firester, Joan
Wanted Rx for the equitable management of parent-school conflict. Ed Digest 35:5-7 Ap '70

FIRESTONE tire and rubber company
See also
Drexel, Firestone (firm)

FIREWORKS
Safe fireworks; There aren't any. W. R. Vath. il Todays Health 48:50-1 Je '70

FIRING ranges. See Bombing and gunnery ranges

FIRSHEIN, William, and Gillmor, R. G.
DNA-membrane complex: macromolecular content and stimulation of enzymatic activity by polyadenylic acid. bibliog il Science 169:66-8 Jl 3 '70

FIRST aid in illness and injury
Accidents on purpose; Casualties union of Great Britain. D. Lampe. il Todays Health 48:35-7 S '70
Bring your first aid up-to-date. W. W. Conner. il Pop Mech 133:S18 My '70
Emergency first aid for summer accidents. il Good H 170:153 Je '70
First aid. C. J. Potthoff. See issues of Today's health
First seconds count; Collision emergency unit, Toms River, N.J. il Am City 85:54 My '70
For use in emergency; Medical self-help training program. Todays Ed 59:73 O '70
Medical self-help: training for emergency. Parents Mag 45:56-7 N '70

FIRST aid in illness and injury—*Continued*
Rescue on the Freeway. J. P. Blank. il Read Digest 96:73-7 My '70
Tips for a safer summer. J. H. Winchester. il Read Digest 97:127-31 Jl '70
See also
Ambulances
Burns and scalds
Respiration, Artificial
FIRST-born children. See Children, First-born
FIRST chamber dance company of New York. See Ballet companies
FIRST committee of the General assembly. See United Nations—Political and security committee
FIRST day; story. See Montagne, R.
FIRST independence national bank. See Detroit—Banks
FIRST international conference of American states. See Inter-American conferences
FIRST national bank of Chicago. See Chicago —Banks
FIRST national city corporation of New York. See Bank holding companies
FIRST Pennsylvania banking and trust company. See Philadelphia—Banks
FISCHBACH, Gerald D.
Synaptic potentials recorded in cell cultures of nerve and muscle. bibliog il Science 169: 1331-3 S 25 '70
FISCHER, Alfred G. and others
Geological history of the western North Pacific. bibliog il Science 168:1210-14 Je 5 '70
FISCHER, Bobby
Enigma tries a new role. L. Evans. Sports Illus 33:85-7 O 12 '70 *
Is Boris good enough? il por Newsweek 75: 130-1 Ap 20 '70 *
FISCHER, George D.
Indian education; a national disgrace; a dialogue. pors Todays Ed 59:24-7 Mr '70
Our nation's schools: desegregation is not enough. por Parents Mag 45:16 S '70
School lunch program and the NEA. pors Todays Ed 59:16-19 Ja '70
Today's teacher: a new breed. por Parents Mag 45:34 Mr '70
(ed) See Harris, F. R. Teacher's political role
(ed) See McNamara, M. C. Reading is FUNdamental
(ed) See Maheu, R. Road to peace and progress
(ed) See Morton, R. C. B. Teacher's political role
FISCHER, John
On the off-beat. A. Rich. Hi Fi 20:secII 7 Je '70 *
FISCHER, John, 1910-
Coming upheaval in Congress. Harper 241: 21-2+ O; 17 D '70
Easy chair. See issues of Harper's magazine
Preface to the catalogue of Curmudgeon college. Harper 240:18+ Je '70; Same abr. with title Cheers for old Curmudgeon! Read Digest 97:188-90 S '70
Why and how to build another U.S.A. Cur 114:9-16 Ja '70
FISCHER, John Henry
Who needs schools? il Sat R 53:78-9+ S 19 '70
FISCHER, Larry G.
Teflon trimmer capacitors. Electr World 83: 51 Ap '70
FISCHER, Robert E. and Walsh, F. J.
What the systems approach means to air conditioning (cont) Arch Rec 147:153-60 Ap '70
FISCHER-WILLIAMS, Barbara
(ed) See Dickie, M. Scotsman
FISH, Hamilton
Where are they now? il pors Newsweek 76:24 D 14 '70 *
FISH, Stewart A. and Feinstein, Phylis
Report on rubella vaccine. Redbook 134:29+ Ap '70
FISH
Memory
See Memory
FISH, Frozen
Frozen fish sticks. il Consumer Rep 35:545-9 S '70
FISH, Pickled
For fancy herring, season your own. Sunset 144:184 My '70
FISH and game commission, Nevada. See Nevada—Fish and game commission
FISH and wildlife service. See United States— Fish and wildlife service
FISH as food
Fish without a friend. R. Petrow. il Pop Mech 134:112-14 Jl '70
How to fillet fish. W. Davis. il Mech Illus 66:54-5 Jl '70
See also
Cookery—Fish
Fish protein concentrate

FISH chowder. See Chowder
FISH culture
Aquaculture: food from the deep. il Time 96:48+ Ag 31 '70
FISH eggs. See Fishes—Eggs
FISH fillets
Blitz fillets. G. Reiger. il Pop Mech 133:155 Ap '70
FISH flour. See Fish protein concentrate
FISH hawks. See Ospreys
FISH in art
Walnut, maple, pine and butternut fish. D. Shiner. il Design 71:30-1 Spr '70
FISH industry and trade
See also
Fisheries
Whitney-Fidalgo seafoods, inc.
FISH poisons
Grim pursuit of quicksilver; tightening of leaks by chlor-alkali producers. il Bsns W p42+ Jl 18 '70
Mad hatter's legacy; Canadian export ban on fish. Newsweek 75:72 Ap 20 '70
Poison roams our coastal seas. R. H. Boyle. il Sports Illus 33:70-4+ O 26 '70
See also
Antimycin
FISH populations
Fish stocks: biochemical and serological identification; report of meeting. A. E. Mourant. Science 167:1760 Mr 27 '70
FISH protein concentrate
Fish protein progress. il Sci N 98:270-1 S 26 '70
Setback for a supplement. il Sci N 97:90-1 Ja 24 '70
Superfood from the sea. il Bsns W p 112+ N 14 '70
FISH sauce. See Sauces
FISH soups. See Chowder
FISHBEIN, Morris
Point of view. Science 167:148 Ja 9 '70
FISHER, A. D.
White rites versus Indian rights. bibliog l) por Trans-Action 7:29-33 N '69
FISHER, Aileen
Standing up for Santa; drama. Plays 30:66-8 D '70
Time for mom; drama; reprint. Plays 29:67-70 My '70
FISHER, Arthur
Science newsfront. See issues of Popular science, January 1970-
Strange world of magnetic bubbles. il Pop Sci 196:65-7 F '70
FISHER, Graham, and Fisher, Heather Anne: Britain's royal swinger. il pors Good H 171:44-6+ Jl '70
FISHER, Harvey I.
Death of Midway's antennas. il Audubon 72: 62-3 Ja '70
FISHER, Heather. See Fisher, G. jt auth.
FISHER, Isabelle
Tax reform act. Dance Mag 44:6 D '70; 45: 83 Ja '71
FISHER, James Maxwell McConnell
Obituary
Audubon 72:132 N '70
Pub W 198:35 O 26 '70
FISHER, Jonathan
Rediscovery: Parson Jonathan Fisher. A. Winchester. il Art in Am 58:92-9 N '70 *
FISHER, M. F. K.
Enclave. New Yorker 46:36-42 S 5; 35-9 O 3; 175-6+ N 14; 48-50 D 12 '70
What is the difference between this photograph and a real frozen TV dinner? il Esquire 74:96-9+ Ag '70
FISHER, Neal F.
Where on earth do you do theology? Chr Cent 87:1291-4 O 28 '70
FISHER, Renée
Spring song. il por Opera N 34:8-13 Ja 31 '70
FISHER, Richard V. and Waters, A. C.
Bed forms in base-surge deposits: lunar implications. bibliog Science 165:1349-52; 167: 1638 S 26 '69, Mr 20 '70
FISHER, Robert
Project Slow Down: the middle-class answer to Project Head Start. Sch & Soc 98:356-7 O '70
FISHER, Roy
Comment. D. Zaiss. Poetry 116:51-2 Ap '70 *
FISHER, Rosaline
(comp) Voting in 1970: some facts and figures. Todays Ed 59:64-5 S '70
FISHER, William H.
Value judgments and neo-behaviorism. bibliog f Sch & Soc 98:106-8 F '70
FISHER foods, inc.
Fantastic Fazios of foodland. il por Bsns W p 146+ F 21 '70

FISHERIES

Food-from-the-sea myth; effects of over-exploitation and pollution. P. R. Ehrlich and A. H. Ehrlich. Sat R 53:53-5+ Ap 4 '70

Marine farming. G. B. Pinchot. il Sci Am 223: 14-21 bibliog (p 140) D '70

We're fishing from outer space. G. Lee. il por Nat Wildlife 8:36-41 F '70

Where have all the fishes gone? J. Hay. il Audubon 72:74-7 N '70

See also
Fishery research
Shellfish fisheries

International aspects

Resources of the sea. J. A. Gulland. il Sea Front 16:211-19 Jl '70

Salmon catchers make a splash; proposed ban on high-seas fishing. il Bsns W p50+ F 7 '70

U.S. and Poland modify agreement on Atlantic coast fisheries. Dept State Bul 63:93 Jl 20 '70

Australia

Australian abalone fisheries. J. Harding. il Sea Front 16:282-5 S '70

Canada

Mad hatter's legacy; Canadian export ban on fish. Newsweek 75:72 Ap 20 '70

Greenland

Danes scourge the seas; decimating Atlantic salmon. C. Gammon. il Sports Illus 31:28-30+ D 15 '69

Threat to salmon fishing; recommended ban on high-seas fishing. H. J. Barnes. il Sci N 97:78 Ja 17 '70

What's happening to Atlantic salmon? G. Beall. il Field & S 75:36-7+ Jl '70

See also
United States—Fish and wildlife service

Nigeria

Food from the sea for Nigeria. C. P. Idyll. il Sea Front 16:340-51 N '70

United States

See also
American fisheries society

FISHERMEN

Big Sur storm. S. Abrams. il Natur Hist 79: 8-10+ Ag '70

FISHERY laws and legislation

Editorial; future of sport fishing off U.S. coastlines. B. Brister. Field & S 75:8 D '70

Fishing laws; United States and Canada (cont) Field & S 74:10+ Ap '70

Fishing seasons (cont) Outdoor Life 145: 48+ Ap '70

U.S. and Canada negotiate draft fisheries agreement; joint statement: February 16, 1970. Dept State Bul 62:434-5 Mr 30 '70

FISHERY products

Preservation

Cured salmon in olive oil. il Sunset 145:107 Ag '70

FISHERY research

Fisheries research: rejuggling of priorities is assailed. L. J. Carter. Science 167:1471-2 Mr 13 '70

Fisheries story at Cape Vincent. A. W. Bromley. il Cons 24:16-17 Ag '69

FISHES

See also
Fisheries
Nervous system—Fishes
also headings beginning Fish; also names of fishes, e.g. Piranhas

Accidents and hazards

Fish and power plants. A. C. Jensen; reply with rejoinder. L. H. Mantell. Cons 24:42-3 Ap '70

Eggs

Mermaid's purse. il Sea Front 16:300-1 S '70

Eye

See Eye (fishes)

Food and feeding

See also
Food chain (ecology)

Habits and behavior

Secret to fish behavior. W. J. Wisby. il Nat Wildlife 8:18-20 Ag '70

Migration

Mullet madness. R. Clancy. il Sea Front 16: 49-50 Ja '70
See also
Salmon

Orientation

See Orientation

Poisoning

See Fish poisons

FISHES, Effect of temperature on

Calefaction of a river. D. Merriman. il Sci Am 222:42-52 My '70

FISHES, Insects, etc, Rain of

Crazy rains or animals that fall from the sky? M. W. Martin. il Sci Digest 67:32-6 Ja '70

Of frogs and floods. Time 97:31 Ja 18 '71

FISHHOOKS

Bottle your hooks and leaders. R. H. Jones. il Outdoor Life 145:104 F '70

FISHING

Anglers of industry. R. Levy. il Duns 96:40-3 S '70

Boys and brooks, a special magic. T. Trueblood. il Field & S 74:6+ Ap '70

Camp wild for best fishing. A. W. Prince. il pors Field & S 75:58-9+ My '70

Cartop boat: an angler's secret weapon. C. Nansen. il Field & S 74:58-9+ Ja '70

Fishing. J. Brooks. See issues of Outdoor life

Fishing; ed. by A. J. McClane. See issues of Field & stream

Fishing with a map; bottom fishing. G. Heinold. il Outdoor Life 146:38+ Ag '70

Floating down the river. W. Davis. il Mech Illus 66:76-7+ Ap '70

For some, minis are the maximum; mini fishing. R. H. Boyle. il Sports Illus 32:54-5 My 18 '70

Gist of it; ed. by H. Moore. See issues of Outdoor life

Greatest fishing secret ever. D. J. Anderson. il Field & S 74:62-5+ Ap '70

How fishermen fool fish and vice versa. H. F. Blaisdell. il Field & S 75:76-7+ Je '70

How to have great fishing with the family. S. Marking. il Field & S 74:68-9+ F '70

Navigation for fishermen. J. A. Emmett. il Outdoor Life 145:22+ Je '70

Retrieve: how fast? G. Heinold. il Outdoor Life 145:30+ Je '70

Sportsman's notebook. H. G. Tapply. See issues of Field & stream

Straight-down fishing vs. the hot lake problem. L. J. Bashline. il Field & S 74:56-7+ F '70

Think like a fish. T. Trueblood. il Field & S 75:14-15+ Jl '70

Water temperature is fishy business. D. Richey. il Field & S 75:40-1+ Jl '70

Where to go; ed. by V. T. Sparano. See issues of Outdoor life

Why don't you take the boy fishing? M. Wilk. il Field & S 74:72-3+ Ap '70

See also
Airplanes in hunting and fishing
Bait
Casting (fishing)
Fisheries
Fishermen
Fishing clubs
Salt water fishing

also Bass fishing and similar headings

Anecdotes, facetiae, satire, etc.

Look your bass in the eye. C. Elliott. il Outdoor Life 145:144 Ap '70

Bibliography

New literature available from fishing tackle manufacturers. il Outdoor Life 146:88-9 N '70

Competitions

Field & stream fishing contest. Field & S 74:18+ Ap '70

Frigid fiesta; annual pike contest. T. Janes. il por Outdoor Life 145:40-3+ Ja '70

Hot on the trail of big mama; Hawaiian international billfish tournament. R. F. Jones. il Sports Illus 33:22-5 Ag 17 '70

1969 winners; Field & stream fishing contest. Field & S 74:14+ Mr '70

Will the real Shinnecock swordfish tournament please stand up? D. Kirkpatrick. il Motor B 125:26 Ap '70

Winning steelhead river. C. F. Waterman. il Field & S 74:42-5+ F '70

Implements and appliances

Fishing floats and currents. E. T. Webber. il pors Sea Front 16:26-31 Ja '70

How to get close to the dam fish; miniature airboat for motor casting. W. Transue. il Pop Mech 134:106-8 N '70

Mothproof fly chest. il Design 72:32-3 Wint '70
See also
Fishing tackle

FISHING—*Continued*

Law
See Fishery laws and legislation

Photographs
Salty balm on the edge of the city. Sports Illus 33:32-7 Jl 20 '70

Quotations, maxims, etc.
Some choice lines on fishing. H. Hoover. il Read Digest 96:135 My '70

Study and teaching
Don't spare the rod; course in flytying and flyfishing. B. Gillette. il Outdoor Life 145: 88-91+ Ap '70
Learning to fish. B. W. Dalrymple. il Outdoor Life 146:74-7+ S '70

Alaska
Wilderness adventure in Alaska; Dolly Varden trout fishing. B. Thomas. il Travel 133: 34-9+ Je '70

Arizona
Arizona, land of built-in fishing. H. Bradshaw. il Field & S 74:37-9+ Ja '70
Make a reservation for trout. J. Tallon. il Outdoor Life 146:72-3+ N '70
Stripers in the desert. B. Grant. il Field & S 75:52-3+ My '70

Arkansas
Ozark crappie jamboree. H. Bradshaw. il Field & S 74:70-1+ Ap '70

Bahama Islands
Bonefish for everybody. G. Heinold. il Outdoor Life 145:12+ Ja '70

British Honduras
Tarpon, snook, and bones. J. Brooks. il Outdoor Life 146:66-7+ S '70

California
Camanche, hot new bass lake. L. Green. il Field & S 74:66-7+ Ap '70
Fly for all season; ant flies. M. W. Fong. il por Outdoor Life 145:56-7+ My '70
Gift of the Gualala; an angler's Christmas. B. Nauheim. il Outdoor Life 146:50-1+ D '70
Family fishing on the Kern. J. Martin il por Outdoor Life 146:56-7+ Ag '70
Ice fishing comes to California. J. Martin. il pors Outdoor Life 145:64-5+ Ja '70
Kings come to the Smith. B. Nauheim. il pors Outdoor Life 146:90-3+ O '70
Largemouths are predictable. J. Brooks. il Outdoor Life 145:76-8+ My '70
March with the kings. M. Hayden. il Outdoor Life 145:52-5+ Mr '70

California, Gulf of
Hap i nes afloat on the Sea of Cortez. J. Rhoades. il Sports Illus 32:64-6+ Mr 30 '70

California, Lower
California's most fabulous fishing grounds. H. Bonner. il Field & S 75:50-1+ D '70
Yellowtails by the ton. L. Miracle. il por Outdoor Life 145:60-3+ F '70

Canada
Challenge of Nova Scotia. J. Brooks. il Outdoor Life 146:90-5 D '70
Crazy way to catch lakers. W. Davis. il por Outdoor Life 146:78-9+ Ag '70
Ice-out lakers. J. O. Cartier. il Outdoor Life 145:72-5+ Ap '70
Island for summer steelhead. J. Gartner. il Field & S 75:22-3+ Jl '70
Nova Scotia's striped sea barse. G. Heinold. il pors Outdoor Life 146:62-4+ Jl '70
River running out of Eden; Restigouche River. P. Ryan. il Sports Illus 32:86-9+ My 25 '70
Rivière Philippe; brook trout stream in Quebec. B. Warner. il pors Outdoor Life 145: 48-51+ Je '70
Roughing it on Smoothrock. B. Scifres. il Outdoor Life 145:64-7+ Je '70
Ten-second salmon. N. Karas. il Field & S 74:66-7+ F '70
This is adventure; char and trout fishing. R. Cochran. il pors Outdoor Life 146:36-9+ Jl '70
Trail of the giant tuna; Notre Dame Bay, Newfoundland. J. Brooks. il Outdoor Life 145:68-71+ Je '70
Troll for early trout. R. Cochran. il Field & S 74:52-3+ F '70
Truth about New Brunswick salmon. L. J. Bashline. il Field & S 75:34-5+ Jl '70

Unspoiled pike of Washington Lake. G. Crittenden. il Field & S 75:60-1+ My '70
Water all white. D. Jarden. il por Outdoor Life 145:45-7+ Mr '70
Winning steelhead river. C. F. Waterman. il Field & S 74:42-5+ F '70

Colorado
Turn left at the porcupine. J. Olsen. il Sports Illus 33:50-8+ Ag 24 '70

Connecticut
Alewives spell action. G. Heinold. il Outdoor Life 145:44+ Ap '70
King saves the day. G. Heinold. il por Outdoor Life 145:96+ My '70
Try jetty jockeying. G. Heinold. il Outdoor Life 145:24+ Mr '70

Costa Rica
New in-spot for tarpon. B. Warner. il Field & S 74:194-7+ Mr '70

Florida
Fishing paradise in the Prairies. W. Davis. il Mech Illus 66:59+ Ja '70
Half a dozen for the pan; bluegills. J. Brooks. il Outdoor Life 146:88-9+ Jl '70
How to think like a bass. J. Robinson and H. Carroll. il Field & S 75:56-7+ N '70
Island-hopping vacation. F. M. Paulson. il Field & S 74:53-5+ Ja '70
Prospecting for Florida bass. G. Laycock. il Field & S 75:56-7+ My '70
Redwing black bass. B. Underwood. il por Outdoor Life 146:48-9+ Jl '70
What the experts taught me; how to catch very big bass. P. Bauer. il por Outdoor Life 146:68-71+ Ag '70

Georgia
Fishing rodeo; annual event in Statesboro. L. C. Barrett. il Parks & Rec 5:27 Jl '70

Great Britain
British bass. D. Fletcher. il Sea Front 16:164-9 My '70
Sex life of the salmon is brief and terrible. W. Humphrey. il Esquire 73:123-8+ Je '70

Great Lakes Region
Salmon potpourri. A. J. McClane. il Field & S 75:88-90 D '70
Surf fishing; Michigan's newest sport. H. F. Zeman. il Field & S 74:150-3+ F '70

Greenland
Greenland salmon. M. Sosin. il Field & S 75: 54-5+ My '70
Last chance for Atlantic salmon? A. Grahame. il Outdoor Life 145:41-3+ Je '70

Idaho
What, no caviar! C. Ormond. il Outdoor Life 146:60-3+ N '70
Whitefish'll get you. B. W. Dalrymple. il pors Outdoor Life 146:60-1+ Jl '70

Indiana
Catch big bass right now. J. Brang. il pors Outdoor Life 145:92-3+ Ap '70
Goggle-eyes'll get you; rock bass fishing in Miami County. B. Scifres. il por Outdoor Life 146:82-3+ O '70

Ireland
Bloodless battle on the Blackwater; protest against private ownership of fisheries. C. Gammon. il Sports Illus 32:49-51 Je 15 '70
In a land of green, a touch of blue; blue Swedish plug. C. Gammon. il Sports Illus 33:64-8+ O 5 '70

Labrador
Labrador's trophy trout country. B. Cairns. il Travel & Camera 33:50-3 Je '70
Lapland salmon, at bargain prices. A. J. McClane.. il Field & S 74:58-9+ F '70

Louisiana
Ah-chaf-ah-lie-ah spells bass. W. Allegood. il Outdoor Life 145:68-9+ Mr '70

Maine
Hot weather hot spot. H. F. Blaisdell. il Field & S 75:36-9+ Jl '70
How to catch big early season trout. J. B. Robinson. il Field & S 74:58-9+ Mr '70
Maine's predictable Saco River stripers. P. McLain. il Field & S 75:72-3+ My '70
Night on the ice J. B. Robinson. il pors Outdoor Life 145:52-5+ F '70

FISHING—*Continued*

Maryland
Meet the streamerettes; shad caught with light fly rod. S. R. Slaymaker, 2d. il pors Outdoor Life 145:98-100+ Ap '70
Rocks on the brain. G. Heinold. il Outdoor Life 145:36+ F '70

Massachusetts
Saving of a river; Squannacook. R. Donnelly. il por Outdoor Life 145:65-7+ Ap '70

Michigan
Beer barrel brownies. C. Nansen. il Field & S 74:82-3+ Mr '70
New: no-hackle dry fly. J. Brooks. il Outdoor Life 146:48-51+ Ag '70
Springtime is steelhead time. J. B. Gleason. il Field & S 74:42-3+ Ja '70

Minnesota
Big fish in town. R. Gilsvik. il por Outdoor Life 145:72-3+ Je '70
Double play in Minnesota. J. Seville. il Motor B 126:58-60 S '70

Mississippi
Bass from the bottom up. B. Brady. il por Outdoor Life 146:56-7+ N '70

Montana
Drive-in grayling. N. Strung. il Field & S 75:74-5+ My '70
This has gotta be paradise. R. J. Whitcomb. il por Outdoor Life 145:46-9+ My '70

Nevada
Most fishermen catch limits of bass in Ruby marshes. il Sunset 145:40 S '70
They're killing Pyramid Lake! D. Lynch. il Field & S 74:10-15 Ja '70

New Hampshire
It's spring for smallmouths. J. B. Robinson. il por Outdoor Life 145:54-5+ My '70
Too many bass. T. Janes. il Outdoor Life 145: 60-1+ Je '70

New Jersey
New Jersey's best bet for smallmouths. J. B. Robinson. il Field & S 74:198-201+ Ap '70
Roll call for carp. J. Stabile. il Outdoor Life 146:42-3+ Jl '70
Spree of cats. D. Pryce. il pors Outdoor Life 146:64-5+ Ag '70

New Mexico
On the upper Rio Grande; brown and rainbow trout. H. Simmons. il Field & S 75: 62-3+ My '70

New York (state)
But at first he did succeed; Richard Hausknecht's record tuna at Montauk. D. Levin. il Sports Illus 33:82-3+ S 21 '70
Finger Lakes turnover trout. E. R. Belak, jr. il Cons 24:14-15 Ag '69
Pike by snowmobile. P. D. Lane. il Field & S 75:36-7+ N '70

New Zealand
Fishing in New Zealand (cont) J. Brooks. il por Outdoor Life 145:56-7+ Ja '70
Twelve New Zealand trout flies. K. Draper. il Field & S 74:84-7+ Mr '70

North Carolina
Carolina blues. K. Osborne. il pors Outdoor Life 146:70-1+ O '70
New hotspot for channel bass. K. Osborne. il por Outdoor Life 145:70-3+ My '70
Where little tuna hit the beach. J. B. Robinson. il Field & S 75:64-5+ My '70

Northeastern states
News: the Northeast; ed. by T. Janes. See issues of Outdoor life

Norway
Gold-plated salmon: Norway's Malangsfoss. J. A. Maxtone-Graham. il Travel & Camera 33:64+ F '70

Oregon
Day on the Deschutes. L. Miracle. il Outdoor Life 145:78-9+ Ap '70
Trouting in solitude. M. W. Fong. il pors Outdoor Life 146:54-7+ S '70

Pacific coast
Action on the color front; new hotspot for longfins. H. Williams. il por Outdoor Life 146:72-5+ Ag '70

Pennsylvania
Marvelous cork bug. R. S. Kommer. il Outdoor Life 146:52-5+ Jl '70
Weekend in Carlisle. J. Brooks. il Outdoor Life 145:76-7+ F '70

Puerto Rico
Fast bass in Puerto Rico; black bass. D. Ladd. il Field & S 75:154-5+ My '70

Rhode Island
Blacks. G. Heinold. il Outdoor Life 146:138-9+ S '70

Scotland
Salmon fishing in Scotland. E. Nabb. il Motor B 125:136-8 Je '70

Southwestern states
Best fishing lake ever built? Toledo Bend Lake. G. Gresham. il Field & S 75:38-9+ D '70

Texas
All this and rainbows, too; Guadalupe River. V. Kraft. il por Sports Illus 32:44+ Mr 2 '70
Bass in the treetops. C. Elliott. il Outdoor Life 146:60-1+ S '70
Now's a time for bass. R. Tinsley. il Outdoor Life 145:66-7+ F '70

United States
Future of sport fishing. J. S. Gottschalk. il Parks & Rec 5:17-19+ N '70

Washington (state)
Are Washington's steelhead facing disaster? L. Johnson. Field & S 75:46-7+ N '70
Clearwater and smallmouth. D. Pryce. il Field & S 75:24-5+ Jl '70
Magnum salmon fishing. D. Stair. il Field & S 74:74-5+ Ap '70

Western states
Big flies for western waters. A. J. McClane. il Field & S 74:98-100+ F '70
Fishing with Fred. T. Trueblood. il pors Field & S 74:20+ Ja '70
Fur bearing trout. N. Strung. il Field & S 74:40-1+ Ja '70

Wisconsin
I'll tell you about muskies. B. Hoeft. il por Outdoor Life 146:58-9+ Ag '70
On the Mississippi ice. A. W. Prince. il por Outdoor Life 146:54-7+ D '70

Wyoming
Honeymoon adventure. J. Clark. il Field & S 74:62-3+ Mr '70

FISHING, Winter
Chug up a laker. J. O. Cartier. il Outdoor Life 145:58-9+ Mr '70
Fishing the deep freeze. T. Kerasote. il por Outdoor Life 146:38-41+ D '70
Fold and trail fish house. H. Bradshaw. il Outdoor Life 146:12-12A N '70
Frigid fiesta; annual pike contest. T. Janes. il por Outdoor Life 145:40-3+ Ja '70
Hottest sport on ice. E. A. Bauer. il por Nat Wildlife 9:54-7 D '70
Ice fishing comes to California. J. Martin. il pors Outdoor Life 145:64-5+ Ja '70
Ice-time fishing. W. Davis. il Mech Illus 66: 61+ F '70
Night on the ice. J. B. Robinson. il pors Outdoor Life 145:52-5+ F '70
Now you can fish through the ice in California. il Sunset 144:52 F '70
On the Mississippi ice. A. W. Prince. il por Outdoor Life 146:54-7+ D '70
Pike by snowmobile. P. D. Lane. il Field & S 75:36-7+ N '70
Rainbows through the ice. H. Bradshaw. il Field & S 75:104-7+ D '70
When the ice is thick, go fishing! il Changing T 24:24 Ja '70
Where the bluegill is king. P. Barrett. il Field & S 75:34-5+ D '70
Winter fishing: through the ice. Bet Hom & Gard 48:28-9 D '70

FISHING boats
Big fish from small boats. C. R. Meyer. il Motor B 125:68-9+ F '70
Biography of a little boat. C. F. Sheppard. il Yachting 128:72-3+ Jl '70
Great red fleet. il Newsweek 75:73-4 F 9 '70
Perfect bass boat. G. Reiger. il Pop Mech 133:113-16 F '70
Small sportfisherman. J. A. Emmett. il Outdoor Life 146:140-1+ S '70
Sportfishermen. J. Hargrave. il por Motor B 125:106-7+ Ja '70

FISHING boats—*Continued*

Design

Classic boats in fiberglass. B. Cobb, jr. il Yachting 129:100-1+ Ja '71
Outrage: new 21-foot Boston Whaler. il Yachting 128:68 Ag '70

Equipment

Rig for fishing. B. Marston. il Motor B 125:152-3 F '70

FISHING boats, Remodeled
When a boat is more than a boat. S. Taylor and R. S. Taylor. il Motor B 125:234-6 Mr '70

Anecdotes, facetiae, satire, etc.

Saga of Happy Adventure; excerpts from The boat who wouldn't float. F. Mowat. il Yachting 128:53-5+ Jl '70
World lay waiting; excerpt from The boat who wouldn't float. F. Mowat. il Yachting 127:54-6+ Ap '70; 77-9+ My '70

FISHING clubs
Fishing on the rivers of the mind; Golden Gate angling and casting club. T. McGuane. il Sports Illus 34:40-3 Ja 4 '71

FISHING derbies. See Fishing—Competitions

FISHING docks and piers
Try jetty jockeying. G. Heinold. il Outdoor Life 145:24+ Mr '70

FISHING flies. See Fishing lures, flies, etc.

FISHING in art
Fishing subjects by Junius Brutus Stearns. M. F. Rogers, jr. il Antiques 98:246-50 Ag '70

FISHING lures, flies, etc.
Ancient lure that stripers can't resist. J. B. Robinson. il Field & S 74:60-1+ Ap '70
Best all-around lure? shad dart. C. B. Pfeiffer. il Field & S 75:68-9+ O '70
Big flies for western waters. A. J. McClane. il Field & S 74:98-100+ F '70
Fly fishing for bass. A. J. McClane. il Field & S 75:62-5 Jl '70
Fly-tying tricks. H. G. Tapply. il Field & S 74:88 Mr '70
How to make a wobbler minnow lure. P. Campaner. il Pop Mech 133:152-4 Ap '70
In a land of green, a touch of blue; blue Swedish plug. C. Gammon. il Sports Illus 33:64-8+ O 5 '70
Jig is up! L. A. Goth. il Pop Mech 133:110-12+ Je '70
Jiggerpoling for lunkers. B. Phillips. il Outdoor Life 145:54-5+ Je '70
Lower the odds on lunker bass. S. Fagerstrom. il Field & S 74:78-9+ Mr '70
Marvelous cork bug. R. S. Kommer. il Outdoor Life 146:52-5+ Jl '70
New: no-hackle dry fly. J. Brooks. il Outdoor Life 146:48-51+ Ag '70
No-nonsense nymph. E. Marsh. il Field & S 74:100-2 Ja '70
Rigging for lakers. B. Adams. il Field & S 74:78-9+ Ap '70
Sculpin and its imitations. D. Whitlock. il Field & S 75:114-16 S '70
Serpent fly, flexible lines. L. Green. il Field & S 75:58-9+ S '70
Spin-cast flies, toothpaste tubes and wire. V. Kraft. il Sports Illus 32:66+ Je 8 '70
Surface plugs for top fishing. W. Davis. il Mech Illus 66:104+ My '70
Tom Loving, pioneer fly man. J. Brooks. il por Outdoor Life 146:118-19+ N '70
Twelve New Zealand trout flies. K. Draper. il Field & S 74:84-7+ Mr '70
Ultralight in salt water. A. J. McClane. il Field & S 74:100-3+ Mr '70
Worm-tailed jig. G. Heinold. il Outdoor Life 146:96-7+ D '70
See also
Fly casting

FISHING reefs. See Reefs, Artificial

FISHING reels. See Fishing tackle

FISHING rods. See Fishing—Implements and appliances

FISHING stories
Why don't you take the boy fishing? M. Wilk. il Field & S 74:72-3+ Ap '70

FISHING tackle
Best fishing rod you ever had. J. Hand. il Pop Sci 196:114+ Mr '70
Cruising's watersport, fishing. D. Kirkpatrick. bibliog il Motor B 125:12-14 Mr '70
$800 reel? G. Reiger. il Pop Mech 133:128-31+ Ap '70

Fishing tackle. Consumer Rep 34:324-35 D '69
Fishing tackle, what you need for various species. V. Evanoff. Motor B 125:130+ Ap '70
Pushbutton fishing. G. Reiger. il Pop Mech 133:100-1 F '70
Right leader. G. Heinold. il Outdoor Life 146:174-6 O '70
Spin-casting tackle: reels and rods. il Consumer Rep 35:648-56 N '70
Spincaster's way. J. Brooks. il pors Outdoor Life 146:96-8+ O '70
Spinning for more fish. J. Brooks. il Outdoor Life 145:84-5+ Ap '70
That unimportant fly reel. A. J. McClane. il Field & S 75:140-4 O '70

FISHING tournaments. See Fishing—Competitions

FISHING with bow and arrow
Carp for the bow. G. H. Gillelan. il por Outdoor Life 145:146+ My '70

FISHLOCK, David
Unifying government research. il Sci N 97:160 F 7 '70

FISHMAN, Charles
At the R movie; poem. Film Q 24:2 Fall '70

FISHNET floats See Fishing—Implements and appliances

FISK graduates. See College graduates, Negro

FISK university, Nashville, Tenn.
Student protest at Fisk university in the 1920's. M. L. Johnson. bibliog il Negro Hist Bul 33:137-40 O '70
Voices of Fisk '70. C. E. Lincoln and C. E. Lincoln. il N Y Times Mag p30-1+ Je 7 '70

FISKE, John
Crispus Attucks; address, 1888. il Negro Hist Bul 33:58-68 Mr '70

FISSION (biology) See Reproduction, Asexual

FISSION, Atomic. See Nuclear fission

FISSION track dating. See Radioactive dating

FITCH, Bill
Low camp in Cleveland. il pors Newsweek 76:33 D 28 '70
Madcap Cavs of Cleveland. P. Carry. por Sports Illus 33:68-9 D 14 '70 *

FITCH, Bob
Nixon: with a little help for his friends. il pors Ramp Mag 8:58-62+ Mr '70
(ed) See Chávez, C. Tilting with the system

FITCH, Charles Marden
Lady of the night orchid. il Horticulture 48:34-5 Jl '70

FITCH, Coy D.
Plasmodium falciparum in owl monkeys: drug resistance and chloroquine binding capacity. bibliog il Science 169:289-90 Jl 17 '70

FITCH, Edwin M. See Shanklin, J. F. jt. auth.

FITCH, John
Old pro tries out the world's most advanced car. il Pop Mech 133:88-91 Ja '70

FITCH, William
Preaching amid smog. Chr Today 15:6-8 D 18 '70

FITCHBURG, Mass.
Town like Fitchburg. por Newsweek 76:46 D 28 '70

FITHIAN, Janet H.
Organization child. il Parents Mag 45:54-5+ Ap '70

FITTING (sewing) See Dressmaking

FITTING out boats. See Boats—Maintenance and repair

FITTS, E. Grant
Building a fortune on LTV's discards. por Bsns W p76-7 O 3 '70 *

FITZ, Grancel
Are hunters murderers? reprint of August 1948 article. il Outdoor Life 146:46-7+ Ag '70

FITZGERALD, Arthur Ernest
Fate of a watchdog. J. Volz. Commonweal 93:341 Ja 8 '71 *

FITZGERALD, Edward, bp
Bishop from Petricula. por Time 96:58+ Jl 27 '70 *

FITZGERALD, Francis Scott Key
Day at the studio: Scott Fitzgerald in Hollywood; excerpt from Crazy Sundays. J. A. Latham. Harper 241:38-9+ N '70 *
Gatsby: false prophet of the American dream. R. L. Pearson. bibliog f Engl J 59:638-42+ My '70 *
Zelda; excerpts. N. W. Milford. pors Ladies Home J 87:117-21 Je '70 *

FITZGERALD, Gerald
(ed) See Melchior, L. Speaking of Wagner

FITZGERALD, Scott. See Fitzgerald, F. S. K.

FITZGERALD, Zelda (Sayre)
Zelda, by N. W. Milford. Review
Atlan 226:104-6 Ag '70. M. Schorer *
Commentary 50:54+ Ag '70. S. Donadio *
Commonweal 92:370-1 Jl 24 '70. R. E.
Long *
Life por 68:24 Je 12 '70. A. Mizener *
Nation 211:123-4 Ag 17 '70. R. Sklar *
New Repub 162:24-7 Je 27 '70. C. T.
Samuels *
Newsweek il pors 75:102+ Je 15 '70. P.
D. Zimmerman *
Sat R il por 553:30-1 Je 13 '70. E. Jane-
way *
Time il por 95:99 Je 15 '70 *
Zelda; excerpts. N. W. Milford. pors Ladies
Home J 87:117-21 Je '70 *
FITZHUGH, Gilbert Wright
In the McNamara vein. A. Harrigan. Nat R
22:1110 O 20 '70 *
Shaping the amorphous lump. il por Time
96:8-10 Ag 10 '70 *
FITZHUGH report on defense procurement and
contracts. See United States—Defense. De-
partment of—Procurement
FITZMYER, Joseph A.
Marinating the mushroom. America 123:206-7
S 26 '70
FITZPATRICK, Donovan
Moon illusions. il Sci Digest 67:66-7 Je '70
FITZPATRICK, John R.
Beehives protect snow-removal salt and pre-
vent water pollution. il Am City 85:81-3 S
'70
FITZPATRICK, Tom
Front-page Fitzpatrick. il por Time 95:69
My 18 '70 *
FITZPATRICK, William J.
Curriculum: the non-life. Clear House 44:333
F '70
FITZSIMMONS, Frank E.
Hoffa's heir fights to keep his job. Bsns W
p28+ My 9 '70 *
Hoffa's stand-in likes the title role. por Bsns
W p 109+ S 19 '70 *
FIVE and ten-cent stores
See also
Woolworth, F. W. and company, ltd.
FIVE on the black hand side; drama.   See
Russell, C. L.
FIVE star saint; drama. See Molloy, E. A.
FIX, John
Woman with a Micro-zoo. il por Sci Digest
67:94-6 F '70
FIXES, Baseball. See Bribery
FIXTURES, Bathroom. See Bathroom fixtures
FIZDALE, Robert. See Gold, A. jt. auth.
FJELD, Asbjørn
Mosaic mutants: absence in a eucaryotic or-
ganism. bibliog il Science 168:843-4 My 15
'70
FJORDS
Benthic life in the fjords of Norway. M.
Berrill. il Natur Hist 79:53-9 N '70
Fjord-hopping by trawler-yacht through
Princess Louisa Inlet. B. Crabtree. il Yacht-
ing 127:54-5+ Mr '70
FLACCA (mutant) See Tomato plants
FLACK, Roberta
Roberta. S. K. Oberbeck. por Newsweek 77:
91 Ja 11 '71 *
FLACKS, Richard
Young intelligentsia in revolt; excerpt from
America: system and revolution, ed. by R.
Aya and N. Miller. il Trans-Action 7:46-55
Je '70
—and Mankoff, Milton
Why they burned the bank. il Nation 210:
337-40 Mr 23 '70
FLAGELLA
Bacterial flagella: polarity of elongation. S. U.
Emerson and others. bibliog il Science 169:
190-2 Jl 10 '70
FLAGELLATES
Transformation of tetramitus amebae into
flagellates. C. Fulton. bibliog il Science
167:1269-70 F 27 '70
See also
Dinoflagellates
Euglena
FLAGLER, Henry Morrison, museum. See Palm
Beach, Fla.—Galleries and museums
FLAGS
See also
Corporations—Flags, insignia, etc.

Cambodia
Stitch in time. il Sr Schol 97:5-6 N 2 '70

United States
Art; Flag show at the Judson memorial
church. L. Alloway. Nation 211:573-4 N 30
'70
Flag and the law. il Sr Schol 97:15-17 O 5 '70
Flag desecration is legal. Time 96:43 Jl 20 '70
Flag fetish. Nation 210:773-4 Je 29 '70
Flagwaving. B. Atkinson. New Repub 162:
13-14 F 14 '70
Love it or leave it; courts reactions to flag
abuse in Texas. New Repub 163:8-9 Ag 1
'70
New Glory. il Newsweek 75:30-2 Je 15 '70
Our flag is still there; reprint. R. L. Duffus.
il Read Digest 97:114-16 S '70
Showing the flag; the People's flag show. P.
Steinfels. il Commonweal 93:295 D 18 '70
Stars and stripes forever; cases involving
defilement or desecration of the flag. E. R.
Cain. Commonweal 92:61-2 Mr 27 '70
Who owns the stars and stripes? il Time 96:
8-15 Jl 6 '70
FLAGS of convenience. See Ships—Registra-
tion and transfer
FLAGSTAD, Kirsten
Duet of the century. W. Zakariasen. il pors
Hi Fi 20:sec1 52-6 Jl '10 *
FLAHERTY, Daniel L.
Of many things. America 123:161, 219 S 19, O
3 '70
FLAHERTY, George A.
Computer upgrades law enforcement, revenue
management. il Am City 85:102-3 O '70
FLAHERTY, Joe
Life sports review. Life 68:12 Je 12; 69:12
Ag 21 '70
FLAHERTY, Peter F.
From the mayor's chair; interview. pors Sr
Schol 96:11 Mr 2 '70
FLAHERTY, Robert Joseph
Bob Flaherty remembered. H. V. Fondiller.
il Pop Phot 66:98+ Mr '70 *
FLAME throwers
Flame gun for the gardener; jet rod model.
il Consumer Bul 53:20-1 Jl '70
Flame thrower goes civilian. il Mech Illus
66:90-1 Ja '70
FLAMENCO
Ciro and his ballet flamenco, Alice Tully hall,
NYC. T. Borek. Dance Mag 44:75 D '70
Flamenco in Spain. M. Baguena. il Sat R 53:
48+ S 12 '70
Triana! whole exciting spectrum of flamenco
dance. V. H. Swisher. il pors Dance Mag
44:22-6 Jl '70
FLAMING fruit sauces. See Sauces
FLAMINGOS
Bird in the hand. il Natur Hist 79:76-9 Ja '69
East Africa's majestic flamingos. M. P. Kahl.
il por Nat Geog 137:276-94 F '70
FLAMMABLE textile fabrics. See Textile fab-
rics, Flammable
FLANAGAN, Brian
Home to the wars. Time 96:15 Ag 31 '70 *
FLANNER, Janet
Letter from Paris. See issues of New York-
er
                    about
[Photograph] B. Brandt. Harp Baz 103:138
F '70
FLANTZ, Richard
Comment. A. Brilliant. Poetry 116:129 My
'70 *
FLAPS, Airplane
747 flap track improvement discussed by
Boeing, airlines. R. G. O'Lone. Aviation
W 93:30 N 9 '70
FLARE stars. See Stars, Variable
FLASH connectors. See Photography—Elec-
tronic equipment
FLASH meters. See Exposure meters
FLASHCUBES. See Electric lamps, Photoflash
FLASHING electric lamps. See Electric lamps,
Flashing
FLASHLIGHTS, Electric
Low-priced flashlights. il Consumer Rep 36:
41-7 Ja '71
FLASHMAN, Harry Paget
At it again. C. Elliott. il Time 96:92+ O 5 '70 *
Up Britannia! A. Clun. Trans-Action 7:57-8
Mr '70 *
FLATTOPS. See Aircraft carriers
FLATWARE. See Tableware
FLATWARE, Stainless steel. See Tableware,
Stainless steel
FLAUMENHAFT, A. S.
Men of letters. il Har Yrs 10:22-3 Je '70
Pampered pooches. il por Har Yrs 10:14-15
S '70
FLAVIN, Dan
Art. L. Alloway. Nation 210:155-6 F 9 '70
Dan Flavin: fiat lux. W. S. Wilson. il por
Art N 68:48-51 Ja '70

FLAVONES
Dimethylbenzanthracene tumorigenesis and aryl hydrocarbon hydroxylase in mouse skin: inhibition by 7,8-benzoflavone. H. V. Gelboin and others. bibliog il Science 170:169-71 O 9 '70

FLAX Pond marine research laboratory. See New York (state)—Environmental conservation, Department of

FLEA markets. See Markets

FLEABANES
Wild daisy and English daisy. il Sunset 144:248-9 My '70

FLEAS
Compleat flea by B. Lehane. Review
Environ 11:55 Jl '69. S. Novick

FLEET, Robert R. See Coon, D. W. jt. auth.

FLEETS, Motor vehicle. See Motor vehicle fleets

FLEISCHER, R. L. and others
Particle track identification: application of a new technique to Apollo helmets. bibliog il Science 170:1189-91 D 11 '70

FLEISHER, Leon
Hand of fate. il por Newsweek 76:64-5 Ag 31 '70 *
Kindling a new flame. il por Time 96:47 S 7 '70 *

FLEISCHER, R. L. and others
Particle track, X-ray, thermal, and mass spectrometric studies of lunar material. bibliog il Science 167:568-71 Ja 30 '70

FLEMER, William, 3d
Narrow trees. il Horticulture 48:24-5+ Ap '70

FLEMING, Alice. See Fleming, T. J. jr, jt. auth.

FLEMING, Bethel
Modern medicine comes to ancient Nepal. E. D. Nadel. il por Todays Health 48:28-33+ My '70 *

FLEMING, Donald
Big science under fire. Atlan 226:96-101 S '70

FLEMING, James G.
Should abortion laws be liberalized? interview, ed. by C. Remsberg and B. Remsberg. pors Good H 170:92-3+ Mr '70

FLEMING, Karl
California on wheels: I'm somebody. il Newsweek 76:64-9 N 30 '70
—and Goldman, Peter
Ronald Reagan story: scenario for a star. il pors Newsweek 76:28-31 N 2 '70

FLEMING, Lawrence
SCR controls for small motors. il Electr World 83:36+ Je '70
Speed control for large d.c. motors. il Electr World 85:78 Ja '71

FLEMING, Ray
Black man looks at Boston; poem. America 122:585 My 30 '70

FLEMING, Robben Wright
Return to campus quiet. por Sch & Soc 98:326 O '70 *

FLEMING, Rodney R.
How to purchase and maintain street equipment. il Am City 85:96+ Ap '70

FLEMING, Shirley
In great mansions: a romantic revival. il Hi Fi 20:MA20-1 O '70
Karajan's modest Creation. Hi Fi 20:sec1 96 Ap '70
Little Vivaldi festival. Hi Fi 20:104 S '70
Musical kidney stone removal and other programmatic delights. Hi Fi 20:122 O '70
Russian Angles in America. il Hi Fi 20:sec1 71-2 My '70

FLEMING, Thomas James, 1927-
Abraham Lincoln's hardest decision. por Read Digest 96:94-9 F '70
Duel that changed our history. il Read Digest 97:190-5 Ag '70
Man who dared the lightning; condensation. il pors Read Digest 97:233-44+ Jl '70
Murder trial of Dr Ossian Sweet; reprint. il pors Ebony 25:106-8+ O '70
Policeman's lot. il Am Heritage 21:4-17+ F '70
West Point cadets now say, "why, sir?" il por N Y Times Mag p 14-18+ Jl 5; 68 Ag 16 '70
—and Fleming, Alice
What kids still don't know about sex. il Look 34:59-60+ Jl 28 '70; Same abr. Read Digest 97:153-6 D '70

FLESCH, Hugo
Son of Why Johnny can't read and what you can do about it, by Hugo Flesch, son of Rudolf Flesch, author of the father of son of Why Johnny can't read and... por Wilson Lib Bul 45:270-1 N '70

FLESCH, Rudolf
Son of Why Johnny can't read and what you can do about it, by Hugo Flesch, son of Rudolf Flesch, author of the father of son of Why Johnny can't read and... H. Flesch. por Wilson Lib Bul 45:270-1 N '70 *

FLETCHER, Arthur Allen
Neither separated nor integrated, but an open society. por Ebony 25:145-7 Ag '70
Sharing the wealth. H. Brandon. Sat R 53:5+ Ap 11 '70 *

FLETCHER, Derek
British bass; with biographical sketch. il Sea Front 16:164-9, 191 My '70

FLETCHER, Janet
Readers miscellany. Library J 95:498-9, 907, 1372-3, 1729-30, 2157, 2446-7 F 1, Mr 1, Ap 1, My 1, Je 1, Jl '70

FLETCHER, John. See Beaumont, F. jt. auth.

FLETCHER, Joseph Francis, 1905-
Genetic enginering. J. Rohler. Chr Today 14:50-1 Ap 10 '70 *

FLETCHER, Joseph O.
Polar ice and the global climate machine. il por Bul Atom Sci 26:40-7 D '70

FLETCHER, Tom
On the boards. W. Como. por Dance Mag 44:24 Ja '70

FLEURAGE. See Pictures

FLEXIBLE lines. See Fishing lures, flies, etc.

FLEXNER, James Thomas
Nineteenth century American painting; excerpts. il Antiques 98:432-5 S '70

FLICKER phenomena
Critical flicker-fusion of solid and annular stimuli. D. N. Robinson. bibliog il Science 167:207-8 Ja 9 '70

Der FLIEGENDE Holländer; opera. See Wagner, R.

FLIES
Behold the hateful housefly. J. B. Shuman. il Read Digest 96:49-50+ Je '70
Environmental and genetical contributions to class difference: a model experiment. J. M. Thoday and J. B. Gibson. bibliog il Science 167:990-2 F 13 '70
See also
Diptera
Dragonflies
Drosophila

FLIES, Artificial. See Fishing lures, flies, etc.

FLIES as carriers of infection
Saurian malaria: development of sporozoites in two species of phlebotomine sandflies. S. C. Ayala and D. Lee. bibliog il Science 167:891-2 F 6 '70

FLIGHT
See also
Aerodynamics
Birds—Flight
Insects—Flight

FLIGHT, Interplanetary. See Space flight

FLIGHT crews. See Airplane crews

FLIGHT directors. See Aeronautic instruments

FLIGHT nurses. See Nurses and nursing

FLIGHT planning by computer. See Computers—Aeronautic use

FLIGHT schools. See Aviation schools

FLIGHT simulators
Flight simulator for super jets. F. W. Holder. il Electr World 84:43+ Ag '70
Grounded; ground-bound pilot-training devices. R. B. Parke. Flying 86:38 F '70
Radar, cockpit views simulated. K. J. Stein. il Aviation W 92:46-7+ Je 8 '70
See also
Space flight simulators

FLINKER, Irving
Teacher recruitment and selection in New York city archaic and costly. il Clear House 44:483-7 Ap '70

FLINN, Sister Patricia
I teach in a racist school. America 123:201-3 S 26 '70

FLINT, Mich
Cold night in Flint. P. Tracy. Commonweal 91:447-50 Ja 23 '70

Education
Toward real teacher power; a single, unified organization. il Sr School 95:Schol Teach 1 N 17 '69

FLINT RIVER regional library, Griffin, Ga.
Three consultants, one county: Clayton County. W. Murphy. il Library J 95:2068+ Je 1 '70

FLIPPEN, J. L. and others
Crystal and molecular structure of a thymine phototrimer. bibliog il Science 169:1084-5 S 11 '70

FLOATING airports. See Airports, Floating

FLOATING hospitals. See Hospital ships

FLOATING instrument platforms. See Oceanographic buoys

FLOATING marinas. See Marinas

FLOATING trips. See Boats and boating

FLOATS, Fishing. See Fishing—Implements and appliances

FLOCCULATION. See Water purification

FLOCH, Jenny
Thrown chuck. il Ceram Mo 18:18-20 S '70
—and Efland, Arthur
Exhibition '70. il Craft Horiz 30:34-5+ O '70

FLOOD, Curt
Curt Flood strikes out. Newsweek 76:62 Ag 24 '70 *
Curt Flood's complaint. il por Newsweek 75:85 Je 1 '70 *
Enter Senator Flood. Newsweek 76:71 N 16 '70 *
Fair or foul? il por Sr Schol 96:14+ F 16 '70 *
Found, an Abe Lincoln of baseball. por Ebony 25:110-11 Mr '70 *
Players go to bat against baseball. il por Bsns W p74+ F 28 '70 *

FLOOD insurance. See Insurance, Flood

FLOOD lighting. See Light projection

FLOOD prevention and control
See also
Rivers—Regulation

United States
Story framed in pines; flood prevention projects. Miss. H. R. Williams. il Am For 76:20-3 Jl '70
U.S. and Mexico to improve Rio Grande flood control; White House announcement, October 7, 1970. Dept State Bul 63:681-2 N 30 '70

FLOODLIGHTING. See Light projection

FLOODS
Italy
After the flood in Genoa. il Life 69:44-5 O 30 '70
Malaysia
Of frogs and floods. Time 97:31 Ja 18 '71
Rumania
Rumania: the crest. il Time 95:40 Je 22 '70

FLOOR coverings
Beautiful floor: bare floors and carpeting. W. Baldwin. House & Gard 137:12-13+ Ap '70
Excitement for floors: color and pattern out of a bucket; Desert marble. il House & Gard 137:106-7 Ap '70
Rolls: floor and wall-covering materials. il Bet Hom & Gard 48:45-5+ Ja '70
See also
Rugs and carpets
Tiles, Floor

FLOOR leaders in Congress. See United States —Congress

FLOORING
Atomic wood, for stomping on. H. Friedman. il Mech Illus 66:72-3 D '70
Flooring. Bet Hom & Gard 48:86+ F '70
From home base; resilient flooring in your kitchen. M. K. Spencer. Am Home 73:44 S '70

FLOORS
Hazards and hurdles in developing standards; a case history. il Arch Rec 147:147-50 My '70
See also
Swine houses—Floors

FLOORS, Concrete
Concrete floor paints. il Consumer Rep 36:36-9 Ja '71

FLORAL design. See Design, Decorative—Plant forms

FLORAL initiation. See Fruit-bud development

FLORAL painting. See Flowers in art

FLORENCE
Art
Sequestered treasure; collection of the late Count Alessandro Contini-Bonacossi. il Time 96:72-5 S 14 '70
Music
Report:
Productions at Teatro comunale. J. C. Adams. Opera N 31:30 Mr 7 '70
Productions of Der fliegende Holländer and Verdi's Masnadieri. J. C. Adams. Opera N 34:30 F 14 '70

FLORENCE agreement. See Duty free importation

FLORES, Adolph R.
C.O.'s private battle. il por Time 96:35 N 23 '70 *

FLORES, Antonio Carrillo
Community and diversity; excerpt from address, April 14, 1970. il pors Américas 22:12-17 Je '70

FLORES, Edmundo
Land reform in Peru. Nation 210:174-7 F 16 '70

FLORICULTURE
Bits of nature and hand-me-downs. G. Alexander. il por Org Gard & Farm 17:53-6 O '70
Gardener's almanac; ed. by E. Haraszty. R. E. Atkinson. il McCalls 97:70-1+ My; 44+ Je; 48+ Jl; 24+ Ag; 26+ S; 98:50+ O; 38+ N; 21+ D '70; 44 Ja '71
Gardener's notes. See issues of House & garden incorporating Living for young homemakers
In your greenhouse. J. U. Crockett. See issues of Horticulture
See also
Annuals (plants)
Bulbs
Flowers
Gardening
Perennials
also names of flowers, e.g. Irises

FLORIDA
Florida. J. M. Zanutto. il Pop Phot 66:101-9 Je '70
See also
Airports—Florida
Architecture, Domestic—Florida
Biscayne Bay
Biscayne National Monument
Conservation of resources—Florida
Crime and criminals—Florida
Ecology—Florida
Education—Florida
Environmental policy—Florida
Everglades
Everglades National Park
Fishing—Florida
Hunting—Florida
Itchetucknee River
Kissimmee River
Oklawaha River
Palm Beach County
Reclamation of land—Florida
Sanibel Island
Ten Thousand Islands
Tourist trade—Florida
Description and travel
Dream called Florida. A. Rankin. il Read Digest 96:152-8 Mr '70
Florida for the boatman in 1970. E. S. Maloney. il Motor B 126:52-4 N '70
Florida West Coast Keys; Sarasota's islands. H. Sutton. Holiday 47:8+ My '70
From tip to top in Florida. G. Bourke. See issues of Travel
Industries
See also
Cattle industry and trade
Parks and reserves
Itchetucknee, Florida's crystal river. J. F. Stanfield. il Nat Parks & Con Mag 44:13-16 My '70
Politics and government
Carswell vs. Cramer: Senate fight with national overtones. pors U S News 69:34-5 S 7 '70
Carswell's fiasco; Republican primary. il pors Newsweek 76:39 S 21 '70
Dent in a hard hat; L. Chiles wins Senate seat. New Repub 163:10 N 14 '70
Having fun with Florida. R. M. Williams. il Nation 211:109-14 Ag 17 '70
Recognition factor; Cramer and Carswell campaign for Senate seat. Nation 210:547-8 My 11 '70
Verdict on the Florida judge. il por Time 96:16-17 S 21 '70

FLORIDA East Coast railway
When a railroad makes the rules. il Bsns W p 109-10 Ja 17 '70

FLORIDA EVERGLADES. See Everglades

FLORIDA flood control district. See Central and southern Florida flood control district

FLORIDA power and light company
Power play over pollution; thermal pollution of Biscayne Bay. il Bsns W p28-9 Mr 21 '70

FLORIDA. University
Libraries
I can't hear the flutes; excessive noise from nonbook learning devices in new Hume library. L. Cassidy. il Am Lib 1:888-9 O '70

FLORIN, A. E. See Rabideau, S. W. jt. auth.

FLORY, Elizabeth De Grunne
Living with antiques. il Antiques 97:730-3 My '70

FLORY, Sheldon
New Year; poem. New Yorker 46:30 Ja 2 '71

FLOTOW, Friedrich von
Martha. W. Botsford. il Am Rec G 36:872-4 Jl '70 *

FLOUR
Flimsy staff of life. J. Lear. Sat R 53:53-4 O 3 '70
Molecular approach to breadmaking. Y. Pomeranz and others. bibliog il Science 167:944-9 F 13 '70
See also
Grain

FLOUR beetles
Flour beetles: responses to extracts of their own pupae. M. F. Ryan and others. bibliog il Science 170:178-80 O 9 '70
Senescence and genetic load: evidence from tribolium. R. R. Sokal. bibliog il Science 167:1733-4 Mr 27 '70

FLOUR industry and trade
See also
Pillsbury company

FLOW charts
Flow chart approach to curriculum study. R. C. Kolz and J. O'Dell. il Clear House 45:72-5 O '70

FLOW of cash. See Cash flow

FLOW of matter. See Rheology

FLOWER arrangements. See Flowers, Arrangement of

FLOWER boxes, planters, etc.
At your nursery, a quiet revolution; use of plastic containers. il Sunset 145:205+ O '70
Big wood planter box. il Sunset 144:86-7 Ja '70
Complete your garden with a planter box. il Home Gard 57:56 F '70
Nursery planter tubs and boxes retrimmed with redwood. il Sunset 144:146 Ap '70
Strawberry jars and other odd pots with balconies, from Mexico. il Sunset 144:100-3 My '70

FLOWER-bud development. See Fruit-bud development

FLOWER City conspiracy trial. See Trials (conspiracy)

FLOWER exhibits
Coming events of interest to gardeners. See issues of Horticulture
Flower shows and garden tours. il House & Gard 137:205+ Mr '70
Garden events. See issues of Home garden & flower grower
Garden events [in month] (title varies) See issues of Sunset
Milking a cow at the flower show. New Yorker 46:34 Mr 21 '70
One orchid show after another. il Sunset 144:226 Ap '70
Twelve upcoming camellia shows. Sunset 144:192 F '70

FLOWER formation. See Fruit-bud development

FLOWER gardening. See Floriculture

FLOWER painting. See Flowers in art

FLOWER photography. See Photography of flowers, plants, trees, etc.

FLOWER pictures. See Pictures

FLOWER shows. See Flower exhibits

FLOWER stands
Bonsai do well on a stage. so do many other potted plants. il Sunset 144:180-1 F '70
Patio-door plant rack. M. Burns. il Org Gard & Farm 17:73 N '70
Plant display along a wall. il Sunset 144:221 Mr '70

FLOWERING crabapples. See Crab apples

FLOWERING dogwood. See Dogwood

FLOWERING maples
It's just great for hanging. il Sunset 144:198 Je '70

FLOWERING onions. See Alliums

FLOWERS, Sir Brian Hilton
Research in Britain: a non-weeping formula for living on tight funds. D. S. Greenberg. Science 167:1596-8 Mr 20 '70 *
Science on a tight budget. Science 170:1361 D 25 '70

FLOWERS, Cora
Basic reference books for writers. Writer 83:27-8+ O '70

FLOWERS, Frank C.
Discovering truth about words. Engl J 59:259-62 F '70

FLOWERS
Flowers of spring at our garden; Home garden of ideas in Sterling Forest garden. il Home Gard 57:20-1 S '70
Flowers shaped for the 70's. E. McDonald. il House B 112:124-5+ Ap '70

Flowers that bloom in the snow. E. McDonald. il House B 112:64-5+ Ja '70
New plants to grow for 1971. M. C. Ohlander. il Home Gard 58:34-40+ Ja '71
See also
Annuals (plants)
Bulbs
Fertilization of plants
Floriculture
Perennials
Pollen
State flowers
Wild flowers
also names of flowers, e.g. Daphnes

All America selections
See Plants—All America selections

FLOWERS, Arrangement of
Flower arranging classics. E. D. Craster and H. Mason. il Bet Hom & Gard 48:66-71 O '70
Please don't eat the flowers. il por House & Gard 137:74-7 F '70
Summer arrangements. Mrs A. H. Smith. il Horticulture 48:38-9+ Je '70
Traditional gladiolus arrangements. A. A. Ascher. il Horticulture 48:38-9 S '70
Using flowers on small tables. il Horticulture 48:32-3 My '70
See also
Bouquets

FLOWERS, Artificial
Flowers from beads. R. Wrenn. il pors Design 71:26-9 Spr '70
See also
Glass flowers

FLOWERS, Dried
Bouquets for winter. R. M. Peters. il Horticulture 48:32-3+ S '70
Fresh look at dried flowers. J. H. Hunter. il House B 112:58-9 Jl '70

FLOWERS, Glass. See Glass flowers

FLOWERS in art
Flowers that run. E. J Dorsey. il Design 71:10-12 Fall '69

FLOWERS in house decoration. See Plants in house decoration

FLOYD, Carlisle
Floyd's Of mice and men. R. Commanday. il Hi Fi 20:secII 28-9 Ap '70 *
Musician of the month. S. Fleming. il por Hi Fi sec II 20:8-9 F '70
Of mice and men. Criticism
Time il 95:51 F 9 '70

FLOYD, Charles Arthur
Oklahoma Robin Hood. K. L. Steckmesser. por Am West 7:38-41 Ja '70 *

FLUID control. See Hydraulic control

FLUID dynamics
Doppler shift is used to study superfluid currents. B. G. Levi. bibliog Phys Today 23:61 F '70

FLUIDICS. See Hydraulic control

FLUIDS
See also
Liquids

FLUIDS, Magnetic. See Magnetic fluids

FLUORENONE
Tilorone hydrochloride: an orally active antiviral agent. R. F. Krueger and G. D. Mayer. il Science 169:1213-14 S 18 '70
Tilorone hydrochloride: mode of action. G. D. Mayer and R. F. Krueger. il Science 170:1214-15 S 18 '70

FLUORENYLACETAMIDE
Reactivity in vivo of the carcinogen N-hydroxy-2-acetylaminofluorene: increase by sulfate ion. J. R. DeBaun and others. bibliog il Science 167:184-6 Ja 9 '70

FLUORESCENCE
Changes in extrinsic fluorescence in squid axons during voltage-clamp. F. Conti and I. Tasaki. bibliog il Science 169:1322-4 S 25 '70
See also
Luminescence
Mössbauer effect

FLUORESCENT antibodies. See Antibodies, Fluorescent

FLUORESCENT lamps in art. See Electric lamps in art

FLUORIDATION. See Water supply—Fluoridation

FLUORINE compounds
See also
Fluorocarbons

FLUORITE lenses. See Lenses, Photographic

FLUOROCARBON-polyol blood substitutes. See Blood substitutes

FLUOROCARBONS
Preparing fluorocarbons, a new method. il Chem 43:30 Ap '70

FLUOROCITRATES
Fluorocitrate inhibition of aconitase: relative configuration of inhibitory isomer by X-ray crystallography. H. L. Carrell and others. bibliog il Science 170:1412-14 D 25 '70

FLUTE
Slip cast ceramic flute. E. Traylor. il Ceram Mo 18:26-7 Mr '70

FLY casting
Fly for all season; ant flies. M. W. Fong. il por Outdoor Life 145:56-7+ My '70
Good bet for spring. J. Brooks. il Outdoor Life 145:76-7+ Mr '70
Honeymoon adventure; Grand Teton National Park. J. Clark. il Field & S 74:62-3+ Mr '70
How to fish flies deep; excerpts from Salt water fly fishing. G. X. Sand. Field & S 74:48-9+ F '70
Short casts, heavy creels. H. G. Tapply. il Field & S 75:82 My '70
Spin-cast flies, toothpaste tubes and wire. V. Kraft. il Sports Illus 32:66+ Je 8 '70
Ten-second salmon. N. Karas. il Field & S 74:66-7+ F '70
Untangling the tangled leader; ed. by A. J. McClane. il Field & S 75:94-8+ My '70

FLY fishing. See Fly casting

FLYING black medics (organization) See Medical service

FLYING boats. See Seaplanes

FLYING bridge. See Navigating bridge

FLYING Dutchman; opera. See Wagner, R.

FLYING machines
Flying platform developed. il Aviation W 93:61 S 28 '70
See also
Aeronautics—History
Autogiros

FLYING platforms. See Flying machines

FLYING saucers
Air force conclusion: spacemen don't fly saucers. il Sr Schol 95:2 Ja 12 '70
Now, a do-it-yourself UFO. D. Heiserman. il Pop Sci 196:109 My '70
Status inconsistency theory and flying saucer sightings. D. I. Warren. bibliog il Science 170:599-603 N 6 '70

FLYING Tiger line, inc.
Fighting off Flying Tiger. Bsns W p 19 Ag 15 '70
New prey for the Flying Tiger. T. J. Murray. il Duns 95:42-6 Mr '70
Robert W. Prescott of Flying Tiger line; interview. R. W. Prescott. il pors Nations Bsns 58:64-8+ O '70

FLYNN, Anne
Contract cities. il Parks & Rec 5:26-7+ Ap '70
New city for the '70s. il Am City 85:84+ O '70

FLYNN, Sean
Bad trip. il por Newsweek 75:101-2 Ap 20 '70 *
Missing in Cambodia. il pors Time 95:43 Ap 20 '70 *

FLYNN, William G.
Town like Fitchburg. por Newsweek 76:46 D 28 '70 *

FLYNN, William James
Watercolor page; with biographical sketch. il por Am Artist 34:60-2 D '70

FLYWHEELS
Another auto entry. il Sci N 98:218 S 12 '70
Cut subway power costs; New York city Metropolitan transportation authority. Am City 85:98 S '70
Fragmentary evidence. B. Lang. il Hot Rod 23:82-3 Ja '70
Super flywheel to power zero-emission car. A. P. Armagnac. il Pop Sci 197:41-3+ Ag '70
Wind up car. K. Hohenemser and J. McCaull. il Environ 12:14-21+ Je '70

FOAM metals. See Metals, Cellular

FOAM plastics in building. See Plastics in building

FOAMED materials
See also
Metals, Cellular

FOCHT, D. D. and Alexander, M.
DDT metabolites and analogs: ring fission by hydrogenomonas. bibliog il Science 170:91-2 O 2 '70

FOCUSING. See Photography—Focusing

FODOR, Denis
(ed) See Socarras Ramírez, A. Stowaway

FOG
Coming of the mist. F. Russell. il Audubon 72:16-25 N '70
See also
Automobile driving—Fog hazards
Aviation—Fog problem

FOG navigation. See Navigation

FOGEL, Howard H.
Swim in your garden this summer. il Home Gard 57:41-8 Ap '70

FOGEL, Yvonne
Laurance S. Rockefeller. il pors Parks & Rec 5:14-17+ Mr '70
Right on! il Parks & Rec 5:24+ N '70
Student designers tackle leisure area. il Parks & Rec 5:24-6 My '70

FOGGERS, Insect. See Spraying apparatus

FOKINE, Michel
Letter to Igor Fedorovitch, August 1940. Dance Mag 44:22 N '70

FOKKER, Royal Netherlands aircraft factory. See Airplane industry and trade—Netherlands

FOLDING doors. See Doors

FOLDING furniture. See Furniture

FOLDING stands. See Stands (furniture)

FOLDING tables. See Tables

FOLIAGE. See Leaves

FOLINSBEE, R. E. and others
Carbon-13 and oxygen-18 in dinosaur, crocodile, and bird eggshells indicate environmental conditions. bibliog il Science 168:1353-6 Je 12 '70

FOLK, Robert L.
Spherical urine in birds: petrography. bibliog Science 166:1516-19; 169:1231; 170:98-9 D 19 '69, S 18, O 2 '70

FOLK art
American folk art. il Good H 171:163 Jl '70
Frightful faces for Halloween; excerpts from Ephemeral folk figures by A. Parker and A. Neal. il Life 69:68-71 O 30 '70
From Chilean hands. J. Gómez-Sicre. il Américas 22:21-6 Ap '70
Made in Japan. R. Mitchell. il Natur Hist 79:60-5 O '70
Rediscovery: a remarkable trade sign; The tin man. il Art in Am 58:90-1 S '70
Shopping tour, Guadalajara to Mexico city and back to Guadalajara. il Sunset 145:64-75 O '70
When shall we three meet again, in thunder, lightning, or in rain? A. Neal. il Am Heritage 21:74-7 Ap '70

Exhibitions
Folk arts, cross-country; exhibition in U.S. pavilion at Expo '70. F. J. Dockstader. il Art in Am 58:74-7 Mr '70
Tinware show at the Museum of American folk art. J. Lipman. il Life 68:10 F 27 '70
Unknown masters; naive American paintings from the collection of E. W. and B. Chrysler Garbisch. il Time 95:54-5 F 9 '70

FOLK dance festivals. See Dance festivals

FOLK dancing
Tamburitzans; Hunter college. N. Mason. Dance Mag 44:96 My '70
See also
Dancing in religion, folklore, etc.

FOLK festivals. See Festivals

FOLK literature
Case for folk literature. A. Korpalski. il Todays Ed 59:63 N '70

FOLK lore. See Folklore

FOLK medicine. See Medicine, Popular

FOLK music
Songs of a people; folk music in opera. N. Payne. il Opera N 34:8-12 F 21 '70
See also
Phonograph records—Folk music

FOLK music, American
Back to the country (again) C. H. Simonds. il Nat R 22:216-17 F 24 '70
Country music. J. Greenway. Nat R 22:842+ Ag 11 '70
Country music gets soul; L. Martell at the Grand ole opry. il pors Ebony 25:66-8+ Mr '70
High noon for Tex Ritter. R. Cleghorn. il pors N Y Times Mag p 10-11+ Jl 12 '70
Kris Kristofferson is the new Nashville sound. P. Hemphill. il pors N Y Times Mag p54-5+ D 6 '70
Nashville sound, by P. Hemphill. Review
    Life il 68:16 My 1 '70. J. McGinnis
    New Repub 162:21-3 Je 27 '70. J. Seelye
Out of my mind on bluegrass. C. Lehmann-Haupt. il por N Y Times Mag p36-7+ S 13 '70
Pickin' and singin'; Bluegrass festival. il por Newsweek 75:85 Je 29 '70
Singing to silent America. P. Dickson. il Nation 210:211-13 F 23 '70

FOLK sculpture, American. See Folk art
FOLK singers. See Singers
FOLK songs, American
Willie York from Big East Fork. D. Snell.
il pors Life 69:53-8 Jl 17 '70
    See also
Ballads, American
FOLK songs, Portuguese
    See also
Fados
FOLK songs, Scottish
Hummel and George Thomson of Edinburgh.
J. Sachs. bibliog f il pors Mus Q 56:270-87
Ap '70
FOLK tales. See Folklore
FOLKLORE
    See also
Animal lore
Fairies
Weather lore
Africa
How men and women came to live together:
Kerebe tale; translation. A. Kitereza. il por
Natur Hist 79:8-9 Ja '70
Asia
Asian folktales: lively, recent editions. R. K.
Carlson. bibliog il por Wilson Lib Bul 45:
372-83 D '70
United States
American folklore in the secondary schools.
H. H. Lee. bibliog f Engl J 59:994-1004 O '70
Pug-nosed Lil and The girl with the blue
velvet band. A. Fife and A. Fife. il pors
Am West 7:32-7 Mr '70
FOLKLORE of birds. See Birds in religion,
folklore, etc.
FOLKLORE of lead. See Lead in religion, folk-
lore, etc.
FOLKLORE of oil. See Oil in religion, folk-
lore, etc.
FOLKLORE of trees. See Trees in religion,
folklore, etc.
FOLKWAYS. See Manners and customs
FOLLAIN, Jean
Comment. S. Berg. Poetry 116:262-4 Jl '70 *
FOLLOW the River Lai; drama. See Winther. B.
FOLLOW through program. See Project Head
Start—Follow through programs
FOLLOWS, Donald S.
Capitol Reef: extended monument. il Nat
Parks & Con Mag 44:4-9 Jl '70
FOLSOM, Theodore R.
Choose a changer. Hi Fi 20:secI 58 Ap '70
FOLSOM, Calif.
Parting shots; two bears named Smokey. S.
Mahoney. il Life 68:72-4 Ap 3 '70
FOLSOM man. See Man, Prehistoric
FOLSTAD, John William. See Levy. G. F. jt.
auth.
FOLTZ, Charles S. Jr
Coup in Cambodia: eyewitness account. il
por U S News 68:19-20 Mr 30 '70
(ed) See Nasser, G. A. New crisis in Mid-
east
FOLTZ, R. L. and others
Metabolite of (—)-trans-Δ⁸-tetrahydrocanna-
binol: identification and synthesis. bibliog
il Science 168:844-5 My 15 '70
FONDA, Henry
Flying Fondas and how they grew; with in-
terview. il pors Time 95:58-63 F 16 '70 *
FONDA, Jane
Jane Fonda talks about. .; interview, ed. by
L. Lerman. pors Mlle 71:328-31 Ag '70
    about
Cause celeb. il por Newsweek 76:65 N 16 '70
Flying Fondas and how they grew; with
interview. il pors Time 95:58-63 F 16 '70 *
Movies: "astonish me!" P. Bosworth. il por
McCalls 97:14+ Ap '70 *
Trade winds. C. Amory. Sat R 53:14 O 10 '70 *
Two young successes: Liza Minnelli and Jane
Fonda. pors Vogue 155:106-7 Je '70 *
FONDA, Peter
Flying Fondas and how they grew; with
interview. il pors Time 95:58-63 F 16 '70 *
FONDILLER, Harvey V.
Film notes. See issues of Popular photog-
raphy
Globe photos: picture agency plus. il Pop
Phot 66:78-9+ F '70
Magnamultiscreen at Expo '70. il Pop Phot
66:102-3+ My '70
Movie camera factories of Europe. il Pop
Phot 67:124-6 N '70
Twelve books for film makers. il Pop Phot
66:91+ Mr '70
FONDUES
Fondues are fun! il Good H 171:122-3 N '70

FONG, Michael W.
Fly for all season. il por Outdoor Life 145:
56-7+ My '70
Trouting in solitude. il pors Outdoor Life
146:54-7+ S '70
FONGER, Hilary
Punishment; story. Redbook 134:90-1 Ap '70
FONO, Paulette, and Stacho, Maria
Great crepe recipes; excerpts from The crepe
cookbook. il Redbook 134:90-3+ F '70
FONSELIUS, Stig H.
Stagnant sea. bibliog il Environ 12:2-11+
Jl '70
FONT, Louis P.
West Point cadets now say, "why, sir?" T.
Fleming. il por N Y Times Mag p 14-18+
Jl 5 '70 *
FONTAINE, André
New climate of coexistence. Cur 122:60-4 O '70
FONTAINE, John Pierceall Kearfott
Ex-owner didn't fit in. pors Bsns W p64+
F 14 '70 *
FONTENOT, Sherrill
Fille en noir; poem. Sat R 53:51 Ag 22 '70
FONTEYN, Dame Margot
Dame Margot; interview. New Yorker 46:
24-5 My 30 '70
    about
Cinderella. W. Terry. il por Sat R 53:58 N 7
'70 *
Dame Margot and her new cavalier. W. Terry.
il pors Sat R 53:62+ F 28 '70 *
Open letter to Dame Margot Fonteyn. K.
Tunney. il Harp Baz 103:162-3 F '70
Stars beyond. il Time 95:68+ My 25 '70 *
Subtract a little tenderness. N. M. Stoop. il
pors Dance Mag 44:32-4 Ag '70 *
FONTINELL, Eugene
If you could make one change in the church,
what would it be? Commonweal 92:166 My
1 '70
FOOD
Food consumption patterns in the seventies;
address, November, 1969. L. P. Ullens-
vang. Vital Speeches 36:240-6 F 1 '70
    See also
Cookery
Diet
Dinners and dining
Nutrition
Nutrition problems
Oils and fats, Edible
Salads
Sandwiches
Vegetarianism
Analysis
    See also
Coloring matter in food
Contamination
    See Food contamination
Drying
    See also
Freeze drying
Fruit—Drying
Fat content
Fats and the heart; recommendations of the
Inter-society commission for heart disease
resources. il Newsweek 76:38-9 D 28 '70
Role of diet; report of Inter-society commis-
sion for heart disease resources. Sci N 98:
461 D 19 '70
Irradiation
    See Food, Effect of radiation on
Marketing
Getting food to the table in hungry lands.
por Bsns W p 134 My 23 '70
Marketing organic foods in the '70's; sympo-
sium. il Org Gard & Farm 17:37-55+ Ag '70
Move to eat natural; with report by E. Lans-
ing. il Life 69:44-50+ D 11 '70
To market, to market for organic food. M.
Franz. il Org Gard & Farm 17:62-4 Ja '70
Where to buy organic foods and products.
J. Olds. Org Gard & Farm 17:64-5 My '70
Preservation
    See Food preservation and preservatives
Prices
A&P's own brand of consumerism. il Bsns W
p32 Ap 11 '70
American farmer: the consumers' real pro-
tector; address, June 23, 1970. C. May. Vital
Speeches 36:625-8 Ag 1 '70
Break for housewives, not for farmers. il
Fortune 82:24 S '70
Food for Americans: prices, safety, new prod-
ucts; interview. C. W. Cook. il pors U S
News 68:74-8 Je 1 '70

FOOD—Prices—*Continued*
Food outlook for 1970. il Camp Mag 42:14 Ap
'70
Food prices: eat your heart out. il Bsns W
p27 F 14 '70
Grocery bills; effect of discount pricing in
Washington, D.C. D. Sanford. New Repub
163:12-14 O 17 '70
How one man tackled his grocery bill; com-
parison in time and money between con-
venience foods and cooking from scratch.
E. J. Dapron, jr. il Bet Hom & Gard 48:26-
7+ Jl '70
Saving graces. F. M. Crawford. Am Home
73:108 O '70
Thought for food. Fortune 81:80 Mr '70
See also
Meat—Prices

Ready-to-cook food

How one man tackled his grocery bill; com-
parision in time and money between con-
venience foods and cooking from scratch.
E. J. Dapron, jr. il Bet Hom & Gard 48:26-7+
Jl '70
How to use convenience foods at camp. W.
Weir. il Camp Mag 42:44-5 Mr '70

Storage

Good ideas for using and storing holiday-
food leftovers. il Good H 171:162 D '70
How to keep foods hot and cold. Bet Hom &
Gard 48:49+ Je '70
See also
Farm produce—Storage
FOOD, Contaminated. See Food contamination
FOOD, Cost of. See Food—Prices
FOOD, Dried
See also
Freeze drying
FOOD, Effect of radiation on
Strawberries, papayas, finfish. Sci N 97:217
F 28 '70
FOOD, Enriched
Chemical breakfast; controversy over forti-
fied cereals. D. Sanford. New Repub 163:
12-15 Ag 22 '70
FOOD, Frozen
Boil a bag or so. E. Gibbs. Motor B 126:
102-4 S '70
Cooking for the freezer; recipes. il Redbook
135:65-6+ S '70
Filling the freezer. il Consumer Rep 34:675-7
N '69
Frozen cake. il Consumer Rep 35:55-8 Ja '70
Is good frozen pie just pie in the sky? Con-
sumer Rep 35:330-1 Je '70
Parties from the freezer; with recipes. M. M.
Hemingway. House & Gard 137:129-32+ My
'70
Soul on ice. Newsweek 75:57 Mr 9 '70
What about instant breakfasts? Swanson
frozen breakfasts. Consumer Rep 35:195 Ap
'70
What is the difference between this photo-
graph and a real frozen TV dinner? M. F.
K. Fisher. il Esquire 74:96-9+ Ag '70
When you leave the dinner to dad; recipes for
main dishes to freeze. il Parents Mag 45:64-
5+ Ag '70
Your freezer; the family treasure chest;
recipes. F. M. Crawford. il Am Home 73:78-
80+ S '70
See also
Fish, Frozen
Freeze drying
Freezers
Freezing of food
Green giant company
Meat, Frozen
Vegetables, Frozen
FOOD, Irradiated. See Food, Effect of radiation
on
FOOD, Organic
Adelle Davis and the new nutrition; inter-
view, ed. by J. Poppy. A. Davis. il pors
Look 34:62+ D 15 '70
Anyone can homestead on two acres. J. Cox.
il Org Gard & Farm 17:81-2+ O '70
Direct-to-customer organic food farm. C. F.
Marley. il Org Gard & Farm 17:45-7 Mr '70
Ecological consumer products listing. J. Olds.
il Org Gard & Farm 17:52-4 Je '70
Health food; why . . . and why not. J. Trager.
Vogue 157:122-3+ Ja 1 '71
Kosher of the counterculture. il Time 96:
59-60+ N 16 '70
Make mine amino acids. M. Ungerer. il Life
68:18 My 22 '70
More farms for organic food. M. C. Goldman.
il Org Gard & Farm 17:68-73 D '70

More organic foods for wise shoppers. M. C.
Goldman. il Org Gard & Farm 17:78-82 Mr
'70
Move to eat natural; with report by E. Lans-
ing. il Life 69:44-50+ D 11 '70
Organic food and health. J. I. Rodale. Org
Gard & Farm 17:103-4+ D '70
Organic food symposium makes history. M.
C. Goldman. il Org Gard & Farm 17:38-45
Ag '70
Organic living for half a million people. J.
Olds. il Org Gard & Farm 17:40-4 Mr '70
Sharp rise in organic food demand. M. C.
Goldman. il Org Gard & Farm 17:66-70 Ap
'70
Stuff of life. il Newsweek 75:100 My 25 '70
See also
Cookery—Organic food
Erewhon trading company
Whole earth cooperative

Marketing
See Food—Marketing
FOOD, Raw
See also
Vegetarianism
FOOD, Synthetic. See Food substitutes
FOOD, Wild
Best food in town. E. Gibbons. Org Gard
& Farm 17:108-11 F '70
Interlude on an unspoiled island; wild vege-
tables for a wild luau. E. Gibbons. Org
Gard & Farm 17:88-91 Jl '70
Love-out on an island. E. Gibbons. il Org
Gard & Farm 17:82-4 Je '70
Nibbling at the edge of a daring adventure.
E. Gibbons. Org Gard & Farm 17:102-5 Ap
'70
Wild parties, Boy scout style. E. Gibbons.
Org Gard & Farm 17:92-4 Ag '70
See also
Plants, Edible
FOOD additives
Balance is all in their favor. F. Stare. por
Life 68:38 Mr 6 '70
Chemical feast, by J. S. Turner. Review
Environ il 12:40-1 O '70. D. Cottrell
Congressman who fights for safe food. M. C.
Goldman. Org Gard & Farm 17:66-70 My '70
Danger of cancer in food; controversy over
repeal of the Delaney clause. J. Carper. il
Sat R 53:47-9+ S 5 '70
Facts on food additives. Good H 170:6 Je '70
Food for Americans: prices, safety, new prod-
ucts; interview. C. W. Cook. il pors U S
News 68:74-8 Je 1 '70
Lessons cyclamates teach. Consumer Rep 35:
59-60 Ja '70
Look at food from the inside. R. Rodale.
il Org Gard & Farm 17:29-32 N '70
Secretary Finch is not alarmed. J. Car-
per. Nation 210:262-5 Mr 9 '70
See also
Monosodium glutamate
FOOD adulteration and inspection
See also
United States—Food and drug administration
FOOD allergy
Of man and milk; milk intolerance. il Time
96:59 Jl 13 '70
FOOD and agriculture organization of the
United Nations
Access to the oceans' wealth. R. L. Tobin.
Sat R 53:24 N 28 '70
Address by the Secretary-General to the sec-
ond World food congress; June 16, 1970.
Thant. UN Mo Chron 7:132-8 Jl '70
Hunger and the preschool child; FAO's dairy
scheme. R. L. Tobin. il Sat R 53:18 Jl 11 '70
Reform, revolution and food; World food
congress. F.W. Detje. il Sci N 98:86 Jl 25
'70
To save the seas; conference. Time 96:40 D
28 '70
UN and the power of food; progress report on
the World food programme. R. L. Tobin.
Sat R 53:20 Ja 31 '70
World agricultural plan. A. H. Boerma. il Sci
Am 223:54-63+ bibliog(p 128) Ag '70
FOOD and drug administration. See United
States—Food and drug administration
FOOD as gifts
Boutique gifts from your kitchen. il McCalls
98:52-3 D '70
Christmas presents made with great spirits.
House & Gard 138:102-4 D '70
Fruit and nut breads. il Sunset 145:158-9 N
'70
Goodies to go. il Bet Hom & Gard 48:58-9+
D '70
Imaginative gifts from your kitchen. fruit
wine cordials. il Sunset 145:129 D '70
Under peek-through plastic, a gift of home-
made sweets. il Sunset 145:158 D '70

FOOD buying. See Purchasing, Household

FOOD buying groups, Cooperative. See Purchasing, Cooperative

FOOD chains (ecology)
Photosynthesis and fish production in the sea. J. H. Ryther; reply with rejoinder. D. L. Alverson and others. bibliog Science 168:503-5 Ap 24 '70
Pyramiding damage; experimental study of DDT movement in the environment. T. J. Peterle. bibliog il pors Environ 11:34-40 Jl '69
Resources of the sea. J. A. Gulland. il Sea Front 16:211-19 Jl '70

FOOD colors. See Coloring matter in food

FOOD contamination
Could you stay in business without additives? carcasses with residues. R. Wilmore. Farm J 94:H28 O '70
How to stay away from drug-residue problems; meat contamination. J. G. Clark. Farm J 94:B28 O '70
Poisons in your food, by R. Winter. Review Environ 11:32-3 S '69. M. Duffy
Pollution, your problem too; food residue control. R. Sanders. il Suc Farm 68:32-3 S '70

FOOD distribution. See Food—Marketing; Nutrition problems—United States

FOOD for peace program. See Food relief

FOOD freezers. See Freezers

FOOD habits
Eat! Says fat little Johnny's mother. C. B. Hicks. il Todays Health 48:48-50+ F '70
Eating and being eaten; excerpt from Jungle in the house. M. Bates. il Sci Digest 68:20-4 Jl '70
Flap over food. il Life 69:44-9 Ag 21 '70
Food book, by J. Trager. Review Newsweek 76:102+ S 21 '70. S. K. Oberbeck
Food consumption patterns in the seventies; address, November, 1969. L. P. Ullensvang. Vital Speeches 36:240-6 F 1 '70

FOOD in the Bible. See Bible—Food

FOOD industry and trade
Fatter outlook for diet foods. il Bsns W p93+ Je 6 '70
Good nutrition? Only in spurts. J. Cross. Nation 211:357 O 19 '70
Hunger and the marketplace; excerpts from Let them eat promises: the politics of hunger in America. N. Kotz. Harper 240:88-92 Ja '70
Poisons in your food, by R. Winter. Review Environ 11:32-3 S '69. M. Duffy
See also
Cadbury Schweppes, ltd.
Canneries
CPC international, inc.
Food—Marketing
Food additives
General foods corporation
Hershey foods corporation
Infants food
McDonald's corporation
Meat, Frozen
Nestlé company
Squibb Beech-nut, inc.
White House conference on food, nutrition, and health

Consolidations and mergers
Bold start for AMK and United fruit. Bsns W p22-3 Jl 4 '70

FOOD labels. See Labels

FOOD laws and legislation
After cyclamates; what's next on the FDA's food target list? Delaney clause. K. N. Anderson. il Sci Digest 67:16-23 F '70
Bladder tumors in rats fed cyclohexylamine or high doses of a mixture of cyclamate and saccharin. J. M. Price and others. bibliog il Science 167:1131-2 F 20 '70
Congressman who fights for safe food; Delaney clause. M. C. Goldman. Org Gard & Farm 17:66-70 My '70
Danger of cancer in food; controversy over repeal of the Delaney clause. J. Carper. il Sat R 53:47-9+ S 5 '70
Flimsy staff of life. J. Lear. Sat R 53:53-4 O 3 '70
See also
United States—Food and drug administration

FOOD mixers, Electric. See Household appliances, Electric

FOOD mixes
Irresistible: cake mix desserts. il Redbook 135:98-9+ Jl '70
Work wonders with biscuit mix. il Ladies Home J 87:80+ F '70

FOOD plants. See Plants, Edible

FOOD poisoning
Food poisoning: salmonellosis and staphylococcus poisoning. il Consumer Bul 53:15-17 Ag '70

FOOD preservation and preservatives
Proper food preservation. E. A. Zadig. il Motor B 126:12-13+ Jl '70
See also
Food, Effect of radiation on
Freeze drying
Freezing of food

FOOD production. See Food supply

FOOD quackery. See Quacks and quackery

FOOD relief
President reports to Congress on 1969 Food for peace program; text of letter, June 18, 1970. R. M. Nixon. Dept State Bul 63:37-8 Jl 13 '70
Regulating compassion. L. K. Tarr. Chr Today 14:37 F 13 '70
See also
Food and agriculture organization of the United Nations

Nigeria
Reports: Washington; bungling Biafran relief. E. B. Drew. Atlan 225:4+ Je '70

United States
Food for thought? college students and federal food stamps. Newsweek 76:107 D 21 '70
Food stamp program changes could help older Americans. Aging 184:22 F '70
Hunger and the marketplace; excerpts from Let them eat promises: the politics of hunger in America. N. Kotz. Harper 240:88-92 Ja '70
Mrs Leavitt lends a hand; demonstrating how to use government-issue commodities. J. E. Roper. por Read Digest 96:132-4 F '70
Nixon's fight against hunger. il U S News 68:24-6 Ja 19 '70
Our food-stamp fiasco. L. Velie. Read Digest 96:103-7 Je '70
Strikers, college students get food stamps too. Farm J 94:39 D '70
TRB from Washington; Congress and the report on food stamp distribution by T. P. Goggin. New Repub 162:4 Je 20 '70
Why can't we just give them food? commodity and food stamp programs. R. Sherrill. il N Y Times Mag p28-9+ Mr 22 '70; Reply with rejoinder. J. Mayer. p32+ Ap 26 '70

FOOD research
See also
Nutrition research

FOOD sensitiveness. See Food allergy

FOOD shopping. See Shopping and shoppers

FOOD stamp plan. See Food relief—United States

FOOD storage. See Food—Storage

FOOD stores
Action's at the Boston area Ecology action center. Org Gard & Farm 17:64-5 Ag '70
Organic supermarket on the grow. il Org Gard & Farm 17:60-3 Ag '70
Southern California: food-shopper's paradise! organic foods. M. C. Goldman. il Org Gard & Farm 17:38-45 N '70
See also
Erewhon trading company
Supermarkets

FOOD substitutes
Beefsteak from bean webs. J. Reinert. il Sci Digest 68:17-22 S '70
Foods of the future; synthetics and vegetable protein food. il Chem 43:25 Je '70
Guide to new meatless meat products. il Good H 171:181 O '70
See also
Milk substitutes

FOOD supply
Human food production as a process in the biosphere. L. R. Brown. il Sci Am 223:160-70 bibliog(p265) S '70
More or less people; thoughts on feeding the hungry. W. H. Davis. il New Repub 162:19-21 Je 20 '70
New wheats and social progress. L. P. Reitz. bibliog il Science 169:952-5 S 4 '70
World hunger: the crisis an expert sees; interview. R. L. Hall. il por U S News 69:66-9 S 28 '70
See also
Fisheries
Food and agriculture organization of the United Nations
Nutrition problems
Production, Agricultural
Underdeveloped areas—Food supply
World food programme

FOOD supply—*Continued*

New sources

See also
Fish protein concentrate

India

Ironies of India's green revolution. W. Ladejinsky. For Affairs 48:758-68 Jl '70

Nigeria

Food from the sea for Nigeria. C. P. Idyll. il Sea Front 16:340-51 N '70

United States

How your market will grow. C. W. Gifford. il Farm J 94:40B-40C Ap '70
See also
Nutrition problems—United States

FOOD technology
Some problems in food technology. Chem 43:5 My '70

FOOD values
Breakfast of what? views of R. B. Choate, jr. Newsweek 76:57-8 Ag 3 '70
Cereal tempest; views of Robert B. Choate, jr. Sr Schol 97:5-6 S 14 '70
Don't be fooled by these food myths. Good H 172:125 Ja '71
Health food: why . . . and why not. J. Trager. Vogue 157:122-3+ Ja 1 '71
Let's talk about food. P. L. White. See issues of Today's health
Preserving vitamins and minerals in food. il Good H 171:153 S '70
See also
Diet
Nutrition

FOOD waste disposers. See Refuse grinders

FOONER, Andrea
House of Anne Frank. Travel & Camera 33: 16+ Je '70

FOOT
I am Joe's foot. J. D. Ratcliff. il Read Digest 97:117-20 S '70

Care and hygiene

How to be a feet snob. Redbook 135:60 il(p88-9) Jl '70
How to step beautifully into summer. P. Van Wagenen. il Parents Mag 45:83-5 My '70
Keep your feet walking. C. Coiro. il Har Yrs 10:48-50 Mr '70
Leg to stand on: feet too. il Mlle 70:254-5 Ap '70
Of course your feet hurt. il Changing T 24: 33-4 F '70
Preventing summer foot-care problems. il Good H 171:153 Ag '70
Your poor tired feet. A. Hamilton. il Sci Digest 68:82-6 N '70

FOOT painting. See Art—Study and teaching

FOOTBALL
Academic approach to the spectacular; Air force academy. P. Putnam. il por Sports Illus 33:60+ O 12 '70
And now the bowl season. il Newsweek 77: 66-7 Ja 4 '71
Archie and the war between the states; University of Mississippi vs Alabama. W. F. Reed. il pors Sports Illus 33:14-17 O 12 '70
Arms against the ogres; Plunkett and Theismann vs Texas and Ohio state in bowl games. D. Jenkins. il Sports Illus 33:28-30+ D 21 '70
Big-time college football is on the skids. S. Padwe. il Look 34:66-9 S 22 '70
Body language, 1970; Texas Longhorns vs Arkansas Razorbacks. D. Jenkins. il Sports Illus 33:20-5 D 14 '70
Brawl in the afternoon. J. C. Smith. Nat R 22:262 Mr 10 '70
College football 1970. il Sports Illus 33:46-76+ S 14 '70
Day of the champion; New Year's day bowl games. il Newsweek 77:55 Ja 11 '71
Devil's devil; Arizona state Sun Devils. il Newsweek 76:56 O 26 '70
Eating high on the hogs; Stanford Indians vs Arkansas Razorbacks. D. Jenkins. il Sports Illus 33:22-5 S 21 '70
End of a season at Syracuse; inability to resolve differences with black football players. P. Putnam. il Sports Illus 33:22-3 S 28 '70
Flying to the bowl games; Orange bowl, Cotton bowl and Rose bowl. il Flying 87:69-72 D '70
Football. See issues of New Yorker
For Easterners, prospecting doesn't pay off; Colorado vs Penn state. D. Jenkins. il Sports Illus 33:46-8 O 5 '70
Green and leafy football; small college answer to big-time madness. S. Isaacs. il Look 34: 68-72+ O 20 '70

Just ask the tailgate set who is no. 1; answer: Dartmouth. E. Shrake. il Sports Illus 33:44-5 N 9 '70
Longhorns and longhairs; football, blacks, and hippies at the University of Texas. J. Toback. Harper 241:70-3 N '70
Mad, mad punter of Louisville: barefoot S. Marcus. J. Underwood. il pors Sports Illus 33:36-41 N 9 '70
Meet Michigan's meanest man; Wolverine coach, B. Schembechler. P. Putnam. il por Sports Illus 33:32-3 N 16 '70
Nebraska skins the 'Cats and earns a bowl; Cornhuskers vs Kansas state. W. F. Reed. il Sports Illus 33:67-8 N 23 '70
Not such a bad scene at all; Kent state vs Ohio university. S. Treadwell. il Sports Illus 33:52+ S 28 '70
Notre Dame goes kicking into the Cotton. S. Myslenski. il Sports Illus 33:70-1 N 30 '70
Out of their league, by D. Meggyesy. Review Bsns W p6 Ja 2 '71. M. Ruby
Please say it ain't so, Joe; Notre Dame vs Southern Cal. J. Tobin. il Sports Illus 33:64+ D 7 '70
Reports of li'l Joe's death were premature; J. Theismann of Notre Dame. P. Putnam. Sports Illus 33:51-2 O 26 '70
Revival and revenge; Ohio state vs Michigan. D. Jenkins. il por Sports Illus 33:16-19 N 30 '70
Round on the ends and hi in the middle: O-hi-o! Ohio state Buckeyes. H. L. Masin. il Sr Schol 95:32 S 29 '69
Sis-boom-bah! choosing the top college team. il Newsweek 76:50+ D 7 '70
Sports; The rhinoceros hypothesis. R. Kahn. Esquire 74:78+ N '70
Tennessee lonesome end; L. McClain. P. Schrag. il Harper 240:59-63+ Mr '70
Texas by an eyelash; Longhorns vs Arkansas Razorbacks. D. Jenkins. il por Sports Illus 31:20-5 D 15 '69
They don't play no mullets down there; small-college football. P. Putnam. il Sports Illus 33:20-5 N 2 '70
Tornado with a new twist; Coaches All-America football game. W. F. Reed. il Sports Illus 33:16-17 Jl 6 '70
Two fast gunslingers were slow on the draw; Jim Plunkett of Stanford and Dennis Dummit of UCLA. D. Jenkins. il Sports Illus 33:51-2 N 2 '70
Two gods too many; Ohio state, Texas and Notre Dame battle for national title. D. Jenkins. il Sports Illus 33:14-17 N 9 '70
Upside down and over with the coast crazies; Stanford vs USC; UCLA vs Oregon. A. Rosenbaum. il Sports Illus 33:48-9 O 19 '70
Week; college football. H. Peterson. Sports Illus 33:71-2+ N 30 '70
Week; college football. P. Putnam. Sports Illus 33:68+ N 23 '70
Week; college football. W. F. Reed, jr. il Sports Illus 33:49-50+ O 19; 52-4 O 26; 45-7 N 9; 67-9 D 7 '70
Week; college football. S. Treadwell. Sports Illus 33:70-1 N 16 '70
With bowls ahead, they're whistling in Dixie; Southeastern conference bowl-happy four teams. W. F. Reed. il Sports Illus 33:66+ N 16 '70
Woo of Texas is upon you; S. Worster of Texas Longhorns. D. Jenkins. il Sports Illus 33:18-19 O 19 '70
See also
Football players
Soccer

Accidents and injuries

Casualty list. Newsweek 76:76 N 2 '70
Casualty list; NFL injuries. Sports Illus 33: 17 N 23 '70
Football knee; report by the National research council. il Newsweek 76:78 S 7 '70
Game that gets a good man down; with photographs by C. Iwasaki. Sports Illus 33:28-35 Ag 17 '70
Mayhem on the line; pro football's linemen. P. Zimmerman. il Look 34:26-31 D 29 '70
What a way to make a living; pro football. il Sports Illus 33:18-22 N 16 '70

Anecdotes, facetiae, satire, etc.

Everything you always wanted to know about football. R. Baker. Read Digest 97: 59-60 O '70

Bibliography

Let's hear it for old hyperbole. J. Newcombe. il Life 69:14 O 2 '70

Finance

He cried all the way to the bank; eleventh game, USC vs Alabama. P. Putnam. Sports Illus 33:78+ S 21 '70

FOOTBALL—*Continued*

Photographs

Man in the middle. Sports Illus 33:56-63 S 21 '70

What a way to make a living. il Sports Illus 33:18-22 N 16 '70

FOOTBALL accidents. See Football—Accidents and injuries

FOOTBALL clubs

Beer cans or bouquets; San Francisco 49ers. il Newsweek 76:76 N 2 '70

Big ifs in big D; Dallas Cowboys. T. Maule. il Sports Illus 33:10-13 Ag 31 '70

Catch-up football; Kansas City Chiefs vs Minnesota Vikings in Super bowl. il Newsweek 75:60-1 Ja 26 '70

Coach wants to see you; ed. by J. Underwood. B. Lusteg. il Sports Illus 33:92-6+ S 21 '70

Cracks in a golden egg. P. Rozelle. il por Forbes 106:23-4 S 15 '70

For the Saints, realignment is a love-in. T. Maule. il Sports Illus 31:62-3+ D 15 '69

Future moves into the past; Minnesota Vikings vs. Kansas City Chiefs. T. Maule. il Sports Illus 33:26-8 S 28 '70

George Blanda is alive and kicking; Oakland Raiders. il por Time 96:74 N 23 '70

Growing weary in their aerie; Philadelphia Eagles. R. F. Jones. il Sports Illus 33:20-2+ O 5 '70

Harvard vs. Patriots. Newsweek 75:58 F 16 '70

He goes where the trouble is; J. Kapp wandering quarterback. J. Olsen. il pors Sports Illus 33:22-4+ O 19 '70

He whistles while he works; NFL referees. W. F. Reed. il pors Sports Illus 33:22-7 Ag 10 '70

How intangible can you get; ed. by M. Cope. A. Hawkins. il pors Sports Illus 33:48-50+ N 23 '70

How the West was, uh, tied; San Francisco 49ers vs Los Angeles Rams. T. Maule. il Sports Illus 33:24-6+ D 7 '70

Into the Pride bowl: the Baltimore Colts and the Dallas Cowboys. il Time 97:44 Ja 18 '71

Jolly Giants. il Newsweek 76:91-2 N 30 '70

Let George do it, and he does; Oakland Raiders vs Denver Broncos. T. Maule. il por Sports Illus 33:30-2+ N 23 '70

Let's hear it for old hyperbole. J. Newcombe. il Life 69:14 O 2 '70

Loose and fun-loving off the field; ed. by M. Cope. A. Hawkins. il Sports Illus 33: 88-90+ N 16 '70

Man of machismo; ed. by J. Olsen. J. Kapp. il pors Sports Illus 33:26-31 Jl 20; 30-7 Jl 27; 20-5 Ag 3 '70

Meet Mr Twinkletoes and his friends; A. Karras of Detroit Lions. G. Plimpton. il por Sports Illus 33:22-4+ O 12 '70

Message from Minnesota: three dots and a dash; Minnesota Vikings vs Chicago Bears. P. Putnam. il Sports Illus 33:28-30+ D 14 '70

Miami gets a miracle worker; Miami Dolphins vs Baltimore Colts. D. Shula. il por Sports Illus 33:16-17 S 7 '70

Mystique of pro football; Time essay. C. Clark. il Time 96:36-7 N 9 '70

No miracle required; Oakland Raiders, western division title winners. T. Maule. il Sports Illus 33:18-23 D 21 '70

Philosophy of a corner linebacker. J. McMurtry. Nation 212:83-4 Ja 18 '71

Pro football '70; scouting reports; National football league, American football league. T. Maule. il Sports Illus 33:34-40+ S 21 '70

Pro football's dazzling new look; Kansas City Chiefs; ed. by D. Anderson. H. Stram. il Look 34:27-34 S 8 '70

Rosenbloom-Robbie bowl; Colts vs Dolphins. J. Olsen. il pors Sports Illus 33:22-4+ N 9 '70

Route of the super Chiefs. il por Time 95:35 Ja 26 '70

Rubies and diamonds; Detroit pro football draft. G. Plimpton. Sports Illus 32:24-6 F 9 '70

Rushing to stake a claim; Super bowl gold. T. Maule. il Sports Illus 34:10-15 Ja 4 '71

Short courageous life of Brian Piccolo; excerpts from I am third, ed. by A. Silverman. G. Sayers. pors Look 34:48-51+ Ag 25 '70

There's gold in them thar spills; San Francisco 49ers. T. Maule. il Sports Illus 33:20-1 O 26 '70

Thinking man's guide to pro football, by P. Zimmerman. Review
Newsweek il 76:55 D 7 '70. P. Axthelm

This man fired Flipper; owner of the Miami Dolphins. M. Kram. il pors Sports Illus 31: 76-8+ D 15 '69

Too small to be overlooked; Oilers star. J. Levias. M. Sharnik. il pors Sports Illus 33: 24-6+ N 30 '70

Trials of a rookie. il pors Newsweek 76:58-60+ O 5 '70

Wham, bam, Stram! Kansas City Chiefs and Minnesota Vikings in Super bowl. T. Maule. il pors Sports Illus 32:10-15 Ja 19 '70

What is a punter's hang time? R. Hickey, scout for Dallas Cowboys. W. B. Furlong. il pors N Y Times Mag p30-2+ Ja 10 '71

You win! You're fired! G. Allen of the L.A. Rams. A. Wright. por Sports Illus 33:34-6+ S 7 '70

See also
American football league
National football league

Ethical aspects
See Sports—Ethical aspects

Organization and administration

Rozelle's taut ship; tampering by J. Robbie. Newsweek 75:67+ Ap 27 '70

FOOTBALL coaches. See Coaches (athletics)

FOOTBALL fans

Mystique of pro football; Time essay. C. Clark. il Time 96:36-7 N 9 '70

FOOTBALL league players association, National. See National football league players association

FOOTBALL players

Black football players in the white South. L. J. Banks. il Ebony 26:131-2+ D '70

Body language, 1970; Texas Longhorns vs Arkansas Razorbacks. D. Jenkins. il Sports Illus 33:20-5 D 14 '70

Coach wants to see you; ed. by J. Underwood. B. Lusteg. il Sports Illus 33:92-6+ S 21 '70

College football 1970. il Sports Illus 33:46-76+ S 14 '70

End of a season at Syracuse; inability to resolve differences with black football players. P. Putnam. il Sports Illus 33:22-3 S 28 '70

Football racket; excerpt from Out of their league. D. Meggyesy. il Look 34:66+ N 17; 64-6+ D 1 '70

For the defense: Barney of the Lions, Detroit's superb cornerback; with report by B. Bruns. il Life 69:34-7 N 6 '70

Growing weary in their aerie: Philadelphia Eagles. R. F. Jones. il Sports Illus 33:20-2+ O 5 '70

Holdouts. il Newsweek 76:80 Ag 17 '70

Hustling the Heisman hopefuls. il Time 96:53 N 16 '70

Jolly Giants. il Newsweek 76:91-2 N 30 '70

Just for starters; starting quarterbacks in the pros. H. L. Masin. il Sr Schol 97:19 N 16 '70

Kick in time; place kickers enjoying their finest season. il Newsweek 76:114 N 23 '70

Man of machismo; ed. by J. Olsen. J. Kapp. il pors Sports Illus 33:26-31 Jl 20; 30-7 Jl 27; 20-5 Ag 3 '70

Mayhem on the line; pro football's linemen. P. Zimmerman. il Look 34:26-31 D 29 '70

Message from Minnesota: three dots and a dash; Minnesota Vikings vs Chicago Bears P. Putnam. il Sports Illus 33:28-30+ D 14 '70

1969 H.S. football All-Americans. H. L. Masin. il Sr Schol 96:27 Mr 2 '70

1970 Look All America. il Look 34:97+ D 15 '70

No miracle required; Oakland Raiders, western division title winners. T. Maule. il Sports Illus 33:18-23 D 21 '70

Parting shots; P. Palinkas first woman on the gridiron. il pors Life 69:63-4 Ag 28 '70

Pro football discovers the black college. A. S. Young. il Ebony 25:116-20 S '70

Pro football '70; scouting reports; National football league, American football league. T. Maule. il Sports Illus 33:34-40+ S 21 '70

Pro quarterback: toughest job in sports. B. Surface. il Read Digest 97:187-8+ N '70

Reports of li'l Joe's death were premature. P. Putnam. Sports Illus 33:51-2 O 26 '70

Rubies and diamonds; Detroit pro football draft. G. Plimpton. Sports Illus 32:24-6 F 9 '70

Rushing to stake a claim; Super bowl gold. T. Maule. il Sports Illus 34:10-15 Ja 4 '71

Second-hand roses: quarterbacks. H. L. Masin. Sr Schol 97:18 O 5 '70

Super All-American (cont) H. L. Masin. Sr Schol 96:17 Ja 26 '70

Tale of two quarterbacks: G. Blanda and D. Lamonica; with report by B. Bruns. il pors Life 69:44-7 D 4 '70

There's gold in them thar spills; San Francisco 49ers. T. Maule. il Sports Illus 33:20-1 O 26 '70

FOOTBALL players—*Continued*
Time's All-America team: prime prospects for the pros. il Time 96:50-1 D 28 '70
Trials of a rookie.   il pors Newsweek 76:58-60+ O 5 '70
Who's no. 1? college passers. H. L. Masin. il Sr Schol 95:27 O 20 '69
You learn the art of invisibliity. R. F. Jones. il Sports Illus 33:22-5 N 16 '70
    See also
National football league players association
Strikes—United States—Football players
    See also names of Football players, e.g. C. Hill

Photographs
Red-letter year for quarterbacks. il Sports Illus 33:48-51 S 14 '70

Recruiting
    See Football scouting
FOOTBALL referees. See Umpires (sports)
FOOTBALL scouting
Gamblers. il Newsweek 75:76+ F 9 '70
Pro football discovers the black college. A. S. Young. il Ebony 25:116-20 S '70
Pro football '70; scouting reports; National football league, American football league. T. Maule. il Sports Illus 33:34-40+ S 21 '70
What is a punter's hang time? R. Hickey, scout for Dallas Cowboys. W. B. Furlong. il pors N Y Times Mag p30-2+ Ja 10 '71
FOOTBALL stadiums. See Stadiums
FOOTE, Emerson
Overpopulation: crisis today, disaster tomorrow. por Parents Mag 45:30 Ja '70
FOOTE, Timothy
Nobel prize winner who deserved it. por Life 69:58 O 23 '70
FOOTPRINTS
    See also
Dermatoglyphics
FOOTSTOOLS. See Stools
FORAGE crops. See Forage plants
FORAGE plants
Forage is their specialty. il Suc Farm 68:B10-11 Ja '70
He feeds quality forage every month. J. R. Borcherding. il Suc Farm 68:no3 34-8 F '70
    See also
Sorghum
FORAKER, David
All shrubs are hardy now. il Org Gard & Farm 17:78-80 F '70
Hollyhocks can be made to please. il Org Gard & Farm 17:96-9 Ja '70
FORAMINIFERA
Differential isotopic fractionation in benthic foraminifera and paleotemperatures reassessed. J. C. Duplessy and others. bibliog il Science 168:250-1 Ap 10 '70
Diversity of planktonic foraminifera in deepsea sediments. W. H. Berger and F. L. Parker. bibliog il Science 168:1345-7 Je 12 '70
Hyalinea baltica and the plio-pleistocene boundary in the Caribbean Sea. W. D. Bock. bibliog il Science 170:847-8 N 20 '70
FORAMINIFERA, Fossil
Oxygen-18 studies of recent planktonic foraminifera: comparisons of phenotypes and of test parts. A. D. Hecht and S. M. Savin. bibliog il Science 170:69-71 O 2 '70
Pleistocene climates in the Atlantic and Pacific Oceans: a reevaluated comparison based on deep-sea sediments. R. W. Morin and others. bibliog il Science 169:365-6 Jl 24 '70
FORBES, Calvin
Chocolate soldiers: Good morning blues; Gabriel's blues; poems. Poetry 116:157-9 Je '70
Noah's dove: poem. Yale R 60:88 O '70
FORBES, Charles
I am an Affiliate artist. il Hi Fi 20:secII 10-11+ Je '70
FORBES, Eric G.
Who discovered longitude at sea? il Sky & Tel 41:4-6 Ja '71
FORBES, James E.
Environmental deterioration and declining species. il Cons 25:21-6 Ag '70
Facts on pesticides today. bibliog il Cons 24:2-4 Ag '69
FORBES, Robert Elliott
Dissent comes to the high school. America 123:177-8 S 19 '70
Up against the wall. America 122:454-5 Ap 25 '70
FORBES (periodical)
Typical Forbes man. Forbes 105:7 F 1 '70

FORCE (violence) See Violence
FORCE and energy
Energy is energy. J. A. Dutton and A. K. Blackadar. Weatherwise 23:231-4+ O '70
Isaac Asimov explains; all for an ounce of matter. I. Asimov. Sci Digest 67:67-8 Ja '70
    See also
Coriolis force
Dynamics
FORCING (plants)
Bulbs bring color indoors. A. J. Hebert. Horticulture 48:18-19 N '70
    See also
Hotbeds
FORD, Amasa B.
Casualties of our time. bibliog il Science 167:256-63 Ja 16 '70
FORD, Barbara
Body language, what it reveals about you. il Sci Digest 68:16-21 Ag '70
ESP in the dream laboratory. il Sci Digest 67:10-18 Ja '70
Games that play with your psyche. il Sci Digest 67:26-32 Mr '70
Garbage: a new raw material? il Sci Digest 68:22-7 D '70
Gout: what causes it and why it's not so funny. il Sci Digest 67:76-81 Mr '70
How they taught a chimp to talk. bibliog il Sci Digest 67:10-17 My '70
My machine loves me. il Sci Digest 68:43-8+ S '70
Noise: it hurts! il Sci Digest 68:34-40 O '70
Portrait of a problem drinker. il Sci Digest 68:20-5 N '70
What today's veterinary medicine can do for your pet. il Sci Digest 67:54-9 F '70
Who's beautiful to whom, and why? il Sci Digest 69:9-15 Ja '71
FORD, Bob. See Rothschild, M. jt. auth.
FORD, Corey
Our German wehrmacht is being stopped by a shadow; excerpts from Donovan of OSS. il por Am Heritage 21:56-7+ F '70
Road to Tinkhamtown; story. Field & S 75:74-5 Je '70
FORD, Daniel
(ed) See Carter, R. Visit with the Cape Codders
FORD, David, 2d
Interesting design may mean back to fundamentals, two University press designers tell AIGA clinic. Pub W 197:45-6 Mr 16 '70 *
FORD, Eileen
Godmother to the world's loveliest girls. J. Mills. il pors Life 69:63-5+ N 13 '70 *
FORD, Elaine
Oklahoma oasis. il Travel 134:28-33+ Ag '70
FORD, George Barry
Pastor ahead of time. S. Hughes. Cath World 211:136 Je '70 *
FORD, Gerald R.
Excerpt from debate, September 16, 199. Cong Digest 49:16+ Ja '70
Representative Ford's charges against Justice Douglas; excerpts from address, April 15, 1970. por U S News 68:67-71 Ap 27 '70
FORD, Glenn, and Redfield, Margaret
Glenn Ford, star gardener; excerpts from Glenn Ford, RFD Beverly Hills. il por Am Home 73:24+ Ap '70
FORD, Henry, 1917-
Five who care. il Look 34:41 Ap 21 '70
Help Russians build trucks? Ford's policy; statement. May 6, 1970. por U S News 68:102 My 18 '70
Young people, the establishment, and the quality of life; excerpt from The human environment and business. Read Digest 97:139-42 Jl '70
    about
Marking time. E. Dahlquist. Motor T 22:6 O '70 *
Mister Ford: they never call him Henry. il por Time 96:66-7 Jl 20 '70 *
Nyet to Ford's future in Russia. por Bsns W p40 My 23 '70 *
FORD, James W.
Rewards from the Kennedy round. por Nations Bsns 58:46 Ja '70
FORD, Leighton
Revolution for heaven's sake; excerpt from One way to change the world. Chr Today 15:14-16 D 4 '70
    about
Reaching the unchurched. Chr Today 14:43 F 13 '70 *
FORD, Norman D.
Autumn in the Rockies. il Har Yrs 10:30-8 Ag '70
Mexico. il Har Yrs 10:14-21+ Je '70
Shunpike tour of Europe. bibliog il Har Yrs 10:6-13+ Ap '70

FORD, Norman D.—*Continued*
South for sunshine! il Har Yrs 10:34-41 O '70
Vacationing in the great outdoors. il Har Yrs 10:6-14 F '70

FORD, Richard I.
Indian in America's closet. Natur Hist 79: 78+ Je '70

FORD, Richard J.
Hermann Hesse: prophet of the pot generation. por Cath World 212:15-19 O '70

FORD, Seabury
Professor gags. Nation 211:454 N 9 '70

FORD agency models. See Models (persons)

FORD foundation
Adapting British school reforms to U.S. needs. Sch & Soc 98:16-17 Ja '70
Berkeley mafia and the Indonesian massacre; with editorial comment. D. Ransom. il Ramp Mag 9:26-9+ O '70
Better idea for endowments. il Bsns W p44 D 26 '70
Ford and la raza: they stole our land and gave us powdered milk. R. Lloyd and P. Montague. il Ramp Mag 9:10-18 S '70
Howe now Ford foundation executive. Sch & Soc 98:340 O '70
Let's solve the endowment crisis; with summary of report. C. D. Ellis. bibliog f il Harvard Bsns R 48:92-102 Mr '70
New means for new music. R. Jacobson. il Sat R 53:65-6+ Ja 31 '70
Tax gremlins hit the Ford grants. Bsns W p40 Ja 24 '70
  See also
Fund for the advancement of education
Fund for the Republic

FORD motor company
Car of the year: product planners. il Motor T 22:39-41+ F '70
Ford in Russia's future? il Time 95:87 Ap 27 '70
Ford must disconnect from Autolite plugs. Bsns W p24 Jl 11 '70
Ford pulls off the track. Bsns W p22 N 28 '70
Ford settlement copies GM model. il Bsns W p 18 D 12 '70
Ford's better idea: collapsing front wheels. Consumer Rep 35:657-8 N '70
Ford's top brass talks about Pinto power; interview, ed. by J. Dunne. J. B. Naughton. il pors Pop Sci 197:54-5+ S '70
Help Russians build trucks? Ford's policy; statement, May 6, 1970. H. Ford, 2d. por U S News 68:102 My 18 '70
How Iacocca won the big one. il por Bsns W p38-9 D 19 '70
Is there a Ford in Russia's future? il Bsns W p41+ Ap 18 '70
Lee's here. por Newsweek 76:83 D 21 '70
Making and selling of the smallest car; Pinto. il Motor T 22:56-7+ S '70
Market research: Ford's gift horse; Pinto project for the academic community. R. J. Bazell. Science 170:953 N 27 '70
Patience rewarded. il por Time 96:66 D 21 '70
Profits and security: Soviet truck plant. Newsweek 75:73-4 My 4 '70
Riding the model T to mass production. A. Nevins. il Nations Bsns 58:72-3 Ja '70
Russians lay out the red carpet for Ford. il Bsns W p27-8 Ap 25 '70
Spoiler: Soviet deal off. Newsweek 75:85-6 My 25 '70
Truck is now; Louisville, Ky. plant. T. J. Murray. il por Duns 95:42+ Ja '70
Wheeling and dealing; lease rates for congressmen. Newsweek 76:66 Ag 17 '70
When an auto plant closes up; Ford's Dallas plant. il Bsns W p24-5 F 14 '70

FORD museum. See Henry Ford museum and Greenfield Village, Dearborn, Mich.

FORDHAM university
Bensalem. I. Taves. il Look 34:28-32 My 19 '70

FORD'S theatre. See Washington, D.C.—Theater

FORECASTING stock prices. See Stocks— Price forecasting

FORECASTS
Black mayors discuss state of the Nation; interviews. il Ebony 25:76-8+ F '70
Can we afford tomorrow? address, November 19, 1970. J. I. Miller. Vital Speeches 37: 190-2 Ja 1 '71
Cloudy crystal balls: rundown on predictions for 1969. Chr Cent 87:95 Ja 21 '70
Evaluating signals of technological change. J. R. Bright. bibliog f il Harvard Bsns R 48:62-70 Ja '70
Forecasters turn to group guesswork; Delphi technique. il Bsns W p 130+ Jl '70
Future of prediction. J. P. Sisk. Commentary 49:65-8 Mr '70; Discussion. 50:6+ Jl '70

Halfway to 1984. L. Malkin. il por Horizon 12:32-9 Spr '70
A look into the 1970s. il Mech Illus 66:39-45 Ja '70
Newsgram. See issues of U.S. news & World report
Parting shots; apocalyptic visions for our fragile little planet. il Life 69:63-6 S 4 '70
Possibilities of transformation: a report on the state of mankind: 1970. F. K. Kelly. Sat R 53:17-19+ Mr 7 '70
Second thought department. Am City 85:8 F '70
Writer in the year: 2001. F. Pohl. il Writers Digest 50:36-9 Ja '70
  See also
Agricultural forecasts
Business forecasting
Nineteen hundred and seventy-one
Political forecasts
Two thousand (year)
Weather forecasts

Anecdotes, facetiae, satire, etc.
Future tense; cartoons. J. Noonan. Cath World 211:224-5 Ag '70

FORECASTS (economics)
As bankers see it: a slow rise in '71. il U S News 69:80-3 D 14 '70
Better 1971? Duns 96:80 D '70
Bleak outlook. P. A. Samuelson. Newsweek 75:64 Mr 2 '70
Computer spies a happier 1971. il Bsns W p 18-19 N 28 '70
Consensus for 1971: good but not great. il Bsns W p66-7+ D 12 '70
Credit shifts but forecasters don't. il Bsns W p43 Mr 28 '70
Depression ahead? M. J. Ulmer. New Repub 163:14-15 Jl 4 '70
Europe thinks the U.S. is steadying; views of OECD staff. il Bsns W p58-9 Ag 8 '70
Good times coming. P. A. Samuelson. Newsweek 76:90 S 14 '70
Great turnaround. il Fortune 82:15-16+ Jl '70
Has Cambodia changed the outlook? R. Lekachman. Duns 95:9 Je '70
How deep a slump coming? what top economists say. il U S News 68:24-7 Mr 2 '70
Inflation is rolling back, at a price. il Newsweek 76:67-8 S 21 '70
Look at the next five years. D. R. Burrus. por Nations Bsns 58:73-4 S '70
Making the turn to a peacetime economy; recession in defense-related industries. S. Rose. il Fortune 82:110-13 S '70
Monetarists enter forecasting sweepstakes. il Bsns W p 100-2 My 2 '70
Mood is inflation gray. il Bsns W p 16-17 N 28 '70
1970: the year of the hangover; outlook for 1971. il Time 96:55-6 D 28 '70
No bust, no boom; views of R. L. Reierson. A. Hershman. por Duns 95:93-4 Je '70
Opportunity of a lifetime? interview. B. W. Sprinkel. por Forbes 106:34 O 1 '70
Pessimists are a growing minority. il Bsns W p33 Je 27 '70
Profit forecast: a jarring note of optimism; with editorial comment. il Bsns W p 14-15, 132 Mr 7 '70
Profit picture brightens; views of business executives. il Nations Bsns 58:30-4 O '70
Rosy hue beyond the gloom. il Bsns W p68 My 23 '70
'70s: a strong economy, but; official preview of the U.S. in 1980. il U S News 68:64 Ap 27 '70
Shape of 1971. C. Morgello. il Newsweek 76:77 D 21 '70
Slow convalescence, but it's real; Wharton econometric model. il Bsns W p20-1 S 12 '70
Slump: will this bottom hold up? il Newsweek 76:51-2 Jl 27 '70
Stronger omens of an upturn, but new worries. Fortune 82:19-20 Ag '70
Trillion-dollar economy. il U S News 68:29 F 9 '70
U.S. economy in 1980: a preview of BLS projections. il Mo Labor R 93:3-34 Ap '70
Wharton's model says it again. il Bsns W p33 F 21 '70
Why inflation goes on and on. il U S News 68:20-1 F 2 '70
  See also
Business forecasting
Computers—Economic use

FORECASTS (social sciences)
Indicators of change in political institutions. N. E. Long. bibliog f Ann Am Acad 388: 35-45 Mr '70

FOREST conservation—*Continued*
View from VISTA; Appalachian volunteers in conservation programs. E. Urvant. il Am For 76:8+ S '70
Wanted: a program for our trees. M. Frome. Field & S 74:48+ Mr '70
See also
Wilderness areas

FOREST ecology
Ecology of fire; excerpt from Sierra Nevada. V. R. Johnston. il Audubon 72:76-81+ S '70
Forest fires: suppression policy has its ecological drawbacks. M. Oberle; discussion. Science 166:552, 945+; 168:420 O 31, N 21 '69, Ap 24 '70
Nutrient cycles of an ecosystem. F. H. Bormann and G. E. Likens. il Sci Am 223:92-101 O '70
Preserving nature in forested wilderness areas and national parks. M. L. Heinselman. il Nat Parks & Con Mag 44:8-14 S '70
See also
Forest fires—Controlled fires
Rain forests

FOREST fire ecology. See Forest fires—Controlled fires

FOREST fire patrol, Aerial
CL-215 getting heavy use in France; water bomber aircraft. D. E. Fink. il Aviation W 93:61-3 Ag 3 '70

FOREST fire protection
Forest fires: suppression policy has its ecological drawbacks. M. Oberle; discussion. Science 166:552, 945+; 168:420 O 31, N 21 '69, Ap 24 '70
See also
Northeastern forest fire protection compact
United States—Forest service

FOREST fires
Preserving nature in forested wilderness areas and national parks. M. L. Heinselman. il Nat Parks & Con Mag 44:8-14 S '70
See also
Brush fires

Controlled fires
Ecology of fire; excerpt from Sierra Nevada. V. R. Johnston. il Audubon 72:76-81+ S '70
Forest fires, a changing philosophy. Chem 43:24 Mr '70
Restoring fire to the Sequoias. B. Kilgore. il Nat Parks & Con Mag 44:16-22 O '70

History
When the Midwest burned. D. A. Haines and E. L. Kuehnast. bibliog il Weatherwise 23:112-19 Je '70

FOREST lookouts. See United States—Forest service

FOREST management
Clearing the air. J. B. Craig. Am For 76:11 D '70
Desert under the trees; tree farms. M. Margolin. il Nat Parks & Con Mag 44:8-13 D '70
More muscle for multiple use; proposal to reduce logging in Oregon. J. B. Craig. Am For 76:7 Ag '70
Myth of multiple use. E. M. Sterling. il Am For 76:25-7 Je '70; Discussion. 76:6 S; 4 O '70
New England's memorial forests; deeding to the New England forestry foundation. R. Applegate. il Am For 76:12-15 Ja '70
Stopping the decline and fall of grouse; use the aspen forest; Cloquet study. G. W. Gullion. il Field & S 75:32-3+ D '70
Timber management: improvement implies new land-use policies. L. J. Carter. il Science 170:1387-90 D 25 '70
Trees for people; questions and answers. K. B. Pomeroy. il Am For 76:8+ Ap; 28-9+ Je '70
See also
Forest conservation
Forest fires—Controlled fires
Forest ownership
Forest thinning
United States—Forest service

FOREST of the Wabash, Ill. See Forests, State

FOREST ownership
Private enterprise reacts to recreation demands; recreation facilities provided by privately owned forest lands. E. J. Hodges. il Parks & Rec 5:36-8+ Ja '70
Smartest fellow around; foresters vs. small landowners. J. M. Vardaman. il Am For 76:8+ N '70
You, too, can have a forest. D. Howlett. il Am For 76:20-3+ Ag '70

FOREST planting
See also
Reforestation

FOREST products industry
Planting the South's third forest: more tree power. F. C. Gragg. il por Am For 76:12-13+ O '70
See also
Boise Cascade corporation

Finance
Forest products & packaging; with yardsticks of management performance. il Forbes 105:189-90 Ja 1 '70; 107:164-5 Ja 1 '71

FOREST protection
See also
Trees—Diseases and pests

FOREST recreation
Impact of man on the Adirondack high country. E. H. Ketchledge and R. E. Leonard. il Cons 25:14-18 O '70
Myth of multiple use. E. M. Sterling. il Am For 76:25-7 Je '70; Discussion. 76:6 S; 4 O '70

FOREST regeneration. See Forest reproduction

FOREST reproduction
Planting the South's third forest: more tree power. F. C. Gragg. il por Am For 76:12-13+ O '70
To regenerate eastern hardwoods: clearcut. W. E. McQuilkin. il Am For 76:20-3+ Je '70; Discussion. 76:3+ Ag; 4-5 S '70

FOREST research. See Forestry research

FOREST service (United States) See United States—Forest service

FOREST thinning
Clear cutting and conservation. il Sci N 98:430 D 5 '70
Clearcutting in West Virginia. Am For 76:49 S '70
Clearcutting probe sought; practice on national forests. Am For 76:37 Jl '70
Esthetics: the sixth value. J. B. Craig. Am For 76:6-7 O '70
Hardwoods in New York; letter. H. S. Kernan. Am For 76:6-7 N '70
Moderation, moderation, moderation! aspects of clearcutting presented at Fontana conservation roundup. K. A. Argow. Am For 76:5-6 S '70
To regenerate eastern hardwoods: clearcut. W. E. McQuilkin. il Am For 76:20-3+ Je '70; Discussion. 76:3+ Ag; 4-5 S '70

FORESTERS
Metro forestry in Atlanta; tree power. A. Shirley. il Am For 76:8-11+ O '70

FORESTRY, industrial. See Forest management

FORESTRY laws and regulations
Saga of a law; how the Multiple use-sustained yield act was enacted by Congress. E. C. Crafts. il Am For 76:12-19+ Je; 28-35 Jl '70
Why we needed the Multiple use bill. R. E. McArdle. il Am For 76:10-11+ Je '70

FORESTRY research
Planting the South's third forest: more tree power. F. C. Gragg. il por Am For 76:12-13+ O '70
Up three flights to the third forest. C. Hathaway and J. B. Craig. il Am For 76:8-11+ Mr '70

FORESTRY schools and education
Cradle of forestry; where tree power started; Biltmore forest school. H. E. Jolley. il Am For 76:16-21 O; 36-9 N; 36-9+ D '70

FORESTRY societies
See also
American forestry association

FORESTS, Memorial. See Forest management

FORESTS, Private. See Forest management; Forest ownership

FORESTS, State
Laura Beall Woods. G. A. Peterson. il Nat Parks 44:24-5 Ja '70

FORESTS and forestry
Hidden forest; excerpts. S. F. Olson. il Nat Wildlife 7:40-7 O '69
How good are you as a forester? quiz. J. Daugherty and M. Daugherty. il Sci Digest 68:78-9+ Ag '70
See also
Chaparral
Forest conservation
Forest fires
Foresters
Lumbering
Rain forests
Timber line
Woodlots
also headings beginning Forest, Forestry

Economic aspects
Up three flights to the third forest. C. Hathaway and J. B. Craig. il Am For 76:8-11+ Mr '70

FORESTS and forestry—*Continued*
Laws and regulations
See Forestry laws and regulations
Study and teaching
See also
Forestry schools and education
Alaska
Loners of Alaska. A. S. Harris. il por Am For 76:20-3+ My '70
Brazil
Brazil's decade of forestry progress. D. M. Knudson. il Am For 76:57-62 O '70
Georgia
Metro forestry in Atlanta: tree power. A. R. Shirley. il Am For 76:8-11+ O '70
Latin America
25000 kinds of trees; increasing forest production in Latin America. G. D. Fox and J. G. Hutchinson. il Américas 22:9-15 My '70
Lebanon
Painful lessons of the cedars of Lebanon. L. Thomas. il por Nat Wildlife 8:50-5 D '69
Mexico
Forestry and the public domain; a Mexican point of view; address (cont) E. Beltran. il Am For 76:36-7+ Ja '70
Montana
Mike Frome; lack of application of scientific forestry. M. Frome. Am For 76:3+ F '70
New England
See also
New England forestry foundation, Boston
New York (state)
Saddled prominent. J. H. Risley. il Cons 24:29-30 Ag '69
Norway
Forest scene in Norway. E. R. Yarham. il Am For 76:28-30+ F '70
Oregon
More muscle for multiple use; prosposal to reduce logging. J. B. Craig. Am For 76:7 Ag '70
Southern states
Planting the South's third forest: more tree power. il por Am For 76:12-13+ O '70
Up three flights to the third forest. C. Hathaway and J. B. Craig. il Am For 76:8-11+ Mr '70
Tropics
See also
Rain forests
United States
Washington lookout. V. Trumbull. See issues of American forests
See also
Forest conservation
National forests
United States—Forest service
West Virginia
Esthetics: the sixth value. J. B. Craig. Am For 76:6-7 O '70
FORGERIES, Art. See Forgery of works of art
FORGERY
See also
Counterfeits and counterfeiting
Forgery of works of art
Musical forgeries and mystifications
FORGERY of antiques
Aspects of fake artifacts. C. Miles. il Hobbies 75:114-15 Ag '70
FORGERY of works of art
Bartlett forgeries: Coke Smyth originals; Royal Ontario museum in Toronto. R. Davidon. il Antiques 97:202+ F '70
Forging a career; case of D. Stein. Newsweek 76:105 O 12 '70
What next, the Mona Lisa? E. de Hory, master faker. il por Life 68:34-5 F 6 '70
See also
Art—Expertising
FORGET, Bernard G. and Jordan, Bertrand
5S RNA synthesized by escherichia coli in presence of chloramphenicol: different 5'-terminal sequences. bibliog il Science 167:382-4 Ja 23 '70
FORGETTING. See Memory
FORGING
See also
Blacksmithing

FORGIVENESS
Albert Speer and the miracle of forgiveness. M. Barth. Chr Cent 87:1537-8 D 23 '70
FORLAND, Katrine Seip
Letter from Africa. il Bul Atom Sci 26:42-5 Ap '70
FORMALDEHYDE
Formaldehyde absorption coefficients in the vacuum ultraviolet (650 to 1850 angstroms) E. P. Gentieu and J. E. Mentall. bibliog il Science 169:681-3 Ag 14 '70
Microwave detection of thioformaldehyde. D. R. Johnson and F. X. Powell. bibliog il Science 169:679-80 Ag 14 '70
Search for the 1_{10}–1_{11} transition of interstellar thioformaldehyde. N. J. Evans, 2d, and others. bibliog il Science 169:680-1 Ag 14 '70
FORMAN, James
Economics of the Black manifesto. M. K. Carney. por Chr Cent 87:171-4 F 11 '70 *
Roundup: the year of the Black manifesto. M. Stone. Chr Cent 87:185-8 F 11 '70 *
FORMAN, Milos
Czechs in exile. il pors Newsweek 76:70-1 Jl 27 '70 *
FORMIC acid
New space molecule. Sci N 98:366 N 7 '70
FORMOSA. See Taiwan
FORMOSAN termites. See Termites
FORMS, Municipal. See Municipal government—Forms, blanks, etc.
FORMS of address
Etiquette of names and titles. A. Vanderbilt. Ladies Home J 87:16 Je '70
FORNASETTI, Piero
Art on four wheels: Louvre show of automotive design. il Life 68:70-3 My 22 '70 *
FORNER, José
Collector's choice: a first for law & order. R. Olmstead. Am West 7:11 Ja '70 *
FORNEY, James S.
Batteries come first! il Mod Phot 34:74-7+ S '70
How good are the automatic electronic flash units? il Mod Phot 34:72-3+ Ap '70
FORNOFF, Frank J.
Survey of the teaching of chemistry in secondary schools. Sch & Soc 98:242-3 Ap '70
FORREST, A. C.
United church observer: no trees for Forrest. L. K. Tarr. Chr Today 14:37 My 22 '70 *
FORRESTER, Eugene
Tarnished medals. Newsweek 76:65 N 2 '70 *
FORSHEE, Lorene
Neither does a rose. il Har Yrs 10:22-3 My '70
FORSTER, Edward Morgan
Aspects of the novelist. por Time 95:82 Je 22 '70 *
E. M. Forster, 1879-1970. P. D. Zimmerman. por Newsweek 75:84+ Je 22 '70 *
Memory of Forster. R. Stern. Nation 210:795-6 Je 29 '70 *
Obituary
Chr Cent 87:894 Jl 22 '70. A. R. Vidler New Repub 162:28 Je 20 '70. R. Whittemore *
FORSTER, Robert
Obstacles to agricultural growth in eighteenth-century France. bibliog f Am Hist R 75:1600-15 O '70
FORSTER-HAHN, Françoise
German painting: the forgotten century. il Art N 69:50-5+ N '70
FORSYTH, William
Let the sunshine in. R. E. Atkinson. il McCalls 98:44 Ja '71
FORSYTHIAS
Let the sunshine in. R. E. Atkinson. il McCalls 98:44 Ja '71
FORT DETRICK, Frederick, Md. See Laboratories, Government
FORT DIX, N.J. See Military training camps
FORT HALL Indian reservation, Idaho. See Indians of North America—Reservations
FORT PIERCE, Fla.
Cemeteries
Soldier's rest; burial of Pondexteur Williams in all-white cemetery. il Newsweek 76:33-4 S 7 '70
FORT SAN LORENZO, Panama Canal Zone
Fort San Lorenzo. R. B. Chardkoff. il Américas 22:2-8 F '70
FORT SUMTER
Gallantry under fire. D. Vestal. il Travel & Camera 33:34-9 F '70
Weatherman and Fort Sumter. H. V. Jaffa. Nat R 22:1403+ D 29 '70
FORT WAYNE, Ind.
Computer to speed traffic flow. Am City 85:59 Je '70

FORT WORTH, Tex.
In-service training enhances a computer system. H. D. McMahan. il Am City 85:126+ S '70

Moral conditions
Fort Worth: happy triumph of a city that once seemed a place to run away from. T. Thompson. il Life 69:24-5 O 2 '70

Social conditions
Fort Worth: happy triumph of a city that once seemed a place to run away from. T. Thompson. il Life 69:24-5 O 2 '70

Water supply
Pigs keep our water mains clean. G. Muller. il Am City 85:112+ O '70

FORT WORTH opera association
Report:
Fledermaus. O. Chism. Opera N 34:33 Mr 7 '70
Verdi's Ballo in maschera. R. Douglass. Opera N 34:26 My 16 '70

FORTE, Charles
Hotelier-at-large. por Bsns W p96 Mr 14 '70 *

FORTH, Jane
Just plain Jane. il pors Life 69:54-7 Jl 4 '70 *

FORTIER, John
Research and discovery at Louisbourg. il Antiques 97:880-7 Je '70

FORTIFICATION
Fort San Lorenzo. R. B. Chardkoff. il Américas 22:2-8 F '70
Louisbourg, the forgotten fortress. J. Lunn. il Antiques 97:872-9 Je '70

FORTIFIED food. See Food, Enriched

FORTIN-MAGANA, R. and others
Intestinal enzymes; indicators of proliferation and differentiation in the jejunum. bibliog il Science 167:1627-8 Mr 20 '70

FORTNEY, David L.
Physicians phone for automatic medical advice. Todays Health 48:18-19 Mr '70

FORTNIGHT lily. See Moraea

FORTS. See Fortification

FORTUNE telling
Dukuns, bomohs and gurus; Asian leaders and soothsayers. il Time 96:31 N 9 '70
See also
Astrology
Tarot

49ers (football club). See Football clubs

42d street. See New York (city)—Streets

FORTY years on; drama. See Bennett, A.

FORUM communications, inc.
Clout bout; license challenge. R. L. Shayon. Sat R 53:59 F 28 '70

FORUM 303 (shopping center) See Arlington, Tex.—Stores

FORUMS (discussion and debate)
1969 student burgesses at colonial Williamsburg (title varies) il Sr Schol 95:8-10+ O 13; 14-16+ O 20 '69
1970 student burgesses at colonial Williamsburg. il Sr Schol 96:18-19 My 4 '70
See also
Center for the study of democratic institutions, Santa Barbara, Calif.
Teach-ins

FORWARDING companies
Forwarders attack small parcel problem. il Aviation W 93:32-4 O 26 '70
Shippers associations gaining. Aviation W 93:131+ O 26 '70

FOSBERG, F. R.
Desert wilderness. il Liv Wildn 34:17-24 Spr '70

FOSKETT, A. C.
Shelf classification, or else. il por Library J 95:2771-3 S 1 '70

FOSSE, Bob
Robert Fosse; interview. ed. by R. Hemming. por Sr Schol 96:14 F 2 '70

FOSSE, Ray
When a Rose ran over a Mule. S. Treadwell. por Sports Illus 33:44 Ag 3 '70

FOSSIL algae; Fossil pollen; etc. See Algae, Fossil; Pollen, Fossil; etc.

FOSSIL man. See Man, Prehistoric

FOSSIL microorganisms. See Micropaleontology

FOSSILS. See Paleontology

FOSTER, Bob
One round of boxing was more than enough. P. Putnam. il pors Sports Illus 33:20-1 N 30 '70 *

FOSTER, Gloria
Star couple. L. Robinson. il pors Ebony 25:142-4+ Mr '70 *

FOSTER, H. Lincoln
Making a wild flower garden. il Nat Wildlife 8:13-16 Ap '70

FOSTER, Helen H.
Cylinder art. il Design 71:4-6 Wint '69
Treasures from a wood scrap bin. il Design 71:13 Fall '69

FOSTER, Howard G.
Nonapprentice sources of training in construction. bibliog il Mo Labor R 93:21-6 F '70

FOSTER, John L.
(tr) Papyrus Harris 500; poems. Poetry 116: 304-12 Ag '70

FOSTER, John Stuart, 1922-
Hedge against the unknown; excerpts from testimony. Aviation W 92:11 Mr 16 '70
Russia vs. U.S; coming crisis in arms; interview. il pors U S News 69:24-6+ N 30 '70
Soviet technological threat; excerpts from address. Aviation W 92:13 Ap 27 '70

FOSTER, Kenneth L.
Student goal centered learning program. Clear House 45:212-15 D '70

FOSTER, Robert
Matchless art of Lucian Bernhard. il Am Artists 34:54-9+ D '70

FOSTER care for mental patients. See Mentally ill—Home care

FOSTER day care
See also
Day nurseries

FOSTER grandparent program
Foster grandparent program seen saving taxpayers money. il Aging 184:24 F '70
Pennsylvania foster grandparent leader: Washington is second. Aging 182:16 D '69

FOSTER parents
Second chance at parenthood. E. Holt. il Todays Health 48:64-5+ Mr '70

FOUCAULT, Michel
Michel Foucault. R. McMullen. por Horizon 11:36-9 Aut '69

FOULKE, Adrienne
(tr) See Arbasino, A. Gae Aulenti: new force in Italian design

FOUNDATION for mind research
Mysticism in the laboratory. il por Time 96: 72+ O 5 '70

FOUNDATION garments
See also
Brassieres

FOUNDATIONS, Charitable and educational
Blue-ribbon panel tells how to avoid charitable crisis. B. Nelson. Science 168:808 My 15 '70
Company builds with a foundation. V. Louviere. Nations Bsns 58:20 D '70
Foundation grants and fellowships for writers; with list of foundations and fellowships. D. Dempsey. il Writers Digest 50:48-53+ Ja; 48-9 F '70
How local projects can get grants from foundations. Good H 170:134 Ja '70
Tax-exempt foundations: their effects on national policy. I. L. Horowitz and R. L. Horowitz. bibliog il Science 168:220-8 Ap 10 '70; Discussion. 168:1041-2 My 29; 169:127 Jl 10 '70
VW foundation; money giver on the European scene. D. S. Greenberg. Science 168: 952-4 My 22 '70
See also
Alfred P. Sloan foundation

Taxation
Foundations and the tax bill; threat to the private sector? L. J. Carter; reply. G. E. Janssen. Science 167:933 F 13 '70
Foundations: taking stock after the tax reform bill. J. Walsh. Science 167:1598+ Mr 20 '70
Tax-exempt litigation: IRS curbs draw widespread opposition. R. J. Bazell. Science 170: 716-17 N 13 '70
Tax gremlins hit the Ford grants. Bsns W p40 Ja 24 '70
Tax reform act (cont) I. Fisher. Dance Mag 44:6 D '70; 45:83 Ja '71

FOUNDING fathers. See Great men

FOUNDRIES
Foundries fail on clear-air laws. il Bsns W p48 Ag 29 '70
Water-powered iron foundry; Knights foundry. il Sunset 145:50 O '70

FOUNDRY practice

Study and teaching
Cast jewelry; pewter pendants. J. D. Kain. il Sch Arts 70:16-18 Ja '71

FOUNTAIN, Leatrice
I am a draft counselor. il McCalls 98:73+ O '70

FOUNTAIN; story. See Merwin, W. S.

FOUNTAIN pens
Fountain pen repair service. Consumer Bul 53:36 Mr '70
  See also
Waterman-Bic pen corporation

FOUNTAINS
Achieving effective collaboration in the design of fountains. R. Chaix. il Arch Rec 148:105-8 D '70
Portland's walk-in waterfall. il Arch Forum 133:56-9 O '70
  See also
Drinking fountains

FOUR-channel broadcasting. See Radio broadcasting—Stereophonic transmission

FOUR-channel sound. See Sound—Stereophonic recording and reproducing

FOUR-day week. See Hours of labor

FOUR letters from Algernon; drama. See Nolan, P. T.

FOUR seasons (restaurant) See New York (city)—Hotels, restaurants, etc.

FOUR seasons nursing centers of America, inc. See Nursing homes

FOUR wheel drive automobiles. See Automobiles—Four wheel drive

FOURAKER, Lawrence Edward
New dean, new era for Harvard B-school. il por Bsns W p58-60+ Ja 24 '70

FOURIER series. See Harmonic analysis

FOURTEENTH amendment. See United States—Constitution—Amendments

FOURTH alarm; story. See Cheever, J.

FOURTH committee of the General assembly. See United Nations—Trusteeship committee

FOURTH market. See Stocks—Marketing

FOURTH of July
Different kind of rally; Honor America day. il U S News 69:19 Jl 6 '70
Fourth of July, in Randolph, Vermont. il Travel & Camera 33:22-5 Jl '70
Fourth: showing the flag. il Newsweek 76:30-1 Jl 13 '70
Games on July 4th; Honor America day in Washington, D.C. T. M. Gannon. America 123:43-4 Jl 25 '70
Gathering in praise of America. il Time 96:9-10 Jl 13 '70
Honor America day. Chr Today 14:33 Jl 3 '70
Religious heritage—Reader's digest—Bob Hope—Billy Graham—Walt Disney productions complex; Honor America day. Chr Cent 87:811 Jl 1 '70; Discussion. 87:1094-5, 1357-8, 1388 S 16, N 11-18 '70
Super salute to God and country; service at Lincoln memorial. D. Kucharsky. Chr Today 14:35 Jl 31 '70
Who owns the stars and stripes? il Time 96:8-15 Jl 6 '70

  Anecdotes, facetiae, satire, etc.
Fourth of July that was. M. McGrory. New Repub 163:7 Jl 4 '70

FOURTH party movement. See Political parties—United States

FOWL. See Poultry

FOWLER, Cleo. See Fowler, H. jt. auth.

FOWLER, Elizabeth M.
Mortgage money is here again. il Am Home 73:32+ O '70

FOWLER, Gene
Amorous Senator; story, excerpt from Timber line. il Am West 7:28-31 Mr '70

FOWLER, Harry, and Fowler, Cleo
Mississippi camping. il Motor B 125:65-7+ F '70

FOWLER, John M. and West, Richard
What our left hand has been doing. bibliog il pors Phys Today 23:24-9+ Mr '70

FOWLER, Leonard
Leonard Fowler ballet, Kaufmann concert hall, NYC. P. G. Richmond. Dance Mag 45:74 Ja '71 *
Leonard Fowler ballet; 92nd street Y. J. Armstrong. il Dance Mag 44:76 Ja '70
Leonard Fowler ballet; 92nd st. Y, NYC. L. Pastore. Dance Mag 44:91-2 My '70 *

FOWLER, Ruth E. See Edwards, R. G. jt. auth.

FOWLES, John
Weeds, bugs, Americans. il Sports Illus 33:84-8+ D 21 '70

  about
French lieutenant's woman's man. R. B. Stolley. il pors Life 68:55-60 My 29 '70 *

FOWLING
Boats for hunters. J. A. Emmett. il Outdoor Life 146:52+ O '70

FOX, Carol
Lady of the Lyric; photographs. S. Jenkins. Opera N 35:13-15 O 31 '70 *

FOX, Frances L.
He thrives on history. il por Har Yrs 10:30-3 Je '70

FOX, Gerald G.
Make information systems work for you. il Am City 85:108+ Mr '70

FOX, Gerald S.
Berrys (twice) with Bernstein: Des knaben wunderhorn. il por Am Rec G 36:544-6 Ap '70
Ormandy's Mahler 1: passionate involvement. Am Rec G 36:800-2+ Je '70
Two perspectives: the Roman trilogy. Am Rec G 37:176-7 N '70

FOX, Gordon D. and Hutchinson, J. G.
25000 kinds of trees. il Américas 22:9-15 My '70

FOX, M. R. Spivey, and Fry, B. E. Jr
Cadmium toxicity decreased by dietary ascorbic acid supplements. bibliog il Science 169:989-91 S 4 '70

FOX, Paul J. and others
Jurassic sandstone from the tropical Atlantic. bibliog il Science 170:1402-4 D 25 '70

FOX, Paula
Bitter-coated sugar pills. Sat R 53:34 S 19 '70

FOX, R. M. and others
Orotidinuria induced by allopurinol. bibliog il Science 168:861-2 My 15 '70

FOX, R. W.
Electronic dice. il Electr World 83:34-5+ F '70
How to putter with the PUT. il Radio-Electr 41:50-2 O '70; 50-1 N '70

FOX, Richard W.
Algeria, Israel and the Al Fatah. Commonweal 92:184-5 My 8 '70

FOX, Sidney W. and Windsor, C. R.
Synthesis of amino acids by the heating of formaldehyde and ammonia. bibliog il Science 170:984-6 N 27 '70
—and others
Bio-organic compounds and glassy microparticles in lunar fines and other materials. bibliog il Science 167:767-70 Ja 30 '70

FOX, Willard, and Jones, R. D.
Plan for evaluation of teacher efficiency through cooperative goal-setting. Clear House 44:541-3 My '70

FOX, William Price
Southern boy writes home about Rome. Holiday 47:86-7+ F '70

FOX, William T. R.
Causes of peace and conditions of war. bibliog f Ann Am Acad 392:1-13 N '70
(ed) How wars end. bibliog f Ann Am Acad 392:1-172 N '70

FOXES
Vixen and the boy. T. Browne. il Nat Parks & Con Mag 44:22-3 Je '70

FOXFIRE (student magazine) See College and school journalism

FOY, Bob
Reaching the unreached. il Todays Ed 59:44-6 Mr '70

FOY, Fred C.
Chairman's chair. por Forbes 105:76 Je 1; 106:70 Jl 15; 70-1 O 1 '70
Some kind words for a new villain; address, January 22, 1970. Vital Speeches 36:343-6 Mr 15 '70
Why bosses should fire themselves. por Forbes 105:93-4 Ap 15 '70

FOYT, Anthony Joseph, 1935-
Foyt wins, Jones wins eighth annual. A. B. Shuman. il pors Motor T 22:74-8 Mr '70 *

FRACCI, Carla
Carla Fracci: American ballet theatre's Giselle. E. Jacob. il pors Dance Mag 44:42-53 N '70 *

FRACTIONATION. See Separation (technology)

FRACTIONATION of blood. See Blood— Analysis and chemistry

FRACTURES
First aid; ankle fracture. C. J. Potthoff. Todays Health 48:74-5 N '70
  See also
Spine—Fracture

FRACTURES (geology) See Faults (geology)

FRADY, Marshall
American innocent in the Middle East. il Harper 241:55-8+ O; 104-6+ N '70 (to be cont)
Growing up a Baptist. Mlle 70:156+ Mr '70
Sweetest finger this side of Midas; with editorial comment. il pors Life 68:52-52B+ F 27 '70
View from Hilton Head. il Harper 240:103-12 My '70

FRAGRANCE. See Odors

FRAKES, Margaret
Indispensable, *st*; expendable, no. Chr Cent 87:63 Ja 14 '70

FRALEY, Elwin E. and others
Spontaneous in vitro neoplastic transformation of adult human prostatic epithelium. bibliog il Science 170:540-2 O 30 '70

FRAME, George W.
On the hunt with the wild dogs of Africa. il Sci Digest 67:33-8 Je '70

FRAME, Helen Dunn
Liechtenstein. il Travel 134:48-9+ S '70

FRAME, Janet
Winter garden; story. New Yorker 45:37-9 Ja 31 '70

FRAMES for pictures. See Picture frames

FRAMINGHAM, Mass.

Gardens
Garden in the woods. J. A. Lynch. il Am For 76:20-3+ Mr '70

FRANCE
See also
Aerospace industries—France
Agriculture—France
Airlines—France
Airplanes, Military—France
Aix-en-Provence
Americans in France
Architecture, Domestic—France
Arts and crafts—France
Ballet—France
Bastille day
Brittany
Business consolidations and mergers—France
Camarque
Carpentras
Censorship—France
Chantilly
Children—France
Civil rights—France
Colleges and universities—France
Crime and criminals—France
Education and state in France
Elections—France
Horse racing—France
Investments, Foreign (in France)
Jews in France
Languedoc
Liquor problem—France
Loire Valley
Moving pictures—France
Munitions industries—France
Music festivals—France
Nancy
Newspapers—France
Opera—France
Paleontology—France
Periodicals—France
Political campaigns—France
Provence
Publishers and publishing—France
Purchasing, Military—France
Railroads—France
Religious thought—France
Restaurants—France
Rhône Valley
Riviera
Science and state—France
Skis and skiing—France
Space research—France
Strikes—France
Student demonstrations—France
Student militants—France
Television broadcasting—France
Theater—France
Trials—France
Women—France
World war, 1939-1945—France

Antiquities, Roman
Tower of mystery: Tour Magne. L. S. De Camp. il Sci Digest 68:15 O '70

Appropriations and expenditures
Civil aviation budget approved in France. il Aviation W 93:23 N 23 '70
French set defense budget at $5 billion. Aviation W 93:19 S 21 '70

Armed forces
Appropriations and expenditures
French assembly votes defense budget. D. E. Fink. Aviation W 93:18-19 O 19 '70
French budget aids strategic forces. Aviation W 93:21 N 2 '70

Army
Foreign legion
Last Beau Geste. il Time 95:32 F 16 '70

Officers
Where are they now? four former OAS generals. il Newsweek 75:16 My 4 '70

Colonies
See also
Guadeloupe (islands)
Martinique
Pentecost Island
Saint Pierre and Miquelon (islands)

Defenses
Debré vs. the brass. Newsweek 75:35-6 Ap 13 '70

Description and travel
See also
Baux, Les

Economic conditions
Changing France: tradition bows to progress. F. C. Painton. il U S News 69:92-4 Ag 17 '70
See also
Money—France

Economic history
See also
Agriculture—France—History

Eonomic policy
Pompidou's France. P. Ben. New Repub 162: 8-9 F 28 '70

Economic relations
Libya
Certain odor; French interest in Libyan oil. Nation 210:131-2 F 9 '70

Foreign relations
France and Germany: less divergent outlooks? A. Grosser. For Affairs 48:235-44 Ja '70
France and the Atlantic community. G. de Carmoy. Cur Hist 58:269-75 My '70
New look at France; interview, ed. by C. Painton. G. Pompidou. il por U S News 68:44-7 Mr 2 '70
Pompidou's France. P. Ben. New Repub 162: 8-9 F 28 '70
Pompidou's trip to America, what he hopes to achieve. il pors U S News 68:16 Mr 2 '70
See also
Military assistance, French

Arab states
Mirage sales key to French Africa policy. E. H. Kolcum. Aviation W 92:20-1 Ap 6 '70

Germany (Federal Republic)
Mission to Moscow and Paris. Time 95:31 F 9 '70

Israel
Israel's new coup; gunboats and oil. T. Land. Nation 210:103-4 F 2 '70
Mirages' storage indicates Israeli-French talks falter. D. E. Fink. Aviation W 92:21 F 2 '70

Middle East
Buying grandeur on the cheap; arms sales. il Newsweek 75:31-2 F 2 '70
Feelings of ambivalence. Newsweek 75:50+ Mr 16 '70
Pompidou line. E. Behr. Newsweek 75:42 F 9 '70
Reports: France and the Middle East. G. G. Stevens. Atlan 226:8+ Ag '70; Reply with rejoinder. J. Kutoy. 226:28-9 O '70

Russia
See Russia—Foreign relations—France

United States
See United States—Foreign relations—France

Foreign service
France: putting scientists into its embassies. Science 167:1230-1 F 27 '70

History
See also
World war, 1939-1945—France

Bibliography
Articles and other books received; comp. by B. F. Hyslop. See issues of American historical review

House of Valois, 1328-1589
See also
John II, king of France

Revolution
Bastille day revisited. A. Bakshian, jr. Nat R 22:734-5+ Jl 14 '70

FRANCE—History—*Continued*

February revolution, 1848
Recollections, by A. de Tocqueville, ed. by J. P. Mayer and A. P. Kerr. Review Sat R 53:38-40 My 9 '70. S. K. Padover

Industries
Reshaping of Saint Gobain. il Bsns W p47 Ja 31 '70
See also
Airplane industry and trade—France
Automobile industry and trade—France
Helicopter industry and trade—France
Liquor industry and trade—France
Machinery industry

Intellectual life
In quest of Kerygma: Catholic intellectual life in nineteenth-century France. H. W. Paul. Am Hist R 75:387-423 D '69

Moral conditions
See also
Prostitution

National center for space studies
Europe shifts goals in funding squeeze. R. F. Coburn. il Aviation W 92:89+ Mr 9 '70
France seeking world use of Diamant B. D. E. Fink. il Aviation W 92:84-5+ Ap 27 '70
French space center operational; Guiana center. D. E. Fink. il Aviation W 92:61-2+ Ap 6 '70

Appropriations and expenditures
French space unit seeks $160-million 1971 budget. Aviation W 92:29 Ap 27 '70

Politics and government
Death of a legendary hero. D. Singer. Nation 211:550-2 N 30 '70
France and Germany: less divergent outlooks? A. Grosser. For Affairs 48:235-44 Ja '70
Pompidou: a new Gallic image. por Time 95:18-19 Mr 2 '70
Pompidou pays a visit. E. Behr. por Newsweek 75:33-4 Mr 2 '70
See also
Communist party (France)
Elections—France
Political campaigns—France
Political parties—France

Religious institutions and affairs
Politics, impolitics and unpolitics; Échanges et dialogue. Chr Cent 87:525 Ap 29 '70

Riots
Maoist summer festival. Time 96:21 Jl 27 '70

Social conditions
See also
Women—France

Social history
Obstacles to agricultural growth in eighteenth-century France. R. Forster. bibliog f Am Hist R 75:1600-15 O '70
FRANCE (yacht) See Yachts—Design
FRANCE and the United States
See also
United States—Foreign opinion—French
FRANCEKEVICH, Al
In the darkroom. See issues of Popular photography
Red eye, TV eye, and other eyes I have shot. il Pop Phot 66:68-70 Mr '70
FRANCES, Evan
Diet 1970: how to lose pounds and find yourself. pors Ladies Home J 87:57+ Ja '70
Room service, extension 1970. il Ladies Home J 87:48+ Mr '70
FRANCHISE. See Suffrage
FRANCHISE system
Franchise fever strikes again. D. Demske. il Mech Illus 66:50-2+ F '70
Franchising, solid gold or quicksilver? H. A. Williams, jr. il Har Yrs 10:19-23 N '70
Franchising's busy helpers; franchiser consultants. il Bsns W p 132-3 F 21 '70
Franchising's troubled dream world. C. G. Burck. il Fortune 81:116-21+ Mr '70
What it takes to succeed in a franchise business. Changing T 24:25-8 My '70
What you need to know before you buy a franchise; questions and answers. C. L. Vaughn. por Pop Mech 133:25-6+ F '70
See also
Basketball teams—Franchise system
Restaurants—Franchise system

Finance
Bookkeepers ask questions. Bsns W p59 Je 27 '70
Franchising: too much, too soon. il Bsns W p54-5+ Je 27 '70

Laws and legislation
Chain of laws for franchising. Bsns W p26 Ap 4 '70
FRANCHISED automobile dealers. See Automobile dealers
FRANCHISED aviation schools. See Aviation schools
FRANCHISED regional basketball team. See Basketball teams
FRANCI, Carlo
Madman; interview, ed. by M. J. Matz. por Opera N 34:17 My 16 '70
FRANCIS, Connie
Lack of signed writing nullifies agreement. H. F. Pilpel and K. P. Norwick. Pub W 198:30-1 O 26 '70 *
FRANCIS, Ed
Winding your own output transformers. il Pop Electr 33:78-82 S '70
FRANCIS, Emile
Flashing blades for a mini-mastermind. G. Ronberg. il por Sports Illus 32:20-3 Mr 2 '70 *
FRANCIS, H. E.
(tr) See Wernicke, E. Gardeners' affairs
FRANCIS A. Countway library of medicine. See Harvard university—Medical school—Library
FRANCIS Bitter national magnet laboratory. See Massachusetts institute of technology, Cambridge
FRANCISCANS
No room for St Francis. Time 95:92 Mr 16 '70
FRANCK, Frederick
In Dutch with Rome. Commonweal 91:502-3 F 6 '70
Pontificate of lost opportunities. Commonweal 92:30-1 Mr 20 '70
FRANCO, Francisco
Franco vs. free unions. A. Rodriguez. America 122:36-7 Ja 17 '70
Homage to the hard-liners. Time 97:34 Ja 4 '71 *
Return of the ultras? il por Time 96:18-19 D 28 '70 *
Turning a page. il por Newsweek 76:26-7 D 28 '70 *
Unlikely savior. il por Newsweek 75:53 Mr 2 '70 *
FRANCO, Marjorie
Poet of Evolution avenue; story. Redbook 135:84-5 My '70
FRANCONIA college, Franconia, N.H.
Experimental president. por Newsweek 76:40 Ag 3 '70
Student as president. por Time 96:32+ Jl 13 '70
FRANEY, Diane
Recipes from a young cook. House B 112:44 F '70
FRANJIEH, Suleiman
President by a squeak. il Newsweek 76:37 Ag 31 '70 *
FRANK, Anne, museum. See Amsterdam, Netherlands—Historic houses, etc.
FRANK, Bonnie, and others
Interanimal memory transfer: results from brain and liver homogenates. bibliog il Science 169:399-402 Jl 24 '70
FRANK, Henry S.
Structure of ordinary water. bibliog il Science 169:635-41 Ag 14 '70
FRANK, Howard, and Frisch, I. T.
Network analysis; with biographical sketches. il Sci Am 223:15, 94-100+ bibliog (p 136) Jl '70
FRANK, Jacob
Holiness of sin; tr. by H. Halkin. G. Scholem. Commentary 51:41-70 Ja '71 *
FRANK, Reuven
Freedom of the broadcast press; address, February 17, 1970. Vital Speeches 36:332-6 Mr 15 '70
FRANK, Yakira H.
Linguistics and poetry. Engl J 59:947-53 O '70
FRANKE, Richard H. See Barrett, G. V. jt. auth.
FRANKEL, Charles L.
Uphill road to black capitalism. il Nations Bsns 58:60-2+ D '70
FRANKEL, Emily
Emily Frankel: coming back for good. E. Jacob. pors Dance Mag 44:68-73 O '70 *
FRANKEL, Fred H.
Perspective on community mental health and community psychiatry. bibliog Ment Hy 54:155-8 Ja '70

FRANKEL, Haskel
  Criminal record. See last issue of each month
    of Saturday review. April 25, 1970-
  How to take the nonsense out of cooking. il
    pors Redbook 135:68-9+ O '70
FRANKEL, Max
  These are the words for Richard Nixon after
    his first year. il pors N Y Times Mag p
    12-13+ Ja 18 '70
FRANKENSTEIN, Alfred
  Exhibition preview: the reality of appear-
    ance. il Art in Am 58:94-9 Mr '70
  Jenufa, the biggest hit. il Hi Fi sec II 20:
    28-9+ F '70
  Sound world of Chou Wen-chung. Hi Fi 20:
    secI 84 Jl '70
  Yankee rhyparography. il Art N 69:50-3+ Mr
    '70
FRANKFORT on the Main

  Description
  To Frankfurt. B. Gillam. Mlle 71:49 Jl '70

  Music
  Report:
    Alban Berg's Lulu. H. McGinnis. Opera
      N 34:30 Mr 7 '70
    Schoenberg's Moses und Aron. D. Graham.
      il Opera N 35:33 Ja 9 '71

  Social history
  Return to Frankfurt. F. Ungeheuer. il Harper
    241:84-90+ Jl '70
FRANKFURT book fair. See Book fairs
FRANKFURT declaration. See Missions
FRANKFURT opera ballet. See Ballet com-
  panies
FRANKFURTERS
  Chickening out on the frankfurter. il Con-
    sumer Rep 35:31-3 Ja '70
  Low-fat hot dog: good but expensive; Mor-
    rell's. Consumer Rep 35:630-1 N '70
    See also
  Cookery—Meat
FRANKLIN, Benjamin
  Man who dared the lightning; condensation.
    T. Fleming. il pors Read Digest 97:233-44+
    Jl '70 *

  Drama
  That Franklin boy. A. C. Martens. Plays 29:
    47-52 Mr '70 *
FRANKLIN, Bonnie
  Futures, great. pors Vogue 156:90-1 Jl '70 *
  Pair from Applause. N. M. Stoop. il pors
    Dance Mag 44:42-6 O '70 *
FRANKLIN, Hugh
  Mechanical cow. J. Hobson. il Sci Digest 67:
    76-8 Je '70 *
FRANKLIN, Marian
  (ed) Thoughts of a dropout. Todays Ed 59:
    15 F '70
FRANKLIN, Paul
  Full-time freelancing in technical writing. il
    Writers Digest 50:20-2+ Ag '70
FRANKLIN book programs, inc.
  Franklin's new emphasis. Pub W 199:33 Ja 4
    '71
FRANKLIN stoves. See Stoves, Franklin
FRANKS, Lucinda, and Powers, Thomas
  Destruction of Diana. Read Digest 97:49-58
    N '70
FRANSON, Al
  Build FM stereo multiplex generator. il
    Radio-Electr 41:63-4+ O '70
FRANSON, Paul
  Curiosity box. il Electr World 84:82-3 S '70
  Panic button. il Electr World 83:41+ My '70
  Power transistors, a status report. il Electr
    World 83:25-9+ My '70
FRANT, M. S. and Ross, J. W. Jr
  Potassium ion specific electrode with high
    selectivity for potassium over sodium. bib-
    liog il Science 167:987-8 F 13 '70
FRANTZ. Andrew G. and Kleinberg, D. L.
  Prolactin: evidence that it is separate from
    growth hormone in human blood. bibliog
    il Science 170:745-7 N 13 '70
FRANTZ, Joe Bertram
  Great age for people; interview. por U S
    News 70:26-8 Ja 11 '70
FRANTZ, John C.
  John Frantz leaves Brooklyn; joins National
    book committee. por Library J 95:1268 Ap
    1 '70 *
FRANZ, Maurice
  Mulching with newspapers is here to stay! il
    Org Gard & Farm 17:34-9 D '70
FRANZA, August
  Abolish English! Engl J 59:798-9 S '70
FRANZGROTE, Ernest J. and others
  Chemical composition of the lunar surface
    in Sinus Medii. bibliog il Science 167:376-9
    Ja 23 '70

FRAREY, Carlyle J.
  Placements & salaries: the 1969 plateau. il
    por Library J 95:2099-103 Je 1 '70
FRASER, Lady Antonia (Pakenham)
  Lively lady was a secret scholar. R. B. Stol-
    ley. il pors Life 68:42-4+ F 20 '70 *
FRASER, H. Russell
  Men who make treasurers tremble. pors
    Forbes 106:19-20 S 1 '70 *
FRASER, Jay
  Holiday guide to European youth hostels. il
    Holiday 47:38-9 Je '70
FRASER, John
  Photography and the city. Yale R 59:228-41
    D '69
FRASER, Kathleen
  Poem from True romances. Harp Baz 103:
    157 Ag '70
FRASER, Kennedy
  On and off the avenue. New Yorker 46:147-8+
    N 14 '70
FRASER, Kirk
  Training project aids black youth. il Camp
    Mag 42:27 Ja '70
FRATANTONI, Joseph C. See Neufeld, E. F.
  jt. auth.
FRATERNAL association of steel haulers. See
  International brotherhood of teamsters,
  chauffeurs, warehousemen and helpers of
  America
FRAUD
  Beware of the freezer-meat frauds. il Good H
    171:155 Ag '70
  Going astray in the yellow pages. Consumer
    Rep 35:74 F '70
  Gyps that thrive at Christmas. il Changing
    T 23:12 D '69
  Home-improvement racket. B. Furness. Mc-
    Calls 97:40+ Ap '70
  How to squelch fraud schemes. Bet Hom &
    Gard 48:30 D '70
  It takes all kinds! dubious business prac-
    tices plaguing Popular electronics readers.
    O. P. Ferrell. Pop Electr 33:7 D '70
  It's a racket! consumer gyps and how to
    spot them. il Sr Schol 96:11-12 Ja 26 '70
    See also
  Advertising, Fraudulent
  Counterfeits and counterfeiting
  Diplomas, Fraudulent
  Forgery of works of art
  Malingering
  Quacks and quackery
FRAUDULENT diplomas. See Diplomas,
  Fraudulent
FRAUDULENT voting. See Elections—Corrupt
  practices
FRAZER, A. pseud.
  Opinion: working freaks. Mlle 71:34+ Jl '70
FRAZIER, George, 4th
  Masculine mystique. Mlle 71:63-4+ Jl '70
FRAZIER, Howard
  Consumer protection; address, November 23,
    1969. Vital Speeches 36:265-70 F 15 '70
FRAZIER, Joe
  Bring on Ali. il por Newsweek 75:94 Mr 2 '70 *
  Free at last? il por Time 95:51+ Mr 2 '70 *
  In the corner, the official heavyweight champ.
    P. Wood. il pors N Y Times Mag p52-3+
    N 15 '70 *
  Joe Frazier, singer and champ. D. Amram.
    Vogue 155:148+ My '70 *
  One round of boxing was more than enough.
    P. Putnam. il pors Sports Illus 33:20-1 N
    30 '70 *
  Power broker. Newsweek 76:92 N 30 '70 *
  Show biz is out, boxing is in. M. Kram. il
    Sports Illus 32:14-15 F 16 '70 *
  World champion nobody knows. M. Kane. il
    pors Sports Illus 33:36-8+ N 16 '70 *
FRAZIER, John
  Changes in the black ghetto: Cleveland; white
    and black Unitarians form separate units.
    J. G. Mearns. il pors Sat R 53:13-14+ Ag
    1 '70 *
FRAZIER, John Linley
  Mass murder in Soquel. il por Time 96:10-11
    N 2 '70 *
  Tarot murders. il pors Newsweek 76:32+ N 2
    '70 *
FREAKS (hippies) See Hippies
FRED, James A.
  Replacing TV circuit breakers. il Radio-Electr
    42:70+ Ja '71
  Wireless lamp. il Mech Illus 66:100 S '70
FREDERIC, Harold
  Books. E. Wilson. New Yorker 46:112-14+
    Je 6 '70 *
FREDERICK II. the Great, king of Prussia
  Boyhood of Frederick the Great. N. Mitford.
    il por Horizon 12:104-10 Wint '70
  Frederick the Great. by N. Mitford. Review
    Vogue 156:34 O 15 '70. J. Stafford *

FREDERICK, Frances
Formosanum, the late-late lily. il House B
112:30 F '70
FREDERICK, Nancy
We did it. il House B 112:10+ N '70
FREDERICK A. Praeger, inc.   See Praeger,
Frederick A, inc.
FREDERICK Douglass home. See Washington,
D.C.—Historic houses, etc.
FREDERICKS, Bob
Oh! Chicago! Bare essentials sell the now
generation by mail. il Pop Phot 67:72-3+ Ag
'70
FREDERICKS, John
Case for the sandtini. il Field & S 74:76-7+
Mr '70
FREDERICKSON, Ronald H.
Kansas to Ketchikan. il Yachting 128:56-7+
D '70
FREDERICKSON, William, Jr
Service through concessions. il Parks & Rec
9:40-2+ S '70
FREDRICKSON, Bruce E.
Selecting sailboats for your camp. il Camp
Mag 42:18 Ap '70
FREDRICKSON, Olive A.
Bears in my hair. il pors Outdoor Life 145:
36-9+ Ja '70
FREDRIKSON, Roger L.
ABC's new prexy. Chr Today 14:37 Je 5 '70 *
FREDRIKSSON, K. and others
Lunar glasses and micro-breccias: properties
and origin. bibliog il Science 167:664-6 Ja
30 '70
FREE, John R.
Electronics in photography. Radio-Electr 41:
33-4 F '70
FREE democratic party. See Political parties—
Germany (Federal Republic)
FREE enterprise
America's heritage of bigness. H. S. Com-
mager. Sat R 53:10-12 Jl 4 '70
Generation gap; youth and the free-market
system. H. C. Wallich. Newsweek 76:98 O
12 '70
Market v. the bureaucrat; excerpts from In-
dividuality and the new society, ed. by A.
Kaplan. M. Friedman. Nat R 22:507-10+
My 19 '70
New right credo: libertarianism. S. Lehr and
L. Rossetto, jr. il N Y Times Mag p24-5+
Ja 10 '71
Synergy that made America grow. il Bsns W
p68-70 O 17 '70

Anecdotes, facetiae, satire, etc.

Little red hen (revisited) D. Smith. il Na-
tions Bsns 58:32-3 Jl '70
FREE food for school children. See School
lunches
FREE lance writers. See Authors
FREE-lance writing. See Authorship
FREE library of Philadelphia. See Philadelphia
free library
FREE masons. See Freemasons
FREE music store (concerts) See Radio broad-
casting—Music
FREE press. See Freedom of the press
FREE radicals (chemistry) See Radicals (chemistry)
FREE schools. See Schools, Experimental
FREE speech
Dissent through the courts. Time 95:65 Ap 27
'70
Free to speak, free to publish. R. L. Tobin.
Sat R 53:53-4 Ap 11 '70
Gofman and Tamplin: harassment charges
against AEC, Livermore. P. M. Boffey. pors
Science 169:838-43 Ag 28 '70
Rational dissent at St John's colleges. Sch &
Soc 98:326-7 O '70
Role of the mass media. Cur 114:44-6 Ja '70
Threat from Spiro. Cur 114:42-4 Ja '70
White House and free speech. W. Roberts.
Sat R 53:26 My 2 '70
See also
Academic freedom
American civil liberties union
Contempt of court
Information, Freedom of
Libel and slander
FREE-stall barns. See Barns and stables
FREE trade and protection
AFL-CIO talks protectionism. il Bsns W p66
Mr 28 '70
Can free traders stave off quotas? with edi-
torial comment. Bsns W p34, 140 My 16 '70
Changing perspectives; world trade and fi-
nance; address, September 8, 1970. A. W.
Clausen. Vital Speeches 36:746-9 O 1 '70
Comeback for protectionism. il Time 95:98+
My 11 '70
Free-for-all over protection. por Bsns W
p20 My 2 '70

Free trade. M. Friedman. Newsweek 76:71
Ag 17 '70
Growing battle of trade barriers. il Newsweek
75:80+ Mr 23 '70
Protection can be dangerous. S. V. Malcuit.
por Nations Bsns 58:47 F '70
Protectionism: should we be afraid to trade?
Sr Schol 97:8-9 S 14 '70
Protectionism versus free trade; address,
September 29, 1970. J. H. Dent. Vital
Speeches 37:47-9 N 1 '70
Protectionists win a vital skirmish. Bsns W
p28-9 Jl 18 '70
Seesaw; findings of Milton L. Godfrey's com-
puter readout. Forbes 106:35 S 1 '70
Why unions fear the multinationals. il Bsns
W p94-5+ D 19 '70
See also
Free enterprise
Import quotas
Tariff
FREE trade area, European. See European free
trade association
FREE universities
What happened to the free university; The
conspiracy of the young; condensation.
P. Lauter and F. Howe. il Sat R 53:80-2+
Je 20 '70
FREE-use-of-land agreements. See Land utili-
zation
FREE verse
Poet's workshop. F. Trefethen. Writer 83:24-
7 Jl '70
FREED, Donald
Inquest. Criticism
Commentary 50:18+ Jl '70.*
Commentary 50:6+ N '70 *
Nation 210:573-4 My 11 '70
New Yorker 46:83-5 My 2 '70 *
Newsweek il 75:89 My 4 '70 *
Time il 95:62 My 4 '70 *
FREED, Richard
Beethoven by the numbers. Sat R 53:67-8 N
28 '70
(comp) Year's best recordings. Sat R 53:78+
N 28 '70
FREEDMAN, Janet
Liberated librarian? bibliog il por Library
J 95:1709-11 My 1 '70
FREEDMAN, Richard
Marschallin without marzipan. il Life 68:18
Mr 6 '70
Videotape explosion. Life 68:22 My 15 '70
FREEDMAN, William
Mr Sammler, can it; poem. Nation 211:24
Jl 6 '70
FREEDMAN'S village, Arlington, Va. See Negro
towns and settlements
FREEDMEN
Establishment of Freedom's village in Ar-
lington, Virginia. F. James. bibliog il Negro
Hist Bul 33:90-3 Ap '70
FREEDOM. See Liberty
FREEDOM (theology)
In bondage to freedom. Chr Today 15:26 O 23
'70
FREEDOM, Intellectual. See Intellectual liberty
FREEDOM house (organization)
Freedom's balance sheet. J. Deedy. Com-
monweal 91:466 Ja 30 '70
FREEDOM of assembly. See Assembly, Right
of
FREEDOM of information. See Information,
Freedom of
FREEDOM of information act. See Informa-
tion, Freedom of
FREEDOM of religion. See Religious liberty
FREEDOM of speech. See Free speech
FREEDOM of teaching. See Academic free-
dom
FREEDOM of the press
ACLU joins Scanlan's in dispute with print-
er. Pub W 198:29 N 2 '70
Censorship and fear; repression in South
America. Time 95:42+ Ap 13 '70
Death at the hospital; Traverse City state
hospital's campaign against Weekender's
advertisers. il Time 96:23 D 28 '70
First amendment; T.V. coverage, Congress
and the Supreme court; address. December
15, 1969. F. Stanton. Vital Speeches 36:234-6
F 1 '70
Free press is on trial. J. Hohenberg. il Sat
R 53:109-10 Mr 14 '70
Freedom of the press, 1970; Jackson, Miss.
underground paper Kudzu. Nation 212:3 Ja
4 '71
If something has to give: protecting sources;
case of M. Knops. por Newsweek 76:74 S 14
'70
Printer as censor. R. H. Smith. Pub W 199:37
Ja 4 '71
Promise on subpoenas. il Time 95:49 F 16 '70
Subpoenas and sources. il Newsweek 75:55-6
F 16 '70

FREEDOM of the press—*Continued*
Voice of reason; reply to Vice President
Agnew. E. Sevareid. Time 96:9 N 2 '70
What's fit to print? G. A. Harrison. Writers Digest 50:54-5 Ja '70
  See also
  Censorship
  Foreign correspondents
  Government and the press
  Information, Freedom of
  Press law
FREEDOM of the seas
  See also
  Territorial waters
FREEDOM to know. See Information, Freedom of
FREEDOM to read. See Intellectual liberty
FREEDOM to read foundation
Board of trustees of the Freedom to read foundation; annual meeting in Detroit. J. F. Krug and J. A. Harvey. Am Lib 1:845 O '70
Freedom to read foundation announces charter membership. il Am Lib 1:653 Jl '70
Freedom to read foundation: membership. Wilson Lib Bul 44:600 F '70
FTR foundation drive asks for members. Library J 95:965 Mr 15 '70
Intellectual freedom in Detroit. S. Havens. il Library J 95:2623-6 Ag '70
Intellectual freedom: realities, capabilities, purposes. J. F. Krug. Am Lib 1:336-8 Ap '70; Reply. F. M. Blake. 1:646 Jl '70
Power to the perverts. J. Berry. Library J 95:1785 My 15 '70
FREEHAN, Bill
Never touch a superstar; excerpt from Behind the mask, ed. by S. Gelman and D. Schaap. il pors Sports Illus 32:54-8+ Mr 2 '70
FREEMAN, A. Myrick, 3d
Pollution tax. New Repub 162:13-15 Je 20 '70
FREEMAN, Arthur
Currents; poem. New Yorker 46:32 Ag 8 '70
FREEMAN, Bud
Father and his flock; interview, ed. by I. Kolodin. il por Sat R 53:15-17 Jl 4 '70
FREEMAN, Frankie (Muse)
Something is wrong; address, November 23, 1969. Vital Speeches 36:364-7 Ap 1 '70
FREEMAN, Gaylord Augustus, 1910-
What's ahead for business; interview. por U S News 68:38-41 Je 29 '70

                  about
Banker who tells it like it is. il por Bsns W p76-8 Je 20 '70 *
FREEMAN, Jean Todd
Who am I? Where did I come from? il Ladies Home J 87:74+ Mr '70
FREEMAN, Jim
Doves for openers. il Field & S 75:40-1+ S '70
FREEMAN, Jo
Four of a kind, yet different. pors Newsweek 75:73 Mr 23 '70 *
FREEMAN, John W.
Bartók's Castle. il por Opera N 35:6-7 O 31 '70
Long line. il Opera N 34:24-5 Ap 4 '70
Play of light and shade. Opera N 34:24-5 F 14 '70
FREEMAN, Norman
Gear and gadgets for the one-design. il Yachting 127:64-5+ My '70
Norm Freeman on the Bruder spar. Yachting 127:102 F '70
FREEMAN, Olive W.
Day the bicycles came. il Har Yrs 10:19-20 Ag '70
FREEMAN, Richard L. See Shockley, D. G. jt. auth.
FREEMAN, Roger A.
Crisis in American education; address, June 19, 1970. Vital Speeches 36:592-7 Jl 15 '70; Excerpts. por U S News 68:72-3 Je 29 '70
Wayward welfare state; address. September 1, 1970. il Vital Speeches 37:16-24 O 15 '70
FREEMAN, Rudy C.
After the great odometer raid. Consumer Rep 35:579-80 O '70 *
FREEMAN, William J. and Craig, A. C.
Turning on bright underachievers. Todays Ed 59:52-3 F '70
FREEMASONS
Segregation in brotherhood; steps to reaffirm legitimacy of Prince Hall masonry. Negro Hist Bul 33:132-3 O '70
FREEMASONS, Negro
Segregation in brotherhood; steps to reaffirm legitimacy of Prince Hall masonry. Negro Hist Bul 33:132-3 O '70

FREEPORT, Grand Bahama Island
Boom town in the Bahamas. P. Fiori. il Holiday 47:56-9 F '70
Freeport that isn't. D. Butwin. il Sat R 53:45-7 Mr 21 '70
Grand Bahama: the big binge is over. il por Bsns W p54-5+ Ag 1 '70
FREEPORT sulphur company
Copper entices Freeport sulphur. il Bsns W p28 N 28 '70
Freeport first? il Forbes 105:34-5 My 1 '70
Where are the fat years? il Forbes 106:40 S 15 '70
FREESE, Arthur S.
Eight-year ice cube. il Mech Illus 66:68-70+ S '70
Laser knife for bloodless surgery. il Pop Mech 133:124-7+ Ja '70
Mechanics of medicine. il Pop Mech 133:110-13+ Ap '70
Mechanics of medicine; automatic breathing monitor, radiosurgery, and tooth transmitter. il Pop Mech 135:92-5+ Ja '71
Now: atomic power to keep your heart beating. il Pop Mech 134:104-7+ S '70
Pump that works like a heart. il por Pop Mech 134:128-31+ N '70
Ultrasonics: the silent sound with see-through eyes for science. il Sci Digest 67:42-51 Mr '70
Yes, you're a blue blood. il Todays Health 48:46-8+ Ag '70
FREEWAYS. See Express highways
FREEZE drying
What's new in freeze-dried foods. Bet Hom & Gard 48:101 Jl '70
FREEZE-etch electron microscopy. See Electron microscope and microscopy
FREEZER food plans. See Food, Frozen; Meat, Frozen
FREEZERS
Freezers. il Consumer Rep 34:667-75 N '69
Keeping food cool. il Redbook 135:90-8 Je '70
Owning a home freezer: convenience? Economy? H. K. Idleman and M. P. Idleman. il Consumer Bul 53:33-6 Ap '70
FREEZING
Hot water freezes fast. Sci Digest 68:13 D '70
Superheated ice formed by the freezing of superheated water. G. Schubert and R. E. Lingenfelter. il Science 168:496-70 Ap 24 '70; Reply. B. Kamb. bibliog 169:1343-4 S 25 '70
Water drop freezing: ejection of microdroplets. R. J. Cheng. bibliog il Science 170:1395-6 D 25 '70
  See also
  Cryobiology
  Frostbite
  Ice—Manufacture
FREEZING of food
Bulk freezing saves time, money and effort. D.-E. Coggins. il Org Gard & Farm 17:110-12 N '70
Freeze-ahead holiday buffet. il McCalls 98:70-1+ D '70
How to help your freezer do its job. M. K. Spencer. Am Home 73:84-5+ S '70
FREIBERG, Peter
Pierre Trudeau's legal overkill. Commonweal 93:292-4 D '70
FREIGHT and freightage
  See also
  Air freight service
  Trucking
FREIGHT handling
Freight handling evolving slowly toward giant jet age. N. Himmel. il Aviation W 93:88-9+ O 26 '70
  See also
  Containerization (freight)
FREIGHT trains. See Railroads—Freight trains
FREIGHT vessels
                 Design
Building ships Detroit-style; standardized design. il Bsns W p 106 My 30 '70
FREIGHTER cruises. See Ocean travel
FREIRE, Nelson
Music to my ears; Philharmonic debut. I. Kolodin. Sat R 53:45 Ja 17 '70
FREITAG, George H.
Garden of flowers; story. New Yorker 45:28-30 F 7 '70
FRELINGHUYSEN, Elizabeth L.
Lyell, Slover, Taylor Phyfe, et al. il Antiques 97:119-20 Ja '70
FRENCH, Charles
Coin quiz. See issues of Hobbies
Numismatics. See issues of Hobbies
FRENCH, David
Coming home to Martha Mitchell. Commonweal 92:156-7 My 1 '70
FRENCH, Janet
Evaluation gap. bibliog il Library J 95:1162-6+ Mr 15 '70

FRENCH, Jere Stuart
Decline and deterioration of the American city park. il Parks & Rec 5:24-8+ Ag '70
FRENCH, Roberts W.
I poems and You poems. Nation 210:695-6+ Je 8 '70
FRENCH academy
Académie française; excerpt from The French: portrait of a people. S. De Gramont. Horizon 11:48-51 Aut '69
Ionesco on Olympus. T. Bishop. por Sat R 53:21-3+ My 16 '70
FRENCH architecture. See Architecture, French
FRENCH art. See Art, French
FRENCH artificial satellites. See Artificial satellites, French
FRENCH CANADA. See Quebec (province)
FRENCH CANADIAN separatist movement. See Front for the liberation of Quebec
FRENCH CANADIANS
Voyageur. R. L. Nelson. il Nat Parks & Con Mag 44:20-4 D '70
See also
Acadians in Louisiana
Quebec (province)
FRENCH castles. See Castles
FRENCH cookery. See Cookery, French
FRENCH drama
See also
Theater—France
FRENCH foreign legion. See France—Army—Foreign legion
FRENCH foreign service. See France—Foreign service
FRENCH fries. See Frying
FRENCH furniture. See Furniture, French
FRENCH house decoration. See House decoration, French
FRENCH language

Study and teaching
Survey of the teaching of French, Spanish, and German in secondary schools. N. W. Austin and J. L. D. Clark. Sch & Soc 98: 250-2 Ap '70
Your foreign language program, is it relevant? C. S. Kersten and V. E. Ott. Ed Digest 35:53-5 Ap '70
FRENCH literature
See also
Philosophy, French
FRENCH painting. See Painting, French
FRENCH philosophy. See Philosophy, French
FRENCH poetry
See also
Troubadours

Translations into English
Alba; tr. by S. Orgel. Giraut de Bornelh. Poetry 116:356 Ag '70
Frugal path; tr. by P. Auster. J. Dupin. Poetry 116:279 Ag '70
Grapes and figs; I would like only to remove; Who will help me? None can come this far; I lifted up my eyes; And I now utterly in the celestial cascade; tr. by C. Corman. P. Jaccottet. Poetry 116:287-91 Ag '70
La houle à bout-portant; Briser le silence; Élans du jour; Chaque trace d'envol; Oublier tout; tr. by D. Wynand. J. Chatard. Poetry 116:374-83 Ag '70
Parallels; Right angle; Acute angle; Rectangle; tr. by T. Savory. E. Guillevic. Poetry 116:358-61 Ag '70
Sens-plastique; tr. by R. Howard. M. de Chazal. Poetry 116:327-9 Ag '70
FRENCH quarter. See New Orleans
FRENCH radical party. See Political parties—France
FRENCH revolution. See France—History—Revolution
FRENCH revolutionists. See Revolutionists, French
FRENCH students
France: the enemy within. E. Behr. il Newsweek 75:42-4 Je 8 '70
See also
Student demonstrations—France
Student militants—France
FRENCH terrorists. See Terrorism
FRENCH visitors in the United States. See Foreign visitors in the United States
FRENCH wines. See Wine
FRENCH women. See Women—France
FRENKEL, J. K. and others
Toxoplasma gondii in cats: fecal stages identified as coccidian oocysts. bibliog il Science 167:893-6 F 6 '70

FRENKIL, Victor
Frenkil and his friends. il por Time 96:12-13 Jl 13 '70 *
FRENN, George
He knows how to throw his weight around. P. Putnam. il por Sports Illus 32:52+ Mr 9 '70 *
FRENZEL, Louis E. jr
Can you learn electronics by home study? il Electr World 84:34-6 S '70
Careers in electronics, blueprint to your future. il Radio-Electr 41:65-7 D '70
Tune up your car with a vom. il Radio-Electr 41:23-5 Ap '70
FREQUENCY allocation, Radio. See Radio frequency allocation
FREQUENCY counters. See Counting machines and devices
FREQUENCY modulation receivers. See Radio receivers—Frequency modulation receivers
FREQUENCY standards
500/50-kHz frequency standard. N. Johnson. il Pop Electr 32:63-4+ My '70
IC experimenter's corner:
Build the 100-kHz standard. D. Lancaster. il Pop Electr 32:56-8+ Ap '70
Portable dual-range IC frequency standard. F. H. Tooker. il Electr World 83:76-7 F '70
Using power line as accurate time standard. R. A. Anderson. il Electr World 83:46-7+ My '70
See also
United States—Standards, National bureau of—Radio stations
FRESCO, Robert M.
Problem of visibility. Nation 211:206-8 S 14 '70
FRESCOES
Cloud-damsels of Sigiriya rescued. D. B. Udalagma. il Art N 69:32-3+ Sum '70
Our first look at Greek wall-painting. M. Napoli. il Horizon 12:22-9 Aut '70
Paestum. M. C. Lacoste. il UNESCO Courier 23:4-9 Ap '70
Treasure at Paestum; Lucanian tomb with Greek frescoes unearthed. il Time 95:46 Ja 26 '70
FRESH fruit. See Fruit
FRESH water biology
Bioresources of shallow water environments; report of a national symposium on hydrobiology. P. E. Greeson. Science 170:355-6 O 16 '70
See also
Fresh water ecology
Limnology
FRESH water ecology
Amateur scientist: how to study the life of a pond and to cultivate aquatic insects. B. S. Settle. il Sci Am 222:131-4 Mr '70
FRESH water fauna
Teeming life of a pond. W. H. Amos. il Nat Geog 138:274-98 Ag '70
See also
Bryozoa
FRESH water flora
Periphyton: autoradiography of zinc-65 adsorption. F. L. Rose and C. E. Cushing. bibliog il Science 168:576-7 My 1 '70
FRESHMEN. See College students
FRESNO, Calif.
EDP cuts equipment maintenance costs. D. Smith. il Am City 85:131-2+ My '70

Fire department
Cut fire protection costs. il Am City 85:92+ Mr '70

Music
See also
Fresno opera association

Parks and playgrounds
Here's a great stop-off in the San Joaquin; Roeding park. il Sunset 145:30 Ag '70
FRESNO opera association
Opera amid the grapes. S. Jenkins. jr. il por Opera N 34:6-7 Mr 14 '70
Report:
Rigoletto in the Martin translation. W. Aguiar. jr. il Opera N 34:25 My 16 '70
FRETWORK
Austrian hand-carved fret-work. S. A. Parvin. il Hobbies 75:112-13+ Ag '70
Ornamental scrollwork you can do at home. J. Burroughs. il Pop Mech 133:192-5 Mr '70
FREUD, Clement
Blues and hangovers on the Nile. il Sports Illus 34:16-19 Ja 4 '71
FREUD, Esti D. and Weiser, Morton
How well does your preschooler speak? il Parents Mag 46:40-1+ Ja '71

FREUD, Sigmund
Dear Father Freud. P. Roazen. Nation 210: 631-2 My 25 '70 *
Freud and philosophy, by P. Ricoeur. Review Nat R 22:635-6 Je 16 '70. R. Berman *
Freud as philosopher. H. W. Brann. bibliog Am Imago 27:122-39 Sum '70 *
Freud, Jung and the collective unconscious. D. Elkind. il pors N Y Times Mag p23-5 O 4 '70 *
Freud on the couch. A. Storr. il Horizon 12:42-7 Wint '70
Freud: political and social thought by P. Roazen. Review
Trans-Action 7:61 Je '70. M. Shapiro *
Freudian psychology and ethical doctrine. M. B. Zweig. bibliog f Am Imago 27:90-106 Spr '70 *
Freud's disturbance on the Acropolis; symposium. bibliog il Am Imago 26:303-78 Wint '69 *
Freud's dreams revisited. L. Shengold. Am Imago 26:242-50 Fall '69 *
FREUDIANISM. See Psychoanalysis
FREUND, Gerhard
Impairment of shock avoidance learning after long-term alcohol ingestion in mice. bibliog il Science 168:1599-601 Je 26 '70
FREY, Fred A. and others
Microtektites and tektites: a chemical comparison. bibliog il Science 170:845-7 N 20 '70
FREYTAG, Elizabeth A.
Great grass clipping controversy. il por Org Gard & Farm 17:38-42 Je '70
Imagine gardening in a new climate! il Org Gard & Farm 17:96-9 Mr '70
FRIARS
See also
Franciscans
FRICKER, John
Foreign accent. See issues of Flying
FRIDEN division. See Singer company
FRIEDAN, Betty
Mother superior to Women's lib. P. Wilkes. il pors N Y Times Mag p27-9+ N 29 '70 *
FRIEDBERG, Judith
Scouting the antique market. Travel & Camera 33:72-3 My '70
FRIEDLAND, Bea
Italy's ottocento: notes from the musical underground. bibliog f il Mus Q 56:27-53 Ja '70
FRIEDLAND, Dennis
Kids at Cannon. il pors Time 96:60 Ag 31 '70 *
FRIEDLANDER, Michael W. and Klarmann, J.
How many children? with excerpts from address, May 1969, by E. Sternglass. bibliog il Environ 11:2-13 D '69
FRIEDLANDER, Paul J. C.
Jet time syndrome. il Sci Digest 67:10-15 Je '70
FRIEDMAN, Benno
Presenting Benno Friedman. il Art in Am 58: 100-5 Mr '70
FRIEDMAN, Bruce Jay
Just back from the coast: story. il Harper 240:68-72 Mr '70

about

Steambath. Criticism
Commonweal 93:95 O 23 '70 *
New Yorker 46:48 Jl 11 '70 *
Newsweek 76:101 Jl 13 '70 *
Sat R 53:28 Ag 8 '70 *
FRIEDMAN, Fredrica S.
Our home on Barbados. il Travel & Camera 33: 24+ Ja '70
FRIEDMAN, Herb
Atomic wood, for stomping on. il Mech Illus 66:72-3 D '70
Installing a burglar alarm. il Mech Illus 66:73-4+ Jl '70
FRIEDMAN, Herbert
Focus on sound. Pop Phot 66:58+ Ja; 67:64+ N '70
How to match your tape to your recorder and vice versa. il Hi Fi 20:secI 46-50 Ag '70
FRIEDMAN, Herman. See Chakrabarty, A. K. jt. auth.
FRIEDMAN, Howard A. and Callahan, W. S.
ESSA research flight facility's support of environmental research in 1969. bibliog il Weatherwise 23:174-81+ Ag '70
FRIEDMAN, Irving, and Smith, G. I.
Deuterium content of snow cores from Sierra Nevada area. bibliog il Science 169:467-70 Jl 31 '70
—and others
Water, hydrogen, deuterium, carbon, carbon-13, and oxygen-18 content of selected lunar material. bibliog il Science 167:538-40 Ja 30 '70
—See Gleason, J. D. jt. auth.

FRIEDMAN, Jacob H. and Spada A. R.
Psychiatric training program for high school students assigned to a geriatric service. bibliog Ment Hy 54:427-9 Jl '70
FRIEDMAN, Milton
[Column on economic questions] See issues of Newsweek
How the slump looks to three experts. pors Newsweek 75:78-9 My 25 '70
Market v. the bureaucrat; excerpts from Individuality and the new society, ed. by A. Kaplan. Nat R 22:507-10+ My 19 '70
Social responsibility of business is to increase its profits. il N Y Times Mag p32-3+ S 13 '70
We must stand firm against inflation. Read Digest 96:202-4+ Je '70

about

Friedmanism, n. doctrine of most audacious U.S. economist. M. Viorst. il pors N Y Times Mag p22-3+ Ja 25 '70
Laissez-faire in a closed biosphere. Chr Cent 87:1403 N 25 '70 *
Little trauma at the Fed. M. Seeger. Esquire 74:36+ S '70 *
FRIEDMAN, Ralph
Out of work. Nation 210:421-2 Ap 13 '70
FRIEDMAN, Saul
Race relations is their business. il N Y Times Mag p44+ O 25 '70
FRIEDRICH, Otto
Would you welcome, please: Otto Friedrich? Esquire 74:32+ D '70
FRIEDRICH, Priscilla
Tarot. il McCalls 97:72-3+ Mr '70
FRIEDRICHSEN, Bruce
Iowa's new wonderland. il Travel 133:70-1+ F '70
FRIEND, Charlotte. See Rossi, G. B. jt. auth.
FRIEND, Milton, and Trainer, D. O.
Polychlorinated biphenyl: interaction with duck hepatitis virus. bibliog il Science 170: 1314-16 D 18 '70
FRIENDLY, Fred W.
Asleep at the switch of the wired city. Sat R 53:58-60 O 10 '70; Same abr. with title Today's short supply of air time. Cur 124:28-33 D '70
State of broadcast journalism. Cur 114:49-54 Ja '70
FRIENDS, Society of
AQAG to protest U.S. navy's test bombing in Caribbean. Chr Cent 88:7 Ja 6 '71
Enclave; being a non-Quaker in Whittier, Calif. M. F. K. Fisher. New Yorker 46:36-42 S 5 '70
In defense of Friends; working party document Search for peace in the Middle East. Chr Cent 88:35 Ja 13 '71
Quiet rebels, by M. H. Bacon. Review Commonweal 91:564-5 F 20 '70. G. P. Fogarty
See also
American Friends service committee
FRIENDS of the library
Friends. Am Lib 1:421, 637-8 My, Jl '70
FRIENDS service committee, American. See American Friends service committee
FRIENDSHIP
Price of friendship; study by D. Wright. Time 95:54 Je 8 '70
FRIENDSHIP clubs. See Clubs
FRIGGENS, Paul
Shame of our teacher pensions. Read Digest 96:167-8+ Mr '70
World war on hail. il Read Digest 96:29-30+ Je '70
World's most versatile police. il Read Digest 97:134-8 Jl '70
FRIGIDITY (psychology)
Female sexual inadequacy. D. Reuben. McCalls 98:50+ N '70
FRIMBO, Ernest M.
Notes and comment; interview. New Yorker 46:25-6 S 26 '70
FRINGE benefits. See Non-wage payments
FRISBEE (game)
It's beer, bratwurst and a guts game. J. Jares. il Sports Illus 33:48-9 Ag 3 '70
FRISCH, David H.
Scientists and the decision to bomb Japan. il por Bul Atom Sci 26:107-15 Je '70
FRISCH, Ivan T. See Frank, H. jt. auth.
FRISCH, Rose E. and Revelle, Roger
Height and weight at menarche and a hypothesis of critical body weights and adolescent events. bibliog il Science 169:379-9 Jl 24 '70
FRISHBERG, Dave
Lingle jingle. Newsweek 76:86 S 7 '70 *
FRITON, Edwin E.
Meteor fragments. R Pop Astron 63:2 Ag '69

FRITS
Frits for the art potter. R. Behrens. Ceram
Mo 18:32-3 Mr '70
FRITSCH, Albert J. See Sullivan, J. B. jt.
auth.
FROBISHER, Martin
Shopping for the underwater boat. il Motor
B 127:136-9 Ja '71
FROGS
Extraoptic celestial orientation in the south-
ern cricket frog acris gryllus. D. H. Taylor
and D. E. Ferguson. bibliog il Science 168:
390-2 Ap 17 '70
Frogs for the lily pool. C. O. Masters. il
Horticulture 48:26-7 Ap '70
Somatic cell mating and segregation in
chimeric frogs. E. P. Volpe and E. M. Ear-
ley. bibliog il Science 168:850-2 My 15 '70;
Reply with rejoinder. J. J. Freed. 169:1229-
30 S 18 '70
See also
Tadpoles
FROGS, Rain of. See Fishes, insects, etc, Rain
of
FROHLICHER, Jean S.
Elementary and secondary education amend-
ments of 1969. Am Ed 6:7-9 Jl '70
FROINES, John
Not guilty, but . . . G. Johnson. New Repub
163:9-10 Jl 25 '70 *
Too dangerous to teach. G. Johnson. New
Repub 163:18-19 S 5 '70; Reply. C. T. Dun-
can. 163:31 O 3 '70 *
FROM this day forward; story. See Duncan,
L.
FROME, Michael
Conservation. See issues of Field & stream
Forest lands and wilderness. Cur Hist 58:343-
8+ Je '70
Mike Frome. See issues of American forests
FROMER, Carl
Amateur scientist. il Sci Am 222:130-4+ Ja
'70
FROMHOLD, Hal
Compartmented bowls. il Ceram Mo 18:29 D
'70
On being a professional potter. il por Ceram
Mo 18:26-7 My; 30-1 Je; 29-30 S '70
FROMKIN, David
Entangling alliances. For Affairs 48:688-700
Jl '70
FROMM, William D.
How planning saves $$$$$. Am City 85:80+
Ag '70
FROMSON, David, and Nemer, Martin
Cytoplasmic extraction: polyribosomes and
heterogeneous ribonucleoproteins without as-
sociated DNA. bibliog il Science 168:266-7
Ap 10 '70
FRONDEL, Clifford, and others
Mineralogy and composition of lunar fines
and selected rocks. il Science 167:681-3 Ja
30 '70
FRONT de libération du Québec. See Front for
the liberation of Quebec
FRONT for the liberation of Quebec
At cross purposes; abduction of J. R. Cross
by separatists. il por Newsweek 76:55 O 19
'70
Canada: end of a bad dream. il por Time
96:29-30 D 14 '70
Canada enters the revolutionary age. il
Newsweek 76:41-4+ N 2 '70
Canada: the answer was murder; War mea-
sures act invoked against the FLQ. il
Newsweek 76:35-6 O 26 '70
Canada: this very sorry moment. il pors
Time 96:33-4 O 26 '70
Crackdown on terrorists; Canada invokes
war powers. il Sr Schol 97:3 N 9 '70
FLQ: blue-collar terrorists. Newsweek 76:36
O 26 '70
Iron law to deal with crisis in Quebec. il Life
69:34-5 O 30 '70
Law, order and Trudeau. D. Coxe. il Nat R
22:1201 N 17 '70
Lives in the balance; abduction of J. R.
Cross. Time 96:40 O 19 '70
Most beautiful sensation; release of J. R.
Cross. il por Newsweek 76:59 D 14 '70
Pierre Trudeau: counterrevolutionary. Nat R
22:1144+ N 3 '70
Quebec: terrorism & separatism. P. Leduc.
Nation 211:422-3 N 2 '70
Specialists in terror: Quebec's FLQ. il U S
News 69:18 N 2 '70
Terrorism in Canada; P. E. Trudeau's re-
action to violence. il U S News 69:17-19
N 2 '70
Trapped like rats; arrest of P. Laporte's sus-
pected kidnap-killers. il Newsweek 77:44+
Ja 11 '71
Violence has economic roots. il Bsns W p36+
O 24 '70

FRONT yards. See Home grounds
FRONTIER and pioneer life
See also
Ranch life
Canada
Boy artist of Red River; with paintings by
P. Rindisbacher. A. M. Josephy, jr. il Am
Heritage 21:30-2+ F '70
United States
Are we losing our pioneer spirit? P. Engle.
il Nat Wildlife 9:5-11 D '70
Aunt Clara's luminous world; with paintings
by C. M. Williamson. il Am Heritage 21:46-
56 Ag '70
Boy artist of Red River; with paintings by
P. Rindisbacher. A. M. Josephy, jr. il Am
Heritage 21:30-2+ F '70
Pioneer trip; Concord stagecoach along Kan-
sas Smoky Hill trail. D. Johnson. il Travel
& Camera 33:30+ Mr '70
Ride for life in a buffalo herd; excerpt from
autobiography. O. C. Marsh. il Am Heri-
tage 21:46-7+ Je '70
Three views of the western experience. J. L.
Shover. Am West 7:49+ Mr '70
See also
Oregon Trail
Overland journeys to the Pacific
Pioneers
FROOK, John
Very special problem. il pors Life 69:54-8+
N 13 '70
FROSCH, Frank
Death of the daring. il pors Time 96:41 N 9
'70 *
FROSH, Maxine B.
Confessions of a jackpot addict. il por Har
Yrs 10:43-5 Ag '70
FROST, David
Perspectives; interview, ed. by S. Nirenberg.
House B 112:14+ Je '70
Trade winds; interview, ed. by C. Amory. Sat
R 53:16+ N 28 '70
—and Cavett, Dick
David Frost & Dick Cavett talk about Frost
& Cavett. pors Redbook 135:94-5+ S '70
about
David Frost rampant. Sedulus. New Repub
163:33-4 O 10 '70 *
David Frost: TV's intercontinental man. H.
Ehrlich. il pors Look 34:64-8 Mr 24 '70 *
People are talking about. . . il por Vogue 155:
200-1 My '70 *
FROST, Joe L. and Rowland, G. T.
The seventies: a time for giant steps; ex-
cerpts from Curricula for the seventies. Ed
Digest 35:1-4 F '70
FROST, Justin
Earth, air, water. bibliog il Environ 11:14-
29+ Jl '69
FROST, Robert
Frost: country poet and cosmopolitan poet.
T. Morrison. Yale R 59:179-96 D '69 *
Frost revised. W. H. Pritchard. Atlan 226:
130+ O '70 *
Robert Frost: an intermittent intimacy; ex-
cerpt from Eloquent April. M. Cane. Am
Scholar 40:158+ Win '70 *
Robert Frost and wilderness. W. Van Dore.
por Liv Wildn 34:47-9 Sum '70 *
Robert Frost: The years of triumph, 1915-
1938, by L. Thompson. Review
Nation 211:185-6 S 7 '70. R. W. French *
Newsweek il por 76:66 Ag 24 '70. G.
Wolff *
Sat R por 53:21-3+ Ag 15 '70. J. W. Ald-
ridge *
Time il pors 96:70 Ag 31 '70 *
Robert Frost: The years of triumph 1915-
1938; excerpts. L. Thompson. il Harp Baz
103:70-3 Jl '70 *
FROST protection
Clearing the air in the orchards; pollution-
free heater. Bsns W p40+ Jl 25 '70
FROST resistance in plants. See Plants—Frost
resistance
FROSTBITE
Frostbite, white peril. Chem 43:5-6 Mr '70
FROZEN breakfasts. See Food, Frozen
FROZEN cake. See Food, Frozen
FROZEN desserts. See Ice cream, ices, etc.
FROZEN dinners. See Food, Frozen
FROZEN fish; Frozen food; etc. See Fish, Fro-
zen; Food, Frozen; etc.
FROZEN food cabinets. See Freezers
FROZEN ground
Getting set for a black gold rush; Trans-
Alaska pipeline. E. Gross. il Sci N 97:177-9
F 14 '70
Permafrost, Alaska's cold, cold ground. S.
Bicknell. il Sci Digest 68:60-5 O '70

FROZEN water pipes. See Water pipes—Freezing

FRUEHAUF corporation
Fruehauf's troubles. Forbes 105:22 Ap 1 '70

FRÜHBECK DE BURGOS, Rafael
Music to my ears; Philharmonic debut. I. Kolodin. Sat R 53:45 Ja 17 '70

FRUIT
Glossary of exotic fruits. Good H 170:186 Ap '70
Tropical fruits. A. F. Smart. il Horticulture 48:28-9+ N '70
    See also
Cookery—Fruit
Fruit culture
    also names of fruits, e.g. Figs

Drying
What's cooking?
A bowlful of seeds 'n raisins, homegrown, that is. M. C. Goldman. il Org Gard & Farm 17:112+ S '70

Preservation
    See also
Canning and preserving

Storage
    See also
Farm produce—Storage

Varieties
New fruits and vegetables. G. Logsdon. Farm J 94:50D Mr '70

FRUIT-bud development
Floral inducing extract from xanthium. H. K. Hodson and K. C. Hamner. bibliog il Science 167:384-5 Ja 23 '70

FRUIT culture
Do you grow rare fruit? il Sunset 145:154-5 Jl '70
Four easy-to-grow fruits. B. Thompson. il Home Gard 57:32-3+ Ap '70
Orchard practices that grow better fruit. J. I. Rodale. Org Gard & Farm 17:106-11 S '70 (to be cont)
    See also
Frost protection
Fruit
Gooseberries

FRUIT desserts. See Desserts

FRUIT diet. See Vegetarianism

FRUIT drinks. See Beverages

FRUIT flies
    See also
Drosophila

FRUIT industry
Fresh fruit from the tropics and from below the equator. il Sunset 144:86-8 F '70
    See also
Citrus fruit industry

FRUIT punch. See Punch (beverage)

FRUIT salads. See Salads

FRUIT sauces. See Sauces

FRUIT syrups. See Syrups

FRUIT trees
    See also
Apricot trees
Fruit culture
Peach trees
Sapote

Pruning
    See Pruning

FRUIT trees, Dwarf
Dwarfs simplify fruit gardening. Suc Farm 68:no5 44 Mr '70

FRUIT trees, Training of
Apple fences. il Sunset 144:58-9 Ja '70

FRUITCAKE. See Cake

FRUITS. See Fruit

FRUITS, vegetables, etc. in decoration
Fall branches. il Bet Hom & Gard 48:128 O '70

FRUM, Bernard
Early example of dramatic procedures in 18th-century keyboard music. il Mus Q 56:230-46 Ap '70

FRUMKIN, Gene
The title of this poem is. Nation 211:572 N 30 '70

FRUTKIN, Arnold W.
International cooperation in space. bibliog il Science 169:333-9 Jl 24 '70

FRY, Bert E. Jr. See Fox, M. R. S. jt. auth.

FRY, C. George
Christ and cosmopolis. Chr Today 14:3-6 Je 5 '70
John Calvin: theologian and evangelist. Chr Today 15:3-6 O 23 '70

FRY, Christopher
Fry in summer. por Newsweek 76:79 Jl 27 '70 *
Yard of sun. Criticism
    Time 96:56 Ag 10 '70 *

FRY, John R.
Books. S. Terkel. Commonweal 92:67-8 Mr 27 '70

FRY, Ray MacNairn
New directions in DLP. Am Lib 1:904-7 O '70

FRYBURG, Estelle L.
Children's attitudes during the New York city school strike of 1968. bibliog Sch & Soc 98:429-33 N '70

FRYE, John
Thermal pollution? with biographical sketch. il por Sea Front 16:85-95, 127 Mr '70

FRYE, John T.
[Monthly article on electronics] See issues of Electronics world

FRYING
Making your own fish and chips. il Sunset 144:213 My '70
Things mother never taught you. il Ladies Home J 87:128 My '70

FRYMIER, Jack R.
Teaching the young to love. Ed Digest 35:9-12 F '70

FRYXELL, Roald, and others
Apollo 11 drive-tube core samples: an initial physical analysis of lunar surface sediment. bibliog il Science 167:734-7 Ja 30 '70

FUCHS, Estelle
Time to redeem an old promise. il Sat R 53:54-7+ Ja 24 '70

FUCHS, Louis H.
Orthopyroxene-plagioclase fragments in the lunar soil from Apollo 12. bibliog il Science 169:866-8 Ag 23 '70

FUCHS, Sir Vivian
Evolution of a venture in Antarctic science; Operation Tabarin and the British Antarctic survey. il por Bul Atom Sci 26:75-80 D '70

FUCHSIAS
How to grow tree fuchsias. J. Machado. il Horticulture 48:24-5+ O '70

FUECHTMANN, Thomas G.
Uncoupling celibacy; Dutch pastoral council V. America 122:102+ Ja 31 '70

FUEL
    See also
Gas, Natural
Petroleum as fuel
    also subhead Fuel under various subjects, e.g. Rockets—Fuel

FUEL consumption of motor boats. See Marine engines—Fuel consumption

FUEL injection systems. See Automobile engines—Fuel feeding

FUEL oil. See Petroleum as fuel

FUEL research
    See also
Coal research

FUEL storage tanks. See Motor fuels—Storage

FUEL supply
Cold winter coming? energy crisis, with cold homes. Nat R 22:1098-9 O 20 '70
Costlier winter for fuel users. il U S News 69:70-2 O 12 '70
Energy shortage worsens. il Time 96:62-3 Ag 31 '70
Fossil fuel crisis. Nation 211:613 D 14 '70
Fuel for a boomlet. C. Morgello. il Newsweek 76:95 O 12 '70
Fuel stocks shrink to the danger point. Bsns W p20 Ag 29 '70
How bad a winter, long-range outlook. il U S News 69:58-9 N 30 '70
Judging the energy crisis. il Sci N 98:379-80 N 14 '70
New strength in energy stocks. il Fortune 82:129-30 D '70
Power and fuel resources. R. W. Holcomb. Cur Hist 58:330-6+ Je '70
Scrounging for fuel. Newsweek 76:89-90 S 14 '70
U.S. looking to Canada for help in fuel crisis. il U S News 69:43-4 N 9 '70
U.S. moves toward a fuel crisis. il U S News 69:26-8 Ag 24 '70
Why the U.S. is in an energy crisis. L. A. Mayer. il Fortune 82:74-7+ N '70

FUEL systems of automobiles. See Automobile engines—Fuel feeding

FUGARD, Athol
Boesman and Lena. Criticism
    Commonweal 93:47-8 O 9 '70 *
    Nation 211:285 S 28 '70 *
    New Repub 163:16+ Jl 25 '70
    New Yorker 46:57 Jl 4 '70 *
    Newsweek il 76:78 Jl 6 '70 *
    Sat R 53:53 S 19 '70 *
    Time 96:63 Jl 13 '70 *

FUGITIVES from Justice
FBI foils flight; Angela Davis case. por Sr
Schol 97:4 N 9 '70
Extradition to the United States of fugitives
from justice; executive order. R. M. Nixon.
Dept Stat Bul 62:528-Ap 20 '70
Fleeing leftists: why they pick Algeria. Il
por U S News 69:36 N 9 '70
Fugitives. il Newsweek 76:17 Ag 31 '70
Home away from home; T. Leary and others
in Algeria. il por Newsweek 76:38+ N 9 '70
How to make a difference. D. Berrigan. Com-
monweal 92:384-6 Ag 7 '70; Discussion. 92:
431; 93:3+, 35+, 78-9 S 4. O 2-16 '70
Life at the edge. D. Berrigan. Chr Cent 87:
787-90 Je 24 '70
Madison bombers. il pors Newsweek 76:28-9
S 14 '70
Notes from the underground; or, I was a
fugitive from the F.B.I. D. Berrigan. por
Commonweal 92:263-5 My 29 '70
On the lam in America; sixteen most wanted
by the F.B.I. J. A. Lukas. il N Y Times
Mag p30-1+ D 13 '70
Taking of Father Dan. il por Newsweek 76:
37 Ag 24 '70
Wanted by FBI. il Time 96:49 N 16 '70
FUGLEBERG, Paul H.
Make your vacation pay for itself. il Writers
Digest 50:28-9 Je '70
FUHRMANN, William
Iron forged. il por Craft Horiz 30:40-1+ O
'70
FUHRO, Warren
Clarify before you buy. il Am City 85:82 Ja
'70
FUJI, Japan
Fuji's frightful example. il Time 96:44 O 12
'70
FUJI photo film company. See Photographic
apparatus industry and trade
FUJICHROME films. See Photography—Films
FUJIKAWA, Gyo
Gyo Fujikawa: an illustrator children love. M.
R. Kraner. il por Pub W 199:45-6+ Ja 4 '71 *
FUJITA, Tetsuya Theodore
Lubbock tornadoes: a study of suction spots.
bibliog il Weatherwise 23:161-73 Ag '70
FUKE, Motohiro. See Inselburg, J. jt. auth.
FUKUDA, Nob
Nob Fukuda: fantasist. il Pop Phot 67:85-9
N '70 *
FULBRIGHT, James William
Arab-Israeli settlement; address, August 24
1970; with an interchange with A. A. Ribi-
coff. New Repub 163:20-3 O 10 '70
Fulbright proposal for peace in the Mideast;
abstract of address, August 24, 1970. il por
U S News 69:43 S 7 '70
Governance of the Pentagon; excerpt from
The Pentagon propaganda machine. Sat R
53:22-5+ N 7 '70
Madness on the grand scale; address, April
2, 1970. New Repub 162:19 Ap 18 '70

about

Dilettante. Nation 211:166 S 7 '70 *
Fulbright converted? K. Crawford. Newsweek
76:34 S 7 '70 *
Fulbright's firing line. por Time 96:9-10 Ag
17 '70 *
Guaranteeing a Mideast peace. D. Lawrence.
U S News 69:80 S 7 '70 *
Imperial role. G. W. Johnson. New Repub
163:9 D 12 '70 *
Junkets are classified; two cases of Congress
being misled by the executive. New Repub
162:8-9 Je 13 '70 *
Mourning becomes Senator Fulbright. C. Mc-
Carry. por Esquire 73:116-19+ Je '70 *
Myths and realities. K. Crawford. Newsweek
75:48 Ap 20 '70 *
One-upmanship. il Newsweek 76:37 Jl 6 '70 *
Tube power. por Newsweek 76:61 Ag 17 '70 *
FULCHER, James
Making of a radical teacher. Engl J 59:384-
6 Mr '70
FULLER, Buckminster. See Fuller. R. B.
FULLER, George C. and Langner, R. O.
Elevation of aortic proline hydroxylase: a
biochemical defect in experimental arterio-
sclerosis. bibliog il Science 168:987-9 My 22
'70
FULLER, Henry Blake
Books. E. Wilson. New Yorker 46:112-16+
My 23 '70 *
FULLER, Hoyt
Digest of rage. il por Time 96:89 S 21 '70 *
FULLER, Marielle. See Kardener, S. H. jt.
auth.

FULLER, Richard Buckminster
Pianetary planning; address, November 13,
1969. il Am Scholar 40:29-63 Wint '70 (to
be cont)

about

America on wheels. R. F. Sayre. Nation 210:
728-30 Je 15 '70 *
Buckminster Fuller gets A.I.A. gold medal.
synergetic spin-offs keep coming. il por
Arch Rec 147:41 F '70 *
Bucks, as in Buckminster. por Forbes 106:
54 D 1 '70 *
FullerAgelFiore: visual-verbal treatment for
I seem to be a verb. M. R. Kraner. il
Pub W 198:42-3 O 19 '70 *
Inside Buckminster Fuller's universe. H. Tay-
lor. por Sat R 53:56-7+ My 2 '70 *
FULLER, Wallace H.
Pollution or profit? Horticulture 48:22-3+ D
'70
FULLER, Warren
The Woods' mighty oak. il Am For 76:28-9
Ag '70
FULTON, Chandler
Transformation of tetramitus amebae into
flagellates. bibliog il Science 167:1269-70 F
27 '70
FULTON fish market. See New York (city)—
Markets
FULVIC acids
Humic substances: fulvic acid-dialkyl phthal-
ate complexes and their role in pollution.
G. Ogner and M. Schnitzer. bibliog Sci-
ence 170:317-18 O 16 '70
FUND, J. R.
For your wagon, build this pop-up camper.
il Pop Sci 196:64-6+ Je '70
FUND for the advancement of education
Investment in innovation, by P. Woodring.
Review
Sat R 53:62-3 D 19 '70. F. M. Hechinger
FUND for the Republic
Freedom and the foundation, by T. C.
Reeves. Review
Nation 210:248-50 Mr 2 '70. F. J. Don-
ner
FUND raising
Girl scout cookies taste of success. Bsns W
p24-5 F 7 '70
Our church gave money away! M. N. Kain.
Good H 171:199 D '70
Raising money for your church or club. il
Changing T 24:15-17 S '70
Three gatherings; parties in Manhattan.
New Yorker 45:31-3 F 14 '70
When Christmas cards can help others. il
Good H 171:186 O '70
See also
Campaign funds
Community chests

Anecdotes, facetiae, satire, etc.
God and Croesus. Chr Cent 88:55 Ja 13 '71
Whom Wahoo should woo. Chr Cent 87:1139
S 23 '70
FUNDAMENTAL particles. See Particles (nu-
clear physics)
FUNDAMENTALISM
Roots of fundamentalism, by E. R. Sandeen.
Review
Chr Cent 87:1565-6 D 30 '70. R. T. Handy
See also
Evangelicalism
FUNDAMENTALIST controversy. See Tennes-
see evolution controversy
FUNDULUS. See Killifishes
FUNERAL parlors. See Undertakers and un-
dertaking
FUNERAL rites and ceremonies
See also
Nasser, G. A.—Funeral rites and ceremonies

Anecdotes, facetiae, satire, etc.
Don't they look natural? R. Drake. Chr Cent
87:1416+ N 25 '70
Heaven can wait; I hope. F. H. E. Wood.
Chr Cent 87:269-70 Mr 4 '70
FUNGI
Fungal endogenous rhythms expressed by
spiral figures. J. A. Bourret and others; re-
ply with rejoinder. B. M. Sweeney. Science
169:1229 S 18 '70
Trisporic acid synthesis in blakeslea trispora.
R. P. Sutter. bibliog il Science 168:1590-2
Je 26 '70
See also
Lichens
Mushrooms
Mycology
Phycomyces
Rusts (botany)
Slime molds
Spores (botany)
Wood decaying fungi

FUNGI—*Continued*
Development
DNA synthesis during yeast sporulation: genetic control of an early developmental event. R. Roth and K. Lusnak. bibliog il Science 168:493-4 Ap 24 '70

Resistance and sensitivity
Colcemid sensitivity of fission yeast and the isolation of colcemid-resistant mutants. S. Lederberg and G. Stetten. bibliog il Science 168:485-7 Ap 24 '70

FUNGI, Effect of light on
Phycomyces: habituation of the light growth response. J. K. E. Ortega and R. I. Gamow. bibliog il Science 168:1374-5 Je 12 '70

FUNGI, Fossil
Fungal attack on rock: solubilization and altered infrared spectra. M. P. Silverman and E. F. Munoz. bibliog il Science 169:985-7 S 4 '70

FUNGI, Pathogenic
See also
Histoplasma

FUNGI, Sex in
Saccharomyces cerevisiae: a diffusible sex factor. W. Duntze and others. bibliog il Science 168:1472-3 Je 19 '70
Sexual reproduction in candida lipolytica. L. J. Wickerham and others. bibliog Science 167:1141 F 20 '70
Sexual reproduction in geotrichum candidum. E. E. Butler and L. J. Petersen. bibliog il Science 169:481-2 Jl 31 '70

FUNGICIDES
Annals of medicine; case of organic mercury poisoning by pork from hogs fed surplus seed grain chemically treated. B. Roueché. New Yorker 46:64-70+ Ag 22 '70
See also
Triazoles

FUNK, Mitchell
Sandwiches, paint, and filters. C. Steinberg. il Pop Phot 67:98-101 D '70 *

FUNK, Peter
It pays to increase your word power. See issues of Reader's digest

FUNKHOUSER, J. G. and others
Gas analysis of the lunar surface. bibliog il Science 167:561-3 Ja 30 '70

FUNNIES. See Comics (books, strips, etc)

FUNNYÉ, Clarence
Zoning; the new battleground; excerpts. Arch Forum 132:62-5 My '70

FUNT, Allen
Five happy moments. il por Esquire 74:140 D '70

FUR
Furs, fashion, and conservation. Vogue 156:144 S 1 '70
See also
Hides and skins

FUR, Artificial
Fashion for fake furs. il Vogue 156:94-103 Jl '70
Furs for the woman with a conscience. il McCalls 98:96-101 O '70
New fake furs; answers to your questions. A. Holmes. il Good H 171:179 D '70

FUR bearing animals
See also
Sea otters

FUR coats, wraps, etc.
Furs are a man's best friend. C. Kriebel. il Harp Baz 104:95 N '70

FUR industry
Mink yes, tiger no. il Time 96:40 Ag 31 '70

FUR seals. See Seals (animals)

FUR trade
Fur flies in defense of the great cats. il Life 68:68-70 F 27 '70
See also
Hudson's Bay company
Trapping

FURLONG, William Barry
Adlai III brand of politics. il pors N Y Times Mag p28-9+ F 22 '70
Astronauts are human too. il Todays Health 49:16-20+ Ja '71
Danger! pesticides at work. il Good H 170:82-3+ Mr '70
Guardsmen's view of the tragedy at Kent state. il N Y Times Mag p 12-13+ Je 21 '70
How Durocher blew the pennant. por Look 34:55-6+ Mr 10 '70
Johnny Bench: supercatcher for the big red machine. il por N Y Times Mag p8-9+ Ag 30 '70
What is a punter's hang time? il pors N Y Times Mag p30-2+ Ja 10 '71

FURLOUGHS
Far from Vietnam; Robert Anderson at home in Castro Valley, Calif. il por Newsweek 77:16 Ja 4 '71

FURNACE closet. See Closets

FURNACES
Protection for an orphaned heating system: Winter watchman. il Consumer Bul 53:22 D '70
See also
Solar furnaces

FURNEAUX, Robin
World's worst animals; excerpts from The Amazon. il Horizon 12:112-17 Wint '70

FURNESS, Betty
Cost of living (cont) por McCalls 97:28+ F; 36+ Mr; 40+ Ap; 58+ My; 20+ Je; 36+ Jl '70

FURNISHINGS, Household. See Household furnishings

FURNITURE
Build the marvelous Fold-A-Majig. H. Wicks. il por Pop Mech 135:140-5 Ja '71
Exciting new casual furniture! il Bet Hom & Gard 48:4+ Je '70
Families on the go: switchables, movables, stackables, adaptables. il Bet Hom & Gard 48:34-57+ Jl '70
Furniture. Bet Hom & Gard 48:90 F '70
Furniture on the go. C. Garner. il Bet Hom & Gard 48:28+ Jl '70
New furniture rounds the curve. V. D. Hahn. il Am Home 73:66-7 S '70
Real finds in new furniture. il Good H 170:114-21 My '70
Space shapers. B. Plumb. il Am Home 73:26+ My '70
See also
Bedroom furniture
Cabinet work
Cabinets (furniture)
Chairs
Chests
Desks
Period rooms
Rattan furniture
Serving carts
Shelves
Sofas
Stands (furniture)
Stools
Tables
Woodworking

Collectors and collecting
Furniture owned by the American antiquarian society. W. D. Garrett. il Antiques 97:402-7 Mr '70

Design
Plastic furniture of Carlos Sansegundo. C. Southern. il Craft Horiz 30:28-31+ D '70
Sitting easy. V. D. Hahn. il Am Home 73.56-9+ F '70
Wharton Esherick 1887-1970. S. Maloof; W. Castle. il por Craft Horiz 30:10-17 Ag '70

Exhibitions
Dateline: Cologne furniture fair. H. Morrison. il House B 112:134-7 My '70
Furniture of nineteenth-century America; exhibition at the Metropolitan museum of art. il Antiques 97:382-91 Mr '70

Finishing
Antiquing paint kits. il Consumer Rep 35:596-8 O '70
Art of glazing. il House & Gard 138:142-3 O '70
Decorating zest; lacquer colors and lacquer looks. il House & Gard 137:102-7 Mr '70
How to apply a finish you'll be proud of. F. L. Greenwald. il Pop Sci 196:120 My '70

History
Classics. il Bet Hom & Gard 48:45-65 O '70
Queen Anne and Chippendale furniture in the Henry Francis du Pont Winterthur museum. C. F. Hummel. il Antiques 97:896-903; 98:900-9 Je, D '70 (to be cont)

FURNITURE, American
American modern. il Bet Hom & Gard 48:62-5 O '70
American traditional. il Bet Hom & Gard 48:52-3 O '70
Charleston furniture. E. M. Burton. il Antiques 97:910-14 Je '70
Clement Conger: diplomatic treasure hunter; effort by State department to collect and preserve americana. M. Evans. por Am Home 73:50+ N '70
Dunlap cabinetmakers. C. S. Parsons and D. S. Brooke. il Antiques 98:224-31 Ag '70
Early American furniture; excerpts. J. T. Kirk. il Antiques 98:428-31 S '70
Furniture of nineteenth-century America; exhibition at the Metropolitan museum of art. il Antiques 97:382-91 Mr '70
Look at colonial American furniture. il Good H 171:148 Jl '70

FURNITURE, American—*Continued*
Masterpieces of early American furniture at the United States Department of state. R. C. Smith. il Antiques 98:766-73 N '70
Queen Anne and Chippendale furniture in the Henry Francis du Pont Winterthur museum. C. F. Hummel. il Antiques 97:896-903; 98:900-9 Je, D '70 (to be cont)
Regional characteristics of western Shaker furniture. J. Neal. il Antiques 98:611-17 O '70
Unusual forms in Shaker furniture. E. R. Pearson and H. L. P. Kealy. il Antiques 98:606-10 O '70
See also
House decoration, American

FURNITURE, Built in
Stocks items. il Bet Hom & Gard 48:36-7 Jl '70

FURNITURE, Childrens
Children's furniture inspired by Dr Seuss characters. il House B 112:80-5 D '70
Saddle-seat homework desk. il Pop Mech 133:170-1 Mr '70
What's great about this table is its size; art table for children. il Sunset 145:110+ N '70

FURNITURE, Chinese
Cargoes of splendor. il Am Home 74:48-51 Ja '71

FURNITURE, English
English Chinese style in furniture. J. Gloag. il Antiques 97:718-23 My '70
Hepplewhite, Sheraton & Regency. il Bet Hom & Gard 48:50-1 O '70
Queen Anne & Chippendale. il Bet Hom & Gard 48:48-9 O '70

FURNITURE, French
Louis XIII cabinet at Toledo. R. Davidson. il Antiques 97:893-5 Je '70
Louis XV & Louis XVI. il Bet Hom & Gard 48:54-6 O '70
Past into present; Norman court, collection by Heritage. il House B 112:102-5 Mr '70

FURNITURE, Inflatable
Inflatables are here. B. Dilenschneider. il Mech Illus 66:44-5 Jl '70

FURNITURE, Italian
Bravissimo! great new Italian chairs. il Redbook 134:117-21 Mr '70
Fantasy comes alive. H. Morrison. il House B 112:74-9 Ja '70

FURNITURE, Lacquer
Lively lilt of lacquer. L. Grundy. il House B 112:60-3 Ja '70

FURNITURE, Mediterranean
Mediterranean. il Bet Hom & Gard 48:46-7 O '70

FURNITURE, Miniature
Austrian hand-carved fret-work. S. A. Parvin. il Hobbies 75:112-13+ Ag '70

FURNITURE, Modern. See Furniture

FURNITURE, Outdoor
All from just one sheet of plywood; table and four stools. il Sunset 145:86-7 Jl '70
Build these now for summer use. il Bet Hom & Gard 48:32-3 F '70
Horseshoe lawn furniture. D. Shiner. il Design 71:24-6 mid-Sum '70
Laminate a lawn-chair frame. R. Capotosto. il Pop Sci 196:79-83+ Ap '70
Our ten most popular outdoor projects. il Bet Hom & Gard 48:12+ Ag '70
Outdoor projects. il Bet Hom & Gard 48:56-7 Jl '70
Patio furniture you can build. J. Doherty. il Mech Illus 66:128-31 Mr '70
Plywood rocker-table. L. Walker. il Pop Sci 197:76-8 Jl '70
See also
Benches
Chaise longues
Tables

FURNITURE, Painted
See also
Furniture, Lacquer

FURNITURE, Paperboard
Could you bend up a chair from foamboard? L. Walker. il Pop Sci 196:106-9 F '70

FURNITURE, Plastic
Caring for acrylic plastic furniture. E. Taylor. il Good H 170:165 My '70
Fantasy comes alive. H. Morrison. il House B 112:74-9 Ja '70
Free-form future. B. Plumb. il N Y Times Mag p50-1 Mr 29 '70
Mobile plastics. il Bet Hom & Gard 48:48-9 Jl '70
Plastic furniture of Carlos Sansegundo. C. Southern. il Craft Horiz 30:28-31+ D '70
Plastic trend in furniture's future. il Bsns W p 112-13 S 26 '70
Pulsating color in new fluorescent plastics. il House & Gard 138:98-9 S '70

FURNITURE, Scandinavian
Scandinavia strikes back. S. G. Lewin. il House B 112:63-9 S '70
Scandinavian. il Bet Hom & Gard 48:60-1 O '70

FURNITURE, Used
Pickups. il Mlle 71:152-3+ Je '70

FURNITURE design. See Furniture—Design

FURNITURE designers
Twelve imaginations at work. S. G. Lewin. il House B 112:23-30 Jl '70

FURNITURE finishing. See Furniture—Finishing; Wood finishing

FURNITURE makers. See Cabinetmakers

FURNITURE stores
On and off the avenue; new Knoll international showroom, D/R international stores. J. Malcolm. New Yorker 46:147-8+ N 7 '70

FURS. See Fur

FURST, Betty
I'm having the time of my life. il Har Yrs 10:6-9 My '70

FURSTENBERG, Frank F. Jr
Premarital pregnancy among black teen-agers. il Trans-Action 7:52-5 My '70

FURY, Kathleen D.
Exasperating art of living with a big-time athlete. il Redbook 135:76-7+ My '70
How to avoid pre-Christmas panic (next year) Redbook 136:83+ D '70

FUSION, Nuclear. See Nuclear fusion

FUSION reaction. See Nuclear fusion

FUSION reactors. See Nuclear reactors

FUSON, Ben W.
At halfway point; state literary maps. bibliog f Engl J 59:87-98 Ja '70

FUTCH, J. D.
1922 all over again? il Nat R 22:354-5 Ap 7 '70

FUTURE
Future shock. by A. Toffler. Review
Fortune il 82:195-6 N '70. J. Zukosky
Newsweek 76:67-8 Ag 24 '70. R. A. Gross
Sat R 53:39-40 D 12 '70. A. A. Rogow
Future that nobody knows? reprint from issue of January 3, 1958. D. Lawrence. U S News 70:68 Ja 4 '71
Futurists and visionaries: hope's partners; conference on religion and the future. G. Fackre. Chr Cent 87:1060-3 S 9 '70
Look symposium: 21 hours toward the future. il Look 34:84 Ja 13 '70
Reflections: new generation in relation to the corporate state and the new consciousness. C. A. Reich. New Yorker 46:42-6+ S 26 '70
Schools in the 1990's; predictions of K. A. Ryan. il por Sch & Soc 98:454+ D '70
See also
Forecasts
Nineteen hundred and ninety-five
Nineteen hundred and ninety-one
Two thousand (year)

FUTURE farmers of America
They're out to revamp vo-ag. J. D. Boyd. il Farm J 93:26-7+ D '69
Three cheers for the boys in blue. Farm J 94:106 F '70

FUTURE life
Time of an idea. V. P. McCorry. America 123:416 N 14 '70
See also
Heaven
Hell
Immortality
Spiritualism

FUTURES. See Commodity exchanges; Hedging

G

G. Schirmer, inc. See Schirmer, G, inc.

GAC corporation
What are earnings? Forbes 105:24-5 Mr 1 '70

GAO. See United States—General accounting office

GARP (global atmospheric research program) See Weather research

GB (nerve gas) See Gases, Asphyxiating and poisonous

GCD (general and complete disarmament) See United Nations—Committee on disarmament

GE. See General electric company

GEE. See Group for environmental education

GHOST (global horizontal sounding technique) balloons. See Balloons, Meteorological

GI bill of rights. See Veterans—Education
GM. See General motors corporation
GMA. See Grocery manufacturers of America
GNP. See Gross national product
GOP. See Republican party
GPO bookstores. See United States—Government printing office
GSA. See United States—General services administration
GABELICH, Gary
Run was a natural gas. G. Ferguson. il por Sports Illus 33:50+ N 9 '70
GABIANELLI, Vincent J.
Water: the fluid of life; with biographical sketch. il Sea Front 16:258-70, 319 S '70
GABLE, Dan
Good littler man wins big. H. Weiskopf. Sports Illus 32:72+ Ap 6 '70 *
GABLER, Milt
My thousand-year man. il por Sat R 53:18-19 Jl 4 '70
GABLIK, Suzi
Double-bind. il Art N 69:43-5 Ja '71
GABON
    See also
Hospitals—Gabon
GABREE, John
Country soul from Hollywood to prison. Hi Fi 20:138 O '70
Looking past the Beatles. il Hi Fi 20:secI 83-4 Ap '70
GABRIEL, Jack P.
Captain's paradise. il Travel 134:60-1 Ag '70
GABRIEL, Sister Louis-. See Louis-Gabriel, Sister
GABRIEL (guided missile) See Guided missiles—Launching from ships
GABRIELSEN, Trygve O. See Taren, J. A. jt. auth.
GABRIELSON, Ira N.
Oil pollution. il Nat Parks 44:4-9 Mr '70
GADDAFI, Muammar. See Qaddafi, M.
GADDUM, Penelope, and Biandau, R. J.
Proteolytic reaction of mammalian spermatozoa on gelatin membranes. bibliog il Science 170:749-51 N 13 '70
GADDY, Hazel Ross
Mother Goose lives on. E. Simpson. il pors Am For 76:44-8 O '70 *
GADDY, Lockhart
Mother Goose lives on. E. Simpson. il pors Am For 76:44-8 O '70 *
GADE, Daniel W.
Brazil's water buffalo. il Américas 22:35-9 My '70
GADOLINIUM earths
Gadolinium: distribution between aqueous and silicate phases. R. L. Cullers and others. bibliog il Science 169:580-3 Ag 7 '70
GADPAILLE, Warren J.
Is there a too soon? il pors Todays Health 48:34-5+ F '70
Myths about childhood homosexuality. Todays Health 49:45-7+ Ja '71
GADZIKOWSKI, Claire
Day before heartbreak; story. Ladies Home J 87:82 My '70
GAEBELEIN, Frank E.
Beethoven: a bicentennial tribute. Chr Today 15:7-8+ D 4 '70
Christian use of the printed page; excerpts from address. Chr Today 14:5-8 Ja 30 '70
Reflections in retrospect. Chr Today 14:9-12 Jl 31 '70
GAERTNER, Kenneth
Song of the jungle soldier. America 122:585 My 30 '70
GAFFURIUS, Franchinus. See Gafori, Franchino
GAFORI, Franchino
Early Gaffuriana: new answers to old questions. C. A. Miller. bibliog f por Mus Q 56:367-88 Jl '70 *
GAGE, Larry
Grooving in the Caribbean. il pors Esquire 73: 95+ F '70
GAGE, Nicholas
Little big man who laughs at the law. il pors Atlan 226:62-9 Jl '70
—and Kulukundis. Elias
Report from Greece: under the junta. Am Scholar 39:475-97 Sum '70
GAGES
Build your own portable water tester; conductivity gauge. P. Emerson. il Pop Sci 197:127-8+ S '70
Why two miter gauges are better than one. R. J. DeCristoforo. il Pop Sci 196:108 Je '70
Woodworking tools that make you an expert. R. J. De Cristoforo. il Pop Sci 197: 93-5 Ag '70
    See also
Indexing (machine work)
Strain gages

GAGLIANO, Frank
Prince of Peasantmania. Criticism Sat R il 53:12+ Mr 21 '70 *
GAGLIARDO, Ruth
Books for children (title varies) See issues of PTA magazine to June 1970
Notable children's books of 1969. PTA Mag 64:22-4 My '70
GAGNÉ, Robert M.
Some new views of learning and instruction. Ed Digest 36:4-7 O '70
GAGOSIAN, Earl
Riches from royal treatment. il por Time 96:87 N 16 '70 *
GAHAGAN, James R.
Market letter from Milwaukee. il Writers Digest 50:28-32 Mr '70
GAINES, Edith
(ed) Collectors' notes. See issues of Antiques
In the service of soup: a great collection. il Antiques 97:109-18 Ja '70
GAINES, Ervin J.
Viewpoint. Library J 95:641, 1455, 2335, 2639, 3452, 4233 F 15, Ap 15, Je 15, Ag, O 15, D 15 '70
    about
Minneapolis librarians defeat censorship move. Library J 95:4090 D 1 '70 *
GAINES, Tilford C.
Money markets and interest rates; address, April 29, 1970. Vital Speeches 36:536-9 Je 15 '70
GAINES, William A. See Glatt, C. A. jt. auth.
GAINSBOROUGH, Thomas
Royal road to art. D. Davis. il Newsweek 75:109 Je 15 '70 *
GALACTIC magnetic fields. See Magnetic fields (cosmic fields)
GALACTIC systems. See Galaxies
GALACTOSIDASES
Fabry's disease: alpha-galactosidase deficiency. J. A. Kint. bibliog il Science 167:1268-9 F 27 '70
Genetic inactivation of the α-galactosidase locus in carriers of Fabry's disease. G. Romeo and B. R. Migeon. bibliog il Science 170:180-1 O 9 '70
GALANTAY, Ervin
Designing the environment. il Nation 211:134-8 Ag 31 '70
GALANTOWICZ, Richard E.
Space preservation, taxes, planning, and talking: the crunch. il Am For 76:36-8+ O '70
GALÁPAGOS ISLANDS
Caldera collapse in the Galápagos Islands, 1968; Isla Fernandina. T. Simkin and K. A. Howard. bibliog il Science 169:429-37 Jl 31 '70
Cruise to islands of wonders and terror. C. Mitchell. il Sports Illus 32:36-43 Je 8 '70
Galapagos. S. Wiedel. il Travel & Camera 33:46-9+ Je '79
    See also
Zoology—Galápagos Islands
GALAXIES
Black holes; elliptical galaxies. Sci Am 223: 54 O '70
Crowded galaxy; study of Seyfert galaxies. il Sci N 97:552 Je 6 '70
Deep-sky wonders. W. S. Houston. See issues of Sky and telescope
Extragalactic distance scale. il Sky & Tel 39: 93-4 F '70
Galaxies and quasars: puzzling observations and bizarre theories. R. W. Holcomb. Science 167:1601-3 Mr 20 '70
Galaxies and the universe. J. H. Oort. bibliog il Science 170:1363-70 D 25 '70
Galaxies with bright infrared cores. il Sky & Tel 39:357-8 Je '70
Galaxy diameters and red shifts. il Sky & Tel 40:353 D '70
Origin of galaxies. M. J. Rees and J. Silk. il Sci Am 222:26-35 bibliog (p 152) Je '70
X-ray survey of Centaurus A. E. T. Byram and others. bibliog il Science 169:366-8 Jl 24 '70
Young or just peculiar? Zw galaxies. il Sci N 99:6 Ja 2 '71
    See also
Magellanic clouds
Milky way
        Spectra
Faint galaxy with an unusual spectrum. Sky & Tel 41:26 Ja '71
GALBRAITH, Georgie Starbuck
Song of sons and daughters. Good H 170:124 Je '70
Wishes for a new child; poem. Good H 171: 180 S '70

GALBRAITH, John Kenneth
Revisionist view. New Repub 162:17-19 Mr 28 '70
To my friends in the affluent society; greetings. por Life 68:20 Mr 27 '70
Wage-price controls: the cure for runaway inflation. il por N Y Times Mag p24-5+ Je 7 '70
Who needs the Democrats? il Harper 241:43-53+ Jl '70
Who prefers Gstaad? Those of us with better taste. il Holiday 47:60-3+ Ja '70
Winning in November is not enough. New Repub 162:13-14 Je 13 '70

about

Galbraith purge. K. Crawford. Newsweek 75:29 F 9 '70
Galbraith was wrong again. E. McDowell. Nat R 22:1108 O 20 '70 *
Other purge. K. Crawford. Newsweek 76:39 N 23 '70 *
Workmanlike job in New Delhi. V. Miller. Nat R 22:39-40 Ja 13 '70
GALEN Martini, Sister. See Martini, G.
GALENA park, Peoria, Ill. See Aged—Housing
GALGOCI, Charles. See Hutton, H. K. jt. auth.
GALIANO, Louis C.
Prologue; poem. Nat R 22:897 Ag 25 '70
GALILEI, Galileo
Today's impress & Galileo's Medicean stars. P. W. Schmidtchen. il Hobbies 75:134-6 Ap '70 *
GALL, Helen Ward
How many autumns? il Nat Wildlife 7:17 O '69
GALL, Joseph G. See Pardue, M. L. jt. auth.
GALL, Norman
Chileans have elected a revolution. il pors N Y Times Mag p26-7+ N 1 '70
Latin America: the church militant. bibliog f Commentary 49:25-37 Ap '70
GALLAGHER, Edward A.
Getting the message across. R. Levy. il por Duns 95:43-4+ Ja '70
GALLAGHER, Michael J.
Carnival revolution. America 122:295-8 Mr 21 '70
GALLAGER, Sheldon M.
Boating instruments you can build from kits. il Pop Mech 134:126-9 Jl '70
GALLAGHER, Thomas
Tragedy at Kent state. il Good H 171:82-3+ O '70
GALLAUDET college, Washington, D.C.
Breaking the sound barrier. A. Eggebroten. Chr Today 15:42 O 23 '70
GALLAWAY, John. See Gallaway, S. jt. auth.
GALLAWAY, Sally, and Gallaway, John
Wind chimes. il Ceram Mo 18:20-2 Ap '70
GALLEN, John
Liturgical reform, again? America 124:20-2 Ja 9 '71
GALLER, David
Marsyas; poem. Poetry 116:92 My '70
Moray eels; poem. New Yorker 45:34 Ja 24 '70
Prodigal son returns; poem. Commonweal 92:13 Mr 13 '70
GALLER, Sol
No glamour, just work. il Am City 85:116+ My '70
GALLEYS, Boat. See Boats—Equipment
GALLICO, Paul
To my daughter, on acquiring her first car. Read Digest 97:100-2 Jl '70
GALLIUM
Gallium-67 localization in rat and mouse tumors. R. L. Hayes and others. bibliog il Science 167:289-90 Ja 16 '70
GALLO, Donald R.
I do as I do, not as you say: using literature research in the classroom. bibliog Engl J 59:509-16 Ap '70
GALLO, Robert C.
Finding a cancer clue. Time 96:41 D 21 '70 *
GALLOWAY, Howard
Howard Galloway begins 25th year as Camping magazine editor-publisher; letters to the editor. Camp Mag 42:34 Ja '70
GALLUP, Donald
T.S. Eliot & Ezra Pound: collaborators in letters. pors Atlan 225:48-62 Ja '70
GALLUP, George
No major trend to either party; interview. por U S News 69:29 N 2 '70
GALLUP, Gordon G. jr
Chimp discovers its self. il Sci Digest 67:67 Ap '70 *
GALLUZZO, Tony
Don't shoot blind, storyboard your films. il Mod Phot 34:94-5+ Je '70
Movie making. il por Mod Phot 34:26+ Ap; 16+ My; 32+ Je; 40+ O '70

GALSTON, Arthur W.
Science in review. See issues of Yale review
Sense of time. Yale R 59:448-54 Mr '70
GALSWORTHY, John
Real scandal behind The Forsyte saga. A. West. il Vogue 155:206-7+ My '70 *
GALTON, Lawrence
New lease on life for heart sufferers. il Read Digest 97:98-102 S '70
GALTSOFF, Paul Simon
Natural gas; excerpts from 1948 report. il Environ 12::22-3 Mr '70
GALUB, Jack
Burglars will get you, if you don't watch out. Am Home 73:108+ S '70
How to get health insurance that's right for your family. il Parents Mag 45:78-9 N '70
GALVANIC corrosion. See Corrosion and anti-corrosives
GALVAO, Henrique
Dictator and the pirate. Nation 211:101 Ag 17 '70 *
GALVESTON BAY
Galveston Bay: test case of an estuary in crisis. L. J. Carter. il Science 167:1102-8 F 20 '70
Galveston: the island that's killing itself. R. Starnes. Field & S 75:6+ Ag '70
GALVESTON-Vera Cruz race. See Yacht racing
GALVIN, Hoyt R. and Asbury, Barbara
Public library building in 1970. il pors Library J 95:4113-34 D 1 '70
GAMBEE, Budd L.
Standards for school media programs. 1920: a lesson from history. bibliog Am Lib 1:483-5 My '70
GAMBIA
Gambia. R. W. Howe. Travel 134:62-3 Ag '70
See also
Tourist trade—Gambia
GAMBINO, Robert B.
Inexpensive greenhouse. il Horticulture 48:26-7 F '70
GAMBLE, Bertin Clyde
Gamble finally finds a man for the top. pors Bsns W p40-1 Ja 9 '71 *
GAMBLE, F. R. and others
Superconductivity in layered structure organometallic crystals. bibliog il Science 168:568-70 My 1 '70
GAMBLE-Skogmo, inc.
Gamble finally finds a man for the top. pors Bsns W p40-1 Ja 9 '71
GAMBLING
Another shadow. il por Time 95:58 Mr 9 '70
Confessions of a jackpot addict; playing the slot machines. M. B. Frosh. il por Har Yrs 10:43-5 Ag '70
Denny the dupe; investigation of D. McLain's activities. il por Time 95:51 Mr 2 '70
Downfall of a hero; D. McLain, pitcher of Detroit Tigers. M. Sharnik. il por Sports Illus 32:16-21 F 23 '70
Government as bookie. Time 96:77-8 N 23 '70
Ideal sucker. il pors Newsweek 75:93 Mr 2 '70
No. 11 off the boards; valuable man to Cosa nostra in the field of betting on college and professional athletics. il por Time 95:16-17 Mr 2 '70
Slap on the wrist; B. Kuhn's handling of the D. McLain affair. P. Axthelm. por Newsweek 75:48 Ap 13 '70
See also
Casinos
Horse race betting

Laws and regulations
Floating casino. Time 95:28+ Ap 20 '70

Psychology
Suckers. F. Trippett. il Look 34:34-5+ My 19 '70

Great Britain
Floating casino. Time 95:28+ Ap 20 '70
Your friendly neighborhood betting shop. G. Astor. il Look 34:54-6 Jl 28 '70

Japan
Foul ball in Japan; investigation into fixes, bribes and gambling. il Newsweek 75:99 Mr 30 '70
GAMBLING stocks. See Stocks
GAME
See also
Cookery—Game
GAME, Dressing of
How to dress a deer. W. Davis. il Mech Illus 66:76-7+ N '70
How to skin a deer with a golf ball. C. M. Marshall. il Field & S 75:98-9 O '70
I've been gypped! hunters' complaints about the meat processors. G. N. Hunter. il por Outdoor Life 146:74-6+ N '70

GAME birds
See also
Shooting
also names of game birds, e.g. Quails

Food and feeding
Stopping the decline and fall of grouse; use the aspen forest; Cloquet study. G. W. Gullion. il Field & S 75:32-3+ D '70

Protection
Limit the duck hunters? J. T. Shields. il Outdoor Life 146:47-9+ S '70

GAME calls. See Animal calling

GAME laws
Face of starvation; hunting and game conservation. J. B. Trefethen. il Nat Wildlife 7:4-8+ O '69
Hunting abroad? Know this law; importing of trophies. E. P. Denson. il Outdoor Life 146:66+ D '70
Hunting seasons (cont) Outdoor Life 146: 20+ S '70
Small game seasons 1969-70. Cons 24:35 Ag '69
See also
Game birds—Protection
Poaching

GAME preserves
Cabeza Prieta, our forgotten wilderness. L. W. Robinson. il Liv Wildn 33:25-8 Aut '69
Pavlov's ducks fly to a last supper; Meadow view wildlife preserve. R. F. Jones. Sports Illus 32:46 Ja 19 '70

GAME protection
Growing worry for Africa; saving its big game. il U S News 69:81-2 N 2 '70
See also
Game laws
Game wardens
Wildlife conservation

GAME wardens
My toughest patrol. D. D. Ellis. il pors Outdoor Life 146:62-5+ D '70
See also
New York (state)—Conservation department —Employees

GAMES
Agon, Ludus and Paidia. R. F. Sayre. Nation 210:281-2 Mr 9 '70
Children's games in street and playground, by I. Opie and P. Opie. Review
New Yorker 46:146+ Mr 14 '70. G. Steiner
Class tells. Newsweek 76:108 O 19 '70
Designed for play. S. G. Lewin. il House B 112:50-3 D '70
Driver-ed, learn while you play. il Consumer Bul 53:23 D '70
Family fun in your own backyard. R. M. Peters. il Home Gard 57:32-40 Je '70
Fun & games. J. A. Roscoe. il Todays Ed 59:78-9 O '70
Games children play. J. Newcombe. il Life 68: 67-8 Mr 6 '70
Games children play. il Time 95:59 Ja 26 '70
Games students play. R. G. Shirts. Sat R 53: 81-2 My 16 '70
Games that play with your psyche. B. Ford. il Sci Digest 67:26-32 Mr '70
Games that teach your children to read. il Bet Hom & Gard 48:44+ My '70
Ghetto; board game. il Newsweek 76:61 D 7 '70
Hit the squirrel. D. Shiner. il Mech Illus 66:116 N '70
Match wits with Danish gamemaster Piet Hein. H. Shuldiner. il por Pop Sci 196:68-71 Ja '70
On a dirty day you can play forever; Smog and Dirty water. D. Zwerdling. New Repub 163:11 Ag 22 '70
Pollution play; Smog and Dirty water. il Newsweek 75:91 Je 22 '70
Summer fun and games. il Bet Hom & Gard 48:35-7+ Je '70
See also
Billiards
Chess
Electronic games
Indians of Mexico—Games
Management games
School athletics
Sports
Word games

History
Revolutions and revelations in games people play. L. M. Bishoff. il Hobbies 74:152-3 Ja: 150-1+ F '70

GAMES, Mathematical. See Mathematical recreations

GAMES, Promotional. See Advertising—Prize contests

GAMETES
See also
Spermatozoa
GAMETOPHYTES
See also
Apogamy
GAMMA-ray spectrometry. See Spectrum analysis
GAMMA rays
See also
Mössbauer effect

GAMMON, Clive
Cymru am byth! il Sports Illus 32:58-64 F 9 '70
Danes scourge the seas. il Sports Illus 31: 28-30+ D 15 '69
Fishing (cont) il Sports Illus 32:49-51 Je 15 '70
In a land of green, a touch of blue. il Sports Illus 33:64-8+ O 5 '70
Nature. il Sports Illus 33:42-3 Jl 6 '70

GAMOW, George
How George Gamow went West; excerpt from My world line. il Sat R 53:51-4 F 7 '70
GAMOW, Rustem Igor. See Ortega, J. K. E. jt. auth.

GAMSON, William A. and McEvoy, James
Police violence and its public support. bibliog f il Ann Am Acad 391:97-110 S '70

GANAPATHY, R. and others
Apollo 12 lunar samples: trace element analysis of a core and the uniformity of the regolith. bibliog il Science 170:533-5 O 30 '70

GANDHI, Indira (Nehru)
We are a people in a hurry for progress; interview. ed. by C. S. Foltz, jr. pors U S News 68:65-7 My 25 '70

about
Indira's big gamble. il Newsweek 77:49 Ja 11 '71 *
Mrs Gandhi's gamble. por Time 97:27-8 Ja 11 '71 *

GANDHI, Mohandas Karamchand
Gandhi: in history as in life, a man of enormous complexity. P. G. Altbach. Commonweal 92:16-17 Mr 13 '70 *
Gandhi's spiritual classic. N. Braybrooke. por Chr Cent 87:423 Ap 8 '70 *
Gandhi's truth. by E. H. Erikson. Review Chr Cent 87:424-6 Ap 8 '70. W. R. Miller *
Harper 240:100+ Ap '70. I. Howe *
New Yorker 46:118-20+ N 14 '70. R. Coles *
Sci Am 222:122+ Ap '70. S. Gopal *
Seeking the relevance of Gandhi. H. A. Jack. Chr Cent 87:427-8 Ap 8 '70 *

GANGS
Ambushes in Chicago. Time 96:13 Ag 24 '70
Aquarius wept; Hell's Angels at Altamont concert. R. J. Gleason. il Esquire 74:84-92+ Ag '70
Chicago: turning against the gangs. il por Time 96:13 Jl 27 '70
Skinheads; British youths. il Time 95:37-8 Je 8 '70
See also
Young Lords (organization)

GANGTOK, Sikkim
Gangtok: cloud wreathed Himalayan capital. J. Scofield. il Nat Geog 138:698-713 N '70
GANN, Ernest K.
Magnificent Apollos. il Flying 87:37-56+ S '70

GANNON, Robert
Alaskan oil dilemma: ecology or prosperity? bibliog il Sci Digest 68:14-19 Jl '70
Doctor Hibben's New Mexican ark. il por Sci Digest 68:23-9 O '70
I saw them crunch through the Northwest Passage. il pors Pop Sci 19:101-5+Ja '70

GANNON, Thomas M.
Adlai Stevenson: a sense-making prophet. America 123:57-9 Ag 8 '70
Breaking the circle of poverty. America 123: 394-5 N 14 '70
Chile turns to Marxism. America 123:321-2 O 24 '70
CICOP 1970: prelude to conscientization. il America 122:214-18 F 28 '70
Games on July 4th. America 123:43-4 Jl 25 '70
Home scene (cont) America 122:476-8; 123: 470-2 My 2, N 28 '70
Renewal: Tennessee model. America 122:152-5+ F 14 '70
—and Hacala, J. R.
Waking up people power. America 123:520-1 D 12 '70

GANS, Carl
How snakes move; with biographical sketch. il Sci Am 222:12, 82-6+ bibliog(p 152) Je '70

GANT, Lisbeth
Sister debates a brother on that black man-white woman thing; interview, ed. by K. Mehlinger. il pors Ebony 25:130-3 Ag '70

GANTRY; musical comedy. See Musical comedies, revues, etc.—Criticisms, plots, etc.

GANZ, Alexander
Future of the central city. il Am City 85:57-9 Ag '70

GAPAY, Les L.
Form sheet on the dark horses. Nation 211: 202-6 S 14 '70
Leaderless majority; seniority in the House. Nation 210:134-6 F 9 '70
Stuck reform. New Repub 163:10-11 S 5 '70

GARAGE doors

Electric control
Electric control for garage doors. J. Capotosto. il Mech Illus 66:114-15 N '70

GARAGE storage. See Storage in the home

GARAGES
Automated parking system speeds cars underground; Rotopark. Arch Forum 133:101 Jl '70
Concrete on steel cuts garage costs; Scranton, Pa. il Am City 85:118 Jl '70
How to add a garage to your garage. il Mech Illus 66:94-5 F '70
1970 workshop & garage; plus a new carport and potting shed. N. Seney and J. Pinkham. il Bet Hom & Gard 48:60-3 F '70
Parking construction hits new high. Am City 85:102 N '70

GARAGES (service stations) See Automobile service stations

GARAGES, Municipal
Great garage at the top; garage for Coliseum and convention center in New Haven, Conn. il Arch Forum 133:42-3 O '70
How to get off-street parking. bibliog il Am City 85:91-3+ Ja '70
Parking design with everyone in mind; Hempstead, N.Y. F. R. Rundle. il Am City 85:100+ Ja '70
Parking garage built to give downtown a lift; Akron, Ohio. J. Alkire. il Am City 85: 65-7 Ag '70
Parking garage exteriors. il Am City 85:105-7 Ja '70
Parking garage helps revitalize a deteriorating downtown; providing parking for regional shopping center; New Rochelle, N.Y. D. Locitzer. il Am City 85:94 Je '70
Portable garage. il Am City 85:108+ Ja '70
Small towns can support a parking authority; Pottsville, Pa. D. N. Howe. il Am City 85: 132 Je '70

Lighting
Innovative lighting dramatizes garage design; Boston. J. F. Mulhern and W. R. McGrath. il Am City 85:114+ Ja '70

GARAUDY, Roger
Christ to a Marxist. J. Deedy. Commonweal 91:522 F 13 '70 *
Clampdown in the West. il por Time 95:24+ F 23 '70 *
Dissent of Roger Garaudy. R. Salloch. New Repub 162:17-19 Mr 7 '70 *
Excommunication of Roger Garaudy. A. Woodrow. Commonweal 92:28-30 Mr 20 '70 *
Girardi and Garaudy. America 122:173 F 21 '70 *
Letter from Paris. Genêt. New Yorker 46:92-3 F 21 '70 *

GARBAGE. See Refuse and refuse disposal
GARBAGE as fertilizer. See Refuse as fertilizer
GARBAGE bags. See Refuse receptacles
GARBAGE cans. See Refuse receptacles
GARBAGE collection and disposal. See Refuse and refuse disposal
GARBAGE compactors. See Refuse and refuse disposal—Apparatus
GARBAGE grinders. See Refuse grinders
GARBARINO, Merwyn S.
(ed) Seminole girl. il Trans-Action 7:40-6 F '70
GARBER, Charles
Holy family; story. New Yorker 46:22-8 Ja 2 '71
GARBISCH, Edgar W. collection. See Art—Private collections
GARBO, Greta
Garbo is 65; excerpts from Garbo. J. Bainbridge. pors Look 34:48-50+ S 8 '70 *
GARCIA, Joaquin Torres-. See Torres-García, J.
GARCIA PRADA, Carlos
Amado Nervo. il por Américas 22:9-14 O '70

GARD, Robert R.
Realistic look at the flexible schedule. Clear House 44:425-9 Mr '70
GARDEN apartments. See Apartment houses—Garden apartments
GARDEN architecture. See Garden houses, shelters, etc.
GARDEN benches. See Benches
GARDEN borders
See also
Garden walls
GARDEN catalogs. See Catalogs, Seed and plant
GARDEN clubs
Garden-club ladies. il Time 95:13 Je 1 '70
GARDEN contests. See Gardening—Competitions
GARDEN design
Walk in an artist's garden. il Sunset 144:93 F '70
See also
Gardening—Planting plans and tables
Landscape gardening
GARDEN drainage. See Drainage
GARDEN equipment. See Garden tools, equipment, and supplies
GARDEN exhibits
Coming events of interest to gardeners. See issues of Horticulture
Garden events [in month] (title varies) See issues of Sunset
GARDEN fences. See Fences
GARDEN houses, shelters, etc.
Behind the fence, her potting center. il Sunset 144:172 F '70
Build this back-yard beauty. B. Snyder. il Pop Mech 133:110-13 My '70
Build this handsome cookout gazebo. W. C. Leckey. il Pop Mech 133:160-3+ Mr '70
Early American garden houses. R. E. Griswold. il Antiques 98:82-7 Jl '70
Gazebo: island of tranquility. il House B 112:80-1 Je '70
Ingenious outdoor storage. il Bet Hom & Gard 48:60-1 Ag '70
Inside the graceful lathhouse is a hard-working work center. il Sunset 145:92 O '70
Pop art in the garden: a red, white, and blue gazebo. il Sunset 145:148 Jl '70
Teahouse by the pool. il Arch Forum 132:52-3 My '70
See also
Sheds
Trellises
GARDEN in the woods. See Framingham, Mass.—Gardens
GARDEN lanterns. See Lanterns
GARDEN lighting. See Gardens—Lighting
GARDEN of flowers; story. See Freitag, G. H.
GARDEN ornaments
Garden sculpture. C. B. Lees. il Horticulture 48:22-3 Jl '70
Glass hanging for the garden. il Sunset 144: 156-7 My '70
Setting hen with river rocks for eggs and other garden sculptures. il Sunset 145:74-5 S '70
See also
Sundials
GARDEN parties. See Lawn parties
GARDEN paths. See Garden walks
GARDEN photography. See Photography of flowers, plants, trees, etc.
GARDEN pools
Delights of water gardening. il Horticulture 48:20-2+ Ag '70
Frogs for the lily pool. C. O. Masters. il Horticulture 48:26-7 Ap '70
See also
Water lilies
GARDEN sculpture. See Garden ornaments
GARDEN seeds. See Seeds
GARDEN shelters. See Garden houses, shelters, etc.
GARDEN stakes and staking
It's July, so your squash need you. il Sunset 145:152 Jl '70
Should you stake and prune your tomato plants? K. F. Polscer. il Org Gard & Farm 17:52-3 Ap '70
Staking tomatoes the easy way. M. M. Crowley. il Org Gard & Farm 17:83 Mr '70
Tomatoes should be up off the ground. il Sunset 144:193 Je '70
GARDEN state ballet. See Ballet companies
GARDEN steps
Garden of steps. il House & Gard 137:64-5 Je '70
Garden steps in redwood 2 by 6's. il Sunset 145:180 S '70

GARDEN tools, equipment, and supplies
Eighteen great tools that make yardwork easier. il Pop Mech 133:162-5 My '70
Have you heard? See issues of Home garden & flower grower
It's tool-up time. E. McDonald. il House B 112:72+ Ap '70
More gift ideas for people interested in natural gardening. il Sunset 145:177 D '70
Power up for more gardening with less effort. B. C. Kilvert, jr. il Home Gard 57:32-40 Mr '70
Preview of new 1971 garden equipment. il Home Gard 58:52-3 Ja '71
What does an ecologically defensive gardener really want for Christmas? il Sunset 145:66-7 D '70
See also
Garden stakes and staking
Lawn tools, equipment and supplies
Tractors
Maintenance and repair
Power equipment. F. Burgmeier. il Horticulture 48:38 Mr '70
Storage
Garden cupboard. il Mech Illus 66:130 F '70
See also
Garden houses, shelters, etc.
GARDEN tours
Flower shows and garden tours. il House & Gard 137:205+ Mr '70
GARDEN tractors. See Tractors
GARDEN umbrellas. See Umbrellas
GARDEN walks
Garden in far-off Bali has interesting pathways. il Sunset 145:76-7 Jl '70
Patterns in paving. il Home Gard 57:48 Jl '70
GARDEN walls
Serpentine brick wall. J. Fanning. il House & Gard 137:202 Mr '70
GARDEN water wheels. See Water wheels
GARDENERS' affairs; story. See Wernicke, E.
GARDENING
Check list for late summer. B. C. Kilvert, jr. il Home Gard 57:40-1 Ag '70
Fall: a good time to plant. B. Thompson. il Home Gard 57:32-9 S '70
Garden calendar. See issues of Organic gardening and farming
Gardener's notebook. E. McDonald. See issues of House beautiful
Gardener's notes. J. Fanning. See issues of House & garden incorporating Living for young homemakers
Gardens, plants and man. by C. B. Lees. Review
  Horticulture 48:14+ D '70. G. H. M. Lawrence
Guide to improved lawns and gardens. il Good H 170:171 My '70
How to create a portable garden. E. McDonald. il House B 112:82-5 Je '70
It's time to finish up planting. il Sunset 145:184-5 D '70
[Month] in your garden. See issues of Sunset
October is a great month to put spring color in the ground. il Sunset 145:90-1 O '70
Stop disease in your garden. Suc Farm 68:no4 59 Mr '70
Vegetables in the rose garden. M. Bennett. il Org Gard & Farm 17:50-1 S '70
What to do in (month) See issues of Horticulture
See also
Bulbs
Childrens gardens
City gardens
Fertilizers and manures
Floriculture
Fruit culture
Gardens
Gardens, Wild
Herbs
Hotbeds
House plants
Indoor gardening
Landscape gardening
Lawns
Mulching
Organic gardening
Plant propagation
Plants, Potted
Pruning
Spraying and dusting
Transplanting
Vegetable gardening
Watering of gardens, lawns, etc.
Weeds
  also headings beginning Garden, Gardens, Plant, Plants

Anecdotes, facetiae, satire, etc.
Glenn Ford, star gardener; excerpts from Glenn Ford. RFD Beverly Hills. G. Ford and M. Redfield. il por Am Home 73:24+ Ap '70
Bibliography
Onward and upward in the garden. K. S. White. New Yorker 46:110+ Mr 28 '70
Speaking of books. See issues of Home garden & flower grower
Competitions
Enter Home garden's $2500 contest now (cont) Home Gard 57:8-9 D '70
Entry deadline for the 1970 Sunset garden contest is June 15. il Sunset 144:202 Je '70
Gardener's achievement in a single season; winners in Sunset's garden contest. il Sunset 144:114-18+ Ap '70
Home garden nursery contest winners. Home Gard 57:54-5 My; 18-19 Jl '70
How to enter Sunset's garden contest for 1970. il Sunset 144:241 Ap '70
Presenting the organic harvest award winners. il Org Gard & Farm 17:35-55 Ja '70
Prize-winners take a priceless trip! St Petersburg, Fla. il Home Gard 57:10 Ja '70
Winners in the 1970 sunflower contest. M. C. Goldman. il Org Gard & Farm 17:74-5 D '70
Youngest gardener was five, the oldest sixteen; winners of Sunset garden contest. il Sunset 144:218-19 Ap '70
See also
Childrens gardens—Competitions
Equipment and supplies
See Garden tools, equipment and supplies
Exhibitions
See Garden exhibits
Planting plans and tables
Color all year. il House B 112:130-1+ O '70
Garden guidelines, from coast to coast; cont of Home garden guide for reluctant gardeners. See issues of Home garden & flower grower
Planning the perennial garden. B. M. Capen. il Horticulture 48:20-1+ N '70
California
Joys of California gardening. il Sunset 144:84-93 Mr '70
Winter gardening in California. T. L. Loving. il por Org Gard & Farm 17:74-6 O '70
Canary Islands
Canary Islanders mulch with volcanic ash. A. Halperin. il Org Gard & Farm 17:52 O '70
Maine
Gardener reflects on Maine in May. P. R. Budd. il Home Gard 57:20-1 My '70
New Zealand
Gardening in New Zealand. B. Halliwell. il Horticulture 48:36-7+ S '70
Vermont
Anyone can homestead on two acres. J. Cox. il Org Gard & Farm 17:81-2+ O '70
GARDENING by children. See Childrens gardens
GARDENS
Personal thoughts on the art of gardens; excerpts from Des Jardins heureux. F. C. d'Harcourt. House & Gard 138:78-80+ O '70
Small walled garden. B. Simpson. il House & Gard 137:60-3 F '70
Very personal garden of Dorothy Hirshon: an old-fashioned country garden. il House & Gard 138:72-5 Ag '70
See also
Bird gardens
Blind, Gardens for the
Botanical gardens
Childrens gardens
City gardens
Gardening—Planting plans and tables
Roof gardens
Store gardens
Color
Annuals for bright summer color. il Home Gard 57:26-7 Ap '70
Color all year. il House B 112:130-1+ O '70
Color from bearded iris. R. P. Merry. il Horticulture 48:28-9+ My '70
Color in the seaside garden. G. Taloumis. il Horticulture 48:28-31+ Ag '70
Color slump coming in your garden? Here are color plants available in nurseries now or soon. il Sunset 144:242-3 Mr '70

GARDENS—Color—*Continued*
Perennial parade of color. L. Grove. il Bet
Hom & Gard 48:60-1 Ap '70
Plan bulb combinations now. B. Miles. il
Horticulture 48:22-5+ My '70
Yellow and white show for a party in Au-
gust. il Sunset 144:229 My '70

Lighting
Cheerful light for a dark pathway. il Sunset
144:144+ Mr '70
Unusual approach to garden lighting. il
Horticulture 48:37 Ag '70
See also
Lanterns

Austria
See also
Vienna—Gardens

Bahama Islands
Bahama Islands. M. Perry. il Home Gard
57:22-5+ O '70

Bali
Garden in far-off Bali has interesting pathways. il Sunset 145:76-7 Jl '70

Bermuda
Bermuda; a large and well-loved garden.
M. Perry. il Home Gard 57:14-16+ N '70

California
Summer is the time to see these historic trees
in Sunset's garden. il Sunset 145:132-3 Ag
'70
Two minutes off Sunset, the look of cool
woods. il Sunset 145:170-1 S '70
See also
San Francisco—Gardens

Canada
Butchart gardens, Victoria, British Colum-
bia. M. F. Bohm. il Horticulture 48:38-9+
Ag '70

Capri
See Gardens—Italy

Colorado
Garden beauty in mountainous Colorado.
L. Burgess. il Home Gard 57:46-7 Jl '70

England
England's cottage gardens. P. Brindley. il
Home Gard 57:16-17+ Ag '70
Gardens of Shakespeare's town. P. Brindley.
il Home Gard 57:26-9 Mr '70
Syon park. J. Kilborn. il Horticulture 48:25-
7+ Mr '70

Europe, Western
Great gardens of Europe. D. L. McFadden. il
Home Gard 57:32-4 Ja '70

Florida
See also
Fairchild tropical garden. Coconut Grove, Fla.
Miami, Fla.—Gardens

Hawaii
See also
Honolulu—Gardens

Italy
Miniature hillside garden; the personal garden
of Margaret Williamez. il House & Gard
137:96-9 Ja '70

Japan
See also
Osaka, Japan—Worlds fair, 1970—Gardens

Long Island, N.Y.
See also
Bayard Cutting arboretum, Long Island, N.Y.

Maryland
Gardens new and old in historic Maryland.
M. Perry. il Home Gard 57:44-5 Je '70
Witty topiary garden. H. Ladew. il House &
Gard 137:88-93 Ap '70
See also
Baltimore—Gardens

Massachusetts
See also
Framingham, Mass.—Gardens

New York (state)
Daffodils: trip with horticultural society of
New York to Brookside, estate of Mrs
Flagler Matthews, in Rye. New Yorker 46:
29-30 My 23 '70
Flowers of spring at our garden; Home gar-
den of ideas in Sterling Forest garden. il
Home Gard 57:20-1 S '70

Very personal garden and house of Mrs
Quaintance Mason. il House & Gard 138:
90-5 N '70

St John Island
St John, a far-away island not too far from
home. M. Perry. il Home Gard 57:30-2 D
'70

St Thomas Island
Set in a sapphire sea; the gardens of St
Thomas. il Home Gard 57:28-31+ Je '70

Scotland
Garden in the Highlands; Inverewe gardens.
J. Robertson. il Am For 76:36-9+ S '70

South Carolina
South Carolina's gardens. E. Cheatham and
P. Cheatham. il Home Gard 57:64-5 F '70

Sweden
See also
Stockholm—Gardens

Virginia
Virginia, a garden paradise. L. A. L. Copersino. il Home Gard 57:20+ Mr '70

Washington (state)
Gig Harbor gardener who couldn't wait. il
Sunset 144:84-7 My '70

GARDENS, Balinese
See also
Gardens—Bali
GARDENS, Childrens. See Childrens gardens
GARDENS, City. See City gardens
GARDENS, Fragrant
See also
Blind, Gardens for the
GARDENS, Hillside
Here's a way to plant ground covers securely
on really steep hillsides; paper collars. il
Sunset 145:212 O '70
Hillside garden success story. il Sunset 144:
250 Ap '70
Trouble with a steep bank. W. Ferguson. il
Org Gard & Farm 17:76-7 F '70
GARDENS, Indoor
Daylighted garden indoors. il Sunset 144:196
F '70
Garden that's right in the house. il Sunset
144:124-5 Ja '70
Mini-garden fun for a shut-in child. M. Rea.
il Todays Health 48:66 F '70
GARDENS, Italian
See also
Gardens—Italy
GARDENS, Japanese
Garden spot in the lobby; art class project.
E. Lee. il Sch Arts 69:35 My '70
Pine and moss garden; Bel Air, Calif. E.
McDonald. il House B 112:70-1 Ag '70
Very personal garden of Jean Arthur; a
whispering garden. il House & Gard 138:
70-3 Jl '70
See also
Osaka, Japan—Worlds fair, 1970—Gardens
GARDENS, Miniature
Dish gardens from the florist. il Sunset 144:
188-9 F '70
Mini desert on a table. K. Adler. il Home
Gard 57:28-9 O '70
See also
Terrariums
GARDENS, Protection of. See Plants, Protec-
tion of
GARDENS, Rock
Rock garden in the fall. D. Richardson. il
Horticulture 48:34-5+ O '70
GARDENS, Roof. See Roof gardens
GARDENS, Seaside
Color in the seaside garden. G. Taloumis. il
Horticulture 48:28-31+ Ag '70
GARDENS, Water. See Water gardens
GARDENS, Watering of. See Watering of gar-
dens, lawns, etc.
GARDENS, Wild
Making a wild flower garden. H. L. Foster.
il Nat Wildlife 8:13-16 Ap '70
See also
Framingham, Mass.—Gardens
GARDENS for the blind. See Blind, Gardens
for the
GARDINER, C. Harvey
Mexico: season of shadow. Cur Hist 58:91-4+
F '70
GARDINER, Glenn N.
Adult school trends in course offerings.
Clear House 45:15-17 S '70
GARDINIER, David E.
(comp) Articles and other books received:
Africa. See issues of American historical
review

GARDNER, D. Bruce
Obviously a lemon. Flying 87:93 D '70
GARDNER, D. R. See Greer, G. L. jt. auth.
GARDNER, Dave
Whatever happened to Brother Dave? L. L. King. il por Harper 241:52-5+ S '70; Discussion. 241:14+ D '70 *
GARDNER, Erle Stanley
Case of the agile ATVs. il pors Pop Sci 196: 70-3+ F '70

about

Case closed. il por Time 95:85 Mr 23 '70 *
Matter of loyalty. por Newsweek 75:114 Mr 23 '70 *
Obituary
  Pub W 197:47 Mr 23 '70 *
GARDNER, Harvey
They put snowmobiles to work. il Mech Illus 66:66-8+ Ja '70
GARDNER, Hugh
Your global alternative: communes, experiments, jails and hidey-holes. il Esquire 74: 106-9 S '70
GARDNER, Jim
Ink rendering. Design il 72:29-31 Fall '70
GARDNER, John
Care and repair of wood boats. il Field & S 75:124-8 N '70
GARDNER, John W.
Common cause: a new citizens' lobby; address, September 11, 1970. Cur 123:3-8 N '70
Crisis of confidence in our leadership. Cur 120:6-9 Ag '70
Failure of leadership; address, December 9, 1969. Vital Speeches 36:217-19 Ja 15 '70
Fresh prescriptions for disengagement in Vietnam; excerpt. pors Newsweek 75:31-2 My 25 '70
Let's say yes to hope; excerpt from The recovery of confidence. Read Digest 96:74-6 Je '70
Undelivered speech; excerpts. por Time 95: 16-17 My 25 '70
Waking in a nightmare; excerpts from address, 1969. Am For 76:6-7 Mr '70

about

Cause célèbre. il pors Time 97:16 Ja 18 '71 *
CC: citizens' lobby in the public interest. H. J. Sievers. America 123:109 S 5 '70 *
Gardner builds a citizens' lobby. il Bsns W p25 O 31 '70 *
Gardner's cause. il por Newsweek 76:23-4 D 7 '70 *
Gardner's common cause. Time 96:10 Ag 10 '70 *
Is business cooling on city problems? il por Bsns W p31-2 My 30 '70 *
GARDNER, Martin
Mathematical games. See issues of Scientific American
GARDNER, R. F. R
Christian choices in a liberal abortion climate. Chr Today 14:6-8 My 22 '70
GARDNER, Richard A.
If your parents are getting divorced...; excerpt from The boys and girls book about divorce. il N Y Times Mag p93+ N 22 '70
GARDNER, Richard Newton
Can the United Nations be revived? For Affairs 48:660-76 Jl '70; Same abr. with title Ten steps for UN reform. Cur 120:47-55 Ap '70
For global initiative. Sat R 53:41+ Jl 4 '70
Quality of life; address, April 21, 1970. Vital Speeches 36:466-70 My 15 '70
GARFIELD, Eugene, and others
Fixed valence and molecular formula verification. bibliog il Chem 43:13-15 O '70
GARFIELD, Sidney R.
Delivery of medical care: with biographical sketch. il Sci Am 222:12. 15-23 bibliog(p 130) Ap '70
GARFUNKEL, Art
Simon and Garfunkel, nothing gauche. R. Goldstein. Vogue 155:110 Ap 1 '70 *
Simon & Garfunkel: the singers and the songs. E. Sander. pors Sat R 53:91+ F 28 '70 *
GARGAN, Edward A.
If you could make one change in the church, what would it be? Commonweal 92:165-6 My 1 '70
GARLAND, Arville, murder trial. See Trials (murder)
GARLAND, Phyllis
Isaac Hayes: Hot buttered soul. il pors Ebony 25:82-4+ Mr '70
Prize winners. il pors Ebony 25:29-32+ Jl '70
Sounds. Ebony 25:24 Jl; 28 Ag; 26 S; 26:28 D '70

GARLIC
Breath that kills; mosquitocide? Newsweek 75:87 Mr 30 '70
GARLITS, Don
I'm the guy who leaves them breathless. Sports Illus 33:27-9 Jl 27 '70
GARMENT, Leonard
Blast from a bishop. pors Time 96:11 Jl 13 '70 *
GARMUS, George G.
Careers in electronics. il Radio-Electr 41: 52-4 N '70
GARNER, C. William
Non-verbal communication and the teacher. bibliog Sch & Soc 98:363-4 O '70
GARNER, James
Motor trend interview. por Motor T 22:54+ O '70
GARNER, L. H.
Four channel amplifier for multi-speaker systems. il Electr World 84:28-30 N '70
GARNER, Louis E. jr
Solid state. See issues of Popular electronics
GARNETS
Garnet: first occurrence in the lunar rocks. R. J. Traill and others. bibliog il Science 169:981-2 S 4 '70
Pyroxene-garnet transformation in Coorara meteorite. J. V. Smith and B. Mason. bibliog il Science 168:832-3 My 15 '70
GAROT, J. C.
(ed) See Sartre, J. P. Intellectuals and revolution: interview with Jean-Paul Sartre
GARRARD, Mimi
Mimi Garrard dance theatre; Henry street settlement playhouse, NYC. N. Mason. Dance Mag 44:74 Jl '70 *
GARRATY, John A.
(ed) Conversations with historians; excerpts from Interpreting American history. pors Am Heritage 21:58-64 F '70
(ed) See Kazin, A. Century of American realism
GARRETT, Banning
Dominoization of Thailand. il Ramp Mag 9:6-8+ N '70
Road to Phnom Penh: Cambodia takes up the gun. il Ramp Mag 9:32-5+ Ag '70
Vietnamization of Laos. il Ramp Mag 8:36-45 Je '70
GARRETT, DeLois
Dream motif in contemporary Negro poetry. bibliog f Engl J 59:767-70 S '70
GARRETT, Mike
Career switch. por Newsweek 75:80 Je 22 '70 *
GARRETT, Peter
Phanerozoic stromatolites: noncompetitive ecologic restriction by grazing and burrowing animals. bibliog il Science 169:171-3 Jl 10 '70
GARRETT, Richard W. See Virts, J. R. jt. auth.
GARRETT, Rodney
Shuffle system. il Farm J 94:55I F '70
GARRETT, W. E.
Canada's heartland, the Prairie provinces. il Nat Geog 138:443-89 O '70
GARRETT, Wendell D.
(ed) Clues and footnotes. See issues of Antiques
Furniture owned by the American antiquarian society. il Antiques 97:402-7 Mr '70
GARRETT COUNTY, Md.
Longest strike. il Newsweek 76:81 N 30 '70
GARRIGUE, Jean
Grounding and the moon; poem. Nation 210: 312 Mr 16 '70
GARRIGUES, George L.
Careers in writing: government public information officer. Writers Digest 50:16-18 Mr '70
GARRISON, Dorothy Joan
Teacher aide and child care program. il Todays Ed 59:32 F '70
GARRISON, Guy
Library education and the public library. por Library J 95:2763-7 S 1 '70
GARRISON, Peter
Back to basics (cont) Flying 86:62-3 Ja; 70-2 F; 58-9 Ap; 87:82-3 Jl '70; 88:44-8 Ja '71
GARRISON, Preston J.
Let your 9-11's enjoy wilderness camping, too. il Camp Mag 42:13+ N '70
GARRISON, Webb B.
Anticigarette crusades that failed. il Todays Health 48:23-5 F '70
Electricity & physiology. il Pop Electr 34: 27-31 Ja '71
Electronics goes CAT catching. il Pop Electr 33:29-34 N '70
He discovered healing in the soil. il por Todays Health 48:42-3+ Mr '70
GARRYA. See Silk tassel bushes

GARTENHAUS, Jacob
Jewish conception of the Messiah. Chr Today 14:8-10 Mr 13 '70
GARTNER, John
Island for summer steelhead. il Field & S 75:22-3+ Jl '70
Recreation vehicles for today and tomorrow. il Field & S 74:66-71+ Mr '70
GARTNER, Mike
Silent generation meets the class of 1970. il Sat R 53:52-3+ Ag 15 '70
GARTNER, Stefan, jr
Sea-floor spreading, carbonate dissolution level, and the nature of horizon A. bibliog il Science 169:1077-9 S 11 '70
GARVAN, Mabel Brady, collections. See Yale university
GARVEY, William D. and others
Communication in the physical and the social sciences. il Science 170:1166-73 D 11 '70
GARVEY, ranch observatory. See Astronomical observatories
GARVIE, James B.
Saga of the rust-resistant ash truck. il Am City 85:88+ O '70
GARWOOD, John D.
Can a nice guy win in Kansas? Nation 211: 272-4 S 28 '70
GARY, Jan
William D. Gorman and Jan Gary. H. Gasser. il pors Am Artist 34:36-42+ O '70 *
GARY, Romain
Ode to the man who was France. il pors Life 69:42-4 N 20 '70
White dog; excerpts. il por Life 69:58-58B+ O 9 '70

about

Affinity for animals and lost causes. R. Graves. por Life 69:3 O 9 '70 *
Letter from Paris. Genêt. New Yorker 46: 116-17 My 2 '70 *
GARY, Ind.

Air pollution

Gary; a game of pin the blame. H. Waters. il Newsweek 75:38-9 Ja 26 '70

Education

Schooling for profit. il Forbes 106:41 N 1 '70
Teaching for profit. il Newsweek 76:58 Ag 17 '70
Where private firm runs public school. il U S News 69:41 O 12 '70
See also
Gary, Ind.—Public schools

Politics and government

Is there a plot to kill Mayor Hatcher? A. Poinsett. il pors Ebony 26:142-4+ D '70

Public schools

What happened to one model high school; Horace Mann school. il U S News 68:37-40 Ap 27 '70

Strikes

See also
Strikes—United States—Teachers
GARY, Ind, public library
Gary branch dispute moves toward crunch. Library J 95:110+ Ja 15 '70
Library action during teachers' strike, a report. K. E. Burgess. Wilson Lib Bul 44:921 My '70
GAS

Prices

See Gas rates

Rates

See Gas rates
GAS, Natural
Fuel shortage that's growing. il U S News 68:29 Mr 30 '70
See also
Gas industry
Liquefied natural gas
Motor fuels

Prices

See Gas rates
GAS and oil engines
One-cylinder engine boasts overhead valves. E. F. Lindsley. il Pop Sci 196:42 Je '70
See also
Airplane engines
Diesel engines
Motor boat engines
Motorcycle engines
Outboard motors
Snowmobile engines
Tractor engines

Fuel

See also
Gasoline

Maintenance and repair

Care & feeding of small engines. il Mech Illus 66:84-6 My '70
Prevent winter engine problems. Suc Farm 68:B24 N '70
GAS and oil engines, Outboard. See Outboard motors
GAS as fuel
See also
Automobile engines—Fuel
Gas, Natural
Liquefied petroleum gas
Motor fuels
GAS chromatography. See Chromatographic analysis
GAS companies
See also
Coastal states gas producing company
Gas rates
Houston natural gas corporation
GAS endarterectomy. See Blood vessels—Surgery
GAS industry
Gas shortage fuels a fight. Bsns W p22 Ag 1 '70
Rising market in rare gases. N. A. Martin. il Duns 95:81-2+ My '70
Wildcatter; Ladd petroleum's natural gas resources. R. Brady. pro Duns 96:67-8 Jl '70
Will nuclear blasts boost gas supplies? Project Rulison. il Bsns W p21-2 Ag 1 '70

Regulation

See also
United States—Federal power commission

Securities

Making money work. S. Meisenberg. il Har Yrs 10:48-50 Ag '70

Europe, Western

Europe battles over a natural gas boom. il Bsns W p 138-9+ Ap 25 '70
GAS leases. See Oil and gas leases
GAS meter reading. See Meter reading
GAS meters
See also
Meter reading
GAS prices. See Gas rates
GAS rates
Gas pricing gets an update. Bsns W p 19 Jl 25 '70
Gas producers find a rate compromise; natural gas rates. Bsns W p24 N 21 '70
Gas producers name their price. Bsns W p18 S 5 '70
GAS stations. See Automobile service stations
GAS stoves
Ranges with self-cleaning ovens. il Consumer Rep 35:691-700 N '70
What to look for in a gas range. il Parents Mag 45:71-4 Ja '70
GAS turbines, Aircraft
JT9D-3A modifications disrupt 747 introductions. Aviation W 92:27 Je 29 '70
Jumbo jet sputters a little; bugs in the JT9D. il Bsns W p28-9 O 10 '70
Longer inspection times sought after JT9D hot section checks. Aviation W 93:28-9 Jl 6 '70
Small gas turbines developed. M. L. Yaffee. il Aviation W 93:40-3 N 2 '70
Turbine program sparks new technology. M. L. Yaffee. il Aviation W 93:53-5+ N 30 '70
See also
Helicopter engines

Air supply

Electronic unit to control inlet for SST. B. M. Elson. il Aviation W 93:44-6 N 2 '70

Blades

RB.211 backup blade under impact tests. Aviation W 93:32 N 9 '70

Design

Adour is prepared for production. D. E. Fink. il Aviation W 92:58-9 My 18 '70
GE1 engine spawns numerous derivatives. M. L. Yaffee. il Aviation W 93:52-4+ Ag 24 '70
JT9D modifications. Aviation W 93:32 O 5 '70
NASA studies small jet engine. M. L. Yaffee. il Aviation W 92:56-7+ Je 1 '70
NASA's quiet engine program focuses antinoise effort. il Aviation W 92:88-9 Je 22 '70
New versions of TF41 designed. M. L. Yaffee. il Aviation W 93:42-3+ O 19 '70

GAS turbines, Aircraft—Design—*Continued*
Nozzle/reverser to cut Concorde weight. D. E. Fink. il Aviation W 92:57-9 Ap 13 '70
Rolls develops engine trouble. Bsns W p32 Je 6 '70
Rolls V/STOL lift fan aim is less noise. H. J. Coleman. il Aviation W 93:48-9 Jl 27 '70
Small aircraft turbofans studied. M. L. Yaffee. il Aviation W 92:43-5+ F 9 '70
Soviet engine detailed. il Aviation W 92:44-7 Je 15 '70
Turbomeca designs new turbofans. D. E. Fink. il Aviation W 92:72-3 My 4 '70
Variable pitch fan designed for low-noise STOL aircraft. il Aviation W 93:66 S 14 '70

Exhaust
Nozzle/reverser to cut Concorde weight. D. E. Fink. il Aviation W 92:57-9 Ap 13 '70

Failure
Assembly cited in engine failure. Aviation W 93:22 O 19 '70
FAA backs 747, JT9D in safety dispute. J. P. Woolsey. Aviation W 93:27-8 O 12 '70
FAA orders inspections for JT9D-3A engines. il Aviation W 92:30-1 Je 8 '70

Fuel
Carriers seek alternatives to turbojet fuel dumping. H. D. Watkins. Aviation W 93: 27-8 N 2 '70

Fuel feeding
Testing
Computer tests jet engine fuel controls. K. J. Stein. Aviation W 93:44-5 Ag 17 '70

Specifications
Leading international gas turbines; tables (cont) Aviation W 92:141-2 Mr 9 '70
U.S. gas turbine engines; tables (cont) Aviation W 92:138-9 Mr 9 '70

Testing
M49 Larzac testing under way. D. E. Fink. il Aviation W 93:40-1+ N 23 '70

Thrust reversers
Jet thrust reverser systems designed for business aircraft. Aviation W 93:78 O 12 '70

GASBUGGY project. See Atomic blasting

GASCOYNE, Steve
How I learned to live with radioactivity and love it, in Colorado. Commonwealth 92: 7-9 Mr 13 '70

GASES
Hofmann apparatus and leak rate of gases. G. Harshman and G. Melville. il pors Chem 43:26 Je '70
Testing Boyle's law. M. S. Spritzer. il por Chem 43:29-30 O '70
See also
Plasma (ionized gases)
also names of gases, e.g. Helium

Liquefaction
See also
Liquefied natural gas

GASES, Asphyxiating and poisonous
Double antidote. Sci N 98:137 Ag 15 '70
Natural gas; irritating substances in Red tide; excerpts from 1948 report. P. S. Galtsoff. il Environ 12:22-3 Mr '70
On the last frontier with VX and GB; opinions of people in Umatilla County on government's plan to store nerve gas. J. Didion. il Life 68:22 F 20 '70
See also
Carbon dioxide
Carbon monoxide
Chemical and biological weapons
Sarin
Tear gas

Accidents
Muckuppery along the Potomac. R. Bongartz. Esquire 73:70+ Je '70

Disposal in the ocean
Death in the deep; chemical warfare agents of World war II in the Baltic Sea. Newsweek 76:33-4 Ag 24 '70
Department makes determination on sea disposal of nerve agent; Department statement; with statement by Mr Rhinelander, and letter to the president of the Senate by U.A. Johnson. Dept State Bul 63:282-3 S 7 '70
Disposal at sea. Sci N 98:113 Ag 8 '70
GB or not GB? il Time 96:10 Ag 17 '70
Matter of 400 coffins; controversy over nerve gas dumping. il Newsweek 76:54 Ag 17 '70

Nerve gas disposal: how the AEC refused to take army off the hook. L. J. Carter. Science 169:1296-8 S 25 '70
Nerve-gas scare: a look at the facts. il U S News 69:32 Ag 17 '70
Rate of decomposition of GB in seawater. J. Epstein. bibliog il Science 170:1396-8 D 25 '70

Storage
Weapons nobody wants; nerve gases. il Time 95:53 Je 8 '70

Transportation
Cut holes and sink 'em. il Time 96:9 Ag 24 '70
Nerve gas; Oregon gas train plan. H. Rogers. New Repub 162:13-14 Mr 7 '70

GASES, Liquefied
See also
Liquefied natural gas

GASES, Poisonous. See Gases, Asphyxiating and poisonous

GASES, Rare
Apollo 11 lunar science conference: stable isotopes, rare gases, solar wind, and spallation products, symposium. bibliog il Science 167:533-82 Ja 30 '70
Rising market in rare gases. N. A. Martin. il Duns 95:81-2+ My '70
See also
Argon

GASES, Solidified
See also
Oxygen, Solid

GASES in warfare
See also
Tear gas

GASOLINE
Lead in the air; lead-free gasoline. il Time 96:51-2 S 14 '70

Additives
Apathy at the pumps; low-lead fuels. Newsweek 76:60-1 S 7 '70
Delayed demise of leaded gasoline. Consumer Bul 53:19-20 My '70
Ethyl's deflated romance; battle over lead in gasoline. il Newsweek 75:84+ Mr 23 '70
Fill 'er up with antismog gasoline. il Bsns W p24 F 7 '70
Get the lead out. Fortune 81:80 Mr '70
Get the lead out: pollution remedy? il Sr Schol 97:5 O 12 '70
Gettin' the lead out. J. Ethridge. il Motor T 22:48-50 My '70
Getting the lead out. B. Behme. il Field & S 75:80-2 D '70
Getting the lead out. J. B. Sullivan and A. J Fritsch. New Repub 163:9-10 N 21 '70
Getting the lead out. il Sci N 97:167-8 F 14 '70
Getting the lead out. il Time 95:81-2 F 23 '70
Getting the lead out of gas, how it will affect you and your car. J. P. Norbye and J. Dunne. il Pop Sci 196:45-7 Je '70
Industry focuses on unleaded gas. E. Gross. il Sci N 98:71-2 Jl 25 '70
Is lead really good for us? il Forbes 106:26-7 S 15 '70
Leaded gasoline: what the argument is about. il U S News 68:55-6 Je 8 '70
New gas cuts smog, cleans engine, too! J. Zmuda. il Pop Mech 133:44+ Ag '70
Oil companies fume over lead. il Bsns W p22 Mr 7 '70
Oilmen cut the lead, before taxes. Bsns W p33 My 23 '70
Surprising facts on unleaded gas. T. Tappett. il Mech Illus 66:88-90+ N '70
Swing to unleaded gas; what's ahead. il U S News 69:35-6 D 28 '70
Who foots the tab for lead-free gas? il Bsns W p 102+ F 14 '70
See also
Ethyl corporation

Anti-knock and anti-knock mixtures
There's more to gasoline quality than octane ratings. F. N. Ikard. por Pop Sci 196:89+ My '70
Why they should tell you the octane rating of the gasoline you buy. R. Nader. por Pop Sci 196:54-5 Ap '70

Marketing
No-lead or low-lead, new gas goes slow. il Bsns W p21 Ag 29 '70

Taxation
Tax on leaded gas scares independents. il Bsns W p29 Je 6 '70
Treasury abandons a dying lead tax. Bsns W p29 S 26 '70

GASOLINE industry.   See Petroleum industry
and trade
GASQUE, W. Ward. See Armerding, C. E. jt.
auth.
GASSER, Henry
William D. Gorman and Jan Gary. il pors
Am Artist 34:36-42+ O '70
GAST, Paul W. and Hubbard, N. J.
Abundance of alkali metals, alkaline and rare
earths, and strontium-87/strontium-86 ra-
tios in lunar samples. bibliog il Science 167:
485-7 Ja 30 '70
GASTON, Thomas E.
Teaching a concept of style for literature
and composition. Engl J 59:65-70 Ja '70
GASTON, Velma S.
Experimental sculpture. il Sch Arts 70:20-1
O '70
GASTONGUAY, Paul R.
Six Catholics to extinction. Cath World 212:
189-93 Ja '71
GASTRIC ulcers. See Peptic ulcers
GATELY, Christopher D.
Improvements in the Moth rig. il por Yacht-
ing 128:37+ D '70
GATES, Judith
Am I in art or English? Engl J 59:988-9 O
'70
GATES, Judith Rae
Bilingually advantaged. il Todays Ed 59:38-
40+ D '70
GATES, Lock. See Locks (hydraulic engineer-
ing)
GATES Learjet corporation. See Lear jet in-
dustries, inc.
GATHA, Ashvin
Ashvin Gatha's colorful world. il Pop Phot
67:87-9 S '70 *
GATORNATIONALS. See Automobile racing
GAUGE, Larry
For Easter, it's Nassau. Travel & Camera
33:8+ F '70
GAUGES. See Gages
GAULLE, Charles de
Charles de Gaulle. 1890-1970. R. Watson. il
pors Newsweek 76:43B-45+ N 23 '70 *
Charles de Gaulle: they remember him well.
R. Bosc. por America 123:563-4 D 26 '70 *
Death of a legendary hero. D. Singer. Nation
211:550-2 N 30 '70 *
De Gaulle: a footnote. S. Alsop. Newsweek
76:140 N 23 '70 *
De Gaulle and three presidents. H. Sidey.
Life 69:4 N 20 '70 *
France: twilight of grandeur. il Time 95:48
My 11 '70 *
Glimpse of glory, a shiver of grandeur. il
pors Time 96:18-22+ N 23 '70 *
Great man, a great warrior. il por Newsweek
76:42-43B N 23 '70 *
How often he was right: some parting
thoughts on de Gaulle. D. Brogan. New
Repub 163:19-20 D 5 '70 *
Irish sketches; reactions of villagers of
Sneem to visit. J. McCarten. New Yorker
46:127-9 O 31 '70 *
Letter from Paris (cont) Genêt. New Yorker
46:111-12 N 21 '70 *
Obituary
Nat R 22:1256-7 D 1 '70
New Repub 163:7 N 21 '70
New Yorker 46:36-7 N 28 '70
Sr Schol por 97:7 D 7 '70
Ode to the man who was France. R. Gary.
il pors Life 69:42-4 N 20 *
Remembrances of things past. il pors Time
96:28 S 28 '70 *
Third person singular; Memoirs of hope. por
Time 96:39 O 19 '70 *
U.S. joins France in mourning death of Gen-
eral de Gaulle; statement, text of letter to
President Pompidou, and remarks at Orly
airport. R. M. Nixon. Dept State Bul 63:
690 D 7 '70 *
Whatever happened to Charles de Gaulle of
France? il pors U S News 69:44 O 12 '70 *
When a nation needs a father. E. Behr.
il por Newsweek 76:48 N 23 '70 *

Funeral rites and ceremonies
Glimpse of glory, a shiver of grandeur. il
pors Time 96:19-20+ N 23 '70

Memorials
Eternal star: changing name of Place de
l'Etoile to Place Charles de Gaulle. il Time
96:28 N 30 '70
GAUR, B. K. See Mishra, S. D. jt. auth.
GAUT, Norman E. See Starr, V. P. jt. auth.
GAVAGAN, James E. See Woldt, A. jt. auth.
GAVER, Mary Virginia
Can library and education groups meet joint-
ly? report. Wilson Lib Bul 44:921-2 My '70

GAVI, Phillipe
Eruption in India; tr. by J. Oringer. il Ramp
Mag 8:8+ Ap '70
GAVRAS, Costa-. See Costa-Gavras
GAY, P. and others
Diffraction and Mössbauer studies of minerals
from lunar soils and rocks. bibliog il Science
167:626-8 Ja 30 '70
GAY, Peter
Enlightenment. il Horizon 12:40-5 Spr '70
History of history. il Horizon 11:112-19 Aut
'69
Weimar resemblance. il Horizon 12:4-15 Wint
'70
GAY liberation front. See Homosexuality
GAY Head, pseud.
Talking it over with Gay Head; questions
and answers. See issues of Senior scholas-
tic
GAYLUSSACIA brachycera. See Box huckle-
berries
GAYNOR, Evelyn, and others
Vascular lesions: possible pathogenetic basis
of the generalized Shwartzman reaction.
bibliog il Science 170:986-8 N 27 '70
GAYNOR, William Jay
Mayor who mastered New York, by L.
Thomas. Review
Sat R 53:29 Mr 7 '70. W. Moscow *
GAZA

Education
Diplomas for Palestinian students in Gaza
Strip. Sch & Soc 98:142 Mr '70
GAZA STRIP
Emerging realities. il Newsweek 75:48+ Mr
23 '70
Strip: a hellhole for the Israelis. P. Young.
il Life 68:30-1 Je 12 '70
GAZEBOS. See Garden houses, shelters, etc.
GAZETTE and daily. See York County, Pa.—
Newspapers
GAZPACHO. See Soups
GEAGAN, Bill
How Indians hunt deer. il Field & S 75:36-
7+ D '70
Merry marathoner. il Field & S 74:44-5+
Ja '70
GEAKE, J. E. and others
Luminescence, electron paramagnetic reso-
nance, and optical properties of lunar ma-
terial. bibliog il Science 167:717-20 Ja 30
'70
GEARING, Frederick O.
Toward a mankind curriculum. il Todays Ed
59:28-30 Mr '70
GEARING
See also
Automobiles—Gearing
Chain gear
Indexing (machine work)
GEBHARD, David
West Coast report. il Art in Am 58:130-3 My
'70
GEDDES, Norman Bel
Restless genius of Norman Bel Geddes. A. J.
Pulos. il por Arch Forum 133:46-51 Jl '70 *
GEE, Peter
Medium is his home. J. Broudy. il por Look
34:30-1 Jl 14 '70 *
GEER, Abbot M. and Hand, A. J.
How science is putting the wind in our
sails. il Pop Sci 197:76-7 S '70
GEESE
Goose on the duck stamp; Ross's geese.
E. N. Layne. il Am Heritage 21:113 Je '70
GEESE, Wild
Carnage at Sand Lake; with editorial com-
ment. G. Sherwood. il Audubon 72:66-73,
140-1 N '70
Goose hunting from underwater. P. McLain.
il Field & S 75:40-3+ N '70
Goose of the Himalayas; bar-headed geese.
L. W. Swan. il Natur Hist 79:68-75 D '70
Goosenappers. H. Simmons. il Field & S 75:
60-1+ O '70
Great gabble over Iowa lakes. D. Levin. il
Sports Illus 32:40-3 My 18 '70
Honker! Canada goose. J. Van Wormer. il
Nat Wildlife 8:12-15 O '70
There are honkers in the valley. D. Holm.
il por Outdoor Life 146:52-3+ D '70
Where the geese beckon. P. Curtis. il Field
& S 75:52-3+ S '70
Where the wild goose flies. A. Russell. il Out-
door Life 146:76-7+ Ag '70
GEHMAN, Richard
Brothers Dorsey. por il Sat R 53:52-3+ Ja
17 '70
GEHRINGER, Charles Leonard
Where are they now? il pors Newsweek 76:8
Jl 20 '70 *

GEHRINGER, Christie Jensen
Helping the disadvantaged youth. Clear House 44:304 Ja '70
GEIGER-Mueller counters. See Counters (electrons, ions, etc)
GEISEL, Theodor Seuss
Children's furniture inspired by Dr Seuss characters. il House B 112:80-5 D '70 *
Mr Brown can moo like a cow! Can you? excerpts. il McCalls 98:78-81 O '70
GEISERT, Arthur F.
Simple way to do large woodcuts. il Sch Arts 70:14-15 D '70
GEISHAS
Geisha 1970. I. Penn. il Vogue 156:84-7+ Jl '70
GEISMAN, Gemma
Epilogue to a dream. Redbook 134:89+ Mr '70
Image of home. Good H 170:32+ Je '70
GEIST, Valerius
Mountain goat mysteries. il Field & S 75:34-5+ Ag '70
GEL permeation chromatography. See Chromatographic analysis
GELATT, Roland
SR goes to the movies. See occasional issues of Saturday review
GELBER, Harry Gregor
Australia as an Indo-Pacific power. bibliog f Cur Hist 58:223-8+ Ap '70
GELBOIN, Harry V. and Levy, H. B.
Polyinosinic-polycytidylic acid inhibits chemically induced tumorigenesis in mouse skin. bibliog il Science 167:205-7 Ja 9 '70
—and others
Dimethylbenzanthracene tumorigenesis and aryl hydrocarbon hydroxylase in mouse skin: inhibition by 7,8-benzoflavone. bibliog il Science 170:169-71 O 9 '70
GELEHRTER, Thomas, and others
Genetic control mechanisms in man and other mammals. Science 169:791-2 Ag 21 '70
GELFAND, Louis I.
Communicate through your supervisors. Harvard Bsns R 48:101-4 N '70
GELINAS, Mary V.
Classroom drug scene. il Am Ed 6:3-5 N '70
GELL-MANN, Murray
Murray Gell-Mann wins Nobel prize for physics. B. G. Levi. bibliog por Phys Today 23:83+ Ja '70
GELLEN, Martin
Making of a pollution-industrial complex. il Ramp Mag 8:22-7 My '70
GELLER, Evelyn
Adrift in new directions. il Library J 95:1169-72 Mr 15 '70
GELLER, Irving
Modern industry. il Duns 95:87-90 Mr; 75-6+ Ap '70
GELLER, Robert E.
Reaching the deaf: report of an in-hospital group. Ment Hy 54:388-92 Jl '70
GELLMAN, Harvey S.
Crime in industry; address, September 9, 1970. Vital Speeches 37:152-5 D 15 '70
GELMAN, Rena. See Hartung, G. jt. auth.
GELMIS, Joseph
Mike Nichols talks about his films; excerpt from The film director speaks. por Atlan 225:71-7 F '70
GELPI, Donald L.
Understanding spirit-baptism. America 122:520-1 My 16 '70
GELSENKIRCHEN ballet. See Ballet companies
GELTMAN, Max
Case for the primacy of Israel. Nat R 22:407-9 Ap 21 '70
Paris again. Nat R 22:1002 S 22 '70
GELZER, David G.
Random notes on black theology and African theology. Chr Cent 87:1091-3 S 16 '70
GEMELLO, Linda, and Wilde, W. E.
Uncommon man. Engl J 59:1266-9 D '70
GEMS
Buying gems and jewelry. G. V. Axon. il Consumer Bul 53:4+ D '70
See also
Diamonds
GENDEL, Milton
Avant-garde Milanese. il Art N 69:41-3+ Sum '70
Beknighted Malta. il Art N 69:44-7+ Sum '70
Venice. Art N 69:63+ S '70
GENDLER, Everett E.
Where have all the beach clubs of old Havana gone? with biographical sketch. il Natur Hist 79:4, 10-14+ My '70
GENEALOGY
Genealogical research: a basic guide. C. L. Miller. Hobbies 75:140-1+ S '70
Genealogy: the well-pruned family tree. J. H. Plumb. il Horizon 12:118-20 Wint '70

Who am I? Where did I come from? adopted girl's search for real mother. J. T. Freeman. il Ladies Home J 87:74+ Mr '70
See also
Registers of births, etc.
GENEEN, Harold Sydney
Financial key at ITT. por Duns 96:24+ D '70 *
ITT takes the profit path to Europe. il por Bsns W p60-2+ My 9 '70 *
GENERAL acceptance corporation. See GAC corporation
GENERAL accounting office. See United States—General accounting office
GENERAL and complete disarmament. See United Nations—Committee on disarmament
GENERAL assembly of the Presbyterian church in the United States (southern) See Presbyterian church in the United States (South)
GENERAL assembly of the United Nations. See United Nations—General assembly
GENERAL association of regular Baptist churches. See Baptists in the United States
GENERAL cable corporation
General cable's transatlantic link. Bsns W p25 F 7 '70
Welcome relief for General cable. Bsns W p23 Ag 22 '70
GENERAL dynamics corporation
Colonel's second battle. il por Time 96:88 N 2 '70
Crown's prince. il por Newsweek 76:93 N 2 '70
David S. Lewis to head General dynamics. Aviation W 93:22 O 26 '70
General dynamics finds a new boss; D. S. Lewis. por Bsns W p33 O 24 '70
Out again, in again; H. Crown's investments. por Forbes 105:17 Mr 15 '70
Real-life drama at General dynamics. il por Bsns W p 17-18 Jl 11 '70
Visit with Colonel Crown; interview. H. Crown. il pors Bsns W p 106+ Mr 21 '70
Who wants General dynamics? Henry Crown, that's who. C. J. Loomis. il por Fortune 81:76-9+ Je '70
GENERAL electric company
Careers in electronics, blueprint to your future; computer maintenance. G. G. Garmus. il Radio-Electr 41:52-4 N '70
Crime fight progress: a police-GE product. V. Louviere. il Nations Bsns 58:19 Ap '70
Fork in the road; a postscript on the G.E. strike. J. Davenport. Fortune 81:82 Mr '70
GE bows out. Newsweek 75:80 Je 1 '70
GE dips into the copper business. il Bsns W p40 Jl 25 '70
GE is unreeling new circuits. il Bsns W p22+ D 12 '70
GE puzzle. A. A. Butkus. il por Duns 96:34-8+ Jl '70
GE strike didn't kill Boulwarism. Bsns W p32 O 24 '70
GE: the empire that subdivided. Bsns W p 116 O 17 '70
GE tries harder on process controls. Bsns W p52 O 17 '70
GE will share a wealth of data; management analysis and projection system. il Bsns W p88+ My 9 '70
G.E.'s costly ventures into the future. A. T. Demaree. il Fortune 82:88-93+ O '70
GE's hookup for business conferees. Bsns W p24+ Jl 11 '70
How a little fish hooked a big one; Biomarine's closed-cycle underwater breathing system. il Bsns W p88+ F 28 '70
Inflationary end to a class war. il Time 95:71-2 F 9 '70
Into the barn, and a lofty future. A. M. Bueche. il Nations Bsns 58:74-5 Ja '70
Keeping in touch during a walkout. V. Louviere. Nations Bsns 58:18 S '70
Rough road to GE's settlement. il Bsns W p28-9 Ja 31 '70
Strike hides GE's light under a bushel. Bsns W p31 Ja 17 '70
What General electric didn't sell. il Forbes 105:38+ Je 15 '70
See also
General learning corporation
Tomorrow productions, inc.
GENERAL electric strike. See Strikes—United States—Electric workers
GENERAL foam division. See Tenneco, inc.
GENERAL foods corporation
Decision that built managers. C. W. Cook. il Nations Bsns 58:76-7 Ja '70
GENERAL Gates house. See York, Pa.—Historic houses, etc.
GENERAL host corporation
General host counts its losses. il Bsns W p35-6 My 23 '70
It's all done with arithmetic. il Forbes 105:22-3 F 15 '70

GENERAL information tests. See information tests

GENERAL instrument corporation
Bush leaguer finally scores. Bsns W p24 N 28 '70

GENERAL learning corporation
After the altar. Forbes 105:17 F 1 '70

GENERAL mills, inc.
Even computers say, me, too! il Forbes 105:44+ Ap 1 '70

GENERAL motors corporation
Accountability; Campaign to make General motors more responsible. J. Featherstone. New Repub 162:9-10 F 28 '70
After GM: outlook for auto peace. U S News 69:72 D 7 '70
After the courtesy, a crisis of costs. por Fortune 81:31 Je '70
As pressures rise in GM strike: some optimistic signs. il U S News 69:78-9 N 9 '70
Auto strike begins to cut deep. il Newsweek 75:83-4+ N 16 '70
Auto strike: what it will do to business. il U S News 69:15-17 S 28 '70
Black for G.M.'s board. por Time 97:72 Ja 18 '71
Blue collar worker's lowdown blues. il Time 96:68-72+ N 9 '70
Boss Kettering's decision: build a better diesel. R. L. Terrell. il Nations Bsns 58:78-9 Ja '70
Campaign GM: a new pitch to university shareholders. L. J. Carter. Science 170:958-9 N 27 '70
Campaign GM: corporation critics seek support of universities. L. J. Carter. Science 168:452-5 Ap 24 '70
Campaign GM: reformers lose on vote but not on influence. L. J. Carter. Science 168:1077-8 My 29 '70; Reply with rejoinder. H. G. Manne. 169:325-6 Jl 24 '70
Commotion at GM; campaign to make General motors responsible. L. J. Carter. New Repub 162:8-9 Je 6 '70
Corporate power and social duty. America 122:625 Je 13 '70
Corporate responsibility campaign. Chr Cent 87:715 Je 10 '70
Cost of getting rolling again. Bsns W p22-3 N 14 '70
Costly end to a costly strike. il Newsweek 76:101-2 N 23 '70
End to obsolescence? changes in the new models. il Time 95:83 My 18 '70
General motors' bumpy road. Time 95:85+ Ap 27 '70
General motors gears for the seventies. il Fortune 81:31 Ap '70
Gerstenberg gets closer to summit. por Bsns W p22-3 Ap 11 '70
GM makes criticism a family affair: forms five-man public policy committee. Bsns W p19 S 5 '70
GM: organizing 2¼ per cent of the GNP. Duns 96:31-2 D '70
GM settlement: impact on other industries. il U S News 69:65-6 N 30 '70
GM starts up and hikes prices. Bsns W p22-3 N 28 '70
GM's critics hail its new director. por Bsns W p 17 Ja 9 '71
GM's new way to save scrap; reconstituted steel. Bsns W p24 Mr 7 '70
GM's ordeal may set the fashion; Campaign to make GM responsible. il Bsns W p84 My 30 '70
Gradual getaway from the GM strike; with editorial comment. il Bsns W p22-3, 124 N 21 '70
Guessing game; who's up at GM? il Bsns W p 16-17 Mr 7 '70
How bitter will the strike be? il Newsweek 76:65-6 S 28 '70
Mighty GM faces its critics. il Bsns W p72-3+ Jl 11 '70
Nader v. G.M. por Time 96:29 Ag 24 '70
Nader's $425,000. Newsweek 76:48 Ag 24 '70
Nader's pitch to GM stockholders. Bsns W p30 F 14 '70
New kind of wheel at GM. B. Yates. il pors Sports Illus 31:39-42+ D 15 '69
Other bumps in the road. por Newsweek 76:82-3 S 14 '70
Our footloose correspondents: annual stockholders meeting. E. J. Kahn, jr. New Yorker 46:40-2+ Je 20 '70
Taking stock; Campaign GM. il Newsweek 75:109 Ap 27 '70
Toughest year. Newsweek 76:89 D 14 '70
Toward a wider constituency; resolutions proposed by Campaign G.M. il Time 95:54+ Je 1 '70
UAW's bill for repairs. B. J. Widick. Nation 211:259-60 S 28 '70
Union puts brakes on GM. il Sr Schol 97:3 O 5 '70

Wankel for GM. il Newsweek 76:87 N 16 '70
What auto strike cost the U.S. il U S News 69:15-17 N 23 '70
What GM's pact means to industry. il Bsns W p96+ N 21 '70
Wheels of fortune; fighting a government suit. Newsweek 76:112 N 23 '70

Chevrolet division
Chevy's top brass talks about Vega: starlet with a future; interview, ed. by J. Dunne. J. Z. DeLorean. il pors Pop Sci 197:56-7+ S '70
GM's John DeLorean: powerhouse behind the Vega. A. Rothenberg. il pors Look 34:54-7 Ag 25 '70
Nuts and bolts; Vega and the automatic car wash. New Repub 163:10-11 N 7 '70

Pontiac motor division
Pontiac slumps as the image ages. il Bsns W p48-9 Mr 28 '70
Producing cars, and good citizens, Nations Bsns 58:16 F '70

GENERAL public utilities corporation
Glutton for punishment. il Forbes 105:34 F 15 '70

GENERAL services administration. See United States—General services administration

GENERAL signal corporation
Out to clean up if peace comes. il por Bsns W p32-3 O 3 '70

GENERAL telephone and electronics corporation
For Motorola, a chance to unload; sale of picture-tube manufacturing facilities. Bsns W p24-5 Ap 11 '70
See also
General telephone company of California

GENERAL telephone company of California
Mea culpa campaign. Time 96:67 Jl 27 '70

GENERALIZATION (psychology)
Neural readout from memory during generalization. E. R. John and others; discussion. bibliog il Science 169:303-5 Jl 17 '70

GENERALS
See also
Davis, B. O. jr

GENERATION gap
Bridging the generation gap; discussion. M. K. Udall. New Repub 163:11-13 N 28 '70
Children of change; address, May 7, 1970. R. G. Reed, 3d. Vital Speeches 36:713-15 S 15 '70
Closing the generation gap; search for a national policy; interview. S. Hess. il por U S News 68:56-9 F 16 '70
Conspiracy against youth. D. M. Broderick. por Library J 95:214-15 Ja 15 '70; Discussion. 95:1139-40 Mr 15 '70
Culture and commitment, by M. Mead. Review
Atlan 225:118-20 Je '70. E. Van Den Haag
Nation 210:373-6 Mr 30 '70. P. Clecak
Decay: blessing in disguise. R. M. Bowman. America 123:114-17 S 5 '70; Discussion. 123:189, 275 S 26, O 17 '70
Exploitation and the generational conflict. D. Elkind. Ment Hy 54:490-7 O '70
For now. C. H. Simonds. por Nat R 23:35+ Ja 12 '71
Generation gap; address, June 7, 1970. E. L. Richardson. Vital Speeches 36:583-6 Jl 15 '70; Same with title Differing perceptions of U.S. foreign policy. Dept State Bul 62:800-3 Je 29 '70
Generation gap and international development; youth movement. F. Herrera. Américas 22:13-20 Ap '70
Generation gap, does it begin at home or school? excerpts from panel discussions. il Sr Schol 95:8-10+ O 13 '69
Generation gap in the western world. E. M. von Kuehnelt-Leddihn. il Cath World 212:9-14 O '70
I was single, unattached, and trapped. B. Krupczak. por Redbook 135:20+ Jl '70
Is the generation gap widening? No, not really; with study-discussion program, by C. Smallenburg and H. Smallenburg. G. Konopka. bibliog il PTA Mag 65:6-8, 35 O '70
Is the generation gap widening? Yes, it is; with study-discussion program by C. Smallenburg and H. Smallenburg. R. D. Cross. bibliog il PTA Mag 65:22-4, 36 S '70
Is there a generation gap in science? AAAS symposium, December 1970. A. H. Esser and V. R. Hannon. Science 170:1336 D 18 '70
Like fathers, like sons. N. Podhoretz, Commentary 50:21 Ag '70; Reply with rejoinder. A. Kazin. 50:28 N '70
Manner of speaking. J. Ciardi. Sat R 53:6 Ag 1 '70

GENERATION gap—*Continued*
Middle age meets the kid ghetto. V. Bourjaily.
il pors N Y Times Mag p46-7+ N 29 '70
Natural enemies? Youth and the conflict of
generations. ed. by A. Klein. Review
New Repub 162:23-4 F 28 '70. J. Yardley
Nixon and the rancid right. S. Alsop. Newsweek 76:132 O 12 '70
Non-generation gap. S. M. Lipset and E.
Raab. Commentary 50:35-9 Ag '70
Plus ça change: twenties through the sixties.
J. H. Shera. il por Library J 95:979-86 Mr 15
'70; Reply. P. Schuman. 95:1781-2 My 15 '70
Protestation and the elders; letter to the editor. R. V. Vaughn. Am Lib 1:112 F '70
Reflections: new generation in relation to
the corporate state and the new consciousness. C. A. Reich. New Yorker 46:42-6+ S 26 '70
Report on the two cultures; Orange County,
Calif. T. Goodhue. New Repub 162:12-13
Je 20 '70
Silent generation meets the class of 1970.
M. Gartner. il Sat R 53:52-3+ Ag 15 '70
Talk with Konrad Lorenz; ed. by F. de
Towarnicki. K. Z. Lorenz. il por N Y Times
Mag p4-5+ Jl 5 '70
War between young and old. A. Miller. il
por McCalls 97:32 Jl '70
We no longer know how to bring our children into the world we have built; interview. ed. by C. Dreyfus. C. Lévi-Strauss.
por Mlle 71:236-7+ Ag '70
What generation gap? J. Adelson. il N Y
Times Mag p 10-11+ Ja 18 '70
What kind of revolution? D. McDonald. Cur
121:28-30 S '70
When the young teach and the old learn. il
Time 96:35-40 Ag 17 '70
Yardsticks for a new era. F. D. Murphy.
il Sat R 53:23-5 N 21 '70
Youth buffs rapped by youth. Library J
95:200 Ja 15 '70

Anecdotes, facetiae, satire, etc.
Father-son rap-in. J. D. Tierney. Nat R 22:
998+ S 22 '70
George tells it to Marvin. R. H. Smith. Nat
R 23:34 Ja 12 '71
GENERATORS, Signal. See Signal generators
GENES
Differentiation of populations: importance of
gene flow. P. R. Ehrlich and P. H. Raven;
discussion. bibliog Science 167:1636-7 Mr 20
'70
Fitness of an escherichia coli mutator gene.
T. C. Gibson and others. bibliog il Science
169:686-8 Ag 14 '70
Gene at last. il por Sci N 97:547 Je 6 '70
Gene makers: first artificial synthesis of a
gene. il por Newsweek 75:91 Je 15 '70
Genetic load. C. Wills. il Sci Am 222:98-107
bibliog(p 146) Mr '70
Genetic repressors. M. Ptashne and W. Gilbert. il Sci Am 222:36-44 bibliog(p 152) Je
'70
Isolated gene. Sci Am 222:50 Ja '70
Isolation of genes. il Chem 43:20 Mr '70
Localization of 5S RNA genes on drosophila
chromosomes by RNA-DNA hybridization
D. E. Wimber and D. M. Steffensen. bibliog il Science 170:639-41 N 6 '70
Making a gene. Sci Am 223:49-50 Jl '70
Molecular biology: moving toward an understanding of genetic control. G. L. Wick.
Science 167:157-9 Ja 9 '70
Secrets of the cell: first artificial synthesis
of a gene. il por Time 95:43-4 Je 15 '70
Susceptibility to an avian leukosis-sarcoma
virus: close association with an erythrocyte
isoantigen. L. B. Crittenden and others.
bibliog il Science 169:1324-5 S 25 '70
Tryptophan operon: structural gene mutation creating a "promoter" and leading
to 5-methyltryptophan dependence. R.
Callahan, 3d. and E. Balbinder. bibliog
il Science 168:1586-9 Je 26 '70
Visualization of bacterial genes in action. O.
L. Miller, jr. and others. bibliog il Science
169:392-5 Jl 24 '70
See also
Heredity of disease
GENESEE COUNTY, Mich. youth and activities center. See Recreation centers
GENESIS, Book of. See Bible—Old Testament
—Genesis
GENET, Jean
Here and now for Bobby Seale; tr. by J.
Oringer. Ramp Mag 8:30-1 Je '70
GENÊT, pseud. See Flanner, J.
GENETIC counseling
Genetic counseling; ed. by S. Olds. G. E.
Sarto. Redbook 136:12+ D '70

GENETIC research
Friendly virus; injections of Shope papilloma
virus to aid arginemia victims. Newsweek
76:88 S 28 '70
Genetic repressors. M. Ptashne and W. Gilbert. il Sci Am 222:36-44 bibliog(p 152)
Je '70
Human gene maps: a first step toward genetic
engineering. B. J. Culliton. il Sci N 98:
176-7 Ag 22 '70
Mouse stage of the new biology. R. W.
Stock. il Sci Digest 67:44-7+ Ap '70
Repression of colony formation reversed by
antiserum to mouse thymocytes. J. E. Till
and others. bibliog il Science 169:1327-9 S
25 '70
Rise and fall of T. D. Lysenko. by Z. A.
Medvedev. Review
Bul Atom Sci 26:54-6 Ap '70. O Hechtler
See also
Mutagenic substances
GENETICS
Genetics activity of mitochondria and chloroplasts. U. W. Goodenough and R. P. Levine.
il Sci Am 223:22-9 N '70
Mechanism of antibody diversity: germ line
basis for variability. L. Hood and D. W.
Talmage. bibliog il Science 168:325-34 Ap
17 '70
Strain C3H-AvyfB mice: ninety percent incidence of mammary tumors transmitted by
either parent. G. Vlahakis and others. bibliog il Science 170:185-7 O 9 '70
See also
Allelomorphism
Chromosomes
Eugenics
Genotype and phenotype
Human genetics
Isolation (biology)
Microbial genetics
Mosaics (biology)
Plant genetics
Variation (biology)

Conferences
Gene regulation in mammalian cells: basel
colloquium. S. Gluecksohn-Waelsch. Science
167:1524+ Mr 13 '70

Research
See Genetic research
GENETICS (botany) See Plant genetics
GENNARO, Peter
Master of jazz forms turns to TV. H. Stern.
il pors Dance Mag 44:44-7 Je '70 *
GENOCIDE
Department supports ratification of the genocide convention; statements, April 24, 1970.
C. W. Yost; R. E. Hauser; G. H. Aldrich.
Dept State Bul 63:9-15 Jl 6 '70
On killing members of one's own species;
tr. by H. Zeisel. K. Lorenz. il por Bul
Atom Sci 26:2-5+ O '70
President Nixon urges Senate advice and consent to ratification of the Treaty on genocide; message to the Senate. February 19,
1970; Secretary Rogers' report; with text of
convention. R. M. Nixon; W. P. Rogers.
Dept State Bul 62:350-3 Mr 16 '70
Why doesn't the U.S. outlaw mass murder?
struggle over signing the UN genocide
treaty. A. D. Morse. Look 34:40 Mr 10 '70
World law. World court: proposed ratification
of the Genocide convention. Commonweal
92:51-2 Mr 27 '70
GENOTYPE and phenotype
Partial reversion in yeast: genetic evidence
for a new type of bifunctional protein. B.
Dorfman and others. bibliog il Science 168:
1482-4 Je 19 '70
GENOVÉS, Juan
Visions of our time. il UNESCO Courier 23:
18-19 Ag '70 *
GENOVESE, Eugene D.
Fortunes of the left. Nat R 22:1266-70 D 1
'70
Massive breakdown. por Newsweek 76:25-7
Jl 6 '70; Same. Cur 120:3-6 Ag '70
GENTELE, Göran
New general manager; interview. New Yorker 46:15-16 D 26 '70

about
Gentele for Bing, or new blood from Sweden.
I. Kolodin. Sat R 53:34 D 26 '70 *
Met's new chief. il por Newsweek 76:67 D
21 '70 *
Musical events; new general manager. W.
Sargeant. New Yorker 46:57-8 D 26 '70 *
New manager for the Met. il por Time 96:51
D 21 '70 *

GENTIEU, E. P. and Mentall, J. E.
Formaldehyde absorption coefficients in the vacuum ultraviolet (650 to 1850 angstroms) bibliog il Science 169:681-3 Ag 14 '70

GENTNER, W. and others
Fission track ages and ages of deposition of deep-sea microtektites. bibliog il Science 168:359-61 Ap 17 '70

GENTRY, R. Cecil
Hurricane Debbie modification experiments, August 1969. bibliog il Science 168:473-5 Ap 24 '70

GENTRY, Robert V.
Giant radioactive halos: indicators of unknown radioactivity? bibliog il Science 169:670-3 Ag 14 '70

GEOCHEMISTRY
Phenolic aldehydes: generation from fossil woods and carbonaceous sediments by oxidative degradation. R. F. Leo and E. S. Barghoorn. bibliog il Science 168:582-4 My 1 '70

GEODES
Geodes. H. D. Brown. il Hobbies 75:157 O '70

GEODESIC domes
Contemporary art lesson; constructing a geodesic dome of styrofoam coffee cups. T. J. McGuire. il Sch Arts 70:19 O '70

GEODUCKS. See Clams

GEODYNAMICS
From the how to the why; Upper mantle project. Sci N 98:9 Jl 4 '70

GEOFFREY, Christopher
Cannery song. New Yorker 46:122 My 9 '70

GEOGRAPHICAL distribution of animals and plants
Monoplacophora in the south Atlantic Ocean. J. Rosewater. bibliog il Science 167:1485 Mr 13 '70
Rangia cuneata on the East coast: thousand mile range extension, or resurgence? S. H. Hopkins and J. D. Andrews. bibliog il Science 167:868 F 6 '70
See also
Animals—Migration
Birds—Geographical distribution

GEOGRAPHICAL medicine. See Medical geography

GEOGRAPHICAL names. See Names, Geographical

GEOGRAPHOS (asteroid) See Asteroids

GEOGRAPHY
See also
Medical geography

GEOGRAPHY, Historical
Maps
See also
Maps, Early

GEOLOGICAL research
See also
International geophysical year

GEOLOGICAL society of America
Earth sciences. Sci N 98:392 N 21 '70

GEOLOGICAL time
See also
Radioactive dating

GEOLOGISTS
See also
DeGolyer, E. L.

GEOLOGY
Mr Rodale becomes a rockhound. R. E. Meyers. Org Gard & Farm 17:73-6 Jl '70
See also
Computers—Geological use
Earth tides
Faults (geology)
Geodes
Geological society of America
Glaciers
Hot springs
Metamorphism (geology)
Submarine geology

Alaska
Bentonite debris flows in northern Alaska. D. M. Anderson and others; reply with rejoinder. D. B. Prior and C. Ho. bibliog il Science 167:1014-15 F 13 '70
Possible bedrock source for obsidian found in archeological sites in northwestern Alaska. W. W. Patton, jr. and T. P. Miller. bibliog il Science 169:760-1 Ag 21 '70

Antarctic Regions
Antarctic geology and Gondwanaland. C. Craddock. il Bul Atom Sci 26:33-9 D '70
Rubidium-strontium date of possibly 3 billion years for a granitic rock from Antarctica. M. Halpern. bibliog il Science 169:977-8 S 4 '70
Soviet research in Antarctica. P. Senko and M. Ravich. il Sci N 98:185-6 Ag 22 '70

California
Borax Lake site revisited. C. W. Meighan and C. V. Haynes. bibliog il Science 167:1213-21 F 27 '70
How the geologist can help your city; geological mapping of hillside areas, Los Angeles. C. A. Richards. il Am City 85:84-6 Je '70

Canada
Precambrian sedimentation in the Canadian shield; report of meeting. G. M. Young. Science 170:1239-40 D 11 '70

Caribbean Region
Rock bottom; floor of the Caribbean. L. Purrett. il Sci N 99:31 Ja 9 '71

Ethiopia
Afar triangle. H. Tazieff. il Sci Am 222:32-40 bibliog(p 126) F '70
Exposed guyot from the Afar Rift, Ethiopia. E. Bonatti and H. Tazieff. bibliog il Science 168:1087-9 My 29 '70

Georgia
Georgia granite. W. A. Bake, jr. il Natur Hist 79:32-7 O '70

Mediterranean Sea
Probing the Mediterranean's hidden geological past; Deep sea drilling project's Mediterranean leg. il Sci N 98:20-1 Jl 4 '70

Oregon
Mantle-derived peridotites in southwestern Oregon: relation to plate tectonics. L. G. Medaris, jr. and R. H. Dott, jr. bibliog il Science 169:971-4 S 4 '70

Pennsylvania
Rock music; ringing rocks of Bucks County. J. Gibbons and S. Schlossman. il Natur Hist 79:36-41 D '70

Russia
Piecing together the past; Uralides. il Sci N 98:285 O 3 '70

Utah
Explaining Moses rock dike; study of kimberlite formations. il Sci N 98:33 Jl 11 '70

Venezuela
Boconó fault, Venezuelan Andes: evidence of postglacial movement. C. Schubert and R. S. Sifontes. bibliog il Science 170:66-9 O 2 '70

Washington (state)
Earthquake at Giza; Hanford atomic products operation; with interview with G. T. Seaborg. S. Novick. bibliog il Environ 12:2-15 Ja '70; Same abr. with title Dangers from radioactive wastes. Cur 118:41-5 My '70

Western states
Why the West is wild; new theory of East Pacific rise. il Time 97:34 Ja 11 '71

GEOLOGY, Stratigraphic

Cenozoic
Central North Atlantic plate motions over the last 40 million years. J. D. Phillips and B. P. Luyendyk. bibliog il Science 170:727-9 N 13 '70

Ordovician
South Pole reaches the Sahara; report of symposium on the Saharan Ordovician ice age. R. W. Fairbridge. Science 168:878+ My 15 '70

Paleozoic
Paleomagnetism and Gondwanaland. M. W. McElhinny and G. R. Luck. bibliog il Science 168:830-2 My 15 '70

Pleistocene
See also
Glacial epochs

Pre-Cambrian
Precambrian sedimentation in the Canadian shield; report of meeting. G. M. Young. Science 170:1239-40 D 11 '70

Tertiary
Antarctic glaciation during the Tertiary recorded in sub-Antarctic deep-sea cores. S. V. Margolis and J. P. Kennett. bibliog il Science 170:1085-7 D 4 '70

GEOLOGY, Structural
Bed forms in base-surge deposits: lunar implications. R. V. Fisher and A. C. Waters. reply with rejoinder. D. R. Grine. bibliog Science 167:1637-8 Mr 20 '70

GEOLOGY, Structural—_Continued_
Bentonite debris flows in northern Alaska. D. M. Anderson and others; reply with rejoinder. D. B. Prior and C. Ho. bibliog il Science 167:1014-15 F 13 '70
Breakup of Pangaea. R. S. Dietz and J. C. Holden. il Sci Am 223:30-41 bibliog(p 144) O '70
Building mountain ranges: a plate tectonics model; studies of J. F. Dewey and J. M. Bird. K. Frazier. il pors Sci N 98:143-5 Ag 15 '70
Continent building. Sci N 97:192 F 21 '70
Earth tides, global heat flow, and tectonics. H. R. Shaw. bibliog il Science 168:1084-7 My 29 '70
Earth's gravity field: relation to global tectonics. W. M. Kaula. bibliog il Science 169:982-5 S 4 '70
Geopolitics of plate tectonics; Soviets reject hypothesis. Sci N 98:29 Jl 11 '70
Global tectonics; Penrose conference of the Geological society of America. W. R. Dickinson. Science 168:1250+ Je 5 '70
Mantle-derived peridotites in southwestern Oregon: relation to plate tectonics. L. G. Medaris, jr. and R. H. Dott, jr. bibliog il Science 169:971-8 S 4 '70
Mountain-building in the Mediterranean. Sci N 98:316 O 17 '70
Transversely aligned seismicity and concealed structures. C. F. Richter; reply. Z. F. Danes. Science 167:396 Ja 23 '70
Turning to the earth's smaller crustal plates. K. Frazier. il Sci N 97:153-5 F 7 '70
See also
Faults (geology)
GEOMAGNETISM. See Magnetism, Terrestrial
GEOMETRY
Megalithic rings: their design construction. T. M. Cowan. bibliog il Science 168:321-5 Ap 17 '70; Reply. N. Grossman. 169:1228-9 S 18 '70
Planetary planning; address, November 13, 1969. R. B. Fuller. il Am Scholar 40:29-63 Wint '70 (to be cont)
See also
Polyhedrons
Triangles
GEOPHYSICAL research
See also
Polar research
GEOPHYSICAL stations
Developing an unmanned Antarctic geophysical station. J. A. Jenny and others. bibliog il Space World G-4-76:9-16 Ap '70
GEOPHYSICS
See also
American geophysical union
Earth—Internal structure
Earth tides
Electronics in geophysics
Energy budget (geophysics)
International geophysical year
Meteorology
Seismology
GEORGADJIS, Polycarpos
Under the threat of guns. il Time 95:37 Mr 30 '70 *
GEORGE III, king of Great Britain
George III and the mad business, by I. Macalpine and R. Hunter. Review
Nation 211:220-1 S 14 '70. M. Byrd *
Newsweek 76:67-8 Ag 3 '70. R. A. Gross
GEORGE, Henry
Overdue business of tax reform. Am City 85:12 O '70 *
GEORGE, J. David
Curious bristle-worms; with biographical sketch. il Sea Front 16:291-9, 319 S '70
GEORGE, Jean (Craighead)
Victory in the Everglades. Read Digest 97:73-7 Ag '70
Wondrous creatures of the night. il Read Digest 96:182-8 Ja '70
GEORGE Eveleigh house. See Charleston, S.C.—Historic houses, etc.
GEORGE Washington Birthplace National Monument
Colgate's gift establishes Morgan horse breeding farm. il por Parks & Rec 5:30-2 F '70
GEORGE Washington masonic museum, Alexandria, Va. See Washington, George—Museums, relics, etc.
GEORGE Washington university, Washington, D.C.
Of lollipops and larynxes; speech and hearing clinic. A. Lewis. il Am Ed 6:29-30 Jl '70
GEORGES-PICOT, Jacques
Gloomy view of the U.S. economy. por Forbes 105:42-3 My 1 '70 *
GEORGETOWN, Colo.
Stopover for skiers, an hour from Denver. il Sunset 144:48 F '70

GEORGETOWN, Md.
Gourmet ashore:
Granary restaurant. J. W. Giles. il Motor B 126:134-5 Jl '70
GEORGIA
See also
Alcovy River
Banks and banking—Georgia
Cumberland Island
Education—Georgia
Fishing—Georgia
Forests and forestry—Georgia
Geology—Georgia
Land—Georgia

Description and travel
See also
Tourist trade—Georgia

Politics and government
Governor and the newspapers. America 122. 624-5 Je 13 '70
Leroy Johnson outslicks Mister Charlie. S. Lesher. il pors N Y Times Mag p34-6+ N 8 '70

Population
Optimum population and environment: a Georgian microcosm. E. P. Odum. il Cur Hist 58:355-9+ Je '70
GEORGIA, STRAIT OF
Racemization of amino acids in sediments from Saanich Inlet, British Columbia. K. A. Kvenvolden and others. bibliog il Science 169:1079-82 S 11 '70
GEORGIA art pottery. See Pottery, American
GEORGIA-Pacific corporation
Generous gift from Georgia-Pacific. il Am For 76:48-50 Mr '70
GEORGIA. University, Athens
Homecoming for the first black girl at the University of Georgia. C. Hunter. il pors N Y Times Mag p24:5+ Ja 25 '70
GEORGYI musical comedy. See Musical comedies, revues, etc.—Criticisms, plots, etc.
GEOTHERMAL energy. See Steam, Natural
GEOTROPISM (botany)
Amateur scientist; the effects of gravity on plant growth; ed. by C. L. Stong. D. Graham. il Sci Am 222:141-3 Je '70
GERACI, Phil
Built-in light meters, eyes that see what you can't. il Pop Mech 135:118-21 Ja '71
Crop those shots for better pictures. il Pop Mech 133:144-7+ F '70
How to choose the right film for the best picture. il Pop Mech 134:132-5 Jl '70
Simple camera checks for good summer shooting. il Pop Mech 133:124-7 Je '70
GERANIUMS
Geranium man. N. C. Gray. il por Am Home 73:22-3 Jl '70
GERBER, Albert B.
Right to receive and possess pornography. por Wilson Lib Bul 44:641-4 F '70
GERBER, Dan
Prelude to summer; poem. Nation 210:312 Mr 16 '70
Yellow; poem. New Yorker 46:171 O 10 '70
GERBER, Gary A.
Handy shelves you peg together. il Mech Illus 66:138-140 O '70
GERBER, Judianne Densen-. See Densen-Gerber, J.
GERBER, Leslie
Folk music. Am Rec G 36:922-3, 996-7; 37:64-5, 130-1, 194-5 Jl-N '70
Peter Serkin: nearly two hours of glorious Mozart. Am Rec G 36:895+ Jl '70
Stunning Schubert by Artur Rubinstein. Am Rec G 36:490-1 Mr '70
—and others
In the pop bag. Am Rec G 36:854-5, 926-7, 998-9; 37:66-9 Je-S '70
—See Summerlin, E. jt. auth.
GERBER, Merrill Joan
Daydreams; story. Ladies Home J 87:106-7 N '70
Forbidden subjects in slick fiction. Writers Digest 50:32-3 Ap '70
Things in their proper order; story. Redbook 135:68-9 Ag '70
Ultimate friend; story. Redbook 134:80-1 Ap '70
GERBER, Rosanna
(tr) See Singer, I. B. Tutor in the village
GERBER, Sophia P.
What's your trademark? il Mech Illus 66:72-3+ F '70
GERBILS
Monosodium glutamate: feeding of large amounts in man and gerbils. G. Bazzano and others. bibliog il Science 169:1208-9 S 18 '70

GERBNER, George
Cultural indicators: the case of violence in television drama. bibliog f il Ann Am Acad 388:69-81 Mr '70
GERDES, R. J. and others
Refractory oxide-metal composites: scanning electron microscopy and X-ray diffraction of uranium dioxide-tungsten. il Science 167:979-80 F 13 '70
GERHARDT, Lillian N. and others
(ed) Best books for spring 1970. il Library J 95:1911-13 My 15 '70
(ed) Book review. See second issue of each month of Library journal
GERIATRIC centers. See Old age homes
GERIATRICS. See Aged—Care and hygiene
GERLACH, Luther P.
Eco-Gemini: two for the teach-in. il Natur Hist 79:70-6 My '70
When people begin making sacrifices, you'll see more militancy. J. Pekkanen. il Life 68:28-30 Ja 30 '70
—and Hine, Virginia
You and the ecology movement; questionnaire. Natur Hist 79:27-9 Je; 8+ O: 16-17+ D '70
GERM free animals. See Germfree life
GERM warfare. See Biological warfare
GERMAN AMERICANS
Furor Teutonicus: Upper Mississippi Abteilung. G. Mann. Yale R 60:306-20 D '70
GERMAN architecture. See Architecture, German
GERMAN art. See Art, German
GERMAN artificial satellites. See Artificial satellites, German
GERMAN automobiles. See Automobiles, Foreign
GERMAN composers. See Composers, German
GERMAN cookery. See Cookery, German
GERMAN language

Foreign words and phrases
Dictionary headed for die bestsellerliste. il Time 96:28 N 23 '70

Study and teaching
Survey of the teaching of French, Spanish, and German in secondary schools. N. W. Austin and J. L. D. Clark. Sch & Soc 98:250-2 Ap '70
GERMAN literature
See also
German poetry
GERMAN mail order business. See Mail order business
GERMAN measles. See Rubella
GERMAN painting. See Painting, German
GERMAN pewter. See Pewter
GERMAN philosophy. See Philosophy, German
GERMAN poetry

Translations into English
Changed landscape; Clearings in the woods; tr. by T. Savory. G. Eich. Poetry 116:362-3 Ag '70
Rest on the flight into Egypt; poem, tr. by M. W. Hess. R. M. Rilke. Cath World 212:118 D '70
Six poems; How long; Chorus of trees; Chorus of invisible things; Chorus of the dead; Birds; Chorus of the wanderers; tr. by R. Mead and M. Mead. N. Sachs. New Yorker 46:48-9 O 31 '70
Song of the traveller at evening; Mignon; Death of a fly; To Charlotte Von Stein; Anacreon's grave; Permanence in change; tr. by J. F. Nims. J. W. von Goethe. Poetry 116:345-52 Ag '70
GERMAN refugees. See Refugees, German
GERMAN spies. See Spies
GERMAN wines. See Wine
GERMAN wirehaired pointers. See Pointers (dogs)
GERMANS in Poland
Grimms' tale. B. van Voorst. il Newsweek 76:50+ N 23 '70
GERMANY
See also
Government, Resistance to—Germany
Jews in Germany
Paleobotany—Germany
Paleontology—Germany
Russians in Germany

Civilization
Notes on the germanization of American youth. J. L. Sammons. Yale R 59:342-56 Mr '70; Same abr. with title American youth and the Germans. Cur 119:10-14 Je '70

Defenses
Dilatory demolition: Siegfried line. Time 95:28 Ja 26 '70

Economic conditions
See also
Money—Germany

Foreign relations
Germany and the Russo-Japanese war. J. Steinberg. bibliog f Am Hist R 75:1965-86 D '70
See also
Prussia—History

History

Bibliography
Articles and other books received; comp. by A. H. Price. See issues of American historical review

1918-1933
Look back at the Weimar republic, the cry was, Down with das system. W. Laqueur. il N Y Times Mag p 12-13+ Ag 16 '70; Reply. D. E. Westlake. p 136 S 13 '70
Revolution at home and abroad; parallels between Germany and U.S; address, September 8 and 9, 1970. K. I. Falk. Vital Speeches 37:58-61 N 1 '70
Weimar analogy. H. S. Levine. Nation 210:684-7 Je 8 '70
Weimar resemblance. P. Gay. il Horizon 12:4-15 Wint '70

1933-1945
In Hitler's service. L. S. Dawidowicz. bibliog f Commentary 50:85-90 N '70)

Intellectual life
Germans and Jews, by G. Mosse. Review Commentary 50:94-6+ O '70. L. D. Wurgaft
See also
Berlin—Intellectual life

National socialist movement
See National socialism

Navy
Germany and the Russo-Japanese war. J. Steinberg. bibliog f Am Hist R 75:1965-86 D '70

Politics and government
See also
National socialism

Reconstruction
See also
Dresden—City planning
GERMANY (Democratic Republic)
Germany we don't know. J. R. Moskin. il Look 34:42-50+ Je 16 '70
One nation, divisible. il Newsweek 75:41-2 Mr 30 '70
See also
Colleges and universities—Germany (Democratic Republic)
Communism—Germany (Democratic Republic)
Political prisoners—Germany (Democratic Republic)

Foreign relations
Germany (Federal Republic)
See Germany (Federal Republic)—Foreign relations—Germany (Democratic Republic)

Industries
Capitalists among Communists. il Time 95:84 Ap 20 '70

Intellectual life
Dragon slayer; work of W. Biermann. por Time 97:28+ Ja 18 '71

Politics and government
See also
Berlin question, 1945-

Religious institutions and affairs
World around us (cont) Chr Cent 87:309-10, 853-4 Mr 11, Jl 8 '70
See also
Evangelical church in Germany
Protestant churches—Germany (Democratic Republic)
GERMANY (Federal Republic)
One nation, divisible. il Newsweek 75:40-1 Mr 30 '70
See also
Airlines—Germany (Federal Republic)
Airplanes, Military—Germany (Federal Republic)
Architecture—Germany (Federal Republic)

GERMANY (Federal Republic)—See also—
  Continued
Automobile industry and trade—Germany
  (Federal Republic)
Ballet—Germany (Federal Republic)
Banks and banking—Germany (Federal Republic)
Church tax—Germany (Federal Republic)
Colleges and universities—Germany (Federal Republic)
Drug trade—Germany (Federal Republic)
Education—Germany (Federal Republic)
Festivals—Germany (Federal Republic)
Government and the press—Germany (Federal Republic)
Heidelberg
Industrial relations—Germany (Federal Republic)
Investments, Foreign (by Germany [Federal Republic])
Jews in Germany
Labor supply—Germany (Federal Republic)
Lübeck
Political parties—Germany (Federal Republic)
Publishers and publishing—Germany (Federal Republic)
Purchasing, Military—Germany, Federal Republic)
Schleswig-Holstein
Security classification (government documents)—Germany (Federal Republic)
Shopping and shoppers—Germany (Federal Republic)
Shopping centers—Germany (Federal Republic)
Television broadcasting—Germany (Federal Republic)
Theological seminaries—Germany (Federal Republic)
Urban transportation—Germany (Federal Republic)

Army

Help for the orphan army: the Bundeswehr. Time 95:37 Je 15 '70

Description and travel

Another tramp abroad; Neckar region. D. Butwin. il Sat R 53:40-1 Je 27 '70
Germany's wine country. H. P. Koenig. il Travel & Camera 33:54-7 O '70
Rhineland is wineland. N. Hazelton. Travel & Camera 33:25-7 O '70
  See also
Rhine River

Economic conditions

German miracle ending? il U S News 68:27-9 F 2 '70

Economic policy

Inflation on the Rhine; Kark Schiller-Willy Brandt dispute. Newsweek 75:89-90 Mr 16 '70

Economic relations

Coup for Bonn? Daimler-Benz and the Russian truck factory deal. Newsweek 76:67 S 7 '70
Politics on wheels. Time 96:33 S 14 '70

Foreign relations

Back on the track. Newsweek 76:50 N 23 '70
France and Germany: less divergent outlooks? A. Grosser. For Affairs 48:235-44 Ja '70
Germany in the era of negotiations. H. Schmidt. For Affairs 49:40-50 O '70
Ostpolitik: the era of negotiation in Europe. R. Bail. il Fortune 82:68-71+ D '70
Reports: Europe; Brandt's new deal. D. Cook. Atlan 226:23+ Jl '70
West German foreign policy in ferment. G. Braunthal. Cur Hist 58:292-7 My '70

Europe, Eastern

Big issue. Newsweek 75:42 F 23 '70
Bonn's diplomatic drive to the East. il Newsweek 75:45-6 Mr 16 '70
On the road to a new reality. il Time 97:6-7+ Ja 4 '71
West Germany turns to the East. M. M. Mestrovic. Commonweal 91:444-5 Ja 23 '70

Europe, Western

German Ostpolitik: appeasement or detente? address, April 22, 1970. R. Dahrendorf. Vital Speeches 36:517-20 Je 15 '70

France

  See France—Foreign relations—Germany (Federal Republic)

Germany (Democratic Republic)

Another Berlin wall. Newsweek 75:52-3 Ja 26 '70
Bonn's diplomatic drive to the East. il Newsweek 75:45-6 Mr 16 '70

Detour to the summit. Newsweek 75:44+ Mr 23 '70
Divided German talk at last. il pors U S News 68:37 Mr 30 '70
Divided Germans; reaching across the border. il U S News 68:29 F 2 '70
End of an era: the German summit. il por Newsweek 75:39 Mr 30 '70
Examining Erfurt. America 122:365 Ap 4 '70
Foxy Red Riding Hood. Newsweek 75:40 F 2 '70
Germany summit. Sr Schol 96:13-14 Ap 6 '70
Germany: the rocky road to recognition; W. Brandt's Ostpolitik. Time 96:22 Ag 3 '70
Hammering at recognition. J. A. Morris, jr. Nation 210:614-16 My 25 '70
Message from Ulbricht. il Time 95:31 Je 29 '70
No wanderer. por Time 95:27 Ja 26 '70
On speaking terms at last: Erfurt summit meeting. il Time 95:38+ Mr 30 '70
Problem of patience. Time 95:19-20 F 2 '70
Return engagement; conference in Kassel. il Newsweek 75:42-3 Je 1 '70
Setback for Ostpolitik; conference in Kassel. il Time 95:29 Je 1 '70
Two Germanys: a beginning; meeting of W. Brandt and W. Stopf. Nation 210:388-9 Ap 6 '70
Two Germanys face to face; Erfurt summit. il pors Time 95:18 Mr 23 '70
West Germany looks to the East. il por Time 95:37-8+ Mr 16 '70
Willy and Willi. Newsweek 75:35 Mr 2 '70
  See also
Berlin question, 1945-

Poland

Sticking point; Warsaw talks. Newsweek 75:42+ F 16 '70
  See also
Germany (Federal Republic)—Treaties—Poland

Russia

  See Russia—Foreign relations—Germany (Federal Republic)

Industries

  See also
Aerospace industries—Germany (Federal Republic)
Automobile industry and trade—Germany (Federal Republic)
Building industry—Germany (Federal Republic)
Chemical industries—Germany (Federal Republic)
Krupp works, Essen
Munitions industries—Germany (Federal Republic)
Phonograph record industry—Germany (Federal Republic)
Photographic apparatus industry and trade

Politics and government

France and Germany: less divergent outlooks? A. Grosser. For Affairs 48:235-44 Ja '70
No wanderer. por Time 95:27 Ja 26 '70
Technical mistake. il por Newsweek 75:61 My 11 '70
Willy's woes. il por Newsweek 76:43-4 Jl 27 '70
  See also
Berlin question, 1945-
Elections—Germany (Federal Republic)
Political parties—Germany (Federal Republic)

Religious institutions and affairs

World around us (title varies) (cont) Chr Cent 87:1433; 88:17-18 N 25 '70, Ja 6 '71
  See also
Evangelical church in Germany
Lutheran church in Germany

Treaties

Poland

Europe: a symbolic act of atonement; Oder-Neisse treaty. il por Time 96:25 D 21 '70
Muted celebration. Chr Cent 88:3 Ja 6 '71
So much history to overcome; Oder-Neisse treaty. il Newsweek 76:50 D 21 '70
Step toward conciliation: Treaty of Warsaw. il Time 96:22 N 30 '70

Russia

  See Russia—Treaties—Germany (Federal Republic)

GERMANY, EASTERN. See Germany (Democratic Republic)
GERMANY, WESTERN. See Germany (Federal Republic)
GERMFREE life
From embryo to adulthood, germ-free. il Sci Digest 68:47-51 Jl '70

GIBBONS, Russell W.
Four score and six years ago. Commonweal 92:285 Je 12 '70
GIBBONS
Gibbon fibrinopeptides: identification of a glycine-serine allelism at position B-3. G. A. Mross and others. bibliog il Science 170: 468-70 O 23 '70
GIBBS, Elizabeth
Gourmet afloat. Motor B 126:102-4 S '70
Gourmet ashore. il Motor B 126:106-7 Ag '70
GIBBS, Gordon E. and Griffin, G. D.
Beta glucuronidase activity in skin components of children with cystic fibrosis. bibliog il Science 167:993-4 F 13 '70
GIBBS, Ronald J.
Mechanisms controlling world water chemistry. bibliog il Science 170:1088-90 D 4 '70
GIBBS, Tony
Boat showcase. il Motor B 126:84-5 Jl; 64-5 S '70
Book shelf. See issues of Motor boating
Cruisers and houseboats '71. il Motor B 126: 54-60+ O '70
Design showcase. il Motor B 126:78-82 Jl; 61-3+ S '70
Sailing films for the hot stove league. il por Motor B 126:11 N '70
What price sailing glory? il Motor B 126:52-3+ Ag '70
World of the flying pint. il Motor B 125:50-3 Je '70
GIBOR, Aharon. See Cloud, P. jt. auth.
GIBRALTAR
Gibraltar. J. Faber. il Travel 133:28-33 Je '70
The Rock. A. Waugh. Nat R 22:413 Ap 21 '70
GIBSON, Bob
In a changing cast, one guy still gives a hoot. W. Leggett. por Sports Illus 33:75-6 S 21 '70 *
GIBSON, Henry
Elements; Ingredients for expedience; Sing me no country airs; Declaration of dependence; Instant archive; Maptrap; poems. il por Nat Wildlife 9:18-19 D '70
Memo. Audubon 72:144-5 S '70
GIBSON, J. B. See Thoday, J. M. jt. auth.
GIBSON, John E.
Test your creativity. Sci Digest 68:23-4+ S '70
GIBSON, Kenneth Allen
Another big city elects a Negro mayor. por U S News 68:46 Je 29 '70 *
Black mayors. il por Newsweek 76:16, 21 Ag 3 '70 *
Double jeopardy in Newark. il pors Time 95:20 Je 15 '70 *
Fresh air in Newark. il por Life 69:42-3 Jl 4 '70 *
Gibson's victory. New Yorker 46:28-9 Je 27 '70 *
Let us enjoy our victory; black victory, white reactions. il pors Newsweek 75:16-19 Je 29 '70 *
New mayor tries for a new Newark. il por Bsns W p36 Je 27 '70 *
Newark signs up a business team. Bsns W p23 Ag 15 '70 *
Visible man; il por Time 95:12-13 Je 29 '70 *
GIBSON, Michael
La jeune peinture. protest and politics. il Art in Am 58:142-5 N '70
GIBSON, Ralph
Dream photographs. R. Hattersley. Pop Phot 67:98-101+ O '70
GIBSON, Thomas C. and others
Fitness of an escherichia coli mutator gene. bibliog il Science 169:686-8 Ag 14 '70
GIDEON, Gene
Fantastic Caverns. il Travel 133:50 F '70
GIDEONSE, Harry D.
Year 2000; address, November 8, 1969. bibliog f Vital Speeches 36:530-6 Je 15 '70
GIDEONSE, Hendrik D.
Policy framework for educational research. bibliog il Science 170:1054-9 D 4 '70
GIEREK, Edward
Poland erupts. Gomulka steps out. il por Newsweek 76:21-2+ D 28 '70 *
Poland: new leaders and old problems. il Newsweek 77:21+ Ja 4 '71 *
Poland's new regime: gifts and promises. il por Time 97:33-4 Ja 4 '71 *
Polish unpleasantness. Nat R 23:20 Ja 12 '71 *
Rough road ahead for Polish leaders. il por U S News 70:64 Ja 4 '71 *
With Gomulka gone a new generation takes over. il pors Newsweek 77:22 Ja 4 '71 *
GIFFEN, Jane C.
Susanna Rowson and her academy. il por Antiques 98:436-40 S '70

GIFFORD, Horace
Three architects speak their minds. pors House & Gard 137:42+ Je '70
GIFFORD, Sanford Robinson
Sanford Robinson Gifford, landscape painter. S. B. Sherrill. il Antiques 98:834 D '70 *
GIFT from a stranger; story. See Anthony, D.
GIFT of tongues
Reassessing glossolalia. W. E. Mills. Chr Cent 87:1217-19 O 14 '70; Discussion. 87: 1389 N 18 '70
GIFT wrappings. See Wrapping of packages
GIFTED child; story. See Cousins. M.
GIFTED children. See Children, Gifted
GIFTS
Dad's handy gift-in. il Seventeen 29:180-1 Je '70
Easy to make gifts. il Design 7:21 mid-Wint '70
Every dad has his day. il Seventeen 29:176-7 Je '70
Hyacinths to feed the soul. C. Amen. Read Digest 96:201-2 Mr '70
Museums offer gifts by mail. il Sunset 145: 60 N '70
To you, now. R. A. Smith. il por Har Yrs 10:42-3 S '70
See also
Christmas gifts
Colleges and universities—Gifts, legacies, etc.
Food as gifts
Giving
Plants as gifts
Presidents—United States—Gifts

Anecdotes, facetiae, satire, etc.
More blessed to get than to give. G. Ace. Sat R 54:6 Ja 2 '71
On unwrapping a parcel. J. D. McAulay. Clear House 45:250 D '70
Wife problem. F. K. Smith. Flying 86:124 My '70
GIFTS, Spiritual
Charismatic and the playful in outdoor recreation. R. Meyersohn. bibliog f il Ann Am Acad 389:35-45 My '70
Understanding spirit-baptism; as Catholic Pentecostals practice it. D. L. Gelpi. America 122:520-1 My 16 '70
GIFTS for children
See also
Christmas gifts for children
GIFTS for service men
People-to-people programs for GI's in Vietnam. il U S News 68:89-91 Mr 23 '70
GIGANTOPITHECUS. See Apes, Fossil
GILBERT, Arthur N.
International relations and the spirit of tragedy. Yale R 60:45-52 O '70
GILBERT, Bil
Exploring the world within. il Read Digest 96:177-8+ F '70
Golf. il Sports Illus 33:49 Jl 13 '70
Great buffalo hunt? Shoot? Slaughter? il Sports Illus 33:36-8+ N 23 '70
Home on the range. il Sports Illus 33:46-8+ Jl 6 '70
Nature. Sports Illus 33:85-7 N 16 '70
GILBERT, Carl J.
Trade expansion expectations; address. November 19, 1969. Dept State Bul 61:564-8 D 15 '69
GILBERT, Celia
Data bankers: poem. Atlan 225:70 Mr '70
GILBERT, David
Music to my ears. I. Kolodin. Sat R 53:18 D 5 '70 *
GILBERT, James
Beech stagger wing; excerpt from Great planes. il Flying 87:68-9+ O '70
Flying visit. il Flying 86:26-7+ Mr '70
GILBERT, Richard
Cassettes: the big news in home music systems. il House B 112:52-3+ Jl '70
GILBERT, Walter. See Ptashne, M. jt. auth.
GILBRETH, Edward S.
Illinois: Stevenson fights TV. il Nation 211: 399-402 O 26 '70
GILBY, A. R. See Atkinson, P. W. jt. auth.
GILDEN, Raymond V. See Oroszlan, S. jt. auth.
GILES, Cynthia Davis
How to create a good home library. il Parents Mag 45:64-5 My '70
GILES, John W.
Gourmet ashore. il Motor B 126:134-5 Jl '70
GILES, John Warren
Let's clear up laws on copyright of plans. Arch Rec 148:39-40 D '70
GILFORD, Barbara
My mountain of leaves. il Org Gard & Farm 17:54-6 N '70
Turtles guard our garden. il Org Gard & Farm 17:92-3 S '70

GILGAMESH
Death of Enkidu; excerpt from Gilgamesh: a verse narrative. H. Mason. Am Scholar 40:138-41 Wint '70
GILKEY, Richard
Instructional media (cont) Clear House 44: 510-12, 567-8; 45:191-2, 255-6 Ap-My, N-D '70
GILL, Brendan
Fat girl; story. New Yorker 46:32-41 S 26 '70
Theatre. See issues of New Yorker
GILL, Donald H.
Bye-bye Babylon. Chr Today 15:17-18+ N 20 '70
GILLAM, Barbara
Gathering of Europe's playgrounds. il Mlle 70:259-64+ F '70
Great American vacation scenes. Mlle 70: 258-61+ Ap '70
Where famous people go. Mlle 71:154-6 Je '70
GILLELAN, G. Howard
Archery. See issues of Outdoor life
GILLEN, Denver
Mexico and the American artist. il por Am Artist 34:32-9+ Ap '70
GILLESPIE, Charles
Dynamite in pollution. Nation 211:455-7, 674 N 9, D 28 '70
Jim Brown comes to Mississippi. Nation 211: 236-9 S 21 '70
GILLESPIE, J. M.
Mammoth hair: stability of α-keratin structure and constituent proteins. bibliog il Science 170:1100-2 D 4 '70
GILLETT, Charlie
Getting it straight. Time 96:47+ S 28 '70 *
GILLETTE, Bill
Don't spare the rod. il Outdoor Life 145:88-91+ Ap '70
GILLETTE, Jeanette L.
Grafting pecan trees, Texas style. il Org Gard & Farm 17:46-9 O '70
Newspaper stringing as a freelance starter. il Writers Digest 50:24-6 Ap '70
Pecans, an extra cash crop. il Org Gard & Farm 17:50-3 My '70
GILLETTE, Virginia M.
Love to share; story. Good H 171:96-7 N '70
Time for caring; story. Good H 171:100-1 O '70
GILLETTE company
You know you're not getting Maudie Frickert. W. Johnson. il Sports Illus 32:30-6 Ja 26 '70
GILLETTE safety razor company. See Gillette company
GILLETTI, Don
Mere alcohol doesn't thrill them at all. P. Knight. il por Sports Illus 33:76-7 N 30 '70 *
GILLHAM, Charles E.
Let's call it like it is. il Field & S 75: 48-9+ N '70
Multiply thy kind and perish. il Field & S 75:8+ Jl '70
Tomorrow's critters. il Audubon 72:41-3 N '70
GILLHAM dam project. See Dams
GILLIAM, Dorothy
My children have a right to feel proud. por Redbook 135:62+ Ag '70
GILLIAM, Harold
Ecology: rhetoric and reality. Ed Digest 36: 35-6 N '70
GILLIATT, Mary
Zest in wall painting. il House & Gard 138: 126-7+ O '70
GILLIATT, Penelope
Antique love story. New Yorker 46:42-8 Ap 4 '70
Current cinema. See issues of New Yorker, April 4 to September 26, 1970
Foreigners; story. New Yorker 46:36-43 Mr 14 '70
Property; story. New Yorker 46:33-9 My 2 '70
GILLIGAN, John Joyce
Going for Gilligan. P. R. Wieck. New Repub 163:10-12 O 17 '70 *
GILLISPIE, Charles Coulston
Authors & Editors. B. A. Bannon. por Pub W 197:23-4 Ap 13 '70 *
GILLMAN, R. W.
One man's theory opens a new door. il Nations Bsns 58:84-5 Ja '70
GILLMOR, Rogene G. See Firshein, W. jt. auth.
GILLOCK, Oliver P. Jr
Spreading state library riches for peanuts. il Wilson Lib Bul 45:354-5+ D '70
GILLON, Hadassah
Detecting deafness early. il Sci N 97:112 Ja 24 '70

GILLS
Habituation and dishabituation in the absence of a central nervous system. B. Peretz. bibliog il Science 169:379-81 Jl 24 '70
Insect eggshells. H. E. Hinton. il Sci Am 223: 84-91 Ag '70
GILLULY, Richard H.
How much, how soon for anti-pollution? New Repub 162:7-8 Ja 24 '70
Sulfur oxide control: a grim future. il Sci N 98:187-8 Ag 22 '70
GILMAN, Dugan
After eating salt fish; poem. Poetry 115:391 Mr '70
GILMARTIN, Frederick G.
Ethnic art gallery. il Sch Arts 69:8 F '70
GILMORE, Artis
Alcindor II? il por Newsweek 75:76 F 9 '70
GILMORE, Clifford F.
Introducing Anthony Newman. Hi Fi sec I 20:94 Ja '70
GILMORE, J. Herbert, Jr
Committed Baptists. Time 96:42 N 9 '70 *
First Baptist, Birmingham: a case study of old wineskins bursting. D. G. Shockley. Chr Cent 87:1462-3 D 2 '70 *
GILMORE, Kathryn
Rooftop of the world; poem. Am For 76:25 D '70
GILMORE, Kenneth O.
Along the infamous Ho Chi Minh trail. il Read Digest 97:146-50 O '70
Let's fence this sacred cow. Read Digest 97: 76-80 S '70
What hope of reforming federal spending? Read Digest 97:83-7 Jl '70
GILMOUR, Robert S.
Private interests and public lands. Cur Hist 59:36-42+ Jl '70
GILOT, Françoise
Newsmakers. il pors Newsweek 75:53 Je 29 '70 *
GILPATRIC, Roswell Leavitt
Dear Ros. il por Time 95:19 F 23 '70 *
From Jackie with love. il por Newsweek 75: 25 F 23 '70 *
Onassis-Gilpatric letters. J. McLaughlin. America 122:252+ Mr 7 '70*
GILPIN, C. R. and Neufeld, Edward
Community cooperation and a shoestring budget: Rx for an activity therapy program. Ment Hy 54:397-400 Jl '70
GILPIN, Robert
Technological strategies and national purpose. bibliog Science 169:441-8 Jl 31 '70
GILSTRAP, James B.
Right night approach. Flying 87:105 S '70
GILSTRAP, Robert, and others
Some questions & answers. Todays Ed 59:39-40 Ap '70
GILSVIK, Robert
Big fish in town. il por Outdoor Life 145:72-3+ Je '70
GIMER, Richard H.
Declaration on principles of friendly relations; statement. September 24, 1970. Dept State Bul 63:623-7 N 16 '70
GINANDES, Shepard C.
Why so many young women steal from stores. S. Blum. il Redbook 135:72-3+ O '70 *
GINASTERA, Alberto
Don Rodrigo. Criticism
New Yorker 46:159 O 17 '70 *
GINDOFF, Bryan
Thalberg didn't look happy. il Film Q 24:3-6 Fall '70
GINGERBREAD lady; drama. See Simon, N.
GINGERICH, Owen
Laboratory exercises in astronomy: spectral classification. il Sky & Tel 40:74-6 Ag '70
GINGRICH, Arnold
Publisher's page. See issues of Esquire
GINOTT, Haim G.
Between parent and child (cont) McCalls 97: 54+ F; 32+ Mr; 32 Ag '70
(ed) How psychotherapists deal with their children. Vogue 155:90-1+ Mr 15 '70
GINSBERG, Allen
Allen Ginsberg and the 60's. M. Dickstein. bibliog f Commentary 49:64+ Ja '70
From Howl to OM. R. Whittemore. New Repub 163:17-18 Jl 25 '70 *
GINSBERG, Leon
Radical view of social welfare and mental health. bibliog Ment Hy 54:44-9 Ja '70
GINSBURG, David
Communication versus polarization. T. Wicker. Cur 114:48-9 Ja '70
GINSBURG, Max
Max Ginsburg: underground & above ground. I. Greenberg. il Am Artist 34:28-34+ S '70 *

GINZBURG, Ralph
Chancellor of the exchequer. por Time 96:73 O 26 '70 *
GIORDANO, Gus
Ritual-D: Gus Giordano & company. M. Perrone. il pors Dance Mag 44:26-7 S '70 *
GIORDANO, Umberto
Fedora. G. L. Mayer. pors Am Rec G 37: 76-9 O '70 *
GIOSEFFI, Daniela
Poem; On the palm of my hand I can taste you. Nation 211:218 S 14 '70
GIPSY moths. See Gypsy moths
GIR wildlife sanctuary. See Wildlife sanctuaries—India
GIRARD avenue bridge. See Philadelphia—Bridges
GIRARDI, Giulio
Girardi and Garaudy. America 122:173 F 21 '70*
GIRAUDOUX, Jean
Madwoman of Chaillot. Criticism
New Yorker 46:64 Ap 4 '70 *
GIRAUT de Bornelh
Alba; poem, tr. by S. Orgel. Poetry 116:356 Ag '70
GIRL athletes. See Women as athletes
GIRL of the golden West; opera. See Puccini, G.
GIRL scouts
Cleveland has nation's only 60+ Girl scout troop, with men as members too! il Aging 186:10-11 Ap '70
Girl scout cookies taste of success. Bsns W p24-5 F 7 '70
Motivated to be better; youth-serving agencies. A. E. Iverson. il Todays Ed 59: 34-5 Mr '70
Retirees, Girl scouts, win in inter-generation exchange. il Aging 186:11-12 Ap '70
Scout power tidies the Hackensack; action by Girl scout troop 127. il Life 68:37-40 Je 12 '70
GIRL who believed in love; story. See Soman, F. J.
GIRL who wouldn't be missed; story. See Boyd, C.
GIRLS
How to get along with boys. D. A. Sugarman and R. Hochstein. il Seventeen 29: 134-5+ F '70
Special season of the young; some of California's beautiful girls. il Life 69:46-53 Jl 10 '70
Young living; questions and answers. A. Wood. See issues of Seventeen
See also
Coeducation
Runaway boys and girls
Sisters
GIRLS, Delinquent
Help for troubled girls; Good Shepherd home in St Paul, Minn. J. Engh. il Parents Mag 45:66-8+ Mr '70
GIRLS clubs
See also
Camp fire girls
Girl scouts
GIRLS reformatories. See Reformatories
GISELLE; ballet. See Ballets—Criticisms
GITT, Josiah William
Jess Gitt's Gazette. J. Higgins. Nation 211: 497 N 16 '70 *
GITTELSON, Natalie
Needles and pins. See issues of Harper's bazaar
GIUSEPPE Panza di Biumo collection. See Art—Private collections
GIVEAWAY games. See Advertising—Prize contests
GIVEN names. See Names, Personal
GIVENS, Richard A.
Technology and mankind's future. America 123:254-6 O 10 '70
GIVING
Americans open pocketbook: giving to charity sets record. il U S News 69:65 Jl 13 '70
To give or not to give? Korean orphan care as big business. W. G. Henderson. Chr Cent 87:294-5 Mr 11 '70
See also
Charities
Church finance
Corporations—Charitable contributions
Gifts
GLACIAL epochs
Convection in the Antarctic ice sheet leading to a surge of the ice sheet and possibly to a new ice age. T. Hughes. bibliog il Science 170:630-3 N 6 '70
GLACIER NATIONAL PARK
Glacier adventure. B. Rockow. il Travel 134: 67-71 Jl '70

GLACIERS
Above the Arctic Circle; 1969 International ice patrol glacier survey. D. A. Smith. il Am Scholar 39:434-44 Sum '70
Ice cores: clues to past climates. L. Purrett. il Sci N 98:369-70 N 7 '70
Ice survey by the U.S. coast guard; Greenland ice sheet. W. S. Carlson. bibliog il Science 168:396-7 Ap 17 '70
Neoglaciation. G. H. Denton and S. C. Porter. il Sci Am 222:100-10 Je '70
See also
Glacial epochs
Icebergs
GLADIATORS
Colosseum: world's bloodiest acre. J. Bryan, 3d. il Read Digest 96:234-6+ Je '70
Most deadly games. J. H. Plumb. il Horizon 1:52-3 Aut '69
GLADIOLUS
Gladiolus, a great cut flower for summer bouquets. il Home Gard 57:14-15+ Mr '70
GLADIOLUS, Arrangement of. See Flowers, Arrangement of
GLADSTONE, Gary
Child's playground of verses; photographs. Life 69:56-9 Jl 24 '70
GLADWIN, Ellis
St Jude: phoenix of the jungle. il Todays Health 48:26-9+ Ag '70
GLADWIN, Thomas
East is a big bird; excerpts, with biographical sketch. il Natur Hist 79:4, 24-35 Ap; 58-69 My '70
GLANDS
See also
Harderian gland
Pituitary body
Diseases
See also
Cystic fibrosis
GLANDS, Ductless
See also
Thymus gland
GLASCO, Sue
Freelance job idea: teaching high school journalism. il Writers Digest 50:28-30 O '70
GLASER, Alice
Farewell to Alice. A. Gingrich. Esquire 74: 8 D '70 *
GLASER, John W.
Anonymous priesthood. Commonweal 93: 271-4 D 11 '70
GLASER, Milton, and Snyder, Jerome
Commercial arts. il Am Artist 34:9+ O; 14 N; 14-15 D '70
GLASER, Peter Edward
How to get sun power for New York. por Bsns W p 128 My 9 '70 *
GLASGOW, Lowell A.
Transfer of interferon-producing macrophages: new approach to viral chemotherapy. bibliog il Science 170:854-6 N 20 '70
—See Overall, J. C. jr, jt. auth.
GLASGOW university. See Colleges and universities—Scotland
GLASS, Bentley. See Glass, H. B.
GLASS, Billy P.
Zircon and chromite crystals in a Muong Nong-type tektite. bibliog il Science 169: 766-9 Ag 21 '70
GLASS, Dick
C.E.T. test. Electr World 83:74 F; 59 Mr; 67 Ap; 67 My; 53 Je; 84:74 Ag; 62 S; 74-5 O; 70 N; 67 D '70; 85:76 Ja '71
GLASS, H. Bentley
Educational obsolescence. Science 170:1041 D 4 '70
Introducing William Bevan. Science 170:21 O 2 '70
GLASS, Malcolm
Death of a holy man; poem. Chr Cent 87: 112 Ja 28 '70
GLASS, Roger
Aid fiasco in Peru. New Repub 163:14 S 19 '70
GLASS
Glass submarines. D. Groves. il Sea Front 16: 286-90 S '70
See also
Glassware
Tektites
Lead content
Simple field test for TV X-radiation; test of glass for lead content. Electr World 84:65 O '70
GLASS, Ornamental
Maurice Heaton's laminated panels; ed. by T. Bayne. M. Heaton. il Craft Horiz 30:24-5+ Ag '70
GLASS, Safety
How safe are glass walls and what can you do to make yours safer? il Sunset 145:62-4 Ag '70

GLASS, Volcanic. See Obsidian
GLASS blowing and working
Ask Rufus. R. Cartwright. Mech Illus 66: 101 D '70
Glass blowing. E. B. Meroney. il Parks & Rec 5:34-5+ Ja '70
GLASS-bottom boats. See Boats—Materials
GLASS bottle industry. See Glass container industry
GLASS construction
   See also
Glass houses
Walls, Glass
GLASS container industry
Return of the returnables? il Newsweek 76: 70-1 S 21 '70
GLASS floats. See Fishing—Implements and appliances
GLASS flowers
Glass flowers; a unique and beautiful plant collection; Ware collection. K. Kaltenbach. il por Horticulture 48:36-7 F '70
GLASS houses
House with a view for the neighbors; glass house, Cambridge, England. il Mech Illus 66:67 N '70
GLASS industry
Improbable genius was Mike Owens. R. H. Mulford. il Nations Bsns 58:96-7 Ja '70
   See also
Eagle glass and manufacturing company
Glass container industry
Libbey-Owens-Ford glass company
Owens-Illinois, inc.
Pilkington brothers, ltd.
GLASS lamps. See Lamps
GLASS manufacture
   See also
Glass blowing and working

History
Glass blowing. E. B. Meroney. il Parks & Rec 5:34-5+ Ja '70
GLASS painting and staining
Play of light through colored glass. il Sunset 144:138 Mr '70
GLASS utensils. See Kitchen utensils
GLASS walls. See Walls, Glass
GLASSER, Ira
Protecting student rights. Cur 115:46-54 F '70
GLASSER, William
Youth in rebellion, why? interview. il por U S News 68:42-6 Ap 27 '70
GLASSES, Musical. See Musical glasses
GLASSMAN, James K.
Flicks in France. Atlan 226:106-8 Jl '70
Reports: students in France. Atlan 226:25-6+ S '70
GLASSOCK, Janet A.
We are a family: man; poem. Negro Hist Bul 32:27 D '69
GLASSWARE
X-Ray pattern glass. A. G. Peterson. il Hobbies 75:68-9 Je '70
   See also
Corning glass center, Corning, N.Y.
Epergnes
Salt and pepper shakers
Tableware

Exhibitions
Great glass: treasures of Toledo, Ohio, museum of art. J. Peter. il Look 34:22-5 S 8 '70

History
Libbey commemorative revival of Amberina, 1917. C. U. Fauster. il Hobbies 75:98J-98L Mr '70
West Virginia glass manufacturing company. A. G. Peterson. il Hobbies 74:106 F '70
GLASSWARE, Ancient
Remnants of a fourth century glass factory; fragments uncovered in northwestern Israel, at the Corning, N.Y. museum. il Hobbies 75:82 Je '70
GLASSY semiconductors See Semiconductors
GLASSY state
Vitreous water: identification and characterization. C. A. Angell and E. J. Sare. bibliog Science 168:280-1 Ap 10 '70
GLATT, Charles A. and Gaines, W. A.
School desegregation: some impediments and solutions. Ed Digest 35:12-15 Mr '70
GLAZE, Andrew
Make room; poem. Sat R 53:100 S 12 '70
Melt-out; poem. Atlan 226:73 D '70
GLAZE, Eleanor
Strolling brink; story. Atlan 225:101-8 Ap '70

GLAZER, Nathan
Campus rights and responsibilities: a role for lawyers? Am Scholar 39:445-62 Sum '70; Same with title What new governance systems? Cur 122:44-55 O '70
On being deradicalized. Commentary 50:74-80 O '70; 51:22-3 Ja '71
GLAZER, Sidney
(comp) Articles and other books received; Near East. See issues of American historical review
GLAZES and glazing
Alkaline glaze. R. Behrens. Ceram Mo 18:26+ O '70
Chromium, the swinging glaze colorant. R. Behrens. Ceram Mo 17:33 D '69
Cobalt blues at cone 9. R. Behrens. il Ceram Mo 18:31 My '70
Dust glazing. R. Behrens. il Ceram Mo 18: 19 F '70
Glazes from barnard slip. R. Behrens. Ceram Mo 18:33 S '70
Hamada legacy. J. Larson. il por Ceram Mo 18:13-15 O '70
Local reduction copper reds; reprint. E. Littlefield. il Ceram Mo 18:31-3 Ja '70
Reduction of raku glazes; excerpts from Raku: art and technique. H. Riegger. il Ceram Mo 18:16-18 Je '70
Volcanic ash bodies and glazes. R. Behrens. il Ceram Mo 18:28 D '70
Yellow glazes. R. Behrens. Ceram Mo 18:31 N '70
   See also
Frits
Furniture—Finishing
GLAZIER, Kenneth M.
Paper pollution. por Wilson Lib Bul 44:856-7 Ap '70
GLAZING (food)
Buttery glazes for your vegetables. il Sunset 145:190 N '70
GLEASON, Jim D. and Friedman, Irving
Deuterium: natural variations used as a biological tracer. bibliog il Science 169:1085-6 S 11 '70
GLEASON, John B.
Springtime is steelhead time. il Field & S 74:32-3+ Ja '70
GLEASON, Ralph J.
Aquarius wept. il Esquire 74:84-92+ Ag '70
GLEKEL, Newton
Up and down with Newton Glekel. il por Forbes 106:37-8 S 15 '70 *
Wrong foot forward. pors Time 96:65 Jl 27 '70 *
GLENMORE distillers company
Zigzagging liquorman. G. Berkwitt. por Duns 96:52 D '70
GLENN, Jack W.
Collectors: Mr and Mrs Jack W. Glenn. M. Amaya. il por Art in Am 58:86-93 Mr '70 *
GLENN, Lynn
Living with uncertainty: the families who wait back home. il pors Time 96:18-19 D 7 '70 *
GLIAL cells. See Nerve cells
GLICK, Phil
Selling the sports article. Writer 84:26-7 Ja '71
GLICKSTEIN, Mitchell, and Millodot, Michel
Retinoscopy and eye size. bibliog il Science 168:605-6 My 1 '70
GLIDE memorial united Methodist church. See San Francisco—Churches
GLIDERS (aeronautics)
Foreign accent: powered sailplanes. J. Fricker. il Flying 87:18-19+ D '70
Q-Star achieves reduced noise; powered sailplane. C. M. Plattner. il Aviation W 92:87-8+ Ap 6 '70
   See also
Gliding and soaring

Military use
Our supersecret, superquiet plane. K. V. Brown. il Pop Mech 133:94-7 Mr '70

Research use
Fighting the Cat that threatens you from a clear blue sky. K. J. Scribner. il por Pop Sci 196:60-3 My '70

Testing
Pilot report:
Schweizer 1-34. D. Lamont. il Flying 87: 62-71 Jl '70
GLIDING and soaring
Red baron in the wild blue yonder; world soaring championship. R. F. Jones. il por Sports Illus 33:18-21 Jl 13 '70
Welcome back, world champion. International soaring championships. G. Moffat. il Flying 87:78-9+ S '70

GLINN, Burt
  Shropshire; photographs. il Holiday 47:32-7 Ja '70
GLIOMAS. See Tumors
GLIXON, David M.
  SR's semi-annual reference book roundup (cont) il Sat R 53:35-40+ My 16; 32+ D 5 '70
  (ed) Your literary I.Q. See issues of Saturday review
GLOAG, John
  English Chinese style in furniture. il Antiques 97:718-23 My '70
GLOBAL atmospheric research program. See Weather research
GLOBAL satellite communications systems. See Communications satellites—International aspects
GLOBE photos, Inc.
  Globe photos: picture agency plus. H. V. Fondiller. il Pop Phot 66:78-9+ F '70
GLOBES, Astronomical
  See also
  Moon—Maps
GLOBETTI, Gerald, and Pomeroy, Grace
  Characteristics of community residents who are favorable toward alcohol education. Ment Hy 54:411-15 Jl '70
GLOBOID leukodystrophy. See Leukodystrophy
GLOBULAR clusters. See Stars—Clusters
GLOBULINS
  See also
  Blood—Proteins
  Concanavalins
GLÖGG. See Punch (beverage)
GLOMAR Challenger (ship) See Ships, Research
GLOMERULONEPHRITIS. See Kidneys—Diseases
GLONEK, Thomas, and others
  Biological phosphonates: determination by phosphorus-31 nuclear magnetic resonance. bibliog il Science 169:192-4 Jl 10 '70
GLORIA and Esperanza; drama. See Bovasso, J.
GLOSSOLALIA. See Gift of tongues
GLOXINIAS
  Gloxinias for brilliant color. A. H. Buell. il Home Gard 57:48-9+ N '70
GLOYE, Eugene E. and Marcus, R. J.
  Drug effect prediction by computer. il Science 169:89-91 Jl 3 '70
GLUCAGON
  δ-Aminolevulinic acid synthetase: induction in embryonic chick liver by glucagon. J. A. Simons. bibliog il Science 167:1378-9 Mr 6 '70
GLUCK, Christoph Willibald
  Melody beyond grief. M. O. Lee. Opera N 35:24-5 Ja 9 '71 *
  Orfeo ed Euridice. Criticism
    Nation 211:350 O 12 '70 *
    New Yorker 46:134+ O 3 '70 *
    Opera N 35:24-5 Ja 9 '71 *
    Opera N il 35:17-20 Ja 9 '71 *
    Sat R 53:41 O 10 '70 *
GLUCK, Louis
  Head start for survival. Time 96:94+ D 7 '70 *
GLUCONEOGENESIS. See Carbohydrate metabolism
GLUCOSE
  Glucose production by lamprey meninges. C. M. Rovainen. bibliog il Science 167:889-90 F 6 '70
GLUCOSE transport. See Biological transport
GLUE
  Barnacle glue. J. Singer. il Sea Front 16:96-103 Mr '70
  See also
  Cements, Adhesive
GLUE guns. See Spraying apparatus
GLUE sniffing
  Glue sniffing causes heart block in mice. G. J. Taylor and W. S. Harris. bibliog il Science 170:866-8 N 20 '70
GLUECK, Grace
  Maxfield Parrish. pors Am Heritage 22:17-18+ D '70
  New York gallery notes. See issues of Art in America
  (ed) See Steinberg, S. Artist speaks
GLUSMAN, Paul
  Behind the Chicago conspiracy trial. il Ramp Mag 8:39-47 Ja '70
GLUTAMIC acid decarboxylase. See Decarboxylase
GLUTAMIC oxaloacetic transaminase. See Transaminases
GLUTAMINE synthetase. See Synthetases

GLUTATHIONE
  Phosphorylation coupled to the transfer of electrons from glutathione to cytochrome c. A. A. Painter and F. E. Hunter, jr. bibliog il Science 170:552-3 O 30 '70
GLUTEN
  Molecular approach to breadmaking. Y. Pomeranz and others. bibliog il Science 167:944-9 F 13 '70
GLUTEN-free diet. See Diet in disease
GLUTETHIMIDE
  White like me; J. W. Finley's suit against government for negligent use of Doriden. il por Newsweek 75:76 Je 22 '70
GLYCERIC acid
  Thyroid hormone control of erythrocyte 2,3-diphosphoglyceric acid concentrations. L. M. Snyder and W. J. Reddy. bibliog il Science 169:879-80 Ag 28 '70
GLYCINE
  Glycine inhibition of asparaginase. W. L. Ryan and H. C. Sornson. bibliog il Science 167:1512-13 Mr 13 '70
GLYCOLIPIDS
  See also
  Cerebrosides
GLYCOSIDES
  See also
  Cardiac glycosides
GLYNDEBOURNE festival. See Music festivals—England
GLYNN, Edward
  Bishops' spring meeting. America 122:496 My 9 '70
  Equal rights for brothers. America 123:64-5 Ag 8 '70
  Faith in focus. America 124:49 Ja 16 '71
  How to unnerve male chauvinists. America 123:144-6 S 12 '70
  (ed) See Dellums, R. V. Enter Ron Dellums: radical
GNAGEY, Tom
  Myth of underachievement. Ed Digest 35:49-52 Mr '70
GNOSTICA bookstore. See Booksellers and bookselling—Minnesota
GNOSTICISM
  Barth on Tillich: neo-gnosticism. R. K. Anderson. pors Chr Cent 87:1477-81 D 9 '70
GOAD, Walter B. See Cann, J. R. jt. auth.
GOAL values. See Value (psychology)
GOALKEEPERS. See Hockey players
GOALS, National. See United States
GOAT hunting
  See also
  Rocky Mountain goat hunting
GOATS
  My friend, the goat. F. W. Townley. il Org Gard & Farm 17:102-4+ Ja '70
GOBAN, Ronald D.
  Watchdog cats! Har Yrs 10:32 Ja '70
GOBLE, Susan
  Matins; story. Mlle 71:250 Ag '70
GOBLETS. See Drinking vessels
GOD
  Did God really say so? Chr Today 14:28 F 27 '70
  Is there a substitute for God? D. R. Klein. Read Digest 96:51-5 Mr '70
  Is your God too big? Chr Today 14:27 F 13 '70
  Rahner's argument for God. J. Donceel. America 123:340-2 O 31 '70
  X marks the mystery. C. F. H. Henry. Chr Today 15:31-2 D 4 '70
  See also
  Atheism
  Christianity
  Holy Spirit
  Jesus Christ
  Theology
  Trinity
      Attributes
  Believe and appropriate! L. N. Bell. Chr Today 14:27-8 My 22 '70
GODARD, Jean Luc
  Current cinema. P. Gilliatt. New Yorker 46:102+ My 2; 81-5 My 30 '70 *
GODBER, Sir George
  Cigarettes and cancer. il UNESCO Courier 23:10-13 My '70
GODDARD, Burton L.
  Crucial issue in Bible translation. Chr Today 14:12-13 Jl 3 '70
GODDARD, G. V. See Gersch, W. jt. auth.
GODDARD, Robert Hutchings
  Strivings of a pioneer. I. M. Holley, jr. Science 170:522-3 O 30 '70 *
GODDARD college, Plainfield, Vt.
  Alternatives; underground media conference. R. Todd. Atlan 226:112+ N '70
  Goddard: genesis, transition and tradition. J. Anderson. il Dance Mag 44:36-40 S '70

GOLDBERG, Arthur Joseph—about—*Continued*
Goldilocks may not be the most exciting fellow in town but he's the only one who can win this year. R. Reeves. il pors N Y Times Mag p7+ Je 14 '70 *
Hello, Arthur? il por Newsweek 76:25 N 2 '70 *
Is the Rock still solid? il pors Time 96:19-20 O 19 '70 *
Judge gets an argument. il por Time 96:18-19 Jl 6 '70 *
Justice triumphs. il por Newsweek 76:37-8 Jl 6 '70 *
Mr Goldberg runs for office. New Yorker 46: 27-9 Je 13 '70 *
This is the battle of the titans? R. Reeves. il pors N Y Times Mag p23-5+ N 1 '70 *
Waiting for Goldberg. por Newsweek 75:32-3 Mr 23 '70 *
GOLDBERG, Dorothy
Woman thing. N. Gittelson. Harp Baz 104: 16+ N '70 *
GOLDBERG, Jerome. See Woloshin, A. A. jt. auth.
GOLDBERG, Leah
On Lea Goldberg & S. Y. Agnon. R. Alter. bibliog f Commentary 49:83-6 My '70 *
GOLDBERG, Margaret F. See Evans, A. S. jt. auth.
GOLDBERG, Norman
Crystal lens: yes, but ... il Pop Phot 66:80-1+ Ja '70
Inside front shutters. il Pop Phot 66:98-100+ Je '70
Lens: a most imperfect eye. il Pop Phot 66: 66-7+ Mr '70
Lenses are for testing. il Pop Phot 66:62-3+ F '70
Little lenses that make space clearer. il Pop Phot 66:114-15+ Je '70
Our men at Oberkochen. il Pop Phot 66:84-5+ Ja '70
Photo tools from toyland. il Pop Phot 66: 76-7+ My '70
Shop talk. See issues of Popular photography
Your camera's built-in margin for error. il Pop Phot 67:69-71+ S '70
GOLDBERG, Richard T. and Stein, Jane
Role of the psychiatric consultant in the state rehabilitation agency. bibliog Ment Hy 54: 553-8 O '70
GOLDBERG, Rube
Obituary
Time il pors 96:52 D 21 '70
GOLDBERG, Steven
Bob Dylan and the poetry of salvation. il pors Sat R 53:43-6+ My 30 '70
GOLDBERG variations; ballet. See Ballets— Criticisms
GOLDBERGER, Marvin L.
How physicists can contribute. il Phys Today 23:26-8+ D '70
GOLDBERGER, Paul
Bookshelf. Sr Schol 96:17 F 16 '70
Girls at Yale. il Todays Ed 59:50-1 O '70
New Haven under siege. Sr Schol 96:18 My 18 '70
Peaceful crowd, a violent few. Sr Schol 95:13 D 1 '69
Some thoughts about teachers and teaching. Todays Ed 59:17-18 F '70
GOLDBLAT, Jozef
Are tear gas and herbicides permitted weapons? il Bul Atom Sci 26:13-16 Ap '70
GOLDBLOOM, Maurice J.
Nixon so far. Commentary 49:29-38 Mr '70
GOLDEN, Harry
Israel and the Christian shrines. il Sat R 53: 15-16 D 19 '70
Remembrance of Chanukah. il House B 112: 58-9 D '70
GOLDEN, L. L. L.
Public relations. See Communications issues of Saturday review
GOLDEN, Rolland
Watercolor page; with biographical sketch. il por Am Artist 35:28-9+ Ja '71
GOLDEN bat; musical comedy. See Musical comedies, revues, etc.—Criticisms, plots, etc.
GOLDEN books. See Childrens literature
GOLDEN bowl hibiscus. See Hibiscus
GOLDEN door resort. See Health resorts, watering places, etc.
GOLDEN eagle aviation (firm)
CAB monitoring charter crash study. Aviation W 93:21 O 19 '70
Colorado crash may spur new regulations. C. E. Schneider. Aviation W 93:23-4 O 12 '70
Days of stillness at Wichita state; football team's plane crash. W. Johnson. Il Sports Illus 33:20-1 O 19 '70
GOLDEN Eagle passports. See Recreation— Fees
GOLDEN Gate angling and casting club. See Fishing clubs

GOLDEN Gate bridge. See San Francisco Bay bridges
GOLDEN Gate park. See San Francisco—Parks and playgrounds
GOLDEN goose; drama. See Holmes, R. V.
GOLDEN mean. See Moderation
GOLDEN plough tavern. See York, Pa.—Historic houses, etc.
GOLDEN press, inc.
Scratching the surface of nosepower: scents applied to the printed page. il Pub W 198: 42-3 Ag 24 '70
GOLDEN seals. See Seals (animals)
GOLDEN thread cypress. See False cypress
GOLDEN West airlines
Golden West seeks trunkline agreements. N. S. Himmel. Aviation W 92:47-9+ F 23 '70
GOLDENSOHN, Barry
Returned utopians; Alert scribe; 13th anniversary; Visual contact: Letter killeth, the letter giveth life; Light; poems. Poetry 117:166-73 D '70 *
Sybil the psychoanalysand in the subways; Aerial photo; New center of gravity; Noli me tangere; Worn bearing cross; Flaubert and Emma Bovary; poems. Poetry 115:263-8 Ja '70 *
GOLDFARB, Ronald L.
Brief for preventive detention. il N Y Times Mag p28-9+ Mr 1 '70
GOLDFARB, Sidney
Comment. A. Williamson. Poetry 115:284-5 Ja '70
GOLDFINGER, Nat
Labor costs and the rise in housing prices. il Mo Labor R 93:60-1 My '70
GOLDFISH
Extinction in goldfish facilitation by intracranial injection of RNA from brains of extinguished donors. W. G. Braud. bibliog il Science 168:1234-6 Je 5 '70
GOLDHAMMER, Keith, and Becker, G. L.
What makes a good elementary school principal? Am Ed 6:11-13 Ap '70
GOLDIN, Amy
Coy women, purple upholstery, cosmic landscapes. il Art N 69:40-5+ My '70
—and Kushner, Robert
Conceptual art as opera. il Art N 69:40-3 Ap '70
GOLDING, William O.
Rediscovery: William O. Golding. il Art in Am 58:84-5 Ja '70
GOLDKNOPF, David
Realism in the novel. Yale R 60:69-84 O '70
GOLDMAN, Albert
Beatles decide to let it be, apart. il Life 68: 38-9 Ap 24 '70
Drugs and death in the run-down world of rock music. il pors Life 69:32-3 O 16 '70
Life music review (cont) Life 68:13 Ja 30; 12 F 6; 17 Mr 20; 10 My 29; 13 Je 19; 69:10 Ag 7; 11 O 2; 18 O 16; 16 N 6 '70
Movies. Vogue 156:40 Ag 1; 34 Ag 15; 55 S 15 '70
Revolt: views from the campus. il Life 68: 18 My 15 '70
Thirty-year loser is a winner. por Life 69:8 Ag 28 '70
about
Scholar hooked on rock. R. Graves. il por Life 68:3 My 29 '70 *
Storm in section two. Newsweek 75:78-9 Ap 13 '70 *
GOLDMAN Don
Sense of wonder in a changing world. Nat Parks & Con Mag 44:25-6 Je '70
GOLDMAN, Eric F.
President, the people and the power to make war. Am Heritage 21:28-35 Ap '70
GOLDMAN, Harvey
New roles for principals. Clear House 45: 135-9 N '70
GOLDMAN, Jerry
Clay bugles. il Ceram Mo 18:27-9 Je '70
GOLDMAN, Judith
Prints of Mauricio Lasansky. il por Am Artist 34:62-8+ Mr '70
GOLDMAN, Leon
Warts and all. il Time 97:60+ Ja 4 '71 *
GOLDMAN, M. C.
Hottest gardeners in the west. Il Org Gard & Farm 17:69-72+ F '70
Organic classrooms are here! il Org Gard & Farm 17:66-72 S '70
GOLDMAN, Marshall I.
Convergence of environmental disruption; excerpts from address. March 1970. bibliog Science 170:37-42 O 2 '70
Costs of fighting pollution. bibliog f il Cur Hist 59:73-81+ Ag '70
Soviet dual economy. bibliog f Cur Hist 59: 232-7 O '70

GOLDMAN, Peter. See Fleming, K. jt. auth.
GOLDMAN, R. D. and Follett, E. A. C.
Birefringent filamentous organelle in BHK-21 cells and its possible role in cell spreading and motility. bibliog il Science 169:286-8 Jl 17 '70
GOLDMANN, Nahum
Future of Israel. For Affairs 48:443-59 Ap '70
Toward Israel's neutralization. Cur 119:53-7 Je '70

about

Doctor Goldmann's initiative. America 122:448 Ap 25 '70 *
GOLDMARK, Karl
Good marks for Goldmark; concert version of The queen of Sheba. I. Kolodin. Sat R 53:47 Ap 11 '70 *
Musical events; performance of the Queen of Sheba by the American opera society. W. Sargeant. New Yorker 46:128-9 Ap 4 '70 *
GOLDNER, Nancy
Dance. Nation 210:188-9, 252-3, 346-7, 477-8, 571-2, 669-70; 211:58-60, 445-6, 505-6, 604, 701-2 F 16, Mr 2, 23, Ap 20, My 11, Je 1, Jl 20, N 2, 16, D 7, 28 '70
GOLDREICH, Gloria
Bird; story. Redbook 135:70-1 O '70
Facts and fallacies about cesarean births. il Parents Mag 45:52-3+ My '70
When will your friend be leaving, Denny? story. Redbook 135:78-9 Ag '70
GOLDRING, Irene P. and others
Pulmonary hemorrhage in hamsters after exposure to proteolytic enzymes of bacillus subtilis. bibliog il Science 170:73-4 O 2 '70
GOLDSCHMIDT, Jean
Letter to the mayor. Atlan 225:58-9 F '70
Message. Atlan 226:104 D '70
GOLDSMITH, Arthur
What you need to know about model releases. il Pop Phot 66:58-9+ F '70
GOLDSMITH, Barbara
Where is the art? il Harp Baz 103:144-7 My '70
(ed) See Nichols, M. Grass, women and sex
GOLDSMITH, Harris
Beethoven on records. il Hi Fi 20:secI 51-6+ Ag; 66-8 S; 63-6+ O '70
Feuermann mementos. Hi Fi 20:secI 112 Ap '70
George Szell; in memoriam. por Hi Fi 20:82-3 N '70
Horowitz vs. Rubinstein. il Hi Fi 20:secI 67-8 Ag '70
Mozart happening with Peter Serkin. Hi Fi 20:secI 86 My '70
Must a great violinist play in tune? Hi Fi Sec I 20:91 Ja '70
Okko Kamu, a conductor to watch. por Hi Fi 20:114 O '70
Piano music of Mozart and Debussy. il Hi Fi 20:secI 81-3 Ap '70
Stokowski's splendid one-disc phase 4 Ninth. Hi Fi 20:secI 74 Ag '70
GOLDSMITH, Maurice
Crisis in Aspen; report on conference on Technology, man and culture. Bul Atom Sci 26:28-30+ N '70
GOLDSMITH, Oliver
She stoops to conquer; drama; adapted by P. T. Nolan. Plays 30:79-91 Ja '71
GOLDSMITH, Virginia G.
Barbershop reading. Ed Digest 35:40-1 My '70
GOLDSTEIN, Abraham S.
Newsmen and their confidential sources. New Repub 162:13-15 Mr 21 '70

about

Yale's new dean. por Time 95:66 Mr 23 '70 *
GOLDSTEIN, Bernard D. and others
Ozone and vitamin E. bibliog il Science 169:605 Ag 7 '70
GOLDSTEIN, R. M.
Mercury: surface features observed during radar studies. il Science 168:467-9 Ap 24 '70
—and Rumsey, H. Jr
Radar snapshot of Venus. il Science 169:974-7 S 4 '70
GOLDSTEIN, Richard
New culture. Vogue 156:99+ Ag 1 '70
Pop music. See occasional issues of Vogue to May, 1970
Randy Newman. il Vogue 157:84 Ja 1 '71
GOLDSTEIN, Shirley. See Christ, J. jt. auth.
GOLDSTEIN, Walter
Europe faces the technology gap. Yale R 59:161-78 D '69
Lessons of the Vietnam war. il Bul Atom Sci 26:41-5 F '70

GOLDSTEIN, William
On seeing through the academic looking glass. Clear House 45:131-4 N '70
GOLDSTON, Eli
New look at urban priorities; address, December 3, 1969. Vital Speeches 36:282-6 F 15 '70
GOLDWATER, Barry Morris, 1909-
Facts on SST; address, October 2, 1970. Vital Speeches 37:40-4 N 1 '70
Federal government; address, July 14, 1970. Vital Speeches 36:642-7 Ag 15 '70
Out West, we trust one another. por Life 69:4 O 9 '70

about

Innocence: the essence of the American heartland. E. J. Hughes. Sat R 53:25-8+ O 17 '70 *
Odd couple. pors Newsweek 76:18-19 S 7 '70 *
Olsen affair. Newsweek 76:76 S 14 '70 *
Olsen affair; objection to appointment. por Time 96:17 S 14 '70 *
Vintage Goldwater. W. A. Rusher. por Nat R 22-1117 O 20 '70 *
GOLES, Gordon G. and others
Instrumental neutron activation analyses of lunar specimens. bibliog il Science 167:497-9 Ja 30 '70
GOLF
Best in the South; interview, ed. by D. Green. S. Snead. il por Travel & Camera 33:46-51 F '70
Golf is not a fair game. H. Baron. il Esquire 73:142-9 Ap '70
How to save ten strokes off your game. A. Palmer. il Look 34:68-70+ Ap 7 '70
Keep your game young; ed. by C. Kirkpatrick. G. Sarazen. il Sports Illus 32:20-7 F 16 '70
King of the flat blade. il por Time 95:53 Ap 27 '70
Where a golf nut is king: Morocco. D. Jenkins. il pors Sports Illus 33:32-9 S 28 '70
See also
Golf courses
Swing (golf)
United States duffers' association

Anecdotes, facetiae, satire, etc.

My tussle with tees. M. Boyle. il Har Yrs 10:17-18 Jl '70

Caricatures and cartoons

Par for the course. Read Digest 97:90-1 S '70

Tournaments

All yours, Billy Boy; Masters champion. D. Jenkins. il pors Sports Illus 32:14-19 Ap 20 '70
Amateur week at the Heritage; professional golf classic at Harbour town golf links. C. Kirkpatrick. il Sports Illus 33:22-3 D 7 '70
Another opening, another tour; with list of golf's 1969 world champions. D. Jenkins. il por Sports Illus 32:18-20+ Ja 19 '70
Arnie's party was a divine affair; National Four-Ball championship at Laurel Valley. M. Mulvoy. pors Sports Illus 33:16-17 Ag 3 '70
Australia's cup runneth (thirty-two) under; World cup matches at Buenos Aires. D. Jenkins. il Sports Illus 33:28-9 N 23 '70
Big amateur shoot-out at generation gap. C. Kirkpatrick. il por Sports Illus 33:98+ S 14 '70
Blind man's buff at Hazeltine. J. Nicklaus. il por Sports Illus 32:40-3 Je 15 '70
British bombers downed by U.S. spitfires; Curtis cup matches. M. Mulvoy. il Sports Illus 32:50+ Ag 17 '70
Can trivia win the U.S. Open? D. Jenkins. il Sports Illus 32:34-6 Je 15 '70
Combat at Hazeltine; T. Jacklin winning U.S. Open. il por Time 96:43 Jl 6 '70
Compleat caddie; Masters championship. il por Newsweek 75:70 Ap 27 '70
Crosby weather. K. G. Richards. bibliog il Weatherwise 22:240-3 D '69
Dow Jones came up with Nichols and dimes; Upper Montclair country club. Clifton N. J. M. Mulvoy. il por Sports Illus 33:54-5 S 7 '70
End of a long, long drought; ed. by M. Mulvoy. J. Nicklaus. il por Sports Illus 33:16-17 Jl 27 '70
Free French strike again. D. Doust. il Sports Illus 33:60+ O 26 '70
Gary's garrison: bogeymen and bodyguards; at Monsanto Open. W. Bingham. il por Sports Illus 32:60+ Mr 23 '70

GONDWANALAND. See Continental drift

GONORRHEA
Stopping gonorrhea. Newsweek 76:61 Jl 6 '70

GONZALES, Laurence
Forgery; poem. Poetry 117:34-5 O '70

GONZALES, Pancho. See Gonzales, R. A.

GONZALES, Richard Alonzo
Big cat on the prowl. R. H. Boyle. il pors Sports Illus 32:14-17 F 9 '70 *
Pancho at forty-one. por Time 95:57 F 16 '70 *

GONZALEZ, Arturo F. jr
Get free help for your articles. Writers Digest 51:37+ Ja '71
How to moonlight as a freelancer. il Writers Digest 50:28-31 F '70

GONZALEZ, Edward
Cuba's recent setbacks. Cur 124:45-52 D '70

GONZALEZ, Henry B.
Excerpt from address, June 9, 1970. Cong Digest 49:240+ O '70

GONZALEZ DE LEDO, Liliana
Señor Augusto; story, tr. by J. Y. Bermúdez. Américas 22:14-15 S '70

GOOCH, Bryan N. S. See Westermark, T. jt. auth.

GOOCH, Robert M.
Old-road rabbits. il Outdoor Life 146:58-9+ D '70

GOOD, Robert A.
David's doctor. il por Newsweek 76:97-8 N 23 '70 *

GOOD and evil
California evil. C. Karpel. il Esquire 73:99-100 Mr '70
Word; good and evil. V. P. McCorry. America 122:228-inside back cover F 28 '70
See also
Sin

GOOD housekeeping (periodical)
This and other times. Good H 170:69 My '70

GOOD manners. See Courtesy

GOOD morning club. See Recreation for the aged

GOOD News convocation of United Methodists for evangelical Christianity. See Religious conferences

GOOD will in business
See also
Advertising, Institutional

GOOD woman of Setzuan; drama. See Brecht, B.

GOODALL, Jane van Lawick-. See Lawick, J. G. van

GOODBODY and company
Another chance for Goodbody. Bsns W p92 O 24 '70
Goodbody runs with the herd. Bsns W p55 D 26 '70
Goodbye to Goodbody? acquisition by Shareholders capital corp. Forbes 106:48 O 1 '70
Last act in the cliff-hanger? Wall Street rescue of brokerage house. il Time 96:78 N 9 '70
Merrill Lynch to the rescue? Bsns W p21 O 31 '70
Thundering Herd to the rescue. il Newsweek 76:73 N 9 '70
Why a broker needs a fund; membership of mutual funds in the NYSE. Bsns W p24 O 3 '70

GOODELL, Charles Ellsworth
After ten years; excerpts from addresses and from Congressional record, ed. by H. Dibble. Nat R 22:948-9 S 8 '70
Bridging the gulf with dissenting youth. Cur 122:32-4 O '70
Excerpt from the Abbott memorial lecture, January 13, 1970. Cong Digest 49:214+ Ag '70
Setting a deadline for withdrawal. Cur 115:30-2 F '70
about
Agnew: purging the GOP? il pors Newsweek 76:36 O 12 '70 *
Conservative upset in the making in liberal New York? il pors U S News 69:30-1 Ag 31 '70 *
Don Quixote rides again in New York; S. T. Agnew vs C. E. Goodell. P. J. Lavin. America 123:279 O 17 '70 *
Exit Goodell. New Repub 163:7 N 28 '70 *
Hoopla. New Yorker 46:26-8 S 26 '70 *
Onward and upward. Nat R 22:827-8 Ag 11 '70 *
Purging the GOP. H. L. Reiter. Nation 212:71-4 Ja 18 '71 *
Special Spiro pin. il por Time 96:17 O 12 '70 *
Vice President and the senator. Nat R 22:1096-7 O 20 '70 *
Who's kidding whom? Agnew's near-psychopathic crusade against Goodell. Commonweal 93:83-4 O 23 '70 *

GOODENOUGH, Ursula W. and Levine, R. P.
Genetic activity of mitochondria and chloroplasts; with biographical sketches. il Sci Am 223:10, 22-9 N '70

GOODFELLOW, Thomas Mackey
Countdown for America's railroads; address, September 22, 1970. Vital Speeches 37:56-8 N 1 '70

GOODHEART, Barbara
Sex in the schools: education or titillation? il Todays Health 48:28-30+ F '70
Winter's unvanquished foe: pneumonia. Todays Health 48:50-2+ N '70
—See Goodheart, C. R. jt. auth.

GOODHEART, Clyde R. and Goodheart, Barbara
New clues in the virus-cancer mystery. il Todays Health 48:32-5 Je '70

GOODHEART, Eugene
Rhetoric of violence. il Nation 210:399-402 Ap 6 '70; Same abr. Cur 118:9-13 My '70

GOODHEART, John
Pots and non-pots. il Sch Arts 70:30-1 Ja '71

GOODHUE, Tom
Report on the two cultures. New Repub 162:12-13 Je 20 '70

GOODING, Judson
Blue-collar blues on the assembly line. il Fortune 82:68-71+ Jl '70
Fraying white collar. il Fortune 82:78-81+ D '70
How Baltimore tamed the highway monster. il Fortune 81:128-9+ F '70
It pays to wake up the blue-collar worker. il Fortune 82:132-5+ S '70

GOODING, Richard
Exile in my own country. il por Look 34:19-23 F 24 '70

GOODMAN, Ernest
American lawyer makes notes. Nation 211:363-5 O 10 '70

GOODMAN, Jack, and Green, Alan
Bottoms up! excerpt from How to do practically anything. il Read Digest 97:173-6+ Ag '70

GOODMAN, Julian
U.S. broadcasting freedom; address, June 23, 1970. Vital Speeches 36:658-9 Ag 15 '70

GOODMAN, Lillian
Juan's right to read. il Am Ed 6:3-6 Jl '70

GOODMAN, Linda
It's not easy to please a virgin; poem. McCalls 98:97 Ja '71

GOODMAN, Mitchell
Conspiracy charges dropped against Coffin, Goodman. Chr Cent 87:655 My 27 '70 *

GOODMAN, Paul
Paul Goodman vis-à-vis; interview, ed. by H. S. Resnik. Sat R 53:44 My 23 '70
The young; poem. Nation 210:794 Je 29 '70
about
Heretic from the mass faith in scientific technology. H. S. Resnik. por Sat R 53:43+ My 23 '70 *
Unless I can think up an alternative or two. E. Goodheart. Nation 211:84-6 Ag 3 '70 *

GOODMAN, Robert
I love the way it sounds like God. il por Newsweek 76:36-7 O 19 '70 *

GOODMAN, Robert L.
TV on a chip. il Radio-Electr 41:69-72 Mr '70

GOODMAN, Ronald
Again and now; poem. Am Scholar 39:473 Sum '70

GOODMAN, Saul
Brief biography. See issues of Dance magazine
Extraordinary anniversary. il pors Dance Mag 44:28-31 N '70

GOODMAN, Walter
Question of repression. Commentary 50:23-8 Ag: 18 N '70
Rosenberg case: an inquest on an inquest. il pors N Y Times Mag p28-9+ My 24 '70
Senate v. Alan and Margaret McSurely. il pors N Y Times Mag p28-9+ Ja 10 '71

GOODNER, Mrs Robert
Goodner's own miniworld. S. A. Parvin. il por Hobbies 75:144+ Mr '70 *

GOODPASTER, Andrew Jackson
Further reductions could destroy stability in Europe; interview. il por U S News 69:61-3 D 7 '70

GOODRICH, B. F, company
B. F. Goodrich co.'s century-old standards. V. Louviere. Nations Bsns 58:13 Je '70

GOODRICH, Jim
Sun finally rises for Connie Hawkins. il pors Ebony 25:36-8+ F '70

GOODRICH, Lloyd
Exhibition preview: retrospective for Georgia O'Keeffe. il Art in Am 58:80-5 S '70
Thomas Nast's grand caricaturama. il Art N 69:58-61 Ap '70

GOODRICH, Samuel Griswold
Peter Parley; address, October 9, 1969. H. S. Canfield. bibliog il Horn Bk 46:135-41, 274-82, 412-18 Ap-Ag '70 *
GOODWIN, Georgie J.
Educational tool for all. il Am Lib 1:164-5 F '70
GOODWIN, Richard Naradof
Day in June. il McCalls 97:38+ Je '70
GOODYEAR, C. Phillip
Terrestrial and aquatic orientation in the starhead topminnow, fundulus notti. bibliog il Science 168:603-5 My 1 '70
GOODYEAR tire and rubber company
How millions were tied to the cord of the future. R. DeYoung. il Nations Bsns 58:80-1 Ja '70
GOOSE. See Geese
GOOSE as food. See Cookery—Poultry
GOOSE barnacles. See Barnacles
GOOSE carving. See Carving (meat, etc)
GOOSE LAKE prairie. See Prairies
GOOSE shooting. See Geese, Wild
GOOSEBERRIES
Gooseberries, culinary prize for northern gardens. L. Hill. il Org Gard & Farm 17:40-2 O '70
See also
Yangtaos
GOOSSEN, Eugene C.
Student of the night. por Vogue 156:96-7+ Ag 15 '70
(ed) See Morris, R. Artist speaks; Robert Morris
GOPALAN, K. and others
Rubidium-strontium, uranium, and thorium-lead dating of lunar material. bibliog il Science 167:471-3 Ja 30 '70
GORDIMER, Nadine
Authors & editors. B. A. Bannon. por Pub W 198:21-2 D 28 '70 *
GORDON, Arthur
Answer at nightfall. il Read Digest 97:143-5 S '70
Birth-control success story no. 1. Read Digest 96:80-4 Ja '70
Stranger who taught magic. Read Digest 96:77-80 Je '70
They go to prison on purpose. Read Digest 97:147-8+ Ag '70
GORDON, Bernard K.
United States policies in Southeast Asia. Cur Hist 59:321-5+ D '70
GORDON, Cyrus H.
New English Bible Old Testament. Chr Today 14:6-8 Mr 27 '70
about
Ancient landings in America. J. Lear. il Sat R 53:18-19+ Jl 18 '70 *
GORDON, Dane R.
Polyphony; poem. Chr Cent 87:361 Mr 25 '70
GORDON, Diane
What faith can do. il PTA Mag 65:6-8 bib-liog(p34) D '70
GORDON, Dudley
Aggressive librarian: Charles Fletcher Lum-mis. bibliog il por Wilson Lib Bul 45:399-405 D '70
GORDON, Edgar S.
High protein diet. House & Gard 137:104+ Ja '70
GORDON, Eileen
To Japan through art. il Sch Arts 69:42-3 Ap '70
GORDON, Ethel Edison
Mrs Marvel's magic carpet; story. Ladies Home J 87:104-5 My '70
GORDON, Harry
Americans are emigrating to Australia. il N Y Times Mag p75+ My 17 '70
GORDON, James S.
R. D. Laing: in search of a new psychiatry. il por Atlan 227:50-3+ Ja '71
GORDON, James Stewart-. See Stewart-Gordon, J.
GORDON, Jean
Editorial; changes in Dance magazine. il por Dance Mag 44:27 Ja '70
GORDON, John
Computerized municipal information system. il Am City 85:96-7+ Je '70
GORDON, Karen
Lying about your age. Harp Baz 103:228 Mr '70
GORDON, Leonard I.
New exercise for a longer life. il Vogue 156:152-3+ N 1 '70
GORDON, Lillian
Beyond the reality principle; illusion or new reality? bibliog f Am Imago 27:160-82 O '70
GORDON, Lincoln
Torture in Brazil. Commonweal 92:378-9+, 451+ Ag 7, S 18 '70

GORDON, Robbie
In my opinon. por Seventeen 29:234 My '70
GORDON, Robert
Novice newsman in the East room. por Time 96:12 D 21 '70 *
GORDON, Rodger W.
Is Dawes' limit out of date? R Pop Astron 63:16-18 Ag '69
GORDON, Sol
Bankruptcy of compensatory education. Ed Digest 36:28-31 D '70
GORDON, Stanley
(ed) See Voight, J. Voight: fresh eye on Hollywood
GORDON, T. J. and LeBleu, R. E.
Employee benefits, 1970-1985. il Harvard Bsns R 48:93-107 Ja '70
GORDON, William M. and others
ImPALLA: a new approach to secondary school language arts. il Engl J 59:534-9 Ap '70
GORDON research conferences
Gordon research conferences; 1970 program. A. M. Cruickshank. Science 167:1390-402+ Mr 6 '70
GORDONE, Charles
From the muthah lode. por Newsweek 75:95 My 25 '70
about
Prize winners. P. Garland. il pors Ebony 25:29-32+ Jl '70 *
GORDY, William D.
Georgia art potter. W. A. Reedy. il pors Ceram Mo 18:19-26 Je '70 *
GORE, Albert Arnold
Excerpt from address, April 30, 1970. Cong Digest 49:205+ Ag '70
about
After the fox. il por Newsweek 76:31 Ag 17 '70 *
Blood and Gore. P. R. Wieck. New Repub 163:11-12 O 24 '70 *
Good-bye Gore? Nat R 22:934 S 8 '70 *
Number one target. New Repub 163:6-7 Ag 22 '70 *
Tennessee: Gore vs. the White House. K. Leiter. Nation 211:396-9 O 26 '70 *
GORE, Daniel
Against the dogmatists: a sceptical view of libraries. bibliog Am Lib 1:953-7 N '70
GOREN, Charles Henry
Bridge. See issues of Sports illustrated
GORES, Joe
Library closes at nine. Writer 83:16-19 Jl '70
el GORESEY, Ahmed. See Ramdohr, P. jt. auth.
GORILLAS
Growing up with Snowflake. A. J. Riopelle. il Nat Geog 138:490-503 O '70
GORKIN, Jess
Needed: a Washington-Peking hot line. Cur 119:58-9 Je '70
GORKIN, Lev
Here is the latest radical plan; interview, ed. by G. Astor. Look 34:78 N 17 '70
GORKY, Maxim
Country people. Criticism
Nation 210:157 F 9 '70
Newsweek il 75:74 Ja 26 '70
Sat R 53:24 F 7 '70
GORMAN, Cliff
Man from The boys in the band. il pors Life 68:49-50 My 8 '70 *
GORMAN, Robert
Those wild watches with the built-in brains. il Pop Sci 197:80-2+ D '70
GORMAN, William D.
William D. Gorman and Jan Gary, H. Gasser. il pors Am Artist 34:36-42+ O '70 *
GORNICK, Vivian
Consciousness 2. il N Y Times Mag p22-3+ Ja 10 '71
GORSKI, Jack. See Clark, J. H. jt. auth.
GORTON, Carl
Carl Gorton pays fine, quits library board. Library J 95:2864+ S 15 '70 *
GORWITZ, Kurt. See Klee, G. D. jt. auth.
GOSHAWKS. See Hawks
GOSHEN, Charles E.
Diagnostic overkill and management of psychiatric problems. Ment Hy 54:306-9 Ap '70
GOSLING, Gordon D.
We hunted down a man-killer. il por Outdoor Life 146:45-7+ N '70
GOSPELS. See Bible—New Testament—Gospels
GOSSAGE, Wayne. See Kulleseid. E. jt. auth.
GOSSENS, Salvador Allende. See Allende Gossens, S.

GOSSET, Pierre, and Gosset, Renée
Tricks and treats for travelers in the U.S.A.
il Read Digest 97:178-80 S '70
GOSSET, Renée. See Gosset, P. jt. auth.
GOSSIP
Delicious morsels, deadly poison. Chr Today
15:35 N 6 '70
Feminine eye. S. Alexander. por McCalls 97:8
F '70
Fine male art. D. Lowe. il McCalls 97:48+
F '70
What gossiping reveals about you. T. I.
Rubin. por Ladies Home J 87:46+ F '70
GOSSIP columnists. See Journalists
GOSSIP columns. See Newspapers—Sections,
columns, etc.
GOSSWILLER, Richard
Social worker: survival expert in urban slums.
il Todays Health 48:59-62 S '70
GOTH, Louis A.
Jig is up! il Pop Mech 133:110-12+ Je '70
GOTHAM book mart. See Booksellers and
bookselling—New York (state)
GOTHIC architecture. See Architecture, Gothic
GOTHIC revival in architecture. See Architecture, Gothic
GOTHS
Barbarians. R. Winston. il Horizon 12:66-81
Sum '70
GOTT, Edwin Hays
Foreign threats to a basic industry; interview. il pors U S News 69:64-8 O 26 '70
GOTTFRIED, Martin
Theatre. Vogue 156:38 Ag 1; 102 N 1 '70
Two remarkable directors. il pors Vogue 155:
204-5+ My '70
GÖTTINGEN Handel festival. See Music festivals—Germany (Federal Republic)
GOTTLIEB, Elaine
(tr) See Singer, I. B. Dr Beeber
GOTTLIEB, Lou
God as landlord. il por Time 96:41+ Jl 20 '70 *
GOTTLIEB, P. and others
Lunar gravity over large craters from Apollo
12 tracking data. bibliog il Science 168:477-
9 Ap 24 '70
GOTTSCHALK, John S.
Future of sport fishing. il Parks & Rec 5:17-
19+ N '70
GOTTSCHALK, Louis Moreau
Forty piano works by Louis Moreau Gottschalk. R. Kammerer. il por Am Rec G
36:570-1 Ap '70 *
Gottschalk, musical Humboldt. M. M. Sterling. il por Américas 22:10-18 Ja '70
GOTTSCHO, Samuel Herman
Flower photographer. il Travel & Camera
33:60-2 Ap '70
Flowers and a lifetime of picture making.
Travel & Camera 33:72 Ap '70

about

Nonagenarian. New Yorker 46:34 Ap 4 '70 *
Sam Gottscho: nonagenarian flower power. J.
Deschin. il Pop Phot 67:80-3+ O '70 *
GÖTZ, Hermann
Holes in the cheese, cantos from the cantons. O. Daniel. Sat R 53:58 O 31 '70 *
GOUGH, Marion
All's fair in Japan. il Harp Baz 103:60-L
F '70
Travel (cont of) How to leave home and
like it. See issues of House beautiful
GOULD, Elliott
Elliott Gould as the entrepreneur. M. Mayer.
il pors Fortune 82:108-11+ O '70 *
Elliott Gould: the urban Don Quixote. il
pors Time 96:35-40 S 7 '70 *
Mallomar kid. J. Morgenstern. il por Newsweek 75:88+ Mr 9 '70
GOULD, Glenn
His country's most experienced hermit
chooses a desert-island discography. por
Hi Fi 20:secI 29+ Je '70
GOULD, Jack
Storm in section two. Newsweek 75:78-9
Ap 13 '70 *
GOULD, James L. and others
Communication of direction by the honey
bee. bibliog il Science 169:544-54 Ag 7 '70
GOULD, Jay, family
Realms of Gould: Lyndhurst. F. Kintrea. il
pors Am Heritage 21:46-65 Ap '70 *
GOULD, Laurence M.
Emergence of Antarctica: the mythical land.
il por Bul Atom Sci 26:5-10 D '70
GOULD, Richard A.
Journey to Pulykara: with biographical
sketch. il Natur Hist 79:6, 56-67 bibliog
(p90) D '70
GOULD, Richard G.
Transmission delays and echoes in satellite communications. il Electr World 84:
34-6+ Ag '70

GOULD, Robert E.
Early steps toward preventing drug abuse. il
PTA Mag 64:6-9 bibliog(p33) Mr '70
Wrong reasons to have children. il N Y
Times Mag p83+ My 3 '70
GOULD, Samuel Brookner
Changes coming in American colleges; interview. il por U S News 68:78-82 Je 8 '70
GOULD, Stephen Jay
Coincidence of climatic and faunal fluctuations in pleistocene Bermuda. bibliog il
Science 168:572-3 My 1 '70
GOULD, Susan
Final moments. il Opera N 34:24-5 Mr 21 '70
Latin expression. por Opera N 35:32 D 19 '70
GOULDEN, Joseph C.
Bell system kids the press. il Nation 210:
167-8 F 16 '70
Cops hit the jackpot. il Nation 211:520-33 N
23 '70
Helicopter bread line. Nation 212:50-2 Ja 11 '71
Military saboteurs. Nation 210:231-3 Mr 2
'70
Real good relationship. Nation 210:646-8 Je
1 '70
Voices from the silent majority. il Harper
240:67-72+ Ap; 241:12 Jl '70
GOULDING, Fred S. and Stone, Yvonne
Semiconductor radiation detectors. bibliog il
Science 170:280-9 O 16 '70
GOULDING, Ray. See Bob and Ray (comedians)
GOUNOD, Charles François
Faust. Criticism
New Yorker 46:107 Mr 7 '70 *
Gounod and Georgina. R. Rushmore. pors
Opera N 34:24-5 Ap 18 '70 *
Romeo and Juliet. Criticism
Opera N il 34:17-20 Ap 18 '70 *
GOURAS, Peter
Trichromatic mechanisms in single cortical
neurons. bibliog il Science 168:489-92 Ap
24 '70
GOURDS
Gourd that kept growing. T. Knolle. il Org
Gard & Farm 17:94+ Je '70
Quick wall cover, then gourds. il Sunset
144:242 My '70
GOURHAN, André Leroi-. See Leroi-Gourhan,
A.
GOURNAY, Marie le Jars de
Montaigne's soul mate. M. Bishop. por Horizon
12:102-3 Spr '70 *
GOUT
Gout and achievement. il Sci N 98:161-2 Ag
22 '70
Gout: what causes it and why it's not so
funny. B. Ford. il Sci Digest 67:76-81 Mr
'70
GOVERNMENT. See Nations; Political science; State, The
GOVERNMENT, Resistance to
Agnew's talk with five students; text of television debate. S. T. Agnew and others. il
pors U S News 69:86-8+ O 12 '70
Beaver 55 group convicted. Chr Cent 87:1059
S 9 '70
Berrigans: jail for the Christian conscience.
il pors Time 95:65-6 My 4 '70
Bulls and Berrigans. por Newsweek 75:106
My 4 '70
How much room is left for dissent? R. H.
Smith. Pub W 198:36 N 9 '70
Lessons from the Czech ordeal; guidelines
for nonviolent opposition. J. Power. il Chr
Cent 87:1011-13 Ag 26 '70
Obligations: essays in disobedience, war, and
citizenship, by M. Walzer. Review
Nation 211:278-80 S 28 '70. C. Cohen
Priest who stayed out in the cold. P. Nobile.
il por N Y Times Mag p8-9+ Je 28 '70
Prison journals of a priest revolutionary, by
P. Berrigan. Review
America 123:127 S 5 '70. T. J. Vittoria
Reflections: civil disobedience. H. Arendt.
New Yorker 46:70+ S 12 '70
Reform or resistance? J. E. Mulligan. Cath
World 212:131-3 D '70
Respect for law, respect for persons. J. B.
Sheerin. Cath World 211:50-1 My '70
Revolution of unreason. A. M. Bickel. New
Repub 163:18-21 O 17 '70
Rips in the fabric of the law. S. Hyman. il
Sat R 53:21-4+ Jl 11 '70
Strategy of nonviolent direct action interpreted by Beaver 55 protesters; interviews,
ed. by M. Stone. J. A. Mulert; T. Trost.
Chr Cent 87:610-12 My 13 '70
See also
Protests, demonstrations, etc.
Revolutions

Germany

Students against tyranny, by I. Scholl. Review
Nation 211:503-4 N 16 '70. C. L. Markmann

GOVERNMENT, Resistance to—*Continued*

Russia

Open conspiracy; presentation of Voices from the Russian underground by CBS news. R. L. Shayon. Sat R 53:62 Ag 22 '70

Wales

How green was my valley; protests against flooding of valleys. il Newsweek 75:48 Ap 6

GOVERNMENT agencies

United States

See Independent regulatory commissions; United States—Executive departments

GOVERNMENT aid. See Subsidies

GOVERNMENT and art. See Art and state

GOVERNMENT and business. See Industry and state

GOVERNMENT and music. See Music and state

GOVERNMENT and science. See Science and state

GOVERNMENT and the arts. See The Arts and state

GOVERNMENT and the press

Appeal for credibility; case of New York times reporter. E. Caldwell. Newsweek 75:74 My 11 '70

Battling Mitchell vs. the media. Nation 210:259-60 Mr 9 '70

Buddy-buddy. J. Aronson. Nation 210:792-4 Je 29 '70

Coordinating the media; dragnet subpoenas served on C.B.S. and other news reporters. Nation 210:163-4 F 16 '70

Equal time for the closed fraternity; excerpt from address. R. Mudd. il por Life 68:4 Mr 13 '70

Flexible guidelines. Newsweek 76:71 Ag 24 '70

How much privilege? San Francisco court rules on the press's rights. il por Newsweek 75:77-8 Ap 13 '70

If something has to give; protecting sources; case of M. Knops. por Newsweek 76:74 S 14 '70

Is right of access coming? G. Cranberg. Sat R 53:48-9+ Ag 8 '70

Journalist's privilege; San Francisco Court of appeals quashes federal subpoenas served on E. Caldwell. il por Newsweek 76:87 N 30 '70

Mitchell and the media; government's right to raw news materials bearing on criminal investigations. Nat R 22:191-2 F 24 '70

Need for a two-way dialogue. M. Lerner. Cur 114:46-7 Ja '70

New threat to the press. P. Hoffman. Nation 210:454 Ap 20 '70

Newsmen and their confidential sources. A. S. Goldstein. New Repub 162:13-15 Mr 21 '70

Notes and comment; government's campaign against the news media. New Yorker 46:29-30 F 28 '70

Objectivity and the American press. il Sr Schol 96:2-7 F 2 '70

Press monopoly; Mr Agnew's oversights. S. R. Barnett. Nation 210:72-5 Ja 26 '70

Privilege for the press; right of newspaper men to keep sources of information confidential. Nation 210:292-3 Mr 16 '70

Reforming the news media. Commonweal 91:467-8 Ja 30 '70

Say it again, Spiro; excerpts from address, 1970. S. T. Agnew. Nat R 22:608-9 Je 16 '70

Spiro Agnew's candles; proposed Newspaper preservation act. M. Mintz. New Repub 162:13-15 Ja 17 '70

Subpoena siege; have the news media become too big to fight? A. M. Adelson. il Sat R 53:106-8 Mr 14 '70

TRB from Washington; off-the-record. New Repub 163:6 O 10 '70

That liberal cabal; questioning the "Eastern-establishment media." Time 95:41 Je 8 '70

When the President meets the press. H. Smith. Atlan 226:65-7 Ag '70

See also

Government information
Presidents—United States—Press conferences

Germany (Federal Republic)

Ahlers affair. por Newsweek 75:68-9 F 23 '70

Russia

Crackdown; Pravda article attacks dissidents and western reporters in Russia. Newsweek 76:24 D 28 '70

GOVERNMENT appropriations and expenditures

See also subhead Appropriations and expenditures under names of countries, e.g. United States—Appropriations and expenditures

GOVERNMENT bonds. See Bonds, Government

GOVERNMENT centralization. See Decentralization in government

GOVERNMENT consultants

See also

Scientists in government

GOVERNMENT consultants, Municipal

Consultant game. Newsweek 76:46 Ag 3 '70

Consultant vs. urban anti-intellectualism. Am City 85:12 S '70

GOVERNMENT contracts. See Contracts, Government

GOVERNMENT corporations

See also

Overseas private investment corporation

GOVERNMENT decentralization. See Decentralization in government

GOVERNMENT documents. See Government publications

GOVERNMENT employees

Bearding Uncle Sam; discontent among federal employees. il Time 96:64-5 Ag 31 '70

Labor turmoil; truce and new threats. il Time 95:8-10 Ap 6 '70

Pandora's box has been opened. il Newsweek 75:25 Ap 6 '70

Postal strike; the effect. il U S News 68:16-19 Ap 6 '70

Reports; Washington; dissenters within. E. B. Drew. Atlan 225:4+ Ja '70

Uncle Sam's finest; National service league awards for the top ten federal employees. il Nations Bsns 58:34-7 S '70

U.S. jobs overseas; fewer of them now. il U S News 69:44 Jl 20 '70

See also

American federation of government employees

American federation of state, county and municipal employees

Bureaucracy

Collective bargaining—Government employees

Negro government employees

Postal employees

Public officers

Strikes—United States—Government employees

Appointment, qualifications, tenure, etc.

Details, transfers of U.S. employees to international organizations, executive order. R. M. Nixon. Dept State Bul 63:394 O 5 '70

Dismissal

Puritanical government; firing of postal clerk N. Mindel. Time 95:60 Ap 27 '70

See also

Layoff systems

Political activities

Dissent and reaction; vigilante activity at NBS labs in Boulder. P. M. Boffey. por Science 169:163-4 Jl 10 '70

Salaries, allowances, etc.

Automatic pay raise for federal workers every year? il U S News 69:19-20 D 21 '70

Automatic raises for federal workers; Nixon's plan. il U S News 69:48-9 Ag 10 '70

Federal pay raise; meaning to you. il U S News 68:30-1 Ap 27 '70

Return of pocketbook politics. H. Sidey. Life 68:4 Ap 3 '70

Training

Opening a new horizon; training the low-skilled for vacant public sector jobs. il Nations Bsns 59:90-2 Mr '70

GOVERNMENT employees unions

Pandora's box has been opened. il Newsweek 75:25 Ap 6 '70

Reflections on the future of bargaining in the public sector; excerpt from address, May 1970. E. W. Bakke. Mo Labor R 93:21-5 Jl '70

Union membership among government employees; with tables. H. P. Cohany and L. M. Dewey. Mo Labor R 93:15-20 Jl '70

Union shop coming for government workers? postal-reform bill. il U S News 68:85-6 Je 22 '70

When cities collide with the unions; with editorial comment. il Bsns W p24-7+, 56 Ja 2 '71

GOVERNMENT entertaining

Americana gets a presidential boost. il U S News 68:8 Mr 2 '70

Enlivening the gray; White House entertaining. il Time 95:20 Mr 30 '70

GOVERNMENT entertaining—*Continued*
Entertaining at the White House: Nixons set a record. il U S News 68:36-40 My 11 '70
Golf, ruffles and flourishes; A. Palmer and B. Casper at the White House after Greater Greensboro Open. P. Ryan. il Sports Illus 32:30-2+ Ap 13 '70
Show at the palace; reception at the presidential palace, Abidjan. H. Sutton. Sat R 53:44-5+ O 31 '70
See also
Washington, D.C.—Social life and customs
GOVERNMENT ethics. See Political ethics
GOVERNMENT finance. See Finance
GOVERNMENT housing projects. See Housing projects, Government
GOVERNMENT information
Blindfolding the Senate; concerning views of S. Symington. Nation 211:291 O 5 '70
Case for candor; Soviet space tests of satellite killer. R. Hotz. Aviation W 93:9 N 30 '70
Communication: the weak link in our foreign relations? address, October 16, 1970. W. D. Blair, jr. Dept State Bul 63:580-6 N 9 '70; Same. Vital Speeches 37:109-13 D 1 '70
Congress's right to know; withholding of military information by the executive branch. S. Symington. il N Y Times Mag p7+ Ag 9 '70; Same abr. Cur 22:36-43 O '70
Government test data are no buyer's guide. Bsns W p26 O 31 '70
Intelligence of Congress: information and public-policy patterns. E. Schneier. bibliog f Ann Am Acad 388:14-24 Mr '70
People's right to know: how much or how little? Time essay. J. L. Steele. Time 97: 16-17 Ja 11 '71
Purloined letter. K. Crawford. il por Newsweek 75:37 Mr 16 '70
Unequal duel; Symington subcommittee and U.S. involvement in Morocco, Libya and Ethiopia. Nation 211:482-4 N 16 '70
Where the bombs weren't. R. Hotz. Aviation W 93:11 N 16 '70
See also
Information, Freedom of
GOVERNMENT information officers. See Public information officers
GOVERNMENT information services. See Information services, Government
GOVERNMENT investigations
Banzhaf's bandits. Time 95:15-16 Mr 2 '70
Indictments for two: investigation of M. Sweig and N. Voloshen. por Time 95:16 Ja 26 '70
McCormack's reapers? Sweig-Voloshen cases. por Newsweek 75:16 Ja 26 '70
U.S's toughest customer: R. Nader & raiders. Read Digest 96:76-80 Mr '70
See also
Commissions of inquiry

Conglomerate corporations
Celler is tempted to call for a law. Bsns W p35 Ja 17 '70
Litton: the shy conglomerate. Bsns W p26 Mr 7 '70

Copper industry and trade
Nixon tackles the copper spiral. Bsns W p34 Ja 17 '70

Drug trade
Pill trial. por Time 95:32+ Mr 9 '70
Plain talk about the pill. il Newsweek 75:93 Mr 16 '70

Franchise system
Law shapes up on franchising. Bsns W p30 Ja 31 '70

Gambling
Eternal vigilance? Sports Illus 32:7 Ja 19 '70

Government contracts
Frenkil and his friends. il por Time 96:12-13 Jl 13 '70

Insurance companies
Insurers brace for federal action. Bsns W p29-30 F 7 '70

My Lai massacre
To the woodshed; the Hébert report. il Newsweek 76:27 Jl 27 '70

Stock exchange
Congress sets out to explore the Street; with editorial comment. Bsns W p 15-16, 56 Ja 2 '71

Spain
National scandal starts to unravel; Matesa affair. por Bsns W p56 My 23 '70
Scandal in the cabinet; the Matesa affair. Newsweek 76:44-5 Jl 27 '70

GOVERNMENT labor policy. See United States —Labor policy
GOVERNMENT laboratories. See Laboratories, Government
GOVERNMENT lending
Warnings of trouble in government lending. il U S News 69:80 D 7 '70
See also
Agricultural credit
GOVERNMENT officials. See Public officers
GOVERNMENT ownership
Nationalist barriers go higher. Bsns W p 126+ D 19 '70
See also
Railroads and state

Chile
Chile starts chasing the capitalists. il por Time 97:68 Ja 4 '71

Great Britain
Going public in the public sector. Fortune 82:45 D '70
Politics of selling off. il Time 97:71-2 Ja 18 '71

Italy
More state control over Montedison. Bsns W p28-9 O 31 '70

Peru
Social reform jolts the mine owners. il Bsns W p26 Ag 29 '70

South Africa
Nationalization strikes again. Fortune 82:190 Ag '70

Zambia
Friendly takeover in the copperbelt. il Bsns W p24+ Ag 22 '70

GOVERNMENT printing office. See United States—Government printing office
GOVERNMENT procurement. See Purchasing, Government
GOVERNMENT publications
Electronics self-study course. K. J. Englert. il Pop Electr 33:45-8 D '70
Historic bundles from Britain; British parliamentary papers, reprinted by the Irish university press. K. Rose. Sat R 53:33+ Je 20 '70
To catch a government document: two magic phrases. F. J. O'Hara; J. W. Brewster. bibliog il pors Wilson Lib Bul 44:940-6 My '70
Uncle Sam's bookstores are on the move. Pub W 197:75-6 Ap 13 '70
See also
America illustrated (periodical)
United States historical documents institute

Bibliography
Congressional documents relating to foreign policy. See issues of Department of state bulletin
Publications of the Department of state. See issues of Department of state bulletin
Selected government publications. F. J. O'Hara. See issues of Wilson library bulletin
Source material; comp. by D. Wasson. See issues of Foreign affairs
GOVERNMENT publicity
See also
Government and the press
Public information officers
GOVERNMENT regulation of industry. See Industry and state
GOVERNMENT scientists. See Scientists in government
GOVERNMENT service. See Public officers
GOVERNMENT spending policy
Back to reality. H. C. Wallich. Newsweek 75:81 F 16 '70
Can't afford what? New Repub 162:7-8 F 7 '70
Inflation and the prospects for prosperity. R. J. Saulnier. Read Digest 96:99-102 Mr '70
New kind of tax bite? Duns 95:108 Je '70
View from San Clemente; summary of news conference by R. M. Nixon. il por Newsweek 76:17 Ag 10 '70
Vote for your future; deficit spending and fiscal responsibility. il Farm J 94:54 N '70
Why federal deficit will get bigger. il U S News 69:70 Ag 10 '70
See also
United States—Appropriations and expenditures
GOVERNMENT statistics
Numbers that cost money. Bsns W p 108 Mr 14 '70
See also
United States—President's commission on federal statistics

GOVERNORS
Election impact: new faces in the national spotlight. il U S News 69:44-6 N 16 '70
Governors: a Democratic blitz. il Newsweek 76:44+ N 16 '70
Inside America: as it looks to the governors. il U S News 68:24-5 My 25 '70
New crop of governors. il Time 96:24+ N 16 '70
See also
Candidates, Political
Republican governors association

Succession
Maddox case: broad impact? por U S News 68:10-11 Ja 19 '70
GOVERNORS conference, 1970
Governors set their goals. U S News 69:16 Ag 24 '70
GOW, Windsor
His farm includes a great garden. A. G. Jensen. il pors Org Gard & Farm 17:107-10 O '70 *
GOWAN, Donald E.
Genesis and ecology: does subdue mean plunder? il Chr Cent 87:1188-91 O 7 '70
GOWLAND, Peter
Glamor by Gowland. Pop Phot 66:22+ Ja; 14 Je '70
GOWON, Yakubu
General Gowon: the binder of wounds. il Time 95:22 Ja 26 '70
Gowon's optimistic views. por Time 95:27-8 F 9 '70
Same Jack Gowon, but now he is the boss. il por Newsweek 75:51 Ja 26 '70
GOYA Y LUCIENTES, Francisco José de
Art: for fun or fulfilment; exhibition in Paris. K. Kuh. por Sat R 53:36-7 D 19 '70 *
Goya: madmen and monarchs; newly discovered paintings and well-known masterpieces at the Orangerie in Paris. J. López-Rey. il Art N 69:56-9+ O '70 *
GOYER, Jane
Hoarders anonymous. Har Yrs 10:31-2 N '70
GOZZI, Raymond, jr
On not becoming revolutionary; excerpt from Ready for the rain. il Nation 211:492-4 N 16 '70
GRABARKEWITZ, Bill
Surprise named Bill. il por Newsweek 75:87 Je 29 '70 *
GRABNER, George John
Man of the year loses a stripe. Bsns W p 17 Ag 8 '70 *
GRACE Patricia, consort of Rainier III, prince of Monaco
Princess Grace: how a royal beauty stays beautiful. R. Mann. il pors Ladies Home J 87:101-3+ My '70
GRACE, Doris
When to put your foot down. il PTA Mag 64:2-4 bibliog(p34) My '70
GRACE, Nancy
Does Amsterdam have the best airport in the world? Holiday 47:16+ Ap '70
GRACE (theology)
God's Grace is amazing. L. N. Bell. Chr Today 14:22-3 Je 5 '70
GRACE, Grace, Grace, Grace; story. See Nissenson. H.
GRACIE, Bill
Alarms stop burglars. il Radio-Electr 41:33-6 N '70
GRADE crossings. See Railroads—Crossings
GRADERS (excavating machinery)
Fresh look at graders, flexible heavyweights; Duluth, Minn. il Am City 85:44 O '70
GRADING and marking (students)
Child left back may leave school. Sr Schol 96:Schol Teach 1 Ap 6 '70
College grades: predictors of what? letter. H. C. Lindgren. Science 169:6-7 Jl 3 '70; Discussion. bibliog 170:491-2 O 30 '70
Contract for grades. E. F. Dash. bibliog il Clear House 45:231-5 D '70
Death of the report card. B. Bard. Ladies Home J 87:160-1 O '70
Evaluation of children's picture making. E. Walton. il Sch Arts 70:6-7 N '70
Grading strikers. Time 95:44 My 25 '70
How much is a Beesworth? R. K. Sparks. Clear House 44:544-6 My '70
Making the grade. L. A. Gutkind. il Schol Teach Sec Teach Sup p6-8+ Ap 6 '70
Marking and reporting pupil progress. Todays Ed 59:55-6 N '70
Self-evaluation; or, How to defang an educational albatross. A. Beck. Sch Arts 70:38-9 S '70
Skipping or repeating school grades: why so controversial? il Good H 172:126 Ja '71
Student evaluation; a design for the middle school. G. F. Vars. il Clear House 45:18-21 S '70
Students grade themselves. C. D. Jackson. il Todays Ed 59:24-5 O '70

Teacher perceptions of correlates of academic achievement. C. J. Dunn and G. T. Kowitz. bibliog f Sch & Soc 98:370-2 O '70
GRADING of pork. See Meat—Grading and standardization
GRADING of swine. See Swine—Grading and standardization
GRADUATE schools. See Colleges and universities—Graduate work
GRADUATE students
Federal aid
See Student aid
GRADUATE work. See Colleges and universities—Graduate work
GRADUATES, College. See College graduates
GRADUATES, High school. See High school graduates
GRADUATION. See Commencements
GRADUATION addresses. See Baccalaureate addresses
GRADY, Roger C.
Colic: a new approach to a common problem. il Parents Mag 45:42-3+ Jl '70
GRAEBNER, Norman A.
NATO; an uneasy alliance. Cur Hist 58:298 303+ My '70
United States and the Soviet Union: the elusive peace. Cur Hist 59:193-8+ O '70
GRAESER, Henry J.
America's drinking water is . . . is not safe il pors Am City 85:77-9+ Je '70
GRAF, Rudolf F. and Whalen, G. J.
Alarm keeps its electric eye out for burglars il Pop Sci 196:94-5 Je '70
Blinker reminds you to gas up. il Pop Sci 196:98+ Ap '70
Build a better battery charger. il Pop Sci 197:101-3+ Jl '70
Build your own indoor-outdoor electronic thermometer. il Pop Mech 133:150-2 F '70
Electronic football lets you play like the pros. il Pop Mech 134:146-50+ O '70
Electronic stethoscope probes the unhearable. il Pop Sci 196:39-101 F '70
Fill 'er up! The blinker says so. il Pop Sci 197:95+ N '70
Instant-on for AC/DC radios. il Mech Illus 66:96-7 N '70
Put a speed control on your windshield wipers. il Pop Mech 133:138-9 Ja '70
—See Rimmer, D.; Whalen, G. J. jt. auths.
GRAFF, M. M.
Crocuses. il Horticulture 48:18-21 O '70
GRAFFITI
Alfresco history; erotic graffiti. il Time 95: 61+ Ap 13 '70
Gordion graffiti. Sci Digest 67:43-4 F '70
Graffiti. J. Ciardi. Sat R 53:10+ My 16 '70
GRAFFITO decoration
Sgraffito with liquid enamels. F. Ball. il Ceram Mo 18:26-8 S '70
White-on-white enameling; liquid enamel for sgraffito work. F. Ball. il Ceram Mo 18:20-1+ O '70
GRAFTING
Grafting pecan trees, Texas style. J. Gillette. il Org Gard & Farm 17:46-9 O '70
GRAFTING (surgery) See Transplantation of organs, tissues, etc.
GRAFTON, Samuel
What you can do about the drug problem. il Parents Mag 45:72-5+ N '70
GRAFTON, Sue
Where does a novel begin? Writer 83:17-19 F '70
GRAGG, Fred C.
Planting the South's third forest: more tree power. il por Am For 76:12-13+ O '70
GRAHAM, Augusta
Parent's manifesto: our grievances. PTA Mag 64:2-5 bibliog(p34) Mr '70
GRAHAM, Billy
Jesus and the liberated woman. por Ladies Home J 87:40+ D '70
Turn, baby, turn: the evangelism of tomorrow. Ladies Home J 86:128 D '69
Unfinished dream: address, July 4, 1970. Chr Today 14:20-1 Jl 31 '70
What the Bible says about sex. por Read Digest 96:117-20 My '70
about
Are sports good for the soul? il por Newsweek 77:51-2 Ja 11 '71 *
Billy Graham and civil religion. D. Kucharsky. Chr Today 15:56+ N 6 '70 *
Billy Graham in Big Orange country. R. L. Love. il por Chr Today 14:33-4 Je 19 '70 *
Black concerns in the White House. Chr Today 14:46+ Ap 10 '70 *

GRAHAM, Billy—about—*Continued*
Charisma of Billy Graham. C. W. Hall. por Read Digest 97:88-92 Jl '70
Euro 70 crusade: never, so many. D. Foster. il por Chr Today 14:24, 38 My 8 '70 *
From tents to stadiums to straw. Chr Today 14:36 Ja 16 '70
Graham Dortmund crusade. D. Foster. Chr Today 14:34 Ap '70 *
Graham in Gotham. D. Kucharsky. Chr Today 14:30-1 Jl 17 '70 *
How Nixon used the media, Billy Graham, and the good Lord to rap with students at Tennessee U. G. Wills. il Esquire 74:119-22+ S '70 *
In praise of youth; East Tennessee crusade. pors Time 95:13 Je 8 '70 *
Notes and comment. New Yorker 46:35-7 O 10 '70 *
Preaching and the power il pors Newsweek 76:50-5 Jl 20 '70 *
Showers of blessing. Baton Rouge crusade. A. Matthews. il Chr Today 15:48-9 N 20 '70 *
GRAHAM, Dale E. See Skinner, D. M. jt. auth.
GRAHAM, Don
Amateur scientist; ed. by C. L. Stong. il Sci Am 222:141-3 Je '70
GRAHAM, Frank, 1925-
Dilemma of Machiasport. il Audubon 72: 106-11 Jl '70
Man behind M.A.S.H. il por Todays Health 48:24-7 D '70
Reports: pesticides. Atlan 226:22+ S; 36+ N '70
Sanctuary on the subway. il Audubon 72: 54-9 My '70
Silent spring: the genesis and the storm; excerpts from Since silent spring. il por Audubon 72:70-2+ Ja '70
Tempest in a nuclear teapot. il Audubon 72: 12-19 Mr '70
That mess on the Prestile. il Am Heritage 21: 106-12 F; 95 Ag '70
GRAHAM, Fred P.
Black crime: the lawless image. il Harper 241:64-5+ S; 14 D '70
Business and the Nixon court. il por Duns 96:40-2 O '70
GRAHAM, Grace
Can the public school survive another ten years? Ed Digest 36:1-3 O '70
GRAHAM, Hugh Davis
Paradox of American violence: a historical appraisal. bibliog f Ann Am Acad 391:74-82 S '70
GRAHAM, James A. Maxtone-. See Maxtone-Graham, J. A.
GRAHAM, Janet
Oberammergau: the village that kept its vow. il Read Digest 97:193-4+ Jl '70
This woman fights the Sahara with trees. il pors Sci Digest 69:20-3 Ja '71
GRAHAM, Jeffrey B. and Rosenblatt, R. H.
Aerial vision: unique adaptation in an intertidal fish. bibliog il Science 168:586-8 My 1 '70
GRAHAM, John L. and Filbert, J. W.
Unconventional approach. il Am City 85:72-5 O '70
GRAHAM, Martha
Dance. N. Goldner. Nation 211:446 N 2 '70 *
In praise of Martha Graham il por Dance Mag 44:68-9 Ja '70
Martha Graham: past, present, future. W. Terry. il por Sat R 53:61-2 O 24 '70 *
GRAHAM, Martha, and dance company. See Martha Graham and dance company
GRAHAM, Patricia Albjerg
Women in academe. bibliog Science 169:1284-90 S 25 '70
GRAHAM, Robert A.
Legacy of conscience. il America 123:312-15 O 24 '70
GRAHAM, Robin Lee
Robin sails home. il pors Nat Geog 138:504-45 O '70
GRAHAM, Saxon. See Gewirtz, H. jt. auth.
GRAHAM magnetics, inc.
Tougher tape for computers. il Bsns W p 124 Je 13 '70
GRAHAME, Arthur
Last chance for Atlantic salmon? il Outdoor Life 145:41-3+ Je '70
GRAHAME, Kenneth
Note on Kenneth Grahame. N. Braybrooke. il Horn Bk 46:504-7 O '70 *
GRAIN
What's cooking?
Inflation, grains and hippies. F. Nusz. il Org Gard & Farm 17:110-11+ Ap '70
See also
Feeding and feeding stuffs—Grain
also names of cereal plants, e.g. Barley

Diseases and pests
See also
Greenbugs
Drying
How low-temperature drying works. il Suc Farm 68:D26 O '70
How to operate a bin dryer without overdrying. P. B. Jones. Suc Farm 68:B2 N '70
Handling
See Grain handling
Harvesting
See also
Wheat—Harvesting
Prices
Is there any future in grain farming? R. Krumme. il Suc Farm 68:no5 19 Mr '70
Storage
Inspect grain in storage. Suc Farm 68:A8 O '70
See also
Corn—Storage
Granaries
GRAIN handling
Grain legs and augers that speed up corn harvest. il Farm J 94:18-19 S '70
Ideas for better grain moving. il Suc Farm 68:41 Je '70
Move grain the easy way. G. L. Earle. il Suc Farm 68:B28 Ja '70
GRAIN trade
Whiplash; corn-blight scare. Forbes 106:58 S 15 '70
GRAINGER, Percy
Percy Grainger posy. R. D. Darrell. por Hi Fi 20:sec1 86 Ag '70 *
GRAMCO international
Adverse tide hits offshore funds. Bsns W p50 O 17 '70
Bonn makes it rough for Gramco. Bsns W p84 O 10 '70
Gramco: the second domino. por Time 96: 79-80 O 19 '70
Gramco's plunge. Newsweek 76:96-7 O 19 '70
Is the game up at Gramco? with editorial comment. J. Ross-Skinner and A. Hershman. il por Duns 96:3, 28-31+ S '70; Reply with rejoinder. R. Garcia-Navarro. 96:15-16 O '70
GRAME, Theodore C.
Music in the Jma al-Fna of Marrakesh. bibliog f il Mus Q 56:74-87 Ja '70
GRAMICIDIN
Conformations at local energy minimums for gramicidin S; optical calculations. E. S. Pysh. bibliog Science 167:290-2 Ja 16 '70
GRAMMAR, English. See English language—Grammar
GRAMMAR schools. See Education, Elementary
GRAMONT, Nancy de. See De Gramont, N.
GRAMONT, Sanche de. See De Gramont, S.
GRAN, Eldon E.
If I have but one life to live, let me live it above the median. Ed Digest 36:32-3 O '70
GRANADOS, Robert R. See Chen, T. A. jt. auth.
GRANARIES
He still cribs his ear corn. il Suc Farm 68: no4 D32 Mr '70
This grain center stays modern. il Suc Farm 68:no5 B6 Mr '70
GRANATELLI, Andy
Rap 'n 'pinion. por Motor T 22:18 My '70
GRANBECK, Marilyn
Stories without plot. Writers Digest 50:45-6 Ja '70
GRAND BAHAMA ISLAND
Black power on the beach. il Time 96:82 O 19 '70
See also
Freeport
GRAND CANYON
Grand Canyon by helicopter. B. Thomas. il Travel 133:46-50 Je '70
Grand Canyon: the world below the rim. D. E. Weaver, jr. il Nat Parks 44:10-14 Ja '70
Heck of a hole in the ground. il Newsweek 75:23 Je 22 '70
Trees on the rim; photographs. P. D. Duncan. Am For 76:12-15 Jl '70
GRAND CANYON NATIONAL PARK
Moods of the North Rim: Grand Canyon National Park. J. Fain. il Nat Parks & Con Mag 44:4-7 My '70
GRAND COULEE power and reclamation project
Grand Coulee: heading toward first place. E. Gross. il Sci N 97:329 Mr 28 '70
GRAND JUNCTION, Colo.
America's most radioactive city. N. Wood. McCalls 97:46+ S '70

GRAND ole opry (radio program) See Radio broadcasting—Music

GRAND PORTAGE NATIONAL MONUMENT
Voyageur. R. L. Nelson. il Nat Parks & Con Mag 44:20-4 D '70

GRAND prix cars. See Automobiles, Racing

GRAND right and left; story. See Kassan, R.

GRAND TETON NATIONAL PARK
Breakfast ride. N Wood il Travel & Camera 33:10+ Jl '70
Cruising the high country. F. M. Paulson. il Field & S 75:44-5+ D '70
How to wreck a national park; overcrowding. C. S. Wren. il Look 34:77-8+ Je 16 '70
There's a water-level way to explore Yellowstone and Grand Teton Parks. il Sunset 144:44-6 Je '70

GRANDMOTHERS. See Grandparents

GRANDO, Michael
Jewelry of Michael Grando. E. Case. il Am Artist 34:38-44+ F '70

GRANDPARENTS
Babies after sixty-five? interview, ed. by K. F. Westfall. I. Boyle. il Har Yrs 10:34-7 Ap '70
Goodbye, grandma. M. M. Weiser. Har Yrs 10:13 N '70
Meddling grandmothers. B. Bettelheim. Ladies Home J 87:26+ S '70
On being a grandmother. M. Mead. il Redbook 135:70-1+ Jl '70
See also
Foster grandparent program

Les GRANDS ballets canadiens. See Ballet—Canada

GRANITE
Boston granite. il Arch Forum 132:64-9 Je '70
Georgia granite. W. A. Bake, jr. il Natur Hist 79:32-7 O '70
Rock bottom; floor of the Caribbean. L. Purrett. il Sci N 99:31 Ja 9 '71
Rubidium-strontium date of possibly 3 billion years for a granitic rock from Antarctica. M. Halpern. bibliog il Science 169:977-8 S 4 '70

GRANT, Bess (Myerson)
(ed) How other women save money in stores. il Redbook 136:68-9+ N '70

GRANT, Bob
Florida bass invade California. il Field & S 74:46-7+ F '70
Ocean paradise. il Field & S 74:55-7+ Mr '70
Stripers in the desert. il Field & S 75:52-3+ My '70

GRANT, Cary
Day at the office with Cary Grant. D. Lilly. por Ladies Home J 87:142-3 N '70 *

GRANT, Gerald
Q. Are parochial schools the answer? A. Well, er, uhh ... Commonweal 92:85-7 Ap 3 '70

GRANT, Mary Kent
Mystery, detective and suspense. See first issue of each month of Library journal

GRANT, Stephen
Second marriage; poem. Poetry 115:232 Ja '70

GRANT, W. Brewer
Patients nobody wants. Ment Hy 54:162-5 Ja '70

GRANT, W. T. company
Great what-is-it il Forbes 105:15 Ja 15 '70

GRANT, W. Vance
Statistical look at education in the United States. il Am Ed 6:13-15 O '70

GRANT, W. Wayne
Rich churches and poor people. Chr Today 14:11-12 F 27 '70

GRANT, William
Where did everyone go to? New Repub 163:20 S 5 '70

GRANT, Zalin B.
Bearing gifts to Greeks. New Repub 162:19-21 Mr 7 '70
Why the Paris talks are getting nowhere. New Repub 163:17-19 O 10 '70

GRANTHAM, Jared J.
Vasopressin: effect on deformability of urinary surface of collecting duct cells. bibliog il Science 168:1093-5 My 29 '70

GRANTS-in-aid
We are embarked on a great new mission of reform; address, July 27, 1970. E. L. Richardson. por U S News 69:57-9 Ag 17 '70
See also
Economic assistance, Domestic

GRANULAR applicators. See Agricultural machinery

GRANULOSIS virus. See Viruses, Insect

GRAPE boycott. See Boycott

GRAPE festival, Naples, N.Y. See Festivals—New York (state)

GRAPE industry. See Viticulture

GRAPE pickers strike. See Strikes—United States—Farm labor

GRAPEFRUIT
See also
Cookery—Fruit

GRAPES
Doctored grapes? J. R. Coyne, jr. il Nat R 22:88 Ja 27 '70
See also
Viticulture
Wine making

GRAPHIC arts
Beauty in the bizarre. il Time 95:74-5+ Ap 27 '70
See also
Prints

Bibliography
Books about the graphic arts (cont) il Pub W 197:56-7 Je 15; 198:40 Ag 17 '70
Graphic art books; illustrated reviews (title varies) (cont) il Am Artist 34:52-6+ My; 26-8+ O '70

Exhibitions
Louvre holds retrospective of Push pin studio's graphics. il Pub W 197:70-2 Ap 13 '70
Two controversial exhibitions; Graphics 1: new dimensions, and Information, at the Museum of modern art, New York. il Pub W 198:48-50 S 21 '70

Study and teaching
Prints of Mauricio Lasansky; the university workshop of printmaker and teacher. J. Goldman. il por Am Artist 34:62-8+ Mr '70

GRAPHIC arts research and engineering council. See Research and engineering council of the graphic arts industry, inc.

GRAPHIC data processing. See Computer graphics

GRAPHIC methods
Find R.M.S. values graphically. W. A. Vincent. il Electr World 84:17 Jl '70
Graphs that look funny but tell you a lot; graphs on semi-log paper. il Changing T 24:34-7 N '70
See also
Flow charts
Organization charts
Regge trajectories

GRAPHIC recorders. See Recording instruments

GRAPHICS, Computer. See Computer graphics

GRAPHITE fibers. See Fibers

GRAPHOLOGY
Is your script showing? N. Olyanova. il Seventeen 29:150-1+ Mr '70

GRAPHOTHERAPY
Pen-and-pencil therapy. il Time 96:51 S 21 '70

GRASS, Günter
Dentist's chair as an allegory of life. il pors Time 95:68-70+ Ap 13 '70 *
Günter Grass' tale of men and molars in a mended Germany. L. Kriegel. Commonweal 92:195-6 My 8 '70 *
View from the dental chair. J. Updike. New Yorker 46:133-6 Ap 25 '70 *

GRASS, Artificial. See Turf, Artificial

GRASS clippers. See Lawn tools, equipment and supplies

GRASS clippings. See Lawn thatch

GRASS cutters. See Lawn tools, equipment and supplies

GRASS grub beetle. See Beetles

GRASS lands. See Prairies

GRASS shears. See Lawn tools, equipment and supplies

GRASS trimmers. See Lawn tools, equipment and supplies

GRASSES
How to stop panic grass in corn. B. Coffman. il Farm J 94:40A Ap '70
See also
Bamboo
Fescue
Lawns
Pangola grass

Diseases and pests
See also
Lawns—Diseases and pests

GRASSLANDS. See Prairies

GRATITUDE
See also
Thanksgiving

GRATZ, Rebecca
Portraits of Rebecca Gratz by Thomas Sully. H. R. London. pors Antiques 98:115-17 Jl '70 *

GRAVEREAUX, Daniel
How important is a level turntable? il Hi Fi
20:sec1 57 Ap '70
GRAVES, Charles N. and Biggers, J. D.
Carbon dioxide fixation by mouse embryos
prior to implantation. bibliog il Science
167:1506-8 Mr 13 '70
GRAVES, Dorothy
Taking the child's emotional temperature. il
PTA Mag 64:5-7 bibliog(p35) F '70
GRAVES, Elizabeth Minot
Selected list of children's books (cont) Com-
monweal 92:245-8+; 93:198-207 My 22, N 20
'70
GRAVES, John
Aunt Clara's luminous world. il Am Herit-
age 21:46-8 Ag '70
GRAVES, Robert
Ambrosia of Dionysus and Semele: poem.
Atlan 225:113 F '70
Brief reunion; poem. New Yorker 46:40 Ap 11
'70
Death of love; poem. Harper 240:28 Mr '70
Judges; poem. New Yorker 46:38 Ap 25 '70
My ghost; poem. Atlan 227:85 Ja '71
Robbers' den; poem. Atlan 225:90 Mr '70
Strayed message; poem. Atlan 226:103 Jl '70

about

Graves yawns. R. Howard. Poetry 116:107-
10 My '70 *
If it looks like Zeus, and sounds like Zeus,
it must be Robert Graves. J. Skow. il Es-
quire 74:144-5+ S '70 *
Keys to ourselves. J. Kessler. pors Sat R 53:
36 My 2 '70 *
Robert Graves: a poet's quest for meaning.
P. L. Sanders. Engl J 59:23-6 Ja '70
GRAVES, Ronald
Once a medic, now a medex. il pors Life 68:
67-8+ Je 12 '70 *
GRAVES, Wallace B.
Strategies for a real academic revolution;
adaptation of address. September 1969. il
Todays Ed 59:26-7 S '70
GRAVESTONES. See Sepulchral monuments
GRAVINA, Peter
Porto Venere and the Cinque Terre. Harp
Baz 103:68+ Ap '70
GRAVITATION
Space age support for Einstein. il Sci N 98:
395 N 21 '70
See also
Relativity (physics)
GRAVITY
Earth's gravity field: relation to global tec-
tonics. W. M. Kaula. bibliog il Science 169:
982-5 S 4 '70
Gravity's tug on the ocean floor. il Sci N
97:191-2 F 21 '70
Lunar gravity over large craters from Apollo
12 tracking data. P. Gottlieb and others.
bibliog il Science 168:477-9 Ap 24 '70
See also
Geotropism (botany)
GRAVITY waves
Defending coincidences. D. E. Thomsen. il
Sci N 97:206 F 21 '70
Experimental relativity hits the big time. G.
B. Lubkin. il Phys Today 23:41+ Ag '70
Far-out waves. il Time 95:66 F 9 '70
Gaining on gravity waves. D. E. Thomsen.
il Sci N 98:44-5 Jl 11 '70
Gravitational waves: the evidence mounts.
G. L. Wick. bibliog il Science 167:1237-9
F 27 '70
Gravity waves may come from black holes.
D. E. Thomsen. il Sci N 98:480-1 D 26 '70
Things that go bump. il Sci Am 222:58 Mr '70
Trying to confirm Weber waves. il Sci N
98:366 N 7 '70
GRAY, Alec
Alec Gray's daffodils. J. Kilborn. il por
Horticulture 48:22-3+ Ap '70 *
GRAY, Allan P.
Should college applicants be selected by lot-
tery? letter. Science 167:1075 F 20 '70
GRAY, Cleve
Marin and music il por Art in Am 58:72-81
Jl '70
GRAY, Darrell
Elephants; Poem: Lightning arranges us: To-
day is water; For the future occupants;
Thought; Planets; poems. Poetry 115:401-10
Mr '70
GRAY, David
Un-hostile park. il Parks & Rec 5:26-8+ F
'70
GRAY, David M.
No place for blue-collars. Commonweal 93:
13-14. 79 O 2, 16 '70
GRAY, Francine du Plessix. See Du Plessix,
F.

GRAY, J. A. and Ball, G. G.
Frequency-specific relation between hippo-
campal theta rhythm, behavior, and amo-
barbital action. bibliog il Science 168:1246-8
Je 5 '70
GRAY, John M.
Rating your school. Todays Ed 59:32-3 D '70
GRAY, Nancy C.
California wine wizard. Am Home 73:42+
N '70
Grand old lady of Coronado. il Am Home 73:
30+ S '70
GRAY, Wood
(comp) Articles and other books received;
United States. See issues of American his-
torical review
GRAYLING fishing
Drive-in grayling; Big Hole River, Mont.
N. Strung. il Field & S 75:74-5+ My '70
GRAYSON, George W. Jr
Peru's military government. bibliog f Cur
Hist 58:65-72+ F '70
GRAYSON, Lawrence P.
Education beyond the horizon. bibliog Sci-
ence 170:1376-82 D 25 '70
GRAZIANO, John
Lupus Hellinck: a survey of fourteen masses.
bibliog f il Mus Q 56:247-69 Ap '70
GRAZIER, Harve
Flying visit. Flying 87:22-3 N '70
GRAZING
Cows on Padre Island; destroying dune
vegetation. C. Cottam. il Nat Parks & Con
Mag 44:27 S '70
Make milk, not bloat; pasturing alfalfa. Farm
J 94:D9 Je '70
Pasture your beef cows year round. Suc
Farm 68:B14 S '70
600 lbs. beef per acre from fertilized grass.
Farm J 94:52K Ap '70
See also
Pastures
GRAZING permits. See Grazing
GREAT ABACO ISLAND. See Bahama Is-
lands
GREAT American management and research
company. See Gramco international
GREAT Americans, Hall of fame for. See New
York university—Hall of fame for great
Americans
GREAT Atlantic and Pacific tea company
A&P's own brand of consumerism. il Bsns W
p32 Ap 11 '70
Mafia war on the A&P. E. H. Methvin. Read
Digest 97:71-6 Jl '70
New teeth for the lion? por Forbes 105:44
F 15 '70
GREAT BRITAIN
See also
Abortion—Laws and legislation—Great Bri-
tain
Aeronautics, Commercial—Great Britain
Aerospace industries—Great Britain
Agricultural administration—Great Britain
Agriculture—Great Britain
Air pollution—Great Britain
Airlines—Great Britain
Airplanes, Military—Great Britain
Astronomical observatories—Great Britain
Atomic power—Great Britain
Automobile industry and trade—Great Brit-
ain
Banks and banking—Great Britain
Birth control—Great Britain
Budget—Great Britain
Building industry—Great Britain
Censorship—Great Britain
Childrens literature—Great Britain
Colleges and universities—Great Britain
Commonwealth of nations
Crime and criminals—Great Britain
Customs service—Great Britain
Education—Great Britain
Fishing—Great Britain
Foreign students in Great Britain
Gambling—Great Britain
Government ownership—Great Britain
Horse racing—Great Britain
Hotels, taverns, etc.—Great Britain
Immigration and emigration—Great Britain
Industrial relations—Great Britain
Industrial research—Great Britain
Investments, Foreign (by Great Britain)
Investments, Foreign (in Great Britain)
Labor and laboring classes—Great Britain
Labor laws and legislation—Great Britain
Liquor industry and trade—Great Britain
Money—Great Britain
Motor vehicle racing—Great Britain
Newspaper publishers and publishing—Great
Britain
Oceanographic research—Great Britain
Opera—Great Britain
Police—Great Britain
Postal service—Great Britain

GREAT BRITAIN—See also—*Continued*
Publishers and publishing—Great Britain
Recreation—Great Britain
Science and state—Great Britain
Seaside resorts—Great Britain
Strikes—Great Britain
Television broadcasting—Great Britain
Theater—Great Britain
Trade unions—Great Britain
Youth—Great Britain

Antiquities
Woodhenges. G. Wainwright. il Sci Am 223:
  30-8 bibliog(p 132) N '70
  See also
Megalithic monuments
Stonehenge, England

Army
Brigade of Ghurkas
Lo, the poor Gurkha; cutback. il Newsweek
  76:46 Ag 17 '70

Forces in Northern Ireland
Yesterday's heroes. M. Kupfer. il Newsweek
  76:30 Jl 20 '70

Atomic energy authority
Getting with it. il Forbes 105:29 Ja 15 '70

Cabinet
Dispossessed; ex-cabinet ministers of the
  Labor party. A. Howard. New Repub 163:
  7-8 Ag 15 '70
From shadow into substance; Tory appoin-
  tees. il Newsweek 75:32-3 Je 29 '70

Colonies
African dream, by B. Gardner. Review
  Sat R 53:26-7 Ag 1 '70. C. Miller
  See also
Anguilla (island)
Gibraltar
Pentecost Island
Seychelles (islands)

Commerce
Boom in British horses. J. Ross-Skinner. il
  Duns 97:44-6+ Ja '71
  See also
European economic community

Constitution
Reports: British constitution. H. Judson.
  Atlan 225:18+ F '70

Defenses
See also
Aeronautics, Military—Great Britain
Atomic warfare—Defenses

Diplomatic and consular service
Classy choice; ambassador to Washington.
  il por Newsweek 76:55-6 N 23 '70

Economic conditions
Aerospace role in U.K. economy cited. H. J.
  Coleman. il Aviation W 93:67+ Ja 13 '70
Britain's comeback: can it last? il U S News
  68:43-4 Ja 19 '70
Britain's struggle with stagflation. il Time
  96:84-5 S 14 '70
Getting back his bite. il Forbes 105:28-31+
  Ap 15 '70
  See also
Labor and laboring classes—Great Britain

Economic policy
Ahead for Britain: less welfare, lower taxes. il
  U S News 69:37 N 9 '70
Britain starts liquidating Labor policy. Bsns
  W p92+ N 7 '70
Counter-revolution. R. J. Korengold. News-
  week 76:49 D 21 '70
Did Harold Wilson save the pound? J. E.
  Powell. il Nat R 22:306-8 Mr 24 '70
Interview with Britain's Prime Minister Ed-
  ward Heath; ed. by J. Fromm. E. Heath.
  il pors U S News 69:24-6+ D 21 '70
Jolly, jolly sixpence. Newsweek 76:43 N 9 '70
Letter from London. M. Panter-Downes. New
  Yorker 46:74-6 Jl 25 '70
No longer the sick man. il por Time 95:83
  Ap 27 '70
Shrinking the welfare state: the Heath gov-
  ernment's plans. il U S News 69:22-3 D 21 '70
Ted Heath's new year. A. Lejeune. Nat R
  22:1393-4 D 29 '70
  See also
Budget—Great Britain
Wage-price policy—Great Britain

Economic relations
Did Harold Wilson save the pound? J. E.
  Powell. il Nat R 22:306-8 Mr 24 '70

Europe, Western
Do the British want to join Europe? A. Howard. New Repub 162:8-9 Ja 24 '70

Exchequer
Filling Macleod's shoes. il pors Newsweek
  76:30 Ag 3 '70
Letter from London; autumn economies. M.
  Panter-Downes. New Yorker 46:158+ N 14
  '70

Foreign opinion
Irish
Yesterday's heroes. M. Kupfer. il Newsweek
  76:30 Jl 20 '70

Foreign relations
Royal navy and the Ethiopian crisis of 1935-
  36. A. Marder. bibliog f Am Hist R 75:1327-
  56 Je '70
  See also
Great Britain—Diplomatic and consular service

Europe, Western
Britain, Europe and the Alliance. M. Stewart.
  For Affairs 48:648-59 Jl '70

Far East
Shanghai crisis of 1932, the basis of British
  policy. C. Thorne. bibliog f Am Hist R 75:
  1616-39 O '70

Middle East
Levantine laugh-in. por Time 95:26 F 2 '70

Spain
  See also
Gibraltar

United States
  See United States—Foreign relations—
  Great Britain

Foreign service
  See also
Great Britain—Diplomatic and consular serv-
  ice

Government publications
  See Government publications

Health education council
Lesson from Casanova; birth-control pamphlets. il Newsweek 77:59 Ja 11 '71

Historic houses, etc.
Britain's stately homes. S. Clark. il Travel
  133:42-7+ My '70

History
Bibliography
Articles and other books received; comp. by
  L. H. Carlson. See issues of American his-
  torical review

Puritan revolution, 1642-1660
Court and the country, by P. Zagorin. Review
  Nation 210:698-700 Je 8 '70. C. Hill

1760-1789
  See also
United States—History—Revolution

Victorian period, 1837-1901
  See also
Victorian period

World war, 1939-1945
  See World war, 1939-1945—Great Britain

History, Naval
Royal navy and the Ethiopian crisis of 1935-
  36. A. Marder. bibliog f Am Hist R 75:1327-
  56 Je '70
  See also
Nile, Battle of the, 1798

Industries
See also
Aerospace industries—Great Britain
Airplane industry and trade—Great Britain
Automobile industry and trade—Great Britain
Babcock and Wilcox, ltd.
Beecham group, ltd.
Defense industries—Great Britain
Electronic apparatus industry and trade—
  Great Britain
Imperial chemical industries, ltd.
Motorcycle industry and trade
Pilkington brothers, ltd.
Pottery industry
Rank Xerox, ltd.

GREAT BRITAIN—*Continued*

Intellectual life
See also
Bloomsbury group
Great Britain—Popular culture

Kings and rulers
See also
Great Britain—Royal family

Labor policy
See also
Labor laws and legislation—Great Britain

Moral conditions
Looking back without anger; whatever became of the angry young men? C. Sigal. il Commonweal 92:186-8 My 8 '70
Young men seeing visions. D. Martin. il Chr Cent 87:1063-6 S 9 '70

Naval history
See Great Britain—History, Naval

Navy
See also
Great Britain—History, Naval

Politics and government
After victory: the Tories' next steps. por Bsns W p50 Je 27 '70
All's right with the world of Harold Wilson. A. Lewis. il pors N Y Times Mag p 14-15+ Je 14 '70
Britain: the quiet revolution. Time 96:28-9 N 9 '70
Britain's new, willful prime minister. A. Howard. New Repub 163:16 Jl 4 '70
Cruel dilemma. T. Beeson. Chr Cent 87:635 Je 3 '70
Dilemma for Heath: how to please all. por U S News 69:60 Jl 6 '70
Heath's coherent design. Nat R 22:1385-6 D 29 '70
Heath's first week. il por Time 96:29 Jl 6 '70
Mandate running out; editorial point of view of New statesman. J. Burnham. Nat R 22: 937 S 8 '70
Moving in. Newsweek 76:42+ Jl 6 '70
Saying no to Labour. R. Williams. Nation 210:710-12 Je 15 '70
Silent majority clues as Britons vote against ins. il por U S News 68:30-1 Je 29 '70
Spring fever. Newsweek 75:61-2 My 11 '70
Surfeit of setbacks. il Time 96:20+ Ag 3 '70
See also
Conservative party (Great Britain)
Elections—Great Britain
Great Britain—Cabinet
Labor party (Great Britain)
Political campaigns—Great Britain
Socialism—Great Britain
Suffrage—Great Britain

Popular culture
Neophiliacs, by C. Booker. Review
America 123:296 O 17 '70. J. Vezeau
Nat R 22:850-1 Ag 11 '70. A. Lejeune
New Repub 163:25-7 Jl 11 '70. J. Seelye

Prime ministers
See also
Heath, E. R. G.

Race problems
Britain and race relations. J. D. Douglas. Chr Today 14:40 Jl 3 '70
British churchmen react to racism. Chr Cent 87:591 My 13 '70
No British blueprint for a nightmare; interview, ed. by C. R. Hughes. E. J. B. Rose. America 122:266-70 Mr 14 '70
Oh, what a lovely bash! skinheads vs Pakistanis in London. il Newsweek 75:58-9 Je 22 '70
Only in England; South African cricket team and the British churches. Chr Cent 87:748 Je 17 '70

Religious institutions and affairs
Alternative church union scheme for Britain. Chr Cent 87:687 Je 3 '70
British churches and the battle of the budget. Chr Cent 87:933 Ag 5 '70
Going underground; new British organization called ONE. T. Beeson. Chr Cent 87: 717 Je 10 '70
Livingston; Scottish venture in unity. Chr Cent 87:580-2 My 6 '70
Tenacious devoutness. T. Beeson. Chr Cent 87:860 Jl 15 '70
See also
Church and state in Great Britain
Church union—Great Britain

Royal air force
Bomber command
Reflections; From schoolboy pacifist to collision expert. F. J. Dyson. New Yorker 46:44-6+ F 21 '70

Chaplains
See Chaplains, Military

Royal family
Year with the Queen; excerpts from The Queen's year. A. Duncan. il por Look 34:34-40+ My 5; 43-6+ My 19 '70
See also
Royal warrant

Science research council
Research in Britain: a non-weeping formula for living on tight funds. D. S. Greenberg. Science 167:1596-8 Mr 20 '70
Science on a tight budget. B. H. Flowers. Science 170:1361 D 25 '70

Social conditions
See also
Labor and laboring classes—Great Britain

Social life and customs
British, by A. Glyn. Review
Sat R 53:37-8 N 7 '70. A. Kendrick

Vital statistics
People of York: 1538-1812. U. M. Cowgill il Sci Am 222:104-10+ Ja '70

GREAT depression. See Business depression, 1929-1939
GREAT DISMAL SWAMP. See Dismal Swamp
GREAT EXUMA ISLAND. See Bahama Islands
GREAT gray owls. See Owls
GREAT horned owls. See Owls
GREAT LAKES
Endangered Great Lakes; pollution by mercury. il Time 95:85 My 4 '70
Lampreys in the Lakes. G. F. Bush. il Sea Front 16:142-7 My '70
New river; sixteen nuclear power plants on the Great Lakes. il Environ 12:36-40 Ja '70
Reviving the Great Lakes; Muskegon project. J. R. Sheaffer. il Sat R 53:62-5 N 7 '70
U.S. and Canada discuss problems of pollution in the Great Lakes. Dept State Bul 63:36-7 Jl 13 '70
Water supply and water management problems of the Great Lakes; AAAS symposium, December 30, 1970. L. A. Heindl. il Science 170:1230-1 D 11 '70
Way to save the Great Lakes? proposed law for containment areas for dredgings. il U S News 68:72 Ap 27 '70
See also
Erie, Lake
Ontario, Lake
Superior, Lake
GREAT LAKES REGION
See also
Fishing—Great Lakes Region
GREAT LAKES-St Lawrence waterway. See St Lawrence Seaway
GREAT men
Higher patriotism; ideas of the Founding fathers. N. Cousins. Sat R 53:20 Jl 4 '70
Men & women who shaped the '60's. il Sr Schol 95:9-11 S 22 '69
100 most important people in the world; with editorial comment. D. Robinson. il Esquire 73:6, 104-7 Ap '70
You say tomentose; I say tomahntose; wisdom of the Founding fathers vs. pettiness of men today. G. Ace. Sat R 53:3 Jl 4 '70
See also
Kings and rulers
Leadership
New York university—Hall of fame for great Americans
GREAT Northern Nekoosa corporation
Actions speak louder. il Forbes 106:26-7 S 15 '70
GREAT PLAINS
See also
Paleobotany—Great Plains
GREAT PLAINS REGION
See also
Prairies
GREAT SALT LAKE
Mining the Great Salt Lake. il Sci N 97:454-5 My 9 '70
GREAT SMOKY MOUNTAINS
Mushrooms of the mountains. M. B. Mellinger. il Nat Parks & Con Mag 44:15-18 S '70
GREAT SMOKY MOUNTAINS NATIONAL PARK
Scientist against Smokies road. Liv Wildn 34:62 Spr '70

GREAT southern trucking-Ryder truck rental merger. See Business consolidations and mergers

GREAT southwest corporation
Great southwest goes back to the well. Bsns W p29 D 5 '70
One hand giveth . . . il Forbes 106:56 O 1 '70
Trials of Penn central's sweetheart. il Bsns W p46-7 O 17 '70

GREAT western civilization caper. story. See Claiborne, S.

GREAT Western united corporation
High flier comes back with a thud. por Bsns W p24 Jl 25 '70

GREATER Rockford (airplane) See Aeronautics —History

GREATEST writing ever wrote; story. See McClanahan, E.

GREAVES, Marsha L. See Coulter, C. L. jt. auth.

GRECHKO, Andrei Antonovich
Grechko: master of the Soviet military colossus. J. G. Hubbell. por Read Digest 97:98-103 O '70 *

GRECO, Constance M.
Barred from the library. bibliog il Am Lib 1:908-10 O '70

GRECO, Emilio
Doors of Orvieto. il Time 96:56-7 Ag 31 '70 *

GREECE, Ancient
See also
Argos
Temples—Greece, Ancient

Antiquities
Marathon mounds. Sci Am 223:52 Jl '70
See also
Athens, Greece—Antiquities

Archeology
Resurrecting the oldest known Greek ship. M. L. Katzev. il Nat Geog 137:840-57 Je '70

GREECE, Modern
See also
Aegean Islands
Architecture. Domestic—Greece, Modern
Cyclades (islands)
Petroleum industry and trade—Greece, Modern
Political prisoners—Greece, Modern
Public opinion—Greece, Modern
Shipping—Greece, Modern
Trials—Greece, Modern

Description and travel
Greece: instant delights. D. Messinesi. Vogue 156:26 Jl '70
Travel. D. Messinesi. Vogue 155:46 F 15 '70

Foreign relations
Greek colonels talk back. America 122:148 F 14 '70
United States
See United States—Foreign relations— Greece, Modern

Politics and government
Bearing gifts to Greeks. Z. B. Grant. New Repub 162:19-21 Mr 7 '70
Conversations in Greece. T. W. Pew. jr. Nation 212:74-80 Ja 18 '71
Democrat; interview. G. Mylonas. New Yorker 46:35-7 Ap 18 '70
Exile; interview. H. Vlachos. New Yorker 46:19-20 Jl 4 '70
Greece, three years after. N. Elias. il N Y Times Mag p30-1+ My 3 '70
Greece under the colonels. C. L. Sulzberger. For Affairs 48:300-11 Ja '70
Lady and the colonels. S. Rousseas. Nation 211:149-50 Ag 31 '70
New men, old mentality. Time 96:36 D 14 '70
Report from Greece: under the junta. N. Gage and E. Kulukundis. Am Scholar 39:475-97 Sum '70
Slight relaxation. Time 96:20 Ag 24 '70
Sop to the critics. il por Time 95:42 Ap 27 '70
Story of Z. il Time 96:23 Ag 17 '70

Religious institutions and affairs
Greek orthodoxy: the junta defied. T. Cosmades. Chr Today 14:38-9 Ja 16 '70

GREEFF fabrics, inc.
Fabrics from the forest. il por Nat Wildlife 8:28-9 Ag '70

GREEK cookery. See Cookery, Greek

GREEK frescoes. See Frescoes

GREEK islands. See Aegean Islands

GREEK Orthodox archdiocese of North and South America. See Orthodox Eastern church in the United States

GREEK Orthodox church in the United States. See Orthodox Eastern church in the United States

GREEK poetry
Translations into English
Homeric hymn to Aphrodite; tr. by D. Hine. Homer. Poetry 116:313-26 Ag '70
Meaning of simplicity; In the barracks; Absence; Suspicious sleep; Not suspecting; Achievement; Minimum delay; tr. by R. Dalven. G. Ritsos. Poetry 116:292-8 Ag '70
On old age; tr. by M. Mesic. Mimnermus. Poetry 116:344 Ag '70

GREEK sculpture. See Sculpture, Greek

GREEK vases. See Vases, Greek

GREELEY, Andrew M.
Intellectuals as an ethnic group. il N Y Times Mag p22-3+ Jl 12 '70
Myths, meaning and vatican III. America 123:538-42 D 19 '70
Redeeming of America according to Charles Reich. America 124:14-17 Ja 9 '71
Take heart from the heartland. New Repub 163:16-19 D 12 '70
Turning off the people. New Repub 162:14-16 Je 27 '70; Same with title War and white ethnic groups. Cur 120:22-7 Ag '70
about
Andrew Greeley, divine sociologist. P. Steinfels. Commonweal 92:286 Je 12 '70 *

GREEN, Alan. See Goodman, J. jt. auth.

GREEN, Alex E. S.
Fundamental nuclear interaction. bibliog il Science 169:933-41 S 4 '70

GREEN, Arthur S.
Beginning writer's bonanza: 2,000 trade journals! il Writers Digest 50:28-31 D '70

GREEN, Beverley R. and Burton, Hugh
Acetabularia chloroplast DNA: electron microscopic visualization. bibliog il Science 168:981-2 My 22 '70

GREEN, Christopher
Léger, purism and the Paris machines. il Art N 69:54-6+ D '70

GREEN, Daniel G.
Testing the vision of cataract patients by means of laser-generated interference fringes. bibliog il Science 168:1240-2 Je 5 '70

GREEN, Douglas
New way to afford a second home. il Mech Illus 66:65-7+ F '70
When should you sue? il Mech Illus 66:46-8+ Ja '70

GREEN, Edith
Education complex. il por Newsweek 76:72-3 S 7 '70 *

GREEN, Fletcher Melvin
Two southern historians. G. M. Fredrickson. Am Hist R 75:1387-92 Je '70 *

GREEN, Hannah
Last of the wine; story. New Yorker 46:38-46 F 28 '70
Summer afternoon, summer afternoon; story. New Yorker 45:30-8 Ja 17 '70

GREEN, Harris
Music (cont) Commonweal 91:586-7 F 27 '70

GREEN, John J.
Where and when to use anecdotes. Writers Digest 50:23-5 Mr '70

GREEN, Larry
Camanche, hot new bass lake. il Field & S 74:66-7+ Ap '70
Serpent fly. il Field & S 75:58-9+ S '70

GREEN, Louis C.
Ordinary stars, white dwarfs, and neutron stars. il Sky & Tel 41:18-20 Ja '71
Pulsars today. il Sky & Tel 40:260-2 N; 357-60 D '70

GREEN, Mark J.
Business in government. New Repub 163:14-16 N 14 '70
Law graduates: the new breed. il Nation 210:658-60 Je 1 '70

GREEN, Percy
Percy Green vs. McDonnell aircraft. L. Barrett. Nation 210:404-5 Ap 6 '70

GREEN, Philip
Can it happen here? Is it already happening? il N Y Times Mag p30-1+ S 20; 12+ O 18 '70

GREEN, Stanley S. and Sell, K. W.
Mixed leukocyte stimulation by normal peripheral leukocytes by autologous lymphoblastoid cells. bibliog il Science 170:989-90 N 27 '70

GREEN, Timothy S.
Last of the desert adventurers; excerpt from
Restless spirit. il pors Horizon 12:104-11
Spr '70
Remarkable woman: Jane Goodall; excerpt
from Restless spirit. il por McCalls 97:46-
7+ Ag '70
GREEN-ARMYTAGE, Stephen
Saratoga gallery; photographs. Sports Illus 33:
28-35 Ag 3 '70
GREEN BAY wildlife sanctuary. See Wildlife
sanctuaries—Wisconsin
GREEN beans. See Beans
GREEN Beret force. See United States—Army
—Special forces—Forces in Vietnam
GREEN giant company
Green giant's red face. il Forbes 105:44 Ap
15 '70
GREEN sea turtles. See Turtles
GREEN thumb, inc.
Green thumb: blight into beauty. il Har Yrs
10:19-21 Ap '70
Muscling out of retirement. il Life 69:38-9
O 16 '70
GREEN torso; story. See Warner. W. S.
GREENACRE, Phyllis
Treason and the traitor. bibliog Am Imago
26:199-232 Fall '69
GREENBANK, John
Springtime in Los Angeles; poem. Am For
76:47 Ap '70
GREENBAUM, Norman
Just plain Norman. H. Saal. il por Newsweek
75:117+ My 25 '70 *
GREENBERG, Daniel
Experimental school. M. S. Rothenberg. il
Phys Today 23:28+ My '70 *
Farewell to Daddario; letter. F. A. Long.
Science 170:1254 D 18 '70 *
GREENBERG, Emanuel
How to stock the bar for a party. il House B
112:50+ N '70
Sherry on the rocks. il House B 112:92-3+
Je '70
GREENBERG, Harvey R.
Rags of time: Ingmar Bergman's Wild straw-
berries. Am Imago 27:66-82 Spr '70
GREENBERG, Irwin
Max Ginsburg; underground & above ground.
il Am Artist 34:28-34+ S '70
GREENBERG, Jerry
Scuba diving for live treasures. il Nat Wild-
life 8:26-31 Ap '70
GREENBLATT, Augusta
Hidden handicaps to learning. il Parents
Mag 45:53-5+ O '70
GREENBLATT, Robert, and Jacobs, Evelyn
Hirsutism. Redbook 136:24+ N '70
GREENBRIER resort, W.Va. See Health re-
sorts, watering places, etc.
GREENBUGS
Greenbugs change their diet to sorghum. Suc
Farm 68:C10 Je '70
GREENE, Bob
Up on two wheels. See issues of Hot rod
GREENE, Christopher
Black continentals. P. Barnett. il Negro Hist
Bul 33:6-10 Ja '70 *
GREENE, Fred
Case for and against military withdrawal
from Vietnam and Korea; address, April
1970, with questions and answers. Ann Am
Acad 390:1-17 Jl '70
GREENE, Gael
Guide to all-star indigestion. il Sports Illus
33:88-92+ O 12 '70
How the world's great beauties stay beauti-
ful. Ladies Home J 87:68-9+ F '70
Indigestion on the turnpike. il Life 69:12 Ag
28 '70
Life food review. il Life 69:12 Ag 28; 8 O
23 '70
GREENE, Gail
Strange obsession? R. Hattersley. il Pop Phot
66:98-101+ Ja '70
GREENE, Graham
Greene, the funny writer, on comedy; in-
terview, ed. by J. Newcombe. Life 68:10
Ja 23 '70
Lowdown from our man in Havana. Vogue
155:94-5+ Ap 15 '70
about
Burnt-out case? J. D. Kellogg. America 122:
273-4 Mr 14 '70 *
Evergreen. L. E. Sissman. New Yorker 46:
110+ F 28 '70 *
GREENE, Holley D. 3d
Developing a balanced insurance program.
Pub W 198:35-6 D 7; 25 D 14 '70

GREENE, Jack P.
Political mimesis; a consideration of the
historical and cultural roots of legislative
behavior in the British colonies in the
eighteenth century. bibliog f Am Hist R
75:337-60, 364-7 D '69
GREENE, Janet
Can you afford, retirement afloat? il pors
Yachting 127:67+ Je '70
GREENE, Martin L. and others
Substrate stabilization: genetically controlled
reciprocal relationship of two human enzy-
mes. bibliog il Science 167:887-9 F 6 '70
GREENE, Pat Ryan
Sensitivity training: fulfillment or freak-out?
il Cath World 211:18-21 Ap '70
GREENE, Sheldon L.
Somebody is always offended. Nation 211:624-
7 D 14 '70
GREENE, Stephen, press
Stephen Greene press. M. Metcalf. il Pub
W 198:20 N 23 '70
GREENE, Wade
Militants who play with dynamite. il N Y
Times Mag p38-9+ O 25 '70
What happened to the attempts to clean up
the majestic, the polluted Hudson? il N Y
Times Mag p28-9+ My 3 '70
Where are the Savios of yesteryear? il N Y
Times Mag p6-9+ Jl 12 '70
GREENE COUNTY, Ala.
Black power comes to Greene County. il
Fortune 81:70-5 Je '70
GREENFELD, Josh
Child called Noah. il Life 69:60-2+ O 23
'70
Conservatives are out to beat: Rockeberg,
Goldfeller, Ottindell and Goodinger. il por
N Y Times Mag p26-7+ O 18 '70
Paul Mazursky in wonderland. il pors Life
69:51-4+ S 4 '70
GREENFIELD, Edward
Behind the scenes. See issues of High fidelity
section I
Cavilli's Calisto; Bennett's Victory. il Hi Fi
20:secII 26-7 Ag '70
Festivals at Aldeburgh, London, Glynde-
bourne. Hi Fi 20:MA27+ O '70
Les Troyens. il Am Rec G 36:936-41 Ag '70
GREENFIELD, Jeff
(comp) See Nixon, R. M. Mr Nixon's sense
of history
GREENFIELD Village. See Henry Ford museum
and Greenfield Village, Dearborn, Mich.
GREENHOUSE, Linda J.
After July 1, an abortion should be as simple
to have as a tonsillectomy, but—. il N Y
Times Mag p7+ Je 28 '70
Constitutional question: is there a right to
abortion? il N Y Times Mag p30-1+ Ja 25
'70
Reincarnation of John Monro. il por N Y
Times Mag p56-7+ Mr 15 '70
GREENHOUSES
Greenhouse built in one afternoon. W. L.
Meachem. il Home Gard 57:42-3 N '70
Greenhouse dreams that all came true; sym-
posium. il Home Gard 57:40-6 O '70
Home greenhouse. J. A. Eaton. See issues of
Home garden & flower grower
In your greenhouse. J. U. Crockett. See is-
sues of Horticulture
Inexpensive greenhouse. R. B. Gambino. il
Horticulture 48:26-7 F '70
Inflated, plastic greenhouse is prototype of
bigger things. il Arch Forum 132:96 My '70
Jungle in the house; excerpts. M. Bates. il
por Sci Digest 67:27-32 Je '70
Low-cost greenhouse for the porch. R. Hen-
drickson. il Org Gard & Farm 17:96-7 Ag
'70
New greenhouse, the second time around. S.
W. Plimpton. il Horticulture 48:42-3+ Mr
'70
Small greenhouse; Raja. il Consumer Bul
53:23 Ja '70
Tilling the desert under plastic skies; inte-
grated power-water-food system. il Bsns W
p92+ My 9 '70
Woman can build a hothouse. M. Wilbur. il
Org Gard & Farm 17:83-5 Ja '70
See also
Cold frames
GREENING, W. E.
Showdown ahead for Spain. il America 123:487-
9 D 5 '70
GREENLAND
See also
Fishing—Greenland
GREENLAND ice sheet. See Glaciers
GREENLAND turbot
See also
Cookery—Fish

GREENLEAF, Warren T.
Humanities and the culture-hungry American. il Am Ed 6:7-11 Ja '70

GREENLEE, Lyman E.
Build the bug shoo. il Pop Electr 33:27-30 Jl '70

GREENMAN, Norman N. and Gross, H. G.
Luminescence of Apollo 11 lunar samples. bibliog il Science 167:720-1 Ja 30 '70

GREENOUGH, Richard
Coeducation as a world trend. Sch & Soc 98: 31-2 Ja '70

GREENS, Edible
Know your salad greens. il Bet Hom & Gard 48:84 My '70
Salad greens in a corner. G. L'Allemand. il Org Gard & Farm 17:40-1 My '70
Winter salad greens by the tubful. J. S. Park. il Org Gard & Farm 17:36-9 O '70
See also
Chicory

GREENSHAW, H. Wayne
Journalist sues Viking, Esquire, over Calley story. Pub W 198:30 O 19 '70 *

GREENSHIELDS, Bruce D.
Traffic and highway research and how it may be improved. bibliog Science 168:674-ö My 8 '70

GREENSPAN, Michael D. and others
Enzyme specificity as a factor in regulation of fatty acid chain length in escherichia coli. bibliog il Science 170:1203-4 D 11 '70

GREENVILLE, S.C.

Education

All desegregation orders obeyed. il U S News 69:26-8 D 7 '70

GREENWALD, Frank L.
Build a better miter jig than you can buy. il Pop Sci 197:98-9 D '70
Marble topped table you can build. il Pop Sci 196:72-3 My '70
New twists on building fine furniture: a marble-topped table. il Pop Sci 196:110+ My '70

GREENWAY, Hugh D. S.
Pendulum of war swings wider in Laos. il Life 68:32-6 Ap 3 '70
Reports: Cambodia. Atlan 226:32+ Jl '70
Which is the Burma road. Ne Win or U Nu? il pors N Y Times Mag p34-5+ My 3 '70

GREENWAY, John
Country music. Nat R 22:842+ Ag 11 '70

GREENWICH observatory. See Astronomical observatories—Great Britain

GREENWICH VILLAGE, New York. See New York (city)—Greenwich Village

GREENWOOD, Edward
Importance of play. por Camp Mag 42:8-9+ Mr '70

GREER, Colin
Public schools: the myth of the melting pot; excerpt from Cobweb attitudes: essays in American education and culture. Ed Digest 35:1-4 Mr '70

GREER, G. L. and Gardner, D. R.
Temperature-sensitive neurons in the brain of brook trout. bibliog il Science 169:1220-2 S 18 '70

GREER, Gordon. See Talbert, W. F. jt. auth.

GREER, Gordon G.
Family health. Bet Hom & Gard 48:42+ Ap '70

GREETING cards
Cartoonist Q's. J. Markow. Writers Digest 50: 19-20 N '70
Hang-up card; sensitivity cards. il Newsweek 76:88 S 7 '70
Humorous greeting cards. C. Goeller. Writer 83:21-4 Mr '70
Look what photography's doing to greeting cards. R. Bruns. il Pop Phot 67:96-7+ O '70
UNICEF greeting cards. il UNESCO Courier 23:33 N '70
See also
Booksellers and bookselling—Greeting cards
Christmas cards
Hallmark cards, inc.
Post cards
Valentines

GREGG, Duane L.
Cars. See issues of Better homes and gardens
—and Lidster, D. M.
Good news. See issues of Better homes and gardens

GREGG, James R.
Sunglasses for sportsmen. il Field & S 74: 50-1+ F '70
Use your eyes for better retirement. il por Har Yrs 10:14-18 Ja '70

GREGOR, Arthur
Indices; poem. Nation 210:728 Je 15 '70

about
Comment. R. B. Shaw. Poetry 117:113-14 N '70 *

GREGORIAN chants. See Chants (Gregorian, plain, etc.)

GREGORY, André
Alice in Wonderland; dramatization of story by L. Carroll. Criticism
Nation 211:443 N 2 '70 *
Newsweek 76:123 O 19 '70 *
Sat R 53:12 O 31 '70 *
Time il 96:93 O 26 '70
Vogue il 156:170-1+ D '70 *
Wild Alice. J. Gruen. il por Vogue 156:170-1+ D '70 *

GREGORY, Cynthia
Cynthia Gregory; an American swan queen. il pors Dance Mag 44:58-63 Je '70 *
Star quality. por Mlle 71:130-3 O '70 *

GREGORY, Dick
Dick Gregory on campus. W. F. Buckley, jr. Nat R 22:1420 D 29 '70 *
Diogenes, put down your lamp! C. E. Douglas. il pors Ebony 25:72-4+ Ap '70 *
Return of the native son. A. Keneas. por Newsweek 75:74 Je 29 '70 *

GREGORY, Gene
Spin-off: the fruit of space research. il UNESCO Courier 23:4-31+ Mr '70

GREGORY, Jack. See Strickland, R. jt. auth.

GREGORY, John D. and Saldera, S. W.
Interference in the Lowry method for protein determination. Science 169:97-8 Jl 3 '70

GREGORY, Myron
How to fish flies deep; excerpts from Salt water fly fishing. G. X. Sand. Field & S 74: 48-9+ F '70

GREGORY, Vernon
What's a film classic without the mighty Wurlitzer? M. Mann. il Pop Phot 66:27-8+ Ja '70

GREGORY, Vincent L.
Vince Gregory's clear bill. il por Forbes 106: 26 N 1 '70 *

GREIG, Howard, and Martineau, P. J.
Instant Italy. Holiday 48:44-5 Jl '70

GREINER, Larry E. and others
Putting judgment back into decisions. il Harvard Bsns R 48:59-67 Mr '70

GRELAK, R. P. and others
Amantadine-dopamine interaction: possible mode of action in Parkinsonism. bibliog il Science 169:203-4 Jl 10 '70

GRENADA
Grenada: the nowhere island. F. Trippett. il Look 34:28 Mr 10 '70

GRENADINES (islands)
See also
Bequia (island)

GRENIER, Mildred
Parent's plight; poem. Farm J 93:44 N '69

GRÈS, Alix
[Photograph] B. Brandt. Harp Baz 103:141 F '70

GRESHAM, Grits
Best fishing lake ever built? il Field & S 75: 38-9+ D '70
Greatest bass boat ever? il por Field & S 74:56-7+ Ja '70

GRETH, Roma
Would-be swingers; drama. Plays 30:1-10 Ja '71

GRETZ, Charles R.
Build this three-way Travelpod. il Pop Mech 133:158-62+ F '70

GREVE, Donald
American Indian; address, December 9, 1969. Vital Speeches 36:276-9 F 15 '70

GREYHOUND corporation
Fighting a doggy image. il Time 96:89 N 2 '70
Piggy in a poke. Newsweek 76:98 O 12 '70

GREYHOUND racing. See Dog racing

GRID-dip meters. See Electric meters

GRID dip oscillators. See Oscillators

GRIDDLE cakes
Breakfast favorites as desserts. Sunset 144: 98 Ja '70
Christmas crêpe. M. Happel. il Ladies Home J 87:82-3+ D '70
Crepes without suzette. C. Claiborne. il N Y Times Mag p74 Ap 19 '70
Great crepe recipes; excerpts from The crepe cookbook. P. Fono and M. Stacho. il Redbook 134:90-3+ F '70
Holiday-makers; seafood crepes. C. Claiborne. il N Y Times Mag p36 D 20 '70
Inside each mandarin pancake flavors assemble. il Sunset 144:158-60 My '70
Ricotta cheese pancakes. il Sunset 145:172 O '70
Strawberry ice cream crêpes. il Sunset 144: 215 My '70

GRIDS (electric distribution) See Electric plants—Interconnection

GRIEDER, Terence
Ecology before Columbus. il Américas 22: 21-8 My '70

GRIEF. See Bereavement

GRIEG, Edvard
Incomparable art of Emanuel Feuermann. D. W. Moore. Am Rec G 37:12-13 S '70 *
Slightly more than ever before; excerpts from the Peer Gynt music. J. Diether. il Am Rec G 36:668+ My '70 *

GRIEVANCE procedures
See also
Teachers grievances

GRIFFE of the master; story. See Steegmuller, F.

GRIFFIN, C. W. Jr
Frontier freedoms and space age cities; excerpt. il Sat R 53:17-19+ F 7 '70

GRIFFIN, Dorothy M.
Dialects and democracy. Engl J 59:551-8 Ap '70

GRIFFIN, Guy D. See Gibbs, G. E. jt. auth.

GRIFFIN, John
Five hundred lime-green islands. il Sat R 53:43-4+ O 24 '70

GRIFFIN, John Howard
Where are they now? il pors Newsweek 76: 10 Ag 31 '70 *

GRIFFIN, M. J. See Carubelli, R. jt. auth.

GRIFFIN, Olva R.
Non-stop gardening. il Org Gard & Farm 17: 86-7 Je '70

GRIFFIN, Rachael
Ken Shores. il Craft Horiz 30:26-9 Ag '70

GRIFFIN, Stuart
In space at last. il Sci N 97:232 F 28 '70
Japan asks for help. il Sci N 97:516 My 23 '70
Macau. il Travel 133:46-9 F '70

GRIFFITH, Beverly
Obituary
Nat R 22:450 My 5 '70. W. F. Rickenbacker *

GRIFFITH, David Wark
Griffith's Russian fans. R. Sklar. Nation 211: 249-50 S 21 '70 *

GRIFFITH, F. H.
Old mechanical banks. See issues of Hobbies

GRIFFITH, John D.
Shoot glareless pictures with polarized light. il Pop Mech 133:128-9 Ja '70

GRIFFITH, Milt
To bag a buck. il Field & S 75:46-7+ O '70

GRIFFITH, Thomas
Putting it back together. il Life 70:85-6+ Ja 8 '71
View of America from Lake Como. Life 68: 26 Je 26 '70

GRIFFITH, William E.
Why American troops should remain in Europe. Read Digest 96:121-5 My '70
Zero hour for the Middle East. Read Digest 96:49-53 Ja '70

GRIFFITH, Winthrop
Isla Vista war; campus violence in a class by itself. il N Y Times Mag p 10-11+ Ag 30 '70

GRIFFITHS, D. J.
Profits from pictures. il Writers Digest 51:26-7 Ja '71

GRIFFITHS, Martha (Wright)
Equal rights for women? Things may never be the same. il por U S News 69:29-30 Ag 24 '70 *
Ladies' day. il por Newsweek 76:15-16 Ag 24 '70
Martha Griffiths: graceful feminist. por Time 96:10-11 Ag 24 '70 *

GRIFFITHS, Thomas
Mission for Mr Wedgwood; excerpts from journal, with introd. and epilogue by H. C. Wedgwood. il Am Heritage 21:64-7 Ag '70

GRIGGS, Lee
Oil and water rebuild an ancient land. il Fortune 82:88-97+ N '70

GRIGORENKO, Petr Grigor'evich
Notes from a Soviet asylum; excerpts. por Time 95:40 Ap 6 '70

GRIGSON, Geoffrey
Scent of women; Incident of wolves and water; Poor Tom, poor scullion; Short history of old art; poems. Poetry 117:174-8 D '70
about
Comment. M. Mott. Poetry 116:46-50 Ap '70 *

GRILLET, Alain Robbe-. See Robbe-Grillet, A.

GRILLS. Barbecue. See Barbecue grills

GRIMES, Glenn
Contract details can cost you. Farm J 94:H15 N '70

GRIMLEY, Oliver
Oliver Grimley: pen draughtsman. H. C. Pitz. il pors Am Artist 34:28-34 Ja '70

GRIMM, Carl J. 3d
Ground fog? Where'd it come from? il Flying 86:82-3 Ap '70

GRIMSBY, Roger
Cheer leaders. J. Morgenstern. Newsweek 77:9 Ja 4 '71 *

GRIMSHAW, Allen D.
Interpreting collective violence: an argument for the importance of social structure. bibliog f Ann Am Acad 391:9-20 S '70

GRIMSLEY, Juliet
Martian chronicles: a provocative study. Engl J 59:1239-42 D '70

GRIN and bare it! drama. See McGuire, K.

GRINAGER, Virginia M.
Unexpected twist. il pors Outdoor Life 145: 22-3 Ja '70

GRINDING
See also
Diamond cutting

GRINDING machines
Grinder gives Norton an edge. il Bsns W p70 O 31 '70
Versatile overarm mirror-grinding machine. P. R. Zurakowski and F. Kolberg. il Sky & Tel 40:382-7 D '70

GRINNELL, George Bird
George Bird Grinnell: grandfather of conservation. M. Frome. Field & S 75:52+ Je '70 *

GRINSPOON, Lester
Marihuana; with biographical sketch. Sci Am 221:15, 17-25 D '69; 222:6-7 F '70

GRINSTEAD, Robert R.
New resource. bibliog il Environ 12:2-17 D '70

GRIST, Reri
Musician of the month. G. Movshon. por(p 1) Hi Fi sec II 20:5 Ja '70

GRISWOLD, Ralph E.
Early American garden houses. il Antiques 98:82-7 Jl '70

GRIZZLY bear hunting. See Bear hunting

GRIZZLY bears. See Bears

GROB, Samuel
Psychiatric social clubs come of age. bibliog Ment Hy 54:129-36 Ja '70

GROCERY manufacturers of America
Hunger and the marketplace; excerpts from Let them eat promises: the politics of hunger in America. N. Kotz. Harper 240:88-92 Ja '70

GROCERY store chains. See Supermarkets

GROCERY stores
See also
Supermarkets

GROCERY trade
Discounting: a food chain reaction. il Bsns W p44-6 S 26 '70
Shoppers' forum bags goodwill; Stop & shop, inc. Bsns W p52 Ja 31 '70
See also
Fisher foods, inc.
Great Atlantic and Pacific tea company
Jewel companies, inc.

GROFF, Patrick
Chall revisited. bibliog por Library J 95:1904-6+ My 15 '70

GROISSER, Leon B. See Negroponte, N. jt. auth.

GROLIER, INC.
Grolier sales subsidiary enjoined in Washington. Pub W 197:62-3 F 9 '70

GROMAN, G.
Speaking of love; story. Har Yrs 10:10-11 Je '70

GROMMON, Alfred H.
Which ways now in the '70s? Engl J 59:692-6 My '70

GROMYKO, Andrei Andreevich
President Kennedy and the Russian fable. N. Cousins. il Sat R 54:20-1 Ja 9 '71 *

GRONER, Alex, and Brall, Carlyn
Part-time teachers. Todays Ed 59:64-5 Ja '70

GROOMING, Personal
Grooming American men is big business. il Bsns W p90-1+ F 21 '70
Spruce yourself up for the holidays. H. Alpert. Har Yrs 10:6-8+ D '70

GROOMING of dogs. See Dog grooming

GROPPE, John D.
Radicalizing liturgy. Cath World 212:30-4 O '70

GROPPER, Esther C.
Literature for the restive: Hermann Hesse's books. Engl J 59:1221-8 D '70

GROPPI, James Edward
Father Groppi freed of contempt charge. Chr Cent 87:471 Ap 22 '70 *

GROSE, Peter
Publishing boom ends Down-Under. Pub W
198:pt2 175-6 S 21 '70
GROSHANS, Werner
Werner Groshans: painter of realism & fan-
tasy. M. Dulac. il por Am Artist 34:54-60+
Je '70 *
GROSKINSKY, Henry
Matisse sculpture; photographs. il pors Life
69:40-9 S 11 '70
GROSS, Amy
Getting together. Mlle 71:154-5+ My '70
Growing up a Jew. Mlle 70:159+ Mr '70
Ibiza: how to drop out without falling. il
Mlle 72:112-13+ D '70
Women's lib loves you. il Mlle 70:232-3+ F
'70
GROSS, Beatrice, and Gross, Ronald
Little bit of chaos. il Sat R 53.71-3+ My 16
'70
GROSS, Bertram M. and Springer, Michael
(eds) Political intelligence for America's
future. bibliog f il Ann Am Acad 388:1-132
Mr '70
GROSS, Beverly
Films. Nation 211:60 Jl 20 '70
GROSS, Cecelia
Navajo children draw. il Sch Arts 70:14-15
N '70
GROSS, Edith Loew
Bringing up people. il pors Vogue 155:88-91+
Je '70
Oh. Genevieve! pors Vogue 155:188-91+ Ap 1
'70
GROSS, H. Gerald. See Greenman, N. N. jt.
auth.
GROSS, Harvey
Hegel, Beethoven, Wordsworth: 1770-1970. Am
Scholar 40:142-56 Wint '70
GROSS, Jane
Track & field (title varies) Sports Illus 33:77
N 23 '70
GROSS, Kenneth G.
Should we tax church wealth? il Look 34:25-7
My 19 '70
GROSS, Leonard
Our uptight troops in Europe. il pors Look
34:14-19 S 8 '70
Why are they smiling? il Look 34:21-7 Mr 24
'70
GROSS, Ronald. See Gross, B. jt. auth.
GROSS, Sid
Coming clean about plastic waste. House B
112:96+ My '70
GROSS national product
Analysis of price changes in the third quarter
of 1969. W. J. Layng and T. Nakayama. il
Mo Labor R 93:44-7 Ja '70
Anatomy of price change: the second quarter,
1970. T. Nakayama. il Mo Labor R 93:
43-5 S '70
Auto strikers take the GNP for a ride. il Bsns
W p 18 O 3 '70
Budget with a bite. il Newsweek 75:65-7 F 9
'70
Celebration of what? il Newsweek 76:55-6 D 28
'70
Economic growth: new doubts about an old
ideal. il Time 95:72-4 Mr 2 '70
Economy: modest hopes, modest gains. il
Time 96:103 O 26 '70
Inflation everywhere, but some real growth
too. L. A. Mayer. il Fortune 82:136-41 Ag
'70
Look at national priorities. K. E. Boulding.
il Cur Hist 59:65-72+ Ag '70
Poverty of affluence. R. Lekachman. Com-
mentary 49:39-44 Mr '70; Reply with re-
joinder. B. Shaicovitch. 50:10+ Jl '70
Race for industrial might: U.S. still ahead,
but—. il U S News 69:78-9 D 7 '70
Slump: will this bottom hold up? second-
quarter figures. il Newsweek 76:51-2 Jl 27
'70
Trillion-dollar economy: with editorial com-
ment. il Bsns W p65-7, 192 O 17 '70
History
How it hit its dazzling pace. il Bsns W
p75 O 17 '70
GROSSBARD, Henry
Gallery; photographs. Life 69:6-7 Jl 24 '70
GROSSE, Aristid V.
Plastic bubbles and how to blow them. bibliog
il pors Chem 43:24-7 N; 25-7 D '70
about
Science's answer to violence: bubbles. il pors
Sci Digest 67:74-7 Ap '70 *
GROSSER, Alfred
France and Germany: less divergent outlooks?
For Affairs 48:235-44 Ja '70

GROSSMAN, Edward
Film. Harper 241:32-4+ D '70
In pursuit of the American woman; or, Gulli-
ver at the gynecologist's. il Harper 240:
47-58+ F '70
GROSSMAN, Ezra
Two players in the E-day action. il pors Bsns
W p30 Ap 25 '70 *
GROSSMAN, Jack J. and others
Surface properties of lunar samples. bibliog
il Science 167:743-5 Ja 30 '70
GROSVENOR, Gilbert M.
Frederick G. Vosburgh retires as editor; Gil-
bert M. Grosvenor succeeds him. M. M.
Payne. il pors Nat Geog 138:838-43 D '70 *
GROSVENOR, Kali
Christmas is what it means to me. Redbook
136:65+ D '70
GROSVENOR, Melville Bell
North through history aboard White Mist.
il pors Nat Geog 138:1-55 Jl '70
Vacationland U.S.A. il Nat Geog 137:734-40
My '70
GROSVENOR, Verta Mae
Soul food. il McCalls 97:72-5 S '70
about
Authors & editors. D. N. Mount. por Pub W
197:49-50 Je 29 '70 *
GROTESQUE in art
See also
Art, Fantastic
GROTH, John
John Groth's addition to the art of sport. A.
Gingrich. Esquire 74:6+ N '70 *
GROTOWSKI, Jerzy
Act of the actor. P. McDermott. Commonweal
91:510-13 F 6 '70
Grotowski: an unsettled American theater
replies; symposium, ed. by S. W. Little.
Sat R 53:20-1 F 7 '70
Grotowski revolution. C. R. Hughes. America
122:44-5 Ja 17 '70
GROUND covers. See Cover plants
GROUND effect machines. See Air cushion
vehicles
GROUND phlox. See Moss pink
GROUND schools. See Aviation schools
GROUND stations (communications satellites)
See Communications satellites—Ground sta-
tions
GROUND support systems (space flight)
Apollo 13 crises spur massive support. E. J.
Bulban. il Aviation W 92:22-5 Ap 27 '70
GROUNDCOVERS. See Cover plants
GROUNDS, Vernon C.
Bombs or Bibles? Get ready for revolution!
Chr Today 15:4-6 Ja 15 '71
GROUP buying. See Purchasing, Cooperative
GROUP conflict. See Social conflict
GROUP counseling
See also
Group guidance in education
Group psychotherapy
GROUP for environmental education
Opening your eyes. il Time 95:41 My 18 '70
GROUP guidance in education
Group counseling. J. A. Thayer. bibliog Clear
House 45:100-3 O '70
GROUP living. See Collective settlements
GROUP Lotus car companies, ltd. See Auto-
mobile industry and trade—Great Britain
GROUP medical practice. See Medicine—Group
practice
GROUP medicine. See Medicine—Group practice
GROUP morale. See Social psychology
GROUP motion. See Dance companies
GROUP plan of piano instruction. See Piano
classes
GROUP psychology. See Groups (sociology)
GROUP psychotherapy
Diagnostic intake: variation on a theme. R.
A. Simons. bibliog Ment Hy 54:101-4 Ja '70
Doctor Baird of East Harlem: conductor of
group therapy sessions for narcotic addicts.
W. F. Buckley. jr. Nat R 22:100 Ja 27 '70
Interagency pooling of resources to establish
new services. G. A. Crow. Ment Hy 54:118-22
Ja '70
Observations on psychiatric services for the
deaf. K. Z. Altshuler and J. D. Rainer. bib-
liog Ment Hy 54:535-9 O '70
Problems and pitfalls of establishing an Op-
erant conditioning-token economy program.
J. Montgomery and R. D. McBurney. Ment
Hy 54:382-7 Jl '70
Psychiatric social clubs come of age. S. Grob.
bibliog Ment Hy 54:129-36 Ja '70
Reaching the deaf: report of an in-hospital
group. R. E. Geller. Ment Hy 54:388-92 Jl
'70

GROUP psychotherapy—*Continued*
School grades and group therapy. S. Tenenbaum. Ment Hy 54:525–9 O '70
See also
Family psychotherapy
Moving pictures in psychotherapy
Neurotics anonymous
GROUP reading. See Reading—Study and teaching
GROUP relations training
Are your sensitivities trained? R. Kirk. Nat R 22:1352 D 15 '70
Behavioral science: is the cure worth it? G. Berkwitt. il Duns 95:38–41 My '70
Can sensitivity training help teach math? H. S. Resnik. Vogue 156:76 N 15 '70
Encounter; by J. Mann. Review
New Repub 162:21–2 My 23 '70. R. Whittemore
Encounter groupers up against the wall. B. L. Maliver. il N Y Times Mag p4–5+ Ja 3 '71
Encounter groups: emotional striptease for women? excerpts from Please touch. J. Howard. Vogue 155:110–11+ Je '70
Face doodles done for fun. il Life 69:68–71 N 6 '70
Getting together; Human potential movement. A. Gross. Mlle 71:154–5+ My '70
Group therapy: a special report. S. Blum. il Redbook 134:102–3+ Mr '70
Having wonderful encounter; singles weekend at Concord hotel, Catskills. J. Klemesrud. il por N Y Times Mag p8–9+ D 20 '70
New hope for the dull: the Encounter group. R. L. Schwartz. Life 68:16 Je 12 '70
Opinion: encounter groups. J. D. Black. Mlle 71:33+ My '70
Potential of human potential. R. Claiborne. Nation 211:373–5 O 19 '70
Sensitivity and sensuality. R. Kirk. Nat R 23:36 Ja 12 '71
Sensitivity modules; to help tear down the wall of unreality between school and life. H. Kirschenbaum. Ed Digest 35:16–18 My '70
Sensitivity training aids our staff development program. R. Brower. por Camp Mag 42:14+ N '70
Sensitivity training: fulfillment or freakout? P. R. Greene. il Cath World 211:18–21 Ap '70
Sensitivity training touch and grow? H. B. Kuhn. Chr Today 15:61–2 N 6 '70
Understanding laboratory education: an overview. C. P. Alderfer. bibliog il Mo Labor R 93:18–27 D '70
Weekend encounter: strength from the group; report of a Cleveland encounter group. L. Jaroff. Time 96:56–7 N 9 '70
You don't have a body; you are your body; excerpt from Please touch. J. Howard. Mlle 71:153+ My '70
See also
Esalen institute, Calif.
Social education

Anecdotes, facetiae, satire, etc.
My (ugh!) sensitivity training. J. Stafford. Horizon 12:112 Spr '70
Touch me, feel me, grunt, growl, purr; excerpt from People I have loved, known, or admired. L. Rosten. Sat R 53:12–13 My 30 '70

Bibliography
Techniques for psychic survival. H. S. Resnik. il Sat R 53:21–4+ Jl 25 '70

Caricatures and cartoons
Sensitivity nonsense; cartoons. J. Noonan. Chr Cent 88:22 Ja 6 '71
GROUP work in education
Individual in the group, an antidote for intellectual loneliness? T. Benfey. Chem 43:4 F '70
Le GROUPE express. See Publishers and publishing—France
GROUPERS
Giant grouper. J. Harding. il Sea Front 16:82–4 Mr '70
GROUPING by ability. See Ability grouping in education
GROUPS (sociology)
Collective violence; symposium, ed. by J. F. Short, jr. and M. E. Wolfgang. bibliog f il Ann Am Acad 391:1–176 S '70
Critical note on conceptions of collective behavior; with reply by N. J. Smelser. E. Currie and J. H. Skolnick. bibliog f Ann Am Acad 391:34–55 S '70
Ethnic consciousness I. T. H. Clancy. America 124:10 Ja 9 '71
Experiments in intergroup discrimination. H. Tajfel. il Sci Am 223:96–102 bibliog(p 132) N '70

Out on a limb. il Time 96:59+ O 5 '70
Violet way, excerpt from The social contract. R. Ardrey. il Life 69:56B–56D+ S 11 '70; Same abr. with title Is man naturally violent? Read Digest 97:115–19 D '70
See also
Social psychology
GROUSE shooting
Extra season for grouse. P. Barrett. il Field & S 75:50–1+ S '70
Greatest game on earth. il Nat Wildlife 8:52–3 O '70
Grouse hunter's scorecard. H. G. Tapply. il Field & S 75:58 N '70
Grouse on the upbeat. J. O. Cartier. il Outdoor Life 146:70–1+ S '70
I-wasn't-ready bird; the ruffed grouse. D. Holland. il Field & S 74:90–1+ Ap '70
Mountain grouse are work. G. X. Sand. il pors Outdoor Life 145:56–7+ F '70
See also
Prairie chicken shooting
GROUTT, John W.
City of (big) brotherly love. Commonweal 92:167–9 My 1 '70
GROVE, Kay
Bye, bye blackboard. il Mlle 72:186–7+ N '70
GROVE, Larry
Landscaping (cont) il Bet Home & Gard 48:34–5 F '70
GROVE, Pearce S.
Live-in in the Southwest: SWLA 1970. il Wilson Lib Bul 45:445–7 Ja '71
GROVE press, inc.
Big headlines, small profits. J. Smith. por Duns 96:66 N '70
Election set at Pyramid, Grove arbitration ends. Pub W 197:129 Je 8 '70
Grove and union agree to arbitration, election. il Pub W 197:55–7 Ap 27 '70
Grove fires union activists. Women's lib seizes officers. Pub W 197:38 Ap 20 '70
Grove loses arbitration; four must be rehired. Pub W 198:248 Ag 31 '70
Union election set at Grove, petition for vote at Pyramid. Pub W 197:36 My 4 '70
Union soundly beaten at Grove press. Pub W 197:22 My 11 '70
GROVER, Robert C.
My life and high times in harness. il Sports Illus 33:36–40 O 5 '70
GROVES, Colin P. See Oakley, K. P. jt. auth.
GROVES, Don
Glass submarines. il Sea Front 16:286–90 S '70
GROVES, Leslie Richard
Some recollections of July 16, 1945. il por Bul Atom Sci 26:21–7 Je '70

about
Builder of the bomb. il por Newsweek 76:63 Jl 27 '70 *
GROWER, Marvin F. and Bransome, E. D. Jr
Adenosine 3',5'-monophosphate, adrenocorticotropic hormone, and adrenocortical cytosol protein synthesis. bibliog il Science 168:483–5 Ap 24 '70
GROWTH
See also
Children—Growth and development
GROWTH (plants)
Maize leaf elongation: continuous measurements and close dependence on plant water status. T. C. Hsiao and others. bibliog il Science 168:590–1 My 1 '70
Starch accumulation associated with growth reduction at low temperatures in a tropical plant. J. H. Hilliard and S. H. West. bibliog il Science 168:494–6 Ap 24 '70
See also
Fungi, Effect of light on
Geotropism (botany)
Phototropism
GROWTH, Economic. See Economic development
GROWTH hormone. See Pituitary hormones
GROWTH inhibiting substances
Inhibition of phosphofructokinase by quinone methide and α-methylene lactone tumor inhibitors. R. L. Hanson and others. bibliog il Science 168:378–80 Ap 17 '70
Reactions of alpha methylene lactone tumor inhibitors with model biological nucleophiles. S. M. Kupchan and others. bibliog il Science 168:376–8 Ap 17 '70
GROWTH inhibiting substances (plants)
Growth inhibitor from young expanding tobacco leaves. H. G. Cutler. bibliog Science 170:856–7 N 20 '70
Leaf-dropping hormone isolated. F. L. Addicott. il Horticulture 48:40 F '70
See also
Abscisic acid

GROWTH inhibiting substances (viruses)
See also
Rhodanine
GROWTH of children. See Children—Growth and development
GROWTH of cities and towns. See Cities and towns—Growth
GROWTH promoting substances
See also
Pituitary hormones
GROWTH promoting substances (plants)
Moon dust may lead to new growth stimulant. Farm J 94:24D Ag '70
See also
Colchicine
Gibberellic acid
GROWTH stocks. See Stocks
GRUBEL, Herbert G.
Foreign scientists in the United States. il Bul Atom Sci 26:9-12 Ap '70
GRUBER, Michael
Finding a hole in the bottom of the sea. il Sea Front 16:309-11 S '70
New Northwest Passage. il Sea Front 16:2-12 Ja '70
Patterns of marine life. il Sea Front 16:194-205 Jl '70
Robot sailor. il Sea Front 16:77-81 Mr '70
GRUEN, John
Art's new originals. il Am Home 73:50+ Ap '70
Movie (cont) Vogue 155:34 Mr 15; 152 My; 156:106 N 1 '70
Movies (cont) Vogue 155:34 Mr 15; 152 My '70
Underground. See occasional issues of Vogue to September 1, 1970
Wild Alice. il por Vogue 156:170-1+ D '70
GRUENBERG, Selma
Pop goes the weaving! il Sch Arts 70:19 Ja '71
GRUENINGER, Walter F.
Phonograph records. See issues of Consumer bulletin
GRUGMANN, Bruce B.
Farewell, free enterprise. P. Barnes. New Repub 163:16-18 O 17 '70 *
GRUMBACH, Doris
American peaceniks, 150 years ago. Commonweal 93:164-5 N 13 '70
Father church and the motherhood of God. Commonweal 93:268-9 D 11 '70
In the works at Mercy. Commonweal 92:356-7 Jl 24 '70
Out of the grooves of academe. Commonweal 91:468-70 Ja 30 '70
GRUMBACH, Melvin M.
Boy or girl? A new pre-birth test can tell; interview. il Good H 170:139 Ja '70
GRUMMAN corporation
F-14 crash shakes Grumman. il Bsns W D 16 Ja 9 '71
Grumman cracks a silence barrier. Bsns W p32 Mr 21 '70
GRUND, Benjamin
What's coming in executive taxes; interview, ed. by G. R. Rosen. il por Duns 95:56-7+ Mr '70
GRUNER, Wayne R.
Why there is a job shortage. bibliog il por Phys Today 23:21-6 Je '70
GRUNFELD, Frederic V.
Enchanted chessmen. il Horizon 12:100-3 Wint '70
Land where lemons grow. Holiday 47:48-9+ Ja '70
La Mancha. il Horizon 11:40-7 Aut '69
Not two flutes, you scoundrels! Two piccolos! Two piccolos! Oh, what brutes! il pors Horizon 12:102-11 Aut '70
Troubadours. il Horizon 12:14-27 Sum '70
GRUTZNER, Charles
How to lock out the Mafia. bibliog f il Harvard Bsns R 48:45-58 Mr '70
GSTAAD, Switzerland
Who prefers Gstaad? Those of us with better taste. J. K. Galbraith. il Holiday 47:60-3+ Ja '70
GUACAMOLE. See Sauces
GUADALAJARA, Mexico
Guadalajara. G. Trotta. Harp Baz 103:46+ Ag '70
Guadalajara is a good place to make an Orozco mural tour. il Sunset 144:36 Mr '70
Sunday market in Guadalajara. il Sunset 145:32 D '70
Teen travel talk; student serenade to Guadalajara and Puerto Vallarta. il Seventeen 29:255 Ap '70
GUADALCANAL
Guadalcanal today. G. E. Allen. il Travel 133:60-6 Ap '70
GUADALUPE ISLAND
Party cruise. C. Pepper. il Travel 135:58-61 Ja '71

GUADELOUPE (islands)
Caribbean hideaways. G. Koretz. il Travel & Camera 33:60-3 Ja '70
France in the Caribbean: Martinique and Guadeloupe. il Harp Baz 103:32L Ap '70
Gallic pizzazz in the West Indies. M. Gough. il House B 112:22+ Ag '70
Guadeloupe: French escape route for swingers; Club Mediterranee. J. Star. il Look 34:22-7 Mr 10 '70
Guadeloupe gamble. D. Teague. il Yachting 128:62-3+ N '70
GUAM
Return to Guam. R. H. Peck. il Travel & Camera 33:66-8 Ja '70
U.N. subcommittee discusses American Samoa and Guam; statements, June 30 and August 17, 1970. F. H. Sacksteder. Dept State Bul 63:336-40 S 21 '70
GUANIDINE hydrochloride. See Guanidines
GUANIDINES
1,3-bis(p-chlorobenzylideneamino)guanidine hydrochloride (robenzidene): new poultry anticoccidial agent. S. Kantor and others. bibliog il Science 168:373-4 Ap 17 '70
GUANO bats. See Bats
GUARANTEED annual income
Can handouts make better wage earners? OEO income-maintenance program experiment. il Bsns W p80-2 F 28 '70
Guaranteed income? experiment findings. R. Lekachman. Duns 95:9 Ap '70
Minimum income for all: a step closer. il U S News 68:76 Ap 27 '70
Nearer: aid for working poor. il U S News 68:36 Mr 9 '70
Trying out the new plan; OEO experimental income maintenance program. il Sci N 97:216-17 F 28 '70
Will work work? OEO income maintenance programs. J. A. Hamilton. il Sat R 53:24-7 My 23 '70
GUARANTEED income. See Guaranteed annual income
GUARANTY. See Warranty
GUARD dogs. See Watchdogs
GUARD service. See Guards
GUARDS
Urban renewal needs a guard service; Milford, Conn. S. Keene. il Am City 85:68 N '70
GUARDS, Papal. See Papal guards
GUARNERI string quartet. See String quartets
GUATEMALA
See also
Arts and crafts—Guatemala
Elections—Guatemala
Guerrillas—Guatemala
Tikal

Politics and government
Power to the gunmen; kidnapping of diplomats in Latin America. New Repub 162:9 Ap 4 '70
Snatch diplomacy. Nat R 22:296-7 Mr 24 '70
See also
Elections—Guatemala
GUATEMALAN pottery. See Pottery, Guatemalan
GUBERNATORIAL candidates. See Candidates, Political
GUCCIONE, Robert
Bunny hunting. il pors Newsweek 75:71 Mr 2 '70 *
GUELFI, Giangiacomo
Man of the law; interview, ed. by F. Stevenson. por Opera N 34:16 Mr 14 '70 *
GUENTHER, John E.
Use of supplemental materials in teaching black history. il Clear House 45:226-30 D '70
GUERIN, Pierre
New ring of Saturn. il Sky & Tel 40:88 Ag '70
GUERIN, Richie
War games. il Newsweek 75:67 Ap 27 '70 *
GUERNSEY, John
Portland's unconventional Adams high. il Am Ed 6:3-7 My '70
GUÉRON, Jules
Atomic energy in continental western Europe. il por Bul Atom Sci 26:62-8+ Je '70
GUERRILLA theater. See Theater, Experimental
GUERRILLA warfare
How to be a terrorist in ten easy lessons. Nat R 22:1036 O 6 '70
GUERRILLAS
Arab states
Arab guerrillas adopt air piracy as tactic. il Aviation W 93:33+ S 14 '70
Arab guerrillas: who are they? Sr Schol 97:10 S 28 '70

GUERRILLAS—Arab states—*Continued*
Arab vs. Arab vs. Israel, new 100-year war? il Sr Schol 95:21 N 17 '69
Arabs their own worst enemy. America 122:604 Je 6 '70
Chaos in the sky; Palestinian guerrillas strike at the big jets; with report of earlier hijacking by L. Khaled. il Life 69:30-7 S 18 '70
Civil war explodes in Jordan; with report by L. Jenkins. il Newsweek 76:35-8+ S 28 '70
Drama on the desert; the week of the hostages. il Time 96:18-20+ S 21 '70
Eretz Israel, or historic Palestine? America 122:666 Je 27 '70
Fedayeen: Israel's fanatic foe. D. Reed. il Read Digest 97:168-73 O '70
Frustrating case of TWA flight 741. il Bsns W p34+ O 10 '70
Guerrilla threat. il Newsweek 76:23 Ag 17 '70
Hidden leader of the Arab guerrillas; interview, ed. by O. Fallaci. Abu Lotuf. il Look 34:24-6 Je 30 '70
Hijack war. il Newsweek 76:20-8 S 21 '70
Jordan: the battle ends; the war begins. il por Time 96:24-7 O 5 '70
Palestine Arab commandos; with report on the Gaza Strip by P. Young and interview with G. Habash, ed. by O. Fallaci. il Life 68:26D-34 Je 12 '70
Palestinians: confused and uncertain. il Newsweek 76:30 Ag 24 '70
War of the long breath. il Time 95:32-7 Mr 30 '70
Why Arab guerrillas are out of control. J. N. Wallace. il U S News 69:24-5 S 21 '70
See also
Fedayeen
Guerrillas—Lebanon

Bolivia
Bolivian guerrilla movement comes to an end. M. Arias. Chr Cent 88:18-19 Ja 6 '71
Che: a myth embalmed in a matrix of ignorance. il pors Time 96:34+ O 12 '70

Brazil
How one pleasant, scholarly young man from Brazil became a kidnapping, gun-toting, bombing revolutionary. S. De Gramont. il pors N Y Times Mag p43-5+ N 15 '70; Discussion. p22+ D 6; 79+ D 13 '70
Politics of violence: the urban guerrilla in Brazil; interview with four revolutionists, ed. by A. Truskier. il Ramp Mag 9:30-4+ O '70

Cambodia
Buying time for FUNK; National united front of Kampuchea. il Newsweek 76:34 Ag 3 '70
Cambodian civil war; Khmer rouge activities. O. Schell. New Repub 162:12-14 Je 6 '70
Road to Phnom Penh: Cambodia takes up the gun. B. Garrett. il Ramp Mag 9:32-5+ Ag '70

Canada
See also
Front for the liberation of Quebec

Colombia
Private war of a guerrilla; D. Aljure. R. L. Maullin. il por Trans-Action 7:45-54 bibliog(p64) Mr '70

Guatemala
Diplomats on the firing line. Sr Schol 96:15 Ap 27 '70
Escalating terror. Newsweek 75:40 Ap 13 '70
Guatemala and the guerrillas. G. A. Geyer. New Repub 163:17-19 Jl 4 '70
Real good relationship: Col. C. Arana Osorio. J. C. Goulden. Nation 210:646 Je 1 '70

India
Indian revolutionaries with a Chinese accent: the Naxalites. D. Moraes. il N Y Times Mag p30-1+ N 8 '70

Indochina
Back to guerrilla warfare. il Time 96:26 Ag 17 '70

Jordan
Arab guerrillas v. Arab governments. il por Time 95:22-3 Je 22 '70
Commando revolution: a hundred years war in the Middle East? Z. B. Grant. New Repub 162:9-11 Ja 24 '70
Explosion in Jordan. il por Newsweek 75:34-5 Je 22 '70
How Hussein met commando crisis. J. Law. por U S News 68:19 Mr 9 '70
Jordan: a nation cracking apart. J. Law. il U S News 69:20-1 S 28 '70
Jordan: the king takes on the guerrillas. il pors Time 96:16-18+ S 28 '70

King under fire. L. Jenkins. il Newsweek 76:51 S 14 '70
Lull in the madness. il Newsweek 75:35 Je 29 '70
Shoring up a shaky calm. il por Time 95:24+ Je 29 '70
Violent men of Ammand. E. Pace. il N Y Times Mag p8-9+ Jl 19 '70
See also
Fedayeen

Latin America
Kidnaping diplomats, what's back of terrorist tactics. il U S News 68:22-3 Ap 20 '70
New terror in Latin America: snatching the diplomats. R. O'Mara. Nation 210:518-19 My 4 '70

Lebanon
If it happens here, it will happen there. il Time 95:35 My 25 '70
Reports: Beirut. G. G. Stevens. Atlan 225:27-8+ F '70
Slap on the wrist: Israelis attack Aita es Shaab. il Newsweek 75:47D+ Mr 16 '70
Waiting for Washington to decide; government order to stop provoking Israelis. il Newsweek 75:39+ Je 8 '70

Middle East
Palestinians and Israel. S. Avineri. bibliog f Commentary 49:31-44 Je '70; Discussion. 50:6+ S; 30+ N; 18+ D '70
Tiger Nasser can't ride; Palestine liberation movement. V. S. Kearney. il America 122:208-11 F 28 '70
See also
Guerrillas—Arab states
Guerrillas—Lebanon

Oman
After the party's over. A. de Borchgrave. il Newsweek 76:29 D 28 '70

Uruguay
And now Uruguay. Chr Cent 87:1009 Ag 26 '70; Reply. E. M. Smith. Chr Cent 87:1287-8 O 28 '70
Hanging tough: ransom demands and political kidnappings. il Newsweek 76:32 Ag 24 '70
It was a terrible scene: kidnappings and deaths by Tupamaros. R. Peter. Nat R 22:1001+ S 22 '70
Kidnap fever. Newsweek 76:45 Ag 17 '70
Murder, Tupamaros-style. il por Time 96:20+ Ag 24 '70

Vietnam (Democratic Republic)
See Vietnamese war, 1957- —Guerrillas

Vietnam (Republic)
See Vietnamese war, 1957- —Guerrillas
GUERRILLAS; drama. See Hochhuth, R.
GUERTIN, Cynthia
Visit to the Cambridge art center. il Sch Arts 69:36-7 Ap '70
GUEST houses
At home with art: the Lawrence Bloedel guesthouse. il Art in Am 58:80-5 My '70
Getting away at home. L. Grundy. il House B 112:57-61 Je '70
It grew from a garden. R. FitzGerald. il House B 112:62-4 Je '70
GUEST ranches. See Ranches
GUEST rooms
Guest room in a ten-inch space. A. Lees and others. il Pop Sci 197:86-7+ S '70
GUESTS
Welcome but warning. E. Klein. Harp Baz 103:84-5 Ag '70
See also
Entertaining

Anecdotes, facetiae, satire, etc.
Well-tempered dinner guest: results of competition on dinner-table conversation starters with uncommunicative partners. N. S. Hazelton. Nat R 22:157 F 10 '70
GUEVARA, Ernesto
Che: a myth embalmed in a matrix of ignorance. il pors Time 96:34+ O 12 '70 *
Death of a revolutionary, by R. Harris. Review
America 123:268-9 O 10 '70. F. P. LeVeness *
Living up to an image: memorial unveiled in Chile. il Newsweek 76:56 N 23 '70 *
GUFFEY, Rand
Fly-ash-by-night conspiracy. il Audubon 72:147-8 N '70
GUGA, Sister Ann Rose M.
Architectural boom in the visual arts. il Sch Arts 69:20-1 Ap '70

GUGGENHEIM, Charles
Electronic politics: the image game. il por Time 96:43-4+ S 21 '70 *
Victory through TV. America 122:546 My 23 '70 *

GUIANA, DUTCH. See Surinam

GUIANA space center. See France—National center for space studies

GUIDANCE. See Personnel service in education; Vocational guidance

GUIDE books. See Guidebooks

GUIDEBOOKS
Mammoth editorial project for an innovative guidebook, Treasures of Britain. M. R. Kramer. il Pub W 197:94-6 Je 29 '70

Bibliography
Traveler's guide to guidebooks. il Changing T 24:31-3 Je '70

GUIDED missile bases
Air force seeks missile rebasing funds. K. Johnsen. Aviation W 93:19-20 Ag 3 '70
Round two on ABM; expansion of Safeguard system. il Time 95:17 Mr 9 '70
Why a new fight looms over missile defense. il U S News 68:8 Mr 9 '70

GUIDED missile bases, Russian
Moscow-on-the-Nile. Time 95:31+ Je 22 '70
New missile sites threat to Israeli air supremacy. Aviation W 93:20 Ag 24 '70
SAM changes force new strategy on Israelis. E. H. Kolcum. il Aviation W 93:16-21 N 16 '70

GUIDED missiles
Army missile becomes a target; Shillelagh vs. Hughes-built TOW missile. Bsns W p 130-1 Mr 28 '70
Buildup on the Suez: Soviet missiles. il Time 96:21 S 14 '70
Harpoon anti-ship missile development to accelerate. B. Miller. Aviation W 94:18-19 Ja 4 '71
How to cope with SAM-3. il Newsweek 75:40 Ap 6 '70
Minuteman 3 deployment slated. Aviation W 92:23 Mr 16 '70
Minuteman III's spring planting. il Bsns W p 130 Mr 28 '70
Politics to pace missile advances. C. Brownlow. il Aviation W 92:220-2+ Je 22 '70
Question of credence; buildup of Soviet missiles. il Newsweek 76:50-1 S 14 '70
Senate marksmen bring down tactical missiles. il Bsns W p 114+ Ja 17 '70
Standard ARM is tested on F-4D, F-105. il Aviation W 93:16-17 Ag 24 '70
Tactical missile advances slowed. il Aviation W 92:226+ Je 22 '70
See also
MIRV

Control
Phoenix fire control unit expanded. B. Miller. il Aviation W 92:51-2+ My 25 '70

Cost
SALT chips and Safeguard. R. E. Lapp. New Repub 163:14-17 Ag 15 '70

Defenses
ABM & MIRV; in the context of SALT; address, June 12, 1970. R. Kilmarx. Vital Speeches 36:602-4 Jl 15 '70
ABM cost rise estimated at $2 billion. D. C. Winston. Aviation W 92:25-6 My 25 '70
ABM debate: who, what, why? il Sr Schol 95:6-11+ S 29 '69
ABM fight heads into second stage. il Bsns W p32-3 F 14 '70
ABM, MIRV, and the arms race. H. F. York. Science 169:257-60 Jl 17 '70
ABM request faces opposition in Senate. D. C. Winston. Aviation W 92:18-19 Mr 2 '70
ABM: Senate approves expansion but hope seen for arms curb. L. J. Carter. Science 169:844-5 Ag 28 '70
Arms control: current prospects and problems. J. B. Wiesner. il Bul Atom Sci 26:6-8+ My '70
Bell labs scaling down. Sci N 97:525 My 30 '70
Citizen looks at the ABM; Safeguard system. H. C. Lodge. Read Digest 96:57-64 Je '70
Conferees agree on limited ABM scope. D. C. Winston. Aviation W 93:20-1 O 5 '70
Go signal for more ABM's: new fight ahead in Congress. il U S News 68:34-5 F 16 '70
How Russia closed missile gap; defense chief's report. il U S News 68:21 My 4 '70
Let's send SABMIS to sea now. W. R. Anderson. Read Digest 96:102-6 F '70
Margin of safety; Cooper-Hart amendment. il Newsweek 76:14-15 Ag 24 '70

Military buildup by Soviet spurs Safeguard growth. Aviation W 92:17-18 F 23 '70
National priorities; are we to become a second rate power? address, April 20, 1970. M. R. Laird. Vital Speeches 36:452-6 My 15 '70
Opponents cite ABM vulnerability to high-altitude nuclear blasts. Aviation W 93:20 Jl 20 '70
President Nixon's news conference of January 30, 1970. R. M. Nixon. Dept State Bul 62:173-7 F 16 '70
Proponents fight to save Safeguard from attacks. Aviation W 93:21 Ag 10 '70
Real issue in the ABM showdown. il U S News 69:19-21 Ag 17 '70
Round two on ABM; expansion of Safeguard system. il Time 95:17 Mr 9 '70
Safeguard prize goes for a bargain. il Bsns W p 31 Ap 4 '70
SALT: a sprinkling of hope. il Time 96:24-5 Jl 20 '70
SALT chips and Safeguard. R. E. Lapp. New Repub 163:14-17 Ag 15 '70
Second strike; ABM program. il Newsweek 75:18-19 Mr 9 '70
Shifting the ground; Safeguard debate. il Sci N 97:548-9 Je 6 '70
Soviet ABM and arms control. J. I. Coffey. il Bul Atom Sci 26:39-43 Ja '70
Spartan operational test scores intercept. il Aviation W 93:17 S 7 '70
Try, try again; ABM phase II. il Newsweek 76:18-19 Ag 10 '70
Underground nuclear testing. il Environ 11:3-6 Jl '69
Verification of nuclear arms limitations: an analysis. H. Scoville, jr. Bul Atom Sci 26:6-11 O '70
Why a new fight looms over missile defense. il U S News 68:8 Mr 9 '70
See also
MIRV
Russia—Defenses
United States—Defenses

Detection
Expectations from SALT. A. De Volpi. il Bul Atom Sci 26:6-8 Ap '70

Electronic equipment
Motorola develops radar seeker. B. Miller. il Aviation W 92:63-4 Mr 16 '70

Ethical aspects
See Atomic warfare—Ethical aspects

Launching
See Guided missile bases

Launching from airplanes
AIM-82A missile proposals for USAF F-15 fighter readied. Aviation W 92:19 Mr 2 '70
Phoenix fire control unit expanded. B. Miller. il Aviation W 92:51-2+ My 25 '70
USAF cancels AIM-82A missile. Aviation W 93:21 S 7 '70
What its like to face tilim. il Time 96:19 Jl 20 '70

Launching from ships
Israel's Gabriel: top defense missile. il Space World H-1-85:23-9 Ja '71
Martel ship-launched version designed. il Aviation W 93:81-2 S 7 '70
Norwegian navy gets Penguin missiles. il Aviation W 94:51 Ja 4 '71
Shipboard launch tests of Exocet started. D. E. Fink. Aviation W 93:21 Jl 20 '70

Launching from submarine boats
Blue water boondoggle; projected Undersea long-range missile system to replace Polaris and Poseidon. S. D'Arazien. il Nation 211:498-500 N 16 '70
Major ULMS funding expected. C. Brownlow. Aviation W 93:14-15 Jl 20 '70

Photographs
Soviet crews simulate Scud firing. Aviation W 92:54-5 Ap 20 '70

Protective measures
Air force fights to save Minuteman. Bsns W p 110+ O 10 '70

Specifications
Leading international missiles; tables (cont) Aviation W 92:112-13 Mr 9 '70
U.S. drones and target missiles; tables (cont) Aviation W 92:111 Mr 9 '70
U.S. missiles; tables (cont) Aviation W 92:103-4 Mr 9 '70
USSR missiles; tables (cont) Aviation W 92:110 Mr 9 '70

GUIDED missiles—*Continued*

Testing

ABM vs. ICBM, round 1; Safeguard test. il Newsweek 76:97 S 14 '70

Franco-German missile is tested; Roland surface-to-air missile. il Aviation W 92: 116-17 Ap 27 '70

Hitting a fly in space: a milestone for America's ABM; Spartan. il U S News 69:31 S 14 '70

Major test of ABM scheduled by army. Aviation W 92:27 Ap 27 '70

Moscow's better mousetrap; testing new ABM system at Sary-Shagan test range. Time 96:33 O 12 '70

Poseidon checkout computerized. B. M. Elson. il Aviation W 92:48-9+ F 16 '70

Spartan operational test scores intercept; first operational ABM test firing from Kwajalein. il Aviation W 93:17 S 7 '70

Tests of ABM missile integration slated for Kwajalein this month. D. C. Winston. Aviation W 92:18-19 Mr 16 '70

GUIDES

How to have a great guided hunt. H. Rate. il Field & S 75:32-3+ Ag '70

See also

Mountaineering

GUIDES, Road. See Road maps, guides, etc.

GUIDI, Eriberto

Gallery; photographs. Life 68:6-9 F 27 '70

GUIDI, V. H.

Unexpected spectacles: U.S. mines and quarries. il Travel 133:64-3+ Mr '70

GUILLET, James E.

Plastic for ecologists. Time 95:86 My 11 '70 *

GUILLEVIC, Eugene

Parallels; Right angle; Acute angle; Rectangle; poems, tr. by T. Savory. Poetry 116:358-61 Ag '70

about

Comment. S. Berg. Poetry 116:260-2 Jl '70 *

GUILLORY, Ferrel

Baton Rouge desegregates. America 122:650-2 Je 20 '70

Louisiana desegregation, and Catholic schools. il America 123:119-21 S 5 '70

GUILT

Guilt and dental mutilation. Sci Digest 67:56 Ap '70

GUILT, Plea of. See Pleas (criminal procedure)

GUIMARD, Hector

Art nouveau designs at new Guimard exhibit. M. R. Kraner. il Pub W 197:51-2 Ap 20 '70 *

Man with the top hat: display at the Museum of modern art. D. Davis. il por Newsweek 75:53+ Mr 30 '70 *

Le style Guimard. R. Reif. il N Y Times Mag p92-3 Mr 8 '70 *

GUINAN, Bridget

Growing up a Catholic. Mlle 70:157+ Mr '70

GUINEA

Cloudy days in Conakry; invasion. il Time 96:46 D 7 '70

What's happening? invasion. Newsweek 76: 33-4 D 7 '70

See also

Ballet—Guinea

GUINEA, PORTUGUESE. See Portuguese Guinea

GUINEA pigs

Genetically controlled total deficiency of the fourth component of complement in the guinea pig. L. Ellman and others. bibliog il Science 170:74-5 O 2 '70

Immunotherapy of cancer: an experimental model in syngeneic guinea pigs. B. S. Kronman and others. bibliog il Science 168:257-9 Ap 10 '70

Pharamacological differentiation of allergic and classically conditioned asthma in the guinea pig. D. R. Justesen and others. bibliog il Science 170:864-6 N 20 '70

Satellite DNA in constitutive heterochromatin of the guinea pig. J. J. Yunis and W. G. Yasmineh. bibliog il Science 168:263-5 Ap 10 '70

GUINIER, Ewart G.

Harvard's Afro-American studies. por Negro Hist Bul 33:20 Ja '70 *

GUINNESS, Gloria

Fashion 1970. Harp Baz 104:76-7 D '70

Money matters! Harp Baz 103:138-9 Ag '70

Those magnificent men. Harp Baz 103:129 My '70

What is chic, what is fashion? Harp Baz 103: 152-3 Ap '70

about

Gloria Guinness. il pors Vogue 155:90-3 Ap 15 '70 *

Gloria, hallelujah. E. Sheppard. Harp Baz 103:142-3 F '70

GUITAR, Mary Anne

Ecology: new cause, new career. il Mlle 70: 190-3+ Ap '70

R for Philip. il Good H 170:12+ My '70

GUITAR

Redesigning the guitar. A. Perlmeter. il por Sci N 98:180-1 Ag 22 '70

Science builds a guitar with the now sound; parabolic-back guitar. P. Wahl. il Pop Sci 196:93 Mr '70

Instruction and study

Guitars for everyone; summer course for ghetto children. S. Lesher. il Parks & Rec 5:22-4+ Jl '70

GUITAR, Electronic. See Musical instruments, Electronic

GULBENKIAN, Calouste

How I didn't get Mr Gulbenkian's art. J. Walker. il por Horizon 12:28-43 Sum '70 *

GULF and Western industries, inc.

Hollywood sells off the splendor. il Life 68:38-43 F 27 '70

GULF OF CALIFORNIA. See California, Gulf of

GULF OF MEXICO. See Mexico, Gulf of

GULF OF TONKIN incident, 1964. See Tonkin Gulf incident, 1964

GULF oil corporation

Activists lay plans for war on Gulf. il Bsns W p23 Ap 11 '70

Gulf oil: pings over Portugal. E. E. Plowman. Chr Today 15:42 Ja 1 '71

Iberian assist helped oil the way; INI take over of Gulf oil operations. Bsns W p28-9 My 2 '70

More heat on Gulf; United church of Christ resolution. Commonweal 93:138 N 6 '70

Poker game where talk was the payoff. E. D. Brockett. il Nations Bsns 58:82-3 Ja '70

GULF specimen company

Panacea for a salty Yankee; collecting marine creatures for scientific study. R. H. Boyle. il por Sports Illus 32:28-30+ Ap 20 '70

GULF STREAM

Bottom velocity observations directly under the Gulf Stream. W. J. Schmitz, jr. and others. bibliog il Science 170:1192-4 D 11 '70

GULLAND, J. A.

Resources of the sea; with biographical sketch. il Sea Front 16:211-19, 255 Jl '70

GULLETTE, Irene. See Hatfield, F. jt. auth.

GULLIBILITY. See Credulity

GULLION, Gordon W.

Stopping the decline and fall of grouse. il Field & S 75:32-3+ D '70

GUMMERE, John F.

Schools, songs, and supplications. Sch & Soc 98:299-300 Sum '70

GUMMERE, Richard M. jr

Art subverts the curriculum. il Nation 211: 368-71 O 19 '70

GUMS (anatomy)

Diseases

Dental care. T. Berland. il Todays Ed 59:59+ My '70

Endotoxin: stimulation of bone resorption in tissue culture. E. Hausmann and others. bibliog il Science 168:862-4 My 15 '70

GUN cabinets. See Cabinets (furniture)

GUN control legislation. See Firearms—Laws and regulations

GUN sights. See Firearms—Sights

GUN thefts. See Firearms, Theft of

GUNDELFINGER, John

John Gundelfinger draws from life; excerpt from On-the-spot drawing. N. Meglin. il Am Artist 35:56-62 Ja '71 *

GUNDERSON, Doris V.

U.S. office of education: report on research projects. Engl J 59:304-7 F '70

GUNITE

Gunite gives new life to an old, failing brick sewer system; Chattanooga, Tenn. W. M. Englerth. il Am City 85:101-2 Jl '70

GUNN, Margaret M.

Desert exotic for northern homes and gardens. il Org Gard & Farm 17:80-2 Jl '70

Herb-drying, tastiest old-fashioned art. il Org Gard & Farm 17:114-18 O '70

GUNN, Moses

Rolling thunder. por Time 95:62+ Ap 6 '70 *

GUNN, Thom

Messenger; Being born; Discovery of the Pacific; poems. Poetry 116:1-5 Ap '70

GUNN effect. See Oscillators, Crystal

GUNNERY ranges. See Bombing and gunnery ranges

GUNS (small arms) See Firearms; Pistols; Revolvers; Shotguns

GUNSTOCK camera supports. See Camera supports

GUNTER, Peter A.
Mental inertia and environmental decay: the end of an era. il Liv Wildn 34:3-7 Spr '70

GUNTHER, John
Inside Down Under. il Read Digest 97:207-10+ O '70

about

Mr Inside. por Newsweek 75:105 Je 8 '70 *
Obituary
Time 95:53 Je 8 '70 *

GUNTHER, Max
Ringing down the curtain. Writer 83:18-22 S '70

GUPTA, Raj K. and Redfield, A. G.
Double nuclear magnetic resonance observation of electron exchange between ferri- and ferrocytochrome c. bibliog il Science 169:1204-6 S 18 '70

GUPTON, James A. jr
Antenna installer's guidebook. il Radio-Electr 41:55-8 S; 59-62 O '70

GURNEY, Alan
Racing-cruising auxiliaries. il por Motor B 125:104-5 Ja '70

GURNEY, Dan
Drivin' with Dan: questions and answers. See issues of Popular mechanics
Motor trend interview; ed. by E. Dahlquist. pors Motor T 22:90+ Ja '70
Trans-Am: the secret word is competition! il Pop Mech 134:74-7+ Jl '70

GURNEY, Ramsdell, jr
Soviet motives and stateside suspicions. Commonweal 93:63-8 O 16 '70

GURR, Ted Robert
Sources of rebellion in western societies: some quantitative evidence. bibliog f il Ann Am Acad 391:128-44 S '70

GUSTAFSON, James M.
(ed) Sixties: radical change in American religion. bibliog f Ann Am Acad 387:1-140 Ja '70

GUSTAFSON, Philip F.
Nuclear power and thermal pollution: Zion, Illinois. il Bul Atom Sci 26:17-23 Mr '70

GUSTAITIS, Rasa
Art of group scrounging. Holiday 47:55+ Mr '70
Pablum in paradise. il Am Home 73:80-5 Jl '70

GUSTAVA, Alice
Landscape with Navajo child; poem. America 122:345 Mr 28 '70

GUSTON, Philip
Art; exhibition at Marlborough. L. Alloway. Nation 211:574 N 30 '70 *
Art world; paintings of Klansmen at the Marlborough. H. Rosenberg. New Yorker 46:136+ N 7 '70 *
Ku klux komix. R. Hughes. il por Time 96:62-3 N 9 '70 *
New Gustons. B. Berkson. il por Art N 69:44-7+ O '70 *

GUSTS. See Winds

GUT, Artificial. See Intestines, Artificial

GUTENBERG Bible. See Bible

GUTH, Hans P.
Monkey on the bicycle: behavioral objectives and the teaching of English; address, November, 1969. Engl J 59:785-92 S '70

GUTHEIM, Frederick
Architecture. Nation 210:446 Ap 13 '70
Roland Wank, 1898-1970. il por Arch Forum 133:58-9 S '70

GUTHMAN, William H.
Surveyors' equipment and the western frontier. il Antiques 98:423-7 S '70

GUTHRIE, A. B. jr
Matter of opinion: microcosm. Am West 7:48 Jl '70; Same with title Day Choteau went dry. il Audubon 72:153 N '70

GUTHRIE, Ramon
Anatomy of the week; poem. Poetry 117:84-8 N '70
Black squirrels and Albert Einstein; poem. New Repub 163:28-9 Jl 11 '70
Fiercer than evening wolves; poem. Nation 210:440 Ap 13 '70
Making of the bear; poem. New Yorker 46:40-1 My 2 '70

GUTIÉRREZ, José L.
Unsung artist of the Mexican renaissance. J. B. Lynch. il por Américas 22:35-9 Je '70 *

GUTKIND, Lee Alan
Making the grade. il Schol Teach Sec Teach Sup p6-8+ Ap 6 '70
No more teachers' dirty looks. il Schol Teach Jr/Sr High p20-1+ N 2 '70
Probing Project Plan. il Schol Teach Jr/Sr High p20-3 O 5 '70

GUTMAN, Judith Mara
More perfect union. Nation 210:250-2 Mr 2 '70

GUTS frisbee. See Frisbee (game)

GUTTMACHER, Alan F.
Pill trial. por Time 95:32+ Mr 9 '70 *

GUY, Ronald
Build this wood planer for $100. il Pop Mech 134:174-9+ Ag '70

GUY, Rosa
Christmas, that blasted season! Redbook 136:81+ D '70

GUYER, David L.
International student and faculty exchange, 1968-69. il Sch & Soc 98:178-81 Mr '70

GUZIE, Tad W.
Celibacy and clericalism. Cath World 211:120-4 Je '70

GUZMAN, Paschal
Downtown ballet company, 92nd St. Y, NYC. T. Borek. Dance Mag 44:81 D '70 *

GUZZWELL, John
In the wake of Captain Cook. il Yachting 128:50-1+ D '70; 129:98-9+ Ja '71
Pacific delivery experienced circumnavigator takes a busman's holiday. il Yachting 127:60-1+ Mr '70

GWINUP, Grant
Energetics; excerpts. il House B 112:50+ O '70
The one sensible way to diet; interview, ed. by R. H. Berg. il Read Digest 96:163-4+ Je '70

GWINUP, Thomas
Causes and consequences. bibliog il por Library J 05:3729-30 N 1 '70

GYARMATHY, L.
TV-technician shortage; excerpts from address. Electr World 83:32 Mr '70

GYLDENDAL (publisher) See Publishers and publishing—Denmark

GYMNASIUMS
Shiny, rich look for the old gym. il Sports Illus 33:32-8 N 30 '70
Thinnest circular concrete plate spans 130 ft to roof a gymnasium. il Arch Rec 147:160-1 Je '70

GYMNASTICS
Sun didn't rise overnight; Japanese, the world's best gymnasts. D. Levin. por Sports Illus 32:28-9 Ap 13 '70
See also
Exercise

GYMNODINIUM. See Dinoflagellates

GYÖRGYI, Albert Szent-. See Szent-Györgyi, A.

GYPSY moths
Potent sex attractant of the gypsy moth: its isolation, identification, and synthesis. B. A. Bierl and others. bibliog il Science 170:87-9 O 2 '70

GYROCOPTERS. See Autogiros

GYROSCOPIC Instruments
See also
Automatic pilot (airplanes)
Automatic pilot (boats)
Inertial guidance systems

H

H-bombs. See Hydrogen bombs

H&R Block, Inc. See Block, H. and R. inc.

HEW. See United States—Health, education and welfare, Department of

HFC. See Household finance corporation

HRFA. See Hudson River fishermen's association

HUD. See United States—Housing and urban development, Department of

HAACK, Robert William
How Wall Street toes its own line. il por Nations Bsns 58:26-8+ S '70
New York stock exchange; address, November 17, 1970. Vital Speeches 37:140-3 D 15 '70
Stock-exchange head speaks out; excerpts from address, November 17, 1970. por U S News 69:76-7 N 30 '70

about

Big board's stand-up president. por Time 96:74 N 30 '70 *

HAACK, Robert William—about——*Continued* .
Market: time for a new broom. il pors Newsweek 76:71-3+ N 30 '70 *
New campaign to repave Wall Street. il Time
96:73-4 N 30 '70 *
Stripping secrecy from the big board; with
editorial comment. il Bsns W p70-2, 94 N
28 '70 *
HAAGEN-SMIT, Arie Jan
Man and his home; address, April 28, 1970.
Vital Speeches 36:572-6 Jl 1 '70; Same. Liv
Wildn 34:38-46 Sum '70
about
Let's hear it for Mr Clean. R. Starnes. Field
& S 75:10+ S '70 *
HABASH, George
Leader of the fedayeen: we want a war like
the Vietnam war; interview, ed. by O. Fallaci. il por Life 68:32-4 Je 12 '70
about
Doctor Habbash's strong medicine. por Newsweek 76:28 S 21 '70 *
Rebellious Palestinians. por Time 96:22 Ag 10
'70 *
HABEEB, Virginia
What's really new in the new appliances. il
Mech Illus 66:63-5+ D '70
HABER, Bernard, and others
L-Glutamic acid decarboxylase: a new type
in glial cells and human brain gliomas.
bibliog il Science 168:598-9 My 1 '70
HABER, Gordon C.
Isle Royale wilderness plan, a job unfinished. il Liv Wildn 34:31-7 Sum '70
HABER, Paul
Champ. por Newsweek 76:49 Ag 31 '70 *
HABER, Ralph Norman
How we remember what we see; with biographical sketch. il Sci Am 222:10, 104-12
My '70
HABIB, Philip Charles
Mr Habib discusses Hanoi's refusal to attend
May 6 meeting on Viet-Nam; transcript of
briefing, May 6, 1970. Dept State Bul 62:650-
1 My 25 '70
[Plenary sessions] on Vietnam held at
Paris. See issues of Department of state
bulletin, December 11, 1969 to July 30, 1970
HABITS of animals. See Animals—Habits and
behavior
HABSBURG, Otto von. See Otto, archduke
of Austria
HACALA, Joseph R. See Gannon, T. M. jt.
auth.
HACHENBERG, O.
New Bonn 100-meter radio telescope. il Sky
& Tel 40:338-43 D '70
HACHETTE. See Publishers and publishing—
France
HACK, Margherita
Stellar rotation and atmospheric motions. il
Sky & Tel 40:84-6, 143-5, 208-9 Ag-O '70
HACKENSACK, N.J.
Clarify before you buy. W. Fuhro. il Am City
85:82 Ja '70
HACKENSACK RIVER
Scout power tidies the Hackensack: action
by Girl scout troop 127. il Life 68:37-40 Je
12 '70
HACKER, Andrew
Violent black minority. il N Y Times Mag
p25+ My 10 '70
We will meet as enemies. por Newsweek 76:
24-5 Jl 6 '70
HACKER, Helen M.
How clergymen view hippiedom. il Chr Cent
87:887-91 Jl 22 '70
HACKETT, Alice Payne
Hardcover best sellers of 1969 in the U.S.
book trade. il Pub W 197:40-3 F 9 '70
HACKETT, Blanche
Are campers slobs? il Am For 76:36-9+ Ap '70
HACKETT, Walter
Christmas carol; dramatization of story by C.
Dickens. Plays 30:83-95 D '70
HACKS, Peter
Amphitryon, tr. by R. Manheim. Criticism
New Yorker 46:92 Je 13 '70 *
HACKSAWS. See Saws
HADDEN, Jeffrey K.
Clergy involvement in civil rights. bibliog
f Ann Am Acad 387:118-27 Ja '70
HADDON, E. P.
Take the whole family on a wilderness escape. il Todays Health 48:35-8 Ag '70
HADLEY, Drummond
Comment. Poetry 116:128 My '70 *
HADLEY, Leila
Shades. il Holiday 47:46-7+ Je '70
HADRONS. See Particles (nuclear physics)

HAFFER, Virna
Photograms: non-stop imagery as art. J.
Deschin. por Pop Phot 67:20+ S '70
HAFLER, David
Adding extra channel for improved hi-fi ambience. il Electr World 84:31 O '70
HAGANS, Orville R.
On time. See issues of Hobbies
HAGANS clock manor museum, Bergen Park,
Colo. See Museums
HAGE, Elizabeth B.
Rebuttal from Prince George; letter to the
editor. Am Lib 1:647-9 Jl '70 *
HAGEMAN, George
Ceramic ladies. il Ceram Mo 18:22-3 N '70
HAGEN, Kenneth S.
Following the ladybug home. il Nat Geog
137:542-53 Ap '70
HAGEN, Natalie
1970 articles contest. Writers Digest 50:35-6 O
'70
HAGEN show. See Festivals—New Guinea
HAGER, David R.
Orbiting junkyard. il Sat R 53:44-6 S 5 '70
HAGERTY, James
Textbook: a guide for its proper use. Clear
House 44:410 Mr '70
HAGGERTY, Patrick Eugene
Haggerty, McElroy, Bromley stress relevance.
T. Johnides. por Phys Today 23:61-2 D '70 *
HAGGERTY, S. E. and others
Iron-titanium oxides and olivine from 10020
and 10071. bibliog il Science 167:613-15 Ja
30 '70
HAGGIN, Bernard H.
New records in review. See issues of Yale
review
HAGUE, The
International court of Justice
See International court of justice, The
Hague
HAHN, Emily
Dar. New Yorker 46:25-9 Jl 18 '70
Pilgrim's progress. New Yorker 46:26-30 Ag
15 '70
T'ang. il Horizon 11:88-103 Aut '69
HAHN, Françoise Forster-. See Forster- Hahn,
F.
HAHN, Reynaldo
Historical records. A. Favia-Artsay. pors
Hobbies 74:35 F '70 *
HAHN, Vera D.
Sitting easy. il Am Home 73:56-9 F '70
Wall magic with fabric. il Am Home 73:68-
73+ Ap '70
—and Evans, Mary
Cargoes of splendor. il Am Home 74:46+ Ja
'71
HAHNIUM. See Chemical elements—Atomic
no. 105
HAIBUN. See Haiku, American
HAIGHT, Philip
Mechanics of bliss. il Esquire 74:166-71 D
'70 *
HAIGHT-Ashbury district. See San Francisco
HAIGNEY, John E.
Rheingold: growth with flavor. R. Levy. por
Duns 96:58 O '70 *
HAIKU, American
Anguilla sojourn; English language *hai-bun.*
R. Spiess. il Travel 134:56-61 D '70
Haiku: pretty punchy poetry. L. Marker. il
Clear House 45:219-20 D '70
HAIL insurance. See Insurance, Hail
HAIL storms. See Storms
HAILE Selassie I, emperor of Ethiopia
Ethiopia and the Pan-African movement,
1945-1963. C. G. Contee. il por Negro Hist
Bul 33:122-5 My '70 *
Ethiopia: storm signals flashing for a U.S.
friend. il por U S News 68:46-8 F 23 '70 *
Long way to go. Newsweek 76:57+ N 16
'70 *
No hard feelings but no obelisk either. il
Time 96:44 N 16 '70 *
HAINES, Aubrey B.
Polarization within the churches. Chr Cent
87:1039-41 S 2 '70
HAINES, Donald A. and Kuehnast, E. L.
When the Midwest burned. bibliog il Weatherwise 23:112-19 Je '70
HAINSWORTH, F. Reed, and Wolf, L. L.
Regulation of oxygen consumption and body
temperature during torpor in a hummingbird. eulampis jugularis. bibliog il Science
168:368-9 Ap 17 '70
HAIR
Great hair hassle. N. Joseph. il Todays
Health 48:30-3 Mr '70

HAIR—*Continued*
Hirsutism. R. Greenblatt and E. Jacobs. Redbook 136:24+ N '70
See also
Baldness
Dandruff
Hairdressing
Keratin
Wigs

Care

And a good head of hair. il Mlle 71:154-5 S '70
Cosmic conditioning of hair. X. Pové. See issues of Harper's bazaar
Glow-getter hair: what the experts say about its wear and care. il Vogue 156:112-17 Jl '70
What (if anything) to do for your hair. il Changing T 24:21-3 O '70
Your hair: back in shape for fall. P. Van Wagenen. il Parents Mag 45:93-6 S '70

Dyeing and bleaching

Age of enlightenment: hair coloring at home. S. Obre. il Ladies Home J 87:116-19 My '70
Bright is the colour of the new-love hair. B. Bergery. il Vogue 156:115-17 O 1 '70
Color digest. L. Blanchard. il pors Harp Baz 104:121 Ja '71
Gentlemen prefer: dyeing to be a blonde. Mlle 71:65-71 Jl '70
Guide to at-home hair coloring. il Good H 170:110-13+ My '70
New easier hair colors. il Redbook 135:80-1+ O '70
Safety of hair bleaching. L. Allen. Todays Health 48:16-17 Mr '70

HAIR; musical comedy. See Musical comedies, revues, etc.—Criticisms, plots, etc.

HAIR, Removal of
Hair that you can do without. il Vogue 155:121-2+ Ap 15 '70

HAIR adornments. See Decoration and ornament, Personal

HAIR bleaching. See Hair—Dyeing and bleaching

HAIR curlers
Electric hair-setters. il Consumer Rep 35:136-42 Mr '70
Instant hairsetter; Heat 'n' curl. il Consumer Bul 53:22 Ja '70

HAIR cutting. See Haircutting

HAIR dressing. See Hairdressing

HAIR loss. See Baldness

HAIR pieces. See Wigs

HAIR preparations
Hair sprays: a checkout of nineteen brands. il Consumer Bul 53:17-18 Je '70

HAIR sprays. See Hair preparations

HAIR styles. See Hairdressing

HAIRCUTTING
Case of the bearded teacher; D. Lucia. por Todays Ed 59:26-7 My '70
Hairy victory; court decision. Time 95:61 Je 15 '70
See also
Barbers and barber shops

HAIRDOS. See Hairdressing

HAIRDRESSERS. See Beauty operators

HAIRDRESSING
Beauty for the new fashions. il Good H 171:82-3 S '70
Co-heads; hair parlors set up just for male/female crops. il Mlle 71:90-1 Jl '70
Cowlick cut. il Mlle 70:208-9 F '70
For evening loveliness: moonlit makeup, cascading curls. T. Pavlik. il Good H 171:84-5+ D '70
From hair to eternity. il Esquire 74:74-5 Ag '70
G. E. encounter: hair. J. Sims. il Mlle 71:307-9 Ag '70
Going ape. il Time 96:62 O 5 '70
Hair: how it shapes up. S. Obre. il Ladies Home J 87:102-5 O '70
Hair levels to turn his head: hair cut in different levels. il McCalls 97:82-5 Mr '70
Hair; styling for men. il Newsweek 76:69-70 Ag 3 '70
Little wigs for little girls. il Life 69:34-6 O 16 '70
Long loving look at hair. il Seventeen 29:136-9+ Ap '70
Military meets the Afro. L. Banks. il pors Ebony 25:86-92 S '70
New cuts for hair with a will of its own. il McCalls 98:68-71+ Ja '71
New great shapes for hair. il Redbook 135:88-95+ My '70
New year, a new hairdo, a new you. il Parents Mag 45:62+ Ja '70

News at the top: topknots! il Seventeen 29:146-7+ F '70
Not with a bang: hair. S. Christie. il por Mlle 70:252-3 Ap '70
Seven easy hairstyles for a cool summer look. il McCalls 97:72-5+ Jl '70
Simple summer hair styles. il Parents Mag 45:66+ Jl '70
Straight A's for hair; styles for children. il McCalls 97:70-3+ Ag '70
Twenty-four new hairdos; notes on the new makeup. il Good H 170:100-9+ Ap '70
Twenty one new hairdos, all the latest makeup looks. il Good H 171:86-95+ O '70
Vogue's eye view: raising hair, 1970. il Vogue 155:53-60 F 15 '70
Wash, cut, blow and go. il Seventeen 29:124-5 My '70

HAIRPIECES. See Wigs

HAIRSTON, Nelson G.
Biological field work. Science 169:8 Jl 3 '70

HAISE, Fred W. jr
Apollo 13: the mission and the meaning. il por PTA Mag 65:14-16 S '70
We had only one choice and took it. il por Life 68:31-3 My 1 '70
about
Brave men of Apollo. il pors Time 95:16-17 Ap 27 '70 *
Fred W. Haise, jr, civilian. por Newsweek 75:63 Ap 13 '70 *
See also
Space flight to the moon—Manned flights—Apollo 13 flight

HAITI
See also
Architecture, Domestic—Haiti
Ethnology—Haiti
Jews in Haiti

Description and travel

Offbeat Caribbean: Haiti. J. Laird. il Yachting 127:58-9+ Mr: 57-9+ Ap '70

History

Great Haitian epic. G. de Zéndegui. il por Américas 22:2-11 Je '70
See also

Kings and rulers

See also
Christophe, Henri, king of Haiti

Politics and government

Comedians revere the Doctor. J. A. Moreau. Nation 211:621-4 D 14 '70
Mangoes don't grow in Brooklyn. B. Thompson. Commonweal 93:347-50 Ja 8 '71

HAITIAN dancing. See Dancing, Haitian

HAITIAN voodoo. See Voodooism

HAITIANS in the United States
Mangoes don't grow in Brooklyn. B. Thompson. Commonweal 93:347-50 Ja 8 '71

HAITINK, Bernard
Man with two bands. H. Saal. por Newsweek 75:87 My 4 '70 *

HAKES, Jay E.
Election year politics in Kenya. bibliog f Cur Hist 58:154-9+ Mr '70

HALABY, Najeeb E.
Pan Am chief hits Concorde initial design. Aviation W 92:21 F 16 '70 *
Shadow of a doubt on the Concorde. il Bsns W p40 F 21 '70 *

HALBERSTAM, David
American notes. Harper 240:124-5 My; 241:30-1 Jl; 22-5 S '70
Questions which tear us apart. il Harper 240:70-2+ F '70

HALBERSTAM, Michael Joseph
Abortion: a startling proposal. Redbook 134:78-9+ Ap '70

HALBOUTY, Michel Thomas
Mr Scripps said it; address, June 18, 1970. Vital Speeches 36:688-92 S 1 '70

HALBREICH, Susan T.
(ed) Books to come. Library J 95:1221-47, 3659-96 Mr 15, O 15 '70
(comp) Children's paperbacks (cont) Library J 95:265-8, 1979-81, 2997-8+ Ja 15, My 15, S 15 '70

HALCROW, John H. See Apostal, R. A. jt. auth.

HALDEMAN, Harry Robbins
How Nixon handles world's biggest job; interview. il pors U S News 69:56-62 S 14 '70; Same abr. with title How the President does his job. Read Digest 97:120-3 D '70
Men who decide what Nixon sees. il pors Bsns W p96-7 Ja 31 '70
about
How Nixon's White House works. il pors Time 95:15-20 Je 8 '70 *

HALE, Daniel
Country doctor looks at conservation and health. il pors Am For 76:16-18+ Ja '70
HALE, Edward Everett
Man without a country; dramatization. See Olfson, L.
HALE, Hanna
Fifth grade makes a movie. il Sch Arts 70: 24-5 D '70
HALE, Irlene W.
October inspiration: school libraries work! excerpt from report. il por Wilson Lib Bul 45:127 O '70
HALE, Lucy Lambert
They all loved Lucy. R. Morcom. il pors Am Heritage 21:12-15 O '70 *
HALE, Robert
Know by the company you keep; poem. Chr Cent 87:1410 N 25 '70
Ordained; poem. Chr Cent 87:1486 D 9 '70
Unoriginal sin; poem. Cath World 210:247 Mr '70
Why; poem. Cath World 212:62 N '70
HALEAKALA NATIONAL PARK
Kipahulu: from cinders to the sea. P. Matthiessen. il Audubon 72:10-23 My '70
HALEY, Harold
Bloody breakout at San Rafael; with editorial comment. il pors Life 69:2A, 30-4 Ag 21 '70 *
Justice: a bad week for the good guys. il pors Time 96:6-9 Ag 17 '70 *
HALF-pint cowboy; drama. See Miller, H. L.
HALICTINE bees. See Bees
HALIFAX, Nova Scotia
Week of group therapy for a region. G. M. Chamberlain. il Am City 85:105-6+ O '70
HALKIN, Hillel
Hebrew as she is spoke. Commentary 48:55-60 D '69; 49-12 Ap '70
(tr) See Scholem, G. Holiness of sin
HALL, Adrian. See Taylor, T. jt. auth.
HALL, Clarence W.
Charisma of Billy Graham. por Read Digest 97:88-92 Jl '70
Ordinary guy in Ethiopia. il por Read Digest 97:157-8+ Jl '70
HALL, Clem
(ed) Writing project applications for funding. Am Lib 1:779-80 S '70
HALL, Durward Gorham
Excerpt from debate, September 17, 1969. Cong Digest 49:13+ Ja '70
HALL, Eric, and Marshall, K. T.
Quest for lightness. il Yachting 128:54-5+ S '70
HALL, Frances
Granada: the grandmothers; poem. America 122:131 F 7 '70
HALL, Gerry
Maritimes. il Travel & Camera 33:42-5 Je '70
HALL, Graham M.
Fireball: flat out for fun. il Yachting 129: 72-3+ Ja '71
Kick-off for college sailing. il Yachting 127: 70-1+ Mr '70
Racing clinic. See issues of Yachting
Swap-boat series sailing. il Yachting 128:63+ Ag '70
Tempest stirs the Olympic teapot. il Motor B 125:16+ Mr '70
HALL, H. Tracy
Sintered diamond: a synthetic carbonado. il Science 169:868-9 Ag 28 '70
HALL, H. W.
S/F: the other side of the coin; ed. by B. Katz. Library J 95:2240-1 Je 15 '70
HALL, Jim
Box? Bar of soap? No, it's a car. B. Yates. il por Sports Illus 33:16-17 Jl 20 '70 *
Vacuum cleaner car. il Newsweek 76:49 Jl 27 '70 *
HALL, John S.
V. M. Slipher's trailblazing career. il pors Sky & Tel 39:84-6 F '70
HALL, Leonard
What price tomorrow? Am For 76:42+ Ja '70
HALL, R. A. and others
Evoked response and behavior in cats. bibliog il Science 170:998-1000 N 27 '70
HALL, Richard
Dilemma of the black cop. il pors Life 69:60-60B+ S 18 '70
HALL, Richard L.
World hunger: the crisis an expert sees; interview. il por U S News 69:66-9 S 28 '70
HALL, Richard W.
Alone with the voice. il Opera N 35:8-11 S 5 '70
Chopsticks and Chopin. il Opera N 34:8-12 Mr 7 '70
Literature: grand opera vs the now sound. Engl J 59:1150-3 N '70

HALL, Ridgway M. Jr
Keeping it cool on the campus. New Repub 162:11-12 Ap 4; 28-9 My 16 '70
Last-minute rescue for legal aid? New Repub 163:13-15 N 21; 24 D 26 '70
HALL, Terry
This soufflé alway falls. H. Weiskopf. Sports Illus 32:49-50+ F 16 '70 *
HALL of fame, Sports. See Sports hall of fame
HALL of fame for great Americans. See New York university—Hall of fame for great Americans
HALL of flame (museum) See Kenosha, Wis. —Galleries and museums
HALL of Mexico and Central America. See American museum of natural history, New York
HALLAH. See Bread
HALLAM, Gene
God save the mule. il Am For 76:4-5+ Ag '70
HALLE and Stieglitz (firm)
Middleweight comes out swinging. il Bsns W p83 Je 20 '70
HALLECK, Charles White
Greening of Halleck. pors Newsweek 76:34+ N 23 '70 *
HALLER, Henry
Leak in the kitchen. Newsweek 76:101 O 19 '70 *
HALLER, Manny
Sketching a personal diary. il Am Artist 34: 40-4+ Ap '70
HALLETT, Douglas L.
Bitter fruit in the vineyards. il pors Nations Bsns 58:80-3 F '70
HALLETT, Stanley
Church union and urban mission. Chr Cent 87:238-9 F 25 '70
HALLEY, Edmond
Edmond Halley at St Helena. J. Ashbrook. bibliog il por Sky & Tel 40:86-7 Ag '70 *
HALLEY'S comet
Halley's comet in 1682. J. Classen. il Sky & Tel 39:102 F '70
HALLIBURTON, John H.
Lord of the Cypress. il Outdoor Life 146:77-80+ N '70
HALLIDAY, E. M.
When the forty-niners went sixty. il Am Heritage 22:75-8 D '70
HALLIDAY, Mark
Agreeable voyage. il pors Am Heritage 21:8-11+ Je '70
HALLIDAY lithograph corporation
Running after the short run book. il Pub W 197:78-9 F 2 '70
HALLIWELL, Brian
Gardening in New Zealand. il Horticulture 48: 36-7+ S '70
HALLMARK cards, Inc.
Greeting cards grow in all seasons. il Bsns W p32-3 D 12 '70
HALLORAN, Donal W.
Creating an effective interpretive program. il Nat Parks 44:10-13 Mr '70
HALLORAN, Kevin C.
On defiling the sanctity of English. Engl J 59:566-8 Ap '70
HALLORAN, Richard
Japan's future on expo-sition. Commonweal 92:109-10 Ap 17 '70
HALLOWEEN
Frightful faces for Halloween; excerpts from Ephemeral folk figures by A. Parker and A. Neal. il Life 69:68-71 O 30 '70
Nowadays, witches don't have to burn! il Consumer Bul 53:27 O '70

Drama
Broomstick beauty. H. L. Miller. Plays 30:23-32 O '70
Magic hat. A. C. Martens. Plays 30:71-7 O '70
Wanted: a house to haunt. H. W. Corson. Plays 30:78-82 O '70

Poetry
Goblin dance. K. Baker. il Horn Bk 46:509 O '70
Halloween couplets. M. Speracio. Good H 171: 230 O '70
HALLOWEEN costumes. See Costume
HALLS of fame
See also
New York university—Hall of fame for great Americans
HALLUCINATION and illusion producing plants
Books: hypothetical identification of a drink called Soma with Amanita muscaria or fly agaric mushroom. W. Sargeant. New Yorker 46:90+ My 30 '70
See also
Soma (drug)

HALLUCINOGENIC drugs
Charlie Manson's home on the range. G. Talese. il por Esquire 73:101-3+ Mr '70
Deceptions in the illicit drug market. F. E. Cheek and others. il Science 167:1276 F 27 '70
Drug abuse and social alienation; address, 1970. A. I. Malcolm. il Todays Ed 59:28-31 S '70
Freaked-out spiders. il Newsweek 76:67 Ag 10 '70
Turned-on spiders spin weird webs. il Sci Digest 67:80-2 Ja '70
See also
Amphetamines
LSD
Mescaline
THC

HALLUCINOGENIC drugs and poetry
Natural highs. J. Jerome. Writers Digest 50: 32-4 Ag '70

HALLWORTH, Gerald L.
More justice to come? America 122:390-1 Ap 11 '70

HALOGENS
Trace elements and accessory minerals in lunar samples. G. W. Reed, jr. and others. bibliog il Science 167:501-3 Ja 30 '70

HALOS (mineralogy)
Giant radioactive halos: indicators of unknown radioactivity? R. V. Gentry. bibliog il Science 169:670-3 Ag 14 '70

HALPER, Joseph W.
Mobile recreation fleet. il Am City 85:100+ S '70

HALPERIN, Morton H.
Reports: Japan. Atlan 225:14+ Ap '70
War termination as a problem in civil-military relations. bibliog f Ann Am Acad 392: 86-95 N '70

HALPERN, Martin
Rubidium-strontium date of possibly 3 billion years for a granitic rock from Antarctica. bibliog il Science 169:977-8 S 4 '70

HALPRIN, Lawrence
Lawrence Halprin: eco-architect. D. Lloyd-Jones. il por Horizon 12:46-55 Sum '70 *

HALSMAN, Philippe
King of covers shoots his hundredth. R. Graves. il por Life 68:3 Ja 23 '70

HALSTED, Robert
Casting with native red clays. il Ceram Mo 18: 24-6 N '70

HALVERSON, Guy
Mediated teaching: does it make a difference? il Schol Teach Sec Teach Sup p 10-12+ N 3 '69

HAM
See also
Cookery—Meat

HAM, Canned. See Meat, Canned

HAM radio stations. See Radio stations, Amateur

HAMACHEK, Don E.
How to be a successful parent. il Parents Mag 45:35-7+ Ag '70

HAMADA, Atsuyu
Hamada legacy. J. Larson il por Ceram Mo 18:13-15 O '70 *

HAMALIAN, Leo
Visible voice: an approach to writing. Engl J 59:227-30 F '70

HAMBLETONIAN race. See Harness racing

HAMBLETONIAN resort. See Health resorts, watering places, etc.

HAMBLIN, Dora Jane
Mad cyclist of Napoli. Life 69:67 O 2 '70
Ulterior motive for Umag. il por Sports Illus 32:14-15 Je 1 '70
Whole town upward bound. il Life 69:14+ Jl 17 '70

HAMBRO, Edvard Isak
Twenty-fifth president; interview. New Yorker 46:27-9 S 19 '70
United Nations day, 24 October 1970; message. UN Mo Chron 7:i O '70

about
Achievement of sorts. il por Newsweek 76: 47 S 28 '70 *
Grateful for small favors. Time 96:30 S 28 '70 *

HAMBURG, Susan
Study fiestas. il Har Yrs 10:40-4 Ap '70

HAMBURG
Music
Behind the scenes. P. Moor. Hi Fi 20:secI 25 Je '70
Ernst Krenek's new opera. That's what happens. P. Moor. il Hi Fi 20:MA19 N '70

Report:
Premiere of Milko Kelemen's State of siege. J. H. Sutcliffe. il Opera N 34:31 Mr 7 '70
Salome. J. H. Sutcliffe. Opera N 35:33 Ja 2 '71
Tannhauser. J. H. Sutcliffe. il Opera N 34:29 F 7 '70
See also
Hamburg state opera company

Transit systems
Urban transit model. H. J. Stueck. Sat R 53:62-3 D 5 '70

HAMBURG state opera company
Report:
Rosenkavalier. J. H. Sutcliffe. il Opera N 34:29 Ap 11 '70

HAMBURGER, Philip
Double vision. New Yorker 46:51-2 D 12 '70

HAMBURGER steak. See Cookery—Meat

HAMBURGERS. See Cookery—Meat

HAMEL, Théophile
Two Quebec painters. S. B. Sherrill. il Antiques 98:674+ N '70 *

HAMER, Fannie Lou
Hunger has no color line. P. Marshall. il por Vogue 155:126-7+ Je '70 *

HAMILL, Pete
People are talking about. . . por Vogue 155:110-11 Ap 15 '70 *

HAMILTON, Alexander
Duel that changed our history. T. Fleming. il Read Digest 97:190-5 Ag '70 *

HAMILTON, Andrew Jackson
Hydropsychotherapy: help for the disturbed on a water couch. il pors Sci Digest 67:59-63 Je '70
Mighty anti-pollution weapon: the honeybee. il pors Sci Digest 68:9-14 O '70
N-ray, miracle tool for science and industry. il Sci Digest 68:68-72 S '70
Solving the traffic nightmare with electronics. il Sci Digest 69:46-8+ Ja '71
Your poor tired feet. il Sci Digest 68:82-6 N '70
(ed) See Knudsen, V. Noise, a major health problem

HAMILTON, Charles, 1913-
By their own hands. por Newsweek 75:82 F 23 '70 *
Penmanship that pays off. il por Bsns W p 116-17 Ap 18 '70 *

HAMILTON, Charles R. and Lund, J. S.
Visual discrimination of movement: midbrain or forebrain? bibliog il Science 170:1428-30 D 25 '70

HAMILTON, Charles Vernon
Silent black majority. il N Y Times Mag p25-6+ My 10 '70

HAMILTON, D. H. jr, and others
Power plants: effects of chlorination on estuarine primary production. bibliog il Science 169:197-8 Jl 10 '70

HAMILTON, David
Anniversary of a dream. il Hi Fi 20:secI 73-4 My '70
Beethoven on records. Hi Fi 20:secI 62-5+ Jl '70
Behind the scenes. il por Hi Fi 20:secI 22 My '70
Berlioz' Les Troyens, conquered at last. il Hi Fi 20:secI 65-7 Ag '70
Best of Baker. Hi Fi 20:secI 86 Je '70
Boulez' Debussy, lucid and illuminating. Hi Fi sec I 20:98 Ja '70
Chamber music from Marlboro. Hi Fi 20:secI 102 Mr '70
Historical treasures from Heliodor. il Hi Fi 20:secI 96-7 Jl '70
Hugo Wolf's masterful miniatures. il Hi Fi 20:85-6 O '70
Landowska as harpsichordist and pianist. Hi Fi 20:secI 80 Je '70
Music (cont) Nation 210:125-6, 253-4, 317-18, 570-1; 211:349-50, 476-7; 212:28-9 F 2, Mr 2, 16, My 11, O 2, N 9, 70, Ja, 4 '71
Ponselle miracle. por Hi Fi 20:81-2 S '70
Prophetic Doktor Faust. il Hi Fi 20:secI 69-70 Jl '70
Recorded legacy of Ferruccio Busoni. por Hi Fi sec I 20:77-8 F '70
Recording Verdi's Requiem. il Hi Fi 20:79-81 N '70
Recordings of Copland's music. Hi Fi 20:64-6+ N '70
Records (cont) Nation 210:61-2, 381-2, 542, 635-6, 797-8; 211:412-13, 602-3 Ja 19, Mr 30, My 4, 25, Je 29, O 26, D 7 '70

HAMILTON, Edward A.
Computer potentials for the graphic designer; excerpts from Graphic design for the computer age. il Pub W 198:40+ Ag 10 '70

HAMILTON, Jack
Son of the Catskills. J. Corry. Harper 241:
79-82 S '70 *
HAMILTON, Jack (editor)
Hollywood: the year you almost couldn't find
it. il Look 34:27-33 N 3 '70
(ed) Movies. il Look 34:27-36+ N 3 '70
(ed) See Welch, R. Raquel Welch, Mae West
talk about men, morals and Myra Breck-
inridge
(ed) See West, M. Raquel Welch, Mae West
talk about men, morals and Myra Breck-
inridge
HAMILTON, James T.
Educational administrators and academic free-
dom. Sch & Soc 98:159+ Mr '70
HAMILTON, John
Feedlot expansion in one jump. il Farm J 94:
B12-13+ F '70
HAMILTON, John A.
Will work work? il Sat R 53:24-7 My 23 '70
(ed) See Stewart, R. E. How to pay for
15,000,000 auto accidents a year
HAMILTON, John David
Canada. Atlan 227:86-91 Ja '71
HAMILTON, Lee David
Nuclear subs: a century after Captain Nemo.
il Todays Health 48:26-31 Ap '70
HAMILTON, Lee Herbert
Over sixty-five; address. May 29, 1970. Vital
Speeches 36:606-8 Jl 15 '70
HAMILTON, Peter Goodwill
Fair-haired boy of the stockers. K. Chapin.
por Sports Illus 32:63+ Je 15 '70 *
Pete Hamilton makes it two in a row at the
big T. il por Motor T 22:106 O '70 *
Yankee Pete and his reb getaway car. R. F.
Jones. il por Sports Illus 32:16-17 Mr 2
'70 *
HAMILTON, Randy
How to catch a dogcatcher. R. Moskowitz. il
Am Ed 6:9-12 O '70 *
HAMILTON, Richard
Richard Hamilton. J. Russell. il Art in Am
58:115-19 Mr '70 *
HAMILTON, Virginia Van Der Veer
Gentlewoman and the robber baron. il pors
Am Heritage 21:78-86 Ap '70
HAMILTON, Walter C.
Revolution in crystallography. bibliog il Sci-
ence 169:133-41 Jl 10 '70
HAMILTON, William W. Jr
Can a rich guy lose in Texas. Nation 211:274-
7 S 28 '70
HAMLET evaluation system. See Vietnamese
war, 1957- —Pacification programs
HAMM, Russell L.
Middle school v. junior high school. Clear
House 44:256 Ja '70
HAMM, Theodore, brewing company
CU files suits against Seagram and Hamm.
Consumer Rep 35:6 Ja '70
CU wins injunction against Hamm. Con-
sumer Rep 35:508 S '70
HAMMEL, Lisa
Home (cont) il N Y Times Mag p74-5 Je 7;
38-9 Ag 2; 50-1 Ag 23; 104-5+ S 13 '70
HAMMER, Armand
Will Oxy make it? il Forbes 106:18-19 Ag 1.
'70 *
HAMMER, Richard
My Lai: did American troops attack the
wrong place? il Look 34:60 F 10 '70
HAMMERS
Add an aluminum hammer to your tool rack.
W. E. Burton. il Pop Mech 133:191 Mr '70
HAMMOCKS
Cotton duck-plastic pipe hammock. il Sun-
set 145:80+ S '70
HAMMONASSETT state park. See Connecticut
—Parks and reserves
HAMMOND, Earl W.
House grandpa built. il Har Yrs 10:30-1 Ap
'70
HAMMOND, Geoffrey F.
America's cup report: a close call for the
cup. il Motor B 127:25-40 Ja '71
Boat show time again. Motor B 126:34 O '70
Cognac derby: bad day at Shrewsbury Rock.
il Motor B 126:50-1+ S '70
Houseboats among the Virgins. il Motor B
126:38-41+ D '70
Luff the outhaul sheet in the halyard! il
Motor B 126:42-5+ O '70
On the water, 1970. il Motor B 127:179-87 Ja
'71
Port Elco rendezvous. il Motor B 126:46+ N '70
HAMMOND, George Simms
Cambodia speech sinks nomination. J. Walsh.
Science 168:1189 Je 5 '70 *
HAMMOND, Lenore Peters
On collecting ornate bells. il(p 1) Hobbies 75:
117 N '70
HAMMOND, Reese
Effective preparation for apprenticeship. Mo
Labor R 93:44-5 Ap '70

HAMMOND, Wayne A.
Scholastic achievement and part-time em-
ployment. Clear House 44:465-7 Ap '70
HAMMOND-INNES, Ralph. See Innes, H
pseud.
HAMNER, K. C. See Hodson, H. K. jt. auth.
HAMPSHIRE, Susan
Hampshire saga. por Time 95:53 Je 22 '70 *
HAMPSHIRE college
Hampshire college: a quest for quality, a bal-
anced budget. J. Walsh. Science 170:954-8
N 27 '70
Jewel in the rough. il Newsweek 76:86 S 28
'70
HAMPTON, Christopher
Philanthropist. Criticism
Nation 211:252 S 21 '70 *
HAMS (radio) See Amateur radio operators
HAMSTERS
Olfactory bulb removal eliminates mating
behavior in the male golden hamster. M.
R. Murphy and G. E. Schneider. bibliog il
Science 167:302-4 Ja 16 '70
Pulmonary hemorrhage in hamsters after
exposure to proteolytic enzymes of bacillus
subtilis. I. P. Goldring and others. bib-
liog il Science 170:73-4 O 2 '70
HANCHETT, George D.
Build modular six-channel stereo mixer
preamp. il Radio-Electr 41:36-9 O '70
HANCOCK, John, mutual life insurance com-
pany. See John Hancock mutual life in-
surance company
HANCOCK, Walker
Mountain in labor. il Time 95:66 My 18 '70 *
HANCOCK, Mass. Shaker community. See Vil-
lages. Restored
HANCOCK center, Chicago. See Chicago—
Buildings
HANCOCK COUNTY, Ga.
Catfish empire; activities of J. L. McCown.
Newsweek 76:48+ O 19 '70
HAND, A. J. See Geer, A. M. jt. auth.
HAND, Jackson
How big is a board? il Pop Sci 196:141+ Ja
'70
How to tell a good used camera from a
bad one. il Mech Illus 66:110-13+ O '70
Up-to-date story on getting your house paint-
ed. il Mech Illus 66:68-70+ Ag '70
HAND
Beauty in hand. C. Bartel. il Am Home 73:
16+ My '70
Keeping kitchen and garden hands living-
room soft. S. Lindsay. il House B 112:14+
F '70
Personality of hands. R. Hattersley. il Pop
Phot 66:90-3+ My '70
See also
Gesture
Manicuring
Palmistry
HAND baggage. See Luggage
HAND bags. See Handbags
HAND care. See Hand
HAND cleaners. See Cleaning compositions
HAND presses. See Printing presses. Hand
HAND puppets. See Puppets and puppet plays
HAND tools. See Tools
HAND weaving. See Weaving
HANDBAGS
How to buy a handbag. Good H 170:144 Mr
'70
HANDBALL
Champ; J. Haber. por Newsweek 76:49 Ag
31 '70
HANDBOOKS
See also subhead Handbooks, manuals,
etc. under various subjects, e.g. Automo-
biles—Handbooks, manuals, etc.
HÄNDEL, Georg Friedrich
Complete Handel for the violin. B. Schwarz.
Sat R 53:84-5 F 28 '70 *
Handel and the opera seria, by W. Dean. Re-
view
Sat R 53:85+ F 28 '70. H. Weinstock *
Handel's Tamerlano: the creation of an op-
era. J. M. Knapp. bibliog f il Mus Q 56:405-
30 Jl '70 *
Judgment on Solomon. S. Lincoln. il Am Rec
G 37:96-8+ O '70 *
Records:
Samson. Opera N 34:36 Ja 24 '70 *
Tamerlano. Criticism
Mus Q il 56:405-30 Jl '70 *
HANDGUNS. See Pistols
HANDICAPPED
See also
Active handicapped (periodical)
Blind
Children. Handicapped
Libraries—Services to physically handicapped
Mentally handicapped

HANDICAPPED—*Continued*

Employment

Handicapped are an asset. V. Louviere. Nations Bsns 58:17 My '70

I struck back at stroke. A Martin. Har Yrs 10:43-5 F '70

Transportation

Special cabs enable handicapped to work; Handicabs of Milwaukee. il Todays Health 48:16 D '70

HANDICAPPED, Apparatus for the
New helps for the handicapped. D. H. Barton. il Har Yrs 10:37-41 S '70

HANDICAPPED children. See Children, Handicapped

HANDICRAFT
Affirmation: the American craftsman 1971. R. Slivka. Craft Horiz 30:10-11 D '70

Bringing it all back home; arts and crafts you can whip up on your own. il Mlle 71: 178-9 O '70

Make it thrifty, sell it nifty! il Seventeen 29:130-1 Je '70
See also
Arts and crafts
Arts and crafts movement
Braiding
Jewelry making
Weaving

HANDKE, Peter
Theater. S. Kauffmann. New Repub 162:19+ F 28 '70 *

HANDLER, Philip
Basic R&D: is the U.S. falling behind? interview. il por Forbes 105:204+ My 15 '70
Science and scientists: obligations and opportunities; excerpts from address, October 21, 1970. por Science 170:837 N 20 '70

HANDLES
Knife handle that really fits your hand. A. Jetter. il Mech Illus 66:94-5 D '70

HANDLEY, Arthur
Meeting the solid wastes problem. il Cons 24:3-8 Ap '70

HANDLEY, Dorothy Curnow
Secret of Mike's mother; story. Good H 170: 84-5 My '70

HANDLEY Page aircraft, ltd.
Foreign accent; we got problems. J. Fricker. il Flying 86:24-5 F '70

Handley Page reorganizing. Aviation W 92: 79+ Ja 19 '70

Handley Page's final grounding. il Bsns W p48 Mr 21 '70

New Jetstream firm founders. Aviation W 92:228 Mr 9 '70

HANDLIN, Oscar
Radical chic in academe. Newsweek 77:58-9 Ja 11 '71 *

HANDPRINTS
See also
Dermatoglyphics

HANDSPICKER, Meredith, and Wagoner, W.D.
Unity: above ground and below. Chr Cent 87: 419-22 Ap 8 '70

HANDWRITING. See Autographs; Penmanship

HANDWRITING analysis. See Graphology

HANDY associates, Inc.
Company officers in striped pants? V. Louviere. Nations Bsns 58:20 Ap '70

HANFF, Helene
84, Charing Cross road; condensation. il Read Digest 97:221-4+ D '70
Trade winds; interview, ed. by C. Amory. Sat R 54:14-15 Ja 9 '71

HANFORD works, Richland, Wash.
Earthquake at Giza: Hanford atomic products operation; with interview with G. T. Seaborg. S. Novick. bibliog il Environ 12: 2-15 Ja '70; Same abr. with title Dangers from radioactive wastes. Cur 118:41-5 My '70

Swords into ploughshares: Hanford makes the switch. L. J. Carter. il Science 167: 1357-8+ Mr 6 '70

HANFSTAENGL, Ernst Franz Sedgwick
Where are they now? il pors Newsweek 76:14 S 28 '70 *

HANGARS
USAF shelters for aircraft in Europe boost survivability. Aviation W 93:25 D 7 '70

HANGEN, Welles
Russians in Asia. Atlan 225:30+ My '70
about
Beyond the checkpoint. il pors Newsweek 75:65 Je 15 '70 *

HANGING
Collector's choice: a first for law & order; execution of J. Forner in San Francisco. R. Olmsted. Am West 7:11 Ja '70

Hanging is dead in Britain. Chr Today 14:37 Ja 16 '70

Throat trouble; photographs. Am West 7: 22-3 Ja '70

HANGING of pictures. See Pictures, Hanging of

HANGING roofs. See Roofs, Suspension

HANGINGS, Wall. See Wall hangings

HANGOVERS. See Alcohol—Physiological effects

HANIN, I. and others
Acetylcholine concentrations in rat brain: diurnal oscillation. bibliog il Science 170:341-2 O 16 '70

HANKE, Jeannette J.
Romeo and Juliet and the disadvantaged. Engl J 59:273-6 F '70

HANKS, David A.
American silver at the Art institute of Chicago. il Antiques 98:418-22 S '70

HANKS, Nancy
Government and the arts. Sat R 53:32 F 28 '70
about
Administration sees leap forward for arts. Pub W 197:62 F 9 '70 *

HANLEY, Tullah
Flamboyant patron. il por Time 95:62-3 Je 8 '70 *

HANLON, Joseph
Snooping on the home front. Nation 211: 305-6 O 5 '70

HANNA, W. W. and others
Apospory in sorghum bicolor (L.) Moench. bibliog il Science 170:338-9 O 16 '70

HANNAH, John Alfred
Interdependence of the world, U.S. and local community; address, October 30, 1970. Dept State Bul 63:672-7 N 30 '70

HANNAN, Philip Matthew, abp
Religion is the extra dimension. Ladies Home J 86:127 D '69

HANNIBAL, Edward
Authors & editors. B. A. Bannon. il por Pub W 198:19-21 S 7 '70 *
Commitment and action. Writer 83:11-14 D '70

HANNIBAL, Mo.
Tom Sawyer boyhood 1970 style. P. Powell. il pors Life 69:50-7 O 9 '70

HANNIGAN, Paul
Contests; poem. Atlan 227:74 Ja '71
Lives of the saints; poem. Atlan 226:125 O '70

HANOVER, Germany

Music

Report:
Premieres of Diether de la Motte's Board of directors and Hans Werner Henze's The end of a world. J. H. Sutcliffe. il Opera N 34:30-1 Mr 28 '70
Production of Le donne curiose. J. H. Sutcliffe. Opera N 35:34-5 N 21 '70
Rossini's Le Comte Ory. J. H. Sutcliffe. il Opera N 34:30 F 7 '70

HANOVER air show. See Aviation—Exhibitions

HANRAHAN, Edward V.
Heavy baggage. Nation 211:37 Jl 20 '70 *

HANSBERRY, Lorraine
Les blancs. Criticism
Nation 211:573 N 30 '70 *
Nation 211:606 D 7 '70 *
New Yorker 46:104 N 21 '70 *
Newsweek 76:98 N 30 '70 *

HANSEN, B. Lyle. See Langway, C. C. jr, jt. auth.

HANSEN, Burdette P.
Computer in education. Clear House 45:195-200 D '70

HANSEN, Clifford Peter
Excerpt from debate, December 22, 1969. Cong Digest 49:83 Mr '70

HANSEN, Dorothy S.
Well-bread woman. Har Yrs 10:31 Ja '70

HANSEN, Erik
Liberated pro. R. Hattersley. il Pop Phot 67:116-19+ D '70 *

HANSEN, H. J. See Sonneborn, D. W. jt. auth.

HANSEN, J. Merrell
Negativism and the hand that feeds us. Clear House 45:204-6 D '70

HANSEN, J. N. and others
Bacterial spore outgrowth: its regulation. bibliog il Science 168:1291-8; 170:872 Je 12, N 20 '70

HANSEN, Lyle M. See Mutchler, C. K. jt. auth

HANSEN, Sally P.
Teaching the poetry of war. bibliog f Engl J 59:497-501 Ap '70

HANSEN, W. Lee
Who benefits from higher education subsidies. il Mo Labor R 93:43-6 Mr '70

HANSER, Richard
Of deathless remarks. il Am Heritage 21:54-9
Je '70
Thomas Mann makes the top forty. Sat R
53:6-8 Mr 21 '70
HANSON, Dick
Across the editor's desk. See issues of Suc-
cessful farming
HANSON, Duane
Presenting Duane Hanson. il Art in Am 58:
86-9 S '70
HANSON, George P. and Stewart, W. S.
Photochemical oxidants: effect on starch
hydrolysis in leaves. bibliog il Science 168:
1223-4 Je 5 '70
HANSON, Howard G.
Against dark angels; poem. Chr Today 15:20
N 20 '70
HANSON, Ronald L. and others
Inhibition of phosphofructokinase by quinone
methide and α-methylene lactone tumor in-
hibitors. bibliog il Science 168:378-80 Ap
17 '70
HANSON, Wallace
Eye-phi and you. il Pop Phot 66:60-1+ Mr '70
How to succeed as a occasional photographer.
il Pop Phot 67:78-9+ O '70
Mystery and magic of photography. il Pop
Phot 66:85-7+ Je '70
Should you keep your color in the dark? il
Pop Phot 66:90-1+ F '70
Stabilization processors. il Pop Phot 66:74-
5+ My '70
Why I take lousy pictures with great cam-
eras. il Pop Phot 67:108-9 Ag '70
HANUKKAH (Feast of lights)
Remembrance of Chanukah. H. Golden. il
House B 112:58-9 D '70
HAPKE, Bruce W. and others
Solar radiation effects in lunar samples.
bibliog il Science 167:745-7 Ja 30 '70
HAPPE, D. L.
Through the lattice, my beloved; poem. Cath
World 211:12 Ap '70
HAPPEL, Margaret, and Harrington, Elsa
Ladies' home journal Handbook of holiday
cuisine; excerpts. il Ladies Home J 87:80-8+
D '70
HAPPENINGS (theater)
On the off-beat. A. Rich. Hi Fi 20:secII 7 Je
'70
HAPPINESS
Pursuit of happiness; symposium. Esquire 74:
133-53+ D '70
See also
Joy
Anecdotes, facetiae, satire, etc.
190 things to avoid. Esquire 74:133-5 D '70
HAPPINESS cage; drama. See Reardon, D. J.
HAPPY birthday, Wanda June; drama. See
Vonnegut, K. jr
HAPPY Hollidays; drama. See Murray, J.
HAPSBURG, Otto von. See Otto, archduke of
Austria
HAPTOGLOBINS. See Blood—Proteins
HARAKIRI
Last samurai. il pors Time 96:32+ D 7 '70
Mishima incident. W. Mensendiek. Chr Cent
88:29-30 Ja 6 '71
Notes and comment; case of Y. Mishima.
New Yorker 46:39-41 D 12 '70
Samurai '70: the death of Mishima. il pors
Newsweek 76:31-2 D 7 '70
HARANGUES; drama. See Walker, J. A.
HARASZTY, Eszter
(ed) See Atkinson, R. E. Gardener's almanac
—See Atkinson, R. E. jt. auth.
HARAYDA, Janice
Guest editors advise. Mlle 71:206 O '70
HARBERT, Guy M. Jr, and others
Diurnal variation of spontaneous uterine ac-
tivity in nonpregnant primates (macaca
mulatta) bibliog il Science 170:82-5 O 2 '70
HARBISON, Frederick H.
Campus revolt from an industrial relations
perspective. Mo Labor R 93:33-6 Mr '70
HARBOR precinct. See New York (city)—Police
department—Harbor precinct
HARBORS
See also
Ports
also subhead Harbor under names of
cities, e.g. Chicago—Harbor

Cleaning
Danger of debris; army engineers combat a
major problem in New York. W. J. Papin.
il Yachting 129:107+ Ja '71
HARBOUR Town golf course. See Golf courses
HARBURG, Edgar Y.
Prospects for a prosperous New Year; poem.
Sat R 53:9 D 19 '70

about
Where are they now? il pors Newsweek 75:10
Je 22 '70 *
HARCOURT, François Charles, duc d'
Personal thoughts on the art of gardens; ex-
cerpts from Des jardins heureux. House &
Gard 138:78-80+ O '70
HARCOURT Brace Jovanovich, inc.
Dismissed Harcourt employee files unfair
labor charges. Pub W 198:41 O 5 '70
HARD-core unemployed
Hard-core hiring is going public. il Bsns W
p29-30 My 16 '70
Hard-core jobs; are there any left? L. Zim-
pel. Chr Cent 87:941-2 Ag 5 '70
In a time of layoffs, trouble for the hard
core. il US News 69:24-6 Jl 13 '70
Meanwhile, back at the zoo. H. Schaden. il
Am Ed 6:18-25 Ag '70
Opening a new horizon; training the low-
skilled for vacant public sector jobs. il Na-
tions Bsns 58:90-2 Mr '70
Picking up the pace of integration. B. L.
Masse. America 122:363 Ap 4 '70
Training hard-core jobless: the record after
two years; interview. D. M. Kendall. il por
US News 68:60-2 Mr 30 '70
See also
COPE program
National alliance of businessmen

Training
Fighting back: Harlem headquarters of on-
the-job training program for blacks and
Puerto Ricans. New Yorker 46:28-30 Ag 22
'70
Hard core unemployment; trainee attitudes.
J. L. Tapp and A. H. Roberts. Trans-Ac-
tion 7:48-9 S '70
Survey of employer attitudes toward training
the disadvantaged; excerpt from Training
programs of private industry in the Greater
Cleveland area. J. L. Iacobelli. il Mo Labor
R 93:51-5 Je '70
HARDENING of the arteries. See Arteriosclerosis
HARDERIAN gland
Harderian gland: an extraretinal photoreceptor influencing the pineal gland in neo-
natal rats? L. Wetterberg and others. bibliog il Science 167:884-5 F 6 '70
Harderian gland: development and influence
of early hormonal treatment on porphyrin
content. L. Wetterberg and others. bibliog
il Science 168:996-8 My 22 '70
Harderian gland: influence on pineal hydroxyindole-O-methyltransferase activity in
neonatal rats. L. Wetterberg and others.
bibliog il Science 170:194-6 O 9 '70
HARDIE, Dee
Christmas is a glorious gift to be shared.
House & Gard 138:22+ D '70
Place to be alone. House & Gard 137:70+ My
'70
HARDIN, Clifford Morris
International cotton advisory committee
meets at Washington; address, October 12,
1970. Dept State Bul 63:678-80 N 30 '70

about
Professor who runs Agriculture. il por Bsns
W p 120-2 My 9 '70 *
HARDIN, Garrett
Parenthood: right or privilege? Science 169:
427 Jl 31 '70
Parenthood: right or privilege? Science 169:
427 170:259+ Jl 31, O 16 '70
To trouble a star: the cost of intervention
in nature. Bul Atom Sci 26:17-20 Ja '70;
Same abr. with title Ecology versus econom-
ics. Cur 116:34-9 Mr '70
HARDING, John
Australian abalone fisheries. il Sea Front 16:
282-5 S '70
Giant grouper. il Sea Front 16:82-4 Mr '70
HARDING, Nelson
Utilizing closed circuit television. il Am Lib
1:165-6 F '70
HARDING, Vincent
Toward the black university. il por Ebony
25:156-9 Ag '70
about
Think tank for black scholars. A. Poinsett.
il por Ebony 25:46-8+ F '70 *
HARDING, Warren
Conquest of El Capitan. il pors Time 96:12 N
30 '70 *
HARDING, Warren Gamaliel
Harding rides again. F. Russell. Nat R 22:
213-14 F 24 '70 *
Is Warren G. Harding really dead? F. M.
Wilhoit. Commonweal 92:181-4 My 8 '70 *

HARDWARE
Bright ideas for dull cabinets. H. A. Dawson.
il Bet Hom & Gard 48:66-7+ Ap '70
See also
Bolts and nuts
Curtain and drapery fixtures
Fastenings
Nails

Exhibitions
Twenty great new ideas from hardware
show; National hardware show. il Pop Mech
133:50-1+ Ja '70
HARDWARE catalogs. See Catalogs, Mail order
HARDWICK, Elizabeth
Books. Vogue 156:42 Ag 1; 306 S 1; 74 N 15
'70
Movies. Vogue 155:118+ F 1 '70
Women re women. Mlle 70:186-7+ F '70
HARDY, Don
Serious funny business. D. Wadley. il pors
Hot Rod 23:76-8 My '70 *
HARDY, Jim
America's cup. il por Newsweek 76:60-3 S 21
'70 *
HARDY, Noah
Revamping priorities. il Sci N 97:492 My 16
'70
Uncertainty about space. Sci N 98:126 Ag 8
'70
HARDY, Rosemary
Dog grooming. J. Kuh. por Ladies Home J
87:118 Ag '70 *
HARDY Holzman Pfeiffer associates
Three new theaters. J. S. Margolies. il Art
in Am 58:88-93 My '70
HARE, F. Kenneth
How should we treat environment? bibliog
Science 167:352-5 Ja 23 '70
HARE, Raymond Arthur
Serious blow to the U.S. peace effort; inter-
view. por U S News 69:20-1 O 12 '70
HARE hunting. See Rabbit hunting
HARES
Changeable snowshoe hare. L. W. Zuidema.
il Cons 24:18-20 F '70
HARGADON, Fred A.
Freshmen in 1970; interview. New Yorker 46:
42-4 D 12 '70
HARGER, El
My no. 1 game. il por Outdoor Life 146:94-
5+ O '70
HARGIS, Billy James
America's other radicals. P. Schrag. il Har-
per 241:35-46 Ag '70 *
HARGRAVE, Jack
Sportfishermen. il por Motor B 125:106-7+
Ja '70
HARGRAVES, R. B. and others
Compositional zoning and its significance in
pyroxenes from three coarse-grained lunar
samples. bibliog il Science 167:631-3 Ja 30
'70
HARGROVES, Vernon Carney
New world Baptist head: bringing together 31
million. por Chr Today 14:38 Ag 21 '70 *
HARIJANS. See Untouchables
HARITHAS, James
American painter-writer. il por Vogue 155:
128-9+ Je '70
Paolo Soleri, genius. il por Vogue 156:96-7+
Ag 1 '70
Retrospective for Alexander Liberman. il Art
in Am 58:106-7 Mr '70
HARK, Mildred, and McQueen, Noel
Father's Easter hat; drama. Plays 29:53-60
Ap '70
Many thanks; drama. Plays 30:39-46 N '70
Minority of millions; drama. Plays 29:71-82
My '70
HARKABI, Yehoshafat
Liberation or genocide? il Trans-Action 7:62-
7+ Jl '70
HARKINS, Paul Donal
Where are they now? il pors Newsweek 75:18
My 25 '70 *
HARKNESS ballet
Mrs Harkness is a rich woman. M. Marks.
il Dance Mag 44:28-30 Ja '70
HARLAN, Jack R. and others
Chromosome pairing within genomes in
maize-tripsacum hybrids. bibliog il Science
167:1247-8 F 27 '70
HARLAN, Louis R.
Booker T. Washington in biographical per-
spective. bibliog f Am Hist R 75:1581-99 O
'70
HARLAN, William F.
Teach it like it is: a stimulating game. Engl
J 59:1146-9 N '70
HARLEM. See New York (city)—Harlem
HARLEM teams for self-help, inc.
Harlem teams on top. K. Aylor. il Am Ed
6:32 My '70

HARLOW, Bryce Nathaniel
Nixon record so far: an inside appraisal; in-
terview. il por U S News 69:74-7 Ag 17 '70
HARLOW, Lewis A.
Know your meter. il Radio-Electr 41:60-4 Jl
'70
—and Pfister, H.R.
Clock that tells the tides. il Pop Sci 196:136-
7+ F '70
HARLOW, William M.
Inside wood; excerpts. il Am For 76:24-7 S
'70
HARMONIC analysis
Fourier analysis and the structure of DNA.
J. Donohue; discussion. bibliog il Science
167:1693-702 Mr 27 '70
HARMONICA (musical glasses) See Musical
glasses
HARMONICAS
I dreamed of playing the organ. M. Vanden-
burgh. il Har Yrs 10:33-4 N '70
HARMS, Ernest
Need for differentiation in rehabilitating the
mentally retarded. Ment Hy 54:457-3 Jl '70
HARNESS racing
Bet O'Brien if he twinkles; International trot.
L. Simross. Sports Illus 34:44+ Jl 27 '70
Country slicker; Hambletonian. il Newsweek
76:124 S 14 '70
Hambo was a family affair. W. F. Reed. il
pors Sports Illus 33:24-5 S 14 '70
Happiness boys at the track; administering
undetectable tranquilizer to horses. R. H.
Boyle. il Sports Illus 33:20-1 O 12 '70
Hot colts and clambakes in the cool Catskills;
Goshen, N.Y. W. F. Reed, jr. il Sports
Illus 33:52-3 Jl 13 '70
Little Joe on the big Red mile. W. F. Reed.
il por Sports Illus 33:58+ O 19 '70
Marlu has a bit of trouble. W. F. Reed. il
por Sports Illus 33:22-3 Ag 24 '70
Marlu upsets the Hambo cart; Dexter cup
winner. W. F. Reed. il Sports Illus 32:56+
Je 22 '70
Max is in luck with Truluck. W. F. Reed, jr.
il por Sports Illus 32:74-6 My 25 '70
Stanley's most happy Jug; Most Happy Fella
winner of $100,000 Little brown jug. W. F.
Reed, jr. il por Sports Illus 33:60+ O 5
'70
HARNEY, Kenneth
Fragments of an interview in the tenth year
of exile; poem. por Atlan 226:56-7 S '70
Two, three, many Indias! Commonweal
92:157-8, 490 My 1, S 25 '70
HARO, Robert P.
How Mexican-Americans view libraries. bib-
liog il Wilson Lib Bul 44:736-42 Mr '70
HARP seals. See Seals (animals)
HARPER, Carroll G.
Singers' friend; interview, ed. by A. M. Lingg.
il por Opera N 34:30 Ap 4 '70
HARPER, Gwen
Adventure: Camp fire girls style. il Parks &
Rec 9:35-6+ S '70
HARPER, Harry
Excuse me, we're looking for Bermuda. il
Yachting 127:60-1+ Je '70
HARPER, Tommy
Leading man without a voice. L. Keith. il
por Sports Illus 33:44 S 7 '70 *
HARPER and Row, publishers, inc.
Harper & Row employees to seek arbitration.
Pub W 197:38-9 Mr 30 '70
Harper trade editors take a walk for a day.
Pub W 197:42 Je 15 '70
Harper trade head leaves in dispute over list.
Pub W 198:33 Jl 6 '70
HARPER'S magazine
South toward home. por Time 95:77 Je 1 '70
HARPSICHORD
Harpsichord boom. R. Evett. Atlan 225:122+
My '70
HARPSICHORD music
See also
Phonograph records—Harpsichord music
HARPSTER, Jack
Exploring the San Juan Islands. il Travel
133:60-5 My '70
HARR, Karl G. jr
Space and tomorrow's society. Space World
G-12-84:30-3 D '70
HARRELL, Lynn
Music to my ears; Carnegie Hall performance.
I. Kolodin. Sat R 53:63 F 28 '70 *
HARRELSON, Bud
..And a mighty Met is he! A. Wright. il por
Sports Illus 33:22-4 S 7 '70 *
HARRIGAN, Anthony
In the McNamara vein. Nat R 22:1110 O 20 '70
SALT talks: round two. Nat R 22:360 Ap 7 '70
HARRIMAN, Jane
In trouble. por Atlan 225:94-8 Mr '70

HARRIMAN, William Averell
Vietnamization is immoral; excerpt from America and Russia in a changing world. Look 34:38+ N 17 '70

HARRINGTON, Elsa. See Happel, M. jt. auth.

HARRINGTON, John J.
Curbing crime: a policeman speaks out; interview. Read Digest 97:202+ D '70

HARRINGTON, Michael
Betrayal of the poor. Atlan 225:71-4 Ja '70
New left and the Arab-Israeli conflict. Cur 118:23-6 My '70
Politics of pollution; why are the corporations cooperating? Commonweal 92:111-14 Ap 17 '70
Radical strategy: don't form a fourth party; form a new first party. il N Y Times Mag p28-9+ S 13; 40+ O 11 '70
Toward legalizing revolution. Cur 122:28-31 O '70
Whatever happened to socialism? Harper 240:99-105 F '70

HARRINGTON, Michael Joseph
Dead hand of seniority. Nation 211:229-32 S 21 '70

about
Vested seniority. Nation 210:356 Mr 30 '70 *

HARRINGTON, Richard
Contented colonies. il Travel 134:60-3 Jl '70
Paddleboat on the Murray. il Travel 135:48-51 Ja '71
Republic of Togo, West Africa. il Travel 133:71-3 Je '70

HARRIS, A. John, and Dennis, M. J.
Acetylcholine sensitivity and distribution on mouse neuroblastoma cells. bibliog il Science 167:1253-5 F 27 '70

HARRIS, A. S.
Loners of Alaska. il por Am For 76:20-3+ My '70

HARRIS, Charles R.
Cigar smoking kid grows up. il pors Ebony 25:58-60+ F '70 *

HARRIS, Dale B. and Harris, Elizabeth
Responsibility is relevant; with study discussion program. bibliog il PTA Mag 64:24-6, 35-6 F '70

HARRIS, David
Letters from prison: Dear Joanie. il por Look 34:64-5 My 5 '70

about
Joan Baez and David Harris: we're just nonviolent soldiers. W. Hedgepeth. il pors Look 34:58-61+ My 5 '70 *

HARRIS, Elizabeth. See Harris, D. B. jt. auth.

HARRIS, Ellen Stern
Mountains are in trouble! por Bsns W p73 Ap 11 '70 *

HARRIS, Fred Roy
Making of a majority; excerpts from Now is the time. Harper 240:49-52 My '70
Teacher's political role; interview, ed. by G. D. Fischer. pors Todays Ed 59:22-4 Ap '70

HARRIS, J. A.
Bat-guano cave environment. bibliog Science 169:1342-3 S 25 '70

HARRIS, Janette Hoston
Beautiful people; poem. Negro Hist Bul 33:126 My '70
Lesson plan, Crispus Attucks. Negro Hist Bul 33:69 Mr '70

HARRIS, LaDonna Crawford
LaDonna Harris: a woman who gives a damn. T. Morris. il Redbook 134:74-5+ F '70 *

HARRIS, Louis
Stock market as people: interview. il por Forbes 105:53+ F 1 '70

HARRIS, Marion Rex
Black courage in Klan country; building of a successful cleaning business. P. Bailey. il pors Ebony 25:136-41 Ap '70 *

HARRIS, Maureen
Interferon: clinical application of molecular biology. bibliog il Science 170:1068-70 D 4 '70

HARRIS, Richard, 1933-
Irishman with impact; interview, ed. by E. Miller. pors Seventeen 29:152-3+ Mr '70

HARRIS, Richard E.
Annals of politics (cont) New Yorker 46:60-4+ D 5; 53-8+ D 12 '70

HARRIS, Robert B.
Multihulls. il por Motor B 125:108-9 Ja '70

HARRIS, Sheldon H.
L.A.'s Scottsboro boys case. Commonweal 91:548-9 F 20 '70

HARRIS, Sherwood
First is to fly; excerpt. il Am Heritage 21:60-9 Je '70

HARRIS, Wayne M.
Wayne M. Harris: citizen pollution fighter. H. G. Jackson, jr. il Field & S 75:12+ My '70 *

HARRIS, Willard S. See Taylor, G. J. jt. auth.

HARRISBURG, Pa.
After one community lost a military base; Olmsted air force base. il U S News 68:33 F 16 '70

HARRISON, C. G. A. See Ball, M. M. jt. auth.

HARRISON, Charles H.
Aerospace education takes off. il Schol Teach Sec Teach Sup p 10-11 Ap 6 '70
Are we educating for tomorrow? Schol Teach Jr/Sr High p 16-17 S 21 '70
City is our classroom. il Schol Teach Sec Teach Sup p 12-13 D 1 '69
Drug epidemic: what's a teacher to do? il Schol Teach Sec Teach Sup p4-6+ My 4 '70
Model schools: blueprint for the future. Schol Teach Sec Teach Sup 18-19+ Mr 9 '70
Schools put a town on the map. Sat R 53:66-8+ F 21 '70
Should the drug education bandwagon be rerouted? il Schol Teach Jr/Sr High p 18-19+ O 5 '70
Who is accountable? il Schol Teach Jr/Sr High p 12-13+ N 2 '70

HARRISON, G. B.
Englishing the new liturgy. America 122:492-5 My 9 '70
What did he mean by etc? il Pub W 197:55-7 Ja 19 '70

about
Of many things; Campion award. D. R. Campion. America 122:inside cover My 9 '70 *

HARRISON, George
Letting George do it; album, All things must pass. W. Bender. il por Time 96:57 N 30 '70 *

HARRISON, George H.
On the trail of bigfoot. il Nat Wildlife 8:4-9 O '70
Yes, we are teaching Johnny conservation. il Nat Wildlife 8:42-7 Ap '70

HARRISON, Gerard A.
Camping needs revival of the fundamental ethic; excerpts from address. por Camp Mag 42:8-10 Je '70

HARRISON, Gilbert A.
What's fit to print? Writers Digest 50:54-5 Ja '70

HARRISON, Gordon
Mess of modern man. il Natur Hist 79:68-9 Ja '70

HARRISON, H. L. and others
Systems studies of DDT transport. bibliog il Science 170:503-8 O 30 '70

HARRISON, Hal H.
Baltimore oriole. il Nat Wildlife 7:16-18 O '69
Beachcomber's paradise. il Nat Wildlife 9:58-63 D '70

HARRISON, Halstead
Stratospheric ozone with added water vapor; influence of high-altitude aircraft. bibliog il Science 170:734-6 N 13 '70

HARRISON, Harry
Science fiction: short story and novel. Writer 83:16-18 My '70

HARRISON, Howard
Primer on light. Travel & Camera 33:68-71 Je '70

HARRISON, Jeffrey L.
Student bargaining. New Repub 163:10-11 N 21; 32 D 12 '70

HARRISON, John
Harrison's timekeepers. il(p 1) Sky & Tel 41:3 Ja '71 *

HARRISON, Walter A.
News from the world of space exploration. Space World G-6-78:54-5 Je '70 *

HARRISON, William
Characterization. Writer 83:21-3+ Je '70
Man who really came to dinner; story. Esquire 74:128-9 S '70

HARRISON, Yolande Heslop-. See Heslop-Harrison, Y.

HARRISS, Robert C. and others
Mercury compounds reduce photosynthesis by plankton. bibliog il Science 170:736-7 N 13 '70

HARRISSY, Louis J.
Nation is moving to the left. Nat R 22:260 Mr 10 '70

HARRITON, Maria
Elaine Summers: new forms, new ideas! il pors Dance Mag 44:66-73 S '70
Looking at dance films: Seafall. il Dance Mag 44:22-3 Ag '70
Looking at television. il Dance Mag 44:72 Jl '70

HARRY X
Case of Harry X. il Newsweek 76:48 Jl 27 '70 *

HARSCH, Joseph C.
Toward an urban guerrilla movement? Cur 118:13-14 My '70

HARSHMAN, James, and Melville, George
Hofmann apparatus and leak rate of gases. il
pors Chem 43:26 Je '70

HART, Gary
Test case in California. W. Seifert. New
Repub 163:8-9 O 31 '70 *

HART, Harold H.
How weather-wise are you? excerpt from
Grab a pencil. il Read Digest 97:143-4 Jl '70

HART, Jeffrey
Gulp: there goes UCal La Jolla. Nat R 22:
1046+ O 6 '70
Secession of the intellectuals. Nat R 22:1278-
82 D 1 '70

HART, Jerry
Bold coasts and castled islands. il Yachting
127:64-6+ Je '70

HART, Joe
Learning to be hypnotized. P. Boyle. Sci Digest 68:71 D '70 *

HART, John Fraser, and Adams, R. B.
Twin Cities. bibliog il Focus 20:1-11 F '70

HART, Michael, and Bonse, Ulrich
Interferometry with X rays. bibliog il pors
Phys Today 23:26-31 Ag '70

HART, Parker T.
American policy toward the Middle East; address, April 1970, with questions and answers. Ann Am Acad 390:98-113 Jl '70

HART, Philip
Perlman and Ashkenazy: a stunning team for
Prokofiev. Hi Fi sec I 20:90 F '70
Symphonic strike season. il Sat R 53:47-9+
S 26; 60-1 O 31 '70
Young performers face young listeners. il
Hi Fi 20:secII 15-17 Jl '70

HART, Philip A.
Motor trend interview. il pors Motor T
22:92+ Ap '70

HART, Sandra
In the wake of Columbus. il Travel 134:28-
33+ O '70

HART, Virginia
We did it; ed. by S. Nirenberg. il por House
B 112:3+ Jl '70

HARTE, John, and Socolow, Robert
(eds) Patient earth; excerpts. il Phys Today
23:28-9 D '70

HARTER, Walter
Don't throw it away! il Har Yrs 10:22 Ja '70
You have to believe. il PTA Mag 64:15 My
'70

HARTFORD, Bill
Can the Can-Am kings blitz the brickyard?
il Pop Mech 133:90-3+ My '70
How I became a racing driver in three easy
lessons. il Pop Mech 135:86-90 Ja '71
Performance tests. Detroit vs. Union oil. il
Pop Mech 133:94-7 Ap '70

HARTFORD, Bruce
(ed) See Browne, R. Ram for the records

HARTFORD, Robert J.
Voluntary mental health association: an innovator of services. Ment Hy 54:97-100 Ja '70

HARTFORD, Conn.
Music
Magda Olivero: worth a journey. G. Mov-
shon. Hi Fi sec II 20:21 Ja '70

HARTLEY, Anthony
U.S. the Arabs & Israel. Commentary 49:45-
50 Mr '70

HARTLEY, Ellen. See Hartley, W. B. jt. auth.

HARTLEY, Fred Lloyd
Luck of the drill bit. Forbes 105:16-17 Ja 15
'70

HARTLEY, William B.
(ed) See Aronow, D. From my ocean racers:
a better boat for you
—and Hartley, Ellen
Experimental surgery fights heart disease. il
Sci Digest 67:10-11+ Ap '70
Ocean full of medicine. il Sci Digest 68:34-40
D '70
Redbook guide to America's Heritage trails.
il Redbook 134:35-42 Ap; 135:51-8 Jl '70
Rescue of Donald and Richard. il Good H 171:
12+ Jl '70
Training school for birds. il Sci Digest 69:
32-6 Ja '71
Your kids may live to be 100+. il Sci Digest
68:38-42 S '70

HARTMAN, J. E.
Manatee: siren of the sea. il Nat Wildlife 7:
38-9 O '69
Prairie jester. il Nat Wildlife 8:35-7 Ap '70

HARTMAN, Karl A. and Thomas, G. J. Jr
Secondary structure of ribosomal RNA. bib-
liog il Science 170:740-1 N 13 '70
—and others
Structure of RNA in ribosomes. bibliog il
Science 170:171-3 O 9 '70

HARTMANN, Ernest L.
Sleep and emotions. Time 95:53 Je 29 '70 *

HARTMANN, Lillian. See Devons, S. jt. auth.

HARTONG, Hendrik J. R. G. Jr
Take-charge guy in venture capital. pors
Bsns W p72 O 24 '70 *

HARTUNG, George, and Gelman, Rena
Something different in in-service education.
il Todays Ed 59:24-5 My '70

HARTUNG, Philip T.
Festival flashback. Commonweal 93:250 D 4
'70

HARTWIG, Marie
Instant camp evaluation. Camp Mag 42:12-13
My '70

HARTWIG C, Fernando
Problems of Chilean national parks. il Nat
Parks 44:14-17 F '70

HARTZ, Frederic R. See Bone, L. E.; Eistein,
H. jt. auths.

HARTZOG, George B. Jr
But why, George? E. N. Layne. il por Am
Heritage 21:113 Je '70 *

HARVARD business review
B-school's link to businessmen. il Bsns W
p59 Ja 24 '70

HARVARD business school. See Harvard university—Graduate school of business administration

HARVARD coop bookstore. See College bookstores

HARVARD dictionary of music. See Music—
Dictionaries and encyclopedias

HARVARD graduates. See College graduates

HARVARD school of education's pre-school
project. See Harvard university—Graduate
school of education

HARVARD university
Blowing my mind at Harvard; experiences of
a Nieman fellow. L. L. King. Harper 241:
95-8+ O '70
Caught in the middle; contract demands more
minority workers in campus building. News-
week 75:65 F 23 '70
Discrimination: women charge universities,
colleges with bias. N. Gruchow. Science
168:559-61 My 1 '70
End of a chapter. por Newsweek 75:67-8 Mr
2 '70
Harvard twenty-three: one for president?
question of Pusey's successor. il Newsweek
76:79 D 14 '70
Harvard's Afro-American studies. por Negro
Hist Bul 33:20 Ja '70
Non humilis mulier triumpho; commencement
address given by female student. Time 95:45
Je 29 '70
President bows out. por Time 95:63 Mr 2 '70
President for Harvard. por Time 97:46 Ja 18
'71
Voices of Harvard '70. R. Todd. il N Y Times
Mag p26-9+ Je 7 '70; Discussion. p56 Je 28
'70
War was two years ago; Harvard after
twenty years. R. Maloney. Atlan 225:61-3
Mr '70

Botanical museum
Glass flowers: a unique and beautiful plant
collection; Ware collection. F. Kaltenbach.
il por Horticulture 48:36-7 F '70

Graduate school of business administration
New dean, new era for Harvard B-school; L.
Fouraker. il por Bsns W p58-60+ Ja 24 '70

Graduate school of design
Harvard graduate school of design. R. Jensen. il Arch Rec 147:140-2 F '70

Graduate school of education
Crucial years for learning; findings of Harvard's pre-school project. C. Lang. il Parents Mag 45:62-3+ S '70

Medical school
Library
Vision information center: a user-oriented
data base. M. M. Eichhorn and R. D. Reinecke. bibliog il Science 169:29-31 Jl 3 '70

HARVESTING
Handy harvest ideas. il Suc Farm 68:36 Je '70
See also
Corn—Harvesting

HARVESTING machinery
How to combine two bu. more soybeans per
acre. G. W. Wormley. il Farm J 94:28E N '70
How to handle combine problems. P. B.
Jones. il Suc Farm 68:32-5 Je '70
Tomato harvesters: bigger in the West,
smaller in the East. R. G. Fowler. il Farm
J 94:54A F '70

Cost of operation
See Agricultural machinery—Cost of operation

HARVESTING machinery—*Continued*

Leasing and renting

To get corn, soybeans out on time, rent a combine. B. Coffman. Farm J 93:36J N '69

Maintenance and repair

Machinery maintenance; combines. il Suc Farm 68:42 Ja '70

HARVEY, A. McGehee
1969 conversation with Khrushchev: the beginning of his fall from power. Life 69:48B D 18 '70

HARVEY, Dodd L. See Kohler, F. D. jt. auth.

HARVEY, Frank
Aerobatics: survival school in the sky. il pors Pop Sci 197:58-60 S '70

HARVEY, Herbert R.
Florentine codex. il Natur Hist 79:42-51+ D '70

HARVEY, James
Screen. Commonweal 92:37-8, 270-2, 343-5, 416-17 Mr 20, My 29, Jl 10, Ag 21 '70

HARVEY, James A. See Krug, J. F. jt. auth.

HARVEY, Paul
If the silent majority could talk, what would it say? T. Ferrell. pors Esquire 73:146-51+ My '70 *

HARVEY, Robert
Poetry in secondary schools. bibliog Engl J 59:308-15 F '70

HARVEY, Robert C.
How Shavian is the Pygmalion we teach? Engl J 59:1234-8 D '70

—and Denby, R. V.
Reference shelf for curriculum planning. Engl J 59:1177-85 N '70

HARVEY, Tad
Bottomless wonder: twenty-story tank stores oil on floor of Arabian Gulf. il Pop Sci 196:80-3 Ja '70

HARVEY; drama. See Chase, M. C.

HARVEY Cushing society
Medical sciences; American association of neurological surgeons meeting. Sci N 97:435 My 2 '70

HARWIT, Martin. See Houck, J. R. jt. auth.

HARWOOD, Richard Lee
Editorial ombudsman. il por Newsweek 76:72 D 14 '70 *

HASCHEMEYER, Rudy H. See Zelazo, P. O. jt. auth.

HASH
ABC's of hash. il Am Home 73:92 O '70

HASHISH. See Marijuana

HASIDIC tales. See Tales, Hasidic

HASIDISM
In praise of the Baal Shem Tov, tr. by D. Ben-Amos and J. R. Mintz. Review
Commentary 50:88-90 S '70. A. A. Cohen

HASKELL, Helen L.
Factors to consider in stimulating and motivating campers; address. il Camp Mag 42:12-13 Mr '70

HASKETT, Thomas R.
Electronics geography quiz. Pop Electr 32:42+ Ap '70
Power tools. il Radio-Electr 41:54-8 N '70
Tools for electronics. See issues of Radio-electronics to June 1970
TV-FM lead-in: what kind to use? il Electr World 83:46-50 Ja '70

HASKIN, Larry A. and others
Rare earth elements in returned lunar samples. bibliog il Science 167:487-90 Ja 30 '70

HASLEY, Louis
Poetry of Phyllis McGinley. por Cath World 211:211-15 Ag '70

HASSAN II, king of Morocco
President Nixon, King Hassan open communications satellite service; exchange of remarks, January 7, 1970. Dept State Bul 62:129 F 2 '70

about

Where a golf nut is king. D. Jenkins. il pors Sports Illus 33:32-9 S 28 '70 *

HASSAN, Farkhonda. See Cohen, A. J. jt. auth.

HASSEL, Odd
Structural aspects of interatomic charge-transfer bonding: Nobel prize lecture, June 9, 1970. bibliog il Science 170:497-502 O 30 '70

HASSELL, Bert
Return of the Rockford. R. E. Carlin. il por Flying 87:52-7 N '70 *

HASTINGS, Anne
Buono da mangiare; story. Harp Baz 103:84 Je '70

HASTINGS college of law, San Francisco. See California. University—Hastings college of law, San Francisco

HASWELL, Anthony
Passenger's friend. por Bsns W p30 Ag 1 '70 *

HAT industry
See also
Stetson, John B. company

HATCH, Anthony P.
Many fronts of Israel. il Nation 210:197-200 F 23 '70

HATCH, Francis W.
Case of Peol Sussep. il Sat R 53:17 Jl 11 '70

HATCH, Robert
Films. See issues of Nation

HATCH, Virginia B.
Chance for identity, integrity, and independence. Ed Digest 35:9-12 Ja '70

HATCHER, Richard Gordon
Black mayors. il por Newsweek 76:17-18 Ag 3 '70 *
Is there a plot to kill Mayor Hatcher? A. Poinsett. il pors Ebony 26:142-4+ D '70 *

HATFIELD, Frances, and Guliette, Irene
Individualized learning in the flexible school. Am Lib 1:169-70 F '70

HATFIELD, Mark Odom
Odd couple. pors Newsweek 76:18-19 S 7 '70 *

HATHAWAY, Caleb, and Craig, J. B.
Up three flights to the third forest. il Am For 76:8-11+ Mr '70

HATHAWAY, Lodene Brown
Christmas pageant will be presented; poem. Chr Cent 87:1535 D 23 '70
Every Sunday they made gods; poem. Chr Cent 87:860 Jl 15 '70
Tottering rebellion; poem. Chr Cent 88:13 Ja 6 '71

HATHAWAY, William Dodd
Excerpt from testimony, May 21,1970. Cong Digest 49:266+ N '70

HATHEWAY house. See Connecticut—Historic houses, etc.

HATTERAS NATIONAL SEASHORE, CAPE. See Cape Hatteras National Seashore Recreation Area

HATTERSLEY, Ralph
Artistry of Max Waldman. il Pop Phot 66:102-11+ Ja '70
Do you have eyes in your skin? il Pop Phot 66:55-9 Mr '70
Don't let critics kill your pictures. il Pop Phot 67:67-9+ Jl '70
Hattersley class. See issues of Popular photography

HATTORI, Shoji
Who's afraid of Vega, Pinto and Gremlin? Not Toyota; interview. pors Motor T 22:65-6+ Ag '70

HAUGH, Gerry Lynn
Case of the Toy Town clown; drama. Plays 30:69-75 D '70

HAUGHEY, John C.
Christian unity, the U.S. scene. il America 123:261-3 O 10 '70
Exodus of Protestant ministers? America 122:243-4 Mr 7 '70
Letter from Holland. America 122:450-2 Ap 25 '70
Loyalty and dissent: lessons from the saints. America 122:682-4 Je 27 '70
Those Black Panthers. America 122:43-4 Ja 17 '70
U.S. sisters organize. America 122:388-90 Ap 11 '70

HAUGHTON, Jerry W.
Incarnational evangelism. Chr Today 14:10-12 Ag 21 '70

HAUNTED houses (amusements) See Amusements

HAUPERT, John S.
Israel. il Focus 20:1-12 Mr '70

HAUPT, Christopher Lehmann-. See Lehmann-Haupt, C.

HAUSE, Lawrence, and others
Cell surface coatings and membrane potentials of malignant and nonmalignant cells. bibliog il Science 169:601-3 Ag 7 '70

HAUSER, Ernest O.
Henry Moore and the shape of things. il por Read Digest 96:136-41 Ap '70
Man who betrayed Christ. il Read Digest 96:214-16+ Ap '70

HAUSER, Philip M.
On population and environment; address, June 8, 1970. Vital Speeches 36:696-701 S 1 '70

HAUSER, Rita E.
Department supports ratification of genocide convention; statement, April 24, 1970. Dept State Bul 63:11-13 Jl 6 '70
United States supports creation of the post of U.N. high commissioner for human rights; statement, December 5,1969. Dept State Bul 62:41-4 Ja 12 '70

HAUSMAN, Leonard J. See Kasper, H. jt. auth.

HAUSMANN, E. and others
Endotoxin: stimulation of bone resorption in tissue culture. bibliog il Science 168:862-4 My 15 '70

HAUSSMAN, Fay
  Brazil: a giant begins to stir. il Sat R 53:62-3+
    O 17 '70
HAUTEFEUILLE, Phillippe
  Europe's creative new breed. il por Time 95:
    90 Mr 16 '70 *
HAUTZIG, Esther
  Endless steppe, for children only? excerpts
    from address, April 8, 1970. E. Hautzig.
    Horn Bk 46:461-8 O '70
HAVARD, Pauline
  On Christmas eve; poem. il Farm J 93:37 D
    '69
HAVASU CANYON
  Down, down, to Havasu. il Sunset 144:80-3
    My '70
  Indian Shangri-LA of the Grand Canyon. J.
    Johnston. il Nat Geog 137:354-73 Mr '70
HAVASU LAKE
  Cove hopping Havasu. M. Rizer. il Motor B
    126:48-9+ N '70
HAVASUPAI Indians
  Indian Shangri-La of the Grand Canyon. J.
    Johnston. il Nat Geog 137:354-73 Mr '70
HAVE you been depressed lately, Mrs Hardy?
  story. See Weisbrod, R. R.
HAVEN, Elizabeth W.
  Curricular innovation and practices in the
    American high school. Sch & Soc 98:239-41
    Ap '70; Same abr. Ed Digest 36:39-41 S '70
HAVERHILL, Mass.
  Child guerrillas? Time 96:81-2 N 23 '70
HAVERSTOCK, Mary Sayre
  American bestiary. il Art in Am 58:38-71 Jl
    '70
HAVIGHURST, Clark C.
  Compensating persons injured in human ex-
    perimentation. bibliog Science 169:153-7 Jl
    10 '70
HAVIGHURST, Walter
  Steamboat to the Rockies. bibliog il Am
    West 7:4-11+ S '70
HAW Par brothers international, ltd. See Drug
  trade—Singapore
HAWAII
  Across Oahu from Honolulu, lively replica
    Polynesia: Polynesian cultural center. il
    Sunset 144:17 Ap '70
  Making waves in Hawaii; group organized
    to save surfing areas. Nation 210:517-18 My
    2 '70
    See also
  Airlines—Hawaii
  Astronomical observatories—Hawaii
  Camping—Hawaii
  Diamond Head
  Festivals—Hawaii
  Haleakala National Park
  Hawaii (island)
  Kavai (island)
  Labor laws and legislation—Hawaii
  Landscape protection—Hawaii
  Law—Hawaii
  Laysan (island)
  Maui (island)
  Molokai (island)
  Railroads—Hawaii

    Description and travel
  Hawaii's historic sites spring from a tur-
    bulent past. R. F. MacMillan. il Travel 133:
    56-9 F '70
  Romantic's Hawaiian guide. J. Hulse. il Tra-
    vel & Camera 33:69-71 Ja '70

    Hotels, restaurants, etc.
  Shoeless life. D. Butwin. il Sat R 53:48+ Ja
    24 '70
    See also
  Honolulu—Hotels, restaurants, etc.

    Industries
    See also
  Amfac, inc.

    Social life and customs
  Football goes Hawaiian. D. Butwin. il Sat
    R 53:46 Ja 17 '70
  How the paniolo came. S. V. Candland. il
    Americas 22:7-9 Ja '70
HAWAII air cargo shippers association
  Hawaiian group stresses service. Aviation W
    93:132 O 26 '70
HAWAII (island)
  Hawaii's Hawaii. H. Sutton. il Travel &
    Camera 33:30-9 Ja '70
HAWAII islanders (baseball) See Baseball clubs
HAWAIIAN airlines. See Airlines—Hawaii
HAWAIIAN cookery. See Cookery, Hawaiian
HAWAIIAN international billfish tournament.
  See Fishing—Competitions
HAWAIIAN ISLANDS national wildlife refuge.
  See Wildlife sanctuaries—Hawaii

HAWK MOUNTAIN sanctuary. See Bird sanc-
  tuaries—Pennsylvania
HAWKES, Alex Drum
  Great vegetables. il House & Gard 137:87-
    9+ F '70
HAWKING, Frank
  Clock of the malaria parasite; with biograph-
    ical sketch. il Sci Am 222:12, 123-31 Je '70
HAWKINS, Alex
  How intangible can you get; ed. by M. Cope.
    il pors Sports Illus 33:48-50+ N 23 '70
  Loose and fun-loving off the field; ed. by M.
    Cope. il Sports Illus 33:88-90+ N 16 '70
HAWKINS, Connie
  Sun finally rises for Connie Hawkins. J.
    Goodrich. il pors Ebony 25:36-8+ F '70 *
HAWKINS, Pat
  Everyone can stand Pat! H. L. Masin. por
    Sr Schol 97:20 N 9 '70 *
HAWKINS, Robert E.
  Workshop Christmas wrap-ups. il Pop Sci
    197:86-7 D '70
HAWKINS, William J.
  Here they are: results of the $25,000 anti-car-
    theft competition. E. A. Zadig. il por Pop
    Sci 196:72-3+ Je '70 *
  —See Bawer, B. jt. auth.
HAWKMOTHS. See Moths
HAWKS
  Killer! goshawk; with painting by G. Cohe-
    leach. H. R. Sass. il Audubon 72:40-1 Ja '70
  Wings over Hawk Mountain. D. S. Heintzel-
    man. il Nat Wildlife 8:22-7 Ag '70
    See also
  Nighthawks
  Ospreys
HAWKS (basketball team) See Basketball teams
HAWN, Goldie
  How golden to be Goldie. il pors Life 68:76-
    9 Je 26 '70 *
HAWORTH, Mary
  As I see youth today; interview. Todays Ed
    59:46 Ja '70
HAWTHORN-juniper rust. See Rusts (botany)
HAWTHORNS
  Hawthorn berry for the heart. J. I. Rodale.
    il Org Gard & Farm 17:112-15 F; 128-30 Mr;
    106-9 Ap; 91-2+ My; 100-1 Je; 77-9 Jl; 98-9
    Ag '70
HAWXHURST, Donna, and Walzer, Hank
  Patients helping patients. bibliog Ment Hy
    54:370-3 Jl '70
HAY, Edwards
  Quiet killer. il Am For 76:16-19 Ap '70
HAY, John
  Where have all the fishes gone? il Audubon
    72:74-7 N '70
HAY fever; drama. See Coward, N.
HAYAKAWA, Samuel Ichiyé
  Real root of student disorder? Read Digest
    97:167-8 N '70
    about
  Hayakawa at Northeastern. D. Brudnoy. Nat
    R 22:202 F 24 '70 *
HAYASAKI, Yoshi
  Sun didn't rise overnight. D. Levin. por Sports
    Illus 32:28-9 Ap 13 '70 *
HAYASHIDA, T. See Herbert, D. C. jt. auth.
HAYCRAFT, Howard
  Howard Haycraft. por Wilson Lib Bul 45:444
    Ja '71 *
HAYDEE, Marcia
  Monologues with meeting places: John Cran-
    ko, Marcia Haydee, ed. by N. M. Stoop.
    Dance Mag 44:35 Ag '70
HAYDEN, Arthur
  Extending camp season offers three benefits.
    Camp Mag 42:11-12 N '70
HAYDEN, Julie
  Walking with Charlie; story. New Yorker
    46:48-50 N 7 '70
HAYDEN, Melissa
  Extraordinary anniversary. S. Goodman. il
    pors Dance Mag 44:28-31 N '70 *
HAYDEN, Mike
  March with the kings. il Outdoor Life 145:
    52-5+ Mr '70
HAYDEN, Thomas Emmett
  Trial; excerpts. il Ramp Mag 9:10-11+ Jl;
    26-7+ S '70
    about
  Judging the Chicago trial. A. M. Bickel. bib-
    liog f Commentary 51:31-40 Ja '71 *
  Tract for our time. Ramp Mag 9:6 Jl '70 *
  Trashing the public. G. Wagner. Nat R 22:1118
    O 20 '70 *
HAYDN, Franz Joseph
  Joseph Haydn, by L. Somfai. Review
    Am Rec G por 36:763 My '70. R. Zar-
    bock *

HAYDN, Franz Joseph—*Continued*
Joseph Haydn: his life in contemporary pictures; comp. by L. Somfai. Mus Q 56:295-9 Ap '70 *
Karajan's Creation. R. Jacobson. Sat R 53:54 Je 27 '70 *
Karajan's modest Creation. S. Fleming. Hi Fi 20:secI 96 Ap '70 *
Particularly exciting Creation. P. L. Miller. Am Rec G 36:572 Ap '70 *
HAYES, D. K. and others
Photoperiod manipulation of insect diapause: a method of pest control? bibliog il Science 169:382-3 Jl 24 '70
HAYES, Denis
Environmental teach-in. il Liv Wildn 34:12-13 Spr '70
HAYES, Isaac
Isaac Hayes: Hot buttered soul. P. Garland. il pors Ebony 25:82-4+ Mr '70 *
HAYES, Melvin L.
Teacher strikes reach record heights. Sch & Soc 98:433-4 N '70
HAYES, R. L. and others
Gallium-67 localization in rat and mouse tumors. bibliog il Science 167:298-90 Ja 16 '70
HAYES, Wayne Woodrow
Revival and revenge. D. Jenkins. il por Sports Illus 33:16-19 N 30 '70 *
HAYES, Woody. See Hayes, W. W.
HAYLOCK, E. F.
Alone on a wide, wide sea. il Motor B 125:36-8+ Mr '70
Great round Britain sailing race. il Motor B 126:38-42+ N '70
Welcome aboard Hedonist. il Motor B 125:78-80+ Je '70
HAYMARKET square riot, 1886. See Chicago—Haymarket square riot, 1886
HAYNE, Arnold
Supply and demand. Look 34:92 D 15 '70
HAYNES, C. Vance, jr
Earliest Americans. bibliog Science 166:709-15; 167:1670 N 7 '69, Mr 27 '70
—See Meighan, C. W. jt. auth.
HAYNES, Lincoln
Begetting of "The begatting" il Writers Digest 50:30-1 Ag '70
HAYNES, Lloyd
Looking & listening; interview, ed. by P. Hudson. il Sr Schol 95:33 S 22 '69
HAYNES, Margaret C. and Helseth, Pam
Art and multi-age grouping. il Sch Arts 70:32-4 Ja '71
HAYNES, Muriel
Other revolution. Nation 211:632-3 D 14 '70
HAYNSWORTH, Clement Furman, 1912-
After the Carswell defeat, Nixon's new strategy. il pors U S News 68:19-21 Ap 20 '70 *
Haynsworth v. the U.S. Senate (1969) J. L. Steele. il por Fortune 81:90-3+ Mr '70 *
Newsmaker. por Sr Schol 95:16 N 3 '69 *
HÄYRY, Pekka, and Defendi, Vittorio
Mixed lymphocyte cultures produce effector cells: model in vitro for allograft rejection. bibliog il Science 168:133-5 Ap 3 '70
HAYS, H. R.
Age? poem. Nation 210:632 My 25 '70
HAYSTACK MOUNTAIN (ski resort) See Winter resorts
HAYWOOD, Spencer
Haywood affair. il por Time 97:44+ Ja 18 '71 *
HAZARD, Patrick
Caribbean: this side of paradise. Nation 210:335-7 Mr 23 '70
HAZARDOUS occupations. See Occupations, Hazardous
HAZARDOUS substances

Disposal in the ocean

Death in the deep: chemical warfare agents of World war II in the Baltic Sea. Newsweek 76:33-4 Ag 24 '70
One small step; proposed legislation to control ocean dumping. Sci N 98:318 O 17 '70
See also
Gases, Asphyxiating and poisonous—Disposal in the ocean

Transportation

Danger! Hazardous materials in transit. D. Robinson. Read Digest 96:177-8+ My '70
Freighted with hazard. E. Albone and J. McCaull. bibliog il Environ 12:18-26+ D '70
See also
Chemicals—Transportation
Gases, Asphyxiating and poisonous—Transportation
HAZELTINE national golf club course. See Golf courses

HAZELTON, Nika Standen
Delectations. See issues of National review
Rhineland is wineland. Travel & Camera 33:25-7 O '70
about
Mrs Hazelton throws a bash. il pors Nat R 22:1296-301 D 1 '70 *
HAZLITT, Henry
Compounding the welfare mess. Nat R 22:205 F 24 '70
Nixon's economic dilemma. Nat R 22:1351 D 15 '70
What the market says. Nat R 22:675+ Je 30 '70
HAZO, Robert G.
P.M. Commentary 49:88-9 Ap '70
HAZO, Samuel
Spills of glimmer; poem. Sat R 53:27 O 24 '70
HÁZY, Erzsébet
Two sopranos: a discovery and an old friend. G. Movshon. pors Hi Fi 20:secI 79 Je '70 *
HEACOCK, Charlene
Heart of New Guinea. il Yachting 127:64-6+ Mr '70
HEACOCK, Robert H.
Choice for offshore. il Yachting 127:106-7+ Ja; 62-4+ F '70
HEACOX, Cecil E.
This is the timberdoodle. il Outdoor Life 146:76-7+ O '70
HEAD, Faye E.
Second shepherd's play; drama. Plays 30:37-42 D '70
Spouse for Susie Mouse; dramatization of a Korean folk tale. Plays 29:61-4, 96 Ap '70
HEAD Start, Project. See Project Head Start
HEADACHE
Annals of medicine; symptom of carbon monoxide poisoning. B. Roueché. New Yorker 45:60-8 Ja 31 '70
Curing modern headaches. Sci Digest 67:57-8 Ja '70
Ten common misconceptions about headaches. G. M. Knox. Bet Hom & Gard 48:36+ Mr '70
Your aching head. D. Schultz. il Ladies Home J 87:56+ S '70
HEADER, the rigger, the captain; story. See Thompson, E.
HEADLEE, Judy Anne
Educational approach to Negro individualism. bibliog f Engl J 59:34-9 Ja '70
HEADLINES, Newspaper. See Newspapers—Headlines
HEADPHONES. See Earphones
HEADS (engines) See Automobile engines
HEADS of state
Parting shots; can you match any of these heads of state to the countries they run? il Life 69:75-8 S 25 '70
Trend setters '71. il Sr Schol 97:16-18 S 21 '70
HEALING, Divine. See Faith cure
HEALTH
Family health. G. M. Knox. See issues of Better homes and gardens
Today's health news. A. L. Blakeslee. See issues of Today's health
What it takes to acquire physical fitness. Consumer Bul 54:27-8 Ja '71
Your health. il Todays Hd 59:54-6 F; 40-1 Mr; 59+ My; 74-5 O; 42-4 N '70
See also
Aged—Care and hygiene
Children—Care and hygiene
Exercise
Hygiene
Infants—Care and hygiene
Longevity
Men—Health and hygiene
Nutrition
Sickness
Sleep
Woman—Health and hygiene
HEALTH, Mental. See Mental hygiene
HEALTH and religion. See Medicine and religion
HEALTH and weather. See Weather—Mental and physiological effects
HEALTH benefit plans. See Insurance, Health
HEALTH centers
Delivery of medical care. S. R. Garfield. il Sci Am 222:15-23 bibliog(p 130) Ap '70
Health care goes into the streets. J. Bockel. il Sci N 97:276-7 Mr 14 '70
New spirit at old Meharry: cooperation with Taborian hospital in Mound Bayou, Miss. il Ebony 25:42-6+ Ap '70
See also
Mental health centers
HEALTH certification of swine. See Swine—Health certification

HEART beat—*Continued*
When two hearts beat as two. Sci Am 223:
60 O '70
See also
Pacemaker, Artificial (heart)
HEART block. See Heart—Diseases
HEART diseases. See Heart—Diseases
HEART muscle. See Heart—Muscle
HEART neuroses. See Neuroses
HEART of the matter; story. See Hodgson,
M. S.
HEART poisons. See Cardenolides
HEART pump. See Hearts, Artificial
HEART rate. See Heart beat
HEARTS, Artificial
Engineering the new mechanical heart. C.
Mitchell. il Pop Sci 196:64-6+ Mr '70
Era of plastic hearts. B. J. Culliton. il por
Sci N 97:375-7 Ap 11 '70
Pump that works like a heart. A. S. Freese.
il por Pop Mech 134:123-31+ N '70
Seventeen year old invents heart-lung
machine. S. V. Jones. il Sci Digest 68:75 S
'70
Steam machine to help your heart. P.
Weissler. il Mech Illus 66:68-9 Ap '70
HEAT
Physiological effects
Limits of microbial existence: temperature
and pH. T. D. Brock and G. K. Darland.
bibliog il Science 169:1316-18 S 25 '70

Radiation and absorption
Apollo 11 lunar science conference; other
physical properties; symposium. bibliog il
Science 167:724-30 Ja 30 '70
Why not green hot? I. Asimov. Sci Digest 68:
78-9 Jl '70
HEAT, Specific. See Specific heat
HEAT, Waste. See Waste heat
HEAT conductivity
Thermal conductivity of lunar and terrestrial
igneous rocks in their melting range. T.
Murase and A. R. McBirney. bibliog il
Science 170:165-7 O 9 '70
Thermal radiation properties and thermal
conductivity of lunar material. R. C. Birke-
bak and others. il Science 167:724-6 Ja 30
'70
HEAT flow. See Heat transmission
HEAT pollution. See Water pollution
HEAT radiation. See Heat—Radiation and ab-
sorption
HEAT resistant materials
New high-temperature materials sought. il
Aviation W 92:37+ Je 22 '70
See also
Refractory materials
HEAT transmission
Earth tides, global heat flow, and tectonics.
H. R. Shaw. bibliog il Science 168:1084-7
My 29 '70
Second sound in solid helium. B. Bertman
and D. J. Sandiford. il Sci Am 222:92-101
My '70
**Tricky metals that cool it; NaK alloy cool-
ant system.** il Bsns W p 112 N 7 '70
HEAT treatment of metals. See Metals—Heat
treatment
HEATERS, Water. See Water heaters
HEATH, Aloise Buckley
It says here... Nat R 22:1395-6 D 29 '70
HEATH, Dwight B.
Costa Rica and her neighbors. Cur Hist 58:
95-101+ F '70
HEATH, Edward Richard George
Interview with Britain's Prime Minister Ed-
ward Heath; ed. by J. Fromm. il pors U S
News 69:24-6+ D 21 '70

about

After victory: the Tories' next steps. por
Bsns W p50 Je 27 '70 *
Britain's new, willful prime minister. A.
Howard. New Repub 163:16 Jl 4 '70 *
Charisma sweepstakes. il pors Newsweek 75:
53 Je 15 '70 *
Counter-revolution. R. J. Korengold. News-
week 76:49 D 21 '70 *
Dark days in Great Britain. il Time 96:26-7
D 21 '70 *
Dilemma for Heath: how to please all. por
U S News 69:60 Jl 6 '70 *
Edward Richard George Heath: the road to
no. 10. por Newsweek 75:31 Je 29 '70 *
Heath's coherent design. Nat R 22:1385-6 D
29 '70 *
Heath's first week. il por Time 96:29 Jl 6 '70 *
Letter from London. M. Panter-Downes. New
Yorker 46:61-2 Jl 4 '70 *

Moving in. Newsweek 76:42+ Jl 6 '70 *
Now or never for Tory Heath? il por U S
News 68:36 Je 1 '70 *
Oiling the machinery. il por Time 96:20 D 28
'70 *
Silent majority clues as Britons vote against
ins. il por U S News 68:30-1 Je 29 '70 *
Ted Heath's new year. A. Lejeune. Nat R
22:1393-4 D 29 '70 *
Tory, Tory, hallelujah. il por Newsweek 75:
30+ Je 29 '70 *
Unexpected triumph. il pors Time 95:16-18+
Je 29 '70 *
HEATH, F. G.
Large-scale integration in electronics; with
biographical sketch. il Sci Am 22:10, 22-31 F
'70
HEATH, James Edward. See Mills, S. H. jt.
auth.
HEATH, Ted. See Heath, E. R. G.
HEATHROW International airport. See London
—Airports
HEATING
How to stretch your fuel this winter. Chang-
ing T 24:4 D '70
See also
Insulation (heat)
School buildings—Heating and ventilation
Solar heating
HEATING equipment
See also
Furnaces
HEATING from central stations
Central plant heats and cools California's cap-
itol. il Arch Rec 147:167-70 Ja '70
HEATON, Maurice
Maurice Heaton's laminated panels; ed. by
T. Bayne. il Craft Horiz 30:24-5+ Ag '70
HEAVEN
What's so great about heaven? C. D. Linton.
Chr Today 15:3-5 N 20 '70
HEAVY water. See Deuterium oxide
HEBBLETHWAITE, Peter
Forty more saints. America 123:399-400 N 14
'70
Nymphs and shepherds. Cath World 211:55-7
My '70
HEBERT, Arnold J.
Bulbs bring color indoors. Horticulture 48:
18-19 N '70
Summer-flowering bulbs. il Horticulture 48:
50-3 Mr '70
HÉBERT, F. Edward
And now, the communications yap; excerpts
from statements. por Time 97:11 Ja 11 '71

about

Hébert: a tough, critical friend. por Bsns W
p 14 Ja 2 '71 *
Powerful committee post for a defense-
minded congressman. por U S News 70:45
Ja 11 '71 *
HEBERT report. See Government investiga-
tions—My Lai massacre
HEBREW authors
See also
Agnon, S. J.
Goldberg, L.
HEBREW language
Hebrew as she is spoke. H. Halkin: discus-
sion. Commentary 49:8+ Ap '70
HEBREW literature
See also
Jewish literature
HEBREW philosophy. See Philosophy, Jewish
HEBREW religion. See Judaism
HEBRIDES
Fighting the Scotch tide; distilleries of Islay.
il Time 95:72 Je 8 '70
See also
Lewis with Harris (island)

Description and travel
Scotland's Outer Hebrides. K. MacLeish. il
Nat Geog 137:676-91+ My '70
HECHINGER, Fred. See Hechinger, G. jt. auth.
HECHINGER, Grace, and Hechinger, Fred
Parent and child. il N Y Times Mag p83+
N 1 '70
HECHT, Alan D. and Savin, S. M.
Oxygen-18 studies of recent planktonic
foraminifera: comparisons of phenotypes
and of test parts. bibliog il Science 170:69-
71 O 2 '70
HECHT, Florence M.
Twin bed bridge; story. Atlan 225:100-4 My
'70
HECHT, George J.
Introducing our new editor. por Parents Mag
46:22 Ja '71
Smaller families: a national imperative. por
Parents Mag 45:24+ Jl '70

HECKLER, Margaret M.
Excerpt from debate, September 16, 1969.
Cong Digest 49:27 Ja '70
HECKMAN, Donald, and others
In the pop bag. See issues of American rec-
ord guide
HECKT, Neil
Build with IC's: three-way waveform gen-
erator. il Radio-Electr 41:62-3+ N '70
HEDDA Gabler; drama. See Ibsen, H.
HEDGEPETH, William
American South: rise of a new confederacy.
il Look 34:19-32+ N 17 '70
America's Indians. il Look 34:23-34 Je 2 '70
Growl to me softly and I'll understand. il
Look 34:46-8+ Ja 13 '70
Joan Baez and David Harris: we're just non-
violent soldiers. il pors Look 34:58-61+ My
5 '70
HEDGES, David
Nijinsky's triple was a lark. il Sports Illus 33:
28-9 S 21 '70
HEDGES, Irwin R.
Process of development; address, January
21, 1970. Vital Speeches 36:290-5 Mr 1 '70
HEDGES
Hedges that solve problems. L. Grove. il Bet
Hom & Gard 48:84-5+ Mr '70
How to start a hedge. il Good H 171:184 O '70
HEDGING
Hedging against money changes. il Bsns W
p94 S 19 '70
How I use the futures market; ed. by R. San-
ders. B. E. Jones. il por Suc Farm 68:33
Ap '70
Managing risks in foreign exchange. B. A.
Lietaer. il Harvard Bsns R 48:127-38 Mr
'70
HEDGPETH, Joel W.
Oceans: world sump. il Environ 12:40-6 Ap '70
HEDIN, Robert S.
Let high-pressure water wash your car. il
Pop Sci 196:106-7 Mr '70
Make your own electronic enlarging meter.
il Pop Mech 135:124-7 Ja '71
HEDLA, Lenore
Slick tricks for cold-country gardening. il
Home Gard 58:54-5+ Ja '71
HEDLEY, Leslie Woolf
Life among the negatives. Chr Cent 87:869-70
Jl 15 '70
HEDLUND, Ronald D. See Tessler, M. A. jt.
auth.
HEDORO. See Water pollution—Japan
HEELEY, Desmond
Love affair; interview, ed. by F. Stevenson.
por Opera N 34:13 Ap 4 '70
HEELS (shoes) See Shoes
HEESACKER, Frank L.
Hitching up the small school districts. il Am
Ed 6:18-21 Ap '70
HEFFERNAN, Helen
Influence on the elementary school. il Todays
Ed 59:41-2 Ap '70
HEFLEY, James C.
Woman doctor is missing in action. il Todays
Health 48:38-41+ Ap '70
—and Hefley, Marti
Babies in question. il Todays Health 48:16-
19+ Ag '70
HEFLEY, Marti. See Hefley, J. C. jt. auth.
HEFNER, Hugh Marston
Hugh M. Hefner; interview; ed. by L. R.
Hills. il pors Esquire 74:141-3+ D '70
What Playboy doesn't know about women
could fill a book; interview, ed. by G.
Steinem. il por McCalls 98:139-40 O '70

about

Bunny hunting. il pors Newsweek 75:71 Mr
2 '70 *
Hugh Hefner's jet black bunny in the sky.
H. Ehrlich. il pors Look 34:62-5 Je 2 '70 *
HEGEL, Georg Wilhelm Friedrich
Hegel, Beethoven, Wordsworth: 1770-1970. H.
Gross. Am Scholar 40:142-56 Wint '70 *
Hegelian dialectic in theology. J. N. Jons-
son. Chr Today 14:3-5 Ag 21 '70 (to be
cont) *
HEIDELBERG, Germany
Home on the Rhine. D. Butwin. il Sat R 53:
56-7 Je 20 '70
HEIGHT of man. See Stature
HEILBRONER, Robert Louis
Priorities for the seventies. Cur 116:11-18 Mr
'70
Socialism and the future. bibliog f Commen-
tary 48:35-45 D '69; 49:16 Ap '70
HEILMAN, Joan Rattner
(ed) See Nidetch, J. Story of weight watchers
HEILMAN, John A.
Coming of age at sea. il Yachting 127:97+
Ja '70

HEILMEIER, George H.
Liquid-crystal display devices; with biograph-
ical sketch. il Sci Am 222:12, 100-6 Ap '70
HEIMANN, Richard
Barn reborn. il House & Gard 137:124-9 Mr
'70 *
HEIMSATH, Clovis
Place for a happening. America 123:149-50
S 12 '70
HEIN, Piet
Match wits with Danish gamemaster Piet
Hein, H. Shuldiner. il por Pop Sci 196:68-71
Ja '70
HEINDEL, Richard H.
Letter of congratulations to a new university
president. Sch & Soc 98:408-10 N '70
HEINEMAN, Ben Walter
Can Heineman peddle a deadhead? por Bsns
W p 19 O 3 '70 *
HEINEMANN, Arthur
Book mark; story. Ladies Home J 87:56 Ag
'70
HEINER, Lou
Binoculars for the boatman. il Yachting 127:
78-80+ Mr '70
HEINITZ, Thomas
Britten and the borough: on the winds of
the North Sea. il Sat R 53:80+ Mr 14 '70
Other side. See issues of Saturday review
HEINL, Robert Debs, Jr
Turmoil; address, December 8, 1969. Vital
Speeches 36:296-9 Mr 1 '70
'Twas the night before Christmas. . . il por
Am Heritage 22:105-9 D '70
HEINOLD, George
Anglerfish, the fisherman with a built-in
lure. il Sci Digest 67:20-4 Ja '70
Just how serious is thermal pollution? il por
Sci Digest 68:62-6 N '70
Nova Scotia's striped sea barse. il pors Out-
door Life 146:62-4+ Jl '70
Salt water. See issues of Outdoor life
HEINRICH, Bernd
Nervous control of the heart during thoracic
temperature regulation in a sphinx moth.
bibliog il Science 169:606-7 Ag 7 '70
Thoracic temperatures stabilization by blood
circulation in a free-flying moth. bibliog il
Science 168:580-2 My 1 '70
HEINRICH, Kurt F. J. and others
Image-formation technique for scanning elec-
tron microscopy and electron probe micro-
analysis. bibliog il Science 167:1129-31 F 20
'70
HEINS, Paul
Coming to terms with criticism; address,
June 19, 1969. Horn Bk 46:370-5 Ag '70
Out on a limb with the critics; address, June
18, 1969. bibliog Horn Bk 46:264-73 Je '70
—and others
(comp) See Booklist (title varies) See issues of
Horn book magazine
HEINSELMAN, Miron L.
Preserving nature in forested wilderness areas
and national parks. il Nat Parks & Con
Mag 44:8-14 S '70
HEINSHEIMER, Hans W.
Beethoven's Vienna. il Opera N 35:6-10 Ja
2 '71
(tr) See Stuckenschmidt, H. H. Beethoven
in retrospect: Germany
HEINTJE (singer)
Flying Dutch boy. por Newsweek 76:99 S 14
'70
HEINTZE, James R.
Music of the Washington family: a little-
known collection. bibliog f por Mus Q 56:
288-93 Ap '70
HEINTZELMAN, Donald S.
Wings over Hawk Mountain. il Nat Wildlife
8:22-7 Ag '70
HEINZ, Gerald F.
Creative writing with a movie camera. il
Schol Teach Sec Teach Sup p20-1 N 3 '69
HEINZ, W. C.
Man who said, they don't have to die. il por
Todays Health 49:26-9+ Ja '71
New eyes for Tom Large Whiskers. il pors
Todays Health 48:30-3+ S '70
HEINZEN, Barbara Brem
Teen tycoon; drama. Plays 29:1-10 Mr '70
HEIPLE, Clark
Our sungods. il Sch Arts 69:22-3 Ap '70
HEIRLOOMS
To you, now. R. A. Smith. il por Har Yrs 10:
42-3 S '70
HEISE, George Franklin
Status in the 80s; letter to the editor. Am
Lib 1:522-4 Je '70
HEISENBERG, Werner
Physics and beyond: encounters and conver-
sations; excerpt. il Bul Atom Sci 26:33-6 N
'70

HEISERMAN, David L.
Chip capacitors for IC's. il Electr World 84: 40-2+ D '70
Computer time sharing. il Electr World 83: 42-4+ Mr '70
Experiments with Schlieren auras. il Sci Digest 69:75-8 Ja '71
Graphic computer terminals. il Electr World 84:34-6+ O; 35-7+ N '70
Now, a do-it-yourself UFO. il Pop Sci 196: 109 My '70
Opportunity mirror; questions and answers. See issues of Popular electronics
Strange Enright illusion. il Sci Digest 68:15-17 N '70

HEISEY, Henry
Farmer-archeologist. G. Logsdon. il por Farm J 93:A4 N '69 *

HEITNER, Paul
Whale of a hand and a player, too. C. Goren. il por Sports Illus 33:104 S 14 '70 *

HEIZER, Edgar F. Jr
What do you do with $81 million? por Forbes 106:42+ Jl 15 '70 *

HELA cells. See Cells

HELEN Therese Nyberg, Sister. See Nyberg, H. T.

HELEN Worth cooking school. See Cookery— Study and teaching

HELENA Brand, Sister. See Brand, H.

HELFANT, Murray H.
Letter to the President. il Look 34:48-53 Jl 28 '70

HELFER, Harold
Prescription; poem. Good H 171:10 N '70

HELGELAND, Glenn B.
California quail, hurry-scurry bird. il Nat Wildlife 8:20-20B O '70
How to pick a marina. il Pop Mech 133:130-5 Mr '70
Owooo... il Nat Wildlife 9:52-3 D '70

HELI-Coil system. See Screw threads

HELICOPTER airlines
See also
Los Angeles airways, inc.
San Francisco and Oakland helicopter airlines

HELICOPTER carriers. See Aircraft carriers

HELICOPTER engines

Testing
Test facility designed for S-64B helicopter. il Aviation W 93:60-1 Jl 6 '70

HELICOPTER flying. See Helicopters—Piloting

HELICOPTER industry and trade

France
Sud broadens helicopter marketing base. E. H. Kolcum. il Aviation W 92:52-3 F 2 '70

Japan
Japan lags in helicopter design. C. Brownlow. il Aviation W 92:49+ Ap 20 '70

United States
Crime issue spurs helicopters. Aviation W 92: 198 Mr 9 '70
Military helicopters get chopped down. il Bsns W p58+ Ag 29 '70

HELICOPTERS
Helicopters move in on home-front jobs. il U S News 69:26-7 Jl 6 '70
How you can own and fly your own whirly-bird. K. V. Brown. il Pop Sci 197:40-2+ Jl '70
Intercity demonstration flights show S-65 helicopter capability. R. S. Kahn. Aviation W 92:23 Je 15 '70
See also
Autogiros

Blades
See Helicopters—Rotors

Design
Bo.105 could spur German production. il Aviation W 92:108 Ap 27 '70
Boeing demonstrates Bo.105 Lamps entry. il Aviation W 92:20-1 Ja 19 '70

Marketing
Ka-26 western market sought. Aviation W 92:54-5 F 16 '70
Sud broadens helicopter marketing base. E. H. Kolcum. il Aviation W 92:52-3 F 2 '70

Military use
AH-56 faces new army tests. W. S. Hieronymus. il Aviation W 93:58-9+ N 16 '70
AH-56 operational requirement revised. C. Brownlow. il Aviation W 93:18 N 9 '70
Army tests nocturnal HueyCobra. P. J. Klass. il Aviation W 93:57-9 O 5 '70

Infrared fire control tests start. B. Miller. il Aviation W 92:53-5 My 11 '70
Kaman Sealite proposed for navy Lamps. il Aviation W 93:20-1 O 12 '70
LAMPS proposal request expected soon. C. Brownlow. il Aviation W 93:19-20 N 30 '70
Lessons U.S. has learned in the helicopter war. il U S News 69:49-50 N 23 '70
New orders bolster helicopter program. il Aviation W 93:63-4+ S 7 '70
Sikorsky testing fast armed helicopter. C. Brownlow. il Aviation W 93:16-18 S 21 '70
See also
Armor plate

Piloting
Could you learn to fly a chopper? N. Aubuchon. il Pop Sci 196:52-3+ Ap '70
Learning to fly a helicopter. P. Garrison. il Flying 87:48-56+ Ag '70

Private ownership
Four ways to beat the 8:55 from Greenwich. il Esquire 73:76-81+ F '70

Rotors
Composite-structure blade spar studied. M. L. Yaffee. Aviation W 93:44+ Jl 27 '70

Specifications
Leading international rotary-wing aircraft; tables (cont) Aviation W 92:123 Mr 9 '70
U.S. rotary-wing aircraft; tables (cont) Aviation W 92:122 Mr 9 '70

Testing
Helicopter test changes planned. E. J. Bulban. Aviation W 93:57+ D 7 '70
Lockheed flight testing AH-56 with modified controls. blades. Aviation W 92:66-7 Mr 30 '70

HELICOPTERS, Ambulance
Helicopter ambulance inaugurated: Palm Beach County, Fla. il Am City 85:16 O '70

HELICOPTERS, Business
Bell 212 noise, vibration reduced. D. A. Brown. il Aviation W 93:59-61 S 28 '70

HELICOPTERS, Military. See Helicopters— Military use

HELICOPTERS, Sight-seeing. See Sight-seeing helicopters

HELICOPTERS in medical service
Copters cut precious minutes in traffic accident aid. il Todays Health 49:14 Ja '71
Helicopter gives citizens a better chance to live; Marion County, Ind. il Am City 85:38 Jl '70
Helicopters tested to fill major civil ambulance role. il Aviation W 93:95+ S 21 '70
Here come the helicopter ambulances. il Flying 87:73-4+ D '70
See also
Helicopters, Ambulance

HELICOPTERS in police work
Helicopters undergo new tests as traffic units; California highway patrol. il Am City 85: 53 Ap '70
Use of helicopters, airplanes by police agencies increasing. il Aviation W 93:91+ S 21 '70

HELICOPTERS in sports
New direction for skiers: up; Sun Valley, Idaho. H. Ehrlich. il Look 34:41-3 F 24 '70

HELIUM
Helium: costs jeopardize future of government conservation program. P. M. Boffey. Science 167:1593-6 Mr 20 '70
Is purity practical? J. H. Hildebrand. il Chem 43:19-20 Ja '70
Strange world of helium. J. Zimmerman. bibliog il Chem 43:14-17 F '70

Isotopes
Helium isotope effect in solution in water and seawater. R. F. Weiss. bibliog il Science 168:247-8 Ap 10 '70

HELIUM, Solid
Second sound in solid helium. B. Bertman and D. J. Sandiford. il Sci Am 222:92-101 My '70

HELL
Hell of a question. J. E. Kokjohn. Commonweal 93:367-70 Ja 15 '71
Is there a hell? Chr Today 15:34 N 20 '70

HE'LL forget by the time he's married; story. See Thaler, S.

HELLA, U. W.
St Croix: a national scenic riverway. il Parks & Rec 5:40-3 D '70

HELLE, Anita
Prowl; poem. Mlle 71:253 Ag '70

HELLER, Celia S.
Chicano is beautiful. Commonweal 91:454-8 Ja 23 '70

HELLER, Michael
 Maro spring; poem. Nation 210:150 F 9 '70
HELLER, Sidney
 Good conglomerates. il Duns 96:39 N '70
HELLER, Walter Wolfgang
 Heller and tax reform. E. S. Herman. New
  Repub 161:30-1 D 6 '69; Discussion. 162:33
  Ja 3; 26+ Ja 17; 33-6 F 14; 29 F 21; 22+ Mr
  14; 35-6 Ap 4 '70
HELLINCK, Lupus
 Lupus Hellinck: a survey of fourteen masses.
  J. Graziano. bibliog f il Mus Q 56:247-69
  Ap '70 *
HELLIWELL, Robert A.
 Upper atmosphere as seen from Antarctica.
  il por Bul Atom Sci 26:55-61 D '70
HELLMAN, Geoffrey T.
 Profiles; B. Powers. New Yorker 46:43-6+ Mr
  7 '70
HELLMAN, Peter
 One in ten shoppers is a shoplifter. il N Y
  Times Mag p34-5+ Mr 15 '70
 Your policy is hereby canceled. il N Y Times
  Mag p32-3+ N 8; 16 N 29 '70
HELL'S Angels. See Gangs
HELLS CANYON
 It's not called Hells Canyon for nothing. R.
  Bongartz. il Holiday 47:52-3+ My '70
 Last great dam. B. Norton. il Audubon 72:
  14-27 Ja '70
 Wilderness and the living Middle Snake.
  R. Mager. il Liv Wildn 33:8-11 Aut '69
HELM, Everett
 ISCM festival: why? Hi Fi 20:MA27 S '70
HELMETS
   See also
 Astronauts—Clothing
HELMS hall, Los Angeles. See Museums
HELMSLEY, Harry Brakmann
 It's the individual investment that counts;
  interview. pors Forbes 106:42-4 N 1 '70
   about
 Shrewd collector. por Bsns W p74 Ja 9 '71 *
HELP, help, the Globolinks! opera. See Menotti,
  G. S.
HELSETH, Pam. See Haynes, M. C. jt. auth.
HELSINKI
   Description
 Stopover in Helsinki. S. Turner. il Schol
  Teach Sec Teach Sup p22-3 Mr 9 '70
   Music
 Report:
 Prokofiev's The love for three oranges.
  A. Swanson. Opera N 34:29 My 16 '70
   Stores
 Ideas and things to bring home from Hel-
  sinki. M. Roche. House & Gard 137:78+ My
  '70
HELSINKI conference, 1970. See Strategic
 arms limitation talks
HELSIVA, Thomas
 How to be weather-wise. il Motor B 125:108-
  10 Mr '70
HELSLEY, Charles E.
 Magnetic properties of lunar dust and rock
  samples. bibliog il Science 167:693-5 Ja 30
  '70
HELSON, Ravenna
 Fantasy and self-discovery. il Horn Bk 46:
  121-34 Ap '70
HELXINE soleirolii. See Babys tears
HELZ, Armin. See Annell, C. jt. auth.
HEMAGGLUTINATION test. See Blood—Test-
  ing
HEMATITE
 Hematite: intrinsic and defect ferromagnet-
  ism. D. J. Dunlop. bibliog il Science 169:
  858-60 Ag 28 '70
HEME
 Heme requirement for reproduction of a free-
  living nematode. W. F. Hieb and others.
  bibliog il Science 168:143-4 Ap 3 '70
 Magnetic resonance in biology: structure-
  function relations in heme proteins. K.
  Wüthrich and R. G. Shulman. bibliog il
  pors Phys Today 23:43-50 Ap '70
HEMENWAY, Arthur
 Effect of wind sheer. il Yachting 127:62-3+
  Je '70
 Expert varnishing. il Yachting 127:74-5+ Ap
  '70
 Helping hand; USCG safety center. il Yacht-
  ing 129:110+ Ja '71
HEMEROCALLIS. See Day lilies
HEMET, Calif.
 Speed up water billing, simply. il Am City
  85:62-3 N '70

HEMICHOLINIUM *
 Regeneration of the amputated amphibian
  limb: retardation by hemicholinium-3. F.
  Hui and A. Smith. bibliog il Science 170:
  1313-14 D 18 '70
HEMINGWAY, Brian
 Enrich your garden with silver pennies. il
  Horticulture 48:43 S '70
HEMINGWAY, Ernest
 Bimini; story; excerpt from Islands in the
  stream. Esquire 74:121-37 O '70
   about
 Books. E. Wilson. New Yorker 46:59-62 Ja 2
  '71 *
 Double life, half told. M. Cowley. Atlan
  226:105-6+ D '70 *
 Great man going down. I. Howe. Harper 241:
  120-5 O '70 *
 Hemingway as Walter Pater. G. Davenport.
  Nat R 22:1214-15 N 17 '70 *
 Hemingway between triumph and disaster.
  J. W. Aldridge. por Sat R 53:23-6+ O 10
  '70 *
 Hemingway's Michigan. W. Paige. il Travel
  & Camera 33:32-7 Jl '70 *
 How papa grew. J. Yardley. New Repub 163:
  25-6+ O 10 '70 *
 Islands in the stream, by E. Hemingway. Re-
  view
  Commonweal 93:99-100 O 23 '70 *
 Notes on Bimini. A. Gingrich. Esquire 74:6+
  O '70 *
 Novel in the drawer. B. Oldsey. Nation 211:
  376+ O 19 '70 *
 Out of the desk. G. Wolff. il por Newsweek
  76:118+ O 12 '70 *
 Out of the vault; Islands in the stream. il
  por Newsweek 75:91-2 Ap 27 '70 *
 Papa watching. T. Foote. por Time 96:90+ O
  5 '70 *
 Trilogy of irony; analysis of Old man at
  the bridge. E. E. Miller. Engl J 59:59-62 Ja
  '70
HEMINGWAY, John
 Out in Hemingway country. H. Bradshaw. il
  pors Field & S 75:70-1+ Je '70 *
HEMINGWAY, Mary (Welsh)
 Journey south to a cold summer. il por
  Sports Illus 33:44-8 N 2 '70
HEMINGWAY, Mary Moon
 How to serve party drinks. House & Gard
  137:128+ My '70
 Notes for the hostess (title varies) See is-
  sues of House & garden incorporating Liv-
  ing for young homemakers
 Parties from the freezer. House & Gard 137:
  129-32+ My '70
HEMINGWAY, Patrick
 Out in Hemingway country. H. Bradshaw.
  il pors Field & S 75:70-1+ Je '70 *
HEMLINE. See Clothing and dress
HEMMIG, Bob
 Vanishing skipjack; with biographical sketch.
  il Sea Front 16:336-9, 383 N '70
HEMMING, Roy
 Art not for art's sake. por Sr Schol 95:19+
  N 17 '69
 DIScussions. See issues of Senior scholastic
HEMMINGSEN, E. A.
 Supersaturation of gases in water: absence
  of cavitation on decompression from high
  pressures. bibliog il Science 167:1493-4 Mr 13
  '70
HEMOGLOBIN
 Hemoglobin interaction: modification of solid
  phase composition in the sickling phenom-
  enon. J. F. Bertles and others. bibliog il
  Science 169:375-7 Jl 24 '70
 Synthetic oxygen-carrying compound. il Chem
  43:21 Mr '70
   See also
 Porphyria
HEMOLYSIS
 Hemolysis near a transversely oscillating wire.
  A. R. Williams and others. bibliog il Science
  169:871-3 Ag 28 '70
 Hemolysis near an ultrasonically pulsating
  gas bubble. J. A. Rooney. bibliog il Science
  169:869-71 Ag 28 '70
HEMORRHAGE
 Hippocrates vindicated; effects of cold on
  bleeding. Time 97:60 Ja 4 '71
 Pulmonary hemorrhage in hamsters after ex-
  posure to proteolytic enzymes of bacillus
  subtilis. I. P. Goldring and others. bibliog
  il Science 170:73-4 O 2 '70
   See also
 Cerebral hemorrhage
HEMP
   See also
 Marijuana

HEMPHILL, Paul
Kris Kristofferson is the new Nashville sound. il pors N Y Times Mag p54-5+ D 6 '70
HEMPSTEAD, N. Y.
Parking design with everyone in mind. F. R. Rundle. il Am City 85:100+ Ja '70
Try a citizen-service plan. il Am City 85: 106-8 N '70
HEMSLEY, Stuart
Scots, wha hae frae Arthur fled. . ; poem. Atlan 225:87 My '70
HENDERSHOTT, Carmen
Proofs and prescriptions. il por Library J 95:3735-8 N 1 '70
HENDERSON, Algo D.
Social change and educating for the professions. Sch & Soc 98:92-5+ F '70
HENDERSON, Charles P. jr
Richard Nixon, theologian. Nation 211:232-6 S 21 '70
HENDERSON, D. S.
White rhino; the road back. il Nat Parks 44: 19-20 Mr '70
HENDERSON, Florence
Tips on winter beauty. por Parents Mag 45: 23 D '70
HENDERSON, George. See Ragan, W. B. jt. auth.
HENDERSON, Hazel
Politics by other means. Nation 211:617-21 D 14 '70
HENDERSON, Norman D.
Brain weight increases resulting from environmental enrichment: a directional dominance in mice. bibliog il Science 169:776-8 Ag 21 '70
HENDERSON, O. E.
My movable three-in-one cold frame. il Org Gard & Farm 17:58 Jl '70
HENDERSON, Robert P.
Record-keeping in the space age; address, June 9, 1970. Vital Speeches 36:585-8 Jl 15 '70
HENDERSON, Skitch
Christmas with the Skitch Hendersons. H. Brown. il pors Am Home 73:40-2 D '70 *
HENDERSON, Stephen
Toward a black university. il por Ebony 25: 108-10+ S '70
HENDERSON, W. Guy
To give or not to give? Chr Cent 87:294-5 Mr 11 '70
HENDERSON, William
Black experience in color. il Ramp Mag 8:33-5 Je '70
HENDIN, Herbert
Racial oppression and black suicide; excerpts from Black suicide. Cur 114:29-36 Ja '70
HENDRICKS, Gary
For jet setters only? Aviation W 93:11 O 19 '70
HENDRICKSON, Robert
Grow a tree on a tree by air-layering. il Org Gard & Farm 17:58-9 My '70
Low-cost greenhouse for the porch. il Org Gard & Farm 17:96-7 Ag '70
HENDRIX, Algie Allen
Employer bargaining; address, December 29, 1969. Vital Speeches 36:317-20 Mr 1 '70
HENDRIX, Jimi
Drugs and death in the run-down world of rock music. A. Goldman. il pors Life 69: 32-3 O 16 '70 *
Of Apollo and Dionysus. Chr Cent 87:1308-9 N 4 '70 *
Transitional sex figures. D. Newman and R. Benton. pors Mlle 71:102 Jl '70 *
HENDRYSON, Elizabeth
Experiment in democracy: the guided-choice curriculum; adaptation of address, June 1970. PTA Mag 65:22-4 N '70
HENGE monuments. See Great Britain—Antiquities
HENISSART, Paul
Easy riding. Travel & Camera 33:16+ Ap '70
HENKEL, Stephen C.
Pipit becomes a yawl. il Yachting 129:108-9+ Ja '71
HENKES, Robert
Emergence of security. il Design 71:34-6 midSum '70
Isolation of a single aspect of nature. il Design 71:20-1 Sum '70
Symbolism, an elusive thing. Design 71:32-3 Wint '69
Tempera and enamel painting. il Design 72: 34-5 Fall '70
HENLE, Fritz
Fritz Henle: four decades at the top. J. Scully. il Mod Phot 34:62-71+ Mr '70 *
HENLE, Werner, and others
Differential reactivity of human serums with early antigens induced by Epstein-Barr virus. bibliog il Science 169:188-90 Jl 10 '70

HENLEY, Arthur
How teens get a head start on health careers. il Todays Health 48:34-5+ My '70
Your child's name could mark him for failure. Ladies Home J 87:137+ Je '70
HENNACY, Ammon
Of many things. D. R. Campion. America 122:inside cover Mr 14 '70 *
Requiem for an anarchist. M. True. Commonweal 91:525 F 13 '70 *
HENNEPIN COUNTY, Minn.
High mounted lights in. il Am City 85:114 Jl '70
HENNEY, Christopher S. and Waldman, R. H.
Cell-mediated immunity shown by lymphocytes from the respiratory tract. bibliog il Science 169:696-7 Ag 14 '70
HENNINGER, Daniel
And now, lettuce. New Repub 163:9-11 O 10 '70
One-eyed slicker. New Repub 162:17-19 My 2 '70
HENRIOT, Peter J.
Theological buzzwords. Cath World 211:180 Jl '70
HENRY, Buck
Diary of planes, pilots and pratfalls. por Life 68:46+ Je 12 '70

about

Bucking the system. P. D. Zimmerman. pors Newsweek 76:111-12 O 19 '70 *
Hollywood's hottest writer: Buck Henry. M. Seligson. il N Y Times Mag p 10-11+ Jl 19 '70 *
I see everything twice. C. Thegze. il Film Q 24:7-17 Fall '70 *
HENRY, Ebenezer Elijah, and Putney, Harrison
Past springs out of a picture; photographs. pors Am Heritage 21:2, 16-27 Je '70
HENRY, George H.
Style of teaching and teacher evaluation. bibliog f Engl J 59:921-7 O '70
HENRY, George J.
Overseas commentary. See issues of Forbes
HENRY, Gerrit
Effete corps of impudent snobs. il Art N 69:34-7+ D '70
HENRY, Mary Roblee
Travel. il Vogue 156:78+ N 15; 96+ D '70; 157:28 Ja 1 '71
HENRY, Omer
Business and trade journal market. Writer 83:24-6 Je '70
HENRY, Richard C. and Carruthers, G. R.
Far-ultraviolet photography of Orion: interstellar dust. bibliog il Science 170:527-31 O 30 '70
HENRY, Vera
Short short. Writers Digest 50:24-6 F '70
HENRY, William E.
When the money runs out. Todays Ed 59: 54-5 Mr '70
—and Sims, J. H.
Actors' search for a self. il Trans-Action 7: 57-62 S '70
HENRY Ford museum and Greenfield Village, Dearborn, Mich.
Flying visit. J. Gilbert. il Flying 86:26-7+ Mr '70
HENRY Francis du Pont Winterthur museum
Queen Anne and Chippendale furniture in the Henry Francis du Pont Winterthur museum. C. F. Hummel. il Antiques 97: 896-903; 98:900-9 Je, D '70 (to be cont)
Unusual opportunity at Winterthur. S. B. Sherrill. il Antiques 98:496+ O '70
HENRY Morrison Flagler museum. See Palm Beach, Fla.—Galleries and museums
HENSLEY, Glenn S.
Keel positioning guide. il Motor B 126:58 D '70
Landlocked no more. il Yachting 129:106-7+ Ja '71
HENTOFF, Margot
Schools we want: a family dialogue. il Sat R 53:75-6 S 19 '70
Television (cont) Vogue 155:114 F 1 '70
Women's liberation, the time is now. Parents Mag 45:44+ D '70
HENTOFF, Nat
Children who hate school. il Parents Mag 45:60-1+ F '70
Looking backwards, and ahead, with Alice. il Wilson Lib Bul 45:169-71 O '70
On tracking down dissent. Cur 121:37-41 S '70
Schools we want: a family dialogue. il Sat R 53:74+ S 19 '70
What I want for my children. il Parents Mag 45:52-3+ S '70
Women's liberation, but how soon will it happen? Parents Mag 45:45+ D '70

HENZE, Hans Werner
Does his music speak for our age? interview, ed. by R. Hemming. il por Sr Schol 96:15-17 My 4 '70
Records:
Raft of the Medusa. Opera N 34:35 Mr 7 '70 *

HENZELL, R. F. and Lowe, M. D.
Sex attractant of the grass grub beetle. bibliog Science 168:1005-6 My 22 '70

HEPATITIS
Australia antigen: distribution during Cohn ethanol fractionation of human plasma. D. D. Schroeder and M. M. Mozen. bibliog il Science 168:1462-4 Je 19 '70
Case of the yellow killer. J. Carper. Todays Health 48:53-4+ S '70
Hemagglutination assay for antigen and antibody associated with viral hepatitis. G. N. Vyas and N. R. Shulman. bibliog il Science 170:332-3 O 16 '70
Hepatitis from transfusions. il Sci Digest 67:55 Je '70
Mysterious hepatitis. Sci Am 223:48 Ag '70
Rapid screening test for detecting hepatitis-associated antigen. C. A. Saravis and others. bibliog il Science 169:298-9 Jl 17 '70
Testing for HAA antigen. Sci N 98:367 N 7 '70
Tests for Australian antigen answer a need; serum hepatitis. J. Bockel. il Sci N 97:584-5 Je 13 '70

HEPATITIS viruses
Polychlorinated biphenyl: interaction with duck hepatitis virus. M. Friend and D. O. Trainer. bibliog il Science 170:1314-16 D 18 '70
Serum hepatitis antigen (SH): rapid detection by high voltage immunoelectroosmophoresis. A. M. Prince and K. Burke. bibliog il Science 169:593-5 Ag 7 '70

HEPATOMA cells. See Tumor cells

HEPBURN, Ethel
War song. Cath World 211:220 Ag '70

HEPBURN, Katharine
McCall's Woman of the year. por McCalls 97:57 F '70 *
Private Kate. G. Kanin. il pors McCalls 97:58-65+ F '70 *

HEPPLEWHITE furniture. See Furniture, English

HER own kind; story. See Pearlman, E.

HERALDRY
At the sign of the crest. H. K. Eilers. See issues of Hobbies

HERB teas. See Tea

HERBACEOUS peonies. See Peonies

HERBER, Lewis, pseud. See Bookchin, M.

HERBERG, Will
Optimism of Dr Will Herberg. Nat R 22:428-9 Ap 21 '70 *

HERBERS, John
Senator Ervin thinks the Constitution should be taken like mountain whisky, undiluted and untaxed. il pors N Y Times Mag p50-1+ N 15 '70

HERBERT, D. C. and Hayashida, T.
Prolactin localization in the primate pituitary by immunofluorescence. bibliog il Science 169:378-9 Jl 24 '70

HERBERT, Donald Jeffry
Mr Wizard revisited. T. Johnides. il pors Phys Today 23:42-5 Mr '70 *

HERBERT, Jay
Books about your house and garden. House & Gard 138:68+ N '70
Books and records to give for Christmas. House & Gard 138:30-2 D '70
New books. House & Gard 137:60+ Ap '70

HERBICIDES
Are tear gas and herbicides permitted weapons? J. Goldblatt. il Bul Atom Sci 26:13-16 Ap '70
Curbs on 2,4,5-T use imposed. N. Gruchow. Science 168:453 Ap 24 '70
Dimethylpropynylbenzamides: a new group of herbicides. K. L. Viste and others. il Science 167:280-1 Ja 16 '70
Herbicides in Vietnam: AAAS study runs into a military roadblock. P. M. Boffey. Science 170:42-5 O 2 '70; Discussion. 170:1034+ D 4 '70
Herbicides: order on 2,4,5-T issued at unusually high level. B. Nelson; discussion. bibliog Science 168:1606-7 Je 26 '70
Kill roots as you clean the sewer. Am City 85:30 Je '70
Reporter at large; defoliation in Vietnam. T. Whiteside. New Yorker 45:32-8+ F 7; 46:124-9 Mr 14; 64-6+ Jl 4 '70
Teratogenic evaluation of 2,4,5-T. K. D. Courtney and others. bibliog il Science 168:864-6 My 15 '70

Weed and insect control guide. E. L. Knake. il Suc Farm 68:no3 43-6+ F '70
Weed killers. il Consumer Rep 35:359-63 Je '70
See also
Weed control—Chemical control

Cost
How much to spend for weed control. M. Hood. il Suc Farm 69:D1 Ja '71

Injurious effects
Department of amplification; dangerous effects of 2,4,5-T. T. Whiteside. New Yorker 46:78+ Je 20 '70
Family likeness; birth defects from 2,4-D and 2,4,5-T. S. S. Epstein. il Environ 12:16-25 Jl '70
Globe's mystery; effects of spraying with Silvex. il Time 95:42 F 23 '70
2,4,5-T; case of abnormal births in South Vietnam. Am For 76:11 Jl '70

Residues
Metobromuron: acetylation of the aniline moiety as a detoxificaton mechanism. B. G. Tweedy and others. Science 168:482-3 Ap 24 '70

HERBS
Best ways to store herbs and spices. il Good H 170:137 Ja '70
Country herb garden. V. Durbin. il Horticulture 48:18-21+ S '70
Discoveries in the mailbox. E. Gibbons. Org Gard & Farm 17:82-4 My '70
Herb-drying, tastiest old fashioned art. M. M. Gunn. il Org Gard & Farm 17:114-18 O '70
Herb power. il Am Home 73:96+ Ap '70
Herbs for all seasons. il Home Gard 57:30-1+ S '70
With Gene Boucher after the opera: herbs and bonsai. E. McDonald. il por House B 112:167-8 F '70
See also
Tansy
Yarrows

HERBS, Medicinal. See Botany, Medical

HERCHENROEDER, John
Ombudsman in Louisville. il por Time 96:44+ Jl 6 '70 *

HERDER correspondence (periodical)
Bell tolls; June issue its last. J. Deedy. Commonweal 92:306 Je 26 '70

HEREDITY
Inheritance of a cardiac arterial asymmetry in mice. J. H. Bruell and others. bibliog il Science 167:199-200 Ja 9 '70
Intelligence and race. W. F. Bodmer and L. L. Cavalli-Sforza. il Sci Am 223:19-29 bibliog(p 144) O '70
Race and intelligence; doctrine called jensenism. R. C. Lewontin. Bul Atom Sci 26:2-8 Mr '70; Discussion. 26:42-3 S '70
See also
Blood groups
Chromosomes
Eugenics
Evolution
Genetics
Mosaics (biology)
Natural selection

HEREDITY of disease
Finding and treating genetic diseases; vitamin-dependency diseases. por Sci N 98:157-8 Ag 22 '70
Genetics of schizophrenic and schizoid disease. L. L. Heston. bibliog il Science 167:249-56 Ja 16 '70
How heredity affects your family's health. G. G. Greer. Bet Hom & Gard 48:42+ Ap '70
Hyperactive children. M. A. Stewart. il Sci Am 222:94-8 Ap '70
Man's decline as a species. A. H. Drummond, jr. bibliog il Sci Digest 68:26-31 Jl '70
Therapy by virus; genetic disease. il Sci N 98:198-9 S 5 '70
See also
Angiokeratoma
Metabolism, Disorders of
Porphyria

HERESY
Subversion in the church. Chr Today 14:16 Jl 31 '70

HERING, Millicent B.
Law and maryjane. bibliog il Am Lib 1:896-9 O '70

HERITAGE (yacht) See Yachts—Design

HERITAGE golf classic. See Golf—Tournaments

HERITAGE trails. See Trails

HERMAN of Alaska, Saint
Herman the Wonderworker. por Time 96:48-9 Ag 24 '70 *

HERMAN, Andrea
Few words of advice. il Har Yrs 10:34-6 S '70
HERMAN, David
Federico Fellini. bibliog Am Imago 26:251-68
Fall '69
HERMAN, Edwards S.
Heller and tax reform. New Repub 161:30-1
D 6 '69; 162:26+ Ja 17 '70
HERMAN, Richard L.
Mr Herman named to U.S.-Canada International boundary commission. Dept State
Bul 61:558 D 15 '69
HERMAN, Woody
Out there forever. por Time 95:57-8 My 11
'70 *
HERMAN, Yvonne
Arctic paleo-oceanography in late cenozoic
time. bibliog il Science 169:474-7 Jl 31 '70
HERMAPHRODITISM
Pseudohermaphrodite rat: end organ insensitivity to testosterone. C. W. Bardin and
others. bibliog il Science 167:1136-7 F 20 '70
Reproductive system of hutchinsoniella macracantha. A. Y. Hessler and others. bibliog
il Science 168:1464 Je 19 '70
HERMITS
Desert hermits. A. J. Toynbee. il Horizon 12:
22-7 Spr '70
King of the Ecrehous: A. Le Gastelois. por
Newsweek 75:38 F 2 '70
HERN, George L. Jr
Chic in '71; Relais de campagne chain. il
Travel 135:62-7 Ja '71
HERN, Warren M.
Family planning and the poor. New Repub
163:17-19 N 14 '70
HERNANDEZ, Arturo D.
Tangarano; story. il Américas 22:31-4 F '70
HERNIA
Infant hernias. Sci Digest 67:55 Ap '70
HERNMARCK, Helena Barynina
Helena Barynina Hernmarck. il por Craft
Horiz 30:20-3 Mr '70 *
HEROES
Anybody see Patton? the President's fascination with the movie, Patton. H. Sidey.
Life 68:2B Je 19 '70
See also
Carnegie hero fund commission
HEROES in literature. See Characters in literature
HEROIN
C21 H23 Nos: a primer for parents and children. L. Edson. il N Y Times Mag p92-3+
My 24 '70
Death from heroin. P. H. Abelson. Science
168:1289 Je 12 '70
Father tells how drugs invaded his family;
anonymous report. Life 68:50-2+ Mr 20 '70;
Same abr. with title Story of my son's
heroin addiction. il Read Digest 97:64-9 Jl
'70
Horrors of heroin: Hunts Point scene. R.
Severo. Read Digest 96:72-5 Ja '70
Kids and heroin: the adolescent epidemic. il
Time 95:16-20+ Mr 16 '70
Life on two grams a day. il Life 68:24-32 F
20 '70
New heroin substitute. il Sci Digest 67:56 Je
'70
There are people who say, Well, business is
business. il Forbes 105:19-22 Ap 1 '70
What the English are doing about heroin.
M. Simons. il Look 34:47-52+ Ap 7 '70
HEROINES in literature. See Women in literature
HEROISM. See Courage
HERPE, Robert
New capitalists of broadcasting. por Forbes
106:40 O 15 '70 *
HERPES simplex virus
Inflammation and herpes simplex virus: release of a chemotaxis-generating factor
from infected cells. A. M. Brier and others.
bibliog il Science 170:1104-6 D 4 '70
HERPESVIRUS
Differential reactivity of human serums with
early antigens induced by Epstein-Barr virus. W. Henle and others. bibliog il Science
169:188-90 Jl 10 '70
New clues in the virus-cancer mystery. C. R.
Goodheart and B. Goodheart. il Todays
Health 48:32-5 Je '70
HERPETOLOGY. See Snakes
HERR, Michael
War correspondent: a reappraisal. il Esquire
73:95-101+ Ap '70
HERR, W. and others
Determination of manganese-53 by neutron
activation and other miscellaneous studies
on lunar dust. bibliog il Science 167:747-9
Ja 30 '70

HERRERA, Felipe
Generation gap and international development. il Américas 22:13-20 Ap '70
HERRERO, Stephen
Human injury inflicted by grizzly bears. bibliog il Science 170:593-8 N 6 '70
HERRESHOFF, A. Sidney D. See Herreshoff,
H. C. jt. auth.
HERRESHOFF, Halsey C. and Herreshoff,
A. S. D.
Herreshoff symposium. il Yachting 129:91+
Ja '71
HERRESHOFF, Nathanael Greene
Nathanael Herreshoff. B. Robinson. il por
Yachting 127:66-7+ My '70 *
HERRNKIND, William F.
Migration of the spiny lobster; with biographical sketch. il Natur Hist 79:4, 36-43
bibliog(p79) My '70
HERSCHELIAN telescope. See Telescopes
HERSEY, John
Are alumni listening? J. Cass. Sat R 53:61-2
N 21 '70 *
HERSEY, M. Leonard
Control points. See issues of Yachting to November 1970
HERSH, Seymour M.
How I broke the Mylai 4 story. il por Sat R
53:46-9 Jl 11 '70
My Lai 4: a report on the massacre and its
aftermath; excerpts. Harper 240:53-84 My;
241-12 Ag '70
about
Painful prize; Pulitzer prize for international
reporting. por Newsweek 75:73-4 My 18
'70 *

HERSHEY, Alfred Day
Idiosyncrasies of DNA structure; Nobel lecture, December 12, 1969. bibliog il Science
168:1425-7 Je 19 '70
HERSHEY, Barbara
Essence of Barbara: interview, ed. by E.
Miller. il pors Seventeen 29:132-3+ F '70
HERSHEY, Constance Vecchione
Mortuary art in Charleston churches. il
Antiques 98:800-7 N '70
HERSHEY, Lewis Blaine
Alternative to the draft. por Time 95:14-15
Mr 2 '70 *
HERSHEY foods corporation
Hershey's sweet tooth starts aching. il por
Bsns W p98-9+ F 7 '70
HERST, Herman, Jr
Stamps. See issues of Hobbies
HERSTEIN, Rosaline
Mother-child workshops. il Sch Arts 69:18-19
Mr '70
HERTER, Christian A. Jr
Mr Herter becomes special assistant for environmental affairs; remarks, January 13,
1970. Dept State Bul 62:213-14 F 23 '70
HERTZ, David B.
Technological imperative, social implications of professional technology. bibliog f
Ann Am Acad 389:95-106 My '70
HERTZ, Kenneth D.
County acts to save its vanishing shorelands.
il Parks & Rec 5:48-9+ F '70
HERTZLER, R. A.
High-power color organ. il Electr World 84:
78-80 S '70
HERZBERG, Joseph. See Bernstein, S. jt. auth.
HERZENBERG, C. L. and Riley, D. L.
Mössbauer spectrometry of lunar samples.
bibliog il Science 167:683-6 Ja 30 '70
HERZENBERG, Leonard A. See Riblet, R. J.
jt. auth.
HERZOG, Arthur
Dozen duds in the canons of youth. Ed Digest
36:37-40 N '70
HERZOG, Frederick
Political gospel. il Chr Cent 87:1380-3 N 18 '70
HERZOG, Marie-Pierre
Lenin and education, science, culture.
UNESCO Courier 23:4-5 Jl '70
HERZOG, Mick
Seminar, or suspension? Education or punishment for teen-age smokers? Clear House 45:
146-9 N '70
HERZOG, Ray E.
New look for television schematics. il Electr
World 84:88 N '70
HESLOP-HARRISON, Yolande
Scanning electron microscopy of fresh leaves
of pinguicula. bibliog il Science 167:172-4 Ja
9 '70
HESS, Andrew C.
Evolution of the Ottoman seaborne empire
in the age of the oceanic discoveries, 1453-
1525. bibliog f il Am Hist R 75:1892-919 D
'70

HICKEL, Walter Joseph—about—*Continued*
Walter Hickel is an endangered species; with editorial comment. P. O'Neil. il pors Life 69:1,48-48B+ Ag 28 '70 *
You never know; risk of prejudgments. Chr Cent 87:653 My 27 '70 *

HICKEY, Red
What is a punter's hang time? W. B. Furlong. il pors N Y Times Mag p30-2+ Ja 10 '71 *

HICKMAN, Geneva
Show me a sick child and I'll show you a very tired mother. il Redbook 134:75+ Ap '70

HICKMAN, Sara
What's relevant in classical literature? address, November 1969. Engl J 59:375-9 Mr '70

HICKORY shad fishing. See Shad fishing

HICKS, Bruce L.
Will the computer kill education? Ed Digest 36:10-12 S '70

HICKS, Clifford B.
Eat! Says fat little Johnny's mother. il Todays Health 48:48-50+ F '70

HICKS, Dan, jr
Two guns and a weekly. il por Time 95:47 Ap 27 '70 *

HICKS, David
David Hicks was here. il Ladies Home J 87:30+ Ja '70
Perspectives. por House B 112:86+ O '70 *
Trade winds. C. Amory. Sat R 53:43 O 17 '70 *

HICKS, Louise (Day)
Breeze that whispered Louise. Nat R 22:1038 O 6 '70 *

HICKS, Sam
Gambling men and honest horses. il Am West 7:40-7+ N '70

HICKS, Wilson
W. Eugene Smith, passionate involvement with Life. il Mod Phot 34:88-93 Ja '70

HIDALGO, Elvira de
Latin festival on L.P. A. Favia-Artsay. pors Hobbies 75:35 S '70 *

HIDES and skins
Fur flies in defense of the great cats. il Life 68:68-70 F 27 '70
See also
Fur

HIEB, W. F. and others
Heme requirement for reproduction of a free-living nematode. bibliog il Science 168:143-4 Ap 3 '70

HIELSCHER, Bill
Mr Bardahl. J. Dianna. il pors Hot Rod 23: 64-6 F '70 *

HIEMENZ, Jack
Classics for the now generation. il por Hi Fi sec I 20:112 Ja '70
Martirano's L's GA; the composer as Politico. Hi Fi 20:secI 100 Ap '70
Musician of the month. il por Hi Fi 20:secII 6-7 Jl '70
Scriabin and his demons. por Hi Fi 20:19-20 S '70
Tureck & Fox play Bach. il Hi Fi 20:MA16-17 S '70

HI-FI speakers. See Loud speaking apparatus

HI-FI systems. See High fidelity sound systems

HIGDON, Hal
Clean air? Color it black! il Todays Health 48:38-41+ S '70
Creepers, floaters and squirmers. il Sports Illus 32:32-7 Ap 27 '70
Marathon and me. il Sports Illus 32:78-80+ Ap 6 '70

HIGDON, Rose M.
How mothers answer: where do babies come from? Todays Health 48:34-5+ O '70

HIGGINS, Alice
Horse shows (cont) Sports Illus 32:76+ Je 8 '70

HIGGINS, Anne
Engineer on the train; poem. Commonweal 93:250 D 4 '70

HIGGINS, Chester
Salute to Joe. il pors Ebony 25:158-62 O '70

HIGGINS, James
Horror takes the stand. Nation 212:6-8 Ja 4 '71
Jess Gitt's Gazette. Nation 211:497 N 16 '70
Philadelphia boomerang. il Nation 211:332-6 O 12 '70

HIGGINS, Jim, and Higgins, S. R.
Scenery behind the shoot-'em-ups. il Todays Health 48:42-7+ Ap '70
See Europe. il Todays Health 48:44-7+ N '70

HIGGINS, Joe
Joe Higgins: Dodge material. il pors Motor T 22:62 Ap '70 *

HIGGINS, Shirley Rose. See Higgins, J. jt. auth.

HIGGINS, V. Louise
Linguistics in the high school? Engl J 59: 559-65+ Ap '70

HIGGINSON, John
Cancer, where we stand. il UNESCO Courier 23:4-9 My '70
International research: its role in environmental biology. bibliog Science 170:935-9 N 27 '70

HIGH altitude, Influence of. See Altitude, Influence of

HIGH blood pressure. See Hypertension

HIGH energy physics. See Nuclear physics

HIGH fidelity shows. See Audio fairs

HIGH fidelity sound systems
All-in-one music centers: your best bet in hi-fi? H. Fantel. il Pop Mech 134:130-3 D '70
Bumper crop of new products. R. Long. il Hi Fi 20:42-4+ O '70
Equipment in the news. See issues of High fidelity section I
Four-channel stereo from cartridge tapes. il Pop Mech 134:144-5 S '70
Hi-fi convenience revolution. I. Berger. Sat R 53:57-8 S 26 '70
New equipment reports. See issues of High fidelity section I
What's watt in choosing a hi-fi? H. Fantel. il Pop Mech 134:143-5+ O '70
See also
Stereophonic sound systems

Control
Balance control tunes your hi-fi to your living room. J. Davis. il Pop Sci 197:79 Jl '70

Maintenance and repair
Testing hi-fi equipment. J. D. Hirsch. il Electr World 84:47-50+ D '70; 85:45-8+ Ja '71

Testing
Torture tracks for your hi-fi system: test records. H. Fantel. il Pop Mech 133:132-4+ Ja '70

HIGH fidelity speakers. See Loud speaking apparatus

HIGH John library, Fairmount Heights, Md.
High John closed by staff walkout. il Library J 95:3861 N 15 '70
High John: closing for openers. A. Plotnik. il Wilson Lib Bul 45:214-15 N '70
Triumph & tragedy: a play in two acts. R. B. Croneberger and J. C. Welbourne, jr. il pors Library J 95:1705-8 My 1 '70; Discussion. 95:2397, 3416-18 Jl, O 15 '70

HIGH MOUNTAIN SHEEP DAM. See Dams

HIGH octane gasoline. See Gasoline—Anti-knock and anti-knock mixtures

HIGH pressure oxygenation. See Hyperbaric oxygenation

HIGH pressure research
Making of metallic hydrogen. E. Gross. il Sci N 97:623:5 Je 27 '70

HIGH school athletes. See Athletes

HIGH school athletics. See School athletics

HIGH school counselors. See Student counselors

HIGH school dropouts. See Dropouts

HIGH school graduates
Employment of high school graduates and dropouts; with tables and charts. H. Hayghe. Mo Labor R 93:35-42 Ag '70
High-school grads: a better world because of them; sampling of opinions of high-school principals. il U S News 68:24-6 Je 1 '70
Nostalgic reunion in Salina, Kansas. W. Friedman. il Time 96:14 Jl 13 '70
Old-fashioned at twenty-seven; Bayonne high school reunion. S. V. Roberts. il pors N Y Times Mag p45-7+ D 6 '70

HIGH school publications. See College and school journalism

HIGH school student militants. See Student militants

HIGH school students
Pregnant teen-agers. il Todays Ed 59:26-9+ O '70
SDS and the high schools: a study in student extremism. J. E. Hoover. il PTA Mag 64: 2-5 Ja; 8-9 F '70; Discussion. 64:19-20 Mr '70
Sensitizing modules; making seniors aware of ghetto problems. S. S. Simon. il Schol Teach Jr/Sr High p28-9+ S 21 '70
Talking it over with Gay Head; questions and answers. Gay Head. See issues of Senior scholastic
Too bad; excerpts from high school underground newspapers. il Esquire 73:61-2 F '70
What's wrong with the high schools? il Newsweek 75:65-6+ F 16 '70
Who's the troublemaker? Sr Schol 96:Schol Teach 1 F 16 '70

HIGH school students—*Continued.*
You don't have to leave school to drop out. P. Schrag; W. Roberts. il Sat R 53:59-64+ Mr 21 '70
See also
High school graduates
School management and organization—Student participation
Self government in education
Student achievements
Student activities

Adjustment

Schoolhouse ombudsman. R. H. Levine. Clear House 44:354-5 F '70

Attitudes

See Students—Attitudes

Clothing

See Clothing and dress—Students

Dating

See Dating

Demonstrations

See Student demonstrations

Employment

See Student employment

Political activities

High school students and the campaign; elections '70 in Maryland. il Sr Schol 97:15 O 26 '70
Politics from the inside; Maryland high school seniors. Sr Schol 97:4 D 14 '70
Story of the posting of the theses; M-day at Irondequoit high. R. Brookhiser. Nat R 22:196-8 F 24 '70
Student campaigners: do they turn on or put off voters? il Sr Schol 97:14 O 12 '70
Students in the Statehouse. J. B. Arone. Todays Ed 59:17 O '70

Reading

Interest rate is rising. G. R. Carlsen. Engl J 59:655-9 My '70
Whoever heard of James Fenimore Cooper? independent guided reading program. J. L. Dobson. Engl J 59:1135-7+ N '70

HIGH school students, Mentally superior
Talent runs free at the Twin Cities institute. C. Watson. il Am Ed 6:3-6 O '70

HIGH school students and smoking. See Smoking and youth

HIGH school teachers. See Teachers

HIGH school textbooks. See Textbooks

HIGH school underground press. See College and school journalism

HIGH schools
As violence spreads in high schools. . . il U S News 69:18-20 N 30 '70
Bold new directions for U.S. high schools. A. Silberman. Read Digest 97:87-91 Ag '70
Case for a small high school. S. Leggett and others. Ed Digest 36:15-18 N '70
Now, focus on high school unrest. M. R. Weisbord. Ed Digest 35:5-8 Ja '70
Student unrest in high schools. Sch & Soc 98:75-6 F '70
Times change; reflections of a high-school student from the class of '40. K. Vonnegut, jr. por Esquire 73:60 F '70
What's going on in schools & colleges. See issues of Changing times
What's wrong with the high schools? il Newsweek 75:65-6+ F 16 '70
See also
Education, Secondary
Schools, Experimental

Administration

See School management and organization

Curriculum

American folklore in the secondary schools. H. H. Lee. bibliog f Engl J 59:994-1004 O '70
Curricular innovation and practices in the American high school. E. W. Haven. Ed Digest 36:39-41 S '70
ETS curriculum study (cont) Sr Schol 95: Schol Teach 2 N 3; 1 N 10 '69
Experiment in democracy: the guided-choice curriculum; adaptation of address, June 1970. E. Hendryson. PTA Mag 65:22-4 N '70
High school curriculum survey; symposium. Sch & Soc 98:239-54 Ap '70
Middle school years and career development. W. A. Stanton. Clear House 44:531-3 My '70

Project mobilization; program for educationally disadvantaged students. D. L. Carl. Clear House 44:519-22 My '70
See also
Correlation (education)
Elective system in education
Junior high schools—Curriculum
Independent study

Desegregation

See Public schools—Desegregation

Personnel service

See Personnel service in education

Summer sessions

See Summer schools

HIGH schools, Experimental. See Schools, Experimental

HIGH SIERRAS. See Sierra Nevada (California)

HIGH society. See Upper classes

HIGH speed ground transportation, Office of. See United States—Transportation, Department of

HIGH speed trains. See Railroads—Passenger service—High speed trains

HIGH temperatures
See also
Solar furnaces

HIGHER education. See College education; Colleges and universities; Junior colleges

HIGHET, Gilbert
Mad world of Hieronymus Bosch. il Horizon 12:66-81. sup(folded reproduction) Spr '70
Whose Satyricon, Petronius's or Fellini's? bibliog f il por Horizon 12:42-7 Aut '70

HIGHLAND games. See Competitions

HIGHLAND pistols. See Pistols

HIGHT, Rebecca
How to tote your tots. il Travel 134:24-5 Ag '70

HIGHTOWER, Jim, and Newton, Verne
Ambush on the Hill. Nation 211:266-70 S 28 '70
—See Berman, J. J. jt. auth.

HIGHTOWER, John B.
From class art to mass art. Art in Am 58:25 S '70
Who are the culturally deprived? Sat R 53:41-2 Jl 18 '70

HIGHWAY, Pan American. See Pan American highway

HIGHWAY accidents. See Traffic accidents

HIGHWAY beautification. See Roadside improvement

HIGHWAY engineering
Street construction & maintenance. See issues of American city
320 billion dollars more for future highways? il U S News 68:34-5 Mr 2 '70
See also
Traffic engineering

HIGHWAY law
See also
Traffic courts

HIGHWAY lighting. See Roads—Lighting

HIGHWAY lobby. See Lobbying

HIGHWAY location. See Roads—Location

HIGHWAY patrol. See Police, State

HIGHWAY planting. See Roadside improvement

HIGHWAY police. See Police, State

HIGHWAY research
Traffic and highway research and how it may be improved. B. D. Greenshields. bibliog Science 168:674-8 My 8 '70

HIGHWAY transportation. See Transportation, Automotive

HIGHWAY trust fund. See United States—Public roads, Bureau of

HIGHWAYS. See Express highways; Roads

HIJACKING. See Robberies and assaults

HIJACKING of airplanes. See Airplane hijacking

HIJACKING of ships. See Ship hijacking

HIKING. See Walking

HILD, Herbert
Guide to buying sails. il Motor B 127:142-3+ Ja '71

HILDEBRAND, Tim
Silver; Her back; Once in the water; poems. Poetry 115:386-8 Mr '70

HILDENBRAND, Barbara
Stigmata: a matter of mind or miracle? il Todays Health 48:57-9+ Ag '70

HILDER, Rowland
Notes on watercolor; excerpt from Starting with watercolor. il Am Artist 34:20-1 S '70

HILL, Calvin
Merriwell by Baldwin. il por Time 95:78-9 Ap 6 '70 *

HILL, Dave
Plain words at Westchester. M. Mulvoy. por Sports Illus 33:12-13 Ag 10 '70 *
HILL, Edward V.
New strides in the ghetto. R. Klein. il por Chr Today 14:46-7 S 11 '70 *
HILL, Gladwin
After Earth day. il Nat Wildlife 8:30-1 Ag '70
HILL, Howard E.
Twelve rules for story dissection. Writers Digest 50:26 F '70
HILL, Joseph, pseud.
From GM to big steel. Commonweal 93:238-9 D 4 '70
Labor loses a leader. Commonweal 92:260-1 My 29 '70
Labor's political kick still there? Commonweal 92:133-4 Ap 24 '70
Labor's split political personality. Commonweal 92:382-3; 93:55 Ag 7, O 9 '70
HILL, Leslie Pinckney
Self-determination; poem. Negro Hist Bul 33: 42 F '70
HILL, Lewis
Gooseberries, culinary prize for northern gardens. il Org Gard & Farm 17:40-2 O '70
HILL, Morton A.
Civil war over smut. J. Witcover. Nation 210: 550-3 My 11 '70 *
HILL, Napoleon
Obituary
Pub W 198:22 N 30 '70
HILL, Norman
Decline and fall of the column item. Sat R 53:53-4 Ag 8 '70
Last of the red hot supplements. il Sat R 53:56-7+ D 12 '70
When journalists become PR men. Sat R 53: 57-60 Je 13 '70
HILL, Phil
Eight years later; interview. il pors Motor T 22:42-3+ N '70
HILL, Robert E. and Spenser, I. D.
Biosynthesis of vitamin B6: incorporation of three-carbon units. bibliog il Science 169: 773-5 Ag 21 '70
HILL, Robin E. T. and Boettcher, A. L.
Water in the earth's mantle: melting curves of basalt-water and basalt-water-carbon dioxide. bibliog il Science 167:980-2 F 13 '70
HILL, Ronald A.
Ferrite-core memories. il por Electr World 84: 49-52 O '70
HILL, Susan
Nothing to say; story. Redbook 135:76-8 Ag '70
HILL, William B.
Fiction (cont) America 122:478-9; 123:464+ My 2, N 28 '70
HILLBILLY music. See Folk music, American; Folk songs, American
HILLENBRAND, Robert
Apollo 12 explorers on the moon. il Sky & Tel 39:95-8 F '70
HILLER, A. J.
Kites over the sea; with biographical sketch. il por Sea Front 16:51-3, 62 Ja '70
HILLESTAD, Robert. See Newton, A. jt. auth.
HILLIARD, Joe H. and West, S. H.
Starch accumulation associated with growth reduction at low temperatures in a tropical plant. bibliog il Science 168:494-6 Ap 24 '70
HILLIARD, Marion
Too tired to love? excerpt from Women and fatigue: a woman doctor's answer. Read Digest 97:65-8 S '70
HILLIKER, Floyd
Presenting Thurston DeHaan, organic gardener. il pors Org Gard & Farm 17:28-31 O '70
HILLIS, Burton
Man next door. See issues of Better homes and gardens
HILLIS, Dick
Challenge of the ministry. Chr Today 15:25 D 18 '70
HILLIS, Richard R.
Toward simplicity. il Design 72:26-8 Fall '70
HILLMAN, Serrell
Flavor and savor of Canada. il Travel & Camera 33:24-39+ Je '70
HILLS, L. Rust
(ed) See Hefner. H. M. Hugh M. Hefner
HILLSIDE architecture
Hillside house; a bargain lot in Maryland. il N Y Times Mag p92-3 My 17 '70
Hillside house in Sherman, Connecticut. il Arch Rec 148:112-13 N '70
House of seven levels. J. DeLong. il House B 112:86-93 S '70
Island of space in a sea of trees; Eugene, Ore. J. Delong. il House B 112:74-9 D '70
Kirk house, Mercer Island, Wash. il Arch Rec 147:76-9 mid-My '70

Lakefront hideaway in the Berkshires. il Am Home 73:62-5 S '70
Private residence, Marin County, Calif. il Arch Rec 147:70-1 mid-My '70
Suspended from a hill. il Am Home 73:48-9+ Ja '70
HILLSIDE Gardens. See Gardens. Hillside
HILLYARD, Kay
Come walk with me; poem. Har Yrs 10:26-9 Ap; 26-9 Je; 26-9 Ag; 26-9 O; 26-9 N '70
Pretty personal Valentines. il Har Yrs 10: 26-7 F '70
They live here, too; with photographs by S. Crouch. Har Yrs 10:26-30 Jl '70
Today is what you make it. por Har Yrs 10: 30-1 N '70
Your 1970 activities almanac. il Har Yrs 10: 23-9 Ja '70
HILSUM, Cyril
Three-level oscillator in indium phosphide. G. B. Lubkin. Phys Today 23:19-20 D '70 *
HILTON, Allan
ACA management study under way. Camp Mag 42:6+ Je '70
HILTON, B. D. and O'Brien, R. D.
Antagonism by DDT of the effect of valinomycin on a synthetic membrane. bibliog il Science 168:841-3 My 15 '70
HILTON, David
Salty dog asleep; Above passion; Furnished cottage; Excursionists; Making love; poems. Poetry 116:13-18 Ap '70
HILTON, Peter
Corporate aviary. il Nations Bsns 58:32-6 F '70
HILTON, T. E.
Ghana. bibliog il Focus 21:1-8 O '70
HILTON HEAD ISLAND
BASF backs off from a beachhead; proposed South Carolina plant. il Bsns W p29-30 Ap 11 '70
Battle of Beaufort; conservation collides with the jobless. A. Simon. New Repub 162: 11-15 My 23 '70
Fight at Hilton Head; BASF project. il Newsweek 75:71-2+ Ap 13 '70
Fight for Hilton Head Island; proposed site of BASF plant. H. Drane. il Am For 76:12-15+ My '70
Introduction to the setting and characters of the tragical farce or farcical tragedy of Victoria Bluffs. SC; BASF corp. in New York city to open plant. A. Ternes. il Natur Hist 79:8-10+ Ap '70
Shrimp boats are a-comin'; protests to BSAF plant. il Am For 76:26-7 Jl '70
Troubled little island; proposed site of American subsidiary of BASF. il Time 95:55+ Ja 26 '70
View from Hilton Head; Badische anilin und soda-fabrik. M. Frady. il Harper 240: 103-12 My '70
HILTS, Len
Tan your way through winter. il Todays Health 48:37-9 D '70
HIMALAYAN cookery. See Cookery, Himalayan
HIMALAYAS
See also
Everest, Mount
Nepal
HIMES, Chester Bomar
Hard-bitten old pro who wrote Cotton. R. Chelminski. il pors Life 69:60-1 Ag 28 '70 *
HIMMELFARB, Milton
Jewish class conflict? Commentary 49:37-52 Ja '70
This Aquarian age. Commentary 49:38-41 Ap '70
Topless tower of Babylon. Commentary 50: 79-81 D '70
HINCHLIFFE, Douglas M.
Interview with three recreation planners. Forbes 105:202-3 Ja 1 '70
HINCKEN, James
Break with tradition: parochial and public schools combine resources to serve their pupils. Clear House 44:315-16 Ja '70
HINCKLE, Warren, 3d
Scanlan's monthly and other diversions. P. Steinfels. Commonweal 92:6 Mr 13 '70 *
Scanlan's reviewed. L. Smith. il por Newsweek 75:66 My 25 '70 *
Scanlon is born. il por Time 95:42 Mr 5 '70 *
HINDEMITH, Paul
Decline and fall of Paul Hindemith. R. Evett. New Repub 162:27-9 F 28 '70
First of Paul Hindemith's full-length operas; Cardillac. P. L. Miller. Am Rec G 36:549 Ap '70 *
Hindemith's Cardillac; recording. R. Jacobson. Sat R 53:44-5 Jl 25 '70 *

HINDENBURG (airship) See Airships

HINDERY, Roderick
Marcuse's eroticized man. por Chr Cent 87:
136-8 F 4 '70

HINDS, Jeanette
Between seasons; poem. Farm J 94:84 Ap
'70

HINDS, Lynn, and Smith, Carolyn
Rhetoric of opposites. Nation 210:172-4 F 16
'70

HINDU dancing. See Dancing. Indian (East
Indian)

HINDUS
See also
India—Hindu-Muslim relations

HINE, Al
Raucous Italy. il Holiday 48:22-7 Jl '70

HINE, Bromfield, and Paolino, R. M.
Retrograde amnesia: production of skeletal
but not cardiac response gradient by electroconvulsive shock. bibliog il Science 169:
1224-6 S 18 '70

HINE, Daryl
Histrionic landscape; poem. Harper 241:109 S
'70
Lines in lieu of a review. Poetry 117:211-15
D '70
(tr) See Homer. Homeric hymn to Aphrodite

HINE, Virginia. See Gerlach, L. P. jt. auth.

HINERMAN, C. Philip
Who is polarizing the church? Chr Today 15:
8-10 N 6 '70

HINES, Jerome
Muzzling atheists. Chr Today 14:35 Je 19 '70 *

HINMAN, Norman D. and Phillips, A. H.
Similarity and limited multiplicity of membrane proteins from rough and smooth
endoplasmic reticulum. bibliog il Science
170:1222-3 D 11 '70

HINRICHS, Marie A.
Doctor, I have a question; questions and answers. See issues of Harvest years

HINTENBERGER, H. and others
Rare gases, hydrogen, and nitrogen: concentrations and isotopic composition in lunar
material. il Science 167:543-5 Ja 30 '70

HINTON, H. E.
Insect eggshells; with biographical sketch.
il Sci Am 223:12, 84-91 Ag '70

HIP culture. See Counter culture

HIP joint
New new hip. il Time 95:68 Ap 27 '70
Surgery that aids arthritis victims. il Bsns W
p 116+ Ap 25 '70
Triumph of Dr Tucker; total hip replace-
ment operation. L. Rockey. il por Todays
Health 48:48-9+ N '70

HIPPIES
Art of group scrounging. R. Gustaitis. Holi-
day 47:55+ Mr '70
Banality of the new evil; games the sur-
vivors play. W. Kloman. il Esquire 73:115-
17+ Mr '70
Bourbon on the rocks; police crackdown on
hippies in the French quarter of New Or-
leans. il Newsweek 76:58-9 Jl 13 '70
Charlie Manson's home on the range. G.
Talese. il por Esquire 73:101-3+ Mr '70
Condemnation and persecution of hippies.
M. E. Brown; reply with rejoinder. A.
Dobrin. Trans-Action 7:71-2 Ja '70
Free clinic for street people; medical care
without a hassle; Cambridgeport medical
clinic. J. Brenner. il por N Y Times Mag
p30-1+ O 11 '70; Discussion. p 114-16 N 8
'70
Health of Haight-Ashbury. D. E. Smith and
others. il Trans-Action 7:35-45 Ap '70
How clergymen view nippiedom. H. M. Hack-
er. il Chr Cent 87:887-91 Jl 22 '70
Just waiting for Charlie; followers of C.
Manson. il por Life 69:40-3 Ag 21 '70
Love among the rattlesnakes; the girls of C.
Manson's colony. J. Stafford. il McCalls 97:
68-9+ Mr '70
M-i-c-k-e-y; confrontation at Disneyland. il
Newsweek 76:34 Ag 17 '70
New Mexico: no mecca for hippies. S. F.
Wheeler. Chr Cent 87:828-30 Jl 1 '70
Opinion: phoniness. P. Miletich. por Mlle
71:30+ Je '70
La raza, the land and the hippies. P. Nabo-
kov. il Nation 210:467-8 Ap 20 '70
Sharon Tate murders. P. Maas. il por Ladies
Home J 87:52+ Ap '70
Street people of Denmark. D. Smith. Nation
211:559-61 N 30 '70
Tripping down Hippie Highway; the freaks
of the coastal highway of California. K.
Fleming. il Newsweek 76:32-4 Jl 27 '70
Very special pair. J. Trelford. il por Mc-
Calls 97:63-5+ Ap '70
Youth unrest: what worldwide survey shows.
il U S News 69:76-9 O 26 '70

Religion
Blessitt is the cross-bearer. J. R. Greisch.
Chr Today 14:31 Jl 17 '70
Evangelical pathbreaking. C. F. H. Henry.
Chr Today 14:34-5 My 8 '70
Good/bad vibes at Glide; Jesus freaks. R. L.
Cleath. Chr Today 15:37 O 23 '70
Jesus freaks; savagery and salvation on Sun-
set strip. P. Tracy. il Commonweal 93:122-5
O 30 '70
Rally round the cross. A. Eggebroten. il Chr
Today 14:42-3 Ag 21 '70
Street Christians: Jesus as the ultimate trip.
il Time 96:31-2 Ag 3 '70

HIPPLE, Theodore W.
Student compositions. Clear House 44:523-6
My '70

HIPPLER, Arthur E.
Game of black & white at Hunters Point.
il Trans-Action 7:56-63 Ap '70

HIRAOKA, Kimitake. See Mishima, Y. pseud.

HIRATA, Arthur A. and Terasaki, P. I.
Cross-reactions between streptococcal M proteins and human transplantation antigens.
bibliog il Science 168:1095-6 My 29 '70

HIRED men. See Farm labor

HIRING. See Recruiting of employees

HIRING halls
Building trades versus the people; with editorial comment. G. Burck. il Fortune 82:
67-8, 94-7+ O '70

HIROSHIMA
A-bombed cities: twenty-five years later.
K. M. Chrysler. il U S News 69:54-6 Ag 10
'70
Hiroshima. N. Cousins. il Look 34:38-45 Ag 11
'70
Hiroshima, August 1945; the camera remem-
bers. M. R. Weiss. il Sat R 53:32-3 Ag 1 '70
Japan: to count the dead. il Time 96:27 Ag 10
'70
Memory and a hope: Hiroshima after a quar-
ter century. D. W. Shriver, jr. il por Bul
Atom Sci 26:32-4 S '70
My God, what have we done? excerpts from
The rising sun. J. Toland. il Look 34:51-
4+ O 6 '70
Scientists and the decision to bomb Japan.
D. H. Frisch. il por Bul Atom Sci 26:107-15
Je '70
Twenty-five years ago two cities two bombs.
il Life 69:30-1 Jl 31 '70
What if Hiroshima had never happened? Time
essay. M. Mohs. il Time 96:28-9 Ag 10 '70
Where are they now? air force men who
triggered the release of the first atomic
bomb. il pors Newsweek 76:10 Ag 10 '70

HIROSHIMA maidens
Hiroshima. N. Cousins. il Look 34:44-5 Ag 11
'70
Way back to life. J. Robbins. il Redbook 135:
76-7+ Jl '70

HIRSCH, Helmut V. B. and Spinelli, D. N.
Visual experience modifies distribution of
horizontally and vertically oriented receptive fields in cats. bibliog il Science 168:869-
71 My 15 '70

HIRSCH, Julian D.
EW lab tests new automatic turntables. il
Electr World 83:23-7+ Je '70
New stereo receivers. il Electr World 84:27-
30+ D '70
Testing hi-fi equipment. il Electr World 84:
47-50+ D '70; 85:45-8+ Ja '71

HIRSCH, Paul M.
Economics of rock. Nation 210:275-6 Mr 9 '70

HIRSCHFELD, Robert A.
Build the Voxor. il Pop Electr 32:81-4 F '70

HIRSCHFIELD, Robert Carl
Israel; the strange sounds of protest. Commonweal 91:607-8 Mr 6 '70
Jerusalem: 1970. il Cath World 212:134-6 D
'70

HIRSCHOWITZ, Ralph G. and others
Psychiatric nurse, fox or hedgehog? bibliog
Ment Hy 54:123-8 Ja '70

HIRSHON, Dorothy
Very personal garden of Dorothy Hirshon. il
House & Gard 138:72-5 Ag '70 *

HIRSUTISM. See Hair

HIRVONEN, T. See Toivanen, P. jt. auth.

HISCOCK, Eric
Designing and building for offshore. il
Yachting 127:76-7+ Ap '70

HISPANIC American history. See Latin America—History

HISPANIOLA
See also
Dominican Republic

HISPANO-American art. See Art, Latin American

HISS, Alger
Odyssey of a friend; letters to W. F. Buckley, jr. 1954-1955. W. Chambers. bibliog f Nat R 22:22-32 Ja 13 '70
Potential of psychoanalytic biography: Zeligs on Chambers and Hiss. G. Bychowski. bibliog f Am Imago 26:233-41 Fall '69 *

HISS, Anthony
Concert records (cont) New Yorker 45:80-5 F 7 '70

HISTAMINE
Histamine production by transplantable argyrophilic gastric carcinoid of praomys (mastomys) natalensis. S. Hosoda and others. bibliog il Science 170:454-5 O 23 '70

HISTOCOMPATIBILITY. See Immunological tolerance

HISTONES
Puffing and histone acetylation in polytene chromosomes. U. Clever and E. G. Ellgaard. bibliog il Science 169:373-4 Jl 24 '70

HISTOPLASMA
Release of protoplasts in the yeast phase of histoplasma capsulatum without added enzyme. M. D. Berliner and M. E. Reca. bibliog il Science 167:1255-7 F 27 '70

HISTORIANS
See also
Jewish historians

HISTORIANS, American
See also
American historical association
Prescott, W. H.

HISTORIANS, English
See also
Gibbon, E.

HISTORIC houses, etc.
Historic houses, landmarks, and museums. See issues of Antiques
See also
Musical landmarks
also subhead Historic houses, etc. under names of countries, states, cities, etc, e.g. Great Britain—Historic houses, etc.

Conservation and restoration
See Architecture—Conservation and restoration

HISTORIC trails. See Trails

HISTORIC trees. See Trees, Historic

HISTORICAL criticism. See History—Historiography

HISTORICAL documents institute. See United States historical documents institute

HISTORICAL literature
Advent of printing in current historical literature: notes and comments on an elusive transformation. E. L. Eisenstein. bibliog f Am Hist R 75:727-43 F '70

HISTORICAL museums
Scott museum in Trinity County. il Sunset 144:56 My '70

HISTORICAL paintings
Death of Captain Cook: two views. J. E. Ayres. il Antiques 97:724-7 My '70

HISTORICAL research
Exclusive interview with T. Harry Williams; ed. by P. A. Brock. T. H. Williams. por Writers Digest 50:26-7+ S '70
Hooks and other matters. C. Miles. Hobbies 75:142-3 My '70

HISTORICAL societies
See also
American historical association
Colfax highway association
Massachusetts historical society

HISTORIOGRAPHY. See History—Historiography

HISTORY
How nations take defeat. C. Barnett. Horizon 12:4-11 Sum '70
Is history dead? M. Himmelfarb. Commentary 50:45-8 Ag '70
It takes all kinds. R. L. Tobin. Sat R 53:18 Ag 15 '70
See also
Civilization
Current events
Historical research
Revolutions
World history
also subheads Antiquities; Foreign relations; History; Politics and government under names of countries, states, etc. e.g. Latin America—History; also subhead History under various subjects, e.g. Science—History

Bibliography
History (cont) C. L. Hohl, jr. America 122: 480-1; 123:468-9 My 2, N 28 '70

Historiography
History of history. P. Gay. il Horizon 11:112-19 Aut '69
See also
United States—History—Historiography

Philosophy
Historical rootlessness and alienation. H. B. Kuhn. Chr Today 14:48 F 13 '70

Psychological aspects
History and human survival, by R. J. Lifton. Review
Sat R 53:35-8 F 21 '70. H. S. Resnik

Sources
See also
Oral history

Study and teaching
History begins at home. G. E. McCully. il Sat R 53:74-5+ My 16 '70
Is our history obsolete? proposal for eliminating ethnocentrism. T. J. Knight. Ed Digest 35:28-31 My '70
Survey of the teaching of history and social studies in secondary schools. E. G. Kimball. Sch & Soc 98:246-9 Ap '70
See also
United States—History—Study and teaching

HISTORY, Ancient
See also
Archeology

Bibliography
Articles and other books received; comp. by T. R. S. Broughton. See issues of American historical review

HISTORY, Medieval. See Middle ages—History

HISTORY, Modern
See also
Nineteen hundred and forties

HISTORY, Naval. See Naval history

HISTORY and science. See Science and civilization

HISTORY in art
See also
Historical paintings

HITACHI, ltd. See Japan—Industries

HITCH hiking. See Hitchhiking

HITCHCOCK, Alfred Joseph
Hitchcock. C. T. Samuels. Am Scholar 39:295-304 Spr '70; Reply with rejoinder. J. Belton. 39:728-32 Aut '70 *
Trade winds. C. Amory. Sat R 53:14-15 F 7 '70

HITCHCOCK, H. Wiley
Vocal ornamentation in Caccini's Nuove musiche. bibliog f il Mus Q 56:389-404 Jl '70

HITCHCOCK, James
Here lies community: R.I.P. America 122:578-81; 123:287-8 My 30, O 17 '70
Revolution in the university. Yale R 60:161-74 D '70

HITCHCOCK, Stephen W.
Day the sea ran out of flounder; with biographical sketch. por Natur Hist 79:4, 28-31+ Mr '70

HITCHENS, Gordon
(ed) See Rocha, G. Way to make a future

HITCHES. See Knots and splices

HITCHES (automobile) See Automobiles—Equipment

HITCHHIKING
Hallelujah, on the bum. E. Abbey. il Am West 7:11-14 Jl '70
Thumbs down on hitchhiking! B. Surface. il Read Digest 96:128-31 Ja '70

HITCHINGS, George P.
Growth versus inflation. por Nations Bsns 58:77-8 Ap '70

HITLER, Adolf
About that Hitler quote. J. D. Lofton, jr. Nat R 22:411 Ap 21 '70 *
After twenty-five years: memory of two dictators. il pors Time 95:54 My 4 '70 *
Design for evil. D. Davis. il Newsweek 76:82 S 28 '70 *
Der Fuehrer dead center. W. H. Hale. Sat R 53:19-21+ Ag 29 '70 *
Hitler as architect. il Time 96:76 O 5 '70 *
Hitler I knew. S. Lorant. il pors Sat R 53:20-3 My 2 '70 *
Inside the Third reich, by A. Speer. Review
Nat R 22:958 S 8 '70. M. L. Kahn *
Time il por 96:58+ S 7 '70. K. R. Johnson *
Long long days with the Fuhrer; excerpts from Inside the Third reich. A. Speer. il pors Life 68:58-58B+ Ap 24 '70 *
Private world of Hitler. il pors Life 68:45-57 Ap 24 '70 *

HO, Hoang. See Hoang Ho
HOAG, Joy Marie
 Middle years of childhood. il Parents Mag 45:56-7+ O '70
HOAG, M. De Koning
 Second choice; story. Seventeen 29:164-5 Ap '70
 Thursday's child; story. Seventeen 29:144-5 My '70
 Your halo is showing; story. Seventeen 29:156-7 Mr '70
HOAGLAND, Edward
 Americana by the acre. il Harper 241:109-14+ O '70
 Home is two places. Commentary 49:70-6 F '70
HOANG Ho
 How to make a martyr. il por Time 95:25 Mr 9 '70 *
HOARDING
 Hoarders anonymous. J. Goyer. Har Yrs 10:31-2 N '70
HOAXES
 Cruelest trick-or-treat hoax. K. Engh. il pors Good H 171:12+ O '70
 Snouters, by H. Stümpke. Review
  Environ 12:34-5 Je '70. K. Shea
  See also
 Musical forgeries and mystifications
 Piltdown forgery
HOBBIES
 Time for self-expression. P. A. Dickinson. il Har Yrs 10:38-47 D '70
  See also
 Collectors and collecting
 Lightner museum of hobbies. St Augustine, Fla.
 Postage stamps—Collectors and collecting
 Bibliography
 Books reviewed. Hobbies 75:106-7+ Ag '70
HOBBS, Allen F.
 Through space astronomy, man will study eras older than time. il Space World G-5-77:26-7 My '70
HOBBS, Cecil
 (comp) Articles and other books received; southern Asia. See issues of American historical review
HOBBS, Helen Morton
 (ed) See King, A. Breast cancer
HOBBY airport. See Houston, Tex.—Airports
HOBSON, J. Allan. See McCarley, R. W. jt. auth.
HOBSON, James Earl
 Race and the GI. il por Newsweek 76:37-8 N 9 '70 *
HOBSON, Joan
 Mechanical cow. il Sci Digest 67:76-8 Je '70
HOBSON, Laura Z.
 Custody; story. Ladies Home J 87:88-9 S '70
 Tenth month; story. Redbook 136:139-61 D '70
HOBSON, Sandra
 Ceramist's odyssey of clay; the Palau Islands. il Craft Horiz 30:16-17 My '70
HOCHBERG, Max
 Max is in luck with Truluck. W. F. Reed, jr. il por Sports Illus 32:74-6 My 25 '70 *
HOCHHUTH, Rolf
 Guerrillas. Criticism
  Nation 211:124-6 Ag 17 '70 *
  Newsweek 75:105 Je 1 '70 *
 Hochhuth's coup d'état (U.S.) G. G. Eckstein. Nation 211:124-6 Ag 17 '70 *
HOCHMAN, Sandra
 Elation after childbirth; poem. McCalls 97:116 Je '70
 Waking in Westchester; poem. New Yorker 46:24 Ag 29 '70
HOCHMAN, Stanley
 (tr) See Koestler, A. Arthur Koestler at sixty-five, a fighter for men's minds now studies their brains
HOCHSTEIN, Rollie
 Many talents of Sheila MacRae. il pors Good H 170:12+ Ap '70
 Six women who care. il Good H 170:72-5+ My '70
 —See Sugarman, D. A. jt. auth.
HOCK, Raymond J.
 Physiology of high altitude; with biographical sketch. il Sci Am 222:10, 52-8+ F '70
HOCKEY
 Making of a hockey slave; from the cradle to the NHL, a Canadian odyssey. L. Shecter. il Look 34:70-4 F 10 '70
 Not so silent minority; San Diego Gulls of Western hockey league. M. Mulvoy. il por Sports Illus 34:54-5 Ja 4 '71
 Only game in town. W. Johnson. il Sports Illus 32:54-6+ F 16 '70
 Tea party for Bobby's Bruins; Chicago Black Hawks in Stanley cup encounter. G. Ronberg. il por Sports Illus 32:18-21 My 4 '70

Caricatures and cartoons
 Game behind the whistle; ice hockey. M. Ramus. il Sports Illus 33:42-7 N 23 '70
HOCKEY players
 Desperate hours; Chicago-Boston hockey race. M. Mulvoy and G. Ronberg. il Sports Illus 32:18-21 Ap 6 '70
 Don't bother hitting a Plager on the head; Plager brothers of St Louis Blues. M. Mulvoy. il Sports Illus 33:58+ N 9 '70
 Hockey's new season. M. Mulvoy. il Sports Illus 33:28-30+ O 19 '70
 Newcomer at the net. il por Time 95:58 Mr 9 '70
 Resurgent Rangers. il Newsweek 75:51 F 2 '70
 Sportsman of the year; Bobby Orr. J. Olsen. il por Sports Illus 33:36-7+ D 21 '70
  See also
 Hockey teams
 Orr, B.
HOCKEY teams
 Chicago! New York! Miltown! NHL's frantic playoffs. M. Mulvoy. Sports Illus 32:96+ Ap 13 '70
 Cup runneth over; B. Orr of Boston Bruins. Time 95:74 My 25 '70
 Desperate hours; Chicago-Boston hockey race. M. Mulvoy and G. Ronberg. il Sports Illus 32:18-21 Ap 6 '70
 Don't bother hitting a Plager on the head; Plager brothers of St Louis Blues. M. Mulvoy. il Sports Illus 33:58+ N 9 '70
 Flashing blades for a mini-mastermind; E. P. Francis of New York Rangers. G. Ronberg. il por Sports Illus 32:20-3 Mr 2 '70
 Got those St Louis Blues. L. Monahan. il Sports Illus 32:58-9 My 18 '70
 Hockey's new season. M. Mulvoy. il Sports Illus 33:28-30+ O 19 '70
 Hunker down and fly right; Chicago Black Hawks in NHL race. G. Ronberg. il Sports Illus 32:56-7 Mr 16 '70
 Kelly's light shines under Pitt's bushel. G. Ronberg. Sports Illus 32:64-5 Ap 20 '70
 Layer cake for the Canucks; Vancouver Canucks vs Buffalo Sabres. M. Mulvoy. il Sports Illus 33:66 D 14 '70
 Maggie the policeman. por Time 97:36 Ja 11 '71
 Mr O and the sack of New York; Boston Bruins vs New York Rangers. M. Mulvoy. il por Sports Illus 32:20-1 Ap 27 '70
 New York on the move again; clamoring for Rangers championship. G. Ronberg. il Sports Illus 31:26-7 D 15 '69
 Newcomer at the net. il por Time 95:58 Mr 9 '70
 Panic was quelled in Boston; Bruins vs Rangers. M. Mulvoy. il Sports Illus 33:18-19 N 9 '70
 Penny-pinching Bruins; resignation of coach S. Sinden. Newsweek 75:85 Je 1 '70
 Punch line gets the last laugh; Toronto Maple Leafs vs Buffalo Sabres. M. Mulvoy. Sports Illus 33:86-7 N 30 '70
 Reluctant dragon torments the Red Wings. G. Ronberg. il por Sports Illus 32:46-7 Ja 26 '70
 Resurgent Rangers. il Newsweek 75:51 F 2 '70
 Should seals wear spats? selling the Oakland Seals. Newsweek 75:87 Je 29 '70
 Soaring Hawkes. il Newsweek 75:130 Ap 20 '70
 Tea party for Bobby's Bruins; Chicago Black Hawks in Stanley cup encounter. G. Ronberg. il por Sports Illus 32:18-21 My 4 '70
 Then there were four; final scramble for Stanley cup. Time 95:60+ Ap 20 '70
 Two worlds against the Black Hawks; Boston Bruins and Montreal Canadiens. M. Mulvoy. il Sports Illus 33:20-1 D7 '70
 Up jump those pore li'l Canucks; Montreal Canadiens. M. Mulvoy. il Sports Illus 32:24-5 Mr 23 '70
HODGE, Gillian
 Hal Riegger. il pors Ceram Mo 18:13-15 Je '70
HODGE, Jane Aiken
 Two wives; story; excerpt from Savannah purchase. Good H 172:55-7 Ja '71
HODGE, John Dennis
 NASA veterans get new U.S. jobs. Aviation W 92:23 Je 1 '70 *
HODGE, Paul W.
 Celestial photography with fiber-optics image tubes. il Sky & Tel 39:234-5 Ap '70
 about
 Pollution watching by telescope. Sci N 98:300 O 10 '70 *
HODGES, Allen
 How not to be a consultant. bibliog Ment Hy 54:147-8 Ja '70

HODGES, Ernest J.
Private enterprise reacts to recreation demands. il Parks & Rec 5:36-8+ Ja '70
HODGES, Johnny
Obituary
New Yorker 46:88+ My 23 '70. W. Balliett *
Sat R por 53:54 My 30 '70. L Kolodin *
HODGES, William H.
Not by white might nor by black power. Chr Today 15:5-10 O 9 '70
HODGIN, Ellis
Constitutional rights of public librarians. R. P. Dwoskin. bibliog por Library J 95:2417-21 Jl '70 *
Ellis Hodgin loses first round. W. R. Eshelman. il Wilson Lib Bul 44:901+ My '70 *
Hodgin loses suit against city manager. Library J 95:1685 My 1 '70 *
HODGINS, Maibelle Dickey
Garden clowns. il Horticulture 48:34-5 S '70
Ways to attract birds to your garden. il Home Gard 57:26-32 N '70
HODGSON, Anthony M. and Dill, W. R.
Programmed case: the misfired missive. bibliog Harvard Bsns R 48:140-2+ S; 105-10 N '70
HODGSON, Gordon W. and others
Search of porphyrins in lunar dust. bibliog il Science 167:763-5 Ja 30 '70
HODGSON, James D.
Changes ahead in Washington's labor policies? interview. il pors Nations Bsns 58:68-72 S '70
Hodgson: the labor outlook; interview. ed. by G. R. Rosen. por Duns 96:8-9+ N '70

about

Businessman the unions like. il por Bsns W p98 Je 20 '70 *
New secretary: same strike policy. por U S News 68:86 Je 22 '70 *
HODGSON, Marion S.
Heart of the matter; story. Good H 171:104-5 O '70
HODIERNE, Robert
How the G.I.'s in Vietnam don't learn about the war. il por N Y Times Mag p28-9+ Ap 12 '70
HODSON, H. Kent, and Hamner, K. C.
Floral inducing extract from xanthium. bibliog il Science 167:384-5 Ja 23 '70
HOECHST a.g. See Chemical industries—Germany (Federal Republic)
HOEFT, Bill
I'll tell you about muskies. il por Outdoor Life 146:58-9+ Ag '70
HOERNI, Jean
Intersil: upstart with talent. il pors Bsns W p70+ S 12 '70 *
HOFE, G. Douglas, Jr
Wild rivers. il por Parks & Rec 5:22-5+ F '70
HOFER, Charles W.
Emerging EDP pattern. bibliog il Harvard Bsns R 48:16-18+ Mr '70
HOFER, Evelyn
Pilgrim with a lens. S. E. Meyer. il Am Artist 34:46-52+ N '70 *
HOFER, Lynne
Films on demand. il Library J 95:3962-4 N 15 '70
HOFER, Myron A.
Physiological responses of infant rats to separation from their mothers. bibliog il Science 168:871-3 My 15 '70
HOFF, Philip Henderson
Vermont Democrats: Hoff's campaign. P. R. Wieck. New Repub 163:11-13 O 3 '70 *
HOFFER, Eric
Whose country is America? excerpt from First things, last things. il N Y Times Mag p30-1+ N 22 '70
HOFFER, William R.
Variable annuities fight inflation. il Har Yrs 10:14-16 Jl '70
HOFFMAN, Abbie
Movement seeks a mass. L. D. Nachman. il Nation 212:39-45 Ja 11 '71 *
Transitional sex figures. D. Newman and R. Benton. pors Mlle 71:103 Jl '70 *
HOFFMAN, Betty Hannah
Joan Kennedy today. il pors Ladies Home J 87:82-3+ Ag '70
Joan Kennedy's story. il pors Ladies Home J 87:57-9+ Jl '70
HOFFMAN, Daniel
Old photo in an old life; poem. Poetry 117:80 N '70
Snatches from Charles Ives; poem. New Yorker 45:32 Ja 17 '70
Snow; poem. Nation 210:124 F 2 '70
This silence; poem. Am Scholar 39:208 Spr '70

about

Aging Autolycus. Nation 210:151-3 F 9 '70
HOFFMAN, Dustin
Old age of Dustin Hoffman; with interview, ed. by R. Meryman. il pors Life 69:75-9 N 20 '70

about

Little big man clings to life. S. Kempton. il Esquire 74:78-81+ Jl '70 *
HOFFMAN, Joseph E. Jr
Keystone Canyon. il Parks & Rec 5:29-31 D '70
HOFFMAN, Julius J.
Behind the Chicago conspiracy trial; with editorial comment. P. Glusman. il Ramp Mag 8:7+. 39-47 Ja '70
Judgment in Chicago. il por Newsweek 75:22-4 Mr 2 '70 *
That riotous trial: end or beginning? Chr Cent 87:260-1 Mr 4 '70 *
What provoked the most-severe contempt citations on record. por U S News 68:6-7 Mr 2 '70 *
HOFFMAN, L. E.
Sapote tree. Horticulture 48:48 Mr '70
HOFFMAN, Lisa
Real Auntie Mame. il pors Har Yrs 10:34-7 Jl '70
HOFFMAN, Martin
Homosexuality. Todays Ed 59:46-8 N '70
HOFFMAN, Marvin
Wishes, feelings, dreams. il Library J 95:3599-601 O 15 '70
HOFFMAN, Paul
New threat to the press. Nation 210:454 Ap 20 '70
HOFFMAN, Rheba
Spaciousness key to Memphis state store. il Pub W 198:58-9 Jl 27 '70
HOFFMAN, Robert
Here come the helicopter ambulances. il Flying 87:83-4+ D '70
HOFFMAN, Thomas
Alessandro Magnasco, "a garden party at Albano" (after 1735); poem. Yale R 60:87-8 O '70
HOFFMAN, Virginia
When will weaving be an art form? il Craft Horiz 30:18-23 Ag '70
HOFFMANN, Bruno
Musical glasses. il por Newsweek 76:58 D 28 '70 *
HOFFMANN, Rita
On the edge of disaster. Mlle 70:222-3+ Ap '70
Who's afraid of the big bad U? il Mlle 71:176-7+ O '70
HOFFMANN, Roald, and Woodward, R. B.
Orbital symmetry control of chemical reactions. bibliog il Science 167:825-31 F 6 '70
HOFHEIMER, Fritz S. inc.
Mail animal. R. Byrne. Sat R 53:4-5 Ag 8 '70
HOFLER, Donald B.
Wanted! Desert sheath for kidnapping. il Todays Ed 59:41 Ja '70
HOFMANN, August Wilhelm von
Missing medal. D. H. Wilcox, Jr. and W. D. Miles. bibliog il Chem 43:13 F '70 *
HOFMANN, Philip B.
Human chemistry at J&J. por Duns 96:30-1 D '70 *
HOFMANN apparatus. See Chemical apparatus and supplies
HOFSTADTER, Richard
Age of rubbish; interview. por Newsweek 76:20-3 Jl 6 '70
Future of American violence; excerpt from American violence. il Harper 240:47-53 Ap '70
—and Wallace, Michael
(eds) America as a gun culture; excerpt from American violence. il Am Heritage 21:4-11+ O '70

about

Obituary
Pub W 198:35 N 9 '70
HOFSTRAND, Richard H.
Wild ricing; with biographical sketch. il por Natur Hist 79:8, 50-5 Mr '70
HOG auctions. See Auctions
HOG cholera
Cholera changes may help pig industry. Farm J 93:H25 O '69
How Canada stays cholera-free. R. Wilmore. il Farm J 93:H8-9+ O '70
Is your state short on cholera indemnity funds? W. R. Prafka. Farm J 94:H12 My '70
HOG contracts. See Contracts, Agricultural
HOG houses. See Swine houses
HOGAN, Ben
Welcome back, Mister Hogan. W. Bingham. il pors Sports Illus 32:18-21 My 18 '70 *

HOGAN, Clarence Lester
Foundation for human survival; address, August 26, 1970. Vital Speeches 36:755-8 O 1 '70
HOGAN, Paul
Double-duty for parking lots. il Parks & Rec 5:51+ My '70
HOGE, Carson H. and Lykes, J. E. Jr
Inventory your streets for better management. il Am City 85:98+ Mr '70
HOGE VELUWE NATIONAL PARK. See National parks and reserves—Netherlands
HOGG, Quintin
Three conservative musketeers. C. Brogan. Nat R 22:148-9 F 10 '70
HOGG, Tony
Passing of the eternal infernal internal combustion engine. Esquire 74:80+ O '70
What this country needs is a good $25,000 car. Esquire 74:82+ Ag '70
HOGS. See Swine
HOHENBERG, John
Free press is on trial. il Sat R 53:109-10 Mr 14 '70
Journalist as missionary. il Sat R 53:76-7 F 14 '70
HOHENEMSER, Kurt H.
Onward and upward. il Environ 12:22-7 My '70
—and McCaull, Julian
Wind up car. il Environ 12:14-21+ Je '70
HOHL, Clarence Leonard, Jr
History (cont) America 122:480-1; 123:468-9 My 2, N 28 '70
HOISTING machinery
Hoist a few. J. Dianna. il Hot Rod 23:42-3 Jl '70
This vacuum has a tender touch. Bsns W p 156 Mr 28 '70
HOISTS, Boat. See Boats—Equipment
HOIT, Elizabeth
Second chance at parenthood. il Todays Health 48:64-5+ Mr '70
HOKE, Franklin
World under a dome. il Am For 76:12-14+ Mr '70
HOKE, Melvin A.
John Arden's Serjeant Musgrave's dance: a highly relevant play for young people. Engl J 59:633-7 My '70
HOLCOMB, Robert W.
Power and fuel resources. Cur Hist 58:330-6+ Je '70
HOLD-ups. See Robberies and assaults
HOLDEN, David
Cairo's war: now you see it, now you don't. il N Y Times Mag p32-3+ My 24 '70
HOLDEN, Joan
Independent female; or, A man has his pride; text of play performed by the San Francisco Mime troupe. il Ramp Mag 9:20-31 D '70
HOLDEN, John C. See Dietz, R. S. jt. auth.
HOLDEN, Stanley
Sleeping Beauty may awake in Los Angeles. V. H. Swisher. il pors Dance Mag 44:62-7 F '70
HOLDER, Fred W.
Color organs & strobe lights enhance music. il Electr World 85:42-4+ Ja '71
Computers that talk. il Electr World 84:38-9+ D '70
Electronic fuel injection reduces air pollution. il Electr World 84:48-9+ S '70
Electronics and the heart. il Electr World 83:25-7 F '70
Flight simulator for super jets. il Electr World 84:43+ Ag '70
Myo-cybernetics. Electr World 85:39+ Ja '71
Seeing with sound. il Pop Sci 196:76-9+ Ja '70
Sonic holography. il Electr World 83:32-5 Je '70
System trend in medical electronics. il Radio-Electr 41:61-3+ Mr '70
—and Springs. R. D.
Testing VW's electronic fuel-injection system. il Electr World 83:88-9 Ja '70
HOLDER, William G. and Siuru. W. D. Jr
Skylab, America's first space station. il Sci Digest 68:70-6 Ag '70
HOLDING companies
See also
Airline holding companies
Bank holding companies
CNA financial corporation
Gramco international
INA corporation
Insurance holding companies
ITC commercial credit card, inc.
Marcor, inc.
NLT corporation
Northwest industries, inc.

HOLDING devices (machine work)
How to machine a boring-bar holder with extra talents. W. E. Burton. il Pop Sci 196:127 My '70
See also
Clamps
Jigs
HOLDREN, John P. See Ehrlich, P. R. jt. auth.
HOLE in the bucket; story. See McMurtry, L.
HOLFORD, D. J.
Air traffic control transponder identifies radar targets. il Electr World 83:36-8+ F '70
HOLIDAY (periodical)
Holiday's choice of North American restaurants. S. Spitzer and H. Spitzer. il Holiday 48:75-82 Jl '70
HOLIDAY (periodical) awards. See Landscape protection—Awards, prizes, etc.
HOLIDAY Home; story. See Litvinov, I.
HOLIDAY parties. See Entertaining
HOLIDAYS
Holiday guidelines for schools urge religious neutrality. Chr Cent 87:1508 D 16 '70
It's time to plan for those stretched weekends. il Nations Bsns 58:81 S '70
1971: the year of the three-day weekend. il Todays Health 49:48-51 Ja '71
There should be a labor-management day. D. Lawrence. U S News 69:88 S 14 '70
See also
Vacations
also names of holidays, e.g. Fourth of July
HOLIFIELD, Chet
New tool for cutting government costs. il por Nations Bsns 58:58-60 F '70
HOLINESS
Conquest of holiness. G. Weckman. Chr Cent 87:595-7 My 13 '70
HOLLAND, Alma Boice
Second thoughts. See issues of Writer's digest
HOLLAND, Anthony
Lekythos; drama. Mlle 72:178-9+ N '70
HOLLAND, Cecelia
Nobody ever learned anything from violence, except how to duck. Mlle 72:177+ N '70
HOLLAND, Dan
I-wasn't ready bird. il Field & S 74:90-1+ Ap '70
HOLLAND, Jerome Heartwell
Holland to Sweden. por Time 95:13-14 Ja 26 '70
Jerome H. Holland sworn in as United States ambassador to Sweden. il Negro Hist Bul 33:131 My '70
HOLLAND, John J. and Kiehn, E. D.
Influenza virus effects on cell membrane proteins. bibliog il Science 167:202-5 Ja 9 '70
HOLLAND, Kenneth
Half-century of the Institute of international education: only a beginning. Sch & Soc 98:426-9 N '70
HOLLAND, Ray P.
Ray P. Holland. T. Trueblood. por Field & S 75:82-3+ Je '70 *
HOLLAND, Robert G.
What does student writing tell us? il Todays Ed 59:37-8+ My '70
HOLLAND. See Netherlands
HOLLAND festival. See Music festivals—Netherlands
HOLLANDER, Jacob H.
Poverty programs: the view from 1914. H. M. Doutp. Mo Labor R 93:69-71 Ap '70
HOLLANDER, John
Curse; poem. Poetry 117:41-2 O '70
Going home; New York; poem. Harper 241:78-81 Ag '70
Let a thousand blooms. Poetry 117:43-5 O '70
To Richard Howard on our birthdays; poem. Yale R 59:549-50 Je '70
HOLLANDER, Lorin
Classics for the now generation. J. Hiemenz. il por Hi Fi sec I 20:112 Ja '70
HOLLANDERS. See Dutch
HOLLEB, Arthur I.
Using the cancer cures we have now; ed. by W. S. Ross. por Todays Health 48:48-9+ Ap '70
HOLLIDAY, Leslie
Early views on forces between atoms; with biographical sketch. il Sci Am 222:10, 116-22 bibliog(p 148) My '70
HOLLIDAY, Richard J.
Let's raise a baby calf! il Org Gard & Farm 17:62-5 Je '70
HOLLINGS, Ernest Frederick
America is fed up; address, September 21, 1970. Vital Speeches 37:37-40 N 1 '70

HOLLINGS, Ernest Frederick—*Continued*
We must wipe out hunger in America! interview, ed. by P. Jablow. il por Good H 170: 68-9+ Ja '70
HOLLINS college, Hollins, Va.
Science building; contemporary yet sedate, for an old southern college. il Arch Rec 147: 110-11 F '70
HOLLISTER, Charlotte Ann
Computer-liaison. M. S. Rothenberg. por Phys Today 23:26-7 My '70 *
HOLLISTER, David
Business of survival. Hi Fi 20:secII 26+ Je '70
HOLLISTER, William G.
Booster shots for personality. il PTA Mag 64:16-19, bibliog(p36) Ja '70
HOLLO, Anselm
For Osip Mandelstam (1891-1938); poem. Nation 211:310 O 5 '70
Sunset with blame; poem. Nation 210:792 Je 29 '70
HOLLOMON, John Herbert
Shake-up Oklahoma. il por Newsweek 76:48-9 Ag 10 '70 *
HOLLOWAY, Bruce Keener
Two worlds; address, January 17, 1970. Vital Speeches 36:262-5 F 15 '70
HOLLOWAY, Irmagene Nevins
Preventing child burns. il PTA Mag 64:14-15 Je '70
HOLLOWAY, Ralph L.
Australopithecine endocast (Taung specimen, 1924): a new volume determination. bibliog il Science 168:966-8 My 22 '70
HOLLOWAY, Ruth Love
How relevant is equality? Ed Digest 35: 19-21 Ja '70
HOLLOWAY, Trevor
Artists of the frozen North. il por Design 72: 4-8 Wint '70
HOLLY
Festive greenery; ed. by E. Haraszty. R. E. Atkinson. il McCalls 98:21+ D '70
Hollies for the holidays. H. Dengler. il Am For 76:20-3 D '70
HOLLYHOCKS
Hollyhocks can be made to please. D. Foraker. il Org Gard & Farm 17:96-9 Ja '70
HOLLYWOOD, Calif.
Trouble in Xanadu; plans to reshape decaying face of the downtown area. Newsweek 77:56-7 Ja 11 '71

Churches
Hope for the homosexual; service of Metropolitan community church. il por Time 96: 46+ Jl 13 '70

Description
Good, tolerant life of the Hollywood hills. J. D. Weaver. il Holiday 47:60-3+ Ap '70

Industries
See also
Moving picture industry—United States
HOLLYWOOD bowl
Music to my ears; new menu at the Bowl. I. Kolodin. Sat R 53:42 S 5 '70
HOLLYWOOD park race track, Inglewood, Calif. See Race tracks
HOLM, Bernard J.
(comp) Articles and other books received; medieval. See issues of American historical review
HOLM, Don
There are honkers in the valley. il por Outdoor Life 146:52-3+ D '70
HOLM, Jane Wang
What's cooking? il pors Org Gard & Farm 17:114-16 N '70
HOLMAN, Ben
Urban Vietnamization; address, November 21, 1969. Vital Speeches 36:246-50 F 1 '70
HOLMAN, John
Rap 'n 'pinion. por Motor T 22:16 S '70
HOLMAN, Ross E.
I was sick and you visited me. il por Har Yrs 10:11 My '70
HOLMDEL TOWNSHIP, N.J.
Beauty, strength and efficiency. il Am City 85:20 Jl '70
HOLMES, Arthur F.
Idea of a Christian college. Chr Today 14:6-8 Jl 31 '70
HOLMES, Doloris
Art for everyday living; survival dome. il Art in Am 58:78-9 S '70
HOLMES, Marion
Star quality. por Mlle 71:130-3 O '70 *
HOLMES, Marjorie
Apron-pocket prayers for Christmas. il Ladies Home J 86:75-8 D '69
Motoring marvels of yesteryear. il Todays Health 48:54-5+ Mr '70
You're a baaad parent! il Todays Health 48: 4+ F '70

HOLMES, Mary
Mary Holmes paints the figure. P. Thompson. il por Am Artist 34:86-93 Mr '70 *
HOLMES, Oliver Wendell, 1809-1894
Memorandum to Oliver Wendell Holmes. C. B. Mitchell. il Am Heritage 21:23-7+ F '70 *
HOLMES, Ruth Vickery
Golden goose; dramatization of Grimm's fairy tales. Plays 29:71-82. 96 Ap '70
HOLMES, Sherlock, stories. See Doyle, A. C.
HOLMES, Theodore
Storm day; Apple tree; poems. Poetry 116: 89-91 My '70
HOLMES, William C.
Current chronicle. il Mus Q 56:478-84 Jl '70
HOLMGREN, Muriel
Exercise saved my life. por Har Yrs 10:16-17 My '70
HOLOGRAMS. See Holography
HOLOGRAPHY
Holography. il Chem 43:25-7 Ap '70
New focus for the hologram. L. Rich. il Duns 96:59-61 Ag '70
Now everyone can make a 3-D hologram. W. F. Wilson. il Pop Phot 67:82-4 N '70
Nth dimension; exhibition at Finch college museum. D. Davis. il Newsweek 75:110 Je 15 '70
Seeing with sound. F. W. Holder. il Pop Sci 196:76-9+ Ja '70
Sonic holography. F. W. Holder. il Electr World 83:32-5 Je '70
Underwater view in 3-D; sonography. S. V. Jones. il Sci Digest 68:80 Ag '70
HOLROYD, Michael
Out of print. Am Scholar 39:310+ Spr '70
Publisher as the mad hatter, or, the writer as Alice. Pub W 197:24-6 Mr 16 '70
Rediscovery; the Bloomsbury painters. il Art in Am 58:116-23 Jl '70
HOLSENDOLPH, Ernest
States join the pollution battle. Fortune 82: 116 O '70
HOLST, Gustav
At the Boar's head. Criticism
New Yorker 45:78 F 7 '70
Heirs and rebels. K. F. Reuling. il pors Opera N 34:12-15 Ja 24 '70
HOLST, Imogen
Heirs and rebels. K. F. Reuling. il pors Opera N 34:12-15 Ja 24 '70
HOLT, Edward R.
Long view. R. Brady. por Duns 95:101-2 Ap '70 *
HOLT, J. Gordon
Stereo scene. il Pop Electr 33:97-9 S; 94-7+ O; 69-71+ N; 71+ D '70; 34:68-70+ Ja '71
HOLT, James
Magicube; flash that works without batteries. il Pop Sci 197:67 S '70
HOLT, John Caldwell
Radicalizing of a guest teacher at Berkeley. il N Y Times Mag p30-1+ F 22; 12+ Mr 15 '70
Why we need new schooling. Look 34:52 Ja 13 '70
HOLTE, Clarence LeRoy
Clarence Holte's search into the black past. il pors Ebony 25:94-6+ Ap '70
HOLTON, A. Linwood
Southern governor dramatizes the push for school integration. il por U S News 69: 52 S 14 '70 *
HOLTON, Gerald
Lessons of the intellectual biography of science. Science 170:933 N 27 '70
Relevance of physics; adaptation of address, June 1970. bibliog il Phys Today 23:40-3+ N '70
HOLTON, Robert R.
Vatican radio. Cath World 211:7-12 Ap '70
HOLWAY, John
(ed) See Bell, J. How to score from first on a sacrifice
HOLY family; story. See Garber, C.
HOLY LAND
Israel and the Christian shrines. H. Golden. il Sat R 53:15-16 D 19 '70
See also
Bethlehem
HOLY Loch
Inside Holy Loch; with report by R. B. Stolley. il Life 68:66-9+ Ap 3 '70
HOLY See. See Papacy
HOLY Spirit
Fellowship of the Holy Spirit. H. A. Snyder. Chr Today 15:4-7 N 6 '70
See also
Pentecost
Trinity
HOLYOAKE, Sir Keith Jacka
U.S. shield is still needed; interview, ed. by C. S. Foltz, jr. por U S News 69:20-1 Ag 31 '70

HOLZMAN, Seymour
180 days vs. the year-round school. il Schol Teach Sec Teach Sup p 18-19 Ap 6 '70

HOLZSCHLAG, Phyllis
Is Catch-22 male chauvinist? Commonweal 93: 69-70 O 16 '70

HOME, Alexander Frederick Douglas-Home, 14th earl of. See Douglas-Home, A F.

HOME
Home is where the head is. C. G. Scully. Cath World 211:78-81 My '70
See also
Family
Family life

HOME; drama. See Storey, D.

HOME accidents. See Accidents

HOME and the school. See School and the home

HOME aquariums. See Aquariums

HOME bars. See Bars for the home

HOME building. See House construction

HOME building industry. See Building industry

HOME building materials. See Building materials

HOME buying. See House buying

HOME construction. See House construction

HOME decoration. See House decoration

HOME economics
Ask Rufus; questions and answers. R. Cartwright. See issues of Mechanix illustrated
Forty great hints for your home and shop. il Pop Mech 134:156-62 D '70
Keeping house with Emily Taylor. E. Taylor. See issues of Good housekeeping
Notes of a happy housekeeper. M. E. Falter. See issues of House & garden incorporating Living for young homemakers
Should you change your housekeeping habits? Good H 170:180+ My '70
See also
Budget, Household
Clothing and dress—Care
Cookery
Domestic finance
Moving
Sewing
Storage in the home

Anecdotes, facetiae, satire, etc.
Washington householder speaks his mind; interview. A. Buchwald. por House & Gard 138:26+ Ag '70

Study and teaching
See also
Cookery—Study and teaching

HOME equipment. See Household appliances

HOME fires. See Fires

HOME freezers. See Freezers

HOME furnishings. See Household furnishings

HOME garden and flower grower garden contest. See Gardening—Competitions

HOME garden contest. See Gardening—Competitions

HOME garden of ideas, Sterling Forest gardens. See Gardens—New York (state)

HOME garden photography contest. See Photography—Competitions

HOME grounds
Fronting! five examples. S. Mead and J. Pinkham. il Bet Hom & Gard 48:50-9 S '70
Surfacing by the yard. il Bet Hom & Gard 48:52-3 Ja '70
What happened in just eighteen months. il Sunset 145:236 N '70
See also
Back yards

HOME-improvement frauds. See Fraud

HOME improvements. See Houses—Maintenance and repair

HOME insurance. See Insurance—All risk policies

HOME labor
Few words of advice; earn money at home schemes. A. Herman. il Har Yrs 10:34-6 S '70

HOME libraries. See Libraries, Private

HOME loan bank board. See United States—Federal home loan bank board

HOME mechanics. See Mechanics, Household

HOME movies. See Moving pictures, Amateur

HOME music. See Music in the home

HOME ownership
Home sweet second home. W. Cross. Read Digest 97:181-2+ S '70
Trends in homeownership and rental costs. R. C. Joiner. il Mo Labor R 93:26-31 Jl '70
See also
Mortgages

HOME playgrounds. See Playgrounds, Home

HOME service industries. See Service industries

HOME sewing. See Sewing

HOME storage. See Storage in the home

HOME study
Home and homework; with study-discussion program, by E. Harris and D. Harris. J. S. Cross. bibliog il PTA Mag 65:14-16+, 34-5 D '70
Homework; symposium. il Todays Ed 59: 16-21 S '70
Realistic view of homework for the ghetto child. R. B. Shuman and H. L. Sublett, jr. bibliog Clear House 45:140-5 N '70

HOME study courses. See Correspondence schools and courses

HOME-swapping vacations. See Vacations

HOME visitations. See School and the home

HOME waste disposal appliances. See Refuse and refuse disposal—Apparatus

HOME work. See Home study

HOME workshops. See Workshops

HOMELESS, The
Hotels without hope: welfare hotels of New York. W. Friedman and R. Anson. il Time 97:28-30 Ja 4 '71
New York city skid row Negro: some research findings. B. M. Levinson. bibliog Ment Hy 54:548-52 O '70

HOMEMAKING. See Home economics

HOMEOWNER policies. See Insurance—All risk policies

HOMER
Homeric hymn to Aphrodite; tr. by D. Hine. Poetry 116:313-26 Ag '70

about
Crime and punishment in the Odyssey. G. Dimock. Yale R 60:199-214 D '70 *
Homer in 2001; comparisons between the Odyssey and 2001: a space odyssey. P. Drake. Engl J 59:1270-1 D '70 *
Odyssey as archetype. A. M. Lowery. Engl J 59:1076-9 N '70 *

HOMER, Sidney
Bonds: lure for savings; interview. por U S News 70:31-2 Ja 4 '71

HOMES, Institutional
New way to raise kids; interview, ed. by J. Whitbread. B. Bettelheim. il por Look 34: 64+ F 24 '70
See also
Children—Institutional care
Nursing homes
Old age homes

HOMES for the aged. See Old age homes

HOMESTEADER stoves. See Stoves

HOMEWORK. See Home study

HOMICIDE. See Murder

HOMING instinct. See Orientation

HOMOLOGY (biology)
On the apparent homology of actin and tubulin. R. E. Stephens. bibliog il Science 168:845-7 My 15 '70

HOMOSEXUALITY
Case for sexual restraint. Chr Today 14:31-2 Mr 13 '70
Gay mecca no. 1; invasion of Gay liberation front in Alpine County, Calif. il Time 96:12 N 2 '70
Gay pride. il Time 96:6 Jl 13 '70
Gays go radical. R. L. Cleath. Chr Today 15: 40-1 D 4 '70
Homo/hetero: the struggle for sexual identity. J. Epstein. il Harper 241:37-44+ S '70; Discussion. 241:6+ N '70
Homosexual church. R. Cleath. Chr Today 14:48-50 S 11 '70
Homosexual church. il por Newsweek 76:107 O 12 '70
Homosexual revolution. G. D. Phillips. America 123:406-7 N 14 '70; Reply. M. V. D. 123: 504 D 12 '70
Homosexuality. M. Hoffman. Todays Ed 59:46-8 N '70
Hope for the homosexual. il por Time 96: 46+ Jl 13 '70
Myths about childhood homosexuality. W. J. Gadpaille. Todays Health 49:45-7+ Ja '71
Parade: first-anniversary celebration of the Gay liberation movement. New Yorker 46: 19-20 Jl 11 '70
Same sex. ed. by R. W. Weltge. Review Commonweal 91:338-9 D 12 '69. W. Gaylin; Reply. L. R. Littlejohn. 91:499+ F 6 '70
Task force on gay liberation meeting. Am Lib 1:1013 D '70

HOMOSEXUALITY—*Continued*
Tearoom trade: impersonal sex in public places; excerpts. L. Humphreys. il Trans-Action 7:10–14+ Ja '70
We're freakin' on in! look at gay power. L. Skir. Mlle 71:150-1+ S '70

HONAN, William H.
Can Teddy Kennedy survive his reputation? il pors N Y Times Mag p25-7+ My 24 '70
Champion tenor defends his title. il pors N Y Times Mag p28-9+ F 8 '70; Same abr. Read Digest 96:83-7 My '70
Japan strikes: 1941. il por Am Heritage 22:12-15+ D '70
Russian and American pilots play chicken. il N Y Times Mag p25-7+ N 22 '70

HONDA (automobile) See Automobiles, Foreign

HONDURAS, BRITISH. See British Honduras

HONE, Howard Russell
Meet the family doctor for the 70's. M. Michaelson. il pors Todays Health 48:50-3+ My '70 *

HONESTY
For they deal honestly. Chr Today 14:23 Jl 17 '70
Simple shortcut will set you free. E. M. Davis. Read Digest 96:165-6+ Ap '70
Who's a phony? B. S. Llamzon. America 123:196-8 S 26 '70

HONESTY (plants)
Enrich your garden with silver pennies. B. Hemingway. il Horticulture 48:43 S '70

HONEY
Glossary of honeys. Good H 170:166 F '70

HONEY bees. See Bees

HONEY HOLLOW watershed. See Watersheds

HONEYMOON
Million dollar honeymoon. G. E. Miller. il Motor B 125:64-5+ My '60
Redbook's guide to honeymoons and other vacations. R. Deardorff. il Redbook 136:35-42 N '70
Winter honeymoon haven. H. P. Koenig. il Travel 135:28-35 Ja '71

HONEYWELL, Inc.
GE and Honeywell test their match. il Bsns W p30-1 My 30 '70
GE bows out. Newsweek 75:80 Je 1 '70
Honeywell tries to make its merger work; acquisition of GE's computer division. il Bsns W p92-3+ S 26 '70
Proxies for protesters; Honeywell project to stop bomb production. il por Time 95:69 Ja 26 '70

HONG KONG
See also
Catholic church in Hong Kong
Police—Hong Kong
Shopping and shoppers—Hong Kong
Temples—Hong Kong
Tourist trade—Hong Kong

Description
China's rear window by tour. L. Barry. il Pop Phot 66:50+ Ap '70
Hong Kong: the Orient's allure and its bargains. Bsns W p69-70 Ag 29 '70

Industries
See also
Boatbuilding

Japanese occupation
Pilgrim's progress: adjustment to home life by an American exchanged prisoner of war. E. Hahn. New Yorker 46:26-30 Ag 15 '70

Photographs
Hong Kong. B. Wolf. il Travel & Camera 33:45-51 Mr '70

Stores
Bargains from Mao. il Newsweek 76:60 Ag 31 '70

Streets
Cat street, Hong Kong. F. Robertson. il Holiday 47:44-5+ F '70

HONOLULU
Booked for travel; Waikiki. Sat R 53:48 Ja 17 '70

Airports
Honolulu airport expansion questioned. R. G. O'Lone. il Aviation W 94:32-5 Ja 4 '71
Hydrofoil boats studied for Honolulu airport/Waikiki link. Aviation W 93:63 Jl 27 '70

City planning
Erosion of Eden. H. Sutton. il Sat R 53:60-1+ Je 6 '70
Trouble in paradise. G. Laycock. il Audubon 72:24-31 My '70

Galleries and museums
Lighting dramatizes Hawaii's royal palace. il Am City 85:92 Ag '70

Gardens
Garden at the East-west center. il Sunset 145:29 N '70

Hotels, restaurants, etc.
Scrapbook of a pink palace in the sand; Royal Hawaiian. J. Didion. il Life 68:26B Ap 24 '70

Mayors
Frank Fasi fights fiercely. Time 95:44+ F 23 '70

Music
Report:
Production of Nozze di Figaro. W. Aguiar, jr. Opera N 34:31 Ap 11 '70

HONOR
See also
Sportsmanship

HONOR America day. See Fourth of July

HONOR thy father and thy mother; story. See Golwarz, S.

HONORARY degrees. See Degrees, Honorary

HOOD, Frederick E.
Sailmaker to the twelves. B. D. Burrill. il por Yachting 128:56-7+ S '70 *

HOOD, Graham
New catalogue of the Mabel Brady Garvan collection of silver at Yale. il Antiques 98:932-5 D '70

HOOD, Leroy E. and Talmage, D. W.
Mechanism of antibody diversity: germ line basis for variability. bibliog il Science 168:325-34 Ap 17 '70

—and others
Immunoglobin structure: amino terminal sequences of kappa chains from genetically similar mice (BALB/c) bibliog il Science 170:1207-10 D 11 '70

HOOD, Warwick
Aussie bid. il Yachting 127:54-5+ Je '70

HOOD ornaments, Automobile. See Automobiles—Equipment

HOOGENSTYN, Donald R. jr
I love it, I love it not. il Hi Fi 20:secI 60-2 Je '70

HOOK, Sidney
What student rights in education? excerpt from Academic freedom and academic anarchy. Cur 17:21-7 Ap '70

HOOK, Thom
All those planes you can build from plans. il Pop Sci 196:98-100+ Je '70

HOOKER, John Jay, jr
Fried chicken that went into politics. il Bsns W p37 S 19 '70 *
Wing and a prayer; Tennessee gubernatorial candidates. pors Bsns W p96 Mr 14 '70 *

HOOKER, Orvel E.
Requirements; address, February 26, 1970. Vital Speeches 36:440-2 My 1 '70

HOOKER, Richard, pseud. See Hornberger, H. R.

HOOKING
How to make a better rug hook. J. Burroughs. il Pop Mech 135:158 Ja '71

HOOKS
Glue-on hooks for household uses. Consumer Bul 53:36 N '70

HOOPER, L. O.
Market comment. See issues of Forbes

HOOPES, Townsend
LBJ's account of March, 1968. New Repub 162:17-19 Mr 14 '70
Legacy of the cold war in Indochina. For Affairs 48:601-16 Jl '70

HOORAY for Thanksgiving; drama. See Churchill, M. P.

HOOVER, Herbert Clark
Some choice lines on fishing. il Read Digest 96:135 My '70

about
Shattered dream, by G. Smith. Review
America 123:300-1 O 17 '70. R. J. Meister*
'Twas the night before Christmas . . . R. D. Heinl, jr. il por Am Heritage 22:105-9 D '70 *

HOOVER, John Edgar
Bull market in stock and bond thefts; interview. il por Nations Bsns 58:28-32 Mr '70

HOOVER, John Edgar—*Continued*
FBI's J. Edgar Hoover reports on a turbulent year; excerpts from report. il U S News 69: 24 Jl 27 '70
J. Edgar Hoover speaks out with vigor; excerpts from interview. por Time 96:16-17 D 14 '70
SDS and the high schools: a study in student extremism. il PTA Mag 64:2-5 Ja; 8-9 F '70

about
Bulldog vs. jellyfish. Newsweek 76:23+ N 30 '70 *
Bureau of vituperation. Time 96:11 N 30 '70 *
Conspiracy group denies charges, denounces Hoover. Chr Cent 87:1508 D 16 '70 *
Full circle; tackling the Catholics. Nation 211: 613-14 D 14 '70 *
Government and Martin Luther King. V. S. Navasky. pors Atlan 226:43-52 N '70 *
Hoover and the Berrigans; East coast conspiracy to save lives organization. America 123:509 D 12 '70 *
Hoover's conspiracy; letter to the editor. D. Kirk and others. Commonweal 93:291+ D 18 '70 *
Hoover's FBI, by W. W. Turner. Review Ramp Mag 9:54+ Ag '70. A. Truskier *
J. Edgar, Dan and Phil. J. Deedy. Commonweal 93:290 D 18 '70 *
Least wanted. il New Repub 63:5-6 N 28 '70 *
Plots and conspiracies. New Repub 163:7 D 12 '70 *
TRB from Washington. New Repub 163:4 N 28 '70 *

HOOVER, Mary B.
How children test a marriage. il Parents Mag 45:39-41+ Ap '70
How important are good manners? il Parents Mag 45:60-1+ Mr '70

HOOVER, Robert A.
Hoover's aerobatics a key factor in Shrike sales increase. C. M. Plattner. il por Aviation W 92:40-4 Mr 2 '70 *

HOOVER company
One man's theory opens a new door. R. W. Gillman. il Nations Bsns 58:84-5 Ja '70

HOOVER DAM
Piece of work for now and doomsday. J. Didion. il Life 68:20 Mr 13 '70

HOPE, Bob
I get a lot more than I give. Read Digest 96: 177-8+ Ja '70
about
This is Bob (politician-patriot-publicist) Hope. J. A. Lukas. il pors N Y Times Mag p28-9+ O 4 '70 *

HOPE, Jack
Parks are for people? il Audubon 72:68-70+ Jl '70
Redwoods forever? il Audubon 72:66-8+ Mr '70

HOPE, Marjorie
Family life in Africa: a look at another culture. il Parents Mag 45:46-7+ Ja '70

HOPE, Norman V.
How Jesus taught. Chr Today 14:8-9 Ag 21 '70

HOPE
Case for hope. N. Cousins. Sat R 53:18 D 26 '70
Coming faith; excerpt. C. Marney. Chr Cent 87:284 Mr 11 '70
Politics and the practice of hope; Christian hope. J. Moltmann. por Chr Cent 87:288-91 Mr 11 '70
Problem of hope; can we judge the theology of hope an unmixed blessing? M. Daly. Commonweal 92:314-17 Je 26 '70; Reply. G. Willenbrink. 92:491 S 25 '70
Then shall be brought to pass; excerpt from Coming faith. C. Marney. Chr Cent 87:260 Mr 4 '70
Trumpet shall sound; excerpt from The coming faith. C. Marney. Chr Cent 87:228 F 25 '70

HOPE (ship) See Hospital ships
HOPITAL Saint-Jean museum. See Bruges, Belgium—Galleries and museums

HOPKINS, Ginny
Private treasure; story. Good H 170:62-3 Ja '70

HOPKINS, Jeannine
Floor tile mosaics. il Sch Arts 70:14-15 Ja '71

HOPKINS, John
Tangier buzzless flies; story. New Yorker 46: 40-5 O 10 '70

HOPKINS, John, d 1570
Sternhold and Hopkins puzzle. H. Byard. Mus Q 56:221-9 Ap '70 *

HOPKINS, Sewell H. and Andrews, J. D.
Rangia cuneata on the East coast: thousand mile range extension, or resurgence? bibliog Science 167:868 F 6 '70

HOPKINS, Minn.
Standpipe proved best. il Am City 85:81 Ja '70

HOPPE, Arthur
I was born here. Holiday 47:60 Mr '70

HOPPE, E. O.
Mercurial swan. por Dance Mag 45:30-1 Ja '71 *

HOPPENSTEDT, Elbert M.
Poet's nightmare; drama. reprint from January 1950 issue. Plays 30:41-8 Ja '70

HOPPER, Dennis
Dennis Hopper saves the movies. T. Burke. Esquire 74:138-41+ S '70 *
Easy rider runs wild in the Andes. B. Darrach. il pors Life 68:48-50+ Je 19 '70 *

HOPSON, James A. See Barghusen, H. R. jt. auth.

HORAI, Ki-iti, and others
Thermal diffusivity and conductivity of lunar material. bibliog il Science 167:730-1 Ja 30 '70

HORAN, Ellen
Long tradition. il Yachting 128:63-6 Jl '70
(ed) With the racing classes. See issues of Yachting

HORENSTEIN, Jascha
Recordings. D. M. Clarke. New Repub 163:27-9 D 12 '70 *

HORGAN, John
Burying Biafra. Commonweal 91:551-3 F 20 '70
Riot act. Sat R 53:4 O 3 '70
Storm on the Holy See. il Sat R 53:19-21+ Mr 28 '70
Theologo '70. Commonweal 93:39 O 9 '70

HORMONAL contraceptives. See Contraceptives
HORMONES
See also
ACTH
Cortisone
Glucagon
Hydrocortisone
Juvenile hormone
Leuteotropin
Oxytocin
Parathyroid hormone
Pituitary hormones
Prostaglandins
Stilbestrols
Thyroid hormones
Thyroxine
Vasopressin

HORMONES, Plant
Interaction of plant hormones. R. E. Drury; reply with rejoinder. B. V. Milborrow. bibliog il Science 168:875-7 My 15 '70
See also
Abscisic acid
Gibberellic acid
Kinins

HORMONES, Sex
Hormones during the menstrual cycle; ed. by S. Olds. R. B. Jaffe. Redbook 134:12 Mr '70
Steroid hormones: effects on adenyl cyclase activity and adenosine 3', 5'-monophosphate in target tissues. M. G. Rosenfeld and B. W. O'Malley. bibliog il Science 168:253-5 Ap 10 '70
See also
Estrogens
Gonadotropins
Trisporic acid

HORN, C. S.
Reunion in Sharon. Nat R 22:1056-7 O 6 '70

HORN, Gunnar
Home visits. il Todays Ed 59:44-6 S '70
Some thoughts about teaching and teachers. il Todays Ed 59:12-15 F '70

HORN, Michael H. and others
Petroleum lumps on the surface of the sea. bibliog il Science 168:245-6 Ap 10 '70

HORN, William A.
To see and to touch. il Am Ed 6:35-6 Ag '70

HORN, CAPE
Third time lucky; Tzu Hang braves Cape Horn (cont) M. Smeeton. il Yachting 127: 100-2+ Ja '70

HORN book magazine
Subject to qualifications. P. Heins. Horn Bk 46:9 F '70

HORNABROOK, R. W.
Institute of human biology of Papua-New Guinea. Science 167:146-7 Ja 9 '70

HORNBERGER, H. Richard
Man behind M.A.S.H. F. Graham, jr. il por Todays Health 48:24-7 D '70 *

HORNBLENDE
Deformation twins in hornblende. T. P. Rooney and others. il Science 169:173-5 Jl 10 '70

HORNE, Alistair
Israel and the credibility gap. Nat R 22:309-10 Mr 24 '70

HORNE, Bryant
Longleaf pine. il Horticulture 49:16+ Ja '71
HORNE, Lena
Harry and Lena off the cuff! il pors Ebony
25:128-9 Mr '70 *
HORNE, M. T.
Coevolution of escherichia coli and bacterio-
phages in chemostat culture. bibliog il Sci-
ence 168:992-3 My 22 '70
HORNE, Marilyn
Marilyn at the Met. il por Time 95:69 Mr 16
'70 *
Marilyn Horne goes to the Met. P. J. Smith.
por Hi Fi 20:secII 13+ My '70 *
Marilyn, Joan and Norma. H. Saal. il pors
Newsweek 75:63 Mr 16 '70 *
Music to my ears; performance in Carnegie
Hall. I. Kolodin. Sat R 53:55 Ja 31 '70
Sutherland-Horne Norma. I. Kolodin. Sat R
53:28 Mr 21 '70 *
Tour of two great throats; interviews, ed. by
R. Meryman. il pors Life 68:63-4+ Je 26 '70
HORNOCKER, Maurice G.
American lion; with biographical sketch. il
Natur Hist 79:6, 40-9+ N '70
HORNSTEIN, Alvin
Liberty trail. il Travel 134:58-9+ Jl '70
HORNYKIEWICZ, O. See Lloyd, K. jt. auth.
HOROSCOPE. See Astrology
HOROSKO, Marian
(ed) See Anderson-Ivantzova, E. In the
shadow of Russian tradition
HOROVITZ, Israel
William Wyman: the rebel in the conserva-
tive. il por Craft Horiz 30:10-15+ O '70
HOROVITZ, Al
Chess corner. See issues of Saturday review
HOROWITZ, David
Bertrand Russell: the final passion. il pors
Ramp Mag 8:36-43+ Ap '70
Making of a revolutionary; introduction by
David Horowitz. por Ramp Mag 9:38-40 Ag
'70
HOROWITZ, Irving Louis
Trade-unionization of students. Cur 122:55-9
O '70
—and Horowitz, R. L.
Journalistic moralizers. Trans-Action 7:5-8
My '70
Tax-exempt foundations: their effects on
national policy. bibliog il Science 168:220-
8 Ap 10 '70
—See Becker, H. S. jt. auth.
HOROWITZ, Mannie
Designing solid-state stereo amplifiers (title
varies) il Radio-Electr 41:38-40+ D '70;
42:61-3 Ja '71 (to be cont)
HOROWITZ, Ruth Leonora. See Horowitz, I. L.
jt. auth.
HORRIGAN, Alfred F.
Diocese and Catholic higher education. il
America 122:342-4 Mr 28 '70
HORROR films. See Moving pictures—Horror
films
HORROR television programs. See Television
broadcasting—Horror programs
HORS d'œuvres. See Appetizers
HORSE, Perry
Man called Perry Horse.   J. Corry. il por
Harper 241:81-4 O '70 *
HORSE breeding
Colgate's gift establishes Morgan horse breed-
ing farm. il por Parks & Rec 5:30-2 F '70
Horses are a household word in New Jersey.
P. Alampi. il Parks & Rec 5:33-5 F '70
HORSE power. See Horsepower (mechanics)
HORSE race betting
Big gamble on gambling; New York's off-track
betting. F. J. Cook. il Nation 211:9-13 Jl 6
'70
Instead of tax hikes, horse parlors. U S News
68:74-5 My 4 '70
Playing the cinco-seis in San Juan; off-track
betting in Puerto Rico. W. Tower. Sports
Illus 33:44-5 Jl 6 '70
HORSE racing
Buddy vs. the moguls; suspension and pro-
secution of B. Jacobson. P. Axthelm. il
por Newsweek 75:87-8 Mr 9 '70
Command performance; Dust Commander
winner of the Kentucky Derby. il Sports
Illus 32:22-7 My 11 '70
Contest among survivors; Belmont stakes.
W. Tower. il Sports Illus 32:63-4 Je 8 '70
Dust Commander's dust; Kentucky Derby. il
Newsweek 75:71+ My 11 '70
Even the very best can blunder; Nijinsky's
defeat. W. Tower. il Sports Illus 33:56-8 O
26 '70
Hip horses with square names: Derby favor-
ites. My Dad George and Corn Off The Cob.
W. Tower. il Sports Illus 32:55 Mr 16 '70

I blew a few big ones, too; ed. by W.
Tower. W. Shoemaker. il Sports Illus 32:32-
4+ F 9 '70
Las Vegas on the Hudson? legalizing off-track
betting. Newsweek 75:58 My 4 '70
Mike and this horse needed each other; jockey
Manganello and Dust Commander. W. Tower.
il pors Sports Illus 32:22-7 My 11 '70
Naskra? You've got to be kidding; winner of
Everglades at Hialeah. W. Tower. Sports
Illus 32:52 Mr 2 '70
100 miles in just one day; Tevis cup ride. il
Sunset 145:38+ Ag '70
One more winner for the Derby list; Native
Royalty. W. Tower. il Sports Illus 32:93-4
Ap 13 '70
Our joint is jumping; international races at
Laurel, Md. and Camden, S.C. W. Tower.
il Sports Illus 33:22-7 N 23 '70
Out of the oven and into the winner's circle;
ed. by W. Tower. W. Shoemaker. il pors
Sports Illus 32:20-5 F 2 '70 (to be cont)
Pick 'em with a pin, and don't give up on
the office pool; Kentucky Derby hopefuls.
W. Tower. il Sports Illus 32:24-6+ Ap 27
'70
Plenty Old, but little else; Derby crop. W.
Tower. il Sports Illus 32:56 Mr 9 '70
Preakness with Personality; Triple crown
event. W. Tower. il Sports Illus 32:26-7 My
25 '70
Race track. A. Minor. See issues of New
Yorker
Royal Ascot. il Travel & Camera 33:54-7 My
'70
Saints and sidewalks; Epsom Downs and
Belmont park. W. Tower. il Sports Illus
32:14-19 Je 15 '70
Saratoga gallery; photographs. S. Green-
Armytage. Sports Illus 33:28-35 Ag 3 '70
Shoe on the way to 6033. J. Olsen. il por
Sports Illus 33:28-30+ S 14 '70
Smiling through at (S)Miles park. J. Mann.
il Look 34:46-9 Ag 11 '70
Sonny sniffs a derby, Silent Screen to Chur-
chill Downs. W. Tower. il por Sports Illus
32:10-11 +F 16 '70
Sports; Bill Veeck. R. Kahn. Esquire 74:34+
O '70
They're still chasing Apaches; Pagosa
Springs, Colo. to Grants, N.Mex. 210-mile
pony express race. A. Napier. il Sports
Illus 32:46+ Je 1 '70
Through a julep glass, darkly; questionable
starters in Kentucky Derby. W. Tower.
Sports Illus 32:61 My 4 '70
Two derbies down, one to go; My Dad
George in the Florida derby at Gulfstream
park. W. Tower. il Sports Illus 32:22-5 Ap
6 '70
Victory for the family of Mann; Staunch
Avenger wins Arch Ward stakes. W. John-
son. il Sports Illus 33:44-5 Ag 31 '70
    See also
Harness racing
Race horses
Race tracks

France
Nijinsky's last dance; Prix de l'Arc de
Triomphe. il por Newsweek 76:73-4 O 19
'70
One head that cost a crown; Sassafras vs
Nijinsky at Prix de l'Arc de Triomphe. W.
Tower. il Sports Illus 33:18-19 O 12 '70
Sporting scene; Prix du jockey club, and
Prix de Diane. F. Feldkamp. New Yorker
46:62+ Je 6 '70

Great Britain
Nijinsky's triple was a lark. D. Hedges. il
Sports Illus 33:28-9 S 21 '70

Ireland
Triumph for the clan O'Brien; Nijinsky, Irish
Sweeps Derby winner. C. Cockburn. il por
Sports Illus 33:14-15 Jl 6 '70

Japan
Off and running in Japan. il Time 95:59 Je 8
'70
HORSE radish. See Horseradish
HORSE shows
Big victory for an old troublemaker; The
Deputy at Spindletop charity horse show,
Beaumont, Tex. A. Higgins. Sports Illus
32:76+ Je 8 '70
Every Sunday afternoon near Pomona you
can watch the elegant Arabians in action.
il Sunset 145:45-6+ N '70
HORSE stables. See Barns and stables
HORSE trainers
Buddy barred again. il por Newsweek 75:68
Je 8 '70

HORSE trainers—*Continued*
Buddy vs. the moguls; suspension and prosecution of B. Jacobson. P. Axthelm. il por Newsweek 75:87-8 Mr 9 '70
   See also
Jacobs, H.
HORSE training
   See also
Horse racing
HORSEBACK riding. See Horsemanship
HORSEBACK trips
Breakfast ride. N. Wood. il Travel & Camera 33:10+ Jl '70
High on a horseback. E. A. Bauer. il Outdoor Life 145:62-5+ Mr '70
Trail riding. G. H. Cardinet, jr. il Parks & Rec 5:43-4 F '70
Yellowstone pack trips. il Sunset 144:80 Ap '70
HORSEMANSHIP
Equestrian husbandry courses. J. Cryderman. Parks & Rec 5:42 F '70
Happiness comes on horseback. C. E. Ball. il Farm J 94:14-15 Je '70
   See also
Rodeos
HORSEPOWER (mechanics)
Armstrong+327 Chevy=572 horsepower. B. Lang. il Hot Rod 23:96-9 My '70
Boosting engine output. E. Nabb. il Motor B 125:88+ Je '70
HORSERADISH
Horse-radish, the three-way plant. E. V. Alfrey. il Org Gard & Farm 17:76-7 Ja '70
HORSES
Horse drive down from Yosemite, late October. il Sunset 145:24+ O '70
Horses and parks; symposium. il Parks & Rec 5:29-44 F '70
   See also
Asses and mules
Horse breeding
Horsemanship
Race horses

Anecdotes, facetiae, satire, etc.
Equus caballus. C. Tomkins. New Yorker 45:28-9 Ja 24 '70
HORSES, Miniature. See Ponies
HORSESHOE crabs. See King crabs
HORSESHOES
Horseshoe lawn furniture. D. Shiner. il Design 71:24-6 mid-Sum '70
HORSTED, Leon R.
Build your own low-cost chicken feeders. il Org Gard & Farm 17:42 D '70
HORTICULTURAL libraries
First conference, horticultural and botanical libraries. Horticulture 48:46-7 Mr '70
Library is more than a collection of books; Massachusetts horticultural society library. G. W. Dillon. Horticulture 49:36+ Ja '71
HORTICULTURAL societies
Members' news. See issues of Horticulture
   See also names of horticultural societies, e.g. American iris society
HORTICULTURAL society of New York
Daffodils: trip with horticultural society of New York to Brookside, estate of Mrs Flagler Matthews, in Rye, N.Y. New Yorker 46:29-30 My 23 '70
HORTICULTURE

Bibliography
Book reviews. See issues of Horticulture
HORTICULTURE (periodical)
Garden club yearbook contest winners (cont) Horticulture 48:49 Jl; 16+ O '70
HORTON, Frank
Privacy, security, and a free America; address, September 15, 1970. Vital Speeches 37:44-7 N 1 '70
HORTON, Lowell, and Horton, Phyllis
Instructional materials centers: an annotated bibliography. Am Lib 1:290-2 Mr '70
HORTON, Phyllis. See Horton, L. jt. auth.
HORTY, John
Consulting the computer. il por Time 95:68 My 4 '70 *
HORVATH, William J.
Parish or perish. Chr Cent 87:790 Je 24 '70
HORY, Elmyr de
What next, the Mona Lisa? il por Life 68:34-5 F 6 '70
HOSIERY
Latest looks in panty hose. il Good H 171:178 D '70
Panty hose and panty/hose combinations. il Consumer Bul 53:37-40 O '70
Pantyhose. il Consumer Rep 35:642-7 N '70
What's happening with panty hose. il Good H 170:6 Ja '70

HOSKINS, Katherine
Two poems: Sounds d'antan; Towards finistere (Eugenio Montale) Yale R 60:256 D '70
HOSKINS, William R.
How to counter expropriation. bibliog f Harvard Bsns R 48:102-12 S '70
HOSMER, Charles B. jr
Preservation history; reprint. Hobbies 75:82 Jl '70
HOSMER, Craig
Nuclear materials; address, May 25, 1970. Vital Speeches 36:635-8 Ag 1 '70
HOSODA, Syun, and others
Histamine production by transplantable argyrophilic gastric carcinoid of praomys (mastomys) natalensis. bibliog il Science 170:454-5 O 23 '70
HOSOKAWA, Bill
Expo '70: super show in Japan. il Read Digest 96:149-53 Ja '70
HOSPITAL aides. See Nurses aides
HOSPITAL and community psychiatry achievement awards. See American psychiatric association
HOSPITAL building. See Building industry
HOSPITAL care
Acute respiratory failure. P. M. Winter and E. Lowenstein; reply with rejoinder. F. J. Dyson. Sci Am 222:6+ Mr '70
Capsules replace hospital rooms. M. Villecco. il Arch Forum 132:55-7 My '70

Cost
Dose of control for health costs. Bsns W p32+ Mr 14 '70
Five patients; excerpt. M. Crichton. Ladies Home J 87:34+ Jl '70
High cost of cure: how a hospital bill grows 17 feet long; excerpt from Five patients. M. Crichton. Atlan 225:49-57 Mr '70; Discussion. 225:40+ Je; 226:38 Ag '70
Hospital that pays patients; self-care. R. C. Davids. il Farm J 94:50R Mr '70
I can afford to be sick. W. A. Nolen. il Esquire 73:118-19+ Ap '70
Medicare deductible and hospital costs will be increased in January. T. Schuchat. Har Yrs 10:4 N '70
HOSPITAL chains. See Hospitals
HOSPITAL garbage. See Rufuse and refuse disposal
HOSPITAL libraries. See Libraries, Hospital
HOSPITAL service, Cost of. See Hospital care —Cost
HOSPITAL service, State. See Medical service, State
HOSPITAL ships
Decade of Hope, legacy of health. R. L. Tobin. Sat R 53:22 Ap 4 '70
Not so ugly American; Laetare medal for Dr Walsh of Project Hope. America 122:288 Mr 21 '70
HOSPITAL supplies. See Hospitals—Equipment and supplies
HOSPITAL visiting. See Hospitals—Visitors
HOSPITALITY
   See also
Guests
HOSPITALLERS. See Malta, Knights of
HOSPITALS
   See also
Hospital ships
Nursing homes

Administration
See Hospitals—Management and regulation

Architecture
Boston city hospital. il Arch Rec 147:119-24 My '70
Building types study. il Arch Rec 148:91-104 D '70
Mental health center revisited to evaluate design effects; Marin County community mental health center. il Arch Rec 147:116-18 Mr '70
Research building programming via client-architect education; research addition to the New York psychiatric institute. il Arch Rec 147:108-9 Mr '70
System-analysis approach to hospital design; St Mark's hospital, Salt Lake City. il Arch Rec 147:112-15 Mr '70

Emergency services
Shock room; traumatic shock treatment at Houston's Ben Taub general; with report by T. Thompson. il Life 69:24-31 N 6 '70

Employees
See Hospitals—Staff

HOSPITALS—*Continued*

Equipment and supplies

Capsules replace hospital rooms. M. Villecco. il Arch Forum 132:55-7 My '70

Disposing of disposables. il Time 95:58 My 18 '70

Life-saving baby mattress. il Sci Digest 67:72-3 F '70

See also
Medical instruments and apparatus

Federal aid

Matter of survival; hospital-construction bill. Newsweek 76:31 Jl 13 '70

Finance

Food man whips up a chain of hospitals. il por Bsns W p44 My 30 '70

Making hospitals pay; chain-operated-for-profit hospitals. il Forbes 106:76+ O 15 '70

Food service

Four stars for hospital food? J. Unger. il Todays Health 49:52-4 Ja '71

Management and regulation

Dose of control for health costs. Bsns W p32+ Mr 14 '70

New blood for tired hospitals. R. G. Wasyluka. bibliog f il Harvard Bsns R 48:65-74 S '70

Nurses

See Hospitals—Staff

Regulation

See Hospitals—Management and regulation

Staff

Who's who in the hospital? V. Anderson. il Todays Health 48:64-5 O '70

See also
Collective bargaining—Hospital employees
Drug and hospital employees union (local 1199)
Hospitals, Psychiatric—Staff

Salaries, pensions, etc.

Earnings of hospital employees. J. C. Bush. il Mo Labor R 93:40-1 O '70

Visitors

I was sick and you visited me. R. E. Holman. il por Har Yrs 10:11 My '70

Volunteer workers

How teens get a head start on health careers. A. Henley. il Todays Health 48:34-5+ My '70

See also
Hospitals, Psychiatric—Volunteer workers

Gabon

Schweitzer hospital may close in 1971. Chr Cent 87:39 Ja 14 '70

St Lucia (island)

St Jude: phoenix of the jungle. E. Gladwin. il Todays Health 48:26-9+ Ag '70

Switzerland

Medical miscellany; hip operation at Wilhelm Schulthess klinik in Zürich. N. S. Hazelton. Nat R 22:845 Ag 11 '70

United States

Five patients. by M. Crichton. Review
Nation 210:725-7 Je 15 '70. M. G. Michaelson

See also
United States—Veterans administration hospitals

HOSPITALS, Childrens. See Children—Hospitals, Psychiatric

HOSPITALS, Military
See also
United States—Veterans administration hospitals

HOSPITALS, Naval and marine
Hey, hero! Vietnam amputees at the Oak Knoll naval hospital. S. Kirkpatrick. il Read Digest 97:71-5 S '70

See also
United States—Veterans administration hospitals

HOSPITALS, Psychiatric
Architecture to help drug addicts calls for speed and inventiveness; Manhattan rehabilitation center. il Arch Rec 147:160-1 Ja '70

Death at the hospital; Traverse City state hospital's campaign against Weekender's advertisers. il Time 96:23 D 28 '70

Effects of the Baltimore riots on psychiatric hospital admissions. G. D. Klee and K. Gorwitz. Ment Hy 54:447-9 Jl '70

New centers at state hospitals designed for rehabilitation, not custody; Rehabilitation center, Middletown state hospital, Middletown, N.Y. il Arch Rec 147:154-6 Ja '70

Problems and pitfalls of establishing an Operant conditioning-token economy program. J. Montgomery and R. D. McBurney. Ment Hy 54:382-7 Jl '70

Release of the chronic psychiatric patient. W. H. Clayton. bibliog Ment Hy 54:407-10 Jl '70

Struggle for patients' rights in a state hospital. L. C. Suchotliff and others. bibliog Ment Hy 54:230-40 Ap '70

Titicut follies revisited: a long range plan for the mentally disordered offender in Massachusetts. A. L. McGarry. Ment Hy 54:20-7 Ja '70

See also
Children—Hospitals, Psychiatric
Mentally ill—Care and treatment

Staff

First-year psychiatric resident and the professional identity crisis. C. M. Worby. bibliog Ment Hy 54:374-7 Jl '70

From psychiatric aide to psychologist. E. W. Williams. bibliog Ment Hy 54:430-2 Jl '70

Mental hospital employees and social action. E. M. Straight and others. Ment Hy 54:241-6 Ap '70

Mental hospital patient-consumer as a determinant of services. T. Ishiyama. Ment Hy 54:221-9 Ap '70

Psychiatric nurse, fox or hedgehog? R. G. Hirschowitz and others. bibliog Ment Hy 54:152-4 Ja '70

Small group experience with psychiatric aides. S. Bernstein and J. Herzberg. bibliog Ment Hy 54:113-17 Ja '70

Training

Stability of attitudes in psychiatric attendants following training. M. K. Distefano, jr. and M. W. Pryer. bibliog Ment Hy 54:433-5 Jl '70

Training nursing assistants for a subprofessional role. G. Krieger. bibliog Ment Hy 54:152-4 Ja '70

Volunteer workers

Catholic seminarians in a secular institution. A. S. Evans and M. F. Goldberg. bibliog Ment Hy 54:559-64 O '70

HOSSACK, Lesma
Amazing Amazonia. il Travel 133:40-5+ Je '70

HOSSMANN, K. A. and Sato, K.
Recovery of neuronal function after prolonged cerebral ischemia. bibliog il Science 168:375-6; 170:1000 Ap 17, N 27 '70

HOSTAGES
At Dawson field: life as a hostage. il Newsweek 76:23B S 21 '70

Drama on the desert: the week of the hostages. il Time 96:18-20+ S 21 '70

Hijack war; Palestinian terrorists hijack four airliners; with report by L. Jenkins. il Newsweek 76:20-8 S 21 '70

Hostage generals: a closed case, but—. il U S News 69:34 N 23 '70

HOSTELS, Youth. See Youth hostels

HOSTESSES, Air. See Airlines—Hostesses

HOSTETTER, Douglas
Need for a new Christian presence in Vietnam. Chr Cent 87:536-7 Ap 29 '70

HOSTICK, King V.
Quarterly notes concerning the Library of Congress manuscripts. Hobbies 75:140 Mr '70

HOSTILITY (psychology)
Hostility; a big expense you can avoid. M. Layden. il Nations Bsns 58:54-5 S '70

HOSTOS, Eugenio Maria de
Hostos community college. por Sch & Soc 98:143 Mr '70 *

HOT crayon painting. See Encaustic painting

HOT Dog (television program) See Television broadcasting—Childrens programs

HOT line (Washington-Peking) (proposed)
Needed: a Washington-Peking hot line. J. Gorkin. Cur 119:58-9 Je '70

HOT springs
Limits of microbial existence: temperature and pH. T. D. Brock and G. K. Darland. bibliog il Science 169:1316-18 S 25 '70

Red Sea hot brines. E. T. Degens and D. A. Ross. il Sci Am 222:32-42 Ap '70

HOT springs—*Continued*
Sulfur isotope distribution in solfataras, Yellowstone National Park. R. Schoen and R. O. Rye. bibliog il Science 170:1082-4 D 4 '70
Where are all the hot springs? il Sunset 145:48 O '70

HOT SPRINGS NATIONAL PARK
Park for people. R. B. Kasparek. il Nat Parks & Con Mag 44:12-15 Ap '70

HOT water
Handling hot water, with a payoff; beneficial uses of thermal discharge. R. Stewart and S. P. Mathur. il Cons 25:16-20 D '70

HOT-water irrigation. See Irrigation
HOT water rockets. See Rockets, Steam

HOTALING, Ed
Age of lucite dawns in Sacramento. il pors Art N 69:50-1+ My '70
Los Angeles. Art N 69:24 Mr; 8 Ap; 16B My; 62 S; 16+ O '70
Rally round the Picasso, boys! il Art N 68: 46-7+ Ja '70

HOTBEDS
Build a mini-hotbed. il Home Gard 57:52-3 Ap '70
See also
Cold frames

HOTEL Oak; drama. See Boiko, C.

HOTELLING, Carole
When toddlers act up. il Parents Mag 45:64-5+ Mr '70

HOTELS, taverns, etc.
Holiday travel handbook. See issues of Holiday
Hotel headliners. See issues of Travel
There's a not-so-small hotel. M. Gough. il House B 112:46+ F '70
World hotels: little room and big boom. il Time 95:92-3 Je 15 '70
Worldwide boom in jet-age hotels; U.S. hotels abroad. il Bsns W p32-4+ Ag 8 '70
See also
Airlines—Hotel operations
Motels
Restaurants
  also subhead Hotels, restaurants, etc. under names of cities, e.g. Paris—Hotels, restaurants, etc.

Brazil
Brazil's Senhor Jose. L. Zalamea. il por Américas 22:8-12 Mr '70

California
See Hotels, taverns, etc.—United States

Canada
Adrift in the Rockies: Baghdad comes to Jasper; Banff springs hotel and Jasper park lodge. D. Butwin. il Sat R 53:57-9 F 28 '70

Europe, Western
Chic in '71; Relais de campagne chain. G. L. Hern, jr. il Travel 135:62-7 Ja '71

Fiji
American seeks to develop Fiji market. Aviation W 93:40 D 21 '70

Great Britain
At home with the barons and earls; Country homes and castles in Great Britain. il Sat R 53:46-7 S 12 '70

Hawaii
Let's travel; Mauna Kea Beach hotel. il Mlle 70:42+ Ja '70

India
See also
Udaipur, India—Hotels, restaurants, etc.

Jamaica
Jamaica: Port Antonio, shiny places. D. Messinesi. Vogue 156:180 N 15 '70
Jamaican dining with a flair; Trident villas. M. Woodward. il Travel 135:14 Ja '71
Variety dining in Jamaica. M. Woodward. il Travel 133:77 Ja '70

Japan
Travel tips for Expo year in Japan. P. Brooks. House & Gard 137:60+ Mr '70

Puerto Rico
Cliff dwellers of Las Croabas; El Conquistador hotel and club. D. Butwin. il Sat R 53: 43-5 D 12 '70

Southern states
See Hotels, taverns, etc.—United States

Switzerland
Secret Swiss ski sites. H. P. Koenig. il Travel 134:30-3 N '70

United States
Golfing Southern style. D. Green. il Travel & Camera 33:71-3 F '70
Great homes away from home: the Ahwahnee of Yosemite National park, Calif. B. Seidler. il Am Home 73:32-3+ Jl '70
Having wonderful encounter; singles weekend at Concord hotel, Catskills. J. Klemesrud. il por N Y Times Mag p8-9+ D 20 '70
Old hotels in the Trinity area; northern California. il Sunset 145:49 S '70
See also
Wyatt corporation
  also subhead Hotels, restaurants, etc. under names of cities, e.g. New York (city)—Hotels, restaurants, etc.

Virgin Islands
What to look for in the Virgin Islands. S. Wiedel. il Travel & Camera 33:57-60 D '70

HOTTELET, Richard C.
Undemonizing the Middle East. Sat R 53:23-5+ Je 6 '70

HOUCK, Carter
New sewing machines: which one for you? il Parents Mag 45:51-4 Ag '70

HOUCK, J. R. and Harwit, Martin
Far-infrared observations of the night sky. bibliog Science 164:1271-3; 167:1277 Je 13 '69, F 27 '70

HOUCK, L. H.
Are you setting aside tax free retirement income as a freelancer? Writers Digest 50: 32-3 D '70
Taxes and the freelance writer. il Writers Digest 50:28-31 Ap '70

HOUGH, Emerson
Stories of the old West. Field & S 75:174+ Je '70

HOUGHTON, Donold E.
Failure of speech in The ox-bow incident. Engl J 59:1245-51 D '70

HOUGHTON Mifflin company
Building of the house, by E. Ballou. Review Pub W il 197:45-7 F 16 '70. J. Tebbel

HOUK, Allen R.
Banker who battled the slums. J. E. Roper. por Read Digest 97:37-8+ O '70 *

HOUK, Judith A.
Libraries involved in government. Am Lib 1:357-9 Ap '70

HOUNDS
How to start a coonhound. D. M. Duffey. il por Outdoor Life 145:158-9+ My '70

HOUNSHELL, Paul B. and West, E. L. Jr
Trends in the teaching of science. Ed Digest 35:25-8 Ap '70

L'HOURLOUPE work. See Art, Modern

HOURS before morning; story. See Polk, D.

HOURS of business. See Store hours

HOURS of labor
Changes in factory workweek as an economic indicator. H. M. Willacy. bibliog f il Mo Labor R 93:25-32 O '70
Coming: the four-day week. Nation 211:549-50 N 30 '70
Day-labor racket. America 122:459-60 My 2 '70
Four-day week. P. A. Samuelson. Newsweek 76:91 N 16 '70
Four-day week. il Newsweek 75:84 Je 15 '70
Four-day work week catches on. il Life 70:96-104 Ja 8 '71
Four days, forty hours, ed. by R. Poor. Review Bsns W p6+ N 14 70. I. Pave
Hours and earnings, private nonagricultural payrolls; tables. See issues of Monthly labor review
New popularity for four-day, forty-hour week. U S News 69:75-6 N 2 '70
Research summaries. See issues of Monthly labor review
Small business eyes the four-day workweek. K. E. Wheeler. il Harvard Bsns R 48:142-7 My '70

Shift schedules
Late-shift employment in manufacturing industries; with tables. C. M. O'Connor. bibliog Mo Labor R 93:37-42 N '70

HOUSE, J. E. Jr
Ionic bonding in solids. bibliog il por Chem 43:18-22 F '70
Substitution reactions in metal complexes. bibliog il por Chem 43:11-14 Je '70

HOUSE agencies, Advertising. See Advertising agencies

HOUSE armed services committee. See United States—Congress—House—Armed services, Committee on

HOUSE boats. See Houseboats

HOUSE building. See House construction

HOUSE building industry. See Building industry
HOUSE building materials. See Building materials
HOUSE buying
Housing picture: grim scene. Bsns W p 123-4 F 21 '70
Housing scene: buyers get a better break. Bsns W p 105 N 21 '70
It pays us to keep the old house. J. J. Dwyer. Har Yrs 10:22-3 Jl '70
Learn to spot what's wrong with a house. il Changing T 24:11-14 F '70
What home buyers are up against now. il U S News 69:22-3 Ag 3 '70
What to consider before buying a house. il Good H 171:156 Ag '70
See also
Mortgages

HOUSE cleaning
Easy ways to clean your bathroom. Redbook 134:68+ Ap '70
Housework system that really works. H. A. Dawson. il Bet Hom & Gard 48:124 My '70
How clean is clean? Bet Hom & Gard 48:20+ S '70
See also
Vacuum cleaning

HOUSE committees. See United States—Congress—House—Committees

HOUSE construction
Can we ever build cheaper houses? il Changing T 24:15-19 O '70
House building: dream or nightmare. S. Schuler. Am Home 73:40+ My '70
House grandpa built. E. W. Hammond. il Har Yrs 10:30-1 Ap '70
Our far-flung correspondents; comparison of house building expenses now with those in Thoreau's time. N. Perrin. New Yorker 46:70+ F 21 '70
Vacation home for $1200. M. Seif. il Mech Illus 66:80-3+ Je '70
We're building what we like; S. Jacob and T. Rice of Plainfield, Vt. J. H. Ingersoll. il House B 112:50-1+ Jl '70
See also
Concrete houses

HOUSE decoration
After too much moving ... cheerful rooms to live in, a private place to work. G. Steinem. il por House & Gard 138:52-5 Jl '70
And still modern; Art Deco interiors. R Reif. il N Y Times Mag p98-9+ N 8 '70
Art of mastering the mix. il House B 112:91-123 O '70
Chicago style: glass-house living at its loftiest; Lake point tower. J. L. O'Neill. il Am Home 73:48-55 +F '70
Dan Rowans: we lead an easy, entertaining life. il por House & Gard 138:48-51 Jl '70
Decorate your walls with leftover paneling. H. Wicks. il Pop Mech 133:160-1 Je '70
Decorating a shell: M. Dwork designing the interior of Long Island residence. N. Skurka. il N Y Times Mag p94-5 D 13 '70
Decorating clinic; questions and answers. See issues of American home
Decorating in the adobe mood; Santa Fe home of Mrs Lois Field. il Am Home 73:64-5 Mr '70
Decorating newsletter. See issues of American home
Decorating that doubles your space. V. D. Hahn. il Am Home 73:90-4 My '70
Decorating to order: the easy way. il Parents Mag 45:78-81 O '70
Decorating to please yourself. il House B 112:61-77 Mr '70
Designer's choice; home of D. L. Roth. N. Skurka. il N Y Times Mag p 102-3 O 11 '70
Diplomatic meeting; townhouse of ambassador to the U.N. and Mrs Mehdi Vakil of Iran. N. Skurka. il N Y Times Mag p 114:15 N 15 '70
Dream house come true; weekend retreat of Henry Glazier. L. Hammel. il N Y Times Mag p 104-5+ S 13 '70
Dune house tailor-made for children. il House & Gard 137:80-3 Je '70
Efficient home can be charming, too. R. Martens. il Farm J 93:62-3 N '69
Environment to stimulate talk and new ideas: Q. Khanh designs for his own family. il House & Gard 138:96-9 N '70
Flower-filled world. il House & Gard 137:100-5 My '70
Forty decorating ideas to make the most of your house. il House & Gard 137:55-63 Ja '70
Four houses in the sun. il House B 112:37-59 Ja '70
From Washington's houses, gardens, parties: ideas you'd love to live with. il House & Gard 138:48-57 Ag '70

Happy world of the Harry Murphys. N. C. Gray. il Am Home 73:42-5 Jl '70
How an expert decorates. S. K. Stone. il Farm J 94:70-1 Mr '70
How five rooms reflect five personalities. W. Baldwin. il House & Gard 138:104-9 O '70
How to decorate with a personal touch; symposium. House & Gard 137:40-59 F '70
How to stretch your decorating dollars. il House & Gard 137:72-87 Ap '70
Impatient decorator. E. Kinard. il House B 112:84-8 Ja '70
In and out: changing status symbols at home. House B 112:138-9 My '70
James Coburns: we live in a house of travel treasures. il pors House & Gard 138:42-7 Jl '70
Joy of beauty at home. il House & Gard 137:84-93 My '70
Joy of summer at home; Eric Mulvanys' house on Long Island. il House & Gard 137:56-61 Je '70
Leslie Uggams; interview, ed. by K. Sohigian. L. Uggams. il pors House B 112:68-9+ F '70
Life at full fling; van Zuylen house in Normandy. V. Lawford. il por Vogue 156:124-9 Ag 15 '70
Living in styles: classical. il Redbook 135:108-11+ S '70
Mica Ertegün's town house: it has just three rooms! il McCalls 97:98-9 Ap '70
Much ado about something; symposium. il House B 112:78-9+ F '70
New design: put-on or pertinent? il House B 112:76-7 F '70
19th century: alive and well. R. Reif. il N Y Times Mag p50-1 Je 21 '70
Pattern power, pattern-splashed fabrics and wallpapers. R. Reif. il N Y Times Mag p68-9 Ag 30 '70
Patterns; the house of Mr and Mrs Pierre S. du Pont IV. S. Stagg. il House & Gard 137:108-15 Mr '70
Personal approach to decorating the new open spaces. il House & Gard 138:130-41 O '70
Personal approach to entertaining: the Stephane Groueff's small barn full of ideas. il House & Gard 138:82-7 N '70
Play of light through colored glass. il Sunset 144:138 Mr '70
Playing the angles; Rhode Island cypress house. B. Plumb. il N Y Times Mag p94-5 F 15 '70
Quick-change artistry in Vermont. H. Brown. il Am Home 73:56-9 Ja '70
Room service, extension 1970: designer-decorated rooms to order. E. Frances. il Ladies Home J 87:48+ Mr '70
Rooms they love to live in:
The David K. E. Bruces. il por House & Gard 138:34-9 Ag '70
Mrs Mellon Byers. il por House & Gard 138:44-7 Ag '70
Mrs Stephenson Mahoney. il House & Gard 138:40-3 Ag '70
Scene-changing; mixing traditional and contemporary. il N Y Times Mag p86-7 O 18 '70
Seduction of color. il House & Gard 137:94-9 My '70
Strength and beauty of Santa Fe style; adobe home of Mrs Sallie Wagner. il Am Home 73:60-3 Mr '70
Summer spruce-up for $200. H. Brown. il Am Home 73:58-61 Je '70
There...stood the house; excerpts from Plant dreaming deep. M. Sarton. il por N Y Times Mag p50-1 Ag 23 '70
To ease the decorating trauma, the handholding store. House B 112:65-6 O '70
Top designers at home. il Am Home 73:68-75 S '70
Twenty-five very smart rooms. P. Rumely. il Bet Hom & Gard 48:44-57+ Ag '70
Walter Matthaus: we've given our house a country look and a country feeling. il por House & Gard 138:38-41 Jl '70
Warm-up of an unfriendly tudor. R. Fitzgerald. il House B 112:116-21 My '70
We did it; place of my own. N. Frederick. il House B 112:10+ N '70
What is environmental decorating? P. Rumely and N. Cordts. il Bet Hom & Gard 48:43-57 F '70
Why didn't I think of that? An architect's beautifully simple ideas for your home. il Redbook 134:94-6+ Ap '70
See also
Antiques
Apartments
Art in the home
Bathrooms
Bedrooms
Bookcases
Ceilings

HOUSE decoration—See also—*Continued*
Childrens rooms
Christmas decorations
Color in house decoration
Curtains and draperies
Display of antiques, art objects, etc.
Furniture, Built in
Guest rooms
Household furnishings
Kitchens
Lighting, Architectural and decorative
Living rooms
Mirrors
Mural painting and decoration
Music rooms and equipment
Painting, Industrial and practical
Period rooms
Pictures, Hanging of
Plants in house decoration
Rooms
Rugs and carpets
Shelves
Slip covers
Tapestry
Wall coverings
Window shades
HOUSE decoration, American
Hunter house: restoration showcase. V. D. Hahn. il Am Home 73:56-9 Ag '70
Living in styles: early American. il Redbook 135:94-7+ Jl '70
Nineteenth-century American rooms at the Metropolitan museum of art. M. D. Schwartz il Antiques 98:400-9 S '70
Period rooms: the sixties and seventies. J. Lipman. il Art in Am 58:126-9 N '70
Wealth of eagles; the diplomatic reception rooms in the Department of state. il Am Home 73:63-9 N '70
HOUSE decoration, Colonial and early American. See House decoration, American
HOUSE decoration, Exterior
See also
House painting
HOUSE decoration, French
Living in styles: *la vie provinciale* (country French) il Redbook 135:88-91+ O '70
HOUSE decoration, Haitian
Bonjour, M'sieu Peabody; designer's home. il por McCalls 97:88-93 Mr '70
HOUSE decoration, Tunisian
Moon house; a vacation house of ideas in Tunisia; interview. G. Berthelot. il House & Gard 137:120-3 Mr '70
HOUSE decoration, Victorian
Brooklyn restoration. L. Hammel. il N Y Times Mag p38-9 Ag 2 '70
HOUSE dust allergy. See Allergy
HOUSE ethics committee. See United States—Congress—House—Standards of official conduct, Committee on
HOUSE expansion. See Houses, Remodeled
HOUSE fires. See Fires
HOUSE fittings. See Building fittings
HOUSE flies. See Flies
HOUSE insulation. See Insulation (heat)
HOUSE internal security committee. See United States—Congress—House—Internal security, Committee on
HOUSE of David
Hairiest team of all. J. Kirshenbaum. il Sports Illus 32:104-6+ Ap 13 '70
HOUSE of leather; musical comedy. See Musical comedies, revues, etc.—Criticisms, plots, etc.
HOUSE of representatives. See United States—Congress—House
HOUSE paint. See Paint
HOUSE painting
How to spot-paint your house. il Bet Hom & Gard 48:44 S '70
Tips on painting; indoors and out. Good H 170:160 Je '70
Up-to-date story on getting your house painted. J. Hand. il Mech Illus 66:68-70+ Ag '70
What if the paint peels? Bet Hom & Gard 48:18+ Ap '70
HOUSE placement. See Building sites
HOUSE plans. See Architecture, Domestic—Designs and plans
HOUSE plants
Bulbs bring color indoors. A. J. Hebert. Horticulture 48:18-19 N '70
Festive greenery; ed. by E. Haraszty. R. E. Atkinson. il McCalls 98:21+ D '70
Gardener speaks her mind; interview. T. Cruso. House & Gard 138:24+ O '70
Gardener's guide to holiday plants. R. M. Peters. il Home Gard 57:38-44 D '70
House plants enjoy summer outdoors but under cooling bamboo. il Sunset 145:172 S '70

Houseplant how-to. H. Mason. il Bet Hom & Gard 48:54-8 N '70
How to get more mileage from house plants. G. Abraham. il Horticulture 48:30-1+ O '70
Lazy way to better houseplants. M. I. Lendle. il pors Org Gard & Farm 17:103-6 O '70
Phyllis Diller: the plant lady? E. McDonald. il pors House B 112:202-3 Ap '70
Twenty-two house plants & how to make them thrive. il Changing T 24:24-5 N '70
Unusual plants for indoor gardens. S. W. Plimpton. Horticulture 48:28 F '70
Your garden indoors. F. S. David. See issues of Home garden & flower grower
See also
African violets
Amaryllis
Artificial light gardening
Cactus
Dieffenbachias
Gloxinias
Plants, Potted
Window gardening
HOUSE prices. See Housing—Costs
HOUSE protection
See also
Burglary protection
HOUSE purchasing. See House buying
HOUSE selling
See also
House buying
Mortgages
HOUSE sparrows. See Sparrows
HOUSE-swapping vacations. See Vacations
HOUSE trailers. See Mobile homes
HOUSE walls. See Walls
HOUSEBOATS
Cruisers and houseboats '71: what's new for the new year? T. Gibbs. il Motor B 126:54-60+ O '70
Floating paradise on a bay. B. Plumb. il Am Home 73:46-7 Je '70
The 'Glades by houseboat. B. Hutchinson. il Yachting 128:64-5+ D '70
Great escape living on Portage Bay. D. Connelly. il Am Home 73:48-9+ Je '70
House boats on busy waters. il Life 69:30-3 Ag 14 '70
Houseboat on the Hudson. V. D. Hahn. il Am Home 73:62-3 Je '70
Houseboats. il Motor B 125:192-7+ Ja '70
Houseboats. D. D. Beach. il por Motor B 125:96-7 Ja '70
Mr and Mrs Jay Tunney weekend in a house afloat, decorated by Jay Steffy. il Vogue 155:250-3 My '70
Tollyhome 36. B. Crabtree. il Yachting 128:40+ D '70
We houseboated down the mighty Miss. P. Snook. il por Nat Wildlife 8:38-42 Ag '70
Women and children afloat and aground. C. Landau. il Motor B 125:104-7 Mr '70

Automobile trailer combination
Down to the sea in a tent trailer. E. H. Arctander. il Pop Sci 197:73 Ag '70
Family fun amphibians: houseboats on water, travel trailers on land. F. K. Coffee. il Mech Illus 66:46-8+ Jl '70
Micro houseboats; Sea Camper. F. M. Paulson. il Field & S 75:74-6+ Jl '70
PS tests the Seacamper, new breed of trailer/houseboat. J. Roe. il Pop Sci 196:68-9 Mr '70

Handling
Docking the houseboat. J. Martenhoff. il Yachting 127:80-1+ My '70

Leasing and renting
All aboard for adventure. E. Sotiriou. il Parents Mag 45:44-5+ Jl '70
Houseboats among the Virgins. G. F. Hammond. il Motor B 126:38-41+ D '70
Just bring the groceries. L. Lindquist. il Har Yrs 10:41-3 My '70

Testing
Thirty day live-aboard houseboat test. T. McCahill. il Mech Illus 66:106-7+ Mr '70
HOUSECLEANING. See House cleaning
HOUSEFLIES. See Flies
HOUSEHOLD accidents. See Accidents
HOUSEHOLD accounts
See also
Domestic finance
HOUSEHOLD appliances
Appliances. Bet Hom & Gard 48:6+ F '70
Exciting new products. C. Bilski. See issues of Popular mechanics

HOUSEHOLD appliances—*Continued*
Is the kitchen a thing of the past? symposium; ed. by N. Craig. il House B 112:68-71 Ja '70
Nine functionaries with award-winning form. il House B 112:77 Ag '70
Preview of 1980 appliances. il Mech Illus 66:84 Ag '70
Productivity in the major household appliance industry. J. E. Henneberger and H. F. Gale. il Mo Labor R 93:39-42 S '70
What's new for living. See issues of House & garden incorporating Living for young homemakers to April, 1970
What's really new in the new appliances. V. Habeeb. il Mech Illus 66:63-5+ D '70
  See also
Bathroom fixtures
Kitchen utensils

Care

See Household appliances—Maintenance and repair

Labels

See Labels

Maintenance and repair

How to save money on appliances and furnishings. R. O'Brien. Read Digest 97:95-7 S '70
Usually on Sunday; what to do when no repairman is available. il Sunset 144:118+ Mr '70

HOUSEHOLD appliances, Electric
Baconer, a new appliance. il Consumer Bul 53:21-2 Jl '70
Big appliances on a small scale. il Redbook 135:100-1+ My '70
Blenders. il Consumer Rep 35:9-14 Ja '70
Broiler that solves some storage problems. il Consumer Rep 35:134-5 Mr '70
Egg cookers; most makes dangerous. il Consumer Bul 54:25 Ja '71
Electric mixers. il Consumer Bul 53:7-14 S '70
[Electric ranges, broilers, coffeemakers, etc] Consumer Rep 34:93-113 D '69
Electric rotisserie broilers. il Consumer Bul 53:17-22 Ap '70
Good electric vertical broiler: Presto vertical broiler. il Consumer Bul 53:4 My '70
Magnetic stirrer. il Mech Illus 66:102-3+ Ap '70
Major appliances, when should you trade? Bet Hom & Gard 48:110-11 O '70
Portable food mixers. il Consumer Rep 35:164-9 Mr '70
Readers sound off about home appliances. il Changing T 24:19-20 Ja '70
Shopping for appliances. C. Klamkin. Nation 212:81-3 Ja 18 '71
Small wonders. M. Davidson. il Ladies Home J 87:42+ Ap '70
This broiler sizzled less, but fizzled: Presto vertical broiler. il Consumer Rep 35:6-7 Ja '70
Trouble shooting electric can openers. R. Graf. il Mech Illus 66:86-7+ S '70
Workhorse in the kitchen, the everready blender. il House B 112:34 D '70
  See also
Whirlpool corporation
  also names of appliances, e.g. Electric toasters

Maintenance and repair

From home base. M. K. Spencer. Am Home 74:24 Ja '71
Home appliance electronics. J. Darr. il Radio-Electr 41:26 D '70
Who pays the bill when your appliance breaks down? M. Spencer. Am Home 73:42+ Mr '70
HOUSEHOLD budget. See Budget, Household
HOUSEHOLD cleaning preparations. See Cleaning compositions
HOUSEHOLD employees
Do whites make the best domestics? il Esquire 74:157-9 O '70
J'etais jeune fille au pair a Paris (I was a mother's helper in Paris) S. Solberg. il Seventeen 29:144-5+ F '70
Mobile maids; employment agencies capitalize on Los Angeles's poor public-transportation system. Newsweek 75:54 F 9 '70
  See also
Visiting housekeepers
HOUSEHOLD expenses. See Domestic finance
HOUSEHOLD finance corporation
More than meets the eye. il Forbes 105:39 F 15 '70
HOUSEHOLD furnishings
Blondes & silvers. il House & Gard 137:78-85 F '70

Cool living. il Vogue 155:116-25 Mr 14 '70
D is for durable; mini-chateau in a Chicago suburb. R. Reif. il N Y Times Mag p82-3 Mr 22 '70
Decorating newsletter. See issues of American home
Decorating zest. il House & Gard 138:116-25 O '70
Decorating zest, white and white with color. il House & Gard 137:108-9 Ap '70
Factory for living in; Christophe de Menil Thurman's New York house. P. Devlin. il por Vogue 155:194-7+ Mr 1 '70
For bath, bedroom and you. il House & Gard 137:142-5 My '70
Ideas and things with decorating zest. il House & Gard 137:84-7 Ja '70
Indian influence in city decorating; furnishing apartments in New Mexico. H. Brown. il Am Home 73:70-1+ Mr '70
Man-made environment; Manhattan penthouse. B. Plumb. il N Y Times Mag p52-3 Ja 18 '70
Metals. il House B 112:140-5 My '70
New Mexican gadfly: John Conron; owner of Santa Fe store Centerline, inc. V. D. Hahn. il Am Home 73:33 Mr '70
No century gap here; Manhattan apartment. R. Reif. il N Y Times Mag p 104-5 Ap 5 '70
Objects you love. W. Baldwin. House & Gard 137:12-13+ My '70
On and off the avenue; Hector Guimard exhibition at the Museum of modern art. J. Malcolm. New Yorker 46:89-92 My 2 '70
On and off the avenue; new Knoll international showroom, D/R international stores. J. Malcolm. New Yorker 46:147-8+ N 7 '70
One stitch led to another; crewelwork designs in an eighteenth-century Connecticut farmhouse. R. Reif. il N Y Times Mag p66-7 Mr 1 '70
Past and present; North Carolina, 18th century-style house. R. Reif. il N Y Times Mag p74-5 My 10 '70
Ready-to-use decorating. il House & Gard 138:64-71 Ag '70
Setting up the second home. S. Lindsay. il House B 112:62-5 Ag '70
Space-age Moorish; the Spanish finca of Ambassador and Mme Hector de Ayala. il pors Vogue 155:198-201 Ap 1 '70
Stowaways; packable, totable, stackable. il Am Home 73:32+ Ja '70
Summer zest; ideas and things to bring the look of summer indoors. il House & Gard 137:62-3 Je '70
Summer zest; natural beauty for parties indoors and out. il House & Gard 137:68-9 Je '70
What the young want to live with. M. Gough. House B 112:48-9+ Jl '70
What's new for living. See issues of House & garden incorporating Living for young homemakers to April, 1970
Your own zone. il Seventeen 29:172-5 Ap '70
  See also
Christmas gifts for the home
Color in house decoration

Exhibitions

Forward! New York Lamp and home furnishings show. New Yorker 45:23-4 Ja 24 '70

History

Eighteenth-century English and American furnishing fashions; excerpts from Printed textiles, English and American cotton and linens, 1700-1850. F. M. Montgomery. il Antiques 97:267-71 F '70
HOUSEHOLD furnishings, Moving of. See Moving
HOUSEHOLD furnishings industry and trade
Home $weet home. il Forbes 106:24-6+ N 15 '70
  See also
Simmons company
HOUSEHOLD linen, Durable press. See Linen, Household
HOUSEHOLD mechanics. See Mechanics, Household
HOUSEHOLD pest control
How to kill household insects like a pro. A. Markovich. il Mech Illus 66:90-2+ Ag '70
HOUSEHOLD purchasing. See Purchasing, Household
HOUSEKEEPERS, Visiting. See Visiting housekeepers
HOUSEKEEPING. See Home economics
HOUSER, John Sherrill
World; an artist's palette. il Am Artist 34:28-34+ Ag '70

HOUSES
See also
Architecture, Domestic
Beach architecture
Cabins
Concrete houses
Farmhouses
Glass houses
Guest houses
Home ownership
Vacation houses

Air conditioning
See Air conditioning

Leasing and renting
It pays us to keep the old house. J. J. Dwyer. Har Yrs 10:22-3 Jl '70

Maintenance and repair
God bless our shimmed-up home. J. Mills. Read Digest 97:59-62 N '70
Help about the house; questions and answers. Am Home 73:110 Ap; 144-5 My; 85-6 Je; 86 Jl '70
Homeowners' clinic; questions and answers. W. C. Lammey. See issues of Popular mechanics
Horrors of home repair; unskilled and inaccessible craftsmen. W. A. McWhirter. il Life 68:58-60+ Je 5 '70
How to get your money's worth on home improvements. il Good H 171:168-9 N '70
How to repair clapboard siding. il Bet Hom & Gard 48:10 S '70
How to save on home-maintenance costs. il Good H 170:140 Ja '70
New ways to get money for home improvements. R. Day. il Mech Illus 66:100-1+ N '70
Seven ways to prepare your house for winter. R. Day. il Mech Illus 66:95-7 O '70
Three good home-repair tips. il Pop Sci 197:127 O '70
Twelve money-saving tips on maintaining your home. R. O'Brien. Read Digest 96:189-90+ Je '70
Twenty great home fix-up ideas. il Mech Illus 66:83-93 F '70
See also
Mechanics, Household

Prices
See Housing—Costs

HOUSES, Air conditioned. See Air conditioning

HOUSES, Dampness in. See Dampness in buildings

HOUSES, Fabricated. See Houses, Prefabricated

HOUSES, Modular. See Houses, Prefabricated

HOUSES, Paperboard
People who live in paper houses. il Sci Digest 67:39-41 Je '70

HOUSES, Photography of. See Photography of buildings and structures

HOUSES, Prefabricated
Aluminum house. il Mech Illus 66:12+ My '70
... And how it grew. M. C. Huntoon, jr. il Am Home 73:58-9+ Ap '70
Factory-built houses will cost less, give you more. J. Hand. il Pop Sci 196:52-5+ Je '70
First aerospace-developed housing built. il Aviation W 93:64-5 D 7 '70
Homes from production lines. il U S News 68:74-5 Mr 23 '70
Modular exhibition of house at the Whitney museum. New Yorker 46:27-8 O 3 '70
New ideas for breaking the house logjam. il U S News 69:72-4 N 23 '70
One-a-day factory-built for $13,500. M. Spires. il Am Home 73:60-3 Ap '70
People who live in paper houses. il Sci Digest 67:39-41 Je '70
Retreat in the trees, ready in two weeks. il House B 112:74-9 S '70
Self-help and beyond; modular housing system. B. Thorne. il Arch Forum 132:52-3 Mr '70
This is prefab? il Bet Hom & Gard 48:38-9 Ja '70
Well-built house; aluminum-skinned design of Philip Brookshire. J. H. Ingersoll. il House B 112:26+ S '70
Where housing will break new ground; Breakthrough competition. il Bsns W p32+ Mr 7 '70
See also
Apartment houses, Prefabricated
Mobile homes
Vacation houses

Transportation
Prebuilt homes come a long way. il Bsns W p27 Jl 18 '70

HOUSES, Remodeled
Architects speak their minds: four architects talk about remodeling. il House & Gard 137:20+ My '70
Art in an old red barn. il House & Gard 137:84-5 Je '70
Articulate house: from boys school to post office to a personal expression. il House B 112:41-4 Ag '70
Barn reborn. il House & Gard 137:124-9 Mr '70
Basic basement beautification. L. Netti. il Mech Illus 66:62-5+ Mr '70
Brainstorming a barn. il N Y Times Mag p94-5+ Ap 26 '70
By the Aegean, the new and the old: an artist splashes color into a white house on ancient Patmos. E. Sverbeyeff. il House B 112:53-9 Ja '70
Congenital builder's itch. M. Davenport. House & Gard 137:56+ My '70
Expert help to remodel your home. il Farm J 93:61-3 N '69
Four home additions you can build; deck covered entry, carport, and fence. il Pop Sci 197:103 S '70
Four ways to build beautiful new rooms. il House & Gard 137:106-13 My '70
Fronting! five examples. S. Mead and J. Pinkham. il Bet Hom & Gard 48:50-9 S '70
Getaway house by an old millstream; a remodeled gristmill. il House & Gard 137:70-3 Je '70
House just for you. V. Jaxon. il Har Yrs 10:14-16 Ag '70
House that owes its life to its setting. S. G. Lewin. il House B 112:48-51 Ag '70
House that time built; library wing of a mansion in the Bronx, converted. B. Plumb. il N Y Times Mag p52-3 F 1 '70
Houston Moorish: 1900s. B. Plumb. il Am Home 73:80-1 My '70
How to slash your remodeling bills. A. J. Maher. Am Home 73:46+ O '70
In Dublin, a two-for-one spectacular: home of architect Sam Stephenson. il House B 112:104-8 My '70
Inside story; Victorian house on Long Island. il N Y Times Mag p32-3 Ja 3 '71
Lively living in a sanctuary; former religious community house near Taos now owned by Lawrence P. Frank family. V. D. Hahn. il Am Home 73:56-9 Mr '70
Memphis Main st: 1910. il Am Home 73:82-5 My '70
Mill of their dreams; eighteenth-century stone mill as a home. B. Plumb. il N Y Times Mag p74-5 F 8 '70
Old Victorian house in San Francisco begins its second life. il Sunset 144:78-9 F '70
Porch to family room for under $900. H. Wicks. il Pop Mech 134:156-9+ S '70
Raising the roof; space gained by pushing roofs up and out. il Sunset 145:96-100+ N '70
Rebirth in the Southwest: an architect and his wife rescue an old adobe. J. De Long. il House B 112:43-9 Ja '70
Rewards of rejecting the obvious. il House B 112:128-9 My '70
Room stretchers! six mini additions you can build yourself. N. Seney. il Bet Hom & Gard 48:50-3 N '70
Successful face lift; three case histories. il Sunset 144:102-4 F '70
Surprising Victorian; renovated townhouse in Brooklyn. il Arch Forum 133:36-9 S '70
They bought a builder's house, then remodeled while it was still new. il Sunset 145:80-1 O '70
Thinking of remodeling the house? il Changing T 24:24-8 S '70
This addition still looks new after ten years. S. K. Stone. il Farm J 94:76-7 Ap '70
Two houses that work as one; 1967 wraparound addition to Allen McNowns' 1850 adobe at Nambe, N.Mex. il Am Home 73:66-9+ Mr '70
Ugly duckling in Portland is done over inside and out. il Sunset 144:80-1 F '70
Very personal garden and house of Mrs Quaintance Mason. il House & Gard 138:90-5 N '70
Victorian for moderns: Brooklyn brownstone. B. Plumb. il N Y Times Mag p 104-5 Mr 15 '70
We did it; two houses into one. R. Kelly and G. Kelly. il House B 112:32+ Je '70
Where the best of yesterday and today meet: East Hampton, N.Y. il House B 112:101-3 My '70
White magic. il House & Gard 137:94-103 Ap '70
Why a major addition could be your only way to have a new house this year. il Bet Hom & Gard 48:49-75 My '70

HOUSES, Remodeled—*Continued*
Yankee barn with a Gallic accent. R. Reif.
il N Y Times Mag p46-7 Ag 9 '70
Yankee original; Irish imprint; remodeling
of Connecticut barn. il House B 112:80-3
Ja '70
See also
Houses, Restored

Anecdotes, facetiae, satire, etc.
Rob and Barbi go brownstoning. T. Meehan.
il N Y Times Mag p32-3+ N 22 '70; Reply.
P. Wilkes and J. Wilkes. p 144 D 6 '70

HOUSES, Restored
Newport; an American treasury; by V. D.
Hahn and B. Plumb. il Am Home 73:39-59
Ag '70
Young approach to restoration; Moravian
home in Old Salem, Winston-Salem, N.C.
R. Reif. il N Y Times Mag p76-7 Ap 19
'70

HOUSES, Seashore. See Beach architecture
HOUSES in art. See Art—Themes
HOUSEWIVES
Woman thing. N. Gittelson. Harp Baz 104:
16+ N '70
See also
Mothers
HOUSEWORK. See Home economics
HOUSING
See also
Aged—Housing
College students—Housing
Discrimination in housing
Slums

Costs
Buy or rent? R. W. Murray, jr. Todays Ed
59:46-8 D '70
Can we ever build cheaper houses? il Chang-
ing T 24:15-19 O '70
House grandpa built. E. W. Hammond. il Har
Yrs 10:30-1 Ap '70
House hunting? Costs you face, city by city.
il U S News 68:81-2 My 18 '70
Housing: the industry that hits you where
you live. il Sr Schol 97:7 O 5 '70
Labor costs and the rise in housing prices.
N. Goldfinger. il Mo Labor R 93:60-1 My '70
Maybe you can afford a second home. R. Day.
il Mech Illus 66:50-2+ Ap '70
Mobile home vs. a house: how the costs com-
pare. il Changing T 25:19-21 Ja '71
Operation Breakthrough; building types study;
with introd. by R. Jensen. il Arch Rec 147:
137-52 Ap '70
Trends in homeownership and rental costs.
R. C. Joiner. il Mo Labor R 93:26-31
Jl '70
What home buyers will face next year. il
U S News 69:59-61 N 9 '70
See also
Vacation houses—Costs

Desegregation
Battle to open the suburbs: new attack on
zoning laws. il U S News 68:39-40 Je 22 '70
Furor over a drive to integrate the suburbs.
il U S News 69:23-4 Ag 10 '70
Man on the spot in housing dispute. por
U S News 69:25 Ag 10 '70
Pressure builds for open housing. il Bsns W
p61 Jl 11 '70
See also
Sponsors of open housing investment

Federal aid
Belated help. il Time 95:61-2 Mr 9 '70
Coming: federal aid in housing for 24 mil-
lion. il U S News 68:74-6 Je 15 '70
Cooling words on a hot issue. Fortune 82:68 O
'70
Ecstasy in Rockford; public-housing experi-
ment aids poor to buy own houses. il News-
week 76:61 N 30 '70
Housing wins big partners. Bsns W p83 F 14
'70
How goes the new federalism? subsidy and
the Curtis amendment. Nat R 22:1148 N 3
'70
How Washington is helping more people buy
homes. il U S News 69:50-2 O 26 '70
Living room: Senate and House bills. New
Repub 163:8 D 19 '70
More help for the poor; 1970 housing bill. il
Time 95:96 Je 15 '70
Pilot project to build 529 apartments; Na-
tional corporation for housing partnerships.
U S News 69:52 O 26 '70
President on construction: hopeful ideas,
hard questions. W. F. Wagner, jr. Arch Rec
147:9-10 My '70
Pumping money into housing. il Bsns W
p66-7 S 26 '70

Subsidized fraud. il Time 97:70-1 Ja 18 '71

Finance
See Housing finance

Netherlands
Profiles. A. Bailey. New Yorker 46:34-40+ Ag
8 '70
Russia
Elbowroom. il Newsweek 76:39+ S 7 '70

United States
Belated help. il Time 95:61-2 Mr 9 '70
Fair market value. S. B. Moser. il pors Am
For 76:20-3+ Ja '70
Great housing crisis. il Newsweek 75:69+
Je 22 '70
Housing: from crisis to disaster? J. Peter.
il Look 34:53-9 F 10 '70
Housing: the swing back to ticky-tacky. il
Time 96:56-7 Ag 17 '70
Housing: this time architects can't just boo
from the stands. W. F. Wagner, jr. Arch
Rec 148:9-10 S '70
Housing: too little, too expensive. R. Diet-
sch. New Repub 162:9-11 Ap 4 '70
Marshaling props for new housing. il Bsns W
p34 F 28 '70
National housing policy; inflation must be
ended; address, January 19, 1970. G. Rom-
ney. Vital Speeches 36:309-12 Mr 1 '70
New government and industry partnership
for building more housing. D. Pellish. il
Arch Forum 133:58-61 Jl '70
New model in housing; interview, ed. by G.
R. Rosen. H. Finger. por Duns 95:10-11+
Je '70
New ideas for breaking the housing logjam.
il U S News 69:72-4 N 23 '70
New mythology of housing. A. M. Stegman.
il Trans-Action 7:55-62 Ja '70; Reply. R. J.
Margolis. 7:10-11 Je '70
Operation Breakthrough; building types study;
with introd. by R. Jensen. il Arch Rec 147:
137-52 Ap '70
U.S. priorities: housing is the number one;
comments by members of Dun's presidents'
panel, ed. by G. R. Rosen. il Duns 96:47+
O '70
Urban housing and transportation: a new
partnership. W. Owen. bibliog f Cur Hist
59:290-5+ N '70
When landlords walk away. il Time 95:88+
Mr 16 '70
See also
Building industry
Housing, Experimental
Housing—Federal aid
Housing projects
Negroes—Housing
United States—Housing and urban develop-
ment, Department of
also subhead Housing under names
of cities, e.g. Boston—Housing
HOUSING, Discrimination in. See Discrimina-
tion in housing
HOUSING, Experimental
Where housing will break new ground;
Breakthrough competition. il Bsns W p32+
Mr 7 '70
HOUSING and development administration. See
New York (city)—Housing and develop-
ment administration
**HOUSING and urban development, Department
of.** See United States—Housing and urban
development, Department of
HOUSING construction. See Building industry
HOUSING development incinerators. See Ref-
use incinerators
HOUSING finance
And now it's housing's turn. il Fortune 81:
18+ Ap '70
Bumping the cost ceiling; upturn in housing.
il Fortune 82:20+ O '70
Great housing crisis. il Newsweek 75:69+ Je
22 '70
Home financing; old approach to mortgages
has to change, here are five new plans.. Bet
Hom & Gard 48:30+ Ag '70
Housing: from crisis to disaster? J. Peter. il
Look 34:53-9 F 10 '70
Housing: the swing back to ticky-tacky. il
Time 96:56-7 Ag 17 '70
Money squeeze on homes. il Newsweek 75:
59 F 2 '70
New ways to get money for home improve-
ments. R. Day. il Mech Illus 66:100-1+ N
'70
Noose tightens on housing. il Bsns W p32
Ja 17 '70
Try negative cash. E. H. Palmer. Am City
85:46 S '70
See also
Connecticut housing investment fund
Federal national mortgage association
Mortgages
United States—Federal home loan bank board

HOUSING laws and legislation
Subsidized housing in foreign countries. il
U S News 68:76 Je 15 '70

United States
See also
Housing—Federal aid

HOUSING projects
Breakthrough? M. Villecco and J. M. Dixon.
Arch Forum 132:50-1 Ap '70
It's not just the cities. A. Mayer. il Arch Rec
148:101-6 Jl '70
Omnibuildings. W. Karp. il Horizon 12:48-
55 Wint '70
Pablum in paradise: California's instant com-
munities. R. Gustaitis. il Am Home 73:80-5
Jl '70
See also
Apartment houses

Site planning
Alternates to suburban sprawl: new processes,
new involvement. W. F. Wagner, jr. Arch
Rec 148:9-10 N '70
Breakthrough sites and site planners. Arch
Rec 147:151 Ap '70
Marines square apartments, Newport Beach,
Calif. il Arch Rec 147:94-5 mid-My '70
Revolution in suburbia? trend toward town
houses and garden apartments. il Forbes
105:24-6+ Ap 1 '70
Snowmass villas, Snowmass at Aspen, Colo.
il Arch Rec 147:96-7 mid-My '70
Westbeth's rehabilitation project: a clue to
improving our cities; with statement by
R. Meier. il Arch Rec 147:103-6 Mr '70

HOUSING projects, Government
Pruitt-Igoe, RIP; St Louis slum. Nat R 22,
1335-6 D 15 '70
Vertical ghetto: Cabrini-Green, Chicago. il
Newsweek 76:76 S 7 '70
See also
New York (state)—Urban development cor-
poration

HOUSING subsidies. See Housing—Federal aid

HOUSLEY, John B.
Ethics and the art of the possible in inter-
American relations. il Chr Cent 87:1283-
5 O 28 '70

HOUSTON, James
Artists of the frozen North. T. Holloway. il
por Design 72:4-8 Wint '70 *

HOUSTON, Jean
Mysticism in the laboratory. il por Time
96:72+ O 5 '70 *

HOUSTON, Walter Scott
Deep-sky wonders. See issues of Sky and
telescope

HOUSTON, Tex.

Airports
Airports that bring the planes to the people.
il Bsns W p98-100 F 14 '70
Bypassed airline hub flourishing; Hobby airport. Z. Strickland. Aviation W 93:59-61 N
9 '70

City planning
Houston: boom in the heart of Texas. il Bsns
W p86+ My 23 '70
Houston seeks the refugees. il Time 95:71
Je 8 '70
Texas-size Houston. il Newsweek 76:52 N 9
'70

Galleries and museums
See also
Houston museum of fine arts

Hospitals
Shock room; traumatic shock treatment; with
report by T. Thompson. il Life 69:24-31 N 6
'70
Texas tornado vs. Dr Wonderful. T. Thompson. il pors Life 68:62B-62D+ Ap 10 '70

Industries
Shell's $25-million trip to Houston. il Bsns
W p68+ S 19 '70

Music
See also
Houston symphony orchestra

Negroes
U.S. journal: thirty year sentence to L. O.
Johnson for giving away one marijuana
cigarette. C. Trillin. New Yorker 46:164+
D 12 '70

Police
Pigs 24, freaks 5; softball game between
hippies and police. il Time 96:22 O 5 '70

Sanitary affairs
Test stainless-steel tubing for aeration pipes.
il Am City 85:46 O '70

Stores
Showdown at Post Oak; Sakowitz vs. Neiman-Marcus. il Bsns W p 124-5 F 28 '70

Streets
How do you drain flat land? il Am City 85:
20 Ag '70

HOUSTON ballet company. See Ballet com-
panies

HOUSTON foundation ballet. See Ballet com-
panies

HOUSTON grand opera association
Report:
Douglas Moore's Ballad of Baby Doe. A.
Holmes. il Opera N 34:30-1 Ap 11 '70
Fidelio. A. Holmes. Opera N 35:29 D 5 '70
Paul and Martha Boesing's Wanderer. A.
Holmes. Opera N 35:22-3 O 10 '70
Report: production of Rigoletto. A. Holmes.
Opera N 34:33 Ja 31 '70
Report: productions of Mascagni's Cavalleria
rusticana and Puccini's Gianni Schicchi. A.
Holmes. Opera N 34:32 F 28 '70

HOUSTON museum of fine arts
Empire style at Bayou bend: new period
rooms in Houston. D. B. Warren. il Antiques 97:122-7 Ja '70

HOUSTON natural gas corporation
We know where we're going. il Forbes
106:38 O 1 '70

HOUSTON Oilers (football club) See Football
clubs

HOUSTON ship channel
Dangerous route to Houston. il Bsns W p26
My 9 '70

HOUSTON space center. See United States—
Manned spacecraft center

HOUSTON symphony orchestra
Uproar: Previn and afterwards. G. Cunningham. Hi Fi 20:secII 25+ Ap '70

HOUTHAKKER, Hendrik Samuel
What goes down must go up, first? por
Forbes 105:36 Mr 1 '70 *

HOVEY, William B.
High pressure snowmaking. il Weatherwise
23:224-7 O '70

HOVHANESS, Alan
Sing, cetacea, sing! performance of And
God created great whales. Time 95:59+
Je 22 '70 *

HOVING, Thomas Pearsall Field
Faces and places, paintings from the Met. il
Art in Am 58:62-5 Mr '70

HOW I met Joseph Mulligan, jr; story. See
Morris, W.

HOW men and women came to live together;
story. See Kitereza, A.

HOW to tell corn fairies if you see 'em; story.
See Sandburg, C.

HOWALD, Ferdinand, collection. See Art—Pri-
vate collections

HOWARD, Alvin W.
Subversion of the school assembly. Clear
House 44:401-3 Mr '70
—and Phillips, William
Junior high schools: results of a four-state
survey. il Clear House 45:120-4 O '70

HOWARD, Anthony
[Report from Britain] (title varies) New
Repub 162:8-9 Ja 24; 12-13 My 30; 163:16 Jl
4; 7-8 Ag 15; 7-8 O 17; 8-9 D 19 '70

HOWARD, Benn
Benn Howard and Elle Johnson: a dance
partnership; interview, ed. by V. H. Swisher.
il pors Dance Mag 4:31-3 Ja '70

HOWARD, Carl
Instant power. il Pop Sci 196:76-7 Ap '70

HOWARD, David L. and others
Biological nitrogen fixation in Lake Erie.
bibliog il Science 169:61-2 Jl 3 '70

HOWARD, David M.
Rise and fall of SVM. Chr Today 15:15-17 N
6 '70

HOWARD, Edward N.
Orbital organization. il por Library J 95:
1712-15 My 1 '70

HOWARD, Elizabeth Jane
Fraud in bed; with excerpt from Something
in disguise. Vogue 156:98-9 S 15 '70

HOWARD, Harriet K.
Face of a child. Todays Ed 59:81-2 O '70

HOWARD, Harry N.
United Nations in the Middle East. bibliog f
Cur Hist 60:7-12+ Ja '71

HOWARD, Jane
Encounter groups: emotional striptease for
women? excerpts from Please touch. Vogue
155:110-11+ Je '70
Free schools. il Life 70:45-6+ Ja 8 '71
Mr Bellow considers his planet. il pors Life
68:57-8+ Ap 3 '70
Springfield. il Life 69:28-9 O 2 '70

HOWARD, Jane—*Continued*
You don't have a body; you are your body;
excerpt from Please touch. Mlle 71:153+
My '70
HOWARD, Jewel L.
Classroom teachers of Dallas. Todays Ed 59:
41 D '70
HOWARD, John Addison
Innovation mirage; address, September 9,
1970. Vital Speeches 36:743-6 O 1 '70
HOWARD, John Arnold
Don't sell the buyer short; interview. por
Nations Bsns 58:34-5 Ag '70

about
New theory on why people buy. il por Bsns
W p70 Ja 24 '70
HOWARD, Keith A. See Simkin, T. jt. auth.
HOWARD, Richard
Chalk cliffs of Rügen; poem. il Harper 241:
102-3 N '70
From Beyoglu; poem. New Yorker 46:30-1
My 30 '70
Giovanni da Fiesole on the sublime, or Fra
Angelico's Last judgement; poem. Poetry
117:1-2 O '70
Graves yawns. Poetry 116:107-10 My '70
Poetry of darkness. Nation 211:634-5 D 14 '70
Sortes Vergilianae. Poetry 117:50-3 O '70
Tate's essays. Poetry 116:43-5 Ap '70
(tr) See Chazal, M. de. Sens-plastique

about
Authors & editors. A. Johnston. por Pub W
197:27-9 Je 1 '70 *
HOWARD, Steven J.
How to fix those newfangled faucets. il Pop
Mech 134:189-92 N '70
Take the sweat out of condensation prob-
lems. il Pop Mech 134:164-6 Ag '70
Well-oiled home runs smoother. il Pop Mech
134:172-4 Jl '70
What you should know about garbage dis-
posers before you buy one. il Pop Mech 133:
156-9 My '70
HOWARD, Thomas
What about unwed mothers? Chr Today 14:
11-12 Mr 13 '70
What not to tell your child about religion.
il Redbook 135:67+ Je '70
HOWE, Charles
Prevalence of bombing. Nation 210:361-3 Mr
30 '70
HOWE, Fanny
Being loved is secondary to loving. Mlle 72:
76-7+ D '70
Framed; poem. Mlle 71:116 S '70
Fresh pond; poem. Atlan 226:89 S '70
HOWE, Florence. See Lauter, P. jt. auth.
HOWE, Harold, 2d
Howe now Ford foundation executive. Sch &
Soc 98:340 O '70 *
HOWE, Irving
Books. See issues of Harper's magazine
New course for the new left; excerpt from
Beyond the new left. Sat R 53:8-11 My 30
'70
Political terrorism: hysteria on the left. il
N Y Times Mag p25-7+ Ap 12; 22+ My 10
'70
HOWE, John W. Jr
Prep-school ministry. Chr Today 14:9-10 F 27
'70
HOWE, Marvine
Fado in Portugal. il Sat R 53:49+ S 12 '70
HOWE, Reuel L.
Training for a time of change. Chr Cent 87:
477-80 Ap 22 '70
HOWE, Russell Warren
Gambia. Travel 134:62-3 Ag '70
One nation, divisible. New Repub 162:15-17
F 7 '70
Taming of the Congo. New Repub 163:15-16
Ag 1 '70
HOWE, Samuel Gridley
First miracle worker. L. Lader. il Todays
Health 48:42-3+ S '70 *
HOWELL, Martin
Our uptight troops in Europe. L. Gross. il
pors Look 34:16-19 S 8 '70 *
HOWELL, Milton M.
Hawaii's doctor of the year. A Rosenthal. il
pors Todays Health 48:56-9 Mr '70 *
HOWELL, Robert A.
Plan to integrate your acquisitions. il Har-
vard Bsns R 48:66-76 N '70
HOWELLS, W. W.
Recent physical anthropology. bibliog f Ann
Am Acad 389:116-26 My '70
HOWERING, Robert
Air tubular trimmer capacitors. por Electr
World 83:52-3 Ap '70

HOWES, Barbara
Letter from Little Tobago: poem. New Yorker
46:42 Mr 14 '70
HOWES, Connie B.
Job travel isn't glamorous for him, or her.
il Todays Health 48:27-9+ S '70
Ski survival for beginners. il Todays Health
49:35-7 Ja '71
HOWES, Helen Claire
Gingerbread mansion. il Design 71:19 mid-
Sum '70
HOWES, Robert G.
Future by design? address, March 17, 1970.
Cath World 211:221-5 Ag '70
HOWES, Virgil
Trouble with Johnny. por Library J 95:1902-3
My 15 '70
HOWIE, Virginia
All about lilies. il Home Gard 57:20-7 Ag '70
HOWLAND, Clare
Diet 1970: how to lose pounds and find your-
self. E. Frances. pors Ladies Home J 87:
57+ Ja '70
HOWLAND, Elton, family
New heart for Becky Howland. A. Lake. il
Good H 170:56-7+ Ja '70
HOWLETT, Barbara W.
Caring for a sick-a-bed child. il Parents Mag
45:88-90+ N '70
HOWLETT, Duncan
You, too, can have a forest. il Am For 76:
76:20-3+ Ag '70
HOWLETT, William Porter
Rehash at Consolidated. pors Newsweek 75:
64+ Ja 26 '70
HOWSE, Derek
Restoration at Greenwich observatory. il Sky
& Tel 40:4-9 Jl '70
HOXHA, Enver
Albania: the first few breezes of change.
A. Tillier. il por Newsweek 76:47-8 S 7 '70 *
HOY, Ronald R. See Bentley, D. R. jt. auth.
HOYDAL, Karsten
White night; Stones; poems, tr. by G. John-
ston. Poetry 116:333-4 Ag '70
HOYER, Linda Grace
Woman's house; story; excerpt from En-
chantment. McCalls 98:91-2 Ja '71
HOYLE, Graham
How is muscle turned on and off? with
biographical sketch. il Sci Am 222:12, 84-
93 bibliog(p130) Ap '70
HOYT, Robert G.
Israel and the Fedayeen: an exchange of
letters. Cath World 211:32-3 Ap '70
HOYT, William R.
Zen Buddhism and western alienation from
nature. Chr Cent 87:1194-6 O 7 '70
HRESHCHYSHYN, Myroslaw M.
Expectant mother; ed. by E. Edelson. Red-
book 135:38+ O '70
HROMÁDKA, Josef Luki
Hromádka as pilgrim. Chr Cent 87:36 Ja 14 '70
Josef Hromadka. Chr Today 14:21-2 Ja 30
'70
HRUSKA, Roman Lee
Excerpt from Senate debate, March 11, 1970.
Cong Digest 49:139+ My '70
HSIAO, Theodore C. and others
Maize leaf elongation: continuous measure-
ments and close dependence on plant water
status. bibliog il Science 168:590-1 My 1 '70
HUANG, Po Fei
Two poems: Tourist's soliloquy; Summer
solstice. Yale R 60:254 D '70
HUANG, Yung-sheng
Army's man. por Time 96:26 Ag 24 '70 *
HUANTES, Margarita
San Antonio's fight against illiteracy. D.
Wright. il Am Ed 6:20-1 N '70 *
HUAYLAS, Callejón de
Town that was, until May 31, 1970. il Amér-
icas 22:16-20 S '70
HUBBARD, Alice Harvey
Instant landscaping, can it be done? il Home
Gard 57:58-60 F '70
HUBBARD, Clarence T.
Connecticut revives the chestnut. il Am For
76:26-8 D '70
HUBBARD, David Graham
Profile of a skyjacker. il por Newsweek 76:
69 Ag 24 '70 *
HUBBARD, Norman J. See Gast, P. W. jt.
auth.
HUBBARD medal
First moon explorers receive the society's
Hubbard medal. il Nat Geog 137:858-61 Je
'70
HUBBELL, John G.
Exploring a new path to a better America.
Read Digest 97:131-4 O '70
Grechko: master of the Soviet military colos-
sus. por Read Digest 97:98-103 O '70

HUBBELL, John G.—*Continued*
President Nixon, Cambodia and new chances for peace. il Read Digest 97:54-63 Jl '70
Sentinel of the Pacific. il Read Digest 96: 203-4+ Mr '70

HUBBELL, John Lorenzo
Hubbell trading post. O. F. Oldendorph. il por Nat Parks & Con Mag 44:6-9 O '70 *

HUBBELL trading post national historic site
Hubbell trading post. O. F. Oldendorph. il por Nat Parks & Con Mag 44:6-9 O '70

HUBERT, Jeanne B.
Junior high image, how can it be improved? Clear House 44:373-7 F '70

HUCK, Susan C. and Denomme, P. A.
Checkpoints for fighting the drug menace in camp. Camp Mag 42:19+ S '70

HUDDLESTON, Silous
Fifth suspect. Newsweek 75:24 Mr 9 '70 *

HUDGINS, H. C. Jr
Are student lockers off limits to principals? Ed Digest 36:14-15 D '70
What the Warren court decided; excerpts from The Warren court and the public schools. Ed Digest 36:44-7 N '70

HUDSON, Howard
Washington market letter. il Writers Digest 50:28-30 My '70

HUDSON, James W.
We can build space age cities now. il Nat Wildlife 8:4-9 Ag '70

HUDSON, Michael
Does economics deserve a Nobel prize? Commonweal 93:296-8 D 18 '70

HUDSON, Peggy
Look and listen. See issues of Scholastic teacher to May 18, 1970
Television (cont of) Looking and listening. See issues of Senior scholastic

HUDSON and Manhattan corporation
What's the hurry? por Forbes 105:54 Mr 1 '70

HUDSON Bay company. See Hudson's Bay company

HUDSON RIVER
Clearwater's cargo is a message: stop pollution. R. Gannon. il Pop Sci 197:70-2+ Ag '70
Creative cruising. R. W. Wilkie. il Yachting 127:66-7+ F '70
Enjoyable run up the Hudson River to historic West Point. B. Schill and B. Schill. il Yachting 127:62-3 Ap '70
Foully flows the Hudson. il Bsns W p 118 Ja 31 '70
Hudson River, by R. H. Boyle. Review
Commonweal 92:488 S 25 '70. D. Cort
Time il 95:94+ Ap 27 '70
Sailing down my dirty river; P. Seeger on the sloop, Clearwater, to point out pollution. P. Richards. il por Nat Wildlife 8:28-9 F '70
Vision on the Hudson; Clearwater sloop. E. Layne. il Am Heritage 21:116 Ap '70
What happened to the attempts to clean up the majestic, the polluted Hudson? Castleton-on-Hudson. N.Y.   W. Greene. il N Y Times Mag p28-9+ My 3 '70

HUDSON RIVER fishermen's association
My struggle to help the President; HRFA in Hudson River cleanup. R. H. Boyle. il Sports Illus 32:32-4 F 16 '70

HUDSON RIVER sloops. See Sloops

HUDSON'S BAY company
Hudson's Bay company; with paintings and photographs. D. Lavender. il Am Heritage 21:4-27 Ap '70

HUÉ, Vietnam
Bitter story of Hué; excerpt from The Vietcong strategy of terror. D. Pike. Read Digest 97:105-9 S '70

HUEBNER, A. L.
Disintegration of charged liquid jets: results with isopropyl alcohol. il Science 168: 118-19 Ap 3 '70

HUEBNER, Louise
Good witch of the West. il pors Life 68: 59-61 Ap 10 '70 *

HUENEFELD, John
Organizing book inventory the A&A way. Pub W 197:90-1 Je 29 '70

HUESSY, Eugen Rosenstock-. See Rosenstock-Huessy, E.

HUESSY, Mark
Ulbricht's prisoners. por Time 96:27 N 9 '70 *

HUFF, Betty Tracy
Ride the Gooberville stage! drama. Plays 29:1-10 Ap '70

HUFF, Darrell
Free tables from cable reels. il por Pop Sci 197:92-3 O '70
New beauty with decorative carvings. il Pop Sci 196:76-7 Mr '70
New fireplaces that solve problems. il Pop Sci 197:90-1+ S '70

Sliding doors that let in the light. il Pop Sci 197:93 S '70
Tuck a mini-sauna into a corner, or a closet. il Pop Sci 197:89 S '70
Vacation homes you buy by mail. il Pop Sci 196:90-3 Mr '70

HUFF, William H. See Brown, N. B. jt. auth.

HUFFMAN, Zella L.
Build with youth for a better world. il Sch Arts 70:20-1 N '70

HUFFNAGEL, Norman P.
Build a RIAA/NAB preamplifier. il Pop Electr 33:61-4 Ag '70

HUGGINS, Charles B. and Urist, M. R.
Dentin matrix transformation: rapid induction of alkaline phosphatase and cartilage. bibliog il Science 167:896-8 F 6 '70

HUGHES, Carroll J.
Hand-me-downs cuts costs for city fleet. il Am City 85:106 Je '70

HUGHES, Catharine R.
Avant-garde Simone Weil. America 122:612 Je 6 '70
Bones beneath the house. America 123:65-6 Ag 8 '70
Broadway hails Britannia. America 124:46-8 Ja 16 '71
Doing in Shakespeare. por America 122:132 F 7 '70
Ends and means in Dublin. Cath World 210: 266-8 Mr '70
Grotowski revolution. America 122:44-5 Ja 17 '70
Paradox of Samuel Beckett. por Cath World 211:26-8 Ap '70
Souping up Shakespeare. America 123:458 N 28 '70
Ulster revisited. il America 122:413-15 Ap 18 '70
(ed) See Rose, E. J. B. No British blueprint for a nightmare

HUGHES, E. See Machta, L. jt. auth.

HUGHES, Edwin L.
Inertial navigation for 747 superjet. il Electr World 84:27-30+ S '70

HUGHES, Emmet John
Innocence: the essence of the American heartland. Sat R 53:25-8+ O 17 '70

HUGHES, Harold Everett
Dark horse. por Newsweek 75:30-1 Mr 2 '70 *
1972? J. Deakin. il pors Esquire 73:55-9+ F '70 *

HUGHES, Howard Robard
Case of the invisible billionaire. il pors Newsweek 76:75-6+ D 21 '70 *
Howard Hughes meets tight money. il Bsns W p20 D 12 '70 *
Hughes caper. il Newsweek 76:56 D 28 '70 *
LAA suing Hughes over merger plan. Aviation W 93:30 O 12 '70 *
Midnight ride with Howard Hughes. F. McCulloch. Time 96:64-5 D 21 '70 *
Shootout at the Hughes corral. il pors Time 96:62-6 D 21 '70 *

HUGHES, James, and Reed, Bob
Community college: review and preview. Arch Rec 147:153 Je '70

HUGHES, Jim
Photographing people. il Travel & Camera 33:90-2 Mr '70

HUGHES, John S.
Insights and oversights in the poetic vision. Sat R 53:33-5 Ag 8 '70

HUGHES, Sister Mary Enda
Celebration; poem. Cath World 211:250 S '70

HUGHES, Richard
Mao makes the trials run on time. il N Y Times Mag p22-3+ Ag 23; 128 N 15 '70

HUGHES, Ronald
Missing Manson lawyer. por Time 96:61 D 21 '70 *

HUGHES, Spike
Take notice of the words... il por Opera N 34:8-13 F 14 '70

HUGHES, T.
Convection in the Antarctic ice sheet leading to a surge of the ice sheet and possibly to a new ice age. bibliog il Science 170:630-3 N 6 '70

HUGHES, Ted
Crowcolor; poem. New Yorker 46:144 N 14 '70
Crow's fall; poem. New Yorker 46:46 D 19 '70
Five poems: Crow tries the media; Magical dangers; Crow frowns; Crow's undersong; Crow and mama. New Yorker 46:30-1 Jl 18 '70
Lovepet; poem. New Yorker 46:24 Ja 2 '71

HUGHES aircraft company
Air West plans stock issue to assure its sale to Hughes. Aviation W 92:29 Mr 23 '70
Hughes plans domestic TV satellites. K. Johnsen. Aviation W 94:16 Ja 4 '71
Hughes purchase of Air West near completion; suit possible. Aviation W 92:27 Mr 30 '70

HUGHES tool company
Hughes caper. il Newswek 76:56 D 28 '70
HUGLIN, Jinnie
Diary of a disaster. il McCalls 97:58+ Je '70
HUGO, Richard F.
Only bar in Dixon; poem. New Yorker 46:48 O 10 '70
HUI, F. and Smith, A.
Regeneration of the amputated amphibian limb: retardation by hemicholinium-3. bibliog il Science 170:1313-14 D 18 '70
HUIE, William Bradford
Trade winds; interview, ed. by C. Amory. Sat R 53:10-11 Je 27 '70
Two months on the lam. il Esquire 73:104-7+ Je '70
HUILA, NEVADO DEL (mountain) See Andes mountains
HUIZENGA, John R.
Nuclear fission revisited. bibliog il Science 168:1405-13 Je 19 '70
HULL, Radia
At ease. por Library J 95:207-8 Ja 15 '70
HULL, Roger, jr
MUST: missionary thrust or bust? Chr Cent 87:665-7 My 27 '70
HULLS (naval architecture)
All about displacement cruisers. F. C. Clark, jr. il Motor B 126:38-41+ S '70
Herreshoff symposium. H. C. Herreshoff and A. S. D. Herreshoff. il Yachting 129:91+ Ja '71
Powerboat hull design. E. A. Zadig. il Motor B 127:130-3 Ja '71
HULME, Denis
When victory was just a broken engine away. C. Koch. il Motor T 22:32-4+ D '70 *
HULME, H. S. jr
All you see is the stream. il Am City 85:77-8 Mr '70
HULSE, Jerry
Romantic's Hawaiian guide. il Travel & Camera 33:69-71 Ja '70
HULSTRUNK, Alfred
You can sample the air around you. il Cons 25:48+ Ag '70
HUMAN auras. See Auras
HUMAN behavior. See Behavior (psychology)
HUMAN beings. See Man
HUMAN body. See Body, Human
HUMAN ecology
Demography and human ecology: some apparent trends. L. F. Schnore. bibliog f il Ann Am Acad 390:120-8 Jl '70
Earth day and after. R. M. Fagley. Chr Cent 87:440-2 Ap 15 '70
Ecology's angry lobbyist. D. M. Rorvik. il por Look 34:42-4 Ap 21 '70
Environmental pollution: an ecological perspective. D. L. Allen. Ed Digest 36:51-4 D '70
Environmental threat and social organization. L. Krader. bibliog f Ann Am Acad 389:11-18 My '70
Five who care. M. Mead. il Look 34:37 Ap 21 '70
Human landscape. R. Dubos. Bul Atom Sci 26:31-7 Mr '70
Making peace with man and nature. A. Berube. Cur 117:3-10 Ap '70
Metropolis and the transformation of resources. R. L. Meier. il Bul Atom Sci 26:2-5+ My '70
Needed land trusteeship, not just ownership. E. P. Odum. por Field & S 75:63+ Je '70
On population and environment; address, June 8, 1970. P. M. Hauser. Vital Speeches 36:696-701 S 1 '70
Overpopulated America. W. H. Davis; discussion. New Repub 162:28-30 Ja 31 '70
Prospects for spaceship man; excerpts from address, 1969. G. L. Stebbins. il Sat R 53:48-50+ Mr 7 '70
Rising population: its effect on environment. S. J. McNaughton. il Cons 24:14-16 Je '70
Struggle for an ecological theology: a case in point: Faith-man-nature group's conference. H. P. Santmire. Chr Cent 87:275-7 Mr 4 '70
Toward an ecological solution. M. Bookchin. il Ramp Mag 8:6-8+ My '70
See also
Ekistics
Environmental policy
Man—Influence on nature
Social psychology

Bibliography
Concerns of our precarious habitat. il Library J 95:1495-8 Ap 15 '70
HUMAN embryo. See Fetus

HUMAN engineering
Engineers of the body. il Bsns W p49 D 5 '70
New twists for old tools. il Life 68:73-4 Je 26 '70
HUMAN environment, United Nations conference on the. See United Nations conference on the human environment (proposed)
HUMAN figure in art
Mary Holmes paints the figure. P. Thompson. il por Am Artist 34:86-93 Mr '70
See also
Human figure in photography
HUMAN figure in photography
Autopolaroid; photographs, with interview. L. Samaras. Art in Am 58:66-83 N '70
Feininger; female nude in photography. A. Feininger. Mod Phot 34:66+ O '70
Nude-o-grams. J. Scully. il Mod Phot 34:96-9 My '70
Seeing pictures; displaying the human form. J. Scully. Mod Phot 34:10+ S '70
HUMAN genetics
Advances in human genetics and their impact on society; AAAS symposium, December 28, 1970. D. S. Borgaonkar and S. A. Shah. Science 170:347-8 O 16 '70
Caucasian genes in American Negroes. T. E. Reed; discussion. Science 166:1353; 167:1388-9 D 12 '69. Mr 6 '70
Heritable fragile site on chromosome 16: probable localization of haptoglobin locus in man. R. E. Magenis and others. bibliog il Science 170:85-7 O 2 '70
Homozygous Hb J Tongariki: evidence for only one alpha chain structural locus in Melanesians. R. K. Abramson and others. bibliog il Science 169:194-6 Jl 10 '70
Isoantigenic variants: isolation from human diploid cells in culture. R. Adman and D. A. Pious. bibliog il Science 168:370-2 Ap 17 '70
Lessons from a primitive people: South American Indians. J. V. Neel. bibliog il Science 170:815-22 N 20 '70
Pepsinogens: genetic polymorphism in man. I. M. Samloff and P. L. Townes. bibliog il Science 168:144-5 Ap 3 '70
Prospects for genetic intervention in man; adaptation of address, December 1969. B. D. Davis. bibliog Science 170:1279-83 D 18 '70
Substrate stabilization: genetically controlled reciprocal relationship of two human enzymes. M. L. Greene and others. bibliog il Science 167:887-9 F 6 '70
See also
Genetic counseling
Heredity
Heredity of disease
HUMAN growth hormone. See Pituitary hormones
HUMAN heredity. See Heredity
HUMAN information processing
How we remember what we see. R. N. Haber. il Sci Am 222:104-12 My '70
HUMAN interaction. See Social interaction
HUMAN milk. See Milk, Human
HUMAN nature. See Man
HUMAN potential movement. See Group relations training
HUMAN race. See Anthropology; Man
HUMAN relations
Beyond survival. J. Poppy. il Look 34:34-5 Ja 13 '70
Essence of Barbara; interview, ed. by E. Miller. B. Hershey. il pors Seventeen 29:132-3+ F '70
Fresh way of understanding yourself; excerpt from Chatelaine. M. Landsberg. Read Digest 97:219-22+ O '70
Honorable behavior. V. P. McCorry. America 122:428 Ap 18 '70
How did he get there? human realization can be facilitated or retarded by others' expectations. D. N. Aspy. Ed Digest 35:49 Ap '70
Need for loving strife; existential communication. A. Deeken. Cath World 211:74-7 My '70
Sweet uses of solitude. J. Mills. Read Digest 96:211-12+ Je '70
Third environment. A. Szent-Gyorgyi. Sat R 53:63 My 2 '70
Try giving yourself away; condensation. D. Dunn. Read Digest 97:98-100 Ag '70
Violence as a defense against intimacy. S. H. Kardener and M. Fuller. bibliog Ment Hy 54:310-15 Ap '70
Who's a phony? B. S. Llamzon. America 123:196-8 S 26 '70
See also
Bores (persons)
Friendship

HUMAN relations—See also—*Continued*
Group relations training
Loneliness
Marriage
Personal space
Popularity
Prejudice
Race relations
Sensitiveness
Sex relations
Women and men

Study and teaching
See also
Esalen institute, Calif.
HUMAN rights. See Civil rights
HUMAN rights, Universal declaration of. See
Universal declaration of human rights
HUMAN rights commission of the United Nations. See United Nations—Commission on human rights
HUMAN rights committee, Russia. See Civil rights organizations—Russia
HUMAN rights day and week
Bill of rights day, Human rights day; proclamation. R. Nixon. Dept State Bul 62:6 Ja 5 '70
HUMAN sacrifice. See Sacrifice, Human
HUMANE treatment of animals. See Animals —Treatment
HUMANISM
China. H. Yu. Chr Cent 87:550 Ap 29 '70
Christianity: the true humanism. W. S. Reid. Chr Today 14:9-11 Je 19 '70
Humanism and the churches. Chr Today 14:32-3 Ap 10 '70
Rahner and the anonymous Christian. D. Maloney. America 123:348-50 O 31 '70
Sowing the wind; a special report from Kent state university. D. Bryant. Chr Today 14: 13-15 Je 5 '70
HUMANISTIC psychology. See Psychology
HUMANITIES
Humanities today. bibliog Clear House 45: 126-8 O '70
Relevance of the humanities. H. J. Muller. Am Scholar 40:103-18 Wint '70
See also
Liberal education
Science and the humanities

Bibliography
Humanities potpourri. il Schol Teach Jr/Sr High p36-8 S 21 '70

Study and teaching
Man's world: an electronic experience in the humanities. S. May. Engl J 59:413-15+ Mr '70
Moral purpose of humanities programs. R. Stackelberg. Engl J 59:1141-5 N '70
Reflections of a humanist. T. H. Briggs. Ed Digest 35:34-7 Ja '70
To preserve humanness: language and literature in the '70s and beyond. J. E. Miller, jr. Engl J 59:1154-6 N '70
HUMBLE oil and refining company
Fine feelings about a refinery. il Nations Bsns 58:15 F '70
Refinery blast that rocked Humble: Linden, N.J. il Bsns W p 17-18 D 12 '70
HUME, David N. See April. R. W. jt. auth.
HUME, Ivor Noël-. See Noël-Hume, I.
HUME, Paul, and Hume, Ruth
Great Chicago piano war. il pors Am Heritage 21:16-21 O '70
HUME, Ruth. See Hume, P. jt. auth.
HUMES, Charles W. jr
Guidance office location aids counselor role. bibliog Clear House 44:506-8 Ap '70
HUMFREY family
Humfrey coat-of-arms. H. K. Eilers. il Hobbies 74:158-9 Ja '70
HUMIC acids
Humic substances: fulvic acid-dialkyl phthalate complexes and their role in pollution. G. Ogner and M. Schnitzer. bibliog Science 170:317-18 O 16 '70
HUMIDIFIERS
Merchants bask in humidity. Bsns W p40+ F 28 '70
HUMIDITY
Physiological effects
Tips for your home and family. Todays Health 48:77-8 F '70
HUMMA, John
Hot weekend sun in Rhode Island, etc; poem. New Repub 162:32 My 9 '70

HUMMEL, Charles F.
Queen Anne and Chippendale furniture in the Henry Francis du Pont Winterthur museum. il Antiques 97:896-903; 98:900-9 Je, D '70 (to be cont)
HUMMEL, Johann Nepomuk
Hummel and George Thomson of Edinburgh. J. Sachs. bibliog f il pors Mus Q 56:270-87 Ap '70 •
HUMMELER, Klaus, and others
Human cystinosis: intracellular deposition of cystine. bibliog il Science 168:859-60 My 15 '70
HUMMERSTONE, Robert G.
I don't hate the guardsmen who shot me. il por Life 69:44-5 O 16 '70
HUMMINGBIRDS
Regulation of oxygen consumption and body temperature during torpor in a hummingbird, eulampis jugularis. F. R. Hainsworth and L. L. Wolf. bibliog il Science 168:368-9 Ap 17 '70
HUMOR
Humor to the rescue. R. Armour. il Parents Mag 45:48-9+ Jl '70
In praise of fools. L. M. Orsy. America 122: 276 Mr 14 '70
Peg Bracken: an exclusive interview; ed. by F. Cameron. P. Bracken. il por Writers Digest 50:24-6 My '70
What can you be funny about? R. Armour. Writer 83:21-3 D '70
See also
Anecdotes
Comedy
Laughter
Limericks
Puns and punning
Radio broadcasting—Humor
Television broadcasting—Humor
also subhead Anecdotes, facetiae, satire, etc. under various subjects, e.g. Animals—Anecdotes, facetiae, satire, etc.
HUMOR, American
We are not amused, and why; Time essay. M. Maddock. il Time 96:30-1 Jl 20 '70
See also
National lampoon (periodical)
HUMOR, Pictorial
See also
Caricatures and cartoons
HUMOR, Russian
Soviets show off their sense of humor; U.S.S.R. photo '70, exhibition. il Life 68: 69-72 Mr 13 '70
HUMOR in science
Is science funny? il Sci Digest 67:40-2 F '70
See also
Worm runner's digest
HUMORISTS
See also
Comedians
HUMPERDINCK, Engelbert
Ladies' men of music; with report by J. Bonfante. il pors Life 69:46-52+ S 18 '70 •
HUMPHREY, Donald R. and others
Predicting measures of motor performance from multiple cortical spike trains. bibliog il Science 170:758-62 N 13 '70
HUMPHREY, Hubert Horatio, 1911-
Top Democrat talks about party's debt; interview. por U S News 68:32-3 Mr 2 '70
We stand on common ground. Read Digest 96:88-92 Mr '70
about
Crawfisher. Nation 211:387-8 O 26 '70 •
For Democrats: a way out of their differences? summary of statements. il por U S News 68:17 F 23 '70 •
Humphrey's comeback. por Newsweek 76:27 S 28 '70 •
Humphrey's imperative. K. Crawford. Newsweek 76:25 Ag 24 '70 •
New Humphrey. A. A. Eisele. New Repub 163:18-19 S 19 '70 •
Still the man who loves to talk, to teach, to preach. R. Wool. il pors N Y Times Mag p25-7+ O 11 '70 •
View from Minnesota. H. Sidey. il por Life 68:4 Ap 17 '70 •
Will it be Senator Humphrey again? il por U S News 69:63 O 12 '70
HUMPHREY, Richard
Boat owner's safety log. Motor B 125:142-3+ Ja '70
Marine communications up-to-date. il Electr World 85:25-7+ Ja '71
Talk ain't cheap no more. il Motor B 125:118-19+ Ja '70
HUMPHREY, William
Ditches are quicker. il por Life 69:58-61 Ag 7 '70
Sex life of the salmon is brief and terrible. il Esquire 73:123-8+ Je '70

HUMPHREYS, David
To the Southern islands. il Yachting 128:61+
O '70
HUMPHREYS, Henry S.
Zoo opera going strong. il Hi Fi 20:MA22-3
O '70
HUMPHREYS, Laud
Tearoom trade: impersonal sex in public
places; excerpts. il Trans-Action 7:10-14+
Ja '70
about
Feedback from our readers. D. H. Wrong.
Trans-Action 7:8 Jl '70 *
Sociological snoopers; with reply by I. L.
Horowitz and L. Rainwater. N. Von Hoff-
man. Trans-Action 7:4-8 My '70 *
HUMPHREYS, Robert
Virtuoso of the political scene. P. M. Crane.
Nat R 22:687-8 Je 30 '70 *
HUMPHRIES, Percy Lund, and company. See
Publishers and publishing—Great Britain
HUMPHRY, John A. and Ferguson, E. A.
State library: institution in transition. bib-
liog il Am Lib 1:949-52 N '70
HUMUS
See also
Humic acids
HUNDLEY, Craig
Teenagers aren't as liberal about music as
they think they are; interview, ed. by P. M.
Jones and R. Hemming. il por Sr Schol
95:21 S 29 '69
HUNGARIAN cookery. See Cookery, Hungarian
HUNGARIAN partridge shooting. See Part-
ridge shooting
HUNGARIAN peppers. See Peppers
HUNGARIAN poetry

Translations into English
Glasses; O Europe; On evening clouds; Fine
summer evenings; tr. by J. Batki. A. József.
Poetry 116:281-4 Ag '70
HUNGARIANS
Hungary today. J. Wechsberg. il Sat R 53:21-
3+ N 28 '70
HUNGARY
See also
Catholic church in Hungary
Communism—Hungary
Communist party (Hungary)
Publishers and publishing—Hungary

Economic conditions
Hungary: quiet changes. T. Land. Nation
211:464-5 N 9 '70

Economic policy
Reports: Hungary. R. Longworth. Atlan 225:
22+ My '70

Politics and government
Hungary: quiet changes. T. Land. Nation
211:464-5 N 9 '70
Hungary's quiet revolution. K. Huszar. il por
Newsweek 76:32 Ag 3 '70
What's going on now behind the iron cur-
tain. R. A. Haeger. il U S News 69:86-8
N 9 '70

Religious institutions and affairs
Hungarians prefer religious over secular rites.
Chr Cent 87:1058 S 9 '70
HUNGATE, William Leonard
Excerpt from debate, September 16, 1969. Cong
Digest 49:25+ Ja '70
HUNGER
Helplessly hungry. Chr Today 14:26-7 Ja 16
'70
HUNNEX, Milton D.
Is the new theology self-defeating? Chr To-
day 15:9-12 Ja 15 '71
HUNNICUTT, C. W. See Goforth, F. jt. auth.
HUNS
Barbarians. R. Winston. il Horizon 12:66-81
Sum '70
HUNSUCKER, Suzanne
Who wants equality? Nation 211:465-8 N 9
'70
HUNT, Graham R. See Logan, L. M. jt. auth.
HUNT, Haroldson Lafayette
Big daddy of sport. E. Shrake. il por Sports
Illus 33:60-2+ S 7 '70 *
HUNT, Irene
Writing for children. Writer 83:17-20 Mr '70
HUNT, John
Dogs, cats, and other living things. il
McCalls 97:30+ Jl '70; 98:39+ Ja '71
HUNT, Lyman C. jr
Lively learning center and the alert librar-
ian. il por Wilson Lib Bul 45:293-7 N '70

HUNT, Morton M.
Gentle art of understanding your parents. il
Seventeen 29:136-7+ My '70
HUNT, R. K. and Jacobson, Marcus
Brain enhancement in tadpoles: increased
DNA concentration after somatotrophin or
prolactin. bibliog il Science 170:342-4 O 16 '70
HUNT, Reed Oliver
Another stab at financial reform. por Bsns
W p97+. 140 Ap 18 '70 *
Biggest reform? il Newsweek 75:84+ Ap 20
'70 *
HUNT, William
Ladder you offer; After a fine day we found
this; This is a way; Two days; poems. Po-
etry 115:311-17 F '70
HUNT commission. See United States—Com-
mission on financial institutions (proposed)
HUNTER, Beatrice Trum
What's cooking? il Org Gard & Farm 17:116-
18+ F; 98-101 Jl '70
HUNTER, Celia
Alaskan wilderness: going, going, gone? il
Nat Parks & Con Mag 44:11-15 N '70
HUNTER, Charlayne A.
Homecoming for the first black girl at the
University of Georgia. il pors N Y Times
Mag p24-5+ Ja 25 '70
HUNTER, Edith
Boy with imagination plus. il Parents Mag
45:42-3+ D '70
HUNTER, F. Edmund, Jr. See Painter, A. A.
jt. auth.
HUNTER, Gilbert N.
I've been gypped! il por Outdoor Life 146:
74-6+ N '70
HUNTER, Guy
New Africa. For Affairs 48:712-25 Jl '70
HUNTER, Hilda
Young music makers; excerpts from Growing
up with music. il Parents Mag 45:58-9+
F '70
HUNTER, Jacqueline H.
Fresh look at dried flowers. il House B 112:
58-9 Jl '70
HUNTER, Neale
Is Chinese communism godless? il Cath World
212:197-9 Ja '71
Working group 7. Commonweal 93:60-1 O 16
'70
HUNTER, Robert Douglas
Sight size, a method of painting; interview,
ed. by R. Goetz. il por Am Artist 34:48-53+
D '70
HUNTER, Robert E.
How Philco lost its chairman. por Bsns W p28
F 14 '70 *
HUNTER, Sam
Josef Albers: prophet and presiding genius of
American op art. il pors Vogue 156:70-3+
O 15 '70
HUNTER-farmer relations. See Farmer- hunter
relations
HUNTER house, Newport. See Newport, R.I.—
Historic houses, etc.
HUNTERS POINT district. See San Francisco
HUNTING
Face of starvation; hunting and game con-
servation. J. B. Trefethen. il Nat Wildlife
7:4-8+ O '69
Gist of it; ed. by H. Moore. See issues of
Outdoor life
Sportsman's notebook. H. G. Tapply. See
issues of Field & stream
Where to go; ed. by V. T. Sparano. See
issues of Outdoor life
See also
Game, Dressing of
Game laws
Hunting with bow and arrow
Poaching
Trapping
Whaling
also Rabbit hunting, and similar headings

Accidents and injuries
How to keep free public hunting; hunter
safety program. B. E. Burgin. il Cons
25:6-7 O '70

Ethical aspects
Are hunters murderers? reprint of August
1948 article; with editorial comment. G.
Fitz. il Outdoor Life 146:45, 46-7+ Ag '70

Safety devices and measures
How to keep free public hunting; hunter
safety program. B. E. Burgin. il Cons
25:6-7 O '70

Statistics
Small game take down last year. H. F. Maguire. il Cons 25:32-3 D '70

HUNTING—*Continued*

Stories

Uncle Al's good deed. J. M. Vance. il Field & S 75:52-3+ N '70

Africa

One-rifle safaris. J. O'Connor. il Outdoor Life 145:88+ Ja '70

Alaska

Angry men; plunder of Alaska's wildlife. B. East. il Outdoor Life 146:31-3+ D '70

High-climb Kodiaks. D. Powell. il pors Outdoor Life 145:58-9+ F '70

Nothing's wrong with Nanook; Alaskan polar bears. W. Page. il Field & S 74:46-7+ Ja '70

Perilous cruise for Alaskan brown bear; reprint. D. J. Singer. il Field & S 75:200-4+ Je '70

Stalk for the book; no. 1 Dall sheep? D. Sykes. il pors Outdoor Life 145:76-7+ Ap '70

Arctic Regions

See also
Hunting—Canada

Arizona

Desert mule deer. J. O'Connor. il Outdoor Life 146:44-5+ D '70

Trophy bucks on the Vermilion cliffs. C. C. Niehuis. il Outdoor Life 146:78-81+ O '70

Watch who you call birdbrain; dove shoots. N. Riley. il Outdoor Life 145:46-7+ Ja '70

Asia

Travel notes. R. Joseph. Esquire 74:46+ Ag '70

Austria

Weidmannsdank! hunting red deer and chamois. W. Page. il Field & S 74:80-3+ Ap '70

California

China Lake chukars. J. Mears. il por Outdoor Life 146:64-5+ N '70

Doves for openers. J. Freeman. il Field & S 75:40-1+ S '70

High climb for blacktails. J. Martin. il Outdoor Life 146:62-5+ S '70

West's hottest deer hunting. W. Curtis. il Field & S 75:44-5+ N '70

Canada

Arctic adventure; seal hunting. H. J. Samuels. il por Outdoor Life 145:68-71+ F '70

Don't shoot the first caribou. G. G. Sikes. il Outdoor Life 146:58-9+ N '70

Ghost billy of Heart Mountain. W. C. Eubank. il por Outdoor Life 145:48-51+ Mr '70

Hotspot for trophy whitetails. J. O. Cartier. il por Outdoor Life 146:66-7+ N '70

I came for bear. G. McKenna. il Outdoor Life 145:50-3+ My '70

Last call for moose. C. Anderegg. il pors Outdoor Life 145:60-3+ Ja '70

Mountain goat mysteries. V. Geist. il Field & S 75:34-5+ Ag '70

New Brunswick: mixed-bag bonanza. D. Knight. il por Field & S 74:84-5+ Ap '70

Presbyterian buck. L. J. Bashline. il Field & S 75:172-3+ O '70

$2,903.55 polar bear. P. Moon. il Audubon 72: 149-52 N '70

Where the wild goose flies. A. Russell. il Outdoor Life 146:76-7+ Ag '70

Woodcock along the salmon rivers. J. B. Robinson and H. Carroll. il Field & S 75: 54-5+ S '70

Colorado

High in the velvet. C. Elliott. il por Outdoor Life 146:60-3+ Ag '70

Europe, Western

High-flown styles of wing shooting; in six countries of Europe. T. Alexander. il Fortune 82:122-31 Ag '70

Florida

Lord of the Cypress. J. H. Halliburton. il Outdoor Life 146:77-80+ N '70

Idaho

Doing the duck crawl; grand tour for mallards. J. J. Platt. il pors Outdoor Life 146: 42-3+ D '70

Mountains of home. C. Conley. il Field & S 75: 66-7+ Je '70

Rules for bagging pheasant. T. Trueblood. il Field & S 75:22+ O '70

Iran

Hunting in Iran. E. A. Bauer. il por Outdoor Life 145:58-61+ My; 146:44-7+ Jl '70

Kansas

Prairie cottontails. D. Pryce. il por Outdoor Life 146:88-9+ O '70

Kentucky

Silver bullet for me; ed. by D. Bowring. D. Lohre. il pors Outdoor Life 145:74-6+ Je '70

Kenya

Henry Poolman story. J. S. Barrett. il pors Outdoor Life 145:68-71+ Ap '70

Mexico

Take me to your pichiguilas. N. Riley. il Outdoor Life 145:64-5+ F '70

Michigan

Fantastic island for whitetail; South Fox Island. J. Chiappetta. il por Field & S 75:38-9+ N '70

Gray ghost; coyote hunting. L. J. Marlatt. il Outdoor Life 146:58-9+ S '70

My no. 1 game. E. Harger. il por Outdoor Life 146:94-5+ O '70

Track of the whitetail. F. H. Struble. il por Outdoor Life 145:48-51+ F '70

Minnesota

Best way to hunt whitetail! C. Nansen. il Field & S 75:30-1+ D '70

Double play in Minnesota. J. Seville. il Motor B 126:58-60 S '70

Grouse on the upbeat. J. O. Cartier. il Outdoor Life 146:70-1+ S '70

Judge of Disappointment Mountain. B. Cary. il por Outdoor Life 146:32-5+ Jl '70

Missouri

Where the geese beckon. P. Curtis. il Field & S 75:52-3+ S '70

Montana

Bettering the odds for bowhunters. C. Nansen. il Field & S 75:34-5+ N '70

Cyanide Creek affair. W. J. McRae. il por Outdoor Life 145:44-7+ Je '70

Ram for the records; ed. by B. Hartford. R. Browne. il por Outdoor Life 146:72-5+ O '70

Mozambique

African safari. P. Buckley. il Harp Baz 103: 118+ S '70

New Mexico

Bachelor bighorns. T. Kelly. il por Outdoor Life 146:50-1+ Jl '70

Goosenappers. H. Simmons. il Field & S 75: 60-1+ O '70

Javelina come high. J. Samson. il Field & S 75:68-71+ My '70

New range for record heads; mule deer hunting. B. Brister. il pors Field & S 75:42-3+ O '70

Spoiled lion. T. J. Lyon. il pors Outdoor Life 145:72-5+ F '70

Trophy bucks are easy; ed. by D. Knight. J. Washburn. il Field & S 75:36-7+ Ag '70

New York (state)

Average deer hunt? Catskill Mountains. J. Walters. il por Outdoor Life 146:68-9+ O '70

Eastern homeland of the hun. J. B. Robinson. il Field & S 75:136-8+ S '70

Extra season for grouse. P. Barrett. il Field & S 75:50-1+ S '70

Small game seasons 1969-70. Cons 24:35 Ag '69

Small game take down last year. H. F. Maguire. il Cons 25:32-3 D '70

This is the timberdoodle. C. E. Heacox. il Outdoor Life 146:76-7+ O '70

North Carolina

Goose hunting from underwater. P. McLain. il Field & S 75:40-3+ N '70

Northeastern states

News: the Northeast; ed. by T. Janes. See issues of Outdoor life

Ohio

Start from the bottoms; squirrel season. E. A. Bauer. il Outdoor Life 146:78-9+ S '70

Oklahoma

Ten million crows? B. W. Dalrymple. il por Outdoor Life 145:52-5+ Ja '70

Oregon

There are honkers in the valley. D. Holm. il por Outdoor Life 146:52-3+ D '70

To bag a buck. M. Griffith. il Field & S 75: 46-7+ O '70

HUNTING—*Continued*

Rhode Island

Citified ducks satisfy. J. B. Robinson. il Outdoor Life 146:52-5+ N '70

South Carolina

Where to hunt in South Carolina. G. X. Sand. Field & S 75:134+ N '70

South Dakota

Late great grouse hunting. H. Bradshaw. il Field & S 74:48-9+ Ja '70

Southern states

Do you really want to be a turkey shooter? C. Elliott. il por Outdoor Life 145:72-5+ Mr '70

Tennessee

Countdown for chucks. C. Vinson. il Outdoor Life 145:86-7+ Ap '70
Cow pasture buck. C. Vinson. il pors Outdoor Life 146:60-1+ D '70
Mountain grouse are work. G. X. Sand. il pors Outdoor Life 145:56-7+ F '70

Texas

Christmas trip to Texas. E. A. Bauer. il pors Outdoor Life 146:34-7+ D '70
For mule deer: look longer; use binoculars. B. W. Dalrymple. il Outdoor Life 146:48-51+ N '70
Hangup on javelina. R. Tinsley. il por Outdoor Life 145:66-7+ Mr '70
No gamebird like it; sandhill crane. B. W. Dalrymple. il Outdoor Life 145:56-9+ Je '70

United States

How to have a great guided hunt. H. Rate. il Field & S 75:32-3+ Ag '70
Old and the new. T. Trueblood. il Field & S 75:24+ N '70

Vermont

Whistlers like it mean. J. B. Robinson. il Outdoor Life 146:84-7+ O '70

Virginia

Old-road rabbits. R. M. Gooch. il Outdoor Life 146:58-9+ D '70

Washington (state)

Can you top this? ed. by E. E. Kurrus, jr. H. M. Oliver. il Outdoor Life 145:94-7+ Ap '70
Walkin' bear. E. E. Kurrus, jr. il por Outdoor Life 146:46-9+ D '70

Wisconsin

Bear for the barbershop. D. D. Kerscher. il por Outdoor Life 145:60-1+ Mr '70
Boat hunting for whitetail. K. Heuser. il Field & S 74:60-1+ Ja '70

Wyoming

Best antelope in seventy years. L. Arce. il por Outdoor Life 145:44-5+ Ja '70
How to get started on elk. J. R. Olt. il Field & S 75:38-9+ Ag '70
Hunt we'll remember. R. Merchant. il Outdoor Life 146:72-3+ S '70
Hunting the desert cottontail. B. Milek. il Field & S 75:42-3+ S '70
New goat country; Beartooth Mountains. R. A. Weidner. il por Outdoor Life 145:52-3+ Je '70
Pronghorn for a pioneer. B. Milek. il Field & S 75:40-1+ Ag '70
Westward the raccoon. J. Stagg. il por Outdoor Life 145:56-7+ Mr '70
Wyoming's first Rocky Mountain goat hunt. C. J. Farmer. il Field & S 75:56-7+ O '70

Zambia

Cliff-hanging lion. J. O'Connor. il Outdoor Life 145:45-7+ F '70
Elephants on the Zambezi. J. O'Connor. il por Outdoor Life 145:33-5+ Ja '70
Two tickets for two lions. W. Page. il Field & S 75:52-3+ D '70

HUNTING clothes. See Clothing and dress—Sports clothes

HUNTING dogs
Bears and bear dogs. D. M. Newell. il Field & S 74:64-5+ Ja '70
Dogs. D. M. Duffey. See issues of Outdoor life
In defense of the versatile dog; the European breeds. J. J. Knap. il Field & S 75:174-5+ My '70
Old-road rabbits. R. M. Gooch. il Outdoor Life 146:58-9+ D '70
Saddleback Bigs. L. Mueller. il Field & S 75:78-9+ My '70

That gunshyness bugaboo. D. M. Duffey. il Outdoor Life 145:136+ F '70
See also
Bird dogs
Hounds

Training
See Dogs—Training

HUNTING guides. See Guides

HUNTING in art
Glories of the hunt; Hunting book of Wolfgang Birkner. il Time 95:54-5+ Ap 20 '70

HUNTING knives. See Knives

HUNTING laws. See Game laws

HUNTING on farm land. See Farmer-hunter relations

HUNTING rifles. See Rifles

HUNTING stories. See Hunting—Stories

HUNTING trophies
Hunting abroad? Know this law; importing of trophies. E. P. Denson. il Outdoor Life 146:66+ D '70
Trophy bowhunting. G. H. Gillelan. il por Outdoor Life 146:36+ S '70

HUNTING with bow and arrow
Archery. G. H. Gillelan. See issues of Outdoor life
Bettering the odds for bowhunters. C. Nansen. il Field & S 75:34-5+ N '70
Blackbeard's booty. J. Morrison. il por Outdoor Life 145:48-51+ Ja '70
Bowhunting's controversial new arrow; tranquilizer arrow. C. Conley. il Field & S 75:50-1+ O '70
Bowman in winter. G. H. Gillelan. il Outdoor Life 146:86+ D '70
Head start on big game. G. H. Gillelan. il Outdoor Life 145:16+ Mr '70
My goat was high. L. Marvin. il Outdoor Life 146:66-7+ Ag '70
New kind of bowhunting; hypodermic arrowheads. G. H. Gillelan. il Outdoor Life 145:132+ Je '70
New Year's resolutions. G. H. Gillelan. il Outdoor Life 145:128+ Ja '70
Stalk for the book; no. 1 Dall sheep? D. Sykes. il pors Outdoor Life 145:76-7+ Ap '70
Trophy bowhunting. G. H. Gillelan. il por Outdoor Life 146:36+ S '70
World record ram; bighorn with a bow. R. Alt. il Outdoor Life 146:68-71+ N '70

HUNTINGTON, Roger
Advance look at Detroit's 1971 models. il Consumer Bul 53:7-12 O '70
How much carburetor do you need? il Pop Mech 134:144-7+ N '70

HUNTINGTON, W.Va.

Education
Step up to reading. D. Marsh. il Am Ed 6:15-17 Ja '70

HUNTLEY, Chet
Chet heads for the hills. T. Thompson. por Life 69:33+ Jl 17 '70 *
Fadeout was shortlived. il por Bsns W p 102 O 10 '70 *
Good night. . . Newsweek 75:72 Mr 2 '70 *

HUNTOON, Maxwell C. Jr
. . .And how it grew. il Am Home 73:58-9+ Ap '70
Dollars and sense of condominiums. il Am Home 73:54-5+ Ja '70

HUNTSMAN, Lee L. See Rushmer. R. J. jt. auth.

HUNTSVILLE, Ala.
Huntsville's return to earth. il Bsns W p 125-6+ F 14 '70

HUOT, M. I. A.
In our fourth year of marriage; story. Good H 170:104-5 Mr '70

HURD, Michael
In my opinion. por Seventeen 29:24 Mr '70

HURLER, syndrome. See Lipochondrodystrophy

HURLEY, Lucille S. and others
Liver mitochondria from manganese-deficient and pallid mice; function and ultrastructure. bibliog il Science 170:1316-18 D 18 '70

HURLEY, Patrick M. and Pinson, W. H. Jr
Rubidium-strontium relations in Tranquillity base samples. il Science 167:473-4 Ja 30 '70

HURLEY, Philip S.
Ideas on trial. America 122:181-2 F 21 '70

HURRICANE control. See Hurricane protection

HURRICANE ISLAND outward bound school. See Outward bound schools

HURRICANE protection
Hurricane Debbie modification experiments, August 1969. R. C. Gentry. bibliog il Science 168:473-5 Ap 24 '70; Reply. B. Vonnegut. 169:7-8 Jl 3 '70

HURRICANE protection—*Continued*
Predicting the fury; National hurricane center in Miami. il Sci N 97:573 Je 13 '70
Spitting in the eye of a hurricane. R. Gannon. il Pop Sci 197:56-8 Ag '70

HURRICANES
Camille's wake lies full of battered hopes. il Bsns W p94+ My 16 '70
Celia at Aransas Pass. R. L. Herndon. il Weatherwise 23:186 Ag '70
Face to face with hurricane Camille. J. P. Blank. il Read Digest 96:62-7 Mr '70
Haunting legacy of Camille. il Life 69:78-83 S 18 '70
Hurricane peak: mid-September? interview. R. H. Simpson. por U S News 69:16 Ag 10 '70
Hurricane season of 1969. A. L. Sugg and L. G. Pardue. il Weatherwise 23:12-17+ F '70
Lady was a killer; hurricane Camille. E. Shrake. il Sports Illus 32:60-4+ Mr 9 '70
No warning on the beach; Northeast coast hurricane of 1938; excerpts from Hurricane. J. McCarthy. il Motor B 126:54-5+ S '70
Storm they still don't believe; hurricane Camille. E. D. Fales, jr. il Pop Mech 134:90-5+ S '70
Tragedy in the wake of Celia. il U S News 69:53 Ag 17 '70
Whatever happened to the area smashed by hurricane Camille? U S News 69:53 Ag 17 '70
See also
Cyclones
Hurricane protection

Names
Hurricane girls of 1970. Weatherwise 23:107 Je '70

HURST, Charles G.
Doctor Charles G. Hurst: the mastermind of Malcolm X college. A. Poinsett. il pors Ebony 25:29-32+ Mr '70 *

HURST, Willard
At the borderland of law and economic history: the contributions of Willard Hurst; address, December 1968. H. N. Scheiber. bibliog f Am Hist R 75:744-56 F '70 *

HURWITZ, Al
Turned-on art. il Am Ed 6:14-17 Mr '70

HURWOOD, David Lyon
Israel: first pilgrimage. Yale R 59:459-80 Mr '70

HUSAK, Gustav
Prague: nothing is forever. D. North. il Nation 211:102-5 Ag 17 '70 *
Return engagement. il Newsweek 75:60 My 18 '70 *

HUSBAND and wife. See Marriage; Wives

HUSBANDS
How to rekindle his fire. S. Lord. Harp Baz 104:102-3 Ja '71
How to support your husband's ego. J. L. Collier. Read Digest 96:108-11 Ja '70
See also
Marriage
Wives

HUSELTON, B. C.
Spare hand who went beyond the dream of Leonardo da Vinci. il pors Nations Bsns 58:50-1 Ja '70

HUSSEIN, king of Jordan
Isolation of a king; interview, ed. by J. Bonfante. il pors Life 69:50-4 N 20 '70
Talk with Hussein; interview, ed. by M. J. Kubic and L. Jenkins. il por Newsweek 76:36 Ag 31 '70 *
about
All alone: a monarch on the spot. il Newsweek 76:38 S 28 '70 *
Arab guerrillas v. Arab governments. il por Time 95:22-3 Je 22 '70 *
Christmas shopping; U.S. visit. Time 96:28 D 21 '70 *
Explosion in Jordan. il por Newsweek 75:34-5 Je 22 '70 *
Fortunes of Hussein. F. Qassim. Nation 212:38-9 Ja 11 '71 *
How Hussein met commando crisis. J. Law. por U S News 68:19 Mr 9 '70 *
Hussein's costly victory. il por Newsweek 76:35 O 5 '70 *
Is Hussein necessary? il por Newsweek 75:35 Je 22 '70 *
Jordan: the battle ends; the war begins. il por Time 96:24-7 O 5 '70 *
Jordan: the king takes on the guerrillas. il pors Time 96:16-18+ S 28 '70 *
Jordan's Hussein: in search of peace. por U S News 69:38 D 21 '70 *
King Hussein's ten-day war. T. Theodoracopulos. Nat R 22:1109 O 20 '70 *
King under fire. L. Jenkins. il Newsweek 76:51 S 14 '70 *

Lull in the madness. il Newsweek 75:35 Je 29 '70 *
Middle East: a secret rendezvous. il pors Time 96:26 N 23 '70 *
Middle East on the Potomac. il pors Newsweek 76:41-2 D 21 '70 *
Shoring up a shaky calm. il por Time 95:24+ Je 29 '70 *

HUSTON, Joseph P. and Bures, Jan
Drinking and eating elicited by cortical spreading depression. bibliog il Science 169:702-4 Ag 14 '70

HUSTON, Tom Charles
Cato v. Publius in the White House. il pors Time 95:18 F 23 '70 *

HUTCHENS, John K.
Happy essence of Frank Sullivan. por Sat R 53:88-9 S 12 '70
One thing and another (cont) il por Sat R 53:35 F 14; 32-3+ Mr 21; 26+ Je 20; 30 D 19 '70

HUTCHES (furniture) See Cabinets (furniture)

HUTCHINS, Edward
Poem with a punch line; reprint. Chr Cent 87:1107 S 16 '70

HUTCHINSON, Bob
The 'Glades by houseboat. il Yachting 128:64-5+ D '70

HUTCHINSON, Ford
Bay that refused to die. il Am For 76:24-7+ Ap '70

HUTCHINSON, G. Evelyn
Biosphere; with biographical sketch. il Sci Am 223:33, 44-53 bibliog(p262) S '70

HUTCHINSON, Jay G.
Orienteering. il Parks & Rec 5:45+ F '70
—See Fox, G. D. jt. auth.

HUTCHINSON, Larry
How to write a rock 'n' roll song. il Sr Schol 97:24 D 14 '70
Solid-body electric guitar. il Sr Schol 97:38-9 N 16 '70

HUTCHINSON, Peter
Back to nature. il pors Time 95:62-3+ Je 29 '70 *

HUTCHINSON, W. H.
Law, order, and survival. Am West 7:4-5 Ja '70
West of Out our way. il Am West 7:18-25 My '70

HUTCHINSONIELLA macracantha. See Crustaceans

HUTCHISON, Ira J. Jr
Changing concepts: citizen safety in parks and recreation. il Parks & Rec 9:43-4+ S '70

HUTNER, Milton
Now the poor can get divorced, too. G. Lichtenstein. il pors N Y Times Mag p30-1+ Ap 26 '70 *

HUTSCHNECKER, Arnold A.
Doctor Hutschnecker's plan. por Newsweek 75:76 Ap 20 '70 *
Notes and comment. New Yorker 46:35-7 O 10 '70 *
Physician, heal thyself. Time 95:8 Ap 20 '70 *

HUTTERITE Brethren
Hutterites, plain people of the West. W. A. Allard. il Nat Geog 138:98-125 Jl '70

HUTTLESTON, Donald G.
Staghorn ferns. il Horticulture 48:26-7+ Je '70

HUTTON, Ginger
How to ball a tree. il Org Gard & Farm 17:98-9 Je '70

HUTTON, Harry K. and Galgoci, Charles
McAndrew case; Britain at the Chicago bar. Sch & Soc 98:112-15 F '70

HUTTON, Virginia
Mothers and daughters. il pors Vogue 155:100 Je '70

HUXLEY, Aldous
Aldous Huxley and the way to reality, by C. M. Holmes. Review
  Nation 211:565-6 N 30 '70. G. Woodcock *
In a world of analysis. B. Gross. Nation 210:693-5 Je 8 '70 *
Later novels of Huxley. J. Bentley. Yale R 59:507-19 Je '70 *
Letters of Aldous Huxley, ed. by G. Smith. Review
  Cath World 212:53 O '70. B. M. LaRosa
  New Yorker 46:81-3 Jl 18 '70. N. Bliven
Prophet and preacher. G. Wolff. por Newsweek 75:101+ My 4 '70 *
Voices and visions of Aldous Huxley. L. Kronenberger. Atlan 226:100-1+ Jl '70 *

HUXTABLE, Ada Louise
Perspectives; interview, ed. by S. Nirenberg. por House B 112:20+ S '70

HUYCK, Dorothy Boyle
Tikal: yesterday and tomorrow. il Am For 76:34-5+ F '70

HYALINE membrane disease
Cancer: battle report; research findings. M. Clark. il Newsweek 75:56 Ap 6 '70
Head start for survival; tests on the fetal lung. Time 96:94+ D 7 '70
HYALINEA baltica. See Foraminifera
HYATT corporation
Hotel chain rises to rival the giants. il Bsns W p 101-2+ S 19 '70
HYBRID corn. See Corn—Hybrids
HYBRID sterility. See Isolation (biology)
HYBRIDIZATION
See also
Allelomorphism
also subhead Hybrids under various subjects, e.g. Wheat—Hybrids
HYDANTOINS
See also
Diphenylhydantoin
HYDRANGEAS
Easy to grow. il Sunset 144:98-100 Je '70
HYDRANTS

Maintenance and repair
Salvage what you can; fire-hydrant maintenance policy, San Antonio, Tex. R. P. Van Dyke. il Am City 85:70-1 O '70
HYDRATES
Carbon dioxide clathrate in the martian ice cap. S. L. Miller and W. D. Smythe. bibliog il Science 170:531-3 O 30 '70
HYDRAULIC control
News from the world of space exploration: Fluidic controller for modulating spacesuit temperatures. il Space World G-3-75:49-50 Mr '70
HYDRAULIC engineering
Dam the rivers, full speed ahead. M. Frome. Field & S 75:58-9+ O; 12+ N '70
See also
Channels (hydraulic engineering)
Dams
United States—Reclamation, Bureau of
HYDRAULIC hammer tampers. See Tamping machines
HYDRAULIC machinery
See also
Liquidonics Industries, Inc.
HYDRAULIC models
Models predict environment; estuaries. il Sea Front 16:352-6 N '70
HYDROBIOLOGY. See Fresh water biology
HYDROCARBONS
Electron-repulsion theory: application to aliphatic and aromatic hydrocarbons. S. Zuffanti. bibliog il por Chem 43:8-13 My '70
Search for alkanes of 15 to 30 carbon atom length. W. G. Meinschein, and others. bibliog Science 167:753 Ja 30 '70
See also
Aldehydes
Olefins

Physiological effects
Long and short of the oil spills. il Sci N 97: 263-4 Mr 14 '70
HYDROCEPHALUS
Hydrocephalus in mice inoculated neonatally by the oronasal route with reovirus type I. P. A. Phillips and others. bibliog il Science 168:858-9 My 15 '70
HYDROCHLORIC acid
Hydrogen bonding in hydrochloric acid solutions. S. C. Lee and R. Kaplow. bibliog il Science 169:477-8 Jl 31 '70
HYDROCORTISONE
Neuraminidase activity in HeLa cells: effect of hydrocortisone. R. Carubelli and M. J. Griffin. bibliog il Science 170:1110-12 D 4 '70
Posttranscriptional control in the steroid-mediated induction of hepatic tyrosine transaminase. I. B. Levitan and T. E. Webb. bibliog il Science 167:283-5 Ja 16 '70
HYDRODYNAMICS
See also
Cavitation
Drops
Jets
Magnetohydrodynamics
Turbulence
Waves
HYDROELECTRIC plants
Digging in; controversy over the Cabora Bassa project. il Newsweek 76:60 N 16 '70
Fish and power plants; Storm King Mountain pumped-storage project. A. C. Jensen; reply with rejoinder. L. H. Mantell. Cons 24:42-3 Ap '70
Hydroelectricity and your electric bill; Government's chance to end private exploitation. il Consumer Rep 35:170-3 Mr '70

Instant power; Northfield Mountain hydroelectric pumped storage facility. C. Howard. il Pop Sci 196:76-7 Ap '70
See also
Grand Coulee power and reclamation project
HYDROELECTRIC power
River idols. A. W. Smith. Nat Parks & Con Mag 44:2 S '70
HYDROFOILS
Hydrofoil boats studied for Honolulu airport/ Waikiki link. Aviation W 93:63 Jl 27 '70
HYDROGEN
Hydrogen atom and its reactions in solution. W. A. Pryor and others. bibliog il Science 169:181-3 Jl 10 '70
Isaac Asimov explains; how can hydrogen be a metal? I. Asimov. Sci Digest 68:87-8 O '70
Making of metallic hydrogen. E. Gross. il Sci N 97:623-5 Je 27 '70
Rare gases, hydrogen, and nitrogen; concentrations and isotopic composition in lunar material. H. Hintenberger and others. il Science 167:543-5 Ja 30 '70
Through a cell of hydrogen. Sci N 99:23-4 Ja 9 '71
Isotopes
See also
Deuterium
HYDROGEN bombs

Ethical aspects
See Atomic warfare—Ethical aspects

Manufacture
Do-it-yourself. S. Novick. il Environ 11:22-5 D '69
HYDROGEN bonds. See Chemical bonds
HYDROGEN ion concentration
Limits of microbial existence: temperature and pH. T. D. Brock and G. K. Darland. bibliog il Science 169:1316-18 S 25 '70
See also
Soils—Analysis
HYDROGEN oxides
Hydrogen trioxide. il Chem 43:20 Je '70
HYDROGEN sulfide
Carbon-13 in Black Sea waters and implications for the origin of hydrogen sulfide. W. G. Deuser. bibliog il Science 168:1575-7 Je 26 '70
HYDROGENOMONAS. See Bacteria
HYDROLASES
Cerebral acid hydrolase activities: comparison in quaking and normal mice. D. J. Kurtz and J. N. Kanfer. bibliog il Science 168:259-60 Ap 10 '70
HYDROLOGIC cycle
Water cycle. H. L. Penman. il Sci Am 223:98-100+ bibliog(p262-3) S '70
HYDROLOGIC research
Pantanal: 400,000 sq. km. of swampland in the Mato Grosso. N. V. Cordeiro. il UNESCO Courier 23:14-15 Je '70
HYDROLYSIS
Photochemical oxidants: effect on starch hydrolysis in leaves. G. P. Hanson and W. S. Stewart. bibliog il Science 168:1223-4 Je 5 '70
Rate of decomposition of GB in seawater. J. Epstein. bibliog il Science 170:1396-8 D 25 '70
HYDRO-MASSAGE pools. See Swimming pools
HYDROMECHANICS
See also
Hydrostatics
HYDROPHONES
Amateur scientist. W. A. Watkins. Sci Am 223:116-17 Ag '70
HYDROPLANE building. See Boat building
HYDROPLANE racing

Photographs
Spray ballet, or practice doesn't necessarily make perfect. Motor B 125:12-13 Ap '70
HYDROPLANES
Sixteen-cylinder revolution. il Hot Rod 23: 110-11 S '70
HYDROPSYCHOTHERAPY. See Psychotherapy
HYDROSOLS. See Colloids
HYDROSTATIC extrusion process. See Extrusion process
HYDROSTATICS
Supersaturation of gases in water: absence of cavitation on decompression from high pressures. E. A. Hemmingsen. bibliog il Science 167:1493-4 Mr 13 '70
HYDROXYAPATITE
Uranium localization on hydroxyapatite by analysis of fission fragment tracks. R. C. Thompson. bibliog il Science 167:1494-7 Mr 13 '70

HYDROXYLASES
Elevation of aortic proline hydroxylase: a biochemical defect in experimental arteriosclerosis. G. C. Fuller and R. O. Langner. bibliog il Science 168:987-9 My 22 '70
HYDROXYTRYPTAMINE. See Serotonin
HYDROXYUREA. See Urea
HYGIENE
I cured myself with wool.... R. Bugg and H. G. Scott. Todays Health 48:56-7 Je '70
See also
Cleanliness
Perspiration
Woman—Health and hygiene
HYGIENE, Mental. See Mental hygiene
HYLA. See Tree frogs and tree toads
HYMAN, Stanley Edgar
Richard Wright reappraised. Atlan 225:127-8+ Mr '70
about
Modest critic. J. Mazzaro. Nation 211:569-70 N 30 '70 *
HYMENOCALLIS calathina. See Basket flowers
HYMENOPTERA
See also
Wasps
HYMER, W. C. and others
DNA synthesis in the anterior pituitary of the male rat: effect of castration and photoperiod. bibliog il Science 167:1629-31 Mr 20 '70
HYMES, James L. jr
Is aggression natural? il PTA Mag 65:2-4 bibliog(p34) O '70
Why programs for young children? il Todays Ed 59:34-6 Ap '70
HYMNS
Fakery of guitar masses. T. Day. il Cath World 211:270-2 S '70; Reply. J. Paulin. 212:174 Ja '71
Our own hymnal. Chr Cent 87:1435, 1467 N 25-D 2 '70
HYPERBARIC oxygenation
Hyperbaric oxygen: effects on metabolism and ionic movement in cerebral cortex slices. P. Joanny and others. bibliog il Science 167:1508-10 Mr 13 '70; Discussion. 169:704-5 Ag 14 '70
World's highest-pressure chamber. S. Carpenter. il por Pop Sci 196:66-7+ Ap '70
HYPERKINESIS
Children with no alternative. C. Ellingson. Sat R 53:67 N 21 '70
Drugs for learning. il Time 96:43-4 Ag 10 '70
Hyperactive children. M. A. Stewart. il Sci Am 222:94-8 Ap '70
Pep pills for pupils; use of stimulants to control hyperactive children in Omaha. Newsweek 76:60-1 Jl 13 '70
Pep pills for youngsters; treatment of hyperactive children in Omaha. il U S News 69:49 Jl 13 '70
Pills for classroom peace? controversy over use of drugs to improve school performance by controlling hyperactivity. E. T. Ladd. il Sat R 53:66-8+ N 21 '70; Discussion. 53:50 D 19 '70
HYPERPHENYLALANINEMIA. See Metabolism, Disorders of
HYPERSENSITIVITY. See Allergy
HYPERSONIC airplanes. See Airplanes Supersonic
HYPERTENSION
Hypertension. Todays Ed 59:48-50 Ja '70
Norepinephrine metabolism in brainstem of spontaneously hypertensive rats. Y. Yamori and others. bibliog il Science 170:544-6 O 30 '70
Perils of muscle beach; weight lifter's blood pressure. il Time 96:46 Jl 20 '70
HYPNOANALYSIS. See Hypnotism—Therapeutic use
HYPNOTICS
See also
Glutethimide
HYPNOTISM
How hypnosis may help you to quit smoking. il Good H 170:164 F '70
Learning to be hypnotized. P. Boyel. Sci Digest 68:71 D '70
Questioning hypnosis. il por Time 96:54-5 Jl 13 '70
Therapeutic use
My Sony, the doctor (William J. Bryan jr, M.D.) D. Slavitt. il Esquire 74:164-5+ O '70
Your emotions: can they influence disease? adaptation of address, November 1, 1969. H. B. Miller. il Sci Digest 68:61-4 Jl '70

HYPOTHALAMUS
Body temperature: possible ionic mechanism in the hypothalamus controlling the set point. R. D. Myers and W. L. Veale. bibliog il Science 170:95-7 O 2 '70
I am Joe's hypothalamus. J. D. Ratcliff. il Read Digest 96:124-7 Mr '70
Lateral hypothalamic control of killing: evidence for a cholinoceptive mechanism. D. E. Smith and others. bibliog il Science 167:900-1 F 6 '70
Microelectrophoresis of biogenic amines on hypothalamic thermosensitive cells. A. L. Beckman and J. S. Eisenman. bibliog il Science 170:334-6 O 16 '70
HYSLOP, Beatrice F.
(comp) Articles and other books received; France. See issues of American historical review
Trends in historical writing about modern western Europe in the last five years. bibliog f Ann Am Acad 387:141-76 Ja '70
HYSTERECTOMY. See Uterus—Surgery
HYSTERESIS synchronous motor. See Electric motors, Synchronous
HYSTERIA (social psychology)
Mass hysteria. Time 95:59-60 Ja 26 '70

I

IAEA. See International atomic energy agency
IA-ECOSOC. See Inter-American economic and social council
IAM. See International association of machinists and aerospace workers
IATA. See International air transport association
IATSE. See International alliance of theatrical stage employees and moving picture machine operators of the United States and Canada
IAU. See International astronomical union
IBM. See International business machines corporation
IBM magnetic tape selectric composer. See Phototypesetting
IBP. See International biological program; Iowa beef packers, inc.
IBRD. See International bank for reconstruction and development
ICAC. See International cotton advisory committee
ICAO. See International civil aviation organization
ICC. See International chamber of commerce; International controls corporation
ICEL. See International committee on English in the liturgy
ICI. See Imperial chemical industries, ltd.
IDS. See Investors diversified service, inc.
I dreamt I dwelt in Bloomingdale's; drama. See Musical comedies, revues, etc.—Criticisms, plots, etc.
IEEE. See Institute of electrical and electronics engineers
IFA (international fighter aircraft) See Airplanes, Military
IFALPA. See International federation of air line pilots associations
IFC. See American library association—Intellectual freedom committee
IFCO. See Interreligious foundation for community organization
IFLA. See International federation of library associations
IFR flying. See Aviation—Instrument flying
IGY. See International geophysical year
IHD. See International hydrological decade
IHM (Immaculate Heart of Mary, Missionary sisters of) See Sisterhoods
IIE. See Institute of international education
ILGB. See International laboratory of genetics and biology
ILO. See International labor organization
ILS (instrument landing system) See Airplanes —Landing
ILWU. See International longshoremen's and warehousemen's union
IMC. See Instructional materials centers
IMF. See International monetary fund
INA corporation
Philadelphia renaissance. il Forbes 106:48 D 15 '70
See also
Insurance company of North America

INBEX (industrialized building exposition and congress) See Building industry—Exhibitions

IOF. See International oceanographic foundation

IOS. See Investors overseas services, ltd.

IPI (individually prescribed instruction) See Individual instruction

IQ. See Intelligence quotient

IQ tests. See Intelligence tests

IRA. See International reading association

IRRA. See Industrial relations research association

IRRI. See International rice research institute

IRRPOS (interdisciplinary research relevant to problems of our society) program. See United States—National science foundation

IRS. See United States—Internal revenue service

ITC commercial credit card, inc.
Finance group hears master plan for foreign sales. Pub W 197:45 Mr 23 '70

I-T-E circuit breaker company. See I-T-E imperial corporation

I-T-E imperial corporation
Why make monuments? il por Forbes 105: 51-2 Mr 15 '70

ITT. See International telephone and telegraph corporation

ITU. See International typographical union

ITV (instructional television) See Television in education

I take care of things; story. See Cady, J.

I thought you were a unicorn; story. See Boles, P. D.

IUD (intra-uterine device) See Contraceptives

IWW. See Industrial workers of the world

I wonder if I have an inner value I don't know about; story. See Ellingson, M.

IACOBELLI, John L.
Survey of employer attitudes toward training the disadvantaged; excerpt from Training programs of private industry in the Greater Cleveland area. il Mo Labor R 93:51-5 Je '70

IACOCCA, Lee Anthony. See Iacocca, Lido Anthony

IACOCCA, Lido Anthony
How Iacocca won the big one. il por Bsns W p38-9 D 19 '70 *
Lee's here. por Newsweek 76:83 D 21 '70 *
Patience rewarded. il por Time 96:66 D 21 '70 *

IACOVETTI, Nicola
Opera amid the grapes. S. Jenkins, jr. il por Opera N 34:6-7 Mr 14 '70 *

IANUZZI, Ralph
(comp) Who won what? Motor B 125:26+ F '70 *

IATROGENIC diseases
Can doctors cause disease? N. Cousins. Sat R 53:30-2 Ag 22 '70; Discussion. 53:23+ O 17 '70

IBARRA, José María Velasco. See Velasco Ibarra, J. M.

IBBOTSON, Eva
Little countess; story. Ladies Home J 87:78-9 Mr '70
Why is this fish smiling? story. Redbook 136:88-9 D '70

IBEN, Icko, jr
Globular-cluster stars; with biographical sketch. il Sci Am 223:15, 26-39 bibliog(p 136) Jl '70

IBERO-AMERICAN art. See Art, Latin American

IBISA. See Iviza (island)

IBIZA. See Iviza (island)

IBN Hakkan al-Bokhari, dead in his labyrinth; story. See Borges, J. L.

IBO tribe. See Nigeria—Native races

IBSEN, Henrik
Enemy of the people; drama, ed. by P. T. Nolan. Plays 29:86-96 Mr '70
Hedda Gabler. Criticism
Nat R 22:852 Ag 11 '70 *
Nation 211:253 S 21 '70 *
Time 95:70 Je 22 '70
Time il 96:45 Jl 20 '70

IBSON, K. G.
We renovated stores and print-shop operations. il Am City 85:116+ Mr '70

ICA, Peru
Politics and government
See Peru—Politics and government

ICARUS complex. See Complexes (psychology)

ICE
Subliming ice surfaces: freeze-etch electron microscopy. J. G. Davy and D. Branton. bibliog il Science 168:1216-18 Je 5 '70
Superdense water ice. A. H. Deisemme and A. Wenger; reply with rejoinder. B. A. Seiber and others. bibliog Science 170:652-4 N 6 '70
See also
Freezing
Glaciers

Manufacture
Tips on easier ice-making. E. Taylor. il Good H 171:197 Ag '70
What about automatic ice-makers? Consumer Rep 35:614-15 O '70

Polar Regions
Antarctic ice sheet: stable isotope analyses of Byrd station cores and interhemispheric climatic implications. S. Epstein and others. bibliog il Science 168:1570-2 Je 26 '70
Polar ice and the global climate machine. J. O. Fletcher. il por Bul Atom Sci 26:40-7 D '70
Stalactite growth beneath sea ice. R. A. Paige. bibliog il Science 167:171-2 Ja 9 '70
See also
Glaciers

ICE age art. See Art, Primitive

ICE ages. See Glacial epochs

ICE boats and ice boating
Say a little prayer, and go; iceboating. D. Levin. il Sports Illus 32:50+ F 9 '70

ICE breaking vessels
I saw them crunch through the Northwest Passage; SS Manhattan. R. Gannon. il pors Pop Sci 196:101-5+ Ja '70
New Northwest Passage; Manhattan's voyage. M. Gruber. il Sea Front 16:2-12 Ja '70
North for oil: Manhattan makes the historic Northwest Passage. B. Keating. il Nat Geog 137:374-91 Mr '70
Supertanker has a hole and Canada fears for Arctic. Audubon 72:117 Ja '70

ICE breaking vessels, Submarine
Submarine icebreaker for Arctic oil? J. F. Pearson. il pors Pop Mech 133:85-9 Mr '70; Same. Sci Digest 67:75-9 My '70

ICE cream, ices, etc.
Homemade ice cream. il Ebony 25:174+ Ag '70
How frozen desserts differ. il Good H 170:150 Je '70
How to make an ice cream bombe. il Sunset 145:117 S '70
Ice cream diet; excerpt. G. Maddox. il Ladies Home J 87:48+ S '70
Ice cream: recipes. M. Happel. il Ladies Home J 87:80-1+ Jl '70
Orange ice cream homemade. il Sunset 145: 120 Jl '70
Sherbet with mint, ginger. il Sunset 145:152 S '70
Simple sundaes with very special syrups. il Sunset 145:146 D '70
Spectacular ice cream bombes. J. Jaffry. il Am Home 73:72-3 Ag '70

ICE cream scoops. See Scoops

ICE cubes
Manufacture
See Ice—Manufacture

ICE drilling. See Drilling and boring (ice)

ICE fishing. See Fishing, Winter

ICE hazards in aviation. See Airplanes—Ice protection

ICE hockey. See Hockey

ICE machinery. See Ice—Manufacture

ICE making. See Ice—Manufacture

ICE sheets. See Glaciers

ICE shows
New ice age packs 'em in. il Bsns W p 104-5 Ja 17 '70

ICEBERGS
Iceberg water. Chem 43:23 Ja '70
Icebergs of West Greenland. C. W. Morgan. il Sea Front 16:328-36 N '70

ICEBOATS. See Ice boats and ice boating

ICED drinks. See Beverages

ICELAND
See also
Airlines—Iceland

Description and travel
Iceland explorations. J. Cowan. Vogue 156:36 O 15 '70

ICELAND poppies. See Poppies

ICELANDIC airlines. See Airlines—Iceland

ICHTHYOSIS. See Skin—Diseases

ICKERINGILL, Nan
Spirited invasion. House B 112:92-3 Ja '70
ICONS
Moscow's godsend. il Newsweek 76:59-61 Ag 10 '70
I'D rather do it myself; drama. See Collins, D. R.
IDAHO
See also
Clearwater River
Craters of the Moon National Monument
Fishing—Idaho
Hells Canyon
Hunting—Idaho
Salmon River
Skis and skiing—Idaho
Wilderness areas—Idaho
Wildlife conservation—Idaho

Description and travel
Rugged Idaho. D. Wharton. il Read Digest 97:138-44 Ag '70
IDAHO caves. See Caves
IDEA engineering. See Ideas in business
IDEAL states. See Utopias
IDEALISM
Another look at the American dream. R. J. Lamont. Chr Today 14:6-8 Ap 24 '70
IDEALISM in art
See also
Realism in art
IDEAS in business
Are you an innovator or operator? C. A. Cerami. il Nations Bsns 58:54-7 Je '70
Outside job fills the product gap: free-lance idea men. il Bsns W p54+ My 16 '70
IDENTIFICATION
See also
Dermatoglyphics
Fingerprints
IDENTITY, Personal. See Personality
IDIOCY
See also
Cretinism
IDLEMAN, Hillis K. and Idleman, M. P.
Owning a home freezer: convenience? Economy? il Consumer Bul 53:33-6 Ap '70
IDLEMAN, Martha P. See Idleman, H. K. jt. auth.
IDRIA columnaris. See Cirios
IDYLL, Clarence P.
Food from the sea for Nigeria. il Sea Front 16:340-51 N '70
IEHSI, Ambilos
Trust Territory of the Pacific Islands; statements, June 3 and 11, 1970. Dept State Bul 63:259-62, 266-8 Ag 31 '70
IERONYMOS, abp
Greek orthodoxy: the junta defied. T. Cosmades. Chr Today 14:38-9 Ja 16 '70
IF you meet a leprechaun; drama. See Feather, J.
IGLEBURGER, Robert
Dayton's mod cops. il por Newsweek 76:51-2 N 9 '70 *
IGNATOW, David
While I live; Waiting inside; Intimations; Baker; Off to the cemetery; poems. Nation 210:58 Ja 19 '70
IGNITION, Automobile. See Automobile engines—Ignition
IGNITION devices. See Automobile engines—Ignition
IGNITION locks, Boat. See Boat locks and keys
IGUANAS
Extraretinal light perception: entrainment of the biological clock controlling lizard locomotor activity. H. Underwood and M. Menaker. bibliog il Science 170:190-3 O 9 '70
IKARD, Frank Neville
Petroleum industry's role in the preservation of the environment. il Parks & Rec 5:18-21+ My '70
There's more to gasoline quality than octane ratings. por Pop Sci 196:89+ My '70
IKEDA, Shig
Shig Ikeda. il Pop Phot 66:78-83 My '70 *
IKEMOTO, Takashi
(tr) See Takahashi, S. Spray of hot air; Canna; Sun through the leaves; Ice
IKLÉ, Max
Dollar's future as Europe sees it: interview. ed. by A. Zanker. il por U S News 68:66-70 Ap 13 '70
ILLEGAL television stations. See Television stations, Illegal
ILLEGITIMACY
Copyright renewal rights of illegitimates cited a recurring problem. Pub W 197:34 My 4 '70

Identity crisis Italian style; children of black GIs. M. Senesi. il Ebony 25:40-6 Jl '70
Larry: case history of a mistake. R. McQueen. Sat R 53:16-19+ S 12 '70; Same abr. il Read Digest 97:133-7 D '70
What kids still don't know about sex. T. Fleming and A. Fleming. il Look 34:59-60+ Jl 28 '70; Same abr. Read Digest 97:153-6 D '70
See also
Mothers, Unmarried
ILLICH, Ivan D.
De-schooling the teaching orders. por America 124:12-14 Ja 9 '71
False ideology of schooling. il Sat R 53:56-8+ O 17 '70
Letter to Pope Paul. Commonweal 92:428-9 S 4 '70
about
Ivan Illich and CIDOC as theater. S. Bliss. Chr Cent 87:1463-6 D 2 '70 *
Profiles. F. Du Plessix. por New Yorker 46:40-4+ Ap 25 '70 *
ILLICK, Joseph E.
Looking westward. See Issues of American west
ILLINOIS
See also
Booksellers and bookselling—Illinois
Education—Illinois
Justice Administration of—Illinois
Landscape protection—Illinois
Paleontology—Illinois
Roads—Illinois
Water supply—Illinois

Legislature
Campus meets legislature. il Time 95:47 Je 8 '70

Politics and government
Adlai III brand of politics. W. B. Furlong. il pors N Y Times Mag p28-9+ F 22 '70
Adlai III; his new politics startle old pros. J. Star. il pors Look 34:82-4+ O 6 '70
Illinois: Stevenson fights TV. E. S. Gilbreth. il Nation 211:399-402 O 26 '70
New Adlai; Senate race. il por Newsweek 76:38+ O 12 '70
New bill of rights for Illinois. Nation 211:421-2 N 2 '70
They're after Adlai. P. R. Wieck. New Repub 163:13-15 S 26 '70
ILLINOIS central railroad company
Derailment at last chance junction? mini-train plan. il Bsns W p68-9+ Mr 28 '70
Mini-trains get a green light. il Bsns W p27-8 Je 13 '70
ILLINOIS. University
Advances in computer-based education; PLATO program. D. Alpert and D. L. Bitzer. bibliog il Science 167:1582-90 Mr 20 '70
Latin for the now generation. Sch & Soc 98:286-70 Sum '70
When college students grade the faculty. T. Dillman. Todays Ed 59:62+ F '70

Chicago campus
New galaxies at Chicago circle. J. Dixon. il Arch Forum 133:24-33 N '70
ILLITERACY
Battle against illiteracy: a Unesco survey. A. Brock. Sch & Soc 98:181+ Mr '70
Combating illiteracy. Har Yrs 10:51 F '70
Illiteracy, abettor of poverty. K. Cole. Focus 20:12 Ja '70
Illiteracy, woman's worldwide burden; UNESCO report. R. L. Tobin. Sat R 53:16 S 5 '70
Literacy librarian: case studies of experiments in Dallas. M. Warren. il por Wilson Lib Bul 45:278-84 N '70
New ideas in an ancient land; national campaign against illiteracy. W. G. Carr. il Todays Ed 59:28-9 N '70
News and the functional illiterate; views of Walter Cronkite; Harvard survey findings. R. L. Tobin. Sat R 53:51-2 Je 13 '70
San Antonio's fight against illiteracy. D. Wright. il Am Ed 6:20-1 N '70
ILLNESS. See Sickness
ILLUMINATED manuscripts. See Illumination of books and manuscripts
ILLUMINATION. See Electric lighting
ILLUMINATION of books and manuscripts
Donald Jackson: calligrapher & illuminator. F. Johnson. il por Am Artist 34:17-23+ My '70
Pride of illuminations; exhibition of medieval and renaissance works at New York headquarters of H. P. Kraus. H. A. La Farge. il Art N 69:58-9 Mr '70

ILLUSION and hallucination producing plants.
See Hallucination and illusion producing
plants
ILLUSION of reality. See Trompe-l'oeil
ILLUSIONS and hallucinations
See also
Flying saucers
Optical illusions
ILLUSTRATED books
Illustrated book, by D. Klemin. Review
Pub W il 197:48-50 My 25 '70
Modern visual concepts create moving Lin-
coln biography. M. R. Kraner. il Pub W
197:48-50 My 4 '70
See also
Picture books
ILLUSTRATION of books and periodicals
Airport becomes a movie. il Good H 170:52+
Ap '70
Business and trade journal market. O. Henry.
Writer 83:24-6 Je '70
Dynamic ink drawings of Charles Shaw. C.
Shaw. il Am Artist 34:61-6 Je '70
Gyo Fujikawa: an illustrator children love.
M. R. Kraner. il por Pub W 199:45-6+ Ja 4
'71
How and where to sell photos and photo-
illustrated articles. R. Arnold. il Writers
Digest 50:24-6 Jl '70
Illustrations of Murray Tinkelman. C. Cor-
cos. il por Am Artist 34:20-5+ O '70
Lesson in spot illustration. L. J. Miller. il
Design 71:14-15 mid-Wint '70
Man who drew Pooh. R. Cowley. il McCalls
97:12+ Ag '70
Price is won; or, How Maurice Sendak dis-
covered where the wild things are; address,
April 4, 1970. il por Pub W 197:30-1 My 25
'70
Virginia Lee Burton's dynamic sense of de-
sign. L. Kingman. il Horn Bk 46:449-60,
593-602 O-D '70
William A. Berry; illustrator/painter. S. E.
Meyer. il Am Artist 34:80-5 Mr '70
See also
Newspapers—Illustrations
Picture books for children
ILLUSTRATORS
See also
Berry, W. A.
Fujikawa, G.
Groth, J.
Sendak, M.
Shepard, E. H.
Steig, W.
Tinkelman, M.
Volk, V.
ILTIS, Hugh H.
Man's forgotten necessity, eco-variety. por
Field & S 75:62+ Je '70
—and others
Criteria for an optimum human environment.
Bul Atom Sci 26:2-6 Ja '70
IMAGE intensifiers
Image-tube observations at Cerro Tololo. M.
F. Walker. bibliog il por Sky & Tel 40:132-8
S '70
Night scopes add extra insight to police work;
Newton, Mass. W. F. Quinn. Am City 85:16
O '70
Seeing-eye scope. il Newsweek 76:60-1 Ag 3
'70
See also
Television camera tubes
IMAGINARY animals. See Animals, Imaginary
IMAGINARY revolutions
Scenario for a military coup d'etat in the
United States. E. Luttwak. il Esquire 74:
60-5+ Jl '70
IMAGINARY societies
Halfway to 1984. L. Malkin. il por Horizon 12:
32-9 Spr '70
Walden two: three? Many more? R. Todd.
il por N Y Times Mag p24-5+ Mr 15 '70
IMAGINATION
Leap to imagination. J. Weston. Writer 83:
12-14 Ag '70
See also
Creative ability
Daydreams
IMAGINE two people who both wear a size
eight shoe just finding each other on the
street; story. See Shyer, M. F.
IMAI, Ryukichi
Japan and the nuclear age. il por Bul Atom
Sci 26:35-9 Je '70
IMBER, Dorot, and Tal, Moshe
Phenotypic reversion of flacca, a wilty mu-
tant of tomato, by abscisic acid. bibliog il
Science 169:592-3 Ag 7 '70
IMBERT BARRERA, Antonio
Where are they now? il por Newsweek 75:22
My 18 '70 *
IMIPRAMINE. See Antidepressants

IMITATION in literature
See also
Plagiarism
IMLACH, George
Punch line gets the last laugh. M. Mulvoy.
Sports Illus 33:86-7 N 30 '70 *
IMMACULATE conception. See Mary, Virgin
IMMACULATE Heart sisters of Los Angeles.
See Sisterhoods
IMMANENCE of God
See also
Transcendence of God
IMMERSION heaters. See Water heaters
IMMIGRANTS in Great Britain
See also
Pakistanis in Great Britain
IMMIGRANTS in the United States
See also
Citizenship
Cubans in the United States
Irish in the United States
Italians in the United States
Jews in the United States
Naturalization

Education
See also
Libraries—Services to foreign born
IMMIGRATION and emigration

Law
See Immigration and emigration law

Australia
Americans are emigrating to Australia. H.
Gordon. il N Y Times Mag p75+ My 17 '70

Canada
Indiana family leaves the U.S. for keeps;
Argast family. il Life 69:42-7 Jl 17 '70

Cuba
See also
Cubans in the United States

Europe
Europe's migrant workers: northward! il
Time 95:38-9 Je 8 '70

Great Britain
Britain: no haven for U.S. deserters. T. Bee-
son. Chr Cent 88:37 Ja 13 '71
Girl without a country. il por Time 95:31-2
F 23 '70
No British blueprint for a nightmare; in-
terview, ed by C. R. Hughes. E. J. B. Rose.
America 122:266-70 Mr 14 '70

Israel
Black migrants to a promised land. il Life
68:65-6+ My 22 '70

Latin America
Migration of scientists from Latin America;
adaptation of address, 1968. H. M. Nussenzveig; discussion. Science 166:820-1;
167:1669-70 N 14 '69, Mr 27 '70
Promised land. G. de Zéndegui. il Américas
22:2-8 O '70

Poland
Reluctant emigrés; Poland's last Jews. M.
Reynolds. New Repub 162:17-19 Mr 21 '70

Russia
Opinion of mankind; Jewish hijacking case.
Nation 212:34 Ja 11 '71

United States
Latest American exodus. il Time 96:13-15 N
30 '70
Melting pot: the ethnic group that blended
the Scotch-Irish; excerpts from Scotch-
Irish: a social history. J. G. Leyburn. il
Am Heritage 22:28-31+ D '70
Pictogram: the new Americans. il U S News
69:70-1 O 5 '70
Promised land. G. de Zéndegui. il Américas
22:2-8 O '70
See also
Brain drain
IMMIGRATION and emigration law
Growing rich on the alien. T. D. Williams.
il Nation 211:614-17 D 14 '70
IMMIGRATION quotas. See Immigration and
emigration—United States
IMMORAL literature and pictures
Books. M. Muggeridge. Esquire 73:206 My '70
Dealing with pornography:
Case against censorship. A. S. Engel.
Cur 123:38-43 N '70
Case for censorship. R. M. Christenson.
Cur 123:31-8 N '70

IMMORAL literature and pictures—*Continued*
Does it have to be dirty to sell? W. Wolfe.
Writer 83:20-2 F '70
End of pornography. H. Gold. Sat R 53:25-7+
O 31 '70
Flag day at Judson memorial church. M.
Geltman. Nat R 22:1252 D 1 '70
How big is the smut industry? il U S News
69:62 O 12 '70
Keep pornography clean; Copenhagen's 1969
porno fair. R. Wolfe. il Holiday 47:18+ Mr
'70
Obscenity. S. Kauffmann. New Repub 163:22+
O 17 '70
Oh! Copenhagen! T. Buckley. il N Y Times
Mag p32-4+ F 8 '70
Porn capital of America; San Francisco. W.
Murray. il N Y Times Mag p8-9+ Ja 3 '71
Pornography and antisocial behavior. Sch
& Soc 98:76+ F '70
Pornography goes public. il Newsweek 76:26-
8+ D 21 '70
Pornography goes public; with report on
attempts of clean up by Mason City, Iowa
group. J. Neary. il Life 69:18-25 Ag 28 '70
Pornography in a free society. Chr Today
14:20-1 My 22 '70
Put the mail-order smut merchants out of
business! G. Denison. Read Digest 96:209-
10+ My '70
Rich pornocopia. il Time 96:92 N 16 '70
Second thoughts about obscenity. A. Holland.
Writers Digest 50:8 Ag '70
Tell all the gang on 42nd street. il Time 96:
21 O 19 '70
What women think of pornography. J. Bro-
thers. il Good H 170:54+ My '70
When pornography curbs are lifted; Den-
mark. A. Zanker. il U S News 69:68 O 19 '70
See also
Booksellers and bookselling—Immoral litera-
ture and pictures
Censorship
Obscenity (law)
Sex in literature
United States—Commission on obscenity and
pornography

Anecdotes, facetiae, satire, etc.

Immodest proposal; Sanitary plan for dis-
placing obscene literature. F. K. Bartz.
Engl J 59:43 Ja '70

IMMORTALITY
Hell of a question. J. E. Kokjohn. Common-
weal 93:367-70 Ja 15 '71
Logic of ultimate hope. J. W. Woelfel. Chr
Cent 87:356-61 Mr 25 '70; Discussion. 87:
734:5, 1041-2 Je 10, S 2 '70
See also
Death
Future life
Reincarnation

IMMORTALS; story. See Borges, J. L. and
Casares, A. B.

IMMUNITIES and privileges See Privileges
and immunities

IMMUNITY
Cell-mediated immunity shown by lympho-
cytes from the respiratory tract. C. S.
Henney and R. H. Waldman. bibliog il Sci-
ence 169:696-7 Ag 14 '70
David's doctor. il por Newsweek 76:97-8 N
23 '70
Mediation of immunity to tumor isografts in
mice by heterologous ribonucleic acid. K.
P. Ramming and Y. H. Pilch. bibliog il
Science 168:492-3 Ap 24 '70
See also
Antigens and antibodies
Antiserum
Complements (immunity)
Inoculation
Phagocytes and phagocytosis

IMMUNITY (exemption) See Privileges and
immunities

IMMUNOASSAY. See Biological assay

IMMUNOELECTROOSMOPHORESIS. See Electrophoresis

IMMUNOFLUORESCENCE. See Antibodies,
Fluorescent

IMMUNOGLOBULINS. See Blood—Proteins

IMMUNOLOGICAL tolerance
Cell interaction in an immune response in
vitro: requirement for theta-carrying cells.
E. L. Chan and others. bibliog il Science
170:1215-17 D 11 '70
Cytotoxicity: specificity after in vitro sensitization. S. Solliday and F. H. Bach. bibliog il Science 170:1406-9 D 25 '70
Immune responses of inbred mice to repeated low doses of antigen: relationship to
histocompatibility (H-2) type. N. M. Vaz
and B. B. Levine. bibliog il Science 168:852-
4 My 15 '70

Immunological surveillance; report of meeting. D. B. Wilson. Science 169:1006+ S 4 '70
Lymphomas in mice: failure of induction
after a graft-versus-host reaction. G. B.
Rossi and C. Friend. bibliog il Science 167:
1383-5 Mr 6 '70
Mixed lymphocyte cultures produce effector
cells: model in vitro for allograft rejection.
P. Häyry and V. Defendi. bibliog il Science 168:133-5 Ap 3 '70
Mixed lymphocyte reactions and tissue
transplantation tolerance. W. K. Silvers
and others. bibliog il Science 167:1264-6 F
27 '70
Ranks of donor-recipient histocompatibility
for human transplantation. F. T. Rapaport and J. Dausset. bibliog il Science 167:
1260-2 F 27 '70
Sex ratio of newborns: preponderance of
males in toxemia of pregnancy. P. Toivanen
and T. Hirovonen. bibliog il Science 170:
187-8 O 9 '70
Tolerance to polyinosinic polycytidylic acid
in NZB/NZW mice. A. D. Steinberg and
others. bibliog il Science 167:870-1 F 6 '70
Transplantation: pairing of donor and recipient. F. H. Bach. bibliog il Science 168:
1170-9 Je 5 '70

IMMUNOLOGY
Bone marrow and spleen: dissociation of im-
munologic properties by cortisone. M. A.
Levine and H. N. Claman. bibliog il Science
167:1515-17 Mr 13 '70
Hominid phylogeny and immunology: a cri-
tical appraisal. D. W. Read and P. E.
Lestrel. bibliog il Science 168:578-80 My 1
'70
Poly I:C moves into a new arena: immunity.
B. J. Culliton. il Sci N 97:323 Mr 28 '70
Vibriolytic antibody-forming cells: a new ap-
plication of the Pfeiffer phenomenon. R. F.
McAlack and others. bibliog il Science 168:
141-2 Ap 3 '70
Vitamin B_{12} binders of chicken serum and
chicken proventriculus are immunologically similar. D. W. Sonneborn and H. J.
Hansen. bibliog il Science 168:591-2 My 1
'70

IMMUNOSUPPRESSIVE agents
L-asparaginase-induced immunosuppression:
effects on antibody-forming cells and se-
rum titers. A. K. Chakrabarty and H.
Friedman. bibliog il Science 167:869-70 F
6 '70
See also
Mercaptopurine

IMPACTED aid. See Education—Federal aid

IMPEACHMENTS
Impeaching Justice Douglas? il por U S
News 68:25-6 Ap 27 '70

IMPEDANCE (electricity)
Bioelectrical impedance; report of Interna-
tional impedance. L. A. Geddes. Science
167:1761 Mr 27 '70
Calculating strip-line impedance. R. L. Car-
roll. il Electr World 84:31 S '70
See also
Electric resistance
Reactance (electricity)

IMPERIAL chemical industries, ltd.
Getting at the root of a labor crisis; ICI's
wage-productivity plan. il Bsns W p56+
O 17 '70

IMPERIALISM
Empire and revolution, by D. Horowitz. Re-
view
Ramp Mag 8:60+ F '70. T. Gitlin
Imperial role. G. W. Johnson. New Repub
163:9 D 12 '70
Imperialism. G. Lichtheim. bibliog Commen-
tary 49:42-75 Ap; 33-58 My '70
See also subhead Colonies under names
of countries, e.g. Great Britain—Colonies

IMPLANTATION. Subcutaneous
Alza's big promise. por Duns 97:53 Ja '71
Now, this won't hurt; implantable drug de-
livery system. il Newsweek 77:59-60 Ja 4 '71

IMPLANTATION in mammals. See Embryology
—Mammals

IMPLEMENTS, utensils, etc.
See also
Indians of North America—Implements
Stone implements and weapons
Tools

IMPORT and export controls. See Foreign trade
regulation

IMPORT quotas
Are imports killing off U.S. industries? with
editorial comment. il Bsns W p76-7, 100
Jl 25 '70
Consumer be damned; import quota system
for oil. W. K. Wyant, jr. New Repub 162:
11-12 Mr 7 '70
Consumerism and trade. H. C. Wallich. Newsweek 76:61 Ag 31 '70

IMPORT quotas—*Continued*
Controls may be necessary; comments by
Dun's presidents' panel; with editorial comment. G. R. Rosen. il Duns 97:38, 80 Ja '71
Evil consequences of quotas. America 123:
34 Jl 25 '70
Fight over quotas; foreign oil into the U.S.
il Time 95:69-70 Ja 26 '70
Government of oil. Commonweal 92:3 Mr 13
'70
Irritated friendship; Japanese textile im-
passe. Chr Cent 87:835 Jl 8 '70
Latin America strives against protectionist
trade policies. Américas 22:44 S '70
Meat import limitations modified for remain-
der of 1970; with proclamation and executive order. R. M. Nixon. Dept State Bul
63:157-9 Ag 3 '70
Mills bill. il Newsweek 75:76 Ap 27 '70
Mills bill; savior or disaster? il Newsweek
76:77-8 D 7 '70
Nettle up for grabs; proposed bill. Newsweek
76:61-2 Jl 27 '70
Nixon opens tap a bit on oil imports. il
Bsns W p37 Je 27 '70
No winners in a trade war, and one is get-
ting started. il U S News 69:46-8 S 14 '70
Oil policy committee discontinues considera-
tion of tariff system; text of letter, August
13, 1970. G. A. Lincoln. Dept State Bul 63:
360-1 S 28 '70
Oil: quotas or tariffs? Duns 95:102 F '70
Oilmen shrug off increase in imports. Bsns
W p 12 Ja 2 '71
On the import quota system; Latin America's
objectives; excerpt from address, April 23,
1970. G. Plaza. Américas 22:1 My '70
President announces assistance to footwear
industry. Dept State Bul 63:91-3 Jl 20 '70
President Nixon amends oil import program;
White House announcement; with proclama-
tion, June 17, 1970. R. M. Nixon. Dept State
Bul 63:7-8 Jl 6 '70
President Nixon modifies oil import program;
proclamation. R. Nixon. Dept State Bul 63:
682-3 N 30 '70
President Nixon receives report of oil im-
port control task force; statement, February
20, 1970. R. M. Nixon. Dept State Bul 62:
427-8 Mr 30 '70
Pressure mounts to tap domestic oil. il Bsns
W p 17-18 Jl 25 '70
Promise paid; restrictions on imports of
foreign-made textiles. il Time 96:61 Jl 6 '70
Protectionist push. Newsweek 76:66-7 Jl 6
'70
Protectionists win a vital skirmish. Bsns W
p28-9 Jl 18 '70
Push for more quotas gets going. il Bsns
W p 17 Jl 4 '70
Quota backfires for steelmakers. il Bsns W
p24 S 12 '70
Reports: Washington; President's pledge to
the textile industry. M. Seeger. Atlan 226:
20+ N '70
Slapping controls on a Niagara of oil; Can-
adian imports. Bsns W p27 Mr 14 '70
Snag in textiles; Japanese proposals. Time
95:74 Je 29 '70
Temporizing; Japanese textiles. il Nat R
22:720 Jl 14 '70
Textile victory for protectionists. il Bsns W
p38 Je 27 '70
Trade: the black comedy that could come
true. il Time 96:97-8 N 23 '70
Trade trap; U.S. policy of trade restriction.
New Repub 163:7 O 31 '70
Trade war? New Repub 163:7 Ag 1 '70
TV set tiff: Japan out of focus? Sr Schol 97:
12 S 28 '70
U.S. establishes formal limitation on oil imports from Canada; White House an-
nouncement; with proclamation by Presi-
dent Nixon. Dept State Bul 62:494-5 Ap 13
'70
Why the growing fight over foreign goods.
il U S News 69:43-4 Jl 6 '70
Why the U.S. is letting in more foreign oil.
il U S News 70:17 Ja 4 '71
IMPORTS
Increases in shipping weights of total U.S.
exports and imports; table. Aviation W 93:
79 O 26 '70
Shipping weights of U.S. exports and im-
ports by air, year 1969; table. Aviation W
93:42 O 26 '70
See also
Dumping (commercial policy)
IMPOSTOR; story. See Crittenden, J.
IMPOSTORS and imposture
See also
Forgery of works of art
IMPOTENCE
Male sexual inadequacy. D. Reuben. McCalls
98:26+ O '70

IMPREGNATION, Artificial. See Artificial in-
semination, Human
IMPRESSIONISM (art)
Bonjour, M Durand-Ruel. B. Berry and L.
Traiger. il por Art N 69:44-7+ Ap '70
IMPRISONMENT of children. See Children—Im-
prisonment
IN-flight movies. See Airlines—Passenger
service
IN-flight periodicals. See Periodicals for air-
line passengers
IN from the islands out from the town; story.
See Delbanco, N.
IN our fourth year of marriage; story. See
Huot, M. I. A.
IN search of Mihailo; story. See Pala, D.
IN search of Nan Page; story. See Kevles, B.
H.
IN-service librarian education. See Librarians
—Education in service
IN-service teacher education. See Teachers—
Education in service
IN-service training of employees. See Employees
—Training
IN the forests of Riga the beasts are very
wild indeed; story. See Brown, M. F.
IN the night; ballet. See Ballets—Criticisms
INAUGURAL addresses. See Speeches, address-
es, etc.
INAUGURAL addresses of the Presidents. See
Presidents—United States—Inaugural ad-
dresses
INBOARD motor boats. See Motor boats
INBOARD motors. See Motor boat engines
INBORN errors of metabolism. See Metabo-
lism, Disorders of
INBREEDING
Immune responses of inbred mice to repeat-
ed low doses of antigen: relationship to
histocompatibility (H-2) type. N. M. Vaz
and B. B. Levine. bibliog il Science 168:852-
4 My 15 '70
INCARNATION
Incarnation unveiled. J. R. Tunnell; discus-
sion. Chr Cent 87:116 Ja 28 '70
See also
Jesus Christ
INCANTATIONS. See Magic
INCAS
Languages
Literate Incas. il Time 96:46+ Ag 17 '70
INCENTIVE pay. See Incentives in industry
INCENTIVES in industry
Big steel workers win a decision. Bsns W
p30 Je 13 '70
Getting at the root of a labor crisis; ICI's
wage-productivity plan. il Bsns W p56+ O 17
'70
Steel burns again over incentives. Bsns W
p42+ F 21 '70
INCINERATORS. See Refuse incinerators;
Sewage incinerators
INCO. See International nickel company of
Canada, ltd.
INCOME
Federal spending: new spur to business; taxes
are cut, pay rates are rising. il U S News
68:24-6 Ap 20 '70
Look at national priorities. K. E. Boulding.
il Cur Hist 59:65-72+ Ag '70
Money income of older people. il Aging 187:
24-7 My '70
Now 1,122 incomes of 1 million or more. U S
News 69:61-2 N 9 '70
Personal income; tables. See occasional is-
sues of Business week
TRB from Washington:
Smith experiment; proposed national
Family allowance program. New Repub
162-8 F 21 '70
See also
Gross national product
Guaranteed annual income
Negative income tax
Retirement income
INCOME tax
See also
Corporations—Taxation
Old age pensions—Taxation
Auditing
See Tax auditing
Capital gains tax
Tough new capital gains law can still save
you tax dollars. F. Bailey, jr. Suc Farm
68:8-9 O '70
Collection
See Tax collection; Withholding tax

INDIA—*Continued*

Nobility

Reprieve for the rajahs. il Time 96:21 D 28 '70

Parliament

Indira's big gamble; dissolution of Parliament. il Newsweek 77:49 Ja 11 '71

Politics and government

Eruption in India; tr. by J. Oringer. P. Gavi. il Ramp Mag 8:8+ Ap '70

Mrs Gandhi's gamble. por Time 97:27-8 Ja 11 '71

World around us. V. Koilpillai. Chr Cent 87:974 Ag 12 '70

See also

Communist party (India)

India—Parliament

Political parties—India

Population

See also

Birth control—India

Relief work

Profiles; Missionaries of charity. Calcutta. V. Mehta. New Yorker 46:97-8+ Mr 21 '70

Religious institutions and affairs

World around us. V. Koilpillai. Chr Cent 87:974 Ag 12 '70

See also

Methodist church in India

Sikhs

Riots

Eruption in India; tr. by J. Oringer. P. Gavi. il Ramp Mag 8:8+ Ap '70

Fire and blood again. Time 95:41-2 My 25 '70

Social conditions

Eruption in India; tr. by J. Oringer. P. Gavi. il Ramp Mag 8:8+ Ap '70

See also

Untouchables

Social life and customs

Indian expatriate rediscovers India. D. Moraes. il pors N Y Times Mag p26-7+ F 15 '70

INDIAN (East Indian) bronzes. See Bronzes

INDIAN affairs, Bureau of. See United States—Indian affairs, Bureau of

INDIAN airlines. See Airlines—India

INDIAN arts and crafts. See Indians of North America—Industries

INDIAN character dolls. See Dolls

INDIAN clothing. See Indians of North America—Costume and adornment

INDIAN clubs. See Clubs (weapons)

INDIAN cookery (East Indian) See Cookery, Indian (East Indian)

INDIAN corn. See Corn

INDIAN Creek reservoir, Calif. See Reservoirs

INDIAN dancing (East Indian) See Dancing, Indian (East Indian)

INDIAN festivals. See Indians of North America—Rites and ceremonies

INDIAN GRINDING ROCK STATE HISTORICAL MONUMENT. See California—Parks and reserves

INDIAN OCEAN

As South Africa pushes for role in West's defense. il U S News 69:74-6 S 7 '70

Suez Canal: key to Soviet strategy in the Mideast? access to the Indian Ocean. il U S News 68:22-4 Je 22 '70

See also

Diego Garcia (atoll)

Seychelles (islands)

INDIAN princes. See India—Nobility

INDIAN reservations. See Indians of North America—Reservations

INDIAN rice. See Wild rice

INDIAN schools. See Indians of North America—Education

INDIAN towns. See Indians of North America—Villages

INDIAN trails

See also

Portages

INDIAN women. See Indians of North America—Women

INDIANA, Robert

Robert Indiana; interview, ed. by E. Sverbeveff and S. Nirenberg. il por House B 112:52-5+ F '70

INDIANA

Wild hemp of Indiana. M. King. Nation 211: 402-3 O 26 '70

See also

Fishing—Indiana

Justice, Administration of—Indiana

Marion County

Social conditions

She fights poverty. D. R. Maxey. il pors Look 34:18-21 Je 16 '70

INDIANA cabinetmakers. See Cabinetmakers

INDIANAPOLIS

Churches

Church of the revised Catholic liturgy; Church of St Thomas Aquinas. il Arch Rec 147:119-22 F '70

Education

Educational tool for all; Southport high school, District of Perry Township. G. J. Goodwin. il Am Lib 1:164-5 F '70

Metropolitan district

Indianapolis consolidates with surrounding Marion County. J. F. Zimmerman. Am City 85:76 Ja '70

Politics and government

Brash mayor stirs Indianapolis. il pors Bsns W p84-5 O 3 '70

Public health

Case history: Indianapolis helicopter ambulance. K. Jaeger. il Flying 87:74-7 D '70

INDIANAPOLIS 500. See Automobile racing

INDIANS

See also

Paleo-Indians

Agriculture

Aboriginal drained-field cultivation in the Americas. W. M. Denevan. bibliog il Science 169:647-54 Ag 14 '70

Education

See also

Indians of North America—Education

Origin

See also

Man, Prehistoric

INDIANS (of India) See East Indians

INDIANS, Treatment of

America's oldest debt: justice for the Indians. J. N. Bell. il Good H 172:78-9+ Ja '71

Case of Peol Sussep. F. W. Hatch. il Sat R 53:17 Jl 11 '70

Freedom equals liberation; Indian population of Latin America. J. L. Klaiber. il America 122:606-9 Je 6 '70

Nixon and the Indian. R. Strickland and J. Gregory. il por Commonweal 92:432-6 S 4 '70; Reply. W. J. Hickel. 93:59+ O 16 '70

Who am I? The Indian sickness; the White Hawk case. R. Bongartz. Nation 210:496-8 Ap 27 '70

INDIANS in art

Boy artist of Red River; with paintings by R. Rindisbacher. A. M. Josephy, jr. il Am Heritage 21:30-2+ F '70

INDIANS in moving pictures

Good guys wear war paint. G. Astor. il Look 34:56-61 D 1 '70

INDIANS of Alaska. See Indians of North America

INDIANS of Canada. See Indians of North America—Canada

INDIANS of Central America

Cuna revolt. R. Chardkoff. il Américas 22: 14-21 Jl '70

See also

Mayas

Antiquities

See also

Mayas

Sculpture, Pre-Columbian

British Honduras

Tumbaga object from the early classic period, found at Altun Ha, British Honduras (Belize) D. M. Pendergast. bibliog il Science 168:116-18 Ap 3 '70

INDIANS of Mexico

World: an artist's palette; Lacandon and Seri Indians. J. S. Houser. il Am Artist 34:28-34+ Ag '70

See also

Aztecs

Antiquities

Early and middle preclassic culture in the Basin of Mexico. P. Tolstoy and L. I. Paradis. bibliog il Science 167:344-51 Ja 23 '70

INDIANS of Mexico—Antiquities—*Continued*
In an Aztec market. A. J. Sadulé. il Américas 22:2-8 My '70
Magnetometer evidence of a structure within the La Venta pyramid. F. Morrison and others. bibliog il Science 167:1488-90 Mr 13 '70
Tlachtli, the roughest game of all. S. S. McKern and T. W. McKern bibliog il Sci Digest 68:26-31 N '70
See also
Mayas
Teotihuacán, Mexico

Costume and adornment
Mexican Indian costumes, by D. Cordry and D. Cordry. Review
Américas il 22:40 My '70. M. W. Laughlin

Culture
Early and middle preclassic culture in the Basin of Mexico. P. Tolstoy and L. I. Paradis. bibliog il Science 167:344-51 Ja 23 '70

Games
Tlachtli, the roughest game of all. S. S. McKern and T. W. McKern. bibliog il Sci Digest 68:26-31 N '70

Religion and mythology
Closed society of the Chamulas. K. O'Connor. il Cath World 211:58-62 My '70

Social life and customs
Zinacantan: a Maya community in the highlands of Chiapas, by E. Z. Vogt. Review
Natur Hist 79:66-72 F '70. H. R. Harvey
See also
Indians of Mexico—Games

INDIANS of North America
America's Indians. W. Hedgepeth. il Look 34:23-34 Je 2 '70
Meanwhile, back at the reservation. E. Witten. Commonweal 91:515-16 F 6 '70
New guide to the Indian country. il Sunset 144:112-13 Ap '70
See also
American Indian movement
Cherokee Indians
Eskimos
Havasupai Indians
Kiowa Indians
Navaho Indians
Paiute Indians
Paleo-Indians
Pueblo Indians
Tewa Indians
Yuchi Indians

Antiquities
Indian relics. C. Miles. See issues of Hobbies

California
Borax Lake site revisited. C. W. Meighan and C. V. Haynes. bibliog il Science 167:1213-21 F 27 '70

Canada
Archaic India cemetery in Newfoundland. J. A. Tuck. il Sci Am 222:112-21 Je '70

Connecticut
Aboriginal trephination: case from southern New England? B. W. Powell. bibliog il Science 170:732-4 N 13 '70

Missouri
Early canid burial from the western Ozark highland. R. B. McMillan. bibliog il Science 167:1246-7 F 27 '70

Architecture
See also
Pueblo architecture

Art
At the Indian fair in Phoenix; Heard museum of anthropology and primitive art. il Sunset 144:74-9 Mr '70
Vanishing Indian. R. Constable. Art in Am 58:45 Ja '70
See also
Institute of American Indian art, Santa Fe

Bibliography
American Indians: a bibliography of sources. J. N. Naumer. il Am Lib 1:861-4 O '70
Indian in America's closet. R. I. Ford. Natur Hist 79:78+ Je '70

Civil rights
American Indians: the right to be themselves. il Sr Schol 95:3-7 O 13 '69
Angry American Indian: starting down the protest trail. il Time 95:14-20 F 9 '70

Custer died for your sins, by V. Deloria, jr. Review
Trans-Action 7:72+ S '70. J. R. Jaquith
Let the Indians run Indian policy. E. M. Kennedy. Look 34:36+ Je 2 '70
Lords of the rock; occupied Alcatraz. J. A. Coleman. America 122:465-7 My 2 '70
This country was a lot better off when the Indians were running it. V. Deloria, jr. il por N Y Times Mag p32-3+ Mr 8 '70

Civilization
See Indians of North America—Culture

Costume and adornment
At the Indian fair in Phoenix; Heard museum of anthropology and primitive art. il Sunset 144:74-9 Mr '70
Indian and Eskimo tools and clothing. C. Miles. il Hobbies 75:142-3+ Mr; 142-3 Ap '70

Culture
Indian values. P. Da. il por Liv Wildn 34:25-6 Spr '70

Dances
See also
Dancing in religion, folklore, etc.
Indians of North America—Rites and ceremonies

Dwellings
Native American homes and equipment. C. Miles. il Hobbies 74:142-5 Ja '70

Economic conditions
Managing cash the tribal way: Jicarilla Apache tribe. il Bsns W p26 D 26 '70
See also
Indians of North America—Employment

Education
American Indians: search for Fort Hall's library service. G. R. Shields and G. Sheppard. bibliog il Am Lib 1:356-60 O '70
Failure in Navaho schooling. D. A. Erickson. il Parents Mag 45:66-8+ S '70
Indian education; a national disgrace; a dialogue. G. D. Fischer; W. F. Mondale. pors Todays Ed 59:24-7 Mr '70
Let the Indians run Indian policy. E. M. Kennedy. Look 34:36+ Je 2 '70
Time to redeem an old promise. E. Fuchs. il Sat R 53:54-7+ Ja 24 '70
To keep the things we love; Follow through projects. S. Moorefield. il Am Ed 6:6-8 Ag '70
Voice for Indians in education decisions. Sch & Soc 98:303 Sum '70
White rites versus Indian rights; dropouts among Canadian Indians. A. D. Fisher. bibliog il por Trans-Action 7:29-33 N '69
See also
Institute of American Indian art, Santa Fe
Navajo community college, Many Farms, Ariz.

History
See also
Carlisle Indian industrial school, Carlisle, Pa.

Employment
American Indian; address, December 9, 1969. D. Greve. Vital Speeches 36:276-9 F 15 '70
Industry invades the reservation. il Bsns W p72-3 Ap 4 '70

Festivals
See Indians of North America—Rites and ceremonies

Government relations
Alcatraz: the Indian uprising that worked. W. Hedgepeth. il Look 34:44-5 Je 2 '70
American Indians: the right to be themselves. il Sr Schol 95:3-7 O 13 '69
Angry American Indian: starting down the protest trail. il Time 95:14-20 F 9 '70
Day on Alcatraz with the Indians. K. Boyle. New Repub 162:10-11 Ja 17 '70
First Americans; proposed legislative package. Newsweek 76:18 Jl 20 '70
LaDonna Harris: a women who gives a damn. T. Morris. il Redbook 134:74-5+ F '70
Lords of the rock; occupied Alcatraz. J. A. Coleman. America 122:465-7 My 2 '70
New Indian. R. Bongartz. il Esquire 74:107-9+ Ag '70
Nixon and the Indian. R. Strickland and J. Gregory. il por Commonweal 92:432-6 S 4 '70; Reply. W. J. Hickel. 93:59+ O 16 '70
None but the brave; government tightens squeeze on the Rock. il Newsweek 76:38-9 Jl 6 '70
Our most silent minority. P. Nabokov. Nation 210:86-8 Ja 26 '70

INDIANS of North America—Government relations—*Continued*

Our shameful failure with America's Indians; excerpts from Our brother's keeper: the Indian in white America. ed. by E. S. Cahn. Read Digest 96:104-9 Ap '70

Red man's burden. P. Collier. il Ramp Mag 8:26-38 F '70; Same abr. Cur 119:22-6 Je '70

Sometimes we feel we're already dead: Arizona's ruined Cocopah. C. Mangel. il Look 34:38-43 Je 2 '70

See also
Indians of North America—Education
Indians of North America—Land tenure
Indians of North America—Reservations
United States—Indian affairs, Bureau of

Habitations

See Indians of North America—Dwellings

Health and hygiene

New Indian war, against suicide. J. L. Bach. il pors Todays Health 48:16-17 O '70

History

Mission for Mr Wedgwood; excerpts from journal, with introd. and epilogue by H. C. Wedgwood. T. Griffiths. il Am Heritage 21: 64-7 Ag '70

Usable history for the red man; University of Utah's Center for studies of the American West. J. Cass. Sat R 53:69 My 16 '70

Historiography

Indians in history. A. M. Josephy, jr. il Atlan 225:67-72 Je '70; Discussion. 226:46-7 S '70

Hunting

How Indians hunt deer. B. Geagan. il Field & S 75:36-7+ D '70

Implements

Aspects of fake artifacts. C. Miles. il Hobbies 75:114-15 Ag '70

Indian & Eskimo drills. C. Miles. il Hobbies 74:142-5 F '70

Indian and Eskimo tools and clothing. C. Miles. il Hobbies 75:142-3+ Mr; 142-3 Ap '70

Native American homes and equipment. C. Miles. il Hobbies 74:142-5 Ja '70

Some tools of the Indian. C. Miles. il Hobbies 75:144-5+ S '70

Tools of the Indian. C. Miles. il Hobbies 75: 142-3 Je '70

Industries

Patterns and things from the American Indians. il House & Gard 137:154-7 Mr '70

Southwest Indian. M. Evans. il Am Home 73: 76+ Mr '70

Land tenure

Matter of Indian giving; question of land rights to Blue Lake watershed. E. Shrake. il Sports Illus 33:42-4 Ag 17 '70

New era in Indian affairs; Taos Pueblo Indians to get Blue Lake land in New Mexico. Time 96:49 D 14 '70

Legal status, laws, etc.

See Indians of North America—Government relations

Libraries

American Indians: search for Fort Hall's library service. G. R. Shields and G. Sheppard. bibliog il Am Lib 1:856-60 O '70

Wind is rising: Navajo community college. B. E. Richardson. bibliog il por Library J 95:463-7 F 1 '70

Medicine

American Indian medicine, by V. J. Vogel. Review
    Am West 7:49 Jl '70. F. Egan
See also
Medicine men

Mixed bloods

Red and black: the Indians and the Africans. L. Bennett, jr. il Ebony 26:70-2+ D '70

Mortuary customs

Archaic Indian cemetery in Newfoundland. J. A. Tuck. il Sci Am 222:112-21 Je '70

Early canid burial from the western Ozark highland. R. B. McMillan. bibliog il Science 167:1246-7 F 27 '70

Museums

Inter-tribal doll museum is one-of-a-kind. il Hobbies 74:44 F '70

Nationalism

New Indian. R. Bongartz. il Esquire 74:107-9+ Ag '70

Relations with Negroes

Red and black: the Indians and the Africans. L. Bennett, jr. il Ebony 26:70-2+ D '70

Reservations

American Indians: search for Fort Hall's library service. G. R. Shields and G. Sheppard. bibliog il Am Lib 1:856-60 O '70

Indian reservations: should they be abolished? arguments on three sides. il Sr Schol 97: 21-3 S 28 '70

Quinault Indian beach closed to whites. Nat Parks 44:28 Ja '70

Red man's burden. P. Collier. il Ramp Mag 8:26-38 F '70; Same abr. Cur 119:22-6 Je '70

Rites and ceremonies

Indian festivals in the Southwest. Sunset 145: 32 Jl '70

Powwow. J. Eastman. il Natur Hist 79:24+ N '70

Social conditions

Red man's burden. P. Collier. il Ramp Mag 8: 26-38 F '70; Same abr. Cur 119:22-6 Je '70

Sometimes we feel we're already dead: Arizona's ruined Cocopah. C. Mangel. il Look 34:38-43 Je 2 '70

This country was a lot better off when the Indians were running it. V. Deloria, jr. il por N Y Times Mag p32-3+ Mr 8 '70

U.S. journal: Los Angeles. C. Trillin. New Yorker 46:92+ Ap 18 '70

See also
Indians of North America—Reservations

Trading posts

See also
Hubbell trading post national historic site

Treatment

See Indians, Treatment of

Tribal government

New deal coming for American Indians? il U S News 69:68-70 S 14 '70

Villages

Eklutna, almost a ghost town. il Sunset 145:32 Ag '70

Wars

See also
Little Big Horn, Battle of the, 1876

Women

Hokahe! a look at the young Indian women. N. A. Comer. il Mlle 71:158-9+ O '70

Promiscuity and prostitution in urbanized Indian communities. R. E. Kuttner and A. B. Lorincz. bibliog Ment Hy 54:79-91 Ja '70

Alaska

Alaska: politicians and natives, money and oil. L. Lapham. il Harper 240:85-102 My '70

Justice for the natives of Alaska. America 122:404 Ap 18 '70

Justice to first inhabitants; native land claims. A. J. Goldberg. Am Heritage 21: 119 Ap '70

Oil rush of '70. R. Zelnick. il N Y Times Mag p26-7+ Mr 1 '70

Canada

Two tactics for ethnic survival: Eskimo & Indian. R. J. Dryfoos, jr. il Trans-Action 7: 51-4 Ja '70

White rites versus Indian rights; dropouts. A. D. Fisher. bibliog il por Trans-Action 7: 29-33 N '69

INDIANS of North America in art. See Indians in art

INDIANS of North America in moving pictures. See Indians in moving pictures

INDIANS of Peru. See Indians of South America—Peru

INDIANS of South America

Lessons from a primitive people. J. V. Neel. bibliog il Science 170:815-22 N 20 '70

See also
Incas

Antiquities

Art of terra-cotta pottery in pre-Columbian Central and South America, by A. von Wuthenau. Review
    Life il 69:12 O 16 '70. K. E. Meyer

Chile

Cluster analysis and multidimensional scaling of archeological sites in northern Chile. D. L. True and R. G. Matson. bibliog il Science 169:1201-3 S 18 '70

Colombia

San Agustin: archaeological mystery of prehistoric Colombia. F. Sanz. il UNESCO Courier 23:20-5 Ap '70

INDIANS of South America—Antiquities—*Cont.*

Peru

Early human cultural and skeletal remains from Guitarrero cave, northern Peru. T. F. Lynch and K. A. R. Kennedy. bibliog il Science 169:1307-9 S 25 '70

Flaking stone with wooden implements. D. E. Crabtree. bibliog il Science 169:146-53 Jl 10 '70

Mystery of the Nazca lines. D. Cohen. il Sci Digest 67:46-8+ My '70

Education

Bilingual jungle school. L. M. Wistrand. il Américas 22:2-8 Ag '70

Religion and mythology

Ecology before Columbus. T. Grieder. il Américas 22:21-8 My '70

Treatment

See Indians, Treatment of

Argentina

Caste and class in the Chaco. L. L. Browne. Nation 211:239-42 S 21 '70

Brazil

Genocide in Brazil. J. Deedy. Commonweal 91:498 F 6 '70; Reply with rejoinder. P. T. F. De Lima. 92:151 Ap 24 '70

Ecuador

Feast of the sun. M. Acosta Solís. il Américas 22:24-30 O '70

Peru

Infrahumans. Nation 211:5 Jl 6 '70

Venezuela

Bruce Olson and the man-killing Motilones S. Seegers and K. Seegers. il Read Digest 96:128-33 Mr '70

INDICATOR tubes. See Electron tubes

INDICATORS, Proximity warning. See Proximity warning indicators

INDIGESTION. See Digestive system—Diseases

INDIGO buntings

Celestial rotation: its importance in the development of migratory orientation. S. T. Emlen. bibliog il Science 170:1198-201 D 11 '70

INDIUM phosphide. See Phosphides

INDIVIDUAL and society

Is the corporation next to fall? A. G. Athos. bibliog f il Havard Bsns R 48:49-61 Ja '70

Politics of authenticity: radical individualism and the emergence of modern society, by M. Berman. Review

Nation 212:23-5 Ja 4 '71. E. Chill

INDIVIDUAL and state

School prayer issue: a perverse paradox. H. M. Engel. il Cath World 211:125-7 Je '70

What government snooping can find out about you. il U S News 68:22-4 My 4 '70

INDIVIDUAL instruction

Computers and adaptive education. H. E. Mitzel. il Am Ed 6:23-6 D '70

Elements of individualized instruction. P. A. O'Donnel and C. W. Lavaroni. Ed Digest 36:17-19 S '70

If I have but one life to live, let me live it above the median. E. E. Gran. Ed Digest 36:32-3 O '70

Individualized learning in the flexible school; elementary schools, Broward County, Fla. F. Hatfield and I. Gullette. Am Lib 1:169-70 F '70

Individualizing study assignments. T. F. Bowman and R. Minge. Clear House 45:230 D '70

New learning center thrives in New York; John Dewey high school. W. E. Williamson. Clear House 45:58-9+ S '70

Prescription for learning. B. Bard. il Parents Mag 45:58-9+ S '70

Probing Project PLAN (Program for learning in accordance with needs) in California. L. A. Gutkind. il Schol Teach Jr/Sr High p20-3 O 5 '70

Wide open for learning; Project SOLVE; schools without walls in New Hampshire. R. C. Wing and P. H. Mack. il Am Ed 6:13-15 N '70

INDIVIDUAL liberty. See Liberty

INDIVIDUALISM

Bitch goddess of individualism; the new left. R. S. Wheeler. Nat R 22:1346+ D 15 '70

What's going to happen to us individuals? address, August 14, 1970. M. Rafferty. Vital Speeches 36:752-5 O 1 '70

See also

Conformity

INDIVIDUALITY

See also

Personality

Temperament

INDIVIDUALIZED Instruction. See Individual instruction

INDIVIDUALIZED reading plan. See Reading —Study and teaching

INDIVIDUALLY prescribed instruction. See Individual instruction

INDOCHINA

Danger and opportunity in Indochina. il Time 95:22-4+ Mr 30 '70

From the Vietnam war to an Indochina war. J. Lacouture. For Affairs 48:617-28 Jl '70

Indochina: the calm before the storm? il Newsweek 75:36-7 Ap 6 '70

New hope: Asianization. il Newsweek 75:34+ Mr 30 '70

Nixon's peace plan. New Repub 163:5-6 O 17 '70

Signal from Moscow? the Malik proposal. Newsweek 75:36 Ap 27 '70

Three-theater war; the war in Indochina. il Time 95:28+ Ap 13 '70

See also

Cambodia

Guerrillas—Indochina

United Nations—Indochina

Vietnamese war, 1957-

Foreign relations

United States

See United States—Foreign relations—Indochina

History

Indochina's curse: ancient enmities. il Newsweek 75:24 My 4 '70

Peoples of Indochina. C. F. Keyes. il Natur Hist 79:40-53+ O '70

Natives races

Peoples of Indochina. C. F. Keyes. il Natur Hist 79:40-53+ O '70

Race problems

Indochina's curse: ancient enmities. il Newsweek 75:24 My 4 '70

INDOCTRINATION

Irish Catholic was beautiful. A. W. Godfrey. America 123:493 D 5 '70

INDONESIA

See also

Anti-Communist movements—Indonesia

Bali

Jakarta

Java

Kotabaru

Motor boat racing—Indonesia

Petroleum industry and trade—Indonesia

Description and travel

Distant sound of flutes. R. Atcheson. il Holiday 47:32-7+ F '70

Economic conditions

Good-will trip with a purpose. il U S News 68:84 Je 8 '70

Indonesia: back from the brink. il Newsweek 75:50-2 My 25 '70

Turnaround in Indonesia. H. P. Jones. il Read Digest 96:184-6+ Mr '70

Foreign relations

United States

See United States—Foreign relations—Indonesia

Politics and government

Berkeley mafia and the Indonesian massacre; with editorial comment. D. Ransom. il Ramp Mag 9:26-9+ O '70

Indonesia: back from the brink. il Newsweek 75:50-2 My 25 '70

Turnaround in Indonesia. H. P. Jones. il Read Digest 96:184-6+ Mr '70

INDOOR gardening

Aids for indoor seed starting. il Home Gard 58:50-1+ Ja '71

Movable garden, indoors and out. W. F. Bowers. il Org Gard & Farm 17:44-6 S '70

You can start gardening in February if you move into the kitchen. il Sunset 144:82-5 F '70

Your garden indoors. F. S. David. See issues of Home garden & flower grower

See also

Artificial light gardening

House plants

Window gardening

INDOOR gardens. See Gardens, Indoor

INDOOR light gardening. See Artificial light gardening

INDOOR plants. See House plants
INDOOR tennis courts. See Tennis courts, Indoor
INDOOR track. See Track athletics
INDUCTANCE
  See also
  Reactance (electricity)
INDUSTRIAL accidents. See Accidents, Industrial
INDUSTRIAL advertising. See Advertising, Industrial
INDUSTRIAL arts
  You can't weld in a mini skirt; case for a unified arts course. W. G. Clark. il Sch Arts 70:22-5 O '70

Study and teaching
New role for industrial arts. D. Maley. Ed Digest 35:42-5 My '70
INDUSTRIAL buildings
  Two industrial buildings: technical center at Cummins engine company, Columbus, Ind, and distribution center for Koret of California. il Arch Rec 148:107-14 Jl '70
  See also
  Factories
  Warehouses
INDUSTRIAL development board of the United Nations. See United Nations industrial development organization
INDUSTRIAL development programs
  Industry's hidden dividends. il Nations Bsns 58:74-7+ O '70
INDUSTRIAL diamonds. See Diamonds, Industrial
INDUSTRIAL districts
  Looking like new; industrial parks. il Nations Bsns 58:93-4+ O '70
  New towns and industrial parks change Europe. Nations Bsns 58:97-8 O '70
INDUSTRIAL diversification. See Diversification in industry
INDUSTRIAL education
  See also
  Apprentices
  Employees—Training
  Industrial arts—Study and teaching
  Vocational education
INDUSTRIAL equality. See Woman—Equal rights
INDUSTRIAL equipment
  In industry, sheer size really pays. il Bsns W p 172-4+ O 17 '70
INDUSTRIAL equipment industry

Finance
Industrial equipment; with yardsticks of management performance. il Forbes 105:194+ Ja 1 '70; 107:120-2 Ja 1 '71
INDUSTRIAL espionage. See Spies, Industrial
INDUSTRIAL expansion
  CEO's role in corporate growth. J. O. Eastlack, jr. and P. R. McDonald. il Harvard Bsns R 48:150-2+ My '70
  See also
  Capital investments
INDUSTRIAL films. See Moving pictures in industry
INDUSTRIAL forecasting. See Business forecasting
INDUSTRIAL forestry. See Forest management
INDUSTRIAL location. See Location in business and industry
INDUSTRIAL management and organization
  Union prospects and programs for the 1970's. A. A. Blum. bibliog f Mo Labor R 93:36-9 Mr '70
  See also
  Business management and organization
  Collective bargaining
  Efficiency, Industrial
  Employment stabilization
  Industrial relations
  Industries, Size of
  Labor productivity
  Personnel management

Russia
Russia wields a capitalist tool: the layoff; Shchekino plant. il Bsns W p 108-10 Ja 31 '70
INDUSTRIAL marketing. See Marketing
INDUSTRIAL mobilization
  See also
  Stockpiling
INDUSTRIAL models. See Factory models
INDUSTRIAL museums
  See also
  Henry Ford museum and Greenfield Village, Dearborn, Mich.
INDUSTRIAL parks. See Industrial districts

INDUSTRIAL pensions. See Pensions, Industrial
INDUSTRIAL production. See Production
INDUSTRIAL products. See Commercial products
INDUSTRIAL psychology. See Psychology, Industrial
INDUSTRIAL purchasing. See Purchasing, Industrial
INDUSTRIAL relations
  Developments in industrial relations. See issues of Monthly labor review
  Employer bargaining; address, December 29, 1969. A. A. Hendrix. Vital Speeches 36:317-20 Mr 1 '70
  Hard bargaining, more strikes; what unions see ahead. il U S News 68:62-4 Mr 2 '70
  How to win at the bargaining table. W. Wingo. il Nations Bsns 58:38-42 F '70
  Labor and the economy in 1969. R. W. Fisher. bibliog il Mo Labor R 93:30-43 Ja '70
  Significant decisions in labor cases. See issues of Monthly labor review
  There should be a labor-management day. D. Lawrence. U S News 69:88 S 14 '70
  Will labor lose its leverage? comments of members of the presidents' panel. G. R. Rosen. Duns 95:34-6 F '70
  See also
  Business management and organization—Employee participation
  Collective bargaining
  Communication in management
  Employees representation in management
  Labor disputes
  Layoff systems
  Personnel management
  Spies, Industrial
  Strikes
  Trade agreements
  United States—Labor policy
  United States—National labor relations board

Germany (Federal Republic)
Relations between management and labor in West Germany. E. M. Bussey. bibliog f Mo Labor R 93:28-34 Ag '70

Great Britain
Peace on the docks; Fred Olsen's contract with dockers. Newsweek 75:87+ Mr 23 '70
INDUSTRIAL relations research association
  IRRA conference papers; excerpts. Mo Labor R 93:33-48 Mr; 44-53 Ap '70
INDUSTRIAL research
  Into the barn, and a lofty future. A. M. Bueche. il Nations Bsns 58:74-5 Ja '70
  Key to success: a scrub pail. B. S. Cross. il por Nations Bsn° 58:90-1 Ja '70
  Research management. W. V. Smith. Science 167:957-9 F 13 '70
  See also
  Battelle memorial institute, Columbus, Ohio
  Coal research
  Products, New
  Technology transfer

Great Britain
Conservative approach to science. L. Miller. Sci N 98:102 Ag 1 '70
INDUSTRIAL revolution
  Next industrial revolution; excerpts from address. A. Spilhaus. Science 167:1673 Mr 27 '70; Same abr. Read Digest 97:169-70 Jl '70
INDUSTRIAL robots. See Machinery, Automatic
INDUSTRIAL safety
  Matter of life and death. il Newsweek 76:64-6 Ag 17 '70
  See also
  Accidents, Industrial

Laws and regulations
At issue: a fair approach to job safety; interview. W. Steiger. pors Nations Bsns 58:47-9 S '70
Impact of job-safety law on employers and workers. il U S News 70:80-1 Ja 11 '71
Job-safety bill breaks new ground. U S News 69:57 D 28 '70
Safety act's hidden bite. Bsns W p 19-20 Ja 9 '71
Safety bill in jeopardy. Bsns W p 112+ S 19 '70
Warning: safety hazard. il Nations Bsns 58:20-2 Je '70
Work at your own risk. D. P. Sachs. Sat R 53:64-5 Je 6 '70
INDUSTRIAL secrets. See Trade secrets
INDUSTRIAL security measures. See Industry—Security measures

INDUSTRIAL stabilization. See Employment stabilization

INDUSTRIAL union department. See American federation of labor and Congress of industrial organizations—Industrial union department

INDUSTRIAL waste. See Trade waste

INDUSTRIAL waste disposal. See Trade waste disposal

INDUSTRIAL workers of the world
Case of the very American militants; notes on the IWW. J. R. Conlin. il Am West 7: 4-10+ Mr '70
We shall be all, by M. Dubofsky. Review
    Cath World 212:165 D '70. D. J. O'Brian

INDUSTRIALIZATION
Man the killer of nature. Thant. il UNESCO Courier 23:46-53 Ag '70
River idols. A. W. Smith. Nat Parks & Con Mag 44:2 S '70
    See also
Economic development
Mexico—Industries
Underdeveloped areas

INDUSTRIALIZED building exposition and congress. See Building industry—Exhibitions

INDUSTRIES, Service. See Service industries

INDUSTRIES, Size of
In industry, sheer size really pays.   il Bsns W p 172-4+ O 17 '70

INDUSTRY
    See also
Industries, Size of
Location in business and industry
Production

Charitable contributions
    See   Corporations—Charitable contributions

Location
    See Location in business and industry

Security measures
Companies besieged. il Time 95:92 Ap 13 '70
Electronics industry gives electrifying testimony; House committee on internal security hearings. Chr Cent 87:781 Je 24 '70
Great game of corporate espionage. J. Perham. Duns 96:30-3+ O '70
House detectives, new style. il U S News 69: 71 Jl 6 '70
Security men thrive on the wages of fear. il Bsns W p 112-14 Je 20 '70
To catch a thief. il Newsweek 76:59-60 Jl 27 '70
    See also
Electronic data processing—Security measures

INDUSTRY, Nationalization of. See Government ownership

INDUSTRY and education. See Business and education

INDUSTRY and state
Business in government. M. J. Green. New Repub 163:14-16 N 14 '70
Businessmen still like Nixon. il Bsns W p31-2 Ap 18 '70
Corporate ambassadors to Washington; excerpts; with portfolio. R. W. Miller and J. D. Johnson. Nations Bsns 58:44-50 Jl '70
How to end giveaways; argument for selling limited rights by auction. M. Friedman. Newsweek 75:84 F 23 '70
News-lines.   See issues of U.S. news & World report
Para-real estate: the handing out of resources. J. Ridgeway. il Ramp Mag 8:28-33 My '70
Top priority: renovating our ideology. G. C. Lodge. bibliog f Harvard Bsns R 48:43-55 S '70
Washington desk. G. R. Rosen. See issues of Dun's
What Congress did for business. il Time 97:68-70 Ja 18 '71
Why an outmoded ideology thwarts the new business conscience. G. C. Lodge. por Fortune 82:106-7+ O '70; Same abr. with title Top priority: renovating our ideology. bibliog f Harvard Bsns R 48:43-55 S '70
Why it's harder to run a business. il U S News 69:29-31 Jl 20 '70
    See also
Contracts, Government
Corporate state
Free enterprise
Government ownership
Military-industrial complex
Strikes—United States—Government intervention
United States—Federal power commission
United States—Federal trade commission
United States—Labor, Department of

United States—Labor policy
United States—President's commission on personnel interchange (proposed)

Italy
GE turns cool to a state partner. Bsns W p23 O 3 '70
More state control; case of Montecatini Edison. Time 96:92 N 2 '70

INDUSTRY and the arts. See The Arts and industry

INDUSTRY and the environmental movement
Consumer; corporate reform programs. E. Marshall. il New Repub 163:27-9 O 31 '70
Earth day broom sweeps in business. il Bsns W p22-4 Ap 18 '70
Eco-establishment. K. Barkley and S. Weissman. Ramp Mag 8:48-9+ My '70
Environment dilemma. il Nations Bsns 58: 50-1+ N '70
For land's sake; Nature conservancy. il Newsweek 75:87B My 18 '70
Making of a pollution-industrial complex. M. Gellen. il Ramp Mag 8:22-7 My '70
Playing games with nature; expansion of the Consolidated Edison plant in Astoria. Commonweal 92:427-8 S 4 '70. Reply. S. A. Mallard. 92:490 S 25 '70
Pollution: puffery or progress? FTC investigation into anti-pollution claims. il Newsweek 76:49-51 D 28 '70
Tax on noise? A tax on congestion? interview. R. Dubos. il pors Forbes 106:64+ S 15 '70
Trade-offs for a better environment. il Bsns W p62-3+ Ap 11 '70
Westinghouse's environment school: combining business with ecology. T. P. Southwick. Science 169:453-4 Jl 31 '70
    See also
Paper making and trade

INDUSTRY wide collective bargaining. See Collective bargaining, Industry wide

INERT gases. See Gases, Rare

INERTIAL guidance systems
Collins to test civil inertial unit. P. J. Klass. il Aviation W 92:59+ F 23 '70
Guidance unit links sensor ideas; miniature floated inertial platform. B. Miller. il Aviation W 92:48-9+ Ap 13 '70
Inertial aids fill primary overwater role. K. J. Stein. il Aviation W 93:56-7+ O 19 '70
Inertial navaids gain pilot favor. K. J. Stein. il Aviation W 93:52-3+ O 12 '70
Inertial navigation for aircraft. C. T. Leondes. il Sci Am 222:80-4+ Mr '70
Inertial navigation for 747 superjet. E. L. Hughes. il Electr World 84:27-30+ S '70
Light, compact navigator designed. B. Miller. il Aviation W 92:51-3+ F 9 '70
MIT device raises inertial reliability. P. J. Klass. il Aviation W 93:81-4 S 14 '70
New inertial aid has many uses. il Aviation W 93:56 D 7 '70
New inertial navaid flight tested. B. Miller. il Aviation W 92:69-71 My 4 '70
New Titan 3C guidance system could reduce program costs. B. Miller. Aviation W 93:55-6 O 5 '70

INFALLIBILITY, Papal. See Popes—Infallibility

INFANCY of animals. See Animals, Infancy of

INFANT feeding. See Infants—Nutrition

INFANT language. See Children—Language

INFANT mortality
Crib deaths: some answers to 20,000 sudden tragedies. E. H. McGough. il Sci Digest 67: 26-30 F '70
How many children? with excerpts from address, May 1969, by E. Sternglass M. W. Friedlander and J. Klarmann. bibliog il Environ 11:2-13 D '69
Infant mortality and nuclear tests. E. J. Sternglass; discussion. Bul Atomic Sci 25: 27 Je; 26-32 O '69; 26:46 Mr; 40-2+ My '70
Professor Sternglass, fallout and infant mortality. Bul Atom Sci 26:46 Mr '70

INFANTS
Cardiac responses on the visual cliff in prelocomotor human infants. J. J. Campos and others. bibliog il Science 170:196-7 O 9 '70
    See also
Adoption

Care and hygiene
Checklist of items for the first baby. il Good H 170:170 My '70
Importance of postnatal care for mother and child. il Good H 171:161 S '70
It wasn't me who wet: toilet training. B. Bettelheim. Ladies Home J 87:62+ Mr '70
More light, less jaundice. il Sci Digest 67: 67-8 Mr '70

INFANTS—Care and hygiene—*Continued*
She who hesitates; toilet training. J. D. Bucher. il por Redbook 136:29+ N '70
Summer fun with baby. il Parents Mag 45:46-7+ Ag '70
When baby steps out. il Parents Mag 45:44-5 Ja '70
Working mothers and their children. M. Mead. il Cath World 212:78-82 N '70
Working mothers: some possible solutions for child care. B. Spock. Redbook 135:34+ S '70
See also
Baby sitters
Children—Care and hygiene
Colic
Infants—Nutrition
Infants, Premature
Mothers

Anecdotes, facetiae, satire, etc.
Dear baby doctor; excerpts from Mothers write funny letters to baby doctors. B. Adler. il Todays Health 48:24-6 S; 75-6 O '70

Clothing
See also
Diapers, Infants

Crying
Sounds of sickness; a recording of infants' cries. Time 96:57 S 21 '70

Exercise
See Exercise

Food
See Infants food

Growth and development
Fit by five; headstart to make your child. J. A. Segal. il Look 34:76-7+ Ap 7 '70
Infant separates himself from his mother. H. L. Rheingold and C. O. Eckerman. bibliog il Science 168:78-83 Ap 3 '70
Jerome Bruner maintains: infants are smarter than anybody thinks. M. Pines. il pors N Y Times Mag gp32-3+ N 29 '70
Malnourished bodies, malnourished minds; with study-discussion program. L. V. Wilder. bibliog il PTA Mag 64:10-12+, 33 Mr '70
See also
Child study

Names
See Names, Personal

Nutrition
Children, food, and sex; questions and answers. D. Reuben. McCalls 97:38+ Ag '70
How to turn table failures into successful eaters. Todays Health 48:74 O '70
When baby is ready for solid foods. il Parents Mag 45:52-3 Ap '70
See also
Breast feeding
Infants food

Physical examinations
See Physical examinations

Surgery
See Children—Surgery
INFANTS, Cost of. See Domestic finance
INFANTS, Newborn
Chromosomal abnormalities in the human population: estimation of rates based on New Haven newborn study. H. A. Lubs and F. H. Ruddle. bibliog il Science 169:495-7 Jl 31 '70
First baby in the house. G. Youcha. il Parents Mag 45:62-3+ O '70
New baby at our house. C. Lang. il por Parents Mag 45:54-5 Mr '70
New medical treatment for high-risk babies. Good H 171:189 O '70

Surgery
Miracle babies. L. David. il Ladies Home J 87:85+ Ap '70
INFANTS, Premature
Good start for the premature baby. il Parents Mag 45:44-5+ Je '70
INFANTS, Travel with. See Travel with children
INFANTS food
Baby foods: can you (and your baby) afford them? R. Nader. McCalls 98:36+ N '70
INFANTS in art. See Children in art
INFANTS supplies
What it costs now to have a baby. S. Porter. il Ladies Home J 87:32-3 Jl '70
INFECTIOUS diseases. See Communicable diseases
INFERTILITY. See Sterility

INFLAMMABLE textile fabrics. See Textile fabrics, Flammable
INFLAMMATION
Inflammation and herpes simplex virus: release of the chemotaxis-generating factor from infected cells. A. M. Brier and others. bibliog il Science 170:1104-6 D 4 '70
Rat thoracic duct lymphocytes: types that participate in inflammation. F. Koster and D. D. McGregor. bibliog il Science 167:1137-9 F 20 '70
INFLATABLE boats. See Boats and boating
INFLATABLE furniture. See Furniture, Inflatable
INFLATABLE structures. See Air-supported structures
INFLATION (finance)
Accentuating the positive. il Nations Bsns 58:34-8 Ap '70
Arthur Burns: the stage has been set for a recovery; address, December 7, 1970. A. F. Burns. por U S News 69:64-8 D 21 '70; Same with title Basis for lasting prosperity. Vital Speeches 37:162-6 Ja 1 '71
As inflation spiral hits Europe—. U S News 69:50-1 Ag 31 '70
Battle against inflation: new initiatives; address, March 9, 1970. D. S. MacNaughton. Vital Speeches 36:437-40 My 1 '70
Bitter medicine for the West's inflation. il Bsns W p92-3 N 21 '70
Budget with a bite. il Newsweek 75:65-7 F 9 '70
Business questions the game plan. Bsns W p28 O 24 '70
Businessmen's worry in '71. il U S News 69:46 N 2 '70
Canada's businessmen shoulder the load. il Nations Bsns 58:63-72 N '70
Capital spending is the key. R. Lekachman. por Duns 95:9 Mr '70
Construction versus inflation. R. M. Young. il Arch Rec 147:69 Ja; 61 F; 85 Ap '70
Controls may be necessary; comments by Dun's presidents' panel; with editorial comment. G. R. Rosen. il Duns 97:37-8, 80 Ja '71
Despite inflation, people living better. il U S News 68:85-6 F 23 '70
Economic clouds girdle the globe. il Bsns W p21 Ja 2 '71
Economy: trying to speed up a recovery. il Time 96:63-4 Ag 3 '70
Europe thinks the U.S. is steadying; views of OECD staff. il Bsns W p58-9 Ag 8 '70
Factors controlling inflation; address, March 19, 1970. F. H. Schott. Vital Speeches 36:561-3 Jl 1 '70
Fighting recession. P. A. Samuelson. Newsweek 75:75 Je 22 '70
Finally, some real slowing of inflation. il U S News 69:29 O 5 '70
Finland's formula for deflating inflation; interview. K. Waris. il por Nations Bsns 58:36-8 Ag '70
Focus on inflation: when more (money) means less (value) il Sr Schol 96:6-10 Ja 26 '70
Game plan goes on, in slow motion; with editorial comment. il Bsns W p94-5, 102 O 31 '70
Generation gap; interviews. T. R. Price; D. Babson. pors Forbes 106:46+ N 15 '70
German miracle ending? il U S News 68:27-9 F 2 '70
Gloomy feeling; a nervous market, a troubled economy. il Life 68:28-35 Je 5 '70
Growth versus inflation. G. P. Hitchings. por Nations Bsns 58:77-8 Ap '70
Hard going for the game plan; with editorial comment. G. Burck. il por Fortune 81:145-6, 152-5+ My '70
Helping shareowners help themselves; address, November 7, 1970. L. R. Boulware. Vital Speeches 37:155-60 D 15 '70
High price of labor peace; open-end escalator clauses. Duns 96:108 N '70
How Canada fights inflation: a step beyond tight money; interview, ed. by A. Jones. pors Forbes 105:36+ Je 1 '70
How families fight inflation. il U S News 68:66-9 F 16 '70
How many times? M. Friedman. Newsweek 76:85 N 30 '70
How to stop inflation: stop raising wages. E. L. Dale, jr. il N Y Times Mag p 10-11+ Ja 3 '71
How you can live with inflation. P. Lindberg. Bet Hom & Gard 48:18+ O '70
Inflation: a call for restraint; R. M. Nixon's new anti-inflation policy. il por Newsweek 75:61-2 Je 29 '70
Inflation and ideology; physicians abuse of medicaid systems. Chr Cent 87:228-9 F 25 '70

INFLATION (finance)—*Continued*
Inflation and the prospects for prosperity.
R. J. Saulnier. Read Digest 96:99-102 Mr
'70
Inflation and wages. M. Friedman. News-
week 76:77 S 28 '70
Inflation, by A. M. Okun and others. Review
New Repub 163:26-7 Jl 4 '70. L. Ross
Inflation control; address. December 5, 1969.
G. Ackley. Vital Speeches 36:200-3 Ja 15 '70
Inflation feeds the jobless figure. il Bsns W
p26-7 My 30 '70
Inflation fighters see a ray of hope. il Bsns W
p 114 Ap 18 '70
Inflation hurts, and stopping inflation hurts.
E. L. Dale, jr. il N Y Times Mag p24-5+
F 22 '70
Inflation: now a worldwide crisis. il U S News
69:22-4 Jl 20 '70
Inflation on the Rhine. Newsweek 75:89-90
Mr 16 '70
Inflation over? not if you're buying. il U S
News 68:40-1 Ap 6 '70
Inflation showdown: new pressures on Nixon.
il U S News 69:15-16 D '70
Inflation talk. W. F. Buckley, jr. Nat R 22:
168-9 F 10 '70
Inflation: the wrong medicine. P. L. Bern-
stein. Nation 210:168-71 F 16 '70
Inflation virus attacks others, too. B. L.
Masse. America 122:403 Ap 18 '70
Inflation's stubborn resistance. il Time 96:82-
4+ D 14 '70
Inflationary pains. Chr Today 14:25 F 13 '70
Is jawboning a joke? M. J. Ulmer. New Re-
pub 162:21-3 My 30 '70
Jawboning's a joke. E. L. Dale, jr. New
Repub 162:17-19 Ap 18 '70
Jolts on the price elevator. H. A. Lewis. por
Nations Bsns 58:65-6 My '70
Learning to live with inflation. il Newsweek
76:87-8 N 2 '70
Let's make a deal. il Newsweek 76:78+ D 21
'70
Mr Nixon on the inflation struggle. America
123:536 D 19 '70
Mood is inflation gray. il Bsns W p 16-17 N
28 '70
National housing policy; inflation must be
ended; address, January 19, 1970. G. Rom-
ney. Vital Speeches 36:309-12 Mr 1 '70
Nation's economic outlook: progress against
inflation; address, December 7, 1970. R. M.
Nixon. Vital Speeches 37:130-3 D 15 '70
New game plan. il por Newsweek 76:15-16 N
30 '70
New timetable for the game plan; Joint economic committee hearings. il Bsns W p 15-
16 Jl 25 '70
Nixon's economic bind. R. Lekachman. Duns
95:7 Ja '70
Nixon's economic dilemma. H. Hazlitt. Nat R
22:1351 D 15 '70
Now the game plan's target is '72. il Bsns W
p 16 N 7 '70
Old champ wins again. Nat R 22:391-2 Ap
21 '70
Our current inflation. J. R. Cammarosano.
America 122:369-72 Ap 4 '70
Picking up the wishbone; anti-inflation mea-
sures of R. M. Nixon. il Time 95:10-11 Je 29
'70
Postwar price cycles: a new chronology;
excerpt from address, September 1970. G.
H. Moore. il Mo Labor R 93:11-17 D '70
Prepare your company for inflation. B. A.
Lietaer. il Harvard Bsns R 48:113-25 S '70
Pressure for new steps to curb inflation. il
U S News 68:37-8 Je 1 '70
Price of ending inflation stays high. il Bsns
W p92 Ja 31 '70
Recession can't cure inflation. M. Shapiro. il
Duns 96:54-6 Jl '70
Relief at last for multiple pains. il Time
96:80 O 5 '70
Retreat on the inflation front? America 122:
364 Ap 4 '70
Richard Nixon, inflation fighter. il por News-
week 76:45-6 D 14 '70
Rising attack on Nixonomics. il Time 95:64-5
F 2 '70
Shifting gears. H. C. Wallich. Newsweek 76:
112 N 23 '70
Sidestepping the money gap; with report by
R. Woodbury. il Life 68:20-7 F 13 '70
Stronger omens of an upturn, but new wor-
ries. Fortune 82:19-20 Ag '70
Task ahead; address, May 14, 1970. J. L.
Robertson. Vital Speeches 36:520-3 Je 15 '70
To combat inflation: what Congress must do.
C. E. Walker. Read Digest 97:74-8 N '70
Tougher tack on inflationary hikes. Bsns W
p23-4 N 21 '70
Tougher talk, and more to come; with edi-
torial comment. il Bsns W p26, 104 D 5
'70

U.S. can't afford what labor wants; with
editorial comment. il Bsns W p 104-8, 134
Ap 11 '70
Washington shifts gears. R. Lekachman. Duns
97:9 Ja '71
We must stand firm against inflation. M.
Friedman. Read Digest 96:202-4+ Je '70
We're still cutting back; comments of mem-
bers of the Dun's presidents' panel. G. R.
Rosen. il Duns 96:27-30 Ag '70
What makes prices rise? il Bsns W p 122 S 19
'70
Where inflation takes its toll: the soaring cost
of services. il U S News 68:30-1 Ja 19 '70
Why dollar looks stronger to world's bankers.
il U S News 69:104-6 O 19 '70
Why inflation goes on and on. il U S News
68:20-1 F 2 '70
Will the cure be worse than the disease? il
Forbes 105:68 My 15 '70
World experts prescribe strong medicine for
inflation; OECD report. il U S News 69:17-
18 D 7 '70
See also
Currency question
Wage-price policy
INFLUENCE of music. See Music. Influence
of
INFLUENZA
Flu: more than expected, but—. U S News
68:10 Mr 2 '70
Pediatrician's guide to colds, grippe, flu; ex-
cerpts from When your child is ill. S
Karelitz. Ladies Home J 87:36+ Ja '70
INFLUENZA, Swine. See Swine—Diseases and
pests
INFLUENZA viruses
Influenza virus effects on cell membrane pro-
teins. J. J. Holland and E. D. Kiehn. bibliog
il Science 167:202-5 Ja 9 '70
INFORMAL education. See Education, Experi-
mental
INFORMATION. See Knowledge
INFORMATION, Freedom of
Letter from Dr Sakharov; democratization
proposals to Russian leaders. A. D. Sakharov
and others. il Newsweek 75:34-5 Ap 13 '70
Need for democratization; letter. A. D. Sak-
harov and others. Sat R 53:26-7 Je 6 '70;
Same abr. with title Letter from Dr Sark-
harov. il Newsweek 75:34-5 Ap 13 '70
Public information act; with text. M. J.
Kerbec. por Library J 95:4229-31 D 15 '70
When officials shackle the news. R. L. Tobin.
Sat R 53:49-50 D 12 '70
See also
Freedom of the press
Government and the press
INFORMATION, Government. See Government
information
INFORMATION agency (United States) See
United States—Information agency
INFORMATION centers. See Information ser-
vices
INFORMATION centers, United Nations. See
United Nations—Information centers
INFORMATION display systems
Liquid-crystal display devices. G. H. Hell-
meier. il Sci Am 222:100-6 Ap '70
Making displays easier to read; liquid-crystal
and cathodochromic technology. il Bsns W
p49 N 21 '70
Oceanic ATC concept uses video displays. B.
M. Elson. il Aviation W 93:60-1+ N 23 '70
See also
Aeronautic instruments—Display systems
INFORMATION industry association
Notes on a triangle: second annual meeting.
K. Nyren. il Library J 95:1803-6 My 15 '70;
Reply. E. Garfield. 95:2854 S 15 '70
INFORMATION processing, Human. See Hu-
man information processing
INFORMATION services
Bells are ringing in St Petersburg; Service
and information center. il Am City 85:130
Mr '70
Four-use visitor center for national sea-
shore; Point Reyes National Seashore, San
Francisco. il Arch Rec 147:138-9 My '70
See also
Agricultural forecasts
Cattle marketing information service, inc.
Science—Information services
INFORMATION services, Government
Census data: tailored to suit you. Nations
Bsns 58:52 Ag '70
Data system for measuring and analyzing
public programs; excerpt from address, De-
cember 1969. C. L. Schultze. Mo Labor R
93:13-15 Mr '70
How far must surveillance go? government
data banks. A. R. Miller. Cur 123:27-30 N
'70

INFORMATION services, Government—*Cont.*
I spy, you spy. E. Marshall. New Repub 163:15-16 O 3 '70
Profit from 1970 census data. A. R. Eckler. il Harvard Bsns R 48:4-6+ Jl '70

INFORMATION storage and retrieval systems
Changing market for serious books. C. J. Duncan. Pub W 198:pt2 188-90 S 21 '70
Data study will watch Big Brother. por Bsns W p34 Mr 14 '70
Editorial game: imagination and technology. S. Rice. Pub W 197:45-6+ Ap 6 '70
Everybody's business, and nobody's. S. Rabinove. Chr Cent 87:843-6 Jl 8 '70
Libraries in miniature: a new era begins. J. Tebbel. il Sat R 54:41-2 Ja 9 '71
Personal privacy v. the print-out: Time essay. il Time 95:38-9 F 16 '70
Psychology: apprehension over a new communications system. P. M. Boffey. Science 167:1228-30 F 27 '70; Discussion. 168:194+ Ap 10 '70
What government snooping can find out about you. il U S News 68:22-4 My 4 '70
See also
Computers
Electronic data processing
Eric
Libraries—Automation
School libraries—Automation

Medicine
Vision information center: a user-oriented data base. M. M. Eichhorn and R. D. Reinecke. bibliog il Science 169:29-31 Jl 3 '70

Psychology
APA information plan funded. C. Holden. Science 170:1385 D 25 '70
NISP: noisy signal in psychology; proposed National information system for psychology. J. Loevinger. Trans-Action 7:10 My '70
Psychology: apprehension over a new communications system. P. M. Boffey. Science 167:1228-30 F 27 '70; Discussion 168:194+, 1041 Ap 10, My 29 '70

Science
Information-program questions; letters. L. J. Creek; A. Herschman. Phys Today 23:13+ D '70
NASA seeks ways to handle data flood. Z. Strickland. il Aviation W 92:135+ Je 22 '70

INFORMATION systems, Management
Blueprint for MIS. W. M. Zani. il Harvard Bsns R 48:95-100 N '70
Intelligence in industry: the uses and abuses of experts; excerpts from Organizational intelligence. H. L. Wilensky. bibliog f Ann Am Acad 388:46-58 Mr '70
Litton's electronic information machine. il Bsns W p 158+ Mr 28 '70
Putting judgment back into decisions; appraising performance. L. E. Greiner and others. il Harvard Bsns R 48:59-67 Mr '70
See also
United States—Management and budget, Office of

INFORMATION tests
Are you a smart money-manager? Take this test. il Changing T 24:46-7 Je '70
Changing times quiz (cont) Changing T 24:47 Ap; 18 Ag; 42 D '70
Checkpoint. K. M. Binkley. See issues of Flying to April 1970
Could you be an April fool? J. Klein. Sci Digest 67:71+ Ap '70
Diabolical quiz. T. Sharkey. Read Digest 97:167+ O '70
Educators' quiz. M. Rosenberg. See issues of Education digest
[Electronics quiz] R. P. Balin. il Pop Electr 32:30+ Je '70; 34:32 Ja '71
[Electronics quiz] V. Bell. Pop Electr 32:32 F '70
End-term review test. Sr Schol 96:27-8 My 11 '70
Family quiz game. C. Levine. See issues of Parents' magazine & better family living
Goren's Christmas quiz (cont) C. Goren. il Sports Illus 33:78-80+ D 21 '70
How much do you know about movies? quiz. H. V. Fondiller. Pop Phot 67:119+ O '70
Is your relationship on the right road? il Seventeen 29:120-1+ Je '70
Midterm review test. Sr Schol 95:23-4 N 3 '69; 96:25-6 Mr 23; 97-23-4 N 9 '70
1969 contemporary affairs test. Sr Schol 95:35-6 S 15 '69
Quiz. J. Daugherty and M. Daugherty. See issues of Science digest

Test yourself: what do you know about reading? J. Bloomfield. il por Wilson Lib Bul 45:242-5 N '70
What is your black culture quotient? Todays Ed 59:27 F '70
Your literary I.Q; ed. by D. M. Glixon. See issues of Saturday review

Anecdotes, facetiae, satire, etc.
Well, I'll be damned! L. Rosten. Look 34:16 F 10 '70

INFORMATION theory
Information theory in biology after eighteen years. H. A. Johnson. bibliog il Science 168:1545-50 Je 26 '70

INFORMERS (law)
Informing by compulsion; TV reporters and interviewers as informers. Nation 210:133 F 9 '70
Violence trap; arranged bombing to catch terrorists in Miss. Nation 210:261 Mr 9 '70

INFRARED detectors. See Detectors, Infrared

INFRARED photography. See Photography, Infrared

INFRARED proximity warning indicators. See Proximity warning indicators

INFRARED rangefinders. See View finders

INFRARED rays
Far-infrared observations of the night sky. J. R. Houck and M. Harwit; reply with rejoinder. D. P. McNutt and P. D. Feldman. bibliog Science 167:1277 F 27 '70

INFRARED spectroscopy. See Spectrum analysis

INFRARED thermography. See Photography, Infrared

INFRASOUND. See Sound waves

INGALLS, Susan R.
Interim: story. il Seventeen 29:138-9 F '70

INGELFINGER, Franz J.
Medical literature: the campus without tumult. bibliog Science 169:831-7 Ag 28 '70

INGERSOLL, Andrew P.
Mars: occurrence of liquid water. bibliog il Science 168:972-3 My 22 '70

INGERSOLL, John E.
Drug menace: how serious? interview. il por U S News 68:38-42 My 25 '70
U.S. proposes new U.N. action program against illicit narcotics; statement. September 28, 1970. Dept State Bul 63:492-7 O 26 '70

INGERSOLL, John H.
Ideas to build on. See issues of House beautiful
Well-built house (cont of) Well-built well-kept house. See issues of House beautiful

INGILS, Chester R.
Let's do away with teacher evaluation. il Clear House 44:451-6 Ap '70

INGLEWOOD, Calif.
Regional fire-training center for small cities. D. W. Ayres. Am City 85:58 S '70

INGRAM, Marylou, and Preston, Kendall, Jr
Automatic analysis of blood cells; with biographical sketches. il Sci Am 223:10, 72-82 bibliog(p 132) N '70

INGRAM. W. C. See Nachmias, V. T. jt. auth.

INHERITANCE
See also
Estate planning
Probate law and practice
Wills

INHERITANCE (biology) See Heredity

INHERITANCE of disease. See Heredity of disease

INHIBITION
On killing members of one's own species; tr. by H. Zeisel. K. Lorenz. il por Bul Atom Sci 26:2-5+ O '70

INHIBITION of enzymes. See Enzymes—Inactivation

INITIALISMS. See Acronyms

INJECTION lasers. See Lasers

INJECTIONS
See also
Inoculation

INJECTIONS, Intravenous
How to give an IV injection easier, safer. J. G. Clark. Farm J 94:B22 S '70

INJUNCTIONS
Court grants injunction in Seven minutes case. H. F. Philpel and K. P. Norwick. Pub W 197:30-1 Ap 6 '70
No-strike pacts now mean what they say. Bsns W p25 Je 6 '70
No-strike reversal by Supreme court. U S News 68:52-3 Je 15 '70

INJURIES. See Accidents; First aid in illness and injury; Traumatism

INJURIES (law) See Accident law; Damages

INK
Fingerprinting the ink in ballpoint pens. Sci Digest 67:68 F '70
Ink blowing. J. Desoto. il Design 72:24-5 Wint '70

INK blowing. See Ink

INK drawing. See Pen drawing

INLAND navigation
See also
River trips
Waterways
Waterways—United States

INLAND steel company
Inland steel's give and take. il Forbes 105: 58 Ap 15 '70
Steel checking out of the supermarket. Bsns W p34+ Mr 14 '70

INLAND surfing. See Surf riding

INLAND waterways. See Intracoastal Waterway; Waterways; Waterways—United States

INLAY
Enamel inlays in wood. P. Rothenberg. il Ceram Mo 18:32-3 Je '70

INMATES of public institutions
Larry: case history of a mistake. R. McQueen. Sat R 53:16-19+ S 12 '70; Same abr. il Read Digest 97:133-7 D '70
Laura's bastille of science. P. Steinfels. Commonweal 93:270 D 11 '70

INNER ear. See Labyrinth (ear)

INNER spring mattresses. See Mattresses

INNES, Hammond, pseud.
Long voyage. Writer 83:25 Mr '70

INNIS, Roy
Black leader's idea for South's schools; interview. il por U S News 68:30-1 Mr 2 '70
We have not shared affluence; interview. U S News 70:29-30 Ja 11 '71

INNOCENTI (firm) See Italy—Industries

INNOVATION, Technological. See Technological change

INNOVATIONS in education. See Educational innovations

INNSBRUCK, Austria
Let's travel: the Alpin-schule; offering hiking courses. R. Rudner. il Mlle 70:124+ Mr '70

INOCULATION
Pediatric immunization procedures. L. W. Sauer. il PTA Mag 64:31-2 Ap '70

INQUEST; drama. See Freed, D.

INQUIRY, Courts of. See Courts martial and courts of inquiry

INSANE
Legal status, laws, etc.
See Mental health laws

Rehabilitation
See Mentally ill—Rehabilitation

INSANE, Criminal and dangerous
Community mental health and the criminal justice system: some issues and problems. S. A. Shah. bibliog Ment Hy 54:1-12 Ja '70

INSANITY
See also
Mental illness
Psychiatry
Schizophrenia

Jurisprudence
See also
Insane, Criminal and dangerous

INSANITY and crime. See Insane, Criminal and dangerous

INSCRIPTIONS
See also
Graffiti
Petroglyphs
Picture writing

INSECT baits and repellants
Bugless boating: Yard Guard. B. Schill and B. Schill. il Motor B 126:103 Ag '70
Insect repellents. il Consumer Rep 35:420-2 Jl '70
Your kitchen is a garden center! G. Abraham. il Org Gard & Farm 17:41-3 F '70

INSECT bites and stings
Not so harmless bee. M. Schultz. Mech Illus 66:4 Je '70

INSECT circulatory system. See Cardiovascular system (insects)

INSECT communication
Bee language. Cons 24:35 Je '70
Communication of direction by the honey bee. J. L. Gould and others. bibliog il Science 169:544-54 Ag 7 '70
Defending the dance of the bees. T. C. Lucey. Sci N 98:150 Ag 15 '70
On with the dance; recruiting behavior of bees. Sci Am 223:60 O '70
What does the bee dance say? Sci Digest 68: 48 N '70

INSECT control
Ant war; the imported fire ant. D. W. Coon and R. R. Fleet. bibliog il Environ 12:28-38 D '70
Can we control pests without pollution? M. C. Goldman. il Org Gard & Farm 17:25-31 Jl '70
Coping with summer insects. il Good H 171: 6 Ag '70
Department fights beech disease and decline; beech bark disease, and insect-fungus complex. W. H. Buzzard, jr. and J. H. Risley. il Cons 24:10-13 Je '70
Insect control: alternatives to the use of conventional pesticides. R. W. Holcomb. Science 168:456-8 Ap 24 '70
Photoperiod manipulation of insect diapause; a method of pest control? D. K. Hayes and others. bibliog il Science 169:382-3 Jl 24 '70
Stopping insects in small grains. Suc Farm 68:C6 Je '70
Weed and insect control guide. E. L. Knake. il Suc Farm 68:no3 43-6+ F '70
See also
Household pest control
Insecticides
Mosquito control
Spraying and dusting

Biological control
Ally to protect elms? il Cons 24:21 F '70
Biological control of Chagas' disease. J. Bockel. il Sci N 97:485 My 16 '70
Cereal leaf beetle continues to spread. L. D. Rawson. il Suc Farm 68:B6 Ja '70
Fighting insects with insects. S. M. Spencer. il Nat Wildlife 9:48-51 D '70; Same abr. with title Alternative to poisonous pesticides? Read Digest 97:57-8+ D '70
Fish to control mosquitoes. D. Valentry. il Sea Front 16:231-3 Jl '70
Helping nature control insects. il Sci N 98: 197-8 S 5 '70
Mantis in action. J. L. Bean. il Org Gard & Farm 17:124-6 Mr '70
Nasturtiums, cukes and tomatoes; controlling black lice. W. Ferguson. il Org Gard & Farm 17:50-1 Mr '70
Not many pests in my patch; using pest-repellent plants. R. Tirrell. il Org Gard & Farm 17:60-3 My '70
Pests' pests. il Newsweek 75:107 Je 8 '70
Sex and aggression among bugs could lead to new pest control methods. Farm J 94:51 My '70
Sterile males for control of insect populations; report of meeting. L. E. LaChance. Science 168:163-4+ Ap 3 '70
Sweet smells. Sci Am 222:46+ Ap '70
Tansy and yarrow, handsome, helpful herbs; pest-repellent plants. R. Tirrell. il pors Org Gard & Farm 17:106-9 Mr '70
Turtles guard our garden. B. Gilford. il Org Gard & Farm 17:92-3 S '70
Wasps help fight the alfalfa weevil. G. Reynolds. il Farm J 94:20-1+ S '70
When it arrives, it will be a killer; hormone analog as ultimate insecticide. il Bsns W p 136+ Je 6 '70

INSECT cuticle. See Cuticle (insects)

INSECT eggs. See Insects—Eggs

INSECT flight. See Insects—Flight

INSECT foggers. See Spraying apparatus

INSECT populations
Changing farm practices affect insect numbers. Suc Farm 68:D8 Ap '70

INSECT repellents. See Insect baits and repellents

INSECT resistance. See Plants—Disease and pest resistance

INSECT sex attractants
Antennal receptors: reactions to female sex attractant in periplaneta americana. J. Boeckh and others. bibliog il Science 168: 589 My 1 '70
Persuasive scents in moth sex life. M. Birch. il Natur Hist 79:34-9+ bibliog(p88) N '70
Potent sex attractant of the gypsy moth: its isolation, identification, and synthesis. B. A. Bierl and others. bibliog il Science 170: 87-9 O 2 '70
Sex attractant of the grass grub beetle. R. F. Henzell and M. D. Lowe. bibliog il Science 168:1005-6 My 22 '70
Sex pheromones: abolition of specificity in hybrid bark beetles. G. N. Lanier. bibliog il Science 169:71-2 Jl 3 '70
Sex pheromones of the southern armyworm moth: isolation, identification, and synthesis. M. Jacobson and others. bibliog Science 170:542-4 O 30 '70
Sweet smells. Sci Am 222:46+ Ap '70

INSECT sounds
Why the cricket chirps. il Time 96:39 Ag 24 '70

INSECT viruses. See Viruses, Insect

INSECTICIDES
DDT-less mosquito control; new larvicide known as Dursban. W. H. Cranford. il Am City 85:109+ Je '70
Name your poison; relative toxicities, with table. Environ 11:30-1 S '69
Old shell game: No-pest insecticide strip, with DDVP. A. Wolff. il Am Heritage 21:112-13 O '70
Pesticide dos and don'ts. R. C. Clement. il Audubon 72:50-1 Mr '70
See also
Aldrin
Chlordane
Dieldrin
Lindane
Spraying and dusting
Zoecon corporation

Conferences
Biochemical toxicology of insecticide action; report of fifth meeting of the U.S.-Japan cooperative science program. I. Yamamoto and R. D. O'Brien. Science 168:154-6+ Ap 3 '70

Disposal
See Pesticides—Disposal

Injurious effects
Air of safety; lindane vapor dispensing devices. J. McCauli and M. Antell. bibliog il Environ 12:2-15+ N '70
Burden of proof; lack of adequate warning on DDVP resin strips. S. Novick. bibliog il Environ 12:16-29 O '70
Death of the bees; use of carbonyl insecticide, Sevin, by vegetable canners in Minnesota. Sci N 98:349-50 O 31 '70
Marine phytoplankton vary in their response to chlorinated hydrocarbons. D. W. Menzel and others. bibliog il Science 167:1724-6 Mr 27 '70
Price of convenience: effects of inhaling vapors from DDVP No-pest strips. bibliog il Environ 12:2-15+ O '70
Shell's No-pest strip; injurious effects of inhaling DDVP vapors. Consumer Rep 35:701-2 N '70

Residues
Chlorinated hydrocarbon insecticides: root uptake versus vapor contamination of soybean foliage. R. G. Nash and M. L. Beall, jr. bibliog il Science 168:1109-11 My 29 '70
Enhancement of photoalteration of cyclodiene insecticide chemical residues by rotenone. G. W. Ivie and J. E. Casida. bibliog il Science 167:1620-2 Mr 20 '70
Formation of photodieldrin by microorganisms. F. Matsumura and others. bibliog il Science 170:1206-7 D 11 '70
See also
DDT (insecticide)—Residues

INSECTICIDES, Resistance to. See Insects, Injurious and beneficial—Resistance to control

INSECTS
Could you be an entomologist? quiz. J. Daugherty and M. Daugherty. il Sci Digest 67:74-5+ F '70
See also
Age (insects)
Insect sounds
Nervous system—Insects
Parasites—Insects
also names of insects, e.g. Moths

Anatomy
See also
Antennae
Sense organs—Insects

Biological control
See Insect control—Biological control

Classification
Batch of bug finders; discoveries of new species. il Life 68:59-60 Mr 20 '70

Control
See Insect control

Development
Photoperiod manipulation of insect diapause; a method of pest control? D. K. Hayes and others. bibliog il Science 169:382-3 Jl 24 '70
Photoperiodic induction and termination of diapause in an insect; response to changing day lengths. M. J. Tauber and C. A. Tauber. bibliog il Science 167:170 Ja 9 '70
Prevention of metamorphosis by exposure of insect eggs to juvenile hormone analogs. L. M. Riddiford. bibliog il Science 167:287-8 Ja 16 '70

Eggs
Insect eggshells. H. E. Hinton. il Sci Am 223:84-91 Ag '70

Flight
Insect flight: lift and rate of change of incidence. L. Bennett. bibliog il Science 167:177-9 Ja 9 '70

Food and feeding
Cardiac glycosides and distastefulness: some observations on the palatability spectrum of butterflies. S. S. Duffey. bibliog il Science 169:78-9 Jl 3 '70
Elm bark derived feeding stimulants for the smaller European elm bark beetle. R. W. Doskotch and others. bibliog il Science 167:380-2 Ja 23 '70
See also
Cannibalism (insects)

Habits and behavior
See also
Courtship of insects
Insect communication
Mimicry (biology)

Migration
Migrating monarchs. Sci Digest 67:30 Ap '70

Molting
See Molting

Physiology
See also
Cardiovascular system (insects)

Protective equipment
See Defense mechanisms (biology)

Resistance to control
See Insects, Injurious and beneficial—Resistance to control

Sight
See Sight (insects)

INSECTS, Age of. See Age (insects)

INSECTS, Injurious and beneficial
See also
Weed control—Biological control
also subhead Diseases and pests under names of crops, trees, plants, etc, e.g. Corn—Diseases and pests; *also* names of insects, e.g. Alfalfa weevils

Biological control
See Insect control—Biological control

Control
See Insect control

Resistance to control
Diminishing returns; increasing resistance to pesticides. bibliog il Environ 11:6-11+ S '69
What's the resistance problem all about? il Suc Farm 68:no4 D18 Mr '70

INSECTS as carriers of infection
See also
Flies as carriers of infection

INSECTS as carriers of plant disease
Barley yellow dwarf virus: phenotypic mixing and vector specificity. W. F. Rochow. bibliog il Science 167:875-8 F 6 '70

INSELBURG, Joseph, and Fuke, Motohiro
Replicating DNA: structure of colicin factor E1. bibliog il Science 169:590-2 Ag 7 '70

INSEMINATION, Artificial. See Artificial insemination, Human

INSERVICE teacher education. See Teachers—Education in service

INSIDE media (newsletter) See News letters

INSIDER trading. See Stocks—Insider trading

INSIGNIA
See also
Emblems

INSITE (Instructional systems in teacher education) See Teachers—Education

INSPECTION of automobiles. See Automobiles—Inspection

INSPECTION of sewers. See Sewer inspection

INSPIRATION consolidated copper company
Inspiration's big blast. Forbes 105:51 F 15 '70

INSPIRATION of the Bible. See Bible—Inspiration

INSTALMENT plan
How to manage time-payment buying. L. David. Mech Illus 66:39-41 Mr '70

Laws and regulations
Finance charges: are they or aren't they interest? il Changing T 24:13-14 Ag '70
Two legal reforms to protect shoppers' rights. il Changing T 24:23-4 Ap '70

INSURANCE, Automobile—*Continued*

Finding fault with no-fault rates. Bsns W p24 Ag 29 '70

Great insurance debate. J. Brokaw. il Motor T 22:72-4+ Ag; 30-1+ S; 38-40+ O '70

How to pay for 15,000,000 auto accidents a year; interview, ed. J. A. Hamilton. R. E. Stewart. il N Y Times Mag p32-4+ My 10 '70

Lawmakers write insurance reform. Bsns W p32 S 19 '70

Motor trend interview; problems facing car owners. P. A. Hart. il pors Motor T 22:92+ Ap '70

New problems in auto insurance. il U S News 69:17-18 Jl 6 '70

New system of auto insurance on the way? il U S News 69:46 S 21 '70

Nobody's fault? Massachusetts adopts plan. il Newsweek 76:51-2 Ag 31 '70

Politics at fault; debacle of no-fault plan in Massachusetts. il Time 96:66 Ag 31 '70

Prospects for reform. Consumer Rep 35: 342-3 Je '70

Rough ride and new roads ahead for auto insurers. il Bsns W p 118 Mr 28 '70

Toward quick payment. il Time 95:76 Mr 2 '70

Why automobile insurance rates keep going up; excerpt from Are you being taken for a ride? G. B. Friedman; discussion. Atlan 225:28 Ja '70

Why you can't buy the insurance you need; with editorial comment. il Bsns W p64-5+, 114 N 7 '70

See also

Insurance. Motor vehicle

INSURANCE, Aviation

Insurance rates for aircraft rise. Aviation W 92:85+ Ja 19 '70

See also

Airlines—Insurance

INSURANCE, Business

State aid for retailers insurance coverage; Buy-Rite's appeal. H. F. Pilpel and K. P. Norwick. Pub W 198:33-4 D 28 '70

See also

Brokers—Insurance

INSURANCE, Casualty

This month's feature: Congress & casualty insurance regulation. Cong Digest 49:33-64 F '70

See also

Insurance, Automobile

Insurance, Property

Insurance, Workmens compensation

INSURANCE, Dental

Coming: a new way to pay dental costs. il U S News 69:92-3 S 21 '70

Dental insurance: a developing success story. L. Joseph. il Todays Health 48:48-9+ Mr '70

INSURANCE, Disability

Insurance that pays you when you can't work. il Changing T 24:31-3 S '70

INSURANCE, Flood

Now, flood insurance you can afford. il Changing T 24:32 Ap '70

INSURANCE, Hail

How to buy crop hail insurance. H. L. Tinley. il Suc Farm 68:23 My '70

INSURANCE, Health

How to get health insurance that's right for your family. J. Galub. il Parents Mag 45:78-9 N '70

Time to check over your health insurance. il Changing T 24:15-18 Je '70

See also

Insurance. Dental

California

See also

Medicaid

Europe, Western

National health care abroad. il U S News 69: 29 Ag 10 '70

Quebec (province)

Crisis in Canada over a new medicare plan. il U S News 69:79-80 N 23 '70

United States

Band-aids and major surgery. Sci N 97:430 My 2 '70

Case for national health insurance. R. Fein. il Sat R 53:27-9+ Ag 22 '70

Changes in health and insurance plans for salaried employees. D. R. Kittner. bibliog il Mo Labor R 93:32-9 F '70

Crisis of health care. America 123:168 S 19 '70

Debate over National health insurance. il Time 96:68 O 12 '70

Growing pains of medical care. F. Anderson. New Repub 162:17-18 Ja 17; 13-16 Ja 24; 17-19 F 7 '70; Discussion. 162:36-9 Mr 21 '70

Health security program; medicine in the free enterprise system; address. September 9, 1970. P. Ashton. Vital Speeches 37: 100-2 D 1 '70

How to buy health insurance. Suc Farm 68:no4 D24 Mr '70

Insurance for the nation's health. il Time 95: 60-1 My 11 '70

Insurance is not enough. G. A. Silver. Nation 210:680-3 Je 8 '70

Is there any way out of our health care mess? F. Bailey. il Bet Hom & Gard 48: 48-9+ N '70

Kaiser: you pay your money and you take your chances. J. M. Carnoy. il Ramp Mag 9:26-31 N '70

Medical justice. Chr Cent 87:883 Jl 22 '70

National health insurance; labors no. 1 legislative goal; adress, September 7, 1970. G. Meany. Vital Speeches 37:14-16 O 15 '70

National health insurance: the next attack on medical costs. il Changing T 25:41-4 Ja '71

NHI is nigh; national health insurance plans. L. Witt. Todays Health 48:26-9+ Jl '70

Prepaid medical care for all. il U S News 69:26-9 Ag 10 '70

$60-billion crisis over medical care; with editorial comment. il Bsns W p50-1+, 118 Ja 17 '70

TRB from Washington; towards socialized medicine. New Repub 162:6 Ja 17 '70

That queasy feeling; health insurance companies and government-supported health insurance. il Forbes 106:42 O 1 '70

Will Finch flinch? prepayment plan. New Repub 162:10-11 My 2 '70

See also

Medicaid

Medicare

INSURANCE, Industrial

See also

Insurance, Unemployment

INSURANCE, Liability

He's insured, sock it to him! il Forbes 105: 63-4+ Ap 15 '70

Liability insurance: is your family fully protected? il Good H 171:162 S '70

See also

Insurance, Automobile

INSURANCE, Life

NEA life insurance dependents' coverage increased. Todays Ed 59:15 Ja '70

Truth in life insurance. J. Carper. il Nation 212:45-8 Ja 11 '71

See also

Annuities

Agents

See Insurance agents

Policies

How should your life insurance pay off? settlement options. il Changing T 24:41-2 My '70

President signs 15 per cent social security rise for 25.4 million. Aging 183:3 Ja '70

When is term insurance the best buy? il Changing T 24:43-5 Mr '70

Wife insurance: how it fits your estate plan. Bsns W p95 O 24 '70

Policy loans

Rise in borrowing on life insurance. U S News 69:79-80 Jl 20 '70

INSURANCE, Marine

Britons waive rule to spare U.S. fleet. Bsns W p21-2 Mr 7 '70

How to buy boat insurance. P. Rockwell. il Mech Illus 66:108-9+ Mr '70

Insuring a small boat, easier now. Sunset 145:119 N '70

INSURANCE, Medical. See Insurance, Health

INSURANCE, Motor vehicle

What you need to know about snowmobile insurance. Suc Farm 68:B22 N '70

INSURANCE, Property

Why it is harder to get insurance. il U S News 69:44-6 S 21 '70

INSURANCE, Sickness. See Insurance, Health

INSURANCE, Social

Worldwide developments in social security, 1967-69. il Mo Labor R 93:43-4 O '70

United States

Bigger pensions, higher tax: coming hike in social security. il U S News 68:74-6 My 18 '70

Coming: changes in social security. il U S News 68:34-6 F 2 '70

Increases ahead in social security. U S News 69:57 D 21 '70

More money for 25 million. R. R. Jalbert. il por Har Yrs 10:49-50 My '70

Now: bigger checks for the elderly. il U S News 68:38 Ap 6 '70

Penalizing the oldsters' earnings. R. L. Masse. America 122:119 F 7 '70; Reply. H. S. Ryan. 122:360 Ap 4 '70

INSURANCE, Social—United States—*Cont.*
Runaway expansion of social security? interview. R. J. Myers. pors Nations Bsns 58: 60-3 M$_r$ '70
Should Congress flunk the retirement test? raising earning power under social security. G. Town. Har Yrs 10:30-1 Ja '70
Social security and medicare explained. R. Krumme. il Suc Farm 68:no5 37-41 Mr '70
Social security at the crossroads. R. J. Myers. Read Digest 96:81-5 Ap '70
Some overlooked benefits in the social security raise. il U S News 68:65-6 Je 29 '70
Twenty million letters a year! R. R. Jalbert. il por Har Yrs 10:42-4 Ja '70
Tying social security to cost of living: the prospects. il U S News 68:57-9 Je 8 '70
Will the elderly rescue the retailers? il Bsns W p32-3 Ap 25 '70
See also
Insurance, Health—United States
Insurance, Unemployment—United States
Social security act, 1935
United States—Social security administration
INSURANCE, Stock exchange
If your broker fails, a new insurance plan. il U S News 68:101-2 Ap 13 '70
INSURANCE, Strike
Strike insurance: employers win; NLRB decision. U S News 70:82 Ja 11 '71
INSURANCE, Travelers
How insurance protects the air traveler. Bsns W p 108 S 26 '70
INSURANCE, Unemployment

United States

Changes in law on jobless benefits. U S News 69:82 Ag 17 '70
Changes in state unemployment insurance during 1969. F. C. Johnson. Mo Labor R 93:62-70 Ja '70
Jobless benefits, for the jobless; unemployment compensation laws. Duns 95:90 Ja '70
Jobless pay is due for overhaul. il Bsns W p35 Jl 4 '70
More generous pay for jobless. Bsns W p25 My 9 '70
Unemployment kitty depleted at Douglas. Bsns W p32 Je 27 '70
Using unemployment insurance wage reports as a data source. M. E. Borus. Mo Labor R 93:66-7 Jl '70
INSURANCE, Workmens compensation
How workmen's compensation laws changed during 1969. F. C. Johnson. Mo Labor R 93:57-61 Ja '70
Work at your own risk. D. P. Sachs. Sat R 53:64-5 Je 6 '70
INSURANCE agents
Making a living selling life insurance. il Changing T 23:15-17 D '69
INSURANCE and state
See also
Insurance companies—Regulation
INSURANCE companies
Auto insurance. il Consumer Rep 35:332-41, 426-33 Je-Jl '70
That queasy feeling; health insurance companies and government-supported health insurance. il Forbes 106:42 O 1 '70
Truth in life insurance. J. Carper. il Nation 212:45-8 Ja 11 '71
Why nobody likes the insurers. J. Main. il Fortune 82:82-7+ D '70
Your policy is hereby canceled. P. Hellman. il N Y Times Mag p32-3+ N 8 '70
See also
American insurance association
American insurance group
Government investigations—Insurance companies
Insurance company of North America
John Hancock mutual life insurance company
Lloyd's. London
New York life insurance company
Overseas private investment corporation
Prudential insurance company of America
Starr, C. V, and company

Accounting

Finance; with yardsticks of management performance. il Forbes 105:140+ Ja 1 '70

Directories

Fifty largest life-insurance companies. Fortune 81:206-7 My '70

Finance

Regulators eye insurers' funds. il Bsns W n36 Ja 2 '71

Why automobile insurance rates keep going up; excerpt from Are you being taken for a ride? G. B. Friedman; discussion. Atlan 225:28 Ja '70
See also
Insurance companies—Investments

Holding companies
See Insurance holding companies

Investments

Billion-dollar insurance caper; fire-and-casualty companies' upstream dividend payouts. il Forbes 106:66-8 O 15 '70
Other pocket. P. Hellman. N Y Times Mag p 124 N 8 '70
Why automobile insurance rates keep going up; excerpts from Are you being taken for a ride? G. B. Friedman; discussion. Atlan 225:28 Ja '70

Mutual fund operations

Insurance men stick to their funds. il Bsns W p72+ N 21 '70

Real estate operations

Future largest landlords in America; life-insurance companies. S. Rose. il Fortune 82: 90-3+ Jl '70

Regulation

Regulators eye insurers' funds. il Bsns W p36 Ja 2 '71
This month's feature: Congress & casualty insurance regulation. Cong Digest 49:33-64 F '70
Why you can't buy the insurance you need; with editorial comment. il Bsns W p64-5+, 114 N 7 '70

Securities

Child of empire: American international group. il Forbes 105:40 Mr 15 '70
INSURANCE company of North America
Fighting for bold ideas. C. K. Cox. il Nations Bsns 58:86-7 Ja '70
INSURANCE holding companies
Billion-dollar insurance caper; fire-and-casualty companies' upstream dividend payouts. il Forbes 106:66-8 O 15 '70
Building a fortune on LTV's discards; Gulf life holding co. por Bsns W p76-7 O 3 '70
INSURANCE law
Lawmakers write insurance reform. Bsns W p32 S 19 '70
See also
Insurance companies—Regulation
INSURANCE offices. See Offices
INSURANCE policies. See Insurance—Policies
INSURANCE tax. See Insurance—Taxation
INSURRECTIONS. See Revolutions
INTEGRATED circuits. See Electronic circuits, Integrated
INTEGRATION (term)
Terms defined. Ebony 25:35 Ag '70
INTEGRATION, Agricultural. See Contracts, Agricultural
INTEGRATION of public schools. See Public schools—Desegregation
INTELLECT
See also
Brain
Reason

Nutritional aspects

Malnourished bodies, malnourished minds; with study-discussion program. L. V. Wilder. bibliog il PTA Mag 64:10-12+, 33 Mr '70
Malnutrition and learning. M. S. Read. Ed Digest 35:8-11 Ap '70
Rats, pigs and children; relationship of malnutrition to mental retardation. Trans-Action 7:15 My '70
INTELLECTUAL cooperation
See also
Educational exchanges
INTELLECTUAL development of children. See Children—Growth and development
INTELLECTUAL liberty
Intellectual freedom jobs asked of major libraries. Library J 95:107-8 Ja 15 '70
1969 in review: freedom to read. il Pub W 197:50-1 F 9 '70
What's fit to print? G. A. Harrison. Writers Digest 50:54-5 Ja '70
See also
Academic freedom
American library association—Intellectual freedom committee
Libraries and intellectual liberty

INTELLECTUAL life
See also
Enlightenment
also subhead Intellectual life under names of countries, states, cities, e.g. New York (city)—Intellectual life
INTELLECTUALS
Cultural transplants. M. Jay. Commentary 49:78+ Mr '70
Dissent cannot be shot down or arrested. P. Young. il pors Life 68:61+ My 1 '70
Dissent in the USSR. Nation 211:389 O 26 '70
Home thoughts from abroad. por Time 95:100+ Je 15 '70
Intellectuals and revolution: interview with Jean-Paul Sartre; ed. by J. C. Garot, tr. by B. Rice. J. P. Sartre. il Ramp Mag 9:52-5 D '70
Intellectuals as an ethnic group. A. M. Greeley. il N Y Times Mag p22-3+ Jl 12 '70
Secession of the intellectuals. J. Hart. Nat R 22:1278-82 D 1 '70
Whose country is America? excerpt from First things, last things. E. Hoffer. il N Y Times Mag p30-1+ N 22 '70; Discussion. p34+ D 13 '70
Young intelligentsia in revolt; excerpt from America: system and revolution, ed. by R. Aya and N. Miller. R. Flacks. il Trans-Action 7:46-55 Je '70
See also
Christians—Intellectual life

Anecdotes, facetiae, satire, etc.
Rules for intellectual experts. P. Steinfels. Commonweal 93:242 D 4 '70
INTELLIGENCE
See also
Intellect
INTELLIGENCE, Artificial. See Artificial intelligence
INTELLIGENCE levels
Intellectual development of children from interracial matings. L. Willerman and others. bibliog il Science 170:1329-31 D 18 '70
Intelligence and race. W. F. Bodmer and L. L. Cavalli-Sforza. il Sci Am 223:19-29 bibliog(p 144) O '70

Negroes
How racists use science to degrade black people. C. T. Rowan. il por Ebony 25:31-4+ My '70
Jensenism: variation on a racial theme. J. Neary. il pors Life 68:58B-58D+ Je 12 '70
Negro intelligence and educational theory. R. A. Lindsey. bibliog f Clear House 45:67-71 O '70
Race and intelligence; doctrine called jensenism. R. C. Lewontin. Bul Atom Sci 26:2-8 Mr '70; Discussion. 26:17-25 My; 42-3 S '70
Race and IQ. il Time 96:27 S 7 '70
INTELLIGENCE of animals. See Animal intelligence
INTELLIGENCE quotient
Can children get smarter? with study-discussion program, by M. M. Conant. E. S. Schaefer. bibliog il PTA Mag 65:10-12+, 35 S '70
Helping children to grow up smart: Syracuse university children's center. B. Asbell. il Redbook 135:34+ Jl '70
Intelligence and race. W. F. Bodmer and L. L. Cavalli-Sforza. il Sci Am 223:19-29 bibliog(p 144) O '70
Intelligence quotient pattern over age: comparisons among siblings and parent-child pairs. R. B. McCall. bibliog il Science 170:644-8 N 6 '70
Jensen vs. Lewontin; a comment. E. Rabinowitch. Bul Atom Sci 26:25-6 My '70
Jensenism: variation on a racial theme. J. Neary. il pors Life 68:58B-58D+ Je 12 '70
Race and intelligence; doctrine called jensenism. R. C. Lewontin. Bul Atom Sci 26:2-8 Mr '70; Discussion. 26:17-25 My; 42-3 S '70
What's the IQ of the IQ test. P. Pine. Ed Digest 35:13-16 F '70
INTELLIGENCE service

United States
Eyes left; J. M. O'Brien charges army with political snooping. Newsweek 76:18 D 28 '70
Keeping tabs on civilians; Army security agency. J. Stout. il Nation 211:681-3 D 28 '70
INTELLIGENCE tests
Can an intelligence test be wrong? G. M. Knox. Bet Hom & Gard 48:45-6 N '70
Children who are tested in an alien language: mentally retarded? M. E. Leary. New Repub 162:17-18 My 30 '70
Pseudo-sacrosanct role of intelligence in education. H. P. Baptiste, jr. Ed Digest 36:24-7 D '70

Race and IQ. il Time 96:27 S 7 '70
What do intelligence tests really tell us? B. Spock. Redbook 135:37-8+ Ag '70
See also
Intelligence quotient
INTELSAT. See International telecommunications satellite consortium
INTENSIFIERS, Image. See Image intensifiers
INTENSITY transportation. See Transportation
—United States
INTENSIVE care units. See Hospital care
INTERACTION, Social. See Social interaction
INTER-AMERICAN conferences
1890; the First international conference of American states. C. Márquez Sterling. il Américas 22:7-12 Ap '70
INTER-AMERICAN cooperation. See Inter-American relations
INTER-AMERICAN council for education, science, and culture
Councils approve draft statutes, budgets. il Américas 22:44 Je '70
INTER-AMERICAN cultural council
Optimistic note; Executive committee approves special fund. Américas 22:1 F '70
INTER-AMERICAN development bank
Board of governors of the Inter-American development bank holds eleventh annual meeting at Punta del Este; statement, with message from President Nixon, April 23, 1970. D. M. Kennedy. Dept State Bul 62:658-61 My 25 '70
Inter-American bank marks tenth anniversary. Américas 22:44 Mr '70
INTER-AMERICAN economic and social council
Councils approve draft statutes, budgets. il Américas 22:44 Je '70
IA-ECOSOC Caracas meeting yields special committee. Américas 22:45 Ap '70
IA-ECOSOC special committee meets at Washington; statement; with Department announcement, November 18, 1969. C. A. Meyer. Dept State Bul 61:631-4 D 29 '69
Inter-American economic and social council holds special meeting at Caracas; text of message from President Nixon and statement by C. A. Meyer, February 5, 1970. R. M. Nixon; C. A. Meyer. Dept State Bul 62:254-9 Mr 2 '70
New mechanism for inter-American negotiations. Américas 22:43 Ja '70
INTER-AMERICAN highway. See Pan American highway
INTER-AMERICAN juridical committee
On the Inter-American juridical level; condemning acts of terrorism: excerpts from address. August 31, 1970. G. Plaza. Américas 22:1 O '70
INTER-AMERICAN relations
Ethics and the art of the possible in inter-American relations. J. B. Housley. il Chr Cent 87:1283-5 O 28 '70
Inter-American cooperation: a prime concern to the United States; statement. October 19, 1970. J. N. Irwin, 2d. Dept State Bul 63:561-5 N 9 '70
Opening to the future. G. Plaza. il America 122:96-8 Ja 31 '70
See also
Alliance for progress
Organization of American states
Pan American day and week
INTER-AMERICAN seminars. See Seminars
INTER-AMERICAN social development institute
New institute for Inter-American social development; statement and White House announcement. August 17, 1970. R. M. Nixon. Dept State Bul 63:301 S 14 '70
INTER-AMERICAN tropical tuna commission
Mr Terry named to Inter-American tropical tuna commission. Dept State Bul 63:355 S 28 '70
INTERARMS. See International armament corporation
INTERCHANGES (highway engineering) See Roads—Interchanges and intersections
INTERCOLLEGIATE football. See Football
INTERCOMMUNICATING systems
Home intercoms. il Consumer Rep 35:659-62 N '70
Keeping track of lawbreakers by radio. S. V. Jones. il Sci Digest 67:76 F '70
See also
Television, Closed circuit
INTERCONNECTED electric utility systems. See Electric plants—Interconnection
INTERCOSMOS (satellite) See Artificial satellites, European
INTERCUTTING of moving pictures. See Moving pictures—Editing

INTERDENOMINATIONAL cooperation. See Religious cooperation

INTERDISCIPLINARY curriculum. See Colleges and universities—Curriculum

INTEREST
As credit eases, new cut in prime rate? U S News 69:49 D 28 '70
Banks join the easier money trend. il Newsweek 75:67 Ap 6 '70
Break in interest rates; hope for borrowers. il U S News 68:93-4 Ap 6 '70
Defense of usury. M. Friedman. Newsweek 75:79 Ap 6 '70
Dip in interest rates: what it means to borrowers. il U S News 69:65-7 Jl 27 '70
Finance charges: are they or aren't they interest? il Changing T 24:13-14 Ag '70
First slice off the prime rate. Bsns W p35 S 19 '70
For borrowers: cheaper credit; cutback in the prime rate. U S News 69:93 O 5 '70
Hope after a dip. C. Morgello. il Newsweek 76:108 N 23 '70
How to earn top dollar from your savings account. R. Krumme. il Suc Farm 68:G8 S '70
Life of lower rates. Times 96:88 D 7 '70
Lower interest rates ahead. Time 96:96 N 23 '70
Lower interest rates ahead: as experts see it now. il U S News 69:64-7 S 21 '70
Man who cut the prime: president of Philadelphia's First Pennsylvania banking & trust co. por Time 96:73 S 28 '70
Markets dance to the new Fed tune. il Bsns W p 17-18 N 28 '70
Money: easier. Time 96:81 O 5 '70
More ease for money. Bsns W p27 D 5 '70
Need a loan? First check these interest rates. il Good H 171:190 O '70
New wave of cuts in interest rates. U S News 69:32 D 7 '70
New way to buy a home, flexible interest rates. il U S News 68:90-2 Ap 27 '70
Nudge toward a lower prime. il Bsns W p24 N 14 '70
On paper, things look a bit looser. il Bsns W p33 F 28 '70
Political interest: U.S. banks cutting prime business-loan rate. Time 95:10 Ap 6 '70
Prime rate: opposing views. U S News 69:63 S 28 '70
Prospects for a downturn in interest rates. il U S News 68:92-3 Mr 16 '70
Spur of credit. C. Morgello. il Newsweek 76:82 O 5 '70
Sternest test. Newsweek 76:51-2+ Ag 31 '70
Welcome drop. il Time 96:83-4 S 14 '70
What about interest rates? W. Parkhurst. Sci Digest 67:85 Je '70
What money costs you. P. Lindberg. il Bet Hom & Gard 48:14+ D '70
Will the Fed now follow the banks? il Bsns W p32 S 26 '70
Word on dips in the monetary rates: excerpts from statement to Senate banking and currency committee, March 18, 1970. A. F. Burns. U S News 68:65-6 Mr 30 '70
See also
Bank deposits—Interest
Discount
Investments
Savings deposits—Interest

INTEREST groups, Political. See Pressure groups

INTERESTED Negroes (organization)
New set of heroes. C. Lewis. il Am Ed 6:23 Ja '70

INTERFACIAL tension. See Surface tension

INTERFAITH committee for religious concerns. See Vocation in religion

INTERFAITH cooperation. See Religious cooperation

INTERFERENCE (light)
Optical interference coatings. P. Baumeister and G. Pincus. il Sci Am 223:58-68+ D '70

INTERFERENCE (psychology)
Tones and numbers: specificity of interference in immediate memory. D. Deutsch. bibliog il Science 168:1604-5 Je 26 '70

INTERFERENCE, Radio. See Radio interference

INTERFEROMETERS
Earth strain measurements with a laser interferometer. J. Berger and R. H. Lovberg. bibliog il Science 170:296-303 O 16 '70

INTERFEROMETRY
Interferometry with X rays. M. Hart and U. Bonse. bibliog il pors Phys Today 23:26-31 Ag '70
Radar interferometric observations of Venus at 70-centimeter wavelength. D. B. Campbell and others. bibliog il Science 170:1090-2 D 4 '70

Radar snapshot of Venus. R. M. Goldstein and H. Rumsey, jr. il Science 169:974-7 S 4 '70

INTERFERON
Fetal response to viral infection: interferon production in sheep. J. C. Overall, jr. and L. A. Glasgow. bibliog il Science 167:1139-41 F 20 '70
Inducing the virus-fighter. Sci N 98:163 Ag 22 '70
Interferon: clinical application of molecular biology. M. Harris. bibliog il Science 170:1068-70 D 4 '70
Transfer of interferon-producing macrophages: new approach to viral chemotherapy. L. A. Glasgow. bibliog il Science 170:854-6 N 20 '70

Conferences
Interferon. J. Vilček. Science 168:398-9 Ap 17 '70

INTERGOVERNMENTAL fiscal relations
Thanks, but no thanks; federal funds, but not federal control. il Nations Bsns 58:56-7 Ag '70

INTERGOVERNMENTAL tax relations
Bill would force state to pay in lieu taxes; New Jersey legislation. Am City 85:40 Ag '70
Governors' big worry: where to get money. il U S News 69:14-16 Ag 24 '70
New pressure for tax sharing. il U S News 69:47-8 D 28 '70
Nixon's new federalism; revenue sharing. D. Mars. Nation 210:435-7 Ap 13 '70
Revenue-sharing lobby mobilizes. Bsns W p82-3 D 5 '70
Sharing wealth and authority. Sci N 97:121-2 Ja 31 '70
Welfare reform and revenue sharing. R. Lekachman. Duns 96:9 O '70
Who'll get what from tax sharing. il U S News 69:56 Ag 17 '70

INTERIM; story. See Ingalls, S. R.

INTERIOR, Department of. See United States—Interior, Department of

INTERIOR decoration
Design of interiors. il Arch Rec 148:89-102 Ag '70
Record interiors; selection of twelve designs. il Arch Rec 147:97-120 Ja '70
See also
House decoration
Yacht decoration

INTERIOR decorators
Mica+Chessy=MAC II. il pors McCalls 97:96-101 Ap '70

INTERIORS, Photography of. See Photography—Interiors

INTERLIBRARY communication
Best laid plan: OLDP, ALSO, and JSHP: with excerpts from the Ohio library development plan. R. H. Donahugh Am Lib 1:973-7 N '70
Informational switching yard. E. J. Gaines. Library J 95:641 F 15 '70; Reply. E. Castagna. 95:2742 S 1 '70
New York library development plan released. il Library J 95:3715 N 1 '70
N-I-H syndrome: creating so-called new techniques or processes. G. R. Brong and E. F. Pasternak. il pors Library J 95:3877-8 N 15 '70
No library is an island: networks conference in Va; Airlie house, facility for meeting. A. Plotnik. il Wilson Lb Bul 45:225+ N '70
N.Y. report puts children services in schools; national media standards recommended as minimum Library J 95:3945 N 15 '70
Public libraries and the network idea: address, April 26, 1968. V. W. Clapp. il Library J 95:121-4 Ja 15 '70
Working library network; established for book processing by Systems development division of IBM. B. M. Wolpert. il Am Lib 1:570-2 Je '70

INTERLÜBKE wall system. See Walls

INTERMARRIAGE of races
Boy, girl, black, white. il Time 95:74 Ap 6 '70
For love or money; Vietnamese-American marriages. il Newsweek 76:50-1 S 7 '70
Sister debates a brother on that black man-white woman thing; interviews. ed. by K. Mehlinger. L. Gant; D. K. Davis. il pors Ebony 25:130-3 Ag '70
See also
Indians of North America—Mixed bloods
Mulattoes

INTERMARRIAGES, Religious. See Marriages, Mixed

INTERMEDIA performances. See Performing arts

INTERNAL combustion engines. See Automobile engines; Gas and oil engines

INTERNAL migration. See Migration, Internal
INTERNAL revenue service. See United States
—Internal revenue service
INTERNAL security
As violence spreads U.S. goes on guard. il
U S News 69:15-16 N 2 '70
Authorization for security checks; Defense
facilities and internal security bill. J.
Walsh. Science 167:1233 F 27 '70
Infrastructure of repression. Nation 210:482-
3 Ap 27 '70
See also
Industry—Security measures
INTERNAL security, Committee on. See United
States—Congress—House—Internal security,
Committee on
INTERNATIONAL agencies
See also
African and Malagasy common organization
United Nations—Non-governmental organiza-
tions
INTERNATIONAL agreements. See Treaties
INTERNATIONAL air line employees asso-
ciation. See Air line employees associa-
tion, International
INTERNATIONAL air transport association
Air net, by K. G. J. Pillai. Review
Sat R 53:59-60 Ap 25 '70. P. J. C. Fried-
lander
Atlantic tariffs snag IATA talks. R. G.
O'Lone. Aviation W 93:25-6 O 12 '70
Carriers urged to improve marketing. E. H.
Kolcum. Aviation W 93:26 N 9 '70
Disapproval of IATA vote plan by CAB
sparks new protests. Aviation W 93:23 S 21
'70
En route charges peril IATA fare pacts.
Aviation W 94:24 Ja 11 '71
Excursion fare will get IATA scrutiny. R. S.
Kahn. Aviation W 93:30-1 Ag 10 '70
IATA chief spurs anti-hijack program. E. H.
Kolcum. il Aviation W 93:32-3 D 7 '70
IATA forecasts ten per cent traffic gain in
1971. Aviation W 94:28 Ja 11 '71
IATA keys advance spade work to avoiding
Honolulu stalemate. Aviation W 92:34 Je 8
'70
IATA, official of Munich airport debate over
anti-hijacking roles. Aviation W 93:29 N 16
'70
IATA to attack fare deadlock at Tehran. R. G.
O'Lone. Aviation W 93:22-3 O 26 '70
Pacific, Asia, Australia fares set. R. G.
O'Lone. Aviation W 93:24-5 O 19 '70
Who sets the plane fares? K. G. J. Pillai. il
Nation 210:177-80 F 16 '70
INTERNATIONAL airport, Amsterdam, Neth-
erlands. See Amsterdam, Netherlands—Air-
ports
INTERNATIONAL alliance of theatrical stage
employees and moving picture machine
operators of the United States and Canada
Movie unions waive rights. U S News 68:72
Ap 6 '70
INTERNATIONAL animal exchange, Inc.
Wild game pays off for Bwana. Don. il Bsns
W p 128+ My 23 '70
INTERNATIONAL armament corporation
Dealers who are cashing in. il Bsns W p 118
My 23 '70
INTERNATIONAL association for the study of
history of religions
Sojourn in Stockholm: history of religions
congress. S. Cain. Chr Cent 87:1328+ N 4 '70
INTERNATIONAL association of machinists
and aerospace workers
IAM sees Braniff cutback keyed to sale. Avi-
ation W 93:28 Jl 6 '70
Portable pensions cover 85,000 IAM members
in forty states, D.C. Aging 188:16 Je '70
INTERNATIONAL astronomical union
Astronomical notes from Brighton. il Sky &
Tel 40:353-6 D '70
IAU Brighton assembly. il Sky & Tel 40:192-
200 O '70
IAU to convene in England. il Sky & Tel 39:
90-1 F '70
Names on the back of the moon; with folded
NASA map. J. Ashbrook. il Sky & Tel 40:
262-6, 291-300 N '70
INTERNATIONAL atomic energy agency
Assembly adopts resolution on IAEA. UN
Mo Chron 7:127-9 Ja '70
General conference of the International
atomic energy agency holds 14th session at
Vienna; statement, September 22, 1970. G.
T. Seaborg. Dept State Bul 63:485-91 O 26
'70
International atom. S. Eklund. il pors Bul
Atom Sci 26:56-61 Je '70
Nuclear materials: security; address, May 25,
1970. C. Hosmer. Vital Speeches 36:635-8 Ag
1 '70
See also
International centre for theoretical physics,
Trieste, Italy

INTERNATIONAL automobile show. See Au-
tomobiles—Exhibitions
INTERNATIONAL balance of payments. See
Balance of payments
INTERNATIONAL ballet competition. Moscow.
See Ballet—Competitions
INTERNATIONAL bank for reconstruction and
development
Boards of governors of the IMF and IBRD
meet at Copenhagen; statement, September
22, 1970. D. M. Kennedy. Dept State Bul 63:
431-5 O 12 '70
Let the sun shine in; World bank-IMF joint
meeting. il Newsweek 76:74+ O 5 '70
New storm hits the World bank. il Bsns W
p 100-1 S 26 '70
Partners in development, by L. B. Pearson
and others. Review
Commonweal 92:65-7 Mr 27 '70. M. Hud-
son
Pearson report: Partners in development. Il
UNESCO Courier 23:4-33 F '70
Second development decade; address, Novem-
ber 13, 1970. R. S. McNamara. Vital Speeches 37:135-40 D 15 '70
World bank and education. Sch & Soc 98:
13-14 Ja '70
World development needs; aid to underde-
veloped countries; address, September 21,
1970. R. S. McNamara. Vital Speeches 37:
7-14 O 15 '70
INTERNATIONAL banking. See Banks and
banking, International
INTERNATIONAL biological program
Advent of big biology. il Time 95:40 Mr 23 '70
Ecology: the biome approach. R. Gilluly. Il
Sci N 98:204-5 S 5 '70
International biological program; AAAS sym-
posium, December 28-29, 1970. J. McKee. il
Science 170:471-2 O 23 '70
Slow progress worldwide; need for global en-
vironmental monitoring network. Sci N 98:
300-1 O 10 '70
Tundra biome program. J. Brown. il Science
167:1278 F 27 '70
INTERNATIONAL book year, 1972
UNESCO: 1972 set for International book
year. H. Lottman. il Pub W 198:pt2 160-1 S
21 '70
INTERNATIONAL boundary and water com-
mission (United States and Mexico)
U.S. and Mexico to improve Rio Grande flood
control; White House announcement, Octo-
ber 7, 1970. Dept State Bul 63:681-2 N 30 '70
INTERNATIONAL boundary commission
(United States and Canada)
Mr Herman named to U.S.-Canada Inter-
national boundary commission. R. L. Her-
man. Dept State Bul 61:558 D 15 '69
INTERNATIONAL brotherhood of police of-
ficers
Blue power? por Newsweek 75:87+ Je 8 '70
INTERNATIONAL brotherhood of teamsters,
chauffeurs, warehousemen and helpers of
America
Chavez and the Teamsters. J. J. Berman and
J. Hightower. Nation 211:427-31 N 2 '70
Hoffa's heir fights to keep his job. Bsns W
p28+ My 9 '70
Hoffa's stand-in likes the title role; Fitz-
simmons, acting head of the teamsters.
pors Bsns W p 109+ S 19 '70
If it breathes, organize it. I. Ross. il Fortune
81:122-5+ Mr '70
Industry pact wins teamster approval; truck-
ing industry. U S News 68:64 Je 1 '70
Labor starts to mend its divided house. il
Bsns W p 17-18 O 31 '70
Listening to America; Fraternal assocation
of steel haulers. B. Moyers. il Harper 241:
52-4+ D '70
Roadblocks continue for the truckers. Bsns
W p40-1 My 23 '70
Steel haulers' rebellion rolls on. Bsns W p57
Je 6 '70
Teamsters: a study in giantism. il Bsns W
p 150 O 17 '70
Teamsters on campus. il Newsweek 76:52 Ag
3 '70
Trucking: passing the buck. il Forbes 105:
20-2+ My 1 '70
Wildcats at the wheel; truck drivers' strike.
il Newsweek 75:85B My 11 '70
INTERNATIONAL business machines corpora-
tion
Copy war. Time 95:92 My 4 '70
Giant rival for the top copier cat. il Bsns W
p33-4 Ap 25 '70
IBM clears way for the big cases. Bsns
W p 19 S 5 '70
IBM programs another winner; success of
System/370. Bsns W p 19-20 Ag 22 '70

INTERNATIONAL business machines corpora-
tion—*Continued*
IBM thinks up a new generation. Bsns W
p32 Je 13 '70
IBM World trade center. il Aviation W 93:129
O 26 '70
IBM's new line confirms the rumors. Bsns
W p21 Jl 4 '70
IBM's surprising new computer. Bsns W p31
S 26 '70
Man who makes it one world for IBM. il
pors Bsns W p90-2 Jl 18 '70
Other IBM; World trade corp. il Forbes 106:
34 Jl 15 '70
Powerhouse growth of IBM. por Duns 96:26-7
D '70
RCA fires a broadside at no. 1. il Bsns W
p82-3 S 19 '70
Taking a recount on the IBM slide. Bsns W
p31 Ja 24 '70
Talking back to IBM; Britain's IBM com-
puter users association. J. Ross-Skinner.
Duns 97:52 Ja '71
TWA reserves space with IBM. Bsns W p88-9
O 31 '70
Two gee-whiz giants go at each other. il
Bsns W p70-1+ Je 13 '70
Why cores could become just a memory. il
Bsns W p60-1 D 26 '70
Wide-open market that IBM unbundled. il
Bsns W p84+ My 2 '70
Working library network; established for
book processing by Systems development
division of IBM. B. M. Wolpert. il Am Lib
1:570-2 Je '70
Xerox vs IBM. il Newsweek 75:74 My 4 '70
INTERNATIONAL centre for theoretical physics,
Trieste, Italy
Memorandum on a world university. A. Salam.
Bul Atom Sci 26:38-9 Mr '70
INTERNATIONAL chamber of commerce

Court of arbitration
Court to settle corporate quarrels. Bsns W
p60+ Mr 28 '70
INTERNATIONAL children's emergency fund.
See United Nations children's fund
INTERNATIONAL Chopin piano competition.
See Music—Competitions
INTERNATIONAL Christian broadcasters
Christian broadcasters tune toward future.
J. Huffman. Chr Today 14:35 My 22 '70
INTERNATIONAL civil aviation organization
ICAO actions may reduce aircraft civil vio-
lence threat. Aviation W 93:24 Jl 13 '70
United States proposal on unlawful seizure of
aircraft for blackmail purposes adopted by
ICAO council; statement with texts of U.S.
resolutions, October 1, 1970. J. A. Volpe.
Dept State Bul 63:449-53 O 1 '70
U.S. sees anti-hijacking support in Soviets'
membership in ICAO. J. P. Woolsey. Avia-
tion W 93:26 N 23 '70
INTERNATIONAL coffee council
Fifth annual report on the International cof-
fee agreement transmitted to the Con-
gress; President's letter of transmittal;
with text of report. R. Nixon. il Dept
State Bul 62:719-25 Je 8 '70
INTERNATIONAL committee on English in the
liturgy
Englishing the new liturgy. G. B. Harrison.
America 122:492-5 My 9 '70
INTERNATIONAL competition. See Competi-
tion, International
INTERNATIONAL conference of Orthodox
theologians. See Religious conferences
INTERNATIONAL conference on the peaceful
uses of atomic energy, 4th Geneva, 1971
Peaceful uses of atomic energy. U N Mo
Chron 7:86-8 Ja '70
INTERNATIONAL conference on the problems
of human environment (proposed) See
United Nations conference on the human
environment (proposed)
INTERNATIONAL conferences
Best of everything; nonaligned summit meet-
ing at Lusaka. Newsweek 76:50+ S 21 '70
Calendar of international conferences. See
issues of Department of state bulletin
JFK at the summit; Kremlinologists views
on first Kennedy-Khrushchev encounter.
il Newsweek 76:32-3 S 7 '70
Lusaka conference; nonaligned summit. W. R.
Lloyd. jr. Nation 211:325 O 12 '70
Tears in Lusaka; conference of nonaligned
nations. Time 96:33-4 S 21 '70
See also
Crimea conference, Yalta, Russia, 1945
INTERNATIONAL congress of gerontology. See
Aging, Conferences on
INTERNATIONAL controls corporation
Dark horse in IOS derby. por Bsns W p23-4
Ag 29 '70
Prize for agility. por Time 96:98 S 21 '70

INTERNATIONAL cookery. See Cookery, Inter-
national
INTERNATIONAL cooperation
Pearson report: Partners in development.
il UNESCO Courier 23:4-33 F '70
Swords into plowshares; business-operated
multinational development programs. R. E.
McGarrah. bibliog f Harvard Bsns R 48:
36-8+ Jl '70
See also
Antarctic treaty, 1959
Communications satellites—International as-
pects
International education
International organization
Meteorology—International cooperation
Nato
Polar research—International aspects
Science—International aspects
Space flight—International aspects
Space research—International aspects
United Nations
INTERNATIONAL copyright. See Copyright
INTERNATIONAL corporations. See Corpora-
tions, International
INTERNATIONAL cotton advisory committee
International cotton advisory committee
meets at Washington; Department an-
nouncement; with address by C. M. Hardin.
and text of statement. Dept State Bul 63:
678-81 N 30 '70
INTERNATIONAL council for bird preservation
Bird preservation; presentation of Delacour
medal. New Yorker 46:27-8 Mr 14 '70
INTERNATIONAL council of scientific unions
See also
International biological program
INTERNATIONAL court of justice, The Hague
Contribution of the principal judicial organ
of the United Nations to the achievement of
the objectives of the organization. M. Zaf-
rulla Khan. UN Mo Chron 7:139-46 Jl '70
Election of officers. UN Mo Chron 7:24 Mr '70
Growing law fullness of the world commun-
ity; address, August 18, 1970. C. S. Rhyne.
Vital Speeches 36:761-4 O 1 '70
Issues communique relating to Namibia. UN
Mo Chron 7:83 Ag '70
Judge Dillard; interview. H. C. Dillard. New
Yorker 46:27-8 Mr 28 '70
Law-and-order issue; nations ignore World
court. N. Cousins. Sat R 53:27 N 21 '70
World law, World court; proposed ratification
of the Genocide convention. Commonweal
92:51-2 Mr 27 '70
INTERNATIONAL date line
Anecdotes, facetiae, satire, etc.
Lost time. E. G. Love. Sat R 53:4+ N 7 '70
INTERNATIONAL day for the elimination of
racial discrimination
International day for the elimination of racial
discrimination 21 March; message, March 21,
1970; with text of appeal. Thant. UN Mo
Chron 7:i-ii, 4 Mr '70
INTERNATIONAL design conference
End of Aspen? il Arch Forum 133:33-4 Jl '70
INTERNATIONAL disputes. See Arbitration,
International
INTERNATIONAL economic relations. See Eco-
nomic relations
INTERNATIONAL education
International studies and the disciplines. C.
C. Wooten. Sch & Soc 98:413-15 N '70
Students must look at the whole world. Sch
& Soc 98:120 F '70
They called it philosophical poppycock; ex-
periment in international education: Atlan-
tic college at St Donat's castle. L. Jonck-
heere. il Schol Teach Jr/Sr High p 16-17 N 2
'70
United world colleges; Atlantic college at St
Donat's castle first in chain. T. Sylte. il
UNESCO Courier 23:28-32 O '70
See also
American institute for foreign study
Institute of international education
International relations—Study and teaching
Students, Interchange of
INTERNATIONAL education year, 1970
Commitment to international education year
1970. R. Maheu. Sch & Soc 98:295-6 Sum '70
IEY begins with more bark than bite. Sr
Schol 96:Schol Teach 2 F 2 '70
International education year, a proclamation.
R. M. Nixon. Dept State Bul 62:349 Mr 16 '70
International education year 1970; statement.
J. E. Allen. Sch & Soc 98:318 Sum '70
1970 international education year; message. R.
Maheu. UN Mo Chron 7:1-2 F '70
Road to peace and progress; interview, ed. by
G. D. Fischer. R. Maheu. il por Todays Ed
59:20-3 My '70

INTERNATIONAL education year, 1970—*Cont.*
Tasks for the International education year.
M. S. Adiseshiah. Sch & Soc 98:296-8 Sum
'70
Toward a better world for all children. C. L.
Bailey. por Parents Mag 45:30 Ag '70
INTERNATIONAL educational exchanges. See
Educational exchanges
INTERNATIONAL emergency children's fund.
See United Nations children's fund
INTERNATIONAL federation of air line pilots
associations
Hijack policy reflects conservative view. H.
J. Coleman. Aviation W 92:43+ Ap 13 '70
Murder on the airlines. R. Hotz. Aviation
W 92:9 Mr 23 '70
INTERNATIONAL federation of chemical and
general workers' unions
Labor's global organizer. J. Ross-Skinner.
por Duns 96:67 N '70
INTERNATIONAL federation of library asso-
ciations
Libraries as a force in education: 36th IFLA.
W. R. Eshelman. il Wilson Lib Bul 45:218-
20+ N '70
Meeting in Moscow and Leningrad. G. R.
Shields. Am Lib 1:1011 D '70
INTERNATIONAL festival of music and
drama, Edinburgh
U.S. youth at Edinburgh. T. Prideaux. Life
69:18 O 9 '70
INTERNATIONAL fighter aircraft. See Air-
planes, Military
INTERNATIONAL film festival, Cannes. See
Cannes international film festival
INTERNATIONAL flower show. See Flower
exhibits
INTERNATIONAL foundation for art research,
inc.
Information please. T. B. Hess. Art N 69:31
My '70
INTERNATIONAL geophysical year
Antarctica since the IGY; symposium. il Bul
Atom Sci 26:2-104 D '70
See also
Antarctic exploration
INTERNATIONAL harvester company
Harvester peeks out of its shell. Bsns W p23
Ap 4 '70
INTERNATIONAL herald tribune
HPT joint venture? The old Paris Herald!
W. B. Kerr. il Sat R 53:61-3 Ja 17 '70
INTERNATIONAL hydrological decade
Man's perpetual quest for water. R. L. Nace.
il UNESCO Courier 23:4-8+ Je '70
INTERNATIONAL ice patrol
See also
United States—Coast guard
INTERNATIONAL institute for peace and con-
flict research
Comprehensive test ban; report of SIPRI
conference. Environ 11:45 Jl '69
INTERNATIONAL institute for the manage-
ment of technology (proposed)
Son of technology gap: European group
setting up an institute. D. S. Greenberg.
Science 167:850-2 F 6 '70
INTERNATIONAL labor organization
Changing role of the International labor or-
ganization. A. Sturmthal. bibliog f Mo La-
bor R 93:41-6 My '70
Cold-war politics; Senate's cancellation of
U.S. contribution. Commonweal 92:452 S
18 '70
Report on the 1970 International labor con-
ference. J. P. Goldberg. bibliog f Mo La-
bor R 93:24-9 S '70
We won't pay. Sr Schol 97:6-7 N 16 '70
INTERNATIONAL laboratory of genetics and
biology
Italy: political turmoil kills plan for first doc-
toral program. D. S. Greenberg. Science 168:
683-4 My 8 '70
INTERNATIONAL language. See Language,
Universal
INTERNATIONAL law
Growing law fullness of the world communi-
ty; address, August 18, 1970. C. S. Rhyne.
Vital Speeches 36:761-4 O 1 '70
Rule of law and the settlement of interna-
tional disputes; address, April 25, 1970. W.
P. Rogers. Dept State Bul 62:623-7 My 18
'70
Safety of diplomats and other people. N.
Cousins. Sat R 53:26 Ap 25 '70
United Nations and the development of in-
ternational law, 1945-1970. C. A. Stavro-
poulos. UN Mo Chron 7:78-84 Je '70
See also
Airspace (international law)
Arbitration, International
Asylum, Right of
Citizenship
Eminent domain (international law)
Exterritoriality

Inter-American juridical committee
International court of justice, The Hague
Intervention (international law)
Maritime law
Nuremberg trials
Sanctions (international law)
Territorial waters
United Nations—Charter
United Nations—International law commis-
sion
United Nations—Legal committee
United Nations—Special committee on prin-
ciples of international law concerning
friendly relations and cooperation among
states
War
War crimes
INTERNATIONAL law commission. See United
Nations—International law commission
INTERNATIONAL license agreements
Japan: now the imitator shows the way. il
Bsns W p88-9+ My 16 '70
Should a license cut out competition? patent
antitrust suit against Westinghouse. Bsns W
p20+ My 2 '70
U.K. electronics makers ask review of co-
operation policy. Aviation W 92:59 My 11 '70
INTERNATIONAL loans. See Loans, Foreign
INTERNATIONAL Lonergan congress. See
Religious conferences
INTERNATIONAL longshoremen's and ware-
housemen's union
Dock workers set tough goals. Bsns W p69
N 28 '70
INTERNATIONAL Mark Twain society
Mark Twain and Richard M. Nixon. C.
Clemens. Hobbies 75:142-3 N '70
INTERNATIONAL monetary fund
Boards of governors of the IMF and IBRD
meet at Copenhagen; statement, September
22, 1970. D. M. Kennedy. Dept State Bul
63:431-5 O 12 '70
Financial setting for 1970; address, February
25-27, 1970. F. A. Southard, jr. Vital
Speeches 36:375-8 Ap 1 '70
IMF may bend a bit on flexible rates. Bsns
W p35 S 19 '70
Let the sun shine in; World bank-IMF joint
meeting. il Newsweek 76:74+ O 5 '70
South African threads among the gold
U.S. agreement with South Africa and the
IMF to support the price of South African
gold. H. S. Reuss. Commonweal 92:32-4
Mr 20 '70
See also
Special drawing rights
INTERNATIONAL nickel company of Canada,
ltd.
Beguiling new economics of nickel. A. F. W.
Liversidge. il Fortune 81:100-3+ Mr '70
INTERNATIONAL oceanographic foundation
Planet ocean; proposed ocean center. il Sea
Front 16:138-41 My '70
INTERNATIONAL officials and employees
See also
United Nations—Secretariat
INTERNATIONAL organization
Pope Paul: world government or slaughter?
J. B. Sheerin. Cath World 212:171-2 Ja '71
Beyond Babel; adaptation of address, Decem-
ber 1969. A. C. Clarke. il UNESCO Courier
23:32-7 Mr '70.
Modern man is obsolete; excerpts; reprint.
Sat R 53:16-18+ Ag 1 '70
See also
World association of world federalists
INTERNATIONAL organizations, Regional
International collaboration concerning south-
east Asia; address, April 1970, with ques-
tions and answers. T. T. B. Koh. bibliog f
Ann Am Acad 390:18-26 Jl '70
See also
Organization of American States
Southeast Asia treaty organization
INTERNATIONAL police academy. See Police
—Training
INTERNATIONAL postal union. See Universal
postal union
INTERNATIONAL publishers association
London notebook. B. Kolins. Pub W 198:28
O 19 '70
What's happening at the Int'l publishers
assn. H. Lottman. Pub W 198:pt2 157 S 21
'70
INTERNATIONAL publishing corporation, ltd.
Back to the Stradivarius. il Time 95:64 Mr 9
'70
INTERNATIONAL radio consultative commit-
tee
U.S. group to help plan for 1971 space tele-
communications meeting; Department an-
nouncement, May 4, 1970. Dept State Bul
62:714-15 Je 8 '70

INTERNATIONAL reading association
IRA: what's in it for you? R. C. Staiger.
  Wilson Lib Bul 45:272 N '70
Why poor readers fail to improve. U S News
  68:80 My 25 '70
INTERNATIONAL recreation association
European congress discusses leisure. G.
  Johansen. il Parks & Rec 5:37+ O '70
INTERNATIONAL relations
America and Europe. Z. Brzezinski. bibliog
  f For Affairs 49:11-30 S 26 '70
Autumn chill; East-West relations. News-
  week 76:36+ O 26 '70
Causes of peace and conditions of war. W. T.
  R. Fox. bibliog f Ann Am Acad 392:1-13 N
  '70
Changing world: today's White House ap-
  praisal. il U S News 69:24-5 Ag 31 '70
Finlandization? J. Burnham. Nat R 22:506 My
  19 '70
Growing gulf between the big two. il Time
  96:30 N 16 '70
In a glass, clearly. J. Burnham. Nat R 22:556
  Je 2 '70
International relations and the spirit of
  tragedy. A. N. Gilbert. Yale R 60:45-52
  O '70
Man's real missing link. D. Behrman. il
  UNESCO Courier 23:24-5 Ag '70
Notes from the other shore. J. Burnham. Nat R
  22:452+ My 5 '70
Our continuing commitment to western Eu-
  rope; address, December 6, 1969. W. P. Ro-
  gers. Dept State Bul 61:622-5 D 29 '69
Reporter at large: some questions about the
  war; interview, ed. by W. Whitworth. E.
  V. Rostow. New Yorker 46:30-46+ Jl 4 '70
Toward the era of negotiations. il Time 96:14
  Ag 17 '70
U.S. and world affairs annual. Directions '70-
  '71. il Sr Schol 97:6-24 S 21 '70
U.S. & world affairs annual, 1969-70 edition.
  il Sr Schol 95:5-25 S 22 '69
War termination and conflict theory: value
  premises, theories, and policies. B. A. Car-
  roll. bibliog f Ann Am Acad 392:14-29 N '70
Wars prolonged by misunderstood signals. G.
  H. Quester. bibliog f Ann Am Acad 392:30-9
  N '70
    See also
Agriculture—International aspects
Alliances
Arbitration, International
Atlantic community
Balance of power
Church and international relations
Crimea conference, Yalta, Russia, 1945
Disarmament
Economic relations
International court of justice, The Hague
International labor organization
International law
International organization
International security
Intervention (international law)
Munitions
Neutrality
Peace
Petroleum—International aspects
Sea power
United Nations
War
    also subhead Foreign relations under
  names of countries, e.g. Russia—Foreign
  relations

Anecdotes, facetiae, satire, etc.
Arsenal of appeasement. S. Thompson. Nat R
  22:769 Jl 28 '70

Bibliography
International relations, 1965-1969. H. J. Morgenthau. bibliog f Ann Am Acad 390:114-19
  Jl '70
Recent books on international relations; comp.
  by J. G. Stoessinger. See issues of Foreign
  affairs
Source material; comp. by D. Wasson. See issues of Foreign affairs
World scene (cont) V. S. Kearney. America
  122:474-6; 123:461-2+ My 2, N 28 '70

Study and teaching
Educating future citizens of the international
  community; address, February 11, 1970. M.
  Collins. Dept State Bul 62:230-3 Mr 2 '70
INTERNATIONAL reply coupons. See Universal
postal union
INTERNATIONAL rice research institute
Trouble in the rice bowl. America 122:487 My 9
  '70
INTERNATIONAL rowing association regatta.
See Regattas

INTERNATIONAL science fair. See Science
fairs
INTERNATIONAL security
Can peace be made and the world unified?
  D. Lawrence. U S News 69:108 O 19 '70
Collective security; address, June 15, 1970.
  L. L. Lemnitzer. Vital Speeches 36:669-71
  Ag 15 '70
Needed: a single alliance to keep world peace.
  D. Lawrence. U S News 68:100 Je 22 '70
Peaceful settlement within nations. Cur 116:51-
  4 Mr '70
Reports: Europe. D. Cook. Atlan 226:22-3+ Jl
  '70
U.S. gives views on strengthening interna-
  tional security, text of a letter, May 1
  1970. C. W. Yost. Dept State Bul 62:732-4
  Je 8 '70
    See also
Disarmament
International relations
Peace
United Nations—Special committee on peace-
  keeping operations
**INTERNATIONAL senior citizens association
conference.** See Aging. Conferences on
INTERNATIONAL soaring championships. See
Gliding and soaring
**INTERNATIONAL society for contemporary
music**
ISCM festival: why? contemporary music's
  jumbo jamboree. E. Helm. Hi Fi 20:MA27
  S '70
INTERNATIONAL studies. See International
education
INTERNATIONAL telecommunication union
Challenge to cooperation. J. d'Arcy. il Sat
  R 53:24-5+ O 24 '70
**INTERNATIONAL telecommunications satellite
consortium**
Assembly deadlocks Intelsat committee. Avia-
  tion W 92:21 Je 8 '70
Cable, satellites battle for key communica-
  tions roles. il Aviation W 92:83 Mr 9 '70
Intelsat agreement awaits procurement poli-
  cy draft. K. Johnsen. Aviation W 93:21-
  2 O 12 '70
Intelsat nations study draft treaty articles.
  Aviation W 92:43+ Je 29 '70
Intelsat on ice? B. Maddox. New Repub 162:
  10-11 My 16 '70
Intelsat's third conference seeks lasting
  agreement. K. Johnsen. Aviation W 92:120-1
  Ap 27 '70
Japan, Australia offer Intelsat compromise.
  K. Johnsen. Aviation W 92:20 Mr 2 '70
Troubles pile up for first business in space.
  il U S News 68:64-5 My 18 '70
U.S. industrial nations disagree on Intelsat
  procurement policy. Aviation W 92:21-2
  Mr 23 '70
**INTERNATIONAL telephone and telegraph
corporation**
Corporate giant stresses individuals; ITT ex-
  ecutive association. V. Louviere. Nations
  Bsns 58:18 S '70
Financial key at ITT. por Duns 96:24+ D '70
ITT takes the profit path to Europe. il por
  Bsns W p60-2+ My 9 '70
INTERNATIONAL trade. See Commerce
INTERNATIONAL trade regulation. See For-
eign trade regulation
INTERNATIONAL traffic in arms. See Muni-
tions
INTERNATIONAL travel. See Travel
INTERNATIONAL trusteeships
    See also
Papua-New Guinea (territory)
United Nations—Trusteeship council
INTERNATIONAL typographical union
New York city's dailies vs. the unions: auto-
  mation's armageddon. A. H. Raskin. il Sat
  R 53:50-2 Jl 11 '70
Profiles: B. Powers. G. T. Hellman. New
  Yorker 46:53-6+ Mr 7 '70
INTERNATIONAL union of crystallography
Eighth congress of the International union
  of crystallography. L. H. Jensen; R. E.
  Marsh. Phys Today 23:117+ Ja '70
**INTERNATIONAL union of electrical, radio
and machine workers**
Rough road to GE's settlement. il Bsns W
  p28-9 Ja 31 '70
**INTERNATIONAL union of official travel or-
ganizations**
Landmark for world travel; conference in
  Mexico City. W. D. Patterson. Sat R 53:
  27 O 24 '70
INTERNATIONAL university (proposed)
Memorandum on a world university. A. Salam.
  Bul Atom Sci 26:38-9 Mr '70
INTERNATIONAL utilities corporation
Driving toward a merger; proposed Ryder-
  PIE merger. il Bsns W p45-6 My 2 '70

INTERNATIONAL whaling commission
Whale of a failure. il Time 96:44+ Jl 13 '70
INTERNSHIP (teaching) See Student teachers
INTERPERSONAL relations
    See also
    Human relations
INTERPLANETARY flight. See Space flight
INTERPRETATION (music) See Music—Analysis, interpretation, etc.
INTERPRETERS. See Translators
INTERPRETERS, United Nations. See United Nations—Employees
INTERRACIAL adoption. See Adoption
INTERRACIAL cooperation
East Palo Alto. W. Stegner. Sat R 53:12+ Ag 1 '70
Freedom for the black; a workable coalition; address, November 7, 1970. G. Jonas. Vital Speeches 37:105-9 D 1 '70
New wind blowing; black-white coalition. P. J. McCaffrey. New Repub 163:10 O 24 '70
INTERRACIAL marriages. See Intermarriage of races
INTERRACIAL relations. See Race relations
INTERRELIGIOUS foundation for community organization
Another Jim Forman? Chr Today 15:44 O 9 '70
INTERSECTION of streets. See Streets—Intersections
INTERSECTIONS (highway engineering) See Roads—Interchanges and intersections
INTERSIL, inc.
Fast switch in semiconductors. il por Bsns W p 16 S 5 '70
Intersil: upstart with talent. il por Bsns W p70+ S 12 '70
INTERSTATE commerce
    See also
    Railroads and state—United States
INTERSTATE commerce commission. See United States—Interstate commerce commission
INTERSTATE highway system. See Express highways
INTERSTATE mobility. See Migration, Internal
INTERSTELLAR matter. See Matter, Interstellar
INTER-TRIBAL doll museum. See Indians of North America—Museums
INTERVENTION (international law)
Air America: flying the U.S. into Laos. por Ramparts 8:39-42+ F '70
American intervention and Catholic fatalism. J. B. Sheerin. Cath World 212:59-60 N '70
Limits to intervention. G. Allison and others. For Affairs 48:245-61 Ja '70
INTERVIEWING
    See also
    Employment interviewing
    Magnetic recorders and recording—Journalistic use
    Reporters and reporting
INTESTINES
Intestinal enzymes; indicators of proliferation and differentiation in the jejunum. R. Fortin-Magana and others. bibliog il Science 167:1627-8 Mr 20 '70
Intestinal hydrolysis and conjugation of a pesticidal carbamate in vitro. J. C. Pekas and G. D. Paulson. bibliog il Science 170:77-8 O 2 '70
    Surgery
Pre-heart trouble surgery. A. J. Snider. Sci Digest 67:66 Mr '70
    Transplantation
Intestinal transplant. il Time 96:94 D 7 '70
INTESTINES, Artificial
Artificial gut new hope for intestinal disease. A. J. Snider. Sci Digest 68:52 Jl '70
Portable intestine; artificial gut. il Newsweek 75:51 Je 8 '70
INTOLERANCE. See Prejudice; Toleration
INTOXICATION. See Liquor problem
INTRACOASTAL WATERWAY
California's-eye view of the ICW. H. M. Rizer. il Motor B 125:72-3+ My '70
Choosing a vacation waterway; ed. by F. M. Paulson. il Field & S 75:122-7 My '70
First time south. T. Kelly. il Yachting 128:66-7+ O '70
Love letter to the big ditch: Intracoastal route to Florida. S. Wilson. Motor B 126:50-1+ N '70
Sans stove; Miami to Ottawa by outboard. J. Charleson. il por Motor B 125:68-9+ Je; 126:58+ Jl '70
INTRACOM (firm)
Intracom started as Int'l communications club. por Pub W 198:18 D 14 '70
INTRA-UTERINE device. See Contraceptives

INTRAVENOUS injections. See Injections, Intravenous
INTROVERSION and extroversion
    See also
    Autism
INTRUDERS; story. See Sturges, P. P.
INVASION of privacy. See Privacy, Right of
INVECTIVE
Mentor for our time; excerpt from radio series The Overstreet outlook. B. W. Overstreet. PTA Mag 65:21 D '70
We all live in a psychological zoo; excerpts from A jungle in the house. M. Bates. il Sci Digest 68:30-3 O '70
You say tomentose; I say tomahntose; name-calling by men in high office and others today. G. Ace. Sat R 53:3 Jl 4 '70
INVENTIONS
Inventions. S. Jones. See issues of Science digest
Just patented. See issues of Popular mechanics
New ideas from the inventors. See issues of Popular science monthly
New inventions from the London show. il Pop Sci 197:80-1 S '70
Thirteen bright ideas from the International investors' showcase. il Pop Sci 197:46-7 Jl '70
Up with Uncle Scrooge; Danish inventor, K. Kroyer. por Newsweek 77:70+ Ja 11 '71
    See also
    Patents
    United States—Patent office
    Anecdotes, facetiae, satire, etc.
Leave my world alone. R. T. Allen. il Read Digest 96:195-8 Ap '70
INVENTORIES
Close watch on inventories. il Fortune 81:56 My '70
Inventories: silver linings in strike clouds. il Fortune 82:20 N '70
Slow times in inventories. S. S. Parker and others. il Fortune 81:34+ F '70
Why inventory buying will firm up. il Fortune 82:24 Ag '70
    See also
    Booksellers and bookselling—Stock
INVENTORIES, Municipal
We renovated stores and print-shop operations; Des Moines. K. G. Ibson. il Am City 85:116+ Mr '70
INVENTORS
Civilization's debt to the watchmaker. O. R. Hagans. il Hobbies 75:124+ My; 124+ Je '70
    See also
    Edison, T. A.
    Koppleman, E.
    Lear, B.
    Sherwood, H. A.
    Smith, K. E.
INVEREWE gardens. See Gardens—Scotland
INVERSION of atmospheric temperature. See Temperature inversions
INVERTEBRATES
    See also
    Crustaceans
    Skeleton (invertebrates)
INVESTIGATIONS, Government. See Government investigations
INVESTMENT. See Investments
INVESTMENT advisory services. See Investments—Advisers
INVESTMENT banking
Investment banking in America by V. P. Carosso. Review
    Bsns W il p6 My 9 '70. G. L. Levy
    See also
    Kleiner, Bell and company
    Oppenheimer and company
    White, Weld and company
INVESTMENT companies. See Investment trusts
INVESTMENT company offices. See Offices
INVESTMENT letter stocks. See Securities—Registration
INVESTMENT offices. See Offices
INVESTMENT tax credit
How to revive capital spending. il Bsns W p58 Ag 22 '70
INVESTMENT trusts
Adverse tide hits offshore funds. Bsns W p50 O 17 '70
Bad review for performance; study by Irwin Friend and others. Bsns W p26 Ag 15 '70
Cold eye on mutual funds. D. Seligman. il Fortune 82:169-70+ O '70
Cool trio runs a hot fund; New York venture fund. il Bsns W p78-9 F 7 '70
Crisis for Cornfeld; mutual funds. il por Newsweek 75:81 My 18 '70

INVESTMENT trusts—*Continued*
Difference between p and P. Forbes 105:7 Je 1 '70
Federated breaks the fund mold. por Bsns W p98+ Jl 11 '70
Fred Mates is one happy man; his Mates fund is thriving. S. Mahoney. il pors Life 68:56B-56D+ My 22 '70
Funds. See issues of Forbes
Goodbye to Goodbody? acquisition by Shareholders capital corp. Forbes 106:48 O 1 '70
Insurance news you ought to know; the rush to mutual funds. il Changing T 24:13-16 Jl '70
Investing: the case for bigness; interview. R. A. M. C. Johnson. por Forbes 105:190+ My 15 '70
Making money work; investing in closed-end funds. S. Meisenberg. il Har Yrs 10:48-50 Jl '70
Memory lingers on; Enterprise fund il Forbes 105:15-17 My 1 '70
Mutual fund for unionists only; American union investment fund. Bsns W p71 Ja 9 '71
Mutual funds: where they fit in your financial picture. Bet Hom & Gard 48:18 Ja '70
New tack for a fund pioneer; Massachusetts investors trust group. il Bsns W p90 N 7 '70
No-loads swing more weight. il Bsns W p94 Je 27 '70
Offshore funds are in dangerous waters. P. Siekman. il Fortune 82:118-21+ Ag '70
Once-heady fund gets a hangover; Enterprise fund. il Bsns W p36-7 F 21 '70
Prudent investing. P. A. Samuelson. Newsweek 76:52 Ag 24 '70
Regulation of investments; interview. H. H. Budge. il pors U S News 69:52-6 S 7 '70
Scotland's canny investment trusts. J. Ross-Skinner. il Duns 96:43-5 Jl '70
Something new in stock for Sears shoppers; Allstate enterprises stock fund. il Bsns W p 120+ Ap 25 '70
Swing in stocks by mutual funds. U S News 69:62 N 16 '70
Tortoise and the hare; Windsor fund. il por Forbes 105:72-3 Ap 1 '70
USI's mortgage trust: no money down; Citizen's mortgage. A. Hershman. il Duns 96:46-8+ S '70
Variable annuities fight inflation. W. R. Hoffer. il Har Yrs 10:14-16 Jl '70
Wall Street:
Slump is mutual. C. Morgello. il Newsweek 75:80 Mr 30 '70
Why a broker needs a fund; membership of mutual funds in the NYSE. Bsns W p24 O 3 '70
See also
Insurance companies—Mutual fund operations
Investors diversified service, inc.
Investors overseas services, ltd.
Oppenheimer fund, inc.
Real estate investment trusts
Small business investment companies
Tracy investment company

Finance

Fallible funds; study findings on mutuals by Irwin Friend and others. C. Morgello. il Newsweek 76:47 Ag 24 '70
Forbes fund ratings: 1970. Forbes 106:51-5+ man. por Duns 95:89-90 F '70
Mutual-fund fees: curbs are readied. U S News 69:81-2 D 7 '70
No way but up; views of F. Alger. A. Hersh-Ag 15 '70
What went wrong with the go-go funds. il Bsns W p86-7 My 30 '70

Regulation

Big get bigger. C. Morgello. Newsweek 75:80 My 4 '70
Mutual funds try to duck lawsuits. Bsns W p37 Ja 31 '70
Nixon; with a little help for his friends. B. Fitch. il pors Ramp Mag 8:58-62+ Mr '70

Securities

Funds' favorites. C. Morgello. il Newsweek 76:54 D 28 '70
Investment funds that specialize. il Changing T 24:37-9 Ja '70

Taxation

Wall Street:
Offbeat funds. C. Morgello. il Newsweek 76:96 N 2 '70
INVESTMENTS
Advice for investors in '71; interviews. R. D. Naess; S. Homer. pors U S News 70:30-2 Ja 4 '71
Bedroom theory; interview. P. Lepercq. pors Forbes 105:62-3 Mr 15 '70

Bold investing. P. A. Samuelson. Newsweek 75:82 My 4 '70
Buy? When? views of K. Smilen. R. Brady. por Duns 96:64-5 Ag '70
Executive investor. See issues of Dun's
Find out how your investments are really doing; new Changing times computer service. il Changing T 24:47-9 Mr '70
Generation gap; interviews. T. R. Price; D. Babson. pors Forbes 106:46+ N 15 '70
Investments: how to manage your portfolio. Bsns W p 105-6 Jl 11 '70
Investor view of 1969: a shocker. il U S News 68:70 Ja 19 '70
Long view; recommendations of E. R. Holt. por Duns 95:101-2 Ap '70
Making money work; questions and answers. E. Merillat. See issues of Harvest years to April 1970
Matter of timing. C. Morgello. il Newsweek 76:55 Ag 10 '70
Mineral search for the wealthy. il Bsns W p24 Ag 8 '70
Outwitting Wall Street: you too can get little rich. J. Fischer. Harper 241:12+ S '70
Personal investing. See issues of Fortune
Playing the horse market. W. Tower. il Sports Illus 33:48-9 Ag 24 '70
Professional opinions. C. Morgello. Newsweek 75:78 F 16 '70
Prudent investing. P. A. Samuelson. Newsweek 76:52 Ag 24 '70
Putting cash to work; short-term investments. il Fortune 81:181-2 F '70
Rally or no, it's not too late to short the frauds. il por Forbes 105:55+ Je 15 '70
Report on American industry. il Forbes 105:43-9+ Ja 1 '70; 107:31-4+ Ja 1 '71
Smart money draws a crowd; venture capital. il Bsns W p92-5 F 28 '70
Some simple truths about the stock market. C. J. Rolo and others. Bet Hom & Gard 48:28 My '70
Time for cyclicals? views of Charles Brunie. C. Morgello. il Newsweek 75:73 F 23 '70
Ways to invest your savings now. il U S News 68:77-8+ F 23 '70
Ways to make your savings earn 7 per cent and up. il Changing T 24:6-10 S '70
When a young man starts investing. il Changing T 23:41-5 D '69
When Richard Carney buys goldfish; investing in little growth companies. por Forbes 106:33-4 Ag 1 '70
Where people are putting their money now. il U S News 69:40-1 N 2 '70
See also
Annuities
Bonds, Government
Brokers
Capital investments
Computers—Investment use
Dividends
Estate planning
Finance, Personal
Hedging
Investment trusts
Investor relations programs
Real estate investment
Saving and savings
Savings and loan associations
Speculation
Stockholders
Stocks
Trusts and trustees
also subhead Investments under various subjects, e.g. Insurance companies—Investments

Advisers

How stocks are valued. P. Lindberg. Bet Hom & Gard 48:4+ N '70
How to keep up with insiders; use of SEC reports. il por Bsns W p 108+ My 9 '70
How to read a stock market letter. M. T. Bloom. il N Y Times Mag p48-9+ N 15 '70; Reply with rejoinder. J. Dines. p58+ D 6 '70
Read the prospectus. R. Brady. por Duns 95:103-4 My '70
See also
Argus research corporation
National investor relations institute
INVESTMENTS, Church. See Church finance
INVESTMENTS, Foreign
American business and international investment flows; address, December 11, 1969. N. Samuels. Dept State Bul 62:33-8 Ja 12 '70. Same Vital Speeches 36:197-200 Ja 15 '70
Nationalist barriers go higher. Bsns W p 126+ D 19 '70
U.S. companies keep up the pace. il Bsns W p24 Ag 15 '70

INVESTMENTS, Foreign—*Continued*
U.S. foreign policy; the reasons why. R. B. Du Boll Commonweal 91:560-2 F 20 '70
Welcome for capitalists; foreigners doing well in Iran. il Time 95:94 My 25 '70
What U.S. companies are doing abroad. See issues of U.S. news & World report
World investment; stability; address, January 29, 1970. G. H. Weyerhaeuser. Vital Speeches 36:312-14 Mr 1 '70
See also
Business—Foreign expansion
Corporations—Foreign subsidiaries
Overseas private investment corporation

INVESTMENTS, Foreign (by Germany [Federal Republic])
Germans are coming. Time 95:72 F 9 '70

INVESTMENTS, Foreign (by Great Britain)
American challenge, from Plessey. J. Ross-Skinner. il Duns 96:42-4 N '70
Bundle from America; Britain's Plessy co. acquisition of alloys. por Time 96:60-1 Ag 10 '70

INVESTMENTS, Foreign (by Japan)
Enter the quiet Japanese, on the run. il Bsns W p22-3 S 5 '70
Mitsubishi made in the U.S. il Bsns W p43 Je 6 '70
Red-hot economy's quest for raw material. il Bsns W p46-7 Ja 24 '70
Tokyo makes Wall Street toe the line. il Bsns W p54 My 23 '70

INVESTMENTS, Foreign (by Russia)
Soviets take a joint venture road west. il Bsns W p73-4 Je 6 '70

INVESTMENTS, Foreign (in Africa)
Up from chaos: black Africa after ten years of freedom. A. J. Meyers. il U S News 69:52-5 Jl 6 '70

INVESTMENTS, Foreign (in Argentina)
Jackpot is a chemical plant; PASA's Argentine petrochemical plant. il Bsns W p48 F 28 '70

INVESTMENTS, Foreign (in Australia)
American bankers hit a new market. Bsns W p42-3 My 30 '70
Steel finds a gold mine Down Under. il Bsns W p58+ Mr 28 '70

INVESTMENTS, Foreign (in Belgium)
Schlitz goes flat in Europe again. por Bsns W p23-4 D 26 '70

INVESTMENTS, Foreign (in Borneo)
Wilds of Borneo lure U.S. lumbermen. il Bsns W p51 Je 27 '70

INVESTMENTS, Foreign (in Canada)
Canada's closing open door. il Forbes 106:22-5+ D 1 '70
Canadian caper; Aquitaine co. of Canada, ltd. N. A. Martin. Duns 96:57-8 Ag '70

INVESTMENTS, Foreign (in Chile)
Who may get hurt in Chile; list of U.S. companies. U S News 69:90 S 28 '70

INVESTMENTS, Foreign (in Congo [capital Kinshasa])
Enter the quiet Japanese, on the run. il Bsns W p22-3 S 5 '70

INVESTMENTS, Foreign (in Fiji)
Where sugar may turn bitter; Colonial sugar refining co. pulling out of Fiji. il Bsns W p46-7 Ap 25 '70

INVESTMENTS, Foreign (in France)
Foreign investors feel new warmth; American companies in France. il Bsns W p23 S 5 '70
Testing France's selective welcome. Fortune 82:75-6 Ag '70

INVESTMENTS, Foreign (in Great Britain)
Investing in Britain. G. J. Henry. Forbes 105:82 Ap 1 '70

INVESTMENTS, Foreign (in India)
From Dustbowl to Saigon: the "Peoples bank" builds an empire. M. Sweeney. il por Ramp Mag 9:44-5 N '70

INVESTMENTS, Foreign (in Iran)
Welcome for capitalists. il Time 95:94 My 25 '70

INVESTMENTS, Foreign (in Ireland)
Irish eyes are smiling at American business. il Nations Bsns 58:28-31 Je '70
Irish way. R. Brady. il Duns 96:74+ N '70

INVESTMENTS, Foreign (in Italy)
Joining the first families; new European mutual fund called the 3-R fund. Time 95:94 Ap 13 '70
Zombanakis plan to counter capital outflow. W. Wynn. il por Fortune 82:39+ Jl '70

INVESTMENTS, Foreign (in Japan)
Big three in Japan. il Newsweek 76:80-1 N 30 '70
No trespassing; report of the Foreign investment council. Newsweek 76:57 Ag 31 '70
Rolling up the welcome mat; foreign banks in Japan. Bsns W p45 O 10 '70

INVESTMENTS, Foreign (in Korea)
Korea: electronics and oil. N. A. Martin. il Duns 95:78-80+ Mr '70

INVESTMENTS, Foreign (in Latin America)
Investor's guide to Latin America. F. C. Foy. Forbes 105:76 Je 1 '70
It isn't easy to make a peso. il Bsns W p48 Ja 24 '70
Kicking the gringo. il Time 95:86+ Mr 30 '70
Latin reformers seek more from business. il Bsns W p 104-5+ S 12 '70

INVESTMENTS, Foreign (in Mexico)
Analysis of Mexico's border industrialization program. A. S. Ericson. il Mo Labor R 93:33-40 My '70
Bond market in Mexico. G. J. Henry. Forbes 105:69 Je 1 '70
Growth & stability in Mexico. G. J. Henry. Forbes 105:56 My 1 '70

INVESTMENTS, Foreign (in Peru)
Social reform jolts the mine owners. il Bsns W p26 Ag 29 '70

INVESTMENTS, Foreign (in Puerto Rico)
Changing Bootstrap. Bsns W p64-5 O 10 '70

INVESTMENTS, Foreign (in Russia)
Russians lay out the red carpet for Ford. il Bsns W p27-8 Ap 25 '70

INVESTMENTS, Foreign (in Singapore)
Boom that fooled everybody. Singapore without the British. J. N. Wallace. il U S News 68:70-2 Mr 30 '70
Magnet for eager manufacturers. il Bsns W p23 Ag 8 '70
Singapore acts to cushion British withdrawal impact. C. Brownlow. il Aviation W 92:66-8 My 11 '70

INVESTMENTS, Foreign (in South Africa)
Builder heaves a brick at apartheid; refusal to do business in South Africa. por Bsns W p36 S 26 '70

INVESTMENTS, Foreign (in Taiwan)
Counterattack base for U.S. companies. il Bsns W p38 Jl 11 '70

INVESTMENTS, Foreign (in the United States)
American challenge, from Plessey. J. Ross-Skinner. il Duns 96:42-4 N '70
Foreign capital heads this way. il Bsns W p56+ Ja 9 '71
Foreign holdings in the U.S.: the quiet invasion. Time 96:61 Ag 10 '70
Invasion from abroad. N. A. Martin. il Duns 95:38-41 Mr '70
Mitsubishi made in the U.S. il Bsns W p43 Je 6 '70
Now foreign firms invade U.S. il U S News 68:70-1 Je 29 '70
Tokyo makes Wall Street toe the line. il Bsns W p54 My 23 '70

INVESTMENTS, Foreign (in underdeveloped areas)
Poor countries turn from buy-less to sell-more. S. Rose. il Fortune 81:90-3+ Ap '70
Swords into plowshares; business-operated multinational development programs. R. E. McGarrah. bibliog f Harvard Bsns R 48:36-8+ Jl '70

INVESTMENTS, Foreign (in Zambia)
We want investors to come, our policies are nonracial; interview. K. D. Kaunda. por U S News 69:55-6 Jl 6 '70

INVESTMENTS literature. See Business literature

INVESTOR relations programs
Crucial role of investor relations. R. H. Savage. il Harvard Bsns R 48:122-30 N '70
See also
National investor relations institute

INVESTORS. See Stockholders

INVESTORS diversified service, inc.
Nixon; with a little help for his friends. B. Fitch. il pors Ramp Mag 8:58-62+ Mr '70

INVESTORS overseas services, ltd.
At IOS, a revelation and a roadblock. Bsns W p34 My 30 '70
Bernie Cornfeld had a friend in Denver, but not many on Wall Street. il Fortune 81:35 Je '70
Bernie Cornfeld: the salesman who believed himself. R. Ball. il por Fortune 82:136-41+ S '70
Can all the King's men put I.O.S. together again? il Time 95:90-1 My 25 '70
Can Cornfeld's IOS rebuild confidence? il Bsns W p21 My 9 '70
Can King sell his IOS rescue plan? Bsns W p36-7 My 23 '70
Comedown for Cornfeld. por Time 95:88 My 4 '70
Cornfeld dumped. Time 96:71 Jl 13 '70
Cornfeld under pressure. Newsweek 75:92 Ap 20 '70
Cornfeld's comeback. Newsweek 76:48+ Ag 24 '70
Cornfeld's new bid for a comeback. por Bsns W p 19-20 Ag 1 '70

INVESTORS overseas services ltd.—*Continued*
Crisis at IOS; the behind-scenes story; with interview with B. Cornfeld, ed. by O. Moore. il Newsweek 76:68-70+ Jl 6 '70
Dark horse in IOS derby. por Bsns W p23-4 Ag 29 '70
Farewell to Cornfeld. il por Time 95:84-6 My 18 '70
How IOS is picking up the pieces. Bsns W p 116-17+ My 16 '70
How IOS lost some luster. il Bsns W p29 Ap 25 '70
IOS: back from an impossible dream. il Bsns W p68-9 Jl 4 '70
IOS may try to go it alone. il Bsns W p30 Je 20 '70
King's gambit. Newsweek 75:80 Je 8 '70
Many woes of Bernie Cornfeld. J. Ross-Skinner. il por Duns 95:32-6 Ja '70
Picking up from Bernie. Newsweek 75:86 My 25 '70
Prize for agility. por Time 96:98 S 21 '70
Reaching bottom. Newsweek 76:82+ Jl 13 '70
Rothschild comes up to bat at IOS. Bsns W p30 Je 6 '70
Those I.O.S. loans. il Time 95:77 Je 22 '70
INVISIBLE nation; story. See Swan, J.
IOMEC, Inc.
More muscle for minicomputers. il Bsns W p 130+ Ap 18 '70
ION bombardment
Ion implantation. G. L. Wick. il Science 170:425-7 O 23 '70
ION engines. See Rocket engines
ION exchange chromatography. See Chromatographic analysis
ION exchange electrodes. See Electrodes
ION implantation. See Ion bombardment
IONARC smelters, ltd.
Plasma: the lab toy that grew up. il Bsns W p74+ Ag 22 '70
IONESCO, Eugéne
Les chaises. Criticism
New Yorker 46:105 My 16 '70 *
Ionesco on Olympus. T. Bishop. por Sat R 53:21-3+ My 16 '70 *
La jeune fille a marier. Criticism
New Yorker 46:105 My 16 '70 *
La lacune. Criticism
New Yorker 46:105 My 16 '70 *
Triumph of death. Criticism
Time il 95:64 F 16 '70
IONIZATION of gases
See also
Plasma (ionized gases)
IONOSPHERE. See Atmosphere, Upper
IONOSPHERIC research
New national facility; incoherent-scatter radar center. Sci N 97:123-4 Ja 31 '70
IONS
Ionic bonding in solids. J. E. House, jr. bibliog il por Chem 43:18-22 F '70
Living polymers: a tool in studies of ions and ion-pairs. M. Szwarc. bibliog il Science 170:23-31 O 2 '70
See also
Cations
Ion bombardment
Plasma (ionized gases)
Thermionic emission
IOVIN, P. J.
Move people efficiently in our center cities; excerpts from address, 1969. il Am City 85:69-71 N '70
IOWA
See also
Music festivals—Iowa
School libraries—Iowa

Description and travel
India? Give me exotic Iowa! S. Stewart. il Har Yrs 10:26-9 S '70
Iowa's new wonderland. B. Friedrichsen. il Travel 133:70-1+ F '70

Population
Where there is no population explosion. il U S News 69:82 S 28 '70
IOWA beef packers, inc.
Winners and losers. il Forbes 105:30+ My 1 '70
IOWA CITY, Iowa
Where have all the writers gone? J. Hess. il Holiday 47:60-3+ Je '70
IOWA state university of science and technology, Ames
Iowa's prairie auditorium; C. Y. Stevens auditorium. R. Jensen. il Arch Rec 148:75-80 D '70

IOWA, University, Iowa City
Dealers roll to a title; Hawkeyes Big Ten championship. J. Jares. Sports Illus 32:47-8 Mr 9 '70
Where have all the writers gone? To Iowa City, that's where. J. Hess. il Holiday 47:60-3+ Je '70
IRA Aldridge award. See Association for the study of Negro life
IRAN
See also
Aeronautics, Military—Iran
Airlines—Iran
Education—Iran
Hunting—Iran
Investments, Foreign (in Iran)
Khuzestan
Music—Iran
Economic conditions
Welcome for capitalists. il Time 95:94 My 25 '70
IRAN national airlines. See Airlines—Iran
IRANIAN art. See Art, Persian
IRAQ
See also
Kurdistan
Kurds
Politics and government
Kurdish truce. L. Jenkins. il por Newsweek 76:41 D 7 '70
IRBID, Jordan
Birth of an Arab Soviet. L. Jenkins. il Newsweek 76:36 S 28 '70
IREDELL, Tex.
Aunt Clara's luminous world; with paintings by C. M. Williamson. J. Graves. il Am Heritage 21:46-56 Ag '70
IRELAND, Innes
Safe at any speed: the Jensen FF. il Pop Mech 133:114-16 Je '70
IRELAND
See also
Airports—Ireland
Aran Islands
Architecture, Domestic—Ireland
Arts and crafts—Ireland
Banks and banking—Ireland
Canals—Ireland
Community development—Ireland
Fishing—Ireland
Horse racing—Ireland
Investments, Foreign (in Ireland)
Kerry
Northern Ireland
Shannon River
Sneem
Tourist trade—Ireland
Description and travel
Ireland: double image. W. Weaver. Harp Baz 103:40-1 Jl '70
Travel notes. R. Joseph. Esquire 74:62+ S '70
Traveling with Mlle; with guest editorial comments. Y. Anaya. il Mlle 71:310-15+, 316+ Ag '70
Economic conditions
See also
Ireland—Industries
History
Bibliography
Articles and other books received; comp. by L. H. Carlson. See issues of American historical review
Sinn Fein rebellion, 1916
Thomas Dillon: chemist & revolutionary. J. A. Schufle. il por Chem 43:18-21 Ap '70
Industries
Irish way. R. Brady. il Duns 96:74+ N '70
Politics and government
Irish vs. Irish: why they keep fighting. il U S News 69:80-1 O 26 '70
See also
Ireland—History—Sinn Fein rebellion, 1916
Northern Ireland—Politics and government
IRELAND, NORTHERN. See Northern Ireland
IRENE, princess of the Hellenes
Artist life. D. J. Soria. il pors Hi Fi secII 4-5 Ag '70 *
IRENE, goodnight; story. See Weesner, T.
IREYS, Alice Recknagel
Needle-leaved evergreens for many purposes. il Horticulture 48:36-9+ Ap '70
IRION, Mary Jean
Sows' ears; poem. Chr Cent 87:1374 N 18 '70
Vivaldi morning; poem. Chr Cent 87:421 Ap 8 '70

IRISES
Color from bearded iris. R. P. Merry. il
Horticulture 48:28-9+ My '70
How to grow a beautiful iris. B. Boss. il
Home Gard 57:24-5 Je '70
In-between irises. L. Eberhardt. il Horticul-
ture 48:30-1+ F '70
Iris: can you improve upon perfection? E.
McDonald. il House B 112:146-7+ My '70
My iris are on a great diet. L. Riotte. il Org
Gard & Farm 17:35-7 Je '70
See also
American iris society
Moraea
IRISH
Irish sketches; reactions of villagers of Sneem
to visit of C. de Gaulle. J. McCarten. New
Yorker 46:127-9 O 31 '70
Irish sketches: Sneem. J. McCarten. New
Yorker 46:109-11 S 12 '70
See also
Scotch-Irish
IRISH AMERICANS
American Irish: a long way from the auld sod.
il Sr Schol 95:8-11 N 10 '69
Irish Catholic was beautiful. A. W. Godfrey.
America 123:493 D 5 '70
IRISH cookery. See Cookery, Irish
IRISH in the United States
Bernadette Devlin: an Irish revolutionary in
Irish America. S. Davidson. il por Harper
240:78-87 Ja '70; Discussion. 240:6+ Mr '70
Why Massachusetts loves the Kennedys. F.
Russell. il Nat R 22:836-9 Ag 11 '70
See also
Irish Americans
IRISH revolt, 1916. See Ireland—History—Sinn
Fein rebellion, 1916
IRISH Sweeps Derby. See Horse racing—Ire-
land
IRIZARRY, Carmen
Young Bolshoi in Spain. il Dance Mag 44:
63-7 O '70
IRON city plan. See Urban renewal—Southern
states
IRON compounds
Synthetic oxygen-carrying compound. il Chem
43:21 Mr '70
IRON curtain. See Europe, Eastern
IRON in diet
Iron-rich answers to tired food. G. Maddox.
il Todays Health 48:60-3 Ap '70
IRON lung
Polio's silent giants: asleep or just napping?
E. Mulligan. il Todays Health 48:44-5 Ag
'70
IRON ores
See also
Hematite
Magnetite
Pyrites
IRON rust. See Corrosion and anticorrosives
IRON silicates
See also
Olivine
IRON stands. See Trivets
IRON sulfides
Cubic FeS, a metastable iron sulfide. R. De
Médicis. bibliog il Science 170:1191-2 D 11 '70
High-pressure polymorph of troilite, FeS.
L. A. Taylor and H. K. Mao. bibliog il Sci-
ence 170:850-1 N 20 '70
Lunar troilite: crystallography. H. T. Evans,
jr. bibliog il Science 167:621-3 Ja 30 '70
See also
Pyrites
IRONING

Anecdotes, facetiae, satire, etc.
Ironing. J. Ferris. Sat R 53:12+ N 21 '70
IRONWORK
Art of the medieval blacksmith. B. Colvin.
il Craft Horiz 30:24-7+ Mr '70
Charleston ornamental ironwork. A. Deas. il
Antiques 97:748-51 My '70
Contemporary blacksmith: 1970. R. Pearson.
il Craft Horiz 30:22-7 D '70
See also
Blacksmithing
IRRADIATED food. See Food, Effect of radia-
tion on
IRRADIATED wood. See Wood, Irradiated
IRRADIATION
Radiation effects and oxygen vacancies in
silicates. A. Chatelain and others. bibliog
Science 168:570-1 My 1 '70
Radioresistance of cooperative function of car-
rier-specific lymphocytes in antihapten anti-
body responses. D. H. Katz and others. bib-
liog il Science 170:462-4 O 23 '70
IRRIGATION
How to know when to irrigate. Suc Farm
68:C8 Ag '70

Some crops like their water hot. G. Lorang.
Farm J 94:50M Mr '70
See also
Irrigation, Overhead
Sewage irrigation

India
Ganges Plain: irrigation potential. H. E.
Thomas. Science 168:1042 My 29 '70

Jordan
East Ghor irrigation project. I. R. Manners.
bibliog il Focus 20:8-11 Ap '70

United States
Corn Belt irrigation: is it for you? R.
Krumme and C. E. Sommers. il Suc Farm
68:41-3 Ag '70
How irrigation is changing the beef business.
G. Lorang. il Farm J 94:26-7+ O '70

Western states
Reclamation; first Irrigation congress, 1891,
Salt Lake City. P. S. Taylor. bibliog il
Am West 7:27-33+ Jl '70
IRRIGATION, Overhead
Solid-set sprinklers that you farm right
under. G. Lorang. il Farm J 94:62B-62C Mr
'70
IRRIGATION, Underground
Water your garden from below. N. H. Berlin.
il Org Gard & Farm 17:127 Mr '70
IRRIGATION farming
Dry lands and desalted water. G. Young.
bibliog il Science 167:339-43 Ja 23 '70; Same
abr. Todays Ed 59:28-30 My '70
IRRIGATION machinery
Center pivot system on tracks. R. Krumme.
il Suc Farm 68:46 Ag '70
Corn Belt irrigation systems that work.
P. B. Jones. Suc Farm 68:44-5 Ag '70
New automatic valve for gated pipe. O. Bay.
il Farm J 94:50S Mr '70
New irrigation ideas that beat the labor
shortage. G. Lorang. il Farm J 94:16-17 Jl
'70
IRVIN, Robert W.
MI unveils the 1971 cars. il Mech Illus 66:39-
42+ Jl '70
1971 cars! il Mech Illus 66:59-63+ O '70
IRVINE, Keith
Storm clouds over the African Horn. il Cur
Hist 58:142-7+ Mr '70
IRVINE company
Irvine case. il por Forbes 105:44-5+ Je 1
'70
IRVING, George W. jr
Agricultural pest control and the environ-
ment. bibliog Science 168:1419-24 Je 19 '70
IRVING, Washington
Washington Irving's Andalusia. V. Condon.
il por Travel 134:52-6+ O '70 *
IRWIN, John Nichol, 1913-
Inter-American cooperation: a prime concern
to the United States; statement, October 19,
1970. Dept State Bul 63:561-5 N 9 '70
IRWIN, Theodore
Better schooling for bright youngsters. il
Parents Mag 45:40-1+ Ja '70
Boy or girl: would you choose your baby's
sex? il Parents Mag 45:67-9+ N '70
Get in the checkbook balancing act. Am
Home 73:78b Ag '70
High-school sports flunk the saliva test. To-
days Health 48:44-6+ O '70
New abortion laws; how are they working? il
Todays Health 48:20-3+ Mr '70
Those smoking statistics: fact or distortion?
il Todays Health 48:34-7+ Ap '70
—See Loyd, F. G. jt. auth.
IS Cupid stupid? drama. See Martens, A. C.
IS it for real? story. See Ackworth, R.
IS this our daughter? story. See Alexander, R.
W.
ISAAC, Ephraim
Black studies: a painful birth. il por Time
95:50+ Ja 26 '70
ISAACS, Kenneth
Modern bowl for sunbathing. il Pop Sci 196:
112-13+ F '70
ISAACS, Stan
Green and leafy football. il Look 34:68-72+
O 20 '70
ISCHEMIA. See Blood—Circulation
ISELIN, Sally
When men were iron. il Yachting 128:58+ S
'70
ISHIYAMA, Toaru
Mental hospital patient-consumer as a de-
terminant of services. Ment Hy 54:221-9 Ap
'70
ISLA VISTA, Calif.
New campus stepchildren. G. H. Wierzynski.
il Time 97:72 Ja 4 '71

ISLAM
Nasser's death as a religious event. J. C.
Haughey. America 123:278 O 17 '70
New thought stirring Islam. T. Cosmades.
Chr Cent 87:1133 S 23 '70
See also
Bahaism
Church and state in Turkey
Dervishes
ISLAM and Christianity. See Christianity and
other religions
ISLAND communities. See Islands
ISLAND of decision; story. See Schweitzer, G.
ISLAND parks
Islands in time; proposed National system
of islands, with text of bill. E. C. Crafts.
il Am For 76:16-19+ D '70
ISLANDS
Adaptive aspects of insular evolution: report
of meeting. R. W. Matthews and J. R. Mat-
thews. Science 167:909-10 F 6 '70
Island earth. M. Mead. por Natur Hist 79:22+
Ja '70
See also
Corsica
ISLANDS of the Pacific
See also
Bikini
Cook Islands
Guadalcanal
Guam
Polynesia
Tuamotu Islands
Tubuai Islands
ISLAY (island) See Hebrides
ISLE AU HAUT
Island images. T. E. Jones. il Nat Parks &
Con Mag 44:11-13 Jl '70
Isle au Haut, Acadia's wildness area. T. E.
Jones. il Nat Parks & Con Mag 44:13-17
Je '70
ISLE ROYALE NATIONAL PARK
Isle Royale wilderness plan, a job unfinished.
G. C. Haber. il Liv Wildn 34:31-7 Sum '70
ISMAILIA, Egypt
Ismailia childhood; Jewish members of the
Suez Canal company. S. Eban. New Yorker
46:174-6+ D 5 '70
ISMENE. See Basket flowers
ISOLATION (biology)
Antimycoplasmal antibiotics and hybrid ster-
ility in drosophila paulistorum. R. P. Ker-
naghan and L. Ehrman. bibliog il Science
169:63-4 Jl 3 '70
ISOLATION, Social. See Social isolation
ISOLATIONISM (United States) See United
States—Foreign relations
ISOMERIZATION
Enhancement of photoalteration of cyclodiene
insecticide chemical residues by rotenone.
G. W. Ivie and J. E. Casida. bibliog il Sci-
ence 167:1620-2 Mr 20 '70
ISOMETRIC exercise
Perils of muscle beach; weight lifter's blood
pressure. il Time 96:46 Jl 20 '70
ISOMETRICS. See Isometric exercise
ISOPODS, Fossil. See Crustaceans, Fossil
ISOPROPYL alcohol. See Alcohols
ISOTENISCOPE. See Chemical apparatus and
supplies
ISOTOPES
Apollo 11 lunar science conference; stable
isotopes, rare gases, solar wind, and spalla-
tion products, symposium. bibliog il Sci-
ence 167:533-82 Ja 30 '70
See also
Radioisotopes
also subhead Isotopes under names of
chemical elements, e.g. Helium—Isotopes
ISOTOPIC power generators
Power from radioisotopes. R. L. Mead and
W. R. Corliss. il Space World G-5-77:41-5
My '70
See also
Space vehicles—Atomic power plants
ISRAEL, Jerry
For God, for China and for Yale: the open
door in action. bibliog f Am Hist R 75:
796-807 F '70
ISRAEL, Lee
Dick and Jane revisited. Sat R 53:12+ F 21
'70
ISRAEL
Between the Rock and the hard place, by
P. Jacobs. Review
Life por 68:14 Mr 20 '70. U. Avnery
Crucial issues in the Mideast. E. R. Chandler.
Chr Today 14:14-15 F 27 '70
Israel. J. S. Haupert. il Focus 20:1-12 Mr '70
Israel: first pilgrimage. D. L. Hurwood. Yale
R 59:459-80 Mr '70; Reply. E. Berger. 59:
637-40 Je '70

Not to kill, but to live. W. D. Patterson. il
Sat R 53:15-16 Jl 25 '70
Thirteen days in an instant country. P.
Siekman. il Fortune 81:43-4+ Ap '70
See also
Airlines—Israel
Airplanes, Military—Israel
Beersheba, Israel
Christmas—Israel
Collective settlements—Israel
Conservation of resources—Israel
Dead Sea
Foreign visitors in Israel
Immigration and emigration—Israel
Jaffa
Jerusalem
Law—Israel
Libraries—Israel
Morale, National—Israel
Music—Israel
Petroleum industry and trade—Israel
Political prisoners—Israel
Public officers—Israel
Public opinion—Israel
Purchasing, Military—Israel
Research—Israel
Secret service—Israel
Sinai (peninsula)
Student demonstrations—Israel
Tourist trade—Israel
United Nations—Israel
War and emergency powers—Israel
Women—Israel
Zionism

Air force
Israel's non-secret weapon; with report by
M. Elkins. il Newsweek 75:39-40 Ap 6 '70
Phantom shape over Suez; with interviews
with pilots, ed. by P. Young. il Life 69:28-34
S 25 '70
Vietnam lessons helped Israel build Mideast
air supremacy. E. H. Kolcum. il Aviation
W 92:18-21 My 25 '70
World's toughest air force: it keeps Israel
alive. G. Astor. il Look 34:17-23 Je 30 '70

Antiquities
Concert shell for a Roman ruin; Caesarea festival theater. G. C. Izenour. il Arch Rec
148:67-74 D '70

Appropriations and expenditures
See also
Budget—Israel

Armed forces
Israel and its enemies. il Time 95:24+ Je 22
'70
Walls of Israel, by J. Lartéguy. Review
Sat R 53:32-3 F 7 '70. D. Kurzman

Procurement
Pledge, by L. Slater. Review
Newsweek il 75:99-99A+ My 11 '70 A.
Keneas

Army
How I didn't make it in the women's army
of Israel. B. Rollin. il por Look 34:68-9 F
24 '70
Survival in Sinai. R. Starnes. Field & S
74:6+ Ja '70

Boundaries
Settling in along the border. M. Clark. il
Time 97:35-6 Ja 4 '71
U.S. and Israel: the built-in conflict. S. Alsop.
Newsweek 76:72 Ag 3 '70

Cabinet
Israel moves right. M. S. Kogan. Nat R 22:
83 Ja 27 '70

Defenses
Arms to Israel: the U.S. moves. il Newsweek
76:17-18 Jl 20 '70
Life on the Bar-Lev line. il Time 95:30 Je 22
'70
Next best thing: new weapons systems. il
Time 95:35 My 18 '70
SAM changes force new strategy on Israelis.
E. H. Kolcum. il Aviation W 93:16-21 N 16
'70
Up in arms; hopes of U.S. aid. il Newsweek
75:53-4 Ja 26 '70
U.S. dilemma in Middle East. il U S News
68:28-30 Je 15 '70
U.S. pledge to Israel: how far does it extend?
il U S News 68:30 Je 15 '70
Why U.S. is worried about Mideast build-
up. il U S News 69:44 O 26 '70

Description and travel
Israel diary. D. Butwin. il Sat R 53:40+ Ap
25; 46+ My 2 '70
Travel. D. Messinesi. Vogue 155:46 F 15 '70

ISRAEL—*Continued*

Economic conditions
Israel on a war footing. G. Yalowitz. il U S News 68:37-40 Ja 19 '70

Economic policy
Harvest in Palestine; investment in occupied territories. H. Krosney. Nation 210:721-4 Je 15 '70
See also
Budget—Israel

Foreign opinion
French
Feelings of ambivalence. Newsweek 75:50+ Mr 16 '70

Foreign relations
Future of Israel. N. Goldmann. For Affairs 48:443-59 Ap '70
Viva Eban. W. F. Buckley, jr. Nat R 22: 1124-5 O 20 '70

Arab states
Israel and its enemies. il Time 95:24+ Je 22 '70

France
See France—Foreign relations—Israel

Lebanon
U.S. calls for end to cycle of violence on Israel-Lebanon border; statements, May 12, 14 and 19, 1970, with texts of resolutions. C. W. Yost. Dept State Bul 62:726-30 Je 8 '70

United States
See United States—Foreign relations—Israel

Industries
Kindest cut of all; polished diamonds. il Time 96:62 Ag 17 '70
See also
Airplane industry and trade—Israel

Military policy
Israel's fiery new message. M. Elkins. il Newsweek 75:32 F 2 '70

Neutrality
Future of Israel; question of neutralization. N. Goldmann. For Affairs 48:443-59 Ap '70

Politics and government
Dissenters. Newsweek 75:36-8 Mr 2 '70
Israeli politics since the 1967 war. N. Safran. Cur Hist 60:19-25+ Ja '71
Israelis believe war is inevitable. A. Elon. il Life 68:46-48B+ F 6 '70
Lion's roar. por Time 95:26-7 Ja 26 '70

Religious institutions and affairs
Israel and the Christian shrines. H. Golden. il Sat R 53:15-16 D 19 '70

Social history
Israel's power elite. R. Rosenzweig and G. Tamarin. il Trans-Action 7:26-33+ Jl '70

Territorial expansion
Points at issue in the hostile Middle East. il Time 96:19 Ag 3 '70

ISRAEL aircraft industries, ltd. See Airplane industry and trade—Israel

ISRAEL philharmonic orchestra
Schoenberg for others; subscribers protest première in Israel of Arnold Schoenberg's twelve-tone violin concerto. por Time 97: 45 Ja 18 '71

ISRAELI-Arab border conflicts
He who lights a fire may be burned. il Newsweek 75:47-8 My 25 '70
Israel's growing gloom. il Time 95:30-1 Je 15 '70
Jitters in Lebanon. il Time 95:24 Je 8 '70
U.S. calls for end to cycle of violence on Israel-Lebanon border; statements, May 12, 14 and 19, 1970, with texts of resolutions. C. W. Yost. Dept State Bul 62:726-30 Je 8 '70
Waiting for Washington to decide; government order to stop provoking Israelis. il Newsweek 75:39+ Je 8 '70
See also
Fedaveen

ISRAELI-Arab relations. See Jewish-Arab relations

ISRAELI-Arab war, 1967-
Arab view; waiting for Russian rescue. J. Law. il U S News 68:48 Mr 2 '70
Controlled tension. il Newsweek 76:32-3 Jl 27 '70

Dangerous situation. il Newsweek 76:43 Jl 13 '70
From victory to war. il Newsweek 75:41-2 Je 15 '70
Great danger from a new direction. H. Sidey. Life 69:2B Jl 17 '70
Is the Middle East about to explode again? interview. J. Law. il U S News 68:53-5 Je 29 '70
Israel and the credibility gap. A. Horne. Nat R 22:309-10 Mr 24 '70
Israeli munitions and the Jewishness of Jesus. Chr Cent 87:164-5 F 11 '70; Discussion. 87:397-8 Ap 1 '70
Israeli view; no intention of letting up. J. Fromm. il U S News 68:49 Mr 2 '70
Israelis believe war is inevitable. A. Elon. il Life 68:46-48B+ F 6 '70
Israel's Bar-Lev; how to cope with the Arab armies. interview. ed. by M. Levin. H. Barlev. il por Time 95:39 Ap 6 '70
Lasting peace in the Middle East: an American view; address, December 9, 1969. W. P. Rogers. Dept State Bul 62:7-11 Ja 5 '70
Many fronts of Israel. A. P. Hatch. il Nation 210:197-200 F 23 '70
Middle East cockpit. Nation 210:708-9 Je 15 '70
Mideast: alarm signals for U.S. and Russia. il U S News 69:11-12 Jl 20 '70
Most dangerous arena; U.S. peace proposals presented by Secretary of State Rogers. il por Time 96:23 Jl 13 '70
New crisis in Mideast; interview. ed. by C. S. Foltz, jr. G. A. Nasser. il por U S News 68:60-3 My 18 '70
New flareup in Middle East. il Sr Schol 95: 17 S 29 '69
To the brink again in the Mideast. il U S News 68:29-30 F 16 '70
War of the long breath. il Time 95:32-7 Mr 30 '70
Why no backdown in Mideast: a report from both sides. J. Law. il U S News 68:53-5 My 4 '70
See also
Arab states—Foreign relations

Aerial operations
Bombs away! Israel's bloody blunder; Abu Zabal incident. il Newsweek 75:37-8 F 23 '70
Electronic summer. il Time 95:38+ Ap 6 '70
In earshot of the front. il Time 95:26-7 F 9 '70
Israel under fire; Egyptian school bombed. il Newsweek 75:54 Ap 20 '70
Italians, Lebanese seek to identify missile that hit Alitalia DC-8. E. H. Kolcum. il Aviation W 93:20 Jl 6 '70
Middle East; civilians as targets. il Time 95: 22-3 F 23 '70
Middle East: that electronic summer. il Time 96:18-19 Jl 20 '70
Mideast: another step closer to explosion; with report by J. Law. il U S News 68:9 F 23 '70
On their own turf; Soviet pilots in Egypt. il Newsweek 75:58+ My 18 '70
Other fronts; Syrian border dogfights. il Newsweek 75:38-40 Ap 13 '70
Phantom shape over Suez; with interviews with pilots, ed. by P. Young. il Life 69:28-34 S 25 '70
Relief for Egypt, anxiety for Israel. il Time 95:43-4 My 11 '70
Sonic booms and a war of nerves. M. J. Kubic. il Newsweek 75:41 F 9 '70
Soviets accelerating Mideast drive; with editorial comment. E. H. Kolcum. il Aviation W 92:9, 14-18 My 18 '70
Soviets shifting Mideast balance. E. H. Kolcum. il Aviation W 92:18-21 My 11 '70
Vietnam lessons helped Israel build Mideast air supremacy. E. H. Kolcum. il Aviation W 92:18-21 My 25 '70
World's toughest air force; it keeps Israel alive. G. Astor. il Look 34:17-23 Je 30 '70

Atrocities
Middle East: in cold blood. il Time 95:19-20 Je 1 '70

Bibliography
Assessing the six-day war. A. Perlmutter. Commentary 49:71-5 Ja '70

Campaigns and battles
Bigger flare-ups in the Mideast. il U S News 68:4 F 2 '70

Casualties
An eye for an eye: who loses? civilian toll. Sr Schol 96:13-14 Mr 23 '70
Innocent dead. il Time 95:28 Ap 20 '70
Middle East: in cold blood. il Time 95:19-20 Je 1 '70

ISRAELI-Arab war, 1967- —*Continued*

Censorship
War of the communiqués. Time 95:33 F 2 '70

Peace and mediation
Arab-Israel hope? U.S's Mideast peace plan. Sr Schol 97:4-5 S 14 '70
Arab-Israeli cease-fire: a pause, or lasting peace? il U S News 69:22-3 Ag 17 '70
Arab-Israeli conflict: an American policy. J. C. Campbell. For Affairs 49:51-69 O '70
Arab-Israeli settlement; address, August 24, 1970; with an interchange with A. A. Ribicoff. J. W. Fulbright. New Repub 163:20-3 O 10 '70
As Arab and Israeli talk. America 123:110-11 S 5 '70
Assistant Secretary Sisco gives observations on the Near East; statement, April 24, 1970. J. J. Sisco. Dept State Bul 62:693 Je 1 70
Assistant Secretary Sisco interviewed on Meet the press; transcript of interview, July 12, 1970. J. J. Sisco. Dept State Bul 63:150-5 Ag 3 '70
Assistant Secretary Sisco interviewed on NBC's Today; television program, October 15, 1970. J. J. Sisco. Dept State Bul 63:566-8 N 9 '70
At last a truce along the Suez. il Life 69:38-9 Ag 21 '70
Back into focus. Nat R 22:17 Ja 13 '70
Back to Jarring. Newsweek 77:43-4 Ja 11 '71
Beleaguered Israel. Chr Today 14:26 Ja 16 '70
Can peace be negotiated. A. Hetherington. il Cur 116:55-64 Mr '70
Can the Mideast truce work? il Newsweek 76:19+ Ag 17 '70
Crucial test for old friends. il Time 96:20-1 S 14 '70
Dangerous deadline for the Middle East. il Time 96:20-1 N 9 '70
De facto settlement? S. Alsop. Newsweek 76:100 O 26 '70
Demanding position; Israel to return to the peace table. Newsweek 76:58+ N 23 '70
Doctor Goldmann's initiative. America 122: 448 Ap 25 '70
Doves in Vietnam, hawks in Israel? J. B. Sheerin. Cath World 211:194-5 Ag '70; Reply. D. R. Cooper. 212:173 Ja '71
Egypt steals a march; U.S. proposal. pors Newsweek 76:26-7 Ag 3 '70
Faint flutterings. il Newsweek 76:41-2 N 30 '70
Faint hope. Nation 211:258 S 28 '70
Father Hesburgh's proposal. Nation 211:356 O 19 '70
Fulbright proposal for peace in the Mideast; abstract of address, August 24, 1970. J. W. Fulbright. il por U S News 69:43 S 7 '70
Guaranteeing a Mideast peace. D. Lawrence. U S News 69:80 S 7 '70
In defense of Friends; working party document Search for peace in the Middle East. Chr Cent 88:35 Ja 13 '71
Inching toward the table. por Time 96:30+ D 14 '70
Israel against the wall. New Repub 163:5-6 S 26 '70
Israel and the US. New Repub 162:7 Je 27 '70
Israel: criticism from within; symposium, ed. by A. de Borchgrave and M. Elkins. il Newsweek 75:56-8 Ap 20 '70
Israel's Dayan: also seeking a solution. por U S News 69:39 D 21 '70 *
Jordan's Hussein: in search of peace. por U S News 69:38 D 21 '70
Let's get on with it. il Newsweek 76:29+ Ag 24 '70
Letter from Washington (cont) R. H. Rovere New Yorker 46:130-2 S 26 '70
Middle East: a secret rendezvous; Hussein-Allon talks. il pors Time 96:26 N 23 '70
Middle East: at last, a way out? il por Time 96:14-16+ Ag 10 '70
Middle East balance? But Russia's gain. W. H. Dorsey, jr. New Repub 163:12-13 Ag 15 '70
Middle East: between hope and menace. il Time 96:16-17 Jl 27 '70
Middle East on the Potomac. il pors Newsweek 76:41-2 D 21 '70
Middle East: peace hopes and new dangers. il Sr Schol 97:10 S 21 '70
Middle East: persuasion amid peril. il Time 96:16-17 S 7 '70
Middle East: statesmen speak and guns answer. il Time 96:22-3 Jl 6 '70
Middle East: toward the start of talks. il Time 96:26+ Ag 31 '70
Mideast peace talks begin. il Newsweek 76: 37-8 S 7 '70
Mideast: Soviets test U.S. il U S News 69:39 S 14 '70

Mideast truce. Nation 211:98 Ag 17 '70
Mideastern maze. Nat R 22:930+ S 8 '70
Missile impasse. il por Time 96:26 S 28 '70
More time to talk; extended cease-fire. il Time 96:33 N 16 '70
Moshe the mild. il por Time 96:25 N 30 '70
Movement in the Middle East? Nat R 23:20-1 Ja 12 '71
On ditching Israel. C. Benson. Nat R 22: 1206-10 N 17 '70; Reply with rejoinder. A. S. Epstein. 23:12+ Ja 12 '71
Our Middle East stance: rejected but still valid. Life 68:28 Ja 23 '70
Phantom peace bid; reactions to U.S. plan. il Newsweek 76:40-1 Jl 6 '70
Plucky peacemakers. Chr Cent 87:983 Ag 19 '70
President gratified at acceptance of U.S. Middle East peace initiative; statement, July 31, 1970. R. M. Nixon. Dept State Bul 63: 218 Ag 24 '70
President Nixon interviewed for CBS television; excerpt from interview, August 29, 1970. R. M. Nixon. Dept State Bul 63:327-9 S 21 '70
President Nixon's news conference, July 20, 1970. R. M. Nixon. Dept State Bul 63:161-4 Ag 10 '70
Quaker appeal for peace; excerpt from Search for peace in the Middle East. Cur 121:59-64 S '70
Question of credence. il Newsweek 76:50-1 S 14 '70
Realpolitik is peace; excerpt from Search for peace in the Middle East. il Trans-Action 7:20-3 Jl '70
Saboteurs of peace. il Newsweek 76:30 S 21 '70
Secretary Rogers and Secretary Laird interviewed on Issues and answers. W. P. Rogers; M. R. Laird. Dept State Bul 63: 542-53 N 2 '70
Secretary Rogers' news conference of June 25, 1970. W. P. Rogers. Dept State Bul 63: 26-8 Jl 13 '70
Secretary Rogers' news conference of October 9, 1970. W. P. Rogers. Dept State Bul 63:471-8 O 26 '70
Shadow over the cease-fire. il Time 96:14-15 Ag 24 '70
Shoring up a shaky calm; Abdel Nasser's cease-fire terms. il por Time 95:29 Je 29 '70
Soviets testing. K. Crawford. Newsweek 76: 46 S 21 '70
Sprig of peace; Jarring mission. A. Tuckerman. Nation 211:167 S 7 '70
Step toward peace. America 123:83-4 Ag 22 '70
Strategic alternative? C. Benson. Nat R 22: 1206-10 N 17 '70
Suez: shalom and salaam. il Time 96:15-16 Ag 17 '70
Talk with Hussein; interview, ed. by M. J. Kubic and L. Jenkins. Hussein. il por Newsweek 76:36 Ag 31 '70
Talking about the talks; resumption of Jarring talks. il por Time 97:25-7 Ja 18 '71
Toward Israel's neutralization. N. Goldmann. Cur 119:53-7 Ja '70
Toward the showdown. il Time 97:20-1 Ja 11 '71
Truce survives a falling-out. il Newsweek 76:34-6 Ag 31 '70
Truncated plank for the Middle East. Nat R 22:824+ Ag 11 '70
Turning from confrontation. New Repub 163: 5-6 Ag 1 '70
Undemonizing the Middle East. R. C. Hottelet. Sat R 53:23-5+ Je 6 '70
U.S. gives views in U.N. General assembly debate on the situation in the Middle East; statements, October 29 and November 4, 1970; with texts of resolution. C. W. Yost. Dept State Bul 63:656-63 N 23 '70
U.S. initiative toward peace in the Middle East; text of letter, June 19, 1970. W. P. Rogers. Dept State Bul 63:178 Ag 10 '70
U.S. initiative toward peace in the Middle East; with text of Rogers letter to U.A.R. Foreign Minister Riad, June 19, 1970. Cur Hist 60:46+ Ja '71
U.S. objectives in the Middle East; address, June 30, 1970. J. J. Sisco. Dept State Bul 63:175-8 Ag 10 '70
U.S. stake in Mideast peace. il U S News 69:11-13 Ag 10 '70
US and Israel. New Repub 162:5-6 Ja 24 '70
Way Egyptians see Israel, Uncle Sam, the SAM's. E. R. F. Sheehan. il N Y Times Mag p28-9+ S 20 '70
What Nasser did. G. G. Stevens. Atlan 227: 45-7 Ja '71
While Jordan burned. il por Newsweek 76: 20-1 S 28 '70
Why peace in Mideast hangs by a thread. il U S News 69:40-3 D 28 '70

ISRAELI-Arab war, 1967- —Peace and mediation—*Continued*
Yes from Nasser, dilemma for Israel. il Time 96:17-18 Ag 3 '70
Yes to a frail Mideast truce. il Newsweek 76:15-16 Ag 10 '70

Personal narratives
Our life on a border kibbutz. C. Abrams and A. Abrams. il pors Nat Geog 138:364-91 S '70

Photography
See also
Aerial reconnaissance

Protests, demonstrations, etc, against
Israel; the strange sounds of protest. R. C. Hirschfield. Commonweal 91:607-8 Mr 6 '70; Reply. J. Segal. 92:127 Ap 17 '70
Now in Israel a fluttering of doves. A. Rubinstein. il N Y Times Mag p8-9+ Jl 26 '70

Public opinion
Cairo's war: now you see it, now you don't. D. Holden. il N Y Times Mag p32-3+ My 24 '70
Inside Israel: uneasy and ready for anything. J. Law. il U S News 69:43-4 O 26 '70
Now in Israel a fluttering of doves. A. Rubinstein. il N Y Times Mag p8-9+ Jl 26 '70

Russian participation
Coming destruction of Israel, by M. S. Kaufmann. Review
Sat R 53:30-1 S 5 70. D. Kurzman
Israel and its enemies. il Time 95:24+ Je 22 '70
Kremlin's Mideast gamble; with reports by A. de Borchgrave; M. Elkins. il Newsweek 75:37-42 Je 1 '70
On ditching Israel. C. Benson. Nat R 22:1206-10 N 17 '70; Reply with rejoinder. A. S. Epstein. 23:12+ Ja 12 '71
Reading Soviet intentions. J. Alsop. New Repub 163:17-19 O 3 '70
Strategic alternative? C. Benson. Nat R 22:1206-10 N 17 '70

War correspondents
Scouting both sides of an angry border. R. Graves. pors Life 68:3 Je 12 '70
ISRAELI dancing. See Dancing, Israeli
ISRAELI designers. See Costume designers
ISRAELI literature
Israel's interest in Jesus. America 123:392 N 14 '70
Jesus in Israeli literature. P. E. Lapide. Chr Cent 87:1248-53 O 21 '70
ISRAELI occupation of Jordan, 1967-. See Jordan—Israeli occupation, 1967-
ISRAELI students
See also
Student demonstrations—Israel
ISRAELI technical assistance. See Technical assistance, Israeli
ISRAELIS
Manchild in the promised land: to Israel and back. P. Schwaber. Am Scholar 39:506+ Sum '70
ISTANBUL

Theater
Love affair: James Baldwin and Istanbul. C. E. Adelsen. il pors Ebony 25:40-2+ Mr '70
ISTOMIN, Eugene
Gallery of great performances. il Hi Fi 20: secI 32+ Ap '70
Three men on a hobby; remarks, ed. by I. Kolodin. il pors Sat R 53:47-9 O 31 '70
IT all looks different on the way back; story. See King, J.
ITALIAN AMERICANS
Bless you, Joe; Unity day. il Newsweek 76: 34 Jl 13 '70
Italian Americans: discovering America the second time around. il Sr Schol 95:12-16 Ja 12 '70
Italian power; demonstrations against the New York headquarters of the FBI. il Newsweek 75:22 Je 22 '70
ITALIAN composers. See Composers, Italian
ITALIAN cookery. See Cookery, Italian
ITALIAN designers. See Designers
ITALIAN furniture. See Furniture, Italian
ITALIAN language
Talking like a native; TV teaching Italians standard Italian. il Newsweek 75:57 Mr 9 '70
ITALIAN literature
See also
Childrens literature—Italy

ITALIAN mulattoes. See Mulattoes
ITALIAN poetry

Translations into English
Days; tr. by B. Swann and R. Feldman. L. Piccolo. Poetry 116:303 Ag '70
Pigeons; tr. by E. Pound. U. Fasolo. Atlan 226:94 N '70
Untitled; tr. by B. Swann and R. Feldman. C. Pavese. Poetry 116:302 Ag '70
ITALIAN pottery. See Pottery, Italian
ITALIAN students
See also
Student demonstrations—Italy
ITALIANS
Raucous Italy. A. Hine. il Holiday 48:22-7 Jl '70
ITALIANS in Libya
Celebrating xenophobia. il Time 96:20 S 7 '70
ITALIANS in the United States
See also
Italian Americans
ITALO-ETHIOPIAN war, 1935-1936
Royal navy and the Ethiopian crisis of 1935-36. A. Marder. bibliog f Am Hist R 75: 1327-56 Je '70
ITALY
See also
Abano Terme
Airlines—Italy
Airplanes, Military—Italy
Automobile driving—Italy
Automobile industry and trade—Italy
Barga
Capri
Cathedrals—Italy
Chemical industries—Italy
Childrens literature—Italy
Communism—Italy
Country estates—Italy
Crime and criminals—Italy
Divorce—Italy
Earthquakes—Italy
Elba (island)
Emilia-Romagna
Family—Italy
Floods—Italy
Gardens—Italy
Government ownership—Italy
Industry and state—Italy
Investments, Foreign (in Italy)
Lotteries—Italy
Money—Italy
Nemi, Lake
Opera—Italy
Parma
Periodicals—Italy
Ponza Island
Porto Ercole
Portovenere
Pozzuoli
Publishers and publishing—Italy
Reggio di Calabria
Sardinia
Science—Italy
Sila, La
Strikes—Italy
Student demonstrations—Italy
Terracina
Trade unions—Italy
Trials—Italy
Venice
Women—Italy
World war, 1939-1945—Italy

Antiquities
See also
Paestum

Description and travel
How to discover a resort. H. P. Koenig. il Travel 133:51-5 F '70
Italian emphasis. B. Diamonstein. Harp Baz 103:112-13+ Ag '70
Italy: everybody's favorite country; symposium. il Holiday 48:20-45+ Jl '70
Porto Venere and the Cinque Terre. P. Gravina. Harp Baz 103:68+ Ap '70
Winter in Italy. W. Weaver. Harp Baz 103:88 O '70

Economic conditions
Economy on the edge of a volcano. il Bsns W p22 Ag 8 '70

Fascist movement
See Fascism—Italy

Foreign relations
Italy in Europe. P. Nazzaro. Cur Hist 58: 281-6 My '70

Ethiopia
See also
Italo-Ethiopian war, 1935-1936

ITALY—Foreign relations—*Continued*

Yugoslavia

Europe: a symbolic act of atonement; Tito cancels visit. il por Time 96:25-6 D 21 '70

History

Bibliography

Articles and other books received; comp. by E. P. Noether. See issues of American historical review

Industries

Innocenti and how they grew. il Bsns W p29 My 2 '70

Innocenti decides not to press on. Bsns W p39-40 Jl 18 '70

See also

Aerospace industries—Italy
Automobile industry and trade—Italy
Boatbuilding
Chemical industries—Italy
Electronic apparatus industry and trade—Italy
Italy—Economic conditions
Liquor industry and trade—Italy
Shoes—Trade and manufacture

Maps

Invitation to explore: a new map of Italy for the traveler. il Nat Geog 137:790-3, sup (folded map) Je '70

Moral conditions

See also
Prostitution

Politics and government

Foreign report: Italy's happy Communists. C. Sterling. Harper 240:24+ F '70

Italy: bent for chaos. A. De Borchgrave. il Newsweek 76:31-2 Ag 10 '70

Italy in Europe. P. Nazzaro. Cur Hist 58:281-6 My '70

Italy: the crisis of governing. A. Levi. For Affairs 49:147-60 O '70

Manning the lifeboats; change to regional councils. il Time 95:38 Je 15 '70

1922 all over again? J. D. Futch. il Nat R 22:354-5 Ap 7 '70

No. 33. Time 96:18 Ag 17 '70

Reports: Italy. I. R. Levine. Atlan 225:22+ Ap '70

Soloists. il Time 95:41 Ap 6 '70

See also
Communist party (Italy)
Elections—Italy
Fascism—Italy

Race problems

Identity crisis Italian style; children of black GIs. M. Senesi. il Ebony 25:40-6 Jl '70

Religious institutions and affairs

See also
Catholic church in Italy

Riots

Italy: no saints in paradise; Reggio's rebellion. il Time 96:35 O 26 '70

Social life and customs

Italian family is a commune. A. Menen. il N Y Times Mag p22-3+ Mr 1 '70

World war, 1939-1945

See World war, 1939-1945—Italy

ITCHETUCKNEE RIVER

Itchetucknee, Florida's crystal river. J. F. Stanfield. il Nat Parks & Con Mag 44:13-16 My '70

ITCHETUCKNEE SPRINGS state park (proposed) See Florida—Parks and reserves

ITO, Yoichiro, and Bowman, R. L.
Countercurrent chromatography: liquid-liquid partition chromatography without solid support. bibliog il Science 167:281-3 Ja 16 '70

IVANTZOVA, Elizaveta Anderson. See Anderson-Ivantzova, E.

IVASK, Ivar
One thing and another. J. K. Hutchens. Sat R 53:32-3+ Mr 21 '70 *

IVERSEN, William
Dog who came in from the cold. il Read Digest 97:127-30 S '70

IVERSON, A. E.
Motivated to be better. il Todays Ed 59:34-5 Mr '70

IVES, Charles Edward
New Ivesian discoveries. A. Frankenstein. Hi Fi 20:secI 92 Mr '70 *
Playing and conducting that simply could not be bettered. A. Cohn. pors Am Rec G 37:148-51 N '70 *

IVES, Ronald L.
Dehumming small receivers. il Pop Electr 32:75-6 Ap '70

IVIE, Glen Wayne, and Casida, J. E.
Enhancement of photoalteration of cyclodiene insecticide chemical residues by rotenone. bibliog il Science 167:1620-2 Mr 20 '70

IVIZA (island)
Ibiza: how to drop out without falling. A. Gross. il Mlle 72:112-13+ D '70
Why-of all places-Ibiza? M. Thomas. il Holiday 47:32-7+ Je '70

IVORY carving
See also
Scrimshaw

IVORY COAST
African Riviera. H. Sutton. il Sat R 53:37-8+ O 24 '70
Show at the palace. H. Sutton. Sat R 53:44-5+ O 31 '70
See also
Tourist trade—Ivory Coast

IVY poisoning. See Poison ivy

IWO JIMA (helicopter carrier) See Aircraft carriers

IZARD, Carroll E.
Cambodian crisis: reason and emotion. Science 168:1157 Je 5 '70

IZEMBEK wilderness area (proposed) See Wilderness areas—Alaska

IZENOUR, George C.
Concert shell for a Roman ruin. il Arch Rec 148:67-74 D '70

J

J. WALTER Thompson company. See Thompson. J. Walter, company

JFP enterprises
Dynamic growth companies. il pors Nations Bsns 58:64-7 Mr '70

JOBS (job opportunities in business sector) See National alliance of businessmen

JPL. See Jet propulsion laboratory

JABLONSKI, Martha
Fiat; poem. Commonweal 92:272 My 29 '70

JABLOW, Paul
(ed) See Hollings, E. F. We must wipe out hunger in America

JACCOTTET, Philippe
Grapes and figs: I would like only to remove; Who will help me? None can come this far; I lifted up my eyes; And I now utterly in the celestial cascade; poems, tr. by C. Corman. Poetry 116:287-91 Ag '70

JACK MacGowran in the works of Samuel Beckett (dramatic reading) See Dramatic readings

JACK the Ripper. See Crime and criminals—Great Britain

JACK: the story of a pretty good donkey; story. See Jay, F. J.

JACKLIN, Tony
Combat at Hazeltine. il por Time 96:43 Jl 6 '70 *
Go to America and learn what the game is all about. C. Kirkpatrick. il Sports Illus 32:18 Je 29 '70 *
New king of England. il por Newsweek 76:55 Jl 6 '70*
Tony's a shark at pasture pool. D. Jenkins. il por Sports Illus 32:14-19 Je 29 '70 *

JACKLING, Daniel Cowan
Mountain that became the richest hole on earth. F. R. Milliken. il Nations Bsns 58:58-88-9 Ja '70

JACKS
Powered car jack that does the job; Lectrojack. il Consumer Rep 35:268 My '70

JACKSON, Andrew
Santa Claus stocks the White House. H. J. Sievers. America 123:556 D 26 '70 *

JACKSON, Charles D.
Students grade themselves. il Todays Ed 59:24-5 O '70

JACKSON, Donald
Memories of Big Country. il Life 68:40-8+ Ap 3 '70
San Mateo. il Life 69:26-7 O 2 '70
Search for recollections of Nixon's younger days. por Life 69:3 N 6 '70
This land is our land. il Life 70:32-43 Ja 8 '71
Young Nixon. il pors Life 69:54-54B+ N 6 '70; Same abr. with title Portrait of the young Nixon. Time 96:18-19 N 9 '70

JACKSON, Donald (calligrapher)
Donald Jackson: calligrapher & illuminator. F. Johnson. il por Am Artist 34:17-23+ My '70 *

JACKSON, Geoffrey Holt Seymour
Machine gun in the lettuce. por Time 97:31 Ja 18 '71 *
JACKSON, George
Soledad brother, by G. Jackson. Review America 123:550-6 D 19 '70. T. M. Gannon *
Soledad brother: the prison letters of George Jackson. D. N. Mount. Pub W 198:19-21 O 26 '70 *
Soledad brothers: how a prison picks its victims. il por Ramp Mag 9:50-2 Ag '70
JACKSON, Glenda
Futures, great. pors Vogue 156:92 Jl '70 *
They hardly ever make passes at Glenda Jackson. H. Ehrlich. il pors Look 34:36-41 D 29 '70 *
JACKSON, Henry Martin
Henry Jackson: a statesman of uncommon quality. R. K. Bennett. por Read Digest 97:110-15 Jl '70 *
War is hell for Senator Jackson. B. Weiner. por Nation 211:138-41 Ag 31 '70 *
JACKSON, Herbert G. jr
Wayne M. Harris: citizen pollution fighter. il Field & S 76:12+ My '70
JACKSON, Howard E.
Towns with wings. il Travel 134:54-9 Ag '70
JACKSON, James P.
Death of a river. il Nat Parks 44:19-22 F '70
Missouri's river of springs. il Travel 133:48-53 Ap '70
People problems on the Riverways. il Nat Parks & Con Mag 44:24-7 Ag '70
What is a songbird worth? il Am For 76:34-5+ Ap '70 *
JACKSON, Jesse L.
Dialogue on separatism. por Ebony 25:62-4+ Ag '70

about

Jesse Jackson: one leader among many. il pors Time 95:14-16+ Ap 6 '70 *
JACKSON, Jonathan
Bloody breakout at San Rafael; with editorial comment. il pors Life 69:2A, 30-4 Ag 21 '70 *
JACKSON, Joseph Harrison
Meaning of the cross. por Time 95:72 Ap 6 '70
JACKSON, Maynard
Atlanta's first vice mayor. Negro Hist Bul 33:49 F '70 *
JACKSON, Paul Gerrard
Christmas: eve and morn; poem. Chr Today 15:44 D 18 '70 *
JACKSON, Richard
At morning she begins to remember him; poem. America 122:585 My 30 '70
JACKSON, Ronald B.
Schools and communities: a necessary relevance. Clear House 44:488-90 Ap '70
JACKSON, Samuel C.
Are American cities obsolete? address, August 10, 1970. Vital Speeches 36:706-10 S 15 '70
JACKSON, T. Sherron
Strange company. Chr Today 14:43 Ag 21 '70 *
JACKSON, Vera Ruth
Weaving with weeds. il Design 71:34-6 Wint '69
JACKSON, W. Keith
New Zealand in the 1970's. Cur Hist 58:217-22+ Ap '70
JACKSON, Miss.

Negroes

Truth at the crossroads. J. P. Adams. il Chr Cent 87:749-50 Je 17 '70
JACKSON COUNTY, Ore.
Medieval faire; children's festival. S. A. Nelson. il Parks & Rec 5:30-1 Jl '70
JACKSON Five (soul group) See Rock 'n' roll groups
JACKSON state college, Jackson, Miss.
Arms and the campus; report on campus unrest. Newsweek 76:49 O 12 '70
Dark day in Jackson. il Newsweek 75:35-6 My 25 '70
Killings in Jackson and Augusta. America 122:577 My 30 '70
Law and disorder. il Ebony 25:96-7 Jl '70
South: death in two cities. il Time 95:22+ My 25 '70
What the tape said; students deaths; hearings before the President's commission on campus unrest. Newsweek 76:22+ Ag 24 '70
JACKSONVILLE, Fla.
Meter enforcement with a smile. P. Atter. il Am City 85:134 My '70

Parks and playgrounds

Parking lot can mean a lot to kids. V. Louviere. il Nations Bsns 58:20 Ap '70

Politics and government

Jacksonvillians like consolidated city government. H. Tanzler. il por Am City 85:79-81 Ap '70
JACOB, Ellen
Carla Fracci: American ballet theatre's Giselle. il pors Dance Mag 44:42-53 N '70
Emily Frankel: coming back for good. pors Dance Mag 44:68-73 O '70
JACOBI, Abraham
Abraham Jacobi, the children's physician. R. Dunlop. il Todays Health 48:58-9+ Ap '70 *
JACOBOWITZ, Martin
Anti-slavery medallions in the Martin Jacobowitz collection. H. Aptheker. bibliog il Negro Hist Bul 33:114-21 My '70 *
JACOBS, Charles J.
King song; poem. Negro Hist Bul 33:125 My '70
JACOBS, Ellen W.
Learning to look. il Dance Mag 44:24+ O '70
JACOBS, Evelyn
(ed) See Rogers, R. E.   Report on venereal disease
—See Carrington, E. R.; Greenblatt, R. jt. auths.
JACOBS, Fenno
Ways of the Orient; with photographs. Motor B 126:42-7 S '70
JACOBS, Florence B.
Old summer, eleventh hour; poem. Horn Bk 46:375 Ag '70
JACOBS, Hayes B.
New York market letter. See issues of Writer's digest
Writer turned salesman: the article query; excerpt from Writing and selling non-fiction. il Writers Digest 50:24-5 Ag '70
JACOBS, Hirsch
Jacobs legacy. P. Axthelm. il por Newsweek 76:61 Ag 24 '70 *
JACOBS, Jane
More babies needed, not fewer; interview, ed. by L. Kent. Vogue 156:86-7 Ag 15 '70
JACOBS, Jay
Architectural blight, and light. Art in Am 58:53+ N '70
Books. See issues of Art in America
Iceman cometh; symptoms of the seventies. il Art in Am 58:62-7 Ja '70
JACOBS, Paul
Israel's early warning system in the Arab world. il N Y Times Mag p23-5+ F 8 '70

about

Super-Jew and super-Arab. U. Avnery. por Life 68:14 Mr 20 '70 *
JACOB'S Pillow dance festival. See Dance festivals
JACOBSEN, Josephine
Arrival; Destinations; The planet; poems. Poetry 117:20-3 O '70
Class; poem. New Repub 162:25 My 16 '70
JACOBSON, Dan
Holy, holy holy. Commentary 50:29-34 Ag '70
Rape of Tamar; story; excerpt from novel. Harper 241:54-70 Ag '70
Surviving word. Commentary 49:92+ Ap '70
JACOBSON, Howard
Buddy barred again. il por Newsweek 75:68 Je 8 '70 *
Buddy vs. the moguls. P. Axthelm. il por Newsweek 75:87-8 Mr 9 '70 *
JACOBSON, Marcus. See Hunt, R. K. jt. auth.
JACOBSON, Martin, and others
Sex pheromones of the southern armyworm moth: isolation, identification, and synthesis. bibliog Science 170:542-4 O 30 '70
JACOBSON, Robert
Berlioz's Les Troyens, Busoni's Doktor Faust, and Hindemith's Cardillac. il pors Sat R 53:44-5 Jl 25 '70
Karajan's Creation. Sat R 53:54 Je 27 '70
Landmark for Rosina Lhevinne. il pors Sat R 53:57-9+ Mr 28 '70
Martha with merits. Sat R 53:51 My 30 '70
Music to my ears. Sat R 53:50 F 21; 35 Ag 1 '70
New light on festival opera. il Sat R 53:80-1 S 12 '70
New means for new music. il Sat R 53:65-6+ Ja 31 '70
Pelléas by Debussy, Maeterlinck, and Boulez. Sat R 53:45 D 26 '70
Rumble of Etna, the lilt of Bellini. il Sat R 53:70+ Mr 14 '70
Spoleto sampler, minus Schippers. il Sat R 53:44 Ag 29 '70
Williams as Thomas. por Sat R 53:74 Ap 25 '70

JACOBY, Susan
Tchaikovsky's Russia: the lingering passion. il por Sat R 53:75-6+ Mr 14 '70
Women in Russia. New Repub 162:16-18 Ap 4 '70

JACQUARD, Jerald
Portrait in steel. il pors Design 71:16-18 Mid-Wint '70 *

JADE plants
Midwinter cheerfulness, the pink-flowering jade plants. il Sunset 144:128-9 Ja '70

JADID, Salah
Golan offensive. Newsweek 75:40-2 F 16 '70 *

JAEGER, Gustav
I cured myself with wool... R. Bugg and H. G. Scott. Todays Health 48:56-7 Je '70 *

JAEGER, Hugo
Private world of Hitler; photographs. Life 68:45-57 Ap 24 '70
about
History preserved in prison and buried for years. R. Graves. por Life 68:3 Ap 24 '70 *

JAEGER, Ken
Case history: Indianapolis helicopter ambulance. il Flying 87:74-7 D '70

JAEGER, Rudolph J. and Rubin, R. J.
Plasticizers from plastic devices: extraction, metabolism, and accumulation by biological systems. bibliog il Science 170:460-2 O 23 '70

JAFFA, Harry V.
Weathermen and Fort Sumter. Nat R 22:1403+ D 29 '70

JAFFA, Israel
Offshore, Greek myth comes alive. L. Barry. il Pop Phot 67:48+ O '70

JAFFE, Dorothea Kahn
Ready, set, go! il Am Ed 6:9-12 Ag '70

JAFFE, Leonard D.
Lunar surface: changes in thirty-one months and micrometeoroid flux. bibliog il Science 170:1092-4 D 4 '70

JAFFE, Robert B.
Hormones during the menstrual cycle; ed. by S. Olds. Redbook 134:12 Mr '70

JAFFE, Stanley R.
We will back film makers with our eyes open il por Life 68:46 F 27 '70

JAFFRY, Jacques
Cooking lesson. See issues of American home

JAGGER, Mick
Mick Jagger and the future of rock. il pors Newsweek 77:44-8 Ja 4 '71 *
People are talking about ... por Vogue 155:168-9 F 1 '70
Transitional sex figures. D. Newman and R. Benton. pors Mlle 71:102 Jl '70 *

JAHN, Ernst A.
Down that Pan American highway. il Travel 133:30-5 Ja; 34-9 F; 44-7+ Mr; 68-70+ Ap '70

JAHR, El
Paper core pottery. R. D. Bonham. il Ceram Mo 18:14-17 My '70 *

JAKARTA, Indonesia
Invisible men: a hard life; driving three-wheeled rickshaws through the streets of Djakarta. B. Krisher. il Newsweek 75:51 My 25 '70

JAKEY fat boy; drama. See Eveling S.

JALBERT, Russell R.
Facts about social security. il por Har Yrs 10:6-10 Jl '70
Medicare's extended facilities. Har Yrs 10:45-6 Mr '70
More money for 25 million. il por Har Yrs 10:49-50 My '70
Twenty million letters a year! il por Har Yrs 10:42-4 Ja '70

JALÉ (native race) See West Irian—Native races

JALÉMO, West Irian
Cannibalistic revenge in Jalé warfare. K. F. Koch. il por Natur Hist 79:40-51 F '70

JAMAICA
Jamaica report. E. J. Kahn, jr. Travel & Camera 33:64-5 Ja '70
See also
Hotels, taverns, etc.—Jamaica

Foreign relations
Overcoming insularity in Jamaica. M. Manley. For Affairs 49:100-10 O '70

Social conditions
Caribbean: this side of paradise. P. Hazard. Nation 210:335-7 Mr 23 '70
Overcoming insularity in Jamaica. M. Manley. For Affairs 49:100-10 O '70

JAMAICA BAY
Environment: journal on Jamaica Bay. A. S. Taormina. il Cons 24:16-20 Ap '70

JAMAICA BAY wildlife refuge. See Wildlife sanctuaries—New York (state)

JAMBRO, Thomas A.
Wax in the art classroom. il Sch Arts 69:26-7 Je '70

JAMES, Carl
Applied institutional linguistics in the classroom. bibliog il Engl J 59:1096-105 N '70

JAMES, Daniel, jr
Chappie James; a new role for an old warrior. C. DuBose. il pors Ebony 25:152-4+ O '70 *
Fourth black general. Negro Hist Bul 33:49 F '70 *

JAMES, Don
Shooting the big surf. il pors Travel & Camera 33:40-5 Ja '70

JAMES, Felix
Establishment of Freedman's village in Arlington, Virginia. bibliog il Negro Hist Bul 33:90-3 Ap '70

JAMES, George S.
Up on the Boundary. il Am For 76:24-7+ N '70

JAMES, Howard
Children in trouble: a national scandal; condensation. il Read Digest 96:257-62+ Je '70
Police enemies or friends? excerpt from Children in trouble. il PTA Mag 64:2-5 Je '70

JAMES, J. C.
Black principal. New Repub 163:17-20 S 26 '70

JAMES, Jeanne S.
Starting a library stamp club. bibliog il por Wilson Lib Bul 44:645-9 F '70

JAMES, Jesse
Jesse James legend. P. Strickler. il pors Life 68:72 Je 12 '70 *

JAMES, Suzanne
(ed) See Kopechne, Mrs. J. Truth about Mary Jo

JAMES, Thomas
Waking up; poem. Poetry 115:248 Ja '70

JAMES, William
Religion and American experience. R. J. Roth. il America 124:43-4 Ja 16 '71 *
William James and the octopus of higher education. J. Lindeman. por Sch & Soc 98:365-7 O '70 *

JAMES S. Gibbes memorial art gallery. See Charleston. S.C.—Galleries and museums

JAMES RIVER plantations. See Plantations

JAMIESON, John
History is fun. Wilson Lib Bul 45:236 N '70

JANÁČEK, Leoš
Jenufa ten years later. H. Weinstock. por Sat R 53:65 Mr 28 '70 *
Makropoulos affair. Criticism
New Yorker 46:199-202 N 14 '70 *
Newsweek 76:96 N 16 '70 *
Sat R 53:28+ N 21 '70 *
Time 96:73 N 16 '70 *

JANECZKO, Paul B. and Skapura, Robert
Poetry is alive and well: a workshop blueprint. Engl J 59:1131-4 N '70

JANER, Arland Frederick Christ-. See Christ-Janer, A. F.

JANES, Ted
Frigid fiesta. il por Outdoor Life 145:40-3+ Ja '70
(ed) See News: the Northeast. See issues of Outdoor life

JANESVILLE, Wis.
New city hall, old site. K. A. Samek. il Am City 85:90+ My '70

JANEWAY, Eliot
A 500 Dow? interview. ed. by G. R. Rosen. Duns 95:10-11+ F '70
about
Profit of gloom. por Bsns W p23 Ja 2 '71 *

JANEWAY, Elizabeth
Happiness and the right to choose; excerpt from Man's world, woman's place. por Atlan 225:118-22+ Mr '70

JANEWAY, Michael
Politics of quackery. Atlan 226:69-73 D '70

JANNSON, Erik
Student vote. New Repub 163:11-12 S 19 '70

JANSEN, Godfrey
(ed) See Khaled, L. This is your new captain speaking

JANSSEN, Peter A.
Education vouchers. Am Ed 6:9-11 D '70

JANUARY sales. See Bargain sales

JAPAN
See also
Aeronautics, Military—Japan
Aerospace industries—Japan
Airlines—Japan
Architecture—Japan
Arts and crafts—Japan
Atomic power—Japan
Automobile industry and trade—Japan
Automobile touring—Japan
Banks and banking—Japan

JAPAN—See also—*Continued*
Baseball—Japan
Birth rate—Japan
Business education—Japan
Business management and organization—Japan
Colleges and universities—Japan
Commodity exchanges—Japan
Conservation of resources—Japan
Consumer protection—Japan
Environmental movement—Japan
Fuji
Gambling—Japan
Hiroshima
Horse racing—Japan
Hotels, taverns, etc.—Japan
Investments, Foreign (by Japan)
Investments, Foreign (in Japan)
Japanese
Kyoto
Libraries—Japan
Miyajima
Museums—Japan
Music—Japan
Nagasaki
Okinawa
Osaka
Photography—Japan
Pollution—Japan
Public officers—Japan
Publishers and publishing—Japan
Railroads—Japan
Recreation—Japan
Research—Japan
Shipping—Japan
Space research—Japan
Sports—Japan
Student militants—Japan
Technology—Japan
Television advertising—Japan
Transportation—Japan
United States—Armed forces—Forces in Japan
United States—Commerce—Japan
Wages—Japan
Water pollution—Japan
Women—Japan
World war, 1939-1945—Japan
Zoology—Japan

Commerce

Dumping: an old ban imposed anew. il Newsweek 76:73 O 5 '70
Free trade. M. Friedman. Newsweek 76:71 Ag 17 '70
Growing battle of trade barriers. il Newsweek 75:80+ Mr 23 '70
How the Japanese mount that export blitz. L. Kraar. il Fortune 82:126-31+ S '70
Japan, salesman to the world. il Newsweek 75:64-8 Mr 9 '70
Pacific basin. il Forbes 106:28-31+ N 1 '70
Protectionist push; U.S. talks collapse. Newsweek 76:66-7 Jl 6 '70
See also
Japan—Industries

Defenses

U.S. steps up troop cuts in Far East. il U S News 70:55 Ja 4 '71

Description and travel

All's fair in Japan. M. Gough. il Harp Baz 103:60+ F '70
Invitation to Japan. B. Rudofsky. il Harp Baz 103:194-5+ Mr '70
Kansai: Japan's historic heartland. T. J. Abercrombie. il Nat Geog 137:295-339 Mr '70
They said I was crazy to drive in Japan. R. P. Crossley. il Pop Mech 134:126-9+ O '70

Diplomatic and consular service

Noble Bolshevik; Tokyo's unofficial ambassador in Peking. por Newsweek 76:48 S 7 '70

Economic conditions

Economic growth of Japan. J. C. Abegglen. il Sci Am 222:31-7 bibliog(p 146) Mr '70
Fraying miracle. Newsweek 76:80-1 N 9 '70
How the Japanese got so rich so fast. J. K. Jessup. il Life 68:44-6 Mr 27 '70
Japan, salesman to the world. il Newsweek 75:64-8 Mr 9 '70
Japanese culture and the business boom. H. F. Van Zandt. For Affairs 48:344-57 Ja '70
Japan's drive to outstrip U.S. il U S News 68:26-8 Ap 6 '70
Japan's remarkable industrial machine. il Bsns W p59-65+ Mr 7 '70
Toward the Japanese century. il Time 95: 20+ Mr 2 '70
See also
Japan—Industries

Economic policy

Emerging Japanese superstate, by H. Kahn. Review
    Bsns W p 10-11 D 5 '70. J. Pearson
    Nat R 22:1216+ N 17 '70. D. Brudnoy
Looking ahead in Asia; interview. S. Okita. il por Forbes 106:35 N 1 '70

Economic relations

New devil figure. Newsweek 75:58+Ap 20 '70

Foreign opinion
Asian

New invasion of greater east Asia. Time 95: 26 Mr 2 '70

Foreign relations

Japan, all Asia watches and wonders. C. T. Rowan. Read Digest 97:103-7 Ag '70
Japan's future on expo-sition. R. Halloran. Commonweal 92:109-10 Ap 17 '70
Reports: Japan. M. H. Halperin. Atlan 225: 14+ Ap '70
See also
Japan—Diplomatic and consular service

China (People's Republic)

See China (People's Republic)—Foreign relations—Japan

United States

See United States—Foreign relations—Japan

History

Rising Sun. D. Brudnoy. Nat R 22:1118-20 O 20 '70
See also
Russo-Japanese war, 1904-1905

Allied occupation, 1945-1952

Twenty-five years ago: how Japan won the war. F. Bowers. il pors N Y Times Mag p5-7+ Ag 30 '70; Discussion. p 136-7 S 13 '70

Industries

Here comes Hitachi, hot for foreign sales. il Bsns W p72-4 Ag 1 '70
Japan: now the imitator shows the way. il Bsns W p88-9+ My 16 '70
Japan, salesman to the world. il Newsweek 75:64-8 Mr 9 '70
Japan's remarkable industrial machine. il Bsns W p59-65+ Mr 7 '70
Wage boom busts Japan's small business. il Bsns W p44 Ag 22 '70
See also
Aerospace industries—Japan
Airplane industry and trade—Japan
Automobile industry and trade—Japan
Computer industry—Japan
Electronic apparatus industry and trade—Japan
Helicopter industry and trade—Japan
Japan—Commerce
Japan—Economic conditions
Milk industry and trade
Office equipment industry—Japan
Petroleum industry and trade—Japan
Photographic apparatus industry and trade
Steel industry and trade—Japan
Television apparatus industry and trade

Military policy

Reports: Japan. M. H. Halperin. Atlan 225: 14+ Ap '70

Nationalism

Japan's future on expo-sition. R. Halloran. Commonweal 92:109-10 Ap 17 '70

Photographs

Henri Cartier-Bresson's Japan. H. Cartier-Bresson. il Travel & Camera 33:36-43 Mr '70

Politics and government

How stable is Japan? G. Niemeyer. Nat R 22:1349-50 D 15 '70
See also
Japan—Nationalism

Popular culture

Japanese culture and the business boom. H F. Van Zandt. For Affairs 48:344-57 Ja '70

Population

See also
Birth rate—Japan

Protests, demonstrations, etc.

Era of friction? demonstrations against the U.S.-Japan security treaty. il Newsweek 76:41-2 Jl 6 '70

JAPAN—*Continued*

Religious institutions and affairs
See also
Soka Gakkai (sect)

Social conditions
Toward the Japanese century. il Time 95: 20+ Mr 2 '70

Social life and customs
Airborne ablutions; Japan's hot-bath cable-car system. il Newsweek 76:79 Jl 6 '70
Going to the fair? How to understand the Japanese. D. L. Osborn. il N Y Times Mag p22-3+ F 22 '70
It's polite to slurp in Japan. B. Rich. il Seventeen 29:30 Mr '70
See also
Geishas

Treaties
United States
See United States—Treaties—Japan
JAPAN air lines. See Airlines—Japan
JAPAN and the United States
How to negotiate in Japan. H. F. Van Zandt. bibliog il Harvard Bsns R 48:45-56 N '70
See also
Hiroshima maidens
JAPAN current. See Ocean currents
JAPAN-United States air agreement. See Aviation—International aspects
JAPAN-United States cooperative medical science committee. See Medical research—International cooperation
JAPAN-United States cooperative science program. See Science—International aspects
JAPANESE
Going to the fair? How to understand the Japanese. D. L. Osborn. il N Y Times Mag p22-3+ F 22 '70
How to negotiate in Japan. H. F. Van Zandt. bibliog f il Harvard Bsns R 48:45-56 N '70
Karsh's Japanese studies; with photographs. M. R. Weiss. Sat R 53:16-18 My 9 '70
JAPANESE architects. See Architects
JAPANESE art. See Art, Japanese
JAPANESE artificial satellites. See Artificial satellites, Japanese
JAPANESE baseball. See Baseball—Japan
JAPANESE baths. See Baths
JAPANESE businessmen. See Businessmen
JAPANESE-Chinese war, 1931-1932. See Chinese-Japanese war, 1931-1932
JAPANESE-Chinese war, 1937-1945. See Chinese-Japanese war, 1937-1945
JAPANESE cookery. See Cookery, Japanese
JAPANESE dolls. See Dolls
JAPANESE folk art. See Folk art
JAPANESE gardens. See Gardens, Japanese
JAPANESE in New York. See Japanese in the United States
JAPANESE in the United States
Nice place to make money: Japanese in New York. il Newsweek 75:67 Mr 9 '70
Tokyo kid brothers: performers in Golden bat, rock revue at the Sheridan square playhouse. New Yorker 46:34-6 S 12 '70
JAPANESE librarians. See Librarians
JAPANESE long-tailed fowls
Scientist studies Japan's fantastic long-tailed fowl. F. X. Ogasawara. il Nat Geog 138: 844-55 D '70
JAPANESE moving pictures. See Moving pictures—Japan
JAPANESE paper folding. See Origami
JAPANESE poetry

Translation into English
Heavenly suicide by hanging; Third patient; Shining hand; Autumn cricket; Small town geisha; Water rite; tr. by G. Wilson. H. Sakutarō. Yale R 59:391-5 Mr '70
Poems by Japanese children; excerpts from There are two lives; ed. by R. Lewis and tr. by H. Kimura. Mlle 72:166-7 N '70
Spray of hot air; Canna; Sun through the leaves; Ice; tr. by L. Stryk and T. Ikemoto. S. Takahashi. Poetry 116:364-7 Ag '70
Zoo; Shadow of my former self; Hagitei inn; Early summer; tr. by G. Wilson. H. Sakutaro. Poetry 116:370-3 Ag '70
JAPANESE pottery. See Pottery, Japanese
JAPANESE quails. See Quails
JAPANESE students
See also
Student militants—Japan
JAPANESE toys. See Toys

JAPONICAS. See Camellias
JAQUES, Jack
Build IC guitar reverb. il Radio-Electr 41: 44-5 F '70
JAQUITH, Lorraine
People, people, people. il Har Yrs 10:32-3+ My '70
JARDEN, David
Water all white. il por Outdoor Life 145:45-7+ Mr '70
JARES, Joe
Baker's dream needs dough. il Sports Illus 33:18-21 S 7 '70
Barnburner in the old barn. il Sports Illus 33:24-5 D 21 '70
College basketball. Sports Illus 32:47-8 Mr 9 '70
Frisbee. il Sports Illus 33:48-9 Ag 3 '70
One-night season. il Sports Illus 33:8-11 Ag 10 '70
Rise of the bossy Ivies. il Sports Illus 32:16-17 F 16 '70
Spiking's the punch at UCLA. il Sports Illus 32:24-5 My 4 '70
Time for the mighty scramble. il Sports Illus 32:22-7 Mr 16 '70
Victory by mystique. il Sports Illus 32:16-19 Mr 30 '70
Water skiing. il Sports Illus 33:48-9 Jl 20 '70
Week; college basketball. Sports Illus 33:56+ D 14 '70; 34:46+ Ja 4 '71
Wrestling. il Sports Illus 32:60-1 Ap 27 '70
JARGON
Murder of English; adaptation of address. W. Carroll. Ed Digest 36:29-31 O '70
See also
English language—Terms and phrases
Slang
JARMAN, Douglas
Some rhythmic and metric techniques in Alban Berg's Lulu. bibliog f il Mus Q 56: 349-66 Jl '70
JARMAN, Walton Maxey
Wing and a prayer; Tennessee gubernatorial candidates. por Bsns W p96 Mr 14 '70 *
JARRELL, Alex
Jarrell's junior stockers. J. Dianna. il Hot Rod 23:78-80 Ja '70
JARRETT, Robert M. and Edmunds, L. N. Jr
Persisting circadian rhythm of cell division in a photosynthetic mutant of euglena. bibliog il Science 167:1730-3 Mr 27 '70
JARRING, Gunnar
Diplomat Gunnar Jarring, the man in the middle. il por Newsweek 76:20 Ag 17 '70 *
Discreet messenger to the Middle East. por Time 96:16 Ag 17 '70 *
Talking about the talks. il por Time 97: 25-7 Ja 18 '71 *
JARROLD, Ernest J.
Solid-state locked oscillator FM limited/detector. il Electr World 84:62-4 Jl '70
JASPER park lodge. See Hotels, taverns, etc. —Canada
JASTROW, Robert
Space odyssey of tomorrow: a trip to Mars. il N Y Times Mag p30-1+ My 10 '70
JAUNDICE
Substrate-induced conjugation of bilirubin in genetically deficient newborn rats. M. M. Thaler. bibliog il Science 170:555-6 O 30 '70
Transfer of bilirubin uridine diphosphate-glucuronyltransferase to enzyme-deficient rats. H. E. Rugstad and others. bibliog il Science 170:553-5 O 30 '70
JAVA
Art and monuments of Java. H. Daifuku. il UNESCO Courier 23:22-7 Jl '70
Java: lush and troubled island. il Life 68:46-57 Je 26 '70

Antiquities
See also
Borobudur
JAVELIN, Muriel C.
Services to the senior citizen. il Am Lib 1: 133-7 F '70
JAVELINA hunting. See Peccary hunting
JAVITS, Jacob Koppel
Congressional presence in foreign relations. For Affairs 48:221-34 Ja '70
Excerpt from address, July 30, 1969. Cong Digest 49:84+ Mr '70
Excerpt from debate, February 17, 1970. Cong Digest 49:112+ Ap '70
Second development decade: international strategy; statement. October 16, 1970. Dept State Bul 63:607-12 N 16 '70

about
Senator Javits reflects. Nation 211:677 D 28 '70 *

JAWORSKI, Leon
How to stop rise in crime; interview. il por U S News 69:40-3 Jl 20 '70

JAWS
Surgery
See Oral surgery
JAWS (animals)
Dentary-squamosal joint and the origin of
mammals. H. R. Barghusen and J. A. Hop-
son. bibliog il Science 168:573-5 My 1 '70
JAXON, Valerie
House just for you. il Har Yrs 10:14-16
Ag '70
Phone calls that care. il Har Yrs 10:38-40 My
'70
What did you get in the mail today? Har
Yrs 10:17-18 D '70
JAY, Frank P.
Jack; the story of a pretty good donkey;
condensation. il Read Digest 96:231-4 Mr
'70
JAYS
Something wonderful happened; meeting
friendly and hungry Whiskey jack, or Can-
ada jay. W. Ferguson. Org Gard & Farm
17:78-9 Ja '70
Woodland tattler; Steller's jay. F. Weddle. il
Am For 76:5+ Ap '70
JAYWALKERS. See Pedestrians
JAZZ bands. See Bands (music)
JAZZ festivals. See Music festivals
JAZZ music
Great jazz revival. A. Goldman. il Life 68:10
My 29 '70
Miles of music; M. Davis at the Fillmore
East. H. Saal. il por Newsweek 75:99-100
Mr 23 '70
Our local correspondents; a day with the
Duke. W. Balliett. New Yorker 46:52-5
Je 27 '70
Preservation Hall. G. Cotler. il Holiday 47:
54-5+ My '70
Professor plays jazz. il pors Ebony 25:104-6+
My '70
Southern comfort; New Orleans jazz at New
York's Philharmonic Hall. S. K. Oberbeck.
il Newsweek 76:86 Jl 20 '70
Soul; the black man and his music. A. G.
Mims. bibliog il Negro Hist Bul 33:141-6
O '70
Teenagers aren't as liberal about music as
they think they are; interview. ed. by P.
M. Jones and R. Hemming. C. Hundley.
il por Sr Schol 95:21 S 29 '69
See also
Blues (songs, etc)
Phonograph records—Jazz music
Rock 'n' roll music (songs, etc)

History
Jazz; New Orleans sound. E. L. Borenstein.
il Travel & Camera 33:32-5+ S '70
JAZZ musicians
Elvin Jones's kinesthetic trip. A. Goldman. il
por Life 68:12 F 6 '70
See also
Armstrong, L.
Evans, B.
Herman, W.
Negro musicians
Williams, T.
JEALOUSY
Confessions of a jealous wife. J. Viorst. il
Redbook 134:92-3+ Mr '70; Same abr. Read
Digest 96:137-40 Je '70
See also
Envy
JEANMAIRE, Zizi
Old-fashioned insouciance. il por Time 96:62
Jl 13 '70
JEANNE, Robert L.
Chemical defense of brood by a social wasp.
bibliog il Science 168:1465-6 Je 19 '70
JEANNERET, Marsh
Be good editors by being good publishers;
excerpts from address, September 18, 1970.
il Pub W 198:24-6 O 19 '70
JEANS. See Clothing and dress—Sports clothes
JEDLICKA, Daniel A.
Avanti still means forward. il por Esquire
73:116-17+ Ap '70
Drag racing goes legit. Esquire 74:66+ S '70
JEDWAB, Jacques, and others
Search for magnetite in lunar rocks and
fines. bibliog Science 167:618-19 Ja 30 '70
JEEP automobiles
Jeep in wolf's clothing; XJ001. B. Hartford.
il Pop Mech 134:120-1 O '70

Steering gear
See Automobiles—Steering gear
JEFFERS, John M.
How to make a better canoe paddle. il Pop
Sci 197:83+ Ag '70

JEFFERSON, Thomas
Higher patriotism. N. Cousins. Sat R 53:20
Jl 4 '70 *
Jefferson and his aristocracy of talent pro-
posal. C. C. Lammers. Ed Digest 35:45-7
Ja '70
JEFFERSON Airplane. See Rock 'n' roll
groups
JEFFERY, Charles Bartley
Liturgical enamels of Charles Bartley Jeffery.
R. D. Bonham. il por Ceram Mo 18:14-17 D
'70 *
JEFFRIES, William
Today's Cuba and U.S. policy. Chr Cent 87:
560-3 My 6 '70
JEHOVAH'S Witnesses
Watchtower on Brooklyn Heights. il Arch
Forum 132:40-1 Mr '70
JEHU, Margaret
Commitment and consciences in children's
services. por Wilson Lib Bul 45:168 O '70
JEJUNUM. See Intestines
JELLICO, John
Spontaneous drawings of Robert L. Pratt.
il por Am Artist 34:44-9 Ag '70
JELLINEK, George
Vienna in 3/4 time, with Lehár, Stolz, and
Strauss. Sat R 53:46 My 30 '70
(tr) See Kroo, G. Beethoven in retrospect:
Hungary
JELLINEK, Hedy D.
(comp) Guide to European music festivals,
1970. Sat R 53:83-4 Mr 14 '70
(comp) Music festivals USA, summer 1970.
Sat R 53:46-8 Je 13 '70
JELLISON, Bill
Can a nice guy win in Kansas? J. D. Gar-
wood. Nation 211:272-4 S 28 '70 *
JELLY, jam, etc.
And then, there's tomato marmalade; lime
marmalade. J. Hewitt. il N Y Times Mag
p68 S 20 '70
How to make and use a jelly bag. il House
B 112:120 S '70
See also
Canning and preserving
JELLY-rolls. See Cake
JELLYFISH
Deadly sea wasp. J. C. Trinca and P. Schiff.
il pors Sea Front 16:32-40 Ja '70
What is the world's deadliest animal? sea
wasp. G. Compton. il Sci Digest 68:24-8
Ag '70
JENCKS, Charles
Student dorms on a Scottish coast. il Arch
Forum 133:55-6 S '70
JENCKS, Christopher
Education vouchers. New Repub 163:19-21
Jl 4 '70
about
Jencks tuition voucher plan. America 122:
644-5 Je 20 '70 *
JENKINS, Alan
Two hundred French horns. il Hi Fi 20:MA20-
1 S '70
JENKINS, Bill
Secrets of Grumpy Jenkins. A. B. Shuman.
il Motor T 22:32-4+ Je '70 *
JENKINS, Dan
All yours, Billy Boy. il pors Sports Illus 32:
14-19 Ap 20 '70
Another nightmare for the year ahead. Sports
Illus 33:46-8 S 14 '70
Arms against the ogres. il Sports Illus 33:
28-30+ D 21 '70
Australia's cup rematch (thirty-two) under.
il Sports Illus 33:28-9 N 23 '70
Body language, 1970. il Sports Illus 33:20-5
D 14 '70
Can trivia win the U.S. Open? il Sports Illus
32:34-6 Je 15 '70
College football (cont) il Sports Illus 33:46-8
O 5; 51-2 N 2 '70
Eating high on the hogs. il Sports Illus 33:
22-5 S 21 '70
Golf. por Sports Illus 32:70+ Je 8 '70
Grab the gold and say goodby. il por Sports
Illus 32:26-9 F 23 '70
Masters; Bobby Jones started it all. il por
Sports Illus 32:44-6 Ap 6 '70
One that got away again. il por Sports Illus
33:12-15 Ag 24 '70
Revival and revenge. il por Sports Illus 33:
16-19 N 30 '70
Skiing (cont) Sports Illus 32:42+ F 16 '70
Tony's a shark at pasture pool. il por Sports
Illus 32:14-19 Je 29 '70
Two gods too many. il Sports Illus 33:14-17 N
9 '70
Virtue in the valley of sin. il pors Sports
Illus 33:12-15 Jl 20 '70
Where a golf nut is king. il pors Sports Illus
33:32-9 S 28 '70
Woo of Texas is upon you. il Sports Illus
33:18-19 O 19 '70

JENKINS, Farish A. Jr
Limb movements in a monotreme (tachyglossus aculeatus): a cineradiographic analysis. bibliog il Science 168:1473-5 Je 19 '70
JENKINS, Felton
Their community needs them. H. Alpert. il pors Har Yrs 10:43-5+ Je '70 *
JENKINS, Ferguson
Pitcher in the cub-board. H. L. Masin. por Sr Schol 95:26 S 15 '69 *
JENKINS, Henry W.
Monster. il Am City 85:146 S '70
JENKINS, Kenneth D.
Renaissance '70. bibliog f Clear House 44: 338-42 F '70
JENKINS, Paul
Graphics '70. D. H. Karshan. il por Art in Am 58:48-51 Ja '70
JENKINS, Roy Harris
No longer the sick man. il por Time 95:88 Ap 27 '70 *
JENKINS, Speight, Jr
Opera amid the grapes. il por Opera N 34:6-7 Mr 14 '70
Saint Anthony's spring. il Opera N 34:6-11 Ap 11 '70
Star vehicle. Opera N 35:14-15 Jl 19 '70
(ed) See Puleo, R. Twilight of a career
(ed) See Nilsson, B. Nilsson on Wagner
JENKINS, William A.
NCTE council letter. Engl J 59:577-8 Ap '70
NCTE presidential address: dreams and realities; November 27, 1969. bibliog f Engl J 59:349-58 Mr '70
JENKINTOWN, Pa.
Why they ran us out of Jenkintown. M. Moore and T. W. Moore. il pors Look 34:98 O 20 '70
JENKS, John H.
Old digesters don't die. il Am City 85:70-1 Ag '70
JENNINGS, Ernie
Academic approach to the spectacular. P. Putnam. il por Sports Illus 33:60+ O 12 '70 *
JENNINGS, Gary
Adventures of a short story. Writer 83:20-2+ Ja '70
JENNISON associates capital corporation
Jennison's stars. A. Hershman. Duns 97:54 Ja '71
JENNY, Jon A. and others
Developing an unmanned Antarctic geophysical station. bibliog il Space World G-4-76:9-16 Ap '70
JENNY LIND ISLAND
Jenny Lind's Island. G. M. Sutton. il Audubon 72:14-35 S '70
JENSEN, A. H.
Other grains perform as well as corn. il Farm J 94:H18-19 N '70
JENSEN, Albert C.
Fish and power plants. Cons 24:2-5 D '69; 42-3 Ap '70
Thermal pollution in the marine environment. il Cons 25:8-13 O '70
JENSEN, Albert G.
His farm includes a great garden. il pors Org Gard & Farm 17:107-10 O '70
JENSEN, Arthur Robert
Race and the genetics of intelligence: a reply to Lewontin. il Bul Atom Sci 26:17-23 My '70

about

Intelligence and race. W. F. Bodmer and L. L. Cavalli-Sforza. il Sci Am 223:19-29 bibliog(p 144) O '70 *
Jensenism: variation on a racial theme. J. Neary. il pors Life 68:58B-58D+ Je 12 '70 *
Negro intelligence and educational theory. R. A. Lindsey. bibliog f Clear House 45: 67-71 O '70 *
Race and intelligence. R. C. Lewontin. Bul Atom Sci 26:2-8 Mr '70; Discussion. 26:23-5 My; 42-3 S '70
JENSEN, Donald D. See Wasserman, E. A. jt. auth.
JENSEN, Eric
Hard lessons on a far slope. il Field & S 74: 12+ F '70
JENSEN, Johannes E. N.
Sign language of the national park system. il Parks & Rec 5:42-3+ N '70
JENSEN, Pennfield
Student manifesto on the environment; with biographical sketch. Natur Hist 79:4, 20-2 Ap '70
JENSEN, Phil
How to build models like a pro. il Pop Mech 134:164-6 N '70
JENSEN, Robert P.
Fork-mounted telescopes with dual eyepiece positions. il pors Sky & Tel 40:313-17 N '70

JEON, K. W. and others
Reassembly of living cells from dissociated components. bibliog il Science 167:1626-7 Mr 20 '70
JERISON, Harry J.
Brain evolution: new light on old principals. bibliog il Science 170:1224-5 D 11 '70
JERNIGAN, William W.
One who DAIRed: a dial access system. il por Wilson Lib Bul 44:653-7 F '70
JEROME, Judson
Epithalamium; poem. Sat R 53:27 Mr 7 '70
Poetry: how and why. See issues of Writer's digest
JEROME, Ariz.
Ghost town that refused to die. N. Deak. il Todays Health 48:56-9 F '70
JERSEY central railroad. See Central railroad company of New Jersey
JERSIG, Harry
All this and rainbows, too. V. Kraft. il por Sports Illus 32:44+ Mr 2 '70 *
JERUSALEM
Jerusalem: 1970. R. C. Hirschfield. il Cath World 212:134-6 D '70
This winter in Jerusalem. H. Krosney. Nation 210:47-51 Ja 19 '70

Antiquities
Death in Jerusalem. il Time 97:64-5 Ja 18 '71

Description
Holy, holy, holy. D. Jacobson. Commentary 50:29-34 Ag '70
Jerusalem. J. S. Haupert. il Focus 20:9-12 Mr '70

Holy places
Eschatological stirrings: madman at the mosque? fire at al Aksa mosque. Chr Today 14:35 F 27 '70

Population
Emerging realities. il Newsweek 75:48+ Mr 23 '70
JERUSALEM artichokes
Growing Jerusalem artichokes with corn. D. Criner. il Org Gard & Farm 17:90-2 Mr '70
JERVIS INLET
Fjord-hopping by trawler-yacht through Princess Louisa Inlet. B. Crabtree. il Yachting 127:54-5+ Mr '70
JESSUP, John Knox
How the Japanese got so rich so fast. il Life 68:44-6 Mr 27 '70
Yale proves dissent doesn't have to turn out that way. il por Life 68:38-40 My 15 '70
JESTES, Edward C.
Little fiche eat big librarians, one whale of a story. il por Wilson Lib Bul 44:650-2 F '70
JESUIT high schools. See Catholic schools
JESUIT universities. See Catholic colleges and universities
JESUITS
Issues of war and peace; Jesuit educators conference. A. Christiansen. America 122: 302-3 Mr 21 '70
Jesuit artists at work; Holy Cross college, Worcester, Mass. C. J. McNaspy. America 123:131 S 5 '70
Jesuits and the Contract buyers league. R. F. Smith. Chr Cent 87:246+ F 25 '70
Jesuits speak. J. Deedy. Commonweal 92:306 Je 26 '70
Spanish Jesuits rebuff their leader. Chr Cent 87:751 Je 17 '70
Waking up people power. T. M. Gannon and J. R. Hacala. America 123:520-1 D 12 '70

See also
Institute for Jesuit community organizers, Chicago

Education
Jesuit high school. R. A. Schroth. Commonweal 91:472-5 Ja 30 '70
JESUS CHRIST
Christology without Jesusolatry. R. Kysar. Chr Cent 87:1035-8 S 2 '70; Discussion. 87: 1201, 1287 O 7, 28 '70
If God be for us; excerpt from The coming faith. C. Marney. Chr Cent 87:316 Mr 18 '70
In what sense is Christ unique? J. A T Robinson. Chr Cent 87:1409-12 N 25 '70; Discussion. 87:1569; 88:19 D 30 '70, Ja 6 '71
Jesus, by D. Flusser. Review
Chr Cent 87:271 Mr 4 '70. M. H. Elovitz
Commentary 49:77-80 Je '70. C. Raphael
Jesus was a sissy after all. T. K. Hearn. jr. Chr Cent 87:1191-2+ O 7 '70
No disappointment in Jesus? E. Elliot. Chr Today 15:11-12 D 18 '70

JESUS CHRIST—*Continued*
Redeeming Christ, by P. J. Riga. Review
Cath World 212:53 O '70. M. J. Gallagher
See also
Messiah

Art
Face of Christ. R. Strong. il Vogue 155:178-
9+ Ap 1 '70

Birth
See Jesus Christ—Nativity

Childhood
Simeon and the Child Jesus. H. J. Ockenga.
Chr Today 15:4-6 D 18 '70

Crucifixion
Cross, it must be. Chr Today 14:30-1 Mr 13
'70

Divinity
Who is Jesus? V. P. McCorry. America 122:
285 Mr 14 '70 •

Iconography
See Jesus Christ—Art

Kingdom
Triumphant king. V. P. McCorry. America
123:446 N 21 '70

Miracles
Food for the hungry. V. P. McCorry. America 122:255-6 Mr 7 '70

Nativity
Christmas day: December 25. R. E. McNally.
America 123:557 D 26 '70
Great light. . . real light. V. P. McCorry.
America 123:570 D 26 '70
Tall tale of Christmas. Chr Cent 87:1527 D
23 '70

Passion
Passion and resurrection of Jesus Christ,
by P. Benoit. Review
Commonweal 91:598-9 F 27 '70. B. Vaw-
ter
Passion of Christ. V. P. McCorry. America
122:313-14 Mr 21 '70
What was the cup that Jesus had to drink?
H. Summerall, jr. Chr Today 14:9-12 Jl
17 '70

Poetry
See also
Christmas poetry

Priesthood
Christ the priest. V. P. McCorry. America 123:
304 O 17 '70

Resurrection and ascension
Easter light on history. W. S. Reid. Chr
Today 14:8-9 Mr 27 '70
Evolution, revolution, or victory. H. O. J.
Brown. Chr Today 14:4-6 Ap 10 '70
Hope in the midst of horror. R. L. Cleath.
Chr Today 14:3-5 Mr 27 '70 •
Total victory; our Lord's ascension. V. P.
McCorry. America 122:484 My 2 '70
See also
Easter

Teachings
Christ: revolutionary or rebel? B. M. Kel-
ley. Chr Today 14:14 My 22 '70 •
Evangelicals and the black revolution; ex-
cerpts from address. T. Skinner. Chr
Today 14:10-12+ Ap 10 '70
How Jesus taught. N. V. Hope. Chr Today
14:8-9 Ag 21 '70
New discovery in the quest of the historical
Jesus: the primacy of food in the Gospel.
G. H. Clark. il Chr Today 15:12-13 Ja 15 '71

JESUS CHRIST in literature
Israel's interest in Jesus. America 123:392 N
14 '70
Jesus in Israeli literature. P. E. Lapide. Chr
Cent 87:1248-53 O 21 '70

JESUS freaks. See Hippies—Religion

JET air travel. See Air travel

JET airplane engines
Engines are main Pan Am 747 problem. W. S.
Hieronymus. il Aviation W 93:44+ Ag 10
'70
Germans face increasing M45H costs; Rolls-
Royce/Snecma engine for the VFW 614. E.
H. Kolcum. Aviation W 93:18 Ag 17 '70
U.S. efforts pace engine advance. M. L.
Yaffee. il Aviation W 92:75+ Je 22 '70
See also
Gas turbines, Aircraft

Exhaust
Concorde intake computerized. Aviation W
93:30 Jl 20 '70

Jet smoke gets the eyeball test. il Bsns W
p46+ D 19 '70
Latest moves on pollution control; new
burners on jets. il U S News 68:5 F 2 '70
SST officials strive to blunt opposition. R. G.
O'Lone. Aviation W 93:16-17 Ag 10 '70
U.S. hands airlines anti-smoke timetable. il
Aviation W 92:33-4 Ja 26 '70

JET airplanes. See Airplanes, Jet

JET propulsion
See also
Jet airplane engines

JET propulsion laboratory
Los Alamos, Livermore, JPL studied. N
Gruchow. Science 169:35 Jl 3 '70
Star is born; Self-testing and repairing com-
puter. Time 96:50 D 7 '70

JETS
Disintegration of charged liquid jets: results
with isopropyl alcohol. A. L. Huebner. il
Science 168:118-19 Ap 3 '70

JETTER, Al
Knife handle that really fits your hand. il
Mech Illus 66:94-5 D '70

JEUNE Afrique (periodical) See Periodicals—
Africa

La JEUNE fille a marier; drama. See Ionesco,
E.

La JEUNE peinture (group) See Painting,
French

JEWEL cases. See Jewelry cases, boxes, etc.

JEWEL companies, inc.
Jewel lets young men make mistakes. il
Bsns W p90-2 Ja 17 '70

JEWELRY
Buying gems and jewelry. G. V. Axon. il
Consumer Bul 53:4+ D '70
Enameled repousse medallions. P. Rothen-
berg. il Ceram Mo 18:24-5 Mr '70
Jewelry making for teens: a new direction;
new metal alloy, called Coolver. M. S. Coo-
ley. il Sch Arts 69:12-13 F '70
Jewelry of Art Smith. il por Craft Horiz 30:
20-3 Ja '70
Jewelry of Michael Grando. E. Case. il Am
Artist 34:38-44+ F '70
$10,000,000 jewels of Elizabeth Taylor & Jac-
queline Onassis. L. Smith. il pors Ladies
Home J 86:64+ D '69
See also
Diamond cutting
Diamonds
Necklaces
Rings

JEWELRY cases, boxes, etc.
Egg carton jewelry boxes. M. Beckton. il
Design 71:40-1 mid-Wint '70

JEWELRY crosses. See Cross and crosses

JEWELRY making
Cast jewelry; pewter pendants. J. D. Kain. il
Sch Arts 70:16-18 Ja '71

JEWELRY trade
Why the fake diamond market glitters. il
Bsns W p 116-17 F 14 '70

JEWELS. See Gems

JEWETT, Don L. and others
Human auditory evoked potentials: possible
brain stem components detected on the
scalp. bibliog il Science 167:1517-18 Mr
13 '70

JEWISH-Arab relations
American innocent in the Middle East. M.
Frady. il Harper 241:55-8+ O '70 (to be
cont)
Arab Palestine: phoenix or phantom? D.
Peretz. For Affairs 48:322-33 Ja '70
Arab vs. Arab vs. Israel, new 100-year war?
il Sr Schol 95:21 N 17 '69
As the Palestinians see it; symposium. ed.
by A. de Borchgrave and M. J. Kubic. il
Newsweek 75:50+ Ap 27 '70
Beirut conference: Zionist racism? L. H.
Dean. Chr Today 14:46 Je 5 '70
Beleaguered Israel. Chr Today 14:27 Je 5 '70
Between the Rock and the hard place, by P.
Jacobs. Review
Life por 68:14 Mr 20 '70. U. Avnery
Close-up of Mideast under a cease-fire. J.
Wallace. il U S News 69:18-20 Ag 24 '70
Crucial issues in the Mideast. E. R. Chand-
ler. Chr Today 14:14-15 F 27 '70
Decision or drift? Nat R 22:604-5 Je 16
'70; Reply. F. S. Meyer. 22:682 Je 30 '70
Fedayeen: Israel's fanatic foe. D. Reed. il
Read Digest 97:168-73 O '70
Grand conspiracy; interview. ed. by A. de
Borchgrave. King Faisal. por Newsweek
76:43 D 21 '70
Harvest in Palestine. H Krosney. Nation
210:721-4 Je 15 '70
Hopeful voices from Israel: interview. ed.
by F. D. Lueking. Z. Werblowsky; J. Raya.
il Chr Cent 87:139-41 F 4 '70

JEWISH-Arab relations—*Continued*
Hotter and hotter. il Nat R 22:69-70 Ja 27 '70
Israel: criticism from within; symposium, ed. by A. de Borchgrave and M. Elkins. il Newsweek 75:56-8 Ap 20 '70
Israel in siege. C. Amory. Read Digest 96: 147-8+ Ap '70
Israel on a war footing. G. Yalowitz. il U S News 68:37-40 Ja 19 '70
Israel seeks neighbors. H. Krosney. Nation 211:457-60 N 9 '70
Israeli view; no intention of letting up. J. Fromm. il U S News 68:49 Mr 2 '70
Israelis believe war is inevitable. A. Elon. il Life 68:46-48B+ F 6 '70
Israel's early warning system in the Arab world. P. Jacobs. il N Y Times Mag p23-5+ F 8 '70
Israel's incoherent response to an incoherent Arab world. M. Halpern. bibliog Sat R 53: 36+ F 14 '70
Lever on Lebanon. il Time 95:32+ Mr 16 '70
Middle east: a stern test. Chr Today 14:32 Mr 13 '70
New left and the Arab-Israeli conflict. M. Harrington. Cur 118:23-6 My '70
Nuclear weapons over the Middle East? Israel's probable capacity for making and delivering a nuclear bomb. M. Lerner. Cur 121:57-9 S '70
One Palestine; two states? America 122:205 F 28 '70; Reply. D. H. Elazar. 122:399 Ap 18 '70
Palestine: a case of right v. right. il Time 96:28-9 D 21 '70
Palestinians and Israel. S. Avineri. bibliog f Commentary 49:31-44 Je '70; Discussion. 50: 6+ S; 30+ N; 18+ D '70
Palestinians: refugees or a people? M. C. Bassiouni. il Cath World 211:257-62 S '70
Permanent war; symposium. il Trans-Action 7:18-84 Jl '70
Sonic booms and a war of nerves. M. J. Kubic. il Newsweek 75:41 F 9 '70
Terror on the home front. Time 95:27 Mr 9 '70
This winter in Jerusalem. H. Krosney. Nation 210:47-51 Ja 19 '70
Tiger Nasser can't ride; Palestine liberation movement. V. S. Kearney. il America 122: 208-11 F 28 '70
Toward Israel's neutralization. N. Goldmann. Cur 119:53-7 Je '70
TRB from Washington: Middle East head on. New Repub 162:4 Je 27 '70
Undemonizing the Middle East. R. C. Hottelet. Sat R 53:23-5+ Je 6 '70
See also
Israeli-Arab border conflicts, 1949-
Palestinian Arabs
United Nations—Israel

JEWISH cantors. See Cantors, Jewish

JEWISH children in literature
34th man: Jewish culture in children's fiction. L. Daniels. bibliog il por Library J 95: 738-43 F 15 '70

JEWISH childrens literature. See Childrens literature

JEWISH commission on law and public affairs. See National Jewish commission on law and public affairs

JEWISH daily forward
Downtown jews, by R. Sanders. Review
Atlan 225:116-18 F '70. J. Kaplan

JEWISH dancing. See Dancing, Jewish

JEWISH defense league
Lapel diplomacy; Moscow's reaction to anti-Soviet demonstrations by U.S. Jews. Time 97:27 Ja 18 '71
Superjew. R. Bongartz. il Esquire 74:110-11+ Ag '70

JEWISH-gentile marriages.   See Marriages, Mixed

JEWISH historians
See also
Roth, C.

JEWISH literature
Discourses of the rabbis; Yale Judaica series. C. Raphael. Commentary 49:77-80 Ap '70
See also
Booksellers and bookselling—Jewish literature

JEWISH merchants. See Merchants, Jewish

JEWISH philosophy. See Philosophy, Jewish

JEWISH question. See Anti-Semitism

JEWISH refugees. See Refugees, Jewish

JEWISH sects
See also
Hasidism
Sabbathaians

JEWISH theology
Arguments and doctrines, ed. by A. A. Cohen. Review
Commentary 50:103-4+ N '70. M. A. Meyer

Jewish theology faces the 1970's. E. B. Borowitz. bibliog f Ann Am Acad 387:22-9 Ja '70

JEWISH way of life
Anecdotes, facetiae, satire, etc.
Hassidic tales, with a guide to their interpretation by the noted scholar. W. Allen. New Yorker 46:31-2 Je 20 '70

JEWS
Ashes & the gold. H. Wouk. il Ladies Home J 87:68+ O '70
Identity problems plague Israel; Halachic definition of Jewishness. R. Chandler. il Chr Today 14:34 F 27 '70
Legislating Jewishness. Newsweek 75:114 Mr 23 '70
Topless tower of Babylon. M. Himmelfarb. Commentary 50:79-81 D '70
Who is a Jew? il por Time 95:50-1 F 2 '70
Who is a Jew? B. Shalit case. G. Astor. il pors Look 34:32-4 Je 16 '70
Who is a Jew? Israeli high court ruling on nationality. il por Newsweek 75:70 F 2 '70
Who's a Jew? Another round for the Orthodox. Chr Cent 87:165-6 F 11 '70
Will Judaism survive the seventies? M. Saltzman. il Chr Cent 87:263-6 Mr 4 '70
See also
Anti-Semitism
Israel
Zionism

Economic conditions
Class struggle in the Pale, by E. Mendelsohn. Review
Commentary 50:98-100 D '70. I. Howe

Education
Gains in Jewish education in Europe. Sch & Soc 98:341+ O '70

History
This land is His land. D. Foster. Chr Today 14:38-9 My 8 '70
Yishuv and Diaspora: a study of history. S. Cain. Chr Cent 87:668-71 My 27 '70
See also
Moses
World war, 1939-1945—Jews

Law
See Jews—Legal status, laws, etc.

Legal status, laws, etc.
Shalit case. R. Alter. Commentary 50:55-61 Jl '70; Reply with rejoinder. L. Bernstein. 50:15-16 N '70
Who is a Jew? synagogue and state in Israel. M. Zeik. Commonweal 92:114-17 Ap 17 '70

Nationalism
Some reflections on the Jewish-Christian dialogue in the light of the six-day war. M. Vogel. bibliog f Ann Am Acad 387:96-108 Ja '70
See also
Zionism

Persecutions
People Israel lives. E. L. Fackenheim. bibliog f por Chr Cent 87:563-8 My 6 '70; Reply. R. L. Rubenstein. 87:921-3 Jl 29 '70
Unlikely savior; F. Franco saving Jews during World war II. il por Newsweek 75:53 Mr 2 '70

Political and social conditions
Deadly innocence of American Jews. E. Raab. Commentary 50:31-9 D '70
Is there a Jewish vote? A. M. Klebanoff. Commentary 49:43-7 Ja '70
Jewish class conflict? M. Himmelfarb. Commentary 49:37-42 Ja '70
See also
Jews—Economic conditions
Zionism

Religion
See Judaism

Rites and ceremonies
See also
Hanukkah (Feast of lights)

JEWS, Negro
Black migrants to a promised land. il Life 68:65-6+ My 22 '70

JEWS and Catholics. See Catholic church—Relations—Jews

JEWS and Christians. See Christianity and other religions

JEWS and Negroes
Confrontation, by M. Geltman. Review
Nat R 22:900-1 Ag 25 '70. W. Herberg

JEWS and the World war. See World war, 1939–
    1945—Jews
JEWS as executives
    Has bias locked up the room at the top?
        Bsns W p38-9 Ja 24 '70
JEWS in Egypt
    Ismailia childhood; members of the Suez
        Canal company. S. Eban. New Yorker 46:
        174-6+ D 5 '70
JEWS in Europe
    Class struggle in the Pale, by E. Mendelsohn.
        Review
        Commentary 50:98-100 D '70. I. Howe
JEWS in France
    Feelings of ambivalence. Newsweek 75:50+
        Mr 16 '70
    Jews in the mind of France. R. Winegarten.
        Commentary 50:64-8 N '70
JEWS in Germany
    Arson returns to Munich. M. L. Kahn.
        America 122:386-8 Ap 11 '70
    Germans and Jews, by G. Mosse. Review
        Commentary 50:94-6+ O '70. L. D. Wur-
        gaft
JEWS in Haiti
    Land without Jews. H. Gold. Commentary
        51:79-86 Ja '71
JEWS in literature
        See also
    Anti-Semitism in literature
JEWS in New York city. See Jews in the
    United States
JEWS in Palestine
        See also
    Zionism
JEWS in Poland
    European scene; anti-Semitic purging. H. R.
        Lottman. Pub W 197:58 Ja 19 '70; Reply. L.
        Slovinsky. 197:30 F 9 '70
    Guests on a winter night; tr. by I. B. Singer
        and D. Straus. New Yorker 45:31-8 Ja 24
        '70
    Reluctant emigrés. M. Reynolds. New Repub
        162:17-19 Mr 21 '70
JEWS in Russia
    Audacious struggle; Russian anti-Zionist
        drive. il Time 95:24+ Mr 23 '70
    Caught in the crossfire. R. Brackman. il Nat
        R 22:564-5+ Je 2 '70
    In quest of justice, ed. by A. Brumberg. Re-
        view
        Commentary 50:100-5 D '70. M. Friedberg
    Lapel diplomacy; Moscow's reaction to anti-
        Soviet demonstrations by U.S. Jews. Time
        97:27 Ja 18 '71
    Legal brutality and the anguish of separation.
        Chr Cent 88:5 Ja 6 '71
    Leningrad eleven. il Newsweek 77:29 Ja 4 '71
    New serfdom in the U.S.S.R: a visit with the
        Jews of audacity. J. J. Sprayregen. Chr
        Cent 87:1326+ N 4 '70
    Nyet is no answer; anti-Zionist drive. il
        Newsweek 75:48 Mr 23 '70
    On the Jewish question in the Soviet Union.
        B. Tzion. il N Y Times Mag p24-5+ My 3 '70
    Soviet Union: limited leniency; fate of the
        Leningrad eleven. il Time 97:19-20 Ja 11 '71
    Why Jews are target of Soviet crackdown.
        il U S News 70:24 Ja 11 '71
JEWS in the Netherlands
    Destruction of the Dutch Jews, by J. Pres-
        ser. Review
        Commentary 49:77-80 Ja '70; H. Boas.
        Reply with rejoinder. R. M. W. Kemp-
        ner. 50:14-15 Jl '70
JEWS in the United States
    Arming of the Jews; report. L. Levitt. il
        Time 97:15 Ja 11 '71
    Deadly innocence of American Jews. E. Raab.
        Commentary 50:31-9 D '70
    Downtown Jews, by R. Sanders. Review
        Atlan 225:116-18 F '70. J. Kaplan
    Growing up a Jew. A. Gross. Mlle 70:159+
        Mr '70
    Intermarriage & Jewish survival. M. Sklare.
        Commentary 49:51-8 Mr '70; Discussion.
        49:4+ Je '70
    Is there a Jewish foreign policy? Time 95:15
        Mr 16 '70
    Motl Weiss and the golden land. T. Marks.
        il Read Digest 97:178-81 D '70
    Notes from a Jewish diary. N. Perlmutter.
        il Nat R 22:670-4 Je 30 '70
    Out of place in America; excerpts. P. Schrag.
        Sat R 53:12-13+ My 9 '70
JICAMAS. See Cookery—Vegetables
JICARILLA Apaches. See Apache Indians
JIGS
    Build a better miter jig than you can buy.
        F. L. Greenwald. il Pop Sci 197:98-9 D
        '70
    Make this dial-a-jig router attachment. W.
        G. Waggoner. il Pop Mech 134:188-9 O '70

Simple jig holds small parts for soldering.
    H. P. Strand. il Pop Sci 196:105 Je '70
They sharpen drills fast. H. Silken. il Mech
    Illus 66:96-7 Ja '70
Woodworking tools that make you an expert.
    R. J. De Cristoforo. il Pop Sci 197:93-5
    Ag '70
JIGS, Fishing. See Fishing lures, flies, etc.
JIGSAW puzzles. See Puzzles
JIM Walter corporation. See Walter, Jim, cor-
    poration
JITNEY buses. See Motor buses
JOANNY, Pierre, and others
    Hyperbaric oxygen: effects on metabolism
        and ionic movement in cerebral cortex
        slices. bibliog il Science 167:1508-10 Mr
        13 '70
JOB, Brian
    Impatience of Mrs Job. R. Blount, jr. il pors
        Sports Illus 33:24-9 Ag 24 '70 *
JOB, Mary
    Impatience of Mrs Job. R. Blount, jr. il pors
        Sports Illus 33:24-9 Ag 24 '70 *
JOB, Book of. See Bible—Old Testament—Job
JOB analysis
    How to catch a dogcatcher. R. Moskowitz. il
        Am Ed 6:9-12 O '70
JOB banks. See Computers—Employment use
JOB contracts. See Labor contracts
JOB discrimination. See Discrimination in em-
    ployment
JOB interviews. See Employment interviewing
JOB opportunities in business sector. See
    National alliance of businessmen
JOB performance. See Employees—Rating
JOB performance standards. See Performance
    standards
JOB satisfaction
    Blue-collar blues on the assembly line. J.
        Gooding. il Fortune 82:68-71+ Jl '70
    Changing careers: five Americans begin again
        in their middle years. A. Bayer. il Life 68:
        50-7 Je 12 '70
    It pays to wake up the blue-collar worker.
        J. Gooding. il Fortune 82:132-5+ S '70
    Motivating people with meaningful work.
        W. J. Roche and N. L. MacKinnon. bib-
        liog il Harvard Bsns R 48:97-110 My '70
JOB training. See Employees—Training; Voca-
    tional education
JOBS. See Occupations
JOCKEYS
    Three stylish jockeys. il Life 68:60-3 F 6 '70
        See also
    Horse racing
    Shoemaker, W.
JODRELL Bank telescopes. See Radio tele-
    scopes
JOE Weatherly stock car racing museum, Dar-
    lington, S.C. See Automobile museums
JOE White and the seven lizards; drama. See
    Boiko, C.
JOEL, Lydia
    Dance. Vogue 155:34 Mr 15; 76 Je '70
JOEL, Yale
    Crisis in power; photographs. il Life 69:
        26F-35 D 11 '70
JOERDEN, Marga
    What I learned from four top fiction editors.
        Writers Digest 50:24-5 S '70
JOFFREY, Robert
    Capricorn combine. A. Fatt. il pors Dance Mag
        44:32-6 O '70 *
JOFFREY ballet. See City center Joffrey ballet
JOHANNESBURG
                        Negroes
    Kaffir society. Newsweek 76:34+ D 7 '70
JOHANSEN, Gladys
    European congress discusses leisure. il Parks
        & Rec 5:37+ O '70
JOHN II, the Good, king of France
    Duty of the prince is magnificence. M. Bish-
        op. il pors Horizon 12:54-79 Aut '70
JOHN, Elton
    Handstands and fluent fusion. W. Bender.
        il Time 96:60 D 14 '70 *
JOHN B. Stetson company. See Stetson, John
    B, company
JOHN Birch society
    America's other radicals: the far right. P.
        Schrag. il Harper 241:35-46 Ag '70
JOHN Cotton Dana publicity awards
    John Cotton Dana publicity awards. il Wil-
        son Lib Bul 45:30 S '70
JOHN D. Rockefeller Asian collection. See Art
    —Private collections
JOHN Dewey high school. See Schools, Experi-
    mental

JOHN F. Kennedy center for the performing
arts, Washington, D.C.
Deadly decor for the lively arts. W. McQuade.
il Life 69:12 N 20 '70
JOHN F. Kennedy international airport. See
New York (city)—Airports
JOHN F. Kennedy library, Cambridge, Mass.
JFK tapes: how it was. il pors Newsweek 76:
23-4+ Ag 31 '70
JOHN F. Kennedy space center. See United
States—John F. Kennedy space center
JOHN Fitzgerald Kennedy college, Wahoo, Neb.
Whom Wahoo should woo. Chr Cent 87:1139
S 23 '70
JOHN Hancock center, Chicago. See Chicago—
Buildings
JOHN Hancock mutual life insurance com-
pany
Tale of two signatures: new chairman G.
Bleicken. Forbes 105:17 Mr 15 '70
JOHN Jay college of criminal justice. See
New York (city). City university—John Jay
college of criminal justice
JOHN Tracy clinic. See Deaf—Education
JOHN XXIII peace prize
Prize for Mother Teresa. Time 97:56 Ja 4
'71
JOHNBOATS. See Boats and boating
JOHNES, Claude
(comp) Children of Vietnam-II. il Ramp Mag
9:32-5 N '70
JOHNIDES, Theodora
Mr Wizard revisited. il pors Phys Today
23:42-5 Mr '70
JOHNS, Mrs Francis. See Jones, Mrs D. jt.
auth.
JOHNS, Jasper
On looking at what isn't. S. Koch. New Re-
pub 163:31-3 O 10 '70
JOHNSON, Al
You can make it. baby; condensation. J. P.
Blank. il por Read Digest 96:219-23+ Ja
'70
JOHNSON, Alex
Avenging Angel. il por Newsweek 76:74-5 S
7 '70 *
JOHNSON, Art
Ektachrome-X print film? il Mod Phot 34:
84-7+ Je '70
JOHNSON, Arte
Want a walnetto. P. Hudson. por Sr Schol
95:18-19 Ja 12 '70 *
JOHNSON, Charles C. jr
People's protector. por Time 95:62 Mr 16
'70 *
JOHNSON, Charles E. jr, and Zappolo, A. A.
Recent trends in U.S. school enrollment. bib-
liog Sch & Soc 98:116-19 F '70
JOHNSON, Charley
Break for Charley. Sports Illus 33:17 N 23
'70 *
JOHNSON, Claudia Alta (Taylor)
White House diary, excerpt. il pors McCalls
98:57-9+ N; 50-1+ D '70
about
Rare Bird. R. A. Sokolov. il por Newsweek
76:114A-114B+ N 2 '70 *
Recollections of the fishbowl. por Time 96:
18 N 9 '70 *
White House diary, by C. A. T. Johnson.
Review
Life 69:12 N 6 '70. W. F. Buckley, jr *
JOHNSON, D. R. See Becker, K. jt. auth.
JOHNSON, Dave
Day I moved Vancouver. Flying 87:87 O '70
JOHNSON, Dennis Edward
Word and the videotape; address. Chr Today
14:8-11 S 25 '70
JOHNSON, Dolores
Pioneer trip. il Travel & Camera 33:30+ Mr
'70
JOHNSON, Don M.
Stretched texture. il Ceram Mo 18:20-2 F '70
JOHNSON, Donald D.
Trust Territory of the Pacific Islands. Cur
Hist 58:233-9+ Ap '70
JOHNSON, Donald E.
Quarter-century of the GI bill. il Sch & Soc
98:226-8 Ap '70
JOHNSON, Donald R. and Powell, F. X.
Microwave detection of thioformaldehyde.
bibliog il Science 169:679-80 Ag 14 '70
JOHNSON, Elaine L.
Art in Latin America. il Art in Am 58:150-
2 N '70
New developments in Buenos Aires. il Art
in Am 58:150-2 N '70
JOHNSON, Elfriede Nemetz
Working in batik. il Design 71:32-3 Spr '70

JOHNSON, Elizabeth, and Merriweather, Thel-
ma
Blind children learn to relate. il Am Lib 1:
168-9 F '70
JOHNSON, Elle
Benn Howard and Elle Johnson: a dance
partnership; interview, ed. by V. H. Swish-
er. il pors Dance Mag 44:31-3 Ja '70
JOHNSON, Eric Folke
Accuses government of neglecting water
supply. Am City 85:41 N '70 *
JOHNSON, Evert
Clay unfired. il Craft Horiz 30:36-9 O '70
JOHNSON, Franklyn A.
No more Vietnams? address, February 4,
1970. Vital Speeches 36:372-4 Ap 1 '70
JOHNSON, Fridolf
Donald Jackson: calligrapher & illuminator.
il por Am Artist 34:17-23+ My '70
JOHNSON, Gerald W.
Dirksen's ghost. New Repub 162:14-15 Mr 7
'70
Our imaginary vice. Am Scholar 39:387-94
Sum '70
Plowshare at the crossroads. il por Bul Atom
Sci 26:83-91 Je '70
JOHNSON, Gilbert
Not guilty, but... New Repub 163:9-10 Jl
25 '70
Too dangerous to teach. New Repub 163:18-
19 S 5 '70
JOHNSON, Harry A.
Educational needs of economically deprived
children. Ed Digest 35:45-8 Mr '70
JOHNSON, Haynes
Glory road leads to exhaustion. il Todays
Health 48:34-7+ N '70
JOHNSON, Horton A.
Information theory in biology after eighteen
years. bibliog il Science 168:1545-50 Je 26
'70
JOHNSON, Howard Wesley
Come squeeze or bust, in Ho-Jo we trust. J.
Davenport. il por Fortune 81:176-9+ My
'70 *
Time enough. por Newsweek 76:81 S 21 '70 *
JOHNSON, J. Stewart
Of time and taste: European clocks in the
Bliss collection. il Antiques 97:90-5 Ja '70
JOHNSON, James A.
New generation of isolationists. For Affairs
49:136-46 O '70
JOHNSON, Jimmy D. See Miller, R. W. jt.
auth.
JOHNSON, John D.
Needle, ball, and no airspeed. Flying 86:88
Mr '70
JOHNSON, Joseph C. and Sublett, H. L. Jr
Judgmental reading and the study of law.
bibliog Clear House 44:559-61 My '70
JOHNSON, Joseph Esrey
U.N. calls for increased efforts to meet needs
of Palestine refugees in the Near East;
statements, November 25 and December 10,
1969. Dept State Bul 62:46-50 Ja 12 '70
JOHNSON, Joy
(ed) See Newton, H. Huey Newton in prison
JOHNSON, Lady Bird. See Johnson, C. A. T.
JOHNSON, Laura S.
If it's fun, it can't be reading! address, No-
vember, 1969. Engl J 59:387-45 S '70
JOHNSON, Lee Otis
U.S. journal: Houston; thirty year sentence
for giving away one marijuana cigarette.
C. Trillin. New Yorker 46:164+ D 12 '70 *
JOHNSON, Leroy Reginald
Leroy Johnson outslicks Mister Charlie. S.
Lesher. il pors N Y Times Mag p34-6+
N 8 '70 *
JOHNSON, Les
Are Washington's steelhead facing disas-
ter? Field & S 75:46-7+ N '70
JOHNSON, Lyndon Baines
President Nixon honors President Diaz Ordaz
of Mexico at a state dinner in California;
remarks, September 3, 1970. Dept State Bul
63:349-50 S 28 '70
about
After the fall: comments on television inter-
view with W. Cronkite. Nat R 22:19, 189
Ja 13, F 24 '70 *
American notes; L. Johnson-W. Cronkite TV
interviews. D. Halberstam. Harper 240:
124-5 My '70 *
Books. M. Muggeridge. Esquire 73:64B+ Mr
'70 *
Camelot's credibility; Kenneth O'Donnell reveals plans of J. F. Kennedy. K. Crawford.
Newsweek 76:36 Ag 17 '70 *
From LBJ a blast at the war's foes. U S
News 68:18 F 16 '70 *
Johnson seeks vindication. Time 95:20 F 23
'70 *

JOHNSON, Lyndon Baines—about—*Continued*
LBJ and the Kennedys; excerpt. K. O'Don-
nell. il pors Life 69:44-9+ Ag 7 '70 *
LBJ on the assassination. Newsweek 75:41
My 11 '70 *
LBJ on the bombing halt. por Newsweek 75:
22-3 F 16 '70 *
LBJ's account of March, 1968. T. Hoopes.
New Repub 162:17-19 Mr 14 '70 *
Making history on the Pedernales. H. Sidey.
il por Life 68:4 F 20 '70 *
Mellower L.B.J. televised reminiscences of
his White House days. Time 95:32+ My 11
'70 *
Memoirs from the tomb; L. John-
son-W. Cronkite TV interviews. R. Kutt-
ner. Commonweal 91:606-7 Mr 6 '70 *
Memories from the Pedernales. H. Sidey. por
Time 95:16 F 16 '70 *
My brother Lyndon, by S. H. Johnson.
Review
Harper 240:40-4 Ap '70. L. L. King *
No hail, no farewell, by L. Heren, and Pres-
ident steps down, by G. Christian. Reviews
Sat R 53:68-70 O 24 '70. A. Cooper *
President steps down, by G. Christian. Re-
view
Newsweek il por 76:68 Ag 24 '70. K. Craw-
ford *
Return of L.B.J. H. Sidey. il por Life 68:4
Ap 24 '70 *
Sentimental journey. il por Newsweek 75:
42+ Ap 20 '70 *
Twilight of the presidency, by G. E. Reedy.
Review
Nation 210:727-8 Je 15 '70. C. Roberts *
Unpredictable LBJ: seems like old times on
the Pedernales. il por U S News 69:28 S 7
'70 *
TRB from Washington; television interview
with W. Cronkite. New Repub 162:4 F 28
'70 *

Birthplace
Visit to Lyndon Johnson's birthplace. L.
Janos. il Time 96:15 Jl 27 '70
JOHNSON, M. J.
Build this early American bedroom set.
il Pop Mech 134:146-9 Jl; 154-7+ Ag '70
JOHNSON, M. W.
Commissioning a new boat. il Motor B 125:
49-51+ Ap '70
Incident from the Venice race. Motor B 125:
186-7 My '70
Southern circuit. il Motor B 125:66-7+ My '70
JOHNSON, Marcia Lynn
Students protest at Fisk university in the
1920's. bibliog il Negro Hist Bul 33:137-40
O '70
JOHNSON, Moses
Shaker meetinghouses of Moses Johnson. M.
B. Péladeau. il Antiques 98:594-9 O '70 *
JOHNSON, Neil
500/50-kHz frequency standard. il Pop Electr
32:63-4+ My '70
JOHNSON, Nicholas
Public channels & private censors. Nation
210:329-32 Mr 23 '70
What do we do about television? il Sat R
53:14-16+ Jl 11 '70

about
How Commissioner Johnson bugs Ma Bell.
il por Bsns W p63-4 N 14 '70 *
Nicholas the terrible. W. F. Buckley, jr. Nat
R 22:220-1 F 24 '70 *
Regulating the regulator. Newsweek 76:53+ O
26 '70 *
Returning the call. por Newsweek 76:88 N
16 '70 *
JOHNSON, Oakley C.
Negro-Caucasian club: a history. il Negro
Hist Bul 33:35-41 F '70
JOHNSON, Oliver
Poster paints on wrapping paper. il Sch Arts
69:40-1 Ap '70
Transferring designs to clay for relief carv-
ing. il Sch Arts 70:16-18 O '70
JOHNSON, Pamela
Brief biography. S. Goodman. il pors Dance
Mag 44:70-1 Je '70 *
JOHNSON, Paul
Pope Paul VI. por Horizon 12:56-9 Wint '70
JOHNSON, Philip Cortelyou
Duke of Xanadu at home. R. Hughes. il por
Time 96:82-3+ O 26 '70 *
JOHNSON, Pyke, Jr
Student strikes and book sales: the Dart-
mouth experience. Pub W 198:265-6 Ag 31
'70
JOHNSON, Richard A. M. C
Investing: the case for bigness; interview.
por Forbes 105:190+ My 15 '70

JOHNSON, Richard D. and Davis, C. C.
Pyrolysis-hydrogen flame ionization detec-
tion of organic carbon in a lunar sample.
bibliog il Science 167:769-60 Ja 30 '70
JOHNSON, Robert H.
Vietnamization: can it work? For Affairs
48:629-47 Jl '70
JOHNSON, Robert L.
Protestant hangups with the counter-culture.
Chr Cent 87:1318-20 N 4 '70
JOHNSON, Rockne H.
Active submarine volcanism in the Austral
Islands. bibliog il Science 167:977-9 F 13
'70
JOHNSON, Ronald V.
Ordeal of L/Cpl. Johnson. R. Oliver. Nation
211:141-6 Ag 31 '70 *
JOHNSON, Rulon E. See Brandreth, D. A. jt.
auth.
JOHNSON, Sam Houston
LBJ's secret brother meditates on history.
L. L. King. Harper 240:38+ Ap '70 *
JOHNSON, Samuel
Doctor's doctors. H. F. Ellis. New Yorker
46:114-16+ S 19 '70 *
18th century student activist. P. W. Schmidt-
chen. il por Hobbies 75:134-6+ O '70 *
JOHNSON, Sandra, and Powell, Judith
Make your own movie. il Am Lib 1:245-7
Mr '70
JOHNSON, Thomas A.
Black progress in a new South. Read Di-
gest 97:144-7 D '70
JOHNSON, Torrence V. See McCord, T. B. jt.
auth.
JOHNSON, U. Alexis
Asia in the decade of the seventies; address,
February 28, 1970. Dept State Bul 62:381-7
Mr 23 '70; Same. Vital Speeches 36:386-9
Ap 15 '70
Role of Japan and the future of American
relations with the Far East; address, April
10, 1970. Dept State Bul 62:537-42 Ap 27 '70
Role of Japan and the future of American
relations with the Far East; address, April
1970, with questions and answers. Ann Am
Acad 390:63-72 Jl '70
Statement on U.S.-Spain agreement submit-
ted to the Senate; August 6, 1970. Dept
State Bul 63:248-50 Ag 31 '70
Under Secretary Johnson interviewed for
Voice of America; July 17, 1970. Dept State
Bul 63:188-93 Ag 17 '70
JOHNSON, Valerie Miner
Nairobi college; East Palo Alto, Calif. il
Mlle 71:290-1+ Ag '70
JOHNSON, Virginia E.
Sex and marriage. Redbook 135:83-90 S '70
Sex, guilt and the double standard. Redbook
135:67+ O '70
—See Masters, W. H. jt. auth.

about
Human sexual inadequacy. M. Clark. pors
Newsweek 75:90+ My 4 '70 *
Masters & Johnson: their new cures for sex
problems. M. Weber. Ladies Home J 87:51+
Jl '70 *
Repairing the conjugal bed. il pors Time 95:
49-52 My 25 '70 *
Sex and the married couple. P. Wilkes. il
Atlan 226:82-4+ D '70 *
Sexual inadequacy: what can be done. W.
Bradbury. il pors Life 68:42-6 My 1 '70;
Same abr. Read Digest 97:63-6 Ag '70
JOHNSON, Wilfred E.
Energy for tomorrow; address, September 22,
1970. Vital Speeches 37:29-32 O 15 '70
JOHNSON, William
Days of stillness at Wichita state. il Sports
Illus 33:20-1 O 19 '70
Down to the sea in $. il Sports Illus 33:16-
21 Ag 17 '70
Handful of Aces. il por Sports Illus 32:68-
72+ Mr 23 '70
Horse racing. Sports Illus 33:44-5 Ag 31 '70
Icy adventures of a Viking grandson. il
Sports Illus 33:54-63 N 16 '70
Look, ma, no hands. il Sports Illus 33:106-
10+ S 14 '70
Name is the name of the game. il Sports
Illus 32:12-17 Mr 9 '70
Only game in town. il Sports Illus 32:54-6+
F 16 '70
Skiing (cont) Sports Illus 31:72+ D 15 '69;
32:58-9 Mr 23; 33:78-9 N 23 '70
Television and sport (cont) Sports Illus 32:24-
31 Ja 19; 30-6 Ja 26 '70
TV's wild world of sports. il Read Digest 96:
33-4+ Ap '70
U.S.A. up, up and away. il Sports Illus 32:22-
7 Je 8 '70
JOHNSON, William B.
Our top priority; address, June 2, 1970. Vital
Speeches 36:615-19 Ag 1 '70

JOHNSON and Johnson (firm)
Human chemistry at J&J. por Duns 96:30-1 D '70
JOHNSON CITY, Tenn.
Industry's hidden dividends. il Nations Bsns 58:86+ O '70
JOHNSON products company, inc.
Making black beautiful. il Time 96:87-8 D 7 '70
JOHNSON Smith catalogue. See Catalogs, Mail order
JOHNSTON, Edward E.
Trust Territory of the Pacific Islands; statements, June 3 and 11, 1970. Dept State Bul 63:254-9, 269-71 Ag 31 '70
JOHNSTON, George
October; Shadowy; Ongoing; Day that would never come; poems. Poetry 117:3-6 O '70
(tr) See Hoydal, K. White night; Stones
(tr) See Matras, C. Company of the blind; So deep, so deep
JOHNSTON, Jay
Indian Shangri-La of the Grand Canyon. il Nat Geog 137:354-73 Mr '70
JOHNSTON, R. W. See Komatsu, S. R. jt. auth.
JOHNSTON, Velda
Strange welcome; story. Redbook 135:161-83 My '70
JOHNSTON, Verna R.
Ecology of fire; excerpt from Sierra Nevada. il Audubon 72:76-81+ S '70
JOHNSTONE, Archie
(tr) See Rza, R. While yet there is time
JOHNSTONE, Margaret Blair
You're braver than you think. Read Digest 97:177-8 N '70
JOHNSTONE, William C.
United States as a Pacific power. Cur Hist 58:193-5+ Ap '70
JOHNTZ, William
Common language. il por Newsweek 75:57-8 My 4 '70 *
JOHR, Wilma
Gifts straight from Mother Nature. il Org Gard & Farm 17:60-1 Mr '70
JOINER, Charles A.
Political processes in the two Vietnams. bibliog f Cur Hist 59:356-61+ D '70
JOINT adventures
Door to Russia's storehouses opens. il Bsns W p32 O 10 '70
How to get along with local partners. il Bsns W p76-7 D 19 '70
Soviets take a joint venture road west. il Bsns W p73-4 Je 6 '70
JOINT African and Malagasy organization. See African and Malagasy common organization
JOINT chiefs of staff. See United States—Joint chiefs of staff
JOINT commission on mental health of children
Mental health and social action programs for children and youth in international perspective. H. P. David. bibliog Ment Hy 54:503-9 O '70
JOINT committee on library services to labor groups. See American library association and American federation of labor and Congress of industrial organizations—Joint committee on library services to labor groups
JOINT committee on society, development and peace
SODEPAX program: guidelines for peace and Christian action. H. A. Jack. Chr Cent 87: 675-7, 709-10 My 27-Je 3 '70
Sodepax studies world finance. America 124: 32 Ja 16 '71
JOINT committee on the environment (proposed) See United States—Congress—Joint committee on the environment (proposed)
JOINT economic committee. See United States—Congress—Joint economic committee
JOINT ventures. See Joint adventures
JOINTERS (woodworking machinery)
Jointers ain't what it used to be. W. C. Leckey. il Pop Mech 134:197 N '70
New jointer attachment for your unimat. W. E. Burton. il Pop Mech 133:48 My '70
JOINTS
See also
Hip joint
Knee
Sprains
Diseases
See also
Arthritis
JOINTS (carpentry)
Fingerlap joint: symbol of the expert woodworker. R. J. De Cristoforo. il Pop Sci 197: 94-6 O '70

JOINTS (engineering)
See also
Universal joints (mechanics)
JOKE; story. See Singer. I. B.
JOKERS. See Cards
JOKES. See Humor
JOLIVET, André
Intelligent trash of Jolivet and Milhaud. J. Ringo. Am Rec G 37:166-7+ N '70 *
JOLLEY, Harley E.
Cradle of forestry: where tree power started. il Am For 76:16-21 O; 36-9 N; 36-9+ D '70
JOLLEY, Thomas Glenn
Man without a country? Newsweek 75:29 Mr 30 '70 *
JOLLY, Govid R.
Shoestring Caesar. A. A. Butkus. por Duns 96:53-4 Ag '70 *
JOLLY, Iva D.
Wild fruits along country roadsides. il Horticulture 48:32-3 Jl '70
JONAH, Book of. See Bible—Old Testament—Jonah
JONAS, George
Circle narrows; poem. Sat R 53:44 F 14 '70
JONAS, Gerald
Mastering the art of Himalayan cooking. Esquire 73:20+ Je '70
Song. New Yorker 46:42 Ap 25 '70
JONAS, Gilbert
Freedom for the black: a workable coalition; address, November 7, 1970. Vital Speeches 37:105-9 D 1 '70
JONATHAN, Joseph Leabua. See Jonathan. L.
JONATHAN, Leabua
Coup for the chief. P. Webb. por Newsweek 75:47 F 16 '70 *
Death in the hills. por Time 95:35 Ap 20 '70 *
JONATHAN Logan, inc. See Logan, Jonathan. inc.
JONATHAN'S Thanksgiving; drama. See Very, A.
JONCKHEERE, Lucy
They called it philosophical poppycock. il Schol Teach Jr/Sr High p 16-17 N 2 '70
Walking around London. il Schol Teach Sec Teach Sup p6-8 Mr 9 '70
JONES, Anissa
For Buffy and Jody, two very special rooms. R. Fitzgerald. il por House B 112:37-41 D '70 *
JONES, Antony Charles Robert Armstrong-, 1st earl of Snowdon. See Snowdon, A. C. R. A.-J.
JONES, Arthur
(ed) See Young, J. H. How Canada fights inflation: a step beyond tight money
JONES, Barret H.
Fire-police communications. il Am City 85: 91+ Jl '70
JONES, Bobby
Masters; Bobby Jones started it all. D. Jenkins. il por Sports Illus 32:44-6 Ap 6 '70
JONES, Byron E.
How I use the futures market; ed. by R. Sanders. il por Suc Farm 68:33 Ap '70
JONES, Clara S.
Black branch librarian gets top Detroit job. Library J 95:1265 Ap 1 '70 *
Librarians rake LJ for Detroit boner. Library J 95:2411-12 Jl '70 *
Of note. il por Am Lib 1:311 Ap '70 *
JONES, Curtis H.
At last: real computer power for decision makers. bibliog f il Harvard Bsns R 48: 75-89 S '70
JONES, David Cadwalader
Tinderbox; dramatization of a fairy tale by H. C. Andersen. Plays 30:61-5, 75 D '70
JONES, David E. H.
Stability of the bicycle. bibliog il pors Phys Today 23:34-40 Ap '70
about
Unridable bicycle. il Time 95:78 Je 8 '70 *
JONES, David Lloyd-. See Lloyd-Jones, D.
JONES, Mrs Denton, and Johns, Mrs Francis
Puppet world. il Sch Arts 69:18-19 Je '70
JONES, Elinor
Colette, Criticism
Nation 210:636 My 25 70 *
New Repub 162:18 Je 13 '70 *
New Yorker 46:105-6 My 16 '70 *
Newsweek 75:121 My 18 '70 *
JONES, Elvin
Elvin Jones's kinesthetic trip. A. Goldman. il por Life 68:12 F 6 '70
JONES, Enid (Bagnold) lady. See Bagnold, E.
JONES, Esther. See Myers, A. jt. auth.

JONES, Evan William Petley-. See Petley-Jones, E. W.

JONES, Fredy
Firing and hiring of Fredy Jones. R. Scott. New Repub 163:12-15 Jl 25 '70 *

JONES, G. R. See Burbank, R. D. jt. auth.

JONES, Gary E. and Mortimer, R. K.
L-Asparaginase-deficient mutants of yeast. bibliog il Science 167:181-2 Ja 9 '70

JONES, Howard Palfrey
Turnaround in Indonesia. il Read Digest 96:184-6+ Mr '70

JONES, John Paul
Agreable voyage. M. Halliday. il pors Am Heritage 21:8-11+ Je '70 *

JONES, Karl P.
Fall care of roses. il Horticulture 48:22-3+ O '70

JONES, LeRoi
Keys to ourselves. J. Kessler. pors Sat R 53:36+ My 2 '70
Slave ship. Criticism
    Nation 210:125 F 2 '70

JONES, Mike
Car of the year; cars panel. por Motor T 23:63 Ja '71 *

JONES, Miles J.
Toward a theology of the black experience. il Chr Cent 87:1088-91 S 16 '70

JONES, Parnelli
Foyt wins, Jones wins eight annual. A. B. Shuman. il pors Motor T 22:74-8 Mr '70 *

JONES, Phil B.
Machinery management (cont of) What's new. See issues of Successful farming
Truck and car news (cont of) What's new. See issues of Successful farming
(ed) See Clark, A. He makes mechanical feeding work

JONES, Richard L. and others
Chemical inducers of oviposition for the corn earworm, heliothis zea (Boddie) bibliog il Science 168:856-7 My 15 '70

JONES, Robert
Corita Kent's serigraph the wedding feast at Cana; poem. Chr Cent 87:1250 O 21 '70

JONES, Robert A.
Wink at the environment. il Nation 210:493-5 Ap 27 '70

JONES, Robert C.
University supervisor: a student teacher's best friend. bibliog Clear House 44:433-6 Mr '70

JONES, Robert F.
Baseball. Sports Illus 33:40-1 Ag 24 '70
Brother Al's turn in the 500. il por Sports Illus 32:30-2+ Je 8 '70
Growing weary in their aerie. il Sports Illus 33:20-2+ O 5 '70
Hot on the trail of big mama. il Sports Illus 33:22-5 Ag 17 '70
Hunting. Sports Illus 32:46 Ja 19 '70
Indy wheels west, fast and fancy. il Sports Illus 33:30-2 S 21 '70
Mom Unser and the Indy chili caper. il por Sports Illus 32:28-9 My 25 '70
Motor sports (cont) Sports Illus 32:57 Mr 30 '70
No way to treat a mystique. il Sports Illus 32:20-3 F 9 '70
Nobody thinks I can talk. por Sports Illus 33:64-9 S 21 '70
Old man and the river. il pors Sports Illus 33:28-34 Ag 10 '70
Red baron in the wild blue yonder. il por Sports Illus 33:18-21 Jl 13 '70
World's first peace pentathlon. il por Sports Illus 32:50-8+ My 11 '70
Yankee Pete and his reb getaway car. il por Sports Illus 32:16-17 Mr 2 '70
You learn the art of invisibility. il Sports Illus 33:23-5 N 16 '70

JONES, Robert L. See Adams, J. B. jt. auth.

JONES, Ronald D. See Fox, W. jt. auth.

JONES, Sara M.
Magic room. Good H 171:83+ D '70

JONES, Stacy V.
Inventions. See issues of Science digest

JONES, Stuart E.
When in Rome. . . il Nat Geog 137:741-89 Je '70

JONES, Thomas E.
Island images. il Nat Parks & Con Mag 44:11-13 Jl '70
Isle au Haut, Acadia's wildness area. il Nat Parks & Con Mag 44:13-17 Je '70

JONES, Thomas O.
Developing the U.S. Antarctic research program. por Bul Atom Sci 26:81-4 D '70

JONES, Tom
You can build your own spiral stairs. il Pop Mech 133:160-3 Ja '70

JONES, Tom, 1940?-
Ladies' men of music; with report by J. Bonfante. il pors Life 69:46-52+ S 18 '70 *

JONES, Wendell P.
Education of the black man in the U.S; excerpt from Foundations of education; ed. by G. F. Kneller. Sch & Soc 98:467-70 D '70

JONES, Win
Watercolor page; with biographical sketch. il por Am Artist 34:56-7+ N '70

JONES and Laughlin steel corporation
At J&L, the auto strike hurts. il Bsns W p27 O 10 '70
Year that ruined J&L's profits. il Bsns W p 110-12 Je 6 '70

JONG, Erica Mann
Student revolution; poem. Mlle 71:196 Ag '70

JONGEN, Antoinette
Gallery; photographs. il Life 69:4-7 Jl 4 '70

JONSEN, Albert R.
Loyalty and dissent: theology and the university. America 122:676-8 Je 27 '70

JONSSON, John N.
Hegelian dialectic in theology. Chr Today 14:3-5 Ag 21; 14-16+ S 11 '70

JOPLIN, Janis
Blues for Janis. por Time 96:54 O 19 '70 *
Drugs and death in the run down world of rock music. A. Goldman. il pors Life 69:32-3 O 16 '70 *
Of Apollo and Dionysus. Chr Cent 87:1308-9 N 4 '70 *
Singing is better than any dope. H. Saal. il por Newsweek 76:124-5 O 19 '70

JORDAN, Bertrand. See Forget, B. G. jt. auth.

JORDAN, David C.
Argentina's new military government. Cur Hist 58:85-90+ F '70

JORDAN, June
Exercise in quits; poem. Harp Baz 103:156 Ag '70
Mississippi black home: a sweet and bitter bluesong. il N Y Times Mag p 64-5+ O 11 '70
Our eyes have grown; poem. por Library J 95:1558-61 Ap 15 '70

JORDAN, Pat
Sam of 1,000 ways. il por Sports Illus 33:36-40 Ag 17 '70
You can't beat the draft. il Sports Illus 33:50-2+ Jl 27 '70

JORDAN, Robert Paul
Yugoslavia. il Nat Geog 137:589-633 My '70

JORDAN, W. Clarence
What is the Negro doing? poem. Negro Hist Bul 33:25 F '70

JORDAN, Walter H.
Nuclear energy: benefits versus risks. bibliog il por Phys Today 23:32-8 My; 11 S; 11 N '70

JORDAN
See also
Americans in Jordan
Dead Sea
Guerrillas—Jordan
Irbid, Jordan
Irrigation—Jordan

Civil war, 1970
Agony of Amman: it was sheer butchery. A. de Borchgrave. il Newsweek 76:38-9 O 5 '70
Arab vs. Arab in Jordan war. il Sr Schol 97:3-4 O 12 '70
Battle of Amman. J. Stork. Ramp Mag 9:14+ D '70
Civil war explodes in Jordan; with report by L. Jenkins. il Newsweek 76:35-8+ S 28 '70
Conflaguration in Jordan. Chr Cent 87:1146 S 30 '70
Dilemmas in the desert: unilateral military support from the United States. Nat R 22:1034+ O 6 '70
Hussein's costly victory. il por Newsweek 76:35 O 5 '70
In the flaming streets of Amman. E. R. F. Sheehan. il N Y Times Mag p26-7+ S 27 '70
Invasion that failed; Syrian troops in Ramtha battle. B. van Voorst. il Newsweek 76:39+ O 5 '70
Isolation of a king; interview, ed. by J. Bonfante. Hussein. il pors Life 69:50-4 N 20 '70
Jordan: the battle ends; the war begins. il por Time 96:24-7 O 5 '70
Jordan: waiting for the next round. B. Van Voorst. il Newsweek 76:61-2 O 12 '70
Jordan's nine-day war. il Newsweek 76:36-7 O 5 '70
King Hussein's ten-day war. T. Theodoracopulos. Nat R 22:1109 O 20 '70
King vs. commandos: Jordan's week of war; chronology of events. il U S News 69:20 O 5 '70

JORDAN—Civil war, 1970—*Continued*
Mideast: big powers sidestep a showdown. il
U S News 69:19-20 O 5 '70
Mid East: search for stability. il Time 96:
10-11+ O 5 '70
Postscript to terror. il Time 96:30+ O 12
'70
U.S. can breathe easier; interview. J. Law.
U S News 69:21 O 5 '70
War flares in Jordan. il Life 69:34-5 O 2 '70
While Jordan burned. il por Newsweek 76:20-
1 S 28 '70

    War correspondents
Agony of Amman: it was sheer butchery.
A. de Borchgrave. il Newsweek 76:38-9 O 5
'70
Incommunicado in Amman; virutual prisoners at the Intercontinental hotel. R. Flam-
ini. il Time 96:38 O 5 '70

    Defenses
Jordan's Hussein: in search of peace. por
U S News 69:38 D 21 '70

    Foreign relations
Fortunes of Hussein. F. Qassim. Nation 212:
38-9 Ja 11 '71

    United States
See United States—Foreign relations—Jordan

    Industries
Jordan. I. R. Manners. bibliog il Focus 20:1-7
Ap '70

    Israeli occupation, 1967–
Harvest in Palestine; investment in occupied
territories. H. Krosney. Nation 210:721-4 Je
15 '70
Time stands still in an Israeli-occupied town;
Ramallah. J. Feron. il N Y Times Mag p30-
3+ My 17 '70

    Politics and government
Arab guerrillas v. Arab governments. il por
Time 95:22-3 Je 22 '70
Explosion in Jordan. il por Newsweek 75:34-
5 Je 22 '70
How Hussein met commando crisis. J. Law.
por U S News 68:19 Mr 9 '70
Jordan: a nation cracking apart. J. Law. il
U S News 69:20-1 S 28 '70
King under fire. K. Jenkins. il Newsweek
76:51 S 14 '70
Lull in the madness. il Newsweek 75:35 Je 29
'70
Mideast stories; the existence of Israel. J.
Burnham. Nat R 22:1045 O 6 '70
Shoring up a shaky calm. il por Time 95:
24+ Je 29 '70
Talk with Hussein; interview, ed. by M. J.
Kubic and L. Jenkins. Hussein. por News-
week 76:36 Ag 31 '70

    Population
Other Jordanians. il Time 96:40+ O 26 '70

    Relief work
U.S. informs United Nations of emergency
relief to Jordan; letter, October 2, 1970.
C. W. Yost. Dept State Bul 63:478 O 26 '70
JORGENSEN, Earle M. company
When management grows old. il Forbes 105:
26-7 My 1 '70
JOSE Limon dance company. See Dance com-
panies
JOSEPH, James
PM tests. il Pop Mech 133:108-11 Je '70
Sixteenth annual Colorado River cruise. il
Motor B 125:68-71 My '70
(ed) See Lytle, J. To the summit by ATV
JOSEPH, Lou
Dental insurance: a developing success story.
il Todays Health 48:48-9+ Mr '70
JOSEPH, Newton
Great hair hassle. il Todays Health 48:30-3
Mr '70
JOSEPH, Richard
Blue heaven for greenbacks. il Esquire 74:206-
9+ D '70
Fare backward, traveler. il Esquire 74:130-5
S '70
Pleasures of the slow pace. il Esquire 74:
166-7+ O '70
Stacked up over Stornoway. Esquire 73:153+
Mr '70
Taiwan; the country and its art. il Travel
& Camera 33:72-5 Mr '70
Travel notes. See issues of Esquire
JOSEPHS, Devereux C. Jr
Race scoring on the computer. Yachting 127:
232+ Je '70

JOSEPHSON, Brian David
How Josephson discovered his effect; adapta-
tion of address, September 1970. P. W. An-
derson. bibliog il por Phys Today 23:23-5+
N '70
JOSEPHSON effect. See Superconductivity
JOSEPHY, Alvin M. Jr
Boy artist of Red River. il Am Heritage 21:
30-2+ F '70
Here in Nevada a terrible crime. il Am
Heritage 21:93-100 Je '70
Indians in history. il Atlan 225:67-72 Je '70
JOSEY, E. J.
Edward Christopher Williams: librarians's li-
brarian; address, June 24, 1968. bibliog Ne-
gro Hist Bul 33:70-7 Mr '70
(ed) See Mapp, E. Invisible librarian
(ed) See Wedgeworth, R. Overdue
—and Blake, F. M.
Educating the academic librarian. bibliog il
pors Library J 95:125-30 Ja 15 '70
JOSHUA B. Powers, inc. See Powers. Joshua
B. inc.
JOSHUA TREE NATIONAL MONUMENT
From low to high desert in rock-ribbed
Joshua Tree. il Sunset 144:66-73 F '70
JOSIAH Smith house. See Charleston. S. C.
Historic houses, etc.
JOSLIN, Jennifer
Black prince; poem. il Horn Bk 46:324 Je
'70
JOURNALISM
New journalism; panel discussion. L. W.
Robinson and others. il por Writers Digest
50:32-5+ Ja '70
   See also
Editorials
Editors and editing
Foreign correspondents
Freedom of the press
Libel and slander
Magnetic recorders and recording—Journalis-
tic use
News
News letters
Newspaper court reporting
Reporters and reporting
Sports journalism
Women as journalists

    Medicine
See Journalism, Medical

    Research
How I broke the Mylai 4 story. S. M.
Hersh. il por Sat R 53:46-9 Jl 11 '70

    Study and teaching
Can journalism schools improve the press?
J. Tebbel. Sat R 53:63-5 Ja 17 '70
Freelance job idea: teaching high school jour-
nalism. S. Glasco. il Writers Digest 50:28-
30 O '70
High school journalism is dead! Dead! Dead!
replacement by live TV news program-
ming class. E. E. Balazs. Engl J 59:1283-
4 D '70
Recruiting in the inner city; Urban journal-
ism workshops. J. Tebbel. Sat R 53:54-5
Jl 11 '70
    Europe, Western
   See also
Newspapers—Europe, Western

    France
   See also
Newspapers—France

    United States
Honors for giants of U.S. journalism. U S
News 68:43 My 4 '70
Journalist as missionary. J. Hohenberg. il
Sat R 53:76-7 F 14 '70
   See also
Newspapers—United States
Periodicals—United States
JOURNALISM, Medical
Medical writing. J. Ellison. il Writers Di-
gest 50:34-5 N '70
JOURNALISM, Religious
Journalistic jeopardies. J. D. Douglas. Chr
Today 15:48 Ja 1 '71
JOURNALISM as a profession
Black journalism moves ahead. Chr Cent
87:836 Jl 8 '70
Magazine jobs U.S.A. N. A. Comer. Mlle 71:
160+ S '70
JOURNALISTIC ethics
Libel and private college newspapers. J. S.
Corcoran. bibliog Sch & Soc 98:354-6 O '70
Onassis-Gilpatric letters. J. McLaughlin.
America 122:252+ Mr 7 '70

JOURNALISTIC photography. See Photography, Journalistic

JOURNALISTS
Antagonists; journalistic brawl in Catholic press. S. J. Adamo. America 123:332 O 24 '70
Black journalism moves ahead. Chr Cent 87: 836 Jl 8 '70
Decline and fall of the column item. N. Hill. Sat R 53:53-4 Ag 8 '70
If the silent majority could talk, what would it say? views of S. Marshall and S. Evans. T. Ferrell. pors Esquire 73:146-51+ My '70
Journalistic moralizers. I. L. Horowitz and L. Rainwater. Trans-Action 7:5-8 My '70
That Cheshire cat; gossip columnist of the Washington post. S. B. Conroy. il pors Ladies Home J 87:80-1+ Mr '70
Unsatisfied newsmen. Time 96:89 S 21 '70
What ever became of the common scolds? super-gossip columnists. G. Eells. il Look 34:90+ N 3 '70
See also
Foreign correspondents
Lyons, L.
National press club
News photographers
Women as journalists

JOURNALS. See Periodicals

JOVA, Joseph John
OAS asked to consider problem of kidnaping and terrorism; statement, April 15, 1970. Dept State Bul 62:662 My 25 '70
OAS in a period of transition; statement, March 17, 1970. Dept State Bul 62:529-34 Ap 20 '70
OAS permanent council honors twenty-fifth anniversary of the U.N; statement. Dept State Bul 63:637-8 N 16 '70

JOWITT, Deborah
Opinion: on dance. por Mlle 72:58+ N '70

JOY, Donald M
Building children's belief. il Chr Today 14: 29-30 Je 19 '70

JOY
Joie de vivre. B. Bergery. il Vogue 155: 130-3 Ap 1 '70
There is no such thing as something for nothing. R. West. Mlle 72:74-5+ D '70

JOY; musical comedy. See Musical comedies, revues, etc.—Criticisms, plots, etc.

JOYE, Harlon E.
Dixie's new left. il Trans-Action 7:50-6+ S '70

JOYNER, Conrad
Pondering the unthinkable. America 123:256-8 O 10 '70

JOYNER, James A.
Make a pantograph for your router. il Pop Sci 197:104-5 O '70

JÓZSEF, Attila
Glasses; O Europe; On evening clouds; Fine summer evenings; poems, tr. by J. Batki. Poetry 116:281-4 Ag '70

JU, Shu Dick
Watercolor page; with biographical sketch. il por Am Artist 34:50-1+ Ag '70

JUAREZ, Mexico
Juarez hell. J. D. Kirwan. Nat R 22:899 Ag 25 '70

JUDAISM
Jewish theology faces the 1970's. E. B. Borowitz. bibliog f Ann Am Acad 387:22-9 Ja '70
Myth of the Judeo-Christian tradition; excerpts. A. A. Cohen; discussion. Commentary 49:4+ Ja; 14+ Mr '70
Religion of ethical nationhood, by M. M. Kaplan. Review
Sat R 53:36-7 Ag 8 '70. J. W. Burrow
Some reflections on the Jewish-Christian dialogue in the light of the six-day war. M. Vogel. bibliog f Ann Am Acad 387:96-108 Ja '70
Will Judaism survive the seventies? M. Saltzman. il Chr Cent 87:263-6 Mr 4 '70
See also
Church and state in Israel
Jewish theology
Messiah
Philosophy, Jewish
Reform Judaism
Women as rabbis

Study and teaching
Judaic studies in college and seminary classrooms. S. S. Bernards. Chr Cent 87:993-4 Ag 19 '70

JUDAISM and Christianity. See Christianity and other religions

JUDAS Iscariot, apostle
Man who betrayed Christ. E. O. Hauser. il Read Digest 96:214-16+ Ap '70 *

JUDAS tree. See Redbud

JUDAY, Paul
We must eliminate overlapping interests. Farm J 94:H14+ F '70

JUDGES
Considering the alternatives. il Time 95:53 Mr 30 '70
Greening of Halleck. pors Newsweek 76:34+ N 23 '70
What to do when the judge is put up against the wall. L. Nizer. il N Y Times Mag p30-1+ Ap 5 '70; Same abr. with title Order in the court! Read Digest 97:95-9 Jl '70; Discussion. N Y Times Mag p 114-15 My 3 '70
See also
Contempt of court
Judicial corruption
United States—Supreme court

Appointment, qualifications, tenure, etc.
Better way to pick Supreme court justices? Time 95:48 Mr 30 '70
Parting shots: some better qualified Supreme court candidates. il Life 68:67-70 Mr 27 '70
Picking judges in Georgia. New Repub 163: 6 Ag 15 '70
Politics of the bench and the bar, by R. A. Watson and R. G. Downing. Review
Trans-Action 7:60-1 F '70. H. Jacob
Verdict against life terms. Nations Bsns 58: 22 My '70
What makes a good Supreme court justice. E. McCarthy. McCalls 97:34+ Ag '70
Why not four years for both the president and Congress? U S News 68:76 F 2 '70

JUDGING of photographs. See Photography—Criticism

JUDGMENT
See also
Attitude change

JUDGMENT (logic)
If not reason, what? address, December 29, 1969. K. Brewster, jr. Am Scholar 39:243-52 Spr '70

JUDGMENT day
Face the alternative. L. N. Bell. Chr Today 14: 15-16 S 25 '70

JUDICIAL corruption
Haynsworth v. the U.S. Senate (1969) J. L. Steele. il por Fortune 81:90-3+ Mr '70

JUDICIAL procedure. See Procedure (law)

JUDO
Men are full of weak points, these gals know where. K. V. Brown. il Todays Health 48: 64-6 N '70

JUDSON, Horace
Reports: British constitution. Atlan 225:18+ F '70

JUDY, Stephen
Search for structures in the teaching of composition. Engl J 59:213-18+ F '70

JUETTNER, Walter R.
Cruising to the cup. il Motors B 126:44-7+ Jl '70
Marine surveyor. il Motor B 125:60+ F '70

JUILLIARD American opera center. See Lincoln Center for the performing arts, New York—Juilliard school

JUILLIARD school. See Lincoln center for the performing arts—Juilliard school

JUILLIARD string quartet. See String quartets

JULIA and the bazooka; story. See Kavan, A.

JULLIAN, Philippe
Extravagant Casati. il pors Vogue 156:378-81+ S 1 '70

JULY fourth. See Fourth of July

JUMPING
See also
Trampolines

JUNE
Two kinds of June. M. Franz. il Org Gard & Farm 17:76-8 Je '70

JUNG, Carl Gustav
Freud, Jung and the collective unconscious. D. Elkind. il pors N Y Times Mag p23-5+ O 4 '70; Reply. V. E. Brooks. p 111 N 1 '70 *

JUNG, Herbert M.
ITV turns students on. il Todays Ed 59:36-7 Ja '70

JUNGERS, Alfred F.
How to use contractors for snow removal. il Am City 85:79-81 O '70

JUNGKUNTZ, Richard Paul
Moderate removed from Missouri Synod post. Chr Cent 87:230 F 25 '70; Discussion. 87:642 My 20 '70 *

JUNGLE. See Rain forests

JUNIOR college graduates. See College graduates

JUNIOR colleges
Building types study. il Arch Rec 147:143 Je '70
College moves off campus to teach; St Petersburg junior college. il U S News 69:46-7 Ag 17 '70
Community college: review and preview. J. Hughes and B. Reed. il Arch Rec 147:153 Je '70
Growth of Raymond Walters branch college; University of Cincinnati's first off-campus college. il Sch & Soc 98:206-7 Ap '70
New role for community colleges; recommendations of the Carnegie commission. il Sat R 53:54-5 Jl 18 '70
Open the doors; two-year community colleges; proposals of the Carnegie commission. il Newsweek 76:77 Jl 6 '70
Opportunities for community college graduates. Sch & Soc 98:396 N '70
These unknown JCs are tomorrow's BMOCs. P. Carry. Sports Illus 32:40 F 23 '70
Two-year college comes of age. V. Block. il Parents Mag 45:52-4 D '70
   See also
American association of junior colleges
New York (city). City university of New York—Borough of Manhattan community college
Piney Woods country life school
Portland community college, Oregon
Ramapo college, Mahwah, N.J.

   Administration
Administrators for community colleges. Sch & Soc 98:209-10 Ap '70

   Attendance
Enrollment trend in junior colleges; Michigan. Sch & Soc 98:207 Ap '70

   Curriculum
Physics in the open-door college. B. G. Aldridge. il por Phys Today 23:46-51 Mr '70

   Enrollment
See Junior colleges— Attendance

   Teaching
Teaching English in the junior college; findings from a national study. M. F. Shugrue. Ed Digest 36:51-4 O '70
JUNIOR colleges, Catholic. See Catholic junior colleges
JUNIOR high school buildings. See School buildings
JUNIOR high schools
Hey, man, you our principal? L. L. Cunningham. Ed Digest 35:5-8 F '70
Junior high image, how can it be improved? J. B. Hubert. Clear House 44:373-7 F '70
Junior high schools: results of a fourstate survey. A. W. Howard and W. Phillips. il Clear House 45:120-4 O '70

   Curriculum
Change can be dynamic. R. J. Roman. Clear House 44:343-6 F '70
JUNIOR librarians. See Librarians
JUNIOR rodeos. See Rodeos
JUNIOR stamp clubs. See Postage stamps—Collectors and collecting
JUNIPER
One-seed juniper; cherrystone or desert juniper. G. W. Kelly. Horticulture 48:40 Je '70
Patriarchs; bristlecone pine, pinus aristata and the western juniper; photographs. Am For 76:32-3 My '70
JUNK
Don't throw it away! restoring, redecorating, and creating new uses for common discards. W. Harter. il Har Yrs 10:22 Ja '70
JUNK cars. See Automobiles—Wrecking
JUNK prints. See Collage
JUNK sculpture. See Metal sculpture
JUNKER, Howard
See the amazing future, beyond television, of video machines. il Vogue 157:87 Ja 1 '71
JUNKIES. See Narcotic addicts
JUPITER (planet)
Jupiter: his limb darkening and the magnitude of his internal energy source. L. M. Trafton and R. L. Wildey. bibliog il Science 168:1214-15 Je 5 '70
Jupiter's convection and its red spot. R. Smoluchowski. bibliog Science 168:1340-2 Je 12 '70
   See also
Space flight to Jupiter

   Atmosphere
Atmosphere of Jupiter. Owen. bibliog il Science 167:1675-81 Mr 27 '70
Jupiter's clouds: structure and composition. J. S. Lewis and R. G. Prinn. bibliog il Science 169:472-3 Jl 31 '70
JUPITER probe. See Space probes
JURASSIC period. See Paleobotany—Jurassic; Paleontology—Jurassic
JURISDICTION, Territorial
Murder in legal limbo; case of U.S. v. Escamilla. il por Time 96:58 S 28 '70
JURISPRUDENCE
American jurisprudence between the wars: legal realism and the crisis of democratic theory. E. A. Purcell, jr. bibliog f Am Hist R 75:424-46 D '69
   See also
Sociological jurisprudence
JURISPRUDENCE, Medical. See Medical jurisprudence
JURY, William
Every man an astronaut. il Space World G-3-75:32-3 Mr '70
JURY
Bias in the jury box. Time 95:61 Ap 6 '70
First integrated jury impaneled in the United States, May, 1867. il Negro Hist Bul 33:134 O '70
Half a jury is better than none; Supreme court ruling on size of jury. Time 96:42 Jl 6 '70
Justice in New Haven; trial of Lonnie McLucas. il Time 96:70 S 14 '70
Minimizing racism in jury trials, ed. by A. F. Ginger. Review
   Ramp Mag 9:52+ S '70. M. Burnstein
Teachers should serve on juries. N. Justin. Todays Ed 59:12 Ja '70
Voir dire; selecting a jury for the Panther 21 trial. New Yorker 46:38-9 O 10 '70
JUST, Ward S.
Americans in Paris. Atlan 225:20+ Ja '70
Soldiers. Atlan 226:59-98 O; 59-90 N '70
JUST back from the coast; story. See Friedman, B. J.
JUST the two of us; story. See Shyer, M. F.
JUSTESEN, Don R. and others
Pharmacological differentiation of allergic and classically conditioned asthma in the guinea pig. bibliog il Science 170:864-6 N 20 '70
JUSTICE
Explanations and excesses. N. Cousins. Sat R 53:20 O 10 '70
   See also
Congressional conference on justice in America
JUSTICE, Administration of
   See also
Criminal procedure
Judges
Justice and politics
Preventive detention
Punishment

   Alabama
Can a black be acquitted? indictment of R. Holloway. N. C. Chriss. Nation 211:690-1 D 28 '70

   Arkansas
Advocate for underdogs; A. Amsterdam taking cases to Supreme court. por Time 95:67 My 25 '70

   California
Imprisoning the poor. D. G. Shockley. Chr Cent 87:1286 O 28 '70

   Illinois
Best traffic court in the Nation. R. Schiller. Read Digest 96:219-20+ Ap '70
Chicago trial: a loss for all. il Time 95:38-9 F 23 '70
Judgment in Chicago. il por Newsweek 75:22-4 Mr 2 '70
Justice in Chicago: an ominous farce. Life 68:34 F 27 '70
Unfinished business of the Chicago trial. il U S News 68:6-7 Mr 2 '70
Verdict on the Chicago seven: from court to country. il Time 95:8-11 Mr 2 '70

   Indiana
Injustice in Indiana. Chr Cent 87:1552-3 D 30 '70

   Maine
Case of Peol Sussep. F. W. Hatch. il Sat R 53:17 Jl 11 '70

   Mississippi
Freedom of the press, 1970; Jackson underground paper Kudzu. Nation 212:3 Ja 4 '71

JUSTICE, Administration of—*Continued*

Texas

Big stick in big D; protracted sentences in Dallas. Newsweek 76:59 Jl 20 '70

Law'n order in Dallas; case of four black students from the University of California. Nation 211:582 D 7 '70

Love it or leave it; courts reactions to flag abuse. New Repub 163:8-9 Ag 1 '70

United States

Behind the turmoil at Yale; black power and the courts. il U S News 68:41-2 My 11 '70

Criminal justice in times of turbulence; excerpt from Crime in America. R. Clark. Sat R 53:21-4+ S 19 '70

Dissent through the courts. Time 95:65 Ap 27 '70

Interview with Chief Justice Warren E. Burger. W. E. Burger. il pors U S News 69:32-6+ D 14 '70; Discussion. 70:66-9 Ja 11 '71

Is justice at bay? il Sr Schol 97:7-10 D 14 '70

Justice in a torn nation; interview, ed. R. Sherrill. R. Clark. il Nation 211:587-91 D 7 '70

Justice: a bad week for the good guys. il pors Time 96:6-9 Ag 17 '70

Lawlessness and disorder. Nation 210:770-1 Je 29 '70

Minding the store; State of the judiciary message. Newsweek 76:19-21 Ag 24 '70

New man: the compleat soldier. D. Berrigan. il Sat R 53:31-4+ F 14 '70

Orangeburg massacre, by J. Nelson and J. Bass. Review
New Repub 16:26-8 N 21 '70. J. Yardley

Same justice can be both a strict and a loose constructionist. A. Lewis. il N Y Times Mag p30-1+ Mv 24 '70

State of the judiciary. il por Time 96:28 Ag 24 '70

There has been a terrible breakdown in criminal justice; excerpts from interview, February 15, 1970; ed. by J. McCaffrey. E. B. Williams. il por U S News 68:20-1 Mr 16 '70

TRB from Washington: one-eyed justice. New Repub 163:4 O 31 '70

Views of the Chief Justice. W. Burger. por Life 69:26 Ag 7 '70
See also
Bail
Congressional conference on justice in America
Courts—United States
Courts martial and courts of inquiry
Jury
Pleas (criminal procedure)
Sacco-Vanzetti case
Trials—United States
United States—Justice, Department of

JUSTICE, Department of. See United States—Justice, Department of

JUSTICE and politics
Judging the Chicago trial. A. M. Bickel. bibliog f Commentary 51:31-40 Ja '71

Legal issues: justice and politics. Time 95:10-11 Mr 2 '70

White House and free speech. W. Roberts. Sat R 53:26 My 2 '70

JUSTICES, Supreme court. See United States—Supreme court

JUSTIN, Neal
Culture conflict and Mexican-American achievement. bibliog Sch & Soc 98:27-8 Ja '70

Teachers should serve on juries. Todays Ed 59:12 Ja '70

JUVENILE courts
Justice denied. A. Eisenberg and H. Eisenberg. Parents Mag 45:48-51 Ap '70

Overkill at the Silver dollar; Chicanos in Los Angeles. E. H. Lopez. il Nation 211:365-8 O 19 '70

JUVENILE delinquency
Child savers, by A. M. Platt. Review
Trans-Action 7:58-60 N '69. G. M. Sykes

Police enemies or friends? excerpt from Children in trouble. H. James. il PTA Mag 64:2-5 Je '70

Rescue of Donald and Richard; boys saved from an adult prison. W. Hartley and E. Hartley. il Good H 171:12+ Jl '70
See also
Detention homes
Juvenile courts
Narcotics and youth
Reformatories

Prevention

Doctor Hutschnecker's plan. por Newsweek 75:76 Ap 20 '70

It's hard to come back; Liaison teacher program to help delinquent children in Milwaukee schools. M. P. Pfeil. il Am Ed 63:3-6 Je '70

Physician, heal thyself; predicting future criminal careers by testing six-year old children. Time 95:8 Ap 20 '70
See also
Police athletic league

Prevention

New lives for troubled youth; Juvenile behavior council of Shawnee, Okla. E. Gravley. Chr Cent 87:1497-8 D 9 '70

JUVENILE hormone
Insect juvenile hormone activity of selected terpenoid compounds. M. Schwarz and others. bibliog il Science 167:191-2 Ja 9 '70

Peptides with juvenile hormone activity. M. Zaoral and K. Slama. bibliog il Science 170:92-3 O 2 '70

Prevention of metamorphosis by exposure of insect eggs to juvenile hormone analogs. L. M. Riddiford. bibliog il Science 167:287-8 Ja 16 '70

Synthetic juvenile hormone and "synthetic juvenile hormone" C. E. Berkoff. bibliog Science 168:1607 Je 26 '70

JUVENILE literature. See Childrens literature

K

KCS. See Kansas City Southern industries
KGB. See Secret service—Russia
KIST. See Korea institute for science and technology
KKK. See Ku Klux klan
KOA. See Kampgrounds of America, inc.
KPTF (radio station) See Radio stations
KQED-TV. See Television stations, Educational

KABATZNICK, Joel
In the beginning. Engl J 59:956-9 O '70

KADAR, Jan
Czechs in exile. il pors Newsweek 76:70-1 Jl 27 '70 *

KÁDÁR, János
Hungary's quiet revolution. K. Huszar. il por Newsweek 76:32 Ag 3 '70 *
Reports: Hungary. R. Longworth. Atlan 225:22+ My '70 *

KADDAFI, Muammar. See Qaddafi, M.

KADEN, Lewis B.
Youth gets out the voters, but the wrong ones. il pors Newsweek 75:28-9 Je 15 '70 *
—See Kheel, T. W. jt. auth.

KAEL, Pauline
Current cinema. See issues of New Yorker to March 28, 1970; October 3, 1970—
about
Moviegoer. J. Morgenstern. por Newsweek 75:100-1 F 23 '70 *
Perils of Renata, pearls of Pauline. R. Corliss. Nat R 22:369-70 Ap 7 '70 *

KAFKA, Franz
Kafka's A hunger artist: the ego in isolation. P. Neumarkt. bibliog Am Imago 27:109-21 Sum '70 *

KAGAN, Jerome
Attention and psychological change in the young child. bibliog il Science 170:826-32 N 20 '70

KAGAWA, Toyohiko
Religious aspects of cosmic consciousness. pors Chr Cent 87:1533-6 D 23 '70 *

KAGEL, Mauricio
Caper by Mauricio Kagel. O. Daniel. il Sat R 53:68 Ja 31 '70

KAHIN, George McT.
Going nowhere in Paris. New Repub 163:11-12 D 26 '70

KAHL, M. Philip
East Africa's majestic flamingos. il por Nat Geog 137:276-94 F '70

KAHLER, Dean
Fifth victim of Kent state: with account by R. G. Hummerstone. il pors Life 69:42-5 O 16 '70 *

KAHN, Ely Jacques, 1916-
Great gazpacho hunt. Travel & Camera 33:50-2 Ap '70
Jamaica report. Travel & Camera 33:64-5 Ja '70
Letter from Osaka. New Yorker 46:88+ Je 6 '70

KAHN, Ely Jacques—*Continued*
Our footloose correspondents. New Yorker 46:40-2+ Je 20 '70
Profiles: Amnesty international. New Yorker 46:44-6+ Ag 22 '70
Queen of the desert. Travel & Camera 33: 48-9+ N '70

KAHN, Hannah
Notation in time; Without compass; poems. Poetry 116:20-1 Ap '70

KAHN, Herman
Issues of thermonuclear war termination; excerpts from War termination, issues and concepts. bibliog f il Ann Am Acad 392:133-72 N '70

KAHN, Louis Isadore
Architectural metaphysic of Louis Kahn. S. Braudy. il pors N Y Times Mag p72-3+ N 15 '70 *

KAHN, Manya
Stretch is the name of the fitness game. C. Bartel. il Am Home 73:14+ Ap '70 *

KAHN, Marcia L.
Arson returns to Munich. America 122:386-8 Ap 11 '70

KAHN, Roger
How about a new TV deal for baseball? il Life 68:10 Mr 20 '70
Perfect toy. il Esquire 74:172-6 D '70
Sports. Esquire 74:32+ Ag; 58+ S; 34+ O; 78+ N; 14+ D '70

KAIN, Jay D.
Cast jewelry. il Sch Arts 70:16-18 Ja '71

KAIN, Mildred Nelson
Our church gave money away! Good H 171: 199 D '70

KAISER, Henry John
Where are they now? il Newsweek 75:16 Ap 6 '70 *

KAISER, Robert Blair
Rediscovery of Elvis. il pors N Y Times Mag p28-9+ O 11; 111 N 1 '70
RFK must die; excerpts. il Ladies Home J 87:163-70+ My '70
Was Sirhan programmed to kill Robert Kennedy? excerpt from RFK must die. il por Ladies Home J 87:66+ O '70

about

Sirhan B. Sirhan literary negotiations, etc, inc. S. V. Roberts. pors Esquire 74:131-4+ N '70 *

KAISER, Robert G.
In Vietnam, a new optimism. Read Digest 96:87-92 Ja '70

KAISER, Walter H.
On the management and use of paperbacks in libraries; address, 1970. il por Library J 95:2875-83 S 15 '70

KAISER foundation health plan. See Insurance, Health—United States

KAISER resources, ltd. See Kaiser steel corporation

KAISER steel corporation
Kaiser's black gold. T. J. Murray. Duns 96:66-7 Jl '70
Mining coal for hungry steel mills; Kaiser resources complex in British Columbia. il Bsns W p 114+ Je 27 '70

KAKOLEWSKI, Jan W. See Deaux, E. jt. auth.

KALAMAZOO, Mich, public library
Library psychedelics stir Kalamazoo fuss; window at East branch library. il Library J 95:3232 O 1 '70

KALES, David
Refugees of Laos. Nation 210:76-7 Ja 26 '70

KALISPELL, Mont.
Communications for the 70's and beyond. G. Baldwin. Am City 85:132 Mr '70

KALKSTEIN, Shawn
Miracle of the beginning: a child is born. il Good H 172:62-5 Ja '71

KALLGREN, Joyce K.
Third party in Chinese-American relations: the need for change. il Bul Atom Sci 26:11-16 My '70

KALMANOFF, Martin
Composers and poodles. Opera N 34:6 Ap 4 '70

KALOUDIS, Nick
American lawyer takes notes. E. Goodman. Nation 211:363-5 O 19 '70 *

KALS, William S.
Dinghy management; excerpt from Practical boating inland and offshore, power and sail. il Motor B 125:102-3+ Mr '70

KALVEN, Harry, Jr
Chicago howler. New Repub 162:21-3 Mr 7 '70

KAMIYA, Shotaro
Shrine for the victims. Time 96:58 Ag 17 '70 *

KAMM, Henry
Lon Nol reads no newspapers and never uses a telephone. il pors N Y Times Mag p28-9+ D 13 '70

KAMMAN, Madeleine
Frankly fancy. il Farm J 94:84-5 F '70

KAMMERER, Rafael
Forty piano works by Louis Moreau Gottschalk. il por Am Rec G 36:570-1 Ap '70
Great recordings of the century from Seraphim: GROC reissues. il Am Rec G 36:336-8 Ja '70
Rapture for the keyboard collector: International piano library's special Limited editions club series. il Am Rec G 36:950-6+ Ag '70
Viable, vibrantly alive, Scharwenka and Henselt. il Am Rec G 37:84-6 O '70

KAMPGROUNDS of America, inc.
Cashing in on campers. il Time 96:62 Jl 6 '70

KAMU, Okko
Okko Kamu, a conductor to watch. H. Goldsmith. por Hi Fi 20:114 O '70 *

KANAMORI, Hiroo, and others
Elastic wave velocities of lunar samples at high pressures and their geophysical implications. bibliog il Science 167:726-8 Ja 30 '70

KANDEL, Eric R.
Nerve cells and behavior; with biographical sketch. il Sci Am 223:15, 57-67+ bibliog(p 136) Jl '70

KANE, Margaret Brassler
Thirty-year sculpture project. il Am Artist 34:38-43+ Ja '70

KANE, Martin
Boxing (cont) Sports Illus 33:56-7 Ag 22 '70
Shooting. Sports Illus 33:56-7 N 9 '70
Welcome back, Ali! il pors Sports Illus 33:20-3 S 14 '70
World champion nobody knows. il pors Sports Illus 33:36-8+ N 16 '70

KANFER, Julian N. See Kurtz, D. J. jt. auth.

KANFER, Stefan
Meistersinger. Atlan 226:108-10 D '70
—and Elson, J. T.
(comps) New American credo. il Time 96:43 S 28 '70

KANGAROOS
Kangaroos, states and conservation. W. Scholes. il Sci N 97:564 Je 6 '70

KANGAS, Lenni W.
Integrated incentives for fertility control. bibliog il Science 169:1278-83 S 25 '70

KANIN, Garson
Private Kate. il pors McCalls 97:58-65+ F '70

KANNY, Mark
Carlo Maria Giulini, in Chicago, a splendid diversity of excellences. il Am Rec G 37:80-2+ O '70
Late Beethoven and Schoenberg by Erich Leinsdorf: first-rate. Am Rec G 36:488-9 Mr '70
Solid gold in Cleveland. il Am Rec G 36:884-5 Jl '70

KANSAS
See also
Hunting—Kansas
Libraries—Kansas

Politics and government

Can a nice guy win in Kansas? J. D. Garwood. Nation 211:272-4 S 28 '70

KANSAS CITY, Kan.

Police

Kansas City's top cop. L. J. Banks. il pors Ebony 25:35-8+ O '70

KANSAS CITY, Mo.

Police

Mobile exhibit takes the police story to the people. J. R. Perry. il Am City 85:46 Ja '70

Sanitary affairs

Our neighbor the sewer plant. D. R. Youngquist. il Am City 85:104+ My '70

Streets

One crew instead of two. il Am City 85:71 Ja '70

Strikes

In Kansas City they couldn't go as far as they wanted; construction workers strike. il Fortune 82:98-101 O '70
One city's ordeal by strike; building industry. U S News 69:64-5 S 14 '70

Theater

Updating Kansas City; Missouri repertory theatre. H. Hewes. Sat R 53:51 O 3 '70

KANSAS CITY Chiefs (football club) See Football clubs
KANSAS CITY Royals (baseball) See Baseball clubs
KANSAS CITY Southern industries
Test case; Kansas City Southern-Lee national fight. il Forbes 105:50 F 15 '70
KANSAS Smoky Hill trail. See Trails
KANSAS state university, Manhattan
Mr Nixon shows the flag. il pors Newsweek 76:22-3 S 28 '70
Nixon: the pursuit of peace and politics; concerning first Landon lecture of the year. il pors Time 96:6-8 S 28 '70
KANSAS state university of agriculture and applied science, Manhattan
Art in situation. il Craft Horiz 30:42-3 My '70
KANSAS. University, Lawrence
Bleeding Kansas; violence at University of Kansas and Lawrence high school. il Time 95:25 My 4 '70
Burning Kansas. il Newsweek 75:57 My 4 '70
Kansas: police-student violence imperils university. B. Nelson. Science 169:567-9 Ag 7 '70
Where will dedicated anarchists focus attention? interview. E. L. Chalmers, jr. por U S News 69:20-2 S 7 '70
KANTOR, MacKinlay
Hamilton County U.S.A; excerpts. il Life 69:17-27 Jl 4 '70
KANTOR, Sidney, and others
1,3-bis(p-chlorbenzylideneamino)guanidine hydrochloride (robenzidene); new poultry anticoccidial agent. bibliog il Science 168:373-4 Ap 17 '70
KANZER, Mark
Sigmund and Alexander Freud on the Acropolis. bibliog Am Imago 26:324-54 Wint '69
KAPITZA, Peter Leonidovich
Interview with Peter Kapitsa; ed. by G. B. Lubkin. il pors Phys Today 23:63+ Ja '70
about
Strange case of Dr Peter Kapitsa. I. D. Talmadge. por Sr Schol 95:12+ O 13 '69 *
KAPLAN, Abraham
Recordings; Camerata chorale. M. Mayer. Esquire 73:88+ Ap '70 *
(ed) See Friedman, M. Market v. the bureaucrat
KAPLAN, Allan
Poem: I don't know whether I am light or heavy. Poetry 115:227 Ja '70
KAPLAN, Andrew
Israel: libraries in a state of siege. il por Wilson Lib Bul 44:1046-53 Je '70
KAPLAN, Gilbert E.
Investment showman. il por Time 95:82+ F 16 '70 *
KAPLAN, Henry K. See Coogan, D. jt. auth.
KAPLAN, Herbert
Equipment that works on the refuse disposal problems. il Arch Rec 148:133-6 Jl '70
KAPLAN, I. R. and Smith, J. W.
Concentration and isotopic composition of carbon and sulfur in Apollo 11 lunar samples. bibliog il Science 167:541-3 Ja 30 '70
—See Smith, J. W. jt. auth.
KAPLAN, Jim
Baseball. Sports Illus 33:36 Ag 31 '70
KAPLAN, Joel H.
Does our army fight on drugs? ed. by C. S. Wren. Look 34:72+ Je 16 '70
KAPLAN, Johanna
Babysitting; story. Commentary 50:60-6 D '70
Dragon lady; story. il Harper 241:78-83 Jl '70
Sudden luck; story. Redbook 136:84-5 D '70
KAPLAN, John
Prohibition of marijuana. il New Repub 163:11-12 N 21 '70
What legal status for marijuana? Cur 123:44-7 N '70
about
If pot were legal. il por Time 96:41 Jl 20 '70 *
KAPLAN, Judith
In my opinion. por Seventeen 29:270 Ap '70
KAPLAN, M. L. and Kelleher, P. G.
Oxidation of a polymer surface with gas-phase singlet ($^1\Delta_g$) oxygen. bibliog il Science 169:1206-7 S 18 '70
KAPLAN and McLaughlin, architects (firm)
Adventures in architectural services on the frontiers of change; with introd. by W. B. Foxhall. il Arch Rec 147:107-18 Mr '70
KAPLOW, Roy. See Lee, S. C. jt. auth.
KAPP, Joe
Man of machismo; ed. by J. Olsen. il pors Sports Illus 33:26-31 Jl 20; 30-7 Jl 27; 20-5 Ag 3 '70

about
He goes where the trouble is. J. Olsen. il pors Sports Illus 33:22-4+ O 19 '70 *
Price cut for Joe. Newsweek 76:72+ O 12 '70 *
KAPPES, Irwin J.
Transylvania. il Travel 133:54-9 My '70
KAPRAL, Richard L.
Pileated woodpecker. il Cons 25:5+ O '70
KAPSTEIN, Sherwin J.
125 years of service to Rhode Island. Todays Ed 59:69 S '70
KARAJAN, Herbert von
Berlin diary. J. H. Sutcliffe. il pors Opera N 35:8-13 N 21 '70 *
Karajan closes the ring. C. L. Osborne. il Hi Fi 20:77-9 S '70 *
Karajan completes the Ring. P. Moor. il por Sat R 53:63-5 Ap 25 '70 *
Karajan completes the Ring cycle. P. Moor. Hi Fi 20:secI 22 Mr '70 *
Karajan's Creation. R. Jacobson. Sat R 53:54 Je 27 '70 *
KARAS, Nicholas
Ten-second salmon. il Field & S 74:66-7+ F '70
KARATE
Black karate: new concept to ancient art; Dravidian school, Chicago. il pors Ebony 25:104-6+ Je '70
Meet Kung Fu, father of Karate. il Mech Illus 66:64-5 Ap '70
Miss Superfist. D. Gerrity. por Atlan 225:92-3 Mr '70
KARDENER, Sheldon H. and Fuller, Marielle
Violence as a defense against intimacy. bibliog Ment Hy 54:310-15 Ap '70
KARDOS, Louis T.
New prospect. bibliog il Environ 12:10-21+ Mr '70
KARELITZ, Samuel
Pediatrician's guide to colds, grippe, flu; excerpts from When your child is ill. Ladies Home J 87:36+ Ja '70
KARL, Jean
Here and beyond. il por Wilson Lib Bul 45:149-55 O '70
KARLEN, Arno
Amsterdam's a surprising city even for those who don't surprise easily. il Holiday 47:42-3+ Ja '70
KARLINSKY, Simon
Red wedge. Nation 210:121-2 F 2 '70
KARLOWICH, Robert A.
(tr) See Rudomino, M. I. Soviet Union: of 370,000 libraries, 2.5 billion volumes, and a treasure house of foreign literature
KARNES, Merle B.
Slow learner, what are his characteristics and needs? il Todays Ed 59:42-4 Mr '70
KARNOW, Stanley
Orient. il Travel & Camera 33:44-59 Mr '70
KAROL, K. S.
Castro on the contradictions in Cuba; excerpt from Guerrillas in power. il Ramp Mag 9:44-8 D '70
Charisma or democratization? Cur 124:52-5 D '70
KARP, Walter
Designer in the desert. il por Horizon 12:30-9 Aut '70
Omnibuildings. il Horizon 12:48-55 Wint '70
KARPAT, Kemal H.
Military and politics in Turkey, 1960-64: a socio-cultural analysis of a revolution. bibliog f Am Hist R 75:1654-83 O '70
KARPEL, Craig
Das hip Kapital. il Esquire 74:184-8+ D '70
How men feel about abortion. Mlle 71:142-3+ Je '70
KARPEL, William
Face to face with a student seaman. por Seventeen 29:32 Je '70
KARR, John
From maverick country. S. Z. Wintroub. Nation 210:293 Mr 16 '70 *
KARRAS, Alex
Meet Mr Twinkletoes and his friends. G. Plimpton. il por Sports Illus 33:22-4+ O 12 '70 *
KARSH, Eileen B.
Fixation produced by conflict. bibliog il Science 168:873-5 My 15 '70
KARSH, Yousuf
Counter-establishment; photographs. il Look 34:68-73 D 15 '70
Karsh's Japanese studies; with photographs. Sat R 53:16-18 My 9 '70
KARSHAN, Donald H.
Graphics '70. il por Art in Am 58:48-51 Ja; 56-9 Mr; 48-51 My; 31-4 Jl; 48-51 S; 48-51 N '70

KARTER, Madeleine B.
Daddy takes over; with photographs by S. Szasz. Good H 170:112-15 Ap '70
KARTUZ, Michael J.
Unusual colorful holiday plants. il Horticulture 48:26-7 D '70
KARUME, Abeid Amani
Take us from this place. Newsweek 76:62+ O 12 '70 *
KASABIAN, Linda Darlene
Linda's punishment. por Newsweek 76:29+ Ag 31 '70 *
Open letter to Linda Kasabian. R. Chandler. Chr Today 14:21 S 11 '70 *
KASE, Judith B.
Informal theater. il Camp Mag 42:16-17+ Mr '70
KASHA, Bernard
Intrusion alarm for your boat. il Motor B 126:80 D '70
KASHA, Michael
Redesigning the guitar. A. Perlmeter. il por Sci N 98:180-1 Ag 22 '70 *
KASHMIR
   See also
Paleontology—Kashmir
KASPAREK, Robert B.
Park for people. il Nat Parks & Con Mag 44:12-15 Ap '70
KASPER, Hirschel, and Hausman, L. J.
Nixon's Family assistance plan. New Repub 162:8-10 Mr 28 '70
KASSAN, Roberta
Grand right and left; story. Redbook 135:70-2 Ag '70
KASSELL, Germany
Music
Report:
Entführung and Lohengrin. J. H. Sutcliffe. il Opera N 35:32-3 Ja 2 '71
Francis Burt's Volpone. J. H. Sutcliffe. Opera N 4:30-1 F 7 '70
Pop-art Parsifal. J. H. Sutcliffe. il Opera N 34:32 Ap 18 '70
KASTRINOS, William
Survey of the teaching of biology in secondary schools. Sch & Soc 98:241-2 Ap '70
KASUN, Jacqueline R.
Real population explosion. il America 123:112-14 S 5 '70
KATAHDIN, MOUNT
Mt Katahdin, Maine. J. M. Leigh. il Holiday 47:68-9 My '70
KATAOKA, Senji
Scarecrow crusader. il Time 96:50 N 9 '70 *
KATEB, George
Political thought of Herbert Marcuse. bibliog f Commentary 49:48-63 Ja '70
KATELEY, Margaret A.
They also read who roll in dough. il por Wilson Lib Bul 45:477-81 Ja '71
KATHMANDU. See Katmandu, Nepal
KATMANDU, Nepal
Kathmandu: where every man's home is his temple. M. Gough. il House B 112:34+ Ja '70
KATZ, Sir Bernard
How the Nobelists won. il pors Newsweek 76:83 O 26 '70 *
Neurobiology: on the research frontier. pors Sci N 98:331 O 24 '70 *
Nobel prize: three share 1970 award for medical research. A. R. Martin. por Science 170:423-4 O 23 '70 *
KATZ, Bill
(ed) Magazines. See issues of Library journal
KATZ, David H. and others
Radioresistance of cooperative function of carrier-specific lymphocytes in antihapten antibody responses. bibliog il Science 170: 462-4 O 23 '70
KATZ, Joseph
Rearing rads, rebs, & regulars. il PTA Mag 64:8-10 bibliog(p33) Ap '70
KATZ, Leon
Dracula: Sabbat; dramatization of novel by B. Stoker. Criticism
   Newsweek 76:87 O 5 '70 *
KATZ, Lucy V.
Nixon's Family assistance bill. New Repub 163:30-1 Jl 18 '70
KATZ, Marilyn
Self-improvement; poem. Good H 171:10 N '70
KATZ, Phyllis B.
(ed) Family clinic. See issues of Parents' magazine & better family living
KATZEV, Michael L.
Resurrecting the oldest known Greek ship. il Nat Geog 137:840-57 Je '70
KATZ-SUCHY, Juliusz
Topless tower of Babylon. M. Himmelfarb. Commentary 50:79-81 D '70 *

KAUFFMAN, Ewing
To the tune of a hickory (well, ash) stick. W. Leggett. il por Sports Illus 34:50-1 Ja 4 '71 *
KAUFFMAN, Mark
New tintype heroes; photographs. Sports Illus 33:26-35 Jl 6 '70
KAUFFMANN, Stanley
Films. See issues of New republic
Theater. See occasional issues of New republic
KAUFMAN, Fern
Beachcomber; poem. Horn Bk 46:77 F '70
KAUFMAN, George S. and Connelly, Marc
Beggar on horseback. Criticism
   Nation 210:668 Je 1 '70 *
   New Yorker 46:73-4 My 23 '70 *
   Newsweek 75:95 My 25 '70 *
KAUFMAN, Irma. See Rosenthal, A. jt. auth.
KAUFMAN, Leon, and others
Chemically induced porphyria: prevention by prior treatment with phenobarbital. bibliog il Science 170:320-2 O 16 '70
KAUFMAN, Max
Phoenix amateur's 12 ½-inch Schmidt-Cassegrain. il Sky & Tel 39:254-60 Ap '70
KAUFMAN, Richard F.
Our national insecurity. Nation 210:186-8 F 16 '70
Who won the debate? military spending. Nation 210:137-42 F 9 '70
KAUFMAN, Shirley
Getting there; Apples; In touch; poems. Poetry 117:28-32 O '70
KAUFMAN, Sue
New Year's eve syndrome. il N Y Times Mag p 10-12+ D 27 '70
KAUFMAN, Wallace
Song of growing up in Queens, N.Y; poem. Nation 210:443 Ap 13 '70
KAUFMAN and Broad building company
Kaufman & Broad's private housing boom. E. Carruth. il Fortune 82:119 Jl '70
KAUFMANN, Carl
Why we need new businessmen. Look 34: 76+ Ja 13 '70
KAULA, William M.
Earth's gravity field: relation to global tectonics. bibliog il Science 169:982-5 S 4 '70
KAUNDA, Kenneth David
We want investors to come, our policies are nonracial; interview. por U S News 69:55-6 Jl 6 '70
   about
Passage of arms. il por Newsweek 76:50 N 2 '70 *
Tears in Lusaka. Time 96:33-4 S 21 '70 *
KAVAI (island)
Sliding down a waterfall, it's great sport on Kauai. il Sunset 144:54 Mr '70
KAVAN, Anna
Julia and the bazooka; story. Harp Baz 104:98-9 Ja '71
KAVANAU, J. Lee, and Ramos, J.
Roadrunners: activity of captive individuals. bibliog il Science 169:780-2 Ag 21 '70
KAY, Charles G. and Meyer, Daniel
Assemble the Popular electronics digi-vista (title varies) il Pop Electr 33:25-32 D '70; 34:71-4 Ja '71
KAYA, Harry K.
Toxic factor produced by a granulosis virus in armyworm larva: effect on apanteles militaris. bibliog il Science 168:251-3 Ap 10 '70
KAYAK racing
Tippy canoe in a wild rapids stew; photographs. D. Mulkey. il Sports Illus 32:26-33 Je 29 '70
KAYAL, Philip M.
Final solution for college unrest. Commonweal 92:53-4, 206-7 Mr 27, My 8 '70
KAYE, Danny
All wok and no play. S. F. Kaye. il pors Vogue 156: 168:168-9+ D '70 *
People are talking about . . . por Vogue 156:166-7 D '70 *
Spicy side of Danny Kaye. il pors Look 34: 36-8 Mr 10 '70 *
KAYE, Sylvia Fine
All wok and no play. il pors Vogue 156:168-9+ D '70
KAYE, William G.
Take in a new partner, the consumer. il Nations Bsns 58:54-7 F '70
KAYE (radio station) See Radio stations
KAYLOR, Paul Evans
In affirming the celebrative, we are saying yes! Mlle 72:80-1+ D '70
Opinion: the new religion of environment. Mlle 70:38+ Ap '70
Religion in America. Mlle 70:154-5 Mr '70

KAYSEN, Carl
Institute advances. por Newsweek 75:54-5 Ap 6 '70
KAZANTZAKIS, Nikos
Fiction. R. Maurer. Sat R 53:42-3 F 21 '70 *
KAZIN, Alfred
Books. Vogue 156:34 Jl; 100 D '70
Century of American realism; interview. ed. by J. A. Garraty. il Am Heritage 21:12-15+ Je '70
Whatever happened to criticism? Commentary 49:58-63 F '70
KEALY, Hinman L. P. See Pearson, E. R. jt. auth.
KEAN, Jim
Murderers ordered him to take their pictures. R. Graves. pors Life 69:2A Ag 21 '70 *
KEANE, Margaret
Lady behind those Keane-eyed kids. il pors Life 69:57-8 N 20 '70 *
KEANE, Walter Stanley
Lady behind those Keane-eyed kids. il pors Life 69:57-8 N 20 '70 *
KEARNEY, Richard David
U.S. accedes to convention on foreign arbitral awards; statement. September 30, 1970. Dept State Bul 63:598 N 9 '70
KEARNEY, Vincent S.
Of many things. America 123:inside cover Ag 8 '70
Tiger Nasser can't ride. il America 122:208-11 F 28 '70
World scene (cont) America 122:474-6; 123: 461-2+ My 2, N 28 '70
KEARNS, Henry
Ex-im's new boss fuels the trade race. il por Bsns W p48+ Mr 7 '70 *
Salesman runs a bank. il por Nations Bsns 58:77-9 Jl '70 *
KEATING, Charles H. jr
Civil war over smut. J. Witcover. Nation 210: 550-3 My 11 '70 *
Court enjoins publication of obscenity report. Pub W 198:37 S 21 '70 *
Odd man in. por Newsweek 76:44 S 21 '70 *
Porno report cleared for publication; with editorial comment. Pub W 198:58-60, 62 S 28 '70 *
KEATLEY, Robert
Is the Middle East Russia's Vietnam? Cur 121:54-7 S '70
KEATON, Buster
Buster Keaton festival. S. Kauffmann. New Repub 163:24+ O 24 '70 *
Buster Keaton's comic world. P. D. Zimmerman. il pors Newsweek 76:96+ O 5 '70 *
Current cinema. P. Gilliatt. New Yorker 46: 118-23 S 26 '70 *
Great stone face. S. Kanfer. il pors Time 96: 94 N 2 '70 *
KEATS, John
Appraising marijuana. il Holiday 47:52-3+ Ap '70
She's the American traveler's best friend. Read Digest 96:39-40+ F '70
You might as well live: the life and times of Dorothy Parker; excerpt. por McCalls 98:125-32+ O '70
KEATS, John, 1795-1821
Dreaming of death. J. Jerome. Writers Digest 40:14+ My '70 *
KEAYS, Reid R. and others
Trace elements and radioactivity in lunar rocks: implications for meteorite infall, solar-wind flux, and formation conditions of moon. bibliog il Science 167:490-3 Ja 30 '70
KECK, George E.
Dogfight downs United's top man. por Bsns W p 16 D 26 '70 *
Loner who lost. pors Time 97:69 Ja 4 '71 *
KECKLEY, Elizabeth
Black woman's view of Mary Todd Lincoln; excerpts from Behind the scenes. il pors Ebony 25:98-100+ Mr '70
KECSKEMETI, Paul
Political rationality in ending war. bibliog f Ann Am Acad 392:105-15 N '70
KEE, S. Janice
Cooperation moves ahead in the Southwest. il por Library J 95:1294-7 Ap 1 '70
KEELAN, Jean
Right pew, wrong church. il Commonweal 92: 359-64 Jl 24 '70
KEELER, Ruby
Busby and Ruby. il por Newsweek 76:63 Ag 3 '70
Ruby Keeler: back to Broadway after forty years. R. C. Roman. il pors Dance Mag 44:62-7 D '70 *
KEELER, William Wayne
If I were twenty-one today; address, April 20, 1970. Vital Speeches 36:539-42 Je 15 '70

about
My time is running out. il Forbes 106:26 Jl 1 '70 *
Theft of a nation: apologies to the Cherokees. P. Collier. il por Ramp Mag 9:35-45 S '70 *
KEEN, James N.
What James Keen taught me. Simon. il Pop Phot 66:52+ Mr '70 *
KEEN, Sam
Gospel of Cluster 39. Ladies Home J 86:129-30 D '69
KEENAN, John J.
Sweep second movement; poem. Commonweal 92:272 My 29 '70
KEENAN, Philip E.
Wonderful world of crabapples. il Horticulture 48:26-9+ O '70
KEENE, Stanley
Urban renewal needs a guard service. il Am City 85:68 N '70
KEENE corporation
Conglomerate bucks a trend. por Bsns W p 110+ Jl 11 '70
KEENEY, Barnaby C.
Bridge of values; adaptation of address, April 28, 1970. Science 169:26-8 Jl 3 '70
Humanities and the culture-hungry American. W. T. Greenleaf. il Am Ed 6:7-11 Ja '70 *
KEENEY, Ralph L.
Assessment of multiattribute preferences. bibliog il Science 168:1491-2 Je 19 '70
KEEP America beautiful, inc.
AFA honored by Keep America beautiful. il Am For 76:5 F '70
Keeping America beautiful. A. H. Seed, jr. il Parks & Rec 9:30-2+ S '70
KEEPMAN, Florence S.
Harriet's crosses. il Hobbies 75:124+ Ap '70
KEETON, William T.
Orientation by pigeons: is the sun necessary? bibliog Science 165:922-8; 168:153 Ag 29 '69, Ap 3 '70
KEHDE, Ned
American right and pamphleteering: recommendations for a radical pamphlet library. il Am Lib 1:965-7 N '70
New left and a new age of pamphlets: recommendations for a radical pamphlet library. il Am Lib 1:873-6 O '70
KEHL, D. G.
Art of writing evaluative comments on student themes. Engl J 59:972-80 O '70
KEIFFER, Elisabeth
Her town. il pors Good H 171:34+ S '70
Woman alone. il pors Good H 171:84-5+ Jl '70
KEIL, Klaus, and others
Mineral chemistry of lunar samples. bibliog il Science 167:597-9 Ja 30 '70
KEILLOR, Garrison
Local family keeps son happy; story. New Yorker 46:39 S 19 '70
Snack firm maps new chip push. New Yorker 46:45 O 10 '70
KEINO, Kipchoge
Neat feet with a Kenya beat. P. Putnam. il por Sports Illus 32:18-19 F 2 '70
KEITH, D. Graeme
English decorative arts at the M. H. de Young memorial museum. il Antiques 97: 712-17 My '70
KEITH, John L.
Electronic overload protection. il Pop Electr 32:54-6 Mr '70
KEITH, Larry
Baseball. il por Sports Illus 33:44 S 7 '70
KEITH, Sandra L.
Redwood reflections. il Nat Parks & Con Mag 44:16-17 Ap '70
KEITH-SPIEGEL, Patricia, and others
Using the discharge interview to evaluate a psychiatric hospital. Ment Hy 54:298-300 Ap '70
KEKKONEN, Urho Kaleva
President Kekkonen of Finland visits the United States; exchange of remarks and toasts, July 23, 1970. Dept State Bul 63:194-7 Ag 17 '70

about
Man on a tightrope; Moscow and Washington visits. Newsweek 76:28 Ag 3 '70 *
Neutrality with a tilt. il por Time 96:19-20 Jl 27 '70 *
KELDYSH, Mstislav
Lenin and the development of science. il UNESCO Courier 23:6-11 Jl '70
KELHAM, Byron E.
Dusk in the Poconos; poem. Liv Wildn 33:32 Aut '69
KELLEHER, P. G. See Kaplan, M. L. jt. auth.
KELLER, Andrew
Long-chain polymer crystals. bibliog il por Phys Today 23:42-50 My '70

KELLER, Charles R.
Toward a new American history. Ed Digest 36:52-4 S '70
KELLER, Charlie
Keeping 'em down on the farm. J. Kirshenbaum. il pors Sports Illus 32:44-7 My 18 '70 *
KELLER, Eugenia
DDT story. il Chem 43:8-12 F '70
Forensic toxicology: poison detection and homicide. il Chem 43:14-17 Ja '70
Photography. bibliog il Chem 43:6-12 O; 8-11 D '70
KELLER, George C.
Cost, and price, of education. Nation 210:242-4 Mr 2 '70
KELLER, O. Lewin, Jr
Predicted properties of elements 113 and 114. bibliog il por Chem 43:8-11 N '70
KELLER, William
Drinker's guide to safe holiday driving; interview. il por Todays Health 48:8+ D '70
KELLEY, Barry M.
Christ: revolutionary or rebel? Chr Today 14:14 My 22 '70
KELLEY, Charles F.
Is galvanic corrosion following you? il Yachting 128:69+ Ag '70
KELLEY, Dean M.
Young Lords and the Spanish congregation. Chr Cent 87:208-11 F 18 '70
KELLEY, James B.
Law and social action. America 124:41-2 Ja 16 '71
Ravaged soil of Vietnam. il Cath World 211:71-3 My '70
KELLEY, William N. and Beardmore, T. D.
Allopurinol: alteration in pyrimidine metabolism in man. bibliog il Science 169:388-90 Jl 24 '70
KELLOGG, Jean D.
Burnt-out case? America 122:273-4 Mr 14 '70
KELLOGG, Karl, and others
Thermochemical remanent magnetization and thermal remanent magnetization: comparison in a basalt. bibliog il Science 170:628-30 N 6 '70
KELLY, Bill, and Kelly, Gertrude
We did it. il House B 112:32+ Je '70
KELLY, Desmond
Brief biography. S. Goodman. il pors Dance Mag 44:66-7 Ja '70
KELLY, Francis X.
Living past. il Parks & Rec 5:48-9 My '70
KELLY, Frank K.
Possibilities of transformation. Sat R 53:17-19+ Mr 7 '70
KELLY, George Edward
Where are they now? pors Newsweek 75:12 F 2 '70
KELLY, George W.
One-seed juniper. Horticulture 48:40 Je '70
What to plant around steps. il Horticulture 48:18-21+ Je '70
KELLY, Gertrude. See Kelly, B. jt. auth.
KELLY, Grace. See Grace Patricia, consort of Rainier III, prince of Monaco
KELLY, Hal
Build this turtle boat for the fun of it! il Pop Mech 134:143-5+ Jl '70
Unsinkable uniboat. il Mech Illus 66:81-2+ Mr '70
Win. . .or else! il por Motor B 126:118-20 S '70
KELLY, Harry Charles
Harry C. Kelly: an extraordinary ambassador to Japanese science. P. M. Boffey. il por Science 169:449-53 Jl 31 '70 *
KELLY, Henry Ansgar
Death of the devil? il Commonweal 93:146-9 N 6 '70
KELLY, James R.
Is ecumenism dead? America 123:258-9 O 10 '70
Possibility of prayer. Commonweal 92:413-15 Ag 21 '70
—and Campion, D. R.
Loyalty and dissent: reflections of two sociologists. America 122:679-80 Je 27 '70
KELLY, James W.
Making the family or group canoe trip. il Cons 24:48+ Ap '70
KELLY, Joe
Make conflict work for you; excerpts from Organizational behaviour. bibliog f il Harvard Bsns R 48:103-13 Jl '70
KELLY, Joe, 1939?–
Joe Kelly has reached his boiling point. R. Rogin. il pors N Y Times Mag p 12-14+ Je 28 '70 *
KELLY, Red
Kelly's light shines under Pitt's bushel. G. Ronberg. Sports Illus 32:64-5 Ap 20 '70 *

KELLY, Steve
Inside Buick's back room. il por Hot Rod 23:32-5 My '70
Openings for everyone. il Hot Rod 23:34-9 Je '70
Roundy-round corner. See issues of Hot rod
KELLY, Ted
First time south. il Yachting 128:66-7+ O '70
First time to the Bahamas. il Yachting 128:56-7+ N '70
KELLY, Thomas
Traditional enmity between Sparta and Argos: the birth and development of a myth. bibliog f il Am Hist R 75:971-1003 Ap '70
KELLY, Tim
Bachelor bighorns. il por Outdoor Life 146:50-1+ Jl '70
KELLY, Virginia
There's nothing gray about the Azores. il Read Digest 97:146-52 S '70
KELMAN, Steven J.
Letter from Stockholm. il New Yorker 46:36-46+ D 26 '70
Youth and foreign policy. For Affairs 48:414-26 Ap '70
KELP
Kelp farming. R. E. Ruff. il Sea Front 16:182-5 My '70
KELSALL, John P.
Migration of the barren-ground caribou; with biographical sketch. il Natur Hist 79:4, 98-106 Ag '70
KELSEY, P. M.
Eucharist; poem. Chr Cent 87:1282 O 28 '70
KELSEY, Paul M. and Tanck, John
Venison: from the freezer to the table. il Cons 24:48-9 F '70
KELSO, James L.
Inspiration of Scripture. Chr Today 14:6-9 Je 5 '70
KELSO, Louis Orth
Louis Kelso: nut or Newton? R. G. Sherrill. Nation 210:234-7 Mr 2 '70 *
Man who would make everybody richer. il por Time 95:72-3 Je 29 '70 *
KELTON, Richard
By sound and smell. il Yachting 128:66-7+ D '70
KEMAL, Mustafa. See Atatürk, K.
KEMBLE, Charles
Charles Kemble, man of the theatre, by J. Williamson. Review
Sat R 53:37 Je 20 '70. R. H. Gaines *
KEMBLE, Penn
Who needs the liberals? Commentary 50:57-64 O '70
KEMENY, John George
Teaching president. il por Newsweek 75:75 F 2 '70
KEMP, Arnold
Harlem to Harvard, and back. por Time 96:64 O 19 '70 *
KEMP, Geoffrey
Arms traffic and third world conflicts. bibliog il por Int Concil 577:5-80 Mr '70
Dilemmas of the arms traffic. For Affairs 48:274-84 Ja '70
KEMP, Jack F.
Making of a quarterback 1970. P. Ryan. il pors Sports Illus 33:82-6+ D 7 '70 *
KEMPADOO, Manghanita
Letters of thanks; excerpts. il Ladies Home J 86:58 D '69
KEMPER, Robert Graham
Now what hath God wrought? Chr Cent 87:1120-3 S 23 '70
KEMPLER, Walter
Uncovering your child's masked messages. il Todays Health 48:54-5+ Ap '70
KEMPNER, Robert D.
Overdue. il por Wilson Lib Bul 44:658-9 F '70
KEMPTON, Sally
Cutting loose. Esquire 74:53-7 Jl '70
Little big man clings to life. il Esquire 74:78-81+ Jl '70
KENAI PENINSULA
Half-day Alaska sampler. il Sunset 144:88 Ap '70
Kenai. R. Belous. il Field & S 75:28-31+ Jl '70
KENDALL, David, and Ross, Leonard
Draft odds. New Repub 162:9-10 Ja 31 '70
KENDALL, Donald McIntosh
Training hard-core jobless: the record after two years; interview. il por U S News 68:60-2 Mr 30 '70
KENDALL, Elizabeth, and Talmey, Allene
What is a nervous breakdown. Vogue 156:144-5 N 15 '70
KENDALL, Jack. See Bowes, A. jt. auth.
KENDRICK, Alexander
Prime time: the life of Edward R. Murrow; excerpts. Todays Ed 59:15-16 F '70

KENNEDY, Lois J.—*Continued*
Ships of the desert. il Motor B 126:138-40 Ag '70
Triumphant youngsters. il Motor B 125:56-7+ Je '70

KENNEDY, Mary
Mary Kennedy's glorified rag dolls; Mother Goose at the Arkansas state college. C. H. Fawcett. il Hobbies 75:41+ Je '70 *

KENNEDY, Robert Francis, 1925-1968
Government and Martin Luther King. V. S. Navasky. pors Atlan 226:43-52 N '70 *
Irish heart, Greek conscience. G. Clarke. il por Time 97:74 Ja 4 '71 *
Kennedyism. M. Decter. Commentary 49:19-27 Ja '70· Discussion. 49:20+ My; 17-18 Je '70 *
Robert F. Kennedy memorial. Ladies Home J 87:98 Ja '70
Under the skin of the Statue of Liberty; tr. by A. C. Todd, jr. E. A. Evtushenko. il por N Y Times Mag p34+ F 15 '70 *
Why I named my son after Robert Kennedy. A. Williams. il pors Ladies Home J 87:50+ Ja '70

Assassination
Day in June. R. N. Goodwin. il McCalls 97:38+ Je '70
R.F.K. must die! by R. B. Kaiser. Review Newsweek il por 76:114+ O 19 '70. G. Wolff
Sat R 53:29-30+ O 17 '70. F. J. Cook
RFK must die; excerpts. R. B. Kaiser. il Ladies Home J 87:163-70+ My '70 *
Sirhan B. Sirhan literary negotiations, etc, inc. S. V. Roberts. pors Esquire 74:131-4+ N '70
Special unit senator, by R. A. Houghton. Review
Life 68:8 F 6 '70. D. Jackson
Was Sirhan programmed to kill Robert Kennedy? excerpt from RFK must die. R. B. Kaiser. il por Ladies Home J 87:66+ O '70

Funeral rites and ceremonies
American journey; interviews by J. Stein. ed. by G. Plimpton. Review
Life 69:22 D 11 '70. B. Bradlee

KENNEDY, Robert Francis, 1954?-
Busting the boys. il pors Newsweek 76:32 Ag 17 '70 *

KENNEDY, Robert F, youth center, Morgantown, W.Va. See Detention homes

KENNEDY, Rose (Fitzgerald)
Giving children the gifts of faith and courage. por Ladies Home J 86:60+ D '69
Rose Kennedy at 80; with interview. ed by S. Wright. il pors Life 69:20-5 Jl 17 '70 *
Rose Kennedy; excerpt from The Kennedy women. P. S. Buck. il pors Good H 170: 68-71+ Je '70 *

KENNEDY, Ted. See Kennedy, E. M.

KENNEDY, Thomas
Freedom to strike is in the public interest. bibliog f il Harvard Bsns R 48:45-57 Jl '70; Same abr. with title Should we abolish all strikes? Cur 121:32-6 S '70

KENNEDY, X. J.
Comment. J. McGann. Poetry 117:197-9 D '70 *
Recurrences. Nation 210:378-80 Mr 30 '70
Singing to spite this hunger. H. Taylor. Nation 210:122-4 F 2 '70

KENNEDY brothers
Why Massachusetts loves the Kennedys. F. Russell. il Nat R 22:836-9 Ag 11 '70

KENNEDY family
Ask not what Ted Sorensen can do for you. . . D. Halberstam; discussion. Harper 240:6+ F '70

KENNEDY, CAPE
Comesin goes to a special launching. M. Wilder. il Yachting 128:60-2+ D '70
Vacation countdown. M. L. Norwood. il Travel 135:42-7 Ja '71

KENNEDY international airport. See New York (city)—Airports

KENNEDY-King community college, Chicago, Ill.
Kennedy-King community college. il Arch Rec 147:154-6 Je '70

KENNEDY library. See John F. Kennedy library, Cambridge, Mass.

KENNEDY space center. See United States— John F. Kennedy space center

KENNELS
Easy money raising dogs? D. M. Duffey. il Outdoor Life 145:110+ Ja '70
Ideas for the two-dog family. il Sunset 145: 94 S '70

Porch for pooch. D. Shiner. il Design 71:37 mid-Sum '70
Quonset-hut dog house. J. R. Aller. il Pop Sci 196:140 Ja '70

KENNER, Hugh
Delectations. il Nat R 22:35+, 790 Ja 13, Jl 28 '70

KENNETH
Kenneth discusses wigs. pors Harp Baz 104: 121 Ja '71

KENNETT, James P. See Margolis, S. V. jt. auth

KENNEY, James E.
New consumerism. America 122:270-2 Mr 14 '70

KENNY, Bik
Apricots by the bucketful, from your own garden! il Org Gard & Farm 17:50-3 D '70

KENNY, John V.
Recollections of a Jersey City childhood. M. Butler. il por Time 97:12 Ja 11 '71 *

KENOSHA, Wis.
Combined sewers may be an advantage. F. I. Vilen. il Am City 85:68-70 Ja '70

Galleries and museums
Hall of flame. H. E. Smith. il Har Yrs 10:19 Ja '70

KENSETH, Arnold
Shout for Christmas; poem. Chr Cent 87: 1548 D 23 '70

KENT, Corita
We need Decembers; poem. Ladies Home J 86:134 D '69

KENT, Edward
Daredevil poetics: Ferlinghetti's definition of a poet. Engl J 59:1243-4+ D '70

KENT, George
Merry squiggles of Joan Miró. il Read Digest 97:165-70 D '70

KENT, H. R.
Through the country; poem. Am Scholar 39: 469 Sum '70

KENT, Leticia
(ed) See Jacobs, J. More babies needed, not fewer
(ed) See Warhol, A. It's hard to be your own script

KENT, Norman
Artist's studio. il Am Artist 34:56-68 Ja '70
Frank N. Wilcox: a review of his last book. il Am Artist 34:30-1+ Ap '70
Student drawing competition. il por Am Artist 34:38-44+ Je '70
Walter Young. landscape painter. il por Am Artist 34:42-7+ D '70
Woodcuts of Robert C. Skelley. il Am Artist 35:44-9+ Ja '71

KENT, William A.
How to keep up with insiders. il por Bsns W p 108+ My 9 '70 *

KENT state university. See Ohio. Kent state university

KENTFIELD, Calvin
Jefferson Airplane is an unscheduled trip. il N Y Times Mag p32-4+ O 18 '70
Turning off the Tijuana grass. Esquire 73: 8+ My '70

KENTUCKY
See also
Architecture, Domestic—Kentucky
Education—Kentucky
Hunting—Kentucky
Music festivals—Kentucky

KENTUCKY Derby. See Horse racing

KENTUCKY fried chicken corporation
Colonel Sanders spreads his wings; franchise in Britain. Bsns W p47 Ja 24 '70
Franchising; too much, too soon. il Bsns W p54-5+ Je 27 '70
Profiles; H. Sanders, founder. W. Whitworth. por New Yorker 45:40-6+ F 14 '70

KENTUCKY opera association
Report:
Madama Butterfly in English. W. Mootz. Opera N 34:33 Mr 28 '70

KENTUCKY. State college, Frankfort
Tall story from the land of Boone; NAIA tournament winner. W. F. Reed. il Sports Illus 33:66-8 N 30 '70

KENYA
See also
Elections—Kenya
Hunting—Kenya
Paleontology—Kenya

Description and travel
Let's travel: safari to Kenya. S. Cuneo. il Mlle 71:88-90+ Je '70
One in the bush: photographic safaris. D. Butwin il Sat R 53:42+ Ap 4 '70
Smart shops and safaris. R. Eiseley. il Travel 134:60-1 S '70

KENYA—*Continued*

Native races

Tribal politics harass Kenya; conflict between Kikuyu and Luo tribes. S. Meisler. For Affairs 49:111-21 O '70

Politics and government

Tribal politics harass Kenya. S. Meisler. For Affairs 49:111-21 O '70
See also
Elections—Kenya

Religious institutions and affairs

Oaths in Kenya. Chr Today 14:40 F 13 '70
See also
Protestant churches—Kenya

KENYATTA, Jomo
Tribal politics harass Kenya. S. Meisler. For Affairs 49:112-21 O '70 *

KENYON college, Gambier, Ohio
Little help from my friends; tutoring in elementary schools by students. D. R. Maxey. il Look 34:22-4 Je 16 '70

KENYON review
End of the Kenyon? Time 95:40+ Mr 9 '70

KEPPLER, Herbert
Keppler on the SLR. See issues of Modern photography

KERALA, India
Reporter at large; Indian journal. V. Mehta. New Yorker 46:118+ Ap 11 '70

KERASOTE, Ted
Fishing the deep freeze. il por Outdoor Life 146:38-41+ D '70

KERATIN
Mammoth hair: stability of α-keratin structure and constituent proteins. J. M. Gillespie. bibliog il Science 170:1100-2 D 4 '70

KERBEC, Matthew J.
Public information act. por Library J 95: 4229-31 D 15 '70

KERBY, Phil
California: Jess Unruh. Populist. Nation 211: 393-6 O 26 '70

KERENSKII, Aleksandr Fedorovich
From the past: Kerensky & Brüning. P. Steinfels. Commonweal 92:310 Je 26 '70 *
Kerensky dies. il por Newsweek 75:40+ Je 22 '70 *
Obituary
Nat R 22:660 Je 30 '70; Reply. E. Lyons. 22:766 Jl 28 '70 *

KERENSKY, Alexander. See Kerenskii, A. F.

KERKORIAN, Kirk
Kerkorian: goodbye to some big chips. il Bsns W p39-40 Ja 24 '70
Kerkorian's cold streak. por Time 96:65 Jl 27 '70 *
Kerkorian's game cramped for cash. il por Bsns W p36 Je 13 '70 *

KERMODE, Frank
Poet in praise of limestone. por Atlan 225:67-71 My '70

KERN, Edward
Good revolution goes on sale: Cassette TV. il Life 69:46-53 O 16 '70

KERN, James A.
Biscayne Bay; photographs. Audubon 72:37-44 S '70

KERN, Lawrence E. jr
Japan: a few thoughts and figures. il Pub W 198:pt2 172-4 S 21 '70

about

Kern stateside. P. Nathan. Pub W 198:71 S 28 '70 *

KERNAGHAN, R. P. and Ehrman, Lee
Antimycoplasmal antibiotics and hybrid sterility in drosophila paulistorum. bibliog il Science 169:63-4 Jl 3 '70

KERNER commission. See United States—National advisory commission on civil disorders

KEROUAC, Jack
Great western bus ride. Esquire 73:136-7+ Mr '70

about

Spontaneous requiem; poem. G. Corso. il Ramp Mag 8:23-5 Mr '70 *
This is how the ride ends. J. McClintock. il por Esquire 73:138-9+ Mr '70 *

KERR, Graham
Lady who makes the gourmet gallop. J. Pascoe. il por McCalls 97:14+ Je '70 *

KERR, James Robert
Diversified and still waiting. il por Bsns W p78+ Ag 29 '70 *

KERR, Jean
How to talk to a baby; excerpt from Penny candy. il Read Digest 97:104-6 O '70
How wives drive husbands crazy; excerpt from Penny candy. il Read Digest 97:85-7 D '70

I want to go down to the sea again. Holiday 47:16-18 Je '70
Marriage: unsafe at any speed. il Read Digest 96:60-2 My '70
Our poetry hour. il McCalls 97:44-5+ Ag '70

KERR, Randolph E.
How to use your snowmobile. il Cons 25:48-9 O '70

KERR, Treena
Lady who makes the gourmet gallop. J. Pascoe. il por McCalls 97:14+ Je '70 *

KERR, Walter
What Simon says. il por N Y Times Mag p6+ Mr 22 '70

KERR, Walter B.
Communicating in Los Alamos: don't call him doctor! Sat R 53:57-8 Ap 11 '70
French television and the control of the news il Sat R 53:72+ F 14 '70
HPT joint venture? The old Paris Herald! il Sat R 53:61-3 Ja 17 '70

KERRIA
Bright stems now, flowers soon. il Sunset 144:174 F '70

KERRY, Ireland
See also
Sneem, Ireland

Photographs

Gaeltacht of West Kerry. L. Stephens. il por Natur Hist 79:44-90 bibliog(p 133) Ag '70

KERSCHER, D. Dean
Bear for the barbershop. il por Outdoor Life 145:60-1+ Mr '70

KERSHAW, J. A. and Mood, A. M.
Resource allocation in higher education. Mo Labor R 93:46-8 Mr '70

KERSTEN, Caesar S. and Ott, V. E.
Your foreign language program, is it relevant? Ed Digest 35:53-5 Ap '70

KERTÉSZ, André
Drooping tulip heralds new business. J. Deschin. il Pop Phot 67:32+ Ag '70 *

KERTESZ, Istvan
Istvan Kertesz; interview, ed. by R. Hemming. por Sr Schol 96:27 Ap 13 '70

KESHET, Sylvie
Sylvie's poison arrows. il por Time 96:44 Jl 6 '70 *

KESSELMAN, Jeff
Librarian vs. publisher. il por Library J 95: 4221-4 D 15 '70

KESSELRING, Albert
Our German wehrmacht is being stopped by a shadow; excerpts from Donovan of OSS. C. Ford. il por Am Heritage 21:56-7+ F '70 *

KESSLER, Edward
Waiting woman; poem. Am Scholar 39:654 Aut '70

KESSLER, Edwin
Thunderstorms over Oklahoma, 22 June 1969. bibliog il Weatherwise 23:56-69 Ap '70

KESSLER, Gary
Flexure of a concrete telescope pier. il Sky & Tel 40:235-6 O '70

KESSLER, Jascha
Keys to ourselves. pors Sat R 53:34-6+ My 2 '70

KESSLER, Milton
The moment of no recovery; poem. Nation 212:88 Ja 18 '71
Willow song. Nation 210:629 My 25 '70

KESSLER, Ruth O.
Lunar visit; poem. Am For 76:11 Ja '70

KESTENBAUM, Richard S. and others
Behavioral measurement of neural poststimulation excitability cycle: pain cells in the brain of the rat. bibliog il Science 167: 393-6 Ja 23 '70

KESTER, Bernard
Laura Andreson. il Craft Horiz 30:12-17 D '70

KESTER, Kay
Today's children and tomorrow's world? Camp Mag 42:20-1 S '70

KETCHES. See Sailing vessels

KETCHIKAN, Alaska

Education

Sea Ed; high school program. C. G. Fader. il Todays Ed 59:30-1 D '70

KETCHLEDGE, Edwin Herbert
New York state's most spectacular environment. il Cons 25:16-20 Ag '70
—and Leonard, R. E.
Impact of man on the Adirondack high country. il Cons 25:14-18 O '70

KETCHUM, Richard M.
Faces from the past. il por Am Heritage 21: 52-3 Je '70
Thankless task of Nicholas Trist. il por Am Heritage 21:12-15+ Ag '70

KETTERING, Charles Franklin
Boss Kettering's decision: build a better diesel. R. L. Terrell. il pors Nations Bsns 58:78-9 Ja '70

KETTNER, Irene
Variations on basic shapes. il Ceram Mo 18: 26-7 D '70

KEVERN, Bob
Wind chill factor. il Sci Digest 68:56-9 D '70

KEVLES, Barbara H.
In search of Nan Page; story. Atlan 226:74-8 Jl '70

KEY, Clyde J.
Underground Toscanini. por Time 95:65 Mr 2 '70 *

KEY cases, holders, etc.
Key cases. il Consumer Bul 53:17-20 Ja '70
KEY holders. See Key cases, holders, etc.

KEY WEST, Fla.
Key West, automatically; new automatic transmission for the Renault 16 sedanwagon. B. Kilpatrick. Mech Illus 66:34+ My '70

KEYE, Donna and Pearlstein. See Advertising agencies

KEYES, Charles F.
Peoples of Indochina; with biographical sketches. il Natur Hist 79:4, 40-53+ O '70

KEYES, Robert W.
Power dissipation in information processing. bibliog il Science 168:796-801 My 15 '70

KEYNES, John Maynard Keynes, 1st baron
Economic consequences of Maynard Keynes. L. Malkin. il pors Horizon 11:104-11 Aut '69

KEYSERLING, Leon H.
Which economists have flunked out? New Repub 163:10-11 O 3; 29-31 O 24 '70

KEYSTONE CANYON state scenic park. See Alaska—Parks and reserves

KHALATNIKOV, Isaak Markovich
Soviet work suggests mixmaster singularity at origin. G. B. Lubkin. pors Phys Today 23:59-60+ Mr '70 *

KHALED, Leila
This is your new captain speaking; interview, ed. by G. Jansen. il por Life 69:34-7 S 18 '70

about

Lady who trained tigers. il por Newsweek 76:25 S 21 '70 *

KHAMA, Sir Seretse
Road to independence. P. Webb. il por Newsweek 76:46 O 26 '70 *

KHAN, Abdul Ghaffar
Where are they now? il pors Newsweek 75: 10 Ja 26 '70

KHAN, Ahsan U.
Singlet molecular oxygen from superoxide anion and sensitized fluorescence of organic molecules. bibliog il Science 168:476-7 Ap 24 '70

KHAN, Sir Muhammad Zafrulla. See Zafrulla Khan, M.

KHANH, Quasar
Environment to stimulate talk and new ideas. il House & Gard 138:96-9 N '70 *

KHARKAR, D. P. See Turekian, K. K. jt. auth.

KHEEL, Theodore Woodrow
Automation house; interview. New Yorker 46: 30-2 Mr 14 '70

about

Profiles. F. C. Shapiro. New Yorker 46:36-44+ Ag 1 '70 *
—and Kaden, L. B.
Plan to resolve impasses in hospital bargaining. Mo Labor R 93:45-8 Ap '70

KHESANH, Battle of, 1968. See Vietnamese war, 1957- —Campaigns and battles

KHMERS
Indochina's curse; ancient enmities. il Newsweek 75:24 My 4 '70
Mysterious Angkor, jungle city of the dead. L. S. De Camp. il Sci Digest 67:18-23 Ap '70

KHORANA, Har Gobind
Gene at last. il por Sci N 97:547 Je 6 '70 *
Gene makers. il por Newsweek 75:91 Je 15 '70 *
Secrets of the cell. il por Time 95:43-4 Je 15 '70 *

KHOROSHILOV, Ivan Ivanovich
Russian grain expert visits U.S. il por Suc Farm 68:no2 A12 F '70 *

KHOURI, Fred J.
Arabs in exile. il Trans-Action 7:52-5+ Jl '70

KHRUSHCHEV, Nikita Sergeevich
Khrushchev remembers; excerpts, ed. and tr. by C. Talbott. il pors Life 69:32-9+ N 27; 48-54+ D 4; 54-58B+ D 11; 16B-25+ D 18 '70

about

Adventures of a survivor. por Newsweek 77: 83 Ja 11 '71 *
Great Khrushchev mystery. il pors Newsweek 76:36+ N 30 '70 *
JFK at the summit; Kremlinologists views on first Kennedy-Khrushchev encounter. il Newsweek 76:32-3 S 7 '70 *
K, K. and K. Nat R 22:1386+ D 29 '70 *
Khrushchev: averting the apocalypse. il por Time 96:31 D 21 '70 *
Khrushchev: notes from a forbidden land. il por Time 96:20-1 N 30 '70 *
Khrushchev: showdown in the Kremlin. il por Time 96:38+ D 14 '70 *
Khrushchev: the illusions of war; reminiscences. il pors Time 96:38+ D 7 '70 *
1969 conversation with Khrushchev: the beginning of his fall from power. A. M. Harvey. Life 69:48B D 18 '70 *
Secrecy veils Time-LB's memoir by Khrushchev. Pub W 198:49 N 16 '70 *
Testament of a Soviet dictator. H. Schwartz. por Sat R 53:21-3+ D 26 '70 *

KHUZESTAN
Oil and water rebuild an ancient land. L. Griggs. il Fortune 82:88-97+ N '70

KIBBUTZIM. See Collective settlements—Israel

KIDD, Billy
Flake and the old man. R. Meryman. il pors Life 68:54-6+ Mr 6 '70 *
Grab the gold and say goodby. D. Jenkins. il por Sports Illus 32:26-9 F 23 '70 *
Kidd comes in from the old cold. D. Jenkins. il por Sports Illus 32:42+ F 16 '70 *
Slippery days on the slopes. il por Time 95: 48 Mr 23 '70 *

KIDDE, Walter, and company
Kidde's new boss tries to get it together. por Bsns W p36 Ja 31 '70 *
Kidde's seagoing days are over. Bsns W p29-30 N 21 '70

KIDDIE cars. See Automobiles, Toy

KIDNAPPING
At Cross purposes; abduction of J. R. Cross by Quebec separatists. il por Newsweek 76:55 O 19 '70
Diplomacy by terror: is it getting out of control? il U S News 69:22-3 Ag 24 '70
Diplomats on the firing line; kidnapping and murder of Karl von Spreti. il Sr Schol 96:15 Ap 27 '70
Escalating terror; West German ambassador in Guatemala. Newsweek 75:40 13 '70
Ethical meditation: kidnapping of West German Ambassador Ehrenfried von Hollenben by Brazilian revolutionaries. Nat R 22:657-8 Je 30 '70
Hanging tough; ransom demands and political kidnappings. il Newsweek 76:32 Ag 24 '70
Helpless hostages; kidnapping and murder of K. von Spreti in Guatemala. il Time 95:30 Ap 20 '70
High cost of blackmail: kidnappings and deaths of hostages at San Rafael, Calif. and Uruguay. Nat R 22:880+ Ag 25 '70
It was a terrible scene; kidnappings and deaths by Tupamaros in Uruguay. R. Peter. Nat R 22:1001+ S 22 '70
Kidnap fever; three cases in Uruguay. Newsweek 76:45 Ag 17 '70
Kidnaping diplomats, what's back of terrorist tactics. il U S News 68:22-3 Ap 20 '70
Kidnapped diplomats: Greek tragedy on a Latin stage. M. M. Alves. Commonweal 92:311-14 Je 26 '70
Lesson learned; case of the West German ambassador to Brazil. Newsweek 75:40 Je 22 '70
Lives in the balance; abduction of J. R. Cross. Time 96:40 O 19 '70
Machine gun in the lettuce; capture of G. Jackson by Uruguay's Tupamaros. por Time 97:31 Ja 18 '71
Nervous in the service; diplomats in Latin America. Newsweek 75:40-1 Ap 6 '70
New approach. W. F. Buckley, jr. Nat R 22: 1016-17 S 22 '70
New terror in Latin America: snatching the diplomats. R. O'Mara. Nation 210:518-19 My 4 '70
New terror tactic; diplomatic kidnaping in Latin America. Time 95:37-8 Ap 6 '70
OAS asked to consider problem of kidnaping and terrorism; statement, April 15, 1970. J. J. Jova. Dept State Bul 62:662 My 25 '70
Parting shots; dangers of being a diplomat in Latin America. il Life 68:81-2 Je 26 '70
Power to the gunmen; kidnapping of diplomats in Latin America. New Repub 162:9 Ap 4 '70

KINETIC art
Art: for fun or fulfillment; exhibition in London. K. Kuh. por Sat R 53:36-7 D 19 '70
Current picture; the Kalliroscope. Time 96: 62 O 5 '70
Fun art; environmental art, tech art, participatory art. T. Meehan. il Horizon 11:4-15 Aut '69
Living wall; Y. Agam's hexagonal mural in Leverkusen, West Germany. il Time 95: 66-7 My 18 '70
    See also
Kinetic light art
KINETIC light art
Mighty machine; reconstruction of L. Moholy-Nagy's light-space modulator. D. Davis. il Newsweek 76:108+ N 16 '70
Next, the sun; O. Piene's sky ballet, Red helium sky line. il Time 95:62 My 4 '70
KING, Alan
Breast cancer; ed. by H. M. Hobbs. Redbook 135:22+ S '70
KING, Allan
Fiction documentary; interview, ed. by A. Rosenthal. il Film Q 23:9-19 Sum '70
KING, Blues Boy. See King, R. B.
KING, Bruce
Yachting interviews; Bruce King; ed. by B. Crabtree. il Yachting 127:77+ Mr '70
KING, David C.
Drugs are your problem. America 122:497-3 My 9 '70
Global corporation is here to stay. il America 123:229-31 O 3 '70
KING, Derek
Exiled from Nigeria. America 122:245 Mr 7 '70
KING, Edward L.
Making it in the U.S. army. New Repub 162: 19-21 My 30 '70
KING, Elbert Aubrey, 1935-, and others
Mineralogy and petrology of coarse particulate material from lunar surface at Tranquillity base. il Science 167:650-2 Ja 20 '70
KING, Helen H.
Hair. il Ebony 25:120-2+ My '70
It's easier to adopt today. il Ebony 26:120-2+ D '70
KING, Joan
It all looks different on the way back; story. Redbook 135:82-3 O '70
KING, John
U.S. and U.K. discuss impact of new U.K. agricultural program; statement, November 4, 1970. Dept State Bul 63:677 N 30 '70
KING, John L.
Consumer and the investor are the same guy. por Forbes 106:43-4 S 1 '70 *
KING, John McCandish
Big John. por Time 95:91 My 25 '70 *
Can King sell his IOS rescue plan? Bsns W p36-7 My 23 '70 *
King shows his colors. R. Brady. por Duns 96:50 D '70 *
Kingdom besieged. por Time 96:66-7 Ag 3 '70 *
King's abdication. por Newsweek 76:48+ Ag 24 '70 *
King's gambit. Newsweek 75:80 Je 8 '70 *
Personal money machine of John King. R. Brady. il pors Duns 95:34-8 Je '70 *
KING, Kendall W.
Malnutrition in the Caribbean. il Natur Hist 79:64-7 Ja '70
KING, Larry
Operations research. M. S. Rothenberg. por Phys Today 23:30 My '70 *
KING, Larry L.
Blowing my mind at Harvard. Harper 241: 95-8+ O '70
Confessions of a white racist. il Harper 240:63-6+ Ja '70
Exploring the Cajun country. il Holiday 47: 70-3+ My '70
LBJ's secret brother meditates on history. Harper 240:38+ Ap '70
Whatever happened to Brother Dave? il por Harper 241:52-5+ S '70
KING, Lawrence T.
Bishops in the vineyard. Commonweal 92:214 My 15 '70
GOP and God. Commonweal 93:37-8 O 9 '70
KING, Martin Luther, 1929-1968
Government and Martin Luther King. V. S. Navasky. pors Atlan 226:43-52 N '70
King God didn't save, by J. A. Williams. Review
    Sat R 53:54 Ag 22 '70. E. Capouya *
King's dream recaptured; documentary of thirteen years in the life of civil-rights leader. Chr Today 14:45 Ap 10 '70 *
Posthumous pillory. il por Time 96:12-13 Ag 17 '70 *
Powerful new movie: King; from Montgomery to Memphis. il pors Ebony 25:172-4+ Ap '70 *

Simple act of sanctity. Chr Cent 87:35 Ja 14 '70
Slur of the year. R. Neuhaus. Chr Cent 87: 1079-80 S 16 '70; Discussion. 87:1358 N 11 '70 *

Assassination
Trade winds; interview, ed. by C. Amory. W. B. Huie. Sat R 53:10-11 Je 27 '70

Memorials
King day: birth date observances. il Newsweek 75:24+ Ja 26 '70

Poetry
M.L.K. N. S. Robins. Nation 210:765 Je 22 '70
KING, Maxwell
Wild hemp of Indiana. Nation 211:402-3 O 26 '70
KING, Morgana
Queen King. H. Saal. por Newsweek 75:81 Ja 26 '70
KING, Nicholas
Do we want environment? il Nat R 22:557-9 Je 2 '70
KING, Phillip
London; one-man show at the Rowan gallery. J. Russell. Art N 69:24+ S '70 *
KING, Riley B.
B. B. and Carla. New Yorker 46:25-6 Je 13 '70 *
Five happy moments. il por Esquire 74:139 D '70
KING, Terry Johnson
Uruguay. il Travel 134:40-5 O '70
KING, William
Telltale gesture. il por Time 95:82 Mr 23 '70 *
KING, Winston L.
Eastern religions: a new interest and influence. Ann Am Acad 387:66-76 Ja '70
KING Arthur and his knights; drama. See Morley, O. J.
KING COUNTY, Wash.
Swimming pools galore; public indoor pools. R. Sigismund. il Parks & Rec 5:35 My '70
KING crabs
Horseshoe crab lactate dehydrogenase: tissue distribution and molecular weight. E. J. Massaro. bibliog il Science 167:994-6 F 13 '70
KING James Bible. See Bible—Versions
KING Karol (shop) See Phonograph record shops
KING Lear; drama. See Shakespeare, W.—Plays
KING resources company
King resources shrinks to survive. Bsns W p33-4 O 24 '70
Kingdom besieged. por Time 96:66-7 Ag 3 '70
King's abdication. por Newsweek 76:48+ Ag 24 '70
Personal money machine of John King. R. Brady. il pors Duns 95:34-8 Je '70
KING salmon fishing. See Salmon fishing
KING who was bored; drama. See Thane, A.
KINGDOM of God
    See also
Jesus Christ—Kingdom
KINGFISH fishing
King saves the day. G. Heinold. il por Outdoor Life 145:96+ My '70
KINGFISHERS
Kingfisher repays her debt. L. F. Addington. il Nat Wildlife 8:36-7 D '69
KINGMAN, Lee
Virginia Lee Burton's dynamic sense of design. il Horn Bk 46:449-60, 593-602 O-D 70
KINGS and rulers
Grim great. A. Campbell. New Repub 163: 23-4 D 5 '70
KINGSTON, N.Y.
Ceremony for citizens: the Zweiflers and others. il Life 68:32B-32D Mr 27 '70
KINGSTON, N.Y. area library
Intellectual freedom; with letter by R. H. Rosichan. J. F. Krug and J. A. Harvey. Am Lib 1:425, 433 My '70
KININS
Cytokinin activity of ureidopurine derivatives related to a modified nucleoside found in transfer RNA. W. H. Dyson and others. bibliog il Science 170:328-30 O 16 '70
    See also
Bradykinin
KINKEAD, Eugene
Is there another life after death? il pors Look 34:84-8+ O 20 '70
Our local correspondents (cont) New Yorker 46:143-6+ O 24 '70
KINLOCH, Bohun B. Jr. and others
White pine blister rust: simply inherited resistance in sugar pine. il Science 167: 193-5 Ja 9 '70

KINNAMON, Keneth
Afro-American literature, the black revolution, and ghetto high schools. bibliog Engl J 59:189-94 F '70

about

Non-black teacher, black literature, and black students. R. A. Shepard. Engl J 59:1071-3 N '70 •

KINNELL, Galway
Night song; poem. Nation 211:158 Ag 31 '70

KINNEY, Jo Ann S. See Luria, S. M. jt. auth.

KINNEY national service, inc.
Kinney national service bids to acquire Simon & Schuster. Pub W 198:29 N 2 '70
Market mystery. Forbes 105:22-3 Je 1 '70; Correction. 106:10 N 1 '70

KINNICK, B. Jo
English teacher conference, California; poem. Engl J 59:26 Ja '70

KINSOLVING, Lester
Irreverent reverend. il Time 97:66 Ja 11 '71 •

KINT, J. A.
Fabry's disease: alpha-galactosidase deficiency. bibliog il Science 167:1268-9 F 27 '70

KINTREA, Frank
Realms of Gould. il pors Am Heritage 21:46-65 Ap '70

KIOWA Indians
Man called Perry Horse. J. Corry. il por Harper 241:81-4 O '70

KIPPLEY, John F.
Parish councils: democratic process or new absolutism? America 123:94-7 Ag 22 '70

KIRCHER, Sylvia Foster
Chaparral. il Audubon 72:4-15 N '70

KIRK, Claude Roy, 1926-
Crisis in Southern schools; excerpts from statements, February 3, 1970. por(p39) U S News 68:43-4 F 16 '70
I, Claudius. Newsweek 75:35 Ap 27 '70

about

Ain't nobody gonna touch king Claude. il por Time 95:16 Ap 20 '70 •
Having fun with Florida. R. M. Williams. il Nation 211:109-14 Ag 17 '70 •
How to win by losing. Time 95:22 Ap 27 '70 •
Kirk's caper. il Newsweek 75:40-2 Ap 20 '70 •
Lesson from the governor. Chr Today 14:25 My 8 '70 •

KIRK, David, and others
Hoover's conspiracy; letter to editor. Commonweal 93:291+ D 18 '70

KIRK, David K.
Tape recording facts and fallacies. il Radio-Electr 41:53+ O '70

KIRK, Gerry
If not Thieu, who? por Nat R 22:667-9 Je 30 '70

KIRK, John J.
Changing of the guard. por Camp Mag 42:4 Mr '70
Ecology comes to camp. por Camp Mag 42:4 N '70
Organized camp: a laboratory for learning. por Camp Mag 42:4 Je '70

KIRK, John T.
Early American furniture; excerpts. il Antiques 98:428-31 S '70

KIRK, Russell
From the academy. See issues of National review

KIRKLAND, Gelsey
First flight of a bright new Firebird. il pors Life 69:32-7 Jl 31 '70 •
Hatching a new Firebird. H. Saal. por Newsweek 75:89 Je 8 '70 •

KIRKPATRICK, Curry
Amateur week at the Heritage. il Sports Illus 33:22-3 D 7 '70
Basketball. il Sports Illus 32:82+ Ap 13 '70
College basketball (cont) Sports Illus 33:55-6 D 14 '70
Even end to an eventful year. il Sports Illus 32:26-8+ Mr 23 '70
Golf (cont) Sports Illus 33:42-3 Ag 10; 98+ S 14 '70
Nontransmogrification of Orville Moody. por Sports Illus 32:34-7 Je 22 '70
Odds on for the pro bowl. Sports Illus 32:47-8 F 9 '70
One more war to go. il Sports Illus 32:12-15 Mr 2 '70
Six days in April: life and hard times of a Masters rookie. il pors Sports Illus 32:50-4+ Ap 6 '70
Toughest kid on anybody's block. il por Sports Illus 34:20-2+ Ja 4 '71
UCLA: simple, awesomely simple. Sports Illus 33:39-43 N 30 '70
(ed) See Sarazen, G. Keep your game young

KIRKPATRICK, Dick
National wildlife visits Arthur Singer. il pors Nat Wildlife 8:58-63 D '69
Will the real Shinnecock swordfish tournament please stand up? il Motor B 125:26 Ap '70

KIRKPATRICK, Miles W.
FTC gets tough. por Time 96:80 O 19 '70 •
Logical choice to head the FTC. Bsns W p21-2 Ag 15 '70 •

KIRKPATRICK, R. B.
National wildlife visits Guy Coheleach. il pors Nat Wildlife 8:41-3 O '70
Trees of yuletide. il Nat Wildlife 9:12-16 D '70

KIRKPATRICK, Sandra
Hey, hero! il Read Digest 97:71-5 S '70

KIRKTON, Carole M.
Reference shelf for curriculum planning. Engl J 59:1306-12 D '70

KIRP, David L.
Race, class, and the limits of schooling. Ed Digest 36:12-15 O '70

KIRPICHNIKOV, Aleksandr
Golden hoard of the Scythians. il UNESCO Courier 23:18-21 O '70

KIRSCH, Wolff M. and others
Bulk isolation in nonaqueous media of nuclei from lyophilized cells. bibliog il Science 168:1592-5 Je 26 '70

KIRSCHENBAUM, Howard
Sensitivity modules. Ed Digest 35:16-18 My '70

KIRSHENBAUM, Jerry
Aaah-eeee-aaah... umgawa. il pors Sports Illus 33:58-60+ Ag 17 '70
Greening of the fighting Irish. il Sports Illus 33:76-8+ D 14 '70
Hairiest team of all. il Sports Illus 32:104-6+ Ap 13 '70
Keeping 'em down on the farm. il pors Sports Illus 32:44-7 My 18 '70
Now look who's an old lady. il pors Sports Illus 33:18-20+ Ag 31 '70
Speed king without a kingdom. il pors Sports Illus 32:64-8+ Ap 27 '70
Top hat, white tie and bare toes. il por Sports Illus 34:30-3 Ja 4 '71
—and Mechem, R. M.
Plenty of air if you know where. Sports Illus 32:63-4 My 25 '70

KIRSHNER, Donnie
Bubble-gum music. A. Goldman. il por Life 68:13 Ja 30 '70

KIRSTEIN, Lincoln
Art books of 1970. Nation 211:695+ D 28 '70

KIRSTEN, Dorothy
Musician of the month. por Hi Fi 20:MA8 O '70 •

KIRSTEN, T. and others
Rare gases in lunar samples: study of distribution and variations by a microprobe technique. il Science 167:571-4 Ja 30 '70

KIRWAN, John D.
Boola-boola 1970; poem. Nat R 22:437 My 19 '70
Juarez hell. Nat R 22:899 Ag 25 '70

KISHI, Hideshi
Religious aspects of cosmic consciousness. pors Chr Cent 87:1533-6 D 23 '70

KISS, Zoltan J.
Photochromics. bibliog il por Phys Today 23:42-9 Ja '70

KISSIMMEE RIVER
River-eater. P. Matthiessen. il Audubon 72:52-3 Mr '70

KISSINGER, Henry Alfred
Henry's wonderful machine. J. Osborne. New Repub 162:11-13 Ja 31 '70
How Nixon decided to invade Cambodia. D. R. Maxey. il Look 34:22-5 Ag 11 '70 •
How Nixon's White House works. il pors Time 95:15-20 Je 8 '70 •
Kissinger, Kennedy and order. W. F. Buckley, jr. Nat R 22:532 My 19 '70 •
Pleasures of global chess. H. Sidey. il por Life 68:4 F 27 '70 •
Who speaks for the United States? il por Newsweek 76:31-2 Jl 27 '70 •

KISTIAKOWSKY, George B. See Rathjens, G. W. jt. auth.

KIT greenhouses. See Greenhouses

KITAGAWA, Daisuke
Obituary
Chr Cent 87:436 Ap 15 '70. A. Geyer •

KITCHEN cabinets
Bright ideas for dull cabinets. H. A. Dawson. il Bet Hom & Gard 48:66-7+ Ap '70
Kitchen's pushed-out side is a new storage wall. il Sunset 144:119 Je '70
Roll-outs in the kitchen. il Sunset 144:117 Mr '70

KITCHEN furniture
Build this kitchen island. H. Wicks. il Pop Mech 134:186-8 N '70
Is this the kitchen island to end all kitchen islands? il Sunset 145:76-7 O '70

KITCHEN furniture—*Continued*
Kitchen cart with swing-up leaves. il Sunset 144:134 Ap '70
Next, your counter tops. il Bet Hom & Gard 48:68-9+ Ap '70
See also
Kitchen cabinets

KITCHEN garbage grinders. See Refuse grinders

KITCHEN gardening. See Vegetable gardening, Home

KITCHEN knives. See Knives

KITCHEN range hoods. See Ventilators

KITCHEN sinks. See Sinks

KITCHEN storage. See Storage in the home

KITCHEN thermometers. See Thermometers, Cooking

KITCHEN towels. See Towels

KITCHEN utensils
Brides equip their kitchens; lists of basic kitchen equipment. M. Davidson. il Ladies Home J 87:30+ Je '70
Ceramic ladles. G. Hageman. il Ceram Mo 18:22-3 N '70
Cooking in clay; with recipes. J. Vetz. il Am Home 73:84+ Mr '70
Cooking with flower power. N. Craig. il House B 112:134-5 N '70
Cooking with glass. M. K. Spencer. il Am Home 74:66+ Ja '71
Different track; foreign accents in the kitchen. il House B 112:3 Ag '70
Easy come easy go cookware: the move outdoors. N. Craig. il House B 112:94-5 Je '70
Equipment to store, prepare, and cook vegetables. il House & Gard 137:95 F '70
For your kitchen: exotic pots, exotic cookery. il Changing T 24:43-5 D '70
Gifts I'd like to give. J. Pépin. il House B 112:47 D '70
How can you beat an egg? equipment for mixing and cooking eggs. il McCalls 97:106-7 Mr '70
In housewares, color is the thing. il Changing T 24:28 Ap '70
New flavor in home cookware. il Bsns W p98-100 Ap 4 '70
Pots and pans. J. R. Cary. il Parents Mag 45:58-61 Je '70
Pots, pans, and gadgets, an international collection. il House & Gard 137:124-7 Ap '70
Surprise her with a cheese slicer? il Sunset 145:58-9 D '70
Twenty-five bright ideas for your kitchen. il Good H 170:124-5+ Mr '70
Western kitchen. See issues of Sunset
Where to find bargains in Paris for your kitchen. il Sunset 144:86-7 Je '70
World of things to help you prepare lunch. il House & Gard 137:146-7 Mr '70
Your cooking is only as good as your tools. J. Jaffry. il Am Home 73:90-2+ N '70
See also
Knives
Molds (cookery)
Scoops

Care

Easier kitchen cleanup. E. Taylor. il Good H 171:181 D '70
Ways to keep pots and pans clean. il Good H 171:157 S '70

KITCHEN ventilators. See Ventilators

KITCHEN ware. See Kitchen utensils

KITCHENS
Always workable but now more inviting. il Sunset 144:136 My '70
Big little kitchen. M. Davidson. il Ladies Home J 87:52+ Mr '70
Design flair rescues a vacation kitchen. il House B 112:67-9 Jl '70
Easy kitchen renewal, with paint and paper. il House B 112:223 O '70
GH updates an old-fashioned kitchen. il Good H 170:108-9 My '70
Heart of this new kitchen is an island that moves. il Sunset 144:127 Mr '70
Is the kitchen a thing of the past? symposium; ed. by N. Craig. il House B 112:68-71 Ja '70
Its design keeps everybody out of the way of the cook. il Sunset 144:104 Je '70
It's the same spacious kitchen, but the work area is tighter. il Sunset 145:84-5 Ag '70
Kid-watcher kitchen. il Bet Hom & Gard 48:60 My '70
Kitchen secrets of five master cooks. J. Wilson. il pors House & Gard 138:74-83 Jl '70
Kitchen with an open-door policy. il House B 112:132-3+ N '70
Kitchen women want. M. Davidson. il Ladies Home J 87:108-11+ O '70
Kitchens just aren't what they used to be. N. Seney. il Bet Hom & Gard 48:68-75 S '70

Lazy woman's kitchen. E. Stuby. il por Farm J 94:77 Mr '70
Mobile help for a new kitchen. N. Craig. il House B 112:148-9 My '70
One-of-a-kind kitchen with ready-to-adapt ideas. il Good H 171:130-1 O '70
Personality lunch in kitchens around the world. il House & Gard 137:131+ Mr '70
She loves her conversation kitchen. J. Gillies. il Farm J 93:50-1 O '69
Sociable family kitchens. M. K. Spencer. il Am Home 73:96-9 My '70
Super kitchen. il House & Gard 137:92-5+ Ja '70
This cheerful kitchen is an open U with an island. il Sunset 145:68-9 S '70
Three kitchens in wood. N. Craig. il House B 112:108-11+ S '70
Transformation by design: new life for five old kitchens. il House B 112:88-97+ F '70
Yes, I painted my new kitchen cabinets! J. Gillies. il Farm J 94:42-3 Ja '70
Your kitchen of tomorrow. M. K. Spencer. il Am Home 73:72-3 O '70

KITEREZA, Aniceti
How men and women came to live together: Kerebe tale; translation: with biographical notes by G. Hartwig and C. Hartwig. il por Natur Hist 79:8-9 Ja '70

KITES
Kites over the sea. A. J. Hiller. il por Sea Front 16:51-3 Ja '70
Kiting! il Bet Hom & Gard 48:52-3 Je '70

KITMAN, Marvin
Kitman's laws. S. K. Oberbeck. por Newsweek 75:123+ Ap 20 '70 *

KITTATINNY MOUNTAINS
Wings over Hawk Mountain. D. S. Heintzelman. il Nat Wildlife 8:22-7 Ag '70

KIWI fruit. See Yangtaos

KJELGAARD, Betty
Few days of summer; story. Seventeen 29:148-9 Mr '70
Nicest part of all; story. Good H 171:64-5 Jl '70

KLAIBER, Jeffrey L.
Freedom equals liberation. il America 122:606-9 Je 6 '70
Pentecostal breakthrough. il America 122:99-102 Ja 31 '70

KLAMKIN, Charles
Shopping for appliances. Nation 212:81-3 Ja 18 '71

KLARE, Michael T.
Great South Asian war. il Nation 210:265-73 Mr 9 '70
Military research network. Nation 211:327-32 O 12 '70
Policing the empire. Commonweal 92:455-61 S 18 '70
Sun never sets on America's empire. Commonweal 92:239-43 My 22 '70

KLARMANN, Joseph. See Friedlander, M. W. jt. auth.

KLAUSNER, Samuel Z.
(ed) Society and its physical environment. bibliog f il Ann Am Acad 389:1-115 My '70
Thinking social-scientifically about environmental quality. Ann Am Acad 389:1-10 My '70

KLAVAN, Gene
Radio-downhill all the way. Nation 212:5 Ja 4 '71 *

KLAW, Barbara
New nostalgia: many happy returns. il Am Heritage 21:34-9 Je '70

KLAW, Spencer
Management psychologists have landed. il Fortune 81:106-9+ Ap '70

KLEBANOFF, Arthur M.
Is there a Jewish vote? Commentary 49:43-7 Ja '70

KLEBANOFF, Seymour J.
Myeloperoxidase: contribution to the microbicidal activity of intact leukocytes. bibliog il Science 169:1095-7 S 11 '70

KLEE, Albert J.
Let DARE make your solid-waste decisions. il Am City 85:100-3 F '70

KLEE, Gerald D. and Gorwitz, Kurt
Effects of the Baltimore riots on psychiatric hospital admissions. Ment Hy 54:447-9 Jl '70

KLEE, Paul
Inward perspectives. R. Hughes. il por Time 96:66-8 N 30 '70 *

KLEIN, Alexander
Toward participatory citizenship; excerpt from Natural enemies? Cur 121:3-11 S '70

KLEIN, David
College & careers. See issues of Seventeen

KLEIN, David C. and Weller, J. L.
Indole metabolism in the pineal gland: a circadian rhythm in N-acetyltransferase. bibliog il Science 169:1093-5 S 11 '70

KLEIN, David C.—*Continued*
—and others
Melatonin synthesis: adenosine 3',5'-monophosphate and norepinephrine stimulate N-acetyltransferase. bibliog il Science 168: 979-80 My 22 '70
Pineal gland: dibutyryl cyclic adenosine monophosphate stimulation of labeled melatonin production. bibliog il Science 167:1738-40 Mr 27 '70
KLEIN, David Raphael
Is there a substitute for God? Read Digest 96:51-5 Mr '70
KLEIN, Edith
How to plan your pre-camp and in-camp staff training. Camp Mag 42:15 Je '70
KLEIN, Elinor
Welcome but warning. Harp Baz 103:84-5 Ag '70
KLEIN, Eloise
Genesis reversing; poem. America 122:131 F 7 '70
KLEIN, Frederick C.
Chemistry of violence. Sci Digest 68:8-12 D '70
KLEIN, Herbert George
Commissar of credibility. D. Bonafede. Nation 210:392-6 Ap 6 '70 *
KLEIN, Jan
Histocompatibility-2 (H-2) polymorphism in wild mice. bibliog il Science 168:1362-4 Je 12 '70
KLEIN, Jerome
Could you be an April fool? Sci Digest 67: 71+ Ap '70
KLEIN, LeRoy, and Currey, J. D.
Echinoid skeleton: absence of a collagenous matrix. bibliog il Science 169:1209-10 S 18 '70
KLEIN, Norma
Apocalypse at the Plaza; story. Mlle 70:240-1 Ap '70
KLEIN, Paul
Dann v. Klein: the best game in town. pors Time 95:98+ My 25 '70 *
Inside TV view stirs media flap. Bsns W p52 Mr 14 '70 *
KLEIN, Richard M.
Bananas in Vermont; with biographical sketch. il Natur Hist 79:8, 10-12+ bibliog(p82) F; 10-12 Mr '70
KLEIN, Roger
Creative editing award in memory of Roger Klein. Pub W 198:30 N 2 '70 *
KLEIN, Thomas D.
Personal growth in the classroom: Dartmouth, Dixon, and humanistic psychology. bibliog f Engl J 59:235-43 F '70
KLEIN and Wagner; story. See Hesse, H.
KLEINBERG, David L. See Frantz, A. G. jt. auth.
KLEINDIENST, Richard G.
Case for pretrial detention; address, January 30, 1970. Vital Speeches 36:354-9 Ap 1 '70
KLEINER, Burt
Kleiner's eclipse. Newsweek 76:51 Ag 24 '70 *
KLEINER, Bell and company
Good-by to a guru. Newsweek 76:90-1 D 14 '70
Hot-shot broker makes a cold exit. Bsns W p 19 Ag 29 '70
Kleiner's eclipse. Newsweek 76:51 Ag 24 '70
KLEMENZ, Hans Peter
Gallery: photographs. Life 69:8-9 O 30 '70
KLEMESRUD, Judy
Coming Wednesday: a herstory-making event. il N Y Times Mag p6+ Ag 23 '70
Having wonderful encounter. il N Y Times Mag p8-9+ D 20 '70
KLEMPERER, Otto
Bearding the lion. A. M. Lingg. il pors Opera N 35:12-15 S 19 '70 *
KLEPPER, Dan
Be your own bird dog. il Field & S 75:46-7+ S '70
KLINTWORTH, Robert J.
Film: an art form il Sch Arts 69:24-6 Mr '70
KLITGAARD, Robert E.
Onward Christian soldiers: dehumanization and the military chaplain. il Chr Cent 87: 1377-80 N 18 '70
KLOMAN, William
Banality of the new evil. il Esquire 73:115-17+ Mr '70
KLOS, Dieter
From Profiteer to choreographer: Dieter Klos of the Gelsenkirchen ballet. N. M. Stoop. il pors Dance Mag 44:40-2 Ag '70 *
KLUGMAN, Jack
Odd squad. il pors Time 96:74+ O 26 '70 *
KLÜVER, Billy
Onward and upward with the arts. C. Tomkins. New Yorker 46:86+ O 3 '70 *
KLYSTRONS
X-ray measurements near high-power klystrons. R. L. Lehman. bibliog il Science 169: 52-4 Jl 3 '70

KNAB, Oscar R.
Making a 6-inch air-spaced visual objective. il por Sky & Tel 40:46-53 Jl '70
KNAP, Jerome J.
In defense of the versatile dog. il Field & S 75:174-5+ My '70
Mercury poisoning; or, The fish you catch can kill you! Field & S 75:44-5+ Jl '70
KNAPP, Dan. See Conway, M. jt. auth
KNAPP, Diane
Nun's search for freedom drives her from the convent. M. Fay. il pors Life 68:26-7 Mr 20 '70 *
KNAPP, J. Merrill
Handel's Tamerlano: the creation of an opera. bibliog f il Mus Q 56:405-30 Jl '70
KNAPP, Sherman Richmond
Nuclear controversy; address, November 16, 1970. Vital Speeches 37:145-9 D 15 '70
KNAPPENBERGER, Dorothy. See Reeves, R. jt. auth.
KNAUER, Virginia Harrington Wright
Magna carta? bill emerging in Congress. Newsweek 75:81+ My 18 '70 *
Virginia Knauer: what she tells the President about consumers. il por Nations Bsns 58: 34-8 Jl '70 *
KNEBEL, Fletcher
Hollywood: broke, and getting rich. il Look 34:50-2 N 3 '70
Why we need new politicians. Look 34:74 Ja 13 '70
KNECHT, Kenneth B.
Chief engineer of a small radio station. il pors Electr World 83:37-40 My '70
Designing a small CCTV system. il Electr World 84:34-7+ D '70
KNEE
Mechanics of medicine; new joints for old. A. S. Freese. il Pop Mech 135:95+ Ja '71

Wounds and injuries

Football knee; report by the National research council. il Newsweek 76:78 S 7 '70
KNEESE, Allen V.
Economic responsibility for the by-products of production. il Ann Am Acad 389:56-62 My '70
KNEPLER, John
Cross-modulation and intermodulation in receiver R.F. amplifiers. il Electr World 83: 55-8 Mr '70
KNETSCH, Jack L. See Krutilla, J. V. jt. auth.
KNICKERBOCKER, Suzy, pseud. See Mehle, A.
KNIFE handles. See Handles
KNIFE sharpening. See Sharpening
KNIGHT, Arthur
Flood of film books. il Sat R 53:15-17 D 26 '70
SR goes to the movies. See issues of Saturday review
Wise in Hollywood. il por Sat R 53:22-5 Ag 8 '70
KNIGHT, Cook
Down and locked? il Flying 88:50-1 Ja '71
KNIGHT, Doug
New Brunswick: mixed-bag bonanza. il por Field & S 74:84-5+ Ap '70
(ed) See Washburn, J. Trophy bucks are easy
KNIGHT, Frances G.
Clash by Knight. por Time 96:17 O 19 '70 *
She's the American traveler's best friend. J. Keats. Read Digest 96:39-40+ F '70 *
KNIGHT, Max. See Fabry, J. jt. auth.
KNIGHT, Pamela
Design for sport (cont) Sports Illus 33:42-6 S 28; 76-7 N 30 '70
KNIGHT, Thomas J.
Is our history obsolete? Ed Digest 35:23-31 My '70
KNIGHT newspapers, Inc.
Why newspapers are making money again. il Bsns W p36-8+ Ag 29 '70
KNIGHTON, David R.
Student's open letter to God. Chr Today 14: 16 Je 5 '70
KNIGHTS foundry. See Foundries
KNIGHTS hospitallers. See Malta, Knights of
KNIGHTS of Columbus

Headquarters

Landmark tower on New Haven's skyline. R. Jensen. il Arch Rec 148:109-15 Ag '70
KNIGHTS of Malta. See Malta, Knights of
KNIGHTS of St John. See Malta, Knights of
KNISELY, Melvin H.
Alcohol and your brain. A. Q. Maisel. Read Digest 96:67-9 Je '70 *
KNIT goods
Cotton knits that won't shrink out of shape. il Good H 172:6 Ja '71

KNITTING
Knit something small & special! il Good H 170: 150+ Ap '70
Loos knit; washcloths. A. Loos. il por McCalls 97:60+ Ap '70
KNIVES
Block party. il McCalls 98:72-3+ Ja '71
Care and choosing of knives. J. Pépin. il House B 112:116 S '70
Kitchen knives and their care. E. Taylor. il Good H 171:145 N '70
Make this one-piece knife sheath. R. W. Berger. il Pop Mech 133:162 Je '70
Number one knife? It's French. il Sunset 144: 110-11 Ap '70
KNIVES, Painting. See Artists materials
KNOCK on the door; drama. See Parrella. L.
KNOEPFLE, John
Now; poem. Nation 212:88 Ja 18 '71
KNOLL, Erwin
Oil lobby is not depleted. il N Y Times Mag p26-7+ Mr 8; 138+ Ap 5 '70
KNOLLE, Tex
Gourd that kept growing. il Org Gard & Farm 17:94+ Je '70
KNOPF, Terry Ann
Race, riots and reporters. il Commonweal 92: 336-40 Jl 10 '70; Same abr. with title Race and the press. Cur 121:20-5 S '70
KNOPS, Mark
If something has to give. por Newsweek 76: 74 S 14 '70 *
KNOTS, Macramé. See Macramé
KNOTS and splices
All about dock lines; a lesson for ladies. R. L. Williamson. il Motor B 125:62-7 Je '70
Indispensable rope. C. B. Colby. il Outdoor Life 145:16+ Ja '70
Knots that everyone ties backwards; bowline knot. A. S. Woodle. il Motor B 126:16 Jl '70
KNOTTING. See Macramé
KNOTT'S berry farm. See Amusement parks
KNOWLEDGE
Indicators of the capacities for societal guidance. A. Etzioni. bibliog f il Ann Am Acad 388:25-34 Mr '70
Initiative in learning. D. S. Seckinger. Sch & Soc 98:24 Ja '70
See also
Intellect
KNOWLEDGE, Theory of
See also
Concepts
Education—Philosophy
Empiricism
KNOWLES, C. Harry
Laser beam communicator. il Pop Electr 32: 27-35+ My '70
KNOWLES, Darold
Little luck would be a relief. D. Delliquanti. Sports Illus 33:92 S 14 '70 *
KNOWLES, John H.
U.S. health: do we face a catastrophe? Look 34:74+ Je 2 '70
Where doctors fail. il Sat R 53:21-3+ Ag 22 '70
KNOX, Gerald M.
Family health. See issues of Better homes and gardens
KNOX, Gregory H. C.
Notes of a young radical. il Sat R 53:48-51+ Ag 15 '70
KNOXVILLE, Tenn.
Historic houses, etc.
History in houses; Craighead-Jackson house. G. R. Dempster. il Antiques 98:110-14 Jl '70
KNUDSEN, Semon Emil
As they see it; interview. por Forbes 106: 63-4 N 15 '70
There's a Ford in my past; interview, ed. by B. Beason. il pors Mech Illus 66:45-7+ F '70
about
Knudsen finds a home on wheels. il por Bsns W p94 N 14 '70 *
KNUDSEN, Vern
Noise, a major health problem; ed. by A. Hamilton. il Parents Mag 45:66-8 F '70
KNUDSON, Douglas M.
Brazil's decade of forestry progress. il Am For 76:57-62 O '70
KNUDSON, Rozanne
Knudson's complaint. il Am Lib 1:776-8 S '70
KNUTSON, Kent S. bp
Bishop Kent Knutson at the ALC helm. por Chr Today 15:43-4 N 20 '70 *
KO, William L.
Watercolor page; with biographical sketch. il por Am Artist 34:46-7+ O '70
KOANGA; opera. See Delius, F.

KOBAYASHI, Lenore. See Kobayashi, Tatsuki, jt. auth.
KOBAYASHI, Tatsuki, and Kobayashi, Lenore
Dolls of Tomoyo Kobayashi. il Hobbies 75: 48-9+ My '70
KOBAYASHI, Tomoyo
Dolls of Tomoyo Kobayashi. T. Kobayashi and L. Kobayashi. il Hobbies 75:48-9+ My '70 *
KOBBE, Jeffrey
Greek colonels' revenge. Nation 210:789 Je 29 '70
KOCH, Edward I.
Politics of conscience. Nation 210:165 F 16 '70 *
KOCH, Herman William
Age of change. bibliog il por Phys Today 23: 27-32 Ja '70
KOCH, Kenneth
On Christmas day no more current events; poems by schoolchildren. il N Y Times Mag p5-7 D 20 '70
(ed) Wishes, lies & dreams; excerpts. il Harp Baz 104:140-1 D '70
about
Ah, poets. il por Time 96:26-7 D 28 '70 *
Juvenile bards. il por Newsweek 75:54 Ap 6 '70 *
On a sailboat of sinking water. B. Farrell. il por Life 68:4 My 15 '70 *
Teaching writing. J. Featherstone. New Repub 163:12-14 Jl 11 '70 *
KOCH, Klaus-Friedrich
Cannibalistic revenge in Jalé warfare; with biographical sketch. il por Natur Hist 79:8, 40-51 F '70
KOCH, Ruth M.
Textile designs with foam rubber. il Sch Arts 69:14-15 F '70
KOCH, Stephen
Cruel, cruel critics. il Sat R 53:12-14+ D 26 '70
KOCH Industries, Inc.
Dynamic growth companies. il Nations Bsns 58:48-53 F '70
KOCIVAR, Ben
New world of air travel. il Mlle 70:215-18 Mr '70
P-38 from Piper? il Pop Mech 133:87-9+ My '70
KODACOLOR films. See Photography—Films
KODAK company. See Eastman Kodak company
KODAK teenage movie contest. See Moving picture photography—Competitions
KODALY, Zoltán
Hárv János. It has stuff to be a popular success. P. L. Miller. Am Rec G 36:362 Ja '70 *
KOEDT, Anne
Five passionate feminists; ed. by M. W. Lear. il pors McCalls 97:54-5+ Jl '70
KOEHLER, George A.
New capitalists of broadcasting. por Forbes 106:40 O 15 '70 *
KOEHLER, Nancy J.
Macramé jewelry; an approach to body ornamentation. il Sch Arts 70:12-13 Ja '71
KOEHLER, W. C.
French research leader receives award for accomplishments in solid state field. por Science 170:606-7 N 6 '70
KOENIG, H. P.
Aran Islands. il Travel 133:42-7+ Ap '70
Chateaux of the Loire. il Travel & Camera 33:68-71 Ap '70
Holland's hinterland. il Travel 134:34-9+ Ag '70
How to discover a resort. il Travel 133:51-5 F '70
North of Hamburg. il Travel 133:34-9+ Mr '70
Secret Swiss ski sites. il Travel 134:28-33 N '70
Winter honeymoon havens. il Travel 135:28-35 Ja '71
Yankeeland winter. il Travel 134:28-33 D '70
Yugoslavia. il Travel & Camera 33:52-63 F '70
KOEPPE, David E. and Miller, R. J.
Lead effects on corn mitochondrial respiration. bibliog il Science 167:1376-8 Mr 6 '70
KOESTLER, Arthur
Arthur Koestler at sixty-five, a fighter for men's minds now studies their brains; interview by the editors of L'Express, tr. by S. Hochman. il pors N Y Times Mag p 12-14+ Ag 30 '70
about
Cassandra revisited, a testament. A. Schlesinger, jr. Vogue 156:40 Ag 15 '70 *
KOETHE, John
Boston. Art N 69:18+ My; 30+ O '70; 12+ Ja '71
Domes; poem. Poetry 117:89-94 N '70
Freely espoused. Poetry 117:54-9 O '70

KOFFLER, Camilla. See Ylla, pseud.
KOGAN, Deen
This is street theater. il Parks & Rec 5:44-6 Ja '70
KOGAN, Michael S.
Israel moves right. Nat R 22:83 Ja 27 '70
KOH, B. C.
Two Koreas. bibliog f Cur Hist 58:209-16+ Ap '70
KOH, T. T. B.
International collaboration concerning southeast Asia; address, April 1970, with questions and answers. bibliog f Ann Am Acad 390:18-26 Jl '70
KOHL, Benjamin, and others
Barriers fall. il Environ 12:40-8 N '70
KOHLER, Carl
Great electron-pedantic project. il Pop Electr 32:48-52 F '70
Kool-keeping kwiz. Pop Electr 32:63-4 Je '70
KOHLER, Foy D.
Mideast outlook: why Russia shuns a showdown; interview. il por U S News 68:25-6 Je 22 '70
Why the Kremlin is testing Nixon; interview. por U S News 69:19-20 O 19 '70
—and Harvey, D. L.
Administering and managing the U.S. and Soviet space programs. bibliog Science 169: 1049-56 S 11 '70
KOHLER, Harrison
What price Vietnam glory? il Chr Cent 87: 113-14 Ja 28 '70
KÖHLER, Heinz, and others
Macroglobulin structure: variable sequence of light and heavy chains. bibliog il Science 169:56-9 Jl 3 '70
KÖHLER, Karl Heinz
Beethoven's conversation books. il Hi Fi sec I 20:56-63 Ja '70
KOHLER, Mariane
Color: a clue to your character. il Seventeen 29:158-9 Mr '70
KOHMAN, Truman P. and others
Lead and thallium isotopes in Mare Tranquillitatis surface material. bibliog il Science 167:481-3 Ja 30 '70
KOHN, Dixie A. See Beltz, G. jt. auth.
KOHN, Sherwood Davidson
Paolo Soleri thinks very big. il por N Y Times Mag p26-7+ Jl 26 '70
Warning: the green slime is here. il N Y Times Mag p26-7+ Mr 22 '70
KOHNE, David E. See Britten, R. J. jt. auth.
KOKJOHN, Joseph E.
Hell of a question. Commonweal 93:367-70 Ja 15 '71
KOLARS, John
Belvedere; poem. Commonweal 93:223 N 27 '70
KOLB, Anne
Glow of candles: for warmth, romance. House B 112:28-9 D '70
KOLBE, Robert
Dawley re-asserts realism. il Am Artist 34: 69-76 Mr '70
KOLBERG, Fritz. See Zurakowski, P. R. jt. auth.
KOLFF, Willem Johan
Era of plastic hearts. B. J. Culliton. il por Sci N 97:375-7 Ap 11 '70 *
Gathering of specialists. B. J. Culliton. il pors Sci N 97:347-9 Ap 4 '70 *
KOLINS, Bill
London notebook. Pub W 197:38-9 Je 15; 198: 26-7 Jl 6; 23-4 Ag 10; pt2 177-8 S 21; 28-9 O 19 '70
KOLLAS, Joseph E.
Build your own easel. il Design 72:13 Wint '70
New use for old prints. il Design 71:14-15 Sum '70
KOLLMAN, Peter A. See Allen, L. C. jt. auth.
KOLODIN, Irving
Berlioz's Les Troyens, Busoni's Doktor Faust, and Hindemith's Cardillac. il pors Sat R 53:43-4 Jl 25 '70
Music to my ears. See issues of Saturday review
Recordings in review. See issues of Saturday review
Recordings reports: miscellaneous LPs. See issues of Saturday review
Recordings reports: orchestral LPs. See issues of Saturday review
Size of Szell. por Sat R 53:33-5+ Ag 29 '70
Three men on a hobby. il pors Sat R 53:47-9 O 31 '70
Twenty years of Schwann. il por Am Rec G 36:540-2 Ap '70
KOLODNEY, David
San Francisco mime troupe. il Ramp Mag 9: 26 Ag '70
(tr) See Beauvoir, S. de. On aging

KOLTUN, Frances L.
Tahiti. il Mlle 71:189-90+ O '70
To put your town on the map. Read Digest 97:31-2+ S '70
KOLZ, Richard C. and O'Dell, John
Flow chart approach to curriculum study. il Clear House 45:72-5 O '70
KOMAIKO, Jean R.
Shocking failure of the School lunch act. Parents Mag 45:56-9 Mr '70
KOMATSU, S. R. and Johnston, R. W.
Tour de force in water-plant design. il Am City 85:60-2 Ag '70
KOMISAR, Lucy
New feminism. Sat R 53:27-30+ F 21 '70
KOMMER, Ronald S.
Marvelous cork bug. il Outdoor Life 146:52-5+ Jl '70
KOMORNY, Annie
September song; poem. Good H 171:146 S '70
KONDO, Allan K.
Children can't think. Ed Digest 35:32-3 Ja '70
KONG Le. See Le, K.
KONIGSBURG, Elaine (Lobl)
Double image, address, 1969. il por Library J 95:731-4 F 15 '70
KONOPKA, Gisela
How to make camping significant in the 1970's. por Camp Mag 42:8-11 Ja '70
Is the generation gap widening? No, not really. il PTA Mag 65:6-8 bibliog(p35) O '70
KOOB, C. Albert
Agents for Christian community. il America 122:335-7 Mr 28 '70
Where is the Catholic school system heading? America 123:169-71 S 19 '70
KOOKABURRAS
Kookiest kook of all. il Am For 76:4-5 D '70
KOON, Judith F.
Cues for teaching the emotionally disturbed: turn on, tune in, drop out. Clear House 44:497-500 Ap '70
KOONTZ, Elizabeth Duncan
Complete integration must be the goal. por Ebony 25:133-41 Ag '70
Liberated, all liberated. il pors Vogue 155: 120-1 Je '70 *
KOOPMAN, John M.
Keep in gear. il Motor B 126:59+ D '70
KOOYMAN, Gerald L. and others
Bronchograms and tracheograms of seals under pressure. bibliog il Science 169:82-4 Jl 3 '70
KOPECHNE, Mrs Joseph
Truth about Mary Jo; ed. by S. James. il pors McCalls 97:65-7+ S '70
KOPECHNE, Mary Jo
Back to Chappaquiddick; grand jury inquiry. Newsweek 75:27-8 Ap 6 '70 *
Chappaquiddick. por Time 95:11 Ap 6 '70
Chappaquiddick: suspicions renewed. il pors Time 95:30+ My 11 '70 *
Grand jury. por Newsweek 75:23-4 Ap 13 '70 *
New look at Kennedy case and a public airing? grand jury probing. il por U S News 68:20-1 Ap 13 '70 *
This case is closed. il Newsweek 75:42 Ap 20 '70 *
Truth about Mary Jo; ed. by S. James. Mrs J. Kopechne. il pors McCalls 97:65-7+ S '70 *
KOPKIND, Andrew
Hard times. Ramp Mag 9:8-9 D '70
Is it revolution? Cur 118:18-21 My '70
—and Lang, Frances
How far repression? Cur 115:36-8 F '70
KOPP, Roger A.
High altitude observatory's 1970 eclipse expedition. il Sky & Tel 39:359-62 Je '70
KOPPLEMAN, Edward
Genius, but not mad. pors Forbes 106:71 N 15 '70 *
KORALL, Burt
Bill Evans aone. il por Sat R 53:46-7 Jl 25 '70
Everybody's talkin' about Nilsson. il por Sat R 53:56 Ja 17 '70
James Taylor: sunshine and... por Sat R 53:83+ S 12 '70
KOREA
Union (proposed)
U.N. reaffirms objectives for reunification of Korea: statements, November 11, 12 and 25, 1969; with text of resolution. W. B. Buffum; J. I. Whalley. Dept State Bul 61:609-15 D 22 '69
KOREA (People's Republic)
Two Koreas. B. C. Koh. bibliog f Cur Hist 58:209-16+ Ap '70
See also
United Nations—Korea (People's Republic)

KRAMER, Hilton
Episodes from the sixties. il Art in Am 58:
56-61 Ja '70
KRAMER, Jane
Letter from Dublin. New Yorker 46:56-65 Jl
25 '70
Profiles; founding cadre: personalities of and
dialogues among some members of a
womens liberation group. New Yorker 46:
52-6+ 28 '70
Reporter at large. New Yorker 46:33-6+ Ag
29; 43-8+ S 5; 112+ S 12 '70
KRAMER, Jerry
We played for Lombardi. il por Life 69:53-4
S 11 '70; Same abr. Read Digest 97:159-62
D '70
KRAMER, Rita
Parent and child (cont) N Y Times Mag
p99-100+ Mr 15 '70
KRAMER, Robert
Current cinema. P. Kael. New Yorker 46:
136-9 O 24 '70 *
KRAUS, Arthur James Israel
Finale, almost. J. Deedy. Commonweal 92:
258 My 29 '70 *
Kraus' vindication. J. Deedy. Commonweal
91:466 Ja 30 '70
KRAUS, Richard
Economics of recreation today. il por Parks
& Rec 5:19-21+ Je '70
KRAUS, Robert
William Steig. il por Horn Bk 46:361-3 Ag '70
KRAUSE, Allison
Death story. E. Segal. il pors Ladies Home
J 87:100-1+ O '70 *
KRAUSE, Bernard
Earth people's pop; In a wild sanctuary. E.
Sander. pors Sat R 53:37 Ag 29 '70 *
KRAUSE, George
Gallery; photographs. Life 69:6-7 O 23 '70
KRAUSE, Harold A.
Dynamic growth companies; American sales-
masters, ltd. il por Nations Bsns 58:68-71 Jl
'70 *
KRAUSE, Richard F.
Build a light garden for winter salads. il
Org Gard & Farm 17:111-12 O '70
KRAWITT, Edward L. and others
Amino acid transport in hepatoma cell cul-
tures during tyrosine aminotransferase in-
duction. bibliog il Science 169:294-6 Jl 17 '70
KREBS, A. V. Jr
Agribusiness in California. Commonweal 93:
45-7 O 9 '70
KREBS, Margaret
Liturgy, the celebration of life. America 123:
147-9 S 12 '70
KREBS, Marguerite, and Krebs, Robert
Are you raising a perfectionist? il Todays
Health 48:39-41 Ag '70
KREBS, Robert. See Krebs, Marguerite, jt.
auth.
KREBS, Robert P. See Pearson, A. D. jt. auth.
KRECH, David
Don't use the kitchen-sink approach to en-
richment: adaptation of address. il Todays
Ed 59:30-2+ O '70
KREIMER, Evered. See Mallas, J. H. jt. auth.
KREISKY, Bruno
Unorthodox route to power. por Time 95:40
Mr 16 '70 *
KRENEK, Ernst
Ernst Krenek's new opera. P. Moor. il Hi Fi
20:MA19 N '70 *
That's what happens. Criticism
Hi Fi il 20:MA19 N '70 *
KRENTS, Harold
What? Laugh at a blind boy? T. Prideaux. il
pors Life 68:57-8 F 6 '70
KRESGE, S. S, company
How Kresge became the top discounter. il
Bsns W p62-3+ O 24 '70
S. S. Kresge: unlikely material. il Forbes
107:27 Ja 1 '71
When 2 cents=$380 million. il Forbes 105:
60-1 Ap 1 '70
KRESSLEY, June
Tribal dolls of South Africa. il Negro Hist
Bul 32:20-1 D '69
KRETCHMER, Jerome
Dream of gas masks. il por Newsweek 76:58+
D 7 '70
KRETTEK, Germaine, and Cooke, E. D.
ALA Washington notes. See issues of Wilson
library bulletin
KREVITSKY, Nik
Crafts today. il Am Artist 35:16 Ja '71
KRICH, Aron, and Blum, Sam
Marriage and the mystique of romance. Red-
book 136:65+ N '70
KRIEBEL, Charles
His bazaar. See issues of Harper's bazaar
KRIEGEL, Leonard
Günter Grass' tale of men and molars in a
mended Germany. Commonweal 92:195-6
My 8 '70

Last stop on the D train: in the land of the
new racists. Am Scholar 39:272-88 Spr '70
KRIEGER, George
Training nursing assistants for a subprofes-
sional role. bibliog Ment Hy 54:152-4 Ja '70
KRILL, John
Mulch-planted onions beat spring mud. il
Org Gard & Farm 17:46-7 F '70
KRINSKY, Norman
Stamping, a new technique for making
prints; interview. il Am Artist 34:38-43 S '70
KRISTAN, William B. Jr, and Gerstein, G. L.
Plasticity of synchronous activity in a small
neural net. bibliog il Science 169:1336-9 S
25 '70
KRISTOFFERSON, Kris
Kris Kristofferson is the new Nashville
sound. P. Hemphill. il pors N Y Times
Mag p54-5+ D 6 '70 *
KRISTOL, Irving
Books & ideas. Fortune 81:191-2 Mr; 197-8
Je '70
Urban civilization & its discontents. Com-
mentary 50:29-35 Jl; 44+ N '70; 51:26 Ja
'71
What business is a university in? N Y Times
Mag p30-1+ Mr 22; 22 Ap 19 '70; Same abr.
with title Toward universities for edu-
cation. Cur 118:51-6 My '70
KROCH'S and Brentano's. See Booksellers and
bookselling—Illinois
KROGAGER, Eilif
Pastor's hobby. il pors Newsweek 76:69 S 21
'70 *
KROHN, Herbert
Grand tour de Saigon; poem. New Yorker
46:36 Mr 7 '70
KROKER, Bruno
Reinventing the NCC. Chr Cent 87:885 Jl 22 '70
KROKODIL (periodical) See Periodicals—Rus-
sia
KROLL, Ernest
Ennui; poem. Sat R 53:26 O 24 '70
Greeting; poem. Chr Cent 87:138 F 4 '70
Nick's place; poem. Sat R 53:61 My 23 '70
Song from the playing fields of Dolores
County. New Repub 162:21 Ap 18 '70
Vantage; poem. Sat R 53:16 D 5 '70
Vantage point; Drag race; poems. Sat R 53:80
Je 6 '70
KROLL, Judith
Poem of the city of New York. New Repub
162:30 Mr 7 '70
KRÖLLER-MÜLLER museum
Dawdling in the Dutch woods. H. Sutton.
Sat R 53:40-1 D 19 '70
KRONENBERGER, John
Push-button movies: the video-cassette revo-
lution. Look 34:94 N 3 '70
KRONENBERGER, Louis
Voices and visions of Aldous Huxley. Atlan
226:100-1+ Jl '70
KRONMAN, Barry S. and others
Immunotherapy of cancer: an experimental
model in syngeneic guinea pigs. bibliog il
Science 168:257-9 Ap 10 '70
KROO, György
Beethoven in retrospect: Hungary; tr. by G.
Jellinek. il Sat R 53:61-2 N 28 '70
KROOP, David C.
Make your own seven segment readout. il Pop
Electr 33:68-70 Ag '70
KROSNEY, Herbert
Harvest in Palestine. Nation 210:721-4 Je 15
'70
Israel seeks neighbors. Nation 211:457-60 N
9 '70
This winter in Jerusalem. Nation 210:47-51
Ja 19 '70
KROTKOV, Iŭrii Vasil'vich
KGB: condensation. J. Barron. il Read Digest
97:201-15 + Ag '70 *
KROYER, Karl
Up with Uncle Scrooge. por Newsweek 77:70+
Ja 11 '71 *
KRUEGER, Henry
Tote road and the pung. il Cons 24:29-31 F
'70
KRUEGER, Russell F. and Mayer, G. D.
Tilorone hydrochloride: an orally active an-
tiviral agent. il Science 169:1213-14 S 18 '70
—See Mayer, G. D. jt. auth.
KRUG, Judith F.
ALA testimony presented to Commission on
obscenity and pornography; statement,
May 4, 1970. Am Lib 1:653-5 Jl '70
Intellectual freedom. Am Lib 1:20-1, 117-18,
212-13, 336-8 Ja-Ap '70
—and Harvey J. A.
Intellectual freedom. Am Lib 1:433, 583-5,
751-2, 843-5, 944-5, 1026-7 My-Je, S-D '70
KRUGER, Juliane
Working to a Latin beat. Mlle 70:128+ Ja '70
KRUGER, W. Stanley
Program auditor: new breed on the education
scene. Am Ed 6:36 Mr '70

KRUGER NATIONAL PARK
How to catch a hippopotamus; or an elephant, or a zebra, or a buffalo. R. P. Crossley. il Pop Mech 133:102-6+ Ja '70; Same. Sci Digest 67:10-16 Mr '70
KRUGMAN, Herbert Ellis
TV vs. print. Newsweek 76:122-3 N 2 '70 *
KRUMME, Richard
Money management (cont of) What's new: money management. See issues of Successful farming
KRUPCZAK, Bobbi
I was single, unattached, and trapped. por Redbook 135:20+ Jl '70
KRUPP, George
Can fighting make a good marriage better? il Redbook 134:62-3+ F '70
Husbands and wives talk frankly about sex. Redbook 135:69+ Jl '70
KRUPP works, Essen
Krupp rises again. il Time 96:67 Ag 3 '70
KRUSZYNSKI, Eugene
Nature of urban education. Sch & Soc 98:166-8+ Mr '70
KRUTCH, Joseph Wood
Coral dunes. il Travel & Camera 33:38-41 Jl '70
If you don't mind my saying so. See issues of American scholar to Autumn 1970
It's a boojum! il por Nat Wildlife 8:36-7 Je '70
Unnatural history. il Audubon 72:36-40 N '70

about

Despairing optimist. R. Dubos. Am Scholar 40:16-20 Wint '70 *
Many worlds of Joseph Wood Krutch. B. Atkinson. il por Sat R 53:17 Jl 25 '70 *
Obituary
Audubon 72:97 Jl '70
Nation 210:677 Je 8 '70 *
Newsweek por 75:105 Je 1 '70 *
Uncommon carrier of truth. J. Barzun. Am Scholar 39:556-7 Aut '70 *
KRUTILLA, John V. and Knetsch, J. L.
Outdoor recreation economics. Ann Am Acad 389:63-70 My '70
KRYLOV, Ivan Andreevich
President Kennedy and the Russian fable. N. Cousins. il Sat R 54:20-1 Ja 9 '71 *
KSANDA, Charles J.
Make this lathe indexing attachment. il Pop Mech 134:179 O '70
KU KLUX klan
Murder in Mississippi; condensation of Attack on terror. D. Whitehead. il Read Digest 97:191-6+ S '70
U.S. journal: Luverne, Ala. G. T. Miller's plan to help Crenshaw County despite trouble with the Klan. C. Trillin. New Yorker 46:53-8 Ag 29 '70
Violence trap; arranged bombing to catch terrorists in Miss. Nation 210:261 Mr 9 '70
KU KLUX klan in art. See Art—Themes
KUBEK, Tony
OEO names retired baseball man, thirty-four, as advisor on aging. Aging 190:21 Ag '70 *
KUBIAK, T. J.
Rhodesia. il Focus 20:1-11 Je '70
KUCHARSKY, David
American ecumenism at the crossroads. Chr Today 15:7-10+ N 20 '70
KUCHEMAN, Clark
Churches and the Viet Nam issue. Chr Today 15:15-16 O 23 '70
KUDELA, Raphael M.
Facing student unrest. bibliog Clear House 44:547-52 My '70
KUDIRKA, Simas
Disobeying orders. Chr Today 15:28 Ja 1 '71 *
KUEHL, F. A. Jr, and others
Prostaglandin receptor site: evidence for an essential role in the action of luteinizing hormone. bibliog il Science 169:883-6 Ag 28 '70
KUEHL, Linda
First novels. Commonweal 93:105-6 O 23 '70
(ed) Novelists for novelists. il Commonweal 92:198-9 My 8 '70
KUEHLER, Stephen
Earthsea; poem. Horn Bk 46:419 Ag '70
KUEHNAST, Earl L. See Haines, D. A. jt. auth.
KUEHNELT-LEDDIHN, Erik Maria, ritter von
Generation gap in the western world. il Cath World 212:9-14 O '70
Letter from Latin America (cont) Nat R 22: 84, 515 Ja 27, My 19 '70
Letter from the Continent (cont) Nat R 22: 891 Ag 25 '70
Mythological and real America. il Cath World 210:208-12 F '70
KUENSTLER, Frank
Living monument; Brinkley show; Red suede stockings; poems. Nation 211:538 N 23 '70
Thumbs (the white Jew); poem. Nation 212:88 Ja 18 '71

KUERZE, Edward. See Stoms, R. K. jt. auth.
KUH, Joyce
How to make money in your spare time. Ladies Home J 87:176 N '70
KUH, Katharine
Art of Sicily. il Sat R 53:16-23 O 3 '70
Clyfford Still, the enigma. il pors Vogue 155: 180-3+ F 1 '70
Fine arts. See issues of Saturday review
KUHLMAN, Kathryn
Miracle woman. il por Time 96:62+ S 14 '70 *
KUHN, Bowie
Boo-boo or baby for Bowie. W. Leggett. il por Sports Illus 32:22-4+ Je 15 '70 *
Ideal sucker. il pors Newsweek 75:93 Mr 2 '70 *
Inside baseball. por Time 95:76-7 Je 15 '70 *
Pitcher in the wry. P. Axthelm. il por Newsweek 75:59 Je 15 '70 *
Slap on the wrist. P. Axthelm. por Newsweek 75:48 Ap 13 '70 *
Time to be frank. Sports Illus 33:11+ S 21 '70 *
KUHN, Harold B.
Consciousness III: greening or withering? Chr Today 15:14+ D 18 '70
Sensitivity training: touch and grow? Chr Today 15:61-2 N 6 '70
KUHN, James W.
Would Horatio Alger need a degree? il Sat R 53:54-5+ D 19 '70
KULLESEID, Eleanor, and Gossage, Wayne
Joint use of collections. il Am Lib 1:173-5 F '70
KULUKUNDIS, Elias. See Gage, N. jt. auth.
KUMIN, Judith
Bread; poem. Mlle 71:253 Ag '70
KUMIN, Maxine (Winokur)
Desert near Palm Springs; poem. Mlle 71:98 Je '70
Making of Mother Rosarine. Writer 83:19-21 Ap '70
Mother Rosarine; poem. Writer 83:20 Ap '70
Night, the paddock, some dreams; poem. Mlle 70:176 Ap '70
KUNC, Patricia
What to do till the baby comes. il Redbook 134:12+ F '70
KUNEN, James Simon
Ecliptic vibrations. Esquire 74:72+ Jl '70
KÜNG, Hans
Küng's publishers reprimanded. Chr Cent 88:8 Ja 6 '71 *
KUNG Fu. See Karate
KUNHARDT, Philip Bradish, 1928-
Christmas at my father's house; excerpt from My father's house. il McCalls 98: 44-5 D '70
Fair Japan waited a century for. il Life 69:8 Jl 17 '70
In and out of the news. Life 68:3 My 22 '70
My father's country; excerpt from My father's house. il Life 69:44-44B+ Jl 4 '70
My father's country; excerpt from My father's house. il Read Digest 97:197-200+ O '70
KUNITZ, Stanley
Around Pastor Bonhoeffer: The plot against Hitler; Next to last things; The extermination camp; poems. Atlan 226:94-5 D '70
King of the river; poem. Atlan 26:54-5 Jl '70
KUNSTLER, William Moses
Brief encounter with a lawyer named Kunstler; interview. ed. by C. R. Sternhell. il por McCalls 98:54-5+ Ja '71
We talk to ..; interview. por Mlle 71:297 Ag '70

about

Kunstler constituency. J. R. Coyne, jr. Nat R 22:467 My 5 '70 *
Love of client, or law? ABA criticisms. Time 95:40 Je 29 '70 *
Right on! With lawyer William Kunstler. V. S. Navasky. il pors N Y Times Mag p30-1+ Ap 19 '70 *
KUNZ, Robert F.
Environmental glossary. Sat R 54:67 Ja 2 '71
KUO, J. T. and others
Transcontinental tidal gravity profile across the United States. bibliog il Science 168: 968-71; 170:1003 My 22, N 27 '70
KUPCHAN, S. Morris, and others
Reactions of alpha methylene lactone tumor inhibitors with model biological nucleophiles. bibliog il Science 168:376-8 Ap 17 '70
KUPFERMANN, Irving, and others
Neuronal correlates of habituation and dishabituation of the gill-withdrawal reflex in aplysia. bibliog il Science 167:1743-5 Mr 27 '70
KURDISTAN
Kurdish truce. L. Jenkins. il por Newsweek 76:41 D 7 '70

KURDS
Fifth foe. il Time 95:23 Mr 23 '70

KURDYBACHA, Lukasz
Comenius documents in Poland. Sch & Soc
98:446 N '70

KURLAND, C. G.
Ribosome structure and function emergent.
bibliog il Science 169:1171–7 S 18 '70

KURLAND, Philip B.
New American university; address, January
22, 1970. Vital Speeches 36:314–17 Mr 1 '70

KURRUS, Elmer E. jr
Walkin' bear. il pors Outdoor Life 146:46–9+
D '70
(ed) See Oliver, H. M. Can you top this?

KURTIN, S. L. and others
Polywater: a hydrosol? bibliog il Science 167:
1720–2 Mr 27 '70

KURTIS, Carol
Drug abuse is your headache, too; excerpts
from Drug abuse as a business problem.
il Nations Bsns 58:38+ N '70

KURTZ, Benjamin
Black studies: time for restructuring. Clear
House 45:201–3 D '70

KURTZ, Donald J. and Kanfer, J. N.
Cerebral acid hydrolase activities: compari-
son in quaking and normal mice. bibliog il
Science 168:259–60 Ap 10 '70

KURTZ, Elaine Shaffer. See Shaffer, E.

KURTZ, Helen G.
Centralized processing: diversified. il por Library J 95:1807–12 My 15 '70

KURTZ, Stephen A.
Can you still become an old master at twenty-eight? il Art N 69:54–7 Mr '70

KURZMAN, Dan
Trade winds. C. Amory. Sat R 53:12–13 Jl
18 '70 *

KURZWEIL, Jack H.
Tenure controversy: rejected San Jose engi-
neer is wed to a red. P. M. Boffey. por
Science 170:420–2 O 23 '70 *

KUSH, Frank
Devil's devil. il Newsweek 76:56 O 26 '70 *

KUSHIRO, ikuo, and others
Crystallization of some lunar mafic magmas
and generation of rhyolitic liquid. bibliog
il Science 167:610–12 Ja 30 '70

KUSHNER, Robert. See Goldin, A. jt. auth.

KUSTOW, Michael
Prague's whispering gallery. il N Y Times
Mag p34–5+ S 13 '70

KUTAKOV, L. N.
United Nations and disarmament. UN Mo
Chron 7:56–61 My '70

KUTTNER, Robert
Many sides of the Chicago conspiracy trial.
Commonweal 93:303–4 D 18 '70

KUTTNER, Robert E. and Lorincz, A. B.
Promiscuity and prostitution in urbanized
Indian communities. bibliog Ment Hy 54:
79–91 Ja '70

KUTTNER, Robert L.
Memoirs from beyond the tomb. Commonweal 91:606–7 Mr 6 '70

KUWANO, Michihiko, and others
Ribonuclease V of escherichia coli: susceptibility of heated ribosomal RNA and
stability of R17 phage RNA. bibliog il Science 168:1225–6 Je 5 '70

KUZMA, Greg
Drowned; poem. Nation 211:316 O 5 '70
In the morning; Hose and iron; poems. Poe-
try 116:160–2 Je '70
Old block; poem. Commonweal 91:619 Mr 6
'70

KUZMANOFF, Leon
Grand prize winner. il por Life 69:107–11 D
25 '70 *

KUZNETSOV, Anatolii Petrovich
Censoring the censor; uncensored version of
Babi Yar. S. K. Oberbeck. il por News-
week 77:62 Ja 4 '71 *
Emerging A. Kuznetsov. H. R. Mayes. Sat R
53:4+ D 12 '70 *

KVAKA, Margaret
Ladies' day at the races; All women's international air race. il Flying 87:62–3 Ag '70

KVENVOLDEN, Keith A. and others
Racemization of amino acids in sediments
from Saanich Inlet, British Columbia. bibliog il Science 169:1079–82 S 11 '70

KWAN, Robert K.
LA school librarian files unfair treatment
complaint. Library J 95:198–200 Ja 15 '70
LA teachers group appealing librarian's
rights. Library J 95:1892 My 15 '70 *

KY, Nguyen-cao-. See Nguyen-cao-Ky

KYNELL, Kermit S.
Love affair, almost. il Yachting 127:56–7+
F '70

KYOTO, Japan
Kyoto, Osaka's exotic neighbor. J. R. Roberson. il Holiday 47:46–9 F '70

KYSAR, Robert
Christology without Jesusolatry. Chr Cent
87:1035–8 S 2 '70

L

L-dopa. See Dopa

LAD. See American library association—Library administration division

LADT. See Los Angeles dance theatre

LEAA. See United States—Justice, Department
of—Law enforcement assistance administration

LED. See American library association—Library education division

LED (light-emitting diodes) See Diodes

LISST. See Library and information science
scholarship today project

**LIST (Library and information science today
project)** See Library and information science scholarship today project

LM (lunar module) See Space vehicles—Landing systems—Moon

LNG. See Liquefied natural gas

LP gas. See Liquefied petroleum gas

LPGA. See Ladies' professional golfers' association

LPGA tournament. See Golf—Tournaments

LRS. See United States—Library of Congress—
Legislative reference service

LSCA (library services and construction act)
See Library laws and legislation

LSD
Acid by accident; case of mass hallucinogenic
poisoning. Time 95:8 Ap 20 '70
Chromosomal aberrations induced in barley by
LSD. M. P. Singh and others. bibliog il Sci-
ence 169:491–2 Jl 31 '70
I can take it or leave it. PTA Mag 64:5–7
My '70
LSD: no teratogenic action in rats, mice,
and hamsters. C. Roux and others. bibliog
il Science 169:588–9 Ag 7 '70; Reply. R.
Auerbach. Science 170:558 O 30 '70
New warning on LSD; defective children.
Newsweek 75:98 My 18 '70
Price of a trip? possibility of chromosome
damage to germ cells by LSD. Time 95:43
F 23 '70
Princess Leda's castle in the air. T. Burke.
il Esquire 73:104–11+ Mr '70

LSI (large-scale integration) See Electronic
circuits, Integrated

LTP. See American library association—Library
technology program

LTV. See Ling-Temco-Vought, inc.

LTV aerospace corporation. See Ling-Temco-
Vought, inc.

LABARRE, Harriet
Facelift; excerpts from Plastic surgery;
beauty you can buy. il Ladies Home J 87:
66+ Mr '70

LABASTILLE, Anne
Conservation careers for women. il por Cons
24:31–4 Je '70

LABELING laws. See Labels—Laws and legislation

LABELS
Are food labels honest? B. Furness. McCalls
97:36+ Jl '70
Code to end labeling mixups. il Bsns W
p53 Jl 4 '70
Importance of textile labels. Good H 170:6 Ap
'70
Informative labeling for effective communi-
cation to consumers. Consumer Bul 53:18–
19 Jl '70
Pesticide labels read them carefully. Suc
Farm 68:no5 B24 Mr '70
Why not collect labels? consumer education
value of collecting food and textile labels.
Consumer Bul 53:15–16 S '70
See also
Drugs—Labeling
Unit pricing

Laws and legislation

Canning the codes. Newsweek 76:68–9 S 21
'70
Clothing-care labels that last. B. Furness. Mc-
Calls 98:46+ O '70
Those exasperating cents-off labels. Con-
sumer Rep 35:509 S '70
See also
Unit pricing

LABOR (obstetrics) See Childbirth

LABOR, Casual
Slave shops: day-labor agencies in Chicago.
il Newsweek 75:53 Mr 9 '70

LABOR, Department of. See United States—
Labor, Department of

LABOR, Migrant. See Migrant labor
LABOR absenteeism. See Absenteeism
LABOR agreements. See Trade agreements
LABOR and laboring classes
Foreign labor briefs. See issues of Monthly labor review
Illness of convenience; absenteeism in auto plants. Newsweek 77:58 Ja 4 '71
  See also
Absenteeism
Alien labor
Automobile factories—Employees
Blacklisting
Employment
Farm labor
Hours of labor
Middle classes
Skilled labor
Trade unions
Unemployment
Woman—Employment

Bibliography
Book reviews and notes. See issues of Monthly labor review

Education
Education of adult workers: projections to 1985; with tables and charts. D. F. Johnston. bibliog f Mo Labor R 93:43-56 Ag '70
Educational attainment of workers, March 1969 and 1970; with tables and charts. W. Deutermann. bibliog f Mo Labor R 93:9-16 O '70

Non-wage payments
See Non-wage payments

Political activities
See Trade unions—Political activities

Statistics
Current labor statistics. See issues of Monthly labor review
  Europe
  See also
Migrant labor
  Europe, Eastern
Communist builders rake in the D-marks. il Bsns W p33 S 12 '70
  Europe, Western
Europe's cutback: made in U.S.A. J. Ross-Skinner. il Duns 96:57-8+ D '70
Italians are coming; western workers in the U.S.S.R. Newsweek 76:81-2 D 21 '70
Workers cool to lures of ownership; Renault and Volkswagen experiment. B. L. Masse. America 122:233 Mr 7 '70
  France
  See also
Wages—France
  Germany (Federal Republic)
  See also
Trade unions—Germany (Federal Republic)
  Great Britain
Passing of the British working class. D. Moraes. il N Y Times Mag p32-3+ Ap 5 '70
  See also
Labor laws and legislation—Great Britain
Strikes—Great Britain
Trade unions—Great Britain
  Italy
  See also
Strikes—Italy
Trade unions—Italy
  Japan
  See also
Labor supply—Japan
Wages—Japan
  Mexico
  See also
Migrant labor
  Russia
Consumers and the commissars. M. Miller. Nation 210:302-5 Mr 16 '70
  See also
Labor supply—Russia
  Spain
Spanish archbishop issues letter in support of workers. Chr Cent 87:1010 Ag 26 '70
  See also
Labor laws and legislation—Spain
  Sweden
  See also
Trade unions—Sweden

United States
Black and blue; the Rosow report on blue-collar workers. New Repub 163:9 Jl 18 '70
Blue-collar blues; report by a White House team. Newsweek 76:34 Jl 13 '70
Blue-collar strategy; the Rosow report. P. Schrag. Sat R 53:18 Jl 25 '70
Blue collar worker's lowdown blues. il Time 96:68-72+ N 9 '70
Determining the labor force status of men missed in the census. D. P. Klein. il Mo Labor R 93:26-32 Mr '70
Ethnic American; interview, ed. by T. H. Clancy. B. Mikulski. America 123:558-9+ D 26 '70
Horrors of home repair; unskilled and inaccessible craftsmen. W. A. McWhirter. il Life 68:58-60+ Je 5 '70
In group of the '70's. il Sci N 98:244 S 19 '70
It pays to wake up the blue-collar worker. J. Gooding. il Fortune 82:132-5+ S '70
Labor month in review. See issues of Monthly labor review
Nixon's plan to win the blue-collar vote. il U S News 69:18-20 Jl 20 '70
Unions aim for the blue-collar vote. il Bsns W p48+ S 5 '70
  See also
American federation of labor and Congress of industrial organizations
Government employees
Industrial workers of the world
Labor disputes
Labor laws and legislation—United States
Labor supply—United States
Migrant labor
Negroes—Economic conditions
Negroes—Employment
Strikes—United States
Trade unions—United States
Unemployment—United States
Wages—United States
  Political activities
  See Trade unions—Political activities
LABOR blacklisting. See Blacklisting
LABOR conferences
  See also
International labor organization
LABOR contracts
Pinning down your job in writing. Bsns W p69 Ag 1 '70
  See also
Trade agreements
LABOR cost
Labor costs and the rise in housing prices. N. Goldfinger. il Mo Labor R 93:60-1 My '70
Recent changes in productivity and unit labor costs. J. A. Mark and S. W. Herman. il Mo Labor R 93:28-32 My '70
LABOR disputes
Unsettlements. Newsweek 75:79+ Ap 20 '70
Wanted: a new way to solve labor woes. il Newsweek 76:84 N 16 '70
  See also
Collective bargaining
Injunctions
Strikes
LABOR ethics
Coal-black shame of the UMW. T. Armbrister. Read Digest 97:135-40 O '70
Decade of Landrum-Griffin. America 123:509-10 D 12 '70
LABOR in politics. See Trade unions—Political activities
LABOR incentives. See Incentives in industry
LABOR injunctions. See Injunctions
LABOR laws and legislation
  See also
Injunctions
Insurance, Workmens compensation
  Great Britain
Britain's Tories to test union strength. U S News 69:82-3 O 19 '70
Coming struggle; proposed industrial-relations bill. Newsweek 76:27-8 D 28 '70
Disarming the stewards; shop stewards and the labor-relations law. Newsweek 76:28 D 28 '70
Labor pains; reform proposals. il Newsweek 76:62 O 19 '70
Law moves in on labor. il Bsns W p26 D 12 '70
Sweeping labor law gains in Britain. U S News 69:56 D 28 '70
Tories and the unions; proposed industrial relations bill and the Parliamentary Labour party. A. Howard. New Repub 163:8-9 D 19 '70
  Hawaii
Recent statutes covering public employees: Hawaii and Pennsylvania statutes. J. P. Goldberg. Mo Labor R 93:31-2 D '70
Right to strike in Hawaii: public employees. W. L. Abbott. Nation 210:756 Je 22 '70

LABOR laws and legislation—*Continued*

Pennsylvania

Recent statutes covering public employees: Hawaii and Pennsylvania statutes. J. P. Goldberg. Mo Labor R 93:31-2 D '70

Spain

Franco vs. free unions. A. Rodriguez. America 122:36-7 Ja 17 '70

United States

Blow to unions. Time 95:60-1 Je 15 '70
Labor and the economy in 1969. R. W. Fisher. bibliog il Mo Labor R 93:30-43 Ja '70
New crime list stirs union ire; amendment to Landrum-Griffin act barring criminals from union office. Bsns W p56 Mr 21 '70
Nixon and labor: the gloves come off. il Bsns W p21-2 Ap 4 '70
Nixon vs. strikes. Newsweek 75:81 Mr 9 '70
Nixon's brand of labor law. Bsns W p35 Ja 24 '70
Notes from a strikebreaker. W. F. Buckley, jr. Nat R 22:428 Ap 21 '70
OE's role in manpower development and training. il Am Ed 6:34-5 Mr '70
Priority switch on labor laws. Bsns W p73 Ja 9 '71
Significant decisions in labor cases. See issues of Monthly labor review
State labor legislation enacted in 1969. O. G. Mitchell and C. T. Sorenson. Mo Labor R 93:48-56 Ja '70
Unhappy parent of new hiring rules; proposed minority hiring regulations. Bsns W p39 Ja 24 '70
Union chiefs hit back at antistrike plans. il U S News 68-87-9 F 23 '70
Young workers: growing problem for unions. il U S News 68:81-3 Ja 26 '70
See also
Insurance, Unemployment—United States
Minimum wage—United States

Taft-Hartley law

Airline strike law hearings set. Aviation W 92:230 Mr 9 '70
New curbs on transportation strikes? il Bsns W p76 Mr 7 '70
Strike ban for rails, is trucking next? il U S News 68:53-4 Mr 16 '70

LABOR leaders. See Trade unions—Officials
LABOR lobby. See Lobbying
LABOR-management relations. See Industrial relations
LABOR mobility
See also
Labor turnover
LABOR officials. See Trade unions—Officials
LABOR output. See Labor productivity
LABOR party (Great Britain)
British labor calls for new synthesis; A. W. Benn's conclusions. B. L. Masse. America 123:309 O 24 '70
Emerging majority? il Newsweek 75:44 Je 1 '70
Labour and labor; annual conference. A. Howard. New Repub 163:7-8 O 17 '70
Remarkable recovery. il por Time 95:47 My 11 '70
Saying no to Labour. R. Williams. Nation 210:710-12 Je 15 '70
Tories and the unions; proposed industrial relations bill and the Parliamentary Labour party. A. Howard. New Repub 163: 8-9 D 19 '70
Up against the odds. R. J. Korengold. por Newsweek 75:36+ F 2 '70
LABOR productivity
ABC's of productivity; its meaning to you. il U S News 69:54-5 Ag 17 '70
It pays to wake up the blue-collar worker. J. Gooding. il Fortune 82:132-5+ S '70
Out of control? il Forbes 106:15-16 Ag 1 '70
Output per man-hour in selected industries. C. S. Fehd. il Mo Labor R 93:39-40 D '70
Output per man-hour in selected industries; with table and chart. C. W. Ardolini. il Mo Labor R 93:54-5 Mr '70
Productivity in the major household appliance industry. J. E. Henneberger and H. F. Gale. il Mo Labor R 93:39-42 S '70
Productivity: tables. See issues of Monthly labor review
Profits: a fruit of productivity. R. Williams. por Nations Bsns 58:101 O '70
Recent changes in productivity and unit labor costs. J. A. Mark and S. W. Herman. il Mo Labor R 93:28-32 My '70
Shortage of workers cramps Soviet muscle. il Bsns W p50+ Mr 21 '70

There'll be less leisure than you think. G. Burck. il Fortune 81:86-9+ Mr '70
Trends in output per man-hour in the sugar industry. J. W. Ferris, jr. and H. Gale. il Mo Labor R 93:32-4 Jl '70
Why it's so tough to boost productivity. il Bsns W p64+ Jl 25 '70
LABOR relations. See Industrial relations
LABOR shortage. See Labor supply
LABOR supply
See also
College graduates—Employment
Manpower

Germany (Federal Republic)
Where companies are crying help. il Bsns W p49 F 28 '70

Japan
Japan: a crowded nation wants to boost its birthrate. P. M. Boffey. Science 167:960-2 F 13 '70; Reply. A. R. Sweezy. 169:97 Jl 3 '70
Shortage of workers changes Japan. il Bsns W p70-2 Ja 31 '70

Mexico
Analysis of Mexico's border industrialization program. A. S. Ericson. il Mo Labor R 93:33-40 My '70

Russia
Shortage of workers cramps Soviet muscle. il Bsns W p50+ Mr 21 '70

United States
Impact of commuters on the Mexican-American border area. A.-S. Ericson. bibliog f il Mo Labor R 93:18-27 Ag '70
Impact of higher unemployment on major labor force groups. P. M. Ryscavage. il Mo Labor R 93:21-5 Mr '70
Marital and family characteristics of the U.S. labor force; with tables. E. Waldman. bibliog f Mo Labor R 93:18-27 My '70
Notes on jobs and people holding them. B. L. Masse. America 123:137 S 12 '70
Story of jobs and workers in the 1960's. B. L. Masse. America 122:108 Ja 31 '70
U.S. labor force of the future. U S News 69:88 N 23 '70
U.S. labor force: projections to 1985. S. C. Travis and others. bibliog f il Mo Labor R 93:3-12 My '70
LABOR turnover
Labor turnover rates; tables. See issues of Monthly labor review
Seven ways to turn off turnover. R. O. Snelling. il Nations Bsns 58:58-60 O '70
LABOR unions. See Trade unions
LABORATORIES
See also
Atomic research laboratories
Research laboratories
Underwater laboratories

Architecture
Corporate headquarters and research laboratories for Burroughs Wellcome & co, inc. il Arch Rec 148:92-3, 95 N '70
Palace on a strip; Avco research labs. il Arch Forum 132:32-7 Je '70
LABORATORIES. Government
Civilian use for biological warfare facility under study; biological complex at Pine Bluff arsenal. J. Walsh. Science 167:1359 Mr 6 '70
Government labs: Britain weighs plan to make them earn their way. D. S. Greenberg. Science 167:964-5 F 13 '70
Job cuts at the national laboratories. Sci N 97:192 F 21 '70
No home for a weapons lab; Ft Detrick. Sci N 97:62 Ja 17 '70
Reflections on national laboratories; with reply by R. B. Duffield. M. J. Moravcsik. il Bul Atom Sci 26:11-16 F '70; Correction. 26:48 O '70
See also
Atomic research laboratories
United States—Langley research center
United States—National aeronautics and space administration—Electronics research center
LABORATORY animals
Last gasp for cigarettes? smoking dogs research. S. M. Spencer. Read Digest 96:92-5 Ap '70
Mouse stage of the new biology. R. W. Stock. il Sci Digest 67:44-7+ Ap '70
Smoking and cancer in dogs. Time 95:48 F 16 '70
Smoking beagles. il Newsweek 75:86 F 16 '70

LABORATORY animals—*Continued*
Taming the killer instinct; investigating rat's murderous behavior. il Time 95:47 Mr 30 '70
Tumors in smoking dogs. Sci N 97:169 F 14 '70
See also
Germfree life
Vivisection
also names of laboratory animals, e.g. Mice
LABORATORY architecture. See Laboratories —Architecture
LABORATORY schools
Let's talk sense about laboratory schools. W. Kuschman. Clear House 45:56 S '70
LABRADA, Emilio B.
(ed) See Arciniegas, G. Word with Germán Arciniegas
LABRADOR
See also
Fishing—Labrador
LABRADOR dogs
Pointing Lab; marsh hen shooting. F. E. Hester. il Field & S 75:148-50 S '70
LABRADOR retrievers. See Labrador dogs
LA BREA, Los Angeles
Marine fossils at Rancho La Brea. J. W. Valentine and J. H. Lipps. bibliog il Science 169:277-8 Jl 17 '70
LABYRINTH (ear)
Adjusting to space; frog otolith. il Sci N 98:397 N 21 '70
Cochlear summating potentials: composition. P, Dallos and others. bibliog il Science 170:641-4 N 6 '70
Orbiting frog otolith. il Space World G-11-83:31-7 N '70
Scanning electron microscopy of the organ of Corti. G. Bredberg and others. bibliog il Science 170:861-3 N 20 '70
Short-latency labyrinthine input to the vestibular nuclei in the pigeon. V. J. Wilson and R. M. Wylie. bibliog il Science 168:124-7 Ap 3 '70
LABYRINTHS
Daedalus and I; sculpted recreation of labyrinth. M. Ayrton. il por Horizon 12:56-65 Spr '70
LA CANADA, Calif.
Zoning law seen banning Bible classes. N. B. Rohrer. Chr Today 14:37 F 13 '70
LACANDON Indians. See Indians of Mexico
LACE and lace making
See also
Macramé
LACEY, Frederick B.
New Jersey: the state of Mafia. F. J. Cook. il Nation 210:560-3+ My 11 '70 *
LACHAPELLE, Edward R.
From snowflake to avalanche; with biographical sketch. il Natur Hist 79:8, 30-8 F '70
LACHENBRUCH, David
Looking ahead. See issues of Radio-electronics
LACONTE, Ronald T.
Who are the real censors? Ed Digest 36:44-6 O '70
LA COSTA, Calif. See Health resorts, watering places, etc.
LACOSTE, Michel Conil-. See Conil-Lacoste, M.
LACOUTURE, Jean
From the Vietnam war to an Indochina war. For Affairs 48:617-28 Jl '70
LACQUER and lacquering
See also
Furniture—Finishing
Furniture, Lacquer
LACROSSE
One team, anyway, says, yes, Virginia; Cavaliers of University of Virginia. P. Carry. Sports Illus 32:78 My 25 '70
They're not going to like it in Maryland; Long Island program produces college stars. P. Carry. il Sports Illus 32:62-3 My 4 '70
LACTATE dehydrogenases. See Dehydrogenases
LACTATION
See also
Luteotropin
LACTONES
Inhibition of phosphofructokinase by quinone methide and α-methylene lactone tumor inhibitors. R. L. Hanson and others. bibliog il Science 168:378-80 Ap 17 '70
Reactions of alpha methylene lactone tumor inhibitors with model biological nucleophiles. S. M. Kupchan and others. bibliog il Science 168:376-8 Ap 17 '70
LACTOSE
Of man and milk; milk intolerance. il Time 96:59 Jl 13 '70
La LACUNE; drama. See Ionesco, E.
LACY, Edward A.
Bonus for CATV subscribers: cable FM. il Pop Electr 34:60-2 Ja '71

LACY, Leslie Alexander
Slave narrative, 1970. C. R. Larson. New Repub 163:24-6 O 3 '70 *
LA DANY, Louis
China: period of suspense. For Affairs 48:701-11 Jl '70
LADBROKE and company
London bookie everyone bets on. il Bsns W p47 Ap 25 '70
LADD, Doyt
Fast bass in Puerto Rico. il Field & S 75:154-5+ My '70
LADD, Edward T.
Pills for classroom peace? il Sat R 53:66-8+ N 21 '70
LADD, J. B.
Wildcatter. R. Brady. por Duns 96:67-8 Jl '70
LADD petroleum corporation
Wildcatter. R. Brady. por Duns 96:67-8 Jl '70
LADDER chairs. See Chairs
LADDERS
Ladder safety around the home. il Bet Hom & Gard 48:34 My '70
LADEJINSKY, Wolf
Ironies of India's green revolution. For Affairs 48:758-68 Jl '70
LADER, Lawrence
First miracle worker. il Todays Health 48:42-3+ S '70
Laws to limit family size. Parents Mag 45:58-61 O '70
National guide to legal abortion. il Ladies Home J 87:73 Jl '70
LADERMAN, Ezra
Ezra Laderman's Quartet no. 2: big, bold, stimulating. A. Cohn. por Am Rec G 36:676-7 My '70 *
LADEW, Harvey
Witty topiary garden. il House & Gard 137:88-93 Ap '70
LADIES
The lady, by E. J. Putnam. Review
Sat R il 53:30 Jl 11 '70. E. G. Davis
LADIES' home journal
Liberating the Journal. il Newsweek 76:44 Ag 3 '70
Woman-power. il Time 95:59 Mr 30 '70
Woman power; feminists storm headquarters. il Newsweek 75:61 Mr 30 '70
LADIES' professional golfers' association
Fine till the nerves go ding; S. Englehorn, Ladies PGA champion. M. Mulvoy. il por Sports Illus 32:48+ Je 29 '70
LADIMER, Irving
Housing: problems and solutions. il Har Yrs 10:38-42 F '70
LADLES. See Kitchen utensils
LADOF, Nina Sydney
Dirty word smokescreen. il por Library J 95:2424-6 Jl '70
LADY of the night orchids. See Orchids
LADYBIRDS
Following the ladybug home; migrating California convergent ladybugs. K. S. Hagen. il Nat Geog 137:542-53 Ap '70
LADYBUGS. See Ladybirds
LAETARE medal
Not so ugly American: Laetare medal for Dr Walsh of Project Hope. America 122:288 Mr 21 '70
LAETRILE
Apricot pit bit. por Sci N 98:55-6 Jl 25 '70
LA FARGE, Henry A.
Félix the Nabi. il por Art N 69:48-9+ Ap '70
First impressions. il Art N 69:37+ O '70
Iranian caviare to the general. il Art N 69:46:51 D '70
Pride of illuminations. Art N 69:58-9 Mr '70
LA FARGE, John
In search of innocence. L. Auchincloss. il pors Am Heritage 21:28-33 Je '70 *
LA FARGE, Phyllis
Keeping going; excerpt. il McCalls 98:49+ Ja '71
Recollections of Christmas past. Redbook 136:63+ D '70
Wisdom of silence. il Redbook 135:74-5+ Jl '70
LA FAY, Howard
Vikings. il Nat Geog 137:492-541 Ap '70
LAFAYETTE college, Easton, Pa.
Lafayette college to admit women. Sch & Soc 98:270-1 Sum '70
LAFAYETTE COUNTY, Miss.
Faulkner country. C. Hesse and S. Hesse. il Travel 134:68-70 D '70
LAFEBER, Walter
China and Japan: different beds, different dreams. Cur Hist 59:142-6+ S '70
LAFFEY, James L.
Some bright children can't read. il PTA Mag 65:9-11+ bibliog(p35) O '70

LAGOONS, Manure. See Manure lagoons
LAGUARDIA airport. See New York (city)—
Airports
LAGUNA BEACH, Calif.
This summer it's Laguna Beach. F. Riley. il
Holiday 47:46-9+ My '70
LAHAINA-Kaanapali and Pacific rail road. See
Railroads—Hawaii
LAHAYE, P. A. and Epstein, Emanuel
Salt toleration by plants: enhancement with
calcium. bibliog Science 166:395-6, 167:1387-
8 O 17 '69, Mr 6 '70
LAHR, John
Choreographers theatre. il Dance Mag 44:
46-51 Mr '70
        about
Apostle to the gentiles. F. Hirsch. Nation
211:600-1 D 7 '70 *
LAIDLAW, Angus
How to buy a safe kiddie seat for your car.
il Mech Illus 66:66-7+ Mr '70
LAING, Alexander
Graffito; poem. Nation 211:701 D 28 '70
Reptile in October; poem. Sat R 53:29 Je 6
'70
LAING, Ronald David
Madness as an existential solution to an ex-
istential situation. W. F. Lynch. pors Com-
monweal 92:484-5 S 25 '70 *
Medicine man. N. N. Holland. Nation 210:
569-70 My 11 '70 *
R. D. Laing: in search of a new psychiatry.
J. S. Gordon. il por Atlan 227:50-3+ Ja
'71 *
Webs of maya; with excerpts from Knots. il
Time 97:38 Ja 18 '71 *
LAIRD, Charlton
Down Giantwife: the uses of etymology.
Engl J 59:1106-12 N '70
LAIRD, Jack
Offbeat Caribbean: Haiti. il Yachting 127:58-
9+ Mr; 57-9+ Ap '70
LAIRD, Melvin R.
Dangers confronting U.S; interview. il pors
U S News 68:64-8+ My 11 '70
Edge of prudent risk; excerpts from address,
April 1970. Nat R 22:449 My 5 '70
National priorities; address, April 20, 1970.
Vital Speeches 36:452-6 My 15 '70
Peace dividend from the Pentagon. il Nations
Bsns 58:40-2 O '70
Secretary Rogers and Secretary Laird inter-
viewed on Issues and answers. Dept State
Bul 63:542-53 N 2 '70
        about
Ahead: faster withdrawal from Vietnam. il
por U S News 68:29-30 F 23 '70 *
Correcting our posture. R. E. Lapp. New
Repub 162:12-15 Mr 28 '70 *
Defense: Laird warns of Soviet technological
threat. A. Hamilton. Science 167:1360 Mr 6
'70 *
Defense's fly before you buy policy. il por
Newsweek 76:53-4 Ag 10 '70 *
Diplomat at the Pentagon. il por Newsweek
76:33-4+ D 14 '70 *
How goes the war? A colloquy in Saigon.
M. Clark and others. il por Time 95:20-1
F 23 '70 *
Laird renews appeal for ABM, MIRV. Avia-
tion W 92:19 My 18 '70 *
Laird seeks industry aid to defeat Mansfield
amendment. A. Hamilton. Science 167:1599
Mr 20 '70 *
Lean times loom for suppliers. il por Bsns W
p 115-16 F 28 '70 *
U.S. defense spending may grow. il Aviation
W 92:16-17 Mr 2 '70*
LAIRD, Wilson M.
Energy; address, March 5, 1970. Vital
Speeches 36:396-9 Ap 15 '70
LAISSEZ faire. See Free enterprise
LAITY
Quiet storm in the churches. H. A. Bosley.
Chr Cent 87:1449-52 D 2 '70
        Catholic church
Lay situation; Work's report. Commonweal
93:140 N 6 '70
Making use of middle age. R. Haughton.
Cath World 210:246-7 Mr '70
Matter of principal; National association of
laymen criticizes management of diocesan
finances. Newsweek 76:101-2 N 30 '70
Needed: more adult education. America 123:
167 S 19 '70; Reply. L. J. Losoncy. 123:275
O 17 '70
Parish councils: democratic process or new
absolutism? J. F. Kippley. America 123:
94-7 Ag 22 '70
See also
Council of the laity

LA JOLLA campus. See California. University
—La Jolla campus
LAKE, Alice
Day-care business. il McCalls 98:60-1+ N
'70
Kienast quints. il Good H 171:84-9+ S '70
Must babies wear religious tags? il Good H
171:78-9+ N '70
New heart for Becky Howland. il Good H
170:56-7+ Ja '70
Vision. il Seventeen 29:140-1+ F '70
What teen-age medicine can do for you. il
Seventeen 29:132-3+ Je '70
Will a new nose make you happier? il Seven-
teen 29:162-3+ Ap '70
LAKE cruises. See Cruising
LAKE ERIE. See Erie, Lake
LAKE HAVASU. See Havasu Lake
LAKE MALAWI. See Malawi, Lake
LAKE MENDOTA. See Mendota, Lake
LAKE MICHIGAN. See Michigan, Lake
LAKE NEMI. See Nemi, Lake
LAKE ONTARIO. See Ontario, Lake
LAKE OSWEGO, Ore.
Right water psychologically. D. Seeger. il
pors Am City 85:79-82 My '70
LAKE pollution. See Water pollution
LAKE POWELL. See Powell, Lake
LAKE SUPERIOR. See Superior, Lake
LAKE TAHOE. See Tahoe, Lake
LAKE trout fishing. See Trout fishing
LAKE WASHINGTON. See Washington, Lake
LAKE WASHINGTON SHIP CANAL. See
Canals—Washington (state)
LAKES
Seeks solution to growth of algae in lakes.
Am City 85:30 My '70
See also
Great Lakes
Limnology
Water pollution

        Temperature
Water temperature is fishy business. D.
Richey. il Field & S 75:40-1+ Jl '70

        New York (state)
Water chemistry and lake productivity. C. L.
Schofield. il Cons 24:9-15+ Ap '70
LAKES, Artificial
Best fishing lake ever built? Toledo Bend
Lake. G. Gresham. il Field & S 75:38-9+
D '70
Landlocked no more; Carlyle Lake, Ill. pro-
viding floating marina. G. S. Hensley. il
Yachting 129:106-7+ Ja '71
Super highway lakes. B. Thomas. il Field &
S 75:66-7+ My '70
See also
Powell, Lake
Reservoirs
LAKES basin recreational area. See Recrea-
tion areas—California
LAKEWOOD, Calif.
City-sponsored glass redemption a huge suc-
cess. Am City 85:29 D '70
LA LANNE, Jack
Easy thirty-day shape-up to keep you fit. il
pors Mech Illus 66:44-7+ Je '70
LALIBERTÉ, Norman
Norman Laliberté: painter, graphic artist &
craftsman. D. W. Boynton. il Am Artist 34:
52-9 F '70
L'ALLEMAND, Gordon
Forty years of farming naturally. il Org Gard
& Farm 17:92-5 N '70
Salad greens in a corner. il Org Gard & Farm
17:40-1 My '70
Sunflowers aren't just for the birds! il Org
Gard & Farm 17:61-3 Ap '70
LALMBA association. See Volunteer service,
International
LA MAMA ETC (Experimental theater club)
See New York (city)—Theater
LA MANCHA. See Mancha, La
LAMAR, South Carolina
Bad day in Lamar; whites attacked school
buses carrying Negro children. il News-
week 75:26 Mr 16 '70
Evenhandedness at home; attack by white
extremists against school buses carrying
Negro children. Nat R 22:296 Mr 24 '70
Rebellion at Lamar. il Time 95:12-13 Mr 16 '70
White violence in Lamar. J. Bass. New
Repub 162:10-12 Mr 23 '70
LAMARQUE, Gerrald T. See Nichols, J. jt.
auth.
LAMB, Carl C.
Last winter; fable. il Nat Parks 44:21-2 Mr
'70

LAMB, Warren
Those telltale executive gestures. J. Ross-Skinner. il Duns 95:66-7 Mr '70 *
LAMB (meat)
See also
Cookery—Meat
LAMB curry. See Curry
LAMBDIN, William
Light touch. Todays Ed 59:25 Ap '70
LAMBERT, Darwin
Alaskan dream. Nat Parks & Con Mag 44:22 N '70
Earthmanship. Nat Parks 44:15-16 Ja '70
Earth's words in the national parks. il Nat Parks & Con Mag 44:16-22 Jl '70
Nature on a broken screen. Nat Parks & Con Mag 44:18 Ap '70
Who has seen the wind? Nat Parks & Con Mag 44:19 D '70
LAMBERT, Ian B. and Wyllie, P. J.
Low-velocity zone of the earth's mantle: incipient melting caused by water. bibliog il Science 169:764-6 Ag 21 '70
LAMBERT, John
For a cleaner Europe. il Sci N 97:280 Mr 14 '70
LAMBERT, Joseph B.
Shapes of organic molecules; with biographical sketch. il Sci Am 222:16, 58-66+ bibliog(p 146) Ja '70
LAMBERT, William
What the senator didn't disclose. pors Life 69:26-9 Ag 28 '70
LAMBORGHINI Jarama (automobile) See Sports cars
LAMBRAKIS, Grigorios
Story of Z. il Time 96:23 Ag 17 '70 *
LAMENTATIONS; story. See Nissenson H.
LAMHUT, Phyllis
Phyllis Lamhut and company in Extended voices; Henry street settlement playhouse, NYC. J. Armstrong. Dance Mag 44:76-7 Je '70 *
LAMINATED plastics. See Plastics, Laminated
LAMM, Michael
Driver education: are we getting our money's worth? il Parents Mag 45:48-9+ Je '70
Fantastic new farm machines. il Pop Mech 133:118-23 Ja '70
How to become a smiling used-car buyer. il Pop Mech 133:85-9+ Je '70
PM owners report:
Dodge challenger. il Pop Mech 133:96-9 Je '70
Studded tires take hold. il Pop Mech 133:112-16+ Ja '70
When birds & beasts went motoring. il Audubon 72:36-9 Ja '70
LAMM, Richard D.
Stork outfiles American eagle; reprint. il Am For 76:4+ Jl '70
LAMMERDING, Heinrich
Lammerding affair. il por Time 97:22 Ja 11 '71 *
LAMMERS, Claude C.
Jefferson and his aristocracy of talent proposal. Ed Digest 35:45-7 Ja '70
LAMMEY, W. Clyde
Homeowners' clinic; questions and answers. See issues of Popular mechanics
Make this handsome banjo barometer. il Pop Mech 134:150-2 Jl '70
LAMONICA, Daryle
Tale of two quarterbacks; with report by B. Bruns. il pors Life 69:44-7 D 4 '70 *
LAMONT, Robert J.
Another look at the American dream. Chr Today 14:6-8 Ap 24 '70
LAMOTT, Kenneth
Bill McGill takes over Columbia's hot campus. il por N Y Times Mag p26-7+ Ag 23 '70
Quiet revolt. por Horizon 12:68-72 Wint '70
Where do San Franciscans play? il Holiday 47:62-3+ Mr '70
LAMOUREUX, Dominique
Zeta-potential plus people potential. il por Am City 85:93-4+ F '70
LAMOUREUX, Doris
ABE and the twentieth century pioneers. il Todays Ed 59:60-1 Ja '70
LAMP bulbs. See Electric lamps
LAMPE, David
Accidents on purpose. il Todays Health 48:34-7 S '70
LAMPPOSTS. See Street lighting fixtures
LAMPREYS
Glucose production by lamprey meninges. C. M. Rovainen. bibliog il Science 167:889-90 F 6 '70
Lamprey larvae survey. il Cons 25:40 Ag '70
Lampreys in the Lakes. G. F. Bush. il Sea Front 16:142-7 My '70

LAMPS
Forward! New York Lamp and home furnishings show. New Yorker 45:23-4 Ja 24 '70
Glass lighting devices. J. S. Shadel. il Antiques 98:916-21 D '70
Projects to keep your workshop humming; telephone table lamp. B. Brightman. il Pop Mech 134:194 O '70
Triplex lamp. il Pop Mech 133:174-6 Mr '70
Wireless lamp. J. Fred. il Mech Illus 66:100 S '70
You can build this candlestand lamp. W. C. Leckey. il Pop Mech 134:168-71 N '70
See also
Electric lamps
LAMSON, Merle
Are we bandwagoneers? (cont) Am Lib 1:530-1 Je '70
LANCASTER, Donald E.
Add-subtract MOS IC decimal counter. il Electr World 83:45-8+ Je '70
Assembling the Popular electronics mini-DVM. il Pop Electr 33:35+ S '70
Build numeric glow tube DCU. il Pop Electr 32:33-5+ F '70
Build the Digital logic microlab. il Pop Electr 32:27-35+ Ap '70
IC experimenter's corner. il Pop Electr 32:29-31 F; 51-3 Mr; 56-8+ Ap; 43-7 My; 43-5 Je '70
Predetermining decimal counter. il Electr World 83:34-6+ My '70
LANCASTER, Rosemary
Our merry-go-round nursery group. il Parents Mag 45:46-7+ Je '70
LANCE Link, secret chimp. See Television broadcasting—Childrens programs
LANCET, Michael S. and Anders, Edward
Carbon isotope fractionation in the Fischer-Tropsch synthesis and in meteorites. bibliog il Science 170:980-2 N 27 '70
LAND, Edwin Herbert
Black and white issue faces Polaroid. Bsns W p32 N 14 '70 *
LAND, Herman W.
How to talk with your teen-ager about drugs: excerpt from What you can do about drugs and your child. Read Digest 97:69-72 Ag '70
LAND, Irene Ellen (Stokvis) See Stokvis, I. E.
LAND, Thomas
Chinese working on the railroad. il Nation 211:371-2 O 19 '70
Hungary: quiet changes. Nation 211:464-5 N 9 '70
Israel's new coup. Nation 210:103-4 F 2 '70
Trial of a dutiful man. il Nation 211:339-40 O 12 '70
LAND
Likely farms, unlikely places. J. Cox. il Org Gard & Farm 17:62-3+ D '70
See also
Land utilization
Real property
Wetlands
Prices
See Land values
Taxation
See Property tax; Single tax
Florida
See also
Reclamation of land—Florida
Georgia
Optimum population and environment: a Georgian microcosm. E. P. Odum. il Cur Hist 58:355-9+ Je '70
United States
See also
Public lands—United States
LAND between the lakes national recreation area. See Recreation areas
LAND contracts
Curse of contract buying; Chicago evictions. C. C. Douglas. il Ebony 25:43-6+ Je '70
LAND crabs. See Crabs
LAND drainage. See Drainage
LAND fills. See Filling (earthwork)
LAND grant colleges
See also
National association of state universities and land grant colleges
LAND management, Bureau of. See United States—Land management, Bureau of
LAND mines. See Mines, Military
LAND planning. See Land utilization
LAND reclamation. See Reclamation of land
LAND reform. See Land tenure
LAND sailboats. See Sand yachts

LAND snail. See Snails
LAND speculation
Prices of land near a plateau. il Bsns W p31 Je 20 '70
LAND tenure
See also
Farm ownership

Alaska
Justice to first inhabitants; native land claims. A. J. Goldberg. Am Heritage 21:119 Ap '70
Landless in Alaska. J. C. Muskrat. il Bul Atom Sci 26:12-16 Mr '70
Legal battle for Alaska. Nat Parks & Con Mag 44:31-4 N '70
Oil rush; native claims. W. K. Wyant, jr. New Repub 162:19-21 F 14 '70

India
Land-grab war; Naxalite movement in West Bengal. il Newsweek 76:31 Ag 3 '70
On the march; land grab by Naxalites. il Time 96:23-4 Ag 24 '70

Peru
Land reform in Peru. E. Flores. Nation 210: 174-7 F 16 '70

Rhodesia
Rhodesian bishops: no apartheid; new Land tenure act. F. M. Sekyewa. Commonweal 92:308-9 Je 26 '70

Spain
Land reform in Spain. P. M. Enggass. il Focus 20:9-12 My '70

United States
California water plan: the most expensive faucet in the world. G. Marine. il Ramp Mag 8:34-41 My '70
Ford and la raza; they stole our land and gave us powdered milk. L. Rees and P. Montague. il Ramp Mag 9:10-18 S '70
Southwest Episcopal diocese to withhold mission funds; the Alianza. Chr Cent 87:38 Ja 14 '70

Vietnam (Republic)
Pursuing the peasantry. il Time 95:37 Ap 6 '70
LAND use. See Land utilization
LAND utilization
Battle for America's crowded coastlines. il U S News 69:44-7 Ag 10 '70
California water plan: the most expensive faucet in the world. G. Marine. il Ramp Mag 8:34-41 My '70
Census of arable lands. R. Lanier. il Cur Hist 58:337-42 Je '70
Dry-farming free-use land. J. R. Coggins. il Org Gard & Farm 17:54-6 S '70
It's not just the cities. A. Mayer. il Arch Rec 147:137-42 Je '70
Land use: Congress taking up conflict over power plants. L. J. Carter. Science 170: 718-19 N 13 '70
Land-use problems in Illinois; AAAS symposium, December 30, 1970. R. E. Bergstrom. il Science 169:1003-4 S 4 '70
Landscaping the Netherlands. I. G. Simmons. il Am For 76:19-21+ F '70
Last frontier. W. E. Towell. il por Am For 76:32-4+ Ja '70
Living space; EQ index. il Nat Wildlife 8:36 O '70; Same. Schol Teach Jr/Sr High pA12 O 5 '70
National resource revenue sharing. W. W. Porter, 2d. il por Am For 76:24-7+ Ja '70
Park program; it's bigger than you think; address, October 1969. R. Rienow. il por Parks & Rec 5:27-8+ Mr '70
Rangelands of the western U.S. R. M. Love. il Sci Am 222:88-94+ bibliog (p126) F '70
Sensible plan for future development; ecological inventory; interview, ed. by J. N. Miller. I. L. McHarg. il Read Digest 97:77-81 Ag '70
Space preservation, taxes, planning, and talking; the crunch. R. E. Galantowicz. il Am For 76:36-8+ O '70
Timber management; improvement implies new land-use policies. L. J. Carter. il Science 170:1387-90 D 25 '70
Which way back to the land? new recreation communities. R. Rodale. il Org Gard & Farm 17:57-60 D '70
See also
Suburbs

History
Forestry and the public domain: a Mexican point of view; address (cont) E. Beltran. il Am For 76:36-7+ Ja '70
LAND values
Farmers report on land prices. D. Hanson. Suc Farm 68:19 N '70
Now: a rush to buy land. il U S News 68: 54-7 Mr 9 '70

Prices of land near a plateau. il Bsns W p31 Je 20 '70
What is a marsh worth? J. T. Starr. il Am For 76:12-15+ Ag '70
LAND yachts. See Sand yachts
LANDAU, Cynthia
Panama. il Motor B 126:55-7+ N '70
Women and children afloat and aground. il Motor B 125:104-7 Mr '70
LANDAU, Genevieve Millet
What every woman should know about abortion. Parents Mag 46:42-3+ Ja '71

about
Introducing our new editor. G. J. Hecht. por Parents Mag 46:22 Ja '71 *
LANDAUER, Carl
Student revolt. Yale R 60:175-84 D '70
LANDAUER, Rolf
Future evolution of the computer; adaptation of address, October 1969. bibliog il por Phys Today 23:22-8 Jl '70
LANDERS, Ann, pseud.
Ann Landers: substitute pastor; interview. il por Chr Today 14:16-17 Mr 13 '70
LANDERS, Clifford E. and Cicarelli, J. S.
Academic recession. New Repub 162:14-16 My 9 '70
LANDFILLS. See Filling (earthwork)
LANDING fees, Airport. See Airports—Finance
LANDING gear, Airplane.   See Airplanes—Landing gear
LANDING sites
Moon
See Moon—Surface
LANDING systems for space vehicles. See Space vehicles—Landing systems
LANDLORD and tenant
In the inner cities; acres of abandoned buildings. il U S News 68:54-6 Ja 26 '70
See also
Rent
LANDMAN, Phyllis
Clay and metal, beautifully compatible. il Sch Arts 70:10-11 Ja '71
People pots. il Sch Arts 69:36-7 Je '70
LANDMARKS, Literary. See Literary landmarks
LANDMARKS, Musical. See Musical landmarks
LANDMARKS preservation commission.   See New York (city)—Landmarks preservation commission
LANDON, Alfred Mossman
Sage of Topeka; interview, ed. by I. Shenker. pors Am Heritage 21:92-6 Ap '70
LANDON, H. C. Robbins
Beethoven; a pictorial essay. il Hi Fi sec I 20:69-76 Ja '70
Beethoven on records. Hi Fi sec I 20:70-2+ F '70
LANDOWSKA, Wanda
Landowska as harpsichordist and pianist. D. Hamilton. Hi Fi 20:secI 80 Je '70
LANDRIEU, Maurice E.
New Moon over New Orleans. S. V. Roberts. Commonweal 91:501 F 6 '70
LANDRIEU, Moon. See Landrieu, M. E.
LANDRUM, Philip Mitchell
Excerpt from debate, April 15, 1970. Cong Digest 49:173+ Je '70
LANDRUM-Griffin act. See Labor laws and legislation—United States
LANDS, Public. See Public lands
LANDSBERG, Helmut E.
Man-made climatic changes. bibliog il Science 170:1265-74 D 18 '70
LANDSBERG, Michele
Fresh way of understanding yourself; excerpt from Chatelaine. Read Digest 97:219-22+ O '70
LANDSCAPE; drama. See Pinter, H.
LANDSCAPE architecture
How to build a view. il House & Gard 137: 104-5 Ap '70
Oakland museum; with introd. by M. F. Schmertz. il Arch Rec 147:115-22 Ap '70
LANDSCAPE drawing
Drawing from the environment. A. Pierce. il Sch Arts 70:22-3 D '70
Drawing landscapes from life and imagination. J. Mugnaini. il Am Artist 34:44-9 S '70
Stimulating perception. P. K. Scholl. il Sch Arts 70:12-13 N '70
LANDSCAPE gardening
All-green garden idea. il Sunset 145:182-3 D '70
Big stones as ground covers. il Sunset 145: 143 Ag '70
Eighteen landscape problems solved. il Home Gard 57:32-40 My '70
Go native, we did! landscaping with native trees, shrubs and flowers. M. Enright. il Org Gard & Farm 17:80-1 Ja '70

LANDSCAPE gardening—*Continued*
Home landscape plants to give quick results. il Home Gard 57:74-5 Mr '70
Instant landscaping, can it be done? A. H. Hubbard. il Home Gard 57:58-60 F '70
Landscape plan is what pulled everything together. il Sunset 145:86-7 Ag '70
Landscaping (cont) L. Grove. il Bet Hom & Gard 48:34-5 F '70
Pocket gardens. H. Mason and L. Grove. il Bet Hom & Gard 48:58-9 Ag '70
Sometimes what old gardens need is a haircut and tailoring. il Sunset 144:104-7 My '70
Trees & shrubs to frame your home. B. C. Kilvert, jr. il Home Gard 57:36-44 Ja '70
Update your front yard. D. Baylis. il Horticulture 48:38-41 My '70
What to plant around steps. G. W. Kelley. il Horticulture 48:18-21+ Je '70
    See also
City gardens
Cover plants
Evergreens
Garden steps
Gardening—Planting plans and tables
Gardens
Gardens, Hillside
Gardens, Japanese
Golf courses
Hedges
Home grounds
Lawns
School grounds
Shrubs
Topiary work
Water gardens

Economic aspects
How to landscape and save money. H. Mason. Bet Hom & Gard 48:48 Ja '70

LANDSCAPE improvement
Ten ways to make your city more attractive. W. H. Whyte. House & Gard 138:100-1 S '70
    See also
Green thumb, Inc.

LANDSCAPE in literature. See Nature in literature

LANDSCAPE painting
American landscape: a changing frontier. D. W. Scott. il Liv Wildn 33:3-13 Wint '69
American visions of wilderness; reprint. W. S. Talbot. bibliog il Liv Wildn 33:14-25 Wint '69
California horizons; the touring exhibition Horizons: a century of California landscape painting. C. N. Stallone. il Art in Am 58:124-5 N '70
Six villages near Salzburg. J. Lipman and M. Pálffy. il Art in Am 58:102-5 Jl '70
Wilderness and the Adirondacks, an historical view. W. K. Verner. il Liv Wildn 33:27-46 Wint '69

LANDSCAPE photography. See Photography—Landscapes

LANDSCAPE protection
Are landmarks part of the environment? reprint. Hobbies 75:50+ My '70
Battle for America's crowded coastlines. il U S News 69:44-7 Ag 10 '70
Camera with a cause; B. Norton's conservation photography. K. Poli. il Pop Phot 67:92-7 D '70
Continent in our hands. C. Ogburn, jr. il Nat Parks & Con Mag 44:22-30 My '70
Erosion of Eden: is tourism creating its own pollution. H. Sutton. il Sat R 53:58-61+ Je 6 '70
How not to make dirty pictures. N. Rothschild. il Pop Phot 66:40+ Ja '70
Key legal victory; new right of citizens' groups to defend natural resources, scenic beauty and historical value. il Time 95:85 My 4 '70
Let's sing Auld lang syne for the upper Brandywine. L. B. Leopold. il Natur Hist 79:4-6+ Je '70
Motorized recreation vehicles: problems, and suggested solutions. D. R. Dunn. il Parks & Rec 5:10-14+ Jl '70
Page forty-eight; a taint from technocrary. L. W. Douglas. Am West 7:48 Mr '70
Seven things you can do to make America beautiful. S. Udall. House & Gard 137:55+ Je '70
Threatened America (cont) il Life 68:52B-54+ Mr 13; 69:58-61 Ag 7 '70
To fit the landscape. J. T. Starr. il Am For 76:12-15+ F '70
    See also
American scenic and historic preservation society
Conservation of resources
Environmental movement
Nature conservancy (organization)
Regional planning
Roadside improvement
Shore protection
Wilderness areas

Awards, prizes, etc.
1970 Holiday awards for a beautiful America. il Holiday 47:28+ My '70

Alaska
Is it TAPS for wild Alaska? B. East. il Outdoor Life 145:43-5+ My '70
Kiss the north slope good-by? G. Laycock. il Audubon 72:68-75 S '70
Letter from the Arctic: Brooks Range; excerpts. S. Wright. Am Heritage 21:97 Ag '70

Arctic Regions
Concern for the Arctic environment. W. Kornberg. il Sci N 97:486-8 My 16 '70

California
Don't fight, negotiate! East Bay regional park district. F. J. Monteagle. il Parks & Rec 9:38-9+ S '70
Great beer can bust. W. Bronson. il Audubon 72:146-7 N '70

Hawaii
Erosion of Eden. H. Sutton. il Sat R 53:60-1+ Je 6 '70
Trouble in paradise. G. Laycock. il Audubon 72:24-31 My '70

Illinois
Preserving a prairie; Goose Lake prairie. G. Leposky. Travel & Camera 33:12+ O '70

Maine
Notes and comment: responsibility for removal of centennial plot for new traffic islands in Kennenbunk, Me. New Yorker 46:19 Jl 4 '70

LANDSLIDES
Death by glacier; Yungay, Peru mudflow. Sci Am 223:46 Ag '70

LANDY, Dick
Dandy Dick Landy; interview, ed. by J. Dianna. il pors Hot Rod 23:58-60 Ja '70

LANE, Sir Allen
Sir Allen Lane dies, sale of Penguin quickly announced. Pub W 198:47-8 Jl 20 '70 *

LANE, Louis
Musical events. W. Sargeant. New Yorker 46:108 Mr 7 '70 *

LANE, Mark
Rush to judgment? Newsweek 77:76-7 Ja 11 '71 *

LANE, Mills B. 1912-
Atlanta banker with a social conscience. il por Bsns W p34+ Jl 25 '70 *
Irrepressible Mills B. Lane. I. Ross. il por Read Digest 96:17+ F '70 *

LANE, Paul D.
Pike by snowmobile. il Field & S 75:36-7+ N '70

LANE, Will
South Dakota's vacation corner. il Travel 134:62-8 S '70

LANE, William
Lying down to sleep; poem. Nation 211:155 Ag 31 '70

LANE, William H.
Riviana expansion. J. Smith. por Duns 95:62+ Ap '70 *

LANE college, Jackson, Tenn.
Up from Uncle Tomism. R. L. Terrell. Commonweal 92:87-8+ Ap 3 '70; Discussion. 92:211+ My 15 '70

LANEY, James T.
New morality and the religious communities. bibliog f Ann Am Acad 387:14-21 Ja '70

LANG, Bud
Chevy's mini-rat. il Hot Rod 23:44-6 Je '70
Wild Willie. il pors Hot Rod 23:52-4 My '70

LANG, Cynthia
Crucial years for learning. il Parents Mag 45:62-3+ S '70
New baby at our house. il por Parents Mag 45:54-5 Mr '70
Parent and child. il N Y Times Mag p66+ O 18 '70

LANG, Daniel
Reporter at large (cont) New Yorker 46:42-6+ My 23 '70

LANG, Donald
Blind justice and a deaf-mute. Time 97:51 Ja 11 '71 *

LANG, Edith
My organic-trench-method potatoes. il Org Gard & Farm 17:49-51 Je '70

LANG, Frances. See Kopkind, A. jt. auth.

LANG, Paul Henry
Don Giovanni done in. il Hi Fi 20:secI 72-3 My '70
Exploring Idomeneo. il Hi Fi 20:secI 75-7 Mr '70
Mozart's symphonic miracles. il Hi Fi 20:secI 71-3 Jl '70

LANGDON, John E.
American silversmiths in Canada; excerpts from Loyalist silversmiths in British North America 1776-1800. Antiques 97:100-1 Ja '70

LANGE, Dorothea
Assignment I'll never forget; reprint from Popular photography, February 1960. il por Am West 7:46-7 My '70

about
Dorothea Lange. M. Mann. il Pop Phot 66:84-5+ Mr '70 *
Migrant mother: 1936. P. Taylor. il Am West 7:41-5 My '70 *

LANGER, Don
Splicing: wet and dry. il Pop Phot 66:118-20 Ja '70

LANGER, Richard W.
Hidden book. Writer 83:24-6 Ag '70

LANGEWIESCHE, Wolfgang
Can our rivers stand the heat? Read Digest 96:76-80 Ap '70
Sky-lift: a great way to move up in the world. il Read Digest 97:170-2+ N '70
Will this be our next tax? Read Digest 97:132-6 S '70

LANGGUTH, A. J.
Dear Prince: since you went away ... il N Y Times Mag p4-5+ Ag 2 '70
1964: exhilaration; 1968: frustration; 1970: hopelessness. il N Y Times Mag p26-7+ O 4 '70
Vietnamization of General Di. il por N Y Times Mag p5+ S 6 '70

LANGLEY, J. Alex
Down Under; photographs. Travel & Camera 33:24-8 N '70

LANGLEY research center. See United States—Langley research center

LANGLOIS, Henri
M Langlois. New Yorker 46:25 Ag 8 '70 *
Movie saver. il por Newsweek 76:64 Ag 24 '70 *

LANGMAN, Betsy
Working with Fellini. il Mlle 70:74-5+ Ja '70

LANGNER, Ronald O. See Fuller, G. C. jt. auth.

LANGRIDGE, Robert, and others
Sulfate-binding protein from salmonella typhimurium: physical properties. bibliog il Science 169:59-61 Jl 3 '70

LANGSETH, M. G. Jr, and others
Apollo 13 lunar heat flow experiment. bibliog il Science 168:211-17 Ap 10 '70

LANGSTAFF, Nancy
Recommended recordings. Horn Bk 46:325, 508, 648 Je, O-D '70

LANGUAGE, Universal
Growl to me softly and I'll understand. W. Hedgepeth. il Look 34:46-8+ Ja 13 '70
Prospects for a global language. M. Pei. Sat R 53:23-5 My 2 '70

LANGUAGE and languages
Catharsis, linguistics & all that. J. Thompson. bibliog f Commentary 50:65-73 O '70
Double image: language as the perimeter of culture; address, 1969. E. L. Konigsburg. il por Library J 95:731-4 F 15 '70
Inarticulate hero. A. L. Theroux. Nat R 22:199-201 F 24 '70
See also
Alphabet
Children—Language
Language, Universal
Sign language
Slang
Translations and translating
also English language; Zulu language, etc.

Psychology
See also
Children—Language

Study and teaching
Does research in linguistics have practical applications? address, November 1969. R. C. O'Donnell. Engl J 59:410-12+ Mr '70
See also
Bilingual instruction
English language—Study and teaching
Languages, Modern—Study and teaching

LANGUAGE arts
Delete English courses from the curriculum. M. H. Beaven. Engl J 59:800-2 S '70

Study and teaching
Reading and writing can be fun for the underachiever! J. P. Anderson. Engl J 59:1119-21+ N '70

LANGUAGE development. See Children—Language

LANGUAGE of animals. See Animal communication

LANGUAGES. See Language and languages

LANGUAGES, Modern

Study and teaching
Fast ways to learn a foreign language. A. Markovich. il Mech Illus 66:48-50+ Mr '70
FL's weak sisters. J. Venti. Clear House 45:44 S '70
Foreign language study: a new rationale. N. A. Poulin. Clear House 44:286-9 Ja '70
Killing living languages; foreign language teaching in France. Time 95:63 My 18 '70
Non-graded, multi-directional approach to the study of foreign languages. F. H. Wood. bibliog f Clear House 44:279-85 Ja '70
See also
English language—Study and teaching

LANGUEDOC, France
Chercher le sandwich. D. Butwin. il Sat R 53:44-6 O 3 '70

LANGWAY, C. C. Jr, and Hansen, B. L.
Drilling through the ice cap; probing climate for a thousand centuries. il pors Bul Atom Sci 26:62-6 D '70

LANHAM, Edwin
Clock at 8:16; story. Redbook 135:149-71 Ag '70

LANIER, Bob
Bonnie lad. H. L. Masin. por Sr Schol 96:18-19 F 16 '70 *
Bonny year for Buffalo Bob. W. F. Reed. il por Sports Illus 32:16-17 Ja 19 '70

LANIER, G. N.
Sex pheromones: abolition of specificity in hybrid bark beetles. bibliog il Science 169:71-2 Jl 3 '70

LANIER, Ray
Census of arable lands. il Cur Hist 58:337-42 Je '70

LANIER, Robin S.
How you can enjoy surround sound now. il Pop Sci 196:146-8+ Mr '70
Join the revolution in stereo headphones. il Pop Sci 197:76-7+ N '70
Multiplying sound with a tape recorder. il Pop Sci 196:102-3+ F '70
Should you consider omnidirectional speakers? il Hi Fi 20:secI 50-3 Ja '70
Stereo without fuss. il Hi Fi 20:secI 54-8 Mr '70
Try the new generation of automatic turntables. il Pop Sci 197:78-9+ N '70

LANING, Edward
Memoirs of a WPA painter; excerpt from The new deal art project, ed. by F. V. O'Connor. il por Am Heritage 21:38-44+ O '70

LANKARD, J. R.
Amateur scientist. C. L. Stong. il Sci Am 222:116-20 F '70 *

LANKTON, G. William
Forget the cook's parade unless—. Camp Mag 42:22-4 N '70

LANNON, Edwin R.
Lannon's fluxions for a technology in flux. V. Strauss. Pub W 198:46-8 O 12 '70 *
Preliminary report of CRT cost study, highlight of American university meeting. Pub W 197:54-5 Mr 30 '70 *

LANNUIER, Charles Honoré
Chairs by Lannuier at New York's city hall. M. M. Craigmyle. il Antiques 97:268-9 F '70 *

LA NOUE, George R.
Freedom and financing; address, April 17, 1970. Vital Speeches 36:563-6 Jl 1 '70

LANSDOWNE, J. Fenwick
Lansdowne, a portfolio; excerpts from Birds of the eastern forest. Audubon 72:56-65 N '70

LANSFORD, Henry
Supercivilized weather and sky show; with biographical sketch. il Natur Hist 79:4, 92-7+ bibliog(p 133) Ag '70

LANSING, Elizabeth
Image to shed, more food to grow. Life 69:52 D 11 '70

LANSING, Mich.
Land-and-water emergency rescue. il Am City 85:115-16 S '70

Fire department
Special-duty fire fighting. il Am City 85:68 Ag '70

LANSKY, Meyer
Little big man who laughs at the law. N. Gage. il pors Atlan 226:62-9 Jl '70 *
Shocking success story of public enemy no. 1. W. Schulz. por Read Digest 96:54-9 My '70 *

LANTERN projection
Past springs out of a picture; with stereopticon photographs by E. E. Henry and H. Putney, details enlarged by D. R. Phillips. pors Am Heritage 21:2, 16-27+ Je '70

LANTERNS
Japanese garden lanterns. L. M. Burgess. il
Horticulture 48:44-5 Mr '70
See also
Electric lanterns
LANTHANIDE elements. See Earths, Rare
LANZAROTE
Lanzarote. F. R. Buckley. Nat R 22:1166 N
3 '70
LAO refugees. See Refugees, Lao
LAOS
And now Laos. New Repub 162:7-8 Mr 7 '70
Battle for the Plain; Plain of Jars. Time 95:38
Mr 2 '70
Brother vs. brother in Laos. il pors U S
News 68:59 Mr 23 '70
Flank attack: chaos in Laos. il Newsweek
75:32-3 Mr 30 '70
Laos and the burden of history. Chr Cent
87:411 Ap 8 '70
Laos: detailing the commitment. il Time 95:
29:30 Mr 16 '70
Laos in the second Indochina war. A. J.
Dommen. Cur Hist 59:326-32+ D '70
Laos scenario; U.S. involvement. il Newsweek
75:29 Mr 9 '70
Laos: where enemy holds trumps. U S News
69:15-16 Jl 20 '70
Once again Laos. Nation 210:258-9 Mr 9 '70
Our Asian war widens. D. Warner. il Look
34:64-71+ My 19 '70
War in Laos; crucial test for Nixon doc-
trine? il U S News 68:10 Mr 9 '70
See also
Americans in Laos
Communism—Laos
Mercenary troops in Laos
United States—Armed forces—Forces in Laos
United States—Foreign relations—Laos

Air force
Day in Laos, and an evening. W. F. Buckley,
jr. Nat R 22:44 Ja 13 '70

Defenses
If reds take Laos. il U S News 68:20-2 Mr 23
'70
Laos: deeper into the other war. il Time 95:
23-4 Mr 9 '70

Foreign relations
Anatomy of a limited war. D. Greenway.
Time 95:30 Mr 16 '70
Souvanna's bid; peace offer to Hanoi. News-
week 75:37 F 16 '70

United States
See United States—Foreign relations—
Laos

Native races
Notes and comment; C.I.A. support of opium-
producing Meo tribe. New Yorker 46:31
Ap 11 '70

Politics and government
And what about Laos & Cambodia? il Sr
Schol 96:11-13 Ap 13 '70
Cambodia's lost patrimony; political reper-
cussion of the fall of Saravane. il News-
week 75:24+ Je 22 '70
Laos: plain and fancy talk; peace proposal
from the Pathet Lao. Newsweek 75:37 Mr 23
'70
Our involvement in Laos. R. Shaplen. il For
Affairs 48:478-93 Ap '70
Peace probes. Newsweek 76:26-7 Ag 24 '70
Toward talks? Time 96:30+ N 9 '70
Vietnamization of Laos. B. Garrett. il Ramp
Mag 8:36-45 Je '70
LAP joints. See Joints (carpentry)
LAPAROSCOPY. See Sterilization, Sexual
LAPHAM, Lewis H.
Alaska: politicians and natives, money and
oil. il Harper 240:85-102 My '70
Attorney General has heard it all before. il
pors Life 68:50-50B+ F 13 '70
Case study of an army star. il pors Life 69:
54-6+ S 25 '70
LAPIDE, Pinchas E.
Jesus in Israeli literature. Chr Cent 87:1248-53
O 21 '70
LAPIDUS, Morris
Architect of joy. D. Davis. il por Newsweek
76:103 N 2 '70 *
LAPLAND
See also
Fishing—Lapland

Description and travel
Winter fun in Finland. P. Patricoff. il Travel
133:52-6 Ja '70

LAPORTE, Pierre
Canada enters the revolutionary age. il
Newsweek 76:41-4+ N 2 '70 *
Canada: this very sorry moment. il pors Time
96:33-4 O 26 '70 *
LAPP, Ralph E.
Can SALT stop MIRV? il N Y Times Mag
p 14-15+ F 1 '70
Correcting our posture. New Repub 162:12-15
Mr 28 '70
Cutting the Pentagon down to size. New Re-
pub 163:16-20 Ag 22 '70
Nuclear weapons: past and present. por Bul
Atom Sci 26:103-6 Je '70
SALT chips and Safeguard. New Repub 163:
14-17 Ag 15 '70
$10 billion more for space? New Repub 162:
16-19 F 21 '70
Where will we get the energy? New Repub
163:17-21 J 11 '70
LAQUEUR, Walter
Look back at the Weimar republic, the cry
was, Down with das system. il N Y Times
Mag p 12-13+ Ag 16 '70
LARCH
Larch. il Cons 25:31 O '70
LARDNER, Rex
What it's like to free-lance. il Sat R 54:47-9
Ja 9 '71
LARDNER, Susan
Current cinema (cont) New Yorker 46:62-4 Je
27 '70
Our local correspondents. New Yorker 46:96+
Je 20 '70
LAREDO cigarette rolling kit. See Cigarette-
making machines
LARGE families. See Family, Size of
LARGE farms. See Farms, Large
LARGE-scale integration. See Electronic cir-
cuits, Integrated
LARGEMOUTH bass fishing. See Bass fishing
LARMOTH, Jeanine
Beauty through the drinking glass. Harp
Baz 103:241+ Mr '70
Portrait of a house. il House B 112:40-1 F
'70
LAROCHELLE, A. and Schwarz, E. J.
Magnetic properties of lunar sample 10048-22.
bibliog il Science 167:700-1 Ja 30 '70
LARSEN, Christian
U.S. business worldwide: Arizona view; in-
terview. pors Forbes 106:50-1 O 1 '70
LARSEN, Jack Lenor
Irish treasury. M. Gough. il House B 112:
98-101 Mr '70 *
LARSEN, Roy E.
Thinking man's medium; excerpt from ad-
dress, September 1970. Sat R 53:71-2 N 14
'70
LARSON, Charles R.
Beowulf's hang-up. Sat R 53:8+ Ja 17 '70
LARSON, Edith
All around the town; drama. Plays 29:63-71
Mr '70
LARSON, Jane W.
Ceramics at Expo '70. il Ceram Mo 18:37 Je
'70
Hamada legacy. il por Ceram Mo 18:13-15 O
'70
LARSON, Richard L.
Theory of the curriculum in composition:
goals and writing assignments. Engl J 59:
393-404+ Mr '70
LARSON, Stephen
Plea for moral resistance. Chr Cent 87:197 F
18 '70
LA RUE, Danny
Danny La Rue? pors Vogue 156:376-7 S 1 '70 *
LARVAE
See also
Caterpillars
Cercaria
LARVICIDES. See Insecticides
LARYNX, Artificial
Good vibrations. il Newsweek 75:46 Mr 9 '70
LASAGNA. See Cookery, Italian
LASANSKY, Mauricio
Prints of Mauricio Lasansky. J. Goldman. il
por Am Artist 34:62-8+ Mr '70 *
LA SCALA opera, Milan. See Milan, Italy—
La Scala
LASCAUX murals. See Cave drawings and
paintings
LASER communication systems. See Light
communication systems
LASER-holography. See Holography
LASER modulators. See Modulators
LASER photography. See Lasers—Photographic
use
LASER strain gages. See Strain gages
LASER surgery. See Lasers—Medical applica-
tions

LATIN AMERICA
New Latins, by G. A. Geyer. Review
  Sat R 53:30-1 S 12 '70. D. Kurzman
Where smuggling is a way of life. il Bsns
  W p24-5 Ag 15 '70
  See also
Aeronautics, Commercial—Latin America
Atlantic community development group for
  Latin America
Birth control—Latin America
Catholic church in Latin America
Church and social problems—Latin America
Church and state in Latin America
Civil rights—Latin America
Community development—Latin America
Ecology—Latin America
Economic assistance in Latin America
Education—Latin America
Forests and forestry—Latin America
Guerrillas—Latin America
Immigration and emigration—Latin America
Investments, Foreign (in Latin America)
Missions—Latin America
Newspapers—Latin America
Performing arts—Latin America
Public health—Latin America
Publishers and publishing—Latin America
Purchasing, Military—Latin America
Science—Latin America
Social change—Latin America
Surinam
Unemployment—Latin America
United States—Economic relations—Latin
  America
United States—Foreign relations—Latin Amer-
  ica

Antiquities
  See also
Indians of South America—Antiquities

Commerce
On the import quota system; excerpt from
  address, April 23, 1970. G. Plaza. Américas 22:1 My '70
Trade, capital, and Latin American development; address, January 19, 1970. N. Samuels. Dept State Bul 62:179-85 F 16 '70

Defenses
Generals sharpen their swords. il Bsns W
  p42 Je 6 '70

Description and travel
Journey into the tropics. R. H. De Rageot.
  il Américas 22:36-42 Jl '70
See the Americas first. G. de Zéndegui. il
  Américas 22:18-28 Mr '70

Discovery and exploration
Art of terra-cotta pottery in pre-Columbian
  Central and South America, by A. von
  Wuthenau. Review
  Life il 69:12 O 16 '70. K. E. Meyer
River of Doubt. T. H. Brown. il pors Améri-
  cas 22:15-23 O '70

Economic conditions
Latin America: toward a new policy; address, April 10, 1970. F. Church. Vital
  Speeches 36:418-23 My 1 '70
Medellin guidelines. M. J. Drinkwater. America 122:258 Mr 14 '70
Medellin guidelines; Latin American episcopal
  conference statement. V. T. Mallon. Amer-
  ica 122:92-6 Ja 31 '70
Opening to the future. G. Plaza. il America
  122:96-8 Ja 31 '70
Quality of life in the Americas; statement,
  by President Nixon with text of the Rocke-
  feller mission report. Dept State Bul 61:493-
  540 D 8 '69
Trade, capital, and Latin American develop-
  ment; address, January 19, 1970. N. Samuels. Dept State Bul 62:179-85 F 16 '70
  See also
Inter-American economic and social council
United Nations—Economic commission for
  Latin America

Economic policy
  See also
Inter-American social development institute

Foreign relations
Latin America; symposium. bibliog f il Cur
  Hist 58:65-117 F '70

United States
  See United States—Foreign relations—
  Latin America

History
Potosi and Charcas; the Spanish colonial
  world. R. P. Romecín. il Américas 22:2-7
  Mr '70

Bibliography
Articles and other books received; comp.
  by D. E. Worcester. See issues of American historical review
Recent developments in Latin American history. R. N. Burr. Ann Am Acad 388:133-44
  Mr '70

Maps
Latin America. Sr Schol 95:15 S 22 '69; 97:7
  S 21 '70

Nationalism
Latin America and the flying buttress pol-
  icy. J. Marías. il pors Américas 22:16-20
  My '70

Politics
Alliance rhetoric versus Latin American re-
  ality. A. F. Lowenthal. For Affairs 48:
  494-508 Ap '70
Center stage for Chile's Marxist president;
  Latins move left, and right. il por Newsweek
  76:52+ N 2 '70
How generals are ruling most of a continent.
  il U S News 68:74-5 Je 22 '70
Kipnapped diplomats: Greek tragedy on a
  Latin stage. M. M. Alves. Commonweal 92:
  311-14 Je 26 '70
Latin America: sitting on a volcano. Sr
  Schol 97:6 S 21 '70
Latin America; symposium. bibliog f il Cur
  Hist 58:65-117 F '70
Latin America: the shrinking middle. il Time
  96:22-3 O 19 '70
Price of stability. E. von Kuehnelt-Leddihn.
  Nat R 22:84 Ja 27 '70
Sweet and sour. New Repub 162:11 F 21 '70

Religious institutions and affairs
  See also
Catholic church in Latin America
Protestant churches—Latin America

Social conditions
Lowering hemisphere. A. Schlesinger, jr. il
  Atlan 225:79-84+ Ja '70
Medellin guidelines; Latin American episcopal
  conference statement. V. T. Mallon. America 122:92-6 Ja 31 '70
Quality of life in the Americas; statement,
  by President Nixon with text of the Rockefeller mission report. Dept State Bul 61:493-
  540 D 8 '69

Treaties
How wars end in Latin America. B. Wood.
  bibliog f Ann Am Acad 392:40-50 N '70

LATIN AMERICA and Spain. See Spain and Latin America
LATIN AMERICA and the United States
  See also
Alliance for progress
Inter-American relations
Pan American day and week
LATIN AMERICAN art. See Art, Latin American
LATIN AMERICAN cookery. See Cookery, Latin American
LATIN AMERICAN literature
Periquillo Sarniento. G. R. Pérez. il Améri-
  cas 22:29-34 My '70
Reading resources and Project LEER. M. D.
  Shepard. bibliog il por Wilson Lib Bul 44:
  743-50 Mr '70
  See also
Argentine literature
LATIN AMERICAN propaganda. See Propa-
  ganda, Latin American
LATIN AMERICAN scientists. See Scientists, Latin American
LATIN AMERICAN terrorists. See Terrorism
LATIN AMERICANS
New Latins, by G. A. Geyer. Review
  Sat R 53:30-1 S 12 '70. D. Kurzman
LATIN AMERICANS in the United States
Libraries and the Spanish-speaking; sym-
  posium, ed. by W. L. Ramirez. bibliog il
  por Wilson Lib Bul 44:714-67 Mr '70
Silent minority starts to speak out. il U S
  News 69:66-9 Jl 13 '70

Religion
Neighbors who moved in: Spanish-Ameri-
  can congress on evangelism. W. G. Marx.
  Chr Today 14:60-3 S 25 '70
LATIN language

Study and teaching
Latin for the now generation; University of
  Illinois. Sch & Soc 98:268-70 Sum '70
Survey of the teaching of Latin in second-
  ary schools. N. W. Austin. Sch & Soc
  98:252-4 Ap '70
Via *latina* to English mastery? J. S. Sherwin;
  J. H. Parks. Todays Ed 59:42-4 F '70

LATIN poetry
Translations into English
Eclogue II; tr. by S. Orgel. Virgil. Poetry 116:
353-5 Ag '70
LATIN school, Chicago. See Private schools
LA TOUR DU PIN GOUVERNET, Henriette
Lucie (Dillon) marquise de
Portrait of a lady. M. Maddocks. por Time
97:76 Ja 18 '71 *
LATTER-day saints. See Mormons and Mor-
monism
LATTICES. See Trellises
LATTMANN, Dieter
Letter from West Germany. Pub W 197:53-4
Mr 2; 37-8 Je 15; 198:pt2 191 S 21 '70
Report from Scandinavia. Pub W 198:16 D
14 '70
LAUBACH, Frank Charles
Obituary
Chr Cent 87:782 Je 24 '70
Chr Today 14:22 Jl 3 '70 *
LAUD, William, abp
Religious medals. C. F. French. il Hobbies
75:132 N '70 *
LAUDER, Leonard
Lauder: the man behind the makeup. por
Bsns W p94 F 21 '70 *
LAUGHING gas. See Nitrous oxide
LAUGHLIN, J. R.
Build an electronic clinical thermometer. il
Pop Electr 34:75-8 Ja '71
LAUGHLIN, Ledlie I
Pewterers of eighteenth-century New York.
il Antiques 98:624-8 O '70
LAUGHTER
Mystery of laughter. il Time 95:60 F 9 '70
See also
Humor
LAUNCHING of space vehicles. See Space ve-
hicles—Launching
LAUNCHING of yachts. See Yachts—Launching
LAUNDRIES
Closet-size laundry centers. H. A. Dawson.
il Bet Hom & Gard 48:82 Ap '70
Wonderful work room. J. Gillies. il Farm J
94:68-9 My '70
LAUNDRY
How to do your bulky items. J. Heckroth.
Bet Hom & Gard 48:26 S '70
Washing the unwashables. M. Davidson and
B. Wadsworth. il Ladies Home J 87:46 Jl '70
See also
Ironing
LAUNDRY cabinets. See Cabinets (furniture)
LAUNDRY detergents. See Detergents
LAUNDRY equipment
See also
Clothes dryers
Washing machines
LAUNDRY products, Enzyme. See Enzyme
laundry products
LAURA Beall Woods, Ill. See Forests. State
LAURA Ingalls Wilder award. See Wilder
award
LAUREL international. See Horse racing
LAURENCE, William L.
Now we are all sons-of-bitches. il por Sci N
98:39-41 Jl 11 '70
LAURENT, Pierre Henri
(comp) Articles and other books received;
Low Countries. See issues of American
historical review
Milestone for the European community. Cur
Hist 58:257-63 My '70
LAUTER, Paul, and Howe, Florence
What happened to the free university. il Sat
R 53:80-2+ Je 20 '70
LAVA tubes (caves) See Caves
LAVARONI, Charles W. See O'Donnell, P. A.
jt. auth.
LAVE, Lester B. and Seskin, E. P.
Air pollution and human health. bibliog il
Science 169:723-33 Ag 21 '70
LAVENDER, David
Hudson's Bay company. il Am Heritage 21:
5-10+ Ap '70
LA VENTA culture. See Indians of Mexico—
Antiquities
LAVER, Rodney George
How to play togetherness tennis. il por La-
dies Home J 87:54 Ag '70
LAVERDIERE, Bruno
Bruno LaVerdiere. W. Tucciarone. il por
Ceram Mo 18:14-17 S '70 *
LAVIN, Patrick J.
Washington front (cont) America 123:279 O 17
'70
LAW, Kenneth L.
Real heart of a negotiated agreement. To-
days Ed 59:36-8 F '70

LAW
See also
American bar association
Jurisprudence
Jury
Justice
Lawyers
Libel and slander
Medical jurisprudence
Probate law and practice
Social contract
Wills
also special branches of law, e.g.
Criminal law; also law on special subjects,
e.g. Game laws; etc.

Jews
See Jews—Legal status, laws, etc.

Philosophy
American jurisprudence between the wars:
legal realism and the crisis of democratic
theory. E. A. Purcell, jr. bibliog f Am Hist
R 75:424-46 D '69

Sociology
See Sociological jurisprudence

Study and teaching
Head Start in legal studies for minority
groups. Sch & Soc 98:135-6 Mr '70
Judgmental reading and the study of law.
J. C. Johnson and H. L. Sublett, jr. bibliog
Clear House 44:559-61 My '70
Soaking up law at leisure; use of cassette
tapes. V. Louviere. Nations Bsns 58:13 Jl
'70
See also
Law schools

Brazil
We have more laws than we can afford. il Bsns
W p48 Ja 24 '70

California
See also
Justice, Administration of—California

Hawaii
Abortion on request; Hawaii. Time 95:34 Mr
9 '70
Abortion unlimited. Newsweek 75:46 Mr 9 '70

Israel
Legislating Jewishness. Newsweek 75:114
Mr 23 '70
Shalit case. R. Alter. Commentary 50:55-61 Jl
'70; Reply with rejoinder. L. Bernstein.
50:15-16 N '70

Maryland
Veto for abortion. Newsweek 75:51-2 Je 8 '70

Massachusetts
Finding fault with no-fault rates. Bsns W
p24 Ag 29 '70

New York (state)
Fathers and sons; abortion reform bill.
Newsweek 75:77 Ap 20 '70
New York's mental hygiene law: a preliminary
evaluation. A. Zitrin and others. bibliog
Ment Hy 54:28-36 Ja '70

Southwestern states
Law & the land: the legal heritage of the
American Southwest. O. B. Faulk. Am
West 7:14-16+ Ja '70
Variations on a theme of law and order;
symposium; with introd. by W. H. Hutch-
inson. il Am West 7:4-47 Ja '70

United States
Canada can, can we? New Repub 163:7-8 O
31 '70
Family legal matters. L. M. Brown. Bet Hom
& Gard 48:26+ Ap; 20 My; 30 Je; 28+ O; 6
N; 18 D '70
Rips in the fabric of the law. S. Hyman. il
Sat R 53:21-4+ Jl 11 '70
See also
Courts—United States
Justice, Administration of—United States
Law enforcement
Negroes—Legal status, laws, etc.
Teachers—Legal status, laws, etc.
Transplantation of organs, tissues, etc.—Legal
aspects
Uniform state laws

History
At the borderland of law and economic history: the contributions of Willard Hurst;
address, December 1968. H. N. Scheiber.
bibliog f Am Hist R 75:744-56 F '70

LAW—*Continued*

Utah

Surprise, surprise: a dirty speech is illegal; violating Utah's obscenity statute. Time 96:63 S 28 '70

LAW, Maritime. See Maritime law

LAW, Sunday. See Sunday legislation

LAW, Usury. See Usury laws

LAW and Christianity. See Religion and law

LAW and ethics
Law and conscience. J. R. Connery. il America 122:178-81 F 21 '70

LAW and religion. See Religion and law

LAW and society. See Sociological jurisprudence

LAW corporations. See Law partnership

LAW enforcement
About that Hitler quote: law and order. J. D. Lofton, jr. Nat R 22:411 Ap 21 '70
Are we moving right? W. F. Buckley, jr. Nat R 22:1125 O 20 '70
Attorney General Mitchell: the tide is turning against crime; interview. J. N. Mitchell. il pors Nations Bsns 58:32-4+ Je '70
Blotter for the first year. il Time 95:15-16 Ja 26 '70
Curbing crime: a policeman speaks out; interview. J. J. Harrington. Read Digest 97:202+ D '70
Law-and-order issue. P. Schrag. Sat R 53:26+ N 21 '70
Let this madness cease; reprint. Camp Mag 42:30 Je '70
Night thoughts of a police chief. J. P. Kimble. il Nation 210:490-2 Ap 27 '70
Notes and comment: extreme-left-wing movement and current administration's response. il New Yorker 46:25-6 Je 27 '70
Page 48; an escape from paranoia. R. M. Brown. Am West 7:48 Ja '70
Protesters, police, and politicians. J. Unruh. Sat R 53:31+ F 21 '70
Real constitutional crisis. F. S. Meyer. Nat R 22:571 Je 2 '70
Repression, U.S.A. W. F. Buckley, jr. Nat R 22:480 My 5 '70
Squelching revolutionaries. D. Lawrence. il U S News 68:96 Ap 6 '70
To stop terror bombing: new laws White House asks. il U S News 68:20+ Ap 6 '70
Tough vs. moderate cops. il Bsns W p38+ D 12 '70
White House and free speech. W. Roberts. Sat R 53:26 My 2 '70
Whose law? Whose order? Nation 211:420-1 N 2 '70
Whose law, whose order? Commission on civil rights report. Commonweal 93:139-40 N 6 '70
See also
Congressional conference on justice in America
Law—United States
Police
United States—Justice, Department of—Law enforcement assistance administration

History

Variations on a theme of law and order; symposium; with introd. by W. H. Hutchinson. il Am West 7:4-47 Ja '70

Europe, Western

Europe's law-and-order syndrome. il Time 95:36+ My 25 '70

LAW enforcement assistance administration. See United States—Justice, Department of—Law enforcement assistance administration

LAW firms. See Law partnership

LAW libraries
See also
Law library company of Philadelphia

LAW library company of Philadelphia
Law library company of Philadelphia; new library administered by Theodore F. Jenkins memorial law library company bar association's new agent. il Library J 95:4146-7 D 1 '70

LAW of relativity. See Relativity (physics)

LAW partnership
Law graduates: the new breed. M. Green. il Nation 210:658-60 Je 1 '70
Muddled approach; tax-exempt status to public-interest law firms. Commonweal 93:212 N 27 '70
Taxing the public interest; tax-exempt status of public-interest law firms. Time 96:94+ N 16 '70

LAW reform. See Legal reform

LAW school deans. See College deans

LAW schools
Black law student. J. A. McPherson. Atlan 225:93-100 Ap '70
See also
Law—Study and teaching
Stanford university—School of law

LAW societies
See also
American bar association

LAW students
Black law student. J. A. McPherson. Atlan 225:93-100 Ap '70
Law graduates: the new breed. M. Green. il Nation 210:658-60 Je 1 '70

LAW students, Women
Portia's complaint. il Newsweek 76:101 D 7 '70

LAW suits. See Actions and defenses

LAWFORD, Valentine
Life at full fling. il por Vogue 156:124-9 Ag 15 '70
Renaissance reborn; villa dei Vescovi. il pors Vogue 156:152-7+ S 15 '70

LAWICK, Jane (Goodall) baroness van
Chimps instead of Spock. il Time 96:51 N 30 '70 *
Remarkable woman: Jane Goodall; excerpt from Restless spirit. T. Green. il por McCalls 97:46-7+ Ag '70 *
Should we ape the chimpanzee? D. Behrman. il UNESCO Courier 23:7-18 Ag '70

LAWICK-GOODALL, Jane, baroness van. See Lawick, J. G. van

LAWLESSNESS
Only the people as a whole can cure crime. D. Lawrence. U S News 68:92 Mr 9 '70

LAWN, Tex.
Entire town in one obsolete missile site. J. Zachry. il Am City 85:87 Jl '70

LAWN edgers. See Lawn tools, equipment and supplies

LAWN fertilizers. See Fertilizers and manures

LAWN furniture. See Furniture, Outdoor

LAWN mowers
Black & Decker's cordless mower. J. M. Liston. il Pop Mech 133:119 Ap '70
Front or rear drive which rotary mower is for you? E. F. Lindsley. il Pop Sci 196:102-4+ Ap '70
Great grass clipping controversy. E. A. Freytag. il Org Gard & Farm 17:38-42 Je '70
Low-cost rotary power mowers. il Mech Illus 66:78 Ap '70
Mighty mo, no-nonsense machine with a sense of humor. J. M. Liston. il Pop Mech 134:128-31 S '70
More tethered mowers make the rounds. il Pop Sci 196:92-3 Je '70
New for the lawn. il Mech Illus 66:80+ Ap '70
One pull, you're off and moving; new no-choke mower. E. F. Lindsley. il Pop Sci 197:16 O '70
Power up for more gardening with less effort. B. C. Kilvert, jr. il Home Gard 57:32-40 Mr '70
Rotary power mowers. Consumer Rep 34:186-9 D '69
Short cuts to a trimmer garden. W. F. Bruning. il Home Gard 57:18-19+ Ag '70
Skil's powerful electric mower. J. M. Liston. il Pop Mech 133:118 Ap '70

Anecdotes, facetiae, satire, etc.

Pink thumbs and brown lawn. H. J. Montgomery. il Todays Health 48:40-1 Jl '70

Maintenance and repair

Keeping your mower on the go. E. F. Lindsley. il Pop Sci 196:106-8+ My '70
Now's the time to check lawn tools. il Home Gard 57:26 Ja '70

LAWN parties
Poolside luau; with recipes. il Bet Hom & Gard 48:56 Je '70

LAWN thatch
Great grass clipping controversy. E. A. Freytag. il por Org Gard & Farm 17:38-42 Je '70

LAWN tools, equipment, and supplies
For the care of your lawn: a cordless electric grass shear. il Consumer Bul 53:34 Ag '70
Good electric grass shears; Disston cordless. il Consumer Rep 35:396 Jl '70
Grass trimmer with the power in the handle. E. F. Lindsley. il Pop Sci 197:85 N '70
Lawn spreaders. il Consumer Rep 35:252-5 Ap '70
No-work way to condition your lawn; Simplicity lawn thatcher. E. F. Lindsley. il Pop Sci 196:101 Ap '70
Previewed at the hardware show: tools to keep your yard in trim this spring. A. Lees. il Pop Sci 196:142-3 Ja '70

LAWN trimmers. See Lawn tools, equipment and supplies

LAWNS

Good tips for summer lawn and garden care. il Good H 171:141 Jl '70

Instant lawns the weed-free way. S. Schuler. il Am Home 73:22+ Ag '70

Lawn care now pays green dividends. R. W. Schery. il Home Gard 57:35+ Ap '70

Lawn care starts this month. R. W. Schery. il Home Gard 57:52-3 Mr '70

Plan next summer's lawn now. Bet Hom & Gard 48:101 F '70

Revitalize your lawn now! il Home Gard 57: 22-3 S '70

Sod versus seed. il Home Gard 57:28-31 Ag '70

Spring handbook on lawns. R. W. Schery. il Horticulture 48:22-4+ Mr '70

Yes, you can still have grass this summer. il Changing T 24:11-12 My '70

Diseases and pests

Spotless summer lawn takes careful planning. R. W. Schery. il Home Gard 57:30-1 Jl '70

LAWNS, Artificial. See Turf, Artificial

LAWRENCE, A. F. R.

Rather odd, to say the least: Sousa sans Sousa! Am Rec G 36:557 Ap '70

LAWRENCE, Daniel

How to shop for a stereo receiver. il Hi Fi 20:50-7 S '70

LAWRENCE, David Herbert

Eliot, Lawrence & the Jews. R. Alter. Commentary 50:81-6 O '70 *

Women in love; novel a classic film. J. Hamilton. il por Look 34:32-7 F 24 '70 *

LAWRENCE, Jacob

Melting pot: its most difficult test: the immigrant within; paintings. il Am Heritage 22:32-9 D '70

LAWRENCE, Jerome, and Lee, R. E.

Night Thoreau spent in jail. Criticism Nat R 23:45-6 Ja 12 '71 *

LAWRENCE, Joe B.

Allegory of Easy rider. Engl J 59:665-6 My '70

LAWRENCE, L. George

Electronics & meteorites. bibliog il Electr World 84:23-6+ Jl '70

Electronics and parapsychology. bibliog il Electr World 83:27-9 Ap '70

LAWRENCE, Louise de Kiriline

Apartment. Audubon 72:4-7 Mr '70

LAWRENCE, Robert

Berlioz from the Tabernacle. il Sat R 53:60 Mr 28 '70

Burst of Berlioz. il Sat R 53:66+ Ap 25 '70

Donizetti, Sills, and Devereux. Sat R 53:83 F 28 '70

Double rich, double good Ludwig-Berry-Bernstein Mahler. il Sat R 53:69 Ja 31 '70

Nilsson-Nilsson Tannhäuser. Sat R 53:47 My 30 '70

LAWRENCE, Ruth

Your boat's interior; excerpts from The woman's guide to boating & cooking. il Yachting 127:103+ Ja '70

LAWRENCE, Ted, and Velleman, Jim

Drugs/teens=alcohol/parents. il pors Sci Digest 68:46-8+ O '70

LAWRENCE, Thomas Edward

Secret lives of Lawrence of Arabia, by P. Knightly and C. Simpson. Review Commonweal 93:100-4 O 23 '70. J. Meyers *

Nat R 22:422-3 Ap 21 '70. F. Russell *

LAWRENCE, Kan.

Education

Bleeding Kansas; violence at University of Kansas and Lawrence high school. il Time 95:25 My 4 '70

Police

Kansas: police-student violence imperils university. B. Nelson. Science 169:567-9 Ag 7 '70

Religious institutions and affairs

Whither unity? A case study; Church of Christ uniting and Bethany Park Christian church. T. Miller. Chr Cent 87:891-3 Jl 22 '70; Discussion. 87:1423-4, 1457-9 N 25-D 2 '70

Riots

Death in Lawrence. il Newsweek 76:41 Ag 3 '70

Kansas: police-student violence imperils university. B. Nelson. Science 169:567-9 Ag 7 '70

Listening to America. B. Moyers. il Harper 241:56-64+ D '70

LAWRENCE hall of science. See California. University—Berkeley campus—Lawrence hall of science

LAWRENCE radiation laboratory, Berkeley, Calif. See California. University—Lawrence radiation laboratories

LAWRENCE radiation laboratory, Livermore, Calif. See California. University—Lawrence radiation laboratories

LAWRENSON, Helen

All about Yves. por Esquire 73:108-9+ Je '70

People inside Peter Sellers. por Esquire 74: 120-3+ N '70

LAWS, William R. Jr

Pastor Laws heads UPUSA. por Chr Today 14:32 Je 19 '70 *

LAWS of nature. See Nature, Laws of

LAWSON, Donna

Constant cup. il Craft Horiz 30:54-7+ D '70

LAWSON, James M.

Methodism under siege. D. Kucharsky. Chr Today 14:36-7 My 8 '70 *

LAWSON, Philip

Clash over urban ministry styles. Chr Cent 87:1507 D 16 '70 *

Methodist uproar. J. S. Tinney. Chr Today 15:39 D 18 '70 *

LAWTON, Florian K.

Watercolor page; with biographical sketch. il por Am Artist 34:52-3+ Ap '70

LAWWILL, Mert

Mert Lawwill: motorcycling's number one fun and games man. B. Greene. il pors Hot Rod 23:112 Jl '70 *

LAWYERS

Campus rights and responsibilities: a role for lawyers? N. Glazer. Am Scholar 39:445-62 Sum '70; Same with title What new governance systems? Cur 122:44-55 O '70

How to choose a lawyer. L. David. Mech Illus 66:65-7+ Jl '70

Law firms go multinational. il Bsns W p36-8 Jl 11 '70

Law professor behind ASH, SOUP, PUMP and CRASH; the new breed of public interest lawyers. J. A. Page. il por N Y Times Mag p32-3+ Ag 23 '70; Reply. R. H. Quinn. p33 S 27 '70

Lawyer's case; liability lawyers. Forbes 105:71 Ap 15 '70

Missing Manson lawyer. por Time 96:61 D 21 '70

Squad-car lawyers. il Newsweek 75:75-6 Mr 16 '70

Troika of torts. il por Time 96:68 D 7 '70

Your lawyer and your will. L. M. Brown. Bet Hom & Gard 48:26+ Ap '70

See also

American bar association

Attorney and client

Bailey, F. L.

Law partnership

LAWYERS assistants. See Legal assistants

LAX, Michael

Top designers at home. il por Am Home 73: 74-5 S '70 *

LAXALT, Robert

New Mexico, the golden land. il Nat Geog 138:299-345 S '70

LAY, Margaret

Scene then & now. Todays Ed 59:37-8 Ap '70; Same abr. with title Early childhood education: the scene then and now. Ed Digest 36:36-8 S '70

LAYCOCK, George

Call it Lake inferior. il Audubon 72:48-53 My '70

Haunted sands of Laysan. il Audubon 72:42-9 Mr '70

Hawaiian Islands of birds. il Audubon 72:44-61 Ja '70

Kiss the north slope good-by? il Audubon 72: 68-75 S '70

Not all is Sanguine in Wisconsin il Audubon 72:104-9 Ja '70

Prospecting for Florida bass. il Field & S 75: 56-7+ My '70

Trails of the Lincoln back country. il Field & S 75:32-3+ Jl '70

Trouble in paradise. il Audubon 72:24-31 My '70

LAYDEN, Milton

Hostility: a big expense you can avoid. il Nations Bsns 58:54-5 S '70

LAYE, Leonard

Darlington stripe. il Motor T 22:82-4 Jl '70

Last stop. il Motor T 22:44-6+ F '70

LAYING up of boats. See Boats—Storage

LAYNE, Elizabeth N.

Environment: notes on the continuing battle. il Am Heritage 21:111-13 Je; 118-19 Ag '70

Field notes (cont) Am Heritage 21:113-15 F; 116-17 Ap '70

LAYOFF systems
Job cuts at the national laboratories. Sci N 97:192 F 21 '70
RIF is a drag on the job market. Bsns W p37 F 21 '70
Where workers opt for a layoff; inverse seniority. il Bsns W p88+ Mr 14 '70
Will layoffs undermine the hard core? with editorial comment. il Bsns W p29-30, 118 Ja 17 '70

LAYOUT and typography, Periodical. See Periodical layout and typography

LAYPORT, Mike
Going nowhere, on wheels. S. Treadwell. il pors Sports Illus 32:30-2 + My 18 '70 *

LAYSAN (island)
Haunted sands of Laysan. G. Laycock. il Audubon 72:42-9 Mr '70

LAYSAN albatrosses, See Albatrosses

LAYTON, Donald H. See Campbell, R. F. jt. auth.

LAZARUS, Charles Y.
Establishment; address, April 15, 1970. Vital Speeches 36:498-502 Je 1 '70

LAZARUS, George
Name of the game. Sat R 53:60 Je 13 '70

LAZARUS, Simon
Defending consumers. New Repub 163:10-11 S 26 '70

LAZY susans
Susan goes round an umbrella. il Sunset 145: 118+ O '70

LE, Kong
Where are they now? il pors Newsweek 76:8 Jl 13 '70 *

LEAD
See also
Plants, Effect of lead on

LEAD additives. See Gasoline—Additives

LEAD in religion, folklore, etc.
Lead in the New Year with lead; tradition of melting lead on New Year's eve to tell fortunes. X. Pové. Harp Baz 104:147 D '70

LEAD industry and trade
See also
St Joseph lead company

LEAD paint. See Paint

LEAD poisoning
Consumers and the earthenware problem. Sci N 98:382 N 14 '70
Demyelinating encephalomyelopathy associated with lead poisoning in nonhuman primates. R. M. Sauer and others. bibliog il Science 169:1091-3 S 11 '70
Earthware pitcher hazard. il Sci N 98:301 O 10 '70
Lead in the air. il Time 96:51-2 S 14 '70
My family is dying! J. L. Block. Read Digest 96:171-2+ Ap '70
Poisoned pottery. Time 96:68 O 12 '70
℞ for Philip; ceramic ware as source of lead poisoning. M. A. Guitar. il Good H 170: 12+ My '70

LEADED gasoline. See Gasoline—Additives

LEADERSHIP
Demand for moral leadership. H. Sidey. il Life 69:2 O 23 '70
Failure of leadership; address, December 9, 1969. J. W. Gardner. Vital Speeches 36:217-19 Ja 15 '70
Looking at leadership. Todays Ed 59:70 Ja '70
1970 student burgesses at colonial Williamsburg; voices of tomorrow, leaders for tomorrow. il Sr Schol 96:18-19 My 4 '70
Three phase program starts leader, training at eight years old; Van Buren youth camp, Mich. K. V. Washburn, jr. il Camp Mag 42:20+ F '70
See also
Christian leadership
Negro leadership

LEAF, Alexander
Social consequences of new developments in medicine. Bul Atom Sci 26:21-2 Ja '70

LEAF cactus. See Cactus

LEAF designs. See Design, Decorative—Plant forms

LEAF gatherers
Blow your leaves and bale them; Canton, Ohio. F. Elaass. il Am City 85:38 O '70
Discarded packer excels in leaf pick-up; North Tarrytown, N.Y. J. A. Biros. Am City 85:28 O '70
Leaf raking gives way to air brooms; Kent state university campus. il Am City 85:27 N '70

LEAF rust. See Rusts (botany)

LEAFLETS. See Pamphlets

LEAGUE of women voters of the United States
Women in league for better education. C. Aaron. Am Ed 6:32-3 Mr '70

LEAKEY, Richard E.
In search of man's past at Lake Rudolf. il pors Nat Geog 137:712-33 My '70

LEAN, David
Current cinema. P. Kael. New Yorker 46: 116-18+ N 21 '70 *
David Lean's big gamble. H. Alpert. por Sat R 53:53+ N 14 '70 *
Lean years. C. L. Westerbeck, jr. Commonweal 93:302-3 D 18 '70 *

LEAR, Edward
On children's literature: a runcible symposium. B. J. Lifton. il Horn Bk 46:255-63 Je '70 *

LEAR, Evelyn, and Stewart, Thomas
Never say never. pors Opera N 34:14-16 Mr 28 '70

LEAR, John
Ancient landings in America. il Sat R 53:18-19+ Jl 18 '70
Enemy is us. il Sat R 53:58-9 Mr 7 '70
Progress report on smogless motoring. Sat R 53:44-5 Ag 1 '70
Science/the endless search. il Sat R 53:39 Mr 7; 41 Mr 14; 48 Mr 21; 44-6 Mr 28; 46-7 Ap 4; 52 Ap 11; 47 Ap 18; 52 Ap 25; 45 My 2; 56 My 9; 62 My 16; 59 My 23 '70

LEAR, Martha Weinman
Rudolf Nureyev: dynamite looking for a match. il Redbook 136:76+ N '70
When college dorms go coed. Read Digest 96:27-8+ F '70
(ed) See Koedt, A. Five passionate feminists

LEAR, William Powell
King Lear. P. Garrison. il pors Flying 86:64-9+ F '70
Lear steams back. Newsweek 76:71-2 S 21 '70 *

LEAR jet Industries, Inc.
Gates Learjet delays helicopter. Aviation W 92:19 Je 1 '70

LEARNING, Psychology of
Don't use the kitchen-sink approach to enrichment; adaptation of address. D. Krech. il Todays Ed 59:30-2+ O '70
Learning in the autonomic nervous system. L. V. DiCara. il Sci Am 222:30-9 bibliog(p 146) Ja '70
Learning to control the uncontrollable; visceral learning. L. Massett. il por Sci N 97: 274-5 Mr 14 '70
Some new views of learning and instruction. R. M. Gagné. Ed Digest 36:4-7 O '70
Train yourself to stay well; visceral learning. M. Pines. il McCalls 97:48+ Je '70
Value judgments and neo-behaviorism. W. H. Fisher. bibliog f Sch & Soc 98:106-8 F '70
What is learning? address, August 3, 1970. M Bundy. Vital Speeches 36:710-13 S 15 '70
See also
Animal learning
Interference (psychology)
Memory
Problem solving
Transfer of training

LEARNING ability, influence of age on. See Ability, Influence of age on

LEARNING and scholarship
See also
Intellectuals
Knowledge

LEARNING disabilities. See Minimal brain dysfunction

LEARNING materials. See Teaching—Aids and devices

LEARNING theory. See Learning, Psychology of

LEARY, Howard R.
Cop quits. il por Newsweek 76:89-90 S 21 '70 *

LEARY, John P.
Ten year term for the bishop. il Cath World 212:194-6 Ja '71

LEARY, Mary Ellen
Children who are tested in an alien language: mentally retarded? New Repub 162:17-18 My 30 '70
Remarkable Mr Riles. New Repub 163:12 D 19 '70
Reports: California. Atlan 226:20+ Ag; 40 N '70
Reports: San Francisco's Chinatown. Atlan 225:32+ Mr '70

LEARY, Timothy
Fleeing leftists: why they pick Algeria. il por U S News 69:36 N 9 '70 *
Home away from home. il por Newsweek 76: 38+ N 9 '70 *
Leary's latest trip. por Newsweek 76:33 S 28 '70 *

LEASCO data processing equipment corporation
Can Leasco come back? A. A. Butkus. il por Duns 95:69-70 Mr '70
Double standard? take-over of Reliance insurance. il Forbes 106:30-1 Jl 15 '70

LEASCO data processing equipment corporation
—*Continued*
Leasco will not bid on Pergamon shares.
Pub W 198:35-6 D 28 '70
Missing millions. pors Time 96:85-6 S 14 '70
Pergamon dispute rekindled; Maxwell's count-
er-bid. Pub W 198:28 Ag 17 '70
LEASE and rental services
Renting almost everything, a new way of
life. il U S News 68:47-8 Mr 30 '70
See also
Airplanes—Leasing and renting
Automobile trailers—Leasing and renting
Automobiles—Leasing and renting
Boats—Leasing and renting
Campers and coaches, Truck—Leasing and
renting
Capital management corporation
CNA nuclear leasing (firm)
Houseboats—Leasing and renting
Snow removal equipment—Leasing and rent-
ing
Yachts—Leasing and renting
LEASES
See also
Houses—Leasing and renting
Oil and gas leases
LEAST squares
Electron population parameters from least-
squares refinement of X-ray diffraction
data. P. Coppens and others. bibliog il
Science 167:1126-8 F 20 '70
LEATHER
See also
Shark leather
LEATHER work
It's a hanging candlestrap, it's cut from
leather. il Sunset 145:102+ D '70
LEATHERBEE, Mary
Through Russian snows with guide, group
and camera. il Life 68:46-9 Mr 20 '70
Timetable tailored to suit myself. il por Life
69:46-46B Ag 14 '70
LEAVENING
What's cooking?
Make your own leavening. B. T. Hunter.
Org Gard & Farm 17:98-101 Jl '70
LEAVENWORTH, Kan.
Past springs out of a picture; with stereop-
ticon photographs by E. E. Henry and H.
Putney, details enlarged by D. R. Phillips.
pors Am Heritage 21:2, 16-27+ Je '70
LEAVES
Ozone uptake by bean leaves. S. Rich and
others. bibliog il Science 169:79-80 Jl 3 '70
Scanning electron microscopy of fresh leaves
of pinguicula. Y. Heslop-Harrison. bibliog
il Science 167:172-4 Ja 9 '70
See also
Color of leaves
Defoliation
Petioles
LEAVING home; story. See Cavanaugh, A.
LEAVING time; story. See Beasley, R. M.
LEAVITT, Peter R. See Wyckoff, C. W. jt.
auth.
LEAVITT, Sophie
Mrs Leavitt lends a hand. J. E. Roper. por
Read Digest 96:132-4 F '70 *
LEBANESE cookery. See Cookery, Lebanese
LEBANON
Arab vs. Arab vs. Israel, new 100-year war?
il Sr Schol 95:21 N 17 '69
Reports: Beirut. G. G. Stevens. Atlan 225:27-
8+ F '70
See also
Forests and forestry—Lebanon
Guerrillas—Lebanon
Israel—Foreign relations—Lebanon
Public opinion—Lebanon

Description and travel

Lebanon, little Bible land in the crossfire
of history. W. S. Ellis. il Nat Geog 137:
240-75 F '70

Foreign relations

U.S. abstains on U.N. resolution on Lebanese
complaint against Israel; statement, September 5, 1970. W. B. Buffum. Dept State
Bul 63:402-3 O 5 '70

Politics and government

President by a squeak. il Newsweek 76:37
Ag 31 '70
LEBANON-United States air agreement. See
Aviation—International aspects
LEBLEU, R. E. See Gordon, T. J. jt. auth.
LECKEY, Wayne C.
Build this handsome electric serving cart. il
Pop Mech 133:118-21+ My '70
LECTIONARIES
Lectionary: a brand-new thing. P. Digan.
America 123:291-2 O 17 '70; Discussion. 123:
362 N 7 '70

LECTURES and lecturing
King of the talkies; American program bureau.
Newsweek 75:69 Ja 26 '70
Lecture team keeps it fast, informal. P. Gow-
land. il Pop Phot 66:22+ Ja '70
Talk industry. S. Birmingham. il Holiday
47:60-1+ F '70
LED Zeppelin. See Rock 'n' roll groups
LEDBETTER, B. G.
Sea level isn't level, it's hilly. il Sci Digest
68:68-72 Jl '70
LEDDIHN, Erik Maria, ritter von Kuehnelt-.
See Kuehnelt-Leddihn, E. M. von
LEDERBERG, Joshua
Biological weapons race: address, August 5,
1970. Vital Speeches 36:740-3 O 1 '70
What controls for genetic engineering? Cur
121:48-51 S '70
LEDERBERG, Seymour, and Stetten, Gail
Colcemid sensitivity of fission yeast and the
isolation of colcemid-resistant mutants.
bibliog il Science 168:485-7 Ap 24 '70
LEDERER, Esther Pauline (Friedman) See
Landers, A. pseud.
LEDERER, Robert F.
Green survival. il Parks & Rec 5:34-6 O
'70
LEDERMAN, Alfred
Switzerland: a comprehensive youth pro-
gram. il Parks & Rec 5:44+ Ap '70
LEDLIE, Joseph M. A.
Another lost image. America 123:122-4 S 5
'70
LE DRUGSTORE. See New York (city)—Stores
LE Duan
Is Hanoi ready to end the Vietnam war? V.
Zorza. Cur 120:27-30 Ag '70 *
LEDUC, Pierre
Quebec: terrorism & separatism. Nation 211:
422-3 N 2 '70
LEE, Al
Devil in red light; poem. Nation 210:348 Mr
23 '70
LEE, Albert
How to talk to Vietnam, free. il Pop Mech
134:108-10 S '70
LEE, Alwyn
Obituary
Time por 96:9 Jl 20 '70
LEE, Barbara. See Lee, J. jt. auth.
LEE, Dwyane. See Ayala, S. C. jt. auth.
LEE, Elizabeth
Garden spot in the lobby. il Sch Arts 69:35
Ap '70
LEE, Elizabeth (dancer)
Brief biography. S. Goodman. pors Dance
Mag 44:70-1 Ap '70 *
LEE, Gary
We're fishing from outer space. il por Nat
Wildlife 8:36-41 F '70
LEE, Gypsy Rose
Obituary
Newsweek il por 75:44 My 11 '70 *
LEE, Hector H.
American folklore in the secondary schools.
bibliog f Engl J 59:994-1004 O '70
LEE, John, and Lee, Barbara
Customs inspectors miss a lot, but don't
count on it. il Holiday 47:36-7+ Ap '70
LEE, Katharine C. See Berkowitz, R. M. jt.
auth.
LEE, Keith
Keith Lee, evening of firsts; Clark center for
the performing arts. T. Borek. Dance Mag
44:88-9 F '70
LEE, M. Owen
Death and transfiguration. il Opera N 34:24-5
Mr 28 '70
Melody beyond grief. Opera N 35:24-5 Ja 9 '71
LEE, Margery R.
Sugar cane train. il Travel 135:52-4 Ja '71
LEE, Patricia Ann
Prints from plastic throw-aways. il Sch Arts
69:22-3 Mr '70
LEE, Peggy
Peggy Lee; interview, ed. by R. Hemming.
por Sr Schol 97:19 O 5 '70
LEE, Richard F. and others
Wax esters in marine copepods. bibliog il
Science 167:1510-11 Mr 13 '70
LEE, Robert E. See Yunis, E. J. jt. auth.
LEE, Robert Edwin. See Lawrence, J. jt. auth.
LEE, Sang C. and Kaplow, Roy
Hydrogen bonding in hydrochloric acid solu-
tions. bibliog il Science 169:477-8 Jl 31 '70
LEE, Sherman Emery
Financial perspicacity. Art in Am 58:14-15 Jl
'70
LEE, William C.
Modern educational development in free China
since 1898. bibliog Sch & Soc 98:416-21 N
'70
LEE national corporation
Test case; Kansas City southern-Lee na-
tional fight. il Forbes 105:50 F 15 '70

LEECH family
Leech coat-of-arms. H. K. Eilers. il Hobbies 75:148 O '70 *
LEEDOM, Joanne
Citizen power: mobilize for scholarships. il Am Ed 6:21 Jl '70
LEEDS, Mary C.
Blastoff bloodbank. Todays Health 49:21 Ja '71
LEEDS, Morton
People and products; address, October 6, 1969. Vital Speeches 36:303-6 Mr 1 '70
LEEK, Sybil
Horoscopes (cont) Ladies Home J 86:41-2 D '69; 87:42-3 Ja; 30 F; 32+ Mr '70
LEEKS
Oklahoma's okay for leeks. L. Riotte. il Org Gard & Farm 17:52-3 F '70
LEEN, Nina
Echolocation in bats; photographs; excerpts from The world of bats. il Natur Hist 79:32-41 Mr '70
Gallery; photographs. Life 69:8-9 N 20 '70
Trade winds. C. Amory. il Sat R 53:12-13 S 12 '70 *
LEEPER, Faye
What is in the name? Engl J 59:63-4 Ja '70
LEES, Al, and Allphin, Willard
Which phone bench for your home? il Pop Sci 196:86-7 Ap '70
LEES, Benjamin
First recordings: Sessions and Lees. A. Cohn Am Rec G 36:298+ D '69
LEES, Carlton
Trade winds; interview, ed. by C. Amory. Sat R 54:8 Ja 2 '71
LEES, Gene
Lees side. See issues of High fidelity section I
LEES, Robert S.
Immunoassay of plasma low-density lipoproteins. bibliog il Science 169:493-5 Jl 31 '70
LEES, Sidney, and others
Dental enamel: detection of surface changes by ultrasound. bibliog il Science 169:1314-16 S 25 '70
LEEUWEN, Arend Th. van
Christocentric world history. R. Ruether. por Commonweal 93:251-3 D 4 '70 *
LEEWARD ISLANDS
Triangular mini-cruise; St Martin's, St Bart's and Anguilla. C. Mitchell. il Yachting 128: 64-5+ N '70
LEFEVER, Grace
What's cooking? il Org Gard & Farm 17:90-3 Je '70
LEFF, David N.
Familiar story. il Environ 12:11-13 My '70
LEFKOWITZ, Louis J.
Chasing a future. il pors Time 96:20-1 O 19 '70 *
LEFKOWITZ, R. J. and others
Radioreceptor assay of adrenocorticotropic hormones: new approach to assay of polypeptide hormones in plasma. bibliog il Science 170:633-5 N 6 '70
LEFRAK, Samuel J.
Lefrak goes to the ghetto. il por Bsns W p28 Ag 15 '70 *
LEFT and right (political science) See Right and left (political science)
LEFT wing (politics) See Right and left (political science)
LEFTOVERS. See Cookery—Leftovers
LEG
How to step beautifully into summer. P. Van Wagenen. il Parents Mag 45:83-4 My '70
Leg to stand on: feet too. il Mlle 70:254-5 Ap '70
LEG exercises. See Exercise
LEGACIES
See also
Wills
LEGAL aid
Law firms move into the ghetto. il Bsns W p 124-5 F 14 '70
Letter to editor; The art emergency fund. Art in Am 58:33 N '70
Somebody is always offended; legal service program. S. L. Greene. Nation 211:624-7 D 14 '70
See also
National consumer law center
LEGAL aid societies
Store front lawyers in San Francisco; San Francisco neighborhood legal assistance foundation. J. E. Carlin. il Trans-Action 7:64-74 Ap '70
LEGAL aid warranty fund
Jail insurance; California organization created to get people out of jail fast. il Newsweek 77:61 Ja 11 '71
LEGAL assistants
Legal aides for busy lawyers. il Bsns W p62 D 26 '70

LEGAL education. See Law—Study and teaching
LEGAL ethics
See also
Attorney and client
Judicial corruption
LEGAL medicine. See Medical jurisprudence
LEGAL philosophy. See Law—Philosophy
LEGAL procedure. See Procedure (law)
LEGAL reform
American law, by J. P. Frank. Review Sat R 53:34-5 Mr 21 '70. M. Mayer
Honest politician's guide to crime control, by N. Morris and G. Hawkins. Review Sat R 53:36-7 Ap 4 '70. F. J. Cook
Only radical reform can save the courts. J. Main. il Fortune 82:110-14+ Ag '70; Same abr. Read Digest 97:106-10 N '70
(Over) due process of law. Sr Schol 97:11-14 D 14 '70
LEGAL research
See also
Computers—Legal use
LEGAL services program. See United States—Economic opportunity, Office of
LE GASTELOIS, Alphonse
King of the Ecrehous. por Newsweek 75:38 F 2 '70
LEGENDRE, Bokara
Food in Vogue. il por Vogue 155:79 Je '70 *
LEGENDS
See also
Folklore
LÉGER, Fernand
Léger, purism and the Paris machines. C. Green. il Art N 69:54-6+ D '70 *
LEGG, Jean
Coordinating library services within the community. Am Lib 1:457-63 My '70
LEGGE, Roger
English language news broadcasts; tables (cont of) English language broadcasts to North America. See issues of Popular electronics to August 1970
LEGGETT, Robert Louis
Representative Leggett intervenes. Nation 211:676 D 28 '70 *
LEGGETT, Stanton, and others
Case for a small high school. Ed Digest 36: 15-18 N '70
LEGGETT, William
Baseball (cont) Sports Illus 32:64+ My 11; 40-1 Je 1; 33:38-9 Ag 10; 75-6 S 21 '70; 34: 50-1 Ja 4 '71
Bird in hand and a burning Busch. il por Sports Illus 32:18-23 Mr 23 '70
Boo-boo or baby for Bowie. il por Sports Illus 32:22-4+ Je 15 '70
Cincy cannonball. il Sports Illus 33:12-17 Jl 13 '70
Denny McLain: ready for his comeback try. il por Sports Illus 32:20-1 Je 29 '70
Flying start for the big bad Birds. il Sports Illus 33:14-17 O 19 '70
Full series for a fleet pair. il pors Sports Illus 33:18-21 Ag 24 '70
Henry raps one for history. pors Sports Illus 32:30-2+ My 25 '70
Red menace from staid Cincy. pors Sports Illus 32:24-7 Ap 20 '70
That big Red machine has developed a few sputters. il Sports Illus 33:18-19 O 5 '70
That black and orange magic. il Sports Illus 33:22-4+ O 26 '70
They're playing those grinders again. il Sports Illus 33:16-21 S 28 '70
Tumultuous spring but a fine season ahead. il Sports Illus 32:48-60+ Ap 13 '70
LEGION, American. See American legion
LEGISLATION
See also
Lobbying

California
Wink at the environment. R. A. Jones. il Nation 210:493-5 Ap 27 '70

Great Britain
See also
Labor laws and legislation—Great Britain

Massachusetts
Massachusetts asks: is the war legal? Sr Schol 96:16 Ap 27 '70
Massachusetts protest; anti-Vietnam. New Repub 162:11 Ap 18 '70
Massachusetts v. Viet Nam. Time 96:77 N 23 '70
Outlawing the war. il Newsweek 75:22 Ap 13 '70
Test on Vietnam war heads for High court. U S News 68:99 Ap 13 '70
Wrath of the doves; law to outlaw war. R. Donway. Nat R 22:568-70 Je 2 '70

LEGISLATION—*Continued*
United States
Belling the cat; proposed measures to oversee the military. Nation 210:37 Ja 19 '70
Carry-over for 92nd Congress. B. L. Masse. America 124:5-6 Ja 9 '71
Congress fights, but it works. Bsns W p27-8 Je 20 '70
Down to business. il Newsweek 76:17-18 N 30 '70
Getting the lame ducks in a row. il Newsweek 76:29-31 N 23 '70
My God, we're back to square one. Newsweek 77:14-15 Ja 4 '71
Nixon's program, its chances in Congress. il U S News 68:17-18 Ap 27 '70
Rating Congress: twenty-four test votes. il New Repub 163:17-23 O 24 '70
Reelection fever hurts major bills. Bsns W p28-9 S 26 '70
Reforming itself; the issue Congress won't face. E. D. Eshleman and R. S. Walker. America 122:124-5 F 7 '70
Report card; 91st Congress, 2d. session. Newsweek 76:29-30 O 26 '70
Saga of a law; how the Multiple use-sustained yield act was enacted by Congress. E. C. Crafts. il Am For 76:12-19+ Je: 28-35 Jl '70
Senate: chaos at the deadline. il Time 96: 6-7 D 28 '70
Which way to the egress? il Newsweek 76: 15-16 D 28 '70
See also
Consumer protection—Laws and legislation
Library laws and legislation
School laws and legislation—United States
United States—Congress
United States—Supreme court
LEGISLATIVE bodies
See also
Caucus
United States
See also
United States—Congress

History
Political mimesis: a consideration of the historical and cultural roots of legislative behavior in the British colonies in the eighteenth century; with a comment by B. Bailyn and reply by Greene. J. P. Greene. bibliog f Am Hist R 75:337-67 D '69
LEGISLATIVE organization act of 1970. See United States—Congress—Reorganization
LEGISLATIVE reference service, Library of Congress. See United States—Library of Congress—Legislative reference service
LEGISLATURES. See Legislative bodies
LEGITIMACY (law) See Illegitimacy
LEGLER, Philip
Roses for you; poem. Commonweal 93:374 Ja 15 '71
LEGS. See Leg
LEGS, Artificial. See Artificial limbs
LEGUM, Colin
Problems of reconstruction. Cur 116:47-51 Mr '70
LEGUMES
See also
Peas
LEHIGH university, Bethlehem, Pa.
Joint student-faculty-administration assembly at Lehigh. Sch & Soc 98:331-2 O '70
LEHMAN, David
Two sonnets: It's hardly there, and then it vanishes; Listen! The garbage pouring down the chutes. Poetry 117:26-7 O '70
LEHMAN, James O.
Professional developments reviewed: choice as a selection tool. bibliog Wilson Lib Bul 44:957-61 My '70
LEHMAN, Richard L.
X-ray measurements near high-power klystrons. bibliog il Science 169:52-4 Jl 3 '70
LEHMAN art collection. See Metropolitan musum of art, New York
LEHMANN, Robert E.
Mike and this horse needed each other. W. Tower. il pors Sports Illus 32:22-7 My 11 '70 *
LEHMANN-HAUPT, Christopher
Out of my mind on bluegrass. il por N Y Times Mag p36-7+ S 13 '70
LEHNER, Andreas P.
Laissez-faire curriculum in the democratic school; address, November, 1969. Engl J 59:803-10 S '70
LEHR, Stan, and Rossetto, Louis, Jr
New right credo: libertarianism. il N Y Times Mag p24-5+ Ja 10 '71
LEHRBAUMMER, Andrew L.
Preference in public bidding. Am City 85:124+ S '70

LEIBOWITZ, H. and others
Ponzo perspective illusion as a manifestation of space perception. Science 166:1174-6; 168:395 N 28 '69, Ap 17 '70
LEIFER, Neil
Man in the middle; photographs. Sports Illus 33:56-63 S 21 '70
LEIGA, Algird G. and others
Polywater: an attempt at synthesis in a gas discharge. bibliog il Science 168:114-16 Ap 3 '70
LEIGH, Joe Michael
Mt Katahdin, Maine. il Holiday 47:68-9 My '70
LEIGHTON, Lauren G.
(tr) See Chukovskii, K. I. Confessions of an old story-teller
LEIGHTON, Robert B.
Surface of Mars; with biographical sketch. il Sci Am 222:10, 26-41 My '70
LEIMBACH, Patricia P.
To a son on Mother's day. Farm J 94:59 My '70
LEIMBACHER, Ed
Crash of the Jefferson Airplane. il Ramp Mag 8:14-16 Ja '70
LEINER, Marvin
Cuba's schools, ten years later. il Sat R 53:59-61+ O 17 '70
LEINSTER, Colin
Nixon's friend Bebe. il pors Life 69:18B-27 Jl 31 '70
LEISURE
Harried leisure class, by S. B. Linder. Review
New Repub 162:27-8 F 21 '70. K. Boulding
How to get more out of your vacation; leisure planning. W. Cross. Read Digest 96: 113-16 Mr '70
Leisure & education; with yardsticks of management performance. il Forbes 105:201 Ja 1 '70; 107:176-8 Ja 1 '71
There'll be less leisure than you think. G. Burck. il Fortune 81:86-9+ Mr '70
What we want from the time we spend. P. A. Dickinson. il Har Yrs 10:19-23 O '70
Why we spend time (the way we do) P. A. Dickinson. il Har Yrs 10:20-4 S '70
See also
Recreation
Retirement
LEISURE class
Harried leisure class, by S. B. Linder. Review
New Repub 162:27-8 F 21 '70. K. Boulding
LEITENBERG, Harold, and others
Reinforcement of competing behavior during extinction. bibliog il Science 169:301-3 Jl 17 '70
LEITENBERG, Milton
So far, so good. bibliog il Environ 12:26-35 Jl '70
LEITER, Kelly
Tennessee: Gore vs. the White House. Nation 211:396-9 O 26 '70
LEITER, Naomi
How easy are you to live with? Ladies Home J 87:102+ Je '70
LEITERMAN, Richard
Fiction documentary; interview, ed. by A. Rosenthal. il Film Q 23:19-28 Sum '70
LEITHEAD, William Ballantyne
Taking drugs through Russia meant two years at hard labor; interview, ed. by J. Fincher. por Life 68:34 Je 26 '70
LEJEUNE, Anthony
Letter from London (cont) Nat R 22:730, 885, 1393-4 Jl 14, Ag 25, D 29 '70
LEJEUNE, Camp. See Military training camps
LEKACHMAN, Robert
Economy. See issues of Dun's
Money in America. Harper 241:29-34 Ag: 16 O '70
Poverty of affluence. Commentary 49:39-44 Mr; 50:10+ Jl '70
LEKYTHOS; drama. See Holland, A.
LELES, Sam
Educational structure, is it capable of innovation? bibliog Clear House 44:368-72 F '70
LELOIR, Luis F.
Divide and honor. pors Newsweek 76:100 N 9 '70 *
Magnetism to metabolism. Sci N 98:348 O 31 '70 *
Nobel prize. E. Cabib. por Science 170:608-9 N 6 '70 *
Plasmas, magnets and sugars. il por Time 96: 39 N 9 '70 *
LELYVELD, Joseph
Will we say "it just happened," when the world overpopulates itself to extinction? il por N Y Times Mag p24-5+ Jl 19 '70
LE MANS Grand prix. See Automobile racing —France

LEMBERGER, Louis, and others
Marihuana: studies on the disposition and
metabolism of delta-9-tetrahydrocannabinol
in man. bibliog il Science 170:1320-2 D 18
'70

LEMBO, Diana
Notes from a semi-darkened room; address,
1969. il por Library J 95:735-7 F 15 '70
Screenings: filmstrips. See occasional issues
of Library journal

LEMKE, Eugene
New modular color-TV receiver. il Electr
World 85:32-3+ Ja '71

LEMMINGS
Lesson of the lemmings. O. D'Aulaire and
E. D'Aulaire. il Read Digest 97:167-9+ Ag
'70

LEMNITZER, Lyman L.
Collective security; address, June 15, 1970.
Vital Speeches 36:669-71 Ag 15 '70

LEMON sky; drama. See Wilson, L.

LEMONE, Evelyn
Records for teachers. See issues of Dance
magazine

LEMONS, Wayne
How color TV works. il Radio-Electr 42:32-5
Ja '71

LENCI, Margaret Zellers
Caribbean island-hopping. Travel & Camera
33:72-5 Ja '70

LENCZOWSKI, George
Arab radicalism: problems and prospects.
Cur Hist 60:32-7+ Ja '71

LENDLE, H. G.
Start shrubs from your own cuttings. il Org
Gard & Farm 17:82-3 N '70
Why we chose black walnuts. il Org Gard &
Farm 17:44-5 Je '70

LENDLE, Mabel I.
Lazy way to better houseplants. il pors Org
Gard & Farm 17:103-6 O '70

LENGTH of life. See Longevity

LENGTH of skirts. See Clothing and dress

LENHER, Samuel
Encourage the seeker, and find nylon. il pors
Nations Bsns 58:68+ Ja '70

LENIN, Vladimir Il'ich
Birthday for Lenin and a boost for Brezh-
nev. il por Time 95:30+ Ap 27 '70 *
Can Lenin's communism survive? Russia at
crossroads. il pors U S News 68:66-70 Ap
20 '70 *
Drive to make Lenin a secular saint. por
Time 95:27 Ap 13 '70 *
History lesson; letter. M. Salvadori. Nat R
22:721 Jl 14 '70 *
Lenin. P. A. Samuelson. Newsweek 76:86 D
7 '70 *
Lenin: a contemporary portrait; reprint from
March 15, 1924 issue. V. Chernov. For Af-
fairs 48:471-7 Ap '70 *
Lenin; address, April 21, 1970. L. I. Brezhnev.
Vital Speeches 36:482-98 Je 1 '70 *
Lenin and education, science, culture; sym-
posium. il pors UNESCO Courier 23:4-21
Jl '70 *
Lenin: communism's charter myth; Time
essay. por Time 95:34-5 Ap 27 '70 *
Lenin (1870-1970) N. D. Roodkowsky. por
Cath World 211:107-11 Je '70 *
Lenin: his legacy. A. B. Ulam. For Affairs
48:460-70 Ap '70 *
Lenin: the making of a revolutionary; ex-
cerpts. I. Deutscher. il pors Ramp Mag
9:40-7 Ag '70 *
Leninism: any number can play. por News-
week 75:39 Ap 27 '70 *
Lenin's secret. J. Burnham. Nat R 22:21 Ja
13 '70
Saint Lenin; honored by United Nations. Chr
Today 14:26 My 8 '70 *
Soviet Union: leadership at the crossroads.
il pors Time 95:33-6 My 4 '70 *
United Nations observes Lenin centenary.
UN Mo Chron 7:62-4 My '70 *

LENINGRAD
Description
Heart of Leningrad is still the Palace square.
il Sunset 144:74+ Ap '70

LENNARD, Henry L. and others
Hazards implicit in prescribing psychoactive
drugs. bibliog Science 169:438-41; 170:929-
30 Jl 31, N 27 '70
—See Brissenden, R. W. jt. auth.

LENNON, Alton Asa
Nerve gas disposal: how the AEC refused to
take army off the hook. L. J. Carter. Science 169:1296-8 S 25 '70 *

LENNON, John
Bag one: opening of the show of erotic
lithographs at the Nordness galleries. New
Yorker 46:29-30 F 21 '70 *
John Rennon's excrusive gloupie. C. McCarry.
il Esquire 74:204-5+ D '70 *

LENNON sisters
Singing Lennon sisters. M. Abramson. il pors
Good H 170:42+ Je '70 *

LENS adapters. See Photography—Apparatus
and supplies

LENSES
Making a 6-inch air-spaced visual objective
O. R. Knab. il por Sky & Tel 40:46-53 Jl
'70
New law for lenses. Newsweek 76:83 O 12 '70

LENSES, Photographic
And some mirror teles are better. B. Sher-
man. il Mod Phot 34:72-5+ Mr '70
Are SLR lenses getting better? B. Sherman.
il Mod Phot 34:90-3+ O '70
Close-up exposure is simple? L. A. Mannheim.
il Mod Phot 34:78-9+ Mr '70
Combining camera lenses for solar photog-
raphy. A. Boyko. il Sky & Tel 39:134-5 F
'70
Crystal lens: yes, but. . ; fluorite makes lenses
smaller, lighter, slower, and costlier. N.
Goldberg. il Pop Phot 66:80-1+ Ja '70
Feininger; human vision vs. camera vision.
A. Feininger. Mod Phot 34:51+ Mr '70
How good are macro lenses? H. Keppler and
B. Sherman. il Mod Phot 34:90-3+ My '70
How to avoid second guessing about second
bodies. N. Rothschild. il Pop Phot 67:78-81
S '70
Is it safe to attach independent brand lenses
to various camera bodies? H. Keppler. Mod
Phot 34:36+ Ag '70
Keppler on the SLR. H. Keppler. il Mod
Phot 33:32+ D '69; 34:12+ Ja; 14+ F '70
Latest close-up lenses are sharper. C. W.
Kennedy. il Pop Phot 66:44+ Ja '70
Lens: a most imperfect eye. N. Goldberg.
il Pop Phot 66:66-7+ Mr '70
Lenses don't take pictures; you do. E. Meyers.
il Pop Phot 66:48+ Ap '70
Little lenses that make space clearer. N.
Goldberg. il Pop Phot 66:114-15+ Je '70
More about those two-zone lenses. C. W.
Kennedy. il Pop Phot 67:36+ O '70
New mirror lenses: short in size but long on
reach. B. Berger. il Pop Mech 134:136-7
Ag '70
Say it with lenses. E. Wildi. il Pop Phot 67:
84-6+ S '70
Shifty fifty. B. Schwalberg. il Pop Phot 67:
72-5+ S '70
Techniques tomorrow. B. Sherman. Mod Phot
34:74+ Ja; 56+ F '70
Telephoto hunting simplified. J. H. Robin-
son. il Field & S 75:154 Je '70
Two lenses are closer than one. C. Lecakes.
il Mod Phot 33:54 D '69
View camera control with 35-mm. E. Meyers.
il Pop Phot 67:32+ S '70
Why 90s are normal. C. W. Kennedy. il Pop
Phot 67:32+ N '70
Wider than wide and super-sharp: the
Hologon with its 15-mm lens. L. Drukker.
il Pop Phot 66:74-6+ Ap '70
You can have it both ways; split-field attach-
ments. C. W. Kennedy. il Pop Phot 67:76-7+
S '70
See also
Zoom lenses

History
How it all began, a brief look at the con-
tributions of lens designers Petzval and
Seidel. B. Sherman. Mod Phot 34:26+ Mr '70

Testing
Lenses are for testing. N. Goldberg. il Pop
Phot 66:62-3+ F '70
Test your lenses the modern way. D. L.
Miller. il Mod Phot 33:40-5 D '69
View from Kramer; reticles. A. Kramer. il
Mod Phot 34:34+ Ap '70

LENT, Arnold L.
New buddy plan aids waterfront safety. il
Camp Mag 42:14+ My '70

LENT
Lent: what else is new? V. P. McCorry.
America 122:142-Inside back cover F 7 '70
Lenten reading suggestions. America 122:
163-6 F 14 '70
Lenten season. Chr Today 14:26 F 13 '70

LENTZ, John J.
Age of the enzyme. il Todays Health 48:
32-3+ Ap '70

LEO X, pope
Great confrontations: Leo X and Luther. L.
B. Smith. il pors Horizon 12:90-5 Spr '70 *

LEO, Richard F. and Barghoorn, E. S.
Phenolic aldehydes: generation from fossil
woods and carbonaceous sediments by oxidative degradation. bibliog il Science 168:
582-4 My 1 '70

LEON, Abelardo Sanchez. See Sanchez Leon,
A.

LEONARD, George B.
  Future of power. Look 34:36+ Ja 13 '70
  Pilgrims' odyssey: a new view. il Look 34:
    22-9 D 1 '70
  Place for snakes as well as naked lovers. il
    Look 34:80-5 Ja 13 '70
  Why we need a new sexuality. Look 34:54 Ja
    13 '70
LEONARD, James F.
  Chemical and biological methods of warfare;
    statement, December 10, 1969. Dept State
    Bul 62:95-7 Ja 26 '70
  Control of chemical and biological weapons;
    statement, August 27, 1970. Dept State
    Bul 63:330-6 S 21 '70
  Geneva disarmament conference agrees on
    text of treaty banning emplacement of
    nuclear weapons on the seabed; statement,
    September 1, 1970. Dept State Bul 63:362-
    4 S 28 '70
  U.S. discusses problem of control of con-
    ventional arms; statement, August 13,
    1970. Dept State Bul 63:310-15 S 14 '70
  U.S. reviews position on general and com-
    plete disarmament; statement, June 23,
    1970. Dept State Bul 63:198-203 Ag 17 '70
  U.S. supports inclusion of toxins in biological
    warfare convention; statement, April 20,
    1970. Dept State Bul 62:731 Je 8 '70
  United States and U.S.S.R. table revised draft
    treaty banning emplacement of nuclear
    weapons on the seabed; statement, April
    23, 1970. Dept State Bul 62:663-5 My 25 '70
  United States explains position on chemical
    and biological weapons; statement, March
    17, 1970. Dept State Bul 62:552-6 Ap 27 '70
LEONARD, John
  Eye of the storm. il Life 68:16 My 8 '70
  Late-night talker who knows how to listen.
    por Life 68:10 F 13 '70
  Life TV review. il Life 69:10 S 4; 24 N 13;
    13 D 4; 8 D 18 '70

                    about
  Book power. R. A. Sokolov. il pors Newsweek
    76:114-114A N 2 '70 *
  Buckley, Berkeley and back. il por Time 96:
    62 N 2 '70 *
  John Leonard named editor of N.Y. times
    book review. il por Pub W 198:31-2 O 19
    '70 *
LEONARD, R. E. See Ketchledge, E. H. jt.
  auth.
LEONARDSON, Evelyn K.
  America's moonscape. il Travel 133:56-9 Je
    '70
LEONCAVALLO, Ruggiero
  Pagliacci. Criticism
    New Yorker 45:54+ Ja 17 '70
    Opera N 34:17-20 F 7 '70
    Sat R 53:21 Ja 24 '70
  Then the music. J. C. Adams. il Opera N
    34:25+ F 7 '70
LEONDES, Cornelius T.
  Inertial navigation for aircraft; with
    biographical sketch. il Sci Am 222:25: 80-
    4+ Mr '70
LEONT'EV, Konstantin Nikolaevich
  Russian aesthete. W. H. Auden. New Yorker
    46:133-8 Ap 4 '70 *
LEOPARD tanks. See Tanks, Military
LEOPARDS
  Killer leopard of Danpur. J. Shepherd. il
    Sports Illus 32:18-19 Mr 2 '70
    See also
  Cheetahs
LEOPOLD, A. Starker
  Weaning grizzly bears; with biographical
    sketch. il por Natur Hist 79:4, 94-101 Ja '70
LEOPOLD, Luna B.
  Let's sing Auld lang syne for the upper Bran-
    dywine; with biographical sketch. il Natur
    Hist 79:3, 4-6+ Je '70
LEPENSKI vir excavations. See Yugoslavia—
    Antiquities
LEPERCQ, Paul Adolphe
  Bedroom theory; interview. pors Forbes 105:
    62-3 Mr 15 '70
LEPIDOPTERA
    See also
  Moths
LEPIS, Cabrini B.
  Another day, another war; story. Cath World
    210:220-3 F '70
LEPOSKY, George
  Preserving the prairie. Travel & Camera 33:
    12+ O '70
LEPROSY research
  Of mice and leprosy. il por Time 95:47-8 Mr
    2 '70
LEPTIS MAGNA
  Leptis Magna. A. Menen. il Holiday 47:66-8
    F '70

LERIDON, Henri
  Fertility in Martinique. il Natur Hist 79:57-9
    Ja '70
LERMAN, Leo
  Catch up with. See issues of Mademoiselle
  Changers. il Mlle 71:146-9 Je '70
  Moviemakers. il Mlle 70:69-73+ Ja '70
  Scene/seen. il Mlle 71:165-9 S; 186-8 O; 72;
    106-11 D '70
  (ed) See Fonda, J. Jane Fonda talks
    about . . .
LERNER, Alan Jay
  Lerner and Duke revisited. I. Kolodin. Sat R
    53:101 Mr 14 '70 *
LERNER, Daniel, and Teich, A. H.
  Internationalism and world politics among
    CERN scientists. il Bul Atom Sci 26:4-10
    F '70
LERNER, Fred
  Ups and downs of a TV stuntman; inter-
    view, ed. by P. Hudson. il Sr Schol 97:42-
    3 S 28 '70
LERNER, Max
  Need for a two-way dialogue. Cur 115:46-7 Ja
    '70
  Nuclear weapons over the Middle East? Cur
    121:57-9 S '70
  Toward an urban guerrilla movement? Cur
    118:14-16 My '70
LERNER, Michael. See Keniston, K. jt. auth.
LEROI-GOURHAN, André
  Adornment: for gods, for love, for war; ex-
    cerpt from Le geste et la parole. Vogue
    156:151+ D '70
LEROY, Mervyn
  Look and listen. P. Hudson. por Sr Schol 96:
    Schol Teach 8 Mr 16 '70 *
LES BAUX. See Baux, Les
LESCAULT, E. G.
  Easy way to determine reflex enclosure dimen-
    sions. il Pop Electr 33:64 D '70
LESCH-Nyhan syndrome
  Biochemically marked lymphocytoid lines:
    establishment of Lesch-Nyhan cells. K. W.
    Choi and A. D. Bloom. bibliog il Science
    170:89-90 O 2 '70
  Lesch-Nyhan syndrome: preventive control
    by prenatal diagnosis. J. A. Boyle and oth-
    ers. bibliog il Science 169:688-9 Ag 14 '70;
    Correction. 170:1333 D 18 '70
LESHER, Stephan
  Guitars for everyone. il Parks & Rec 5:22-
    4+ Jl '70
  Leroy Johnson outslicks Mister Charlie. il
    pors N Y Times Mag p34-6+ N 8 '70
LESHNIOWSKY, Walter O. and others
  Aldrin: removal from lake water by flocculent
    bacteria. bibliog il Science 169:993-5 S 4 '70
LESIONS, Brain. See Brain damage
LESLEY, Jayne, and Dutton, R. W.
  Antigen receptor molecules: inhibition by
    antiserum against kappa light chains. bib-
    liog il Science 169:487-8 Jl 31 '70
LESLIE, Alfred
  Return of the real. D. Davis. il Newsweek
    75:105 F 23 '70 *
LESLIE, John E.
  Bache's ledgerman. A. Hershman. por Duns
    96:68 N '70 *
LESLIE, Larry L. and Bigelow, R. C.
  Black studies: a practical alternative. bibliog
    f Clear House 44:479-82 Ap '70
LESLIE, Peter
  Bahamian cruise-regatta. il Yachting 128:59+
    N '70
LESOTHO
  Coup for the chief. P. Webb. por Newsweek
    75:47 F 16 '70
  Crisis in Lesotho. P. A. Crane. America 122:
    212-13 F 28 '70; Reply with rejoinder. B.
    Reed. il 122:559-62 My 23 '70
  Death in the hills. por Time 95:35 Ap 20
    '70

           Religious institutions and affairs
    See also
  Church and state in Lesotho
LESSA, Tony
  Dinosaurs finally win one. il pors Life 69:73-4
    D 11 '70 *
LESSER, R. H.
  Evangelization crisis in India: a missionary's
    view. il Cath World 211:166-71 Jl '70
LESSING, Doris May
  Back-of-the-book. S. Lydon. Ramp Mag 8:48+
    Ja '70
LESSING, Lawrence
  Great hopes from Ovshinsky's little switches
    grow. il por Fortune 81:110-14+ Ap '70

LESSING, Lawrence—*Continued*
New ways to more power with less pollution. il Fortune 82:78-81+ N '70
Satellites to steer by. il Fortune 82:115-17+ Ag '70

LESSINGER, Leon M.
Accountability in public education. Todays Ed 59:52-3 My '70

LESTER, David, and Benson, G. D.
Alcohol oxidation in rats inhibited by pyrabole, oximes, and amides. bibliog il Science 169:282-4 Jl 17 '70

LESTER, Elenore
La MaMa is a lady. il por Holiday 47:22+ My '70

LESTER, Julius
Interview with Julius Lester; ed. by P. Meras. Nation 210:762-3 Je 22 '70
Kinds of books we give children: whose nonsense? il por Pub W 97:86-8 F 23 '70
Necessity for separation. por Ebony 25:166-9 Ag '70

LESTREL, Pete E. See Read, D. W. jt. auth.

LESURE, Thomas B.
Hawaii's Molokai. il Travel 134:62-7 O '70

LETTER boxes. See Mailboxes

LETTER carriers. See Postal service—Letter carriers

LETTER carriers of the United States of America, National association of. See National association of letter carriers

LETTER stocks. See Securities—Registration

LETTERING
Ben Shahn's lettering; excerpts from address. B. Shahn. il Pub W 198:38+ D 7 '70
Gallery: Simon Nathan's alphabet photographs. Life 69:8-9 Jl 10 '70
Letters and imagination. M. Glaser and J. Snyder. il Am Artist 34:14 N '70
See also
Calligraphy

LETTERS
See also
Chain letters

LETTERS from servicemen
See also
Vietnamese war, 1957- —Personal narratives

LETTERS to children
Your letters can help a child. A. L. Von Tungeln. Har Yrs 10:16+ S '70

LETTERS to congressman. See Lobbying

LETTERS to mayors. See Lobbying

LETTERS to the editor. See Newspapers—Letters to the editor; Periodicals—Letters to the editor

LETTERS to the president. See Presidents—United States—Correspondence

LETTUCE
Cold frame salads; buttercrunch. K. McReynolds. il Org Gard & Farm 17:86 F '70
Keep lettuce fresh; lettuce crispers. il Consumer Bul 53:22 S '70

Storage
See Vegetables—Storage

LETTUCE boycott. See Boycott

LEUCINE
Marine sediments: dating by the racemization of amino acids. J. L. Bada and others. bibliog il Science 170:730-2 N 13 '70

LEUKEMIA
Finding a cancer clue; RNA-dependent DNA polymerase. Time 96:41 D 21 '70
Formation of virus-like particles by bone cells in mice with a high incidence of spontaneous leukemia. B. H. Schofield and others. bibliog il Science 168:588-9 My 1 '70
Hopeful signs in the battle against cancer. il U S News 69:67 D 7 '70
Teminism marches on; RNA-dependent DNA polymerase. Sci N 98:432 D 5 '70

Therapy
Leukemia: we're starting to use the word cure. W. S. Ross. il Todays Health 48:49-51+ O '70; Same abr. with title They're gaining on leukemia. Read Digest 97:148-52 D '70
New gains in the battle against leukemia in children. Good H 170:177-9 Ap '70
Small victory against leukemia. A. J. Snider. Sci Digest 68:66 D '70
Very special problem. J. Frook. il pors Life 69:54-8+ N 13 '70
We have a chance to beat leukemia now. R. H. Berg. il Look 34:26-8+ My 5 '70

Vaccines
Double duty; Canadian research findings on BCG. Newsweek 76:83-4 O 26 '70

LEUKEMIA cells. See Cancer cells

LEUKEMIA viruses
Demonstration of biological activity of a murine leukemia virus of New Zealand black mice. J. A. Levy and T. Pincus. bibliog il Science 170:326-7 O 16 '70
Feline leukemia and sarcoma viruses; susceptibility of human cells to infection. P. S. Sarma and others. bibliog il Science 168:1098-100 My 29 '70

LEUKOCYTES
Mixed leukocyte stimulation of normal peripheral leukocytes by autologous lymphoblastoid cells. S. S. Green and K. W. Sell. bibliog il Science 170:989-90 N 27 '70
Myeloperoxidase: contribution to the microbicidal activity of intact leukocytes. S. J. Klebanoff. bibliog il Science 169:1095-7 S 11 '70
Neutrophils: their role in the formation of a tick feeding lesion. R. J. Tatchell and D. E. Moorhouse. bibliog il Science 167:1002-3 F 13 '70
See also
Phagocytes and phagocytosis

LEUKODYSTROPHY
Tubules of globoid leukodystrophy: a right-handed helix. E. J. Yunis and R. E. Lee. bibliog il Science 169:64-6 Jl 3 '70

LEUTZE, Emanuel Gottlieb
That bitter night in '76; famous painting Washington crossing the Delaware. B. Hibbs. il Read Digest 96:174-8 Mr '70

LE VAILLANT, Yvon
Opus Dei: Spain on the cross; tr. by L. Bensky. il Ramp Mag 8:14+ F '70

LEVARIE, Siegmund
Epochs of opera (cont) il Opera N 34:24-9 Ja 24; 26-31 Ja 31 '70

LEVATIN, Isobella
(tr) See Lysohorsky, O. pseud. Poet; Room for all; At the circus; Trees in courtyards

LEVEL of aspiration. See Aspiration level

LEVENSON, Sam
Men in mama's life. il Ladies Home J 87:24+ My '70; Same abr. Read Digest 97:41-4 S '70
Oh, doctor! il Ladies Home J 87:64+ O '70
Sense about sex; excerpts from address. 1970. PTA Mag 65:5 O '70

LEVENSON, William B.
School principal: on the cross-fire line? bibliog Clear House 45:216-18 D '70

LEVERS
New theory of pyramid building; use of weight arm. O. Tellefsen. il Natur Hist 79:10-12+ N '70; Discussion. 79:8-10+ D '70

LÉVESQUE, René
Temporary reprieve. il por Newsweek 75:60-1 My 11 '70 *

LEVI, Arrigo
Italy: the crisis of governing. For Affairs 49:147-60 O '70

LEVI, Barbara G.
Novel applications of computers. bibliog il Phys Today 23:49-52 Jl '70
Physicists teach minority students. il Phys Today 23:53-6 Mr '70

LEVI, Edward H.
University and the modern condition; excerpt from Point of view: talks on education. Science 170:1263 D 18 '70

LEVI, Josef
In the eye of the beholder. W. S. Wilson. il por Art N 68:52-3+ F '70 *

LEVI, Peter
Comment. R. Magowan. Poetry 116:201-2 Je '70 *

LÉVI-STRAUSS, Claude
We no longer know how to bring our children into the world we have built; interview, ed. by C. Dreyfus. por Mlle 71:236-7+ Ag '70
about
Claude Levi-Strauss, by E. Leach. Review Nation 211:692-4 D 28 '70. B. Bendow *

LEVI Strauss and company. See Strauss, Levi, and company

LEVIAS, Jerry
Too small to be overlooked. M. Sharnik. il pors Sports Illus 33:24-6+ N 30 '70 *

LEVIN, Dan
Fishing. il por Sports Illus 31:66+ D 15 '69; 32:48-9 Mr 16; 82-3+ S 21 '70
Great gabble over Iowa lakes. il Sports Illus 32:40-3 My 18 '70
Rugby. il Sports Illus 33:76+ D 7 '70
Runningest bloke alive. il Read Digest 96:196-200 Ja '70
Sailing. il Sports Illus 32:50+ F 9 '70
Sun didn't rise overnight. por Sports Illus 32:28-9 Ap 13 '70
Swimming. il Sports Illus 33:56+ S 7 '70
Upon a peak in Delaware. il pors Sports Illus 33:34-6+ D 14 '70

LEVIN, Harry
  Charles Dickens (1812-1870) Am Scholar 39:
  670-6 Aut '70
  William Carlos Williams and the old world.
  Yale R 59:520-31 Je '70
LEVIN, Henry M.
  Why ghetto schools fail. il Sat R 53:68-9+
  Mr 21 '70
LEVIN, Howard S.
  Stunning coup. por Time 95:68 F 2 '70
LEVIN, Irving
  Nursing homes: the real problems; interview,
  by H. Alpert. por Har Yrs 10:6-12 N '70
LEVIN, Martin
  (ed) Phoenix nest. See issues of Saturday
  review
LEVIN, N. Gordon, jr
  Nixon, the Senate & the war. Commentary
  50:69-84 N '70
LEVIN, Nora
  Arab refugees. il Cath World 211:256+ S '70
  Letter from Israel. il Bul Atom Sci 26:46-52
  Ap '70
LEVIN Townsend computer corporation
  Stunning coup. por Time 95:68 F 2 '70
LEVINE, Bernard B. See Vaz, N. M. jt. auth.
LEVINE, Carol
  Family quiz game. See issues of Parents'
  magazine & better family living
  —See Silberstein, R. M. jt. auth.
LEVINE, Daniel U.
  Stratification, segregation, and children in
  the inner-city school. bibliog Sch & Soc
  98:84-9 F '70
LEVINE, Harris
  Radioactive scientist. Time 95:68 Mr 2 '70 *
LEVINE, Herbert S.
  Dissent or anarchy. il Nation 210:520-2 My 4
  '70
  Weimar analogy. Nation 210:684-7 Je 8 '70
LEVINE, Irving R.
  Reports: Italy. Atlan 225:22+ Ap '69
  Reports: the Mediterranean. Atlan 225:4+ F
  '70
  Reports: the Vatican. Atlan 226:5-6+ S '70
  Venice. Atlan 227:16+ Ja '71
LEVINE, Julius
  Laser-beam communicator. il Electr World
  84:46-8 N '70
LEVINE, Marilyn
  My daughter hears with her eyes. il por
  Redbook 134:10+ Ap '70
LEVINE, Mark A. and Claman, H. N.
  Bone marrow and spleen: dissociation of
  immunologic properties by cortisone. bib-
  liog il Science 167:1515-17 Mr 13 '70
LEVINE, Philip
  Later still; poem. New Yorker 46:38 Je 27
  '70
LEVINE, R. P. See Goodenough, U. W. jt.
  auth.
LEVINE, Richard H.
  Reaching out to Danny. il Am Ed 6:10-14 Jl
  '70
  Schoolhouse ombudsman. Clear House 44:
  354-5 F '70
LEVINE, Ruth J.
  Question of focus. Engl J 59:40-2 Ja '70
LEVINSON, Boris M.
  New York city skid row Negro: some re-
  search findings. bibliog Ment Hy 54:548-
  52 O '70
LEVINSON, Charles
  Labor's global organizer. J. Ross-Skinner.
  por Duns 96:67 N '70 *
LEVINSON, Harry
  Management by whose objectives? bibliog f
  Harvard Bsns R 48:125-34 Jl '70
  Psychologist diagnosis merger failures. bib-
  liog f Harvard Bsns R 48:139-47 Mr '70
LEVISON, Teddi
  Atlanta's dynamic duo. pors Time 95:73 My
  4 '70 *
LEVITAN, Irwin B. and Webb, T. E.
  Posttranscriptional control in the steroid-
  mediated induction of hepatic tyrosine trans-
  aminase. bibliog il Science 167:283-5 Ja 16 '70
LEVITIN, Anatolii
  Revival in Russia? D. Kucharsky. Chr Today
  15:44 D 18 '70 *
LEVITT, I. M.
  Grand tour of the planets. il Space World
  G-8-80:23-7 Ag '70
LEVITT, Irving
  Collectors: Dr and Mrs Irving Levitt. M.
  Esterow. il Art in Am 58:72-7 My '70 *
LEVITT, Morton
  University and society. bibliog Sch & Soc
  98:342-6 O '70
LEVITT, Theodore
  Morality (?) of advertising. il Harvard Bsns
  R 48:84-92 Jl '70
LEVITT and sons, inc.
  Housing enters the era of the superbuilder.
  il Bsns W p50-3 D 26 '70

LEVY, Alan
  Peter Ustinov plays Santa to the children
  of many nations. il pors Good H 171:38-40+
  D '70
LEVY, Fred
  Photo center sets pace for nation. J. Deschin.
  il Pop Phot 66:34+ Ap '70 *
LEVY, Gerald F. and Folstad, J. W.
  Swimmer's itch. bibliog il Environ 11:14-16+
  D '69
LEVY, H. A. See Narten, A. H. jt. auth.
LEVY, Howard J.
  P.P.A. authors' press conference; excerpts.
  il pors Pub W 197:27-9 Mr 23 '70
LEVY, Jacques
  Two remarkable directors. M. Gottfried. il pors
  Vogue 155:204-5+ My '70 *
LEVY, Jay A. and Pincus, Theodore
  Demonstration of biological activity of a
  murine leukemia virus of New Zealand
  black mice. bibliog il Science 170:326-7 O
  16 '70
LEVY, Marvin David
  Music to my ears; piano concerto presented
  by Chicago symphony. I. Kolodin. Sat R
  53:35 D 19 '70 *
LEVY, Natalie
  Cactus to starboard. il Yachting 128:58-9+
  D '70
  Whittlin' on a whale. il Har Yrs 10:30-3 F '70
LEVY, Sheldon G.
  Psychology of political activity. bibliog f il
  Ann Am Acad 391:83-96 S '70
LEVY, Uriah Phillips
  Uriah Levy: the common sailor's skipper. por
  Sr Schol 95:12 D 1 '69 *
LEWIE, Reva G.
  Creative uses of scrap materials. il Sch Arts
  69:11 F '70
LEWIN, Nathan
  Justice cops out. New Repub 162:14-18 Je 6 '70
LEWIN, Seymour Z.
  Lalibela's ancient churches saved by a new
  preservative. il Sci Digest 68:84-5 Ag '70 *
LEWIN, Susan Grant
  House that owes its life to its setting. il
  House B 112:48-51 Ag '70
LEWINE, Frances
  Washington witch hunt. il por Time 96:34 Ag
  3 '70 *
LEWIS, Anne
  Of lollipops and larynxes. il Am Ed 6:29-30
  Jl '70
LEWIS, Anthony
  All's right with the world of Harold Wilson.
  il pors N Y Times Mag p 14-15+ Je 14 '70
  How pointless it all seems now. il N Y Times
  Mag p26-7+ F 8 '70
  Jungle drum of the British establishment.
  Esquire 74:52+ N '70
  Same justice can be both a strict and a loose
  constructionist. il N Y Times Mag p30-1+
  My 24 '70
LEWIS, Arthur J.
  Continuing education for world affairs; earth
  survival centers; address, October 15, 1970.
  bibliog Vital Speeches 37:116-21 D 1 '70
LEWIS, Carroll
  Bootstrap library drive succeeds in Puerto
  Rico. il por Library J 95:1813-15 My 15 '70
LEWIS, Clarence E.
  Persimmon. Horticulture 48:40+ Ag '70
LEWIS, Claude
  New set of heroes. il Am Ed 6:23 Ja '70
LEWIS, Cyrus
  Man asks. . . Har Yrs 10:34-6 F '70
LEWIS, David
  Ancient star paths; excerpts from journal. il
  por Yachting 127:62-3+ Mr '70
LEWIS, David L.
  In voting on great Americans, business gets
  the business. il Nations Bsns 58:88-9 Mr
  '70
LEWIS, David Sloan, 1917-
  David S. Lewis to head General dynamics.
  Aviation W 93:22 O 26 '70 *
  General dynamics finds a new boss. por Bsns
  W p33 O 24 '70 *
LEWIS, Elma
  Black art's amazing fund-raiser. P. Bailey. il
  pors Ebony 25:70-2+ Je '70 *
LEWIS, Flora
  Nixon doctrine. Atlan 226:6+ N '70
  Rumble at Camp Lejeune. Atlan 225:35-41 Ja
  '70
LEWIS, Golda
  Golda Lewis: from collage to compage. il
  Craft Horiz 30:52-3 Ag '70
LEWIS, Harry
  Gossip (for Charles Olson): poem. Nation
  210:665 Je 1 '70
LEWIS, Henry, 1932-
  Conductor as listener. il por Hi Fi sec I 20:
  26 F '70

LEWIS, Herbert A.
Jolts on the price elevator. por Nations Bsns 58:65-6 My '70
LEWIS, Jerry
Five happy moments. por Esquire 74:137 D '70
LEWIS, John S. and Prinn, R. G.
Jupiter's clouds: structure and composition. bibliog il Science 169:472-3 Jl 31 '70
LEWIS, Oscar
Obituary
   Pub W 198:39 D 28 '70
LEWIS, Richard
(ed) Poems by Japanese children; excerpts from There are two lives; tr. by H. Kimura. Mlle 72:116-7 N '70
LEWIS, Richard S.
Antarctic research and the relevance of science. il Bul Atom Sci 26:2-4 D '70
Evolution in NASA: loss and cost of transition. il Bul Atom Sci 26:28-9 Ap '70
Painless path to Mars. il Bul Atom Sci 26: 44-5 Ja '70
SALT in Vienna: the waltz of the powers. il Bul Atom Sci 26:19-21 S '70
LEWIS, Ted
Where are they now? pors Newsweek 76:6 S 7 '70 *
LEWIS, Theophilus
Theatre. See occasional issues of America to August 22, 1970
LEWIS, Walter H.
Chromosomal drift, a new phenomenon in plants. bibliog il Science 168:1115-16 My 29 '70
LEWIS, Wilbert W.
Child advocacy and ecological planning. Ment Hy 54:475-83 O '70
LEWIS, William H.
Tanzania: commitment to self reliance. Cur Hist 58:160-4+ Mr '70
LEWIS, Wyndham
Standpoint of genius. H. Kenner. Nat R 22: 846-7 Ag 11 '70 *
LEWIS with Harris (island)
Enchanted chessmen. F. V. Grunfeld. il Horizon 12:100-3 Wint '70
LEWISTON, Pa.
Swinging playground at no cost. il Am City 85:66 Je '70
LEWITZKY, Bella
Bella. W. Terry. por Sat R 53:22 S 12 '70 *
LEWONTIN, Richard C.
Race and intelligence. Bul Atom Sci 26:2-8 Mr; 23-5 My '70
Race and the genetics of intelligence. A. R. Jensen. il Bul Atom Sci 26:17-23 My '70 *
LEXINGTON, Ky. public library
Library vs. commissioners: fight to the finish? il Wilson Lib Bul 44:990-1 Je '70
LEXINGTON, N.C.

Education

Unshackled education; modular scheduling. D. Cooper. Clear House 45:22-5 S '70
LEYBURN, James G.
Scotch-Irish excerpts. il Am Heritage 22:28-31+ D '70
LEYDA, Jay
Between explosions. Film Q 23:33-8 Sum '70
LEYHAUSEN, Paul
Sane community: a density problem? il UNESCO Courier 23:26-32 Ag '70
LEYLAND motor corporation. See British Leyland motor corporation
LEYTON, Robert A. and Ullrick, W. C.
Z disc ultrastructure in scutal depressor fibers of the barnacle. bibliog il Science 168:127-8 Ap 3 '70
L'HEUREUX, John
Being and becoming; Exegesis; poems. Atlan 225:92 My '70
Night letter to Regina; poem. Atlan 227:70 Ja '71
Something missing; story. Atlan 226:79-84 Ag '70
Thing about cats; poem. Atlan 226:112 D '70
LHEVINNE, Rosina
Landmark for Rosina Lhevinne. R. Jacobson. il pors Sat R 53:57-9+ Mr 28 '70 *
LI, Choh Hao
Controlling human growth. por Time 97:35 Ja 18 '71 *
—See Bewley, T. A. jt auth.
LIABILITY (law)
Demise of accountability; with editorial comment. Chr Today 14:14-16, 33 Ap 10 '70
How liable are you for your child's misdeeds? L. M. Brown. Bet Hom & Gard 48: 6 N '70
Punishing parents; four Detroit-area communities. Time 96:60-1 N 9 '70
When should you sue? D. Green. il Mech Illus 66:46-8+ Ja '70
   See also
Damages
Insurance, Liability

LIABILITY insurance. See Insurance, Liability
LIAT, Lim Boo. See Muul, I. jt. auth.
LIBARLE, Marc, and Seligson, Tom
(eds) High school revolutionaries; excerpts. il Look 34:70+ Mr 24 '70
LIBBEY-Owens-Ford glass company
Libbey commemorative revival of Amberina, 1917. C. U. Fauster. il Hobbies 75:98J-98L Mr '70
Strengthening the weaker sex. Time 96:43-4 Ag 3 '70
LIBBY, McNeill and Libby (firm)
Libby says aloha to its old life-style. Bsns W p39-40 Ja 17 '70
LIBEL and slander
Libel and private college newspapers. J. S. Corcoran. bibliog Sch & Soc 98:354-6 O '70
Proceedings privileged against libel actions. Pub W 198: 34 D 28 '70
Reports of secret cases denied libel privilege. H. F. Pilpel and K. P. Norwick. Pub W 198:33-4 S 7 '70
Times libel rule is issue in recent court cases. H. F. Pilpel and K. P. Norwick. Pub W 197:54-6 Mr 2 '70
Two faces of malice. H. F. Pilpel and K. P. Norwick. Pub W 198:31-2 Ag 3 '70
Press law
LIBERAL arts colleges. See Liberal education
LIBERAL education
Liberal education and campus activists; excerpts from address. G. Stade. por Sch & Soc 98:459 D '70
Plight of the Christian liberal-arts college. S. R. Obitts. Chr Today 14:8-10 Ap 24 '70
Revolution in the university. J. Hitchcock. Yale R 60:161-74 D '70
   See also
Humanities
LIBERAL party (South Africa) See Political parties—South Africa
LIBERALISM
After liberalism, what? symposium. ed. by J. Burnham. Nat R 22:1263-89 D 1 '70
Continuing claims of liberalism. C. Frankel. Nat R 22:1274-7 D 1 '70
Decade of the great liberal death wish. M. Muggeridge. il Esquire 74:154-9 D '70
Decline of liberal politics. W. Pfaff; discussion. Commentary 49:16+ F '70
Sound liberalism is still the answer; reprint. D. Lawrence. U S News 69:88+ N 2 '70
Struggle over the liberal heritage. F. S. Meyer. Nat R 22:207 F 24 '70
Who needs the liberals? views of John Kenneth Galbraith and Samuel Lubell. P. Kemble. Commentary 50:57-64 O '70
Year of the losers. W. C. McWilliams and others. Commonweal 93:214-16 N 27 '70
   See also
Conservatism
Right and left (political science)

History

Myths the liberals live by. P. McGouldrick. il Nat R 22:151-3+ F 10 '70
LIBERALISM (theology) See Modernism
LIBERATION front for Quebec. See Front for the liberation of Quebec
LIBERATION news service. See News agencies
LIBERMAN, Alexander
Great-circle route. L. Campbell. il por Art N 69:52-7+ Ap '70 *
Retrospective for Alexander Liberman; exhibition at the Corcoran gallery of art, Washington, D.C. J. Harithas. il Art in Am 58: 106-7 Mr '70 *
LIBERTY
Four essays on liberty, by I. Berlin. Review Commonweal 91:492-3 Ja 30 '70. A. Nebolsine
   Harper 241:92-8 Ag '70. I. Howe
Freedom to destroy freedom. Chr Today 14: 25 F 13 '70
Is America moral? American moral tradition of freedom. R. J. Neuhaus. Commonweal 92:341-3 Jl 10 '70
Is freedom dying in America? H. S. Commager. il il por Look 34:16-21 Jl 14 '70
Repression in the mirror. B. Farrell. Life 68: 22B Ap 3 '70
What's right with America: lack of liberty in North Vietnam. H. R. Perot. il por Nations Bsns 58:20-1+ Jl '70
   See also
American civil liberties union
Civil rights
Democracy
Dictatorship
Free speech
Liberalism
Religious liberty

LIBERTY (periodical)
Liberty cont'd. P. S. Nathan. Pub W 199:50 Ja 4 '71
Liberty's heirs. P. Nathan. Pub W 197:54 Je 1 '70
Massmags and microcult. S. O'Connell. Nation 210:310-11 Mr 16 '70

LIBERTY, Religious. See Religious liberty

LIBERTY lobby
America's other radicals: the far right. P. Schrag. Harper 241:35-46 Ag '70

LIBERTY of the press. See Freedom of the press

LIBRAIRIE Hachette. See Publishers and publishing—France

LIBRARIANS
Above politics: how U.S. and Japanese librarians cleared the way for true professional exchange. Y. Suzuki. bibliog il Wilson Lib Bul 44:1054-9 Je '70
Foreign library manpower raises basic new issues; LED institute. Library J 95:3722 N 1 '70
Intellectual freedom; question of insurance against intellectual freedom problems. J. F. Krug. Am Lib 1:20-1, 117-18 Ja, F '70
Let your son shine in: giving younger ones a chance in running ALA. E. M. Oboler. Am Lib 1:747 S '70
Library front-liners. il Wilson Lib Bul 45:200-1, 330-1, 424-5, 458-9 O '70-Ja '71
Mister Carnegie's library; a librarian's memories of her librarian mother in Moberly, Mo. C. E. Werkley. il por Am Heritage 21:65-8 F '70
Tomorrow people. K. Nyren. Library J 95:3421 O 15 '70
See also
Childrens librarians
College librarians
Library assistants
National freedom fund for librarians
Negro librarians
School librarians

Anecdotes, facetiae, satire, etc.
Captain Catalog; comic strip. il Wilson Lib Bul 44:834-8 Ap '70
Personnel work at Irvine: astrology and a chaplain; reprint. Library J 95:3233-4 O 1 '70

Caricatures and cartoons
State of the image. A. Wittig. il Am Lib 1:710-12 Jl '70

Civil rights
Constitutional rights of public librarians. R. P. Dwoskin. bibliog por Library J 95:2417-21 Jl '70

Education
See Library schools and education

Education in service
Continuing education in librarianship: ideas for action. E. W. Stone. Am Lib 1:543-51 Je '70; Reply. V. L. Parker. 1:739-40 S '70
Human element: a retrospective evaluation of the OSUL internship program. D. J. Netz and D. E. Wood. Am Lib 1:253-4 Mr '70
Taking the full ride; routes to continuing education. L. E. Bone and F. R. Hartz. bibliog il pors Library J 95:3244-6 O 1 '70

Placement
See Librarians—Selection and appointment

Political activities
Silence, exile and cunning: libraries' defense against extremism at ALA in Detroit. E. J. Gaines. Library J 95:2639 Ag '70
Voices of experience: what makes a social issue a library issue? opinions of librarians in the field. il Wilson Lib Bul 45:45-53 S '70

Qualifications
Back to the baccalaureate! question of a master's degree for library work. R. C. Thompson; R. D. Aldrich. Library J 95:430-1 F 1 '70
From Roswell to Richmond, to your town. G. McShean. il pors Library J 95:627-31 F 15 '70; Discussion. 95:2035+, 2585-6 Je 1, Ag '70

Rating
Performance ratings and librarians rights. D. Peele. il Am Lib 1:595-600 Je '70; Discussion. 1:740-2 S '70

Recruiting
Dawning or the age of librarius; third annual Student leadership conference for library aides. il Wilson Lib Bul 45:130-2 O '70

Proofs and prescriptions; job crisis. C. Hendershott. il por Library J 95:3735-8 N 1 '70
See also
American library association—Office for recruitment

Salaries
Disadvantaged majority: women employed in libraries. A. R. Schiller. bibliog il Am Lib 1:345-9 Ap '70; Discussion. 1:644 Jl '70
Editor's choice. G. R. Shields; R. E. Berry. Am Lib 1:335 Ap '70
Placements & salaries: the 1969 plateau. C. J. Frarey. il por Library J 95:2099-103 Je 1 '70
Women and blacks; letter to the editor. E. D. Murphy. Library J 95:959 Mr 15 '70
See also
College librarians—Salaries

Selection and appointment
Death of the manpower shortage: the job crisis; symposium. bibliog il Library J 95:3711, 3735-44 N 1 '70
Detroit conference placement center. il por Am Lib 1:311 Ap '70
Editor's choice. G. R. Shields; R. E. Berry. Am Lib 1:335 Ap '70
Intellectual freedom jobs asked of major libraries. Library J 95:107-8 Ja 15 '70
Job placement service at ALA midwinter reduced. Library J 95:4084 D 1 '70
Liberated librarian? second sex in the library profession. J. Freedman. bibliog il por Library J 95:1709-11 My 1 '70; Discussion. 95:2853, 3704+ S 15, N 1 '70
Overdue; jobless in Gotham. J. A. Bernstein. por Wilson Lib Bul 44:1065 Je '70
Placements & salaries: the 1969 plateau. C. J. Frarey. il por Library J 95:2099-103 Je 1 '70
Status of women in libraries: task force meets in Detroit; SRRT. P. Schuman. Library J 95:2635 Ag '70

Supply and demand
Death of the manpower shortage: the job crisis; symposium. bibliog il Library J 95:3711, 3735-44 N 1 '70
Library education and manpower; ALA policy proposal. Am Lib 1:341-4 Ap '70; Reply. G. M. Casey. 1:706-9 Jl '70
Library manpower in the Detroit metropolitan region. G. Casey. il Am Lib 1:787-9 S '70
No more shortage? letter to the editor. B. L. Wimble. Library J 95:607 F 15 '70
See also
Librarians—Recruiting
School librarians—Supply and demand

Tenure
See also
College librarians—Tenure

Trade unions
See Librarians unions

LIBRARIANS as authors
Overdue; death by clearance. Wilson Lib Bul 44:769 Mr '70

LIBRARIANS strike (Canada) See Strikes—Canada

LIBRARIANS unions
Just dirt: a whole lot of it; ALA pre-conference institute on collective bargaining. W. Doak. Library J 95:2631 Ag '70
L.A. library union opposes commission: new director for LAPL. Library J 95:112 Ja 15 '70
London, Ontario strike ends with settlement. il Library J 95:2602-4 Ag '70

LIBRARIANSHIP
Aware. J. A. McCrossan. Am Lib 1:87, 187-8, 396, 493-4, 618-20, 713-14 Ja-F, Ap-Jl '70
Editor's choice; issues offered for ALA Detroit conference. G. R. Shields. Am Lib 1:431 My '70
Faddism: over-commitment of libraries, resulting in inadequate service. E. J. Gaines. il Library J 95:2235 Je '70; Discussion. 95:3215-16 O 1 '70
Librarian and the teaching of reading; symposium, ed. by. A. Plotnik. bibliog il Wilson Lib Bul 45:239-307 N '70
Library front-liners. il Wilson Lib Bul 45:200-1, 330-1, 424-5, 458-9 O '70-Ja '71
Library response to a restive world; address, July 3, 1970. L. M. Bradshaw. por Am Lib 1:688-90 Jl '70
Quality librarianship the day after tomorrow. J. Z. Nitecki. bibliog Am Lib 1:130-1 F '70
Shoe on the other foot: from library administrator to user; address, March 1970. L. C. Powell. por Wilson Lib Bul 45:384-9 D '70
Varieties of social involvement: ten recent case histories. il Wilson Lib Bul 45:64-7 S '70

LIBRARIANSHIP—*Continued*

Voices of experience: what makes a social issue a library issue? opinions of librarians in the field. il Wilson Lib Bul 45:45-53 S '70

Who speaks for the concern of library service? address, 1970. J. F. Anderson. bibliog il Am Lib 1:1062-8 D '70

Anecdotes, facetiae, satire, etc.

LJ's non-awards. J. Berry, 3d, and others. Library J 95:4207 D 15 '70

Yippie librarianship. D. Roberts. il Am Lib 1:1046-51 D '70

LIBRARIANSHIP as a profession

ALA: a professional or a library association. C. M. Weisenberg. Am Lib 1:1060-1 D '70

Dawning of the age of librarius; third annual Student leadership conference for library aides. il Wilson Lib Bul 45:130-2 O '70

Disadvantaged majority: women employed in libraries. A. R. Schiller. bibliog il Am Lib 1:345-9 Ap '70; Discussion. 1:644 Jl '70

Liberated librarian? second sex in the library profession. J. Freedman. bibliog il por Library J 95:1709-11 My 1 '70; Discussion. 95:2853, 3704+ S 15, N 1 '70

Library education and manpower; ALA policy proposal. Am Lib 1:341-4 Ap '70; Reply. G. M. Casey. 1:706-9 Jl '70

Overdue; the women's liberation movement. E. G. Detlefsen; P. Schuman; G. W. Hathaway. il Wilson Lib Bul 44:962-5+ My '70

Plus ça change: twenties through the sixties. J. H. Shera. il por Library J 95:979-86 Mr 15 '70; Reply. P. Schuman. 95:1781-2 My 15 '70

Silence, exile and cunning: libraries' defense against extremism at ALA in Detroit. E. J. Gaines. Library J 95:2639 Ag '70

Status in the 80s; letter to the editor. G. F. Heise. Am Lib 1:522-4 Je '70

Status of women in libraries: task force meets in Detroit; SRRT. P. Schuman. Library J 95:2635 Ag '70

Women and blacks; letter to the editor. E. D. Murphy. Library J 95:959 Mr 15 '70

Anecdotes, facetiae, satire, etc.

Nightmares along the Tallahatchie bridge. J. M. Carter. Library J 95:2889 S 15 '70

LIBRARIES

Against the dogmatists: a sceptical view of libraries. D. Gore. bibliog Am Lib 1:953-7 N '70

Library as arbiter. F. Patterson. Am Lib 1:254-5 Mr '70

Quiet stir of thought, or. What the computer cannot do; adaptation of address. May 1969. J. H. Shera; reply. K. W. Jaffe. Library J 95:101-2 Ja 15 '70

See also
College libraries
School libraries

Acquisitions

See also
College libraries—Acquisitions

Administration

See Library administration

Advertising

See Library publicity

Architecture

See Library architecture

Audio-visual materials

See Libraries and audio-visual materials

Automation

Centralized processing: diversified; Rhode Island. H. G. Kurtz. il por Library J 95:1807-12 My 15 '70

Hurdles, problems, rewards: a total system concept at work; Boulder public library. A. Mathews. il Am Lib 1:151-3 F '70

Informational switching yard. E. J. Gaines. Library J 95:641 F 15 '70; Reply. E. Castagna. 95:2742 S 1 '70

Old and new design philosophies used in library automation. T. K. Burgess; discussion. Am Lib 1:110-11, 425 F, My '70

One who DAIRed: a dial access system; Oral Roberts university, Tulsa, Okla. W. W. Jernigan. il por Wilson Lib Bul 44:653-7 F '70

Public libraries and the network idea; address, April 26, 1968. V. W. Clapp. Library J 95:121-4 Ja 15 '70

Spreading state library riches for peanuts: Micro-automated catalog system. O. P. Gillock, jr. il Wilson Lib Bul 45:354-5+ D '70

Texas tech circulation speeded by Xerox system. il Library J 95:3729 N 1 '70

Typewriters in libraries; a short history of mechanization. A. M. Beagles. bibliog por Library J 96:46-7 Ja 1 '71

Working library network; established for book processing by Systems development division of IBM. B. M. Wolpert. il Am Lib 1:570-2 Je '70

See also
College libraries—Automation
Information storage and retrieval systems
School libraries—Automation

Book losses

See also
Library thefts

Book selection

See Book selection

Censorship

Carl Gorton pays fine, quits library board; Farmingdale public library, New York. Library J 95:2864+ S 15 '70

Confrontation in Memphis. C. L. Wallis; discussion. Library J 94:4102-3; 95:189-90 N 15 '69, Ja 15 '70

From Roswell to Richmond, to your town. G. McShean. il pors Library J 95:627-31 F 15 '70; Discussion. 95:2035+, 2585-6 Je 1, Ag '70

From whitest Africa: a dark tale of censorship. B. Lunn. bibliog il por Library J 95:131-3 Ja 15 '70; Reply. S. Berman. 95:2399-400 Jl '70

Institutional censorship. J. G. Burke and H. P. Bowers. il pors Library J 95:468-9 F 1 '70

Intellectual freedom; report from Farmingdale. J. F. Krug. Am Lib 1:118, 212-13 F-Mr '70

Lawyer looks at libraries and censorship; address, 1970. T. R. Asher. por Library J 95:3247-9 O 1 '70; Discussion. 95:4204 D 15 '70

Minneapolis librarians defeat censorship move. Library J 95:4090 D 1 '70

Misuse of libraries: Soviet Union. W. C. Jackson. Am Lib 1:940 N '70

Overdue: death by clearance. Wilson Lib Bul 44:769 Mr '70

Overdue: deselection policy: how to exclude everything. M. Crush. por Wilson Lib Bul 45:180-1 O '70

Rebuttal from Prince George; removal of Washington free press; letters to the editor. Am Lib 1:647-9 Jl '70

Right to receive and possess pornography; an attorney foresees the end of legal restrictions. A. B. Gerber. por Wilson Lib Bul 44:641-4 F '70

Spiro and the nitrogen cycle. K. Nyren. Library J 95:433 F 1 '70

State libraries and intellectual freedom; ed. by J. F. Krug and J. A. Harvey. P. B. Cors. Am Lib 1:944-5 N '70

See also
American library association—Intellectual freedom committee
Library bill of rights
School libraries—Censorship

Childrens rooms

See Libraries, Childrens

Circulation, loans, etc.

Mail order/phone order moves books in Kansas. Library J 95:1430+ Ap 15 '70

Sorry, it's charged out. R. M. Pierson. il por Wilson Lib Bul 44:951-6 My '70

See also
College libraries—Circulations, loans, etc.
Libraries—Fines

Classification

See Classification

Cooperative service

See Library cooperation

Equipment and supplies

See Library furniture and equipment

Extension work

See Library extension

Federal aid

Crucial education vote due February 6. Library J 95:435 F 1 '70

Dorothy S. McAllister, library trustee. il pors Wilson Lib Bul 45:330-1 N '70

Equalization is keyword of new HEA title 11-B. Library J 95:3716+ N 1 '70

Federal funding for fiscal 1970 set. Library J 95:1417 Ap 15 '70

LIBRARIES—Federal aid—*Continued*
Financing discrimination; services to the disadvantaged. E. Geller. Library J 95:3943 N 15 '70
HEW holding USOE funds; LSCA amendments of 1970. G. Krettek and E. D. Cooke. Wilson Lib Bul 45:324-5 N '70
Library funds released. C. Krettek and E. D. Cooke. Am Lib 1:1054 D '70
New directions in DLP. R. M. Fry. Am Lib 1:904-7 O '70
1971 education appropriations. Wilson Lib Bul 44:903 My '70
U.S. funds for library programs released. G. Krettek and E. D. Cooke. Wilson Lib Bul 45:429 D '70
Writing project applications for funding; with guide by HEW, ed. by C. Hall. Am Lib 1:779-80 S '70
  See also
College libraries—Federal aid
Libraries, Institution—Federal aid
School libraries—Federal aid

Fiction collections
Risking the first novel. J. Berry. Library J 95:3219 O 1 '70

Film programs
See Libraries and moving pictures

Finance
Accreditation of public libraries: yes or no? W. K. Selden. por Wilson Lib Bul 45:394-8 D '70
Architects' fees: their place in library planning. J. Orne. il por Library J 95:4099-106 D 1 '70
Causes and consequences; job crisis. T. Gwinup. bibliog il por Library J 95:3729-30 N 1 '70
Chill of recession settles on libraries. Library J 95:2405 Jl '70
Fear of real costs: some financial aspects of the PLA systems study. R. Rohlf. Am Lib 1:242-4 Mr '70
501 (C) (3) protect us; Internal revenue code of 1954: our tax-exempt status. J. Berry. Library J 95:837 Mr 1 '70
Northeast city libraries: some feasting, some famine. Library J 95:3226-8 O 1 '70
Politics and tax exemption: educators issue guidelines. Library J 95:2749 S 1 '70
2½ percent box. E. J. Gaines. il Library J 95:3452 O 15 '70
  See also
Libraries—Federal aid
Libraries—Statistics

Fines
Law and order in people orientation; letter to the editor. A. H. Rineer, jr. Am Lib 1:527-8 Je '70

Foreign language collections
Chinatown's library; Chatham square, branch of the New York public library. M. H. Cole. il por Wilson Lib Bul 45:482-4 Ja '71
Libraries and the Spanish-speaking; symposium. ed. by W. L. Ramirez. bibliog il por Wilson Lib Bul 44:714-67 Mr '70

Furniture
See Library furniture and equipment

Hours of opening
Day the library closed its doors; Peterboro, N.H. town library. E. Yates. Am Lib 1:179-80 F '70
Sunday hours popular says LJ mail. Library J 95:442+ F 1 '70
Sunday; Mass. letter to the editor. L.-J. Roberts. Library J 95:2739-40+ S 1 '70

Information service
See Libraries—Reference work

Instruction in use
Integrated library instruction. J. R. Kennedy, jr. il por Library J 95:1450-3 Ap 15 '70

Intermediate departments
See also
Libraries—Services to young people

International aspects
At the newsfronts of the world; symposium. bibliog il Wilson Lib Bul 44:1020-63 Je '70
International library statistics. Wilson Lib Bul 45:224-5 N '70
Reading resources and Project LEER. M. D. Shepard. bibliog il por Wilson Lib Bul 44:743-50 Mr '70
School libraries and international development; ed. by J. E. Lowrie. Am Lib 1:182-3 F '70

Layout
See Library architecture

Legislation
See Library laws and legislation

Management
See Library administration

Microfilm collections
Little fiche eat big librarians, one whale of a story. E. C. Jestes. il por Wilson Lib Bul 44:650-2 F '70
Microimages and the library. J. G. Veenstra. bibliog il por Library J 95:3443-7 O 15 '70; Reply. P. G. Zurkowski. 95:3855-6 N 15 '70
New microfilms for old books. Am Lib 1:137 F '70

Moving picture collections
See also
United States—Library of Congress—National film collection

Organization
See Library administration

Pamphlet collections
New left and a new age of pamphlets: recommendations for a radical pamphlet library. N. Kehde. il Am Lib 1:873-6 O '70

Paperback books
On the management and use of paperbacks in libraries; address, 1970. W. H. Kaiser. il por Library J 95:2875-83 S 15 '70

Periodicals
See Library science—Periodicals

Poetry
Overdue; poem. Wilson Lib Bul 45:86-7 S '70
  See also
School libraries—Poetry

Public relations
Changing library; experimenting with new techniques. il Newsweek 75:33 F 16 '70
Faddism: over-commitment of libraries, resulting in inadequate service. E. J. Gaines. il Library J 95:2235 Je 15 '70; Discussion. 95:3215-16 O 1 '70
New interest in library-community study. J. A. McCrossan. Am Lib 1:618 Je '70
Overdue; library public relations: a backward glance. Los Angeles public library. C. M. Weisenberg. por Wilson Lib Bul 45:406-7 D '70
  See also
Adult education—Library participation

Reading rooms
Library addition has garden-like reading room; Westminster, Colo. il Am City 85:81 O '70

Reference work
CATV+NCPL=VRS: Video reference service over a community TV system at Natrona County public library. K. E. Dowlin. il pors Library J 95:2768-70 S 1 '70
Specialized investment services. R. S. Burgess. il por Library J 95:867-9 Mr 1 '70
  See also
Libraries—Foreign language collections
United States—Library of Congress—National film collection
United States—Library of Congress—Special collections

Services to children
See Libraries, Childrens

Services to foreign born
Chicanos and libraries; letter to the editor. R. P. Haro. Am Lib 1:932-3 N '70
Libraries and the Spanish speaking; symposium. ed. by W. L. Ramirez. bibliog il por Wilson Lib Bul 44:714-67 Mr '70

Services to groups
Community finds its forum; Tulsa city-county library. R. G. Swartz. il Am Lib 1:554-61 Je '70

Services to hospitals
Prisoners, patients, and public libraries; Buffalo and Erie County public service. D. C. Rittenhouse. il por Wilson Lib Bul 45:490-3 Ja '71

LIBRARIES—*Continued*

Services to mentally handicapped children

Library response to the challenge of mental retardation. B. H. Baskin. bibliog Am Lib 1:65-8 Ja '70

Services to physically handicapped

Barred from the library; architectural barriers. C. M. Greco. bibliog il Am Lib 1:908-10 O '70

Consider the confined; methods of reaching in; Los Angeles public library program. J. G. Sutton. il Wilson Lib Bul 45:485-9 Ja '71

Extending public library services to the home bound. J. A. McCrossan. Am Lib 1:485-90 My '70

Services to prisons

Books behind bars; American institute of discussion program at El Reno federal reformatory, Okla. il Am Ed 6:28-9 D '70

Prisoners, patients, and public libraries; Buffalo and Erie County public library service. D. C. Rittenhouse. il por Wilson Lib Bul 45:490-3 Ja '71

Services to schools

See Libraries and schools

Services to socially handicapped

Changing library; experimenting with new techniques. il Newsweek 75:33 F 16 '70

Chicanos and libraries; letter to the editor. R. P. Haro. Am Lib 1:932-3 N '70

Community control of the libraries; a philosophical position; excerpt from A study of library services for the disadvantaged in Buffalo, Rochester, and Syracuse. Am Lib 1:610-11 Je '70

Failure of libraries: a call to action; a model library for community action. M. Owens. il por Library J 95:1701-4 My 1 '70

Financing discrimination. E. Geller. Library J 95:3943 N 15 '70

John Ferguson, outreach librarian; Atlanta PL, branches in poverty areas. il pors Wilson Lib Bul 45:424-5 D '70

Libraries and the inner city. D. Dempsey. il Sat R 53:22-3 Ap 18 '70

Libraries and the Spanish-speaking; symposium, ed. by W. L. Ramirez. bibliog il por Wilson Lib Bul 44:714-67 Mr '70

Life is short, death is sure; Brooklyn public library, Coney Island branch; excerpts from annual report. S. Schickler. il Am Lib 1:35-8 Ja '70

Literacy librarians: case studies of experiments in Dallas. M. Warren. il por Wilson Lib Bul 45:278-84 N '70

Pre-college program for the disadvantaged; SEEK's library. S. H. Wright. il por Library J 95:2884-7 S 15 '70

Slum storefront library serves San Francisco poor. il Library J 95:1798 My 15 '70

Talking inner-city at the U. of Illinois. A. Plotnik. il Wilson Lib Bul 44:910-11 My '70

Time of the Gringo; southwestern states. B. E. Sheldon. bibliog il Am Lib 1:123-7 F '70

Toy libraries featured in preschool experiments. Library J 95:2958-9 S 15 '70

Two-day Maryland meet weighs urban libraries. P. Schuman. Library J 95:438+ F 1 '70

Services to the aged

Guidelines for library service to the institutionalized aging. D. Romani. Am Lib 1:286-9 Mr '70

Reading and the aged; with essay by M. Shapiro. C. H. Buswell. bibliog il por Wilson Lib Bul 45:467-76 Ja '71

Services to the senior citizen. M. C. Javelin. il Am Lib 1:133-7 F '70

Services to the blind

See also
School libraries—Services to blind

Services to young people

Common vibration; with discography. J. Santella. il por Library J 95:3967-70 N 15 '70

Conspiracy against youth. D. M. Broderick. por Library J 95:214-15 Ja 15 '70; Discussion. 95:1139-40 Mr 15 '70

Day the library closed its doors, Peterboro, N.H. town library. E. Yates. Am Lib 1:179-80 F '70

Films on demand; Moviebox in New York city. L. Hofer. il Library J 95:3962-4 N 15 '70

Listen, Miss, Mrs, Mr Librarian; with discography. D. Roberts. il Library J 95:3965-7 N 15 '70

Overdue; who speaks for silence? R. D. Kempner. il por Wilson Lib Bul 44:658-9 F '70

See also
Libraries and students

Shelving systems

Rapid & efficient; student assistant Marlin Dieter's method of shelf reading; letter to the editor. D. K. Hosler. Library J 95:2201 Je 15 '70

Shelf classification, or else. A. C. Foskett. il por Library J 95:2771-3 S 1 '70

Special collections

Joint use of collections; Bank street college of education, N.Y. E. Kulleseid and W. Gossage. il Am Lib 1:173-5 F '70

Notes and comment; offers by libraries to promote future works and private papers of living authors. New Yorker 46:19-20 Jl 25 '70

See also
Libraries—Foreign language collections
United States—Library of Congress—National film collection
United States—Library of Congress—Special collections

Standards

Accreditation of public libraries: yes or no? W. K. Selden. por Wilson Lib Bul 45:394-8 D '70

On the development of libraries and information centers. G. Salton. bibliog il por Library J 95:3433-42 O 15 '70

What good are public library standards? J. L. Wheeler. bibliog il por Library J 95:455-62, 2739 F 1, S 1 '70

See also
School libraries—Standards

Statistics

International library statistics. Wilson Lib Bul 45:224-5 N '70

Public library building in 1970. H. Galvin and B. Asbury. il pors Library J 95:4113-34 D 1 '70

What good are public library standards? J. L. Wheeler. bibliog il por Library J 95:455-62, 2739 F 1, S 1 '70

Student assistants

See Library assistants

Technical processes

Centralized processing; diversified; Rhode Island. H. G. Kurtz. il por Library J 95:1807-12 My 15 '70

Is work simplification alive and well someplace? R. M. Dougherty. Am Lib 1:969-71 N '70

N-I-H syndrome; creating so-called new techniques or processes. G. R. Brong and E. F. Pasternak. il pors Library J 95:3877-8 N 15 '70

Working library network; established for book processing by Systems development division of IBM. B. M. Wolpert. il Am Lib 1:570-2 Je '70

Terminology

Overdue; who's circulating 'round the reference desk's vertical file? R. Fink. por Wilson Lib Bul 45:308-9 N '70

Trustees, boards, committees, etc.

Dorothy S. McAllister, library trustee. il pors Wilson Lib Bul 45:330-1 N '70

Gary branch dispute moves toward crunch. Library J 95:110+ Ja 15 '70

Library system trustee. S. Whitney. bibliog por Library J 95:636-9 F 15 '70

Quality of community life. D. D. Corrigan. Am Lib 1:1081-2 D '70

See also
American library trustee association

Africa

See also
East African library association

California

How Mexican-Americans view libraries; East Los Angeles and Sacramento. R. P. Haro. bibliog il Wilson Lib Bul 44:736-42 Mr '70

See also
Los Angeles public library
Oakland, Calif. public library
San Francisco—Libraries
San Francisco public library
San Joaquin Valley library system, Fresno, Calif.
San Jose, Calif. public library

Canada

See also
Canadian library association
Toronto public library

LIBRARIES—*Continued*

Colorado

See also
Boulder, Colo, public library
Colorado library association
Denver public library

Connecticut

See also
Bridgeport, Conn, public library
Connecticut state library, Hartford

Denmark

What Americans can learn from the Danes. F. J. Mosher; reply, P. Birkelund. Wilson Lib Bul 44:1011+ Je '70

Egypt

In search of the Nile; the challenge to libraries in Egypt. S. M. Matta. bibliog il por Wilson Lib Bul 44:1040-5 Je '70

England

See also
London—Libraries

Florida

See also
Coral Gables, Fla, public library
Miami, Fla, public library

France

See also
American library in Paris

Georgia

See also
Atlanta public library
Chestatee regional library, Gainsville, Ga.
Flint River regional library, Griffin, Ga.

Illinois

See also
Chicago public library

Indiana

See also
Evansville, Ind, public library
Gary, Ind, public library
New Albany-Floyd County, Ind, public library
Vigo County, Ind, public library, Terre Haute

Iowa

See also
Davenport, Ia, public library

Israel

Israel: libraries in a state of siege. A. Kaplan. il por Wilson Lib Bul 44:1046-53 Je '70

Japan

Above politics: how U.S. and Japanese librarians cleared the way for true professional exchange. Y. Suzuki. bibliog il Wilson Lib Bul 44:1054-9 Je '70

Kansas

Mail order/phone order moves books in Kansas. Library J 95:1430+ Ap 15 '70

Kentucky

See also
Lexington, Ky, public library
Louisville free public library

Maryland

See also
Enoch Pratt free library, Baltimore
High John library, Fairmount Heights

Massachusetts

Sunday: Mass. letter to the editor. L.-J. Roberts. Library J 95:2739-40+ S 1 '70

Michigan

Help for VERY small libraries. J. A. McCrossan. Am Lib 1:493 My '70
See also
Detroit—Libraries
Detroit public library
Kalamazoo, Mich, public library

Minnesota

See also
Minneapolis public library

Missouri

Missouri paradox; letter to the editor. E Arthur. Library J 95:4077+ D 1 '70
See also
Missouri state library, Jefferson City
St Charles County, Mo, library, St Charles

Montana

See also
Billings, Mont, public library

New Hampshire

See also
Peterboro, N.H, town library

New Jersey

See also
New Jersey state library, Trenton

New York (state)

Community control of the libraries: a philosophical position; excerpt from A study of library services for the disadvantaged in Buffalo, Rochester, and Syracuse. Am Lib 1:610-11 Je '70
Minimum wages for pages denied in N.Y. Library J 95:614 F 15 '70
New York library development plan released. il Library J 95:3715 N 1 '70
See also
Buffalo and Erie County, N.Y, public library
Farmingdale, N.Y, public library
Kingston, N.Y, area library
New York library association
New York public library
Niagara Falls, N.Y, public library
Scarsdale, N.Y, public library
Yonkers, N.Y, public library

Nigeria

Recorded knowledge: a war casualty. B. U. Nwafor.il por Library J 96:42-5 Ja 1 '71

Northeastern states

Northeast city libraries: some feasting, some famine. Library J 95:3226-8 O 1 '70

Ohio

Best laid plan: OLDP, ALSO, and JSHP; with excerpts from the library development plan. R. H. Donahugh. Am Lib 1:973-7 N '70
Ohio's BOOKS/JOBS program. J. F. Shubert and C. E. Dowlin. il pors Library J 95:3239-43 O 1 '70
See also
Akron, Ohio, public library
Elyria, Ohio, public library

Ontario

See also
London, Ontario—Public library and art museum
Toronto public library

Pennsylvania

See also
Altoona, Pa. public library
Pennsylvania state library, Harrisburg
Philadelphia free library
Uniontown, Pa, public library

Puerto Rico

See also
San Juan, Puerto Rico—Libraries

Rhode Island

Centralized processing: diversified. H. G. Kurtz. il por Library J 95:1807-12 My 15 '70

Russia

Bibliographic sputnik? steps toward cataloging at source in the U.S.S.R. E. Buist. bibliog il por Wilson Lib Bul 44:1033-9 Je '70
Misuse of libraries. W. C. Jackson. Am Lib 1:940 N '70
Soviet Union: of 370,000 libraries, 2.5 billion volumes, and a treasure house of foreign literature; tr. by R. A. Karlowich. M. I. Rudomino. il por Wilson Lib Bul 44:1022-32 Je '70

South Africa

From whitest Africa: a dark tale of censorship. B. Lunn. bibliog il por Library J 95: 131-3 Ja 15 '70; Reply. S. Berman. 95:2399-400 Jl '70

Southern states

See also
Southeastern library association

Southwestern states

Time of the Gringo. B. E. Sheldon. bibliog il Am Lib 1:123-7 F '70

Texas

See also
Dallas public library

United States

Aware. J. A. McCrossan. Am Lib 1:87, 187-8, 396, 493-4, 618-20, 713-14 Ja-F, Ap-Jl '70
Editor's choice; big valentine to a small library. G. R. Shields. Am Lib 1:115 F '70
From Roswell to Richmond, to your town. G. McShean. il pors Library J 95:627-31 F 15 '70; Discussion. 95:2035+, 2585-6 Je 1, Ag '70
Happy new decade! J. M. Carter. Library J 95:135 Ja 15 '70
Library forecast: blustery, partly clear. Library J 95:3423 O 15 '70

LIBRARIES—United States—*Continued*
News report: 1970. K. Nyren. il Library J
  96:27–41 Ja 1 '71
Week in April. il Am Lib 1:388–94 Ap '70
  See also
Friends of the library
Indians of North America—Libraries
Libraries—Statistics
Libraries and state
Library surveys
National library week
School libraries
Special libraries association

History
Rich man's burden, and how Andrew Carnegie unloaded it; excerpts from Andrew
Carnegie. J. F. Wall. il pors Am Heritage
21:58–67+ O '70

Virginia
  See also
Martinsville, Va, public library

Wisconsin
  See also
Milwaukee public library

Wyoming
  See also
Natrona County, Wyo, public library, Casper

LIBRARIES, Childrens
Commitment and conscience in children's ser-
vices. M. Jehu. por Wilson Lib Bul 45:168
O '70

Book selection
See Book selection

Projects
Starting a library stamp club. J. S. James.
bibliog il por Wilson Lib Bul 44:645–9 F
'70

LIBRARIES, College. See College libraries
LIBRARIES, Hospital
If we are serious; response to the library ed-
ucation and manpower policy proposal. G.
M. Casey. Am Lib 1:706–9 Jl '70
  See also
Libraries—Services to hospitals
LIBRARIES, Institution
If we are serious; response to the library ed-
ucation and manpower policy proposal. G.
M. Casey. Am Lib 1:706–9 Jl '70
Institutional library service at the state level.
B. Wang. Am Lib 1:781–5 S '70
Libraries in the therapeutic society; ed. by
G. Casey. bibliog Am Lib 1:65–8 Ja '70

Federal aid
Correctional libraries and LSCA title IV-A. G.
Brinkman. bibliog Am Lib 1:380–3 Ap '70
LIBRARIES, Instruction in use. See Libraries
—Instruction in use
LIBRARIES, National
National libraries: a proposal. K. Nyren. Li-
brary J 95:3859 N 15 '70
LIBRARIES, Negroes. See Libraries and Ne-
groes
LIBRARIES, Private
How to create a good home library. C. D.
Giles. il Parents Mag 45:64–5 My '70
LIBRARIES, School. See School libraries
LIBRARIES, Special
  See also
Botanical libraries
Horticultural libraries
Special libraries association
LIBRARIES, State
Administering our state library agencies. G.
DuFrane. Am Lib 1:23–6 Ja '70
Institutional library service at the state level.
B. Wang. Am Lib 1:781–5 S '70
State libraries and intellectual freedom; ed.
by J. F. Krug and J. A. Harvey. P. B.
Cors. Am Lib 1:944–5 N '70
State library: institution in transition. J. A.
Humphry and E. A. Ferguson. bibliog il
Am Lib 1:949–52 N '70
  See also
New Jersey state library, Trenton
Pennsylvania state library, Harrisburg
LIBRARIES, Thefts from. See Library thefts
LIBRARIES, Traveling
  See also
Bookmobiles
LIBRARIES, University. See College libraries
LIBRARIES and adult education. See Adult
education—Library participation
LIBRARIES and audio-visual materials
AV task force survey report; with reply by
J. Brown. C. W. Stone. Am Lib 1:40–5 Ja '70
Bridgeport's audiovisual story hours. J. A.
McCrossan. Am Lib 1:493 My '70

Can't see and won't listen: ALA AV committee proposal for an office of audio-
visual services, not funded; letter to the
editor. R. L. Ducote. Am Lib 1:836–7 O '70
I can't hear the flutes; excessive noise from
nonbook learning devices in new Hume
library at University of Florida. L. Cassidy.
il Am Lib 1:888–9 O '70
Memo to ALA/LTP; new media. J. Berry.
Library J 95:2857 S 15 '70
One who DAIRed: a dial access system; Oral
Roberts university, Tulsa, Okla. W. Jer-
nigan. il Wilson Lib Bul 44:653–7 F '70
  See also
School libraries and audio-visual materials
LIBRARIES and authors
Notes and comment; offers by libraries to
promote future works and private papers
of living authors. New Yorker 46:19–20
Jl 25 '70
LIBRARIES and communication. See Interli-
brary communication
LIBRARIES and intellectual liberty
Box score on confidentiality of library circu-
lation records. J. F. Krug and J. A. Harvey.
Am Lib 1:944 N '70
Card-carrying reader; probe by the IRS into
what people read. New Repub 163:7 Jl 25
'70
Editor's choice; sanctity: libraries, clients,
IRS, ALA. G. R. Shields. Am Lib 1:749–50
S '70
Ellis Hodgin loses first round. W. R. Eshelman.
il Wilson Lib Bul 44:901+ My '70
Hodgin loses suit against city manager. Li-
brary J 95:1685 My 1 '70
Intellectual freedom. J. F. Krug. Am Lib
1:20–1, 117–18 Ja–F '70
Intellectual freedom; Kingston, N.Y, area
library; with letter by R. H. Rosichan. J.
F. Krug and J. A. Harvey. Am Lib 1:425,
433 My '70
Librarian demonstrators march on IRS of-
fice. Library J 95:2749 S 1 '70
Library still free in Philly; vote to retain
Jerry Rubin's Do it! on open shelves. Wil-
son Lib Bul 45:450 Ja '71
Like Jack's magic beans: controversy at the
Detroit conference over IRS's inspection
of private reading habits. J. F. Krug and
J. A. Harvey. Am Lib 1:843–5 O '70
Litmus test of tyranny. T-men vs. librarians.
W. R. Eshelman. Wilson Lib Bul 45:5–7 S
'70
Missouri paradox; letter to the editor. E.
Arthur. Library J 95:4077+ D 1 '70
National press and television coverage: IRS
incident. J. F. Krug and J. A. Harvey. Am
Lib 1:1026–7 D '70
Obscenity and pornography statement further
justified; incidents in Milwaukee and Atlan-
ta. J. F. Krug and J. A. Harvey. Am Lib 1:
751–2 S '70
Of note: Atlanta public library's policy on in-
vestigations by IRS and other law enforce-
ment agencies. Am Lib 1:729 S '70
Of note: investigation of what people read by
Treasury agents. G. R. Shields. Am Lib
1:633 Jl '70
Reader interest in bombs checked by T-men;
with editorial comment. il Library J 95:
2591, 2593 Ag '70
Snoopers in the public libraries: representa-
tives of the Internal revenue service. R. H.
Smith. Pub W 198:33 Ag 10 '70
When readers become suspect. R. Cleghorn.
Cur 121:42–6 S '70
Will school libraries be next? views of the
National education association. Cur 211:47
S '70
  See also
American library association—Intellectual
freedom committee
Freedom to read foundation
Library bill of rights
National freedom fund for librarians

Anecdotes, facetiae, satire, etc.
Smith/Jones. D. DeCamp. Library J 95:3451
O 15 '70
LIBRARIES and mentally handicapped children.
See Libraries—Services to mentally handi-
capped children
LIBRARIES and moving pictures
Feature films in your library; with list of
distributors, cinema periodicals, and out-
standing films. P. Spehr. il Wilson Lib Bul
44:848–55 Ap '70
Films on demand; Moviebox in New York
city. L. Hofer. il Library J 95:3962–4 N 15 '70
  See also
School libraries and audio-visual materials

LIBRARIES and music
Common vibration; with discography. J. Santella. il por Library J 95:3967-70 N 15 '70
Listen, Miss, Mrs, Mr Librarian; with discography. D. Roberts. il Library J 95:3965-7 N 15 '70

LIBRARIES and Negroes
Bibliographies on social issues; St Charles County library, Mo. on the Black manifesto. A. Webb. il Wilson Lib Bul 45:65-6 S '70
Counterfeit service: creating slum libraries in slums. E. J. Gaines. Library J 95:4233 D 15 '70
Gary branch dispute moves toward crunch. Library J 95:110+ Ja 15 '70
High John closed by staff walkout; Fairmount Heights, Md. il Library J 95:3861 N 15 '70
High John: closing for openers; Fairmount Heights, Md. A. Plotnik. il Wilson Lib Bul 45:214-15 N '70
In search of soul; pre-conference institute, sponsored by the Social responsibilities round table, at ALA in Detroit. P. Schuman. il Library J 95:2632-4 Ag '70
Touch of bramble, glimpse of beauty: In search of soul preconference institute of SRRT. H. H. Eason. Am Lib 1:1018 D '70
Triumph & tragedy: a play in two acts; High John, Fairmount Heights, Md. R. B. Croneberger and J. C. Welbourne, jr. il pors Library J 95:1705-8 My 1 '70. Discussion. 95: 2397, 3416-18 Jl, O 15 '70
What now? address, July 2, 1970. J. Bond. Am Lib 1:847-8 O '70
Woodlawn: a photographic essay; with photos taken by children under the direction of S. Rush. M. A. Fitzharris. il Am Lib 1:892-5 O '70
    See also
School libraries and Negroes

LIBRARIES and politics
Merit and importance; ALA taking a stand on political issues. J. Forman. Am Lib 1:745-6 S '70

LIBRARIES and publishers
    See also
College libraries and publishers
Royalties

LIBRARIES and readers
Can this marriage be saved? D. Bass; discussion. Library J 94:4321-2; 95:429 D 1 '69, F 1 '70
Extending public library services to the homebound. J. A. McCrossan. Am Lib 1: 485-90 My '70
Our other customers; symposium. bibliog il Wilson Lib Bul 45:465-93 Ja '71
Quality of community life; trustees' relationship. D. D. Corrigan. Am Lib 1:1081-2 D '70
Sacred or secular: the context of culture. B. Chase. il por Library J 95:3871-6 N 15 '70
Sorry, it's charged out. R. M. Pierson. il por Wilson Lib Bul 44:951-6 My '70
They also read who roll in dough: observations based on activities of Scarsdale public library. M. A. Kateley. il por Wilson Lib Bul 45:477-81 Ja '71
Whither public service in America? A. P. Sable. il Wilson Lib Bul 45:390-3 D '70

Anecdotes, facetiae, satire, etc.
Hooper and the very rich. K. Nyren. Library J 95:2745 S 1 '70

LIBRARIES and research
Librarian and the scholar: eternal enemies; address, February 20, 1970. R. H. Logsdon. il por Library J 95:2871-4 S 15 '70
October inspiration: school libraries work! excerpt from report. I. W. Hale. il por Wilson Lib Bul 45:127 O '70

LIBRARIES and schools
Getting along with reading teachers. S. I. Fenwick. bibliog il por Wilson Lib Bul 45: 273-7 N '70
Libraries and education. H. H. Punke and C. H. Cantrell. Ed Digest 36:8-10 D '70
Vision transplanted: NYLA reports on lack of school-library cooperation. E. Geller. Library J 95:4307 D 15 '70
    See also
School libraries

LIBRARIES and social and economic problems
Bureaucracy or commitment? school libraries. G. Clark. por Library J 95:209-10 Ja 15 '70
Community finds its forum; Tulsa city-county library. R. G. Swartz. il Am Lib 1: 554-61 Je '70
Education for sensibility in the house of facts; address, March 28, 1969. K. Molz. il Am Lib 1:28-32 Ja '70

Library as a social planetarium. H. D. Lasswell. Am Lib 1:142-3 F '70
Library education and the public library. G. Garrison. por Library J 95:2763-7 S 1 '70; Discussion. 95:3855; 96:5 N 15 '70, Ja 1 '71
New left and a new age of pamphlets: recommendation for a radical pamphlet library. N. Kehde. il Am Lib 1:873-6 O '70
Ohio's BOOKS/JOBS program. J. F. Shubert and C. E. Dowlin. il pors Library J 95: 3239-43 O 1 '70
Overdue; the irrelevance of relevance. E. M. Oboler. por Wilson Lib Bul 44:869+ Ap '70
Plus ça change; twenties through the sixties. J. H. Shera. il por Library J 95:979-86 Mr 15 '70; Reply. P. Schuman. 95:1781-2 My 15 '70
Urban library dilemma. E. J. Gaines; discussion. Library J 95:101 Ja 15 '70
When is a social issue a library issue? symposium, ed. by D. Bendix. bibliog il Wilson Lib Bul 45:42-85 S '70
When is a social issue a school library issue? R. Young; R. L. Darling. Wilson Lib Bul 45:62-3 S '70
    See also
American library association—Social responsibilities of libraries round table
Libraries—Services to foreign born
Libraries—Services to socially handicapped
Libraries and Negroes

LIBRARIES and state
Libraries involved in government; councils of government (COGs) J. A. Houk. Am Lib 1:357-9 Ap '70
Veto, post office, and NCLIS lead September news; Porno commission, ALA and IRS in news. Library J 95:2859 S 15 '70
    See also
Libraries—Federal aid
School libraries and state

LIBRARIES and students
Library service for commuting students, by M. A. Gocek. Review
    Am Lib 1:713-14 Jl '70. J. A. McCrossan
Student voices: what makes a social issue a library issue? student opinions; ed. by E. Zaremba. il Wilson Lib Bul 45:54-61 S '70
Students use the public library; Lincoln Heights branch of the Los Angeles public library. J. A. McCrossan. Am Lib 1:87 Ja '70
    See also
Libraries—Services to young people

LIBRARIES and television
CATV+NCPL=VRS: Video reference service over a community TV system at Natrona County public library. K. E. Dowlin. il pors Library J 95:2768-70 S 1 '70
Coming through your front door: prerecorded video cassettes. J. G. Burke and M. C. Lux. il Am Lib 1:1069-73 D '70
Sesame street; what next? il Library J 95: 3958-61 N 15 '70

LIBRARIES and the Cambodian-Vietnamese conflict. See Libraries and the Vietnamese war

LIBRARIES and the environmental movement
Earth day. K. Nyren. Library J 95:1415 Ap 15 '70
Editor's choice; more abandon: Earth day push. G. R. Shields. il Am Lib 1:539 Je '70
Libraries, environment, and earth day. il Wilson Lib Bul 44:808-9 Ap '70
New OE bureau: BLET for library programs. Library J 95:1266-7 Ap 1 '70
Of note; suggestions and plans for environmental day. Am Lib 1:201 Mr '70

LIBRARIES and the physically handicapped. See Libraries—Services to physically handicapped

LIBRARIES and the public. See Libraries—Public relations

LIBRARIES and the Vietnamese war
Massacre and invasion: the library reaction. Library J 95:2047-8 Je 1 '70; Discussion. 95:2397-8 Jl '70
New York library assn. bans Vietnam statement; reply. W. M. Forman. Library J 95:607 F 15 '70
Of note: results of troops into Cambodia and deaths at Kent state university. Am Lib 1: 633 Jl '70

LIBRARIES and unemployment. See Libraries and social and economic problems

LIBRARIES and war
Recorded knowledge: a war casualty; library devastation during the Nigerian civil war. B. U. Nwafor. il por Library J 96:42-5 Ja 1 '71
    See also
Libraries and the Vietnamese war

LIBRARY administration
Administering our state library agencies. G. DuFrane. Am Lib 1:23-6 Ja '70
Administration experiment tried in Elyria, Ohio. Library J 95:1430 Ap 15 '70

LIBRARY administration—*Continued*
Comfortable pullman: administrative creativity on the siding. D. Sager. il Am Lib 1:587-92 Je '70
Community control of the libraries: a philosophical position; excerpt from A study of library services for the disadvantaged in Buffalo, Rochester, and Syracuse. Am Lib 1:610-11 Je '70
Fear of real costs: some financial aspects of the PLA systems study. R. Rohlf. Am Lib 1:242-4 Mr '70
On the development of libraries and information centers. G. Salton. bibliog il por Library J 95:3433-42 O 15 '70
Orbital organization; Vigo County public library, Terre Haute, Ind. E. N. Howard. il por Library J 95:1712-15 My 1 '70
Organizational problems in library cooperation. T. L. Minder. il por Library J 95:3448-50 O 15 '70
Overdue; who speaks for silence? R. D. Kempner. il por Wilson Lib Bul 44:658-9 F '70
Performance ratings and librarians rights. D. Peele. il Am Lib 1:595-600 Je '70; Discussion. 1:740-2 S '70
See also
College library administration
Librarians—Selection and appointment
Libraries—Trustees, boards, committees, etc.
School libraries—Supervisors and supervision

Anecdotes, facetiae, satire, etc.
Personnel work at Irvine: astrology and a chaplain; reprint. Library J 95:3233-4 O 1 '70

LIBRARY administration division of ALA. See American library association—Library administration division

LIBRARY advertising. See Library publicity

LIBRARY and information science scholarship today project
Birth of LIST; seminar at the University of Maryland School of library and information services. P. Wasserman and E. Daniel. bibliog il pors Library J 95:3879-83 N 15 '70

LIBRARY architecture
Akron gets beautiful new library in downtown area. il Library J 95:967+ Mr 15 '70
Architectural issue (cont) il Library J 95: 4099-147 D 1 '70
Articulated library; Yeshiva university library. il Arch Forum 133:56-9 N '70
Barred from the library; architectural barriers to use by the physically handicapped. C. M. Greco. bibliog il Am Lib 1:908-10 O '70
Bricks and mortar. See occasional issues of Library journal
Central library, Niagara Falls, N.Y. il Arch Rec 148:89-91, 94 N '70
Clark's Goddard library: a mod solution. T. Barron. il Library J 95:2412-13 Jl '70
Coral Gables library keeps Spanish flavor. il Library J 95:446+ F 1 '70
Counterfeit service: creating slum libraries in slums. E. J. Gaines. Library J 95: 4233 D 15 '70
Fifth library buildings awards. il Am Lib 1: 578-83 Je '70
Five-story bonanza for Billings. S. Hake. il Library J 95:620+ F 15 '70
New Altoona library features color, space and comfort. Library J 95:843 Mr 1 '70
North Texas solution: installment building. il Library J 95:3235-6 O 1 '70
Northside residents achieve success in Evansville. il Library J 95:844 Mr 1 '70
Northwestern university library by Walter Netsch of SOM. il Arch Rec 148:89-96 Jl '70
Northwestern's new library. G. R. Shields. il Am Lib 1:443-5 My '70
Sarah Lawrence library-instructional center. R. Jensen. il Arch Rec 147:143-6 F '70
Southern Utah state college adds a jewel. il Library J 95:849-50 Mr 1 '70
Three consultants, one county: Clayton County, Ga. W. Murphy. il Library J 95: 2068+ Je 1 '70
Trouble-free library planning and construction. M. Tatum. il Am Lib 1:878-83 O '70

LIBRARY assistants
See also
Library staffs

Education
Canadian workshop on library technicians; sponsored by the Canadian library association. R. C. Ellsworth. Wilson Lib Bul 45:9+ S '70
Dawning of the age of librarius; third annual Student leadership conference for library aides. il Wilson Lib Bul 45:130-2 O '70
Library assistants: letter to the editor. M. A. Crush. Library J 95:3701-2 N 1 '70

Library education and manpower; ALA policy proposal. Am Lib 1:341-4 Ap '70; Reply. G. M. Casey. 1:706-9 Jl '70

Wages and hours
Minimum wages for pages denied in N.Y. Library J 95:614 F 15 '70

LIBRARY associations
Dues problem; survey of state library associations and the District of Columbia. K. M. Cottam. il Am Lib 1:574-5 Je '70
See also names of library associations, e.g. Catholic library association

LIBRARY bill of rights
ALA testimony presented to Commission on obscenity and pornography; statement, May 4, 1970. J. F. Krug. Am Lib 1:653-5 Jl '70
Intellectual freedom: statement of ALA Intellectual freedom committee to Activities committee on new directions for ALA. J. F. Krug and J. A. Harvey. Am Lib 1:533-5 Je '70
Proceedings and findings; J. Bodger and Library bill of rights; ALA report. E. Castagna and others. bibliog Am Lib 1:694-704 Jl '70

LIBRARY boards. See Libraries—Trustees, boards, committees, etc.

LIBRARY budgets. See Libraries—Finance

LIBRARY building consultants. See Library consultants

LIBRARY buildings. See Library architecture

LIBRARY catalogs. See Catalogs, Library

LIBRARY censorship. See Libraries—Censorship

LIBRARY classification. See Classification

LIBRARY conferences
Calendar. See issues of Library journal
Can library and education groups meet jointly? report. M. V. Gaver. Wilson Lib Bul 44:921-2 My '70
Meetings (title varies) See issues of Wilson library bulletin
No library is an island: networks conference in Va; Airlie house, facility for meeting. A. Plotnik. il Wilson Lib Bul 45:225+ N '70
Taking inner-city at the U. of Illinois. A. Plotnik. il Wilson Lib Bul 44:910-11 My '70
Two-day Maryland meet weighs urban libraries. P. Schuman. Library J 95:438+ F 1 '70

LIBRARY consultants
Three consultants, one county: Clayton County, Ga. W. Murphy. il Library J 95: 2068+ Je 1 '70
Trouble-free library planning and construction. M. Tatum. il Am Lib 1:878-83 O '70

LIBRARY cooperation
Above politics: how U.S. and Japanese librarians cleared the way for true professional exchange. Y. Suzuki. bibliog il Wilson Lib Bul 44:1054-9 Je '70
California librarians debate new association. Library J 95:4085 D 1 '70
California model. J. Berry. Library J 95:4081 D 1 '70
Centralized processing: diversified; Rhode Island. H. G. Kurtz. il por Library J 95: 1807-12 My 15 '70
Cooperation moves ahead in the Southwest. S. J. Kee. il por Library J 95:1294-7 Ap 1 '70
Coordinating library services within the community. J. Legg. Am Lib 1:457-63 My '70
Library service for commuting students. by M. A. Gocek. Review
Am Lib 1:713-14 Jl '70. J. A. McCrossan
Library system trustee. S. Whitney. bibliog por Library J 95:636-9 F 15 '70
New directions; excerpts from CLA report, ed. by G. R. Shields. P. Ackerman and others. Am Lib 1:1021-2 D '70
On the development of libraries and information centers. G. Salton. bibliog il por Library J 95:3433-42 O 15 '70
Organizational problems in library cooperation. T. L. Minder. il por Library J 95: 3448-50 O 15 '70
See also
Interlibrary communication

LIBRARY discipline. See Library administration

LIBRARY education. See Library schools and education

LIBRARY education division. See American library association—Library education division

LIBRARY employees. See Library assistants; Library staffs

LIBRARY equipment. See Library furniture and equipment

LIBRARY exhibits
Editor's choice; libraries and the national teach-in on pollution. G. R. Shields. Am Lib 1:19 Ja '70
Library display. See issues of Wilson library bulletin

LIBRARY extension
Consider the confined; methods of reaching in; Los Angeles public library program. J. G. Sutton. il Wilson Lib Bul 45:485-9 Ja '71
Extending public library services to the homebound. J. A. McCrossan. Am Lib 1: 485-90 My '70
See also
Bookmobiles

LIBRARY finance. See Libraries—Finance

LIBRARY furniture and equipment
Buyer's guide; ed. by T. W. McConkey. See (usually) first issue of each month of Library journal
Multimedia shelving. R. Muller. Library J 95:750 F 15 '70
Purchasing guide 1970; ed. by T. W. McConkey. Library J 95:1307+ Ap 1 '70

LIBRARY institutes and workshops
Best laid plan: OLDP, ALSO, and JSHP: with excerpts from the Ohio library development plan. R. H. Donahugh. Am Lib 1:973-7 N '70
Federally-supported institutes. Am Lib 1:315-17 Ap '70
Librarianship institutes announced for 1970-71; school, children's and young adult instruction. Library J 95:1153-4 Mr 15 '70
Meetings (title varies) See issues of Wilson library bulletin
1970-71 HEA institutes for training announced. Library J 95:1268 Ap 1 '70

LIBRARY instruction. See Libraries—Instruction in use

LIBRARY journal
Librarians rake LJ for Detroit boner. Library J 95:2411-12 Jl '70
What's new in LJ. J. Berry. Library J 96:9 Ja 1 '71

LIBRARY laws and legislation
Renewed hope for LSCA extension. il Am Lib 1:961-2 N '70
Senate passes extension of Library services act. S. Wagner. Pub W 198:38+ O 5 '70
See also
United States—National commission on libraries and information services

LIBRARY loans. See Libraries—Circulation, loans, etc.

LIBRARY management. See Library administration

LIBRARY of Congress. See United States—Library of Congress

LIBRARY of Congress catalog cards. See Catalog cards

LIBRARY of presidential papers. See New York (city)—Libraries

LIBRARY pages. See Library assistants

LIBRARY patrons. See Libraries and readers

LIBRARY periodicals. See Library science—Periodicals

LIBRARY personnel. See Librarians; Library staffs

LIBRARY programs, Division of. See United States—Education, Office of—Libraries and educational technology, Bureau of—Library programs, Division of

LIBRARY publicity
Editor's choice; libraries and the national teach-in on pollution. G. R. Shields. Am Lib 1:19 Ja '70
Library roundup in pictures: mini-revolution in the general image. il Wilson Lib Bul 44: 596-7 F '70
See also
National library week

Anecdotes, facetiae, satire, etc.
Hooper and the very rich. K. Nyren. Library J 95:2745 S 1 '70

LIBRARY reading rooms. See Libraries—Reading rooms

LIBRARY research. See Library science—Research

LIBRARY resources, inc.
Microbooks: a new library medium? il Pub W 198:48-50 N 9 '70

LIBRARY revenue. See Libraries—Finance

LIBRARY schools and education
Accreditation of programs of education for librarianship; ALA report. bibliog Am Lib 1:62-5 Ja '70
Back to the baccalaureate! question of a master's degree for library work. R. C. Thompson; R. D. Aldrich. Library J 95:430-1 F 1 '70

Continuing education in librarianship: Ideas for action. E. W. Stone. Am Lib 1:543-51 Je '70; Reply. V. L. Parker. 1:739-40 S '70
Course descriptions in library science: a report on a survey. B. Myatt. Am Lib 1:865-7 O '70
Educating the academic librarian. E. J. Josey and F. M. Blake. bibliog il pors Library J 95:125-30 Ja 15 '70
Graduate library school programs accredited by the American library association. il Am Lib 1:997-9 N '70
Library education and the public library. G. Garrison. por Library J 95:2763-7 S 1 '70; Discussion. 95:3855, 4079; 96:5 N 15-D 1 '70, Ja 1 '71
Library education, relevance to the future; letter to the editor. M. Boaz. bibliog Am Lib 1:937-8 N '70
Meetings (title varies) See issues of Wilson library bulletin
Minority L.S. grads still a trickle. Library J 95:616-17 F 15 '70
Part of the solution? new ideas of library school students. J. Berry. Library J 95:2205 Je 15 '70
Practical usefulness; letter to the editor. K. Parke. Am Lib 1:323-4 Ap '70
Professional adaptation: library education mandate. P. Wasserman. il por Library J 95:1281-8 Ap 1 '70
Proofs and prescriptions; job crisis. C. Hendershott. il por Library J 95:3735-8 N 1 '70
Taking the full ride; routes to continuing education. L. E. Bone and F. R. Hartz. bibliog il pors Library J 95:3244-6 O 1 '70
See also
Library assistants—Education
Library institutes and workshops
also names of library schools, e.g. Ohio, Kent state university—School of library science

Canada
Canadian workshop on library technicians; sponsored by the Canadian library association. R. C. Ellsworth. Wilson Lib Bul 45:9+ S '70

Denmark
What Americans can learn from the Danes. F. J. Mosher; reply. P. Birkelund. Wilson Lib Bul 44:1011+ Je '70

LIBRARY science
See also
Cataloging
Librarianship

Bibliography
Professional reading. See issues of Library journal
Publications checklist. Am Lib 1:88-91, 188-90, 298-9, 397-400, 494-7, 620-1, 715-18, 815-16, 912-13, 1001-2, 1089-91 Ja-D '70

Periodicals
Simple and plain; letter to the editor. H. Bliss. Am Lib 1:742-3 S '70
See also
ALA bulletin
American libraries (periodical)
Wilson library bulletin

Anecdotes, facetiae, satire, etc.
Library germule. il Wilson Lib Bul 44:839-47 Ap '70

Research
Birth of LIST; seminar at the University of Maryland School of library and information services. P. Wasserman and E. Daniel. bibliog il pors Library J 95:3879-83 N 15 '70
Library research: using what we have. J. G. Fetros. bibliog il Am Lib 1:360-4 Ap '70

Study and teaching
See Library schools and education

LIBRARY service to the socially handicapped. See Libraries—Services to socially handicapped

LIBRARY services and construction act. See Library laws and legislation

LIBRARY shelving. See Library furniture and equipment

LIBRARY shelving systems. See Libraries—Shelving systems

LIBRARY staffs
ALA: a professional or a library association. C. M. Weisenberg. Am Lib 1:1060-1 D '70
See also
Librarians unions

LIBRARY standards. See Libraries—Standards; School libraries—Standards

LIBRARY statistics. See Libraries—Statistics

LIBRARY surveys
Course descriptions in library science: a report on a survey. B. Myatt. Am Lib 1:865-7 O '70
Dues problem; survey of state library associations and the District of Columbia. K. M. Cottam. il Am Lib 1:574-5 Je '70
Library manpower in the Detroit metropolitan region. G. Casey. il Am Lib 1:787-9 S '70
New interest in library-community study. J. A. McCrossan. Am Lib 1:618 Je '70
Northeast city libraries: some feasting, some famine. Library J 95:3226-8 O 1 '70
Placements & salaries: the 1969 plateau. C. J. Frarey. il por Library J 95:2099-103 Je 1 '70
Sunday: Mass. letter to the editor. L.-J. Roberts. Library J 95:2739-40+ S 1 '70
See also
Libraries—Standards
School library surveys

LIBRARY technology program. See American library association—Library technology program

LIBRARY thefts
Book bugging: a possible answer to library thefts? M. Mueller. Science 167:361-2 Ja 23 '70

LIBRARY trustees. See Libraries—Trustees, boards, committees, etc.

LIBRARY week. See National library week

LIBRARY workers. See Librarians; Library assistants

LIBRARY workshops. See Library institutes and workshops

La LIBRERIA, New York. See Booksellers and bookselling—New York (state)

LIBRETTISTS
See also
Schikaneder, E.
Sondheim, S.

LIBRETTO
Belle epoque; between the 1880's and World war I. H. Peyre. il Opera N 35:8-13 D 12 '70
How to read a libretto. P. J. Smith. il Opera N 34:13-15 Mr 7 '70
Long, long road; Plough and the stars. E. Siegmeister. il por Opera N 34:26-9 Mr 14 '70
Mailer's opera. C. Matz. il por Opera N 34:14-16 F 21 '70

LIBYA
See also
Aeronautics, Military—Libya
Arab federation (proposed)
Italians in Libya
Petroleum industry and trade—Libya
Purchasing, Military—Libya
Sports—Libya
Defenses
Mirage sales key to French Africa policy. E. H. Kolcum. Aviation W 92:20-1 Ap 6 '70
Economic relations
France
See France—Economic relations—Libya
Nationalism
Celebrating xenophobia. il Time 96:20 S 7 '70
Libya's lot: half a loaf. M. J. Kubic. por Newsweek 76:38-9 S 7 '70
Politics and government
Libya: oasis of oil. O. Martinez. Nation 210:744-7 Je 22 '70
Political jack-in-the-box. por Time 97:21 Ja 11 '71
Reports: Libya. D. Kiker. Atlan 225:30+ Je '70

LICE
See also
Plant lice

LICENSE agreements, international. See International licence agreements

LICENSES
How to end giveaways; argument for selling limited rights by auction. M. Friedman. Newsweek 75:84 F 23 '70
Licensing: for cars and babies. B. M. Russett. Bul Atom Sci 26:15-19 N '70
Should mechanics have to have a license? M. Schultz. il Pop Mech 135:73-5 Ja '71

LICHENS
In a mini-world of lichens. N. Ames. il Nat Wildlife 8:48-9 Ap '70
Lichens, mirror to the universe; with photographs by B. Ratcliffe. D. McKinley. Audubon 72:44-55 N '70

LICHT, Kenneth F.
School liability and safety education. Ed Digest 36:22-4 N '70

LICHTENSTEIN, Grace
Now the poor can get divorced, too. il pors N Y Times Mag p30-1+ Ap 26 '70

LICHTENSTEIN, Harvey
Academy. New Yorker 46:44 N 14 '70 *

LICHTENSTEIN, Jack
In search of the impossible dream. Ed Digest 35:34-5 My '70

LICHTHEIM, George
Imperialism. bibliog Commentary 49:42-75 Ap; 33-58 My '70

LICKO, Pavel
Attack on Solzhenitsyn. por Time 96:18 D 28 '70 *

LIDSTER, Douglas M.
New facts on dog nutrition. il Bet Hom & Gard 48:4+ Ap '70
Tooth care for your dog. il Bet Hom & Gard 48:120+ My '70
When your dog has puppies. il Bet Hom & Gard 48:20+ Mr '70
—See Gregg, D. L. jt. auth.

LIEBER, Charles S. and DeCarli, L. M.
Reduced nicotinamide-adenine dinucleotide phosphate oxidase: activity enhanced by ethanol consumption. bibliog il Science 170:78-80 O 2 '70

LIEBER, Harvey
Water pollution. Cur Hist 59:23-30 Jl '70

LIEBERMAN, E. James
Parent and child. il N Y Times Mag p86+ Mr 8 '70

LIEBERMAN, Laurence
Lobsters in the brain coral; poem. Poetry 117:81-3 N '70
Poet-critics and scholar-critics. Poetry 115:346-52 F '70

LIEBERMANN, Rolf
Rolf Liebermann; interview. R. Liebermann. New Yorker 46:21-2 Ag 29 '70
about
Artist life. D. J. Soria. il por Hi Fi 20:MA4-6 O '70 *

LIEBERSTEIN, Stanley H.
Computer and the law. il Duns 95:58-60 Mr '70

LIEBES, Dorothy
Dorothy Liebes. N. Znamierowski. il por Craft Horiz 30:34-41+ Ag '70 *

LIEBFRAUMILCH. See Wine

LIEBMAN, Arthur
Mexican justice. New Repub 162:12-13 Ap 25 '70

LIEBMAN, Paul A. See Laties, A. M. jt. auth.

LIEBOW, Elliot
No man can live with the terrible knowledge that he is not needed. il N Y Times Mag p28-9+ Ap 5 '70

LIEBSON, Malvina
Businessmen's expectations. il Duns 95:105 Je; 96:99 S; 76 D '70

LIECHTENSTEIN
Liechtenstein. H. D. Frame. il Travel 134:48-9+ S '70

LIEDER, Ruth
Sporting look (cont) il Sports Illus 32:40-3 Ap 20; 33:52-5 O 5 '70

LIENER, Martin
Seven step program helps to integrate camp. il Camp Mag 42:14-15 S '70

LIES. See Lying

LIETAER, Bernard A.
Managing risks in foreign exchange. il Harvard Bsns R 48:127-38 Mr '70
Prepare your company for inflation. il Harvard Bsns R 48:113-25 S '70

LIFE
Right to live. J. R. Quinn. America 123:56-7 Ag 8 '70
See also
Conduct of life
Death

LIFE (biology)
Biosphere; symposium. il Sci Am 223:44-74+ bibliog(p262-6) S '70
Search for viable organisms in a lunar sample. V. I. Oyama and others. bibliog il Science 167:773-5 Ja 30 '70
Origin
Amateur scientist; experiments in generating the constituents of living matter from inorganic substances. C. Fromer. il Sci Am 222:130-4+ Ja '70
Clues to creation. Newsweek 76:56 Jl 20 '70
Step toward life; catalyst of genesis. il Time 95:52 My 11 '70
Test tubes and scripture. F. Stockwell. Chr Cent 87:528-31 Ap 29 '70

LIFE (periodical)
Announcing Life's new photographic contest. R. Graves. Life 68:3 Ap 3 '70
Art direction enters new age as Life begins layout by machine. il Pub W 198:28-9 Jl 6 '70
First world publication of a unique historical document: Khrushchev remembers. il Life 69:30-1 N 27 '70
Great Khrushchev mystery. il pors Newsweek 76:36+ N 30 '70
Introducing a new staffer who's really plugged in; computerized layout machine. R. Graves. il Life 69:3 Ag 14 '70
Jones project; preparation of reminiscences of N. Khrushchev for publication. R. Graves. il pors Life 69:3 N 27 '70
Khrushchev: the illusions of war; story behind the story. il pors Time 96:40+ D 7 '70
Life cuts back. Newsweek 76:130 O 12 '70
Life's sixties. Nat R 22:16-17 Ja 13 '70
Old friend leaves our staff. R. Graves. por Life 68:3 Je 5 '70
Photography contest; prizewinning pictures. il Life 69:5-8+ D 25 '70
Revolution in layout. J. Tebbel. il Sat R 53:93-4 S 12 '70
Situation report on the biggest photo contest ever. R. Graves. il Life 69:1 O 23 '70
Some of our reporters who covered Women's lib. R. Graves. il Life 69:2A S 4 '70
Why a Life cover seldom makes everybody happy. R. Graves. il Life 69:3 N 20 '70

Covers
See Periodical covers
LIFE, Duration of. See Longevity
LIFE and times of Sigmund Freud; drama. See Wilson, R.
LIFE expectancy. See Longevity
LIFE extension. See Longevity
LIFE insurance. See Insurance, Life
LIFE insurance companies. See Insurance companies
LIFE on other planets
NASA studies planetary habitation methods. Aviation W 93:62-3 N 30 '70
Persons, by R. Puccetti. Review
Commonweal 91:592-4 F 27 '70. B. Murchland
Space: a barrier to the species. J. P. Wiley, jr. il Natur Hist 79:70-3 Ja '70
LIFE saving. See rescue work
LIFE saving equipment
Land-and-water emergency rescue; Lansing, Mich, police department. il Am City 85:115-16 S '70
See also
Fire escapes, Portable
First aid in illness and injury
LIFE span. See Longevity
LIFE support systems (space environment)
Handling spacecraft waste. Space World G-4-76:44 Ap '70
LIFE support systems (submarine environment)
Controlling breathing atmospheres. N. W. Rakestraw. il Chem 43:18-23 O '70
LIFSCHUTZ, Joseph E.
Privacy and the psychiatrist. por Time 95:60+ Ap 27 '70 *
LIFTING. See Weight lifting
LIFTING bodies. See Space vehicles—Landing systems
LIFTON, Betty Jean
On children's literature: a runcible symposium. il Horn Bk 46:255-63 Je '70
LIFTON, Robert Jay
False God; excerpt from Boundaries: psychological man in revolution. il Atlan 226:104-6+ O '70
Scars of Vietnam. Commonweal 91:554-6 F 20 '70
Student of death's symbols. il por Newsweek 75:82 Ap 6 '70 *
Why civilians are war victims in Vietnam; interview. il Sci Digest 67:40-5 My '70
LIFTS. See Hoisting machinery
LIGHT
Monomolecular layers and light. K. H. Drezhage. il Sci Am 222:108-19 Mr '70
See also
Fluorescence
Interference (light)
Luminescence
Photochemistry
Photochromic substances
Photography—Light
Polarization (light)
Raman effect

Physiological effects
Adenosine 3',5'-monophosphate in rat pineal gland: increase induced by light. M. S. Ebadi and others. bibliog il Science 170:188-90 O 9 '70
More light, less jaundice. il Sci Digest 67:67-8 Mr '70
See also
Photoperiodism

Scattering
Spectra of backscattered light from the sea obtained from aircraft as a measure of chlorophyll concentration. G. L. Clarke and others. bibliog il Science 167:1119-21 F 20 '70

Transmission thru water
Chopped pulses; underwater laser optical system. Sci Am 223:41 D '70
LIGHT, Colored
Alison has her own light show. il Sunset 144:110-11 F '70
See also
Christmas tree lights
LIGHT airplanes. See Airplanes, Light
LIGHT and sound. See Sound and light programs
LIGHT bulbs. See Electric lamps
LIGHT bulbs in art. See Electric lamps in art
LIGHT communication systems
Assemble an LED communicator, the opticom. F. M. Mims, 3d and H. E. Roberts. il Pop Electr 33:45-50+ N '70
Laser beam communicator. C. H. Knowles. il Pop Electr 32:27-35+ My '70
Laser-beam communicator; navy ship-to-ship communications system. J. Levine. il Electr World 84:46-8 N '70
Laser link uses stabilized binoculars; experimental optical communicator. B. M. Elson. il Aviation W 92:42-3 Je 29 '70
Optical communications research progress. S. E. Miller. bibliog il Science 170:685-95 N 13 '70
Wideband laser link test planned. B. M. Elson. il Aviation W 92:50-2 Je 1 '70
LIGHT control films. See Films
LIGHT displays. See Information display systems; Stroboscopic lighting
LIGHT-emitting diodes. See Diodes
LIGHT filters
Filters: they only take away. D. B. Eisendrath. il Pop Phot 66:18+ My '70
Shoot glareless pictures with polarized light. J. D. Griffith. il Pop Mech 133:128-9 Ja '70
LIGHT in art
Sparkling decorations of light. il House & Gard 138:60-7 D '70
See also
Kinetic light art
LIGHT intensification. See Image intensifiers
LIGHT meters. See Exposure meters
LIGHT modulators. See Modulators
LIGHT projection
Alison has her own light show. il Sunset 144:110-11 F '70
Lights add new life to Lincoln memorial; new lighting system with concealed floodlights. il Am City 85:112+ Jl '70
LIGHTED make-up mirrors. See Mirrors
LIGHTING
See also
Electric lighting
Lamps
Light projection
Opera—Stage lighting
Stroboscopic lighting
also subhead Lighting under various subjects, e.g. Photography—Lighting
LIGHTING, Architectural and decorative
Bright ideas in lighting. M. Kraft. il Good H 172:96-101 Ja '71
Engineers develop lighting design from model tests. il Arch Rec 147:147-52 F '70
How to turn your house on with lighting. W. Baldwin. House & Gard 137:12-13 Ja '70
Lighting dramatizes Hawaii's royal palace. il Am City 85:92 Ag '70
LIGHTING, Outdoor
For nighttime beauty, illuminate! R. Capotosto. il Mech Illus 66:90-2+ Je '70
How to install a yard lamp. il Mech Illus 66:132-3 Mr '70
Lights that match the elegance of a civic center; Amarillo, Tex. T. Abrahamson. il Am City 85:128+ Ap '70

LIGHTING, Outdoor—*Continued*
Outdoor lighting. See issues of American city
See also
Christmas decorations, Outdoor
Light projection
also subhead Lighting under various subjects, e.g. Race tracks—Lighting
also subhead Lighting under names of cities, e.g. Boston—Lighting

Control
See Electric lighting—Control
LIGHTING fixtures
High mounted lights in; Hennepin County, Minn. il Am City 85:114 Jl '70
Lights up. il Redbook 134:76-9+ F '70
See also
Street lighting fixtures
LIGHTING in house decoration. See Lighting, Architectural and decorative
LIGHTNER, Otto C.
Americana page; reprint. por Hobbies 75:100+ Jl '70 *
Americana page; with excerpts from August 1947 article. il(p 1) por Hobbies 75:100-1 Ag '70 *
LIGHTNER museum of hobbies, St Augustine, Fla.
Americana page; with excerpts from August 1947 article. il(p 1) por Hobbies 75:100-1 Ag '70
LIGHTNING
Facts about thunder and lightning. il Good H 170:173 My '70
Lightning-warning system for NASA launches. Space World G-6-78:40 Je '70
See also
Aviation—Lightning hazards
Electricity, Injuries from
Thunderstorms
LIGHTNING protection
Automatic lightning protection; antenna system. H. Phillips. il Pop Electr 33:61-4 Jl '70
Could lightning strike your boat? J. Martenhoff. il Pop Mech 134:100-3+ Jl '70
LIGNIN
Polymeric structure of spruce lignin. H. I. Bolker and H. S. Brenner. bibliog il Science 170:173-6 O 9 '70
LIKENS, Gene E. See Bormann, F. H. jt. auth.
LIKES and dislikes
See also
Musical preferences
LILAC garden; ballet. See Ballets—Criticisms
LILIES
All about lilies. V. Howie. il Home Gard 57:20-7 Ag '70
Choose your lilies now. il Bet Hom & Gard 48:84 Ag '70
Formosanum, the late-late lily. F. Frederick. il House B 112:30 F '70
Propagating liliums from scales. A. V. Pike. il Horticulture 48:28-9 Ap '70
Three seasons of lilies. G. H. Pride. il Horticulture 48:30-3+ Mr '70
See also
Day lilies
Tiger lilies
LILLEY, E. M. See Stephens, D. R. jt. auth.
LILLQUIST, Kenneth
Rosemount; Realization; Outside mattoon; Macoupin County; poems. Poetry 115:228-31 Ja '70
LILLY, Doris
Day at the office with Cary Grant. por Ladies Home J 87:142-3 N '70
Jackie's fabulous Greek; excerpts from Those fabulous Greeks. pors Look 34:30-6+ Je 30 '70
LILLY, Eli, and company
Duel over Elizabeth Arden. il Bsns W p48 O 17 '70
Tweedle dee. Forbes 105:65-6 Mr 1 '70
LILLY endowment, inc.
Ecology comes to camp. J. J. Kirk. por Camp Mag 42:4 N '70
LILY pools. See Garden pools
LIMA, Alceu Amoroso
Brazil's revolution six years later. il America 122:646-9 Je 20 '70
LIMA, Peru
History
Lima through British eyes; the early 1800's. S. S. Triflo. bibliog il Américas 22:27-34 Je '70
LIMBACHER, James L.
On the record: Words. See issues of Library journal
Recordings. See second issue of each month of Library journal

LIMBURG, A. W.
Flotation tests. il Motor B 125:172-5 Ap '70
LIME
See also
Plants, Effect of calcium on
LIMERICKS
There was a young lady. . . Good H 170:230 Mr '70
LIMITATION of armaments. See Disarmament
LIMITATION of population. See Birth control
LIMITED partnership
Investing with tax dollars. il Bsns W p66+ Ja 17 '70
LIMITERS, Electric current. See Electric current limiters
LIMITS of national jurisdiction. See United Nations—Committee on the peaceful uses of the seabed and the ocean floor
LIMNOLOGY
Alkalinity and formation of zeolites in saline alkaline lakes. R. H. Mariner and R. C. Surdam. bibliog il Science 170:977-80 N 27 '70
Lakes which produce too much. R. T. Oglesby. il Cons 24:18-21 Je '70
Phosphorus, nitrogen, and algae in Lake Washington after diversion of sewage. W. T. Edmondson. bibliog il Science 169:690-1 Ag 14 '70
Water chemistry and lake productivity. C. L. Schofield. il Cons 24:9-15+ Ap '70
LIMON, Jose, dance company. See Dance companies
LIMULUS. See King crabs
LINCK, Norman
Educational media and independent study. Ed Digest 35:29-31 Ap '70
LINCOLN, Abraham
Abraham Lincoln's hardest decision. T. Fleming. por Read Digest 96:94-9 F '70 *
Modern visual concepts create moving Lincoln biography. M. R. Kraner. il Pub W 197:48-50 My 4 '70 *
See also
Lincoln memorial, Washington, D.C.

Assassination
Guns of the Lincoln murder. C. Worman. il Hobbies 75:158 My '70 *
Lights are up at Ford's theatre. L. Aikman. il Nat Geog 137:392-401 Mr '70 *

Bibliography
Lincolniana in 1969; related Civil war activities. B. E. Wheeler. il Hobbies 74:116-19 F '70 *

Statues, portraits, etc.
Lincoln: a picture story of his life, by S. Lorant. Review
Sat R il por 53:25-7+ F 14 '70. M. R. Weiss *
LINCOLN, Cecil Eric. See Lincoln, Charles Eric, jt. auth.
LINCOLN, Charles Eric, and Lincoln, C. E.
Voices of Fisk '70. il N Y Times Mag p30-1+ Je 7 '70
LINCOLN, George A.
Oil policy committee discontinues consideration of tariff system; text of letter, August 13, 1970. Dept State Bul 63:360-1 S 28 '70
LINCOLN, Marshall
How to use an FM mike for remote tape recordings. il Pop Sci 197:89+ Ag '70
LINCOLN, Mary (Todd)
Black woman's view of Mary Todd Lincoln; excerpts from Behind the scenes. E. Keckley. il pors Ebony 25:98-100+ Mr '70 *
LINCOLN, Nancy
Very special problem. J. Frook. il pors Life 69:54-8+ N 13 '70 *
LINCOLN, Stoddard
Judgment on Solomon. il Am Rec G 37:96-8+ O '70
LINCOLN, Tom
Very special problem. J. Frook. il pors Life 69:54-8+ N 13 '70 *
LINCOLN, Neb.
Mobile homes granted residential zoning. Am City 85:34 S '70

Lighting
Lighting keeps downtown the focal point. il Am City 85:90 Ag '70

Public buildings
Two level government. one building. L. Scherer. il Am City 85:111 O '70

Streets
Businessmen transform an alley to a walkway. il Am City 85:40 Ap '70
LINCOLN back country-Scapegoat Mountain wilderness (proposed) See Wilderness areas —Montana

LINCOLN cathedral model. See Architectural models
LINCOLN Center festival. See Music festivals—New York (state)
LINCOLN Center for the performing arts, New York
Lincoln Center; an all-purpose guide. il Holiday 47:82-3 F '70

Juilliard school
Juilliard school. il Arch Rec 147:121-30 Ja '70
Lincoln Center's great little opera theater; Stravinsky's The rake's progress. I. Kolodin. Sat R 53:48 My 9 '70
Mercadante's Giuramento at the Juilliard theater. I. Kolodin. Sat R 53:35 My 30 '70
Music; Stravinsky's Rake's progress. D. Hamilton. Nation 210:570-1 My 11 '70
Music to my ears; concert performance of Beethoven's Fidelio. I. Kolodin. Sat R 53:55 Ja 31 '70
Musical events: Mercadante's Il giuramento, by Juilliard American opera center. W. Sargeant. New Yorker 46:76 My 23 '70
Musical events: out of the mouths of babes; concert performance of Fidelio, at Philharmonic Hall, Leonard Bernstein conducting with Juilliard students participating. W. Sargeant. New Yorker 45:79 Ja 24 '70
Musical events; Stravinsky's The rake's progress. W. Sargeant. New Yorker 46:118+ My 2 '70
Report:
Rake's progress. F. Merkling. il Opera N 34:22-3 Je 13 '70
Young performers face young listeners. P. Hart. il Hi Fi 20:secII 15-17 Jl '70
LINCOLN Center repertory theater company
Synge's wake. T. E. Kalem. il Time 97:37 Ja 18 '71
LINCOLN memorial, Washington, D.C.
Lights add new life to Lincoln memorial. il Am City 85:112+ Jl '70
LINCOLN park. See Long Beach, Calif.—Parks and playgrounds
LINCOLN train museum. See Railroad museums
LIND, Jenny
Jenny Lind's 150th anniversary; concert and exhibition in London. W. P. Ware. il Hobbies 75:142-3+ O '70 *
Jenny Lind's 150th anniversary, 1820-1970. W. P. Ware. il por Hobbies 75:48-50 O '70 *
Rare glimpse of Jenny Lind. W. P. Ware. il por Hobbies 75:124+ O '70 *
LIND ISLAND. See Jenny Lind Island
LINDANE
Air of safety; lindane vapor dispensing devices. J. McCaull and M. Antell. bibliog il Environ 12:2-15+ N '70
LINDAUER, Martin
What does the bee dance say? Sci Digest 68:48 N '70 *
LINDBERG, Peter
(ed) Family money management. See issues of Better homes and gardens
LINDBERGH, Anne (Morrow)
Harmony with the life around us; adaptation of address. il por Good H 171:62-3+ Jl '70
What I learned from the sea; excerpt from Gift from the sea. il Nat Wildlife 9:24-5 D '70
LINDBERGH, Charles Augustus, 1902-
Wartime journals of Charles A. Lindbergh; excerpts. Am Scholar 39:577-613 Aut '70
Wartime journals of Charles A. Lindbergh; excerpts. il pors Am Heritage 21:32-7+ O '70

about
Adventure in honesty. J. Chamberlain. por Nat R 22:1213-14 N 17 '70 *
Flyer and the Yahoos. R. Whittemore. New Repub 163:21-3 O 3 '70 *
Lindy and the war. S. K. Oberbeck. il pors Newsweek 76:96+ S 28 '70 *
Lone Eagle's concern for the Bald Eagle. B. Goldwater. por Sat R 53:31-2+ O 3 '70 *
Old debate. W. F. Buckley, jr. Nat R 22:1017 S 22 '70 *
LINDE division. See Union carbide corporation—Linde division
LINDELL, Thomas J. and others
Specific inhibition of nuclear RNA polymerase II by α-amanitin. bibliog il Science 170:447-9 O 23 '70
LINDEMAN, Bard
Louis Russell: man with a stout heart. il pors Todays Health 48:32-4+ D '70
LINDEMAN, Jack
Flag; poem. Nation 210:312 Mr 16 '70
William James and the octopus of higher education. por Sch & Soc 98:365-7 O '70
LINDENWOOD college, St Charles, Mo.
Position paper on dormitory intervisitation; statement. J. A. Brown. Sch & Soc 98:379-81 O '70

LINDFORS, Bernth
West African literature in English in the sixties. Negro Hist Bul 33:80-1 Mr '70
LINDGREN, Raymond E.
(comp) Articles and other books received; northern Europe. See issues of American historical review
LINDLEY, Daniel A. Jr
Teaching is a science, not an art. Engl J 59:960-3 O '70
LINDMARK, Arne
Arne Lindmark: master of the watercolor scene. M. Malmstrom. il Am Artist 35:38-43+ Ja '71 *
LINDQUIST, Lynn
Just bring the groceries. il Har Yrs 10:41-3 My '70
LINDSAY, John Vliet
Conspiracy against American cities. il Redbook 135:78-9+ O '70
Notes and comment; excerpts from address, May 1970. New Yorker 46:33 My 16 '70

about
Around city hall (cont) A. Logan. New Yorker 46:101-4+ F 28; 106+ Ap 18; 104-8 Je 6; 120-2+ S 19; 126+ N 21 '70 *
Black hole of Manhattan. il Time 96:28-9 Ag 24 '70 *
Broader base now for Mayor Lindsay. il por U S News 68:9 Ja 19 '70
His honor revisited. R. C. Lee. New Repub 162:20-2 Mr 28 '70 *
John V. Lindsay: a political portrait. R. Starr. Commentary 49:25-46 F '70
John Lindsay's idealism. Nat R 22:245 Mr 10 '70 *
Letter to the mayor. J. Goldschmidt. Atlan 225:58-9 F '70
Lindsay: a political fantasy. Time 94:13 F 16 '70 *
Lindsay and the gateway to oblivion. S. Alsop. Newsweek 76:104 N 30 '70 *
Lindsay: eying the White House in '72? il por U S News 69:48 Jl 20 '70 *
Lindsay idea. New Repub 163:5-6 O 3 '70 *
Lindsay scenario. R. Scammon. il pors Newsweek 76:44-5 O 12 '70 *
Lindsay's promise, by W. Klein. Review Commentary 50:90-3 S '70. J. Zukosxy * Time il por 95:60-1 Je 29 '70 *
Politics of fear. Commonweal 93:163-4 N 13 '70 *
TRB from Washington: Lindsay and Muskie. New Repub 162:4 Je 13 '70 *
Thanks to Governor Reagan. Nation 210:324-5 Mr 23 '70 *
Why Lindsay's toughest job is hiring. il por Bsns W p51+ Je 20 '70 *
LINDSAY, Sally
(comp) Earth watch. Sat R 53:60-1 My 2; 66-7 Je 6; 46-7 Jl 4; 50-1 Ag 1; 54-5 S 5; 60-1 O 3; 70-1 N 7; 64-5 D 5 '70; 54:70-1 Ja 2 '71
LINDSAY, Seton
Beauty and the bath. See issues of House beautiful
LINDSAY, Vachel
Vachel Lindsay by A. Massa. Review Sat R 53:39-41 Je 20 '70. L. Untermeyer *
LINDSELL, Harold
COCU: a critique. Chr Today 15:3-5 O 9; 8-10+ O 23 '70
Crisis of the church. Chr Today 14:4-6 S 11 '70
Sex, SIECUS, and the schools. Chr Today 14:10-13 Ja 30 '70
LINDSEY, Richard A.
Negro intelligence and educational theory. bibliog f Clear House 45:67-71 O '70 *
LINDSLEY, Donald H. and Burnham, C. W.
Pyroxferroite: stability and X-ray crystallography of synthetic $Ca_{0.5}$ $Fe_{0.83}$ SiO_3 pyroxenoid. bibliog il Science 168:364-7 Ap 17 '70
LINDSLEY, E. F.
Recreation roundup. il Pop Sci 196:22 Ap '70
LINDSTROM, P. J. See Albert, R. D. jt. auth.
LINDSTROM, Pamela Tyler
Egg machine; with biographical sketch. il por Natur Hist 79:8, 52-5 F '70
LINDSTROM, Paul D.
Pastor Paul. il por Newsweek 76:70 Jl 13 '70 *
LINE, Les
In praise of weeds. il Am Heritage 21:102-6 O '70
World of Sally lightfoot; photographs. Audubon 72:52-5 Jl '70
LINE-of-credit. See Credit
LINE of least existence; drama. See Drexler, R.
LINEAR accelerators. See Accelerators (electrons, etc)
LINEAR integrated circuits. See Electronic circuits, Integrated

LINEAWEAVER, Marion
  Other one; poem. Nation 210:346 Mr 23 '70
LINEN, Household
  Durable-press sheets and pillow cases. il
    Consumer Rep 35:26-9 Ja '70
    See also
  Sheets
  Towels
  Washcloths
LINEN prints, Photographic. See Photography on glass, metal, pottery, etc.
LINERS. See Ocean liners
LING, James Joseph
  Conglomerates will come back; interview. pors
    Forbes 107:111-12 Ja 1 '71
              about
  Battered Ling tries a comeback. por Bsns W
    p23-4 D 5 '70 *
  Creditor's grip on Ling and LTV. Bsns W p54
    O 17 '70 *
  End of something. por Forbes 106:50 D 15 '70 *
  Jim Ling forced out. il por Time 95:56 Je
    1 '70 *
  Ling's new lesson in how to go public. Bsns
    W p21 Ja 9 '71 *
  Luck of Jim Ling. por Time 95:89 My 4 '70 *
  New pilot at LTV. il por Time 96:64 Jl 27 '70 *
LING, Michael F.
  Tougher SEC shuts broker Ling. Bsns W p 19
    Ja 9 '71 *
LING-Temco-Vought, inc.
  Banker replaces Ling at LTV, plans to restructure company. E. J. Bulban. Aviation
    W 92:26-7 My 25 '70
  Braniff purchase offer rejected. Aviation W
    93:28 My 11 '70
  Can Jim Ling and LTV pull through? il
    Newsweek 75:72-4 Je 1 '70
  Creditor's grip on Ling and LTV. Bsns W p54
    O 17 '70
  Fate worse than bankruptcy? Forbes 106:17-
    18 Ag 15 '70
  Jim Ling forced out. il por Time 95:56 Je 1
    '70
  Jim Ling turns to demerging. il Bsns W
    p36-7 F 28 '70
  Ling chops up the meatball. Time 95:74 F 9
    '70
  Ling sticks with steel. Time 95:75 Mr 2 '70
  Ling's shuffle. il Newsweek 75:87 Mr 23 '70
  LTV acquires a new boss. il por Bsns W p34-
    5 My 23 '70
  LTV proposing modified F-8 for export. il
    Aviation W 92:85 Ap 6 '70
  LTV recounts its many ills. por Bsns W p42
    D 19 '70
  L-T-V's lost year. Fortune 81:275 My '70
  Luck of Jim Ling. por Time 95:89 My 4 '70
  New pilot at LTV. il por Time 96:64 Jl 27 '70
  Thayer assumes leadership at LTV. Aviation
    W 93:60-1 Jl 27 '70
  Tough pilot takes the stick at LTV. por
    Bsns W p26-7 Jl 18 '70
  Vought plans civil aircraft move. E. J. Bulban.
    Aviation W 92:54-5 Je 29 '70
LINGENFELTER, Richard E. See Schubert,
  G. jt. auth.
LINGG, Ann M.
  Bearding the lion. il pors Opera N 35:12-15 S
    19 '70
  J.P. il por Opera N 34:6-7 F 7 '70
  Musical tanner. il Opera N 34:26-8 F 14 '70
  One-man band. por Opera N 35:12-13 Ja 2 '71
    (ed) See Harper, C. G.   Singers' friend
LINGUISTICS. See Language and languages
LINING of reservoirs. See Reservoirs—Lining
LINKE, Dick
  How to merchandise an actor on TV. J. Barthel. il por N Y Times Mag p 14+ O 25 '70 *
LINKLETTER, Art
  Outback. il por Travel & Camera 33:29-33+
    N '70
  We must declare war on drugs; ed. by J. N.
    Bell. il pors Good H 170:94-5+ Ap '70
  We must fight the epidemic of drug abuse!
    Read Digest 96:56-60 F '70
LINKLETTER, Diane
  We must declare war on drugs; ed. by J. N.
    Bell. A. Linkletter. il pors Good H 170:
    94-5+ Ap '70 *
The LINKS, inc.
  Links take care of business. il Ebony 25:93-
    6+ S '70
LINOWITZ, Sol Myron
  Tensions on the campus. por Sch & Soc
    98:115-16 F '70
LINSKY, Jack
  Forty-four years on the upswing. il por Fortune
    81:163 Je '70 *
LINSLEY, Richard
  War machine vs. the peace machinist. il
    Esquire 73:82-3 F '70

LINTON, Calvin D.
  What's so great about heaven? Chr Today
    15:3-5 N 20 '70
LINVILLE, Kasha
  Howald's American line. il Art N 69:52-5
    Sum '70
LION hunting
  Cliff-hanging lion. J. O'Connor. il Outdoor
    Life 145:45-7+ F '70
  Henry Poolman story. J. S. Barrett. il pors
    Outdoor Life 145:68-71+ Ap '70
  Spoiled lion. T. J. Lyon. il pors Outdoor
    Life 145:72-5+ F '70
  Two tickets for two lions; Luangwa Valley,
    Zambia. W. Page. il Field & S 75:52-3+
    D '70
LION in the lei shop; story. See Starbird, K.
LION rock, Ceylon. See Sigiriya, Ceylon
LIONDOS, Demetrius
  Greek Orthodox priest: 123 years old; interview, ed. by T. Cosmades. il Chr Today
    14:39 Je 5 '70
LIONNI, Leo
  Lionni's artichokes: an interview; ed. by R.
    Agree. bibliog il por Wilson Lib Bul 44:
    947-50 My '70
LIONS
  Cat's whiskers; system of identifying lions
    by whisker patterns. Sci Am 223:94 S '70
  Last stand of the Asiatic lion; Gir wildlife
    sanctuary. P. Tilden. il Nat Parks & Con
    Mag 44:14-18 D '70
  Lion's whiskers. il Chem 43:4 O '70
LIONS (football) See Football clubs
LIONS, Mountain. See Pumas
LIOTTA, Domingo
  Pump that works like a heart. A. S. Freese.
    il por Pop Mech 134:128-31+ N '70 *
LIP prints. See Dermatoglyphics
LIPATTI, Dinu
  Immortal Lipatti. W. F. Rickenbacker. Nat R
    22:579-80 Je 2 '70 *
LIPIDS
  Calorimetric detection of a membrane-lipid
    phase transition in living cells. J. C. Reinert
    and J. M. Steim. bibliog il Science 168:1580-2
    Je 26 '70
  Drosophila melanogaster: identity of male
    lipid in reproductive system. G. Brieger and
    F. M. Butterworth. bibliog Science 167:1262
    F 27 '70
    See also
  Lipoproteins
  Phosphatides
LIPKIN, Mack, jr
  Young scientists and the AAAS. Science 170:
    683 N 13 '70
LIPMAN, Jean
  Money for money's sake. il Art in Am 58:
    76-83 Ja '70
  Period rooms: the sixties and seventies. il
    Art in Am 58:126-9 N '70
  Tinware show at the Museum of American
    folk art. il Life 68:10 F 27 '70
  —and Pálffy, Martin
  Six villages near Salzburg. il Art in Am 58:
    102-5 Jl '70
LIPMAN, Sidney
  Capitalist stenographers. por Time 95:68 My
    4 '70 *
LIPOCHONDRODYSTROPHY
  Scheie and Hurler syndromes: apparent identity of the biochemical defect. U. Wiesmann
    and E. F. Neufeld. bibliog il Science 169:
    72-4 Jl 3 '70
LIPOPROTEINS
  Identity of very low density lipoprotein apoproteins of plasma and liver Golgi apparatus. R. W. Mahley and others. bibliog
    il Science 168:380-2 Ap 17 '70
LIPPERT, Marion
  Music to my ears. I. Kolodin. Sat R 53:40
    Mr 7 '70 *
LIPPINCOTT, Barbara B. See Lippincott, J.
  A. jt. auth.
LIPPINCOTT, James A. and Lippincott, B. B.
  Lysopine and octopine promote crown-gall
    tumor growth in vivo. bibliog il Science
    170:176-7 O 9 '70
LIPPMANN, Walter
  After the war is over. il por Newsweek 76:
    32-3 D 14 '70
  What the V.P. should learn. il por Newsweek
    77:19 Ja 11 '71
              about
  Clear, calm voice that stayed relevant. C.
    Gardner. por Bsns W p6 Jl 11 '70 *
  Early Lippmann. S. W. Little. il Sat R 53:53 Jl
    11 '70 *
  Example of Lippmann. P. Roazen. Nation
    211:184-5 S 7 '70 *
  So smart so soon. J. Reston. New Repub
    163:25-6 Ag 1 '70 *
  Young Lippmann. R. A. Gross. por Newsweek
    76:78+ Jl 20 '70 *

LIPPS, Jere H. See Valentine, J. W. jt. auth.

LIPSET, Seymour Martin
Socialism of fools: the new left calls it anti-Zionism. il N Y Times Mag p6-7+ Ja 3 '71
—and Raab, Earl
Non-generation gap. Commentary 50:35-9 Ag '70

LIPSKY, S. R. and others
Analysis of lunar material for organic compounds. Science 167:778-9 Ja 30 '70

LIPTON, Dean
Mixed-up genes & pure-bred dogs. il Sci Digest 68:41-6 D '70

LIQUEFIED natural gas
Expanding future for a clean fuel. il Bsns W p54+ S 26 '70

LIQUEFIED petroleum gas
Camper's guide to butane-propane. il Pop Mech 133:S22+ My '70
Propane power, now it's for every kind of camping. E. H. Arctander. il Pop Sci 196:58-9+ Je '70
See also
Automobile engines—Fuel
Motor fuels

LIQUEURS
Imaginative gifts from your kitchen. fruit wine cordials. il Sunset 145:129 D '70

LIQUID assets. See Liquidity (economics)

LIQUID crystals
Liquid-crystal display devices. G. H. Heilmeier. il Sci Am 222:100-6 Ap '70
Liquid crystals, light wonder of the world. L. Buckwalter. il Mech Illus 66:57-9+ Mr '70

LIQUID fire guns. See Flame throwers

LIQUID jets. See Jets

LIQUID metals. See Metals, Liquid

LIQUIDATION
Using liquidation as a strategy. Bsns W p34 O 3 '70
Watch that waistline! il Forbes 105:214+ My 15 '70

LIQUIDITY (economics)
Constant search for more capital. il Bsns W p 102-3+ D 19 '70
Does your firm face a liquidity crisis? G. N. Morris. Nations Bsns 58:59 D '70
Liquidity fears crease the paper market. il Bsns W p90+ Jl 11 '70
Liquidity problem. C. Morgello. il Newsweek 76:64 Jl 6 '70
Oversupply of stocks. il Fortune 81:171-2+ Je '70
Suddenly, business in a bind: operating cash is short. il U S News 69:33-5 Jl 6 '70
When the Fed won the liquidity battle. il Bsns W p50+ O 24 '70

LIQUIDITY, International
See also
Special drawing rights

LIQUIDONICS industries, inc.
When a mouse tries to swallow an elephant ... il Forbes 105:42+ Mr 1 '70

LIQUIDS
Slippery liquids; Toms effect. Sci Am 223:60 O '70
See also
Hydrostatics
Surface tension
Viscosity
Diffusion
See Diffusion

LIQUOR industry and trade
Distillers worry about the youngsters. il Bsns W p 126+ Mr 7 '70
See also
Glenmore distillers company
Heublein, inc.
Seagram, Joseph E. and sons
Securities
Scotch whiskey, a costly blend. A. Hershman. il Duns 95:42-3+ Ap '70
France
Bartender for the Common market; Ricard. il Bsns W p36 My 9 '70
Champagne taste stimulates mergers. il Bsns W p22 Ja 2 '71
Great Britain
Let's drink to that! Distillers co. ltd. Forbes 106:45 S 1 '70
Italy
Wife who listened; president of Davide Campari-Milano company. N. Willatt. il Duns 95:53-4+ Ja '70

LIQUOR laws and regulations
Texas
Texans take a shot at state's bar ban. Bsns W p28 N 14 '70

LIQUOR problem
See also
Alcohol and youth
Alcoholism
France
Bitter harvest. il Newsweek 76:30 D 28 '70
United States
Portrait of a problem drinker. B. Ford. il Sci Digest 68:20-5 N '70
Why we let go when we drink. S. Blum. Redbook 135:96+ My '70

LIQUOR traffic
Great Britain
See also
Bars and barrooms

LIQUORI, Marty
Monkey rides the easy runner. S. Myslenski. il pors Sports Illus 32:30-1+ Mr 2 '70 *
Revenge can be sour. S. Myslenski. il pors Sports Illus 32:22-5 My 25 '70

LIQUORS
Aperitif. W. Clifford. il Holiday 47:64-5+ F '70
Before-and after-dinner drinks. Bet Hom & Gard 48:24+ S '70
Boating man's drink book. il Motor B 126:60-4 Jl '70
High spirits from white alcohols; eau de vie. H. McNulty. House & Gard 137:116+ Ap '70
How to serve party drinks. M. M. Hemingway. House & Gard 137:128+ My '70
How to stock the bar for a party. E. Greenberg. il House B 112:50+ N '70
Kentucky's nectar; mint juleps. W. R. Scott. Travel & Camera 33:14 Je '70
Little red bottles; Campari soda. S. Spitzer. il Holiday 48:38-9 Jl '70
Sherry on the rocks and other sins of summer. E. Greenberg. il House B 112:92-3+ Je '70
Spirited invasion. N. Ickeringill. House B 112:92-3 Ja '70
To enjoy outdoors: cooling drinks. House & Gard 137:96+ Je '70
Top liquor brands of 1969. il Bsns W p 127 Mr 7 '70
Unusual party drinks from a great party giver. M. Williams. il House & Gard 138:126+ N '70
What famous people like to drink. House & Gard 138:89 Jl '70
White spirits. J. T. Elson. Travel & Camera 33:12+ S '70
See also
Alcohol
Champagne
Cocktails
Cookery—Liquors
Whiskey

LIRA. See Money—Italy

LISAGOR, Peter
(ed) See DuBridge, L. A. Clearing the air: we can end pollution
about
Horizontal in Washington. por Time 96:42 Ag 17 '70 *

LISBON, Portugal
Music
Fado in Portugal. M. Howe. il Sat R 53:49+ S 12 '70

LISK, Donald J.
Analysis of pesticide residues: new problems and methods. bibliog il Science 170:589-93 N 6 '70

LISLE, Larry
Short-wave converter. il Radio-Electr 41:50-2 Mr '70
Single-signal S.W. receiver. il Electr World 83:64 Ap '70

LISSAMAN, P. B. S. and Shollenberger, C. A.
Formation flight of birds. il Science 168:1003-5 My 22 '70

LISTEN to the Hodja; drama. See Winther, B.

LISTENING
Anecdotes. facetiae. satire. etc.
Talk of the town; speed listening. P. Steinfels. il Commonweal 91:422+ Ja 16 '70

LISTER, E. Darlene
To measure the moo; poem. Chr Cent 87:890 Jl 22 '70

LISTER, Merle
Merle Lister dance company, the Hudson guild theatre. N. M. Stoop. Dance Mag 44:88 Ag '70

LISTON, James M.
How to carve a mountain. il por Pop Mech 133:76-9+ Je '70
Why Winnebago is number one. il Pop Mech 133:120-5+ My '70

LITERATURE—Themes—*Continued*
My reluctant magician. R. Powell. Writer 83:
11-14+ F '70
Regional poetry. P. S. Curry. Writer 83:21-3
Ag '70
White trap: a motif; R. Wright's Native
son. D. M. Donlan. Engl J 59:943-4 O '70
See also
Anti-Semitism in literature
Chemistry in literature
Childrens literature—Themes
Drama—Themes
Dreams in literature
Jesus Christ in literature
Nature in literature
Negroes in literature
Science fiction—Themes
Sex in literature
LITERATURE, Childrens. See Childrens literature
LITERATURE, Immoral. See Immoral literature and pictures
LITERATURE, Influence of
See also
Children's literature, Influence of
LITERATURE, Medieval
See also
Romances
Troubadours
LITERATURE and art. See Art and literature
LITERATURE and morals
Must the novelist crusade? E. Welty. il Writers Digest 50:32-5+ F '70
LITERATURE and music. See Music and literature
LITERATURE and politics
Literary revolutionism. R. Winegarten. Commentary 49:67-74 Je '70; Discussion. 50:
16-18 S '70
LITERATURE and science
See also
Science fiction
LITERATURE as a profession. See Authorship
LITHIUM carbonate
Controversial drug approved. Sci N 97:390
Ap 18 '70
Help for manic highs. Newsweek 75:77 Ap 20
'70
Help for the manic-depressive. por Time 95:46
Ap 20 '70
LITHIUM fluoride
Controversial bond in the F shell; chemical
bonding between neutrons and electrons.
il Sci N 97:92-3 Ja 24 '70
LITHIUM in the body
Antidotal thirst: a response to intoxication.
D. F. Smith and others. bibliog il Science
167:297-8 Ja 16 '70
LITHOGRAPHS
Graphics '70. D. H. Karshan. il por Art in
Am 58:48-51 Ja; 56-9 Mr; 48-51 My; 31-4
Jl; 48-51 S; 48-51 N '70
Lithographs by Rembrandt Peale. J. A.
Mahey. il Antiques 97:236-42 F '70
Original art, hot off the presses. il Life 68:57-
61 Ja 23 '70
LITHOGRAPHY
Form of lithography; cellulose gum and nitric
acid. J. G. Cecere. il Sch Arts 70:28-9 D '70
Tamarind lithography workshop. M. N. Tabak. il Craft Horiz 30:28-33+ O; 50-3+ D '70
See also
Color printing
Printing, Offset
LITIGATION. See Actions and defenses
LITTELL, Browne
You too can match race. il Yachting 128:73+
S '70
LITTER. See Refuse and refuse disposal
LITTKE, Lael J.
Eternal life of Kerry Magill; story. Ladies
Home J 87:72-3 Je '70
LITTLE, Brian W. and Meyer, W. L.
Ribonuclease-inhibitor system abnormality
in dystrophic mouse skeletal muscle. bibliog il Science 170:747-9 N 13 '70
LITTLE, Cleavon
Prize winners. P. Garland. il pors Ebony 25:
29-32+ Jl '70 *
LITTLE, Doyle. See Brower, M. jt. auth.
LITTLE, James P.
Garvey ranch observatory. il R Pop Astron
63:28-9 Ag '69
LITTLE, Malcolm. See Malcolm X
LITTLE, Nina Fletcher
New light on Joseph H. Davis, left hand
painter. il Antiques 98:754-7 N '70
LITTLE, Robert, and Robinson, L. J.
With the eclipse expeditions in Mexico. il
Sky & Tel 39:280-4 My '70
LITTLE, Royal
As they see it; interview, ed. by James
Cook. pors Forbes 106:38-41 D 15 '70
Restless world of Royal Little. R. Levy. por
Duns 95:38-40 F '70 *

LITTLE, Stuart W.
Books in communications. See issues of
Saturday review
Celebrity commercials industry. il Sat R 53:
55-6+ Ap 11 '70
From A to Z on Sesame street. il Sat R 53:
62-4 My 9 '70
(ed) Grotowski; an unsettled American theater replies. Sat R 53:20-1 F 7 '70
Joshua B. Powers, inc; from comic strips
to mass technology. Sat R 53:59-61+ Ja
17 '70
Sponsored films are better than ever. il Sat R
53:90-2 S 12 '70
LITTLE BIG HORN, Battle of the, 1876
Haunting new vision of the Little Big Horn;
with drawings by L. Baskin. il Am Heritage
21:101-3 Je '70
LITTLE, Brown and company
Secrecy veils Time-LB's memoir by Khrushchev. Pub W 198:49 N 16 '70
LITTLE countess; story. See Ibbotson, E.
LITTLE leagues
Don't let your son play small-fry football.
F. Tarkenton. il por Ladies Home J 87:
146-7 O '70
Let your son play little league ball? il Changing T 24:41-3 Jl '70
Little league can hurt kids. D. F. Schwertley.
il Todays Ed 59:40-1 My '70
Surgeon raps little league. il Sci Digest 67:
55-6 Ja '70
LITTLE Lord Fauntleroy (literary character)
See Characters in literature
LITTLE minister; drama. See Thane, A.
LITTLE orchestra society, New York
Music to my ears; concert performance of
Weber's Euryanthe. I. Kolodin. Sat R 53:48
N 14 '70
Musical events; K. M. von Weber's Euryanthe. W. Sargeant. New Yorker 46:169-70
N 7 '70
Musical events; Williams' Riders to the sea
and Holst' At the Boars head. W. Sargeant. New Yorker 45:78 F 7 '70
Report:
Vaughan Williams' Riders to the sea and
Holst's At the boar's head. F. Merkling.
Opera N 34:32 Mr 7 '70
Weber's Euryanthe. F. Merkling. Opera
N 35:29 D 5 '70
LITTLE players theater company. See Puppets
and puppet plays
LITTLE red schoolhouse. See School buildings
LITTLE review (periodical)
Exuberance and ecstasy. J. M. Edelstein.
New Repub 162:19-22 Je 13 '70
LITTLE ROCK, Ark.

Architecture

Big bank in Little Rock; Worthen bank
building. il Arch Rec 148:105-8 N '70

Education

Little Rock thirteen years later: how integration is working. il U S News 68:82-4 Je
22 '70

Sanitary affairs

Tunneling solves tough sewer-construction
problem. T. W. Clapham. il Am City 85:
105+ F '70
LITTLE wrens and robins; story. See Kiely,
B.
LITTLEFIELD, Edgar
Local reduction copper reds; reprint. il Ceram
Mo 18:31-3 Ja '70
LITTLER, Frank
Terms of reference. Sat R 53:24 N 14 '70
LITTLER, Gene
Sporting scene. H. W. Wind. New Yorker
46:94-101 My 2 '70 *
LITTLEST elf; drama. See Watts, F. B.
LITTON industries, inc.
Calculated risk in Pascagoula. il Fortune
82:31 Ag '70
Litton's electronic information machine. il
Bsns W p158+ Mr 28 '70
Litton's ship is still leaking. Bsns W p35-6
Ja 17 '70
Litton's ships come in; navy contract to Ingalls shipbuilding division. Time 96:62 Jl 6
'70
Modern times; navy destroyers contract.
Newsweek 76:75-6 Jl 6 '70
Nixon likes Litton's system; proposed Office of management & budget. Management
information systems division. Bsns W p
162+ Mr 28 '70
Struggle over a destroyer contract. Bsns W
p31-2 Je 27 '70
LITURGICAL art. See Christian art and symbolism

LITURGICAL language
　See also
International committee on English in the
　liturgy
LITURGICAL movement
　　　　　Catholic church
Is there any hope for liturgy? G. S. Sloyan.
　Commonweal 92:56-60 Mr 27 '70; Discus-
　sion. 92:155+ My 1 '70
Liturgy; dioceses and parishes and liturgical
　reform. Commonweal 92:403 Ag 21 '70
LITURGICAL music. See Church music
LITURGICAL week
No liturgical week. America 122:149 F 14 '70
LITURGIES
Radicalizing liturgy; experiment in exposure
　education. J. D. Groppe. Cath World 212:30-4
　O '70
LITURGY, Catholic. See Catholic church—Lit-
　urgy and ritual
LITVINOV, Ivy
Apartheid; story. New Yorker 46:35-9 S 19
　'70
Boy who laughed; story. New Yorker 46:43-7
　O 31 '70
Bright shores; story. New Yorker 46:28-33 Ag
　1 '70
Holiday Home; story. New Yorker 46:42-51
　N 28 '70
LITZ, Katherine
Katherine Litz and dance company; Judson
　memorial church. J. Anderson. Dance Mag
　44:88 F '70
LIU, K. L.
Chinese nine-inch semiportable reflector. il
　Sky & Tel 40:110-12 Ag '70
LIVE bait. See Bait
LIVER
　　　　　Diseases
Cirrhosis: a growing threat to life. J. Carper.
　Todays Health 48:26-7+ F '70
Increase of liver disease; cirrhosis of the
　liver. Sci Digest 67:57 Je '70
Pyrazole and induction of fatty liver by a
　single dose of ethanol. G. O. Bustos and
　others. bibliog il Science 168:1598-9 Je 26
　'70
　See also
Hepatitis
Jaundice
　　　　　Transplantation
Liver: outer limit of the state of the art.
　J. Bockel. il pors Sci N 97:202-3 F 21 '70
LIVER enzymes. See Enzymes
LIVER mitochondria. See Mitochondria
LIVERIGHT, Horace Brisbin
Hearing about the publishers. S. W. Little.
　Sat R 53:56 Ag 8 '70 *
Horace Liveright, by W. Gilmer. Review
　Newsweek il por 76:82-3 Jl 6 '70. R. A.
　Sokolov *
LIVERSIDGE, Anthony F. W.
Beguiling new economics of nickel. il Fortune
　81:100-3+ Mr '70
LIVERWORTS
Hydroxy-L-proline- and 2,2'-dipyridyl-induced
　phenovariations in the liverwort Nowellia
　curvifolia. D. V. Basile. bibliog il Science
　170:1218-20 D 11 '70
LIVESTOCK
Getting your share of the livestock action?
　C. W. Gifford. Farm J 94:54+ Ap '70
Livestock management guide; symposium. il
　Suc Farm 68:47-9+ O '70
　See also
Swine
　　　Diseases and pests
　See also
Bloating
　　　　　Marketing
Check that bounces. W. Kester. il Farm J
　94:B16+ O '70
Marketing management. R. W. Sanders. Suc
　Farm 68:34 Ag '70
　　　　　Prices
Livestock prices: up again in '70. Farm J
　94:52N Ap '70
LIVESTOCK, Weight and measurements of
　See also
Cattle, Weight and measurements of
LIVESTOCK auctions. See Auctions
LIVESTOCK feed. See Feeding and feeding
　stuffs
LIVESTOCK markets
Terminal markets fight back. il Farm J 93:
　B12-13 N '69
　See also
Chicago—Stockyards

LIVESTOCK shows
American royal. il Travel & Camera 33:42-7
　O '70
LIVING. See Conduct of life; Life
LIVING, Cost of. See Cost of living
LIVING expenses. See Cost of living
LIVING history farms. See Agricultural
　museums
LIVING rooms
Family room and an apartment for parents.
　il Bet Hom & Gard 48:62-3 My '70
Getaway kind of family room. il Bet Hom &
　Gard 48:65 My '70
Living room that spills outdoors. il Bet Hom
　& Gard 48:68-9 My '70
New kind of living room. il Bet Hom &
　Gard 48:58-9 My '70
New space for family living. il Bet Hom &
　Gard 48:72-3 My '70
Room that does it all; family room addition.
　il Bet Hom & Gard 48:70 My '70
Two with sociable airs. il House B 112:98-9
　N '70
Versatile, all-season family room. il Bet Hom
　& Gard 48:51-3 My '70
Warm, inviting family room. il Bet Hom &
　Gard 48:71 My '70
LIVING trust funds. See Trusts and trustees
LIVINGSTON, A. D.
New batteries for sportsmen. il Field & S 75:
　26-7+ Jl '70
LIVINGSTON, Jane
West coast report (cont) il Art in Am 58:126-
　31 S '70
LIVINGSTON, M. Stanley
Atom smasher. il por Newsweek 75:56 Je 22
　'70 *
LIVINGSTON college. See Rutgers university,
　New Brunswick, N.J.—Livingston college
LIZARD malaria. See Malaria
LIZARDS
　See also
Iguanas
LLAMZON, Benjamin S.
Who's a phony? America 123:196-8 S 26 '70
LLANO, George A.
Survey of Antarctic biology: life below freez-
　ing. il por Bul Atom Sci 26:67-74 D '70
LLERAS RESTREPO, Carlos
Biggest little man in Columbia. S. Seegers
　and K. Seegers. por Read Digest 96:159-64
　Ja '70
LLOYD, Edward F.
God and man in Oregon. Chr Cent 87:1239 O 14
　'70 *
LLOYD, John
Washington report. See issues of Scholastic
　teacher to May 4, 1970
LLOYD, K. and Hornykiewicz, O.
Parkinson's disease: activity of L-dopa
　decarboxylase in discrete brain regions. bib-
　liog il Science 170:1212-13 D 11 '70
LLOYD, Rees, and Montague, Peter
Ford and la raza: they stole our land and
　gave us powdered milk. il Ramp Mag 9:10-
　18 S '70
LLOYD, Trevor
Canada's Arctic in the age of ecology. il For
　Affairs 48:726-40 Jl '70
LLOYD family
Lloyd coat-of-arms. H. K. Eilers. il Hobbies
　75:148-9+ Mr '70 *
LLOYD-JONES, David
Lawrence Halprin: eco-architect. il por Hori-
　zon 12:46-55 Sum '70
LLOYD'S, London
Lloyds reinsures its own future. il Fortune
　82:86-7 D '70
LLOYD'S register of American yachts
Who's on what? M. E. Slate. il Motor B 125:
　120-1+ Ja '70
LOADERS, Municipal. See Municipal equipment
LOADING and unloading
Truck-mounted loading boom; South Miami,
　Fla. il Am City 85:85 Ja '70
LOADING of cameras. See Cameras—Loading
LOAN, Nguyen-ngoc-. See Nguyen-ngoc-Loan
LOAN associations. See Savings and loan as-
　sociations
LOAN companies. See Finance companies
LOAN sharks
Let's compete with loan sharks. J. M. Seidl.
　bibliog f il Harvard Bsns R 48:69-77 My '70
LOANE, Marcus L.
Questions of truth. por Newsweek 76:59 O 26
　'70 *

LOANS
Private lenders yank the welcome mat. il Bsns W p78 D 12 '70
See also
Credit
Credit unions
Insurance, Life—Policy loans
Interest
Mortgages
Student loans
Usury laws

LOANS, Art. See Art loans

LOANS, Bank
Banks share in fight against pollution. V. Louviere. Nations Bsns 58:19 D '70
Banks start ungluing consumer loan rates. Bsns W p 16 D 12 '70
No more waiting at the loan window. il Bsns W p24 O 3 '70
Pollution foes find a friend at the bank. Bsns W p 19-20 Jl 4 '70
Prime rate cut may not be enough. Bsns W p 19 D 26 '70

LOANS, Foreign
Zombanakis plan to counter capital outflow. W. Wynn. il por Fortune 82:39+ Jl '70
See also
Export-import bank of the United States of America
International bank for reconstruction and development

LOANS, Government. See Government lending

LOANS, Personal
Let's compete with loan sharks. J. M. Seidl. bibliog f il Harvard Bsns R 48:69-77 My '70
See also
Credit unions
Household finance corporation
Savings and loan associations

LOBAN, Walter
Literature and the examined life. bibliog f Engl J 59:1086-90 N '70

LOBB, John Cunningham
John Lobb's orphan asylum; interview. por Forbes 106:24-5 Jl 1 '70

LOBBIES (architecture)
Meet me in the lobby. R. Lynes. por Art in Am 58:27 My '70

LOBBYING
Ambush on the Hill; McGovern-Hatfield and Cooper-Church amendments. J. Hightower and V. Newton. Nation 211:266-70 S 28 '70
Business in government. M. J. Green. New Repub 163:14-16 N 14 '70
Citizen enterprise; political movements to end the war. New Repub 162:7 Je 20 '70
Detroit's battle with Washington. Bsns W p28 D 5 '70
Ecology fans show their muscle. il Bsns W p26-7 N 14 '70
Haynsworth v. the U.S. Senate (1969) labor opposition. J. L. Steele. il por Fortune 81:90-3+ Mr '70
Letters that legislate. L. Spruill. Har Yrs 10:15 O '70
Oil lobby is not depleted. E. Knoll. il N Y Times Mag p26-7+ Mr 8 '70; Reply with rejoinder. F. N. Ikard. p 136+ Ap 5 '70
Plot to pave America; highway lobbying. R. Starnes. Field & S 75:6+ N '70
Power of the purse; Operation pursestrings. Nation 210:674 Je 8 '70
Private interests and public lands. R. S. Gilmour. Cur Hist 59:36-42+ Jl '70
Some NIH, NIMH scientists lobby to end the war. L. J. Carter. Science 168:1191 Je 5 '70
Toward participatory citizenship; proposal for a national citizens lobby; excerpt from Natural enemies? A. Klein. Cur 121:3-11 S '70
Your right to write. B. Barr. il Nations Bsns 58:84-7 Ap '70
Youth on the Hill; up against the marble wall; anti-war activities. D. Blackburn. Nation 210:719-21 Je 15 '70
See also
Common cause (political organization)
Lobbyists
Pressure groups

Anecdotes, facetiae, satire, etc.
Floto letters: Dear Mayor Floto. R. Angel. New Yorker 46:34-7 F 21 '70
When kids write their congressman. P. Brooks. America 122:341-2 Mr 28 '70

LOBBYISTS
Corporate ambassadors to Washington; excerpts; with portfolio. R. W. Miller and J. D. Johnson. Nations Bsns 58:44-50 Jl '70
Peace politics; youthful peace movement. New Repub 163:8 S 26 '70
Youth wants to know; student delegations on mission to Washington. il Newsweek 75: 33 My 25 '70

LOBELIAS
Two showy lobelias. T. L. Cahalan. Horticulture 48:52-3 My '70

LO BELLO, Nino
When the Krokodil arrives, watch out! il Read Digest 96:101-3 Ap '70

LOBSENZ, Norman M.
Importance of childhood memories. il Read Digest 97:127-30 N '70
Loving message in a touch. Read Digest 96: 132-4 My '70
Mini-midi-maxi madness. il Good H 171:61+ Ag '70

LOBSTER trapping
Face to face with a Maine lobsterman. L.-L. Barton. por Seventeen 29:14 F '70

LOBSTERS
Migration of the spiny lobster. W. F. Herrnkind. il Natur Hist 79:36-43 bibliog(p79) My '70
See also
Cookery—Shellfish

LOCAL educational associations. See Educational associations

LOCAL 1199 of the Drug and hospital employees union. See Drug and hospital employees union (local 1199)

LOCAL family keeps son happy; story. See Keillor, G.

LOCAL finance
See also
Municipal finance

LOCAL government
See also
Metropolitan government
Municipal government

Canada
See also
Town meeting

United States
See also
Town meeting

LOCAL news. See Newspapers—Local news

LOCAL service airlines
Local service airline support scrutinized. H. D. Watkins. Aviation W 92:41+ My 25 '70
Locals, trunks vie for short-haul traffic. H. D. Watkins. il Aviation W 93:33-4+ Jl 13 '70
See also
Air taxi service
Air West, inc.
Airlines—Non-scheduled operations
Pacific Southwest airlines

Federal aid
West seeks air route study funds. N. S. Himmel. Aviation W 92:25 Mr 30 '70

Finance
Economic problems of locals resist jets, new authority. H. D. Watkins. il Aviation W 92: 168-9+ Mr 9 '70
Regional airlines run into debt storms. il Bsns W p74 D 12 '70

Regulations
See Aviation—Laws and regulations

Routes
Locals expand with mixed results. H. D. Watkins. il Aviation W 93:24-6 Jl 6 '70
West seeks air route study funds. N. S. Himmel. Aviation W 92:25 Mr 30 '70

Statistics
Supplemental airline revenues and expenses, year 1969; table. Aviation W 92:47 Ap 27 '70

LOCAL-state fiscal relations. See Inter-governmental fiscal relations

LOCAL taxation
Protection tax wins voter yes; Bloomington, Ill. il Am City 85:100+ Ag '70
Rise in local taxes; growing worry for business. il U S News 69:63-5 N 23 '70
State & local taxes: how they compare. city to city. Changing T 24:46 S '70
Why are they smiling? system in Stockholm. L. Gross. il Look 34:21-7 Mr 24 '70
See also
Libraries—Finance

LOCAL transit
Fewer riders, rising deficits: woes of the transit industry. il U S News 68:6 Ja 19 '70
Getting blue-collar workers to use buses; Santa Clara County, Calif. H. K. Evans. il Am City 85:94+ Ag '70
How to get nowhere; need for modern mass transit systems. N. Cousins. Sat R 53:49 Ap 4 '70
New towns are our mandate for urban innovations. S. Myers and R. Schwartz. il Arch Forum 132:38-41 Je '70
Reduced senior transit fares now available in fifty cities. Aging 188:17 Je '70

LOCAL transit—*Continued*
They're finally doing something about traffic.
il Changing T 24:31-2 O '70
Untangling big-city traffic: the big push
for mass transit. il U S News 68:48-9 My 25
'70
See also
Motor bus lines
Motor buses
Moving platforms
Railroads
Subways
    also subhead Transit systems under
names of cities and metropolitan areas,
e.g. Detroit—Transit systems

Fares
Nickel still goes a long way; reduced transportation fare. F. C. Weed. il Har Yrs 10:
19-21+ My '70
Thirty-four cities from coast to coast now
have low senior fares: savings average
10-15 cents. Aging 186:9 Ap '70
See also
New York (city)—Transit systems—Fares

Federal aid
Aid for transit, a step ahead. U S News
68:15 F 16 '70
First, find the mice; UMTA policies. News-
week 76:58+ S 28 '70
Here come the buses. Forbes 105:62-3 Je 1 '70
1970, the year of the traveler. J. Carlson.
Arch Rec 148:43 D '70
Policy on aged, handicapped, inserted in mass
transit bill. Aging 193:7 N '70

Finance
Battle over the driver's dollar. R. T. Gray.
il Nations Bsns 58:38-40+ S '70
LOCANTE, Salvatore
Composting octogenarian. V. L. Rinelli. il
por Org Gard & Farm 17:54-5 My '70*
LOCATION in business and industry
Do's and don't's for wooing industry. B. M.
Conboy. Nations Bsns 58:92 O '70
Exodus from New York city: what makes
businesses leave. il U S News 69:50-3 D 7
'70
Flight from the cities. il Newsweek 76:58+
N 30 '70
Lessons from Vermont; lowering antipollution
standards when competing for industry.
Time 96:50 N 9 '70
New jobs for your community. R. J. Gangel.
Farm J 94:32H Ja '70
Northeast cuts its losses. il Bsns W p82+ Je
6 '70
Payrolls and pickerel in Maine; proposed oil
refinery potential disaster to fishing and
tourism industries. il Time 95:52 F 16 '70
Shell's $25-million trip to Houston. il Bsns
W p68+ S 19 '70
When companies go suburban. il Bsns W
p58+ D 12 '70
Would industry do this to your town? D.
Seim. il Farm J 94:32A-32B O 10 '70
See also
Chemical plants—Location
Power plants—Location
LOCATIONS, Moving picture. See Moving pic-
tures—Setting and scenery
LOCH NESS, Scotland. See Ness, Loch
LOCH NESS monster
Pieces of the frame. J. McPhee. il Atlan
225:42-7 Ja '70
LOCHMAN, J. M.
Radical secularity and radical grace. por Chr
Cent 87:911-14 Jl 29 '70
LOCHRY, Marie A.
Careful planning of a patio. il Home Gard
57:48-9 Ja '70
LOCITZER, Daniel
Parking garage helps revitalize a deteriora-
ting downtown. il Am City 85:94 Je '70
LOCK gates. See Locks (hydraulic engineering)
LOCKABEY, Almon
L'Allegro wins Mazatlan race. il Yachting
129:61 Ja '71
LOCKERBIE, D. Bruce
Is summer reading itself an old adage?
Engl J 59:573-6 Ap '70
Theater of deceit. Chr Today 14:5-7+ Jl 3 '70
LOCKERS
Are student lockers off limits to principals?
H. C. Hudgins, jr. Ed Digest 36:14-15 D '70
LOCKHART Gaddy's wild goose refuge. See
Bird sanctuaries—North Carolina
LOCKHEED aircraft corporation
Bailing out Lockheed. Newsweek 77:66 Ja 11
'71
Blueprint for keeping the C-5A going. Bsns
W p 19 Ag 29 '70
Can Lockheed's pilots avoid the crash? il
Bsns W p23-5 Mr 14 '70

Care and feeding of Lockheed. B. Newman.
New Repub 163:11-13 O 10 '70
Complex problems hit Lockheed. B. Miller.
il Aviation W 92:56-60 Mr 30 '70
Defense cuts mirage. Nation 210:323-4 Mr
23 '70
Delivery stretch asked for C-5. Aviation W
92:20 F 16 '70
Inquiry on C-5A cost disclosures could spur
stricter SEC rules. Aviation W 92:19 Je 8
'70
Lockheed asks DOD fiscal help. Aviation W
92:224-5 Mr 9 '70
Lockheed cautious on JetStars. D. A. Brown.
Aviation W 93:88 N 16 '70
Lockheed flies into heavier flak. il Bsns W
p28 My 30 '70
Lockheed gains some financial lift. Bsns W
p36 S 19 '70
Lockheed hits heavy head winds. il Bsns W
p46-8 F 14 '70
Lockheed joins the bread line. Nation 211:
68 Ag 3 '70
Lockheed mass cargo system (cont) D. A.
Brown. il Aviation W 92:32-4 Ja 19 '70
Lockheed objections stall SEC inquiry. D. C.
Winston. Aviation W 93:21 Jl 13 '70
Lockheed plans litigation, rejects fixed C-5A
loss. C. Brownlow. Aviation W 94:17-18
Ja 11 '71
Lockheed reports earnings dip. Aviation W
93:23 N 9 '70
Lockheed scandal; C-5A cost overrun affair.
J. G. Phillips. New Repub 163:19-23 Ag 1 '70
Lockheed seeks a place to land. il Bsns W p23-
4 Jl 11 '70
Lockheed sets goal for Watts facility. Avia-
tion W 92:65 My 18 '70
Lockheed stock; SEC investigation. New
Repub 162:9-10 Ap 25 '70
Lockheed threatens to die. P. D. H. Stock-
ton. il Nations 210:402-4 Ap 6 '70
Lockheed's earnings fall, but sales rise. il
Aviation W 93:22 Ag 10 '70
Lockheed's lament. il Time 95:82 My 18 '70
One up and away; air-bus battle. il News-
week 76:62+ S 7 '70
Partner in trouble. il Newsweek 75:87+ Mr 16
'70
Pentagon plans aid to Lockheed; financiers
fear L-1011 problems. Aviation W 92:22-3
Mr 16 '70
Pity curve; relations with the military. Na-
tion 210:101-2 F 2 '70
Poverty pocket; lack of funds to fill order
for C5A planes. New Repub 162:7-8 Mr 28
'70
SEC to make public a portion of Lockheed's
C-5A cost data. Aviation W 93:15 S 21 '70
Shock waves of Lockheed's gamble. il Bsns W
p14-15 Ja 9 '71
Striving to maintain Drew Pearson's stan-
dards. W. F. Buckley, jr. Nat R 23:50-1 Ja
12 '71
LOCKS (hydraulic engineering)
Other side of the locks; Lake Washington
Ship Canal; ed. by E. Crimmin. il Motor B
126:54-5+ Jl '70
LOCKS, Wooden
Early American stock locks. D. Streeter. il
Antiques 98:251-5 Ag '70
LOCKS and keys
Build a cryptolock. J. G. Busse. il Pop Electr
34:42-4+ Ja '71
Change your lock, improve your security. P.
Wahl. il Pop Sci 196:93 Ap '70
Combination time lock. il Radio-Electr 41:
93 S '70
How to make locks last and last and last.
R. Capotosto. il Mech Illus 66:93 Ag '70
See also
Automobile locks and keys
Boat locks and keys
Locks, Wooden

Collectors and collecting
Old locks & keys collected by young Califor-
nian. il pors Hobbies 75:72+ Jl '70
LOCKSPEISER, Edward
Baudelaire and music. Yale R 59:498-506 Je
'70
Debussy's dream House. il pors Opera N 34:
8-12 Mr 21 '70
LOCKTON, David
Motor trend interview. pors Motor T 22:94-
8+ Mr '70
LOCKWOOD, Edgar
Director resigns; letter, with reply by the
editors. il Ramp Mag 9:50+ O '70
LOCKWOOD, W. B.
Long life of a great lady. il Motor B 125
60-1+ Ap '70
LOCKWOOD-Mathews mansion. See Norwalk,
Conn.—Historic houses, etc.
LOCOMOTION
See also
Animal locomotion

LOCOMOTIVE models. See Railroad models

LOCUSTS, Seventeen year. See Cicadas

LODGE, George Cabot
Ideology, interests and foreign policy in the 1970's; address, November 18, 1970. Vital Speeches 37:181-6 Ja 1 '71
Top priority: renovating our ideology. bibliog f Harvard Bsns R 48:43-55 S '70
Why an outmoded ideology thwarts the new business conscience. por Fortune 82:106-7+ O '70; Same abr. with title Top priority: renovating our ideology. bibliog f Harvard R 48:43-55 S '70

LODGE, Henry Cabot, 1902-
Ambassador Lodge reports on visit to the Vatican; transcript of news conference, August 6, 1970. Dept State Bul 63:277-8 S 7 '70
Citizen looks at the ABM. Read Digest 96: 57-64 Je '70
U.S. reaffirms willingness to negotiate on Viet-nam; statement, November 24, 1969. Dept State Bul 61:549 D 15 '69

about
Ambassador Lodge resigns as head of U.S. delgation to Paris meetings; White House announcement; with exchange of letters by Lodge and President Nixon. Dept State Bul 61:549-50 D 15 '69
Henry Cabot Lodge goes to the Vatican. Chr Today 14:22 Jl 3 '70 *
Lodge to the Vatican. Chr Cent 87:779 Je 24 '70 *
New emissary to the Pope. por Time 96:46 Jl 13 '70 *
President's man at the Vatican. America 122: 640 Je 20 '70 *

LOEB, Armin, and others
Three methods of contacting employers to obtain jobs for the rehabilitated psychiatric patient. il Ment Hy 54:137-9 Ja '70

LOENGARD, John
Gallery; photographs. Life 69:6-9 Jl 31 '70
Haunting legacy of Camille; photographs. Life 69:78-83 S 18 '70

LOESCHEN, John
Filthy-minded reflections on theological method. Chr Cent 87:108-12 Ja 28 '70

LOESER, Cornelius. See Tirtha, R. jt. auth.

LOEVINGER, Jane
NISP: noisy signal in psychology. Trans-Action 7:10 My '70

LOEWENSTEIN, Werner R.
Intercellular communication; with biographical sketch. il Sci Am 222:10, 78-84+ bibliog(p 148) My '70

LOFTON, John D. Jr
About that Hitler quote. Nat R 22:411 Ap 21 '70

LOFTS, Norah (Robinson)
Getting to know them. Writers 83:9-10+ N '70
Lovers all untrue; story. Redbook 135:147-69 Je '70
Man on the telephone; story. Good H 171: 68-9 Ag '70

LOG drives. See Lumbering

LOGAN, Andy
Around city hall (cont) New Yorker 46: 101-4+ F 28; 106+ Ap 18; 104-8 Je 6; 120-2+ S 19; 126+ N 21 '70

LOGAN, Carolyn
Myth and method. Engl J 59:548-50+ Ap '70

LOGAN, Edgar
Retirement years. Ed Digest 36:29-31 N '70
Teachers who know their onions vacation in Bermuda. il Schol Teach Sec Teach Sup p28-9 F 2 '70

LOGAN, Fred, Jr
Death of an Anglo. il por Newsweek 76:21 Jl 27 '70 *

LOGAN, Jonathan, inc.
Helping a competitor, at a price. il pors Bsns W p48+ Ap 18 '70

LOGAN, Lloyd M. and Hunt, G. R.
Infrared emission spectra: enhancement of diagnostic features by the lunar environment. bibliog il Science 169:865-6 Ag 28 '70

LOGBOOKS (ships)
Log keeping for the cruising man. E. S. Maloney. il pors Motor B 125:100-1 Mr '70

LOGGERHEAD turtles. See Turtles

LOGGING. See Lumbering

LOGIC
See also
Dilemma

LOGIC, Symbolic and mathematical
Build the Digital logic microlab. D. Lancaster. il Pop Electr 32:27-35+ Ap '70

LOGIC circuits. See Computers—Circuits

LOGICAL positivism
Ernst Mach: the unconscious motives of an empiricist. L. S. Feuer. bibliog Am Imago 27:12-40 Spr '70

LOGOS bookstore, Ann Arbor. See Booksellers and bookselling—Michigan

LOGS, Ships. See Logbooks (ships)

LOGSDON, Gene
Are we feeding those hungry Americans? il Farm J 94:34-5+ D '70
Why dairymen are glad you're not in dairying. Farm J 94:20+ Ap '70

LOGSDON, Richard H.
Librarian and the scholar: eternal enemies; address, February 20, 1970. il por Library J 95:2871-4 S 15 '70

LOGUE, Edward J.
New York's Mr Urban Renewal. R. Schickel. il pors N Y Times Mag p30-4+ Mr 1 '70 *
Notes from the underground; excerpts from book. J. Fischer. Harper 240:12+ F '70 *

LOH, Jules
Soul of the Navajo. il Esquire 74:162-7+ N '70

LOHRE, Dick
Silver bullet for me; ed. by D. Bowring. il pors Outdoor Life 145:74-6+ Je '70

LOIRE VALLEY
Wine-lover's tour of the Loire. R. A. De Groot. il House B 112:74-5+ Jl '70

Photographs
Loire Valley. B. Barbey. il Travel & Camera 33:40-7 Ap '70

LOLLI, Antonio
Antonio Lolli's letters to Padre Martini. A. Mell. bibliog f il Mus Q 56:463-77 Jl '70 *

LOMAS and Nettleton financial corporation
Master builder of real estate deals. il Bsns W p 128+ S 12 '70

LOMBA, Laurie
Unrecognized professional. Ment Hy 54:149-51 Ja '70

LOMBARD, Alain
Eager to know; interview, ed. by S. Gould. por Opera N 34:16 Ap 18 '70

LOMBARDI, Joan
Starbird. N. Russell. pors Dance Mag 44:20-1 O '70 *

LOMBARDI, Vince
Obituary
Nat R 22:990 S 22 '70. V. Gold
Sports Illus 33:17 S 14 '70
Proud father, proud sons. il pors Time 96: 61 S 14 '70 *
Special madness. por Newsweek 76:123 S 14 '70 *
We played for Lombardi. J. Kramer. il por Life 69:53-4 S 11 '70; Same abr. Read Digest 97:159-62 D '70 *

LOMEO, Angelo. See Bullaty, S. jt. auth.

LON Nol
What Cambodia wants from U.S; interview, ed. by C. S. Foltz, jr. il por U S News 68: 30-1 Ap 13 '70

about
Lon Nol and Sihanouk speak out. il pors Time 96:27 S 28 '70 *
Lon Nol reads no newspapers and never uses a telephone. H. Kamm. il pors N Y Times Mag p28-9+ D 13 '70 *
Turnabout in Cambodia. il por Newsweek 76: 57 O 12 '70 *

LONDON, Hannah R.
Portraits of Rebecca Gratz by Thomas Sully. pors Antiques 98:115-17 Jl '70

LONDON, Herbert
Notes from a campus ombudsman. Ed Digest 36:32-4 N '70

LONDON, Kurt L.
Soviet Union and west Europe. bibliog f Cur Hist 59:199-205+ O '70

LONDON
London particular; clean air. T. Dozier. Travel & Camera 33:46-7 My '70
Voyage autour de ma chambre; Bloomsbury set. C. Brogan. Nat R 22:897 Ag 25 '70

Air pollution
Smoake of London: two prophecies. Review Environ il 12:36-7 Jl '70
Smog threat over the Thames. il Bsns W p58 O 24 '70

Airports
Thieves thriving at bustling Heathrow. H. J. Coleman. Aviation W 92:30 Mr 2 '70

American colony
See Americans in England

Art
London. J. Russell. See issues of Art news
New names in London: A to Z. J. Russell. il Art in Am 58:96-9 S '70

British museum
See British museum

LONDON—*Continued*

Churches

Financial crisis at St Margaret's. T. Beeson. Chr Cent 87:956 Ag 12 '70

City planning

If only other cities were like London. il Bsns W p64-6 My 30 '70

Clubs

See also
Night clubs—England

Covent Garden

See also
Royal opera, Great Britain

Crime

Mr Bumble, the burglar. il Newsweek 77:43 Ja 4 '71

Description

She's got style: London. M. Cantwell. il Mlle 71:106+ Je '70
Walking around London. L. Jonckheere. il Schol Teach Sec Teach Sup p6-8 Mr 9 '70

Galleries and museums

Royal road to art; Gainsborough exhibition in the Queen's gallery at Buckingham palace. D. Davis. il Newsweek 75:109 Je 15 '70
See also
British museum
Royal academy of arts, London

Hotels, restaurants, etc.

See also
Night clubs—England

Intellectual life

See also
Bloomsbury group

Libraries

Penny's worth. H. R. Mayes. Sat R 53:20-1+ Je 6 '70

Markets

Hail and ta-ta; Covent Garden. il Newsweek 75:84+ My 18 '70

Music

Behind the scenes. E. Greenfield. See issues of High fidelity section I
Other side; operatic and musical offerings. T. Heinitz. Sat R 53:65 F 14 '70
Report:
  Productions of Carmen and Salome. F. G. Barker. il Opera N 35:26 S 5 '70
  Royal opera's Don Giovanni and The love of three oranges by Sadler's Wells. F. G. Barker. Opera N 34:34 Mr 14 '70
See also
Royal opera, Great Britain
Sadlers Wells opera

Newspapers

Newsplay in London. W. F. Buckley, jr. Nat R 22:1230 N 17 '70
See also
Times, London

Sanitary affairs

Fetid streets and fouled rivers. il Time 96:28 N 9 '70

Social conditions

Unfinished battle in London; community action. C. Holmes. Chr Cent 87:1236-7 O 14 '70

Social history

Public and private Pepys. J. H. Plumb. por Sat R 53:29-31+ O 24 '70

Street traffic

London's maze craze. Newsweek 75:92 Je 15 '70

Theater

Broadway hails Britannia. C. R. Hughes. America 124:46-8 Ja 16 '71
Player's the thing. C. Porterfield. il Time 96:46 S 14 '70
Theatre. H. Clurman. Nation 211:28+, 252-3 Jl 6, S 21 '70
West End story. C. Barnes. il Sat R 53:52+ S 12 '70

LONDON, Ontario

Public library and art museum

London, Ontario strike ends with settlement. il Library J 95:2602-4 Ag '70

LONDON antiques fair and exhibition. See Antiques—Exhibitions
LONDON opera society. See Opera—Great Britain

LONDON philharmonic orchestra

Man with two bands; program at Carnegie Hall. H. Saal. por Newsweek 75:87 My 4 '70
LONDON-Sydney marathon. See Automobile racing
LONDON Times. See Times, London
LONE Star steel company
Square, or foursquare for his country? V. Louviere. il Nations Bsns 58:19 D '70
LONELINESS
Human cry; excerpts from radio broadcast. B. W. Overstreet. PTA Mag 64:23 F '70
To a man: the terrain of love. S. Agnelli. por Vogue 156:112-13+ N 15 '70
See also
Solitude
LONERGAN, Bernard Joseph Francis
Achievement of Bernard Lonergan, by D. Tracy. Review
  Cath World 211:276-7 S '70. E. L. Donahue *
  Chr Cent 87:1096 S 16 '70. G. A. Lindbeck
Answer is the question. por Time 95:58-9 Ap 20 '70 *
Bernard J. F. Lonergan; a name to remember. J. K. Ostling. Chr Today 14:38 Ap 24 '70 *
First International Lonergan congress; a report. F. E. Crowe. America 122:452-3 Ap 25 '70 *
Great Christian mind. por Newsweek 75:75 Ap 20 '70 *
Phenomenon of Bernard Lonergan. B. J. Tyrrell. America 122:298-300 Mr 21 '70 *
LONERGAN conference. See Religious conferences
LONEY, Glenn
Germany after the fall. il Dance Mag 44:28-42 Ag '70
Opera festival. il Hi Fi 20:MA28-9 O '70
Sons and mothers: Niklas Ek and Birgit Cullberg. il pors Dance Mag 44:32-7 Ap '70
Towards the sun. Mot solen. il Dance Mag 44:62-5 N '70
(ed) See Boulton, L. Urge to dance
(ed) See O'Horgan, T. Like, madness
LONG, Augustus C.
Texaco's fire chief. A. A. Butkus. il por Duns 97:26-9 Ja '71 *
Texaco's master returns to the helm. il por Bsns W p36-7 S 19 '70 *
LONG, Norton E.
Indicators of change in political institutions. bibliog f Ann Am Acad 388:35-45 Mr '70
LONG, Robert
Bumper crop of new products. il Hi Fi 20:42-4+ O '70
Challenge of the changers. il Hi Fi 20:secI 54-6+ Ap '70
New designs in headphones. il Hi Fi sec I 20:56-61 F '70
—and Eisenberg, Norman
Tape recording at twenty-five. il Hi Fi 20:secI 40-5 Ag '70
LONG, William R.
Expectations in Chile. New Repub 163:8-9 N 28 '70
LONG BEACH, Calif.
Berth of the blues; woes of the Queen Mary. il Time 96:56 S 7 '70

Airports

Renovate runways before resurfacing. il Am City 85:74-5 Ag '70

Parks and playgrounds

Un-hostile park; Lincoln park. D. Gray. il Parks & Rec 5:26-8+ F '70

Sanitary affairs

Downtown merchants beat dirty-sidewalk problems. il Am City 85:50 My '70
LONG BEACH-Hennessy race. See Motor boat racing
LONG distance telephone. See Telephone, Long distance
LONG ISLAND, N.Y.
Beach life at ebb tide. J. H. Loret. Cons 24:22-8+ Ag '69
See also
Architecture, Domestic—Long Island
Jamaica Bay
Nassau County, N.Y.

Moral conditions

Long Island: we just stare politely at each other until the damn planes pass. L. Wainwright. il Life 69:32-3 O 2 '70
LONG ISLAND railroad
Mandel's complaint; damages suit. Newsweek 75:82+ F 23 '70
Uneasy riders. Newsweek 75:59 F 9 '70

LONG leaf pine. See Pine
LONG live the lion; story. See Rohde, B.
LONG range navigation. See Loran
LONG-tailed fowls. See Japanese long-tailed fowls
LONGEVITY
Greek Orthodox priest: 123 years old; interview, ed. by T. Cosmades. D. Liondos. il Chr Today 14:39 Je 5 '70
Life expectancy and life cycles. H. L. Browning. Cur 114:55-62 Ja '70
Mae West tells her secrets on staying young. Vogue 155:28 Je '70
Nine steps to a longer life. B. Clark. Read Digest 97:84-7 O '70
Prospects for living even longer. Time 96:52 Ag 3 '70
Rise of the elders. H. Wheeler. il Sat R 53: 14-15+ D 5 '70
Smoker's paradise; life expectancy in the U.S. Sci Am 223:53 O '70
    See also
Aging
Centenarians
LONGFIN tuna fishing. See Albacore fishing
LONGITUDE
Who discovered longitude at sea? E. G. Forbes. il Sky & Tel 41:4-6 Ja '71
LONGLEAF pine. See Pine
LONGSHOREMEN
    See also
International longshoremen's and warehousemen's union
LONGSHOREMEN'S strike, Great Britain. See Strikes—Great Britain
LONGUEUIL, Quebec

Water supply
Zeta-potential plus people potential. D. Lamoureux. il Am City 85:93-4+ F '70
LONGWORTH, Richard
Reports: Hungary. Atlan 225:22+ My '70
LONSDALE, Richard C.
Education in a changing society. Ed Digest 36:6-9 S '70
LOOK (periodical)
Another Look. Newsweek 75:64 My 4 '70
Down on farm grew nation's no. 1 teacher. il por Sr Schol 96:Schol Teach 1-2 My 18 '70
Inside Look. il por Newsweek 76:73-4 S 14 '70
Look: ahead. W. Attwood and W. B. Arthur. Look 34:86 Ja 13 '70
1970 Look All America. W. J. McKean. il Look 34:97+ D 15 '70
Teacher of the year 1970. W. J. McKean. il pors Look 34:50-2+ Je 2 '70
    See also
All-America cities
LOOK to the lilies; musical comedy. See Musical comedies, revues, etc.—Criticism, plots, etc.
LOOKOUTS, Forest. See United States—Forest service
LOOMIS, Carol J.
Capital mess on Wall Street. il Fortune 82: 141+ Jl '70
Living it up in a Salomon-sized world. il Fortune 81:72-5+ Ap '70
Wall Street on the ropes. il Fortune 82:62-7+ D '70
Who wants General dynamics? Henry Crown, that's who. il por Fortune 81:76-9+ Je '70
LOOMIS, W. F.
Rickets; with biographical sketch. il Sci Am 223:10, 76-82+ bibliog(p 140) D '70
LOOS, Anita
Loos knit. il por McCalls 97:60+ Ap '70
LOOTING. See Pillage
LOPEZ, Enrique Hank
Overkill at the Silver dollar. il Nation 211:365-8 O 19 '70
Papa and Pancho Villa. il Am Heritage 21: 57-63 Ag '70
LOPEZ, Lillian
New York: the south Bronx project. il Wilson Lib Bul 44:757-60 Mr '70
LOPEZ, Martin
Papa and Pancho Villa. E. H. Lopez. il Am Heritage 21:57-63 Ag '70 *
LOPEZ, Robert S.
Pirandello old and new. Yale R 60:228-40 D '70
LÓPEZ PELLÓN, Nivio
R for aging art. il Américas 22:31-7 Ag '70
LÓPEZ-REY, José
Goya: madmen and monarchs. il Art N 69: 56-9+ O '70
LOPEZ SEPULVEDA, José Patricio
Papa and Pancho Villa. E. H. Lopez. il Am Heritage 21:57-63 Ag '70 *

LOPEZ TIJERINA, Reies. See Tijerina, R. L.
LORAN
Bistatic-radar observation of long-period, directional ocean-wave spectra with loran A. A. M. Peterson and others. bibliog il Science 170:158-61 O 9 '70
Marine electronics; power & sail. il Motor B 125:102-4 My '70
Military expands interest in Loran. B. Miller. il Aviation W 93:55+ Jl 13 '70
LORANT, Stefan
Hitler I knew. il pors Sat R 53:20-3 My 2 '70
Man who knows Lincoln. il pors Sat R 53: 25-7+ F 14 '70 *
LORD, Robert J. See Dory, J. P. jt. auth.
LORD, Shirley
Conversation about being in love. Harp Baz 103:60 My '70
How to live with your husband when he retires. Harp Baz 103:104-5 Je '70
How to rekindle his fire. Harp Baz 104:102-3 Ja '71
LORDS Supper
Trends to intercommunion. C. J. Armbruster; discussion. America 121:575; 122:29 D 15 '69, Ja 17 '70

Anecdotes, facetiae, satire. etc.
Demons also believe; works of Albee, Arrabal and Buñel. S. Terrien. Chr Cent 87: 1481-3+ D 9 '70
LOREN, Sophia
Questions at Radio City; news conference, October 1, 1970. New Yorker 46:30-1 O 3 '70
Sophia Loren. il pors Vogue 156:124-36+ D '70 *
LORENZ, Clarissa
Call it misadventure. por Atlan 225:106-10+ Je '70
LORENZ, Konrad Zackarias
On killing members of one's own species; tr. by H. Zeisel. il por Bul Atom Sci 26:2-5+ O '70
Talk with Konrad Lorenz; ed. by F. de Towarnicki. il por N Y Times Mag p4-5+ Jl 5 '70
    about
Bird preservation; presentation of Delacour medal. New Yorker 46:27-8 Mr 14 '70 *
LORENZEN, Frederick C.
It's easy with miniature roses. il Org Gard & Farm 17:62-4 F '70
LORENZINI, Carlo
Pinocchio; dramatization. See Mahlmann, L.
    about
Puppet's progress. M. Bacon. il Atlan 225: 88-90+ Ap '70 *
LORET, John H.
Beach life at ebb tide. il Cons 24:22-8+ Ag '69
LORINCZ, Albert B. See Kuttner, R. E. jt. auth.
LORIOD, Yvonne
Birds of heaven. H. Saal. pors Newsweek 76:138 N 23 '70 *
LORR, John S.
How to live with a brush. il Design 71:25 Wint '69
Let's ramble with a scramble. il Design 72:20-1 Wint '70
LORSCH, Jay W. See Morse, J. J. jt. auth.
LOS ALAMOS, N.Mex.
Communicating in Los Alamos: don't call him doctor! W. B. Kerr. Sat R 53:57-8 Ap 11 '70
LOS ALAMOS laboratory. See Atomic research laboratories
LOS ANGELES
    See also
Hollywood, Calif.
La Brea

Air pollution
Los Angeles has a cough. R. Rapoport. il Esquire 74:83-5+ Jl '70
Quiet killer. E. Hay. il Am For 76:16-19 Ap '70

Airports
Aerospace firms design cars for Los Angeles transit link. N. S. Himmel. Aviation W 92: 18 Je 15 '70
Airlines expand Los Angeles facilities. N. S. Himmel. il Aviation W 92:44-6 My 4 '70

Architecture
L.A, the stuccoed box. D. Gebhard. il Art in Am 58:130-3 My '70

Art
Four Los Angeles artists. J. Livingston. il Art in Am 58:126-31 S '70

LOS ANGELES—Art—*Continued*
L.A. trip. N. R. Piene. il Art in Am 58:138-41 Mr '70
Los Angeles. E. Hotaling. Art N 69:24 Mr; 8 Ap; 16B My; 62 S; 16+ O '70
Los Angeles artists' studios. B. A. Bengston. il Art in Am 58:100-9 N '70

Banks

Blowup in Basel; scandal of the Swiss affiliate of the United California bank. Newsweek 76:81 O 5 '70
California bank with a Swiss puzzle · United California bank. Bsns W p27-8 S 12 '70
Scandal in Basel. Time 96:86 O 5 '70

Churches

Homosexual church. R. Cleath. Chr Today 14:48-50 S 11 '70
Homosexual church. il por Newsweek 76:107 O 12 '70

City planning

How the geologist can help your city. C. A. Richards. il Am City 85:84-6 Je '70
How to plan for the urban spirit. A. C. Martin. il Am City 85:82+ F '70

Education

LA school librarian files unfair treatment complaint; R. K. Kwan. Library J 95:198-200 Ja 15 '70
Western city, pattern for North? il U S News 68:32-3 Mr 16 '70

Foreign population

How Mexican-Americans view libraries. R. P. Haro. bibliog il Wilson Lib Bul 44:736-42 Mr '70

Geology

See Geology—California

Hotels, restaurants, etc.

Back to elegance; renovated Alexandria. Newsweek 75:74 Je 29 '70
Folk art and fine food; The egg and the eye gallery-restaurant. V. D. Hahn. il pors Am Home 73:46-7 Jl '70
Perino's of Los Angeles. Esquire 73:36 My '70

Immigrants

See Los Angeles—Foreign population

Libraries

See also
Los Angeles public library

Music

Behind the scenes. A. Segal. il Hi Fi 20:secI Jl 15 '70
Music to my ears; new menu at the Bowl. I. Kolodin. Sat R 53:42 S 5 '70
See also
Los Angeles philharmonic orchestra

Negroes

... And a touch of pride; WLCAC projects in Watts. il por Newsweek 75:83 Mr 23 '70
Mobile maids; employment agencies capitalize on Los Angeles's poor public-transportation system. Newsweek 75:54 F 9 '70
Watts: everything has changed, and nothing. J. Dotson and N. Proffitt. il Newsweek 76:58-60 Ag 24 '70

Newspapers

See also
Los Angeles free press

Parks and playgrounds

Reduce park maintenance costs. C. V. Clarke. Am City 85:132+ O '70

Public library

See Los Angeles public library

Religious institutions and affairs

Quiet revolt; archdiocese of Los Angeles. K. LaMott. por Horizon 12:68-72 Wint '70

Riots

Chicano riot; unrest in East Los Angeles. il Time 96:11 S 7 '70
Death in the barrio. il Newsweek 76:35 S 14 '70
Killing of Ruben Salazar: nothing has really changed in the barrio. D. F. Gomez. Chr Cent 88:49-52 Ja 13 '71
When it started; Chicano rebellion. Nation 211:261 S 28 '70

Schools

Why are we afraid of these children? Mirman school for academically gifted children. J. Fincher. il McCalls 97:41+ Ag '70

Social conditions

U.S. journal: Indian population. C. Trillin. New Yorker 46:92+ Ap 18 '70

Social life and customs

Trade winds. C. Amory. Sat R 53:12 Ja 24 '70

Strikes

See also
Strikes—United States—Teachers

Theater

Los Angeles's Company theatre; energy. M. Gottfried. Vogue 156:102 N 1 '70
Love play in Braille; avant-garde group, The company, producing theater of touch called James Joyce memorial liquid theatre. il Time 95:68 F 23 '70
West Coast scene. W. I. Scobie. Nat R 22:1173-4 N 3 '70

Transit systems

Aerospace firms design cars for Los Angeles transit link. N. S. Himmel. Aviation W 92:18 Je 15 '70

Transportation, Bureau of

Tiny E-cell monitors your equipment. il Am City 85:22 Jl '70

LOS ANGELES airways, inc.
Los Angeles airways costly strike ends. Aviation W 92:26 My 11 '70
LAA suing Hughes over merger plan. Aviation W 93:30 O 12 '70

LOS ANGELES archdiocese. See Catholic church—Dioceses

LOS ANGELES COUNTY, Calif.

Parks and recreation, Department of

Contract cities; county-city teamwork. A. Flynn. il Parks & Rec 5:26-7+ Ap '70

Police

California: the besieged; actions of the sheriff's riot squad in Isla Vista. J. Larsen. il Time 95:16-17 Je 22 '70

LOS ANGELES dance theatre
Loring discloses LADT plans. V. H. Swisher. il Dance Mag 44:91 F '70

LOS ANGELES Dodgers (baseball) See Baseball clubs

LOS ANGELES free press
L.A. free press is rich. W. Murray. Esquire 73:54+ Je '70

LOS ANGELES freeways. See Express highways—California

LOS ANGELES Lakers (basketball team) See Basketball teams

LOS ANGELES philharmonic orchestra
Hit it, Zubin; odd musical conjunction between rock and the classics. il por Time 95:72 Je 1 '70
Music to my ears; Oistrakh in Los Angeles. I. Kolodin. Sat R 53:54 Mr 28 '70
Musical events; concert in Carnegie Hall, conducted by Z. Mehta. W. Sargeant. New Yorker 46:170-1 N 7 '70

LOS ANGELES public library
Aggressive librarian: Charles Fletcher Lummis. D. Gordon. bibliog il por Wilson Lib Bul 45:399-405 D '70
Consider the confined; methods of reaching in. J. G. Sutton. il Wilson Lib Bul 45:485-9 Ja '71
L.A. library union opposes commission. Library J 95:112 Ja 15 '70
Overdue; library public relations: a backward glance. C. M. Weisenberg. por Wilson Lib Bul 45:406-7 D '70

Branches

Students use the public library; Lincoln Heights branch. J. A. McCrossan. Am Lib 1:87 Ja '70

LOS ANGELES Rams (football club) See Football clubs

LOS ANGELES times
Chicano columnist. il por Newsweek 75:61 Je 22 '70
New Times. por Bsns W p43 D 26 '70

LOSING. See Failure (psychology)

LOSS of appetite. See Appetite

LOST chapters of Trout fishing in America; story. See Brautigan, R.

LOST friend; story. See Proulx, E. A.

LOST persons. See Missing persons

LOT of cowboys; story. See Rascoe, J.

LOTHROP, Eaton S. Jr, and Zucker, Harvey (comps) Antique camera sampler. il Pop Phot 67:94-7 N '70

LOTIONS. See Cosmetics

LOTT, James
Prodigal son; poem. Chr Cent 87:1033 S 2 '70
LOTTERIES
Who wins the sweepstakes? Sr Schol 96:17
Ap 27 '70

Italy
Lotteries to keep the lire home. Bsns W
p48 Ja 31 '70
LOTTERY, Draft. See Military service, Compulsory
LOTTMAN, Herbert R.
European scene. See occasional issues of
Publishers' weekly
Feltrinelli: there is no more personal a publisher. pors Pub W 197:60-2 F 2 '70
LOTZ, Wolfgang
Champagne spy. il por Time 96:27-8 N 23
'70 *
LOUD speaking apparatus
Adding extra channel for improved hi-fi ambience. D. Hafler. il Electr World 84:31 O
'70
Buck up bass response with a super woofer.
E. Pavlak. il Pop Electr 32:62 Je '70
Cadillac quality in Volkswagen space; Bose
speakers. I. Kolodin. Sat R 53:53 Je 27 '70
Direct vs reverberant sound for stereo speakers. G. L. Augspurger. il Electr World 84:
40-1+ S '70
How I hooked up my center-channel speaker.
G. Movshon. il Hi Fi 20:secI 71 Mr '70
Is omnidirectionality desirable in a loudspeaker. D. Davis. il Electr World 84:44-5+
Ag '70
Loudspeakers. il Consumer Rep 35:272-8 My
'70
Numbers game; multiple-cheap speaker systems. D. B. Weems. bibliog il Pop Electr 33:
64-8 N '70
Omni-eight speaker system. D. B. Weems.
il Pop Electr 32:69-73+ F '70
One speaker stereo sound. F. Shunaman. il
Radio-Electr 41:90-1 Mr '70
PA system you sling over your shoulder. E.
Ortner. il Pop Sci 196:91 My '70
Phasing P.A. speakers. H. Stratman. il
Electr World 84:31+ D '70
Portable speaker you can plug in anywhere.
G. J. Whalen and R. F. Graf. il Pop Mech
134:126-9 Ag '70
Public-address do's & dont's. W. C. Salm. il
Radio-Electr 41:33-5 Jl '70
Remote speakers for car stereo. H. L. Davidson. il Radio-Electr 41:53 Ap '70
Should you consider omnidirectional speakers? R. Lanier. il Hi Fi 20:secI 50-3 Je '70
Sound all around: the new multi-directional speakers. I. Berger. il Pop Sci 196:86-8
Mr '70
Speaker for your patio. il Mech Illus 66:76-7
Ag '70
Stereo scene. J. G. Holt. il Pop Electr 33:
94-7+ O '70
What should you pay for a hi-fi speaker system? il Electr World 84:12-14+ S '70
Wire your backyard for stereo. L. Feldman.
il Hi Fi 20:secI 54-9 Je '70

Cabinets
Build bookshelf speaker system. A. N. Retsoff. il Radio-Electr 41:43-5 Mr '70
Easy way to determine reflex enclosure dimensions E. G. Lescault. il Pop Electr 33:
64 D '70
Frisky four speaker system. D. B. Weems. il
Pop Electr 32:43-7 Ap '70
Mini-speaker from a spray-can cap. R. F.
Graf and G. J. Whalen. il Pop Mech 134:
123 Jl '70
Novel ultra-low-frequency woofer enclosure.
R. Dones. il Electr World 83:43-5 My '70

Testing
Hi-fi product report:
Advent loudspeaker system. il Electr
World 83:18+ Je '70
Altec 892A Madera speaker. il Electr
World 84:18 Jl '70
Altec-Lansing 729A Acousta-Voicette. il
Electr World 85:13-14 Ja '71
Empire 7000 speaker system. il Electr
World 83:16-17 Mr 21 '70
Jensen stereo I (S-100) speaker system.
il Electr World 83:7-8 My '70
KLH model 33 speaker system. il Electr
World 84:14-15 Ag '70
Scott S-15 speaker system. il Electr
World 83:58-9 Ja '70
Philosophy, fidelity, and sonic pleasure;
acoustic research AR-3a, and the rectilinear
III. I. Berger. Sat R 53:69 Mr 28 '70
Speaker tests can be relevant to the listening experience. B. Bauer. il Hi Fi 20:secI
42-9 Je '70

Tuning
Equalizing the sound system to match the
room. D. Davis and D. Palmquist. il Electr
World 83:34-6 Ja '70
LOUGH, Thomas
Indicted professor. New Repub 163:15 N 7 '70 *
LOUIS, Arthur M.
Chrysler's private hard times. il por Fortune
81:102-5+ Ap '70
Fat maverick stirs up the accounting profession. il Fortune 82:96-9+ D '70
Hidden jokers in the new tax deck. il Fortune 82:100-2+ Jl '70
Year of the executive axing. il Fortune 82:
142-5+ S '70
LOUIS, Joe
Salute to Joe. C. Higgins. il pors Ebony 25:
158-62 O '70 *
LOUIS, Morris
Morris Louis: veiled illusions. E. C. Baker.
il Art N 69:36-9+ Ap '70 *
LOUIS, Victor
Who is Mr X? S. Alsop. Newsweek 77:68 Ja
4 '71 *
LOUIS-GABRIEL, Sister
Gospels and the Oberammergau passion play.
il Cath World 211:13-17 Ap '70
LOUISBOURG fortress. See Cape Breton
Island—Historic houses, etc.
LOUISIANA
See also
Acadians in Louisiana
Education—Louisiana
Fishing—Louisiana
Negroes—Louisiana
Politics, Corruption in—Louisiana

Description and travel
Exploring the Cajun country. L. L. King. il
Holiday 47:70-3+ My '70
Joy in Mudville. D. Butwin. il Sat R 53:42-
4 S 26 '70

Politics and government
See also
Politics, Corruption in—Louisiana

History
Remarks; reprint. O. J. Dunn. por Negro
Hist Bul 33:18 Ja '70
LOUISIANA family planning program. See
Birth control
LOUISIANA land and exploration company
Pumping money at Louisiana land. Fortune
81:194 Je '70
LOUISVILLE

Libraries
See also
Louisville free public library

Music
See also
Kentucky opera association

Newspapers
Ombudsman in Louisville; investigating
newspaper readers' complaints. il por Time
96:44+ Jl 6 '70
LOUISVILLE free public library
Louisville: a library turnabout. il Library J
95:4138 D 1 '70
LOURIE, Dick
Comment. A. Billiant. Poetry 116:125-7 My
'70 *
LOUTHAN, William T.
LP-gas cuts police car costs, improves performance. il Am City 85:87-8 Je '70
LOUVIERE, Vernon
Panorama of the Nation's business. See issues
of Nation's business
LOUVRE, Paris
Art on four wheels; show of automotive design. il Life 68:70-3 My 22 '70
LOVBERG, R. H. See Berger, J. jt. auth.
LOVE, Edmund G.
Lost time. Sat R 53:4+ N 7 '70
LOVE, Harry
Black knight of the Zayante. R. H. Dillon. por
Am West 7:20-1 Jl '70 *
LOVE, Iris Cornelia
Archeologist: interview. New Yorker 46:28-
31 Mr 28 '70
about
Love affair. il Time 96:52+ N 23 '70 *
LOVE, J. Spencer
Threading your way to the top. E. R. Callaway. il Nations Bsns 58:62-3 Ja '70
LOVE, R. Merton
Rangelands of the western U.S. with biographical sketch. il Sci Am 222:10, 88-94+
bibliog(p 126) F '70

LOVE, Rose Leary
Obituary
Negro Hist Bul 32:24-5 D '69
LOVE
Men on love; ideas of celebrities. il Harp
Baz 103:112-13+ F '70
Opinion: phoniness. P. Miletich. por Mlle 71:
30+ Je '70
Pablo Casals: the meaning of love; excerpts
from Joys and Sorrows. il pors McCalls
97:70-3+ Ap '70
Scientific look at romantic love. Sci Digest
67:91 My '70
Why men can't say I love you. T. I. Rubin.
Ladies Home J 87:36 Je '70
Yes begins with a no; theories of R. May.
il por Time 95:66+ Je 22 '70
See also
Jealousy
Marriage

Anecdotes, facetiae, satire, etc.
Conversation about being in love. S. Lord.
Harp Baz 103:60 My '70
Cost of conducting an affair. A. Mehle.
Vogue 155:70-1 F 15 '70
LOVE (charity) See Charity
LOVE (theology)
Love, law and conduct. Chr Today 14:28 Je 5
'70
LOVE, Maternal
To a son on Mother's day. P. P. Leimbach.
Farm J 94:59 My '70
See also
Mothers
LOVE affair; story. See Richler, M.
LOVE and death; story. See Oates, J. C.
LOVE and maple syrup; revue. See Musical
comedies, revues, etc.—Criticisms, plots,
etc.
LOVE field airport. See Dallas—Airports
LOVE in literature
See also
Love poetry
LOVE poetry
Poet's workshop. F. Trefethen. Writer 83:
21-4 My '70
LOVE song; story. See Coffer, H. L.
LOVE sounds of a wife; story. See Sheehy, G.
LOVE story; story. See Segal, E.
LOVE to share; story. See Gillette, V. M.
LOVECRAFT'S follies; drama. See Schevill,
J. E.
LOVEJOY, Esther (Clayson) Pohl
Doctor was an adventuress. J. L. Block. il
Todays Health 48:20-1+ Ag '70 *
LOVELAND, Colo.
Air and electronics save pavement. il Am
City 85:10 D '70
LOVELIDGE, Brian
Sewage plant designed for livestock wastes.
il Farm J 94:54B-54C F '70
LOVELL, James A. 1928-
I was a good target for the law of averages. il
pors Life 68:24-8 My 1 '70

about
Brave men of Apollo. il pors Time 95:16-17 Ap
27 '70 *
Captain James A. Lovell, jr (USN) por
Newsweek 75:63 Ap 13 '70 *
See also
Space flight to the moon—Manned flights—
Apollo 8 flight
Space flight to the moon—Manned flights—
Apollo 13 flight
LOVERING, J. F. See Ware, N. G. jt. auth.
LOVERS all untrue; story. See Lofts, N.
LOVING, Rush, jr
How Cortes Randell drained the fountain of
youth. il por Fortune 81:94-7+ Ap '70
Penn central bankruptcy express. il pors
Fortune 82:104-9+ Ag '70
What the U.S. textile industry really needs.
il Fortune 82:84-7+ O '70
LOVING, Taylor Leroy
Winter gardening in California. il por Org
Gard & Farm 17:74-6 O '70
LOVING, Tom
Tom Loving, pioneer fly man. J. Brooks. il por
Outdoor Life 146:118-19+ N '70 *
LOVING, Walter Howard
Walter Howard loving, military band con-
ductor. J. Davis. il Negro Hist Bul 33:127
My '70 *
LOVOOS, Janice
James Trittico, designer for television. il por
Am Artist 34:30-5+ O '70
Quarter century of American ceramic art. il
Am Artist 34:20-5 F '70

LOVRIĆ, Ante
Planting in Pag. J. W. Duffield. il Am For
76:22-4+ F '70 *
LOW, George Michael
Soviet space gains cited by Low to sena-
tor. Aviation W 93:20 D 7 '70 *
LOW, Jacqueline
Everything is going to be all right; story.
Redbook 135:96-7 S '70
LOW COUNTRIES. See Belgium; Netherlands
LOW-sodium diet. See Diet in disease
LOW-temperature physics. See Low tempera-
tures
LOW temperatures
Cryogenics: new superconducting materials
announced at Dallas. R. W. Holcomb. Sci-
ence 168:103 Ap 3 '70
Low-temperature physics runs both hot and
cold. H. L. Davis. il Phys Today 23:17-18
D '70
Optical spectra of molecules at low tempera-
ture. B. Meyer. bibliog il Science 168:783-9
My 15 '70
See also
Cryobiology
LOWDERMILK'S secondhand bookstore. See
Booksellers and bookselling—Washington,
D.C.
LOWE, Arbon Jack
Mexico's metro. il Américas 22:30-5 Jl '70
LOWE, David
Fine male art. il McCalls 97:48+ F '70
Sight & sound. McCalls 98:16+ O '70
LOWE, M. D. See Henzell, R. F. jt. auth.
LOWELL, Robert
Comment. K. Spivack. Poetry 116:191-3 Je
'70 *
Comment. A. Williamson. Poetry 115:281-2
Ja '70
LOWEN, Alexander
You don't have a body; you are a body; ex-
cerpts from Please touch. J. Howard. Mlle
71:153+ My '70 *
LOWENSTEIN, Allard Kenneth
Lame duck; interview. New Yorker 46:51-2
N 21 '70
about
Pied Piper of the new children's crusade.
G. Astor. il por Look 34:36-8 Ag 25 '70 *
LOWENSTEIN, Edward. See Winter, P. M. jt.
auth.
LOWENSTEIN, James G. and Moose, R. M.
Prospect for Vietnamization. Cur 116:9-10 Mr
'70
LOWENTHAL, Abraham F.
Alliance rhetoric versus Latin American re-
ality. For Affairs 48:494-508 Ap '70
LOWER CALIFORNIA. See California, Lower
LOWERY, Alice M.
Odyssey as archetype. Engl J 59:1076-9 N '70
LOWERY, John M.
End that bites. il Flying 86:84-5 F '70
LOWI, Theodore J.
Apartheid U.S.A; excerpts from The end of
liberalism. il Trans-Action 7:32-9 F '70
Artificial majority. il Nation 211:91-4 D 7
'70
LOWREY, Bette
Statistics say the average voter is Bette
Lowrey of Ohio. il pors Life 69:30-2 O 30
'70 *
LOWREY, Joseph
'70 1/2 Sunbeam Avenger. il Motor T 22:
98+ Ap '70
LOWRIE, Jean E.
(ed) School libraries and international de-
velopment. Am Lib 1:182-3 F '70
LOWRY, David
Back to basics. Flying 87:82-3 N '70
LOWRY, Malcolm
Call it misadventure. C. Lorenz. por Atlan
225:106-10+ Je '70 *
LOWRY, William H. and Reilley, R. R.
Life problems and interests of adolescents.
bibliog il Clear House 45:164-8 N '70
LOYALTY
See also
Americanism
Patriotism
LOYALTY, Oaths of
Do we need a new pledge of allegiance?
L. A. Stevens. Look 34:19-21 D 1 '70
How odd! dropping of requirement by Civil
service commission. Nation 210:69 Ja 26
'70

Anecdotes, facetiae, satire, etc.
Loyalty begins at home; ALA midwinter
meeting in Daleyland. K. Nyren. Library
J 95:963 Mr 15 '70

LOYD, F. Glen
Jack Armstrong is dead. Todays Health 48:
47-8+ O '70
Why unfit men are drafted. il Todays Health
48:50-3 Ap '70
—and Irwin, Theodore
How quackery thrives on the occult. il Todays
Health 48:20-3+ N '70
LUAU. See Cookery, Hawaiian
LUBBOCK, Tex.
Tornado fails to darken sports lighting pro-
ject. il Am City 85:100 N '70
Tornado with a new twist; Coaches All-
America football game. W. F. Reed. il
Sports Illus 33:16-17 Jl 6 '70
LUBBOCK tornadoes. See Tornadoes
LüBECK
Lübeck's ancient skyline of steeples. L.
Barry. il Pop Phot 67:34+ S '70
LUBELL, Samuel
Our contemporary hidden crisis; excerpt from
Hidden crisis in American politics. Cur 123:
9-13 N '70
LUBENOW, Gerald
Enough of Reagan? New Repub 162:14-15
F 14 '70
LUBKIN, Gloria B.
(ed) See Kapitza, P. L. Interview with Peter
Kapitsa
LUBOLD, Joyce Kissock
What to do if the doctor comes. il Good H
171:59+ Jl '70
LUBOVITCH, Lar
Choreography by Lar Lubovitch; 92nd street Y.
D. Hering. il Dance Mag 44:86-7 F '70
Ecstasy; body and being. W. Terry. il por
Sat R 53:45 O 10 '70 *
Lar Lubovitch and company; American
theatre laboratory. N. M. Stoop. il por
Dance Mag 44:74 Jl '70 *
LUBRICANTS. See Lubrication and lubricants
LUBRICATION and lubricants
Well-oiled home runs smoother. S. J. Howard.
il Pop Mech 134:172-4 Jl '70
What those new motor oil letters mean.
Suc Farm 69:D5 Ja '71
    See also
Airplane engines—Lubrication
Automobiles—Lubrication
LUBRIZOL
Lucky Lubrizol. il Forbes 105:30-1 Ja 15 '70
LUBS, H. A. and Ruddle, F. H.
Chromosomal abnormalities in the human
population: estimation of rates based on
New Haven newborn study. bibliog il Sci-
ence 169:495-7 Jl 31 '70
LUCA, Giuseppe de
Giuseppe De Luca. A. Favia-Artsay. por Hob-
bies 75:35-6 N '70 *
LUCAL, John A.
United Nations and the Holy See. il America
123:315-17 O 24 '70
LUCAS, Christopher
Lilliput in the South Pacific. il Read Digest
96:211-12+ Ja '70
LUCAS, Dione
Dione and her cooking kids; with recipes.
E. Alston. il pors Look 34:50-2 Ag 11 '70 *
Kitchen secrets of five master cooks; with
recipes. J. Wilson. il pors House & Gard
138:80-1+ Jl '70 *
—and Robbins, A. R.
Dione Lucas meat and poultry cookbook;
excerpt. il por Ladies Home J 87:98-103+
S '70
LUCAS, Jerry
Mellow wine in a new bottle. P. Carry. il
pors Sports Illus 33:16-19 D 7 '70 *
LUCAS, Joseph Richard
Setback for safety. il por Newsweek 75:80+
Je 8 '70 *
LUCAS, Lawrence E.
If you could make one change in the church,
what would it be? Commonweal 92:162-3
My 1 '70
LUCAS, Leo
How to avoid feet and leg problems. il Farm
J 94:H26 Mr '70
LUCCHESI, Bruno
Bronze realists. il Time 95:74 Je 1 '70 *
LUCE, Charles Franklin
Con Ed's Charles Luce: all power (sometimes)
to the people. S. Brownmiller. il pors N Y
Times Mag p34-5+ Ap 12 '70 *
Power-short winter? interview. il por U S
News 69:38-42 N 9 '70
LUCE, Clare (Boothe)
Doll's house 1970; text. il pors Life 69:54-6+
O 16 '70
Two books on abortion. Nat R 23:27-8+ Ja 12
'71
LUCE, Don
Expelling the exposer. Time 96:76 N 16 '70 *
How Thieu rules. New Repub 162:17-18 F 28
'70
Not welcome; harassment in South Vietnam.
por Newsweek 76:99B N 23 '70 *

LUCE, Henry Robinson
Passion for ideas and order; ed. by J. K.
Jessup. por Time 95:56 Mr 9 '70
    about
Media master. R. D. Heffner. Sat R 53:37-8
Mr 7 '70 *
LUCE, W. G.
You can feed wheat. il Farm J 93:H16 N '69
LUCEY, James D.
Can you state your story in a sentence?
Writers Digest 50:27+ D '70
LUCEY, Thomas C.
Defending the dance of the bees. Sci N 98:150
Ag 15 '70
LUCIA, David
Case of the bearded teacher. por Todays Ed
59:26-7 My '70 *
LUCIA di Lammermoor; opera. See Donizetti,
G.
LUCIENTES, Francisco José de Goya y. See
Goya y Lucientes, F. J. de
LUCILLA'S proposal; drama. See Reed, D.
LUCK, G. R. See McElhinny, M. W. jt. auth.
LUCKIEST girl in Iowa; story. See Williams,
L. and Espy, H. C.
LUCKINBILL, Laurence
Oh, you Sundance Kid! il por Esquire 74:
160-3+ O '70
LUCKMAN, Sidney
Where are they now? il pors Newsweek 76:16
O 5 '70 *
LUCY Faciane, Sister. See Faciane, L.
LUDLUM, David M.
Espy-Redfield dispute. pors Weatherwise 22:
224-9+ D '69
Snowfall season of 1968-69. il Weatherwise
23:24-31 F '70
LUDOWICI, Ga.
American scene: Ludowici, Ga; speed-trap
warning. J. Kane. il Time 95:28 Ap 27 '70
Town without pity? il Newsweek 75:35 Ap
27 '70
LUDVIGSEN, Karl E.
Cerv II: Corvette experimental (non) racing
vehicle. il Motor T 22:47-50+ N '70
Corvettes in Chevy's closet are the most
interesting of all! il Motor T 22:32-7+ Ja
'70
EFI: a squirt in the right direction. il Motor
T 22:60-3 N '70
Every man his own reactor. il Motor T 23:
44-6+ Ja '71
For America only. il Motor T 22:44-6+ Ap
'70
Lamborghini Jarama. il Motor T 22:56-7
Jl '70
Next ten years. il Motor T 22:62-5+ Ja '70
Objective: Ontario. il Motor T 22:72+ S '70
Travel in the '70s. Mech Illus 66:44-5 Ja '70
    about
Car of the year; cars panel. por Motor T 23:
63 Ja '71 *
LUDVIGSON, H. Wayne. See Morrison, R. R.
jt. auth.
LUDWIG, Daniel K.
Twilight of a tycoon. il por Time 96:76-8 N 30
'70 *
LUECKE, Richard Henry
Protestant clergy: new forms of ministry,
new forms of training. bibliog f Ann Am
Acad 387:86-95 Ja '70
LUEHRS, Armin F.
Values of camping. por Camp Mag 42:4 My
'70
LUEKING, F. Dean
(ed) See Raya, J. Hopeful voices from Israel
(ed) See Werblowsky, Z. Hopeful voices from
Israel
LUFKIN, Dan W.
Is the corporation dead? address, September
22, 1970. Vital Speeches 37:90-3 N 15 '70
    about
Lufkin pursues his conscience. por Bsns W
p95-6 Ja 24 '70
LUFTHANSA. See Airlines—Germany (Federal
Republic)
LUGAR, Richard G.
Brash mayor stirs Indianapolis. il pors
Bsns W p84-5 O 3 '70 *
LUGGAGE
Consumer's guide to luggage. il Mech Illus
66:102 F '70
Packing up for Expo. C. Kriebel. Harp Baz
103:68-9 Mr '70
LUGGAGE handling, Airlines. See Airlines—
Luggage handling
LUHN, David Ryan
Mercy general; poem. Am Scholar 39:470
Sum '70

LUIS, Earlene
How not to teach English in high school.
Engl J 59:964-6 O '70

LUITJENS, Helen
Sculpture can be fun. il Sch Arts 70:28-9 O
'70

LUKACS, György
Marxism of George Lukacs. D. Gross. por
Commonweal 93:224-5 N 27 '70 *

LUKACS, John Adalbert
Bourgeois interior; excerpt from The passing
of the modern age. Am Scholar 39:616-30
Aut '70
Emancipation or degradation? excerpts from
The passing of the modern age. Nat R
22:833-5 Ag 11 '70
Paradox of prosperity; excerpt from The pass-
ing of the modern age. Commentary 49:64-9
F '70

LUKAS, J. Anthony
On the lam in America. il N Y Times
Mag p30-1+ D 13 '70
Second confrontation in Chicago. il N Y
Times Mag p 10-11+ Mr 29 '70
This is Bob (politician-patriot-publicist)
Hope. il pors N Y Times Mag p28-9+ O 4
'70

LUKE
To come to you and say; poem. America 123:
260 O 10 '70

LUKENBILL, L.
Un-tapped research source. il Writers Digest
50:29 Ag '70

LULL, Ramón
Great moments in chemisty; tr. by R. E.
Oesper. F. Szabadvary. il Chem 43:5-7 D
'70 *

LULLUS, Raimundus. See Lull, R.

LULU
Lulu. C. Mangel. il pors Look 34:68-70 Jl
28 '70

LULU; opera. See Berg, A.

LUMACHI, Ronald
Low-cost tools for your lathe. il Mech Illus
66:96-7+ D '70
Making your own springs. il Mech Illus 66:
71 Ag '70

LUMBER
Fair market value. S. B. Moser. il pors Am
For 76:20-3+ Ja '70
See also
Wood

Grading and standardization
How big is a board? J. Hand. il Pop Sci 196:
141+ Ja '70

LUMBER industry and trade
Habit of waste. M. Margolin. Nation 210:
238-40 Mr 2 '70
Mike Frome; National timber supply act. M.
Frome. Am For 76:3+ Ap '70
NPA in action; National timber supply act
postponed. Nat Parks & Con Mag 44:32-
3 My '70
Raiding the forests; timber supply act. M.
McCloskey; reply. H. Rogers. New Repub
162:11 F 7 '70
View from VISTA; Appalachian volunteers
in conservation programs. E. Urvant. il
Am For 76:8+ S '70
Wilds of Borneo lure U.S. Lumbermen. il
Bsns W p51 Je 27 '70
See also
Georgia-Pacific corporation
Timber

LUMBERING
Last log drive; Clearwater River, Idaho.
A. Tussing. il Am For 76:16-19 Jl '70
To regenerate eastern hardwoods; clearcut.
W. E. McQuilkin. il Am For 76:20-3+ Je '70;
Discussion. 76:3+ Ag; 4-5 S '70

LUMINAIRES. See Lighting fixtures; Street
lighting fixtures

LUMINESCENCE
Apollo 11 lunar science conference: other
physical properties; symposium. bibliog il
Science 167:713-24 Ja 30 '70
Cathodoluminescence properties of lunar
rocks. R. F. Sippel and A. B. Spencer. bib-
liog Science 167:677-9 Ja 30 '70
See also
Thermoluminescence

Conferences
Delaware luminescence meeting covers organ-
ics and inorganics. R. B. Murray. Phys Today 23:87+ F '70

LUMMIS, Charles Fletcher
Aggressive librarian: Charles Fletcher
Lummis. D. Gordon. il por Wilson Lib
Bul 45:399-405 D '70 *

LUNA flights. See Space flight to the moon—
Luna flights

LUNAR bases
See also
Moon—Exploration

LUNAR communication systems. See Space
flight—Communication systems

LUNAR eclipses. See Eclipses, Lunar

LUNAR ephemeris. See Ephemerides

LUNAR exploration. See Moon—Exploration

LUNAR geology
Aerospace; preliminary studies of Apollo 12
moon rocks. Sci N 97:269 Mr 14 '70
Apollo 11 lunar science conference; papers,
with editorial comment. bibliog il Science
167:447, 449-784 Ja 30 '70; Correction. 167:
1759 Mr 27 '70
Apollo 12 lunar samples: trace element analysis of a core and the uniformity of the
regolith. R. Ganapathy and others. bibliog il
Science 170:533-5 O 30 '70
Apollo 12 seismic experiment links red lunar
glow to quakes. Z. Strickland. Aviation W
93:57 Ag 10 '70
Apollo samples spur lunar debate. Z.
Strickland. il Aviation W 92:46-8 Ja 26
'70
As moon yields its secrets; official findings
from Apollo. il U S News 68:28-9 Ja 19
'70
Back to time one. il Sci N 97:428-9 My 2
'70
Bed forms in base-surge deposits; lunar im-
plications. R. V. Fisher and A. C. Waters;
reply with rejoinder. D. R. Grine. bibliog
Science 167:1637-8 Mr 20 '70
Catch two; Apollo 12 rocks. Sci Am 222:56
My '70
Chemical composition of the lunar surface
in a terra region near the crater Tycho. J.
H. Patterson and others. bibliog il Science
168:825-8 My 15 '70
Dating the moon. J. Lear. il Sat R 53:52
Ap 11 '70
Findings from a sample of lunar material.
R. N. Watts. jr. il Sky & Tel 39:144-7 Mr
'70
Garnet: first occurrence in the lunar rocks.
R. J. Traill and others. bibliog il Science
169:981-2 S 4 '70
Glowing jewels from the moon: rocks under
the microscope. il Life 68:30-2 Ja 23 '70
Lunar anorthosites: rare-earth and other ele-
mental abundances. H. Wakita and R. A.
Schmitt. bibliog il Science 170:969-74 N 27
'70
Lunar soil. J. A. Wood. il Sci Am 223:14-23
bibliog(p 128) Ag '70
Moon: major questions still remain. K. Fra-
zier. il Sci N 97:99-101 Ja 24 '70
Moon rock distribution; Apollo 12 samples. il
Space World G-6-78:44 Je '70
Moon rock identified with tektites. Space
World G-12-84:13 D '70
Moon rock resembles meteorites. Space World
G-4-76:31 Ap '70
Orthopyroxene-plagioclase fragments in the
lunar soil from Apollo 12. L. H. Fuchs.
bibliog il Science 169:866-8 Ag 28 '70
Potassium-argon ages of lunar rocks from
Mare Tranquillitatis and Oceanus Procel-
larum. O. A. Schaeffer and others. bibliog
il Science 170:161-2 O 9 '70
Preliminary examination of lunar samples
from Apollo 12. il Science 167:1325-38 Mr
6 '70
Properties and composition of lunar ma-
terials: earth analogies. E. Schreiber and
O. L. Anderson. bibliog il Science 168:
1579-80 Je 26 '70
Radioactivity induced in Apollo 11 lunar
surface material by solar flare protons. H.
R. Heydegger and A. Turkevich. bibliog
il Science 168:575-6 My 1 '70
Results of Apollo 11 research. R. N. Watts,
jr. il Sky & Tel 39:226-7 Ap '70
Rock of ages. il Newsweek 75:106 Je 8 '70
Stones with a story. il Space World G-8-80:
4-13 Ag '70
Stories the moon rocks tell. il Space World
G-4-76:4-8 Ap '70
Surprising facts we're learning from the
moon landings. W. Von Braun. il Pop Sci
196:62-4+ F '70
Tektite glass in Apollo 12 sample. J. A.
O'Keefe. bibliog il Science 168:1209-10 Je 5
'70; Reply with rejoinder. E. A. King, jr.
and others. 170:199-200 O 9 '70
Thermal conducitivity of lunar and terres-
trial igneous rocks in their melting range.
T. Murase and A. R. McBirney. bibliog
bibliog il Science 170:165-7 O 9 '70
U.S. presents moon stone to the United Na-
tions. T. O. Paine. Dept State Bul 63:179 Ag
10 '70
Viscosity of lunar lavas. T. Murase and A.
R. McBirney. bibliog il Science 167:1491-3
Mr 13 '70

LUNAR geology—*Continued*
What the moon is made of. il Chem 43:22-4 S '70
What the moon rocks reveal. F. Warshofsky. il Read Digest 97:157-60+ Ag '70

Anecdotes, facetiae, satire, etc.
Notes and comment. New Yorker 46:25 Je 13 '70

Conferences
Letter from the space center; Apollo 11 lunar science conference. H. S. F. Cooper, jr. New Yorker 46:80+ Ap 4 '70

LUNAR gravity. See Gravity

LUNAR landing sites. See Moon—Surface

LUNAR magnetic fields. See Magnetic fields (cosmic physics)

LUNAR module. See Space vehicles—Landing systems—Moon

LUNAR names. See Names, Lunar

LUNAR receiving laboratory. See United States—Manned spacecraft center—Lunar receiving laboratory

LUNAR rocks
Analysis
See Lunar geology

LUNAR roving vehicle. See Lunar vehicles

LUNAR seismology. See Seismology

LUNAR soil. See Soils

LUNAR vehicles
Buggy on the moon; Lunokhod. il Newsweek 76:50 N 30 '70
First car on the moon; Lunar Rover. il Space World G-5-77:38-40 My '70
Giant step for Lunokhod; Luna 17 and Lunokhod I. il Time 96:63 N 30 '70
Lunokhod 1 vehicle, Luna 17 shown on moon and in assembly. il Aviation W 93:14-15 N 30 '70
Lunokhod resumes lunar travel; extricated from steep crater. Aviation W 93:21 D 21 '70
Lunokhod tests French laser reflector. il Aviation W 93:18-20 D 7 '70
Lunokhod to reactivate after lunar night. il Aviation W 93:16-17 N 30 '70
Moon car. D. Wells. il Motor T 22:55-9+ Ag '70
Moon cars that didn't make it. il Motor T 22:60-1 Ag '70
News from the world of space exploration; lunar roving vehicle. Space World G-3-75:45 Mr '70
News from the world of space exploration; pogo-stick. il Space World G-6-78:53 Je '70
Putting robots on the planets. il U S News 69:45 N 30 '70
Robot on moon; Lunokhod 1. Sci N 98:397 N 21 '70
Rover initiates Soviet applied lunar work. il Aviation W 93:19-20 N 23 '70
Unknowns force Apollo 15 crew to be cautious on lunar rover. Aviation W 93:85 N 16 '70
Unveiling a 1970 model: the Lunar Rover. E. Diamond. il N Y Times Mag p34-5+ Ap 5 '70
Wheels
Markow lunar roving vehicle wheel, earth-applications spin-off. il Space World G-9-81:16-17 S '70

LUNARIA. See Honesty (plants)

LUNCHEONS
Cooking is just like making music; Bobby Short's luncheon menu; with recipes. il pors House B 112:112+ Mr '70
Personality lunch in kitchens around the world. il House & Gard 137:131+ Mr '70
See also
Brunches

LUNCHES
Brown bag lunch; with recipes. il Sunset 145:94-5 N '70
Hi, mom, what's for lunch? R. M. Fabio. See issues of Parents' magazine & better family living
Lunchbox menus for dieting school children; excerpts from Help your child lose weight. G. Mason. Ladies Home J 87:116-17 Mr '70
School's out, good nutrition isn't. G. Maddox. il Todays Health 48:52-5 Je '70
You and your children's diet. B. Newman. il Good H 171:133-5 Ag '70

LUNCHES, School. See School lunches

LUND, Jennifer S. See Hamilton, C. R. jt. auth.

LUND, Morten
Lonely cruise on Long Island Sound. il Holiday 47:44-5+ Je '70

LUND, Robert
Detroit listening post. See issues of Popular mechanics
Easy-to-fix cars. il Pop Mech 133:83-5+ F '70

LUND Humphries, Percy, and company. See Publishers and publishing—Great Britain

LUNDBORG, Louis Billings
War and big business. L. L. L. Golden. Sat R 53:95 S 12 '70 *

LUNDSTEDT, Sven
Conflict management: preeminent challenge. Ment Hy 54:584-8 O '70

LUNDY, Joseph R.
Mitchell tests the Constitution. Nation 210:205-7 F 23 '70

LUNG cancer. See Cancer

LUNGFISHES
When life moved ashore. il Chem 43:5 O '70

LUNGS
Pulmonary surfactant and evolution of the lungs. J. A. Clements and others. bibliog il Science 169:603-4 Ag 7 '70

Diseases
Lungs in health and in disease. L. W. Sauer. il PTA Mag 65:31-2 S '70
Obstructive lung disease and O-antitrypsin deficiency gene heterozygosity. F. Kueppers and others; discussion. bibliog il Science 167:1015-16 F 13 '70
See also
Cystic fibrosis
Emphysema
Pneumonia

LUNGWORMS
How to diagnose and treat lungworm infections. J. G. Clark. Farm J 94:B23 N '70

LUNN, Sir Arnold
Olympics and modern philosophy. Nat R 22:840 Ag 11 '70

LUNN, Betty
From whitest Africa: a dark tale of censorship. bibliog il por Library J 95:131-3 Ja 15 '70

LUNN, John
Louisbourg, the forgotten fortress. il Antiques 97:872-9 Je '70

LUNNY, Ray
Chip off the old redwood. il por Sports Illus 33:44-5 Ag 10 '70 *

LUNOKHOD (moon vehicle) See Lunar vehicles

LUO tribe. See Kenya—Native races

LUPINES
Trouble with a steep bank. W. Ferguson. il Org Gard & Farm 17:76-7 F '70

LUPSHA, Peter A.
Obstacles to urban change. Cur Hist 59:296-9+ N '70

LUPTON, Mary Jane
Rime of the ancient mariner: the agony of thirst. bibliog f Ann Imago 27:140-59 Sum '70

LUPUS erythematosus
Antibody to nuclear material eluted from isolated spleen vessels in systemic lupus erythematosus. K. H. Svec and S. T. Allen. bibliog il Science 170:550-1 O 30 '70

LURES, Fishing. See Fishing lures, flies, etc

LURIA, A. R.
Functional organization of the brain; with biographical sketch. il Sci Am 222:25, 66-72+ bibliog(p 146) Mr '70

LURIA, Salvador Edward
Phage, colicins, and macroregulatory phenomena. bibliog Science 168:1166-70 Je 5 '70
Recognition of DNA in bacteria; with biographical sketch. il Sci Am 222:16, 88-92+ bibliog(p 146) Ja '70

LURIA, Saul Martin, and Kinney, J. A. S.
Underwater vision. bibliog il Science 167:1454-61 Mr 13 '70

LURIE, Diana
Sargent Shriver: what happens to a man who marries a Kennedy. il pors Ladies Home J 87:96-7+ Ap '70

LURIE, Raanan
He commutes from paint to pen and back. R. Graves. por Life 68:3 Mr 27 '70 *

LURIE, Sidney B.
Market outlook. See issues of Forbes

LUSAKA conference, 1970. See International conferences

LUSNAK, Karin. See Roth, R. jt. auth.

LUSTEG, Booth
Coach wants to see you; ed. by J. Underwood. il Sports Illus 33:92-6+ S 21 '70

LUTÈCE (restaurant) See New York (city)—Hotels, restaurants, etc.

LUTEINIZING hormone. See Gonadotropins

LUTEN, C. J.
From the Arturo Toscanini society: memorable Strauss. il Am Rec G 36:330-1 Ja '70
Giselle, all of it for the first time on records. por Am Rec G 36:868-9 Jl '70
Götterdämmerung. il Am Rec G 37:4-6+ S '70

LUTEOTROPIN
Brain enhancement in tadpoles: increased DNA concentration after somatotrophin or prolactin. R. K. Hunt and M. Jacobson. bibliog il Science 170:342-4 O 16 '70
Prolactin: evidence that it is separate from growth hormone in human blood. A. G. Frantz and D. L. Kleinberg. bibliog il Science 170:745-7 N 13 '70
Prolactin localization in the primate pituitary by immunofluorescence. D. C. Herbert and T. Hayashida. bibliog il Science 169:378-9 Jl 24 '70

LUTHER, Martin
Great confrontations: Leo X and Luther. L. B. Smith. il pors Horizon 12:90-5 Spr '70 *
In-communication of Martin Luther. Chr Cent 87:101 Ja 28 '70
Luther and erotic love; in reply to Reinhold Niebuhr. C. Lindberg. Chr Cent 87:456-7 Ap 15 '70 *
Young man Luther, by E. H. Erikson. Review New Yorker 46:84+ N 14 '70. R. Coles *

LUTHERAN church
See also
Lutheran world federation

LUTHERAN church in America. See Lutheran Church in the United States

LUTHERAN church in Brazil
Brazil and the Lutherans; LWF's fifth assembly. Chr Cent 87:523 Ap 29 '70

LUTHERAN church in Germany
Worldly religious community; Bavaria's Casteller Ring. G. Weckman. Chr Cent 87: 1513-15 D 16 '70

LUTHERAN church in the United States
ALC leans closer to LCA. R. Durham. Chr Today 15:43 N 20 '70
Division=Lutheran unity? Chr Today 14:33 Mr 27 '70
Hunting Lutheran heretics. il Newsweek 76: 47 Ag 3 '70
Lutheran sex code: covenant above contract. R. Chandler. Chr Today 14:32-3 Jl 31 '70
Lutheran youth: caring in the wilderness. A. Eggebroten. Chr Today 14:50-1 S 11 '70
Lutherans in America: drawing together or pulling apart? R. Chandler. Chr Today 14:33-4 Jl 17 '70
Marriage covenant: promises, promises. Chr Today 14:17 Jl 31 '70
Moderate removed from Missouri Synod post. Chr Cent 87:230 F 25 '70; Discussion 87:642 My 20 '70
See also
Lutheran world federation

Names
See Churches—Names

LUTHERAN world federation
Adeus, Porto Alegre; bonjour, Evian-Les-Bains! new site for fifth assembly. Chr Cent 87:884-5 Jl 22 '70
Atrocities charged: Brazil loses Lutheran assembly. Chr Today 14:36 Jl 3 '70
Brazil and the Lutherans; LWF's fifth assembly. Chr Cent 87:523 Ap 29 '70
LWF assembly: uncertain trumpet. D. McCurry. Chr Cent 87:1100-3 S 16 '70
World Lutherans: unequal standards; with editorial comment. Chr Today 14:29, 40-1 Ag 21 '70

LUTHERANS in the United States
Lutherans and American Indians: a confrontation. E. R. Trexler. Chr Cent 87:1103-5 S 16 '70

LUTSKY, Valery
236-inch Soviet reflector. il Sky & Tel 39:99 F '70

LUTTGE, William G. See Whalen, R. E. jt. auth.

LUTTWAK, Edward
Scenario for a military coup d'etat in the United States. il Esquire 74:60-5+ Jl '70

LUTZ, Carroll
After the sale. il Yachting 127:114+ Ja '70

LUTZ, Charles P.
Middle America: theologically formed. Chr Cent 87:323-5 Mr 18 '70

LUTZ, Loren L.
Bighorns: wild sheep of California. il Am For 76:28-31 My; 30-1+ Je '70

LUXEMBOURG
Luxembourg, the quiet fortress. R. L. Conly. il Nat Geog 138:68-97 Jl '70

LUXURY
Status symbols are changing, too. J. Smith. il Duns 95:52-4+ My '70
See also
Leisure class

LUYENDYK, Bruce P. See Phillips, J. D. jt. auth.

LYCOPENE
Changing the color of fruit. il Chem 43:26 S '70
Lycopene accumulation induced by 2-(4-chlorophenylthio)-triethylamine hydrochloride. C. W. Coggins, jr. and others. bibliog Science 168:1589-90 Je 26 '70

LYCORIS
Surprising lycoris. M. G. Stewart. Horticulture 48:40 S '70

LYDON, Michael
Rolling Stones, a play in the Apocalypse. il Ramp Mag 8:26-53 Mr '70
Top beats the bottom: Carl Perkins and his music; excerpt from Rock folk. il por Atlan 226:96-8+ D '70

LYING
On being a woman: little white lies. J. Brothers. Good H 170:54+ F '70
Truth about lying; excerpt from Lies and truth. M. Eck. il N Y Times Mag p87+ Ap 26 '70

LYKES, J. E. jr. See Hoge, C. H. jt. auth.

LYKES-Youngstown corporation
Steelmaker casts an eye on the Gulf. il Bsns W p22 Jl 25 '70

LYLE, Margaret E.
Traveler's choice. Travel 133:13 Ja '70

LYMAN, Donald Joseph
Era of plastic hearts. B. J. Culliton. il por Sci N 97:376-7 Ap 11 '70 *

LYMAN, Richard Wall
New order for Stanford. por Time 96:50+ O 12 '70 *

LYMAN, Stanford M.
Red guard on Grant avenue. il Trans-Action 7:20-34 Ap '70

LYMPHOCYTES
Cell-mediated immunity shown by lymphocytes from the respiratory tract. C. S. Henney and R. H. Waldman. bibliog il Science 169:696-7 Ag 14 '70
Inhibition of cytotoxicity of lymphocytes by concanavalin A in vitro. P. Perlmann and others. bibliog il Science 168:1112-15 My 29 '70
Lymphocytic responses to streptococcal antigens in glomerulonephritic patients. J. B. Zabriskie and others. bibliog il Science 168:1105-8 My 29 '70
Mixed lymphocyte cultures produce effector cells: model in vitro for allograft rejection. P. Häyry and V. Defendi. bibliog il Science 168:133-5 Ap 3 '70
Radioresistance of cooperative function of carrier-specific lymphocytes in antihapten antibody responses. D. H. Katz and others. bibliog il Science 170:462-4 O 23 '70
Rat thoracic duct lymphocytes: types that participate in inflammation. F. Koster and D. D. McGregor. bibliog il Science 167: 1137-9 F 20 '70
Specificity of antigen recognition by human lymphocytes in vitro. D. C. Zoschke and F. H. Bach. bibliog il Science 170:1404-6 D 25 '70

LYNCH, Ann Q.
Quit teaching students. Todays Ed 59:58-9 N '70

LYNCH, Don
They're grabbing our hunting land. Field & S 75:12+ Ag '70
They're killing Pyramid Lake. il Field & S 74:10-15 Ja '70

LYNCH, J. Barry
Peace corps intrigue in the Philippines. G. H. Anderson; discussion. Chr Cent 87:184, 538 F 11, Ap 29 '70

LYNCH, James B.
Unsung artist of the Mexican renaissance. il por Américas 22:33-9 Je '70

LYNCH, John A.
Batter up! il Am For 76:32-5+ N '70
Garden in the woods. il Am For 76:20-3+ Mr '70
Nature's jewels; photographs. Am For 76: 44-5 S '70

LYNCH, Thomas F. and Kennedy, K. A. R.
Early human cultural and skeletal remains from Guitarrero cave, northern Peru. bibliog il Science 169:1307-9 S 25 '70

LYNCH, Vincent. See Felig, P. jt. auth.

LYNCH, William F.
Madness as an existential solution to an existential situation. pors Commonweal 92:484-5 S 25 '70

LYND, Robert S.
Obituary
Nation 211:517 N 23 '70
Pub W 198:22 N 30 '70
LYND, Staughton
Again, don't tread on me. por Newsweek
76:30-2 Jl 6 '70
LYNDEN, Patricia
What day care means to the children: the
parents, the teachers, the community, the
President. il N Y Times Mag p30-1+ F 15;
60+ Mr 15 '70
LYNDHURST (historic house) See New York
(state)—Historic houses, etc.
LYNDON B. Johnson state park. See Texas—
Parks and reserves
LYNDS, C. Roger. See Burbidge, E. M. jt.
auth.
LYNES, Russell
After hours. Harper 240:32+ Ap '70
Artist as uneconomic man. il Sat R 53:25-8+
F 28 '70
Square peg in a square hole. il pors Art in
Am 58:80-5 Mr '70
State of taste (cont) por Art in Am 58:21
Ja; 27 Mr; 27 My; 11 Jl; 21 S; 39 N '70
LYNN, Janet
Many-faceted champion. pors Sports Illus 32:
20-4 Ja 26 '70
LYNN, Mass.
Our crash street-cleaning program. J. R.
Casey. il Am City 85:63-5 Jl '70
LYNTON, Norbert
Intimations of mortality. Art in Am 58:43
N '70
LYNXES
See also
Bobcats
LYON, Danny
Conversations with the dead. M. Kozloff. il
pors Art N 69:24-7+ D '70 *
LYON, Ninette
Cook as communicator. Vogue 156:197+ N 1
'70
Food in Vogue. See issues of Vogue to April,
1970
Garden speedway. Vogue 156:432 S 1 '70
LYON, T. J.
Spoiled lion. il pors Outdoor Life 145:72-5+
F '70
LYONS, Charles H.
Nigeria. bibliog il Focus 21:1-7 D '70
LYONS, Daniel J.
Lyons' dropping stock. J. Deedy. Common-
weal 93:210 N 27 '70 *
Lyons goes full circle. Chr Today 14:47 S 11
'70
LYONS, Leonard
Jack and Charlie's hideaway house. il Holi-
day 47:77-9 Ja '70
There's no accounting for houses. House &
Gard 138:28 Jl '70

about

See Lennie run. il pors Time 95:44 F 23 '70 *
LYONS, Nathan
Survival in the Zaharah Desart; poem. Yale
R 60:85-7 O '70
LYONS, Richard
Garden of the (dead) gods; poem. Nation 210:
726 Je 15 '70
LYONS, France

Hotels, restaurants, etc.
Weekend of incredible gluttony. R. A. De
Groot. il Esquire 73:135-9+ My '70
LYRIC opera of Chicago
Lyric opera breaks the jinx. R. C. Marsh. il
Hi Fi sec II 20:24-5 Ja '70
Lyric today and yesterday: annals and pic-
tures. Opera N 35:17-20 O 31 '70
Report:
Benjamin Britten's Billy Budd. J. W.
Freeman. il por Opera N 35:36 D 19 '70
Italiana in Algeri. C. Cassidy. il Opera
N 35:29 Ja 2 '71
Production of Rosenkavalier. C. Cassidy. il
Opera N 35:26 O 31 '70
Productions of Cavalleria rusticana,
El amor brujo and Il barbiere di Si-
viglia. J. Stedman and G. McElroy.
Opera N 34:32 Ja 24 '70
Turandot, Lucia di Lammermoor and
La Traviata. C. Cassidy. il Opera N
35:30 D 12 '70
LYRICS. See Music, Popular (songs, etc); Songs
LYSENKO, Trofim Denisovich
Rise and fall of T. D. Lysenko, by Z. A.
Medvedev. Review
Bul Atom Sci 26:54-6 Ap '70. O. Hechtler.*
New Yorker 45:85-6+ Ja 24; 46:93-4 Je 13
'70. J. Bernstein *

LYSERGIC acid diethylamide. See LSD
LYSIS (bacteriology) See Bacteriolysis
LYSOHORSKY, Ondra, pseud.
Poet; Room for all; At the circus; Trees in
courtyards; poems, tr. by I. Levatin and
W. H. Auden. Poetry 116:273-8 Ag '70
LYSOZYME
Mouse lysozyme production by a monocytoma:
isolation and comparison with other
lysozymes. R. J. Riblet and L. A. Herzen-
berg. bibliog il Science 168:1595-7 Je 26 '70
LYSTROSAURUS. See Reptiles, Fossil
LYTLE, Jim
To the summit by ATV; interview, ed. by
J. Joseph. il Pop Mech 133:102-5+ F '70

M

M-16 rifle. See Rifles
MAC. See United States—Military airlift com-
mand
MAI-3. See Submarine research vehicles
MAILS (multiple-antenna instrument landing
system) See Airplanes—Landing
MAP (management analysis and projection
system) See Computers—Business use
MARS (military affiliated radio system) See
Radio telephone
MAST (manned astronomical space telescope)
See Artificial satellites—Astronomical use
MCPL. See Members of Congress for peace
through law
MDTA (Manpower development and training
act) See Labor laws and legislation—
United States
MESBIC (minority enterprise small business
investment companies) See Small business
investment companies
M. H. De Young memorial museum, San Fran-
cisco
English decorative arts at the M. H. de
Young memorial museum. D. G. Keith. il
Antiques 97:712-17 My '70
Flamboyant patron; gift of Edward Hanley
collection by widow. il por Time 95:62-3
Je 8 '70
MIRV
ABM & MIRV; in the context of SALT;
address, June 12, 1970. R. Kilmarx. Vital
Speeches 36:602-4 Jl 15 '70
ABM, MIRV, and the arms race. H. F. York.
Science 169:257-60 Jl 17 '70
Arms control at the crossroads; Vienna talks.
il Newsweek 75:53-4 Ap 20 '70
Can SALT stop MIRV? R. E. Lapp. il N Y
Times Mag p 14-15+ F 1 '70
Disarmament problems. H. A. Bethe. por Bul
Atom Sci 26:99-102 Je '70
Expectations from SALT. A. De Volpi. il Bul
Atom Sci 26:6-8 Ap '70
Minuteman III's spring planting. il Bsns W
p 130 Mr 28 '70
MIRV, Gorgon Medusa of the nuclear age. A.
De Volpi. Bul Atom Sci 26:35-8+ Ja '70
SALT: a sprinkling of hope. il Time 96:24-5
Jl 20 '70
Was it a slip? announcement of deployment.
Nation 210:354-5 Mr 30 '70
Why our defenses are down. M. B. Schneider.
Nat R 22:512-13 My 19 '70
MIS (management information systems) See In-
formation systems, Management
MIT. See Massachusetts institute of technol-
ogy, Cambridge
MLA. See Modern language association of
America
MMA (mastitis-metritis-agalactia complex) See
Swine—Diseases and pests
MNC. See Movement for a new congress
MOS circuits. See Electronic circuits, Integrated
MP. See United States—Army—Corps of mili-
tary police
MRA. See Moral rearmament
MSA. See Museum storage association
MSG. See Monosodium glutamate
MSU. See Michigan state university, East Lans-
ing
MTA. See Metropolitan transportation author-
ity
MUST (metropolitan urban service training)
See Religious cooperation
MAAS, Peter
Sharon Tate murders. il por Ladies Home J
87:52+ Ap '70

MAAZEL, Lorin
Bow, baton, and bows by Lorin Maazel. I. Kolodin. Sat R 53:26 My 16 '70 *
Musical events; violinist and conductor at Philharmonic concert in Philharmonic Hall. W. Sargeant. New Yorker 46:151-2 My 9 '70 *
Schumann's die peri with Janowitz, Brilioth, Engen, Smith. I. Kolodin. Sat R 53:55 Je 6 '70 *

MABEL Brady Garvan collections. See Yale university

MACACA mulatta. See Monkeys

MCADAMS, Richard P. jr
Avoiding court cases. Clear House 45:45-7 S '70

MCALACK, Robert F. and others
Vibriolytic antibody-forming cells: a new application of the Pfeiffer phenomenon. bibliog il Science 168:141-2 Ap 3 '70

MCALISTER, James E.
Nomogram aids voltage-drop calculations. il Electr World 84:46 D '70
Understanding random-access memories. il Electr World 84:34 N '70

MCALISTER, Virginia
Decoupage: the art of cut and paste. il Har Yrs 11:38-9 Ap '70

MCALLISTER, Dorothy S.
Dorothy S. McAllister, library trustee. il pors Wilson Lib Bul 45:330-1 N '70 *

MACANDREW, Craig
Rules of drunkenness. il Time 95:54 Je 8 '70 *

MCANDREW, William
McAndrew case: Britain at the Chicago bar. H. K. Hutton and C. Galgoci. Sch & Soc 98:112-15 F '70 *

MACAO
Macao. B. Wolf. il Travel & Camera 33:55-7 Mr '70
Macau. S. Griffin. il Travel 133:46-9 F '70

MCARDLE, R. E.
Why we needed the Multiple use bill. il Am For 76:10-11+ Je '70

MACARONI
Farm journal's fabulous pasta dishes. E. W. Manning. il Farm J 94:40-1+ Ja '70
Pasta revolution; spaghetti carbonara and rotelle. C. Claiborne. il N Y Times Mag p50 Jl 26 '70
Pasta; with recipes. D. Eby. il Bet Hom & Gard 48:76-84+ S '70
Spaghetti alla Yankee. C. Claiborne in N Y Times Mag p 102 Ap 5 '70

MACARTHUR, Douglas
Twenty-five years ago: how Japan won the war. F. Bowers. il pors N Y Times Mag p5-7+ Ag 30 '70 *
Years of MacArthur, by D. C. James. Review
Sat R 53:39-40 S 19 '70. F. C. Pogue *

MACARTHUR, John Donald
Stockholder, by W. Hoffman. Review *
Bsns W p6 Ag 1 '70. E. Bernstein *
Sweeter options of John D. MacArthur and Truman Capote. T. Burke. il pors Esquire 74:210-14+ D '70 *

MCARTHUR, Norma
Demography of primitive populations. bibliog Science 167:1097-101 F 20 '70

MACAU. See Macao

MACBEAN, James Roy
La hora de los hornos. il Film Q 24:31-7 Fall '70
(tr) See Solanas. F. Fernando Solanas: an interview

MCBEE, Susanna
Health, education, and welfare of Robert Finch. il pors McCalls 97:58-9+ Jl '70
Pat Nixon and the first-lady watchers. il por McCalls 97:76-7+ S '70
Scientist looks at ESP. McCalls 97:50+ Mr '70
Who needs Martha Mitchell? pors McCalls 98:61+ Ja '71

MACBETH, George Mann
Comment. R. B. Shaw. Poetry 117:109-10 N '70 *
MACBETH; drama. See Shakespeare, W.—Plays

MACBETH (literary character) See Shakespeare, W.—Characters

MCBIRNEY, Alexander R. See Murase, T. jt. auth.

MCBRIDE, Joseph
Welles before Kane. Film Q 23:19-22 Spr '70
Welles's Chimes at midnight. il pors Film Q 23:11-20 Fall '69
—and Wilmington, Michael
Private life of Billy Wilder. il por Film Q 23:2-9 Sum '70

MCBRIEN, Richard P.
Meaningful survival for the church. Ladies Home J 86:130 D '69

MCBROWN, Gertrude Parthenia
Paul Robeson world renowned actor, singer and scholar. por Negro Hist Bul 33:128-9 My '70

MCBURNEY, Raymond D. See Montgomery, J. jt. auth.

MCCABE, Bernard
Grand passions and grander talent, in a grandly romantic time. Commonweal 92:119-20 Ap 17 '70

MCCABE, James Dabney. See Martin. E. W. pseud.

MCCAFFERTY, Phil
Special wood fasteners make the job easier. il Pop Sci 197:96-7 D '70

MCCAFFERY, James F. and Turner, D. S.
Discipline in the innovative school. Clear House 44:491-6 Ap '70; Same abr. Ed Digest 36:16-19 O '70

MCCAFFREY, Neil
Jazz. Nat R 22:1414-16 D 29 '70

MCCAFFREY, Patrick J.
New wind blowing. New Repub 163:10 O 24 '70

MCCAHILL, Tom
Mail for McCahill. See issues of Mechanix illustrated
MI tests. See issues of Mechanix illustrated

MCCAIN, Jerry
Country cads. pors Newsweek 75:84-6 Ap 13 '70 *

MCCAIN, John Sidney, 1911-
Sentinel of the Pacific. J. G. Hubbell. il Read Digest 96:203-4+ Mr '70

MCCALL, Robert B.
Intelligence quotient pattern over age: comparisons among siblings and parent-child pairs. bibliog il Science 170:644-8 N 6 '70

MCCALLISTER, Lois
Tell me what you had in mind. Engl J 59:231-4 F '70

MCCALL'S (periodical)
Feminine eye; McCall's editor's views of women's liberation. S. Alexander. por McCalls 97:8+ Jl '70
McCall's and the new woman. D. McKinney. Writer 83:9-11 Ag '70

MCCARLEY, Robert W. and Hobson, J. A.
Cortical unit activity in desynchronized sleep. bibliog il Science 167:901-3 F 6 '70

MCCARRAN airport. See Las Vegas, Nev.—Airports

MCCARRY, Charles
Home to the enduring Berkshires. il Nat Geog 138:196-221 Ag '70
John Rennon's excrusive gloupie. il Esquire 74:204-5+ D '70
Mourning becomes Senator Fulbright. por Esquire 73:116-19+ Je '70
Ol' man Rivers. il por Esquire 74:168-71+ O '70

MCCARTEN, John
Irish sketches (cont) New Yorker 46:109-11 S 12; 127-9 O 31 '70

MCCARTHY, Abigail (Quigley)
McCarthy campaign. Atlan 226:60-3 Ag '70

MCCARTHY, Barbara Powell
Jobs for boys and girls? il Parents Mag 45:42-3+ Ja '70

MCCARTHY, Eugene Joseph
One man's America (title varies) (cont) por McCalls 97:18+ F; 26 Mr; 28 Ap; 30 Je; 34+ Ag; 98:10 O '70
One must be very careful of Christmas. McCalls 98:4 D '70
Third party may be a real force in '72. il por N Y Times Mag p6+ Je 7 '70; Excerpts. Cur 120:31-2 Ag '70

about

Exit Eugene McCarthy. por Time 97:8 Ja 11 '71 *
McCarthy campaign. A. McCarthy. Atlan 226:60-3 Ag '70 *
McCarthy's call for a third party. New Repub 162:5-6 Je 20 '70; Same abr. with title Not necessarily so. Cur 120:33-4 Ag '70 *
No ordinary senator. Nation 212:37 Ja 11 '71 *
Nobody knows, by J. Larner. Review Commonweal 92:418-19 Ag 21 '70. R. H. Miller *
Time il 95:78 Mr 2 '70 *
People, by R. T. Stout. Review
Newsweek il por 76:98+ S 21 '70. G. Wolff *
Purity, power and politics. E. Schneier. Nation 210:119-21 F 2 '70

MCCARTHY, Glenn
Where are they now? R. Levy. pors Duns 95:42 Je '70 *

MCCARTHY, James H.
Interview with three recreation planners. Forbes 105:202-3 Ja 1 '70

MCCARTHY, Joe
How to buy a diamond. il Read Digest 96: 188-90+ My '70
No warning on the beach; excerpts from Hurricane. il Motor B 126:54-5+ S '70

MCCARTHY, John J.
Running against Teddy. il pors Newsweek 76: 22 Ag 24 '70 *

MCCARTHY, John P.
Hilaire Belloc, Edwardian radical. America 123:66-9 Ag 8 '70

MCCARTHY, Joseph Raymond
Enforced conformitq; address, June 9, 1970. N. M. Pusey. Vital Speeches 36:588-92 Jl 15 '70 *
McCarthy to the rescue. W. F. Buckley, jr. Nat R 22:804-5 Jl 28 '70 *
Odyssey of a friend; letters to W. F. Buckley, jr, 1954-1965. W. Chambers. bibliog f Nat R 22:22-32 Ja 13 '70

MCCARTHY, Mary
Battle of Rocky Port; story; excerpt from Birds of America. McCalls 98:87-90 Ja '71
Reflections. New Yorker 45:39-40+ Ja 24 '70
Thanksgiving in Paris, 1964; story; excerpt from Birds of America. Atlan 226:43-52 Ag '70

about
Books. E. Hardwick. Vogue 156:306 S 1 '70 *
Mary à la mode. E. Grossman. Commentary 49:81-5 Je '70 *
Moral vitamins. L. Coxe. New Repub 162: 20+ F 28 '70 *

MCCARTNEY, Tom
How they're making beef cows pay. il Suc Farm 68:A4-5 N '70
Real Little Lord Fauntleroy. il pors Am Heritage 21:50-5+ F '70

MCCARTHY, Tom (photographer)
Florida; photographs. il Pop Phot 66:101-8 Je '70

MCCARTNEY, Paul
Beatles minus one. H. Saal. il por Newsweek 75:95 Ap 20 '70 *
Hello, goodby, hello. il por Time 95:57 Ap 20 '70 *
McCartney on his own. E. Sander. il por Sat R 53:53-4 My 30 '70 *
Newsmakers. por Sr Schol 95:15 N 10 '69 *

MCCAUL, Robert L.
Twentieth century books influencing American education. Ed Digest 36:28-31 S '70

MCCAULL, Julian
Who owns the water? il Environ 12:30-9 O '70
—and Antell, Mark
Air of safety. bibliog il Environ 12:2-15+ N '70
—See Albone, E; Hohenemser, K. H. jt. auths.

MCCLAIN, Lester
Tennessee lonesome end. P. Schrag. il Harper 240:59-63+ Mr '70 *

MCCLANAHAN, Ed
Greatest writing ever wrote; story. Esquire 73:146-8 Mr '70
—and Norman, Gurney
Whole Whole earth catalog. Esquire 74: 95-6+ Jl '70

MCCLANE, A. J.
Field & stream hat trick. il por Field & S 75:72-3+ Je '70
(ed) Fishing. See issues of Field & stream

MCCLARREN, Robert
Tax-exempt status. Am Lib 1:607 Je '70

MCCLEARY, Elliott H.
Wanted for fraud: professional patients. il Todays Health 49:30-1+ Ja '71

MCCLELLAN, John Little
Excerpt from address, August 11, 1969. Cong Digest 49:77+ Mr '70

about
Leader in drive to cut crime. por U S News 68:12 F 2 '70
Weak link in our war on the Mafia. Read Digest 96:56-61 Mr '70

MCCLELLAN committee. See United States— Congress—Senate—Government operations, Committee on

MCCLINTOCK, Jack
This is how the ride ends. il por Esquire 73: 138-9+ Mr '70

MCCLOSKEY, Mark
God; poem. Commonweal 92:117 Ap 17 '70
Pig; Too dark; poems. Poetry 116:94-5 My '70

MCCLOSKEY, Michael
Confrontation: battle over our forests. House B 112:55+ Jl '70

MCCLOSKEY, Robert James
Crisis spokesman. por Newsweek 76:106 O 5 '70 *

MCCLUGGAGE, Denise
Getting a grip on things. Am Home 73:34+ Ag '70
Hubcap gap. il Am Home 73:50+ S '70
Leave the driving lessons to mother. Am Home 73:64+ My '70

Package house full of surprises. il por Am Home 73:64-7+ Ap '70
Slippery road, don't hit the brakes. il por Am Home 73:22+ Ja '70
Woman beside the man behind the wheel. il Am Home 73:24+ F '70

MCCLURE, Billie B.
Sex in the army. Chr Today 15:40-1 O 9 '70 *

MCCLURE, Michael
They lick the platter clean. R. J. Griffin. Nation 211:54 Jl 20 '70 *

MCCLURE'S magazine
McClure's magazine and the muckrakers, by H. S. Wilson. Review
New Repub 163:20-1 D 19 '70. J. Walt

MCCLUSKEY, Neil G.
Rome replies (act II) il America 122:330-4 Mr 28 '70

MACCOBY, Eleanor
Women re women. Mlle 70:180-1+ F '70

MCCOMBS, Philip A.
How can we lose in Vietnam, having won? il Nat R 22:1399-402 D 29 '70

MCCONKEY, Thomas W.
(ed) Buyers' guide. See (usually) first issue of each month of Library journal
(ed) Purchasing guide 1970. Library J 95: 1307+ Ap 1 '70

MCCONNELL, Dan R.
Microwave ovens, revolution in cooking. il Electr World 84:25-9+ Ag; 37-9+ S '70

MCCONNELL, James Vernon
"When I get through explaining this to you, you will know even less than before I started" il Horizon 12:112-13 Sum '70

about
Wackiest worm runner. J. S. Shaw. il por Sci Digest 67:82-6 My '70 *

MACCONNELL, John G. and others
Alkaloid from fire ant venom: identification and synthesis. bibliog il Science 168:840-1 My 15 '70

MCCOOL, Gerald A.
Rahner's anthropology. America 123:342-4 O 31 '70

MCCORD, David
Excerpts from Write me another verse. Horn Bk 46:364-9 Ag '70
Suddenly; poem. McCalls 98:115 D '70

MCCORD, Howard
Bear that came to the wedding; poem. Nation 210:312 Mr 16 '70
Reptiles; poem. Nation 210:540 My 4 '70

MCCORD, Thomas B. and Johnson, T.V.
Lunar spectral reflectivity (0.30 to 2.50 microns) and implications for remote mineralogical analysis. bibliog Science 169:855-8 Ag 28 '70
—and others
Asteroid vesta: spectral reflectivity and compositional implications. bibliog il Science 168:1445-7 Je 19 '70

MCCORMACK, George R.
Griggsby station revisited; poem. il Har Yrs 10:33-7 Ja '70

MCCORMACK, Helen G.
Expatriate portraits. il Antiques 98:787-93 N '70

MCCORMACK, John William
America: today and yesterday; interview. il pors U S News 69:58-62 Jl 27 '70
Excerpt from debate, September 15, 1969. Cong Digest 49:10+ Ja '70

about
End of an era in Congress. pors U S News 68:35 Je 1 '70 *
House: changing of the guard. P. S. Templin. America 123:421 N 21 '70 *
House speaker; target of rebels. por U S News 68:18 Mr 2 '70 *
Indictments for two. por Time 95:16 Ja 26 '70
McCormack: a symbol retires. por Time 95:14 Je 1 '70 *
McCormack's reapers? por Newsweek 75:16 Ja 26 '70
Mr Speaker yields the gavel. il por Newsweek 75:26-7 Je 1 '70 *
Such ingratitude! Nation 210:195-6 F 23 '70 *
TRB from Washington: sapless branch. New Repub 162:4 Ja 24 '70

MCCORMICK, Bernard
War of the cops. il N Y Times Mag p 23-5+ O 18 '70

MCCORMICK, Richard A.
Loyalty and dissent: the magisterium, a new model. America 122:674-6 Je 27 '70
—and others
Brussels hosts the theologians. il America 123:232-4 O 3 '70

MCCORMICK, Richard A.—*Continued*
about
Paging the unbandaged. D. Callahan. America 123:143 S 12 '70 *
MCCORMICK tract, Mich. See Wilderness areas —Michigan
MCCORRY, Vincent P.
Word. See issues of America
MCCOWN, John L.
Catfish empire. Newsweek 76:48+ O 19 '70 *
MCCOY, Charles Breisford
Lighting a fire under the sleeping giant. il por Bsns W p40-1 S 12 '70 *
MCCOY, Dan
Gallery: photographs. Life 69:6-7 Jl 17 '70
MCCOY, Kid
Real McCoy. R. Cantwell. por Sports Illus 32:52-6+ Je 1 '70 *
MCCRACKEN, Paul Winston
Excerpt from testimony. February 16. 1970. Cong Digest 49:245+ O '70
about
Hard going for the game plan; with editorial comment. G. Burck. il por Fortune 81:145-6, 152-5+ My '70 *
How fast should money grow? pors Bsns W p59-60 Ag 8 '70 *
Why economists flunk out. M. J. Ulmer. New Repub 163:6-7 S 19 '70 *
MCCRACKEN, Robert A.
Audiovisuals in reading. bibliog Library J 95: 1907-8 My 15 '70
MCCRARY, Bill
Rap 'n 'pinion. por Motor T 22:18 F '70
MCCRILLIS, John O. C.
Interesting design may mean back to fundamentals. two University press designers tell AIGA clinic. Pub W 197:45-6 Mr 16 '70 *
MCCRORY corporation
Shutdowns stalk big city stories. il Bsns W p28 O 10 '70
MCCROSKY, Richard E.
Lost City meteorite fall. il por Sky & Tel 39: 154-8 Mr '70
MCCROSSAN, John A.
Aware. Am Lib 1:87, 187-8, 396, 493-4, 618-20, 713-14 Ja-F, Ap-Jl '70
Extending public library services to the homebound. Am Lib 1:485-90 My '70
MCCULLOCH, William M.
Excerpts from debate, September 10 and 17, 1969. Cong Digest 49:21+ Ja '70
MCCULLOUGH, David G.
(ed) American land (cont) il Am Heritage 21:97-115+ F; 97-117 Ap '70
Epitaph for an American landmark. il Am Heritage 21:110-13 Ap '70
MCCULLOUGH, Robert F.
Arnold Crane: photographic materials collector extraordinary. il por Pop Phot 66:96-7+ Ap '70
Fragments of the past. il Pop Phot 66:82-3 Ja '70
MCCULLY, George E.
History begins at home. il Sat R 53:74-5+ My 16 '70
MCCULLY, Helen
Nobody ever tells you these things; questions and answers. See issues of House beautiful
MCCUNE, Billy
Conversations with the dead. M. Kozloff. il pors Art N 69:24-7+ D '70 *
MCCUTCHEN, C. W.
Surface films compacted by moving water: demarcation lines reveal film edges. bibliog il Science 170:61-4 O 2 '70
MCDANIEL, Paul W.
Current state of physics: AEC's view; interview, ed. by G. B. Lubkin. il por Phys Today 23:55-8 My '70
Visit with Paul McDaniel of the AEC: interview, ed. by G. B. Lubkin. il por Phys Today 23:56-7+ Ap '70
MCDANIELS, Jim
Big Mac fills a tall order. W. F. Reed. Sports Illus 34:46 Ja 4 '71 *
MACDANIELS, L. H.
Landscaping with nut trees. il Horticulture 48:42-3+ F '70
MCDERMOTT, Patrick
Act of the actor. Commonweal 91:510-13 F 6 '70
MCDERMOTT, Stephen W.
Supering with the Royal ballet. il Dance Mag 44:62-9 Ap '70
MCDEVITT, Charles Francis
Wrong foot forward. pors Time 96:65 Jl 27 '70 *
MCDEVITT, Thomas J.
My family is dying! J. L. Block. Read Digest 96:171-2+ Ap '70 *

MACDONALD, Don
Cars of the '70s. Mech Illus 66:42-3 Ja '70
MCDONALD, Donald
What kind of revolution? Cur 121:28-30 S '70
MCDONALD, Elvin
Flowers shaped for the 70's. il House B 112: 124-5+ Ap '70
Gardner's notebook. See issues of House beautiful
It's tool-up time. il House B 112:72+ Ap '70
MCDONALD, Gerald Doan
Obituary
Library J por 95:2219 Je 15 '70 *
MACDONALD, Gordon J. F.
How man endangers the climate. Cur 114: 17-24 Ja '70
MCDONALD, Henry Stewart, 3d
Top hat, white tie and bare toes. J. Kirshenbaum. il por Sports Illus 34:30-3 Ja 4 '71 *
MACDONALD, Jack R.
Doppler shift measurements of nuclear lifetimes. bibliog il Science 167:1339-47 Mr 6 '70
MACDONALD, Jeffrey
Captain MacDonald's ordeal il pors Time 97: 50+ Ja 11 '71 *
MACDONALD, John
How social responsibility fits the game of business. il Fortune 82:104-6+ D '70
(ed) See Brooker, R. Strategy that saved Montgomery Ward
MACDONALD, Joseph A.
Those were the days. il por Yachting 127: 50-2+ F '70
MACDONALD, Mari-Lou
Anything you can do, Mari-Lou can do better. il pors Life 69:70-3 S 25 '70 *
MCDONALD, P. T. and Rai, K. S.
Aedes aegypti: origin of a new chromosome from a double translocation heterozygote. bibliog il Science 168:1229-30 Je 5 '70
MCDONALD, Philip R. See Eastlack, J. O. jr. jt. auth.
MACDONALD, Robert
True hi-fi speaks for itself. Pop Electr 32:82-4 Mr '70
MCDONALD, Stew. See McDonald, H. S. 3d
MCDONALD'S corporation
Mirror, mirror on the wall. Forbes 106:21 N 1 '70
MCDONNELL, J. A. M. See Berg, O. E. jt. auth.
MCDONNELL, Kilian
Catholic looks at evangelical Protestantism. Commonweal 92:408-13 Ag 21 '70
Religious life in low profile. il America 123: 16-20 Jl 11 '70
MCDONNELL Douglas corporation
Control of plant for minority workers being transferred. Aviation W 93:61 N 9 '70
Douglas hams it up to sell seven DC-9s. il Bsns W p60 Mr 28 '70
From underdog to top dog. il Forbes 106: 31+ Jl 1 '70
McDonnell Douglas production approach for DC-10 stresses early systems installation. W. S. Hieronymus. il Aviation W 93:38-41 Jl 27 '70
New titles at McDonnell. Bsns W p26 N 7 '70
One up and away; air-bus battle. il Newsweek 76:62+ S 7 '70
Percy Green vs. McDonnell aircraft. L. Barrett. Nation 210:404-5 Ap 6 '70
Unemployment kitty depleted at Douglas. Bsns W p32 Je 27 '70
MCDONOUGH, Jean
Tenerife. il Harp Baz 103:112+ Mr '70
MCDONOUGH, Patrick J.
Assistant principal: educational leader? bibliog f Clear House 45:97-9 O '70
—See Dugan, W. E. jt. auth.
MACDOUGAL, Gary E. and Malek, F. V.
Master plan for merger negotiations. il Harvard Bsns R 48:71-82 Ja '70
MACDOUGALL, David
Prospects of the ethnographic film. il Film Q 23:16-30 Wint '69
MACDOUGALL, Ruth Doan
Morning man; story. Redbook 135:80-1 S '70
MCDOWELL, Bart
Orissa: past and promise in an Indian state. il Nat Geog 138:546-77 O '70
MCDOWELL, Charles, Jr
Better living with machinery; excerpt from What did you have in mind? il Read Digest 97:113-14 Ag '70
MCDOWELL, Edwin
Galbraith was wrong again. Nat R 22:1108 O 20 '70
MCDOWELL, Leroy
Court-martial: the trial of one GI for murder. il por Newsweek 76:21 Ag 31 '70 *
MCDOWELL, Sam
Sam of 1,000 ways. P. Jordan. Sports Illus 33:36-40 Ag 17 '70 *

MACDOWELL (writers colony) See Authors colonies

MCDYER, James
Commissar is a priest. J. Roddy. il pors Look 34:56-8 Mr 24 '70 *

MCEACHERN, Margaret
Town meeting is not dead, it's alive and well on radio. il Todays Health 48:32-3+ Jl '70

MCELHINNY, M. W. and Luck, G. R.
Paleomagnetism and Gondwanaland. bibliog il Science 168:830-2 My 15 '70

MCELREATH, Jim
500 miles into history. S. Kelly. il por Hot Rod 23:48-50 N '70 *

MCELROY, David
Spawning in northern Minnesota; poem. Nation 210:278 Mr 9 '70

MCELROY, M. B. See Dalgarno, A. jt. auth.

MCELROY, Neil H.
Neil McElroy of Procter & Gamble; interview. il pors Nations Bsns 58:58-63 Ag '70

MCELROY, William David
Antarctic research: a pattern of science management. il por Bul Atom Sci 26:85-8 D '70
Point of view; excerpts from address, October 12, 1970. por Science 170:517 O 30 '70

about

Haggerty, McElroy, Bromley stress relevance. T. Johnides. por Phys Today 23:62 D '70 *
Mission: relate science to society. il por Bsns W p72+ My 23 '70 *

MCENTEE, Howard G.
Build your own R.P.M. counter. il Pop Sci 196:146-7+ Ja '70
World's biggest little airplane meet. il Pop Sci 197:108-9 Jl '70

MCEVOY, James. See Gamson, W. A. jt. auth.

MCEWEN, Tom
Mongoose. J. Thawley. il por Hot Rod 23:66-8 Ag '70 *

MCFADDEN, Dorothy Loa
See it made, in Europe. il Travel 133:54-9+ Ap '70
See it made-in Japan. il Travel 133:51-5 Je '70
See it made in the Caribbean (plus Bermuda and the Bahamas) il Travel 134:53-9 S '70

MCFANN, Howard L.
Air controller's radar sees through weather. il Electr World 83:32-3 Ap '70
Radar in air traffic control. il Electr World 84:32-4 Jl '70
Taming radar weather clutter. il Electr World 83:44-5 Ja '70

MCFARLAND, Gary
Mirrors of our time; interview, ed. by R. Hemming. por Sr Schol 96:17 My 23 '70

MCFARLAND, Jim
(ed) See Conze, V. Man who collects Offenhausers

MCFEGGAN, James
Bagged refuse brings better service. il Am City 85:69-72 Mr '70

MCGAHERN, John
Recruiting officer; story. Atlan 226:56-61 Jl '70

MCGANN, Jerome
Blake and a tradition. Poetry 117:45-9 O '70
Poetry and truth. Poetry 117:195-203 D '70

MCGANNON, Donald Henry
Group W president rocks broadcasters. por Bsns W p24 Ap 11 '70 *
McGannon's haymaker. J. McLaughlin. America 122:397 Ap 11 '70 *

MCGARRAH, Robert E.
Swords into plowshares. bibliog f Harvard Bsns R 48:36-8+ Jl '70

MCGARRY, A. Louis
Titicut follies revisited: a long range plan for the mentally disordered offender in Massachusetts. Ment Hy 54:20-7 Ja '70

MCGAVRAN, Donald
Crisis of identity for some missionary societies. Chr Today 14:10-12+ My 8 '70
Frankfurt declaration. Chr Today 14:3-4 Je 19 '70

MCGEE, A. E. Jr
VHF-UHF drain-dip oscillator. il Pop Electr 33:69-76 O '70

MCGILL, William James
City vs. campus violence. il por Am City 85:78+ N '70

about

Bill McGill takes over Columbia's hot campus. K. Lamott. il por N Y Times Mag p26-7+ Ag 23 '70 *
Columbia gets its man. por Time 95:40 F 16 '70 *
Homecoming. por Newsweek 75:69 F 16 '70 *

MCGINLEY, Phyllis
Poetry of Phyllis McGinley. L. Hasley. por Cath World 211:211-15 Ag '70 *

MCGINNIS, R. C. See Dubuc, J. P. jt. auth.

MCGINNISS, Joe
Yablonski murders. il Life 68:36-7 Ja 23 '70

MCGINTY, G.
Inside portable VTR's. il Radio-Electr 41:9-12+ Ag '70

MCGOUGH, Elizabeth H.
Crib deaths: some answers to 20,000 sudden tragedies. il Sci Digest 67:26-30 F '70

MCGOULDRICK, Paul
Myths the liberals live by. il Nat R 22:151-3+ F 10 '70

MCGOVERN, George Stanley
Federal government and the environment. Cur Hist 59:82-3+ Ag '70
Lessons of 1968. Harper 240:43-7 Ja '70

about

TRB from Washington. New Repub 162:6 My 16 '70 *

MCGOVERN, John P. See Barkin, G. D. jt. auth.

MCGOWAN, J. William
Some three-body atomic systems; adaptation of address, February 3, 1969. bibliog il Science 167:1083-92 F 20 '70

MACGOWRAN, Jack
Jack MacGowran in the works of Samuel Beckett. Criticism
Nation 211:605-6 D 7 '70 *
New Repub 163:20 D 12 '70 *
New Yorker 46:142 N 28 '70 *
Time 95:62+ My 11 '70
Time il por 96:48 N 30 '70 *

MCGRADY, Martin
Big man who wasn't there. P. Putnam. il por Sports Illus 32:72-3 My 11 '70 *
King of the 600. il por Newsweek 75:94 Mr 16 '70 *
McGrady's game, deck, deal. P. Putnam. il por Sports Illus 32:48-9 F 23 '70 *

MCGRADY, Mike
Trade winds. C. Amory. Sat R 53:6 Jl 25 '70 *

MCGRATH, Lee Parr, and Scobey, Joan
What is a brother? excerpts. il Good H 170:74-5 F '70

MCGRATH, Thomas
Beyond the red river; Route song and epitaph; Rose of bankruptcy; Sound of one hand; After I'm gone (da da da da da) poems. Nation 211:509 N 16 '70
Lineaments of unsatisfied desire; poem. Nation 211:380 O 19 '70

MACGRAW, Ali
Ali McGraw. P. Wilkes. il pors Look 34:26-30 Ag 11 '70 *
Ali MacGraw: a return to basics. il pors Time 97:40-5 Ja 11 '71 *
Five young beauties & how they get that way. il pors Mlle 72:135-41 N '70 *

MCGRAW, Eloise Jarvis
Cure for halfwayitis. Writer 83:18-20+ Ag '70

MCGRAW-Hill, inc.
McGraw-Hill jumps into bidding for Penguin. Pub W 198:33 Ag 3 '70
McGraw-Hill picketed by women in publishing. Pub W 198:35 Jl 6 '70
McGraw-Hill withdraws; Penguin goes to Longman. Pub W 198:247-8 Ag 31 '70
Time for a change; purchase of Time, inc. broadcasting operation. Newsweek 76:69 N 9 '70
TV looks tempting to McGraw-Hill. Bsns W p24 N 7 '70

MCGRAW-Hill book company. See McGraw-Hill, inc.

MCGRAW-Hill company of Canada. See Publishers and publishing—Canada

MCGRAW-Hill publishing company. See McGraw-Hill, inc.

MACGREGOR, Clark
Excerpt from debate, September 11, 1969. Cong Digest 49:23+ Ja '70

MCGREGOR, D. D. See Koster, F. jt. auth.

MCGREGOR, Donald C.
New life for Felicity Ann. il Yachting 128:64-5+ Ag '70

MCGREGOR, Douglas
Beyond Theory Y. J. J. Morse and J. W. Lorsch. bibliog f il Harvard Bsns R 48:61-8 My '70 *

MACGREGOR, I. D. See Carter, J. L. jt. auth.

MCGRORY, Mary
Fourth of July that was. New Repub 163:7 Jl 4 '70
Washington front. See issues of America

MCGUANE, Thomas
Fishing on the rivers of the mind. il Sports Illus 34:40-3 Ja 4 '71

MCGUCKIN, Floyd, and Payne, Jack
Redwood canoe goes sailing. il Pop Sci 197:80-2 Ag '70
Three-way redwood canoe. il Pop Sci 197: 89-91 Jl '70

MCGUIRE, Al
Maravich vs. McGuire. il pors Newsweek 75: 98-9 Mr 30 '70 *

MCGUIRE, Dennis
Affirmative eye. R. Hattersley. il Pop Phot 67:94-7+ Jl '70 *

MCGUIRE, Ken
Grin and bare it! adaptation of play by T. Cushing. Criticism
New Yorker 46:81 Mr 28 '70 *

MCGUIRE, Mabelle B.
Quadra's and Vancouver's island. il por Américas 22:2-8 Jl '70

MCGUIRE, Margaret. See Keane, M.

MCGUIRE, Thomas J.
Contemporary art lesson. il Sch Arts 70:19 O '70

MACH, Ernst
Ernst Mach: the unconscious motives of an empiricist. L. S. Feuer. bibliog Am Imago 27:12-40 Spr '70 *

MACHADO, Joseph
How to grow tree fuchsias. il Horticulture 48: 24-5+ O '70

MCHALE, Tom
Why we gave up kidnapping. il McCalls 98: 40+ D '70

MCHARG, Ian L.
Sensible plan for future development; interview, ed. by J. N. Miller. il Read Digest 97: 77-81 Ag '70

MACHIASPORT, Me.
Dilemma of Machiasport. F. Graham, jr. il Audubon 72:106-11 Jl '70

MACHIAVELLI, Niccolò
Machiavelli; by S. Anglo. Review
Sat R 53:38+ Ap 18 '70. G. Gersh *
Murderous Machiavel. S. Hughes. Nation 212: 26-8 Ja 4 '71 *

MACHINE operators. See Machinists

MACHINE shop practice
See also
Indexing (machine work)
Pantographs

MACHINE stands. See Machinery—Stands

MACHINE tool industry and trade
Tool builders grapple for markets. Bsns W p33 S 26 '70
Tool makers renew the systems approach. il Bsns W p86+ My 9 '70
Toolmen put on a show of hope. il Bsns W p25 Jl 18 '70
See also
Cincinnati milling machine company
Norton company

MACHINE tool operators. See Machinists

MACHINE tool stands. See Machinery—Stands

MACHINE tools
Flexible-shaft machine rolls to the job. W. G. Waggoner. il Pop Mech 134:172-3 Ag '70
Machine research aims at shaving costs. E. J. Bulban. il Aviation W 92:232-9+ Je 22 '70
See also
Cutting tools
Grinding machines
Holding devices (machine work)

Control
Brains of automation. J. W. Dietrich. il Radio-Electr 41:94+ S '70
Computers move into the machine shop. il Bsns W p88-90 S 19 '70

Numerical control
See Machine tools—Control

MACHINE work
See also
Indexing (machine work)

MACHINERY
Lonely efficiency of new machines; portfolio. Fortune 81:160-7 My '70
See also
Clutches (machinery)
Machine tools
Tamping machines

Stands
Stand for belt sanders. il Mech Illus 66:75 S '70
Table extensions for your radial saw. il Pop Mech 134:180 Ag '70

Transportation
Spares for machinery are major aid items. il Aviation W 93:119-20 O 26 '70

MACHINERY, Automatic
Made in Ohio by robots; General motors' unimates. R. Lund. il Pop Mech 134:81-3+ S '70
Robots take a bigger stride; use in assembly lines. il Bsns W p50+ Ap 4 '70

MACHINERY and civilization. See Technology and civilization

MACHINERY industry
Shovel maker digs up profits; Poclain. il Bsns W p36 O 10 '70
See also
Agricultural machinery industry and trade
Machine tool industry and trade

MACHINES. See Machinery

MACHINES, Copying. See Copying processes

MACHINISTS
My friend the machine; survey findings of E. Mueller. il Newsweek 75:79 F 23 '70
War machine vs. the peace machinist. R. Linsley. il Esquire 73:82-3 F '70

MACHTA, Lester, and Hughes E.
Atmospheric oxygen in 1967 to 1970. bibliog il Science 168:1582-4 Je 26 '70

MCHUGH, Vincent
Denver: the old roaring capital of the mountain West. il Holiday 47:50-1+ My '70
Golden Gate park: everything from hippie hill to superb Oriental art. il Holiday 47:61+ Mr '70

MACIAS, Ysidro Ramon
Chicano movement. il por Wilson Lib Bul 44: 731-5 Mr '70

MCILHANY, Sterling
Art and the life of feeling. Am Artist 34:5 D '70
Art as an answer. Am Artist 34:6 Ag; 5 S '70
Art for everyone. Am Artist 34:5 O '70
Art: its frame and nature. Am Artist 34:5 My '70
Art of travel. Am Artist 34:5 Ap '70
Artist and the city. Am Artist 34:5 N '70
Close look at optical art. il Am Artist 34:32-7 Je '70
Crafts and nature. Am Artist 34:5 F '70
Look at learning. Am Artist 34:5 Mr '70
Matting, mounting, and frames. il Am Artist 34:42-7 My '70
Pop goes the easel. il Am Artist 34:46-51+ F '70
Time to draw the line. Am Artist 34:5 Je '70
University art student. il Am Artist 34:52-8 Mr '70

about
Sterling McIlhany: the new editor. R. J. Riedinger. Am Artist 34:5 Ja '70

MCILWAIN, James T. and Fields, H. L.
Superior colliculus: single unit responses to stimulation of visual cortex in the cat. bibliog il Science 170:1426-8 D 25 '70

MCINERNY, Ralph
Past love, present danger; story. Redbook 134:64-5 F '70
Vices of a perfect couple; story. Redbook 134:86-7 Ap '70

MACINKO, John
Tailpipe problem. bibliog il Environ 12:6-13 Je '70

MCINTIRE, Carl
Behind the row over Ky's visit to U.S. il pors U S News 69:71 S 28 '70 *
Carl McIntire's victory: in this sign conquer. W. Willoughby. il Chr Today 14:25, 35 Ap 24 '70 *
Fairness doctrine. Chr Today 14:17 Jl 31 '70 *
McIntire-O'Hair debate: bruised but unbowed. M. Moss. il Chr Today 14:42-3 Mr 13 '70 *
McIntire shuns prophecy. Chr Today 15:45-6 N 6 '70 *
McIntire's victory march. R. Chandler. il Chr Today 15:36-7 O 23 '70 *
Military-ecclesiastical complex. Chr Today 15: 39 O 9 '70 *
TRB from Washington. New Repub 163:4 S 26 '70 *
Welcome General; Ky's proposed visit to US. Nation 211:293 O 5 '70 *
Will the real ACCC please come to order? N. Rohrer. Chr Today 15:44-5 N 20 '70 *

MCINTOSH, Sandy
America before the revolution; poem. Nation 211:566 N 30 '70

MCINTYRE, Alice T.
Cure; poem. New Yorker 46:38 Ag 8 '70
Deathwatch; poem. New Yorker 46:165 N 7 '70

MACINTYRE, Ferren
Why the sea is salt; with biographical sketch. il Sci Am 223:11, 104-15 bibliog (p 132) N '70

MCINTYRE, James Francis, cardinal
New archbishop. pors Newsweek 75:70-1 F 2 '70
On borrowed time. por Time 95:49 F 2 '70
Quiet revolt. K. LaMott. por Horizon 12: 68-72 Wint '70

MCINTYRE, Loren
Colombia, from Amazon to Spanish Main.
il Nat Geog 138:234-73 Ag '70
MCINTYRE, Lynda
Eat. Mlle 71:140+ Ag '70
MCINTYRE, Peter
With pen and ink and paintbrush New Zea-
land's leading artist does a book on the
American West. il por Sunset 145:90-3 N
'70 *
MACK, Herbert. See Cook, A. jt. auth.
MACK, Patricia H. See Wing, R. C. jt. auth.
MACK, Sally Sears
Saratoga school of modern dance. il Dance
Mag 44:40-1 Jl '70
MACKAY, Anna (Case) See Case, A.
MCKAY, David, company
Authors & editors. B. A. Bannon. il Pub W
197:19-22 Ap 20 '70
MCKAY, David Oman
New prophet. pors Newsweek 75:71 F 2 '70
Prophet, seer and innovator. por Time 95:
49-50 F 2 '70
MCKAY, David S. and others
Morphology and related chemistry of small
particles from Tranquillity base. bibliog
il Science 167:654-6 Ja 30 '70
MACKAY, Margaret R.
Lepidoptera in cretaceous amber. bibliog il
Science 167:379-80 Ja 23 '70
MCKEAN, William J.
All America basketball. il Look 34:53-4 Mr
24 '70
Meanwhile...back at Vassar. il Look 34:28+
F 24 '70
1970 Look All America. il Look 34:97+ D 15
'70
MCKEE, Gladys
Recompense; poem. Good H 171:170 S '70
MCKEE, Russell
Different America. il Audubon 72:9-17 Jl '70
MCKEEN, Laurence W.
Separating lanthanides by ion exchange chro-
matography. bibliog il por Chem 43:28-31
My '70
MCKENDRICK, Norman
Shore; poem. America 122:345 Mr 28 '70
MCKENDRY, Maxime
Food gazette. il Vogue 156:43 Jl; 47+ Ag 1;
311 S 1; 107 O 1; 111 N 1; 105 D '70; 157:
43 Ja 1 '71
MCKENNA, David L.
Changing partnerships in Christian higher ed-
ucation. Chr Today 14:5-7 Ag 21 '70
MCKENNA, George
I came for bear. il Outdoor Life 145:50-3+
My '70
MCKENNA, Horace
Of many things. D. R. Campion. America
123:inside cover O 10 '70; Discussion. 123:
364 N 7 '70
MCKENNA, Richard
Seeing with new eyes; The sand pebbles. D.
Stoen. Engl J 59:1256-8 D '70 *
MCKENZIE, John Lawrence
Lessons from history and elsewhere. por
Chr Cent 87:839-42 Jl 8 '70
MACKENZIE, Osgood Hanbury
Garden in the Highlands. J. Robertson. il
Am For 76:36-9+ S '70 *
MACKENZIE, Rachel
Risk; story. New Yorker 46:56-64 N 21 '70
MCKENZIE, Richard B.
Economic literacy of elementary school pu-
pils. Ed Digest 36:41-3 N '70
MCKENZIE, Robert A.
Odyssey from liberal to radical. Chr Cent
87:362-3 Mr 25 '70
MCKEON, Matthew C.
Where are they now? il pors Newsweek 76:12
Ag 17 '70 *
MCKEOWN, Bill
Boating (title varies) See issues of Mechanix
illustrated
Camping out of your pocket. il Mech Illus
66:58-60 Je '70
Camping with a snowmobile. il Mech Illus
66:32-3+ D '70
MCKEOWN, Tom
In a summer field; poem. Nation 210:469 Ap
20 '70
Phantasma of women; poem. Commonweal
91:587 F 27 '70
MCKERN, Sharon S.
Radiography: new tool for retrieving the
wealth of the pharaohs. il Sci Digest 68:
8-13 Jl '70
Solving the mystery of ancient Tikal. il Sci
Digest 69:67-71 Ja '71
—and McKern, T. W.
Brain surgery in the stone age. il Sci Digest
67:32-7 F '70
Tlachtli, the roughest game of all. bibliog il
Sci Digest 68:26-31 N '70

MCKERN, Thomas W. See McKern, S. S. jt.
auth.
MCKERNAN, John
Two poems: May day soliloquy of the Chinese
bullet; Negation. Nat R 22:1104 O 20 '70
MACKERRAS, Charles
Mozart with a flourish. il Opera N 34:24-5
Ap 11 '70
MACKEY, Eugene Joseph
Obituary
Wilson Lib Bul 45:451 Ja '71. S. Brown *
MCKIM, E.
Poem: Horses move across unlighted land-
scapes. Poetry 117:38 O '70
MCKIMMEY, James
Kiss, a gun, a tear, a smile. Writer 83:15-17 S
'70
Visitors; story. Good H 171:80-1 N '70
MCKINLEY, Daniel
Lichens, mirror to the universe. il Audubon
72:44-55 N '70
MCKINNEY, Don
McCall's and the new woman. Writer 83:
9-11 Ag '70
MCKINNEY, Laurence O.
Private enterprise and dope. W. F. Buckley,
jr. Nat R 22:964 S 8 '70 *
MCKINNIS, Paul Willis
Light touch. Todays Ed 59:41 F '70
MACKINNON, Neil L. See Roche W. J. jt.
auth.
MACKINTOSH, Malcolm
Clues to Soviet policy; interview; ed. by J.
Fromm. il pors U S News 69:66-9 N 2 '70
MCKISSICK, Floyd Bixler
Soul City's need is green power. il por Bsns
W p 106 Ja 17 '70
MCKNIGHT, Albert J.
To be somebody someday. J. Smith. il por
Redbook 135:86-7+ My '70 *
MACKO, V. and others
Self-inhibitor of bean rust uredospores: me-
thyl 3,4-dimethoxycinnamate. bibliog Sci-
ence 170:539-40 O 30 '70
MCKUEN, Rod
Rod McKuen; interview. ed. by S. Nirenberg.
il pors House B 112:70-1+ F '70
MCLAIN, Denny
Another shadow. il por Time 95:58 Mr 9 '70 *
Denny McLain: ready for his comeback
try. W. Leggett. il por Sports Illus 32:20-1
Je 29 '70 *
Denny the dupe. il por Time 95:51 Mr 2 '70 *
Downfall of a hero. M. Sharnik. il por Sports
Illus 32:16-21 F 23 '70 *
Ideal sucker. il pors Newsweek 75:93 Mr 2
'70 *
McLain: with love and hisses. P. Carry. il
por Sports Illus 33:42-3 Jl 13 '70 *
Never touch a superstar; excerpt from Be-
hind the mask, ed. by S. Gelman and D.
Schaap. B. Freehan. il pors Sports Illus
32:54-8+ Mr 2 '70 *
Second coming. il por Newsweek 76:69 Jl
13 '70 *
Slap on the wrist. P. Axthelm. por News-
week 75:48 Ap 13 '70 *
Time to be frank. Sports Illus 33:11+ S 21
'70 *
MCLAIN, Pete
Goose hunting from underwater. il Field &
S 75:40-3+ N '70
Maine's predictable Saco River stripers. il
Field & S 75:72-3+ My '70
MCLAREN, Bruce
Don't take that extra risk; interview. ed. by
D. Bacon. por Life 69:34 Ag 7 '70
Obituary
Motor T por 22:6 Ag '70. E. Dahlquist
MCLAUGHLIN, Elinor
When your parents grow old. il Parents
Mag 45:66-7+ O '70
MCLAUGHLIN, John
Communication (cont) America 122:140, 252+,
397, 482 F 7, Mr 7, Ap 11, My 2 '70
          about
He wanted to be Senator McLaughlin, S.J.
P. J. Donaldson. America 123:428-32 N 21
'70; Reply. V. A. Lapomarda. 124:2 Ja 9 '71 *
Of many things. D. R. Campion. America
122:inside cover My 9 '70 *
Priest vs. Pastore. S. Cunneen. Chr Cent
87:1067-8 S 9 '70 *
MCLAUGHLIN, Lorrie
Reflections on fashion; poem. Good H 171:11
S '70
MCLAUGHLIN, P. J. and Dayhoff, M. O.
Eukaryotes versus prokaryotes: an estimate
of evolutionary distance. bibliog il Science
168:1469-71 Je 19 '70
MCLAURIN, Dunbar S.
Short-range separatism. il por Ebony 25:
123-5 Ag '70

MCLEAN, William
Alfresco history. il Time 95:6+ Ap 13 '70 *
MACLEAR, Frank
Offshore cruisers, power & sail. il por Motor
B 125:110-11 Ja '70
MACLEISH, Archibald
Festival of freedom. il Sat R 53:16 Ag 29 '70
State funeral; poem. Atlan 225:63 Ap '70
Thrush on the island of Barra; poem. por
Nat Geog 137:692-3 My '70
Trustee of the culture; excerpt from address.
Sat R 53:18-19 D 19 '70
MACLEISH, Kenneth
Scotland's Outer Hebrides. il Nat Geog 137:
676-91+ My '70
MCLENDON, Winzola
(ed) See Mitchell, M. Amazing Martha
Mitchell
—and Smith, S. F.
Don't quote me! excerpt. il Ladies Home J
87:90+ N '70
MCLENNAN, Kenneth. See Moskow. M. H. jt.
auth.
MACLEOD, Iain Norman
Filling Macleod's shoes. il pors Newsweek
76:30 Ag 3 '70 *
MCLOUTH steel corporation
Perils of pioneering. il Forbes 105:34 Mr 15 '70
MCLUCAS, Lonnie, trial. See Trials (murder)
MCLUHAN, Herbert Marshall
Avenging eye. R. L. Shayon. Sat R 53:58 My
16 '70 *
Linear teacher and the non-linear McLuhan.
H. R. Smith. bibliog Clear House 45:126-8
O '70 *
McLuhan on religion. Chr Today 14:34 F 13
'70 *
MCLUHAN, Marshall. See McLuhan. H. M.
MCLURE, John
Social science laboratory. Clear House 44:
407-10 Mr '70
MCMAHAN, Howard D.
In-service training enhances a computer sys-
tem. il Am City 85:126+ S '70
MCMAHAN, Ian
School records: invasion of privacy? il
Parents Mag 45:64-5+ S '70; Same abr. Ed
Digest 36:5-7 D '70
MCMAHON, Frank
Borstal boy; dramatization of memoirs, by
B. Behan. Criticism
America 122:483 My 2 '70 *
Life il 68:16 My 22 '70 *
Nation 210:473 Ap 20 '70 *
New Yorker 46:81-2 Ap 11 '70 *
Newsweek 75:83 Ap 13 '70 *
Sat R 53:26 Ap 18 '70 *
Time il 95:97 Ap 13 '70 *
MACMAHON, James R.
Fall onions down south. il Org Gard & Farm
17:68+ Ag '70
MCMANUS, Benjamin
Get it together! poem. Horn Bk 46:323 Je
'70
MCMANUS, Patrick
Dog for all seasons. il Field & S 75:50-1+
Ag '70
Imaginary pistol. il Field & S 75:78-9+ Je
'70
Penthouse in the wilderness. Read Digest 96:
201-2+ My '70
MCMANUS, Richard W.
(ed) See Reischauer, E. O. Danger of the
Cambodian expansion
MCMICHAEL, James
Vegetables; poem. Poetry 117:71-8 N '70
MCMILLAN, Ann
Listening eye. il Craft Horiz 30:14-19 Ja '70
MCMILLAN, D. E. and others
1-Δ⁹-Trans-tetrahydrocannabinol in pigeons:
tolerance to the behavioral effects. bibliog
il Science 169:501-3 Jl 31 '70
MACMILLAN, Harold
P.M. R. G. Hazo. Commentary 49:88-9 Ap
'70 *
MCMILLAN, Polly
Nostalgia; poem. Sat R 53:10 S 12 '70
MCMILLAN, R. Bruce
Early canid burial from the western Ozark
highland. bibliog il Science 167:1246-7 F 27
'70
MACMILLAN, Richard F.
Hawaii's historic sites spring from a turbu-
lent past. il Travel 133:56-9 F '70
MCMILLEN, Tom
All-star named Tom is the most Dapper Dan.
C. Kirkpatrick. il Sports Illus 32:82+ Ap 13
'70 *
If you want Tom, easy does it. P. Carry. il
pors Sports Illus 32:28-31 F 16 '70
MCMULLEN, Richard E.
Rivers; poem. Commonweal 93:150 N 6 '70

MCMULLEN, Roy
Chopin and Sand: in the wake of that Major-
can winter. il Sat R 53:78-9+ Mr 14 '70
Delacroix in Africa. il por Horizon 11:60-75
Aut '69
EMI's new spoken/sung Carmen. Hi Fi sec I
20:20+ Ja '70
Michel Foucault. por Horizon 11:36-9 Aut '69
MCMURTRY, John
Philosophy of a corner linebacker. Nation
212:83-4 Ja 18 '71
MCMURTRY, Larry
Hole in the bucket; story; excerpt from Mov-
ing on. il Harper 240:113-15 My '70
Trade winds. C. Amory. Sat R 53:12+ Je 13
'70 *
MCNAIL, Stanley
Great birds passing; poem. Commonweal 92:
60 Mr 27 '70
MCNALLY, Dave
Three Birds who mainly stay; Baltimore's big
three pitching staff. R. Blount, jr. il pors
Sports Illus 33:30-2+ O 12 '70 *
MC NALLY, Robert E.
Christmas day: December 25. America 123:
557 D 26 '70
MCNAMARA, Margaret Craig
Reading is FUN-damental; interview, ed. by
G. D. Fischer. il pors Todays Ed 59:20-3 F
'70
MCNAMARA, Patrick H.
Bishops, PADRES and the barrios. Common-
weal 93:116-17 O 30 '70
MCNAMARA, Robert Strange
Foreign aid; address, February 20, 1970. Vi-
tal Speeches 36:338-41 Mr 15 '70
Second development decade; address. Novem-
ber 13, 1970. Vital Speeches 37:135-40 D
15 '70
World development needs; address, Septem-
ber 21, 1970. Vital Speeches 37:7-14 O 15 '70
about
Changing role of Robert McNamara. por U S
News 68:100 Ap 13 '70 *
In the McNamara vein. A. Harrigan. Nat R
22:1110 O 20 '70 *
New storm hits the World bank. il Bsns W
p 100-1 S 26 '70 *
Where the bombs weren't. R. Hotz. Avia-
tion W 93:11 N 16 '70 *
MCNASPY, Clement J.
Fine arts. See issues of America to Septem-
ber 5, 1970
Liturgical music for today. America 123:401-4
N 14 '70
Missions for today. America 122:416-18 Ap 18
'70
about
Of many things. D. R. Campion. America 123:
inside cover S 5 '70 *
MACNAUGHTON, Donald Sinclair
Battle against inflation; address, March 9,
1970. Vital Speeches 36:437-40 My 1 '70
MCNAUGHTON, S. J.
Rising population: its effect on environment.
il Cons 24:14-16 Je '70
—and Wolf, L. L.
Dominance and the niche in ecological sys-
tems. bibliog il Science 167:131-9; 170:
1335 Ja 9, D 18 '70
MCNAY, J. L. and Dayton, P. G.
Placental transfer of a substituted pteridine
from fetus to mother. bibliog il Science
167:988-90 F 13 '70
MACNEICE, Louis
Prayer before birth; poem. Mlle 72:108 D '70
MCNEILL, Don
End of the trip. R. A. Gross. por Newsweek
75:94-5 Ap 13 '70 *
MACNEISH, R. S. and others
Megafauna and man from Ayacucho, highland
Peru. bibliog il Science 168:975-7 My 22 '70
MACNELLY, C. L.
C. L. MacNelly: portrait painter. F. Taubes.
il por Am Artist 34:24-9+ My '70 *
MCNELLY, Willis E.
Science fiction, the modern mythology. il
America 123:125-7 S 5 '70
MCNULTY, Faith
Reporter at large. il New Yorker 46:40-2+ Je
13 '70
MCNULTY, Henry
High spirits from white alcohols. House &
Gard 137:116+ Ap '70
Scotch and what? House & Gard 138:116+ S
'70
MACOMBER, William B.
Management strategy: a program for the
seventies; address, January 14, 1970. Dept
State Bul 62:130-41 F 2 '70
New sprint in foggy bottom. S. Simpson. Na-
tion 210:296-302 Mr 16 '70 *

MACONDE sculpture. See Sculpture, African
MACOR, inc.
See also
Montgomery Ward and company
MCPHEE, John
Our far-flung correspondents. New Yorker 46:141-7 O 10 '70
Pieces of the frame. il Atlan 225:42-7 Ja '70
Scotch malt whiskey. il Holiday 47:66-7+ Ja '70
Sporting scene. New Yorker 46:126+ Mr 21 '70
MCPHERSON, Aimee Semple
Storming heaven, by L. Thomas. Review Sat R il por 53:35-6 N 21 '70. D. Poling * Time il por 96:88+ O 12 '70. B. Darrach *
MCPHERSON, James Alan
Black law student. Atlan 225:93-100 Ap '70
(ed) See Ellison, R. Indivisible man
MCPHERSON, James M.
White liberals and black power in Negro education, 1865-1915. bibliog f il Am Hist R 75:1357-86 Je '70
MCPHERSON, Sandra
His body; Some meanings of silence; Eschatology; poems. Poetry 116:31-4 Ap '70
Peter rabbit; poem. New Repub 162:25 Je 20 '70
MCQUADE, Walter
Books & ideas. Fortune 82:140-1 D '70
Caution! Si Ramo at work. il pors Fortune 82:104-7+ N '70
Deadly decor for the lively arts. il Life 69:12 N 20 '70
Downtown is looking up. il Fortune 81:132-6+ F '70
Global earth-shapers in complex competition. il Fortune 81:78-81+ Ap '70
Innocent idea for a '76 fair. il Life 69:10 Jl 4 '70
Photo show of old New York. il Life 69:18-19 D 11 '70
Rise of an American architecture; exhibition at Metropolitan museum. il Life 69:14 Ag 14 '70
Why are they running, stretching, starving? il Fortune 82:132-5+ Ag '70
MCQUEEN, Jim
One man's career. il por Yachting 127:80-1+ Ja '70
MCQUEEN, Noel. See Hark, M. jt. auth.
MCQUEEN, Robert
Larry; case history of a mistake. Sat R 53:16-19+ S 12 '70; Same abr. il Read Digest 97:133-7 D '70
Look over the shoulder of a scholarship committee chairman. Todays Ed 59:44-6 Ja '70
MCQUEEN, Steve
Bullitt in the boondocks. A. B. Shuman. il por Motor T 22:70-1 Jl '70 *
Steve McQueen: Mr Mansmanship. B. Rollin. il pors Look 34:48-52 Ja 27 '70
MCQUILKIN, William E.
To regenerate eastern hardwoods: clearcut. il Am For 76:20-3+ Je '70
MACRAE, Julia
Timely response; address, November 1969. Horn Bk 46:189-94 Ap '70
MACRAE, Norman
Foreign report; what will destroy apartheid? Harper 240:30+ Mr '70; Same abr. with title What will destroy apartheid? Cur 118:57-64 My '70
MACRAE, Sheila (Stephens)
Many talents of Sheila MacRae. R. Hochstein. il pors Good H 170:12+ Ap '70 *
MCRAE, William J.
Cyanide Creek affair. il por Outdoor Life 145:44-7+ Je '70
Elk drama in autumn. il Outdoor Life 146:40-1 Jl '70
MACRAMÉ
Macrame. M. W. Phillips. il Design 72:34-7 Wint '70
Macramé; ancient African-Arabic art form goes mod. il Ebony 25:108-10+ Jl '70
Macramé jewelry: an approach to body ornamentation. N. J. Koehler. il Sch Arts 70:12-13 Ja '71
MCREYNOLDS, Karman
Cold frame salads. il Org Gard & Farm 17:86 F '70
No-work vegetable garden. il Org Gard & Farm 17:76-7 Ag '70
MACRO lenses. See Lenses, Photographic
MACROBERTS, Barbara R. and MacRoberts, M. H.
Gulls of Walney Island; with biographical sketches. il pors Natur Hist 79:3, 64-9 Mr '70
MACROBERTS, Michael H. See MacRoberts, B. R. jt. auth.

MACROBIOTIC diet. See Diet
MACROPHAGES
Macrophage membranes view through a scanning electron microscope. A. H. Warfel and S. S. Elberg. bibliog il Science 170:446-7 O 23 '70
Transfer of interferon-producing macrophages: new approach to viral chemotherapy. L. A. Glasgow. bibliog il Science 170:854-6 N 20 '70
MCSHEA, William P.
Who does he think he was? poem. Chr Cent 87:526 Ap 29 '70
MCSHEAN, Gordon
From Roswell to Richmond, to your town. il pors Library J 95:627-31, 2585-6 F 15, Ag '70
MCSLOY, Tom
Music to jangle your insides. Nat R 22:680-1+ Je 30 '70
MCSORLEY, Harry J.
On disowning an expert. America 123:537 D 19 '70
MCSORLEY'S old ale house. See Bars and barrooms
MCSURELY, Alan
Senate v. Alan and Margaret McSurely. W. Goodman. il pors N Y Times Mag p28-9+ Ja 10 '71 *
TRB from Washington. New Repub 163:4 O 31 '70 *
MCSURELY, Margaret
Senate v. Alan and Margaret McSurely. W. Goodman. il pors N Y Times Mag p28-9+ Ja 10 '71 *
TRB from Washington. New Repub 163:4 O 31 '70 *
MCVICKER, James H.
How to weld with your lathe. il Pop Sci 196:67 Je '70
MCVIE James A.
Tacking through the rapids. il Motor B 126:51 Ag '70
MACWEENEY, Alen
Gallery; photographs. il Life 68:8-9 Mr 20 '70
MCWHIRTER, William A.
Horrors of home repair. il Life 68:58-60+ Je 5 '70
Up the organization man. il pors Life 68:61-2+ Ap 17 '70
MCWILLIAMS, Carey
Lucky Democrats. Nation 211:485-7 N 16 '70
Man, a place, and a time. Am West 7:4-8+ My '70
MCWILLIAMS, Donald E.
(ed) See Wiseman, F. Frederick Wiseman
MCWILLIAMS, Nancy R.
Feminism and femininity. Commonweal 92:219-21 My 15 '70
MCWILLIAMS, Wilson Carey, and others
Year of the losers. Commonweal 93:214-16 N 27 '70
MACY, John Williams, 1917-
Critics of television; address, January 15, 1970. Vital Speeches 36:286-8 F 15 '70
MAD (periodical)
MAD magazine in the remedial English class. B. Sanders. Engl J 59:266-7+ F '70
MAD Bear (Tuscarora Indian)
New Indian. R. Bongartz. il Esquire 74:107-9+ Ag '70 *
MADAME Butterfly; opera. See Puccini, G.
MADDEN, Stuart. See Rosen, R. jt. auth.
MADDOCKS, Melvin
Just another face in a rearview mirror. il Sports Illus 33:42-4+ N 16 '70
Life book review. il Life 68:10 F 6; 12 Je 5; 69:6-7 Ag 7; 16-17 O 23; 10 D 4 '70
MADDOX, Brenda
Intelsat on ice? New Repub 162:10-11 My 16 '70
MADDOX, Gaynor
Ice cream diet; excerpt. il Ladies Home J 87:48+ S '70
[Monthly column on cookery] See issues of Today's health to June 1970
MADDOX, Lester G.
Crisis in Southern schools; interview. por(p39) U S News 68:42 F 6 '70

about

American scene: Ludowici, Ga. J. Kane. il Time 95:28 Ap 27 '70 *
Give 'em the ax. il por Newsweek 75:20 Mr 9 '70 *
Governor and the newspapers. America 122:624-5 Je 13 '70 *
Mad as a Maddox. il por Time 95:80 Je 15 '70 *
Maddox case; broad impact? por U S News 68:10-11 Ja 19 '70

MADEIRA
Description and travel
Travel notes. R. Joseph. Esquire 73:8+ Je '70
Traveler's choice: Funchal. R. M. Vansickle. Travel 133:17 Mr '70

MADELINE DeFrees, Sister. See DeFrees, M.
MADEMOISELLE (periodical)
Top people: the Mile awards; twenty-five great hopes for the '70s. il Mile 70:56-9 Ja '70

MADISON, D. M. and Shoop, C. R.
Homing behavior, orientation, and home range of salamanders tagged with tantalum-182. bibliog il Science 168:1484-7 Je 19 '70

MADISON, Dolly, industries, Inc. See Dolly Madison industries, inc.

MADISON, Wis.
Life in Wisconsin, 1948 and today. R. Graves. il Life 69:3 S 18 '70

Housing
Squatters of Miffland; report. R. Rein. il por Time 96:19 N 9 '70

MADISON Square Garden corporation
Unusual twist; battle for Roosevelt raceway. il Forbes 106:43-4 S 15 '70

MADOCS, Rita
Whole Madeline; story. Redbook 135:78-9 My '70

MADONNAS. See Mary, Virgin—Art

MADRID
Description
Spain: fresh flashes. D. Messinesi. Vogue 156:102+ O 1 '70
Galleries and museums
See also
Prado museum
Theater
European literary scene; Buero Vallejo's El sueño de la razón. R. J. Clements. Sat R 63:33 My 2 '70

MADRIGALS
See also
Phonograph records—Madrigals

MADSEN, Edna
Add action to your papier-mâché il Sch Arts 70:14-15 O '70

MADSON, John
Prairie blizzard. il Audubon 72:54-6+ Mr '70

MADWOMAN of Chaillot; drama. See Giraudoux, J.

MAELSTROMS. See Whirlpools

MAEROFF, Gene I.
Robert Taft vs. Howard Metzenbaum. il pors N Y Times Mag p32-4+ O 4 '70
Stinging the corporations. Nation 210:753-6 Je 22 '70

MAERSK-MOLLER, Hans
How to flatten your film for sharper pictures. il Mod Phot 34:78-9+ Ap '70

MAFFEI, Lamberto, and Campbell, F. W.
Neurophysiological localization of the vertical and horizontal visual coordinates in man. bibliog il Science 167:386-7 Ja 23 '70
—See Fiorentini, A. jt. auth.

MAFIA
Defamation by wire tap; release of transcript of recorded New Jersey Mafia conversations. Nation 210:66-7 Ja 26 '70
Harder they fall; attempted assassination of F. DePaula. il pors Newsweek 75:67-8 Je 8 '70
How the Mafia preys on the poor. E. H. Methvin. Read Digest 97:49-55 S '70
How to lock out the Mafia. C. Grutzner. bibliog f il Harvard Bsns R 48:45-58 Mr '70
Legal weapon the Mafia fears most. G. Denison. Read Digest 96:81-5 Je '70
Louisiana still jumps for mobster Marcello. D. Chandler. il pors Life 68:30-7 Ap 10 '70
Mafia. Chr Today 14:25 Ja 16 '70
Mafia and the law; release of FBI transcripts of recorded conversations of the New Jersey Mafia. Commonweal 91:444 Ja 23 '70
Mafia war on the A&P. E. H. Methvin. Read Digest 97:71-6 Jl '70
Mayor, the Mob and the lawyer; two-faced crime fight in St. Louis. D. Walsh. il pors Life 68:24-31 My 29 '70
New Jersey: the state of Mafia; attempt to discredit F. B. Lacey. F. J. Cook. il Nation 210:560-3+ My 11 '70
Organized crime. D. Cressey. New Repub 163:12-13 Jl 18 '70
Organized crime: is it America's other government? il Sr Schol 96:5-9 Ap 6 '70
Parting shots: one golf outing that won't be seen again. il Life 68:82-3 Je 12 '70
People v. the mob; or, Who rules New Jersey? F. J. Cook. il N Y Times Mag p9-11+ F 1 '70
Portrait of a mobster: Marcello the boss in Louisiana. W. Schulz. por Read Digest 97:58-62 Ag '70

Story of T; New York Mafia boss F. Mari. N. Pileggi. il por N Y Times Mag p 12-13+ Mr 29 '70
Weak link in our war on the Mafia. J. L. McClellan. Read Digest 96:56-61 Mr '70

Anecdotes, facetiae, satire, etc
A look at organized crime. W. Allen. New Yorker 46:24-5 Ag 15 '70

MAGANA, R. Fortin-. See Fortin-Magana, R.
MAGAZINE advertising. See Advertising mediums—Periodicals
MAGAZINE art. See Illustration of books and periodicals
MAGAZINE articles. See Periodical articles
MAGAZINE stands, racks, etc.
Easy to make magazine rack. D. Shiner. il Design 71:19-21 Spr '70
MAGAZINES. See Periodicals
MAGDALANY, Philip
Criss-crossing. Criticism
New Yorker 45:56 Ja 31 '70
Watercolor. Criticism
New Yorker 45:56 Ja 31 '70
MAGDALEN, Sister Mary. See Mary Magdalen, Sister
MAGEE, James J.
Early Christians on sex. il Cath World 211:208-10 Ag '70
MAGEE, James S.
ECA and the paradox of African cooperation. bibliog f por Int Concil 580:5-64 N '70
MAGELLANIC clouds
Polarization and magnetism. il Sci N 97:477 My 16 '70
Test for Magellanic cloud members. il Sky & Tel 39:160 Mr '70
MAGENIS, R. Ellen, and others
Heritable fragile site on chromosome 16: probable localization of haptoglobin locus in man. bibliog il Science 170:85-7 O 2 '70
MAGER, Russ
Wilderness and the living Middle Snake. il Liv Wildn 33:8-11 Aut '69
MAGES, Loren J.
Safeguard your city with standby power. il Am City 85:73 N '70
MAGGID, Michael
Discovery: Michael Maggid. J. Dreyfuss. il Mod Phot 34:74-5+ Ap '70 *
MAGGIO musicale fiorentino. See Music festivals—Italy
MAGHREB
Maghreb: a different path. il Newsweek 75:40-1 F 16 '70
MAGI
Why the Wise men came to worship Christ. il Good H 171:158 D '70
MAGIC
If all else fails, try these; magic spells to get a man. S. L. Morrison. Mile 72:156-7+ N '70
See also
Witchcraft
MAGIC box; drama. See Peterson, M. N.
MAGIC flute; opera. See Mozart, J. C. W. A.
MAGIC hat; drama. See Martens, A. C.
MAGIC man; story. See O'Connor, E.
MAGIC mountain (Calif.) See Amusement parks
MAGIC time; story. See Weston, C.
MAGIC words; story. See Bittle, C. R.
MAGNAVOX company
Technician training. il Radio-Electr 41:26 Je '70
MAGNET, Myron
Paranoia at the movies. Commentary 49:80-3 Ap '70
MAGNET laboratory, MIT. See Massachusetts institute of technology, Cambridge
MAGNETIC bubbles. See Domain structure
MAGNETIC catheters. See Catheters
MAGNETIC disk memory devices. See Memory devices (computers)
MAGNETIC domains. See Domain structure
MAGNETIC fields (cosmic physics)
Apollo 12 magnetometer: measurement of a steady magnetic field on the surface of the moon. P. Dyal and others. bibliog il Science 169:762-4 Ag 21 '70
Astrophysics: model proposed for galactic magnetic field. R. W. Holcomb. Science 168:811 My 15 '70
Chromosphere-Corona transition region. G. W. Pneuman. il Sky & Tel 39:148-51 Mr '70
Exploring the nature of galactic fields. D. E. Thomsen. il Sci N 97:557-9 Je 6 '70
Kicking the gong; unexpected lunar information. Sci Am 222:49-50 Ja '70
Polarization and magnetism. il Sci N 97:477 My 16 '70

MAGNETIC fluids
Mobile magnets. Newsweek 75:67 Mr 16 '70
MAGNETIC head corporation
Maverick maker of magnetic heads. il Bsns W p81+ Mr 14 '70
MAGNETIC materials
Permanent magnets. J. J. Becker. il Sci Am 223:92-100 bibliog(p 140) D '70
See also
Ferrites (magnetic materials)
MAGNETIC measurements
See also
Magnetometers
MAGNETIC memory (computers) See Memory devices (computers)
MAGNETIC monopoles. See Particles (nuclear physics)
MAGNETIC poles. See Magnetism, Terrestrial
MAGNETIC recorders and recording
All about tape recorder bias. N. H. Crowhurst. il Radio-Electr 41:40-2 Mr '70
Carter's virtuoso concerto. D. Hamilton. il por Hi Fi 20:secI 22 My '70
Cassette recorders. il Consumer Bul 54:31-7 Ja '71
Cassette tape systems: now they're hi-fi. H. Fantel. il Pop Sci 197:70-3+ N '70
Constant-speed motors for tape recorders; hysteresis synchronous motor. A. Williams. il Radio-Electr 41:49 O '70
Hi-fi product report; Concord Mark III tape recorder. il Electr World 83:18 Je '70
Hi-fi product report; Tandberg model 11 tape recorder. il Electr World 83:14-16 Ap '70
How to match your tape to your recorder and vice versa. H. Friedman. il Hi Fi 20:secI 46:50 Ag '70
How to use an FM mike for remote tape recordings. M. Lincoln. il Pop Sci 197:89+ Ag '70
Hunting with a tape recorder. C. Perkins and G. Perkins. il por Field & S 74:86-7 Ap '70
New trends in sight and sound systems. R. Berkovitz. il Pop Sci 197:68-9+ N '70
Record pirates. il Newsweek 76:70-1 O 5 '70
Recording techniques. D. Molner. Schol Teach Sec Teach Sup p 18-19 F 2 '70
Tape deck with built-in Dolby; KLH 41. I. Berger. il Pop Sci 197:80 N '70
Tape recording at twenty-five. R. Long and N. Eisenberg. il Hi Fi 20:secI 40-5 Ag '70
Tape recording facts and fallacies. D. K. Kirk. il Radio-Electr 41:53+ O '70
What's your recorder's tape bias? H. Friedman. il Pop Phot 66:49+ F '70
See also
Automobiles—Tape equipment
Magnetic head corporation
Tape recordings
Video recorders and recording

Aeronautic applications
Taming radar weather clutter. H. L. McFann. il Electr World 83:44-5 Ja '70

Equipment
Build an audio multicoupler. D. M. Wherry. il Pop Electr 33:31-4 Jl '70
For more recording fun, add a middle mike; panpot control. W. G. Salm. il Pop Mech 134:130-1 Ag '70
How to keep your tape recorder humming happily. W. Salm. il Pop Mech 133:160-3+ Ap '70
Syncro slide adds sound to your slide show. P. Blaire. il Radio-Electr 41:73-4 Ap '70
Tape noise-reducer for audio hobbyists; Dolby noise reduction unit. il Consumer Rep 35:576-7 O '70

Journalistic use
I got it right here on tape! il Forbes 105:7 Ap 1 '70
Mastering mike fright. R. Angus. il Pop Phot 67:33+ O '70
What the writer should know about tape recorders. S. D. Bykofsky. il Writers Digest 50:31-3+ O '70

Maintenance and repair
How to keep your tape recorder humming happily. W. Salm. il Pop Mech 133:160-3+ Ap '70

Stereophonic recorders
Consumer electronic show: observations and reservations about four-channel. I. Berger. il Sat R 53:51 Jl 25 '70
Dolby and four channel: two interim reports. I. Berger. Sat R 53:73 Ap 25 '70
Four-channel system you can buy; Wollensak's model 6154. I. Berger. il Pop Sci 197: 80 N '70

Hi-fi product report: Ferrograph 72A/P tape recorder. il Electr World 83:15-17 Mr '70
How you can enjoy surround sound now. R. Lanier. il Pop Sci 196:146-8+ Mr '70

Tape changers
Cassette changers are coming up fast. J. R. Free. il Pop Sci 197:72-3 N '70
Slot-loading cassette transport. A. Zuckerman. il Electric World 84:44-5 D '70

Testing
Hi-fi product report; Wollensak 6250 tape recorder. il Electr World 84:23 D '70

Visual recording and recordings
See Video recorders and recording
MAGNETIC recorders and recording, Portable
Are cassettes fulfilling their promise? L. Zide. il Hi Fi 20:73-7 N '70
Cassette tape recorders. il Consumer Rep 34:625-9 N '69
Cassettes: the big news in home music systems. R. Gilbert. il House B 112:52-3+ Jl '70
How toying about led to a discovery; cheaper cassette player. il por Bsns W p68 O 31 '70
Pleasures of portables. F. Petras. il Hi Fi 20: secI 46-52 My '70
MAGNETIC resonance
Magnetic resonance properties of some lunar material. R. A. Weeks and others. bibliog il Science 167:704-7 Ja 30 '70
Magnetic resonance studies of lunar samples. S. L. Manatt and others. bibliog il Science 167:709-11 Ja 30 '70
Proton magnetic resonance spectrum of polywater. G. A. Petski. il Science 167:171 Ja 9 '70
See also
Nuclear magnetic resonance
MAGNETIC semiconductors. See Semiconductors
MAGNETIC stirrers. See Household appliances, Electric
MAGNETIC tape
Are cassettes fulfilling their promise? L. Zide. il Hi Fi 20:73-7 N '70
How cassettes compare with tapes and discs. Consumer Rep 35:396-7 Jl '70
How to buy audio tape. B. G. Wels. il Radio-Electr 41:43-4 O '70
How to match your tape to your recorder and vice versa. H. Friedman. il Hi Fi 20:secI 46-50 Ag '70
Magnetic tape; handle with care. C. H. Dodson. il Pop Electr 32:85-7+ F '70
See also
Graham magnetics, inc.
Tape recordings

Care
Sound is only skin-deep. H. Friedman. il Pop Phot 67:64+ N '70
MAGNETIC trains. See Air cushion vehicles
MAGNETISM
Apollo 11 lunar science conference: magnetic and electrical properties; symposium. bibliog il Science 167:691-711 Ja 30 '70
French research leader receives award for accomplishments in solid state field. W. C. Koehler. por Science 170:606-7 N 6 '70
Hematite: intrinsic and defect ferromagnetism. D. J. Dunlop. bibliog il Science 169: 858-60 Ag 28 '70
Testing magnetic theory; structure of TMMC, antiferromagnetic substance. il Sci N 98: 411 N 28 '70
See also
Magnets
MAGNETISM, Stellar
Celestial supermagnet. D. E. Thomsen. il Sci N 98:290-1 O 3 '70
Magnetic dwarf in Draco. il Time 96:45 S 14 '70
MAGNETISM, Terrestrial
Age of the Bay of Biscay: evidence from seismic profiles and bottom samples. E. J. W. Jones and J. I. Ewing; reply. N. D. Watkins and A. Richardson. bibliog Science 167:209 Ja 9 '70
Geomagnetic intensity: changes during the past 3000 years in the western hemisphere. V. Bucha and others. bibliog il Science 168: 111-14 Ap 3 '70
Magnetic havoc; findings of James D. Hays and Neil Opdyke. il Time 96:63-4 N 30 '70
Paleomagnetism and Gondwanaland. M. W. McElhinny and G. R. Luck. bibliog il Science 168:830-2 My 15 '70
South Pole reaches the Sahara; report of symposium on the Saharan Ordovician ice age. R. W. Fairbridge. Science 168:878+ My 15 '70
See also
Van Allen radiation belts

MAGNETITE
Search for magnetite in lunar rocks and fines. J. Jedwab and others. bibliog il Science 167:618-19 Ja 30 '70
MAGNETIZATION
Thermochemical remanent magnetization and thermal remanent magnetization: comparison in a basalt. K. Kellogg and others. bibliog il Science 170:628-30 N 6 '70
MAGNETOHYDRODYNAMICS
How much, how soon for anti-pollution? R. H. Gilluly. New Repub 162:7-8 Ja 24 '70
Magnetism to metabolism; physics, chemistry Nobels. Sci N 98:348 O 31 '70
  See also
Van Allen radiation belts
MAGNETOMETERS
Magnetometer evidence of a structure within the La Venta pyramid. F. Morrison and others. bibliog il Science 167:1488-90 Mr 13 '70
MAGNETS
New alloy shows promise as high-field superconducting magnet. G. B. Lubkin. il Phys Today 23:55 Ja '70
Permanent magnets. J. J. Becker. il Sci Am 223:92-100 bibliog(p 140,) D '70
Super superconducting magnets? Sci Am 222:56-7 My '70
MAGNUSON, Keith
Maggie the policeman. por Time 97:36 Ja 11 '71 *
MAGNUSON, Roger P.
Pupil control in English and French schools. Ed Digest 35:25-7 My '70
MAGNUSON, Warren Grant
Excerpt from address, May 23, 1969. Cong Digest 49:44+ F '70
How our new warranty law would protect you. por Pop Sci 197:56-7 N '70
Needed: a national dental health plan for children. por Parents Mag 45:44 F '70
MAGOON, Bob
Magoon on the bounding main. H. D. Whall. il Sports Illus 33:76-7 N 16 '70 *
MAGOWAN, Robin
Pancakes for you and me. Poetry 116:193-202 Je '70
MAGRUDER, William
Excerpt from testimony before the Senate committee on appropriations, August 27, 1970. Cong Digest 49:302+ D '70
MAGRUDER Corridor wilderness area (proposed) See Wilderness areas—Nevada
MAGUIRE, Francis
Dazzle; poem. Cath World 211:246 S '70
Growing; poem. Commonweal 92:221 My 15 '70
Little love, a little wit; poem. Cath World 212:14 O '70
Once on a black morning; poem. Chr Today 14:14 Je 5 '70
One joy; poem. Chr Today 15:12 O 23 '70
Plants in the bathtub; poem. Chr Today 15:10 O 9 '70
Strange memorial; poem. Chr Cent 87:1119 S 23 '70
Sunwards; poem. Chr Today 14:9 Mr 13 '70
MAGUIRE, H. F.
Small game take down last year. il Cons 25:32-3 D '70
MAGUIRE, John W.
Professional negotiations: state or federal legislation? Sch & Soc 98:176-7 Mr '70
MAHAN, Joseph B.
Canaanite Columbus? il por Newsweek 76:65 O 26 '70 *
MAHAN, Paul E.
What's cooking? Org Gard & Farm 17:99 D '70
MAHAGONNY; opera. See Weill, K.
MAHANAY, C. E.
Mall that communications built. il Am City 85:76+ O '70
MAHARAJAS. See India—Nobility
MAHBOUBIAN art collection. See Art—Private collections
MAHER, Arthur J.
How to slash your remodeling bills. Am Home 73:46+ O '70
Is your money going up in smoke? Am Home 73:34+ N '70
MAHEU, René
Commitment to international education year 1970. Sch & Soc 98:295-6 Sum '70
1970 international education year; message. UN Mo Chron 7:1-2 F '70
Road to peace and progress; interview. ed. by G. D. Fischer. il por Todays Ed 59:20-3 My '70
Tenth anniversary of U.N. declaration on the independence of colonial peoples; excerpts from address, 1970. UNESCO Courier 23:14 N '70

MAHEU, Robert A.
Case of the invisible billionaire. il pors Newsweek 76:75-6+ D 21 '70 *
Hughes caper. il Newsweek 76:56 D 28 '70 *
Shootout at the Hughes corral. il pors Time 96:62-6 D 21 '70 *
MAHEY, John A.
Lithographs by Rembrandt Peale. il Antiques 97:236-42 F '70
MAHLER, Gustav
Berrys (twice) with Bernstein: Des knaben wunderhorn. G. S. Fox. il por Am Rec G 36:544-6 Ap '70 *
Double rich, double good Ludwig-Berry-Bernstein Mahler. R. Lawrence. il Sat R 53:69 Ja 31 '70
Jascha Horenstein's matchless Mahler 1. J. Diether. por Am Rec G 36:796-9 Je '70 *
Mahler in Utah. R. C. Marsh. Hi Fi 20:secI 84 My '70 *
Music to my ears; New York Philharmonic performs the Ninth symphony. I. Kolodin. Sat R 53:41 O 10 '70 *
Ormandy's Mahler 1: passionate involvement. G. S. Fox. Am Rec G 36:800-2+ Je '70 *
RCA's great Philadelphia orchestra recording. R. C. Marsh. il Hi Fi 20:80 S '70 *
Records:
Des knaben wunderhorn; Rückert songs; Symphony no. 5; and Symphony no. 2 (Resurrection) Opera N 34:30 My 16 '70 *
Two new recordings of the Mahler Sixth. J. Diether. il Am Rec G 37:34-5+ S '70 *
MAHLEY, R. W. and others
Identity of very low density lipoprotein apoproteins of plasma and liver Golgi apparatus. bibliog il Science 168:380-2 Ap 17 '70
MAHLMANN, Lewis
Pinocchio; dramatization of story by C. Collodi. Plays 30:47-54 N '70
MAHMOOD, David J.
Playing card maker does a neat trick. il por Bsns W p40+ Jl 11 '70 *
MAHONEY, Charles A.
Watercolor page; with biographical sketch. il por Am Artist 34:46-7+ Mr '70
MAHONEY, David Joseph, 1923-
Salesman in the executive suite. A. A. Butkus. por Duns 96:34-8 O '70 *
MAHONEY, J. Daniel
Conservatives are out to beat: Rockeberg, Goldfeller, Ottindell and Goodinger. J. Greenfeld. il por N Y Times Mag p26-7+ O 18 '70 *
MAHONEY, Stephen
Fred Mates is one happy man. il pors Life 68:56B-56D+ My 22 '70
MAHONEY, Mrs Stephenson
Rooms they love to live in. il House & Gard 138:40-3 Ag '70
MAHONIAS
Mahonias: some just grow, some look as though they were designed. il Sunset 144:214-15 Mr '70
MAIL advertising. See Advertising, Direct mail
MAIL boats
Mailboat to Exuma. H. Reussille. il Travel 134:52-5 N '70
MAIL boxes. See Mailboxes
MAIL carriers. See Postal service—Letter carriers
MAIL censorship. See Postal censorship
MAIL lobbying. See Lobbying
MAIL order business
Mail-order items for the hobbyist. il Consumer Bul 53:31-2 Ja '70
Put the mail-order smut merchants out of business! G. Denison. Read Digest 96:209-10+ My '70
Riding the sex wave; West Germany. Newsweek 75:108 Ap 20 '70
  See also
Booksellers and bookselling
Montgomery Ward and company
Postal service—Unordered merchandise
Sears, Roebuck and company
MAIL order catalogs. See Catalogs, Mail order
MAIL robberies. See Robberies and assaults
MAILBOXES
Country and suburban mail: here are ideas. il Sunset 144:110+ Mr '70
Even mailboxes can be charming. il Design 71:34-5 Spr '70
When your mailbox flunks. D. Williamson. Sat R 53:20 Ag 15 '70
MAILER, Norman
Mailer's opera. C. Matz. il por Opera N 34:14-16 F 21 '70 *
Managing Mailer, by J. Flaherty. Review
Commentary 50:89-92 O '70. C. W. Brooks *
Nat R por 22:688-9 Je 30 '70. G. F. Will *
Sat R 53:36 Je 6 '70. A. Cooper *

MAILING lists
    See also
Hofheimer, F. S, inc.
MAILMEN. See Postal service—Letter carriers
MAIMONIDES mental health center, Brooklyn.
    See Mental health centers
MAIN, Jeremy
    Conservationists at the barricades. il Fortune 81:144-7+ F '70
    Only radical reform can save the courts. il Fortune 82:110-14+ Ag '70; Same abr. Read Digest 97:106-10 N '70
    Why nobody likes the insurers. il Fortune 82:82-7+ D '70
MAINE
    See also
Acadia National Park
Conservation of resources—Maine
Fishing—Maine
Gardening—Maine
Isle au Haut
Justice, Administration of—Maine
Katahdin, Mount
Landscape protection—Maine
Wassataquoik Stream
Wilderness areas—Maine

    Description and travel
Relax on Maine's inland waterways. D. Becker. il Travel 133:68-70 Je '70

    Industries
Case of sour sugar. il por Time 95:12 F 9 '70
    See also
Petroleum industry and trade—Maine
MAISEL, Albert Q.
    Alcohol and your brain. Read Digest 96:65-9 Je '70
MAISEL, Jay
    Gallery; photographs. il Life 68:6-9 Je 26 '70
MAISONROUGE, Jacques Gaston
    Man who makes it one world for IBM. il pors Bsns W p90-2 Jl 18 '70 *
MAITLAND, Alastair
    Workman can master his tools. Sat R 53:22 N 14 '70
MAJCHROWICZ, Edward, and Mendelson, J. H.
    Blood concentrations of acetaldehyde and ethanol in chronic alcoholics. bibliog il Science 168:1100-2 My 29 '70
MAJORCA
    Chopin and Sand: in the wake of that Majorcan winter. R. McMullen. il Sat R 53:78-9+ Mr 14 '70
    Majorca: where European girls are. R. Atcheson. il Holiday 47:64-5+ Ja '70
MAJUMDAR, Sachindra K.
    Beauty as personality. Vogue 156:123+ O 1 '70
    Meditation: open way to serenity of mind and body. Vogue 156:105+ Jl '70
MAKARIOS III, abp
    No cheers. Newsweek 75:42+ Ap 6 '70 *
    Wounded soul. il por Time 95:23 Mr 23 '70 *
MAKAROVA, Natalya
    Big leap. il por Newsweek 76:86 S 21 '70 *
    Little Juggernaut. il por Time 97:57 Ja 4 '71 *
    Musical events; Giselle at the New York city center. W. Sargeant. New Yorker 46:57 Ja 2 '71 *
    Natalya Makarova: a Russian Giselle in exile. O. Maynard. il pors Dance Mag 44:54-9 N '70 *
    Russian ballerina. W. Terry. por Sat R 53:52 D 5 '70 *
MAKE-up
    Beauty advice from the experts. P. Van Wagenen. il Parents Mag 46:60-3 Ja '71
    Beauty for busy young mothers. P. Van Wagenen. il Parents Mag 45:23+ Ap '70
    Beauty-to-be. il Mlle 71:125-9 O '70
    Beauty today; questions & answers on the new makeup trends. il Good H 170:90-3 F '70
    Color play. il Mlle 71:140-1 Je '70
    Colourquake. il Vogue 155:172-7 Mr 1 '70
    Easy on the eyes. il Mlle 70:200-1 Mr '70
    Eye to beauty. P. Van Wagenen. il Parents Mag 45:37 F '70
    Eyes of March. il Mlle 70:180-1 Mr '70
    Face doodles done for fun. il Life 69:68-71 N '70
    Face of America; six beauty types. il Mlle 71:156-9 S '70
    For evening loveliness: moonlit makeup, cascading curls. T. Pavlik. il Good H 171:84-5+ D '70
    G.E. encounter: beauty. J. Sims. il Mlle 71:304-6 Ag '70
    Great new look for a girl on the go. S. Obre. il Ladies Home J 87:108-9 N '70
    Joie de makeup. il Vogue 155:138-43 Ap 1 '70
    Long loving look at hair. il Seventeen 29:139 Ap '70
    Make-up for a new fall face. il Redbook 135:98-101 S '70

New makeup colors; which ones for you? il Good H 170:106-9 Je '70
New party makeup: an applied art. C. Bartel. il Am Home 73:14+ N '70
On and off the avenue. K. Fraser. New Yorker 46:147-8+ N 14 '70
Psycho-power of make-up. il Harp Baz 103:218-19 S '70
Ski do's. il Mlle 72:192-3 N '70
Twenty-four new hairdos: notes on the new makeup. il Good H 170:100-9+ Ap '70
Twenty one new hairdos, all the latest make-up looks. il Good H 171:86-95+ O '70
What meets the eye. S. Obre. il Ladies Home J 87:100-1 Ap '70
    See also
Beauty, Personal
Cosmetics
MAKE-up, Theatrical
    Old age of Dustin Hoffman; with interview, ed. by R. Meryman. D. Hoffman. il pors Life 69:75-9 N 20 '70
MAKE-up mirrors. See Mirrors
MAKMAN, Maynard H.
    Adenyl cyclase of cultured mammalian cells: activation by catecholamines. bibliog il Science 170:1421-3 D 25 '70
MAKOFF, Stephen J.
    Preparing groups for weekend camp programs. il Camp Mag 42:46-7 Mr '70
MAKONDE (Bantu tribe) See Mozambique—Native races
MAKROPOULOS affair; opera. See Janáček, L.
MALACOLOGY. See Mollusks
Le MALADE imaginaire; drama. See Molière, J. B. P.
MALAKOFF diggins state historic park. See California—Parks and reserves
MALAMUD, Bernard
    Analysis of The prison by Bernard Malamud. D. Wechsler. Engl J 59:782-4 S '70 *
MALARIA
    Malaria resistance: artificial induction with a partially purified plasmodial fraction. L. E. D'Antonio and others. bibliog il Science 168:1117-18 My 29 '70
    Saurian malaria: development of sporozoites in two species of phlebotomine sandflies. S. C. Ayala and D. Lee. bibliog il Science 167:891-2 F 6 '70
    Sickle cell anemia and malaria. il Chem 43:22 Je '70

    Prevention and control
    See also
Antimalarials
Atabrine
Chloroquine
MALARIAL parasites. See Plasmodium (parasite)
MALAS, Spiro
    Greeks bearing gifts. Q. Eaton. por Opera N 34:12 My 16 '70 *
MALAWI, LAKE
    Malawi: portrait of a lake. G. Ross. il Travel 134:34-9+ N '70
MALAYSIA
    Creeping self-reliance in Malaysia. S. A. Douglas. Cur Hist 59:345-50+ D '70
    New man on a troubled scene. il por Time 96:35 O 5 '70
    Tunku steps down. Newsweek 76:58+ S 14 '70
MALAYSIA-Singapore airlines. See Airlines—Asia, Southeastern
MALAYSIA-United States air agreement. See Aviation—International aspects
MALCOLM, Andrew I.
    Drug abuse and social alienation; address, 1970. il Todays Ed 59:28-31 S '70
MALCOLM, Janet
    Help! New Repub 163:15-17 O 10 '70
    On and off the avenue. New Yorker 46:89-92 My 2; 63-4+ Je 20; 62-5 Ag 8; 67-9 S 5; 147-8+ N 7 '70
MALCOLM X
    Malcolm X, ed. by J. H. Clarke. Review
        Chr Cent 87:177 F 11 '70. W. Hamilton *
    Malcolm X: history as hope. por Time 95:88+ F 23 '70 *
MALCUIT, Stanley V.
    Protection can be dangerous. por Nations Bsns 58:47 F '70
MALDEN, Mass.
    People prefer trash bags. il Am City 85:52 S '70
MALE coiffure. See Hairdressing
MALE cosmetics. See Cosmetics for men
MALE embroiderers. See Embroidery workers
MALEK, Frederick Vincent
    At battle stations. J. Osborne. New Repub 163:10-11 D 12 '70 *
    —See MacDougal, G. E. jt. auth.

MALENA, Dave
Beef management (cont of) What's new. See issues of Successful farming
MALEY, Donald
New role for industrial arts. Ed Digest 35: 42-5 My '70
MALFATTI, Franco Maria
Bold view of a transformed Europe by 1980; interview, ed. by A. de Borchgrave. por Newsweek 76:51 Ag 17 '70
MALFORMATIONS. See Deformities
MALIK, [Akov Aleksandrovich
Signal from Moscow? Newsweek 75:36 Ap 27 '70 *
MALINGERING
Wanted for fraud: professional patients. E. H. McCleary. il Todays Health 49:30-1+ Ja '71
MALISCH, Ward R. and others
Streets of glass. il Am City 85:104+ Jl '70
MALIVER, Bruce L.
Encounter groupers up against the wall. il N Y Times Mag p4-5+ Ja 3 '71
MALKIN, Lawrence
Economic consequences of Maynard Keynes. il pors Horizon 11:104-11 Aut '69
Halfway to 1984. il por Horizon 12:32-9 Spr '70
MALKOC, Anna Maria, and Roberts, A. H.
Bilingual education: a special report from CAL/ERIC. Engl J 59:721-9+ My '70
MALLALIEU, H. B.
Lines to an ambassador; poem. Poetry 117: 36-7 O '70
Samothrace; poem. Poetry 116:76 My '70
MALLAS, John H.
Selected objects from the Mallas Observer's catalogue. See issues of Review of popular astronomy to August 1969
—and Kreimer, Evered
Messier album. See issues of Sky and telescope to September 1970
MALLECZEWEN, Friedrich Percyval Reck-.
See Reck-Malleczewen, F. P.
MALLEY, Jean
Quilt; Stale piece; Untitled; Past; Strength; Ghost; poems. Poetry 115:337-42 F '70
MALLON, Mary
Case of the disappearing cook. M. Sufrin. il pors Am Heritage 21:37-43 Ag '70 *
MALLON, Vincent T.
Medellin guidelines. America 122:92-6 Ja 31 '70
MALLORY, H. R.
Universal manganese-alkaline battery charger. il Radio-Electr 41:52-3 Ag '70
MALLS, Shopping. See Business districts
MALMSTROM, Margit
Arne Lindmark: master of the watercolor scene. il Am Artist 35:38-43+ Ja '71
Charles Umlauf, sculptor of the living form. il por Am Artist 69:52-9+ S '70
MALNUTRITION. See Children—Nutrition; Nutrition problems
MALOFF, Saul
Beware of "literature boys"? Commonweal 93:96-8 O 23 '70
Fiedler on the Woolf. Commonweal 92:189-91 My 8 '70
Poetry and power. Commonweal 93:352-4 Ja 8 '71
Stage. Commonweal 92:38-9, 222 Mr 20, My 15 '70
Writers & writing (cont) Commonweal 91:513-15 F 6 '70
MALONE, Art
Sun Devil no. 1. H. L. Masin. por Sr Schol 95:inside back cover N 3 '69 *
MALONE, Eric V.
Topiary in Britain. il Am For 76:44-5+ N '70
MALONE, Hank
Underground Detroit for SLA and ALA conventioneers. il por Wilson Lib Bul 44:931-9 My '70
MALONEY, Donald
Rahner and the anonymous Christian. America 123:348-50 O 31 '70
MALONEY, Elbert S.
Compass for your boat. il Motor B 126:22+ D '70
Florida for the boatman in 1970. il Motor B 126:52-4 N '70
Log keeping for the cruising man. il pors Motor B 125:100-1 Mr '70
New charts. See issues of Motor boating to July 1970
Notices to boatmen. Motor B 126:30+ O; 24+ D '70
Skipper and his charts. Motor B 125:146-7 Ja '70
MALONEY, Phyllis Church
Fleurage. il por Horticulture 48:48-9+ F '70

MALONEY, Ralph
God out of the machinery. Atlan 226:144-5 O '70
Vinum omnia vincit. Atlan 225:114-16 F '70
War was two years ago. Atlan 225:61-3 Mr '70
Way it all comes loose; story. Atlan 226:70-2 Jl '70
MALOOF, Sam
Wharton Esherick 1887-1970. il pors Craft Horiz 30:10-11 Ag '70
MALPRACTICE
Malpractice mess. il Time 96:36+ N 2 '70
See also
Trials (malpractice)
MALRAUX, André
Portrait of André Malraux, by R. Payne. Review
Commonweal 93:280-1 D 11 '70. J. Meyers *
Sat R il por 54:30 Ja 9 '71. L. LeSage *
MALTA, Knights of
Beknighted Malta; council of Europe's exhibition. M. Gendel. il Art N 69:44-7+ Sum '70
Catholic nobility. il Newsweek 76:70-1 Jl 13 '70
MALTHUSIANISM
Constraints on the species. Natur Hist 79: 63 Ja '70
MAMA, La. See New York (city)—Theater
MAMMALIAN ecology. See Zoology—Ecology
MAMMALS
Dentary-squamosal joint and the origin of mammals. H. R. Barghusen and J. A. Hopson. bibliog il Science 168:573-5 My 1 '70
Social subordination, population density, and mammalian evolution. J. J. Christian. bibliog Science 168:84-90 Ap 3 '70; Reply with rejoinder. M. D. F. Udvardy. 170:344-6 O 16 '70
See also
Anteaters
Bats
Embryology—Mammals
Marsupials
Primates
Whales
MAMMALS, Fossil
Fossil sea mammal: paleoparadoxia. H. P. Zuidema. il Sea Front 16:20-4 Ja '70
MAMMARY tumors. See Tumors
MAMMEL, Richard
From pipe to pot. il Ceram Mo 18:16-18 Mr '70
MAMMOTH cave, Idaho. See Caves
MAMMOTHS
Mammoth hair: stability of α-keratin structure and constituent proteins. J. M. Gillespie. bibliog il Science 170:1100-2 D 4 '70
Those mysterious woolly mammoths. D. Cohen. il Sci Digest 67:44-8+ Ja '70
MAN
Biological cages; D. Morris and his colleagues. G. Stade. bibliog Nation 210:566-8 My 11 '70
Erik Erikson's eight ages of man. D. Elkind. il N Y Times Mag p25-7+ Ap 5 '70
Hand and the head. P. A. Cuadra. il Américas 22:27-9 S '70
Human zoo, by D. Morris. Review
Natur Hist il 79:104-6 Ja '70. R. Fox
Modern man is obsolete; excerpts; reprint. Sat R 53:16-18+ Ag 1 '70
Possibilities of transformation: a report on the state of mankind: 1970. F. K. Kelly. Sat R 53:17-19+ Mr 7 '70
Quiet in the night. H. Borland. il Audubon 72:26-7 N '70
Social contract, by R. Ardrey. Review
Nation 211:469-70 N 9 '70. B. Bendow
Sat R 53:32-4 O 24 '70. M. M. Tumin
Star dragon; excerpt from The invisible pyramid. L. Eiseley. il Natur Hist 79:18+ Je '70
State of the species; symposium. il Natur Hist 79:43-74 Ja '70
Technology and mankind's future. R. A. Givens. America 123:254-6 O 10 '70
Three Damoclean swords; annual meeting of American association for advancement of science. J. R. Nelson. Chr Cent 87:69-71 Ja 21 '71
Unexpected universe, by L. Eiseley. Review
New Yorker 46:118+ F 21 '70. W. H. Auden
See also
Anthropology
Ethnology
Evolution
History
Humanism
Human relations
Longevity
Manners and customs

MAN—*Continued*

Constitution

Body build and heart attacks. A. J. Snider.
il Sci Digest 69:57 Ja '71

Food habits

See Food habits

Influence of environment

Environmental threat and social organiza-
tion. L. Krader. bibliog f Ann Am Acad 389:
11-18 My '70
Exploring earthman's world. See issues of
National parks & Conservation magazine
Inside Buckminster Fuller's universe. H.
Taylor. por Sat R 53:56-7+ My 2 '70
Property and the person. Chr Cent 87:716 Je
10 '70
Thinking social-scientifically about environ-
mental quality. S. Z. Klausner. Ann Am
Acad 389:1-10 My '70
See also
Altitude, Influence of
Environmental health

Influence on nature

America the raped, by G. Marine. Review
Am West 7:50+ Mr '70. J. E. Illick
Confessions of a polluter. A. Godfrey. por
Read Digest 97:60-4 S '70
Crud; excerpt from A jungle in the house.
M. Bates. il Sci Digest 68:34-8 Ag '70
Cultural basis for our environmental crisis;
adaptation of address. April 16, 1970. L.
W. Moncrief. bibliog Science 170:508-12 O
30 '70
Current ecological problems; the place of
technology and design; address, August 19,
1970. M. Tribus. Vital Speeches 36:717-20 S
15 '70
Different 2001; excerpts from address. F. El-
der. Cath World 211:63-6 My '70
Environmental pollution; an ecological
perspective. D. L. Allen. Ed Digest 36:
51-4 D '70
Environmental stewardship; with editorial
comment. H. B. Kuhn. Chr Today 14:25,
46-7 My 8 '70
Exploring earthman's world. See issues of
National parks & Conservation magazine
Frontier freedoms and space age cities; excerpt. C. W. Griffin, jr. il Sat R 53:17-19+
F 7 '70
Genesis and ecology: does subdue mean
plunder? D. E. Gowan. il Chr Cent 87:1188-
91 O 7 '70
Genius of the place. R. J. Dubos. il por Am
For 76:16-19+ S '70
Global environment: M.I.T. study looks for
danger signs. L. J. Carter. Science 169:660-
2 Ag 14 '70
Good earth and the golden rule. L. Sumner.
il Nat Parks 44:4-9 Ja '70
How man endangers the climate. G. J. F.
MacDonald. Cur 114:17-24 Ja '70
Human energy production as a process in
the biosphere. S. F. Singer. il Sci Am 223:
174-6+ bibliog(p265) S '70
If you don't mind my saying so. J. W.
Krutch. Am Scholar 39:202+ Spr '70
Impact of man on the Adirondack high
country. E. H. Ketchledge and R. E.
Leonard. il Cons 25:14-18 O '70
Island images. T. E. Jones. il Nat Parks &
Con Mag 44:11-13 Jl '70
Man and his environment; excerpts from ad-
dress. A. Godfrey. il PTA Mag 65:2-5 S '70
Man is the endangered species; interview. P.
R. Ehrlich. por Nat Wildlife 8:38-9 Ap '70
Man-made climatic changes. H. E. Lands-
berg. bibliog il Science 170:1265-74 D 18 '70
Man's forgotten necessity eco-variety. H. H.
Iltis. por Field & S 75:62+ Je '70
Mental inertia and environmental decay: the
end of an era. P. A. Gunter. il Liv Wildn
34:3-7 Spr '70
Mess of modern man. G. Harrison. il Natur
Hist 79:68-9 Ja '70
Mortgaging the old homestead. Lord Ritchie-
Calder. For Affairs 48:207-20 Ja '70; Same.
il Sports Illus 32:44-51 F 2 '70
No deposit-no return, ed. by H. D. Johnson.
Review
Am For 76:29+ D '70. M. Bush
Our ecological crisis. C. Quigley. Cur Hist
59:1-12 Jl '70
Our vandal ideology. S. Paradise. Cur 115:
55-60 F '70
Park program: it's bigger than you think: ad-
dress, October 1969. R. Rienow. por Parks &
Rec 5:27-8+ Mr '70
Parting shots; apocalyptic visions for our
fragile little planet. il Life 69:63-6 S 4 '70

People pollution. P. R. Ehrlich. il Audubon
72:4-9 My '70
People-power and pollution: what can I do?
C. E. Randall. il Am For 76:28-35+ O '70
People problem. P. R. Ehrlich and J. P.
Holdren. Sat R 53:42-3 Jl 4 '70
Project survival; symposium, with editorial
comment. bibliog il Environ 12:2-47 Ap '70
Prospects for space ship man; excerpts from
address, 1969. G. L. Stebbins. il Sat R 53:
48-50+ Mr 7 '70
Raping Alaska; ecology of oil. B. Weisberg.
il Ramp Mag 8:25-33 Ja '70
Ravaged environment. il Newsweek 75:30-
40+ Ja 26 '70
Russian roulette? P. Cloud. Science 167:1323
Mr 6 '70
Science and the quality of our environment;
adaptation of address, June 1970. W. T.
Pecora. il Bul Atom Sci 26:20-3 O '70
Technological imperative, social implications
of professional technology. D. B. Hertz.
bibliog f Ann Am Acad 389:95-106 My '70
Theology for ecology. J. B. Shepherd. il Cath
World 211:172-5 Jl '70
To trouble a star: the cost of intervention
in nature. G. Hardin. Bul Atom Sci 26:17-20
Ja '70; Same abr. with title Ecology versus
economics. Cur 116:34-9 Mr '70
View from dead men's shoulders. R. C.
Cook. il Nat Parks 44:10 F '70
We have met the enemy, and he is us. W.
Stegner. il Life 69:10-11 Jl 10 '70
Weeds, bugs, Americans. J. Fowles. il Sports
Illus 33:4-8+ D 21 '70
What price tomorrow? L. Hall. Am For 76:
42+ Ja '70
Will the world come to a horrible end? S.
F. Singer. bibliog Science 170:125 O 9 '70
See also
Pollution
United Nations conference on the human
environment (proposed)

Anecdotes, facetiae, satire, etc.

Adam and Eve, ltd; an ecological fable. W. B.
Park. il Look 34:67-8 Ap 21 '70
Desecrate with howls so jolly. F. Deford.
il Sports Illus 31:48-50 D 15 '69

Migrations

Ancient landings in America; findings of C
H. Gordon. J. Lear. il Sat R 53:18-19+ Jl 18
'70
Canaanite Columbus? the Metcalf stone. il
por Newsweek 76:65 O 26 '70
Early man in America. il Sci N 98:364 N
7 '70

Origin and antiquity

Origin of man. C. L. Brace. il Natur Hist 79:
46-9 Ja '70
See also
Evolution

Periodicity

See Biology—Periodicity

Survival

Battle for earth; the supreme challenge to
modern education; address, August 1, 1970.
H. J. Zitko. Vital Speeches 36:692-6 S 1 '70
Bomb shelters, arks and ecology. R. Moses.
il Nat R 22:938-42 S 8 '70
Crisis of transformation. J. Platt. Cur 115:3-
17 F '70
Earthmanship. D. Lambert. Nat Parks 44:
15-16 Ja '70
History and human survival, by R. J. Lifton.
Review
Sat R 53:35-8 F 21 '70. H. S. Resnik
Mankind's last, best chance. J. Poppy. il
Look 34:17-21 Ja 13 '70
Man's real missing link. D. Behrman. il
UNESCO Courier 23:24-5 Ag '70
Mere survival is not enough for man. R.
Dubos. por Life 69:2 Jl 24 '70; Same abr.
with title Why survival is not enough.
Read Digest 97:111-12 O '70
Notes and comment. New Yorker 46:27-9 My
23 '70
Peace research; the science of survival; re-
print. B. V. A. Röling. il UNESCO Courier
23:21-2+ N '70

MAN (theology)

Aspects of a theology of play. J. V. Schall.
il Cath World 212:69-73 N '70
Back to the real world. J. V Schall. America
123:8-10, 77-8 Jl 11, Ag 22 '70
Barrier; man's fall. L. N. Bell. Chr Today
15:34-5 O 9 '70
Christianity: the true humanism. W. S. Reid
Chr Today 14:9-11 Je 19 '70
Crisis of the church. H. Lindsell. Chr Today
14:4-6 S 11 '70
Myth of primitive religion. M. Douglas. bib-
liog il Commonweal 93:41-4 O 9 '70

MAN (theology)—*Continued*
Not by white might nor by black power.
W. H. Hodges. Chr Today 15:5-10 O 9 '70
Rahner's anthropology. G. A. McCool.
America 123:342-4 O 31 '70
MAN, Effect of altitude on. See Altitude, Influence of
MAN, Prehistoric
Ancient man in Kow swamp. L. Bickel. il
Sci N 97:254-5 Mr 7 '70
Australopithecine endocast (Taung specimen, 1924): a new volume determination.
R. L. Holloway. bibliog il Science 168:
966-8 My 22 '70
Creativity of ancient man. E. Keller and
J. Zimmerman. il Chem 43:14-21 Jl '70
Drying out a discovery; flooding of Marmes
man site. il Sci N 97:91-2 Ja 24 '70
Early man in America. il Sci N 98:364 N 7
'70
Man's bag. Sci Am 222:52 Ja '70
Rise of ancient man. E. Keller. il Chem
43:8-13 Jl '70
Social contract, by R. Ardrey. Review
Nat R 22:1358-60 D '70. J. Greenway
Song of man; Folsom culture. C. L. Camp.
il Am West 7:18-23 S '70
Who's who at Swartkrans. Sci Am 222:52 Je
'70
See also
Cave drawings and paintings
Neanderthal race
Paleo-Indians
Petroglyphs
Piltdown forgery

Bibliography
Suggested readings on ancient man. Chem
43:47 Jl '70
MAN and his world cultural exhibition. See
Montreal—Exhibitions
MAN and nature. See Man—Influence on nature
MAN-made fabrics. See Textile fabrics, Synthetic
MAN-made lakes. See Lakes, Artificial
MAN of the year distinguished service award
See American forestry association
MAN on the telephone; story. See Lofts, N.
MAN on the threshold; story. See Borges, J. L.
MAN power. See Manpower
MAN-powered airplanes. See Airplanes, Light
MAN who really came to dinner; story. See
Harrison, W.
MAN without a country; drama. See Olfson, L.
MANAGEMENT
See also
Business management and organization
Farm management
MANAGEMENT analysis and projection system. See Computers—Business use
MANAGEMENT and budget, Office of. See
United States—Management and budget,
Office of
MANAGEMENT costs. See Cost
MANAGEMENT games
Games can teach the boss his business. il
Changing T 24:45-7 N '70
MANAGEMENT information systems. See Information systems, Management
MANAGEMENT information systems division.
See United States—Management and budget,
Office of
MANAGEMENT of children. See Children—
Management and training
MANAGEMENT programs. See Executives—
Training
MANAGEMENT psychology. See Psychology,
Industrial
MANAGERS. See Executives
MANAGERS, Baseball. See Baseball managers
MANATEE COUNTY, Fla.
Education
Ain't nobody gonna touch king Claude; school
busing case. il por Time 95:16 Ap 20 '70
I, Claudius; C. Kirk yields. Newsweek 75:35
Ap 27 '70
Kirk's caper. il Newsweek 75:40-2 Ap 20 '70
MANATEES
Manatee: siren of the sea. J. E. Hartman. il
Nat Wildlife 7:38-9 O '69
MANATT, Stanley L. and others
Magnetic resonance studies of lunar samples. bibliog il Science 167:709-11 Ja 30 '70
MANCHA, La, Spain
La Mancha. F. V. Grunfeld. il Horizon 11:40-
7 Aut '69

MANCHESTER, Harland
New campus hero; the computer. il PTA
Mag 64:2-4 F '70; Same abr. Read Digest
96:33-4+ Mr '70
MANCHESTER, Conn.
How to build a town ski slope. W. D. O'Neill.
il Am City 85:84+ Ag '70
Night tennis and basketball. W. D. O'Neill.
il Am City 85:28 N '70
MANCHESTER, N.H.

Historic houses, etc.
Epitaph for an American landmark; Amos-
keag textile mills. D. G. McCullough. il Am
Heritage 21:110-13 Ap '70
Parting shots; demolition of the Willows for
parking space. il Life 68:69 F 20 '70
MANCOTT, Anatol
Use of alligation alternate in chemistry. Chem
43:37 Jl '70
MANDEL, Burton H.
Mandel's complaint. Newsweek 75:82+ F 23
'70 *
MANDEL, George
(ed) See Puzo, M. Wealthy father of The god-
father
MANDEL'SHTAM, Nadezhda
Buried life. R. Z. Sheppard. Time 97:76+
Ja 18 '71 *
Poetry and power. S. Maloff. Commonweal
93:352-4 Ja 8 '71 *
MANDEL'SHTAM, Osip Emil'evich
Hope against hope, by N. Mandelstam. Re-
view
Nat R 22:1411-12 D 29 '70. G. Davenport *
Nation 211:309-11 O 5 '70. A. Hollo *
New Yorker 46:59-63 D 26 '70. G. Steiner. *
Time 97:76+ Ja 18 '71. R. Z. Sheppard *
Russia's courageous dissenters. A. Alvarez.
Sat R 53:29+ N 28 '70 *
MANDELSTAM, Janet
Grinds on the grand tour. il Sat R 53:77-9 F
21 '70
MANDER, John
Future of social democracy. Commentary 50:
57-64 S '70
MANDL, Matthew
Build solid state power supplies. il Radio-
Electr 41:49-51 D '70
Computers, how they read. il Radio-Electr
41:50-2 F '70
MANELOVEG, Herbert D.
Is the agency in trouble? Sat R 53:73-4 N
14 '70
MANET, Eduardo
Nuns (Les nonnes) Criticism
Nation 210:766 Je 22 '70 *
MANGANELLO, Mike
Mike and this horse needed each other. W.
Tower. il pors Sports Illus 32:22-7 My 11
'70 *
MANGANESE
Magnetic particles extracted from manga-
nese nodules: suggested origin from stony
and iron meteorites. R. B. Finkelman. bib-
liog il Science 167:982-4 F 13 '70
Vacuuming the Atlantic floor. il Sci N 98:
134-5 Ag 15 '70

Isotopes
Determination of manganese-53 by neutron
activation and other miscellaneous studies on lunar dust. W. Herr and others. bib-
liog il Science 167:747-9 Ja 30 '70
MANGANESE chlorides
Testing magnetic theory; structure of TMMC,
antiferromagnetic substance. il Sci N 98:
411 N 28 '70
MANGANESE in the body
Liver mitochondria from manganese-defi-
cient and pallid mice: function and ultra-
structure. L. S. Hurley and others. bibliog
il Science 170:1316-18 D 18 '70
MANGEL, Charles
Sometimes we feel we're already dead. il Look
34:38-43 Je 2 '70
MANGER groups. See Christmas cribs
MANGIERI, Adolph A.
Building a printing exposure lightmeter. il
Pop Electr 33:60-1+ O '70
One second metronome timer. il Pop Electr
32:58-60 F '70
Remote camera shutter release. il Pop Electr
33:65-8 Jl '70
MANGLONA, Benjamin T.
Trust Territory of the Pacific Islands; state-
ments, June 3 and 11, 1970. Dept State Bul
63:262-5, 268-9 Ag 31 '70
MANGOES
See also
Cookery—Fruit
MANGOLD, Robert
To be continued. H. Rosenstein. il Art N
69:63-5+ O '70 *

MANHATTAN (tanker) See Ice breaking vessels
MANHATTAN community college. See New York (city). City university—Borough of Manhattan community college
MANHATTAN project. See Atomic bombs—History
MANHATTAN rehabilitation center. See Narcotic addicts—Rehabilitation
MANHATTAN school of music
Report:
Mascagni's Amico Fritz. S. Jenkins. Opera N 34:23 Je 13 '70
Mozart's Cosi fan tutte. H. E. Phillips. Opera N 34:32 Ja 31 '70
MANHEIM, Frank T. and Sayles, F. L.
Brines and interstitial brackish water in drill cores from the deep Gulf of Mexico. bibliog il Science 170:57-61 O 2 '70
—and others
Suspended matter in surface waters of the Atlantic continental margin from Cape Cod to the Florida Keys. bibliog il Science 167:371-6 Ja 23 '70
MANHEIM, Ralph
(tr) See Hacks, P. Amphitryon
Trials of a translator. Time 95:73 Ap 13 '70 *
MANIC-depressive psycoses. See Psychoses
MANICOTTI. See Cookery, Italian
MANICURING
Good hand; nail care. il Mlle 71:153+ S '70
Project: you, the manicure. Ladies Home J 87:86 Je '70
See also
Hand
Nails (anatomy)
MANIFOLDS
Manifold mods. B. Lang. il Hot Rod 23:100-1 N '70
MANILA

Description
Manila: capital of many cultures. P. Brooks. Travel & Camera 33:88 Mr '70
MANIPULATORS
Rivet: the acrobatic tractor; remote-controlled manipulator. D. Scott. il Pop Sci 197:83 O '70
MANITOBA
See also
Dauphin
MANKA, R. H. and Michel, F. C.
Lunar atmosphere as a source of argon-40 and other lunar surface elements. bibliog il Science 169:278-80 Jl 17 '70
MANKER, Don
Oh little town; poem. Ladies Home J 87:107 D '70
MANKOFF, Milton. See Flacks, R. jt. auth.
MANKS, Dorothy S.
Christmas tree. Horticulture 48:25+ D '70
MANLEY, Fletcher
Gallery: photographs. Life 68:8-9 Ja 23 '70
MANLEY, Merlin
Antidote: when teaching sours. Clear House 45:112-15 O '70
MANLEY, Michael
Overcoming insularity in Jamaica. For Affairs 49:100-10 O '70
MANN, Dewey
Data transmission network speeds customer service. il Am City 85:98-9 F '70
MANN, Georg
Furor Teutonicus: Upper Mississippi Abteilung. Yale R 60:306-20 D '70
MANN, George V. and Crofford, O. B.
Insulin levels in primates by immunoassay. bibliog il Science 169:1312-13 S 25 '70
MANN, Jack
Smiling through at (S)Miles park. il Look 34:46-9 Ag 11 '70
MANN, John L.
Victory for the family of Mann. W. Johnson. il Sports Illus 33:44-5 Ag 31 '70 *
MANN, Margery
Children and cameras. il Pop Phot 66:64-5 F '70
Dorothea Lange. il Pop Phot 66:84-5+ Mr '70
Marvella, is that you? il Pop Phot 67:100-1+ Ag '70
View from the Bay. See Issues of Popular photography
Wynn Bullock: in the midst of life we are in death. il Pop Phot 67:92-3+ Jl '70
MANN, Mary Louise
(ed) Casebook of school library services; symposium. il Am Lib 1:162-75 F '70
Do's and don'ts for librarians and administrators. Todays Ed 59:23 O '70
MANN, Milton
Teacher's guide to Polynesia. il Schol Teach Sec Teach Sup p 16-17+ Mr 9 '70

MANN, Murray Gell-. See Gell-Mann, M.
MANN, Peggy
Swap that view. Travel & Camera 33:8+ D '70
MANN, Roderick
Princess Grace: how a royal beauty stays beautiful. il pors Ladies Home J 87:101-3+ My '70
MANN, Thomas Clifton
Clean air and the automobile. il Parks & Rec 5:16-18+ Je '70
MANNED astronomical space telescope. See Artificial satellites—Astronomical use
MANNED space center. See United States—Manned spacecraft center
MANNED undersea research stations. See Underwater laboratories
MANNEQUINS. See Models (display figures)
MANNERS, David X.
Bathroom revolution. il Am Home 73:124+ My '70
MANNERS, Ian R.
Jordan. bibliog il Focus 20:1-11 Ap '70
MANNERS. See Etiquette
MANNERS and customs
Doing it in the road: folkways vs. mores. E. Schoenfeld. Ment Hy 54:450-2 Jl '70
From one humble servant to another; exchange of letters. J. B. Radnor; G. Washington. il pors Am Heritage 22:112 D '70
Instinct and the origins of love. M. Mead. Redbook 136:39-40 D '70
Masks: linkage between cultures. R. L. Asch. il Sch Arts 69:20-1 Je '70
See also
Clothing and dress
Costume
Dating
Rites and ceremonies
also subhead Social life and customs under names of countries, states, cities, etc, e.g. United States—Social life and customs
MANNES, Marya
Television: the splitting image. Sat R 53:66-8 N 14 '70
MANNHEIM, L. Andrew
Close-up exposure is simple? il Mod Phot 34:78-9+ Mr '70
How far is sharp? il Mod Phot 34:78-83+ Je '70
MANNHEIM, Germany

Music
Report:
Handel's Radamisto and Der junge lord. D. Graham. Opera N 35:33-4 Ja 2 '71
MANNING, Archie
. . .And the best of them all is Archie. W. F. Reed. il por Sports Illus 33:52-5 S 14 '70 *
Archie and the war between the states. W. F. Reed. il pors Sports Illus 33:14-17 O 12 '70 *
MANNING, Bayless Andrew
Stanford's dean steps down. por Time 96:69 O 5 '70 *
MANNING, Gordon P.
Customizing stock cruisers. il Motor B 125:56-9+ Ap '70
How to select a marina. il Motor B 125:124-5 Mr '70
Make a good boat sanding board. il Motor B 126:23 Ag '70
Wall mounted memo pad. il Motor B 125:180-1 My '70
Wonderful world of trim tabs. il Motor B 126:14+ Jl '70
MANNING, Jack
He gets to the core of a story fast. J. Deschin. por Pop Phot 67:24+ D '70 *
MANNING, Timothy J. abp
New archbishop. pors Newsweek 75:70-1 F 2 '70
On borrowed time. por Time 95:49 F 2 '70
MANNINO, Fortune V. and others
Distance and the use of the mental health clinic by community professionals. bibliog il Ment Hy 54:73-8 Ja '70
MANNLICHER rifle. See Rifles
MANO, Nori-ichi
Changes of simple and complex spike activity of cerebellar Purkinje cells with sleep and waking. bibliog il Science 170:1325-7 D 18 '70
MANOLSON, Frank
Everything you always wanted to know about your pet's sex life. Ladies Home J 87:82+ N '70
MANPOWER
Tangling with the manpower tangle. il Nations Bsns 58:64-6+ F '70
See also
Labor supply—United States
United States—Armed forces

MANPOWER development and training act. See
　Labor laws and legislation—United States
MANSAGER, Felix Norman
　One man's theory opens a new door. R. W.
　　Gillman. il Nations Bsns 58:84-5 Ja '70
MANSFIELD, D. Bruce
　More electric power: how on earth do we get
　　it? Look 34:51+ D 1 '70
MANSFIELD, Harvey C. See Goetcheus, V.
　M. jt. auth.
MANSFIELD, Michael Joseph
　Excerpt from Senate debate, March 12, 1970.
　　Cong Digest 49:138+ My '70
　Inflation, unemployment, war: a Democratic
　　reply to Nixon; address, June 24, 1970. por
　　U S News 69:68-70 Jl 6 '70; Same with title
　　Nation's economy. Vital Speeches 36:581-3 Jl
　　15 '70
MANSON, Charles
　Charlie Manson's home on the range. G.
　　Talese. il por Esquire 73:101-3+ Mr '70 *
　Fragments from the shooting gallery. M.
　　Singer. pors Ramp Mag 8:16-18 Ap '70 *
　Just waiting for Charlie. il por Life 69:40-3
　　Ag 21 '70 *
　Love among the rattlesnakes. J. Stafford.
　　il McCalls 97:68-9+ Mr '70 *
　Manson wins! A fantasy. F. Conroy. il Harper
　　241:53-9 N '70 *
　Sharon Tate murders. P. Maas. il por Ladies
　　Home J 87:52+ Ap '70 *
　Sing along with Manson. il por Newsweek
　　75:36-7 Mr 16 '70 *
MANSON, Charles, trial. See Trials (murder)
MANTELLO, Dennis
　Prop tip. Flying 87:89 Jl '70
MANTIS, Praying. See Praying mantis
MANUFACTURED houses. See Houses, Pre-
　fabricated
MANUFACTURES
　Labor turnover rates; tables. See issues of
　　Monthly labor review
　　See also
　Quality of products
　　also subhead Manufacture under various
　　subjects, e.g. Electronic circuits, Integrated
　　—Manufacture

Statistics
Ratios of manufacturing; with table (cont)
　Duns 96:70-3 N '70

Wages and hours
Late-shift employment in manufacturing in-
　dustries; with tables. C. M. O'Connor. bib-
　liog Mo Labor R 93:37-42 N '70
Relationship between changes in wage rates
　and in hourly earnings. V. J. Sheifer. bib-
　liog f il Mo Labor R 93:10-17 Ag '70
Wage developments in manufacturing, 1969;
　with tables. J. Kinyon. Mo Labor R 93:35-9
　Jl '70
MANUFACTURING plants. See Factories
MANURE handling. See Fertilizers and manures
　—Handling
MANURE lagoons
　Ducks and gas stir lagoons. T. B. Gray. il
　　Farm J 94:62G Mr '70
　Lagoon takes care of his feedlot runoff.
　　W. Waltner. il Suc Farm 68:B20 Ja '70
MANURES. See Fertilizers and manures
MANUSCRIPT division. See United States—
　Library of Congress—Manuscript division
MANUSCRIPTS
　Quarterly notes from the manuscript division
　　of the Library of Congress (cont) K. V.
　　Hostick. Hobbies 74:140 F '70
MANUSCRIPTS, Authors. See Authorship
MANUSCRIPTS, Illumination of. See Illumina-
　tion of books and manuscripts
MANUSCRIPTS of Pauline Archange; story.
　See Blais, M. C.
MANWELL, Reginald D. See Stone, W. B. jt.
　auth.
MANY happy returns; musical comedy. See
　Musical comedies, revues, etc.—Criticisms,
　plots, etc.
MANY thanks; drama. See Hark, M. and
　McQueen, N.
MAO, H. K. See Taylor, L. A. jt. auth.
MAO, Tse-tung
　Day in the life of the Chairman. M. Conway
　　and D. Knapp. il por Esquire 73:120-3+ Ap
　　'70 *
　Deification of Mao. H. Welch. il por Sat R
　　53:25+ S 19 '70 *
　New religion in Mao's China. America 123:
　　249-50 O 10 '70 *
　What makes Mao a Maoist. S. R. Schram. il
　　N Y Times Mag p36-7+ Mr 8 '70 *
MAO, Tse-tung, Mme
　Madame Mao's concerto. il Newsweek 75:46
　　Je 8 '70

MAOISM. See Communism—China (People's Re-
　public)
MAP reading
　Woman beside the man behind the wheel;
　　useful skill. D. McCluggage. il Am Home 73:
　　24+ F '70
MAPES, Carol A. and others
　Enzyme replacement in Fabry's disease, an
　　inborn error of metabolism. bibliog il Sci-
　　ence 169:987-9 S 4 '70
MAPLE
　Black maple. L. J. Uttal. Horticulture 48:
　　61-3 Mr '70

Diseases and pests
Sugar maple: another endangered species? il
　Sci Digest 67:82-3 Je '70
MAPLE Leafs (hockey team) See Hockey teams
MAPLE sugar
　Spring is maple-sugar time. T. Anderson. il
　　Org Gard & Farm 17:116-18 Mr '70
　Sugar maple: another endangered species? il
　　Sci Digest 67:82-3 Je '70
MAPLES, Flowering. See Flowering maples
MAPP, Edward
　Invisible librarians; excerpt from The black
　　librarian in America, ed. by E. J. Josey.
　　il por Library J 95:3745-7 N 1 '70
MAPPING, Aerial
　　See also
　Photogrammetry
MAPS
　At halfway point: state literary maps. B. W.
　　Fuson. bibliog f Engl J 59:87-98 Ja '70
　Sensible plan for future development; eco-
　　logical inventory; interview, ed. by J. N.
　　Miller. il. L. McHarg. il Read Digest 97:
　　77-81 Ag '70
　　See also
　Orienteering (sport)
　World maps
　　also subhead Maps under names of
　　countries, states, cities, e.g. Italy—Maps
MAPS, Aerial
　Aerial maps can help you plan. Suc Farm
　　68:36 N '70
MAPS, Early
　Discovery of a world: early maps showing
　　America (cont) D. Pratt. il Antiques 97:128-
　　34 Ja '70
MAPS, Road. See Road maps, guides, etc.
MARAN, Stephen P. and others
　Electronic pulsarium. il Sky & Tel 40:17-19
　　Jl '70
MARASCO, Robert
　Child's play. Criticism
　　America 122:312-13 Mr 21 '70 *
　　Commonweal 92:62-3 Mr 27 '70 *
　　Life il 68:18 Ap 10 '70 *
　　Nation 210:285 Mr 9 '70 *
　　New Yorker 46:77 F 28 '70 *
　　Newsweek il 75:77-8 Mr 2 '70 *
　　Sat R 53:26 Mr 14 '70 *
　　Time 95:69 Mr 2 '70 *
MARATHON dancing. See Dancing
MARATHON races. See Running
MARATHON running. See Running
MARAVICH, Pete
　Louisiana hot-shot. il por Time 95:57 F 16
　　'70 *
　Maravich vs. McGuire. il pors Newsweek 75:
　　98-9 Mr 30 '70 *
　Merger, madness and Maravich. F. Deford.
　　il por Sports Illus 32:28-3+ Ap 6 '70 *
　Pistol Pete now is up against the pros. N.
　　Sanders. il pors N Y Times Mag p32-3+
　　O 11 '70 *
　We have a slight delay in show time. P.
　　Carry. il por Sports Illus 33:28-9 O 26 '70 *
MARBLE, Artificial
　New man-made marble for your home; corian.
　　A. Lees. il Pop Sci 197:78-9+ Ag '70
MARCEAU, Marcel
　Marcel Marceau; New York city center. N.
　　Mason. Dance Mag 44:76 Je '70 *
MARCELLO, Carlos
　Louisiana still jumps for mobster Marcello.
　　D. Chandler. il pors Life 68:30-7 Ap 10 '70 *
　Portrait of a mobster. W. Schulz. por Read
　　Digest 97:58-62 Ag '70 *
MARCERE, Norma Snipes
　Genteel violence. Good H 170:89+ Ap '70
MARCH, Saturday, 2 p.m.-3 p.m. story.
　See Stevenson, J.
MARCHETTI, Nick
　Nick Marchetti's spaghetti boats. A. Zidock,
　　jr. il pors Motor B 125:14+ Ap '70 *
MARCIANO, Rocky
　Clay vs. Marciano: the super fight. il pors
　　Life 68:42-3 Ja 30 '70
MARCINIAK, Edward A.
　Catholic social action: where do we go from
　　here? il America 123:511-16 D 12 '70

MARIJUANA—*Continued*

Private enterprise and dope; Creative learning group, distributor of scientific educational materials on drug damage. W. F. Buckley, jr. Nat R 22:964 S 8 '70

Prohibition of marijuana. J. Kaplan. il New Repub 163:11-12 N 21 '70

Pursuit of pot; Nixon eases proposals. il Sr Schol 95:14 N 10 '69

Sparks fly over pot. Nations Bsns 58:24 Mr '70

To parents: plain talk on marijuana. Bsns W p 121 Mr 21 '70

Turning off the Tijuana grass; Operation Intercept. C. Kentfield. Esquire 73:8+ My '70

Turning on in society. M. Zane. il Nation 211:595-6 D 7 '70

Washington report; a new look at marijuana. J. Lloyd. Sr Schol 95:Schol Teach 2 O 20 '69

What legal status for marijuana? J. Kaplan. Cur 123:44-7 N '70

What? Pot? Not Laredo. il Forbes 106:48 N 1 '70

What we have forgotten about pot, a pharmacologist's history; cannabis sativa. S. H. Snyder. il N Y Times Mag p26-7+ D 13 '70

What's it like to smoke marijuana? il Sci Digest 68:18-19 O '70

Wild hemp of Indiana. M. King. Nation 211:402-3 O 26 '70

See also

THC

MARIN, John

Marin and music; with excerpts from Marin's writings. C. Gray. il por Art in Am 58:72-81 Jl '70 •

New look at Marin. D. Davis. il Newsweek 76:68+ Jl 27 '70 •

MARIN, Peter

Children of the apocalypse. il Sat R 53:71-3+ S 19 '70

MARIN COUNTY, Calif.

Marin County: San Francisco's Connecticut. il Holiday 47:64-7 Mr '70

MARIN COUNTY court. See San Rafael, Calif.—Courts

MARINAS

How to pick a marina. G. Helgeland. il Pop Mech 133:130-5 Mr '70

How to select a marina. G. P. Manning. il Motor B 125:124-5 Mr '70

Landlocked no more; Carlyle Lake, Ill. providing floating marina. G. S. Hensley. il Yachting 129:106-7+ Ja '71

MARINATED meat. See Cookery—Meat

MARINE, Gene

California water plan. il Ramp Mag 8:34-41 My '70

Politics of the environment. Nation 210:82-4 Ja 26 '70

Trees on the back lot. Nat Parks & Con Mag 44:4-6 Ag '70

MARINE aquariums. See Aquariums

MARINE biology

Patterns of marine life. M. Gruber. il Sea Front 16:194-205 Jl '70

Sea and me. E. Chan. il por Seventeen 29:154-5+ Ap '70

Threat to life in the sea; excerpt from The doomsday book. G. R. Taylor. Sat R 53:40-2 Ag 1 '70

See also

Benthos

Fresh water biology

Marine resources

Marine sediments

Plankton

Seashore biology

MARINE cookery. See Cookery, Marine

MARINE corrosion. See Corrosion and anticorrosives

MARINE deposits. See Marine sediments

MARINE diesel engines. See Diesel engines, Marine

MARINE ecology

Ecology and the canal; possible effects of a sea-level Isthmian canal across Panama. il Sci N 97:364-5 Ap 11 '70

Lesson from the hidden sea; with photographs by D. Faulkner. Audubon 72:47-57 S '70

Thermal pollution in the marine environment. A. C. Jensen. il Cons 25:8-13 O '70

MARINE education. See Nautical education

MARINE electronics. See Boats—Electronic equipment

MARINE engineers' beneficial association. See National marine engineers' beneficial association

MARINE engines

Compleat company. M. Crook. il Yachting 127:64-6+ Ap '70

Marine engines. E. Nabb. See issues of Motor boating

Power plants. il Motor B 125:198-205+ Ja '70

Progress in power; 1945-1970. M. Crook. il Yachting 127:70-1+ Ja '70

What kind of engine? T. Bottomley. il Motor B 127:140-1+ Ja '71

Yachting's boat show in print. il Yachting 127:127-37+ Ja; 211-12+ F; 220+ Mr '70

See also

Cylinders (engines, etc)

Motor boat engines

Outboard motors

Fuel consumption

Foolproof fuel supplies. E. Slepian. Motor B 125:14+ Je '70

Fuel feeding

Inspect your boat's fuel system, now! C. Miller. il Motor B 126:10-12+ Ag '70

Gearing

Keep in gear. J. M. Koopman. il Motor B 126:59+ D '70

Maintenance and repair

Is galvanic corrosion following you? problem of stern drives. C. F. Kelley. il Yachting 128:69+ Ag '70

Why is your motor missing? M. Schultz. il Pop Mech 134:124-5 Jl '70

Starting

Hard starting made easy. E. Nabb. Motor B 126:78-9 D '70

MARINE engines, Used

Buying a used motor. C. R. Meyer. il Yachting 127:75+ Je '70

MARINE fauna

See also

Barnacles

Corals

Foraminifera

Marine worms

Mollusks

Octopus

Sea anemones

Sea otters

Sea pens

Shrimps

Sponges

Starfishes

MARINE fauna, Conservation of. See Wildlife conservation

MARINE geology. See Submarine geology

MARINE insurance. See Insurance, Marine

MARINE midland banks, inc.

Country bank & the city bank. il Forbes 105:54+ Ap 15 '70

MARINE paint. See Paint

MARINE painting

Elusive ocean. il Time 96:46 Ag 24 '70

For those who look but do not see; field trip to paint seascape. T. Stevens. il Sch Arts 70:10-11 N '70

MARINE parks. See Marinas

MARINE photography. See Moving picture photography—Marines; Photography—Marines

MARINE pollution

Bad times for a multinational sea; Baltic Sea. H. J. Barnes. il Sci N 97:356 Ap 4 '70

Death of the oceans; pesticides; address, March 13, 1970. D. Epel. Vital Speeches 36:411-14 Ap 15 '70

Dying ocean? dirt in the deep. Sr Schol 97:6 O 12 '70

Dying oceans. il por Time 96:64 S 28 '70

Heat waste; study of Turkey Point plant's effect on Biscayne Bay. B. Stearns. il Sea Front 16:154-63 My '70

Marine environment and pollution control; address, February 19, 1970. G. Nelson. Vital Speeches 36:325-9 Mr 15 '70

NATO experts recommend international action on ocean oil spills; White House announcement; with statement by J. A. Volpe, and text of resolution. Dept State Bul 63:665-9 N 30 '70

New York's dead sea. il Newsweek 75:86 F 23 '70

Ocean pollution: findings at Woods Hole oceanographic institution. New Yorker 45:27-30 Ja 31 '70

Power play over pollution; thermal pollution of Biscayne Bay. il Bsns W p28-9 Mr 21 '70

MARINE pollution—*Continued*
President Nixon asks Senate approval of conventions on pollution of the sea by oil; message, May 20, 1970, and Secretary Rogers report, May 7, 1970. R. M. Nixon; W. P. Rogers. Dept State Bul 62:756-9 Je 15 '70
Saving the oceans. J. Deedy. Commonweal 93:82 O 23 '70
Threat to life in the sea; excerpt from The doomsday book. G. R. Taylor. Sat R 53:40-2 Ag 1 '70
To save the seas; FAO conference. Time 96:40 D 28 '70
U.S. opposes unilateral extension by Canada of high seas jurisdiction; Department statement, April 15, 1970. Dept State Bul 62:610-11 My 11 '70
　See also
Gases, Asphyxiating and poisonous—Disposal in the ocean
Mercury pollution of rivers, lakes, etc.
Oil pollution of rivers, harbors, etc.
Waste disposal in the ocean

Laws and legislation
　See Water pollution—Laws and legislation
MARINE radar. See Radar in navigation
MARINE radiotelephone. See Radiotelephone on ships, boats, etc.
MARINE refrigerators. See Refrigeration on boats
MARINE resources
Can the sea feed us? M. Bush. Am For 76: 40+ N '70
Food-from-the-sea myth; effects of overexploitation and pollution. P. R. Ehrlich and A. H. Ehrlich. Sat R 53:53-5+ Ap 4 '70
Marine science and ocean politics. D. S. Cheever. il Bul Atom Sci 26:22+ F '70; Reply. M. Leitenberg. 26:47-8 O '70
Ocean full of medicine. W. Hartley and E. Hartley. il Sci Digest 68:34-40 D '70
Ocean resources. E. A. Perry, jr. bibliog f il Cur Hist 58:349-54+ Je '70
Ocean resources; address, January 24, 1970. W. B. Spong, jr. Vital Speeches 36:261-2 F 15 '70
Ore search on land and in the ocean; Japanese survey. S. Griffin. il Sci N 98:46 Jl 11 '70
Our new worlds below: the sea frontier. il Sr Schol 96:8-10 Mr 16 '70
Pacem in maribus; international conference in Malta. W. Wynn. il Time 96:34-5 Jl 20 '70
Photosynthesis and fish production in the sea. J. H. Ryther; reply with rejoinder. D. L. Alverson and others. bibliog Science 168:503-5 Ap 24 '70
　See also
Fisheries

International aspects
Access to the oceans' wealth. R. L. Tobin. Sat R 53:24 N 28 '70
Oceans: whose hunting preserve? il Forbes 105:22-4+ Mr 15 '70
Who should control deep-seabed resources? P. A. Rona. Focus 20:12 F '70
MARINE sediments
Black Sea: recent sedimentary history. D. A. Ross and others. bibliog il Science 170: 163-5 O 9 '70
Brines and interstitial brackish water in drill cores from the deep Gulf of Mexico. F. T. Manheim and F. L. Sayles. bibliog il Science 170:57-61 O 2 '70
Composition of interstitial waters of marine sediments: temperature of squeezing effect. J. L. Bischoff and others. bibliog il Science 167:1245-6 F 27 '70
Diversity of planktonic foraminifera in deepsea sediments. W. H. Berger and F. L. Parker. bibliog il Science 168:1345-7 Je 12 '70
Early holocene oöids in modern littoral sands reworked from a coastal terrace, southern Tunisia. F. H. Fabricius and others. bibliog il Science 169:757-60 Ag 21 '70
Fission track ages and ages of deposition of deep-sea microtektites. W. Gentner and others. bibliog il Science 168:359-61 Ap 17 '70
Fossil membranes and cell wall fragments from a 7000-year-old Black Sea sediment. E. T. Degens and others. bibliog il Science 168: 1207-8 Je 5 '70
High-magnesian calcite: leaching of magnesium in the deep sea. D. N. Gomberg and E. Bonatti. bibliog il Science 168:1451-3 Je 19 '70
Jurassic sandstone from the tropical Atlantic. P. J. Fox and others. bibliog il Science 170:1402-4 D 25 '70

Marine sediments: dating by the racemization of amino acids. J. L. Bada and others. bibliog il Science 170:730-2 N 13 '70
Pleistocene climates in the Atlantic and Pacific Oceans: a comparison based on deepsea sediments. D. B. Ericson and G. Wollin. bibliog il Science 167:1483-5 Mr 13 '70
Racemization of amino acids in sediments from Saanich Inlet, British Columbia. K. A. Kvenvolden and others. bibliog il Science 169:1079-82 S 11 '70
Red Sea hot brines. E. T. Degens and D. A. Ross. il Sci Am 222:32-42 Ap '70
Sterols in recent marine sediments. D. Attaway and P. L. Parker. bibliog il Science 169:674-6 Ag 14 '70
MARINE service technicians. See Electronic technicians
MARINE superstition. See Superstition
MARINE surveyors. See Surveyors, Marine
MARINE terminals. See Terminals
MARINE worms
Asexual reproduction in a sipunculan worm. M. E. Rice. bibliog il Science 167:1618-20 Mr 20 '70
　See also
Annelids
MARINE zoological specimens. See Zoological specimens
MARINER, Robert H. and Surdam, R. C.
Alkalinity and formation of zeolites in saline alkaline lakes. bibliog il Science 170:977-80 N 27 '70
MARINER probes. See Space probes
MARINERS compass. See Compass
MARININ, Yuri
Soviet Luna 16. Space World G-12-84:21-2 D '70
MARION, Ohio
How to calculate refuse collection and disposal costs. L. Finley and R. Mucha. Am City 85:88+ S '70
Pumps speed sewer cleaning. il Am City 85: 30 My '70
MARION COUNTY, Ind.
Helicopter gives citizens a better chance to live. il Am City 85:38 Jl '70
MARIONETTES. See Puppets and puppet plays
MARITAL infidelity. See Sexual ethics
MARITIME administration. See United States—Maritime administration
MARITIME law
U.S. gives views on convening conference on law of the sea, text of note, June 12, 1970. W. P. Rogers. Dept State Bul 63: 38-9 Jl 13 '70
　See also
Boats and boating—Laws and regulations
Territorial waters
MARITIME meteorology. See Meteorology, Maritime
MARITIME PROVINCES, Canada
Maritimes. G. Hall. il Travel & Camera 33:42-5 Je '70
MARITIME workers
　See also
Collective bargaining—Maritime workers
MARK, Charles C.
Originality and tradition in American culture. il UNESCO Courier 23:16-17+ Je '70
MARK, Hans Michael
Space agency urged to consider student ideas on space station. R. G. O'Lone. Aviation W 93:58 S 28 '70 *
MARK, R. F. and others
Reinnervated eye muscles do not respond to impulses in foreign nerves. bibliog il Science 170:193-4 O 9 '70
MARK, Gospel of. See Bible—New Testament—Mark
MARK (coin) See Money—Germany
MARK Trail (cartoon character) See Caricatures and cartoons
MARK Twain, pseud. See Clemens, S. L.
MARK Twain society, international. See International Mark Twain society
MARKALL, Francis, abp
Crisis of conscience. por Time 95:58 Ap 13 '70 *
MARKER, Mrs Floyd
Church must change or die. il Redbook 136: 70+ N '70
MARKER, Linda
Haiku: pretty punchy poetry. il Clear House 45:219-20 D '70
MARKET letters. See Investments—Advisers
MARKET research
Market research: Ford's gift horse; Pinto project for the academic community. R. J. Bazell. Science 170:953 N 27 '70
New hope for market research; report of meeting. il Pub W 197:27-9 My 25 '70
New theory on why people buy; Howard-Sheth theory. il por Bsns W p70 Ja 24 '70

MARKET research—*Continued*
Outside job fills the product gap; free-lance idea men. il Bsns W p54+ My 16 '70
Putting customer demands first; changing image of Reliance electric co. il Bsns W p62-3 N 28 '70
Ten years is long enough; lack of cooperative research support by all publishers concerned. C. B. Grannis. Pub W 197:43 Je 22 '70
See also
Nielsen, A. C, company

MARKETING
Corporate models: better marketing plans. P. Kotler. bibliog f il Harvard Bsns R 48:135-49+ Jl '70
Marketing and the vocal minority. W. Weir. il Sat R 53:113 Mr 14 '70
Marketing planning that gets things done. W. F. Christopher. il Harvard Bsns R 48:56-64 S '70
Mismarketing, by T. L. Berg. Review
Bsns W p6 Je 6 '70. D. Dunn
Selling to the hottest market ever. il Bsns W p 124-6+ O 17 '70
Trappings vs. substance in industrial marketing. B. C. Ames. il Harvard Bsns R 48:93-102 Jl '70
Why a global market doesn't exist. il Bsns W p 140-2+ D 19 '70
See also
Advertising
Mail order business
Old age market
Salesmen and salesmanship
Supermarkets
also subhead Marketing under various subjects. e.g. Farm produce—Marketing
MARKETING research. See Market research

MARKETS
Bay area flea markets. il Sunset 145:3-4 Jl '70
See also subhead Markets under names of cities, e.g. Paris—Markets
MARKETS, Black. See Black markets
MARKETS for authors. See Authors and publishers

MARKING, Syl
How to have great fishing with the family. il Field & S 74:68-9+ F '70
MARKING (students) See Grading and marking (students)

MARKLEY, Herbert Emerson
Manufacturing by the numbers; address, September 16, 1970. Vital Speeches 37:143-5 D 15 '70

MARKOVA, Dame Alicia
World of dance. W. Terry. por Sat R 53:34 My 30 '70 *

MARKOVICH, Alexander
Fast ways to learn a foreign language. il Mech Illus 66:48-50+ Mr '70
Finally, they really are improving our roads. il Mech Illus 66:70-2+ N '70
How to kill household insects like a pro. il Mech Illus 66:90-2+ Ag '70
So you think you are a safe driver, eh? il Mech Illus 66:68-70+ F '70
Those sensible station wagons. il Pop Mech 134:134-9+ S '70
What you need in a roadside emergency kit. il Pop Mech 134:120-2 Jl '70

MARKOVITS, Andrew S.
How to cope with your allergy. il Mech Illus 66:65-7 My '70

MARKOW, Jack
Cartoonist Q's. See issues of Writer's digest

MARKS, Alvin
U.S. business worldwide: Arizona view; interview. pors Forbes 106:50-1 O 1 '70

MARKS, Jane
College women 1970: a whole new can of worms. Mlle 70:258+ F '70
Off the do-gooders! Mlle 72:126-7+ D '70
Paper tiger, with teeth. Mlle 71:226-7+ Ag '70
Tell the "why why trippers" the answer will come. Mlle 71:188-9+ My '70
Three-ring classroom. il Mlle 72:184-5+ N '70

MARKS, Johnny
Where are they now? il pors Newsweek 76:8 D 28 '70 *

MARKS, Sue
Open letter to a concerned parent. Engl J 59:667-8 My '70

MARKS, Theodore
Motl Weiss and the golden land. il Read Digest 97:178-81 D '70

MARKS, Potters. See Pottery—Marks

MARLAND, Sidney Percy, 1914-
Education complex. il por Newsweek 76:72-3 S 7 '70 *
Embattled commissioner. por Newsweek 76:67 O 5 '70 *

MARLATT, Leo J.
Gray ghost. il Outdoor Life 146:58-9+ S '70

MARLEY, C. F.
Direct-to-customer organic food farm. il Org Gard & Farm 17:45-7 Mr '70

MARLEY, Doone
Off-beat British Virgin Islands. il Harp Baz 104:56+ D '70

MARLIN-fishing tournament. See Fishing—Competitions

MARLOW, Foster
What's your bag? il Sch Arts 69:24-5 Je '70

MARLOWE, John
Marlowe 48. W. Juettner. il Motor B 126:62-3+ D '70 *

MARMALADE. See Jelly, jam, etc.

MARMOSETS
ST-feline fibrosarcoma virus: induction of tumors in marmoset monkeys. F. Deinhardt and others. bibliog il Science 167:881 F 6 '70

MARNEY, Carlyle
Coming faith; excerpts. Chr Cent 87:196, 228, 260, 284, 316, 348 F 18, 25, Mr 4, 11, 18, 25 '70

MAROTTA, Albert J.
Homework on tape. Todays Ed 59:21 S '70

MARQUEZ STERLING, Carlos
1890; the First international conference of American states. il Américas 22:7-12 Ap '70

MARQUIS, Arnold
Famous Civil war band lives again. il Hobbies 75:48-9+ S '70

MARR, Dave
Golfing's pro of 52nd street. D. Jenkins. il por Sports Illus 32:32-5 F 2 '70

MARRIAGE
Can fighting make a good marriage better? G. Krupp. il Redbook 134:62-3+ F '70
Can this marriage be saved? case histories; ed. by D. C. Disney. See issues of Ladies' home journal
Has monogamy failed? H. A. Otto. Sat R 53:23-5+ Ap 25 '70
How children test a marriage. M. B. Hoover. il Parents Mag 45:39-41+ Ap '70
How good is your marriage? T. I. Rubin. Ladies Home J 87:34 Ag '70
Husbands and wives talk frankly about sex. G. Krupp. Redbook 135:69+ Jl '70
Life expectancy and life cycles. H. L. Browning. Cur 114:55-62 Ja '70
Man talk; toting up a bill of goods. D. Newman and R. Benton. il Mlle 71:96 S '70
Marriage and the mystique of romance. A. Krich and S. Blum. Redbook 136:65+ N '70
Marriage covenant: promises, promises; Lutheran church's statement. Chr Today 14:17 Jl 31 '70
Marriage that beat the odds; eight famous couples tell how they've stayed happily married. M. Davidson. il Good H 171:72-5 Jl '70
New young marrieds. C. Bird; L. J. Robb. il por Ladies Home J 87:70-1 Je '70
On being a woman: little white lies. J. Brothers. Good H 170:54+ F '70
Overzealous helpmate. il Good H 170:36+ My '70
Thorny question. V. P. McCorry. America 123:246 O 3 '70
Till death us do part? B. L. Smith. Chr Today 14:5-8+ Ja 16 '70
Twenty-year fracture; long-term marriages. K. Donelson and I. Donelson. Har Yrs 10:19-21+ F '70
What a husband's business trips do to a marriage. L. Tornabene. Ladies Home J 87:75-6+ My '70
When married love is disappointing. C. Vincent. il Redbook 134:82-3+ Ap '70
Young wife's world. H. Valentine. See issues of Good housekeeping
See also
Child marriage
Divorce
Family
Honeymoon
Intermarriage of races
Sex relations
Sexual ethics
War marriages
Weddings
Wives

Anecdotes, satire, facetiae, etc.
Marriage: unsafe at any speed. J. Kerr. il Read Digest 96:60-2 My '70

Annulment (canon law)
Debate over Catholic marriage; simplification of annulment procedures. il Time 96:64+ Jl 6 '70

MARRIAGE—*Continued*

Handbooks, manuals, etc.

Sex: how to read all about it; From art to diagrams: a history of love books. il Newsweek 76:38-43 Ag 24 '70

United States

See Marriage

MARRIAGE (canon law)

Debate over Catholic marriage; simplification of annulment procedures. il Time 96:64+ Jl 6 '70

Farewell to the tribunal. L. M. Croghan. il America 123:227-9 O 3 '70

Love over law; dispensation of an unconsummated marriage. T. Beeson. Chr Cent 87:748 Je 17 '70

New norms for marriage cases. America 123:32 Jl 25 '70

Rethinking the marriage bond. P. F. Palmer. America 122:39-42 Ja 17 '70; Discussion. 122:229, 379, 513 Mr 7, Ap 11, My 16 '70

MARRIAGE counseling

Can this marriage be saved? case histories; ed. by D. C. Disney. See issues of Ladies' home journal

MARRIAGE customs and rites

"Old country" weddings: Italian, Greek, Polish, and Danish. il McCalls 97:96-103 Je '70

Korea (Republic)

Mass matrimony in Seoul. il Time 96:33 N 2 '70

Nepal

Marriage of convenience; Crown Prince Birendra and Princess Aishwarya of Nepal. il por Time 95:29 Mr 9 '70

Nepal: come, let us marry. il pors Newsweek 75:46-47D Mr 16 '70

Nepal's right royal wedding. il por Life 68:34-5 Mr 13 '70

MARRIAGE law

See also

Marriage (canon law)

Tanzania

Take us from this place; forced interracial marriages in Zanzibar. Newsweek 76:62+ O 12 '70

Ties that bind; Tanzanian women protesting new marriage bill. il Time 95:35 Ap 20 '70

Zanzibar

See Marriage law—Tanzania

MARRIAGE lesson; story. See Rodgers, M. A.

MARRIAGE manuals. See Marriage—Handbooks, manuals, etc.

MARRIAGE of a young stockbroker; story. See Webb, C.

MARRIAGE of Figaro; opera. See Mozart, J. C. W. A.

MARRIAGE of priests

Dutch priests defy Alfrink. Chr Cent 87:1246 O 21 '70

Fragile marriage of an ex-priest. W. H. DuBay. il por McCalls 97:70-1+ S '70

Kicking the habit. il Esquire 74:124-7 N '70

Reflections on priesthood and marriage. G. Grudzen; discussion. Cath World 210:244-5, 211-4 Mr-Ap '70

Why priests marry. J. A. O'Brien. il Chr Cent 87:415-19 Ap 8 '70; Reply. J. R. Hertel. 87:768 Je 17 '70

MARRIAGE proposals

Man talk. D. Newman and R. Benton. il Mlle 71:100 My '70

MARRIAGE tribunal. See Ecclesiastical courts

MARRIAGES, Mixed

Behind Pope's decree on marriages. U S News 68:77 My 11 '70

Easier on mixed marriages. Time 95:77 My 11 '70

How to marry a Catholic; new papal rules. Newsweek 75:79 My 11 '70

Intermarriage & Jewish survival. M. Sklare. Commentary 49:51-8 Mr '70; Discussion. 49:4+ Je '70

Lifting the veil on mixed matches. J. R. Greisch. Chr Today 14:33 My 22 '70

Matrimonia mixta: mixed blessing. Chr Cent 87:588 My 13 '70

Mixed marriage mixture. America 122:515 My 16 '70

Strict mixed marriage rules set for English and Welsh Catholics. Chr Cent 87:1375 N 18 '70

Vatican and mixed marriages; *matrimonia mixta*. R. W. Rousseau. Chr Cent 87:963-4+ Ag 12 '70

When groups intermarry. America 122:385 Ap 11 '70

MARRIED women

Happiness and the right to choose; excerpt from Man's world, woman's place. E. Janeway. por Atlan 225:118-22+ Mr '70

See also

Mothers

Wives

Education

See Education of women

Employment

Changes in the labor force activity of women. E. Waldman. bibliog f il Mo Labor R 93:10-18 Je '70

Does it pay for a mother to work? GH poll. il Good H 170:40+ Mr '70

Economic status of families headed by women; AFDC program. R. L. Stein. il Mo Labor R 93:3-10 D '70

Ellie was a tired working wife. D. C. Disney. Ladies Home J 87:16+ N '70

Facts about fifty good part-time jobs for women. il Good H 170:187-9 Mr '70

Go-go mother; Boston's catalyst program. N. Gittelson. Harp Baz 103:25+ Ap '70

How to trade your mop for a typewriter. M. A. Ralston. Todays Health 48:53-5 F '70

Marital and family characteristics of the U.S. labor force; with tables. E. Waldman. bibliog f Mo Labor R 93:18-27 My '70

Two-paycheck family. B. Davidson. il Good H 170:86-7+ My '70

What a second income really means. P. Lindberg. il Bet Hom & Gard 48:49+ Mr '70

Why working mothers have happier children. B. Bettelheim. Ladies Home J 87:24+ Je '70

Working mothers and their children. M. Mead. il Cath World 212:78-82 N '70

Working mothers: some possible solutions for child care. B. Spock. Redbook 135:34+ S '70

See also

Part time employment

MARROW

Bone marrow and spleen: dissociation of immunologic properties by cortisone. M. A. Levine and H. N. Claman. bibliog il Science 167:1515-17 Mr 13 '70

Bone marrow colonies: stimulation in vitro by supernatant from incubated human blood cells. P. A. Chervenick and D. R. Boggs. bibliog il Science 169:691-2 Ag 14 '70

Bone marrow histogenesis: a comparison of fatty and red marrow. M. Tavassoli and W. H. Crosby. bibliog il Science 169:291-3 Jl 17 '70

Heterozygous beta thalassemia: balanced globin synthesis in bone marrow cells. E. Schwartz. bibliog il Science 167:1513-14 Mr 13 '70

Transplantation

David's doctor. il por Newsweek 76:97-8 N 23 '70

MARS, David

Nixon's new federalism. Nation 210:435-7 Ap 15 '70

MARS (planet)

Carbon dioxide clathrate in the martian ice cap. S. L. Miller and W. D. Smythe. bibliog il Science 170:531-3 O 30 '70

Is ozone trapped in the solid carbon dioxide polar cap of Mars? H. P. Broida and others. bibliog Science 170:1402 D 25 '70

Mars: occurrence of liquid water. A. P. Ingersoll. bibliog il Science 168:972-3 My 22 '70

See also

Space flight to Mars

Space vehicles—Landing systems—Mars

Atmosphere

Mariner 6: origin of Mars ionized carbon dioxide ultraviolet spectrum. A. Dalgarno and others. bibliog il Science 167:1490-1 Mr 13 '70

Mars: detection of atmospheric water vapor during the southern hemisphere spring and summer season. E. S. Barker and others. bibliog il Science 170:1308-10 D 18 '70

Mars: is nitrogen present? A. Dalgarno and M. B. McElroy. bibliog il Science 170:167-8 O 9 '70

Red snowflakes on Mars? il Time 95:52 Mr 23 '70

Mass

Martian mass and earth-moon mass ratio from coherent S-band tracking of Mariners 6 and 7. J. D. Anderson and others. bibliog il Science 167:277-9 Ja 16 '70

Photographs

Surface of Mars. R. B. Leighton. il Sci Am 222:26-41 My '70

MARS (planet)—*Continued*

Photographs from space

Mariner 6 television pictures: first report. R. B. Leighton and others; discussion. bibliog il Science 167:906-8 F 6 '70

Mars photo album. Space World G-9-81:23-33 S '70

Radiation

Bright flares on Mars. Sky & Tel 39:83 F '70

Satellites

See Satellites

Surface

Hills and dales of Mars. Sci Am 222:60+ Mr '70

Mars surface processes studied. B. M. Elson. il Aviation W 92:61+ F 9 '70

Radar measures Martian heights. il R Pop Astron 63:15 Ag '69

Red plastic snow. Sci Am 222:46 F '70

Red snowflakes on Mars? il Time 95:52 Mr 23 '70

Surface on Mars. R. B. Leighton. il Sci Am 222:26-41 My '70

MARS probes. See Space probes

MARSEILLES

Provençal weekend. D. Butwin. il Sat R 53:44+ O 17 '70

MARSH, Corinna

Getting down to mass tax; poem. Nat R 22:927 S 8 '70

MARSH, Don

Step up to reading. il Am Ed 6:15-17 Ja '70

MARSH, Ed

No-nonsense nymph. il Field & S 74:100-2 Ja '70

MARSH, James T. and others

Auditory frequency-following response: neural or artifact? il Science 169:1222-3 S 18 '70

MARSH, Othniel C.

Ride for life in a buffalo herd; excerpt from autobiography. il Am Heritage 21:46-7+ Je '70

MARSH, Richard Oglesby

Cuna revolt. R. Chardkoff. il Américas 22:14-21 Jl '70 *

MARSH, Richard R.

Choose-&-use capacitor guide. il Radio-Electr 41:23-5 F '70

MARSH, Robert C.

Beethoven on records. il Hi Fi 20:secI 60-8+ My '70

Behind the scenes. il Hi Fi 20:secI 14 Jl '70

Berio's Opera premiere. il por Hi Fi 20:MA12-13+ N '70

Lyric opera breaks the jinx. il Hi Fi sec II 20:24-5 Ja '70

Mahler in Utah. Hi Fi 20:secI 84 My '70

Must a great violinist play in tune? Hi Fi sec I 20:91 Ja '70

RCA's great Philadelphia orchestra recording. il Hi Fi 20:80 S '70

Ravinia: success and problems. il Hi Fi 20:MA14-15 N '70

Raymond Lewenthal and Anton Rubinstein: two irresistible Victorians. Hi Fi 20:secI 90 Jl '70

Records for a critic's holiday. por Hi Fi 20:secI 26+ Mr '70

MARSH, Tracy H.

American presidents in glass sulphides. il Hobbies 75:102+ Jl '70

Identification & attribution of the Railroad train bread plate. il Hobbies 74:116-18 Ja

MARSH hens. See Rails (birds)

MARSHACK, Alexander

Baton of Montgaudier; with biographical sketch. il por Natur Hist 79:8, 56-63 Mr '70

about

Symbols in the stone age. il por Sci N 97:242 Mr 7 '70 *

MARSHAK, Robert E.

Rochester conferences. il por Bul Atom Sci 26:92-8 Je '70

MARSHALL, Calvin

Peace and power. por Time 95:71-2 Ap 6 '70

MARSHALL, Charles M.

How to skin a deer with a golf ball. il Field & S 75:98-9 O '70

MARSHALL, Eliot

Consumer. il New Repub 163:27-9 O 31 '70

I spy, you spy. New Repub 163:15-16 O 3 '70

Scott of Pennsylvania. New Repub 163:11 Ag 1 '70

MARSHALL, James A.

Photochemically induced ionic reactions of cycloalkenes. bibliog il Science 170:137-41 O 9 '70

MARSHALL, K. T. See Hall, E. jt. auth.

MARSHALL, Lenore

Comment. M. Van Duyn. Poetry 115:436 Mr '70 *

MARSHALL, Marvin L.

Focus on leadership in group decision making. Clear House 45:41-4 S '70

MARSHALL, P. Anthony. See Healy, J. H. jt. auth.

MARSHALL, Paule

Fannie Lou Hamer: hunger has no colour line. il por Vogue 155:126-7+ Je '70

MARSHALL, Robert L.

How J. S. Bach composed four-part chorales. bibliog f il Mus Q 56:198-220 Ap '70

MARSHALL, Yale

Center opera goes way out. J. Gerstel. il Hi Fi sec II 20:26-7 F '70 *

MARSHALL COUNTY, Miss.

Jim Brown comes to Mississippi; Black economic union helps residents. C. Gillespie. Nation 211:236-9 S 21 '70

MARSHALL gold discovery state historical park. See California—Parks and reserves

MARSHALL ISLANDS

See also

Bikini

MARSHES

PYE in the face of pollution; club at Thomas school, Rowayton, Conn, called Protect your environment. il Sr Schol 97:16 N 16 '70

River-eater; destruction of the Kissimmee. P. Matthiessen. il Audubon 72:52-3 Mr '70

What is a marsh worth? J. T. Starr. il Am For 76:12-15+ Ag '70

Why not create a marsh? R. Badaracco. il Parks & Rec 5:29-30 Je '70

Wilderness or wasteland? the blights to channelization. B. B. Blackburn. il Liv Wildn 34:27-32 Spr '70

Winter marsh. F. Russell. il Read Digest 96:135-41 F '70

See also

Bogs

Dismal Swamp

Salt marshes

MARSHFIELD, Mass.

Big loader offsets burning ban. E. Williams. il Am City 85:60-1 D '70

MARSICANO, Merle

Merle Marsicano dance company; the Cubiculo, NYC. D. Hering. Dance Mag 44:74 Je '70 *

MARSTON, Bob

Rig for fishing. il Motor B 125:152-3 F '70

MARSTON, David W.

Seychelles. il Travel 133:48-53 Mr '70

MARSTON, R. M.

Build! Lights-on reminder. il Radio-Electr 41:60-1 Ap '70

Experimenters, thirty IC circuits you can use. il Radio-Electr 41:62-3+ F '70

Solid-state tach & add-on speed alarm. il Radio-Electr 41:33-8 Ap '70

Stay-awake alarm. il Radio-Electr 41:52-4 S '70

Thirty new IC circuits you can use. il Radio-Electr 41:22+ Ag; 37-40+ N '70

Twenty triac circuits. il Radio-Electr 41:51-3+ Je; 49-53 Jl '70

MARSTON, Red

Charlie Morgan: the Dixie gambler. il Motor B 126:65-70+ Ag '70

80,000 miles by outboard. il Yachting 127:67+ Ap '70

His southern belle. il Motor B 126:65-70+ Ag '70

SORC's most challenging competition. il Motor B 125:28-30+ Ap '70

MARSUPIALS

Reproductive physiology of marsupials; viviparity in therian mammals. G. B. Sharman. bibliog il Science 167:1221-8 F 27 '70

See also

Kangaroos

MARTELL, E. A. and others

Fire damage. il Environ 12:14-21 My '70

MARTELL, Linda

Country music gets soul. il pors Ebony 25:66-8+ Mr '70 *

MARTELL, Lizabeth K.

Their community needs them. H. Alpert. il pors Har Yrs 10:43-5+ Je '70 *

MARTENHOFF, Jim

Could lightning strike your boat? il Pop Mech 134:100-3+ Jl '70

Docking the houseboat. il Yachting 127:80-1+ My '70

Outboard auxiliary power. il Yachting 129:104-5+ Ja '71

Outboarding finesse. il Yachting 128:69+ D '70

Quick cures for compass error. il Pop Sci 196:148-9 Ja '70

Shakedown cruise. il Yachting 127:72-3+ Mr '70

MARTENS, Anne Coulter
Dragon with the squeaky roar; drama. Plays 30:55-9 N '70
Is Cupid stupid? drama. Plays 29:1-10 F '70
Magic hat; drama. Plays 30:71-7 O '70
Springtime for Dan; drama. Plays 29:30-40 Ap '70
That Franklin boy; drama. Plays 29:47-52 Mr '70

MARTHA Graham and dance company
And tomorrow? What did the Martha Graham dance company, without Miss Graham, tell us about her art and its future? D. Hering. il Dance Mag 44:24-9 D '70
Martha Graham: past, present, future; engagement at the Brooklyn academy of music. W. Terry. il por Sat R 53:61-2 O 24 '70

MARTHA'S VINEYARD
Alfred Eisenstaedt's Martha's Vineyard; photographs. A. Eisenstaedt. Travel & Camera 33:17-25 S '70
Island consciousness. B. B. Chamberlain. il Natur Hist 79:114-15+ Ag '70

MARTI, Kurt, and others
Solar wind gases, cosmic ray spallation products, and the irradiation history. bibliog il Science 167:548-50 Ja 30 '70

MARTIN, A. R.
Nobel prize: three share 1970 award for medical research. por Science 170:423-4 O 23 '70

MARTIN, Alastair
Advantage, Mr Martin. Time 95:53 Ap 27 '70 *

MARTIN, Albert C.
How to plan for the urban spirit. il Am City 85:82+ F '70

MARTIN, Art
I struck back at stroke. Har Yrs 10:43-5 F '70
Writing and selling fillers. il Writers Digest 50:24-6 N '70

MARTIN, Bill
Peace in Middle Earth; paintings. il Ramp Mag 9:35-8 O '70

MARTIN, C. F. and Van Flandern, T. C.
Secular changes in the lunar elements. bibliog il Science 168:246-7 Ap 10 '70

MARTIN, Charles
Four for Theodore Roethke; Remembering the box; Heroic attitudes; poems. Poetry 115:249-56 Ja '70

MARTIN, David
Basic power cruisers. il por Motor B 125:112-13 Ja '70

MARTIN, David A.
Young men seeing visions. il Chr Cent 87:1063-6 S 9 '70

MARTIN, David C.
My Lai massacre, the prosecution rests. New Repub 163:13 N 7 '70

MARTIN, David Thomas
Excerpt from debate, July 30, 1970. Cong Digest 49:237+ O '70

MARTIN, Donald B. and Carter, J. R. Jr
Insulin-stimulated glucose uptake by subcellular particles from adipose tissue cells. bibliog il Science 167:873-4 F 6 '70

MARTIN, Edward Winslow, pseud.
Fun city one hundred years ago; excerpts from The secrets of the great city, comp. by G. M. Naimark. Holiday 47:92+ F '70

MARTIN, Edwin W.
New outlook for education of handicapped children. il Am Ed 6:7-10 Ap '70

MARTIN, George, 1926-
Another turn. il Opera N 34:6-7 Mr 7 '70
Benjamin Britten: twenty-five years of opera. Yale R 60:24-44 O '70
Eternal nightingale. il Hobbies 75:98M-98N Ag '70

MARTIN, Harold
Mad hatter visits Alice's restaurant. il Todays Health 48:39-43+ O '70

MARTIN, Jeanne G. M.
Traveler's choice. Travel 133:15 F '70

MARTIN, Jim
Family fishing on the Kern. il por Outdoor Life 146:56-7+ Ag '70
High climb for blacktails. il Outdoor Life 146:62-5+ S '70
Ice fishing comes to California. il pors Outdoor Life 145:64-5+ Ja '70

MARTIN, John B.
AoA backs aging visibility in planning for model cities; excerpts from interview. Aging 182:11 D '69
Full citizenship for aging urgently needed, Martin says; excerpts from address, February 23, 1970. Aging 186:13 Ap '70
1971 White House conference on aging: a message to older Americans. Aging 184:3 F '70
Quotations from the commissioner. Aging 182:10 D '69; 183:9 Ja; 187:8 My; 188:8 Je; 190:10-11 Ag '70
Transport for elderly problem now and for future, Martin says; excerpts from testimony. Aging 186:6 Ap '70

about

Martin hails Texas, Oklahoma programs. Aging 182:12 D '69

MARTIN, Joseph B. and Reichlin, Seymour
Thyrotropin secretion in rats after hypothalamic electrical stimulation or injection of synthetic TSH-releasing factor. bibliog il Science 168:1366-8 Je 12 '70

MARTIN, Kingsley
Editor describes himself. S. W. Little. Sat R 53:61 D 12 '70 *

MARTIN, M. W.
Crazy rains or animals that fall from the sky? il Sci Digest 67:32-6 Ja '70
Transplants that help disfigured faces. il Sci Digest 68:81-3 Jl '70

MARTIN, Madelyn H.
Building the slow learner's self-estem. Todays Ed 59:46-7 Mr '70

MARTIN, Michael M.
Biochemical basis of the fungus-attine ant symbiosis. bibliog il Science 169:16-20 Jl 3 '70

MARTIN, Mildred Crowl
Helping children cope with sorrow. Parents Mag 45:42-3+ Ag '70

MARTIN, Neil A
International business. il Duns 95:62-4+ F; 78-80+ Mr; 96:57-8 Ag '70; 97:62-4+ Ja '71
Matsushita knows how to do it. il Duns 95:62-4+ F '70
Modern industry. il Duns 95:81-2+ My; 96:63-5 Jl; 75+ O '70

about

Digging at Kidd Creek. Duns 95:3 Ap '70 *

MARTIN, Preston
Outlook for home buyers; interview. il pors U S News 68:70-3 Mr 23 '70

MARTIN, Ralph P.
Some new directions in New Testament study. Chr Today 14:10-13 F 13 '70

MARTIN, Robert A.
Line and grade in the extinct medius medius species group of sigmodon. bibliog il Science 167:1504-6 Mr 13 '70

MARTIN, Vicky
Last go-round with Max; story. Redbook 135:73-4 Ag '70

MARTIN, W. Richard
New capitalists of broadcasting. por Forbes 106:40 O 15 '70 *

MARTIN, William C.
God-hucksters or radio. il Atlan 225:51-6 Je '70

MARTIN, William McChesney, 1906-
Bill Martin. P. A. Samuelson. Newsweek 75:73 F 9 '70
Little trauma at the Fed. M. Seeger. Esquire 74:36+ S '70 *
Martin era. por Time 95:66 F 2 '70
Martin years. por Newsweek 75:59-60 F 2 '70
Swan song for a good public servant. Bsns W p 120 Ja 31 '70
Well done, Mr Martin. Nat R 22:127-8 F 10 '70

MARTIN Luther King foundation
M. L. King foundation in Britain names minister as director. Chr Cent 87:72 Ja 21 '70

MARTIN Luther King square. See San Francisco—Housing

MARTINEAU, Patty J.
Shopping: from Gump's to Jax. il Holiday 47:70-1+ Mr '70
—See Greig, H. jt. auth.

MARTINELLI, Giovanni
Martinelli on Edison. A. Favia-Artsay. por Hobbies 75:35 Mr '70 *

MARTINEZ, Elizabeth
Profile leaps to view. Nation 211:262-6 S 28 '70

MARTINEZ, Joan Smith
Lessons; poem. Negro Hist Bul 32:27 D '69

MARTINEZ, Orlando
Libya: oasis of oil. Nation 210:744-7 Je 22 '70

MARTINI, Sister Galen
Livin is no easy thing, man; poem. Cath World 211:150 Jl '70

MARTINIQUE
Fertility in Martinique. H. Leridon. il Natur Hist 79:57-9 Ja '70
France in the Caribbean Martinique and Guadeloupe. il Harp Baz 103:32L Ap '70
Gallic pizzazz in the West Indies. M. Gough. il House B 112:22+ Ag '70

MARTINS
Nest parasitism, productivity, and clutch size in purple martins. W. W. Moss and J. H. Camin. bibliog il Science 168:10000-3 My 22 '70; Discussion. 170:112 D 4 '70
What is a songbird worth? purple martins. J. P. Jackson. il Am For 76:34-5+ Ap '70

MARTINSVILLE, Va, public library
Ellis Hodgin loses first round. W. R.
  Eshelman. il Wilson Lib Bul 44:901+ My '70
Hodgin loses suit against city manager.
  Library J 95:1685 My 1 '70
MARTIRANO, Salvatore
Martirano's L's GA; the composer as Politi-
  co. J. Hiemenz. Hi Fi 20:secI 100 Ap '70 *
MARTY, Martin E.
Perishing publishers. Commonweal 91:580-2
  F 27 '70
Problem of God. Ladies Home J 86:128 D '69
MARTYN, Jack
Market's lonely man; caller at the New
  York coffee and sugar exchange. R. Levy.
  il Duns 96:60 O '70 *
MARTYRS
Are martyrs relevant? T. H. Clancy. Ameri-
  ca 123:320 O 24 '70
MARUYAMA, Magoroh
Walk-in exposure projects in the ghetto.
  Ment Hy 54:261-70 Ap '70
MARVIN, Lee
Saturday at Lee . . . ing Marvin's. R. Ebert.
  por Esquire 74:148-9+ N '70 *
MARVIN, Lelia. See Olson, T. A. jt. auth.
MARVIN, Lowell
My goat was high. il Outdoor Life 146:66-7+
  Ag '70
MARX, Anne
December current; poem. Good H 171:133 D
  '70
MARX, Gary T.
Issueless riots. bibliog f il Ann Am Acad
  391:21-33 S '70
MARX, Hans Joachim
Some corelli attributions assessed; tr. by L.
  Wallach. bibliog f il Mus Q 56:88-98 Ja '70
MARX, Leo
American institutions and ecological ideals;
  adaptation of address, December 29, 1969.
  bibliog Science 170:945-52 N 27 '70
MARX, Robert
New science of hunting underwater treasure.
  il Pop Mech 133:102-5+ Je '70
MARX, Werner G.
Neighbors who moved in: Spanish-American
  congress on evangelism. Chr Today 14:60-
  3 S 25 '70
MARXISM. See Communism; Socialism
MARY, Virgin
Welcome occasion; feast of the Immaculate
  conception. V. P. Mc Corry. America 123:
  502 D 5 '70

Art

Anecdotes, facetiae, satire, etc.
Bunny and the Madonna. R. J. Mouw. Chr
  Today 14:12 Mr 27 '70

Theology
Devotion of Mary. V. P. McCorry. America
  122:55-6 Ja 17 '70
MARY, queen of Scots
Lively lady was a secret scholar; Lady A.
  Fraser, author of Mary queen of Scots R. B.
  Stolley. il pors Life 68:42-4+ F 20 '70 *
MARY Ellen, Sister
Seventeenth year; poem. Commonweal 92:417
  Ag 21 '70
Untitled; poem. Commonweal 91:483 Ja 30
  '70
MARY Enda Hughes, Sister. See Hughes, M. E.
MARY Magdalen, Sister
Blotter prints. il Design 71:34-6 Fall '69
MARY Stuart, queen of the Scots. See Mary,
  queen of Scots
MARYANNA Childs, Sister. See Childs M.
MARYLAND
  See also
  Anacostia River
  Architecture, Domestic—Maryland
  Assateague Island
  Baltimore County
  Camps—Maryland
  Chesapeake Bay
  Education—Maryland
  Fishing—Maryland
  Gardens—Maryland
  Law—Maryland
  Smith Island

Politics and government
Maryland microcosm. S. Alsop. Newsweek 76:
  126 O 19 '70
Out gunning; Citizens against Tydings. New
  Repub 163:7 N 28 '70
MARYLAND academy of sciences, Baltimore
Events of 1971 in the Graphic time table. il
  Sky & Tel 41:33-5 Ja '71

MARYLAND. University, College Park
School of library and information
  services
Birth of LIST. P. Wasserman and E. Daniel.
  bibliog il pors Library J 95:3879-83 N 15 '70
Maryland L.S. info center meets Cambodia
  crisis. Library J 95:2208 Je 15 '70
MARYVILLE, Tenn.
Make a playground a challenge. F. T. Brad-
  ley. il Am City 85:28+ Ap '70
MASARYK, Jan Garrigue
Masaryk case, by C. Sterling. Review
  Life por 68:16 Ja 23 '70. E. Ambler
MASCAGNI, Pietro
Cavalleria rusticana. Criticism
  New Yorker 45:54+ Ja 17 '70
  Opera N 34:17-20 F 7 '70
  Sat R 53:21 Ja 24 '70
First the words. . . D. Stivender. il Opera N
  34:24+ F 7 '70
MASCULINITY (psychology)
How to appeal to women. J. Brothers. por
  Mech Illus 66:35-7+ Ag '70
Jesus was a sissy after all; new conception of
  being a male. T. K. Hearn, jr. Chr Cent
  87:1191-2+ O 7 '70
MASIN, Herman L.
(P)rhyme time; poem. Sr Schol 97:32 D 14
  '70
Sports. See issues of Senior scholastic
MASKED ball; opera. See Verdi, G.
MASKED bobwhite quail. See Quails
MASKEY, Jacqueline
Dance. il Hi Fi 20:secII 9+ My; 9+ Jl; MA10-
  11 S; MA10-11 O; MA8-9 N '70
MASKING tape. See Adhesive tape
MASKS (for the face)
Behind the mask. F. Bowers. il Opera N
  34:8-12 Ap 18 '70
Exploring the world behind a mask. il
  UNESCO Courier 23:27 O '70
Faces and masks and auxiliary deceptions.
  D. Shapiro. il Craft Horiz 30:36-45+ D '70
Masks: linkage between cultures. R. L. Asch.
  il Sch Arts 9:20-1 Je '70
Masks; primitive mask making. S. G. Stevens.
  il Sch Arts 69:6-7 Je '70
MASKS (sculpture)
Twentieth century masks. P. Berg. il Sch
  Arts 69:18-19 F '70
MASON, Birny, Jr
Birny Mason of Union carbide; interview.
  por Nations Bsns 58:60-5 S '70
MASON, Brian, and others
Mineralogy and petrography of lunar sam-
  ples. bibliog il Science 167:656-9 Ja 30 '70
—See Smith, J. V. jt. auth.
MASON, Clifford
Black fiction: a second look. pors Life 68:18
  My 8 '70
MASON, George
Antifederalist. C. Wilson. Nat R 22:849-50 Ag
  11 '70 *
Papers of George Mason, ed. by R. A. Rut-
  land. Review
  Sat R 53:48+ Je 20 '70. R. B. Morris *
MASON, Gussie
Lunchbox menus for dieting school children;
  excerpts from Help your child lose weight.
  Ladies Home J 87:116-17 Mr '70
MASON, H. M. Jr
America's deadly new bomber. il Mech Illus
  66:74-6+ O '70
MASON, Herbert
Death of Enkidu; excerpt from Gilgamesh;
  a verse narrative. Am Scholar 40:138-41
  Wint '70
MASON, Linda
Computer dating. il Nation 210:530-2 My 4
  '70
MASON, Raymond
What the senator didn't disclose. W. Lambert.
  pors Life 69:26-9 Ag 28 '70 *
MASON CITY, Ia.
Is Main Street still there? P. Schrag. il Sat
  R 53:20-5 Ja 17 '70
There's trouble right here in Mason City;
  Concerned community citizens' move to
  ban blue movies. J. Neary. il Life 69:22-5
  Ag 28 '70
MASONIC orders. See Freemasons
MASONS, Free. See Freemasons
MASS
Cathedral alive: Clowns, mass theme at Oak-
  land cathedral, Calif. C. J. McNaspy. Amer-
  ica 123:159-60 S 12 '70
Is there any hope for liturgy? G. S. Sloyan.
  Commonweal 92:56-60 Mr 27 '70; Discus-
  sion. 92:155+ My 1 '70

MASS—*Continued*
New liturgy. M. Ward; H. Smith. America 122:589-92 My 30 '70
New mass; more variety for Catholics. il Time 95:76+ Ja 26 '70
Opportunity for priests and people; the new Ordinary of the mass. America 122:290 Mr 21 '70
Right-wing underground; to preserve a liturgy that will safeguard the unity of the church. America 122:62 Ja 24 '70
  See also
International committee on English in the liturgy

MASS (music)
Beethoven's Missa solemnis. R. Thibodeau. por Commonweal 93:328-9 D 25 '70
Fakery of guitar masses. T. Day. il Cath World 211:270-2 S '70; Reply. J. Paulin. 212:174 Ja '71
Lupus Helinck: a survey of fourteen masses. J. Graziano. bibliog f il Mus Q 56:247-69 Ap '70
  See also
Phonograph records—Mass

MASS behavior. See Group (sociology)
MASS communication. See Mass media
MASS culture. See Popular culture
MASS hysteria. See Hysteria (social psychology)

MASS media
Agnew's effect; attack on news media. J. Osborne. New Repub 162:13-15 F 28 '70
American press; address, February 20, 1970. H. D. Bentley. Vital Speeches 36:329-32 Mr 15 '70
Coming age of news monopoly; symposium, with editorial comment. Sat R 53:51-4+ O 10 '70; Same abr. Cur 124:27-8 D '70
Communicating in Los Alamos: don't call him doctor! W. B. Kerr. Sat R 53:57-8 Ap 11 '70
Covering the foreign news; news agencies, print and electronic media. H. Schwartz. For Affairs 48:741-57 Jl '70
Critic babbles of green fields. Sedulus. New Repub 163:28-9 O 24 '70
Do news media overplay disorder? Press power revisited. J. Tebbel. Sat R 53:53-4 Je 13 '70
Lady tells it like it is; H. D. Bentley's brand of Americanism. H. J. Sievers. America 123:5 Jl 11 '70
Mike Frome. M. Frome. Am For 76:5+ Ja '70
People and the press. il Newsweek 76:22-5 N 9 '70
Reforming the news media. Commonweal 91: 467-8 Ja 30 '70
Role of the mass media; symposium. Cur 114: 41-54 Ja '70
Studying the mass media; report of study groups set up by the National commission on the causes and prevention of violence. J. Tebbel. Sat R 53:69-71 F 14 '70
TV vs. print; study findings of H. Krugman. Newsweek 76:122-3 N 2 '70
Year after Des Moines; Agnew's attack on the broadcasting media. Nation 211:549 N 30 '70
  See also
Center for media study (proposed)
Moving pictures

International aspects
  See also
Intracom (firm)

Moral aspects
Cultural indicators: the case of violence in television drama. G. Gerbner. bibliog f il Ann Am Acad 388:69-81 Mr '70
Violence and the mass media. il UNESCO Courier 23:21 Ag '70

Multiple ownership question
Communications monopolies. R. H. Smith. Pub W 197:37 Ap 6 '70
FCC's bomb for the broadcasters. il Bsns W p25 Ap 4 '70
One to a customer? FCC proposal. Newsweek 75:64 Ap 6 '70

Social aspects
Mass media & their impact on society. il Sr Schol 95:4-11 D 1 '69
Mass media as educators. W. W. Brickman. Sch & Soc 98:78-9 F '70
Media revolution: its educational implications. R. Pratte. Clear House 45:207-11 D '70
Super bowl. F. Bardacke. Ramp Mag 8:6 Mr '70

MASS media in religion
Christian broadcasters tune toward future. J. Huffman. Chr Today 14:35 My 22 '70
Mastering the media: the bishops go to school. R. Shaw. il America 122:158-60 F 14 '70
Moving upon the mass media; address. S. E. Wirt. Chr Today 14:3-6 My 22 '70
Rainbow for religion? Religious communication congress; with editorial comment. D. Kucharsky. Chr Today 14:25, 41 My 8 '70

MASS spectrometry
Amateur scientist; how to construct a molecular-beam apparatus and a mass spectrometer. C. L. Stong. il Sci Am 223:120-2+ Jl '70
Search for organic material in lunar fines by mass spectrometry. R. C. Murphy and others. il Science 167:755-7 Ja 30 '70

MASS transit. See Local transit

MASSACHUSETTS
  See also
Architecture, Domestic—Massachusetts
Berkshire Hills
Booksellers and bookselling—Massachusetts
Camps—Massachusetts
Cape Cod
Colleges and universities—Massachusetts
Concord River
Express highways—Massachusetts
Legislation—Massachusetts
Libraries—Massachusetts
Martha's Vineyard
Merrimack River
Nantucket Island
Squannacook River
Unemployment—Massachusetts

History
Pioneers in Massachusetts. F. L. Phelps. il Américas 22:21-30 F '70
  See also
Plymouth

Politics and government
New politics and old; Democratic primary. il por Time 96:12 S 28 '70
Speaker's seat. Nation 211:36 Jl 20 '70

MASSACHUSETTS general hospital, Boston. See Boston—Hospitals

MASSACHUSETTS historical society
Collecting for Clio. T. B. Adams. il Sat R 53:16-17 Je 20 '70

MASSACHUSETTS horticultural society
First conference, horticultural and botanical libraries. Horticulture 48:46-7 Mr '70
Library is more than a collection of books. G. W. Dillon. Horticulture 49:36+ Ja '71

MASSACHUSETTS institute of technology, Cambridge
Come squeeze or bust, in Ho-Jo we trust. J. Davenport. il por Fortune 81:176-9+ My '70
Controversy at MIT; reply. R. M. Byers. Aviation W 92:66 Mr 2 '70
Low-field room built at high-field magnet lab. G. B. Lubkin. il Phys Today 23:56-7 Je '70
M.I.T. administration makes public its intentions on disposition of Draper and Lincoln laboratories. V. K. McElheny. Science 168:1074-5 My 29 '70
M.I.T: March 4 revisited amid political turmoil. A. Hamilton. il Science 167:1475-6 Mr 13 '70
New left v. national security; objections to research at Instrumentation laboratory. Nat R 22:18 Ja 13 '70
Project Cambridge: another showdown for social sciences? J. Coburn; discussion. Science 167:819-20 F 6 '70
Time enough; H. Johnson to resign. por Newsweek 76:81 S 21 '70

MASSACHUSETTS investors trust. See Investment trusts

MASSACHUSETTS, University, Amherst
School of education
Frenzy at U. Mass. por Time 96:34 D 21 '70

MASSAGE
Help is on the way; Alfred Kagan and Anne Benné. Vogue 156:176-7 N 1 '70
Massage: the low-down on the rub-down. Vogue 155:210 Ap 1 '70

MASSAQUOI, Hans J.
Elijah Muhammad: prophet and architect of the separate nation of Islam. il pors Ebony 25:78-80+ Ag '70

MASSARO, Edward J.
Horseshoe crab lactate dehydrogenase: tissue distribution and molecular weight. bibliog il Science 167:994-6 F 13 '70

MASSE, Benjamin Louis
Social front. See issues of America
Testing black capitalism. America 123:491-2
D 5 '70
Washington front. America 122:33, 547 Ja 17,
My 23 '70
MASSENET, Jules
Massenet's Manon, and Puccini's. P. L. Miller. por Am Rec G 36:326-7 Ja '70 *
Werther. P. L. Miller. il Am Rec G 36:324-5
Ja '70 *
MASSEY, Jack C.
Food man whips up a chain of hospitals. il
por Bsns W p44 My 30 '70 *
MASSEY, Robert
Artist's ideal studio. il Am Artist 35:30-4
Ja '71
Painting, drawing, and printmaking supports.
il Am Artist 34:22-6 S '70
MASSIE, Samuel P.
George Washington Carver story. il pors
Chem 43:18-21 S '70
St Elmo Brady: the lengthened shadow. il
Chem 43:7 N '70
MASSINE, Leonide
Leonide Massine, a protean vitality. L. Joel.
Vogue 155:34 Mr 15 '70 *
MASSON, Charles
Please don't eat the flowers. il por House &
Gard 137:74-7 F '70 *
MASTECTOMY. See Breasts—Surgery
MASTER charge cards. See Credit cards
MASTER mariners race regatta. See Regattas
MASTER photodealers and finishers association trade shows. See Photography—Exhibitions
MASTERS, Charles O.
Frogs for the lily pool. il Horticulture 48:26-7
Ap '70
MASTERS, Isabell
College is a family affair. il pors Ebony 25:
50-2+ Mr '70 *
MASTERS, Robert Edward Lee
Mysticism in the laboratory. il por Time 96:
72+ O 5 '70 *
MASTERS, William Howell
Sex and marriage. Redbook 135:82-90 S '70
Sex, guilt and the double standard. Redbook
135:67+ O '70
—and Johnson, V. E.
Sex and married woman. McCalls 97:68-9+
My '70
about
Human sexual inadequacy. M. Clark. pors
Newsweek 75:90+ My 4 '70 *
Masters & Johnson: their new cures for sex
problems. M. Weber. Ladies Home J 87:51+
Jl '70 *
Repairing the conjugal bed. il pors Time 95:
49-52 My 25 '70 *
Sex and the married couple. P. Wilkes. il
Atlan 226:82-4+ D '70 *
Sexual inadequacy: what can be done. W.
Bradbury. il pors Life 68:42-6 My 1 '70;
Same abr. Read Digest 97:63-6 Ag '70 *
MASTERS degrees. See Degrees, Academic
MASTERS golf tournament. See Golf—Tournament
MASTICS, Al
Helping hand: Ohio's South shore CC. il
Yachting 129:110+ Ja '71
MASTITIS-metritis-agalactia complex. See
Swine—Diseases and pests
MASTODONS
Mastodons at sea. A. H. Drummond, jr. il
Sea Front 16:151-3 My '70
MASTOMYS. See Rats
MASTS and rigging
Dilemma of rod; stainless steel rod rigging on
ocean racers. il Motor B 126:72-3 D '70
Improvements in the Moth rig. C. D. Gately.
il por Yachting 128:37+ D '70
Norman Freeman on the Bruder spar. N.
Freeman. Yachting 127:102 F '70
See also
Sails
Maintenance and repair
Maintenance for sailors. il Motor B 125:
79 Ap '70
MATADORS. See Bullfighters
MATAMOROS, A. G.
What hangs in balance on budgets? por Nations Bsns 58:82-3 Jl '70
MATARAZZO, Joseph D.
National mental health manpower showcase
conference: NAMH leads the way. bibliog
Ment Hy 54:333-6 Jl '70
MATCH-making by computers. See Computers
—Social use
MATCHETT, William H.
Nature of the beast; poem. New Repub
162:29 Mr 7 '70

MATCHING pair: story. See Conaway, R.
MATERER, Timothy
Merton and Auden. pors Commonweal 91:
577-80; 92:71 F 27, Mr 27 '70
MATERIALISM
Ego and instinct, by D. Yankelovich and W.
Barrett. Review
Nation 210:564-6 My 11 '70. R. Sampson
So who needs liberation? R. Dickinson. Chr
Cent 88:43-6 Ja 13 '71
MATERIALS
See also
Building materials
Composite materials
Heat resistant materials
Raw materials
MATERIALS centers. See Instructional materials centers
MATERIALS handling
See also
Freight handling
Grain handling
Pallets
MATERIALS research
Materials behavior experiments studied.
Aviation W 93:53 N 2 '70
Materials science & engineering, a modern
multidiscipline. J. Andrade. il por Chem
43:13-15 Ap '70
MATERNAL behavior. See Mothers
MATERNAL deprivation
Physiological responses of infant rats to separation from their mothers. M. A. Hofer.
bibliog il Science 168:871-3 My 15 '70
MATERNAL love. See Love, Maternal
MATERNITY. See Mothers
MATES, Frederic S.
Fred Mates is one happy man. S. Mahoney.
il pors Life 68:56B-56D+ My 22 '70 *
MATES, Leo
Nonalignment and the great powers. For
Affairs 48:525-36 Ap '70
MATES investment fund. See Investment trusts
MATESA company. See Textile machinery industry—Spain
MATHEMATICAL instruments
See also
Abacus
Slide rule
MATHEMATICAL models
Corporate models: one-line, real-time systems.
J. B. Boulden and E. S. Buffa. il Harvard
Bsns R 48:65-83 Jl '70
MATHEMATICAL physics
See also
Equation of motion
Statistical mechanics
MATHEMATICAL recreations
Mathematical games. M. Gardner. See issues
of Scientific American
Mathematics with a light touch. J. Frye.
Electr World 83:51-2 My '70
Not-so-amazing calendar trick; or, You,
too, can be an idiot-savant. T. S. O'Bannon. il Sci Digest 67:86-9 F '70
MATHEMATICAL statistics
See also
Least squares
MATHEMATICS
See also
Coordinates
Geometry
Mathematical recreations
Probabilities

Courses of study
Secondary school math in five cities. Todays
Ed 59:50-1 My '70

Study and teaching
Continuing the math revolution; excerpts
from interviews, ed. by M. N. Suydam.
Am Ed 6:26-30 Ja '70
Improvement in teaching mathematics; using
modern mass communications techniques
to introduce the new math. Sch & Soc 98:
266+ Sum '70
Mathematical education: yesterday and today: interview. J. R. Clark. Todays Ed
59:50-1 D '70
Survey of the teaching of mathematics in
secondary schools. S. I. Williams. Sch &
Soc 98:244-6 Ap '70
See also
Arithmetic—Study and teaching
MATHER, Stephen Tyng
Conservation hall of fame. H. M. Albright.
il por Nat Wildlife 7:10-11 O '69 *
MATHESON, Craig, and others
War and pieces. il Todays Ed 59:20-3 Mr '70
MATHEWS, Anne
Hurdles, problems, rewards: a total system
concept at work. il Am Lib 1:151-3 F '70

MATHEWS, Charles W.
Future progress of space transportation. il
Space World G-7-79:18-21 Jl '70
MATHEWS, H. C.
Save those grapes! il Org Gard & Farm 17:84
Ag '70
MATHEWS, Richard K.
Seal harems in the Pribilofs; with biographi-
cal sketch. il por Natur Hist 79:4, 32-41 Ja
'70
MATHEWS, Virginia H.
Making the right to read real. Schol Teach
Jr/Sr High p6-8 D 7 '70
MATHIS, Bonnie
Brief biography. S. Goodman. pors Dance
Mag 44:74-5 Mr '70 *
MATHIS, Edith
Fresh faces; interview, ed .by S. Jenkins.
por Opera N 34:30-1 F 21 '70
MATHIS, Tex.
Death of an Anglo; F. Logan killed by po-
lice. il por Newsweek 76:21 Jl 27 '70
MATHUR, S. P. See Stewart, R. jt. auth.
MATING behavior. See Sexual behavior in ani-
mals
MATINS; story. See Goble, S.
MATISSE, Henri
Henri Matisse: the further side of joy. P.
Schneider. il Vogue 156:113-19+ D '70 *
Letter from Paris; exhibition at the Grand
palais. Genêt. New Yorker 46:86-8 My 30
'70 *
Matisse; exhibition in Paris celebrates 100th
birthday; with report on meeting with the
artist by G. L. K. Morris. il pors Life 69:
30-44+ Ag 28 '70 *
Matisse's final flowering. R. W. Murphy. il
por Horizon 12:26-41 Wint '70
Matisse's imprint upon an age. il por Time
96:50-3 Jl 13 '70
Most beautiful exhibition in the world. T. B.
Hess. il por Art N 69:28-31+ Sum '70 *
Painter's painter; Paris exhibition at the
Grand palais. il por Newsweek 75:68-70
My 11 '70 *
Sculpture of Matisse H. Groskinsky. il pors
Life 69:40-9 S 11 '70 *
MATISSE, Paul
Current picture. Time 96:62 O 5 '70 *
MATO GROSSO, Brazil
Pantanal: 400,000 sq. km. of swampland in
the Mato Grosso. N. V. Cordeiro. il UNES-
CO Courier 23:14-15 Je '70
MATRAS, Christian
Company of the blind; So deep, so deep; po-
ems, tr. by G. Johnston. Poetry 116:330-2
Ag '70
MATRIMONIA mixta. See Encyclicals
MATRIX management. See Business manage-
ment and organization
MATS, Table. See Table mats, tiles, etc.
MATSON, R. G. See True, D. L. jt. auth.
MATSON navigation company
Matson alters its course. Bsns W p74 S 26 '70
MATSUDA, Morihiro
Where are they now? il por Newsweek 75:18
Je 15 '70 *
MATSUMOTO, Takuo
Twenty-five years later: no more Hiroshimas!
W. Reed. por Chr Today 14:39 Ag 21 '70 *
MATSUMURA, Fumio, and others
Formation of photodieldrin by microorga-
nisms. bibliog il Science 170:1206-7 D 11 '70
MATSUSHITA, Konosuke
Quotations from chairman Matsushita. il por
Time 96:73 O 12 '70 *
MATSUSHITA electric industrial company, Ja-
pan. See Electric apparatus industry
MATSUYAMA, Mutsushi, and Suzuki, Harumi
Differentiation of immature mucous cells into
parietal, argyrophil, and chief cells in stom-
ach grafts. bibliog il Science 169:385-7 Jl 24
'70
MATTA, Seoud M.
In search of the Nile; the challenge to li-
braries in Egypt. bibliog il por Wilson Lib
Bul 44:1040-5 Je '70
MATTEL, inc.
Diversification is Mattel's game. il Bsns W
p32-3 Jl 25 '70
Hot pace in a big mini-race; great toy auto
race between Mattel and Topper. R. H.
Boyle. il Sports Illus 33:38-44 D 7 '70
MATTER
See also
Atoms
Compressibility
Critical point
Force and energy

MATTER, Interstellar
Clues to creation. Newsweek 76:56 Jl 20 '70
Far-ultraviolet photography of Orion: in-
terstellar dust. R. C. Henry and G. R.
Carruthers. bibliog il Science 170:527-31
O 30 '70
Interstellar clouds: a new kind of chemis-
try. D. E. Thomsen. il Sci N 98:124-5 Ag
8 '70
Interstellar hydrogen molecules found. Sky
& Tel 40:139 S '70
Interstellar molecules and chemistry; AAAS
symposium. December 30, 1970. B. Donn.
Science 170:1116-17 D 4 '70
Interstellar molecules: chemicals in the sky.
G. L. Wick. Science 170:149-50 O 9 '70
Material to make stars; discovery of mole-
cular hydrogen in space. il Sci N 97:595 Je
20 '70
Microwave detection of thioformaldehyde. D.
R. Johnson and F. X. Powell. bibliog il
Science 169:679-80 Ag 14 '70
Molecules between the stars. Time 95:78+ Je
8 '70
Molecules in space. Chem 43:28 O '70
Molecules in the interstellar medium. L. E.
Snyder and D. Buhl. bibliog il Sky & Tel
40:267-70 N; 345-8 D '70
More interstellar chemistry. Sci Am 222:49+
Je '70
New space molecule. Sci N 98:366 N 7 '70
Search for the $1_{10} \leftarrow 1_{11}$ transition of interstel-
lar thioformaldehyde. N. J. Evans, 2d. and
others. bibliog il Science 169:680-1 Ag 14 '70
Toward life between the stars. il Sci N
98:299 O 10 '70
MATTHAU, Walter
Walter Matthaus: we've given our house a
country look and a country feeling. il por
House & Gard 138:38-41 Jl '70 *
MATTHEWS, John
Stutterers, speak for yourselves. il Sci Di-
gest 67:62-6 Ap '70
MATTHEWS, Mary, and Sherman, Steve
How to computerize your serials and period-
icals when you don't know how; pors
Wilson Lib Bul 44:861-4 Ap '70
MATTHEWS, T. S.
Rite of summer. Am Scholar 39:463-7 Sum '70
MATTHEWS, William
Explorer; Sandlot basketball; Example;
Apathy; poems. Poetry 117:160-1 D '70
May day; poem. Nation 210:90 Ja 26 '70
MATTHIESSEN, Peter
Kipahulu: from cinders to the sea. il Audu-
bon 72:10-23 My '70
River-eater. il Audubon 72:52-3 Mr '70
MATTINGLY, Debra
Muffin. il por Newsweek 75:21+ Ja 26 '70
MATTINGLY, Thomas Ken, 2d
High-resolution camera to assist Apollo 13
topographical mapping. il por Aviation W
92:19 Mr 23 '70 *
Lieutenant Commander T. K. Mattingly, 2d
(USN) por Newsweek 75:63 Ap 13 '70 *
MATTIX, William W.
Woods of mine; poem. il Am For 76:19 My '70
MATTO GROSSO. See Mato Grosso, Brazil
MATTOLE road. See Roads—California
MATTRESSES
Innerspring mattresses. Good H 170:152 Ja
'70
Mattresses and box springs. Consumer Rep
34:46-50 D '69
MATURE Temps, inc.
Older workers hired, easily placed in contract
jobs by Mature Temps. il Aging 188:10-11 Je
'70
MATURITY
What's your maturity quotient? excerpts
from Power of maturity. L. Binstock.
Read Digest 96:122-3 Mr '70
MATURITY, Sexual. See Puberty
MATZ, Charles
Battle of Wagner. pors Opera N 34:6-7 Ja
31 '70
Mailer's opera. il por Opera N 34:14-16 F
21 '70
MATZ, Mary Jane
First ladies of the Puccini premieres. il pors
Opera N 34:22-3 Ja 24 '70
(ed) See Franci, C. Madman
MATZINGER, Keith R.
Sure, I can fly a '51. il Flying 86:80-1 Ja '70
MATZKIN, Myron A.
Can a super 8 be worth over $500? il Mod
Phot 34:76-7+ Ap '70
Matzkin on movies. See issues of Modern
photography to March 1970
MAUER, Anthony
Gallery; photographs. il Life 68:8-9 Ap 3 '70
MAUER, Irving, and others
Acetylsalicylic acid: no chromosome damage
in human leukocytes. bibliog il Science 169:
198-201 Jl 10 '70

MAUGHAN, Walter L.
  Hail, the ferocious lion! il Américas 22:4-6
    Ap '70
MAUI (island)
  Escape to Maui. D. Butwin. il Sat R 53:30-1
    Ag 29 '70
  Kipahulu: from cinders to the sea. P. Mat-
    thiessen. il Audubon 72:10-23 My '70
  On the Lahaina Kaanapali & Pacific. il Sun-
    set 145:43-4 S '70
MAULE, Tex
  Big ifs in big D. il Sports Illus 33:10-13
    Ag 31 '70
  Chelsea almost won the cup. il Sports Illus
    32:20-3 Ap 20 '70
  Future moves into the past. il Sports Illus
    33:26-8+ S 28 '70
  How the West was, uh, tied. il Sports Illus
    33:24-6+ D 7 '70
  Let George do it, and he does. il por Sports
    Illus 33:30-2+ N 23 '70
  Lew turns small change to big Bucks. il pors
    Sports Illus 32:20-2+ Mr 9 '70
  Miami gets a miracle worker. il por Sports
    Illus 33:16-17 S 7 '70
  No miracle required. il Sports Illus 33:18-23
    D 21 '70
  Pelé and pals retire the Cup. il por Sports
    Illus 32:24-5 Je 29 '70
  Pro football. il Sports Illus 31:62-3+ D 15 '69
  Pro football '70. il Sports Illus 33:34-40+ S
    21 '70
  Rushing to stake a claim. il Sports Illus 34:
    10-15 Ja 4 '71
  Soccer. Sports Illus 32:78 My 11 '70
  Soccer is a frenzy. il Sports Illus 32:12-17 Je 22
    '70
  There's gold in them thar spills. il Sports
    Illus 33:20-1 O 26 '70
MAULLIN, Richard L.
  Private war of a guerrilla. il por Trans-Action
    7:45-54 bibliog(p64) Mr '70
MAUNA KEA observatory. See Astronomical
  observatories—Hawaii
MAUNEY, Michael
  Under spring's green spell; photographs. il
    Life 68:48-55 My 1 '70
MAURA, Sister
  Grief: poem. Commonweal 91:529 F 13 '70
MAUREEN Cronin, Sister. See Cronin, M.
MAURIAC, François
  Death comes to a Nobel prize winner. H. J.
    Cargas. il America 123:234-6 O 3 '70 *
  Francois Mauriac. J. Finn. Commonweal 93:
    320-2+ D 25 '70 *
  Mauriac, the splendor of sin. il por Time
    96:34 S 14 '70 *
  Taking sides: Mauriac, polemicist. A. Wood-
    row. por Commonweal 93:322-3 D 25 '70 *
MAURITIUS
  Into the vacuum. il Time 95:39 Je 15 '70
MAURO, Brother
  Fra Mauro, he inspired Columbus and the
    Apollo astronauts. il Space World G-9-81:
    22 S '70 *
MAURY, Matthew Fontaine
  Matthew Fontaine Maury, Cyrus Field and
    the physical geography of the sea. R. H.
    Charlier and P. S. Charlier. il pors Sea
    Front 16:272-81 S '70
MAURY, Reuben
  President's editorialist. por Time 96:45 Ag 31
    '70 *
MAUTZ, R. K. and Neumann, F. L.
  Effective corporate audit committee. bibliog
    f il Harvard Bsns R 48:57-65 N '70
MAX, Peter
  Peter Max, the ubiquitous designer and his
    book publishing debut. M. R. Kraner. il
    por Pub W 197:70-1 Ap 27 '70 *
  Peter Max: the wizard of ahs paints a
    vivid self-portrait; interview. pors Seven-
    teen 29:236 Ap '70
MAXEY, Carl
  War is hell for Senator Jackson. B. Weiner.
    por Nation 211:138-41 Ag 31 '70 *
MAXEY, David R.
  All-Republican Senate? Jim Allison's work-
    ing on it. il por Look 34:34-6+ O 20 '70
  Bureau of Indian affairs: America's colonial
    service. Look 34:35 Je 2 '70
  How Nixon decided to invade Cambodia. il
    Look 34:22-5 Ag 11 '70
  Mr President, bring us together again. il
    Look 34:15-21 Ja 27 '70
  Volunteers. il Look 34:17-24+ Je 16 '70
MAXIMOV, Gennady
  Along the earth-cosmos route. Space World
    G-7-79:34-5 Jl '70
MAXTONE-GRAHAM, James A.
  Fourth of June. il Travel & Camera 33:38-45
    My '70
  Gold-plated salmon. il Travel & Camera 33:
    64+ F '70
  Measures. Sports Illus 33:47 Ag 24 '70

MAXWELL, Arthur E. and others
  Deep sea drilling in the South Atlantic. bib-
    liog il Science 168:1047-59 My 29 '70
MAXWELL, C. G.
  Real pussy willows. il Design 71:18 Spr '70
MAXWELL, Jess E.
  Scintillating Stowe. il Travel 134:44-51 N '70
MAXWELL, John A. and others
  Chemical composition of lunar material. bib-
    liog il Science 167:530-1 Ja 30 '70
MAXWELL, Robert
  Missing millions. pors Time 96:85-6 S 14
    '70 *
  Pergamon dispute rekindled; Maxwell's
    counter-bid. Pub W 198:28 Ag 17 '70 *
MAXWELL, William Lee
  Delay on the death penalty. il por Time
    95:60 Je 15 '70 *
MAY, Andrew James
  Fifty years at 1/20th of a second. H. Sidey.
    il por Life 69:4 N 27 '70 *
MAY, Buck. See May, A. J.
MAY, Catherine Dean
  American farmer; address, June 23, 1970. Vital
    Speeches 36:625-8 Ag 1 '70
MAY, Rollo
  Finding yourself: the bread-and-butter ques-
    tion; interview, ed. by B. T. Blackwell.
    Mlle 71:152+ My '70
  Yes begins with a no. il por Time 95:66+
    Je 22 '70 *
MAY, Steve
  Man's world: an electronic experience in
    the humanities. Engl J 59:413-15+ Mr '70
MAY, William Frederic
  Dent in American can. A. A. Butkus. il por
    Duns 95:38-41 Ap '70 *
MAY, Wong
  Comment. M. Van Duyn. Poetry 115:437-8
    Mr '70
  Report I; Report II; poems. Am Scholar
    39:473-4 Sum '70
MAYALL, Margaret W.
  Director reports. See issues of Review of
    popular astronomy to August 1969
MAYAS
  Age of frightened men; exhibition in Hall of
    Mexico and Central America. D. Davis. il
    Newsweek 75:103 Je 1 '70
  Tumbaga object from the early classic period,
    found at Altun Ha, British Honduras
    (Belize) D. M. Pendergast. bibliog il Sci-
    ence 168:116-18 Ap 3 '70
  Zinacantan; a Maya community in the high-
    lands of Chiapas, by E. Z. Vogt. Review
    Natur Hist 79:66-72 F '70. H. R. Harvey
      See also
  Tikal, Guatemala
MAYER, Albert
  It's not just the cities (cont) il Arch Rec
    147:137-42 Je; 148:101-6 Jl '70
MAYER, Frank C.
  Internal communications. Clear House 44:290-
    5 Ja '70
MAYER, George Louis
  Bonynge's Don Giovanni. Sat R 53:67+ Ap 25
    '70
  Caballé sings Salome. il Am Rec G 36:402-4
    F '70
  Fedora. pors Am Rec G 37:76-9 O '70
  Dvorak's Requiem by Kertesz. Sat R 53:59
    S 26 '70
  Nilsson: Venus and Elisabeth. Am Rec G
    36:522-3 Mr '70
MAYER, Gerald D. and Krueger, R. F.
  Tilorone hydrochloride: mode of action. il
    Science 169:1214-15 S 18 '70
  —See Krueger, R. F. jt. auth.
MAYER, Grace M.
  Edward Steichen. il Mod Phot 34:82-7+ Jl
    '70
MAYER, Jean
  How to murder your husband. Read Digest
    97:132-4 Ag '70
  Message from the President's nutrition con-
    sultant. Todays Health 48:51 F '70
  On the life sciences; address, March 5, 1970.
    Vital Speeches 36:402-7 Ap 15 '70
  Simple secrets of losing weight. Read Digest
    96:136-9 Ja '70
  —See Arees, E. A. jt. auth.
MAYER, Johann Tobias. See Mayer, T.
MAYER, Lawrence A.
  Inflation everywhere, but some real growth
    too. il Fortune 82:136-41 Ag '70
  Mobile homes move into the breach.   il
    Fortune 81:126-30+ Mr '70
  U.S. population growth: would slower be
    better? il Fortune 81:80-3+ Je '70
  Why the U.S. is in an energy crisis. il For-
    tune 82:74-7+ N '70
MAYER, Leo Meinrad
  Biography of an artist. il Design 72:12-16
    Fall '70 *

MAYER, Martin
Brilliance of Spiro Agnew. pors Esquire 73: 117-19+ My '70
Elliott Gould as the entrepreneur. il pors Fortune 82:108-11+ O '70
Loneliness of the short-distance dialer. il Esquire 74:154-6+ O '70
Man in box 13. il por Opera N 35:6-10 S 19 '70
Recordings. See issues of Esquire
Where the dollars go. il Sat R 53:22-4+ F 28 '70

MAYER, Milton
Thou shalt not. Cur 117:62-4 Ap '70

MAYER, Paul
Diary of a dissenting priest. Commonweal 92:78-9 Ap 3 '70

MAYER, Ralph
Ralph Mayer's technical question & answer page. See issues of American artist

MAYER, Tobias
Who discovered longitude at sea? E. G. Forbes. il Sky & Tel 41:4-6 Ja '71 *

MAYES, Herbert R.
London letter. Sat R 53:13-14 F 7; 14+ Ap 4; 20-1+ Je 6; 10-11+ Jl 25; 4+ O 17; 6+ N 14; 4+ D 12 '70

MAYFLOWER (ship)
See also
Pilgrim fathers

MAYNARD, Fred
Build digisyntone-new music synthesizer. il Radio-Electr 41:47-51 S '70
Electronic strobotuner. il Electr world 83:74-7 Mr '70
Ten emitter-coupled oscillator circuits. il Radio-Electr 41:33-5 My '70

MAYNARD, G. Lafayette
Crustal layer of seismic velocity 6.9 to 7.6 kilometers per second under the deep oceans. bibliog il Science 168:120-1 Ap 3 '70

MAYNARD, Joyce
In my opinion. por Seventeen 29:232 F '70

MAYNARD, Richard
Films can end those social studies doldrums! il Schol Teach Sec Teach Sup p 14-16+ Ap 6 '70

MAYNARD, Robert C.
Black nationalism and community schools; excerpts from Community control of schools. bibliog Sch & Soc 98:121-5 F '70

MAYO, Robert Porter
Budget bureau wields a powerful ax. il por Bsns W p80-3 Ja 17 '70
Budget director responds. Science 169:39 Jl 3 '70
Robert Mayo: calling signals on history's biggest budget. il por U S News 68:10 Ja 19 '70

MAYO clinic, Rochester, Minn.
Nine steps to a longer life. B. Clark. Read Digest 97:84-7 O '70

MAYORS
From the mayor's chair; interview. J. P. Cavanagh; P. Flaherty. pors Sr Schol 96: 10-11 Mr 2 '70
Mayors: do they have America's toughest jobs? il Sr Schol 96:4-9 Mr 2 '70
See also
Negro mayors
Nuns as public officers
United States conference of mayors

MAYR, Otto
Origins of feedback control; with biographical sketch. il Sci Am 223:15, 110-18 O '70

MAYR, Simone
Report: production of Medea in Corinto in Lincoln Center's new Alice Tully Hall. Opera N 34:32 Ja '70

MAYS, Willie
Yea, Mr Mays. R. Blount, jr. il pors Sports Illus 33:10-13 Jl 27 '70 *

MAYTAG company
How to change without really changing. il Forbes 106:18-19 Ag 1 '70

MAZATLAN, Mexico
Just two driving days below Arizona, there is Mazatlán. il Sunset 144:70+ My '70

MAZE tests
Math lesson from racing rats. il Sci Digest 68:90-1 O '70

MAZER, Milton
Psychiatric disorders in young women: the public health implications. bibliog Ment Hy 54:436-9 Jl '70

MAZES. See Labyrinths

MAZLISH, Bruce
Mills: father and son. il pors Horizon 12: 106-11 Sum '70

MAZUR, Peter
Cryobiology: the freezing of biological systems. bibliog il Science 168:939-49 My 22 '70

MAZURSKY, Paul
Paul Mazursky in wonderland. J. Greenfeld. il pors Life 69:51-4+ S 4 '70 *
Portrait of the artisan. J. Cocks. il Time 97: 75-6 Ja 18 '71 *

MAZZI, Enzo
Isolotto: test case for Italian Catholicism. J. J. Carey. Chr Cent 87:336+ Mr 18 '70 *

MAZZO, Kay
Impressions of Kay Mazzo. V. L. Warren; A. Fatt. il pors Dance Mag 44:60-5 Ja '70

MBOYA, Thomas Joseph

Assassination
Tribal politics harass Kenya. S. Meisler. For Affairs 49:111-21 O '70

The ME nobody knows; musical comedy. See Musical comedies, revues, etc.—Criticisms, plots, etc.

MEAD, Clare
Mysticism in the laboratory. il por Time 96: 72+ O 5 '70 *

MEAD, Emerson Ernest
Take-over attempt was the turning point. il por Nations Bsns 58:106-7 Ja '70

MEAD, Lynda Lee
Where are they now? pors Newsweek 76:22 S 14 '70 *

MEAD, Margaret
Five who care. il Look 34:37 Ap 21 '70
Island earth; with biographical sketch. por Natur Hist 79:4, 22+ Ja '70
[Monthly column] See issues of Redbook
Presenting: the very recent past. il N Y Times Mag p28-32 Mr 15 '70
Working mothers and their children. il Cath World 212:78-82 N '70

about
Growing apart in Manhattan. D. Brudnoy. Nat R 22:552 Je 2 '70 *
Mead and her message. D. Dempsey. il por (p 1) N Y Times Mag p23+ Ap 26 '70; Same abr. with title Provocative, prophetic Margaret Mead. Read Digest 97:127-31 Ag '70
New longings abroad in the land. B. DeMott. Sat R 53:23-4 Jl 4 '70 *
Remarkable woman: Margaret Mead. J. Sakol. il por McCalls 97:80-1+ Je '70 *

MEAD, Matthew
(tr) See Sachs, N. Six poems

MEAD, Robert L. and Corliss, W. R.
Power from radioisotopes. il Space World G-5-77:41-5 My '70

MEAD, Ruth
(tr) See Sachs, N. Six poems

MEAD, Sidney E.
In quest of America's religion. por Chr Cent 87:752-6 Je 17 '70

MEADE, David
Gag rule: ominous trend. Chr Cent 87:589-90 My 13 '70

MEADE, James P. jr
Long return of Warrant officer Meade. J. P. Blank. il por Read Digest 97:73-7 D '70 *

MEADE, Richard A. and Ellis, W. G.
Paragraph development in the modern age of rhetoric. bibliog f il Engl J 59:219-26 F '70

MEADOW mice. See Mice

MEADOW view wildlife preserve. See Game preserves

MEAGHER, Robert E.
Church as a family. America 122:37-9 Ja 17 '70

MEALS
Eat; three meals for fall nights. M. Cantwell. Mlle 72:100+ N '70
One-dish meals for the long, cold winter; with recipes. F. M. Crawford. il Am Home 74:52-3+ Ja '71
Twice as much good eating from your food dollar starting with beef; chicken; bologna; ground beef; tuna and ham. il Bet Hom & Gard 48:56-68+ Ja '70
See also
Breakfasts
Buffet meals
Christmas meals
Cookery
Diet
Dinners and dining
Hospitals—Food service
Luncheons
Lunches
Menus
Outdoor meals
Snacks
Thanksgiving dinners
Wedding meals

MECHANICS, Household
Ask Rufus; questions and answers. R. Cartwright. See issues of Mechanix illustrated
How to be a Mrs Fixit. il Redbook 134:53-4+ F '70
    See also
Repairing
MECHANIZATION, Agricultural. See Farm mechanization
MECHEM, Rose Mary. See Kirshenbaum, J. jt. auth.
MECHOULAM, Raphael
Marihuana chemistry. bibliog il Science 168: 1159-66 Je 5 '70
—and others
Chemical basis of hashish activity. bibliog Science 169:611-12 Ag 7 '70
MECKLENBURGER, James A.
Poetry pickle: some reflections. Engl J 59: 263-5 F '70
MECKLIN, John M.
Asia's great leap in textiles. il Fortune 82: 76-83+ O '70
Fire and steel for Palestine. il Fortune 82:84-9+ Jl '70
MECOM, John W.
Oilman Mecom taps the Chapter 10 field. por Bsns W p24 D 5 '70 *
MEDAL of freedom
Honors for giants of U.S. journalism.   U S News 68:43 My 4 '70
MEDALLIONS. See Medals
MEDALLIONS (costume jewelry) See Jewelry
MEDALS
Missing medal; commemoration of A. W. Hofmann's visit. D. H. Wilcox, jr. and W. D. Miles. bibliog il Chem 43:13 F '70
Religious medals; rare silver medal of first English archbishop. C. F. French. il Hobbies 75:132 N '70
    See also
Decorations of honor
    also names of medals, e.g. Caldecott medal

Collectors and collecting
Anti-slavery medallions in the Martin Jacobowitz collection. H. Aptheker. bibliog il Negro Hist Bul 33:114-21 My '70
MEDARIS, L. G. jr, and Dott, R. H. jr
Mantle-derived peridotites in southwestern Oregon; relation to plate tectonics. bibliog il Science 169:971-4 S 4 '70
MEDARY, Marjorie
Simplest clue. Horn Bk 46:635-41 D '70
MEDEIROS, Ethel Bauzer
Brazil: land of contrasts. il Parks & Rec 5:36-7 Ap '70
MEDEIROS, Humberto Sousa, abp
Change of the guard. il por Time 96:61 S 21 '70
    about
Passing the hat. il pors Newsweek 76:82 S 21 '70 *
MEDEROS, Rene
Cuban artist views North Vietnam. K. Wald. il Ramp Mag 8:21-7 Ap '70 *
MEDIATION, International. See Arbitration, International
MEDICAID
Commercializing the aged; nursing homes. R. E. Burger. il Nation 210:557-60 My 11 '70
Growing pains of medical care. F. Anderson. New Repub 162:17-18 Ja 17 '70 (to be cont)
High cost of health. il Sci N 97:170 F 14 '70
Medicare in trouble: Senate study of high costs, abuses; excerpts from report of the Senate finance committee. il U S News 68: 70-2 F 16 '70
MEDICAL art. See Medicine and art
MEDICAL assistants. See Medical workers
MEDICAL botany. See Botany, Medical
MEDICAL care. See Medical service
MEDICAL centers
    See also
Health centers
MEDICAL colleges
Grim diagnosis for medical schools. il Bsns W p82+ Jl 25 '70
Medical schools: portents of national health insurance. J. Walsh. Science 169:267-8 Jl 17 '70
Our ailing medical schools. L. Baker. il Sat R 53:56-7 D 19 '70
Threat to doctor supply: medical colleges going broke. il U S News 69:38-9 N 2 '70
    See also
Meharry medical college, Nashville, Tenn.
MEDICAL conferences
Peace corps physicians: reflections on the future. J. Walsh. il Science 169:1293-6 S 25 '70

MEDICAL consultants
    See also
Psychiatric consultants
MEDICAL delusions
Copper bracelets are a put-on. M. Michaelson. il Todays Health 48:27-9+ Je '70
Copper bracelets for arthritis: fraud or cure? Good H 171:181 O '70
Curious case of the copper band. G. Cant. il Sports Illus 33:37-41 Ag 3 '70
Music in the Jma al-Fna of Marrakesh. T. C. Grame. bibliog f Mus Q 56:74-87 Ja '70
MEDICAL education
Blueprint for reform of medical education; Carnegie commission report. il Sci N 98:363-4 N 7 '70
Calling Dr reform; proposals of the Carnegie commission on higher education. Newsweek 76:70 N 9 '70
Curing the doctor shortage; Carnegie commission plan. Time 96:38+ N 9 '70
Medical education: Carnegie panel urges expansion, acceleration. J. Walsh. Science 170:713-14 N 13 '70
Medical literature: the campus without tumult. F. J. Ingelfinger. bibliog Science 169: 831-7 Ag 28 '70
Revolution in medical care; address, June 24, 1970. W. C. Bornemeier. Vital Speeches 36: 632-4 Ag 1 '70
When a doctor needs a doctor; continuing education. B. Scott. il Todays Health 48: 54-5+ My '70
    See also
Medical colleges
Paramedical education
MEDICAL electronics
Benefits to medicine; bioastronautics. G. Gregory. il UNESCO Courier 23:16-24 Mr '70
Electronics and the heart. F. W. Holder. il Electr World 83:25-7 F '70
Myo-sybernetics; pacemaker-like device for muscle stimulation. F. W. Holder. il Electr World 85:39+ Ja '71
System trend in medical electronics. F. W. Holder. il Radio-Electr 41:61-3+ Mr '70
Will electronics solve the doctor shortage? il U S News 68:87-9 Je 15 '70
MEDICAL engineering. See Biomedical engineering
MEDICAL ethics
Larry: case history of a mistake. R. McQueen. Sat R 53:16-19+ S 12 '70; Same abr. il Read Digest 97:133-7 D '70
Open letter to American doctors: the abortion responsibility. America 122:490-1 My 9 '70
Privacy and the psychiatrist. por Time 95: 60+ Ap 27 '70
    See also
Embryology, Experimental—Moral and religious aspects
MEDICAL examinations. See Physical examinations
MEDICAL fees. See Medical service, Cost of
MEDICAL genetics. See Heredity of disease
MEDICAL geography
Hidden factors in the geography of cancer. N. Willard. il UNESCO Courier 23:27-9 My '70
Multiple sclerosis problem. G. Dean. il Sci Am 223:40-6 bibliog(p 136) Jl '70
MEDICAL hypnosis.   See Hypnotism—Therapeutic use
MEDICAL instruments and apparatus
Engineers apply skills to medical devices; heat transfer projects. il Todays Health 48:13 Ag '70
Machines to help the doctor. il U S News 69:20-1 Jl 6 '70
Mechanics of medicine. A. Freese. il Pop Mech 133:110-13+ Ap '70
    See also
Medical electronics
Respiratory apparatus

Standards
Medical devices: an unhealthy situation. Consumer Rep 35:256-9 Ap '70
Regulating medical devices. Sci N 97:500 My 23 '70
MEDICAL insurance. See Insurance, Health
MEDICAL journalism. See Journalism, Medical
MEDICAL jurisprudence
Controversy over the pill. B. Surface. il por Good H 170:64-5+ Ja '70
    See also
Malpractice
MEDICAL laws and legislation
    See also
Transplantation of organs, tissues, etc.—Legal aspects

MEDICAL libraries
See also
Harvard university—Medical school—Library
United States—National library of medicine
MEDICAL literature
See also
Medicine—Periodicals
MEDICAL news
Medical briefs. See issues of Today's health
Medical literature: the campus without tumult.
F. J. Ingelfinger. bibliog Science 169:831-7
Ag 28 '70; Reply. F. Silber. 170:388-9 O 23
'70
Point of view. M. Fishbein. Science 167:148
Ja 9 '70
Today's health news. A. L. Blakeslee. See
issues of Today's health
MEDICAL personnel. See Medical workers
MEDICAL photography. See Photography, Med-
ical
MEDICAL practice. See Medicine—Practice
MEDICAL relief work

Nigeria

Good news from Nigeria; SR's mobile medical program. N. Cousins. il Sat R 53:22 Mr
14 '70
Last flight out of Biafra; Saturday review's
Aid to Biafran children and the evaluation
project. N. Cousins. Sat R 53:22+ Ja 24
'70

Vietnam (Republic)

Beyond the call of duty in Vietnam. K. Y.
Tomlinson. il Read Digest 96:97-102 Je '70
Woman doctor is missing in action. J. C.
Hefley. il Todays Health 48:38-41+ Ap '70
MEDICAL research
Fighting disease: the latest advances. il U S
News 69:46 D 14 '70
More progress against the killer diseases.
U S News 69:20-1 Jl 6 '70
On the life sciences; address, March 5, 1970.
J. Mayer. Vital Speeches 36:402-7 Ap 15
'70
Primate populations and biomedical research.
C. H. Southwick and others. bibliog il Sci-
ence 170:1051-4 D 4 '70
Social consequences of new developments in
medicine. A. Leaf. Bul Atom Sci 26:21-2 Ja
'70
See also
Cancer research
Dental research
Diabetes research
Drugs, Experimental

Experimentation on man

Compensating persons injured in human experimentation. C. C. Havighurst. bibliog
il Science 169:153-7 Jl 10 '70
Should experimentation on prisoners be
stopped? pro and con discussion. il Sr Schol
95:11-12 N 3 '69

Anecdotes, facetiae, satire, etc.
Up the laboratory. N. Gittelson. Harp Baz
103:16-17+ Je '70

International cooperation

U.S.-Japan medical science committee meets
at Tokyo. Dept State Bul 63:388 O 5 '70
U.S.-Japan medical science program report
transmitted to Congress; President Nixon's
letter of transmittal; March 31, 1970. R.
Nixon. Dept State Bul 62:637 My 18 '70
MEDICAL schools. See Medical colleges
MEDICAL science. See Medicine
MEDICAL secretaries
Unrecognized professional; community mental
health secretary. L. Lomba. Ment Hy 54:
149-51 Ja '70
MEDICAL self-help training. See First aid in
illness and injury
MEDICAL service
Crisis in health care. il Time 95:54 Mr 30 '70
Delivery of medical care. S. R. Garfield. il
Sci Am 222:15-23 bibliog(p 130) Ap '70
Egeberg says health plan in works. J. Walsh.
Science 169:1295 S 25 '70
Flying black medics. il Ebony 25:81-4+ Je
'70
Growing pains of medical care. F. Anderson.
New Repub 162:15-18 Ja 17; 13-16 Ja 24;
17-19 F 7 '70; Discussion. 162:36-9 Mr 21 '70
Health care Rx for change; symposium. il
Sat R 53:17-32+ Ag 22 '70; Discussion. 53:
23+ O 17 '70
Health crisis. E. T. Chase. Commonweal 92:
243-5 D 4 '70; Reply. J. M. Langone. 93:
363 Ja 15 '71
In sickness and in health; definitions of ill-
ness, disease and medical care. E. J.
Cassell. Commentary 49:49-66 Je '70

Insurance is not enough. G. A. Silver. Na-
tion 210:680-3 Je 8 '70
Is there any way out of our health care mess?
F. Bailey. il Bet Hom & Gard 48:48-9+ N '70
Patient as non-starter. G. A. Silver. Na-
tion 212:55-6 Ja 11 '71
Revamping health care; planning ambulatory
service. Sci N 97:267-8 Mr 14 '70
Senate health care report. Sci N 97:480 My 16
'70
Surge in surgery. Sci Am 222:60 Mr '70
Why you really can't get good medical care.
C. Remsberg and B. Remsberg. Good H
170:68-71+ F '70
See also
Helicopters in medical service
United States—Public health service

Bibliography

Failure of American medicine. M. G. Michaelson. Am Scholar 39:694+ Aut '70

Russia

Soviet medicine: the world's most socialized
health system; with a report on the sur-
geon-general, A. A. Vishnevsky, by R.
Chelminski. B. Ray. il Life 68:38-48 Ja 23
'70
MEDICAL service, Cost of
Behind rising cost of health care. il U S
News 68:63 Mr 16 '70
Health care costs; the need for drug research;
address, April 8, 1970. J. J. Powers, jr.
Vital Speeches 36:478-80 My 15 '70
I can afford to be sick. W. A. Nolen. il Esquire 73:118-19+ Ap '70
Inflated health insurance costs. America 122:
177 F 21 '70; Reply. T. J. Weiler. 122:285
Mr 21 '70
Inflation and ideology; physicians abuse of
medicaid systems. Chr Cent 87:228-9 F
25 '70; Discussion. 87:538 Ap 29 '70
Medical inflation goes under the knife. Bsns
W p26-7 Ap 4 '70
Move abroad and live. Nation 210:68-9 Ja 26
'70
$60-billion crisis over medical care; with edi-
torial comment. il Bsns W p50-1+, 118 Ja 17
'70
65+ medical costs $590, 21 per cent rise: non-
elderly bill $195, up 10 per cent. Aging 182:
12 D '69
See also
Hospital care—Cost
Mental health service, Cost of

Anecdotes, facetiae, satire, etc.

Archaic bellyaches about doctors' fees; ex-
cerpt from Curiosities of medical ex-
perience. J. G. Millingen. il Todays Health
48:32-4 Ag '70
MEDICAL service, State
$60-billion crisis over medical care; with edi-
torial comment. il Bsns W p50-1+, 118 Ja
17 '70
TRB from Washington; towards socialized
medicine. New Repub 162:6 Ja 17 '70
See also
Medicaid
Medicare
MEDICAL social work
See also
Health centers
MEDICAL societies
See also names of medical societies, e.g.
American cancer society
MEDICAL specialists. See Specialization in
medicine
MEDICAL students
See also
Negro medical students
MEDICAL students, Women
Medical sexists; study findings of Harold I.
Kaplan. il Newsweek 76:82 O 19 '70
MEDICAL superstitions. See Medical delusions
MEDICAL supplies
Medical supplies. Consumer Rep 34:357-9 D
'69
See also
Hospitals—Equipment and supplies
MEDICAL technologists. See Medical workers
MEDICAL ultrasonics. See Ultrasonic waves—
Medical use
MEDICAL workers
Once a medic, now a medex; new medical
program in the state of Washington. il
pors Life 68:67-8+ Je 12 '70
Paramedics: new doctors' helpers; training
programs for doctors' assistants. il Time 96:
38 N 9 '70

MEDICAL workers—*Continued*
℞ for the family-doctor shortage; the Medex proposal. W. C. Bornemeier. Read Digest 97:103-7 Jl '70
Will your next doctor be a doctor? M. Michaelson. il Todays Health 48:37-41+ Mr '70

Training

Health care: fund shortage impedes training of medical aides. J. Kramer. Science 169: 956-60 S 4 '70

MEDICARE
Alive but not well. M. Schechter.   New Repub 163:15-17 Jl 11 '70
Cheaper medicare, latest official plan; health-maintenance contracts. il U S News 68:62 Ap 13 '70
Commercializing the aged; nursing homes. R. E. Burger. il Nation 210:557-60 My 11 '70
High cost of health. il Sci N 97:170 F 14 '70
Limiting medicare costs. Sci N 97:241 Mr 7 '70
Medicare deductible and hospital costs will be increased in January. T. Schuchat. Har Yrs 10:4 N '70
Medicare in trouble: Senate study of high costs, abuses; excerpts from report of the Senate finance committee. il U S News 68: 70-2 F 16 '70
Medicare kills off its cost predictor. il por Bsns W p27 Je 6 '70
Medicare payments go to $5.30 this month. Har Yrs 10:5 Je '70
Medicare's extended facilities. R. R. Jalbert. Har Yrs 10:45-6 Mr '70
New medicare regulations tighten hospital standards, ease payments. T. Schuchat. Har Yrs 10:4 O '70
Scandal in medicare? il U S News 68:6 F 9 '70
Social security and medicare explained. R. Krumme. il Suc Farm 68:no5 42-3 Mr '70
MEDICATED feed. See Feeding and feeding stuffs—Medicated feed
MÉDICI, Emilio Garrastazú
Affluent cage. Newsweek 76:56+ N 23 '70 *
MEDICINAL plants. See Botany, Medical
MEDICINE
Keep up with medicine. B. Yuncker. See issues of Good housekeeping
Medical sciences. See issues of Science news
Medicine. A. J. Snider. See issues of Science digest
Medicine today. P. Wright and D. R. Zimmerman. See issues of Ladies' home journal
News from the world of medicine. See issues of Reader's digest
What's ahead in medicine? M. R. Swift. il Parents Mag 45:25-7+ Ja '70
See also
Atomic medicine
Biomedical engineering
Diagnosis
Indians of North America—Medicine
Information storage and retrieval systems—Medicine
Medical research
Physiology
Radio in medicine
Space medicine
Specialization in medicine
Television in medicine

Bibliography

Books to come: ed. by J. Donathan. Library J 95:919-35+, 2552-71 Mr 1, Jl '70
Books to come. Library J 95:3813-15+ N 1 '70
Scientific, technical, business and medical highspots; international list. Pub W 198: pt2 146-56 S 21 '70

Group practice

Growing pains of medical care. F. Anderson. New Repub 162:13-16 Ja 24 '70
Solving the doctor shortage. C. M. Cobb. il Sat R 53:24-6+ Ag 22 '70

Periodicals

Medical literature: the campus without tumult. F. J. Ingelfinger. bibliog Science 169:831-7 Ag 28 '70; Reply. F. Silber. 170:388-9 O 23 '70

Practice

Can doctors cause disease? N. Cousins. Sat R 53:30-2 Ag 22 '70; Discussion. 53:23+ O 17 '70
Meet the family doctor for the 70's. M. Michaelson. il pors Todays Health 48:50-3+ My '70
See also
Malpractice
Medical service
Physicians and patients

Social aspects

Social consequences of new developments in medicine. A. Leaf. Bul Atom Sci 26:21-2 Ja '70

Study and teaching

See also
Medical education
Moving pictures in medicine

Superstitions

See Medical delusions

Brazil

Retreads in Rio; world capital of vanity surgery. Time 95:71 Mr 23 '70

Mexico

Healing in the Sierra Madre. D. Werner. il pors Natur Hist 79:60-7 N '70

Nepal

Modern medicine comes to ancient Nepal. E. D. Nadel. il por Todays Health 48:28-33+ My '70

Russia

State of Soviet medicine. J. Schecter. il Time 96:43-4 O 5 '70

Switzerland

Medical miscellany; hip operation at Wilhelm Schulthess klinik in Zürich. N. S. Hazelton. Nat R 22:845 Ag 11 '70

United States

Country's no. 1 health problem; interview. R. Egeberg. il pors U S News 68:68-73 F 23 '70
Looking at medicine. W. C. Alvarez. Look 34:8 Ag 11; 12-13 S 22; 42 D 15 '70
See also
American medical association
MEDICINE, Adolescent. See Youth—Health and hygiene
MEDICINE, Atomic. See Atomic medicine
MEDICINE, Military
See also
United States—Army—Medical and sanitary affairs
Vietnamese war, 1957- —Medical and sanitary affairs
MEDICINE, Popular
Curanderismo, Mexican-American folk psychiatry, by A. Kiev. Review
Américas 22:42 Mr '70. J. Philips
MEDICINE, Preventive
Can companies reduce heart attacks? J. Smith. il Duns 95:51-2+ Ap '70
Growing pains of medical care. F. Anderson. New Repub 162:13-16 Ja 24 '70
See also
Heart—Diseases—Prevention
MEDICINE, Primitive
Antitumor activity in mice of tentacles of two tropical sea annelids. F. L. Tabrah and others. bibliog il Science 170:181-3 O 9 '70
Healing in the Sierra Madre. D. Werner. il pors Natur Hist 79:60-7 N '70
See also
Medicine men
MEDICINE, Psychosomatic
Say it with a stomachache. S. Olds. il Todays Health 48:41-3+ N '70
Your emotions: can they influence disease? adaptation of address, November 1, 1969. H. B. Miller. il Sci Digest 68:61-4 Jl '70
MEDICINE, State. See Medical service, State
MEDICINE, Veterinary. See Veterinary medicine
MEDICINE and art
Checkup; interpretation of a medical checkup by a conceptual artist. D. Burgy. il pors Art in Am 58:108-11 Mr '70
MEDICINE and geography. See Medical geography
MEDICINE and religion
Violence and nonviolence in the cure of disease and the healing of patients. M. Wilson. Chr Cent 87:756-8 Je 17 '70
MEDICINE men
New eyes for Tom Large Whiskers. W. C. Heinz. il pors Todays Health 48:30-3+ S '70
MEDICINES, Patent, proprietary, etc.
Tiger oil tries to treat the world; Haw Par brothers international, ltd. il Bsns W p52 F 21 '70
See also
Richardson-Merrell, inc.
MEDIEVAL art. See Art, Medieval
MEDIEVAL music. See Music, Medieval

MEDINA, Ernest L.
And then there were ten. Newsweek 75:37+
Mr 23 '70 *
How the war is fought? il por Newsweek 76:
18-20 D 28 '70 *
My Lai chain. por Time 95:13 Mr 23 '70 *

MEDINA, Johnnie. See Barker, C. jt. auth.

MEDINA-SIDONIA, duchess of
Eight months in Franco's jail. Nation 210:
396-9 Ap 6 '70

MEDITATION
Making brain waves; findings of Japanese
scientists. il Newsweek 75:92-3 Mr 23 '70
Marcuse's eroticized man: a new synthesis of
action-contemplation. R. Hindery. por Chr
Cent 87:136-8 F 4 '70
Meditation: an open way to serenity of mind
and body. S. K. Majumdar. Vogue 156:
105+ Jl '70
Physiological effects of transcendental meditation. R. K. Wallace. bibliog il Science
167:1751-4 Mr 27 '70
Your very own meditator; dodecahedral structure. K. Isaacs. il Pop Sci 197:92-4+ N '70

MEDITERRANEAN furniture. See Furniture,
Mediterranean

MEDITERRANEAN REGION
Bold coasts and castled islands; Gibraltar to
Sardinia in Mercator. J. Hart. il Yachting
127:64-6+ Je '70
Russia: toward a global reach. il Time 96:29-
30 O 5 '70
Russian and American pilots play chicken;
maneuvers of the Sixth fleet in the Medi-
terranean. W. H. Honan. il N Y Times
Mag p25-7+ N 22 '70
Russians in the Mediterranean. E. von Kueh-
nelt-Leddihn. Nat R 22:891 Ag 25 '70; Re-
ply. I. C. Kidd, jr. 22:1192 N 17 '70
Soviet Mediterranean push deepens; with edi-
torial comment. E. H. Kolcum. il Aviation
W 92:9; 14-18 Mr 30 '70
Top fleet in the Mediterranean: U.S. or Rus-
sian? il U S News 69:19 O 12 '70
See also
Communism—Mediterranean Region
Middle East

Description and travel
Land where lemons grow. F. Grunfeld. il
Holiday 47:48-9+ Ja '70

MEDITERRANEAN SEA
Any port in a showdown; pact with Spain;
U.S. Sixth fleet. L. Fernsworth. il Nation
211:489-91 N 16 '70
Mediterranean may dry up. Sci Digest 69:72
Ja '71
Mountain-building in the Mediterranean. Sci
N 98:316 O 17 '70
See also
Aegean Islands
Corsica
Geology—Mediterranean Sea

MEDIUMS
See also
Brown, R.

MEDNICK, Sarnoff A.
Breakdown in individuals at high risk for
schizophrenia: possible predispositional
perinatal factors. bibliog il Ment Hy 54:50-
63 Ja '70
Prenatal and birth complications linked by
schizophrenia research. J. Moriarty and L.
Massett. il por Scn N 98:15-16 Jl 4 '70 *

MEDVEDEV, Zhores Aleksandrovich
Scientific breakdown. il por Newsweek 75:
44+ Je 15 '70 *
Very special case; release. il por Newsweek
75:47 Je 29 '70 *

MEEHAN, Thomas
Flight from reason. Il Horizon 12:4-10 Spr '70
Fun art. il Horizon 11:4-15 Aut '69
Let 'em eat coquilles Saint-Jacques. il N Y
Times Mag p6-7+ D 27 '70
Pied Piper. New Yorker 46:25-8 Jl 4 '70
Rob and Barbi go brownstoning. il N Y Times
Mag p32-3+ N 22 '70
Washington society isn't exactly swinging.
il N Y Times Mag p30-1+ Mr 8 '70

MEEK, George
(comp) Hemisphere. See issues of Américas

MEEK, Russell
Black karate: new concept of ancient art. il
pors Ebony 25:104-6+ Je '70 *

MEEKER, John J.
Aristocrat of the winter crops. il pors Org
Gard & Farm 17:34-8 S '70
Bountiful shallots. il Org Gard & Farm 17:
48-50 F '70

MEEKS family
Meekses west and south. E. Gaines. il
Antiques 98:127 Jl '70

MEETING; story. See Borges, J. L.

MEETINGHOUSES, Shaker. See Churches,
Shaker

MEETINGS
See also
Parliamentary practice
Stockholders meetings

MEEUS, Jean
Some bright visual binary stars. il Sky & Tel
41:21-5 Ja '71 (to be cont)

MEFISTOFELE; opera. See Boito, A.

MEGALITHIC monuments
Megalithic plan underlying Canterbury cathe-
dral. L. B. Borst; discussion. bibliog Sci-
ence 164:769-70; 166:772-4; 167:333 My 16,
N 7 '69, Ja 23 '70
Megalithic rings: their design construction.
T. M. Cowan. bibliog il Science 168:321-5
Ap 17 '70; Reply. N. Grossman. 169:1228-9
S 18 '70
Superhenge; ritual significance of British
superhenges. Sci Am 222:58 My '70
See also
Stonehenge, England

MEGALOPOLIS. See Metropolitan areas

MEGGYESY, Dave
Football racket; excerpt from Out of their
league. il Look 34:66+ N 17; 64-6+ D 1 '70
Rebel with a cause. P. Axthelm. il pors Newsweek 76:68+ N 16 '70 *

MEGLIN, Nick
John Gundelfinger draws from life; excerpt
from On-the-spot drawing. il Am Artist 35:
56-62 Ja. '71

MEHARRY medical college, Nashville, Tenn.
New spirit at old Meharry. il Ebony 25:42-
6+ Ap '70

MEHDI Mahboubian art collection. See Art—
Private collections

MEHL, Hermann
Chaplain's politics. por Newsweek 76:70 Ag
10 '70 *

MEHLE, Aileen
Cost of conducting an affair. Vogue 155:70-1
F 15 '70
Suzy. L. Hershey. il por Ladies Home J 87:
80-1+ S '70 *

MEHLINGER, Kermit
(ed) See Davis, D. K. Sister debates a brother on that black man-white woman thing
(ed) See Gant, L. Sister debates a brother
on that black man-white woman thing

MEHTA, Ved
Profiles. Calcutta. New Yorker 46:47-52+ Mr
21 '70
Reporter at large (cont) New Yorker 45:
62+ F 14: 46:94+ Ap 11 '70

MEHTA, Zubin
Hit it. Zubin. il por Time 95:72 Je 1 '70 *
Musical events; concert by Los Angeles Phil-
harmonic in Carnegie Hall. W. Sargeant.
New Yorker 46:170-1 N 7 '70 *

MEIER, Donna
Fabric candles. il Design 71:36-7 Sum '70

MEIER, Richard
Westbeth and flexible code interpretations;
statement. il Arch Rec 147:106 Mr '70

MEIER, Richard L.
Metropolis and the transformation of resources. il Bul Atom Sci 26:2-5+ My '70

MEIGHAN, Clement W. and Haynes, C. V. Jr
Borax Lake site revisited. bibliog il Science
167:1213-21 F 27 '70

MEILACH, Dona Z.
(ed) See Engel, E. L. Postpartum care

MEINERTZHAGEN, Richard
Trade winds. C. Amory. Sat R 53:7 D 26 '70 *

MEINKE, Peter
Monkey's paw; poem. New Repub 162-21
Je 27 '70
Ode to good men fallen before hero come.
New Repub 162:19 Mr 28 '70
Surfaces: poem. New Repub 163:22 S 26 '70

MEINSCHEIN, W. G. and others
Search for alkanes of 15 to 30 carbon atom
length. bibliog Science 167:753 Ja 30 '70

MEIOSIS. See Cell division (biology)

MEIR, Golda
Dissenters. Newsweek 75:36-8 Mr 2 '70 *
Missile impasse. il por Time 96:26 S 28 '70 *
Most dangerous arena. il por Time 96:23 Jl
13 '70 *
Visitors from Israel. Time 96:14 S 21 '70 *
While Jordan burned; U.S. visit. il por News-
week 76:20-1 S 28 '70 *

MEISENBERG, Sheldon
Making money work. See issues of Harvest
years, May 1970-

MEISLER, Stanley
Reports: Kenya. Atlan 225:26+ Mr '70
Tribal politics harass Kenya. For Affairs 49:
111-21 O '70
Zambia. Atlan 226:32+ S '70

MEISSNER, William W.
Loyalty and dissent: a psychiatrist's report.
America 122:681-2 Je 27 '70

MEISTRICH, Marvin L. and others
Phototropism in phycomyces as investigated by focused laser radiation. bibliog il Science 169:370-1 Jl 24 '70
MELAMED, Monte
Day camp busing. il Camp Mag 42:17-18 My '70
Transportation guide for camp directors. il Camp Mag 42:18+ Mr '70
MELANCHOLY
Anatomy of melancholy. A. Burgess. il por Horizon 12:48-53 Aut '70
MELANCHTHON, Philipp
Melanchthon and Bucer, ed. by W. Pauck. Review
Chr Cent 87:273 Mr 4 '70. W. H. Lazareth
MELANIE
Warm welcome for a human campfire. A. Goldman. por Life 69:18 O 16 '70 *
MELANIN
Crabs that change color overnight; fiddler crab. il Chem 43:27 Ap '70
MELARO, Constance
Mass communication. Sat R 53:9-10 D 19 '70
MELATONIN
Melatonin synthesis adenosine 3',5'-monophosphate and norepinephrine stimulate N-acetyltransferase. D. C. Klein and others. bibliog il Science 168:979-80 My 22 '70
Pineal gland: dibutyryl cyclic adenosine monophosphate stimulation of labeled melatonin prodction. D. C. Klein and others. bibliog il Science 167:1738-40 Mr 27 '70
Pituitary serotonin content: effects of melatonin or deprivation of water. R. S. Piezzi and R. J. Wurtman. bibliog il Science 169:285-6 Jl 17 '70
MELBOURNE, Australia
Airports
Melbourne seeking gateway role. B. Miller. il Aviation W 93:71-2 Ag 24 '70
Description
Kangaroos, Koalas, and me. D. Butwin. il Sat R 53:34-5 Ag 15 '70
MELCHIOR, Lauritz
Speaking of Wagner; interview, ed. by G. Fitzgerald. por Opera N 34:6-9 Mr 28 '70
about
Duet of the century. W. Zakariasen. il pors Hi Fi 20:secI 52-6 Jl '70 *
MELGES, Frederick T. and others
Marihuana and temporal disintegration. bibliog il Science 168:1118-20 My 29 '70
MELL, Albert
Antonio Lolli's letters to Padre Martini. bibliog f il Mus Q 56:463-77 Jl '70
MELLAN, Olivia
Black English. New Repub 163:15-17 N 28 '70
MELLINGER, Frederick
Passion fashion. il por Time 96:31 Ag 17 '70 *
MELLINGER, Marie B.
Mushrooms of the mountains. il Nat Parks & Con Mag 44:15-18 S '70
MELLON, Paul
Man of arts and letters. P. Ryan. il por Sports Illus 32:58-62+ Mr 16 '70 *
Powerhouse. il Newsweek 76:102 O 12 '70 *
Trophy of tenacity. il por Time 96:64 O 12 '70 *
MELLON, Richard King
Death of a king. il por Time 95:96 Je 15 '70 *
MELLOW, James R.
Exhibition preview: four Americans in Paris. il pors Art in Am 58:84-91 N '70
MELNICK, Norman
Twenty years by the sea: the Music academy of the West. il Opera N 34:8-12 F 7 '70
Two against Rafferty. New Repub 162:11-12 Mr 21 '70
MELODRAMA
Dissolves by gaslight: antecedents to the motion picture in nineteenth-century melodrama. J. L. Fell. bibliog il Film Q 23:22-34 Spr '70
MELONS
Put your melons in new ground. S. Fenell. il Org Gard & Farm 17:72-3 Ap '70
See also
Watermelons
MELSON, William G.
America's sleeping volcanoes. il Nat Wildlife 8:39-47 D '69; Same. Sci Digest 68:40-4 Ag '70
—and Thompson, Geoffrey
Layered basic complex in oceanic crust, Romanche fracture, equatorial Atlantic Ocean. bibliog il Science 168:817-20 My 15 '70
MELTON, Ellen
(ed) See Gernreich, R. Fashion will go out of fashion

MELTON, George E. and Stanavage, John
Job specifications for principals. Ed Digest 36:25-8 O '70
MELTON, Marjorie L. See Sheffield. H. G. jt. auth.
MELTZER, Herbert. See Engel. W. K. jt. auth.
MELVILLE, George.   See Harshman, J. jt. auth.
MELVILLE, Herman
Art of Herman Melville: the author of Pierre. R. J. Nelson. Yale R 59:197-214 D '69 *
MELVILLE shoe corporation
Melville shoe: selling excitement, not shoe leather. il Forbes 107:26 Ja 1 '71
More for Melville; Chess King clothing store. A. A. Butkus. por Duns 95:64+ My '70
MELVIN, A. Gordon
Natural history. See issues of Hobbies
MELVIN, Kenneth
Democracy on the brain. Nat R 22:410+ Ap 21 '70
MELVIN, Robert
Corporate n*gg*r. J. Sack. il por Esquire 74:90-4+ Jl '70 *
MEMBERS of Congress for peace through law
Cutting the Pentagon down to size; 1970 report. R. E. Lapp. New Repub 163:16-20 Ag 22 '70
MEMBERS of Parliament
Don't call us; former Labor party members. il Newsweek 76:37-8 Ag 31 '70
MEMBRANE lipids. See Lipids
MEMBRANE transport systems. See Biological transport
MEMBRANES (biology)
Acetylcholine sensitivity of muscle fiber membranes: mechanism of regulation by motoneurons. D. M. Fambrough. bibliog il Science 168:372-3 Ap 17 '70
Adenohypophysial transmembrane potentials: polarity reversal by elevated external potassium ion concentration. J. V. Milligan and J. Kraicer. bibliog il Science 167:182-4 Ja 9 '70
Cancer and electrical voltage. il Chem 43:24 Je '70
Charges on the cell membrane. Sci N 97:312-13 Mr 28 '70
Colicin-tolerant mutants of escherichia coli: resistance of membranes to colicin El. P. Bhattacharyya and others. bibliog il Science 168:998-1000 My 22 '70
Expanding on a classic view; role of cell membranes in cancer. B. J. Culliton. il Sci N 97:509-10 My 23 '70
Human glomerular basement membrane: chemical alteration in diabetes mellitus. P. J. Beisswenger and R. G. Spiro. bibliog il Science 168:596-8 My 1 '70
Influenza virus effects on cell membrane proteins. J. J. Holland and E. D. Kiehn. bibliog il Science 167:202-5 Ja 9 '70
Inside-out red cell membrane vesicles: preparation and purification. T. L. Steck and others. bibliog il Science 168:255-7 Ap 10 '70
Intercellular communication. W. R. Loewenstein. il Sci Am 222:78-84+ bibliog(p 148) My '70
Junctional membrane permeability: restoration by repolarizing current. R. Birgit. bibliog il Science 169:607-9 Ag 7 '70
Macrophage membranes viewed through a scanning electron microscope. A. H. Warfel and S. S. Elberg. bibliog il Science 170:446-7 O 23 '70
Moving molecules across membranes. B. J. Culliton. il Sci N 98:42-3 Jl 11 '70
Plasmalemmal and subsurface complexes in human leukemic cells: membrane bonding by zipperlike junctions. F. T. Sanel and A. A. Serpick. bibliog il Science 168:1458-60 Je 19 '70
Proteins in excitable membranes. D. Nachmansohn. bibliog il Science 168:1059-66 My 29 '70; Discussion 170:1228-9, 1332-3 D 11-18 '70
Similarity and limited multiplicity of membrane proteins from rough and smooth endoplasmic reticulum. N. D. Hinman and A. H. Phillips. bibliog il Science 170:1222-3 D 11 '70
Vacuolar perfusion technique for nitella internodal cells. T. H. Strunk. bibliog il Science 169:84-7 Jl 3 '70
See also
Blood-brain barrier
MEMBRANES (technology)
Antagonism by DDT of the effect of valinomycin on a synthetic membrane. B. D. Hilton and R. D. O'Brien. bibliog il Science 168:841-3 My 15 '70; Reply. F. Matsumura. 169:1343 S 25 '70
Bimolecular (black) lipid membranes: study of lipid-protein interactions. E. Smekal and others. bibliog il Science 168:1108-9 My 29 '70

MEMBRANES (technology)—*Continued*
Charge-mosaic membranes: dialytic separation of electrolytes from nonelectrolytes and amino acids. J. N. Weinstein and R. S. Caplan. bibliog il Science 169:296-8 Jl 17 '70
Gathering of specialists; tackling the problems of artificial organs. B. J. Culliton. il pors Sci N 97:347-9 Ap 4 '70
Hindered diffusion in microporous membranes with known pore geometry. R. E. Beck and J. S. Schultz. bibliog il Science 170:1203-5 D 18 '70
Ice sandwich: functional semipermeable membrane. R. D. Miller. il Science 169:584-5 Ag 7 '70
Keeping track of planes by 3-D; membrane mirror. S. V. Jones. Sci Digest 67:87 My '70

MEMO pads. See Memorandum pads

MEMOIR in the form of a novel; story. See Vidal, G.

MEMORANDUM pads
Wall mounted memo pad. G. Manning. il Motor B 125:180-1 My '70

MEMOREX corporation
Danger: handle with care. il Forbes 106:26-7 O 15 '70

MEMORIAL arches. See Arches, Triumphal and memorial

MEMORIAL concerts. See Concerts

MEMORIAL day
U.S.A. up, up and away; Decoration day weekend. W. Johnson. il Sports Illus 32:22-7 Je 8 '70

MEMORIAL forests. See Forest management

MEMORIAL sculpture. See Sepulchral monuments

MEMORIAL tablets. See Sepulchral monuments

MEMORIALS
See also
Crazy Horse (Sioux Indian)—Statues, portraits, etc.
Lincoln memorial, Washington, D.C.
Monuments
Sepulchral monuments
Washington, G.—Memorials

MEMORY
Can chemicals stimulate learning capacity? L. Ernst. Ed Digest 35:32-3 My '70
Forgetting: trace erosion or retrieval failure? R. M. Shiffrin. bibliog il Science 168:1601-3 Je 26 '70
How we remember what we see. R. N. Haber. il Sci Am 222:104-12 My '70
Incubation effects in behavior induction in rats. A. M. Golub and others. bibliog il Science 168:392-5 Ap 15 '70; Reply with rejoinder. J. A. Corson. 169:1342 S 25 '70
Interanimal memory transfer: results from brain and liver homogenates. B. Frank and others. bibliog il Science 169:399-402 Jl 24 '70
Interference and forgetting in bird and fish. E. R. Behrend and others. bibliog il Science 167:389-90 Ja 23 '70
Lack of coincidence between neural and behavioral manifestations of cortical spreading depression. T. J. Carew and others. bibliog il Science 169:1339-42 S 25 '70
Marihuana and temporal disintegration. F. T. Melges and others. bibliog il Science 168:1118-20 My 29 '70
Mind research: the promise and the peril; protein synthesis in the brain. F. Warshofsky. Read Digest 96:119-23 Ap '70
Of mice and memory; isolation of memory-activating substance from brain. Newsweek 75:86 F 23 '70
See also
Amnesia
Aphasia
Attention
Eidetic imagery
Past, The
Recognition (psychology)
Reminiscence

MEMORY bank; drama. See Duberman, M.

MEMORY devices (computers)
All at a glance; optical memory elements. il Sci N 98:477-8 D 26 '70
Bubble memories start taking shape. Bsns W p26-7 N 21 '70
Computer memories; symposium. il Electr World 84:37-60 O '70
IC memories, growth and future. D. Mrazek. bibliog il Electr World 83:25-9+ Mr; 34-6+ Ap '70
Monolithic mass memory design studied. B. M. Elson. Aviation W 92:62+ F 23 '70
More muscle for minicomputers; Iomec's disk drive. il Bsns W p 130+ Ap 18 '70
New tape devices cut cost of speed. Bsns W p70 O 31 '70

Semiconductor memories evolve. B. M. Elson. il Aviation W 92:38-40 Je 15 '70
Speed-of-light computer memory; electro-optical memories. Bsns W p49 Ap 4 '70
Understanding random-access memories. J. E. McAlister. il Electr World 84:34 N '70
Why cores could become just a memory. il Bsns W p60-1 D 26 '70
See also
Precision instrument company
Technitrol, inc.

MEMORY expert; story. See Stanley, E.

MEMORY tree; story. See Chidester, A.

MEMPHIS, Tenn.

Education
Behind the bad behavior; Elementary guidance and psychological services project. J. Chisum. il Am Ed 6:32-4 Ag '70
Hub of the instructional program; Sheffield high school. R. Clay. il Am Lib 1:170-2 F '70

Parks and playgrounds
Overton park. J. L. Franson. il Audubon 72:121 Ja '70

MEMPHIS, Tenn. public library
Confrontation in Memphis. C. L. Wallis; discussion. Library J 94:4102-3; 95:189-90 N 15 '69. Ja 15 '70

MEMPHIS state university book store. See College bookstores

MEN
The enemy. D. Newman and R. Benton. il Mlle 70:222-3 F '70
Gents' auxiliary; a men's liberation movement. Newsweek 76:75-6 Jl 20 '70
Mademoiselle; features and fiction special issue. il Mlle 71:57+ Jl '70
Male in crisis by K. Bednarik. Review Sat R 53:31-3+ Je 6 '70. H. Gold
See also
Boys
Businessmen
Christmas gifts for men
Cookery by men
Great men
Sex differences

Clothing
See Clothing and dress—Men

Health and hygiene
How to murder your husband. J. Mayer. Read Digest 97:132-4 Ag '70
How to shape up your husband; Golden door for men's weeks. C. Duhé. il Vogue 155:160-1+ Je '70
Steps in the right direction; fitness in woodsplitting, walking and running. R. F. Capon. il Sports Illus 33:46-8+ Ag 31 '70; Same abr. Read Digest 97:124-6 D '70
See also
Businessmen—Health and hygiene

Psychology
How to support your husband's ego. J. L. Collier. Read Digest 96:108-11 Ja '70
Men in groups, by L. Tiger. Review Trans-Action 7:57-8 My '70. R. J. Simon
What it's really like to be a man. A. Brien. Mlle 71:57+ Jl '70
What makes a man lovable? T. I. Rubin. Read Digest 96:21-4 Ja '70
See also
Masculinity (psychology)

MEN and women. See Women and men

MENAKER, Michael. See Underwood, H. jt. auth.

MENARCHE. See Puberty

MENDEL, Arthur
Reviews of records. il Mus Q 56:133-42 Ja '70

MENDELS, Franklin F.
Recent research in European historical demography. Am Hist R 75:1065-73 Ap '70

MENDELS, Ora
New help for children who stutter. il Parents Mag 45:80-1+ N '70

MENDELSON, Jack H. See Majchrowicz, E. jt. auth.

MENDELSON, Joseph, and Chillag, Dana
Tongue cooling: a new reward for thirsty rodents. bibliog il Science 170:1418-21 D 25 '70

MENDELSSOHN, Felix
As nearly perfect as anything. G. S. Fox. Am Rec G 36:332 Je '70 *
For once, early Mendelssohn with all his youthful enthusiasm. D. W. Moore. Am Rec G 36:286-8 D '69
More impressive than most: the disc debut of Pinchas Zukerman. M. N. Kanny. Am Rec G 36:436 F '70 *
Spring song. R. Fisher. il por Opera N 34:8-13 Ja 31 '70

MENDEZ, C. See Wulff, V. J. jt. auth.

MENDEZ, Louis G. jr
Right to read leaders and a message from Louis G. Mendez, jr, director. por Wilson Lib Bul 45:240-1 N '70

MÉNDEZ ARCEO, Sergio, bp
Profiles; I. Illich. F. Du Plessix. por New Yorker 46:49-50+ Ap 25 '70 *

MENDING tape
Mending tapes. il Consumer Rep 35:602-3 O '70

MENDOTA, LAKE
Lake that ate too much. M. Michaelson. il Todays Health 48:42-3+ Ag '70

MENDOZA Y AMOR, Benjamin
Apostle endangered. il pors Time 96:55 D 7 '70 *
Pope's perilous journey. il por Newsweek 76:44+ D 7 '70 *
Would-be killer: an avenging angel. Newsweek 76:47 D 7 '70 *

MENEN, Aubrey
Italian family is a commune. il N Y Times Mag p22-3+ Mr 1 '70
Leptis Magna. il Holiday 47:66-8 F '70
Quiet Italy. il Holiday 48:28-9+ Jl '70
Taj Mahal: monument to love? il Holiday 47:64-5+ Ap '70
Why French students riot; situation at Nanterre. il N Y Times Mag p26-7+ Ap 26 '70

MENÉNDEZ PIDAL, Ramón
Menéndez Pidal, J. de M. de Carvalho. il pors Américas 22:2-6 Ja '70

MENHART, Oldrich
Oldrich Menhart, outstanding Czech type designer; excerpts from address. P. Standard. il por Pub W 197:52-4 Ja 12 '70

MENINGES
Glucose production by lamprey meninges. C. M. Rovainen. bibliog il Science 167:889-90 F 6 '70

MENINGITIS
Vaccines
Closing in on three killers. il Bsns W p 107+ O 24 '70

MENINGOENCEPHALITIS. See Encephalitis

MENN, Gregory
Gifts of Gregory Menn. J. P. Blank. Read Digest 97:108-12 Ag '70 *

MENNONITES
Amishville U.S.A. tourist farm near Berne, Ind. B. Thomas. il Travel 134:46-51 O '70
Pioneer nonconformists. R. Chandler. Chr Today 14:44-6 S 11 '70
Regulating compassion. L. K. Tarr. Chr Today 14:37 F 13 '70

MENOPAUSE
Menopause, something to look forward to? S. Olds. il Todays Health 48:48-9+ My '70

MENOTTI, Gian Carlo
Help, help, the Globolinks! Criticism
Dance Mag 44:86 Mr '70 *

MENS beauty shops. See Beauty shops
MENS clothes. See Clothing and dress—Men
MENS hairdressing. See Hairdressing
MENS liberation movement. See Men
MENS parties. See Entertaining
MENS underwear. See Underwear

MENSTRUATION
Hormones during the menstrual cycle; ed. by S. Olds. R. B. Jaffe. Redbook 134:12 Mr '70
Cessation
See Menopause

MENSWEAR industry. See Clothing industry
MENTAL arithmetic. See Arithmetic, Mental
MENTAL depression. See Depression, Mental
MENTAL development of children. See Children—Growth and development
MENTAL development of infants. See Infants—Growth and development
MENTAL health. See Mental hygiene
MENTAL health, National association for. See National association for mental health, inc.
MENTAL health centers
Community accountability and mental health services. S. K. Schiff. bibliog Ment Hy 54:205-14 Ap '70
Distance and the use of the mental health clinic by community professionals. F. V. Mannino and others. bibliog il Ment Hy 54:73-8 Ja '70
How not to be a consultant. A. Hodges. bibliog Ment Hy 54:147-8 Ja '70
Mental health center revisited to evaluate design effects; Marin County community mental health center. il Arch Rec 147:116-18 Mr '70

New centers at state hospitals designed for rehabilitation, not custody; Rehabilitation center, Middletown state hospital, Middletown, N.Y. il Arch Rec 147:154-6 Ja '70
Patients helping patients; friendship club at Boulder mental health center. D. Hawxhurst and H. Walzer. bibliog Ment Hy 54:370-3 Jl '70
Perspective on community mental health and community psychiatry. F. H. Frankel. bibliog Ment Hy 54:155-8 Ja '70
Storefront psychiatry: Maimonides mental health center, Brooklyn. il Sci Digest 68:35-6 Jl '70

MENTAL health clinics. See Psychiatric clinics
MENTAL health consultation. See Psychiatric consultation
MENTAL health counselors
Mental health professionals' hang-ups in training mental health counselors. D. S. Shapiro. bibliog Ment Hy 54:364-9 Jl '70
MENTAL health laws
Development of community mental health programs in the civil area. A. A. Woloshin and J. Goldberg. bibliog Ment Hy 54:13-19 Ja '70
New York's mental hygiene law: a preliminary evaluation. A. Zitrin and others. bibliog Ment Hy 54:28-36 Ja '70
Struggle for patients' rights in a state hospital. L. C. Suchotliff and others. bibliog Ment Hy 54:230-40 Ap '70

Bibliography
Law and the mentally ill. H. A. Davidson. Ment Hy 54:180-5 Ja '70
MENTAL health secretaries. See Medical secretaries
MENTAL health service
Clergyman's role and community mental health. W. G. Scarlett. Ment Hy 54:378-81 Jl '70
Community in community mental health. E. B. Back. bibliog Ment Hy 54:316-20 Ap '70
Community mental health: a new search for social orientation. J. S. Bockoven. Ment Hy 54:172-9 Ja '70
Correlating the Fifteen indices with hospital achievement awards. A. D. Pokorny. Ment Hy 54:575-6 O '70
Developing an inner city mental health association. L. B. Bower and B. Elam. Ment Hy 54:215-20 Ap '70
Development of community mental health programs in the civil area. A. A. Woloshin and J. Goldberg. bibliog Ment Hy 54:13-19 Ja '70
Mental hospital employees and social action. E. M. Straight and others. Ment Hy 54:241-6 Ap '70
Organization of mental health services and its effect on the treatment of career of the patient. R. W. Brissenden and H. L. Lennard. bibliog Ment Hy 54:416-20 Jl '70
Program evaluation: a proposed model for mental health services. A. M. Wellner and others. bibliog il Ment Hy 54:530-4 O '70
Solving problems in living: the citizen's viewpoint. W. B. Eddy and others. bibliog il Ment Hy 54:64-72 Ja '70
Starting a mental health association. C. Baron. Ment Hy 54:247-50 Ap '70
Store-front churches in the inner city; helping recently arrived migrants adapt to urban living. L. S. Sata and others. bibliog Ment Hy 54:256-60 Ap '70
Voluntary mental health association: an innovator of services. R. J. Hartford. Ment Hy 54:97-100 Ja '70
See also
Psychiatric clinics

International aspects
Mental health and social action programs for children and youth in international perspective. H. P. David. bibliog Ment Hy 54:503-9 O '70

MENTAL health service, Cost of
Fees and mental health services: attitudes of the professional. C. D. Dightman. bibliog Ment Hy 54:401-6 Jl '70
MENTAL health workers. See Health workers
MENTAL health workers, Volunteer. See Health workers, Volunteer
MENTAL hospital achievement awards. See American psychiatric association
MENTAL hospitals. See Hospitals, Psychiatric

MENTAL hygiene
Mental health library offers looseleaf service. Library J 95:1432-3 Ap 15 '70
Primary prevention: a challenge to mental health associations. M. VanAntwerp. bibliog Ment Hy 54:453-6 Jl '70
Solving problems in living: the citizen's viewpoint. W. B. Eddy and others. bibliog il Ment Hy 54:64-72 Ja '70
    See also
Adjustment, Social
Businessmen—Health and hygiene
Child guidance clinics
Child psychiatry
College students—Adjustment
Joint commission on mental health of children
Neurotics anonymous
Psychiatric clinics
Psychotherapy
School children—Adjustment
Worry

Bibliography
Book reviews. See issues of Mental hygiene

History
Mental health in and out of public health. D. A. Berlin. bibliog Ment Hy 54:288-94 Ap '70
Romance and rodomontade of comprehensive community mental health. A. A. Woloshin and E E. Dennis. bibliog Ment Hy 54:280-7 Ap '70

Study and teaching
Case studies of volunteer programs in mental health. L. J. Cowne. Ment Hy 54:337-46 Jl '70
Education of the community mental health assistant: dovetailing theory with practice. M. E. Danzig. Ment Hy 54:357-63 Jl '70
MENTAL hygiene as a profession
New professionals. A. F. Willcox. bibliog Ment Hy 54:347-56 Jl '70
MENTAL illness
Mental illness' leading cause. il Sci Digest 67:55-6 Ap '70
Postpartum psychiatric reactions: time of onset and sex ratio of newborns. F. T. Melges; reply. M. A. Taylor. Science 168:151-2 Ap 3 '70
Twin to witchcraft. D. Brudnoy. Nat R 22:469-70 My 5 '70
What is a nervous breakdown? E. Kendall and A. Talmey. Vogue 156:144-5 N 15 '70
    See also
Mental hygiene
Neuroses
Paranoia
Psychiatry
Psychoses
Schizophrenia

Diagnosis
Identifying emotional disturbance in persons seen in industrial dispensaries. B. M. Rosen and others. bibliog Ment Hy 54:271-9 Ap '70

Terminology
    See also
Psychiatry—Terminology

Therapy
    See Psychotherapy
MENTAL suggestion. See Suggestion
MENTAL tests. See Intelligence tests
MENTALL, J. E. See Gentieu, E. P. jt. auth.
MENTALLY handicapped

Rehabilitation
Need for differentiation in rehabilitating the mentally retarded. E. Harms. Ment Hy 54:457-8 Jl '70
MENTALLY handicapped children
    See also
Brain damaged children
Mentally ill children
Slow learning children

Education
Art for the mentally retarded child. M. N. Steinhauser. il Sch Arts 69:30-1 Mr '70
Unscarred wounded; aphasic children. J. W. Purcell. il PTA Mag 64:18-20+ F '70
    See also
Libraries—Services to mentally handicapped
Slow learning children—Education
MENTALLY ill
Patients nobody wants. W. B. Grant. Ment Hy 54:162-5 Ja '70
Personality characteristics of mental health center patients classified by referral source. R. A. Apostal and J. H. Halcrow. bibliog Ment Hy 54:295-7 Ap '70

Release of the chronic psychiatric patient. W. H. Clayton. bibliog Ment Hy 54:407-10 Jl '70
Social adequacy of state mental hospital patients. C. Bentinck and others. bibliog Ment Hy 54:421-4 Jl '70

Care and treatment
Beer for the aged. il Time 95:53 Je 29 '70
Four techniques in dealing with psychotic disorders in the outpatient clinic. J. Christ and S. Goldstein. Ment Hy 54:105-8 Ja '70
From psychiatric hospital to nursing home. M. K. Cunningham and others. Ment Hy 54:109-12 Ja '70
Is basket weaving harmful? Time 96:57 O 12 '70
Mental hospital patient-consumer as a determinant of services. T. Ishiyama. Ment Hy 54:221-9 Ap '70
B for a short beer; treating elderly mental patients. il Newsweek 75:72 My 25 '70
Using the discharge interview to evaluate a psychiatric hospital. P. Keith-Spiegel and others. Ment Hy 54:298-300 Ap '70
    See also
Hospitals, Psychiatric
Mentally ill—Home care

History
Looking back; excerpts from articles. W. H. Stokes. Ment Hy 54:170-1 Ja '70

Civil rights
Radical view of social welfare and mental health. L. Ginsberg. Ment Hy 54:44-9 Ja '70

Employment
Three methods of contacting employers to obtain jobs for the rehabilitated psychiatric patient. A. Loeb and others. il Ment Hy 54:137-9 Ja '70

Home care
Foster mothers and mental patients W. S. Smitson. bibliog il Ment Hy 54:251-5 Ap '70

Legal status, laws, etc.
    See Mental health laws

Rehabilitation
Ex-patient as change agent. D. Blumberg. Ment Hy 54:159-60 Ja '70
Problems and needs in rehabilitation. S. S. Rosner. Ment Hy 54:144-6 Ja '70
Using an education model in a sheltered workshop program. D. Safier. Ment Hy 54:140-3 Ja '70
We need sheltered workshops for former mental patients. A. H. Cristol. Ment Hy 54:444-6 Jl '70
    See also
Group psychotherapy
MENTALLY ill children
Child called Noah. J. Greenfeld. il Life 69:60-2+ O 23 '70
    See also
Child psychiatry

Care and treatment
Developing a unified theory of residential treatment: development of treatment centers on the model of Pioneer house, Detroit. J. K. Whittaker. bibliog Ment Hy 54:166-9 Ja '70
Hospitalizing the young: is it for their own good? H. H. Weiss and E. F. Pizer. bibliog Ment Hy 54:498-502 O '70
Training child care staff: pitfalls and promises. J. K. Whittaker. Ment Hy 54:516-19 O '70

Rehabilitation
Moving the hard to move. D. Coogan and H. K. Kaplan. Ment Hy 54:520-4 O '70
MENTALLY retarded

Rehabilitation
    See Mentally handicapped—Rehabilitation
MENTOR; story. See Singer, I. B.
MENUHIN, Jeremy
Music to my ears; performance of Beethoven's C-minor concerto. Sat R 53:34 D 26 '70 *
MENUS
Classic meals that really please a man. il Good H 170:94-109 F '70
Eight festive menus. House B 112:136+ N '70
Menu magic; with recipes. M. Happel. il Ladies Home J 87:106-8+ Ap '70
[Month] menus; with recipes. See issues of Sunset

MENUS—_Continued_
Parties from the freezer; with recipes. M. M. Hemingway. House & Gard 137:129-32+ My '70
Poppy Cannon's meal-a-day menus. P. Cannon. See issues of Ladies' home journal
Things mother never taught you; menu planning. il Ladies Home J 87:84 Jl '70
See also
Breakfasts
Buffet meals
Camp cookery
Dinners and dining
Luncheons
Lunches
Thanksgiving dinners

MENZEL, David W. and others
Marine phytoplankton vary in their response to chlorinated hydrocarbons. bibliog il Science 167:1724-6 Mr 27 '70

MENZEL, Donald H. and Pasachoff, J. M.
Solar eclipse: nature's super spectacular. il Nat Geog 138:222-33 Ag '70

MEOLA, Eric
Gallery; photographs. il Life 69:8-9 S 18 '70
MEOS (native race) See Laos—Native races
MERAMEC RIVER
Death of a river. J. P. Jackson. il Nat Parks 44:19-22 F '70

MERAS, Phyllis L.
(ed) See Lester, J. Interview with Julius Lester

MERCADANTE, Saverio
Ozymandias of opera. F. Rizzo. il por Opera N 34:18-19 My 16 '70 *
MERCALLI scale. See Seismometry
MERCAPTANS
Reactions of alpha methylene lactone tumor inhibitors with model biological nucleophiles. S. M. Kupchan and others. bibliog il Science 168:376-8 Ap 17 '70
MERCAPTOPURINE
In vitro lymphocyte reactivity during depression of tuberculin hypersensitivity by 6-mercaptopurine. B. Zweiman and S. M. Phillips. il Science 169:284-5 Jl 17 '70
MERCE Cunningham dance company
Dance; Signals at the Brooklyn academy of music. N. Goldner. Nation 211:604 D 7 '70
Merce Cunningham and dance company, Brooklyn academy of music. D. Hering. il Dance Mag 45:70 Ja '71
Scenes from an unreachable world. M. Marks. il Dance Mag 44:30-3 Mr '70
MERCEDES (automobile) See Automobiles, Foreign
MERCENARY troops in Laos
Laos; next step in the Big Muddy. A. Cranston. Nation 210:363-6 Mr 30 '70
MERCER, Harry E.
Opals, anybody? il Travel 134:24+ Jl '70
Winning the west in Australia. il Travel 134:34-41 S '70
MERCHANDISE, Quality of. See Quality of products
MERCHANT, Jane
For many hearts; poem. Farm J 93:44 N '69
Very private world of Princess Anne. por Seventeen 29:122-3+ Je '70
MERCHANT, Larry
Bill Veeck is off to the races. il pors Look 34:68+ Je 30 '70
MERCHANT, Robert
Hunt we'll remember. il Outdoor Life 146:72-3+ S '70
MERCHANT marine
See also
Seamen
Training ships
Russia
Soviet bid for maritime power. il U S News 69:34-5 Jl 20 '70
United States
Britons waive rule to spare U.S. fleet. Bsns W p21-2 Mr 7 '70
Gambling on a sea change. Fortune 82:58 D '70
Merchant marine; address, May 12, 1970. H. D. Bentley. Vital Speeches 36:569-72 Jl 1 '70
Merchant navy gets a military role. il Bsns W p24 O 31 '70
300 new American ships coming. il U S News 69:37 N 2 '70
See also
United States—Maritime administration
MERCHANT of Venice; drama. See Shakespeare, W.—Plays

MERCHANTS, Jewish
Anecdotes, facetiae, satire, etc.
Men in mama's life. S. Levenson. il Ladies Home J 87:24+ My '70; Same abr. Read Digest 97:41-4 S '70
MERCKX, Eddy
Fast Eddy. il por Newsweek 76:49 Jl 27 '70 *
King of the road. il por Time 96:36-6 Ag 24 '70 *
MERCURY
Endangered Great Lakes; pollution by mercury. il Time 95:85 My 4 '70
Mercury; major new environmental problem. C. E. Parker. il Cons 25:6-9 Ag '70
New focus on mercury. il Chem 43:18-20 N '70
MERCURY (planet)
Mercury: the dark side temperature. T. L. Murdock and E. P. Nevy. bibliog il Science 170:535-7 O 30 '70
Surface
Mercury: surface features observed during radar studies. R. M. Goldstein. il Science 168:467-9 Ap 24 '70
MERCURY (planet), **Transit of**
Coming transit of Mercury. il Sky & Tel 39:232-3 Ap '70
Findings from Mercury's transit. J. Ashbrook. il Sky & Tel 40:20-4 Jl '70
Transit of Mercury. J. Stokley. il Sci N 97:418 Ap 25 '70
Transit of the planet Mercury. S. P. Opie. il Chem 43:23-4 D '70
Transit of the planet Mercury; with photographs by J. S. Korintus. S. P. Opie. Science 169:350-1 Jl 24 '70
MERCURY pesticides. See Pesticides
MERCURY poisoning
Annals of medicine; case of organic poisoning by pork from hogs fed surplus seed grain chemically treated. B. Roueché. New Yorker 46:64-70+ Ag 22 '70
Mad hatter visits Alice's restaurant. H. Martin. il Todays Health 48:39-43+ O '70
Mercury poisoning; prevention by spironolactone. H. Selye. bibliog il Science 169:775-6 Ag 21 '70
MERCURY pollution of rivers, lakes, etc.
And now, mercury. D. Zwerdling. New Repub 163:17-18 Ag 1 '70
Deadly mercury. Sports Illus 33:9 Jl 20 '70
Environmental mercury: rapid determination in water at nanogram levels. R. W. April and D. N. Hume. il Science 170:849-50 N 20 '70
Facts behind the mercury menace. J. T. Parker. il Pop Sci 197:62-3+ D '70
Grim pursuit of quicksilver; tightening of leaks by chlor-alkali producers. il Bsns W p42+ Jl 18 '70
Legal antidote for mercury pollution. Bsns W p31 Ap 25 '70
Mad hatter's legacy; Canadian export ban on fish. Newsweek 75:72 Ap 20 '70
Meddlesome mercury. il Sci N 99:7 Ja 2 '71
Mercury and mud. Sci Am 223:82+ S '70
Mercury compounds reduce photosynthesis by plankton. R. C. Harriss and others. bibliog il Science 170:736-7 N 13 '70
Mercury in Lake St Clair. Sci N 97:388 Ap 18 '70
Mercury; major new environmental problem. C. E. Parker. il Cons 25:6-9 Ag '70
Mercury mess. il Time 96:64 S 28 '70
Mercury poisoning; or, The fish you catch can kill you! Lake St Clair. J. J. Knap. Field & S 75:44-5+ Jl '70
Methyl mercury. P. H. Abelson. Science 169:237 Jl 17 '70
Poison roams our coastal seas. R. H. Boyle. il Sports Illus 33:70-4+ O 26 '70
Quicksilver crisis. il Newsweek 76:61 Ag 3 '70
Tainted tuna. Newsweek 76:42 D 28 '70
Ubiquitous mercury; in the sea. Sci N 98:366 N 7 '70
MERCURY probes. See Space probes
MERCURY switches. See Electric switches
MERCY college, Dobbs Ferry, N.Y.
In the works at Mercy. D. Grumbach. Commonweal 92:356-7 Jl 24 '70
MERCY killing. See Euthanasia
MEREDITH, Don
Don and Howard show. pors Time 96:59 D 14 '70 *
MEREDITH, George
George Meredith and English comedy, by V. S. Pritchett. Review
New Yorker 46:77-8 Ag 29 '70. W. Maxwell *

MEREDITH, Jeff
On with the dance at NYU: Jean Erdman seeks roots of style. il por Dance Mag 44: 44-9 Ap '70
MEREDITH, Nancy G.
When parents divorce. il Parents Mag 46: 44-5+ Ja '71
MEREDITH, Scott
Positive view of literary auctions. Pub W 198:27-8 O 26 '70
MEREDITH, Scott, literary agency
Positive view of literary auctions. S. Meredith. Pub W 198:27-8 O 26 '70
MEREDITH, William
I poems and You poems. R. W. French. Nation 210:695-6+ Je 8 '70 *
Reading my poems from World war II; poem. Poetry 115:343 F '70
MERGERS.   See Business consolidations and mergers
MERILLAT, Emile, pseud.
Making money work; questions and answers. See issues of Harvest years to April 1970
MERIMEE, Thomas J. See Fineberg, S. E. jt. auth.
MERINGUE
It's sweet up on top, it's tart down below. il Sunset 145:192+ N '70
M-m-m-m-meringue; Spanish wind torte. C. Claiborne. il N Y Times Mag p88 My 17 '70
MERIT for leadership awards. See American city (periodical)
MERIT pay. See Teachers—Salaries, allowances etc.
MERIT rating of employees. See Employees— Rating
MERIWETHER, Louise
Daddy was a number runner; excerpts. il por Ebony 25:98-103 Jl '70
MERMELSTEIN, Neil H.
Sweat is almost obsolete. Todays Health 48: 40-1+ Je '70
MERONEY, Elmo B.
Glass blowing. il Parks & Rec 5:34-5+ Ja '70
MEROVKA, Larry
Hunting our all-American bird. il Field & S 74:74-5+ Mr '70
MERRELL, Jack G.
No shortcuts; excerpts from address. Aviation W 92:13 Ap 6 '70
MERRETT, Anthony
Dow 1000? Forget it. por Forbes 106:51-2 S 15 '70 *
MERRIAM, John H.
Idaho White Clouds: wilderness in trouble. il Liv Wildn 34:33-7 Spr '70
MERRIAM, Lawrence C. Jr
Potential for parks in Paraguay. il Nat Parks & Con Mag 44:10-12 Je '70
MERRICK, David
Must smut smother the stage? Read Digest 96:103-5 Mr '70
What's needed to revive Broadway; interview. pors U S News 68:83-4 My 4 '70
MERRILL, James
In nine sleep valley; poem. New Yorker 46:34-5 Ag 1 '70
Syrinx; poem. Harper 241:93 S '70
MERRILL, Robert
Merrill's milestone. H. E. Phillips. il por Opera N 35:14-16 Ja 9 '71 *
Musician of the month. por Hi Fi 20:MA8 O '70 *
MERRILL Lynch, Pierce, Fenner and Smith, inc.
Last act in the cliff-hanger? Wall Street rescue of brokerage house. il Time 96:78 N 9 '70
Merrill Lynch still wants small investors. il Bsns W p90-4 Ap 4 '70
Merrill Lynch to the rescue? Bsns W p21 O 31 '70
Thundering Herd to the rescue. il Newsweek 76:73 N 9 '70
MERRIMACK RIVER
If Mr Thoreau calls, tell him I've left the country. R. Mungo. il Atlan 225:72-82+ My '70
MERRIMAN, Daniel
Calefaction of a river; with biographical sketch. il Sci Am 222:10, 42-52 My '70
MERRIMAN, John. See Dahlstrom, M. jt. auth.
MERRITT, James D.
Harlot form. il Opera N 35:6-7 Ja 9 '71
MERRITT, LeRoy Charles
Obituary
Am Lib por 1:638 Jl '70
MERRITT, Vernon, 3d
Tom Sawyer boyhood, 1970 style; photographs. pors Life 69:50-7 O 9 '70
Victory for beauty; photographs. il Life 68: 48-55 Ap 10 '70

MERRIWEATHER, Thelma. See Johnson, H. jt. auth.
MERRY, Ruth Peirce
Color from bearded iris. il Horticulture 48: 28-9+ My '70
Evergreen daylilies. Horticulture 48:26-7 Ag '70
MERRY-go-rounds
Antique carousel revived; Magic mountain, Calif. il Design 72:14-16 Wint '70
MERRYMAN, Donald
Mobile educational technology. il Am Lib 1:162-4 F '70
MERTES, Ivan
Television's built-in test signals. il Electr World 83:38-41 Mr '70
MERTON, Thomas
Holy child's song. Vogue 156:111-12 D '70

about

Keys to ourselves. J. Kessler. pors Sat R 53:34-5 My 2 '70 *
Merton and Auden. T. Materer. pors Commonweal 91:577-80 F 27 '70; Reply with rejoinder. M. G. Walsh. 92:51+ Mr 27 '70 *
Two cities of Thomas Merton. J. T. Baker. Cath World 211:151-5 Jl '70 *
MERTZ, Edwin T. See Deutsch, D. G. jt. auth.
MERWIN, W. S.
Fear; poem. New Yorker 46:35 Ag 22 '70
Five poems: Judgment of Paris; Mountains; Black plateau; Now it is clear; Hands. New Yorker 46:38-9 Je 6 '70
Forebears; poem. Harper 241:6 D '70
Fountain; story. New Yorker 46:28-31 Jl 11 '70
Four poems: Cerements; Web; Letter; Shore. New Yorker 46:40-1 S 12 '70
Four poems: The place of backs; Spring; Letter to the heart; The borrowers. Nation 211:378 O 19 '70
Gardens of Zuñi; Homeland; Western country; poems. Harp Baz 103:110-11 Je '70
Inscription facing western sea; Calling under the breath; Sunset after rain; In the time of the blossoms; Sadness; poems. Poetry 116:71-5 My '70
Late night in autumn; poem. Harper 241: 75 Jl '70
Looking back; Something I've not done; At the same time; Tool; Memory of the loss of wings; poems. Poetry 117:179-82 D '70
Old story about a path; story. New Yorker 46:42-3 My 2 '70
On each journey; poem. Harper 240:51 My '70
Removal; poem. Harp Baz 103:138-9 Ap '70
Roofs. New Yorker 46:89-90 Ap 18 '70
Snowfall; poem. New Yorker 46:34 Mr 14 '70
Three stories: The visitor; Ethel's story; June couple. New Yorker 46:31-2 Jl 25 '70
We have nothing to fear; story. New Yorker 46:34-6 F 28 '70
Wedding march; story. New Yorker 45:39 F 14 '70
(tr) See Ghalib. Ghazals

about

Poetry of darkness. R. Howard. Nation 211: 634-5 D 14 '70 *
MERYMAN, Richard
Flake and the old man. il pors Life 68:54-6+ Mr 6 '70
Mood and feeling. Mlle 72:190+ N '70
(ed) See Hoffman, D. Old age of Dustin Hoffman
(ed) See Horne, M. Tour of two great throats
(ed) See Sutherland, J. Tour of two great throats
MESCALINE
Banality of the new evil; games the survivors play. W. Kloman. il Esquire 73:115-17+ Mr '70
MESELSON, Matthew S.
Behind the Nixon policy for chemical and biological warfare; excerpts from testimony before the Senate committee on foreign relations, April 30, 1969. Bul Atom Sci 26:23-4+ Ja '70
Chemical and biological weapons; with biographical sketch. il Sci Am 222:10, 15-25 My '70

about

Herbicides in Vietnam: AAAS study runs into a military roadblock. P. M. Boffey. Science 170:42-5 O 2 '70 *
MESIC, Michael
(tr) See Mimnermus. On old age
(tr) See Pushkin, A. S. Echo

MESINGER, Maxine
(ed) See Piazza, M. Struggle for life itself
MESONS
Fundamental nuclear interaction. A. E. S.
Green. bibliog il Science 169:933-41 S 4 '70
Puzzle of the A2 meson. P. Schübelin. bibliog
il Phys Today 23:32-8 N '70
Puzzle of two-pion production: is the pion a
point charge? G. B. Lubkin. il Phys Today
23:17+ D '70
Trouble from N*. Sci N 98:96 Ag 1 '70
US-Soviet collaboration to measure pion
charge radius. B. G. Lubkin. Phys Today
23:18-19 S '70
MESQUITE, Tex.

Stores
TownEast: the integration of shopping and
entertainment. il Arch Rec 147:124-7 Mr '70
MESSERSMITH, Andy
Lots of stuff and no nonsense. R. Blount, jr.
il por Sports Illus 32:22-4+ My 18 '70 *
MESSIAEN, Olivier
Birds of heaven. H. Saal. pors Newsweek 76:
138 N 23 '70 *
MESSIAH
Jewish conception of the Messiah. J. Garten-
aus. Chr Today 14:8-10 Mr 13 '70
Martin Buber on Jesus: a Jewish reading. D.
J. Moore. il America 122:630-3 Je 13 '70
MESSICK, Tom
Tiny wonders. il Design 72:9 Wint '70
MESSIER catalog. See Stars—Catalogs
MESSINESI, Despina
Travel. See occasional issues of Vogue
MESSMER, Richard P.
Polywater: possibility of p-electron delocali-
zation. bibliog Science 168:479-80 Ap 24 '70
MESTER, Jorge
Why I didn't become a heart specialist. por
Hi Fi 20:31 O '70

about
Musician of the month. S. Fleming. il por
Hi Fi 20:secII 8-9 Ag '70 *
MESTHENE, Emmanuel G.
Technology, change and the citizen; ex-
cerpts from Technological change. Cur
119:32-6 Je '70
MESTROVIC, Matthew M.
Changing the guard in Poland. Commonweal
93:364-5 Ja 15 '71
Tito & the Pope. Commonweal 93:36-7 O 9 '70
West Germany turns to the East. Common-
weal 91:444-5 Ja 23 '70
METABOLISM
Allopurinol: alteration in pyrimidine metab-
olism in man. W. N. Kelley and T. D.
Beardmore. bibliog il Science 169:388-90
Jl 24 '70
Intestinal hydrolysis and conjugation of a
pesticidal carbamate in vitro. J. C. Pekas
and G. D. Paulson. bibliog il Science 170:77-
8 O 2 '70
Magnetism to metabolism; physics, chem-
istry Nobels. Sci N 98:348 O 31 '70
Proinsulin: metabolic effects in the human
forearm. S. E. Fineberg and T. J. Merimee.
bibliog il Science 167:998-9 F 13 '70
Weight and the weed; research at Temple
university school of medicine. il Newsweek
76:62 Jl 27 '70
See also
Bacteria—Metabolism
Bioenergetics
Calcium metabolism
Carbohydrate metabolism
Deficiency diseases
Drugs—Metabolism
Oxidation, Physiological
METABOLISM, Disorders of
Hyperphenylalaninemia: disaggregation of
brain polyribosomes in young rats. K. Aoki
and F. L. Siegel. bibliog il Science 168:129-30
Ap 3 '70
Inborn errors of mucopolysaccharide meta-
bolism. E. F. Neufeld and J. C. Fratan-
toni. bibliog il Science 169:141-6 Jl 10 '70
Lactosyl ceramidosis: catabolic enzyme de-
fect of glycosphingolipid metabolism. G.
Dawson and A. O. Stein. bibliog il Science
170:556-8 O 30 '70
Orotidinuria induced by allopurinol. R. M.
Fox and others. bibliog il Science 168:861-2
My 15 '70
Scheie and Hurler syndromes: apparent
identity of the biochemical defect. U.
Wiesmann and E. F. Neufeld. bibliog il
Science 169:72-4 Jl 3 '70
See also
Angiokeratoma
Diabetes
Goiter
Gout
Lesch-Nyhan syndrome
Porphyria

METAL cleaning
See also
Sand blast
Ultrasonic cleaning
METAL coating
Applied aluminum finishes: guidelines for
specifiers. W. W. Binger; R. C. Spooner:
A. H. Bushey. il Arch Rec 147:151-2 My '70
See also
Teflon
METAL crystals
Filamentary crystal growth associated with
impact craters from hypervelocity micropar-
ticles. O. E. Berg and J. A. M. McDonnell.
il Science 168:320-2 My 15 '70
METAL cutting tools
Snips story. R. J. De Cristoforo. il Mech Illus
66:70-1+ D '70
Toothbrushes keep cutters clean. W. E.
Burton. il Pop Mech 134:177 Jl '70
METAL detectors
How science will foil the skyjackers. P.
Wahl. il Pop Sci 197:58-60+ N '70
Metal locators. il Consumer Bul 53:29-33+ Mr
'70
New, light, ultra-sensitive treasure finder.
il Pop Sci 197:47 Ag '70
Searching for weapons. Sci N 98:271 S 26 '70
METAL fibers
Fiber composite alloys: preparation by con-
trolled dissociation of metallic solid solu-
tions. A. Fesolowich and others. bibliog il
Science 167:1374-6 Mr 6 '70
METAL finishing
Applied aluminum finishes: guidelines for
specifiers. W. W. Binger; R. C. Spooner:
A. H. Bushey. il Arch Rec 147:151-2 My '70
How to put the right finish on lathe proj-
ects. W. E. Burton. il Pop Mech 133:194-
8+ Ap '70
METAL foam. See Metals, Cellular
METAL industry and trade
Metal men tune up for homebuilding. il Bsns
W p42-3 Ja 9 '71

Finance
Metals: with yardsticks of management per-
formance. il Forbes 105:133-4+ Ja 1 '70; 107:
85+ Ja 1 '71
METAL locators. See Metal detectors
METAL oxide semiconductor integrated cir-
cuits. See Electronic circuits, Integrated
METAL protection
See also
Corrosion and anticorrosives
METAL scrap. See Scrap metal
METAL sculpture
Closing the gaps; work of A. Caro. J. Rus-
sell. il Art N 69:37-9 My '70
Critic's choice: Serra. E. C. Baker. il Art N
68:26-7 F '70
Miro's bronze age. J. Ashbery. il Art N 69:
34-6 My '70
Parking lot sculptor. por Design 71:41 Spr
'70
Portrait in steel. J. Jacquard. il pors De-
sign 71:16-18 mid-Wint '70
Sculpture by order: T. Smith's Snake. il por
Time 96:72 S 14 '70
METAL trade. See Metal industry and trade
METAL work
Iron forged. W. Fuhrmann. il por Craft Horiz
30:40-1 O '70
Solder, braze, or weld? Motor B 125:176-7
My '70
See also
Art metal work
Brass work
Ironwork
Tinware
Welding
METALLIC films. See Films, Metallic
METALLOORGANIC compounds. See Organo-
metallic compounds
METALLOPHONE
It's not a xylophone, it's a metallophone. il
Sunset 145:90 D '70
METALLURGY
See also
Alloys
Extrusion process
Metals—Heat treatment
Powder metallurgy
METALLURGY, Prehistoric
Creativity of ancient man. F. Keller and
J. Zimmerman. il Chem 43:17-19 Jl '70
METALS
See also
Alloys
Transition metals
also names of metals, e.g. Antimony

Coating
See Metal coating

METALS—*Continued*

Heat treatment
Heat treating metals. E. Nabb. Motor B 126: 14+ N '70

METALS, Cellular
Foam metals finally rise to the surface. Bsns W p24 S 12 '70

METALS, Liquid
Tricky metals that cool it; NaK alloy coolant system. il Bsns W p 112 N 7 '70

METALS, Nonferrous
Metals; with yardsticks of management performance. il Forbes 105:133-4+ Ja 1 '70; 107:85+ Ja 1 '71

Prices
Nonferrous prices start to corrode. il Bsns W p21-2 Jl 18 '70

METALS in building
Metal men tune up for homebuilding. il Bsns W p42-3 Ja 9 '71

METALS in the body
Concern about pollution of toxic metals. Chem 43:21 N '70
See also
Manganese in the body

METAMORPHIC rocks. See Rocks, Crystalline and metamorphic

METAMORPHISM (geology)
Apollo 11 lunar science conference: fine particles, glasses, and shock effects; symposium. bibliog il Science 167:641-79 Ja 30 '70
Metamorphic waters from the Pacific tectonic belt of the West coast of the United States. I. Barnes. bibliog il Science 168:973-5 My 22 '70

METAMORPHOSIS
Biochemical differentiation during amphibian metamorphosis. P. P. Cohen. bibliog il Science 168:533-43 My 1 '70
Magic of metamorphosis. E. M. Reilly, jr. il Cons 24:22-6+ F '70
Teacher tips: metamorphosis. J. A. Weeks. bibliog il Cons 24:27-8+ F '70
Those remarkable two-animal animals. R. Platt. il Read Digest 97:33-4+ Jl '70

METAMORPHOSIS (insects) See Insects—Development

METAPHYSICS
See also
Consciousness

METCALF, Mary
Stephen Greene press. il Pub W 198:20 N 23 '70

METCALF, Robert L.
Bug as garbage man. Time 96:36 D 21 '70 •
—See Booth, G. M. jt. auth.

METEOR spectroscopy. See Astronomical spectroscopy

METEORITES
Amino acids in a meteorite. Sci N 98:429 D 5 '70
Amino acids in a meteorite. Sky & Tel 41: 27 Ja '71
April meteorite coincidences. Sky & Tel 40: 138 S '70
Carbon isotope fractionation in the Fischer-Tropsch synthesis and in meteorites. M. S. Lancet and E. Anders. bibliog il Science 170:980-2 N 27 '70
Electronics & meteorites. L. G. Lawrence. bibliog il Electr World 84:23-6+ Jl '70
Endogenous carbon in carbonaceous meteorites. J. W. Smith and I. R. Kaplan. bibliog il Science 167:1367-70 Mr 6 '70
Go, and catch a falling star; Smithsonian astrophysical observatory's Prairie network. Sci N 97:60 Ja 17 '70
Life out there. il por Newsweek 76:118 D 14 '70
Lost City meteorite, a deep-space probe for cosmic rays. E. L. Fireman. il Sky & Tel 39:158 Mr '70
Lost City meteorite fall. R. E. McCrosky. il por Sky & Tel 39:154-8 Mr '70
Magnetic particles extracted from manganese nodules: suggested origin from stony and iron meteorites. R. B. Finkelman. bibliog il Science 167:982-4 F 13 '70
Mars Viking mission given new impetus; amino acids in meteorite. R. G. O'Lone. Aviation W 93:21 D 7 '70
Matter of life: finding amino acids in meteorites. por Time 96:68-9 D 14 '70
Oklahoma asteroid: Lost City meteorite. Sci Am 222:59-60 Mr '70
On meteorites. il Chem 43:21 Je '70
Pyroxene-garnet transformation in Coorara meteorite. J. V. Smith and B. Mason. bibliog il Science 168:832-3 My 15 '70
Traces of life in meteorites claimed. Chem 43:24-5 F '70
See also
Tektites

METEOROLOGICAL buoys. See Oceanographic buoys

METEOROLOGICAL instruments
See also
Barometers

METEOROLOGICAL research
Antarctic meteorology. M. J. Rubin. il por Bul Atom Sci 26:48-54 D '70
See also
Artificial satellites—Meteorological use
Balloons, Meteorological
Polar research
Rain making
Weather control
Weather research

METEOROLOGISTS
See also
Wragge, C. L.

METEOROLOGY
Analyzing atmospheric behavior. H. Panofsky. bibliog il Phys Today 23:32-3+ D '70
See also
Atmosphere, Upper
Atmospheric nucleation
Auroras
Balloons, Meteorological
Climate
Clouds
Computers—Meteorological use
Electronics in meteorology
Radar meteorology
Snow
Television in meteorology
Thunderstorms
Tornadoes
United States—National weather service
Weather
Weather forecasts
Winds

History
Espy-Redfield dispute. D. M. Ludlum. pors Weatherwise 22:224-9+ D '69

International cooperation
Antarctic meteorology. M. J. Rubin. il por Bul Atom Sci 26:48-54 D '70

METEOROLOGY, Aeronautic
Meteorology and the supersonic transport. F. G. Finger and R. M. McInturff; reply. A. A. Few. Science 168:1011 My 22 '70
Pro's nest; getting the weather. T. H. Block. Flying 87:94-5 D '70
Whence weather wisdom. A. Trammell. Flying 87:30 S '70
See also
Radar meteorology
United States—Federal aviation administration—Weather message switching center

METEOROLOGY, Agricultural
See also
Plants, Effect of climate on

METEOROLOGY, Maritime
Effect of wind sheer. A. Hemenway. il Yachting 127:62-3+ Je '70
Fetching Bermuda; how meteorology and oceanography helped Robin win in 1968. J. Chase. il Yachting 127:56-7+ Je '70
How to be weather-wise, without being a meteorologist. T. Helsiva. il Motor B 125: 108-10 Mr '70
On the heavy weather race; interview, ed. by E. Horan. D. Clark. il por Yachting 128:82+ Jl '70
Wind & weather. See issues of Motor boating to May 1970
See also
Ocean-atmosphere interaction

METEORS
Geminid meteors in 1969. il Sky & Tel 39:202-3 Mr '70
Meteor fragments. E. E. Friton. R Pop Astron 63:2 Ag '69
Meteor heights and meteor streams. il Sky & Tel 40:89 Ag '70
Meteor showers at the turn of the year. Sky & Tel 40:398 D '70
Notes on the 1970 Perseid shower. J. Ashbrook. il Sky & Tel 40:325-9 N '70
2,304,333 meteors. il Sky & Tel 39:223 Ap '70

METER (standard of length) See Metric system

METER, Musical. See Musical meter and rhythm

METER maids. See Parking meter inspectors

METER reading
How they'll read your utility meter by phone. S. Shatavsky. il Pop Sci 196:100 Ap '70
Meter reading by telephone. Bsns W p86 D 12 '70
Meters: Victor Lombardo, Con Ed reader on his rounds. New Yorker 45:21-4 Ja 17 '70

METER reading—*Continued*
600 meters per day; Ontario, Ohio. R. Berry-hill. il Am City 85:107-8 S '70
Speed up water billing, simply; Eastern municipal water district, Hemet, Calif. il Am City 85:62-3 N '70

METERS
See also
Electric meters
Exposure meters
Odometers
Photographic meters
Radiometers

METHADONE
Cracks in the panacea. Sci N 97:366-7 Ap 11 '70
Help from methadone. Newsweek 75:52 Je 8 '70
Lesser evil. il Time 97:60 Ja 4 '71
Methadone: a drug to lick a drug? F. Warshofsky. Read Digest 96:88-92 My '70
Methadone and heroin addiction: rehabilitation without a cure. J. Walsh. Science 168:684-6 My 8 '70
Methadone: the law and the clinics. R. O'Mara. Nation 211:242-4 S 21 '70
On treating drug addiction with methadone. Cur 120:35-8 Ag '70

METHEDRINE. See Amphetamines

METHODIST church
See also
United Methodist church

METHODIST church in England
At the Center. T. Beeson. Chr Cent 87:1553-4 D 30 '70
See also
Church union—Great Britain

METHODIST church in India
Some Methodists reject union. J. V. Koilpillai. Chr Cent 87:1397-8 N 18 '70

METHODIST church in the United States
Holiness in Cincinnati; first national Wesleyan gathering. J. Adams. Chr Today 14:37 Ja 30 '70
Kansas City Methodists: horse of a different color; missions to the Black Panthers. J. S. Tinney. Chr Today 14:41 Ap 24 '70
See also
United Methodist church

METHODIST church of Great Britain. See Methodist church in England

METHODOLOGY
See also
Problem solving

METHOTREXATE
Prescribing without approval; use of methotrexate in treatment of psoriasis. Sci N 97:549 Je 6 '70

METHVIN, Eugene H.
How the Mafia preys on the poor. Read Digest 97:49-55 S '70
Mafia war on the A&P. Read Digest 97:71-6 Jl '70
Time to say no to big-farm subsidies. Read Digest 96:78-82 My '70

METHYLENE lactones. See Lactones

METOBROMURON. See Herbicides

METRIC system
Alas, poor England! Metrication is coming. J. A. Maxtone-Graham. Sports Illus 33:47 Ag 24 '70
Conversion to the metric system. Lord Ritchie-Calder. il Sci Am 223:17-25 bibliog(p 136) Jl '70
Farewell to the barleycorn inch. J. H. Bailey. il Sci Digest 69:26-30 Ja '71
First step toward U.S. adoption of the metric system. U S News 69:88 O 19 '70
Metric system: status of adoption by the United States; AAAS symposium, December 28, 1970. R. W. Mattoon. il Science 170:1337-8 D 18 '70
Metrication in America. Sci Am 223:52 O '70
News from the world of space exploration; metric system for NASA. Space World H-1-85:47 Ja '71
Should the U.S. go metric? il Sr Schol 96:11-12 Mr 16 '70
Take me to your liter. Nations Bsns 58:18 Je '70
Ten years to metric; Australian conversion. Sci N 97:340 Ap 4 '70

METRO, Charlie
Tale of the derailed Metro. R. Blount, jr. Sports Illus 32:43 Je 22 '70 •

METRO foresters. See Foresters

METRO-Goldwyn-Mayer, inc.
Dreams for sale. K. Fleming. il Newsweek 75:36-7 My 4 '70
Memories on the block; MGM auctions. il Life 68:42-8+ My 22 '70
MGM is cutting more than film. il por Bsns W p23 My 9 '70

METROLINER (train) See Railroads—Passenger service—High speed trains

METROMEDIA, inc.
Seeing and believing; TV program on the ecology crisis. R. L. Shayon. Sat R 53:32-3 Je 27 '70

METRONOMES
Metronomes. il Consumer Rep 34:649-52 N '69

METROPOLITAN areas
Evolution of a super-urban nation. il Bsns W p76+ O 17 '70
Richest U.S. markets for the '70s. il U S News 69:61 O 5 '70
See also
Metropolitan government
Suburbs
Urban renewal
also subhead Metropolitan district under names of cities, e.g. Indianapolis—Metropolitan district

METROPOLITAN community church. See Hollywood, Calif.—Churches

METROPOLITAN government
Metropolitan government gets a boost; study by CED. Bsns W p71 F 21 '70

Canada
Ontario maps the way to metro reform. il Bsns W p80+ N 21 '70

METROPOLITAN magazines. See Periodicals—United States

METROPOLITAN museum of art, New York
Art: The year 1200. L. Alloway. Nation 210:285-6 Mr 9 '70
Burning issues; Museum's master plan. T. B. Hess. Art N 69:29 Sum '70
Centennial ball. New Yorker 46:29 Ap 25 '70
Coy women, purple upholstery, cosmic landscapes; exhibition of American 19th-century art. A. Goldin. il Art N 69:40-5+ My '70
Furniture of nineteenth-century America; exhibition. il Antiques 97:382-91 Mr '70
Going on 200: the Metropolitan museum. B. Rose. Vogue 156:164-6+ S 15 '70
Growing pains. il Time 95:74 Ap 27 '70
High style; exhibition of 19th century American art, architecture and decoration. il Time 95:82-3 My 25 '70
In the grand manner; centennial ball. il Newsweek 75:70-3 Ap 27 '70
Journey to the year 1200; exhibition of medieval art. C. R. Baldwin. il Art N 69:30-5+ Ap '70
Lehman collection. R. Davidson. il Antiques 97:86+ Ja '70
Medieval men; Style 1200 exhibition. il Newsweek 75:64-9 Mr 23 '70
Meeting; public opinion on expansion plan into Central park. New Yorker 46:25-7 Je 20 '70
Merchants and masterpieces, by C. Tomkins. Review
  Art in Am 58:27+ S '70. J. Jacobs
  Newsweek il por 75:36A-36B Je 22 '70. A. Keneas
Metropolitan celebrates: 1870-1970. E. P. Birk. il Antiques 97:310+ Mr '70
Metropolitan museum, 1870-1970-2001; symposium. il Art N 68:27-45 Ja '69; 69:26-7+ Mr '70
Metropolitan museum of art's fabulous fakes. il Har Baz 104:174-5 N '70
Museum: 100 years and the Metropolitan museum of art, by L. Lerman. Review
  Am Artist 34:48+ Mr '70. F. Johnson
Museum that is testing the future. House B 112:127 Ap '70
Museum turns one hundred. il Arch Forum 132:42-7 Je '70
19th century America at the Met. R. Phelps. il Life 68:10 Je 19 '70
Nineteenth-century American rooms at the Metropolitan museum of art. M. D. Schwartz. il Antiques 98:400-9 S '70
Our nineteenth-century architectural heritage; Rise of an American architecture, exhibition. S. B. Sherill. il Antiques 97:784 Je '70
Paintings of nineteenth-century America; exhibition. il Antiques 97:392-7 Mr '70
President: C. Douglas Dillon. New Yorker 46:35-6 Ap 4 '70
Rise of an American architecture; exhibition at Metropolitan museum. W. McQuade. il Life 69:14 Ag 14 '70
Rooms; acquisition of two eighteenth-century interiors. New Yorker 46:31-3 Ap 11 '70
Spectacular decorating for a great party; the Metropolitan museum centennial ball. il House & Gard 138:60-3 Jl '70
Sweet wind out of the dark; The year 1200 exhibition. il Time 95:62 F 23 '70

METROPOLITAN museum of art, New York
—*Continued*
1200 and all that; Metropolitan museum's exhibition. C. J. McNaspy. America 122:254-5 Mr 7 '70
Wrightsman rooms at the Metropolitan museum of art. J. Parker. il Antiques 97:102-8 Ja '70

Cloisters
Cloisters. B. Black. il Horticulture 49:34-5 Ja '71

METROPOLITAN opera association
Advocates three; Metropolitan opera board of directors. il Opera N 35:6 S 5 '70
Gentele for Bing, or new blood from Sweden. I. Kolodin. Sat R 53:34 D 26 '70
Man in box 13; R. Bing. M. Mayer. il por Opera N 35:6-10 S 19 '70
Matter of national concern. J. Boutwell. il Opera N 34:6-13 Je 13 '70
Met's new chief; G. Gentele. il por Newsweek 76:67 D 21 '70
Multiplied man. por Forbes 105:16-17 Ja 15 '70
Musical events; new general manager. G. Gentele. W. Sargeant. New Yorker 46:57-8 D 26 '70
Musings on the Met. H. C. Schonberg. Harper 241:130-2 D '70
New general manager; interview. G. Gentele. New Yorker 46:15-16 D 26 '70
New manager for the Met; G. Gentele. il por Time 96:51 D 21 '70

METROPOLITAN opera ballet
Prime mover; interview, ed. by J. Boutwell. M. Sparemblek. il por Opera N 35:12-13 Ja 9 '71
Two by Sparemblek, Metropolitan opera. D. Hering. Dance Mag 44:77-80 N '70

METROPOLITAN opera club
Penguins. il Newsweek 75:99 Mr 9 '70

METROPOLITAN opera company
How long can the Met survive? I. Kolodin; reply. H. A. Gray. Sat R 53:79+ Ja 31 '70
Matter of national concern. J. Boutwell. il Opera N 34:6-13 Je 13 '70
Met looks for a new boss. H. Saal. il por Newsweek 75:108+ My 18 '70
Metropolitan opera (cont) il Hi Fi 20:secII 13 Mr; 11-13 Ap; 10-12+ My; 13 Je '70
Metropolitan opera repertory 1970-71. Opera N 35:16 S 19 '70
Metropolitan opera roster 1970-71. Opera N 35:17 S 19 '70
Music to my ears; Cossotto in Norma. I. Kolodin. Sat R 53:58 O 24 '70
Music to my ears; production of Parsifal. I. Kolodin. Sat R 53:18 D 5 '70
Music to my ears; remarriage of Figaro. I. Kolodin. Sat R 53:44 Ap 18 '70
New sounds for the new Met season. I. Kolodin. Sat R 53:47-8 O 3 '70
Puckers for Tucker. il pors Life 68:73-4 My 15 '70

METROPOLITAN opera guild
Board; annual meeting to elect directors. F. Merkling. il Opera N 34:22-3 My 16 '70
Gala party. il Opera N 35:18-19 S 5 '70
Report; performance of Barber of Seville at the Brooklyn academy of music. S. Jenkins. Opera N 34:32 Ja 31 '70
Sponsors' salute; Mr Bing feted. il por Opera N 35:26-7 D 5 '70
See also
Metropolitan opera studio

METROPOLITAN opera national council
Singers' friend; interview, ed. by A. M. Lingg. C. G. Harper. il por Opera N 34:30 Ap 4 '70
See also
Central opera service

METROPOLITAN opera on the air. See Radio broadcasting—Operas

METROPOLITAN opera studio
Little project; Guild-sponsored opera performances. R. Zachary. il Opera N 35:26-9 Ja 9 '71
New audience; with student performance calendar 1970-71. R. A. Tuggle. il Opera N 35:17-24 N 21 '70

METROPOLITAN transportation authority
Cut subway power costs. Am City 85:98 S '70
Mandel's complaint; damages suit. Newsweek 75:82+ F 23 '70
Wholly Ronan empire. F. C. Shapiro. il pors N Y Times Mag p34-6+ My 17 '70

METROPOLITAN urban service training. See Religious cooperation

METS (baseball) See Baseball clubs

METZENBAUM, Howard Morton
Ohio race; Taft vs. man with an image. pors U S News 69:52 S 28 '70 *
Red herring. il por Newsweek 76:29 O 26 '70 *
Robert Taft vs. Howard Metzenbaum. G. I. Maeroff. il pors N Y Times Mag p32-4+ O 4 '70 *

METZGER, H. Peter
Project Gasbuggy and catch-85. il N Y Times Mag p26-7+ F 22 '70

METZGER, Peter. See Metzger, H. P.

METZKER, Ray K.
Gallery; photographs. il Life 68:8-9 Ap 10 '70

MEUDT, Edna
Surplus blanket sale; poem. Chr Cent 87:533 Ap 29 '70

MEUTE, Jason P.
Four-channel stero FM, from one station. il Hi Fi 20:secI 72-3 Mr '70

MEXICAN AMERICAN students
Children who are tested in an alien language; mentally retarded? M. E. Leary. New Repub 162:17-18 My 30 '70
Culture conflict and Mexican-American achievement. N. Justin. bibliog Sch & Soc 98:27-8 Ja '70
Physicists teach minority students; Stanford's summer program. B. G. Levi. il Phys Today 23:53-6 Mr '70

MEXICAN AMERICANS
Bicultural Americans with a Hispanic tradition. A. D. Trejo. il por Wilson Lib Bul 44:716-20 Mr '70
Bishops, PADRES and the barrios. P. H. McNamara. Commonweal 93:116-17 O 30 '70
Chicanos and libraries; letter to the editor. R. P. Haro. Am Lib 1:932-3 N '70
Chicano is beautiful. C. S. Heller. Commonweal 91:454-8 Ja 23 '70
Chicano movement. Y. R. Macias. il por Wilson Lib Bul 44:731-5 Mr '70; Discussion. 44:925-6 My '70
Chicano power. S. Steiner. New Repub 162:16-18 Je 20 '70
Chicano riot; unrest in East Los Angeles. il Time 96:11 S 7 '70
Culture conflict and Mexican-American achievement. N. Justin. bibliog Sch & Soc 98:27-8 Ja '70
Curanderismo, Mexican-American folk psychiatry. by A. Kiev. Review
    Américas 22:42 Mr '70. J. Philips
Death in the barrio. il Newsweek 76:35 S 14 '70
Death of an Anglo; F. Logan killed by police in Mathis, Tex. il por Newsweek 76:21 Jl 27 '70
Ford and la raza; they stole our land and gave us powdered milk. L. Rees and P. Montague. il Ramp Mag 9:10-18 S '70
Houston's MAYO clinic; complicated chemistry; Mexican-American youth organization. R. Durham. Chr Today 14:42-3 My 8 '70
How Mexican-Americans view libraries; East Los Angeles and Sacramento, Calif. R. P. Haro. bibliog il Wilson Lib Bul 44:736-42 Mr '70
How to make a depressed area. Trans-Action 7:4+ Ap '70
Impact of commuters on the Mexican-American border area. A.-S. Ericson. bibliog f il Mo Labor R 93:18-27 Ag '70
Juan's right to read; Whisman, Calif, reading/learning clinic. L. Goodman. il Am Ed 6:3-6 Jl '70
Killing of Ruben Salazar; nothing has really changed in the barrio. D. F. Gomez. Chr Cent 88:49-52 Ja 13 '71
No mañanas for today's Chicanos. J. Rechy. il Sat R 53:31-4 Mr 14 '70
North from Mexico, by C. McWilliams. Review
    Trans-Action 7:82-4 Ap '70. P. D. Ortego
Oakland, Calif, la Biblioteca latino americana. B. L. Wynn. il Wilson Lib Bul 44:751-6 Mr '70
Overkill at the Silver dollar; Chicanos in Angeles. E. H. Lopez. il Nation 211:365-8 O 19 '70
La raza in revolt. R. Bongartz. Nation 210:664-6 Je 1 '70
La raza, the land and the hippies. P. Nabokov. il Nation 210:464-8 Ap 20 '70
San Joaquin Valley, California; la Biblioteca ambulante. M. B. Reynolds. Wilson Lib Bul 44:767 Mr '70
Schools fail Chicanos. America 123:136 S 12 '70
Texas Baptists warned of rising Chicano power. Chr Cent 87:1508 D 16 '70
Tío Taco is dead. il Newsweek 75:22-4+ Je 29 '70
When it started; Chicano rebellion. Nation 211-261 S 28 '70

MEXICAN art. See Art, Mexican

MEXICAN children in the United States. See Mexicans in the United States

MEXICAN cookery. See Cookery, Mexican
MEXICAN folk art. See Folk art
MEXICAN maid; story. See Silverton, D.
MEXICAN 1000. See Motor vehicle racing—
Mexico
MEXICAN sculpture. See Sculpture, Mexican
MEXICAN students
Mexican justice; student prisoners. A. Lieb-
man. New Repub 162:12-13 Ap 25 '70
See also
Student demonstrations—Mexico
MEXICAN-United States boundary and water
commission. See International boundary and
water commission (United States and
Mexico)
MEXICAN war, 1845-1848. See United States—
History—War with Mexico, 1845-1848
MEXICANOS. See Mexican Americans
MEXICANS
Social character in a Mexican village, by
E. Fromm and M. Macoby. Review
Sat R il 53:21-2 D 5 '70. R. F. Murphy
MEXICANS in the United States
Three times lonely; address, October 1968.
T. DeGerez. il Horn Bk 46:66-73 F '70
See also
Mexican Americans
MEXICO
See also
Acapulco
Automobile touring—Mexico
Birth control—Mexico
California, Lower
Camping—Mexico
Cozumel Island
Divorce—Mexico
Elections—Mexico
Festivals—Mexico
Guadalajara
Guadalupe Island
Investments, Foreign (in Mexico)
Juarez
Mazatlán
Medicine—Mexico
Mulegé
Oaxaca (city)
Peasantry—Mexico
Periodicals—Mexico
Political parties—Mexico
Political prisoners—Mexico
Puerto Vallarta
Shopping and shoppers—Mexico
Student demonstrations—Mexico
Tapalapa
Teotihuacán
Tijuana
Zinacantán

Antiquities
See Indians of Mexico—Antiquities

Boundaries
Agreement to conclude treaty to resolve boundary problems. Dept State Bul 63:296-300 S
14 '70
Settling a border. il Sr Schol 97:3 S 21 '70
South of the adjusted border. il por Time
96:12 Ag 31 '70

Commerce
See also
United States—Commerce—Mexico

Description and travel
Hap i nes afloat on the Sea of Cortez. J.
Rhoades. il Sports Illus 32:64-6+ Mr 30 '70
Help in planning a Mexico trip. Sunset 144:57
Mr '70
In the pink in Mexico. G. Christy. Mlle 70:
126-7+ Ja '70
Mexico. P. S. Parr. il Home Gard 57:16-17+
Jl '70
Mexico and the American artist. D. Gillen. il
por Am Artist 34:32-9+ Ap '70

Economic conditions
Down Mexico way. W. F. Buckley, jr. Nat
R 22:910 Ag 25 '70
"Revolutionary" establishment. L. Fenster.
il Nation 211:13-17 Jl 6 '70
Spoils of the Mexican revolution. J. Wo-
mack, jr. For Affairs 48:677-87 Jl '70

Economic policy
New leader in Mexico: meaning to U.S. il
U S News 69:74 Jl 13 '70

Foreign relations
Mexico: season of shadows. C. H. Gardiner.
Cur Hist 58:91-4+ F '70

United States
See United States—Foreign relations—
Mexico

History
1910-1946
Papa and Pancho Villa. E. H. Lopez. il Am
Heritage 21:57-63 Ag '70
Spoils of the Mexican revolution. J. Wo-
mack, jr. For Affairs 48:677-87 Jl '70
Zapata and the Mexican revolution, by J.
Womack, jr. Review
Trans-Action 7:69-72 S '70. K. M. Cole-
man

American punitive expedition, 1916
See United States—History—Punitive
expedition to Mexico, 1916

Industries
Analysis of Mexico's border industrialization
program. A. S. Ericson. il Mo Labor R 93:
33 My '70
See also
Cattle industry and trade—Mexico
Electronic apparatus industry and trade—
Mexico
Mexico—Economic conditions

Native races
See Indians of Mexico

Politics and government
Down Mexico way. W. F. Buckley, jr. Nat
R 22:910 Ag 25 '70
Mexican justice; student prisoners. A. Lieb-
man. New Repub 162:12-13 Ap 25 '70
Mexico: season of shadows. C. H. Gardiner.
Cur Hist 58:91-4+ F '70
"Revolutionary" establishment. L. Fenster. il
Nation 211:13-17 Jl 6 '70
See also
Elections—Mexico
Political parties—Mexico

Religious institutions and affairs
See also
Catholic church in Mexico

Social conditions
Digging out. Time 96:42 D 14 '70

Social life and customs
Mexico's street minstrels. G. L. Reitze. il
Américas 22:36-7 Ja '70
MEXICO (city)
Description
South to the Tamales. H. Sutton. il Sat R
53:34+ Je 13 '70

Education
Open-air school. il Américas 22:9-11 F '70

Hotels, restaurants, etc.
South to the Tamales. H. Sutton. Sat R 53:
39-40 Je 13 '70
Music
Report:
Fall season of the Asociación musical
Daniel. L. Frick. Opera N 35:32 D 5 '70
Productions of Fidelio and Die Walküre.
L. Frick. Opera N 35:30 O 31 '70

Subways
Mexico's metro. A. J. Lowe. il Américas
22:30-5 Jl '70
Notes and comment. New Yorker 45:21 Ja 17
'70
Viva el metro! il Newsweek 77:57 Ja 11 '71

Transit systems
See also
Mexico (city)—Subways
MEXICO, GULF OF
Brines and interstitial brackish water in drill
cores from the deep Gulf of Mexico. F. T.
Manheim and F. L. Sayles. bibliog il Science
170:57-61 O 2 '70
Challenger in the Gulf. Sci N 97:429 My 2
'70
See also
Galveston Bay
Sanibel Island
MEXICO and the United States
See also
Americans in Mexico
MEXICO-United States air agreement. See
Aviation—International aspects
MEYER, Agnes Elizabeth (Ernst)
Obituary
Newsweek por 76:67 S 14 '70
MEYER, Beat
Optical spectra of molecules at low tempera-
ture. bibliog il Science 168:783-9 My 15 '70

MEYER, Charles A.
IA-ECOSOC special committee meets at Washington; statement, November 18, 1969. Dept State Bul 61:631-4 D 29 '69
Inter-American economic and social council holds special meeting at Caracas, statement, Febraury 5, 1970. Dept State Bul 62: 256-9 Mr 2 '70
U.S. supports completion of Pan American highway; statement; December 10, 1969. Dept State Bul 62:38-40 Ja 12 '70

MEYER, Charles R.
Big fish from small boats. il Motor B 125: 68-9+ F '70
Buying a used motor. il Yachting 127:75+ Je '70
Jeep Gladiator. il Pop Sci 197:22 Ag '70
Posh pad for family safari. il Pop Sci 196: 80-1+ Mr '70
Snowmobile safari. il Field & S 74:62-3+ Ja '70
Take your winter vacation on a snowmobile. il por Pop Sci 196:40-3 Ja '70

MEYER, Daniel
Assemble a digital measurements lab (title varies) il Pop Electr 33:51-3+ N '70; 34: 63-7+ Ja '71
Assembling a universal tiger. il Pop Electr 33:31-5+ O '70
One-step motion detector. il Pop Electr 32: 57-61+ Mr '70
—See Kay, C. G. jt. auth.

MEYER, David
Wanting Jolinda; story. Redbook 135:171-93 O '70

MEYER, Debbie
Now look who's an old lady. J. Kirshenbaum. il pors Sports Illus 33:18-20+ Ag 31 '70 *

MEYER, Frank S.
Future of the Republican party. Nat R 22: 1271-3 D 1 '70
Open question. Nat R 22:682 Je 30 '70
Principles and heresies. See issues of National review

MEYER, Henry T.
Magnetic tape, drum, disc memories. por Electr World 84:40-3 O '70

MEYER, Karl E.
Hello, Columbus. il Art N 69:46-9+ N '70

MEYER, Pearl
How to read a resumé. Duns 96:49-50+ O '70

MEYER, Philip
If Hitler asked you to electrocute a stranger, would you? il Esquire 73:72-3+ F '70

MEYER, Richard J.
ITV in the ghetto. Todays Ed 59:35 Ja '70

MEYER, Russ
Porn and man at Yale. F. Schickel. Harper 241:34+ Jl '70 *

MEYER, Susan E.
Elaine Morfogen, illustrator & painter. il por Am Artist 34:54-60 O '70
Evelyn Hofer, pilgrim with a lens. il Am Artist 34:46-52+ N '70
Sketching from life. il Am Artist 34:62-7+ My '70
William A. Berry; illustrator/painter. il Am Artist 34:80-5 Mr '70

MEYER, Ursula
How to explain pictures to a dead hare. il Art N 68:54-7+ Ja '70

MEYER, Vesta G.
Facultative gymnosperm from an interspecific cotton hybrid. bibliog il Science 169:886-8 Ag 28 '70

MEYER, William L. See Little, B. W. jt. auth.

MEYERBEER, Giacomo
At last, Les Huguenots and Meyerbeer. H. Weinstock. Sat R 53:75 N 28 '70 *

MEYERLE, George
Assemble a frequency equalizer. il Pop Electr 33:51-9 O '70
Automatic burglar alarm. il Pop Electr 32:59-61+ Ap '70

MEYEROWITZ, Jan
Do we overestimate Beethoven? Hi Fi sec I 20:77-80 Ja '70

MEYERS, Bruce
Buggymaster of the roaring dunes. B. Yates. il por Sports Illus 32:52-3 Je 29 '70 *

MEYERS, Charles R.
Automatic pilot for outboards. il Pop Sci 197: 80-1 Jl '70

MEYERS, Edward
Getting 1:1 with an eyeball. il Pop Phot 66: 62-3+ Mr '70
Protechniques. See issues of Popular photography

MEYERS, Harold B. See Alexander, H. E. jt. auth.

MEYERS, Marvin
Bitterness at Brandeis. il por Newsweek 76: 54-5 N 9 '70 *

MEYERS, Richmond E.
Mr Rodale becomes rockhound. Org Gard & Farm 17:73-6 Jl '70

MEYERSOHN, Rolf
Charismatic and the playful in outdoor recreation. bibliog f il Ann Am Acad 389:35-45 My '70

MEYERSON, Martin
Wanted man. por Newsweek 75:55-6 F 9 '70

MEYERSON, Michael
Puerto Rico: our backyard colony. il Ramp Mag 8:50-1+ Je '70

MEYNER, Helen (Stevenson)
Helen Meyner: my miracle pregnancy at forty-one. P. Battelle. il por Ladies Home J 87:36+ F '70 *

MEZEY, Robert
Going for a walk at night; I am here; poems. Mlle 71:120+ O '70

MIAMI, Fla.
See also
South Miami

Gardens
Gardens of Vizcaya. G. Taloumis. il Horticulture 48:38-9 F '70

Harbor
Half-mile gangplank; passenger terminal to cruise shipping. P. Blake. il Arch Forum 132:54-7 Mr '70

Music
Report:
Miami opera guild's Traviata. D. Reno. Opera N 34:30 Mr 14 '70

Riots
Meat riot; Brownsville. il Newsweek 75:20-1 Je 29 '70

MIAMI, Fla, public library
Miami, Florida; work with Cuban refugees. H. H. Eason. Wilson Lib Bul 44:760-3 Mr '70

MIAMI, Okla.
It hasn't been easy; serpentine downtown. C. Allonby. il Am City 85:47-8 D '70

MIAMI BEACH, Fla.

Description
Miami Beach: summer resort. E. Wilson. il Travel & Camera 33:14+ Jl '70

Parks and playgrounds
We tried new types of playground equipment. J. Woody. il Am City 85:22 F '70

MIAMI Dolphins (football club) See Football clubs

MIAMI LAKES, Fla.
Miami Lakes new town. J. O. Simonds. il Parks & Rec 5:29-33 O '70

MIAMI-Nassau powerboat race. See Motor boat racing

MICE
Antigen-binding cells in normal mouse thymus. F. Modabber and others. bibliog il Science 170:1102-4 D 4 '70
Brain weight increases resulting from environmental enrichment: a directional dominance in mice. N. D. Henderson. bibliog il Science 169:776-8 Ag 21 '70
Calhoun's horrible mousery; effects of overcrowding. S. Alsop. Newsweek 76:96 Ag 17 '70
Cerebral acid hydrolase activities; comparison in quaking and normal mice. D. J. Kurtz and J. N. Kanfer. bibliog il Science 168:259-60 Ap 10 '70
Formation of virus-like particles by bone cells in mice with a high incidence of spontaneous leukemia. B. H. Schofield and others. bibliog il Science 168:588-9 My 1 '70
Histocompatibility-2 (H-2) polymorphism in wild mice. J. Klein. bibliog il Science 168: 1362-4 Je 12 '70
Hydrocephalus in mice inoculated neonatally by the oronasal route with reovirus type I. P. A. Phillips and others. bibliog il Science 168:858-9 My 15 '70
Immunoglobin structure: amino terminal sequences of kappa chains from genetically similar mice (BALB/c) L. E. Hood and others. bibliog il Science 168:1207-10 D 11 '70
Impairment of shock avoidance learning after long-term alcohol ingestion in mice. G. Freund. bibliog il Science 168:1599-601 Je 26 '70
Inheritance of a cardiac arterial asymmetry in mice. J. H. Bruell and others. bibliog il Science 167:199-200 Ja 9 '70
Moving carpet; field mice plague in Australia. il Time 95:39 Mr 30 '70
Mutagenicity of trimethylphosphate in mice. S. S. Epstein and others. bibliog il Science 168:584-6 My 1 '70
Strain C3H-AvfB mice: ninety percent incidence of mammary tumors transmitted by either parent. G. Vlahakis and others. bibliog il Science 170:185-7 O 9 '70

MICE—*Continued*
Tolerance to polyinosinic polycytidylic acid in NZB/NZW mice. A. D. Steinberg and others. bibliog il Science 167:870-1 F 6 '70
Unexplained Australian plague; mouse eruption. Sci N 97:290 Mr 21 '70
Unilateral inhibition of sound-induced convulsions in mice. R. L. Collins. bibliog il Science 167:1010-11 F 13 '70

Control
How to control mouse damage in conifers; meadow mice. J. W. Caslick and W. R. Eadie. il Cons 24:48-9 Ag '69
Poison in Tennessee; vole eradication. M. Frome. Field & S 74:30+ Ja '70

Extermination
See Mice—Control
MICE as laboratory animals. See Laboratory animals
MICHAEL, George A.
Computer display systems. bibliog il por Phys Today 23:30-6 Jl '70
MICHAEL, Jakob
Mysterious Mr Michael. A. A. Butkus. il por Duns 96:29-31 N '70 *
MICHAEL, James R.
Inspect that toy. New Repub 163:15 D 12 '70
MICHAEL, John A.
Use of video tape in the preparation of art teachers. il Sch Arts 69:36-8 F '70
MICHAELS, Howard
Can you really photograph Africa? il Field & S 75:38-9+ Jl '70
MICHAELS, Leonard
Robinson Crusoe Liebowitz; story. Esquire 73:140-1 Mr '70
MICHAELSON, Michael G.
Failure of American medicine. Am Scholar 39:694+ Aut '70
MICHAELSON, Mike
Copper bracelets are a put-on. il Todays Health 48:27-9+ Je '70
Healing our sick environment. il Todays Health 48:20-5+ Ap '70
Is ICE on the rocks? il Todays Health 48:53-4+ N '70
Lake that ate too much. il Todays Health 48:42-3+ Ag '70
Meet the family doctor for the 70's. il pors Todays Health 48:50-3+ My '70
Sweden's youth says *nej* to pollution. il Todays Health 49:22-5+ Ja '71
Time to tame the abominable snowmobiler. il Todays Health 48:46-9+ D '70
Will your next doctor be a doctor? il Todays Health 48:37-41+ Mr '70
(ed) See Musselman, M. M. In search of sanity; man in the middle
MICHAUD, Mitch
Upon a peak in Delaware. D. Levin. il pors Sports Illus 33:34-6+ D 14 '70 *
MICHEAUX, Oscar
Black film; God's step children. filmed in 1938, black director. New Yorker 46:34-5 Ap 18 '70 *
MICHEL, F. C. See Manka, R. H. jt. auth.
MICHEL, Joan Hess
Charles Apt in Portugal. il por Am Artist 34:54-62 Ap '70
(ed) See Copeland, L. Children: the drawings of Lila Copeland
MICHELANGELO Buonarroti
Ceiling on the wall; exhibition of photographs of the Sistine ceiling. M. R. Weiss. il Sat R 53:50-1 D 5 '70 *
MICHELSON, Annette
Screen. Commonweal 92:63-5 Mr 27 '70
MICHELSON, Peter
'Lascivious ungodly love'. Nation 210:245-7 Mr 2 '70
MICHENER, James Albert
Can a sixty-two-year-old writer with a history of heart trouble find fulfillment running with the bulls in the streets of Pamplona? il Esquire 74:177-81 D '70
Drifters; story. Ladies Home J 87:161-8 N '70
Seven theories why anyone, including a sixty-two-year-old writer with a history of heart trouble, seeks fulfillment running with the bulls in the streets of Pamplona. il Esquire 74:182-3 D '70
Soccer's wild World cup scramble. il Read Digest 96:173-4+ Je '70
What to do about the Palestinian refugees? il N Y Times Mag p22-5+ S 27 '70
Why I collect art. il Read Digest 96:147-52 My '70

MICHIGAN
See also
Architecture, Domestic—Michigan
Booksellers and bookselling—Michigan
Camps—Michigan
Fishing—Michigan
Hunting—Michigan
Libraries—Michigan
Wilderness areas—Michigan

Description and travel
Hemingway's Michigan. W. Paige. il Travel & Camera 33:32-7 Jl '70

Parks and reserves
Michigan. R. O. Dodge. il Parks & Rec 5:37-9+ D '70

Politics and government
Ahead: uphill pull for Lenore Romney. il pors U S News 69:60 Ag 17 '70
Lenore fights alone. A. Rothenberg. il pors Look 34.111+ O 20 '70
Secretary's wife; Republican senatorial primary. por Newsweek 76:26+ Ag 17 '70
MICHIGAN, LAKE
Cooling it; federal policy on pollution. Newsweek 75:123 My 18 '70
Cruising is where you find it. R. M. Withrow. il Yachting 128:58-9+ Jl '70
MICHIGAN education association
Teachers who won't be dragooned; withdrawal of the Detroit education association over agency-shop clause. R. Kirk. Nat R 22:261 Mr 10 '70
MICHIGAN general corporation
Nuts and bolts and no nonsense. il Bsns W p 138+ F 21 '70
MICHIGAN state university, East Lansing
Negro president at Michigan state university. por Sch & Soc 98:145-6 Mr '70
New boss takes over at Michigan state. il pors Ebony 25:60-2+ Jl '70
Ready access to higher ignorance; President C. R. Wharton's open enrollment policy. R. Kirk. Nat R 22:514 My 19 '70
MICHIGAN. University, Ann Arbor
Carnival revolution. M. J. Gallagher. America 122:295-5+ Mr 21 '70
Negro-Caucasian club: a history; the American students' first inter-racial organization. O. C. Johnson. il Negro Hist Bul 33:35-41 F '70
U. of Michigan: black activists win a change in priorities. L. J. Carter. il Science 168:229-31 Ap 10 '70

Conference on aging
See Aging, Conferences on

School of education
First educational gerontology program starting in Michigan. Aging 190:16 Ag '70
MICHIGAN university environmental teach-in.
See Environmental movement—Teach-ins
MICKA, Helen K.
Gift from our seniors. il Todays Ed 59:53 Ja '70
MICKELSON, Sig
First eight years. il Sat R 53:21-3 O 24 '70
MICROBES. See Microorganisms
MICROBIAL genetics
Recognition of DNA in bacteria. S. E. Luria. il Sci Am 222:88-92+ bibliog(p 146) Ja '70
Sunlight ultraviolet and bacterial DNA base ratios. C. E. Singer and B. N. Ames. bibliog il Science 170:822-6 N 20 '70
MICROBIOLOGY
René Dubos. A. Bailey. il por Horizon 12:56-61 Sum '70
See also
Air microbiology
Microbial genetics
MICROBIOLOGY, Space. See Space biology
MICROCRYSTALLINE polymers. See Polymers
MICROELECTRONICS
Large-scale arrays add capabilities; semiconductor microcircuits. B. M. Elson. il Aviation W 92:195-8+ Je 22 '70
Space-age electronics and pocket computers. G. Gregory. UNESCO Courier 23:29-30 Mr '70
See also
Electronic circuits, Integrated
MICROELECTROPHORESIS. See Electrophoresis
MICROENCAPSULATION. See Capsules
MICROFICHE. See Microforms
MICROFILMS
See also
Libraries—Microfilm collections

MICROFORMS
Libraries in miniature: a new era begins. J. Tebbel. il Sat R 54:41-2 Ja 9 '71
Little fiche eat big librarians, one whale of a story. E. C. Jestes. il por Wilson Lib Bul 44:650-2 F '70
Microbooks: a new library medium? il Pub W 198:48-50 N 9 '70
Microfiche inserts may be useful in book publishing. Pub W 197:97 Je 29 '70
Microform in junior colleges. Sch & Soc 98:400 N '70
    See also
Publishers and publishing—Microforms

MICROMINIATURIZATION (electronics) See Microelectronics

MICRONESIA
Micronesia award creates dilemma for administration. L. Doty. Aviation W 92:27-8 Je 1 '70

MICROORGANISMS
How your body keeps you well. R. Brecher and E. Brecher. Read Digest 96:89-93 F '70
    See also
Air microbiology
Microbiology
Protozoa
        Genetics
    See Microbial genetics

MICROORGANISMS, Pathogenic
    See also
Mycoplasma
        Conferences
Food-borne toxic microorganisms. C. La-Manna. Science 168:167-8+ Ap 3 '70

MICROPALEONTOLOGY
Fossil membranes and cell wall fragments from a 7000-year-old Black Sea sediment. E. T. Degens and others. bibliog il Science 168:1207-8 Je 5 '70
Fungal attack on rock: solubilization and altered infrared spectra. M. P. Silverman and E. F. Munoz. bibliog il Science 169:985-7 S 4 '70
Microfossils and the sea floor. W. B. Charm. il Sea Front 16:71-6 Mr '70
Micropaleontological studies of lunar samples. J. W. Schopf. bibliog il Science 167:779-80 Ja 30 '70
Micropaleontological study of lunar material. E. S. Barghoorn and others. il Science 167:775 Ja 30 '70

MICROPHONES
Build the Voxor; voice-operated microphone. R. A. Hirschfeld. il Pop Electr 32:81-4 F '70
How to use an FM mike for remote tape recordings. M. Lincoln. il Pop Sci 197:89+ Ag '70
Microphones. il Consumer Rep 35:34-43 Ja '70
Ten steps to best mike use. W. Wokoun. il Radio-Electr 41:23-6+ Jl '70
Which mikes for what jobs? W. Salm. il Pop Mech 133:92-5+ Je '70

MICROSCOPE and microscopy
Amateur scientist; phase-contrast microscopy is simulated. P. C. Diegenback. il Sci Am 223:123-5 N '70
Molecular microscopy: fundamental limitations. J. R. Breedlove, jr. and G. T. Trammell. bibliog il Science 170:1310-13 D 18 '70
Woman with a Micro-zoo. J. Fix. il por Sci Digest 67:94-6 F '70
    See also
Electron microscope and microscopy

MICROSOMAL oxidation. See Oxidation, Physiological

MICROSOMES
Insulin-stimulated glucose uptake by subcellular particles from adipose tissue cells. D. B. Martin and J. R. Carter, jr. bibliog il Science 167:873-4 F 6 '70

MICROSTRIP. See Microwave wiring

MICROTEACHING. See Teachers—Education in service

MICROTEKTITES. See Tektites

MICROWAVE circuits. See Radio circuits

MICROWAVE ovens. See Electronic ovens

MICROWAVE radiometers. See Radiometers

MICROWAVE wiring
Microstripline parameters. L. Sales. il Electr World 83:66-7 Ja '70

MICROWAVES
Microwaves, the miracle tool for science and industry. A. S. Freese. il Sci Digest 67:44-52 Je '70
Vote counts by microwave; Riverside County, Calif. H. F. Sammis. il Am City 85:76+ Jl '70
    See also
Microwave wiring

Physiological effects
Microwaves: the next health hazard? il Bsns W p122+ Je 20 '70
Mystery. T. Aaronson. bibliog il Environ 12:2-10 My '70
    See also
Electronic ovens—Radiation hazards

MIDAS-International corporation
Separate roads for Midas and son. por Bsns W p32-3 O 10 '70

MIDDENDORF, John H.
Refresher in English grammar. Writers Digest 50:36-7 Jl '70

MIDDLE age
Changing careers: five Americans begin again in their middle years. A. Bayer. il Life 68:50-7 Je 12 '70
Making use of middle age. R. Haughton. Cath World 210:246-7 Mr '70
    See also
Society for creative anachronism

Anecdotes, facetiae, satire, etc.
Pooped generation. il Changing T 23:7-11 D '69

MIDDLE ages
    See also
Art, Medieval
Troubadours
        History
        Bibliography
Articles and other books received; comp. by B. J. Holm. See issues of American historical review

MIDDLE class Americans. See Americans

MIDDLE classes
Blacks' progress: a story of opportunities grasped. il U S News 68:19-21 Je 1 '70
Bourgeois interior; excerpt from The passing of the modern age. J. Lukacs. Am Scholar 39:616-30 Aut '70
Middle-class values; excerpts from article. E. A. Roberts, jr; T. B. Roberts. il Todays Ed 59:20-3 Ja '70
Whose country is America? excerpt from First things, last things. E. Hoffer. il N Y Times Mag p30-1+ N 22 '70; Discussion. p34+ D 13 '70

MIDDLE EAST
Israel's incoherent response to an incoherent Arab world. M. Halpern. bibliog Sat R 53:36+ F 14 '70
    See also
Aeronautics, Military—Middle East
Arab states
Foreign visitors in the Middle East
Guerrillas—Middle East
Jordan
Kurds
Petroleum industry and trade—Middle East
Suez Canal
United Nations—Middle East
United Nations relief and works agency for Palestine refugees in the Near East

Defenses
Buying grandeur on the cheap; arms sales by France. il Newsweek 75:31-2 F 2 '70
Controlled tension. il Newsweek 76:32-3 Jl 27 '70
Firepower grows in the tinderbox. il Bsns W p72-3 Jl 18 '70
Israel and its enemies. il Time 95:24+ Je 22 '70
Middle East: the supersalesman. Time 95:18-19 F 2 '70
Middle East: war without end; Kosygin-Nixon correspondence. il Newsweek 75:39-40 F 16 '70

Foreign relations
        Russia
    See Russia—Foreign relations—Middle East
        United States
    See United States—Foreign relations—Middle East
        History
Emergence of the Middle East, 1914-1924, by H. M. Sachar. Review
Nation 210:90-2 Ja 26 '70
        Bibliography
Articles and other books received; comp. by S. Glazer. See issues of American historical review
        Maps
Middle East. Sr Schol 95:17 S 22 '69; 97:11 S 21 '70

MIDDLE EAST—*Continued*

Nationalism

Palestinians and Israel. S. Avineri. bibliog f
Commentary 49:31-44 Je '70; Discussion. 50:
6+ S; 30+ N; 18+ D '70

Politics

After Nasser. . .what next for the Middle
East? il Newsweek 76:34-5 O 12 '70
Controlled tension. il Newsweek 76:32-3 Jl
27 '70
Leveling and balancing. Nation 210:130-1 F
9 '70
Mid East: search for stability. il Time 96:10-
11+ O 5 '70
Middle East: balancing on the brink. il Time
95:18-19 F 16 '70
Middle East, 1971; symposium. bibliog f il Cur
Hist 60:1-45+ Ja '71
Nasser: despite failures, his prestige with
Arabs stays high. il por U S News 68:14 Ja
26 '70
Other fronts. il Newsweek 75:38-40 Ap 13 '70
Real meaning of Nixon trip. il pors U S News
69:17-19 O 12 '70
Turmoil; address, December 8, 1969. R. D.
Heinl, jr. Vital Speeches 36:296-9 Mr 1 '70
United States changing Mideast policy; ad-
dress, January 13, 1970. B. Roth. Vital
Speeches 36:442-8 My 1 '70
While Jordan burned. il por Newsweek 76:20-1
S 28 '70
Zero hour for the Middle East. W. E. Griffith.
Read Digest 96:49-53 Ja '70
See also
Arab states—Politics
Israeli-Arab war, 1967-
Jewish-Arab relations
Russia—Foreign relations—Middle East

Religious institutions and affairs

Middle East trends toward ecumenism. G.
Fitch, reply. J. R. Butler. Chr Cent 87:212
F 18 '70

MIDDLE EAST crisis, 1967
See also
Israeli-Arab war, 1967-
MIDDLE EASTERN cookery. See Cookery,
Middle Eastern
MIDDLE schools. See Education—Organization
by years
MIDDLE WEST
See also
Great Lakes

Description and travel

Historical tour of the Midwest. il Travel
135:55-7 Ja '71

Economic conditions

Life on the Mississippi, 1970. P. Schrag. il
Sat R 53:19-23 D 12 '70

Photographs

Fragments of the past; exhibition of historical Midwestern photographs at the Chicago art institute. R. F. McCullough. il Pop
Phot 66:82-3 Ja '70

Politics

Political trends in key area: latest survey of
Midwest. il U S News 69:37-40 O 19 '70
MIDDLETOWN, N.J.
Difference is inside the cab. D. Jackson. il
Am City 85:52 Ja '70
MIDDLETOWN state hospital, Middletown,
N. Y. See Hospitals, Psychiatric
MIDGET automobile racing
Old midgets never die; USAC midget race.
S. Kelly. il Hot Rod 23:42-4 F '70
MIDGET racing car engines. See Automobile
engines
MIDGETS. See Dwarfs
MIDISKIRTS. See Clothing and dress
MIDLAND, Mich.
Admixture increases freeze-thaw durability
of concrete. il Am City 85:34 My '70
MIDONICK, Millard
Society's child. por Newsweek 77:60-1 Ja
11 '70 *
MIDRASH
Pesikta rabbati, tr. by W. G. Braude. Review
Commentary 49:77-80 Ap '70. C. Raphael
MIDSUMMER night's dream; drama. See
Shakespeare, W.—Plays
MIDWAY (islands)
Death of Midway's antennas. H. I. Fisher. il
Audubon 72:62-3 Ja '70
MIDWAY airport. See Chicago—Airports
MIDWEST. See Middle West

MIDWESTERNERS
U.S. journal: Missouri; trip home with Sena-
tor T. F. Eagleton. C. Trillin. New Yorker
46:108+ My 16 '70
MIDWOOD, Barton
Short visits with five writers one friend.
il pors Esquire 74:150-3 N '70
MIFFLAND, Wis. See Madison, Wis.
MIFFLIN COUNTY, Pa.
Are we feeding those hungry Americans? G.
Logsdon. il Farm J 94:34-5+ D '70
MIGEON, Barbara Ruben. See Romeo. G. jt.
auth.
MIGLIAVACCA, Angiola Maria
Wife who listened. N. Willatt. il por Duns
95:53-4+ Ja '70
MIGRANT labor
Candor that refreshes; Coca-Cola to improve
living conditions of workers in Florida
citrus groves. il Time 96:59 Ag 10 '70
Coke's migrants get a new deal. il Bsns W
p 109-10 N 14 '70
Europe's guest workers: objects of concern.
T. Cosmades. Chr Cent 87:1333-4 N 4 '70
Europe's migrant workers: northward! il
Time 95:38-9 Je 8 '70
Grapes of wrath; Senate subcommittee hear-
ings. Newsweek 76:15 Ag 3 '70
Migrant mother: 1936. P. Taylor. il Am West
7:41-5 My '70
Migrant workers. M. Friedman. Newsweek
76:60 Jl 27 '70
Poverty at the border; Mexican labor brought
in by greedy U.S. employers. L. Velie. il
Read Digest 97:92-7 Ag '70
See also
American federation of labor and Congress
of industrial organizations—United farm
workers organizing committee
Children of migrant laborers
MIGRATION, Internal
Americans on the move: new patterns. il U S
News 68:66-7 Mr 16 '70
Lord of the ghettos. R. Coles. il Common-
weal 93:167-74 N 13 '70; Reply. R. J.
Neuhaus. 93:287 D 11 '70
See also
Cities and towns—Growth
Negroes—Migration
Rural-urban migration
MIGRATION from cities. See Migration, In-
ternal
MIGRATION of animals. See Animals—Migra-
tion
MIGRATION of birds. See Birds—Migration
MIGRATION of crustaceans. See Crustaceans—
Migration
MIGRATION of insects. See Insects—Migration
MIGRATION of man. See Man—Migrations
MIGRATION of Negroes. See Negroes—Mi-
gration
MIKASA, prince of Japan. See Takahito
MIKLOS, Laszlo D. See Miklos, M. O. jt. auth.
MIKLOS, Mary Oellerich, and Miklos, L. D.
Student council: useful or useless? bibliog
Clear House 45:236-9 D '70
MIKULSKI, Barbara
Ethnic American; interview, ed. by T. H.
Clancy. America 123:558-9+ D 26 '70
MIKUTA, John J.
Uterine tumors; ed. by E. Edelson. Redbook
135:10+ Jl '70
MIKVA, Abner J.
Excerpt from debate, September 17, 1969. Cong
Digest 49:31 Ja '70
MILAGE indicators. See Odometers
MILAN, Italy

Art

Avant-garde Milanese. M. Gendel. il Art N
69:41-3+ Sum '70

La Scala

La Scala's scalpers. S. Von Buchau. il Opera
N 35:6-7 D 12 '70

Music

Report:
Donizetti, Lucia di Lammermoor and
Lucrezia Borgia. P. Hoffer. Opera N
34:26 Je 13 '70
Ernani. P. Hoffer. Opera N 34:30 F 14 '70
MILANESE designers. See Designers
MILAZZO, Charles J.
Syndicated poet: Ben Burroughs. por Writers
Digest 50:27+ O '70
MILBRODT, Richard
County unifies thirty-five sewerage agencies.
il Am City 85:64-5+ N '70

MILEK, Bob
Go alone, but safely! il Field & S 75:40-1+ D '70
Hunting the desert cottontail. il Field & S 75: 42-3+ S '70
Pronghorn for a pioneer. il Field & S 75:40-1+ Ag '70

MILES, Bebe
Plan bulb combinations now. il Horticulture 48:22-5+ My '70
Some uncommon bulbs. il Horticulture 48: 22-5+ N '70

MILES, Charles
Indian relics. See issues of Hobbies

MILES, Dick
Bloodthirsty tennis, anyone? il Sports Illus 33:32-4+ N 2 '70

MILES, F. A.
Centrifugal effects in the avian retina. bibliog il Science 170:992-5 N 27 '70

MILES, Mary P.
Simple weaving to create wall hangings. il Sch Arts 70:20-3 Ja '71

MILES, Richard
Moving; poem. Harp Baz 104:88 N '70

MILES, Wyndham D. See Wilcox, D. H. jr, jt. auth.

MILES college, Birmingham, Ala.
Reincarnation of John Munro. L. Greenhouse. il por N Y Times Mag p56-7+ Mr 15 '70

MILES park race track, Louisville. See Race tracks

MILETICH, Phyllis
Opinion: phoniness. por Mlle 71:30+ Je '70

MILFORD, Nancy Winston
Zelda; excerpts. pors Ladies Home J 87:117-21 Je '70

MILFORD, Conn.
From flood rescue work to snow removal. K. Ryan. il Am City 85:89-90 Ap '70
Hand-me-downs cut costs for city fleet. C. J. Hughes. il Am City 85:106 Je '70
Urban renewal needs a guard service. S. Keene. il Am City 85:68 N '70

MILFORD, N.H.

Newspapers

News from Milford. M. L. Stein. il por Sat R 54:43-6 Ja 9 '71

MILGO electronic corporation
Profitable way to translate computer talk; high speed modems. il Bsns W p 124+ My 16 '70

MILGRAM, Stanley
Experience of living in cities; adaptation of address, September 2, 1969. bibliog il Science 167:1461-8 Mr 13 '70

about

If Hitler asked you to electrocute a stranger, would you? P. Meyer. il Esquire 73:72-3+ F '70 *
Would you obey a Hitler? J. Reinert. il Sci Digest 67:34-9 My '70 *

MILHAUD, Darius
Intelligent trash of Jolivet and Milhaud. J. Ringo. Am Rec G 37:166-7+ N '70 *

MILI, Gjon
Gallery; photographs. il Life 68:6-9 F 20 '70
Gallery; photographs; excerpts from Picasso's third dimension Life 69:8-9 D 4 '70
The me nobody knows; photographs. il Life 69:34-41 S 4 '70

MILIO, Nancy
Invisible woman. R. A. Sokolov. por Newsweek 75:92+ Mr 30 '70 *

MILITARISM
How generals are ruling most of a continent. il U S News 68:74-5 Je 22 '70
Rule of thumb for politicians; metapolitical perspective. F. X. Winters. America 123:11-12 Jl 11 '70
War: who wants it? Nation 210:706 Je 15 '70
See also
War
also subhead Military policy under names of countries, e.g. United States— Military policy

MILITARY airlift. See Transportation, Military
MILITARY airlift command. See United States —Military airlift command
MILITARY airplanes. See Airplanes, Military
MILITARY alliances. See Alliances
MILITARY art and science
See also
Mines, Military
Strategy
War

MILITARY assistance, American
Americans bearing gifts; aid to Greece. Commonweal 92:330 Jl 10 '70
Arms runaround. New Repub 162:7 Je 6 '70
Arms to Israel: the U.S. moves. il Newsweek 76:17-18 Jl 20 '70

Dilemmas of the arms traffic. G. Kemp. For Affairs 48:274-84 Ja '70
Firepower grows in the tinderbox. il Bsns W p72-3 Jl 18 '70
Laos: deeper into the other war. il Time 95: 23-4 Mr 9 '70
Laos: detailing the commitment. il Time 95: 29-30 Mr 16 '70
Mideast: alarm signals for U.S. and Russia. il U S News 69:11-12 Jl 20 '70
Price of a pullout: Asians' message to Agnew. il U S News 69:29-30 S 7 '70
Stacking up arms as talk runs out. il Bsns W p38 S 19 '70
U.S. and Cambodia sign agreement regulating military assistance; text of note. Dept State Bul 63:387 O 5 '70
US and Israel. New Repub 162:5-6 Ja 24 '70
U.S. dilemma in Middle East. il U S News 68: 28-30 Je 15 '70
U.S. lifts partial arms embargo against Greece; Department announcement. Dept State Bul 63:413 O 12 '70
Untimely aid and comfort; the resumption of aid to Greece. Chr Cent 87:1245 O 21 '70
Vietnamization spells more aid. il Bsns W p 112 O 24 '70
Washout; Peterson report. New Repub 162:11 Mr 21 '70
Why Nixon wants another $1 billion for aid to allies; text of message to Congress, November 18, 1970. R M. Nixon. il U S News 69:60-2 N 30 '70; Same with title Strong friends and the balance of peace. Dept State Bul 63:685-9 D 7 '70

MILITARY assistance, British
Passage of arms; K. Kaunda's mission to the West. il por Newsweek 76:50 N 2 '70
Pesky question; sales to South Africa. il Newsweek 76:28+ Ag 3 '70

MILITARY assistance, French
Another fifty Mirages sold to Libya in surprise maneuver by France. Aviation W 92: 20 Ja 26 '70
Buying grandeur on the cheap. il Newswek 75:31-2 F 2 '70
French embargo on arms undefined. D. E. Fink. il Aviation W 93:55 N 2 '70

MILITARY assistance, Russian
Buildup on the Suez: Soviet missiles. il Time 96:21 S 14 '70
Firepower grows in the tinderbox. il Bsns W p72-3 Jl 18 '70
Growing Soviet commitment; training programs and missile sites in Egypt. il Time 95:33 Ap 13 '70
Kremlin's Mideast gamble; with reports by A. de Borchgrave; M. Elkins. il Newsweek 75:37-42 Je 1 '70
Meanwhile, in Cuba, increased Russian activity. Time 96:17 Jl 27 '70
Middle East: new danger from old foes; Soviet involvement in Egypt. il Time 95:23-4 Je 8 '70
Mideast: alarm signals for U.S. and Russia. il U S News 69:11-12 Jl 20 '70
Moscow-on-the-Nile. Time 95:31+ Je 22 '70
Of mosques and MIG's; Moscow's growing military role in Egypt. il Time 95:19-20 Je 1 '70
On their own turf; Soviet pilots in Egypt. il Newsweek 75:58+ My 18 '70
Pattern of Soviet-UAR buildup of missiles at Suez emerges. Aviation W 93:21 S 28 '70
Relief for Egypt, anxiety for Israel. il Time 95:43-4 My 11 '70
Russia moves deeper into Mideast conflict. il U S News 68:54-5 Ap 6 '70
Russia: toward a global reach. il Time 96:29-30 O 5 '70
Russians fly defense missions for Egypt in Middle East conflict. Aviation W 92:27 My 4 '70
Russians in Egypt. New Repub 162:9 My 16 '70
Russians in Egypt: important but invisible. il U S News 69:20 Ag 24 '70
SAM's, MIG's, Russians; Soviet troops in Egypt. il Newsweek 75:59-60 My 11 '70
Soviet, Arab aircraft strength in Mideast tops Israel's 4 to 1. il Aviation W 92:16-17 Je 1 '70
Soviet Mediterranean push deepens; with editorial comment. E. H. Kolcum. il Aviation W 92:9, 14-18 Mr 30 '70
Soviets accelerating Mideast drive; with editorial comment. E. H. Kolcum. il Aviation W 92:9, 14-18 My 18 '70
Soviets deploy new Suez defenses. il Aviation W 93:14-16 Jl 13 '70
Soviets shifting Mideast balance. E. H. Kolcum. il Aviation W 92:18-21 My 11 '70
U.S. dilemma in Middle East. il U S News 68: 28-30 Je 15 '70
Why Moscow risks new Mideast war. U S News 68:33 My 11 '70

MILK—*Continued*

Production

Are we headed for a milk surplus? D. Braun and J. Carlson. Farm J 94:15+ S '70
See also
Cows—Testing

Sanitation
See Milk hygiene

MILK, Human
DDT in mother's milk. C. F. Wurster. Sat R 53:58-9 My 2 '70

MILK, Synthetic. See Milk substitutes

MILK containers
Whose fingers are in the milk? Consumer Rep 35:271 My '70

MILK hygiene
Ways to keep milk quality high. D. Murray. Suc Farm 68:C2 Je '70
Whose fingers are in the milk? Consumer Rep 35:271 My '70

MILK industry and trade
Morinaga exports its milky way. il Bsns W p44-5 Je 20 '70
NFO milk contracts worry big co-ops. N. Reeder. Farm J 94:71 F '70
See also
Carnation company
Milk—Marketing

MILK production. See Milk—Production

MILK products. See Dairy products

MILK sanitation. See Milk hygiene

MILK substitutes
Coming on fast: more milk substitutes. N. Reeder. Farm J 93:D7+ D '69
Mechanical cow: producing milk from plant materials. J. Hobson. il Sci Digest 67:76-8 Je '70

MILK supply
See also
Milk hygiene

MILKEREIT, John E.
Building takeover at the University of Akron. Sch & Soc 98:374-5 O '70

MILKING parlors
Four new ones from Europe. F. E. Breth. il Farm J 94:D8-9+ D '70

Equipment
Add-on automation in the milking parlor. N. Reeder. il Farm J 94:72-3 F '70
Dawning: a new era in parlor milking. D. Braun. il Farm J 93:D8-11+ D '69
Rototandem target: one man, 120 cows per hour; milk producer Derek Powell in England. T. Fellows. il Farm J 93:D12 D '69

MILKMAIDS
Milkmaids are back. L. M. Palmer. Farm J 94:23 S '70

MILKY way
Movie of the Milky way's hydrogen clouds. il Sky & Tel 39:92-3 F '70
See also
Stars

MILL, James
Mills: father and son. B. Mazlish. il pors Horizon 12:106-11 Sum '70 *

MILL, John Stuart
Mills: father and son. B. Mazlish. il pors Horizon 12:106-11 Sum '70 *

MILL VALLEY, Calif.
Happy sound in Mill Valley; a teacher and her third-grade chorus. il pors Life 69:50-2 S 25 '70

MILLAR, T. B.
Soviet policies south and east of Suez. For Affairs 49:70-80 O '70

MILLER, Arthur
Bangkok prince. Harper 241:32-3 Jl '70
War between young and old. il por McCalls 97:32 Jl '70
about
Arthur Miller, by B. Nelson. Review Sat R 53:35 Jl 25 '70. T. F. Driver *

MILLER, Arthur R.
Detour to 1984. Nation 210:648-51 Je 1 '70
How far must surveillance go? Cur 123:27-30 N '70

MILLER, Carolynne L.
Genealogical research: a basic guide. Hobbies 75:140-1+ S '70

MILLER, Catherine Lanham
At my age? il Harp Baz 103:180-3 Mr '70
(ed) See Young, R. G. We did it

MILLER, Clement A.
Early Gaffuriana: new answers to old questions. bibliog f por Mus Q 56:367-88 Jl '70

MILLER, Conrad
Galley refrigerator. il Motor B 126:22 S '70
Help your boat fight corrosion. il Motor B 126:66-70+ O '70
How it works: the outboard motor. il Motor B 126:16 Ag '70
Inspect your boat's fuel system, now! il Motor B 126:10-12+ Ag '70
(ed) Marine electronics; power and sail. See issues of Motor boating
Sun is your compass. il Motor B 126:34-5+ Jl '70

MILLER, David E.
No way out. Flying 87:72 N '70

MILLER, Donald G.
Toward a theology of evangelism. Chr Today 14:5-8+ My 8; 9-12 My 22 '70

MILLER, Drino
Motor trend interview. por Motor T 22:98+ Je '70

MILLER, Ed Mack
In the jump seat. Flying 86:122 Ap '70

MILLER, Eddie
Cabinet and the tool box; address, March 19, 1970. Vital Speeches 36:475-8 My 15 '70

MILLER, Edward B.
Changes ahead in Washington's labor policies? interview. il pors Nations Bsns 58:68-72 S '70
about
Dark horse for the NLRB. por Bsns W p35 F 21 '70 *
Nixon's NLRB man rankles labor. por Bsns W p27-8 My 9 '70 *

MILLER, Edwin
Spotlight! See issues of Seventeen

MILLER, Evelyn E.
Trilogy of irony. Engl J 59:59-62 Ja '70

MILLER, Everett L.
Build with IC's; electronic umpire. il Radio-Electr 41:46-7 D '70

MILLER, Floyd
Back from drugs: the triumph of Johnny Cash. por Read Digest 97:85-9 S '70
Emergency whistle on Block Island. il Read Digest 96:121-6 Je '70
L-dopa has set me free. Read Digest 97:115-19 Ag '70

MILLER, Fred
New look in one-designs. il Yachting 127:68-9+ Ap '70

MILLER, G. T.
U.S. journal: Luverne, Ala. C. Trillin. New Yorker 46:53-8 Ag 29 '70 *

MILLER, Gary E.
Million dollar honeymoon. il Motor B 125:64-5+ My '70

MILLER, Gerrit S.
Piltdown man: the realization of fraudulence. K. P. Oakley and C. P. Groves. bibliog Science 169:789 Ag 21 '70 *

MILLER, Hannah
Screenings: 16mm. il Library J 95:756-7 F 15 '70

MILLER, Harry
Cobra, India's good snake. il Nat Geog 138:392-409 S '70

MILLER, Helen Louise
Beany's private eye; drama. Plays 30:21-32 Ja '71
Broomstick beauty; drama. Plays 30:23-32 O '70
Case of the silent caroler; drama. Plays 30:1-12 D '70
Cupid's golden key ring; drama. Plays 29:75-82 F '70
Half-pint cowboy; drama. Plays 30:73-8 Ja '71
Open house for Shakespeare; drama. Plays 30:25-37, 60 N '70
Pin-up pals; drama. Plays 29:31-8 F '70
Rabbits who changed their minds; drama. Plays 29:75-9 Mr '70
Surprise for mother; drama. Plays 29:35-44 My '70

MILLER, Henry
There are so many idiots among my fans that I wonder who the hell I'm writing for; interview. ed. by J. Burns. Mlle 71:162-3+ My '70

MILLER, Howard B.
Your emotions: can they influence disease? adaptation of address, November 1, 1969. il Sci Digest 68:61-4 Jl '70

MILLER, I. and sons, inc.
I. Miller's new line; new president. por Newsweek 75:74-5 Je 22 '70

MILLER, J. Irwin
Can we afford tomorrow? address, November 19,1970. Vital Speeches 37:190-2 Ja 1 '71

MILLER, J. Jefferson, 2d
Ceramics from an eighteenth-century wilderness fort. il Antiques 97:888-92 Je '70

MILLER, Jack
Excerpt from Senate debate, March 11, 1970.
Cong Digest 49:145 My '70
MILLER, James E. jr
Linguistic imagination. Engl J 59:477-83+
Ap '70
To preserve humanness: language and litera-
ture in the '70s and beyond. Engl J 59:
1154-6 N '70
MILLER, James Nathan
Rape on the Oklawaha. il Read Digest 96:54-
60 Ja '70
Should parochial schools get public funds?
Read Digest 96:113-16 F '70
(ed) See McHarg, I. L. Sensible plan for
future development
—and Simmons, Robert
Crisis on our rivers. il Read Digest 97:78-83
D '70
MILLER, Jason
Nobody hears a broken drum. Criticism
New Yorker 46:84+ Mr 28 '70 *
MILLER, Jeffrey Glenn
Notes and comment. New Yorker 46:34 My
16 '70 *
MILLER, Joan
Joan Miller and associates: the Chamber
arts dance players; the Cubiculo. M. Marks.
Dance Mag 44:86 Ap '70 *
MILLER, John B.
Paper sleeping paraphernalia. il Consumer
Bul 53:23-6 Ap '70
MILLER, John N.
William of Ockham approaches heaven; poem.
Chr Cent 87:868 Jl 15 '70
MILLER, Kemp
Changes in the black ghetto: East Palo
Alto. W. Stegner. por Sat R 53:12+ Ag 1
'70 *
MILLER, Kenneth F.
Glass piston trimmer capacitors. por Electr
World 83:45-8 Ap '70
MILLER, L. L. and Narang, R. S.
Induced photolysis of DDT. bibliog il Science
169:368-70 Jl 24 '70
MILLER, Larry
Conservative approach to science. Sci N 98:
102 Ag 1 '70
Wanted: a policy for science in the sea. il
Sci N 97:256 Mr 7 '70
MILLER, Leon
We need more custom feedlots in the North-
west; interview. ed. by G. Lorang. il por
Farm J 94:B40 F '70
MILLER, Leonard A. See Oppenheimer, J. C.
jt. auth.
MILLER, Louis J.
Creating with torn paper. il Design 71:24-5
Fall '69
Decorative drawings. il Design 72:30-1 Wint
'70
Junk prints. il Design 72:17-19 Fall '70
Lesson in spot illustration. il Design 71:14-15
mid-Wint '70
Modern sculpture in soap. il Design 71:30-1
Wint '69
Printing from cardboard cuts. il Design 71:
20-2 mid-Sum '70
Welding with wax. il Design 71:24-5 mid-
Wint '70
MILLER, Maggi
Two sculptures in wood. il House B 112:
30-6 Ag '70
MILLER, Margaret
Consumers and the commissars. Nation 210:
302-5 Mr 16 '70
MILLER, Merle
Mr Truman's hometown. il Holiday 47:40-5+
My '70
MILLER, Mike
How to develop a good Indian lore program.
il Camp Mag 42:12-13 Ap '70
MILLER, Neal E.
Learning to control the uncontrollable. L.
Massett. il por Sci N 97:274-5 Mr 14 '70 *
MILLER, O. L. jr, and others
Visualization of bacterial genes in action.
bibliog il Science 169:392-5 Jl 24 '70
MILLER, Paul R.
Revolutionists among the Chicago demon-
strators. il Bul Atom Sci 26:16-21 F '70
MILLER, Peter
Skiing the French Alps. il Travel & Camera
33:18-31 D '70
MILLER, Philip L.
Anna Pashley. one of the exciting events of
the year. Am Rec G 37:16-17 S '70
Doktor Faust. il Am Rec G 36:864-5+ Jl '70
Five centuries of Englishry in song. Am Rec
G 36:480-4 Mr '70
Johann Sebastian Bach. il Am Rec G 36:
554-6 Ap '70
On the record: Music. See issues of Li-
brary journal to June, 1970

On twenty-five records: forty hours of Schu-
bert lieder. il por Am Rec G 37:142-6 N '70
Recordings from CRI, Odyssey, Westminster,
and Desto; the music of Ned Rorem. por
(p249) Am Rec G 36:252-4 D '69
Werther. il Am Rec G 36:324-5 Ja '70
MILLER, R. Alden
Gardening with plastic mulch. Horticulture
48:36+ Ag '70
Why and how of soil testing. Horticulture
48:20-1+ My '70
MILLER, R. D.
Ice sandwich: functional semipermeable
membrane. il Science 169:584-5 Ag 7 '70
MILLER, Ralph D.
He was the champion of hobbyists. J.
Deschin. il por Pop Phot 66:44+ F '70 *
MILLER, Raymond J. See Koeppe, D. E. jt.
auth.
MILLER, Richard I.
School reorganization and the process of ed-
ucational change; adaptation of address,
June 29, 1967. bibliog Sch & Soc 98:346-9 O
'70
Teacher education and preparation for the
21st century; adaptation of address, No-
vember 8, 1967. Sch & Soc 98:278-81 Sum
'70
MILLER, Robert B.
Dilemma of child care. America 122:125-8 F
7 '70
Sex, sex, sexxzzzzzz. Commonweal 93:192-7
N 20 '70
MILLER, Robert W. and Johnson, J. D.
Corporate ambassadors to Washington; ex-
cerpts. Nations Bsns 58:44+ Jl '70
MILLER, Robert Watt
Robert Watt Miller, Oakland, California, Oc-
tober 10, 1899—San Francisco, February 19,
1970. K. H. Adler. por Opera N 34:13 Ap 18
'70 *
MILLER, S. E.
Optical communications research progress.
bibliog il Science 170:685-95 N 13 '70
MILLER, S. M. and others
Creaming the poor. il Trans-Action 7:38-45
Je '70
MILLER, Stanley L. and Smythe, W. D.
Carbon dioxide clathrate in the martian ice
cap. bibliog il Science 170:531-3 O 30 '70
MILLER, Stephen M.
More tricks for waterfowl. il Outdoor Life
145:24-5+ Ja '70
MILLER, Stuart C.
Our Mylai of 1900; Americans in the Philip-
pine insurrection. il Trans-Action 7:19-28
S '70
MILLER, Thomas P. See Patton, W. W. jr. jt.
auth.
MILLER, Timothy
Whither unity? A case study. Chr Cent 87:
891-3 Jl 22 '70
MILLER, Walter Michael, 1923-
Theme of responsibility in Miller's A can-
ticle for Leibowitz. M. A. Bennett. Engl
J 59:484-9 Ap '70 *
MILLER, William Robert
Power of Pentecost: we need it now more
than ever. Chr Cent 87:592-4 My 13 '70
MILLETT, Kate
Furious young philosopher who got it down
on paper. M.-C. Wrenn. il pors Life 69:22-3
S 4 '70 *
How now, Kate? E. Van Den Haag. Nat R
22:1004-5 S 22 '70 *
Liberation of Kate Millett. por Time 96:18-19
Ag 31 '70 *
MILLIGAN, J. V. and Kraicer, Jacob
Adenohypophysial transmembrane potentials;
polarity reversal by elevated external potas-
sium ion concentration. bibliog il Science
167:182-4 Ja 9 '70
MILLIGAN, Jerry L. See Dale, E. L. jt. auth.
MILLIKEN, Frank R.
Mountain that became the richest hole on
earth. il por Nations Bsns 58:88-9 Ja '70
MILLIKEN, J. Gordon. See Coddington, D. C.
jt auth
MILLINGEN, John Gideon
Archaic bellyaches about doctors' fees;
excerpt from Curiosities of medical experi-
ence. il Todays Health 48:32-4 Ag '70
MILLIOHMMETERS. See Ohmmeters
MILLION, Guy P.
Manpower training goes to college. il Am Ed
6:23-5 N '70
MILLIONAIRES
Manchild caper; giveaway stunt of M. J.
Brody. il por Newsweek 75:21-2 F 2 '70
Now, 1,122 incomes of 1 million or more.
U S News 69:61-2 N 9 '70
Twilight of a tycoon: the quiet billionaire,
D. Ludwig. il por Time 96:76-8 N 30 '70
World is one big put-on: M. J. Brody gives
away thousands of dollars. il por Time 95:
13 F 2 '70
See also
Michael, J.

MILLIVOLTMETERS. See Voltmeters

MILLODOT, Michel. See Glickstein, M. jt. auth.

MILLON, René
Teotihuacán: completion of map of giant ancient city in the valley of Mexico. bibliog il Science 170:1077-82 D 4 '70

MILLS, Allan
New theory on the moon craters. M. Priestly. il Sci Digest 68:57-8 O '70 *

MILLS, Curtis
Mills brothers. il por Newsweek 75:59-60 Je 15 '70 *
These Mills bros. are in the record business, too. P. Putnam. il pors Sports Illus 32:57-8 My 4 '70 *

MILLS, Enos
Enos Mills, Columbus of the Rockies. I. Ross. il por Nat Wildlife 9:26-8 D '70 *

MILLS, Gordon
Ladies' men of music; with report by J. Bonfante. il pors Life 69:46-52+ S 18 '70 *

MILLS, Grace Evelyn
Christmas comes to Hamelin; drama. Plays 30:53-60, 96 D '70

MILLS, James
Godmother to the world's loveliest girls. il pors Life 69:63-5+ N 13 '70

MILLS, Joan
Christmas coming! il Read Digest 97:69-72 D '70
God bless our shimmed-up home. Read Digest 97:59-62 N '70
Just for fun, and love. Read Digest 96:145-8 Ja '70
Sweet uses of solitude. Read Digest 96:211-12+ Je '70
There must be some kinda trick to this. Read Digest 96:82-4 F '70

MILLS, Marvin
Mills brothers. il por Newsweek 75:59-60 Je 15 '70 *
These Mills bros. are in the record business, too. P. Putnam. il pors Sports Illus 32:57-8 My 4 '70 *

MILLS, Nicolaus C.
Eagle over the lettuce fields. Commonweal 93:140-1 N 6 '70

MILLS, Stephanie
Miss Stephanie Mills vs. motherhood. A. Wolff. il por Look 34:58-9 Ap 21 '70 *

MILLS, Steven H. and Heath, J. E.
Thermoresponsiveness of the preoptic region of the brain in house sparrows. bibliog il Science 168:1008-9 My 22 '70

MILLS, Thomas B.
FET dual-trace scope switch. il Radio-Electr 41:36-8 Jl '70

MILLS, Watson E.
Reassessing glossolalia. Chr Cent 87:1217-19 O 14 '70

MILLS, Wilbur Daigh
Excerpts from debate, April 15, 1970. Cong Digest 49:172+ Je '70
Runaway federal deficits: a warning from Wilbur Mills; excerpts from address, October 21, 1970. il por U S News 69:68-9 N 9 '70
about
Mills bill. il Newsweek 75:76 Ap 27 '70 *
Ways and means chairman. Trans-Action 7: 7 Ja '70
Wilbur the shrewd. Time 95:15 Mr 23 '70 *

MILLS (buildings) See Factories

MILLS brothers (singers) See Negro singers

MILLS college, Oakland, Calif.
Center for contemporary music. A. Earle. il Hi Fi 20:MA24-5 S '70

MILLVILLE, N. J.
Double the life of your landfill. W. E. Shaw. il Am City 85:64 Je '70

MILNE, Alan Alexander
Man who drew Pooh. R. Cowley. il McCalls 97:12+ Ag '70 *

MILNE, Lorus J. and Milne, Margery
Evergreen review; with biographical sketches. il pors Natur Hist 79:4, 80-91 Ja '70

MILNE, Margery. See Milne, L. J. jt. auth.

MILNER, Art
Eat. Mlle 71:20+ Jl 70

MILNER, Christina
Pimping game. il por Time 97:54-5 Ja 11 '71 *

MILNES, Sherrill
Marlboro man as Macbeth. por Time 95:57 My 11 '70 *
Sherrill Milnes; interview, ed. by R. Hemming. por Sr Schol 96:18 My 11 '70

MILO
Can use milo to fight rootworms. il Suc Farm 68:45 Je '70

MILOSH, Joseph
Supplement for teaching Beowulf. Engl J 59:646-54 My '70

MILSTEIN, George
Chant on the plant. il por Newsweek 76:82 Ag 17 '70 *

MILSTEIN, Tom
Perspective on the Panthers. bibliog f Commentary 50:35-43 S '70; 51:16+ Ja '71

MILTON, John, 1608-1674
Milton's dialogue with the epic: Paradise regained and the tradition. R. W. Condee. Yale R 59:357-75 Mr '70 *

MILTZ, Robert J.
Paraprofessional: slave or aide? Clear House 44:390 Mr '70

MILWAUKEE
Good interchange design can make downtown viable. R. C. Greaves. Am City 85: 148-9 Je '70

Education
It's hard to come back; liaison teacher program to help delinquent children. M. P. Pfeil. il Am Ed 6:3-6 Je '70
Milwaukee teachers' education association. J. R. Colter. Todays Ed 59:64 N '70

Hotels, restaurants, etc.
Movable feast. R. A. De Groot. Esquire 74: 98+ N '70

Libraries
See also
Milwaukee public library

Newspapers
See also
Milwaukee journal

Sanitary affairs
Easy-switch spreader removal. il Am City 85:74-5 Ja '70

Theater
Big adventures: presentation of The Prince of Peasantmania by the Milwaukee repertory theater company. H. Hewes. il Sat R 53:12+ Mr 21 '70

MILWAUKEE Brewers (baseball) See Baseball clubs

MILWAUKEE journal
Going for the jugular; political cartoons of W. W. Sanders. il por Newsweek 76:55 S 28 '70

MILWAUKEE public library
Obscenity and pornography statement further justified. J. F. Krug and J. A. Harvey. Am Lib 1:751-2 S '70

MILWAUKEE repertory theater. See Milwaukee—Theater

MILWAUKIE, Ore.

Education
Their own week: pupils planning their own curriculum. J. M. Brown and D. Emberlin. Todays Ed 59:12 My '70

MILWEE, William I. Jr. See Rainnie, W. O. jt. auth.

MIMICRY (biology)
Multiple mimetic forms in an ant-mimicking clubionid spider. J. Reiskind. il Science 169: 587-8 Ag 7 '70

MIMIEUX, Yvette
Yvette Mimieux. il pors Look 34:48-51+ N 17 '70 c

MIMNERMUS
On old age; poem, tr. by M. Mesic. Poetry 116:344 Ag '70

MIMS, A. Grace
Soul: the black man and his music. bibliog il Negro Hist Bul 33:141-6 O '70

MIMS, Forrest M. 3d
Light-emitting diodes. il Pop Electr 33:35+ N '70
—and Roberts, H. E.
Assemble an LED communicator, the opticom. il Pop Electr 33:45-50+ N '70

MIND. See Intellect

MIND, inc.
Education and industry: troubled partnership. E. Carlson. il Sat R 53:46-7+ Ag 15 '70

MIND-altering drugs. See Hallucinogenic drugs

MIND and body
Monkey see, monkey do, as Not George helps science study you. il Todays Health 48:18 O '70
See also
Consciousness
Faith cure
Medicine, Psychosomatic
Mental hygiene
Psychology, Physiological
Stigmatization

MIND reading. See Clairvoyance

MINDER, Thomas L.
Organizational problems in library cooperation. il por Library J 95:3448-50 O 15 '70

MINE accidents and explosions
See also
Coal mines and mining—Accidents and explosions
Coal mines and mining—Safety devices and measures
MINE drainage
Acidic mine drainage: the rate-determining step. P. C. Singer and W. Stumm. bibliog il Science 167:1121-3 F 20 '70; Discussion. 169:98. 504 Jl 3. 31 '70
Problems underfoot; Environmental effects of underground mining and of mineral processing. T. Aaronson. bibliog il Environ 12:16-29 N '70
MINE fires
Problems underfoot; Environmental effects of underground mining of mineral processing. T. Aaronson. bibliog il Environ 12:16-29 N '70
MINE safety appliances company
Tricky metals that cool it; NaK alloy coolant system. il Bsns W p 112 N 7 '70
MINE subsidences
Problems underfoot; Environmental effects of underground mining and of mineral processing. T. Aaronson. bibliog il Environ 12:16-29 N '70
MINE water
See also
Mine drainage
MINER, Lisbeth
Stitch in time. Motor B 126:16 S '70
MINER, Virginia Scott
Of reminder books; poem. Good H 170:184 F '70
MINERAL King recreation area (propsed) See Recreation areas—California
MINERAL metabolism
Mineral cycles. E. S. Deevey, jr. il Sci Am 223:148-58 bibliog(p264-5) S '70
MINERAL waters
Things are hard at the petrifying well; Knaresborough, Yorkshire. il Sci Digest 67:24-5 F '70
MINERALIZATION
Things are hard at the petrifying well; Knaresborough, Yorkshire. il Sci Digest 67:24-5 F '70
MINERALOGY
Apollo 11 lunar science conference: general mineralogy; symposium. bibliog il Science 167:583-604 Ja 30 '70
Apollo 11 lunar science conference: special mineral studies; symposium. bibliog il Science 167:605-40 Ja 30 '70
How good are you as a mineralogist? quiz. J. Daugherty and M. Daugherty. il Sci Digest 67:74-5+ Je '70
See also
Halos (mineralogy)
Meteorites
MINERALS. See Mineralogy
MINERALS in diet
See also
Iron in diet
MINERALS in sea water. See Sea water
MINERALS in the body
See also
Mineral metabolism
Trace elements
MINERS
See also
Coal miners
United mine workers of America
MINES, Bureau of. See United States—Mines, Bureau of
MINES, Military
Why the death toll; land mines and booby traps in Vietnam. N. Horrock. il Newsweek 76:32 Ag 31 '70
MINES and mineral resources
See also
Coal mines and mining
Mining industry and finance
Prospecting
Raw materials
Salt
Sulfur

Alaska
Mining the public lands. E. N. Layne. il Am Heritage 21:118 Ag '70

Australia
Opals, anybody? H. E. Mercer. il Travel 134:24+ Jl '70
Our far-flung correspondents. J. Colebrook. New Yorker 46:70+ S 5 '70
See also
Mining industry and finance—Australia

Canada
See also
Coal mines and mining—Canada

Russia
Door to Russia's storehouse opens. il Bsns W p32 O 10 '70

South Africa
See also
Diamond mines and mining

United States
Minerals aplenty: technology gap. il Sci N 97:288-9 Mr 21 '70
Minerals EQ index. il Nat Wildlife 8:35 O '70; Same. Schol Teach Jr/Sr High pA11 O 5 '70
National resource revenue sharing. W. W. Porter, 2d. il por Am For 76:24-7+ Ja '70
Unexpected spectacles; U.S. mines and quarries; with list of tours. V. H. Guidi. il Travel 133:64-8+ Mr '70
See also
Mining industry and finance—United States

Utah
Mining the Great Salt Lake. il Sci N 97:454-5 My 9 '70

Western states
Fire in the hole! excerpts from Western mining. O. E. Young, jr. bibliog il Am West 7:15-19 Jl '70
Mining the public lands. E. N. Layne. il Am Heritage 21:118 Ag '70
MINES and mineral resources, Submarine. See Ocean mining
MING porcelain. See Pottery, Chinese
MINIATURE cameras. See Cameras
MINIATURE computers. See Computers—Miniaturization
MINIATURE furniture. See Furniture, Miniature
MINIATURE gardens. See Gardens, Miniature
MINIATURE objects
Tiny wonders; Chinese silver spoons inside cherry pit. T. Messick. il Design 72:9 Wint '70
See also
Furniture, Miniature
Models of cities, towns, etc.
MINIATURE rooms. See Rooms, Miniature
MINIATURE roses. See Roses
MINIATURE trees. See Trees, Dwarf
MINI-BICYCLES. See Bicycles
MINI-BIKE racing. See Motorcycle racing
MINIBIKES. See Motorcycles
MINICHIELLO airplane hijacking trial.   See Trials—Italy
MINICK, Roger
Gallery; photographs. Life 69:8-9 S 25 '70
MINI fishing. See Fishing
MINIMAL brain dysfunction
Hidden handicaps to learning. A. Greenblatt. il Parents Mag 45:53-5+ O '70
Secondary emotional reactions in children with learning disabilities. R. F. Wagner. Ment Hy 54:577-9 O '70
MINIMUM wage

United States
Another boost in minimum wage? U S News 68:71 Mr 9 '70
Would lower pay mean more jobs? question of a minimum wage for teen-agers. U S News 68:23 Mr 30 '70
Youth unemployment and minimum wages. T. W. Gavett. il Mo Labor R 93:3-12 Mr '70
MINING claims
Let's stop mining in our national parks and wilderness areas; with editorial comment. R. D. Butcher. il Am For 76:11, 28-31+ S '70
MINING engineering
See also
Blasting
MINING industry and finance
Natural-resource stocks. G. J. Henry. Forbes 106:54 Jl 1 '70
See also
Patino mining corporation

Australia
Mining stocks take a wild ride Down Under il Bsns W p45 Mr 14 '70

Belgium
Mining company without a mine; Union minière. il Forbes 106:44-5 Jl 1 '70

United States
Mineral search for the wealthy. il Bsns W p24 Ag 8 '70
See also
United States—Mines, Bureau of

MINING law
Mining law of 1872 must be scrapped. S. L. Udall. il Nat Wildlife 8:9-11 Je '70
  See also
Mining claims

MINING machinery
  See also
Dredging machinery

MINING towns
  See also
Virginia City, Nev.

MINISTERS of the gospel. See Clergy

MINISTRY, Doctor of. See Degrees, Academic

MINK, Patsy (Takemoto)
Hormones in the White House. pors Time 96:13 Ag 10 '70 *

MINKS
Transmissible mink encephalopathy: experimental transmission to the squirrel monkey. R. J. Eckroade and others. bibliog il Science 169:1088-90 S 11 '70

MINNAERT, Marcel Gilles Jozef
Outstanding solar astronomer. J. Ashbrook. il pors Sky & Tel 40:344 D '70 *

MINNEAPOLIS
Twin Cities. J. F. Hart and R. B. Adams. bibliog il Focus 20:1-7 F '70

City planning
Aerial walkways: big plans for the future. il Bsns W p48-9 D 26 '70
Minneapolis businessmen bring new life to downtown area. il Parks & Rec 5:33 My '70
  See also
Twin Cities metropolitan council

Community centers
Neighborhood center with a difference. G. M. Soule. il Parks & Rec 5:32-4 Ap '70

Education
Talent runs free at the Twin Cities institute. C. Watson. il Am Ed 6:3-6 O '70

Hotels, restaurants, etc.
International chef; Rosewood room of the Northstar inn. M. Woodward. il Travel 134:16 Jl '70

Libraries
  See also
Minneapolis public library

Music
Report: American premiere of Werner Egk's burlesque opera. 17 days and 4 minutes. P. Gainsley. Opera N 34:32 F 28 '70
  See also
Center opera company

Politics and government
God is my adviser. il por Newsweek 76:58 Jl 20 '70

Streets
Repair paving cracks faster, for less money. E. Larson. il Am City 85:60 S '70

Transit systems
People look at transit. H. R. Orth and W. Cherwony. il Am City 85:126+ Je '70

MINNEAPOLIS center opera company. See Center opera company, Minneapolis

MINNEAPOLIS public library
Minneapolis librarians defeat censorship move. Library J 95:4090 D 1 '70

MINNELLI, Liza
Liza. S. Blum. il por Redbook 134:66-7+ F '70 *
Liza, gasping for breath. por Time 95:43 Mr 9 '70 *
Two young successes: Liza Minnelli and Jane Fonda. pors Vogue 155:106 Je '70 *

MINNESOTA
Wild ricing. R. H. Hofstrand. il por(p8) Natur Hist 79:50-5 Mr '70
  See also
Architecture, Domestic—Minnesota
Booksellers and bookselling—Minnesota
Camping—Minnesota
Education—Minnesota
Fishing—Minnesota
Grand Portage National Monument
Hennepin County
Hunting—Minnesota
Wilderness areas—Minnesota

Capitol
Dome lighting turns night into day. Am City 85:142 S '70

Politics and government
Humphrey's comeback. por Newsweek 76:27 S 28 '70
New Humphrey. A. A. Eisele. New Repub 163:18-19 S 19 '70
Palmer's pumpkin. il por Time 97:14-15 Ja 18 '71
Still the man who loves to talk, to teach, to preach: H. H. Humphrey. R. Wool. il pors N Y Times Mag p25-7+ O 11 '70
Will it be Senator Humphrey again? il por U S News 69:36 O 12 '70

MINNESOTA mining and manufacturing company. See 3M company

MINNESOTA multiphasic personality inventory. See Personality tests

MINNESOTA. University, Minneapolis
Criminal justice studies: a quietly emerging field. N. Gruchow. Science 167:1474 Mr 13 '70
Who's afraid of the big bad U? R. Hoffmann. il Mlle 71:176-7+ O '70

MINNESOTA Vikings (football club) See Football clubs

MINNICH, Jerry
Campus whole earth co-op. il Org Gard & Farm 17:73-7 S '70

MINNIE (operatic character) See Characters in opera

MINNIE Pearl's fried chicken system. See Restaurants—Franchise system

MINNIE'S boys; musical comedy. See Musical comedies, revues, etc.—Criticisms, plots, etc.

MINNOWS
Terrestrial and aquatic orientation in the starhead topminnow. fundulus notti. C. P. Goodyear. bibliog il Science 168:603-5 My 1 '70

MINOGUE, K. R.
On the fashionable idea of national guilt. Am Scholar 39:211-18, 726-7 Spr, Aut '70

MINOR, Audax, pseud.
Race track. See issues of New Yorker

MINOR planets. See Asteroids

MINORITIES
Ethnic American: interview. ed. by T. H. Clancy. B. Mikulski. America 123:558-9+ D 26 '70
Lenin and cultural rights of minorities. L. A. Posti. il UNESCO Courier 23:16-21 Jl '70
Minorities are hard to live with. Trans-Action 7:7-8 Ja '70
Minorities in American history. il Sr Schol 95:3-7 O 13; 8-11 N 10 '69; 12-16 Ja 12; 96: 11-13 My 11 '70
New minority: the churches' concern. America 123:253 O 10 '70
Obligations of oppressed minorities. M. Walzer. bibliog f Commentary 49:71-80 My '70; Discussion. 50:14-16 Ag '70
Rising cry: ethnic power; American minorities. C. Roberts. il Newsweek 76:32-3+ D 21 '70
What's going to happen to us individuals? address, August 14, 1970. M. Rafferty. Vital Speeches 36:752-5 O 1 '70
  See also
Race discrimination
United Nations—Sub-commission on prevention of discrimination and protection of minorities

Employment
Helping the hard-core adjust to the world of work. L. Nadler. il Harvard Bsns R 48:117-26 Mr '70
It's not a matter of choice: searching out potential black and Spanish-speaking employees. L. L. L. Golden. Sat R 53:67 My 9 '70

MINORITIES in textbooks. See Textbooks

MINORITY enterprise small business investment companies. See Small business investment companies

MINORITY of millions; drama. See Hark, M. and McQueen, N.

MINORS (law) See Children—Law

MINOTAUR; ballet. See Ballets—Criticisms

MINSKY, Hyman P.
Passage to Pakistan. il Trans-Action 7:27-31 F '70

MINSTRELS
  See also
Troubadours

MINT 400 race. See Motor vehicle racing

MINT juleps. See Liquors

MINTON, Frank
Need for a theology of death. Chr Cent 87: 352-5 Mr 25 '70

MINTON, R. B.
Hints on planetary photography for amateurs. il Sky & Tel 40:56-9, 116-18 Jl-Ag '70

MINTON, Robert, and Rice, Stephen
Using racism at San Quentin. il Ramp Mag
8:18-24 Ja '70
MINTZ, Edward N.
Celebrity spotlight. See issues of Travel
MINTZ, Morton
Confusion on the pill. New Repub 162:10-11
Ja 31 '70
Spiro Agnew's candles. New Repub 162:13-15
Ja 17 '70
MINTZ, Walter
Wall Street view. por Forbes 106:160 O 15 '70
MINUDRI, Regina
(ed) Adult books for young adults (cont) Li-
brary J 95:259-62, 792-8, 1210-16, 1659-65,
1969-75, 2318-20, 2545-50, 3076-8+, 3649-55,
4065-70, 4385-90 Ja 15, F 15, Mr 15, Ap 15,
My 15, Je 15-Jl, S 15, O 15, N 15, D 15 '70
MINUTEMAN (guided missile) See Guided mis-
siles
MINUTEMEN (organization)
DePugh and the Minutemen: wonderland of
the mind. W. Turner. pors Ramp Mag 8:
10+ Je '70
MIQUELON. See Saint Pierre and Miquelon
(islands)
MIRABELLI, Eugene, Jr
Flashbacks and flashforwards. Writer 83:
15-17+ D '70
MIRACLE, Leonard
Day on the Deschutes. il Outdoor Life 145:
78-9+ Ap '70
Yellowtails by the ton. il por Outdoor Life
145:60-3+ F '70
MIRACLES
See also
Faith cure
Jesus Christ—Miracles
Stigmatization
MIRANDA, Gary
For J.C.R. in his eightieth year: poem. Am
Scholar 39:242 Spr '70
Gardener; poem. Mlle 72:210 N '70
MIRANDA sensorex cameras. See Single-lens
reflex cameras
MIRÓ, Joan
Merry squiggles of Joan Miró. G. Kent. il
Read Digest 97:165-70 D '70 *
Miro's bronze age. J. Ashbery. il Art N 69:34-
6 My '70 *
MIRROR lenses. See Lenses, Photographic
MIRRORS
Don't let a mirror set your house on fire!
il Consumer Bul 53:35 N '70
Lighted makeup mirrors. il Consumer Rep
35:676-80 N '70
Mirror, mirror on the wall, who is the fairest
one of all? lighted make-up mirrors. il Con-
sumer Bul 53:7-11 My '70
Nothing makes a room sparkle like mirror.
W. Baldwin. House & Gard 138:12-13+ O '70
Spot-check mirrors that reflect the total you.
il McCalls 98:38 O '70
MIRRORS, Automobile. See Automobiles—
Equipment
MIRRORS for cameras
Up, down & around; candid photos with
Spiratone Circo-Mirrotach. J. Scully. il
Mod Phot 34:84-5 F '70
MIRRORS for telescopes
On making a channeled pitch lap. J. T.. Carle.
il Sky & Tel 39:186-90 Mr '70
Sky's the limit with this 200-power telescope.
R. Brightman. il Pop Mech 134:166-73+ D
'70
Versatile overarm mirror-grinding machine.
P. R. Zurakowski and F. Kolberg. il Sky
& Tel 40:382-7 D '70
MIRV. See MIRV
MISCONDUCT in office
See also
Judicial corruption
MISHIMA, Yukio, pseud.
Last samurai. il pors Time 96:32+ D 7 '70 *
Mishima incident. W. Mensendiek. Chr Cent
88:29-30 Ja 6 '71 *
Notes and comment. New Yorker 46:39-41 D
12 '70 *
Obituary
Nat R 22:1389-90 D 29 '70. D. Brudnoy
People are talking about. . . il por Vogue 156:
144-5 N 1 '70 *
Samurai '70: the death of Mishima. il pors
Newsweek 76:31-2 D 7 '70 *
Samurai who committed hara-kiri. J. Schec-
ter. il pors Life 69:36-7 D 11 '70 *
You've heard of Yukio Mishima. P. Shabe-
coff. il N Y Times Mag p6-7+ Ag 2 '70 *
MISHKIN, Kirsten
Non humilis mulier triumpho. Time 95:45 Je
29 '70 *
MISHRA, S. D. and Gaur, B. K.
Senescence in detached betel leaves: role of
the petiole. bibliog il Science 167:387-8 Ja
23 '70

MISPRONUNCIATION. See English language—
Pronunciation
MISREPRESENTATION. See Fraud
MISS America contests. See Beauty contests
MISS Teen-age America contests. See Beauty
contests
MISSA brevis; ballet. See Ballets—Criticisms
MISSILE bases. See Guided missile bases
MISSING persons
Tom Cat and the Colonel; T. Riha mystery.
pors Time 95:13 F 9 '70
MISSION BAY park, San Diego. See San Diego,
Calif.—Parks and playgrounds
MISSION control (space flight) See United
States—Manned spacecraft center
MISSION of the church
Ancient word for modern churches. M. M.
Shideler. Chr Cent 87:1509-13 D 16 '70
Beyond sectarianism; COCU and Roman
Catholicism. W. B. Blakemore. Chr Cent
87:237 F 25 '70
Church in search of mission. H. Kraemer.
Chr Today 15:10-13 Ja 1 '71
Church, the university and social policy, by
K. Underwood and others. Review
Chr Cent 87:506-7+ Ap 22 '70. F. T. Trotter
Church union and urban mission. S. Hallett.
Chr Cent 87:238-9 F 25 '70
Counterfeit religion. L. N. Bell. Chr Today
14:27 Jl 31 '70
Gospel of the dynamic middle. G. M. Docher-
ty. Chr Cent 87:863-6 Jl 15 '70
Karl Rahner, an interview; ed. by W. V.
Dych. K. Rahner. America 123:356-9 O 31
'70
Night questions. V. Fiddes. Chr Today 14:
3-5 Jl 31 '70
Polarization. L. N. Bell. Chr Today 15:34-5
Ja 1 '71
Purpose of church. J. Burtchaell. Common-
weal 92:437-41 S 4 '70
Training for a time of change. R. L. Howe.
Chr Cent 87:477-80 Ap 22 '70
See also
Church and the world
MISSIONARIES
Agnostic meets missionary. J. D. Douglas.
Chr Today 14:29 S 25 '70
Evangelization crisis in India: a missionary's
view. R. H. Lesser. il Cath World 211:166-
71 Jl '70
Exiled from Nigeria. D. King. America 122:
245 Mr 7 '70
MISSIONARY conferences
Youth on the march; Inter-varsity mission-
ary convention. Chr Today 15:27 D 18 '70
MISSIONARY societies
Converting tent-trailers into missionaries;
Bethany fellowship, Bloomington, Minn. M.
Parrish. il Chr Today 14:25-6 S 25 '70
MISSIONS
Crisis of identity for some missionary so-
cieties. D. McGavran. Chr Today 14:10-12+
My 8 '70
Frankfurt declaration; with text of the De-
claration and editorial comment. D. Mc-
Gavran. Chr Today 14:3-6, 21 Je 19 '70
See also
Catholic church—Missions
Evangelistic work

Africa
See also
Christians in Africa

Cambodia
Missionary work to resume in Cambodia.
Chr Today 14:38 Je 5 '70

Latin America
Pentecostal breakthrough. J. L. Klaiber. il
America 122:99-102 Ja 31 '70

Nigeria
See also
Catholic church—Missions

United States
Rescue missions broaden ministries. D.
Kucharsky. Chr Today 14:41-3 F 13 '70

Vietnam (Republic)
Woman doctor is missing in action. J. C.
Hefley. il Todays Health 48:38-41+ Ap '70
MISSISSIPPI
See also
Education—Mississippi
Fishing—Mississippi
Justice, Administration of—Mississippi
Lafayette County
Negroes—Mississippi
Police—Mississippi

Economic conditions
Camille's wake lies full of battered hopes. il
Bsns W p94+ My 16 '70

MISSISSIPPI—Continued

History

Public opinion and the passage of the Mississippi black codes. M. M. Bigelow. bibliog Negro Hist Bul 33:11-16 Ja '70

Race problems

Yazoo: notes on survival. W. Morris. il Harper 240:43-50+ Je '70

MISSISSIPPI college, Clinton, Miss.
Point and (sob) counterpoint. D. Russell. Sports Illus 32:42-3 Mr 2 '70

MISSISSIPPI council on aging
Senior activity program survives hurricane Camille in Biloxi, Miss. il Aging 190:6-7 Ag '70

MISSISSIPPI hurricane. See Hurricanes

MISSISSIPPI RIVER
Life on the Mississippi, 1970. P. Schrag. il Sat R 53:19-23 D 12 '70
We houseboated down the mighty Miss. P. Snook. il por Nat Wildlife 8:38-42 Ag '70

MISSISSIPPI state university, State College
Return of the boll weevil; C. Evers. J. M. Carter. Library J 95:1817 My 15 '70

MISSISSIPPI test facility. See Proving grounds

MISSISSIPPI. University
Ole Miss enters the '60s. J. B. Cumming, jr. Newsweek 75:83 Mr 30 '70

MISSOURI
  See also
  Booksellers and bookselling—Missouri
  Camps—Missouri
  Current River
  Education—Missouri
  Festivals—Missouri
  Hunting—Missouri
  Libraries—Missouri
  Meramec River
  Ozark Mountains

Antiquities

See Indians of North America—Antiquities—Missouri

State library commission

Dirty word smokescreen; trial of the students involved in J. Bodger incident. N. Ladof. il por Library J 95:2424-6 Jl '70
Joan Bodger vindicated by ALA investigation. por Library J 95:3221 O 1 '70
Proceedings and findings; J. Bodger and Library bill of rights; ALA report. E. Castagna and others. bibliog Am Lib 1:694-704 Jl '70

MISSOURI library association
Proceedings and findings; J. Bodger and Library bill of rights; ALA report. E. Castagna and others. bibliog Am Lib 1:694-704 Jl '70

MISSOURI library commission. See Missouri—State library commission

MISSOURI Pacific railroad
Mop gap. il Forbes 106:30+ S 1 '70

MISSOURI repertory theatre. See Kansas City, Mo.—Theater

MISSOURI RIVER
Steamboat to the Rockies. W. Havighurst. bibliog il Am West 7:4-11+ S '70

MISSOURI state library, Jefferson City, Mo.
Proceedings and findings; J. Bodger and Library bill of rights; ALA report. E. Castagna and others. bibliog Am Lib 1:694-704 Jl '70

MISSOURI. University, Columbia
ALA investigating team slaps U. of Mo. wrist. Library J 95:4211 D 15 '70
Dirty word smokescreen; trial of the students involved in J. Bodger incident. N. Ladof. il por Library J 95:2424-6 Jl '70
Proceedings and findings; J. Bodger and Library bill of rights; ALA report. E. Castagna and others. bibliog Am Lib 1:694-704 Jl '70
Tenure investigation: library administration division's report concerning nonrenewal of contracts of five librarians. Am Lib 1:983-4 N '70

MIST. See Fog

MR Travel award
16th annual Mr Travel award: Apollo 11 crew. il Travel 134:54-7 Jl '70

MISTLETOE
Who started kissing under the mistletoe? il Good H 171:161 D '70

MRS Marvel's magic carpet; story. See Gordon, E. E.

MISUNDERSTANDINGS, International. See International relations

MITCHELL, Albert
In defense of the deer drive. il Field & S 75:48-9+ O '70

MITCHELL, Arthur
Arthur Mitchell & the Dance theater of Harlem. O. Maynard. il pors Dance Mag 44:52-64 Mr '70 *
Ballet with soul. il por Newsweek 76:64 Ag 31 '70 *

MITCHELL, C. Bradford
Memorandum to Oliver Wendell Holmes. il Am Heritage 21:23-7+ F '70

MITCHELL, Carleton
Apres vous, Gretel. il Sports Illus 33:12-15 S 7 '70
Aussies and French hook up. il Sports Illus 33:14-15 Ag 31 '70
Capri: Italy's enchanted rock. il Nat Geog 137:794-809 Je '70
Cruise to islands of wonders and terror. il Sports Illus 32:36-43 Je 8 '70
Grim week for a battling lady. il Sports Illus 33:24-5 S 28 '70
Land of cactus and sunshine. il Motor B 125:94-9+ Mr '70
No cup for the lady. il Sports Illus 33:12-15 O 5 '70
Northland memory. il Yachting 129:66-9+ Ja '71
Rift in the curtain. il Yachting 128:50-2+ Jl; 53-5+ Ag '70
Triangular mini-cruise. il Yachting 128:64-5+ N '70

MITCHELL, Charles I.
Los Alamos: from weapon shop to scientific laboratory. il Bul Atom Sci 26:24-7 N '70

MITCHELL, Curtis
Engineering the new mechanical heart. il Pop Sci 196:64-6+ Mr '70

MITCHELL, David
Mitchell case. il por Newsweek 76:30-1 O 26 '70 *
My Lai massacre, the prosecution rests. D. C. Martin. New Repub 163:13 N 7 '70 *
My Lai trials begin. Time 96:11-12 N 2 '70 *
One not guilty for My Lai. il por Time 96:10 N 30 '70 *
Prosecution rests. Newsweek 76:37-8 N 2 '70 *

MITCHELL, Don
Taking some with Mister Vic; story. Esquire 73:110-12 Je '70
Thelma; story. Atlan 225:73-5 Je '70

MITCHELL, Harold
Islands of the Caribbean. bibliog f Cur Hist 58:107-10+ F '70

MITCHELL, John G.
Bitter struggle for a national park. il Am Heritage 21:97-109 Ap '70

MITCHELL, John Newton
Attorney General Mitchell: the tide is turning against crime; interview. il pors Nations Bsns 58:32-4+ Je '70
Excerpt from address, September 22, 1969. Cong Digest 49:76+ Mr '70
How long Congress how long? address, June 19, 1970. Vital Speeches 36:610-12 Ag 1 '70
John Mitchell on marijuana; interview, ed. by H. Hubbard. por Newsweek 76:22 S 7 '70
Newsmakers; alleged remarks at Women's national press club. Newsweek 76:50 S 28 '70
Respecting the Supreme court. Cur 122:34-5 O '70
Supreme court; address, May 1, 1970. Vital Speeches 36:514-16 Je 15 '70
Wage and price controls? Forget about them; address, May 19, 1970. il por U S News 68:39-41 Je 1 '70
Wire tapping: constitutionality and efficiency; address, October 5, 1970. Vital Speeches 37:34-7 N 1 '70

  about

Attorney General has heard it all before. L. H. Lapham. il pors Life 68:50-50B+ F 13 '70
Battling Mitchell vs. the media. Nation 210:259-60 Mr 9 '70 *
Being candid with Kandy. Time 96:9 S 28 '70 *
Justice, by R. Harris. Review
  Life il por 68:16 Mr 13 '70. W. Sheed *
A look at John Mitchell. J. Osborne. New Repub 162:12-15 F 7 '70 *
Mitchell and the media. Nat R 22:191-2 F 24 '70 *
Mitchell should go. Life 68:38 Ap 17 '70 *
Mitchell tests the Constitution. J. R. Lundy. Nation 210:205-7 F 23 '70 *
Mitchell's answer to critics: look at the facts. por U S News 68:17 F 16 '70 *
New Mitchell? news conference. il por Newsweek 76:14 Jl 27 '70 *
Quiet voice: business suit; Mitchell's program for repression. Nation 210:451-2 Ap 20 '70 *
TRB from Washington: Marse Mitchell. New Repub 163:4 Jl 25 '70 *
Who's delinquent? Nation 210:100-1 F 2 '70

MITCHELL, Joni
Joni Mitchell. G. Astor. il pors Look 34:33-4
Ja 27 '70
MITCHELL, Martha (Beall)
Amazing Martha Mitchell; interview, ed. by
W. McLendon. il pors Look 34:22-6 Jl 28
'70
Most liberated woman in the world; some
Marthaisms. por Newsweek 76:20 N 30 '70
about
And now, the Spiro and Martha show. J.
Austin. il pors Time 96:10 N 23 '70 *
I don't like a plebeian existence. A. Gould.
por Life 68:50B F 13 '70
Life in Washington isn't that much fun. il
pors Life 69:37-41 O 2 '70
Martha Mitchell's view from the top. il pors
Time 96:31-4+ N 30 '70 *
Washington's own Martha. il pors Newsweek
76:18-20+ N 30 '70 *
Who needs Martha Mitchell? S. McBee. pors
McCalls 98:61+ Ja '71 *
MITCHELL, Rodger
Made in Japan; with biographical sketch. il
Natur Hist 79:5, 60-5 O '70
MITCHELL, Roger
For the campus casualties; poem. New Repub
162:26 Je 13 '70
MITCHELL, Wade
On-the-go camping. See issues of Popular
mechanics
MITCHELL, Wanda B.
Teacher's role in ITV. Todays Ed 59:34 Ja
'70
MITCHELL, William R.
By the waters of Zion; poem. Chr Cent 87:
383 Ap 1 '70
MITCHUM, Robert
Robert Mitchum: put on and put down. M.
Ronan. il por Sr Schol 96:22 Ap 27 '70 *
MITER gages. See Gages
MITER jigs. See Jigs
MITES
Mites and commercial extracts of house dust.
G. W. Wharton. bibliog il Science 167:
1382-3 Mr 6 '70
Nasal mites parasitic in nasal and upper
skull tissues in the baboon (papio sp.) C.
S. Kim and B. G. Bang. bibliog il Science
169:372-3 Jl 24 '70
Tiny wolves of the water. D. Barr. il Natur
Hist 79:40-5 Je '70
MITFORD, Jessica
Let us now appraise famous writers. il Atlan
226:45-54 Jl '70
about
Queen of muckrakers. il por Time 96:52 Jl 20
'70 *
MITFORD, Nancy
Boyhood of Frederick the Great. il por Hori-
zon 12:104-10 Wint '70
MITHRAMYCIN. See Antibiotics
MITOCHONDRIA
Cigarette smoke: the effect of residue on
mitochondrial structure. J. R. Kennedy and
A. M. Elliott. bibliog il Science 168:1097-8
My 29 '70
Genetic activity of mitochondria and chloro-
plasts. U. W. Goodenough and R. P. Levine.
il Sci Am 223:22-9 N '70
Liver mitochondria from manganese-deficient
and pallid mice: function and ultrastruc-
ture. L. S. Hurley and others. bibliog il
Science 170:1316-18 D 18 '70
Mitochondrial RNA synthesis during mitosis.
H. Fan and S. Penman. bibliog il Science
168:135-8 Ap 3 '70
Multiple origin for plastids and mitochondria.
P. H. Raven. bibliog Science 169:641-6 Ag
14 '70; Reply. D. L. Taylor. 170:1332 D 18
'70
Ochratoxin A: inhibition of mitochondrial
respiration. J. H. Moore and B. Truelove.
bibliog il Science 168:1102-3 My 29 '70
MITOSIS
See also
Cell division (biology)
MITRIONE, Daniel A.
Murder, Tupamaros-style. il por Time 96:20+
Ag 24 '70 *
Unanswered questions about a tragedy; ex-
cerpts from interview. L. Colonnese. Com-
monweal 92:456-7 S 18 '70 *
U.S. mourns tragic death of Mr Mitrione.
White House statement and Secretary
Rogers' statement, August 10, 1970. W. P.
Rogers. Dept State Bul 63:246-7 Ag 31 '70 *
MITSUI, Takakimi, baron
Where are they now? pors Newsweek 75:10
Mr 9 '70 *
MITTELMAN, Allen
Money loses in bookbuyer's battle. il Pub W
198:26 D 14 '70 *

MITZEL, Harold E.
Computers and adaptive education. il Am Ed
6:23-6 D '70
MIXED bloods (American Indians) See Indians
of North America—Mixed bloods
MIXED marriages. See Marriages, Mixed
MIXED media performances. See Performing
arts
MIXERS
Rancher invents new liquid proportioner.
J. Carlson. Farm J 94:33 Je '70
Revolutionary new mixer has no moving
parts; Static mixer. il Pop Sci 196:62-3 Mr
'70
MIXERS, Electric. See Household appliances,
Electric
MIXERS, Electronic. See Sound—Apparatus
MIXES, Food. See Food mixes
MIXTURES
Use of alligation alternate in chemistry. A.
Mancott. Chem 43:37 Jl '70
MIYAJIMA, Japan
Escape to peaceful Miyajima after the
crowds of Expo '70. il Sunset 144:60+ Mr
'70
MIYAKO hotel. See San Francisco—Hotels, res-
taurants, etc.
MIZENER, Arthur
Edmund Wilson's New republic. New Repub
162:28-30 My 9 '70
MOAB, Utah
Canyonlands by night. F. A. Barnes. il Trav-
el 134:64-6 Ag '70
MOATS, Alice-Leone
Film that shook France. Nat R 22:1406 D 29
'70
MOB violence
Bad day in Lamar; whites attack school
buses carrying Negro children. il News-
week 75:26 Mr 16 '70
Real constitutional crisis. F. S. Meyer. Nat
R 22:571 Je 2 '70
Where we are. Nat R 22:549 Je 2 '70
MOBERLY, Mo.
Mister Carnegie's library; a librarian's
memories of her librarian mother. C. E.
Werkley. il por Am Heritage 21:65-8 F '70
MOBIL oil corporation
One man's poison. il Forbes 105:56 Ap 1 '70
MOBILE crime prevention exhibit. See Exhi-
bitions, Traveling
MOBILE home building industry. See Building
industry
MOBILE home living
Only way to live; Huntington-by-the-Sea mo-
bile village, Calif. N. Proffitt. Newsweek 76:
78-9 Jl 6 '70
People, people, people. L. Jaquith. il Har Yrs
10:32-3+ My '70
MOBILE home parks
Plans mobile-home communities; Intertherm
inc, St Louis. Am City 85:52 Ap '70
MOBILE homes
Mobile home sales roll toward $3-billion. il
Bsns W p74-6 Ja 24 '70; Correction. p7
F 28 '70
Mobile home vs. a house: how the costs com-
pare. il Changing T. 25:19-21 Ja '71
Mobile homes move into the breach. L. A.
Mayer. il Fortune 81:126-30+ Mr '70
Mobile homes one solution to the high cost
of building. Consumer Bul 52:23-4 F '70
Mobile homes: transportable slums of the
future? Trans-Action 7:12-13 F '70
Most home for the money: the mobile home.
il Good H 171:104-9 Jl '70
One housing boom that keeps growing. il
U S News 68:58 F 2 '70
MOBILE libraries. See Bookmobiles
MOBILE servers. See Serving carts
MOBILES
Birth of the Sculp-mobile. A. Wolter. il De-
sign 71:13 mid-Wint '70
Making mobiles. A. Moorey and C. Moorey.
il Design 71:22-6 Sum '70
MOBILITY, Occupational. See Occupational
mobility
MOBIN-UDDIN, Kazi
Great little umbrella. il por Sci Digest 67:
12-13 Ap '70 *
MOBIUS strip; drama. See Boiko, C.
MOBS
See also
Crowds
Mob violence
MOBUTU, Joseph Désiré
President Mobutu of the Congo visits the
United States; exchange of greetings and
toasts, August 4, 1970. Dept State Bul 63:
279-82 S 7 '70
about
Heart specialist. Time 96:31 Jl 6 '70 *
Something to celebrate. il por Newsweek 76:
50+ Jl 13 '70 *
Taming of the Congo. R. W. Howe. New Re-
pub 163:15-16 Ag 1 '70 *

MOCINE, John F.
Case of the illogical ghoti. il Todays Ed 59:
71-2 O '70
MOCKLER, Robert J.
Theory and practice of planning. bibliog
Harvard Bsns R 48:148-50+ Mr '70
MOCKUPS of airplanes. See Airplane models
MOCZAR, Mieczyslaw
With Gomulka gone a new generation takes
over. il pors Newsweek 77:22 Ja 4 '71 *
MOD Donna; musical comedy. See Musical com-
edies, revues, etc.—Criticisms, plots, etc.
MODABBER, Farrokh, and others
Antigen-binding cells in normal mouse thy-
mus. bibliog il Science 170:1102-4 D 4 '70
MODEL airplane engines. See Airplane models
—Engines
MODEL cities program. See Urban renewal
MODEL engines. See Engine models
MODEL farms. See Farms, Model
MODELING
Modeling in clay; helping students learn the
initial study of the human figure. T. S.
Dahood. il Design 71:13 Sum '70
See also
Snow modeling
Soap sculpture
Wax modeling
MODELMAKING
How to build models like a pro. P. Jenscen.
il Pop Mech 134:164-6 N '70
Noah's ark. S. A. Parvin. il por Hobbies 75:
158 O '70
MODELS
Noah's ark. S. A. Parvin. il por Hobbies 75:
158 O '70
See also specific types of models, e.g.
Automobile models; Ship and boat models;
etc.
MODELS (display figures)
Faces for the best places. il por Life 68:76-9
My 15 '70
Special treat for window-shoppers; display
animations. il Design 71:28-9 mid-Sum '70
MODELS (persons)
Godmother to the world's loveliest girls;
model agent E. Ford. J. Mills. il pors Life
69:63-5+ N 13 '70
Have black models really made it? il Ebony
25:152-4+ My '70
See also
Children as models
Forth, J.
MODELS of cities, towns, etc.
Outdoor miniature village. S. A. Parvin. il
por Hobbies 75:144-5+ Jl '70
Sleepy Hollow; an American village of the
1800's in miniature. S. A. Parvin. il Hobbies
75:144-6 My '70
Victorian village in miniature. S. A. Parvin.
il Hobbies 74:148+ Ja '70
MODERATION
Golden mean. K. Crawford. Newsweek 76:
36 D 21 '70
MODERN architecture. See Architecture, Mod-
ern
MODERN art. See Art, Modern
MODERN art museum, New York. See Museum
of modern art, New York
MODERN civilization. See Civilization
MODERN dance. See Dancing
MODERN design. See Design
MODERN foreign language study. See Lan-
guages, Modern—Study and teaching
MODERN furniture. See Furniture
MODERN language association
Radical chic in academe; annual meeting.
Newsweek 77:58-9 Ja 11 '71
MODERN language association of America
Out of the grooves of academe; dissent at
annual meetings. D. Grumbach. Common-
weal 91:468-70 Ja 30 '70
MODERN music. See Music
MODERN photography (periodical)
Annual guide to forty-seven top cameras.
il Mod Phot 33:85-132 D '69
MODERN poetry. See Poetry
MODERNE, Jacques
Jacques Moderne, by S. F. Pogue. Review
Mus Q 56:485-8 Jl '70. L. L. Perkins *
MODERNISM
And that's the way it is. A. H. Leitch. Chr
Today 14:64 S 25 '70; Discussion. 15:39-40
N 6 '70
Beyond belief, by R. N. Bellah. Criticism
Commonweal 93:177-8 N 13 '70. E. Fon-
tinell
Irrationality of modern thought; excerpt from
The church at the end of the twentieth
century. F. A. Schaeffer. Chr Today 15:10-
14 D 4 '70

Manifesto for a theology of the present. R.
Avens. Cath World 212:20-3 O '70
Messianic core; the left tradition in church
and society. R. Ruether. il Commonweal
91:423-5 Ja 16 '70; Reply. A. M. Farrell. 91:
499 F 6 '70
MODERNISM (art)
See also
Art, Modern
Surrealism (art)
MODERNIZATION. See Social change
MODERNIZATION, Housing. See Houses, Re-
modeled
MODERNIZATION of buildings. See Remodel-
ing (architecture)
MODERNIZATION of houses. See Houses, Re-
modeled
MODIFIED Mercalli scale. See Seismometry
MODULAR houses. See Houses, Prefabricated
MODULATION (electronics)
Cross-modulation and intermodulation in re-
ceiver R.F. amplifiers. J. Knepler. il Electr
World 83:55-8 Mr '70
MODULATORS
Amateur scientist; modulator is constructed
for laser light. C. L. Stong. il Sci Am 223:
120-3 N '70
MOE, Ronald C.
Let's keep the electoral college. il Nat R 22:
356-9+ Ap 7 '70
MOELLER, Gregory
Who would ever go to West Point today?
J. R. Moskin. il pors Look 34:31-8 O 6 '70 *
MOFFAT, Donald W.
Nomograms for resonant-circuit Q. il Electr
World 83:30-1 My '70
MOFFAT, George
Welcome back, world champion. il Flying 87:
78-9+ S '70
MOFFAT, Samuel
Parent and child. il N Y Times Mag p97+
N 29 '70
MOFFETT, James P.
Coming on center; address. Engl J 59:528-33
Ap '70
MOFFETT, Samuel H.
What is the evangel? address. Chr Today 14:
3-6 Mr 13 '70
MOFFITT, Ernestine
Student for a day. Schol Teach Jr/Sr High
p 10-11 D 7 '70
MOFFITT, John
(comp) Undergraduate poems. America 122:
444-5 Ap 25 '70
MOFFO, Anna
Anna Moffo; interview, ed. by E. McDonald.
il pors House B 112:60-3 F '70
Anna Moffo; interview, ed. by R. Hemming.
Sr Schol 95:17 Ja 12 '70
Other Moffo; interview, ed. by E. Rizzo. por
Opera N 34:16 Ap 11 '70
MOFFORD, Juliet. See Mofford, T. jt. auth.
MOFFORD, Thomas, and Mofford, Juliet
Come to the Store-front learning center. il
Schol Teach Sec Teach Sup p 13-15 F 2 '70
MOHAMMEDANISM. See Islam
MOHAMMEDANISM and Christianity. See
Christianity and other religions
MOHAN, M. S. See Rechnitz, G. A. jt. auth.
MOHAWK airlines, inc.
Captains capricious. Time 97:70 Ja 4 '71
Mohawk seeks delay on interest payment.
Aviation W 93:30 D 7 '70
MOHIT, Behzad. See Sox, H. C. jr, jt. auth.
MOHNEN, Volker A.
5,000 join in air pollution survey. il por Cons
25:10-15 Ag '70
MOHOLY-NAGY, László
Factory art vs. studio art. B. Rose. Vogue
155:68 Je '70 *
Mighty machine. D. Davis. il Newsweek 76:
108+ N 16 '70 *
MOHOLY-NAGY, Sibyl
Arcology of Paolo Soleri. il Arch Forum 132:
70-5 My '70
Cesar Pelli, public architect. il por Arch
Forum 132:42-7 Mr '70
MOHR, Richard
Curious girl. Opera N 34:24-5 Mr 14 '70
MOIRÉ method
Putting moiré to work. il Chem 43:27 O '70
MOISEYEV dance company
Exalted kitsch; U.S. tour. J. T. Elson. il
Time 96:56-7 Jl 27 '70
Moiseyev and us; fourth American tour. A.
Croce. Atlan 226:128-30+ N '70
Moiseyev dance company, the Metropolitan
opera house, NYC. N. Mason. Dance Mag
44:80 S '70
Russians return. S. K. Oberbeck. il Newsweek
76:87 Jl 20 '70
MOISTURE
See also
Soil moisture

MOISTURE control in buildings. See Dampness in buildings

MOISTURIZERS. See Cosmetics

MOK, Michael
Losing fight for game parks. il Life 69:56-7 N 27 '70

MOLDING machines
What you can do with an injection molding machine. W. C. Leckey. il Pop Mech 134:184-6 S '70

MOLDS (botany)
See also
Slime molds

MOLDS (cookery)
Western kitchen. il Sunset 145:167 D '70

MOLDS (for ceramic products)
From pipe to pot. R. Mammel. il Ceram Mo 18:16-18 Mr '70

MOLECULAR arc lamp. See Electric lamps, Arc

MOLECULAR association
Bimodal sedimenting zones due to ligand-mediated interactions. J. R. Cann and W. B. Goad. bibliog il Science 170:441-5 O 23 '70

MOLECULAR beams
Amateur scientist; how to construct a molecular-beam apparatus and a mass spectrometer. C. L. Stong. il Sci Am 223:120-2+ Jl '70

MOLECULAR biology
Deciphering proteins. il Sci N 97:366 Ap 11 '70
Molecular biology: moving toward an understanding of genetic control. G. L. Wick. Science 167:157-9 Ja 9 '70
Origins of molecular biology. E. L. Hess. bibliog Science 168:664-9 My 8 '70

Conferences
History of biochemistry and molecular biology. J. T. Edsall. Science 170:349-51 O 16 '70

MOLECULAR dynamics
See also
Quantum theory

MOLECULAR formulas. See Chemistry—Notation

MOLECULAR microscopy. See Microscope and microscopy

MOLECULAR orbitals
Chemistry by computer. A. C. Wahl. il Sci Am 222:54-8+ bibliog(p 130) Ap '70
Orbital symmetry control of chemical reactions. R. Hoffmann and R. B. Woodward. bibliog il Science 167:825-31 F 6 '70

MOLECULAR rotation
See also
Conformational analysis

MOLECULES
Monomolecular layers and light. K. H. Drexhage. il Sci Am 222:108-19 Mr '70
Optical spectra of molecules at low temperature. B. Meyer. bibliog il Science 168:783-9 My 15 '70
See also
Molecular orbitals
Polymers

Models
Solution conformation of valinomycin-potassium ion complex. M. Ohnishi and D. W. Urry. bibliog il Science 168:1091-2 My 29 '70

MOLECULES, interstellar. See Matter, Interstellar

MOLESWORTH, Charles
Full count. Nation 210:217-19 F 23 '70
Name Pacific foam is easy; Series; poems. Poetry 115:238-9 Ja '70

MOLIÈRE, Jean Baptiste Poquelin
Amphitryon. Criticism
New Yorker 45:57-8+ F 14 '70 *
Dom Juan; tr. by K. Cavender. Criticism
New Repub 162:19 F 28 '70 *
New Yorker 45:57-8+ F 14 '70 *
Newsweek il 75:95-6 My 25 '70 *
Time il 95:87 Je 15 '70 *
Les femmes savantes. Criticism
New Yorker 46:60+ F 21 '70 *
Life of Monsieur de Moliere, by M. Bulgakov. Review
Nation 211:537-40 N 23 '70. D. Fanger *
Le malade imaginaire. Criticism
New Yorker 46:60+ F 21 '70 *

MOLINA, José
José Molina bailes espanoles. Carnegie Hall. NYC. P. G. Richmond. Dance Mag 45:71 Ja '71 *
World of dance; concert in Carnegie Hall. W. Terry. por Sat R 53:58 N 21 '70 *

MOLINE malleable iron company
Grime doesn't pay, but clean air does. Nations Bsns 58:15 F '70

MOLLENHOFF, Clark
Atrocity story. il Newsweek 75:67 Je 1 '70 *
Blowup. R. L. Shayon. Sat R 53:16 Je 6 '70 *
Ins and outs. J. Osborne. New Repub 162:11-12 My 9 '70 *
Mr 1040. por Newsweek 75:34-5 Ap 27 '70 *
No privacy for 1040. Time 95:19 Ap 27 '70 *
Security leak at the 1040 level. por Bsns W p32+ Ap 18 '70 *

MOLLENKOTT, Virginia Ramey
Literature and the now generation. Todays Ed 59:64-7 O '70
Teachers, students, and selfishness in the seventies. Chr Today 14:6-8+ Ap 10; 13-15 Ap 24 '70

MOLLER, Hans Maersk-. See Maersk-Moller. H.

MÖLLER, Karl D. See Rothschild, W. G. jt. auth.

MOLLISON, Richard Devol
Troubled men of Texas Gulf sulphur. N. A. Martin. il Duns 95:32-3+ Ap '70 *

MOLLO, Victor
Sky-high stakes on London bridge. il Sports Illus 32:18-19 Ja 26 '70

MOLLOY, Edward A.
Five star saint. Criticism
America 122:227-8 F 28 '70 *

MOLLUSKS
Antarctic pelecypod faunal peculiarities. D. Nicol. bibliog Science 168:1248-9 Je 5 '70
How good are you as a malacologist? quiz. J. Daugherty and M. Daugherty. il Sci Digest 68:82-3+ S '70
Monoplacophora in the south Atlantic Ocean. J. Rosewater. bibliog il Science 167:1485 Mr 13 '70
See also
Clams
Nervous system—Mollusks
Paper nautilus
Shells (conchology)

MOLNAR, Charles E. See Pfeiffer. R. R. jt. auth.

MOLNAR, Thomas
Shape of the future. Commonweal 92:365-7 Jl 24 '70

MOLNER, Don
A-V clinic; questions and answers. Schol Teach Jr/Sr High p39 S 21; 34 O 5; 21 D 7 '70
AV products roundup. il Schol Teach Sec Teach Sup p22-4 N 3 '69; 22-3 Ap 6 '70
A-V roundup. Schol Teach Jr/Sr High p40-1 S 21; 31 N 2 '70
Do-it-yourself developing. Schol Teach Jr/Sr High p25-6 O 5 '70

MOLOKAI (island)
Hawaii's Molokai. T. B. Lesure. il Travel 134:62-7 O '70

MOLONEY, Judy
Goodwill ambassador. J. Kuh. por Ladies Home J 87:117 F '70 *

MOLTING
Molting in land crabs: stimulation by leg removal. D. M. Skinner and D. E. Graham. bibliog il Science 169:383-5 Jl 24 '70
Neuroendocrine control of ecdysis in silkmoths. J. W. Truman and L. M. Riddiford. bibliog il Science 167:1624-6 Mr 20 '70

MOLTMANN, Jürgen
Politics and the practice of hope. por Chr Cent 87:288-91 Mr 11 '70

MOLZ, Kathleen
Education for sensibility in the house of facts: address, March 28, 1969. il Am Lib 1:28-32 Ja '70

MONAHAN, Leo
Hockey. il Sports Illus 32:58-9 My 18 '70

MONARCH butterflies. See Butterflies

MONASTERIES
Boquen; interview. ed. by M. Alcott. B. Besret. por Cath World 212:143-5 D '70
Worldly religious community; Bavaria's Casteller Ring. G. Weckman. Chr Cent 87:1513-15 D 16 '70

MONASTICISM
Boquen; interview. ed. by M. Alcott. B. Besret. por Cath World 212:143-5 D '70
On mystifying contemplatives. America 122:146 F 14 '70
See also
Contemplative orders
Hermits

MONCRIEF. Lewis W.
Cultural basis for our environmental crisis; adaptation of address. April 16, 1970. bibliog Science 170:508-12 O 30 '70

MONDALE, Walter Frederick
Excerpt from debate, February 9 and 17, 1970. Cong Digest 49:119+ Ap '70
Indian education; a national disgrace; a dialogue. pors Todays Ed 59:24-7 Mr '70

MONDALE, Walter Frederick—*Continued*
Tax exemption for private schools: what officials plan. pors U S News 69:70-4 Ag 31 '70
Think of these children. New Repub 163:15-17 D 26 '70

about

Mondaleism; appearances on TV. R. L. Shayon. Sat R 53:33 Ag 15 '70 *

MONDAY holiday movement. See Holidays

MONET, Claude
Readers' choice; Monet's La terrasse. D. Douglas. il por Art in Am 58:25 Ja '70

MONETARY fund. See International monetary fund

MONETARY policy
See also
Currency question

MONEY
See also
Capital
Coins
Credit
Depreciation
Foreign exchange
Inflation (finance)
Interest
Investments
Liquidity (economics)
Paper money
Stock exchange

International aspects

American business; international investment flows; address, December 11, 1969. N. Samuels. Vital Speeches 36:197-200 Ja 15 '70
Canada waives the rules. il Time 95:94 Je 15 '70
Dollar's future as Europe sees it; interview, ed. by A. Zanker. M. Iklé. il por U S News 68:66-70 Ap 13 '70
Floating dollar; Canada. Newsweek 75:83-4 Je 15 '70
Gold, the dollar and the American economy; address, July 11, 1970. P. Cortney. Vital Speeches 36:725-9 S 15 '70
Money international. by F. Hirsch. Review Commentary 49:72+ Mr '70. L. Malkin
New gold crisis? C. A. Cerami. il Nations Bsns 58:38-41 My '70
New rival to the dollar? il Time 96:108+ O 26 '70
New sign points to monetary union; European monetary units. Bsns W p28 N 28 '70
Pressures on the dollar. E. H. Yeo, 3d. por Nations Bsns 58:81 D '70
Switzerland in Singapore; Asian dollar market. il Time 96:55-6 S 7 '70
Why dollar looks stronger to world's bankers. il U S News 69:104-6 O 19 '70
See also
Currency question
Eurodollar market
International monetary fund

Psychological aspects

Money matters! G. Guinness. Harp Baz 103: 138-9 Ag '70
What spending money reveals about you. T. I. Rubin. Ladies Home J 87:44 O '70

Canada

Canada waives the rules. il Time 95:94 Je 15 '70
Canada's floating dollar hits tourists, businesses. il U S News 68:69-72 Je 15 '70
Floating dollar. Newsweek 75:83-4 Je 15 '70
Trade tide lifts the floating dollar. il Bsns W p51-2 O 17 '70
See also
Finance—Canada
Paper money—Canada

France

Franc comes back. Newsweek 76:67+ S 7 '70

Germany

Germany 1923: when inflation overshot the mark. il Sr Schol 96:8-9 Ja 26 '70

Great Britain

Our-far-flung correspondents. J. Brooks. New Yorker 46:182-4+ N 21 '70
Preparing for D day; decimalization publicity campaign. Newsweek 76:55 D 28 '70
See also
Paper money—Great Britain

Italy

Flight of the lira. il Time 95:86 Mr 16 '70
Lira wins again. il Time 97:64 Ja 11 '71

United States

Credit drag. S. S. Parker and others. il Fortune 81:30+ F '70
Dollar up, gold down: story of a U.S. comeback. il U S News 68:79-80 F 16 '70
A 500 Dow? interview ed. by G. R. Rosen. E. Janeway. por Duns 95:10-11+ F '70
Money. by L. Ritter and W. Silber. Review Bsns W il p 10 Mr 14 '70. G. Hauge
Will the dollar be devalued via the back door? C. A. Cerami. il Nations Bsns 58: 98-100 N '70
See also
Paper money—United States
Silver as money

History

Understanding signs and symbols on currency. Good H 71:188 O '70

MONEY, Counterfeit. See Counterfeits and counterfeiting

MONEY in art. See Art—Themes

MONEY management. See Budget, Household; Budget, Personal; Domestic finance

MONEY market
Is our financial mechanism adequate for the 70s? address, April 2, 1970. A. W. Clausen. Vital Speeches 36:428-31 My 1 '70

MONEY raising campaigns. See Fund raising

MONEY rates. See Interest

MONGOL Peoples Republic. See Mongolia

MONGOLIA
How to create an international scandal in Ulan Bator. S. Turner. il Sr Schol 95:18-19+ N 17 '69
Mongolia. A. J. K. Sanders. bibliog il Focus 20:1-7 Ja '70
See also
Transportation—Mongolia

MONICA; story. See Soman, F. J.

MONIGLE, Martha
How to write a play. Writers Digest 50:40 Ja '70

MONK, Meredith
Meredith Monk's Juice. D. Hering. il Dance Mag 44:34-7 F '70

MONKEY trial. See Tennessee evolution controversy

MONKEYS
Cancer viruses in primates. R. Kinard. bibliog Science 169:828-31 Ag 28 '70
Diurnal variation of spontaneous uterine activity in nonpregnant primates (macaca mulatta) G. M. Harbert, jr. and others. bibliog il Science 170:82-5 O 2 '70
Monkeys as therapists; pathological behavior induced by isolation. J. Moriarty. il Sci N 98:100 Ag 1 '70
Plasmodium falciparum in owl monkeys: drug resistance and chloroquine binding capacity. C. D. Fitch. bibliog il Science 169: 289-90 Jl 17 '70
Snowbound monkeys of Japan; with photographs by C. Rentmeester. Life 68:36-41 Ja 30 '70
Transmissible mink encephalopathy: experimental transmission to the squirrel monkey. R. J. Eckroade and others. bibliog il Science 169:1088-90 S 11 '70
Trichromatic mechanisms in single cortical neurons. P. Gouras. bibliog il Science 168: 489-92 Ap 24 '70
Visual discrimination of movement: midbrain or forebrain? C. R. Hamilton and J. S. Lund. bibliog il Science 170:1428-30 D 25 '70
See also
Baboons
Chimpanzees

MONKS. See Monasticism

MONNET, Jean
What chance for a United States of Europe? interview. por Read Digest 97:158-62 O '70

about

Wartime journals of Charles A. Lindbergh; excerpts. C. A. Lindbergh. Am Scholar 39: 587-602 Aut '70 *

MONOD, Noël
Unflappable N. Monod. por Forbes 106:82 O 15 '70 *

MONOGAMY. See Marriage

MONOLA, G. Davis
Excerpt from address, February 25, 1970. Cong Digest 49:220+ Ag '70

MONOLITHIC amplifiers. See Amplifiers

MONONUCLEOSIS, Infectious
Facts (for a change) on mononucleosis. il Changing T 24:29-31 Ag '70

MONOPLACOPHORA. See Mollusks

MONOPOLES. See Particles (nuclear physics)

MONOPOLIES
See also
Trusts, Industrial

MONOPRINTS. See Monotypes

MONORAIL railroads. See Railroads, Single rail

MONOSODIUM glutamate
Brain lesions in an infant rhesus monkey treated with monosodium glutamate. J. W. Olney and L. G. Sharpe; discussion. Science 167:1016-17 F 13 '70
Facts about monosodium glutamate. Good H 170:162 F '70
Monosodium glutamate: feeding of large amounts in man and gerbils. G. Bazzano and others. bibliog il Science 169:1208-9 S 18 '70
Monosodium glutamate-induced brain lesions: electron microscopic examination. E. A. Arees and J. Mayer. bibliog il Science 170:549-50 O 30 '70
Monosodium glutamate lack of effects on brain and reproductive function in rats. N. J. Adamo and A. Ratner. bibliog il Science 169:673-4 Ag 14 '70
Monosodium glutamate; under suspicion as a mutagen. Consumer Bul 53:16-19 Mr '70

MONOTYPES
Double monoprints? H. B. Cote. il Sch Arts 70:38-9 Ja '71

MONRO, John U.
Reincarnation of John Monro. L. Greenhouse. il por N Y Times Mag p53-7+ Mr 15 '70 *

MONROE, Bill
Pickin' and singin'. il por Newsweek 75:85 Je 29 '70 *

MONROE, George E. See Talmage. H. jt. auth.

MONROE, James
Library acquires James Monroe letters; text of letter with introd. by K. V. Hostick. Hobbies 75:140-1 My '70

MONROE, Jay
Chase gets caught in a crossfire. il Bsns W p38-9 Ja 17 '70

MONROE, Tenn.
Newspapers
Two guns and a weekly; Monroe County democrat. il por Time 95:47 Ap 27 '70

MONROE COUNTY democrat (newspaper) See Monroe, Tenn.—Newspapers

MONSANTO company
First DDT, now PCB. Sci N 98:332 O 24 '70

MONSANTO Open golf tournament. See Golf—Tournaments

MONSER, George
No snow in June. il Pop Electr 32:27-9 Je '70

MONSKY, John B.
Using liquidation as a strategy. Bsns W p34 O 3 '70 *

MONSON, Curt
Dilemma of the black cop. R. Hall. il pors Life 69:60-60B+ S 18 '70 *

MONSTER mania. See Fads

MONSTERS
See also
Loch Ness monster

MONT BLANC (dessert) See Desserts

MONT PELERIN society
Galbraith was wrong again. E. McDowell. Nat R 22:1108 O 20 '70

MONTAGE
See also
Collage

MONTAGNE, Richard
Boy in a red tie; story. Redbook 136:86-7 D '70
First day; story. Redbook 135:92-3 S '70

MONTAGNES, James
Canada's ten capitals. il Travel 133:28-35 My '70

MONTAGUE, Peter. See Lloyd, R. jt. auth.

MONTAIGNE, Michel Eyquem de
Montaigne's soul mate. M. Bishop. por Horizon 12:102-3 Spr '70 *

MONTANA
See also
Fishing—Montana
Forests and forestry—Montana
Glacier National Park
Hunting—Montana
Taxation—Montana

History
See also
Little Big Horn, Battle of the, 1876

MONTANA earthquake. See Earthquakes—United States

MONTE CARLO
Music
Report:
Production of Jean Michel Damase's operetta. D. Stevens. Opera N 35:29 S 5 '70

MONTEAGLE, Frederick J.
Don't fight, negotiate! il Parks & Rec 9:38-9+ S '70

MONTECATINI Edison. See Chemical industries—Italy

MONTEIRO, José Antonio
Priest tells of torture. Chr Today 15:50+ O 9 '70 *

MONTEREY, Calif.
Climate
Crosby weather. K. G. Richards. bibliog il Weatherwise 22:240-3 D '69

MONTEREY cypress. See Cypress

MONTEROS M, A. Espinosa de los. See Espinosa de los Monteros M, A.

MONTE-SANO, Bizzy
Aboard a defender: in the crew. il Yachting 128:52+ S '70

MONTESSORI method of education
Montessori revival. K. Ahlfeld. Ed Digest 35:18-21 Ap '70

MONTEVERDI, Claudio
Monteverdi's magnificent musical drama. S. T. Sommer. Hi Fi sec I 20:102+ Ja '70
Records:
L'Orfeo. il Opera N 34:35 F 7 '70

MONTEZUMA DE CARVALHO Joaquim de. See Carvalho, J. de M. de

MONTGOLFIERS. See Balloons

MONTGOMERY, Bernard Law, 1st viscount Montgomery of Alamein. See Montgomery of Alamein, B. L. M.

MONTGOMERY, Charlotte
Speaker for the house. See issues of Good housekeeping

MONTGOMERY, Florence M.
Eighteenth-century English and American furnishing fashions; excerpts from Printed textiles, English and American cottons and linens, 1700-1850. il Antiques 97:267-71 F '70

MONTGOMERY, Herbert J.
Pink thumbs and brown lawn. il Todays Health 48:40-1 Jl '70

MONTGOMERY, Jacqueline, and McBurney, R. D.
Problems and pitfalls of establishing an Operant conditioning-token economy program. Ment Hy 54:382-7 Jl '70

MONTGOMERY, Roger
Building for the arts. il Arch Forum 132:81-9 Ja '70
Center of action. il Arch Forum 132:64-71 Ap '70
Pattern language. il Arch Forum 132:52-9 Ja '70
Synanon city. il Arch Forum 133:52-5 N '70

MONTGOMERY of Alamein. Bernard Law Montgomery, 1st viscount
Montgomery: the field marshall, by R. W. Thompson. Review
Nat R 22:1063-4 O 6 '70. G. F. Eliot *

MONTGOMERY COUNTY, Ala.
Need a bridge in a hurry? il Am City 85:119-20 S '70

MONTGOMERY COUNTY, Pa.
How to doctor a quarry for landfill. J. A. McHenry. il Am City 85:38 D '70

MONTGOMERY Ward and company
Like, wow, Montgomery Ward! il Bsns W p47-8 Mr 28 '70
Oh! Chicago! Bare essentials sell the now generation by mail; Ward's latest catalogue. B. Fredericks. il Pop Phot 67:72-3+ Ag '70
Strategy that saved Montgomery Ward; interview, ed. by J. McDonald. R. Brooker. il por Fortune 81:168-71+ My '70
Ward's stores go modular. Bsns W p21 N 28 '70
See also
Marcor, inc.

MONTICELLO (historic house)
South to spring. D. Butwin. il Sat R 53:38-9 My 30 '70

MONTREAL
Montreal: by underground. D. McCluggage. il Travel & Camera 33:62 Je '70
Montreal's continuing festival. J. Drapeau. il Travel & Camera 33:40-1 Je '70
Run it up the flagpole, Johnny; Expo, big-league baseball and the Olympics. F. Deford. il por Sports Illus 33:74-6+ S 28 '70

City planning
Multilevel man. il por Time 96:52-3 O 19 '70

Elections
Canada: a landslide for law and order. il U S News 69:96 N 9 '70

Exhibitions
Why Montreal keeps its fair. il U S News 69:43 Jl 27 '70

MONTREAL—*Continued*

Hotels, restaurants, etc.

Dining on pheasant in Montreal; Queen Elizabeth hotel. M. Woodward. il Travel 133:25 Je '70

Housing

Nun's Island, Phase 1, Montreal, Quebec. il Arch Rec 147:100-2 mid-My '70

Riots

Day the Montreal police went on strike. G. Clark. il Read Digest 96:107-12 F '70

Sanitary affairs

Montreal's combined incinerator-power plant. E. F. Spitzer. il Am City 85:86-9 My '70

MONTRESOR, Beni

Pasta, e basta. Vogue 155:208-9+ Mr 1 '70

MONTROSE, Colo.

Life begins at forty-two. M. Bingham. il por Am City 85:111 Jl '70

MONUMENT VALLEY, Utah and Arizona

Traveler's choice. J. G. M. Martin. Travel 133:15 F '70

MONUMENTS

Memories in stone. D. B. Warnick. il Travel 133:66-71 Ja '70

See also

Crazy Horse (Sioux Indian)—Statues, portraits, etc.

Sepulchral monuments

Washington, G.—Memorials

also subhead Monuments, statues, etc. under names of cities. e.g. Boston—Monuments, statues, etc.

MONUMENTS, Megalithic. See Megalithic monuments

MONZÓN, Carlos

Night Carlos made a no-no out of Ni-no. W. Wynn. il pors Sports Illus 33:80-2 N 16 '70 •

MOOBERRY, Eleanore

Pistol in the parlor. il por Har Yrs 10:13+ Mr '70

MOOD, A. M. See Kershaw, J. A. jt. auth.

MOOD-changing drugs. See Psychopharmacology

MOODS

Changing moods in mid-scream. H. G. Ginott. McCalls 97:32 Ag '70

MOODY, Orville

Nontransmogrification of Orville Moody. C. Kirkpatrick. por Sports Illus 32:34-7 Je 22 '70 •

MOODY Bible Institute, Chicago

Mood at Moody. il Newsweek 75:51 Mr 9 '70

MOOG, Robert A.

Moog is more than a vogue. C. S. Wren. il por Look 34:24+ Ap 7 '70 •

MOOLTEN, Frederick L. and Cooperband, S. R.

Selective destruction of target cells by diphtheria toxin conjugated to antibody directed against antigens on the cells. bibliog il Science 169:68-70 Jl 3 '70

MOON, Eric

Freedom fund on the stand; letter to the editor. Wilson Lib Bul 45:462 Ja '71

MOON, Peter

$2,903.55 polar bear. il Audubon 72:149-52 N '70

MOON

Apollo samples spur lunar debate. Z. Strickland. il Aviation W 92:46-8 Ja 26 '70

Five unexpected new discoveries about the moon. J. Reinart. il Sci Digest 68:9-14 N '70

Lunar sciences. Sci N 97:64+ Ja 17 '70

Sun, moon, and planets this month. See issues of Sky and telescope

Water on the moon? E. Anders. bibliog Science 169:1309-10 S 25 '70

Where was the moon formed? S. F. Singer and L. W. Bandermann. bibliog il Science 170:438-9 O 23 '70

See also

Eclipses, Lunar

Lunar geology

Space flight to the moon—Manned flights

Age

Back to time one. il Sci N 97:428-9 My 2 '70

Dating the moon. J. Lear. il Sat R 53:52 Ap 11 '70

Moon's old age and uniqueness confirmed. Space World G-5-77:33 My '70

Oldest moon rock. Sky & Tel 40:3 Jl '70

Primordial rock found on moon. Aviation W 92:23 Je 1 '70

Atmosphere

Lunar atmosphere as a source of argon-40 and other lunar surface elements. R. H. Manka and F. C. Michel. bibliog il Science 169:278-80 Jl 17 '70

News from the world of space exploration; theories about the dry, airless moon. il Space World G-9-81:46+ S '70

Exploration

ALSEP provides massive data but fragmented picture of moon. Aviation W 93:20 N 23 '70

Lunar science and planetary history. P. Cloud. Science 169:1159 S 18 '70

Moon, earth's book of life? Apollo lunar exploration missions. il Space World G-3-75:24-9 Mr '70

See also

Space flight to the moon—Manned flights—Extravehicular activity

Equipment

ALSEP: the first 100 days. il Space World G-7-79:38-9 Jl '70

Apollo 13 lunar heat flow experiment. M. G. Langseth, jr. and others. bibliog il Science 168:211-17 Ap 10 '70

Automatic devices for space exploration; with comments by Georgi Petrov and Alexei Yeliseyev. V. Shvarev and V. Bulekov. Space World H-1-85:33-7 Ja '71

How lunar drill will work. il Space World G-9-81:12-15 S '70

Maps

Names on the back of the moon; with folded NASA map. J. Ashbrook. il Sky & Tel 40:262-6, 291-300 N '70

USSR's map and globe of the moon. Space World G-10-82:11-12 O '70

Mass

Martian mass and earth-moon mass ratio from coherent S-band tracking of Mariners 6 and 7. J. D. Anderson and others. bibliog il Science 167:277-9 Ja 16 '70

Names

See Names, Lunar

Orbit

Secular changes in the lunar elements. C. F. Martin and T. C. Van Flandern. bibliog il Science 168:246-7 Ap 10 '70

Photographs

Apollo 11 photo album. R Pop Astron 63:4-6 Ag '69

Apollo 12 explorers on the moon. R. Hillenbrand. il Sky & Tel 39:95-8 F '70

Lunar landslides. P. J. Cannon. il Sky & Tel 40:215-18 O '70

Radiation

Alpha radioactivity of the lunar surface at the landing sites of Surveyors 5, 6, and 7. A. L. Turkevich. bibliog il Science 167:1722-4 Mr 27 '70

Lunar ray systems. Sky & Tel 39:80 F '70

Surface

Apollo 11 lunar science conference; papers, with editorial comment. bibliog il Science 167:447, 449-784 Ja 30 '70; Correction. 167:1759 Mr 27 '70

Apollo 11 observations of a remarkable glazing phenomenon on the lunar surface. T. Gold; discussion. bibliog Science 168:608-11 My 1 '70

Apollo 12 lunar module impact: laboratory simulation and possible downrange ballistic effects. H. F. Swift and others. bibliog il Science 169:851-4 Ag 28 '70

Apollo 12 seismic experiment links red lunar glow to quakes. Z. Strickland. Aviation W 93:57 Ag 10 '70

Blowholes. Sci Am 223:45-6 N '70

Chemical composition of the lunar surface in Sinus Medii. E. J. Franzgrote and others. bibliog il Science 167:376-9 Ja 23 '70

Lunar gravity over large craters from Apollo 12 tracking data. P. Gottlieb and others. bibliog il Science 168:477-9 Ap 24 '70

Lunar landslides. P. J. Cannon. il Sky & Tel 40:215-18 O '70

Lunar surface: changes in thirty-one months and micrometeoroid flux. L. D. Jaffe. bibliog il Science 170:1092-4 D 4 '70

Moon bubbles. il Chem 43:7 My '70

New theory on the moon craters. M. Priestly. il Sci Digest 68:57-8 O '70

News from the world of space exploration; theories about the dry, airless moon. il Space World G-9-81:46+ S '70

Tycho is tantalizing; lunar landing sites. Sci N 98:247-8 S 19 '70

Why the moon is gray. Chem 43:22-3 My '70

MOON—*Continued*

Temperature

Apollo 13 lunar heat flow experiment. M. G. Langseth, jr. and others. bibliog il Science 168:211-17 Ap 10 '70

Specific heats of lunar surface materials from 90 to 350 degrees Kelvin. R. A. Robie and others. bibliog il Science 167: 749-50 Ja 30 '70

Summary of arguments for a hot moon. R. B. Baldwin. bibliog Science 170:1297-300 D 18 '70

MOON, Distance to. See Astronomical distances

MOON illusion. See Optical illusions

MOON landing, July 20, 1969. See Space flight to the moon—Manned flights—Apollo 11 flight

MOON soil. See Soils

MOON vehicles. See Lunar vehicles

MOONEY, Elina
Elina Mooney, the Cubiculo, NYC. M. Marks. Dance Mag 45:72 Ja '71 *

MOONEY, Maureen
Star quality. por Mlle 71:130-3 O '70 *

MOONEY, Thomas J.
Mooney case, by R. H. Frost. Review Am West 7:49 Ja '70. J. P. Kindregan *

MOONEY trail. See Trails—California

MOONLIGHTING. See Supplementary employment

MOOR, Paul
Bacchanal in Bavaria. il Sat R 53:62+ S 12 '70
Bayreuth: even the Kartoffelknoedel is Wagnerian. il por Sat R 53:52-3+ Mr 14 '70
Behind the scenes. Hi Fi 20:secI 22 Mr; 25 Je; 25-6 O '70
Ernst Krenek's new opera. il Hi Fi 20:MA 19 N '70
Karajan completes the Ring. il por Sat R 53: 63-5 Ap 25 '70
Must Venice die? il Holiday 47:46-9+ Ap '70
Porgy comes to Germany. Hi Fi 20:secII 28-9 Ag '70
Something called six days of music. Hi Fi 20:secII 27+ Je '70
Stockhausen versus Beethoven. Hi Fi 20:secII 27 Mr '70

MOORADIAN, A.
Laser Raman spectroscopy. bibliog il Science 169:20-5 Jl 3 '70

MOORE, Billie
Dizzyland of show and tell. Todays Ed 59: 57 N '70

MOORE, Blake W. See Cicero, T. J. jt. auth.

MOORE, Brian
Bloody Ulster: an Irishman's lament. il Atlan 226:58-62 S '70

MOORE, Carleton B. and others
Total carbon and nitrogen abundances in lunar samples. bibliog il Science 167:495-7 Ja 30 '70

MOORE, Carman
Music. Vogue 155:58 Ap 15; 156:38 Ag 15 '70

MOORE, David W.
Four records, the sophisticated writing of Rodion Shchedrin. il por Am Rec G 36: 410-12 F '70
Incomparable art of Emanuel Feuermann. Am Rec G 37:12-13 S '70
Sound of brass across four centuries. il Am Rec G 37:92-4 O '70

MOORE, Donald J.
Martin Buber on Jesus: a Jewish reading. il America 122:630-3 Je 13 '70

MOORE, Douglas
New raid on Nader. Chr Cent 87:1176 O 7 '70 *

MOORE, Edward H.
Governor appoints state's first parks and recreation commissioner. por Cons 25:19+ O '70

MOORE, George Stevens
Multiplied man. por Forbes 105:16-17 Ja 15 '70

MOORE, Gerald
Mike sr. keeps a gun he trusts and worries about his son. Life 69:35-36D N 13 '70

about

Cop turned journalist goes back on the beat. R. Graves. il por Life 69:4 N 13 '70 *

MOORE, Henry
(ed) Gist of it. See issues of Outdoor life

MOORE, Henry Spencer
Henry Moore and the shape of things. E. O. Hauser. il por Read Digest 96:136-41 Ap '70 *
It's nice to be a pioneer: visit to H. Moore's studio. J. P. Anderson. il pors Sch Arts 70:30-3 D '70 *
Mellow master. il Time 95:72-3 My 11 '70 *

MOORE, Jack H. and Trueblood, Bryan
Ochratoxin A: inhibition of mitochondrial respiration. bibliog il Science 168:1102-3 My 29 '70

MOORE, Janet Gaylord
How an artist holds our attention: line, color & form: excerpt from The many ways of seeing. il Design 71:4-9 mid-Wint '70
Seeing eye, the thinking hand; excerpts from The many ways of seeing. il Design 71:4-9 Spr '70

MOORE, John, and Pamperin, John
Abortion and the Church. Chr Cent 87:629-31 My 20 '70

MOORE, John W. See Cox. M. M. jt. auth.

MOORE, Marcena, and Moore, T. W.
Why they ran us out of Jenkintown. il pors Look 34:98 O 20 '70

MOORE, Marianne
Enough; poem. New Yorker 45:28 Ja 17 '70
Magician's retreat; poem. New Yorker 46: 40 F 21 '70

MOORE, Mary Lou
Mother goes back to school. il Parents Mag 45:44-5+ Ap '70

MOORE, Mary Tyler
Bright new world of Mary Tyler Moore. M. Davidson. il pors Good H 172:58-9+ Ja '71 *
Woman's role on TV. J. Leonard. il por Life 69:8 D 18 '70 *

MOORE, Melba
Five young beauties & how they get that way. il pors Mlle 72:135-41 N '70 *
Futures, great. pors Vogue 156:90-1 Jl '70 *
Prize winners. P. Garland. il pors Ebony 25: 29-32+ Jl '70 *

MOORE, Michele
(comp) Audiovisual guide. Library J 95:1583-4+, 3973-5+ Ap 15, N 15 '70

MOORE, Richard E. M.
Mosaic ruler. il Science 167:1385 Mr 6 '70

MOORE, Robert H. jr, and Boland, John
Better refuse service with bags. il pors Am City 85:76+ Ag '70

MOORE, Trevor Wyatt
Art. il Chr Cent 87:396-7 Ap 1 '70
Divine dissonance. il por Chr Cent 87:1455-7 D 2 '70
Records (title varies) Chr Cent 87:608-9, 768 My 13, Je 17 '70
—See Moore, M. jt. auth.

MOORE, Virginia Bennett
So long, duck. il Read Digest 96:124-8 Ap '70

MOORE, William C.
Cambodia plus two months: a military appraisal. il por U S News 69:31-2 S 7 '70
Hanoi has suffered a crippling blow. por U S News 68:46-7 Je 22 '70

MOORE, William Harreld
New man at the throttle. Newsweek 76:90 S 14 '70 *
Penn Central: a new chief with new plans. il por Bsns W p48+ Ag 22 '70 *
Railroad man for the Penn central. por Fortune 82:31 S '70 *

MOOREFIELD, Story
Morgan follows through. il Am Ed 6:31-3 Ja '70
To keep the things we love. il Am Ed 6:6-8 Ag '70

MOORER, Thomas Hinman
Attack aircraft carrier: address, March 4, 1970. Vital Speeches 36:392-4 Ap 15 '70
Change of command. por Time 96:16 Jl 6 '70 *
Navy way. il por Newsweek 75:34 Ap 27 '70 *

about

With an admiral at the defense helm. il por U S News 68:32 Ap 27 '70 *

MOOREY, Anne, and Moorey, Christopher
Making mobiles. il Design 71:22-6 Sum '70

MOOREY, Christopher. See Moorey, A. jt. auth.

MOORHOUSE, D. E. See Tatchell, R. J. jt. auth.

MOORHOUSE, Edith
Philosophy underlying the British primary school: excerpts from Teaching in the British primary school. Sch & Soc 98:35-40+ Ja '70

MOORING of airplanes. See Airplanes—Mooring

MOORS (people)
Africa in medieval Spanish literature: its appearance in el Caballero Cifar. M. Sampson. bibliog il Negro Hist Bul 32:14-19 D '69

MOOSE, Richard M. See Lowenstein, J. G. jt. auth.

MOOSE
Ferdinand, the friendly bull moose. A. S. Fick. il Cons 25:2-3 D '70

MOOSE hunting
Last call for moose. C. Anderegg. il pors Outdoor Life 145:60-3+ Ja '70

MOOT, Robert C.
Pentagon cuts: the worst is yet to come: interview. il por Bsns W p94+ S 12 '70

MOR, Nathan Yalin-. See Yalin-Mor, N.
MORAEA
Blooms every fortnight or so. Is that
enough? il Sunset 144:236 My '70
MORAES, Dom
Bombay: wealth, shantytowns, speakeasies. il
N Y Times Mag p34-5+ O 11 '70
East Pakistan: the wave. il N Y Times Mag
p26-7+ Ja 10 '71
Indian expatriate rediscovers India. il pors
N Y Times Mag p26-7+ F 15 '70
Indian revolutionaries with a Chinese accent.
il N Y Times Mag p30-1+ N 8 '70
Passing of the British working class. il N Y
Times Mag p32-3+ Ap 5 '70
Walk on London's wild side. il N Y Times
Mag p 100+ S 13 '70
MORAIS, Herbert Montfort
Obituary
Negro Hist Bul por 33:100 Ap '70 *
MORAL attitudes
Doing it in the road: folkways vs. mores. E.
Schoenfeld. Ment Hy 54:450-2 Jl '70
Generation gap in the western world. E. M.
von Kuehnelt-Leddihn. il Cath World 212:
9-14 O '70
On the fashionable idea of national guilt. K.
R. Minogue. Am Scholar 39:211-18 Spr '70
Pollution. L. N. Bell. Chr Today 14:27-8 Ja
30 '70
Sex, virginity, money; interview, ed. by A.
Talmey. B. Bettelheim. Vogue 156:94-5+
Ag 1 '70
MORAL conditions
Crippled conscience; symposium. Nation 212:
6-22 Ja 4 '71
Reflections: permissiveness and rectitude. L.
Tyrmand. New Yorker 46:85-96 F 23 '70
See also
Moving pictures—Moral aspects
Television broadcasting—Moral aspects
MORAL education
Decay: blessing in disguise. R. M. Bow-
man. America 123:114-17 S 5 '70; Discussion.
123:189, 220, 275 S 26-O 3, 17 '70
Ethical values, education, and the morality
crisis. W. W. Brickman. Sch & Soc 98:456-
7 D '70
Helping your teens to handle sex. H. Bottel.
Read Digest 96:140-2 Mr '70
Jesuit high school. R. A. Schroth. Common-
weal 91:472-5 Ja 30 '70
Should morality be taught in school? excerpts
from Decent and indecent. B. Spock. Red-
book 134:27+ Mr '70
Teach your child to behave morally. M. Pines.
Read Digest 97:163-6 O '70
Teaching morality: a parent's most difficult
challenge; interviews, ed. by R. Coles.
Redbook 136:82+ D '70
MORAL leadership. See Leadership
MORAL obligation. See Duty
MORAL rearmament
Moral re-armament RIP. Nat R 22:1099 O 20
'70
MORAL theology. See Christian ethics
MORAL values. See Worth
MORALE
See also
United States—Armed forces—Morale
United States—Army—Morale
MORALE, National
Czechoslovakia
Prague: nothing is forever. D. North. il Na-
tion 211:102-5 Ag 17 '70
Prague, two years after. K. C. Cole. il N Y
Times Mag p7-9+ Ag 16 '70; Reply. N. E.
Hildes-Heim. p56+ O 18 '70
Dominican Republic
So Balaguer won. G. A. Geyer. New Repub
162:13-14 My 30 '70
Egypt
Where Egypt stands. H. Smith. il Atlan 227:
39-45 Ja '71
Israel
Six days plus three years; Israel asks, ma
thieh hassof? What will be the end? A.
Rubinstein. il N Y Times Mag p5-7+ My 31
'70
Sweden
Sweden's troubled mood; with views of intel-
lectuals. R. J. Korengold. il Newsweek 75:40-
2+ Mr 23 '70
United States
Agony lingers on. H. Brandon. Sat R 53:4+
Mr 14 '70
Clean break with the past. J. Brooks. il Am
Heritage 21:4-7+ Ag '70

Crisis of confidence in our leadership. J. W.
Gardner. Cur 120:6-9 Ag '70
Defusing the bombs. New Repub 162:5-6 Mr
28 '70
Don't blame the system! R. M. Christenson.
Chr Cent 87:784-7 Je 24 '70
End of the American era, by A. Hacker. Re-
view
Commentary 50:85-6+ S '70. M. Cun-
liffe
Failure of leadership; address, December 9,
1969. J. W. Gardner. Vital Speeches 36:217-
19 Ja 15 '70
Finding the American direction. M. Ways. il
Fortune 82:70-5+ O '70; Same abr. with
title What hope for the future? Cur 124:3-16
D '70
Harlem, rebellion and resurrection. W. String-
fellow. Chr Cent 87:1345-8 N 11 '70
Iceman cometh. Nat R 22:240 Mr 10 '70
Is America really sick? D. J. Boorstin. Read
Digest 97:92-4 S '70
Life among the negatives. Chr Cent 87:869-70
Jl 15 '70
Massive breakdown we face. E. D. Genovese.
Cur 120:3-6 Ag '70
Military viewpoint; excerpts from address.
J. Ferguson. Aviation W 92:11 Ja 19 '70
Mr President, bring us together again. D. R.
Maxey. il Look 34:15-21 Ja 27 '70
Mood of America today. U S News 68:17-18
Ap 20 '70
Out of place in America; excerpts. P. Schrag.
Sat R 53:12-13+ My 9 '70
Place for snakes as well as naked lovers. G.
B. Leonard. il Look 34:80-5 Ja 13 '70
Putting it back together. T. Griffith. il Life
70:85-6+ Ja 8 '71
Recovery of confidence, by J. W. Gardner.
Review
Bsns W p6 Je 27 '70. J. J. Corson
Report from middle America. il Sr Schol 97:8-
12 O 5 '70
Spirit of '70: six historians reflect on what
ails the American spirit; symposium. il
Newsweek 76:18-34 Jl 6 '70
Thoughts on a troubled El Dorado; Time es-
say. H. Grunwald. il Time 95:18-21 Je 22 '70
What's right. and what's wrong with Ameri-
ca? il Sr Schol 95:6-15 S 15 '69
Which way is right? C. F. H. Henry. Chr
Today 14:37-8 Mr 13 '70

Vietnam (Republic)
1964: exhilaration; 1968: frustration; 1970:
hopelessness. A. J. Langguth. il N Y Times
Mag p26-7+ O 4 '70
MORALES, Hilda
Brief biography. S. Goodman. il pors Dance
Mag 44:68-9 Jl '70 *
MORALES, Jane
Make your own pretzels. il Parents Mag 45:
82 Je '70
MORALES-ALANO, Roberto
Episcopal church's economy dismissals pro-
tested. Chr Cent 87:559 My 6 '70 *
MORALITY. See Ethics
MORALS and literature. See Literature and
morals
MORALS and war. See War and morals
MORAN, Gabriel
Catechetics. R. I. P. Commonweal 93:299-
302 D 18 '70
MORÁN, H. Fernández-. See Fernández-Mo-
rán, H.
MORAN, James S.
Amateur scientist. il Sci Am 223:124-9 O '70
MORATORIUM day. October 15, 1969. See Viet-
namese war, 1957- —Protests, demonstra-
tions, etc. against—Moratorium day, Octo-
ber 15, 1969
MORATORIUM fast. April 13-15, 1970. See Viet-
namese war, 1957- —Protests, demonstra-
tions, etc, against
MORAVCSIK, Michael J.
Meson factories and the two-nucleon prob-
lem. bibliog il Phys Today 23:40-4+ O '70
Reflections on national laboratories. il Bul
Atom Sci 26:11-15 F; 48 O '70
MORAVIA, Alberto
Federico Fellini on Satyricon: tr. by S. Mori-
ni. il por Vogue 155:168-71+ Mr 1 '70
MORAVIANS
Old Salem: morning star of Moravian faith.
R. Findley. il Nat Geog 138:818-37 D '70
MORAVIANS in Pennsylvania
History
Bringing up the next generation; communal
rearing of children. Trans-Action 7:10 Jl '70

MORAY eels. See Eels

MORCOM, Richmond
They all loved Lucy. il pors Am Heritage 21:12-15 O '70

MORE, Joseph
Prophet Jonah: the story of an intrapsychic process. Am Imago 27:3-11 Spr '70

MOREAU, Jeanne
Vogue à la Moreau. por Time 96:23 D 28 '70 *

MOREAU, John Adam
Comedians revere the Doctor. Nation 211: 621-4 D 14 '70

MORENCY, Jean
On the boards. pors Dance Mag 44:24 Mr '70 *

MORETON, Ann
Amazing spider woman. B. Strohm. il por Nat Wildlife 7:12-15 O '69 *

MORFOGEN, Elaine
Elaine Morfogen, illustrator & painter. S. E. Meyer. il por Am Artist 34:54-60 O '70 *

MORGAN, Berry
Pier glass; story. New Yorker 46:73-6 Ag 29 '70

MORGAN, Charles, Jr
Integration or national retreat? Cur 118:38-40 My '70

MORGAN, Charles W.
Icebergs of West Greenland; with biographical sketch. il Sea Front 16:328-36, 383 N '70

MORGAN, Charley
One man's million-dollar gamble: Heritage to race for the America's cup. il por Life 68: 56-8 My 15 '70 *

MORGAN, George B. and others
Air pollution surveillance systems. bibliog il Science 170:289-96 O 16 '70

MORGAN, H. R.
Next river to die. il Nat Wildlife 8:20-1 Je '70

MORGAN, Henry
Automobile, history of (1896-1984) Sat R 53: 6+ S 19 '70

MORGAN, James
Big jamboree at Johnston City. Ill. il Atlan 225:64-7 Ag '70

MORGAN, Jim
Showdown on the Salmon River range. R. Woodbury. il pors Life 68:54-56A My 22 '70 *

MORGAN, John
Twenty-six years war; Keeping up with the dead; USS Argonaut; poems. Poetry 117: 156-9 D '70

MORGAN, John Pierpont, 1837-1913
J.P. A. M. Lingg. il por Opera N 34:6-7 F 7 '70

MORGAN, John W. See Ehmann, W. D. jt. auth.

MORGAN, Justina
Day in fun city; story. Ladies Home J 87:82-3 Mr '70

MORGAN, Pete
My enemies have sweet voices; poem. Poetry 115:261-2 Ja '70

MORGAN, Robert P.
Bartok's extraordinary quartets. por Hi Fi 20:58-61 S '70
Beethoven on records. Hi Fi 20:secI 73-6+ Ap '70
Early Carter expertly performed. Hi Fi sec I 20:84 F '70

MORGAN, Robin
Invisible woman; poem. Atlan 225:93 Mr '70

MORGAN, Tom
Tom Morgan's two-way gift. J. P. Blank. por Read Digest 96:71-5 Ap '70 *

MORGAN (automobile)   See Automobiles, Foreign

MORGAN (sports car) See Sports cars

MORGELLO, Clem
Wall Street. See issues of Newsweek

MORGENS, Howard Joseph
P&G: still the master marketer. por Duns 96:32-3 D '70 *

MORGENSTERN, Joseph
[Column] por Newsweek 76:21 N 23; 14 D 7; 14 D 21 '70; 77:9 Ja 4 '71

MORGENTHAU, Hans Joachim
International relations, 1965-1969. bibliog f Ann Am Acad 390:114-19 Jl '70
Mr Nixon's foreign policy. New Repub 162:23-5 Mr 21 '70
Mr Nixon's gamble. New Repub 162:15-17 My 23 '70

MORGENTHAU, Robert Morris
Famous prosecutor talks about crime; interview, ed. by V. S. Navasky. il pors N Y Times Mag p32-3+ F 15 '70
Secret bank accounts; address, May 27, 1970. Vital Speeches 36:553-5 Jl 1 '70

MORIMOTO, Nobuo, and others
Pyrrhotites: stoichiometric compounds with composition $Fe_{n-1}S_n (n>8)$ bibliog il Science 165:964-6 My 22 '70

MORIN, Ronald W. and others
Pleistocene climates in the Atlantic and Pacific Oceans: a reevaluated comparison based on deep-sea sediments. bibliog il Science 169:365-6 Jl 24 '70

MORINAGA milk industry company. See Milk industry and trade

MORINI, Simona
Face architecture. il Vogue 156:98-101 Ag 15 '70
Finnish delight: fun, people, saunas. il Vogue 155:127+ Ap 15 '70
Importance of noses. il Vogue 156:138-9 O 1 '70
(tr) See Fellini, F.   Federico Fellini on Satyricon
(tr) See Moravia, A.   Federico Fellini on Satyricon

MORISHITA, Yoko
Girl who loves Jerome Robbins. O. Maynard. il pors Dance Mag 44:27-9 Jl '70 *
World of dance; New York debut at the 92nd street YM-YWHA. W. Terry. Sat R 53:44 My 2 '70 *

MORISON, Bradley G.
Artist as teacher. il Sat R 53:51-3+ D 19 '70

MORISON, Robert S.
Agnew, alcohol, automobiles, and assessment. Science 169:819; 170:1156 Ag 28, D 11 '70

MORKIN, Eugene
Postnatal muscle fiber assembly: localization of newly synthesized myofibrillar proteins. bibliog il Science 167:1499-501 Mr 13 '70

MORLEY, Charles
(comp) Articles and other books received; eastern Europe. See issues of American historical review

MORLEY, John
Theatre. Vogue 156:308 S 1 '70

MORLEY, Mike
Golf's lower depths: the rabbits on tour. L. Shecter. il pors Look 34:84+ My 19 '70*

MORLEY, Olive J.
King Arthur and his knights; drama. Plays 29:83-95 Ap '70

MORMON architecture.   See Architecture, American

MORMON art. See Art, American

MORMONS and Mormonism
For his was the kingdom, and the power, and the glory, briefly; J. J. Strang. R. P. Weeks. il pors Am Heritage 21:4-7+ Je '70
Mormon items. L. L. Quihuis. il Hobbies 75: 48-9 Ag '70
Mormon society, a photo story; with a note by K. Young. il Art in Am 58:70-1 My '70
Mormons; contribution to American art. C. Carmer; M. S. Young. il Art in Am 58:52-71 My '70
Morrisite war. M. H. Cannon. bibliog il Am West 7:4-9+ N '70
New prophet. pors Newsweek 75:71 F 2 '70
Prophet, seer and innovator. por Time 95: 49-50 F 2 '70
See also
Reorganized church of Jesus Christ of Latter day saints

MORMONS and Mormonism, Negro
Mary. J. Adamson. Chr Cent 87:175-6 F 11 '70
Mormons and blacks; doctrine forbidding black males from becoming priests. Chr Today 14:22 Ja 30 '70
Mormons stand pat; forbid black males to become priests. J. Rohler. Chr Today 14: 34-5 F 13 '70
Other side of the Y; attitude toward Negroes of the Church of Jesus Christ of Latter-day saints. W. F. Reed. il Sports Illus 32: 38-9 Ja 26 '70
Pigskin justice and Mormon theology. Chr Cent 87:67 Ja 21 '70

MORNING man; story. See MacDougall, R. D.

MOROCCAN cookery. See Cookery, Moroccan

MOROCCAN music. See Music, Moroccan

MOROCCO
See also
Divorce—Morocco
Women—Morocco

Description and travel
Morocco. C. Connelly. il Travel & Camera 33:38-47+ S '70
Morocco. G. Trotta. il Harp Baz 103:38+ Je '70
Morocco: surrender to a country. M. W. Schwartz. por Travel & Camera 33:82-3 S '70

Politics and government
Reporter at large; honor to the bride. J. Kramer. New Yorker 46:33-6+ Ag 29; 43-8+ S 5; 112+ S 12 '70

MOROCCO—*Continued*

Religious institutions and affairs
Reporter at large; honor to the bride. J. Kramer. New Yorker 46:33-6+ Ag 29; 43-8+ S 5; 112+ S 12 '70

Social conditions
See also
Women—Morocco

Social life and customs
See also
Women—Morocco

MOROCCO in art
Delacroix in Africa. R. McMullen. il por Horizon 11:60-75 Aut '69

MOROCCO-United States air agreement. See Aviation—International aspects

MOROS
Floating gypsies of the Pacific; photographs. Travel 134:62-7 N '70

MOROVITZ, Barney
P.O.N.Y. farm. il por Good H 170:52-3+ Mr '70 *

MORPHINE
Catecholamine biosynthesis in brains of rats treated with morphine. D. H. Clouet and M. Ratner. bibliog il Science 168:854-6 My 15 '70

Morphine: radioimmunoassay. S. Spector and C. W. Parker. bibliog il Science 168:1347-8 Je 12 '70

Tolerance to morphine-induced increases in [^{14}C]catecholamine synthesis in mouse brain. C. B. Smith and others. bibliog il Science 170:1106-8 D 4 '70

MORPHOLOGY
See also
Homology (biology)

MORRILL, George P.
Vermont: of green, glory and granite. il Read Digest 97:145-52 Jl '70

MORRILL, John E.
Industrial advertising pays off. il Harvard Bsns R 48:4-6+ Mr '70

MORRILL, Justin Smith
Senator Morrill's Gothic cottage at Strafford, Vermont. L. Wodehouse. il Antiques 98:237-41 Ag '70 *

MORRIS, Barry
Dollars and sense of the standards. il Library J 95:1568-9 Ap 15 '70

MORRIS, Colin
Cross over Africa. Chr Cent 87:688-91 Je 3 '70

MORRIS, Dan, and Morris, Inez
Pennysaver cookbook; excerpts. il Ladies Home J 87:96-7+ Mr '70

MORRIS, Daniel Luzon
Bronsted-Lowry acid-base theory, a brief survey. por Chem 43:18-19 Mr '70

MORRIS, Desmond
Scientist looks at the human zoo. il por US News 68:38 My 2 '70

MORRIS, George L. K.
Brief encounter with Matisse. Life 69:44+ Ag 28 '70

MORRIS, George N.
Does your firm face a liquidity crisis? Nations Bsns 58:59 D '70

MORRIS, Inez. See Morris, D. jt. auth.

MORRIS, James, 1926-
Salamanca. Holiday 47:40-1+ Ja '70
Venice: the past; the most triumphant city. il Horizon 12:76-91 Wint '70

MORRIS, Joe Alex, jr
Hammering at recognition. Nation 210:614-16 My 25 '70

MORRIS, John
Something old, something new ... America 123:459-60 N 28 '70

MORRIS, John E. and Moscona, A. A.
Induction of glutamine synthetase in embryonic retina: its dependence on cell interactions. bibliog il Science 167:1736-8 Mr 27 '70

MORRIS, John N.
Hating your life; poem. New Repub 162:31 Ja 24 '70
House hunting; poem. Harper 241:75 Ag '70

MORRIS, Joseph
Morrisite war. M. H. Cannon. bibliog il Am West 7:4-9+ N '70 *

MORRIS, Leon
Two hundred years of Australia. Chr Today 14:10-12 Jl 3 '70

MORRIS, M. D.
New towns in the desert. il Am City 85:94+ N '70

MORRIS, Mary Louise
Many heads of Armand Marseille. il Hobbies 75:48-9+ N '70

MORRIS, Nelson
World of darkness. il Travel & Camera 33:82-6 F '70

MORRIS, Philip, inc.
Philip Morris: unconventional wisdom. il Forbes 107:27 Ja 1 '71

MORRIS, Robert
Art; exhibition at the Castelli. L. Alloway. Nation 210:222 F 23 '70 *
Art; exhibition at the Whitney museum. L. Alloway. Nation 210:541 My 4 '70 *
Artist speaks: Robert Morris; interview, ed. by E. C. Goossen. il por Art in Am 58:104-11 My '70
Maximizing the minimal. il por Time 95:54 Ap 20 '70 *
Parking lot sculptor. por Design 71:41 Spr '70 *

MORRIS, Steven W.
How blacks view mankind's giant step. il Ebony 25:33-6+ S '70
Legal speedster. il pors Ebony 26:48-50+ D '70

MORRIS, Terry
LaDonna Harris: a woman who gives a damn. il Redbook 134:74-5+ F '70

MORRIS, William
Dictionary as a tool in vocabulary development programs. Engl J 59:669-71 My '70

MORRIS, Willie
South toward home. por Time 95:77 Je 1 '70 *
Yazoo: notes on survival. il Harper 240:43-50+ Je '70

MORRIS, Wright
Fight between a white boy and a black boy in the dusk of a fall afternoon in Omaha, Nebraska; story. New Yorker 46:109-11 Je 6 '70
Fiona; story. Esquire 74:106 Jl '70
How I met Joseph Mulligan. jr; story. Harper 240:82-5 F '70

MORRIS, Xenophon
Playgrounds in orbit. il Parks & Rec 5:31+ Mr '70

MORRISITES. See Mormons and Mormonism

MORRISON, C. V. and Morrison, D. N.
Help found: team care for disturbed children. il Todays Health 48:34-6+ Mr '70

MORRISON, Charles C. jr
New environmental conservation tool. il Cons 25:10-13 D '70 (to be cont)

MORRISON, Dorothy N. See Morrison, C. V. jt. auth.

MORRISON, Frank, and others
Magnetometer evidence of a structure within the La Venta pyramid. bibliog il Science 167:1488-90 Mr 13 '70

MORRISON, George H. and others
Multielement analysis of lunar soil and rocks. il Science 167:505-7 Ja 30 '70

MORRISON, Gordon
Peanuts. il Horticulture 48:40+ Ap '70
Peas for your garden. il Horticulture 48:40-1+ Mr '70

MORRISON, Jim
Blackbeard's booty. il por Outdoor Life 145:48-51+ Ja '70

MORRISON, Philip, and Morrison, Phylis
Annual survey of books about science for young readers (and their parents) Sci Am 223:122-6+ D '70

MORRISON, Phylis. See Morrison, Philip, jt. auth.

MORRISON, Robert R. and Ludvigson, H. W.
Discrimination by rats of conspecific odors of reward and nonreward. bibliog il Science 167:904-5 F 6 '70

MORRISON, Sarah Lyddon
If all else fails, try these. Mlle 72:156-7+ N '70

MORRISON, Theodore
Frost: country poet and cosmopolitan poet. Yale R 59:179-96 D '69

MORRISSEY, Paul
Current cinema. P. Kael. New Yorker 46:132+ O 10 '70 *

MORRISTOWN, N.J. municipal airport. See Airports—New Jersey

MORRO BAY
Port and park at Morro Bay. il Sunset 144:35 My '70

MORROW, Willie Lee
Military meets the Afro. L. Banks. il pors Ebony 25:86-92 S '70 *

MORSE, Arthur D.
Why doesn't the U.S. outlaw mass murder? Look 34:40 Mr 10 '70

MORSE, David
At home with the barons and earls. B. Bishop. il Sat R 53:46-7 S 12 '70 *

MORSE, Joan. See Morse, T.

MORSE, John J. and Lorsch, J. W.
Beyond Theory Y. bibliog f il Harvard Bsns R 48:61-8 My '70

MORSE, O. C. and Singer, J. R.
Blood velocity measurements in intact subjects. bibliog il Science 170:440-1 O 23 '70

MORSE, Robert
New year; poem. Poetry 117:193-4 D '70

MORSE, Stephen
Streetfight; poem. Sat R 53:67 Ja 24 '70
MORSE, Tiger
Tiger Morse's loft fantasy. J. Gruen. Vogue 155:74 Je '70 *
MORTALITY
Psychogenic death: a reappraisal. G. V. Barrett and R. H. Franke. bibliog il Science 167:304-6 Ja 16 '70
    See also
Death
Heart—Diseases—Mortality
MORTENSON, Robert R.
Tap only the best water in your well. il Am City 85:49-51 D '70
MORTGAGE bankers of America, United. See United mortgage bankers of America
MORTGAGE banks
    See also
Lomas and Nettleton financial corporation
MORTGAGE investment trusts. See Investment trusts
MORTGAGES
Coming: flexible, inflatable mortgages? il Changing T 24:21-4 D '70
Home financing; old approach to mortgages has to change, here are five new plans. Bet Hom & Gard 48:30+ Ag '70
Home-loan rates & terms, city by city; table. Changing T 24:6 Jl; 6 N '70
Housing: too little, too expensive. R. Dietsch. New Repub 162:9-11 Ap 4 '70
How & why of taking over a mortgage. il Changing T 24:21-3 Ja '70
How points hike the interest rate on your mortgage; with table. il Changing T 24:12 Je '70
How to finance a house in today's credit crunch. J. H. Ingersoll. House B 112:38+ S '70
Marshaling props for a new housing. il Bsns W p34 F 28 '70
More mortgages are past due. U S News 69:48 D 28 '70
More steps to aid mortgage lending. U S News 68:80-1 Mr 2 '70
Mortgage money is here again. E. M. Fowler. il Am Home 73:32+ O '70
New way to buy a home, flexible interest rates. il U S News 68:90-2 Ap 27 '70
Outlook for home buyers; interview. P. Martin. il pors U S News 68:70-3 Mr 23 '70
Will variable rates cure S&Ls' woes? il Bsns W p33-4 Jl 4 '70
    See also
Federal national mortgage association
Land contracts
United States—Federal home loan bank board
MORTIMER, Charles Greenough
Where are they now? R. Levy. pors Duns 95:40-1 Je '70 *
MORTIMER, Robert K. See Jones, G. E. jt. auth.
MORTON, Donald L. See Wood, W. C. jt. auth.
MORTON, Frederic
Film. il Harper 240:115-16 Ap '70
MORTON, Louis
World war II: a survey of recent writings. bibliog Am Hist R 75:1987-2008 D '70
MORTON, Rogers Clark Ballard
Teacher's political role; interview, ed. by G. D. Fischer. pors Todays Ed 59:20-1+ Ap '70
    about
Next Interior secretary. por Time 96:46+ D 14 '70 *
Reasons behind the firing of Hickel. pors U S News 69:29 D 7 '70 *
MORTUARY art. See Sepulchral monuments
MORTUARY customs. See Indians of North America—Mortuary customs
MORTUARY sculpture. See Sepulchral monuments
MOSAICON. See Color organ
MOSAICS
Floor tile mosaics. J. Hopkins. il Sch Arts 70:14-15 Ja '71
Mosaic in wood. P. Rothenberg. il Design 71:13-15 mid-Sum '70
Social sermon in stone. G. B. Curran. il Design 71:18-20 Fall '69
Torn tissue becomes tradition. F. A. Barkley. il Sch Arts 70:19 D '70
MOSAICS (biology)
Mosaic mutants: absence in a eucaryotic organism. A. Fjeld. bibliog il Science 168:843-4 My 15 '70
Somatic cell mating and segregation in chimeric frogs. E. P. Volpe and E. M. Earley. bibliog il Science 168:850-2 My 15 '70; Reply with rejoinder. J. J. Freed. 169:1229-30 S 18 '70

MOSCHELES, Ignaz
Assimilating the artistic past, Ignaz Moscheles. D. Dubal. por Am Rec G 37:90-1 O '70 *
MOSCONA, A. A. See Morris, J. E. jt. auth.
MOSCOW university. See Colleges and universities—Russia
MOSEMAN, Verne R.
Brother, you can spare the time. il Nations Bsns 58:34-5 F '70
MOSER, Stephen B.
Fair market value. il pors Am For 76:20-3+ Ja '70
MOSES
Moses in Midian: the burning bush. D. F. Zeligs. bibliog Am Imago 26:379-400 Wint '69 *
MOSES, Richard B.
Detroit as drama; or, Is the process the only payoff? Am Lib 1:841-2 O '70
MOSES, Robert, 1888-
Bomb shelters, arks and ecology. il Nat R 22:938-42 S 8 '70
Man in charge. J. B. Burnham. por Nat R 22:317-18 Mr 24 '70 *
Master builder. G. Wolff. por Newsweek 75:102 F 23 '70 *
Personal history. H. Mitgang. il Sat R 53:35-6 Mr 14 '70 *
MOSK, Stanley
Justice in violent times. Nation 211:431-4 N 2 '70
MOSKIN, J. Robert
Drugs: we are just plain ignorant. Look 34:108+ O 6 '70
Exclusive report from Hanoi; the hard-line demand: victory. il Look 34:20-2+ D 29 '70
Germany we don't know. il Look 34:42-50+ Je 16 '70
Memo from Warsaw: while Asia burns, talk, talk, talk. Look 34:74-5 My 19 '70
Who would ever go to West Point today? il pors Look 34:31-8 O 6 '70
(ed) See Brandt, W. Don't pull the GI's out of Europe
MOSKOS, Charles C. Jr
Why men fight. bibliog il por Trans-Action 7:13-23 N '69
MOSKOW, Michael H.
Trade unions in the performing arts; excerpt from Labor relations in the performing arts. il Mo Labor R 93:16-20 Mr '70
—and McLennan, Kenneth
Impact of school decentralization on collective bargaining. Mo Labor R 93:51-3 Ap '70
MOSKOWITZ, Ronald
How to catch a dogcatcher. il Am Ed 6:9-12 O '70
Leaving the drug world behind. il Am Ed 6:3-6 Ja '70; Same. Ed Digest 35:5-7 My '70
MOSLEY, Jean Bell
Ever hear a bluebell? il Read Digest 96:76-9 Ja '70
MOSLEY, John Brooke, bp, 1915-
Non-scholar. por Newsweek 75:86 Ap 13 '70 *
Our man at Union. Chr Cent 87:468 Ap 22 '70 *
Union finds a president; Manhattan's union theological seminary. por Time 95:58+ Ap 13 '70 *
Union's new president. Chr Today 14:40 Ap 24 '70 *
MOSQUES
    See also
Jerusalem—Holy places
MOSQUITO control
Aedes aegypti; origin of a new chromosome from a double translocation heterozygote. P. T. McDonald and K. S. Rai. bibliog il Science 168:1229-30 Je 5 '70
Build the bug shoo. L. E. Greenlee. il Pop Electr 33:27-30 Jl '70
DDT-less mosquito control; new larvicide known as Dursban. W. H. Cranford. il Am City 85:109+ Ja '70
Fish to control mosquitoes. D. Valentry. il Sea Front 16:231-3 Jl '70
Menacing mosquitoes; California pasture mosquito. il Time 96:44+ O 12 '70
Supression and elimination of an island population of culex pipiens quinquefasciatus with sterile males. R. S. Patterson and others. bibliog il Science 168:1368-70 Je 12 '70
MOSQUITO repellents. See Insect baits and repellents
MOSQUITOES
Aedes aegypti; origin of a new chromosome from a double translocation heterozygote. P. T. McDonald and K. S. Rai. bibliog il Science 168:1229-30 Je 5 '70
Allure of the mosquito. C. B. Worth. il Audubon 72:60-2+ My '70
Amateur scientist; how to study the life of a pond and to cultivate aquatic insects. H. Abernathey. il Sci Am 222:135-6 Mr '70
Menacing mosquitoes; California pasture mosquito. il Time 96:44+ O 12 '70

MOSQUITOES—*Continued*

Extermination

See Mosquito control

MOSS, Frank Edward
Senator Moss gets AAHA honor: urges stricter U.S. standards. por Aging 182:9 D '69

MOSS, Frank T.
Legend in their own time. il Yachting 129: 88-90+ Ja '71
With the sport fishermen. See issues of Yachting

MOSS, Howard
Advisers; poem. New Repub 162:28 F 7 '70
Hand; poem. New Yorker 46:42 S 5 '70
North Sea; poem. New Yorker 46:40 Mr 7 '70
Radical departures; poem. New Yorker 46: 42 My 16 '70

MOSS, Mike
Whale of a hand and a player, too. C. Goren. il por Sports Illus 33:104 S 14 '70 •

MOSS, Norman
War in North Ireland. New Repub 163:13-14 Ag 15 '70

MOSS, W. Wayne, and Camin, J. H.
Nest parasitism, productivity and clutch size in purple martins. bibliog il Science 168: 1000-3; 170:1112 My 22, D 4 '70

MOSS pink
This ground cover is a blooming mulch. M. J. Rozell. Org Gard & Farm 17:89 S '70

MÖSSBAUER effect
Apollo 11 lunar science conference: Mössbauer studies; symposium. bibliog il Sciencee 167: 681-90 Ja 30 '70
Diffraction and Mössbauer studies of minerals from lunar soils and rocks. P. Gay and others. bibliog il Science 167:626-8 Ja 30 '70

MOSSE, George L.
History, anthropology, and mass movements. bibliog f Am Hist R 75:447-52 D '69

MOSSES
See also
Lichens

MOSTERT, Noel
Suez Canal: the broken link. il Read Digest 96:136-41 My '70

MOT solen; ballet. See Ballets—Criticisms

MOTELS
Motel room at bargain rates; F. B. Roedel's Chalet Susse establishments. il Bsns W p20 Ag 22 '70
Motels: quaint, corny and capricious. R. Lynes. Art in Am 58:11 Jl '70
Riches from royal treatment; California-based chain of Royal inns. il por Time 96:87 N 16 '70

MOTHER-child relationship. See Parent-child relationship

MOTHER Goose dolls. See Dolls

MOTHER love. See Love, Maternal

MOTHER-of-pearl
Microarchitecture and deposition of gastropod nacre. S. W. Wise, jr. bibliog il Science 167:1486-8 Mr 13 '70

MOTHER participation in school activities. See Volunteer workers in education

MOTHER tiger; story. See Cain, E.

MOTHERHOOD. See Mothers

MOTHERHOOD; story. See Ullian, R.

MOTHERS
Is there a perfect mother? J. Brothers. Good H 170:52+ Je '70
Mod, mod mamas. Chr Today 14:25 My 8 '70
Motherhood: who needs it? B. Rollin. Look 34:15-17 S 22 '70
New baby at our house; six years between first child and second. C. Lang. il por Parents Mag 45:54-5 Mr '70
Perfect mother. Tiny Tim. por Esquire 74: 144-5+ D '70
Pregnancy quiz: is this the time to have a baby? G. W. Perkin and E. M. Nash. il Good H 170:68+ Ap '70
Take the lilies and the lace; excerpt from The Judy Collins songbook. J. Collins. il pors McCalls 97:66-7+ Ap '70
Young mothers story. See issues of Redbook
See also
Love, Maternal
Parent education

Employment

See Married women—Employment

MOTHERS, Unmarried
Giving unwed schoolgirl mothers a second chance. J. Daniel. il PTA Mag 64:8-10+ Je '70; Same abr. with title Case of the pregnant schoolgirl. Read Digest 97:169-73 S '70
In trouble: the story of an unmarried woman's decision to keep her child. J. Harriman. por Atlan 225:94-8 Mr '70

Larry: case history of a mistake. R. McQueen. Sat R 53:16-19+ S 12 '70; Same abr. il Read Digest 97:133-7 D '70
Premarital pregnancy among black teen-agers. F. F. Furstenberg, jr. il Trans-Action 7:52-5 My '70
What about unwed mothers? T. Howard. Chr Today 14:11-12 Mr 13 '70

MOTHERS against drugs (organization) See Narcotics, Control of

MOTHERS and daughters. See Parent-child relationship

MOTHERS day

Drama

Surprise for mother; drama. H. L. Miller. Plays 29:35-44 My '70
Time for mom; drama; reprint. A. Fisher. Plays 29:67-70 My '70

MOTHER'S day; story. See West, J.

MOTHERS milk. See Milk, Human

MOTHERWELL, Robert
Universal language of children's art, and modernism; address, April 29, 1970. Am Scholar 40:24-7 Wint '70

MOTHNER, Ira
Canada's Trudeau: after the kissing stops. il pors Look 34:47-51 F 24 '70
How can you tell if your child is taking drugs? il Look 34:42+ Ap 7 '70
Odd alliance: Moynihan and the robber barons. il pors Look 34:18-23 Ap 7 '70
When you get mugged: give up, shut up, pay up. il Look 34:66-8 Ag 25 '70

MOTHS
Chemical inducers of oviposition for the corn earworm, heliothis zea (Boddie) R. L. Jones and others. bibliog il Science 168:856-7 My 15 '70
Distal lobe of the pilifer: an ultrasonic receptor in choerocampine hawkmoths. K. D. Roeder and others. bibliog il Science 170: 1098-9 D 4 '70
Last days of polyphemus. C. B. Worth. il Audubon 72:22-30 Mr '70
Life cycle of a moth. N. Smith. il Nat Wildlife 8:18 O '70
Nervous control of the heart during thoracic temperature regulation in a sphinx moth. B. Heinrich. bibliog il Science 169:606-7 Ag 7 '70
Neuroendocrine control of ecdysis in silkmoths. J. W. Truman and L. M. Riddiford. bibliog il Science 167:1624-6 Mr 20 '70
Persuasive scents in moth sex life. M. Birch. il Natur Hist 79:34-9+ bibliog(p88) N '70
Sex pheromones of the southern armyworm moth: isolation, identification, and synthesis. M. Jacobson and others. bibliog Science 170:542-4 O 30 '70
Thoracic temperature stabilization by blood circulation in a free-flying moth. B. Heinrich. bibliog il Science 168:580-1 My 1 '70
See also
Caterpillars
Gypsy moths

MOTILONE Indians. See Indians of South America—Venezuela

MOTION
See also
Equation of motion

MOTION pictures. See Moving pictures

MOTION sculpture. See Mobiles

MOTION study
See also
Movement, Psychology of

MOTIVATION (education)
Building the slow learner's self-esteem; support and encouragement through Achiever program. M. H. Martin. Todays Ed 59:46-7 Mr '70
Experimenting with tempera. C. J. Alkema. il Design 71:26-30 mid-Wint '70
Motivation. S. R. Rainey. il Sch Arts 70:8-9 Ja '71
Pleasure principle; excerpt from A child's mind. M. Beadle. il N Y Times Mag p75+ Mr 22 '70
Project mobilization; program for educationally disadvantaged students. D. L. Carl. Clear House 44:519-22 My '70
See also
Aspiration level

MOTIVATION (psychology)
Fixation produced by conflict. E. B. Karsh. bibliog il Science 168:873-5 My 15 '70
Motivating people with meaningful work. W. J. Roche and N. L. MacKinnon. bibliog il Harvard Bsns R 48:97-110 My '70
Psychogenic death: a reappraisal. G. V. Barrett and R. H. Franke. bibliog il Science 167:304-6 Ja 16 '70
See also
Conflict (psychology)
Reward (psychology)

MOTIVATION research. See Market research

MOTO-CROSS racing. See Motorcycle racing

MOTONEURONS. See Nerve cells

MOTOR boat engines
Outboard or sterndrive? J. A. Emmett. il
Outdoor Life 146:22-3+ Jl '70
See also
Outboard motors

Maintenance and repair
Give your stern drive a mid-season lift. M.
Schultz. il Pop Mech 134:123-5+ Ag '70
Inboard engine maintenance. C. Miller. il
Motor B 125:70-1 Ap '70
New hope for mechanical morons. S. Wilson.
Motor B 126:56-7 D '70

MOTOR boat racing
Closed course racing. E. Crimmin. il Motor B
126:54-9+ Ag '70
Cognac derby; bad day at Shrewsbury Rock;
racing for Hennessy Grand prix. G. F.
Hammond. il Motor B 126:50-1+ S '70
How can you beat two Don Aronows? T. Bot-
tomley. il por Motor B 125:10-11+ F '70
Long Beach-Hennessy. L. Kennedy. il Motor
B 126:10-12+ D '70
Looking back on the year, and ahead at the
future. T. Bottomley. il Motor B 125:12-14+
F '70
Magoon on the bounding main; Miami-Nas-
sau race. H. D. Whall. il Sports Illus 33:
76-7 N 16 '70
Magoon wins Hennessy Key West race. M.
Crook. il Yachting 128:42 D '70
Memo from '69; ed. by F. Rohr. jr. il Motor
B 125:25-40 Ja '70
Miami-Nassau race. L. Evans. Yachting 128:
42 D '70
Month in yachting. See issues of Yachting
More power to you. M. Crook. See issues of
Yachting
Outboards victorious; Bahamas 500. T. Bot-
tomley. il Motor B 126:47-9+ Ag '70
Racing's rewards. M. Crook. il Yachting 128:
68+ O '70
Rooster tales. E. Rickman. See issues of
Hot rod to November 1970
Sirois wins Havasu race. M. Crook. il
Yachting 129:60 Ja '71
$60,000 Outboard world championship. G. F.
Hammond. il Motor B 126:34-5 N '70
Water sports; ed. by F. Rohr. jr. See issues
of Motor boating to April 1970
World championship of outboard racing; Lake
Havasu. M. Crook. il Yachting 127:70-1+ F
'70
Year in yachting. il Yachting 129:76-83 Ja
'71

Anecdotes, facetiae, satire, etc.
Tin boats of Scrog Lake. D. R. Van Volkenburg. il Motor B 126:52-5+ D '70

Indonesia
Win...or else! H. Kelly. il por Motor B 126:
118-20 S '70

MOTOR boats
All-American racing team, 1969; Yachting's
21st annual. M. Crook. il Yachting 127:67-9+
Mr '70
By boat around the tip of Florida. G. Reiger.
il Pop Mech 133:106-9+ Je '70
Fino; America's answer to the Riva. il Motor
B 125:82-3 My '70
Fishing with a gypsy. G. Reiger. il Pop Mech
134:120-2 S '70
High performance powerboats. J. H. Deknatel.
il por Motor B 125:100-1 Ja '70
It's a wet ride on an AquaDart. E. H.
Arctander. il Pop Sci 197:24 O '70
Legend in their own time; Bertram Moppies.
F. T. Moss. il Yachting 129:8-90+ Ja '71
Miami's glamour boats. P. Smyth. il Motor B
125:48-55+ F '70
New boats. See issues of Yachting
New boats for '70. il Pop Mech 133:120-3 Mr '70
Power boats. il Motor B 127:196-215+ Ja '71
Preview of the 1971 boats. B. McKeown. il
Mech Illus 66:50-2+ D '70
Rooster tales. E. Rickman. See issues of
Hot rod to November 1970
Runabouts and utilities. il Motor B 125:206-
13+ Ja '70
Runabouts and utility boats. R. C. Cole. il por
Motor B 125:98-9 Ja '70
Trio of sports boats for men who like 'em
hot. J. Roe. il Pop Sci 197:60-1 Ag '70
What's your thing? J. Roe. il Pop Sci 196:
74-7 F '70
Yachting's boat show in print. il Yachting
127:127-37+ Ja; 211-12+ F; 220+ Mr '70
See also
Cruisers (pleasure boats)
Fishing boats
Hydrofoils
Hydroplanes
Outboard motor boats

Accidents
See Boats and boating—Accidents

Design
Designs. B. D. Barker. 3d. See issues of Yacht-
ing
From my ocean racers; a better boat for you;
ed. by W. B. Hartley. D. Aronow. il por
Pop Sci 196:80-3 F '70

Electric equipment
Anatomy of a powerboat; electrical loads and
batteries. J. West. il Yachting 128:52-3+
D '70
Electrical system maintenance. C. Miller. il
Motor B 125:74-5 Ap '70

Electronic equipment
Modern electronics package. W. Robberson.
il Yachting 127:78-9 Ap '70

Equipment
Commissioning a new boat. M. W. Johnson.
il Motor B 125:49-51+ Ap '70
Yachting's boat show. il Yachting 129:121-2+
Ja '71
Yachting's boat show in print. il Yachting
127:127-37+ Ja; 211-12+ F; 220+ Mr '70

Exhibitions
See Boats—Exhibitions

Gasoline engines
Inside the '70 engines; new features for go
and durability. J. Roe. il Pop Sci 196:82-3 F
'70

Maintenance and repair
Commissioning a new boat. M. W. Johnson.
il Motor B 125:49-51+ Ap '70
Stopping topside leaks. J. Duffet. il Motor
B 125:80 Ap '70
Ten tips for faster performance. B. Mc-
Keown. il Mech Illus 66:98+ Mr '70

Motors
See Motor boat engines

Speed
Speed on the water. T. Bottomley. il Motor B
125:61-4+ F '70
Ten tips for faster performance. B. Mc-
Keown. il Mech Illus 66:98+ Mr '70

Testing
Be your own boat tester. B. Whittier. il
Pop Mech 133:126-9+ Mr; 156-9+ Ap; 140-3
My '70
PM tests Wellcraft's new air-slot hull. G.
Reiger. il Pop Mech 134:106-9 Ag '70

Water supply
Plumbing maintenance. J. Duffet il Motor
B 125:78 Ap '70

**MOTOR boats, Outboard. See Outboard mot-
or boats**

MOTOR bus engines
Progress report on smogless motoring; California's contracts for construction of experimental steambuses. J. Lear. Sat R 53:44-
5 Ag 1 '70

MOTOR bus lines
See also
Carey transportation, inc.
Greyhound corporation

Fares
Whatever happened to the rash of bus robberies? il U S News 68:16 F 23 '70

Radio communication
Automated bus system; Chicago transit authority. il Am City 85:130+ S '70

MOTOR bus travel
Great western bus ride. J. Kerouac. Esquire
73:136-7+ Mr '70

MOTOR buses
Taxis, jitneys & poverty; adaptation of address. S. Rosenbloom. il Trans-Action 7:
47-54 F '70

MOTOR buses, Electric
Mercedes-Benz tests electric zero-emission
city bus. J. P. Norbye. il Pop Sci 196:58 Ja
'70
Ohmsmobile; Mercedes electric bus. E. Dahlquist. il Motor T 22:86-7 Mr '70

MOTOR buses on rails
New York city's rail bus. il Sci Digest 67:88-
9 Ja '70

MOTOR camping. See Camping

MOTOR cycle racing. See Motorcycle racing

MOTOR cycles. See Motorcycles

MOTOR fuels
Compressed natural gas: another clean-air fuel. J. Zmuda. il Pop Sci 197:30 Ag '70
Driving with gas. Newsweek 75:57 F 9 '70
Natural gas as motor fuel. Chem 43:25 My '70
See also
Automobile engines—Fuel

Storage
Five fuel storage ideas you can borrow. il Suc Farm 68:M6 Ap '70

MOTOR homes. See Campers and coaches. Truck

MOTOR response
Predicting measures of motor performance from multiple cortical spike trains. D. R. Humphrey and others. bibliog il Science 170:758-62 N 13 '70

MOTOR transportation. See Transportation, Automotive

MOTOR trend awards
Auto tech winners. il Motor T 22:96-7 O '70
Car of the year: candidates. il Motor T 22:42-3 Ja '70
Car of the year: nominees. il Motor T 22:80-1 D '70
Car of the year: 1970 Ford Torino. il Motor T 22:30-3 F '70
Import car of the year. il Motor T 22:54 My '70
Motor trend's import car of the year. il Motor T 22:106-7 Ap '70

MOTOR trend 500. See Automobile racing
MOTOR trend-Riverside 500. See Automobile racing

MOTOR truck drivers
Song of the open road, 1970. W. Friedman. il Time 96:19 S 14 '70
See also
International brotherhood of teamsters, chauffeurs, warehousemen and helpers of America
Strikes—United States—Truck drivers

MOTOR truck engines
Perk up your pickup. J. Dianna. il Hot Rod 23:116-17 S '70
Truck packs 110 volts under its hood. il Pop Sci 196:56 Ja '70

MOTOR truck industry and trade
See also
Ford motor company
White motor corporation

MOTOR truck lines
See also
Pacific intermountain express company

Consolidations and mergers
Driving toward a merger; proposed Ryder-PIE merger. il Bsns W p45-6 My 2 '70

MOTOR truck robberies. See Robberies and assaults

MOTOR trucking. See Trucking

MOTOR trucks
Jeep Gladiator: a surefooted workhorse to carry your camper. C. R. Meyer. il Pop Sci 197:22 Ag '70
Light truck story for 1971. P. Weissler. il Mech Ilus 66:56-8+ D '70
New trucks for 1971; photographs. Farm J 94:35 O '70
Pickup trucks for use with camper boxes. il Consumer Rep 35:490-7 Ag '70
They grow trucks bigger in Minsk. il Bsns W p48 F 28 '70
Tom McCahill reports on light trucks. T. McCahill. il Mech Illus 66:115-18+ F '70

Engines
See Motor truck engines

Equipment
Truck-mounted loading boom; South Miami, Fla. il Am City 85:85 Ja '70

Exhibitions
Talk about trucks! Internationale automobil-ausstellung in Frankfurt. R. P. Crossley. il Pop Mech 133:134-7 F '70

Laws and legislation
Big-rig truckers roll into battle; AAA vs supertrucks. il Bsns W p 136 Mr 21 '70

Leasing and renting
What to consider when renting a moving van. il Good H 170:190-1 Mr '70

Loading and unloading
See Loading and unloading

Testing
Tom McCahill tests (title varies)
Chevy Blazer. T. McCahill. il Mech Illus 66:57-9+ Ap '70

MOTOR trucks, Electric
Uncle Sam's juice wagon. il Mech Illus 66:75+ Ja '70

MOTOR trucks, Military
Army bogs down over a new truck. il Bsns W p92 N 28 '70
Uncle Sam's juice wagon. il Mech Illus 66:75+ Ja '70

MOTOR trucks, Toy. See Toys

MOTOR trucks in agriculture
Meet the kid. il Mech Illus 66:10+ Je '70

MOTOR vehicle engines

Fuel
See Motor fuels

MOTOR vehicle fleets
GM and Ford cut fleet discounts. il Bsns W p30 Je 13 '70

MOTOR vehicle insurance. See Insurance, Motor vehicle

MOTOR vehicle mountain climbing. See Mountaineering

MOTOR vehicle racing
All-terrain takes in snow; Mount Snow winter rally. G. Reiger. il Pop Mech 135:34D-34E Ja '71
ATV racing, rambunctious new sport. E. H. Arctander. il Pop Sci 197:90-1 Ag '70
C'mon in the mud's fine! four-wheel-drive Grand prix. J. Thawley. il Hot Rod 23:68-9 Jl '70
Dirty, dirty Mint 400. A. B. Shuman. il Motor T 22:60-2+ Je '70
Muddy-er the merrier. B. Kilpatrick. il Pop Mech 134:100-1 Ag '70
SNORE 250; Southern Nevada off-road enthusiasts. J. Thawley. il Hot Rod 23:46-7 D '70
They came, they saw, they conquered, or, they broke; Inaugural national sand championship. il Hot Rod 23:54-5 F '70
293 start; twelve finish; Mint 400. J. Thawley. il Hot Rod 23:40-3 Je '70

Great Britain
England on the move; National drag racing club. M. Lintern. il Hot Rod 23:122 Ap '70

Mexico
Baja 1000. A. B. Shuman. il Motor T 22:56-61+ Ja '70
Drive ya buggy; Mexican 1000. J. Thawley. il Hot Rod 23:126 O '70
Mexican 1000. J. Thawley. il Hot Rod 24:80-3 Ja '71
Motor trend interview. E. Carlsson. por Motor T 22:85-6+ F '70
To finish is a feat, to win is incredible! Mexican 1000. J. Thawley. il Hot Rod 23:42-5 Ja '70
Very fast 500; Baja 500. J. Thawley. il Hot Rod 23:106-8 Ag '70

MOTOR vehicle service centers, Municipal
More than just a building; vehicle service center, Canton, Ohio. L. C. Dubs. il Am City 85:119+ Je '70

MOTOR vehicles
Drive ya buggy. J. Thawley. See issues of Hot rod
Dune buggy or sports car? Both! the Virgo. M. Lamm. il Pop Mech 134:78-80 Jl '70
Incredible no-torque walking machine; Rotoped. D. Scott. il por Pop Sci 196:61-3+ Ja '70
When dune buggies bug-in. J. Davis. il Pop Sci 196:46 Ja '70
See also
Automobiles
Crawler vehicles
Electric vehicles
Jeep automobiles
Motorcycles
Recreational vehicles
Snowmobiles

Bodies
Rebirth of the roadsters; multitude of dune buggies and kits. J. Thawley. il Hot Rod 23:34-41 S '70

Corrosion
See Corrosion and anticorrosives

Design
The Box: all wheels steer and drive. J. Davis. il Pop Sci 197:66-7 N '70

Fuel
See Motor fuels

Skidding
See also
Pavements—Slipperiness

Statistics
100 million cars, trucks, buses; and more on the way. il U S News 68:50-1 My 25 '70

MOTOR vehicles—*Continued*

Testing
PM tests:
Snow Eagle, first of the fast ATVs. J.
Joseph. il Pop Mech 133:108-11 Ja '70
MOTOR vehicles, Amphibious
All terrain vehicles. il Bet Hom & Gard 48:
37 Ap '70
All terrain vehicles in the 70's. B. Behme. il
Field & S 75:44-7+ Ag '70
ATV will take you almost anywhere. K. Pren-
tiss. il Holiday 47:66-7+ My '70
ATV with 4WS. J. Joseph. il Mech Illus 66:
96+ F '70
ATV you make from a kit. E. F. Lindsley.
il Pop Sci 196:102 Je '70
ATV's: invincible vehicles that go any-
where. il Changing T 24:13-15 My '70
Bug-like buggy for all terrains. il Bsns W
p 27 Mr 21 '70
Camping with an ATV? C. B. Colby. il Out-
door Life 146:12+ S '70
Case of the agile ATVs. E. S. Gardner. il pors
Pop Sci 196:70-3+ F '70
Churning into tomorrow on six chubby tires,
all-terrain vehicles. B. Yates. il Sports Illus
33:56-8 N 2 '70
Funmobiles. B. Thomas. il Travel 134:40-3+
Ag '70
Hustler; a new breed of Arkansas traveler.
G. Reiger. il Pop Mech 133:98-100 My '70
Meet the kid. il Mech Illus 66:10+ Je '70
Now! Build your own ATV. il Mech Illus
66:76-81+ Ja '70
One hand controls new cone-drive ATV. il
Pop Sci 196:106-7+ Ja '70
Quiet one; an ATV that runs off batteries.
E. F. Lindsley. il Pop Sci 197:64-5 N '70
Racing in the rough; all-terrain vehicles. il
Mech Illus 66:56-7 Jl '70
Six flats and a cloud of dust. J. Lamm. il
Motor T 22:86-90+ My '70
To the summit by ATV; interview. ed. by J.
Joseph. J. Lytle. il Pop Mech 133:102-5+ F
'70
Tom McCahill tests 3 ATVs. il Mech Illus 66:
48-51+ Ag '70
Tracker, an ATV for all seasons. D. N. Wen-
ner. il Pop Sci 197:62-3 S '70
Your first ride in an ATV. E. H. Arctander. il
Pop Sci 196:44+ Mr '70
MOTOR vehicles, Municipal
See also
Automobiles, Municipal

Maintenance and repair
How to maintain municipal equipment. Am
City 85:39 Je '70
MOTOR vehicles, Police
Plastic shields protect police vehicles; Phila-
delphia. il Am City 85:36 D '70
MOTOR vehicles, Racing
How the Bronco builder beats the Bronco
busters; or, Why Motor trend's project
Bronco won the Baja 1000. A. B. Shuman.
il Motor T 22:70-1 F '70
MOTORBOATS. See Motor boats
MOTORCYCLE camping. See Camping
MOTORCYCLE engines
Who needs a motorcycle battery? Lucas 2MC
capacitor. J. Davis. il Pop Sci 196:95 Mr '70
MOTORCYCLE industry and trade
Then came Kawasaki; new boom. il News-
week 76:84+ S 14 '70
Uneasy rider in the U.S. market; BSA motor-
cyles. il Bsns W p44 Je 20 '70
Vrrooom, skrroww, braap. il Forbes 105:75-6
Je 15 '70
MOTORCYCLE racing
Berkshire; like ducks to water. B. Greene.
il Hot Rod 23:104-5 D '70
Bonneville. T. Murphy. il Hot Rod 23:126-9
N '70
Cycling; the Daytona 200; with comments by
I. Dolin. C. Neilson. il Travel & Camera 33:
48-52 O '70
Hell's Cherubim; racing at Indian Dunes park,
Valencia, Calif. il Time 96:56-7 N 2 '70
Just another face in a rearview mirror. M.
Maddocks. il Sports Illus 33:42-4+ N 16
'70
Midnight run. B. Greene. il Hot Rod 23:
144-5 Ap '70
Mighty and the high. B. Greene. il Hot Rod
23:114-15 Ja '70
Mini-motor nationals. C. Sims. il Hot Rod
23:134-5 Mr '70
Moto-cross invades America. T. Murphy. il
Hot Rod 23:64-6 Mr '70
NHRA bike blast. B. Greene. il Hot Rod 23:
102-3 My '70

Turning on the Trident. T. Murphy. il Hot
Rod 23:102-3 Jl '70
You win the nicest races on a Honda: Day-
tona! B. Greene. il Hot Rod 23:120-2 Je
'70
MOTORCYCLE riding. See Motorcycling
MOTORCYCLES
All about owning a cycle. il Bet Hom &
Gard 48:46+ S '70
All-American Honda. B. Greene. il Hot Rod
23:104-5 S '70
At last; a kick starter for minibikes. J. Davis.
il Pop Sci 197:64 N '70
Bikes get bigger. W. Thoms. il Mech Illus
66:62-4+ Je '70
Bronco Apache 100. T. Murphy. il Hot Rod
24:94-5 Ja '71
Engineering triumph. B. Greene. il Hot Rod
23:96-7 Mr '70
Family guide to mini-bikes. B. Hartford. il
Pop Mech 133:117-21+ F '70
Honda's rugged minibike; out of your trunk
onto the trail. J. Davis. il Pop Sci 197:63 S
'70
Kawasaki's adjustable 350; ready for road
or rough. J. Davis. il Pop Sci 197:82-3 O
'70
King of the royal mounted; Electra Glide.
B. Greene. il Hot Rod 23:108-9 Ap '70
Mini scene. il Mech Illus 66:70 Je '70
Minibikes; dangerous toys. il Consumer Bul
53:27-30 D '70
Minibikes; supertoys or safety hazards? il
Good H 171:159 S '70
My first year on a motorcycle. B. Hartford.
il Pop Mech 133:100-3+ Ap '70
New trail bikes; tough, versatile, and easy-
riding. J. Davis. il Pop Sci 197:58-9 Jl
'70
Night train to 'Frisco; Harley-Davidson Super
glide. B. Greene. il Hot Rod 23:104-5 N '70
Riding Yamaha's first big bike. J. Davis. il
Pop Sci 197:53 Ag '70
Saddle up for dirt! D. Richmond. il Pop Mech
134:138-41+ O '70
Scramble two! AJS Moto-Crossers. B.
Greene. il Hot Rod 23:82-3 D '70
Supercycles. W. Thoms. il Mech Illus 66:66-
7 Je '70
Testing Moto Guzzi's newest V-twin. J.
Davis. il Pop Sci 196:94-5 Ja '70
Three new minibikes with lots of options.
E. F. Lindsley. il Pop Sci 197:44 O '70
Trail bikes on the farm. Suc Farm 68:62
Ap '70
Up on two wheels. B. Greene. See issues of
Hot rod
You're never without wheels with this cycle
in a suitcase. J. Davis. il Pop Sci 196:68-9
F '70
See also
Motorcycling

Maintenance and repair
What to do when your motorcycle conks out.
J. Davis. il Pop Sci 197:96-7 N '70

Testing
Big Horn country; Kawasaki's 350 Enduro.
B. Greene. il Hot Rod 23:90-1 Ag '70
Bulletproof two-stroke; Yamaha 175cc En-
duro bike. B. Greene. il Hot Rod 23:96-7 F
'70
Testing the all-new BMW motorcycle, that
is! B. Hartford. il Pop Mech 133:90-1 Je '70
MOTORCYCLES, Foreign
Sachs. B. Greene. il Hot Rod 23:94-5 Ja '70
MOTORCYCLING
Motorcycle syndrome; psychological studies
of college cyclists. il Time 96:65 D 7 '70
My first year on a motorcycle B. Hartford.
il Pop Mech 133:100-3+ Ap '70
See also
Motorcycle racing

Stunt cycling
Mad cyclist of Napoli; A. Mellino. D. J.
Hamblin. il Life 69:67 O 2 '70
What's an E. J. Potter? S. Kelly. il pors Hot
Rod 23:88-90 S '70
MOTORING. See Automobile touring
MOTOROLA, inc.
Apprentice president makes the grade. il por
Bsns W p60+ S 19 '70
Bouncing back fast. il Forbes 106:39 Jl 1
'70
For Motorola, a chance to unload; sale of
picture-tube manufacturing facilities. Bsns
W p24-5 Ap 11 '70
MOTORS. See Automobile engines; Diesel en-
gines; Outboard motors; etc.
MOTORS, Outboard. See Outboard motors
MOTORSAILERS. See Cruisers (pleasure boats)

MOTT, Michael
Islanders, inlanders; Danaides; Pastoral; poems. Poetry 116:28-30 Ap '70
Seen in clear: Geoffrey Grigson's poems. Poetry 116:46-50 Ap '70
MOTT, N. F. See Austin, I. G. jt. auth.
MOTT, William Penn, Jr
Recreation for forty million people. il Arch Rec 147:132-3 My '70
MOTT transition. See Phase transitions
MOTTA, João Pedro de Almeida. See Almeida Motta, J. P. de
MOULDS, George Henry
Lines addressed to her twelfth birthday; poem. Am For 76:41 Ja '70
MOULTHROP, John F.
Ceramic disc trimmer capacitors. por Electr World 83:49-51 Ap '70
MOUND BAYOU, Miss.

Hospitals
New spirit at old Meharry; cooperation with Taborian hospital. il Ebony 25:42-6+ Ap '70
MOUNT, Rick
Count for Mount. H. L. Masin. por Sr Schol 96:25 F 2 '70 *
MOUNT ARARAT. See Ararat, Mount
MT BEULAH center. See Edwards, Miss.—Community centers
MOUNT EVEREST. See Everest, Mount
MOUNT FALCON white house. See Presidents—United States—Homes
MOUNT HAGEN festival. See Festivals—New Guinea
MOUNT HAMILTON RANGE. See Diablo Range
MOUNT JOY, Pa.
Inflated cover keeps water clean. B. Wells. il Am City 85:40 Je '70
MOUNT KATAHDIN. See Katahdin, Mount
MOUNT LEBANON, Pa.

Education
Suburbia reaches out; race relations program. V. A. Elliott. Engl J 59:660-4+ My '70
MOUNT RAINIER. See Rainier, Mount
MOUNTAIN building. See Geology, Structural
MOUNTAIN cabins. See Cabins
MOUNTAIN climbing. See Mountaineering
MOUNTAIN ecology
Impact of man on the Adirondack high country. E. H. Ketchledge and R. E. Leonard. il Cons 25:14-18 O '70
MOUNTAIN goat hunting. See Rocky Mountain goat hunting
MOUNTAIN grouse shooting. See Grouse shooting
MOUNTAIN lions. See Pumas
MOUNTAIN sculpture
See also
Crazy Horse (Sioux Indian)—Statues, portraits, etc.
Stone Mountain memorial
MOUNTAIN sheep
Bighorns: wild sheep of California. L. L. Lutz. il Am For 76:28-31 My; 30-1+ Je '70
Showdown on the Salmon River range; attempt to save Idaho's bighorns. R. Woodbury. il pors Life 68:54-56A My 22 '70

Protection
See Animals—Protection
MOUNTAIN sheep hunting
Bachelor bighorns; San Andres Range, N.Mex. T. Kelly. il por Outdoor Life 146:50-1+ Jl '70
Hunting in Iran. E. A. Bauer. il por Outdoor Life 145:58-61+ My; 146:44-7+ Jl '70
Ram for the records; ed. by B. Hartford. R. Brown. il por Outdoor Life 146:72-5+ O '70
Stalk for the book; no. 1 Dall sheep? D. Sykes. il pors Outdoor Life 145:76-7+ Ap '70
World record ram: bighorn with a bow. R. Alt. il Outdoor Life 146:68-71+ N '70
MOUNTAINEERING
Conquest of El Capitan. il pors Time 96:12 N 30 '70
Conquest of Hulla. P. C. Ritterbush. il por Américas 22:19-27 Ja '70
Enos Mills, Columbus of the Rockies. I. Ross. il por Nat Wildlife 9:26-8 D '70
Ordeal on El Capitan. il Life 69:46-8 N 20 '70
Reporter at large; trekking expedition to base of Everest. J. Bernstein. New Yorker 46:46-8+ My 9 '70
To the summit by ATV; interview, ed. by J. Joseph. J. Lytle. il Pop Mech 133:102-5+ F '70

Upon a peak in Delaware. D. Levin. il pors Sports Illus 33:34-6+ D 14 '70
West Virginia's mountain climbing; reaching the summit of Seneca Rock. B. Thomas. il Travel 133:28-33+ F '70

Study and teaching
Let's travel: the Alpin-schule Innsbruck; offering hiking courses. R. Rudner. il Mlle 70:124+ Mr '70
MOUNTAINS
See also
Adirondack Mountains
Geology, Structural
Timber line
Volcanoes
MOUNTAINS, Undersea. See Ocean bottom
MOUNTAINS in art
See also
Adirondack Mountains in art
MOUNTFORD, Frances
Among the Welsh mountains. il Travel 134:50-3 Ag '70
MOUNTINGS, Telescope. See Telescope mountings
MOURNING; story. See Bingham, S.
MOURNING dove shooting
Doves for openers. J. Freeman. il Field & S 75:40-1+ S '70
Great dove gun. T. Trueblood. il Field & S 75:24+ S '70
Watch who you call birdbrain; dove shoots. N. Riley. il Outdoor Life 145:46-7+ Ja '70
MOUSSAKA. See Cookery, Greek
MOUSTERIAN culture. See Neanderthal race
MOUTH
Surgery
See Oral surgery
MOUTH organs. See Harmonicas
MOUTH-to-mouth respiration. See Respiration, Artificial
MOUTHWASHES
Are mouthwashes really any good? il Changing T 23:49-51 D '69
MOVABLE partitions. See Partitions, Movable
MOVABLE room dividers. See Partitions, Movable
MOVEMENT, Psychology of
See also
Communication, Nonverbal
MOVEMENT for a new congress
How goes the second children's crusade? organizing M.N.C. student power. il Time 96:14-15 Jl 20 '70
MOVEMENT speakers bureau
LSD and SDS and little lambs eat ivy. P. Krassner. Ramp Mag 8:48 Ja '70
MOVIE censorship. See Moving picture censorship
MOVIE critics. See Critics
MOVIE props. See Moving picture properties
MOVIE shorts. See Moving pictures—Short subject films
MOVING
America on the move. M. Davidson. il Ladies Home J 87:46+ Ag '70
ICC sets new rules on household moving. Har Yrs 10:5 My '70
Learn the new rules on long-distance moving. il Changing T 24:13-14 O '70
New rules to make moving easier. J. S. Wilson. Bet Hom & Gard 48:8 N '70
Plan for a near-painless house move. il Good H 170:165 F '70
Those moving day blues. C. Stark. il Parents Mag 45:62-3+ F '70
See also
Moving and storage companies
MOVING and storage companies
He earns $30,000 a year behind the wheel. E. D. Fales, jr. il pors Pop Mech 133:79-82+ My '70
Moving man cometh (maybe) il Consumer Rep 35:302-4 My '70
MOVING objects, Photography from. See Photography from moving objects
MOVING of structures, etc.
See also
Houses, Prefabricated—Transportation
MOVING of trees. See Tree planting
MOVING picture actors and actresses
Actresses who are real people; interviews with ten starlets, ed. by D. Lurie. il Life 68:40-7 My 29 '70
Airport becomes a movie. il Good H 170:52+ Ap '70
New movies. il Newsweek 76:71-4 D 7 '70
Now faces. I. Mothner. il Look 34:72-7 N 3 '70
Spotlight! E. Miller. See issues of Seventeen
Thalberg didn't look happy; or, With Antonioni at Zabriskie Point. B. Gindoff. il Film Q 24:3-6 Fall '70

MOVING picture actors and actresses—*Cont.*
Where, oh where are the beautiful girls?
J. Hamilton. il Look 34:62-7 N 3 '70
Zanuck: last of the red hot star-makers; interview, ed. by H. Ehrlich. il por Look 34: 69-71 N 3 '70
See also
Academy awards (moving pictures)
Negro actors and actresses
   also names of moving picture actors and actresses, e.g. R. Mitchum
MOVING picture adaptations. See Film adaptations
MOVING picture authorship
But who wrote the movie? H. Alpert. il Sat R 53:8-11 D 26 '70
Day at the studio: Scott Fitzgerald in Hollywood; excerpt from Crazy Sundays. J. A. Latham. Harper 241:38-9+ N '70
Hollywood's hottest writer: Buck Henry. M. Seligson. il pors N Y Times Mag p 10-11+ Jl 19 '70
Television and film writing. N. Vogel. por Writers Digest 50:42+ Ap '70
MOVING picture awards
See also
Academy awards (moving pictures)
MOVING picture cameras
Added attractions; camera features you may or may not need. D. Sutherland. Travel & Camera 33:74-5 S '70
Camera compromise; various means of focusing and of zooming. D. Sutherland. Travel & Camera 33:68-9 O '70
Cameras for G-rated movies: super 8 movie cameras. il Consumer Bul 53:7-14 Jl '70
Can a super 8 be worth over $500. M. A. Matzkin. il Mod Phot 34:76-7+ Ap '70
Matzkin on movies; super 8. M. A. Matzkin. Mod Phot 34:36+ F '70
Test reports. See issues of Travel & camera

Purchasing
Consumer's guide to movie cameras. il Mech Illus 66:111 N '70

Sound equipment
Matzkin on movies; Synchronex. M. A. Matzkin. il Mod Phot 34:36+ Ja '70
Movie making; simple sound systems. T. Galluzzo. il Mod Phot 34:32+ Je '70
Super 8 sound systems. D. Sutherland. Travel & Camera 33:88+ My '70
Test reports:
   Synchronex sound-on-film movie system. D. Sutherland. il Travel & Camera 33: 98-9 Ja '70
MOVING picture censorship
Defense against dirt; Maryland's Board of motion picture censors. il Time 95:20 Mr 9 '70
Witness for obscenity; trial in Jackson, Miss. of theater manager and projectionist for showing The fox. J. M. Carter. Library J 95:2431 Jl '70
See also
Moving pictures—Moral aspects
MOVING picture conferences. See Moving picture industry—United States
MOVING picture criticism
Cruel, cruel critics; movie critics. S. Koch. il Sat R 53:12-14+ D 26 '70
Films; film critic for the New York times. J. Brackman. Esquire 73:26+ Mr '70
Going steady, by P. Kael. Review
   Commentary 50:93-5 S '70. J. Epstein
Movie critic on movie critics. R. Schickel. Harper 240:97-9 Ja '70
MOVING picture criticisms. See Moving picture plays—Criticisms, plots, etc.
MOVING picture critics. See Critics
MOVING picture directors
By Orson Welles: but where are we going? O. Welles. il pors Look 34:34-6 N 3 '70
Czechs in exile; directors in the U.S. il pors Newsweek 76:70-1 Jl 27 '70
Good days, good years; John Ford, Allan Dwan, and Raoul Walsh. R. Schickel. Harper 241:44-8+ O '70
Moviemakers. L. Lerman. il Mlle 70:69-73+ Ja '70
See also
Arkin, A.
Bergman, I.
Brakhage, S.
Brown, B.
Buñuel, L.
Cassavetes, J.
Downey, R.
Eames, C.
Fellini, F.
Godard, J. L.
Griffith, D. W.
Lean, D.

Mazursky, P.
Meyer, R.
Micheaux, O.
Peckinpah, S.
Penn, A.
Ray, S.
Visconti, L.
Wajda, A.
Welles, O.
Wise, R.
MOVING picture editing. See Moving pictures —Editing
MOVING picture festivals
Buster Keaton festival. S. Kauffmann New Repub 163:24+ O 24 '70
Esquire presents the winners of its first International college film festival; with editorial comment. il Esquire 74:6, 155 Ag '70
Festival felicities; New York film festival. R. Gelatt. il Sat R 53:50 O 3 '70
Festival flashback; eighth New York film festival. P. T. Hartung. Commonweal 93: 250 D 4 '70
Festivals; New York film festival. il Time 96:100 S 21 '70
Film festival; New York film festival. H. Clurman. Nation 211:315-17, 347-9 O 5, 12 '70
Film festival party; New York. New Yorker 46:30-1 S 19 '70
Filmmakers of tomorrow: Kinetic art program at Lincoln Center. T. Galluzzo. Mod Phot 34:50+ Ag '70
Garlic and sapphires; New York film festival. il Time 96:74+ S 28 '70
Lively arts; criticism at annual New York film festival. R. Hemming. Sr Schol 97:21 N 9 '70
Mar del Plata's festival of film. G. Nogués. il Américas 22:18-26 Je '70
New York film festival no. 8. R. A. Sokolov. il Newsweek 76:93-4+ S 21 '70
New York film festival: 1970. G. D. Phillips. il Cath World 212:146-9 D '70
See also
Cannes international film festival
MOVING picture film collections
Movie saver; Cinémathèque française. Paris and the U.S. Cinémathèque. il por Newsweek 76:64 Ag 24 '70
MOVING picture films
Matzkin on movies; super 8. M. A. Matzkin. Mod Phot 34:36+ F '70
Movie loops or cartridge feed? il Mod Phot 34:82+ S '70
Movie making; proper film care. T. Galluzzo. Mod Phot 34:48+ Jl '70
MOVING picture industry
See also
Moving picture production and direction

Advertising
For adults only. G. Lees. il Hi Fi 20:secl 104+ My '70
Employees
See also
International alliance of theatrical stage employees and moving picture machine operators of the United States and Canada
Finance
Elliott Gould as the entrepreneur. M. Mayer. il pors Fortune 82:108-11+ O '70
Hollywood: broke, and getting rich. F. Knebel. il Look 34:50-2 N 3 '70

Czechoslovakia
Czechs in exile; directors in the U.S. il pors Newsweek 76:70-1 Jl 27 '70

Great Britain
See also
Rank organisation, ltd.

United States
Confrontation in cinema city; Aspen film conference. M. A. Callahan. America 122: 392-4 Ap 11 '70
Dollars in the desert; New Mexico, location for filmmakers. il Newsweek 76:78 O 26 '70
Hollywood: broke, and getting rich. F. Knebel. il Look 34:50-2 N 3 '70
Hollywood: shivering in the sun. W. Fadiman. New Repub 162:17-19 Je 27 '70
Hollywood: the year you almost couldn't find it. J. Hamilton. il Look 34:27-33 N 3 '70
Hollywood: will there ever be a 21st Century-Fox? il Time 95:57-8 F 9 '70
How much do you know about movies? quiz. H. V. Fondiller. Pop Phot 67:119+ O '70
M*A*S*H notes; economics of the new movie. I. Preminger. il Esquire 74:60-1+ Ag '70
New movies; independent producers and directors. il Newsweek 76:62-74 D 7 '70

MOVING picture plays—Criticisms, plots, etc.
—Single works—*Continued*
Alice's restaurant
  Commentary 49:79-80 F '70
  Film Q 23:3-16 Wint '69
  Sr Schol il 95:28 S 29 '69
Andromeda strain
  Sat R 53:22-5 Ag 8 '70
Angel Levine
  Esquire 74:67 O '70
  Newsweek 76:65 Ag 3 '70
  Sat R 53:20 Ag 1 '70
  Sr Schol il 97:24-5 S 28 '70
  Time 96:68 Ag 3 '70
Anne of the thousand days
  America 122:170 F 14 '70
  Look il 34:12-13 F 24 '70
  New Yorker 45:77-8 Ja 24 '70
  Newsweek 75:75+ Ja 26 '70
  Time il 95:70 F 2 '70
  Vogue 155:108 Ap 1 '70
  Sr Schol il 96:22-3 Ap 6 '70
Antonio das mortes
  Film Q il 24:27-30 Fall '70
  Film Q il 23:42-7 Wint '69
  New Yorker 46:136-7 Ap 18 '70
Arrangement
  Film Q 23:52-4 Sum '70
Au hasard Balthazar
  Newsweek 75:102+ Mr 16 '70
L'aveu
  Atlan 226:106-7 Jl '70
Baby maker
  America 123:303 O 17 '70
  New Yorker 46:137 O 10 '70
  Sat R 53:60-1 O 24 '70
Ballad of Cable Hogue
  America 122:570 My 23 '70
  Commonweal 92:369 Jl 24 '70
  Esquire 73:68 Je '70
  Holiday 47:34-5 My '70
  Life 68:11 Mr 27 '70
  New Repub 162:19+ Je 6 '70
  Newsweek il 75:102+ Mr 23 '70
  Sat R 53:42 Ap 11 '70
  Time il 95:81 Mr 16 '70
Belle de jour
  Film Q il 23:38-41 Fall '69
Beneath the planet of the apes
  New Yorker 46:55 Je 20 '70
  Sr Schol 97:20-1 S 14 '70
  Time 96:70 Jl 27 '70
Beyond the valley of the dolls
  New Repub 163:22 Jl 18 '70
  Newsweek 76:85 Jl 6 '70
  Sat R 53:40 Jl 11 '70
  Time 96:70 Jl 27 '70
Bird with the crystal plumage
  New Yorker 46:70 Ag 1 '70
Black God and white devil
  Film Q il 23:59-62 Wint '69
Bloody mama
  Film Q 23:60 Sum '70
  Newsweek il 75:102 My 25 '70
Bombay talkie
  Nation 211:571 N 30 '70
  New Yorker 46:172+ N 28 '70
  Sr Schol 97:18 D 7 '70
Born yesterday
  New Yorker 46:54 Jl 25 '70
Borsalino
  Commonweal 93:128 O 30 '70
  New Repub 163:22 Ag 15 '70
  Newsweek il 76:72 Ag 31 '70
  Time il 96:69 Ag 31 '70
Le boucher
  Time 96:100 S 21 '70
Boys in the band
  America 122:398 Ap 11 '70
  Chr Cent 87:944 Ag 5 '70
  Life 68:12 Ap 10 '70
  Mlle 71:120+ My '70
  New Repub 162:20+ Ap 18 '70
  New Yorker 46:166-7 Mr 21 '70
  Newsweek 75:91 Mr 30 '70
  Sat R 53:24 Ap 4 '70
  Time il 95:97+ Mr 30 '70
  Vogue 155:152 My '70
Brand X
  New Yorker 46:115-16 My 16 '70
  Newsweek 75:94 Je 8 '70
Brewster McCloud
  Newsweek il 76:67 D 28 '70
Bronco bullfrog
  New Yorker 46:161-2 N 14 '70
Brotherly love
  America 122:456 Ap 25 '70
  Look il 34:66 Je 2 '70
  New Repub 162:24+ My 9 '70
  Sat R 53:53 Ap 25 '70
  Time 95:90 Ap 20 '70

Burn!
  America 123:414 N 14 '70
  Atlan 227:100-2 Ja '71
  Commonweal 93:223 N 27 '70
  Life 69:20 N 27 '70
  New Repub 163:20+ N 14 '70
  New Yorker 46:159-62 N 7 '70
  Newsweek il 76:112+ N 2 '70
  Sat R 53:56 N 21 '70
  Time 96:94 N 2 '70
Butch Cassidy and the Sundance Kid
  Chr Cent 87:221-2 F 18 '70
  Sr Schol 95:18 N 3 '69
C.C. and company
  Commonweal 93:176 N 13 '70
  New Yorker 46:132+ O 31 '70
  Newsweek il 76:108+ N 2 '70
Cabinet of Dr Caligari
  Horizon 12:4-15 Wint '70
Cactus flower
  America 122:113 Ja 31 '70
Catch-22
  Cath World 211:199-202 Ag '70
  Chr Cent 87:1129-30 S 23 '70
  Commentary 50:25 S '70
  Commonweal 92:416-17 Ag 21 '70
  Commonweal 93:69-70 O 16 '70
  Esquire 74:12+ S '70
  Film Q il 24:7-17 Fall '70
  Harper 241:32-4+ D '70
  Life il 69:12 Jl 4 '70
  Look il 34:55-9 Je 30 '70
  Nat R 22:959 S 8 '70
  Nation 211:60 Jl 20 '70
  New Repub 163:22+ Jl 4 '70
  New Yorker 46:62-3 Je 27 '70
  Newsweek il 75:81 Je 22 '70
  Sat R 53:24 Je 27 '70
  Time il 95:66-8+ Je 15 '70
  Vogue 156:40 Ag 1 '70
Cheyenne social club
  Newsweek il 76:92 S 28 '70
Chikamatzu Monogatari
  Time 96:74 S 28 '70
Chimes at midnight
  Film Q il 23:11-20 Fall '69
Chisum
  Commonweal 92:441 S 4 '70
  Nat R 22:798+ Jl 28 '70
  Newsweek 76:86 Ag 17 '70
  Time 96:68 Ag 3 '70
Christmas tree
  Sr Schol il 95:18 N 3 '69
Circus
  New Repub 162:23+ Ja 24 '70
Colossus. See Forbin project, below
Confession
  Nation 211:698-9 D 28 '70
  New Repub 163:16+ D 19 '70
  New Yorker 46:119-20 My 16 '70
  New Yorker 46:172+ D 12 '70
  Newsweek 76:98 D 21 '70
  Time il 97:59 Ja 4 '71
Conformist
  Commonweal 93:129 O 30 '70
  Vogue 156:74 N 15 '70
Cotton comes to Harlem
  Chr Cent 87:1454-5 D 2 '70
  Esquire 74:67 O '70
  Life il 69:58-9 Ag 28 '70
  Newsweek il 75:82 Je 22 '70
  Sat R 53:22 Jl 18 '70
  Time 96:70 Jl 6 '70
Cover me babe
  Life il 69:11 N 6 '70
Cromwell
  America 123:414 N 14 '70
  Atlan 227:99-100 Ja '71
  Look 34:84-5 D 15 '70
  New Yorker 46:163-4 N 7 '70
  Newsweek il 76:92 N 9 '70
Cross and the switchblade
  Chr Today 14:34 Je 19 '70
Damned
  Chr Cent 87:366 Mr 25 '70
  Harper 240:115-16 Ap '70
  Nat R 22:269 Mr 10 '70
  Nation 210:60 Ja 19 '70
  Opera N il 34:32 F 14 '70
  Vogue 155:110 F 1 '70
Darling Lili
  America 123:74-5 Ag 8 '70
  Nat R 22:959 S 8 '70
  New Repub 163:22+ Jl 18 '70
  New Yorker 46:70 Ag 1 '70
  Newsweek 76:71 Jl 27 '70
  Sat R 53:22 Jl 18 '70
  Time 96:68+ Jl 27 '70
David Holzman's diary
  Film Q 23:50-2 Sum '70
Days and nights in the forest
  Nation 211:315-16 O 5 '70
Death in Venice
  Sat R 53:16-18 Ag 8 '70
Destroy, she said
  New Yorker 46:135-6 Ap 18 '70

MOVING picture plays—Criticisms, plots, etc.
—Single works—*Continued*
Diary of a chambermaid
    Commonweal 92:63-4 Mr 27 '70
Diary of a mad housewife
    America 123:131-2 S 5 '70
    Atlan 226:127-8 N '70
    Commonweal 93:222-3 N 27 '70
    Life il 69:8 Ag 7 '70
    Look il 34:70 S 22 '70
    New Repub 163:22+ S 5 '70
    New Yorker 46:68-9 Ag 15 '70
    Newsweek il 76:72 Ag 10 '70
    Sat R 53:36 Ag 15 '70
    Time il 96:34 Ag 17 '70
    Vogue 156:34 Ag 15 '70
Dirty Dingus Magee
    Sat R 53:56 N 21 '70
Downhill racer
    Sr Schol il 95:16 Ja 5 '70
Dream of kings
    America 122:113 Ja 31 '70
Dreamers
    Sat R 53:53 Ap 25 '70
Easy rider
    Atlan 226:90-5 S '70
    Commentary 49:78-9 F '70
    Engl J 59:665-6 My '70
    Film Q 23:3-16 Wint '69
    Film Q il 23:22-4 Fall '69
End of a priest
    New Yorker 46:112-13 Ap 25 '70
End of the road
    Commonweal 92:270-2 My 29 '70
    Nation 210:253 Mr 2 '70
    New Repub 162:31 F 21 '70
    New Yorker 45:117-18 F 14 '70
    Newsweek il 75:87+ F 16 '70
    Newsweek 75:100+ Mr 16 '70
    Time 95:74 F 23 '70
L'enfant sauvage
    America 123:244 O 3 '70
    Atlan 226:118+ D '70
    Commonweal 93:20-1 O 2 '70
    Life il 69:16 O 16 '70
    Nat R 22:1361 D 15 '70
    Nation 211:285-6 S 28 '70
    New Repub 163:20+ O 3 '70
    New Yorker 46:67-9 S 12 '70
    New Yorker 46:144 Mr 21 '70
    Newsweek 76:14 D 21 '70
    Time 96:100 S 21 '70
Entertaining Mr Sloane
    New Yorker 46:69-70 Ag 1 '70
    Newsweek 76:64-5 Ag 3 '70
    Time il 96:32+ Ag 17 '70
An event
    Vogue 155:34 Mr 15 '70
Events
    New Yorker 46:71-2 Jl 4 '70
Everything for sale
    Film Q il 23:37-41 Wint '69
Fando and Lis
    Vogue 155:34 Mr 15 '70
Fellini Satyricon
    Am Scholar 39:679-80 Aut '70
    America 122:376 Ap 4 '70
    Film Q il 23:38-42 Sum '70
    Holiday 47:32 Mr '70
    Horizon il 12:42-7 Aut '70
    Nat R 22:521+ My 19 '70
    Nation 210:347 Mr 23 '70
    New Repub 162:24+ Ap 4 '70
    New Yorker 46:134+ Mr 14 '70
    Newsweek il 75:102 Mr 23 '70
    Sat R il 53:42+ Mr 14 '70
    Time il 95:76-9+ Mr 16 '70
    Vogue 155:58 Ap 15 '70
Une femme douce
    Film Q 23:54-6 Sum '70
La femme infidele
    Film Q il 23:56-8 Sum '70
First love
    New Repub 163:30 O 31 '70
    New Yorker 46:157-8 O 17 '70
    Newsweek 76:112+ O 19 '70
    Sat R 53:60 O 24 '70
    Time 96:88 O 19 '70
Five easy pieces
    America 123:244 O 3 '70
    Commentary 51:92 Ja '71
    Esquire 74:68+ N '70
    Life il 69:16 S 18 '70
    New Repub 163:21+ S 26 '70
    New Yorker 46:101-3 S 19 '70
    Newsweek 76:14 D 21 '70
    Sat R il 53:40-1 S 26 '70
    Time il 96:89 S 14 '70
    Vogue 156:106 N 1 '70
Five philosophical fables
    Film Q il 23:58-9 Sum '70
Flap
    Sat R 53:38 D 19 '70
Float like a butterfly, sting like a bee
    Sr Schol 95:18,19 Ja 12 '70
Fly hunt
    Film Q il 23:37-41 Wint '69

Forbin project
    New Yorker 46:114-15 My 16 '70
    Vogue 156:41 Ag 1 '70
Gaily, gaily
    America 122:82-3 Ja 24 '70
Games
    Time 96:69 Ag 31 '70
Garden of delights
    Time 96:74+ S 28 '70
Generation
    America 122:113 Ja 31 '70
Getting straight
    Atlan 226:140-4 O '70
    Chr Cent 87:1160+ S 30 '70
    Commentary 50:30 S '70
    Esquire 74:10+ Ag '70
    Film Q 24:56-7 Fall '70
    Holiday 48:16-17 Jl '70
    Life 68:14 My 29 '70
    Nation 210:700 Je 8 '70
    New Repub 162:24 My 30 '70
    New Yorker 46:108+ My 23 '70
    Newsweek il 75:103-4+ My 18 '70
    Sat R 53:57 My 23 '70
    Sr Schol il 97:48 S 28 '70
    Time il 95:91+ My 18 '70
    Vogue 155:66 Je '70
Goin' down the road
    Nation 211:477-8 N 9 '70
    New Yorker 46:130-1 O 31 '70
    Newsweek 76:112 N 2 '70
    Time il 96:112+ O 26 '70
Goodbye, Columbus
    Film Q 23:34-8 Fall '69
Goodbye, Mr Chips
    Holiday 47:26 Ja '70
    Sr Schol il 95:28 D 8 '69
Good times, bad times
    Film Q 23:58-9 Spr '70
Grasshopper
    Holiday 48:18 Jl '70
    Sat R 53:54 Je 6 '70
Great white hope
    Life il 69:10 N 6 '70
    Look 34:45 N 17 '70
    New Repub 163:30+ O 31 '70
    New Yorker 46:155-7 O 17 '70
    Newsweek il 76:89+ O 26 '70
    Sat R 53:50 O 17 '70
    Sr Schol il 97:18 D 7 '70
    Time il 96:87 O 19 '70
Hail, hero!
    Sr Schol 95:20 D 1 '69
Halls of anger
    America 122:569-70 My 23 '70
    Sat R 53:52 My 2 '70
    Sr Schol il 96:24-5 My 11 '70
Hamlet
    America 122:170 F 14 '70
    New Yorker 45:66+ Ja 17 '70
    Sat R 53:44 Ja 17 '70
Happy ending
    Film Q 24:57-8 Fall '70
    Holiday 47:25-7 F '70
    Time 95:70+ F 2 '70
Hearts of age
    Film Q 23:19-22 Spr '70
Hello, Dolly!
    America 122:113 Ja 31 '70
    Dance Mag il 44:80-2 Mr '70
    Vogue 155:44 F 15 '70
Hello-goodbye
    America 123:75 Ag 8 '70
    New Yorker 46:46 Jl 18 '70
Hi, mom!
    America 122:512 My 9 '70
    Life il 68:14 Je 5 '70
    New Repub 162:20+ My 16 '70
    New Yorker 46:118+ My 9 '70
Hoa-Binh
    New Yorker 46:132-3 Ap 18 '70
Honeymoon killers
    Nat R 22:523 My 19 '70
    Nation 210:221 F 23 '70
    New Yorker 45:93-4 F 7 '70
Husbands
    Nation 211:570-1 N 30 '70
    New Yorker 46:48-51 Ja 2 '71
    Newsweek il 76:100 D 21 '70
    Sat R 53:26 D 12 '70
    Time il 96:72 D 7 '70
I am curious (blue)
    Chr Cent 87:1022 Ag 26 '70
I love my wife
    Newsweek 76:66-7 D 28 '70
    Sat R 54:38 Ja 9 '71
I never sang for my father
    America 123:473 N 28 '70
    Life il 69:16 O 30 '70
    Look il 34:114 O 6 '70
    Nat R 22:960 S 8 '70
    New Yorker 46:130 O 31 '70
    Newsweek 76:108 N 2 '70
    Sat R 53:50 N 7 '70
    Time il 96:113 O 26 '70

MOVING picture plays—Criticisms, plots, etc.
—Single works—*Continued*
I walk the line
   New Yorker 46:168-9 D 5 '70
Ice
   Nation 211:442 N 2 '70
   New Yorker 46:136-9 O 24 '70
   Newsweek il 76:104+ N 16 '70
If
   Commentary 49:77-8 F '70
Immortal story
   Film Q il 23:44-7 Fall '69
Investigation of a citizen above suspicion
   Life 69:20 N 27 '70
   Nation 211:699-700 D 28 '70
   New Yorker 46:48 Ja 2 '71
   Newsweek il 77:61 Ja 4 '71
   Sat R 53:35 D 26 '70
Je t'aime, je t'aime
   New Yorker 46:103-4 S 19 '70
Jenny
   Sat R 53:45 Mr 7 '70
Joe
   Atlan 226:124-7 N '70
   Commentary 51:93-4 Ja '71
   Esquire 74:60+ D '70
   Life il 69:13 Ag 21 '70
   Life il 69:69-70 O 16 '70
   New Repub 163:33 Ag 22 '70
   New Yorker 46:65-6 Ag 15 '70
   Newsweek il 76:71 Jl 27 '70
   Sat R 53:35 S 5 '70
   Time il 96:68 Jl 27 '70
John and Mary
   Chr Cent 87:638-9 My 20 '70
   Esquire 73:14+ F '70
Joke
   New Repub 162:20+ My 16 '70
   New Yorker 46:110-11 Ap 25 '70
Journey to the far side of the sun
   Sr Schol il 95:24-5 O 20 '69
Julius Caesar
   Sr Schol 97:25 S 28 '70
Kelly's heroes
   Esquire 74:8+ S '70
Kes
   New Repub 163:20+ O 3 '70
   New Yorker 46:124-6 S 26 '70
   Sr Schol 97:18 D 7 '70
   Time il 96:100 S 21 '70
Krakatoa, east of Java
   Sr Schol il 95:30-1 S 15 '69
Kremlin letter
   Commentary 50:91-2 N '70
   New Yorker 45:91-3 F 7 '70
   Sr Schol il 96:22 Mr 16 '70
Landlord
   America 122:618 Je 6 '70
   Esquire 74:67 O '70
   Newsweek 75:99-100 Je 1 '70
   Sat R 53:37 My 30 '70
Last of the mobile hot-shots
   Holiday 47:37 Mr '70
   Newsweek il 75:75 Ja 26 '70
Laughter in the dark
   Film Q il 23:45-8 Spr '70
Lawyer
   America 122:312 Mr 21 '70
   Time 95:88 Mr 23 '70
Learning tree
   Sr Schol 95:26 S 29 '69
Leo the last
   America 122:570 My 23 '70
   Esquire 74:67 O '70
   Sat R 53:37 My 30 '70
   Time il 95:92+ Je 1 '70
Let it be
   New Yorker 46:86-7 Je 6 '70
   Time 95:74+ Je 8 '70
Liberation of L. B. Jones
   America 122:376 Ap 4 '70
   Nation 210:412-13 Ap 6 '70
   Newsweek il 75:88+ Mr 30 '70
   Sat R 53:48 Mr 28 '70
Little big man
   Look 34:56-61 D 1 '70
   New Repub 163:18 D 26 '70
   New Yorker 46:50-2 D 26 '70
   Newsweek 76:98A-98B+ D 21 '70
   Sat R 54:60 Ja 2 '71
   Time il 96:56-7 D 21 '70
Little Fauss and Big Halsy
   Commonweal 93:177 N 13 '70
   Life il 69:20 N 20 '70
   Look il 34:14 D 1 '70
   New Yorker 46:132 O 31 '70
   Newsweek il 76:89A O 26 '70
   Sat R 53:24 O 31 '70
   Time 96:95 N 2 '70
Little murders
   Sat R 53:19-21 Ag 8 '70
Little theatre of Jean Renoir
   New Yorker 46:58-60 Ag 8 '70
Looking glass war
   New Yorker 46:99-100 F 21 '70
   Sat R 53:16+ F 14 '70

Lord thing
   Film Q 24:58-9 Fall '70
Love is a funny thing
   Nation 210:413 Ap 6 '70
   New Yorker 46:116+ Ap 4 '70
   Time 95:109 Ap 13 '70
Love story
   New Yorker 46:52-4 D 26 '70
   Newsweek il 76:66 D 28 '70
   Sat R 54:60 Ja 2 '71
   Time il 96:55-6 D 21 '70
   Time il 97:40-5 Ja 11 '71
Lovers and other strangers
   New Yorker 46:68 Ag 15 '70
   Sat R 53:61 Ag 22 '70
   Time 96:69 Ag 31 '70
Loving
   Commonweal 92:118-19 Ap 17 '70
   Film Q 24:59-60 Fall '70
   Holiday 47:32+ Mr '70
   New Repub 162:30-1 Mr 28 '70
   New Yorker 46:92-3 Mr 7 '70
   Newsweek il 75:84 Mr 2 '70
   Sat R 53:45 Mr 7 '70
   Time il 95:87 Mr 23 '70
Ma nuit chez Maud. See My night at Maud's,
  below
Machine gun McCain
   Time il 96:105 N 23 '70
McMasters
   Commonweal 92:441-2 S 4 '70
   New Yorker 46:61-2 Ag 22 '70
Madwoman of Chaillot
   Sr Schol 95:34 S 22 '69
Magic Christian
   Commonweal 92:14-15 Mr 13 '70
   Nation 210:253 Mr 2 '70
   New Yorker 46:95 Mr 7 '70
   Newsweek 75:84+ Mr 2 '70
   Time il 95:74 F 23 '70
Magic garden of Stanley Sweetheart
   Chr Cent 87:945 Ag 5 '70
   New Yorker 46:64 Je 27 '70
   Newsweek 75:93 Je 8 '70
Mahanagar
   Commonweal 93:71-2 O 16 '70
Man called Horse
   America 122:538+ My 16 '70
   Commonweal 92:318 Je 26 '70
   New Yorker 46:118 My 9 '70
   Newsweek il 75:102+ My 25 '70
   Sat R 53:52 My 2 '70
   Sr Schol il 96:24-5 My 4 '70
   Time il 95:103 My 11 '70
Mandabi
   Film Q il 23:48-50 Sum '70
   Newsweek il 75:94 Ap 6 '70
Marooned
   Sr Schol il 96:20-1 Ja 26 '70
M*A*S*H
   America 122:227 F 28 '70
   Atlan 225:127-9 My '70
   Chr Cent 87:795-7 Je 24 '70
   Commentary 50:25-6+ S '70
   Commonweal 92:343-5 Jl 10 '70
   Film Q 23:38-41 Spr '70
   Harper 241:32-4+ D '70
   Holiday 47:25 Ap '70
   Life 68:12 Ap 10 '70
   Life il 68:12 F 20 '70
   Nation 210:158 F 9 '70
   New Repub 162:30-1 Ja 31 '70
   New Yorker 45:74+ Ja 24 '70
   Newsweek il 75:83 F 2 '70
   Pop Phot 66:128+ Je '70
   Time 96:63 Jl 13 '70
   Time il 95:78 Ja 26 '70
Me
   Newsweek 75:90+ Mr 9 '70
   Sat R 53:45 Mr 7 '70
   Time il 95:101 Mr 30 '70
Me, Natalie
   Sr Schol il 95:21 O 13 '69
Meat rack. See Street rack, below
Medea
   Holiday 47:20 Je '70
   New Yorker 46:90 F 21 '70
Medium cool
   Commentary 49:79 F '70
   Film Q 23:3-16 Wint '69
   Film Q il 23:47-57 Wint '69
   Nat R 22:41-3 Ja 13 '70
Midnight cowboy
   Film Q 23:3-16 Wint '69
   Film Q il 23:20-2 Fall '69
Milky way
   America 122:170 F 14 '70
   Commonweal 92:64-5 Mr 27 '70
   Nat R 22:523 My 19 '70
   Nation 210:188 F 16 '70
   New Repub 162:26+ F 7 '70
   New Yorker 45:91 F 7 '70
   Newsweek il 75:85 F 9 '70
Mind of Mr Soames
   America 123:474 N 28 '70

MOVING picture plays—Criticisms, plots, etc.
—Single works—*Continued*
Mississippi mermaid
    Am Scholar 39:680-2 Aut '70
    Life il 68:16 My 8 '70
    Nation 210:509 Ap 27 '70
    New Repub 162:20+ My 2 '70
    New Yorker 46:134 Ap 18 '70
    Newsweek il 75:96+ My 4 '70
    Sat R 53:53 Ap 25 '70
    Time il 95:93+ Ap 27 '70
Molly Maguires
    America 122:200 F 21 '70
    Life 68:12 F 13 '70
    New Repub 162:20+ F 21 '70
    New Yorker 45:91 F 7 '70
    Newsweek 75:87 F 16 '70
    Sat R 53:61 F 14 '70
    Sr Schol 96:22 Mr 9 '70
    Time il 95:76 F 23 '70
    Vogue 155:42 F 15 '70
Monte Walsh
    New Yorker 46:157 O 17 '70
    Sat R 53:50+ O 17 '70
    Time il 96:114 O 26 '70
Move
    Newsweek 76:73 Ag 10 '70
    Time 96:61 Ag 24 '70
    Vogue 156:55 S 15 '70
My night at Maud's
    America 122:397 Ap 11 '70
    Commonweal 92:169-70 My 1 '70
    Film Q il 23:57-9 Wint '69
    Nation 210:509-10 Ap 27 '70
    New Yorker 46:115-16 Ap 4 '70
    Newsweek 75:101 F 23 '70
    Sat R 53:41 F 7 '70
Myra Breckinridge
    Commentary 50:92 N '70
    Life il 68:50-2 Mr 6 '70
    McCalls il 98:16+ O '70
    Nat R 22:906+ Ag 25 '70
    New Repub 163:22 Jl 18 '70
    Newsweek il 76:85 Jl 6 '70
    Sat R 53:40 Jl 11 '70
    Time il 96:70 Jl 6 '70
Ned Kelly
    Chr Cent 87:1386 N 18 '70
    Commentary 50:90 N '70
    Time 96:61 Ag 24 '70
Norwood
    Look il 34:36 Je 16 '70
    Sat R 53:26 Je 13 '70
Number one
    Sr Schol 95:24 O 20 '69
Oh! What a lovely war
    Chr Cent 87:274 Mr 4 '70
    Sr Schol 95:16 N 10 '69
On a clear day you can see forever
    America 123:74 Ag 8 '70
    Holiday 48:17-18 Jl '70
    New Repub 163:22 Jl 18 '70
    Newsweek il 75:78+ Je 29 '70
    Sat R 53:22 Jl 4 '70
    Time il 95:81 Je 29 '70
One day in the life of Ivan Denisovich
    Time il 95:77 Mr 2 '70
Only game in town
    America 122:284 Mr 14 '70
    Holiday 47:32+ My '70
    New Yorker 46:93-4 Mr 7 '70
    Time il 95:72+ Mr 9 '70
Othon
    Nation 211:315 O 5 '70
Out of it
    Esquire 73:40+ My '70
    New Repub 163:23+ Ag 22 '70
    New Yorker 46:60-1 Ag 22 '70
    Newsweek il 76:64-5 Ag 24 '70
    Time 95:72 Mr 9 '70
Out-of-towners
    America 122:637 Je 13 '70
    New Repub 162:31-2 My 30 '70
    Newsweek 75:99 Je 15 '70
    Sat R 53:26 Je 13 '70
    Time il 95:74 Je 8 '70
    Vogue 156:41 Ag 1 '70
Owl and the pussycat
    Life il 69:10 N 6 '70
    Look 34:12+ D 1 '70
    New Repub 163:22 D 5 '70
    New Yorker 46:165-6 N 14 '70
    Newsweek 76:101 N 16 '70
    Time il 96:96+ N 16 '70
Paint your wagon
    Holiday 47:24+ Ja '70
    Sr Schol 96:23 F 2 '70
Passenger
    New Yorker 46:85-6 Je 6 '70
Passion of Anna
    Am Scholar 39:682+ Aut '70
    America 122:660 Je 20 '70
    Chr Cent 87:1426-7 N 25 '70
    Nat R 22:798 Jl 28 '70
    Nation 210:765 Je 22 '70
    New Repub 162:22+ Je 20 '70
    New Yorker 46:103-4+ Je 13 '70
    Newsweek il 75:98+ Je 15 '70
    Time il 95:74 Je 8 '70

Patton
    America 122:226-7 F 28 '70
    Chr Cent 87:455 Ap 15 '70
    Chr Today 15:50-1 O 23 '70
    Commonweal 92:37-8 Mr 20 '70
    Harper 241:32-4+ D '70
    Holiday 47:24-5 Ap '70
    Nat R 22:797-8 Jl 28 '70
    New Repub 162:24+ Mr 7 '70
    New Yorker 45:73-5 Ja 31 '70
    Newsweek il 75:91-2 F 16 '70
    Sat R 53:59+ Ja 31 '70
    Sr Schol 96:22 Mr 16 '70
    Time il 95:78 F 9 '70
People next door
    America 123:186 S 19 '70
    Chr Cent 87:1227-8 O 14 '70
    Sat R 53:79 S 12 '70
    Sr Schol 97:20-1 O 12 '70
    Time il 96:89 S 14 '70
Perfect Friday
    Time 96:105 N 23 '70
Performance
    America 123:132 S 5 '70
    Commentary 50:91 N '70
    Life 69:6 O 2 '70
    Newsweek il 76:85+ Ag 17 '70
    Sat R 53:61 Ag 22 '70
    Time il 96:61 Ag 24 '70
    Vogue 156:55 S 15 '70
Pizza triangle
    New Yorker 46:170+ N 28 '70
    Sat R 53:38 D 19 '70
Pound
    New Yorker 46:50-2 Ag 29 '70
    Sat R 53:35 S 5 '70
    Time il 96:64+ S 7 '70
Private life of Sherlock Holmes
    New Yorker 46:168 N 14 '70
    Newsweek il 76:108 N 2 '70
    Sat R 53:44 D 5 '70
Quackser Fortune has a cousin in the Bronx
    McCalls 98:119 O '70
    New Yorker 46:55 Jl 25 '70
    Time il 96:44 Jl 20 '70
Quiet days in Clichy
    Sat R 53:79 S 12 '70
Quiet place in the country
    Newsweek 76:106+ S 14 '70
    Time il 96:85 O 12 '70
R.P.M.
    Newsweek 76:92 S 28 '70
    Sr Schol il 97:18-19 N 9 '70
Rain people
    Commentary 49:80-1 F '70
    Film Q il 23:3-16 Wint '69
Raven's end
    New Yorker 46:80-1 My 30 '70
    Newsweek 75:98B+ Je 15 '70
Reivers
    America 122:82-3 Ja 24 '70
Revolutionary
    Commonweal 92:390-2 Ag 7 '70
    Nation 211:93-4 Ag 3 '70
    New Repub 163:23 Ag 22 '70
    New Yorker 46:45-6 Jl 18 '70
    Newsweek il 76:77 Jl 20 '70
    Sat R 53:37 Jl 25 '70
    Sr Schol il 97:48 S 28 '70
    Time il 96:71 Jl 20 '70
Rider on the rain
    America 122:660 Je 20 '70
    Chr Cent 87:1323 N 4 '70
    Nation 210:734 Je 15 '70
    New Yorker 46:56 Je 20 '70
    Newsweek 75:82 Je 22 '70
    Time il 95:89+ Je 22 '70
Rise of Louis XIV
    America 123:245 O 3 '70
    Nation 211:157-8 Ag 31 '70
    New Repub 163:20+ S 19 '70
    New Yorker 46:58-60 Ag 22 '70
    Newsweek il 76:72 Ag 31 '70
riverrun
    America 122:511-12 My 9 '70
    New Repub 162:20+ My 16 '70
    New Yorker 46:120+ My 9 '70
    Sat R 53:50 My 9 '70
    Time il 95:103 My 11 '70
Royal hunt of the sun
    Atlan 225:102-3 Ja '70
    Chr Cent 87:56 Ja 14 '70
Ryan's daughter
    America 123:529 D 12 '70
    Commonweal 93:302-3 D 18 '70
    New Yorker 46:116-18+ N 21 '70
    Newsweek il 76:123 N 23 '70
    Sat R 53:53+ N 14 '70
    Time il 96:96 N 16 '70
Scavengers
    Nation 211:316 O 5 '70

MOVING picture plays—Criticisms, plots, etc.
—Single works—*Continued*
Scrooge
  Commonweal 93:327 D 25 '70
  Look 34:28-32 D 15 '70
  New Yorker 46:175 N 28 '70
  Newsweek il 76:104A+ D 14 '70
  Sat R 53:44 D 5 '70
  Sr Schol 97:17 D 14 '70
  Time il 96:73 D 7 '70
Secret of Santa Vittoria
  Atlan 225:101-2 Ja '70
  Sr Schol il 95:18 Ja 12 '70
Shame
  Film Q il 23:32-4 Fall '69
Sicilian clan
  Chr Cent 87:920-1 Jl 29 '70
  Life il 68:11 Ap 17 '70
  New Yorker 46:165 Ap 11 '70
  Sat R 53:24 Ap 4 '70
  Time 95:90 Ap 20 '70
Le Socrate
  Film Q il 23:29-32 Fall '69
Une simple histoire
  Time il 96:74 S 28 '70
Signs of life
  Newsweek il 75:99 Je 1 '70
Soldier blue
  America 123:185-6 S 19 '70
  Commonweal 92:441-2 S 4 '70
  Esquire 74:58+ D '70
  Newsweek il 76:65 Ag 24 '70
  Sat R 53:6 Ag 29 '70
  Sr Schol il 97:20-1 O 5 '70
  Time il 95:71 F 2 '70
Some like it hot
  Film Q il 23:2-9 Sum '70
Something for everyone
  America 123:132 S 5 '70
  Newsweek 76:65-6 Ag 3 '70
  Sat R 53:20 Ag 1 '70
  Time 96:34 Ag 17 '70
Song of Norway
  America 123:473 N 28 '70
  Dance Mag il 44:50-9 Ja '70
  Look il 34:33 D 29 '70
  New Yorker 46:168-9 N 14 '70
  Time il 96:103+ N 23 '70
Spider's stratagem
  Nat R 22:1362 D 15 '70
  Vogue 156:74 N 15 '70
Start the revolution without me
  New Yorker 46:94 Mr 7 '70
  Time il 95:82 Mr 2 '70
  Vogue 155:108 Ap 1 '70
Sterile cuckoo
  Film Q il 23:52-8 Spr '70
Strawberry statement
  Atlan 226:140-4 O '70
  Chr Cent 87:1129 S 23 '70
  Commentary 50:102+ O '70
  Commonweal 92:390-2 Ag 7 '70
  Esquire 74:60+ D '70
  Newsweek il 75:78 Je 29 '70
  Sat R 53:24 Je 27 '70
  Sr Schol il 97:48 S 28 '70
  Time 95:98 My 25 '70
  Time 96:70 Jl 6 '70
  Vogue 156:40 Ag 1 '70
Street rack
  Commonweal 92:223-4 My 15 '70
Sunflower
  America 123:304 O 17 '70
  Newsweek 76:114 O 12 '70
  Time il 96:65+ O 5 '70
Sympathy for the devil
  Chr Cent 87:702+ Je 3 '70
  New Repub 162:19 Je 6 '70
  Newsweek il 75:88 Mr 30 '70
  New Yorker 46:104-6+ My 2 '70
Take a girl like you
  Life il 69:10-11 N 6 '70
Take the money and run
  Chr Cent 87:122-3 Ja 28 '70
Tchaikovsky
  Time 95:56-7 Ap 27 '70
Tell me that you love me, Junie Moon
  New Yorker 46:54+ Jl 11 '70
  Newsweek il 76:92 Jl 13 '70
  Sat R 53:22 Jl 4 '70
  Sr Schol 97:20-1 S 14 '70
  Time il 96:71 Jl 20 '70
Tell them Willie Boy is here
  America 122:284 Mr 14 '70
  Film Q 23:60-1 Spr '70
  Holiday 47:26-7 Ja '70
  Nat R 22:41-3 Ja 13 '70
  Sr Schol il 96:24 Mr 2 '70
Teorema
  Film Q 23:24-9 Fall '69
Thanos and Despina
  Nation 210:541-2 My 4 '70
There was a crooked man
  Newsweek il 77:60 Ja 4 '71
There's a girl in my soup
  Newsweek 76:67 D 28 '70
  Sat R 53:38 D 19 '70

They call me Mister Tibbs!
  Esquire 74:68 O '70
  New Yorker 46:47 Jl 18 '70
  Newsweek 76:77 Jl 20 '70
They shoot horses, don't they?
  Chr Cent 87:850 Jl 8 '70
  Commentary 49:80-3 Ap '70
  Dance Mag il 44:68-71 F '70
  Film Q il 23:42-7 Sum '70
  Life il 68:15 Ja 23 '70
  New Repub 162:19+ Ja 17 '70
  Sr Schol il 96:22-3 F 2 '70
  Vogue 155:118+ F 1 '70
Thief of Paris
  Film Q 23:47-8 Fall '69
Things of life
  Nation 211:222 S 14 '70
  New Yorker 46:64-6 S 5 '70
This man must die
  Life il 69:16 Ag 14 '70
  Nation 211:478 N 9 '70
  New Repub 163:20 N 14 '70
  New Yorker 46:131-2 O 31 '70
  Time il 96:63-4 S 7 '70
Tick ... tick ... tick
  America 122:284 Mr 14 '70
  Sr Schol 96:24-5 Mr 2 '70
  Time 95:82 Mr 2 '70
Time in the sun
  America 122:170 F 14 '70
Too late the hero
  America 122:637 Je 13 '70
  Time 95:76 Je 8 '70
  Vogue 156:40 Jl '70
Topaz
  Film Q 23:41-4 Spr '70
  Holiday 47:36 Mr '70
  Sr Schol 96:21 F 16 '70
Tora! Tora! Tora!
  Life 69:20 O 23 '70
  Newsweek il 76:91-2 S 28 '70
  Sat R 53:22 O 10 '70
  Sr Schol il 97:20-1 N 2 '70
  Time il 96:65 O 5 '70
Trash
  New Repub 163:30 O 31 '70
  New Yorker 46:132+ O 10 '70
Traveling executioner
  Newsweek 76:124 N 23 '70
Trilogy
  Chr Cent 87:546 Ap 29 '70
Tristana
  Life 69:11 N 6 '70
  Nat R 22:1362 D 15 '70
  Nation 211:316 O 5 '70
  New Repub 163:24 O 10 '70
  New Yorker 46:123-4 S 26 '70
  Newsweek il 76:112+ O 12 '70
  Time il 96:74 S 28 '70
  Vogue 156:100 N 1 '70
Tropic of Cancer
  Life 68:12 Ap 10 '70
  New Repub 162:39 Mr 7 '70
  New Yorker 46:95-8 Mr 7 '70
  Newsweek il 75:86 Mr 2 '70
  Sat R 53:51 Mr 21 '70
  Time 95:82 Mr 2 '70
True grit
  Sr Schol il 95:30 S 15 '69
Twelve chairs
  New Yorker 46:162-3 N 7 '70
  Newsweek 76:92 N 9 '70
Two mules for Sister Sara
  Commonweal 92:368-9 Jl 24 '70
  New Repub 163:24+ Ag 1 '70
  New Yorker 46:56 Jl 11 '70
  Time il 96:72 Jl 13 '70
Two or three things I know about her
  New Repub 162:24+ My 9 '70
  New Yorker 46:102+ My 2 '70
  Newsweek 75:107A+ My 18 '70
Up in the cellar
  New Yorker 46:50-2 Ag 29 '70
  Sat R 53:61 Ag 22 '70
Virgin and the gypsy
  New Repub 163:24 Ag 1 '70
  New Yorker 46:71 Jl 4 '70
  Newsweek 76:92 Jl 13 '70
  Sat R 53:37 Jl 25 '70
  Time il 96:72 Jl 13 '70
  Vogue 156:40 Jl '70
Viva and Louis
  Film Q 23:41-4 Fall '69
Viva Max
  Time 95:71 F 2 '70
WUSA
  Commentary 51:93 Ja '71
  Life 69:20 N 27 '70
  New Repub 163:32 N 14 '70
  New Yorker 46:164-5 N 7 '70
  Newsweek il 76:91 N 9 '70
  Sat R 53:24 O 31 '70
  Time il 96:95-6 N 2 '70
Walk in the spring rain
  Time 95:81 Je 29 '70
Walk with love and death
  Sr Schol 95:21 O 13 '69

MOVING picture plays—Criticisms, plots, etc.
—Single works—*Continued*
Watermelon man
America 122:618 Je 6 '70
Esquire 74:68 O '70
New Yorker 46:85 Je 6 '70
Newsweek 75:102 My 25 '70
Sat R 53:26 Je 13 '70
Way we live now
Esquire 74:14+ Jl '70
Newsweek 75:93 Je 8 '70
What do you say to a naked lady?
Time 95:72 Mr 9 '70
Where's poppa?
New Repub 163:22 D 5 '70
New Yorker 46:166-8 N 14 '70
Newsweek il 76:123-123A+ N 23 '70
Sat R 53:56 N 28 '70
Time il 96:102 D 14 '70
Wild bunch
Esquire 73:68 Je '70
Film Q il 23:2-11 Fall '69
Wild child. See L'enfant sauvage, previous page
Winter wind
New Repub 162:16+ Mr 28 '70
Women in love
America 122:456 Ap 25 '70
Chr Cent 87:1099 S 16 '70
Commonweal 92:223 My 15 '70
Film Q il 24:43-7 Fall '70
Holiday 47:21 Je '70
Life il 68:14 Mr 6 '70
Look il 34:32-7 F 24 '70
Mlle il 71:120 My '70
New Repub 162:20 Ap 18 '70
New Yorker 46:97-101 Mr 28 '70
Newsweek 75:97 Ap 6 '70
Sat R il 53:50 Mr 21 '70
Time il 95:106+ Ap 13 '70
Vogue 155:114 Mr 1 '70
Z
Chr Cent 87:366 Mr 25 '70
Commentary 49:26+ My '70
Look il 34:36 F 10 '70
Sr Schol 96:19 F 9 '70
Zabriskie Point
Am Scholar 39:686+ Aut '70
America 122:199-200 F 21 '70
Chr Cent 87:607 My 13 '70
Commonweal 91:620-1 Mr 6 '70
Esquire 73:38+ My '70
Film Q il 23:35-8 Spr '70
Holiday 47:34 My '70
Nat R 22:524 My 19 '70
Nation 210:220-1 F 23 '70
New Repub 162:20+ Mr 14 '70
New Yorker 46:95-9 F 21 '70
Newsweek il 75:87 F 16 '70
Sat R 53:34 F 21 '70
Time il 95:76 F 23 '70
Vogue 155:116+ Ap 1 '70

Themes
See Moving pictures—Themes
MOVING picture production and direction
Antonioni; interview, ed. by C. T. Samuels. il por Vogue 155:96-7+ Mr 15 '70
Bob Rafelson; interview. B. Rafelson. New Yorker 46:41-2 O 24 '70
Cotton cashes in; all-black comedy is a box office bonanza. il Life 69:58-9 Ag 28 '70
Death in Venice: at the end of the path of beauty lies Eros. K. Tynan. Vogue 156:165+ D '70
Dennis Hopper saves the movies; making of Last movie. T. Burke. Esquire 74:138-41+ S '70
Diary of a dead Bavarian; three days with Dalton Trumbo. J. Zinnamon. Esquire 74:68+ D '70
Directors at work; the making of Death in Venice, Little murders and The Andromeda strain. H. Alpert; L. Cohen; A. Knight. il Sat R 53:16-25 Ag 8 '70; Reply with rejoinder. H. Alpert. 53:20 D 19 '70
Downey's Pound. New Yorker 46:30-2 F 28 '70
Easy rider runs wild in the Andes. B. Darrach. il pors Life 68:48-50+ Je 19 '70
Federico Fellini on Satyricon: a talk with Alberto Moravia; tr. by S. Morini. F. Fellini; A. Moravia. il por Vogue 155:168-71+ Mr 1 '70
Fellini he shoots dreams on film; filming of Satyricon. B. Rollin. il pors Look 34:48-53 Mr 10 '70
Frantic filming of a crazy classic; with report by B. Henry. il por Life 68:44-6+ Je 12 '70
Great white hope hits the movies. R. Daley. Vogue 155:90+ Ap 1 '70
Happy Jack; J. Nicholson interviews nudes for Drive, he said. J. Fayard. il pors Life 68:36A-36C Mr 27 '70

Hard way to go; motorcycle racing in Little Fauss and Big Halsy. il Mech Illus 66:72+ Je '70
Hollywood east; moviemakers leaving Hollywood. M. Ronan. il Sr Schol 95:18 D 1 '69
I see everything twice; an examination of Catch-22. C. Thegze. il Film Q 24:7-17 Fall '70
Invitation to the masquerade; spoof of a society charity ball. H. V. Fondiler. il Pop Phot 66:105-7 Ap '70
It's hard to be your own script; interview. ed. by L. Kent. A. Warhol. Vogue 155:167+ Mr 1 '70
Korty: writer, photographer and director of riverrun; interview. J. Korty. New Yorker 46:27-8 Je 6 '70
McLuhan's child: producer and director of Goin' down the road; interview. D. Shebib. New Yorker 46:47-9 N 21 '70
M*A*S*H; interview, ed. by G. Trotta. I. Preminger. il Harp Baz 103:200-1 Mr '70
Mike Nichols talks about his films; interview, ed. by J. Gelmis. por Atlan 225:71-7 F '70
Mike Nichols tries the impossible: a movie of Catch 22. J. M. Flagler. il por Look 34:55-9 Je 30 '70
Moviemakers. L. Lerman. il Mlle 70:69-73+ Ja '70
Movies: and everybody's doing it. J. Hamilton. il Look 34:41-7 N 3 '70
New movies; independent producers and directors. il Newsweek 76:62-74 D 7 '70
On location with Edvard Grieg; Lee Theodore choreographs Song of Norway. S. Robin. il Dance Mag 44:50-9 Ja '70
Paul Mazursky in wonderland; shooting of Alex in wonderland. J. Greenfeld. il pors Life 69:51-4+ S 4 '70
Peckinpah's return; interview, ed. by S. Farber. S. Peckinpah. il Film Q 23:2-11 Fall '69
Real anger was backstage; racial tensions during shooting of Halls of anger. B. Schulberg. il pors Life 69:50-2+ Ag 21 '70
Rome, B.C, A.F. il por Time 95:76-9+ Mr 16 '70
Seismic moment in cinematic history. H. S. Resnik. il Sat R 53:25-8+ Ap 4 '70
Some are more Yossarian than others. il pors Time 95:66-8+ Je 15 '70
Thalberg didn't look happy: or, With Antonioni at Zabriskie Point. B. Gindoff. il Film Q 24:3-6 Fall '70
Thirty skills make the scene. H. V. Fondiller. il Pop Phot 66:106-7 F '70
Through the muck with Myra. C. Trillin. il Life 68:50-2 Mr 6 '70
Tora! Tora! Tora! H. Ehrlich. il Look 34:27-32 S 22 '70
We are curious (Esquire); symposium. il Esquire 74:59-73+ Ag '70
Will Mia's sister make it? D. Chapman. il pors Look 34:48-53 S 22 '70
Working with Fellini; filming of Satyricon. B. Langman. il Mlle 70:74-5+ Ja '70
See also
Moving picture directors
Moving pictures—Setting and scenery
Paramount pictures corporation
MOVING picture projectors
B&H takes on Kodak's cartridge projector. T. Galluzzo. il Mod Phot 34:99-100+ O '70
Movie loops or cartridge feed? il Mod Phot 34:82+ S '70
New cartridge super 8 projectors: easiest way yet to show your home movies. H. Shuldiner. il Pop Sci 196:84-7 Ja '70
New magic for home movies; instant-loading projectors. B. Murphy. il Pop Mech 134:152-5 O '70
New super 8 projectors accept 400-ft. cartridges. H. V. Fondiller. il Pop Phot 67:114-15 N '70
Super 8 and dual 8 movie projectors. il Consumer Bul 53:17-21 D '70
Zeiss Ikon Movilux DS8 projector. D. Sutherland. il Travel & Camera 33:98-9 F '70

Equipment
Matzkin on movies; projection cartridge. M. A. Matzkin. il Mod Phot 33:56-7 D '69
MOVING picture properties
Dreams for sale; MGM auction. K. Fleming. il Newsweek 75:36-7 My 4 '70
MOVING picture scripts
See also
Publishers and publishing—Moving picture scripts
MOVING picture sets. See Moving pictures—Setting and scenery
MOVING picture studios
Hollywood sells off the splendor. il Life 68:38-43 F 27 '70

MOVING picture theaters
Money in mini-theaters. R. Levy. il Duns 96: 63-4+ O '70
Moving theater gets cut to size; mini-theaters. il Bsns W p29 Mr 14 '70
Snorkel theater; Paramount theater, New York. il Arch Forum 133:54-5 O '70

MOVING picture theaters, Open air
Hillside movies: series of short films in Central park, near 79th street. New Yorker 46:18-19 Jl 18 '70

MOVING pictures
Film orgy; program at the Fillmore East, in New York. New Yorker 46:37 Mr 21 '70
Going to the movies. A. Birstein. Vogue 155:210-11+ Mr 1 '70
Screenings: 16mm (cont) il Library J 95:244-6, 756-7, 1575-7, 3612 Ja 15, F 15, Ap 15, O 15 '70
Year's best films. Time 97:58 Ja 4 '71
See also
Advertising mediums—Moving pictures
Airplanes in moving pictures
Moving picture photography
Moving picture production and direction
Negroes in moving pictures
Osaka, Japan—Worlds fair, 1970—Moving pictures
Realism in moving pictures
Television broadcasting—Moving pictures

Abstract films
Stan Brakhage, the courage of perception. A. Sainer. Vogue 156:298 S 1 '70

Advertising
See Moving picture industry—Advertising

Animated cartoons
Criticisms, plots, etc.
Boy named Charlie Brown
Chr Cent 87:1356 N 11 '70
Look 34:68 Ja 27 '70
New Yorker 45:72-3 Ja 17 '70
Sat R 53:44 Ja 17 '70
Fantasia
Life il 68:15 Ap 3 '70

Bibliography
Books. See issues of Film quarterly

Censorship
See Moving picture censorship

Children, Effect on
See Moving pictures and children

Classification
M-rating dies to help films live; new GP rating. Bsns W p 104+ F 7 '70
Movies and the sexual revolution: should the ratings be revised? G. N. Boyd. Chr Cent 87:1124-5 S 23 '70
Problems in film rating. America 124:31 Ja 16 '71
Rating game. G. Shalit. il Look 34:82+ N 3 '70
Whatever became of the family movie? R. Schickel. il Life 69:10 S 11 '70

Costume
See Costume, Theatrical

Dance films
Looking at dance films: Seafall. M. Harriton. il Dance Mag 44:22-3 Ag '70

Detective and mystery films
Hitchcock. C. T. Samuels. Am Scholar 39: 295:304 Spr '70; Reply with rejoinder. J. Belton. 39:728-32 Aut '70

Documentary films
Clark's tour; film series called Civilization. Time 95:53 Mr 9 '70
Fiction documentary; interviews, ed. by A. Rosenthal. A. King; R. Leiterman; A. Saare. il Film Q 23:9-33 Sum '70
Film reviews. Ment Hy 54:328, 469 Ap-Jl '70
Frederick Wiseman; interview, ed. by D. E. McWilliams. F. Wiseman. il Film Q 24: 17-26 Fall '70
King: from Montgomery to Memphis. il pors Ebony 25:172-4+ Ap '70
Mine eyes have seen the glory; sex education documentaries. H. Alpert. Sat R 53:56 My 16 '70
Public privates; porno films from Denmark. S. Kauffmann. New Repub 163:22+ Jl 11 '70
Screenings: 8mm (cont) A. Cohen. Library J 95:228, 762, 1183, 1924-5 Ja 15, F 15, Mr 15, My 15 '70
Son of gangbusters; Treasury's anti-gun film. R. Starnes. Field & S 74:8+ Mr '70

This land is His land. D. Foster. Chr Today 14:38-9 My 8 '70
True blue. A. Keneas. il Newsweek 76:91-2 Jl 13 '70
See also
Moving pictures—Environmental films
Moving pictures—Short subject films
Newsreel (organization)

Criticisms, plots, etc.

Carry it on
Life 69:18 S 25 '70
Sat R 53:58 S 19 '70
Time 96:61 Ag 24 '70
Censorship in Denmark
Time 96:44+ Jl 20 '70
Eldridge Cleaver
New Repub 163:24 O 10 '70
Newsweek il 76:106 S 14 '70
Sat R 53:58 S 19 '70
Fidel
Film Q 23:59-60 Spr '70
Gimme shelter
Commonweal 93:350-1 Ja 8 '71
Nat R 22:1420-1 D 29 '70
Nation 212:30 Ja 4 '71
New Yorker 46:112-15 D 19 '70
Time il 96:101+ D 14 '70
Groupies
New Repub 163:22+ D 5 '70
New Yorker 46:167 D 5 '70
Newsweek il 76:102+ N 16 '70
High school
Film Q 23:48-51 Spr '70
La hora de los hornos
Film Q il 24:31-7 Fall '70
Hospital
Atlan 225:139-42 Mr '70
New Yorker 45:75-6 Ja 31 '70
Newsweek il 75:85-6 F 9 '70
In the year of the pig
Film Q il 24:43-7 Fall '70
Inside North Vietnam
Chr Cent 87:87 Ja 21 '70
King: a filmed record, Montgomery to Memphis
Chr Cent 87:412 Ap 8 '70
Chr Today 14:45 Ap 10 '70
Married couple
Film Q il 23:9-33 Sum '70
Life 68:12 Ap 10 '70
New Repub 162:20+ Ja 31 '70
New Yorker 45:114+ F 14 '70
Newsweek il 75:83-4 F 2 '70
Sat R 53:47 Ja 24 '70
Time il 95:79 Ja 26 '70
Other voices
Time 95:74 F 23 '70
Pravda
New Yorker 46:81-5 My 30 '70
See you at Mao
New Repub 162:19 Je 6 '70
New Yorker 46:81-5 My 30 '70
Street scenes 1970
Time 96:76 S 28 '70
36
New Yorker 46:90-1 Mr 7 '70
Woodstock
America 122:425-6 Ap 18 '70
Chr Cent 87:733-4 Je 10 '70
Commonweal 92:191-3 My 8 '70
Life il 68:12 Ap 24 '70
New Repub 162:20+ My 2 '70
New Yorker 46:161-2+ Ap 11 '70
Newsweek il 75:97 Ap 6 '70
Ramp Mag 9:60-2+ O '70
Sat R 53:42-3 Ap 18 '70
Sr Schol 96:24 My 18 '70
Time il 95:100+ Ap 13 '70
You are on Indian land
Film Q 24:62 Fall '70

Editing
Fiction documentary; interviews, ed. by A. Rosenthal. A. King; R. Leiterman; A. Saare. il Film Q 23:9-33 Sum '70

Educational aspects
See Moving pictures in education

Educational films
See Moving pictures in education

Environmental films
16mm environmental film sampler. Sat R 53: 60 Ap 4 '70

Ethnographic films
See Moving pictures—Ethnological films

Ethnological films
Prospects of the ethnographic film. D. Mac-Dougall. il Film Q 23:16-30 Wint '69

MOVING pictures—*Continued*

History

Between explosions; prerevolutionary cinema.
J. Leyda. Film Q 23:33-8 Sum '70

Horror films

Fright on! M. Ronan. il Sr Schol 97:30-1
O 26 '70
Movies: ghouls, ghosts, and banshees. il Mc-
Calls 97:12+ Mr '70

Industrial use

See Moving pictures in industry

Moral aspects

Fright on! M. Ronan. il Sr Schol 97:30-1
O 26 '70
Losing it at the movies. D. Brudnoy. Nat
R 22:1309-11 D 1 '70 *
Of pot and pigs; the new cinema. G. Wag-
ner. il Nat R 22:96-7 Ja 27 '70
Popular mechanics of sex; Language of love
and U.S. obscenity laws. Time 96:58+ S 28
'70
Year at the movies. P. C. Rule. America
124:11 Ja 9 '71
See also
Moving picture censorship
Moving pictures—Classification
Sex in moving pictures

Music

What's a film classic without the mighty
Wurlitzer? Avenue photoplay society in San
Francisco presenting weekly programs of
early films and concerts. M. Mann. il Pop
Phot 66:27-8+ Ja '70

Musical films

Movie time at the opera. R. T. Jones. il
Time 96:56 Jl 27 '70
Opera on film: pitfalls aplenty. P. G. Davis.
il Hi Fi 20:MA12-13 O '70
Opera on film; Weber's Freischütz, Lortzing's
Zar und zimmermann and Henze's Young
lord. R. Zachary. il Opera N 35:21 S 5 '70
Rolf Liebermann, creator of operatic films;
interview. R. Liebermann. New Yorker 46:
21-2 Ag 29 '70
Weber and Wagner at the Lincoln Center operafest. I. Kolodin; R. Jacobson. Sat R 53:
35 Ag 1 '70

Opera films

See Moving pictures—Musical films

Political films

Fernando Solanas: an interview; tr. by J.
R. MacBean, reprinted from Cinéthique
No. 3, 1969. F. Solanas. Film Q 24:37-43
Fall '70
Film that shook France; L'áveu, or, The
confession. A.-L. Moats. Nat R 22:1406 D
29 '70
La hora de los hornos. J. R. MacBean. il
Film Q 24:31-7 Fall '70
Perils of politics on film. R. Schickel. Life
69:20 N 27 '70

Renting

Movies were better than ever; Sharon, Conn,
Old movie enthusiasts. P. L. Buckley.
Nat R 22:1059 O 6 '70

Science films

Films of the week. See issues of Science news
Mr Wizard revisited. T. Johnides. il pors
Phys Today 23:42-5 Mr '70

Setting and scenery

America as film, film as America. L. Cohen.
il Art in Am 58:68-73 S '70
Dollars in the desert; New Mexico, location
for filmakers. il Newsweek 76:78 O 26 '70
Easy rider runs wild in the Andes. B. Dar-
rach. il pors Life 68:48-50+ Je 19 '70
Memories on the block; MGM auctions. il
Life 68:42-8+ My 22 '70
Nameless village; seventeenth-century vil-
lage created in Austria for A last valley.
il Travel 133:73 My '70
Scenery behind the shoot-'em-ups. J. Higgins
and S. R. Higgins. il Todays Health 48:42-7+
Ap '70
Simulating Siberia; filming of One day in
the life of Ivan Denisovich, in Norway.
il Time 95:77 Mr 2 '70
Thalberg didn't look happy: or, With An-
tonioni at Zabriskie Point. B. Gindoff. il
Film Q 24:3-6 Fall '70

Sex films

See Sex in moving pictures

Short subject films

Sponsored films are better than ever; projecting the corporate image. S. W. Little.
il Sat R 53:90-2 S 12 '70

Study and teaching

Elementary filmmaking. J. Burgner. il Sch
Arts 69:20-3 F '70
Fifth grade makes a movie. H. Hale. il Sch
Arts 70:24-5 D '70
Make your own movie; Waterville, Me, senior
high school model library. S. Johnson and J.
Powell. il Am Lib 1:245-7 Mr '70
New Ph.D. program in cinema; New York
university. Sch & Soc 98:460 D '70
The scene; ed. by E. Farrell and L. Ruth-
Engl J 59:284-90 F '70

Suspense films

See Moving pictures—Detective and mystery films

Themes

Ali MacGraw: a return to basics. il pors
Time 97:40-5 Ja 11 '71
Ars gratia guano. J. Cocks. il Time 97:58
Ja 4 '71
Bang! Apocalypse for sale. J. Morgenstern.
il Newsweek 75:97-97A+ Ap 27 '70
Comparative anatomy of folk-myth films;
Robin Hood and Antonio das Mortes. E.
Callenbach. il Film Q 23:42-7 Wint '69
Nine bike movies in seven vroom! Days. J.
Didion. il Life 68:4 My 8 '70
Techniques of trickery. B. Nichols. Common-
weal 93:375-6 Ja 15 '71
Way to make a future; interview, tr. by
E. Stein and ed. by G. Hitchens. G. Rocha.
il Film Q 24:27-30 Fall '70
Year at the movies. P. C. Rule. America
124:11 Ja 9 '71
See also
Indians in moving pictures
Moving pictures, Amateur—Themes
Old age in moving pictures
Youth in moving pictures

Therapeutic aspects

See Moving pictures in psychotherapy

Travel films

Filming Paris without the Eiffel tower.
I. Berger. il Pop Phot 66:82-3+ Je '70
Why I film my travels. D. Sutherland. Travel
& Camera 33:77-8+ Ja '70

War films

Bloody popcorn. E. Grossman. Harper 241:
32-4+ D '70
Funny face of war. H. V. Fondiller. il Pop
Phot 66:128+ Je '70
Man behind M.A.S.H. F. Graham, jr. il
por Todays Health 48:24-7 D '70

Argentina

Fernando Solanas: an interview; tr. by J.
R. MacBean, reprinted from Cinéthique
No. 3, 1969. F. Solanas. Film Q 24:37-43
Fall '70
La hora de los hornos. J. R. MacBean. il
Film Q 24:31-7 Fall '70

Brazil

Way to make a future; interview, tr. by
E. Stein and ed. By G. Hitchens. G.
Rocha. il Film Q 24:27-30 Fall '70

France

Flicks in France. J. K. Glassman. Atlan 226:
106-8 Jl '70
Paris theater: the cinema. J. W. Montgomery. Chr Today 14:39 Jl 17 '70
Truffaut; interview. F. Truffaut. New Yorker
46:35-7 O 17 '70

Japan

Samurai to *shomin-geki;* Museum of modern
art retrospective. S. K. Oberbeck. il Newsweek 75:96+ My 11 '70

Poland

Wajda redivivus. K. T. Toeplitz. il pors Film
Q 23:37-41 Wint '69

Russia

Between explosions; prerevolutionary cinema.
J. Leyda. Film Q 23:33-8 Sum '70

United States

Cinema of secession? Film Q 24:1-2+ Fall
'70
Current cinema. P. Kael. New Yorker 46:74+
O 3 '70

MOVING pictures—United States—*Continued*
End of the road? new American cinema. S.
Farber. il Film Q 23:3-16 Wint '69
Movies; symposium, ed. by J. Hamilton. il
Look 34:27-36+ N 3 '70
New movie crash. A. Sarris. Vogue 157:82
Ja 1 '71
New movies. il Newsweek 76:62-74+ D 7 '70
Secrets of the Hollywood establishment. S.
David. il por Esquire 74:64-5+ Ag '70
See also
American film institute
Moving picture industry—United States
Paramount pictures corporation

MOVING pictures, Amateur
Don't shoot blind, storyboard your films. T.
Galluzzo. il Mod Phot 34:94-5+ Je '70
Filming Paris without the Eiffel tower. I.
Berger. il Pop Phot 66:82-3+ Je '70
Fish story on film. B. Duncan. il Pop Phot
67:110-13 Jl '70
How not to make a movie. A. Golino and
others. il Seventeen 29:154-5+ Mr '70
It's fun to make home movies; even five-
year-olds can do it. D. Babcock. il Parents
Mag 46:50-2 Ja '71
Old-time movies; the roaring '20s make for a
roaring affair! il Bet Hom & Gard 48:51 Je
'70
Selling recreation; super 8 techniques. M. E.
Day. il por Parks & Rec 5:27-8+ My '70
See also
Moving picture photography

Editing
Build your movies for speed. E. Wildi. il
Mod Phot 34:94+ F '70
Folding table speeds film editing. W. Fitz. il
Pop Phot 66:106 Mr '70
Seeing machines for movie makers. I. Ber-
ger. il Pop Phot 66:98-100+ Ap '70
Splicing: wet and dry. D. Langer. il Pop
Phot 66:118-20 Ja '70

Sound effects
Never describe the obvious. B. Evans. il Pop
Phot 66:42+ Mr '70
Sounds you want and how to get them. D.
Sutherland. il Travel & Camera 33:76+ Je
'70

MOVING pictures, Experimental
Movies: and everybody's doing it. J. Hamil-
ton. il Look 34:41-7 N 3 '70
Stan Brakhage, the courage of perception.
A. Sainer. Vogue 156:298 S 1 '70
Underground film: a critical history, by P.
Tyler. Review
Commonweal 91:623-4 Mr 6 '70. W. Fow-
lie

MOVING pictures, Realism in. See Realism in
moving pictures

MOVING pictures and children
Whatever became of the family movie? R.
Schickel. il Life 69:10 S 11 '70
See also
Moving pictures—Moral aspects

MOVING pictures and libraries. See Libraries
and moving pictures

MOVING pictures and morals. See Moving pictures—Moral aspects

MOVING pictures and youth
Bang! Apocalypse for sale. J. Morgenstern.
il Newsweek 75:97-97A+ Ap 27 '70
Current cinema. P. Kael. New Yorker 46:74+
O 3 '70
Nine bike movies in seven vroom! Days. J.
Didion. il Life 68:4 My 8 '70
With-it movies. W. S. Pechter. Commentary
49:77-81 F '70

MOVING pictures for children
Family movie guide; ed. by J. Ripp. See issues of Parents' magazine & better family
living

MOVING pictures in art education
Film: an art form. R. J. Klintworth. il Sch
Arts 69:24-6 Mr '70

MOVING pictures in education
Entertainment film in education. B. Crowther.
il por Library J 95:1555-7 Ap 15 '70
Film: a share in the great tradition. J. G.
Boyum and A. Scott. il Schol Teach Jr/Sr
High p24-5 N 2 '70
Film invasion. N. DeMarco. Clear House 45:
61-4 S '70
Films can end those social studies doldrums!
R. Maynard. il Schol Teach Sec Teach Sup
p 14-16+ Ap 6 '70
Our new and dynamic educational films. R.
Gilkey. Clear House 44:567-8 My '70
See also
Libraries and moving pictures
Moving pictures—Documentary films
Moving pictures—Study and teaching

MOVING pictures in health education
See also
Moving pictures—Documentary films

MOVING pictures in industry
How to keep the unions out of the plant;
use of film, Labor unions in America. il
Bsns W p78 Ap 18 '70

MOVING pictures in medicine
Matter of opportunity; AMA-commissioned
film to recruit Negro students. F. G. Loyd.
il Todays Health 48:18-19 Ap '70

MOVING pictures in psychotherapy
Film reviews. Ment Hy 54:328, 469 Ap-Jl '70

MOVING pictures in public relations
Sponsored films are better than ever: projecting the corporate image. S. W. Little.
il Sat R 53:90-2 S 12 '70

MOVING pictures in science
See also
Moving pictures—Science films

MOVING pictures in science education
Mr Wizard revisited. T. Johnides. il pors
Phys Today 23:42-5 Mr '70

MOVING pictures on airplanes. See Airlines—
Passenger service

MOVING platforms
Move people efficiently in our center cities;
excerpts from address, 1969. P. J. Iovin. il
Am City 85:69-71 N '70

MOVSHON, George
Beethoven on records. il Hi Fi sec I 20:81-5+
Ja '70
Callas and Tebaldi, yesterday and today. il
pors Hi Fi sec I 20:89-90 Ja '70
Caramoor: Idomeneo and a U.S. premiere.
il Hi Fi 20:MA18-19 S '70
Fresh appeal of Bidú Sayão. por Hi Fi
20:secI 107 Je '70
How I hooked up my center-channel speaker.
il Hi Fi 20:secI 71 Mr '70
Joanna Simon. por Hi Fi 20:secII 8-9 Ap '70
Karajan closes the Ring. il Hi Fi 20:secII
28-30 Je '70
Magda Olivero: worth a journey. Hi Fi sec
II 20:21 Ja '70
Otello: a new Karajan spectacular. il Hi Fi
20:MA24-7 N '70
Peter Grimes on NET. Hi Fi 20:secII 12 Ag
'70
Superlative Rosenkavalier from London rec-
ords. il Hi Fi sec I 20:75-7 F '70
Two sopranos: a discovery and an old friend.
pors Hi Fi 20:secI 79 Je '70
Video revolution. il Sat R 53:50-2 Ag 8 '70
Wolfgang is not Wieland. il Hi Fi 20:MA24-6
O '70

MOVSHON, J. Anthony
Seraphim's music course, a review from the
campus. Hi Fi 20:106 N '70

MOWAT, Farley
Boat who wouldn't float; excerpts. il Yachting
127:54-6+ Ap; 77-9+ My; 128:53-5+ Jl '70

MOWBRAY, A. Q.
Steam car may save us. il Nation 210:207-11
F 23 '70

MOXLEY, Alison
Real thing: what will it be? bibliog il Wilson
Lib Bul 45:160-2 O '70

MOXNESS, Ron
Long pipe. bibliog il Environ 12:12-23+ S '70

MOYAL, Maurice
Living museum pieces. il Am For 76:25-7+
F '70

MOYER, Donald
Opinion: an English voice. por Mlle 70:26+
Mr '70

MOYERS, Bill D.
Listening to America. il Harper 241:47-54+
D '70
about
Newsday notice. Newsweek 75:65-6 My 25
'70 *
Other side of the fence. por Time 95:33 F 2
'70

MOYES, Patricia
Writing a mystery. Writer 83:11-14 Ap '70

MOYLES, Lois
He knows what he's doing; poem. New Yorker 46:42 Mr 21 '70

MOYNIHAN, Daniel Patrick
For benign neglect. Cur 118:28 My '70
Moynihan memo and civil rights. America
122:264 Mr 14 '70; Reply. B. Hardin. 122:
399 Ap 18 '70
Moynihan memo: Negroes are making great
progress, but—; excerpts. March 1. 1970.
il pors U S News 68:57-8 Mr 16 '70
NATO environmental committee holds second
session; remarks, April 13, 1970. Dept State
Bul 62:636 My 18 '70
Nixon's Family assistance bill. New Repub
163:31-3 Jl 18; 33-4 Ag 1 '70

MOYNIHAN, Daniel Patrick—*Continued*
One step we must take. il Sat R 53:20-3 My 23 '70
What role for social science elites? Cur 124: 17-22 D '70
What's wrong with welfare; answers from Nixon's adviser; interview. pors U S News 68:64-8 Je 15 '70

about

Ambassador Moynihan. por Newsweek 76:26 N 30 '70 *
Are we faced with a new aristocracy? W. B. Cannon. Cur 124:22-6 D '70 *
At battle stations. J. Osborne. New Repub 163:10-11 D 12 '70 *
At half time; shifting the bodies around. il por Time 96:6-8 N 30 '70 *
Benign neglect. Am City 85:8 Ap '70 *
Case of benign neglect. il por Newsweek 75: 25+ Mr 16 '70 *
Democrat leaves the White House. H. Sidey. il Life 69:2 D 18 '70 *
Faithful servant. J. Osborne. New Repub 162:12-13 Mr 14 '70 *
Levitation of Moynihan; reports of his becoming ambassador to the UN. Nation 211:581 D 7 '70 *
Memorandum to Moynihan. Nation 210:291 Mr 16 '70 *
Moynihan memo and civil rights. America 122:264 Mr 14 '70 *
Moynihan's farewell. por Time 97:30 Ja 4 '71 *
Moynihan's memo fever. por Time 95:15-16 Mr 23 '70 *
Neglect, but what kind? recommendation to President Nixon. Commonweal 92:28 Mr 20 '70 *
New look. il pors Newsweek 77:17 Ja 4 '71 *
Odd alliance: Moynihan and the robber barons. I. Mothner. il pors Look 34:18-23 Ap 7 '70 *
Purloined letter. K. Crawford. il por Newsweek 75:37 Mr 16 '70 *
Unmaking of a liberal. J. Deedy. Commonweal 92:60 Mr 27 '70 *
Victim of benign neglect? M. McGory. America 122:327 Mr 28 '70 *
Whig in the White House: Daniel P. Moynihan; Time essay. por Time 95:26-7 Mr 16 '70 *

MOYNIHAN, Rodrigo
Odd American. il Art N 69:50-3 Ja '71

MOZAMBIQUE
See also
Dams—Mozambique
Hunting—Mozambique
Malawi, Lake

Native races
Makonde sculpture. M. Shore-Bos. il por(p4) Natur Hist 79:42-9 Mr '70

MOZARABIC rite. See Catholic church—Mozarabic rite

MOZART, Johann Chrysostom Wolfgang Amadeus
Boynge's Don Giovanni. G. L. Mayer. Sat R 53:67+ Ap 25 '70 *
Don Giovanni done in. P. H. Lang. il Hi Fi 20:secI 72-3 My '70 *
Exploring Idomeneo. P. H. Lang. il Hi Fi 20:secI 75-7 Mr '70 *
Magic flute (Die zauberflöte) Criticism
Hi Fi sec I il 20:66-9 F '70 *
Sat R 53:55 Ja 31 '70
Marriage of Figaro (Le nozze di Figaro) Criticism
New Yorker 46:90-1 Ap 11 '70 *
Opera N il 34:18-20 Ap 11 '70 *
Opera N il 34:24-5 Ap 11 '70 *
Sat R 53:44 Ap 18 '70 *
Mozart, by W. J. Turner. Review
Am Rec G 36:748+ My '70. R. W. Gutman *
Mozart and the Amadeus. S. Fleming. Hi Fi 20:secI 98 Je '70 *
Mozart happening with Peter Serkin. H. Goldsmith. Hi Fi 20:secI 86 My '70 *
Mozart with a flourish. C. Mackerras. il Opera N 34:24-5 Ap 11 '70 *
Mozart's symphonic miracles. P. H. Lang. il Hi Fi 20:secI 71-3 Jl '70 *
Peter Serkin: nearly two hours of glorious Mozart. L. Gerber. Am Rec G 36:895+ Jl '70 *
Piano music for Mozart and Debussy. H. Goldsmith. il Hi Fi 20:secI 81-3 Ap '70 *
Records:
Abduction from the seraglio. Opera N 34:35 Mr 14 '70 *
Idomeneo. Opera N 34:35 Mr 21 '70 *
Lucio Silla. Opera N 34:34 Ja 31 '70
Riddle of the Magic flute. A. Williamson. il Hi Fi sec I 20:66-9 F '70 *

Several big three's; Karl Böhm's forty-six symphonies. C. J. McNaspy. America 122: 353-6 Mr 28 '70 *
Short happy months of Mozart's Prague. J. Wechsberg. il Sat R 53:60-1 Mr 14 '70 *

MOZART festivals. See Music festivals—New York (state)

MOZEN, Milton M. See Schroeder, D. D. jt. auth.

M'POKO, Benjamin
Congo student mediates youth-establishment battle. il pors Ebony 25:90-2+ Je '70 *

MRAZEK, Dale
IC memories, growth and future. bibliog il Electr World 83:25-9+ Mr; 34-6+ Ap '70

MROSS, George A. and others
Gibbon fibrinopeptides: identification of a glycine-serine allelism at position B-3. bibliog il Science 170:468-70 O 23 '70

MTSHALI, B. V.
Zambia's foreign policy. bibliog f Cur Hist 58:148-53+ Mr '70

MUBEEM, Maureen
Psychedelic tie-dye look. il por Time 95:36-9 Ja 26 '70

MUCHA, Ronald. See Finley, L. jt. auth.

MUCK, Karl
Prisoner: 1337; occupation: conductor, Boston symphony orchestra. J. J. Badal. il pors Hi Fi 20:55-60 O '70 *

MUCKRAKERS
McClure's magazine and the muckrakers, by H. S. Wilson. Review
New Repub 163:20-1 D 19 '70. J. Walt

MUCOPOLYSACCHARIDES
Inborn errors of mucopolysaccharide metabolism. E. F. Neufeld and J. C. Fratantoni. bibliog il Science 169:142-3 Jl 10 '70
Rapid axonal transport of sulfated mucopolysaccharide proteins. J. S. Elam and others. bibliog il Science 170:458-60 O 23 '70

MUCOPOLYSACCHARIDOSES. See Metabolism, Disorders of

MUCOUS cells. See Cells

MUD slides. See Landslides

MUDD, Roger Harrison
Equal time for the closed fraternity; excerpt from address. il por Life 68:4 Mr 13 '70

MUELLER, Andrew J.
(comp) CB troubleshooter's casebook (cont) Radio-Electr 41:14 F; 85 Mr; 66+ Ap; 81 Jl '70
Fix CB fast (cont) Radio-Electr 41:78 Mr '70

MUELLER, Elaine
Smile; a memoir. Mlle 72:96-7+ D '70

MUELLER, Eva
My friend the machine. il Newsweek 75:79 F 23 '70 *

MUELLER, Gene
Videotape for self-evaluation. il Todays Ed 59:39 Ja '70

MUELLER, George E.
Moon program's business brain trust; Apollo executive group. E. Clark. il pors Nations Bsns 58:32-4+ My '70 *

MUELLER, Larry
Saddleback Bigs. il Field & S 75:78-9+ My '70
Two ways to train. il Field & S 74:216-17+ Mr '70

MUELLER, Lisel
Life of a queen; Poem about the hounds and the hares; Web; for richer, for poorer; poems. Poetry 115:324-9 F '70

MUELLER, Marti. See White, J. jt. auth.

MUELLER-Lyer illusion. See Optical illusions

MUENCH, David
Flowers of Rainier. il Nat Wildlife 8:22-7 Je '70
Patriarchs; photographs. Am For 76:32-3 My '70
Winter in Yosemite; photographs. il Nat Wildlife 8:44-7 F '70

MUFFLERS. See Automobile engines—Mufflers

MUGGERIDGE, Malcolm
Books. See issues of Esquire
Decade of the great liberal death wish. il Esquire 74:154-9 D '70

about

Muggeridge manhandled. J. Roddy. por Look 34:60 Mr 24 '70 *

MUGGING (crime) See Assault and battery

MUGNAINI, Joseph
Drawing landscapes from life and imagination. il Am Artist 34:44-9 S '70

MUHAMMAD, Elijah
Elijah Muhammad: prophet and architect of the separate nation of Islam. H. J. Massaquoi. il pors Ebony 25:78-80+ Ag '70 *

MUHAMMAD Ali. See Clay, C.

MUHLEN, Norbert
  Willy Brandt turns East. Nat R 22:676-7 Je 30 '70
MUHLENBERG, Frederick Augustus Conrad
  Joseph Wright's portrait of Frederick Muhlenberg. M. H. Fabian. il por Antiques 97:256-7 F '70 *
MUIR, A. H. Jr, and others
  Mössbauer spectroscopy of moon samples. bibliog il Science 167:688-90 Ja 30 '70
MUIR, John
  Rise of American esthetic conservation. D. H. Strong. il pors Nat Parks 44:4-9 F '70 *
MUJIBUR Rahman
  Step in the right direction. Time 96:29-30 D 21 '70 *
  Two-man sweep. il pors Newsweek 76:44 D 21 '70 *
MULATAS ISLANDS
  Cuna revolt. R. Chardkoff. il Américas 22:14-21 Jl '70
MULATTOES
  Identity crisis Italian style; children of black GIs. M. Senesi. il Ebony 25:40-6 Jl '70
  Intellectual development of children from interracial matings. L. Willerman and others. bibliog il Science 170:1329-31 D 18 '70
MULCHING
  Aluminum foil foils aphids. N. J. Smith. il Farm J 94:28H N '70
  Canary Islanders mulch with volcanic ash. A. Halperin. il Org Gard & Farm 17:52 O '70
  Gardening with plastic mulch. R. A. Miller. Horticulture 48:36+ Ag '70
  Happy mulch, organic, natch. R. Stout. il Org Gard & Farm 17:52-5 Jl '70
  Mulch-planted onions beat spring mud. J. Krill. il Org Gard & Farm 17:46-7 F '70
  Mulch your garden this year with newspapers. Org Gard & Farm 17:76-7 My '70
  Mulching with newspapers is here to stay! M. Franz. il Org Gard & Farm 17:34-9 D '70
  My mountain of leaves. B. Gilford. il Org Gard & Farm 17:54-6 N '70
  Putting the garden to bed for the winter. W. Bowers and L. Bowers. il Org Gard & Farm 17:25-7 O '70
  Slick tricks for cold-country gardening. L. Hedla. il Home Gard 58:54-5+ Ja '71
MULE deer hunting. See Deer hunting
MULEGÉ, Mexico
  Traveler's choice. A. C. Wagner. Travel 134:12 O '70
MULERT, Jo Ann
  Strategy of nonviolent direct action interpreted by Beaver 55 protesters; interview, ed. by M. Stone. Chr Cent 87:610-12 My 13 '70
MULES. See Asses and mules
MULFORD, Raymon H.
  Improbable genius was Mike Owens. il pors Nations Bsns 58:96-7 Ja '70
MULHERIN, Kathy
  Memories of a (latter-day) Catholic girlhood. il Commonweal 91:610-19 Mr 6 '70
MULLER, Edward
  Musicians don't look and dancers don't listen. Dance Mag 45:26-7 Ja '71
MULLER, George
  Pigs keep our water mains clean. il Am City 85:112+ O '70
MULLER, Herbert Joseph
  P.P.A. authors' press conference; excerpts. il pors Pub W 197:27-9 Mr 23 '70
  Relevance of the humanities. Am Scholar 40:103-18 Wint '70
MULLER, Kal
  Land diving with the Pentecost Islanders. il Nat Geog 138:799-817 D '70
MULLER, Robert
  Multimedia shelving. Library J 95:750 F 15 '70
MULLETS
  Mullet madness. R. Clancy. il Sea Front 16:49-50 Ja '70
MULLIGAN, Elizabeth
  Polio's silent giants: asleep or just napping? il Todays Health 48:44-5 Ag '70
MULLIGAN, James H.
  Talent lies hidden in the Delta. il Am Ed 6:13-16 My '70
MULLIGAN, Joseph E.
  Better than looking on. America 122:468-9; 123:69-70 My 2, Ag 8 '70
  Death machine. Nation 212:21-2 Ja 4 '71
  Reform or resistance? Cath World 212:131-3 D '70
MULLONEY, Brian
  Structure of the giant fibers of earthworms. bibliog il Science 168:994-6 My 22 '70
MULLOY, John J.
  Cultural understanding. R. Kirk. Nat R 22:363 Ap 7 '70 *

MULTI-media performances. See Performing arts
MULTINATIONAL corporations. See Corporations—International
MULTINATIONAL marketing. See Marketing
MULTIPLE choice tests. See Educational tests and measurements
MULTIPLE exposure photography. See Photography, Trick
MULTIPLE independently-targeted re-entry vehicle. See MIRV
MULTIPLE jobholding. See Supplementary employment
MULTIPLE use plans. See Forest management
MULTIPLEX radio broadcasting. See Radio broadcasting—Multiplex system
MULTIPURPOSE furniture. See Furniture
MULTIVIBRATORS
  Getting to know the JK flip-flop; bistable multivibrator. F. H. Tooker. il Pop Electr 33:67-72+ S '70
  Silicon controlled switch multivibrator. F. H. Tooker. il Electr World 83:60 Je '70
MULVANEY, D. J.
  Prehistory Down Under; with biographical sketch. il Natur Hist 79:6, 44-51 Ap '70
MULVANY, Robert L.
  How to choose the right light pole. il Am City 85:84-5 S '70
MULVOY, Mark
  Arnie's party was a divine affair. pors Sports Illus 33:16-17 Ag 3 '70
  Baseball (cont) il Sports Illus 33:38-9 Jl 6 '70
  Golf (cont) il Sports Illus 32:48+ Je 29; 33:50+ Ag 17; 42-3 Ag 31; 54-5 S 7 '70
  Hockey (cont) Sports Illus 32:96+ Ap 13; 33:58+ N 9; 86-7 N 30; 66 D 14 '70; 34:54-5 Ja 4 '71
  It's gotta be Orr, or else. il Sports Illus 33:28-30+ O 19 '70
  Mr O and the sack of New York. il por Sports Illus 32:20-1 Ap 27 '70
  Panic was quelled in Boston. il Sports Illus 33:18-19 N 9 '70
  Plain words at Westchester. por Sports Illus 33:12-13 Ag 10 '70
  Team that eats managers. il por Sports Illus 32:20-1 Mr 16 '70
  Two worlds against the Black Hawks. il Sports Illus 33:20-1 D 7 '70
  Up jump those pore li'l Canucks. il Sports Illus 32:24-5 Mr 23 '70
  (ed) See Sinden, H. No room at the top for me
  —and Ronberg, Gary
  Desperate hours. il Sports Illus 32:18-21 Ap 6 '70
MUMFORD, Lawrence Quincy
  Technology's assessors. J. Lear. Sat R 53:52 Ap 25 '70 *
MUMFORD, Lewis
  Pentagon of power; excerpts. New Yorker 46:50-2+ O 10; 48-50+ O 17; 55-8+ O 24; 50-2+ O 31 '70
  Pentagon of power; excerpts. il Horizon 12:4-21 Aut '70
    about
  Higher ignorance. Nat R 23:22 Ja 12 '71 *
  Men of letters. A. Trachtenberg. Nation 211:117-20 Ag 17 '70 *
  Some words for the young. J. J. Thorndike. por Horizon 12:2-3 Aut '70 *
  Van Wyck Brooks-Lewis Mumford letters, ed. by R. E. Spiller. Review
    New Repub 163:21-2+ S 19 '70. H. Kramer *
    Newsweek pors 76:82+ S 7 '70. R. A. Gross *
    Sat R 53:48-9 Ag 22 '70. D. Littlejohn *
MUMMIES
  Radiography: new tool for retrieving the wealth of the pharaohs. S. S. McKern. il Sci Digest 68:8-13 Jl '70
MUMS. See Chrysanthemums
MUNCH, Edvard
  Toward the sun. Mot solen. G. Loney. il Dance Mag 44:62-5 N '70 *
MUNCK, L. and others
  Gene for improved nutritional value in barley seed protein. bibliog il Science 168:985-7 My 22 '70
MUNDELL, William D.
  After logging; poem. Am For 76:50 F '70
  Chance of diamond; poem. Am For 76:39 My '70
  Cunning frost; poem. Am For 76:56 N '70
  In windy autumn; poem. Am For 76:53 O '70
  Old tree falls; poem. Am For 76:48 Ja '70
  Swamp; poem. Am For 76:55 Mr '70
MUNDINGER, Paul C.
  Vocal imitation and individual recognition of finch calls. bibliog il Science 168:480-2 Ap 24 '70

MÜNEMANN, Rudolf
Juggler slips. il por Newsweek 75:68 F 9 '70
MUNGO, Raymond
If Mr Thoreau calls, tell him I've left the country. il Atlan 225:72-82+ My '70

about

Take to the hills. A. H. Norman. il por Newsweek 76:76B Ag 10 '70 *
MUNICH
Munich in October. F. Spelman. il Travel & Camera 33:30-5 O '70

Hotels, restaurants, etc.

Dining in Munich. S. J. Reichman. il Travel & Camera 33:28-9 O '70

Music

Behind the scenes. P. G. Davis. il Hi Fi sec 1 20:20 Ja '70
Behind the scenes. P. Moor. Hi Fi 20:25-6 O '70
Report:
Ballo in maschera. D. Graham. il Opera N 34:34 Ap 18 '70
Carmen and La Bohème. D. Graham. il Opera N 34:34 Ja 24 '70
Carmina burana in the Bavarian state opera. H. E. Reed. il Opera N 35:40 D 19 '70
Fledermaus and Rameau's Platée. D. Graham. Opera N 34:33 F 28 '70
Günther Bialas Die geschichte von Aucassin und Nicolette. D. Graham. Opera N 34:29-30 F 7 '70
Janácek's Jenufa in Max Brod's German translation. D. Graham. il Opera N 34:28-9 My 16 '70
Strauss, Mozart and Wagner. D. Graham. Opera N 35:24 S 19 '70
Tannhäuser. D. Graham. Opera N 35:27 S 5 '70

Social life and customs

Oktoberfest, mit chaser. H. Kenner. il Nat R 22:35+ Ja 13 '70
MUNICH festival. See Music festivals—Germany (Federal Republic)
MUNICH opera ballet. See Ballet companies
MUNICH summer festival of opera. See Music festivals—Germany (Federal Republic)
MUNICIPAL accounting
See also
Billing
MUNICIPAL administration. See Municipal government
MUNICIPAL advertising
City tells its story; ed. by P. D. Eimon. See issues of American city
MUNICIPAL and federal relations. See Federal and municipal relations
MUNICIPAL annexations. See Cities and towns —Growth
MUNICIPAL art. See Art, Municipal
MUNICIPAL automobiles. See Automobiles, Municipal
MUNICIPAL bonds
Municipal finance. See issues of American city
Suppose the bond issue fails; planned civic center complex, Pomona, Calif. il Am City 85:88+ Mr '70
Voters on spending: schools down, environment up. il U S News 69:60-2 N 16 '70
MUNICIPAL buildings
Life begins at forty-two; converting old library structure into municipal administration building; Montrose, Colo. M. Bingham. il por Am City 85:111 Jl '70
See also
City halls
Municipal centers
MUNICIPAL centers
Try a paint-in at construction site of new civic center; Norfolk, Va. J. B. Oliver. il Am City 85:126+ O '70
MUNICIPAL consultants. See Government consultants, Municipal
MUNICIPAL contracts
Contract street sweeping removes more than dirt; cities in the Los Angeles area. il Am City 85:46 Je '70
How to use contractors for snow removal; Baltimore County, Md. A. F. Jungers. il Am City 85:79-81 O '70
Look before you leap into total-cost billing; Bangor, Me. L. E. Donnelly. il Am City 85:89+ F '70
Plans and specs affect construction costs. Am City 85:159 S '70
Preference in public bidding. A. L. Lehrbaummer. Am City 85:124+ S '70
Vendor looks at low-bid buying. G. D. Arnold. il por Am City 85:107+ Ap '70

MUNICIPAL corporations
Legal notes and decisions; prepared by National institute of municipal law officers. See issues of American city
See also
Municipal incorporation
MUNICIPAL dumps
See also
Filling (earthwork)
Refuse and refuse disposal
MUNICIPAL elections
See also
New York (city)—Elections
Newark, N.J.—Elections
MUNICIPAL employees
See also
Collective bargaining—Municipal employees
Public safety officers
Strikes—United States—Municipal employees

Salaries, allowances, etc.

Cities in trouble: strapped and facing wage strikes. il U S News 69:27-8 D 28 '70
MUNICIPAL employees' associations. See Employees associations
MUNICIPAL equipment
Big loader offsets burning ban; Marshfield, Mass. E. Williams. il Am City 85:60-1 D '70
From flood rescue work to snow removal; model 545 loader. K. Ryan. il Am City 85:89-90 Ap '70
New products and processes. See issues of American city
Small cities can use big machines; model 2000 Trojan loader. C. Carlan. il Am City 85:117+ Ap '70
See also
Life saving equipment
Salt spreaders
Snow removal equipment, Municipal
Street cleaning apparatus

Maintenance and repair

EDP cuts equipment maintenance costs; Fresno, Calif. D. Smith. il Am City 85:131-2+ My '70
Four public agencies pool equipment maintenance. il Am City 85:105 N '70
MUNICIPAL exhibits, Traveling. See Exhibitions, Traveling
MUNICIPAL finance
Financial noose draws tighter. il Bsns W p31-2 Ja 2 '71
Hard times; economy wave. Newsweek 76:61 D 7 '70
Municipal finance. See issues of American city
New directions in urban financing. D. G. Alexander. bibliog f Cur Hist 59:278-82+ N '70
On the brink of bankruptcy. il Time 97:13-14 Ja 11 '71
See also
Local taxation
Municipal bonds
also subhead Finance under names of cities, e.g. New York (city)—Finance

Federal aid

See Federal and municipal relations
MUNICIPAL foresters. See Foresters
MUNICIPAL garages. See Garages, Municipal
MUNICIPAL government
Cities can work; reorganization proposals. E. N. Costikyan. il Sat R 53:19-21+ Ap 4 '70
City tells its story; ed. by P. D. Eimon. See issues of American city
COGs vs chaos. R. A. Bibler. bibliog il Am City 85:94+ S '70
Cybernetics in city hall; adaptation of address, 1968. E. S. Savas. bibliog il Science 168:1066-71 My 29 '70; Discussion. 169:1155 S 18 '70
Obstacles to urban change. P. A. Lupsha. Cur Hist 59:296-9+ N '70
Urban administration, a new ball game. L. P. Cookingham. il por Am City 85:63-6 Ja '70
See also
Cities and towns
Cities and towns—Consolidation
Fire departments
Metropolitan government
Municipal finance
Police departments
also subhead Politics and government under names of cities, e.g. Jacksonville, Fla.—Politics and government

Forms, blanks, etc.

We renovated stores and print-shop operations; Des Moines. K. G. Ibson. il Am City 85:116+ Mr '70

MUNICIPAL government—*Continued*

Public relations

Bells are ringing in St Petersburg; Service and information service. il Am City 85:130 Mr '70

Million dollar bus trip; Tacoma centennial bus caravan. il Am City 85:108 F '70

Try a citizen-service plan; Hempstead, N.Y. il Am City 85:106-8 N '70

Urban focus 1970: people! il Am City 85: 116+ F '70

Canada

See also
Town meeting

United States

See Municipal government

MUNICIPAL improvement

Parting shots: orchids for eyepleasers, onions for eyesores. il Life 69:85-7 S 18 '70

See also
All-America cities
Art, Municipal
Business districts
City planning
Green thumb, inc.
Parks
Playgrounds
Urban renewal
also subhead Municipal improvement under names of cities, e.g. Minneapolis—Municipal improvement

MUNICIPAL incinerators. See Refuse incinerators

MUNICIPAL incorporation

Incorporation: a new tactic for saving black areas. C. C. Douglas. il pors Ebony 25: 100-2+ Ag '70

MUNICIPAL information service. See Information services

MUNICIPAL inventories. See Inventories, Municipal

MUNICIPAL officers

See also
Mayors
New York (city)—Public officers

MUNICIPAL ordinances

Legal notes and decisions: prepared by National institute of municipal law officers. See issues of American city

See also
Snow and ice removal—Laws and regulations

MUNICIPAL parks. See Parks

MUNICIPAL public opinion polls. See Public opinion polls

MUNICIPAL public relations. See Municipal government—Public relations

MUNICIPAL publications

Bibliography

Book reviews and reports. See issues of American city

MUNICIPAL purchasing. See Purchasing, Municipal

MUNICIPAL revenue. See Local taxation

MUNICIPAL service buildings. See Municipal buildings

MUNICIPAL services

Creeping capitalism; private operation of public services. il Forbes 106:22-6+ S 1 '70

Do-it-yourself solves some problems of rapid growth; Shaler Township. W. L. Crawford. il Am City 85:90+ S '70

MUNICIPAL signs. See Signs and signboards

MUNICIPAL swimming pools. See Swimming pools

MUNICIPAL taxation. See Local taxation

MUNICIPAL transportation. See Urban transportation

MUNITIONS

Arms traffic and third world conflicts. G. Kemp. bibliog il por Int Concil 577:5-80 Mr '70

Booming world trade in arms. il Bsns W p 114-16+ My 23 '70

History's greatest dead end; world spending. F. Blackaby. il Sat R 53:19-21+ Mr 14 '70

Symbols of acceptance; U.S. arms for Greece. Time 96:28+ S 21 '70

Uncle cries "uncle"; Greek arms embargo lifted by U.S. Nation 211:356 O 19 '70

See also
Vietnamese war, 1957- —Equipment and supplies

MUNITIONS industries

See also
Firearms industry and trade
International armament corporation

Finance

Myth of war profiteering. G. E. Berkley; reply. V. Perlo. New Repub 162:23-5 F 7 '70

France

Why French arms makers sell so well. il Bsns W p46+ F 28 '70

Germany (Federal Republic)

Leopard tanks roll up the sales. Bsns W p23 O 3 '70

Switzerland

Fines wound a gun maker; Oerlikon arms works. Bsns W p35 D 5 '70

United States

Ammo plant shuts its doors; study by the Midwest research institute. Bsns W p44 S 5 '70

Boom is fading in munitions making. il Bsns W p25 N 21 '70

See also
Firearms industry and trade

MUNITIONS purchasing. See Purchasing, Military

MUNITIONS trade. See Munitions

MUNOZ, Elaine F. See Silverman, M. P. jt. auth.

MUNRO, Eleanor C.

Orient express. il Art N 69:48-51+ Sum '70

MUNSON, Donald

Trane formula. V. Lewis. por Duns 95:61-2 Ap '70 *

MUNSON, Russell

Super Cub. il Flying 86:56-9 F '70

MUNTJACS. See Deer

MUNVES, J. A.

United Nations village. il Holiday 47:28-9+ Ap '70

Virgin Islands. il Travel & Camera 33:36-45 D '70

MURAL painting and decoration

Living wall; Y. Agam's hexagonal mural in Leverkusen, West Germany. il Time 95:66-7 My 18 '70

Memoirs of a WPA painter; excerpt from The new deal art project, ed. by F. V. O'Connor; with paintings. E. Laning. il por Am Heritage 21:38-57+ O '70

Psychedelic ceiling. A. L. Schott. il Sch Arts 70:38 N '70

School mural. N. K. Rockwell. il Sch Arts 69:16-17 F '70

Zest in wall painting. M. Gilliatt. il House & Gard 138:126-7+ O '70

See also
Cave drawings and paintings
Frescoes
Mosaics

MURAL painting and decoration, Exterior

Art; outdoor wall murals in New York. L. Alloway. Nation 211:253-4 S 21 '70

Painting the town. il Life 69:60-3 Jl 17 '70

Up against the walls; Climax club mural; Siddhartha of Beverly Hills by the Fine Arts Squad. il Newsweek 76:86-7 S 7 '70

MURALS, Photographic. See Photographic murals

MURASE, Tsutomu, and McBirney, A. R.

Thermal conductivity of lunar and terrestrial igneous rocks in their melting range. bibliog il Science 170:165-7 O 9 '70

Viscosity of lunar lavas. bibliog il Science 167:1491-3 Mr 13 '70

MURATA, Steve

Keeping healthy at 30,000 feet. il Todays Health 48:20-3+ My '70

MURCHISON, William, Jr

Where conservatives can't lose. Nat R 22: 1164 N 3 '70

MURCHLAND, Bernard

Between solitude and solidarity. Commonweal 93:91-5 O 23 '70

MURDER

Ben Chaney at eleven and at seventeen; with report by M. Mok. il pors Life 68:36-9 Je 19 '70

Big-city murders· clues to why they keep rising. il U S News 68:13 F 16 '70

Bloody breakout at San Rafael; with editorial comment. il pors Life 69:2A, 30-4 Ag 21 '70

Charlie Manson's home on the range. G. Talese. il por Esquire 73:101-3+ Mr '70

Courthouse shoot-out; San Rafael, Calif. il Newsweek 76:34+ Ag 17 '70

Crime that shocked the Nation; the murder of J. Yablonski. D. Lawrence. U S News 68:80 Ja 19 '70

Dead man's finger; J. A. Yablonski murder suspects held. il por Newsweek 75:22 F 2 '70

Fifth suspect; murder of UMW executive J. A. Yablonski. Newsweek 75:24 Mr 9 '70

Fragments from the shooting gallery; Sharon Tate murders. M. Singer. pors Ramp Mag 8:16-18 Ap '70

Hand from the grave; murder of Yablonski family. il Time 95:11 F 2 '70

MURDER—*Continued*
Helpless hostages; kidnapping and murder of K. von Spreti in Guatemala. il Time 95:30 Ap 20 '70
High cost of blackmail: kidnappings and deaths of hostages at San Rafael, Calif. and Uruguay. Nat R 22:880+ Ag 25 '70
Insulin murders. L. B. Taylor, jr. Todays Health 48:50-3+ D '70
Just friends; Yablonski murders. New Repub 162:10-11 F 21 '70
Manson wins! A fantasy. F. Conroy. il Harper 241:53-9 N '70
Mass murder in Soquel; case of Ohta family. il por Time 96:10-11 N 2 '70
Muffin; daughter charged with murder of Richard Mattingly, sr. il por Newsweek 75:21+ Ja 26 '70
Murder in legal limbo; case of U.S. v. Escamilla. il por Time 96:58 S 28 '70
Murder New Jersey style; Judy Kavanaugh case. C. S. Wren and M. English. il Look 34:43-7 Mr 10 '70
Murder with a union link? U S News 68:6 Ja 19 '70
Professor's guns; gun battle at Marin County courthouse, San Rafael, Calif. il por Time 96:13 Ag 24 '70
Sharon Tate murders. P. Maas. il por Ladies Home J 87:52+ Ap '70
Tarot murders; case of the Ohta family. il pors Newsweek 76:32+ N 2 '70
U.S. journal: West Chester, Pennsylvania; undercover police officer, John Mervin arrested for murder. C. Trillin. New Yorker 46:42-4+ Je 27 '70
Vicarious murder; ruling of California supreme court in A. Taylor case. Time 96:61 D 21 '70
Who killed Alex Rackley? por Newsweek 75:22 Mr 30 '70
Why blacks kill blacks; psychiatrist on ghetto violence. A. F. Poussaint. il por Ebony 25:143-6 O '70
Yablonski murders; a challenge to union leadership among mine workers. J. McGinniss. il Life 68:36-7 Ja 23 '70
   See also
Assassination
Capital punishment
Poisons
Trials (murder)
MURDER of Jeremy Harlowe; story. See Teixeira, C.
MURDER trials. See Trials (murder)
MURDER trials, Military. See Courts martial and courts of inquiry
MURDERERS. See Crime and criminals; Murder
MURDEROUS angels; drama. See O'Brien, C. C.
MURDOCH, Faith T.
Commitment to achievement. il Am Lib 1:758-61 S '70
MURDOCH, Keith Rupert
New headliner rocks Fleet Street. il por Bsns W p32 S 12 '70 *
MURDOCK, Gordon
Mini music hall. il Time 97:53 Ja 4 '71 *
MURDOCK, Steve
Dissident varsity. Nation 210:305-8 Mr 16 '70
MURDOCK, T. L. and Ney, E. P.
Mercury: the dark-side temperature. bibliog il Science 170:535-7 O 30 '70
MURIE, Margaret E.
Wilderness concept; excerpt from address, April 4, 1970. Liv Wildn 34:63 Sum '70
MURIEL, Amador
Brain drain in the Philippines: a case study. Bul Atom Sci 26:38-9 S '70
MURINE leukemia virus. See Leukemia viruses
MURINE sarcoma virus. See Tumor viruses
MURPHEY, John A. Jr
Corpus Christi, Texas. Wilson Lib Bul 44:763-5 Mr '70
MURPHY, Austin S.
Anatomy of affluence; address, November 7, 1969. Vital Speeches 36:207-9 Ja 15 '70
MURPHY, Burt
Biggest little camera in the world. il Pop Mech 133:106-9+ My '70
How to stretch your camera lenses. il Pop Mech 134:123-7+ D '70
New magic for home movies: instant-loading projectors. il Pop Mech 134:152-5 O '70
MURPHY, C. Gordon
Fortune's wheel; new president. por Newsweek 75:74 Je 22 '70 *
MURPHY, Calvin
Super midget. H. L. Masin. por Sr Schol 95:23 Ja 5 '70
   about
Court magician. il por Time 95:48+ Mr 23 '70 *

MURPHY, Cornelius F. Jr
Modern song of praise. Cath World 211:62 My '70
MURPHY, Sister Ellen
First thaw; poem. Commonweal 93:370 Ja 15 '71
MURPHY, Franklin D.
Yardsticks for a new era. il Sat R 53:23-5 N 21 '70
MURPHY, George Lloyd
Murphy's fee. por Newsweek 75:31 Mr 23 '70 *
MURPHY, Geraldine
Teaching fiction through visual and verbal art. Engl J 59:502-8 Ap '70
MURPHY, James F.
Recreation education: a social concern. bibliog f il Parks & Rec 9:57-8+ S '70
MURPHY, James T. See Boyd, R. W. jt. auth.
MURPHY, Mary Kay
PECE corps: career exploration. il Schol Teach Jr/Sr High p24-5 S 21 '70
SUCCESS in early counseling. il Am Ed 6:3-7 Mr '70
   —See Branan, K. jt. auth.
MURPHY, Michael
Bas-relief paper sculpture. il Sch Arts 70:12-13 S '70
MURPHY, Michael R. and Schneider, G. E.
Olfactory bulb removal eliminates mating behavior in the male golden hamster. bibliog il Science 167:302-4 Ja 16 '70
MURPHY, Paula
Funny girl. S. Kelly. il pors Hot Rod 23:68-70 Mr '70 *
MURPHY, Richard W.
Matisse's final flowering. por Horizon 12:26-41 Wint '70
MURPHY, Robert C. and others
Search for organic material in lunar fines by mass spectrometry. il Science 167:755-7 Ja 30 '70
MURPHY, Tom
Advertising copywriting. Writers Digest 51:32-3 Ja '71
MURPHY, Tony
Bonneville. il Hot Rod 23:126-9 N '70
MURPHY, Walter
Three consultants, one county. il Library J 95:2068+ Je 1 '70
MURRAY, Albert
African culture and black identity; excerpt from Omni-Americans. Cur 121:26-7 S '70
MURRAY, David J.
Nigeria after Biafra. il Cur Hist 58:135-41+ Mr '70
MURRAY, John
Happy Hollidays; drama. Plays 30:13-24 D '70
Healthy, wealthy and wild; drama. Plays 29:13-24 My '70
Publisher's choice; drama. Plays 30:1-13 N '70
Sixth juror; drama. Plays 30:33-45 N '70
Swiss chalet mystery; drama. Plays 29:23-34 Mr '70
—and Boretz, Allen
Room service. Criticism
   America 122:638 Je 13 '70 *
   Nation 210:701-2 Je 8 '70 *
   New Yorker 46:73 My 23 '70 *
   Time il 95:62 My 25 '70 *
MURRAY, Madalyn E.
Bishop Madalyn; founding Poor Richard's universal life church. Time 95:44 F 9 '70
McIntire-O'Hair debate: bruised but unbowed. M. Moss. il Chr Today 14:42-3 Mr 13 '70 *
MURRAY, Robert W. Jr
Buy or rent? Todays Ed 59:46-8 D '70
MURRAY, William
L.A. free press is rich. Esquire 73:54+ Je '70
Porn capital of America. il N Y Times Mag p8-9+ Ja 3 '71
MURRAY Louis dance company
Murray Louis dance company in Chicago. A. Barzel. il Dance Mag 44:40-3 Je '70
Murray Louis dance company; New York city center. M. Marks. Dance Mag 44:76-7 Jl '70
MURRAY RIVER
Paddleboat on the Murray. R. Harrington. il Travel 135:48-51 Ja '71
MURRISH, David E. and Schmidt-Nielsen, Knut
Water transport in the cloaca of lizards: active or passive? bibliog il Science 170:324-6 O 16 '70
MURROW, Edward R.
Prime time: the life of Edward R. Murrow; excerpts. A. Kendrick. Todays Ed 59:15-16 F '70 *
MURTAGH, John Martin
Justice Murtagh's formula. Nation 210:260 Mr 9 '70 *
MURTAUGH, Danny
No disgruntlements round here. R. Blount, jr. il por Sports Illus 33:18-21 Ag 10 '70 *

MURTHY, V. Rama, and others
Rubidium-strontium age and elemental and isotopic abundance of some trace elements in lunar samples. bibliog il Science 167:476-9 Ja 30 '70

MURTON, Thomas O'Rhelius
Vindication for Murton. Nation 210:357 Mr 30 '70 *

MUSCAT and Oman. See Oman

MUSCLE
Catch property in single mammalian motor units. R. E. Burke and others. bibliog il Science 168:122-4 Ap 3 '70
How is muscle turned on and off? G. Hoyle. il Sci Am 222:84-93 bibliog(p 130) Ap '70
Striated muscle fibers: inactivation of contraction induced by shortening. S. R. Taylor and R. Rüdel. bibliog il Science 167:882-4 F 6 '70
Z disc ultrastructure in scutal depressor fibers of the barnacle. R. A. Leyton and W. C. Ullrick. bibliog il Science 168:127-8 Ap 3 '70
See also
Heart—Muscle

Proteins
On the apparent homology of actin and tubulin. R. E. Stephens. bibliog il Science 168:845-7 My 15 '70
Postnatal muscle fiber assembly: localization of newly synthesized myofibrillar proteins. E. Morkin. bibliog il Science 167:1499-501 Mr 13 '70
See also
Actomyosin

MUSCLE fibers. See Muscle
MUSCLE power. See Muscle strength
MUSCLE strength
Be a take-charge blaster! H. Weiskopf. il por Sports Illus 32:34-6+ Ap 6 '70
MUSCLEBUILDING. See Muscle strength
MUSCLES
See also
Muscle strength

Diseases
Histochemical abnormalities of skeletal muscle in patients with acute psychoses. W. K. Engel and H. Meltzer. bibliog il Science 168:273-6 Ap 10 '70
See also
Dystrophy, Muscular

Wounds and injuries
What can you do about stiff, aching muscles? Bet Hom & Gard 48:32 Je '70

MUSCULAR dystrophy. See Dystrophy, Muscular
MUSCULAR sense
See also
Movement, Psychology of

MUSES dil oro. See Bogota, Columbia—Galleries and museums
MUSEUM; story. See Tomkins, C.
MUSEUM concerts
Echoes from the East garden court; concert series at the National gallery of art, Washington, D.C. R. Evett. New Repub 163:24-6 Ag 15 '70

MUSEUM education
See also
Childrens museums

MUSEUM loans. See Art loans
MUSEUM of contemporary crafts, New York
Automation house, fun and knowledge in a modern museum. il Sci Digest 67:22-3 Je '70
Designed for contemplation; exhibition. G. Zoghby. il Craft Horiz 30:12-19+ Mr '70
Hark, hark! The art at heaven's gate sings. il Esquire 73:140-5 My '70
Listening eye. A. McMillan. il Craft Horiz 30:14-19 Ja '70

MUSEUM of fine arts, Houston. See Houston museum of fine arts
MUSEUM of modern art, New York
Ars gratia artis? AWC protest at MOMA. il Newsweek 75:80 F 9 '70
Art; open letter sent by Art workers coalition to Picasso suggesting he remove Guernica from the museum. L. Alloway. Nation 210:221-2 F 23 '70
Art theft; movie from actual bank robberies. il Newsweek 76:87 S 7 '70
Frank Stella: perspectives. E. C. Baker. il por Art N 69:46-9+ My '70
Mr Processionary at the conceptacle; information show. D. Shapiro. il Art N 69:58-61 S '70

MUSEUM of natural history. See American museum of natural history, New York

MUSEUM of science and industry, Chicago
On the museum trail in Chicago. L. Barry. il Pop Phot 67:40+ D '70
MUSEUM of the Confederacy. See Richmond, Va.—Galleries and museums
MUSEUM of the media. See New York (city)—Galleries and museums
MUSEUM of wildflowers. See Museums
MUSEUM store association
Among the artifacts, museum bookstores thrive. Pub W 198:37-8 Ag 17 '70
MUSEUM stores
Museum finds. il McCalls 98:38 D '70
Seaport bookshop lures readers downtown in New York. il Pub W 198:29-30 N 23 '70
MUSEUM villages. See Villages, Restored
MUSEUM workers
Culturettes. R. Lynes. por Art in Am 58:21 Ja '70

MUSEUMS
Baker's dream needs dough; Helms hall, Los Angeles. J. Jares. il Sports Illus 33:18-21 S 7 '70
Hellmut-Kienzle clock and watch museum, Black Forest, Germany. O. R. Hagans. il Hobbies 75:125-7 S; 125-6 O; 125-7 N; 125-7+ D '70
Mexico's new shell museum. A. G. Melvin. il Hobbies 75:146-7 N; 158-9 D '70
Museum world. J. L. Stoughtenburgh. See issues of Hobbies
Museums for moderns. D. F. Cameron. il UNESCO Courier 23:22-6+ O '70
Museums: great places to buy offbeat gifts. il Changing T 24:13-15 N '70
Museums offer gifts by mail. Sunset 145:60 N '70
New state of the American museum. E. Kinard. House B 112:126-7+ Ap '70
Obscure museums; western European. D. Ardrey. Travel & Camera 33:18-20 N '70
Unusual clocks in the collection of Clyde N. Fahrney; photographic collection at Hagans clock manor museum, Bergen Park, Colo. O. R. Hagans. il Hobbies 74:126-7+ F '70 (to be cont)
Wildflower and history museum; Tiburon, Calif. il Sunset 144:52 Ap '70
See also
Agricultural museums
Art—Galleries and museums
Astronomical museums
Childrens museums
Historical museums
Railroad museums
also subhead Galleries and museums under names of cities, e.g. New York (city)—Galleries and museums; also names of museums, e.g. Henry Francis du Pont Winterthur museum

Architecture
Art machine for the 70's; Feigen gallery in Manhattan. J. S. Margolies. il Arch Forum 132:44-51+ Ja '70
Oakland museum; with introd. by M. F. Schmertz. il Arch Rec 147:115-22 Ap '70
Ontario's participatory museum; Ontario science center. il Arch Rec 148:103-8 Ag '70
Pinwheel museum; West Germany. il Arch Forum 132:60-3 Mr '70

Work with children
Museum designs exhibition for children; Worcester art museum Exploring art. J. Connor. il Sch Arts 69:28-9 Je '70

Belgium
See also
Bruges, Belgium—Galleries and museums

Japan
Report from Japan. P. Brooks. il Art in Am 58:122-4 Mr '70
MUSEUMS and Negroes
Museums and the ghetto. il Newsweek 76:93 Ag 17 '70
MUSEUMS and politics
Art world; dilemmas of a new season. H. Rosenberg. New Yorker 46:149-54 O 10 '70
MUSEUMS and social and economic problems
Art world; dilemmas of a new season. H. Rosenberg. New Yorker 46:149-54 O 10 '70
See also
Museums and Negroes
MUSEUMS and the socially handicapped
See also
Museums and Negroes
MUSGRAVE, Clifford
Firle Place, Sussex. il Antiques 97:260-6 F '70
MUSHAM, William C.
Why make monuments? il por Forbes 105:51-2 Mr 15 '70 *

MUSHROOMS

Mushroom culture. il Chem 43:26 F '70
Mushrooms. P. Young. il Natur Hist 79:66-71 Je '70
Mushrooms of the mountains. M. B. Mellinger. il Nat Parks & Con Mag 44:15-18 S '70
See also
Cookery—Mushrooms

MUSHROOMS in religion, folklore, etc.

Allegro troppo; views of J. M. Allegro. Newsweek 76:66 Ag 31 '70
Books; hypothetical identification of a drink called Soma with Amanita muscaria or fly agaric mushroom. W. Sargeant. New Yorker 46:90+ My 30 '70
Jesus as mushroom; views presented in Sacred mushroom and the cross. il Time 95:49 Je 8 '70
Sacred mushroom and the cross, by J. M. Allegro. Review
    Sat R 53:42-4 S 19 '70. R. Patai
Soma, by G. Wasson. Review
    Atlan il 225:109-13 F '70. R. Graves

MUSIC

Artist life. D. J. Soria. See issues of High fidelity section II
Does his music speak for our age? interview, ed. by R. Hemming. H. W. Henze. il por Sr Schol 96:15-17 My 4 '70
Here & there. See issues of High fidelity section II
Music; YM-YWHA gallery of new music. H. C. Schonberg. Harper 240:132+ My '70
Musical events; avant-garde music. W. Sargeant. New Yorker 46:156+ Mr 21 '70
Musical events; mysticism. W. Sergeant. New Yorker 45:119 F 14 '70
See also
Bands (music)
Chamber music
Chimes
Church music
Ensemble playing
Folk music
Instrumental music
Jazz music
Moving pictures—Musical films
Musical meter and rhythm
Negro music
Radio broadcasting—Music

Analysis, interpretation, etc.

Ebb and flow: fate of Aida's lovers. R. D. Daniels. il Opera N 35:30-1 D 19 '70
Final moments; expiring heroines in Rigoletto, Trovatore and Traviata. S. Gould. il Opera N 34:24-5 Mr 21 '70
Vocal ornamentation in Caccini's Nuove musiche. H. W. Hitchcock. bibliog f il Mus Q 56:389-404 Jl '70
See also
Conducting (music)
Virtuosity in music

Appreciation

Conductor as listener. H. Lewis. il por Hi Fi sec I 20:26 F '70
Leave the message for Western Union. G. Lees. il Hi Fi 20:secII 108 Jl '70
See also
Music—Philosophy and aesthetics

Bibliography

Book reviews. See issues of American record guide
Book reviews; ed. by P. J. Smith (cont) il Hi Fi 20:secII 29-30 My; 28-30 Jl; MA29-31 S: MA30-2 N '70
Quarterly book-list. J. Newsom. See issues of Musical quarterly

Competitions

Chopin with pow; International Chopin competition. il por Time 96:57 N 30 '70
Key victory; G. Ohlsson wins Chopin piano contest. il Newsweek 76:87 N 9 '70
Winners; High fidelity's electronic music contest. il Hi Fi 20:secI 48-51+ Jl '70

Dictionaries and encyclopedias

Harvard dictionary of music, by W. Apel. Review
    New Repub 162:22-4 Ja 31 '70. J. H. Baron

Historiography

Music in honor of St Thomas of Canterbury; with list of hymns. D. Stevens. bibliog f il Mus Q 56:311-48 Jl '70

History and criticism

Battle of Wagner. C. Matz. pors Opera N 34:6-7 Ja 31 '70
Early example of dramatic procedures in 18th-century keyboard music. B. Frum. il Mus Q 56:230-46 Ap '70

Music. W. F. Rickenbacker. Nat R 22:1120+ O 20 '70
On the off-beat. A. Rich. il Hi Fi sec II 20; 12+ F '70
Realism as preached and practiced: the Russian opera dialogue. R. Taruskin. bibliog f il Mus Q 56:431-54 Jl '70
Some Corelli attributions assessed; tr. by L. Wallach. H. J. Marx. bibliog f il Mus Q 56:88-98 Ja '70
See also
Music, Medieval
Opera—History and criticism

Instruction and study

Center for contemporary music; Mills college, Oakland, Calif. A. Earle. il Hi Fi 20:MA24-5 S '70
Discovery through rock; with discography. B. Scoppa. il Schol Teach Jr/Sr High p 14-15 O 5 '70
General music in the schools. A. J. Apicella and A. J. Giampa. Ed Digest 35:52-3 Ja '70
Two hundred French horns; French horn workshop, Tallahassee, Fla. H. Jenkins. il Hi Fi 20:MA20-1 S '70
See also
Guitar—Instruction and study
Music schools
Opera—Instruction and study
Piano—Instruction and study
School music

Jews

See also
Cantors, Jewish

Moving pictures

See Moving pictures—Music

Periodicals

See also
Opera news (periodical)
Perspectives of new music (periodical)

Philosophy and aesthetics

Early example of dramatic procedures in 18th-century keyboard music. B. Frum. il Mus Q 56:230-46 Ap '70

Psychology

See also
Music, Influence of

Study and teaching

See Music—Instruction and study

Argentina

See also
Buenos Aires—Music

Austria

See also
Salzburg—Music
Salzburg festival
Vienna—Music

Belgium

See also
Brussels—Music

England

Calendar for June events. il Travel & Camera 33:70-1 My '70

Europe

Europe on a musical scale; symposium. il Sat R 53:49-54+ Mr 14 '70

Finland

See also
Helsinki—Music

France

See also
Bordeaux—Music
Paris—Music

Germany (Democratic Republic)

See also
Berlin (East Berlin)—Music

Germany (Federal Republic)

See also
Berlin (West Berlin)—Music
Bonn—Music
Cologne, Germany—Music
Dortmund, Germany—Music
Frankfort on the Main—Music
Hamburg—Music
Hanover, Germany—Music
Kassel, Germany—Music
Mannheim, Germany—Music
Munich—Music
Nuremberg—Music
Stuttgart, Germany—Music
Wuppertal, Germany—Music

Great Britain

See also
Opera—Great Britain

MUSIC—*Continued*

Hawaii
See also
Honolulu—Music

Iran
Attitudes towards Persian music in Tehran, 1969. B. Nettl. bibliog f Mus Q 56:183-97 Ap '70

Israel
In Israel, it's everybody's thing. I. Perlman. Harp Baz 103:90+ O '70
See also
Israel philharmonic orchestra

Italy
See also
Opera—Italy
Parma, Italy—Music
Rome (city)—Music
Siena, Italy—Music
Trieste—Music

Japan
Chopsticks and Chopin; western music in Japan. R. W. Hall. il Opera N 34:8-12 Mr 7 '70
See also
Tokyo—Music

Korea (Republic)
See also
Opera—Korea (Republic)
Seoul, Korea—Music

Mexico
See also
Mexico (city)—Music

Middle East
See also
Music—Iran

Monaco
See also
Monte Carlo—Music

Netherlands
See also
Amsterdam, Netherlands—Music

Portugal
See also
Lisbon, Portugal—Music

Russia
Tchaikovsky's Russia: the lingering passion. S. Jacoby. il por Sat R 53:75-6+ Mr 14 '70
See also
Opera, Russian

South Africa
See also
Pretoria—Music

Spain
See also
Barcelona—Music

Sweden
See also
Stockholm—Music

United States
Current chronicle (cont) il Mus Q 56:116-24, 478-84 Ja, Jl '70
Emphasis. B. Diamonstein. Harp Baz 103: 184-5 Mr; 98-9+ Je; 103 O '70
Live and the canned. R. Evett. Atlan 225: 134+ Mr '70
Music; crisis of confidence in the future of serious music. D. Hamilton. Nation 210: 317-18 Mr 16 '70
Music is what's happening; recreation programs. M. Egbert. il Parks & Rec 5:22-4+ Je '70
See also
Jazz music
also subhead Music under names of cities, e.g. New York (city)—Music

MUSIC, American
See also
Folk songs, American
Jazz music
Music—United States
Negro music
Songs, American

MUSIC, Arabian
See also
Music, Moroccan

MUSIC, Baroque
Ornament and structure; excerpt from Baroque ornamentation in France, Italy and Germany. F. Neumann. bibliog f il Mus Q 56:153-61 Ap '70
Tradition and popular elements in Polish music of the baroque era. Z. M. Szweykowski. bibliog f il Mus Q 56:99-115 Ja '70

MUSIC, Church. See Church music

MUSIC, Czech
See also
Phonograph records—Czech music

MUSIC, Electronic
Debasement of new music. M. Powell. il por Hi Fi 20:MA14-15 S '70
Moog is more than a vogue; synthesizer. C. S. Wren. il por Look 34:24+ Ap 7 '70
Music since Hiroshima: the electronic age begins. H. Russcol. Am Scholar 39:289-93 Spr '70
Music to my ears; Gershon Kingsley's first moog quartet performs in Carnegie Hall. I. Kolodin. Sat R 53:58 F 14 '70
Musical events; Moogs at Carnegie Hall. W. Sargeant. New Yorker 45:80 F 7 '70
See also
Phonograph records—Electronic music

Competitions
See Music—Competitions

MUSIC, Hindu
See also
Shankar, R.

MUSIC, Incidental
See also
Phonograph records—Incidental music

MUSIC, Influence of
Rock, violence, and Spiro T. Agnew. G. Lees. il Hi Fi sec I 120:108+ F '70

MUSIC, Italian
See also
Composers, Italian

MUSIC, Medieval
Performance of the Old Hall descant settings. A. B. Scott. bibliog f il Mus Q 56:14-26 Ja '70

MUSIC, Modern. See Music

MUSIC, Moroccan
Music in the Jma al-Fna of Marrakesh. T. C. Grame. bibliog f il Mus Q 56:74-87 Ja '70

MUSIC, Negro. See Negro music

MUSIC, Polish
Tradition and popular elements in Polish music of the baroque era. Z. M. Szweykowski. bibliog f il Mus Q 56:99-115 Ja '70

MUSIC, Popular (songs, etc)
Coughing up Ludwig; A song of joy. H. Saal. Newsweek 75:85 Je 29 '70
Country cads; the Welfare cadilac controversy. pors Newsweek 75:84-6 Ap 13 '70
Fifties; singers at the Felt forum. New Yorker 46:37 Ap 4 '70
Happy sound in Mill Valey; a teacher and her third-grade chorus. il pors Life 69:50-2 S 25 '70
In the pop bag. D. Heckman and others. See issues of American record guide
Lingle jingle; lyrics of Van Lingle Mungo. Newsweek 76:86 S 7 '70
Modest proposal; responsibility of record industry. G. Lees. Hi Fi 20:secI 116 Je '70
Peggy Lee; interview, ed. by R. Hemming. P. Lee. por Sr Schol 97:19 O 5 '70
Pet teacher; Mill Valley. il por Newsweek 76: 86-7 Jl 20 '70
Pop music. R. Goldstein. See occasional issues of Vogue to May, 1970
Profiles; R. Charles. W. Balliett. por New Yorker 46:44-6+ Mr 28 '70
Profiles; B. Short. W. Balliett. New Yorker 46:28-35 D 26 '70
Simon & Garfunkel: the singers and the songs. E. Sander. pors Sat R 53:91+ F 28 '70
See also
Blues (songs, etc)
Phonograph records—Music, Popular (songs, etc)
Rock 'n' roll music (songs, etc)
Songs, American

Russia
Dean who? Dean Reed. S. Turner. il por Sr Schol 96:12+ Ap 6 '70

MUSIC, Portuguese
See also
Phonograph records—Portuguese music

MUSIC, Russian
See also
Songs, Russian

MUSIC, School. See School music

MUSIC, Scottish
See also
Folk songs, Scottish

MUSIC, Swiss
See also
Phonograph records—Swiss music

MUSIC academy of the West. See Music schools
MUSIC and art. See Art and music
MUSIC and children. See Children and music

MUSIC and color
See also
Color organ
MUSIC and libraries. See Libraries and music
MUSIC and literature
Baudelaire and music. E. Lockspeiser. Yale R 59:498-506 Je '70
MUSIC and moving pictures. See Moving pictures—Music
MUSIC and society
Belle epoque; between the 1880's and World war I. H. Peyre. il Opera N 35:8-13 D 12 '70
Rock, violence, and Spiro T. Agnew. G. Lees. il Hi Fi sec I 20:108+ F '70
Something is rotten in rock. E. Sander. Sat R 53:49 O 10 '70
MUSIC and state
Major musical precedent; totally subsidized by government. J. Gerstel. Hi Fi 20:secII 25 Ag '70
Then the music. J. C. Adams. il Opera N 34:25+ F 7 '70
MUSIC and war
Where were you the night of November 20, 1805? premiere of Fidelio. G. R. Marek. il Opera N 35:24-6 Ja 2 '71
MUSIC conductors. See Conductors (music)
MUSIC contests. See Music—Competitions
MUSIC critics
Critics and the public. R. Evett. Atlan 226: 117-18+ S '70; Discussion. 226:38-40 N '70
Critics criticized; excerpt from Critical affairs: a composer's journal. N. Rorem. Harper 241:90-2 Ag '70
On the firing line. A. Rich. por Opera N 35:8-11 Ja 9 '71
MUSIC festivals
Festivals around the world. il Newsweek 75: 94+ Je 1 '70
Travel, with Beethoven on the side; with guide to Festivities, 1970, comp. by H. D. Jellinek. I. Kolodin. Sat R 53:44-5 Ap 11 '70
See also
International society for contemporary music

Finance
Rock festivals: groovy, but no gravy; investors woes. il Bsns W p20-1 Ag 8 '70

Alabama
Our far-flung correspondents; fifth annual Mobile jazz festival. W. Balliett. New Yorker 46:114-18+ Ap 25 '70

Alaska
Alaska's fifteenth festival. J. D. Car. Hi Fi 20:MA26+ S '70

Austria
Report:
Bregenz festival Norma. G. Loney. il Opera N 35:24 O 10 '70
Rossini's Die Italienerin in Algier, and Beethoven's Fidelio. F. Merkling. il Opera N 35:24 S 5 '70
See also
Salzburg festival

California
Aquarius wept; after Woodstock and love came Altamont and disaster. R. J. Gleason. il Esquire 74:84-92+ Ag '70
Contempo '70; Boulez at Ojai. M. Bernheimer. il Hi Fi 20:secII 22-3 Ag '70
Debasement of new music. M. Powell. il por Hi Fi 20:MA14-15 S '70
Music to my ears; Concord festival, San Francisco. I. Kolodin. Sat R 53:42 S 5 '70

Colorado
Report:
Carlisle Floyd's Of mice and men at Central City. Q. Eaton. Opera N 35:27-8 S 19 '70
Contemporary music conference at Aspen. Q. Eaton. Opera N 35:27 S 19 '70

Connecticut
Festival of life dies at Powder Ridge; with report by W. Abruzzi, ed. by R. Stokes. il Life 69:34-7 Ag 14 '70
Peace and pot on Powder Ridge. il Time 96: 11 Ag 10 '70
Who killed Woodstock? Powder Ridge rock festival. il Newsweek 76:19 Ag 10 '70

Denmark
Report:
Productions at Copenhagen festival. J. H. Sutcliffe. il Opera N 35:24-5 S 19 '70

England
Britten and the borough: on the winds of the North Sea; Adelburgh festival. T. Heinitz. il Sat R 53:80+ Mr 14 '70
Cavalli's Calisto; Bennett's Victory. il Hi Fi 20:secII 26-7 Ag '70
Festivals at Aldeburgh, London, Glyndebourne. E. Greenfield. Hi Fi 20:MA27+ O '70
Phoenix at Snape, festival of Britten; Aldeburgh festival. T. Heinitz. Sat R 53:55 Jl 25 '70
Report:
Britten's Rape of Lucretia at Aldeburgh festival. R. A. Tuggle. Opera N 35:22 S 19 '70
Francesco Cavalli's Calisto at Glyndebourne. F. G. Barker. il Opera N 35:22-3 S 19 '70

Europe
Guide to European music festivals, 1970; comp. by H. D. Jellinek. Sat R 53:83-4 Mr 14 '70

Europe, Western
Summer evenings (cont) Opera N 34:33-4 Ap 4 '70

France
Report:
Rossini's Italiana in Algeri at Aix-en-Provence festival. M. E. Davies. Opera N 35:31 O 31 '70

Germany (Federal Republic)
Opera festival; Munich's annual summer fest. G. Loney. il Hi Fi 20:MA28-9 O '70
Report:
Celebration of Göttingen Handel festival. J. H. Sutcliffe. il Opera N 35:30-1 O 31 '70
See also
Bayreuth festival

Illinois
See also
Ravinia festival

Iowa
When a rock festival moved in on an Iowa town. il U S News 69:46-8 Ag 31 '70

Italy
Maggio musicale & Spoleto: both work. W. Weaver. il Hi Fi 20:MA30-1 O '70
Report:
Maggio musicale. W. Weaver. Opera N 35:25-6 S 5 '70
Productions at Barga opera festival. L. W. Frey. Opera N 35:26-7 O 10 '70

Kentucky
Pickin' and singin'; Bluegrass festival. il por Newsweek 75:85 Je 29 '70

Latin America
Summer evenings (cont) Opera N 34:33 Ap 4 '70

Netherlands
Current chronicle; Holland festival. E. Schwartz. Mus Q 56:119-24 Ja '70
Report:
Haydn's La fedelta premiata. J. Mindszenthy. il Opera N 35:28 S 5 '70

New York (state)
Caramoor festival: twenty-fifth anniversary on weekends from mid-June to mid-July. New Yorker 46:23-4 Jl 4 '70
Caramoor: Idomeneo and a U.S. premiere: Malcolm Williamson's The growing castle. G. Movshon. il Hi Fi 20:MA18-19 S '70
Mostly Mozart means merry musicmaking; August festival at Philharmonic Hall. H. W. Simon. il Hi Fi 20:MA10-11 N '70
Report:
Katonah, N. Y, productions of Mozart's Idomeneo and Malcolm Williamson's Growing castle. J. W. Freeman. il Opera N 35:22 S 5 '70
Rock festival's instant city; Woodstock festival. il Sr Schol 95:26+ S 22 '69
Three festivals: Pop festival on Randall's Island, Little Richard and his band, Staten Island's Open air jazz-o-rama. New Yorker 46:22-3 Ag 1 '70
Why there can't be another Woodstock. T. Barry. Look 34:28+ Ag 25 '70
Woodstock and beyond, why? E. Kiester, jr. il Todays Health 48:20-5+ Jl '70

Puerto Rico
1970 festival Casals, Puerto Rico. I. Kolodin. Sat R 53:45 Ap 11 '70

MUSIC festivals—*Continued*

Rhode Island

In great mansions: a romantic revival; Newport. S. Fleming. il Hi Fi 20:MA20-1 O '70
Musical events; Newport notes. W. Balliett. New Yorker 46:66-9 Jl 25 '70
Report:
Productions at Newport festival. A. M. Lingg. il Opera N 35:28-9 S 19 '70

Texas

Report:
Aida and Don Giovanni. J. Ardoin. Opera N 34:24 Je 13 '70
San Antonio grand opera festival. O. Chism. Opera N 34:24 Je 13 '70
San Antonio grand opera festival 1945-70. Opera N 34:17 Ap 11 '70

United States

Music festivals USA, summer 1970; comp. by H. D. Jellinek. Sat R 53:46-8 Je 13 '70
Summer evenings (cont) Opera N 34:33 Ap 4 '70
Summer music festivals '70 (title varies) Hi Fi 20:secII 9-12 Mr; 22-4 Ap '70
U.S. calendar. See issues of Opera news published during opera season
Who killed Woodstock? summer rock festivals on the rocks. il Newsweek 76:19-21 Ag 10 '70

Vermont

Current chronicle: Burdock festival. J. Appleton. Mus Q 56:116-19 Ja '70

MUSIC for children
See also
Phonograph records—Childrens records
MUSIC halls (variety theaters, etc)
Old-fashioned insouciance; Casino de Paris. il por Time 96:62 Jl 13 '70
See also
Discotheques, etc.
MUSIC in schools. See School music
MUSIC in the home
Enclave; music in school, at home and around town in Whittier, Calif. M. F. K. Fisher. New Yorker 46:35-9 O 3 '70
See also
Music rooms and equipment
MUSIC patronage
See also
Opera patronage
MUSIC pavilions
Soil studies help create music; pavilion near Cuyahoga Falls, Ohio. il Am City 85:64 My '70
See also
Orchestra shells
MUSIC printing
Jacques Moderne, by S. F. Pogue. Review Mus Q 56:485-8 Jl '70. L. L. Perkins
MUSIC publishing
See also
Schirmer, G. inc.

Finance

New means for new music; Ford foundation aid project. R. Jacobson. il Sat R 53:65-6+ Ja 31 '70

History

Printed editions of Andre Campra's L'Europe *galante*. J. R. Anthony. bibliog f il Mus Q 56:54-73 Ja '70
MUSIC rooms and equipment
How two musicians live with music. il por House & Gard 138:56-9 Jl '70
MUSIC schools
Summer campus on the S.S. Carina; music study-cruise. S. Willetts. il Hi Fi sec II 20:10-11 F '70
Twenty years by the sea; the Music academy of the West. N. Melnick. il Opera N 34:8-12 F 7 '70
See also
Manhattan school of music
North Carolina school of the arts, Winston-Salem
MUSIC shells. See Orchestra shells
MUSIC study-cruise. See Music schools
MUSIC subsidies. See Music and state
MUSIC teachers
See also
Lhevinne, R.
Singing teachers
MUSIC workshops. See Music—Instruction and study
MUSIC writing. See Composition (music)
MUSICAL comedies, revues, etc.
See also
Musical comedy, revue, etc.
Phonograph records—Musical comedies, revues, etc.

Criticisms, plots, etc.

Akokawe
New Yorker 46:90 Je 13 '70
Applause
Dance Mag il 44:84-5 Je '70
Life il 68:54A-54D Ap 3 '70
Nation 210:473-4+ Ap 20 '70
New Repub 162:20+ My 23 '70
New Yorker 46:81 Ap 11 '70
Newsweek il 75:83 Ap 13 '70
Sat R 53:26 Ap 18 '70
Time il 95:97 Ap 13 '70
Billy Noname
Dance Mag 44:89-91 My '70
New Yorker 46:122 Mr 14 '70
Blood red roses
New Yorker 46:82+ Mr 28 '70
Boy friend
America 122:509-10 My 9 '70
Dance Mag 44:84 Je '70
Nation 210:574 My 11 '70
New Yorker 46:95 Ap 25 '70
Newsweek il 75:64 Ap 27 '70
Time 95:59 Ap 27 '70
Coco
America 122:54-5 Ja 17 '70
Commonweal 91:558-9 F 20 '70
Dance Mag 44:84-5 Mr '70
Dance Mag il 44:72-8 F '70
Life il 68:12 Ja 30 '70
Nat R 22:370-1 Ap 7 '70
Nation 210:61 Ja 19 '70
Company
America 122:568 My 23 '70
Dance Mag il 44:85-6+ Je '70
Life 68:20 Je 26 '70
Nat R 22:905-6 Ag 25 '70
Nation 210:572-3 My 11 '70
New Repub 162:20 My 23 '70
New Yorker 46:83 My 2 '70
Newsweek il 75:79 My 11 '70
Sat R 53:4-5 My 9 '70
Time il 95:62 My 11 '70
Cry for us all
New Yorker 46:79-80 Ap 18 '70
Time 95:51 Ap 20 '70
Don't bother me, I can't cope
New Yorker 46:144 O 17 '70
Drunkard
New Yorker 46:97 Ap 25 '70
Gantry
New Yorker 46:62+ F 21 '70
Sat R 53:61 F 28 '70
Georgy!
New Yorker 46:83 Mr 7 '70
Golden bat
Commonweal 93:278 D 11 '70
Dance Mag 44:81 N '70
Nation 211:285 S 28 '70
New Yorker 46:59 Ag 1 '70
Newsweek il 76:77 Ag 31 '70
Sat R 53:53 S 19 '70
Time 96:68-9 Ag 3 '70
Hair
Ebony il 25:120-2+ My '70
Life il 68:83-6 Ap 17 '70
Nat R 22:319 Mr 24 '70
House of leather
New Yorker 46:86+ Mr 28 '70
I dreamt I dwelt in Bloomingdale's
New Yorker 46:67 F 21 '70
Joy
Newsweek il 75:95 F 9 '70
Time il 95:63 Mr 30 '70
Last sweet days of Isaac
Nation 210:284 Mr 9 '70
New Yorker 45:73-4+ F 7 '70
Newsweek 75:95 F 9 '70
Look to the lilies
New Yorker 46:61-2 Ap 4 '70
Time 95:98 Ap 13 '70
Love and maple syrup
New Yorker 45:52 Ja 17 '70
Many happy returns
Life il 69:14 Jl 31 '70
The me nobody knows
America 122:638 Je 13 '70
Dance Mag 44:80 S '70
Life il 69:34-42 S 4 '70
Nation 210:701 Je 8 '70
New Repub 162:312 Je 13 '70
New Yorker 46:70+ My 30 '70
Newsweek il 75:104 Je 1 '70
Minnie's boys
Commonweal 92:222 My 15 '70
Dance Mag 44:84 Je '70
New Yorker 46:61 Ap 4 '70
Newsweek il 75:98-9 Ap 6 '70
Sat R 53:20 Ap 11 '70
Time il 95:98+ Ap 13 '70
Mod Donna
Harp Baz 103:6+ Jl '70
New Yorker 46:107 My 16 '70
Newsweek il 75:121 My 18 '70
Time il 95:62 My 25 '70

MUSICAL comedies, revues, etc.—Criticisms, plots, etc.—*Continued*
ODODO
  New Yorker 46:162 D 5 '70
Purlie
  America 122:510 My 9 '70
  Dance Mag 44:89-90 My '70
  Life il 68:18 Ap 24 '70
  Nation 210:414 Ap 6 '70
  New Yorker 46:81 Mr 28 '70
  Newsweek il 75:84 Mr 30 '70
  Time il 95:77 Mr 30 '70
Rothschilds
  Dance Mag 45:77-8 Ja '71
  Nation 211:506 N 16 '70
  New Yorker 46:101 O 31 '70
  Newsweek il 76:104 N 2 '70
  Sat R 53:6+ N 28 '70
  Time 96:77 N 2 '70
Salvation
  Commonweal 91:534-5 F 13 '70
Sensations
  New Yorker 46:135 N 7 '70
1776
  Read Digest il 96:199-200+ F '70
Show me where the good times are
  America 122:398 Ap 11 '70
  New Yorker 46:122 Mr 14 '70
So proudly we hail
  Time il 96:83 N 2 '70
Sound of music
  America 123:104 Ag 22 '70
Stomp
  Commonweal 91:534-5 F 13 '70
  Dance Mag 44:93 F '70
Touch
  Nation 211:542 N 23 '70
  New Yorker 46:132 D 12 '70
Two by two
  New Yorker 46:103 N 21 '70
  Newsweek il 76:137 N 23 '70
  Sat R 53:12 N 28 '70
  Time il 96:100 N 23 '70
Unfair to Goliath
  America 122:228 F 28 '70
  New Yorker 45:76 F 7 '70
Whispers on the wind
  New Yorker 46:90+ Je 13 '70
MUSICAL comedy production. See Theatrical production and direction
MUSICAL comedy, revue, etc.
  Broadway musical: getting away with murder. H. C. Schonberg. Harp 241:106+ Jl '70
  Goings on about town. See issues of New Yorker
  Is Broadway singing it like it is? S. Green. Sat R 53:36+ Ag 29 '70
  Musicals wanted and wanting. H. Hewes. Sat R 53:61 F 28 '70
  Theater. S. Kauffmann. New Repub 162:20+ My 23 '70
MUSICAL composition. See Composition (music)
MUSICAL education
  Ignoring rock won't make it go away; Youth music institute at University of Wisconsin. E. R. Sarig. Ed Digest 35:34-7 Mr '70
    See also
  Children and music
  Music—Appreciation
  Music—Instruction and study
  School music
MUSICAL festivals. See Music festivals
MUSICAL films. See Moving pictures—Musical films
MUSICAL forgeries and mystifications
  Opus posthumous; ghosts of famous composers and Rosemary Brown. il por Newsweek 77:90 Ja 11 '71
  Rosemary's babies; recording of R. Brown. I. Kolodin. por Sat R 53:53 O 31 '70
  Voices of silence. il por Time 96:68 Jl 6 '70
MUSICAL glasses
  Musical glasses. il por Newsweek 76:58 D 28 '70
MUSICAL historiography. See Music—Historiography
MUSICAL instruments
  Wire music. N. A. Steiner. il Pop Electr 33: 35+ Jl '70
    See also
  Musical glasses
  Stringed instruments
    also names of musical instruments, e.g. Flute
MUSICAL instruments, Electric
  Solid-body electric guitar. L. Hutchinson. il Sr Schol 97:38-9 N 16 '70
MUSICAL instruments, Electronic
  Adventures with a musical erector set; the Putney synthesizer. I. Berger. il por Sat R 53:40-1 D 26 '70
  Build digisyntone-new music synthesizer. F. Maynard. il Radio-Electr 41:47-51 S '70

Build this electronic banjo. R. L. Clough, jr. il Pop Mech 134:175-7+ O '70
Touch-a-tone. C. D. Rakes. il Pop Electr 32:66-72+ Mr '70

Equipment
Build IC guitar reverb. J. Jaques. il Radio-Electr 41:44-5 F '70
Modify your electronic guitar sound; delay unit. J. S. Simonton, jr. il Pop Electr 32: 53+ Je '70
Multi-tone; guitarist's tone control. I. A. Ashdown. il Electr World 85:68-9 Ja '71
Thumpa-thumpa box. J. S. Simonton, jr. il Pop Electr 32:53-7 F '70
MUSICAL landmarks
  Europe on a musical scale; symposium. il Sat R 53:49-54+ Mr 14 '70
MUSICAL meter and rhythm
  Some rhythmic and metric techniques in Alban Berg's Lulu. D. Jarman. bibliog f il Mus Q 56:349-66 Jl '70
MUSICAL pitch
  How to tune in on RPMs. P. E. Fiechter and R. J. De Cristoforo. il Pop Sci 196: 104-5 F '70
MUSICAL preferences
  I love it, I love it not. D. R. Hoogenstyn, jr. il Hi Fi 20:secI 60-2 Je '70
MUSICAL research. See Musicology
MUSICAL societies
    See also
  Metropolitan opera club
MUSICAL taste. See Music—Appreciation
MUSICIANS
  Artist life. D. J. Soria. See issues of High fidelity section II
  Debuts & reappearances; New York concerts. See issues of High fidelity section II
  Face behind the performer. G. Lees. il Hi Fi 20:secI 108 Ag '70
  Here & there. See issues of High fidelity section II
  Musical whirl; photographs. See issues of High fidelity and Musical America section II
  Winners; High fidelity's electronic music contest. il Hi Fi 20:secI 48-51+ Jl '70
  Young artists, 1970; photographs. Hi Fi 20: secII 10-13 Jl '70
    See also
  Conductors (music)
  Negro musicians
  Street musicians
  Strikes—United States—Musicians
  Women as musicians

Bibliography
Book reviews. See issues of American record guide
Salaries, allowances, etc.
Symphonic strike season. P. Hart. il Sat R 53:47-9+ S 26 '70; Discussion. 53:60-1 O 31 '70
MUSICIANS, Amateur
  Greedy amateur. C. Contos. il Hi Fi sec II 20:13-15 F '70
MUSICIANS, American
    See also
  Cliburn, V.
  Ellington, D.
  Negro musicians
MUSICIANS, Finnish
    See also
  Kamu, O.
MUSICIANS, French
    See also
  Berlioz, H.
MUSICIANS, Israeli
    See also
  Perlman, '
MUSICIANS, Polish
    See also
  Paderewski, I. J.
MUSICIANS, Rumanian
    See also
  Lipatti, D.
MUSICIANS, Russian
    See also
  Piatigorsky, G.
  Shostakovich, D. D.
MUSICIANS, Spanish
    See also
  Casals, P.
MUSICIANS autographs. See Autographs
MUSICOLOGY
  Italy's ottocento: notes from the musical underground. B. Friedland. bibliog f il Mus Q 56:27-53 Ja '70
    See also
  Music—Historiography
MUSK oxen
  Domesticating the wild and woolly musk ox. J. J. Teal, jr. il Nat Geog 137:862-79 Je '70
  Prolific musk ox. il Cons 25:39 D '70

MUSKAT, Irving
How tough can a plastic get? il por Bsns W
p48 Ap 11 '70 *
MUSKELLUNGE fishing
I'll tell you about muskies. B. Hoeft. il por
Outdoor Life 146:58-9+ Ag '70
MUSKIE, Edmund Sixtus
Environment: a national mission for the
seventies. pors Fortune 81:93 F '70
Excerpts from addresses, December 1969, and
February 3, 1970. Cong Digest 49:209+ Ag
'70
Fresh water: a diminishing supply. il Cur
Hist 58:329+ Je '70
From pollution abatement to quality control.
Cur 117:10-13 Ap '70
Importance of being Muskie; interview, ed.
by H. Gorey. por Time 96:9 N 30 '70
Muskie's timetable: out of Indochina in
eighteen months. il N Y Times Mag p8-13
Jl 5 '70
No clear-cut mandate: it's a mixed bag;
interview. por U S News 69:32-4 N 16 '70
Our polluted America: what women can do.
por Ladies Home J 87:59+ F '70

about

Agonies of a front runner. D. Nevin. il pors
McCalls 97:82-5 My '70 *
Air pollution: Muskie throws down the gaunt-
let. L. J. Carter. Science 169:841 Ag 28 '70 *
As Muskie opens fire on Agnew... pors U S
News 69:33 S 28 '70 *
Democratic unity. New Repub 163:8-9 N 21
'70 *
Ed Muskie, and the pack. il por Newsweek
76:33-5+ N 16 '70 *
Front runner. Nation 211:579-80 D 7 '70 *
Is Muskie the one? New Repub 163:5-6 D
12 '70 *
Job facing Muskie. R. M. Scammon. News-
week 76:35 N 16 '70 *
Muskie hits the trail. il por Time 97:13
Ja 18 '71 *
Muskie running. K. Crawford. Newsweek 76:
25 D 7 '70 *
Muskie's mission. il por Newsweek 76:27-8 O
5 '70 *
Muskie's peace plan. New Repub 163:5-6 Jl
25 '70 *
Old doc Muskie. S. Alsop. Newsweek 76:108 D
21 '70 *
Pro: he's a nice guy. S. Sheehan. il pors N Y
Times Mag p28-9+ N 22 '70 *
Rebuttal. por Newsweek 75:18 F 2 '70 *
TRB from Washington. New Repub 163:6 N
14 '70 *
TRB from Washington: Lindsay and Muskie.
New Repub 162:4 Je 13 '70 *
TRB from Washington: quality of Muskie.
New Repub 163:4 N 21 '70 *
Will the real Ed Muskie please shut up?
Nat R 22:240+ Mr 10 '70 *
MUSKIE fishing. See Muskellunge fishing
MUSKMELONS. See Melons
MUSKOXEN. See Musk oxen
MUSKRAT, Joseph C.
Landless in Alaska. il Bul Atom Sci 26:12-16
Mr '70
MUSLIMS
See also
Islam
MUSLIMS (Negro cult) See Black Muslims
MUSLIMS, Black. See Black Muslims
MUSLIMS in India
See also
India—Hindu-Muslim relations
MUSLIMS in the Philippines
See also
Moros
MUSSELMAN, Merle McNeil
In search of sanity: man in the middle; in-
terview, ed. by M. Michaelson. il por To-
days Health 48:31-3+ F '70
MUSSELS
See also
Cookery—Shellfish
MUSSOLINI, Benito
After twenty-five years: memory of two
dictators. il pors Time 95:54 My 4 '70 *
Fascist modernization in Italy: traditional or
revolutionary? R. Sarti. bibliog f Am Hist
R 75:1029-45 Ap '70 *
MUSTARD, Prepared
See also
Cookery—Mustard
MUTAGENIC substances
Toxicity and mutagens. Sci N 97:314-15 Mr
28 '70
See also
Caffeine
Monosodium glutamate
Trimethylphosphate

MUTATION (biology)
Diploid azaguanine-resistant mutants of
cultured human fibroblasts. R. J. Albertini
and R. DeMars. bibliog il Science 169:482-
5 Jl 31 '70
Evolution by pollution. il Time 96:54+ O 5 '70
Genetic load. C. Wills. il Sci Am 222:98-107
bibliog(p 146) Mr '70
Mosaic mutants: absence in a eucaryotic organism. A. Fjeld. bibliog il Science 168:843-
4 My 15 '70
Non-Darwinian evolution. J. L. King and
T. H. Jukes; reply. B. Clarke. Science 168:
1009-11 My 22 '70
Temperature-sensitive mutations in drosophila
melanogaster; adaptation of address, August 1969. D. T. Suzuki. bibliog il Science
170:695-706 N 13 '70
Tryptophan operon: structural gene mutation
creating a ":promoter" and leading to 5-
methyltryptophan dependence. R. Callahan,
3d. and E. Balbinder. bibliog il Science 168:
1586-9 Je 26 '70
MUTATION (botany)
Mutation in internode length affects wheat
plant-type. C. O. Qualset and others. bibliog il Science 169:1090-1 S 11 '70
Phenotypic reversion of flacca, a wilty mutant of tomato, by abscisic acid. D. Imber
and M. Tal. bibliog il Science 169:592-3 Ag
7 '70
MUTATION (fungi)
L-Asparaginase-deficient mutants of yeast. G.
E. Jones and R. K. Mortimer. bibliog il
Science 167:181-2 Ja 9 '70
MUTATOR genes. See Genes
MUTCHLER, Calvin K. and Hansen, L. M.
Splash of a waterdrop at terminal velocity.
bibliog il Science 169:1311-12 S 25 '70
**MUTED language. See Communication, Non-
verbal**
MUTINY
Unlawful concert: an account of the Presidio
mutiny case, by F. Gardner. Review
Nation 210:628-30 My 25 '70. E. F. Sher-
man
MUTT, Viktor. See Said, S. I. jt. auth.
**MUTUAL aid pact, Airline. See Strikes—United
States—Airlines**
**MUTUAL assistance, Pacts of. See Interna-
tional security**
MUUL, Illar
Mammalian ecology and epidemiology of
zoonoses. bibliog Science 170:1275-9 D 18
'70
—**and Liat, L. B.**
Vertical zonation in a tropical rain forest in
Malaysia: method of study. bibliog il Sci-
ence 169:788-9 Ag 21 '70
**MY grandpa's lump of five wasted years; story.
See Burgess, W. V.**
**MY hearts in the highlands; opera. See Bee-
son, J.**
**MY LAI massacre. See Vietnamese war, 1957- —
Atrocities—My Lai massacre**
MY son, the prince; drama. See Olfson, L.
MYATT, Barbara
Course descriptions in library science: a report
on a survey. Am Lib 1:865-7 O '70
MYCOBACTERIUM
Tumor immunity produced by the intradermal
inoculation of living tumor cells and living
mycobacterium bovis (strain BCG) B. Zbar
and others. bibliog il Science 170:1217-18 D
11 '70
MYCOLOGY
How good are you as a mycologist? quiz. J.
Daugherty and M. Daugherty. il Sci Digest
67:68-9+ My '70
MYCOPLASMA
Calorimetric detection of a membrane-lipid
phase transition in living cells. J. C. Reinert
and J. M. Steim. bibliog il Science 168:1580-2
Je 26 '70
Control of acute mycoplasmal and viral respiratory tract disease. R. M. Chanock. bibliog il Science 169:248-56 Jl 17 '70
Plant-pathogenic mycoplasma like organism:
maintenance in vitro and transmission to
zea may L; corn stunt. T. A. Chen and
R. R. Granados. bibliog il Science 167:1633-
6 Mr 20 '70
Thermophilic, acidophilic mycoplasma isolated
from a coal refuse pile. G. Darland and
others. bibliog il Science 170:1416-18 D 25 '70
Vaccine for a pneumonia. Sci N 98:317-18 O
17 '70
MYELOPEROXIDASE. See Peroxidases
MYER, Maree
Song of freedom; poem. Negro Hist Bul 33:
147 O '70
MYER, Violet
Screenings: 16mm. il Library J 95:224-6 Ja 15
'70

MYERS, Audrey, and Jones, Esther
Why write confessions? Writer 83:14-17 Je '70
MYERS, David G. and Bishop, G. D.
Discussion effects on racial attitudes. bibliog il Science 169:778-9 Ag 21 '70
MYERS, Franklin G.
Plan for all seasons: independent study in an English electives program. Engl J 59: 244-6+ F '70
MYERS, Gloria J.
3-D ink designs. il Design 72:36-8 Fall '70
MYERS, John Bernard
Exercises in taste. il Craft Horiz 30:50-3 My; 7 Ag '70
Puppets of Kurt Seligmann: an homage. il Craft Horiz 30:32-5+ D '70
MYERS, John J.
Sanity from the sea? il America 123:318-19 O 24 '70
MYERS, Odell
No...the bitter is sweet; poem. Chr Cent 88:12 Ja 6 '71
MYERS, R. D. and Veale, W. L.
Body temperature: possible ionic mechanism in the hypothalamus controlling the set point. bibliog il Science 170:95-7 O 2 '70
MYERS, Robert J.
Runaway expansion of social security? interview. pors Nations Bsns 58:60-3 Mr '70
Social security at the crossroads. Read Digest 96:81-5 Ap '70

about

Medicare kills off its cost predictor. il por Bsns W p27 Je 6 '70 *
MYERS, Sumner, and Schwartz, Robert
New towns are our mandate for urban innovations. il Arch Forum 132:38-41 Je '70
MYLAI massacre. See Vietnamese war, 1957––Atrocities––My Lai massacre
MYLONAS, George
Democrat; interview. New Yorker 46:35-7 Ap '70
MYOFIBRILS. See Muscle
MYOMECTOMY. See Uterus––Surgery
MYOPATHIES. See Muscles––Diseases
MYRDAL, Gunnar. See Myrdal, K. G.
MYRDAL, Jan
New look into Mao's China. il Look 34:19-26 F 10 '70
MYRDAL, Karl Gunnar
Professor Gunnar Myrdal returns to the South; interview. ed. by K. Prager. por Time 96:12 N 23 '70
MYRES, John W.
Schools in a spa. Clear House 45:186-8 N '70
MYRTLE, Crape. See Crape myrtle
MYSLENSKI, Skip
College football. Sports Illus 33:70-1 N 30 '70
Cross-country (cont) Sports Illus 33:73-4 D 7 '70
Monkey rides the easy runner. il pors Sports Illus 32:30-1+ Mr 2 '70
Revenge can be sour. il pors Sports Illus 32: 22-5 My '25 '70
MYSORE
Mysore: images of South India. G. Trotta. Harp Baz 104:112-13 Ja '71
MYSTERIOUS case of R; story. See Conroy, F.
MYSTERY
Behold I show you a mystery; excerpt from The coming faith. C. Marney. Chr Cent 87:196 F 18 '70
MYSTERY stories. See Detective and mystery stories
MYSTERY writers of America, inc.
Mystery writers of America awards announced. Pub W 197:23-4 My 11 '70
MYSTIC seaport museum, Mystic, Conn.
Tall ships of Mystic. P. Benchley. il Travel & Camera 33:26-31 Jl '70
MYSTICISM
Musical events. W. Sargeant. New Yorker 45:119 F 14 '70
Thinking with your blood. H. Bowser. Sat R 53:26 S 19 '70
Visions of a new religion. M. Cavell. il Sat R 53:12-14+ D 19 '70
MYSTROMYS
Meet the mystromys albicaudatus. il Sci Digest 68:65-6 Jl '70
MYTHICAL animals. See Animals, Mythical
MYTHOLOGY
Claude Levi-Strauss, by E. Leach. Review Nation 211:692-4 D 28 '70. B. Bendow
Myths, meaning and Vatican III. A. M. Greeley. America 123:538-42 D 19 '70; Reply. W. L. Dolan. 124:29 Ja 16 '71
Revival of ritual on campus. J. W. Goetz. il Cath World 212:24-8+ O '70

MYTHOLOGY, Assyro-Babylonian
See also
Gilgamesh
MYTHOLOGY in art
Daedalus and I; sculpted recreation of labyrinth. M. Ayrton. il por Horizon 12:56-65 Spr '70
Mary Holmes paints the figure. P. Thompson. il por Am Artist 34:86-93 Mr '70
MYTHOLOGY in sculpture. See Mythology in art
MYTHS. See Mythology
MYXOMYCETES. See Slime molds

N

N-radiography. See Radiography
NAACP. See National association for the advancement of colored people
NAB. See National alliance of businessmen; National association of broadcasters
NACS. See National association of college stores
NADA. See National automobile dealers association
NAE. See National academy of engineering
NAEP. See National assessment of educational progress
NAIA. See National association of intercollegiate athletics
NALC. See National association of letter carriers
NAMH. See National association for mental health, inc.
NAPCA. See United States––National air pollution control administration
NAPTC. See United States––Naval air propulsion test center
NARCE. See National association of retired civil employees
NARP. See National association of railroad passengers
NAS. See National academy of sciences
NASA. See United States––National aeronautics and space administration
NASCAR (National association for stock car auto racing) See Automobile racing
NATO. See National association of theater owners; Nato
NBA. See National basketball association; National book awards
NBC. See National broadcasting company
NBER. See National bureau of economic research
NBS. See United States––Standards, National bureau of
NCAA. See National collegiate athletic association
NCC. See National council of churches
NCCB. See National citizens committee for broadcasting; National conference of Catholic bishops
NCCIJ. See National Catholic conference for interracial justice
NCCJ. See National conference of Christians and Jews
NCEA. See National Catholic educational association
NCOA. See National council on the aging
NCR. See National cash register company
NCSC. See National council of senior citizens, inc.
NCTE. See National council of teachers of English
NDT (nondestructive testing) See Testing
NEA. See National education association; National electronic associations
NEA (National endowment for the arts) See United States––National foundation on the arts and the humanities
NEED (national environmental education development) program. See United States––National park service
NEGRO. See National economic growth and reconstruction organzation
NEMO (naval experimental manned observatory) See Underwater laboratories
NESA (national environmental study area) program. See United States––National park service
NET. See National educational television network
NFL. See National football league
NFO. See National farmers organization
NFPC See National federation of priests councils

NHRA springnationals. See Automobile racing
NHRA summernationals. See Automobile racing
NHRA winternationals. See Automobile racing
NIMH. See United States—National institute of mental health
NIRI. See National investor relations institute
NLF. See National liberation front (Vietnam)
NLM. See United States—National library of medicine
NLRB. See United States—National labor relations board
NLT corporation
Rebel money bags. il Forbes 105:32-3 Ja 15 '70
NLW. See National library week
NOAA. See United States—National oceanic and atmospheric administration
NPA. See National pilots association; National planning association
NPCA. See National parks and conservation association
NPPC. See National pork producers council
NRPA. See National recreation and park association
NRTA. See National retired teachers association
NSF. See United States—National science foundation
NSMC. See National student marketing corporation
NTA. See Nitrilotriacetic acid
NTIS. See United States—Commerce, Department of—National technical information service
NWRO. See National welfare rights organization
NYLA. See New York library association
NYPL. See New York public library
NYSE (New York stock exchange) See Stock exchange—New York (city)
NYU. See New York university
NAB, Herb
Lee Roy's secret weapon. B. Kilpatrick. il pors Pop Mech 133:86-8+ F '70 *
NABB, Edward H.
Cruise back in time. il Motor B 126:50-3 Jl '70
High performance propellers. il Yachting 128: 64-5+ O; 68-9+ N '70
Marine engines. See issues of Motor boating
Salmon fishing in Scotland. il Motor B 125: 136-8 Je '70
NABOKOV, Peter
Caribbean: this side of paradise. Nation 210: 322-5 Mr 23 '70
Our most silent minority. Nation 210:86-8 Ja 26 '70
La raza, the land and the hippies. il Nation 210:464-8 Ap 20 '70
NABOKOV, Vladimir
(tr) How I love you; poem. New Yorker 46:44 My 23 '70
            about
Memory's defense: the real life of Vladimir Nabokov's Berlin. R. C. Williams. Yale R 60:241-50 D '70
Profit without honor. il por Time 96:42 D 21 '70
Tale of a tub for our time. A. Alvarez. Sat R 53:27-9+ Je 13 '70 *
NACE, Raymond L.
Man's perpetual quest for water. il UNESCO Courier 23:4-8+ Je '70
NACHATANK RIVER. See Anacostia River
NACHMAN, Larry David
Movement seeks a mass. il Nation 212:39-45 Ja 11 '71
Political meaning of Chicago. il Nation 210: 326-9 Mr 23 '70
NACHMAN, Marvin, and others
Alcohol aversion in the rat: behavioral assessment of noxious drug effects. bibliog il Science 168:1244-6 Je 5 '70
NACHMANSOHN, David
Proteins in excitable membranes. bibliog il Science 168:1059-66; 170:1229, 1333 My 29, D 11-18 '70
NACHMIAS, V. T. and Ingram, W. C.
Actomyosin from physarum polycephalum: electron microscopy of myosin-enriched preparations. bibliog il Science 170:743-5 N 13 '70
NACRE. See Mother-of-pearl
NADEL, Evelyn De Wolfe
Modern medicine comes to ancient Nepal. il por Todays Health 48:28-33+ My '70
NADER, Laura
Another Nader. por Newsweek 76:40-1 Jl 20 '70 *

NADER, Ralph
Baby foods: can you (and your baby) afford them? McCalls 98:36+ N '70
Why they should tell you the octane rating of the gasoline you buy. por Pop Sci 196: 54-5 Ap '70
Yablonski's unfinished business. il Nation 210: 70-2 Ja 26 '70
            about
Campaign GM: corporation critics seek support of universities. L. J. Carter. Science 168:452-5 Ap 24 '70 *
Irate consumer. il por Newsweek 75:63 Ja 26 '70
Nader v. G.M. por Time 96:29 Ag 24 '70 *
Nader v. nursing homes. il Time 96:48 D 28 '70 *
Nader's biggest raid. il por Newsweek 75:67-8 Je 29 '70 *
Nader's $425,000. Newsweek 76:48 Ag 24 '70 *
Nader's pitch to GM stockholders. Bsns W p30 F 14 '70 *
Nader's raiders. America 122:491 My 9 '70 *
Nader's raiders on the FDA: science and scientists misused. P. M. Boffey. Science 168: 349-52 Ap 17 '70 *
Nader's raiders strike again. il por Time 95: 88 Mr 30 '70 *
New raid on Nader. Chr Cent 87:1176 O 7 '70 *
Other bumps in the road. por Newsweek 76: 82-3 S 14 '70 *
Ralph Nader becomes an organization. il por Bsns W p86-8 N 28 '70 *
U.S.'s toughest customer. Read Digest 96:76-80 Mr '70 *
Up against the wall, FDA! por Time 95:18+ Ap 20 '70 *
Wheels of fortune. Newsweek 76:112 N 23 '70 *
NADLER, Leonard
Helping the hard-core adjust to the world of work. il Harvard Bsns R 48:117-26 Mr '70
NAEGLERIA. See Amebas
NAESS, Ragnar D.
Stocks: greater confidence; interview. por U S News 70:30-1 Ja 4 '71
NAGASAKI
A-bombed cities: twenty-five years later. K. M. Chrysler. il U S News 69:54-6 Ag 10 '70
My God, what have we done? excerpts from The rising sun. J. Toland. il Look 34:54+ O 6 '70
Twenty five years ago two cities two bombs. il Life 69:30-1 Jl 31 '70
What if Hiroshima had never happened? Time essay. il Time 96:28-9 Ag 10 '70
NAGATA, T. and others
Magnetic properties of the lunar crystalline rock and fines. bibliog il Science 167:703-4 Ja 30 '70
NAGEL, Myra
Seniors strike for fun. il Har Yrs 10:40-1 Ja '70
NAGENDA, John
Prick the cuckoo; poem. Mlle 71:98 Je '70
NAGLE, John M. See Cross, J. S. jt. auth.
NAGRIN, Daniel
Daniel Nagrin's magnet: the Peloponnesian war. G. Loney. il Dance Mag 44:68-71 Ag '70 *
Lamentations and cheers. W. Terry. il pors Sat R 53:57 F 14 '70 *
NAGY, Bartholomew, and others
Organic compounds in lunar samples: pyrolysis products, hydrocarbons, amino acids. bibliog il Science 167:770-3 Ja 30 '70
NAGY, László Moholy-. See Moholy-Nagy, L.
NAGY, Sibyl Moholy-. See Moholy-Nagy, S.
NAHAT, Dennis
Brief biography. S. Goodman. il pors Dance Mag 44:64-5 S '70 *
NAILS
Primer on nails. il Mech Illus 66:92-4 Ja '70
NAILS (anatomy)
Good nails: how to give them a hand. il Vogue 156:128-9+ O 1 '70
NAIMARK, George M.
(comp) See Martin, E. W. pseud. Fun city one hundred years ago
NAIRN, Ronald C.
Prescott kids go wild. P. Snook. il por Nat Wildlife 8:4-11 F '70 *
NAIROBI, Kenya
            Hotels, restaurants, etc.
Modern eating in an ancient country; Amboseli grill room at the Nairobi Hilton hotel. M. Woodward. il Travel 134:16 S '70

NAIROBI college
Nairobi college; East Palo Alto, Calif. V. M. Johnson. il Mlle 71:290-1+ Ag '70
NAITAMBA (island)
My Naitauba. R. Burr. il pors Travel Camera 33:46-9 Ja '70
NAITAUBA (island) See Naitamba (island)
NAKAMURA, Kimpei
Tradition and vitality. il Craft Horiz 30:10-11 My '70
NAKAMURA, Koji. See Axelbank, A. jt. auth.
NAKASHIMA, George
Meditations on trees and the life of the spirit. Life 68:78 Je 12 '70

about

Nakashima, the craftsman. il pors Life 68:74-7 Je 12 '70 *
NAKEDNESS. See Nudity
NALBANDIAN, Robert
Discriminating disease. il Time 96:41 D 21 '70 *
NAMATH, Joe Willie
Game that gets a good man down. il pors Sports Illus 33:28-35 Ag 17 '70 *
Jet age hero. H. L. Masin. por Sr Schol 95: 32 N 17; 24 D 1 '69
Move over, Valentino. il pors Life 69:42-3 Ag 7 '70 *
NAME calling. See Invective
NAMES
See also subhead Names under various subjects e.g. Hurricanes—Names
NAMES, Geographical
Where's that again? excerpts from A dictionary of American place-names. G. R. Stewart. Am Heritage 21:116 O '70
See also
United Nations conference on the standardization of geographical names
NAMES, Lunar
Names on the back of the moon; with folded NASA map. J. Ashbrook. il Sky & Tel 40: 262-6, 291-300 N '70
NAMES, Personal
East is East but West is best; surnames. R. Armour. Sat R 53:4 O 3 '70
Name your son Tunku? T. O. Echewa. America 122:185-7 F 21 '70
Real names of Edison cylinder performers. J. Walsh. il Hobbies 75:37-9 Je '70
Word people; excerpts, with drawings by E. Sorel. N. Sorel. il pors Horizon 12:112-20 Aut '70
Your child's name could mark him for failure. A. Henley. Ladies Home J 87:137+ Je '70

Anecdotes, facetiae, satire, etc.

Men of letters. A. S. Flaumenhaft. il Har Yrs 10:22-3 Je '70
NAMES of horses. See Horses—Names
NAMES of products. See Trade marks and trade names
NAMIAS, Jerome
Climatic anomaly over the United States during the 1960's. bibliog il Science 170:741-3 N 13 '70
NAMIBIA
See also
United Nations—Namibia
United Nations council for Namibia
NAMPA, Idaho
U.S. journal: O. Campbell, negative and controversial editor of the Idaho free press. C. Trillin. New Yorker 46:104+ O 31 '70
NANA Opoku Ware II, king of Ashanti

Coronation

Golden enstoolment. il por Time 96:26 Ag 10 '70 *
King on a stool of gold. il por Life 69:36-7 Ag 21 '70
NANCY, France
Letter from Paris; J.-J. Servan-Schreiber winner of by-election for deputy. Genêt. New Yorker 46:50 Jl 11 '70
NANDA, Ved P.
Revolution on the Burma trail? il Commonweal 91:530-1 F 13 '70
NANSEN, Charles
Beer barrel brownies. il Field & S 74:82-3+ Mr '70
Best way to hunt whitetail! il Field & S 75: 30-1+ D '70
Bettering the odds for bowhunters. il Field & S 75:34-5+ N '70
Cartop boat: an angler's secret weapon. il Field & S 74:58-9+ Ja '70
NANTUCKET ISLAND
Life's tempo on Nantucket. P. Benchley. il Nat Geog 137:810-39 Je '70

NAPHTHOQUINONE
Energy transduction: inhibition of cockroach feeding by naphthoquinone. D. M. Norris and others. bibliog il Science 170:754-5 N 13 '70
NAPHTHYLAMINES
Bladder cancer induction by aromatic amines: role of N-hydroxy metabolites. J. L. Radomski and E. Brill. bibliog il Science 167: 992-3 F 13 '70
NAPIER, Arch
Horse racing. il Sports Illus 32:46+ Je 1 '70
NAPIER, John
On spirals and social responsibility. il Chem 43:6-7 Mr '70 *
NAPIER, William John
Tremble! Intensely tremble! excerpts from The dragon wakes. C. Hibbert. il por Horizon 12:114-19 Sum '70 *
NAPLES
Mad cyclist of Napoli; A. Mellino. D. J. Hamblin. il Life 69:67 O 2 '70

Music

Report:
Lohengrin sung in Italian. E. Tellini. Opera N 34:28-9 Ap 11 '70
La Traviata and Norma. E. Tellini. Opera N 34:34 Mr 14 '70
NAPOLES, José
Viva Mantequilla. M. Crawford. il pors Ebony 25:58-60+ Mr '70 *
NAPOLES, Mantequilla. See Napoles, J.
NAPOLI, Mario
Our first look at Greek wall-painting. il Horizon 12:22-9 Aut '70
NARANG, R. S. See Miller, L. L. jt. auth.
NARCISSUS
Alec Gray's daffodils. J. Kilborn. il por Horticulture 48:22-3+ Ap '70
Daffodils; trip with Horticultural society of New York to Brookside, estate of Mrs Flagler Matthews in Rye, N.Y. New Yorker 46:29-30 My 23 '70
NARCOLEPSY
Narcolepsy: the sleep disease. il Sci Digest 68:29-30 Ag '70
NARCOTIC addiction control commission of New York state. See New York (state)—Narcotic addiction control commission
NARCOTIC addicts
Banality of the new evil; games the survivors play. W. Kloman. il Esquire 73:115-17+ Mr '70
Does our army fight on drugs? ed. by C. S. Wren. J. H. Kaplan. Look 34:72+ Je 16 '70
Drug scene. S. M. Spencer; R. Severo. Read Digest 96:67-75 Ja '70
Junkie personality. A. J. Snider. il Sci Digest 68:62 D '70
Marijuana: it's big business now; House select committee on crime report. U S News 68:103 Ap 20 '70
Princess Leda's castle in the air. T. Burke. il Esquire 73:104-11+ Mr '70

Rehabilitation

Addicts and zealots; chaotic war against drug abuse in New York city. M. K. Sanders. il Harper 240:71-3+ Je '70; Same abr. with title Encounter at Phoenix house. Read Digest 97:95 D '70
Architecture to help drug addicts calls for speed and inventiveness: Manhattan rehabilitation center. il Arch Rec 147:160-1 Ja '70
Community where drug addicts grow up; Phoenix houses in New York city. A. W. Birch. il PTA Mag 65:2-5 N '70; Same abr. with title Where addicts become adults. Read Digest 97:92-6 D '70
Cracks in the panacea. Sci N 97:366-7 Ap 11 '70
Eighteen narcotic-addiction buildings in eighteen months; Arthur Kill rehabilitation center, Staten Island. il Am City 85:152+ Je '70
How addicts are treated. Time 95:20 Mr 16 '70
How can you tell if your child is taking drugs? I. Mothner. il Look 34:42+ Ap 7 '70
Junior junkie; youthful drug addicts at Odyssey house, New York. il Time 95:36 F 16 '70
Leaving the drug world behind; results from the Awareness house project. R. Moskowitz. il Am Ed 6:3-6 Ja '70; Same. Ed Digest 35: 5-7 My '70
Lifeboat; Phoenix house survival therapy. il Motor B 126:42-3 D '70
Menace and the malady. Nation 211:228-9 S 21 '70

NARCOTIC addicts—Rehabilitation—*Continued*
Narcotic antagonists in opiate dependence;
report of meeting. M. Fink. bibliog Science
169:1005-6 S 4 '70
Opinion: Phoenix house, a celebration of
life. F. Natale. por Mile 72:46+ D '70
Role of therapeutic communities. Cur 120:38-
43 Ag '70
TV soliloquies help young drug users. il To-
days Health 48:64-5 Ap '70
What the English are doing about heroin.
M. Simons. il Look 34:47-52+ Ap 7 '70
    See also
Methadone
Synanon foundation, inc.

NARCOTIC habit
C21 H23 No3: a primer for parents and chil-
dren. L. Edson. il N Y Times Mag p92-3+
My 24 '70
Confronting the drug peril. Chr Today 14:
24-5 Ap 24 '70
Drugs raise a specter. il Bsns W p80-2 My
9 '70
Grams and damns. H. Beckelhymer. Chr Cent
87:267-8 Mr 4 '70
Rising problem of drugs on the job. il Time
95:70 Je 29 '70
    See also
Heroin
Mescaline
Narcotics and youth

Terminology
Drug glossary. Sat R 53:21 N 14 '70
NARCOTIC laws
Addiction, medicine and the law. Sci Am
223:50 Jl '70
Greener grass, grimmer jails; the scene
abroad. il Newsweek 75:51+ Je 15 '70
Hassle over narcotics control. il Sci N 97:
339 Ap 4 '70
How long Congress how long? features of
the Controlled dangerous substance bill;
address, June 19, 1970. J. N. Mitchell. Vital
Speeches 36:610-12 Ag 1 '70
If pot were legal. il por Time 96:41 Jl 20 '70
Moving forward: drug-abuse bill. U S News
68:4 F 9 '70
New look; the Dodd drug bill. Newsweek 75:
24 F 9 '70
No knock? W. F. Buckley, jr. Nat R 22:
220 F 24 '70
No knock drug bill. il Time 95:11-12 F 9 '70
Of plumbing and privacy; no-knock drug
raids. il Ebony 25:154-5 Ap '70
Pot and the law; the legalization of mari-
juana on a provisional basis. Chr Cent 87:
1275 O 28 '70; Discussion. 87:1461 D 2 '70
Pot, hard drugs and the law. G. Samuels.
il por N Y Times Mag p4+ F 15 '70
Pot in prison. W. F. Buckley, jr. Nat R 22:
221 F 24 '70
Pursuit of pot; Nixon eases proposals. il Sr
Schol 95:14 N 10 '69
Some ambiguities for research in Senate's
drug bill. J. Walsh. Science 167:849 F 6
'70
Sparks fly over pot. Nations Bsns 58:24 Mr
'70
Tough bill plus research; Comprehensive drug
abuse and control act of 1970. Sci N 98:332-3
O 24 '70
U.S. journal: Houston; thirty year sentence
to L. O. Johnson for giving away one
marijuana cigarette. C. Trillin. New Yorker
46:164+ D 12 '70
NARCOTIC smuggling. See Smuggling
NARCOTIC trade. See Narcotics, Control of
NARCOTIC traffic. See Narcotics, Control of
NARCOTICS
What you should know about the major
mind-affecting drugs. Good H 171:148-9 Ag
'70
    See also
Heroin
Morphine
United Nations—Commission on narcotic
drugs
NARCOTICS, Control of
Americans abroad; the jail scene. il Time
95:36 Ap 13 '70
Blacks declare war on dope; Mothers against
drugs. il Ebony 25:31-4+ Je '70
Booming traffic in drugs: the government's
dilemma. il U S News 69:40-1 D 7 '70
Broader attack on drug abuse, to dry up the
flow of drugs. il U S News 68:38 Mr 23 '70
Declaration by the Attorneys General on the
narcotics traffic; United States-Mexico joint
cooperation. Dept State Bul 63:300 S 14 '70
Department warns of penalties for drug violations abroad; announcement, March 31,
1970. Dept State Bul 62:549-51 Ap 27 '70

Drugs: ten years to doomsday? H. Sutton. il
Sat R 53:18-21+ N 14 '70
Getting heroin into U.S: how the smugglers
operate; excerpts from What everyone needs
to know about drugs. il U S News 69:41-4 D
7 '70
Greener grass, grimmer jails; the scene
abroad. il Newsweek 75:51+ Je 15 '70
Heroin and crime in the streets. America
122:34 Ja 17 '70
Narcotics: the customs service; address, June
23, 1970. M. J. Ambrose. Vital Speeches 36:
612-15 Ag 1 '70
Paraphernalia, inc. Time 96:15 Jl 20 '70
Pursuit of the poppy. il Time 96:28+ S 14 '70
Smugglers of misery. W. Schulz. Read Digest 96:49-54 Ap '70
Strengthened programs of international cooperation for halting the illicit supply of
drugs; address, April 2, 1970. E. L. Richardson. Dept State Bul 62:544-9 Ap 27 '70
There are people who say, Well, business
is business. il Forbes 105:19-22 Ap 1 '70
U.S. and Mexico continue talks on control
of narcotics; Department announcement
with joint communique. Dept State Bul 62:
527 Ap 20 '70
U.S. journal: West Chester, Pennsylvania;
undercover police officer, John Mervin
arrested for murder. C. Trillin. New Yorker
46:42-4+ Je 27 '70
Vacationing in jail. il Sr Schol 96:19 My 18
'70
War on drugs; its meaning to tourists. il U S
News 69:68 S 7 '70
    See also
Narcotic addicts—Rehabilitation
Narcotic laws
United Nations—Commission on narcotic
drugs
NARCOTICS and athletes. See Doping in sports
NARCOTICS and service men
Another checkup on drug use by GI's. il U S
News 69:33 Ag 31 '70
Fresh disclosures on drugs and GI's; Senate
investigation into marijuana smoking. il
U S News 68:32-3 Ap 6 '70
NARCOTICS and youth
Blacks declare war on dope; Mothers against
drugs. il Ebony 25:31-4+ Je '70
Busting the boys. il pors Newsweek 76:32 Ag
17 '70
Can this marriage be saved? D. C. Disney.
Ladies Home J 87:12+ D '70
Confronting the drug peril. Chr Today 14:
24-5 Ap 24 '70
Do drugs lead to violence? D. M. Rorvik.
il Look 34:58-61 Ap 7 '70
Doctor Baird of East Harlem; conductor
of group therapy sessions for narcotic ad-
dicts. W. F. Buckley, jr. Nat R 22:100 Ja
27 '70
Dope about dope; publications of the Stu-
dent association for the study of hallucino-
gens. Sat R 53:80 S 19 '70
Dope(s) G. Lees. il Hi Fi 20:134 O '70
Drug abuse: newest and most dangerous
challenge. P.C. Barrins. Ed Digest 35:24-6
Ja '70
Drug addicts getting younger; with study-
discussion program, by E. Harris and D.
Harris. C. Winick. bibliog il PTA Mag 65:
6-8, 35-6 S '70
Drug epidemic: what's a teacher to do? C. H.
Harrison. il Schol Teach Sec Teach Sup p4-
6+ My 4 '70
Drug menace: how serious? interview. J. E.
Ingersoll. il por U S News 68:38-42 My 25
'70
Drug scene: high schools are higher now. il
Newsweek 75:66-7 F 16 '70
Drug scene in East Egg. E. Diamond. il
N Y Times Mag p28-9+ My 17 '70; Dis-
cussion. p56-7 Je 28 '70
Drugs and death in the run-down world of
rock music; J. Hendrix and J. Joplin. A.
Goldman. il pors Life 69:32-3 O 16 '70
Drugs and our children: a White House re-
port; questions and answers. il Ladies
Home J 87:112-13+ My '70
Drugs are your problem. D. C. King. America
122:497-8 My 9 '70
Drugs/teens=alcohol/parents. T. Lawrence
and J. Velleman. il pors Sci Digest 68:46-
8+ O '70
Drugs: ten years to doomsday? H. Sutton. il
Sat R 53:18-21+ N 14 '70
Drugs: the landscape of grass and snow. H.
S. Resnik. Sat R 53:23-5+ Ag 15 '70
Each other's victim's; excerpts. M. Travers.
il McCalls 97:70-1+ Je '70
Early steps toward preventing drug abuse;
with study-discussion program, by E. Har-
ris and D. Harris. R. E. Gould. bibliog il
PTA Mag 64:6-9, 33 Mr '70

NARCOTICS and youth—*Continued*
Father tells how drugs invaded his family; anonymous report. Life 68:50-2+ Mr 20 '70; Same abr. with title Story of my son's heroin addiction. il Read Digest 97:64-9 Jl '70

Fathers and sons. il pors Newsweek 75:24+ F 9 '70

Growing menace of pep pills. B. Surface. Seventeen 29:146-7+ My '70

Heroin in the schools. Chr Today 14:32 Mr 13 '70

High-school sports flunk the saliva test. T. Irwin. Todays Health 48:44-6+ O '70

Hotline for troubled teen-agers; Los Angeles. J. N. Bell. Read Digest 97:41-6 N '70

How can you tell if your child is taking drugs? I. Mothner. il Look 34:42+ Ap 7 '70

How I faced my son's drug arrest. G. Astor. Look 34:87-8+ D 15 '70

How to talk with your teen-ager about drugs; excerpt from What you can do about drugs and your child. H. W. Land. Read Digest 97:69-72 Ag '70

Junior junkie. il Time 95:36 F 16 '70

Kids and heroin: the adolescent epidemic. il Time 95:16-20+ Mr 16 '70; Same abr. Read Digest 96:88-92 Je '70

Law and maryjane. M. B. Hering. bibliog il Am Lib 1:896-9 O '70

Leaving the drug world behind; results from the Awareness house project. R. Moskowitz. il Am Ed 6:3-6 Ja '70; Same. Ed Digest 35:5-7 My '70

Life on two grams a day; heroin in the high schools. il Life 68:24-32 F 20 '70

Moderation in drug use at Michigan. Sch & Soc 98:134-5 Mr '70

Modest proposal; responsibility of record industry. G. Lees. Hi Fi 20:secI 116 Je '70

No D for dull. Sr Schol 96:17 My 11 '70

No marijuana for adolescents. K. Angel; discussion. il N Y Times Mag p9+ Ja 25 '70

On campus: drugs vs. drinking. Mlle 70:230 Mr '70

One father's war on marijuana. W. F. Buckley, jr. Nat R 22:1072 O 6 '70

Open season on drug-smugglers; with interview by W. B. Leithead, ed. by J. Fincher. R. Chelminski. il Life 68:28-35 Je 26 '70

Pot bust. il Newsweek 75:92+ My 11 '70

Pot, pills and people; Camp JCA, California. M. Schlesinger. Camp Mag 42:10-11+ Mr '70

Readers, experts examine drug problems; findings from survey; ed. by A. Rosenthal. il Todays Health 48:19-23+ S '70

Rock doctor tells about 985 freakouts; ed. by R. Stokes. W. Abruzzi. il por Life 69:37 Ag 14 '70

Singing is better than any dope. H. Saal. il por Newsweek 76:124-5 O 19 '70

Some straight talk about drugs. il Sr Schol 96:4-10 Mr 9 '70

Tell the "why why trippers" the answer will come; counseling and rehabilitation services. J. Marks. Mlle 71:188-9+ My '70

To parents: plain talk on marijuana. Bsns W p 121 Mr 21 '70

To youth, with love; White House conference on the drug problem. R. L. Shayon. Sat R 53:57 N 21 '70

Town deals sternly with its own; six young drug offenders sent to prison in Rupert, Idaho. L. Wainwright. il Life 69:40-2+ N 6 '70

Walk on London's wild side. D. Moraes. il N Y Times Mag p 100+ S 13 '70

We must declare war on drugs; ed. by J. N. Bell. A. Linkletter. il pors Good H 170:94-5+ Ap '70

We must fight the epidemic of drug abuse! A. Linkletter. Read Digest 96:56-60 F '70

What the English are doing about heroin. M. Simons. il Look 34:47-52+ Ap 7 '70

What you can do about the drug problem. S. Grafton. il Parents Mag 45:72-5+ N '70

Youngsters and drugs: making sense of what's happening. Bet Hom & Gard 48:34+ O '70

Anecdotes, facetiae, satire, etc.
Young names makes news. G. Ace. Sat R 53:12 O 10 '70

NARCOTICS commission, United Nations. See United Nations—Commission on Narcotic drugs

NARCOTICS education
Checkpoints for fighting the drug menace in camp; education program at Camp Narrin, Mich. S. C. Huck and P. A. Denomme. Camp Mag 42:19+ S '70

Classroom drug scene; training sessions for educators. M. V. Gelinas. il Am Ed 6:3-5 N '70

Drugs are not the problem; drug education in schools. V. A. Dohner. Ed Digest 36:25-8 N '70

Narcotics: a crucial area of secondary school responsibility; fully credited courses needed. R. Elliott. Ed Digest 36:44-7 S '70

Should the drug education bandwagon be rerouted? C. H. Harrison. il Schol Teach Jr/Sr High p 18-19+ O 5 '70

Strengthening drug education. Sch & Soc 98:400 N '70

NARDI, Marcia
Senior citizen; poem. Nation 210:438-40 Ap 13 '70

NARROW gage railroads. See Railroads, Narrow gage

NARTEN, A. H. and Levy, H. A.
Observed diffraction pattern and proposed models of liquid water. bibliog Science 165:447:54; 167:1521 Ag 1 '69, Mr 13 '70

NASA. See United States—National aeronautics and space administration

NASCIMENTO, Edson Arantes do. See Arantes do Nascimento, E.

NASCOM system. See United States—National aeronautics and space administration—Communications network

NASH, Douglas B. and others
Luminescence and reflectance of Tranquillity samples: effects of irradiation and vitrification. bibliog il Science 167:721-4 Ja 30 '70

NASH, Ethel Miller. See Perkin, G. W. jt. auth.

NASH, Ogden
At least I'm not the kind of fool who sobs, what kind of fool am I? poem. Holiday 47:22 Ap '70

Gossip that never should be unloosed is gossip that can't come home to roost; poem. McCalls 97:131 F '70

H'ave, Caesar, or, Boadicea's revenge; poem. Travel & Camera 33:35 Ap '70

One man's opiate; poem. New Yorker 46:56 D 5 '70

Please remind me before I forget; poem. New Yorker 45:44 F 14 '70

Thank you, Lord; poem. Ladies Home J 87:65 My '70

Who, sir? Me, sir? No sir, the Times sir! poem. Atlan 225:66 Je '70

NASH, Ralph G. and Beall, M. L. Jr
Chlorinated hydrocarbon insecticides: root uptake versus vapor contamination of soybean foliage. bibliog il Science 168:1109-11 My 29 '70

NASH, Ted
Quakers pull a swift on the Charles. H. D. Whall. il por Sports Illus 32:74+ My 11 '70

NASHVILLE, Tenn.

Education
Warner school is the place to come. F. Sutherland and R. W. Bogen. Todays Ed 59:48-9 F '70

Music
Country music gets soul; L. Martell at the Grand ole opry. il pors Ebony 25:66-8+ Mr '70

NASSAU, Bahama Islands
For Easter, it's Nassau. L. Gauge. Travel 33:8+ F '70

NASSAU COUNTY, N.Y.
Lilliputian town to teach kids rules of roads. Am City 85:126 Mr '70

Mobile recreation fleet. J. W. Halper. il Am City 85:100+ S '70

NASSER, Gamal Abdel
New crisis in Mideast; interview, ed. by C. S. Foltz, jr. il por U S News 68:60-3 My 18 '70

about
Death of Nasser. il pors Newsweek 76:31-5 O 12 '70 *

Egypt steals a march. pors Newsweek 76:26-7 Ag 3 '70 *

From country boy to epic hero. W. Wynn. Time 96:26 O 12 '70 *

Game of nations, by M. Copeland, 3d. Review Sat R por 53:39-41 My 23 '70. D. Kurzman *

Instrument of history; reprint. J. Morris. Nation 211:323-4 O 12 '70 *

Nasser: despite failures, his prestige with Arabs stays high. il por U S News 68:14 Ja 26 '70

Nasser era. Chr Cent 87:1207 O 14 '70 *

Nasser's death haunts U.S. oilmen. il por Bsns W p 15-16 O 3 '70 *

Nasser's legacy: hope and instablity. il pors Time 96:20-6+ O 12 '70

On-the-spot report: Egypt's goodbye to Nasser. S. Turner. Sr Schol 97:3 N 2 '70 *

NASSER, Gamal Abdel—about—*Continued*
Sadat takes over in Egypt. Sr Schol 97:3-4 N 2 '70 *
Serious blow to the U.S. peace effort; interview. R. Hare. por U S News 69:20-1 O 12 '70 *
Shout of Arab grief; with report by M. Copeland. il pors Life 69:28-37 O 9 '70 *
Tributes to Gamal Abdel Nasser. UM Mo Chron 7:13-15 O '70 *
Truncated plank for the Middle East. Nat R 22:824+ Ag 11 '70 *
What Nasser did. G. G. Stevens. Atlan 227: 45-7 Ja '71 *
With Nasser gone, new dangers in Mideast. J. Law. il por U S News 69:20-1 O 12 '70 *

Funeral rites and ceremonies
Nasser's death as a religious event. J. C. Haughey. America 123:278 O 17 '70
NAST, Thomas
Thomas Nast's grand caricaturama. L. Goodrich. il Art N 69:58-61 Ap '70 *
NASTURTIUMS
Nasturtiums, cukes and tomatoes; controlling black lice. W. Ferguson. il Org Gard & Farm 17:50-1 Mr '70
Nice enough to eat. R. E. Atkinson and E. Haraszty. il McCalls 97:44+ Je '70
NATALE, Frank
Opinion; Phoenix house. por Mlle 72:46+ D '70
NATHAN, Paul
Rights and permissions. See issues of Publishers' weekly
NATHAN, Simon
Gallery; photographs. Life 69:8-9 Jl 10 '70
Simon says. See issues of Popular photography
NATHAN Cummings collection. See Art—Private collections
NATHANIEL; story. See Shomon, J. J.
NATHANS, Alan A.
Keep on top of maintenance with this monthly calendar; excerpts from Maintenance for camps and other outdoor recreation facilities. Camp Mag 42:11-13 S '70
NATHNESS, Sarah
Tell it to the marines. Opera N 35:20 S 5 '70
NATION of shopkeepers loses three of them through contact with a nation of violence; story. See Trillin, C.
NATION-wide auto auctions, ltd.
Disposers. il Newsweek 76:60-1 Jl 27 '70
NATIONAL academy of engineering
National academy of engineering selects new members. Science 168:556 My 1 '70
Odd couple: strains in science, engineering academies. D. S. Greenberg. Science 170: 513 O 30 '70
NATIONAL academy of sciences
Academy of sciences selects new members. Science 168:681 My 8 '70
Assessment of technology. H. Brooks and R. Bowers. il Sci Am 222:13-21 F '70
Confronting change. il Sci N 97:453-4 My 9 '70
Life sciences: whistling in the dark for another $250 million. R. J. Bazell. Science 170:1285-7 D 18 '70
NAS again says no to Shockley. L. J. Carter. Science 168:685 My 8 '70
Odd couple: strains in science, engineering academies. D. S. Greenberg. Science 170:513 O 30 '70
On the road to advocacy. B. J. Culliton. il Sci N 98:146-7 Ag 15 '70
NATIONAL accelerator laboratory
Batavia: accelerating people as well as particles. P. M. Boffey. Science 168:1185-7 Je 5 '70
Experimenters vie for first crack at Batavia. G. B. Lubkin. Phys Today 23:17-18 S '70
Massive smasher at a bargain price. Bsns W p56 Ag 22 '70
More power sooner for Batavia. il Sci N 98: 111-13 Ag 8 '70
NATIONAL advisory commission on civil disorders. See United States—National advisory commission on civil disorders
NATIONAL agricultural library. See United States—National agricultural library
NATIONAL air pollution control administration. See United States—National air pollution control administration
NATIONAL airlines, inc.
Airlines stress food service competition. H. D. Watkins. il Aviation W 93:30-1+ N 23 23 '70
Competition slows National traffic return. il Aviation W 93:35+ Ag 17 '70
Lagging traffic sparks trimming in National schedules, personnel. Aviation W 93:24 O 26 '70
National strives to overcome strike loss. Aviation W 93:25 Jl 13 '70

National will resume operations despite complex labor problems. Aviation W 92:32 My 25 '70
National reports January dip. Aviation W 92:37 F 2 '70
National's labor problems ease. Aviation W 92:31 Ap 13 '70
Post-strike service provides challenges. H. D. Watkins. il Aviation W 93:37+ Ag 10 '70
NATIONAL alliance of businessmen
Hard-core hiring is going public. il Bsns W p29-30 My 16 '70
Hard-core jobs; are there any left? L. Zimpel. Chr Cent 87:941-2 Ag 5 '70
Hard times for JOBS. il Time 95:68 Je 8 '70
Townsend takes a hard-core job. Bsns W p23-4 Mr 7 '70
Training hard-core jobless: the record after two years; interview. D. M. Kendall. il por U S News 68:60-2 Mr 30 '70
Will layoffs undermine the hard core? with editorial comment. il Bsns W p29-30, 118 Ja 17 '70
NATIONAL arboretum. See Washington, D.C. —National arboretum
NATIONAL assessment of educational progress
Are we educating for tomorrow? C. H. Harrison. Schol Teach Jr/Sr High p 16-17 S 21 '70
Education assessment: results a step toward accountability. T. P. Southwick. Science 169:358-9 Jl 24 '70
How educated are Americans? What two surveys show. il U S News 69:62-3 Jl 20 '70
Measuring knowledge. il Newsweek 76:40 Jl 20 '70
National assessment: a history and sociology; excerpt from New models for American education; ed. by J. Guthrie. R. W. Tyler. bibliog Sch & Soc 98:471-7 D '70
National assessment: first returns. W. D. Boutwell. PTA Mag 65:17-19 S '70
National educational assessment: initial report, reactions, and benefits. Ed Digest 36: 1-5 S '70
Report card for Americans. il Time 96:58 Jl 20 '70
Testing education. Sci N 98:60 Jl 25 '70
What good are the schools? Sat R 53:54 Ag 15 '70
NATIONAL association for mental health, inc.
National mental health manpower showcase conference: NAMH leads the way. J. D. Matarazzo. bibliog Ment Hy 54:333-6 Jl '70
On helping the disadvantaged. J. E. Chapman. Ment Hy 54:589-90 O '70
Wider field of work of the national committee for mental hygiene. Ment Hy 54:425-6 Jl '70
NATIONAL association for the advancement of colored people
Blast from a bishop; denunciation of the administration's racial policies. pors Time 96:11 Jl 13 '70
End to patience; annual convention. Newsweek 76:36 Jl 13 '70
NAACP legal defense and education fund has achieved fantastic record in major breakthroughs in securing constitutional rights for Negroes. J. W. Davis. por Negro Hist Bul 33:135-6 O '70
Nixon anti-Negro? A charge, a reply. il U S News 69:72-3 Jl 13 '70
NATIONAL association of broadcasters
Kidvid ghetto; reactions to proposal to ban commercials from children's programs. R. L. Shayon. Sat R 53:21 Je 20 '70
NATIONAL association of college stores
As student tempers rise, AEPI and NACS huddle on tactics. Pub W 197:37 Ap 20 '70
NACS convention theme proves to be prophetic. il Pub W 197:14-17 My 18 '70
1969 in review: book trade organizations. il Pub W 197:55 F 9 '70
NATIONAL association of evangelicals
NAE: bringing evangelicals together; with editorial comment. D. Tinder. Chr Today 14: 26, 42 My 8 '70
NATIONAL association of intercollegiate athletics
Tall story from the land of Boone. W. F. Reed. il Sports Illus 33:66-8 N 30 '70
NATIONAL association of laymen. See Laity—Catholic church
NATIONAL association of letter carriers
National association of letter carriers. W. L. Tillery. Mo Labor R 93:36-7 O '70
NATIONAL association of manufacturers
Unhappy parent of new hiring rules. Bsns W p39 Ja 24 '70
NATIONAL association of professional bureaucrats
Maximizing NATAPROBU. il Time 96:44+ N 23 '70
NATIONAL association of railroad passengers
Passenger's friend. por Bsns W p30 Ag 1 '70

NATIONAL association of retired civil employees
NARCE re-elects Walters president; may revert to old name of NARFE. Aging 190:15 Ag '70

NATIONAL association of state universities and land grant colleges
Higher education: administration silent on institutional aid. L. J. Carter. Science 170: 832-3 N 20 '70

NATIONAL association of theater owners
For adults only. G. Lees. il Hi Fi 20:secI 104+ My '70

NATIONAL association of travel organizations. See Discover America organization

NATIONAL Audubon society
Education for survival: conservation comes first. S. S. Donohue. por Parents Mag 45: 18 Je '70
Seattle notebook. A. Young. il Audubon 72: 140-3 S '70
See also
Audubon medal

NATIONAL automobile dealers association
Dealers feel shortchanged. il Bsns W p33-4 Ja 24 '70

NATIONAL ballet
National ballet in Cinderella; Lisner auditorium, Washington, D.C. J. B. Lewis. Dance Mag 44:22 Je '70
National ballet with Margot Fonteyn in Cinderella, Brooklyn college, NY. N. Mason. Dance Mag 44:77 D '70

NATIONAL Baptist convention, USA, inc. See Baptists in the United States

NATIONAL basketball association
East is Knicks but west is West; the NBA playoffs. F. Deford. il Sports Illus 32:30-2+ My 11 '70
Haywood affair. il por Time 97:44+ Ja 18 '71
Meanwhile back at the NBA. H. L. Masin. il Sr Schol 97:20 D 7 '70

NATIONAL bibliography. See Bibliography, National

NATIONAL black economic development conference
Black manifesto's birthday: frosting on the cake? Chr Today 14:37 My 22 '70
On Dow and calico. B. Thompson. Chr Cent 86:1571-2 D 10 '69; Correction. 87:83 Ja 21 '70
South Bend echoes; suit to bar transferring $200,000. Chr Today 14:37-8 Ja 16 '70

NATIONAL boat show. See Boats—Exhibitions

NATIONAL book awards
Children's literature NBA goes to Isaac B. Singer. Library J 95:1542 Ap 15 '70
Judges appointed for National book awards. Pub W 198:20 N 30 '70
National book award winners. il Library J 95:1352 Ap 1 '70
National book awards. il Newsweek 75:104 Mr 16 '70
NBA week: a little heat, a little light; with editorial comment. il Pub W 197:24-7, 48 Mr 23 '70
1969 National book awards presented to seven writers. il Pub W 197:57 Mr 9 '70
Nominating method revised for National book awards. Pub W 198:31 O 19 '70
Nominees announced for national book awards. Pub W 197:127 F 23 '70
Trade winds. J. Beatty, jr. Sat R 53:18 Mr 21 '70

NATIONAL book committee
Book committee cites role in major reading projects. Pub W 198:33 O 26 '70
Book committee elects officers, honors Warren. il Pub W 198:17-18 D 14 '70
Ideal AV exam centers scarce, says National book committee. Library J 95:3950-1 N 15 '70
NBA week: a little heat, a little light; with editorial comment. il Pub W 197:24-7, 48 Mr 23 '70
Selection centers for educational materials. Pub W 198:35 S 7 '70

NATIONAL broadcasting company
Dann v. Klein: the best game in town. pors Time 95:98+ My 25 '70
Good night ... Newsweek 75:72 Mr 2 '70
Troika at NBC; news anchor man. il Newsweek 75:69 Mr 16 '70

Anecdotes, facetiae, satire, etc.
Till it be morrow; future goodnights from John Chancellor, Frank McGee, David Brinkley and NBC news. R. W. O'Donnell. New Yorker 46:29 Jl 4 '70

NATIONAL budget. See Budget—United States

NATIONAL bureau of economic research
Cycle riders take a new turn. il Bsns W p66-7 O 3 '70

NATIONAL bureau of standards. See United States—Standards. National bureau of

NATIONAL cash register company
Mr Chairman..; excerpts from transcript of NCR annual meeting. R. S. Oelman. il por Forbes 105:21 Je 1 '70
Moment of truth for NCR. J. Poindexter. il Duns 95:29-31+ Ja '70
Self-service rings up a billion dollar sale. R. S. Oelman. il Nations Bsns 58:92-3 Ja '70

NATIONAL Catholic conference for interracial justice
Presbyterian minister appointed to Project Equality post. Chr Cent 87:559 My 6 '70
Project Equality today. M. Stone. Chr Cent 87:79-82 Ja 21 '70

NATIONAL Catholic educational association
Catholic schools seek data, help. Sr Schol 96: Schol Teach 1 Ap 6 '70

NATIONAL Catholic office for motion pictures
NCOMP issues film reports. America 122:31-2 Ja 17 '70

NATIONAL Catholic register (newspaper) See Catholic press

NATIONAL cemeteries
United States
Ten long minutes in Punchbowl; National memorial cemetery of the Pacific. J. Didion. il Life 68:26D Ap 10 '70
See also
Arlington, Va.—National cemetery

NATIONAL center for atmospheric research
Prototype for global network. Sci N 99:24 Ja 9 '71

NATIONAL center for educational communication. See United States—Education, Office of—National center for educational communication

NATIONAL center for space studies. See France—National center for space studies

NATIONAL center for voluntary action
National focus on volunteers. A. E. Todd. Parks & Rec 5:25 Je '70

NATIONAL center of Afro-American artists
Black art's amazing fund-raiser; E. Lewis of Boston. P. Bailey. il pors Ebony 25:70-2+ Je '70

NATIONAL characteristics
Conversations with historians; excerpts from Interpreting American history, ed. by J. A. Garraty. H. S. Commager. il por Am Heritage 21:58-60 F '70

NATIONAL cherry blossom festival. See Washington, D.C.—National cherry blossom festival

NATIONAL children's book week. See Book week

NATIONAL citizens committee for broadcasting
Baiting the giants. R. L. Shayon. Sat R 53: 57 N 28 '70

NATIONAL civil service league
Spotlight on top career workers for the U.S: nominees for Career service awards. Nations Bsns 58:94-5 Mr '70
Uncle Sam's finest; awards for the top ten federal employees. il Nations Bsns 58:34-7 S '70

NATIONAL collegiate athletic association
Old law, new turn. Sports Illus 3i:12+ D 15 '69
Time for the mighty scramble; UCLA favored to win NCAA basketball championship. J. Jares. il Sports Illus 32:22-7 Mr 16 '70

NATIONAL collegiate basketball championship. See Basketball tournaments

NATIONAL commission on libraries and information science. See United States—National commission on libraries and information science

NATIONAL commission on product safety. See United States—National commission on product safety

NATIONAL commission on productivity. See United States—National commission on productivity

NATIONAL commission on the causes and prevention of violence. See United States —National commission on the causes and prevention of violence

NATIONAL committee for a sane nuclear policy
Offbeat policemen: peace petition in response to SANE ad. New Yorker 46:22-3 Ag 8 '70

NATIONAL committee for mental hygiene. See National association for mental health, inc.

NATIONAL committee of Black churchmen
Africa and Afro-Americans; report of conversations between NCBC officials and members of the All Africa conference of churches. G. S. Wilmore, jr. Chr Cent 87: 686 Je 3 '70; Reply. G. M. Daniels. 87:1201-2 O 7 '70
Black church. T. Kilgore, jr. il por Ebony 25:106-8+ Ag '70

NATIONAL education association—*Continued*

National foundation for the
improvement of education
National foundation for the improvement of
education; interview. H. Bain. Todays Ed
59:24-5 N '70

NATIONAL education week. See American
education week

NATIONAL educational television network
Courtroom drama; Trial: the city and county
of Denver v. Lauren R. Watson. il Time
95:90 Mr 30 '70
Hats off to NET; Who invited US? Nation
210:228-9 Mr 2 '70
Musical events; NET opera production of
Jack Beeson's My heart's in the highlands.
W. Sargeant. New Yorker 46:108 Mr 28 '70
Musical events; NET opera production of
Mozart's The abduction from the seraglio.
W. Sargeant. New Yorker 46:142 O 31 '70
Sweet corn; music programs. Sedulus. New
Repub 163:34 O 17 '70
Television in court; the City and county of
Denver v. Lauren R. Watson. Nation 210:
421 Ap 13 '70
See also
Educational broadcasting corporation

NATIONAL elections. See Elections—United
States

NATIONAL electronic associations
C.E.T. test. D. Glass. Electr World 83:74 F;
59 Mr; 67 Ap; 67 My; 53 Je; 84:74 Ag; 62 S;
74-5 O; 70 N; 67 D '70; 85:76 Ja '71

NATIONAL endowment for the arts. See United
States—National foundation on the arts
and the humanities

NATIONAL endowment for the humanities. See
United States—National foundation on the
arts and the humanities

NATIONAL environmental education development program. See United States—National
park service

NATIONAL environmental study area. See
United States—National park service

NATIONAL environmental teach-in. See Teach-
ins

NATIONAL extinction. See Genocide

NATIONAL farm bureau federation. See American farm bureau federation

NATIONAL farmers organization
Is the NFO changing directions? interview,
ed. by L. Palmer. O. L. Staley. il por Farm
J 93:28-9+ O '69
NFO doesn't sound quite like NFO anymore.
G. Logsdon. Farm J 94:58+ F '70
NFO milk contracts worry big co-ops. N.
Reeder. Farm J 94:71 F '70
NFO's new drive for $3.50 spuds. G. Lorang.
il Farm J 94:49 My '70
Potato growers protest with fire. il Bsns W
p29-30 Ap 4 '70

NATIONAL federation of priests councils
At the synod. Commonweal 93:36 O 9 '70
NFPC meets in San Diego. America 122:
325-6 Mr 28 '70; Reply. F. Bonnike. 122:
458 My 2 '70
Priests' union: talking tougher. Chr Today
14:68+ Ap 24 '70

NATIONAL film collection. See United States
—Library of Congress—National film collection

NATIONAL flowers
See also
State flowers

NATIONAL football league
Fuel for the feud. il Time 96:41 O 12 '70
Sporting scene; P. Rozelle, NFL's commissioner. H. W. Wind. New Yorker 46:154+ D
12 '70

NATIONAL football league players association
One-night season; K.S. vs. College All-Stars.
J. Jares. il Sports Illus 33:8-11 Ag 10 '70
Owners and players fumble in Philly; Su-
per bowl champs vs. College All-Stars. A.
Wright. il Sports Illus 33:46-7 Ag 3 '70
Player power. il Newsweek 76:48-9 Ag 3 '70
Pro gridders cross the gold line. U S News
69:83 Ag 17 '70
Put 'er there, Judas! strike ends. Newsweek
76:79-80 Ag 17 '70
Rozelle referees a strike settlement. il Bsns
W p 19 Ag 8 '70

NATIONAL foreign policy conference for editors and broadcasters, San Francisco
National foreign policy conference for editors and broadcasters held at San Francisco; address, with transcript of ques-
tions-and-answers, June 29, 1970. W. P.
Rogers. Dept State Bul 63:78-85 Jl 20 '70

NATIONAL foreign policy conference for editors and broadcasters, Washington, D.C.
National foreign policy conference for editors and broadcasters; remarks, January
15, 1970; with address by Secretary Rogers.
M. Collins; E. L. Richardson. Dept State
Bul 62:113-24 F 2 '70

NATIONAL forests
Confrontation. R. Pardo. il Am For 76:32-5+
S '70
Court blocks timber sale. Liv Wildn 34:62-3
Sum '70
Cradle of forestry; where tree power started;
Biltmore forest school. H. E. Jolley. il Am
For 76:16-21 O '70 (to be cont)
French Pete for people; Willamette national
forest, Ore. A. Netboy. il Am For 76:16-18+
My '70
Mike Frome; National timber supply act. M.
Frome. Am For 76:3+ Ap '70
More than meets the eye; different interpre-
tations on the Wilderness act. J. B. Craig.
Am For 76:7 Je '70
Timber battle is far from over; government-
owned timberland. il Bsns W p30 Mr 14 '70
Timber bill draws fire; proposed National
timber supply act, later retitled the Na-
tional forest timber conservation and man-
agement act. Liv Wildn 34:58 Spr '70
Up on the Boundary; Boundary water canoe
area, Superior national forest. G. S. James.
il Am For 76:24-7+ N '70
U.S. plywood's forest of trouble: sale of
timber from Tongass national forest. il
Bsns W p39 F 21 '70
See also
National parks and reserves—United States

NATIONAL foundation for the improvement of
education. See National education association—National foundation for the improvement of education

NATIONAL foundation on the arts and the humanities. See United States—National foundation on the arts and the humanities

NATIONAL freedom fund for librarians
Freedom fund on the stand; letters to the
editor. Wilson Lib Bul 45:462-3 Ja '71

NATIONAL gallery of art, Washington, D.C.
Cummings event in Washington. D. Cooper.
il Art N 69:34-7+ Sum '70
Echoes from the East garden court; concert
series. R. Evett. New Repub 163:24-6 Ag
15 '70
Powerhouse; purchase of Cézanne's The artist
father. il Newsweek 76:102 O 12 '70
Square peg in a square hole. R. Lynes. il
pors Art in Am 58:80-5 Mr '70
Trophy of tenacity; P. Mellon's gift of Cézanne's portrait of the artist's father. il
por Time 96:64 O 12 '70

NATIONAL gallery of Switzerland, Winterthur
Introducing the National gallery of Switzerland; Oskar Reinhart collection bequeathed
to the Swiss state. J. Russell. il Art N 69:
50-1+ Ap '70

NATIONAL geographic magazine
Frederick G. Vosburgh retires as editor; Gil-
bert M. Grosvenor succeeds him. M. M.
Payne. il pors Nat Geog 138:838-43 D '70
With the National geographic on its endless,
cloudless voyage. T. Buckley. il N Y Times
Mag p 10-11+ S 6 '70

NATIONAL geographic society
See also
Hubbard medal

NATIONAL goals commission. See United
States—President's commission on national
goals

NATIONAL goals. See United States

NATIONAL guard (United States) See United
States—National guard

NATIONAL hardware show. See Hardware—
Exhibitions

NATIONAL health insurance. See Insurance,
Health—United States

NATIONAL heart institute. See United States
—National heart institute

NATIONAL hockey league
Hands across Bering Strait. Sports Illus
31:9 D 15 '69

NATIONAL holidays. See Holidays

NATIONAL income. See Income

NATIONAL industrial materials commission
(proposed) See United States—National industrial materials commission (proposed)

NATIONAL industries, inc.
Wild ride of Stanley Yarmuth. il pors Bsns W
p41 Ag 8 '70

NATIONAL information system for psychology
(proposed) See Information storage and retrieval systems—Psychology

NATIONAL institute of arts and letters
National institute literary awards announced.
Pub W 197:19 My 18 '70

NATIONAL institute of education (proposed)
See United States—National institute of education (proposed)
NATIONAL institute of mental health. See United States—National institute of mental health
NATIONAL institute of senior centers
National institute of senior centers inaugurated at March conference. il Aging 187: 4-5 My '70
NATIONAL institutes of health library. See United States—National institutes of health —Library
NATIONAL investor relations institute
Chilling touts with cold facts. il Bsns W p79 Ap 25 '70
NATIONAL invitation tournament. See Basketball tournaments
NATIONAL Jewish commission on law and public affairs
Defenders of the faith. por Newsweek 76:60 D 28 '70
NATIONAL labor relations board. See United States—National labor relations board
NATIONAL laboratories. See Laboratories, Government
NATIONAL lampoon (periodical)
Lampoon's big new laugh; Harvard lampoon goes national. il Bsns W p53-4 Ja 31 '70
Postgraduate humor. Newsweek 75:94 Mr 23 '70
NATIONAL league of women voters. See League of women voters of the United States
NATIONAL liberation front (Vietnam)
Three documents of the National liberation front, ed. by G. Kolko. Review
Ramp Mag il 8:19-20 Ap '70. F. Schurman
NATIONAL libraries. See Libraries, National
NATIONAL library of medicine. See United States—National library of medicine
NATIONAL library week
Ecology takes limelight for coming week. il Library J 95:1266 Ap 1 '70
National library week: the thirteenth year. Library J 95:2053+ Je 1 '70
NATIONAL liturgical week. See Liturgical week
NATIONAL livestock and meat board
Pork industry committee
Exciting new ways to sell your pork; National pork promotion/education workshop. R. Wilmore. Farm J 94:H36 N '70
NATIONAL marine engineers beneficial association
Air controllers may fly with the AFL-CIO. il Bsns W p 112+ My 16 '70
Marine engineers seek big growth. U S News 68:56 My 25 '70
Marine union comes shoreside. Bsns W p98 Ja 17 '70
NATIONAL mediation board. See United States —National mediation board
NATIONAL memorial cemetery of the Pacific. See National cemeteries—United States
NATIONAL mental health foundation. See National association for mental health, inc.
NATIONAL monuments
Living history in your national parks. il Parks & Rec 5:40-1 Je '70
See also names of national monuments, e.g. Craters of the Moon National Monument
NATIONAL morale. See Morale, National
NATIONAL municipal league
See also
All-America cities
NATIONAL neighbors (organization) See Sponsors of open housing investment
NATIONAL oceanic and atmospheric administration. See United States—National oceanic and atmospheric administration
NATIONAL organization for women
Equal rights NOW. Newsweek 75:75 Mr 2 '70
President of NOW socks it to WNBA. Pub W 199:34-5 Ja 4 '71
NATIONAL parents and teachers association. See National congress of parents and teacher
NATIONAL park service (United States) See United States—National park service
NATIONAL parks and conservation association
Conservation center program announced. Nat Parks 44:27-8 F '70
NPA at work; going to bat for Everglades National Park. il Nat Parks & Con Mag 44:28-30 Je '70
NPA in action; National timber supply act postponed. Nat Parks & Con Mag 44:32-3 My '70
NPCA at work. Nat Parks & Con Mag 44: 29-31 Jl '70
Report of president and general counsel, May 22, 1970. A. W. Smith. Nat Parks & Con Mag 44:17-20 My '70

NATIONAL parks and conservation magazine
Environmental challenge. A. W. Smith. Nat Parks & Con Mag 44:2 Ap '70
NATIONAL parks and reserves
See also
Wilderness areas
History
1870-1970. il Parks & Rec 5:33-4 Je '70
Roads
Scientist against Smokies road. Liv Wildn 34:62 Spr '70
Waterways
Outboard the untamed Everglades. F. M. Paulson. il Field & S 75:152-4+ O '70
Arkansas
See also
Hot Springs National Park
California
See also
Point Reyes National Seashore
Yosemite National Park
Canada
Auto tape tours. il Travel 133:26 My '70
Canada's mountain parks. E. Ogle. il Travel & Camera 33:57-9 Je '70
Chile
Problems of Chilean national parks. F. Hartwig C. il Nat Parks 44:14-17 F '70
Cuba
Where have all the beach clubs of old Havana gone? a glimpse of national parks in revolutionary Cuba. E. Gendler. il Natur Hist 79:10-14+ My '70
Ethiopia
Rarities of Ethiopia; with report by M. Mok. il Life 69:46-57 N 27 '70
Florida
See also
Biscayne National Monument
Everglades National Park
Hawaii
See also
Haleakala National Park
Maine
See also
Acadia National Park
Minnesota
See also
Grand Portage National Monument
Montana
See also
Glacier National Park
Netherlands
Dawdling in the Dutch woods; De Hoge Veluwe National Park. H. Sutton. il Sat R 53:39-41 D 19 '70
New York (state)
See also
Saratoga National Historical Park
North Carolina
See also
Cape Hatteras National Seashore Recreation Area
Oklahoma
See also
Platt National Park
Oregon
See also
Crater Lake National Park
Paraguay
Potential for parks in Paraguay. L. C. Merriam, jr. il Nat Parks & Con Mag 44:10-12 Je '70
South Africa
See also
Kruger National Park
Tanzania
Poacher hunt; Serengeti National Park. J. Brenner. il Newsweek 76:38+ Ag 31 '70
Texas
See also
Padre Island National Seashore
United States
Are campers slobs? B. Hackett. il Am For 76:36-9+ Ap '70
Auto tape tours. il Travel 133:26 My '70
Coming: national parks for city dwellers. il U S News 69:76-7 N 23 '70

NATIONAL parks and reserves—United States
—*Continued*
Future & the parks. A. W. Smith. Nat Parks & Con Mag 44:2 O '70
Human injury inflicted by grizzly bears. S. Herrero. bibliog il Science 170:593-8 N 6 '70
Islands in time; proposed National system of islands; with text of bill. E. C. Crafts. il Am For 76:16-19+ D '70
Let's stop mining in our national parks and wilderness areas; with editorial comment. R. D. Butcher. il Am For 76:11, 28-31+ S '70
National park wilderness reviews (lost in the wilderness) E. M. Dickerman. il Liv Wildn 34:40-9 Spr '70
National parks association; report of the president and general counsel, May 22, 1970. A. W. Smith. Nat Parks & Con Mag 44:17-20 My '70
National seashores. E. Welke. il Bet Hom & Gard 48:131-6 N '70
Our national parks: a living heritage; with statements by W. J. Hickel and G. B. Hartzog, jr. il Parks & Rec 5:31-46 Je '70
People, parks, and traffic. A. W. Smith. Nat Parks & Con Mag 44:2 My '70
Should the eagle live? admission fees. Newsweek 75:91 Je 22 '70
Sign language of the national park system. J. E. N. Jensen. il Parks & Rec 5:42-3+ N '70
They're grabbing our hunting land; Calif.-Nevada land swap. D. Lynch. Field & S 75:12+ Ag '70
See also
National forests
United States—National park service
    also names of national parks and reserves, e.g. Bryce Canyon National Park

Washington (state)
See also
North Cascades National Park

Wyoming
See also
Grand Teton National Park
Yellowstone National Park
NATIONAL parks association.   See National parks and conservation association
NATIONAL pastoral council (proposed)
Do we want a national pastoral council? America 123:83 Ag 22 '70
Feasibility of a national Catholic pastoral council to be studied. Chr Cent 87:1147 S 30 '70
Step forward, at Mundelein. T. E. Clarke. il America 123:198-200 S 26 '70
NATIONAL pilots association
We fly an NPA proficiency race, and lose. P. Garrison. il Flying 86:42-4+ My '70
NATIONAL planning

United States
See United States—Social policy
NATIONAL planning association
Rosy hue beyond the gloom. il Bsns W p68 My 23 '70
NATIONAL pork industry conference
Hogmen plan biggest meeting ever. J. Russell. Farm J 94:50F Mr '70
NATIONAL pork producers council
Hogmen plan biggest meeting ever. J. Russell. Farm J 94:50F Mr '70
Research summaries zero in on major pork problems. J. Russell. il Farm J 93:H24 N '69
Your nickels have helped plenty and will do more in '70. D. Seim. il Farm J 94:H28 Mr '70
NATIONAL press club
Breakfast with Godfrey. il Time 95:72 Mr 16 '70
For love or money? Newsweek 76:130 O 12 '70
NATIONAL psychology. See National characteristics
NATIONAL railroad passenger corporation
Green signal for better rail travel. il U S News 69:24 O 26 '70
Now the Railpax row will begin. Bsns W p38 N 28 '70
One last try; proposed National railroad passenger corporation. Newsweek 76:75 O 26 '70
Railpax plan. il Newsweek 76:84+ D 14 '70
Starting signal for better trains; Railpax bill. Bsns W p35-6 O 24 '70
Step to nationalization. Time 96:104+ O 26 '70
Trying it on the cheap; Railpax scheme. il Forbes 106:31 D 1 '70

NATIONAL recreation and park association
Manpower crises: as others see us. H. D. Sessoms. il Parks & Rec 5:39-41+ Ja '70
NRPA: model cities. Parks & Rec 5:53-6 Jl '70
NRPA model cities contract ends. Parks & Rec 5:55-6 D '70
NRPA national awards. il Parks & Rec 9:60-1+ S '70
NRPA news. See issues of Parks & recreation
Meetings, 1970
Changing concepts: citizen safety in parks and recreation; national forum. I. J. Hutchison, jr. il Parks & Rec 9:43-4+ S '70
Highlights: 1970 congress for recreation and parks. il Parks & Rec 5:25-35 N '70
Law enforcement: citizen safety in parks and recreation; National forum series. Parks & Rec 5:11 N '70
1970 congress for recreation and parks. il Parks & Rec 9:45-56 S '70
Right on! Youth forum on the environment. Y. Fogel. il Parks & Rec 5:24+ N '70
NATIONAL recreation areas. See Recreation areas
NATIONAL recreation association. See National recreation and park association
NATIONAL register (periodical) See Catholic press
NATIONAL resource lands. See Public lands—United States
NATIONAL responsibility. See Responsibility
NATIONAL retired teachers association
AARP, NRTA, hold biennial meetings; report big growth; late start plan continued by $251,880 grant. il Aging 190:12-13 Ag '70
NATIONAL review
Clinton Rossiter. W. F. Buckley. Nat R 22:775 Jl 28 '70
In the beginning . . . W. F. Buckley, jr. Nat R 22:1263-5 D 1 '70
Inside story. il Nat R 22:1290-1 D 1 '70
Mrs Hazelton throws a bash; fifteenth birthday. il pors Nat R 22:1296-301 D 1 '70
National review's little war. P. Steinfels. Commonweal 93:213 N 27 '70
Notes asides; letter to W. F. Buckley with comments by members of editorial board. T. McSloy. Nat R 22:347-51 Ap 7 '70
Notes on a fifteenth anniversary. P. L. Buckley. Nat R 22:1260+ D 1 '70
Odyssey of a friend: letters to W. F. Buckley, jr, 1957-1961. W. Chambers. bibliog f Nat R 22:132-7+ F 10 '70
Profile in courage: Ted Sorensen's finest hour. Nat R 22:345-7 Ap 7 '70
NATIONAL sand championship. See Motor vehicle racing
NATIONAL school lunch program. See School lunches
NATIONAL science foundation.   See United States—National science foundation
NATIONAL seashores. See National parks and reserves—United States
NATIONAL secretaries association
Do you drive your secretary up the wall? annual convention. il Nations Bsns 58:50-3 D '70
NATIONAL security. See Internal security
NATIONAL security council. See United States—National security council
NATIONAL semiconductor corporation
Avionics offers prime target for air cargo expansion. Aviation W 93:123-6 O 26 '70
Confounding an industry on prices. il por Bsns W p44+ N 21 '70
NATIONAL sex and drug forum of San Francisco
National sex and drug forum; another viewpoint. P. Tracy. Commonweal 93:194-5 N 20 '70
Sex, sex, sexxzzzzzz. R. B. Miller. Commonweal 93:192-7 N 20 '70
NATIONAL shooting dog championship.   See Field trials (dogs)
NATIONAL socialism
About that Hitler quote: law and order. J. D. Lofton, jr. Nat R 22:411 Ap 21 '70
In Hitler's service. L. S. Dawidowicz. bibliog f Commentary 50:85-90 N '70
Inside the Third reich, by A. Speer. Review Bsns W p6-7 Ag 29 '70. O. Friedrich Nat R 22:958 S 8 '70. M. L. Kahn Time il por 96:58+ S 7 '70. K. R. Johnson
Measures against Nazism and racial intolerance; with text of resolution. UN Mo Chron 7:107 Ja '70
Red fascism; the merger of Nazi Germany and Soviet Russia in the American image of totalitarianism, 1930's-1950's. L. K. Adler and T. G. Paterson. bibliog f Am Hist R 75:1046-64 Ap '70; Discussion. 75:2155-64 D '70

NATIONAL songs
United States
Schools, songs, and supplications. J. F. Gummere. Sch & Soc 98:299-300 Sum '70
See also
State songs
NATIONAL speed centers
Fried chicken and speed equipment. il Hot Rod 23:108 Jl '70
NATIONAL student marketing corporation
How Cortes Randell drained the fountain of youth. R. Loving, jr. il por Fortune 81:94-7+ Ap '70
Pied Piper of Wall Street. il por Time 95:94 Ap 13 '70
NATIONAL symbols. See Symbolism
NATIONAL system of islands (proposed) See National parks and reserves—United States
NATIONAL teacher corps. See United States—National teacher corps
NATIONAL technical information service. See United States—Commerce, Department of —National technical information service
NATIONAL theatre company of Great Britain. See Theater—Great Britain
NATIONAL tobacco spitting contest. See Competitions
NATIONAL trust for historic preservation
Twenty-one years for the Historic trust. J. Prendergast. il Parks & Rec 5:12-13+ N '70
NATIONAL united front of Kampuchea. See Guerrillas—Cambodia
NATIONAL urban coalition. See Urban coalition (organization)
NATIONAL urban league
Strategy for the seventies: unity, coalition, negotiation; address, July 19, 1970. W. M. Young, jr. Vital Speeches 36:732-6 S 15 '70
Whitney Young: black leader or "Oreo cookie"? T. Buckley. il pors N Y Times Mag p32-3+ S 20 '70
NATIONAL weather service. See United States —National weather service
NATIONAL welfare rights organization
Champion of welfare rights. C. P. DuBose. il Ebony 25:31-4+ Ap '70
Now it's welfare lib; Concerned parents for adequate welfare. R. Rogin. il N Y Times Mag p30-1+ S 27 '70
NATIONAL wildlife federation
Awards for conservation achievement. il Nat Wildlife 8:13 Je '70
Conservation summit. il Nat Wildlife 8:20-1 F '70
Do-or-die decade; report of 34th annual meeting. J. Strohm. il Nat Wildlife 8:28-31 Je '70
EQ critical list. See issues of National wildlife
1970 National EQ index. il Nat Wildlife 8:25-40 O '70; Same. Schol Teach Jr/Sr High pA1-16 O 5 '70
Trees for the Arch; project of Future trees foundation. il Nat Wildlife 8:56-7 D '69
NATIONAL woman's Christian temperance union. See Woman's Christian temperance union
NATIONAL woman's party
Where are they now? pors Newsweek 75:18 Mr 23 '70
NATIONAL youth service (proposed) See Service, Compulsory non-military
NATIONAL zoological park, Washington, D.C.
Meanwhile, back at the zoo. H. Schaden. il Am Ed 6:18-25 Ag '70
NATIONALISM
See also subhead Nationalism under names of countries, e.g. Libya—Nationalism; *also* under groups of people, e.g. Negroes—Nationalism

Negro race
See Negroes—Nationalism
NATIONALITY. See Citizenship
NATIONALIZATION of alien property. See Eminent domain (international law)
NATIONALIZATION of industry. See Government ownership
NATIONALIZATION of railroads. See Railroads and state
NATIONS
Facts & figures of nations & states; tables. Sr Schol 95:12-14+ S 22 '69; 97:19-22 S 21 '70
NATIVITY groups. See Christmas cribs
NATIVITY of Christ. See Jesus Christ—Nativity
NATO
Britain, Europe and the Alliance. M. Stewart. For Affairs 48:648-59 Jl '70
Defense or détente? il Time 95:36 Je 8 '70
Europe: of defense and détente. il Time 96:24+ D 14 '70

Europe revises startegic planning basis. E. H. Kolcum. il Aviation W 92:49-50+ Mr 9 '70
Germany in the era of negotiations. H. Schmidt. For Affairs 49:40-50 O '70
NATO: an uneasy alliance. N. A. Graebner. Cur Hist 58:298-303+ My '70
NATO burden-sharing; its ups and downs. B. M. Russett. America 122:586-7 My 30 '70
Nato, by H. Cleveland. Review
    Sat R 53:31-2 S 5 '70. N. King
NATO force level study sought. Aviation W 92:22 My 18 '70
NATO in the coming decade; address, April 21, 1970. R. F. Pedersen. Dept State Bul 62:633-6 My 18 '70
NATO satcom nears operational status. D. E. Fink. Aviation W 92:20-1 Je 1 '70
Non-military dimensions of NATO. M. Cronin. America 123:89-90 Ag 22 '70
North Atlantic council meets at Rome; text of final communique; with text of declaration, May 27, 1970. Dept State Bul 62:772-5 Je 22 '70
North Atlantic council ministerial meeting held at Brussels; text of final communique and declaration, December 1969. Dept State Bul 61:627-30 D 29 '69
Our continuing commitment to western Europe; address, December 6, 1969. W. P. Rogers. Dept State Bul 61:622-5 D 29 '69
Proposed European security conference; excerpts from Brussels declaration. Cur Hist 58:305+ My '70
Reports. D. Cook. Atlan 225:14+ Ja '70
Secretary attends NATO meeting at Rome; visits Madrid and Lisbon; Department announcement with Secretary Rogers' arrival remarks and text of joint U.S.-Spain communique, May 24, 28 and 29, 1970. Dept State Bul 62:775-7 Je 22 '70
Secretary Rogers attends NATO ministerial meeting, Department announcement; with statement by Secretary Rogers, December 2, 1969. Dept State Bul 61:625-6 D 29 '69
Soviet Mediterranean push deepens; with editorial comment. E. H. Kolcum. il Aviation W 92:9, 14-18 Mr 30 '70
We're paying too much for NATO. C. H. Percy. Read Digest 97:115-18 N '70
Withdrawal symptoms; Foreign ministers meeting. il Newsweek 75:41 Je 8 '70
See also
Atlantic community

Armed forces
Harriers readied for NATO role. H. J. Coleman. il Aviation W 94:13-15 Ja 4 '71
United States forces in Europe; address, April 10, 1970. S. R. Resor. Vital Speeches 36:456-9 My 15 '70
What Nato did to ease load on U.S. U S News 69:53 D 14 '70
Why U.S. will not take GI's out of Europe now; with interview with Gen. A. J. Goodpaster. il U S News 69:59-63 D 7 '70

Committee on the challenges of modern society
NATO environmental committee holds second session; remarks, April 13, 1970. D. P. Moynihan. Dept State Bul 62:636 My 18 '70
NATO environmental committee meets at Brussels; message. R. M. Nixon. Dept State Bul 63:647 N 23 '70
NATO experts recommend international action on ocean oil spills; White House announcement; with statement by J. A. Volpe, and text of resolution. Dept State Bul 63:665-9 N 30 '70
NATRONA COUNTY, Wyo, public library, Casper
CATV+NCPL-VRS: Video reference service over a community TV system. K. E. Dowlin. il pors Library J 95:2768-70 S 1 '70
NATURAL areas. See Wilderness areas
NATURAL childbirth. See Childbirth
NATURAL gas. See Gas, Natural
NATURAL gas industry. See Gas industry
NATURAL history
Naturalist at large. See issues of Natural history
See also
Nature study
Wildlife conservation

Study and teaching
See also
Nature study
NATURAL history museums
See also
American museum of natural history, New York

NATURAL law (science) See Nature, Laws of
NATURAL monuments
See also
Wilderness areas
NATURAL resources
Beyond survival. J. Poppy. il Look 34:22-9 Ja 13 '70
Human materials production as a process in the biosphere. H. Brown. il Sci Am 223:194-8+ bibliog(p266) S '70
Metropolis and the transformation of resources. R. L. Meier. il Bul Atom Sci 26:2-5+ My '70
Resources and social structure: some conditions of stability and change. W. R. Burch, jr. bibliog f il Ann Am Acad 389:27-34 My '70
See also
Conservation of resources
Marine resources
Mines and mineral resources
Power resources
Raw materials
Water supply
Wildlife conservation

Bibliography
Reading about resources. M. Bush. See issues of American forests

Laws and legislation
Timber battle is far from over; government-owned timberland. il Bsns W p30 Mr 14 '70

Alaska
See also
Conservation of resources—Alaska

Antarctic Regions
Antarctic: any economic future? N. Potter. il por Bul Atom Sci 26:94-9 D '70

Ghana
Ghana. T. E. Hilton. bibliog il Focus 21:1-8 O '70

Jordan
Jordan. I. R. Manners. bibliog il Focus 20:1-7 Ap '70

Nigeria
Nigeria. C. H. Lyons. bibliog il Focus 21:1-7 D '70

Rhodesia
Rhodesia. T. J. Kubiak. il Focus 20:1-11 Je '70

Spain
Spain. P. M. Enggass. bibliog il Focus 20:1-8 My '70

Surinam
Surinam. R. Tirtha and C. Loeser. bibliog il Focus 21:1-11 S '70

Thailand
Thailand. L. Unger. bibliog il Focus 21:1-9 N '70

United States
Symposium on the shape of tomorrow. F. S. Forsberg. Field & S 75:55 Je '70
U.S. resources: a tally sheet; symposium. bibliog(p360+) il Cur Hist 58:321-59+ Je '70
Washington lookout. V. Trumbull. See issues of American forests
NATURAL resources council of America
Natural resources council of America welcomed at White House. il Am For 76:5 My '70
NATURAL selection
Control of population; excerpt from The social contract. R. Ardrey. il Life 68:48-52+ F 20 '70; Same abr. with title Nature and the case for birth control. Read Digest 96:116-20 Je '70
Dominance and the niche in ecological systems. S. J. McNaughton and L. L. Wolf. bibliog il Science 167:131-9 Ja 9 '70; Reply with rejoinder. H. H. Shugart, jr. 170:1335 D 18 '70
Man's decline as a species. A. H. Drummond, jr. bibliog il Sci Digest 68:26-31 Jl '70
Social subordination, population density, and mammalian evolution. J. J. Christian. bibliog Science 168:84-90 Ap 3 '70; Reply with rejoinder. M. D. F. Udvardy. 170:344-6 O 16 '70
NATURAL steam. See Steam, Natural
NATURAL theology
Struggle for an ecological theology: a case in point; Faith-man-nature group's conference. H. P. Santmire. Chr Cent 87:275-7 Mr 4 '70
NATURALISM in art. See Realism in art
NATURALISM in literature. See Realism in literature

NATURALISTS
Naturalist at large. See issues of Natural history
See also
Lawick, J. G.
Sielmann, H.
NATURALIZATION
Ceremony for citizens; the Zweiflers and others in Kingston, N.Y. il Life 68:32B-32D Mr 27 '70
See also
Citizenship
NATURE
Declare a moratorium on the war against nature. E. Gibbons. il Org Gard & Farm 17:112-15 Mr '70
You have to believe. W. Harter. il PTA Mag 64:15 My '70
See also
Man—Influence on nature
Outdoor life
Smithsonian institution—Center for short-lived phenomena
Winter

Bibliography
Books in review. See issues of Natural history
Naturalist's bookshelf. See issues of Audubon

Religious interpretations
Mike Frome. M. Frome. Am For 76:3+ Jl '70
NATURE (aesthetics)
Art: its frame and nature. S. McIlhany. Am Artist 34:5 My '70
Isolation of a single aspect of nature. R. Henkes. il Design 71:20-1 Sum '70
Letter to a nature lover; nature-study-art. K. Kuh. Sat R 53:50-1 Ap 25 '70
NATURE, Laws of
Forces of nature: testing their strength. G. L. Wick. bibliog il Science 168:1329-31 Je 12 '70
NATURE and art. See Nature (aesthetics)
NATURE and man. See Man—Influence on nature
NATURE centers
Cincinnati nature center. M. F. Bohm. Horticulture 48:26-7+ My '70
Face to face with nature. il Sunset 145:54-9 S '70
New equation: Nature center, community involvement. L. K. Daniels. il Am For 76:20-3+ N '70
No time to talk. J. J. Shomon. il Parks & Rec 9:37+ S '70
NATURE conservancy (organization)
For land's sake. il Newsweek 75:87B My 18 '70
Generous gift from Georgia-Pacific. il Am For 76:48-50 Mr '70
NATURE conservation. See Conservation of resources
NATURE conservation year. See Conservation of resources—Europe, Western
NATURE in art
Feel of winter. il Design 71:8-9 Wint '69
Reflections. M. McCarthy. New Yorker 45:39-40+ Ja 24 '70
See also
Birds in art
Landscape painting
NATURE in literature
Reflections. M. McCarthy. New Yorker 45:39-40+ Ja 24 '70
NATURE in poetry
Robert Frost and wilderness. W. Van Dore. por Liv Wildn 34:47-9 Sum '70
NATURE of man. See Man
NATURE of the crime; drama. See Cohen, L.
NATURE photography
Camera with a cause; B. Norton's conservation photography. K. Poli. il Pop Phot 67:92-7 D '70
Extend the pleasure of gardening through photography. F. J. Pratson. il Horticulture 48:32-3+ Ag '70
Fragile beauty all about us. H. S. C. Yen. il Nat Geog 138:784-95 D '70
Many faces of nature. il Nat Wildlife 9:29-35 D '70
Meadow morning; photographs. D. Cavagnaro. Audubon 72:28-35 N '70
Take a camera camping. C. B. Colby. il Outdoor Life 146:14-16+ Jl '70
Two winners revel in nature's minutiae. il Life 69:83-9 D 25 '70
Wynn Bullock; tracing the roots of man in nature. B. Bullock; J. N. Uelsmann. il Mod Phot 34:84-9+ My '70
See also
Photography of animals
Photography of birds
Photography of flowers, plants, trees, etc.

NATURE study
Conservation summit; plans for a week at Estes Park, Colo. for members of National wildlife federation. il Nat Wildlife 8:20-1 F '70
Conservationists turn on for children of the concrete. A. Dennis. il Nat Parks & Con Mag 44:4-9 Je '70
Creating an effective interpretive program; Bryce Canyon National Park. D. W. Halloran. il Nat Parks 44:10-13 Mr '70
Earth's words in the national parks. D. Lambert. il Nat Parks & Con Mag 44:16-22 Jl '70
Exploring the great outdoors. K. Davis. il Parents Mag 45:62-3+ Mr '70
Race between education and catastrophe. J. R. Vanderzicht. il Parks & Rec 5:29-32+ Ja '70
To build nature interest, use what you have! T. Stinson. il Camp Mag 42:13 Ja '70
See also
Bird study
Botany—Study and teaching
Childrens gardens
Nature
Nature centers
NATURE trails. See Trails
NATURE trails for the blind. See Trails
NAUER, Barbara J.
Day after aggiornamento. il America 124: 36-40 Ja 16 '71
NAUGHTON, James M.
I'm an ordinary man. . . il pors N Y Times Mag p8-9+ D 27 '70
NAUGHTON, John B.
Clever cars, these Pintos; interview. il pors Motor T 22:52-5+ S '70
Ford's top brass talks about Pinto power; interview, ed. by J. Dunne. il pors Pop Sci 197:54-5+ S '70
NAUGHTON, Patience Jarvis
Susan Hill is having a baby; story. Ladies Home J 87:48 Je '70
NAUHEIM, Bob
Gift of the Gualala. il Outdoor Life 146:50-1+ D '70
Kings come to the Smith. il pors Outdoor Life 146:90-3+ O '70
NAUMER, Janet Noll
American Indians: a bibliography of sources. il Am Lib 1:861-4 O '70
Lilliput in the South Pacific. C. Lucas. il Read Digest 96:211-12+ Ja '70
NAUTICAL astronomy
See also
Longitude
NAUTICAL charts
Charts. Motor B 127:169-70+ Ja '71
New charts. E. S. Maloney. See issues of Motor boating to July 1970
Notices to boatmen. Motor B 126:32-3+ Ag; 34+ S; 30+ O; 30+ N; 24+ D '70; 127:13+ Ja '71
Skipper and his charts. E. S. Maloney. Motor B 125:146-7 Ja '70
NAUTICAL education
Face to face with a student seaman. por Seventeen 29:32 Je '70
Return of the dropouts; Florida ocean science institute. B. Robinson. il Motor B 126:44-5 D '70
Sea Ed; high school program. C. G. Fader. il Todays Ed 59:30-1 D '70
See also
Training ships
NAUTICAL instruments
See also
Automatic pilot (boats)
Compass
NAUTILUS, Paper. See Paper nautilus
NAUVOO, Ill.
Mormon items. L. L. Quihuis. il Hobbies 75: 48-9 Ag '70
NAVA, Julian
Two against Rafferty. N. Melnick. New Repub 162:11-12 Mr 21 '70 *
NAVAHO Indians
Failure in Navaho schooling. D. A. Erickson. il Parents Mag 45:66-8+ S '70
Industry invades the reservation. il Bsns W p72-3 Ap 4 '70
Mom, Michael & the five little Indians; adoption of Navahos by newlyweds Lynn and Mike Milot. W. J. McKean. il Look 34:76-80 Je 30 '70
Navajo children draw. C. Gross. il Sch Arts 70:14-15 N '70
New eyes for Tom Large Whiskers. W. C. Heinz. il pors Todays Health 48:30-3+ S '70
Soul of the Navajo. J. Loh. il Esquire 74: 162-7+ N '70

NAVAHO willow planting. See Tree planting
NAVAJO community college, Many Farms. Ariz.
Wind is rising. B. E. Richardson. bibliog il por Library J 95:463-7 F 1 '70
NAVAJO Indians. See Navaho Indians
NAVAL air propulsion test center. See United States—Naval air propulsion test center
NAVAL airplanes. See Airplanes, Military
NAVAL architects. See Architects
NAVAL architecture
See also
Boatbuilding
Hulls (naval architecture)
Masts and rigging
Yachts—Design
NAVAL art and science
See also
Seamanship
NAVAL bases. See Navy yards and naval stations
NAVAL battles
See also
United States—History—Revolution—Naval operations
NAVAL history
Evolution of the Ottoman seaborne empire in the age of the oceanic discoveries, 1453-1525. A. C. Hess. bibliog f il Am Hist R 75:1892-919 D '70
Germany and the Russo-Japanese war. J. Steinberg. bibliog f Am Hist R 75:1965-86 D '70
NAVAL museums
Seafarers' serenity: Europe's maritime museums. L. M. Rhodes. il Travel 133:60-4+ F '70
See also
Mystic seaport museum, Mystic, Conn.
NAVAL offenses
United States
See United States—Navy—Crimes and misdemeanors
NAVAL power. See Sea power
NAVARRO, Rafael G.
Gramco: the second domino. por Time 96:79-80 O 19 '70 *
NAVASKY, Victor S.
Government and Martin Luther King. pors Atlan 226:43-52 N '70
Right on! With lawyer William Kunstler. il pors N Y Times Mag p30-1+ Ap 19 '70
(ed) See Morgenthau, R. M. Famous prosecutor talks about crime
NAVIDI, Marjorie H. and others
Inorganic liquid photovoltaic cell: tetravalent molybdenum in water. il Science 169:980-1 S 4 '70
NAVIES
See also
Sea power
also subhead Navy under names of countries, e.g. Russia—Navies
NAVIGATING bridge
Can your boat take a flying bridge? H. C. Rickborn. il Motor B 126:68-70+ N '70
NAVIGATION
Basic position finding. E. A. Zadig. il Motor B 125:30-2+ Je '70
By sound and smell. R. Kelton. il Yachting 128:66-7+ D '70
Navigation and piloting; power and sail (title varies) See issues of Motor boating
Navigation for fishermen. J. A. Emmett. il Outdoor Life 145:22+ Je '70
See also
Artificial satellites—Navigational use
Azimuth
Boats and boating
Compass
Knots and splices
Logbooks (ships)
Longitude
Loran
Masts and rigging
Nautical charts
Pilots and pilotage
Radar in navigation
Radio in navigation
Sailing
Seamanship
Seamen
Winds

Aids and devices
Easy-to-make time/distance/speed scales. D. Van Volkenburg. il Motor B 126:34 Ag '70
See also
Buoys
Electronics in navigation
Radio in navigation

NAVIGATION—*Continued*

Competitions

Control points. M. L. Hersey. See issues of Yachting

Predict & win; Predicted log competitions. G. Byrnes. il Motor B 126:60-1+ Ag '70

NAVIGATION, Aerial

Day I moved Vancouver. D. Johnson. Flying 87:87 O '70

See also

Inertial guidance systems

Loran

Aids and devices

DC-10 navigation system decision nears; area navigation system. il Aviation W 93:32-3 Ag 31 '70

New roller map navaid developed. C. E. Schneider. il Aviation W 93:77+ N 23 '70

Varied navaids ease transatlantic flights. K. J. Stein. il Aviation W 93:52+ D 14 '70

See also

Decca navigator company, ltd.

NAVIGATION, Primitive

Ancient star paths; excerpts from journal. D. Lewis. il por Yachting 127:62-3+ Mr '70

East is a big bird; excerpts. T. Gladwin. il Natur Hist 79:24-35 Ap; 58-69 My '70

NAVRATIL, James D.

Niobium: space age metal. bibliog il por Chem 43:13-15 S '70

NAVY department. See United States—Navy department

NAVY yards and naval stations

Another test for U.S: threat of a Russian sub base in Cuba; submarine base at Cienfuegos. il U S News 69:22-3 O 12 '70

Inside Holy Loch; with report by R. B. Stolley. il Life 68:66-9+ Ap 3 '70

Soviets boost Caribbean presence. C. Brownlow. il Aviation W 93:16-17 D 21 '70

Sub fuss; base at Cienfuegos. Newsweek 76:41 O 26 '70

Subs of Cienfuegos. il Time 96:20 D 28 '70

NAXALITES (organization) See Communist party (India)

NAXOS (island)

Ariadne's island. F. Stevenson. il Opera N 34:10-13 Mr 28 '70

NAYAR, Anil

Spicy day at Penn. R. Blount, jr. il por Sports Illus 32:58-9 Mr 9 '70 *

NAZARETH, Israel

Nazareth elections: anything good? D. Baker. Chr Today 15:30 Ja 15 '71

NAZCA lines. See Petroglyphs

NAZI spies. See Spies

NAZISM. See National socialism

NAZZARO, Pellegrino

Italy in Europe. Cur Hist 58:281-6 My '70

NDONGMO, Albert, bp

Church and state in Cameroon. J. Derrick. il por America 124:18-20 Ja 9 '71 *

NE Win

Which is the Burma road. Ne Win or U Nu? H. D. S. Greenway. il pors N Y Times Mag p34-5+ My 3 '70 *

NEAGLE, David

In pursuit of duty. G. L. Roberts. il pors Am West 7:26-33+ S '70 *

NEAL, Avon

Graven images: sermons in stones. il Am Heritage 21:18-29 Ag '70

When shall we three meet again, in thunder, lightning, or in rain? il Am Heritage 21:74-7 Ap '70

NEAL, Charles V.

How to budget. il Todays Ed 59:48-9 S '70

NEAL, G.

FET's as audio switches. il Electr World 84:46+ Ag '70

NEAL, Julia

Regional characteristics of western Shaker furniture. il Antiques 98:611-17 O '70

NEANDERTHAL race

Ghar-i-Mordeh Gusfand (Cave of the dead sheep): a new Mousterian locality in north Afghanistan. L. Dupree and others. bibliog il Science 167:1610-12 Mr 20 '70

NEAR EAST. See Middle East

NEARING, Helen (Knothe)

—and Nearing, Scott

Our ten-year strawberry bed. il Org Gard & Farm 17:44-5 F '70

about

Prophets of the good life. Newsweek 76:100+ S 14 '70 *

Up on the farm. C. Elliott. il por Time 97:78 Ja 18 '71 *

NEARING, Scott

—See Nearing, H. K. jt. auth.

about

Away from it all. J. Thompson. Harper 241:120-2 N '70 *

Nation congratulates. Nation 211:485 N 16 '70 *

Prophets of the good life. Newsweek 76:100+ S 14 '70 *

Up on the farm. C. Elliott. il por Time 97:78 Ja 18 '71 *

NEARY, John

Blight blossoms on the highway. Life 69:34 Jl 24 '70

Jensenism: variation on a racial theme. il pors Life 68:58B-58D+ Je 12 '70

Pornography goes public. il Life 69:18-25 Ag 28 '70

Two girls from no. 18. il pors Life 68:26-9 Mr 27 '70

NEARY, Patricia

Patricia Neary arrives. J. Reibstein. il pors Dance Mag 44:38-41 F '70

NEATNESS

Anecdotes, facetiae, satire, etc.

Note from my real office. L. Conger. Writer 83:9-10 O '70

NEBRASKA

Politics and government

Matter of money. Newsweek 75:44 My 11 '70

NEBULAE

Dissecting the Crab. G. Burbidge. il Natur Hist 79:66-73 O '70

Far-ultraviolet photography of Orion: interstellar dust. R. C. Henry and G. R. Carruthers. bibliog il Science 170:527-31 O 30 '70

Planetary nebulae. L. H. Aller. See issues of Sky and telescope to July 1970

See also

Magellanic clouds

NECK exercises. See Exercise

NECKER, Robert

Dream stuff; poem. Sat R 53:16 Ap 11 '70

NECKLACES

Neck deep in dog collars. il Life 69:58-9 S 18 '70

NECTARINES

Apricots, nectarines and almonds. G. L. Slate. il Horticulture 48:42-3+ My '70

NEDERHOOD, Joel H.

Christians and revolution. Chr Today 15:7-9 Ja 1 '71

NEEDHAM, James Joseph

Accounting and the SEC; interview. por Duns 96:10-11+ O '70

NEEDHAM, Mass.

Looking like new; industrial parks. il Nations Bsns 58:93-4+ O '70

NEEDLEPOINT

Crafty animal patterns. A. Wiglama. il House B 112:98-9 S '70

Gift of needlepoint. il House & Gard 138:86-7 D '70

NEEDLEWORK

Beginner's view of basic needlework arts. il Good H 170:152 Je '70

Needlework in private hands. il McCalls 97:68-77+ F '70

Pillows to prize. il Redbook 134:106-7 Mr '70

Susanna Rowson and her academy. J. C. Giffen. il por Antiques 98:436-40 S '70

See also

Crewel work

Crocheting

Embroidery

Knitting

Macramé

Needlepoint

Quilts

Tapestry

NEEL, James V.

Lessons from a primitive people. bibliog il Science 170:815-22 N 20 '70

NÉEL, Louis Eugène Félix

Divide and honor. pors Newsweek 76:100 N 9 '70 *

Magnetism to metabolism. Sci N 98:348 O 31 '70 *

Nobel laureates for 1970; Hannes Alfvén and Louis Néel. G. B. Lubkin. pors Phys Today 23:61-3 D '70 *

Nobel prize. W. C. Koehler. por Science 170:606-7 N 6 '70 *

Plasmas, magnets and sugars. il por Time 96:39 N 9 '70 *

NEFF, John

Tortoise and the hare. il por Forbes 105:72-3 Ap 1 '70 *

NEGATIVE cash. See Depreciation

NEGATIVE differential conductivity. See Electric conductivity

NEGATIVE income tax
Toward an ultimate solution. Y. Brozen. il
Sat R 53:30-1+ My 23 '70
NEGATIVE option sales plans. See Postal
service—Unordered merchandise
NEGATIVES, Photographic. See Photography
—Negatives
NEGLIGENCE
See also
Liability (law)
NEGOTIABLE instruments
Fed watchers spot a hint of ease; two
changes in reserve requirements. Bsns W
p21 Ag 22 '70
Highly volatile paper; commercial paper. il
Time 96:60 Jl 6 '70
Liquidity fears crease the paper market. il
Bsns W p90+ Jl 11 '70
NEGOTIATION, International. See Internation-
al relations
NEGRI, Pola
Where are they now? pors Newsweek 75:26
Ap 20 '70 *
NEGRITUDE. See Negroes—Nationalism
NEGRO (organization) See National economic
growth and reconstruction organization
NEGRO actors and actresses
Hair; controversial musical is biggest outlet
for black actors in U.S. stage history. H.
H. King. il Ebony 25:120-2+ My '70
Real anger was backstage; racial tensions
during shooting of Halls of anger. B.
Schulberg. il por Life 69:50-2+ Ag 21 '70
See also
Foster, G.
Gunn, M.
Haynes, L.
Little, C.
Moore, M.
Negroes in moving pictures
Robeson, P.
Williams, C. 3d
NEGRO advertising agencies
Gray skies for black admen. il Bsns W p81-2
O 31 '70
NEGRO air pilots
He helps jockey the jumbo. il pors Ebony 25:
54-6+ S '70
NEGRO ambassadors
Holland to Sweden. por Time 95:13-14 Ja 26
'70
See also
Holland, J. H.
NEGRO architects
Minorities in the profession. E. P. Berkeley.
Arch Forum 132:56-9 Je '70
NEGRO art. See Art, Negro (American)
NEGRO artists
Black creativity in quest of an audience. H.
Ghent. Art in Am 58:35 My '70
Focus on black artists: a project for schools
and community. R. J. Craig. il Sch Arts
70:30-3 N '70
Object: diversity. il Time 95:80-7 Ap 6 '70
See also
Art, Negro (American)
Golding, W. O.
National center of Afro-American artists
Negroes in art
NEGRO associations. See Negroes—Clubs, soci-
eties, etc.
NEGRO athletes
Black athlete in the golden age of sports
(title varies) (cont) A. S. Young. il Ebony
25:116-20 S; 56-8 O; 26:108-10+ D '70
No! Not John Smith! national AAU track and
field championship winner. P. Putnam. il
pors Sports Illus 33:10-13 Jl 6 '70
These Mills bros. are in the record business,
too. P. Putnam. il pors Sports Illus 32:57-
8 My 4 '70
See also
Mills, C.
Owens, J.
Robinson, F.
NEGRO authors
Indivisible man; interview, ed. by J. A.
McPherson. R. Ellison. por Atlan 226:45-
60 D '70
See also
Baldwin, J.
Ellison, R.
Himes, C. B.
Lester, J.
Negro poets
Wright, R.
NEGRO automobile dealers. See Automobile
dealers
NEGRO automobile mechanics. See Automo-
bile mechanics (persons)
NEGRO bands. See Bands (music)
NEGRO bankers
See also
United mortgage bankers of America

NEGRO banks. See Banks and banking, Negro
NEGRO baseball managers. See Baseball man-
agers
NEGRO baseball players. See Baseball players
NEGRO basketball players. See Basketball
players
NEGRO boxers. See Boxers
NEGRO boys. See Negro youth
NEGRO businessmen
Athlete in business. A. S. Young. il Ebony
26:108-10+ D '70
Major break for a minority member. Nations
Bsns 58:58 Mr '70
Mini-giant of the bindery industry. il Ebony
25:128-30+ My '70
Opening doors to opportunity; OIC. il pors
Nations Bsns 58:48-9+ Ap '70
See also
Black capitalism
Harris, M. R.
Negro executives
NEGRO camp counselors. See Camp counselors
NEGRO-Caucasian club. See College clubs and
societies
NEGRO celebrities
Do whites make the best domestics? il Es-
quire 74:157-9 O '70
NEGRO children
Child is father to the man; growth of polit-
ical knowledge and feeling among school
children. Trans-Action 7:9 Je '70
How racists use science to degrade black
people. C. T. Rowan. il por Ebony 25:31-
4+ My '70
My children have a right to feel proud. D.
Gilliam. por Redbook 135:62+ Ag '70
See also
Socially handicapped children
NEGRO children as authors. See Children as
authors
NEGRO children as photographers. See Chil-
dren as photographers
NEGRO children in literature
Black book power. Z. Sutherland. il Sat R
53:41 My 9 '70
NEGRO childrens literature. See Childrens lit-
erature
NEGRO church. See Negroes—Religion
NEGRO churches
Black church: three views. C. Marshall; J.
H. Jackson; S. W. Williams. il Time 95:71-3
Ap 6 '70
NEGRO clergy
Black ministry institute rises from Conwell
center. Chr Today 14:47 S 11 '70
See also
National committee of Black churchmen
NEGRO clubs. See Negroes—Clubs, societies,
etc.
NEGRO college graduates. See College grad-
uates, Negro
NEGRO college professors and instructors
See also
Brady, S.
NEGRO college students. See Negro students
NEGRO college students and business. See
Negro students and business
NEGRO colleges and universities
Brain drain at Negro colleges. A. Poinsett.
il Ebony 25:74-6+ O '70
Doctor Charles G. Hurst: the mastermind of
Malcolm X college. A. Poinsett. il pors
Ebony 25:29-32+ Mr '70
Ignorant armies. J. Stevenson; discussion.
Atlan 225:29-30 Ja '70
Nairobi college: East Palo Alto, Calif. V. M.
Johnson. il Mlle 71:290-1+ Ag '70
Reports: black colleges. J. Nelson. Atlan 226:
22-4+ O '70
Toward a black university. S. Henderson. il
por Ebony 25:108-10+ S '70
Toward the black university. V. Harding. il
por Ebony 25:156-9 Ag '70
White liberals and black power in Negro edu-
cation, 1865-1915. J. M. McPherson. bibliog
f il Am Hist R 75:1357-86 Je '70
See also
Fisk university, Nashville, Tenn.
Jackson state college, Jackson, Miss.
Kentucky. State college, Frankfort
Lane college, Jackson, Tenn.
Meharry medical college, Nashville, Tenn.
Miles college, Birmingham, Ala.
Piney Woods country life school
South Carolina. State college, Orangeburg

Federal aid
Aid for black colleges. America 123:308 O
24 '70
Backing black colleges. Chr Today 15:32 O
9 '70

NEGRO comedians
See also
Gregory, D.
Wilson, F.
NEGRO companies
Black capitalism: real, or imagined dollar power. il Sr Schol 95:11-15 Ja 5 '70
White help for black business. M. Brower and D. Little. Harvard Bsns R 48:4-6+ My '70
See also
Alliance ventures, inc.
Black capitalism
Black educational services, inc.
Ethnic enterprizes (firm)
Johnson products company, inc.
Watts manufacturing company
NEGRO conferences
See also
Congress of African people
National black economic development conference
NEGRO congresswomen
See also
Chisholm, S.
NEGRO cowboys. See Cowboys
NEGRO criminals. See Negroes—Crime
NEGRO culture. See Negroes—Culture
NEGRO dancers
Black dance. W. Terry. il Sat R 53:26+ S 26 '70
See also
Alvin Ailey American dance theater
Crutchfield, D.
Mitchell, A.
NEGRO dialect. See Negro-English dialects
NEGRO diplomats
Is the State department color-blind? R. P. Straus. Sat R 54:12-13+ Ja 2 '71
NEGRO drama
Black hopes; presentations in New York city. H. Hewes. Sat R 53:30 F 14 '70
Theatre. J. Novick. Nation 210:733-4 Je 15 '70
See also
Television broadcasting—Drama
NEGRO education. See Negroes—Education
NEGRO educators
See also
Riles, W.
Washington, B. T.
Wharton, C. R. jr
NEGRO employees
Training
See Employees—Training
NEGRO-English dialects
Bi-dialectalism: the linguistics of white supremacy. J. Sledd; reply. J. C. Maxwell. Engl J 59:1158-9 N '70
Black English. O. Mellan. New Repub 163:15-17 N 28 '70
Should ghettoese be accepted? W. Raspberry. Todays Ed 59:30-1+ Ap '70
Slang and profanity: their uses in English composition. D. P. Demarest, jr. Clear House 45:76-80 O '70
NEGRO entertainers
Communicating with laughter. il Time 95:56+ Ap 6 '70
Mecca for blackness; Chicago's Affro-arts theater. il Ebony 25:96-8+ My '70
Miss Black America takes soul to Vietnam. il pors Ebony 25:88-90+ My '70
See also
Gregory, D.
Negro actors and actresses
NEGRO evangelical association. See Evangelistic work
NEGRO executives
Corporate n*gg*r. J. Sack. il por Esquire 74:90-4+ Jl '70
See also
Association for the integration of management
NEGRO family life. See Negroes—Social conditions
NEGRO fiction
Black fiction: a second look. C. Mason. pors Life 68:18 My 8 '70
NEGRO football players. See Football players
NEGRO gangs. See Gangs
NEGRO girls. See Negro youth
NEGRO government employees
Negroes in federal jobs: moving upward. il U S News 68:68 My 25 '70
NEGRO hairdressing. See Hairdressing
NEGRO heroes (periodical) See Comics (books, strips, etc)
NEGRO history. See Negroes—History
NEGRO history week
[Proclamation] R. P. Shafer. il Negro Hist Bul 33:102-3 Ap '70

NEGRO institutions. See Negroes—Clubs, societies, etc.
NEGRO intelligence. See Intelligence levels—Negroes
NEGRO Jews. See Jews, Negro
NEGRO journalists. See Journalists
NEGRO judges
See also
Alexander, R. P.
Crockett, G. W. jr
Smith, O. M.
NEGRO junior colleges. See Negro colleges and universities
NEGRO labor. See Negroes—Employment
NEGRO law students. See Law students
NEGRO lawyers
See also
Billingsley, O.
NEGRO leadership
Jesse Jackson: one leader among many. il pors Time 95:14-16+ Ap 6 '70
NEGRO librarians
Invisible librarian; excerpt from The black librarian in America, ed. by E. J. Josey. E. Mapp. il por Library J 95:3745-7 N 1 '70
Overdue; ALA and the black librarian; strategy for midwinter and beyond, excerpts from The black librarian in America, ed. by E. J. Josey. R. Wedgeworth. por Wilson Lib Bul 45:495-7 Ja '71
See also
Williams, E. C.
NEGRO life and history, Association for the study of. See Association for the study of Negro life and history
NEGRO literature
Book reviews. See issues of Negro history bulletin
Ebony book shelf. See issues of Ebony
Educational approach to Negro individualism. J. A. Headlee. bibliog f Engl J 59:34-9 Ja '70
Humanistic tradition of Afro-American literature; address, July 2, 1970. M. Walker il Am Lib 1:849-54 O '70
Interview with Julius Lester; ed. by P. Meras. J. Lester. Nation 210:762-3 Je 22 '70
See also
African literature
Negro poetry
Negroes in literature
Publishers and publishing—Negro literature
Bibliography
Black literature for the culturally deprived curriculum. J. Alexander. Engl J 59:1229-33 D '70
Study and teaching
Affective aspects of black literature. B. D. Stanford. Engl J 59:371-4 Mr '70
Afro-American literature, the black revolution, and ghetto high schools. K. Kinnamon. bibliog Engl J 59:189-94 F '70
Black literature for the culturally deprived curriculum. J. Alexander. Engl J 59:1229-33 D '70
Non-black teacher, black literature, and black students. R. A. Shepard. Engl J 59:1071-3 N '70
NEGRO marines. See United States—Marine corps—Negroes
NEGRO mayors
Black mayors. il por Newsweek 76:16-18+ Ag 3 '70
Black mayors discuss state of the Nation; interviews. il Ebony 25:76-8+ F '70
See also
Evers, C.
Gibson, K. A.
Washington, W. E.
NEGRO medical students
Matter of opportunity; AMA-commissioned film to recruit Negro students. F. G. Loyd. il Todays Health 48:18-19 Ap '70
NEGRO middle class. See Middle classes
NEGRO migration. See Negroes—Migration
NEGRO militants
Black militancy in balmy waters; Caribbean black-power movement. il Newsweek 75:40 My 4 '70
Black mood: more militant, more hopeful, more determined; Time-Louis Harris poll. il Time 95:28-9 Ap 6 '70
Black protests: new voices, new forms. il U S News 68:21 Je 1 '70
Fugitive: A. Davis. il por Time 96:14 Ag 31 '70
Path of Angela Davis. il pors Life 69:20D-27 S 11 '70
Price of repression; interpretation of the shoot-out at the San Rafael courthouse. Nation 211:130-1 Ag 31 '70

NEGRO militants—*Continued*
Rising clamor for black separatism: Revolutionary people's constitutional convention in Philadelphia. il U S News 69:82-3 S 21 '70
Who's irresponsible? views of K. Brewster. New Repub 162:10 My 9 '70
See also
Black Panther party
Jackson, G.
Negro student militants
NEGRO militants and churches
Money for all-black groups: granting the separatists? Chr Today 14:34 Mr 27 '70
NEGRO ministers. See Negro clergy
NEGRO models. See Models (persons)
NEGRO Mormons. See Mormons and Mormonism, Negro
NEGRO municipal officers
See also
Negro mayors
NEGRO music
New thing. il Time 95:87-8 Ap 6 '70
Soul: the black man and his music. A. G. Mims. bibliog il Negro Hist Bul 33:141-6 O '70
See also
Jazz music
Phonograph records—Negro music
NEGRO musicians
Integrated trio goes south: Baumel-Booth-Smith trio's southern tour. R. B. Baumel. il Hi Fi 20secII 26-7+ Jl '70
New thing. il Time 95:87-8 Ap 6 '70
See also
Armstrong, L.
Baker, D.
Ellington, D.
Negro singers
NEGRO nurses. See Nurses and nursing
NEGRO organizations. See Negroes—Clubs, societies, etc.
NEGRO periodicals
See also
Amistad (periodical)
Black world (periodical)
Essence (periodical)
NEGRO photographers. See Photographers
NEGRO physicians
Flying black medics. il Ebony 25:81-4+ Je '70
NEGRO poetry
Dream motif in contemporary Negro poetry. D. Garrett. bibliog f Engl J 59:767-70 S '70
How to read black, in poetry. J. F. Cotter. America 123:264-5 O 10 '70
Undaunted pursuit of fury. il Time 95:98+ Ap 6 '70
NEGRO poets
Undaunted pursuit of fury. il Time 95:98+ Ap 6 '70
NEGRO police
Anguish of blacks in blue. il Time 96:13-14 N 23 '70
Dilemma of the black cop. R. Hall. il pors Life 69:60-60B+ S 18 '70
Kansas City's top cop. L. J. Banks. il pors Ebony 25:35-8+ O '70
Top cop in Tallulah. por Time 95:17 Mr 2 '70
NEGRO political candidates. See Candidates, Political
NEGRO politicians. See Negroes—Politics and suffrage
NEGRO preaching. See Preaching
NEGRO presidents. See Negro public officers
NEGRO priests
Trust for black Catholics? the Black Catholic clergy caucus. R. Rashke. Commonweal 92:35-7 Mr 20 '70
NEGRO principals. See School superintendents and principals
NEGRO prisoners
Anguish of Martin Sostre. W. Worthy. il pors Ebony 25:122-4+ O '70

Treatment
See Prisoners—Treatment
NEGRO public officers
Black policy-makers: an edge for Nixon. il Life 69:61-2 Jl 24 '70
Black power at the polls: gains for Negro candidates. il U S News 69:20 N 16 '70
Black victories. New Repub 163:10 D 5 '70
Blacks in top federal jobs: the Nixon record. il U S News 69:13 Ag 3 '70
Blacks who work for Nixon. M. Viorst. il N Y Times Mag p66-7+ N 29 '70
Chappie James; a new role for an old warrior. C. DuBose. il pors Ebony 25:152-4+ O '70
Political gains by Negroes. il U S News 69:40-1 Jl 13 '70
Why we need a black president in 1980. W. F. Buckley, jr. Look 34:59 Ja 13 '70
NEGRO public opinion. See Public opinion—United States

NEGRO public relations consultants. See Public relations consultants
NEGRO recreation centers. See Recreation centers
NEGRO reporters
Beyond ghetto sniffing. il Time 95:88-9 Ap 6 '70
Black sportswriter. A. S. Young. il Ebony 25:56-8+ O '70
NEGRO schools
Ghetto schools are different. B. E. Patrick. Nat R 22:401-4 Ap 21 '70
See also
Negro colleges and universities
NEGRO scientists
How blacks view mankind's giant step. S. Morris. il Ebony 25:33-6+ S '70
See also
Carver, G. W.
NEGRO singers
Baby, baby, where did Diana go? Supremes. pors Time 96:30-1 Ag 17 '70
Eternal Mills brothers. L. Robinson. il Ebony 25:60-3+ S '70
Farewell, more or less, to the Supremes. B. Farrell. por Life 68:18B F 13 '70
Why Diana Ross left the Supremes. L. Robinson. il pors Ebony 25:120-6 F '70
See also
Belafonte, H.
Broonzy, B.
Hayes, I.
Horne, L.
Martell, L.
Pride, C.
Simone, N.
Smith, B.
Turner, T.
Warwick, D.
Weathers, F.
NEGRO slum clearance. See Urban renewal
NEGRO social workers. See Social workers
NEGRO societies. See Negroes—Clubs, societies, etc.
NEGRO songs
Soul: the black man and his music. A. G. Mims. bibliog il Negro Hist Bul 33:141-6 O '70
NEGRO spirituals. See Negro songs
NEGRO student demonstrations
Ole Miss enters the '60s. J. B. Cumming, jr. Newsweek 75:83 Mr 30 '70
U. of Michigan: black activists win a change of priorities. L. J. Carter. il Science 168:229-31 Ap 10 '70
Up from Uncle Tomism; demonstrations at Lane college, Jackson, Tenn. R. L. Terrell. Commonweal 92:87-8+ Ap 3 '70; Discussion. 92:211+ My 15 '70

History
Student protest at Fisk university in the 1920's. M. L. Johnson. bibliog il Negro Hist Bul 33:137-40 O '70
NEGRO student militants
Building takeover at the University of Akron; shots fired in Buchtel Hall. J. E. Milkereit. Sch & Soc 98:374-5 O '70
Up from Uncle Tomism; demonstrations at Lane college, Jackson, Tenn. R. L. Terrell. Commonweal 92:87-8+ Ap 3 '70; Discussion. 92:211+ My 15 '70
NEGRO students
Black professor says: colleges are skipping over competent blacks to admit authentic ghetto types. T. Sowell. il N Y Times Mag p36-7+ D 13 '70
Black studies at Cornell: the troubled path to understanding. C. Childs. il Life 68:56-60+ Ap 17 '70
Black studies: more than soul courses. S. V. Roberts. Commonweal 91:478-9 Ja 30 '70
Blacks in Christian colleges. Chr Today 14:34-5 S 11 '70
Brain drain at Negro colleges; loss of students to white schools. A. Poinsett. il Ebony 25:74-6+ O '70
Getting it together; the young blacks. il Time 95:45-7 Ap 6 '70
Homecoming for the first black girl at the University of Georgia. C. Hunter. il pors N Y Times Mag p24-5+ Ja 25 '70
Ignorant armies. J. Stevenson; discussion. Atlan 225:29-30 Ja '70
Negro-Caucasian club: a history; the American students' first-inter-racial organization. O. C. Johnson. il Negro Hist Bul 33:35-41 F '70
Straight talk; views of A. Heard and J. Cheek. Newsweek 76:40-1 Ag 3 '70
Two nations at Wesleyan university. R. J. Margolis. il N Y Times Mag p9+ Ja 18 '70; Discussion. p 12+ F 22; 19+ Mr 8 '70
See also
Negro medical students
Negro student militants

NEGRO students—*Continued*

Aid

King scholars at C. W. Post college. E. Arden. Todays Ed 59:72 S '70

NEGRO students and business
Help wanted: must be black; College placement services program. il Bsns W p93 Ja 17 '70

NEGRO students in South Africa. See Foreign students in South Africa

NEGRO suffrage.   See Negroes—Politics and suffrage

NEGRO teachers
Ignorant armies. J. Stevenson; discussion. Atlan 225:29-30 Ja '70

NEGRO television programs. See Television broadcasting—Negro programs

NEGRO theater. See Theater, Negro

NEGRO theology. See Negroes—Religion

NEGRO towns and settlements
Establishment of Freedman's village in Arlington, Virginia. F. James. bibliog il Negro Hist Bul 33:90-3 Ap '70
See also
Mound Bayou, Miss.
Roosevelt City, Ala.
Soul City, N.C.

South Africa

What is it like to be a black South African? life in Soweto, Johannesburg. il Newsweek 75:48 Ap 27 '70

NEGRO universities. See Negro colleges and universities

NEGRO veterans
Black veterans return. J. Fendrich and M. Pearson. il Trans-Action 7:32-7 Mr '70

NEGRO vote. See Negroes—Politics and suffrage

NEGRO-white relations. See Black power; Race relations

NEGRO women
Authors & editors; A. Walker's books and beliefs on the black woman. B. A. Bannon. por Pub W 198:195-7 Ag 31 '70
Liberation struggle generates tension on race, sex issues; interview, ed. by M. Stone. J. Brown; P. Way; H. Fannings. il Chr Cent 87:736-9 Je 10 '70
See also
The Links, inc.
Single women

Employment

Changes in the labor force activity of women. E. Waldman. bibliog f il Mo Labor R 93:10-18 Je '70
Marital and family characteristics of the U.S. labor force; with tables. E. Waldman. bibliog f Mo Labor R 93:18-27 My '70
Working women in urban poverty neighborhoods. H. M. Willacy and H. J. Hilaski. bibliog f il Mo Labor R 93:35-8 Je '70

NEGRO women as athletes. See Women as athletes

NEGRO youth
Daddy was a number runner; excerpts. L. Meriwether. il por Ebony 25:98-103 Jl '70
Ghetto schools are different. B. E. Patrick. Nat R 22:401-4 Ap 21 '70
Horatio Alger is dead. Trans-Action 7:8+ Ap '70
Kids will decide and more power to them. P. Wilcox. il por Ebony 25:134-7 Ag '70
New set of heroes; Interested Negroes organization in Philadelphia. C. Lewis. il Am Ed 6:23 Ja '70
Premarital pregnancy among black teenagers. F. F. Furstenberg, jr. il Trans-Action 7: 52-5 My '70
You can make it, baby! condensation. J. P. Blank. il por Read Digest 96:219-23+ Ja '70

NEGROES
Africa and Afro-Americans; report of conversations between NCBC officials and members of the All Africa conference of churches. G. S. Wilmore, jr. Chr Cent 87: 686 Je 3 '70; Reply. G. M. Daniels. 87: 1201-2 O 7 '70

America's racial crisis; symposium. Cur 118: 27-40 My '70

Black mood: more militant, more hopeful, more determined; Time-Louis Harris poll. il Time 95:28-9 Ap 6 '70

Caucasian genes in American Negroes. T. E. Reed; discussion. Science 166:1353; 167: 1388-9 D 12 '69. Mr 6 '70

Current history. See issues of Negro history bulletin

Indivisible man; interview, ed. by J. A. McPherson. R. Ellison. por Atlan 226:45-60 D '70

Nixon anti-Negro? A charge, a reply. il U S News 69:72-3 Jl 13 '70
What's wrong with welfare: answers from Nixon's adviser; interview. D. P. Moynihan. por U S News 68:64-8 Je 15 '70
See also
Black capitalism
Black Muslims
Black power
Freedmen
Freemasons, Negro
Interracial cooperation
Mulattoes
National association for the advancement of colored people
National urban league
Race relations
Revivals
Slavery—United States
Suburbs—Negroes
United   States—History—Civil   war—Negro troops
also subhead Negroes under names of cities, e.g. Cairo, Ill.—Negroes

Bibliography

Books by and about the American Negro. Library J 95:218-19+ Ja 15 '70
Nobody knows: books on the black experience in America. Schol Teach Sec Teach Sup p26+ Ap 6 '70

Caricatures and cartoons

Humor in black and white. Ebony 25:128-9 Ag '70

Civil rights

Advance and retreat; four events. Time 96:12 D 28 '70
Black America 1970; symposium. il Time 95: 13-16+ Ap 6 '70
Black protests: new voices, new forms. il U S News 68:21 Je 1 '70
Case of benign neglect; the Moynihan memo. il por Newsweek 75:25+ Mr 16 '70
Civil rights and the Warren court. il pors Ebony 25:27-30+ F '70
Civil rights and white textbooks. Negro Hist Bul 33:4-5 Ja '70
Dead silence on human rights. H. Sidey. il Life 68:4 Mr 6 '70
Echoes of benign. neglect. il Sat R 53:87 Je 20 '70
Heart of the racial crisis; Agnew's opinions. B. L. Masse. America 122:547 My 23 '70
Huey Newton in prison: an interview, ed. by J. Johnson. H. Newton. il Ramp Mag 9:4-6 S '70
I expect more Jacksons; remarks, ed. by P. Range. H. Williams. por Time 95:11 Je 1 '70
Invisible blacks. Nation 210:642 Je 1 '70
Moynihan memo and civil rights. America 122:264 Mr 14 '70; Reply. B. Hardin. 122:399 Ap 18 '70
Moynihan memo: Negroes are making great progress, but—; excerpts, March 1, 1970. D. P. Moynihan. il pors U S News 68:57-8 Mr 16 '70
Moynihan's memo fever. por Time 95:15-16 Mr 23 '70
Neglect, but what kind? Moynihan recommendation to President Nixon. Commonweal 92:28 Mr 20 '70
New nullification race; regression toward pre-1954 levels of racial accommodation. Chr Cent 87:283 Mr 11 '70
Nixon and blacks: substance and symbol. New Repub 163:7-8 Jl 18 '70
Racism in white America; excerpts from Beyond racism: building an open society. W. M. Young, jr. Read Digest 96:167-72 F '70
Return of the boll weevil; C. Evers at Mississippi state university. J. M. Carter. Library J 95:1817 My 15 '70
These truths should be self-evident. il Ebony 25:102-3 Je '70
TRB from Washington; progress report. New Repub 163:4 D 26 '70
Which way black America? Separation? Integration? Liberation? il Ebony 25:35-8+ Ag '70
See also
Civil rights act of 1964
Civil rights demonstrations
Race relations

History

Changing the African-American image through history. W. S. Robinson. Negro Hist Bul 33:44-6 F '70
Public opinion and the passage of the Mississippi black codes. M. M. Bigelow. bibliog Negro Hist Bul 33:11-16 Ja '70

NEGROES—*Continued*

Clubs, societies, etc.

Black pioneer period. L. Bennett. jr. il Ebony 25:46-8+ O '70
See also
Association for the study of Negro life and history
Interested Negroes (organization)
National association for the advancement of colored people
National economic growth and reconstruction organization
Southern consumers cooperatives

Crime

Ben Chaney at eleven and at seventeen; with report by M. Mok. il pors Life 68:36-9 Je 19 '70
Black crime: the lawless image. F. P. Graham. il Harper 241:64-5+ S '70; Discussion. 241:6+ D '70
Ghetto schools are different. B. E. Patrick. Nat R 22:401-4 Ap 21 '70

Culture

African culture and black identity; excerpt from Omni-Americans. A. Murray. Cur 121: 26-7 S '70
Interview with Topper Carew; programs of the New thing art and architecture center; ed. by W. Roberts. T. Carew. il Sat R 53: 46-8 Jl 18 '70
Omni-Americans, by A. Murray. Review
New Yorker 46:185-6+ O 17 '70. R. Coles
What is your black culture quotient? Todays Ed 59:27 F '70

Economic conditions

Beyond the ghetto. R. C. Weaver. il por Ebony 25:148-51 Ag '70
Blacks' progress: a story of opportunities grasped. il U S News 68:19-21 Je 1 '70
Economics of the Black manifesto. M. K. Carney. por Chr Cent 87:171-4 F 11 '70
Failure of black separatism. B. Rustin. il Harper 240:25-32+ Ja '70; Same abr. with title What black revolution? Cur 116:19-33 Mr '70; Discussion. Harper 240:6+ Ap '70
Freedom for the black: a workable coalition; address, November 7, 1970. G. Jonas. Vital Speeches 37:105-9 D 1 '70
Negro economic gains, impressive but precarious. C. E. Silberman. il Fortune 82:74-7+ Jl '70
Real story of Negro gains. il U S News 68:30-1 Mr 30 '70
Sharing the wealth; views of A. Fletcher. H. Brandon. Sat R 53:5+ Ap 11 '70
Short-range separatism. D. S. McLaurin. il por Ebony 25:123-5 Ag '70
To blacks, ecology is irrelevant. il Bsns W p49 N 14 '70
Working in the white man's world. il Time 95:92-5 Ap 6 '70
See also
Black capitalism
Negroes—Migration

Education

Benjamin Banneker: he didn't fit the image. por Sr Schol 95:24 S 15 '69
Black leader's idea for South's schools; interview. R. Innis. il por U S News 68:30-1 Mr 2 '70
Black Ph.D.s. Trans-Action 7:14 My '70
Commitment to achievement: Detroit's neighborhood educational project. F. T. Murdoch. il Am Lib 1:758-61 S '70
Does integration still matter to blacks? il Time 95:14 Mr 9 '70
Education of the black man in the U.S; excerpt from Foundations of education; ed. by G. F. Kneller. W. P. Jones. Sch & Soc 98:467-70 D '70
Getting it together: the young blacks. il Time 95:45-7 Ap 6 '70
Learn baby learn; address, May 24, 1970. M. T. Bowie. Vital Speeches 36:604-6 Jl 15 '70
New threat to public schools. il Ebony 25: 84-5 S '70
Parallels of Negro and women's education. B. W. Newell. Sch & Soc 98:357-9 O '70
Pseudo-sacrosanct role of intelligence in education. H. P. Baptiste, jr. Ed Digest 36:24-7 D '70
Recruiting in the inner city; Urban journalism workshops. J. Tebbel. Sat R 53:54-5 Jl 11 '70
Special college entry programs for Afro-Americans. B. A. Rhodes. bibliog Sch & Soc 98:360-2 O '70

Stratification, segregation, and children in the inner-city school. D. U. Levine. bibliog Sch & Soc 98:84-9 F '70
Turn from integration. il U S News 68:29-31 Mr 9 '70; Same abr. with title Will busing make them better? Read Digest 96:95-7 My '70
See also
Catholic schools—Desegregation
Education—Mississippi
Miles college, Birmingham, Ala.
Negro colleges and universities
Private schools—Desegregation
Public schools—Desegregation
Socially handicapped children—Education

History

Booker T. Washington in biographical perspective. L. R. Harlan. bibliog f Am Hist R 75:1581-99 O '70
White liberals and black power in Negro education, 1865-1915. J. M. McPherson. bibliog f il Am Hist R 75:1357-86 Je '70

Employment

Alexander's plan: Harvard minority hiring more ambitious than Philadelphia plan. il Time 95:17 F 23 '70
Batavia: accelerating people as well as particles. P. M. Boffey. Science 168:1185-7 Je 5 '70
Black college forum gives new insights; career opportunities in parks and recreation. Parks & Rec 5:44-5 Jl '70
Caught in the middle: Harvard contract demands more minority workers in campus building. Newsweek 75:65 F 23 '70
Economic rights take a front seat. il Bsns W p22-3 Mr 21 '70
How blacks view mankind's giant step. S. Morris. il Ebony 25:33-6+ S '70
It's not a matter of choice. L. L. L. Golden. Sat R 53:67 My 9 '70
Jobs for Negroes: battle goes on. U S News 68:83 Ja 26 '70
Learning how to help the ghetto help itself; EG&G's Roxbury subsidiary. Bsns W p 107 Ja 31 '70
Negro economic gains impressive but precarious. C. E. Silberman. il Fortune 82:74-7+ Jl '70
Philadelphia plan survives test. America 122: 325 Mr 28 '70
Philadelphia problem. Time 96:61-2 Ag 17 '70
This month's feature: Congress & minority employment policy; controversy over the Philadelphia plan. Cong Digest 49:67-96 Mr '70
Unemployment by region and in ten largest states; with tables. P. M. Schwab. bibliog Mo Labor R 93:3-12 Ja '70
Unions open fire on Nixon over jobs, civil rights. il U S News 68:69-70 Mr 9 '70
Wanted: black air traffic controllers. il Ebony 25:54-6+ Ap '70
Working in the white man's world. il Time 95:92-5 Ap 6 '70
See also
Discrimination in employment
Negro government employees
Negro women—Employment
Negroes—Occupations
Opportunities industrialization centers, inc.

Health and hygiene

Racially rationed health. il Time 95:90-1 Ap 6 '70

History

American Negro, ed. by W. L. Katz. Review
Commentary 49:85-8 Ap '70. D. Donald
Black history gaps revealed in AFT encyclopedia survey. Library J 95:4312 D 15 '70
Choice is ours. Ebony 25:172-3 Ag '70
Making of black America. L. Bennett, jr. il Ebony 25:70-2+ Ag; 46-8+ O; 26:70-2+ D '70
What America would be like without blacks; Time essay. R. Ellison. il Time 95:54-5 Ap 6 '70
See also
Association for the study of Negro life and history
Slavery—United States
United States—History—Revolution—Negroes

Sources

Clarence Holte's search into the black past. il pors Ebony 25:94-6+ Ap '70

NEGROES—History—*Continued*

Study and teaching

Enigma of Negro history. L. J. Alilunas and W. Chazanof. Clear House 45:29-31 S '70; Same abr. Ed Digest 36:38-9 D '70
Lesson plan, Crispus Attucks. J. H. Harris. Negro Hist Bul 33:69 Mr '70
Use of supplemental materials in teaching black history. J. E. Guenther. il Clear House 45:226-30 D '70
See also
Afro-American studies

Study and teaching—Audio-visual aids

New materials on black heritage; the unmaking of a myth. H. D. Weaver, jr. Schol Teach Sec Teach Sup p 12-13 Ja 5 '70

Housing

Apartheid U.S.A: Iron city; excerpts from The end of liberalism. T. J. Lowi. il Trans-Action 7:32-9 F '70
Beyond the ghetto. R. C. Weaver. il por Ebony 25:148-51 Ag '70
Curse of contract buying; Chicago evictions. C. C. Douglas. il Ebony 25:43-6+ Je '70
See also
Connecticut housing investment fund
Discrimination in housing
Housing—Desegregation

Intelligence

See Intelligence levels—Negroes

Language

See Negro-English dialects

Legal status, laws, etc.

Bias in the jury box. Time 95:61 Ap 6 '70
Can a black man get a fair trial in this country? H. Burns. il N Y Times Mag p5+ Jl 12 '70; Same abr. with title Race and fair trial. Cur 121:12-19 S '70; Discussion. N Y Times Mag p54 Ag 9; 21+ S 27 '70

Libraries

See Libraries and Negroes

Migration

Melting pot: its most difficult test; the immigrant within; excerpts from The American people, with paintings by J. Lawrence. B. A. Weisberger. il Am Heritage 22:32-9+ D '70

Nationalism

Black consciousness and the black church: a historical-theological interpretation. J. H. Cone. bibliog f Ann Am Acad 387:49-55 Ja '70
Black nationalism and community schools; excerpts from Community control of schools. R. C. Maynard. bibliog Sch & Soc 98:121-5 F '70
Kids will decide and more power to them; Pan-African liberation and restoration movement. P. Wilcox. il por Ebony 25:134-7 Ag '70
Rediscovery of black nationalism. by T. Draper. Review
Nat R 22:1102 O 20 '70. J. Burnham
Toward a theology of the black experience. M. J. Jones. il Chr Cent 87:1088-91 S 16 '70
Which way black America? Separation? Integration? Liberation? il Ebony 25:35-8+ Ag '70
Wyatt T. Walker takes issue with Cleage's black nationalism. Chr Cent 87:471 Ap 22 '70
See also
Black Muslims
Black power
Congress of African people

Occupations

Blacks in the mills. il Newsweek 76:88+ N 2 '70
Speaking of people. See issues of Ebony
See also
Negro businessmen
Negro librarians
Negro teachers

Photographs

Beautiful people of James Van Derzee. il pors Ebony 25:85-8+ O '70

Politics and suffrage

Black Americans want in; Negroes and the GOP. V. S. Baker. Nat R 22:892-3 Ag 25 '70
Black power at the Dixie polls. il Time 95:17 Je 15 '70
Fifteenth amendment and black America in the century 1870-1970. il Negro Hist Bul 33:28-31 F '70

Fifteenth amendment and the white primary. Negro Hist Bul 33:88-9 Ap '70
Political gains by Negroes. il U S News 69:40-1 Jl 13 '70
Political self-help. Nation 210:771-2 Je 29 '70
Politics of leadership; relationship of blacks with the administration. Nation 212:5 Ja 4 '71
Voting victory. il Time 95:12 Mr 16 '70
See also
Black power
Negro public officers

Psychology

Black hang-ups; White hang-up. il Time 95:64-6 Ap 6 '70
Blackness and madness. T. S. Szasz. Yale R 59:333-41 Mr '70
Pitfalls of black pride. il Time 97:38 Ja 18 '71
Racial oppression and black suicide; excerpts from Black suicide. H. Hendin. Cur 114:29-36 Ja '70
Toward a black psychology. J. White. il por Ebony 25:44-5+ S '70
Why blacks kill blacks; psychiatrist on ghetto violence. A. F. Poussaint. il por Ebony 25:143-6 O '70

Relations with Indians

See Indians of North America—Relations with Negroes

Religion

Black church. T. Kilgore, jr. il por Ebony 25:106-8+ Ag '70
Black churchmen: renouncing and denouncing. Chr Today 14:34 Jl 31 '70
Black consciousness and the black church: a historical-theological interpretation. J. H. Cone. bibliog f Ann Am Acad 387:49-55 Ja '70
Black theology and black liberation; address. J. H. Cone. il Chr Cent 87:1084-8 S 16 '70
Black worship and hermeneutic. R. N. Soulen. Chr Cent 87:168-71 F 11 '70
Cranking up Christian living. C. E. Lincoln. Sat R 53:69-71 F 28 '70
Examining black theology. H. B. Kuhn. Chr Today 14:34 Mr 27 '70
For authentic freedom; COCU and black churches. J. H. Satterwhite. Chr Cent 87:236 F 25 '70
Random notes on black theology and African theology. D. G. Gelzer. Chr Cent 87:1091-3 S 16 '70
Toward a black theology. J. H. Cone. il por Ebony 25:113-16 Ag '70
Toward a theology of the black experience. M. J. Jones. il Chr Cent 87:1088-91 S 16 '70
See also
Black Muslims
National committee of Black churchmen
Negro churches

Reparations

Black manifesto, ed. by R. S. Lecky and H. E. Wright. Review
Commonweal 91:626 Mr 6 '70. J. Deedy
Economics of the Black manifesto. M. K. Carney. por Chr Cent 87:171-4 F 11 '70
Roundup: the year of the Black manifesto. M. Stone. Chr Cent 87:185-8 F 11 '70

Segregation

Advances in segregation. Sci Am 222:46 Ap '70
Segregation in brotherhood. Negro Hist Bul 33:132-3 O '70
Southern integrationists feel betrayed by the North. P. Watters. il N Y Times Mag p26-7+ My 3 '70; Discussion. p83 Je 7 '70
Which way black America? Separation? Integration? Liberation? il Ebony 25:35-8+ Ag '70
See also
Church and race problems
Public schools—Desegregation
Segregation in education

Social conditions

Daddy was a number runner; excerpts. L. Meriwether. il pors Ebony 25:98-103 Jl '70
Failure of black separatism. B. Rustin. il Harper 240:25-32+ Ja '70; Same abr. with title What black revolution? Cur 116:19-33 Mr '70; Discussion. Harper 240:6+ Ap '70
Ghetto ethic. B. N. Odell. il Cath World 210:213-15 F '70
Journey through two Americas. J. Cook and P. Hathaway. il Time 95:30+ Ap 6 '70
Lord of the ghettos. R. Coles. il Commonweal 93:167-74 N 13 '70; Reply. R. J. Neuhaus. 93:287 D 11 '70
Memorandum to Moynihan. Nation 210:291 Mr 16 '70

NEGROES—Social conditions—*Continued*
Nations' two societies; Kerner commission report. Negro Hist Bul 33:112-14 My '70
Silent black majority. C. V. Hamilton. il N Y Times Mag p25-6+ My 10 '70
Stratification, segregation, and children in the inner-city school. D. U. Levine. bibliog Sch & Soc 98:34-9 F '70
Toward a black psychology. J. White. il por Ebony 25:44-5+ S '70
Violent black minority. A. Hacker. il N Y Times Mag p25+ My 10; 12 My 24 '70
See also
United States—National advisory commission on civil disorders

Social status
Theory of the lower class: Edward Banfield, the maverick of urbanology. R. Todd. Atlan 226:51-5 S '70

Societies
See Negroes—Clubs, societies, etc.

Suffrage
See Negroes—Politics and suffrage

Suicide
See Suicide

Trade union membership
See Trade unions—Negro membership

Louisiana
Boondocks jail the future; Homer, La. N. C. Chriss. il Nation 211:495-6 N 16 '70
To be somebody someday. J. Smith. il por Redbook 135:86-7+ My '70

Mississippi
Civil rights conference center in Mississippi endangered; case of the Mt Beulah center, Edwards, Miss. Chr Cent 87:525-6 Ap 29 '70; Discussion. 87:704-5 Je 3 '70
Fannie Lou Hammer: hunger has no colour line. P. Marshall. il por Vogue 155:126-7+ Je '70
Jim Brown comes to Mississippi; Black economic union helps residents of Marshall County. C. Gillespie. Nation 211:236-9 S 21 '70
Mississippi black home: a sweet and bitter bluesong. J. Jordan. il N Y Times Mag p64-5+ O 11 '70

Northern states
See also
Detroit—Negroes
New York (city)—Harlem

Southern states
American South: rise of a new confederacy. W. Hedgepeth. il Look 34:19-32+ N 17 '70
Black progress in a new south. T. A. Johnson. Read Digest 97:144-7 D '70
Dealing with Wallace. New Repub 162:8 Je 27 '70
Integration or national retreat? C. Morgan, jr. Cur 118:38-40 My '70
New South creed, by P. M. Gaston. Review New Repub 163:23-5 S 26 '70. B. W. Eggler
Professor Gunnar Myrdal returns to the South; interview, ed. by K. Prager. G. Myrdal. por Time 96:12 N 23 '70
South revisited after a momentous decade. K. Fleming. il Newsweek 76:25-8 Ag 10 '70
Unquiet schools; segregation disputes. New Repub 163:8 O 3 '70
Where are they now? J. H. Griffin, author of Black like me. il pors Newsweek 76:10 Ag 31 '70
See also
Atlanta—Negroes
Mississippi—Race problems
Negroes—Politics and suffrage

Tennessee
Renewal: Tennessee model. T. M. Gannon. America 122:152-5+ F 14 '70

Western states
Black West; Black frontier series. R. L. Shayon. Sat R 53:54 N 14 '70
NEGROES, Discrimination against. See Race discrimination
NEGROES and advertising. See Advertising and Negroes
NEGROES and libraries. See Libraries and Negroes
NEGROES and museums. See Museums and Negroes
NEGROES and radio. See Radio broadcasting and Negroes
NEGROES and television. See Television broadcasting and Negroes

NEGROES and trade unions. See Trade unions —Negro membership
NEGROES in Africa

Religion
Random notes on black theology and African theology. D. G. Geizer. Chr Cent 87:1091-3 S 16 '70
To deepen understanding. O. W. Okite. Chr Today 15:18-19 O 23 '70
NEGROES in art
Black experience in color. W. Henderson. il Ramp Mag 8:33-5 Je '70
See also
Negro artists
NEGROES in business. See Negro businessmen
NEGROES in Canada
Canada's Negroes: an untold story. il U S News 68:46-8 My 11 '70
NEGROES in Cuba
Black man in red Cuba, by J. Clytus. Review Nat R 23:43-5 Ja 12 '71. L. Stearns
NEGROES in drama. See Negroes in literature
NEGROES in literature
Before the colors fade: Green pastures recalled; interview, ed. by J. L. Phillips. il pors Am Heritage 21:28-9+ F '70
Book reviews. See issues of Negro history bulletin
Ebony book shelf. See issues of Ebony
Filling the void: the black in American literature. R. A. Ross. Engl J 59:31-3 Ja '70
NEGROES in moving pictures
Black film: God's step children, filmed in 1938, black director O. Micheaux. New Yorker 46:34-5 Ap 18 '70
Era of dummies and darkies. S. Fay. Commonweal 93:125-8 O 30 '70
NEGROES in South Africa
Kaffir society. Newsweek 76:34+ D 7 '70
What is it like to be a black South African? life in Soweto, Johannesburg. il Newsweek 75:48 Ap 27 '70
See also
South Africa—Race problems
NEGROES in television
Looking & listening: interview, ed. by P. Hudson. L. Haynes. il Sr Schol 95:33 S 22 '69
NEGROES in the United States army. See United States—Army—Negroes
NEGROES in the Virgin islands
Struggle for paradise. C. L. Sanders. il Ebony 25:66-8+ O '70
NEGROES in the West Indies
See also
Negroes in the Virgin Islands
NEGROES in trade unions. See Trade unions—Negro membership
NEGROPONTE, Nicholas, and Groisser, L. B.
Semantics of architecture machines. il Arch Forum 133:38-41 O '70
NEHAMKIN, Lester
Indy '70. il Motor T 22:34-7+ My '70
NEIGHBORHOOD fairs. See Fairs
NEIGHBORHOOD health centers. See Health centers
NEIGHBORHOOD law office plan. See Legal aid
NEIGHBORHOOD services programs. See Community service
NEIGHBORHOODS
For house hunters: sizing up the neighborhood. il Changing T 24:45-7 Jl '70
NEIHARDT, John G.
Their community needs them. H. Alpert. il pors Har Yrs 10:43-5+ Je '70 *
NEILL, Thomas P.
Of many things. D. R. Campion. America 123:inside cover Jl 25 '70 *
NEILSON, Cook
Cycling. il Travel & Camera 33:48-52 O '70
NEIMAN-Marcus store. See Houston, Tex.—Stores
NEISSER, Edith G. and Bauling, Fay
Crucial preschool years. il Parents Mag 45:49-51+ F '70
NEISWENDER, Mary
Manson watch. il por Newsweek 76:65-6 Ag 31 '70 *
NEIZVESTNY, Ernst
Red wedge. S. Karlinsky. Nation 210:121-2 F 2 '70
NEKOOSA-Edwards paper company. See Great Northern Nekoosa corporation
NELSEN, Ervin N.
Media industry: its growth, structure, and role in education; address, June 1969. por Library J 95:1159-61 Mr 15 '70
NELSON, Bryce
HEW's security. Trans-Action 7:5-6 Ja '70

NELSON, E. and Rennels, M.
Neuromuscular contacts in intracranial arteries of the cat. bibliog il Science 167:301-2 Ja 16 '70

NELSON, Gaylord Anton
Five who care. il Look 34:32-3 Ap 21 '70
Marine environment and pollution control; address, February 19, 1970. Vital Speeches 36:325-9 Mr 15 '70
National teach-in on the crisis of the environment. Am Lib 1:140-1 F '70
Pollution and a concerned public. Cur Hist 59:31-5+ Jl '70
Teach-in to save the earth. Read Digest 96: 110-12 Ap '70
We're making a cesspool of the sea. il Nat Wildlife 8:14-16 Ag '70
Youth to the rescue? Cur 114:24-6 Ja '70

about
Pill trial. por Time 95:32+ Mr 9 '70 *

NELSON, George J.
To what French restaurant in N.Y. do you take your wife? Your mistress? il Holiday 47:70-1 Je '70

NELSON, Horatio Nelson, viscount
Battle of the Nile; excerpts from Mediterranean; portrait of a sea. E. Bradford. il pors Horizon 12:84-95 Aut '70 *

NELSON, J. Robert
Ecumenism in Sofia and Bucharest. Chr Cent 87:437-9 Ap 15 '70
Plague on three houses. Chr Cent 87:232-3 F 25 '70
Three Damoclean swords. Chr Cent 87:69-71 Ja 21 '70

NELSON, Jack
Reports: black colleges. Atlan 226:22-4+ O '70

about
Muckraker's progress. Time 96:73 O 26 '70 *

NELSON, Kay
Down memory lane; poem. Good H 171:10 O '70

NELSON, Paul
Dylan. pors Sr Schol 97:22-3+ D 14 '70

NELSON, Phillip L.
Environment and establishment, a student letter. Nat Parks & Con Mag 44:11-12 My '70

NELSON, Raymond J.
Art of Herman Melville: the author of Pierre. il Yale R 59:197-214 D '69

NELSON, Raymond L.
Voyageur. il Nat Parks & Con Mag 44:20-4 D '70

NELSON, Shirley W.
Anniversary; Songmy; poem. Chr Cent 87: 660 My 27 '70
Sallman's head of Christ; poem. Chr Cent 87:817 Jl 1 '70

NEMATODES
Heme requirement for reproduction of a free-living nematode. W. F. Hieb and others. bibliog il Science 168:143-4 Ap 3 '70
Soybean cyst nematodes are moving North. C. E. Sommers. Suc Farm 68:no2 A16 F '70

NEMER, Martin. See Fromson, D. jt. auth.

NEMEROV, Howard
Being of three minds; Embarrassment lives! On TV, anyhow; Solipsism & solecism; Item; Prism; Behavior; Quaerendo invenietis; poems. Poetry 117:149-53 D '70
Brueghel: the triumph of time; poem. New Yorker 46:48 Ap 18 '70
Most expensive picture in the world; poem. New Repub 162:17 Mr 28 '70
Myth & ritual; poem. New Repub 163:21 N 21 '70
On being asked for a peace poem; poem. Sat R 53:74 Mr 28 '70
One moment in eternity; poem. New Repub 162:25 My 30 '70
September, the first day of school; poem. New Yorker 46:42 S 19 '70
Theory and practice of what. Poetry 116:35-9 Ap '70

NEMI, LAKE
Mysterious ships of Lake Nemi. L. S. De Camp. il Sci Digest 67:68-72 Je '70

NEMSER, Cindy
Presenting Charles Close. il pors Art in Am 58:98-101 Ja '70

NEO-GOTHIC architecture. See Architecture, Gothic

NEOLOGISMS. See Words, New

NEON lamps in art. See Electric lamps in art

NEOSHO, Mo.
Autumn leaves that blossom in the spring. C. Allonby. il Org Gard & Farm 17:40-3 S '70

NEPAL
Nepal: come, let us marry. il pors Newsweek 75:46-47D Mr 16 '70
Reporter at large. J. Bernstein. il New Yorker 46:44-6 My 2; 46-8+ My 9 '70
Reports: Nepal. M. l. White. Atlan 226:26+ Ag '70
See also
Katmandu
Marriage customs and rites—Nepal
Medicine—Nepal

Royal family
Marriage of convenience; Crown Prince Birendra and Princess Aishwarya of Nepal. il por Time 95:29 Mr 9 '70
Nepal's right royal wedding. il por Life 68: 34-5 Mr 13 '70
See also
Birendra, crown prince of Nepal

NEPALESE weddings. See Marriage customs and rites

NEPERUD, Ronald W.
Artist at work. Ed Digest 35:49-51 My '70

NEPODAL, Virginia
Fabrics from the forest. il por Nat Wildlife 8:28-9 Ag '70 *

NEPTUNE (planet)
Diameter of Neptune. Sky & Tel 39:160 Mr '70

NERVA engine. See Rockets, Atomic powered

NERVE cells
Acetylcholine sensitivity of muscle fiber membranes: mechanism of regulation by motoneurons. D. M. Fambrough. bibliog il Science 168:372-3 Ap 17 '70
Behavioral measurement of neural poststimulation excitability cycle: pain cells in the brain of the rat. R. S. Kestenbaum. bibliog il Science 167:393-6 Ja 23 '70
Changes of simple and complex spike activity of cerebellar Purkinje cells with sleep and waking. N. I. Mano. bibliog il Science 170:1325-7 D 18 '70
Dendritic-tree anatomy codes form-vision physiology in tadpole retina. B. Pomeranz and S. H. Chung. bibliog il Science 170: 983-4 N 27 '70
Early experience effects upon cortical dendrites: a proposed model for development. S. Schapiro and K. R. Vukovich. bibliog il Science 167:292-4 Ja 16 '70
Echo-ranging neurons in the inferior colliculus of bats. N. Suga. bibliog il Science 170:449-52 O 23 '70
L-Glutamic acid decarboxylase: a new type in glial cells and human brain gliomas. B. Haber and others. bibliog il Science 168: 598-9 My 1 '70
Motoneuron morphology and synaptic contacts: determination by intracellular dye injection. W. J. Davis. bibliog il Science 168: 1358-60 Je 12 '70
Nerve cells and behavior. E. R. Kandel. il Sci Am 223:57-67+ bibliog (p 136) Jl '70
Neuroglia: biophysical properties and physiologic function. M. C. Trachtenberg and D. A. Pollen. bibliog il Science 167:1248-52 F 27 '70
Neuroglia: gliosis and focal epilepsy. D. A. Pollen and M. C. Trachtenberg. bibliog Science 167:1252-3 F 27 '70
Neuronal soma and whole neuroglia of rat brain: a new isolation technique. W. T. Norton and S. E. Poduslo. bibliog il Science 167:1144-6 F 20 '70
Number coding in association cortex of the cat. R. F. Thompson and others. bibliog il Science 168:271-3 Ap 10 '70
Penicillin as epileptogenic agent: its effect on an isolated neuron. G. F. Ayala and others. bibliog il Science 167:1257-60 F 27 '70
Trichromatic mechanisms in single cortical neurons. P. Gouras. bibliog il Science 168: 489-92 Ap 24 '70
Unified account of the variable effects of carbon dioxide on nerve cells. J. L. Walker, jr. and A. M. Brown. bibliog il Science 167: 1502-4 Mr 13 '70

NERVE conduction. See Electrophysiology

NERVE gases. See Gases, Asphyxiating and poisonous

NERVE regeneration. See Regeneration (biology)

NERVES
Neuromuscular contacts in intracranial arteries of the cat. E. Nelson and M. Rennels. bibliog il Science 167:301-2 Ja 16 '70
See also
Electrophysiology
Nerve cells
Olfactory nerves
Synapses

NERVES—*Continued*

Transplantation

Now it's nerve transplants. Sci Digest 68:22 O '70

NERVO, Amado
Amado Nervo. C. García Prada. il por Américas 22:9-14 O '70 *

NERVOUS breakdown. See Mental illness

NERVOUS system
Improvement of learning in the aged by modification of autonomic nervous system activity. C. Eisdorfer and others. bibliog il Science 170:1327-9 D 18 '70
Learning in the autonomic nervous system. L. V. DiCara. il Sci Am 222:30-9 bibliog (p 146) Ja '70
Learning to control the uncontrollable; visceral learning. L. Massett. il por Sci N 97:274-5 Mr 14 '70
Train yourself to stay well; visceral learning. M. Pines. il McCalls 97:48+ Je '70
See also
Electrophysiology
Meninges
Psychology, Physiological
Shock
Spinal cord
Synapses

Annelids

Structure of the giant fibers of earthworms. B. Mulloney. bibliog il Science 168:994-6 My 22 '70

Conferences

Brain mechanisms and vision: subcortical systems. D. J. Ingle and G. E. Schneider. Science 168:1493-4 Je 19 '70

Crustaceans

Habituation: occurrence at a neuromuscular junction. J. Bruner and D. Kennedy. bibliog il Science 169:92-4 Jl 3 '70

Diseases

Demyelinating encephalomyelopathy associated with lead poisoning in nonhuman primates. R. M. Sauer and others. bibliog il Science 169:1091-3 S 11 '70
See also
Brain—Diseases
Lesch-Nyhan syndrome
Sclerosis, Multiple

Fishes

Reinnervated eye muscles do not respond to impulses in foreign nerves. R. F. Mark and others. bibliog il Science 170:193-4 O 9 '70
Temperature-sensitive neurons in the brain of brook trout. G. L. Greer and D. R. Gardner. bibliog il Science 169:1220-2 S 18 '70

Insects

Postembryonic development of adult motor patterns in crickets: a neural analysis. D. R. Bentley and R. R. Hoy. bibliog il Science 170:1409-11 D 25 '70

Mollusks

Changes in extrinsic fluorescence in squid axons during voltage-clamp. F. Conti and I. Tasaki. bibliog il Science 169:1322-4 S 25 '70
Habituation and dishabituation in the absence of a central nervous system. B. Peretz. bibliog il Science 169:379-81 Jl 24 '70
Habituation and dishabituation of the gill-withdrawal reflex in aplysia. H. Pinsker and others. bibliog il Science 167:1740-2 Mr 27 '70
Nerve cells and behavior. E. R. Kandel. il Sci Am 223:57-67+ bibliog(p 136) Jl '70
Neuronal correlates of habituation and dishabituation of the gill-withdrawal reflex in aplysia. I. Kupfermann and others. bibliog il Science 167:1743-5 Mr 27 '70
Neuronal mechanisms of habituation and dishabituation of the gill-withdrawal reflex in aplysia. V. Castellucci and others. bibliog il Science 167:1745-8 Mr 27 '70
Plasticity of synchronous activity in a small neural net. W. B. Kristan, jr. and G. L. Gerstein. bibliog il Science 169:1336-9 S 25 '70
Visual receptor potential: modification by injected current in the limulus lateral eye. V. J. Wulff and C. Mendez. bibliog il Science 168:1351-3 Je 12 '70

Reptiles

Extraretinal light perception: entrainment of the biological clock controlling lizard locomotor activity. H. Underwood and M. Menaker. bibliog il Science 170:190-3 O 9 '70

Surgery
See also
Harvey Cushing society

NERVOUS tension. See Stress (physiology)

NERVOUSNESS
Hope and help for your nerves; excerpt. C. Weekes. Read Digest 97:138-41 D '70
See also
Stage fright

NESS, LOCH
Scotland's monster lake. B. Bell. il Travel 133:60-2 Je '70

NESSEN, Ron
From dump to glaring dump. il Todays Health 48:20-3+ Je '70

NESTLÉ company
Secret giant. il Forbes 106:24-7 O 1 '70

NET worth statements. See Financial statements

NETBOY, Anthony
French Pete for people. il Am For 76:16-18+ My '70
Salmon situation; excerpts from Man and the salmon. il Am For 76:24-7 Mr '70

NETHERBY, Steve
Pollution with a solution. il Field & S 75:62 D '70

NETHERLANDS
See also
Airplanes, Military—Netherlands
Americans in the Netherlands
Amsterdam
Catholic church in the Netherlands
Cities and towns—Netherlands
Jews in the Netherlands
Music festivals—Netherlands
National parks and reserves—Netherlands
Pollution—Netherlands
Reclamation of land—Netherlands
Youth—Netherlands

Description and travel

Dawdling in the Dutch woods. H. Sutton. il Sat R 53:39-41 D 19 '70
Holland's hinterland. H. P. Koenig. il Travel 134:34-9+ Ag '70

History
Bibliography

Articles and other books received; comp. by P. H. Laurent. See issues of American historical review

Industries
See also
Airplane industry and trade—Netherlands
Shipbuilding

Moral conditions

Amsterdam's a surprising city even for those who don't surprise easily. A. Karlen. il Holiday 47:42-3+ Ja '70

Religious institutions and affairs

Ecumenical breakthrough, by H. A. Fiolet. Review
Chr Today 15:24 N 6 '70. J. L. Garrett
See also
Catholic church in the Netherlands

Social conditions

Profiles. A. Bailey. New Yorker 46:32-8+ Ag 15 '70
See also
Housing—Netherlands

NETHERLANDS chamber choir. See Choirs

NETHERLANDS-United States air agreement. See Aviation—International aspects

NETHERLANDS WEST INDIES
See also
Curaçao (island)

NETSCH, Walter Andrew, 1920-
New galaxies at Chicago circle. J. Dixon. il Arch Forum 133:24-33 N '70 *

NETSCHERT, Bruce C.
Economic impact of electric vehicles: a scenario. il Bul Atom Sci 26:29-35 My '70

NETSILIK Eskimos. See Eskimos

NETTI, Larry
Build a parsons table. il Mech Illus 66:111-13 Ja '70

NETTL, Bruno
Attitudes towards Persian music in Tehran, 1969. bibliog f Mus Q 56:183-97 Ap '70

NETWORK analysis (planning)
Network analysis. H. Frank and I. T. Frisch. il Sci Am 223:94-100+ bibliog (p 136) Jl '70

NETWORK cinema corporation
Money in mini-theaters. R. Levy. il Duns 96:63-4+ O '70

NETZ, David J. and Wood, D. E.
Human element: a retrospective evaluation of the OSUL internship program. Am Lib 1:253-4 Mr '70

NEUFELD, Edward. See Gilpin, C. R. jt. auth.

NEUFELD, Elizabeth F. and Fratantoni, J. C.
In born errors of mucopolysaccharide metabolism. bibliog il Science 169:141-6 Jl 10 '70
—See Wiesmann, U. jt. auth.

NEUFELD, Jacob
To amend refereeing; letter, with reply by S. A. Goudsmit. Phys Today 23:9 Ap '70

NEUGEBOREN, Jay
Your suburban alternative. Esquire 74:113 S '70

NEUHAUS, Richard John
Good sense of amnesty. Nation 210:145-8 F 9 '70
Is America moral? Commonweal 92:341-3 Jl 10 '70
War, the churches, and civil religion. bibliog f Ann Am Acad 387:128-40 Ja '70

about

Politics of conscience. Nation 210:165 F 16 '70 *

NEUMANN, Bill
Smoother approach. il Hot Rod 23:62-4 Je '70

NEUMANN, F. L. See Mautz, R. K. jt. auth.

NEUMANN, Frederick
Ornament and structure; excerpt from Baroque ornamentation in France, Italy and Germany. bibliog f il Mus Q 56:153-61 Ap '70

NEUMANN, Vera
Top designers at home. il pors Am Home 73: 72-3 S '70 *

NEUMARKT, Paul
Kafka's A hunger artist: the ego in isolation. bibliog Am Imago 27:109-21 Sum '70

NEUMEIER, John
Chipping the stone: John Neumeier begins to shape the Frankfurter opern ballett. N. M. Stoop. il por Dance Mag 44:36-9 Ag '70 *

NEURAMINIDASE
Neuraminidase activity in HeLa cells: effect of hydrocortisone. R. Carubelli and M. J. Griffin. bibliog il Science 170:1110-12 D 4 '70

NEUROBIOLOGY
Physicist's renewed look at biology: twenty years later; Nobel lecture, December 10, 1969. M. Delbrück. bibliog Science 168:1312-15 Je 12 '70

Conferences

Oral-facial and motor mechanisms. R. Dubner. Science 170:1130-2 D 4 '70

NEUROBLASTOMA cells. See Cancer cells

NEUROCHEMISTRY
Cell communication, calcium ion, and cyclic adenosine monophosphate. H. Rasmussen. bibliog il Science 170:404-12 O 23 '70
How the Nobelists won. il por Newsweek 76:83 O 26 '70
Neurobiology: on the research frontier. pors Sci N 98:331 O 24 '70
Neuromuscular synapse: stochastic properties of spontaneous release of transmitter. S. Rotshenker and R. Rahamimoff. bibliog il Science 170:648-9 N 6 '70
Nobel prize: three share 1970 award for medical research. S. Udenfriend; A. R. Martin. pors Science 170:422-4 O 23 '70
See also
Brain—Analysis and chemistry

NEUROGLIA. See Nerve cells

NEUROLOGY
See also
Developmental neurology
Electrophysiology
Nervous system
Neurobiology
Neurochemistry
Psychology, Physiological

NEURONS. See Nerve cells

NEUROSES
Diagnostic overkill and management of psychiatric problems. C. E. Goshen. Ment Hy 54:306-9 Ap '70
False heart attack symptoms. il Sci Digest 67:68 Mr '70
Psychiatric disorders in young women: the public health implications. M. Mazer. bibliog Ment Hy 54:436-9 Jl '70
See also
Phobias
Psychoses

NEUROTICS. See Neuroses

NEUROTICS anonymous
Now it's Neurotics anonymous. por Time 95:58 Mr 2 '70

NEUSNER, Jacob
Radical Judaism. Ladies Home J 86:133 D '69

NEUTRA, Richard Joseph
Richard Neutra: survival through design. W. Von Eckardt. il Sat R 53:62-3 Je 6 '70 *

NEUTRAL particles. See Particles (nuclear physics)

NEUTRALITY
Nonalignment and the great powers. L. Mates. For Affairs 48:525-36 Ap '70

NEUTRON activation analysis. See Radioactivation analysis

NEUTRON-induced autoradiography. See Autoradiography

NEUTRON radiography. See Radiography

NEUTRON stars. See Stars—Evolution

NEUTRONS
Controversial bond in the F shell; chemical bonding between neutrons and electrons. il Sci N 97:92-3 Ja 24 '70
See also
Nucleons

NEUTROPHILS. See Leukocytes

NEVADA
See also
Birds—Nevada
Booksellers and bookselling—Nevada
Fishing—Nevada
Pyramid Lake
Wilderness areas—Nevada

Fish and game commission

Here in Nevada a terrible crime; Pyramid Lake. A. M. Josephy, jr. il Am Heritage 21:93-100 Je '70

History

Comstock country. il Am West 7:34-43 S '70
Taken by the wind; excerpt from Nevada ghost towns and mining camps. S. W. Paher. il Am West 7:9-17 My '70

Parks and reserves

Into Nevada's Valley of Fire. il Sunset 145: 30 O '70

NEVADO DEL HUILA (mountain) See Andes mountains

NEVELSON, Louise
Do your work. il Art N 69:41+ Ja '71

NEVER touch a butterfly; story. See Batki, J.

NEVIN, David
Agonies of a front-runner. il pors McCalls 97:82-5 My '70
Powerless students. il McCalls 97:44-5+ Jl '70

NEVINS, Allan
Riding the model T to mass production. il por Nations Bsns 58:72-3 Ja '70

NEW ALBANY-FLOYD COUNTY, Ind, public library
New Albany-Floyd County: cultural focus for a community. il Library J 95:4140 D 1 '70

NEW American Bible. See Bible—Versions

NEW American cinema. See Moving pictures —United States

NEW American review
NAL vehemently denies Times account of NAR demise. Pub W 197:77 Je 29 '70

NEW art association
Arise you prisoners of art history. T. B. Hess. Art N 69:35 N '70
Art. L. Alloway. Nation 211:508+ N 16 '70
See also
College art association of America

NEW business enterprises. See Business enterprises, New

NEW CALEDONIA
See also
Nickel mines and mining—New Caledonia

NEW CANAAN, Conn.
Our newest snowfighter works all year. L. Wood and E. Peck. il Am City 85:54-5 D '70

NEW careers programs. See Socially handicapped—Education

NEW Christian (periodical)
Good will and high hurdles. A. Geyer. Chr Cent 87:619-20 My 20 '70
Journalism for *oikoumene*; New Christian will merge with the Christian century. Chr Cent 87:315-16 Mr 18 '70

NEW cities and towns
Belconnen town center. R. Jensen. il Arch Rec 147:132-5 F '70
Brave new towns that aged awkwardly; Radburn, N.J. and Greenbelt, Md. il Bsns W p22+ Ja 9 '71
Can new cities remake America? Changing T 24:19-22 My '70
New cities: a look at the future. il U S News 68:64-5 Ja 26 '70
New towns, a boon to the quality of life. Parks & Rec 5:13 O '70
New towns and industrial parks change Europe. Nations Bsns 58:97-8 O '70
New towns are our mandate for urban innovations. S. Myers and R. Schwartz. il Arch Forum 132:38-41 Je '70

NEW cities and towns—*Continued*
New towns in the desert; Israel. M. D.
Morris. il Am City 85:94+ N '70
Nordwest Zentrum: ad-hoc heart for a city?
new town near Frankfurt, Germany. L.
Ungers and O. M. Ungers. il Arch Forum
133:30-7 O '70
Omnibuildings. W. Karp. il Horizon 12:48-55
Wint '70
Pablum in paradise: California's instant com-
munities. R. Gustaitis. il Am Home 73:80-5
Jl '70
Why and how to build another U.S.A. J.
Fischer. Cur 114:9-16 Ja '70
See also
Columbia, Md.
Eden, N.C.
Miami Lakes, Fla
Nun's Island
Reston, Va.
Roosevelt City, Ala.
Seward's Success, Alaska
Soul City, N.C.
Sunriver, Ore.
Synanon City, Calif.
Valencia, Calif.

Laws and legislation

Firmer foundation for new towns; new
housing authorization bill. Bsns W p22
Ja 9 '71
New towns rise on the Hill. il Bsns W p96-
7 F 7 '70
NEW deal. See United States—History—
1933-1945
NEW Democratic coalition. See Democratic
party
NEW education. See Education, Experimental
NEW ENGLAND
See also
Connecticut River
Education—New England
Roads—New England

Description and travel

New England's fall fantasia. M. Perry. il
Home Gard 57:24-7 S '70
Yankeeland winter. H. P. Koenig. il Travel
134:28-33 D '70

History

Peaceable kingdoms, by M. Zuckerman. Re-
view
Newsweek il 75:118D Ap 20 '70. R. A.
Gross
Colonial period
Pioneers in Massachusetts. F. L. Phelps. il
Américas 22:21-30 F '70
See also
Pilgrim fathers
Puritans
Social history
Pilgrims' progress. J. E. Illick. Nation 211:
90-3 Ag 3 '70
Social life and customs
See also
Old Sturbridge village, Sturbridge, Mass.
NEW ENGLAND aquarium. See Aquariums
NEW ENGLAND book festival. See Book fairs
NEW ENGLAND cookery. See Cookery,
American
NEW ENGLAND dance theatre. See Dance
companies
NEW ENGLAND forestry foundation, Boston
New England's memorial forests. R. Apple-
gate. il Am For 76:12-15 Ja '70
NEW ENGLAND villages. See Villages
NEW ENGLAND witchcraft. See Witchcraft
NEW ENGLANDERS
Letter from Leete's Island: the puritan ethic
is alive and hard at work in Connecticut.
J. Fischer. Harper 240:12+ Ja '70
NEW English Bible. See Bible—Versions
NEW GUINEA
See also
Costume—New Guinea
Paleontology—New Guinea
West Irian
Description and travel
Greatest show on earth: New Guinea. M.
R. Henry. il Vogue 156:96+ D '70
Native races
More on nitrogen fixing; diet of New Guinea
natives. Sci N 98:161 Ag 22 '70
With the stone age men in New Guinea. L.
Thomas. il por Read Digest 96:154-7+ F
'70
See also
Papua-New Guinea (territory)—Native races

Social conditions
Presenting: the very recent past. M. Mead.
il N Y Times Mag p28-32 Mr 15 '70
NEW GUINEA, Territory of. See Papua-New
Guinea (territory)
NEW HAMPSHIRE
See also
Education—New Hampshire
Fishing—New Hampshire
Merrimack River
NEW HAMPSHIRE cabinetmakers. See Cabi-
netmakers
NEW HAMPSHIRE, University, Durham
Expressionist forms on a budget; new resi-
dence hall. il Arch Rec 148:101-4 N '70
NEW HAVEN, Conn.
Students design a play machine. il Am City
85:28 N '70
Architecture
Great garage at the top; garage for Coliseum
and convention center. il Arch Forum 133:
42-3 O '70
Landmark tower on New Haven's skyline;
Knights of Columbus building. R. Jensen.
il Arch Rec 148:109-15 Ag '70
Negroes
Black Panthers and white radicals. P. Starr.
Commonweal 92:294-7 Je 12 '70
Theater
Theater; productions of the Long Wharf
theatre and the Yale repertory theatre. J.
Kroll. il Newsweek 75:74 Ja 26 '70
NEW HEBRIDES
Demography of primitive populations. N. Mc-
Arthur. bibliog il Science 167:1099-101 F
20 '70
See also
Pentecost Island
NEW HOPE and Ivyland railroad
What hope for the New Hope? il Bsns W p21
Jl 25 '70
NEW JERSEY
See also
Airports—New Jersey
Camps—New Jersey
Conservation of resources—New Jersey
Crime and criminals—New Jersey
Fishing—New Jersey
Kittatinny Mountains
Paleontology—New Jersey
Police—New Jersey
Politics, Corruption in—New Jersey
Trials—New Jersey
Historic houses, etc.
See also
Paterson, N.J.—Historic houses, etc.
History
Melancholy case; order by G. Washington
to hang Capt C. Asgill in reprisal for Tory
atrocity. A. L. Damon. il por Am Heritage
21:18-19+ F '70
Politics and government
Guide for Nixon in '72; New Jersey's '69 elec-
tion. il pors US News 68:32-3 Ja 19 '70
See also
Politics, Corruption in—New Jersey
NEW JERSEY standard oil company. See Stan-
dard oil company (New Jersey)
NEW JERSEY state library, Trenton
Spreading state library riches for peanuts.
O. P. Gillock, jr. il Wilson Lib Bul 45:
354-5+ D '70
NEW JERSEY symphony orchestra
Musical events; concert given in Carnegie
Hall. W. Sargeant. New Yorker 45:79+ Ja
24 '70
NEW left (politics) See Right and left (political
science)
NEW MEXICO
American treasury of Southwest living;
symposium. il Am Home 73:49-72+ Mr '70
See also
Architecture, Domestic—New Mexico
Automobile touring—New Mexico
Fishing—New Mexico
Hunting—New Mexico
Pueblo Indians
Description and travel
New Mexico, the golden land. R. Laxalt. il
Nat Geog 138:299-345 S '70
Traveler's choice; Wingate Valley. P. J.
Pesek. Travel 133:22 My '70
Economic conditions
Dollars in the desert; location for filmmakers.
il Newsweek 76:78 O 26 '70

NEW MEXICO—*Continued*

Land tenure
See Land tenure—United States

Social conditions
New Mexico: no mecca for hippies. S. F. Wheeler. Chr Cent 87:828-30 Jl 1 '70

NEW MEXICO arts and crafts. See Arts and crafts—United States

NEW mobilization committee to end the war in Vietnam
Secret link between Nixon and the New Mobe kids. W. Rogers. Look 34:78 Ja 27 '70

NEW ORLEANS
Bourbon on the rocks; police crackdown on hippies in the French quarter. il Newsweek 76:58-9 Jl 13 '70

Crime
Trouble in New Orleans; violence during Mardi Gras week. Newsweek 75:58-9 F 23 '70
See also
Mafia

Description
Croissants, beignets, and O.J. D. Butwin. il Sat R 53:47-9 S 19 '70
New Orleans. L. Dowty. il Travel & Camera 33:26-31 S '70
Walking tour of the French quarter. E. Galligan. il Travel & Camera 33:70-2 S '70

Hotels, restaurants, etc.
Creole cuisine. A. Gold and R. Fizdale. il Travel & Camera 33:36-7+ S '70
New Orleans' Pontchartrain. G. Cotler. il por Holiday 47:54-7 Je '70
Restaurants of New Orleans. E. Galligan. Travel & Camera 33:69 S '70

Music
Jazz. E. L. Borenstein. il Travel & Camera 33:32-5+ S '70
Music seeker's stroll. E. L. Borenstein. Travel & Camera 33:72 S '70
Preservation Hall. G. Cotler. il Holiday 47: 54-5+ My '70
See also
New Orleans philharmonic-symphony orchestra

Negroes
Death in Desire. il Time 96:13 S 28 '70
Desire under the guns. il Newsweek 76:28+ S 28 '70

Police
Death in Desire. il Time 96:13 S 28 '70
Desire under the guns. il Newsweek 76:28+ S 28 '70

Politics and government
New Moon over New Orleans. S. V. Roberts. Commonweal 91:501 F 6 '70

NEW ORLEANS opera house association
Report:
Production of Gounod's Faust. J. Belsom. il Opera N 35:29 N 21 '70
Richard Strauss' Arabella. J. Belsom. Opera N 34:34 F 7 '70
Tosca. J. Belsom. Opera N 34:30 Ap 11 '70
Verdi's Ballo in maschera. J. Belsom. Opera N 34:25 My 16 '70

NEW ORLEANS philharmonic-symphony orchestra
Business of survival. D. Hollister. Hi Fi 20:secII 26+ Je '70

NEW PALTZ teachers college. See New York (state). State university—College at New Paltz

NEW products. See Products, New

NEW republic (periodical)
Edmund Wilson's New republic. A. Mizener. New Repub 162:28-30 My 9 '70

NEW right (politics) See Right and left (political science)

NEW ROCHELLE, N.Y.

City planning
Parking garage helps revitalize a deteriorating downtown. D. Locitzer. il Am City 85:94 Je '70

NEW school for social research, New York
Undergraduate: selecting a course. New Yorker 45:25-7 Ja 31 '70

NEW school of Decatur. See Schools, Experimental

NEW schools. See Schools, Experimental

NEW statesman (periodical)
Changing of the guard. il por Newsweek 76: 58 Jl 6 '70
Mandate running out. J. Burnham. Nat R 22: 937 S 8 '70

NEW stock issues. See Stocks

NEW thing art and architecture center. See Washington, D.C.—Community centers

NEW towns. See New cities and towns

NEW TRIER township high schools. See Winnetka, Ill.—Education

NEW words. See Words, New

NEW World man. See Man, Prehistoric

NEW YEAR
Chinese New Year in San Francisco. il Sunset 144:37 F '70
Lead in the New Year with lead; tradition of melting lead on New Year's eve to tell fortunes. X. Pové. Harp Baz 104:147 D '70

Anecdotes, facetiae, satire, etc.
New Year's eve syndrome. S. Kaufman. il N Y Times Mag p 10-12+ D 27 '70

NEW YEARS resolutions
My best wishes for the New Year. E. Sheppard. Harp Baz 104:66 Ja '71

NEW YORK (city)
For executives, fun city can be a hardship. il Bsns W p64-9 F 7 '70
How to live in the city and stay sane. L. Lerman. Mlle 70:250-1+ Ap '70
See also
Bronx
Staten Island

Air pollution
Airborne lead and carbon monoxide at 45th street, New York city. J. L. Bové and S. Siebenberg. il Science 167:986-7 F 13 '70
New York's fight against pollution. N. Cousins. il Sat R 53:53-4+ Mr 7 '70
Notes and comment. New Yorker 46:21-2 Ag 8 '70
Smog goes global: a bad week in the cities. il Time 96:37-9 Ag 10 '70
Storms and polluted air caused airline delays around New York. Aviation W 93:28 Ag 10 '70
See also
New York (city)—Air resources, Department of

Air pollution control, Department of
See New York (city)—Air resources, Department of

Air resources, Department of
Commissioner Rickles; interview. R. N. Rickles. New Yorker 46:33-4 My 9 '70
Verdict. New Yorker 46:18-20 Ja 2 '71

Airports
Jackals at J.F.K. F. J. Cook. il N Y Times Mag p30-1+ Ap 12 '70
New runway de-icer termed effective after LaGuardia test. R. S. Kahn. Aviation W 92:34 Mr 30 '70
Pan Am-Carey pact approved; bus service to Kennedy airport. Aviation W 92:34 Ja 19 '70

Anecdotes, facetiae, satire, etc.
Fun city one hundred years ago; excerpts from The secrets of the great city, comp. by G. M. Naimark. E. W. Martin. Holiday 47:92+ F '70

Architecture
Bulwark in lower Manhattan; Manufacturers Hanover trust's new operations center. J. M. Dixon. il Arch Forum 132:62-7 Ja '70
New York's culture in the round. il UNESCO Courier 23:18-19 Je '70
New York's doomed palaces of iron. il Life 69:56-61 Ag 14 '70
Snorkel theater; Paramount theater. New York. il Arch Forum 133:54-5 O '70
Warehouse too handsome to remain one; Westyard building. il Arch Rec 147:113-18 My '70
See also
New York (city)—Buildings

Anecdotes, facetiae, satire, etc.
Rob and Barbi go brownstoning. T. Meehan. il N Y Times Mag p32-3+ N 22 '70; Reply. P. Wilkes and J. Wilkes. p 144 D 6 '70

NEW YORK (city)—Continued

Art

Art. L. Alloway. Nation 211:573-4 N 30 '70
Art; outdoor wall murals. L. Alloway. Nation 211:253-4 S 21 '70
Art world (cont) H. Rosenberg. New Yorker 45:62+ Ja 24; 46:82+ F 21; 90+ Mr 28; 103-4+ My 9; 48-52 Jl 18; 149-54 O 10; 136+ N 7 '70
New York season. H. Aach. il Craft Horiz 30: 49-51+ Ag '70
Painting the town. il Life 69:60-3 Jl 17 '70

Banks

Chase gets caught in a crossfire. il Bsns W p38-9 Ja 17 '70
Window on the world; Allied bank international. il Forbes 106:34-5 Ag 15 '70

Bookstores

See   Booksellers and bookselling—New York (state)

Buildings

One hundred buildings: high-rise office buildings designed by Emery Roth & sons. New Yorker 46:37 O 10 '70
Perils of concentration; New York city planning commission calls for more office construction. W. Von Eckardt. il Sat R 53: 62-3 My 2 '70
Times square news: sign around the Allied chemical tower, written by the Associated press. New Yorker 46:20-2 Ag 1 '70
Why offices stay unrented. il Bsns W p83+ D 5 '70

Chinatown

Chinatown's library; Chatham square, branch of the New York public library. M. H. Cole. il por Wilson Lib Bul 45:482-4 Ja '71

Churches

All nite soul: ceremony in St Peter's Lutheran church. New Yorker 46:38-9 O 31 '70
Flag day at Judson memorial church. M. Geltman. Nat R 22:1252 D 1 '70
Rock, business, and Trinity church. New Yorker 46:20-1 Jl 18 '70
Tourist's guide to New York churches. T. Early. Chr Cent 87:1017-18 Ag 26 '70; Discussion. 87:1287 O 28 '70
Young Lords and the Spanish congregation. D. M. Kelley. Chr Cent 87:208-11 F 18 '70
See also
New York (city)—St Patrick's cathedral

City planning

Model cities, model for failure; East New York section of Brooklyn. D. Stoloff. Arch Forum 132:78-9+ Ja '70
Perils of concentration; New York city planning commission calls for more office construction. W. Von Eckardt. il Sat R 53: 62-3 My 2 '70
Urban design as part of the governmental process. J. Barnett. il Arch Rec 147:131-50 Ja '70
Zoning is a three-dimensional word. E. P. Berkeley. il Arch Forum 133:48-51 N '70
See also
Bronx, N.Y.—City planning

Clubs

Ship society: visit to the Oceanic by New York branch of the World ship society. New Yorker 46:34-5 O 17 '70

Columbia-Presbyterian medical center

Research building programming via client-architect education; research addition to the New York psychiatric institute. il Arch Rec 147:108-9 Mr '70

Courts

Getting busted in New York; night court is easily the greatest show in town. P. Tracy. Commonweal 93:371-2 Ja 15 '71
Logjam in our courts; with editorial comment. D. Wittner. il Life 69:2A, 18-25 Ag 7 '70
Scandal of court congestion. il Time 96:60 N 9 '70

Crime

Easy marks; holdups of taxi drivers. il Time 96:84 S 21 '70
Famous prosecutor talks about crime; interview. ed. by V. S. Navasky. R. M Morgenthau. il pors N Y Times Mag p32-3+ F 15 '70
Requiem for a cabbie. il Newsweek 76:83 O 12 '70
See also
Mafia
New York (city)—Explosions

Description

Day in the city. 1970. L. E. Sissman. Atlan 226:22-5 D '70
Traveltips. Schol Teach Jr/Sr High p37-8 N 2 '70
Upper East side: safe haven in Manhattan. Bsns W p57-8 D 26 '70

Economic conditions

Exodus from New York city: what makes businesses leave. il U S News 69:50-3 D 7 '70
Hard times in Manhattan. P. Benchley. il N Y Times Mag p8-9+ S 6 '70

Education

Citizen power: P.S. 109's man in the pin-striped suit. K. Branan. il Am Ed 6:14-17 Ap '70
Different library, different school! City and country school library. M. B. Piel. il Pub W 198:78-81 Jl 13 '70
Hostos community college. por Sch & Soc 98:143 Mr '70
Instead of Molotov cocktails; constructive action to improve conditions in their community. L. Rich. il Am Ed 6:11-15 Je '70
New learning center thrives in New York; John Dewey high school. W. E. Williamson. Clear House 45:26-8 S '70
New York city principals: on the razor's edge. B. Bard. il Sat R 53:58-9+ Ja 24 '70
Once upon a time: a fable of student power. N. Postman. il N Y Times Mag p 10-11 Je 14 '70
Self-made college; two-year College for human services. il por Time 96:53-4 Jl 6 '70
Suit seeks to smash standards; NAACP legal defense and educational fund to challenge constitutionality system of licensing principals. Sat R 53:72 N 21 '70
Teacher recruitment and selection in New York city archaic and costly. I. Flinker. il Clear House 44:483-7 Ap '70
Who gets the power? il Newsweek 76:121-2 S 14 '70
Young performers face young listeners. P. Hart. il Hi Fi 20:secII 15-17 Jl '70
See also
Bank street college of education
Finch college
New school for social research
New York (city). City university

Elections

Is there a Jewish vote? A. M. Klebanoff. Commentary 49:43-7 Ja '70
Jewish class conflict? M. Himmelfarb. Commentary 49:37-42 Ja '70
Our local correspondents; 40th assembly district of Brooklyn. S. Lardner. New Yorker 46:96+ Je 20 '60

Electric power

Smog goes global: a bad week in the cities: power shortage in New York. il Time 96:37-9 Ag 10 '70
There goes the power. il Newsweek 76:65 Ag 10 '70
See also
Consolidated Edison company of New York

Employees

Militant civil servants in New York city. F. F. Piven. il por Trans-Action 7:24-8+ N '69

Environmental protection administration

Dream of gas masks. il por Newsweek 76:58+ D 7 '70
Environmental protection in the city of New York. M. Eisenbud. bibliog il Science 170: 706-12 N 13 '70

Explosions

Bomb jitters. Newsweek 75:23-4 Mr 30 '70
Bombing: a way of protest and death; bombs exploding at the Manhattan headquarters of Mobil oil, IBM and General telephone and electronics. il Time 95:8-11 Mr 23 '70
Close to home; police headquarters. il Newsweek 75:22 Je 22 '70
House on 11th street. il pors Newsweek 75: 29-30 Mr 23 '70
Ted Gold: education for violence. J. K. Sale. Nation 210:423-9, 514+ Ap 13, My 4 '70
Two girls from no. 18. J. Neary. il pors Life 68:26-9 Mr 27 '70

Festivals

See Festivals—New York (state)

Finance

Is New York hopeless? An official report. il U S News 68:53-4 Mr 23 '70

NEW YORK (city)—*Continued*

Financial district
See Wall Street

Fire department
Around city hall. A. Logan. New Yorker 46:120-2+ S 19 '70
Fireman Smith: Dennis E. Smith of New York fire department, a student of Irish poetry. New Yorker 46:18-19 Ag 29 '70

Foreign population
See also
Puerto Ricans in the United States

Galleries and museums
Art; current exhibitions of modern art. L. Alloway. Nation 210:92-3 Ja 26 '70
Art machine for the 70's; Feigen gallery in Manhattan. J. S. Margolies. il Arch Forum 132:44-51+ Ja '70
Humanizing automation; Automation house. il Arch Forum 133:74-5 Jl '70
Museum of the media makes waves. N. Rothschild. il Pop Phot 67:18+ O '70
New dealing. E. H. Varian. il Art in Am 58:68-73 Ja '70
New York gallery notes. G. Glueck. See issues of Art in America
Reviews and previews. See issues of Art news
Soho in New York. D. Davis. il Newsweek 75:101-2 F 16 '70
Street of ships; historic water front preserved by South street seaport museum. S. B. Sherrill. il Antiques 98:156+ Ag '70
See also
American museum of natural history
Finch college. New York—Museum of art
Metropolitan museum of art
Museum of contemporary crafts
Museum of modern art
New York historical society
Whitney museum of American art

Gardens
See also
Brooklyn botanic garden

Greenwich Village
House on 11th street. il Time 95:10 Mr 23 '70

Fiction
Three likely lads of limbo. E. Waldron. New Yorker 46:38-9 Mr 21 '70

Harbor
Danger of debris; army engineers combat a major problem in New York. W. J. Papin. il Yachting 129:107+ Ja '71
Precision controlled flames fight air pollution. R. G. Burns and R. E. Newton. il Am City 85:98+ My '70
See also
New York (city)—Police department—Harbor precinct

Harlem
At home in East Harlem; interview, ed. by M. R. Weiss. B. Davidson. il Sat R 53:54-5 S 19 '70
Daddy was a number runner; excerpts. L. Meriwether. il por Ebony 25:98-103 Jl '70
Day in Harlem; the Penny sightseeing tours. D. Butwin. il Sat R 53:40-1 Jl 25 '70
Fighting back; headquarters of on-the-job training program for blacks and Puerto Ricans. New Yorker 46:28-30 Ag 22 '70

Photographs
Beautiful people of James Van Derzee. il pors Ebony 25:85-8+ O '70
East 100th street, by B. Davidson. Review New Yorker 46:188+ D 12 '70. L. E. Sissman

Historic houses, etc.
See also
Brooklyn—Historic houses, etc.
New York (city)—Landmarks preservation commission

Hospitals
Abortion in New York. il Newsweek 76:52 O 5 '70
Abortion in New York. il Time 96:48 S 7 '70
After July 1, an abortion should be as simple to have as a tonsillectomy, but—. L. Greenhouse. il N Y Times Mag p7+ Je 28 '70
See also
New York (city)—Columbia-Presbyterian medical center

Hotels, restaurants, etc.
Best bartender in New York: Tony Tisi of Wilby's. J. Corry. por Harper 241:47-51 Ag '70
La dolce dining: Four Seasons and La Seine. N. S. Hazelton. Nat R 22:364+ Ap 7 '70
Eat. L. McIntyre. Mlle 71:140+ Ag '70
Elaine's. J. O'Reilly. il Holiday 47:69-70 Ap '70
Goings on about town. See issues of New Yorker
House beautiful designs a celebrity suite at the Waldorf. R. Fitzgerald and others. il House B 112:122-7 N '70
Jack and Charlie's hideaway house: 21 club. L. Lyons. il Holiday 47:77-9 Ja '70
McSorley's old ale house. R. Burgheim. il Holiday 47:84-6 My '70
New York restaurants. Q. Crewe. Vogue 155:154+ My '70
Random harvest of Albert Stockli. R. A. De Groot. il por Esquire 74:150-1+ O '70
Romantic dining in New York; Chez Vito. M. Woodward. il Travel 134:18 N '70
Sam's; Oyster bar at The Plaza; Yellowfingers. Esquire 73:224-5 My '70
Slump du jour. il Time 95:100 My 11 '70
To what French restaurant in N.Y. do you take you wife? Your mistress? Lutèce, Caravelle, Toque blanche; winners of poll. G. J. Nelson. il Holiday 47:70-1 Je '70
See also
Night clubs

Housing
Around city hall. A. Logan. New Yorker 46:106+ Ap 18 '70
Lefrak goes to the ghetto; target of Justice dept. il por Bsns W p28 Ag 15 '70
Westbeth; artists in residence. E. P. Berkeley. il Arch Forum 133:44-9 O '70
Westbeth's rehabilitation project: a clue to improving our cities; with statement by R. Meier. il Arch Rec 147:103-6 Mr '70
Wildfire of abandonment. il Bsns W p57+ Ap 4 '70
See also
Bronx, N.Y.—Housing

Housing and development administration
Urban design as part of the governmental process. J. Barnett. il Arch Rec 147:131-50 Ja '70

Intellectual life
Split in the family? Nat R 22:1334-5 D 15 '70

Labor and laboring classes
Profiles; T. W. Kheel. F. C. Shapiro. New Yorker 46:36-44+ Ag 1 '70

Landmarks preservation commission
Street of ships. S. B. Sherrill. il Antiques 98:156+ Ag '70

Libraries
Films on demand; Moviebox. L. Hofer. il Library J 95:3962-4 N 15 '70
Presidential caper; The library of presidential papers. il Time 95:21-2 Ap 13 '70
See also
New York public library

Markets
Street of ships; preservation of Fulton fish market. S. B. Sherrill. il Antiques 98:156+ Ag '70

Mayors
New York's other mayor; Deputy Mayor R. Aurelio. il por Newsweek 76:65-6 Jl 27 '70

Metropolitan museum of art
See Metropolitan museum of art

Music
Alexander Schneider's Christmas present; Christmas string seminar. R. S. Brown. il por Hi Fi 20:secII 24-5 Mr '70
Behind the scenes. D. Hamilton. il por Hi Fi 20:secI 22 My '70
Debuts & reappearances. See issues of High fidelity section II
Jazz. W. Balliett. New Yorker 46:110+ Mr 7 '70
Jazz: New York notes. W. Balliett. New Yorker 46:78+ My 23 '70
Lively arts. R. Hemming. il Sr Schol 96:28 My 18 '70
Music. D. Hamilton. Nation 211:476-7; 212:28-9 N 9 '70, Ja 4 '71
Music to my ears. I. Kolodin. See issues of Saturday review
Musical events. W. Sargeant. See issues of New Yorker

NEW YORK (city)—Music—*Continued*
New concert procedures, the walk-around. C.
  Moore. Vogue 156:38 Ag 15 '70
Nowhere to go. I. Stravinsky. Harper 240:
  32+ F '70
On the off-beat. A. Rich. Hi Fi 20:secII 7 Ag
  '70
Pleni sunt celli; P. Casals conducting all-
  cello orchestra at Philharmonic Hall. il por
  Time 95:48 Ap 27 '70
Puccini's pot of gold: 1907 visit to New
  York. H. Bailey. Opera N 34:16 Mr 7 '70
Report:
  Concert performances of three one-act
    operas by the Ruffino opera at Town
    Hall. J. Honig. Opera N 34:33 F 7 '70
  Opera orchestra's concert version of
    Rigoletto at Tully Hall. S. Gould. Opera
    N 34:30 Mr 14 '70
Which one is Joe? English blues singer J.
  Cocker. il por Time 95:67 Ap 13 '70
  See also
Little orchestra society
Metropolitan opera club
Metropolitan opera company
New York city opera company
Philharmonic-symphony society of New York

Negroes
New York city skid row Negro: some research findings; homeless men in the
  Bowery. B. M. Levinson. bibliog Ment Hy
  54:548-52 O '70

Newspapers
Blackout in New York? Newsweek 75:77 Ap
  13 '70
New York city's dailies vs. the unions: auto-
  mation's armageddon. A. H. Raskin. il Sat
  R 53:50-2 Jl 11 '70
Newspapers; two new projects: Daily planet
  and Weekday. New Yorker 46:27-30 Mr 14
  '70
  See also
New York times
Village voice (newspaper)

Noise
Cities lend an ear to noise control. Bsns W
  p 108 Ja 17 '70

Parks and playgrounds
Escape: hornbill's escape from Central park
  zoo. New Yorker 46:23-5 Ag 8 '70
Hillside movies: series of short films in
  Central park, near 79th street. New Yorker
  46:18-19 Jl 18 '70
Meeting: public opinion on Metropolitan's
  expansion plan into Central park. New
  Yorker 46:25-7 Je 20 '70
Nature trails in a wild park in New York
  city; Inwood hill park. il Arch Rec 147:140-1
  My '70
New York: a city going to the dogs? C.
  Berman. il N Y Times Mag p92+ S 27 '70;
  Discussion. p58+ O 18 '70
P.O.N.Y. farm, where city youngsters have
  fun sharing the care of animals; corral in
  dock district. il por Good H 170:52-3+ Mr
  '70
The park; project of an ecology-action group.
  New Yorker 46:25-6 S '70
Playground: adventure playground in Cen-
  tral park. New Yorker 46:30 Ag 22 '70
Shelter: first of six rebuilt by Friends of
  Central park. New Yorker 46:26-7 Je 13 '70
Yes: festival on the Central park mall called
  The people, yes! New Yorker 46:42-3 O 24
  '70
  See also
New York (city)—Washington square

Photographs
Photo show of old New York; exhibition at
  the New York historical society. W.
  McQuade. il Life 69:18-19 D 11 '70

Planning, design and research, Office of
  See New York (city)—Housing and development administration

Poetry
Poem of the city of New York. J. Kroll.
  New Repub 162:30 Mr 7 '70

Police
Bomb scare; removal of bomb from Portuguese government tourist information
  bureau by Bomb squad. New Yorker 46:
  19-20 Jl 18 '70
Compassionate cop; Manhattan's 30th police
  precinct's Family crisis intervention unit.
  il Time 95:58 Mr 23 '70

Cops up against the wall; tactical patrol
  force and Preventive enforcement patrol.
  il Look 34:17-21 Jl 28 '70
John Jay: college for cops. F. J. Cook. il
  Nation 211:555-8 N 30 '70
Offbeat policemen: peace petition in response
  to SANE ad. New Yorker 46:22-3 Ag 8 '70
Police mentality; IQ levels. Newsweek 76:45
  Ag 3 '70
$2 misunderstanding; brutality against L.
  Blutcher. A. Cooper. Newsweek 76:45 Ag
  3 '70
Wall Street lunch. New Yorker 46:30-1 My
  23 '70
Why real-life detective stories so often end
  with a rubber stamp. P. Wilkes. il N Y
  Times Mag p32-3+ Ap 19 '70
  See also
Police athletic league

Police department
Around city hall. A. Logan. New Yorker 46:
  120-2+ S 19 '70
Cop quits; Commissioner H. R. Leary. il por
  Newsweek 76:89-90 S 21 '70

Harbor precinct
Cruise. New Yorker 46:20-3 Jl 4 '70

Politics and government
Around city hall (cont) A. Logan. New
  Yorker 46:101-4+ F 28; Ap 18; 104-8 Je 6;
  120-2+ S 19; 126+ N 21 '70
Broader base now for Mayor Lindsay. il por
  U S News 68:9 Ja 19 '70
Candidates: T. Sorensen for the Democratic
  nomination to the Senate; H. Samuels for
  governor. New Yorker 46:27-30 Je 20 '70
The city, by J. V. Lindsay. Review
  Bsns W p9 Ap 18 '70. F. W. Richmond
  New Repub 162:20-2 Mr 28 '70. R. C. Lee
  Sat R 53:25-6 Ap 11 '70. H. Lavine
Consultants vs. urban anti-intellectualism.
  Am City 85:12 S '70
Managing Mailer, by J. Flaherty. Review
  Nat R por 22:688-9 Je 30 '70. G. F. Will

Poor
Hotels without hope. W. Friedman and R.
  Anson. il Time 97:28-30 Ja 4 '71

Popular culture
New York's culture in the round. il
  UNESCO Courier 23:18-19 Je '70

Prisons and reformatories
Anger in the cells. il Newsweek 76:102 O 19
  '70
Black hole of Manhattan; the Tombs. il Time
  96:28-9 Ag 24 '70
City's island of the damned: Rikers Island.
  H. Swados. il N Y Times Mag p24-5+ Ap
  26 '70; Discussion. p 118-19 My 17 '70
No one cares; suicides at Rikers Island pen-
  itentiary. il Newsweek 75:51-2 Mr 2 '70
Rampage in New York. il Time 96:44 O 19
  '70
Riot against the law's delay; the Tombs. il
  Newsweek 76:20 Ag 24 '70

Protests, demonstrations, etc.
Around city hall. A. Logan. New Yorker
  46:104-8 Je 6 '70
Hard hats: demonstrations around Wall
  Street and city hall. il Newsweek 75:34-5
  My 25 '70
Hard-hats: the rampaging patriots. F. J.
  Cook. il Nation 210:712-19 Je 15 '70
Italian power; demonstrations against the
  New York headquarters of the FBI. il News-
  week 75:22 Je 22 '70
Joe Kelly has reached his boiling point; why
  the construction workers holler, U.S.A. all
  the way! R. Rogin. il pors N Y Times Mag
  p 12-14+ Je 28 '70
N.Y.A.S.A.R.S.R.W; New York artists strike
  against racism, sexism, repression and war.
  il Time 95:62 Je 15 '70
Sudden rising of the hardhats: construction
  workers vs. antiwar student demonstrators.
  il Time 95:20-1 My 25 '70
Three days that shook the establishment:
  building workers and longshoremen vs.
  antiwar protestors in Manhattan. il Bsns
  W p24 My 16 '70
Wall Street lunch. New Yorker 46:30-1 My 23
  '70
Why the clerks join the hardhats. il Bsns W
  p42 My 23 '70
Workers' Woodstock. il Time 95:12 Je 1 '70

Public health
Legal abortion mess. A. Barry. McCalls 98:
  30+ Ja '71
New York: a city going to the dogs? C.
  Berman. il N Y Times Mag p92+ S 27 '70;
  Discussion. p58+ O 18 '70

NEW YORK (city)—*Continued*

Public officers

Aristocrat in local politics. R. Starr. Commentary 51:87-91 Ja '71
Why Lindsay's toughest job is hiring. il por Bsns W p51+ Je 20 '70

Public welfare

Hotels without hope. W. Friedman and R. Anson. il Time 97:28-30 Ja 4 '71
See also
New York (city)—Welfare, Department of

Public works

Public works, by R. Moses. Review
Harper 240:126-9 My '70. J. Thompson

Recreation

Floating swimming pools; proposed use of Liberty ships. Y. Fogel. il Parks & Rec 5:30-1 Ap '70
New York's new pool/play centers. il Arch Rec 148:162-3 O '70
Portable talent scout; summer project in New York's PAL play streets. il Am City 85:64 My '70
See also
New York (city)—Parks and playgrounds

Religious institutions and affairs

See also
Council of churches of the city of New York
New York (city)—Churches

Restaurants

See New York (city)—Hotels, restaurants, etc.

Rockefeller Center

Tree. New Yorker 46:32-4 D 19 '70

St Patrick's cathedral

Cathedral: preparations for May 25, 1979, hundredth anniversary. New Yorker 46:17-19 D 26 '70

Sanitary affairs

Hope for the best; plan for the worst; snow program. il Am City 85:74+ N '70
New York city approves refuse sacks. Am City 85:37 Ja '70
New York city to use Unox system. Am City 85:24 S '70
No glamour, just work. S. Galler. il Am City 85:116+ My '70
See also
New York (city)—Environmental protection administration

Shops

See New York (city)—Stores

Social conditions

Jug jug jug jug jug tu-whit tu-whoo; end of one of the city's most pleasant ways of life. J. Ferris. Sat R 53:4 Jl 11 '70
See also
Bronx, N.Y.—Social conditions
New York (city)—Harlem

Social history

Arrogance of virtue (in old New York) R. Starr. New Repub 163:19-21 D 26 '70

Social life and customs

Four gatherings: openings of barber shop for men at Bonwit Teller; the drama, Home; Film forum, and Anthology film archives. New Yorker 46:48-52 D 5 '70
See also
Night clubs

SoHo

Bohemia's last frontier; artists and galleries in SoHo. il Time 95:82 My 25 '70
SoHo. New Yorker 46:28-9 Je 6 '70

Stock exchange

See Stock exchange—New York (city)

Stores

Balmy day on Herald square; Christmas display windows. D. Butwin. Sat R 53:32-3 D 26 '70
Books enter a third world at F.A.O. Schwarz. il Pub W 197:71-2 Mr 2 '70
Le Drugstore; Manhattan's newest divertissement. il Time 96:56 N 2 '70
Le Drugstore (not a pharmacy) New Yorker 46:35 O 31 '70
Naked on Fifth; Best & co. closes. il Newsweek 76:86 O 19 '70
On and off the avenue; new Knoll international showroom, D/R international stores. J. Malcolm. New Yorker 46:147-8+ N 7 '70

Shutdowns stalk big-city stores; Best & co's closing. il Bsns W p28 O 10 '70
State aid for retailers insurance coverage; Buy-Rite's appeal. H. F. Pilpel and K. P. Norwick. Pub W 198:33-4 D 28 '70
See also
Cartier, inc.

Street traffic

Ban-the-car movement. il Newsweek 77:42 Ja 4 '71
Power to pedestrians; banning autos in New York and Tokyo. il Time 96:36 Ag 24 '70
See also
New York (city)—Traffic, Department of

Streets

Fifth avenue turns into a mall. il Bsns W p22 Jl 13 '70
Pedestrian malls have their day in New York city. Pub W 198:38-9 O 19 '70
Sidewalk's potential; the Calder sidewalk on upper Madison avenue. il Time 96:44 O 5 '70
Tell all the gang on 42nd street. il Time 96:21 O 19 '70

Strikes

See also
Strikes—United States—Actors and actresses
Strikes—United States—Teachers

Subways

Little sand; general deterioration. Nation 211:69 Ag 3 '70
New York's sick subways. il Newsweek 76:79 Ag 31 '70

Theater

After innocence, what? J. Chaikin's off-off-Broadway Open theater. il Time 95:63 Je 1 '70
American chickens; Commune production of Richard Schechner's Performance group. J. Kroll. Newsweek 76:61 D 28 '70
Another reprise of Broadway blues. il Bsns W p34 S 19 '70
Broadway hails Britannia. C. R. Hughes. America 124:46-8 Ja 16 '71
Eleven experimentalists in the theatre; Ellen Stewart's La Mama conglomerate. il Vogue 155:172-3 F 1 '70
Goings on about town. See issues of New Yorker
How the theater season shapes up. il Newsweek 76:104-5 S 21 '70
La MaMa is a lady. E. Lester. il por Holiday 47:22+ My '70
New season; fall offerings. H. Hewes. Sat R 53:18 S 5 '70
Nowhere to go. I. Stravinsky. Harper 240:32+ F '70
Off Broadway; New Lafayette production of The devil catchers by an anonymous hand. E. Oliver. New Yorker 46:132 D 12 '70
Off Broadway; the Open theatre, an off off Broadway troupe exploration called Terminal. E. Oliver. New Yorker 46:50 Je 6 '70
Off Broadway; The serpent: Open theatre's variations on the Book of Genesis. E. Oliver. il New Yorker 46:90 Je 13 '70
Reflections on subscription theatres. T. Lewis. America 123:26-7 Jl 11 '70
Sick Broadway tries two potions; 7:30 curtain and limited gross plan. il Bsns W p 16 Ja 2 '71
Spotlight! E. Miller. See issues of Seventeen
Stage-struck; strike, closing down sixteen off-Broadway shows. Time 96:58 N 30 '70
Theater. See issues of Newsweek
Theater in '70. H. Hewes. il Sat R 53:19-23+ Je 13 '70
Theater; off and off-off-Broadway offerings. H. Hewes. Sat R 53:20 D 26 '70
Theatre; off-Broadway's economic dilemma. H. Clurman. Nation 210:348-9 Mr 23 '70
Tokyo kid brothers; performers in Golden bat, rock revue at the Sheridan square playhouse. New Yorker 46:34-6 S 12 '70
What's needed to revive Broadway; interview. D. Merrick. pors U S News 68:83-4 My 4 '70
Year's best plays. Time 97:54 Ja 4 '71
See also
Brooklyn—Theater
New York drama critics circle

Traffic, Department of

School-crossing sign without words. il Am City 85:76 D '70

Transit systems

New York city's rail bus. il Sci Digest 67:88-9 Ja '70
See also
Hudson and Manhattan corporation
New York (city)—Subways

NEW YORK (city)—Transit systems—*Cont.*

Fares

500,000 older New Yorkers get 1/2 fare; OFTA has paper. Aging 182:13 D '69

Outrage and opportunity. Nation 210:35-6 Ja 19 '70

Shell game. W. F. Buckley, jr. Nat R 22 100-1 Ja 27 '70

Transportation

Bike to work: Sixtieth street and Fifth avenue to Battery park. New Yorker 46:28-9 S 26 '70

See also
New York (city)—Subways

Washington square

Arch. New Yorker 46:19-21 Ag 29 '70

Water supply

See also
New York (city)—Environmental protection administration

Welfare, Department of

Anecdotes, facetiae, satire, etc.

Letter to the mayor. J. Goldschmidt. Atlan 225:58-9 F '70

World trade center

Aiding trade in a big way. il Nations Bsns 58:60D F '70

Zoological park

See New York zoological park

NEW YORK (city). City university

College for all. il Newsweek 76:85 S 28 '70

Dick, Jane and CUNY. Nat R 22:1039-40 O 6 '70

Gambling on open admissions. il Time 96:36-8 S 28 '70

Harlem to Harvard, and back; credit to City university's SEEK program. por Time 96:64 O 19 '70

Jesuit scholar new CUNY vice chancellor. por Sch & Soc 98:144 Mr '70

Open admissions: American dream or disaster? il Time 96:63-6 O 19 '70

Open admissions: emerging concept in higher education; new experiment in New York city. C. F. Stoerker. Chr Cent 87:1013-17 Ag 26 '70

Borough of Manhattan community college

Manhattan community college. il Arch Rec 147:148-52 Je '70

John Jay college of criminal justice

College for cops. il Newsweek 76:59 D 28 '70

John Jay: college for cops. F. J. Cook. il Nation 211:555-8 N 30 '70; Reply. A. J. Ajay. 212:2 Ja 4 '71

Libraries

Pre-college program for the disadvantaged; SEEK's library. S. H. Wright. il por Library J 95:2884-7 S 15 '70

NEW YORK (state)

See also
Adirondack Mountains
Airports—New York (state)
Architecture, Domestic—New York (state)
Birds—New York (state)
Booksellers and bookselling—New York (state)
Camps—New York (state)
Cayuga Lake
Conservation of resources—New York (state)
Courts—New York (state)
Environmental policy—New York (state)
Festivals—New York (state)
Finger Lakes
Fire Island
Fishing—New York (state)
Forests and forestry—New York (state)
Gardens—New York (state)
Hudson River
Hunting—New York (state)
Jamaica Bay
Kingston
Kittatinny Mountains
Lakes—New York (state)
Law—New York (state)
Libraries—New York (state)
Long Island
Music festivals—New York (state)
Nassau County
Public health—New York (state)
Roads—New York (state)
School libraries—New York (state)
Unemployment—New York (state)
Wilderness areas—New York (state)
Wildlife conservation—New York (state)
Wildlife sanctuaries—New York (state)

Conservation department

Aquarium opened at department's Cape Vincent fisheries research station. W. A. Pearce. il Cons 25:20 O '70

Employees

Conservation officer's job. L. R. Fendrick. il Cons 24:8-10 Ag '69

New York's snow patrol. L. R. Fendrick. il Cons 25:21-2 D '70

Council on the arts

Editorial; Governor Rockefeller's appeal for additional funds. W. Como. il Dance Mag 44:29 Mr '70

Description and travel

Extravagant tour that's everything, except expensive. M. Cohen. Redbook 134:71-2+ Mr '70

Education, Department of

Nyquist new Commissioner of education of New York state. Sch & Soc 98:209 Ap '70

Elections

See New York (state)—Politics and government

Environmental conservation, Department of

Department of environmental conservation activated on July 1st at Albany ceremony; excerpts from address, ed. by J. E. Gavagan. H. L. Diamond. il pors Cons 25:4-5 Ag '70

Diamond appoints first deputy commissioner. por Cons 25:7+ O '70

Governor appoints six citizen experts to new State environmental board. J. E. Gavagan. il Cons 25:2-3+ Ag '70

Governor creates Department of environmental conservation; Office of parks and recreation set up in new law; with editorial comment. N. A. Rockefeller. por Cons 24:1-3 Je '70

New marine research laboratory. il Cons 25: 37 Ag '70

Historic houses, etc.

Ghost of Sagamore Hill. A. B. Roosevelt, jr. il por Am Heritage 21:70-3 Ap '70

Philipsburg manor, Upper Mills at North Tarrytown, New York. J. T. Butler. il Antiques 97:864-71 Je '70

Realms of Gould; Lyndhurst. F. Kintrea. il por Am Heritage 21:46-65 Ap '70

Visit an early Dutch manor; Philipsburg manor. J. P. Fairhurst. il Home Gard 57: 42+ My '70

See also
Cooperstown, N. Y.—Historic houses, etc.

Labor, Department of

Youth opportunity program

Psychiatric training program for high school students assigned to a geriatric service. J. H. Friedman and A. R. Spada. bibliog Ment Hy 54:427-9 Jl '70

Mental hygiene, Department of

Health facilities: improvement through management and money for architecture; building types study. il Arch Rec 147:151-66 Ja '70

Metropolitan transportation authority

See Metropolitan transportation authority

Narcotic addiction control commission

Eighteen narcotic-addiction buildings in eighteen months; Arthur Kill rehabilitation center, Staten Island. il Am City 85:152+ Je '70

Parks and recreation, Office of

Governor appoints state's first parks and recreation commissioner. E. H. Moore. por Cons 25:19+ O '70

Politics and government

Agnew and The prince; attack upon Senator Goodell. Nation 211:357 O 19 '70

Bring on the tumblers! The clowns! Nat R 22:659-60 Je 30 '70

Conservative upset in the making in liberal New York? il pors U S News 69:30-1 Ag 31 '70

Conservatives are out to beat: Rockeberg, Goldfeller, Ottindell and Goodinger. J. Greenfeld. il por N Y Times Mag p26-7+ O 18 '70

First hurrah? U.S. Senate seat. Nat R 22: 601 Je 16 '70

NEW YORK (state)—Politics and government
—*Continued*

Goldberg jumps in. Nat R 22:342 Ap 7 '70

Goldilocks may not be the most exciting fellow in town but he's the only one who can win this year. R. Reeves. il pors N Y Times Mag p7+ Je 14 '70

Hello, Arthur? mayoral endorsement of A. Goldberg. il por Newsweek 76:25 N 2 '70

Hi, there! Your next senator. J. L. Buckley campaign. J. J. Kilpatrick. il Nat R 22: 1154-8 N 3 '70

Hoopla: election campaign of Senator C. Goodell. New Yorker 46:26-8 S 26 '70

How Buckley won New York. il por Newsweek 76:37-8+ N 16 '70

Is New York going conservative? senatorial candidates. P. R. Wieck. New Repub 163: 13-15 O 10 '70

Is the Rock still solid? il pors Time 96:19-20 O 19 '70

Judge gets an argument; Goldberg's victory in New York state primary. il por Time 96:18-19 Jl 6 '70

Justice triumphs; Democratic gubernatorial nomination. il por Newsweek 76:37-8 Jl 6 '70

Lame duck; interview. A. K. Lowenstein. New Yorker 46:51-2 N 21 '70

New York: drama on the political stage. il U S News 69:40-2 O 26 '70

New York election. Nat R 22:749 Jl 14 '70

New York primary. Nation 211:3-4 Jl 6 '70

Notes and comment: latest election. New Yorker 46:35-6 N 28 '70

Ottinger: study of a quiet candidate. T. Buckley. pors N Y Times Mag p40-1+ O 25 '70

Perils of quantification; classes of voters. Nation 211:227-8 S 21 '70

Rock of ages. il por Newsweek 76:43-4 O 19 '70

Senator Javits reflects; senator-elect Buckley's bid to join the Republican caucus. Nation 211:677 D 28 '70

Something new is added; election of J. Buckley. Nat R 22:1198-9 N 17 '70

Swing to the right? E. G. Romm. New Repub 163:9-10 N 28 '70

This is the battle of the titans? Rockefeller vs. Goldberg. R. Reeves. il pors N Y Times Mag p23-5+ N 1 '70

Urban development corporation

Buffalo waterfront development, Buffalo. il Arch Rec 148:96-100 N '70

New York's Mr Urban Renewal; E. Logue. R. Schickel. il pors N Y Times Mag p30-4+ Mr 1 '70

New York's UDC launches housing technology program. Arch Forum 132:78 Je '70

Notes from the underground; excerpts from book. J. Fischer. Harper 240:12+ F '70

Superagency for urban superproblems. il Bsns W p96+ Mr 7 '70

NEW YORK (state). State university

Buffalo campus

Buffalo war. il Newsweek 75:83-4 Mr 30 '70

Dissent or anarchy: common front at Buffalo. H. S. Levine. il Nation 210:520-2 My 4 '70

End of the multiversity. J. R. Coyne, jr. Nat R 22:560-1+ Je 2 '70

Six college complex; flexible but stable, communal though private, useful yet beautiful. il Arch Rec 147:102-5 F '70

Student unrest and the library. M. B. Cassata. bibliog il por Wilson Lib Bul 45:78-85 S '70

School of information and library studies

How a library school got buffaloed; School of information and library studies (SILS) A. Plotnik. il Wilson Lib Bul 44:904-6 My '70

SUNY-Buffalo L.S. students fight to save school. il Library J 95:1418+ Ap 15 '70

College at New Paltz

Large campus residential complex designed to achieve a small-scaled residential character. il Arch Rec 147:106-9 F '70

College at Old Westbury

Your suburban alternative. J. Neugeboren. Esquire 74:113 S '70

College at Purchase

Academic village. J. Dixon. il Arch Forum 133:34-41 N '70

Stony Brook campus

Practice in the 1970's: the response to change; construction management. W. B. Foxhall. il Arch Rec 148:160-1+ O '70

NEW YORK (periodical)

Making it. il Newsweek 76:77 Jl 27 '70

New York copes with New York. Bsns W p71 My 2 '70

NEW YORK archdiocese. *See* Catholic church—Dioceses

NEW YORK automobile show. *See* Automobiles—Exhibitions

NEW YORK better business bureau. *See* Better business bureaus

NEW YORK city ballet

Accent on youth. il Sat R 53:58-9 Ja 31 '70

Dance. N. Goldner. Nation 210:346-7 Mr 23 '70

Dance; Firebird. J. Maskey. il Hi Fi 20:MA10-11 S '70

Dear Julia, a spot check of the New York city ballet's November 18-February 5 season. D. Hering. il Dance Mag 44:26-31+ Ap '70

Extraordinary anniversary; 20th anniversary of M. Hayden and J. D'Amboise. S. Goodman. il pors Dance Mag 44:28-31 N '70

Musical events:
Who cares? W. Sargeant. New Yorker 45: 123 F 14 '70

NYC ballet, NY state theater. J. Anderson. Dance Mag 44:74+ Ag '70

Stars in search of a heaven. A. Rich. il Time 96:51 Jl 20 '70

World of dance; spring season. W. Terry. il Sat R 53:33 Jl 4 '70

NEW YORK city council of churches. *See* Council of churches of the city of New York

NEW YORK city employees. *See* New York (city)—Employees

NEW YORK city in art

Max Ginsburg: underground & above ground. I. Greenberg. il Am Artist 34:28-34+ S '70

NEW YORK city in literature

N.Y, N.Y, 1970: Cock Robbins opens in New York; First N.Y. showing; Lieder eines fahrenden Gesellen; poems. L. E. Sissman. Atlan 227:48-9 Ja '71

NEW YORK city in poetry. *See* New York city in literature

NEW YORK city off-track betting corporation. *See* Off-track betting corporation, New York

NEW YORK city opera company

Fountain of youth; production of the Makropoulos affair. H. Saal. il Newsweek 76:96 N 16 '70

Music to my ears; André Jobin and Pélleas. I. Kolodin. Sat R 53:48 Ap 4 '70

Music to my ears; production of Donizetti's Roberto Devereux. I. Kolodin. Sat R 53: 41+ O 31 '70

Musical events:
A. Ginastera's Don Rodrigo. W. Sargeant. New Yorker 46:159 O 17 '70

Boito's Mefistofele. W. Sargeant. New Yorker 46:105 S 19 '70

Britten's The turn of the screw. W. Sargeant. New Yorker 46:144-5 Mr 14 '70

Debussy's Pelléas et Mélisande. W. Sargeant. New Yorker 46:107 Mr 28; 153-4 Ap 18; 143-4 O 31 '70

Donizetti's Roberto Devereux. W. Sargeant. New Yorker 46:161 O 24 '70

L. Janáček's The Makropoulos affair. W. Sargeant. New Yorker 46:199-202 N 14 '70

Performance of G. Donizetti's Lucia di Lammermoor. W. Sargeant. New Yorker 46:80+ F 28 '70

Performance of Gounod's Faust. W. Sargeant. New Yorker 46:107 Mr 7 '70

Performance of La Cenerentola. W. Sargeant. New Yorker 46:89 Ap 11 '70

New York city opera (cont) il Hi Fi 20: secII 8-10 Ja; 14-15 My; 14-15+ Je '70

Niska makes news in The Makropoulos affair. I. Kolodin. Sat R 53:28+ N 21 '70

Queen high; production of Donizetti's Roberto Devereux. H. Saal. il por Newsweek 76:99 O 26 '70

Report:
Britten's The turn of the screw. J. W. Freeman. Opera N 34:30 Ap 11 '70

Gian Carlo Menotti's Help, help, the Globolinks! S. Jenkins. il Opera N 34: 32-3 F 7 '70

Janáček's Makropoulos affair. F. Merkling. il Opera N 35:37-8 D 19 '70

Pelléas et Mélisande. F. Merkling. il Opera N 34:30 Ap 13 '70

Roberto Devereux. F. Merkling. il Opera N 35:28 N 21 '70

Rossini's Cenerentola. S. Jenkins. il Opera N 34:24 My 16 '70

NEW YORK city summer dance festival. *See* Dance festivals

NEW ZEALAND—*Continued*

Description and travel

In the wake of Captain Cook. J. Guzzwell. il Yachting 128:50-1+ D '70; 129:98-9+ Ja '71

Little sheepish in New Zealand. D. Butwin. il Sat R 53:40-2 Ag 8 '70

Sheep station vacation. Travel 134:18 D '70

Religious institutions and affairs

World around us. Chr Cent 87:1362, 1520-1 N 11, D 16 '70
See also
Church of England in New Zealand

NEWARK, N.J.

Sand blast with a tractor? il Am City 85:66 Je '70

Airports

Engineers develop lighting design from model tests. il Arch Rec 147:147-52 F '70

City planning

How businessmen pitched in to save a city. il pors Nations Bsns 58:44-8 D '70

Economic conditions

Newark signs up a business team. Bsns W p23 Ag 15 '70

Elections

Another big city elects a Negro mayor. por U S News 68:46 Je 29 '70

Gibson's victory. New Yorker 46:28-9 Je 27 '70

Heirs to disaster; Newark's mayoralty race. il Newsweek 75:63+ My 25 '70

Let us enjoy our victory; black victory, white reactions. il pors Newsweek 75:16-19 Je 29 '70

Visible man; K. Gibson's mayoral victory. il por Time 95:12-13 Je 29 '70

Music

Report:
Opera theatre of New Jersey's production of Aida. H. E. Phillips. Opera N 34:33 Mr 7 '70
Tosca. S. Jenkins. Opera N 35:38 D 19 '70

Parks and playgrounds

To walk a different way; Weequahic and Branch Brook parks. J. T. Cunningham. il Parks & Rec 5:26-8+ Ja '70

Politics and government

Black mayors. il Newsweek 76:21-2 Ag 3 '70

Double jeopardy in Newark. il pors Time 95:20 Je 15 '70

Fresh air in Newark; K. Gibson takes over as mayor. il por Life 69:42-3 Jl 4 '70

New chance for Newark. Chr Cent 87:837 Jl 8 '70

New mayor tries for a new Newark. il por Bsns W p36 Je 27 '70
See also
Newark, N.J.—Elections

NEWARK museum

Of time and taste: European clocks in the Bliss collection. J. S. Johnson. il Antiques 97:90-5 Ja '70

NEWBERY medal

Newbery acceptance; address, June 30, 1970. W. H. Armstrong. il Horn Bk 46:352-5 Ag '70

Newbery and Caldecott winners announced Pub W 197:66 F 2 '70

Newbery and Caldecott winners for 1969 books. il por Pub W 197:125-6 F 23 '70

Newbery-Caldecott and Ingalls awards. il Wilson Lib Bul 44:692 Mr '70

Newbery-Caldecott-Wilder awards. il Library J 95:1173 Mr 15 '70

Newbery/Caldecott/Wilder winners. Pub W 198:27 Ag 17 '70

NEWBORN infants. See Infants, Newborn

NEWCOMBE, Jack

Games children play. il Life 68:67-8 Mr 6 '70

NEWCOMBE, John

It almost came up roses for Rosewall. W. Bingham. il pors Sports Illus 33:50-1 Jl 13 '70 *

NEWELL, Barbara W.

Parallels of Negro and women's education. Sch & Soc 98:357-9 O '70

NEWELL, Colin

Just another face in a rearview mirror. M. Maddocks. il Sports Illus 33:42-4+ N 16 '70 *

NEWELL, David M.

Bears and bear dogs. il Field & S 74:64-5+ F '70

NEWFIELD, Jack

Myopia of the inside dopesters. Nation 211:336-9 O 12 '70

NEWFOUNDLAND

Antiquities

See Indians of North America—Antiquities—Canada

NEWLIN, Henry H.

Needed: more urban affairs courses. Am City 85:154-5+ S '70

NEWLOVE, Donald

Beautiful soup; story. Esquire 74:93-5 Ag '70

NEWMAN, Anthony

Introducing Anthony Newman. C. F. Gilmore. Hi Fi sec I 20:94 Ja '70

NEWMAN, Barbara

Care and feeding of Lockheed. New Repub 163:11-13 O 10 '70

NEWMAN, Barnett

Culture collision. B. Rose. Vogue 156:98 O 1 '70 *

Most with the least. il por Time 96:54 Jl 20 '70 *

Obituary
Art N 69:29 S '70. T. B. Hess
Newsweek por 76:47-8 Jl 20 '70. D. Davis

NEWMAN, David, and Benton, Robert

Man talk. See issues of Mademoiselle

NEWMAN, David R.

Air pollution. Cur Hist 59:18-22 Jl '70

NEWMAN, Leslie

Wife of Man talk. Mlle 70:44 F '70

NEWMAN, Paul

Motor trend interview: Paul Newman; ed. by D. Wells. por Motor T 22:86+ Ag '70

NEWMAN, Paul Baker

Child; poem. Chr Cent 87:530 Ap 29 '70

New England town; poem. Chr Cent 87:230 F 25 '70

On another garden; poem. Chr Cent 87:910 Jl 29 '70

Slow heart's courage; poem. Chr Cent 87:590 My 13 '70

NEWMAN, Randy

Randy Newman. R. Goldstein. il Vogue 157:84 Ja 1 '71 *

Randy's blues. H. Saal. por Newsweek 76:86+ S 21 '70 *

Records: rock, etc. E. Willis. New Yorker 46:155+ Ap 18 '70 *

Two solo troubadours. por Time 96:56 Jl 13 '70 *

NEWNHAM, Blaine

Wow, like let's really try to win. il pors Sports Illus 33:50-4 O 12 '70

NEWPORT, R.I.

Center of it all. il Yachting 127:53+ Je '70

Hospitable Newport. F. M. Crawford. il Am Home 73:60-1 Ag '70

Architecture

Today's Newport revolution. B. Plumb. il Am Home 73:47-50 Ag '70

Description

Romantic Newport. M. Evans. il Am Home 73:51-4 Ag '70

Historic houses, etc.

Hunter house: restoration showcase. V. D. Hahn. il Am Home 73:56-9 Ag '70

Newport; An American treasury; by V. D. Hahn and B. Plumb. il Am Home 73:39-59 Ag '70

NEWPORT, R.I, jazz festival. See Music festivals—Rhode Island

NEWPORT-Bermuda race. See Yacht racing

NEWPORT-Ensenada race. See Yacht racing

NEWS

All I don't know is what I read in the newspapers. G. Ace. Sat R 53:5 Jl 25 '70

Coming age of news monopoly; symposium, with editorial comment. Sat R 53:51-4+ O 10 '70; Same abr. Cur 124:27-8 D '70

Worst-covered stories: what's the news? J. Tebbel. il Sat R 53:111-12 Mr 14 '70
See also
Current events
Foreign correspondents
Government and the press
News letters
Newspapers
Newspapers—Local news
Radio broadcasting—News
Reporters and reporting
Television broadcasting—News
War news

Anecdotes, facetiae, satire, etc.

Day in the life: believer of all he reads and hears. Nat R 22:933 S 8 '70

NEWS agencies

Policing the movement; Liberation news service. J. Deedy. Commonweal 92:2 Mr 13 '70
See also
Associated press

NEWSPAPERS—*Continued*

Society news
Sign of the Times. il Newsweek 76:71 Ag 24 '70

Sport news
See Sports journalism

Study and teaching
Five dozen ideas for teaching the newspaper unit. H. F. Decker. Engl J 59:268-70 F '70

Sunday supplements
See Newspapers—Magazine sections

Europe, Western
Journalists win power and profits. Bsns W p49 Ja 17 '70

France
Print, and be seized; case of La Cause du peuple. il por Time 96:76+ N 16 '70

Germany (Federal Republic)
Ferment in Frankfurt; putsch at the Frankfurter allgemeine zeitung. il por Newsweek 75:56 Je 29 '70

Great Britain
See also
London—Newspapers
Sunday telegraph
Times, London

Latin America
Censorship and fear; repression in South America. Time 95:42+ Ap 13 '70

Puerto Rico
See also
San Juan star

United States
Alternatives; underground media conference at Goddard college. R. Todd. Atlan 226:112+ N '70
Another lost image. J. M. A. Ledlie. America 123:122-4 S 5 '70
Can printed news save a free society? H. Brucker. Sat R 53:52-4+ O 10 '70
Censorship by harassment; underground journals in San Diego. K. Widmer. Nation 210: 366-9 Mr 30 '70
Not so free press; underground paper, Street journal & San Diego free press. Time 95: 38 Mr 23 '70
Ombudsman in Louisville; investigating newspaper readers' complaints. il por Time 96: 44+ Jl 6 '70
Slammin' Spiro. il por Newsweek 75:30 Je 1 '70
Stories the newspapers do cover. J. Tebbel. Sat R 53:66-7 Ap 11 '70
Stronger voice for reporters. Time 95:57 My 25 '70
Underground press in America, by R. J. Glessing. Review
  Nation 211:410-12 O 26 '70. K. Widmer
  See also names of newspapers, e.g. Newsday (newspaper); *also* subhead Newspapers under names of cities, e.g. New York (city) —Newspapers

NEWSPAPERS, Immoral. See Immoral literature and pictures
NEWSPAPERS, Publishing of. See Newspaper publishers and publishing
NEWSPAPERS, Student. See College and school journalism
NEWSPAPERS in education
No provision for now; address, October 13, 1970. T. R. Peters. Vital Speeches 37:75-9 N 15 '70
NEWSREEL (organization)
News newsreel. P. Tracy. il Commonweal 91: 532-3 F 13 '70
NEWSTRAND, Clyde F.
How to build a stone stoop. il Pop Sci 197: 92 S '70
NEWSWEEK (periodical)
Woman-power. il Time 95:59 Mr 30 '70
NEWTON, Audrey, and Hillestad, Robert
Textile designs. il Design 72:9-11 Fall '70
NEWTON, Huey P.
Huey Newton in prison: an interview, ed. by J. Johnson. il Ramp Mag 9:4-6 S '70

about

Free Huey. por Newsweek 75:30 Je 15 '70 *
Huey freed. il por Newsweek 76:33 Ag 17 '70 *
Panthers go to Temple. R. Rosen and S. Madden. Commonweal 93:6-7 O 2 '70 *
This side of justice. Nation 210:709 Je 15 '70 *

NEWTON, Jack B.
Spectroscope attachment for viewing solar prominences. il Sky & Tel 39:120-3 F '70
NEWTON, Robert E. See Burns, R. G. jt. auth.
NEWTON, Roger G.
Particles that travel faster than light? bibliog il Science 167:1569-74 Mr 20 '70
NEWTON, Verne. See Hightower, J. jt. auth.
NEWTON, Wayne
What ever happened to baby Wayne? il por Time 95:55 Je 29 '70 *
NEWTON, Mass.

Housing
Liberalism in the suburbs; squabble over proposed low-income housing project. il Newsweek 76:57 Jl 6 '70

Police department
Night scopes add extra insight to police work. W. F. Quinn. Am City 85:16 O '70
NEWTS
Changeable newt. R. G. Arndt. il Cons 24: 11-13+ Ag '69
NEY, E. P. See Murdock, T. L. jt. auth.
NG, K. Y. and others
L-Dopa-induced release of cerebral monoamines. bibliog il Science 170:76-7 O 2 '70
NGUYEN-cao-Ky
Nguyen cao Ky: flying high; interview, ed. by M. Parker. il por Newsweek 75:49 Je 1 '70

about

Behind the row over Ky's visit to U.S. il pors U S News 69:71 S 28 '70 *
Controversial Ky; why he came to U.S. il por U S News 69:23 N 30 '70 *
New Ky; U.S. visit. Time 96:37 D 7 '70 *
TRB from Washington; proposed visit to U.S. New Repub 163:4 S 26 '70 *
Welcome General; Ky's proposed visit to United States. Nation 211:293 O 5 '70 *
NGUYEN-ngoc-Loan
Where are they now? il pors Newsweek 75: 10-11 F 9 '70
NGUYEN-thi-Binh, Mme
Oenologist's dilemma. Time 96:28 S 28 '70 *
Re-enter Mme Binh; new Communist plan. il por Newsweek 76:49 S 28 '70 *
NGUYEN-van-Thieu
Can Vietnam go it alone? interview, ed. by W. S. Merick and J. N. Wallace. il por U S News 68:71-5 Mr 16 '70
Finally their own way out? il por Newsweek 75:38-9 F 9 '70
View from Saigon: Thieu speaks out; interview, ed. by O. Elliott. por Newsweek 75: 26-7 My 11 '70

about

How Thieu rules. D. Luce. New Repub 162: 17-18 F 28 '70 *
If not Thieu, who? G. Kirk. por Nat R 22:667-9 Je 30 '70 *
Saigon: the tail wags the dog. Nation 210: 322-3 Mr 23 '70 *
NIAGARA FALLS
Niagara Falls. J. H. Winchester. il Travel 133:63-7 Je '70
Parting shots; Niagara Falls, the scenic and the seamy. il Life 68:81-4 My 15 '70
NIAGARA FALLS, N.Y., public library
Central library, Niagara Falls, N.Y. il Arch Rec 148:89-91, 94 N '70
NIARCHOS, Evghenia (Livanos)
Lion in winter. pors Newsweek 76:43 Ag 31 '70 *
Spetsopoula incident. il por Time 96:34 Ag 31 '70 *
Tragic shadow over Niarchos' island kingdom. R. B. Stolley. il pors Life 69:36-41 Ag 7 '70 *
NIARCHOS, Stavros Spyros
Lion in winter. pors Newsweek 76:43 Ag 31 '70 *
Spetsopoula incident. il por Time 96:34 Ag 31 '70 *
Tragic shadow over Niarchos' island kingdom. R. B. Stolley. il pors Life 69:36-41 Ag 7 '70*
NICARAGUA CANAL (proposed)
Senate asked to approve convention terminating Bryan-Chamorro treaty; message, September 23, 1970. R. M. Nixon. Dept State Bul 63:460 O 19 '70
U.S. and Nicaragua agree to discuss future of Bryan-Chammorro treaty; Department announcement with exchange of notes. Dept State Bul 62:560-1 Ap 27 '70
U.S. and Nicaragua terminate Bryan-Chamorro treaty with text of convention. Dept State Bul 63:183 Ag 10 '70

NIGERIA—Civil war, 1967-1970—*Continued*
Secession that failed. il Time 95:18-24 Ja 26 '70
What follows war. J. Blashill. Time 95:17-18 F 2 '70
White and green and the rising sun. B. J. Oudes. il Nation 210:149-51 F 9 '70

Children
Last flight out of Biafra; Saturday review's Aid to Biafran children and the evaluation project. N. Cousins. Sat R 53:22+ Ja 24 '70

Damage to property
See Nigeria—Civil war, 1967-1970—Destruction and pillage

Destruction and pillage
Recorded knowledge: a war casualty. B. U. Nwafor. il por Library J 96:42-5 Ja 1 '71

Reconstruction
How pointless it all seems now. A. Lewis. il N Y Times Mag p26-7+ F 8 '70
Problems of reconstruction. C. Legum. Cur 116:47-51 Mr '70

Relief work
Last flight out of Biafra; Saturday review's Aid to Biafran children and the evaluation project. Sat R 53:22+ Ja 24 '70
Troubled peace comes to Biafra. America 122: 64 Ja 24 '70

War correspondents
Nightmare junket; covering the collapse of Biafra. il Newsweek 75:74 F 2 '70

Economic conditions
Good news from Nigeria. N. Cousins. il Sat R 53:22 Mr 14 '70
With war over, a new chance for Nigeria. il U S News 68:26-7 Ja 26 '70

History
Nigeria. C. H. Lyons. bibliog il Focus 21: 1-7 D '70
Selected dates in history of Nigeria. Negro Hist Bul 32:11 D '69

Native races
Biafra; a people betrayed. K. Vonnegut, jr. il McCalls 97:68-9+ Ap '70
Dreadful costs of nationhood. Chr Cent 87: 100 Ja 28 '70
Unconquerable Ibos. il Time 96:26 Jl 27 '70

Politics and government
Nigeria after Biafra. D. J. Murray. il Cur Hist 58:135-41+ Mr '70
One nation, divisible. R. W. Howe. New Repub 162:15-17 F 7 '70
Political evolution and the civil war. J. E. Willmer. il Focus 21:7-12 D '70

Reconstruction
See Nigeria—Civil war, 1967-1970—Reconstruction

Relief work
Biafra still in focus. America 123:106 S 5 '70
Biafra: the scramble for life in a dead country. R. Chelminski. il Life 68:32-5 Ja 30 '70
Frustration and delay. Newsweek 75:44+ F 9 '70
Gowan's optimistic view; excerpts, ed. by J. Wilde. Time 95:27-8 F 9 '70
Relief and rehabilitation in Nigeria; statements, January 21, 1970. D. D. Newsom; C. C. Ferguson, jr. Dept State Bul 62:185-8 F 16 '70
Ripon charges State; the threat of mass famine in Biafra. J. Deedy. Commonweal 92:50 Mr 27 '70
War-torn Nigeria on the mend; church aid by Christian council of Nigeria. A. Millard. Chr Cent 87:1300 O 28 '70
See also
Medical relief work—Nigeria

Religious institutions and affairs
See also
Christian council of Nigeria

Social conditions
Civil war aftermath: return to life. W. H. Fuller. Chr Today 14:40+ Je 5 '70
NIGHT animals. See Animals—Habits and behavior

NIGHT clubs
Five in spots for the midnight chic; New York. P. Benchley. il N Y Times Mag p25-7+ N 8 '70
In New York, it's Raffles. E. Sheppard. il Holiday 47:38+ Ap '70
U.S. journal: west Forty-fourth street; showcase for comedians of limited talent at the Improvisation. C. Trillin. New Yorker 46:148+ O 17 '70

England
In London, it's Annabel's. A. Waugh. il Holiday 47:39+ Ap '70

Europe, Western
Discos that swing; European discothèques. T. Sternberg. Travel & Camera 33:16+ My '70
NIGHT court. See Courts, Municipal
NIGHT flying. See Aviation—Night flying
NIGHT photography. See Photography, Night
NIGHT Thoreau spent in jail; drama. See Lawrence, J. and Lee, R. E.
NIGHTCLUBS. See Night clubs
NIGHTHAWKS
Nighthawks. il Audubon 72:inside cover My '70
NIGUT, William C.
Meet the little lady who buys your pork. il Farm J 94:H8-9+ Ap '70
Will the real American meat shopper please stand up? il Farm J 94:B8-9 Ap '70
NIHILISM (philosophy)
Never nothing. G. P. Elliott. il Harper 241: 83-90+ S '70
Nihilism: a philosophical essay, by S. Rosen. Review
Nat R 22:214-16 F 24 '70. H. Caton
Nihilism, by H. Thielicke. Review
Cath World 211:141 Je '70. R. K. King
NIJINSKY, Waslaw
Evening of a faun. F. Robinson. il pors Opera N 34:26-9 F 21 '70
NIKODIM, abp
Diplomatic Russian. por Newsweek 75:96+ My 25 '70 *
Nikodim criticizes boycott of C.P.C. meeting in Prague. Chr Cent 87:351 Mr 25 '70 *
NIKOLAIS, Alwin
Choreography, music, costumes, sets, etc, etc, by Alwin Nikolais. H. C. Schonberg. il por N Y Times Mag p56-7+ D 6 '70 *
NIKOLAIS, Alwin, dance company. See Alwin Nikolais dance company
NILE, Battle of the, 1798
Battle of the Nile; excerpts from Mediterranean: portrait of a sea. E. Bradford. il pors Horizon 12:84-95 Aut '70
NILE boat race. See Regattas
NILE RIVER
See also
Aswan High Dam
NILES, Daniel Thambyrajah
Obituary
Chr Cent por 87:957 Ag 12 '70. B. Thompson
NILES, Henry Edward
Businessmen against the war (sic) S. Weissman. il Ramp Mag 9:32-3 D '70 *
NILSON, Margot
School libraries in Scandinavia. Am Lib 1: 183-5 F '70
NILSSON, Birgit
Nilsson on Wagner; interview, ed. by S. Jenkins, jr. por Opera N 35:16-18 O 10 '70

about
Music to my ears; performance of Elektra. I. Kolodin. Sat R 53:46 D 12 '70 *
Music to my ears; recital in Grace Rainey Rogers auditorium. I. Kolodin. Sat R 53: 28+ Mr 21 '70 *
Nilsson-Nilsson Tannhäuser. R. Lawrence. Sat R 53:47 My 30 '70 *
Records. Opera N 34:35 F 7 '70
NILSSON, Harry
Everybody's talking about Nilsson; interview, ed. by D. Finkle and R. Hemming. por Sr Schol 95:22 D 8 '70

about
Everybody's talkin' about Nilsson. B. Korall. il por Sat R 53:56 Ja 17 '70
Two solo troubadours. por Time 96:56 Jl 13 '70 *
NILSSON, I. M. and others
Δ¹-Tetrahydrocannabinol: structure of a major metabolite. bibliog il Science 168:1228 Je 5 '70
NIMBUS satellites. See Artificial satellites—Meteorological use

NIMS, John Frederick
Lab research (sex); poem. Sat R 53:29 S 12
'70
(tr) See Goethe, J. W. von. Song of the
traveller at evening; Mignon; Death of a
fly; To Charlotte Von Stein; Anacreon's
grave; Permanence in change
NIN, Anaïs
Portrait of Anaïs Nin. S. Edmiston. por
Mlle 71:134-5+ O '70 *
NINE (the number)
Many quirks of no. 9. W. Parkhurst. il Sci
Digest 68:95-6 O '70
NINETEEN hundred and twenties
Teenager's world: the 1920's; normalcy, non-
sense, and all that jazz. il Sr Schol 97:3-6 O
19 '70
NINETEEN hundred and thirties
Teenager's world: the 1930's; from depression
to recovery. il Sr Schol 97:7-10 O 19 '70
NINETEEN hundred and forties
Teenager's world: the 1940's; a world at war,
and an uneasy peace. il Sr Schol 97:11-13
O 19 '70
NINETEEN hundred and fifties
Generation not for barricades. J. Didion. Life
68:26 Je 5 '70
Memories of a (latter-day) Catholic girl-
hood. K. Mulherin. il Commonweal 91:610-
19 Mr 6 '70
1950 was more than twenty years ago. J.
Didion. Life 68:20B Ja 30 '70
Task force report. Commonweal 92:77-8 Ap
3 '70
Teenager's world: the 1950's; from Korea to
Kennedy. il Sr Schol 97:14-16 O 19 '70
NINETEEN hundred and sixties
Editor's choice; last corner. G. R. Shields;
reply. W H. Carlson. Am Lib 1:325 Ap '70
Harsh facts of the 1960s. M. S. Adiseshiah.
il UNESCO Courier 23:4-10 O '70
Memories of a (latter-day) Catholic girl-
hood. K. Mulherin. il Commonweal 91:610-
19 Mr 6 '70
Radical turn in theology and ethics: why it
occurred in the 1960's. S. E. Ahlstrom. bib-
liog f Ann Am Acad 387:1-13 Ja '70
'60s: decade of tumult and change; reply. Nat
R 22:16-17 Ja 13 '70
Smiling through the apocalypse. A. Gingrich.
Esquire 73:12 Mr '70
Staged sixties; excerpts. Deadman. il Ramp
Mag 8:43-51 F '70
Story of jobs and workers in the 1960's. B. L.
Masse. America 122:108 Ja 31 '70
Summing up the '60's. il Sr Schol 95:5-8 S 22
'69
Task force report. Commonweal 92:77-8 Ap
3 '70
Teenager's world: the 1960's; new frontiers and
new divisions. il Sr Schol 97:17-19 O 19 '70
Two cheers for the sixties. Nat R 22:14+
Ja 13 '70
NINETEEN hundred and sixty-nine
Cloudy crystal balls; rundown on predictions
for 1969. Chr Cent 87:95 Ja 21 '70
History as junk: what we left behind at noted
historic scenes. il Am Heritage 21:120 F '70

Anecdotes, facetiae, satire, etc.
Notes & asides. W. F. Buckley, jr. Nat R
22:20 Ja 13 '70
Recalling 1969. J. D. Douglas. Chr Today
14:44 Ja 16 '70
NINETEEN hundred and seventies
Asia in the decade of the seventies; address,
February 23, 1970. U. A. Johnson. Dept
State Bul 62:381-7 Mr 23 '70; Same. Vital
Speeches 36:386-9 Ap 15 '70
Facing the '70's. il Sr Schol 95:4-8 D 8 '69
Happy new decade! J. M. Carter. Library J
95:135 Ja 15 '70
Life in the '70's. il Sr Schol 95:9-14 D 8 '69
A look into the 1970s. il Mech Illus 66:39-45
Ja '70
New decade: changes to come in the 70's. il
Changing T 24:6-10 Ja '70
On the threshold of a new decade: thoughts
for 1970. E. Rabinowitch. il por Bul Atom
Sci 26:2-3+ F '70
The seventies: a time for giant steps; ex-
cerpts from Curricula for the seventies. J.
L. Frost and G. T. Rowland. Ed Digest 35:
1-4 F '70
70's: symposium. il Look 34:17-36+ Ja 13
'70

NINETEEN hundred and seventy
As the Nation enters 1970. B. L. Masse.
America 122:33 Ja 17 '70
Images '70; photographs. Time 97:8-11 Ja 4
'71
Issue of the year: the environment. il Time
97:21-2 Ja 4 '71
1971's unfinished business; symposium. Amer-
ica 124:3-11 Ja 9 '71
Welcome 1970! Am City 85:10 Ja '70

NINETEEN hundred and seventy-one
1971 just may be better. il Time 97:9 Ja 11
'71
Outlook now. il U S News 70:7 Ja 4 '71

Anecdotes, facetiae, satire, etc.
Here it comes... Nat R 23:24 Ja 12 '71
NINETEEN hundred and eighty
America in 1980: a challenge now. il U S
News 69:40 Jl 27 '70
'70s: a strong economy, but; official preview
of the U.S. in 1980. il U S News 68:64 Ap
27 '70
U.S. economy in 1980: a preview of BLS
projections il Mo Labor R 93:3-34 Ap '70
NINETEEN hundred and ninety-one
1991; concerning N. M. Amosoff's Notes from
the future. G. St George. il Look 34:54-8+
Jl 14 '70
NINETEEN hundred and ninety-five
Rise of the elders. H. Wheeler. il Sat R 53:
14-15+ D 5 '70
92nd infantry division. See United States—
Army—Infantry
NIOBIUM
Niobium: space age metal. J. D. Navratil.
bibliog il por Chem 43:13-15 S '70
NIPPON Kogaku company. See Photographic
apparatus industry and trade
NIPPON steel corporation. See Steel industry
and trade—Japan
NISBET, Robert A.
Epistle to the Americans. Commentary 50:40-
5 D '70
Grand illusion. Commentary 50:40-4 Ag '70
NISKA, Maralin
Only way; interview, ed. by R. D. Daniels.
por Opera N 34:13 Ap 11 '70
NISSAN motor company. See Automobile in-
dustry and trade—Japan
NISSENSON, Hugh
Charity; story. Esquire 73:140-1 Ap '70
Grace, Grace, Grace, Grace; story. Esquire
73:192-6 Je '70
Lamentations; story. New Yorker 46:32-4 S
19 '70
NITECKI, Joseph Z.
Quality librarianship the day after tomorrow.
bibliog Am Lib 1:130-1 F '70
NITELLA. See Stoneworts
NITRILOTRIACETIC acid
NTA in for phosphates. Sci N 97:408 Ap 25
'70
NTA; possible substitute for phosphates in
detergents. S. S. Epstein. bibliog il En-
viron 12:2-11 S '70
Phosphate stand-in goes down the drain. Bsns
W p 17 D 26 '70
Solution becomes a problem; dangerous sub-
stitute for phosphates in detergents. il Sci
N 98:475 D 26 '70
NITROGEN
Rare gases, hydrogen, and nitrogen: concen-
trations and isotopic composition in lunar
material. H. Hintenberger and others. il
Science 167:543-5 Ja 30 '70
Total carbon and nitrogen abundances in
lunar samples. C. B. Moore and others.
bibliog il Science 167:495-7 Ja 30 '70

Fixation
Biological nitrogen fixation in Lake Erie. D.
L. Howard and others. bibliog il Science
169:61-2 Jl 3 '70
More on nitrogen fixing; diet of New Guinea
natives. Sci N 98:161 Ag 22 '70
Nitrogen cycle. C. C. Delwiche. il Sci Am
223:136-46 bibliog(p264) S '70
Nitrogen fixation at room temperature.
Chem 43:21 D '70
NITROGEN content of soils. See Soils—Nitro-
gen content
NITROGEN fixation. See Nitrogen—Fixation
NITROGENASE. See Enzymes
NITROUS oxide

Anecdotes, facetiae, satire, etc.
Not with a bang but a hiccup. P. Bracken.
Sat R 53:3 D 26 '70
NIX, Harry
Colorful cannas. Horticulture 48:34-5 Je '70
NIXON, Agnes
TV: Agnes Nixon, soapland's queen. R.
Busch. il por McCalls 97:14+ My '70 *
NIXON, Patricia (Ryan)
Bidding to help the Peruvians. il por Time
96:10 Jl 13 '70 *
Nixon ladies and their summer dresses. il
Life 68:42-3 My 8 '70 *
Nixon touch in the White House. il por U S
News 69:24-6 D 28 '70 *
Pat Nixon and the first-lady watchers. S.
McBee. il por McCalls 97:76-7+ S '70 *

NIXON, Patricia (Ryan)—*Continued*

Pat Nixon is the ultimate good sport. J. Viorst. il pors N Y Times Mag p25-7+ S 13 '70 *

Pat Nixon's answer to the generation gap. il pors U S News 68:40 Mr 16 '70 *

Pat's bandwagon. il por Time 95:13-14 Mr 16 '70 *

Pattie, Pattie, Pattie! visit to Peru. il por Newsweek 76:45-6 Jl 13 '70 *

Travels with Pat. il por Newsweek 75:35 Mr 16 '70 *

NIXON, Richard Milhous

Action for progress; message to OAS. Américas 22:1 Ap '70

Actions to deal with the menace of air piracy; statement, September 11, 1970. Dept State Bul 63:341-2 S 28 '70

African ambassadors honored by President Nixon; exchange of toasts, March 23, 1970. Dept State Bul 62:522-3 Ap 20 '70

Amendment to U.S.-U.K. atomic energy agreement transmitted to the Congress, message, January 26, 1970. Dept State Bul 62:361 Mr 16 '70

Annual report on foreign assistance program transmitted to Congress; letter, March 4, 1970. Dept State Bul 62:499-500 Ap 13 '70

Budget message of the President; excerpts. Dept State Bul 62:234-6 Mr 2 '70

Call for co-operation; excerpts from message to Congress, September 11, 1970. il por U S News 69:71-3 S 21 '70

Chemical and biological defense policies and programs; statement, November 25. 1969. Dept State Bul 61:541-3 D 15 '69

Colonel Borman undertakes mission relating to prisoners of war; statement, August 7, 1970. Dept State Bul 63:276 S 7 '70

Communications satellite program; message to the Congress, February 26, 1970. Dept State Bul 62:534 Ap 20 '70

Congress, Vietnam, Mideast: the President's appraisal; excerpts from radio and TV interview, July 1, 1970. il por U S News 69:20-2 Jl 13 '70

Conversation with the President; transcript of radio and TV interview, July 1, 1970. Dept State Bul 63:101-13 Jl 27 '70; Same abr. with title Congress, Vietnam, Mideast: the President's appraisal; excerpts from radio and TV interview, July 1, 1970. il por U S News 69:20-2 Jl 13 '70

Destiny of the public lands; telegram. por Am For 76:19 Ja '70

Economic report of the President. il Dept State Bul 62:240-1 Mr 2 '70

Environment: a national mission for the seventies. por Fortune 81:92 F '70

Exchange of toasts at Belgrade, September 30; with joint communique, October 1, 1970. Dept State Bul 63:519-21 N 2 '70

Expressing the American spirit; address, December 10, 1969. Opera N 34:6-7 Ja 24 '70

Faith of nations; summary of address at the United Nations. il Time 96:27-8 N 2 '70

Foreign assistance act of 1969 signed into law; statement, December 31, 1969. Dept State Bul 62:86 Ja 26 '70

Foreign assistance for the 'seventies, message to Congress, September 15, 1970. Dept State Bul 63:369-78 O 5 '70

Geneva protocol on gases and bacteriological warfare resubmitted to the Senate; message, August 19, 1970. Dept State Bul 63:273 S 7 '70

Helping the needy go to college; the President's plan; text of message to Congress. March 19, 1970. il por U S News 68:51-4 Mr 30 '70; Same. Am Ed 6:28-31 My '70

How Nixon interprets the election; summary of statements. Time 96:16-17 N 16 '70

In the President's words; what U.S. is doing in Laos; statement, March 6, 1970. por U S News 68:86-8 Mr 16 '70; Same with title Scope of the U.S. involvement in Laos. Dept State Bul 62:405-9 Mr 30 '70

Inter-American economic and social council holds special meeting at Caracas; message, February 5, 1970. Dept State Bul 62:254-5 Mr 2 '70

Message on education reform. il Am Ed 6:30-4 Ap '70

Message to the Senate, February 19, 1970. Dept State Bul 62:350 Mr 16 '70

Mr Nixon's sense of history; quotations, comp. by J Greenfield. il por Harper 241:66-7 N '70

My daughter Tricia; interview, ed. by P. F Healy. il pors Ladies Home J 87:57-63+ Je '70

Nation's economic outlook; address, December 7, 1970. Vital Speeches 37:130-3 D 15 '70

NATO environmental committee meets at Brussels; message. Dept State Bul 63:647 N 23 '70

New institute for Inter-American social development; statement, August 19, 1970. Dept State Bul 63:301 S 14 '70

Nixon on desegregation: text of statement, March 24, 1970. por U S News 68:80-7 Ap 6 '70; Same abr. Cur 118:27 My '70

Nixon on peace, inflation, taxes, student unrest; excerpts from news conference, July 30, 1970. il por U S News 69:32-4 Ag 10 '70

Nixon plan for ending the draft; text of message, April 23, 1970 il U S News 68:25-7 My 4 '70

Nixon: this is the critical moment; address, December 4, 1970. por U S News 69:70-2 D 14 '70

Nixon's new warning to Hanoi: bombing could be resumed; excerpts from news conference, December 10, 1970. U S News 69:79 D 21 '70

Nixon's plea: stop making heroes out of criminals; excerpts from remarks, August 3, 1970. il por U S News 69:70 Ag 17 '70

Offshore oil pollution: message to Congress. May 20, 1970. Dept State Bul 62:754-6 Je 15 '70

Peaceful competition; address, October 23, 1970. Vital Speeches 37:66-9 N 15 '70; Same with title World interest: a generation of peace. Dept State Bul 63:601-6 N 16 '70

President acts on ICAO resolution to deter aircraft hijacking; letter, October 13, 1970. Dept State Bul 63:541 N 2 '70

President appoints youth members to U.N. anniversary commission; statement and White House announcement. Dept State Bul 63:393-4 O 5 '70

President asks Senate approval of protocol II to Treaty for the prohibition of nuclear weapons in Latin America; message, August 13, 1970. Dept State Bul 63:305 S 14 '70

President explains his decision on Indo-China; address. April 30, 1970. il por U S News 68:22-4 My 11 '70; Same with title Cambodia. Vital Speeches 36:450-2 My 15 '70; Same abr. with title Cambodia strike; defensive action for peace. Dept State Bul 62:617-21 My 18 '70

President gratified at acceptance of U.S. Middle East peace initiative; statement, July 31, 1970. Dept State Bul 63:218 Ag 24 '70

President Kekkonen of Finland visits the United States; exchange of remarks and toasts, July 23, 1970. Dept State Bul 63:194-7 Ag 17 '70

President Mobutu of the Congo visits the United States; exchange of greetings and toasts, August 4, 1970. Dept State Bul 63:279-80 S 7 '70

President Nixon and British Prime Minister Wilson hold talks at Washington; exchange of greetings and toasts. January 27, 1970. Dept State Bul 62:207-11 F 23 '70

President Nixon and Chancellor Brandt hold talks at Washington; exchange of greetings and toasts, April 10, 1970. Dept State Bul 62:573-7 My 4 '70

President Nixon and President Diaz Ordaz of Mexico, meet at Puerto Vallarta; remarks, and toasts. August 20-21, 1970. Dept State Bul 63:289-94 S 14 '70

President Nixon and Prime Minister Sato of Japan hold talks at Washington. Dept State Bul 61:551-8 D 15 '69

President Nixon approves policy statement on international air transportation; statement, June 22, 1970, text of policy statement. Dept State Bul 63:86 Jl 20 '70

President Nixon asks Senate approval of conventions on pollution of the sea by oil; message, May 20, 1970. Dept State Bul 62:756-7 Je 15 '70

President Nixon calls for passage of trade bill; text of letter, May 11, 1970. Dept State Bul 62:697-9 Je 1 '70

President Nixon delineates authority of American ambassadors; letter, December 9, 1969. Dept State Bul 62:30 Ja 12 '70

President Nixon discusses reaction to peace initiative; remarks, October 8, 1970. Dept State Bul 63:463-70 O 26 '70

President Nixon greets Mexico-U.S. interparliamentary conference; exchange of remarks. May 5, 1970. Dept State Bul 62:656-7 My 25 '70

President Nixon holds talks with prime minister of Denmark. Dept State Bul 62:632 My 18 '70

President Nixon honors President Diaz Ordaz at Mexico at a state dinner in California; exchange of greetings and remarks. September 3, 1970. Dept State Bul 63:347, 350-2 S 28 '70

NIXON, Richard Milhous—*Continued*
President Nixon hosts dinner for U.N.'s twenty-fifth anniversary; toast at White House dinner, October 24, 1970. Dept State Bul 63:606 N 16 '70
President Nixon interviewed for CBS television; excerpt from interview, August 29, 1970. Dept State Bul 63:327-9 S 21 '70
President Nixon, King Hassan open communications satellite service; exchange of remarks, January 7, 1970. Dept State Bul 62:129 F 2 '70
President Nixon makes nine day visit to Europe; remarks, September 27-October 5, 1970. Dept State Bul 63:506-41 N 2 '70
President Nixon meets with President Caldera of Venezuela; exchange of greetings, toasts, June 2-5, 1970. Dept State Bul 62: 793, 794-5 Je 29 '70
President Nixon meets with President Ceausescu of Romania; exchange of greetings and toasts, October 26, 1970. Dept State Bul 63: 648-50 N 23 '70
President Nixon ratifies nuclear nonproliferation treaty; remarks, November 24, 1969. Dept State Bul 61:544 D 15 '69
President Nixon receives declaration by ICAO against aircraft hijacking; letter, August 10, 1970. Dept State Bul 63:302 S 14 '70
President Nixon receives report of oil import control task force; statement, February 20, 1970. Dept State Bul 62:427-8 Mr 30 '70
President Nixon's news conference:
December 8, 1969. Dept State Bul 61:617-20 D 29 '69
January 30, 1970. Dept State Bul 62:173-7 F 16 '70; Same. il por U S News 68:21 F 9 '70
March 21, 1970. Dept State Bul 62:437-40 Ap 6 '70
May 8, 1970. Dept State Bul 62:641-5 My 25 '70
July 20, 1970. Dept State Bul 63:161-4 Ag 10 '70
July 30, 1970. Dept State Bul 63:185-7 Ag 17 '70
President Nixon's white paper on Cambodia; text, June 30, 1970. il U S News 69:81-6 Jl 13 '70; Same with title Report on the conclusion of the Cambodian operation. Dept State Bul 63:65-75 Jl 20 '70
President pledges rededication of U.S. support for the U.N; text of reply, January 9, 1970. Dept State Bul 62:358 Mr 16 '70
President Pompidou of France visits the United States; exchange of toasts, remarks, February 24-March 2, 1970. Dept State Bul 62:413-22 Mr 30 '70
President reaffirms U.S. concern for prisoners in North Viet-Nam; remarks, December 12, 1969. Dept State Bul 62:3 Ja 5 '70
President recommends contribution to Asian special fund; message, February 25, 1970. Dept State Bul 62:397-8 Mr 23 '70
President replies to Soviet letter on Potsdam conference anniversary; exchange of letters. Dept State Bul 63:388 O 5 '70
President reports on the war in Cambodia; address, June 3, 1970. il por U S News 68: 77-9 Je 15 '70; Same with title Cambodian sanctuary operation: an interim report. Dept State Bul 62:761-4 Je 22 '70
President Soeharto of Indonesia visits the United States; exchange of greetings and toasts, May 26, 1970. Dept State Bul 62:743-6 Je 15 '70
President's message on Indo-China; address, April 20, 1970. por U S News 68:61-2 My 4 '70; Same with title Report on progress in Viet-Nam. Dept State Bul 62:601-4 My 11 '70
Progress report on our plan for peace in Viet-Nam; address, December 15, 1969. Dept State Bul 62:1-3 Ja 5 '70
Protection of all U.S. citizens reaffirmed by President Nixon; remarks, September 17, 1970. Dept State Bul 63:410-12 O 12 '70
Quality of life in the Americas; statement. Dept State Bul 61:493-4 D 8 '69
Reorganizing White House; Nixon describes the plan; excerpts from message to Congress il U S News 68:80-1 Je 22 '70
Report on trade agreements program transmitted to the Congress; message, December 16, 1969. Dept State Bul 62:62 Ja 19 '70
Rescuing the environment: the President's program; excerpt from a message to Congress, February 10, 1970. U S News 68: 93-7 F 23 '70; Cur Hist 58:362-4 Je '70
Responsible university leadership; address, September 16, 1970. Vital Speeches 36:738-40 '70; Excerpts. il por U S News 69:27-8 S 28 '70

Safe boating week; proclamation. il Motor B 125:149 Je '70
Senate asked to approve convention terminating Bryan-Chamorro treaty; message, September 23, 1970. Dept State Bul 63:460 O 19 '70
Senate urged to act on convention on U.N. privileges and immunities; message, December 19, 1969. Dept State Bul 62:61 Ja 19 '70
State of the Union; address, January 22, 1970. il pors U S News 68:63-7 F 2 '70; Same. Vital Speeches 36:226-9 F 1 '70; Excerpts. Dept State Bul 62:145-7 F 9 '70; Parks & Rec 5: 22+ Mr '70
State of the Union between man and nature. por Field & S 75:56-7+ Je '70
Strategic arms limitation talks open at Helsinki; text of message. November 17, 1969. Dept State Bul 61:543-4 D 15 '69
Strategy for peace in Nixon's own words; address, October 7, 1970. por U S News 69: 62-3 O 19 '70; Same with title New peace initiative for all Indochina. Dept State Bul 63:465-7 O 26 '70; Same with title President Nixon's proposal for Indochina peace. Cur Hist 59:362+ D '70
Study of ocean dumping of wastes transmitted to the Congress, message, October 7, 1970. Dept State Bul 63:669-70 N 30 '70
This appointment signifies something fundamental; excerpts from news briefing, December 14, 1970. U S News 69:10 D 28 '70
Toward price stability; address, June 17, 1970. il por U S News 68:61-4 Je 29 '70; Same with title Inflation and economic policy. Vital Speeches 36:546-9 Jl 1 '70
Trade act of 1969; message to the Congress, November 18, 1969. Dept State Bul 61:559-63 D 15 '69
Treaty on the nonproliferation of nuclear weapons enters into force; remarks, March 5, 1970. Dept State Bul 62:411-12 Mr 30 '70
Twenty-fifth anniversary of the United Nations marked at White House dinner; exchange of toasts, July 10, 1970. Dept State Bul 63:166-8 Ag 10 '70
U.S. assists Peru in meeting emergency relief needs; statement, June 8, 1970. Dept State Bul 62:803 Je 29 '70
U.S. foreign assitance in the 1970's: a new approach; statement, March 8, 1970. Dept State Bul 62:447 Ap 6 '70
U.S. foreign policy for the 1970's; a new strategy for peace; report to the Congress, February 18, 1970. Dept State Bul 62:273-332 Mr 9 '70
U.S. joins France in mourning death of General de Gaulle; statement, text of letter to President Pompidou, and remarks at Orly airport. Dept State Bul 63:690 D 7 '70
U.S.-Mexico archeological treaty transmitted to the Senate; message. Dept State Bul 63:587 N 9 '70
U.S. supports completion of Pan American highway; statement; December 10, 1969. Dept State Bul 62:40 Ja 12 '70
United States foreign policy for the 1970s; text of introduction of message to Congress. February 18, 1970. il por U S News 68:65-8 Mr 2 '70
United States policy for the seabed; statement, May 23, 1970. Dept State Bul 62: 737-8 Je 15 '70
Vice President Agnew meets with Asian leaders; remarks, August 22, 1970. Dept State Bul 63:379 O 5 '70
We expect the economy to be moving upward; excerpts from news conference. July 20, 1970. il por U S News 69:36-7 Ag 3 '70
What's right about America; excerpts from address, June 25, 1970. il por U S News 69: 45 Jl 6 '70
Why Nixon wants another $1 billion for aid to allies; text of message to Congress. November 18, 1970. il U S News 69:60-2 N 30 '70; Same with title Strong friends and the balance of peace. Dept State Bul 63: 685-9 D 7 '70

about

Advantage: Mr President; Conversation with the President on TV. il por Time 97:36 Ja 18 '71 *
After Cambodia: the fight to save face. J. J. Stone. Commonweal 92:381-2 Ag 7 '70 *
Anatomy of San Jose. Nation 211:482 N 16 '70 *
And so we leave Cambodia... il Newsweek 76:16-22 Jl 13 '70 *
Anti-Nixon outburst caps a violent week. il U S News 69:52 N 9 '70 *
Anybody see Patton? the President's fascination with the movie, Patton. H. Sidey. Life 68:2B Je 19 '70 *

NIXON, Richard Milhous—about—*Continued*

Nixon crisis: advice but no consent. il pors Newsweek 75:35-40 Ap 20 '70 *

Nixon enigma. K. Crawford. Newsweek 75:28 F 16 '70 *

Nixon goes South for integration. il por Time 96:7-8 Ag 24 '70 *

Nixon in a crisis of leadership. H. Sidey. il por Life 68:28-9 My 15 '70 *

Nixon is shifting to a harder-hitting game; with editorial comment. il Bsns W p 14-15, 92 D 12 '70 *

Nixon on the schools. Chr Today 14:26 Ap 24 '70 *

Nixon so far. M. J. Goldbloom. Commentary 49:29-33 Mr '70 *

Nixon starts moves for 1971, and 1972. il por U S News 69:9-10 D 28 '70 *

Nixon supremacy. J. Kraft. Harper 240:45-51 Mr '70 *

Nixon the crime fighter; reckless statement regarding C. Manson. Nation 211:98-9 Ag 17 '70 *

Nixon: the pursuit of peace and politics; concerning Kansas state's first Landon lecture of the year. il pors Time 96:6-8 S 28 '70 *

Nixon to the left of himself. S. Alsop. Newsweek 77:92 Ja 11 '71 *

Nixon turns a campaign into a crusade. il Bsns W p29 O 24 '70

Nixon watch; behavior on May 10. J. Osborne. New Repub 162:9-11 My 23 '70 *

Nixon watch: paying for integration. J. Osborne. New Repub 162:10-12 Je 6 '70 *

Nixon watch; rage at the White House. J. Osborne. New Repub 162:11-12 My 2 '70 *

Nixon watcher; views of J. Osborne. il por Newsweek 75:60 Je 22 '70 *

Nixon; with a little help for his friends. B. Fitch. il pors Ramp Mag 8:53-62+ Mr '70 *

Nixon's big gamble: no more rule by minorities. R. Wilson. por Look 34:21-5 My 5 '70 *

Nixon's blueprint for a new America. il U S News 68:66-7 F 23 '70 *

Nixon's dilemma; the war and the 1972 elections. Nation 211:578-9 D 7 '70 *

Nixon's first year. T. Wicker. New Repub 162:17-20 Ja 24 '70

Nixon's friend Bebe. C. Leinster. il pors Life 69:18B-27 Jl 31 '70 *

Nixon's last-minute push for a Republican victory. il pors U S News 69:20-1 N 2 '70 *

Nixon's new federalism. D. Mars. Nation 210:435-7 Ap 15 '70 *

Nixon's new plan to run the government; balance sheet on Nixon after two years. pors U S News 68:17-18 Je '70 *

Nixon's outer South strategy. Nat R 22:986+ S 22 '70 *

Nixon's peace plan. New Repub 163:5-6 O 17 '70 *

Nixon's plea to end the killing. il por Time 96: 15-16 O 19 '70 *

Nixon's strategy for '72. il U S News 69:21-4 N 23 '70 *

Nixon's turnabout. M. J. Ulmer. New Repub 163:10-11 Ag 15 '70 *

Nixon's vision of peace. H. Sidey. il por Life 69:4 S 25 '70 *

Nixon's youth corps. D. R. Maxey. il por Look 34:48-51 F 10 '70

Not whether, how. S. Alsop. Newsweek 76:88 Jl 6 '70 *

Notes and comment (cont) New Yorker 46:31-2 My 9; 31-2 My 16; 35-7 O 10 '70; Same as My 16 issue. Forbes 105:17-18 Je 15 '70 *

Now do it! campaigning. J. Osborne. New Repub 163:11-12 O 31 '70 *

Now is the time for all good men to come to the aid of their President. Nat R 22:500-1 My 19 '70 *

On looking back at Cambodia; reprint. P. Worsthorne. Nat R 22:825 Ag 11 '70 *

On the beach with an old friend. H. Sidey. pors Life 68:2 Je 26 '70 *

On the President's yellow pad. S. Alsop. Newsweek 75:106 Je 1 '70 *

One man alone, by R. de Toledano. Review Nat R 22:37+ Ja 13 '70. M. S. Evans

One observer's changed feeling. J. Osborne. New Repub 162:11-13 Ja 17 '70

Our Sharpeville. J. Deedy. Commonweal 92: 234 My 22 '70 *

Perilous path in southeast Asia. il Bsns W p94+ Ap 25 '70 *

Phone calls that didn't get through. H. Sidey. Life 68:4 My 29 '70 *

Picking up the wishbone; anti-inflation measures. il Time 95:10-11 Je 29 '70 *

Politics of Mr Nixon's economics. Life 68:28 F 13 '70

Presidency: looking to '72. T. M. Gannon. America 124:4-5 Ja 9 '71 *

President as educator. C. E. Silberman. Fortune 81:150 My '70 *

President Nixon, Cambodia and new chances for peace. J. G. Hubbell. il Read Digest 97:54-63 Jl '70 *

President Nixon's own crisis syndrome. il pors Newsweek 75:24-5 Je 8 '70 *

President who runs for Congress. il pors Newsweek 76:24-5 N 2 '70 *

President working. K. Crawford. Newsweek 76:50 O 19 '70 *

Presidential bowstring. G. W. Johnson. New Repub 162:12 F 7 '70 *

President's too-secret weapon. S. Alsop. Newsweek 76:124 N 2 '70 *

President's war powers. il Time 95:36-7 Je 1 '70 *

Prestidigitator; Vietnamization plan. Nation 210:162-3 F 16 '70 *

Questions which tear us apart. D. Halberstam. il Harper 240:70-2+ F '70 *

Reclusive President. Nation 210:388 Ap 6 '70 *

Reports: Washington. R. D. Novak. Atlan 225:4+ Ap '70 *

Rescue of Bob Finch. J. Newcombe. il pors Life 68:32-3 Je 19 '70 *

Resurrection of Richard Nixon, by J. Witcover. Review
  Life 69:8 Jl 24 '70. K. Hess *
  New Repub 163:9-10 S 5 '70. J. Osborne *

Reunion with Whittier '34. il por Life 69: 24-5 Jl 24 '70 *

Rhetoric of opposites. L. Hinds and C. Smith. Nation 210:172-4 F 16 '70

Richard Nixon, Apollo watcher. il Newsweek 75:27-8 Ap 27 '70 *

Richard Nixon, inflation fighter. il por Newsweek 76:45-6 D 14 '70 *

Richard Nixon's ten days; decision on Cambodia. il por Newsweek 75:36+ My 18 '70 *

Richard Nixon's very personal White House. J. Cameron. il por Fortune 82:56-9+ Jl '70 *

Save the visual aids for the profs; use of edited film during televised address, June 3, 1970. Sedulus. New Repub 163: 29-30 Jl 4 '70 *

Scenario for '72. C. McWilliams. Nation 212: 66-8 Ja 18 '71 *

Self-inflicted advice. H. C. Wallich. Newsweek 77:58 Ja 4 '71 *

Selling of the President 1968, by J. McGinniss. Review
  Esquire il 73:8+ F '70. M. Muggeridge *

Selling the President, 1970; election eve TV address. Newsweek 76:77-8 N 16 '70 *

Seventh crisis of Richard Nixon: Senate's rejection of G. H. Carswell. il pors Time 95:8-15 Ap 20 '70 *

'70 campaign takes a new turn. il por U S News 69:15-16 O 26 '70 *

Shaken faith in Nixon; Fortune 500-Yankelovich survey. R. S. Diamond. il Fortune 81:60-2 Je '70 *

Shattered trust. Chr Cent 87:587 My 13 '70 *

Southern comfort; press conference on school desegregation. J. Osborne. New Repub 163:13-14 Ag 1 '70 *

Staying alive until 1973. New Repub 162:1+ My 16 '70 *

Story of a peace initiative. H. Sidey. por Life 69:2 O 16 '70 *

Strains in the Nixon team: is the President isolated? il U S News 68:28-30 My 25 '70 *

Sweet 'n' sour encounter. Chr Cent 87:1547 D 23 '70 *

These are the words for Richard Nixon after his first year. M. Frankel. il pors N Y Times Mag p 12-13+ Ja 18 '70

Three strategies of a master politician. R. B. Semple, jr. il pors N Y Times Mag p32-3+ N 1 '70 *

To the polls; permissiveness v. purse. il pors Time 96:6-7 N 2 '70 *

TRB from Washington. See occassional issues of New Repub

Undelivered speech; excerpts. J. Gardner. por Time 95:16-17 My 25 '70 *

Understanding understandings; Vietnam policy statement. Time 96:12-13 D 21 '70 *

Very good day; New Orleans visit. J. Osborne. New Repub 163:7-9 Ag 22 '70 *

Very late, late show in Washington. H. Sidey. il por Life 68:4 Ja 23 '70

Violent end to a vitriolic campaign. il por Time 96:14-15 N 9 '70 *

Weatherman Wicker; President Nixon's Kansas state university speech. Nat R 22:1039 O 6 '70 *

Weekend everyone went to school. N. Cousins. Sat R 53:33 My 23 '70 *

What was it all about? M. McGrory. America 122:547 My 23 '70 *

What's missing in Nixon's welfare program. E. Van Den Haag. Nat R 22:85-7+ Ja 27 '70 *

White House hits the road. il por Newsweek 76:13 Ag 3 '70 *

NIXON, Richard Milhous—about—*Continued*
Who speaks for the United States? il por
Newsweek 76:31-2 Jl 27 '70 *
Why Cambodia? J. Osborne. New Repub
163:7-9 Jl 11 '70 *
**Year of Murray Chotiner. M. Novak. Com-
monweal 93:217-21 N 27 '70 ***

Birthplace

In search of a missing past. H. Sidey. Life
69:2B S 4 '70

Correspondence

Dear Mr President: the people speak out on
the race issue; excerpts from letters. il
U S News 68:30-1 Mr 9 '70 *

Health

Checkup. Newsweek 77:18+ Ja 11 '71
Nixon's health, his doctor's report. il pors
U S News 70:25 Ja 11 '71

Homes

Nixon's movable White House. il pors News-
week 76:16-19 Ag 24 '70
Richard Nixon slept here; White House in
San Clemente. il Time 96:13-14 S 7 '70

Messages

Benign neglect for education too. M. R.
Berube. Commonweal 92:52-3 Mr 27 '70 *
Cleanup campaign; Nixon sets targets; summary of message to Congress July 9, 1970.
il U S News 69:54 Jl 20 '70
Delayed impact; message on education reform. Newsweek 75:113-14 Mr 16 '70 *
From the general to the particular; analysis
of foreign policy message. Nat R 22:244 Mr
10 '70 *
Mr Nixon's foreign policy; report to Con-
gress on the state of the world. H. J. Mor-
genthau. New Repub 162:23-5 Mr 21 '70 *
More words; analysis of foreign affairs mes-
sage. Nation 210:227 Mr 2 '70 *
Nixon doctrine; analysis of foreign policy
message. New Repub 162:5-6 F 28 '70 *
Nixon plan for U.S. in the world during the
1970s. il U S News 68:22-3 Mr 2 '70 *
Nixon way; school desegregation. il por
Newsweek 75:28+ Ap 6 '70 *
Nixon's answers on desegregation. il U S
News 68:15 Ap 6 '70 *
Pleasures of global chess. H. Sidey. il por
Life 68:4 F 27 '70 *
Slowdown on desegregation. P. Woodring
and others. Sat R 53:57 Ap 18 '70 *
State of the planet address. J. B. Sheerin.
Cath World 210:242-3 Mr '70 *
State of the world. il por Newsweek 75:29-30
Mr 2 '70 *
U.S. policy: a new strategy for peace. Amer-
ica 122:234-6 Mr 7 '70 *
World of Richard Nixon. il Time 95:13-14
Mr 2 '70 *

Press conferences

**Backfire; session with nine selected column-
ists. Newsweek 76:99B N 23 '70**
Behind the news conference. Newsweek 76:23
D 21 '70
Climbing out of the trough; press conference, December 8, 1970. Time 96:12 D
21 '70
Direct communication; regional briefings. il
por Newsweek 76:57 S 7 '70
Mr Nixon and the press. Nation 211:675-6 D
28 '70
Nixon and the press. il por U S News 69:12-
14 D 28 '70
Novice newsman in the East room; high
school student's impressions of con-
ference, December 8, 1970. por Time 96:12
D 21 '70
Thank you, Mr President; December 8, 1970.
il por Newsweek 76:22-3 D 21 '70
This is conciliation? conference, December
8, 1970. J. Osborne. New Repub 163:7-9 D
26 '70
View from San Clemente; June 30, 1970. il por
Newsweek 76:17 Ag 10 '70

Public relations

Businessmen still like Nixon. il Bsns W p31-
2 Ap 18 '70 *
Climbing out of the trough. Time 96:11 D 21
'70
Commissar of credibility; communications
director. H. Klein. D. Bonafede. Nation
210:392-6 Ap 6 '70 *
Ending the war. P. A. Samuelson. Newsweek
75:78 Je 1 '70
Equal time for the closed fraternity; excerpt
from address. R. Mudd. il por Life 68:4 Mr
13 '70 *

Government in the heartland. il pors **Time**
95:10-12 F 16 '70 *
Impossible importation: candor like Castro's.
Nation 211:100 Ag 17 '70
Isolation of Pope and President. J. B. Shee-
rin. Cath World 211:146-7 Jl '70
Kent and Cambodia. Commonweal 92:235-6
My 22 '70 *
Listen to youths, Hickel writes Nixon. il
pors U S News 68:34 My 18 '70*
Loose talk from an old lawyer; President's
remark on Charles Manson's guilt. H. Sidey.
Life 69:4 Ag 14 '70 *
Making points with civility. H. Sidey. Life
68:4 Ap 10 '70 *
Newsweek poll: Mr Nixon holds up. il News-
week 75:30 My 25 '70 *
Nixon and the anti-kid vote. S. Alsop. News-
week 75:112 Je 15 '70 *
Nixon: the beach and the budget. por Time
96:7 Ag 10 '70
Nixon's campaign for confidence. il pors
Time 95:15-16 My 25 '70 *
Nixon's stock; on the rebound? il por News-
week 75:23-4 Je 8 '70
On tour with the White House. il por U S
News 68:12 F 16 '70 *
President is listening. il Time 96:8-9 Ag 3 '70
Record of a highly visible president. il por
U S News 70:19 Ja 4 '71
Report card on the President; A. Heard's re-
port. M. McGrory. America 123:53 Ag 8 '70
Secret link between Nixon and the New
Mobe kids. W. Rogers. Look 34:78 Ja 27 '70
Voices from the silent majority. J. C.
Goulden. il Harper 240:67-72+ Ap '70; Dis-
cussion. 241:8+ Jl '70
War gloom and market jitters; business-
men's attitude. il por Bsns W p 19-20 My
9 '70 *
We are going to make America better. il
por Time 96:6-7 Jl 6 '70
Westward the isolation booth. H. Sidey. Life
69:2B Ag 7 '70
Who talks to the President? Bsns W p26 My
16 '70 *
Will Dr Heard be heard? the attitudes and
concerns of college youth. America 123:55 Ag
8 '70

Recreation

Richard Nixon, moviegoer. il Newsweek 76:
25 Ag 17 '70

Relations with Congress

Advise and consent and fireworks. M. Mc-
Grory. America 122:443 Ap 25 '70
Annals of politics; nomination of G. H. Cars-
well to the Court. R. E. Harris. New York-
er 46:60-4+ D 5; 53-8+ D 12 '70
Big spender debate; Nixon vs. Congress. il
U S News 69:57 Ag 24 '70
Collision with Congress? il Newsweek 75:35-6
My 18 '70 *
Congress gets ready to battle Nixon. il Bsns
W p66-70 Ja 9 '71
Congress v. the President. Time 95:16-17 My
25 '70 *
Congress vs Nixon; the big issues of '70. il
por U S News 68:22-5 Ja 26 '70
Double veto, a pair of cuff links. il por
Newsweek 76:13-14 Ag 24 '70
Duel over the power to make war. il por
Newsweek 75:29-31 My 25 '70 *
End of the 91st. Time 97:23-4 Ja 4 '71
Gloves are off for a partisan clash. Bsns W
p33-4 Ja 17 '70
Having it both ways. il por Time 96:8-9 Ag
24 '70
It was a bad week. K. Crawford. News-
week 76:39 Jl 13 '70
Nixon: the beach and the budget. por Time
96:7 Ag 10 '70
Nixon, the Senate & the war. N. G. Levin,
jr. Commentary 50:69-84 N '70
Nixon to Congress: the war's my business.
New Repub 163:5-6 Jl 4 '70
Nixon's program, its chances in Congress. il
U S News 68:17-18 Ap 27 '70 *
POW Congress. New Repub 163:7-9 D 5 '70
Powers and dominations. Nat R 22:550+ Je
2 '70
President and a balky Congress. H. J. Sievers.
America 122:33 Ja 17 '70
Showdown on war: Congress vs. Nixon. il
U S News 68:35 My 25 '70*
War policy splits Congress; U.S. and Cam-
bodia. il Sr Schol 97:2-3 S 21 '70
Washington desk. G. R. Rosen. Duns 95:5-6
My '70 *
We are going to make America better. il por
Time 96:6-7 Jl 6 '70
Welfare and muscle; Family assistance act.
J. Osborne. New Repub 163:11-12 N 7 '70

NIXON, Richard Milhous—*Continued*

Religion

Prototype of heaven? Presidential prayer breakfasts. D. Kucharsky. Chr Today 14:39 F 27 '70 *

Richard Nixon, theologian. C. P. Henderson, jr. Nation 211:232-6 S 21 '70

White House religion: a tricky business. M. Novak. Chr Cent 87:1112 S 23 '70; Discussion. 87:1559 N 11 '70

Speeches, addresses, etc.

Anecdotes, facetiae, satire, etc.

What Nixon might have said; rewriting his Phoenix speech. Time 96:28 N 16 '70

Sports

Parting shots; the President as a sportsman. H. Sidey. il pors Life 68:65-8 Ja 30 '70

State of the Union message, January 22, 1970

As Nixon sees the future. por U S News 68: 17 F 2 '70

Aseptic society. Commonweal 91:499-500 F 6 '70

Dream vs. reality. K. Crawford. Newsweek 75:23 F 2 '70

Nixon's spirit of '76. il por Newsweek 75:17-18 F 2 '70

State of the Union address. America 122:120 F 7 '70

State of the Union from 37,000 feet. H. Sidey. il por Life 68:2 F 6 '70

Summons to a new cause. il por Time 95:7 F 2 '70

TRB from Washington. New Repub 162:4 Ja 31 '70

Turning point for the Nation. Bsns W p 120 Ja 31 '70

State of the world message

See Nixon, R. M.—Messages

Travel

Presidential mileage: Nixon sets a record. il por U S News 68:48-9 Ap 13 '70 *

Visit to Asia and Rumania, 1969

Nixon's earth tour. il por Sr Schol 96:22 S 15 '69

Visit to Europe, 1970

Cui mare? Nixon's trip and American commitment in the Mediterranean and its basin. Nat R 22:1094+ O 20 '70

Mr Nixon makes a trip, and a point. il por Newsweek 76:22-3 O 5 '70

Mr Nixon shows the flag. il pors Newsweek 76:22-3 S 28 '70

Nixon abroad: applause and admonitions. il por Time 96:12-14 O 12 '70

Nixon tour: dizzying pace. il pors Sr Schol 97: 21 O 19 '70

No innocent abroad; reasons for visit to Ireland. Nation 211:324-5 O 12 '70

Presidency as viewed from abroad. H. J. Sievers. America 123:224 O 3 '70

President Nixon makes nine day visit to Europe; September 27-October 5, 1970. R. M. Nixon. Dept State Bul 63:505-41 N 2 '70

Presidential power aboard the Sixth fleet; with report by H. Sidey. il pors Life 69:38-40 O 8 '70

President's circuit of Europe. America 123:280 O 17 '70

President's goal in Europe. il U S News 69: 22-3 O 5 '70

President's progress. il pors Newsweek 76:26-9 O 12 '70

Real meaning of Nixon trip. il pors U S News 69:17-19 O 12 '70

Reasons for Nixon's next trip. il U S News 69:53 S 28 '70

Vietnam cooker. J. Osborne. New Repub 163:11 S 26 '70

With Dick in Europe. J. Osborne. New Repub 163:8-10 O 17 '70

Visit to Mexico, 1970

President Nixon and President Diaz Ordaz of Mexico, meet at Puerto Vallarta; remarks, and toasts, August 20-21, 1970. R. M. Nixon: G. Diaz Ordaz. Dept State Bul 63:289-300 S 14 '70

Settling a border. il Sr Schol 97:3 S 21 '70

South of the adjusted border: il por Time 96:12 Ag 31 '70

Stepping lively. il pors Newsweek 76:15 Ag 31 '70

Youth

Young Nixon. D. Jackson. il pors Life 69: 54-54B+ N 6 '70; Same abr. with title Portrait of the young Nixon. Time 96:18-19 N 9 '70

NIXON, Tricia

My daughter Tricia; interview. ed. by P. F. Healy. R. M. Nixon. il pors Ladies Home J 87:57-63+ Je '70 *

Nixon ladies and their summer dresses. il Life 68:44 My 8 '70 *

Outgoing introvert. il por Time 95:13 Je 8 '70 *

President's daughters. pors Vogue 155:98-9 Je '70 *

Tricia and Eddie. pors Newsweek 77:18 Ja 4 '71 *

NIZER, Louis

Professor Terry and the lady in brown. il Read Digest 97:96-100 N '70

What to do when the judge is put up against the wall. il N Y Times Mag p30-1+ Ap 5; 114-15 My 3 '70; Same abr. with title Order in the court! Read Digest 97:95-9 Jl '70

NO-load mutual funds. See Investment trusts

NO-pest strip insecticide. See Insecticides

NO tillage system for corn. See Corn—Cultivation

NOAH'S ark

Expedition seeks to recover remains of Noah's ark. Chr Cent 87:72 Ja 21 '70

In the wake of the ark. il Sci N 97:574-5 Je 13 '70

Uncovering the mystery; expedition to Mount Ararat. Chr Today 14:39 F 13 '70

NOAH'S ark model. See Models

NOBEL prizes

Dissent in the USSR. Nation 211:389 O 26 '70

Divide and honor; physics and chemistry prize winners. pors Newsweek 76:100 N 9 '70

Does economics deserve a Nobel prize? M. Hudson. Commonweal 93:296-8 D 18 '70

Economics: Nobel prize for 1970 awarded to Samuelson of M.I.T. L. Hurwicz. por Science 170:720-1 N 13 '70

How the Nobelists won; prizes in medicine. il por Newsweek 76:83 O 26 '70

I accept the prize; 1970 prize for literature awarded to A. I. Solzhenitsyn. G. Wolff. por Newsweek 76:67 O 19 '70

Laureate of new economics. por Bsns W p90 O 31 '70

Magnetism to metabolism; physics, chemistry Nobels. Sci N 98:348 O 31 '70

Murray Gell-Mann wins Nobel prize for physics. B. G. Levi. bibliog por Phys Today 23:83+ Ja '70

Neurobiology: on the research frontier. pors Sci N 98:331 O 24 '70

1969 Nobel prizes in science. il Chem 43:20-1 Ja '70

Nobel for greening; peace prize awarded to N. E. Borlaug. il por Newsweek 76:50-1 N 2 '70

Nobel for outcast; A. I. Solzhenitsyn. por Sr Schol 97:5 N 2 '70

Nobel laureates for 1970: Hannes Alfvén and Louis Néel. G. B. Lubkin. pors Phys Today 23:61-3 D '70

Nobel peace prize: developer of high-yield wheat receives award. L. R. Brown. por Science 170:518-19 O 30 '70

Nobel prize: three share 1970 award for medical research. S. Udenfriend; A. R. Martin. pors Science 170:422-4 O 23 '70

Nobel prize winner who deserved it: Russian novelist, A. Solzhenitsyn. T. Foote. por Life 69:58 O 23 '70

Nobel prizes; broadening the range of both the scientific and the peace awards. Sci Am 223:38-40 D '70

Nobel prizes: 1970 awards honor three in physics and chemistry. A. J. Dessler; W. C. Koehler; E. Cabib. pors Science 170:604-9 N 6 '70

Nobel understanding; prize for physiology or medicine. Time 96:99 O 26 '70

Peace and the green revolution. il por Sci N 98:347 O 31 '70

Plasmas, magnets and sugars; prizes in physics and chemistry. il por Time 96:39 N 9 '70

Prize and a dilemma; A. Solzhenitsyn wins Nobel prize for literature. por Time 96:38-9 O 19 '70

Science; P. A. Samuelson winner of Alfred Nobel memorial prize for economics. Time 96:39 N 9 '70

Sowing a green revolution; 1970 Nobel peace prize to N. E. Borlaug. por Time 96:42 N 2 '70

Wheat breeder who won the Peace prize; with editorial comment. C. P. Streeter. il pors Farm J 94:16-17+, 46 D '70

Wheat whiz wins: peace prize to N. E. Borlaug. por Sr Schol 97:8 N 16 '70

NOBILE, Philip
Priest who stayed out in the cold. il por
N Y Times Mag p8-9+ Je 28 '70
Stage (cont) Commonweal 91:558-9 F 20 '70
NOBLE, Joseph V.
Some trick Greek vases. il Ceram Mo 18:18-23
Ja '70
NOBLE gases. See Gases, Rare
NOBODY hears a broken drum; drama. See
Miller, J.
NOCHLIN, Linda
Ugly American. il Art N 69:55-7+ S '70
Why have there been no great women art-
ists? excerpts from Woman in sexist so-
ciety: studies in power and powerlessness.
bibliog il Art N 69:22-39+ Ja '71
NOCTURNAL animals. See Animals—Habits
and behavior
NOEL-BAKER, Philip John
Arms race, escalation of total madness. il
UNESCO Courier 23:4-5+ N '70
NOËL-HUME, Ivor
Rise and fall of English white salt-glazed
stoneware. il Antiques 97:248-55, 408-13 F-
Mr '70
NOETHER, Emiliana P.
(comp) Articles and other books received;
Italy. See issues of American historical re-
view
NOGG, Judy
We won't cop out. por Redbook 134:42+ Mr '70
NOGUÉS, Germinal
Mar del Plata's festival of film. il Américas
22:18-26 Je '70
NOISE
Are academic libraries too noisy? J. A.
McCrossan. Am Lib 1:396 Ap '70
I can't hear the flutes; excessive noise from
nonbook learning devices in new Hume li-
brary at University of Florida. L. Cassidy.
il Am Lib 1:888-9 O '70
Noise; excerpt from The tyranny of noise. R.
A. Baron. Vogue 156:150-1+ N 1 '70
Transportation noises, ed by J. D. Chalupnik.
Review
Environ 12:44-5 N '70
See also
Airports—Noise
New York (city)—Noise

Physiological effects
Breaking the sound barrier. Sr Schol 97:15
D 7 '70
Noise, a major health problem; ed. by A.
Hamilton. V. Knudsen. il Parents Mag 45:
66-8 F '70
Noise: it hurts! B. Ford. il Sci Digest 68:34-40
O '70
Noise: polluting the environment. B. J. Culli-
ton. il Sci N 97:132-3 Ja 31 '70
Privacy: there's too little. Noise: there's too
much. M. Drury. House B 112:74-6 Ag '70
We're poisoning ourselves with noise. J.
Stewart-Gordon. Read Digest 96:187-90+ F
'70

Psychological effects
Louder, please; noiseless products distract-
ing. Time 95:92 My 4 '70
Privacy: there's too little. Noise: there's too
much. M. Drury. House B 112:74-6 Ag '70
NOISE, Electric. See Electric noise
NOISE, Radio. See Radio interference
NOISE control
Cities lend an ear to noise control. Bsns W
p 108 Ja 17 '70
Fundamental noise research emphasized;
aircraft turbine engines. Aviation W 92:90
Je 22 '70
Hazards and hurdles in developing stan-
dards: a case history. il Arch Rec 147:147-50
My '70
Let quiet be public policy; excerpt from The
tyranny of noise. R. A. Baron. Sat R 53:
66-7 N 7 '70
Noise, a major health problem; ed. by A.
Hamilton. V. Knudsen. il Parents Mag 45:
66-8 F '70
Quiet: what you can do to preserve it; ex-
cerpts from The tyranny of noise. R. A.
Baron. House & Gard 138:128-9 O '70
Shhh; retrofitting of jets. il Forbes 105:31
Mr 15 '70
Silencing invisible pollution; anti-noise or-
ganizations. T. Berland. il Todays Health
48:16-18+ Jl '70
See also
Soundproofing
NOISE generator. See Sound—Apparatus
NOISE prevention. See Noise control
NOJIMA, Minoru
Musical events; concert in Carnegie Hall. W.
Sargeant. New Yorker 46:122-3 My 16 '70*

NOL, Lon. See Lon Nol
NOLAN, Grace
My china cabinet; poem. Hobbies 75:71 Je
'70
NOLAN, Martin
Report from Washington. Atlan 226:6+ D
'70
NOLAN, Paul T.
Awakening of Granville; drama. Plays 30:12,
25-35 D '70
Four letters from Algernon; drama. Plays
29:19-29 F '70
Proposal of marriage; dramatization of story
by Anton Chekhov. Plays 29:83-92 My '70
She stoops to conquer; adaptation. See Gold-
smith, O.
(ed) See Ibsen, H. Enemy of the people
NOLAN, William F.
From the land of me... to the land of you.
Writer 83:18-20 Je '70

about
Multi-media man. M. Renz. il por Writers
Digest 50:24-6+ D '70 *
NOLD, Julianne G. and others
Collagen molecules: distribution of alpha
chains. bibliog il Science 170:1096-8 D 4 '70
NOLEN, William A.
I can afford to be sick. il Esquire 73:118-19+
Ap '70
Making of a surgeon. por Newsweek 76:77-8
D 14 '70 *
Making of a surgeon; condensation. il Read
Digest 97:209-12+ N '70
Tell me, doctor, what about sex after my
operation? Ladies Home J 87:162-4 O '70
NOLL, Mark
Hymn to God on my way to Him. Chr Today
14:6 Jl 3 '70
NOLLER, David
We really need only three ways to sell hogs.
Farm J 94:H7 Mr '70
NOMADS
The Danakil: nomads of Ethiopia's waste-
land. V. Englebert. il Nat Geog 137:186-211
F '70
NOME, Alaska
Eskimo. W. Bronson. il Am West 7:34-47 Jl '70

Water supply
Water distribution on wheels. il Am City
85:20 Jl '70
NOMINATION expenditures. See Campaign
funds
NOMINATIONS for office
Advice and consent, power to select, too?
D. Lawrence. U S News 68:104 Ap 13 '70
NOMOGRAMS. See Charts, Calculating
NONAGGRESSION pacts. See Treaties
NON-ALIGNED nations, Conferences of. See
International conferences
NONALIGNMENT. See Neutrality
NONCOMMERCIAL television. See Television
broadcasting, Noncommercial
NONCONFORMISTS. See Dissenters
NONFERROUS metals. See Metals, Non-
ferrous
NON-GOVERNMENT organization of the
United Nations. See United Nations—Non-
governmental organizations
NONGRADED classes. See Ungraded classes
Les NONNES; drama. See Manet, E.
NON-OBJECTIVE art. See Art, Abstract
NON-PROLIFERATION treaty. See Atomic
weapons—International control
NONSKID tape. See Adhesive tape
NONVERBAL communication. See Communica-
tion, Nonverbal
NONVIOLENCE
Encounter in Recife. B. Tyson. il por Chr
Cent 87:720-2 Je 10 '70
Lessons from the Czech ordeal; guidelines
for nonviolent opposition. J. Power. il Chr
Cent 87:1011-13 Ag 26 '70
Seeking the relevance of Gandhi. H. A.
Jack. Chr Cent 87:427-8 Ap 8 '70
Ways of violence. E. W. Ranly. America 123:
140-3 S 12 '70

Anecdotes, facetiae, satire, etc.
Two thoughts of school. G. Ace. Sat R 53:4
N 28 '70
NON-WAGE payments
Analysis of changes in wages and benefits
during 1969. J. E. Talbot, jr. il Mo Labor R
93:45-50 Je '70
Changes in health and insurance plans for
salaried employees. D. R. Kittner. bibliog il
Mo Labor R 93:32-9 F '70
Employee benefits, 1970-1985. T. J. Gordon
and R. E. LeBleu. il Harvard Bsns R 48:
93-107 Ja '70

NON-WAGE payments—*Continued*
Employees' extra benefits soar. il Nations Bsns 55:84-5 S '70
Measuring employee compensation in U.S. industry. A. Bauman. bibliog f il Mo Labor R 93:17-24 O '70
Union bargaining goals in the 1970's. R. A. Oswald. bibliog f Mo Labor R 93:40-2 Mr '70

NOONAN, Joseph
Credit; cartoons. Cath World 211:128-9 Je '70
Ecology, why must you torture me? cartoons. il Cath World 211:82-3 My '70
Future tense; cartoons Cath World 211:224-5 Ag '70
Hijack! cartoons. Cath World 212:211-12 Ja '71
Sensitivity nonsense; cartoons. Chr Cent 88: 22 Ja 6 '71
Women's liberation in historical perspective; cartoons. Cath World 212:95-6 N '70

NORA'S friends; story. See Cullinan, E.

NOREPINEPHRINE
Amphetamine: differentiation by d and e isomers of behavior involving brain norepinephrine or dopamine. K. M. Taylor and S. H. Snyder. bibliog il Science 168: 1487-9 Je 19 '70
Brain norepinephrine: enhanced turnover after rubidium treatment. J. M. Stolk and others. bibliog il Science 168:501-3 Ap 24 '70
Intracranial self-stimulation and wakefulness: effect of manipulating ambient brain catecholamines. S. K. Roll. bibliog il Science 168:1370-2 Je 12 '70
Norepinephrine metabolism in brainstem of spontaneously hypertensive rats. Y. Yamori and others. bibliog il Science 170:544-6 O 30 '70
Norepinephrine turnover and metabolism in rat brain after long-term administration of imipramine. J. J. Schildkraut and others. bibliog il Science 168:867-9 My 15 '70
Tobacco-alcohol link. il Newsweek 76:77 Ag 17 '70

NORFOLK, Va.
City planning
Try a paint-in at construction site of new civic center. J. B. Oliver. il Am City 85:126+ O '70
What urban redevelopment has done for Norfolk, Va. F. Sullivan. il Am City 85:60-1+ N '70

Education
Education association of Norfolk. R. R. Richards. Todays Ed 59:39 My '70

NORMA; opera. See Bellini, V.

NORMAL love; story. See Oates, J. C.

NORMAN, Gurney. See McClanahan, E. jt. auth.

NORMAN, is that you? drama. See Clark, R. and Bobrick, S.

NORMAN furniture. See Furniture, French

NORODOM Sihanouk, king of Cambodia (abdicated 1955)
From Peking: Sihanouk talks to Americans; questions and answers. ed. by W. Attwood. Look 34:102+ O 20 '70
Future of Cambodia. For Affairs 49:1-10 O '70
Let my people go. Nation 211:198-9 S 14 '70

about
Cambodia: runaway *coup d'etat.* M. Osborne. Nation 210:678-80 Je 8 '70 *
Cambodian puzzle. il por Newsweek 75:39 Mr 23 '70 *
Changing Cambodia. D. P. Chandler. bibliog f Cur Hist 59:333-8+ D '70 *
Coup in Cambodia: how Sihanouk lost out; with eyewitness account by C. S. Foltz, jr. il por U S News 68:18-20 Mr 30 '70 *
Dear Prince: since you went away... A. J. Langguth. il N Y Times Mag p4-5+ Ag 2 '70 *
From Vietnam to Indochina. il por Newsweek 75:31-2 Mr 30 '70 *
Lon Nol and Sihanouk speak out. il pors Time 96:27 S 28 '70 *
Prince falls in Asia and U.S. troubles rise. il pors Life 68:30-1 Ap 3 '70 *
Reports: Cambodia. H. D. S. Greenway. Atlan 226:32+ Jl '70 *
Road to Phnom Penh: Cambodia takes up the gun. B. Garrett. il Ramp Mag 9:32-5+ Ag '70 *
Royal jugglers of southeast Asia. il pors Time 95:30 Mr 30 '70 *

NORRIS, Dale M. and others
Energy transduction: inhibition of cockroach feeding by naphthoquinone. bibliog il Science 170:754-5 N 13 '70

NORRIS, Kenneth S.
Third fish. New Repub 162:16-18 My 9 '70

NORRIS, Leslie
Burning the bracken; poem. New Yorker 46: 130 O 17 '70
Deerhound; poem. Atlan 226:84 Ag '70
Early frost; poem. Atlan 226:110-11 N '70
Fishing the Teifi; poem. Atlan 225:91 Ja '70
Plus fours. Atlan 225:120-2 Je '70

NORTH, David
Headhunters lop one of their own. il por Bsns W p28-9 F 14 '70 *

NORTH, Don
Prague: nothing is forever. il Nation 211: 102-5 Ag 17 '70

NORTH, Sandie
Reporting the movement. por Atlan 225:105-6 Mr '70

NORTH AFRICA. See Africa, North

NORTH AFRICAN cookery. See Cookery, North African

NORTH AMERICAN car corporation
Fighting off Flying Tiger. Bsns W p 19 Ag 15 '70

NORTH AMERICAN Christian convention
NACC: involved. Chr Today 14:31 Jl 31 '70; Reply. H. M. Bledsoe. 15:33 O 23 '70

NORTH AMERICAN Indians. See Indians of North America

NORTH AMERICAN Rockwell corporation
Aerospace industry hits some bumpy air. il Newsweek 75:62-4 Mr 2 '70
At North American more of the same. Bsns W p37 F 28 '70
Cheers and tears; contract for the B-1 bomber. Nation 210:740 Je 22 '70
Happy days for North American. il Bsns W p28-9 Je 13 '70
NASA plans orbital utility vehicle; space tug concept. Z. Strickland. il Aviation W 93: 73+ Jl 13 '70
North American seeks aerospace rebound. W. S. Hieronymus. Aviation W 92:63-5 Ap 13 '70
One more chance bomber; B-1 contract. Fortune 82:27 Jl '70
Rockwell game plan starts to work. Bsns W p80+ S 26 '70
Rockwell trims North American. por Bsns W p 112 Ja 31 '70
Subcontract competition for B-1 beginning. il Aviation W 93:59+ S 14 '70
Why a company buys itself. il Bsns W p35 Ap 25 '70

NORTH AMERICAN yacht racing union
Where the action is! il Yachting 128:46-51+ O '70

NORTH AMERICANS for peace in southeast Asia movement. See Vietnamese war, 1957- —Protests, demonstrations, etc, against

NORTH ATLANTIC community. See Atlantic community

NORTH ATLANTIC council. See Nato

NORTH ATLANTIC treaty organization. See Nato

NORTH CAROLINA
See also
Architecture, Domestic—North Carolina
Bird sanctuaries—North Carolina
Booksellers and bookselling—North Carolina
Camps—North Carolina
Cape Hatteras National Seashore Recreation Area
Fishing—North Carolina
Hunting—North Carolina

History
Mission for Mr Wedgwood; excerpts from journal, with introd. and epilogue by H. C. Wedgwood. T. Griffiths. il Am Heritage 21:64-7 Ag '70

Industries
Firing and hiring of Fredy Jones; anti-union practices of textile companies in North Carolina. R. Scott. New Repub 163:12-15 Jl 25 '70

NORTH CAROLINA pageants. See Pageants

NORTH CAROLINA school of the arts, Winston-Salem
North Carolina school in Italy. W. Weaver. Hi Fi 20:MA18+ N '70

NORTH CASCADES NATIONAL PARK
Cruising the Cascades. G. W. Reiger. il Pop Mech 134:132-7+ N '70
North Cascades, a wilderness plan. J. V. Morris. il Nat Parks & Con Mag 44:10-15 O '70
North Cascades National Park. il Sunset 145: 48-57 Jl '70

NORTH CASCADES wilderness area (proposed)
See Wilderness areas—Washington (state)

NORTH DAKOTA
See also
Education—North Dakota
Sheyenne River

Photographs

May day in North Dakota: prairie blizzard.
E. Bry. Audubon 72:57-64 Mr '70

Politics and government

Fit to be tied; Republican congressional primary. Newsweek 76:39+ S 21 '70
NORTH DAKOTA. University, Grand Forks
North Dakota observatory and weather station.
J. R. Eyton. il Sky & Tel 40:201 O '70
NORTH SEA
Age of reason; oil discoveries. il Forbes 106:
21 N 15 '70
Beneath the beautiful sea: oil. il Newsweek
75:81 Je 15 '70
Gushing expectations around the North Sea.
il Fortune 82:178 Ag '70
North Sea. T. Smith. il Travel 133:28-33 Mr
'70
Striking it rich in the North Sea. il Bsns W
p45 My 16 '70
See also
Baltic Sea
NORTH TARRYTOWN, N.Y.
Discarded packer excels in leaf pick-up. J.
A. Biros. Am City 85:28 O '70
NORTH TEXAS state university, Denton

Library

North Texas solution; installment building.
il Library J 95:3235-6 O 1 '70
NORTH VIETNAM. See Vietnam (Democratic
Republic)
NORTHEAST AFRICA. See Africa, Northeast
NORTHEAST airlines, inc.
Northeast loses part of its dowry. Bsns W
p 16 Ja 9 '71
NORTHEAST coast hurricane of 1938. See Hurricanes
NORTHEAST regional ballet festival. See
Dance festivals
NORTHEASTERN forest fire protection compact
Quebec joinder. A. E. Eckes. il Am For 76:
6-7+ Ap '70
NORTHEASTERN states
See also
Fishing—Northeastern states
Hunting—Northeastern states
Libraries—Northeastern states

Politics

Close-up of '70 campaign; at stake in ten
Northeastern states. il U S News 69:25-8
O 5 '70
NORTHEASTERN university, Boston
Hayakawa at Northeastern. D. Brudnoy. Nat
R 22:202 F 24 '70
NORTHERN, Harry. See Harry X
NORTHERN Illinois gas company
Challenge of consumerism. Duns 95:112 Ap
'70
NORTHERN IRELAND
See also
Belfast
Catholics in Northern Ireland
Civil rights—Northern Ireland
Elections—Northern Ireland
Protestants in Northern Ireland
Public opinion—Northern Ireland

Economic conditions

See also
Unemployment—Northern Ireland

Politics and government

Bloody Ulster: an Irishman's lament. B.
Moore. il Atlan 226:58-62 S '70
Divided Ireland: continued agony. J. Rockwell. Chr Cent 87:613-14 My 13 '70
Irish vs. Irish: why they keep fighting. il
U S News 69:80-1 O 26 '70
Letter from Dublin. J. Kramer. New Yorker
46:56-65 Jl 25 '70
Ne plus Ulster? A. Boyd. Nation 211:35-6
Jl 20 '70
Nothing to stop them. Newsweek 75:42+ F
9 '70
On the left, Bernadette Devlin. W. F. Buckley, jr. Nat R 22:856-7 Ag 11 '70
Paisley in Parliament. A. Boyd. Nation 210:
549-50 My 11 '70
Rebel in Armagh jail, the hater in the pulpit.
A. Carthew. il pors N Y Times Mag p 12-
13+ Ag 9 '70
Religion and politics in Northern Ireland. D.
Clark; A. Boserup. il Trans-Action 7:14-31
bibliog(p64) Mr '70

Six counties at the UN; New York talks of
British and Irish prime ministers. Nation
211:452 N 9 '70
Tinder-dry. Newsweek 76:30 Jl 20 '70
Ulster revisited. C. R. Hughes. il America
122:413-15 Ap 18 '70
War in North Ireland. N. Moss. New Repub
163:13-14 Ag 15 '70
What it's like in Belfast. A. Cockburn. il
Ramp Mag 9:8+ O '70
See also
Elections—Northern Ireland

**Religious institutions and
affairs**

Life in Belfast: guarded streets, but aid to
children. J. Rockwell. Chr Cent 87:1024-5
Ag 26 '70
Religion and politics in Northern Ireland.
D. Clark; A. Boserup. il Trans-Action 7:
14-13 bibliog(p64) Mr '70

Riots

Classic scene of Irish violence. il Life 69:48-
48B S 4 '70
Danger and hope. il Newsweek 76:46+ Jl 13
'70
Devil's own timing. il por Time 96:29 Jl 6 '70
Divided Ireland: the North aflame again. J.
Rockwell. Chr Cent 87:901 Jl 22 '70
Letter from Dublin. J. Kramer. New Yorker
46:56-65 Jl 25 '70
On the left, Bernadette Devlin. W. F. Buckley, jr. Nat R 22 856-7 Ag 11 '70
Shoot them down before tea. il Time 96:17+
Jl 13 '70
War in North Ireland. N. Moss. New Repub
163:13-14 Ag 15 '70

Anecdotes, facetiae, satire, etc.

Riot act. J. Horgan. Sat R 53:4 O 3 '70
NORTHERN states power company
Enlightenment strikes a utility. il Bsns W
p 142+ Mr 28 '70
Question of jurisdiction; federal vs. state
control. il Sci N 97:406 Ap 25 '70
NORTHERN TERRITORY, Australia
Inside Down Under. J. Gunther. il Read Digest 97:207-10+ O '70
NORTHFIELD Mountain hydroelectric pumped
storage facility. See Hydroelectric plants
NORTHMEN
See also
Vikings
NORTHROP corporation
Balancing act. il Forbes 105:33 My 1 '70
Early study of users aided F-5 program;
supersonic fighter. W. S. Hieronymus. il
Aviation W 92:46-7+ Mr 16 '70
Northrop fighter takes off again. il Bsns
W p24 N 28 '70
Small contract with lots of clout; air force
sponsored International fighter. il Bsns W
p 19 Mr 7 '70
NORTHWEST

Economic conditions

Out of work. R. Friedman. Nation 210:421-2
Ap 13 '70
NORTHWEST, CANADIAN
See also
British Columbia
Frontier and pioneer life—Canada
NORTHWEST airlines, inc.
Court vetoes antistrike tactic. Bsns W p78+
N 7 '70
Northwest, clerks union resume talks. Aviation W 93:24 O 19 '70
Northwest expects 1970 profits despite 159-
day strike losses. Aviation W 93:29 D 21
'70
Northwest weighs merger ruling options. J.
P. Woolsey. Aviation W 94:26 Ja 11 '71
Rail-air clerks: long strike, and now—. U S
News 69:47-8 D 21 '70
NORTHWEST industries, inc.
Can Heineman peddle a deadhead? proposed
sale of Chicago & North Western railway to
employees. por Bsns W p 19 O 3 '70
Gandy dancers' line North Western employees transportation co. to acquire railroad.
Time 96:79 O 19 '70
NORTHWEST mounted police. See Canada—
Royal Canadian mounted police
NORTHWEST PASSAGE
I saw them crunch through the Northwest
Passage; SS Manhattan. R. Gannon. il pors
Pop Sci 196:101-5+ Ja '70
Icebreaker: saga of Northwest Passage; interview, ed. by N. J. Margolis. T. C. Pullen.
il por U S News 68:72-5 F 9 '70
New Northwest Passage: Manhattan's voyage. M. Gruber. il Sea Front 16:2-12 Ja '70
North for oil; Manhattan makes the historic
Northwest Passage. B. Keating. il Nat Geog
137:374-91 Mr '70

NORTHWEST PASSAGE—*Continued*
Northwest Passage. B. Skovbo. il Natur Hist 79:56-65 Je '70
Testing more than the Arctic ice; Manhattan's voyages. W. Kornberg. il Sci N 97:420 Ap 25 '70
NORTHWEST TERRITORIES, Canada
See also
Jenny Lind Island
NORTHWESTERN university, Evanston, Ill.

Libraries
Northwestern university library by Walter Netsch of SOM. il Arch Rec 148:89-96 Jl '70
Northwestern's new library. G. R. Shields. il Am Lib 1:443-5 My '70
NORTON, Boyd
Last great dam. il Audubon 72:14-27 Ja '70
about
Camera with a cause. K. Poli. il Pop Phot 67:92-7 D '70 •
NORTON, Eloise
Papier-mâché book characters. il Sch Arts 69:28-9 Mr '70
NORTON, M. Scott
School-community relations. Clear House 44:538-40 My '70
NORTON, William T. and Poduslo, S. E.
Neuronal soma and whole neuroglia of rat brain: a new isolation technique. bibliog il Science 167:1144-6 F 20 '70
NORTON company
Grinder gives Norton an edge. il Bsns W p70 O 31 '70
NORTON Simon, inc. See Simon, Norton, inc.
NORWALK, Conn.

Education
Utilizing closed circuit television. N. Harding. il Am Lib 1:165-6 F '70

Historic houses, etc.
History in houses; Lockwood-Mathews mansion in Norwalk. M. D. Schaack. il Antiques 97:378-81 Mr '70

Hotels, restaurants, etc.
Gourmet ashore; great waterfront restaurants:
Pier restaurant. E. Gibbs. il Motor B 126:106-7 Ag '70
NORWAY
See also
Fishing—Norway
Forests and forestry—Norway
Voss

Description and travel
Golden day in Norway. M. Gough. il House B 112:84+ Ap '70
NORWEGIAN breads. See Bread
NORWEGIAN cookery. See Cookery, Norwegian
NORWICK, Kenneth P. See Pilpel, H. F. jt. auth.
NORWOOD, Mary Lou
Vacation countdown. il Travel 135:42-7 Ja '71
NOSE
Importance of noses. S. Morini. il Vogue 156:138-9 O 1 '70
Your nose is a sleep monitor. A. J. Snider. il Sci Digest 67:52-3 Ap '70
See also
Olfactory nerves
Smell
NOSSITER, Bernard Daniel
Does foreign aid really aid? Atlan 225:61-3 F '70
NOSTALGIA
Nostalgia. il Newsweek 76:34-8 D 28 '70
NOTABLE books council. See American library association—Adult services division
NOTABLES. See Celebrities; Great men
NOTHING to say; story. See Hill, S.
NOTRE DAME college of Staten Island
Final solution for college unrest. P. Kaval. Commonweal 92:53-4 Mr 27 '70; Discussion. 92:179+, 303 My 8, Je 12 '70
NOTRE DAME, Ind. University
Greening of the fighting Irish. J. Kirshenbaum. il Sports Illus 33:76-8+ D 14 '70
Notre Dame goes kicking into the Cotton. S. Myslenski. il Sports Illus 33:70-1 N 30 '70
See also
Laetare medal
NOTTEBOHM, Fernando
Ontogeny of bird song. bibliog il Science 167:950-6: 170:1334 F 13, D 18 '70
NOUWEN, Henry
Generation without fathers. Commonweal 92:287-94 Je 12 '70

NOVA SCOTIA
See also
Halifax
Historic houses, etc.
See also
Cape Breton Island—Historic houses, etc.
NOVAE, See Stars, New
NOVAK, Michael
Are universities babysitters or what? Cur 117:16-18 Ap '70
Do students want education? Commonweal 92:10-13 Mr 13 '70
Greening of a con-III-man. Commonweal 93:245-9 D 4 '70
Lonergan explosion. Commonweal 92:268-70 Mr 29 '70
Politics of resentment. Commonweal 92:481-3 S 25 '70; Same. Cur 123:13-18 N '70
Society of lonely people. Ladies Home J 86:129 D '69
White House religion: a tricky business. Chr Cent 87:1112 S 23 '70
Year of Murray Chotiner. Commonweal 93:217-21 N 27 '70
NOVAK, Robert D.
Reports: Washington. Atlan 225:4+ Ap '70
NOVELISTS
Can the U.S. absorb 130 first novelists a year? il Time 95:75 Je 29 '70
First novelists; spring-summer-fall 1970; statements by the writers. ed. by I. E. Stokvis. il Library J 95:516-22, 2290-9, 3309-11 F 1, Je 15, O 1 '70
First novels, the threat of originality. L. Kuehl. Commonweal 93:105-6 O 23 '70
Novelists for novelists; ed. by L. Kuehl. il Commonweal 92:198-9 My 8 '70
NOVELISTS, American
Century of American realism; interview, ed. by J. A. Garraty. A. Kazin. il Am Heritage 21:12-15+ Je '70
See also
Alger, H. jr
Barthelme, D.
Bellow, S.
Cather, W. S.
Clark, W. V.
Faulkner, W
Fiedler, L. A.
Hemingway, E.
McCarthy, M.
McMurtry, L.
Miller, W. M. jr
Nabokov, V.
O'Hara, J.
Porter, K. A.
Potok, C.
Price, R.
Vonnegut, K. jr
NOVELISTS, English
See also
Durrell, L.
Forster, E. M.
Fowles, J.
Huxley, A.
Lessing, D. M.
NOVELISTS, German
See also
Grass, G.
NOVELISTS, Irish
See also
O'Brien, E.
NOVELISTS, Japanese
See also
Mishima, Y. pseud.
NOVELS. See Fiction
NOVICK, Alvin
Echolocation in bats; excerpts from The world of bats. il Natur Hist 79:32-41 Mr '70
NOVICK, Julius
Theatre (cont) Nation 210:189-90, 733-4: 211:189-90, 317-18 F 16, Je 15, S 7, O 5 '70
NOVICK, Sheldon
Burden of proof. bibliog il Environ 12:16-29 O '70
Do-it-yourself. il Environ 11:22-5 D '69
Earthquake at Giza. bibliog il Environ 12:2-13 Ja '70: Same abr. with title Dangers from radioactive wastes. Cur 118:41-5 My '70
NOW. See National organization for women
NOWACK, Dorothy R. and Conant, M. M.
Sex education, K through 6. il PTA Mag 65:6-9 bibliog(p33) N '70
NOYCE, Robert N.
MOSFET semiconductor IC memories. il por Electr World 84:46-8 O '70
NOYES, Judy
Making good guy ads work. il Pub W 197:147-9 Je 8 '70

Le NOZZE di Figaro; opera. See Mozart, J. C. W. A.

NU, 1907-
Revolution on the Burma trail? V. P. Nanda. Commonweal 91:530-1 F 13 '70 *
Voice from the jungle. il por Time 96:31-2 D 7 '70 *
Which is the Burma road, Ne Win or U Nu? H. D. S. Greenway. il pors N Y Times Mag p34-5+ My 3 '70 *
NUCLEAR age. See Atomic age
NUCLEAR boilers. See Pressure vessels
NUCLEAR energy. See Atomic power
NUCLEAR engineering
Nuclear sciences. Sci N 97:97 Ja 24 '70
See also
Atomic blasting
Atomic power industry
NUCLEAR excavation. See Atomic blasting
NUCLEAR excited states. See Energy levels (quantum mechanics)
NUCLEAR fission
Nuclear fission revisited. J. R. Huizenga. bibliog il Science 168:1405-13 Je 19 '70
NUCLEAR fuels
Nuclear fuel runs scarce. il Bsns W p84-5 Mr 21 '70
See also
Plutonium
NUCLEAR fusion
Controlled fusion: plasma heating with lasers. R. Holcomb. Science 167:1112-13 F 20 '70; Reply. J. M. Thorne. 169:893-4 Ag 28 '70
Controlled nuclear fusion: energy for the distant future. L. A. Artsimovich. il por Bul Atom Sci 26:47-55 Je '70
From the H-bomb: power without pollution; with editorial comment. il Bsns W p80+, 134 S 12 '70
H-bomb power for a peaceful future. S. V. Jones. il Sci Digest 67:83 Ap '70
Hot new promise of thermonuclear power. T. Alexander. il Fortune 81:94-7+ Je '70
Isaac Asimov explains: controlled fusion. I. Asimov. Sci Digest 68:89-90 S '70
Mach 3,200 and fusion. il Sci N 98:217 S 12 '70
Note on nuclear fusion. il Chem 43:29 Ap '70
Power for the people; control research in the U.S. and Russia. Newsweek 76:101-2 S 28 '70
Secret patent applications; new method for containing thermonuclear plasma. Sci N 98: 136 Ag 15 '70
NUCLEAR industries. See Atomic power industry
NUCLEAR laboratories. See Atomic research laboratories
NUCLEAR magnetic resonance
Biological phosphonates: determination by phosphorus-31 nuclear magnetic resonance. T. Glonek and others. bibliog il Science 169: 192-4 Jl 10 '70
Blood velocity measurements in intact subjects. O. C. Morse and J. R. Singer. bibliog il Science 170:440-1 O 23 '70
Double nuclear magnetic resonance observation of electron exchange between ferri- and ferrocytochrome c. R. K. Gupta and A. G. Redfield. bibliog il Science 169:1204-6 S 18 '70
Magnetic resonance in biology: structure-function relations in heme proteins. K. Wüthrich and R. G. Shulman. bibliog il pors Phys Today 23:43-50 Ap '70
Nuclear magnetic resonance spectroscopy, an outline. J. J. Wagner. il por Chem 43: 13-15 Mr '70
NUCLEAR medicine. See Atomic medicine
NUCLEAR non-proliferation treaty. See Atomic weapons—International control
NUCLEAR phase transitions. See Phase transitions
NUCLEAR physicists. See Physicists
NUCLEAR physics
Charting the small world. il Newsweek 75:55-6 Je 22 '70
Current state of physics: AEC's view; interview, ed. by G. B. Lubkin. P. McDaniel; W. A. Wallenmeyer. il por Phys Today 23:55-8 My '70
Fundamental nuclear interaction. A. E. S. Green. bibliog il Science 169:933-41 S 4 '70
Physics and beyond: encounters and conversations; excerpt. W. Heisenberg. il Bul Atom Sci 26:33-6 N '70
See also
California. University—Lawrence radiation laboratories
Cosmic rays
Energy levels (quantum mechanics)
Mössbauer effect
Nuclear fission
Parity nonconservation
Particles (nuclear physics)
Quantum electrodynamics
Transmutation (chemistry)

Conferences
Rochester conferences: the rise of international cooperation in high energy physics. R. E. Marshak. il por Bul Atom Sci 26:92-8 Je '70

History
Three decades of fast-neutron experiments; adaptation of address, 1968. H. H. Barschall; reply. L. Cranberg. Phys Today 23: 9+ Mr '70

International aspects
East-West physics; UCLA-Dubna-Serpukhov collaboration. Sci N 98:30-1 Jl 11 '70
Pooling brains to study the atom; Soviet-CERN. il Bsns W p56-7 Ag 22 '70
NUCLEAR power plants. See Atomic power plants
NUCLEAR propulsion. See Rockets, Atomic powered
NUCLEAR reactions
See also
Nuclear fission
Nuclear fusion
NUCLEAR reactors
Alcator, son of Tokamak. Sci Am 222:60 Mr '70
Bombs or reactors? L. Fermi. por Bul Atom Sci 26:28-9 Je '70
Fast breeder reactors. G. T. Seaborg and J. L. Bloom. il Sci Am 223:13-21 N '70
From the H-bomb: power without pollution; with editorial comment. il Bsns W p80+, 134 S 12 '70
Fusion power to fight the trash glut; self-sustaining fusion reactor. D. E. Thomsen. il Sci N 97:249-50 Mr 7 '70
Getting on the Tokamak bandwagon. D. E. Thomsen. il Sci N 97:373-4 Ap 11 '70
Scyllac: toward pulsed fusion. D. E. Thomsen. il por Sci N 98:321-3 O 17 '70
See also
Rockets, Atomic powered
Space vehicles—Atomic power plants

Fuel
See Nuclear fuels
NUCLEAR research. See Atomic research
NUCLEAR rockets. See Rockets, Atomic powered
NUCLEAR weapons. See Atomic weapons
NUCLEASES
Kinetics of folding of staphylococcal nuclease. A. N. Schechter and others. bibliog il Science 167:886-7 F 6 '70
See also
Ribonucleases
NUCLEATION. See Condensation
NUCLEATION, Atmospheric. See Atmospheric nucleation
NUCLEIC acids
Nucleic acid structure function relations; United States-Japan science cooperation seminar. R. M. Bock. Science 170:351+ O 16 '70
See also
DNA
Nucleoproteins
RNA
NUCLEONS
Meson factories and the two-nucleon problem. M. J. Moravcsik. bibliog il Phys Today 23:40-4+ O '70
NUCLEOPROTEINS
Hyperphenylalaninemia: disaggregation of brain polyribosomes in young rats. K. Aoki and F. L. Siegel. bibliog il Science 168:129-30 Ap 3 '70
Ribosome structure and function emergent. C. G. Kurland. bibliog il Science 169:1171-7 S 18 '70
Ribosomes from spores of bacillus cereus T. F. M. Feinsod and H. A. Douthit. bibliog il Science 168:991 My 22 '70
Structure of RNA in ribosomes. K. A. Hartman and others. bibliog il Science 170:171-3 O 9 '70
See also
Interferon
NUCLEOTIDES
Double-helical polynucleotides: immunochemical recognition of differing conformations. B. D. Stollar. bibliog il Science 169:609-11 Ag 7 '70
Nucleotide sequence of an RNA from cells infected with adenovirus. K. Ohe and S. M. Weissman. bibliog il Science 167:879-81 F 6 '70
Oligodeoxyribonucleotides: chemical synthesis in anhydrous base. R. Von Tigerstrom and M. Smith. bibliog il Science 167:1266-8 F 27 '70
See also
Adenosine monophosphate
Adenosine triphosphate

NUDE in photography. See Human figure in photography

NUDISM
Here she comes, Miss Nude America. C. Remsberg and B. Remsberg. il Esquire 73:160+ My '70
Skin trade; Valata nudist camp, Yugoslavia. K. Huszar. il Newsweek 75:52+ My 25 '70

NUDIST colonies. See Nudism

NUDITY
Better mousetrap; topless customers at Pampelonne, France. il Newsweek 76:27-8 Ag 3 '70
Man talk; less the top. D. Newman and R. Benton. Mlle 71:101 O '70
Pink strangers; nude bathers at Gambia's beaches. il Time 95:44-5 Mr 9 '70
Right to be nude. G. F. Will. Nat R 22:832 Ag 11 '70

NUDITY, Theater of. See Theater, Experimental

NUDITY cult. See Nudism

NUECHTERLEIN, Louis
Records. Chr Cent 87:330+, 1488-9 Mr 18, D 9 '70

NUGENT, Randolph
Randolph Nugent: new look for missions? Chr Cent 87:412-13 Ap 8 '70 *

NUMBERS
See also
Nine (the number)

NUMBERS, Theory of
See also
Diophantine analysis

NUMERICAL indicator tubes. See Electron tubes

NUMERICALLY controlled machine tools. See Machine tools—Control

NUMISMATICS
Numismatics. C. French. See issues of Hobbies
See also
Coins
Medals

NUNLIST, Frank J.
Conglomerates will come back; interview. pors Forbes 107:110 Ja 1 '71

NUNS
And then there were nun. Chr Today 14:39 F 27 '70
Immaculate Heart rebels. por Time 95:49-50 F 16 '70
Indian cloister-filling. J. J. van Capelleveen. Chr Today 15:44+ O 9 '70
Nuns' story; exploitation of Keralan nuns in Europe. il Newsweek 76:53 S 7 '70
On the recruitment of nuns. Chr Cent 87:1114 S 23 '70
Scandal in the convents; Indian girls in European convents. America 123:135 S 12 '70
Secular sisterhood; Sisters of the Immaculate Heart of Mary in Los Angeles to abandon religious life. por Newsweek 75:84-5 F 16 '70
Trafficking in nuns? Indian novices from Kerala in European convents. il Time 96:30 S 7 '70
See also
Contemplative orders
Ex-nuns, priests, etc.
Sisterhoods

NUNS; drama. See Manet, E.

NUNS as public officers
This mayor is Sister. Am City 85:51 D '70

NUNS as teachers
De-schooling the teaching orders. I. Illich. por America 124:12-14 Ja 9 '71

NUNS' ISLAND
New town on an island. il Am City 85:110+ S '70

NUREEV, Rudolf
Rudolf Nureyev: dynamite looking for a match. M. Lear. il Redbook 136:76+ N '70 *
Ultimate dancer. H. Saal. il por Newsweek 75:117 My 25 '70 *

NUREMBERG
Description
Curse of Nuremberg. D. Butwin. il Sat R 53:34-5+ Jl 4 '70
Music
Report:
Donizetti's Lucrezia Borgia. D. Graham. Opera N 34:33 Mr 21 '70

NUREMBERG trials
Judgment at Nuremberg. il Sr Schol 97:13 N 2 '70

NURSERIES (horticulture)
Home landscape plants to give quick results. il Home Gard 57:74-5 My '70
Visit to some very old trees; California nursery, Fremont. Sunset 145:177 S '70
See also
Conrad-Pyle company

NURSERIES, Day. See Day nurseries

NURSERY catalogs. See Catalogs, Seed and plant

NURSERY rhymes
Mary and her little lamb. D. F. Brown. il Hobbies 75:128-9 Mr '70

NURSERY schools
Our merry-go-round nursery group. R. Lancaster. il Parents Mag 45:46-7+ Je '70
See also
Day nurseries

NURSERY tale trio; drama. See Barker, C. and Medina, J.

NURSES aides
How teens get a head start on health careers. A. Henley. il Todays Health 48:34-5+ My '70

NURSES and nursing
Miraculous U-shaped table. T. O'Donnell. il Read Digest 97:89-92 O '70
Misuse of nursing talent. il Sci Digest 67:56 Ja '70
Psychiatric nurse, fox or hedgehog? R. G. Hirschowitz and others. bibliog Ment Hy 54:123-8 Ja '70
Samaritans on wings; nurses fly transoceanic missions evacuating injured GIs from Vietnam. il Ebony 25:60-2+ My '70
Teen-age Civil war nurse Susie King Taylor. il Ebony 25:96-8+ F '70
See also
School nurses

Supply and demand
Shortage of nurses: no solution in sight. il U S News 69:37-8 N 30 '70

Training
Superprofessionals ride again, or How to perpetuate a nursing shortage. Trans-Action 7:8 Je '70

NURSING (infant feeding) See Breast feeding

NURSING homes
Commercializing the aged. R. E. Burger. il Nation 210:557-60 My 11 '70
Fight over where to sue Four seasons. Bsns W p20 O 3 '70
Four seasons: unhappy ending. Forbes 106:55 Jl 15 '70
From psychiatric hospital to nursing home. M. K. Cunningham and others. Ment Hy 54:109-12 Ja '70
Money runs out for Four seasons. Bsns W p 16 Jl 4 '70
Nader v. nursing homes; report to the Senate special committee on aging. il Time 96:48 D 28 '70
Nursing homes show disturbing symptoms. il Bsns W p 110-11 Je 27 '70
Nursing homes: the real problems; interview. ed. by H. Alpert. I. Levin. por Har Yrs 10:6-12 N '70
Troubles ahead for nursing homes. il U S News 69:37-8 Jl 20 '70
Un-tapped research source. L. Lukenbill. il Writers Digest 50:29 Ag '70
When a relative requires nursing-home care. il Good H 171:185 O '70
Where we put the aged. D. H. Pryor. New Repub 162:15-17 Ap 25 '70

NUSSBAUM, Albert F.
Verisimilitude in the crime story. Writer 84:13-15+ Ja '71

NUSZ, Frieda
What's cooking? il Org Gard & Farm 17:110-11+ Ap '70

NUT trees
Landscaping with nut trees. L. H. MacDaniels. il Horticulture 48:42-3+ F '70
See also
Chestnut trees
Pecan trees

NUTCRACKER; ballet. See Ballets—Criticisms

NUTDRIVERS (tools) See Wrenches

NUTRITION
ABC's of family meal planning. C. Brock. il Parents Mag 45:72-3+ F '70
Adelle Davis and the new nutrition; interview. ed. by J. Poppy. A. Davis. il pors Look 34:62+ D 15 '70
Chemical breakfast; controversy over fortified cereals. D. Sanford. New Repub 163:12-15 Ag 22 '70
Food for the road. J. I. Rodale. Org Gard & Farm 17:108-11 Ja '70
Heat's on bread. Sr Schol 97:7 N 16 '70
Let's talk about food. P. L. White. See issues of Today's health

NUTRITION—*Continued*
What's behind those breakfast-cereal head-
lines? il Good H 171:215-16 N '70
What's for breakfast? Moss subcommittee
debate. il U S News 69:45 Ag 17 '70
See also
Aged—Nutrition
Breakfasts
Children—Nutrition
Diet
Food habits
Food values
Infants—Nutrition
Iron in diet
Starvation
NUTRITION and intellect. See Intellect—Nutri-
tional aspects
NUTRITION problems
Dual challenge of health and hunger: a
global crisis; reprint. G. A. Borgstrom.
il Bul Atom Sci 26:42-6 O '70
See also
Food and agriculture organization of the
United Nations

Biafra

See Nutrition problems—Nigeria

Caribbean Region
Malnutrition in the Caribbean. K. W. King.
il Natur Hist 79:64-7 Ja '70

Nigeria
Biafra: howling for food. A. Jaffe. il Newsweek 75:33+ F 2 '70

United States
Are we feeding those hungry Americans? G.
Logsdon. il Farm J 94:34-5+ D '70
Balance is all in their favor. F. Stare. por
Life 68:38 Mr 6 '70
Good nutrition? Only in spurts. J. Cross. Na-
tion 211:357 O 19 '70
TRB from Washington; national nutrition
survey. New Repub 162:6 My 16 '70
We must wipe out hunger in America! inter-
view, ed. by P. Jablow. E. F. Hollings. il
por Good H 170:68-9+ Ja '70
See also
White House conference on food, nutrition,
and health
NUTRITION research
More on nitrogen fixing, diet of New Guinea
natives. Sci N 98:161 Ag 22 '70
Trace elements are for people, too; Inter-
national symposium on newer trace ele-
ments in nutrition. D. Seim. Farm J 94:
34 N '70
NUTS
See also
Cookery—Nuts
Nut trees
Peanuts
Pecans
NUTS (machinery) See Bolts and nuts
NUZZO, Ferruccio
Behind the scenes. Hi Fi 20:21 N '70
NWAFOR, B. U.
Recorded knowledge: a war casualty. il por
Library J 96:42-5 Ja 1 '71
NYASA, LAKE. See Malawi, Lake
NYBERG, Sister Helen Therese
Schizophrenia, the body's chemical mistake.
bibliog il por Chem 43:14-17 My '70
NYE, Joseph S.
Better buy bonds, long-term bonds; inter-
view. por Forbes 105:52-3 F 15 '70
NYMPHS, Artificial. See Fishing lures, files,
etc.
NYQUIST, Ewald B.
Nyquist new Commissioner of education of
New York state. Sch & Soc 98:209 Ap '70 *
NYRO, Laura
Funky madonna of New York soul. M. Paley.
il pors Life 68:44-7 Ja 30 '70
NYSTRAND, Martin, and Zeiser, Sue
Dewey, Dixon, and the future of creativity.
Engl J 59:1138-40 N '70

O

OAO (orbiting astronomical observatory) See
Artificial satellites—Astronomical use
OAS. See Organization of American states
OAU. See Organization of African unity
OCAM (Organisation commune africaine et
malgache) See African and Malagasy com-
mon organization

OCAW. See Oil, chemical and atomic workers
international union
OECD. See Organization for economic coopera-
tion and development
OEO. See United States—Economic opportunity,
Office of
OFCC. See United States—Labor, Department
of—Federal contract compliance, Office of
OIC. See Opportunities industrialization cen-
ters, inc.
OMB. See United States—Management and
budget, Office of
OMBE. See United States—Minority business
enterprise, Office of
OPE (orbiting primate experiment) See Space
flight—Physiological aspects
OPIC. See Overseas private investment corpo-
ration
OPS. See United States—Agency for interna-
tional development—Office of public safety
OSS. See United States—Strategic services,
Office of
OST. See United States—Science and technol-
ogy, Office of
OSTS. See United States—Commerce, Depart-
ment of—State technical services, Office of
OTB. See Off-track betting corporation, New
York
OTC trading. See Stocks—Marketing
OAK
The Woods' mighty oak; privately owned
tree in Michigan Bluff, Calif. W. Fuller.
il Am For 76:28-9 Ag '70
OAK KNOLL naval hospital. See Hospitals.
Naval and marine
OAK PARK, III.
Try an opinion survey. C. T. Osborn. il Am
City 85:80+ D '70
OAKDALE state reformatory for women,
Dwight, III. See Reformatories
OAKELEY, John D. A.
Centerboards; excerpts from Winning. il por
Yachting 128:68+ D '70
OAKES, Philip
Guarantee; poem. Mlle 71:50 Jl '70
OAKLAND, Calif.
Is Oakland there? il Newsweek 75:100 My 18
'70

Description
Oakland: that troubled town across the Bay.
S. Stern. il Holiday 47:74-5+ Mr '70

Galleries and museums
Lead kindly blight; Oakland museum's Pol-
lution show. D. Antin. il Art N 69:36-9+
N '70
Oakland museum; with introd. by M. F.
Schmertz. il Arch Rec 147:115-22 Ap '70
Walk through California; dioramas at new
Oakland museum. N. C. Gray. il Am Home
73:18+ F '70

Parks and playgrounds
Program called Workreation; Oakland park
dept. boys program. W. P. Mott. Parks &
Rec 5:72 Je '70
OAKLAND, Calif. public library
Oakland, California: la Biblioteca latino amer-
icana. B. L. Wynn. il Wilson Lib Bul 44:
751-6 Mr '70
OAKLAND Athletics (baseball) See Baseball
clubs
OAKLAND Raiders (football club) See Foot-
ball clubs
OAKLAND Seals (hockey team) See Hockey
teams
OAKLEY, Francis
Figgis, Constance, and the Divines of Paris;
excerpts from address. December 30, 1966.
bibliog f Am Hist R 75:368-86 D '69
OAKLEY, Kenneth P. and Groves, C. P.
Piltdown man: the realization of fraudulence.
bibliog Science 169:789 Ag 21 '70
OAKS, Howard A.
Lights. il Parks & Rec 5:42-3+ Ja '70
OARSMANSHIP. See Rowing
OASES
Pancake oases in the desert; Sahara Desert.
il UNESCO Courier 23:8-11 Je '70
OATES, Joyce Carol
Bodies; story. Harp Baz 103:122-5 F '70
Fact is: we like to be drugged. McCalls 97:
69 Je '70
Love and death; story. Atlan 225:57-66 Je
'70
Madness; poem. Sat R 53:45 F 7 '70
Normal love; story. Atlan 227:80-5 Ja '71
Puzzle; story. Redbook 136:72-3 N '70
Wednesday; story. Esquire 74:80-1 Ag '70
What Herbert Breuer and I did to each oth-
er; story. McCalls 97:102-3 Ap '70
What is the connection between men and
women? story. Mlle 70:244-5 F '70
Wild Saturday; story. Mlle 71:136-7 S '70

OATES, Joyce Carol—*Continued*

about

Comment. J. McGann. Poetry 117:199-200 D '70 *

Hunger for dreams. P. D. Zimmerman. il por Newsweek 75:109A+ Mr 23 '70 *

Sunday dinner. Criticism
  Nation 211:508 N 16 '70 *

OATES, Merrill Ernest
Tied up and undone; poem. Horn Bk 46: 647 D '70

OATHS of loyalty. See Loyalty, Oaths of

OATS
Somatic association in avena sativa. L. J. P. Dubuc and R. C. McGinnis. bibliog il Science 167:999-1000 F 13 '70

OAXACA (city), Mexico
Music, *buñuelos*, radishes. Oaxaca in December. il Sunset 145:48+ D '70

O'BANNON, Thomas S.
Not-so-amazing calendar trick; or, You, too, can be an idiot-savant. il Sci Digest 67: 86-9 F '70

O'BAR, P. R. See Woods, A. H. jt. auth.

OBEDIENCE
If Hitler asked you to electrocute a stranger, would you? P. Meyer. il Esquire 73: 72-3+ F '70

Would you obey a Hitler? J. Reinert. il Sci Digest 67:34-9 My '70

OBEDIENCE (canon law)
Wright's writ; Roman Catholic priests invited to renew ordination promises. il por Newsweek 76:88-9 F 23 '70

OBERAMMERGAU passion play
Bad scene at Oberammergau. Chr Cent 87: 651 My 27 '70; Discussion. 87:995 Ag 19 '70

Current passions. H. O. J. Brown. il Nat R 22:890 Ag 25 '70

Gospels and the Oberammergau passion play. Sister Louis-Gabriel. il Cath World 211: 13-17 Ap '70

Oberammergau: is it anti-Semitic? with editorial comment. H. O. J. Brown. Chr Today 14:22, 24 Je 19 '70

Oberammergau: the village that kept its vow. J. Graham. il Read Digest 97:193-4+ Jl '70

Oberammergau's year. il Travel & Camera 33:11 Mr '70

Passion at Oberammergau. il Time 95:79 Je 1 '70

Passion's the thing. il Newsweek 75:82 Je 1 '70

OBERBECK, S. K.
Elba. il Travel & Camera 33:50-2+ N '70

OBERG, Arthur
Begin, again; poem. Yale R 60:89 O '70

OBERLIN, Abe
Knit-picking for profits. R. Levy. por Duns 96:67-8 N '70 *

OBERLIN college, Oberlin, Ohio
Co-ed dorms, an intimate revolution in campus life; with report by K. Thorsen. il Life 69:32-41 N 20 '70

OBESITY. See Corpulence

OBITTS, Stanley R.
Plight of the Christian liberal-arts college. Chr Today 14:8-10 Ap 24 '70

OBJECTIVE lenses. See Lenses

OBJECTIVES in education. See Education—Aims and objectives

OBJECTS, Miniature. See Miniature objects

OBLIGATION, Moral. See Duty

OBOLER, Eli M.
Overdue. por Wilson Lib Bul 44:869+ Ap '70

Politics of pornography. il Library J 95:4225-8 D 15 '70

O'BOYLE, Patrick Aloysius, cardinal
Plea for reconciliation. America 122:446 Ap 25 '70 *

O'BRIEN, Conor Cruise
Dublin barfly's book of etiquette. il Sat R 53:44-5+ S 12 '70

Murderous angels. Criticism
  Cath World 210:266-8 Mr '70 *
  Nation 210:219-220 F 23 '70 *
  Newsweek 75:103 F 16 '70 *
  Time 95:64+ F 16 '70 *

O'BRIEN, Donald K.
Forage hybrids can make top dairy feed. il Farm J 94:45 My '70

How to blow a tractor engine and $1000 in 30 seconds flat. il Farm J 94:18-19+ Ag '70

Stretched-out silage harvest. il Farm J 94: B8-9 My '70

O'BRIEN, Edna
Authors & editors. B. A. Bannon. Pub W 197: 21-2 My 25 '70 *

O'BRIEN, George
Table-setting advice for the party season from a Tiffany expert; interview, ed. by V. D. Hahn. il por Am Home 73:22 N '70

O'BRIEN, Joe
Bet O'Brien if he twinkles. L. Simross. Sports Illus 33:44+ Jl 27 '70 *

Little Joe on the big Red mile. W. F. Reed. il por Sports Illus 33:58+ O 19 '70 *

O'BRIEN, John A.
Suenens calls for a new deal. Chr Cent 87: 818-21 Jl 1 '70

Why priests marry. il Chr Cent 87:415-19 Ap 8 '70

O'BRIEN, John M.
Eyes left. Newsweek 76:18 D 28 '70 *

O'BRIEN, Lawrence Francis
War: keynote for Democrats in '70? address, May 9, 1970. por U S News 68:97-9 My 25 '70

about

Democrats' new strategy for a comeback this year. il por U S News 68:40-1 Mr 23 '70 *

Larry looks at television. America 123:225-6 O 3 '70 *

Loyal opposition. por Newsweek 76:73 Jl 20 '70 *

Mission impossible? il por Newsweek 75:35-6 Mr 16 '70 *

Reluctant chief. por Bsns W p56+ F 21 '70 *

Return of the pro. por Time 95:16 Mr 2 '70 *

O'BRIEN, R. D. See Hilton, B. D. jt. auth.

O'BRIEN, Robert
How to save money: in the clothing store. Read Digest 96:65-8 Ap '70

How to save money on appliances and furnishings. Read Digest 97:95-7 S '70

To combat inflation. il Read Digest 97:78-81 N '70

Twelve money-saving tips on maintaining your home. Read Digest 96:189-90+ Je '70

Twenty ways to save money at the supermarket. Read Digest 96:68-70 My '70

Wally Hickel; activist from Anchorage. por Read Digest 96:119-23 F '70

O'BRIEN, Vincent
Triumph for the clan O'Brien. C. Cockburn. il por Sports Illus 33:14-15 Jl 6 '70 *

OBSCENE literature. See Immoral literature and pictures

OBSCENE telephone calls. See Telephone calls

OBSCENITY (law)
Booksellers seek support for appeal of porno bust. Pub W 198:21 N 23 '70

Courts again seek definition of obscenity. Pub W 198:17 N 30 '70

Federal court ruling democratizes obscenity. H. F. Pilpel and K. P. Norwick. Pub W 197:65 F 2 '70

Fructification fulguration; Dirksen bill. J. M. Carter. Library J 95:1001 Mr 15 '70

House passes smut mail bill. S. Wagner. Pub W 197:23 My 11 '70

Intellectual freedom: are you a moralist, a libertarian, or a Clorist? J. F. Krug and J. A. Harvey. Am Lib 1:433 My '70

Intellectual freedom; new laws in California. J. F. Krug. Am Lib 1:212-13 Mr '70

New anti-obscenity bill introduced in Congress. S. Wagner. Pub W 197:39-40 Ap 20 '70

New rules for obscenity? il Time 95:78 My 11 '70

Popular mechanics of sex; Language of love and U.S. obscenity laws. Time 96:58+ S 28 '70

Right to receive and possess pornography; an attorney foresees the end of legal restrictions. A. B. Gerber. por Wilson Lib Bul 44: 641-4 F '70

Supreme court leaves obscenity issues unresolved. S. Wagner. Pub W 198:50 Jl 27 '70

Surprise, surprise: a dirty speech is illegal; violating Utah's obscenity statute. Time 96:63 S 28 '70

Two faces of obscenity. H. F. Pilnel and K. P. Norwick. Pub W 198:30-1 Jl 6 '70

Washington busily debates the aspects of pornography. S. Wagner. Pub W 198:26-7 D 7 '70

See also
Postal censorship
Trials (obscenity)
United States—Commission on obscenity and pornography

OBSERVATION cars. See Railroads—Cars

OBSERVATIONS, Astronomical. See Astronomy—Observations

OBSERVATORIES
See also
Astronomical observatories

OBSERVATORIES, Geophysical. See Geophysical stations

OBSIDIAN
Possible bedrock source for obsidian found in archeological sites in northwestern Alaska. W. W. Patton. jr and T. P. Miller. bibliog il Science 169:760-1 Ag 21 '70

OBSTETRICS
Importance of postnatal care for mother and child. il Good H 171:161 S '70
Postpartum care; ed. by D. Z. Meilach. E. L. Engel. Redbook 135:14+ Ag '70
See also
Abortion
Cesarean section
Childbirth

OCCIDENTAL petroleum corporation
Will Oxy make it? il Forbes 106:18-19 Ag 1 '70

OCCULT literature
See also
Booksellers and bookselling—Occult literature

OCCULT sciences
Beyond reason; with photographs by D. Snyder. Horizon 12:11-19 Spr '70
Cult of the occult. il Newsweek 75:96-7 Ap 13 '70
Flight from reason. T. Meehan. il Horizon 12:4-10 Spr '70
How quackery thrives on the occult. F. G. Loyd and T. Irwin. il Todays Health 48: 20-3+ N '70
Occult. N. Pileggi. il McCalls 97:62-5+ Mr '70
Style of evil. il Esquire 73:118-21 Mr '70
Thinking with your blood. H. Bowser. Sat R 53:26 S 19 '70
Trend to the occult. il Sr Schol 97:7-12 N 2 '70
See also
Astrology
Fortune telling
Satanism
Spiritualism
Witchcraft

OCCULTATIONS
Favorable grazing occultations, September-December, 1969. D. W. Dunham. il R Pop Astron 63:25-6 Ag '69
Occultation highlights (cont) D. W. Dunham. il Sky & Tel 40:184; 41:64 S '70, Ja '71
Occultation highlights. H. R. Povenmire. il Sky & Tel 39:336 My '70
Occultations during the February eclipse. R. Abileah. il Sky & Tel 41:57 Ja '71

OCCULTISM. See Occult sciences

OCCUPANCY
See also
Squatters

OCCUPATION, Choice of. See Occupations

OCCUPATIONAL education. See Vocational education

OCCUPATIONAL guidance. See Vocational guidance

OCCUPATIONAL literature. See Vocational literature

OCCUPATIONAL mobility
Are you ready for a new career? F. K. Coffee. il Mech Illus 66:60-2+ D '70
They'd rather switch. il Newsweek 75:83 Je 8 '70
See also
Labor turnover

OCCUPATIONAL therapy
Community cooperation and a shoestring budget: Rx for an activity therapy program. C. R. Gilpin and E. Neufeld. Ment Hy 54:397-400 Jl '70
Effect of work therapy on patients' responses to other hospital therapies. M. S. Barbee and others. bibliog il Ment Hy 54:92-6 Ja '70

OCCUPATIONS
Careers without college. il Ebony 25:120-2+ Jl '70
Changing careers: five Americans begin again in their middle years. A. Bayer. il Life 68:50-7 Je 12 '70
Job guide for next ten years. il U S News 68:54 Je 15 '70
Job in the great outdoors. W. Davis. bibliog il Mech Illus 66:71-3+ My '70
Jobs: an updated look into the future. il Changing T 24:33-6 O '70
21,741 choices for a career. M. Brenton. N Y Times Mag p72+ O 25 '70
Vocations of the '70s. L. David. Mech Illus 66:40-1 Ja '70
What do you want to be when you grow up? N. E. Scofield. il Parents Mag 45:40-1+ Je '70
Where the jobs will be in the next ten years. il U S News 69:73 N 2 '70
See also
Business
Negroes—Occupations
Professions
Woman—Occupations

Anecdotes, facetiae, satire, etc.
Five worst jobs. L. Buckwaiter. il Mech Illus 66:84-6+ O '70

OCCUPATIONS, Choice of. See Occupations

OCCUPATIONS, Hazardous
Matter of life and death. il Newsweek 76:64-6 Ag 17 '70

OCEAN
Ocean: a natural source of carbon monoxide. J. W. Swinnerton and others. bibliog il Science 167:984-6 F 13 '70
Questions about the oceans; excerpts. il Pop Mech 134:121-4 N '70
Why the sea is salt. F. MacIntyre. il Sci Am 223:104-15 bibliog(p 132) N '70
See also
Atlantic Ocean
Icebergs
Marine biology
Oceanographic research
Oceanography
Sea level
Shore lines
Tides
Waves

Economic aspects
See Marine resources

OCEAN-atmosphere interaction
Computing the link between sea and air; studying ocean's effects on climate. K. Frazier. il Sci N 97:533-5 My 30 '70
Energy cycle of the earth. A. H. Oort. il Sci Am 223:54-63 bibliog(p262) S '70
Ocean-atmosphere model. il Phys Today 23:34 D '70
Sea-air explanation; causes of cooler weather. Sci N 98:412 N 28 '70

OCEAN bottom
Building mountain ranges: a plate tectonics model; studies of J. F. Dewey and J. M. Bird. K. Frazier. il pors Sci N 98:143-5 Ag 15 '70
Depth-finding by eye-ball; water's depth is color coder. E. S. Maloney. Motor B 126:29-30 N '70
Diving into the blue holes of the Bahamas. G. J. Benjamin. il Nat Geog 138:346-63 S '70
Gravity's tug on the ocean floor. il Sci N 97:191-2 F 21 '70
Jigsaw of the primeval world; Glomar Challenger's findings. il Life 68:60-3 Ja 30 '70
Mountain-building in the Mediterranean. Sci N 98:316 O 17 '70
Old and mobile; Glomar Challenger's eleventh voyage. Sci N 97:547-8 Je 6 '70
Sea-floor spreading, carbonate dissolution level, and the nature of horizon A. S. Gartner, jr. bibliog il Science 169:1077-9 S 11 '70
Viscosity of the Atlantic Ocean bottom. C. H. Cramer. bibliog il Science 167:1123-4 F 20 '70
Why the West is wild; new theory of East Pacific rise. il Time 97:34 Ja 11 '71
See also
Benthos
Faults (geology)
Marine sediments
Oceanographic research
Submarine geology

International aspects
Common heritage. Sci N 98:476 D 26 '70
International law and the oceans; the seabeds; address, February 18, 1970. J. R. Stevenson. Vital Speeches 36:367-9 Ap 1 '70
Oceans treaty; President's proposal for an international agency. A. W. Smith. Nat Parks & Con Mag 44:2 Ag '70
Politics of marine research. L. Purrett. il Sci N 99:9-11 Ja 2 '71
Prospects for peace in the oceans; summary of the Pacem in Maribus convocation. E. M. Borgese. il Sat R 53:15-22 S 26 '70
Seeking oceanic peace; Malta meeting. Sci N 97:613 Je 27 '70
See also
Seabed treaty (proposed)
United Nations—Committee on the peaceful uses of the seabed and the ocean floor

OCEAN currents
Fishing boats and currents. E. T. Webber. il pors Sea Front 16:26-31 Ja '70
Models of oceanic circulation. D. J. Baker, jr. il Sci Am 222:114-21 Ja '70
See also
Gulf Stream

OCEAN dumping. See Hazardous substances—Disposal in the ocean; Waste disposal in the ocean

OCEAN fishing. See Salt water fishing

OCEAN floor. See Ocean bottom

OCEAN holes. See Ocean bottom

OCEAN in art
See also
Marine painting

OCEAN life. See Marine biology

OCEAN liners
At sea with the Union Jacks; aboard the Oriana. H. Sutton. il Sat R 53:43-5 F 7 '70
Berth of the blues; woes of the Queen Mary and Queen Elizabeth. il Time 96:56 S 7 '70
Dining while at sea; M. S. Europa. M. Woodward. il Travel 133:73 F '70
Ignoble end of Elizabeth. G. Walter. il Life 69:32-6 S 11 '70
Money runs thin for Cunard sisters; Queen Elizabeth on the auction block, Fort Lauderdale, Fla. il Bsns W p 17 S 5 '70
Monument to stupidity; Queen Mary. il Forbes 106:31 Ag 15 '70
Parting shots. W. Zinsser. il Life 68:68-6 Ja 23 '70
Ship society; visit to the Oceanic by New York branch of the World ship society. New Yorker 46:34-5 O 17 '70
Vanishing flag. il Time 96:88+ D 7 '70
Whatever happened to America's luxury liners? il U S News 68:7 F 9 '70
See also
Ocean travel

OCEAN mining
Vacuuming ores from the ocean floor. il Bsns W p60+ Je 6 '70
Vacuuming the Atlantic floor. il Sci N 98:134-5 Ag 15 '70
See also
Diamond mines and mining, Submarine

OCEAN pollution. See Marine pollution

OCEAN science and engineering, inc.
Pumping money out of the sea; manned underwater dredge. il Bsns W p54-5 Jl 11 '70

OCEAN space center. See Oceanography—Exhibitions

OCEAN spray cranberries, inc.
Comeback for cranberries. Fortune 81:176 Je '70

OCEAN travel
1969 U.S. air, sea passengers; table. Aviation W 93:39 N 23 '70
Pleasures of the slow pace; freighter travel. R. Joseph. il Esquire 74:166-7+ O '70
See also
Cruising
Ocean liners
Voyages
Voyages around the world

Anecdotes, facetiae, satire, etc.
I want to go down to the sea again. J. Kerr. Holiday 47:16-18 Je '70

OCEAN yacht racing. See Yacht racing

OCEANARIUMS. See Aquariums

OCEANIA
See also
Fiji
Micronesia
Midway (islands)
Nauru (island)
New Hebrides
South Pacific commission
Tahiti

OCEANIC (ship) See Ocean liners

OCEANOGRAPHERS
See also
Oceanography as a profession

OCEANOGRAPHIC aides
Floating classroom. il Ebony 25:86-8+ F '70

OCEANOGRAPHIC buoys
Robot sailor; SKAMP. M. Gruber. il Sea Front 16:77-81 Mr '70
Skamp, robot boat with rigid sails patrols ocean beat. B. Smith. il Pop Sci 196:70-1+ My '70

OCEANOGRAPHIC institution, Woods Hole. See Woods Hole, Mass, oceanographic institution

OCEANOGRAPHIC instruments
See also
Oceanographic buoys

OCEANOGRAPHIC research
Oceans: coming industrial frontier; with interview with S. Carpenter. il U S News 68:38-40 Mr 30 '70
Our new worlds below; the sea frontier. il Sr Schol 96:8-10 Mr 16 '70
Politics of marine research. L. Purrett. il Sci N 99:9-11 Ja 2 '71
Room at the bottom; Tektite project. E. Peer. il Newsweek 76:66-7 Jl 13 '70
Tektite: a blueprint for cooperative undersea scientific programs. E. Ray and R. M. Cohen. il Bul Atom Sci 26:35-40 F '70; Discussion. 26:47-8 O '70

Tektite 1, man-in-the-sea project: marine science program. H. E. Clifton and others. bibliog il Science 168:659-63 My 8 '70; Discussion. 169:1264-5 S 25 '70
See also
Plankton research
Underwater drilling
Underwater exploration
Underwater laboratories
United States—National oceanic and atmospheric administration
Woods Hole, Mass, oceanographic institution

Equipment
See also
Submarine research vehicles
Underwater laboratories

Federal aid
More research, few ships. Sci N 97:149-50 F 7 '70

Great Britain
Wanted: a policy for science in the sea. L. Miller. il Sci N 97:256 Mr 7 '70

India
India eyes the ocean's resources. S. K. Ghaswala. il Sci N 98:22 Jl 4 '70

OCEANOGRAPHY
Future prospects for physical oceanography. H. Stommel. bibliog Science 168:1531-7 Je 26 '70; Reply. W. S. Wooster. 170:387 O 23 '70
Oceanography. Sci N 98:296 O 10 '70
See also
Marine pollution
Marine resources
Meteorology, Maritime
Ocean
Ocean-atmosphere interaction
Sea level
United States—National oceanic and atmospheric administration

Bibliography
Science of the sea in books. See issues of Sea frontiers

Conferences
Prospects for peace in the oceans; summary of the Pacem in Maribus convocation. E. M. Borgese. il Sat R 53:15-22 S 26 '70

Exhibitions
Planet ocean; proposed ocean center. il Sea Front 16:138-41 My '70
Water: the fluid of life; Ocean space center, IOF's new museum. V. J. Gabianelli. il Sea Front 16:258-70 S '70

History
Matthew Fontaine Maury, Cyrus Field and the physical geography of the sea. R. H. Charlier and P. S. Charlier. il pors Sea Front 16:272-81 S '70

Study and teaching
Floating classroom; training oceanographic aides. il Ebony 25:86-8+ F '70

OCEANOGRAPHY as a profession
Those alluring careers in ocean sciences. il Changing T 24:41-3 Ap '70

OCHOA, Severo
Biochemist sues Ochoa and NYU. R. J. Bazell. Science 170:957 N 27 '70 *

OCHRATOXIN. See Toxins and antitoxins

OCHS, Sidney, and Ranish, N.
Metabolic dependence of fast axoplasmic transport in nerve. bibliog il Science 167:878-9 F 6 '70

OCKENGA, Harold John
Simeon and the Child Jesus. Chr Today 15:4-6 D 18 '70

O'COLLINS, Gerald
Tübingen revisited. America 122:275-6 Mr 14 '70

O'CONNELL, Jean
Art of bonsai trees. il Sci Digest 67:34-8 Mr '70
Holy cats and sacred cows. il Sci Digest 67:57-61 My '70
Something's strange at the Smithsonian. il Sci Digest 68:78-82 O '70

O'CONNELL, Richard
Pot song; poem. Nat R 22:206 F 24 '70
TV tears; poem. Nat R 22:83 Ja 27 '70

O'CONNELL, Shaun
Bringing it all back home. Atlan 225:92-5 Ja '70
Massmags and microcult. Nation 210:310-11 Mr 16 '70

O'CONNOR, Edwin
Magic man; story. McCalls 97:90-1 F '70

about

Best and the last of Edwin O'Connor. ed.
by A. Schlesinger, jr. Review
Commonweal 93:107+ O 23 '70. E. R. F.
Sheehan *

O'CONNOR, Flannery
Barber; story. Atlan 226:111-12 O '70
Writing short stories; excerpts from Mystery
and manners. Writer 83:17-19+ Ja '70

about

World of Flannery O'Connor, by J. Hendin.
Review
Sat R 53:29-30 Jl 18 '70. B. Weber *

O'CONNOR, Francis V.
(ed) See Laning, E. Memoirs of a WPA painter

O'CONNOR, Frank
Analysis of O'Connor's First confession. B.
C. Finnegan. Engl J 59:48-51 Ja '70
Sister Agatha and the milkman; story. Red-
book 135:82-3 My '70

O'CONNOR, Jack
Big cats in trouble. il Outdoor Life 146:63-7+
O '70
Desert mule deer. il Outdoor Life 146:44-5+
D '70
Elephants on the Zambezi. il por Outdoor
Life 145:33-5+ Ja '70
Getting the range. See issues of Outdoor life
Shooting. See issues of Outdoor life

O'CONNOR, James J.
Getting food to the table in hungry lands.
por Bsns W p 134 My 23 '70 *

O'CONNOR, Kate
Closed society of the Chamulas. il Cath
World 211:58-62 My '70

OCTAHEDRONS. See Polyhedrons

OCTANE rating. See Gasoline—Anti-knock
and anti-knock mixtures

OCTOPUS
Mating games octopi play. il Life 69:48-53 N
6 '70
Venomous octopus. W. Deas. il Sea Front 16:
357-9 N '70
See also
Paper nautilus

ODARTCHENKO, Nicolas
Probing the secret of the cell. il UNESCO
Courier 23:17-22 My '70
—and Pavillard, M.
Late DNA replication in male mouse meiotic
chromosomes. bibliog il Science 167:1133-4
F 20 '70

ODD lot sales. See Stocks—Odd lots

ODD lots securities, ltd.
Discount shop on Wall Street. il Bsns W p98
Jl 11 '70

ODELL, Brian Neal
Ghetto ethic. il Cath World 210:213-15 F '70

O'DELL, John. See Kolz, R. C. jt. auth.

ODER-Neisse line. See Poland—Boundaries

ODESSA, Tex. Shakespeare festival. See Shakespeare festivals

ODETS, Clifford
Awake and sing! Criticism
New Yorker 46:52 Je 6 '70 *
Time il 95:76 Je 8 '70 *

ODINGA, Oginga
Tribal politics harass Kenya. S. Meisler. For
Affairs 49:112-21 O '70 *

ODODO; musical comedy. See Musical comedies,
revues, etc.—Criticisms, plots, etc.

O'DOHERTY, Brian
Brian O'Doherty whispers in ogham. J. G.
Bowles. il por Art N 69:34-5+ S '70 *

ODOMETERS
After the great odometer raid; peddling resetting keys. Consumer Rep 35:579-80 O
'70

O'DONNEL, Patrick A. and Lavaroni, C. W.
Elements of individualized instruction. Ed
Digest 36:17-19 S '70

O'DONNELL, Bernard
NCTE/ERIC summaries & sources. Engl J
59:134-8 Ja '70
Priority projects for the teaching of English:
1970. Engl J 59:68-74 S '70

O'DONNELL, Kenneth
LBJ and the Kennedys; excerpt. il pors Life
69:44-8+ Ag 7 '70

O'DONNELL, Richard W.
How to assemble a Christmas toy. Sat R
53:4+ D 5 '70
Till it be morrow. New Yorker 46:29 Jl 4 '70

O'DONNELL, Roy C.
Does research in linguistics have practical
applications? address, November 1969. Engl
J 59:410-12+ Mr '70

O'DONNELL, Terence
Miraculous U-shaped table. il Read Digest
97:89-92 O '70
Pilgrimage; story. Atlan 226:85-9 S '70
Trip for wood; story. Atlan 225:68-72 Ap '70

O'DONOGHUE, Joseph
Bishops open the new season. Commonweal
92:236-7 My 22 '70

ODORS
Olfactory stimuli and the pseudo-extinction
effect. E. A. Wasserman and D. D. Jensen;
reply with rejoinder. M. E. Deutsch. Science 169:402 Jl 24 '70
Scratching the surface of nosepower: scents
applied to the printed page. il Pub W 198:
42-3 Ag 24 '70
See also
Deodorants
Pheromones

ODORS of animals
Discrimination by rats of conspecific odors
of reward and nonreward. R. R. Morrison
and H. W. Ludvigson. bibliog il Science
167:904-5 F 6 '70

ODUM, Eugene P.
Needed land trusteeship, not just ownership.
por Field & S 75:63+ Je '70
Optimum population and environment: a
Georgian microcosm. il Cur Hist 58:355-9+
Je '70

ODYSSEY. See Homer

ODYSSEY house. See Narcotic addicts—Rehabilitation

OEDIPUS; drama. See Sloan, A.

OEDIPUS complex
Self-destruction in Oedipus Rex. M. D. Faber.
bibliog Am Imago 27:41-51 Spr '70

OELMAN, Robert Schantz
Mr Chairman. . ; excerpts from transcript of
NCR annual meeting. il por Forbes 105:21
Je 1 '70
Self-service rings up a billion dollar sale. il
por Nations Bsns 58:92-3 Ja '70

OERLIKON arms works. See Munitions industries—Switzerland

OERTLE, V. Lee
How to match a trailer to your car. il Pop
Mech 134:71-2+ Jl '70
How to travel safely in the wilds. il Pop Sci
197:82-3 Jl '70

OESPER, Ralph E.
Michael Faraday: an informal sketch. pors
Chem 43:16-17 Mr '70
(tr) See Szabadvary, F. Great moments in
chemistry

OF mice and men; opera. See Floyd, C.

OFF-Broadway theater. See New York (city)
—Theater

OFF off Broadway theater. See New York
(city)—Theater

OFF-road racing. See Motor vehicle racing;
Motorcycle racing

OFF-track betting. See Horse race betting

OFF-track betting corporation, New York
Howie the horse. il por Newsweek 77:69 Ja
11 '71
No. 1 bookie makes his play. il por Bsns W
p50+ N 14 '71

OFFENBACH, Jacques
Tales of Hoffmann (Les contes d'Hoffmann)
Criticism
New Yorker 46:114 S 26 '70 *

OFFENHAUSER, Fred
Four cylinder, twin cam, sixteen valve American dream. G. Borgeson. il pors Motor T
22:56-61+ My '70 *

OFFENSES against the person
See also
Assault and battery

OFFICE, Divine. See Divine office

OFFICE appliances
See also
International business machines corporation

OFFICE buildings
Dual space for a union; St Louis. il Arch
Forum 133:68-71 Jl '70
Having fun with harsh reality. J. M. Dixon.
il Arch Forum 132:66-9 My '70
Oh! San Francisco! world headquarters of
Transamerica corporation. A. Zelver. il Arch
Forum 132:68-71 Jl '70
Soaring skylines: Chicago's new entry; the
Sears tower. il U S News 69:65 Ag 10 '70
See also
Bank buildings
New York (city)—Buildings

Designs and plans

Building in the Doric tradition: MacMillan
Bloedel building. Vancouver, B.C. il Arch
Rec 147:123-8 Ap '70
Building types study. il Arch Rec 148:119-32
Jl '70

OFFICE buildings—Designs and plans—*Cont.*
Landmark tower on New Haven's skyline; Knights of Columbus building. R. Jensen. il Arch Rec 148:109-15 Ag '70
Thirty-story slab of ingenuity: Time-Life building in Chicago. J. M. Dixon. il Arch Forum 133:20-7 S '70
Twin towers in Canada. J. S. Margolies. il Arch Forum 132:42-7 Ap '70

Leasing and renting
See Offices—Leasing and renting

OFFICE buildings, Remodeled
Offices for the American field service, New York city. il Arch Rec 147:104-5 Ja '70

OFFICE equipment and supplies
See also
Calculating machines, Electronic

OFFICE equipment industry
See also
Victor comptometer corporation

Finance
Information processing; with yardsticks of management performance. il Forbes 105: 92-4 Ja 1 '70

Japan
Yen for business machines. il Forbes 106: 19-20 D 15 '70

OFFICE for intellectual freedom. See American library association—Office for intellectual freedom

OFFICE for recruitment. See American library association—Office for recruitment

OFFICE furniture showrooms. See Showrooms

OFFICE holders. See Public officers

OFFICE management
Financial paper: variation on themes of Mc-Luhan. G. T. Dunne. bibliog f Harvard Bsns R 48:90-6 My '70

OFFICE of economic opportunity. See United States—Economic opportunity, Office of

OFFICE of environmental affairs. See United States—State, Department of—International scientific and technological affairs, Office of

OFFICE of minority business enterprise. See United States—Minority business enterprise, Office of

OFFICE of public safety. See United States—Agency for international development—Office of public safety

OFFICE of science and technology. See United States—Science and technology, Office of

OFFICE of state technical services. See United States—Commerce, Department of—State technical services, Office of

OFFICE of strategic services. See United States Strategic services, Office of

OFFICE of students and youth. See United States—Education, Office of—Students and youth, Office of

OFFICE of systems analysis. See United States—Defense, Department of—Systems analysis, Office of

OFFICE workers
Fraying white collar. J. Gooding. il Fortune 82:78-81+ D '70
Measuring how office workers work. il Bsns W p54+ N 14 '70
See also
Secretaries

Salaries, allowances, etc.
1970: a banner year for white-collar pay. il U S News 69:70 D 7 '70
White-collar pay in private industry; with tables. W. M. Smith. Mo Labor R 93:59-62 Ap '70
White collar workers: what they're paid now. il Nations Bsns 58:40-1 Ag '70

OFFICERS, Military. See United States—Armed forces—Officers

OFFICES
Artful offices; investment management firm. J. M. Dixon. il Arch Forum 132:48-51 Mr '70
Branch offices for Shearson Hammill & company, Newport Beach, Calif. il Arch Rec 147:110-11 Ja '70
How to save time in your farm office. J. Carlson. il Farm J 94:66 Mr '70
MFB insurance offices, Atlanta, Ga. il Arch Rec 147:100-1 Ja '70
Offices for W. A. Di Giacomo associates, New York city. il Arch Rec 147:118-20 Ja '70

Leasing and renting
High office rents in a low-profile city; London. il Bsns W p67 My 30 '70
Landlords fall prey to the Street's woes. il Bsns W p 17-18 My 2 '70
Why offices stay unrented; Manhattan. il Bsns W p83+ D 5 '70

OFFICES, Display. See Showrooms

OFFICIAL scorers (sports) See Sports officiating

OFFICIAL secrets
See also
Defense information, Classified
Government information
Security classification (government documents)

OFFICIALISM. See Bureaucracy

OFFSET printing. See Printing, Offset

OFFSHORE boundaries. See Territorial waters

OFFSHORE mutual funds. See Investment trusts

OFFSHORE oil fields. See Petroleum in submerged lands

OFFSHORE oil well drilling. See Oil well drilling, Submarine

OGASAWARA, Frank X.
Scientist studies Japan's fantastic long-tailed fowl. il Nat Geog 138:844-55 D '70

OGAWA, Takayuki
Gallery; photographs. Life 69:4-5 Ag 7 '70

OGBURN, Charlton, Jr
Continent in our hands. il Nat Parks & Con Mag 44:22-30 My '70
First discovery of America. il Horizon 12: 92-9 Wint '70
Motorcar vs. America. il Am Heritage 21: 104-10 Je '70

OGDEN, Anne
Artful renter. House B 112:31-2 Ap '70

OGDEN, Eugene C.
Pollination, vital link in plant life. bibliog il Cons 24:21-7+ Ap '70

OGDEN, Samuel R.
Cold-country corn. il pors Org Gard & Farm 17:36-9 Mr '70
Send your beans up a pole. il por Org Gard & Farm 17:32-5 O '70

OGDEN corporation
City in the sky; U.S. railroads interest in real estate development. Time 95:64 Mr 9 '70

OGDEN family
Ogden coat-of-arms. H. K. Eilers. il Hobbies 75:150-1 Jl '70

OGILVIE, Elisabeth
Suspense in fiction. Writer 83:11-14 Ja '70

OGLESBY, Ray T.
Lakes which produce too much. il Cons 24: 18-21 Je '70

OGNER, Gunnar, and Schnitzer, Morris
Humic substances: fulvic acid-dialkyl phthalate complexes and their role in pollution. bibliog Science 170:317-18 O 16 '70

O'GRADY, Desmond
Love; Childhood one; poems. McCalls 97:16 My '70

O'GRADY, Diana
Mrs O'Grady is a widow; statement; ed. by C. S. Wren. por Look 34:67 My 5 '70

O'HAIR, Madalyn E. Murray. See Murray, M. E.

O'HANLON, Michael J.
New York porno shops booming on borrowed time. il Pub W 198:45-6 D 28 '70

O'HARA, Frank
Tomb of Arnold Schoenberg; Unicorn; Note to Harold Fondren; Dolce colloquio; Dido; Homosexuality; Poem: I am not sure there is a cure; poems. Poetry 116:99-106 My '70

O'HARA, Frederic James
Selected government publications. See issues of Wilson library bulletin
Su docs. bibliog il Wilson Lib Bul 44:940+ My '70

O'HARA, John
Appointment in Samarra. R. Boeth. por Newsweek 75:129 Ap 20 '70 *
John O'Hara; excerpts from eulogy. B. Cerf. Pub W 197:21-3 Je 22 '70 *
John O'Hara: the rage is stilled. pors Time 95:38 Ap 20 '70 *
Obituary
Nat R 2:449-50 My 5 '70. J. Hart *
Pub W 197:41 Ap 20 '70 *

O'HARA, Michael J. and others
Experimental petrology of lunar material: the nature of mascons, seas, and the lunar interior. bibliog il Science 167:605-7 Ja 30 '70

O'HARE international airport. See Chicago—Airports

OHE, K. and Weissman, S. M.
Nucleotide sequence of an RNA from cells infected with adenovirus 2. bibliog il Science 167:879-81 F 6 '70

O'HIGGINS, Patrick
Time off (cont) il McCalls 97:38+ F; 24+ Mr '70

OHIO

See also
Booksellers and bookselling—Ohio
Camps—Ohio
Canals—Ohio
Courts—Ohio
Education—Ohio
Festivals—Ohio
Hunting—Ohio
Libraries—Ohio
Reclamation of land—Ohio
Taxation—Ohio

Industries

Where new plants don't cure tax ills. il Bsns
W p89-90 Je 6 '70

Parks and reserves

Ohio parks pay off. Travel 134:11 D '70

Politics and government

Decline of Ohio. D. Hess. Nation 210:429-33
Ap 13 '70
Going for Gilligan. P. R. Wieck. New Repub
163:10-12 O 17 '70
Ohio race: Taft vs. man with an image. pors
U S News 69:52 S 28 '70
Primaries. il Time 95:16-17 My 18 '70
Robert Taft vs. Howard Metzenbaum. G. I.
Maeroff. il pors N Y Times Mag p32-4+
O 4 '70
Season openers: primaries. il Time 95:19 My
4 '70
Surprises in Ohio. il Newsweek 75:42+ My 18
'70

OHIO education association

When the money runs out. W. E. Henry.
Todays Ed 59:54-5 Mr '70

OHIO. Kent state university

Arms and the campus; report on campus un-
rest. Newsweek 76:44-5+ O 12 '70
Build-up to tragedy at Kent state. il U S
News 68:19 My 25 '70
Close-up of the Kent state 25. il U S News
69:46 N 23 '70
Costly blessings at Kent state? Chr Cent 87:
620 My 20 '70
Death story; Allison Krause. E. Segal. il pors
Ladies Home J 87:100-1+ O '70
Double focus on Kent state: findings of
grand jury at odds with those of Scranton
commission. Nat R 22:1146 N 17 '70
Fifth victim of Kent state: D. Kahler, with
account by R. G. Hummerstone. il pors Life
69:42-5 O 16 '70
Four random, pointless deaths. il Newsweek
75:34 My 18 '70
Front-porch America; views of Kent state
students in New York times interview. Na-
tion 210:612 My 25 '70
Gag comes off Kent; grand jury's findings.
New Repub 163:7 N 21 '70
Graduation day at Kent state. il Newsweek
75:20-1 Je 22 '70
Guard fired in self-defense; excerpts from
Ohio grand jury report. il U S News 69:33-5
N 2 '70
Guardsmen's view of the tragedy at Kent
state. W. B. Furlong. il N Y Times Mag p
12-13+ Je 21 '70
Happenings at Kent state; fifth annual Crea-
tive arts festival. A. Rich. il Hi Fi 20:secII
27+ My '70
In the aftermath of Kent state indictments.
il U S News 69:32-3 N 2 '70
Inevitable American tragedy. il Sci N 97:451-2
My 9 '70
Investigations: the Kent state case. il News-
week 75:33-4 My 25 '70
Judgment on Kent state; Department of jus-
tice summary of the FBI's report. il Newsweek 76:14 Ag 3 '70
Jury indicts twenty-five. Sr Schol 97:5-6 N
16 '70
Kent arrests. Newsweek 76:37 N 2 '70
Kent state: another view. il Time 96:27 O
26 '70
Kent state continued; Justice department
summary of FBI investigation. il Time 96:
16 N 9 '70
Kent state: four deaths at noon. il Life 68:30-5
My 15 '70
Kent state gag; report of the Ohio special
grand jury. D. Sanford. New Repub 163:
14-17 N 7 '70
Kent state: martyrdom that shook the coun-
try; killing of four students by Ohio na-
tional guardsmen. il Time 95:12-14 My 18 '70
Kent state: what happened? contradictory
judgments among the three reports. il
Newsweek 76:32-3 N 23 '70
Kent state's continuing battle; reports on
shootings. il Sat R 53:58 D 19 '70
Kent's response; letters to the editor. Library
J 95:2397-8 Jl '70

Man in the middle; President R. I. White.
por Time 96:31 N 23 '70
Mockery of justice. Commonweal 93:211-12
N 27 '70
My God! They're killing us. il Newsweek 75:
31-33F My 18 '70
New verdict on Kent state: special Ohio grand
jury report. Newsweek 76:25 O 26 '70
Notes and comment; funeral service for J.
G. Miller. New Yorker 46:34 My 16 '70
Of many things; the death of four young men
and women. D. R. Campion. America 122:
inside cover My 16 '70
Politics of manslaughter. Nation 210:578-9 My
18 '70
Professor gags; naming of S. Ford to pre-
side at academic hearings. Nation 211:454
N 9 '70
Report on Kent state; Knight newspapers
findings on killing of students. Newsweek
75:67 Je 1 '70
Sowing the wind; a special report from Kent
state university. D. Bryant. Chr Today 14:
13-15 Je 5 '70
Town turns on its children; grand jury report. R. T. Cooper. Nation 211:517-19 N 23
'70
Tragedy at Kent state. T. Gallagher. il Good
H 171:82-3+ O '70

School of library science

More from Kent; letter to the editor. A. R.
Rogers. Library J 95:2586-7 Ag '70

OHIO library association

OLA anniversary conference. R. H. Donahugh. Am Lib 1:1017 D '70

OHIO national guard. See United States—Na-
tional guard

OHIO primaries. See Primaries

OHIO RIVER

Unoxidized nitrogen is the key; exacting
standards of purity set for the Ohio River.
G. Seymour. Am City 85:49 F '70

OHIO state university, Columbus

Libraries

Human element: a retrospective evaluation
of the OSUL internship program. D. J.
Netz and D. E. Wood. Am Lib 1:253-4 Mr
'70

OHLANDER, Margaret C.

New plants to grow for 1971. il Home Gard
58:34-42+ Ja '71

OHLES, John F.

Revised contract for college students. Sch
& Soc 98:23-4 Ja '70
Writing for publication. Clear House 45:245-
9 D '70

OHLHUS, George

Five-point program to keep roses blooming.
il Home Gard 57:12-13 Jl '70

OHLSSON, Garrick

Garrick Ohlsson; interview. New Yorker 46:
16-18 Ja 2 '71
about
Chopin with pow. W. Bender. il por Time 96:
57 N 30 '70 *
Key victory. Newsweek 76:87 N 9 '70 *
Music to my ears. I. Kolodin. Sat R 53:54 N
28 '70 *

OHMANN, O. A.

Skyhooks; reprint from May-June 1955 issue.
bibliog f Harvard Bsns R 48:4-6+ Ja '70

OHMMETERS

Practical expanded scale milliohmmeter. D.
R. Corbin. il Pop Electr 33:77-80 O '70
Simple linear laboratory-quality ohmmeter.
R. L. Carroll. il Electr World 83:60 My '70
See also
Voltohmmeters

OHM'S law

C.E.T. test. D. Glass. Electr World 82:67 My
'70

OHNISHI, M. and Urry, D. W.

Solution conformation of valinomycin potassium ion complex. bibliog il Science
168:1091-2 My 29 '70

O'HORGAN, Tom

Like, madness! interview, ed. by G. Loney.
por Opera N 35:6 N 21 '70
Two remarkable directors. M. Gottfried. il
pors Vogue 155:204-5+ My '70 *

OHTA, Victor, family

Mass murder in Soquel. il por Time 96:10-11
N 2 '70
Tarot murders. il pors Newsweek 76:32+ N
2 '70

OIL and gas leases

Good news for Santa Barbara; proposed
cancellation of twenty federal oil leases.
Time 95:54 Je 22 '70
Hickel v. oil polluters; Gulf of Mexico. Time
95:49 Ap 13 '70

OIL and gas leases—*Continued*
Nixon orders more oil. il Bsns W p 16-17 D
  12 '70
Nixon proposes channel sanctuary. N. Gru-
  chow. Science 168:1438 Je 19 '70
Nixon's oil plan causes friction; canceling
  leases. il Bsns W p33-4 Je 20 '70
Pressure mounts to tap domestic oil; Gulf
  of Mexico drainage leases sale. il Bsns W
  p 17-18 Jl 25 '70
OIL, chemical and atomic workers international
  union
Job hazards hit the bargaining table. Bsns
  W p88 D 12 '70
OIL companies. See Petroleum industry and
  trade
OIL fields, Offshore. See Petroleum in sub-
  merged lands
OIL fuel. See Petroleum as fuel
OIL imports. See Import quotas
OIL in religion, folklore, etc.
Why of chrism. M. L. Tietjen. il Cath World
  212:92-4 N '70
OIL industries
  See also
Petroleum industry and trade
OIL lands
Keeping shale under wraps. C. Welles. il Na-
  tion 211:51-2 Jl 20 '70
Oil shale: ace in the hole for U.S. il U S
  News 68:54 Je 8 '70
OIL leases. See Oil and gas leases
OIL lobby. See Lobbying
OIL participation funds. See Petroleum indus-
  try and trade—Finance
OIL pollution of coastal waters. See Oil pollu-
  tion of rivers, harbors, etc.
OIL pollution of rivers, harbors, etc.
Diary of a disaster; Santa Barbara oil slick.
  J. Huglin. il McCalls 97:58+ Je '70
Dirty dilemma of oil spills; Tampa Bay. il
  Life 68:28-35 Mr 6 '70
Fresh fears spil out of the Gulf; trouble from
  failure to replace defective safety valves.
  il Bsns W p28 Mr 21 '70
Gooey sickness smears the Gulf; Gulf of
  Mexico. P. Ryan. il Sports Illus 32:47-8+
  Mr 30 '70
Gulf tides turn against oilmen il Bsns W
  p 114 Je 6 '70
Long and short of the oil spills. il Sci N 97:
  263-4 Mr 14 '70
Mop-up off Nova Scotia. Sci N 97:551 Je 6
  '70
My struggle to help the President; HRFA in
  Hudson River cleanup. R. H. Boyle. il
  Sports Illus 32:32-4 F 16 '70
Mystery in the Gulf; tar balls. Sci N 97:550-1
  Je 6 '70
Natural oil seepage at Coal Oil Point, Santa
  Barbara, California. A. A. Allen and oth-
  ers. bibliog il Science 170:974-7 N 27 '70
Nervous oilmen scour the Gulf. il Bsns W
  p27 Mr 14 '70
Nixon's oil plan causes friction; canceling
  leases. il Bsns W p33-4 Je 20 '70
Offshore oil pollution; message to Congress
  May 20, 1970. R. M. Nixon. Dept State Bul
  62:754-6 Je 15 '70
Oil discovers Maine. L. Spiker. il Nation
  210:656-8 Je 1 '70
Oil on the waters. R. W. Dietsch. New Repub
  162:10-11 F 28 '70
Oil on troubled waters; Santa Barbara
  beaches. por Time 95:46 F 9 '70
Oil pollution. I. N. Gabrielson. il Nat Parks
  44:4-9 Mr '70
Oil threatens Acadia. F. Davisson. il Nat
  Parks & Con Mag 44:4-7 D '70
Petroleum lumps on the surface of the sea.
  M. H. Horn and others. bibliog il Science
  168:245-6 Ap 10 '70; Reply. F. R. Fosberg.
  168:917 My 22 '70
Precautions and liability. Sci N 97:290 Mr 21
  '70
Sea anemones survive oil spill. Sci Digest
  68:34 O '70
Spilled oil: growing hazard to coasts. il U S
  News 68:42 Mr 16 '70
Ugly new footprint in the sand; polluted
  beach in the Bahamas. A. B. C. Whipple.
  Life 68:20B Mr 20 '70
U.S. oil policy and the environment. E. N.
  Layne. Am Heritage 21:115 Ag '70

Control

Anti-pollution aid keyed to air drop. C. E.
  Schneider. il Aviation W 92:92-3+ My 25
  '70
Anti-pollution machine laps up oil slicks. C.
  Cocking. il Pop Sci 196:56-8+ Ap '70
Bug as garbage man. Time 96:36 D 21 '70
Floating pollution-barrier can confine oil
  slicks. Am City 85:38 F '70

Moving belts skim oil from river; Little
  Cuyahoga River. il Am City 85:18 N '70
Pollution crackdown hits industry. il U S
  News 68:23-5 Ap 6 '70
Putting the lid on oil spills. J. F. Pearson.
  il Pop Mech 135:82-5+ Ja '71

Laws and legislation

  See Water pollution—Laws and legislation

Measurement

Oil spills: method for measuring their extent
  on the sea surface. J. E. Estes and B.
  Golomb. bibliog il Science 169:676-8 Ag 14
  '70
OIL pumps
  See also
Automobiles—Lubrication
OIL shale lands. See Oil lands
OIL spills. See Oil pollution of rivers, harbors,
  etc.
OIL tankers. See Tank ships
OIL tanks
Bottomless wonder: twenty-story tank stores
  oil on floor of Arabian Gulf. T. Harvey. il
  Pop Sci 196:80-3 Ja '70
Underwater giant stores oil. il Sci Digest 67:
  60-1 Ja '70
OIL well drilling, Submarine
Gooey sickness smears the Gulf; Gulf of
  Mexico. P. Ryan. il Sports Illus 32:47-8+
  Mr 30 '70
Gulf tides turn against oilmen. il Bsns W p
  114 Je 6 '70
Hunt for sunken treasure. il Time 95:86+
  Ap 20 '70
Underwater satellites to tap offshore oil.
  A. P. Armagnac. il Pop Sci 197:60-1 D '70
  See also
Petroleum in submerged lands

Safety devices and measures

Crude on troubled waters; Chevron case. il
  Newsweek 75:77-8 Ap 6 '70
Fresh fears spill out of the Gulf; trouble from
  failure to replace defective safety valves. il
  Bsns W p28 Mr 21 '70
OIL workers union. See Oil, chemical and
  atomic workers international union
OILS, Lubricating. See Lubrication and lubri-
  cants
OILS and fats, Edible
Do animal fats cause heart attacks? D. Braun.
  il Farm J 93:24-5+ O '69
Fat debate: saturated vs. polyunsaturated
  fats. il Newsweek 76:98 N 23 '70
Selecting fats and oils for cooking. Good H
  170:148-9 Je '70
  See also
Food—Fat content
OISTRAKH, David
Music to my ears; Oistrakh in Los Angeles.
  I. Kolodin. Sat R 53:54 Mr 28 '70 *
OJAI festival. See Music festivals—California
OJANPERA, Pentti. See Wiik, H. B. jt. auth.
OJUKWU, Chukwuemeka Odumegwu
O captain, my captain. il por Newsweek 75:
  49B Ja 26 '70
OKAI, John
Freedom symphony; poem. Atlan 225:60 F
  '70
OKEECHOBEE, LAKE
Fire one; taking limestone from Lake Okee-
  chobee. W. F. Buckley, jr. Nat R 22:1367
  D 15 '70
O'KEEFE, John A.
Tektite glass in Apollo 12 sample. bibliog il
  Science 168:1209-10; 170:200 Je 5, O 9 '70
O'KEEFFE, Georgia
Art; retrospective at the Whitney museum.
  L. Alloway. Nation 211:637-8 D 14 '70 *
Exhibition preview: retrospective for Georgia
  O'Keeffe. L. Goodrich. il Art in Am 58:80-5
  S '70 *
Georgia is a state of mind; exhibition at the
  Whitney museum. D. Crimp. il Art N 69:
  48-51+ O '70 *
Loner in the desert. R. Hughes. il por Time
  96:64-5+ O 12 '70 *
Return of the native. D. Davis. il por News-
  week 76:104-5 O 12 '70 *
O'KELLEY, G. Davis, and others
Elemental compositions and ages of lunar
  samples by nondestructive gamma-ray spec-
  trometry. bibliog il Science 167:580-2 Ja 30
  '70
OKINAWA
Japan drafts five-year force plan. C. Brown-
  low. il Aviation W 92:37+ F 9 '70
Okinawa: the poison gas issue. E. E. Bollin-
  ger. Chr Cent 87:897 Jl 22 '70
OKITA, Saburo
Looking ahead in Asia; interview. il por
  Forbes 106:35 N 1 '70

OKLAHOMA
Okie: honorary citizenship program. N. A. Martin. Duns 95:52 Je '70
Oklahoma 1970: the dust bowl of the '30s revisited. D. DeVoss. il Time 95:16-17 Ja 26 '70
    See also
Cimarron County
Platt National Park
Recreation areas—Oklahoma

Description and travel
Oklahoma oasis. E. Ford. il Travel 134:28-33+ Ag '70

Industries
Governor is a businessman. N. A. Martin. por Duns 95:50-2+ Je '70

OKLAHOMA CITY

Stores
Crossroads: uniting the living-working-shopping environment. il Arch Rec 147:128-9 Mr '70

OKLAHOMA. University, Norman
Shake-up at Oklahoma. il por Newsweek 76: 48-9 Ag 10 '70

OKLAHOMANS
Okie: honorary citizenship program. N. A. Martin. Duns 95:52 Je '70

OKLAWAHA RIVER
The beautiful and the dammed. H. Bloomfield. il Am For 76:12-15+ S '70
Oklawaha, the fight is on again! W. M. Partington. il Liv Wildn 33:19-23 Aut '69
Oklawaha: the sweetest water-lane in the world. P. Brooks. il Audubon 72:34-6+ Jl '70
Rape on the Oklawaha. J. N. Miller. il Read Digest 96:54-60 Ja '70

OKMULGEE rodeo. See Rodeos

O'KONSKI, Chester T.
Covalent polymers of water. bibliog il Science 168:1089-91 My 29 '70

OKRA
Give us vine okra any time. O. Raney. il por Org Gard & Farm 17:74-5 My '70

OKTOBERFEST. See Festivals—Germany (Federal Republic)

OKUN, Arthur M.
If Nixon had kept the jawbone. il Bsns W p93 Ja 31 '70

O'LAGUE, Paul, and others
Electrical coupling: low resistance junctions between mitotic and interphase fibroblasts in tissue culture. bibliog il Science 170:464-6 O 23 '70

OLAH, George A.
Stable carbonium ions in solution. bibliog il Science 168:1298-311 Je 12 '70

OLCESE, Giuliana, contessa
Renaissance reborn; villa dei Vescovi. V. Lawford. il pors Vogue 156:152-7+ S 15 '70 *

OLCOTT, Chauncey
Chauncey Olcott. J. Walsh. por Hobbies 75: 37-9 Ag; 37-9 S '70 *

OLCOTT, Henry Steel
Mysterious Madame Blavatsky. K. Vonnegut, jr. il por McCalls 97:66-7+ Mr '70 *

OLD age
Letter from Paris; S. de Beauvoir's La vieillesse. Genêt. New Yorker 46:87-90 Mr 7 '70
Neither does a rose. L. Forshee. il Har Yrs 10:22-3 My '70
Terrors of old age; interview, ed. by S. Saler. S. de Beauvoir. por Newsweek 75:54 F 9 '70
    See also
Aged
Aging
Centenarians
Gerontological society
Gerontology
Old age assistance
Retirement

OLD age annuities. See Annuities

OLD age assistance
Bar association committee urges actions to aid elderly. Aging 134:26 F '70
Full citizenship for aging urgently needed, Martin says; excerpts from address, February 23, 1970. J. B. Martin. Aging 186:13 Ap '70
Model cities workshop discusses planning programs for elderly. il Aging 184:4-6 F '70
News of federal agencies. See issues of Aging
News of state agencies. See issues of Aging
Number of recipients of cash payments under social security, old-age assistance, or both, per 1,000 persons aged 65+, by state, February 1969. il Aging 187:23 My '70
Older Americans act programs serving a million older people. il Aging 187:10-13 My '70
Over sixty-five; address, May 29, 1970. L. H. Hamilton. Vital Speeches 36:606-8 Jl 15 '70

Quotations from the commissioner. J. B. Martin Aging 183:9 Ja '70
Seattle's Model cities program develops services for elderly. Aging 184:7-8 F '70
Senate committee holds hearings on rural aged. il Aging 182:6-7 D '69
Strategic Pacific islands now under Older American act. il Aging 190:17 Ag '70
Task force on aging urges change, sends action program to President. T. Schuchat. Har Yrs 10:4-5 Ag '70

OLD age centers. See Senior centers

OLD age homes
Nebraska town makes congregate living a reality for older people. il Aging 184:20-1 F '70
Ohio to relocate 3,000 elderly patients in new geriatric centers. il Aging 183:14 Ja '70
    See also
Nursing homes

OLD age in moving pictures
Old age of Dustin Hoffman; with interview, ed. by R. Meryman. D. Hoffman. il pors Life 69:75-9 N 20 '70
Rags of time: Ingmar Bergman's Wild strawberries; with reply by S. Bach. H. R. Greenberg. Am Imago 27:66-89 Spr '70

OLD age market
Money in old folks; California. T. J. Murray. il Duns 95:75-6 Mr '70
Will the elderly rescue the retailers? il Bsns W p32-3 Ap 25 '70

OLD age pensions
    See also
Pensions, Industrial
Retirement income

Taxation
Treasury finds many retirees overpay taxes; remedy sought. Aging 188:9 Je '70

United States
Treasury finds many retirees overpay taxes; remedy sought. Aging 188:9 Je '70
    See also
Social security act, 1935

OLD airplanes

Collectors and collecting
    See Airplanes—Collectors and collecting

OLD Baba Yage; drama. See Winther, B.

OLD Glory. See Flags—United States

OLD Ironsides (ship) See Constitution (frigate)

OLD LYME, Conn.
Living with antiques. W. T. Donoho. il Antiques 98:922-6 D '70

OLD Order Amish. See Mennonites

OLD people. See Aged

OLD SALEM village. See Winston-Salem, N.C.

OLD story about a path; story. See Merwin, W. S.

OLD STURBRIDGE village, Sturbridge, Mass.
Flying visit. H. Grazier. Flying 87:22-3 N '70

OLD Testament. See Bible—Old Testament

OLD woman who lived in a vinegar bottle; story. See Godden, R.

OLDENBURG, Claes
Making the gallery scene. B. Wasserman. il Sch Arts 70:30-3 O '70 *
Modern museum's soft book for Oldenburg's soft sculptures. il Pub W 198:52 N 9 '70 *

OLDENDORPH, O. F.
Hubbell trading post. il por Nat Parks & Con Mag 44:6-9 O '70

OLDER Americans act. See United States—Aging, Administration on

OLDER persons advisory council. See United States—Economic opportunity, Office of—Older persons advisory council

OLDFIELD, Barney
Or more precisely, the legend of Barney Oldfield. L. W. Steinwedel. il Motor T 23:38-40+ Ja '71 *

OLDHAM, Esther
Fans of the Napoleonic era. il Antiques 97:135-9 Ja '70

OLDS, Glenn A.
United States supports reforms to strengthen UNDP; statement, March 18, 1970. Dept State Bul 62:582-4 My 4 '70

OLDS, Sally
Menopause, something to look forward to? il Todays Health 48:48-9+ My '70
Say it with a stomachache. il Todays Health 48:41-3+ N '70
(ed) See Jaffe, R. B. Hormones during the menstrual cycle
(ed) See Sarto, G. E. Genetic counseling
—and Witt, Linda
New man in the delivery room: the father. il Todays Health 48:52-6 O '70

O'LEARY, Brian T.
  Rebellion among the astronauts; excerpt from
    The making of an ex-astronaut. il por
    Ladies Home J 87:143-6 Mr '70
  Science in space. il Nation 210:522-6 My 4 '70
OLEFINS
  Photochemically induced ionic reactions of
    cycloalkenes. J. A. Marshall. bibliog il Sci-
    ence 170:137-41 O 9 '70
OLFACTORY nerves
  Response of olfactory bulb neurons to X-rays
    as a function of nasal oxygen concentra-
    tion. G. P. Cooper. bibliog il Science 167:
    1726-7 Mr 27 '70
  Three fleeing bullheads. J. Bardach and T.
    Villars. il Natur Hist 79:36-41 bibliog(p 133)
    Ag '70
OLFACTORY organs
  Amygdaloid nucleus: new afferent input from
    the vomeronasal organ. S. S. Winans and
    F. Scalia. bibliog il Science 170:330-2 O 16
    '70
OLFSON, Lewy
  Man without a country; dramatization of
    novel by E. E. Hale. Plays 29:41-6 Ap '70
  My son, the prince; drama. Plays 30:92-6 Ja
    '71
  Spying high; drama. Plays 30:61-5 O '70
  Ten-year-old detective; drama. Plays 29:57-61
    My '70
OLIGODEOXYRIBONUCLEOTIDES. See Nu-
    cleotides
OLITZKA, Rosa
  Rosa Olitzka. A. Favia-Artsay. por Hobbies
    75:35 O '70 *
OLIVA, Tony
  Full series for a fleet pair. W. Leggett. il pors
    Sports Illus 33:18-21 Ag 24 '70 *
OLIVARES, Ruben
  For Mexico (and the world) P. Putnam. il
    pors Sports Illus 32:18-19 Ap 27 '70 *
OLIVEIRA SALAZAR, António de. See Sala-
    zar, A. de O.
OLIVER, Andrew
  Portraits of John Quincy Adams and his
    wife; excerpts. pors Antiques 98:748-53 N
    '70
OLIVER, Chip
  Wow, like let's really try to win; life at a
    commune. B. Newnham. il pors Sports Illus
    33:50-4 O 12 '70 *
OLIVER, Edith
  Theatre. See issues of New Yorker
OLIVER, Elizabeth
  Personal bookshop succeeds in shopping
    center area. Pub W 197:48-9 Ap 20 '70
OLIVER, Hugh M.
  Can you top this? ed. by E. E. Kurrus, jr.
    il Outdoor Life 145:94-7+ Ap '70
OLIVER, James B.
  Try a paint-in. il Am City 85:126+ O '70
OLIVER, Raymond
  La cuisine; excerpts. il por Ladies Home
    J 86:92+ D '69
OLIVER, Richard
  Ordeal of L/Cpl. Johnson. Nation 211:141-6
    Ag 31 '70
OLIVER, Sy
  Sy Oliver, bandleader; with discography. S.
    Dance. il pors Sat R 53:64-5+ My 16 '70 *
OLIVER Twist; drama. See Bland, J.
OLIVERO, Magda
  Fedora; new recording. G. L. Mayer. pors
    Am Rec G 37:76-9 O '70 *
  Magda Olivero: worth a journey. G. Mov-
    shon. Hi Fi sec II 20:21 Ja '70
OLIVES
  Olives. H. McCully. il House B 112:10-11+ Mr
    '70
OLIVIER, Sir Laurence
  Sir says; interview. ed. by H. Ehrlich. il pors
    Look 34:22-6 Ja 27 '70

                    about
  Sir Laurence. por Newsweek 75:57 F 2 '70
OLIVINE
  Iron-titanium oxides and olivine from 10020
    and 10071. S. E. Haggerty and others. bib-
    liog il Science 167:613-15 Ja 30 '70
OLKOWSKI, Helga
  Ecology and the child. il Org Gard & Farm
    17:57-61 N '70
OLMSTED, Roger
  San Francisco and the vigilante style. il Am
    West 7:6-11+ Ja; 20-7+ Mr '70
OLNEY, John W. and Sharpe, L. G.
  Brain lesions in an infant rhesus monkey
    treated with monosodium glutamate. bib-
    liog Science 166:386-8; 167:1017 O 17 '69, F 13
    '70
OLNEY, Richard
  French menu cookbook; excerpts. il Ladies
    Home J 87:88-9+ Ag '70

OLOFSON, Shirley
  On the vagaries of child-care books. il Am
    Lib 1:1036-44 D '70
OLSEN, Arthur J.
  Olsen affair; B. Goldwater objects to ap-
    pointment. Newsweek 76:74+ S 14 '70 *
  Olsen affair; B. Goldwater's objection to ap-
    pointment. por Time 96:17 S 14 '70 *
OLSEN, Edward G.
  City, suburbs, and education; address. De-
    cember 12, 1969. Vital Speeches 36:253-6 F 1
    '70
OLSEN, Jack
  Bad show out in the cold snow. il Sports
    Illus 32:28-30+ Mr 16 '70; Same abr. with
    title Time to control snowmobiles. Read
    Digest 97:174-7 D '70
  He goes where the trouble is. il pors Sports
    Illus 33:22-4+ O 19 '70
  Rosenbloom-Robbie bowl. il pors Sports Illus
    33:22-4+ N 9 '70
  Shoe on the way to 6033. il por Sports Illus
    33:28-30+ S 14 '70
  Sportsman of the year. il por Sports Illus
    33:36-7+ D 21 '70
  Turn left at the porcupine. il Sports Illus 33:
    50-8+ Ag 24 '70
  (ed) See Kapp, J. Man of machismo
OLSEN, Paul
  Dinosaurs finally win one. il pors Life 69:73-4
    D 11 '70 *
OLSON, Bruce
  Bruce Olson and the man-killing Motilones. S.
    Seegers and K. Seegers. il Read Digest 96:
    128-33 Mr '70 *
OLSON, Charles
  Comment. G. Sorrentino. Poetry 116:117-20
    My '70 *
  On verse. R. Whittemore. New Repub 162:21
    Ap 25 '70 *
OLSON, Harry F.
  Experiment that saved hi-fi. D. B. Weems.
    bibliog il por Pop Electr 33:29-34+ S '70 *
OLSON, John M.
  Evolution of photosynthesis. bibliog il Science
    168:438-46 Ap 24 '70
OLSON, Mancur
  Analytic framework for social reporting and
    policy analysis. bibliog f Ann Am Acad
    388:112-26 Mr '70
OLSON, Marlene
  Tahoe's king-size winter. il Travel 135:
    68-70 Ja '71
OLSON, Rodney A.
  Microtubular spherulites: development and
    growth in solutions of bacteriochlorophyll
    protein. bibliog il Science 169:81-2 Jl 3 '70
OLSON, Sigurd F.
  Hidden forest; excerpts. il Nat Wildlife 7:40-
    7 O '69
  Wilderness besieged. il Audubon 72:28-33 Jl
    '70
  Wilderness challenge. il Liv Wildn 34:3-7 Sum
    '70
OLSON, Ted
  Green thumbs down; poem. Sat R 53:50 F 21
    '70
OLSON, Thomas A. and Marvin, Lelia
  Evaluation: one state's approach. Am Ed 6:33
    My '70
OLT, James R.
  How to get started on elk. il Field & S 75:38-
    9+ Ag '70
OLYANOVA, Nadya
  Is your script showing? il Seventeen 29:150-1+
    Mr '70
OLYMPIA press
  S&S asks $4-million in damages, injunctive
    relief. Pub W 197:127-8 F 23 '70
  S&S will sue Olympia over Original seven
    minutes. Pub W 197:48-9 F 16 '70
OLYMPIC games
  Amateurs on the skids? future of winter
    Olympics. il por Newsweek 77:55-6 Ja 11
    '71
  Most deadly games. J. H. Plumb. il Horizon
    11:52-3 Aut '69
  Name is the name of the game; amateurism
    and Olympics. W. Johnson. il Sports Illus
    32:12-17 Mr 9 '70
  Olympics and modern philosophy; amateur
    status of Soviet skiers. A. Lunn. Nat R 22:
    840 Ag 11 '70
OLYMPIC games, 1972
  Only ornery recruits for this boot camp;
    Olympic basketball development camp. P.
    Carry. il Sports Illus 33:50-1 Jl 20 '70
OLYMPIC games, 1976
  Run it up the flagpole, Johnny; Expo, big-
    league baseball and the Olympics. F. Deford.
    il por Sports Illus 33:74-6+ S 28 '70
OLYMPIC NATIONAL PARK
  Winter walk on the Washington coast; Olym-
    pic National Park's wilderness beach. D.
    Birkner. il Nat Parks 44:23-4 F '70

OMAHA, Neb.

Music

Report:
Faust. P. Gainsley. il Opera N 34:31 Mr 21
'70

O'MALLEY, B. W. See Rosenfeld, M. G. jt.
auth.

O'MALLEY, Mary Pat
On campus: the crisis in consciousness. Mlle
71:48 My '70

OMAN
Family coup. Time 96:25-6 Ag 10 '70
Sultan's sulky son; coup. il por Newsweek
76:37B Ag 10 '70
See also
Anti-Communist movements—Oman
Guerrillas—Oman

Foreign relations
United States
See United States—Foreign relations—
Oman

O'MARA, Richard
Methadone: the law and the clinics. Nation
211:242-4 S 21 '70
New terror in Latin America. Nation 210:518-19
My 4 '70

OMBUDSMAN (education)
Campus ombudsman: an emerging role. H. R.
Rowland. Ed Digest 35:28-31 F '70
Notes from a campus ombudsman. H. Lon-
don. Ed Digest 36:32-4 N '70

OMEGA system. See Radio in navigation

OMER, Mordechai
Pot can be more than just a pot: a rebuttal.
Craft Horiz 30:9 Ag '70

OMNIBUILDING. See Architecture, Modern

ON a wagon; story. See Singer, I. B.

ON the desert; story. See Zelver, P.

ON-the-job training. See Employees—Training

ONAGO-dori. See Japanese long-tailed fowls

ONASSIS, Aristotle Socrates
In the swim at Skorpiós with Jackie and Ari.
il pors Life 68:58-60 Je 26 '70 *
Jackie's fabulous Greek; excerpts from Those
fabulous Greeks. D. Lilly. pors Look 34:30-
6+ Je 30 '70 *
No one danced in the aisle; Olympic airways
Boeing 727. il Newsweek 76:27 Ag 3 '70 *
$20,000,000 honeymoon of Jackie Onassis; ex-
cerpt. F. Sparks. il Ladies Home J 87:122-4
Je '70 *

ONASSIS, Athina (Livanos) See Blandford,
A. L. O. S.-C.

ONASSIS, Jacqueline Lee (Bouvier) Kennedy
Dear Ros. il por Time 95:19 F 23 '70 *
From Jackie with love. il por Newsweek 75:25
F 23 '70 *
Happy Jackie, the sad Jackie, the bad Jackie,
the good Jackie. S. Sheehan. il pors N Y
Times Mag p 14-15+ My 31 '70 *
In the swim at Skorpiós with Jackie and Ari.
il pors Life 68:58-60 Je 26 '70 *
Jackie's fabulous Greek; excerpts from Those
fabulous Greeks. D. Lilly. pors Look 34:
44-6 Je 30 '70 *
New York life of Jacqueline Onassis. L.
Smith. il por Ladies Home J 87:56+ F '70 *
Onassis-Gilpatric letters. J. McLaughlin.
America 122:252+ Mr 7 '70 *
$10,000,000 jewels of Elizabeth Taylor &
Jacqueline Onassis. L. Smith. il pors La-
dies Home J 86:64+ D '69
$20,0000,00 honeymoon of Jackie Onassis; ex-
cerpt. F. Sparks. il Ladies Home J 87:122-4
Je '70 *

ONCOGENIC viruses. See Tumor viruses

ONCOGENS. See Cancer producing substances

ONE-bank holding companies. See Bank holding companies

ONE-dish meals. See Meals

ONE hundred words; drama. See Boiko, C.

ONE night stands of a noisy passenger; drama.
See Winters, S.

ONEIDA, N.Y.
Working city hall. il Am City 85:73 Ja '70

O'NEIL, Paul
Hottest candidate in either party. il pors
Life 69:26-9 O 30 '70
Little gift from your friendly banker. il Life
68:48-50A Mr 27 '70
Parting shots; Clarence the Ripper? il pors
Life 69:85-8 N 13 '70
Seattle. il Life 69:30-1 O 2 '70
Walter Hickel is an endangered species. il
pors Life 69:48-48B+ Ag 28 '70
You make so many friends here. il Life 68:46-
50 My 15 '70

about
He knows an iron fraudator when he sees
one. R. Graves. por Life 69:1 Ag 28 '70 *

O'NEILL, Jeanne Lamb
Chicago style: glass-house living at its lofti-
est. il Am Home 73:48-55+ F '70
Columbia, gem of America's new towns. il
Am Home 73:95+ My '70
Housewife's dilemma. Am Home 74:26+ Ja
'71
Ladies of the lanes. il Am Home 73:34+
S '70

O'NEILL, John William
Calculated risk; excerpts from address. Aviation W 92:13 My 25 '70

O'NEILL, Michael
Catholic schools and religious education.
America 122:338-41 Mr 28 '70
Education without schools. Ed Digest 36:
1-4 N '70
Giving Americans a choice; alternatives to
public education. America 122:66-70 Ja 24
'70
Religious education for all: finding the
means. il America 122:626-30 Je 13 '70

O'NEILL, William D.
How to build a town ski slope. il Am City
85:84+ Ag '70

ONGANIA, Juan Carlos
Coup no. 8. il por Newsweek 75:38+ Je 22
'70 *
Fall of a corporate planner. il Time 95:38 Je
22 '70 *

ONION buns. See Bread

ONION soufflés. See Soufflés

ONIONS
Fall onions down south. J. R. MacMahon.
il Org Gard & Farm 17:68+ Ag '70
Mulch-planted onions beat spring mud. J.
Krill. il Org Gard & Farm 17:46-7 F '70
Onions. Chem 43:22 N '70
See also
Alliums
Cookery—Vegetables
Shallots

ONO, Yoko
John Rennon's excrusive gloupie. C. McCarry.
il Esquire 74:204-5+ D '70 *

ONSTOTT, Elmer L.
Put celery in your garden. il Org Gard &
Farm 17:35-7 F '70

ONTARIO
See also
Timmins

Highways, Department of
Beehives protect snow-removal salt and pre-
vent water pollution. J. R. Fitzpatrick. il
Am City 85:81-3 S '70

ONTARIO, LAKE
Protecting a natural beach. J. E. Wilson. il
Cons 24:28-31 Ap '70

ONTARIO, Ohio
600 meters per day. R. Berryhill. il Am City
85:107-8 S '70

ONTARIO 500. See Automobile racing

ONTARIO motor speedway. See Speedways

ONUMA, Naoki, and others
Oxygen isotope fractionation between minerals and an estimate of the temperature
of formation. bibliog il Science 167:536-8 Ja
30 '70

OORT, Abraham H.
Energy cycle of the earth; with biographical
sketch. il Sci Am 223:33, 54-63 bibliog(p262)
S '70

OORT, J. H.
Galaxies and the universe. bibliog il Science
170:1363-70 D 25 '70

OOSTERHUIS, Huub
Prayer. Cath World 212:203-5 Ja '71

OP amps. See Amplifiers

OP art. See Art, Modern

OPAL
Opals, anybody? H. E. Mercer. il Travel 134:
24+ Jl '70

OPAQUE projectors. See Projectors

OPAVA, Czechoslovakia
Report:
Jaroslav Kricka's Czech Bethlehem. R.
Roucek. Opera N 35:40 D 19 '70

OPEL (automobile) See Automobiles, Foreign

OPEN admissions by colleges and universities.
See Colleges and universities—Entrance requirements

OPEN-air concerts. See Concerts

OPEN air moving picture theaters. See Moving
picture theaters, Open air

OPEN-air museums
See also
Agricultural museums

OPEN-air schools
Open-air school; Mexico city's Chapultepec park. il Américas 22:9-11 F '70
OPEN-air theater. See Theater, Open-air
OPEN fire cookery. See Cookery, Outdoor
OPEN house for Shakespeare; drama. See Miller, H. L.
OPEN sandwiches. See Sandwiches
OPEN space planning. See Land utilization
OPEN theater. See New York (city)—Theater
OPERA
Like, madness! interview, ed. by G. Loney. T. O'Horgan. por Opera N 35:6 N 21 '70
    See also
Libretto
Operas
Moving pictures—Musical films

Anecdotes, facetiae, satire, etc.
Enough of Stiffelio. E. V. Epstein. Opera N 34:16 F 14 '70
Tell it to the marines. S. Nathness. Opera N 35:20 S 5 '70

Appreciation
    See also
Opera—Student performances

Benefit performances
Music to my ears; Metropolitan presentation on behalf of benevolent and retirement funds. I. Kolodin. Sat R 53:28 Ap 25 '70

History and criticism
Bartók's Castle. J. W. Freeman. il por Opera N 35:6-7 O 31 '70
Benjamin Britten: twenty-five years of opera. G. Martin. Yale R 60:24-44 O '70
Curious girl; Puccini's girl, Minnie. R. Mohr. Opera N 34:24-5 Mr 14 '70
Death and transfiguration; Ariadne auf Naxos. M. O. Lee. il Opera N 34:24-5 Mr 28 '70
Druids of Gaul; Bellini's Norma. O. S. Rachleff. il Opera N 34:8-12 Ap 4 '70
Ebb and flow; fate of Aida's lovers. R. D. Daniels. il Opera N 35:30-1 D 19 '70
Epochs of opera:
    England and America. S. Levarie. il Opera N 34:26-31 Ja 31 '70
    Slavic countries. S. Levarie. il Opera N 34:24-9 Ja 24 '70
Fourth riddle; Puccini's Turandot. G. R. Marek. Opera N 34:24-5 F 21 '70
Handel and the opera seria. by W. Dean. Review
    Sat R 53:85+ F 28 '70. H. Weinstock
Harlot form. J. D. Merritt. il Opera N 35:6-7 Ja 9 '71
Melody beyond grief; Gluck's Orfeo ed Euridice. M. O. Lee. Opera N 35:24-5 Ja 9 '71
Play of light and shade; in Don Carlo. J. W. Freeman. Opera N 34:24-5 F 14 '70
Riddle of the Magic flute. A. Williamson. il Hi Fi sec I 20:66-9 F '70
Shocker at fifty-nine; Der Rosenkavalier. G. R. Marek. Opera N 34:24-5 F 28 '70
Sin city comes to Fun city; Mahagonny, the Brecht-Weill twenties shocker. R. Zachary. il por Opera N 34:8-12 Mr 14 '70
Star vehicle; Bellini's Norma. S. Jenkins. Opera N 35:14-15 D 19 '70

Instruction and study
Opera off the beat; Opera Barga. P. Elvins. il Opera N 34:14-16 My 16 '70
Teacher Tourel. E. Burns. il pors Opera N 34:20-1 Je 13 '70
    See also
North Carolina school of the arts, Winston-Salem

Stage lighting
How to light the stage. F. Bowers. il Opera N 34:26-9 Ap 4 '70
New light on festival opera. R. Jacobson. il Sat R 53:80-1 S 12 '70

Stage mechanism
Big wheel; Metropolitan opera's revolving stage. il Opera N 34:14-15 Ja 31 '70

Stage setting and scenery
Boris Aronson sketchbook. S. Jenkins. il por Opera N 35:21-3 Ja 2 '71
Floor plan for Figaro. il Opera N 34:21-3 Ap 11 '70
Whence a production? interview, ed. by F. Rizzo. T. Capobianco. il pors Opera N 34:26-9 Mr 21 '70

Stories
    See Libretto

Student performances
New audience; with student performance calendar 1970-71. R. A. Tuggle. il Opera N 35:17-24 N 21 '70
Points of view; student performances in this country and Canada. il Opera N 35:22 N 2 '70

Czechoslovakia
Epochs of opera: Slavic countries. S. Levarie. il Opera N 34:24-9 Ja 24 '70
Report; productions at Olomouc and Ostrava. R. Roucek. il Opera N 34:31 F 14 '70

France
Paris opera crisis. il Newsweek 75-85 F 2 '70
    See also
Opera, French

Germany (Federal Republic)
    See also
Bayreuth festival
Hamburg state opera company

Great Britain
Epochs of opera: England and America. S. Levarie. il Opera N 34:26-31 Ja 31 '70
Harlot form. J. D. Merritt. il Opera N 35:6-7 Ja 9 '71
It was great while it lasted; impresario of London opera society. M. R. Scott. il por Opera N 35:14-16 D 5 '70
New English Wotan; Figaro by Klemperer. T. Heinitz. Sat R 53:70 Mr 28 '70
    See also
Royal opera. Great Britain
Sadler's Wells opera

Italy
Arias and intermissions. W. Weaver. il Sat R 53:42-3 S 12 '70
First the words... D. Stivender. il Opera N 34:24+ F 7 '70
Then the music. J. C. Adams. il Opera N 34:25+ F 7 '70
    See also
Milan, Italy—La Scala

Korea (Republic)
Seoul first; opera version of R. E. Kim's The martyred. J. Wade. il por Opera N 35:14-17 S 5 '70

Russia
Epochs of opera: Slavic countries. S. Levarie. il Opera N 34:24-9 Ja 24 '70
    See also
Opera, Russian

United States
Does opera have a future? C. L. Osborne. Hi Fi 20:secI 60-5+ Mr '70
Epochs of opera: England and America. S. Levarie. il Opera N 34:26-31 Ja 31 '70
Loose lady; Bay area opera ACTION. S. Von Buchau. Opera N 35:6-7 O 10 '70
Plus ça change; U.S. opera survey. M. F. Rich. il Opera N 35:14-16 N 21 '70
U.S. calendar. See issues of Opera news published during opera season
War of Klitticlamma County. D. C. Daheim. il Opera N 34:8-11 Ja 24 '70
    See also
American opera society
Clarion music society, inc.
Metropolitan opera company
Metropolitan opera guild
New York city opera company
Opera society of Washington
Radio broadcasting—Operas
San Francisco opera company
Santa Fe opera company
Television broadcasting—Operas

History
Sopranos and six-guns; the frontier opera house as a cultural symbol. R. L. Davis. il Am West 7:10-17+ N '70
OPERA; opera. See Berio, L.
OPERA, French
Printed editions of André Campra's L'Europe galante. J. R. Anthony. bibliog f il Mus Q 56:54-73 Ja '70
OPÉRA, Paris. See Opera houses
OPERA, Russian
Realism as preached and practiced; the Russian opera dialogue. R. Taruskin. bibliog f il Mus Q 56:431-54 Jl '70
OPERA and society. See Music and society
OPERA and state. See Music and state
OPERA audiences. See Audiences
OPERA broadcasts. See Radio broadcasting—Operas
OPERA club, Metropolitan. See Metropolitan opera club

OPERA company of Boston
Report:
Flying Dutchman. H. Neville. il Opera N 34:30 Mr 21 '70
OPERA conducting. See Conducting (music)
OPERA critics. See Music critics
OPERA dancing. See Dancing
OPERA festivals. See Music festivals
OPERA films. See Moving pictures—Musical films
OPERA houses
Change in Buenos Aires; modernization of Teatro Colón. B. F. Carruthers. il Opera N 34:20-1 My 16 '70
Letter from Paris; the Opéra to be closed for repairs. Genêt. New Yorker 46:69 Ag 8 '70
Paris opera crisis. il Newsweek 75:85 F 2 '70
See also
Bayreuth festspielhaus
OPERA news (periodical)
Twenty questions: results of an Opera news reader survey. F. Merkling. il Opera N 35: 6-7 D 5 '70
OPERA patronage
Composers and poodles. M. Kalmanoff. Opera N 34:6 Ap 4 '70
OPERA quiz. See Radio broadcasting—Operas
OPERA singers
Alone with the voice. R. W. Hall. il Opera N 35:8-11 S 5 '70
Anna Moffo; interview. ed. by E. McDonald. A. Moffo. il pors House B 112:60-3 F '70
How to say it: a pronunciation guide for the Metropolitan opera's 1970-71 broadcasts. Opera N 35:28-9 D 12 '70
Making love to the public. W. Bender. pors Time 96:86 O 26 '70
Sherrill Milnes; interview. ed. by R. Hemming. S. Milnes. por Sr Schol 96:18 My 11 '70
Star vehicle: Bellini's Norma. S. Jenkins. Opera N 35:14-15 D 19 '70
Take notice of the words ... S. Hughes. il por Opera N 34:8-13 F 14 '70
Unique singers' dictionary; A concise biographical dictionary of singers. A. Favia-Artsay. il Hobbies 75:35-6+ Ap '70
See also
Singing
also names of opera singers, e.g. S. Milnes

Anecdotes, facetiae, satire, etc.
Mme X. J. W. Tomlinson. Opera N 34:16 Ja 31 '70
OPERA society of Washington
Ante bellum Aida; production of Koanga. il Time 97:56 Ja 4 '71
Le Comte Ory, with verve. P. J. Smith. il Hi Fi sec II 20:26 Ja '70
Koanga; F. Delius' slave opera. F. Stevenson. il Opera N 35:34-5 D 19 '70
Report: production of Britten's Turn of the screw. F. C. Smith. il Opera N 34:30 Ja 24 '70
OPERA tickets
La Scala's scalpers. S. Von Buchau. il Opera N 35:6-7 D 12 '70
OPERANT conditioning. See Conditioned responses
OPERAS
See also
Phonograph records—Operas

Analysis
Another turn: B. Britten's The turn of the screw. G. Martin. il Opera N 34:6-7 Mr 7 '70
Long line: classical melody carries romantic drama; Bellini's operas. J. W. Freeman. il Opera N 34:24-5 Ap 4 '70

Criticisms, plots, etc.
See name of composer for full entry
Aida. G. Verdi
Ariadne auf Naxos. R. Strauss
Un ballo in maschera. See Masked ball, below
Bluebeard's castle. B. Bartók
La Bohème. G. Puccini
Carmen. G. Bizet
Cavalleria rusticana. P. Mascagni
La Cenerentola. G. Rossini
Les contes d'Hoffman. See Tales of Hoffmann, below
Don Carlo. G. Verdi
Don Pasquale. G. Donizetti
Don Rodrigo. A. Ginastera
Elektra. R. Strauss
Ernani. G. Verdi
La fanciulla del West. See Girl of the golden West, below
Faust. C. F. Gounod
Fidelio. L. van Beethoven

Der fliegende Holländer. See Flying Dutchman, below
Flying Dutchman. R. Wagner
Girl of the golden West. G. Puccini
Help, help, the Globolinks! G. C. Menotti
Koanga. F. Delius
Lucia di Lammermoor. G. Donizetti
Lulu. A. Berg
Madame Butterfly. G. Puccini
Magic flute. J. C. W. A. Mozart
Mahagonny. K. Weill
Makropoulos affair. L. Janáček
Marriage of Figaro. J. C. W. A. Mozart
Masked ball. G. Verdi
Mefistofele. A. Boito
My heart's in the highlands. J. Beeson
Norma. V. Bellini
Le nozze di Figaro. See Marriage of Figaro, above
Of mice and men. C. Floyd
Opera. L. Berio
Orfeo ed Euridice. C. W. Gluck
Otello. G. Verdi
Pagliacci. R. Leoncavallo
Parsifal. R. Wagner
Pelléas et Mélisande. C. Debussy
Peter Grimes. B. Britten
Riders to the sea. R. Vaughan Williams
Roberto Devereux. G. Donizetti
Romeo and Juliet. C. F. Gounod
Der Rosenkavalier. R. Strauss
Tales of Hoffmann. J. Offenbach
Tamerlano. G. F. Händel
That's what happens. E. Krenek
Tosca. G. Puccini
La Traviata. G. Verdi
Turandot. G. Puccini
Turn of the screw. B. Britten
Die zauberflöte. See Magic flute, above
OPERATIC coaches. See Singing teachers
OPERATIC composition. See Composition (music)
OPERATIC costume. See Costume, Theatrical
OPERATIC direction. See Operatic production and direction
OPERATIC production and direction
Artists and lovers; photographs of La Bohème. Opera N 34:21 Ja 24 '70
Church and state; photographs of Don Carlo. Opera N 34:21-3 F 14 '70
Different Don; interview. ed. by H. E. Phillips. R. Tobin. por Opera N 34:12 Ap 11 '70
Division in Gaul; photographs of Norma. Opera N 35:16-18 D 19 '70
Easter passion; photographs of Mascagni's Cavalleria rusticana. il Opera N 34:21 F 7 '70
Fable from Venice; photographs of Turandot. Opera N 34:21-3 F 21 '70
Fidelio in action; photographs of Fidelio by G. Fitzgerald. Opera N 35:14-15 Ja 2 '71
Hello, Minnie! photographs of the Girl of the golden West. Opera N 34:21-3 Mr 14 '70
How to light the stage. F. Bowers. il Opera N 34:26-9 Ap 4 '70
Lady of fashion; photographs of La Traviata. il Opera N 34:21-3 Mr 21 '70
Last laugh; photographs of Leoncavallo's Pagliacci. il Opera N 34:22-3 F 7 '70
Loss of identity; 1967 New York city opera version of Puccini's Madama Butterfly. il Opera N 34:21-3 Mr 7 '70
Magic in the air; new Parsifal. S. Jenkins, jr. il Opera N 35:11 S 19 '70
Mirror of nobility; photographs of Der Rosenkavalier. Opera N 34:21-3 F 28 '70
Music to my ears; productions of Cavalleria rusticana and Pagliacci at the Metropolitan. I. Kolodin. Sat R 53:21 Ja 24 '70
New light on festival opera. R. Jacobson. il Sat R 53:80-1 S 12 '70
Old bachelor and the young widow; photographs of Donizetti's Don Pasquale. Opera N 35:21-3 D 5 '70
On with the show; photographs of Ariadne auf Naxos. Opera N 34:21-3 Mr 28 '70
Price of freedom; photographs of Tosca. Opera N 35:21-3 D 12 '70
Sacred grove; photographs of Norma. Opera N 34:21-3 Ap 4 '70
Sweet sorrow; photographs of Gounod's Roméo et Juliette. Opera N 34:21-3 Ap 18 '70
Take notice of the words ... S. Hughes. il por Opera N 34:8-13 F 14 '70
Triangle by the pyramids; photographs of Aida. Opera N 35:27-9 D 19 '70
Triumph of love; photographs of Gluck's Orfeo ed Euridice. Opera N 35:21-3 Ja 9 '71
Wagner line; photographs of Chicago lyric opera's Flying Dutchman. il Opera N 34:21-3 Ja 31 '70
What a conductor does. E. Buckley. il por Opera N 34:26-9 Mr 28 '70

OPERATIC production and direction—*Cont.*
Whence a production? interview, ed. by F. Rizzo, T. Capobianco. il pors Opera N 34: 26-9 Mr 21 '70
Zeffirelli rides again; photographs of Mets Cavalleria rusticana and Pagliacci rehearsals. il Opera N 34:14-16 F 7 '70
See also
College operas, revues, etc.
OPERATIC training. See Opera—Instruction and study
OPERATION Breakthrough. See United States —Housing and urban development, Department of
OPERATION Deep Freeze. See Antarctic exploration
OPERATION Green Thumb. See Green thumb, inc.
OPERATION SEEK. See New York (city). City university
OPERATION Sidewinder; drama. See Shepard, S.
OPERATION Tabarin. See Antarctic exploration
OPERATIONAL amplifiers. See Amplifiers
OPERATIONS, Surgical. See Surgery
OPERATIONS research
See also
Network analysis (planning)
OPHIUCHUS (constellation) See Constellations
OPIE, Iona (Archibald)
Games children play. il por Time 95:59 Ja 26 '70
OPIE, Peter
Games children play. il por Time 95:59 Ja 26 '70
OPINION, Public. See Public opinion
OPINION, Student. See Student opinion
OPINION research. See Public opinion polls
OPIUM; drama. See Brynner, R.
OPIUM trade
China
Tremble! Intensely tremble! excerpts from The dragon wakes. C. Hibbert. il por Horizon 12:114-19 Sum '70
OPORTO, Portugal
North of Lisbon. J. H. Winchester. il Travel 134:34-9 Jl '70
OPPEN, George
Election; poem. Nation 210:126 F 2 '70
OPPENHEIM, Dennis
Artist under stress. D. Davis. il Newsweek 75: 119 My 25 '70 *
Back to nature. il pors Time 95:62-3+ Je 29 '70 *
Sound enclosed land area, Milano, Italy. J. Gruen. Vogue 156:33 Ag 15 '70 *
OPPENHEIMER, Frank
Doctor Oppenheimer's exploratorium. A. Richmond. il Nation 211:6-9 Jl 6 '70 *
OPPENHEIMER, Jack C. and Miller, L. A.
Environmental problems and legislative responses. il Ann Am Acad 389:77-86 My '70
OPPENHEIMER, Joel
They lick the platter clean. R. J. Griffin. Nation 211:53-4 Jl 20 '70 *
OPPENHEIMER, Julius Robert
Great weapons heresy, by T. W. Wilson, jr. Review
America 123:266 O 10 '70. J. B. Kelley *
Life 68:12 F 27 '70. R. E. Lapp *
Telling it like it isn't. J. Burnham. Nat R 22: 129 F 10 '70
Tiger by the tail. A. Weinstein. Nation 210: 501-3 Ap 27 '70 *
OPPENHEIMER and company
Oppenheimer treads a venturesome path. il Bsns W p42+ Ap 11 '70
OPPENHEIMER fund, inc.
How one fund swam upstream. Bsns W p85 Jl 18 '70
OPPORTUNITIES industrialization centers, inc.
Opening doors to opportunity. il pors Nations Bsns 58:48-9+ Ap '70
OPPRESSION
Obligations of oppressed minorities. M. Walzer. bibliog f Commentary 49:71-80 My '70; Discussion. 50:14-16 Ag '70
OPTICAL art. See Art, Modern
OPTICAL communication systems. See Light communication systems
OPTICAL illusions
Distortions of apparent velocity: a new optical illusion. J. T. Enright. bibliog il Science 168:464-7 Ap 24 '70
Moon illusion explained on the basis of relative size. F. Restle. bibliog il Science 167: 1092-6 F 20 '70
Moon illusions. D. Fitzpatrick. il Sci Digest 67:66-7 Je '70

Mueller-Lyer illusion; effect of age, lightness contrast, and hue. R. H. Pollack. bibliog il Science 170:93-5 O 2 '70
Of optical illusions, from figures that are undecidable to hot dogs that float. M. Gardner. il Sci Am 222:124-7 My '70
Ponzo perspective illusion as a manifestation of space perception. H. Leibowitz and others; reply with rejoinder. W. Schiff. Science 168:395 Ap 17 '70
Strange Enright illusion. D. L. Heiserman. il Sci Digest 68:15-17 N '70
OPTICAL instruments
See also
Lenses
Measuring instruments, Optical
Microscope and microscopy
Schlieren apparatus
Telescopes
OPTICAL interference. See Interference (light)
OPTICAL memory devices. See Memory devices (computers)
OPTICAL modulators. See Modulators
OPTICAL tracking of space vehicles. See Space vehicles—Tracking
OPTICAL trade
See also
Photographic apparatus industry and trade
OPTICS
See also
Electron optics
Electrooptics
Interference (light)
Perspective
Photographic optics
Resolving power (optics)
Spectrum analysis
OPTICS, Physiological
See also
Optical illusions
Phosphenes
Sight
OPTIONS
See also
Put and call transactions
Stock purchase options
OPTOELECTRONICS. See Electron optics
OPTON, Edward M. jr. and Duckles, Robert
Mental gymnastics on Mylai. il New Repub 162:14-16 F 21 '70
—and Sanford, Nevitt
Toward a critical social science. Trans-Action 7:4-7 Mr '70
OPUS Dei (secular institute)
Opus Dei; Spain on the cross; tr. by L. Bensky. Y. Le Vaillant. il Ramp Mag 8:14+ F '70
ORA, John P. See Tinsley, D. G. jt. auth.
ORAISON, Marc
Father Marc Oraison assaulted outside Paris church. Chr Cent 87:287 Mr 11 '70 *
Strange voyage, by M. Oraison. Review
America 123:150-1 S 12 '70. T. H. Clancy *
ORAL contraceptives. See Contraceptives
ORAL history
JFK at the summit; Kremlinologists views on first Kennedy-Khrushchev encounter. il Newsweek 76:32-3 S 7 '70
JFK tapes: how it was. il pors Newsweek 76: 23-4+ Ag 31 '70
When America was singing Buddy, can you spare a dime? H. S. Resnik. Sat R 53:27-30 Ap 18 '70
ORAL reading. See Books and reading—Reading aloud
ORAL Roberts university, Tulsa, Okla.
One who DAIRed: a dial access system. W. W. Jernigan. il por Wilson Lib Bul 44:653-7 F '70
Oral Roberts: small but oh, my! R. H. Boyle. il Sports Illus 33:64-5 N 30 '70
ORAL surgery
Face architecture: how oral surgery can remake your face. S. Morini. il Vogue 156:98-101 Ag 15 '70
ORANGE COUNTY, Calif.
Report on the two cultures. T. Goodhue. New Repub 162:12-13 Je 20 '70
ORANGE peel, Candied. See Confectionery
ORANGEBURG, S.C.
See also
South Carolina. State college
Riots
Orangeburg massacre, by J. Nelson and J. Bass. Review
Commonweal 93:331-2 D 25 '70. L. H. Madaras
ORATORIOS
Divine dissonance; Penderecki's Utrenja. T. W. Moore. il por Chr Cent 87:1455-7 D 2 '70
See also
Phonograph records—Oratorios

ORBACH, Jerry
Jerry Orbach; interview. ed. by M. Sutphen.
il pors House B 112:64-7 F '70
ORBITAL workshop. See Space stations
ORBITALS, Molecular. See Molecular orbitals
ORBITING primate experiment. See Space
flight—Physiological aspects
ORBITS
See also
Moon—Orbit
ORCHARD heating. See Frost protection
ORCHARDS. See Fruit culture
ORCHESTRA shells
Concert shell for a Roman ruin; Caesarea
festival theater, Israel. G. C. Izenour. il
Arch Rec 148:67-74 D '70
ORCHESTRAL conductors. See Conductors
(music)
ORCHESTRAL music
See also
Phonograph records—Orchestral music
ORCHESTRAS
Debuts & reappearances; New York concerts.
See issues of High fidelity section II
Music to my ears; visit to Carnegie Hall of
the Rotterdam philharmonic. N. Cousins.
Sat R 53:44-5 Ap 18 '70
Report:
Concert performance of Alessandro Scar-
latti's Eraclea. N. Zaslow. Opera N 34:
25 Je 13 '70
See also
Ensemble playing
also names of orchestras, e.g. Boston
symphony orchestra

Finance
Silent spring of our symphonies. A. Ames. il
Sat R 53:81-3 F 28 '70
Symphonic strike season. P. Hart. il Sat R
53:47-9+ S 26 '70; Discussion. 53:60-1 O 31
'70
ORCHID exhibits. See Flower exhibits
ORCHIDS
Lady of the night orchid. C. M. Fitch. il
Horticulture 48:34-5 Jl '70
Orchids around the year. G. J. Sessler. il
Horticulture 48:34-5+ Mr; 32-3+ Je; 22-3+
S '70
Specialists in sex: orchids; with photographs
by I. Penn. A. West. il Vogue 156:136-42+
D '70
ORDAZ, Gustavo Díaz. See Díaz Ordaz, G.
ORDER of St John of Jerusalem. See Malta,
Knights of
ORDER processing
See also
Publishers and publishing—Order processing
ORDNANCE
See also
Weapons systems
ORDÓÑEZ, Cayetano
Perhaps not great, but hardly gutless. J.
McCormick. il por Sports Illus 32:58-9 Je
29 '70 *
Sun also sets. S. Adams. il Sports Illus 32:
56-60+ Je 29 '70 *
ORDOVICIAN formation. See Geology, Strat-
igraphic—Ordovician
ORE deposits
See also
Prospecting
O'REGAN, Brendan
Irishman with chutzpah. por Duns 96:75 N
'70 *
OREGON
Sand for the people; Oregon decision on pub-
lic use of beachland. Nation 210:196 F 23 '70
See also
Architecture, Domestic—Oregon
Camps—Oregon
Columbia River
Conservation of resources—Oregon
Crater Lake National Park
Education—Oregon
Fishing—Oregon
Forests and forestry—Oregon
Geology—Oregon
Hells Canyon
Hunting—Oregon
Skis and skiing—Oregon
Umatilla County

Industries
Industry answers a governor's challenge. V.
Louviere. Nations Bsns 58:21 N '70

Theater
See Theater—United States

OREGON, State university, Portland
Convenient clubbing; findings of Human
rights commission on police action against
demonstrators. Nation 211:358 O 19 '70
OREGON TRAIL
Emigrants' guide for women. T. Brown. il
Am West 7:12-17+ S '70
History comes alive along the road to Ore-
gon. R. Dunlop. il Todays Health 48:44-9+
S '70
OREGON, University, Eugene
Not guilty but. . ; case of J. Froines. G.
Johnson. New Repub 163:9-10 Jl 25 '70
Too dangerous to teach; J. Froines and Irv-
ing Wainer. G. Johnson. New Repub 163:18-
19 S 5 '70; Reply. C. T. Duncan. 163:31 O 3
'70
O'REILLY, Jane
Elaine's. il Holiday 47:69-70 Ap '70
ORFEO ed Euridice; opera. See Gluck, C. W.
ORFIELD, Antonia
People are talking about. . . il por Vogue 156:
88-9 Ag 1 '70 *
ORFIELD, Gary
People are talking about. . . il por Vogue
156:88-9 Ag 1 '70 *
ORGAN
Electronic organs. il Consumer Bul 54:7-14
Ja '71
Mighty theater organ sounds again. R. W.
Schaaf. il Hi Fi 20:MA16+ O '70
Organ as synthesizer. il por Time 95:60 Je 8
'70
Theater organs make a comeback; San Fran-
cisco-Sacramento area. il Sunset 145:50+ S
'70
What's a film classic without the mighty
Wurlitzer? Avenue photoplay society in
San Francisco presenting weekly programs
of early films and concerts. M. Mann. il
Pop Phot 66:27-8+ Ja '70
ORGAN, Color. See Color organ
ORGAN music
See also
Church music
Phonograph records—Organ music
ORGAN of corti. See Labyrinth (ear)
ORGANELLES. See Cells
ORGANIC chemistry. See Chemistry, Organic
ORGANIC farms. See Farms, Organic
ORGANIC fertilizers. See Fertilizers and man-
ures
ORGANIC food. See Food, Organic
ORGANIC food stores. See Food stores
ORGANIC gardening
Anyone can homestead on two acres. J. Cox.
il Org Gard & Farm 17:81-2+ O '70
Choose plants that will grow for you! R. J.
Wyndham. il Org Gard & Farm 17:102-3 S
'70
City gardeners beat pollution and inflation.
M. Franz. il Org Gard & Farm 17:26-33 Ag
'70
Education of an organic farmer. C. White-
head. il pors Org Gard & Farm 17:33-7
N '70
Enough life to support new fruit. G. Shearer.
il por Org Gard & Farm 17:52-3 S '70
Environmentalist's response to the Organic
food symposium. D. Orvis. Org Gard &
Farm 17:46-7 Ag '70
Forty years of farming naturally. G. L'Al-
lemand. il Org Gard & Farm 17:92-5 N '70
Fred Jenkins' incredible organic gardens. M.
Brandies. il Org Gard & Farm 17:49-51 Ap
'70
Garden calendar. See issues of Organic gard-
ening and farming
Good life on one acre, continued. O. Saba-
tine. il pors Org Gard & Farm 17:34-9 My
'70
Happy gardening on a hilltop. B. Kennard. il
Org Gard & Farm 17:48-9 D '70
Help farmers become organic. J. Olds. Org
Gard & Farm 17:38-9 Je '70
His farm includes a great garden. A. G.
Jensen. il pors Org Gard & Farm 17:107-10
O '70
Hottest gardeners in the west. M. C. Gold-
man. il Org Gard & Farm 17:69-72+ F '70
How organic farming can save our air. E.
Gibbons. Org Gard & Farm 17:106+ N '70
How to get an experiment station to test
organic gardening. J. Olds. Org Gard &
Farm 17:100-1 N '70
In 1970, the topics are all organic. J. Olds. il
Org Gard & Farm 17:32-4 Ja '70
New England sodbusting, second time
around. J. Vivian. il pors Org Gard &
Farm 17:32-7 Jl '70
New ideas for homesteading. R. Rodale. il
Org Gard & Farm 17:31-5 Mr '70

ORGANIC gardening—*Continued*
Non-stop gardening. O. R. Griffin. il Org Gard & Farm 17:86-7 Je '70
Organic gardening idea goes back a long way. R. Rodale. Org Gard & Farm 17:29-31 Ja '70
Organic growing of vegetables, a success story. il Sunset 144:188-9 Je '70
Organic living for half a million people. J. Olds. il Org Gard & Farm 17:40-4 Mr '70
Organic revolution goes to college. M. C. Goldman. il Org Gard & Farm 17:56-61 Ja '70
Our homestead just grew like crabgrass! J. Belanger. il Org Gard & Farm 17:96-9 N '70
Putting the garden to bed for the winter. W. Bowers and L. Bowers. il Org Gard & Farm 17:25-7 O '70
You'll find the better gardeners in the smaller towns. M. Franz. il Org Gard & Farm 17:46-9 N '70
See also
Compost
Food, Organic
Mulching
Vegetable gardening, Home
Whole earth cooperative

Competitions
See Gardening—Competitions

Study and teaching
Organic classrooms are here! M. C. Goldman. il Org Gard & Farm 17:66-72 S '70
We can do the impossible; organic gardening course at University of California at Berkeley. il Org Gard & Farm 17:23-6 Je '70

ORGANIC gardening and farming (periodical)
Presenting the organic harvest award winners. il Org Gard & Farm 17:35-55 Ja '70

ORGANISATION commune africaine et malgache. See African and Malagasy common organization

ORGANIZATION, Social. See Social organization

ORGANIZATION charts
RSVP cycles, by L. Halprin. Review
Arch Forum 133:78 N '70. G. Clay

ORGANIZATION for economic cooperation and development
Bitter medicine for the West's inflation. il Bsns W p92-3 N 21 '70
Europe thinks the U.S. is steadying; views of OECD staff. il Bsns W p58-9 Ag 8 '70
OECD, its economic outlook for the 1970's. Mo Labor R 93:45-7 O '70
OECD ministerial meeting held at Paris; statement; with text of communique, May 22, 1970. N. Samuels. Dept State Bul 62:811-14 Je 29 '70
World experts prescribe strong medicine for inflation. il U S News 69:17-18 D 7 '70
See also
International institute for the management of technology (proposed)

ORGANIZATION for European nuclear research. See European organization for nuclear research

ORGANIZATION of African unity
African ambassadors honored by President Nixon; exchange of toasts, March 23, 1970. R. M. Nixon; S. E. Peal. Dept State Bul 62:522-5 Ap 20 '70
Ethiopia and the Pan-African movement, 1945-1963. C. G. Contee. il por Negro Hist Bul 33:122-5 My '70
Lusaka manifesto; excerpts from statement; April 14-16, 1969. Cur Hist 58:173-5 Mr '70
Money has no color; question of dialogue with South Africa. il Newsweek 76:47 N 30 '70
Seventh anniversary of the OAU; text of message, May 25, 1970. W. P. Rogers. Dept State Bul 62:752 Je 15 '70
See also
African and Malagasy common organization

ORGANIZATION of American states
Action for progress; message to the Secretary General of the Organization of American states. R. M. Nixon. Américas 22:1 Ap '70
Ambassadors of Guatemala and Ecuador new OAS council officers. il Américas 22:43 Ja '70
Amended OAS charter goes into effect. il Américas 22:43-5 Ap '70
Community and diversity; excerpt from address, April 14, 1970. A. C. Flores. il pors Américas 22:12-17 Je '70
Hemisphere; comp. by G. Meek. See issues of Américas
How wars end in Latin America. B. Wood. bibliog f Ann Am Acad 392:40-50 N '70
New council officers installed on Pan American day. il Américas 22:44 My '70
New OAS; eightieth anniversary message. G. Plaza. por Américas 22:2-3 Ap '70

OAS in a period of transition; statement, March 17, 1970. J. J. Jova. Dept State Bul 62:529-34 Ap 20 '70
OAS permanent council honors twenty-fifth anniversary of the U.N; statement. J. J. Jova. Dept State Bul 63:637-8 N 16 '70
Repression in Brazil: protest vs. protocol. T. Quigley. Commonweal 93:366 Ja 15 '71
Streamlined structure for the General Secretariat. il Américas 22:43-4 F '70
See also
Inter-American cultural council

General assembly
First OAS General assembly held. Américas 22:44 S '70
First special session of the OAS General assembly held at Washington; address, with text of resolution. W. P. Rogers. Dept State Bul 63:115-19 Jl 27 '70
OAS General assembly. F. Amiama-Tió. il pors Américas 22:2-5 S '70

Special training program (PEC)
For Latin Americans: a rural development course in Italy. il Américas 22:28-30 Ja '70

ORGANIZATIONS. See Associations, institutions, etc.

ORGANIZED crime. See Crime and criminals—United States; Mafia; Racketeering

ORGANIZED crime control act of 1970. See Crime prevention

ORGANIZED labor. See Trade unions

ORGANOMETALLIC compounds
Lab bench; ferrocene; a molecular sandwich. J. H. J. Peet. bibliog il por Chem 43:31-4 Ap '70
Superconductivity in layered structure organometallic crystals. F. R. Gamble and others. bibliog il Science 168:568-70 My 1 '70

ORGANS. See Organ

ORGEL, Stephen
(tr) See Giraut de Bornelh. Alba
(tr) See Virgil. Eclogue II

ORIANS, Gordon H. and Pfeiffer, E. W.
Ecological effects of the war in Vietnam. bibliog il Science 168:544-54; 169:1030 My 1, S 11 '70

ORIENT. See Asia; Far East

ORIENTAL art. See Art, Oriental

ORIENTAL astronomical association. See Astronomical societies

ORIENTAL cookery. See Cookery, Oriental

ORIENTAL poppies. See Poppies

ORIENTAL religions. See Religions

ORIENTAL rugs. See Rugs and carpets, Oriental

ORIENTATION
Celestial rotation: its importance in the development of migratory orientation. S. T. Emlen. bibliog il Science 170:1198-201 D 11 '70
Extraoptic celestial orientation in the southern cricket frog acris gryllus. D. H. Taylor and D. E. Ferguson. bibliog il Science 168:390-2 Ap 17 '70
Homing behavior, orientation, and home range of salamanders tagged with tantalum-182. D. M. Madison and C. R. Shoop. bibliog il Science 168:1484-7 Je 19 '70
Orientation by pigeons: is the sun necessary? W. T. Keeton; reply with rejoinder. K. Schmidt-Koenig and D. L. McDonald. Science 168:152-3 Ap 3 '70
Terrestrial and aquatic orientation in the starhead topminnow, fundulus notti. C. P. Goodyear. bibliog il Science 168:603-5 My 1 '70
See also
Echolocation (physiology)

ORIENTATION (architecture)
McCune house, Londonderry. Vt. il Arch Rec 147:74-5 mid-My '70

ORIENTATION of teachers. See Teachers—Adjustment

ORIENTEERING (sport)
Orienteering. J. G. Hutchinson. il Parks & Rec 5:45+ F '70

ORIGAMI
Paper magic of origami. L. Stowe. il pors Read Digest 97:196-200 Ag '70
Playful art of origami. il Good H 170:162 F '70

ORIGIN of life. See Life (biology)—Origin

ORIGIN of man. See Man—Origin and antiquity

ORIGIN of species. See Species

ORINASE. See Tolbutamide

ORINGER, Judy
(tr) See Beauvoir, S. de. On aging
(tr) See Gavi, P. Eruption in India

ORIOLES
Baltimore oriole. H. H. Harrison. il Nat Wild-
life 7:16-18 O '69
ORIOLES (baseball) See Baseball clubs
ORION nebula. See Nebulae
ORISSA
Orissa: past and promise in an Indian state.
B. McDowell. il Nat Geog 138:546-77 O '70
ORKIN, Samuel
Sam Orkin's navy. il por Am Heritage 21:120
Ap '70 *
ORLANDO, Fla.
Disney world wakes sleepy Orlando. il Bsns
W p42-4 N 14 '70

Music

Report:
Offenbach's Tales of Hoffmann. M. E.
Peltz. Opera N 34:32 Mr 21 '70

Negroes

Ghetto youth are this doctor's bag; Wash-
ington shores association for recreation
center. il pors Ebony 25:100-2+ S '70
ORLANDO furioso; drama. See Ronconi, L.
ORLAREY, Maurice
Build a hydraulic lift for your tractor. il Pop
Mech 133:172-5 Je '70
ORLEANS, Leo A. and Suttmeier, R. P.
Mao ethic and environmental quality. bibliog
Science 170:1173-6 D 11 '70
ORLEANS COUNTY, Vt.
Americana by the acre; county fair.   E.
Hoagland. il Harper 241:109-14+ O '70
ORLEN, Steven
Keeping watch; poem. Poetry 117:165 D '70
November; poem. Poetry 116:19 Ap '70
ORLY airport. See Paris—Airports
ORME, J. E.
Multirange transistor checker. il Electr World
83:82-3 Ap '70
ORMEROD, J. G. See Sirevag, R. jt. auth.
ORMOND, Clyde
What, no caviar! il Outdoor Life 146:60-3+
N '70
ORMOND, John
Comment. R. B. Shaw. Poetry 117:110-11 N
'70 *
ORNAMENTAL gardening. See Topiary work
ORNAMENTAL glass. See Glass, Ornamental
ORNAMENTS (music) See Embellishment (mu-
sic); Embellishment (vocal music)
ORNE, Jerrold
Academic library building in 1970. il Library
J 95:4107-12 D 1 '70
Architects' fees; their place in library plan-
ning. il por Library J 95:4099-106 D 1 '70
Undergraduate library. il por Library J 95:
2230-3 Je 15 '70
ORNITHINE decarboxylase. See Decarboxylase
ORNITHOLOGY
Biology of the way-out. J. Eastman. Natur
Hist 79:24-9 My '70
Could you be an ornithologist? quiz. J.
Daugherty and M. Daugherty. il Sci Digest
67:78-9+ Ja '70
ORÓ, J. and others
Organogenic elements and compounds in sur-
face samples from the Sea of Tranquillity.
bibliog il Science 167:765-7 Ja 30 '70
OROSZLAN, Stephen, and Gilden, R. V.
Immune virolysis: effect of antibody and
complement on C-type RNA virus. bibliog
il Science 168:1478-80 Je 19 '70
O'ROURKE, John
Sourdough Jack's garden bonanza. il pors
Org Gard & Farm 17:46-8 Je '70
O'ROURKE, John J.
Freelance job idea: public relations service.
il Writers Digest 50:28-31 N '70 (to be cont)
ORPHANED swimming pool; story. See Up-
dike, J.
ORPHANS and orphan asylums
To give or not to give? Korean orphan care
as big business. W. G. Henderson. Chr Cent
87:294-5 Mr 11 '70
ORR, Bobby
Cup runneth over. Time 95:74 My 25 '70 *
It's gotta be Orr, or else. M. Mulvoy. il Sports
Illus 33:28-30+ O 19 '70 *
Mr O and the sack of New York. M. Mulvoy.
Sports Illus 32:20-1 Ap 27 '70 *
Phenomenal Mr Orr. il por Newsweek 75:94
My 18 '70 *
Sportsman of the year. J. Olsen il por Sports
Illus 33:36-7+ D 21 '70 *
Tea party for Bobby's Bruins. G. Ronberg.
il por Sports Illus 32:18-21 My 4 '70 *
To save or score, try Orr. il pors Life 68:30-3
F 27 '70
Top-rated, under-rated, over-rated! H. L.
Masin. por Sr Schol 96:21 Mr 16 '70 *

ORR, John B. and Nichelson, F. P.
Radical suburb and expansive man; excerpt
from The radical suburb. Cur 122:3-10 O
'70
ORR, William I.
Care and handling of coaxial connectors the
quick foolproof way. il Pop Electr 33:47-9
Ag '70
ORSY, Ladislas M.
Faith in focus. America 122:162, 189, 221, 246,
276, 303-4 F 14-Mr 21 '70
Questions for pilgrims. America 123:59-63 Ag
8 '70
ORTEGA, Joseph K. E. and Gamow, R. I.
Phycomyces: habituation of the light growth
response. bibliog il Science 168:1374-5 Je 12
'70
ORTH, Debbie
Time has somehow lost me: poem. Horn Bk
46:77 F '70
ORTH, H. Richard, and Cherwony, Walter
People look at transit. il Am City 85:126+
Je '70
ORTHODONTICS
Urges orthodontic care at a tender age. To-
days Health 48:85 O '70
ORTHODOX Eastern church
Orthodox theologians reassess their tradition;
International conference of Orthodox theo-
logians. C. B. Ashanin. Chr Cent 87:1392-4
N 18 '70
See also
Ethiopic church
ORTHODOX Eastern church, Russian
Diplomatic Russian; replacement of patriarch
of Moscow and of all Russia. por Newsweek
75:96+ My 25 '70
Orthodox harmony. America 122:402 Ap 18 '70
Patriarch Alexei. Chr Cent 87:555 My 6 '70
Soviet archbishop released from prison, re-
instated by church. M. Bourdeaux. Chr
Cent 87:674 My 27 '70
**ORTHODOX Eastern church, Russian, in the
United States.** See Orthodox Eastern church
in the United States
**ORTHODOX Eastern church in the United
States**
American orthodoxy? il Time 95:92+ Mr 16
'70
Americanizing Greek Orthodoxy. A. Egge-
broten. il Chr Today 14:30-1 Jl 31 '70
Herman the Wonderworker; first American
saint of the Orthodox church. por Time
96:48-9 Ag 24 '70
Orthodox church in America. T. G. Styliano-
poulos. bibliog f Ann Am Acad 387:41-8 Ja
'70
Orthodox crisis; American Russian Orthodox
church. America 122:177 F 21 '70
Patriarchate to permit independent Orthodox
church of America. Chr Cent 87:199 F 18 '70
Russian Orthodox union; with editorial comment. D. Tinder. Chr Today 14:26, 37 F 27
'70
Russians and Greeks: the costs of unilateral
ecumenism. il Chr Cent 87:284-5 Mr 11 '70
Schism in orthodoxy? il Newsweek 75:84 F 16
'70
ORTHODOX Eastern church in Turkey
Succession to Eastern Orthodox patriarchy, a
problem in Turkey. L. Hansen. Chr Cent
87:547 Ap 29 '70
ORTHOPEDIA
Good news for broken bones. Sci Digest
67:58 Je '70
New new hip; ball-and-socket arrangement
with stainless steel ball in polyethylene
socket. il Time 95:68 Ap 27 '70
Surgery that aids arthritis victims. il Bsns W
p 116+ Ap 25 '70
See also
American academy of orthopedic surgeons
ORTHOPEDIC surgery. See Orthopedia
ORTHOPTERA
See also
Stick insects
ORTHWINE, Rudolf
Rudolf Orthwine. W. Como. il pors Dance
Mag 44:20-2 S '70 *
ORTMANN, Jon. See Day, R. jt. auth.
ORTON, Joe
What the butler saw. Criticism
Commonweal 93:95 O 23 '70 *
New Yorker 46:106 My 16 '70 *
Newsweek il 75:121 My 18 '70 *
Time 95:72 My 18 '70 *
ORVIETO cathedral. See Cathedrals—Italy
ORVIS, Deonne
Environmentalist's response to the Organic
food symposium. Org Gard & Farm 17:46-7
Ag '70

ORWELL, George, pseud.
Halfway to 1984. L. Malkin. il por Horizon 12:32-9 Spr '70 *
OSAKA, Japan

Explosions

Mass slaughterhouse. il Time 95:27 Ap 20 '70

Gardens
See also
Osaka, Japan—Worlds fair, 1970—Gardens

Worlds fair, 1970

All's fair for youth at Expo '70. J. Rich. il Seventeen 29:146-7+ Mr '70
All's fair in Japan. M. Gough. il Harp Baz 103:60+ F '70
Businessman's guide to Japan's Expo 70. Bsns W p 139-40 Mr 14 '70
Designing the environment. E. Galantay. il Nation 211:134-8 Ag 31 '70
Electronics at Expo. D. Lachenbruch. Radio-Electr 41:4 Jl '70
Expo '70. M. F. Schmertz. il Arch Rec 147:115-28 Je '70
Expo '70. M. Suntag. il Electr World 83:36-7 Mr '70
Expo '70: East meets West. il Newsweek 75:68-78 Mr 9 '70
Expo '70: Osaka's $2 billion blowout. il Time 95:20-4 Mr 2 '70
Expo '70: super show in Japan. B. Hosokawa. il Read Digest 96:149-53 Ja '70
Expo '70, the curtain goes up. R. Yung. Travel & Camera 33:23-6 Mr '70
Expo '70: U.S. vs. Russia at the fair. il U S News 68:50-2 Mr 2 '70
Fair Japan waited a century for. P. Kunhardt. il Life 69:8 Jl 17 '70
Glitter in Osaka. Sr Schol 96:17 Mr 2 '70
Going to visit EXPO '70? il U S News 68:69 Je 1 '70
Japan's Expo '70, it's a sampler of all the Far East. il Sunset 144:88-91 My '70
Kansai: Japan's historic heartland. T. J. Abercrombie. il Nat Geog 137:295-339 Mr '70
Letter from Osaka. E. J. Kahn, jr. New Yorker 46:88+ Je 6 '70
Mysterious, jet-age East. L. Barry. il Pop Phot 66:46+ Mr '70
One colossal binge. il Time 95:32 Mr 23 '70
Preview peek: Expo '70. il Travel 133:66-8 F '70
World's fair, Asian style. il Time 95:68-71 Ap 20 '70

Art
Ceramics at Expo '70. J. W. Larson. il Ceram Mo 18:37 Je '70
Expo '70: Japan's world fair at Osaka. J. Vanderwall. il Am Artist 34:22-6+ Ap '70
Improbable marriage; Art and technology exhibit. D. Davis. il Newsweek 75:100-1 Ap 20 '70
Orient express. E. C. Munro. il Art N 69:48-51+ Sum '70
Osaka fair: Expo '70. J. Plaut. il Craft Horiz 30:12-13 My '70
U.S. pavilion at Expo '70; symposium. il Art in Am 58:60-79 Mr '70

Gardens
Visit to Japan's Expo '70. S. Kolb. Home Gard 57:36 Jl '70
Water gardens, Japan Expo '70. il House & Gard 138:58-63 Ag '70

Moving pictures
Magnamultiscreen at Expo '70. H. V. Fondiller. il Pop Phot 66:102-3+ My '70

Music
Yesterday & tomorrow at Expo '70. E. Cunningham. il Hi Fi 20:MA22-3 N '70

Pavilions
Expo 70. P. Blake. il Arch Forum 132:30-41 Ap '70
Expo '70. L. Burrows. il Life 68:37-43 Mr 27 '70
Expo '70. M. F. Schmertz. il Arch Rec 147:118-27 Je '70
Expo '70: Japan's world fair at Osaka. J. Vanderwall. il Am Artist 34:22-6+ Ap '70
Glimpse of the future; Takara Beautilion. R. Boyd. il Arch Forum 132:32-5 Mr '70
Onward and upward with the arts; EAT and the Pepsi pavilion at Expo '70. C. Tomkins. New Yorker 46:83-4+ O 3 '70

Religious exhibits
Expo 70: few mindful of what is man? J. Huffman. Chr Today 14:40 My 8 '70
Trouble with the fair; youthful protesters trying to block Christian pavilion. J. Huffman. Chr Today 14:52 Mr 13 '70

OSBORN, Clifford T.
Try an opinion survey. il Am City 85:80+ D '70
OSBORN, David Lawrence
Going to the fair? How to understand the Japanese. il N Y Times Mag p22-3+ F 22 '70
OSBORN, Elburt F.
Bureau of mines: long search for new director ends. L. J. Carter. por Science 170:309-10 O 16 '70 *
Coal producers breathe easier. Bsns W p26 N 7 '70 *
Honeymooner. pors Forbes 106:53 D 1 '70 *
OSBORNE, Conrad L.
Does opera have a future? Hi Fi 20:secI 60-5+ Mr '70
Karajan closes the ring. il Hi Fi 20:77-9 S '70
Naked Carmen laid bare. Hi Fi 20:120 S '70
OSBORNE, John, 1907-
Nixon watch. See issues of New republic

about
Nixon watcher. il por Newsweek 75:60 Je 22 '70 *
OSBORNE, John, 1929-
Looking back without anger. C. Sigal. il Commonweal 92:186-8 My 8 '70 *
OSBORNE, Karl
Carolina blues. il pors Outdoor Life 146:70-1+ O '70
New hotspot for channel bass. il por Outdoor Life 145:70-3+ My '70
OSBORNE, Milton
Cambodia: runaway coup d'etat. Nation 210:678-80 Je 8 '70
OSBORNE, Vera Cook
Reading do's and don'ts. il Todays Ed 59:48-9 Mr '70
OSCAR Reinhart collection. See Art—Private collections
OSCARS (prizes) See Academy awards (moving pictures)
OSCILLATORS
Amateur scientist: curious oscillators that involve salt water, flame and hot wire; ed. by C. L. Stong. il Sci Am 223:221-2+ S '70; Reply. A. D. Moore. 223:129 O '70
Build a stable ham VFO. I. Queen. il Radio-Electr 41:69 S '70
Ten emitter-coupled oscillator circuits. F. Maynard. il Radio-Electr 41:33-5 My '70
VHF-UHF drain-dip oscillator. A. E. McGee, jr. il Pop Electr 33:69-76 O '70
See also
Multivibrators
OSCILLATORS, Crystal
Solid-state technology invades microwave frequencies; Gunn effect devices. il Aviation W 92:204-5+ Je 22 '70
Three-level oscillator in indium phosphide. G. B. Lubkin. Phys Today 23:19-20 D '70
OSCILLOGRAPHS
FET dual-trace scope switch. T. B. Mills. il Radio-Electr 41:36-8 Jl '70
Leader model LBO-501 oscilloscope. il Electr World 84:58 Jl '70
OSCILLOSCOPES. See Oscillographs
OSING, Olga
Maelstrom of the Arctic. il Sea Front 16:104-9 Mr '70
OSLO

Music
Report:
Norwegian opera's production of Wagner's Fliegende Holländer. W. Shank. Opera N 34:30 Mr 28 '70
Production of Lars Johan Werle's Dream about Thérèse. W. Shank. il Opera N 35:24 O 10 '70
OSMAN, Osman Ahmed
Osman the efficient. il por Time 96:69 Jl 13 '70 *
OSMOSIS
See also
Biological transport
Dialysis
Permeability
OSMUNSON, Robert Lee
Higher education as viewed by college and university presidents. bibliog Sch & Soc 98:367-70 O '70
OSORIO, Carlos Manuel Arana. See Arana Osorio, C. M.
OSPREYS
Notes and comment: ospreys in danger from DDT. New Yorker 46:19 Ag 15 '70
OSRIN, Ray
The thinker. il Am For 76:11 Ap '70
OSTEOGENESIS imperfecta
Epilogue to a dream. G. Geisman. Redbook 134:89+ Mr '70

OSTEOPOROSIS. See Bones—Diseases

OSTEOSPERMUM. See Cape marigolds

OSTER, Gerald
Phosphenes; with biographical sketch. il Sci Am 222:10, 82-7 bibliog (p 126) F '70

OSTHAUS, Edmund H.
Dogs that live forever. K. Evans and G. Evans. il por Field & S 75:234-5+ Je '70 *

OSTRANDER, Sheila, and Schroeder, Lynn
Russian farmer's big joke on communism. Farm J 93:30A O '69

OSTRICH farms and farming
On the raising of ostriches for little fun and less profit. J. Fabry and M. Knight. il Am West 7:22-6 Jl '70

OSTROM, John H.
Archaeopteryx: notice of a new specimen. bibliog il Science 170:537-8 O 30 '70
How birds began to fly. il Time 96:50 D 7 '70 *

O'SULLIVAN, Maureen
Umbrella: story. Ladies Home J 87:60-1 Ja '70

OSWALD, Lee Harvey
Assassination of John F. Kennedy, by A. H. Newman. Review
   Nat R 22:606 Je 16 '70 *
   Sat R 53:29-30+ O 17 '70. F. J. Cook *
Marina Oswald Porter: seven years after Dallas. J. West. il pors Redbook 135:57-9+ Ag '70 *

OSWALD, Marina
Marina Oswald Porter: seven years after Dallas. J. West. il pors Redbook 135:57-9+ Ag '70 *

OSWALD, Rudolph A.
Union bargaining goals in the 1970's. bibliog f Mo Labor R 93:40-2 Mr '70

OSWEGO, LAKE. See Lake Oswego, Ore.

OTELLO; opera. See Verdi, G.

OTHELLO; drama. See Shakespeare, W.—Plays

OTHMER, Donald F.
Water and life. bibliog il por Chem 43:12-17 N '70

OTIS elevator company
Blood, sweat, but no miracles. il Forbes 106:18-19 O 1 '70
Otis goes on an acquisition ride. il Bsns W p132+ Je 6 '70

OTOLITHS. See Labyrinth (ear)

OTSEGO Hall (historic house) See Cooperstown, N. Y.—Historic houses, etc.

OTT, George
Is the bald eagle doomed? il Nat Wildlife 8:4-9 Ap '70
Mighty mouse hunters. il Nat Wildlife 8:22-7 F '70
Vicious genius of the woods. il Nat Wildlife 8:14-16 Je '70

OTT, Vesperella E. See Kersten, C. S. jt. auth.

OTTERS
   See also
   Sea otters

OTTINGER, Richard Lawrence
Conservative upset in the making in liberal New York? il pors U S News 69:30-1 Ag 31 '70 *
Ottinger: study of a quiet candidate. T. Buckley. pors N Y Times Mag p40-1+ O 25 '70 *

OTTO, archduke of Austria
Where are they now? il por Newsweek 75:20 Mr 16 '70 *

OTTO, Frei
To Moma, from Germany. N. R. Piene il Art in Am 58:118-19 My '70 *

OTTO, Herbert A.
Has monogamy failed? Sat R 53:23-5+ Ap 25 '70

OTTO and Bruno; story. See Strong, J.

OUACHITA MOUNTAINS
Death row; Gillham dam project on the Cossatot River. W. Jack, jr. il Audubon 72:139 S '70

OUDES, Bruce J.
Press-card disguise. il Nation 211:561-4 N 30 '70
White and green and the rising sun. Nation 210:149-51 F 9 '70

OUGHTON, Diana
Destruction of Diana. L. Franks and T. Powers. Read Digest 97:49-58 N '70
Memories of Diana. il por Time 95:21 Mr 30 '70 *

OUR town; drama. See Wilder, T. N.

OURAY, Colo.
Ouray: last of the great silver boom towns. il Holiday 47:78-9 My '70

OUT island regatta, Great Exuma Island. See Regattas

OUT of print books. See Books—Out of print books

OUT our way (cartoons) See Cowboys—Caricatures and cartoons

OUTBOARD motor boat racing. See Motor boat racing

OUTBOARD motor boats
80,000 miles by outboard. R. Marston. il Yachting 127:67+ Ap '70
Greatest bass boat ever? G. Gresham. il por Field & S 74:56-7+ Ja '70
Outboarding finesse. J. Martenhoff. il Yachting 128:69+ D '70
Shakedown cruise. J. Martenhoff. il Yachting 127:72-3+ Mr '70
Vest-pocket fishermen; photographs. E. Schweikardt. Sports Illus 32:28-33 Je 22 '70

OUTBOARD motors
Fifty horses from 41.5 cubic inches. J. Roe. il Pop Sci 197:74-5 Jl '70
How it works: the outboard motor. C. Miller. il Motor B 126:16 Ag '70
New boats and motors. J. A. Emmett. il Outdoor Life 145:66-72+ Ja '70
New outboards for '71. G. W. Reiger. il Pop Mech 134:92-5+ O '70
1971 outboard preview. B. McKeown. il Mech Illus 66:78-81 O '70
Outboard auxiliary power. J. Martenhoff. il Yachting 129:104-5+ Ja '71
Outboard gallery '71. E. Nabb. Motor B 126:86-8+ O '70
Outboard motors: the sweet, elusive sound of speed. J. Roe. il Pop Sci 197:56-8 D '70
Outboard parade for '71. F. M. Paulson. il Field & S 75:92-6 D '70
Outboards for fishing boats. J. A. Emmett. il Outdoor Life 145:28+ My '70
Outboards for '71. M. Crook. il Yachting 128:52-4+ O '70
Outstanding outboard; pioneer inventors. F. M. Paulson. il Field & S 75:80-1+ Je '70
Small outboard motors. il Consumer Rep 35:364-71 Je '70
So you want a quiet outboard? G. Reiger. il Pop Mech 133:142-3 F '70
Testing the new shipmates: 85-hp, 4-cycle outboard on the Whaler's big brother. J. Roe. il Pop Sci 196:90-1 My '70

Exhaust
Scavenging to provide high performance. E. Nabb. il Motor B 126:75-6 Ag '70

History
Four-cycle engine. E. Nabb. il Motor B 126:73-4 S '70

Maintenance and repair
Controls maintenance. C. Miller. il Motor B 125:73 Ap '70
Outboard motor maintenance. C. Miller. il Motor B 125:70-1 Ap '70
Power train maintenance. C. Miller. il Motor B 125:72 Ap '70

Purchasing
Buying a used outboard motor. B. Weis. il Mech Illus 66:120-1+ Mr '70

OUTDOOR Christmas decorations. See Christmas decorations, Outdoor

OUTDOOR cookery. See Cookery, Outdoor

OUTDOOR education
   See also
   Camping—Educational aspects
   Conservation of resources—Study and teaching
   Nature study
   Outward bound schools

OUTDOOR furniture. See Furniture, Outdoor

OUTDOOR games. See Games

OUTDOOR life
Gifts that last forever, love of the outdoors. T. Trueblood. il Field & S 75:14-15+ D '70
I'm worried about E. B. Wittich. R. Starnes. Field & S 75:12+ Je '70
Outdoors with Wynn Davis. W. Davis. See issues of Mechanix illustrated
Vacationing in the great outdoors. N. D. Ford. il Har Yrs 10:6-14 F '70
   See also
   Camping
   Camps
   Fishing
   Houseboats
   Hunting
   Mountaineering
   Nature
   Picnics
   Vacations
   Walking
   Wilderness survival

Bibliography
Books & flicks (cont) Field & S 74:26+ Ja; 38+ Mr; 75:24 My; 22+ Jl; 109 Ag; 32, 71 S; 34 O '70

OUTDOOR lighting. See Lighting, Outdoor

OUTDOOR meals
Best ways to handle food out-of-doors. il Good H 171:145 Jl '70
Cooking and eating outdoors; with recipes, menus and equipment. L. S. Pappas. il House & Gard 137:97+ Je '70
Dinner at 8:00, twice as romantic in the garden; with summer party recipes. il Bet Hom & Gard 48:34+ Je '70
Dinner on the tailgate. E. W. Manning. il Farm J 94:64-5 My '70
Summer take-outs. il Ladies Home J 87:74-5+ Je '70
See also
Barbecue cookery
Clambakes
Cookery, Outdoor
Picnics

OUTDOOR moving picture theaters. See Moving picture theaters, Open air

OUTDOOR occupations. See Occupations

OUTDOOR parties. See Lawn parties

OUTDOOR recreation. See Recreation

OUTDOOR rooms
Build a beautiful patio. V. Troiano. il Mech Illus 66:84-6+ Jl '70
Careful planning of a patio. M. A. Lochry. il Home Gard 57:48-9 Ja '70
Deck for summer living; at Sterling Forest gardens. il Home Gard 57:24-5 Mr '70
Enjoy the wide outdoors on an open deck. il Pop Mech 133:140-5+ Je '70
From sixteen church pews, a spacious deck. il Sunset 144:226 My '70
House in a sunken garden. il House & Gard 137:86-9 Je '70
How to turn all outdoors into an enchanting summer room. W. Baldwin. House & Gard 138:10-12 Jl '70
Instead of a patio, a new ground-level deck. il Sunset 144:94-5 Je '70
Living room that spills outdoors. il Bet Hom & Gard 48:68-9 My '70
Outdoor living in an entry court. il Bet Hom & Gard 48:57 My '70
She built it herself, in just five weeks. il Sunset 144:246+ Ap '70
Slopes to level with. il Bet Hom & Gard 48:50-1 Ja '70
See also
Roof gardens

OUTDOOR schools. See Open-air schools

OUTDOOR showers. See Shower baths

OUTDOOR survival. See Wilderness survival

OUTDOOR theater. See Theater, Open-air

OUTER HEBRIDES. See Hebrides

OUTER seven (trade area) See European free trade association

OUTER space. See Space, Outer

OUTER space committee. See United Nations—Committee on the peaceful uses of outer space

OUTLAWS
Black knight of the Zayante. R. H. Dillon. por Am West 7:20-1 Jl '70
Quick & the dead; photographs. il Am West 7:36-7 Ja '70
Ringo. J. Burrows. Am West 7:17-21 Ja '70
Sam Bass & the myth machine. H. H. Smith. por Am West 7:31-5 Ja '70

OUTLER, Albert C.
Agenda for a new generation. J. C. Evans. Chr Cent 87:382-3 Ap 1 '70 *

OUTPUT (production) See Production

OUTPUT of workers. See Labor productivity

OUTWARD bound schools
Bald Island revisited, and loved again; Hurricane Island school. E. Gibbons. Org Gard & Farm 17:90-3 D '70
Way to the top; program for executives. J. L. Dotson, jr. il Newsweek 75:80 Ap 27 '70

OUTWATER, Eric B.
Our effluent society. il Nat R 22:203-4 F 24 '70

OVEN cleaners. See Cleaning compositions

OVENS
How to test your own oven. Sunset 144:152+ F '70
See also
Electronic ovens

OVER-the-counter market. See Stocks—Marketing

OVERALL, James C. Jr, and Glasgow, L. A.
Fetal response to viral infection: interferon production in sheep. bibliog il Science 167:1139-41 F 20 '70

OVERDRIVE transmission. See Automobiles—Transmission

OVERDUE books. See College libraries—Circulation, loans, etc; Libraries—Circulation, loans, etc.; Libraries—Fines

OVERHEAD irrigation. See Irrigation, Overhead

OVERLAND journeys to the Pacific
Emigrants' guide for women; preparations for the arduous five-month journey along the Oregon Trail. T. Brown. il Am West 7:12-17+ S '70
See also
Donner party

OVERLAND PARK, Kan.
Everyone into the pool, and a pool for everyone. D. E. Pipes. il Am City 85:91-2 N '70

OVERPOPULATION. See Population—Overpopulation

OVERSEAS employees. See Americans in foreign countries—Employment

OVERSEAS forces. See United States—Armed forces—Forces in foreign countries

OVERSEAS private investment corporation
Birth pains. Forbes 106:44 S 15 '70

OVERSEAS shipholding group. See Shipowners

OVERSEAS telephone. See Telephone, Long distance

OVERSEAS weekly
Inspector General. Newsweek 76:74 S 14 '70

OVERSTREET, Bonaro W.
Different-and the same; excerpt from radio series The Overstreet outlook. PTA Mag 64:19 Je '70
Human cry; excerpts from radio broadcast. PTA Mag 64:23 F '70
Mentor for our time; excerpt from radio series The Overstreet outlook. PTA Mag 65:21 D '70
One teaching experience. PTA Mag 64:21 Ap '70
We and our unwanted experiences. PTA Mag 65:21 O '70

OVERSTREET, Harry Allen
Obituary
Pub W 198:249 Ag 31 '70

OVERTIME
Changes in factory workweek as an economic indicator. H. M. Willacy. bibliog f il Mo Labor R 93:25-32 O '70

OVERTON park. See Memphis, Tenn.—Parks and playgrounds

OVERWEIGHT. See Corpulence

OVIPOSITION
Chemical inducers of oviposition for the corn earworm, heliothis zea (Boddie) R. L. Jones and others. bibliog il Science 168:856-7 My 15 '70
Pineal function and oviposition in Japanese quail: superior cervical ganglionectomy and photoperiod. C. L. Ralph and others. bibliog il Science 170:995-7 N 27 '70

OVSHINSKY, Stanford R.
Great hopes from Ovshinsky's little switches grow. L. Lessing. il por Fortune 81:110-14+ Ap '70 *

OWEN, Christopher
Weekend house must be simple to run; interview. por House & Gard 138:26+ D '70

OWEN, E. Ken
Ten-inch Newtonian with counterpoised canopy. il Sky & Tel 40:169-74 S '70

OWEN, Jean Z.
First aid for story-sag. Writer 83:14-17 O '70

OWEN, Nathan Richard
Out to clean up if peace comes. il por Bsns W p32-3 O 3 '70 *

OWEN, Robert H.
Night pastor dies. Chr Cent 87:350 Mr 25 '70 *

OWEN, Tobias
Atmosphere of Jupiter. bibliog il Science 167:1675-81 Mr 27 '70
—and Roberts, D. L.
New horizon in space exploration. il Bul Atom Sci 26:23-9 F '70

OWEN, Wilfred
Urban housing and transportation: a new partnership. bibliog f Cur Hist 59:290-5+ N '70

OWENS, Gwinn, and Blumberg, S. A.
Planes of Penn central. Nation 211:404 O 26 '70

OWENS, Jesse
My life as a black man; excerpts from Blackthink. por Read Digest 96:126-31 My '70

OWENS, Major
Failure of libraries. il por Library J 95:1701-4 My 1 '70

OWENS, Michael Joseph
Improbable genius was Mike Owens. R. H. Mulford. il pors Nations Bsns 58:96-7 Ja '70

OWENS, Steve
Czar of all the rushers. H. L. Masin. por Sr Schol 95:25 O 13 '69

OWENS-Illinois, inc.
Bottle-maker bids to blunt can's edge. Bsns W p86 Mr 14 '70

OWINGS, Larry
Good littler man wins big. H. Weiskopf. Sports Illus 32:72+ Ap 6 '70 *

OWINGS, Nathaniel Alexander
Mass transit and the cities: mobility and place in America's future. Cur Hist 59:95-9+ Ag '70

OWL monkeys. See Monkeys

OWL on every post; story. See Babb, S.

OWLS
Great horned owl. P. M. Kelsey. il Cons 24:32 F '70
Marsh owl. E. H. Forbush. il Audubon 72: 20-1 Mr '70
Mighty mouse hunters. G. Ott. il Nat Wild-life 8:22-7 F '70
Unknown owl; great gray owl; painting. G. Coheleach. Audubon 72:56-7 Jl '70

OWYHEE project, Idaho. See United States—Land management, Bureau of

OXFORD, England

Galleries and museums

Oxford line; selection of Italian drawings belonging to the Ashmolean museum, on exhibition at the Wildenstein gallery. J. Russell. il Art N 69:34-6+ O '70

OXFORD pendaflex corporation
Oxford file. R. Levy. por Duns 96:52-3 Ag '70

OXFORD, University
Opinion: an English voice; American student at Oxford. D. Moyer. por Mlle 70:26+ Mr '70

OXFORD university press
Homographics, quaternions and notations. il Forbes 106:35-6 D 1 '70

OXIDATION
Acidic mine drainage: the rate-determining step. P. C. Singer and W. Stumm. bibliog il Science 167:1121-3 F 20 '70; Discussion. 169:98, 504 Jl 3, 31 '70
Autoxidation of insect lipids: inhibition on the cuticle of the American cockroach. P. W. Atkinson and A. R. Gilby. bibliog Science 168:992 My 22 '70
Oxidation of a polymer surface with gas-phase singlet($^1\Delta g$) oxygen. M. L. Kaplan and P. G. Kelleher. bibliog il Science 169: 1206-7 S 18 '70

OXIDATION, Physiological
Alcohol oxidation in rats inhibited by pyra-zole, oximes, and amides. D. Lester and G. D. Benson. bibliog il Science 169:282-4 Jl 17 '70
Hepatic microsomal mixed function oxidase; report of International symposium on mi-crosomes and drug oxidations. J. B. Schenkman. Science 168:612-13 My 1 '70
Metabolic dependence of fast axoplasmic transport in nerve. S. Ochs and N. Ranish. bibliog il Science 167:878-9 F 6 '70
Oxygen cycle. P. Cloud and A. Gibor. il Sci Am 223:110-18+ bibliog(p263) S '70
Reduced nicotinamide-adenine dinucleotide phosphate oxidase: activity enhanced by ethanol consumption. C. S. Lieber and L. M. DeCarli. bibliog il Science 170:78-80 O 2 '70
See also
Cytochromes

OXIDES
Metallic and nonmetallic behavior in transi-tion metal oxides. I. G. Austin and N. F. Mott. bibliog il Science 168:71-7 Ap 3 '70
Singlet molecular oxygen from superoxide anion and sensitized fluorescence of organ-ic molecules. A. U. Khan. bibliog il Sci-ence 168:476-7 Ap 24 '70
See also
Hydrogen oxides

OXIMES
See also
Butyraldoxime

OXYGEN
Atmospheric oxygen in 1967 to 1970. L. Machta and E. Hughes. bibliog il Sci-ence 168:1582-4 Je 26 '70
Breathing easy; amount of oxygen in the at-mosphere. Sci Am 223:54 O '70
Man's oxygen reserves. W. S. Broecker. bibliog Science 168:1537-8 Je 26 '70; Same with title Enough air. il Environ 12:26-31 S '70; Discussion. 12:40-3 D '70
Oxygen cycle. P. Cloud and A. Gibor. il Sci Am 223:110-18+ bibliog(p263) S '70
Oxygen in the air and water. Chem 43:3 O '70

Singlet molecular oxygen from superoxide anion and sensitized fluorescence of or-ganic molecules. A. U. Khan. bibliog il Sci-ence 168:476-7 Ap 24 '70
Substitute for breathing. A. J. Snider. Sci Digest 67:54 Je '70
Synthetic oxygen-carrying compound. il Chem 43:21 Mr '70
See also
Hyperbaric oxygenation

Industrial applications

Oxygen can replace aeration to lower waste-water purification costs; Unox system. il Am City 85:90 Je '70

Isotopes

Oxygen isotope fractionation between minerals and an estimate of the temperature of for-mation. N. Onuma and others. bibliog il Science 167:536-8 Ja 30 '70
Solar activity index: validity supported by oxygen isotope dating. J. R. Bray. bibliog il Science 168:571-2 My 1 '70

OXYGEN, Solid
Solid oxygen. A. Trammell. il Flying 87:78-9 Jl '70

OXYGEN apparatus
Inflight oxygen generator studied. N. S. Him-mel. il Aviation W 93:62-3 O 12 '70
See also
Repiratory apparatus

OXYGEN in the body
Response of olfactory bulb neurons to X-rays as a function of nasal oxygen concentration. G. P. Cooper. bibliog il Science 167:1726-7 Mr 27 '70

OXYGEN utility dome (proposed) See Domes

OXYGENATION, Hyperbaric. See Hyperbaric oxygenation

OXYTOCIN
Birth by appointment. il Newsweek 76:85 Jl 20 '70

OYAMA, Vance I. and others
Search for viable organisms in a lunar sam-ple. bibliog il Science 167:773-5 Ja 30 '70

OYSTER culture
Oysters are going places. J. G. Niemeier. il Sea Front 16:13-19 Ja '70
Oysters: planning the environment for an industry. D. H. Wallace. il Cons 25:28-30 O '70

OYSTER fisheries. See Shellfish fisheries

OYSTER-shell scale
Department fights beech disease and de-cline; beech bark disease, an insect-fun-gus complex. W. H. Buzzard, jr. and J. H. Risley. il Cons 24:10-13 Je '70

OYSTERS
Comeback of the oyster. S. Davenport, jr. il N Y Times Mag p22-4+ D 20 '70
Oysters are going places. J. G. Niemeier. il Sea Front 16:13-19 Ja '70
See also
Cookery—Shellfish

OZARK MOUNTAINS
Ozarks: fragments of the American wilder-ness. L. Payton. il Am Lib 1:256-65 Mr '70
Through Ozark hills and hollows. M. W. Ed-wards. il Nat Geog 138:656-89 N '70

OZARK NATIONAL SCENIC RIVERWAYS
People problems on the Riverways. J. P. Jackson. il Nat Parks & Con Mag 44:24-7 Ag '70

OZAWA, Seiji
Far out in S.F. por Newsweek 76:117 D 14 '70 *

OZONE
Is ozone trapped in the solid carbon dioxide polar cap of Mars? H. P. Broida and others. bibliog Science 170:1402 D 25 '70
Stratospheric ozone with added water vapor: influence of high-altitude aircraft. H. Har-rison. bibliog il Science 170:734-6 N 13 '70
See also
Plants, Effect of ozone on

Physiological effects

Ozone and vitamin E. B. D. Goldstein and others. bibliog il Science 169:605 Ag 7 '70

P

PADF. See Pan American development founda-tion

PADRES (Padres asociados para derechos re-ligiosos eclesiasticos) See Priests—Associa-tions, institutions, etc.

PAL. See Police athletic league

PAM. See Pyridine aldoxime methiodide

PBC (Public broadcasting corporation) See
   Corporation for public broadcasting
PC flash connectors. See Photography—Elec-
   tronic equipment
PCB (polychlorinated biphenyls) See Diphenyl
   compounds
PCCI. See United States—President's commit-
   tee on consumer interests
PCPA (para-chlorophenylalanine) See Phenyl-
   alanine
PGF² alpha. See Prostaglandins
pH. See Hydrogen ion concentration
Ph.D degrees. See Degrees, Academic
PIE. See Pacific intermountain express company
PLA. See Pennsylvania library association
PLA (People's liberation army) See China
   (People's Republic)—Armed forces
PMC. See Patino mining corporation
PPA. See Publishers' publicity association
PRI (party of the institutional revolution)
   See Political parties—Mexico
PTA. See Parents and teachers associations
PUT (programmable unijunction transistor)
   See Transistors
PAAN, Ming-to
   Christianity lives on in China. Chr Today 14:
   3-5 F 27 '70
PAANANEN, Roy
   How to power a bicycle with a car battery.
   il por Pop Sci 197:79+ O '70
PABST, Augie
   Pabst's blue ribbon. J. Lamm. il por Motor T
   22:46-8 D '70 *
PACE, Eric
   Violent men of Amman. il N Y Times Mag
   p8-9+ Jl 19 '70
PACEMAKER, Artificial (heart)
   Atom-powered heartbeats. Time 95:58 My 18
   '70
   Atomic heart. il Newsweek 75:91-2 My 11 '70
   Now: atomic power to keep your heart beat-
   ing. A. S. Freese. il Pop Mech 134:104-7+ S
   '70
PACIFIC coast
   Long curving shore from Alaska to Baja; with
   excerpts from Edge of a continent, by D. G.
   Kelley. T. H. Watkins. il Am West 7:18-31
   N '70
      See also
   Fishing—Pacific coast
PACIFIC countries
      See also
   Anzus council
   United States—Commerce—Pacific countries
         Politics
   Nations of the Pacific; symposium. bibliog f
   Cur Hist 58:193-246 Ap '70
PACIFIC Far East line, inc.
   Trucker's oceangoing partner. Bsns W p48
   O 3 '70
PACIFIC intermountain express company
   Driving toward a merger; proposed Ryder-
   PIE merger. il Bsns W p45-6 My 2 '70
PACIFIC ISLANDS. TRUST TERRITORY OF.
   See Trust Territory of the Pacific Islands
PACIFIC NORTHWEST. See Northwest
PACIFIC radio fire; story. See Brautigan, R.
PACIFIC REGION
      See also
   Paul VI, pope—Visit to Asia and the Pacific
   Region
PACIFIC regional ballet festival. See Dance
   festivals
PACIFIC rocket society
   World's first steam rocket mail flight. il
   Space World G-9-81:35-9 S '70; Discussion.
   G-12-84:47-8 D '70
PACIFIC Southwest airlines
   Local growth benefits Pacific Southwest. W.
   S. Hieronymus. il Aviation W 92:36-7 My 11
   '70
   Pacific Southwest plans to buy five L-1011s
   for $75 million. N. S. Himmel. Aviation W
   93:29 S 7 '70
PACIFIC studies center
   Black Monday's Sunday allies. il Ramp Mag
   8:34-8 Ja '70
PACIFIC TRUST TERRITORY. See Trust Ter-
   ritory of the Pacific Islands
PACIFICA foundation
   Barron's pacification. J. Deedy. Common-
   weal 92:210 My 15 '70
PACIFICATION programs in Vietnam. See Vi-
   etnamese war, 1957- —Pacification programs
PACIFISM
   Christians and Caesar's taxes. F. Zahn. il
   Cur Cent 87:1349-52 N 11 '70
   Do pacifists harm peace? E. Van Den Haag.
   il Nat R 22:1344-5+ D 15 '70

Domestic origins of peace. R. Randle. Ann
   Am Acad 392:76-85 N '70
Power: the enshrined heresy. R. Samson.
   Nation 212:14-20 Ja 4 '71
War termination as a problem in civil-mili-
   tary relations. M. H. Halperin. bibliog f Ann
   Am Acad 392:86-95 N '70
      See also
   Conscientious objectors
   Peace
   Vietnamese war, 1957- —Protests, demonstra-
   tions, etc, against

         History
   World war I and the liberal pacifist in the
   United States. C. Chatfield. bibliog f Am
   Hist R 75:1920-37 D '70
PACIFISTS. See Pacifism
PACINI, Giuseppe
   Recording Pacinis; G. Farrar and A.
   Granforte. A. Favia-Artsay. il Hobbies
   75:35-6+ Jl '70
PACK, Robert
   Apocalypse in black and white; poem. Sat R
   53:40 Mr 7 '70
   Pack rat; poem. Harper 240:40 Ap '70
         about
   Comment. N. Sullivan. Poetry 116:123 My
   '70 *
   Recurrences. X. J. Kennedy. Nation 210:378-
   80 Mr 30 '70 *
PACK mules. See Asses and mules
PACK transportation
   God save the mule; effect of mechanization
   on pack mules. G. Hallam. il Am For 76:
   4-5+ Ag '70
PACK trips. See Horseback trips
PACKAGE tours. See Travel
PACKAGES, Wrapping of. See Wrapping of
   packages
PACKAGING
   Cost of living; supermarket's bewildering ar-
   ray of sizes, shapes, and prices. B. Furness.
   por McCalls 97:36+ Mr '70
   Package design, its art and function; analysis
   of ten olive oil cans. M. Glaser and J. Sny-
   der. il Am Artist 34:14-15 D '70
   Real reason farmers buy in bulk. H. Fretz.
   il Farm J 94:19 My '70
   Shrink packaging adapted for palletizing. il
   Aviation W 93:94 O 26 '70
      See also
   Pressure packaging

      Laws and legislaton
   One of our bouillon cubes is missing. il Con-
   sumer Rep 35:248-51 Ap '70
      See also
   Labels—Laws and legislation
   Unit pricing
PACKARD, David
   Challenge to industry; excerpts from address.
   Aviation W 93:7 Ag 31 '70
   Military spending; impact on business; inter-
   view. il por U S News 69:44-8 Ag 3 '70
   Packard: defense on a diet; interview. ed. by
   A. A. Butkus. por Duns 96:10-14 Ag '70
   Packard details milestone plan; excerpts.
   Aviation W 92:7 Je 15 '70
   What's the cost? excerpts from address. Avi-
   ation W 92:9 Je 1 '70
         about
   Packard urges defense decentralization; with
   excerpts from address. W. S. Hieronymus.
   Aviation W 93:7, 15-16 Ag 31 '70 *
   Pentagon's powerful no. 2 man. il por Bsns W
   p94-5+ Mr 21 '70 *
PACKARD, Frederick
   Le tourisme euphonique; poem. New Yorker
   46:90 My 23 '70
PACKARD, George V.
   Pick up your purse, coach, and let's go. il
   Sports Illus 33:88-90+ N 30 '70
PACKARD, Vance
   Packard on Vance Packard. Trans-Action 7:
   10 Je '70
PACKING for shipment
   Wrap-up on packaging; excerpts from ad-
   dress. M. Townsend. Pub W 198:46-7 Jl 27 '70
PACKING industry. See Meat industry and
   trade
PACKING of luggage
   Tips on packing a car for travel. il Good
   H 171:147 Ag '70
PACKWOOD, Robert W.
   Senator for ZPG. K. Crawford. Newsweek
   75:33 Mr 23 '70 *
PACTS of mutual assistance. See International
   security
PADDLE steamers. See Steamships and steam
   boats

PADDLES, Canoe. See Canoe paddles
PADEREWSKI, Ignace Jan
Great Chicago piano war. P. Hume and R. Hume. il pors Am Heritage 21:16-21 O '70 *
PADOW, Judy
Dances by Judy Padow; Emanu-el midtown Y, NYC. L. Pastore. Dance Mag 44:80 Jl '70 *
PADRE ISLAND NATIONAL SEASHORE
Cows on Padre Island; destroying dune vegetation. C. Cottam. il Nat Parks & Con Mag 44:27 S '70
Wilderness potential of Padre Island. A. Dexter and L. Dexter. il Nat Parks & Con Mag 44:14-19 Ag '70
PADUANO, Donato
Petit Marcel and la grande mystique. pors Time 95:74 My 25 '70 *
PADUCAH, Ky.
Why we went to computerized billing. B. Gibbons. il por Am City 85:67+ Ja '70
PADWE, Sandy
Big-time college football is on the skids. il Look 34:66-9 S 22 '70
PAELLA. See Cookery, Spanish
PAESTUM
Our first look at Greek wall-painting. M. Napoli. il Horizon 12:22-9 Aut '70
Paestum. M. C. Lacoste. il UNESCO Courier 23:4-9 Ap '70
Treasure at Paestum; Lucanian tomb with Greek frescoes unearthed. il Time 95:46 Ja 26 '70
PAG (island)
Planting in Pag. J. W. Duffield. il Am For 76:22-4+ F '70
PAGE, Joseph A.
Law professor behind ASH, SOUP, PUMP and CRASH. il por N Y Times Mag p32-3+ Ag 23 '70
PAGE, Warren
Colorful bunch; Field and stream shooting editors. il Field & S 75:68-9+ Je '70
(ed) Shooting. See issues of Field & stream
PAGEANTS
North Carolina: enchanting land of gardens and dramas. E. Cheatham and P. Cheatham. il Home Gard 57:56-7 Ap '70
PAGES, Library. See Library assistants
PAGET'S disease
Hope for Paget's disease cure; mithramycin. A. J. Snider. Sci Digest Digest 69:59 Ja '71
PAGLIACCI; opera. See Leoncavallo, R.
PAGODAS
Closed door to Burma is beginning to open; Shwedagon. il Sunset 145:33-4+ O '70
PAGOPHAGIA. See Pica (pathology)
PAGOSA SPRINGS, Colo. to Grants, N.Mex. race. See Horse racing
PAHER, Stanley W.
Taken by the wind; excerpt from Nevada ghost towns and mining camps. il Am West 7:9-17 My '70
PAIGE, Russell A.
Stalactite growth beneath sea ice. bibliog il Science 167:171-2 Ja 9 '70
PAIGE, Whitney
Hemingway's Michigan. il Travel & Camera 33:32-7 Jl '70
PAIK, Nam June
Electronic wallpaper. D. Davis. il por Newsweek 76:54 Ag 24 '70 *
Nam June Paik: he composes pictures on TV. W. F. Wilson. il por Pop Phot 66:102+ F '70 *
PAIN
What can you do about stiff, aching muscles? Bet Hom & Gard 48:32 Je '70
See also
Suffering
PAIN; ballet. See Ballets—Criticisms
PAIN killing drugs. See Analgesics
PAINE, Thomas O.
Space in the 1970s. Aviation W 92:11 F 9 '70
U.S. presents moon stone to the United Nations. Dept State Bul 63:179 Ag 10 '70
What lies ahead in space? address, September 14, 1970. Vital Speeches 37:26-9 O 15 '70
about
Exit the spaceman. por Newsweek 76:67 Ag 10 '70 *
Future of NASA. por Time 96:44+ Ag 10 '70 *
Paine resigns. Sci N 98:93 Ag 1 '70 *
PAINT
Concrete floor paints. il Consumer Rep 36:36-9 Ja '71
High-gloss paints. il Consumer Rep 35:149-53 Mr '70
How to choose the right paint. il Motor B 125:68 Ap '70

Paints as poisoners. Consumer Rep 35:153 Mr '70
Pick a Newport color for your home. V. D. Hahn. il Am Home 73:26-7 Ag '70
See also
Enamel and enameling
PAINT, Fire resisting
Fighting fire with a paintbrush. J. Hand. il Pop Sci 197:98-9 S '70
PAINT brushes
Brushes: their variety and uses. F. Taubes. il Am Artist 34:24-7 Ag '70
Consumer's guide to paint brushes, pads and rollers. il Mech Illus 66:85 S '70
How to live with a brush. J. Lorr. il Design 71:25 Wint '69
PAINT rollers
Consumer's guide to paint brushes, pads and rollers. il Mech Illus 66:85 S'70
PAINT spraying
Right way to paint with spray guns. il Pop Mech 134:168-70 O '70
PAINTED shrimp. See Shrimps
PAINTER, Audrey A. and Hunter, F. E. Jr
Phosphorylation coupled to the transfer of electrons from glutathione to cytochrome c. bibliog il Science 170:552-3 O 30 '70
PAINTING
See also
Animals in art
Color
Cubism
Decoration and ornament
Encaustic painting
Expressionism (art)
Frescoes
Impressionism (art)
Landscape painting
Marine painting
Mural painting and decoration
Portrait painting
Realism in art
Tempera painting
Water color painting

Competitions
See Art—Competitions

Exhibitions
See Art—Exhibitions

Psychology
See Art—Psychology

Study and teaching
Tempera and enamel painting; drip method. R. Henkes. il Design 72:34-5 Fall '70
See also
Water color painting—Study and teaching

Technique
Color as system. L. Finkelstein. il Craft Horiz 30:42-3+ Mr '70
Experimenting with tempera. C. J. Alkema. il Design 71:26-30 mid-Wint '70
Flowers that run. E. J. Dorsey. il Design 71:10-12 Fall '69
Painting watercolors in acrylic; demonstration. J. Rogers. il Am Artist 34:39-41 D '70
Sponge and starch painting. il Design 71:28-9 Sum '70
See also
Perspective
Water color painting

Themes
See Art—Themes
PAINTING, Abstract. See Art, Abstract
PAINTING, American
American bestiary. M. S. Haverstock. il Art in Am 58:38-71 Jl '70
American landscape: a changing frontier. D. W. Scott. il Liv Wildn 33:3-13 Wint '69
American nineteenth century. R. Berenson. il Nat R 22:636-7 Je 16 '70
American painting of the nineteenth century. by B. Novak. Review
Antiques 97:322+ Mr '70. J. Wilmerding
American paintings in the Reynolda house collection. B. B. Lassiter. il Antiques 98:758-65 N '70
American visions of wilderness; reprint. W. S. Talbot. bibliog il Liv Wildn 33:14-25 Wint '69
Art world: 19th century America exhibition at the Metropolitan. H. Rosenberg. New Yorker 46:48-52 Jl 18 '70
Century of art: Century of California painting exhibition. il Design 72:10-12 Wint '70
Early America's artless art; Garbisch collection. W. A. H. Birnie. il Read Digest 96:142-8 F '70

PAINTING, American—*Continued*
Elusive ocean. il Time 96:46 Ag 24 '70

Exhibition preview: the reality of appearance; nineteenth century trompe-l'oeil paintings at the National gallery. A. Frankenstein. il Art in Am 58:94-9 Mr '70

Faces and places, paintings from the Met; exhibition in U.S. pavilion at Expo '70. T. P. F. Hoving. il Art in Am 58:62-5 Mr '70

Howald's American line. K. Linville. il Art N 69:52-5 Sum '70

New color painters; Lyrical abstraction exhibition at the Aldrich museum of contemporary art, Ridgefield, Conn. D. Davis. il Newsweek 75:84-6 My 4 '70

New informalists; young New York painters. C. Ratcliff. il Art N 68:46-50 F '70

Nineteenth century American painting; excerpts. J. T. Flexner. il Antiques 98:432-5 S '70

Paintings of nineteenth-century America; exhibition at Metropolitan museum of art. il Antiques 97:392-7 Mr '70

Panorama of nineteenth-century America. K. Kuh. il Sat R 53:40-2 My 30 '70

Return of the real; 22 realists on view at New York's Whitney. D. Davis. il Newsweek 75:105 F 23 '70

Unknown masters; naive American paintings from the collection of E. W. and B. Chrysler Garbisch. il Time 95:54-5 F 9 '70

Wilderness and the Adirondacks, an historical view. W. K. Verner. il Liv Wildn 33:27-46 Wint '69

Yankee rhyparography; exhibition of 19th century trompe-l'oeil paintings at National gallery. A. Frankenstein. il Art N 69:50-3+ Mr '70

See also
Albers, J.
Anuszkiewicz, R.
Apt, C.
Avery, M.
Bell, L.
Biederman, C. J.
Blackburn, M.
Bolotowsky, I.
Burchfield, C. E.
Burlin, P.
Cassatt, M.
Christensen, C. C. A.
Close, C.
Close, M.
Curtis, P. C.
Davis, J. H.
Dawley, J.
Eakins, T.
Fisher, J.
Gary, J.
Gifford, S. R.
Gorman, W. J.
Groshans, W.
Guston, P.
Holmes, M.
Jenkins, P.
Johns, J.
Keane, M.
Keane, W. S.
La Farge, J.
Leutze, E. G.
Levi, J.
Liberman, A.
Louis, M.
MacNelly, C. L.
Mangold, R.
Marin, J.
Martin, B.
Morfogen, E.
Nast, T.
Newman, B.
O'Keeffe, G.
Parker, R.
Parrish, M.
Peale, C. W.
Pearlstein, P.
Pereira, I. R.
Perlis, D.
Pollock, J.
Porter, R.
Portrait painting
Portraits, American
Rauschenberg, R.
Ray, M.
Reinhardt, A.
Rivers, L.
Rockwell, N.
Rothko, M.
Ryder, A. P.
Sargent, J. S.
Stearns, J. B.
Stella, F.
Still, C.
Sully, T.
Tobey, M.
Tyler, P.

Walton, H.
Warhol, A.
West, B.
Whitney museum of American art, New York
Wiener, I.
Wyeth, A.
Young, W.

PAINTING, Austrian
Six villages near Salzburg. J. Lipman and M. Pálffy. il Art in Am 58:102-5 Jl '70

PAINTING, British
New names in London: A to Z. J. Russell. il Art in Am 58:96-9 S '70
Rediscovery; the Bloomsbury painters. M. Holroyd. il Art in Am 58:116-23 Jl '70
Victorian painters, by J. Maas. Review
Art in Am 58:135+ Ja '70. J. Jacobs
Vogue 155:110+ Mr 1 '70. A. West
Victorians unbuttoned. J. H. Plumb. il Horizon 11:16-35 Aut '69

See also
Bacon, F.
Bartlett, W. H.
Hamilton, R.
Smyth, J. R. C.
Wright, J. 1734-1797

PAINTING, Canadian
Canada's group of seven; exhibition of their work at the Art gallery of Toronto. M. Amaya. il Art in Am 58:122-5 My '70
See also
Chambers, J.
Hamel, T.
Plamondon, A. S.

PAINTING, Childrens. See Childrens art

PAINTING, Dutch
Rembrandt and his circle (cont) B. A. Rifkin. il Art N 69:58-61+ My '70
See also
Bosch, H.
Gogh, V. van
Saenredam. P. J.

PAINTING, English. See Painting, British

PAINTING, French
La jeune peinture, protest and politics. M. Gibson. il Art in Am 58:142-5 N '70
Letter from Paris; Salon des independants, now showing at the Grand palais. Genêt. New Yorker 46:130-2 Ap 18 '70
Paris: the new surrealists. C. Cutler. il Art in Am 58:129-32 Mr '70
See also
Boudin, E. L.
Cézanne, P.
Charlot, J.
Cocteau, J.
Delacroix, E.
Dubuffet, J.
Duchamp, M.
Léger, F.
Matisse, H.
Monet, C.
Picabia, F.
Redon, O.
Vallotton, F. E.
Vasarely, V.
Villon, J. pseud.

PAINTING, German
German painting: the forgotten century; traveling exhibition of 19th-century German masters. F. Forster-Hahn. il Art N 69:50-5+ N '70

Maturity and a touch of madness; German expressionist exhibition at the Marlborough-Gerson gallery. K. Kuh. il Sat R 53:64-5 F 28 '70

Vision group from the backwater; exhibit of German painting in the 19th century at the Yale university art gallery. R. Hughes. il Time 96:84-6 N 23 '70
See also
Bauer, R.
Beuys, J.

PAINTING, Industrial and practical
Tips on painting: indoors and out. Good H 170:160 Je '70
See also
House painting
Paint spraying

Equipment and supplies
See also
Paint brushes

PAINTING, Italian
Rococo misto all' italiana; 18th-century paintings show. J. J. Rishel. il Art N 69:40-3+ O '70
See also
Florence—Art

PAINTING, Mexican
See also
Gutiérrez, J. L.
Rivera, D.

PAINTING, Modern. See Art, Modern

PAINTING, Non-objective. See Art, Abstract

PAINTING, Scottish
 Nineteenth-century Scottish painting. W. Buchanan. il Antiques 98:394-9 S '70

PAINTING, Spanish
 See also
 Dali, S.
 Genoves, J.
 Goya y Lucientes, F. J. de
 Miró, J.
 Picasso, P.
 Velázquez, D. R. de S. y

PAINTING, Symbolic. See Symbolism in art

PAINTING and photography. See Art and photography

PAINTING knives. See Artists materials

PAINTING materials. See Artists materials

PAINTING on textiles. See Textile painting

PAINTINGS
 Paintings from the Phillips collection. il Atlan 226:61-8 D '70
 See also
 Art—Expertising
 Forgery of works of art
 Historical paintings

Circulation, loans, etc.
 See Art loans

Collections
 See Art—Private collections

Prices
 See Art—Prices

PAINTINGS, Reproduction of. See Reproductions of works of art

PAINTINGS, Theft of. See Art thefts

PAINTINGS in the home. See Art in the home

PAISLEY, Ian Richard Kyle
 Australia to bar Ian Paisley during Pope's visit. Chr Cent 87:1279 O 28 '70 *
 Big fella wins. por Newsweek 75:61 Ap 27 '70 *
 Extremist triumph. Time 95:43 Ap 27 '70 *
 On the left, Bernadette Devlin. W. F. Buckley, jr. Nat R 22:856-7 Ag 11 '70 *
 Paisley in Parliament. A. Boyd. Nation 210:549-50 My 11 '70 *
 Paisley's progress. J. D. Douglas. Chr Today 14:40 My 8 '70 *
 Rebel in Armagh jail, the hater in the pulpit. A. Carthew. il pors N Y Times Mag p12-13+ Ag 9 '70 *

PAIUTE Indians
 Here in Nevada a terrible crime; Pyramid Lake. A. M. Josephy, jr. il Am Heritage 21:93-100 Je '70
 They're killing Pyramid Lake! D. Lynch. il Field & S 74:10-15 Ja '70

PAKISTAN
 Blast of a killer typhoon. il Sr Schol 97:3 D 14 '70
 East Pakistan: the politics of catastrophe. il Time 96:28+ D 7 '70
 East Pakistan: the wave. D. Moraes. il N Y Times Mag p26-7+ Ja 10 '71
 Night of terror. P. Parshall. Chr Today 15:40-1 D 18 '70
 Pakistan: when the demon struck. il Time 96:16+ N 30 '70
 Pakistani tragedy; cyclone; with report and interviews. M. Parker. il Newsweek 76:34-6 N 30 '70
 Portrait of a deadly pinwheel; storm ravages East Pakistan. il Life 69:41-2 N 27 '70
 Tragic aftermath in Pakistan. il Life 69:26-35 D 4 '70
 Walk through a deathly quiet countryside. H. Ellithorpe. il por Life 69:5 D 4 '70
 See also
 Economic assistance in Pakistan
 Elections—Pakistan

Economic conditions
 Passage to Pakistan. H. P. Minsky. il Trans-Action 7:27-31 F '70

Foreign relations
 United States
 See United States—Foreign relations—Pakistan

Politics and government
 Pakistan, East and West, after the flood. B. Stevens. Commonweal 93:319 D 25 '70
 Vote from chaos? Newsweek 76:60 D 14 '70
 See also
 Elections—Pakistan

Relief work
 Beshi . . .beshi; with report by M. Parker. il Newsweek 76:32-3 D 7 '70
 Calamity in Pakistan. Chr Cent 87:1442 D 2 '70
 Churches rally to aid Pakistan. il Chr Today 15:40-1 D 18 '70
 East Pakistan and the U.S. N. Cousins. Sat R 53:24+ D 12 '70; Reply with rejoinder, R. D. Murphy. 54:22 Ja 9 '71
 HELP for manpura; Heartland emergency lifesaving project. il Newsweek 77:25 Ja 4 '71
 Pakistan, East and West, after the flood. B. Stevens. Commonweal 93:319 D 25 '70
 Pakistani tragedy. Newsweek 76:36 N 30 '70

Religious institutions and affairs
 See also
 Church of Pakistan

PAKISTANI cookery. See Cookery, Pakistani

PAKISTANIS in Great Britain
 Oh, what a lovely bash! skinheads vs Pakistanis in London. il Newsweek 75:58-9 Je 22 '70

PAL, Pratapaditya
 Rockefeller bronzes: the Indian tradition. il Art N 69:48-9+ S '70

PALA, Dolores
 In search of Mihailo: story. Redbook 134:137-59 F '70

PALACE of arts and sciences, San Francisco
 Doctor Oppenheimer's exploratorium. A. Richmond. il Nation 211:6-9 Jl 6 '70

PALACES
 Gingerbread mansion: Brighton pavilion. H. C. Howes. il Design 71:19 mid-Sum '70
 See also
 Castles

PALARDY, J. Michael
 Needed: requiem for a structure. bibliog f Clear House 44:360-3 F '70

PALAU (islands)
 Unseen glories of the reef. il Life 69:50-7 O 23 '70

PALAUAN pottery. See Pottery, Palauan

PALEN, Cole
 World war I aircraft fly again in Rhinebeck's rickety rendezvous. H. Arden. il por Nat Geog 138:578-87 O '70 *

PALEOANTHROPOLOGY. See Man, Prehistoric

PALEOBIOLOGY
 See also
 Paleoecology

PALEOBOTANY
 See also
 Trees, Fossil

Eocene
 Chlorophyll derivatives in middle eocene sediments. D. L. Dilcher and others. bibliog il Science 168:1447-9 Je 19 '70

Jurassic
 Palmoxylon simperi and palmoxylon pristina: two pre-cretaceous angiosperms from Utah. W. D. Tidwell and others. bibliog il Science 168:835-40 My 15 '70
 Pre-cretaceous flowering plants: further evidence from Utah. W. D. Tidwell and others. bibliog il Science 170:547-8 O 30 '70

Permian
 Petrified peat from a Permian coal bed in Antarctica. J. M. Schopf. bibliog il Science 169:274-7 Jl 17 '70

Pleistocene
 Postglacial vegetational history of the Great Plains. P. V. Wells. bibliog il Science 167:1574-82 Mr 20 '70

Quaternary
 Pollen sequence from late quaternary sediments in Yellowstone Park. R. G. Baker. bibliog il Science 168:1449-50 Je 19 '70

Antarctic Regions
 Petrified peat from a Permian coal bed in Antarctica. J. M. Schopf. bibliog il Science 169:274-7 Jl 17 '70

Germany
 Chlorophyll derivatives in middle eocene sediments. D. L. Dilcher and others. bibliog il Science 168:1447-9 Je 19 '70

Great Plains
 Postglacial vegetational history of the Great Plains. P. V. Wells. bibliog il Science 167:1574-82 Mr 20 '70

PALEOBOTANY—*Continued*

Utah

Palmoxylon simperi and palmoxylon pristina: two pre-cretaceous angiosperms from Utah. W. D. Tidwell and others. bibliog il Science 168:835-40 My 15 '70

Pre-cretaceous flowering plants: further evidence from Utah. W. D. Tidwell and others. bibliog il Science 170:547-8 O 30 '70

Wyoming

Pollen sequence from late quaternary sediments in Yellowstone Park. R. G. Baker. bibliog il Science 168:1449-50 Je 19 '70

PALEOCLIMATOLOGY

Antarctic glaciation during the tertiary recorded in sub-Antarctic deep-sea cores. S. V. Margolis and J. P. Kennett. bibliog il Science 170:1085-7 D 4 '70

Antarctic ice sheet: stable isotope analyses of Byrd station cores and interhemispheric climate implications. S. Epstein and others. bibliog il Science 168:1570-2 Je 26 '70

Astronomical theory of climate change: support from New Guinea. H. H. Veeh and J. Chappell. bibliog il Science 167:862-5 F 6 '70

Differential isotopic fractionation in benthic foraminifera and paleotemperatures reassessed. J. C. Duplessy and others. bibliog il Science 168:250-1 Ap 10 '70

Pleistocene climates in the Atlantic and Pacific Oceans: a comparison based on deep-sea sediments. D. B. Ericson and G. Wollin. bibliog il Science 167:1483-5 Mr 13 '70

Pleistocene climates in the Atlantic and Pacific Oceans: a reevaluated comparison based on deep-sea sediments. R. W. Morin and others. bibliog il Science 169:365-6 Jl 24 '70

Pleistocene paleotemperatures. C. Emiliani. bibliog il Science 168:822-5 My 15 '70

PALEOECOLOGY

Phanerozoic stromatolites: noncompetitive ecologic restriction by grazing and burrowing animals. P. Garrett. bibliog il Science 169:171-3 Jl 10 '70

PALEO-INDIANS

Earliest Americans. C. V. Haynes, jr; discussion. Science 167:1670 Mr 27 '70

First discovery of America; the Beringians. C. Ogburn, jr. il Horizon 12:92-9 Wint '70

Megafauna and man from Ayacucho, highland Peru. R. S. MacNeish and others. bibliog il Science 168:975-7 My 22 '70

PALEOMAGNETISM. See Magnetism, Terrestrial

PALEONTOLOGY

How good are you as a paleontologist? quiz. J. Daugherty and M. Daugherty. il Sci Digest 68:80-1+ N '70

See also
Algae, Fossil
Birds, Fossil
Mammals, Fossil
Man, Prehistoric
Mastodons
Micropaleontology
Paleobotany

Conferences

North American paleontological convention. E. L. Yochelson. Science 167:398-400 Ja 23 '70

Cenozoic

Arctic paleo-oceanography in late cenozoic time. Y. Herman. bibliog il Science 169:474-7 Jl 31 '70

Hyalinea baltica and the plio-pleistocene boundary in the Caribbean Sea. W. D. Bock. bibliog il Science 170:847-8 N 20 '70

Cretaceous

Lepidoptera in cretaceous amber. M. R. MacKay. bibliog il Science 167:379-80 Ja 23 '70

Devonian

Soft parts of cephalopods and trilobites: some surprising results of X-ray examinations of Devonian slates. W. Stuermer. bibliog il Science 170:1300-2 D 18 '70

Jurassic

Archaeopteryx: notice of a new specimen. J. H. Ostrom. bibliog il Science 170:537-8 O 30 '70

Jurassic sandstone from the tropical Atlantic. P. J. Fox and others. bibliog il Science 170:1402-4 D 25 '70

Permian

Mixed Permian-Triassic fauna, Guryul Ravine, Kashmir. C. Teichert and others. bibliog il Science 167:174-5 Ja 9 '70

Pleistocene

Coincidence of climatic and faunal fluctuations in pleistocene Bermuda. S. J. Gould. bibliog il Science 168:572-3 My 1 '70

Marine fossils at Rancho La Brea. J. W. Valentine and J. H. Lipps. bibliog il Science 169:277-8 Jl 17 '70

Pleistocene climates in the Atlantic and Pacific Oceans: a reevaluated comparison based on deep-sea sediments. R. W. Morin and others. bibliog il Science 169:365-6 Jl 24 '70

Pleistocene paleotemperatures. C. Emiliani. bibliog il Science 168:822-5 My 15 '70

Quaternary

Oxygen-18 studies of recent planktonic foraminifera: comparisons of phenotypes and of test parts. A. D. Hecht and S. M. Savin. bibliog il Science 170:69-71 O 2 '70

Tertiary

Ages of fossil penguins in New Zealand. G. G. Simpson. bibliog Science 168:361-2 Ap 17 '70

Triassic

Bones on Coalsack Bluff: a story of drifting continents. J. Lear. il Sat R 53:46-51 F 7 '70

Dentary-squamosal joint and the origin of mammals. H. R. Barghusen and J. A. Hopson. bibliog il Science 168:573-5 My 1 '70

Mixed Permian-Triassic fauna, Guryul Ravine, Kashmir. C. Teichert and others. bibliog il Science 167:174-5 Ja 9 '70

Triassic tetrapods from Antarctica: evidence for continental drift. D. H. Elliot and others. bibliog il Science 169:1197-201 S 18 '70

Antarctic Regions

Bones on Coalsack Bluff: a story of drifting continents. J. Lear. il Sat R 53:46-51 F 7 '70

Horizons for Antarctic paleontology. K. Frazier. il Sci N 97:350-2 Ap 4 '70

Triassic tetrapods from Antarctica: evidence for continental drift. D. H. Elliot and others. bibliog il Science 169:1197-201 S 18 '70

Whole fossils in Antarctica. il Sci N 98:428 D 5 '70

World of Antarctic paleontology: Coalsack fossils. K. Frazier. il Sci N 97:324-6 Mr 28 '70

Arctic Regions

Arctic paleo-oceanography in late cenozoic time. Y. Herman. bibliog il Science 169:474-7 Jl 31 '70

Bahama Islands

Phanerozoic stromatolites: noncompetitive ecologic restriction by grazing and burrowing animals. P. Garrett. bibliog il Science 169:171-3 Jl 10 '70

Bermuda

Coincidence of climatic and faunal fluctuations in pleistocene Bermuda. S. J. Gould. bibliog il Science 168:572-3 My 1 '70

California

Fossil sea mammal: paleoparadoxia. H. P. Zuidema. il Sea Front 16:20-4 Ja '70

See also
La Brea, Los Angeles

Canada

Lepidoptera in cretaceous amber. M. R. MacKay. bibliog il Science 167:379-80 Ja 23 '70

China

Gigantopithecus. E. L. Simons and P. C. Ettel. il Sci Am 222:76-85 bibliog(p 146) Ja '70

France

Baton of Montgaudier; engraved art on the reindeer antler from stone age France. A. Marshack. il por(p8) Natur Hist 79:56-63 Mr '70

Symbols in the stone age; analysis of ice age art. il por Sci N 97:242 Mr 7 '70

Germany

Soft parts of cephalopods and trilobites: some surprising results of X-ray examinations of Devonian slates. W. Stuermer. bibliog il Science 170:1300-2 D 18 '70

Illinois

Isopod from the Pennsylvanian of Illinois: Hesslerella shermani. F. R. Schram. bibliog il Science 169:854-5 Ag 28 '70

India

Gigantopithecus. E. L. Simons and P. C. Ettel. il Sci Am 222:76-85 bibliog(p 146) Ja '70

PALEONTOLOGY—*Continued*

Kashmir

Mixed Permian-Triassic fauna, Guryul Ravine, Kashmir. C. Teichert and others. bibliog il Science 167:174-5 Ja 9 '70

Kenya

In search of man's past at Lake Rudolf. R. E. Leakey. il pors Nat Geog 137:712-33 My '70

New Guinea

Astronomical theory of climate change: support from New Guinea. H. H. Veeh and J. Chappell. bibliog il Science 167:862-5 F 6 '70

New Jersey

Dinosaurs finally win one; P. Olsen and T. Lessa efforts to save fossil-bearing acres for an educational park. il pors Life 69:73-4 D 11 '70

New Zealand

Ages of fossil penguins in New Zealand. G. G. Simpson. bibliog Science 168:361-2 Ap 17 '70

Peru

Megafauna and man from Ayacucho, highland Peru. R. S. MacNeish and others. bibliog il Science 168:975-7 My 22 '70

PALEOOCEANOGRAPHY. See Paleontology

PALEOPARADOXIA. See Mammals, Fossil

PALEOPATHOLOGY
Java man's jeopardy; bony growth from volcanic fluorine poisoning. Sci Am 222:48 Ap '70

PALEOTEMPERATURE. See Paleoclimatology

PALEOZOIC period. See Geology, Stratigraphic—Paleozoic

PALERMO, Angelo
New cash control and data collection system. il por Parks & Rec 5:32-3 Mr '70

PALERMO

Music

Report: production of Spontini's Vestale. E. Tellni. Opera N 34:28 F 7 '70

PALESTINE
See also
Israel
Jerusalem

History

Legacy of Abraham's children. il Time 96:29 D 21 '70

PALESTINE-Jewish-Arab relations. See Jewish-Arab relations

PALESTINE refugees. See Refugees, Arab

PALESTINIAN Arabs
Algeria, Israel and the Al Fatah. R. W. Fox. Commonweal 92:184-5 My 8 '70; Discussion. 92:331+, 475+; 93:83+ Jl 10, S 25, O 23 '70
American innocent in the Middle East; Jordan. M. Frady. Harper 241:104-6+ N '70
Arab guerrillas v. Arab governments. il por Time 95:22-3 Je 22 '70
Arabs their own worst enemy. America 122:604 Je 6 '70
Emerging realities. il Newsweek 75:48+ Mr 23 '70
Eretz Israel, or historic Palestine? America 122:666 Je 27 '70
Explosion in Jordan. il por Newsweek 75:34-5 Je 22 '70
Fire and steel for Palestine. J. M. Mecklin. il Fortune 82:84-9+ Jl '70
Hidden leader of the Arab guerrillas; interview, ed. by O. Fallaci. Abu Lotuf. il Look 34:24-6 Je 30 '70
Lull in the madness. il Newsweek 75:35 Je 29 '70
Palestine: a case of right v. right. il Time 96:28-9 D 21 '70
Palestine Arab commandos; with report on the Gaza Strip by P. Young and interview with G. Habash, ed. by O. Fallaci. il Life 68:26D-34 Je 12 '70
Palestine's Arabs. D. Peretz. il Trans-Action 7:43-9 Jl '70
Palestinian refugees. G. A. Geyer. New Repub 163:15-18 N 21 '70; Reply. E. Cooper. 163:30-1 D 12 '70
Palestinians and Israel. S. Avineri. bibliog f Commentary 49:31-44 Je '70; Discussion. 50:6+ S; 30+ N; 18+ D '70
Palestinians: refugees or a people? M. C. Bassiouni. il Cath World 211:257-62 S '70
Shoring up a shaky calm. il por Time 95:24+ Je 29 '70
Synagogue council head rebukes "Christians for Palestine"; Pro-Arab Christian conference. Chr Cent 87:783 Je 24 '70

Syria and the Palestinians. il Newsweek 76:42 O 5 '70
Terrorism & preventive detention: the case of Israel. A. M. Dershowitz. bibliog f Commentary 50:67-78 D '70
Tiger Nasser can't ride. V. S. Kearney. il America 122:208-11 F 28 '70
Undemonizing the Middle East. R. C. Hottelet. Sat R 53:23-5+ Je 6 '70
Winter of discontent. L. Jenkins. il Newsweek 76:43 D 21 '70

PALESTINIAN resistance movement. See Fedayeen

PALEY, Grace
Short visits with five writers and one friend. B. Midwood. il pors Esquire 74:150-3 N '70 *

PALEY, Maggie
Funky madonna of New York soul. il pors Life 68:44-7 Ja 30 '70

PALEY, William
Classification of trivets (cont) il Hobbies 75:122 Mr '70

PALFFY, Martin. See Lipman, J. jt auth.

PALINDROMES. See Word games

PALINKAS, Patricia
Parting shots. il pors Life 69:63-4 Ag 28 '70 *

PALISA, Johann
Story of a lost planet: 155 Scylla. J. Ashbrook. il por Sky & Tel 40:361-2 D '70 *

PALLADIUM
Palladium: preparation and catalytic properties of particles of uniform size. J. Turkevich and G. Kim. bibliog il Science 169:873-9 Ag 28 '70

PALLANSCH, Michael J. See Posati, L. P. jt. auth.

PALLETS
Shrink packaging adapted for palletizing. il Aviation W 93:94 O 26 '70

PALM BEACH, Fla.

Galleries and museums

Mansion-museum in Florida: Whitehall, the Henry Morrison Flagler museum. il Antiques 97:180+ F '70

PALM BEACH COUNTY, Fla.
Helicopter ambulance inaugurated. il Am City 85:16 O '70

PALM SPRINGS, Calif.
Golf capital of the world. il Travel 133:65 F '70

PALME, Olof
Sweden; address, June 5, 1970. Vital Speeches 36:578-80 Jl 15 '70
Why Sweden is critical of U.S. role in Vietnam; interview. il por U S News 68:48-9 Je 22 '70

about

Coping with change. por Bsns W p29 N 7 '70 *
Letter from Stockholm. S. Kelman. il New Yorker 46:36-46+ D 26 '70 *
Neutralist's equilibrium. il por Time 95:18 Je 15 '70 *
Palme's picnic; U.S. visit. il por Newsweek 75:44+ Je 22 '70 *
Swedish leader on a tightrope. il por U S News 68:58 Je 15 '70 *
Together again. il por Time 96:32 O 5 '70 *

PALMER, Arnold
How to save ten strokes off your game. il Look 34:68-70+ Ap 7 '70

about

Arnie's party was a divine affair. M. Mulvoy. pors Sports Illus 33:16-17 Ag 3 '70 *

PALMER, Charlene
Misunderstandings; poem. Chr Cent 87:1252 O 21 '70

PALMER, Jeff
How to catch more bass. il Field & S 75:48-9+ Ag '70
Strange way to fool pheasant. il Field & S 75:48-9+ S '70

PALMER, Jim
Three Birds who mainly stay; Baltimore's big three pitching staff. R. Blount, jr. il pors Sports Illus 33:30-2+ O 12 '70 *

PALMER, John D.
Many clocks of man; with biographical sketch. il Natur Hist 79:6, 52-9 Ap '70

PALMER, Paul F.
Rethinking the marriage bond. America 122:39-42, 513 Ja 17, My 16 '70

PALMER, Raymond A.
Bubble up boating. il Pop Mech 134:148-50+ N '70

PALMER, Richard
Palmer's pumpkin. il por Time 97:14-15 Ja 18 '71 *

PALMER, Tyler
Flake and the old man. R. Meryman. il pors Life 68:54-6+ Mr 6 '70 *

PALMISTRY
Would you put your life in this man's hands?
M. Fiel. Mlle 71:86-7+ Jl '70

PALMQUIST, Don. See Davis, D. jt. auth.

PALMS, Fossil. See Trees, Fossil

PALO ALTO, Calif.
Changes in the black ghetto: East Palo Alto.
W. Stegner. Sat R 53:12+ Ag 1 '70
Respectable rioter. il por Time 96:14 Jl
27 '70

PALOMAKI, D. W.
Second guessing the Heathkit IG-72. il Pop
Electr 33:65-6 D '70

PALOS VERDES, Calif, library district
Group programs revive dying branch library:
Malaga Cove plaza branch library. J. A.
McCrossan. Am Lib 1:619-20 Je '70

PALTER, Michael H.
Songmy: poem. New Repub 162:27 F 7 '70

PAMBRUM, Audra
New Indian war, against suicide. J. L. Bach.
il pors Todays Health 48:16-17 O '70 *

PAMPERIN, John. See Moore, J. jt. auth.

PAMPHLETS
Best in booklets. See issues of House & gard-
en incorporating Living for young home-
makers
Booklet bonanza: before you build, buy or
decorate (title varies) House B 112:84+
My; 70+ O '70
Booklets worth writing for. See issues of Good
housekeeping
Publications worth writing for. C. Bilski. Pop
Mech 34:69 O; 55 N '70
Things to write for. See issues of Changing
times
Worth writing for (cont) Motor B 125:89 Ap;
143 Je '70
See also
Libraries—Pamphlet collections

PAMPHLETS, Political. See Political pamphlets

PAMPLONA, Spain
Can a sixty-two-year-old writer with a history of heart trouble find fulfillment running with the bulls in the streets of
Pamplona? J. A. Michener. il Esquire 74:
177-81 D '70
Seven theories why anyone, including a sixty-
two-year-old writer with a history of heart
trouble, seeks fulfillment running with the
bulls in the streets of Pamplona. J. A.
Michener. il Esquire 74:182-3 D '70

PAN-AFRICAN liberation and restoration
movement. See Negroes—Nationalism

PAN-AFRICANISM
Ethiopia and the Pan-African movement,
1945-1963. C. G. Contee. il por Negro Hist
Bul 33:122-5 My '70

PANAGHOULIS, Alexandros
Greek colonels' revenge. J. Kobbe. Nation
210:789 Je 29 '70 *

PANALBA. See Antibiotics

PAN AM (airline) See Pan American world
airways

PANAMA
See also
Panama Canal
Portobelo
School libraries—Panama

Description and travel
Panama, link between oceans and continents.
J. B. Billard. il Nat Geog 137:402-40 Mr '70
Pocket-size Panama. L. Zalamea. il Travel
134:72 S '70
Two exotic, off-beat winter vacations. C.
Landau; E. Crimmin. il Motor B 126:55-7+
N '70

Politics and government
Panama cracks the grip of graft. Bsns W
p41-2 F 7 '70

PANAMA CANAL
New canal in Panama. il Time 96:40 D 14 '70
No big blast. Sr Schol 97:5 D 14 '70

PAN AMERICAN airways. See Pan American
world airways

PAN AMERICAN conferences. See Inter-American conferences

PAN AMERICAN day and week
Pan American day and Pan American week,
1970; proclamation, April 10, 1970. R. M.
Nixon. Dept State Bul 62:696 Je 1 '70

PAN AMERICAN development foundation
Pennies for progress. Américas 22:1 Ag '70

PAN AMERICAN highway
Down that Pan American highway. E. A.
Jahn. il Travel 133:30-5 Ja; 34-9 F; 44-7+
Mr; 68-70+ Ap '70
New tourist milestone; the approaching com-
pletion of the Pan American highway.
Américas 22:1 Mr '70
U.S. supports completion of Pan American
highway; statements; December 10, 1969. C.
A. Meyer; R. M. Nixon. Dept State Bul 62:
38-40 Ja 12 '70

PAN AMERICAN union
Hemisphere art. See issues of Américas

PAN AMERICAN world airways
Baggage system. Aviation W 93:30 Jl 6 '70
Board grants tentative approval to Eastern-
Caribair merger step. H. D. Watkins. Avia-
tion W 93:30 N 16 '70
... But not out. il Forbes 105:20-1 Mr 15 '70
Computer helps deploy reservations staff. il
Aviation W 93:38-9 Ag 3 '70
Engine problems curtail flight of 747 in Eu-
rope. H. J. Coleman. Aviation W 92:27-8
Ja 19 '70
Engines are main Pan Am 747 problem. W. S.
Hieronymus. il Aviation W 93:44+ Ag 10 '70
How the 747 came to fly; inaugural flight. il
Bsns W p78-9 Ja 31 '70
Intercity demonstration flights show S-65
helicopter capability. R. S. Kahn. Aviation
W 92:23 Je 15 '70
Late tape. R. Brady. Duns 96:105 N '70
New data link may lessen communication
workload. B. M. Elson. il Aviation W 93:
44+ N 30 '70
Pan Am devises new maintenance control.
L. Doty. il Aviation W 92:56-8 Mr 23 '70
Pan Am easing 747 into operation. R. S.
Kahn. il Aviation W 92:32-3 F 2 '70
Pan American inaugurates 747 service; with
editorial comment. il Aviation W 92:11, 31-2
Ja 26 '70
Pan Am 1969 loss $25.2 million; American re-
ports profit gain. il Aviation W 92:26 F 16
'70
Pan Am seeks Falcon use contracts. C. E.
Schneider. Aviation W 94:52-3 Ja 4 '71
Pan Am seeks Micronesian route support. L.
Doty. Aviation W 93:24 Ag 31 '70
Pan American 747 operation shown during
first week of New York-London service. il
Aviation W 92:24-31 F 2 '70
Pan American traffic rebound credited to
747. il Aviation W 92-35 My 11 '70
Passenger service fixes planned for 747. W.
H. Gregory. Aviation W 93:24-5 Ag 3 '70
Price of pioneering: 747 inaugural flight. il
Newsweek 75:67+ F 2 '70
Stewardesses help promote Pan Am 747s. R.
S. Kahn. il Aviation W 94:30-1 Ja 11 '71
Who will pay for the burned-out 747? il
Bsns W p64+ D 5 '70

PANARABISM
See also
Arab federation (proposed)

PANCAKES. See Griddle cakes

PANCREAS
Diseases
See also
Cystic fibrosis

PANDAS
Where have all the pandas gone? P. M.
Williams. il Sci Digest 68:76-81 S '70

PANELING
Decorate your walls with leftover paneling.
H. Wicks. il Pop Mech 133:160-1 Je '70
New beauty with decorative carvings. D.
Huff. il Pop Sci 196:76-7 Mr '70
Panels. il Bet Hom & Gard 48:42-3+ Ja '70

PANETTA, Leon E.
Law, says the man who was fired for enforc-
ing it, is the law. por Life 68:30-1 Mr 13 '70

about
End of reconstruction. il pors Time 95:12-13
Mr 2 '70 *
Leon Panetta: first casualty. por Newsweek
75:20 Mr 2 '70 *

PANGAEA. See Continental drift

PANGOLA grass
Starch accumulation associated with growth
reduction at low temperatures in a tropical plant. J. H. Hilliard and S. H. West.
bibliog il Science 168:494-6 Ap 24 '70

PANICUM grass. See Grasses

PANIOLOS. See Cowboys

PANNENBERG, Wolfhart
Theology of zigzags. C. F. H. Henry. Chr
Today 14:36-7 S 11 '70

PANOFSKY, Hans A.
Analyzing atmospheric behavior. bibliog il
Phys Today 23:32-3+ D '70
—See Dutton, J. A. jt. auth.

PANORAMIC photography. See Photography,
    Panoramic
PANSHIN, Alexei
    Basic science fiction collection. por Library
        J 95:2223-9 Je 15 '70
    Science fiction. bibliog il por Wilson Lib Bul
        44:616-20 F '70
    Science fiction bibliography and criticism. Am
        Lib 1:884-5 O '70
PANSIES
    Pick your own pansy seeds. C. Sauerland. il
        Org Gard & Farm 17:55 Je '70
PANTER-DOWNES, Mollie
    Letter from London. New Yorker 46:75-7 My
        30; 61-2 Jl 4; 74-6 Jl 25; 158+ N 14; 55-6 D 26
        '70
PANTHERS
        See also
    Pumas
PANTOGRAPHS
    Make a pantograph for your router. J. A.
        Joyner. il Pop Sci 197:104-5 O '70
PANTOMINE
    Theater on the Balustrade of Prague, Hunter
        college playhouse, NYC. L. Pastore. Dance
        Mag 45:78-9 Ja '71
PANTRIES
    In these pantries things are very visible. il
        Sunset 145:88-9 Ag '70
PANTS. See Trousers
PANTS suits. See Clothing and dress
PANTY hose. See Hosiery
PANZA collection. See Art—Private collections
PANZA DI BIUMO, Giuseppe, conte
    At home with art: the villa of Count Giuseppe
        Panza di Biumo. T. Trini. il por Art in Am
        58:102-9 S '70 *
PAOLI, Ind.
    Portrait of a small town: Paoli, Indiana.
        J. Mandelstam. il Sr Schol 97:13-14 O 5 '70
PAOLINO, Ronald M. See Hine, B. jt. auth.
PAPACY
    New look at Vatican I. T. Early. il Chr Cent
        87:815-18 Jl 1 '70
    Roman legions. C. F. H. Henry. Chr Today
        14:29-30 Jl 3 '70
    Storm on the Holy See. J. Horgan. il Sat
        R 53:19-21+ Mr 28 '70
        History
    Papacy since Peter. X. Rynne. il Horizon 12:
        60-7 Wint '70
PAPAL audiences
    Vatican's noisy family; Pope's general audi-
        ence in St Peter's. J. Bell. il por Time 95:
        50+ Je 15 '70
PAPAL guards
    Cutting the Vatican guard. il Time 96:30 S
        28 '70
    Of many things; disbanding of papal troops.
        D. L. Flaherty. America 123:219 O 3 '70
PAPAL infallibility. See Popes—Infallibility
PAPALEO, Joseph
    Word to go; story. Harper 241:74-6 N '70
PAPATAKIS, Nico
    Films. R. Hatch. Nation 210:541-2 My 4 '70 *
PAPAVER nudicaule. See Poppies
PAPER
        See also
    Waste paper
        Preservation
    Record papers and their preservation. W. K.
        Wilson. bibliog il por Chem 43:8-12 Mr '70
PAPER, Polyethylene
    Embossing Arabic letters and numbers on
        new raised-line polyethylene paper; an aid
        for the blind. R. L. Barr. bibliog il Science
        169:94-5 Jl 3 '70
PAPER, Waste. See Waste paper
PAPER cutting. See Paper work
PAPER decoration. See Paper work
PAPER decorations. See Decoration and orna-
    ment
PAPER diapers. See Diapers, Infants
PAPER folding, Japanese. See Origami
PAPER furniture. See Furniture, Paperboard
PAPER houses. See Houses, Paperboard
PAPER making and trade
    Costly cure; environmental cleanup. Forbes
        107:165+ Ja 1 '71
    Record papers and their preservation. W. K.
        Wilson. bibliog il por Chem 43:8-12 Mr '70
    Stick and carrot; study of pollution control.
        Nation 212:4 Ja 4 '71
        See also
    Great Northern Nekoosa corporation
    Scott paper company
        Consolidations and mergers
    Papermakers aim for strength through union;
        Nekoosa and Great northern. il Bsns W
        p64 My 16 '70

PAPER mobiles. See Mobiles
PAPER money
        Canada
    Queen's image suffers a setback. Bsns W p48
        Ja 31 '70
        Great Britain
    Crisp commentary on inflation; Britain's
        new £ 20-note. il Time 96:29 Jl 20 '70
        United States
    Insulate with a cool $50 million? disposal
        of worn paper money. Nations Bsns 58:41
        D '70
    Whatever happened to silver coins and certi-
        ficates? il U S News 68:14 F 16 '70
PAPER mill sludge. See Trade waste
PAPER mosaics. See Mosaics
PAPER mulching. See Mulching
PAPER nautilus
    Argonaut octopus: rare find from the sea.
        G. W. Compton. il Sci Digest 68:32-4 Jl '70
    Rare gift from the sea. W. Zeiller and G.
        Compton. il Sea Front 16:322-7 N '70
PAPER products
    Cardboard carpentry. G. J. Brady. il Design
        71:30-1 Fall '69
PAPER sculpture
    Bas-relief paper sculpture. M. Murphy. il Sch
        Arts 70:12-13 S '70
    Fantasy, form and fun. L. Walker and K.
        Price. il por Sch Arts 70:38-40 O '70
PAPER sleeping bags. See Sleeping bags
PAPER trees. See Christmas trees
PAPER work
    Christmas decorations. il Good H 171:118-19+
        D '70
    Creating with torn paper. L. J. Miller. il De-
        sign 71:24-5 Fall '69
    Golda Lewis: from collage to compage. G.
        Lewis. il Craft Horiz 30:52-3 Ag '70
    Monster in the imagination; fantasy doodles,
        collages and paper cutouts by H. C. Ander-
        sen. il por Time 96:60-1 O 19 '70
    More quillwork and waxwork; ed. by E.
        Gaines. il Antiques 97:272-4 F '70
    Parthenon made of paper. P. Zakroff. il De-
        sign 71:40-1 Sum '70
        See also
    Collage
    Decoupage
    Origami
    Paper sculpture
    Papier-mâché
PAPER work, Office. See Office management
PAPERBACK books
    Paperback best sellers of the year 1969. il
        Pub W 197:44-7 F 9 '70
        See also
    Booksellers and bookselling—Paperback books
    Libraries—Paperback books
    Publishers and publishing—Paperback books
        Bibliography
    Books to come; childrens and adult; comp. by
        S. T. Halbreich; J. P. Donathan. Library J
        95:265-97, 1979-2001, 2997-8+ Ja 15, My 15,
        S 15 '70
    Current and choice in paperbacks (cont)
        America 123:522-5 D 12 '70
    Paperback bookshelf See issues of Changing
        times
    Paperbacks. See issues of Publishers' weekly
    Pick of the paperbacks. R. W. Saal. See issues
        of Saturday review
    Please don't squeeze the paperbacks! G.
        Stanford and B. D. Stanford. il Schol
        Teach Jr/Sr High p 12-13+ D 7 '70
PAPIER-MÂCHÉ
    Add action to your papier-mâché. E. Mad-
        sen. il Sch Arts 70:14-15 O '70
    Great big paper animal for all the family. il
        Sunset 145:64-5 D '70
    Papier-mâché animals for an animal tree. il
        Sunset 145:62-3 D '70
    Papier-mâché book characters. E. Norton.
        il Sch Arts 69:28-9 Mr '70
PAPILLON, pseud. See Charrière, H.
PAPIN, Warren J.
    Danger of debris. il Yachting 129:107+ Ja '71
PAPISH, Dan
    Couple; poem. Nation 211:442 N 2 '70
PAPP, Joseph
    Whores and wars. N. Gittelson. Harp Baz 103:
        6+ Jl '70 *
PAPPAS, Lou Seibert
    Cooking and eating outdoors. il House & Gard
        137:97+ Je '70
PAPUA-NEW GUINEA (territory)
        See also
    Cruising—Papua-New Guinea (territory)

PAPUA-NEW GUINEA (territory)—*Continued*
Native races
Institute of human biology of Papua-New Guinea. R. W. Hornabrook. Science 167: 146-7 Ja 9 '70
Presenting the very recent past; Hagen show. M. Mead. il N Y Times Mag p28-32 Mr 15 '70
Waiting for Lyndon, or LBJ all the way. Trans-Action 7:13-14 Jl '70

PAPUANS
See also
West Irian—Native races

PARACHUTES
See also
Airdrop
Parachuting

PARACHUTING
Don't make a move or he'll chute; G. Amoretti record attempts. il por Life 68:62-5 My 29 '70
Steel city skydiver aids troubled teens. il pors Ebony 25:72-4+ Jl '70
Surviving at sea. il Mech Illus 66:78 S '70
Where and how to watch skydiving. il Sunset 144:71-2 Ap '70

Anecdotes, facetiae, satire, etc.
My life and high times in harness. R. C. Grover. il Sports Illus 33:36-40 O 5 '70

PARADE (periodical) See Newspapers—Magazine sections

PARADES
That gr-r-a-a-nd day; St Patrick's day. il Newsweek 75:55-6 Mr 23 '70
See also
Chicago—Parades
Pasadena, Calif.—Parades
Washington D.C.—Parades

PARADIS, H. James
Teaching to throw, the hand-guiding technique. il Ceram Mo 18:16-19 O '70

PARADIS, Louise I. See Tolstoy, P. jt. auth.

PARADISE, Scott
Beyond a strategy of conservation. Cur 119: 27-31 Je '70
Our vandal ideology. Cur 115:55-60 F '70

PARADISE. See Heaven

PARADOX
On the cyclical curves generated by wheels that roll along wheels. M. Gardner. il Sci Am 223:210-12+ S '70

PARAFFINIC hydrocarbons. See Hydrocarbons

PARAGE, Helene
On the boards. pors Dance Mag 44:24 Mr 70 *

PARAGUAY
See also
Parks—Paraguay

Religious institutions and affairs
See also
Church and state in Paraguay

PARALYSIS
Correcting facial paralysis. il Time 96:57-8 S 21 '70
I struck back at stroke. A. Martin. Har Yrs 10:43-5 F '70
Spinal cord regeneration. B. J. Culliton. il Sci N 98:337-8 O 24 '70
See also
Parkinson's disease

PARAMEDICAL education
Paramedics: new doctors' helpers; training programs for doctors' assistants. il Time 96:38 N 9 '70

PARAMEDICS. See Medical workers

PARAMOUNT pictures corporation
Hollywood sells off the splendor. il Life 68: 38-43 F 27 '70

PARAMUS, N.J.
Let the camera be your eyes. J. J. Tedesco, jr. il Am City 85:86+ Ja '70

PARANOIA
How's your paranoia? Sci Digest 68:75 N '70

PARANOIA; story. See Williams, T.

PARAPLEGIA. See Paralysis

PARAPSYCHOLOGY
Scientist looks at ESP; visit with J. Pratt of Unversity of Virginia. S. McBee. McCalls 97:50+ Mr '70
Techniques and status of modern parapsychology; AAAS symposium, December 27, 1970. E. D. Dean. il Science 170:1237-8 D 11 '70
See also
Electronics in parapsychology
Spiritualism

PARASITES
Medical sciences; second International congress of parasitology. Sci N 98:280 O 3 '70
See also
Cercaria
Mites
Nematodes
Plasmodium (parasite)
Sarcocystis
Symbiosis
Ticks
Worms, Intestinal and parasitic

Birds
In competition for bird life: parasites. W. B. Stone and R. D. Manwell. il Cons 24:14-17 F '70
Nest parasitism, productivity, and clutch size in purple martins. W. W. Moss and J. H. Camin. bibliog il Science 168:1000-3 My 22 '70; Discussion. 170:1112 D 4 '70

Blood
See Blood—Parasites

Fishes
See also
Lampreys

Insects
Toxic factor produced by a granulosis virus in armyworm larva: effect on apanteles militaris. H. K. Kaya. bibliog il Science 168: 251-3 Ap 10 '70
Trail odors: recognition by insects parasitic on cocoons. P. W. Price. bibliog il Science 170:546-7 O 30 '70

Livestock
They won't kill hogs, but. . .parasites are costing you money. W. R. Prafka. Farm J 94:H38 S '70

Swine
See Parasites—Livestock

PARASITIC diseases
See also
Schistosomiasis
Trypanosomiasis

PARATHYROID hormone
Parathyroid stimulates discussion. il Sci N 98:396-7 N 21 '70

PARCEL post
Parcel post by private enterprise? D. Lawrence. U S News 69:80 Ag 24 '70

PARCEL post rates. See Postal rates—United States

PARDO, Richard
Confrontation. il Am For 76:32-5+ S '70

PARDUE, Leonard G. See Sugg, A. L. jt. auth.

PARDUE, Mary Lou, and Gall, J. G.
Chromosomal localization of mouse satellite DNA. bibliog il Science 168:1356-8 Je 12 '70

PARENT and child (law)
Society's child; child support decision of Judge M. Midonick in a New York city court. por Newsweek 77:60-1 Ja 11 '71

PARENT-child relationship
Between parent and child (cont) H. G. Ginott. McCalls 97:32 Ag '70
Can children get smarter? with study-discussion program, by M. M. Conant. E. S. Schaefer. bibliog il PTA Mag 65:10-12+, 35 S '70
Christmas at my father's house; excerpt from My father's house. P. B. Kunhardt, jr. il McCalls 98:44-5+ D '70
Day I was proudest of my child; symposium, ed. by D. Robinson. il Good H 170:70-3+ Ja '70
Generation of tyrants. H. Van Horne. il Good H 170:102-3+ Mr '70
Gentle art of understanding your parents. M. Hunt. il Seventeen 29:136-7+ My '70
Honoring parents. Chr Today 14:23 Ja 30 '70
How well do you know your children? K. Davis. il Parents Mag 45:39-41+ Jl '70
Infant separates himself from his mother. H. L. Rheingold and C. O. Eckerman. bibliog il Science 168:78-83 Ap 3 '70
Manner of speaking. J. Ciardi. Sat R 53:60 Ag 22 '70
Mills: father and son. B. Mazlish. il pors Horizon 12:106-11 Sum '70
Mothers and daughters. B. Bettelheim. Ladies Home J 87:30+ N '70
Mothers and daughters: a new freedom to be themselves. L. Robb. il por Ladies Home J 87:98-9+ N '70
Mothers and daughters: we love being together. il pors Vogue 155:100-1 Je '70
My father's country; excerpt from My father's house. P. B. Kunhardt, jr. il Life 69:44-44B+ Jl 4 '70; Same abr. Read Digest 97:197-200+ O '70
New heart for Becky Howland. A. Lake. il Good H 170:56-7+ Ja '70

PARENT-child relationship—*Continued*
Parent's manifesto: our grievances; with study-discussion program. by C. Smallenburg and H. Smallenburg. A. Graham. bibliog il PTA Mag 64:2-5. 34 Mr '70
Some tips on coping with parents. H. Muller. Time 96:38 Ag 17 '70
Some words on the generation gap. R. Haughton. Cath World 211:5-6 Ap '70
Truth about lying; excerpt from Lies and truth. M. Eck. il N Y Times Mag p87+ Ap 26 '70
Using a child as a weapon. il Good H 170:12+ Je '70
Very special pair. J. Trelford. il por McCalls 91:63-5+ Ap '70
What generation gap? D. M. Duffey. il pors Outdoor Life 145:58-9+ Ja '70
Why so many women can't stand their own mothers; interviews, ed. by S. Basescu. il Redbook 135:78-9+ Je '70
Wisdom of silence. P. La Farge. il Redbook 135:74-5+ Jl '70
See also
Children—Management and training
Children of divorced parents
Family life
Fathers
Generation gap
Love, Maternal
Mothers
Youth—Management and training

PARENT education
How to talk to your children; parent effectiveness training. J. Fincher. il McCalls 98:16+ Ja '71
Play schools for parents. il Time 97:55 Ja 11 '71
Teaching parents to teach. H. S. Resnik. Vogue 156:96 O 1 '70

PARENT effectiveness training. See Parent education

PARENT participation in school management. See School management and organization—Parent participation

PARENT-teacher cooperation. See School and the home

PARENTE, William J.
College deans discern the times. America 123: 176-7 S 19 '70

PARENTEAU, Shirley
Better boating with the stars. il Motor B 127:82-3 Ja '71

PARENTHOOD, Planned. See Birth control

PARENTS
Schools we want: a family dialogue. N. Hentoff; M. Hentoff. il Sat R 53:74-7 S 19 '70
Wrong reasons to have children. R. E. Gould. il N Y Times Mag p83+ My 3 '70
You're a baaad parent! parent participantitis. M. Holmes. il Todays Health 48:4+ F '70
See also
Family
Family life
Fathers
Mothers
Parent education
School and the home

PARENTS and teachers associations
Getting through to the establishment. M. Essex. Ed Digest 35:42-4 Ja '70
How to's for leaders and members. M. M. Conant. PTA Mag 65:37 S; 36 O; 34 N; 36 D '70
Membership proclamation. P. B. Price. PTA Mag 65:13 O '70
Men speak out for the PTA. il PTA Mag 64: 10-13 F '70
PTA in the seventies. P. B. Price. PTA Mag 64:17 F '70
PTA: where the action is. See issues of PTA magazine
People who appreciate; teachers and members of the PTA. P. B. Price. PTA Mag 64:13 Je '70
Quest for a quality program. P. B. Price. PTA Mag 64:20-1 Ja '70
See also
National congress of parents and teachers

PARENTS and teachers conferences. See School and the home

PARENTS letters to children. See Letters to children

PARENTS liability. See Liability (law)

PARENTS' magazine
Introducing our new editor. G. J. Hecht. por Parents Mag 46:22 Ja '71
Parents' magazine's awards for outstanding service to children. il Parents Mag 45:24 Ja '70
See also
Youth group achievement awards

PARENTS quarrels. See Quarrels

PARENTS responsibility (law) See Liability (law)

PARENTS school visiting. See School and the home

PARIS, James D.
APBA action report. See issues of Motor boating

PARIS
Airports
City of flight; Orly airport. Time 95:48+ Mr 16 '70
Architecture
See also
Unesco—Headquarters
Art
Paris. M. Conil-Lacoste. See issues of Art news
Paris: unrolling the red carpet. J. Russell. il Art in Am 58:114-15 My '70
Description
Author in search of a background. I. Wallace. il pors Holiday 47:52-5 F '70
Paris again. M. Geltman. Nat R 22:1002 S 22 '70
Paris on a sentimental note. J. Barry. il Sat R 53:64-5+ Mr 14 '70
Paris when it sizzles. H. Sutton. il Sat R 53: 36-7 Jl 18 '70
Galleries and museums
Paris burgeoning? A. Bower. il Art in Am 58:112-13 S '70
See also
Louvre
Historic houses, etc.
Paris on a sentimental note. J. Barry. il Sat R 53:64-5+ Mr 14 '70
Hotels, restaurants, etc.
Paris restaurants. Q. Crewe. Vogue 156:38 O 15 '70
Paris Ritz: world's greatest hotel? W. Root. il Holiday 47:38-9+ Ja '70
Libraries
See also
American library in Paris
Markets
Shopper-watching at a Paris street market; Rue Mouffetard. il Sunset 144:40 Ap '70
Metropolitan district
Gallic answer to urban congestion; satellite city, Quartier de la Défense. il Bsns W p74+ N 7 '70
Music
Behind the scenes. R. McMullen. il Hi Fi sec I 20:20+ Ja '70
Letter from Paris; Verdi's Falstaff. Genêt. New Yorker 46:88-9 My 30 '70
Report: new versions of Cavalleria rusticana and Pagliacci in Opéra comique. D. Stevens. Opera N 34:33 F 28 '70
See also
Bastille
Prisons
Riots
Letter from Paris; Left Bank student riots in Latin Quarter and Saint-Germain-des-Prés. Genêt. il New Yorker 46:97-8 Je 13 '70
Social conditions
Letter from Paris: the quality of life. R. Gomer. Bul Atom Sci 26:55-6 F '70
Social life and customs
Ad-lib fashion show at a Paris bistro. il Life 68:48-50 F 27 '70
Streets
Most glamorous half mile in the world; Faubourg St Honore. J. Barry. il Sat R 53:59-60+ S 12 '70
Subways
Letter from Paris; la Défense station. Genêt New Yorker 46:86-7 Mr 7 '70
Theater
Arrabal. panic plays. T. Bishop. Vogue 155: 32 Mr 15 '70
Letter from Paris; Teatro libero di Roma medieval version of Ariosto's Orlando furioso. Genêt. New Yorker 46:88 My 30 '70
Paris season. H. Judson. il Time 96:80 D 7 '70
Paris theater: the stage. J. W. Montgomery. Chr Today 15:35-6 Ja 15 '71
See also
Comédie Française

PARIS auto show. See Automobiles—Exhibitions
PARIS Opéra. See Opera houses
PARIS opera ballet. See Ballet—France
PARIS peace talks. See Vietnamese war, 1957-
—Peace and mediation—Negotiations meetings, May 1968-
PARIS Vogue. See Periodicals—France
PARISH registers. See Registers of births, etc.
PARISHES
Do we want a national pastoral council?
America 123:83 Ag 22 '70
Parish councils: democratic process or new absolutism? J. F. Kippley. America 123:94-7 Ag 22 '70
Parish or perish. W. J. Horvath. Chr Cent 87:790 Je 24 '70
PARITY nonconservation
Parity-violating nuclear forces. G. L. Wick. bibliog il Science 168:104-5 Ap 3 '70
PARK, David C.
Therapeutic program: a community responsibility. Parks & Rec 5:25-6+ Jl '70
PARK, John S.
How to fertilize growing crops organically during the summer. Org Gard & Farm 17:42-3 Jl '70
Winter salad greens by the tubful. il Org Gard & Farm 17:36-9 O '70
PARK, W. B.
Adam and Eve. ltd. il Look 34:67-8 Ap 21 '70
PARK administration. See Parks—Management
PARK and recreation departments
Pull! shooting facilities for P&R departments. W. E. Talley. il Parks & Rec 5:18-20+ O '70
PARK management. See Parks—Management
PARK moving pictures. See Moving picture theaters, Open air
PARK shelters. See Shelters
PARK signs. See Signs and signboards
PARKE-Bernet galleries, inc.
Auction. New Yorker 46:37 N 28 '70
History is today, grown old: auction of photo rarities. K. Poli. il Pop Phot 66:60-1+ F '70
Parke-Bernet photographic auction, a $61,870 bonanza. J. Schneider. il Mod Phot 34:129-30 My '70
PARKE, Davis and company
Back to the wars; merger proposal from Warner-Lambert. Newsweek 76:61 Ag 10 '70
Drug industry catches the fever. Bsns W p 18-19 Ag 8 '70
Peculiar success of Chloromycetin. il Consumer Rep 35:616-19 O '70
Wheeling and dealing; auction of contemporary American art. il Newsweek 76:89 N 30 '70
PARKER, Bruce C.
Life in the sky; with biographical sketch. il Natur Hist 79:5, 54-9 O '70

about
Life in the clouds. Newsweek 76:57 O 5 '70 *
Life in the clouds. por Time 96:42 N 2 '70 *
PARKER, Carl E.
Mercury: major new environmental problem. il Cons 25:6-9 Ag '70
PARKER, Charles W. See Spector, S. jt. auth.
PARKER, Denise
Face to face with a resolute renovator. por Seventeen 29:62 Ap '70 *
PARKER, Dorothy (Rothschild)
Constant reader, by D. Parker, and You might as well live, by J. Keats. Reviews
Sat R por 53:30-2 O 10 '70. E. Janeway *
Tragedy of backchat and bons mots. B. Darrach. por Life 69:17 O 16 '70 *
Wittiest woman. R. A. Sokolov. por Newsweek 76:124+ O 12 '70 *
You might as well live, by J. Keats. Review
Commentary 51:96-8+ Ja '71. J. Epstein *
Vogue 156:100 D '70. A. Kazin *
You might as well live: the life and times of Dorothy Parker; excerpt. J. Keats. por McCalls 98:125-32+ O '70 *
PARKER, Elaine M.
Decade of letters. il Am Lib 1:614-15 Je '70
PARKER, Frances L. See Berger, W. H. jt. auth.
PARKER, Franklin
Biafra and the Nigerian civil war. il Negro Hist Bul 32:7-11 D '69
1970 as a centennial year in the history of education. Sch & Soc 98:110-12 F '70

PARKER, Garland G.
Fifty years of collegiate enrollments: 1919-20 to 1969-70. bibliog il Sch & Soc 98:148-59, 215-24, 282-7+ Mr-Sum '70
Statistics of attendance in American universities and colleges, 1969-70. Sch & Soc 98:41-58 Ja '70
Supplementary report on collegiate enrollments for 1969-70. Sch & Soc 98:119-20 F '70
PARKER, Harold K.
On making incorrigible youths corrigible. Ed Digest 35:22-4 My '70
PARKER, James
Wrightsman rooms at the Metropolitan museum of art. il Antiques 97:102-8 Ja '70
PARKER, James T.
Facts behind the mercury menace. il Pop Sci 197:62-3+ D '70
PARKER, Judith Ann
Art and the special child. il Sch Arts 69:32-3 Mr '70
PARKER, Michael J.
Out gunning. New Repub 163:7 N 28 '70 *
PARKER, P. L. See Attaway, D. jt. auth.
PARKER, Raymond
Ray Parker. D. H. Karshan. il por Art in Am 58:48-51 S '70 *
PARKER, Sanford S. and others
Business roundup. See issues of Fortune
PARKER, Seymour. See Rokeach, M. jt. auth.
PARKER, Wes
Second, without any motion. por Sports Illus 33:38-9 Ag 10 '70 *
PARKER street 470, Boston. See Art dealers
PARKING garages. See Garages; Garages, Municipal
PARKING lots. See Automobile parking
PARKING meter inspectors
Federal aid for meter maids; Toledo, Ohio. il Am City 85:96-7 Ag '70
Meter enforcement with a smile; Jacksonville, Fla. P. Atter. il Am City 85:134 My '70
PARKINSON, C. Northcote
Rise and fossilization of socialism; address, October 14, 1970. Vital Speeches 37:149-52 D 15 '70
PARKINSON'S disease
Amantadine-dopamine interaction: possible mode of action in Parkinsonism. R. P. Grelak and others. bibliog il Science 169:203-4 Jl 10 '70
L-Dopa has set me free. F. Miller. Read Digest 97:115-19 Ag '70
L-dopa: limited approval. Newsweek 75:91 Je 15 '70
My hands are free again. G. Astor. il Look 34:49-50 Jl 14 '70
Parkinson's disease: activity of L-dopa decarboxylase in discrete brain regions. K. Lloyd and O. Hornykiewicz. bibliog il Science 170:1212-13 D 11 '70
Relief from Parkinson's; L-dopa approved by FDA subject to safeguards. Time 95:56 Je 15 '70
PARKMAN, Robertson, and others
Murine sarcoma virus: the question of defectiveness. bibliog il Science 168:387-9 Ap 17 '70
PARKS, Gordon, 1912-
(ed) See Cleaver, E. Eldridge Cleaver in Algiers, a visit with Papa Rage
PARKS, Gordon, 1935?-
Exploring a campus in transition. R. Graves. il pors Life 68:3 Ap 17 '70 *
PARKS, John H.
Via *latina* to English mastery? Yes. Todays Ed 59:43-4 F '70
PARKS, Rosa
Founding mothers. il pors Vogue 155:112-13 Je '70 *
PARKS, Valerie E.
World of sin; poem. Negro Hist Bul 33:77 Mr '70
PARKS
Parks and recreation. See issues of American city
See also
Amusement parks
National parks and reserves
Playgrounds
Recreation
Zoological gardens

Administration
See Parks—Management

Concessions
See Concessions (food, etc)

Equipment
Trends. il Parks & Rec 5:29-42+ My '70

PARKS—*Continued*

Fees
See Recreation—Fees

Maintenance
Park maintenance operations; Topeka, Kan. D. Showalter. por Am City 85:84+ Mr '70
Reduce park maintenance costs; Los Angeles. C. V. Clarke. Am City 85:132+ O '70

Management
Changing concepts: citizen safety in parks and recreation. I. J. Hutchison, jr. il Parks & Rec 9:43-4+ S '70
Law enforcement: citizen safety in parks and recreation. Parks & Rec 5:11 N '70

Paraguay
Potential for parks in Paraguay. L. C. Merriam, jr. il Nat Parks & Con Mag 44:10-12 Je '70

United States
Decline and deterioration of the American city park. J. S. French. il Parks & Rec 5: 24-8+ Ag '70
More wildlife for urban America. J. J. Shomon. il Cons 24:2-7 F '70
Placing a dollar sign on urban parks; highway location. D. G. Brauer. il Parks & Rec 5:14-16 N '70
Urban conservation; adaptation of address. D. F. Rettie. Parks & Rec 9:33-4+ S '70
See also
Camping—United States
National parks and conservation association
National parks and reserves—United States
also subhead Parks and reserves under names of states, e.g. California—Parks and reserves; also subhead Parks and playgrounds under names of cities, e.g. Los Angeles—Parks and playgrounds

PARKWAY program. See Philadelphia—Education

PARLEY, Peter, pseud. See Goodrich, S. G.

PARLIAMENT, Members of. See Members of Parliament

PARLIAMENTARY Labor party. See Labor party (Great Britain)

PARLIAMENTARY papers, British. See Government publications

PARLIAMENTARY practice
Authors & editors; story of Robert's rules of order. B. A. Bannon. por Pub W 197: 15-16 Mr 16 '70
See also
United States—Congress—Rules and practice

PARLOR feminist; story. See Feydy, A.

PARMA, Italy
Man on the thousand-lire note. W. Weaver. il por Sat R 53:66+ Mr 14 '70

Music
Report:
Magyar state opera of Cluj performing Béla Bartók's Miraculous mandarin. E. Rizzo. Opera N 34:28 Ap 11 '70

PARMELEE, David M.
Top designers at home. V. D. Hahn. il pors Am Home 73:68-71 S '70 *

PAROCHIAL schools. See Church schools

PAROCHIAL schools, Catholic. See Catholic schools

PARODY (music)
See also
Phonograph records—Musical parody

PAROLE
Parole board; excerpts from hearings at the Connecticut correctional institution, Somers, Conn. D. Jackson. il Life 69:54-548B+ Jl 10 '70

PARR, Peggy Sullivan
Mexico. il Home Gard 57:16-17+ Jl '70

PARRELLA, Ida
Knock on the door; drama. Plays 30:65-8, 91 Ja '71

PARRILLA, Antulio, bp
Prelate and the prisoners. W. J. Davis. il Commonweal 91:527-9 F 13 '70 *

PARRILLA-BONILLA, Antulio, bp
If you could make one change in the church, what would it be? Commonweal 92:162 My 1 '70

PARRIS, Martha
Radio astronomy. il Space World G-4-76:32-41 Ap '70

PARRISH, Maxfield
Maxfield Parrish; with paintings. G. Glueck. pors Am Heritage 22:16-27+ D '70 *

PARRY, Albert
Samizdat is Russia's underground press. il N Y Times Mag p64-5+ Mr 15 '70

PARSHALL, Phil
Night of terror. Chr Today 15:40-1 D 18 '70

PARSIFAL; opera. See Wagner, R.

PARSONS, Charles S. and Brooke, D. S.
Dunlap cabinetmakers. il Antiques 98:224-31 Ag '70

PARSONS, Donald Holcombe
Parsons's downfall. Newsweek 76:51 Ag 24 '70 *

PARSONS, Talcott
Coming crisis in western sociology, by A. W. Gouldner. Review
Commentary 50:96-7 D '70. S. Rothman *

PARSONS college, Fairfield, Ia.
Parsons college bubble, by J. Koerner. Review
Sat R 53:56 Ag 15 '70. L. B. Mayhew

PARSONS tables. See Tables

PART time employment
Best bets in part-time jobs. il Changing T 24:14 S '70
Facts about fifty good part-time jobs for women. il Good H 170:187-9 Mr '70
Go-go mother; Boston's catalyst program. N. Gittelson. Harp Baz 103:25+ Ap '70
How to make money in your spare time (cont) J. Kuh. Ladies Home J 86:143 D '69; 87:117 F; 132 Mr; 68 Ap: 19 My; 54 Je; 118 Ag; 143 S; 145 O; 176 N '70
Where to get part-time harvest help. R. Krumme and R. Sanders. il Suc Farm 68: 30-1 Je '70
See also
Student employment

PART time farming
Good town job and countryside living. D. Seim. il Farm J 94:22-3+ Ag '70

PART time teachers. See Teachers, Part time

PARTCH, Harry
Concert records. A. Hiss. New Yorker 45:80-5 F 7 '70

PARTHENOGENESIS (plants)
See also
Apogamy

PARTHENON, Model of. See Architectural models

PARTICIPATORY art. See Art, Modern

PARTICLES
Palladium: preparation and catalytic properties of particles of uniform size. J. Turkevich and G. Kim. bibliog il Science 169: 873-9 Ag 28 '70
See also
Colloids

PARTICLES (nuclear physics)
Antihelium. Chem 43:21 Je '70
Building exotic atoms. D. E. Thomsen. il Sci N 98:385-6 N 14 '70
Evidence for partons il Sci N 98:333 O 24 '70
Hadron bootstrap: triumph or frustration? G. F. Chew. bibliog il Phys Today 23:23-8 O '70
More on tachyons; letters. E. H. Kerner and others. bibliog Phys Today 23:13+ My '70
No sign found in search for neutral tachyons. B. G. Levi. Phys Today 23:56 Je '70
Particles that go faster than light. G. Feinberg. il Sci Am 222:68-73+ bibliog(p 126) F '70
Particles that travel faster than light? R. G. Newton. bibliog il Science 167:1569-74 Mr 20 '70
Physical sciences; excerpts from reports at Coral Gables conference on fundamental interactions at high energy. Sci N 97:126 Ja 31 '70
Quests and questions concerning quarks. B. G. Levi. bibliog Phys Today 23:57-8 Je '70
Search for magnetic monopoles in the lunar sample. L. W. Alvarez and others. bibliog il Science 167:701-3 Ja 30 '70
Searching for monopoles. D. E. Thomsen. il Sci N 98:183-4 Ag 22 '70
Surprises at Serpukhov. D. E. Thomsen. il Sci N 97:437-8 My 2 '70
Three-body success; antihelium 3. Sci N 97: 218-19 F 28 '70
Three steps in the structure of matter. V. F. Weisskopf. il por Phys Today 23:17-22+ S '70
What is a quark? I. Asimov. Sci Digest 68: 89-90 N '70
See also
Mesons
Nucleons
Polarization of particles
Protons
Regge trajectories
Tunneling (physics)
Van Allen radiation belts

Acceleration
AGS's second decade; more precise experiments. H. L. Davis. Phys Today 23:20 O '70

PARTICLES (nuclear physics)—*Continued*

Conferences

Particles, meet the fields; conference on fundamental interactions at high energy. il Sci N 97:119-20 Ja 31 '70

PARTIDO revolucionario institucional. See Political parties—Mexico

PARTIES. See Balls (parties); Entertaining

PARTINGTON, William M.
Oklawaha, the fight is on again! il Liv Wildn 33:19-23 Aut '69

PARTITIONS
$51.85 room divider. R. Winblad. il Mech Illus 66:104-5 F '70

PARTITIONS, Movable
Movable room divider. R. Brightman. il Mech Illus 66:70-1 Mr '70
See also
Screens (furniture)

PARTNERSHIP
Owning in partnership. R. H. Rice. il Yachting 127:92-3+ Ja '70
See also
Farm partnership
Joint adventures
Limited partnership

PARTNERSHIPS, Farm family. See Father-son farm operating agreements

PARTONS. See Particles (nuclear physics)

PARTRIDGE shooting
China Lake chukars. J. Mears. il por Outdoor Life 146:64-5+ N '70
Eastern homeland of the hun. J. B. Robinson. il Field & S 75:136-8+ S '70
Super-segmental chukar-checker. J. F. Adams. il Field & S 75:56-7+ S '70
What makes chukar run? C. Conley. il Field & S 74:54-5+ F '70

PARTY funds. See Campaign funds

PARTY menus. See Menus

PARVIN, Stuart A.
Miniaturia. See issues of Hobbies

PARVIN-Dohrmann company
Parvin lives. Newsweek 75:64+ Mr 2 '70

PASACHOFF, Jay M. See Menzel, D. H. jt. auth.

PASADENA, Calif.

Galleries and museums

Until April 26: the great Bauhaus show in Pasadena's new art museum. il Sunset 144:68 Ap '70

Parades

La vie en rose; Pasadena's New Year's parade. A. Wright. il Sports Illus 34:56-65 Ja 4 '71

PASCHAL, Justin
Prophet; poem. Chr Cent 88:10 Ja 6 '71

PASCOE, Jean
Lady who makes the gourmet gallop. il por McCalls 97:14+ Je '70

PASQUALINI, Jean
Christmas mass of Father Hsia. il Read Digest 96:140-4 Ja '70

PASS-throughs
Wall that works. J. Gillies. il Farm J 94:32 S '70

PASSANO, William Moore
How photocopying pollutes sci-tech publishing; excerpts from address, January 13, 1970. il por Pub W 197:63-4 F 2 '70

PASSELL, Peter, and Ross, Leonard
Everybody's money worries. il Trans-Action 7:30-2 My '70

PASSENGER fares. See Airlines—Fares

PASSENGER service on airlines. See Airlines—Passenger service

PASSER, Jerry E.
Regional approach to conservation education. il Cons 24:8-9 Je '70

PASSING through from exotic places; drama. See Ribman, R.

PASSINO, Jacque
Rap 'n 'pinion. por Motor T 22:24 Jl '70

PASSINO, Roberto
Industrial Europe faces the challenge of pollution. il UNESCO Courier 23:61-4 Ag '70

PASSION music
See also
Phonograph records—Passion music

PASSION plays
See also
Oberammergau passion play

PASSIVE resistance to government
See also
Tax evasion

PASSPORT restrictions. See Travel regulations

PASSPORTS
Secretary Rogers receives report of Committee to facilitate travel; Department announcement; with statement by Secretary Rogers, June 9, 1970. Dept State Bul 62:809-10 Je 29 '70
U.S. unlocks door on executive visas. Bsns W p30+ Ap 11 '70

PAST, The
On the passage of time. P. Berlinrut. Commentary 50:44-54 Jl '70

PAST love, present danger; story. See McInerny, R.

PASTA. See Cookery, Italian; Macaroni

PASTAN, Ira, and Perlman, Robert
Cyclic adenosine monophosphate in bacteria. bibliog il Science 169:339-44 Jl 24 '70

PASTED pictures. See Collage

PASTEL drawing
What is pastel? il Design 71:8-12 Sum '70

PASTEL painting. See Pastel drawing

PASTER, Howard G.
Water and air. il New Repub 163:24-6 O 31 '70

PASTER, Zvi, and Abbott, B. C.
Gibberellic acid: a growth factor in the unicellular alga gymnodinium breve. bibliog il Science 169:600-1 Ag 7 '70

PASTERNAK, Elizabeth F. See Brong, G. R. jt. auth.

PASTON, Herbert S.
Paper as a personal medium. il Design 72:29 Wint '70
Puppets are personalities. il Sch Arts 70:28-9 N '70

PASTOR, Blanca
Secrets of the stones il Américas 22:32-7 Ap '70

PASTORAL counseling
Case studies. A. H. Leitch. Chr Today 14:38-9 Mr 27 '70
Clergyman's role and community mental health. W. G. Scarlett. Ment Hy 54:378-81 Jl '70
Conference on pastoral counseling: life and death. C. J. Edson. Chr Cent 87:1545-6 D 23 '70
Focus for pastoral counseling. L. O. Caldwell. Chr Today 15:34-5 O 23 '70
Minister's workshop. See issues of Christianity today
Reform of penance. C. Kiesling. il America 122:652+ Je 20 '70

PASTORAL letters
Not fit to print; New York bishops' on abortion. S. J. Adamo. America 123:568-70 D 26 '70

PASTORAL literature
American institutions and ecological ideals; adaptation of address, December 29, 1969. L. Marx. bibliog Science 170:949-51 N 27 '70

PASTORAL psychology
See also
Pastoral counseling

PASTORAL theology
Missions for today. C. J. McNaspy. America 122:416-18 Ap 18 '70; Discussion. 122:544, 661 My 23, Je 27 '70
Pico Rivera's picnicking pastor. Chr Cent 87:855 Jl 8 '70
Today's priest, GP or more? A. O. Sigur. America 122:237-40 Mr 7 '70; Discussion. 122:320+, 636 Mr 28, Je 13 '70
Unresponsive pew. J. Richie; discussion. Chr Cent 86:1458+, 1549; 87:123-5 N 12, D 3 '69, Ja 28 '70

PASTORE, John O.
Agnew and the Pastore bill. S. Cupps. il Chr Cent 87:77-9 Ja 21 '70
Christmas list. J. Fischer; reply. J. Vacca. Harper 240:10+ Mr '70 *
Making FCC's mission impossible. Consumer Rep 35:109-11 F '70 *
Priest vs. Pastore. S. Cunneen. Chr Cent 87:1067-8 S 9 '70 *

PASTRY
Almond tart, quickly made; gateau pithiviers. il Sunset 144:206 Mr '70
Butter-bright pastries. E. W. Manning. il Farm J 94:26-7 D '70
Cream puff valentine. E. W. Manning. il Farm J 94:86 F '70
Italian cheese pies for Easter. il Sunset 144:199 Mr '70
Kitzbühel confections. F. M. Crawford. il Am Home 73:78-80+ Ja '70
Meat comes in in a crisp and tasty overcoat. il Sunset 144:90-1 Ja '70
Norse treat; krum kake. J. Hewitt. il N Y Times Mag p 107 Mr 15 '70
Pirog and piroshki. il Sunset 144:162-4 My '70
Puff paste. J. Jaffry. il Am Home 73:82-3+ Mr '70
Sweet snack from Mexico: sopapillas. il Sunset 144:186 Mr '70

PASTRY—*Continued*
This easy pastry makes into turnovers or cooky treats. il Sunset 145:160 N '70
Viennese pastry cookbook; excerpts. L. J. Reich. il Ladies Home J 87:104-5+ Ap '70
What these strudels have inside is beef or chicken. il Sunset 145:147-8 O '70
  See also
Pie
Shortcake
Tarts
PASTURE mosquito. See Mosquitoes
PASTURES
Get the most from your pastures. Suc Farm 68:D6 O '70
Horse drive down from Yosemite, late October. il Sunset 145:24+ O '70
How irrigation is changing the beef business. G. Lorang. il Farm J 94:26-7+ O '70
Latest way to put in pasture fast. J. D. Boyd. il Farm J 94:16 N '70
Why a western cowman chose the Corn Belt. R. Sanders. il Suc Farm 68:28-9 My '70
  See also
Grazing
PATAGONIA
Patagonian journey. R. Weekley. il Américas 22:29-35 Mr '70
PATCH, Margaret Merwin
Travelogue (title varies) (cont) il Craft Horiz 30:30-5+ Ja '70
PATCHWORK
West Virginia's super sewing bee; turning patchwork designs into fashions. il Life 69:58-62 Jl 31 '70
PATCO. See Professional air traffic controllers organization
PATÉ maison. See Cookery, French
PATENT cooperation treaty. See Patents—International aspects
PATENT office (United States) See United States—Patent office
PATENTS
Got a bright idea? Read up on patents. il Changing T 24:43-5 S '70
  See also
United States—Patent office

Infringement
Copy war. Time 95:92 My 4 '70
Giant rival for the top copier cat; Xerox suing IBM. il Bsns W p33-4 Ap 25 '70
Magnetic disks go to court. Bsns W p88 Ja 17 '70
Xerox vs. IBM. il Newsweek 75:74 My 4 '70

International aspects
Agreeing on prior art. Patent cooperation treaty. il Sci N 97:614-15 Je 27 '70
Lowering the patent barriers; Patent cooperatiton; treaty. il Nations Bsns 58:78-80 D '70
Signing the treaty; Patent cooperation treaty. Sci N 97:575-6 Je 13 '70
U.S. delegation to conference on Patent cooperation treaty. Dept State Bul 62:715 Je 8 '70
Washington diplomatic conference approves Patent cooperation treaty; summary, address, and remarks; with text of treaty. Dept State Bul 63:40-64 Jl 13 '70
PATER, Walter Horatio
Hemingway as Walter Pater. G. Davenport. Nat R 22:1214-15 N 17 '70 *
PATERNO, Joe
Winningest coach takes his lumps. J. Newcombe. il por Life 69:44-6 O 9 '70 *
PATERSON, Basil A.
Mr Goldberg runs for office. New Yorker 46:27-9 Je 13 '70 *
PATERSON, Thomas G. See Adler, L. K. jt. auth.
PATERSON, N.J.

Historic houses, etc.
Proposal for Paterson. A. Chatfield-Taylor il Arch Forum 132:72-7 Ja '70
PATHOLOGICAL psychology. See Psychology, Pathological
PATHOLOGY
  See also
Diagnosis
PATHS. See Garden walks; Trails
PATIENCE, C. Edgar
Coal-black art. il pors Ebony 25:92-4+ Mr '70 *
PATIENTS and physicians. See Physicians and patients
PATIÑO, Simón Iturri
From rags to Rolls-Royces. il por Forbes 106:36 Ag 1 '70 *
PATIÑO family
Empire reborn. Forbes 106:35-6 Ag 1 '70

PATINO mining corporation
Empire reborn. Forbes 106:35-6 Ag 1 '70
PATIO furniture. See Furniture, Outdoor
PATIOS. See Outdoor rooms
PATMAN, Wright
One bank holding companies; address, April 28, 1970. Vital Speeches 36:523-6 Je 15 '70
Excerpt from debate, July 31, 1970. Cong Digest 49:232+ O '70

    about
Big days for the scourge of the banks. por Time 95:68-9 Ja 26 '70
Prime rate: opposing views. U S News 69:63 S 28 '70 *
PATRICIA Flinn, Sister. See Flinn, P.
PATRICK, B. E. pseud.
Ghetto schools are different. Nat R 22:401-4 Ap 21 '70
PATRICK, J. Milton
For America; address, January 5, 1970. Vital Speeches 36:341-3. Mr 15 '70
PATRICK, James E.
Decade of crisis for education. Vital Speeches 36:502-5 Je 1 '70
PATRICK, Richard K.
Garden of azaleas. il Horticulture 48:32-4 F '70
PATRICOFF, Pat
Winter fun in Finland. il Travel 133:52-6 Ja '70
PATRIOTISM
Manner of speaking; defense against accusation by HISC of being a radical. J. Ciardi. Sat R 53:12+ N 7 '70
  See also
Allegiance
Americanism
Nationalism

  Anecdotes, facetiae, satire, etc.
Oh, say can't you see? G. Ace. Sat R 53:8 D 5 '70
TRB from Washington; imaginary conversation with the Washington monument Executive mansion and Memorial. New Repub 163:4 Jl 4 '70
PATRIOTS (football club) See Football clubs
PATROL cars. See Automobiles, Police
PATRONAGE, Art. See Art patronage
PATRONAGE of opera. See Opera patronage
PATTEN, Edward James
Youth gets out the voters, but the wrong ones. il pors Newsweek 75:28-9 Je 15 '70 *
PATTERN glass. See Glassware
PATTERN pictures. See Photography, Artistic
PATTERSON, Franklin
Library as arbiter. Am Lib 1:254-5 Mr '70
PATTERSON, Howard W. Jr
Building types study. il Arch Rec 148:128-34 N '70
PATTERSON, James H. and others
Chemical composition of the lunar surface in a terra region near the crater Tycho. bibliog il Science 168:825-8 My 15 '70
PATTERSON, R. S. and others
Suppression and elimination of an island population of culex pipiens quinquefasciatus with sterile males. bibliog il Science 168:1368-70 Je 12 '70
PATTERSON, Walter G.
How to obtain a principalship. Clear House 44:310-14 Ja '70
PATTERSON, William D.
Not to kill, but to live. il Sat R 53:15-16 Jl 25 '70
PATTI, Charles
Sea otter returns to Canada; with biographical sketch. il Sea Front 16:220-2, 255 Jl '70
PATTON, Arch
Are stock options dead? Harvard Bsns R 48:20-2+ S '70
PATTON, Debbie
To smoke or not to smoke; excerpts from address, March 1970. por PTA Mag 64:6-7 Je '70
PATTON, George Smith, 1885-1945
Anybody see Patton? H. Sidey. Life 68:2B Je 19 '70 *
Patton, J. W. Montgomery. Chr Today 15:50-1 O 23 '70 *
Power and the gory. H. Alpert. Sat R 53:59+ Ja 31 '70
PATTON, Robert
Vocation profile; marine electronics servicing. il Electr World 84:23-5+ N '70
PATTON, William W. Jr, and Miller, T. P.
Possible bedrock source for obsidian found in archeological sites in northwestern Alaska. bibliog il Science 169:760-1 Ag 21 '70
PAUKER, John
Grandfatherly poem: Avuncular poem. New Repub 162:20, 22 F 28 '70

PAUL, Saint
Gospel of Christian freedom, by Q. Quesnell.
Review
Cath World 212:154-5 D '70. K. P. Coyle *

Teachings
Incarnational evangelism. J. W. Haughton.
Chr Today 14:10-12 Ag 21 '70 *

PAUL VI, pope
How can we persuade modern man to pray?
por Ladies Home J 87:77 Mr '70

about
Brazil and the Pope. Commonweal 92:284 Je
12 '70 *
Cardinal Suenens: a plea for dialogue; inter-
view, ed. by H. Fesquet. L. Suenens. por
Cath World 211:216-20 Ag '70 *
Church torn between dogma and dissent; with
report by J. Cogley. il pors Life 68:22-31
Mr 20 '70 *
Day after aggiornamento. B. J. Nauer. il
America 124:36-40 Ja 16 '71 *
Ecclesiastics and lucre. T. Beeson. Chr Cent
87:884 Jl 22 '70 *
Isolation of Pope and President. J. B.
Sheerin. Cath World 211:146-7 Jl '70 *
Letter to Pope Paul; with reference to police
torture in Brazil. I. Illich. Commonweal 92:
428-9 S 4 '70; Reply. J. J. Kaufmann. 93:55
O 9 '70 *
Papal fallibility. Chr Cent 87:1309 N 4
'70; Discussion. 88:21 Ja 6 '71 *
Place in the country. il Time 96:64 S 14 '70 *
Pope and the Cardinal. America 122:576-7 My
30 '70 *
Pope Paul VI. P. Johnson. por Horizon 12:
56-9 Wint '70
Proposal for next Christmas; an appropriate
time for a trip. Commonweal 93:315-16 D
25 '70 *
Reports: the Vatican. I. R. Levine. Atlan 226:
5-6+ S '70 *
Vatican's noisy family. J. Bell. il por Time
95:50+ Je 15 '70 *

Visit to Asia and the Pacific Region
Apostle endangered; assassination attempt. il
pors Time 96:55 D 7 '70
Asian journey of Paul VI; Contact with
non-Christians. America 123:505 D 12 '70
Hazards of a papal trip abroad. il pors U S
News 69:77 D 7 '70
Image of Christ in the East. Chr Cent 87:
1531 D 23 '70
Journey to the left. il pors Newsweek 76:68-
68B D 14 '70
Papal visit anticipated. C. M. Ferrer. Chr
Cent 87:1134 S 23 '70
Papal visit sets stage for Philippine revolu-
tion. N. Ramientos. Chr Today 15:41 Ja
1 '71
Peripatetic Pope: Philippine peregrinations.
J. Novotney. il Chr Today 15:38 D 18 '70
Political pilgrimage. il por Newsweek 76:101
N 30 '70
Pope's perilous journey; assassination at-
tempt. il Newsweek 76:44+ D 7 '70
Pope's stature enhanced by Pacific visit. C.
M. Ferrer. Chr Cent 88:47 Ja 13 '71
To discover the church. il pors Time 96:66-9
D 14 '70
Traveling Pope: his Far East goals. il por
U S News 69:52 N 30 '70

Visit to Sardinia
Upside-down visit. il por Time 95:53 My 4
'70 *

PAUL, Alice
Where are they now? pors Newsweek 75:18
Mr 23 '70 *

PAUL, Harry W.
In quest of Kerygma: Catholic intellectual life
in nineteenth-century France. Am Hist R
75:387-423 D '69

PAUL, Jan S.
Radiation from color TV receivers, where
lies the danger? il Consumer Bul 53:43+
D '70

PAUL Taylor dance company
Musical events; performance at City center.
W. Sargeant. New Yorker 46:122 My 16 '70
Paul Taylor dance co; New York city center.
J. Anderson. Dance Mag 44:81-3 F '70
Paul Taylor dance company; New York city
center. T. Borek. Dance Mag 44:75 Jl '70

PAULING, Linus
Genetic and somatic effects of high-energy
radiation. il Bul Atom Sci 26:3-8 S '70

about
Case of vitamin C. por Sci N 98:477 D 26
'70 *
Vitamin C, anyone? por Newsweek 76:63-4
N 30 '70 *

PAULSEN, Jane
Playing cards & their diverse effects on man.
il Hobbies 75:150-1 Ap ; 150-1 My '70

PAULSON, F. M.
(ed) Boating. See Issues of Field & stream
Cruising the high country. il Field & S 75:
44-5+ D '70
Outstanding outboard. il Field & S 75:80-1+
Je '70

PAULSON, G. D. See Pekas, J. C. jt. auth.

PAULUCCI, Jeno Francis
Dynamic growth companies. il pors Nations
Bsns 58:64-7 Mr '70 *

PAVALON, Wes
Perfect toy. R. Kahn. il Esquire 74:172-6
D '70 *

PAVEMENT markings. See Traffic markings
PAVEMENTS

Maintenance and repair
Air and electronics save pavement; Love-
land, Colo. il Am City 85:10 D '70
See also
Pavements—Surface treatment
Streets—Maintenance and repair

Slipperiness
Testing
Make pavements skid resistant; Evanston,
Ill. F. X. Schwartz. il Am City 85:121+
My '70

Surface treatment
Make pavements skid resistant; Evanston,
Ill. F. X. Schwartz. il Am City 85:121+ My
'70
One crew instead of two; Kansas City, Mo.
il Am City 85:71 Ja '70
Resurface with old asphalt and save two ways.
il Am City 85:60 O '70
Second try was slurry seal; Contra Costa
County's airport. R. S. Latchaw. il Am
City 85:68+ D '70
Slurry seal proves itself; San Diego, Calif.
W. M. Davis. il Am City 85:120+ S '70

PAVEMENTS, Asphalt
Computer-designed asphalt pavement; experi-
ment near San Diego, Calif. J. F. Shook. il
Am City 85:68+ F '70
One crew instead of two; Kansas City, Mo.
il Am City 85:71 Ja '70
Resurface with old asphalt and save two ways.
il Am City 85:60 O '70

PAVEMENTS, Concrete
It stamps out concrete bricks; imprinting.
il Sunset 145:106+ N '70
Remove old concrete the easy way. il Am
City 85:88 N '70

PAVESE, Cesare
Untitled; poem, tr. by B. Swann and R. Feldman. Poetry 116:302 Ag '70

about
Pavese, in the long run. R. Koffler. Nation
211:283-4 S 28 '70 *

PAVIA, Raphael
Parting shots. il pors Life 68:81 Je 12 '70 *

PAVILIONS
All-weather pavilion for all kinds of play;
gymkhana. Elisabeth Morrow school. Engle-
wood, N.J. il Arch Rec 147:135 My '70
New world in the works; Ontario pavilion.
il Arch Forum 133:26-9 O '70
Tent pavilion for flower show at state fair;
California's new state exposition and fair.
il Arch Rec 147:142-3 My '70
See also
Music pavilions

PAVILLARD, M. See Odartchenko, N. jt. auth.

PAVLAK, Eric
Buck up bass response with a super woofer. il
Pop Electr 32:62 Je '70

PAVOLA, Anna
Mercuria swan. E. O. Hoppe. por Dance
Mag 45:30-1 Ja '71 *

PAWN shops. See Pawnbroking
PAWNBROKING
Of rags and iron roses; the Dorotheum, Viennese pawn-shop-cum-auction house. il Newsweek 76:96+ O 12 '70

PAX Romana

Anecdotes, facetiae, satire, etc.
I was a Catholic for the PAX. P. Steinfels.
Commonweal 92:454 S 18 '70

PAXTON, Tom
People are talking about... por Vogue 155:
174-5 Ap 1 '70 *

PAY differentials. See Wage differentials
PAY telephones. See Telephone
PAY television. See Television broadcasting—
Subscription programs

PAYMENT
See also
Debtor and creditor
PAYMENTS, Balance of. See Balance of payments
PAYNE, Jack. See McGuckin, F. jt. auth.
PAYNE, Melvin M.
Frederick G. Vosburgh retires as editor; Gilbert M. Grosvenor succeeds him. il pors Nat Geog 138:838-43 D '70
PAYNE, Nicholas
Songs of a people. il Opera N 34:8-12 F 21 '70
PAYROLL robberies. See Robberies and assaults
PAYSON, Joan (Whitney)
Joan Whitney Payson. J. Durso. il por Vogue 155:92-3+ Je '70 *
PAYTON, Leland
Ozarks: fragments of the American wilderness. il Am Lib 1:256-65 Mr '70
PAZ, Nestor
Bolivian guerrilla movement comes to an end. M. Arias. Chr Cent 88:18-19 Ja 6 '71 *
PAZ, Octavio
Books. N. Bliven. New Yorker 46:91-2 Ag 15 '70 *
Octavio Paz; tr. by E. Weinberger. Review
Commonweal 92:148-50 Ap 24 '70. R. Christ *
PEABODY, Lawrence
Bonjour, M'sieu Peabody. il por McCalls 97: 88-93 Mr '70 *
PEABODY, Mrs Malcolm
Five passionate feminists. il pors McCalls 97: 52-3+ Jl '70
PEABODY coal company
Outsmarting themselves. Forbes 106:80 O 15 '70
PEACE
Asia and the prospects for world order; address, April 1970. J. S. Clark. bibliog f Ann Am Acad 390:27-37 Jl '70
How wars end; symposium, ed. by W. T. R. Fox. bibliog f Ann Am Acad 392:1-172 N '70
Nixon's vision of peace. H. Sidey. il por Life 69:4 S 25 '70
Pax atomica. J. Burnham. Nat R 22:729 Jl 14 '70
Peace of Bethlehem escapes us. B. L. Masse. America 123:535 D 19 '70
Peace research: the science of survival; reprint. B. V. A. Röling. il UNESCO Courier 23:21-2+ N '70
Peaceful competition; address, October 23, 1970. R. M. Nixon. Vital Speeches 37:66-9 N 15 '70; Same with title World interest: a generation of peace. Dept State Bul 63: 601-6 N 16 '70
Toward peace. J. West. Redbook 135:75+ S '70
Ways to peace in our troubled world. D. Lawrence. US News 69:108 O 12 '70
Whatever happened to mankind's dream of peace? W. B. Arthur. il Look 34:13-17 D 29 '70
See also
Arbitration, International
Disarmament
International relations
International security
United Nations—Special committee on peacekeeping operations
War
World war, 1939-1945—Peace and mediation

Bibliography
Peace: a publishers for peace bibliography. il Library J 95:3602-3+ O 15 '70
PEACE and happiness through prosperity (periodical)
Quotations from chairman Matsushita; PHP (Peace and happiness through prosperity) most popular magazine in the Japanese language. il Time 96:73 O 12 '70
Success stories. il por Newsweek 77:77 Ja 11 '71
PEACE candidates. See Candidates, Political
PEACE conferences
CPC's eleventh hour. A. Geyer. Chr Cent 87:1404-5 N 25 '70
Conversations with Marxists. H. B. Kuhn. Chr Today 14:39 Jl 31 '70
Dream of generations: World conference on religion and peace. Chr Cent 87:1177 O 7 '70
Future for the CPC? D. M. Paton. Chr Cent 87:718 Je 10 '70; Reply. P. Verghese. 87:1353 N 11 '70
Integrity of dialogue: the Christian peace conference, Prague. Chr Cent 87:1007 Ag 26 '70
Nikodim criticizes boycott of C.P.C. meeting in Prague. Chr Cent 87:351 Mr 25 '70

PEACE corps. See United States—Peace corps
PEACE movement
Terrorism for peace and justice. G. C. Zahn. Commonweal 93:84-5 O 23 '70
PEACE pacts. See Treaties
PEACE pentathlon. See Pentathlon
PEACE symbol. See Symbols
PEACE treaties. See Treaties
PEACEFUL coexistence. See World politics, 1945-
PEACEFUL uses of atomic power. See Atomic power—Economic aspects
PEACH trees
My peach trees take the winter. R. Tirrell. il por Org Gard & Farm 17:54-6 D '70
PEACHES
See also
Cookery—Fruit
Nectarines
PEAKALL, David B.
p,p'-DDT: effect on calcium metabolism and concentration of estradiol in the blood. bibliog il Science 168:592-4 My 1 '70
Pesticides and the reproduction of birds; with biographical sketch. il Sci Am 222:12, 72-8 bibliog(p 130) Ap '70
PEAL, S. Edward
African ambassadors honored by President Nixon; exchange of toasts, March 23, 1970. Dept State Bul 62:523-5 Ap 20 '70
PEALE, Charles Willson
Artist of the revolution. P. W. Schmidtchen. il por Hobbies 75:104+ Ag '70 *
Charles Willson Peale, by C. C. Sellers. Review
Sat R 53:39 Ja 17 '70. J. T. Flexner
PEALE, Norman Vincent
Hang-ups that haunt us. Read Digest 96:133-6 Je '70
about
Dais: testimonial dinner. New Yorker 46:34-5 My 9 '70 *
PEALE, Rembrandt
Lithographs by Rembrandt Peale. J. A. Mahey. il Antiques 97:236-42 F '70 *
PEANUT butter
Peanut butter; with list of suppliers of freshground butter. il Consumer Bul 53:4+ N '70
PEANUTS
Peanuts. G. Morrison. il Horticulture 48:40+ Ap '70
There's nothing wrong about working for peanuts. B. Rozell. il Org Gard & Farm 17:58-60 Ap '70
PEARCE, Donn
How to take off your pants while wearing chains. il Esquire 73:98-9 F '70
Oh, that Ahmed. Poor, poor Ahmed. They're going to fry his black, skinny ass. il Esquire 73:138-35+ Mr '70
PEARCE, William A.
Aquarium opened at department's Cape Vincent fisheries research station. il Cons 25: 20 O '70
PEARL, Jack
I'm a fiction ghost. Writers Digest 50:30-2 Je '70
PEARL HARBOR, Attack on, 1941
Japan strikes: 1941; prophesies in books by H. C. Bywater. W. H. Honan. il por Am Heritage 2:12-15+ D '70
Tora! Tora! Tora! H. Ehrlich. il Look 34: 27-32 S 22 '70
PEARLMAN, Edith
Her own kind; story. Seventeen 29:148-9 My '70
PEARLSTEIN, Philip
Eyewitness. D. Davis. il Newsweek 76:110+ N 16 '70 *
Hello and goodbye, Francis Picabia. il Art N 69:52-4+ S '70
Ugly American. L. Nochlin. il Art N 69:55-7+ S '70 *
PEARS
See also
Cookery—Fruit
PEARSON, Allen D. and Krebs, R. P.
Tornado season of 1969. il Weatherwise 23:18-23 F '70
PEARSON, E. Ray, and Kealy, H. L. P.
Unusual forms in Shaker furniture. il Antiques 98:606-10 O '70
PEARSON, Hank
Hobby from the sea. il Design 72:39-41 Fall '70
PEARSON, James Blackwood
Excerpt from memorandum on environmental control, April 23, 1970. Cong Digest 49:204+ Ag '70

PEARSON, John F.
Putting the lid on oil spills. il Pop Mech 135:82-5+ Ja '71
Science worldwide. See issues of Popular mechanics
Submarine icebreaker for Arctic oil? il pors Pop Mech 133:85-9 Mr '70; Same. Sci Digest 67:75-9 My '70
—and Albino, Joseph
Defusing Canada's sunken time bomb. il Pop Mech 134:116-20 N '70
PEARSON, Lester Bowles
New strategy for global development: address. por UNESCO Courier 23:4+ F '70
On human survival; excerpts from letter. Sat R 53:24+ Je 13 '70
U.N. at twenty-five. il Sat R 53:16-18+ Je 27 '70
PEARSON, Michael. See Fendrich, J. jt. auth.
PEARSON, Roger L.
Gatsby: false prophet of the American dream. bibliog f Engl J 59:638-42+ My '70
PEARSON, Ronald
Contemporary blacksmith: 1970. il Craft Horiz 30:22-7 D '70
PEARSON, Rufus Judson, 1915-
How to stay healthy; interview. il por U S News 68:60-3 Ap 6 '70
PEAS
Peas for your garden. G. Morrison. il Horticulture 48:40-1+ Mr '70
PEASANTRY
    See also
Land tenure

                    India
Land-grab war; Naxalite movement in West Bengal. il Newsweek 76:31 Ag 3 '70

                    Mexico
Social character in a Mexican village, by E. Fromm and M. Maccoby. Review Sat R il 53:21-2 D 5 '70. R. F. Murphy

                    Peru
Rural Peru: peasants as activists. W. F. Whyte. il por Trans-Action 7:37-47 N '69

                    Tunisia
Change at Shebika, by J. Duvignaud. Review Cath World 212:164 D '70. W. J. Wilson Commonweal 92:373-4 Jl 24 '70. R. W. Fox

                    Vietnam
    See also
Vietnamese war, 1957- —Pacification programs
PEAT, Fossil
Petrified peat from a Permian coal bed in Antarctica. J. M. Schopf. bibliog il Science 169:274-7 Jl 17 '70
PEBBLE mosaics. See Mosaics
PECAN trees
Grafting pecan trees, Texas style. J. Gillette. il Org Gard & Farm 17:46-9 O '70
Pecan tree. F. B. Widmoyer and D. T. Sullivan. Horticulture 48:20-1 Mr '70
Pecans, an extra cash crop. J. L. Gillette. il Org Gard & Farm 17:50-3 My '70
PECANS
Pecans, an extra cash crop. J. L. Gillette. il Org Gard & Farm 17:50-3 My '70
PECCARY hunting
Hangup on javelina. R. Tinsley. il por Outdoor Life 145:66-7+ Mr '70
Javelina come high. J. Samson. il Field & S 75:68-71+ My '70
PECHET, Maurice M. See Rasmussen, H. jt. auth.
PECHTER, William S.
Movies (title varies) Commentary 49:77-81 F; 50:25-6+ S; 90-2 N '70; 51:92-4 Ja '71
Screen. Commonweal 93:71-2 O 16 '70
PECK, Ernest. See Wood, L. jt. auth.
PECK, Lee C. and Smith, V. C.
Quantitative chemical analysis of lunar samples. Science 167:532 Ja 30 '70
PECK, Ralph H.
Return to Guam. il Travel & Camera 33:66-8 Ja '70
PECK order. See Animals—Habits and behavior
PECKINPAH, Sam
Peckinpah's return; interview, ed. by S. Farber. il Film Q 23:2-11 Fall '69
                    about
Films. J. Brackman. Esquire 73:68 Je '70 *
Unkindest cut. A. Knight. Sat R 53:42 Ap 11 '70 *
PECORA, W. T.
Science and the quality of our environment; adaptation of address, June 1970. il Bul Atom Sci 26:20-3 O '70

PEDA bread. See Bread
PEDEN, Katherine
Decade of the woman; interview. U S News 70:30-1 Ja 11 '71
PEDERSEN, Richard F.
NATO in the coming decade; address, April 21, 1970. Dept State Bul 62:633-6 My 18 '70
PEDERSEN, Ronald W.
Diamond appoints first deputy commissioner. por Cons 25:7+ O '70 *
PEDESTALS
    See also
Garden ornaments
PEDESTRIANS
How to plan for the urban spirit; Los Angeles. A. C. Martin. il Am City 85:82+ F '70
Needed: pedestrian safeguards for ambling oldsters. il Todays Health 48:64-5 F '70
Pedestrian roulette. il Newsweek 76:102+ O 19 '70
Power to pedestrians; banning autos in New York and Tokyo. il Time 96:36 Ag 24 '70
Some pedestrian observations; Manhattan's 42nd street. il Time 95:66 My 11 '70
PEDIATRICIANS
    See also
Jacobi, A.
PEDIATRICS
                    History
Abraham Jacobi, the children's physician. R. Dunlop. il Todays Health 48:58-9+ Ap '70
PEELE, David
Performance ratings and librarians rights. il Am Lib 1:595-600 Je '70
PEERMAN, Dean
Tlatelolco: massacre and aftermath. Chr Cent 87:1503-6 D 16 '70
PEERS report. See Vietnamese war, 1957- —Atrocities—My Lai massacre
PEET, Creighton
Fascinating career in archaeology. il Sci Digest 68:42-6 Jl '70
PEET, J. H. John
Ferrocene: a molecular sandwich. bibliog il por Chem 43:31-4 Ap '70
PEI, Ieoh Ming
House must make people feel good; interview. pors House & Gard 138:114+ N '70
                    about
Making cities better places to live. il por(cover) Bsns W p36-9 Ag 22 '70 *
PEI, Mario
Prospects for a global language. Sat R 53: 23-5 My 2 '70
PEIERLS, Sir Rudolf Ernst
Britain in the atomic age. il por Bul Atom Sci 26:40-6 Je '70
PEISER, H. Steffen. See Wichers, E. jt. auth.
PEKAS, J. C. and Paulson, G. D.
Intestinal hydrolysis and conjugation of a pesticidal carbamate in vitro. bibliog il Science 170:77-8 O 2 '70
PEKING
China: the siege of the ants; celebrating 21st anniversary of Communist victory. il Time 96:36-44 N 16 '70
PEKKANEN, John
Boy who was just there watching it and making up his mind. il pors Life 68:36-7 My 15 '70
When people begin making sacrifices, you'll see more militancy. il Life 68:28-30 Ja 30 '70
PÉLADEAU, Marius B.
Shaker meetinghouses of Moses Johnson. il Antiques 98:594-9 O '70
PELARGONIUMS. See Geraniums
PELÉ. See Arantes do Nascimento, E.
PELECYPODS. See Mollusks
PELEGRINO, Donald
Joy of discovery through camping; address. Camp Mag 42:14 Mr '70
PELFREY, William G.
Face down: climax to the hardship tour. New Repub 163:13-14 Jl 18 '70
No laurels for legionnaires. New Repub 163: 18-20 N 21 '70
PELICANS
Nevada's endangered pelicans. A. Amaral. il Nat Parks & Con Mag 44:23-7 Jl '70
Where have all the pelicans gone? il Chem 43:5 Mr '70
PELL, Claiborne
U.S. discusses U.N. scale of assessments; statement, October 26, 1970. Dept State Bul 63:709-11 D 7 '70
PELL, Eve
Soledad brothers: how a prison picks its victims. il Ramp Mag 9:31+ Ag '70
PELLÉAS et Mélisande; opera. See Debussy, C.

PELLEGRINI, Marion
Just friends. New Repub 162:10-11 F 21 '70 •
PELLI, Cesar
Cesar Pelli, public architect. S. Moholy-Nagy.
il por Arch Forum 132:42-7 Mr '70 *
PELLISH, David
New government and industry partnership
for building more housing. il Arch Forum
133:58-61 Jl '70
PELLÓN, Nivio López. See López Pellón, N.
PELOPONNESIAN war; ballet. See Ballets—
Criticisms
PEN drawing
Oliver Grimley: pen draughtsman. H. C. Pitz.
il pors Am Artist 34:28-34 Ja '70

Study and teaching

Ink rendering. J. Gardner. il Design 72:29-31
Fall '70
PENAL colonies
See also
Devils Island
PENAL reform. See Prisons
PENANCE, Sacrament of. See Confession
PENCE, Roy J.
Mighty anti-pollution weapon: the honeybee.
A. Hamilton. il pors Sci Digest 68:9-14 O
'70 *
PENDANTS. See Jewelry
PENDER, Jane
Alaskan natives, time of crisis. il Nat Parks
& Con Mag 44:23-7 N '70
PENDERECKI, Krzysztof
Divine dissonance. T. W. Moore. il por Chr
Cent 87:1455-7 D 2 '70 *
Music to my ears; performance of Utrenja.
I. Kolodin. Sat R 53:24 O 17 '70 *
Musical events; Utrenja performed by Phila-
delphia orchestra in Philharmonic Hall.
W. Sargeant. New Yorker 46:138-9 O 10 '70 *
PENDERGAST, David M.
Tumbaga object from the early classic
period, found at Altun Ha, British Hon-
duras (Belize) bibliog il Science 168:116-18
Ap 3 '70
PENDLETON, Clarence M. Jr
Community involvement. Parks & Rec 5:21-
2+ O '70
PENDLETON, Edrie
Ghosts in the library; drama. Plays 30:73-84
N '70
PENDLETON round-up. See Rodeos
PENFOLD, Joseph W.
Credit where credit is due. por Am For 76:6
My '70 *
PENG, Ming-min
China policy. J. A. Cohen. Atlan 227:14+ Ja
'71 *
Exile; interview, ed. by R. J. Korengold. por
Newsweek 75:42 F 16 '70 *
PENGUIN books, ltd.
McGraw-Hill jumps into bidding for Penguin.
Pub W 198:33 Ag 3 '70
McGraw-Hill withdraws; Penguin goes to
Longman. Pub W 198:247-8 Ag 31 '70
Report from England; projects of Puffin
books. Z. Sutherland. Sat R 53:52 Ag 22
'70
Sir Allen Lane dies, sale of Penguin quickly
announced. Pub W 198:47-8 Jl 20 '70
PENGUINS
Parting shots; prejudice among the penguins.
il Life 68:77-80 My 1 '70
PENGUINS, Fossil
Ages of fossil penguins in New Zealand. G.
G. Simpson. bibliog Science 168:361-2 Ap
17 '70
PENICILLIN
Penicillin as epileptogenic agent: its effect on
an isolated neuron. G. F. Ayala and others.
bibliog il Science 167:1257-60 F 27 '70
PENITENCE. See Repentance
PENMAN, H. L.
Water cycle; with biographical sketch. il Sci
Am 223:33, 98-100+ bibliog(p262-3) S '70
PENMAN, Sheldon. See Fan, H. jt. auth.
PENMANSHIP
New slant on the second R. R. Goforth and
C. W. Hunnicutt. Todays Ed 59:45-6 F '70
Story of handwriting, by A. Fairbank. Review
Pub W il 197:72-4 Ap 13 '70. P. Standard *
See also
Calligraphy
Graphology
Graphotherapy
PENN, Arthur
Current cinema. P. Kael. New Yorker 46:
50-4 D 26 '70 *
PENN, Irving
Geisha 1970; four new photographic studies. il
Vogue 156:84-7+ Jl '70
Specialists in sex; orchids; photographs. il
Vogue 156:136-42 D '70
Spectacular highlanders of New Guinea, South
Pacific; photographs. Vogue 156:146-57 D
'70

PENN, Matthew
Learning in camp: the fourth force in total
education; excerpts from address. il Camp
Mag 42:13-14 Je '70
PENN, William
Mentor for our time; excerpt from radio
series The Overstreet outlook. B. W. Over-
street. PTA Mag 65:21 D '70 •
PENN central company
After Penn central, who next? il Newsweek
76:63+ Jl 6 '70
Are railroads doomed? il U S News 69:12-13
Jl 6 '70
As I see it; interview. J. W. Barriger. por
Forbes 106:38+ Ag 15 '70
Bankrupt. New Repub 163:6 Jl 4 '70
Biggest bankruptcy ever. il Time 96:58+ Jl 6
'70
Bizarre case of Executive jet. il pors Bsns
W p80-2+ O 24 '70
Candy butcher; Samuel Jacobs, vendor. New
Yorker 46:17-19 Jl 11 '70
Color them red. Newsweek 76:68+ Jl 20 '70
Elephant saw a ghost. Nation 211:4-5 Jl 6 '70
Even bankruptcy doesn't end Penn central's
problems. U S News 69:57 O 5 '70
Fate worse than death. Newsweek 76:78-80 D
7 '70
Federal fuel for Penn central. il Bsns W p26-
7 Je 13 '70
First aid for a shaky giant. il Newsweek 75:
63-4 Je 22 '70
Getting on the route to corporate health.
W. A. Lashley. il pors Nations Bsns 58:98-
9 Ja '70
Hard way to run a railroad; Metroliner ex-
periment. il Bsns W p64-5 Ap 4 '70
High-cost money hurts the Penn central. il
Bsns W p 106-7 Je 6 '70
How to keep up on the Penn central; cor-
porate reorganization report and S&C
news. Bsns W p32 N 21 '70
New man at the throttle. Newsweek 76:90 S
14 '70
Notes and comment: collapse; interview. E.
M. Frimbo. New Yorker 46:25-6 S 26 '70
One hand giveth . . . il Forbes 106:56 O 1 '70
Passenger nightmare. il Time 95:67 F 2 '70
Penn central: a new chief with new plans;
appointment of W. H. Moore to Penn cen-
tral transportation co. il por Bsns W p48+
Ag 22 '70
Penn central bankruptcy express. R. Loving
jr. il pors Fortune 82:104-9+ Ag '70; Reply.
W. E. Hanson. 82:87-8 S '70
Penn Central gets its new engineers. Bsns W
p20 Jl 25 '70
Penn central is still hungry for help. Bsns
W p21 Ja 9 '71
Penn central: Pandora's box; findings of in-
vestigators. il por Newsweek 76:74+ N 9
'70
Penn central sees a hope in Congress. Bsns
W p25 N 14 '70
Penn central, the unanswered question. Forbes
106:18-19 Jl 15 '70
Penn central's misguided gamble; with edi-
torial comment. il Bsns W p96+, 128 Je 27
'70
Penn central's noose draws tighter. Bsns W
p 18 O 3 '70
Penn central's troubles branch out. il Bsns W
p92+ Je 20 '70
Railroad man for the Penn central. por For-
tune 82:31 S '70
Railroads' new worry: looters. il U S News
69:20-1 Jl 27 '70
Rescue derailed. il Newsweek 75:62 Je 29 '70
Rough riding at Penn central. il Bsns W p37-
8 Ja 17 '70
Senate report bares links of railroad, Ex-
ecutive jet. J. P. Woolsey. Aviation W 94:
28 Ja 4 '71
Story behind the commuter crisis. il Bsns W
p60-6+ Mr 14 '70
Taken, by train. R. Sherrill. il Nation 210:
786-8 Je 29 '70
Tiny railroad pulls a switch; demerger of Pro-
vidence & Worcester railroad co. from
Penn central. il Bsns W p84 My 23 '70
Trials of Penn central's sweetheart. il Bsns
W p46-7 O 17 '70
Uncle, can you spare some millions? il por
Time 95:74-6 Je 22 '70
When the Fed won the liquidity battle. il
Bsns W p50+ O 24 '70
Who's hit by biggest bankruptcy. il U S News
69:26 Jl 20 '70
See also
Executive jet aviation, inc.
PENNA, Carlos Victor
School libraries in Panama. Am Lib 1:182-3
F '70
PENNANT, Edmund
Forebloom; poem. Commonweal 93:221 N 27
'70

PENNATULACEA. See Sea pens

PENNEY, Monte M.
Looking deep into the reading process. il
Am Ed 6:24-5 Mr '70

PENNIES. See Coins

PENNSYLVANIA
See also
Architecture, Domestic—Pennsylvania
Bird sanctuaries—Pennsylvania
Brandywine Creek
Education—Pennsylvania
Express highways—Pennsylvania
Fishing—Pennsylvania
Geology—Pennsylvania
Kittatinny Mountains
Labor laws and legislation—Pennsylvania
Mifflin County
Taxation—Pennsylvania

Description and travel
Liberty trail. A. Hornstein. il Travel 134:58-
9+ Jl '70

Historic houses, etc.
At home in a national landmark: Andalusia,
Bucks County. R. Reif. il N Y Times Mag
p84-5+ O 25 '70

Religious institutions and affairs
New ecumenical vehicle in southwest Penn-
sylvania; Christmas associates. J. P. Park.
Chr Cent 87:548-9 Ap 29 '70
See also
Protestant Episcopal church

PENNSYLVANIA ballet company
Pennsylvania ballet; Academy of music, Phila-
delphia. S. Smoliar. Dance Mag 44:80+ Ja
'70
Pennsylvania ballet, Experimental dance the-
atre; Locust street theatre, Phila, Pa. S.
Smoliar. Dance Mag 44:80 N '70
Pennsylvania ballet in Carmina burana; New
York city opera; N.Y. state theater. J.
Armstrong. Dance Mag 44:94-5 My '70
Pennsylvania ballet; Whitman auditorium,
Brooklyn college. M. Marks. Dance Mag
44:77 Je '70

PENNSYLVANIA German crafts. See Arts
and crafts—United States

PENNSYLVANIA library association
Penn. L.A. conference: experiment in format.
J. Berry. Library J 95:4086+ D 1 '70

PENNSYLVANIA New York central transportation company. See Penn central company

PENNSYLVANIA state library, Harrisburg
Law and order in people orientation; letter
to the editor. A. H. Rineer, jr. Am Lib
1:527-8 Je '70

PENNZOIL united, inc.
First things first. il Forbes 106:70+ O 15 '70

PENOLOGY. See Punishment

PENSACOLA, Fla.
Small cities can use big machines. C. Carlan.
il Am City 85:117+ Ap '70

PENSION funds and funding. See Pensions—
Finance

PENSIONS
See also
College professors and instructors—Pensions
Old age pensions
Scientists—Pensions
Teachers—Pensions
World war, 1939-1945—Compensation of non-
combatants

Finance
Ahead: tighter rules on pension funds. il
U S News 68:64-5 Mr 30 '70
Changes in pension plans: tax rules the Trea-
sury wants. il U S News 69:32-4 S 14 '70
Jennison's stars. A. Hershman. Duns 97:54
Ja '71
Pinch on the pension funds. A. Hershman.
il Duns 96:27-9 O'70
Private pensions: promise and problem. Amer-
ica 122:328-9 Mr 28 '70
These people can be dangerous; private pen-
sion funds. il Forbes 106:15-17 O 1 '70

Laws and regulations
Ahead: tighter rules on pension funds. il
U S News 68:64-5 Mr 30 '70
Changes in pension plans: tax rules the Trea-
sury wants. il U S News 69:32-4 S 14 '70
Plans to protect retirement pay. il U S News
70:58-60 Ja 11 '71
Private pensions: promise and problem. Amer-
ica 122:328-9 Mr 28 '70

PENSIONS, Industrial
Benefit security in private pension plans, a
review article. M. W. Latimer. il Mo Labor R 93:47-50 My '70
Plans to protect retirement pay. il U S News
70:58-60 Ja 11 '71

Portable pensions cover 85,000 IAM members
in forty states. D.C. Aging 188:16 Je '70
Private pension plans, 1960 to 1969: an
overview; with tables. H. E. Davis and A.
Strasser. Mo Labor R 93:45-56 Jl '70

PENSTEMONS
Flower fishing in Fishlake forest. D. E. Rose.
Horticulture 48:44-6 Jl '70

PENTATHLON
World's first peace pentathlon; super hippie D. Smith's crusade against competition. R. F. Jones. il pors Sports Illus 32:
50-8+ My 11 '70

PENTAX cameras. See Single-lens reflex cameras

PENTECOST
Gifts of the Spirit. V. P. McCorry. Ameri-
ca 122:541-2 My 16 '70
Power of Pentecost: we need it now more
than ever. W. R. Miller. Chr Cent 87:592-4
My 13 '70

PENTECOST ISLAND
Land diving with the Pentecost Islanders.
K. Muller. il Nat Geog 138:799-817 D '70

PENTECOSTAL churches
Pentecostals celebrate their world flame. J.
S. Tinney. Chr Today 15:36 D 4 '70
Theology of the Holy Spirit, by F. D. Bruner.
Review
Chr Today 15:16-18 Ja 15 '71. W. E. Mills
Understanding spirit-baptism; as Catholic
Pentecostals practice it. D. L. Gelpi.
America 122:520-1 My 16 '70

PENTECOSTAL churches in Brazil
Pentecostals make marked gains in Brazil.
Chr Cent 88:7 Ja 6 '71

PENTECOSTAL churches in Latin America
Pentecostal breakthrough. J. L. Klaiber. il
America 122:99-102 Ja 31 '70
World council of churches and Latin America.
T. Tschuy. Chr Cent 87:320-3 Mr 18 '70

PENTECOSTAL movement. See Pentecostal
churches

PENTHOUSE (periodical)
Bunny hunting. il pors Newsweek 75:71 Mr 2
'70

PENTHOUSE international, ltd.
Bunny hunting. il pors Newsweek 75:71 Mr 2
'70

PENZIAS, A. A. and Wilson, R. W.
Microwave noise from rainstorms. il Science
169:583-4 Ag 7 '70

PEOLE (satellite) See Artificial satellites,
French

PEONIES
Peonies are forever. G. Taloumis. il Home
Gard 57:30-1+ O '70

PEOPLE'S liberation army. See China (People's Republic)—Armed forces

PEP pills. See Amphetamines

PEPE and the cornfield bandit; drama. See
Boiko, C.

PÉPIN, Jacques
House beautiful chef. il por House B 112:73
Jl; 84-5 Ag; 116 S; 128-9+ N; 90 D '70
—See Ernoult, V. jt. auth.

PEPIN, R. O. and others
Isotopic composition of rare gases in lunar
samples. bibliog il Science 167:550-3 Ja 30 '70

PEPPER, Choral
1970 traveler's zodiac. il Travel 133:57-9 Ja
'70
Party cruise. il Travel 135:58-61 Ja '71
West coast wanderings. See issues of Travel

PEPPER, Curtis Bill
Curious split life of Dr Christiaan Barnard.
Vogue 156:124-5+ S 15 '70

PEPPER, G. Willing
Fifty-fifty empire that Scott built. il por Bsns
W p27 Ag 29 '70 *

PEPPER and Tanner (firm) See Advertising
agencies

PEPPERS
Sweet banana: prince of peppers. M. Rozell.
il Org Gard & Farm 17:94-5 Mr '70
Try some peppery Hungarian peppers. B.
Wahlfeldt. Org Gard & Farm 17:82 Ja '70
See also
Cookery—Vegetables

PEPSICO, inc.
Competition changes flavor, too. il Bsns W
p71 Ap 25 '70
Onward and upward with the arts; EAT and
the Pepsi pavilion at Expo '70. C. Tomkins.
New Yorker 46:83-4+ O 3 '70

PEPSI-COLA company. See PepsiCo, inc

PEPSIN
See also
Pepsinogens

PEPSINOGENS
Pepsinogens: genetic polymorphism in man.
I. M. Samloff and P. L. Townes. bibliog il
Science 168:144-5 Ap 3 '70

PEPTIC ulcers
Complex causes of indigestion. K. Anderson. Har Yrs 10:31-2+ Jl '70
Peptic ulcer and an on-off switch. Chem 43:24 F '70

PEPTIDES
Gibbon fibrinopeptides: identification of a glycine-serine allelism at position B-3. G. A. Mross and others. bibliog il Science 170:468-70 O 23 '70
Mechanism of antibody diversity; germ line basis for variability. L. Hood and D. W. Talmage. bibliog il Science 168:325-34 Ap 17 '70
Of mice and memory; isolation of memory-activating substance from brain. Newsweek 75:86 F 23 '70
Peptides with juvenile hormone activity. M. Zaoral and K. Slama. bibliog il Science 170: 92-3 O 2 '70
Polypeptide with broad biological activity; isolation from small intestine. S. I. Said and V. Mutt. bibliog Science 169:1217-18 S 18 '70
See also
Bradykinin
Glutathione
Kinins

PEPYS, Samuel
And so to bed. R. A. Sokolov. por Newsweek 76:117-18 N 2 '70 *
Letter from London; exhibition at the National portrait gallery. M. Panter-Downes. New Yorker 46:56 D 26 '70 *
Public and private Pepys. J. H. Plumb. por Sat R 53:29-31+ O 24 '70 *

PEQUANNOCK, N.J.
Canine Hilton; township dog pound. B. R. Evans. il Am City 85:125-6 Ap '70

PERAINO, Carl, and others
Automated continuous culture of mammalian cells in suspension. bibliog il Science 169: 204-5 Jl 10 '70

PERAZA SARAUSA, Fermin
National bibliographer in exile: Fermin Peraza Sarausa of Cuba, 1907-1969. I. Zimmerman. il pors Wilson Lib Bul 44:1060-3 Je '70 *

PERBROMATES
Perbromate problem. M. M. Cox and J. W. Moore. bibliog il pors Chem 43:15-19 Je '70

PERCEPTION
Cardiac responses on the visual cliff in pre-locomotor human infants. J. J. Campos and others. bibliog il Science 170:196-7 O 9 '70
Creativity takes over; Attleboro, Mass. visual arts program. L. Rich. il Am Ed 6:16-22 D '70
Do you have eyes in your skin? R. Hattersley. il Pop Phot 66:55-9 Mr '70
Drawing from the environment. A. Pierce. il Sch Arts 70:22-3 D '70
Seeing eye, the thinking hand; excerpts from The many ways of seeing. J. G. Moore. il Design 71:4-9 Spr '70
Stimulating perception; eliminating visual clichés. P. K. Scholl. il Sch Arts 70:12-13 N '70
Underwater vision. S. M. Luria and J. A. S. Kinney. bibliog il Science 167:1454-61 Mr 13 '70
See also
Body image
Concepts
Consciousness
Gestalt theory
Human information processing
Sound perception
Space perception
Threshold (perception)
Time perception

PERCHIK, Simon
Poem: Without their spring trees too. Poetry 117:164 D '70

PERCUSSION instruments
See also
Metallophone

PERCY, Charles Harting
Excerpt from debate, December 22, 1969. Cong Digest 49:90+ Mr '70
We're paying too much for NATO. Read Digest 97:115-18 N '70

PERCY Lund Humphries and company. See Publishers and publishing—Great Britain

PEREGRINE falcons. See Falcons

PEREIRA, Irene Rice
American painter-writer. J. Harithas. il por Vogue 155:128-9+ Je '70 *

PERELMAN, Sidney Joseph
Grifter, stay 'way from my door. New Yorker 46:40-2 O 31 '70
Missing; two lollapaloozas, no reward. New Yorker 46:39-41 O 17 '70
Pen is mightier, and also pricier. New Yorker 46:21-2 D 26 '70

Slow down, dangerous footlights ahead. New Yorker 46:53-5 N 21 '70
Who stole my golden undies? New Yorker 46:30-2 Je 6 '70
about
Flinty eye behind the humor. W. Sheed. por Life 69:12 S 18 '70 *
Meisterzinger. S. Kanfer. Atlan 226:108-10 D '70

PERENNIALS
Perennial parade of color. L. Grove. il Bet Hom & Gard 48:60-1 Ap '70
Perennials & biennials, save money by growing them from seed. il Home Gard 57:14-15 Jl '70
Perennials for cover-up jobs. W. Ferguson. il Org Gard & Farm 17:90-1 S '70
Perennials that take care of themselves. R. Webber. il Home Gard 57:10-11 Mr '70
Planning the perennial garden. B. M. Capen. il Horticulture 48:20-1+ N '70
See also
Astilbes
Chrysanthemums
Tansy
Yarrows

PERETZ, Bertram
Habituation and dishabituation in the absence of a central nervous system. bibliog il Science 169:379-81 Jl 24 '70

PERETZ, Don
Arab Palestine: phoenix or phantom? For Affairs 48:322-33 Ja '70
Palestine's Arabs. il Trans-Action 7:43-9 Jl '70

PÉREZ, Galo René
Periquillo Sarniento. il Américas 22:29-34 My '70

PEREZ, Rudy
Rudy Perez dance theatre. J. Anderson. il por Dance Mag 44:89 Mr '70 *
Rudy Perez dance theatre; NYU school of education auditorium. J. Anderson. Dance Mag 44:84-5 Ap '70 *
Rudy Perez dance theatre; the Cubiculo NYC. E. Jacob. Dance Mag 44:82 Ag '70 *

PEREZ, Tony
Big red machine. il por Time 96:35 Ag 24 '70 *
Real red menace. H. L. Masin. por Sr Schol 97:22 S 14 '70 *
Vet-rookie duo sparks Cincinnati machine. L. J. Banks. il pors Ebony 25:70-1+ S '70 *

PERFECTION (psychology)
Are you raising a perfectionist? M. Krebs and R. Krebs. il Todays Health 48:39-41 Ag '70

PERFECTIONISM. See Perfection (psychology)

PERFORMANCE appraisal. See Employees—Rating

PERFORMANCE contracts (education)
Accountability in public education; performance contracts. L. M. Lessinger. Todays Ed 59:52-3 My '70
Customers pass the test or else. Bsns W p42+ S 12 '70; Same. Ed Digest 36:5-7 N '70
Free enterprise for schools. il Time 96:58+ Ag 24 '70
New angle on accountability; performance contract program in the Texarkana schools. M. J. Filogamo. Todays Ed 59:53 My '70
Profit and loss in education. J. Cass. Sat R 53:39-40 Ag 15 '70
Satisfaction guaranteed or money back. Sat R 53:54-5 Ag 15 '70
Schooling for profit. il Forbes 106:41 N 1 '70
Teaching for profit; Gary, Ind. il Newsweek 76:58 Ag 17 '70
What is performance contracting as applied to schools? W. D. Boutwell. PTA Mag 65:31-2 O '70
Where private firm runs public school. il U S News 69:41 O 12 '70
Who is accountable? private industry; teachers. C. H. Harrison. il Schol Teach Jr/Sr High p 12-13+ N 2 '70
Who will be accountable for accountability? address, June 1970. T. B. Dolmatch. por Library J 95:3955-7 N 15 '70

PERFORMANCE standards
Putting judgment back into decisions; appraising performance. L. E. Greiner and others. il Harvard Bsns R 48:59-67 Mr '70
Would Horatio Alger need a degree? J. W. Kuhn. il Sat R 53:54-5+ D 19 '70

PERFORMANCE trials. See Automobile engines—Fuel consumption

PERFORMING animals. See Animals—Training

PERFORMING arts
Anatomy of pretentiousness. R. Evett. Atlan 227:75-9 Ja '71
Celebrity spotlight. E. N. Mintz. See issues of Travel

PERFORMING arts—*Continued*
Elaine Summers: new forms, new ideas! M. Harriton. il pors Dance Mag 44:66-73 S '70
Expanding arts in the U.S.A. UNESCO Courier 23:21 Je '70
Nowhere to go. I. Stravinsky. Harper 240:32+ F '70
Quintessentially American; eleven performers. L. Lerman. il Mlle 70:218-21 Ap '70
Tip sheet to the new season. A. Talmey. Vogue 156:394-7 S 1 '70
See also
Sex in the performing arts

Benefit performances
Notes of a young radical; arts festival at Columbia university to benefit political prisoners. G. H. C. Knox. il Sat R 53:48-51+ Ag 15 '70

Exhibitions
Yuma County schools fine arts festival. M. Elliott. il Sch Arts 69:28-30 F '70

Finance
Agnes De Mille speaks to Congress on the state of the arts; address, with excerpts from testimony, February 9, 1970. A. De Mille. por Dance Mag 44:34-5+ My '70
Where the dollars go. M. Mayer. il Sat R 53:22-4+ F 28 '70

Moral and religious aspects
Theater of deceit. D. B. Lockerbie. Chr Today 14:5-7+ Jl 3 '70

Czechoslovakia
Art of innuendo. K. Huszar. il Newsweek 75:45-6+ Ap 6 '70

Latin America
Multi-media in South America. E. Salzman. il Hi Fi 20:secII 10-11+ Ag '70

Russia
Art not for art's sake. R. Hemming. por Sr Schol 95:19+ N 17 '69
PERFORMING arts festivals. See Performing arts—Exhibitions
PERFUME industry and trade

Consolidations and mergers
French perfume goes American; Rochas-Rubinstein deal. Bsns W p 132 My 23 '70
PERFUMES
Beauty & the bath. S. Lindsay. House B 112:24+ D '70
Everything you always wanted to know about perfume. Vogue 156:180-1 N 1 '70
Fragrances. Redbook 136:99+ D '70
How to give a garden of Eden for Christmas this year. R. Warfield. House & Gard 138:16+ D '70
In celebration of scent. S. Harney. il Ladies Home J 86:54+ D '69
Seasons of scent. il Harp Baz 104:130-1 N '70
Still making scents. il Mlle 70:274 F '70
PERGAMON press, ltd.
Audit claims Pergamon '68 profit far below estimate. Pub W 198:37-8 S 21 '70
Leasco will not bid on Pergamon shares. Pub W 198:35-6 D 28 '70
Missing millions. pors Time 96:85-6 S 14 '70
Pergamon dispute rekindled; Maxwell's counter-bid. Pub W 198:28 Ag 17 '70
Pergamon will pull out of joint venture with BPC. Pub W 197:56 Mr 9 '70
PERIDOTITE
Explaining Moses rock dike; study of kimberlite formations. il Sci N 98:33 Jl 11 '70
Mantle-derived peridotites in southwestern Oregon; relation to plate tectonics. L. G. Medaris, jr. and R. H. Dott, jr. bibliog il Science 169:971-4 S 4 '70
PERINT, Gladys
I declare; an Englishwoman's Christmas list. Harp Baz 104:144 D '70
PERIOD rooms
Empire style at Bayou bend; new period rooms in Houston. D. B. Warren. il Antiques 97:122-7 Ja '70
Louis XIII cabinet at Toledo. R. Davidson. il Antiques 97:893-5 Je '70
Period rooms: the sixties and seventies. J. Lipman. il Art in Am 58:126-9 N '70
Wrightsman rooms at the Metropolitan museum of art. J. Parker il Antiques 97:102-8 Ja '70
PERIODIC tables. See Chemical elements
PERIODICAL advertising. See Advertising mediums—Periodicals

PERIODICAL articles
Article research sources. I. Doig. Writers Digest 50:41-2 Ja '70
As-told-to article. J. Stocker. il Writers Digest 50:20-2 Ap '70
Audience-directed writing; magazines and personae. H. Rank. Engl J 59:405-8 Mr '70
Eight types of how-to-articles and how to write them. H. C. Sherwood. Writers Digest 50:36-7+ N '70
From amateur to pro in the article market. K. Smith. Writer 83:22-3+ Ap '70
Get free help for your articles. A. Gonzalez. Writers Digest 51:37+ Ja '71
How to moonlight as a freelancer. A. F. Gonzalez, jr. il Writers Digest 50:28-31 F '70
How to turn newspaper items into article checks! C. Cunningham. il Writers Digest 50:20-1 S '70
Idea a day. F. A. Dickson. Writers Digest 50:26-7 Je; 11-12+ Ag '70
In-depth magazine article ideas. Writers Digest 50:40-1+ O '70
Make your vacation pay for itself. P. H. Fugleberg. il Writers Digest 50:28-9 Je '70
1970 articles contest. N. Hagen. Writers Digest 50:35-6 O '70
Ringing down the curtain. M. Gunther. Writer 83:18-22 S '70
Tiresome toils of a writer; making an article on testing tires exciting. M. Spiegel. Sr Schol 97:30-1 D 14 '70
Where and when to use anecdotes. J. J. Green. Writers Digest 50:23-5 Mr '70
Writer turned salesman: the article query; excerpt from Writing and selling non-fiction. H. B. Jacobs. il Writers Digest 50:24-5 Ag '70
PERIODICAL cicadas. See Cicadas
PERIODICAL columns. See Periodicals—Sections, columns, etc.
PERIODICAL covers
King of covers shoots his hundredth: P. Halsman's portraits for Life covers. R. Graves. il por Life 68:3 Ja 23 '70
Voices from the past; cover of November 16, 1929 issue of The Saturday review of literature. il Sat R 53:37 Ja 24 '70
Why a Life cover seldom makes everybody happy. R. Graves. il Life 69:3 N 20 '70
PERIODICAL fillers
Writing and selling fillers. A. Martin. il Writers Digest 50:24-6 N '70
PERIODICAL layout and typography
Art direction enters new age as Life begins layout by machine. il Pub W 198:28-9 Jl 6 '70
Introducing a new staffer who's really plugged in; computerized layout machine. R. Graves. il Life 69:3 Ag 14 '70
Revolution in layout; Life's new editorial layout display system. J. Tebbel. il Sat R 53:93-4 S 12 '70
PERIODICAL literature
Detroit market letter. H. Ellis. il Writers Digest 50:34-5 D '70
Forbidden subjects in slick fiction. M. J. Gerber. Writers Digest 50:32-3 Ap '70
Market letter from Milwaukee. J. R. Gahagan. il Writers Digest 50:28-32 Mr '70
New York market letter. H. B. Jacobs. See issues of Writer's digest
Writer's market; late news! See issues of Writer's digest
See also
Fiction in periodicals and newspapers
Religious newspapers and periodicals
Sex in literature
Trade journals
PERIODICAL postal rates. See Postal rates—United States
PERIODICALS
Thinking man's medium; news magazines; excerpt from address, September 1970. R. E. Larsen. Sat R 53:71-2 N 14 '70
See also
Catholic press
Freedom of the press
Illustration of books and periodicals
also subhead Periodicals under various subjects, e.g. Medicine—Periodicals; *also* names of periodicals, e.g. Saturday review

Bibliography
Magazines, ed. by B. Katz. See issues of Library journal

Catalogs
How to computerize your serials and periodicals when you don't know how; experience of University of Alaska library. M. Matthews and S. Sherman. pors Wilson Lib Bul 44:861-4 Ap '70

Circulation
Another Look. Newsweek 75:64 My 4 '70

PERIODICALS—*Continued*

Indexes
See also
Readers' guide to periodical literature

Letters to the editor
Decade of letters; a study of letters to the editor in the ALA bulletin. E. M. Parker. il Am Lib 1:614-15 Je '70

Prices
Price indexes for 1970: U.S. periodicals H. W. Tuttle. Library J 95:2427-8 Jl '70

Sections, columns, etc.
Easy chair. J. Fischer. Harper 240:22-3+ My '70

Africa
African magazines for American libraries. S. Berman. il por Library J 95:1289-93 Ap 1 '70
Telling it to Africa; advertising in Jeune Afrique. il Bsns W p84-5 O 31 '70

France
Express to success; L'Express. il por Newsweek 76:55-6 S 28 '70
In defense of violence; trial of two former editors of La Cause du peuple. il por Newsweek 75:57 Je 8 '70
Vogue à la Moreau. por Time 96:23 D 28 '70

Great Britain
See also
New statesman (periodical)
Penthouse (periodical)

Italy
Women, not girls; Playmen. il por Time 97: 36+ Ja 18 '71

Japan
See also
Peace and happiness through prosperity (periodical)

Mexico
"Revolutionary" establishment; Por qué? affair. L. Fenster. il Nation 211:15-16 Jl 6 '70

Russia
European literary scene; authors views of Soviet literature. R. J. Clements. Sat R 53: 23 S 5 '70
When the Krokodil arrives, watch out! N. Lo Bello. il Read Digest 96:101-3 Ap '70

United States
Hot magazines aim at special targets. il Bsns W p64-5+ My 2 '70
Metropolitan magazines. il Pub W 197:36-7 Mr 30 '70
Shrink; smaller magazines. Time 97:37 Ja 18 '71
Washington market letter. H. Hudson. il Writers Digest 50:28-30 My '70
Where to sell manuscripts. See issues of Writer
See also names of periodicals, e.g. Liberty (periodical)

PERIODICALS, Counter culture. See Counter culture literature
PERIODICALS, Immoral. See Immoral literature and pictures
PERIODICALS, Trade. See Trade journals
PERIODICALS for airline passengers
Those magnificent magazines in the flying machines. G. Evans. il Writers Digest 50: 28-30+ Jl '70
PERIODICALS for men
See also
Penthouse (periodical)
Playboy (periodical)
PERIODICALS for the handicapped
See also
Active handicapped (periodical)
PERIODICALS for women
See also
Ladies' home journal
McCall's (periodical)
PERIODICITY
See also
Biology—Periodicity
PERIODONTAL disease. See Gums (anatomy)—Diseases
PERIPHYTON. See Fresh water flora
PERIPLANETA. See Cockroaches
PERKIN, Gordon W. and Nash, E. M.
Pregnancy quiz: is this the time to have a baby? il Good H 170:68+ Ap '70
PERKIN, Sir William Henry
Mauve not improved. il Chem 43:5 My '70 *

PERKINS, Bradford
Computerized cost estimating is ready now, almost. Arch Rec 147:65-6 F '70
Cost knowledge: tool for budget, program and design. Arch Rec 147:83-4 Je '70
Evaluating hidden cost factors. Arch Rec 148:60-1 Jl '70
Guidelines for early planning estimates. il Arch Rec 147:81-2 Ap '70
Some common errors in cost control programs. Arch Rec 147:61-2 Ja '70
PERKINS, Carl
Top beats the bottom: Carl Perkins and his music; excerpt from Rock folk. M. Lydon. il por Atlan 226:96-8+ D '70 *
PERKINS, Carroll, and Perkins, Gwen
Hunting with a tape recorder. il por Field & S 74:86-7+ Ap '70
—See Perkins, G. jt. auth.
PERKINS, Gwen, and Perkins, Carroll
Want bird close-ups? Call them with tape. il Pop Phot 67:74-5+ Jl '70
—See Perkins, C. jt. auth.
PERKINS, James A.
Five crises of the university; address, February 1970. il UNESCO Courier 23:28-32 Je '70
PERKINS, James Monroe
Ephraim Byram, versatile nineteenth-century craftsman. il por Antiques 97:746-7 My '70
PERKINS, Lawrence A.
Caesar's head; poem. Cath World 211:179 Jl '70
PERKINS, Richard W. and others
Cosmogenic and primordial radionuclides in lunar samples by nondestructive gamma-ray spectrometry. bibliog il Science 167: 577-80 Ja 30 '70
PERKINS, Stuart
Who's afraid of Vega, Pinto and Gremlin? Not VW; interview. pors Motor T 22:65-6+ Ag '70
PERL, Martin L.
New critique of science. Cur 119:39-43 Je '70
PERLEA, Ionel
Obituary
Hi Fi 20:MA32 O '70
Opera N por 35:29 O 10 '70. G. Fitzgerald
PERLIS, Don
Can you still become an old master at twenty-eight? S. A. Kurtz. il Art N 69:54-7 Mr '70 *
PERLMAN, Alfred Edward
Penn central bankruptcy express. R. Loving, jr. il pors Fortune 82:104-9+ Ag '70 *
PERLMAN, Anne S.
Shelter: poem. Mlle 70:156 F '70
PERLMAN, Itzhak
In Israel, it's everybody's thing. Harp Baz 103:90+ O '70
Musician of the month. S. Fleming. il por Hi Fi 20:MA6-7 N '70 *
PERLMAN, Robert. See Pastan, I. jt. auth.
PERLMANN, Peter, and others
Inhibition of cytotoxicity of lymphocyts by concanavalian A in vitro. bibliog il Science 168:1112-15 My 29 '70
PERLMETER, Alan
Redesigning the guitar. il por Sci N 98:180-1 Ag 22 '70
PERLMUTTER, Amos
Big power games, small power wars. il Trans-Action 7:70-8+ Jl '70
PERLMUTTER, Nathan
Notes from a Jewish diary. il Nat R 22:670-4 Je 30 '70
PERMAFROST. See Frozen ground
PERMANENT subcommittee on investigations. See United States—Congress—Senate—Government operations, Committee on
PERMEABILITY
Vasopressin: effect on deformability of urinary surface of collecting duct cells. J. J. Grantham. bibliog il Science 168:1093-5 My 29 '70
PERMIAN period. See Paleobotany—Permian; Paleontology—Permian
PERMITS, Grazing. See Grazing
PEROT, H. Ross
What's right with America. il por Nations Bsns 58:20-1+ Jl '70

about

Hand from Dallas. il por Newsweek 76:85-6 D 7 '70 *
Perils of Perot. por Time 95:88-9 My 4 '70 *
Perot zeroes in on F. I. duPont. por Bsns W p39-40 D 19 '70 *
Ross Perot: billionaire patriot. C. S. Wren. il pors Look 34:28-32 Mr 24 '70 *
Ross Perot: Dallas crusader. il pors Newsweek 75:68-9+ Ap 13 '70 *
What ties Perot to Wall Street. il por Bsns W p78 D 5 '70 *

PEROXIDASES
Myeloperoxidase: contribution to the microbicidal activity of intact leukocytes. S .J. Klebanoff. bibliog il Science 169:1095-7 S 11 '70
Peroxidase-mediated virucidal systems. M. E. Belding and others. bibliog il Science 167: 195-6 Ja 9 '70

PERREAULT, John
Andy Warhol disguised here as Andy Warhol. il por Vogue 155:164-6+ Mr 1 '70
Andy Warhola, this is your life. il por Art N 69:52-3+ My '70

PERRIN, Noel
Our far-flung correspondents. New Yorker 46:70+ F 21; 53-8 Jl 18 '70

PERRIN, Ursula
You can't buy a baby with trading stamps; story. Redbook 135:72-3 Je '70

PERRONE, Glenn
Businessmen's expectations (cont) Duns 95: 121 Mr '70

PERRONE, Miriam
Ritual-D: Gus Giordano & company. il pors Dance Mag 44:26-7 S '70

PERRUCCI, Robert
Potential of sociology as a liberating curriculum; excerpt from Social science in the schools; ed. by I. Morrissett. bibliog Sch & Soc 98:478-9+ N '70

PERRY, Bernard T.
Unscrambling a conglomerate. por Bsns W p 118+ Je 13 '70 *

PERRY, Edward A. Jr
Ocean resources. bibliog f il Cur Hist 58:349-54+ Je '70

PERRY, Eleanor
Collaboration also sets the scene at home. S. Nirenberg. il pors House B 112:72-3+ Ag '70 *
People are talking about. . . pors Vogue 156: 374-5 S 1 '70 *

PERRY, Frank
Collaboration also sets the scene at home. S. Nirenberg. il pors House B 112:72-3+ Ag '70 *
People are talking about. . . pors Vogue 156: 374-5 S 1 '70 *

PERRY, Herbert A.
New training plan in Britain's construction industry. il Mo Labor R 93:27-31 F '70

PERRY, John
Plan to pay you for voting. D. R. Maxey. Look 34:56 D 29 '70 *

PERRY, Margaret
Bahama Islands. il Home Gard 57:22-5+ O '70
Florida's favorite, the Fairchild tropical garden. il Home Gard 58:46-8 Ja '71
Many parks and gardens of Stockholm. il Home Gard 57:28-30 F '70
New England's fall fantasia. il Home Gard 57: 24-7 S '70
Set in a sapphire sea: the gardens of St Thomas. il Home Gard 57:28-31+ Je '70

PERRY, Matthew Calbraith
Walrus and the commodore, a puzzle in scrimshaw. R. W. Updike. il Antiques 98: 263-5 Ag 70 *

PERRY, Richard
Achieving a meeting of minds. Todays Ed 59:34-5 F '70

PERRY, Troy
Homosexual church. il por Newsweek 76:107 O 12 '70
Hope for the homosexual. il por Time 96:46+ Jl 13 '70 *

PERRY, Wes
Telling Paul; story. Redbook 134:72-3 F '70

PERSECUTION
Christianity lives on in China. M. T. Paan. Chr Today 14:3-5 F 27 '70
Russian revolution yields bitter fruit. D. E. Kucharsky. Chr Today 14:42 Ap 24 '70
See also
Jews—Persecutions
Martyrs

PERSECUTION, Political
Oaths in Kenya. Chr Today 14:40 F 13 '70

PERSEIDS. See Meteors

PERSELS, Debbie
Batik. il Sch Arts 70:26-7 N '70

PERSIA. See Iran

PERSIAN art. See Art, Persian

PERSIAN GULF
Persian Gulf Region. R. E. Thoman. bibliog f il Cur Hist 60:38-45+ Ja '71

PERSIANS; drama. See Aeschylus

PERSIMMONS
How to ripen persimmons. il Sunset 145:162 O '70
Persimmon. C. E. Lewis. Horticulture 48:40+ Ag '70

PERSONAL airplanes. See Airplanes, Private
PERSONAL beauty. See Beauty, Personal
PERSONAL credit. See Consumer credit
PERSONAL criticism. See Self evaluation
PERSONAL finance. See Finance, Personal
PERSONAL grooming. See Grooming, Personal
PERSONAL Injuries
See also
Damages
PERSONAL loans. See Loans, Personal
PERSONAL names. See Names, Personal
PERSONAL responsibility. See Responsibility
PERSONAL rights. See Civil rights
PERSONAL space
Art for everyday living: survival dome; oxygen utility dome. D. Holmes. il Art in Am 58:78-9 S '70
Sane community: a density problem? P. Leyhausen. il UNESCO Courier 23:26-32 Ag '70

PERSONALITY
Five young beauties & how they get that way. il Mlle 72:135-41 N '70
How to be absolutely charming; excerpt from How to talk with practically anybody about practically anthing. B. Walters. il McCalls 98:48+ N '70
Identifications and identities: development through childrens literature. L. Alexander. bibliog il por Wilson Lib Bul 45:144-8 O '70
Mystery of inner beauty; views of celebrities, ed. by B. Wysor. Harp Baz 103:128-9 Ag '70
Origin of personality. A. Thomas and others. il Sci Am 223:102-9 bibliog (p 128) Ag '70
See also
Body image
Human relations
Leadership
Self

PERSONALITY, Disorders of
See also
Autism
Schizophrenia

PERSONALITY tests
How easy are you to live with? N. Leiter. Ladies Home J 87:102+ Je '70
Men of the sea; a description of a psychiatric population of merchant seamen using the M.M.P.I. L. H. Tuft and M. I. Berman. bibliog Ment Hy 54:440-3 Jl '70
Now it's the P.Q. test. il Sci Digest 67:38 Ja '70
See also
Character tests

PERSONIFICATION in literature
Poet's workshop. F. Trefethen. Writer 83:22-6 Ja '70

PERSONNEL management
Beyond Theory Y. J. J. Morse and J. W. Lorsch. bibliog f il Harvard Bsns R 48:61-8 My '70
Drug abuse is your headache, too; excerpts from Drug abuse as a business problem. C. Kurtis. il Nations Bsns 58:38+ N '70
Drug threat in business. Nation 211:484 N 16 '70
Drugs raise a specter. il Bsns W p80-2 My 9 '70
Executives in ferment. G. J. Berkwitt. il Duns 97:23-5 Ja '71
Fraying white collar. J. Gooding. il Fortune 82:78-81+ D '70
How to make executives behave. M. R. Feinberg and J. J. Tarrant. il Nations Bsns 58: 72-4 Ap '70
Psychic wages; new trends in personnel management. J. P. Dessauer. Pub W 198:27-9 D 28 '70
Rising problem of drugs on the job. il Time 95:70 Je 29 '70
See also
Employee counseling
Incentives in industry
Layoff systems
Library administration

PERSONNEL service in education
Behind the bad behavior; Memphis elementary guidance and psychological services project. J. Chisum. il Am Ed 6:32-4 Ag '70
Denver doesn't quit on problem students. Z. Von Ende. il Am Ed 6:18-22 Je '70
Schoolhouse ombudsman. R. H. Levine. Clear House 44:354-5 F '70
SUCCESS in early counseling; Cobb County, Ga. Project SUCCESS for elementary school students. M. K. Murphy. il Am Ed 6:3-7 Mr '70
See also
Group guidance in education
Student counselors
Talent Search programs (education)

PERSONNEL service in industry. See Employee counseling

PERSONS, Wallace R.
Emerson's new disarmament policy. il por Bsns W p 110+ Ja 24 '70

PERSPECTIVE
Sight size, a method of painting; interview, ed. by R. Goetz. R. D. Hunter. il por Am Artist 34:48-53+ D '70
What is a painting? the Pozzo phenomenon. M. Polanyi. il Am Scholar 39:655-69 Aut '70

PERSPECTIVES of new music (periodical)
New music. R. Kostelanetz. Yale R 59:314-20 D '69

PERSPIRATION
Sweat is almost obsolete. N. H. Mermelstein. Todays Health 48:40-1+ Je '70

PERSUASION. See Argument; Rhetoric

PERU
See also
Americans in Peru
Arts and crafts—Peru
Birth control—Peru
Community development—Peru
Copper mines and mining—Peru
Earthquakes—Peru
Government ownership—Peru
Huaylas, Callejón de
Investments, Foreign (in Peru)
Land tenure—Peru
Paleontology—Peru
Peasantry—Peru
Shopping and shoppers—Peru
Yungay

Antiquities
See Indians of South America—Antiquities—Peru

Expropriation policy
Day of the generals. S. Rodman. il Nat R 22:1105-7 O 20 '70

History
Truce negotiations of San Martín; winning the independence of Peru. R. C. Smith, 3d. il por Américas 22:31-3 O '70

Native races
See Indians of South America—Peru

Politics and government
Day of the generals. S. Rodman. il Nat R 22:1105-7 O 20 '70
Peru's military government. G. W. Grayson, jr. bibliog f Cur Hist 58:65-72+ F '70
Urban Peru: political action as sellout; case study of Ica. D. L. Bayer. il por Trans-Action 7:36+ N '69

Relief work
Aid fiasco in Peru; United States' effort. R. Glass. New Repub 163:14 S 19 '70
Bidding to help the Peruvians. il por Time 96:10 Jl 13 '70
Churches step up aid to Peru. J. R. Greisch. Chr Today 14:33 Jl 31 '70
OAS countries, employees rush aid to earthquake-stricken Peru. il Américas 22:44 Jl '70
OAS Peruvian relief efforts to center on housing. Américas 22:45 S '70
Puppy for Peru; relief from religious sources. Chr Today 14:46 Ag 21 '70
United in sorrow. Américas 22:1 S '70
U.S. assists Peru in meeting emergency relief needs; statement, June 8, 1970. R. M. Nixon. Dept State Bul 62:803 Je 29 '70
What U.S. companies are doing abroad. U S News 68:88 Je 22 '70

Religious institutions and affairs
World around us. Chr Cent 87:876-8 Jl 15 '70

Social conditions
Target in Peru: social transformation. P. L. Ruggere. America 122:160-1 F 14 '70

PERUTZ, Kathrin
Teenage America; engagement in Fort Worth. il Harper 240:96-102+ Mr; 16 Je '70

PERUVIAN daffodils. See Basket flowers

PERUVIAN Indians. See Indians of South America—Peru

PERUVIAN poetry

Translations into English
Poem: Why did that have to be the only answer? tr. by D. Tipton. A. Sanchez Leon. Poetry 116:368 Ag '70

PESCHKA, Francis
Mini music hall. il Time 97:53 Ja 4 '71 •

PESEK, Ludek
Voyage to the planets; paintings. Nat Geog 138:147-93 Ag '70

PESEK, Patti Jo
Traveler's choice. Travel 133:22 My '70

PEST control
Agricultural pest control and the environment. G. W. Irving, jr. bibliog Science 168:1419-24 Je 19 '70
Co-evolutionary race. P. R. Ehrlich and J. P. Holdren. Sat R 53:66 D 5 '70
What's new for pest control. Suc Farm 68: Ml Ap '70
See also
Household pest control
Insect control

PESTICIDE labels. See Labels

PESTICIDE pollution. See Pesticides and the environment

PESTICIDES
Government's plan to phase out persistent chemicals. il Farm J 94:20-1+ Ja '70
Handy guide for diluting pesticides. Suc Farm 68:D10 Ap '70
Intestinal hydrolysis and conjugation of a pesticidal carbamate in vitro. J. C. Pekas and G. D. Paulson. bibliog il Science 170:77-8 O 2 '70
Weeding out the pesticides. Bsns W p59+ S 26 '70
What canceling a pesticide could mean to you. Suc Farm 68:46 Ap '70
See also
Herbicides
Insecticides

Disposal
How to discard chemicals. Suc Farm 68:B8 Ag '70
Insecticide disposal: the heat's on. il Pop Sci 197:32 O '70
Safe disposal of home pesticides. Consumer Bul 53:26 O '70

Injurious effects
Co-evolutionary race. P. R. Ehrlich and J. P Holdren. Sat R 53:66 D 5 '70
Danger! pesticides at work. W. B. Furlong. il Good H 170:82-3+ Mr '70
Death of the oceans; pesticides; address, March 13, 1970. D. Epel. Vital Speeches 36:411-14 Ap 15 '70
Fighting the fire ant; toxic side effects from Mirex. il Time 96:40 N 2 '70
Mad hatter visits Alice's restaurant; mercury poisoning. H. Martin. il Todays Health 48:39-43+ O '70
Nerve gas in the orchards. R. B. Taylor. Nation 210:751-3 Je 22 '70

Laws and legislation
Birds and bees. D. Zwerdling. il New Repub 163:17-20 O 31 '70
Governor announces strict controls on harmful pesticides; with text of commissioner's order. il Cons 25:4-6 D '70
Public hearings express pros and cons of pesticide use. R. H. Smith. il Cons 25:2-4 O '70
Will EPA take away your pesticides? G. W Wormley. Farm J 94:32 N '70
See also
United States—Agricultural research service—Pesticides regulation division

Research
Bugging out? Newsweek 76:94+ N 2 '70

Residues
Analysis of pesticide residues: new problems and methods. D. J. Lisk. bibliog Science 170:589-93 N 6 '70
Annals of medicine; case of organic mercury poisoning by pork from hogs fed surplus seed grain chemically treated. B. Roueché. New Yorker 46:64-70+ Ag 22 '70
Let's not kill ourselves; mercury residues in game birds. B. East. Outdoor Life 145:4 Ja '70
Pollution is a dirty word. R. Sanders. il Suc Farm 68:23-5 Ag '70
Pollution, your problem too; food residue control. R. Sanders. il Suc Farm 68:32-3 S '70
Real villains: Pesticides regulation division and the mercury pesticide industry. R. Sherrill. Nation 211:208-12 S 14 '70

PESTICIDES and the environment
Birds and bees. D. Zwerdling. il New Repub 163:17-20 O 31 '70
Dead stream; Crooked Creek in Missouri. K P. Shea. il Environ 12:12-15 Jl '70
Earth, air, water. J. Frost. bibliog il Environ 11:14-29+ Jl '69
Pesticides: prescribing for the ecosystem. R. Van Den Bosch. il Environ 12:20-5 Ap '70
Pyramiding damage: experimental study of DDT movement in the environment. T. J. Peterle. bibliog il pors Environ 11:34-40 Ji '69

PESTICIDES and the environment—*Continued*
Remembering Rachel Carson. S. A. Briggs. il
por Am For 76:8-11 Jl '70
Since silent spring, by F. Graham, jr. Review
Environ il 12:30-1 My '70. K. P. Shea
PESTICIDES and wildlife
Butterflies, yes! fate of harmless or beneficial
insects. A. W. Smith. Nat Parks 44:2 Mr
'70
Facts on pesticides today. J. E. Forbes. bibliog il Cons 24:2-4 Ag '69
p-p'-DDT: effect on calcium metabolism and
concentration of estradiol in the blood.
D. B. Peakall. bibliog il Science 168:592-4
My 1 '70
Pesticides and the reproduction of birds. D.
B. Peakall. il Sci Am 222:72-8 bibliog(p 130)
Ap '70
Unwanted harvest. K. P. Shea. bibliog il Environ 11:12-17+ S '69
Where have all the pelicans gone? il Chem
43:5 Mr '70
PESTICIDES regulation division. See United
States—Agricultural research service—Pesticides regulation division
PESTO. See Sauces
PESTS
   See also
Agricultural pests
PET caskets. See Coffins
PET food
   See also
Cats—Food and feeding
Dogs—Food and feeding
PETER III, emperor of Russia
Domestic policies of Peter III and his overthrow. M. Raeff. bibliog f Am Hist R 75:
1289-310 Je '70 *
PETER, Paul and Mary (folk singers) See
Singers
PETER, John
Housing: from crisis to disaster? il Look
34:53-9 F 10 '70
PETER, Klaus J.
High-quality AM section in new hi-fi receiver. il Electr World 83:30-1 Je '70
PETER, Robert
It was a terrible scene. Nat R 22:1001+ S 22
'70
PETER Grimes; opera. See Britten, B.
PETER Scott's Wildfowl trust, Slimbridge, England. See Bird sanctuaries—England
PETERBORO, N.H. town library
Day the library closed its doors. E. Yates.
Am Lib 1:179-80 F '70
PETERBOROUGH, Cyril Eastaugh, bp. of.
See Eastaugh, C.
PETERLE, Tony J.
Pyramiding damage. bibliog il pors Environ
11:34-40 Jl '69
PETERS, Leslie K. See Sinclair, W. jt. auth.
PETERS, Muriel, and Peters, William
How college students feel about love, sex
and marriage. il Good H 170:84-5+ Je '70
PETERS, Ruth Marie
Bouquets for winter. il Horticulture 48:32-3+
S '70
Family fun in your own backyard. il Home
Gard 57:32-40 Je '70
Joy from a window greenhouse. il Home Gard
57:42-3+ S '70
Poppy clan. il Horticulture 48:28-31+ Je '70
Spectacular amaryllis. il Horticulture 48:30-
1+ D '70
Woodland gardens under glass. il Home Gard
57:46-7 N '70
PETERS, Svetlana. See Stalina, S. I.
PETERS, Thomas R.
Descent to wisdom; address, December 2, 1969.
Vital Speeches 36:394-6 Ap 15 '70
No provision for now; address, October 13,
1970. Vital Speeches 37:75-9 N 15 '70
PETERS, William. See Peters, M. jt. auth.
PETERS, William Wesley
Newsmakers. il por Newsweek 75:69 Ap 20
'70 *
PETERSEN, L. J. See Butler, E. E. jt. auth.
PETERSEN, Marjorie
Stornoway progress report. il por Motor B
125:122-3+ Ja '70
PETERSON, Allen M. and others
Bistatic-radar observation of long-period, directional ocean-wave spectra with loran
A. bibliog il Science 170:158-61 O 9 '70
PETERSON, Arthur G.
Eagle glass and manufacturing company. il
Hobbies 75:112-13 Ap; 82-3 My '70
Glass salt shakers: twelve rarities. il(p 1)
Hobbies 74:114-15 Ja '70
X-Ray pattern glass. il Hobbies 75:68-9 Je '70
PETERSON, Bob
Gallery; photographs. Life 69:8-9 N 6 '70

PETERSON, Eugene H.
Morning prayers; poem. Chr Today 14:4 S
25 '70
PETERSON, Eugene K.
Atmosphere: a clouded horizon. il Environ
12:32-9 Ap; 44-5 D '70
PETERSON, Fritz
Dreamy times for Mini-bombers. P. Carry. il
por Sports Illus 32:20-2+ Je 22 '70 *
PETERSON, George A.
Discovery. J. Dreyfuss. il Mod Phot 34:84-5+
Mr '70 *
PETERSON, Gunnar A.
Laura Beall Woods. il Nat Parks 44:24-5 Ja
'70
PETERSON, Harold
Baseball. Sports Illus 32:50 My 4; 50+ My
18; 56 Je 8 '70
Lift, liberty and the pursuit of happiness. il
Sports Illus 33:64-7+ O 19 '70
Moving in for a land grab. il Sports Illus 33:
22-4+ Jl 13 '70
Week. See occasional issues of Sports illustrated published during baseball season
Week; college football. Sports Illus 33:71-2+
N 30 '70
PETERSON, Malcolm
Space available; excerpts from testimony before the Joint congressional committee on
atomic energy, January 29, 1970. bibliog il
Environ 12:2-9 Mr '70
PETERSON, Mary Nygaard
Magic box; dramatization of an Italian folk
tale. Plays 29:39-45 F '70
PETERSON, Richard B.
Worker participation in Swedish enterprise;
excerpt from Worker participation in the
enterprise: the Swedish experience. Mo
Labor R 93:48-50 Ap '70
PETERSON, Robert
Boston stranglers; or, How to pack a pack
of Cub scouts in a Bonanza. il Flying 86:
72-5 Ja '70
How to get a multi-engine rating. il Flying
86:64-70+ Je '70
Say again everything after ATC clears . . .
il Flying 88:62-4 Ja '71
PETERSON, Roger Tory
Where have all the ospreys gone? interview,
ed. by J. Hess. il Nat Wildlife 9:36-7 D '70
PETERSON, Rudolph Arvid
Birth pains. Forbes 106:44 S 15 '70 *
Jumping into a pool. por Time 95:16 Mr 23
'70 *
PETERSON, Tyrone
Counsel for the G.I. defense. Time 96:44-5
O 19 '70 *
PETIOLES
Senescence in detached betel leaves: role of
the petiole. S. D. Mishra and B. K. Gaur.
bibliog il Science 167:387-8 Ja 23 '70
PETITT, Dorothy
(ed) Professional publications. See issues of
English journal
PETLEY-JONES, Evan William
Scrimshaw. il Antiques 98:256-62 Ag '70
PETRAS, Fred
Pleasures of portables. il Hi Fi 20:secI 46-52
My '70
PETRIFIED peat. See Peat, Fossil
PETROCHEMICAL plants. See Chemical plants
PETROGLYPHS
Ancient landings in America; findings of
C. H. Gordon. J. Lear. il Sat R 53:18-19+
Jl 18 '70
Canaanite Columbus? the Metcalf stone. il por
Newsweek 76:65 O 26 '70
Mystery of the Nazca lines. D. Cohen. il Sci
Digest 67:46-8+ My '70
Secrets of the stones; Argentine Northwest.
B. Pastor. il Américas 22:32-7 Ap '70
   See also
Cave drawings and paintings
PETROLEUM
   See also
Gasoline
Hydrocarbons
Oil lands
   International aspects
Mr Scripps said it; control of world petroleum; address, June 18, 1970. M. T. Halbouty. Vital Speeches 36:688-92 S 1 '70
   See also
Petroleum industry and trade—Middle East
   Pipe lines
Alaska: money v. law. il Time 95:84 My
11 '70
Blocking that line; ruling on Alaskan project.
il Newsweek 75:78 Ap 27 '70
Breathing spell; Trans-Alaska pipeline system.
Sci N 97:389 Ap 18 '70
Canada's bid for Arctic oil. W. Kornberg.
il Sci N 97:442-3 My 2 '70

PETROLEUM—Pipe lines—*Continued*
Changing design for TAPS. Sci N 97:432
My 2 '70
Chill for a fever; Alaskan project. Newsweek
75:83+ My 11 '70
Concern for the Arctic environment. W.
Kornberg. il Sci N 97:486-8 My 16 '70
Court enjoins oil pipeline road. Liv Wildn 34:
58-9 Sum '70
Delays gum up Alaska pipeline. Bsns W p28
Ap 18 '70
Getting set for a black gold rush; Trans-
Alaska pipeline. E. Gross. il Sci N 97:177-9
F 14 '70
Go or no go for the Trans-Alaskan pipeline?
W. E. Towell. Am For 76:11 N '70
Hauling and pulling in the Arctic. R. B. Wee-
den. il Liv Wildn 34:8-16 Sum '70
Hot oil on the tundra. C. H. Callison. Audu-
bon 72:104 Jl '70
Israel's bet on oil. il Time 95:87 F 23 '70
Long pipe; Trans-Alaska pipeline system. R.
Moxness. bibliog il Environ 12:12-23+ S '70
Oil rush. W. K. Wyant, jr. New Repub 162:
19-21 F 14 '70
On this side, nothing but virgin wilderness;
on that side, nothing but virgin wilder-
ness; down the middle, the Trans Alaska
pipeline. D. J. Chasan. Esquire 73:129+ Je
'70
Our last great wilderness; Trans-Alaska pipe-
line system or TAPS. W. Sullivan. il Am
Heritage 21:114-17 Ag '70
Pipelines fear a poor bargain; trading state
for federal safety rules. il Bsns W p68-9
Ja 31 '70
Report from Alaska. R. B. Weeden. il Liv
Wildn 34:50-1 Spr '70
Trans-Alaska oil pipeline. Liv Wildn 33:34-5
Aut '69

Prices
Applied economics: increases in price of
crude oil. Nat R 22:1383-4 D 29 '70

Prospecting
100-billion-dollar oil rush, worldwide. il U S
News 68:50-4 Je 8 '70
Report from southeast Asia; hunt for oil off
the coasts of Indonesia and neighboring
countries. L. Kraar. il Fortune 81:45-6 Mr
'70
See also
Louisiana land and exploration company

Transportation
Arctic oil is still beyond reach. il Bsns W
p23 N 28 '70
Biologist explains: why we must plan now
to protect the Arctic. L. C. Bliss. il Bul
Atom Sci 26:34-8 O '70
Can the Arctic be saved? R. Starnes. Field
& S 75:16-17+ Jl '70
See also
Petroleum—Pipe lines
Tank ships

Alaska
Alaska: politicians and natives, money and
oil. L. Lapham. il Harper 240:85-102 My '70
Alaskan oil dilemma: ecology or prosperity?
R. Gannon. bibliog il Sci Digest 68:14-19 Jl
'70
Arctic oil is still beyond reach. il Bsns W
p23 N 28 '70
Biologist explains: why we must plan now to
protect the Arctic. L. C. Bliss. il Bul Atom
Sci 26:34-8 O '70
Can the Arctic be saved? R. Starnes. Field &
S 75:16-17+ Jl '70
North Slope: oil rush. L. J. Carter; discus-
sion. Science 166:1220+; 168:64-5 D 5 '69,
Ap 3 '70
Oil & the Arctic tundra; with editorial com-
ment. J. C. Reed. il Nat Parks & Con Mag
44:2, 4-7 N '70
Oil rush. W. K. Wyant, jr. New Repub 162:19-
21 F 14 '70
Oil rush of '69. il Sr Schol 95:19 S 29 '69
Oil rush of '70. R. Zelnick. il N Y Times Mag
p26-7+ Mr 1 '70
Our last great wilderness; oil and the eco-
logical balance of Alaska's North Slope. W.
Sullivan. il Am Heritage 21:98-117 Ag '70

Arctic Regions
See also
Petroleum—Alaska
Petroleum—Canada

Asia, Southeastern
Report from southeast Asia; hunt for oil off
the coasts of Indonesia and neighboring
countries. L. Kraar. il Fortune 81:45-6 Mr
'70
Sea of oil. F. Jaeger. Nation 211:2 Jl 6 '70

Canada
Canada makes her play. W. Kornberg. il Sci
N 97:466-7 My 9 '70
Canada's bid for Arctic oil. W. Kornberg.
il Sci N 97:442-3 My 2 '70
Oil fever spreads it glow in the Arctic. il
Bsns W p 124-5+ Ap 18 '70
U.S. looking to Canada for help in fuel
crisis. il U S News 69:43-4 N 9 '70

Tennessee
Luck of roaring Oneida; oil boom in Scott
County. il Time 96:74+ N 30 '70

Venezuela
Polar game where talk was the payoff. E. D.
Brockett. il Nations Bsns 58:82-3 Ja '70
PETROLEUM as fuel
Energy shortage worsens. il Time 96:62-3 Ag
31 '70
Fuel oil users feel the drought. Bsns W p21
Ag 22 '70
PETROLEUM engineering
Getting set for a black gold rush; Trans-
Alaska pipeline. E. Gross. il Sci N 97:177-9
F 14 '70
PETROLEUM equipment industry
See also
Zapata Norness, inc.
PETROLEUM in submerged lands
Age of reason; North Sea oil discoveries. il
Forbes 106:21 N 15 '70
Beneath the beautiful sea; oil in the North
Sea. il Newsweek 75:81 Je 15 '70
Find in a treacherous sea: oil in the North
Sea. Time 95:94 Je 15 '70
Gushing expectations around the North Sea.
il Fortune 82:178 Ag '70
Natural oil seepage at Coal Oil Point, Santa
Barbara, California. A. A. Allen and oth-
ers. bibliog il Science 170:974-7 N 27 '70
Report from southeast Asia; hunt for oil off
the coasts of Indonesia and neighboring
countries. L. Kraar. il Fortune 81:45-6 Mr
'70
Stormy debate over North Sea oil. il Bsns W
p35 N 14 '70
Striking it rich in the North Sea. il Bsns
W p45 My 16 '70
See also
Oil well drilling, Submarine
PETROLEUM industry and trade
See also
Royal Dutch-Shell group

Finance
Energy; with yardsticks of management performance. il Forbes 105:151-2+ Ja 1 '70;
107:144+ Ja 1 '71
Oil-well action for the near-rich; oil participation funds. il Bsns W p 120+ Mr 14
'70

International aspects
See Petroleum—International aspects

Law
See Petroleum laws and legislation

Securities
New strength in energy stocks. il Fortune
82:129-30 D '70
Oils show some of the old pizzazz. il Bsns
W p24 S 5 '70

Alaska
Is it TAPS for wild Alaska? B. East. il Out-
door Life 145:43-5+ My '70
Kiss the north slope good-by? G. Laycock.
il Audubon 72:68-75 S '70
Oil rush of '70. R. Zelnick. il N Y Times Mag
p26-7+ Mr 1 '70
Raping Alaska; ecology of oil. B Weisberg. il
Ramp Mag 8:25-33 Ja '70
Rushing the oil gear to Alaska. il Bsns W
p22-3 Jl 11 '70

Bolivia
Iberian assist helped oil the way; INI take
over of Gulf oil operations. Bsns W p28-9
My 2 '70

Canada
U.S. establishes formal limitation on oil
imports from Canada; White House announcement, with proclamation by President Nixon. Dept State Bul 62:494-5 Ap
13 '70

Ecuador
Counting on oil to pay for a spending orgy.
il Bsns W p46-7 Ja 31 '70

France
Canadian caper; Aquitaine co. of Canada, ltd.
N. A. Martin. Duns 96:57-8 Ag '70

PETROLEUM industry and trade—*Continued*

Great Britain

See also
British petroleum company

Greece, Modern

Feud of titans; Aristotle Onassis-Stavros Niarchos refinery contest. Newsweek 75:60 F 2 '70

Indonesia

Attack on corruption; use of Pertamina's funds. il por Time 96:36 Ag 31 '70

Israel

Israel's new coup; gunboats and oil. T. Land. Nation 210:103-4 F 2 '70

Japan

Oil for the lamps of Japan. S. Griffin. Sci N 97:588 Je 13 '70

Libya

Libya pressures the oil producers. il Bsns W p37 Ja 31 '70
Oil in ferment. il Forbes 106:23-5 O 15 '70
U.S. oil companies feel the heat. por Bsns W p42-3 Je 13 '70

Maine

Oil discovers Maine. L. Spiker. il Nation 210: 656-8 Je 1 '70
Payrolls and pickerel in Maine; proposed oil refinery potential disaster to fishing and tourism industries. il Time 95:52 F 16 '70

Middle East

Little throat cutting Arabs and U.S. planes for Israel. il Time 35:73-4 Je 29 '70
Nasser's death haunts U.S. oilmen. il por Bsns W p 15-16 O 3 '70
Oil companies wait for the worst. il Bsns W p24-5 S 26 '70
Political power of Mideast oil. il Time 96:81-2 O 19 '70

Nigeria

Nigeria snaps back. il Newsweek 75:78 Mr 9 '70
Rush for oil. il Time 95:74 F 9 '70

United States

Consumer be damned; import quota system for oil. W. K. Wyant, jr. New Repub 162: 11-12 Mr 7 '70
Nixon opens tap a bit on oil imports. il Bsns W p37 Je 27 '70
Nixon orders more oil. il Bsns W p 16-17 D 12 '70
Oil companies fume over lead. il Bsns W p22 Mr 7 '70
Oil lobby is not depleted. E. Knoll. il N Y Times Mag p26-7+ Mr 8 '70; Reply with rejoinder. F. N. Ikard. p 136+ Ap 5 '70
Oil policy committee discontinues considera-tion of tariff system; text of letter, August 13, 1970. G. A. Lincoln. Dept State Bul 63:360-1 S 28 '70
Oil: quotas or tariffs? Duns 95:102 F '70
Oil taking over the energy business. il Bsns W p54-6 N 7 '70
Oil: the politics of an economic resource. il Sr Schol 95:6-11 Ja 12 '70
Petroleum industry's role in the preservation of the environment. F. N. Ikard. il Parks & Rec 5:18-21+ My '70
President Nixon receives report of oil im-port control task force; statement, February 20, 1970. R. M. Nixon. Dept State Bul 62: 427-8 Mr 30 '70
Pressure mounts to tap domestic oil. il Bsns W p 17-18 Jl 25 '70
Tax on leaded gas scares independents. il Bsns W p29 Je 6 '70
Two-front war. il Forbes 106:40 +S 1 '70
Uncivil servants; purge of public interest types in government resource programs. D. Sanford. New Repub 162:13-14 My 16 '70
U.S. establishes formal limitation on oil im-ports from Canada; White House announce-ment, with proclamation by President Nix-on. Dept State Bul 62:494-5 Ap 13 '70
Why the U.S. is letting in more foreign oil. il U S News 70:17 Ja 4 '71
See also
Collective bargaining—Petroleum industry
also names of oil companies, e.g. Atlantic Richfield company

Venezuela

New way to squeeze the oil companies; oil-service contract. il Bsns W p44-5 My 16 '70

PETROLEUM laws and legislation
Pipelines fear a poor bargain; trading state for federal safety rules. il Bsns W p68-9 Ja 31 '70
See also
Oil and gas leases

PETROLEUM pipe lines. See Petroleum—Pipe lines

PETROLEUM products

Additives

See also
Lubrizol corporation

PETROLEUM refineries
Dilemma of Machiasport. F. Graham, jr. il Audubon 72:106-11 Jl '70
DuPont writes off a refinery plan. Bsns W p33 S 19 '70

PETROLOGY
Apollo 11 lunar science conference; general mineralogy; symposium. bibliog il Science 167:583-604 Ja 30 '70

PETRONE, Rocco A.
Where are they now? por Newsweek 76:8 Jl 27 '70 *

PETRONIUS Arbiter
Whose Satyricon, Petronius's or Fellini's? G. Highet. bibliog f il por Horizon 12:42-7 Aut '70 *

PETROUCHKA; ballet. See Ballets—Criticisms

PETROV, Boris
Astronautics: past and future; interview. Space World G-11-83:38-9 N '70
Intercosmos 1. il Space World G-3-75:30-1 Mr '70

PETROW, Richard
Fish without a friend. il Pop Mech 134:112-14 Jl '70

PETS
Dogs, cats, and other living things. il Mc-Calls 97:30+ Jl; 52+ S; 98:16+ N '70; 39+ Ja '71
Easter pets not to bring home. il Good H 170:182 Ap '70
Not all wild pets like captivity, but some do if you treat them right. il Sunset 145:150-1 Jl '70
Pet news. See issues of Ladies' home jour-nal
White House pets; excerpts. M. Truman. il Ladies Home J 87:110-12 Ja '70
See also names of animal pets, e.g. Dogs

PETSKO, Gregory A.
Proton magnetic resonance spectrum of poly-water. il Science 167:171 Ja 9 '70

PETTER, Mariam, and Bloomquist, Lillian
Library goes to camp. Am Lib 1:166-8 F '70

PETTEYS, D. F.
Roots; poem. Commonweal 93:197 N 20 '70
Synopsis; poem. Yale R 60:255 D '70

PETTICOAT revolution; drama. See Boiko, C.

PETTINGELL, Phoebe
Ode on zero; Transport o Patmos; poems. Poetry 117:183-4 D '70

PETTIT, Terry
Birthright; poem. Chr Cent 87:910 Jl 29 '70

PETTY, Richard
Rap 'n' pinion. por Motor T 22:18 Mr '70

PETZVAL, Josef Max
How it all began, a brief look at the con-tributions of lens designers Petzval and Seidel. B. Sherman. Mod Phot 34:26+ Mr '70 *

PEUGEOT (automobile) See Automobiles, For-eign

PEW, Thomas W. jr.
Chicago seven. Nation 210:38-40 Ja 19 '70
Conversations in Greece. Nation 212:74-80 Ja 18 '71

PEWAUKEE, Wis.
Bio-disc plant confirms test data on new process. il Am City 85:14 Jl '70

PEWTER
Continental pewter epergnes, cruet stands, and sugar bowls. R. M. Vetter. il Antiques 98:88-93 Jl '70
Pewterers of eighteenth-century New York. L. I. Laughlin. il Antiques 98:624-8 O '70

PEWTER casting. See Foundry practice

PEYRE, Henri
Belle epoque. il Opera N 35:8-13 D 12 '70

PFAFF, William
Confessions of a Green Beret. Commentary 49:28-34 Ja '70
Decline of liberal politics. Commentary 48:45-51 O '69; 49:22 F '70
Grand strategy: for 1960. Commonweal 92:55 Mr 27 '70

PFEFFER, Leo
Ready, aim, pray! Commonweal 93:274-6 D 11 '70

PFEIFFER, C. Boyd
Best all-around lure? il Field & S 75:68-9+ O '70

PFEIFFER, E. W. See Orians, G. H. jt. auth.

PFEIFFER, Russell R. and Molnar, C. E.
Cochlear nerve fiber discharge patterns: relationship to the cochlear microphonic. bibliog il Science 167:1614-16 Mr 20 '70

PFEIL, Mary Pat
Computer harvests migrant records. il Am Ed 6:6-9 N '70
It's hard to come back. il Am Ed 6:3-6 Je '70
Off the shelf and into the classroom. il Am Ed 6:13-16 Ag '70

PFISTER, Herbert R. See Harlow, L. A. jt. auth.

PFIZER, Beryl
Poor woman's almanac. See issues of Ladies' home journal

PFOUTZ, Daniel R.
(comp) Sci-tech books '69. il por Library J 95:855-62 Mr 1 '70

PHAGE. See Bacteriophage

PHAGOCYTES and phagocytosis
Plasmalemmal and subsurface complexes in human leukemic cells: membrane bonding by zipperlike junctions. F. T. Sanel and A. A. Serpick. bibliog il Science 168:1458-60 Je 19 '70
See also
Macrophages

PHAKAVALI dancers. See Dancing, Thai

PHANTOM of the opera's friend; story. See Barthelme, D.

PHARMACEUTICAL industry. See Drug trade

PHARMACISTS
Price of a generic Rx drug; druggists' practices. Consumer Rep 35:397-8 Jl '70

Anecdotes, facetiae, satire, etc.
Man of medicine. G. Ace. Sat R 53:10 N 7 '70

PHASE-contrast microscopy. See Microscope and microscopy

PHASE rule and equilibrium
See also
Critical point

PHASE transitions
Magic even-even nuclei show phase transition. G. B. Lubkin. il Phys Today 23:17-18 N '70
Mott transition? It all depends on what you mean. G. B. Lubkin. Phys Today 23:20 D '70

PHASED array radar. See Radar—Antenna and scanning mechanisms

PHASES (chemistry)
Calorimetric detection of a membrane-lipid phase transition in living cells. J. C. Reinert and J. M. Steim. bibliog il Science 168:1580-2 Je 26 '70
Superheated ice formed by the freezing of superheated water. G. Schubert and R. E. Lingenfelter. il Science 168:469-70 Ap 24 '70; Reply. B. Kamb. bibliog 169:1343-4 S 25 '70

PHEASANT calling. See Bird calling

PHEASANT shooting
Rules for bagging pheasant. T. Trueblood. il Field & S 75:22+ O '70
Strange way to fool pheasant. J. Palmer. il Field & S 75:48-9+ S '70

PHEASANTS
See also
Cookery—Game

PHELAN, William D. Jr
Is constitutional democracy doomed? Cur 116:40-6 Mr '70

PHELPS, Flora L.
Pioneers in Massachusetts. il Américas 22:21-30 F '70

PHELPS, Robert
Austere and the earnestly ghastly. il Life 68:10 Je 19 '70
Colette, Cocteau, and Proust. il Mlle 72:124-5+ D '70
This, in fact, is where affirmation begins. Mlle 72:78-9+ D '70
Undying fascination of Colette. il pors McCalls 97:12+ S '70

PHENOBARBITAL
Chemically induced porphyria: prevention by prior treatment with phenobarbital. L. Kaufman and others. bibliog il Science 170:320-2 O 16 '70

PHENOVARIATION. See Variation (botany)

PHENYLALANINE
Alcohol aversion in the rat: behavioral assessment of noxious drug effects. M .Nachman and others. bibliog il Science 168:1244-6 Je 5 '70
p-Chlorophenylalanine methyl ester; an aphrodisiac? R. E. Whalen and W. C. Luttge. bibliog il Science 169:1000-1 S 4 '70
Clues from a chemical; PCPA's effects on serotonin. L. Campbell. il Sci N 98:287-9 O 3 '70

Hypersexuality and behavioral changes in cats caused by administration of p-chlorophenylalanine. J. Ferguson and others. bibliog il Science 168:499-501 Ap 24 '70
Sexual behavior of male cats after administration of parachlorophenylalanine. A. Zitrin and others. bibliog il Science 170:868-70 N 20 '70
Side effect; PCPA as aphrodisiac. Sci Am 222:44 F '70
See also
Dopa

PHENYLTHIOACETATE. See Acetates

PHEROMONES
Pheromone response in pine bark beetles: influence of host volatiles. G. B. Pitman: reply. W. D. Bedard. bibliog il Science 167:1638-9 Mr 20 '70
Pheromone transport and reception in an amphipod. E. Dahl and others. il Science 170:739 N 13 '70
See also
Insect sex attractants

PHILADELPHIA
Great Scott, it's Philadelphia! il Newsweek 76:22-3 Ag 3 '70
Philadelphia: host to the spirit of '76. Bsns W p21-2 Jl 4 '70

Banks
Fast on his feet in Philadelphia; First Pennsylvania banking & trust co. il Bsns W p76+ F 14 '70
First slice off the prime rate; First Pennsylvania banking & trust co. Bsns W p35 S 19 '70
Man who cut the prime: president of First Pennsylvania banking & trust co. por Time 96:73 S 28 '70

Bridges
Bridge replaced in halves to avoid closing river crossing; Girard avenue bridge over Schuykill River. il Am City 85:28 Je '70

City planning
You need good maps. A. K. Strobl. bibliog il por Am City 85:83+ Jl '70

Description
Philadelphia. H. Pollack. il Parks & Rec 5:18-21 Jl '70

Education
Break with tradition: parochial and public schools combine resources to serve their pupils. J. Hincken. Clear House 44:315-16 Ja '70
Can the public schools be saved? M. Polner. Commonweal 93:15-17 O 2 '70
City is our classroom; Parkway program. C. H. Harrison. il Schol Teach Sec Teach Sup p12-13 D 1 '69
High school with no walls; Parkway program. J. Bremer. Ed Digest 35:16-19 Mr '70
Parkway experiment. il por Time 95:55 Mr 23 '70
Pennsylvania advancement school; no game for radicals. H. S. Resnik. il Sat R 53:49-51+ Jl 18 '70
See also
Philadelphia free library

Municipal improvement
Philadelphia wins clean up contest; National award of excellence. Parks & Rec 5:74-5 Ap '70

Music
Shostakovich's unlucky 13th. R. S. Brown. Hi Fi 20:secI 26+ Ap '70
See also
Philadelphia orchestra

Negroes
New set of heroes; Interested Negroes organization in Philadelphia. C. Lewis. il Am Ed 6:23 Ja '70

Parks and playgrounds
Recreation growth in the Congress city. H. Pollack. il Parks & Rec 5:29-30+ Ag '70

Police
City of (big) brotherly love. J. Groutt. Commonweal 92:167-9 My 1 '70
Philadelphia boomerang; police panic over Panthers. J. Higgins. il Nation 211:332-6 O 12 '70
Philadelphia's guerrilla war. il Newsweek 76:30-1 S 14 '70
Plastic shields protect police vehicles. il Am City 85:36 D '70
War of the cops. B. McCormick. il N Y Times Mag p23-5+ O 18 '70; Reply. J. Levine. p50 N 22 '70

PHILADELPHIA—*Continued*

Politics and government

Philadelphia's battered mayor. il por Bsns W p40-1 F 21 '70

Recreation department

One more time! Recreation Commissioner R. W. Crawford. V. Kendrick. il por Parks & Rec 5:26-8 Je '70

Recreation growth in the Congress city. H. Pollack. il Parks & Rec 5:29-30+ Ag '70

Sanitary affairs

Winter housecleaning; cleanup order mixed up by sanitation crew. Time 95:15 Ja 26 '70

Theater

On the lam. J. Kroll. Newsweek 75:95 F 9 '70

This is street theater; Society hill playhouse street theatre. D. Kogan. il Parks & Rec 5:44-6 Ja '70

Water supply

That abandoned quarry may be a water asset; Philadelphia suburban water company. J. M. Ballengee. il Am City 85:69-71 F '70

PHILADELPHIA bar association library. See Law library company of Philadelphia

PHILADELPHIA Eagles (football club) See Football clubs

PHILADELPHIA free library

Library still free in Philly; vote to retain Jerry Rubin's Do it! on open shelves. Wilson Lib Bul 45:450 Ja '71

PHILADELPHIA orchestra

Music to my ears; Penderecki's Utrenja. I. Kolodin. Sat R 53:24 O 17 '70

Musical events; concerts in Philharmonic Hall (cont) W. Sargeant. New Yorker 46:178-9 N 21 '70

Musical events; K. Penderecki's Utrenja in Philharmonic Hall. W. Sargeant. New Yorker 46:138-9 O 10 '70

Musical events; Shostakovich's Thirteenth symphony in Philarmonic Hall. W. Sargeant. New Yorker 45:80-1 Ja 31 '70

PHILADELPHIA Phillies. See Baseball clubs

PHILADELPHIA photo show. See Photography—Exhibitions

PHILADELPHIA symphony orchestra. See Philadelphia orchestra

PHILADELPHIA track classic. See Running

PHILANTHROPIST; drama. See Hampton, C.

PHILANTHROPISTS

See also

Perot. H. R

PHILANTHROPY. See Charities; Giving

PHILATELY. See Postage stamps

PHILBIN, Philip J.

Excerpt from remarks, May 19, 1970. Cong Digest 49:211+ Ag '70

PHILBIN, Tom

Why most people fail at dieting. il Mech Illus 66:43-5+ S '70

PHILBY, Harold Adrian Russell

Mr Philby, I presume? E. Sparn. pors Sr Schol 96:6-7 F 9 '70 *

PHILBY, Kim. See Philby, H. A. R.

PHILCO-Ford corporation

Aerospace activities combined. Aviation W 92:65 My 18 '70

Ford reorganizes Philco operations. Aviation W 92:85 F 23 '70

How Philco lost its chairman. por Bsns W p28 F 14 '70

Philco-Ford gets satellite award. Aviation W 93:22 Ag 10 '70

PHILHARMONIC-symphony society of New York

Music; performance of Elliott Carter's Concerto for orchestra. D. Hamilton. Nation 210:253-4 Mr 2 '70

Music to my ears; Bernstein's Fidelio. I. Kolodin. Sat R 53:55 Ja 31 '70

Music to my ears; concert version of Götterdämmerung. I. Kolodin. Sat R 53:40 F 7 '70

Music to my ears; concerts in Philharmonic Hall. I. Kolodin. Sat R 53:45 Ja 17 '70

Music to my ears; performance of Sinfonia. I. Kolodin. Sat R 53:58-9 O 24 '70

Music to my ears; Stravinsky's Les noces. I. Kolodin. Sat R 53:24 O 17 '70

Musical events:

Excerpts from Götterdämmering in Philharmonic Hall. W. Sargeant. New Yorker 45:79 Ja 31 '70

L. Maazel, violinist and conductor at concert in Philharmonic Hall. W. Sargeant. New Yorker 46:151-2 My 9 '70

Performance of Bruckner's First symphony in Philharmonic Hall. W. Sargeant. New Yorker 46:108 Mr 7 '70

Two opening programs conducted by L. Bernstein. W. Sargeant. New Yorker 46: 137-8 O 3 '70

Report:

Leonard Bernstein's Fidelio. S. Jenkins. Opera N 34:32 F 28 '70

Performance of Bluebeard's castle. S. L. Fogel. Opera N 34:32 Ja 31 '70

Scenes from Götterdämmerung. S. Jenkins. Opera N 34:32 Mr 7 '70

PHILIBERT, V.

Cesium-beam atomic clock. il Electr World 83:40-1+ Je '70

PHILIP, consort of Elizabeth II, queen of Great Britain

Luck of Prince Philip; excerpts from Wildlife crisis. il por Look 34:29-33 O 20 '70

PHILIP Morris, inc. See Morris, Philip, inc.

PHILIPPINE constabulary band. See Bands (music)

PHILIPPINES

See also

Baguio

Evangelistic work—Philippines

Moros

Research—Philippines

Student demonstrations—Philippines

Tourist trade—Philippines

Description and travel

Philippines. il Travel & Camera 33:70-1+ Mr '70

Foreign relations

Philippines under Marcos. R. Butwell. bibliog f Cur Hist 58:196-201+ Ap '70

United States

See United States—Foreign relations—Philippines

History

Insurrection, 1899-1901

Our Mylai of 1900; Americans in the Philippine insurrection. S. C. Miller. il Trans-Action 7:19-28 S '70

Politics and government

Marcos besieged. il Time 95:21 F 16 '70

Philippines under Marcos. R. Butwell. bibliog f Cur Hist 58:196-201+ Ap '70

Rebirth of the revolution. R. Blackburn. il Nation 211:582-7 D 7 '70

Shark's fin. il Time 95:30+ Mr 16 '70

Storm warnings in the Philippines. C. T. Rowan. Read Digest 97:193-4+ N '70

To find itself: a young nation's mission. H. de la Costa. America 123:542-4 D 19 '70

Religious institutions and affairs

Papal visit anticipated; Philippine national council of churches statement. C. M. Ferrer. Chr Cent 87:1134 S 23 '70

World around us (cont) Chr Cent 87:372-3 Mr 25 '70

See also

Catholic church in the Philippines

Christians in the Philippines

Treaties

Letter from Washington; Senate foreign relation subcommittee hearings. R. H. Rovere. New Yorker 45:63-5 Ja 17 '70

PHILIPS, Mack

Hard-top tent camper rides dual-use trailer. il Pop Sci 196:88-91+ Ap '70

Treasure guides for workshoppers. il Pop Sci 196:128-31+ Ja '70

PHILIPSBURG manor, North Tarrytown. See New York (state)—Historic houses, etc.

PHILIPSON, Morris

What's in it for us? excerpts from address. il por Pub W 198:38-40 Jl 27 '70

PHILLIPS, Alvah H. See Hinman, N. D. jt. auth.

PHILLIPS, Arthur, and Phillips, L.

In search of retirement. il Har Yrs 10:14-16 N '70

PHILLIPS, Bill

Jiggerpoling for lunkers. il Outdoor Life 145: 54-5+ Je '70

PHILLIPS, Christopher H.

Draft U.N. convention on the international seabed area; statement, August 3, 1970. Dept State Bul 63:210-13 Ag 24 '70

Letter from Ambassador Phillips to U.N. seabed committee chairman; May 25, 1970. Dept State Bul 62:741 Je 15 '70

United Nations force in Cyprus extended through June 1970; statement, December 11, 1969. Dept State Bul 62:71-3 Ja 19 '70

United Nations headquarters accommodation; statement, December 17, 1969. Dept State Bul 62:107-8 Ja 26 '70

U.S. explains its votes on seabed resolutions; statements, December 2 and 15, 1969. Dept State Bul 62:89-93 Ja 26 '70

PHILLIPS, David R.
Past springs out of a picture; photographs.
pors Am Heritage 21:2,16-27 Je '70
PHILLIPS, Gene D.
Homosexual revolution. America 123:406-7 N
14 '70
New York film festival: 1970. il Cath World
212:146-9 D '70
PHILLIPS, Harold Ross. See Phillips, L.
PHILLIPS, Harvey E.
(ed) See Tobin, R. Different Don
PHILLIPS, Howard
Automatic lightning protection. il Pop Electr
33:61-4 Jl '70
PHILLIPS, J. D. and Luyendyk, B. P.
Central North Atlantic plate motions over
the last 40 million years. bibliog il Science
170:727-9 N 13 '70
PHILLIPS, James
Whooping promise. il Sat R 53:59 O 3 '70
PHILLIPS, James Charles
Bonds and bands in semiconductors. bibliog
il Science 169:1035-42; 170:1432 S 11, D 25
'70
Chemical bond and solid-state physics; adap-
tation of address, March 1969. bibliog il
por Phys Today 23:23-30 F '70
PHILLIPS, James G.
Lockheed scandal. New Repub 163:19-23 Ag
1 '70
PHILLIPS, James Gilbert
Hot tips for cold days. V. Kraft. il por
Sports Illus 32:48-9 Ja 26 '70
PHILLIPS, James W.
Geoduck hunting. il Sea Front 16:246-50 Jl '70
PHILLIPS, John
How it goes in Rhodesia. Nat R 22:894-5 Ag
25 '70
PHILLIPS, John L.
(ed) See Connelly, M. Before the colors
fade: green pastures recalled
PHILLIPS, Kevin P.
Is constitutional democracy doomed? W. D.
Phelan, jr. Cur 116:40-6 Mr '70 *
Making of a majority; excerpts from Now is
the time. F. R. Harris. Harper 240:49-52
My '70 *
Marx goes statistical. Nat R 22:719-20 Jl 14
'70 *
Nixon's southern strategy; it's all in the
charts. J. Boyd. il pors N Y Times Mag
p25+ My 17 '70 *
PHILLIPS, Lefty
Lefty makes the Angels sing. R. Blount, jr.
por Sports Illus 32:28-9 Je 8 '70 *
PHILLIPS, Louise. See Phillips, A. jt. auth.
PHILLIPS, Mary Walker
Macrame. il Design 72:34-7 Wint '70
PHILLIPS, P. A. and others
Hydrocephalus in mice inoculated neonatally
by the oronasal route with reovirus type 1.
bibliog il Science 168:858-9 My 15 '70
PHILLIPS, Paul E. and Christian, C. L.
Myxovirus antibody increases in human con-
nective tissue disease. bibliog il Science
168:982-4 My 22 '70
PHILLIPS, S. Michael. See Zweiman, B. jt.
auth.
PHILLIPS, William. See Howard, A. W. jt.
auth.
PHILLIPS memorial gallery, Washington, D.C.
Paintings from the Phillips collection. il Atlan
226:61-8 D '70
PHILLIPS petroleum company
Beneath the beautiful sea; oil in the North
Sea. il Newsweek 75:81 Je 15 '70
Find in a treacherous sea: oil in the North
Sea. Time 95:94 Je 15 '70
My time is running out. il Forbes 106:26 Jl
1 '70
Stormy debate over North Sea oil. il Bsns W
p35 N 14 '70
Theft of a nation: apologies to the Chero-
kees. P. Collier. il por Ramp Mag 9:35-45 S
'70
PHILOSOPHERS
Philosophers as critical thinking consultants.
E. D'Angelo. Sch & Soc 98:166 Mr '70
See also
Buber, M.
Lonergan, B. J. F.
Royce, J.
PHILOSOPHY
Must we mean what we say? by S. Cavell.
Review
Commonweal 93:131-3 O 30 '70. W. Ar-
nold
See also
Atheism
Atomism
Chance
Christianity
Civilization
Gnosticism

Humanism
Liberty
Materialism
Music—Philosophy and aesthetics
Mysticism
Nihilism (philosophy)
Reality
Thought and thinking
Universe
also subhead Philosophy under various
subjects, e.g. Education—Philosophy
PHILOSOPHY, African
Antibiotic Christ. E. G. Dalbey, jr. Chr Cent
87:695-8 Je 3 '70
PHILOSOPHY, American
Religion and American experience.   R. J.
Roth. il America 124:43-4 Ja 16 '71
PHILOSOPHY, English
See also
Russell, B. R.
PHILOSOPHY, French
Michel Foucault. R. McMullen. por Horizon
11:36-9 Aut '69
See also
Simon, Y.
PHILOSOPHY, German
Notes on the germanization of American
youth. J. L. Sammons. Yale R 59:342-56 Mr
'70; Same abr. with title American youth
and the Germans. Cur 119:10-14 Je '70
See also
Hegel, G. W. F.
Pannenberg, W.
PHILOSOPHY, Hebrew. See Philosophy, Jew-
ish
PHILOSOPHY, Jewish
Birth control and Jewish law, by D. M. Feld-
man. Review
Chr Cent 87:632-3 My 20 '70. J. M. Gustaf-
son
Jewish philosophy in modern times, by N.
Rotenstreich. Review
Commentary 49:100-4 My '70. M. Fox
Notes from a Jewish diary. N. Perlmutter. il
Nat R 22:670-4 Je 30 '70
People Israel lives. E. L. Fackenheim. bib-
liog f por Chr Cent 87:563-8 My 6 '70; Reply.
R. L. Rubenstein. 87:921-3 Jl 29 '70

Anecdotes, facetiae, satire, etc.
Hassidic tales, with a guide to their inter-
pretation by the noted scholar. W. Allen.
New Yorker 46:31-2 Je 20 '70
PHILOSOPHY and religion
Hegelian dialectic in theology. J. N. Jonsson.
Chr Today 14:3-5 Ag 21; 14-16+ S 11 '70
See also
Existentialism
PHILOSOPHY of education. See Education—
Philosophy
PHILPOTTS, John A. and Schnetzler, C. C.
Potassium rubidium, strontium, barium, and
rare-earth concentrations in lunar rocks
and separated phases. bibliog il Science
167:493-5 Ja 30 '70
PHINIZY, Coles
Buddy is everybody's buddy. il pors Sports
Illus 33:30-2+ D 7 '70
Dredging money from the Bank. il Sports Illus
33:22-5 Jl 6 '70
(ed) See Counsilman, J. E. As easy as taking
a stroll
PHLOX
Dependable perennial for color. M. M. Leister
il Home Gard 57:12-13+ Ag '70
See also
Moss pink
PHNOM, Penh. See Pnompenh, Cambodia
PHNOMPENH. See Pnompenh, Cambodia
PHOBIAS
Flying fraidycats fight fear in the sky. K. V.
Brown. il Todays Health 48:24-6+ Je '70
See also
School phobia
PHOBOS. See Satellites
PHOENIX, Ariz.

Galleries and museums
At the Indian fair in Phoenix; Heard museum of anthropology and primitive art.
il Sunset 144:74-9 Mr '70

Religious institutions and affairs
Nun to head corporate ministry in Phoenix.
M. H. Walling. Chr Cent 87:902 Jl 22 '70
PHOENIX (guided missile) See Guided missiles
—Launching from airplanes
PHOENIX house programs. See Narcotic ad-
dicts—Rehabilitation
PHOENIX Suns (basketball team) See Basket-
ball teams
PHONIC method.   See Reading—Study and
teaching

PHONO viewers.   See Phonograph—Projector
  combination
PHONOGRAPH
Sound ideas. L. Zide. See issues of American
  record guide

Pickup

EW lab tested. Shure V-15 type II (improved)
  cartridge. il Electr World 83:8+ My '70
New phono pickup. F. Shunaman. il Radio-
  Electr 41:4+ Mr '70
What should you pay for a phono cartridge?
  with lab tests of the complete line of Shure
  cartridges. il Electr World 84:13-16+ N '70
  See also
Phonograph—Stereophonic pickup

Projector combination

Show 'n tell; phono viewers. il Consumer
  Bul 54:29-30 Ja '71

Record changers

Challenge of the changers; automatic turn-
  tables. R. Long. il Hi Fi 20:secI 54-6+ Ap
  '70
EW lab tests new automatic turntables. J.
  D. Hirsch. il Electr World 83:23-7+ Je '70
Hi-fi product report; Dual 1219 automatic
  turntable. il Electr World 83:68-9 F '70
Try the new generation of automatic turn-
  tables. R. S. Lanier. il Pop Sci 197:78-9+
  N '70
Turntables with arms. il Consumer Rep 35:
  681-7 N '70

Stereophonic pickup

Hi-fi product report; B&O SP-12 phono
  cartridge. il Electr World 85:14+ Ja '71
How to pick a phono pickup. H. Fantel. il
  Pop Mech 133:144-7+ Mr '70

Turntables

How important is a level turntable? D.
  Graveraux. il Hi Fi 20:secI 57 Ap '70
  See also
Phonograph—Record changers
PHONOGRAPH, Portable
Portable phonographs. il Consumer Bul 53:7-
  10 Ja '70
PHONOGRAPH cartridges. See Phonograph—
  Pickup
PHONOGRAPH needles
Stylus timer saves your records; elapsed-
  time meter. T. R. Sear. il Pop Sci 197:81+
  N '70
PHONOGRAPH record industry
Classical-record crisis. il Newsweek 76:78-9
  Ag 10 '70; Reply. S. M. Clarke. New Repub
  163:28-9 S 26 '70
Dope(s) G. Lees. il Hi Fi 20:134 O '70
Made in America, courtesy of Europe. R. C.
  Marsh; A. Segal; M. Steinberg. il Hi Fi 20:
  secI 14-16 Jl '70
Modest proposal. G. Lees. Hi Fi 20:secI 116
  Je '70
  See also
Capitol records, inc.
Columbia records, inc.
Phonograph records—Recording
Pickwick international, inc.

Finance

Music; decline of classical music. H. C. Schonberg. Harper 241:132+ O '70; Reply A
  Venitt. 241:19 D '70
New means for new music; Ford foundation
  aid project. R. Jacobson. il Sat R 53:65-
  6+ Ja 31 '70

Canada

Canadian Rococo. P. G. Davis. il Hi Fi 20:131-
  2 O '70

Germany (Federal Republic)

Historical treasures from Heliodor. D. Hamilton. il Hi Fi 20:secI 96-7 Jl '70

Poland

New additions to the Polish repertory; con-
  cert performances on records within forty-
  eight hours after each concert. K. Blaukopf.
  Hi Fi Sec I 20:22+ Ja '70
PHONOGRAPH record shops
World's most complete record store? New
  York's King Karol. P. G. Davis. il Hi Fi 20:
  62-3 S '70
PHONOGRAPH records
Beethoven by the numbers. R. Freed. Sat R
  53:67-8 N 28 '70
Best buys in Beethoven records. il Chang-
  ing T 24:37-8 D '70
Burst of Berlioz. R. Lawrence. il Sat R 53:
  66+ Ap 25 '70

Classical-record crisis. il Newsweek 76:78-9
  Ag 10 '70; Reply. D. M. Clarke. New Repub
  163:28-9 S 26 '70
Concert records (cont) A. Hiss. New York-
  er 45:80-5 F 7 '70
Convenient omnibus; collections of great
  composers. Time 95:62+ Mr 30 '70
Discussions. R. Hemming; D. Finkle; B.
  Scoppa. See issues of Senior scholastic
Favorite pioneer recording artists. J. Walsh.
  See issues of Hobbies
Four records, the sophisticated writing of
  Rodion Shchedrin. D. W. Moore. il por Am
  Rec G 36:410-12 F '70
Fruits of industry, or What AR hath
  wrought. O. Daniel. Sat R 53:47-8 D 26 '70
Gallery of great performances; learning music
  by listening to records. E. Istomin. il Hi Fi
  20:secI 32+ Ap '70
Guide to low-priced classical records, by H.
  Russcol. Review
  Am Rec G 36:706-7 My '70. M. Kanny
His country's most experienced hermit choos-
  es a desert-island discography. G. Gould.
  por Hi Fi 20:secI 29+ Je '70
Historical records. A. Favia-Artsay. See is-
  sues of Hobbies
Historical treasures from Heliodor. D. Hamilton. il Hi Fi 20:secI 96-7 Jl '70
In brief. See issues of High fidelity section I
Lighter side. M. Ames and others. See is-
  sues of High fidelity section I
Lively arts; special albums for Beethoven's
  200th anniversary. R. Hemming. il Sr Schol
  97:22-3 D 7 '70
Mid-month recordings (cont) il Sat R 53:52-
  3+ Ja 17; 62-3 F 14; 98-9 Mr 14; 64-5+ My
  16; 80-1 S 12 '70
Music. D. Hamilton. Nation 210:125-6 F 2 '70
Music from a waffle iron; how a phonograph
  record is pressed. H. Fantel. il Opera N
  34:17-19 Je 13 '70
Music in the round. Discus. See issues of
  Harper's magazine
New basic record collection. Consumer Rep
  34:210-21 D '69
New records in review. B. H. Haggin. See
  issues of Yale review
On the record: Music. See issues of Library
  journal beginning June 15, 1970
On the record: Music. P. L. Miller. See is-
  sues of Library journal to June 1, 1970
Other reviews. See issues of American record
  guide
Other side. T. Heinitz. See issues of Saturday
  review
Phonograph records. W. F. Grueninger. See
  issues of Consumer bulletin
Record reviews. See issues of Consumer re-
  ports
Recordings. M. Mayer. See issues of Esquire
Recordings from CRI, Odyssey, Westminster,
  and Desto: the music of Ned Rorem. P. L.
  Miller. por(p249) Am Rec G 36:252-4 D '69
Recordings in review. I. Kolodin. See issues
  of Saturday review
Recordings of Copland's music. D. Hamilton.
  Hi Fi 20:64-6+ N '70
Recordings reports: miscellaneous: LPs. I.
  Kolodin. See issues of Saturday review
Records:
  Bach, Handel arias; C. P. E. Bach:
    Magnificat; Handel: Two italian can-
    tatas. Opera N 34:34 F 14 '70
  Mahler: Des knaben wunderhorn; Rückert
    songs; Symphony no. 5; and Symphony
    no. 2 (Resurrection) Opera N 34:30 My
    16 '70
Records (cont) D. Hamilton. Nation 210:61-2,
  381-2, 542, 635-6, 797-8; 211:412-13, 602-3
  Ja 19, Mr 30, My 4, 25, Je 29, O 26, D 7 '70
Records for a critic's holiday. R. C. Marsh.
  por Hi Fi 20:secI 26+ Mr '70
Records (title varies) (cont) W. F. Ricken-
  backer. Nat R 22:579-80, 690-1 Je 2, 30 '70
Reviews of records. See issues of Musical
  quarterly
Seraphim's music course, a review from the
  campus. J. A. Movshon. Hi Fi 20:106 N '70
Sight & sound. See issues of McCall's
Sir Thomas Beecham; concluding a nine-
  part discography. W. Botsford. por Am Rec
  G 36:258-65+ D '69
Sound world of Chou Wen-chung. A. Frank-
  enstein. Hi Fi 20:secI 84 Jl '70
Speaking of records. See issues of High fide-
  lity and Musical America
Spoleto sampler, minus Schippers. R. Jacob-
  son. il Sat R 53:44 Ag 29 '70
Spotlight! E. Miller. See issues of Seventeen
Stunning clarity: Pierre Boulez proves his
  point; conducting Bartók: Music for strings,
  Percussion, and Celesta, and Stravinsky:
  Firebird suite. M. N. Kanny. Am Rec G
  36:416+ F '70

PHONOGRAPH records—*Continued*
Very special: the music of Chou Wenchung.
A. Cohn. por Am Rec G 36:886 Jl '70
Year's best LPs. Time 97:56 Ja 4 '71
Year's best recordings; comp. by R. Freed.
Sat R 53:78+ N 28 '70
See also
Columbia records, inc.

Arias

Callas and Tebaldi, yesterday and today. G.
Movshon. il pors Hi Fi sec I 20:89-90 Ja '70
Duet of the century: Flagstad and Melchior.
W. Zakariasen. il pors Hi Fi 20:secI 52-6 Jl
'70
Feast for francophiles; with Joan Suther-
land. P. L. Miller. Am Rec G 37:182 N '70
Fresh appeal of Bidú Sayão. G. Movshon. por
Hi Fi 20:secI 107 Je '70
Giuseppe De Luca, A. Favia-Artsay. por Hob-
bies 75:35-6 N '70
Great voices of old, a program for the neo-
phyte vocal collector. P. L. Miller. il Am
Rec G 36:341-2 Ja '70
Latin festival on L.P. A. Favia-Artsay. pors
Hobbies 75:35-6+ S '70
Nilsson: Venus and Elisabeth; roles in Tann-
häuser. G. L. Mayer. Am Rec G 36:522-3
Mr '70
Phenomenon that was Kirsten Flagstad. A.
Sperber. Am Rec G 36:440 F '70
Ponselle miracle. D. Hamilton. por Hi Fi 20:
81-2 S '70
Recording Pacinis; G. Farrar and A. Gran-
forte. A. Favia-Artsay. il Hobbies 75:35-6+
Jl '70
Records:
    Alexander Kipnis. Opera N 34:35 Mr 21
        '70
    Birgit Nilsson. Opera N 34:35 F 7 '70
    Cristina Deutekom. Opera N 35:38 N 21
        '70
    Dietrich Fischer-Dieskau. Opera N 34:
        35 Mr 14 '70
    Eleanor Steber; Bidú Sayao and Lily
        Pons. Opera N 34:30 Je 13 '70
    Elisabeth Schwarzkopf. Opera N 34:35 F
        7 '70
    Ezio Pinza. Opera N 34:34 Ja 31 '70
    Franco Corelli. Opera N 34:35 F 7 '70
    Fritz Wunderlich. Opera N 34:35 F 7 '70
    Lauritz Melchior and Joseph Schmidt.
        Opera N 35:30 S 19 '70
    Leontyne Price, Volume 3. Opera N 35:34
        D 5 '70
    Marcella Reale. Opera N 35:35 Ja 9 '71
    Maria Callas. Opera N 34:35 F 7 '70
    Montserrat Caballé and Shirley Verrett
        duets. Opera N 35:30 S 5 '70
    Nicolai Gedda. Opera N 34:34 F 14 '70
    Renata Tebaldi. Opera N 34:35 F 7 '70
    Richard Crooks; John McCormack. Op-
        era N 34:4-5 Mr 28 '70
    Rosa Ponselle; Gladys Swarthout, and
        Maria Cebotari. Opera N 35:35 O 31 '70
    Sylvia Geszty and Bozena Ruk-Focic.
        Opera N 34:35 Ap 4 '70
    Tribute to Gerald Moore. Opera N 34:
        35 Mr 28 '70
Top tenors, on L.P. A. Favia-Artsay. pors
Hobbies 75:35-6+ Je '70
Two sopranos: a discovery and an old friend.
G. Movshon. pors Hi Fi 20:secI 79 Je '70
Vocal bonanza on Canadian LP. A. Favia-
Artsay. il Hobbies 75:35-6 D '70

Ballet music

Anniversary of a dream: Mehta's first, Bou-
lez' second recording of The rite of spring.
D. Hamilton. il Hi Fi 20:secI 73-4 My '70
Giselle, all of it for the first time on records.
C. J. Luten. por Am Rec G 36:868-9 Jl '70
Musically, in the same vein; Burgmüller's La
Péri. G. L. Mayer. Am Rec G 36:869 Jl '70
Must for balletomanes, especially; Swan lake.
G. L. Mayer. Am Rec G 36:906-7 Jl '70
Recharting the muddled waters of Swan
lake. R. D. Darrell. il Hi Fi 20:secI 79-81
Ap '70

Band music

Rather odd, to say the least: Sousa sans
Sousa! A. F. R. Lawrence. Am Rec G
36:557 Ap '70
Sweet and swinging. F. Reynolds. See oc-
casional issues of American record guide to
August 1970

Blues (songs, etc)

Big Bill reconsidered; recordings of B.
Broonzy. P. Welding. il por Sat R 53:62-3
F 14 '70
Empress still reigns; B. Smith. S. Dance. por
Sat R 53:41+ Ag 29 '70

First lady of the blues: B. Smith. M. Ames.
por Hi Fi 20:86-7 O '70
Miss Bessie's blues. por Time 96:40 Ag 3 '70
Resurgence of country blues. M. Cuscuna. il
Sat R 53:67 My 16 '70

Cantatas

Johann Sebastian Bach. P. L. Miller. il Am
Rec G 36:554-6 Ap '70
Records:
    Magnificat; cantata no. 10. Opera N 34:
        35 Mr 21 '70
    Mahler: Das klagende lied. Opera N 35:
        34-5 Ja 9 '71
    Netania Davrath, Max van Egmond. Opera
        N 34:35 Ap 18 '70
    Orff's Carmina burana. Opera N 35:34 D
        5 '70
    Rinaldo, Schicksalslied. Opera N 34:35 F
        28 '70

Care

Sound is only skin-deep. H. Friedman. il Pop
Phot 67:64+ N '70

Catalogs

Monumental catalog of Edison cylinders. J.
Walsh. il Hobbies 74:38-40+ Ja '70
Twenty years of Schwann. I. Kolodin. il por
Am Rec G 36:540-2 Ap '70

Cello music

Feuermann mementos. H. Goldsmith. Hi Fi
20:secI 112 Ap '70
Incomparable art of Emanuel Feuermann.
D. W. Moore. Am Rec G 37:12-13 S '70

Chamber music

Beethoven on records. R. C. Marsh. il Hi
Fi 20:secI 60-8 My '70
Chamber music from Marlboro. D. Hamilton.
Hi Fi 20:secI 102 Mr '70
First recordings of works by Leon Kirchner
and Henry Weinberg, a celebration of
newness. A. Cohn. il Am Rec G 36:552-3
Ap '70

Childrens records

On and off the avenue (cont) New Yorker
46:151-3 D 12 '70
Recommended recordings. N. Langstaff. Horn
Bk 46:325, 508, 648 Je. O-D '70
Recordings. J. L. Limbacher. See second is-
sue of each month of Library journal

Choral music

Beethoven on records. H. C. R. Landon. Hi Fi
sec I 20:70-2+ F '70
Berkshire boy choir. P. L. Miller. il Am Rec
G 36:486 Mr '70
New Ivesian discoveries. A. Frankenstein.
Hi Fi 20:secI 92 Mr '70
Records:
    Berlioz: Te deum. Opera N 34:30 Je 13
        13 '70
    Handel: Acis and Galatea. il Opera N
        35:42 D 19 '70

Christmas music

Choice caroling. L. Nuechterlein. Chr Cent
87:1488-9 D 9 '70

Church music

Records:
    Petite messe solennelle. Opera N 34:35
        Mr 14 '70

Collectors and collecting

Basso, the mighty. A. Favia-Artsay. il Hob-
bies 75:35-6 Ag '70
Collectors' releases. A. Favia-Artsay. il Hob-
bies 75:35-6 My '70
Where do you start? symposium, ed. by R.
Hemming (cont) il Sr Schol 95:18 N 10 '69

Concertos

Above all others at any price: Beethoven's
Violin concerto with Yehudi Menuhin. M.
N. Kanny. Am Rec G 36:648 My '70
Assimilating the artistic past, Ignaz Mos-
cheles. D. Dubal. por Am Rec G 37:90-1
O '70
Beethoven on records. H. Goldsmith. il Hi
Fi 20:secI 51-6+ Ag; 66-8 S '70
First recordings by Nelson Freire, exception-
ally exciting; piano concertos by Tchaikov-
sky, Grieg and Schumann. M. N. Kanny.
Am Rec G 36:406 F '70
First recordings: Sessions and Lees. A. Cohn.
Am Rec G 36:298+ D '69
Forgotten romantics remembered. H. C.
Schonberg. il Hi Fi sec I 20:87-9 Ja '70
In the grand manner: Lewenthal's Rubin-
stein (Anton) and Scharwenka. W. Bots-
ford. por Am Rec G 36:690-1 My '70

PHONOGRAPH records—Concertos—*Continued*
Incomparable Landowska; Haydn harpsichord and Mozart Piano Concertos. R. Kennedy. Am Rec G 36:342 Ja '70
Intelligent trash of Jolivet and Milhaud. J. Ringo. Am Rec G 37:166-7+ N '70
Landowska as harpsichordist and pianist. D. Hamilton. Hi Fi 20:secI 80 Je '70
Little Vivaldi festival. S. Fleming. Hi Fi 20:104 S '70
More impressive than most: the disc debut of Pinchas Zukerman. M. N. Kanny. Am Rec G 36:436 F '70
Music in the round; Ignaz Moscheles, G minor piano concerto. Discus. Harper 240:117-18 Ap '70
Must a great violinist play in tune? R. C. Marsh; H. Goldsmith. Hi Fi sec I 20:91 Ja '70
One to own Graffman's Tchaikovsky: piano concerto No. 1. M. N. Kanny. il Am Rec G 36:588 Ap '70
Raymond Lewenthal and Anton Rubinstein: two irresistible Victorians. R. C. Marsh. Hi Fi 20:secI 90 Jl '70
Record to wake up to; Johann Christian Bach and Johann Ludwig Krebs. E. L. Johnson. Am Rec G 37:172 N '70
Russian Angels in America; Oistrakh and Rostropovich meet Szell and the Clevelanders. S. Fleming. il Hi Fi 20:secI 71-2 My '70
Schnabel: coherence, conviction; Piano concerto no. 4. Am Rec G 37:20+ S '70
Six concertos. R. Kammerer. il Am Rec G 36:336-8 Ja '70
Solid gold in Cleveland. M. Kanny. il Am Rec G 36:884-5 Jl '70
Two Beethoven pupils: Karl Czerny and Ferdinand Ries. W. Botsford. il Am Rec G 37:88-90 O '70
Viable, vibrantly alive, Scharwenka and Henselt. R. Kammerer. il Am Rec G 37:84-6 O '70
Virtuosic crackerjack: Corigliano's piano concerto. A. Cohn. il por Am Rec G 36:656-7 My '70

Czech music
Czech music from Kempe; what a joy! G. S. Fox. Am Rec G 36:301 D '69

Dance music
Records for teachers. E. Le Mone. See issues of Dance magazine
Sweet and swinging. F. Reynolds. See occasional issues of American record guide to August 1970
See also
Phonograph records—Ballet music

Documentary records
Sound of the sixties: I can hear it now, by W. Cronkite and F. W. Friendly. R. L. Tobin. Sat R 53:41+ D 26 '70

Easter music
For Lent and Eastertide. L. Nuechterlein. Chr Cent 87:330+ Mr 18 '70

Electronic music
Caper by Mauricio Kagel. O. Daniel. il Sat R 53:68 Ja 31 '70
Earth people's pop; In a wild sanctuary. E. Sander. pors Sat R 53:37 Ag 29 '70
First recordings of works by Leon Kirchner and Henry Weinberg, a celebration of newness. A. Cohn. il Am Rec G 36:552-3 Ap '70
Son of Switched-on Bach; or, What went wrong in the delivery room; letter to Glenn Gould. L. Marcus. il Hi Fi sec I 20:78-9 F '70

Folk music
Folk music. H. Yurchenco and others. See issues of American record guide
Higher country; Hedge and Donna Capers' music. R. D. Campbell. Chr Cent 87:1355-6 N 11 '70
Percy Grainger posy; London records tribute. R. D. Darrell. por Hi Fi 20:secI 86 Ag '70

Harpsichord music
Grandeur of Couperin. P. H. Lang. Hi Fi 20:secI 86 Mr '70
See also
Phonograph records—Concertos

History
Records. D. Hamilton. Nation 210:381-2 Mr 30 '70

Humorous records
Funniest put-on: Jonathan and Darlene Edwards in Paris. G. Lees. pors Hi Fi 20:120 N '70

Incidental music
Slightly more than ever before; excerpts from the Peer Gynt music. J. Diether. il Am Rec 36:668+ My '70

Instrumental music
See also
Phonograph records—Chamber music

Jazz music
Bill Evans alone. B. Korall. il por Sat R 53:46-7 Jl 25 '70
For the silent majority. N. McCaffrey. Nat R 22:1414-16 D 29 '70
Jazz. J. S. Wilson. Hi Fi 20:secI 132-3 Ap '70
Liberation music orchestra. P. Elwood. il Ramp Mag 8:54-5 Je '70
Recordings reports: jazz LPs. S. Dance. See issues of Saturday review
Records: rock, etc. R. Newman. E. Willis. New Yorker 46:155+ Ap 18 '70
Swing era. A. Goldman. il Life 69:10 Ag 7 '70

Madrigals
Records:
Gesualdo: madrigals. Opera N 35:35 D 12 '70

Mass
Carrillo from CRI, an important release on several counts. P. L. Miller. Am Rec G 36:274 D '69
Sardinian hipsters sound off; Mass for peace. T. M. Moore. Chr Cent 87:608-9 My 13 '70; Reply with rejoinder. M. Slusser. 87:768 Je 17 '70
See also
Phonograph records—Requiems

Music, Popular (songs, etc)
Bath time for Ernie; success of Rubber duckie. Time 96:58 S 14 '70
Bob Dylan and the poetry of salvation. S. Goldberg. il pors Sat R 53:43-6+ My 30 '70
Country soul from Hollywood to prison. J. Gabree. Hi Fi 20:138 O '70
Dylan, P. Nelson. por Sr Schol 97:22-3+ D 14 '70
McCartney on his own. E. Sander. il por Sat R 53:53-4 My 30 '70
Pop minstrelsy: madrigal blues. E. Sander. Sat R 53:47 Je 27 '70
Popular records (cont) D. Watt. New Yorker 46:74-6 Jl 11; 163-4+ O 24 '70
Rock, etc. B. Dylan revisited. E. Willis. New Yorker 46:181-2+ D 12 '70
Simon and Garfunkel, nothing gauche; Bridge over troubled water. R. Goldstein. Vogue 155:110 Ap 1 '70

Musical comedies, revues, etc.
Is Broadway singing it like it is? S. Green. Sat R 53:36+ Ag 29 '70
Lerner and Duke revisited; selections from old shows. I. Kolodin. Sat R 53:101 Mr 14 '70
Lerner-Loewe (and Previn's) Paint your wagon. I. Kolodin. Sat R 53:53 Ja 17 '70
Musical musical: Stephen Sondheim's Company. G. Lees. il Hi Fi 20:secI 68-9 Ag '70
Popular records: Company. D. Watt. New Yorker 46:74-5 Jl 11 '70

Musical parody
Siegfried waltz? W. Zakariasen. il Hi Fi 20:secI 66-70 Mr '70

Negro music
Sounds. P. Garland. Ebony 25:24 Jl; 28 Ag; 26 S; 26:28 D '70

Negro songs
Magnificent voice, Eugene Holmes. P. L. Miller. Am Rec G 36:487 Mr '70

Operas
At last, Les Huguenots and Meyerbeer. H. Weinstock. Sat R 53:75 N 28 '70
Beethoven on records. G. Movshon. il Hi Fi sec I 20:81-5+ Ja '70
Berlioz' Les Troyens, conquered at last. D. Hamilton. il Hi Fi 20:secI 65-7 Ag '70
Berlioz's Les Troyens, Busoni's Doktor Faust, and Hindemith's Cardillac. I. Kolodin; R. Jacobson. il pors Sat R 53:43-5 Jl 25 '70
Best of Baker: Berlioz: les Troyens. D. Hamilton. Hi Fi 20:secI 86 Je '70
Bonynge's Don Giovanni. G. L. Mayer. Sat R 53:67+ Ap 25 '70
Busoni's Doktor Faust. P. L. Miller. il Am Rec G 36:864-5+ Jl '70
Caballé sings Salome. G. L. Mayer. il Am Rec G 36:402-4 F '70
Don Giovanni done in; Bonynge's mannered, comic-opera approach. P. H. Lang. il Hi Fi 20:secI 72-3 My '70

PHONOGRAPH records—Operas—*Continued*

Donizetti, Sills, and Devereux. R. Lawrence. Sat R 53:83 F 28 '70

Exploring Idomeneo; Colin Davis' recording. P. H. Lang. il Hi Fi 20:sec1 75-7 Mr '70

Fedora; new recording with M. Olivero. G. L. Mayer. pors Am Rec G 37:76-9 O '70

Finer Forza, optional Requiems. H. Weinstock. Sat R 53:50 O 31 '70

First of Paul Hindemith's full-length operas; Cardillac. P. L. Miller. Am Rec G 36:549 Ap '70

La forza del destino. A. Sperber. il Am Rec G 36:948-9+ Ag '70

From George Szell, simply stunning Wagner; excerpts from the Ring. M. N. Kanny. Am Rec G 36:593 Ap '70

From the Arturo Toscanini society; memorable Strauss, and Brahms German requiem in English. C. J. Luten. il Am Rec G 36:330-1 Ja '70

Gold of Troy: Berlioz's Les Troyens and Busoni's Doktor Faust. R. T. Jones. il Time 96:58-9 Ag 31 '70

Götterdämmerung; H. von Karajan conducting. C. J. Luten. il Am Rec G 37:4-6+ S '70

Historical records. A. Favia-Artsay. pors Hobbies 74:35-7+ F '70

Irreplaceable artifacts from musical ages past; Der Rosenkavalier. W. Botsford. Am Rec G 36:339-40 Ja '70

Jenufa ten years later. H. Weinstock. por Sat R 53:65 Mr 28 '70

Karajan closes the Ring: DGG's Götterdämmerung. C. L. Osborne. il Hi Fi 20:77-9 S '70

Karajan closes the Ring: recording of Götterdämmerung. G. Movshon. il Hi Fi 20:sec11 28-30 Je '70

Karajan completes the Ring. P. Moor. il por Sat R 53:63-5 Ap 25 '70

Kodály's Háry János, it has stuff to be a popular success. P. L. Miller. Am Rec G 36:362 Ja '70

Maria Barrientos. A. Favia-Artsay. por Hobbies 75:36+ Mr '70

Martha. W. Botsford. il Am Rec G 36:872-4 Jl '70

Martha with merits. R. Jacobson. Sat R 53:51 My 30 '70

Martinelli on Edison. A. Favia-Artsay. por Hobbies 75:35 Mr '70

Massenet's Manon, and Puccini's same heroine in two perspectives. R. L. Miller. por Am Rec G 36:326-7 Ja '70

Monteverdi's magnificent musical drama; Orfeo. S. T. Sommer. Hi Fi sec I 20:102+ Ja '70

Naked Carmen laid bare. C. L. Osborne. Hi Fi 20:120 S '70

New Troyens, in print and in sound. T. Heinitz. Sat R 53:76 Ap 25 '70

Nilsson-Nilsson Tannhäuser. R. Lawrence. Sat R 53:47 My 30 '70

Not to be missed: new Berlioz and Busoni; The Trojans and Doctor Faust. Discus. Harper 241:135-6 N '70

O.A.S.I. releases. A. Favia-Artsay. il Hobbies 74:35-7 Ja '70

Opera we won't hear at the Met; Der freischütz. Discus. Harper 240:117-18 Ap '70

Pelléas by Debussy, Maeterlinck, and Boulez. R. Jacobson. Sat R 53:45 D 26 '70

Pop testament: rock opera, Jesus Christ superstar. H. Saal. il por Newsweek 76:96-7 N 16 '70

Postscript: a souvenir of Janet Baker's Dido at Covent Garden. P. L. Miller. Am Rec G 36:941 Ag '70

Prophetic Doktor Faust, Busoni's opera. D. Hamilton. il Hi Fi 20:sec1 69-70 Jl '70

Real Carmen; Angel's recording. P. G. Davis. Hi Fi 20:83-4 N '70

Records:
Abduction from the seraglio. Opera N 34:35 Mr 14 '70

Beethoven: Fidelio. Opera N 34:35 Ap 4 '70

Bellini: Norma; Puccini: Manon Lescaut; Handel: Solomon. Opera N 34:35 F 14 '70

Berlioz: Damnation of Faust; Trojans and Death of Cleopatra. Opera N 35:34 Ja 9 '71

Berlioz: Les Troyens. Opera N 35:30 S 19 '70

Ferruccio Busoni's Doktor Faust. Opera N 35:34 O 31 '70

Flotow: Martha. Opera N 35:30 S 5 '70

Francesca da Rimini. Opera N 34:35 F 28 '70

Der freischütz. Opera N 34:35 Mr 7 '70

Giordano: Fedora. Opera N 34:30 Je 13 '70

Idomeneo. Opera N 34:35 Mr 21 '70

Janacek: Jenufa. Opera N 34:35 Ap 18 '70

Lucio Silla. Opera N 34:34 Ja 31 '70

Meyerbeer: Les Huguenots. il Opera N 35:35 Ja 2 '71

Mozart: Ascanio in Alba. Opera N 35:34 Ja 9 '71

Mozart: Don Giovanni. Opera N 34:32 Ap 11 '70

Paul Hindemith's Cardillac. Opera N 34:34 Mr 28 '70

Renata Tebaldi. Opera N 34:35 F 7 '70

Der Rosenkavalier. Opera N 34:34 F 14 '70

Rosenkavalier (abridged) Opera N 34:36 Ja 24 '70

Strauss: Ariadne auf Naxos. Opera N 35:35 D 12 '70

Tannhäuser. il Opera N 34:34 F 21 '70

Tchaikovsky: Eugene Onegin. Opera N 35:34 D 5 '70

La Traviata (excerpts) Opera N 34:34 Ja 31 '70

Verdi: La forza del destino. Opera N 35:38 N 21 '70

Verdi: Il Trovatore. il Opera N 34:30 My 16 '70

Wagner: Götterdämmerung. Opera N 35:30 O 10 '70

Records; Wagner's Siegfried. D. Hamilton. Nation 210:61-2 Ja 19 '70

Religious rock; première at St Peter's Lutheran church of Decca album Jesus Christ, superstar. New Yorker 46:39 N 7 '70

Return of Magda Olivero; recording of Zandonai's Francesca da Rimini. P. G. Davis. Hi Fi 20:sec1 77-8 Mr '70

Roberto Devereux; with Beverly Sills. A. Sperber. il Am Rec G 36:660-3 My '70

Rock passion. W. Bender. il pors Time 96:47 N 9 '70

Der Rosenkavalier. R. Freedman. il Life 68:18 Mr 6 '70

Der Rosenkavalier; London recording. W. Botsford. il Am Rec G 36:396-401 F '70

Rostropoviches in Onegin. I. Kolodin. Sat R 53:53 S 26 '70

Superlative Rosenkavalier from London records. G. Movshon. il Hi Fi sec I 20:75-7 F '70

Superstar: haunting questions; Jesus Christ Superstar rock opera. C. A. Forbes. Chr Today 15:38-9 D 4 '70

Superstar is dead. G. Clanton. Chr Cent 88:25-6 Ja 6 '71

Tchaikovsky's musical novel; Eugene Onegin. P. G. Davis. il Hi Fi 20:87-8 O '70

Il Trovatore. A. Sperber. il Am Rec G 36:792-4+ Je '70

Les Troyens. E. Greenfield. il Am Rec G 36:936-41 Ag '70

Two (and a half) cheers for Anna Bolena. H. Weinstock. Sat R 53:39 D 26 '70

Unconventional Mozart; Bonynge's Don Giovanni. Discus. Harper 240:115-16 Je '70

Vocal gold for Trovatore. P. G. Davis. Hi Fi 20:sec1 100 Ja '70

Werther. P. L. Miller. il Am Rec G 36:324-5 Ja '70

Women's lib Carmen; The naked Carmen. il pors Time 96:28 Ag 17 '70

Oratorios

Judgment on Solomon. S. Lincoln. il Am Rec G 37:96-8+ O '70

Karajan's Creation. R. Jacobson. Sat R 53:54 Je 27 '70

Karajan's modest Creation. S. Fleming. Hi Fi 20:sec1 96 Ap '70

Particularly exciting Creation. P. L. Miller. Am Rec G 36:572 Ap '70

Records:
Haydn: The creation and Creation mass. Opera N 35:30 S 5 '70

Raft of the Medusa. Opera N 34:35 Mr 7 '70

Samson. Opera N 34:36 Ja 24 '70

Orchestral music

As nearly perfect as anything; Hebrides overture. G. S. Fox. Am Rec G 36:832 Je '70

Back again: Joseph Keilberth's lustrous documentation of the Hiller variations by Max Reger. L. Richmond. il por Am Rec G 36:332-3 Ja '70

Beethoven on records. D. Hamilton. Hi Fi 20:sec1 62-5+ Jl '70

Best Sacre on records today: Cleveland orchestra conducted by P. Boulez. W. Botsford. il Am Rec G 37:10-11+ S '70

Boulez' Debussy, lucid and illuminating. D. Hamilton. Hi Fi sec I 20:98 Ja '70

Carlos Maria Giulini, in Chicago, a splendid diversity of excellences. M. Kanny. il Am Rec G 37:80-2+ O '70

PHONOGRAPH records—Orchestral music—
  Continued
Excellent new recordings; *Le sacre du printemps*. L. Trimble. New Repub 163:28 Jl
  4 '70
Furtwängler archive; Beethoven: symphony
  no. 3 and Brahms: concerto for piano and
  orchestra. D. Hamilton. il Hi Fi 20:secI 78-9
  Mr '70
In the Venusberg, orgiastic abandon. G. S.
  Fox. Am Rec G 36:909 Jl '70
Playing and conducting that simply could
  not be bettered; Ruggles and Ives by
  Boston symphony under Michael Tilson.
  A. Cohn. por Am Rec G 37:148-51 N '70
Recordings reports; orchestral LPs. I. Kolodin.
  See issues of Saturday review
Underground Toscanini; Arturo Toscanini
  society offering members recordings. por
  Time 95:65 Mr 2 '70
Wagner: the majesty that can be achieved;
  conducted by Wilhelm Furtwängler. M.
  N. Kanny. Am Rec G 37:180-1 N '70
  See also
Phonograph records—Symphonic poems

Organ music
Introducing Anthony Newman. C. F. Gilmore.
  Hi Fi sec I 20:94 Ja '70

Passion music
Portuguese passion. H. Weinstock. Sat R 53:
  53 Jl 25 '70
Reviews of records; Schütz: the Seven last
  words. A. Mendel. il Mus Q 56:133-42 Ja '70

Piano music
Alfred Cortot, poet with a soul. W. Botsford. Am Rec G 36:340 Ja '70
Art of Schnabel. R. Kennedy. il Am Rec G
  36:344-5 Ja '70
Chopin by Ivan Moravec, perverse, and yet
  fascinating. L. Gerber. Am Rec G 36:424
  F '70
Classics for the now generation; L. Hollander's electronic piano recital at Fillmore
  East. J. Hiemenz. il Hi Fi sec I 20:112 Ja
  '70
Claudio Arrau: virtuosity of the mind and the
  spirit. R. Kennedy. Am Rec G 37:25 S '70
David Bean: mostly sensational. L. Gerber.
  Am Rec G 36:972 Ag '70
Davis, protean pianist. I. Kolodin. Sat R 53:
  71 Ja 31 '70
Extraordinary clarity, Gary Graffman's
  Paganini variations. M. N. Kanny. Am Rec
  G 36:354-5 Ja '70
Forty piano works by Louis Moreau Gottschalk. R. Kammerer. il por Am Rec G
  36:570-1 Ap '70
From the tough (for composers) twenties;
  Dane Rudhyar and Ruth Crawford Seeger.
  A. Cohn. Am Rec G 36:688+ My '70
Horowitz vs. Rubinstein; Schumann's Kreisleriana recordings. H. Goldsmith. il Hi Fi
  20:secI 67-8 Ag '70
Immortal Lipatti: records of Chopin's music.
  W. F. Rickenbacker. Nat R 22:579-80 Je 2
  '70
On DGG, an exquisite Debussy recital; performance of Tamás Vàsàry. L. Gerber. Am
  Rec G 36:826 Je '70
Outstanding release in every respect. M. N.
  Kanny. Am Rec G 36:966 Ag '70
Peter Serkin: nearly two hours of glorious
  Mozart. L. Gerber. Am Rec G 36:895+ Jl '70
Piano music of Mozart and Debussy; Angel/
  Seraphim with Walter Gieseking. H. Goldsmith. il Hi Fi 20:secI 81-3 Ap '70
Rapture for the keyboard collector; International piano library's special Limited editions club series. R. Kammerer. il Am Rec
  G 36:950-6+ Ag '70
Real thing: Satie and William Masselos. J.
  Ringo. por Am Rec G 36:692-4 My '70
Recorded legacy of Ferruccio Busoni. D.
  Hamilton. por Hi Fi sec I 20:77-8 F '70
Two metamorphosis night; J. Cage. W. F.
  Rickenbacker. Nat R 22:690-1 Je 30 '70
Voice of the poet, Walter Gieseking; Beethoven: Piano concerto no. 4. M. N. Kanny.
  Am Rec G 36:496 Mr '70
  See also
Phonograph records—Concertos
Phonograph records—Sonatas

Poetry
See Phonograph records—Spoken records

Portuguese music
Portuguese passion. H. Weinstock. Sat R 53:
  53 Jl 25 '70

Prices
Quality records at cut rates. Bsns W p
  117 F 14 '70

Program music
Musical kidney stone removal and other programmatic delights. S. Fleming. Hi Fi 20:
  122 O '70

Recording
Alessandro Scarlatti's Pretty pastoral. P.
  Moor. Hi Fi 20:secI 25 Je '70
Barbirolli's last sessions; Appalachia and
  Brigg fair by Delius. E. Greenfield. il Hi Fi
  20:18+ N '70
Beethoven treat with Zukerman and the
  Barenboims. E. Greenfield. il Hi Fi 20:secI
  24+ Ap '70
Berio's exhilarating Epifanie. E. Greenfield.
  il Hi Fi 20:18-19 S '70
Berlin diary; how Karajan recorded Götterdämmerung. J. H. Sutcliffe. il pors Opera
  N 35:8-13 N 21 '70
Berlioz' Les Troyens, complete at least. E.
  Greenfield. Hi Fi sec I 20:20+ F '70
Caballe and the pirates. F. Nuzzo. Hi Fi 20:
  21 N '70
EMI's new spoken/sung Carmen. R. McMullen. Hi Fi sec I 20:20+ Ja '70
For Beethoven's birthday, the Mass in C
  from DGG. P. G. Davis. il Hi Fi sec I 20:20
  Ja '70
For Mozart's Magic flute, international stars
  and an Austrian lion. K. Blaukopf. Hi Fi
  sec I 20:25 F '70
Henze's curious Savage. J. Buckley. Hi Fi
  20:21+ N '70
Karajan closes the Ring; recording of Götterdämmerung. G. Movshon. il Hi Fi 20:secII
  28-30 Je '70
Karajan completes the Ring cycle. P. Moor.
  Hi Fi 20: secI 22 Mr '70
Klemperer's Die Walkure project. E. Greenfield. il Hi Fi 20:secI 18+ Mr '70
Kubelik and Mahler's mighty Eighth symphony; Deutsche grammophon's recording.
  P. Moor. Hi Fi 20:25-6 O '70
Made in America, courtesy of Europe. R. C.
  Marsh; A. Segal; M. Steinberg. il Hi Fi 20:
  secI 14-16 Jl '70
Music is where the money is. E. Dunbar. il
  Look 34:13-17 Ag 25 '70
Musical comedies from Klemperer and Bonynge. E. Greenfield. il Hi Fi 20:secI 22+
  My '70
Porgy showed the way to the Ring. J. Culshaw. por Hi Fi 20:secI 20 Ag '70
Scriabin and his demons; session with H.
  Somer at Mercury's New York studio. J.
  Hiemenz. por Hi Fi 20:19-20 S '70
Shostakovich's unlucky 13th. R. S. Brown.
  Hi Fi 20:secI 26+ Ap '70
Stereo scene. J. G. Holt. il Pop Electr 34:
  68:70+ Ja '71
Taping Tippett's Midsummer marriage. E.
  Greenfield. il por Hi Fi 20:22+ O '70

Unauthorized recording
Record pirates. il Newsweek 76:70-1 O 5 '70

Reissues
Great recordings of the century from Seraphim; GROC reissues. il Am Rec G 36:336-45
  Ja '70
Historical records. A. Favia-Artsay. pors
  Hobbies 74:35-7+ F '70
Repeat performance. P. G. Davis. See issues of High fidelity section I

Requiems
Berlioz from the Tabernacle; Grande messe
  des morts. R. Lawrence. il Sat R 53:60
  Mr 28 '70
Dvorak's Requiem by Kertesz. G. L. Mayer.
  Sat R 53:59 S 26 '70
Finer Forza, optional Requiems. H. Weinstock. Sat R 53:50 O 31 '70
From the Arturo Toscanini society; memorable Strauss, and Brahms German requiem
  in English. C. J. Luten. il Am Rec G 36:
  330-1 Ja '70
Recording Verdi's Requiem; new versions by
  Bernstein and Barbirolli. D. Hamilton. il
  Hi Fi 20:79-81 N '70
Records:
  Verdi: Requiem. Opera N 35:42 D 19 '70
Requiem of consolation. P. G. Davis. Hi Fi
  20:secI 94 Ap '70

Rock 'n' roll groups
Jefferson Airplane: where we've been today.
  E. Sander. Sat R 53:76-7 Ja 31 '70
Looking past the Beatles. J. Gabree. il Hi
  Fi 20:secI 83-4 Ap '70
Massive impact; Beatle record, Abbey road.
  C. E. Fager. Chr Cent 87:54+ Ja 14 '70
Mellow harvest: The Band's latest album
  Stage fright. J. Cocks. il Time 96:58 Ag 31
  '70
Spector of the Beatles. Time 95:64 My 18 '70

PHONOGRAPH records—*Continued*

Rock 'n' roll music (songs, etc)

Bubble-gum music. A. Goldman. il por Life 68:13 Ja 30 '70

Chilling outrage; Ohio by Crosby Stills Nash & Young. C. E. Fager. Chr Cent 87:999 Ag 19 '70

Everybody's talkin' about Nilsson. B. Korall. il por Sat R 53:56 Ja 17 '70

Friends and neighbors alive, alive-O. E. Sander. il Sat R 53:71+ Ap 25 '70

In the pop bag. D. Heckman and others. See issues of American record guide

Letting George do it; G. Harrison's album, All things must pass. W. Bender. il por Time 96:57 N 30 '70

Medley; The overture to Tommy. C. E. Fager. Chr Cent 87:1566-7 D 30 '70

Music is where the money is. E. Dunbar. il Look 34:13-17 Ag 25 '70

Prime rock, a quality report from Crosby, Stills, Nash, and Young. M. Ames. il Hi Fi 20:secI 70-1 Jl '70

Records for freaks and critics alike. R. Goldstein. Vogue 155:104 Mr 1 '70

Rock, etc. E. Willis. New Yorker 46:112+ F 21 '70

Rock 1970: a level of excellence. E. Sander. il Sat R 53:37-9 D 26 '70

When the saints go walking out. A. Goldman. il Life 69:16 N 6 '70
    See also
Phonograph records—Rock 'n' roll groups

Rock operas
See Phonograph records—Operas

Sonatas

Beethoven on records: Piano sonatas. H. Goldsmith. il Hi Fi 20:63-6+ O '70

Dinu Lipatti: more to be venerated than criticized. L. Gerber. Am Rec G 36:566 Ap '70

Early Carter expertly performed. R. P. Morgan. Hi Fi sec I 20:84 F '70

Elie Siegmeister: a record of more than ordinary importance. A. Cohn. por Am Rec G 36:520-1 Mr '70

Mozart happening with Peter Serkin. H. Goldsmith. Hi Fi 20:secI 86 My '70

Perlman and Ashkenazy: a stunning team for Prokofiev. P. Hart. Hi Fi sec I 20:90 F '70

Probity and wisdom: Barenboim's Beethoven; Piano sonatas. M. N. Kanny. Am Rec G 36:350 Ja '70

Record the musical world has been waiting for: Piano sonata of Paul Dukas. L. Gerber. Am Rec G 36:827 Je '70

Stunning Schubert by Artur Rubinstein; Sonata in B flat. L. Gerber. Am Rec G 36:490-1 Mr '70

Very different impression of Elliott Carter. D. W. Moore. Am Rec G 36:498 Mr '70

Virtue and virtuosity in Bach. B. Schwarz. Sat R 53:55 O 31 '70

Songs

Again, the Berrys, together and otherwise. P. L. Miller. Am Rec G 36:547-8 Ap '70

Anna Pashley, one of the exciting events of the year. P. L. Miller. Am Rec G 37:16-17 S '70

Beardslee: old music, too; Eighteenth-century vocal recital. G. L. Mayer. Am Rec G 36:484 Mr '70

Beethoven on records. G. Movshon. il Hi Fi sec I 20:81-5+ Ja '70

Berrys (twice) with Bernstein: Des knaben wunderhorn. G. S. Fox. il por Am Rec G 36:544-6 Ap '70

Chauncey Olcott: recordings of Irish songs. J. Walsh. por Hobbies 75:37-9 Ag '70 (to be cont)

Double rich, double good Ludwig-Berry-Bernstein Mahler. R. Lawrence. il Sat R 53:69 Ja 31 '70

Five centuries of Englishry in song. P. L. Miller. Am Rec G 36:480-4 Mr '70

Getting to the heart; The art of Aksel Schiøtz. W. Botsford. por Am Rec G 36:343 Ja '70

Hugo Wolf's masterful miniatures. D. Hamilton. il Hi Fi 20:85-6 O '70

Irreplaceable artifacts from musical ages past; Strauss songs. W. Botsford. Am Rec G 36:339-40 Ja '70

Late romantic rediscovered: the unfashionable music of Karl Weigl. P. L. Miller. Am Rec G 36:376-7 Ja '70

Like a breath of fresh air: Souzay and Baldwin. A. Sperber. Am Rec G 36:434-5 F '70

Masterly singing: Hans Hotter. P. L. Miller. Am Rec G 36:344 Ja '70

On twenty-five records: forty hours of Schubert lieder. P. L. Miller. il por Am Rec G 37:142-6 N '70

Recitals (cont) P. L. Miller and others. Am Rec G 36:478-9 Mr '70

Records:
  Brahms: Deutsche volkslieder; Strauss: Songs. Opera N 34:35 N 14 '70
  Britten: Blake & Donne songs. Opera N 34:35 Ap 18 '70
  Christa Ludwig, Walter Berry; Hermann Prey; Dietrich Fischer-Dieskau and Evelyn Lear. Opera N 34:32 Ap 11 '70
  Delius: Songs of sunset, etc; Rimsky-Korsakov: Songs of Oleg the wise. Opera N 34:34 F 21 '70
  Ezio Pinza. Opera N 34:34 Ja 31 '70
  Gérard Souzay. Opera N 34:34 Ja 31 '70
  Hans Hotter. Opera N 34:35 Mr 21 '70
  Heinrich Schlusnus: songs by Mahler, Brahms, Schubert, Strauss, Wolf and Aksel Schiotz: Schubert's Die schöne müllerin. Opera N 35:35 Ja 9 '71
  Marilyn Horne. Opera N 35:30 S 19 '70
  Songs. Opera N 34:36 Ja 24 '70

Seven bygone Edison singers. J. Walsh. il Hobbies 75:37-9+ O; 37-8+ N; 37-9+ D '70

Two sopranos: a discovery and an old friend. P. G. Davis. pors Hi Fi 20:secI 79 Je '70
    See also
Phonograph records—Arias

Spoken records

Manner of speaking; Spoken arts Treasury of 100 American poets. J. Ciardi. Sat R 53:16 S 19 '70

On the record: Words. J. L. Limbacher. See issues of Library journal

Recommended recordings. N. Langstaff. Horn Bk 46:325, 508, 648 Je, O-D '70

Recordings. J. L. Limbacher. See second issue of each month of Library journal

Words only. S. Potter. See issues of American record guide
    See also
Phonograph records—Documentary records

Stereophonic records

Other reviews. See issues of American record guide

Phonograph records. W. F. Grueninger. See issues of Consumer bulletin

Records reviews. See issues of Consumer report

String octet music

For once, early Mendelssohn with all his youthful enthusiasm. D. W. Moore. Am Rec G 36:286-8 D '69

String quartet music

Bartók's extraordinary quartets. R. P. Morgan. por Hi Fi 20:58-61 S '70

Beethoven on records. R. P. Morgan. Hi Fi 20:secI 73-6+ Ap '70

Ezra Laderman's Quartet no. 2: big, bold, stimulating. A. Cohn. por Am Rec G 36:676-7 My '70

Mozart and the Amadeus. S. Fleming. Hi Fi 20:secI 98 Je '70

Swiss music

Holes in the cheese, cantos from the cantons. O. Daniel. Sat R 53:58-9 O 31 '70

Switzerland, another musical tour through the cantons. P. G. Davis. Hi Fi 20:92 S '70

Symphonic poems

Respighi in two perspectives: the Roman trilogy. G. S. Fox. Am Rec G 37:176-7 N '70

Symphonies

Bernstein's Beethoven Nine. M. N. Kanny. Am Rec G 36:964 Ag '70

Borodin Second symphony: five views. M. N. Kanny. por Am Rec G 36:420-1 F '70

Ernest Ansermet, his last recordings; conducting Honegger, Stravinsky and Magnard. R. S. Brown. por Hi Fi sec I 20:95 F '70

Excellent new recordings; Shostakovich's Thirteenth symphony. L. Trimble. New Repub 163:28-9 Jl 4 '70

First recordings: Sessions and Lees. A. Cohn. Am Rec G 36:298+ D '69

First Steinberg-BSO recording: Symphony no. 9 in C. M. N. Kanny. Am Rec G 36:981 Ag '70

Jascha Horenstein's matchless Mahler 1. J. Diether. por Am Rec G 36:796-9 Je '70

Late Beethoven and Schoenberg by Erich Leinsdorf: first-rate. M. Kanny. Am Rec G 36:488-9 Mr '70

Mahler in Utah; M. Abravanel conducting Symphony no. 3 and Symphony no. 9. R. C. Marsh. Hi Fi 20:secI 84 My '70

PHONOGRAPH records—Symphonies—*Cont.*
Mozart's symphonic miracles; Karl Böhm conducts. P. H. Lang. il Hi Fi 20:secI 71-3 Jl '70
One of the great Ninths. M. N. Kanny. Am Rec G 36:651-2 My '70
Ormandy's Mahler 1: passionate involvement. G. S. Fox. Am Rec G 36:800-2+ Je '70
Outstanding: from Decca, a pair of discs by Max Rudolf. M. N. Kanny. Am Rec G 37:32 S '70
RCA's great Philadelphia orchestra recording; Ormandy's Mahler Second. R. C. Marsh. il Hi Fi 20:80 S '70
Records:
Bells. Opera N 34:35 F 28 '70
Shostakovich: Babi Yar. Opera N 35:34-5 O 31 '70
Reviews of records; Bach's four Hamburg symphonies. P. H. Lang. Mus Q 56:300-2 Ap '70
Several big three's; Karl Böhm's forty-six symphonies by Mozart. C. J. McNaspy. America 122:353-6 Mr 28 '70
Shostakovich's banned Babi Yar symphony in the original version. R. S. Brown. il por Hi Fi 20:secI 77-8 Je '70
Stokowski's splendid one-disc phase 4 Ninth. H. Goldsmith. Hi Fi 20:secI 74 Ag '70
Two new recordings of the Mahler Sixth: conducted by Rafael Kubelik and Bernard Haitink. J. Diether. il Am Rec G 37:34-5+ S '70
Uncensored at last: Babi Yar. J. Diether. il por Am Rec G 36:944-6+ Ag '70

Test records
Torture tracks for your hi-fi system: test records. H. Fantel. il Pop Mech 133:132-4+ Ja '70

Violin music
Complete Handel for the violin. B. Schwarz. Sat R 53:84-5 F 28 '70
See also
Phonograph records—Concertos

Violoncello music
See Phonograph records—Cello music

Vocal music
Canadian Rococo. P. G. Davis. il Hi Fi 20:131-2 O '70
See also
Phonograph records—Cantatas
Phonograph records—Songs

Wind ensembles
Sound of grass across four centuries: 1570-1970. D. W. Moore. il Am Rec G 37:92-4 O '70
PHOSPHATES
Chemical to fight tooth decay. J. Bockel. il Sci N 97:536-7 My 30 '70
See also
Cytidine phosphates
Phosphorylation
Sewage disposal—Phosphate removal
Trimethylphosphate
PHOSPHATIDES
Phosphonolipids: localization in surface membranes of tetrahymena. K. E. Kennedy and G. A. Thompson, jr. bibliog il Science 168:989-91 My 22 '70
PHOSPHENES
Phosphenes. G. Oster. il Sci Am 222:82-7 bibliog(p 126) F '70
PHOSPHIDES
Three-level oscillator in indium phosphide. G. B. Lubkin. Phys Today 23:19-20 D '70
PHOSPHOGLYCERIC acid. See Glyceric acid
PHOSPHOLIPIDS. See Phosphatides
PHOSPHONATES
Biological phosphonates: determination by phosphorus-31 nuclear magnetic resonance. T. Glonek and others. bibliog il Science 169:192-4 Jl 10 '70
PHOSPHONOLIPIDS. See Phosphatides
PHOSPHORUS
See also
Plants. Effect of phosphorus on
PHOSPHORYLATION
Phosphorylation coupled to the transfer of electrons from glutathione to cytochrome c. A. A. Painter and F. E. Hunter, jr. bibliog il Science 170:552-3 O 30 '70
PHOTO aerial reconnaissance. See Aerial reconnaissance
PHOTO finishing. See Photographic finishing, Commercial
PHOTOBIOLOGY. See Light—Physiological effects

PHOTOCHEMISTRY
Atmospheric photochemistry. R. D. Cadle and E. R. Allen. bibliog il Science 167:243-9 Ja 16 '70
Induced photolysis of DDT. L. L. Miller and R. S. Narang. bibliog il Science 169:368-70 Jl 24 '70
Photochemically induced ionic reactions of cycloalkenes. J. A. Marshall. bibliog il Science 170:137-41 O 9 '70
See also
Photosynthesis
PHOTOCHROMIC substances
Photochromics. Z. J. Kiss. bibliog il por Phys Today 23:42-9 Ja '70
PHOTOCOMPOSITION. See Phototypesetting
PHOTODIELDRIN. See Dieldrin
PHOTOELECTRIC cells
Inorganic liquid photovoltaic cell: tetravalent molybdenum in water. M. H. Navidi and others. il Science 169:980-1 S 4 '70
Milady's garage parking director. il Radio-Electr 41:48 D '70
See also
Photoelectric multipliers

Control use
See also
Electric motors—Control
PHOTOELECTRIC multipliers
Digital scan used in flat TV display; dynode controlled multiple beam device suitable for future air force fighters. B. Miller. il Aviation W 92:53-5 Mr 2 '70
PHOTOELECTRICITY
See also
Image intensifiers
PHOTOGRAMMETRY
Try photogrammetrisizing; Fairfield, Calif. J. L. Shilts. il por Am City 85:66-7 D '70
PHOTOGRAMS. See Shadowgrams
PHOTOGRAPHERS
Beautiful people of James Van Derzee. il pors Ebony 25:85-8+ O '70
Campus photo boom! photographs by ten San Francisco state college students; with introd. by J. Scully. Mod Phot 34:54-63 S '70
Classics of photography See issues of Modern photography to January, 1970
Do you have eyes in your skin? R. Hattersley. il Pop Phot 66:55-9 Mr '70
Four kinds of photographers show and talk about their work; E. Haas. P. Turner. J. Maisel, W. McBride. J. Scully. Mod Phot 34:12+ Ag '70
How to live with a photographic hang-up. R. Hattersley. il Pop Phot 66:88-91+ Ap '70
Kent state: four deaths at noon; with photographs taken by students and editorial comment by R. Graves. il Life 68:3, 30-5 My 15 '70
Keppler on the SLR: charlatans. H. Keppler. il Mod Phot 34:12+ O '70
Roy DeCarava: thru black eyes. A. D. Coleman. il Pop Phot 66:68-71+ Ap '70
See also
News photographers
also names of photographers, e.g. A. J. May
PHOTOGRAPHERS agents
See also
Globe photos, inc.
PHOTOGRAPHIC apparatus industry and trade
How Rollei plans to snap back. il Bsns W p99-100 O 24 '70
Japanese color invades the U.S; Fuji photo film company. il Bsns W p36 Je 20 '70
Keppler on the SLR: charlatans. H. Keppler. il Mod Phot 34:12+ O '70
Movie camera factories of Europe. H. V. Fondiller. il Pop Phot 67:124-6 N '70
Nikon click; Nippon Kogaku company. N. A. Martin. il Duns 97:62-4+ Ja '71
Oldies-but-goodies; where one can buy photographic junk. S. Nathan. il Pop Phot 67:66+ N '70
Phototronics; making electronic flash units at Matsushita. E. Farber. Mod Phot 34:56+ Jl '70
Pre-photokina news from Germany. N. Rothschild and B. Schwalberg. Pop Phot 67:28 D '70
Venerable cameras get a fresh image: German-Japanese rivalry. il Bsns W p27 Jl 4 '70
See also
Eastman Kodak company
Polaroid corporation

PHOTOGRAPHIC auctions. See Auctions

PHOTOGRAPHIC chemistry
Critical eye; overcoming the limitations of silver in photography. A. Rothstein. Travel & Camera 33:90 Ja '70
How to salvage outdated print paper. C. W. Kennedy. il Pop Phot 66:40+ F '70
Photography; images in silver. E. Keller. bibliog il Chem 43:6-12 O '70
View from Kramer; gum bichromate. A. Kramer. il Mod Phot 34:46+ Ja '70
See also
Photography—Developing and developers
Photography—Processing

PHOTOGRAPHIC Christmas cards. See Christmas cards

PHOTOGRAPHIC copying. See Photography—Copying

PHOTOGRAPHIC enlargers. See Photography—Enlargers and enlarging

PHOTOGRAPHIC equipment. See Photography—Apparatus and supplies

PHOTOGRAPHIC exhibitions. See Photography—Exhibitions

PHOTOGRAPHIC films. See Photography—Films

PHOTOGRAPHIC finishing, Commercial
Photofinishing at home; ratings of mail-order processors. il Consumer Bul 54:15-18 Ja '71

PHOTOGRAPHIC greeting cards. See Greeting cards

PHOTOGRAPHIC illustration. See Illustration of books and periodicals

PHOTOGRAPHIC industry. See Photographic apparatus industry and trade

PHOTOGRAPHIC lectures. See Lectures and lecturing

PHOTOGRAPHIC lenses. See Lenses, Photographic

PHOTOGRAPHIC memory. See Eidetic imagery

PHOTOGRAPHIC meters
Assembling a camera shutter speed meter. W. Coomes. il Pop Electr 33:73-7+ S '70
See also
Exposure meters

PHOTOGRAPHIC murals
How the pros mount murals. A. Francekevich. il Pop Phot 67:34+ O '70

PHOTOGRAPHIC optics
Do your specs and viewfinder get along? N. Goldberg. il Pop Phot 66:48+ F '70
How far is sharp? L. A. Mannheim. il Mod Phot 34:78-83+ Je '70
How light travels inside your camera. N. Goldberg. il Pop Phot 67:71-3 N '70
Little lenses that make space clearer. N. Goldberg. il Pop Phot 66:114-15+ Je '70
Our men at Oberkochen; a dual report on the Zeiss optics symposium. B. Schwalberg; N. Goldberg. il Pop Phot 66:84-5+ Ja '70
Techniques tomorrow. B. Sherman. Mod Phot 34:74+ Ja '70
Techniques tomorrow; lens-vs-film sharpness race. B. Sherman. il Mod Phot 34:38+ Jl '70

PHOTOGRAPHIC paper
Out-dated papers and films: are they safe? W. Hanson. Pop Phot 67:89+ D '70

PHOTOGRAPHIC processing. See Photography—Processing

PHOTOGRAPHIC reconnaissance systems
Air force using line-scan camera. B. Miller. il Aviation W 92:51-3+ Ja 26 '70

PHOTOGRAPHIC reproduction. See Photography—Copying

PHOTOGRAPHIC silk screen printing. See Silk screen printing

PHOTOGRAPHIC slides. See Transparencies

PHOTOGRAPHIC supplies. See Photography—Apparatus and supplies

PHOTOGRAPHIC supplies industry. See Photographic apparatus industry and trade

PHOTOGRAPHIC themes. See Photography—Themes

PHOTOGRAPHS
Ashvin Gatha's colorful world. il Pop Phot 67:87-9 S '70
Gallery:
Abstracts by Aaron Siskind. Life 69:6-7 S 11 '70
Alen MacWeeney's Irish tinkers. il Life 68:8-9 Mr 20 '70
Alfred Eisenstaedt's harborscape. il Life 68:8-9 Mr 6 '70
Alfred Gescheidt's combination pictures. Life 69:6-7 Ag 28 '70
Anthony Mauer's child on a swing. il Life 68:8-9 Ap 3 '70
Ballet of skates' eggs by Nina Leen. Life 69:8-9 N 20 '70
Berenice Abbott's New York newsstand circa 1935. Life 69:8-9 D 11 '70
Bill Binzen's photographic sandwiches. il Life 68:6-9 F 13 '70

Bill Powers' Brooklyn bridge. il Life 68:8-9 Ja 30 '70
Bob Peterson's quiet life among the flowers. Life 69:8-9 N 6 '70
Brett Weston's dramatic abstracts. il Life 68:8-9 Je 12 '70
Burk Uzzle finds Liverpool cold and gloomy. il Life 68:4-7 F 6 '70
Color impressions by Jay Maisel. il Life 68:6-9 Je 26 '70
Devastated landscapes in Hawaii by Jack Ward. Life 69:4-5 O 2 '70
E. Guidi's Umbrian hills. Life 68:6-9 F 27 '70
Eisenstaedt's Martha's Vineyard. il Life 68:6-9 Je 19 '70
Ellen Rogin's strange still lifes. Life 69:4-5 Ag 21 '70
Elliot Erwitt's delicate ironies. il Life 68:8-11 My 15 '70
F. Manley's snowscape. il Life 68:8-9 Ja 23 '70
The fountains of New York by Antoinette Jongen. Life 69:4-7 Jl 4 '70
G. Krause's own touches of fantasy. Life 69:6-7 O 23 '70
Harald Sund's Pacific Northwest. Life 68:8-11 My 22 '70
Harry Callahan's images in black. Life 68:6-9 Mr 27 '70
Henry Grossbard's gloomy images. Life 69:6-7 Jl 24 '70
Imogene Cunningham's testament to realism. il Life 68:8-9 My 1 '70
Jan Weborg's lithographic magic. il Life 68:8-11 Mr 13 '70
John Loengard in England. Life 69:6-9 Jl 31 '70
Josef Sudek, poet of Prague. Life 68:6-9 My 29 '70
A leaf from P. T. Barnum's album. il por Life 68:8-9 Ap 17 '70
Medical photographer, Sam Ehrlich, tries landscapes. Life 69:12-15 N 13 '70
Nudes abstracted by Eric Meola. il Life 69:8-9 S 18 '70
Philip Simkins' weathered wood. il Life 68:8-9 My 8 '70
Photographer Marie Cosindas on the set of Scrooge. Life 69:8-11 N 27 '70
Picasso draws on Gjon Mili's film. Life 69:8-9 D 4 '70
Racing dinghys photographed from helicopter by G. Silk. Life 69:8-9 O 9 '70
Ray Metzker's photocomposition. il Life 68:8-9 Ap 10 '70
Roads by Dan McCoy. Life 69:6-7 Jl 17 '70
Simon Nathan's alphabet photographs. Life 69:8-9 Jl 10 '70
Steve Wilson's sea gulls. il Life 68:8-9 Ap 24 '70
Stroboscopic nudes by Gjon Mili. il Life 68:6-9 F 20 '70
Study of hands by Roger Minick. Life 69:8-9 S 25 '70
Swiss children by Hans Peter Klemenz. Life 69:8-9 O 30 '70
Takayuki Ogawa's illustration for New York is. Life 69:4-5 Ag 7 '70
Vietnam combat photographs; excerpt from War without heroes, by D. D. Duncan. Life 69:4-5 D 18 '70
Visual mysteries by Dave Thomas. il Life 68:8-11 Je 5 '70
W. Eugene Smith's suspenseful pictures. Life 69:4-7 S 4 '70
Walker Evans' flavor of the past. Life 69:6-9 Ag 14 '70
Ken Whitmore: for him, photography is a magic box. il Pop Phot 66:66-75 F '70
Parting shots; pictures that show just what happened next. il Life 68:79-82 Je 5 '70
Readers' gallery. See issues of Travel & camera
See also
Daguerreotypes

Collectors and collecting
Fragments of the past; exhibition of historical Midwestern photographs at the Chicago art institute. R. F. McCullough. il Pop Phot 66:82-3 Ja '70
History is today, grown old. K. Poli. il Pop Phot 66:60-1+ F '70
See Photography—Collectors and collecting

Conservation and restoration
Archival processing is a talk fest. A. Francekevich. Pop Phot 67:36+ N '70
Concatenation of contaminants; meeting at the Smithsonian Institution. J. Deschin. il Pop Phot 67:30+ O '70
New lease on life for daguerreotypes; Enyeart process. J. Deschin. il por Pop Phot 67:42+ N '70

PHOTOGRAPHS—*Continued*

Exhibitions
See Photography—Exhibitions

Framing
See Photographs—Trimming, mounting, etc.

Marketing
Writers with a camera. R. Arnold. por Writers Digest 50:46-8 S; 50+ N '70

Mounting
See Photographs—Trimming, mounting, etc.

Trimming, mounting, etc.
Add 3-D to your photo display. H. Shaman. il Pop Mech 134:134-5 D '70
Crop those shots for better pictures. P. Geraci. il Pop Mech 133:144-7+ F '70
Dress up your prints with beveling. C. W. Kennedy. il Pop Phot 66:36+ My '70
For neat photo trimming, add a hold-down arm. R. S. Hedin. il Pop Mech 135:128 Ja '71
Hang-up, frame-up, round-up. il Mod Phot 34:68-9 Ap '70
How the pros mount murals. A. Francekevich. il Pop Phot 67:34+ O '70

PHOTOGRAPHS, Hanging of. See Pictures, Hanging of

PHOTOGRAPHS, Judging of. See Photography—Criticism

PHOTOGRAPHS in books and periodicals. See Illustration of books and periodicals

PHOTOGRAPHY
Answers by Arnold. R. Arnold. See issues of Travel & camera
B&W problems, and how to solve them. N. Rothschild. il Pop Phot 66:94-7+ Je '70
Critical eye; truth in photography. A. Rothstein. Travel & Camera 33:108 F '70
Feininger. A. Feininger. See issues of Modern photography
Finding a style; work J. Applebaum. R. Hattersley. il Pop Phot 67:102-5 N '70
For better holiday pictures; open your mind first. K. Poli. il Pop Phot 66:78-9+ Ja '70
Give yourself direction by setting up a photographic project that will swing you free. A. Feininger. Mod Phot 34:104+ F '70
Have we really made any progress? N. Rothschild. il Pop Phot 67:18+ Jl '70
Locked in the camera's eye, some instants last an eternity. il Life 68:75-8 Mr 6 '70
Mystery and magic of photography. W. Hanson. il Pop Phot 66:85-7+ Je '70
People, pictures, and paraphernalia. N. Rothschild. il Pop Phot 67:20+ N '70
Photo fun on a budget; special issue. il Pop Phot 67:79-83+ D '70
Picture came out, so what? N. Rothschild. il Pop Phot 66:24+ Ap '70
Special London report. il Travel & Camera 33:74-5 My '70
Tips for the occasional shooter. E. Meyers. il Pop Phot 67:38+ O '70
Tools & techniques. C. W. Kennedy. See issues of Popular photography
Travel guide. R. Joseph. See issues of Travel & camera
Vagabond camera. F. Rohr. See issues of Travel
When B/W is better. J. Scully. il Mod Phot 34:102-3 Ja '70
See also
Astronomical photography
Color photography
Creative photography
Electronics in photography
Moving picture photography
Photosculpture
Radiography
Shadowgrams
Stereophotography
Telephotography
Tintypes
Travel photography
Vietnamese war, 1957- —Photography

Apparatus and supplies
Adapt oddball lenses for better tele shots. H. G. Ross. il Mod Phot 34:82-3+ My '70
Bag of gadgets. B. Pierce. il Pop Phot 67:96-7+ S '70
Behind the scenes. See issues of Modern photography
Blow it up big; lens adapter for 35-mm SLR camera. R. Capotosto. il Pop Mech 134:155-7 N '70
Camera news. See issues of Travel & camera
Cut costs with imagination. E. Meyers. il Pop Phot 67:46+ D '70

First look. See issues of Popular photography
How to stretch your camera lenses; low-cost extenders. B. Murphy. il Pop Mech 134:123-7+ D '70
Lab report. See issues of Popular photography
Once over lightly. See issues of Modern photography
Photo tools from toyland. N. Goldberg. il Pop Phot 66:76-7+ My '70
Pre-photokina news from Germany. N. Rothschild and B. Schwalberg. Pop Phot 67:28+ D '70
Rollei show new products for 1970. B. Schwalberg. il Pop Phot 66:50 F '70
Soft-touch grippers and shirt whiteners. E. Meyers. il Pop Phot 66:34+ F '70
Special German report. R. Arnold. Travel & Camera 33:58-60 O '70
Tools & techniques. C. W. Kennedy. See issues of Popular photography
Twenty-five stocking stuffers and every one sells for under $10; comp. by L. Drukker. il Pop Phot 67:102-3 D '70
See also
Camera cases
Camera stands
Camera supports
Camera tripods
Eastman Kodak company
Exposure meters
Lenses, Photographic
Mirrors for cameras
Moving picture photography—Apparatus and supplies
Photography—Electronic equipment
Photography—Enlargers and enlarging
Photography—Processing—Apparatus and supplies
View finders

Collectors and collecting
Start collecting. H. Zucker. il Mod Phot 34:90-3 F '70

Design
Are they building cameras upside down? N. Rothschild. il Pop Phot 66:55-7+ F '70

Exhibitions
See Photography—Exhibitions

Maintenance and repair
How to keep your equipment in shape. N. Goldberg. il Pop Phot 67:84-7+ D '70
Where for repairs? services recommended by readers. See issues of Modern photography to June, 1970

Testing
Modern tests. See issues of Modern photography
Test reports. See issues of Travel & camera

Bibliography
Book bonanza for the pennypincher. R. Bruns. il Pop Phot 67:104-5+ D '70
Books in review. See issues of Modern photography
Photo books of 1970. F. Kappler. Life 69:12 D 18 '70

Christmas cards
See Christmas cards

Cold weather conditions
Snow might signal putting swim suit away, but not camera. F. Rohr. il Travel 135:72-5 Ja '71

Collectors and collecting
Arnold Crane; photographic materials collector extraordinary. R. F. McCullough. il por Pop Phot 66:96-7+ Ap '70
Drooping tulip heralds new business; offerings of limited editions of fine prints. J. Deschin. il Pop Phot 67:32+ Ag '70
Old cameras: a new bag; Parke-Bernet auction. K. Poli. il Pop Phot 66:58 My '70
Start collecting. H. Zucker. il Mod Phot 34:90-3 F '70

Competitions
Announcing Home garden's 1970 color photography contest. Home Gard 57:50 Jl '70
Announcing Life's new photographic contest. R. Graves. Life 68:3 Ap 3 '70
Announcing the winners of our photography contest. il Home Gard 57:19-21 O '70
How do you judge work of the young? Intercollegiate photography contest. N. Rothschild. il Pop Phot 67:14+ S '70
In focus; Travel & camera's first annual Travel photography contest results. Travel & Camera 33:4 Je '70
Mirror with a memory. il Motor B 125:56-9 F '70
Monthly report. See issues of Modern photography

PHOTOGRAPHY—Competitions—*Continued*
1970 color photo-contest. Home Gard 57:31 My '70
1970 Scholastic awards. il Sr Schol 96:12, 31 My 18 '70
Photo contest winners. il Home Gard 57:10-11 N '70
Photo contests. Pop Phot 66:34 Ja; 158 F; 42 Je; 67:36+ Ag '70
Photography contest; prizewinning pictures. il Life 69:5-8+ D 25 '70
Situation report on the biggest photo contest ever. R. Graves. il Life 69:1 O 23 '70
Winners; Travel & camera's 1970 photography contest. il Travel & Camera 33:54-60 S '70
World travel photo contest: the lens at large. M. R. Weiss. il Sat R 54:46-50 Ja 2 '71

Composition
See Composition (photography)

Copying
Ed Scully on color; black-and-white slides. E. Scully. il Mod Phot 34:38+ Ja '70
Which from what? E. Scully. il Mod Phot 34: 82-3+ F '70
See also
Transparencies—Copying

Criticism
Art is life, not critics' choice. N. Rothschild. il Pop Phot 67:16+ Ag '70
Don't let critics kill your pictures. R. Hattersley. il Pop Phot 67:67-9+ Jl '70
Pictures to argue about. il Mod Phot 34:70-9 My '70
Seeing pictures. J. Scully. See issues of Modern photography
What does photogenic really mean? A. Feininger. Mod Phot 34:30+ Ag '70

Darkroom technique
See Photography—Processing

Darkrooms
See Photography—Studios and darkrooms

Developing and developers
Do-it-yourself developing; color slides without a darkroom! D. Molner. Schol Teach Jr/Sr High p25-6 O 5 '70
Film that tops your best lens. A. Francekevich. il Pop Phot 66:72+ Ja '70
How to develop sheet film. A. Kramer. il Mod Phot 34:146-51 F '70
View from Kramer; advantage of large format sheet film with special developers. A. Kramer. Mod Phot 34:40+ Mr '70
View from Kramer: Beers print developer. A. Kramer. il Mod Phot 33:58+ D '69
See also
Photographic chemistry
Photography—Negatives

Drying (films and prints)
Let blotters dry prints while you sleep. C. W. Kennedy. il Pop Phot 66:36+ Ap '70

Electronic equipment
Electronic flash units. il Consumer Rep 35: 352-7 Je '70
How good are the automatic electronic flash units? J. Forney. il Mod Phot 34:72-3+ Ap '70
Photographic electronics '70. J. R. Free. il Radio-Electr 41:41-3 My '70
Phototronics. E. Farber. See issues of Modern photography
Phototronics; PC flash connectors. E. Farber. il Mod Phot 34:64+ Je '70
Variable-rate repeating strobe light you can build. S. Daniels. il Pop Sci 196:130-1 My '70
What's a top buy electronic flash? Kako Hi-beam II strobe unit. Consumer Rep 36:7 Ja '71
See also
Camera shutters—Control

Bibliography
Phototronics. E. Farber. Mod Phot 34:53+ Ja '70

Enlargers and enlarging
Four projectors with slide preview, three with automatic focus, enlargers that project reflex target. il Pop Phot 66:96-7 Ja '70
Past springs out of a picture; with stereopticon photographs by E. E. Henry and H. Putney, details enlarged by D. R. Phillips. pors Am Heritage 21:2, 16-27+ Je '70
Photographic enlargers. il Consumer Rep 35: 89-96 F '70
Processing tube for murals. A. Francekevich. il Pop Phot 67:20+ Jl '70
Three clever new aids for making color prints. J. A. Linkletter and S. M. Gallager. il Pop Mech 133:136-7 Ja '70

Equipment
See Photography—Apparatus and supplies

Exhibitions
Annual trade show; compact 35s, grown-up super 8s; highlights of MPDFA show. il Pop Phot 66:66 My '70
Best of twenty years? ASMP members exhibition at Gallery of modern art. J. Scully and J. Dreyfuss. il Mod Phot 34:60-7 Ap '70
Boston museum runs 360-degree show to save historic Back Bay area. L. Drukker. il Pop Phot 66:60 Ap '70
Ceiling on the wall; Sistine ceiling seen for the first time at the New York cultural center. M. R. Weiss. il Sat R 53:50-1 D 5 '70
Conversations with the dead; prisoner B. McCune and photographer, D. Lyon at the Institute for the arts, Rice university, Houston. M. Kozloff. il pors Art N 69: 24-7+ D '70
Elliott Erwitt at the Smithsonian. S. Callahan. il por Life 68:12 My 15 '70
From wispets of soul to the garish flea market; De Young museum. M. Mann. il Pop Phot 66:22+ F '70
Gallery snooping. See issues of Modern photography
Marvella, is that you? MOMA's Photography into sculpture show. M. Mann. il Pop Phot 67:100-1+ Ag '70
Multiple tie-in; book and exhibit; Israel: the reality. il Pub W 197:38-9 Ja 12 '70
No thrills from Philly; MPDFA show; symposium. il Pop Phot 66:70+ Je '70
Our man in Prague; new auto-focus system winner of Interkamera technical prize. M. Edelson. il por Pop Phot 67:78-80 Ag '70
Photo show of old New York; exhibition at the New York historical society. W. McQuade. il Life 69:18-19 D 11 '70
Photokine preview from Japan. E. Meyers and S. Nathan. il Pop Phot 67:78-81 N '70
Roy DeCarava: thru black eyes. A. D. Coleman. il Pop Phot 66:66-71+ Ap '70
Russia on display; U.S.S.R. photo '70 in Washington. il Newsweek 75:74 Mr 2 '70
Russians are here! USSR photo '70. A. D. Coleman. il Pop Phot 66:88-91+ Je '70
Shows to see. See issues of Popular photography
Shows we've seen. See issues of Popular photography
Soviets show off their sense of humor; U.S.S.R. photo '70, exhibition. il Life 68:69-72 Mr 13 '70
Spatial effects: more shapes than flats; photography into sculpture. M. R. Weiss. il Sat R 53:36-7 Jl 11 '70
Teeny Philly photo show! il Mod Phot 34: 88-9+ Je '70
Ten photographers tell the story; exhibition in U.S. pavilion at Expo '70. J. Szarkowski. il Art in Am 58:66-9 Mr '70
12,000 Russian shots! USSR photo '70; with photographs. J. Dreyfuss. il Mod Phot 34: 70-7 Je '70
Twenty years of photoshowmanship; photokina 70. B. Schwalberg. il Pop Phot 67:104-5+ S '70
View from the Bay. M. Mann. il Pop Phot 66:25-6+ Je; 67:22+ Jl; 25-6 Ag; 23-4+ O; 29-30+ N; 37+ D '70

Exposure
Basic guide to exposure. H. Birnbaum. il Travel & Camera 33:77-9 My '70
Close-up exposure is simple? L. A. Mannheim. il Mod Phot 34:78-9+ Mr '70
Exposure information printed with a published photograph won't help you one tiny bit. A. Feininger. il Mod Phot 34:50-2 Ja '70
Make exposure work! J. Scully. il Mod Phot 34:62-9 Jl '70
Primer on light. H. Harrison. Travel & Camera 33:68-71 Je '70
See also
Exposure meters

Films
Agfachrome 25S film. N. Rothschild. il Pop Phot 67:94-5 O '70
Camera collector; film sizes in danger of extinction. J. Schneider. il Mod Phot 34: 106+ S '70
Can Kodacolor-X stand the GAF? H. Keppler. il Mod Phot 34:88-9 Jl '70
Don't get caught with the wrong film. A. Francekevich. il Pop Phot 66:30+ My '70
Eclipse photography with a new color film. C. W. Wyckoff and P. R. Leavitt. il Sky & Tel 40:72-3 Ag '70
Ed Scully on color; make your own color negative film. E. Scully. il Mod Phot 34:29-30+ My '70

PHOTOGRAPHY—Films—*Continued*

Ektachrome-X print film? A. Johnson. il Mod Phot 34:84-7+ Je '70

Ektacolor-S; has Kodacolor-X finally had it? E. Scully. il Mod Phot 34:86-7+ Ja; 44+ Je '70

Facts about black and white film. D. Vestal. Travel & Camera 33:84-7 Ap '70

Film that tops your best lens. A. Francekevich. il Pop Phot 66:72+ Ja '70

How good are Japanese color films. N. Rothschild. il Pop Phot 67:78-81+ Jl '70

How to choose the right film for the best picture. P. Geraci. il Pop Mech 134:132-5 Jl '70

Instant art; Pola-color print. il Travel & Camera 33:54-5 Je '70

Is the film plane in your camera doing its job? B. Sherman. il Mod Phot 34:80-1+ F '70

Japanese color invades the U.S; Fuji photo film company. il Bsns W p36 Je 20 '70

Out-dated papers and films: are they safe? W. Hanson. Pop Phot 67:89+ D '70

Stuck on one film? Don't be, try them all! E. Meyers. il Pop Phot 66:54+ Ja '70

35mm slide films compared. E. Scully. il Mod Phot 34:82-3+ O '70

See also
Cameras—Loading
Moving picture films

Holders

View from Kramer; used cut film holders. A. Kramer. Mod Phot 34:16+ O '70

Storage

Should you keep your color in the dark? W. Hanson. il Pop Phot 66:90-1+ F '70

Testing

Ed Scully on color; testing color films. E. Scully. Mod Phot 33:16+ D '69

How they pre-test your film. W. F. Wilson. il Pop Phot 66:80-1 F '70

Focusing

Diffuse as you like it. C. W. Kennedy. il Pop Phot 67:26+ Jl '70

Feininger; human vision vs. camera vision. A. Feininger. Mod Phot 34:51+ Mr '70

How deep can you get? L. A. Mannheim. il Mod Phot 34:72-5+ Jl '70

How far is sharp? L. A. Mannheim. il Mod Phot 34:78-83+ Je '70

Lenses don't take pictures, you do. E. Meyers. il Pop Phot 66:48+ Ap '70

What's so good about optimum? aperture and sharpness. N. Goldberg. il Pop Phot 67:48+ S '70

See also
Lenses, Photographic
Moving picture photography—Focusing

Anecdotes, facetiae, satire, etc.

Shutter shudders. D. Williamson. Sat R 53:4 D 5 '70

History

Photography. E. Keller. bibliog il Chem 43:6-12 O; 8-11 D '70

Snapshot: family record or social document? M. Mann. il Pop Phot 67:29-30 S '70

Techniques tomorrow; sensational 60's. B. Sherman. Mod Phot 34:48+ Ap '70

That 35-mm fad that did last; memories. J. Deschin. Pop Phot 66:32+ My '70

Interiors

Christmas on camera: tips from six professional photographers on capturing your house in its very best light. D. McCluggage. Am Home 73:34+ D '70

Landscapes

Classic images of our land; winners in Life's photography contest. il Life 69:14-30 D 25 '70

Grand prize winner; with photographs by L. Kuzmanoff. il por Life 69:107-11 D 25 '70

When to shoot. J. Scully. il Mod Phot 34:84-5 Ap '70

See also
Nature photography

Law

What you need to know about model releases. A. Goldsmith. il Pop Phot 66:58-9+ F '70

Light

Ed Scully on color; daylighting. E. Scully. Mod Phot 34:10+ Jl '70

Primer on light. H. Harrison. Travel & Camera 33:68-71 Je '70

Techniques tomorrow; how light travels and what it does to your film. B. Sherman. Mod Phot 34:52+ My '70

When to shoot. J. Scully. il Mod Phot 34:84-5 Ap '70

Your enemy, the sun; rays, dangerous to eyes, pictures, and equipment. N. Rothschild. il Pop Phot 67:67-9+ Ag '70

Lighting

Fiat lux! except for fluorescents. D. B. Eisendrath. Pop Phot 66:18+ F '70

Gels for a new look. E. Scully. il Mod Phot 34:82-3+ Mr '70

Lights for tight budgets. N. Rothschild. il Pop Phot 67:82-3 D '70

Phototronics; fluctuating voltage. E. Farber. Mod Phot 34:36+ S '70

See also
Photography—Exposure
Photography, Flashlight

Marines

Mirror with a memory. il Motor B 125:56-9 F '70

Vagabond camera. F. Rohr. il Travel 134:76-7 D '70

See also
Moving picture photography—Marines
Photography of ships

Negatives

Negative-positive color processes may prove to be the wave of the future. A. Rothstein. Travel & Camera 33:90 Ap '70

News

See Photography, Journalistic

Philosophy

Soul-side must not be neglected. N. Rothschild. il Pop Phot 66:18+ Je '70

Portraits

Affirmative eye. R. Hattersley. il Pop Phot 67:94-7+ Jl '70

Autopolaroid; photographs, with interview. L. Samaras. Art in Am 58:66-83 N '70

Discovery: Bob Bailey. J. Dreyfuss. il Mod Phot 34:80-1+ My '70

Encounters with strangers; winners in Life's photography contest. Life 69:35-51 D 25 '70

Gallery; excerpts from Richard M. Ketchum's Faces from the past. Life 69:6-9 O 16 '70

Gallery: photographer Marie Cosindas on the set of Scrooge. Life 69:8-11 N 27 '70

Gels for a new look. E. Scully. il Mod Phot 34:82-3+ Mr '70

Glamor by Gowland. P. Gowland. Pop Phot 66:22+ Ja; 14 Je '70

Handy portrait props! J. Dreyfuss. il Mod Phot 34:70-1 Ap '70

Karsh's Japanese studies; with photographs. M. R. Weiss. Sat R 53:16-17 My 9 '70

Keppler on the SLR. H. Keppler. il Mod Phot 34:40+ My '70

Michael Semak: a photographer involved with life's human drama. M. Edelson. il Pop Phot 67:98-101+ N '70

Photo sketch prints. H. J. Croze. il Design 71:36-7 Spr '70

Photographing people. J. Hughes. il Travel & Camera 33:90-2 Mr '70

Simple scenes lit with tenderness; winners in Life's photography contest. Life 69:70-8+ D 25 '70

Up, down & around; candid photos with Spiratone Circo-Mirrotach. J. Scully. il Mod Phot 34:84-5 F '70

What the eyes don't tell. N. Rothschild. il Pop Phot 66:64-5+ Mr '70

What you need to know about model releases. A. Goldsmith. il Pop Phot 66:58-9+ F '70

See also
Moving picture photography—Portraits
Woman—Photographs

Printing processes

Ed Scully on color; Colorval II. Mod Phot 34:10+ S '70

Ever-changing faces of Naomi Savage. J. Scully. il Mod Phot 34:80-5 Ja '70

Getting started in color printing for $100. G. Reid. il por Pop Phot 67:90-1+ D '70

How to print richer blacks. C. W. Kennedy. il Pop Phot 67:42+ D '70

Make yourself a color sandwich; posterization technique using Color key. A. Francekevich. il Pop Phot 67:18+ Ag '70

Negative side of color prints. E. Scully. il Mod Phot 34:78-9+ S '70

Now, transparencies to enlargements, electrostatically. il Pop Sci 196:62-3 Mr '70

Parting shots; the camera's illusion and delusion. il Life 68:81-4 Ap 24 '70

PHOTOGRAPHY—Printing processes—*Cont.*
Print permanence: yes or no? E. Meyers. il
Pop Phot 67:40+ Jl '70
Turn your snapshots into poster art with
Color key. A. J. Hand. il Pop Sci 197:88-9
N '70
View from Kramer; gum bichromate. A. Kramer. il Mod Phot 34:46+ Ja '70
View from Kramer; temperature control. A.
Kramer. Mod Phot 34:34+ S '70
Wolfman on printing. See issues of Modern
photography
See also
Solarization

Processing

Archival processing is a talk fest. A.
Franckevich. Pop Phot 67:36+ N '70
Ed Scully on color; make your own color
negative film. E. Scully. il Mod Phot 34:
29-30+ My '70
Now there's a pocket-sized darkroom. E.
Meyers. il Pop Phot 66:30+ Mr '70
Stabilization processors. W. Hanson. il Pop
Phot 66:74-5+ My '70
Techniques tomorrow; question of correcting
a negative. B. Sherman. il Mod Phot 34:
40+ Je '70
View from Kramer; washers. A. Kramer. Mod
Phot 34:16+ F '70
See also
Photographic finishing. Commercial

Apparatus and supplies

Build a photographic wash tester. A. Brosnac.
il Pop Electr 32:65-6 My '70
Darkroom timers. il Consumer Rep 35:97-9 F
'70
Daylight print processors. E. Meyers. il Pop
Phot 67:84-6+ O '70
Digital timer for the darkroom. W. F. Wilson.
il Pop Phot 67:104+ O '70
Half-hour interval timer. F. H. Tooker. il
Radio-Electr 41:57-8+ My '70
Making that darkroom handy and safe. E.
Meyers. il Pop Phot 66:42+ My '70
One second metronome timer; visual and
audible indications for your darkroom. A.
A. Mangieri. il Pop Electr 32:58-60 F '70
Print dryer dry-mounts 'em, too. A. J. Hand.
il Pop Sci 197:62 O '70
Pulsed-light darkroom timer. F. H. Tooker.
il Radio-Electr 41:44 S '70
Rotary print washer anyone can build. K.
Adler. il Pop Mech 134:146 S '70
Stabilization processors. W. Hanson. il Pop
Phot 66:74-5+ My '70
This color-print drum works like a film tank.
A. J. Hand. il Pop Sci 197:107 Ag '70
This darkroom travels in your pocket. P.
Wahl. il Pop Sci 196:90 Je '70
Three bright ideas for the darkroom. il Pop
Sci 197:125 O '70
Three clever new aids for making color prints.
J. A. Linketter and S. M. Gallager. il Pop
Mech 133:136-7 Ja '70
Two easy ways to make borderless prints.
il Pop Mech 133:142-3 Mr '70
Wolfman on printing; special easels. A. Wolfman. il por Mod Phot 33:30+ D '69; 34:32+
Ja; 57-8+ Mr '70
See also
Exposure meters

Retouching

How to bleach without blobs. C. W. Kennedy.
il Pop Phot 67:24+ S '70

Scientific use

Photography: a wall, a Bible, an etcher.
N. Goldberg. il Pop Phot 66:66+ Ja '70

Social aspects

Pictures to make you think twice; winners in
Life's photography contest. il Life 69:90-
101+ D 25 '70

Still life

Vagabond camera. F. Rohr. il Travel 134:72-
3+ Jl '70

Studios and darkrooms

Make your pictures spotless: have a darkroom clean-up. N. Rothschild. il Pop Phot
66:72-3 Ap '70
Studio on a shoestring. A. Zayat. il Pop
Phot 67:108-9 D '70
Your first darkroom. P. Farber. Travel &
Camera 33:68-70+ Jl '70

Study and teaching

Diploma hunting with a camera. R. Bruns. il
Pop Phot 66:110-13+ Je '70
Hattersley class. R. Hattersley. See issues
of Popular photography

Look around like a stranger. E. Meyers. il
Pop Phot 67:38+ Ag '70
Photo education. Mod Phot 34:53-4 O '70
Seeing pictures. J. Scully. Mod Phot 34:12+
Ap '70

Themes

Are you passing up good pictures? N. Rothschild. il Pop Phot 66:26+ F '70
Discovery; ideas of George A. Peterson. J.
Dreyfuss. il Mod Phot 34:84-5+ Mr '70
Egg comes first. J. Dreyfuss. il Mod Phot
34:96-9 Ja '70
For better holiday pictures; open your mind
first. K. Poli. il Pop Phot 66:78-9+ Ja '70
Meaning, impact and graphic quality combine with stopping power to make a photograph good. A. Feininger. Mod Phot 33:
72+ D '69
Must that social landscape be horizontal? M.
Mann. il Pop Phot 66:25-6+ Je '70
Mystery. il Pop Phot 66:88-95 Ja '70
Retrieving the past; find yourself in your
photographs. R. Hattersley. il Pop Phot 67:
94-7+ Ag '70
Roy DeCarava: thru black eyes. A. D. Coleman. il Pop Phot 66:66-71+ Ap '70
Tugboat test. R. Hattersley. il Pop Phot 66:
116-19 Je '70
Who says no time for photography? N. Rothschild. il Pop Phot 66:18+ Mr '70

Great Britain

Britain no longer leads in photography. A.
Rothstein. Travel & Camera 33:72 N '70

Japan

Field day for 60,000 cameras. F. Saito. il Mod
Phot 34:78-9 Ag '70
PHOTOGRAPHY, Aerial
Kites over the sea. A. J. Hiller. il por Sea
Front 16:51-3 Ja '70
See also
Aerial reconnaissance
Photogrammetry
PHOTOGRAPHY, Artistic
Artistry with a camera. il Design 71:26-8
Wint '69
Backyard scenics? J. Scully. il Mod Phot 34:
86-7 F '70
Beauty is uninhabitable; G. Thorp. il Pop
Phot 67:90-3 N '70
Beauty is where he finds it. R. Hattersley. il
Pop Phot 67:98-101 S '70
Color and design are all around us. il Pop Phot
67:84-7 Jl '70
Discovery: Michael Maggid. J. Dreyfuss. il
Mod Phot 34:74-5+ Ap '70
Evelyn Hofer, pilgrim with a lens. S. E.
Meyer. il Am Artist 34:46-52+ N '70
Ever-changing faces of Naomi Savage. J.
Scully. il Mod Phot 34:80-5 Ja '70
Focus on photo display. A. Wiglama and A.
Ogden. il House B 112:100+ Je '70
Fritz Henle: four decades at the top. J.
Scully. il Mod Phot 34:62-71+ My '70
Instant art; Pola-color print. il Travel & Camera 33:54-5 Je '70
Make light of it. J. Dreyfuss. il Mod Phot
34:80-1 Mr '70
Modern art around you; photographs. T.
Borland. Farm J 94:44-5 Mr '70
Nob Fukuda: fantasist. il Pop Phot 67:85-9
N '70
Persistence of beauty, by the Friends of
photography in Carmel. Review
Pop Phot 66:22+ Ap '70. M. Mann
Peter Dechar. D. H. Karshan. il por Art in
Am 58:31-4 Jl '70
Photography takes shape; Photography into
sculpture exhibit. J. Scully. il Mod Phot 34:
76-7 Jl '70
Seen with a designer's eye; photographs by
R. Elber. Pop Phot 67:92-3 O '70
Shig Ikeda. il Pop Phot 66:78-83 My '70
Wynn Bullock: tracing the roots of man in
nature. B. Bullock; J. N. Uelsmann. il Mod
Phot 34:84-9+ My '70
See also
Composition (photography)
PHOTOGRAPHY, Close-up
Close-up exposure is simple? L. A. Mannheim. il Mod Phot 34:78-9+ Mr '70
Getting 1:1 with an eyeball. E. Meyers. il
Pop Phot 66:62-3+ Mr '70
More about those two-zone lenses. C. W.
Kennedy. il Pop Phot 67:36+ O '70
Move in for close-ups! M. Duitz. il Pop Phot
66:94+ Mr '70
Photographs can be deceiving. il Design 71:
16-17 Wint '69
Red eye, TV eye, and other eyes I have shot.
A. Francekevich. il Pop Phot 66:68-70 Mr '70

PHOTOGRAPHY, Close-up—*Continued*
Two lenses are closer than one. C. Lecakes. il Mod Phot 33:54 D '69
You can have it both ways; split-field attachments. C. W. Kennedy. il Pop Phot 67:76-7+ S '70

PHOTOGRAPHY, Cold weather. See Photography—Cold weather conditions

PHOTOGRAPHY, Commercial
Seeing pictures; fads, fashions and gimmicks. J. Scully. il Mod Phot 34:44+ Ja '70
See also
Photography, Journalistic
Photography as a profession
Photography in advertising

PHOTOGRAPHY, Composite. See Photomontage

PHOTOGRAPHY, Documentary
Boston museum runs 360-degree show to save historic Back Bay area. L. Drukker. il Pop Phot 66:60 Ap '70
Camera at the boiling point; current upheavals. J. Dreyfuss. il Mod Phot 34:72-9 F '70
Dorothea Lange. M. Mann. il Pop Phot 66:84-5+ Mr '70
Florida. J. M. Zanutto. il Pop Phot 66:101-9 Je '70
Get the pictures, and be ready to run! photographing a political demonstration. E. Meyers. il Pop Phot 66:46+ Je '70
Photographing people. J. Hughes. il Travel & Camera 33:90-2 Mr '70
Photography and the city. J. Fraser. Yale R 59:228-41 D '69
Revolutions in medium, but what about message? snapshot as a medium for social comment. M. Mann. il Pop Phot 67:25-6 Ag '70
Seeing pictures; help a cause. J. Scully. il Mod Phot 34:40+ F '70
Tugboat test. R. Hattersley. il Pop Phot 66:116-19 Je '70

PHOTOGRAPHY, Flashlight
Electronic flash, strobe. by H. Edgerton. Review
Mod Phot 34:38+ O '70. E. Farber
Phototronics; electronic flash ratings. E. Farber. Mod Phot 34:60+ F '70
Phototronics; flash manufacturer's claim about color temperature. E. Farber. il Mod Phot 34:130-1 Mr '70
Try flash with an available-light look. C. W. Kennedy. il Pop Phot 66:32+ Je '70
World of darkness; photographing night animals at the Bronx zoo. N. Morris. il Travel & Camera 33:82-6 F '70

Electronic equipment
See Photography—Electronic equipment

PHOTOGRAPHY, Infrared
Color your island infra-red. H. Weber. il Travel & Camera 33:84-9+ Ja '70
Thermography; coloring with heat. il Time 96:46-8 Ag 17 '70
See also
Photography, Medical

PHOTOGRAPHY, Journalistic
Fifty years at 1/20th of a second; photographer Buck May. H. Sidey. il por Life 69:4 N 27 '70
Freelance job idea: slide presentations. R. Arnold. il Writers Digest 51:34-6+ Ja '71
Globe photos: picture agency plus. H. V. Fondiller. il Pop Phot 66:78-9+ F '70
He gets to the core of a story fast; J. Manning. J. Deschin. por Pop Phot 67:24+ D '70
How and where to sell photos and photo-illustrated articles. R. Arnold. il Writers Digest 50:24-6 Jl '70
Murderers ordered him to take their pictures; shoot-out at San Rafael, Calif. Civic center. R. Graves. pors Life 69:2A Ag 21 '70
Rodeo blues: photographing the Pendleton. 33:78+ Jl '70
Selling pix to newspapers. L. Payne. il Writers Digest 50:22+ S '70
This little free lance stayed home. D. J. Cipnic. il Pop Phot 66:71-3+ My '70
W. Eugene Smith, passionate involvement with Life. W. Hicks. il Mod Phot 34:88-93 Ja '70
What James Keen taught me. Simon. il Pop Phot 66:52+ Mr '70

PHOTOGRAPHY, Laser. See Lasers—Photographic use

PHOTOGRAPHY, Marine. See Photography—Marines

PHOTOGRAPHY, Medical
Thermography; coloring with heat. il Time 96:46-8 Ag 17 '70
Thermography in the home. Sci Digest 68:75-6 N '70

PHOTOGRAPHY, Military
See also
Aerial reconnaissance

PHOTOGRAPHY, Nature. See Nature photography

PHOTOGRAPHY, Night
Color after dark. C. Purcell. il Pop Phot 67:90-5 S '70
World of darkness; photographing night animals at the Bronx zoo. N. Morris. il Travel & Camera 33:82-6 F '70

PHOTOGRAPHY, Panoramic
That Simon/wide, and how it grew; self-made camera to take wide-field pictures. il Pop Phot 66:58+ Ap '70

PHOTOGRAPHY, Stereoscopic. See Stereophotography

PHOTOGRAPHY, Streak. See Photography of moving objects

PHOTOGRAPHY, Submarine
Douglas Faulkner: his beautiful sea and its creatures. M. Edelson. il Pop Phot 67:87-91 O '70
Scuba diving for live treasures. il Nat Wildlife 8:26-31 Ap '70
Tips for travelers with snorkel and camera. F. Rohr. il Travel 133:71+ My '70

PHOTOGRAPHY, Theatrical
Artistry of Max Waldman. R. Hattersley. il Pop Phot 66:102-11+ Ja '70

PHOTOGRAPHY, Three dimensional. See Stereophotography

PHOTOGRAPHY, Travel. See Travel photography

PHOTOGRAPHY, Trick
Go off-beat: try squiggles; multiple exposures. C. W. Kennedy. il Pop Phot 67:20+ Ag '70
Make yourself a color sandwich; posterization technique using Color key. A. Francekevich. il Pop Phot 67:18+ Ag '70
Mystery. il Pop Phot 66:88-95 Ja '70
Parting shots; how these familiar faces would have looked 100 years ago. il por Life 68:66A-68 Je 19 '70
Sandwiches, paint, and filters; the vivid vision of M. Funk. C. Steinberg. il Pop Phot 67:98-101 D '70
Shoot it again, and again, and again. N. Rothschild. il Pop Phot 66:88-9+ My '70
See also
Moving picture photography, Trick

PHOTOGRAPHY and art. See Art and photography

PHOTOGRAPHY as a profession
Fritz Henle: four decades at the top. J. Scully. il Mod Phot 34:62-71+ Mr '70
He put the nude on the Coca-Cola chair. J. Deschin. il Pop Phot 66:22+ Mr '70
How to deal with editors like a pro. D. J. Cipnic. il Pop Phot 67:71-3+ O '70
I was a minor domo for Mayfield. Simon. il Pop Phot 67:62+ Ag '70
Ken Whitmore; for him, photography is a magic box. il Pop Phot 66:66-75 F '70
Turning silver images into gold. E. Meyers. il Pop Phot 67:44+ N '70

PHOTOGRAPHY by children. See Children as photographers

PHOTOGRAPHY center, San Francisco. See San Francisco—Photography center

PHOTOGRAPHY from moving objects
How to take photos on the go. F. Rohr. il Travel 134:75-7 O '70

PHOTOGRAPHY in advertising
Oh! Chicago! Bare essentials sell the now generation by mail; Ward's latest catalogue. B. Fredericks. il Pop Phot 67:72-3+ Ag '70

PHOTOGRAPHY in medicine. See Photography, Medical

PHOTOGRAPHY in science. See Photography—Scientific use

PHOTOGRAPHY in sewer inspection. See Sewer inspection

PHOTOGRAPHY of animals
Artistry with a camera. il Design 71:26-8 Wint '69
Camera safaris: the civilized way. L. Barry. il Pop Phot 67:54+ Jl '70
Can you really photograph Africa? H. Michaels. il Field & S 75:38-9+ Jl '70
Filming at the zoo. R. Pinney. il Pop Phot 67:116-17+ O '70
No license . . . no limit; big and small game hunting. G. Barrus. il Field & S 75:46-7+ D '70
Pets put personality in pictures. F. Rohr. il Travel 133:22-3+ Je '70
Safari trophies are most rewarding when captured on film. F. Rohr. il Travel 134:76-7 S '70
Shooting big game with a camera. C. Purcell. il por Pop Phot 66:98-101+ My '70
Stalk your cats. il Pop Phot 66:86-9 F '70
World of darkness; photographing night animals at the Bronx zoo. N. Morris. il Travel & Camera 33:82-6 F '70

PHOTOGRAPHY of birds
Businessman in the bush. F. K. Truslow. il
pors Nat Geog 137:634-75 My '70
Freeze action with AG-1 flash! M. A. Matzkin. il Mod Phot 34:60 Ja '70
Luck of Prince Philip; excerpts from Wildlife crisis. Prince Philip. il por Look 34:
29-33 O 20 '70
Telephoto hunting simplified. J. H. Robinson.
il Field & S 75:154 Je '70
Want bird close-ups? Call them with tape. G.
Perkins and C. Perkins. il Pop Phot 67:74-
5+ Jl '70

PHOTOGRAPHY of boats. See Photography of
ships

PHOTOGRAPHY of buildings and structures
Christmas on camera: tips from six professional photographers on capturing your
house in its very best light. D. McCluggage. Am Home 73:34+ D '70
How to photograph your home. B. Berger.
il Mech Illus 66:112-13 N '70

PHOTOGRAPHY of children
Catching Christmas candidly saves it for
year-round pleasure. F. Rohr. il Travel 134:
72-4+ N '70
Great pictures, no! Great kids, yes! N. Roths-
child. il Pop Phot 67:70-3+ Jl '70
More than one way to see! with series of
pictures by Stephen Green-Armytage. J.
Dreyfuss. Mod Phot 34:76-7 Mr '70
Youngsters are where the action is! D. Pin-
ney. il Pop Phot 67:128-9+ D '70
See also
Children—Photographs

PHOTOGRAPHY of dancing
Let your camera follow the dance. W. Lane.
il Travel 133:79 Ja '70

PHOTOGRAPHY of eclipses. See Astronomical
photography

PHOTOGRAPHY of emotions
Artistry of Max Waldman. R. Hattersley.
il Pop Phot 66:102-11+ Ja '70
Dorothea Lange. M. Mann. il Pop Phot 66:
84-5+ Mr '70
Dream photographs; R. Gibson. Pop Phot
67:98-101+ O '70
Strange obsession? photograph your com-
pulsions, and maybe your pictures will
make them disappear. R. Hattersley. il
Pop Phot 66:98-101+ Ja '70
What the eyes don't tell. N. Rothschild. il
Pop Phot 66:64-5+ Mr '70

PHOTOGRAPHY of flowers, plants, trees, etc.
Ed Scully on color. E. Scully. il Mod Phot 34:
54+ Ap '70
Flower fishing in Fishlake forest. D. E. Rose.
Horticulture 48:44-6 Jl '70
Flower photographer. S. Gottscho. il Travel
& Camera 33:60-2 Ap '70
Flowers and a lifetime of picture making.
S. H. Gottscho. Travel & Camera 33:72 Ap
Sam Gottscho: nonagenarian flower power.
J. Deschin. il Pop Phot 67:80-3+ O '70

PHOTOGRAPHY of moving objects
Andy, take me along at Indy. Simon. il Pop
Phot 66:60+ Je '70
How I broke the reality barrier; streak
photography. A. Davidhazy. il Pop Phot 67:
74-7 O '70
Stopping the action; winners of Life's pho-
tography contest. il Life 69:58-68 D 25 '70

PHOTOGRAPHY of nature. See Nature photography

PHOTOGRAPHY of planets. See Astronomical
photography

PHOTOGRAPHY of rain and rainfall
It's raining pictures! R. Donaldson's photography of raindrops. il Pop Phot 67:81-3 Ag
'70

PHOTOGRAPHY of reptiles
Snake safari with camera and courage. K.
Severin. il por Sci Digest 68:38-47 N '70

PHOTOGRAPHY of rodeos. See Photography of
sports

PHOTOGRAPHY of ships
Powerful and beautiful. il Motor B 125:124-33
Ja '70

PHOTOGRAPHY of sports
Andy, take me along at Indy. Simon. il Pop
Phot 66:60+ Je '70
In focus; ski photography. Travel & Camera
33:4 Jl '70
Rodeo blues: photographing the Pendleton,
Ore. round-up. D. Budnik. Travel & Camera
33:78+ Jl '70

PHOTOGRAPHY of the human figure. See Human figure in photography

PHOTOGRAPHY of the sun. See Astronomical
photography

PHOTOGRAPHY of winter sports. See Photography of sports

PHOTOGRAPHY on glass, metal, pottery, etc.
Wolfman on printing; sensitized linen prints.
A. Wolfman. Mod Phot 34:50+ Ap '70

PHOTOISOMERIZATION. See Isomerization

PHOTOJOURNALISM. See Photography, Journalistic

PHOTOKINA. See Photography—Exhibitions

PHOTOLYSIS (chemistry) See Photochemistry

PHOTOMECHANICAL processes
See also
Phototypesetting

PHOTOMETRY
See also
Spectrophotometry

PHOTOMETRY, Astronomical
Jupiter: his limb darkening and the magnitude of his internal energy source. L. M.
Trafton and R. L. Wildey. bibliog il Science
168:1214-15 Je 5 '70
Optimum sizes for infrared photometric
telescopes. Sky & Tel 40:15 Jl '70

PHOTOMICROGRAPHY
Unbelievable world of photo-micrography.
il Nat Wildlife 8:42-3 Je '70

PHOTOMONTAGE
Gallery: Ray Metzker's photocomposition. il
Life 68:8-9 Ap 10 '70
New use for old prints. J. E. Kollas. il Design
71:14-15 Sum '70
Real pussy willows. C. G. Maxwell. il Design
71:18 Spr '70
Texturize your color slides. N. Rothschild.
il Pop Phot 66:86-7+ Ja '70

PHOTOPERIODISM
Circadian clock in insect photoperiodism. D.
S. Saunders. bibliog il Science 168:601-3 My
1 '70
DNA synthesis in the anterior pituitary of
the male rat: effect of castration and photoperiod. W. C. Hymer and others. bibliog il
Science 167:1629-31 Mr 20 '70
Photoperiodic induction and termination of
diapause in an insect: response to changing day lengths. M. J. Tauber and C. A.
Tauber. bibliog il Science 167:170 Ja 9 '70
Photoperiodically significant photoreception in sparrows: is the retina involved? H.
Underwood and M. Menaker. bibliog il Science 167:298-301 Ja 16 '70; Reply with rejoinder. D. F. Lott. 169:892-3 Ag 28 '70
Pineal function and oviposition in Japanese
quail: superior cervical ganglionectomy
and photoperiod. C. L. Ralph and others.
bibliog il Science 170:995-7 N 27 '70

PHOTORECEPTOR cells. See Rod and cone
cells

PHOTORESPIRATION. See Plants—Respiration

PHOTOSCULPTURE
Spatial effects: more shapes than flats; photography into sculpture exhibit. M. R. Weiss.
il Sat R 53:36-7 Jl 11 '70

PHOTOSYNTHESIS
Evolution of photosynthesis. J. M. Olson. bibliog il Science 168:438-46 Ap 24 '70
Mercury compounds reduce photosynthesis
by plankton. R. C. Harriss and others. bib-
liog il Science 170:736-7 N 13 '70
Photosynthesis and fish production in the
sea. J. H. Ryther; reply with rejoinder.
D. L. Alverson and others. bibliog Science
168:503-5 Ap 24 '70
Power plants: effects of chlorination on es-
tuarine primary production. D. H. Hamil-
ton, jr. and others. bibliog il Science 169:
197-8 Jl 10 '70
What part of the photosynthesis process
causes leaves to change colors in the fall?
Sci Digest 68:88-9 O '70
See also
Chlorophyll
Chloroplasts

PHOTOSYNTHETIC bacteria. See Bacteria,
Photosynthetic

PHOTOTROPISM
Phototropism in phycomyces as investigated
by focused laser radiation. M. L. Meistrich and others. bibliog il Science 169:370-1
Jl 24 '70

PHOTOTYPESETTING
Betwixt cup and lip. V. Strauss. Pub W 197:
263-5 Ja 26 '70
Everybody's hot for it; Colonial press's use
of CRT composition. il Pub W 197:146-8
F 23 '70
IBM selectric composition system. V. Strauss.
il Pub W 198:31-5 N 30 '70
Lannon's fluxions for a technology in flux. V.
Strauss. Pub W 198:46-8 O 12 '70
Look at two low-cost photocomp systems. V.
Strauss. Pub W 198:45-6+ Jl 6 '70
Preliminary report of CRT cost study, high-
light of American university meeting. Pub
W 197:54-5 Mr 30 '70

PHOTOTYPESETTING—*Continued*
Publishing by cathode ray tube. R. L. Tobin. il Sat R 53:61-2 O 10 '70
Super-fast typsetting machine. S. V. Jones. il Sci Digest 67:73 Je '70
You don't have to be big to be fast; adaptation of address. H. Sperr. Pub W 197:42-4 Mr 16 '70
See also
CompuComp corporation

PHOTOVOLTAIC cells. See Photoelectric cells

PHRASES. See English language—Terms and phrases

PHU TAM, Vietnam
Following the script. Newsweek 76:27 Jl 20 '70

PHYCOMYCES
Phototropism in phycomyces as investigated by focused laser radiation. M. L. Meistrich and others. bibliog il Science 169:370-1 Jl 24 '70
Phycomyces: habituation of the light growth response. J. K. E. Ortega and R. I. Gamow. bibliog il Science 168:1374-5 Je 12 '70

PHYLOGENY
Hominid phylogeny and immunology: a critical appraisal. D. W. Read and P. E. Lestrel. bibliog il Science 168:578-80 My 1 '70

PHYSARUM. See Slime molds

PHYSICAL anthropology. See Anthropology

PHYSICAL astronomy. See Astrophysics

PHYSICAL directors
See also
Coaches (athletics)

PHYSICAL education and training
Vietnam: recreational leadership training. B. Bush. il Parks & Rec 5:40-2+ Ap '70
See also
Sports

PHYSICAL examinations
Medical testing; a lighthearted look at screening procedures. G. M. Rourke. il Todays Ed 59:54-6 F '70
When your baby gets his first physical. il Changing T 24:21-3 S '70

PHYSICAL exercise. See Exercise

PHYSICAL fitness
See also
Exercise
Health
Military service—Physical and mental fitness
Muscle strength

PHYSICAL geography
See also
Climate
Craters
Lakes
Man—Influence on nature

PHYSICAL measurements
Fundamental physical constants. B. N. Taylor and others. il Sci Am 223:62-70+ O '70
See also
Doppler effect
Radiation—Measurement

PHYSICAL oceanography. See Oceanography

PHYSICAL therapy
Thanks to Doug Crutchfield Fru Nilsen can dance again. il pors Ebony 25:86-91 Ap '70

PHYSICALLY handicapped
See also
Libraries—Services to physically handicapped

PHYSICIANS
Family doctor: medicine's newest specialty. E. J. Kowalewski. il Parents Mag 45:40-1+ Ag '70
R for the family-doctor shortage. W. C. Bornemeier. Read Digest 97:103-7 Jl '70
See also
American medical association
Hospitals—Staff
Malpractice
Medical education
Medical ethics
Medical service
Medicine
Medicine—Group practice
Medicine—Practice
Negro physicians
Psychiatrists
Specialization in medicine
Surgeons
Women as physicians

Fees
See Medical service. Cost of

Supply and demand
Country's no. 1 health problem; interview. R. Egeberg. il pors U S News 68:68-73 F 23 '70
Curing the doctor shortage; Carnegie commission plan. Time 96:38+ N 9 '70

Dilemma in Dyersville; doctors needed in Iowa town with a brand-new hospital. L. Wainwright. il Life 68:48-50+ My 29 '70
Let's give foreign doctors a fair shake; ed. by W. Cole. J. C. Serrato. il por Todays Health 48:36-9 F '70
R for the family-doctor shortage; the Medex proposal. W. C. Bornemeier. Read Digest 97:103-7 Jl '70

PHYSICIANS advisory committee on radio, television, and motion pictures. See American medical association

PHYSICIANS and patients
Hearts and palms. il Newsweek 76:103 S 14 '70
How to treat your doctor. F. Casey. il Mech Illus 66:57-9+ N '70
Parting shots: what doctors think of their patients. il Life 69:68-72 O 2 '70
Seductive patients. il Time 96:46+ Jl 20 '70
What to do if the doctor comes; difficulty of getting in touch with doctors. J. K. Lubold. il Good H 171:59+ Jl '70

Anecdotes, facetiae, satire, etc.
Oh, doctor! S. Levenson. il Ladies Home J 87: 64+ O '70

PHYSICIANS assistants. See Medical workers

PHYSICIANS in literature
Doctor did it; Sherlock Holmes, the canny detective. B. Scott. il Todays Health 48:57-9+ O '70

PHYSICISTS
Ph.D. physicists in high school jobs. Sch & Soc 98:394-5 N '70
Physicists with unusual careers. M. S. Rothenberg. il Phys Today 23:23-8+ My '70
Scientists and the decision to bomb Japan. D. H. Frisch. il por Bul Atom Sci 26:107-15 Je '70
Who finds the job? R. H. Ellis, jr; discussion. Phys Today 22:9 S; 9+ N '69; 23:9+ F '70
See also
American physical society
Kapitsa, P
Livingston, M. S.

Supply and demand
Down and out along route 128. B. Rice. il N Y Times Mag p28-9+ N 1 '70; Discussion. p48+ N 22 '70
Quantum shrink. Newsweek 75:71 My 4 '70
Squeeze gets personal. il Sci N 97:171-2 F 14 '70
Supply and demand for physicists. A. A. Strassenburg. bibliog il por Phys Today 23:23-8 Ap '70
Why there is a job shortage. W. R. Gruner. bibliog il por Phys Today 23:21-6 Je '70; Discussion. 23:96 Je; 9+ O '70

PHYSICS
Frontiers of physics today (cont) il Phys Today 23:35-41 Je; 44-9 S; 32-8 N '70
Future of physics; adaptation of address, March 1970. F. J. Dyson. bibliog il Phys Today 23:23-6+ S '70
Physics & society. Phys Today 23:23-8 Ap; 23-8+ My; 21-6 Je '70
Physics in the twentieth century; adaptation of address, April 1969. V. F. Weisskopf. Science 168:923-30 My 22 '70
See also
American institute of physics
Astrophysics
Atomic theory
Biological physics
Compressibility
Cosmic physics
Dynamics
Gravitation
Hydrostatics
Magnetism
Nuclear physics
Quantum theory
Relativity (physics)
Rheology
Sound
Sound waves
Statistical mechanics
Units
Viscosity

Bibliography
Books. See issues of Physics today

History
History-of-physics laboratory. S. Devons and L. Hartmann. il pors Phys Today 23:44-9 F '70
Physics in the great depression. C. Weiner. bibliog il Phys Today 23:31-6+ O '70

International aspects
See Science—International aspects

PHYSICS—*Continued*

Periodicals

New journals. J. T. Scott. bibliog Phys Today 23:54-5 Ag '70
See also
Physics today (periodical)

Research

Forces of nature: testing their strength. G. L. Wick. bibliog il Science 168:1329-31 Je 12 '70
Judging the value of physics research; letter. W. Zernik. il Phys Today 23:9+ D '70
Search and discovery. See issues of Physics today

Social use

IRRPOS looks for relevance to society's problems. J. B. Phelps. il por Phys Today 23:61-2 N '70
Physics and environment; symposium, with editorial comment. Phys Today 23:23-4+, 80 D '70

Study and teaching

Computers in physics instruction. G. Schwarz and others; reply. D. L. Shirer. il Phys Today 23:15+ Ap '70
History-of-physics laboratory. S. Devons and L. Hartmann. il pors Phys Today 23:44-9 F '70
Physics for the nonscience major; symposium. bibliog il Phys Today 23:23-9+ Mr '70
Relevance of physics; adaptation of address, June 1970. G. Holton. bibliog il Phys Today 23:40-3+ N '70
Reshaping the image of physics. J. S. Rigden. bibliog il Phys Today 23:48-53 O '70
Studying physics at Moscow state university; adaptation of address, April 18, 1969. L. A. Artsimovich. il por Phys Today 23:34-40 Ja '70
Survey of the teaching of physics in secondary schools. R. E. Thompson. Sch & Soc 98:243-4 Ap '70
See also
Commission on college physics
International centre for theoretical physics, Trieste, Italy

Russia

Interview with Peter Kapitsa; ed. by G. B. Lubkin. P. L. Kapitza. il pors Phys Today 23:63+ Ja '70

PHYSICS literature
Books & journals: a special report. il Phys Today 23:51-7+ Ag '70

PHYSICS teachers
See also
American association of physics teachers

PHYSICS today (periodical)
Introducing our new look. H. L. Davis. Phys Today 23:92 S '70
Physics today has new editor; Davis replaces Ellis as head; with editorial comment H. W. Koch. il Phys Today 23:125, 152 Ja '70

PHYSIOLOGICAL apparatus
See also
Hearts, Artificial

PHYSIOLOGICAL effects of cold; Physiological effects of noise. See Cold—Physiological effects; Noise—Physiological effects

PHYSIOLOGICAL oxidation. See Oxidation, Physiological

PHYSIOLOGICAL psychology. See Psychology, Physiological

PHYSIOLOGICAL research
See also
Space flight—Physiological aspects

PHYSIOLOGISTS
See also
Bernard, C.
Purkyně, J. E.

PHYSIOLOGY
How good are you as a physiologist? quiz. J. Daugherty and M. Daugherty. il Sci Digest 67:62-3+ Mr '70
See also
Corpulence
Electrophysiology
Metabolism
Reproduction
Stress (physiology)
Weight (physiology)
also names of organs of the body, e.g. Kidneys

History

Purkyne symposium. C. D. Leake. Science 167:210+ Ja 9 '70

PHYTOPLANKTON. See Plankton

PIAGET, Jean
Of time and the child. D. Elkind. il N Y Times Mag p90+ O 11 '70 *

PIANISTS
Artist life; Princess Irene of Greece. D. J. Soria. il pors Hi Fi 20:secII 4-5 Ag '70
Musicians don't look and dancers don't listen; role of dance accompanist. E. Muller. Dance Mag 45:26-7 Ja '71
See also
Barenboim, D.
Cliburn, V.
Ellington, D
Evans, B.
Fleisher, L.
Vásáry, T.

PIANO
See also
Harpsichord

Instruction and study

Landmark for Rosina Lhevinne. R. Jacobson. il pors Sat R 53:57-9+ Mr 28 '70
See also
Piano classes
Piano playing

PIANO classes
Music lessons today: more play than work; group classes. il House B 112:68 O '70

PIANO contests. See Music—Competitions

PIANO industry and trade
See also
Steinway and sons, New York

PIANO music
See also
Phonograph records—Piano music
Piano playing
Sonatas

PIANO playing
Garrick Ohlsson: art of playing Chopin; interview. G. Ohlsson. New Yorker 46:16-18 Ja 2 '71
See also
Ensemble playing
Piano—Instruction and study

PIATIGORSKY, Gregor
Gregor the great; anniversary concert with the Philharmonic in New York. H. Saal. il por Newsweek 76:87 N 9 '70 *

PIAZZA, Marguerite
Struggle for life itself; ed. by M. Mesinger. pors McCalls 97:88-9+ F '70

PIAZZAS. See Plazas

PICA (pathology)
Pagophagia in the albino rat. S. C. Woods and R. S. Weisinger. bibliog il Science 169:1334-6 S 25 '70

PICABIA, Francis
Art; retrospective at the Guggenheim. L. Alloway. Nation 211:314-15 O 5 '70 *
Big Dada; retrospective at the Guggenheim museum. D. Davis. il por Newsweek 76:81-2 S 28 '70 *
Hello and goodbye, Francis Picabia. P. Pearlstein. il Art N 69:52-4+ S '70 *
Metaphysical nose-thumber; exhibition at the Guggenheim museum, New York. K. Kuh. il Sat R 53:54-5 N 21 '70 *

PICASSO, Pablo
Art; open letter sent by Art workers coalition suggesting he remove Guernica from the museum. L. Alloway. Nation 210:221-2 F 23 '70 *
From Pablo, with love. Time 95:82 Mr 23 '70 *
Gallery; photographs; excerpts from Picasso's third dimension. G. Mili. Life 69:8-9 D 4 '70 *
Gift of the master. il por Newsweek 75:64 Mr 23 '70 *
Picasso; excerpt from Selected writings of Gertrude Stein. G. Stein. il por Vogue 157:88-9+ Ja 1 '71 *
Rally round the Picasso, boys! E. Hotaling. il Art N 68:46-7+ Ja '70 *
Thirty years old, going on ninety. il pors Time 96:49 D 7 '70 *

PICCAVER, Alfred
Top tenors, on L.P. A Favia-Artsay. pors Hobbies 75:36 Je '70 *

PICCOLO, Brian
Short courageous life of Brian Piccolo; excerpts from I am third, ed. by A. Silverman. G. Sayers. pors Look 34:48-51+ Ag 25 '70 *

PICCOLO, Lucio
Days; poem, tr. by B. Swann and R. Feldman. Poetry 116:303 Ag '70

PICHINCHA (province)
See also
San Antonio de Pichincha

PICKLE, J. J.
Excerpts from debate, September 16 and 17, 1969. Cong Digest 49:30 Ja '70

PICKLE dishes
Victorian pickle castors. V. K. Schnadig. il Hobbies 75:119 Mr '70

PICKLED fish. See Fish, Pickled

PICKLED herring. See Fish, Pickled

PICKLES and relishes
Canning the late-summer harvest; recipes. J. Uetz. il Am Home 73:90-2+ S '70
Four relishes with zing. E. W. Manning. il Farm J 94:38-9 S '70
What's cooking?
Strong taste of spring. M. C. Goldman. il Org Gard & Farm 17:98-103 My '70
Work wonders with pickles. il Ladies Home J 87:90+ Ag '70

PICKUP, Phonograph. See Phonograph—Pick-up

PICKUP campers. See Campers and coaches, Truck

PICKUP trucks. See Motor trucks

PICKWICK International, inc.
Quality records at cut rates. Bsns W p 117 F 14 '70

PICNIC cookery. See Cookery, Outdoor

PICNICS
Alfresco: the picnic comes of age; with recipes. il McCalls 97:76-81+ Jl '70
At-home picnics; salad and sandwiches go into the garden. il Sunset 145:118-19 S '70
Easter picnic. E. Alston. il Look 34:84-5 Mr 24 '70
Four instant car picnics. il Sunset 145:96-7 Ag '70
Make it a Christmas picnic: Puerto Rico; with recipes. E. Alston. il Look 34:60-2 D 29 '70
Moroccan picnic in the U.S.A. M. McKendry. il Vogue 156:43 Jl '70
Park outing; with recipes. il Bet Hom & Gard 48:43-5+ Je '70
Picnic for Thanksgiving. E. Alston. il Look 34:82-3 N 17 '70
Picnic for the truth; with recipes. E. Alston. il Look 34:62-3 Je 30 '70
Picnics Pacific style; with recipes. il Am Home 73:60-1+ Jl '70
Pontoon picnic; with recipes. il Bet Hom & Gard 48:47 Je '70
Potluck fly-in; with recipes. E. W. Manning. il Farm J 94:37 Je '70
What a day! Let's have a picnic! H. McCully. House B 112:78-9+ Ag '70
See also
Clambakes

PICOT, Jacques Georges-. See Georges-Picot, J.

PICTORIAL tapestries. See Tapestry

PICTURE books
See also
Illustrated books

Bibliography
Bibliography of budget picture books. il Mod Phot 33:48-9+ D '69
Big format gift books. California, the North-west, Hawaii, the West. il Sunset 145:24+ D '70
In place of the real thing; coffee-table books. R. A. Sokolov. il Newsweek 76:106+ D 14 '70

PICTURE books for children
Choosing and using picture books. Z. Sutherland. Sat R 53:33 N 14 '70
Focusing the picture book. M. Calhoun. il Writer 83:20-3 Jl '70
Lionni's artichokes: an interview; ed. by R. Agree. L. Lionni. bibliog il por Wilson Lib Bul 44:947-50 My '70
Ylla: she never shot a hippogriff. J. Deschin. il por Pop Phot 66:38+ Ja '70
See also
Caldecott medal

Bibliography
Some rare picture books. il Pub W 198:39 N 23 '70

PICTURE frames
Frame opening. M. Vogel. il Design 71:17 Fall '69
Matting, mounting, and frames. S. McIlhany. il Am Artist 34:42-7 My '70
Uptight clamp for all picture frames. R. C. Barnes. il Pop Sci 197:111 S '70

PICTURE post cards. See Post cards

PICTURE safes. See Safes

PICTURE windows. See Windows

PICTURE writing
Baton of Montgaudier; engraved art on the reindeer antler from stone age France. A. Marshack. il por(p8) Natur Hist 79:56-63 Mr '70
Symbols in the stone age; analysis of ice age art. il por Sci N 97:242 Mr 7 '70

PICTURES
Fleurage. P. C. Maloney. il por Horticulture 48:48-9+ F '70
See also
Assemblage (art)
Drawings

Framing
See Picture frames

Prices
See Art—Prices

PICTURES, Framing of. See Picture frames

PICTURES, Hanging of
Arrange a family frame-up; ways to display photographs. L. L. Ball. il Am Home 73:28+ Jl '70
Focus on photo display. A. Wiglama and A. Ogden. il House B 112:100+ Je '70

PICTURES, Immoral. See Immoral literature and pictures

PICTURES, Theft of. See Art thefts

PICTURES in education
Effect of pictures on learning to read; also effects on comprehension and attitudes. S. J. Samuels. Ed Digest 36:48-51 N '70
See also
Moving pictures in education

PIDAL, Ramón Menéndez. See Menéndez Pidal, R.

PIE
Cream pie mixes. Consumer Rep 35:175-6 Mr '70
Danes, the Italians, and the Germans all use poached apple rings or slices. il Sunset 145:221+ N '70
Fast and fancy winter fruit pies. il Bet Hom & Gard 48:71-2 Ja '70
It's sweet up on top, it's tart down below. il Sunset 145:192+ N '70
Key lime pie. E. Alston. il Look 34:90-1 My 5 '70
Perfect pie. il Am Home 74:54-6+ Ja '71
Pie and potable; brandy Alexander pie. C. Claiborne. il N Y Times Mag p42 Ja 18 '70
Pie! excerpts. P. H. White. il Ladies Home J 87:70-1+ Ja '70
Two citrus pies: lemon or lime. Sunset 145:130 Jl '70

PIE, Frozen. See Food, Frozen

PIEL, Mary Bird
Different library, different school! il Pub W 198:78-81 Jl 13 '70

PIENE, Nan R.
Art under $500. il Art in Am 58:94-101 My '70
How and where to buy contemporary prints. House & Gard 137:54+ Mr '70
How to collect primitive art. House & Gard 137:48-9+ Ja '70
How to place and light sculpture. House & Gard 137:18+ F '70
L.A. trip. il Art in Am 58:138-41 Mr '70
Living with art. House & Gard 138:40+ S '70
To Moma, from Germany. il Art in Am 58:118-19 My '70

PIENE, Otto
Next the sun. il Time 95:62 My 4 '70 •

PIER glass; story. See Morgan, B.

PIERCE, Albert R.
HUD aid makes the difference. il Am City 85:80-1 Je '70

PIERCE, Arthur
Drawing from the environment. il Sch Arts 70:22-3 D '70

PIERCE, Bill
Bag of gadgets. il Pop Phot 67:96-7+ S '70

PIERCE, Charles H.
Boston's heaviest snowstorm of record. il Weatherwise 22:230-5 D '69

PIERCE, Edith Lovejoy
At Easter; poem. Chr Cent 87:355 Mr 25 '70
Illumination; poem. Chr Cent 87:102 Ja 28 '70
Not one; poem. Chr Cent 87:439 Ap 15 '70
This kneeling-receiving; poem. Chr Cent 87:1179 O 7 '70
Wisdom of God; poem. Chr Cent 87:1554 D 30 '70

PIERCE, Larry M.
Ten quick checks to improve your boat's performance. il Pop Sci 196:76-7 Je '70

PIEROVICH, Andrew L.
School of divinity: St Louis university. Cath World 210:253-5 Mr '70

PIERRE (literary character) See Characters in literature

PIERS
See also
Terminals

PIERS, Fishing. See Fishing docks and piers

PIERSON, Jean
How to stay 10 lbs. thinner. Vogue 155:158-9
Je '70
PIERSON, Robert M.
Sorry, it's charged out. il por Wilson Lib Bul
44:951-6 My '70
PIES. See Pie
PIETROFESA, John J. and Van Hoose, W. H.
Student dissent. Clear House 44:395-400 Mr '70
PIETSCH, William H.
American presence. pors Newsweek 75:49-50
Je 29 '70 *
True believer. S. Alsop. Newsweek 76:104 Jl
13 '70 *
PIEZZI, R. S. and Wurtman, R. J.
Pituitary serotonin content: effects of me-
latonin or deprivation of water. bibliog
il Science 169:285-6 Jl 17 '70
PIG pen; drama. See Bullins. E.
PIGEON man; story. See Woodall, M.
PIGEON population

Control
See Bird populations—Control
PIGEONS
Amateur scientist; the color vision of pigeons
is tested in a Skinner box. J. S. Moran.
il Sci Am 223:124-9 O '70
Orientation by pigeons: is the sun necessary?
W. T. Keeton; reply with rejoinder. K.
Schmidt-Koenig and D. L. McDonald. Sci-
ence 168:152-3 Ap 3 '70
The pill: pigeon control Italian style. il Sci
Digest 67:29-31 Ja '70
1-Δ^9-Trans-tetrahydrocannabinol in pigeons:
tolerance to the behavioral effects. D. E.
McMillan and others. bibliog il Science
169:501-3 Jl 31 '70
PIGMENTS
Creativity of ancient man. E. Keller and J.
Zimmerman. il Chem 43:19-20 Jl '70
See also
Chlorophyll
PIGMENTS (biology)
See also
Bile pigments
Cytochromes
Heme
Lycopene
Melanin
Porphyrins
PIGS. See Swine
PIGS, Wild. See Woods hogs
PIKE, Albert V.
Propagating liliums for scales. il Horticulture
48:28-9 Ap '70
PIKE, Diane (Kennedy)
Bishop Pike's message from beyond the
grave. por Ladies Home J 87:97+ N '70
Search; excerpts. pors Ladies Home J 87:
105-9 Ja; 70-1+ F '70
PIKE, Douglas
Bitter story of Hué; excerpt from The Viet-
cong strategy of terror. Read Digest 97:105-
9 S '70
PIKE, James Albert
Bishop Pike's message from beyond the
grave. D. K. Pike. por Ladies Home J 87:
97+ N '70 *
Bishop Pike's triumph over death; excerpts
from Search. D. K. Pike. il Ladies Home
J 87:70-1+ F '70 *
Desert ordeal of Bishop Pike; excerpts from
Search. D. K. Pike. por Ladies Home J
87:105-9 Ja '70
PIKE, Marian
New way; poem. Chr Cent 87:813 Jl 1 '70
PIKE fishing
Pike by snowmobile. P. D. Lane. il Field &
S 75:36-7+ N '70
Unspoiled pike of Washahigan Lake. G. Crit-
tenden. il Field & S 75:60-1+ My '70
PIKES PEAK auto hill climb. See Automobile
racing
PILATUS aircraft. See Airplane industry and
trade—Switzerland
PILCH, Yosef H. See Ramming, K. P. jt. auth.
PILCHER, Carl B. and others
Saturn's rings: identification of water frost.
bibliog il Science 167:1372-3 Mr 6 '70
PILCHER, Frederick
Observing the asteroids. il R Pop Astron
63:23 Ag '69
—and Boss, L. J.
Geographos swings past earth. il R Pop
Astron 63:11-13 Ag '69
PILE of wood. See Woodpiles
PILEATED woodpeckers. See Woodpeckers
PILEGGI, Nicholas
Occult. il McCalls 97:62-5+ Mr '70
Story of T. il por N Y Times Mag p 12-13+
Mr 29 '70

PILFERING. See Stealing
PILGRIM fathers
Pilgrims all; 350th anniversary celebration. F.
Shemanski. il Schol Teach Jr/Sr High p44-
5 S 21 '70
Pilgrims' odyssey: a new view. G. B. Leon-
ard. il Look 34:22-9 D 1 '70
Pilgrims: unshakable myth. il Time 96:69 N
30 '70
Real Pilgrims. Chr Today 15:28+ N 20 '70
PILGRIM fathers in art
Early depictions of the landing of the Pil-
grims. C. L. Crossman and C. R. Strick-
land. il Antiques 98:776-81 N '70
PILGRIM village. See Plymouth, Mass.
PILGRIMAGE; story. See O'Donnell, T.
PILGRIMS and pilgrimages
Canterbury pilgrims today. R. Wickerd and
F. Wickerd. il Travel 134:34-9+ D '70
Pious come marching in; Italian towns. il
Time 96:96+ S 21 '70
PILGRIMS' progress; story. See Dowty L.
PILIFER. See Sense organs—Insects
PILKINGTON, Betty
Unhappy birthday. Commonweal 93:174-5 N
13 '70
Youth has its day at the UN. Commonweal
92:405-6 Ag 21 '70
PILKINGTON brothers, ltd.
Cracks in the glass. il Newsweek 75:74 Je 1
'70
Glass dynasty lets some light in. il Bsns W
p28 N 28 '70
There's brass in that glass. il Forbes 106:
51-2 N 1 '70
PILL (birth control) See Contraceptives
PILLAGE
Railroads' new worry: looters. il U S News
69:20-1 Jl 21 '70
U.S. and Mexico sign treaty on archeologi-
cal properties: Department announcement,
with text of treaty. Dept State Bul 63:206-7
Ag 17 '70
PILLAI, C. A. Joachim
Roots of clerical restlessness. Cath World 211:
176-9 Jl '70
PILLAI, K. G. J.
Who sets the plane fares? il Nation 210:
177-80 F 16 '70
PILLOW-fighting (game) See Competitions
PILLOWS
Bright pillows for poolside. il Sunset 145:107 O
'70
How to make ribbon-trimmed pillows. il Red-
book 136:124 D '70
Pillows. Good H 171:162 Jl '70
Pillows to prize. il Redbook 134:106-7 Mr '70
PILLSBURY, Charles Alfred
Proxies for protesters. il por Time 95:69
Ja 26 '70
PILLSBURY company
Communicate through your supervisors. L. I.
Gelfand. Harvard Bsns R 48:101-4 N '70
Even computers say, me, too! il Forbes 105:
44+ Ap 1 '70
Pillsbury's best: Committee to end the war.
New Repub 162:8-9 Je 27 '70
PILLSBURY grand national bake-off. See
Cookery—Competitions
PILOT ejection seats, capsules, etc. See Air-
planes—Escape devices
PILOT training. See Air pilots—Training
PILOTS and pilotage
Pencil piloting; practice in plotting. E. A.
Zadig. bibliog il Motor B 125:118-22 Mr '70
See also
Submarine pilots
PILPEL, Harriet F. and Norwick, K. P.
But can you do that? See issues of Publi-
shers' weekly
PILTDOWN forgery
Piltdown man: the realization of fraudulence.
K. P. Oakley and C. P. Groves. bibliog
Science 169:789 Ag 21 '70
PIMLOTT, Douglas H.
Canada in the 70's, make or break. por
Field & S 75:61+ Je '70
PIN-up pals; drama. See Miller, H. L.
PINA, J.
Build Security I. il Pop Electr 32:27-33 Mr
'70
PINCHOT, Gifford
Gifford Pinchot; by H. T. Pinkett. Review
Sat R il 53:74 N 7 '70. P. Borrelli *
He remembers Pinchot. A. Netboy. Am For 76:
47-8 Ag '70 *
Rise of American esthetic conservation. D.
H. Strong. il pors Nat Parks 44:4-9 F '70 *

PINCHOT, Gifford Bryce
Marine farming; with biographical sketch. il Sci Am 223:10, 14-21 bibliog(p 140) D '70
PINCUS, Gerald. See Baumeister, P. jt. auth.
PINCUS, Theodore. See Levy, J. A. jt. auth.
PINDLING, Lynden Oscar
Mr Pindling; interview. New Yorker 46:28-30 O 3 '70

about

Grand Bahama: the big binge is over. il por Bsns W p54-5+ Ag 1 '70 *
PINE, Patricia
Summer is for reading. il Am Ed 6:26-7 Ag '70
What's the IQ of the IQ test? Ed Digest 35:13-16 F '70
You can see the change in Prince Edward. il Am Ed 6:24-8 Jl '70
Young professionals put it all together. il Am Ed 6:16-19 N '70
PINE
Aleppo, a useful pine with many faces. il Sunset 144:240-1 Mr '70
Longleaf pine. B. Horne. il Horticulture 49: 16+ Ja '71
Patriarchs; bristlecone pine, pinus aristata and the western juniper; photographs. Am For 76:32-3 My '70
Story framed in pines; flood prevention projects, Miss. H. R. Williams. il Am For 76: 20-3 Jl '70
Umbrella pine is for the patient. il Sunset 144:220 Ap '70

Diseases and pests

White pine blister rust: simply inherited resistance in sugar pine. B. B. Kinloch, jr. and others. il Science 167:193-5 Ja 9 '70
PINE blister rust. See Pine—Diseases and pests
PINE BLUFF laboratory. See Laboratories. Government
PINE cones, Fossil
One of the world's most remarkable fossils. H. D. Brown. il Hobbies 74:156 F '70
PINEAL body
Adenosine 3',5' -monophosphate in rat pineal gland: increase induced by light. M. S. Ebadi and others. bibliog il Science 170:188-90 O 9 '70
Harderian gland: an extraretinal photoreceptor influencing the pineal gland in neonatal rats. L. Wetterberg and others. bibliog il Science 167:884-5 F 6 '70
Harderian gland: influence on pineal hydroxy-indole-O-methyltransferase activity in neonatal rats. L. Wetterberg and others. bibliog il Science 170:194-6 O 9 '70
Indole metabolism in the pineal gland: a circadian rhythm in N-acetyltransferase. D. C. Klein and J. L. Weller. bibliog il Science 169:1093-5 S 11 '70
Pineal function and oviposition in Japanese quail; superior cervical ganglionectomy and photoperiod. C. L. Ralph and others. bibliog il Science 170:995-7 N 27 '70
Pineal gland: dibutyryl cyclic adenosine monophosphate stimulation of labeled melatonin production. D. C. Klein and others. bibliog il Science 167:1738-40 Mr 27 '70
PINEAPPLE
See also
Cookery—Fruit
PINEAPPLE Poll; ballet. See Ballets—Criticisms
PINEHURST, N.C.
Pinehurst for golf. Southern Pines for horses. S. Birmingham. il Holiday 47:30-5+ Ap '70
PINELLAS COUNTY, Fla.
U.S. journal; attractions. C. Trillin. 46:52-6 Ja 2 '71
PINERO, Sir Arthur Wing
Trelawny of the Wells. Criticism
Commonweal 93:149-50 N 6 '70 *
Nation 211:444 N 2 '70 *
New Repub 163:20 N 28 '70
New Yorker 46:129-30 O 24 '70 *
Newsweek 76:86 O 26 '70 *
Sat R 53:59 N 14 '70 *
PINES, Maya
Jerome Bruner maintains: infants are smarter than anybody thinks. il pors N Y Times Mag p32-3+ N 29 '70
Teach your child to behave morally. Read Digest 97:163-6 O '70
Train yourself to stay well. il McCalls 97:48+ Je '70
PINES. See Pine
PINEY WOODS country life school
Simplest clue. M. Medary. Horn Bk 46:635-41 D '70
PING pong tables. See Tables
PINILLA, Gustavo Rojas. See Rojas Pinilla, G.

PINKERTON, Jan
Wallace Stevens in the tropics: a conservative protest. Yale R 60:215-27 D '70
PINKVILLE massacre. See Vietnamese war, 1957- —Atrocities—My Lai massacre
PINNEY, Doris
Youngsters are where the action is! il Pop Phot 67:128-9+ D '70
PINNEY, Roy
Filming at the zoo. il Pop Phot 67:116-17+ O '70
PINNOCK, Clark H.
Harrowing of heaven. Chr Today 14:7-8 Je 19 '70
PINOCCHIO; drama. See Mahlmann, L.
PINOLE, Calif.
Rattlesnakes of Pinole. il Time 95:15 Je 29 '70
PINSKER, Harold, and others
Habituation and dishabituation of the gill-withdrawal reflex in aplysia. bibliog il Science 167:1740-2 Mr 27 '70
PINSON, Penelope
(comp) Books for parents. See issues of Parents' magazine & better family living
PINSON, W. H. jr. See Hurley, P. M. jt. auth.
PINTER, Harold
Landscape. Criticism
New Repub 162:20+ Ap 25 '70 *
New Yorker 46:84 Ap 11 '70 *
Sat R 53:16 Ap 25 '70 *
Roomer, T. E. Kalem. por Time 96:60+ O 12 '70 *
Silence. Criticism
New Repub 162:20 Ap 25 '70 *
New Yorker 46:84 Ap 11 '70 *
Sat R 53:16 Ap 25 '70 *
PINUS aristata. See Pine *
PINZA, Ezio
Records. Opera N 34:34-5 Ja 31 '71
PION cancer therapy. See Cancer—Therapy
PIONEER life. See Frontier and pioneer life
PIONEER probes. See Space probes
PIONEER systems, inc.
Dynamic growth companies. il Nations Bsns 58:36-8 O '70
PIONEERS
Pioneers in Massachusetts. F. L. Phelps. il Américas 22:21-30 F '70
See also
Frontier and pioneer life—United States
PIONS. See Mesons
PIOUS, D. A. See Adman, R. jt. auth.
PIPE joints
Extra steps cut complaints on two sewer jobs; Greater Vancouver district. il Am City 85:68-9 Jl '70
PIPE laying
Extra steps cut complaints on two sewer jobs; Greater Vancouver district. il Am City 85:68-9 Jl '70
Fast way to put pipe under walks and driveways. il Pop Mech 133:183 Mr '70
How to make an outfall in San Francisco Bay mud. R. G. Bezzant. il Am City 85:83-5 My '70
Huge sewage outfall shipped in 80' lengths; Rochester, N.Y. il Am City 85:24 S '70
Mile of sewer in five hours. il Am City 85: 92 N '70
Out-of-the-ordinary sewer job; Santa Monica, Calif. il Am City 85:84-5 Ap '70
Tunneling solves tough sewer-construction problem; Little Rock, Ark. T. W. Clapham. il Am City 85:105+ F '70
PIPE lines
See also
Petroleum—Pipe lines
Water pipes
Cleaning
See also
Water pipes—Cleaning
PIPE organ. See Organ
PIPE smoking. See Smoking
PIPER, Thomas E.
Case of the embattled banker. il Harvard Bsns R 48:144-6+ N '70
PIPER, William Thomas
From the tower. R. L. Collins. Flying 86:4 Ap '70
PIPER aircraft corporation
Piper faces fiscal, internal hurdles. C. E. Schneider. Aviation W 93:67-9 O 19 '70
PIPES, Donald E.
Everyone into the pool, and a pool for everyone. il Am City 85:91-2 N '70
PIPES, Richard Edgar
Historian's reflections; address, March 18, 1970. Vital Speeches 36:729-32 S 15 '70

PIPES
See also
Water pipes
PIPES, Plastic
Brewster's pipe scheme; to carry rods safely in boat or canoe. H. G. Tapply. il Field & S 75:46 Jl '70
Plastic piping makes you an instant plumber. R. Day. il Pop Mech 134:172-5+ S '70
PIPESTEM resort area. See Recreation areas—West Virginia
PIRANDELLO, Luigi
Pirandello old and new. R. S. Lopez. Yale R 60:228-40 D '70 *
PIRANHAS
Seeking the truth about the feared piranha. P. A. Zahl. il por Nat Geog 138:714-33 N '70
Who's watching whom? il Sci Digest 67:59 Ja '70
World's worst animals; excerpts from The Amazon. R. Furneaux. il Horizon 12:112-17 Wint '70
PIRATE television. See Television stations, Illegal
PIRATES (baseball) See Baseball clubs
PIRELLI, Thomas R.
How a tiny store keeps the books. il por Bsns W p80-1 Ja 9 '71 *
PIROSHKI. See Cookery, Russian
PIRTLE, Caleb
Big Texas Thicket. il Travel 134:28-33 S '70
PISANO, Giovanni
Giovanni Pisano, by M. Ayrton. Review
Sat R il 53:29-31 My 9 '70. J. White *
PISAR, Samuel
East-West trade: wielding a tender sword. il por Time 96:88+ N 16 '70 *
PISGAH national forest, N.C. See National forests
PISMO clams. See Clams
PISTOLS
Four-barreled handgun. K. Warner. il Pop Mech 134:244 O '70
Highland pistols. C. Worman. il Hobbies 75:158-9 Je '70
Springfield "trapdoor" pistols. C. Worman. il Hobbies 75:158-9 Jl '70
See also
Revolvers
PISTON airplane engines See Airplane engines
PISTONS
What about forged pistons? opinions of four manufacturers; ed. by J. Dianna. il Hot Rod 23:84-7 F '70
PIT barbecues. See Barbecue cookery
PITCH, Musical. See Musical pitch
PITCHERS
Victorian ice water pitchers. V. Schnadig. il Hobbies 75:121-2 Ap '70
PITCHERS, Baseball. See Baseball players
PITNEY-Bowes, inc.
Life begins at forty, for a corporation. J. O. Nicklis. il Nations Bsns 58:100-1 Ja '70
Walter H. Wheeler of Pitney-Bowes; interview. W. H. Wheeler. por Nations Bsns 58:72-8 F '70
PITT, William
Younger Pitt, by. J. Ehrman. Review
New Repub 162:21-2 Ja 31 '70. P. Gay
PITTMAN, Joanna, and Thomasson, Clyde
Local association of the month. Todays Ed 59:80 O '70
PITTS, John
Genius of Charles Haddon Spurgeon. Chr Today 14:6-8 F 27 '70
PITTSBURGH Pirates (baseball) See Baseball clubs
PITTSBURGH
City planning
Lighting on the mall. il Am City 85:116 Ja '70
Specter of an unbuilt road; decay of Pittsburgh neighborhood along I-79 planned route. il Bsns W p104+ My 2 '70
Housing
Second East Hills park, Pittsburgh, Pa. il Arch Rec 147:88-9 mid-My '70
Lighting
Lighting reflects a city's image. il Am City 85:112 F '70
Music
Report:
Madama Butterfly. R. Croan. Opera N 35:29 D 5 '70
See also
Pittsburgh opera company

Transit systems
Transit expressway gets green light. Am City 85:50 Ap '70
Water supply
Curious-yellow. J. D. Beck. il Am City 85:73-6 Mr '70
PITTSBURGH Catholic. See Catholic press
PITTSBURGH opera company
Report:
Barber of Seville. C. Apone. Opera N 34:32 Ja 24 '70
Montemezzi's Amore dei tre re. R. Croan. il Opera N 34:25 My 16 '70
Tosca. R. Croan. Opera N 34:30 Mr 14 '70
PITTSBURGH Penguins (hockey team) See Hockey teams
PITTSBURGH symphony orchestra
Music to my ears; concert performance of Bluebeard's castle. Sat R 53:58 F 14 '70
Musical events; concert in Carnegie Hall. W. Sargeant. New Yorker 46:180-1 N 21 '70
PITUITARY body
Adenohypophysial transmembrane potentials: polarity reversal by elevated external potassium ion concentration. J. V. Milligan and J. Kraicer. bibliog il Science 167:182-4 Ja 9 '70
DNA synthesis in the anterior pituitary of the male rat: effect of castration and photoperiod. W. C. Hymer and others. bibliog il Science 167:1629-31 Mr 20 '70
Pituitary serotonin contents: effects of melatonin or deprivation of water. R. S. Piezzi and R. J. Wurtman. bibliog il Science 169:285-6 Jl 17 '70
Prolactin localization in the primate pituitary by immunofluorescence. D. C. Herbert and T. Hayashida. bibliog il Science 169:378-9 Jl 24 '70
See also
Gonadotropins
Thyrotropin
PITUITARY hormones
Brain enhancement in tadpoles: increased DNA concentration after somatotrophin or prolactin. R. K. Hunt and M. Jacobson. bibliog il Science 170:342-4 O 16 '70
Controlling human growth: synthesis of somatotropin. por Time 97:35 Ja 18 '71
Giants and midgets. A. J. Snider. il Sci Digest 69:62-6 Ja '71
Primary structures of human pituitary growth hormone and sheep pituitary lactogenic hormone compared. T. A. Bewley and C. H. Li. bibliog il Science 168:1361-2 Je 12 '70
PITZ, Henry C.
Morris Blackburn back on nature's trail. il por Am Artist 34:20-4+ N '70
Oliver Grimley; pen draughtsman. il pors Am Artist 34:28-34 Ja '70
PITZER, Kenneth S.
Brief encounter. Newsweek 76:77 Jl 6 '70 *
Stanford: why Pitzer resigned as president. P. M. Boffey. por Science 169:561-2+ Ag 7 '70 *
PIVEN, Frances Fox
Militant civil servants in New York city. il por Trans-Action 7:24-8+ N '69
PIZER, Evan F. See Weiss, H. H. jt. auth.
PLACE for Polly; drama. See Coleman, L.
PLACE mats. See Table mats, tiles, etc.
PLACE names. See Names, Geographical
PLACE without doors; drama. See Duras, M.
PLACENTA
Placental transfer of a substituted pteridine from fetus to mother. J. L. McNay and P. G. Dayton. bibliog il Science 167:988-90 F 13 '70
PLACES of retirement. See Retirement, Places of
PLAGEMANN, Bentz
Crisis; story. Good H 170:80-1 F '70
PLAGIARISM
Thomas Mann makes the top forty; pop lyricists steal from classics. R. Hanser. Sat R 53:6-8 Mr 21 '70
PLAGIOCLASES. See Feldspar
PLAIN song. See Chants (Gregorian, plain, etc)
PLAINS
See also
Prairies
Tundras
PLAMONDON, Antoine Sébastien
Two Quebec painters. S. B. Sherrill. il Antiques 98:674+ N '70 *
PLAMONDON, George J.
Build an electrolytic restorer. il Pop Electr 33:46-50 O '70

PLANTING of corn. See Corn—Seeding
PLANTING plans and tables. See Gardening—Planting plans and tables
PLANTMILK. See Milk substitutes
PLANTS
Good plants for hot dry places. R. Webber. Home Gard 57:50-1 Ag '70
Green survival; ability of plants to counter environmental degradation. R. F. Lederer. il Parks & Rec 5:34-6 O '70
Hard-to-find plants go on sale in San Francisco; third annual plant sale. il Sunset 144:244 Mr '70
Have you thanked a green plant today? way plants help to improve our environment. R. Rodale. il Org Gard & Farm 17:27-30 My '70
[Month] in your garden. See issues of Sunset
More new plants for 1970. il Horticulture 48:25 F '70
New plants to grow in 1970. il Home Gard 57:30-1+ Ja '70
New plants to grow for 1971. M. C. Ohlander. il Home Gard 58:34-42+ Ja '71
Plant collector's corner:
Succulent shrub, the spurge olive, a native iris, a carpeting daisy. il Sunset 145:246-7 N '70
Plant ideas to help make a dream garden. Home Gard 57:9-16 D '70
See also
Annuals (plants)
Berry bearing plants
Bulbs
Fertilization of plants
Flowers
Herbs
Perennials
Pollen
Succulent plants
Transplanting
Weeds
Woody plants
also names of plants, e.g. Sunflowers; also headings beginning Plant

Absorption of water
See also
Plants—Water requirements

All America selections
All-star flowers for 1970. G. Logsdon. il Farm J 94:50 Ja '70

Breeding
See Plant breeding

Chemical analysis
Put plant analysis to work. J. B. Jones, jr. and others. Suc Farm 68:B16 N '70

Cold resistance
See Plants—Frost resistance

Disease and pest resistance
Not many pests in my patch; using pest-repellent plants. R. Tirrell. il Org Gard & Farm 17:60-3 My '70
White pine blister rust: simply inherited resistance in sugar pine. B. B. Kinloch, jr. and others. il Science 167:193-5 Ja 9 '70

Diseases and pests
How weather affects plant diseases. Suc Farm 68:B10 N '70
Man-made plant diseases. C. E. Yarwood. bibliog Science 168:218-20 Ap 10 '70
Plants vs. pests: this plant wins; marigolds reduce nematodes. Sunset 144:229 Ap '70
Why we need disease. R. Rodale. il Org Gard & Farm 17:21-4 Jl '70
See also
Plant lice
Tumors, Plant

Drought resistance
Plants that don't get thirsty. R. J. Wyndham. Org Gard & Farm 17:97 D '70

Evolution
Facultative gymnosperm from an interspecific cotton hybrid. V. G. Meyer. bibliog il Science 169:886-8 Ag 28 '70

Fertilization
See Fertilization of plants

Frost resistance
Cold resistance and injury in woody plants. C. J. Weiser. bibliog il Science 169:1269-78 S 25 '70

Growth
See Growth (plants)

Hardiness
See also
Plants—Drought resistance
Plants—Frost resistance

Metabolism
See also
Plants—Respiration

Nutrition
Nutrient balance is important for crops, too! Suc Farm 68:B1 S '70
See also
Plants, Effect of calcium on

Protection
See Plants, Protection of

Pruning
See Pruning

Purchasing
Native plant sale, October 24 in Berkeley. il Sunset 145:214 O '70

Reproduction
See also
Apogamy

Resistance to insects
See Plants—Disease and pest resistance

Respiration
Reversal of photosynthesis; photorespiration. il Chem 43:23 F '70

Transpiration
Leaf hydraulic system: rapid epidermal and stomatal responses to changes in water supply. K. Raschke. bibliog il Science 167:189-91 Ja 9 '70
See also
Plants—Water requirements

Water requirements
Maize leaf elongation: continuous measurements and close dependence on plant water status. T. C. Hsiao and others. bibliog il Science 168:590-1 My 1 '70
PLANTS, Cover. See Cover plants
PLANTS, Edible
Cactus as food. L. P. Bell. Horticulture 48:8+ F '70
Food plants America gave the world. B. Black. il Horticulture 48:24-7+ Jl '70
Stalking the food for four wild feasts; with recipes. E. Gibbons. il House & Gard 138:149:51+ O '70
Wild fruits along country roadsides. I. D. Jolly. il Horticulture 48:32-3 Jl '70
See also
Food, Wild
Greens, Edible
Vegetables
PLANTS, Effect of air pollution on
City v. forest; smog from Los Angeles killing ponderosa pines. il Time 95:49 Ap 13 '70
Photochemical oxidants: effect on starch hydrolysis in leaves. G. P. Hanson and W. S. Stewart. bibliog il Science 168:1223-4 Je 5 '70
Quiet killer; ponderosa pine trees being killed in San Bernardino national forest. E. Hay. il Am For 76:16-19 Ap '70
PLANTS, Effect of aluminum on
Solution to aluminum toxicity. J. Williams. Suc Farm 68:no5 B12 Mr '70
PLANTS, Effect of calcium on
Phosphorus and lime needed for top yields. Suc Farm 68:C4 Ag '70
Salt toleration by plants: enhancement with calcium. P. A. LaHaye and E. Epstein; discussion. bibliog Science 167:1387-8 Mr 6 '70
PLANTS, Effect of climate on
How weather affects plant diseases. Suc Farm 68:B10 N '70
PLANTS, Effect of drought on. See Plants—Drought resistance
PLANTS, Effect of gravity on. See Geotropism (botany)
PLANTS, Effect of lead on
Lead effects on corn mitochondrial respiration. D. E. Koeppe and R. J. Miller. bibliog il Science 167:1376-8 Mr 6 '70
PLANTS, Effect of light on
Corn research worth watching. Suc Farm 68:C12 Je '70
Light could be limiting your corn yields. C. E. Sommers. il Suc Farm 68:no5 24-5+ Mr '70
See also
Artificial light gardening
Fungi, Effect of light on
Phototropism
PLANTS, Effect of noise on. See Plants, Effect of sound on

PLANTS, Effect of ozone on
Ozone uptake by bean leaves. S. Rich and others. bibliog il Science 169:79-80 Jl 3 '70
PLANTS, Effect of phosphorus on
Phosphorus and lime needed for top yields. Suc Farm 68:C4 Ag '70
PLANTS, Effect of propane on
How propane looks now. Suc Farm 68:B7 My '70
PLANTS, Effect of radiation on
Effects of pollution on the structure and physiology of ecosystems. G. M. Woodwell. bibliog il Science 168:429-33 Ap 24 '70
Woody plants: changes in survival in response to long-term (8 years) chronic gamma irradiation. A. H. Sparrow and others. bibliog il Science 169:1082-4 S 11 '70
PLANTS, Effect of salt on
Salt toleration by plants: enhancement with calcium. P. A. LaHaye and E. Epstein; discussion. bibliog Science 167:1387-8 Mr 6 '70
PLANTS, Effect of sound on
What noise does to plants. il Sci Digest 68:60-1 D '70
See also
Plants, Effect of ultrasonic waves on
PLANTS, Effect of temperature on
See also
Plants—Frost resistance
PLANTS, Effect of ultrasonic waves on
Chant of the plant; G. Milstein's disc of vibrations. il por Newsweek 76:82 Ag 17 '70
PLANTS, Flowering of
See also
Fruit-bud development
PLANTS, Food. See Plants, Edible
PLANTS, Fossil. See Paleobotany
PLANTS, Growth. See Growth (plants)
PLANTS, Hallucinogenic. See Hallucination and illusion producing plants
PLANTS, Indoor. See House plants
PLANTS, Industrial. See Industrial buildings
PLANTS, Medicinal. See Botany, Medical
PLANTS, Ornamental
See also
Asparagus
Berry bearing plants
PLANTS, Poisonous. See Poisonous plants
PLANTS, Potted
How to care for the flowering plants. House & Gard 138:100-1, 248-9 N '70
How to create a portable garden. E. McDonald. il House B 112:82-5 Je '70
Put them in special pots, then brings them indoors. il Sunset 144:74-5 F '70
Slick tricks for cold-country gardening. L. Hedla. il Home Gard 58:54-5+ Ja '71
Unusual colorful holiday plants. M. J. Kartuz. il Horticulture 48:26-7 D '70
See also
House plants
PLANTS, Protection of
Fall care of roses. K. P. Jones. il Horticulture 48:22-3+ O '70
Here's a way to plant ground covers securely on really steep hillsides; paper collars. il Sunset 145:212 O '70
How I protect my harvest from the birds. M. L. Coonse. Home Gard 57:74 Ja '70
Protect plants now for a more beautiful springtime. il Home Gard 57:44-5 N '70
Protecting shrubs and plants in cold weather. Good H 171:168-9 N '70
Wind-breaks for vegetable protection. F. D. Schales. il Org Gard & Farm 17:66-7 Je '70
See also
Frost protection
Mulching
Windbreaks
PLANTS, Sex in
See also
Fungi, Sex in
PLANTS, Shade
Shaded garden. D. A. Brown. il Home Gard 57:20-7 Jl '70
Shademaker and shade plants. il Home Gard 57:48-9 My '70
Two plants for shade: hosta and caladium. il Home Gard 57:62 Ap '70
PLANTS, Space arrangement of
Have narrow rows been oversold? interviews. ed. by C. E. Sommers. D. Duvick; W. Colville. il pors Suc Farm 68:28-31+ S '70
PLANTS, State. See State flowers
PLANTS, Training of
How to prune and train grape vines for good looks and a good crop. il Sunset 144:182-5 F '70
Informal espaliers. il Sunset 145:64-7 S '70
PLANTS, Water requirements of. See Plants—Water requirements

PLANTS as gifts
Dwarf citrus as gifts. il Sunset 145:174 D '70
Gardener's guide to holiday plants. R. M. Peters. il Home Gard 57:38-44 D '70
Plant gift giving can be an art. il Sunset 145:76-8 D '70
Unusual colorful holiday plants. M. J. Kartuz. il Horticulture 48:26-7 D '70
PLANTS in design. See Design, Decorative—Plant forms
PLANTS in house decoration
Flowers and prints in the apartment of Mr and Mrs John C. Moore III. il House & Gard 137:50-3 F '70
Joy of living with flowers and art: the very personal collection of Enid Haupt. il House & Gard 138:70-9 D '70
Miniature hillside garden; the personal garden of Margaret Willaumez. il House & Gard 137:96-9 Ja '70
Put life in any room with a rock-garden waterfall. R. Capotosto. il Pop Mech 134: 148-51 D '70
PLANZ, Allen
Comment. R. Watson. Poetry 117:208-9 D '70 •
PLAQUES, plaquettes
Make a birthdate plaque. il Design 72:20-1 Fall '70
PLASMA (ionized gases)
Alcator, son of Tokamak. Sci Am 222:60 Mr '70
Controlled fusion: plasma heating with lasers. R. Holcomb. Science 167:1112-13 F 20 '70; Reply. J. M. Thorne. 169:893-4 Ag 28 '70
From the H-bomb: power without pollution; with editorial comment. il Bsns W p80+, 134 S 12 '70
Getting on the Tokamak bandwagon. D. E. Thomsen. il Sci N 97:373-4 Ap 11 '70
Hot new promise of thermonuclear power. T. Alexander. il Fortune 81:94-7+ Je '70
MIT Tokomak has anomalous-resistivity heating and 130 kG; Alcator. G. B. Lubkin. il Phys Today 23:55-6 Je '70
Mach 3,200 and fusion. il Sci N 98:217 S 12 '70
Plasma: the lab toy that grew up. il Bsns W p74+ Ag 22 '70
Practice leads theory. il Sci N 98:380 N 14 '70
Scyllac: toward pulsed fusion. D. E. Thomsen. il por Sci N 98:321-3 O 17 '70
See also
Van Allen radiation belts
PLASMA fractination. See Blood—Analysis and chemistry
PLASMA lipoproteins. See Blood—Proteins
PLASMA proteins. See Blood—Proteins
PLASMINOGEN
Plasminogen: purification from human plasma by affinity chromatography. D. G. Deutsch and E. T. Mertz. bibliog il Science 170:1095-6 D 4 '70
PLASMODIUM (parasite)
Altered dihydrofolate reductase associated with drug-resistance transfer between rodent plasmodia. R. Ferone and others. bibliog il Science 167:1263-4 F 27 '70
Clock of the malaria parasite. F. Hawking. il Sci Am 222:123-31 Je '70
Fine structure of the exoerythrocytic stage of plasmodium cynomolgi. T. Sodeman and others. bibliog il Science 170:340 O 16 '70
Malaria resistance: artificial induction with a partially purified plasmodial fraction. L. E. D'Antonio and others. bibliog il Science 168:1117-18 My 29 '70
Plasmodium falciparum in owl monkeys: drug resistance and chloroquine binding capacity. C. D. Fitch. bibliog il Science 169: 289-90 Jl 17 '70
PLASTER casts
Ghost maker; G. Segal. il por Time 95:72 My 11 '70
Revival! il House B 112:73-3 F '70
PLASTER work (craft)
Making plaster bats. P. Rothenberg. il Ceram Mo 18:21-3 D '70
PLASTIC airplanes. See Airplanes, Light—Materials
PLASTIC bags
Inflate and float; the Water walk peoplesized plastic bag. il Life 68:76-9 Ap 10 '70
PLASTIC boats. See Boats—Materials
PLASTIC bubbles. See Bubbles
PLASTIC carving. See Carving (art industries)
PLASTIC cement. See Cements, Adhesive
PLASTIC containers. See Containers
PLASTIC furniture. See Furniture, Plastic
PLASTIC garbage. See Refuse and refuse disposal

PLASTIC greenhouses. See Greenhouses
PLASTIC hearts. See Hearts, Artificial
PLASTIC mulch. See Mulching
PLASTIC pipes. See Pipes, Plastic
PLASTIC product industry. See Plastics industry and trade
PLASTIC roofs. See Roofs
PLASTIC sculpture
Fantastics on plastics. il Design 71:36-7 mid-Wint '70
PLASTIC surgery. See Surgery, Plastic
PLASTIC teeth. See Teeth, Artificial
PLASTIC windows. See Windows, Plastic
PLASTICIZERS
Plasticizers from plastic devices: extraction, metabolism, and accumulation by biological systems. R. J. Jaeger and R. J. Rubin. bibliog il Science 170:460-2 O 23 '70
PLASTICS
Fantastic plastic light shows, with polarizers. R. Kouhoupt. il Pop Sci 197:73+ Jl '70
Getting along without plastic. il Org Gard & Farm 17:86-8+ My '70
Plastic for ecologists; research on means to decompose plastics. Time 95:86 My 11 '70
See also
Plasticizers
Polymers
Resinous products

Reinforcement
See Plastics, Reinforced
PLASTICS, Laminated
How to work with plastic laminates. H. Wicks. il Pop Mech 133:154-9+ Mr '70
PLASTICS, Reinforced
How tough can a plastic get? il por Bsns W p48 Ap 11 '70
PLASTICS as an art form
Inflate and float; the Water walk people sized plastic bag. il Life 68:76-9 Ap 10 '70
Maurice Heaton's laminated panels; ed. by T. Bayne. M. Heaton. il Craft Horiz 30:24-5+ Ag '70
PLASTICS as art material
Age of lucite dawns in Sacramento; sculpture by B. Beasley. E. Hotaling. il pors Art N 69:50-1+ My '70
Making the gallery scene. B. Wasserman. il Sch Arts 69:32-5 Je '70
Painting a watercolor in acrylic. A. J. Barbour. il Am Artist 34:48-53+ Je '70
Painting watercolors in acrylic; excerpts from Acrylic watercolor painting. W. Blake. il Am Artist 34:36-41+ D '70
PLASTICS in art. See Plastics as art material
PLASTICS in building
Flowing space that's sprayed on burlap; Littlejohn's house in Maple Plain, Minn. il Life 68:64-7 Mr 13 '70
How to work with plastic laminates. H. Wicks. il Pop Mech 133:154-9+ Mr '70
PLASTICS industry and trade
Plastics: promises, promises. L. Rich. il Duns 95:59-60+ Ja '70

Wages and hours
Wages in miscellaneous plastics products plants. S. L. Mason. il Mo Labor R 93:41-2 O '70
PLASTICS work
Chez Mlle: making it clear; do-it-yourself plexiglas. P. Bartlett. il Mlle 71:76-7 My '70
Good tricks for bending sheet acrylics. J. Hand. il Pop Sci 196:94-5 Ap '70
How to make a plastic cube. il House & Gard 138:91 Jl '70
How to work with plexiglass. W. C. Leckey. il Pop Mech 133:176-80 Je '70

Projects
Three pop-together home accessories; wine rack, pipe rack, and lamp. A. J. Hand. il Pop Sci 197:90-1+ N '70
PLASTIDS
Multiple origin for plastids and mitochondria. P. H. Raven. bibliog Science 169:641-6 Ag 14 '70; Reply. D. L. Taylor. 170:1332 D 18 '70
PLATA, Rio de la
Step toward progress; survey of five-country River plate basin. Américas 22:1 Je '70
PLATE RIVER. See Plata, Rio de la
PLATE tectonics. See Geology, Structural
PLATED silverware. See Silverware
PLATES (dishes) See Pottery

PLATFORMS, Moving. See Moving platforms
PLATH, Sylvia
Gigolo. poem. New Yorker 46:54 N 21 '70
PLATING
See also
Electroplating
PLATT, J. J.
Doing the duck crawl. il pors Outdoor Life 146:42-3+ D '70
PLATT, John
Crisis of transformation. Cur 115:3-17 F '70
Hierarchical growth. Bul Atom Sci 26:2-4+ N '70
PLATT, Rutherford
Those remarkable two-animal animals. il Read Digest 97:33-4+ Jl '70
PLATT NATIONAL PARK
Oklahoma's wee wonder. B. Thomas. il Travel 133:40-3 Mr '70
PLAUT, James
Osaka fair: Expo '70. il Craft Horiz 30:12-13 My '70
PLAY
How much and what kinds of play do babies need? B. Spock. Redbook 136:31+ D '70
Play and ritual. C. J. McNaspy. America 122:426-8 Ap 18 '70
See also
Childrens amusements
Sports
PLAY accidents. See Accidents
PLAY apparatus. See Playgrounds—Equipment
PLAY by Aleksandr Solzhenitsyn; drama. See Solzhenitsyn, A. I.
PLAY houses. See Playhouses
PLAY production. See Theatrical production and direction
PLAY schools
See also
Nursery schools
PLAY streets. See New York (city)—Recreation
PLAY writing. See Drama—Technique
PLAY yards. See Playgrounds, Home
PLAYBOY (periodical)
Bunny hunting. il pors Newsweek 75:71 Mr 2 '70
Hugh Hefner's jet black bunny in the sky. H. Ehrlich. il pors Look 34:62-5 Je 2 '70
Male and female; war between the sexes in the media. il Newsweek 75:74+ My 18 '70
What Playboy doesn't know about women could fill a book; with interview, ed. by G. Steinem. H. Hefner. il por McCalls 98:76-7+ O '70
PLAYBOY building. See Chicago—Buildings
PLAYBOY of the western world; drama. See Synge, J. M.
PLAYER, Gary
Gary's garrison: bogeymen and bodyguards. W. Bingham. il por Sports Illus 32:60+ Mr 23 '70
PLAYGROUND and recreation association of America. See National recreation and park association
PLAYGROUND apparatus. See Playgrounds—Equipment
PLAYGROUNDS
Double-duty for parking lots. P. Hogan il Parks & Rec 5:51+ My '70
Parks and recreation. See issues of American city

Equipment
Designing playground equipment. R. L. Asch. il Sch Arts 69:16-17 Ap '70
For preschoolers: walkway, poles, slide, shelter; Eugene, Ore. il Sunset 144:134 Mr '70
Make a playground a challenge; use of wood structures in Maryville, Tenn. parks. F. T. Bradley. il Am City 85:28+ Ap '70
Students design a play machine; New Haven, Conn. il Am City 85:28 N '70
Students repaint playground equipment; Ector County-City of Odessa parks and recreation department. J. H. Tschauner. Parks & Rec 5:55 Mr '70
We tried new types of playground equipment; Miami Beach. Fla. J. Noody. il Am City 85:22 F '70
See also
Swings
PLAYGROUNDS, Home
Art of play yard planning. Sunset 145:84-5 S '70

Equipment
Please, father, check the gym set! il Consumer Bul 53:22 Jl '70
See also
Playhouses

PLAYHOUSES
Boys command topside, the girls are first below. il Sunset 145:68-9 Ag '70
Build this back-yard beauty. B. Snyder. il Pop Mech 133:110-13 My '70
For a quick getaway there's a slide tunnel and a fireman's pole. il Sunset 144:60-1 Ja '70
Six youngsters put a new playhouse over the jumps. il Sunset 145:72-3 S '70

PLAYING cards. See Cards

PLAYROOMS
Built-ins kids like. J. Gillies. il Farm J 94: 78-9 F '70

PLAYTEN, Alice
Awake and sing. il pors Time 96:41 Jl 27 '70 *

PLAYTHINGS. See Toys

PLAYWRITING. See Drama—Technique

PLAZA, Galo
In tune with the times; remarks, February 27, 1970. Américas 22:44 Ap '70
New OAS. por Américas 22:2-3 Ap '70
On the import quota system; excerpt from address, April 23, 1970. Américas 22:1 My '70
On the Inter-American juridical level; excerpts from address, August 31, 1970. Américas 22:1 O '70
Opening to the future. il America 122:96-8 Ja 31 '70

PLAZAS
Back Bay's sedate square; Boston's rebuilt Copley square. il Arch Forum 133:60-3 O '70
Boston's open center: City hall plaza. J. M. Dixon. il Arch Forum 132:24-31 Je '70
Giving the piazzas back to the people. il Bsns W p 126 Je 27 '70

PLEAS (criminal procedure)
More justice to come? the use of the guilty plea. G. L. Hallworth. America 122:390-1 Ap 11 '70

PLEASANT HILL, Ky. See Shakertown, Ky.

PLEASURE
See also
Joy

PLEDGE of allegiance. See Loyalty. Oaths of

PLEISTOCENE period. See Paleontology—Pleistocene

PLEROMA (flower) See Princess flower

PLESSEY company, ltd.
American challenge, from Plessey. J. Ross-Skinner. il Duns 96:42-4 N '70

PLESSEY, Inc.
Bundle from America; acquisition of alloys. por Time 96:60-1 Ag 10 '70

PLIMPTON, George
Meet Mr Twinkletoes and his friends. il por Sports Illus 33:22-4+ O 12 '70
Rubies and diamonds. Sports Illus 32:24-6 F 9 '70
Watching the man in the mirror. il por Sports Illus 33:80-3+ N 23 '70

about
George Plimpton: the professional amateur; Time essay. G. Clarke. il pors Time 96:66-7 S 21 '70 *

PLIMPTON, Susan W.
New greenhouse, the second time around. il Horticulture 48:42-3+ Mr '70
Unusual plants for indoor gardens. Horticulture 48:28 F '70

PLOSS, Ken
On the boards. por Dance Mag 45:20 Ja '71 *

PLOTS (drama, novel, etc)
See also
Dramas—Criticisms, plots, etc.
Moving picture plays—Criticisms, plots, etc.
Moving pictures—Themes

PLOTNIK, Arthur
(ed) Librarian and the teaching of reading. bibliog il Wilson Lib Bul 45:239-307 N '70

PLOTTING (graphs) See Graphic methods

PLOWDEN, David
See America first. il Audubon 72:46-51 Jl '70

PLOWING. See Tillage

PLOWS
Why slow down the planter with chemicals? il Farm J 94:20-1 Je '70
See also
Snow plows

PLOWSHARE project. See Atomic blasting

PLUG cutters. See Cutting tools

PLUGS (fishing lures) See Fishing lures, flies, etc.

PLUMB, Barbara
Home. See issues of New York times magazine to April 5, 1970
Plumb line. Am Home 73:40+ S; 50+ O; 32-3 N; 31+ D '70

PLUMB, J. H.
Genealogy: the well-pruned family tree. il Horizon 12:118-20 Wint '70
King's new clothes. il Horizon 12:12-13 Sum '70
Most deadly games. il Horizon 11:52-3 Aut '69
Perspective. See occasional issues of Saturday review to August 1, 1970.
Public and private Pepys. por Sat R 53:29-31+ O 24 '70
Victorians unbuttoned. il Horizon 11:16-35 Aut '69
Were they right? il Horizon 12:40-1 Aut '70

PLUMBING
Now, an indestructible water valve. S. J. Howard. il Pop Mech 134:147 D '70

Maintenance and repair
How to fix those newfangled faucets. S. J. Howard. il Pop Mech 134:189-92 N '70

PLUNKETT, Eugenia
Night between Springfield and Boston; poem. Am Scholar 40:64-5 Wint '70

PLUNKETT, Jim
Arms against the ogres. D. Jenkins. il Sports Illus 33:28-30+ D 21 '70 *
Indian giver. H. L. Masin. il por Sr Schol 97: 18 N 2 '70 *
Saturday's hero. il por Time 96:78 D 7 '70
Subject is roses. il por Newsweek 76:72 O 12 '70 *
Upside down and over with the coast crazies. A. Rosenbaum. il Sports Illus 33:48-9 O 19 '70 *

PLURALISTIC university. See College education

PLUTO (planet), Transit of
Pluto will transit two galaxies in October. J. W. Young. il Sky & Tel 40:245 O '70

PLUTONIUM
Catch 24,400; or, Plutonium is my favorite element; fire at Rocky Flats plant. R. Rapoport. il Ramp Mag 8:16-21 My '70
Nuclear materials: security; address, May 25, 1970. C. Hosmer. Vital Speeches 36: 636-8 Ag 1 '70
Plutonium and formation of the solar system. Chem 43:28 Ap '70
Plutonium; economy of the future; address, October 5, 1970. G. T. Seaborg. Vital Speeches 37:69-75 N 15 '70
Plutonium, the lively element (cont) J. M. Cleveland. bibliog il por Chem 43:10-13 Ja '70

PLYMOUTH, Mass.
Pilgrims all; 350th anniversary celebration. F. Shemanski. il Schol Teach Jr/Sr High p44-5 S 21 '70

PLYWOOD
Plywood grades, and those specials. Bet Hom & Gard 48:98+ F '70

PNEUMAN, G. W.
Chromosphere-Corona transition region. il Sky & Tel 39:148-51 Mr '70

PNEUMONIA
Winter's unvanquished foe: pneumonia. B. Goodheart. Todays Health 48:50-2+ N '70

Vaccines
Closing in on three killers. il Bsns W p 107 O 24 '70
Vaccine for a pneumonia. Sci N 98:317-18 O 17 '70

PNOMPENH, Cambodia
Pattern of terror. il Time 96:40 D 14 '70
Phnom-Penh: what is going on? D. Neff. Time 96:24 Jl 6 '70

POACHING
Case of the outfoxed poacher. Cons 24:40 F '70
Poacher hunt; Serengeti National Park. J. Brenner. il Newsweek 76:38+ Ag 31 '70
Wild-goose man; M. Thorpe of Lincolnshire, England. por Time 96:48-9 D 21 '70

POAGE, William Robert
Time to say no to big-farm subsidies. E. H. Methvin. Read Digest 96:78-82 My '70 *

POCAHONTAS
Founding mothers. il pors Vogue 155:112-13 Je '70 *

POCLAIN (firm) See Machinery industry

PODAIR, Simon
If you're worried about your child's growth. il Parents Mag 45:70-1+ N '70

PODELL, Bertram L.
Excerpt from address, August 5, 1969. Cong Digest 49:46+ F '70

PODHORETZ, Norman
Issues. Commentary 49:26+ Je; 50:27 Jl; 21 Ag; 23 S; 30-1 O; 4 N; 5-6 D '70; 51:4+ Ja '71

PODUSLO, Shirley E. See Norton, W. T. jt. auth.

POE, Edgar Allan
Debussy's dream House. E. Lockspeiser. il pors Opera N 34:8-12 Mr 21 '70 *
Deceit and violence; motifs in The narrative of Arthur Gordon Pym. J. P. Campbell. Engl J 59:206-12 F '70 *

POEM forgotten; ballet. See Ballets—Criticisms

POÈME de l'extase; ballet. See Ballets—Criticisms

POESE, Bill
Plant names are fun. il Home Gard 57:18-19+ Mr '70

POET of Evolution avenue; story. See Franco, M.

POETICS
Catharsis, linguistics & all that. J. Thompson. bibliog f Commentary 50:65-73 O '70
Doctor Williams; beautiful blood, beautiful brain; excerpt from introd. to Imaginations. W. Schott. Am Scholar 39:305-9 Spr '70
Excerpts from Write me another verse. D. McCord. Horn Bk 46:364-9 Ag '70
How to write good poetry and get it published. L. E. Sissman. Writer 83:18-21 O '70
Making of Mother Rosarine. M. W. Kumin. Writer 83:19-21 Ap '70
On Christmas day no more current events; poems by schoolchildren. K. Koch. il N Y Times Mag p5-7 D 20 '70
Poet and the laundry list. I. W. Sherwood. Engl J 59:824-5 S '70
Poetry; how and why. J. Jerome. See issues of Writer's digest
Poet's workshop. F. Trefethen. See issues of Writer
Regional poetry. P. S. Curry. Writer 83:21-3 Ag '70
See also
Poetry—Authorship
Rime

POETRY
Does poetry have an audience? J. F. Cotter. America 122:187-8 F 21 '70
Obscurity; unintelligible contemporary poetry. J. Jerome. Writers Digest 50:16+ D '70
Poet tries to make a kind of order; excerpt from Self-interviews, ed. by J. Reiss and B. Reiss. J. Dickey. Mlle 71:142-3+ S '70
Poetry; how and why J. Jerome. See issues of Writer's digest
Poetry place. See issues of Mademoiselle
Todays poetry is protest. J. Wheatcroft. Todays Ed 59:26-9 Ap '70
Truth of poetry, by M. Hamburger. Review
Commonweal 93:381-2 Ja 15 '71. B. Wallenstein
Sat R 53:52+ My 23 '70. S. Burnshaw
Words without song; excerpt from address. N. Rorem. Am Rec G 36:468-9+ Mr '70
See also
Childrens poems (by children)
Childrens poetry
Christmas poetry
College verse
Free verse
Limericks
Love poetry
Nature in poetry
Negro poetry
Nursery rhymes
Poetics
Poets
Religious poetry
Symbolism in literature
also American poetry; Canadian poetry, etc; *also* subhead Poetry under various subjects, e.g. War—Poetry

Appreciation
Our poetry hour. J. Kerr. il McCalls 97:44-5+ Ag '70
Poetry in the classroom: "Ex-basketball player." V. Busha. Engl J 59:643-5 My '70

Authorship
Decade of my poetry. J. Carrera Andrade. il por Américas 22:9-13 Jl '70
Poetry; how and why. J. Jerome. See issues of Writer's digest

Bibliography
Poetry quarterly. Sat R 53:34-5 Ja 17; 34-6 My 2; 33-5 Ag 8; 24-6 D 26 '70

Competitions
970 poetry contest. J. Chimsky. Writers Digest 50:36-7+ O '70
l70 Scholastic awards; writing. Sr Schol 96: 14 My 18 '70

History and criticism
Interpretation of poetry; excerpt from The pursuit of poetry. L. Untermeyer. Writers Digest 50:24-6 O '70
Poet-critics and scholar-critics. L. Lieberman. Poetry 115:346-52 F '70

Periodicals
Black mountaineering. G. Sorrentino. Poetry 116:110-12 My '70
See also
Little review (periodical)
New York quarterly

Study and teaching
Juvenile bards; how K. Koch turned children on. il por Newsweek 75:54 Ap 6 '70
Haiku: pretty punchy poetry. L. Marker. Clear House 45:219-20 D '70
Linguistics and poetry. Y. H. Frank. Engl J 59:947-53 O '70
Parable of poetry and pedagogy. W. P. Blakely. Engl J 59:945-6 O '70
Pegasus and six blind Indians. M. Defrees. Engl J 59:928-37 O '70
Poetry in a scientific world. M. Sweetkind. Engl J 59:359-66 Mr '70
Poetry in secondary schools. R. Harvey. bibliog Engl J 59:308-15 F '70
Poetry pickle; some reflections. J. A. Mecklenburger. Engl J 59:263-5 F '70
Structure signals in The hunchback in the park. H Brand. Engl J 59:195-200 F '70
Writing song lyrics. L. W. Coffin. Engl J 59:954-5 O '70

Aids and devices
Rock poetry, relevance, and revelation. H. W. English. bibliog Engl J 59:1122-7 N '70

Anecdotes, facetiae, satire, etc.
Basic competencies for teaching poetry. T. Westermark and B. N. S. Gooch. Engl J 59:517-19+ Ap '70

Technique
See Poetics

Themes
See Literature—Themes

POETRY (periodical)
Announcement of prize awards for 1970. Poetry 117:123-5 N '70

POETRY, Canadian. See Canadian poetry

POETRY and hallucinogenic drugs. See Hallucinogenic drugs and poetry

POETRY and music. See Music and literature

POETRY and war. See War and literature

POETRY contests. See Poetry—Competitions

POETRY magazines. See Poetry—Periodicals

POETRY phonograph records. See Phonograph records—Spoken records

POETRY workshops. See Educational workshops

POETS
Daredevil poetics: Ferlinghetti's definition of a poet. E. Kent. Engl J 59:1243-4+ D '70
See also
Negro poets
Women as poets

POETS, American
New sounds, new silences. P. Davison. Atlan 227:96-8 Ja '71
Poetry as merchandise. A. Caruba; reply. A. Brilliant. Pub W 197:29 F 9 '70
See also
American poetry
Ammons, A. R.
Ashbery, J.
Bell, M.
Berry, W.
Berryman, J.
Boer, C.
Brautigan, R.
Burroughs, B.
Crane, H.
Crane, S.
Creeley, R.
Cumberlege, M.
Deutsch, B.
Dickey, J.
Dickinson, E.
Duncan, R.
Elliott, G. P.
Ferlinghetti, L.
Flantz, R.
Frost, R.
Gregor, A.
Hadley, D.
Howard, R.
Kennedy, X. J.
Levi, P.
Lourie, D.
Lowell, R.

POETS, American—See also—*Continued*
McGinley, P.
Merwin, W. S.
Niedecker, L.
Oates, J. C.
Olson, C.
Pack, R.
Pound, E.
Riccio, O.
Riley, J. W.
Robinson, E. A.
Rudnik, R.
Ruggles, K.
Schuyler, J.
Sissman, L. E.
Stein, G.
Stevens, W.
Tate, A.
Van Doren, M.
Van Duyn, M.
Weiss, T.
Wilbur, F.
Williams, W. C.
Zukofsky, L.
POETS, Argentine
   See also
Borges, J. L.
POETS, Canadian
   See also
Atwood, M.
Birney, E.
Souster R.
POETS, English
   See also
Auden, W. H.
Blake, W.
Browning, R.
Brownjohn, A.
Byron, G. G. N. B.
Chaucer, G.
Coleridge, S. T.
Donne, J.
Eliot, T. S.
Graves, R.
Grigson, G.
Milton, J.
Sillitoe, A.
Smith, S.
Wordsworth, W.
POETS, French
   See also
Baudelaire, C. P.
Follain, J.
POETS, Irish
   See also
Heaney, S.
Yeats, W. B.
POETS, Israeli
Israel of the poets. M. L. Rosenthal. Nation
   211:630-2 D 14 '70
   See also
Amichai, Y.
POETS, Mexican
   See also
Nervo, A.
Paz, O.
POETS, Puerto Rican
   See also
Cruz, V. H.
POETS, Russian
   See also
Mandel'shtam, O. E.
Tvardovskii, A. T.
POETS, Scottish
   See also
Macbeth, G. M.
POETS, Welsh
   See also
Ormond, J.
Thomas, D.
Vaughan, H.
POET'S nightmare; drama. See Hoppenstedt,
   E. M.
POFF, Richard H.
Excerpt from debate, September 11, 1969.
   Cong Digest 49:22+ Ja '70
POGREBIN, Letty Cottin
It's still a man's world. il Good H 171:73-5 N
   '70
POGROMS. See Jews—Persecutions
POHL, Frederik
Writer in the year: 2001. il Writers Digest 50:
   36-9 Ja '70
POINDEXTER, David R. Jr
Angela Davis case. il pors Newsweek 76:19
   O 26 '70 *
Enigmatic Angela. il pors Time 96:28 O 26
   '70 *
POINSETT, Alex
Brain drain at Negro colleges. il Ebony 25:
   74-6+ O '70
Doctor Charles G. Hurst: the mastermind of
   Malcolm X college. il pors Ebony 25:29-
   32+ Mr '70

Is there a plot to kill Mayor Hatcher? il
   pors Ebony 26:142-4+ D '70
It's nation time! il Ebony 26:98-100+ D '70
Think tank for black scholars. il por Ebony
   25:46-8+ F '70
POINT, Critical. See Critical point
POINT REYES NATIONAL SEASHORE
New parks that aren't. P. Farb. il Audubon
   72:28-35 Ja '70
Point Reyes seashore authority boosted,
   again. Nat Parks & Con Mag 44:31 My '70
POINTERS (dogs)
Honest gun dog; German wirehaired pointers.
   D. M. Duffey. il Outdoor Life 146:184+ O
   '70
Pointer or setter. J. R. Falk. il Field & S
   75:184-6+ O '70
POISON ivy
How (and how not) to treat poison ivy.
   Consumer Rep 35:372-4 Je '70
POISONING. See Poisons
POISONOUS gases. See Gases, Asphyxiating and
   poisonous
POISONOUS plants
Plant-contact poisoning. C. J. Potthoff. To-
   days Health 48:62 Je '70
Poisonous plants to avoid. il Good H 170:185
   Ap '70
POISONS
Forensic toxicology: poison detection and
   homicide. E. Keller. il Chem 43:14-17 Ja '70
   See also
Arsenic
Carbon monoxide
Fish poisons
Lead poisoning
Pesticides
Sarin
Venom
POISONS, Industrial
   See also
Cadmium poisoning
Carbon tetrachloride
POKORNY, Alex D.
Correlating the Fifteen indices with hospital
   achievement awards. Ment Hy 54:575-6 O
   '70
POKORNY, Theodore R. Jr
Art and English. il Sch Arts 69:40 Je '70
POLAND, Fred
Foreign aid turns to research. Sci N 97:332
   Mr 28 '70
New science body for Canada. il Sci N 97:136
   Ja 31 '70
POLAND
Caught between East and West. B. van
   Voorst. il Newsweek 75:42-4 Je 15 '70
   See also
Communism—Poland
Communist party (Poland)
Germans in Poland
Immigration and emigration—Poland
Jews in Poland
Moving pictures—Poland
Phonograph record industry—Poland
Skis and skiing—Poland
Trials—Poland
Youth—Poland

Boundaries

Drawing the line; Oder-Neisse boundary
   negotiations with West Germany. Newsweek
   75:60+ My 18 '70

Economic conditions

Behind the new outbreaks in Poland. il U S
   News 69:23 D 28 '70
Hard lot of the Poles. Nation 212:4-5 Ja 4 '71
Threshold of change. il Time 96:35-6 N 16
   '70
Why Communist Poland looks to the West.
   R. A. Haeger. il U S News 68:49-50 Mr 30
   '70

Economic policy

Economic plan that failed. por Bsns W p23
   D 26 '70
Poland: new leaders and old problems. il
   Newsweek 77:21+ Ja 4 '71
   See also
Wage-price policy—Poland

Politics and government

Changing the guard in Poland. M. M. Mestro-
   vic. Commonweal 93:364-5 Ja 15 '71
Long road from Poznan to Gdansk. il News-
   week 76:23 D 28 '70
Poland: new leaders and old problems. il
   Newsweek 77:21+ Ja 4 '71
Poland's new regime: gifts and promises. il
   por Time 97:33-4 Ja 4 '71
   See also
Communist party (Poland)

POLAND—*Continued*

Religious Institutions and affairs
See also
Protestants in Poland

Riots
Behind the new outbreaks in Poland. il U S News 69:23 D 28 '70
Hard lot of the Poles. Nation 212:4-5 Ja 4 '71
How's your ostpolitik? J. Burnham. Nat R 23:26 Ja 12 '71
Poland erupts; Gomulka steps out. il por Newsweek 76:21-2+ D 28 '70
Polish eruption: a nation in flames. il Time 96:14-17 D 28 '70
Polish unpleasantness. Nat R 23:20 Ja 12 '71

Social conditions
Threshold of change. il Time 96:35-6 N 16 '70

Treaties
Germany (Federal Republic)
See Germany (Federal Republic)—Treaties—Poland

POLAND, Ohio
Well water ends icing problem; Poland, Ohio, water softening plant. il Am City 85:60 Ap '70

POLAND and the United States
See also
United States—Foreign opinion—Polish

POLANYI, Michael
What is a painting? il Am Scholar 39:655-69 Aut '70

POLAR bear hunting. See Bear hunting

POLAR bear tagging. See Animal tagging

POLAR bears. See Bears

POLAR exploration
See also
Antarctic exploration

POLAR ice. See Ice—Polar Regions

POLAR REGIONS
See also
Antarctic Regions
Glaciers
Ice—Polar Regions

POLAR research
Antarctic research: a pattern of science management. W. D. McElroy. il por Bul Atom Sci 26:85-8 D '70
Antarctic research and the relevance of science. R. S. Lewis. il Bul Atom Sci 26:2-4 D '70
Before the deluge; Arctic environmental research. il Sci N 97:218 F 28 '70
Developing an unmanned Antarctic geophysical station. J. A. Jenny and others. bibliog il Space World G-4-76:9-16 Ap '70
Developing the U.S. Antarctic research program; Operation Deep Freeze. T. O. Jones. por Bul Atom Sci 26:81-4 D '70
Drilling through the ice cap: probing climate for a thousand centuries. C. C. Langway, jr. and B. L. Hansen. il pors Bul Atom Sci 26:62-6 D '70
Getting together on Arctic research. il Sci N 97:405-6 Ap 25 '70
President Nixon announces review of U.S. policy for Antarctica. Dept State Bul 63:572-3 N 9 '70
United States and Canada discuss Arctic research problems. Dept State Bul 62:657 My 25 '70
Upper atmosphere as seen from Antarctica. R. A. Helliwell. il por Bul Atom Sci 26:55-61 D '70

International aspects
Antarctica: experimental proving ground for peaceful coexistence and international collaboration. E. K. Fedorov. il por Bul Atom Sci 26:22-8 D '70
International cooperation in Antarctica, the next decade. P. M. Smith. il por Bul Atom Sci 26:29-32 D '70
Political experiment in Antarctica. F. Sollie. il Bul Atom Sci 26:16-21 D '70

POLARIS missiles. See Guided missiles—Launching from submarine boats

POLARIS submarines. See Submarine boats, Atomic powered

POLARIZATION (light)
Fantastic plastic light show, with polarizers. R. Kouhoupt. il Pop Sci 197:73+ Jl '70
Polarizing light. I. Asimov. Sci Digest 67:72-3 Mr '70

POLARIZATION of particles
New polarized-electron source; letter. R. J. Krisciokaitis. Phys Today 23:15+ F '70

POLARIZED light. See Polarization (light)

POLARIZERS
Filter that drives colors wild. N. Rothschild. il Pop Phot 67:84-9 Ag '70

POLARIZING filters. See Light filters

POLAROGRAPH and polarography
How to build and operate an inexpensive polarograph. G. Birrell and others. bibliog il pors Chem 43:26-9 Mr '70

POLAROID color film. See Photography—Films

POLAROID corporation
Black and white issue faces Polaroid. Bsns W p32 N 14 '70
Kodak and Polaroid: an end to peaceful coexistence. P. Siekman. il Fortune 82:82-7+ N '70

POLAROID Land cameras
Cut loose with your Colorpack. A. Vance. il Pop Phot 67:98-9+ Ag '70
Is this Polaroid's next camera? S. M. Gallager. il Pop Mech 134:78-80 Ag '70

POLAROID photography. See Photography

POLE beans. See Beans

POLES
See also
Electric lines—Poles

POLHEMUS, Marjorie
Americano retires to Puerto Rico. il por Har Yrs 10:6-11+ S '70

POLI, Kenneth
For better holiday pictures: open your mind first. il Pop Phot 66:78-9+ Ja '70
History is today, grown old. il Pop Phot 66:60-1+ F '70

POLICANSKY, David, and Ellison, John
Sex ratio in drosophila pseudoobscura: spermiogenic failure. bibliog il Science 169:888-9 Ag 28 '70

POLICE
See also
Automobiles, Police
Detectives
Negro police

Electronic equipment
See Electronics in criminal investigation, espionage, etc.

Equipment and supplies
Danish rolls for crooks; plastic roadblock system to catch hit-and-run motorist or thief. il Mech Illus 66:63 F '70
Humane gun. il Time 96:14 S 28 '70
Newest antiriot weapon; bullets of wood. il U S News 69:36 Jl 20 '70
Vietnamization on Main Street: the dumdum bullet. R. Wells. il Nation 211:38-41 Jl 20 '70
See also
Life saving equipment

Public relations
Bobby's lot. il Newsweek 75:40 Mr 9 '70
Citizens' war on crime; spreading across U.S. il U S News 68:55-8 Mr 23 '70; Same abr. with title America's citizen crime fighters. Read Digest 96:225-6+ Je '70
City of (big) brotherly love; F. Rizzo's Philadelphia. J. Groutt. Commonweal 92:167-9 My 1 '70
Condemnation and persecution of hippies. M. E. Brown; reply with rejoinder. A. Dobrin. Trans-Action 7:71-2 Ja '70
Dayton's mod cops. il por Newsweek 76:51-2 N 9 '70
Dilemma of the black cop. R. Hall. il pors Life 69:60-60B+ S 18 '70
Gentle gendarmes; proposals of George Berkley. H. Bowser. Sat R 53:22 Mr 28 '70
Love letter to the law. Nations Bsns 58:19 Mr '70
Mobile exhibit takes the police story to the people; Mobile crime prevention exhibit, Kansas City, Mo. J. R. Perry. il Am City 85:46 Ja '70
Pigs 24, freaks 5; softball game in Houston between hippies and police. il Time 96:22 O 5 '70
Police enemies or friends? excerpt from Children in trouble. H. James. il PTA Mag 64:2-5 Je '70
Young people who hate the police. B. Bettelheim. Ladies Home J 87:52+ F '70

Recruiting
Police recruiting with an up beat; Washington, D.C. il Bsns W p79 Ja 24 '70
Why don't you guys become cops? R. Daley. il por Life 68:38A-38B+ Mr 20 '70
Young arm of law; lowering the minimum age. Sr Schol 96:15-17 Mr 2 '70

POLICE—*Continued*

Training

Mental health training program prompts police policy. Todays Health 48:34 F '70
Policing the empire. M. T. Klare. Commonweal 92:455-61 S 18 '70

California

See also
Los Angeles County, Calif.—Police

Canada

See also
Canada—Royal Canadian mounted police

Great Britain

Bobby's lot. il Newsweek 75:40 Mr 9 '70

Hong Kong

Creative restraint; riot control tactics of Hong Kong police. il Newsweek 75:66 My 18 '70

Mississippi

Hotheads and professionals; Mississippi highway safety patrol. il Time 96:42 Ag 10 '70

New Jersey

Big brother in New Jersey. il Time 95:60 Je 15 '70

Russia

See also
Secret service—Russia

South Africa

Black African in white prisons. I. Robertson and P. Whitten. Commonweal 93:239-41 D 4 '70

Underdeveloped areas

Policing the empire. M. T. Klare. Commonweal 92:455-61 S 18 '70

United States

Bolder cop killers hitting more often. il U S News 69:26 S 14 '70
Community control of the police. A. I. Waskow; discussion. Trans-Action 7:92-3 Ap '70
Kill the pig. il Newsweek 76:29-31 S 14 '70
Killing cops: signs of a nationwide plot. il U S News 69:61 O 19 '70
Killing cops: the new terror tactics. il U S News 69:11-13 Ag 31 '70
Law and disorder. il Ebony 25:96-7 Jl '70
Local political leadership and popular discontent in the ghetto. P. H. Rossi and R. A. Berk. bibliog f il Ann Am Acad 391:111-27 S '70
New York: Tommy the traveler; undercover agent. Time 95:16 Je 22 '70
Panthers and pigs. Chr Today 14:25 Ja 16 '70
Parting shots; the country's cops finally discover that pigs are ... il Life 69:64-6 Jl 31 '70
Police, fact & fancy. il Sr Schol 96:6-10 My 18 '70
Police in our changing cities. R. W. England, jr. bibliog f Cur Hist 59:273-7+ N '70
Police mob: meeting force with superior force. Nation 211:68 Ag 3 '70
Police under attack, but standing fast. il U S News 69:38 S 21 '70
Police violence and its public support. W. A. Gamson and J. McEvoy. bibliog f il Ann Am Acad 391:97-110 S '70
Politics of repression? symposium. W. H. Ferry. Cur 115:33-45 F '70
Press-card disguise; police posing as newsmen. B. J. Oudes. il Nation 211:561-4 N 30 '70
Snipers in ambush; police under the gun. il Time 96:13-15 S 14 '70
U.S. journal: West Chester, Pennsylvania; undercover police officer, John Mervin arrested for murder. C. Trillin. New Yorker 46:42-4+ Je 27 '70
Unpoliced police. Nation 211:548 N 30 '70
War against the police: officers tell their story; testimony before Senate subcommittee. il U S News 69:82-6 O 26 '70
War on the law. il Newsweek 76:16 Ag 31 '70
We've always wanted to be cops; with report by G. Moore. il pors Life 69:32-7 N 13 '70
What the police can, and cannot do about crime. il Time 96:34-6+ Jl 13 '70
See also
Colleges and universities—Security measures
United States—Justice, Department of—Law enforcement assistance administration
also subhead Police under names of cities, e.g. Cleveland—Police

History

Policeman's lot. T. J. Fleming. il Am Heritage 21:4-17+ F '70

Vietnam (Republic)

Saigon's secret police. D. G. Porter. Nation 210:498-500 Ap 27 '70

POLICE, Military
See also
United States—Army—Corps of military police

POLICE, Mounted
See also
Canada—Royal Canadian mounted police

POLICE, State
Helicopters undergo new tests as traffic units; California highway patrol. il Am City 85:58 Ap '70
See also
Police—Mississippi

POLICE airplanes. See Airplanes in police work

POLICE athletic league
Portable talent scout; summer project in New York's PAL play streets. il Am City 85:64 My '70

POLICE automobiles. See Automobiles, Police

POLICE chaplains. See Chaplains, Police

POLICE communication systems
Fire-police communications; St Joseph, Mo. B. H. Jones. il Am City 85:91+ Jl '70

POLICE departments
Tough vs. moderate cops. il por Bsns W p38+ D 12 '70

POLICE exhibits, Traveling. See Exhibitions, Traveling

POLICE-fire officers. See Public safety officers

POLICE helicopters. See Helicopters in police work

POLICE motor vehicles. See Motor vehicles, Police

POLICE power
See also
Congressional conference on justice in America

POLICE records
Big brother in New Jersey. il Time 95:60 Je 15 '70

POLICE recruiting. See Police—Recruiting

POLICE-school cooperation
Police in the schools; with discussion. D. W. Robinson. Todays Ed 59:18-20 O '70; Same abr. Ed Digest 36:11-13 D '70

POLICE spies. See Police—United States; Spies

POLICE uniforms. See Uniforms, Police

POLICE unions
See also
International brotherhood of police officers

POLICEMEN. See Police

POLICIES, Insurance. See Insurance—Policies

POLICY loans. See Insurance, Life—Policy loans

POLIOMYELITIS
Conquest of polio. Time 96:46 Jl 20 '70
See also
Iron lung

POLISH art. See Art, Polish

POLISH music. See Music, Polish

POLISH poetry

Translations into English

From the Nile to . . ; tr. by R. K. Wilson. J. Słowacki. il Harp Baz 104:78-9 D '70

POLISHES. See Polishing materials

POLISHING
See also
Diamond cutting
Tumbling barrels

POLISHING materials
Cleaners and polishes for aluminum and two rust removers for metal. il Consumer Bul 53:31-2 Ag '70
Silver cleaners and polishes. il Consumer Bul 53:19-22 N '70

POLITBURO. See Communist party (Russia)—Political bureau

POLITICAL activists. See Pressure groups

POLITICAL advertising. See Advertising, Political; Political campaigns

POLITICAL attitudes
Bringing biology into the political picture. C. Behrens. Sci N 98:434 D 5 '70
Child is father to the man; growth of political knowledge and feeling among school children. Trans-Action 7:9 Je '70
Income and ideology. Trans-Action 7:12 N '69
Learning the political facts of life. M. Beadle. il N Y Times Mag p60+ S 20 '70
Like fathers, like sons. N. Podhoretz. Commentary 50:21 Ag '70; Reply with rejoinder. A. Kazin. 50:28 N '70

POLITICAL attitudes—*Continued*
Nixon's southern strategy; it's all in the charts. J. Boyd. il pors N Y Times Mag p25+ My 17 '70
Non-generation gap. S. M. Lipset and E. Raab. Commentary 50:35-9 Ag '70
Political thinking and consciousness, by R. E. Lane. Review
Trans-Action 7:60-1+ My '70. P. W. Sperlich
Psychology of political activity. S. G. Levy. bibliog f il Ann Am Acad 391:83-96 S '70
See also
Public opinion

POLITICAL bureau of the Communist party. See Communist party (Russia)—Political bureau

POLITICAL campaigns
After the primaries: how key races shape up. il U S News 69:31-2 S 28 '70
Agnew on the warpath. B. Brower. il pors Life 69:26-31 O 16 '70
Agnew: purging the GOP? il pors Newsweek 76:36 O 12 '70
Agnew's task, and task force. por U S News 69:21 S 14 '70
All-Republican Senate? Jim Allison's working on it. D. R. Maxey. il por Look 34:34-6+ O 20 '70
Anatomy of San Jose. Nation 211:482 N 16 '70
Antiwar Congress; groups working for peace candidates. New Repub 162:5-7 My 23 '70
As go the suburbs, so goes U.S. politics. A. J. Reichley. il Fortune 82:104-9+ S '70
Assessing the campaigners. Sci N 98:381-2 N 14 '70
At the campaign kickoff: strategy of both parties. il U S News 69:19-21 S 14 '70
Campaign costs. J. McLaughlin. America 122:482 My 2 '70
Campaign wind-up; pre-election survey. il U S News 60:23-6 N 2 '70
Campaigner; electioneering in four states by R. M. Nixon. il por Newsweek 76:25 O 26 '70
Campaigns and the new technology. J. Moriarity. il Sci N 98:229-30 S 12 '70
Campus politics; guidelines from the American council on education. New Repub 163:10 Ag 1 '70
Close-up of '70 campaign: At stake in ten Northeastern states. il U S News 69:25-8 O 5 '70
Conservative is the way to sound; with report on R. Reagan by P. O'Neil and views of the average voter. il Life 69:24-32 O 30 '70
Democrats: defensive politics. il Time 96:11 S 28 '70
Election outlook in Far West. il U S News 69:16-19 O 26 '70
Great Tunney-Brown fight; California Democratic senatorial primary campaign. D. Neff. il por Time 95:15 Je 15 '70
He wanted to be Senator McLaughlin. S. J. P. J. Donaldson. America 123:428-32 N 21 '70; Reply. V. A. Lapomarda. 124:2 Ja 9 '71
Helping win elections; reminders to campaign volunteers. M. E. Talisman. New Repub 162:10-12 Je 20 '70
Hi, there! Your next senator: J. L. Buckley. J. J. Kilpatrick. il por 22:1154-8 N 3 '70
How George did it; Alabama's Democratic gubernatorial primary. il Newsweek 75:27-9 Je 15 '70
How George did it: dirty primary campaign in Alabama. il por Time 95:16 Je 15 '70
Law and order politics; President Nixon's approach. H. Sidey. Life 69:4 O 30 '70
Making of a quarterback 1970. P. Ryan. il pors Sports Illus 33:82-6+ D 7 '70
Middle America's Mr America; S. T. Agnew. il pors Newsweek 76:23-7 S 28 '70
Missiles from the Michelle Ann; S. Agnew begins mission in the West; with excerpts from his addresses. il pors Time 96:14-16 S 21 '70
Mr Nixon and the politics of danger. il Newsweek 76:21-2 N 9 '70
Mood before the vote. P. R. Wieck. New Repub 163:9-11 O 31 '70
New politics in '70; plans of Referendum '70 and Vietnam Moratorium. New Repub 162:9 Ja 17 '70
Nixon's last-minute push for a Republican victory. il pors U S News 69:20-1 N 2 '70
Now do it! R. M. Nixon's campaign. J. Osborne. New Repub 163:11-12 O 31 '70
Opinion: politicizing the university. J. Rudman. por Mlle 71:92+ Ag '70
Other purge; efforts to expel lapdogs of the Pentagon. K. Crawford. Newsweek 76:39 N 23 '70

Our local correspondents; 40th assembly district of Brooklyn. S. Lardner. New Yorker 46:96+ Je 20 '70
People, by R. T. Stout. Review
Newsweek il por 76:98+ S 21 '70. G. Wolff
Political mood: right on. il Newsweek 76:32-3 O 19 '70
Political trends in key area: latest survey of Midwest. il U S News 69:37-40 O 19 '70
President who runs for Congress. il pors Newsweek 76:24-5 N 2 '70
President's too-secret weapon. S. Alsop. Newsweek 76:124 N 2 '70
Republican assault on the Senate. il Time 96:18-22+ O 26 '70
Reverend father congressman; citizens' caucus helps R. F. Drinan. T. M. Gannon. America 123:424-8 N 21 '70; Discussion. 123:531 D 19 '70
'70 campaign: battle for Congress. il Nations Bsns 58:18-23 Ag '70
'70 campaign takes a new turn; barnstorming by President Nixon. il por U S News 69:15-16 O 26 '70
'70 political trends in the South. il U S News 69:37-40 O 12 '70
Skilful campaign. Nat R 22:1253+ D 1 '70
So you're not a politician! E. W. Chandler. Har Yrs 10:13-14 O '70
Special Spiro pin. il por Time 96:17 O 12 '70
Spiro Agnew vs. the radic-libs. il por Newsweek 76:35-6 S 21 '70
Student moves into the 14th C.D. T. Buckley. il pors N Y Times Mag p 10-11+ Je 21 '70
There's a whiff of politics in the air. Changing T 24:6 O '70
Time out for students; Princeton plan. New Repub 163:7 O 17 '70
Time to listen. K. Crawford. Newsweek 75:28 Je 29 '70
To the polls: permissiveness v. purse. il pors Time 96:6-7 N 2 '70
TRB from Washington; R. M. Nixon's unprecedented election gamble. New Repub 163:6 N 14 '70
Violent end to a vitriolic campaign. il por Time 96:14-15 N 9 '70
White House hard hats. E. B. Drew. il por Atlan 226:51-7 O '70
Year of the losers. W. C. McWilliams and others. Commonweal 93:214-16 N 27 '70
Youth gets out the voters, but the wrong ones; New Jersey's Fifteenth congressional district. il pors Newsweek 75:28-9 Je 15 '70
See also
Campaign funds
Campaign issues
Candidates, Political
Radio in politics
Presidential campaigns
Television in politics
also subhead Politics and government under names of countries, states, cities, e.g. Florida—Politics and government

Anecdotes, facetiae, satire, etc.

Changing your spots. P. Steinfels. Commonweal 93:166 N 13 '70

Chile

Backlash in Chile. P. E. Sigmund. Commonweal 92:387-9 Ag 7 '70
Chile turns to Marxism; Allende's Popular unity coalition. T. M. Gannon. America 123:321-2 O 24 '70
Fateful election. il Newsweek 76:36+ Ag 10 '70
October revolution in Chile? S. Rodman. Nat R 22:1053-5 O 6 '70
Tearing up Chile. G. A. Geyer. New Repub 163:9-10 Ag 22 '70

France

Political chicken; Bordeaux by-election. il por Newsweek 76:50 S 21 '70

Great Britain

Britain: the odds on labor. il Time 95:37-8 Je 22 '70
Charisma sweepstakes. il pors Newsweek 75:53 Je 15 '70
Doffing the cloth cap. il Time 95:31-2 Je 15 '70
Down to the wire. il Newsweek 75:36 Je 22 '70
Elections in plain English. I. Ross. Read Digest 97:25+ N '70
Lesser evil? campaign for June 18 elections. Time 95:29-30 Je 1 '70
Letter from London; June 18th elections. M. Panter-Downes. New Yorker 46:75-7 My 30 '70

Sweden

Letter from Stockholm. S. Kelman. il New Yorker 46:36-46+ D 26 '70

POLITICAL candidates. See Candidates, Political

POLITICAL cartoons. See Caricatures and cartoons

POLITICAL clubs and associations
California club movement: the palsy of the CDC. F. Carney. Nation 210:526-30 My 4 '70
Ripon charges State; the threat of mass famine in Biafra. J. Deedy. Commonweal 92:50 Mr 27 '70
      See also
Freedom house (organization)

POLITICAL conventions
      See also
National conventions, Democratic

POLITICAL crimes and offenses
      See also
Assassination
Government, Resistance to
Terrorism
Treason

Greece, Modern
      See also
Political prisoners—Greece, Modern

POLITICAL defectors. See Defectors, Political

POLITICAL ethics
Ethics for everyone. Time 95:18 My 18 '70
Impeaching Justice Douglas? with excerpts from address by G. R. Ford, April 15, 1970. il por U S News 68:25-6, 67-71 Ap 27 '70
Public's ethics. Nation 210:357 Mr 30 '70
We can't depend on Congress to keep Congress honest. R. Sherrill. il N Y Times Mag p5-7+ Jl 19 '70
What the senator didn't disclose; J. Tydings hasn't met the standards he has set. W. Lambert. pors Life 69:26-9 Ag 28 '70
Whose law? Whose order? Commonweal 91: 605-6 Mr 6 '70
      See also
Government, Resistance to
Patriotism
Politics, Corruption in
Subversive activities

POLITICAL films. See Moving pictures—Political films

POLITICAL forecasts
Changes in the House: a prediction. R. W. Boyd and J. T. Murphy. New Repub 163: 12-14 O 24 '70
From here to '72; symposium. Commonweal 93:214-21 N 27 '70
Game plan for November. S. Alsop. Newsweek 76:80 Ag 10 '70
How the polls made out; 1970 election forecasts. U S News 69:21 N 16 '70
How the races look in the homestretch. il Newsweek 76:26-7 N 2 '70
Mood before the vote. P. R. Wieck. New Repub 163:9-11 O 31 '70
Nixon's southern strategy: it's all in the charts. J. Boyd. il pors N Y Times Mag p25+ My 17 '70
No major trend to either party; interview. G. Gallup. por U S News 69:29 N 2 '70
      See also
Public opinion polls

POLITICAL fundamentalism. See Conservatism

POLITICAL ghost writing. See Authorship—Collaboration

POLITICAL kidnapping. See Kidnapping

POLITICAL leadership. See Leadership

POLITICAL liberty. See Liberty

POLITICAL literature
American right and pamphleteering: recommendations for a radical pamphlet library. N. Kehde. il Am Lib 1:965-7 N '70
Innovations and trends in the study of American politics. V. M. Goetcheus and H. C. Mansfield. bibliog f Ann Am Acad 391:177-87 S '70

POLITICAL obligations. See Citizenship

POLITICAL parties
      See also
Communist parties

Austria
Terrors no longer. Time 95:40+ Mr 16 '70

Canada
While Canada waited: Quebec's National union party tactics. M. M. Dorcy. America 122:525-6 My 16 '70

Chile
Backlash in Chile. P. E. Sigmund. Commonweal 92:387-9 Ag 7 '70
Chile: the expanding left; from Christian democrats to anarchic urban terrorists. il pors Time 96:23-4+ O 19 '70

Chile turns to Marxism; Allende's Popular unity coalition. T. M. Gannon. America 123: 321-2 O 24 '70
Christian democracy in Chile. A. Angell. bibliog f Cur Hist 58:79-84+ F '70

France
Radical change; plan to reconstruct the Radical party. il por Newsweek 75:34 Mr 2 '70
      See also
Communist party (France)

Germany (Federal Republic)
On the rocks; Free democratic party. Newsweek 76:49 Jl 6 '70
Willy Brandt turns East; leader of the Social democratic party. N. Muhlen. Nat R 22: 676-7 Je 30 '70

Great Britain
      See also
Conservative party (Great Britain)
Labor party (Great Britain)

Hungary
      See also
Communist party (Hungary)

India
Two, three, many Indias! K. Harney. Commonweal 92:157-8 My 1 '70; Discussion. 92: 326-7, 423, 490 Je 26, Ag 21, S 25 '70

Italy
Soloists. il Time 95:41 Ap 6 '70

Mexico
Upward and onward. il por Time 96:27 Jl 13 '70

Philippines
Rebirth of the revolution. R. Blackburn. il Nation 211:582-7 D 7 '70

Quebec (province)
      See Political parties—Canada

South Africa
Relaxing a bit. Newsweek 75:45 My 4 '70
South Africa's lonely liberal: H. Suzman. il pors Life 68:58C-59D My 15 '70
Step toward the center. il Time 95:47 My 4 '70

Sweden
Letter from Stockholm. S. Kelman. il New Yorker 46:36-46+ D 26 '70

United States
Black candidates: which party? il Sr Schol 97:13 O 12 '70
Comeback of the two-party system. il U S News 68:44-5 Mr 9 '70
Irrelevance of American politics. A. C. Brownfeld. Yale R 60:1-13 O '70
Let's keep the electoral college: bulwark of our two-party system. R. C. Moe. il Nat R 22:356-9+ Ap 7 '70
Lindsay idea; third party. New Repub 163: 5-6 O 3 '70
McCarthy's call for a third party. New Repub 162:5-6 Je 20 '70; Same abr. with title Not necessarily so. Cur 120:33-4 Ag '70
Radical strategy: don't form a fourth party; form a new first party. M. Harrington. il N Y Times Mag p28-9+ S 13 '70
Third party may be a real force in '72. E. J McCarthy. il por N Y Times Mag p6+ Je 7 '70; Excerpts. Cur 120:31-2 Ag '70
What wins elections today? Sr Schol 97:15-17 O 12 '70
What's in a name? Nations Bsns 58:24 D '70
      See also
Democratic party
National woman's party
Party government
Republican party

POLITICAL persecution. See Persecution, Political

POLITICAL philosophy
Indicators of change in political institutions. N. E. Long. bibliog f Am Ann Acad 388: 35-45 Mr '70
Odyssey from liberal to radical. R. A. McKenzie. Chr Cent 87:362-3 Mr 25 '70
Political sciences. by H. Stretton Review Nation 210:277-9 Mr 9 '70. B. Mazlish
Repression in the mirror. B. Farrell. Life 68:22B Ap 3 '70

POLITICAL philosophy—*Continued*
Shape of the future; are there new political concepts in the world today? T. Molnar. Commonweal 92:365-7 Jl 24 '70
See also
Communism and democracy
Conservatism
Democracy
Liberalism
National socialism
Political thought
Racism

POLITICAL posters. See Posters

POLITICAL pressure. See Pressure groups

POLITICAL prisoners
See also
Conscientious objectors

Bolivia
Debray's release. il por Newsweek 77:29-30 Ja 4 '71

Cambodia
Bad trip; U.S. newsmen captured. il por Newsweek 75:101-2 Ap 20 '70
Missing in Cambodia. il Time 95:43 Ap 20 '70

Germany (Democratic Republic)
Ulbricht's prisoners: American and western students. por Time 96:27 N 9 '70

Greece, Modern
Flight to freedom; release of M. Theodorakis. il por Newsweek 75:56+ Ap 27 '70
Greek colonels' revenge. J. Kobbe. Nation 210:789 Je 29 '70
Greek talk; case of N. Vardikos. W. F. Buckley, jr. Nat R 22:272-3 Mr 10 '70
Inquisition Greek style; excerpts from Barbarism in Greece. J. Becket. il Ramp Mag 8:44-8 Ap '70
Monday of Mikis Theodorakis; reprint. J. Boetsch. il pors Sat R 53:14-15+ My 9 '70
Theodorakis; interview. M. Theodorakis. New Yorker 46:22-3 Ag 15 '70

Israel
Terrorism & preventive detention: the case of Israel. A. M. Dershowitz. bibliog f Commentary 50:67-78 D '70

Mexico
Quiet day in Mexico; letter. R. Crespi. Nation 211:277 S 28 '70
Tlatelolco: massacre and aftermath. D. Peerman. Chr Cent 87:1503-6 D 16 '70
Tyranny and soccer. Nation 210:101 F 2 '70
Vatican receives appeal from ninety-one Mexican political prisoners. Chr Cent 87:135 F 4 '70

Russia
Political malpractice; use of insane asylums for dissenters. Newsweek 75:43-4 Je 1 '70
Protesting spiritual murder; scientists and intellectuals protest confinement of dissidents in mental institutions. il por Time 95:30-1 Je 29 '70
Scientific breakdown; arrest of Z. Medvedev. il por Newsweek 75:44+ Je 15 '70
Soviet dissenter; visit from the KGB; arrest of A. Amalrik. il por Newsweek 75:43 Je 1 '70
Televised Samizdat; CBS's filmed interviews of dissident intellectuals. por Newsweek 76:43 Ag 10 '70
Very special case; release of Z. Medvedev. il por Newsweek 75:47 Je 29 '70

Spain
Eight months in Franco's jail. Duchess of Medina-Sidonia. Nation 210:396-9 Ap 6 '70

Uruguay
And now Uruguay. Chr Cent 87:1009 Ag 26 '70; Reply. E. M. Smith. Chr Cent 87:1287-8 O 28 '70

POLITICAL psychology
Election economics. P. A. Samuelson. Newsweek 76:75 O 26 '70
Personality and politics, by F. I. Greenstein. Review
Trans-Action 7:88-90 Jl '70. E. V. Wolfenstein
See also
Political attitudes
Public opinion

POLITICAL publicity. See Radio in politics; Television in politics

POLITICAL rhetoric. See Rhetoric

POLITICAL rumor. See Rumor

POLITICAL science
Biopolitics, by T. L. Thorson. Review
Nation 211:88-90 Ag 3 '70. W. Anderson
Political order in changing societies, by S. P. Huntington. Review
Trans-Action 7:56-8 N '69. R. A. Packenham
See also
American political science association
Civilization
Communism
Corporate state
Decision making (political science)
Democracy
Fascism
Government, Resistance to
Imperialism
Liberalism
Liberty
Minorities
Nations
Political ethics
Political philosophy
Political psychology
Politics
Power (social sciences)
Revolution
Socialism
State, The
State governments

Methodology
Indicators for America's linkages with the changing world environment. B. M. Russett. bibliog f il Ann Am Acad 388:82-96 Mr '70

POLITICAL science research
Bringing biology into the political picture. C. Behrens. Sci N 98:434 D 5 '70
See also
Political science—Methodology

POLITICAL theory. See Political philosophy; Political science

POLITICAL thought
Grand illusion; an appreciation of Jacques Ellul. R. A. Nisbet. Commentary 50:40-4 Ag '70
Myth of the rad decade. P. Steinfels. Commonweal 93:62 O 16 '70
Political thought of Herbert Marcuse. G. Kateb. bibliog f Commentary 49:48-63 Ja '70

POLITICIANS
Take heart from the heartland. A. M. Greeley. New Repub 163:16-19 D 12 '70
Why we need new politicians. F. Knebel. Look 34:74 Ja 13 '70

POLITICS
See also
Conservatism
Liberalism
Political campaigns
Political ethics
Political science
Politicians
Presidential campaigns
Television in politics
Women and politics
Women in politics
also subhead Politics and government under names of countries, states, etc. e.g. France—Politics and government

Terminology
Politics and the name game; Time essay. M. Ways. il por Time 96:14-15 N 2 '70
Words in the news. Sr Schol 95:25 S 22 '69; 97:24 S 21 '70

POLITICS, Corruption in
See also
Conflict of interests (public office)

Louisiana
Louisiana still jumps for mobster Marcello. D. Chandler. il pors Life 68:30-7 Ap 10 '70

New Jersey
Bartles of New Jersey. por Time 97:12-13 Ja 11 '71

POLITICS and art. See Art and politics

POLITICS and business. See Business—Political aspects

POLITICS and Christianity. See Church and politics

POLITICS and economics. See Economics and politics

POLITICS and education
McAndrew case: Britain at the Chicago bar; incident of 1927. H. K. Hutton and C. Gaigoci. Sch & Soc 98:112-15 F '70
See also
College professors and instructors—Political activities
College students—Political activities
Colleges and universities—Political control
High school students—Political activities
Teachers—Political activities
POLITICS and justice. See Justice and politics
POLITICS and libraries. See Libraries and politics
POLITICS and literature. See Literature and politics
POLITICS and museums. See Museums and politics
POLITICS and religion
Churches and the Viet Nam issue. C. Kucheman. Chr Today 15:15-16 O 23 '70
Preaching and the power; B. Graham and the White House. il pors Newsweek 76:50-5 Jl 20 '70
White House religion: a tricky business. M. Novak. Chr Cent 87:1112 S 23 '70; Discussion. 87:1359 N 11 '70
See also
Church and politics
Church and state
Clergy—Political activities
Priests—Political activities
POLITICS and science. See Science and state
POLITICS and war
Domestic origins of peace. R. Randle. Ann Am Acad 392:76-85 N '70
Domestic politics and peacemaking: reconciling incompatible imperatives. R. Rothstein. bibliog f Ann Am Acad 392:62-75 N '70
Political rationality in ending war. P. Kecskemeti. bibliog f Ann Am Acad 392:105-15 N '70
To remember Hiroshima. Chr Cent 87:932-3 Ag 5 '70
POLITZER, Jerome F.
Episcopal church convention. il Chr Today 43-5 N 6 '70
POLK, Duvan
Hours before morning; story. Good H 171:76-7 Ag '70
POLK, James Knox
Thankless task of Nicholas Trist. R. M. Ketchum. il por Am Heritage 21:12-15+ Ag '70 *
POLK, Louis Frederick, 1930–
Wunderkind in venture land. por Bsns W p88 N 28 '70 *
POLL, Heinz
Dream for three. D. Hering. il pors Dance Mag 44:72-6 Ap '70 *
POLLACK, Harvey
Philadelphia. il Parks & Rec 5:18-21 Jl '70
Recreation growth in the Congress city. il Parks & Rec 5:29-30+ Ag '70
POLLACK, Jack Harrison
Dreams that never fade. il Nations Bsns 58:48-51 Ag '70
I want out. il Todays Health 49:32-4+ Ja '71
They're cracking down on the telephone nuts, and you can help! il Todays Health 48:24-7+ My '70
POLLACK, Robert H.
Mueller-Lyer illusion: effect of age, lightness contrast, and hue. bibliog il Science 170:93-5 O 2 '70
POLLACK fishing
Case for the Boston blue. D. Levin. il Sports Illus 32:48-9 Mr 16 '70
Winter king; pollock fishing. G. Heinold. il Outdoor Life 146:114+ N '70
POLLEN, Daniel A. and Trachtenberg, M. C.
Neuroglia: gliosis and focal epilepsy. bibliog Science 167:1252-3 F 27 '70
—See Trachtenberg, M. C. jt. auth.
POLLEN
Pollination, vital link in plant life. E. C. Ogden. il Cons 24:21-7+ Ap '70
POLLEN, Fossil
Pollen sequence from late quaternary sediments in Yellowstone Park. R. G. Baker. bibliog il Science 168:1449-50 Je 19 '70
POLLINATION. See Fertilization of plants
POLLOCK, Jackson
Art; psychoanalytic drawings at the Whitney museum. Nation 211:444-5 N 2 '70
about
Behind the veil. C. L. Wysuph. bibliog il Art N 69:52-5+ O '70 *
Demon drawings. D. Davis. il Newsweek 76:104 N 2 '70 *

POLLOCK fishing. See Pollack fishing
POLLS, Public opinion. See Public opinion polls
POLLUTION
Clash of gloomy prophets. por Time 97:56 Ja 11 '71
Confessions of a polluter. A. Godfrey. por Read Digest 97:60-4 S '70
Earth watch; comp. by S. Lindsay. Sat R 53:60 Mr 7; 58 Ap 4; 60-1 My 2; 66-7 Je 6; 46-7 Jl 4; 50-1 Ag 1; 54-5 S 5; 60-1 O 3; 70-1 N 7; 64-5 D 5 '70; 54:70-1 Ja 2 '71
Effects of pollution on the structure and physiology of ecosystems. G. M. Woodwell. bibliog il Science 168:429-33 Ap 24 '70
Environment: a national mission for the seventies; symposium, and statements by R. M. Nixon and E. S. Muskie. il pors Fortune 81:98-148+ F '70; Discussion. 81:91-3 F; 51+ Ap '70
Environmental sciences. See Issues of Science news
Fighting to save the earth from man. il Time 95:56-7+ F 2 '70; Same abr. with title Last chance for mother earth. Read Digest 96:63-7 My '70
Good earth and the golden rule. L. Sumner. il Nat Parks 44:4-9 Ja '70
Man and his environment; excerpts from address. A. Godfrey. il PTA Mag 65:2-5 S '70
Man the killer of nature. Thant. il UNESCO Courier 23:46-53 Ag '70
More letters in the wind; PCB contamination of the environment. R. Risebrough and V. Brodine. bibliog il Environ 12:16-27 Ja '70
Mortgaging the old homestead. Lord Ritchie-Calder. For Affairs 48:207-20 Ja '70; Same. il Sports Illus 32:44-51 F 2 '70
New conservation poll. Nat Wildlife 8:18-19 D '69
Nicest people protest pollution. J. Olds. il Org Gard & Farm 17:56-9 F '70
No. 1 endangered species: you! B. East. il Outdoor Life 145:32-4+ Ap '70
Of concern now. Bet Hom & Gard 48:28+ Ag '70
Organic gardener's guide to complaining in the name of the environment. J. Olds. Org Gard & Farm 17:60-3 Jl '70
Pollution by organic chemicals. P. H. Abelson. Science 170:495 O 30 '70
Pollution; excerpts from address. L. L. Terry. il Todays Ed 59:26-9 Ja '70
Pollution is caused by people! Consumer Bul 53:15-16 Ap '70
Pollution, threat to man's only home; with map-and-painting supplement. G. Young. il Nat Geog 133:738-83 D '70
Product pushers vs. the people. C. F. Wurster. por Field & S 75:60+ Je '70
Project survival; symposium, with editorial comment. bibliog il Environ 12:2-47 Ap '70
Reports: environmental disaster, acts of nature and man; symposium. il Bul Atom Sci 26:17-41 O '70
Science and the gross national pollution. G. M. Woodwell. Ramp Mag 8:51-4 My '70
Side effects of man. Sci Am 223:78-9 S '70
Small errors. Cons 25:1 O '70
Teacher tips: environmental deterioration and declining species. J. A. Weeks. Cons 25:27+ Ag '70
This is the way the world ends. R. Starr. il Am Heritage 21:94-101 O '70
Toward an ecological solution. M. Bookchin. il Ramp Mag 8:6-8+ My '70
Trace elements in air and water. R. H. Gilluly. il Sci N 97:538-9 My 30 '70
Values! address. R. W. Allin. il Parks & Rec 5:20-3+ N '70
What's happening to Mother Earth: a warning. J. Randolph. il por U S News 69:59-60 N 23 '70
See also
Air pollution
Pesticides and the environment
Radioactive fallout
Soil pollution
Space pollution
Water pollution

Caricatures and cartoons
No laughing matter. il Nat Wildlife 8:32-3 Ap '70
The thinker. R. Osrin. il Am For 76:11 Ap '70

Control
America's polluted environment; symposium. bibliog Cur Hist 59:1-54 Jl '70
Battle plan. il Newsweek 75:23-4 F 23 '70
Business fights pollution, and the Nation profits. il Nations Bsns 58:29-30 F '70

POLLUTION—Control—*Continued*

Cleaning up on pollution. il Time 95:75 Mr 2 '70

Cleaning up the national mess: how great the cost? Who will pay? Time 95:60-1 F 2 '70

Clearing the air: we can end pollution; interview. ed. by P. Lisagor. L. A. DuBridge. il PTA Mag 64:14-16 F '70

Criteria for an optimum human environment. H. H. Iltis and others. Bul Atom Sci 26:2-6 Ja '70

Dirty dilemma of oil spills. il Life 68:28-35 Mr 6 '70

Ecological Christmas. il Nat Parks & Con Mag 44:25 D '70

Ecology: rhetoric and reality. H. Gilliam. Ed Digest 36:35-6 N '70

Ecology: the new religion? R. L. Schueler. America 122:292-5 Mr 21 '70

Editor's choice; libraries and the national teach-in. G. R. Shields. Am Lib 1:19 Ja '70

Energy for man and environmental protection. P. Sporn; discussion. Science 166:1459-60+; 167:1439 D 19 '69, Mr 13 '70

Environmental questions that nobody likes to hear. Am City 85:8 Mr '70

Environmental renewal or oblivion; quo vadis? policies of the Coca-Cola company; address, April 16, 1970. J. P. Austin. Vital Speeches 36:470-5 My 15 '70

Everyday ways to cut down pollution. il Changing T 24:17-19 D '70

Executive investor: pollution and profits. Duns 95:93-6 F '70

Forty ways you can depollute the earth. Mlle 70:112+ Ap '70

Global monitor. Newsweek 75:87 F 23 '70

Green survival. R. F. Lederer. il Parks & Rec 5:34-6 O '70

Housewife's dilemma. J. L. O'Neill. Am Home 74:26+ Ja '71

How organic farming can save our air. E. Gibbons. Org Gard & Farm 17:106+ N '70

How to control pollution; interview. L. A. DuBridge. il por U S News 68:48-52 Ja 19 '70

How to stop pollution; interview. R. E. Train. il pors U S News 69:54-8 N 23 '70

Local wars against pollution. il U S News 68:22-5 F 9 '70

Long, littered path to clean air and water. G. Bylinsky. il Fortune 82:112-15+ O '70

Notes and comment: disposal without pollution. New Yorker 46:17 Ag 29 '70

Now a boom in devices to fight pollution. il U S News 69:43-4 Ag 31 '70

Our polluted America: what women can do. E. S. Muskie. por Ladies Home J 87:59+ F '70

Paying for the cleanup. H. C. Wallich. Newsweek 75:72 Ja 26 '70

People need advocates. V. J. Yannacone. il Am For 76:20-3+ Ap '70

People-power and pollution: what can I do? C. E. Randall. il Am For 76:28-35+ O '70

Petroleum industry's role in the preservation of the environment. F. N. Ikard. il Parks & Rec 5:18-21+ My '70

Politics of pollution; why are the corporations cooperating? M. Harrington. Commonweal 92:111-14 Ap 17 '70

Pollution crackdown hits industry. il U S News 68:23-5 Ap 6 '70

Pollution fighters' newsletter. See issues of Popular mechanics, July 1970-

Pollution is a dirty word. R. Sanders. il Suc Farm 68:23-5 Ag '70

Pollution: puffery or progress? FTC investigation into anti-pollution claims. il Newsweek 76:49-51 D 28 '70

Pollution solutions you can use; antipollution ideas. M. Michaelson. il Todays Health 48:19+ Jl '70

Profits before pollution abatement. Nat Parks 44:29 Ja '70

Ravaged environment. il Newsweek 75:30-40+ Ja 26 '70

Setting the alarm; worldwide network of warning stations. Sr Schol 96:15 Mr 9 '70

Solving the power problem. il Time 95:54-5 Je 22 '70

That little spaceship called earth. il Sr Schol 97:12+ S 14 '70

Wayne M. Harris: citizen pollution fighter. H. G. Jackson, jr. il Field & S 75:12+ My '70

What can I do? R. Rodale. il Org Gard & Farm 17:31-4 F '70

Will pollution win the public lands? address; with remarks by J. P. Saylor. E. C. Crafts. il por Am For 76:28-31+ Ja '70

Wink at the environment; California legislative proposals. R. A. Jones. il Nation 210:493-5 Ap 27 '70

See also

Aerospace industries—Pollution control activities

Electronics in pollution control

Environmental movement

Industry and the environmental movement

New York (city)—Environmental protection administration

United States—Environmental protection agency

Economic aspects

Antipollution squeeze. Nat R 22:1150-1 N 3 '70

Banks share in fight against pollution. V. Louviere. Nations Bsns 58:19 D '70

Cloud nine. D. Sanford. il New Repub 163:13-14 O 31 '70

Costly cure; environmental cleanup bill for forest products and packaging companies. Forbes 107:165+ Ja 1 '71

Costs of fighting pollution; eliminating environomental disruption. M. I. Goldman. bibliog f il Cur Hist 59:73-81+ Ag '70

Economics of environmental quality. S. Rose. il Fortune 81:120-3+ F '70

High cost of cleaner air. il Bsns W p 16-17 D 26 '70

How to buy a cleaner environment; adaptation of address, June 16, 1970. M. L. Weidenbaum. Bul Atom Sci 26:19-21 N '70

Open letter to President Nixon. T. L. Kimball. il Nat Wildlife 8:34-5 Ag '70

Opportunity, thy name is pollution; legislation to let commercial banks underwrite water and sewage bonds. il Forbes 105:21-2 Mr 1 '70

Pollution foes find a friend at the bank. Bsns W p 19-20 Jl 4 '70

Pollution price tag: 71 billion dollars. il U S News 69:38-42 Ag 17 '70

Who pays for anti-pollution? Nat R 22:124 F 10 '70

See also

United States—Environmental financing authority (proposed)

Water pollution—Control—Economic aspects

Economic aspects

Chemistry and cost of contamination. R. S. Berry; N. F. Ramsey. il Bul Atom Sci 26:2-5+ Ap '70

Dynamite in pollution; Jacksonville, Fla. TV station WJXT reports on local polluters. C. Gillespie. Nation 211:455-7 N 9 '70; Reply with rejoinder. J. T. Lynch. 211:674 D 28 '70

Economics of pollution. E. L. Dale, jr. il N Y Times Mag p27-9+ Ap 19 '70

If you don't mind my saying so. J. W. Krutch. Am Scholar 39:378+ Sum '70

Politics of ecology, by J. Ridgeway. Review Nation 211:568-9 N 30 '70. C. W. Griffin

Pollution and affluence. K. Cole. Focus 20:12 Je '70

Pollution and the profit motive. il Bsns W p82+ Ap 11 '70

Treating pollution as a business cost. il Bsns W p88+ O 17 '70

Who owns the environment? P. Schrag. Sat R 53:6-9+ Jl 4 '70

International control

See Pollution—Control

Laws and legislation

Action toward cleaner air. il Sci N 99:22-3 Ja 9 '71

Against pollution; clean air bill. Sci N 98:477 D 26 '70

Air pollution: Muskie throws down the gauntlet. L. J. Carter. Science 169:841 Ag 28 '70

Airlines cautious about smoke law in Los Angeles. Aviation W 93:30 D 7 '70

Chevron indicted; toughest federal action against a polluter. Time 95:41 My 18 '70

Detroit's battle with Washington. Bsns W p28 D 5 '70

Environmental degradation and legal action. A. A. D'Amato. Bul Atom Sci 26:24-6 Mr '70

Environmental protection act of 1970; text of bill. Cur Hist 59:48+ Jl '70

Federal government and the environment. G. S. McGovern. Cur Hist 59:82-3 Ag '70

Federal penalties for polluters. Cur Hist 59:84 Ag '70

High cost of cleaner air: 1970 National air quality standards act. il Bsns W p 16-17 D 26 '70

New right to sue polluters. Time 96:37 Ag 24 '70

People need advocates. V. J. Yannacone. il Am For 76:20-3+ Ap '70

POLLUTION—Laws and legislation—*Cont.*
People vs. the polluters. J. Smith. Duns 96: 52 D '70
Pollution politics; IRS clampdown to stop environmentalists' class action suits. New Repub 163:5-6 O 31 '70
Somebody fouled up; symposium. il New Repub 163:13-29 O 31 '70
States join the pollution battle. E. Holsendolph. Fortune 82:116 O '70
Victory for clean air; National air quality standards act of 1970. Time 96:44+ O 5 '70
See also
Water pollution—Laws and legislation

Measurement
Prototype for global network. Sci N 99:24 Ja 9 '71
Slow progress worldwide; need for global environment monitoring network. Sci N 98: 300-1 O 10 '70
See also
Air pollution—Measurement
Oil pollution of rivers, harbors, etc.—Measurement

Moral and religious aspects
Christians and the crisis of environment. B. L. Masse. America 123:82 Ag 22 '70

Physiological effects
First victims. C. Remsberg and B. Remsberg. il Good H 171:74-5+ Ag '70
Pollution invites disease. B. W. Carnow. il Sat R 53:38-40+ Jl 4 '70
See also
Environmental health

Protests, demonstrations, etc, against
See Environmental movement—Marches, rallies, etc.

Taxation
We need a pollution tax! N. F. Ramsey. il Bul Atom Sci 26:3-5 Ap '70

Colorado
For purple mountains' travesty above polluted plain; groups fighting pollution in Colorado. L. Witt. il Todays Health 48:56-9+ D '70

Europe
Industrial Europe faces the challenge of pollution. R. Passino. il UNESCO Courier 23: 61-4 Ag '70

Japan
Student to premier: clean up Japan. il Sr Schol 97:11 O 26 '70

Netherlands
Automatic sentry to warn of pollution. Bsns W p40 My 9 '70

Russia
Communist pollution. Time 96:54 N 30 '70
Convergence of environmental disruption, excerpts from address,. March 1970. M. I. Goldman. bibliog il Science 170:37-42 O 2 '70
Russians worry too. V. Zora. Cur 117:13-15 Ap '70
Sniffing trouble. il Newsweek 75:62 My 11 '70

POLLUTION control industries
See also
General signal corporation

Securities
Glamor in sludge and smog; antipollution stocks. Bsns W p94-5 Ja 24 '70
Growth stocks for the 70's: companies that make pollution-control equipment. il Changing T 24:7-11 Je '70
Pollution control, a new industry. W. A. Stocklin. por Electr World 83:6 My '70

POLLUTION control teach-ins. See Environmental movement—Teach-ins
POLLUTION-Industrial complex. See Industry and the environmental movement
POLLUTION of lakes. See Water pollution
POLLUTION of streams. See Water pollution
POLLUTION policy. See Environmental policy
POLLUTION probe (organization) See Environmental movement—Canada
POLNER, Murray
Can the public schools be saved? Commonweal 93:15-17 O 2 '70
POLO
See also
Water polo
POLSBY, Nelson W.
Strengthening Congress in national policymaking. Yale R 59:481-97 Je '70

POLSCER, Kenneth F.
How to keep your trees healthy. il Org Gard & Farm 17:38-40 F '70
Should you stake and prune your tomato plants? il Org Gard & Farm 17:52-3 Ap '70
POLY I:C
Poly I:C moves into a new arena: immunity. B. J. Culliton. il Sci N 97:323 Mr 28 '70
Polyinosinic acid-polycytidylic acid: inhibition of DNA synthesis stimulated by isoproterenol. F. T. Serota and R. Baserga. bibliog il Science 167:1379-80 Mr 6 '70
POLYADENYLIC acid
DNA-membrane complex: macromolecular content and stimulation of enzymatic activity by polyadenylic acid. W. Firshein and R. G. Gillmor. bibliog il Science 169:66-8 Jl 3 '70
POLYAMIDES
New fiber to clean water; reverse osmosis permeator. il Bsns W p83 D 12 '70
POLYCHAETA. See Annelids
POLYCHLORINATED biphenyls. See Diphenyl compounds
POLYCHROIC film. See Films
POLYETHYLENE paper. See Paper, Polyethylene
POLYGAMY
Ties that bind; Tanzanian women protesting new marriage bill. il Time 95:35 Ap 20 '70
POLYHEDRONS
Roomful of one-room schoolhouses; truncated octahedrons. il Life 69:32-3 N 6 '70
Your very own meditator; dodecahedral structure. K. Isaacs. il Pop Sci 197:92-4+ N '70
POLYINOSINIC-polycytidylic acid. See Poly I:C
POLYMERASE
DNA polymerase activities associated with smooth membranes and ribosomes from rat liver and hepatoma cytoplasm. E. F. Baril and others. bibliog il Science 169:87-9 Jl 3 '70
Finding a cancer clue; RNA-dependent DNA polymerase. Time 96:41 D 21 '70
Specific inhibition of nuclear RNA polymerase II by α-amanitin. T. J. Lindell and others. bibliog il Science 170:447-9 O 23 '70
Teminism marches on; RNA-dependent DNA polymerase. Sch N 98:432 D 5 '70
POLYMERS
Bring future for a serendipitous chemical discovery; microcrystalline polymers. E. Gross. il Sci N 97:378-9 Ap 11 '70
Covalent polymers of water. C. T. O'Konski. bibliog il Science 168:1089-91 My 29 '70
Living polymers: a tool in studies of ions and ion-pairs. M. Szwarc. bibliog il Science 170:23-31 O 2 '70
Long-chain polymer crystals. A. Keller. bibliog il por Phys Today 23:42-50 My '70
New plastic to beat the heat; Ekonol. Bsns W p36 Mr 7 '70
Water-degradable polymers for controlled release of herbicides and other agents. M. L. Beasley and R. L. Collins. Science 169:769-70 Ag 21 '70
See also
Plastics
Polyamides
POLYMORPHISM
High-pressure polymorph of troilite, FeS. L. A. Taylor and H. K. Mao. bibliog il Science 170:850-1 N 20 '70
Polymorphism in benzene, naphthalene, and anthracene at high pressure. S. Block and others. bibliog il Science 169:586-7 Ag 7 '70
POLYMORPHISM (biology)
Genetic polymorphisms of human mitochondrial glutamic oxaloacetic transaminase. R. G. Davidson and others. bibliog il Science 169:391-2 Jl 24 '70
Histocompatibility-2 (H-2) polymorphism in wild mice. J. Klein. bibliog il Science 168: 1362-4 Je 12 '70
POLYNESIA
In search of innocence; H. Adams and J. LaFarge in the South Seas. L. Auchincloss. il pors Am Heritage 21:28-33 Je '70
See also
Education—Polynesia
Tubuai Islands
POLYNESIAN cultural center. See Hawaii
POLYNESIANS
In search of innocence; H. Adams and J. LaFarge in the South Seas. L. Auchincloss. il pors Am Heritage 21:28-33 Je '70
POLYNUCLEOTIDES. See Nucleotides
POLYOL-fluorocarbon blood substitutes. See Blood substitutes
POLYOX. See Resinous products
POLYPEPTIDES. See Peptides
POLYPHEMUS moths. See Moths
POLYPLOIDY. See Chromosomes

POLYPS (tumors) See Tumors
POLYRIBOSOMES. See Nucleoproteins
POLYSACCHARIDES
   See also
   Mucopolysaccharides
POLYTENE chromosomes. See Chromosomes
POLYTETRAFLUOROETHYLENE. See Teflon
POLYUNSATURATED fats. See Oils and fats,
   Edible
POLYWATER. See Water
POMARE, Eleo, dance company. See Dance
   companies
POMERANZ, B. and Chung, S. H.
   Dendritic-tree anatomy codes form-vision
   physiology in tadpole retina. bibliog il Sci-
   ence 170:983-4 N 27 '70
POMERANZ, Y. and others
   Molecular approach to breadmaking. bibliog
   il Science 167-944-9 F 13 '70
POMEROY, Grace. See Globetti, G. jt. auth.
POMEROY, Kenneth B.
   Trees for people; questions and answers. il
   Am For 76:44-5 Ja; 8+ Ap; 28-9 Je '70
POMEROY, Ruth Fairchild
   Christmas is for children too. il Redbook
   136:66-74 D '70
POMMY-VEGA, Janine
   Poem to David, the psalmster. Mlle 72:140
   D '70
POMONA, Calif.

   Public buildings
Suppose the bond issue fails. il Am City 85:
   88+ Mr '70
POMPIDOU, Claude (Cahour)
   Madame Pompidou; interview. ed. by S.
   Dadolle. il Harp Baz 103:76-7 Jl '70

   about
Away from the palace, a fine touch for pinball
   and politicking. il pors Life 68:38-41 F 20
   '70 *
Claude and the long look. pors Time 95:44
   Mr 9 '70 *
France's Madame Pompidou: first lady with
   pizzaz. L. Bergquist. il pors Look 34:40-7
   Ja 27 '70
French visitor with fashion power. il pors
   U S News 68:14 Mr 9 '70 *
POMPIDOU, Georges
   Man from France; interview. ed. by R. B.
   Stolley. il pors Life 68:34-7 F 20 '70
   New look at France; interview. ed. by C.
   Painton. il por U S News 68:44-7 Mr 2 '70

   about
Away from the palace, a fine touch for pin-
   ball and politicking. il pors Life 68:38-41
   F 20 '70 *
Equal time; visit to Russia. il por Newsweek
   76:54-5 O 19 '70 *
France's Madame Pompidou: first lady with
   pizzaz. L. Bergquist. il pors Look 34:40-7
   Ja 27 '70
France's model President. il por Time 95:86
   Ap 20 '70 *
Georges Pompidou: general manager of
   France's household. Y. Chabas. Chr Cent
   87:277-8 Mr 4 '70 *
Pompidou: a new Gallic image. por Time 95:
   18-19 Mr 2 '70 *
Pompidou line. E. Behr. Newsweek 75:42 F
   9 '70
Question of intentions. il por Time 96:37-8
   O 19 '70 *
Remembrances of things past. il pors Time
   96:28 S 28 '70 *
Staking a claim. il Newsweek 76:41-2 O 26
   '70 *

   Visit to the United States, 1970
Bad day in Chicago. Nation 210:292 Mr 16
   '70 *
Coup in Chicago. il por Newsweek 75:30+
   Mr 16 '70 *
France and the U.S. agree to disagree. il por
   Newsweek 75:17-18 Mr 9 '70 *
Pompidou pays a visit. E. Behr. por News-
   week 75:33-4 Mr 2 '70 *
Pompidou postscripts. il Time 95:14-15 Mr
   16 '70 *
Pompidou's trip to America, what he hopes
   to achieve. il pors U S News 68:16 Mr 2 '70 *
President Pompidou of France visits the
   United States; exchange of toasts, re-
   marks, with address to Congress. February
   24-March 3, 1970. G. Pompidou. Dept State
   Bul 62:413-22 Mr 30 '70 *
Sauce and ceremony; President Pompidou's
   three-day Washington visit. il por Time
   95:18 Mr 9 '70 *

POND ecology. See Fresh water ecology
POND life. See Fresh water fauna
POND lilies. See Water lilies
PONIES
   Living museum pieces; Camargue ponies.
   M. Moyal. il Am For 76:25-7+ F '70
PONNAMPERUMA, Cyril
   Life out there. il por Newsweek 76:118 D 14
   '70 *
   Matter of life. por Time 96:68-9 D 14 '70 *
   —and others
   Search for organic compounds in the lunar
   dust from the Sea of Tranquillity. bibliog
   il Science 167:760-2 Ja 30 '70
PONSELLE, Rosa
   Ponselle miracle. D. Hamilton. por Hi Fi
   20:81-2 S '70 *
PONTCHARTRAIN hotel. See New Orleans—
   Hotels, restaurants, etc.
PONTE, Lowell
   Notes on the proliferation non-treaty. il Nat
   R 22:1340-3+ D 15 '70
PONTE, Vincent de Pasciuto
   Multilevel man. il por Time 96:52-3 O 19 '70 *
PONTECORVO, Gillo
   Current cinema. P. Kael. New Yorker 46:159-
   62 N 7 '70 *
PONTIAC, Mich.

   Education
Teacher aide and child care program. D. J.
   Garrison. il Todays Ed 59:32 F '70

   Urban renewal
Design for regenerating a city; human re-
   sources center. W. W. Chase. il Am Ed 6:
   8-13 Mr '70
PONTIAC motor division. See General motors
   corporation—Pontiac motor division
PONTIFICAL commission for studies on jus-
   tice and peace
   See also
   Joint committee on society, development and
   peace
PONY. See Ponies
PONZA ISLAND
   Undiscovered Italy. P. Fiori. il Holiday 48:
   40-1+ Jl '70
POOL, Ithiel de Sola
   Paradox of nonviolent war in Vietnam. por
   Life 69:2 Jl 4 '70
POOL, (game) See Billiards
POOL tables. See Billiard tables
POOLHOUSES. See Bathhouses
POOLMAN, Henry
   Henry Poolman story. J. S. Barrett. il pors
   Outdoor Life 145:68-71+ Ap '70 *
POOLS. See Swimming pools
POOR
   See also
   Homeless, The
   Slums

   Health and hygiene
Doctor and newcomers to the ghetto; excerpt
   from Children of crisis. R. Coles. Am Scholar
   40:66-80 Wint '70

   United States
Architects design for a new client: the poor.
   J. Hale. il Arch Rec 148:144-7 O '70
Combating poverty; plan of U.S. Catholic
   conference. Commonweal 93:60 O 16 '70
Culture and poverty, by C. A. Valentine. Re-
   view
   Trans-Action 7:60-2 N '69. C. I. Waxman
Extension's big push; better nutrition for
   low-income families. J. Gillies. Farm J
   94:74 F '70
Family planning and the poor. W. M. Hern.
   New Repub 163:17-19 N 14 '70
Farm programs don't help the rural poor. B.
   L. Masse. America 122:623 Je 13 '70
How the Mafia preys on the poor. E. H.
   Methvin. Read Digest 97:49-55 S '70
If you were on welfare. R. M. Elman. il Sat
   R 53:27-9+ My 23 '70
Labor day statement, 1970; U.S. Catholic
   conference devoted to the white ethnic
   working class. America 123:111 S 5 '70
Pollution and the poor. W. Barthelmes. Com-
   monweal 91:549-50 F 20 '70; Discussion. 92:
   3+, 107+ Mr 13, Ap 17 '70
Poverty: a losing war; report on urban pov-
   erty. il Newsweek 76:117 N 23 '70
Poverty down your road; Kosciusko County,
   Ind. E. Logsdon. il Farm J 94:52-4 F '70
Poverty programs: the view from 1914. H.
   M. Douty. Mo Labor R 93:69-71 Ap '70
Profile of the poor. Sat R 53:23 My 23 '70

POOR—United States—*Continued*
Values as social indicators of poverty and race relations in America. M. Rokeach and S. Parker. bibliog f il Ann Am Acad 388: 97-111 Mr '70
We must wipe out hunger in America! interview. ed. by P. Jablow. E. F. Hollings. il por Good H 170:68-9+ Ja '70
Working women in urban poverty neighborhoods. H. M. Willacy and H. J. Hilaski. bibliog f il Mo Labor R 93:35-8 Je '70
See also
Church and social problems
Economic assistance, Domestic
National welfare rights organization
Negroes—Social conditions
Public welfare—United States
White House conference on food, nutrition, and health
also subhead Poor under names of cities, e.g. New York (city)—Poor
POOR laws
See also
Public welfare—Law

United States
See also
Public welfare—United States
POOR man's clever daughter; drama. See Feather, J.
POOR relief. See Public welfare
POOR whites. See Poor—United States
POP art. See Art, Modern
POP lyrics. See Music, Popular (songs, etc)
POP music. See Music, Popular (songs, etc)
POPE, Alexander
Harlot form. J. D. Merritt. il Opera N 35: 6-7 Ja 9 '71 *
POPE, James D.
Comenius speaks to modern man. bibliog Sch & Soc 98:440-5 N '70
POPE John XXIII peace prize. See John XXIII peace prize
POPES
Next Pope; Cardinal Villot, rumored as Pope Paul's successor. J. Deedy. Commonweal 93:338 Ja 8 '71
See also
Papacy
Papal audiences
Election
Burden of age; voting ban on cardinals over eighty. Newsweek 76:47 D 7 '70
Infallibility
Bishop from Petricula. por Time 96:58+ Jl 27 '70
Infallibility revisited. L. M. Orsy. America 122:246 Mr 7 '70
Papal infallibility. Chr Today 14:23 Jl 17 '70
Primacy
Council over Pope? Towards a provisional ecclesiology, by F. Oakley. Review Commonweal 91:490-2 Ja 30 '70. R. P. McBrien
Residence
Place in the country: Castel Gandolfo. il Time 96:64 S 14 '70
POPOLIZIO, Vincent J.
Art as communication. il Sch Arts 70:8-9 D '70
POPPER, Samuel H.
What about the middle school? Ed Digest 35:17-18 Ja '70
POPPIES
How poppies bloom. R. E. Atkinson and E. Haraszty. il McCalls 97:48+ Jl '70
Its ancestors were wildlings, and the ancestry shows; Iceland poppies. il Sunset 145:70-1 S '70
Poppy clan. R. M. Peters. il Horticulture 48: 28-31+ Je '70
Queen of the perennials, the oriental poppy. B. Brinhart. il Org Gard & Farm 17:66-8 Mr '70
POPPY, John
The band; music from home. il Look 34:22-7 Ag 25 '70
Beyond survival. il Look 34:22-35 Ja 13 '70
(ed) See Davis, A. Adelle Davis and the new nutrition religion
POPULAR culture
History, anthropology, and mass movements. G. L. Mosse. bibliog f Am Hist R 75:447-52 D '69
See also
United States—Popular culture
POPULAR democratic front for the liberation of Palestine. See Fedayeen

POPULAR electronics (periodical)
New look. O. P. Ferrell. Pop Electr 33:7-8 S '70
POPULAR front for the liberation of Palestine. See Fedayeen
POPULAR mechanics (periodical)
1970 racing guide. il Pop Mech 133:S1+ Ja '70
1971 auto racing guide. il Pop Mech 135:S3-4+ Ja '71
POPULAR music. See Music, Popular (songs, etc)
POPULAR songs. See Music, Popular (songs, etc)
POPULAR unity coalition (Chile) See Political parties—Chile
POPULARITY
When you want to be popular. J. Brothers. Good H 171:50+ O '70
POPULATION
Drive to stop population growth; Zero population growth plan. il U S News 68:36-8 Mr 2 '70
Safeguarding the quality of life. America 122: 548 My 23 '70
See also
Birth control
Birth rate
Census
also subhead Population under names of countries, states, cities, e.g. United States —Population

Anecdotes, facetiae, satire, etc.
Small solution. R. Armour. Sat R 53:24 N 14 '70
Conferences
Reducing the environmental impact of population growth; AAAS symposium, December 26-30, 1970. S. F. Singer. Science 169: 1233 S 18 '70

Overpopulation
Affluence and effluence; U.S. N. Cousins. Sat R 53:53 My 2 '70
Are there too many of us? P. R. Ehrlich. il McCalls 97:46-7+ Jl '70
Big city syndrome. D. Behrman. UNESCO Courier 23:20+ Ag '70
Calhoun's horrible mousery; effects of overcrowding on mice. S. Alsop. Newsweek 76:96 Ag 17 '70
Dual challenge of health and hunger: a global crisis; reprint. G. A. Borgstrom. il Bul Atom Sci 26:42-6 O '70
Ecological destruction is a condition of American life; interview. ed. by P. Collier. P. Ehrlich. il Mlle 70:188-9+ Ap '70
Economic growth: new doubts about an old ideal. il Time 95:72-4 My 2 '70
Hidden effects of overpopulation. P. R. Ehrlich and J. P. Holdren. Sat R 53:52 Ag 1 '70
In my opinion; we must stop multiplying! R. Gordon. por Seventeen 29:234 My '70
Laws to limit family size. L. Lader. Parents Mag 45:58-61 O '70
Man is the endangered species; interview. P. R. Ehrlich. por Nat Wildlife 8:38-9 Ap '70
More or less people; thoughts on feeding the hungry. W. H. Davis. il New Repub 162:19-21 Je 20 '70
Nonsense explosion. B. Wattenberg. il New Repub 162:18-23 Ap 4 '70; Discussion. 162: 24-6+ My 2; 44-6 My 9; 29-31 My 16 '70
Overpopulated America. W. H. Davis; discussion. New Repub 162:28-30 Ja 31 '70
Overpopulation: crisis today, disaster tomorrow. por Parents Mag 45:30 Ja '70
People pollution; excerpt from The doomsday book. G. R. Taylor. il Ladies Home J 87:74+ O '70
Population and the dignity of man. R. L. Shinn. Chr Cent 87:442-8 Ap 15 '70
Population; EQ index. il Nat Wildlife 8:38-9 O '70; Same. Schol Teach Jr/Sr High pA14-15 O 5 '70
Population overgrowth, the fertile curse. P. R. Ehrlich. por Field & S 75:58+ Je '70
Population problem: in search of a solution. J. J. Spengler; discussion. Science 167:1438-9 Mr 13 '70
Problem of the people bomb. il Sr Schol 97-19-20 S 28 '70
Quality of life: a proposed program for global action by the UN; address, April 21, 1970. R. N. Gardner. Vital Speeches 36:466-70 My 15 '70
Rising population: its effect on environment. S. J. McNaughton. il Cons 24:14-16 Je '70
Scientist looks at the human zoo. D. Morris. il por U S News 68:38 Mr 2 '70
Smaller families: a national imperative. G. J. Hecht. por Parents Mag 45:24+ Jl '70
Starvation or plenty? by C. Clark. Review Nat R 22:631-2 Je 16 '70. G. Wills

POPULATION—Overpopulation—*Continued*
Third fish. K. S. Norris. New Repub 162:16-18 My 9 '70
We're standing on the edge of the earth. P. Ehrlich. Nat Wildlife 8:16-17 O '70
Why the population bomb is a Rockefeller baby. S. Weissman. il Ramp Mag 8:42-7 My '70
  See also
Population, Increase of

  Anecdotes, facetiae, satire, etc.
International mortality lottery. W. D. Dean. Chr Cent 87:449-50 Ap 15 '70
Last winter; fable. C. C. Lamb. il Nat Parks 44:21-2 Mr '70
Stork outflies American eagle; reprint. R. D. Lamm. il Am For 76:4+ Jl '70

  Statistics
World population. Natur Hist 79:60-2 Ja '70
POPULATION, Distribution of
Advances in segregation. Sci Am 222:46 Ap '70
Portrait of a decade. D. H. Wrong. il N Y Times Mag p22-3+ Ag 2 '70
'70 census: how many Americans and where they are. il U S News 69:22-5 S 14 '70
Surprises in the '70 census. il U S News 69:17 Ag 31 '70
What U.S. will be like by 1980: meaning of population shifts. il U S News 70:38-40 Ja 11 '71
Why do people move? P. R. Ehrlich and J. P. Holdren. Sat R 53:51 S 5 '70
POPULATION, Increase of
Drive to stop population growth. il U S News 68:36-8 Mr 2 '70
Economy, ecology, and zero population growth; conditions affecting construction industry. J. E. Carlson. Arch Rec 148:59-60 Ag '70
If population stops growing; impact on U.S. il U S News 69:80-2 S 28 '70
Latin America's unemployment problem. I. Beller. Mo Labor R 93:8 N '70
Multiply thy kind and perish. C. E. Gillham. il Field & S 75:8+ Jl '70
On population and environment; address, June 8, 1970. P. M. Hauser. Vital Speeches 36:696-701 S 1 '70
People pollution. P. R. Ehrlich. il Audubon 72:4-9 My '70
People problem. P. R. Ehrlich and J. P. Holdren. Sat R 53:42-3 Jl 4 '70
Product pushers vs. the people. C. F. Wurster. por Field & S 75:60+ Je '70
Twice as many people in next thirty-six years. il U S News 69:29-30 N 9 '70
United States population policy, origins and development; address, August 21, 1970. P. P. Claxton, jr. Dept State Bul 63:317-26 S 21 '70
U.S. population growth: would slower be better? L. A. Mayer. il Fortune 81:80-3+ Je '70
World population. il Natur Hist 79:60-2 Ja '70
ZPG; new movement challenges the U.S. to stop growing. il Life 68:32-7 Ap 17 '70
  See also
Human ecology
POPULATION pressure. See Population—Overpopulation
POPULATIONS, Animal. See Animal populations
POR qué? (periodical) See Periodicals—Mexico
PORCELAIN. See Pottery
PORCELAIN, Chinese. See Pottery, Chinese
PORCELAIN berry. See Ampelopsis
PORCELAIN figurines. See Figurines
PORCH, William M. and others
Atmospheric aerosol: does a background level exist? bibliog il Science 170:315-17 O 16 '70
PORCHES
How to build a stone stoop. C. F. Newstrand. il Pop Sci 197:92 S '70
PORCUPINES
Peculiar porcupine. N. Smith. il Nat Wildlife 7:20-1 O '69
PORCUPINES at the university; story. See Barthelme, D.
PORIFERA. See Sponges
PORK
  See also
Cookery—Meat
National pork producers council
Swine
  Advertising
  See Meat industry and trade—Advertising
  Marketing
  See Meat—Marketing

PORK cutting. See Meat cutting
PORK grading. See Meat—Grading and standardization
PORK industry. See Meat industry and trade
PORK industry committee. See National livestock and meat board—Pork industry committee
PORNOGRAPHY. See Immoral literature and pictures; Obscenity (law); Sex in moving pictures
PORPHYRIA
Chemically induced porphyria: prevention by prior treatment with phenobarbital. L. Kaufman and others. bibliog il Science 170:320-2 O 16 '70
George III and the mad-business, by I. Macalpine and R. Hunter. Review
  Newsweek 76:67-8 Ag 3 '70. R. A. Gross
Safe from the sun; beta-carotene treatments. Newsweek 75:76-7 Je 22 '70
PORPHYRINS
Fluorometric examination of a lunar sample. J. H. Rho and others. Science 167:754-5 Ja 30 '70
Harderian gland: development and influence of early hormonal treatment on porphyrin content. L. Wetterberg and others. bibliog il Science 168:996-8 My 22 '70
Search for porphyrins in lunar dust. G. W. Hodgson and others. bibliog il Science 167:763-5 Ja 30 '70
PORPOISES. See Dolphins (mammals)
PORSCHE, Ferry
Young Dr Porsche. E. Seidler. por Motor T 22:52-4 Jl '70 *
PORSCHE (automobile) See Automobiles, Foreign
PORT ELCO club. See Boat clubs
PORT-OF-SPAIN, Trinidad
Loss of El Dorado, by V. S. Naipaul. Review
  Nation 211:311-12 O 5 '70. A. Cheuse
PORT terminals. See Terminals
PORT WASHINGTON, N.Y.
Drug scene in East Egg. E. Diamond. il N Y Times Mag p28-9+ My 17 '70; Discussion. p56-7 Je 28 '70
PORTABLE clothes washers. See Washing machines
PORTABLE electric saws. See Saws
PORTABLE pensions. See Pensions, Industrial
PORTABLE phonograph. See Phonograph, Portable
PORTABLE radio receivers. See Radio receivers, Portable
PORTABLE radio telephone. See Radio telephone, Portable
PORTABLE schools. See School buildings, Portable
PORTAGES
Voyageur. R. L. Nelson. il Nat Parks & Con Mag 44:20-4 D '70
PORTER, Cole
New kick out of you. Newsweek 76:102-3 Jl 13 '70 *
PORTER, D. Gareth
Saigon's secret police. Nation 210:498-500 Ap 27 '70
PORTER, Eliot
Smokies spring; excerpts from Southern wilderness. il Audubon 72:32-9 My '70
PORTER, James A.
Obituary
  Negro Hist Bul por 39:99 Ap '70 *
PORTER, Katherine Anne
Belles-lettres. G. Culligan. il Sat R 53:29-30 Mr 28 '70 *
Miss Porter. G. Wolff. por Newsweek 75:91 Ap 6 '70 *
Placing Miss Porter. C. T. Samuels. New Repub 162:25-6 Mr 7 '70 *
PORTER, Marina Oswald. See Oswald, M.
PORTER, Rufus
Yankee da Vinci. il Time 96:45 S 7 '70 *
PORTER, Sheila
(comp) Opera at Covent Garden: 1946-1970. Sat R 53:44-5 Je 27 '70
PORTER, Stephen C. See Denton, G. H. jt. auth.
PORTER, Sylvia
Spending your money; questions and answers. See issues of Ladies' home journal
PORTER, Willard H.
Craziest cruise afloat. il Motor B 126:46-7+ O '70
PORTER, William W. 2d
National resource revenue sharing. il por Am For 76:24-7+ Ja '70
PORTERFIELD, Jeanne, and Chickering, Lisa
Making travel films; with biographical sketches. il pors Travel & Camera 33:6, 62-7 N '70

PORTERFIELD, Nolan
Cross my father's ground; story. il Harper
240:79-84 Ap '70
PORTIS, Charles
Portis' True grit: adventure story or ent-
wicklungsroman? R. B. Shuman. Engl J
59:367-70 Mr '70 *
PORTLAND, Me.
Finance
Computer upgrades law enforcement, revenue
management; traffic ticket collections dou-
ble. G. A. Flaherty. il Am City 85:102-3
O '70
PORTLAND, Ore.
Education
Adams high: best around; John Adams high
school. Portland, Ore. il Newsweek 75:68-9
F 16 '70
Portland's unconventional Adams high. J.
Guernsey. il Am Ed 6:3-7 My '70
Elections
Backlash on law and order. Nation 211:515
N 23 '70
Fountains
See Fountains
Music
See also
Portland opera association
Water supply
Portland water bureau grows as regional sup-
plier. il Am City 85:96 N '70
PORTLAND community college, Ore.
Portland community college. il Arch Rec 147:
144-7 Je '70
PORTLAND opera association
Report:
Lucia di Lammermoor. F. Kinkaid. Op-
era N 34:26 My 16 '70
Rossini's Barbiere di Siviglia. F. Kinkaid.
Opera N 34:30 Mr 14 '70
PORTLAND state university. See Oregon. State
university, Portland
PORTNOY, Armand
Portnoy complains. por Time 96:33 O 12 '70 *
PORTO, S. P. S. See Rousseau, D. L. jt. auth.
PORTOBELO, Panama
Portobelo. G. de Zéndegui. il Américas 22:
20-30 Ag '70
PORTO CERVO. See Sardinia
PORTO ERCOLE, Italy
1970: the year of Porto Ercole. il Holiday 47:
52-5 Ja '70
PORTO VENERE, Italy. See Portovenere,
Italy
PORTOVENERE, Italy
Porto Venere and the Cinque Terre. P. Gra-
vina. Harp Baz 103:68+ Ap '70
PORTRAIT painting
Bettina Steinke, a painter of people. F. Whit-
aker. il por Am Artist 35:20-7+ Ja '71
C. L. MacNelly: portrait painter. F. Taubes.
il por Am Artist 34:24-9+ My '70
Nelson Shanks: interview, ed. by R. Goetz.
N. Shanks. il por Am Artist 34:58-65+ N
'70
New light on Joseph H. Davis, left hand
painter. N. F. Little. il Antiques 98:754-7
N '70
Painting watercolor portraits. E. A. Whitney.
il Am Artist 34:38-43 Ag '70
Portraiture: the face you owe it all to.
Bsns W p87 Ap 4 '70
See also
Gainsborough, T.
PORTRAIT sculpture
Man and his mountain; carving a statue
of Chief Crazy Horse out of a solid granite
mountain, the South Dakota Black Hills.
il por Design 71:22-3 mid-Wint '70
Portrait head in clay. D. Preiss. il Am Artist
34:30-5+ F '70
PORTRAITS
See also
Photography—Portraits
Portrait painting
PORTRAITS, American
American paintings in the Reynolda house
collection. B. B. Lassiter. il Antiques 98:
758-65 N '70
Expatriate portraits: Charlestonians in muse-
ums outside of Charleston. H. G. McCormack. il Antiques 98:787-93 N '70
Henry Walton, American artist. L. Rehner.
il Antiques 97:414-17 Mr '70
Joseph Wright's portrait of Frederick Muh-
lenberg. M. H. Fabian. il por Antiques 97:
256-7 F '70
Paintings in the council chamber of Charleston's city hall. A. W. Rutledge. il Antiques
98:794-9 N '70

Portraits of John Quincy Adams and his wife;
excerpts. A. Oliver. pors Antiques 98:748-
53 N '70
Portraits of Rebecca Gratz by Thomas Sully.
H. R. London. pors Antiques 98:115-17 Ji
'70
PORTRAITS of children. See Children in art
PORTRAITURE. See Photography—Portraits
PORTS
Caribbean's great ports of call. F. Rohr, jr.
il Travel & Camera 33:50-4+ Ja '70
See also
Harbors
also subhead Harbor under names of
cities, e.g. New York (city)—Harbor
PORTUGAL
See also
Albufeira
Church and state in Portugal
Estoril
Oporto
United Nations—Portugal
Colonies
Portugal's drang nach osten. C. R. Boxer.
Am Hist R 75:1684-91 O '70
U.S. abstains on U.N. resolution on Portu-
guese territories; statement, November 14,
1969. S. M. Finger. Dept State Bul 61:641-2
D 29 '69
See also
Macao
Commerce
Portugal's drang nach osten. C. R. Boxer.
Am Hist R 75:1684-91 O '70
Description and travel
Charles Apt in Portugal. J. H. Michel. il por
Am Artist 34:54-62 Ap '70
Travel notes. R. Joseph. Esquire 74:86+ D
'70
Economic conditions
See also
Cost of living—Portugal
Foreign relations
Spain and Portugal: continuity and change.
A. P. Whitaker. Cur Hist 58:287-91+ My
'70
History
Evolution of the Ottoman seaborne empire
in the age of the oceanic discoveries, 1453-
1525. A. C. Hess. bibliog f il Am Hist R 75:
1892-919 D '70
Bibliography
Articles and other books received; comp. by
C. J. Bishko. See issues of American his-
torical review
Politics and government
Salazar's legacy survives in Portugal. W. E.
Greening. Chr Cent 87:708-9 Je 3 '70
Thaw in Portugal. D. L. Wheeler. For Affairs
48:769-81 Jl '70
Religious institutions and affairs
See also
Protestant churches—Portugal
PORTUGUESE cookery. See Cookery, Portu-
guese
PORTUGUESE GUINEA
Our army is our whole people; excerpts from
remarks; ed. by R. Levine. A. Cabral. il por
Newsweek 75:38-9 Mr 9 '70
PORTUGUESE man-of-war
What is the world's deadliest animal? G.
Compton. il Sci Digest 68:24-8 Ag '70
PORTULACA
Portulaca is a summer dazzler. Sunset 144:238
My '70
POSATI, Linda P. and Paliansch, M. J.
Bradykinin inhibition by butylated hydro-
xyanisole. il Science 168:121-2 Ap 3 '70
POSITIONS, Applications for. See Applications
for positions
POSITIVISM
See also
Logical positivism
POSNER, David
Dialogue between two hunters; poem. Yale
R 59:398 Mr '70
POSSESSION (law)
See also
Real property
POST, Troy Victor
Rich way to make a getaway. E. Shrake.
il por Sports Illus 33:26-33 Ag 31 '70 *
POST, Washington. See Washington post
POST boxes. See Mailboxes

POST cards
Early bohemians; picture postcards of La Bohème. il Opera N 34:16 Ja 24 '70
French sentimentals and embroidered cards. M. Skillicorn. il Hobbies 75:153 Ap '70
Writer with a camera. R. Arnold. por Writers Digest 50:46-8 S '70

POST office department (United States) See United States—Post office department

POSTAGE stamps
American history through commemorative stamps. H. S. Gloomgarden. Review Hobbies 74:131+ F '70. H. Herst. jr
Most expensive bit of printing in the world: the 1856 British Guiana one cent. P. W. Schmidtchen. il Hobbies 75:134-6+ Jl '70
One cent; sale of the British Guiana one-cent magenta. New Yorker 46:33-4 Ap 4 '70
Photos on stamps. R. Arnold. por Writers Digest 50:50+ N '70
Stamps. H. Herst, jr. See issues of Hobbies
See also
Computers—Philatelic applications
Postmarks

Collectors and collecting
Ageless lure of stamp collecting. il Changing T 24:41-2 N '70
Like moths to flame. Forbes 106:40-1 Jl 1 '70
New look in stamp collecting. W. A. H. Birnie. il Read Digest 97:174-9 O '70
One-cent treasure. il Life 68:73-4 Ap 24 '70
Specimen stamps. H. Herst, jr. Hobbies 75:131 Ap '70
Stamp history. H. Herst, jr. Hobbies 75:131+ Jl '70
Starting a library stamp club; children from about seven to fourteen. J. S. James. bibliog il por Wilson Lib Bul 44:645-9 F '70

History
Stamp history. H. Herst, jr. Hobbies 75:131+ Je '70

POSTAL censorship
Et tu, Burger! Supreme court decision on direct-mail advertising. Nation 210:645 Je 1 '70
Stretching pornography. Chr Today 14:26 Je 5 '70
Supreme court upholds bar to erotic mail. S. Wagner. Pub W 197:18 My 18 '70
Unwanted mail: a verdict for privacy. Consumer Rep 35:456-7 Ag '70
Washington busily debates the aspects of pornography. S. Wagner. Pub W 198:26-7 D 7 '70

POSTAL employees
Untangling the mess in the post office. il Bsns W p78-80+ Mr 28 '70
See also
Strikes—United States—Postal employees
United federation of postal clerks

Salaries, allowances, etc.
Mailman's overtime doesn't go through. Bsns W p50 D 19 '70

POSTAL laws and regulations. See Postal service—Laws and regulations

POSTAL rates
United States
Book and library rates rest on Senate action. S. Wagner. Pub W 197:76 Je 29 '70
Fate of postal rates still uncertain. S. Wagner. Pub W 198:122 Jl 13 '70
Higher rates expected for fourth-class mail. S. Wagner. Pub W 198:31 Ag 10 '70
Pending bills threaten postal rates for books. S. Wagner. Pub W 197:128 Je 8 '70
Postal rates and periodicals. R. L. Tobin. Sat R 53:63-4 N 14 '70
Postal rates will go through. il Bsns W p36 Ap 25 '70
Postal reform threatens special book rates. S. Wagner. Pub W 197:23 My 11 '70
10 cents to mail a first-class letter? U S News 68:40 Ap 13 '70

POSTAL service
Tentative obituary. G. A. Codding, jr. Nation 211:307 O 5 '70
See also
Mail boats
Rocket mail
Universal postal union

Laws and regulations
Air transport section cut from postal bill. Aviation W 92:26 Je 29 '70
See also
Postal censorship

Letter carriers
Day the mail stopped. il Newsweek 75:14-17 Mr 30 '70
Strike that stunned the country. il pors Time 95:10-16 Mr 30 '70

Anecdotes, facetiae, satire, etc.
Sack of corn candy. R. A. Smith. il Har Yrs 10:14-15 Ap '70

Unordered merchandise
AAP proposes alternative to negative option ban. S. Wagner. Pub W 198:33 N 9 '70
FTC challenges negative option mail sale. S. Wagner. Pub W 197:33-4 My 25 '70
FTC hears pros and cons on negative option plans. S. Wagner. Pub W 198:21-2 N 30 '70
FTC moves to ban unordered merchandise. S. Wagner. Pub W 198:47 Jl 20 '70
FTC postpones hearing on negative option. S. Wagner. Pub W 198:49 Jl 27 '70
Further comment on negative option. C. B. Grannis. Pub W 197:45 Je 15 '70
Provisional consent order on negative option. S. Wagner. Pub W 197:76-7 Je 29 '70
What did you get in the mail today? V. Jaxon. Har Yrs 10:17-18 D '70

Great Britain
Going concern. H. R. Mayes. Sat R 53:13-14 F 7 '70
Some countries have it in the bag. il Bsns W p83 Mr 28 '70

Sweden
Some countries have it in the bag. il Bsns W p83 Mr 28 '70

United States
As new mail service gets set: changes you can expect. il U S News 69:44-5 O 19 '70
Better mail service soon? il U S News 69:33-4 Ag 17 '70
Dividends from the postal strike; business for facsimile and mailing services. Bsns W p36+ Ap 25 '70
Enduring mail mess. Time 95:14 Mr 30 '70
Express mail: how it works. U S News 69:69 D 14 '70
Fall in for mail call; with report by reservist. F. Von Moschzisker. il Life 68:26-9 Ap 3 '70
How a post office corporation would work. il Changing T 24:17-20 F '70
If postal system is reformed. il U S News 68:34-5 Ap 27 '70
Miracle of Christmas. Newsweek 77:70-4 Ja 11 '70
Overhauling the mails; interview. W. Blount. il por U S News 68:46-51 My 4 '70
Post office blues. D. Sanford. New Repub 162:19-22 Mr 21 '70
Postal reformers finally deliver; with editorial comment. Bsns W p20, 76 Ag 8 '70
Service of efficiency? proposed postal corporation. R. G. Sherrill. Nation 210:386-8 Ap 6 '70
Stopping junk mail. Time 95:49 My 18 '70
Toward postal reorganization. J. G. Butler. il Chr Cent 87:104-8 Ja 28 '70
Untangling the mess in the post office. il Bsns W p78-80+ Mr 28 '70
What the new postmen will deliver. il Bsns W p22-3 O 31 '70
Why United parcel admits its size. il Bsns W p94+ Jl 18 '70
See also
Air mail service
American courier corporation
Parcel post
Postal censorship
Postal rates—United States
United States—Post office department
United States postal service (proposed)

Vietnam (Republic)
Viet-Nam's mail delivery hazardous. Hobbies 75:96 Je '70

POSTAL unions. See Government employees unions

POSTCARDS. See Post cards

POSTCARDS; drama. See Prideaux, James

POSTELLE, Yvonne
Migrant youngsters: our forgotten children. il Parents Mag 45:60-3 My '70

POSTERIZATION. See Photography—Printing processes

POSTERS
Malvenido Rockefeller! anti-American posters in Latin America. D. Horowitz. il Ramp Mag 8:20-5 F '70
Matchless art of Lucian Bernhard. R. Foster. il Am Artist 34:54-9+ D '70
Power to the poster. D. Preiss. il Am Artist 34:33-41+ My '70

POSTI, Lauri A.
Lenin and cultural rights of minorities. il UNESCO Courier 23:16-21 Jl '70

POSTMAN, Neil
Once upon a time: a fable of student power. il N Y Times Mag p 10-11 Je 14 '70

POSTMARKS
Paquebot and packet boat mail. Hobbies 74:131+ Ja '70
POSTMEN. See Postal service—Letter carriers
POSTNATAL exercises. See Exercise
POSTNATAL treatment. See Obstetrics
POSTON, Patricia
This is my daughter; story. Good H 170:72-3 F '70
POSTPARTUM depression. See Depression, Mental
POSTPARTUM mental illness. See Mental illness
POSTPARTUM schizophrenia. See Schizophrenia
POT. See Marijuana
POTASSIUM-argon dating. See Radioactive dating
POTASSIUM in the body
Fetal kidney in organ culture: abnormalities of development induced by decreased amounts of potassium. J. F. S. Crocker and R. L. Vernier. bibliog il Science 169:485-7 Jl 31 '70
Potassium ion specific electrode with high selectivity for potassium over sodium. M. S. Frant and J. W. Ross, jr. bibliog il Science 167:987-8 F 13 '70
POTATO salads. See Salads
POTATOES
From desert sand, $1000 an acre the first year; Grant County, Wash. G. Lorang. il Farm J 94:A22-3 F '70
My organic-trench-method potatoes. E. Lang. il Org Gard & Farm 17:49-51 Je '70
Why I plant the whole potato. J. R. Coggins. il Org Gard & Farm 17:58-9 Mr '70
See also
Cookery—Vegetables
Sweet potatoes

History
Potato. D. Ugent. bibliog il Science 170:1161-6 D 11 '70

Prices
NFO's new drive for $3.50 spuds. G. Lorang. il Farm J 94:49 My '70
Potato growers protest with fire. il Bsns W p29-30 Ap 4 '70
POTENCY, Sexual. See Impotence
POTENTIAL, Electric
Charge-coupled devices would be cheap, compact. G. B. Lubkin. il Phys Today 23:17-18 O '70
POTENTIAL, Theory of
See also
Tunneling (physics)
POTOK, Chaim
Jews of the 1970's. Ladies Home J 86:134 D '69
about
What is in the name? analysis of The chosen. F. Leeper. Engl J 59:63-4 Ja '70
POTOMAC electric power company of Washington, D.C.
Making money work. S. Meisenberg. il Har Yrs 10:48-9 S '70
POTOMAC RIVER
Potomac River dams; testimony and excerpts from remarks of other witnesses at Senate hearings. A. W. Smith. il Nat Parks & Con Mag 44:23-6 S '70
POTOSÍ, Bolivia
Potosí and Charcas. R. P. Romecín. il Américas 22:2-7 Mr '70
POTS and pans. See Kitchen utensils
POTSDAM declaration, 1945
President replies to Soviet letter on Postdam conference anniversary; exchange of letters. R. M. Nixon; A. N. Kosygin. Dept State Bul 63:388-9 O 5 '70
POTTED plants. See Plants, Potted
POTTER, David Morris
Two southern historians. G. M. Fredrickson. Am Hist R 75:1387-92 Je '70 *
POTTER, E. J.
What's an E. J. Potter? S. Kelly. il pors Hot Rod 23:88-90 S '70 *
POTTER, Marjorie H.
Recreation in Asia. il Parks & Rec 5:44-6+ N '70
POTTER, Neal
Antarctic: any economic future? il por Bul Atom Sci 26:94-9 D '70
POTTER, Stephen
Words only. See issues of American record guide
POTTER, V. R. and others
Purpose and function of the university. bibliog Science 167:1590-3 Mr 20 '70

POTTERS
Ceramactivities. See issues of Ceramics monthly
On being a professional potter. H. Fromhold. il por Ceram Mo 18:26-7 My; 30-1 Je; 29-30 S '70
See also
Andreson, L.
Gordy, W. D.
Hamada, A.
Jahr, E.
LaVerdiere, B.
Prieto, E.
Riegger, H.
Staffel, B.
Wyman, W.
POTTERS marks. See Pottery—Marks
POTTERS workshops. See Workshops
POTTERY
Ceramic stitchery; clay birds on stitched backdrops. R. Wrenn. il pors Design 71:38-41 mid-Sum '70
Consumers and the earthenware problem; lead hazard. Sci N 98:382 N 14 '70
Pots and non-pots. J. Goodheart. il Sch Arts 70:30-1 Ja '71
R for Philip; ceramic ware as source of lead poisoning. M. A. Guitar. il Good H 170:12+ My '70
Sectioned plates. R. F. Eilenberger. il Ceram Mo 18:28-9 N '70
See also
Ceramic sculpture
Cloisonné
Cups
Drinking vessels
Glazes and glazing
Tableware
Tureens
Vases

Collectors and collecting
In the service of soup: a great collection; Campbell collection. E. Gaines. il Antiques 97:109-18 Ja '70
Japanese porcelains in American and Canadian collections. R. S. Cleveland. il Antiques 98:927-31 D '70

Decoration
Creating facade forms. R. F. Ellenberger. il Ceram Mo 17:30-2 D '69
Stretched texture. D. M. Johnson. il Ceram Mo 18:20-2 F '70

Exhibitions
Boston centennial exhibition. il Ceram Mo 18:24-5 F '70
Ceramic symposium at Bechyne. L. D. Synder. il Ceram Mo 18:14-17 N '70
Ceramics/Northwest. il Ceram Mo 18:24-5 O '70
Coffee, tea, and other cups; exhibition at the Museum of contemporary crafts, New York. il Ceram Mo 18:24-5 D '70
Constant cup; exhibition at the Museum of contemporary crafts, New York. D. Lawson. il Craft Horiz 30:54-7+ D '70
Exhibition '70; fifth biennial competition sponsored by the Beaux arts for the Columbus, Ohio gallery of fine arts. il Ceram Mo 18:27 N '70
Itinerary. See issues of Ceramics monthly
Michigan artist-craftsmen; twenty-first exhibition at the Detroit institute of arts, November 19-December 28, 1969. il Ceram Mo 18:31 F '70
Michigan ceramics; invitational exhibition of Michigan ceramics. il Ceram Mo 18:32 F '70
Nut art in quake time; kookie California ceramics in Objects U.S.A. D. Zack. il Art N 69:38-41+ Mr '70
Objects USA; the Johnson collection of contemporary crafts. il Ceram Mo 17:19-26 D '69
Quarter century of American ceramic art; Scripps college exhibit. J. Lovoos. il Am Artist 34:20-5 F '70
Show time; Toledo area annual; Arts and crafts festival, Louisiana; Southern tier show, Corning, N.Y; Collegiate ceramics; 1970, Cypress, Calif. il Ceram Mo 18:24-5 S '70

Firing
Cobalt blues at cone 9. R. Behrens. il Ceram Mo 18:31 My '70

History
Ceramics from an eighteenth-century wilderness fort: Fort Michilimackinac. J. J. Miller, 2d. il Antiques 97:888-92 Je '70
Identification & attribution of the Railroad train bread plate. T. H. Marsh. il Hobbies 74:116-18 Ja '70
Rise and fall of English white salt-glazed stoneware. I. Noël-Hume. il Antiques 97:248-55, 408-13 F-Mr '70

POULTRY—*Continued*
Diseases and pests
See also
Coccidiosis
Prices
Is a chicken breast really a luxury? il Consumer Bul 53:36 Mr '70
POULTRY feeders
Build your own low-cost chicken feeders. L. R. Horsted. il Org Gard & Farm 17:42 D '70
POUND, Ezra
Life of Ezra Pound, by N. Stock. Review
Atlan 226:108-10 Jl '70. E. Weeks *
Nat R 22:956-8 S 8 '70. P. P. Witonski *
Nation 211:122-3 Ag 17 '70. H. N. Schneidau *
New Repub 163:30-2 O 17 '70. K. Kenner *
Newsweek il pors 76:72 Jl 27 '70 G. Wolff
Sat R por 53:27-9 Jl 18 '70. A. Alvarez *
T.S. Eliot & Ezra Pound: collaborators in letters. D. Gallup. pors Atlan 225:48-62 Ja '70
(tr) See Fasolo, U. Pigeons
POUND cake. See Cake
POUNDS
Canine Hilton: Pequannock, N.J. dog pound. B. R. Evans. il Am City 85:125-6 Ap '70
POURED floors. See Floor coverings
POURING vessels. See Pitchers
POUSSAINT, Alvin F.
Dialogue on separatism. por Ebony 25:62-4+ Ag '70
Why blacks kill blacks. il por Ebony 25:143-6+ O '70
POVÉ, Xavora
Cosmic conditioning of hair. See issues of Harper's bazaar
Eye on the sky. See issues of Harper's bazaar
Lead in the New Year with lead. Harp Baz 104:147 D '70
POVENMIRE, Harold R.
Occultation highlights. il Sky & Tel 39:336 My '70
POVERTY
See also
Slums
United States
See Poor—United States
POWDER metallurgy
Powdered steel: a tough customer. il Bsns W p37 Ja 2 '71
See also
Dispersion strengthening
POWDER RIDGE rock festival. See Music festivals—Connecticut
POWDERED steel. See Steel, Powdered
POWELL, Bernard W.
Aboriginal trephination: case from Southern New England? bibliog il Science 170:732-4 N 13 '70
Build this fire-wood shed. il Pop Mech 133:164-5 Je '70
POWELL, Cecil Frank
Obituary
Bul Atom Sci 26:48 My '70. E. Rabinowitch *
POWELL, Dick
High-climb Kodiaks. il pors Outdoor Life 145:58-9+ F '70
POWELL, Enoch
Did Harold Wilson save the pound? il Nat R 22:306-8 Mr 24 '70
about
Britain's new household word. por Time 95:21 Je 29 '70 *
Most English of the English. P. P. Witonski. Nat R 22:263-4 Mr 10 '70 *
Odd men out; Great Britain. il por Newsweek 75:36+ Je 22 '70 *
Three conservative musketeers. C. Brogan. Nat R 22:148-9 F 10 '70
Understanding Powell. W. F. Buckley, jr. Nat R 22:1230-1 N 17 '70 *
POWELL, Evan
Meter that doctors home appliances. il Pop Sci 197:110+ N '70
POWELL, Francis X. See Johnson, D. R. jt. auth.
POWELL, J. Enoch. See Powell, Enoch
POWELL, Judith. See Johnson, S. jt. auth.
POWELL, Lawrence Clark
Shoe on the other foot: from library administrator to user; address, March 1970. por Wilson Lib Bul 45:384-9 D '70
POWELL, Mel
Debasement of new music. il por Hi Fi 20:MA14-15 S '70

POWELL, Patrick
Tom Sawyer boyhood, 1970 style. il pors Life 69:50-7 O 9 '70
POWELL, Paul
Paul Powell's nest egg. il por Time 97:15 Ja 18 '71 *
POWELL, Ralph L.
Power of the Chinese military. bibliog f Cur Hist 59:129-33+ S '70
POWELL, Richard Pitts
My reluctant magician. Writer 83:11-14+ F '70
POWELL, Robert
Robert Powell: he's got feet down below his knees. M. Last. pors Dance Mag 44:32-5 N '70 *
POWELL, Robert S. jr
Participation is learning. Ed Digest 35:39-42 Ap '70
POWELL, LAKE
Exploring Lake Powell. C. L. Cadieux. il Yachting 128:72-3+ N '70
POWER, Anne
Spanish resistance grows bolder. Commonweal 92:332-5 Jl 10 '70
POWER, Jonathan
Lessons from the Czech ordeal. il Chr Cent 87:1011-13 Ag 26 '70
POWER, Katherine
Bank-heist tactic. il pors Newsweek 76:29-30 O 5 '70 *
Radical bank job. il por Time 96:21-2 O 5 '70 *
POWER, Lawrence V.
Ten trees: best buys. il Am Home 74:43-5 Ja '71
POWER (mechanics)
See also
Compressed air
POWER (social sciences)
Future of power. G. B. Leonard. Look 34:36+ Ja 13 '70
More power to everybody. M. Ways. il Fortune 81:172-5+ My '70
Power and politics in organizational life. A. Zaleznik. il Harvard Bsns R 48:47-60 My '70
Power, by A. A. Berle. Review
Nation 210:54-6 Ja 19 '70. C. B. Macpherson
Sat R 53:26-8 Ap 11 '70. C. J. Friedrich
Power: the enshrined heresy. R. Sampson. Nation 212:14-20 Ja 4 '71
Radical Saul Alinsky: prophet of power to the people; Time essay. por Time 95:56-7 Mr 2 '70
POWER amplifiers. See Amplifiers
POWER boat racing. See Motor boat racing
POWER boats. See Motor boats
POWER cruisers. See Cruisers (pleasure boats)
POWER drills. See Drilling and boring machinery
POWER failures. See Electric power failures
POWER garden tools. See Garden tools, equipment and supplies
POWER gliders. See Gliders (aeronautics)
POWER lawn mowers. See Lawn mowers
POWER line poles. See Electric lines—Poles
POWER plants
Solving the power problem. il Time 95:54-5 Je 22 '70
See also
Atomic power plants
Electric plants
Steam power plants
Location
Land use: Congress taking up conflict over power plants. L. J. Carter. Science 170:718-19 N 13 '70
POWER resources
Crisis in power; with editorial comment by R. Graves. il Life 69:3, 26F-35 D 11 '70
Energy; a scarcity of all kinds; address, March 5, 1970. W. M. Laird. Vital Speeches 36:396-9 Ap 15 '70
Energy crisis: environmental issue exacerbates power supply problem. P. M. Boffey. Science 168:1554-9 Je 26 '70
Energy for tomorrow; coordinated planning; address, September 22, 1970. W. E. Johnson. Vital Speeches 37:29-32 O 15 '70
Energy; with yardsticks of management performance. il Forbes 105:151-2+ Ja 1 '70
Human energy production as a process in the biosphere. S. F. Singer. il Sci Am 223:174-6+ bibliog(p265) S '70
Impact of energy demands. A. B. Cambel. bibliog il Phys Today 23:38-43+ D '70
Is the cupboard bare? il Forbes 107:147 Ja 1 '71
Judging the energy crisis. il Sci N 98:379-80 N 14 '70

POWER resources—*Continued*
Outlook for energy supplies; address, September 24, 1970. P. H. Trezise. Dept State Bul 63:479-83 O 26 '70
Plutonium; economy of the future; address, October 5, 1970. G. T. Seaborg. Vital Speeches 37:69-75 N 15 '70
Power and fuel resources. R. W. Holcomb. Cur Hist 58:330-6+ Je '70
Scarcity of energy. P. H. Abelson. Science 169:1267 S 25 '70
Scrounging for fuel. Newsweek 76:89-90 S 14 '70
Space available; excerpts from testimony before the Joint congressional committee on atomic energy, January 29, 1970. M. Peterson. bibliog il Environ 12:2-9 Mr '70
Where will we get the energy? R. E. Lapp. New Repub 163:17-21 Jl 11 '70
Why the U.S. is in an energy crisis. L. A. Mayer. il Fortune 82:74-7+ N '70
See also
Fuel supply
Solar energy

POWER saws. See Saws
POWER shovels. See Excavating machinery
POWER supply. See Power resources
POWER supply, Electric. See Electric power
POWER tools. See Electric tools

POWER transmission
See also
Electric transmission

POWERBOAT (periodical)
Full speed ahead for Powerboat. Bsns W p90 My 9 '70

POWERED hand tools. See Electric tools, Portable

POWERS, Bertram Anthony
New York city's dailies vs. the unions: automation's armageddon. A. H. Raskin. il Sat R 53:50-2 Jl 11 '70 *
Profiles. G. T. Hellman. New Yorker 46:43-6+ Mr 7 '70 *

POWERS, Bill
Gallery; photographs. il Life 68:8-9 Ja 30 '70

POWERS, Charles W. See Dittes, J. E. jt. auth.

POWERS, Francis Gary
Francis Gary Powers tells his story; excerpt from Operation overflight. il por N Y Times Mag p36-7+ Ap 19 '70

POWERS, Jessica
Siesta in color; poetry. Poetry 115:385 Mr '70

POWERS, John J. Jr
Health care costs; address, April 8, 1970. Vital Speeches 36:478-80 My 15 '70

POWERS, Joshua, B, inc.
Joshua B. Powers, inc: from comic strips to mass technology. S. W. Little. Sat R 53:59-61+ Ja 17 '70

POWERS, Kathy
Dostoievsky in Waltham. Nat R 22:1098 O 20 '70 *

POWERS, Murray
Ideas on trial. America 122:509 My 9 '70

POWERS, Thomas. See Franks. L. jt. auth.

POWIANSKY, Josef
Kremlin will get you if you don't watch out. Nat R 22:784-5 Jl 28 '70

POWILLS, Dorothy
Playing cards. See issues of Hobbies

POWLEDGE, Fred
Going home to Raleigh. Harper 240:54-8+ Ap '70
Learning to live with the credit card. Esquire 74:210-17+ N '70
1652 pages of the American dream. il Esquire 74:190-3+ D '70
Walden III. il Esquire 73:100-3+ Je '70

POWWOWS. See Indians of North America—Rites and ceremonies

POZZO phenomenon (perspective) See Perspective

POZZUOLI, Italy
Rise and fall. il Newsweek 75:53-4 Mr 16 '70
What's up in Pozzuoli? il Time 95:51 Mr 16 '70
Whole town upward bound. D. J. Hamblin. il Life 69:14+ Jl 17 '70

PRADA, Carlos Garcia. See Garcia Prada, C.

PRADO museum, Madrid
Iberian hegira. C. J. McNaspy. America 123:27 Jl 11 '70

PRAEGER, Frederick A. inc.
Praeger series contends with federal changes. Pub W 198:40 O 5 '70

PRAFKA, W. R.
Hog health. See issues of Farm Journal

PRAGUE
Czechoslovaks: between hope and fear. F. Ungeheuer. il Harper 241:71-7 Ag '70

Description
Short happy months of Mozart's Prague. J. Wechsberg. il Sat R 53:60-1 Mr 14 '70

PRAIRIE chicken shooting
Late great grouse hunting. H. Bradshaw. il Field & S 74:48-9+ Ja '70

PRAIRIE dogs
Prairie jester. J. E. Hartman. il Nat Wildlife 8:35-7 Ap '70
Reporter at large; controlling the prairie dog and protecting the blackfooted ferret, in South Dakota. F. McNulty. New Yorker 46:40-2+ Je 13 '70

PRAIRIE provinces, Canada
Canada's heartland, the Prairie provinces. W. E. Garrett. il Nat Geog 138:443-89 O '70

PRAIRIES
Death by the plow. R. Brewer. il Natur Hist 79:28-35+ bibliog(p 133) Ag '70
Prairie blizzard. J. Madson. il Audubon 72:54-6+ Mr '70
Preserving the prairie; Goose Lake prairie. G. Leposky. Travel & Camera 33:12+ O '70
See also
Prairie provinces, Canada
Tundras

PRAOMYS. See Rats

PRASHKER, Ivan
Shirt talk; story. Harper 240:59-62 Ja '70

PRATSON, Frederick John
Extend the pleasure of gardening through photography. il Horticulture 48:32-3+ Ag '70

PRATT, Christopher J.
Sulfur; with biographical sketch. il Sci Am 222:10, 62-7+ My '70

PRATT, Dallas
Discovery of a world: early maps showing America (cont) il Antiques 97:128-34 Ja '70

PRATT, Joseph Gaither
Scientist looks at ESP. S. McBee. McCalls 97:50+ Mr '70 *

PRATT, Robert L.
Spontaneous drawings of Robert L. Pratt. J. Jellico. il por Am Artist 34:44-9 Ag '70 *

PRATTE, Richard
Media revolution: its educational implications. Clear House 45:207-11 D '70

PRAXITELES. See Sculpture, Greek

PRAYER
Book of uncommon prayer. Chr Cent 87:1335, 1367, 1399 N 4-18 '70
Heaven on earth; Unity school of Christianity. R. Rhodes. il Harper 240:116-22 My '70
House of prayer experiments. America 123:451 N 28 '70
How can we persuade modern man to pray? Paul VI. por Ladies Home J 87:77 Mr '70
Missing demonstration. D. Lawrence. U S News 68:96 Je 8 '70
Possibility of prayer. J. R. Kelly. Commonweal 92:413-15 Ag 21 '70
Prayer. H. Oosterhuis. Cath World 212:203-5 Ja '71
Prayer is practical. L. N. Bell. Chr Today 15:22-3 D 4 '70
Praying the space heroes home; with editorial comment. Chr Today 14:27, 37 My 8 '70
That priceless hour. L. N. Bell. Chr Today 14:31-2 My 8 '70
See also
Divine office

Anecdotes, facetiae, satire, etc.
More things are wrought ... Chr Cent 87:255 F 25 '70

PRAYER, Day of. See Day of prayer

PRAYER in the schools. See Public schools and religion

PRAYERS
Apron-pocket prayers for Christmas. M. Holmes. il Ladies Home J 86:75-8 D '69
Send, we pray thee O God; excerpt from Prayers of the spirit. J. W. Suter. il Good H 171:59 D '70

PRAYING mantis
Mantids. H. Borland. il Audubon 72:inside cover Jl '70
Mantis in action. J. L. Bean. il Org Gard & Farm 17:124-6 Mr '70

PRAZER, Stanley J.
Rubber keeps water in and debris out. il Am City 85:70-80 S '70

PREACHING
Black preaching, by H. H. Mitchell and The art of the American folk preacher, by B. A. Rosenberg. Reviews
Commonweal 93:330-1 D 25 '70. R. J. Neuhaus
Genius of Charles Haddon Spurgeon. J. Pitts. Chr Today 14:6-8 F 27 '70

PREACHING—*Continued*
How dare the preacher preach? J. Torrens.
il Cath World 211:251-5 S '70
Preaching amid smog. W. Fitch. Chr Today
15:6-8 D 18 '70
See also
Bible—Homiletical use
Christian preaching conference
Communication (theology)
Sermons
PREADOLESCENCE. See Adolescence
PREAKNESS horse race. See Horse racing
PREAMPLIFIERS. See Amplifiers
PREBIOTIC synthesis. See Biosynthesis
PRE-CAMBRIAN period. See Geology, Strati-
graphic—Pre-Cambrian
PRECAST concrete houses. See Concrete houses
PRECESSION
Interglacial high sea levels and the control
of Greenland ice by the precession of the
equinoxes. C. Emiliani; reply with rejoind-
er. J. H. Mercer. bibliog Science 168:1605-
6 Je 26 '70
PRECIOUS stones
Gems and minerals. H. D. Brown. See issues
of Hobbies
See also
Diamonds
Gems
PRECIOUS stones, Artificial
See also
Diamonds, Artificial
PRECIPITATION (chemistry)
Bimodal sedimenting zones due to ligand-
mediated interactions. J. R. Cann and W. B.
Goad. bibliog il Science 170:441-5 O 23 '70
PRECIPITATION (meteorology)
See also
Rain and rainfall
Snow
PRECISION instrument company
Memory maker gets some help. Bsns W p 124
Je 20 '70
PRE-COLUMBIAN drainage. See Drainage
PRE-COLUMBIAN terraces. See Terraces
(agriculture)
PRECONDITIONING of cattle. See Cattle, Beef
—Preconditioning
PRECOOKED food, Frozen. See Food, Frozen
PREDATION (zoology)
Clutch size in birds: outcome of opposing
predator and prey adaptations. R. E. Rick-
lefs. bibliog il Science 168:599-600 My 1 '70;
Reply with rejoinder. J. Ghiselin. 170:649-51
N 6 '70
PREDATOR control. See Animals, Predatory —
Control
PREDICTED log competitions. See Naviga-
tion—Competitions
PREDICTIONS. See Forecasts; Forecasts (eco-
nomics)
PREFAB fireplaces. See Fireplaces
PREFABRICATED bathrooms. See Bathrooms
PREFABRICATED houses. See Houses, Pre-
fabricated
PREFABRICATED shelters. See Shelters
PREFABRICATION
See also
Houses, Prefabricated
PREFERENCE, Commercial. See Tariff—
United States
PREFERENCES (psychology)
Assessment of multiattribute preferences.
R. L. Keeney. bibliog il Science 168:1491-
2 Je 19 '70
Rat's preference for earned in comparison
with free food. B. Carder and S. N. Berko-
witz. il Science 167:1273-4 F 27 '70; Discus-
sion. 169:503-4; 170:1229 Jl 31, D 11 '70
PREFERENTIAL tariff. See Tariff—United
States
PREFONTAINE, Steve
Freshman and the great guru. P. Putnam. il
pors Sports Illus 32:28-31 Je 15 '70 *
PREGNANCY
Baby on the way. J. L. Arehart. il Parents
Mag 46:48-9+ Ja '71
Expectant mother:
How chronic health problems affect preg-
nancy; ed. by B. R. Boylan. J. J. Ro-
vinsky. Redbook 135:14+ Je '70
How the fetus is nourished. E. R. Car-
rington and E. Jacobs. Redbook 134:
24+ F '70
Postpartum care; ed. by D. Z. Meilach.
E. L. Engel. Redbook 135:14+ Ag '70
Report on rubella vaccine. S. A. Fish and
P. Feinstein. Redbook 134:29+ Ap '70
Helen Meyner: my miracle pregnancy at for-
ty-one. P. Battelle. il por Ladies Home J
87:36+ F '70

Pleasingly pregnant; National academy of
obstetricians on weight control. il News-
week 76:66 Ag 10 '70
Pregnant? Gain 24 lbs. A. J. Snider. Sci
Digest 68:65-6 D '70
Pregnant teen-agers; with teacher opinion
poll. il Todays Ed 59:26-9+ O '70
Starvation in human pregnancy; hypoglyce-
mia, hypoinsulinemia, and hyperketone-
mia. P. Felig and V. Lynch. bibliog il
Science 170:990-2 N 27 '70
Weight and toxemia. Sci N 98:95-6 Ag 1 '70
What to do till the baby comes. P. Kunc.
il Redbook 134:12+ F '70
See also
Abortion
Amniotic liquid
Childbirth
Fetus
Sex determination and control

Signs and diagnosis
Expectant mother: pregnancy tests; ed. by
E. Edelson. M. M. Hreshchyshyn. Redbook
135:38+ O '70
PREGNANCY, Complications of
Facts and fallacies about cesarean births. G.
Goldreich. il Parents Mag 45:52-3+ My '70
Sex ratio of newborns: preponderance of males
in toxemia of pregnancy. P. Toivanen and
T. Hirvonen. bibliog il Science 170:187-8 O 9
'70
PREGNANCY in animals
Intromission pattern and species vaginal code
in relation to induction of pseudopreg-
nancy. M. Diamond. bibliog il Science 169:
995-7 S 4 '70
PREGNANCY test. See Pregnancy—Signs and
diagnosis
PREHISTORIC agriculture. See Agriculture,
Prehistoric
PREHISTORIC archeology. See Archeology
PREHISTORIC geometry. See Geometry
PREHISTORIC man. See Man, Prehistoric
PREHISTORIC metallurgy. See Metallurgy,
Prehistoric
PREHISTORIC monuments. See Megalithic
monuments
PREISS, David
Portrait head in clay. il por Am Artist 34:
30-5+ F '70
Power to the poster. il Am Artist 34:33-41+
My '70
PREJUDICE
Let's have the courage of our doubts. R.
K. Price, jr. Read Digest 97:219-20 Jl '70
Visiting feminine eye; prejudice against wo-
men. S. Chisholm. por McCalls 97:6 Ag '70
Who hates whom? il Esquire 74:160-3 D '70
Worldliness according to James. Chr Today
14:27 My 8 '70
See also
Race prejudice
PREMACK, David
Education of Sarah. il Time 96:51-2 S 21
'70 *
PREMATURE infants. See Infants, Premature
PREMIER quartet. See Choral groups and
societies
PREMINGER, Ingo
M*A*S*H; interview, ed. by G. Trotta. il
Harp Baz 103:200-1 Mr '70
M*A*S*H notes. il Esquire 74:60-1+ Ag '70
PREMIUMS
Giveaway binge. il Newsweek 76:62+ Jl 20
'70
Wigs and blenders: banks' latest gifts. U S
News 69:60-1 Ag 3 '70
PREMIXED cocktails. See Cocktails
PRENATAL care. See Pregnancy
PRENATAL exercises. See Exercise
PRENATAL sex determination. See Sex deter-
mination and control
PRENDERGAST, Joseph
Twenty-one years for the Historic trust. il
Parks & Rec 5:12-13+ N '70
PRENTIS, Henning Webb, 1884-1959
Theme of success: let the buyer have faith.
J. H. Binns. il pors Nations Bsns 58:53-4
Ja '70
PRENTISS, Karl
ATV will take you almost anywhere. il Holi-
day 47:66-7+ My '70
Day they dug up Babs. il Holiday 47:62-3 F
'70
Drama at the Brickyard. il Holiday 47:58-9+
Ap '70
Like a collapsed balloon. por Holiday 47:26-8
Mr '70
Replicars: the ultimate luxury. il Holiday 48:
56-8 Jl '70

PRENTISS, Stanton R.
Vector-scope on the Quasar. il Radio-Electr 41:88-9+ Je '70
What's new in modular and IC color TV for '71. il Radio-Electr 41:62-4+ D '70
PRENTISS, Tina
In space. il Sch Arts 69:4 Je '70
PREPARATION for college. See Colleges and universities—Entrance requirements
PREPARATORY schools. See Private schools
PREPAREDNESS, Military

Russia

Reading Soviet intentions. J. Alsop. New Repub 163:17-19 O 3 '70
PREPAYMENT dental plans. See Insurance, Dental
PRESBYTERIAN church in Canada
Ontario; the Presbyterian and the United church surveys. J. R. Mutchmor. Chr Cent 87:429-30 Ap 8 '70
Presbyterian church in Canada: general assembly convenes. D. H. Rayner. Chr Cent 87:975-6 Ag 12 '70
PRESBYTERIAN church in the United States

Names

See Churches—Names
PRESBYTERIAN church in the United States (general)
Opposition to Presbyterian union mounts in South. A. Matthews. Chr Today 15:45-6 N 20 '70
Presbyterians North and South. Nation 210: 165-6 F 16 '70
Which way Presbyterians? R. Love. Chr Today 14:46 F 13 '70
See also
United Presbyterian church in the U.S.A.
PRESBYTERIAN church in the United States (South)
On being Presbyterian in the South. J. H. Smylie. Chr Cent 87:936-40 Ag 5 '70
Parallels and progress at the southern Presbyterian assembly. T. M. McMillan, jr. Chr Cent 87:946-8 Ag 5 '70
Southern Presbyterians: clashing in Memphis; the Consultation on church union plan. J. F. Nelson. Chr Today 14:35 Jl 3 '70
Southern Presbyterians: cooler in Memphis. Chr Today 14:36 Jl 17 '70
PRESBYTERIAN church in the United States of America
Reaction to reaction. Chr Today 15:27-8 D 18 '70
PRESCHOOL children
When toddlers act up. C. Hotelling. il Parents Mag 45:64-5+ Mr '70
See also
Child study
Readiness for school
Socially handicapped children

Education

At last: a TV show good for children; Sesame street. E. M. Wylie. il PTA Mag 64:12-14+ My '70
Community planning for preprimary education; with study-discussion program. R. H. Anderson and R. Selbert. bibliog il PTA Mag 64:8-10+, 34 My '70
Crucial preschool years. E. G. Neisser and F. Bauling. il Parents Mag 45:49-51+ F '70
Early childhood education; symposium. il Todays Ed 59:34-44+ Ap '70
Early childhoold education: the scene then and now. M. Lay. Ed Digest 36:36-8 S '70
Early education: still in its infancy. M. S. Stearns. il Am Ed 6:3-5 Ag '70
Helping children to grow up smart: Syracuse university children's center. B. Asbell. il Redbook 135:34+ Jl '70
How smart do you want your child to be? J. V. Tunney. McCalls 98:62+ O '70
Preschool enrollment. Sch & Soc 98:11-12 Ja '70
Preschool prospect. W. D. Boutwell. PTA Mag 64:9-10 Ja '70
Preschoolers pose some tough questions. P. Thomson. il Am Ed 6:16-19 O '70
Prospects for growth in preprimary education. J. N. Hedges. il Mo Labor R 93:40-4 Jl '70
Toy libraries featured in preschool experiments. Library J 95:2958-9 S 15 '70

Anecdotes, facetiae, satire, etc.

Project Slow Down: the middle-class answer to Project Head Start. R. Fisher. Sch & Soc 98:356-7 O '70

Nutrition

See Children—Nutrition

PRESCHOOL education. See Preschool children—Education
PRESCOTT, Katherine
Crazy Willie and the choco-bars; story. il Redbook 136:78-9 N '70
PRESCOTT, Peter S.
Authors & editors. B. A. Bannon. por Pub W 198:31+ S 28 '70 *
PRESCOTT, Robert William
Robert W. Prescott of Flying Tiger line; interview. il pors Nations Bsns 58:64-8+ O '70
PRESCOTT, William Hickling
William Hickling Prescott, by C. H. Gardiner. Review
    Américas 22:42 F '70. W. R. Lux *
PRESCOTT college, Prescott, Ariz.
Prescott kids go wild. P. Snook. il por Nat Wildlife 8:4-11 F '70
PRESCRIBED burning. See Forest fires—Controlled fires
PRESENT, The
See also
Past, The
PRESERVATION Hall concerts. See New Orleans—Music
PRESERVATION of architecture. See Architecture—Conservation and restoration
PRESERVATION of food. See Food preservation and preservatives; Canning and preserving
PRESERVATION of landmarks, scenery, etc. See Landscape protection
PRESERVATION of photographs. See Photographs—Conservation and restoration
PRESERVATION of stone. See Stone—Preservation
PRESERVATION of wood. See Wood—Preservation
PRESERVING. See Canning and preserving
PRESIDENTIAL advisers. See Public officers
PRESIDENTIAL campaigns
See also
Campaign funds
Campaign management
National conventions, Democratic
Presidential candidates
Television in politics

1968

McCarthy campaign; survey of campaign books. A. McCarthy. Atlan 226:60-3 Ag '70
Nobody knows: reflections on the McCarthy campaign of 1968. by J. Larner. Review
    Time il 95:78 Mr 2 '70
Purity, power and politics. E. Schneier. Nation 210:119-21 F 2 '70
Still the man who loves to talk, to teach, to preach: H. H. Humphrey. R. Wool. il pors N Y Times Mag p25-7+ O 11 '70

1972

Nixon starts moves for 1971, and 1972. il por U S News 69:9-10 D 28 '70
Nixon's strategy for '72. il U S News 69:21-4 N 23 '70
Strategy for Democrats; excerpts from The real majority. R. M. Scammon and B. J. Wattenberg. New Repub 163:17-21 Ag 15 '70; Same abr. with title Strategy for the outs. Cur 122:14-20 O '70; Reply with rejoinder. P. F. Rousselot and R. E. Vickery, jr. New Repub 163:30-1 S 26 '70
PRESIDENTIAL candidates
Adlai Stevenson: a sense-making prophet. T. M. Gannon. America 123:57-9 Ag 8 '70
See also
Presidential campaigns

1968

New left reconsidered. Trans-Action 7:6+ Je '70

1972

Build-up for a Kennedy comeback. il pors U S News 68:54-6 Ap 27 '70
Darker than dark; possible Democratic candidates. il Newsweek 76:26 Ag 17 '70
Democratic doldrums. Nat R 22:770+ Jl 28 '70
Ed Muskie, and the pack. il por Newsweek 76:33-5+ N 16 '70
Front runner: E. Muskie. Nation 211:579-80 D 7 '70
Gentlemen, start your engines. Nat R 22:1200 N 17 '70
Is Muskie the one? New Repub 163:5-6 D 12 '70
Muskie running. K. Crawford. Newsweek 76: 25 D 7 '70
Nixon v. Kennedy in '72? Time 96:9 N 23 '70
Odds on Muskie; New republic poll. New Repub 162:10 Ap 25 '70
Scenario for '72. C. McWilliams. Nation 212: 66-8 Ja 18 '71

PRESIDENTIAL candidates—1972—*Continued*
Who but Ted? S. Alsop. Newsweek 75:100 Ap 13 '70
Who vs. Nixon in '72? il U S News 69:37-9 N 16 '70
PRESIDENTIAL commissions. See Commissions of inquiry
PRESIDENTIAL communication. See Communication in government
PRESIDENTIAL duties. See Presidents—United States—Powers and duties
PRESIDENTIAL elections. See Presidents—United States—Election
PRESIDENTIAL entertaining. See Government entertaining
PRESIDENTIAL ghost writing. See Authorship—Collaboration
PRESIDENTIAL government. See Presidents—United States
PRESIDENTIAL libraries
See also
John F. Kennedy library, Cambridge. Mass.
PRESIDENTIAL medal of freedom. See Medal of freedom
PRESIDENTIAL power. See Presidents—United States—Powers and duties
PRESIDENTIAL veto. See Presidents—United States—Powers and duties
PRESIDENTS

Egypt
See also
Sadat, A.

United States
Change in atmosphere. H. Sidey. Life 69:4 S 18 '70
Does the U.S. need a king? G. E. Reedy. Look 34:32-5 Mr 10 '70
How Senate dean judges six presidents; excerpts from remarks, February 1970. R. B. Russell il pors U S News 68:18 F 23 '70
Other presidential pals. il Life 69:26 Jl 31 '70
Personal glimpses of the presidents. C. Clemens. Hobbies 75:142-3 Jl '70
Twilight of the presidency, by G. E. Reedy. Review
  Nation 210:727-8 Je 15 '70. C. Roberts
See also
United States—Executive office of the president
White House

Archives
Memoirs come to market. H. Sidey. il Life 68:2 F 13 '70

Birthplaces
See also
George Washington Birthplace National Monument
Johnson, L. B.—Birthplace
Nixon, R. M.—Birthplace

Communication
See Communication in government

Correspondence
Tell it to Nixon; letters of protest lumped with letters of approval. Nation 210:741 Je 22 '70
See also
Nixon, R. M.—Correspondence

Election
Bad idea whose time has come; direct election of the President. I. Kristol and P. Weaver; discussion. N Y Times Mag p4+ D 21 '69; 101-2 F 8 '70
Direct election of the president; House proposal and the Tydings-Griffin amendment. A. M. Bickel. New Repub 163:9 S 26 '70
Direct elections: an invitation to national chaos. T. H. White. por Life 68:4 Ja 30 '70
Great 1972 election rumor. P. Steinfels. Commonweal 92:407 Ag 21 '70
Matter of sides. por Time 96:14-15 Jl 27 '70
Real majority, by R. M. Scammon and B. J. Wattenberg. Review
  Newsweek 76:33-4 S 14 '70. D. M. Alpern
Teacher opinion poll; methods of electing the president. Todays Ed 59:5 F '70
Toward a new system for choosing a president. il U S News 68:26-9 My 11 '70
Voting for president; direct election vs. the Federal system plan. M. P. Curzan. New Repub 162:14-16 Ap 18 '70
See also
Apportionment (election law)
Electoral college
Presidential campaigns
Presidential candidates

Gifts
What happens when the White House goes gift-shopping? S. Nirenberg. il House B 112:6+ D '70

Health
See also
Nixon, R. M.—Health
Roosevelt, F. D.—Health

Homes
Summer white house; J. B. Walker's dream of Mount Falcon white house. E. Bluemel. il por Am West 7:24-5 S '70
See also
Nixon, R. M.—Homes

Inaugural addresses
Measuring presidents. il Time 96:52 Ag 31 '70

Messages
See also
Nixon, R. M.—Messages
Nixon, R. M.—State of the Union message, January 22, 1970

Pets
See Pets

Powers and duties
Advice and consent, power to select, too? D. Lawrence. U S News 68:104 Ap 13 '70
And so we leave Cambodia.... il Newsweek 76:16-22 Jl 13 '70
Congress didn't make war; can it make peace? il Newsweek 75:29 Je 1 '70
Congress vs. Nixon: ABC's of war debate. il U S News 68:44-5 Je 22 '70
Cooking time; question of the Cooper-Church amendment. il Newsweek 75:28 Je 1 '70
Cooper-Church amendment: is it constitutional? C. D. Williams. Nat R 23:731-3 Jl 14 '70; Reply with rejoinder. J. Lotterman. 22:1031+ O 6 '70
Deserving better; choice of a Supreme court justice. il Life 68:38 Ap 17 '70
Dictating the agenda; Nixon's veto of the labor-HEW appropriation. Time 95:9-10 F 9 '70
Keep the presidency free. H. J. Sievers. America 122:603 Je 6 '70
Looking for the outer limits; Byrd amendment voted down. il Newsweek 75:19 Je 22 '70
Making the veto stick. il Newsweek 75:20-1 F 9 '70
Nixon to Congress: the war's my business. New Repub 163:5-6 Jl 4 '70
No confidence on Cambodia; Byrd amendment voted down. Time 95:15 Je 22 '70
Notes and comment; power to declare war or raise armies. il New Yorker 46:31-2 My 16 '70; Same. Forbes 105:17-18 Je 15 '70
One-upmanship; Tonkin Gulf resolution repealed. il Newsweek 76:37 Jl 6 '70
Powers and dominations; war power of Congress and the President. Nat R 22:550+ Je 2 '70
President as commander in chief. Time 96: 8 Jl 13 '70
President, the people and the power to make war. E. F. Goldman. Am Heritage 21:28-35 Ap '70
President's war powers: what Senate finally voted; Cooper-Church amendment. il U S News 69:29 Jl 13 '70
Senate stammers; the Byrd amendment. K. Crawford. Newsweek 76:39 Jl 6 '70
Showdown on war: Congress vs. Nixon. il U S News 68:35 My 25 '70
Veto sustained; bill to limit campaign spending on TV and radio. il Newsweek 76:21-2 D 7 '70
War debate rises in Congress. il U S News 68: 33 Je 15 '70
War-making machinery. R. J. Bresler. il Nation 211:105-9 Ag 17 '70
War-making power. New Repub 162:5-6 Je 6 '70
Warrior-in-chief counts the cost. H. J. Sievers. America 122:489 My 9 '70
Who makes our foreign policy? R. L. Tobin. Sat R 53:28 F 14 '70
Why an undeclared war is constitutional. D. Lawrence. U S News 68:100 My 11 '70

Powers and duties—History
President's war powers. il Time 95:36-7 Je 1 '70

Press conferences
Nixon and the press; history of the presidential news conference. il por U S News 69:12-14 D 28 '70
See also
Nixon, R. M.—Press conferences

Protection
Anatomy of San Jose. Nation 211:482 N 16 '70
As violence spreads U.S. goes on guard. il U S News 69:15-16 N 2 '70

PRESIDENTS—United States—Protection—
—*Continued*
How government would limit protesters near
White House. il U S News 69:25 Jl 27 '70
Threatening the President; Fourth circuit
court of appeals' ruling. Time 96:51 S 7 '70
See also
Secret service—United States

Public relations
See also
Nixon, R. M.—Public relations

Relations with Congress
Blindfolding the Senate; concerning views of
S. Symington. Nation 211:291 O 5 '70
Congress's right to know; withholding of
military information by the executive
branch. S. Symington. il N Y Times Mag
p7+ Ag 9 '70; Same abr. Cur 122:36-43 O
'70
Cooper-Church amendment: is it constitu-
tional? C. D. Williams. Nat R 22:731-3 Jl 14
'70; Reply with rejoinder. J. Lotterman. 22:
1031+ O 6 '70
How it looks from the colonies. D. Brogan.
Esquire 73:36+ F '70
Responsible system of government: when?
proposals for assuring support of Presi-
dent by Congress. D. Lawrence. U S
News 69:88 Jl 13 '70
Responsible system, when? D. Lawrence. U S
News 69:96 N 16 '70
See also
Nixon, R. M.—Relations with Congress

Relations with the press
See Government and the press

Religion
Preaching and the power; B. Graham and
the White House. il pors Newsweek 76:
50-5 Jl 20 '70
See also
Nixon. R. M.—Religion

Salaries, allowances, etc.
Library acquires James Monroe letters; text
of letter with introd. by K. V. Hostick. J.
Monroe. Hobbies 75:140-1 My '70

Speeches, addresses, etc.
What presidents once said about racial equal-
ity. D. Lawrence. U S News 68:76 F 9 '70
See also
Nixon, R. M.—Speeches, addresses, etc.

Speechwriters
See Public officers

Travel
Presidential mileage: Nixon sets a record. il
por U S News 68:48-9 Ap 13 '70

Youth
See also
Nixon, R. M.—United States—Youth
PRESIDENTS, College. See College presidents
PRESIDENTS, Company. See Executives
PRESIDENTS' advisory commission on civil
disorders. See United States—National
advisory commission on civil disorders
PRESIDENT'S commission on campus unrest.
See United States—President's commission
on campus unrest
PRESIDENT'S commission on federal statis-
tics. See United States—President's commis-
sion on federal statistics
PRESIDENT'S commission on international
trade and investment policy. See United
States—President's commission on international trade and investment policy
PRESIDENT'S commission on personnel interchange (proposed) See United States—President's commission on personnel interchange
(proposed)
PRESIDENT'S commission on the assassination of President Kennedy. See United
States—President's commission on the assassination of President Kennedy
PRESIDENT'S committee on consumer interests. See United States—President's committee on consumer interests
PRESIDENT'S council of economic advisers.
See United States—Council of economic advisers
PRESIDENTS pets. See Pets
PRESIDENTS press conferences. See Presidents—United States—Press conferences
PRESIDENTS representatives. See Public officers

PRESIDENT'S task force on aging. See United
States—President's task force on aging
PRESIDIO stockade. See United States—Army
—Prisons
PRESLEY, Elvis
Elvis Presley at Las Vegas. A. Goldman.
por Life 68:17 Mr 20 '70 *
Rediscovery of Elvis. R. B. Kaiser. il pors
N Y Times Mag p28-9+ O 11 '70; Reply
with rejoinder. E. Sonderling. p 111 N 1
'70 *
PRESNALL, Lewis F.
Behavioral problems; address, July 31, 1970.
Vital Speeches 37:79-83 N 15 '70
PRESS
Covering the foreign news; news agencies,
print and electronic media. H. Schwartz.
For Affairs 48:741-57 Jl '70
See also
Freedom of the press
Periodicals
PRESS and government. See Government and
the press
PRESS club, National. See National press club
PRESS conferences
TRB from Washington: off-the-record. New
Repub 163:6 O 10 '70
See also
Presidents—United States—Press conferences

Anecdotes, facetiae, satire, etc.
Press conference. J. Ferris. Sat R 53:4 S 5 '70
PRESS law
Is right to access coming? G. Cranberg. Sat
R 53:48-9+ Ag 8 '70
Right of reply for non-actionable injuries. H.
F. Pilpel and K. P. Norwick. Pub W 197:
32 My 25 '70
PRESS photography. See Photography. Jour-
nalistic
PRESS relations. See Publicity
PRESS secretaries. See Public officers
PRESSER, Jacob
Documenting the holocaust. H. Boas. Com-
mentary 49:77-80 Ja '70
PRESSURE
See also
High pressure research
PRESSURE, Political. See Pressure groups
PRESSURE cookery
Here is dinner, in 3 minutes flat. Sunset 145:
114 Ag '70
PRESSURE groups
Establishment; social responsibilities of citi-
zens; address, April 15, 1970. C. Y. Lazarus.
Vital Speeches 36:498-502 Je 1 '70
Honoring America; political and social acti-
vist groups. New Repub 163:5-6 Jl 11
'70
Out gunning; Citizens against Tydings. New
Repub 163:7 N 28 '70
Senior power. Newsweek 76:101 O 12 '70
Senior power breaks the barriers. C. Coiro. il
Har Yrs 10:6-12 O '70
Teaching in the big school; activities of the
Coalition against the SST. J. Lear. Sat R
54:63-6 Ja 2 '71
See also
Art emergency fund
Common cause (political organization)
Lobbying
Protests, demonstrations, etc.
Universities national anti-war fund

Anecdotes, facetiae, satire, etc.
Party line. P. Silverman. Sat R 53:10 S 12 '70
PRESSURE of population. See Population—
Overpopulation
PRESSURE packaging
Aerosol products: caution. A. Rosenthal and
I. Kaufman. il Todays Health 48:36-8 O '70
Aerosols: $3 billion-a-year success story. S.
Schuler. Am Home 73:34+ Ap '70
Bag inside a can. il Pop Sci 196:118 Je '70
Spray for May; for sports use. C. Conley.
il Field & S 75:143 My '70
PRESSURE suits
Down to the mine in space suits. il Bsns W
p83-4 D 12 '70
News from the world of space exploration;
pressure suit stops internal bleeding. il
Space World G-3-75:48 Mr '70
PRESSURE vessels
Babcock and Wilcox feels the heat. il Bsns W
p43 My 30 '70
PRESTIGE
Status symbols are changing, too. J. Smith.
il Duns 95:52-4+ My '70
PRESTOLITE company
Ford must disconnect from Autolite plugs.
Bsns W p24 Jl 11 '70

PRESTON, Jane
Use the whole outdoors for vegetable storage over winter. il Org Gard & Farm 17:39 S '70
PRESTON, Kendall, Jr. See Ingram. M. jt. auth.
PRESTON, Patsy
Mothers and daughters. il pors Vogue 155:101 Je '70 *
PRETORIA
Music
Report:
  Productions of Wagner's Flying Dutchman and Donizetti's Don Pasquale. S. R. Karnovsky. Opera N 35:26 O 10 '70
PRETRIAL detention. See Preventive detention
PRETZELS
Make your own pretzels. J. Morales. il Parents Mag 45:82 Je '70
PREUS, Jacob A. O.
Hunting Lutheran heretics. il Newsweek 76:47 Ag 3 '70 *
PREVENTION of accidents. See Accidents—Prevention
PREVENTION of crime. See Crime prevention
PREVENTIVE detention
Brief for preventive detention. R. L. Goldfarb. il N Y Times Mag p28-9+ Mr 1 '70
Case for pretrial detention; address, January 30, 1970. R. G. Kleindienst. Vital Speeches 36:354-9 Ap 1 '70
Terrorism & preventive detention: the case of Israel. A. M. Dershowitz. bibliog f Commentary 50:67-78 D '70
PREVENTIVE enforcement patrol. See New York (city)—Police
PREVENTIVE medicine. See Medicine, Preventive
PREVENTIVE psychiatry. See Mental hygiene
PREVIN, André
Uproar: Previn and afterwards. C. Cunningham. Hi Fi 20:secII Ap '70 *
PREVIN, Dory
Odyssey of Dory Previn. J. Rascoe. por McCalls 98:6+ Ja '71 *
Woman's song. por Newsweek 76:86-7 Jl 6 '70 *
PREVOTS, Naima Wallenrod
Teaching the classroom teacher to teach dance. il Dance Mag 45:28-9+ Ja '71
PREY, Hermann
Hermann Prey. P. J. Smith. por Hi Fi 20: MA17 N '70 *
PREZIOSO, Sal J.
Governor appoints state's first parks and recreation commissioner. E. H. Moore. por Cons 25:19+ O '70 *
Prezioso accepts Rockefeller post; with letter by W. Brown. il por Parks & Rec 9:24-5 S '70 *
PRICE, Arnold H.
(comp) Articles and other books received; Germany, Austria, and Switzerland. See issues of American historical review
PRICE, Harrison A.
Interview with three recreation planners. Forbes 105:202-3 Ja 1 '70
PRICE, J. M. and others
Bladder tumors in rats fed cyclohexylamine or high doses of a mixture of cyclamate and saccharin. bibliog il Science 167:1131-2 F 20 '70
PRICE, Karen. See Walker, L. jt. auth.
PRICE, Molly
Day-lilies. il Home Gard 57:28-9+ Jl '70
PRICE, Monty A. See Stephens, E. R. jt. auth.
PRICE, Nancy
On a globe turning; poem. America 122:562 My 23 '70
Tintype; poem. Commonweal 93:351 Ja 8 '71
PRICE, Pearl B.
Editorial. See issues of PTA magazine
PRICE, Peter W.
Trail odors: recognition by insects parasitic on cocoons. bibliog il Science 170:546-7 O 30 '70
PRICE, Raymond K. Jr
Let's have the courage of our doubts. Read Digest 97:219-20 Jl '70
PRICE, Reynolds
Waiting at Dachau; story. Esquire 73:130-3 Ap '70
about
Reynolds Price who outgrew the southern pastoral. T. Solotaroff. Sat R 53:27-9+ S 26 '70 *
PRICE, T. Rowe
Generation gap; interview. por Forbes 106:46 N 15 '70
PRICE calculators. See Calculating devices

PRICE control. See Price regulation by government
PRICE cutting
See also
Discount houses (retail trade)
Dumping (commercial policy)
PRICE earnings ratios. See Stocks—Price earnings ratios
PRICE indexes
Analysis of price changes in the third quarter of 1969. W. J. Layng and T. Nakayama. il Mo Labor R 93:44-7 Ja '70
Anatomy of price change: the second quarter, 1970. T. Nakayama. il Mo Labor R 93:43-5 S '70
Consumer price index and all that. B. L. Masse. America 123:480 D 5 '70
Does the price index tell a straight story? wholesale price index. il Bsns W p46+ Jl 11 '70
First quarter, 1970. T. Nakayama. il Mo Labor R 93:61-3 Je '70
Price pressures ease, by a hair. il Bsns W p22 My 9 '70
Prices (cont of) Consumer prices; tables; Wholesale prices; tables. See issues of Monthly labor review
Third quarter, 1970. T. Nakayama. il Mo Labor R 93:35-7 D '70
PRICE maintenance by industry
Controls. H. C. Wallich. Newsweek 75:81 Mr 9 '70
Canada
Business takes a price pledge. il Bsns W p33-4 F 14 '70
PRICE marks
See also
Unit pricing
PRICE policies
See also
Unit pricing
PRICE regulation by government
See also
Wage-price policy
Canada
Business takes a price pledge. il Bsns W p33-4 F 14 '70
See also
Wage-price policy—Canada
United States
Controls. H. C. Wallich. Newsweek 75:81 Mr 9 '70
PRICE supports, Agricultural. See Agricultural administration—United States
PRICE-wage policy. See Wage-price policy
PRICES
See also
Cost of living
Gas rates
Index numbers
Inflation (finance)
  also subhead Prices under various subjects, e.g. Gold—Prices; also headings beginning Price
Economic aspects
First signs of softer prices. il Bsns W p 14 S 5 '70
See also
Wage-price policy
Statistics
Price trends in fourteen countries. P. Capdevielle. il Mo Labor R 93:66-7 My '70
Canada
Price regulation by government—Canada
United States
As prices climb, where bargains are. il U S News 69:25 Jl 20 '70
Back on the treadmill. Time 96:88 N 2 '70
Inflation, to slow down soon? il U S News 68:17-19 Je 15 '70
Just look where prices are heading! list of randomly selected items. il Changing T 24: 24 Mr '70
Learning to live with inflation. il Newsweek 76:87-8 N 2 '70
More discount sales for shoppers. il U S News 69:14-15 Ag 31 '70
Prices (cont of) Consumer prices; tables; Wholesale prices; tables. See issues of Monthly labor review
Prices: slowdown in prospect. il Fortune 81: 16+ Ap '70
Prices: what to expect now; leading economists interviewed on price and wage outlook. il U S News 68:17-19 Ap 13 '70
Rising attack on Nixonomics. il Time 95:64-5 F 2 '70

PRICES—United States—*Continued*
Slowdown and the consumer. il Time 95:67 Ja 26 '70
What makes prices rise? il Bsns W p 122 S 19 '70
Wholesale prices; tables. See issues of Monthly labor review
See also
Cost of living—United States
Price indexes
Price regulation by government—United States
also subhead Prices under various subjects, e.g. Automobiles—Prices
PRICES and incomes commission (Canada) See Canada—Prices and incomes commission
PRIDE, Charley
Black Pride. por Newsweek 76:82 Ag 17 '70 *
PRIDE, George H.
Three seasons of lilies. il Horticulture 48:30-3+ Mr '70
PRIDE and vanity
Autonomous man. Chr Today 14:27 Ja 16 '70
Pride. L. N. Bell. Chr Today 14:36-7 Ap 10 '70
PRIDEAUX, James
Postcards. Criticism
New Yorker 46:81 Mr 28 '70 *
PRIDEAUX, Tom
Life theater review. See issues of Life
Parting shots: Hair, that play is sprouting everywhere. il Life 68:83-6 Ap 17 '70
What? Laugh at a blind boy? il pors Life 68:57-8 F 6 '70
PRIESAND, Sally
Rabbi Sally. por Newsweek 75:89 F 23 '70 *
PRIEST, Ivy Maude (Baker)
Rich flow from a pool. V. Louviere. Nations Bsns 58:14 Ag '70 *
PRIEST, Roger
Priest's progress. il por Time 95:78+ My 11 '70 *
Seaman Priest. P. M. Stern. New Repub 162:12-13 F 14 '70 *
PRIESTHOOD. See Priests
PRIESTLEY, Joseph
Chemists' involvement in society. R. Ferreira. bibliog il pors Chem 43:16-17 O '70 *
PRIESTLEY, Michael
Pteranodon: first of the hot-blooded flappers. il Sci Digest 68:86-7 S '70
PRIESTS
Anonymous priesthood. J. W. Glaser. Commonweal 93:271-4 D 11 '70
Catholic church professionals. J. H. Fichter. bibliog f Am Am Acad 387:77-85 Ja '70
Christ the priest. V. P. McCorry. America 123:304 O 17 '70
Credit due; Catholic churchmen on presidential and national commissions. Commonweal 93:138 N 6 '70
Critical shortage of Spanish-speaking priests cited by bishop. Chr Cent 87:1034 S 2 '70
Future is for priests; address, October 16, 1969. J. J. Egan. il Cath World 210:262-5 Mr '70
Ideas on trial; first promotion, at age 50? M. Powers. America 122:509 My 9 '70
Of many things; excerpts from address. P. A. Schweitzer. America 122:inside cover Je 13 '70
Rise and fall of the Roman image. I. M. Sussman. America 122:500-2 My 9 '70
Roots of clerical restlessness. C. A. J. Pillai. Cath World 211:176-9 Jl '70; Discussion. 212:5, 61-2 O-N '70
Today's priest, GP or more? A. O. Sigur. America 122:237-40 Mr 7 '70; Discussion. 122:320+, 636 Mr 28, Je 13 '70
Uncoupling celibacy; Dutch pastoral council. V. T. G. Fuechtmann. America 122:102+ Ja 31 '70
Vocations and celibacy. J. Deedy. Commonweal 91:522 F 13 '70
Waiting game; Vatican warfare against dissenting priests. Chr Cent 87:261 Mr 4 '70
What is a priest? V. P. McCorry. America 123:inside back cover O 24 '70
What makes priests leave. America 122:63 Ja 24 '70
See also
Celibacy
Chaplains. Military
Ex-nuns, priests, etc.
Marriage of priests
Women as priests

Associations, institutions, etc.
Bishops, PADRES and the barrios. P. H. McNamara. Commonweal 93:116-17 O 30 '70
Boston priests at grips with the diaspora; Association of Boston urban priests. T. D. Corrigan. Cath World 212:35-6 O '70
Counsels on priest councils. America 122:574 My 30 '70

Free ministry. E. C. Bianchi. Commonweal 91:450-3 Ja 23 '70; Reply with rejoinder. P. J. Murnion. 91:566-7 F 20 '70
Padres and bishops. America 122:380 Ap 11 '70
See also
National federation of priests' councils

Political activities
As clergymen enter politics: the new trend. il por U S News 69:19-21 Ag 10 '70
Chaplain's politics. por Newsweek 76:70 Ag 10 '70
Clerical candidates. il Time 95:22 Je 8 '70
Collars in the ring. il Newsweek 75:105 My 4 '70
Conspiracy of clerics. il Newsweek 76:68+ D 14 '70
Father runs for Congress. W. Kennedy. il pors Look 34:18-22 S 22 '70
Is there a priest in the house? Chr Today 15:25 D 4 '70
Priest candidates and the U.S. Congress. America 123:422 N 21 '70; Reply. J. P. Boland. 123:504 D 12 '70
Priest, law school dean, candidate for Congress; interview, ed. by C. E. Fager. R. Drinan. por Chr Cent 87:1069-72 S 9 '70
Priest vs. Pastore. S. Cunneen. Chr Cent 87:1067-8 S 9 '70
Priests in politics; Latin American controversy. Sr Schol 97:20-1 O 19 '70
Priests, politics and canon law. America 123:110 S 5 '70
PRIESTS as political candidates. See Candidates, Political
PRIESTS as teachers
De-schooling the teaching orders. I. Illich. por America 124:12-14 Ja 9 '71
PRIESTS in literature
Rise and fall of the Roman image. I. M. Sussman. America 122:500-2 My 9 '70
PRIETO, Eunice
Ceramics by Eunice Prieto. il Ceram Mo 18:31 Mr '70 *
PRIMARIES
Early primaries; Alabama, Texas, Ohio. New Repub 162:9-10 My 16 '70
Election returns. New Repub 162:7 Je 13 '70
Humphrey's comeback; Minnesota; Massachusetts; Maryland. por Newsweek 76:27 S 28 '70
In seven statewide primaries. il U S News 68:23 Je 15 '70
Out of nine primaries, fresh clues to November. il U S News 69:50-1 S 21 '70
Political almanac for the year 1970. U S News 68:38-9 My 4 '70
Political indicators to watch; 1970 midterm election. il U S News 68:37 My 4 '70
Politics '70: crosscurrents. il Newsweek 75:26-7 Je 15 '70
Primaries: leaning toward the right. il Time 95:14+ Je 15 '70
Primary results in three states; Arkansas, Oklahoma, Alaska. il U S News 69:35 S 7 '70
Returns. Nation 210:580-1 My 18 '70
'70 election trends: the first clues; Alabama, Ohio and Texas. il U S News 68:40-1 My 18 '70
Uncertain soundings; Vermont, Wisconsin, Florida. Nation 211:226-7 S 21 '70
Undercurrents; Washington, Wyoming, Minnesota, New York. Nation 211:165 S 7 '70
What the primaries tell about voters' mood. il U S News 69:15-16 Jl 6 '70
What voters are saying. il U S News 69:17-18 Ag 17 '70
When the war issue was raised-. il U S News 68:22-3 Je 15 '70
See also subhead Politics and government under names of states, cities, etc. e.g. Ohio—Politics and government
PRIMARY campaigns. See Political campaigns
PRIMARY education. See Education, Elementary
PRIMARY elections. See Primaries
PRIMATES
Primate populations and biomedical research. C. H. Southwick and other. bibliog il Science 170:1051-4 D 4 '70
See also
Chimpanzees
PRIME rate. See Interest
PRIMITIVE and early church. See Church history—Primitive and early church
PRIMITIVE areas. See Wilderness areas
PRIMITIVE art. See Art. Primitive
PRIMITIVE geometry. See Geometry
PRIMITIVE medicine. See Medicine, Primitive

PRIMITIVE navigation. See Navigation, Primitive

PRIMITIVE religion. See Religion, Primitive

PRIMITIVES, American. See Painting, American

PRINCE, Alain Wood
Camp wild for best fishing. il pors Field & S 75:58-9+ My '70
On the Mississippi ice. il por Outdoor Life 146:54-7+ D '70

PRINCE, Alfred M. and Burke, Kathleen
Serum hepatitis antigen (SH): rapid detection of high voltage immunoelectroosmophoresis. bibliog il Science 169:593-5 Ag 7 '70

PRINCE and the pauper; drama. See Bland, J.

PRINCE EDWARD COUNTY, Va.

Education
You can see the change in Prince Edward. P. Pine. il Am Ed 6:24-8 Jl '70

PRINCE GEORGES COUNTY library system
Rebuttal from Prince George; removal of Washington free press; letters to the editor. Am Lib 1:647-9 Jl '70
See also
High John library, Fairmount Heights, Md.

PRINCE Hall Masons. See Freemasons, Negro

PRINCE of Peasantmania; drama. See Gagliano, F.

PRINCESS flower
For the climate privileged. il Sunset 144:224 Je '70

PRINCESS Louisa Inlet. See Jervis Inlet

PRINCETON, N.J.

Institute for advanced study
Institute advances. por Newsweek 75:54-5 Ap 6 '70

PRINCETON university
Advice to Princeton alumni; excerpts from address, 1970. A. Capp. il Nat R 22:994-6+ S 22 '70
Princeton commitment: a race against mace. J. Shepherd. il Look 34:12+ Je 16 '70
Princeton's glass pavilion; Prospect faculty center. M. Villecco. il Arch Forum 132:60-3 Je '70
Two parts into one whole; Fine Hall and Jadwin Hall. il Arch Forum 133:52-7 Jl '70
What Princeton really needed; excerpt from Andrew Carnegie. J. F. Wall. il pors Am Heritage 21:91-2 Je '70
Working from within; Princeton movement for a new Congress. il Newsweek 75:69-70 My 25 '70

PRINCIPALS, School. See School superintendents and principals

PRINN, Ronald G. See Lewis, J. S. jt. auth.

PRINT collections. See Prints—Collectors and collecting

PRINT dryers. See Photography—Processing—Apparatus and supplies

PRINT films. See Photography—Films

PRINTED circuits
Design your own printed circuits. A. W. Burawa. il Pop Electr 32:59-62+ My '70
How to make etchless circuits. B. G. Wels. il Radio-Electr 41:59 S '70

PRINTERS
See also
International typographical union

PRINTERS slowdown. See Strikes—United States—Newspapers

PRINTING
See also
Block printing
Color printing
Computers—Printing use
Lithography
Music printing
Proofreading
Type and typefounding

Design
See also
Type and typefounding

History
Advent of printing in current historical literature: notes and comments on an elusive transformation. E. L. Eisenstein. bibliog f Am Hist R 75:727-43 F '70
Christian use of the printed page: excerpts from address. F. E. Gaebelein. Chr Today 14:5-8 Ja 30 '70

PRINTING (photography) See Photography—Printing processes

PRINTING, Offset
Driography. Pub W 198:57 S 14 '70

PRINTING industry
Profiles; G. Mardersteig, printer of Officina Bodoni and Stamperia Valdonega editions in Verona. Italy. W. Sargeant. por New Yorker 46:32-6+ Jl 11 '70
Technological changes in the printing and publishing industry. R. V. Critchlow. il Mo Labor R 93:3-9 Ag '70
See also
Bowne and company
Halliday lithograph corporation

PRINTING paper (photography) See Photographic paper

PRINTING presses, Hand
Printing with the handpress; excerpts. L. M. Allen. il Pub W 198:58-60 Jl 20 '70

PRINTMAKING. See Prints—Technique

PRINTS
On and off the avenue. J. Malcolm. New Yorker 46:63-4+ Je 20 '70
Prints by four New York painters: H. Frankenthaler, J. Johns, R. Motherwell, B. Newman. il Am Scholar 39:425-33 Sum '70
Revival of prints. R. Hughes. il Time 97:56-7 Ja 18 '71
See also
Lithographs
Monotypes
Shadowgrams

Collectors and collecting
Convertible play in original prints. il Fortune 82:177-8+ N '70
How and where to buy contemporary prints. N. R. Piene. House & Gard 137:54+ Mr '70
How to buy old prints. N. R. Piene. House & Gard 138:40+ S '70

Exhibitions
Danube mannerists; exhibition of Danube school prints and drawings. B. A. Rifkin. il Art N 68:56-8+ F '70
Masques and massacres; Callot's prints. Rhode Island school of design museum, Providence. H. Zerner. il Art N 68:59-61+ F '70

Technique
Blotter prints. Sister Mary Magdalen. il Design 71:34-6 Fall '69
Embossing without a press. J. Comins. il Sch Arts 70:26-7 D '70
Emphasis: printmaking. V. G. Timmons. il Sch Arts 70:4 D '70
Finger paint printing. il Design 71:38-9 mid-Wint '70
Graphics '70: Alexander Calder. D. H. Karshan. il por Art in Am 58:48-51 My '70
How and where to buy contemporary prints. N. R. Piene. House & Gard 137:54+ Mr '70
Mimeographics. M. J. Acosta. il Design 71:38-40 Spr '70
Photo sketch prints. H. J. Croze. il Design 71:36-7 Spr '70
Plasticene prints. H. T. Thomas. il Design 71:21 Fall '69
Printing from cardboard cuts. L. J. Miller. il Design 71:20-2 mid-Sum '70
Prints from plastic throw-aways. P. A. Lee. il Sch Arts 69:22-3 Mr '70
Prints of Mauricio Lasansky. J. Goldman. il por Am Artist 34:62-8+ Mr '70
Prints without cutting. G. F. Brommer. il Sch Arts 70:10-11 D '70
Sponge double-printing. C. Tefft. il Sch Arts 70:12-13 D '70
Stamping a new technique for making prints; interview. N. Krinsky. il Am Artist 34:38-43 S '70

PRINTS, Drying of. See Photography—Drying (films and prints)

PRISON bands
Prison records; Sonny Brown and his Fallen Sparrows. por Time 96:64+ N 2 '70

PRISON camps

China (People's Republic)
Mao makes the trials run on time. R. Hughes. il N Y Times Mag p22-3+ Ag 23 '70; Reply with rejoinder. A. S. Whiting. p41+ N 15 '70

PRISON education. See Education of prisoners

PRISON escapes. See Escapes

PRISON libraries
See also
Libraries—Services to prisons

PRISON recreation
Prison games and other escapes. M. Braly. il Sports Illus 33:48-55 Ag 10 '70

PRISON reform. See Prisons

PRISON riots
Anger in the cells; New York city. il News-week 76:102 O 19 '70
Black hole of Manhattan; the Tombs. il Time 96:28-9 Ag 24 '70
Rampage in New York. il Time 96:44 O 19 '70
Riot against the law's delay; the Tombs. il Newsweek 76:20 Ag 24 '70
Using racism at San Quentin. R. Minton and S. Rice. il Ramp Mag 8:18-24 Ja '70

PRISON ships
Rebels, turn out your dead! detention aboard British prison ship Jersey, moored in the East River. A. B. Tourtellot. il Am Heritage 21:16-17+ Ag '70

PRISON visits. See Prisons—Visits with inmates

PRISONERS
Death row: a new kind of suspense. il Newsweek 77:23-4+ Ja 11 '71
From killers to priests: six men behind the bars; famous U.S. inmates. il Time 97:54-5 Ja 18 '71
Going to jail: a day in the life of a prisoner. N. Horrock. il Newsweek 76:42 S 14 '70
Parting shots: their last move is up to the Supreme court. il Life 68:84 Je 12 '70
See also
Escapes
Libraries—Services to prisons
Negro prisoners
Political prisoners
Prison ships
Prisons—Visits with inmates

Anecdotes, facetiae, satire, etc.

How to take off your pants while wearing chains. D. Pearce. il Esquire 73:98-9 F '70

Legal status, laws, etc.

Inmate manuscripts; class action suit by the Berrigan brothers. R. H. Smith. Pub W 198:29 D 7 '70

Recreation
See Prison recreation

Rehabilitation

California plan: how one state is salvaging its convicts. il U S News 69:44-7 Ag 24 '70
For whom the bell tolls; penal reform; address, February 17, 1970. W. E. Burger. Vital Speeches 36:322-5 Mr 15 '70
Halfway help. Chr Today 15:35 N 6 '70
Producing cars, and good citizens. Nations Bsns 58:16 F '70
Rehabilitation v. revenge. il Time 95:66 Mr 2 '70
See also
Prisoners, Women—Rehabilitation

Treatment

Berrigans in prison. K. L. Woodward. Commonweal 92:428-30 S 4 '70
Black Africans in white prisons; South Africa's police assaults. I. Robertson and P. Whitten. Commonweal 93:239-41 D 4 '70
Eye for an eye, by H. J. Griswold and others. Review
New Repub 163:23-4 Jl 4 '70. M. King
Johnny Cash on prison reform. D. G. Shockley and R. L. Freeman. Chr Cent 87:1157 S 30 '70
Price of repression; interpretation of the shoot-out at the San Rafael courthouse. Nation 211:130-1 Ag 31 '70
Prison debate: where does abuse end and coddling begin? il Sr Schol 95:5-10 N 3 '69
Seize the time; excerpts. B. Seale. pors Ramp Mag 8:17-29 Je '70
Shame of the prisons. il Time 97:48-50+ Ja 18 '71
Should experimentation on prisoners be stopped? pro and con discussion. il Sr Schol 95:11-12 N 3 '69
Soledad brothers: how a prison picks its victims; racial hostilities. E. Pell. il Ramp Mag 9:31+ Ag '70
Soledad story. il por Newsweek 76:21 Ag 24 '70
Using racism at San Quentin. R. Minton and S. Rice. il Ramp Mag 8:18-24 Ja '70

PRISONERS, Discharged
See also
Parole

PRISONERS, Education of. See Education of prisoners

PRISONERS, Political. See Political prisoners

PRISONERS, Women

Rehabilitation

New life for women inmates; Oakdale state reformatory for women, Dwight, Ill. il Ebony 25:105-6+ Ap '70

PRISONERS as artists
See also
McCune, B.

PRISONERS as authors
Inmate manuscripts; class action suit by the Berrigan brothers. R. H. Smith. Pub W 198:29 D 7 '70

PRISONERS of war
See also
United States—History—Revolution—Prisoners and prisons
Vietnamese war, 1957- —Prisoners and prisons

PRISONERS of war, Families of. See Servicemens families

PRISONERS of war, Returned
Forty days; release of Elizabeth Pond, Richard Dudman and Mike Morrow. il Newsweek 75:55 Je 29 '70
Three come back; release of three American correspondents. il Time 95:60 Je 29 '70

PRISONERS of war in China
Small price to pay. il por Time 96:23 Jl 20 '70

PRISONS
Crime and punishment: a new approach; British Quakers report, Why prison? Chr Cent 87:931 Ag 5 '70
See also
Prison riots
Prisoners
Punishment
Reformatories

Visits with inmates

They go to prison on purpose. A. Gordon. Read Digest 97:147-8+ Ag '70

Arkansas

Vindication for Murton. Nation 210:357 Mr 30 '70

Brazil

From the parrot's perch. il Time 96:27 Jl 27 '70

California

California plan; how one state is salvaging its convicts. il U S News 69:44-7 Ag 24 '70
Soledad brothers: how a prison picks its victims; racial hostilities E. Pell. il Ramp Mag 9:31+ Ag '70
Soledad story. il por Newsweek 76:21 Ag 24 '70
Using racism at San Quentin. R. Minton and S. Rice. il Ramp Mag 8:18-24 Ja '70

France

See also
Bastille

New York (state)

See also
New York (city)—Prisons and reformatories
Sing Sing prison, Ossining, N.Y.

Spain

Eight months in Franco's jail. Duchess of Medina-Sidonia. Nation 210:396-9 Ap 6 '70

United States

Crime of prison. B. N. Odell. Cath World 212:43-4 O '70
Prison debate: where does abuse end and coddling begin? il Sr Schol 95:5-10 N 3 '69
Prisons in turmoil. il Newsweek 76:36+ S 14 '70
Shame of the prisons. il Time 97:48-50+ Ja 18 '71
See also subhead Prisons and reformatories under names of cities, e.g. New York (city)—Prisons and reformatories

Vietnam (Republic)

Cages of Con Son Island. il Time 96:20+ Jl 20 '70
Con Son: school for revolutionaries. Tranvan-Dinh. Chr Cent 87:1135-7 S 23 '70
Good collaborators; deplorable South Vietnamese penal system. Nation 211:66 Ag 3 '70
How they unearthed the tiger cages. R. Graves. Life 69:2A Jl 17 '70
Prisoners and prisoners; Con Son prison. Nat R 22:773 Jl 28 '70
Tiger cages; conditions at Con Son prison. il Newsweek 76:27 Jl 20 '70
Tiger cages of Con Son. il Life 69:26-9 Jl 17 '70

Wisconsin

Return of the felon; Waupun prison life. J. Forest. Commonweal 92:334-5 Jl 10 '70

PRISONS, Military
See also
European war, 1914-1918—Prisoners and prisons
United States—Army—Prisons

PRITCHARD, Errol
  Perfenestration; poem. Commonweal 91:475 Ja 30 '70
PRITCHETT, Victor Sawdon
  Fall; story. New Yorker 46:34-9 Je 20 '70
PRIVACY
  Place to be alone; a room for the wife-and-mother. D. Hardie. House & Gard 137:70+ My '70
  What's happening to sexual privacy? F. Trippett. Look 34:50 O 20 '70
PRIVACY, Right of
  Assault on privacy. R. Boeth. il Newsweek 76:15-17+ Jl 27 '70; Same abr. with title is Privacy dying? Read Digest 97:93-7 O '70
  Atlanta public library's policy on investigations by IRS and other law enforcement agencies. Am Lib 1:729 S '70
  Box score on confidentiality of library circulation records. J. F. Krug and J. A. Harvey. Am Lib 1:944 N '70
  Card-carrying reader; probe by the IRS into what people read. New Repub 163:7 Jl 25 '70
  Data study will watch Big Brother. por Bsns W p34 Mr 14 '70
  Data system for measuring and analyzing public programs; excerpt from address, December 1969. C. L. Schultze. Mo Labor R 93:13-15 Mr '70
  Death of privacy. R. Clark. por McCalls 97:66-7+ F '70
  Detour of 1984; credit bureau files. A. R. Miller. Nation 210:648-51 Je 1 '70
  Editor's choice; sanctity: libraries, clients, IRS, ALA. G. R. Shields. Am Lib 1:749-50 S '70
  Everybody's business, and nobody's. S. Rabinove. Chr Cent 87:843-6 Jl 8 '70
  Head-counting time is here again. il Bsns W p80+ Mr 7 '70
  How far must surveillance go? government data banks. A. R. Miller. Cur 123:27-30 N '70
  I spy, you spy. E. Marshall. New Repub 163:15-16 O 3 '70
  Librarian demonstrators march on IRS office. Library J 95:2749 S 1 '70
  Like Jack's magic beans: controversy at the Detroit conference over IRS's inspection of private reading habits. J. F. Krug and J. A. Harvey. Am Lib 1:843-5 O '70
  Litmus test of tyranny. T-men vs. librarians. W. R. Eshelman. Wilson Lib Bul 45:5-7 S '70
  National press and television coverage: IRS incident. J. F. Krug and J. A. Harvey. Am Lib 1:1026-7 D '70
  No-wash whitewash; army intelligence spying on civilians. Nation 212:2 Ja 4 '71
  Obscenity and pornography statement further justified; incidents in Milwaukee and Atlanta. J. F. Krug and J. A. Harvey. Am Lib 1:751-2 S '70
  Of note: investigation of what people read by Treasury agents. G. R. Shields. Am Lib 1:633 Jl '70
  On tracking down dissent. N. Hentoff. Cur 121:37-41 S '70
  Personal privacy v. the print-out: Time essay. il Time 95:38-9 F 16 '70
  Personal tragedy held matter of public interest. H. F. Pilpel and K. P. Norwick. Pub W 198:36 O 5 '70
  Privacy, security, and a free America; address, September 15, 1970. F. Horton. Vital Speeches 37:44-7 N 1 '70
  Privacy: there's too little. Noise: there's too much. M. Drury. House B 112:74-6 Ag '70
  Reader interest in bombs checked by T-men; with editorial comment. il Library J 95:2591, 2593 Ag '70
  Snoopers in the public libraries: representatives of the Internal revenue service. R. H. Smith. Pub W 198:33 Ag 10 '70
  Snooping on the home front; army surveillance of civilians. J. Hanlon. Nation 211:305-6 O 5 '70
  Sociological snoopers; with reply by I. L. Horowitz and L. Rainwater. N. Von Hoffman. Trans-Action 7:4-8+ My '70
  When readers become suspect. R. Cleghorn. Cur 121:42-6 S '70
  Will school libraries be next? views of the National education association. Cur 121:47 S '70
    See also
  Confidential communications
  Wire tapping

    Anecdotes, facetiae, satire, etc.
  Smith/Jones. D. DeCamp. Library J 95:3451 O 15 '70

PRIVATE airplanes. See Airplanes, Private
PRIVATE bills. See Bills, Private

PRIVATE collections of art. See Art—Private collections
PRIVATE colleges and universities. See Colleges and universities
PRIVATE enterprise. See Free enterprise
PRIVATE experimental schools. See Schools, Experimental
PRIVATE flying
  Boston stranglers; or, How to pack a pack of Cub scouts in a Bonanza. R. Peterson. il Flying 86:72-5 Ja '70
  Crazy, tricky, wonderful sport of island hopping. N. Aubuchon. il Pop Sci 196:71-3+ Mr '70
  Flying to the bowl games; Orange bowl, Cotton bowl and Rose bowl. il Flying 87:69-72 D '70
  Follow me through; why practice? R. Blodget. il Flying 87:14-15 N '70
  Piper cub vs. the 747. B. Bernstein. il N Y Times Mag p34-5+ Mr 8 '70; Reply with rejoinder. K. Bailey and J. West. p34+ Mr 22 '70
  Richard Bach. R. Bach. See issues of Flying to April 1970
  St Pierre by air. S. Wilkinson. il Flying 87:50-8 O '70
  Weekend pilot. F. K. Smith. See issues of Flying to July 1970
  Will you lose your right to fly? F. A. Tinker. il Pop Mech 134:88-91+ O '70
    See also
  Airplanes, Private
  Airplanes in business
PRIVATE forests. See Forest ownership
PRIVATE helicopters. See Helicopters—Private ownership
PRIVATE hospitals. See Hospitals
PRIVATE libraries. See Libraries, Private
PRIVATE lives; drama. See Coward, N.
PRIVATE rights. See Civil rights
PRIVATE schools
  Authors & editors; writing about Choate in A world of our own. B. A. Bannon. por Pub W 198:31+ S 28 '70
  Boarding-school blues. il Time 96:49 S 7 '70
  Box full of school; Latin school, Chicago. il Arch Forum 132:58-61 My '70
  Creed and color in the school crisis. Chr Today 14:32-3 Mr 27 '70
  Dance at St Paul's school; Concord, N.H. K. S. Cunningham. il Dance Mag 44:24-5 Je '70
  Here come the girls; new trend among boys' prep schools. Newsweek 75:70 My 25 '70
  Instant schools; segregationists open private, all-white schools. il Newsweek 75:59 Ja 26 '70
  John Dewey is alive and well in New England; free schools. R. H. De Lone and S. T. De Lone. il Sat R 53:69-71+ N 21 '70
  Preparing youth for a world of unprecedented complexity; excerpt from address, March 7, 1970. M. Collins. Dept State Bul 62:425-6 Mr 30 '70
  Preppies, then and now. Trans-Action 7:13 F '70
  Private prep schools. J. Deedy. Commonweal 93:2 O 2 '70
  Segregation by tax exemption. R. Cleghorn. Nation 210:785-6 Je 29 '70
  Tax status of exempt organizations; address, August 24, 1970. R. W. Thrower. Vital Speeches 37:2-5 O 15 '70
  Westside, an exciting new concept in education. K. Branan. il Parents Mag 45:64-5+ F '70
  What a parent faces in finding a private school. Bsns W p93-4 F 7 '70
  Who needs schools? need for independent schools. J. H. Fischer. il Sat R 53:78-9+ S 19 '70
  World of our own, by P. S. Prescott. Review Bsns W p8-9 O 24 '70. J. C. Esty, jr. Newsweek il 76:92-4 O 26 '70. G. Wolff
    See also
  Education and state
  Finch college, New York

    Desegregation
  Court rules out tax exemption for Mississippi's segregated academies. Chr Cent 87:103 Ja 28 '70
  Pastoral pilgrimage; protest segregated private schools. W. Henley. Chr Today 14:33 Mr 27 '70
  Tax blow at white private schools. U S News 68:53 Ja 26 '70
  Tax exemption for private schools: what officials plan. R. W. Thrower; W. Mondale. pors U S News 69:70-4 Ag 31 '70
  Will private schools no longer be private? D. Lawrence. il U S News 69:80 Ag 3 '70

PRIVATE schools—*Continued*

Federal aid

New threat to public schools. il Ebony 25: 84-5 S '70

Nonpublic schools and educational reform. D. A. Erickson. Ed Digest 35:1-4 My '70

Public aid for nonpublic schools? PTA votes no. C. Ryan. il PTA Mag 65:16-18 O '70

PRIVATE schools and religion
Prep-school ministry. J. W. Howe, jr. Chr Today 14:9-10 F 27 '70

PRIVATE secretaries. See Secretaries

PRIVATE treasure; story. See Hopkins, G.

PRIVATELY owned forests. See Forest ownership

PRIVETTE, Mari
We did it. House B 112:46-7 S '70

PRIVILEGED communications. See Confidential communications

PRIVILEGES and immunities
Businessmen lose some immunity. Bsns W p24 N 7 '70

Proceedings privileged against libel actions. Pub W 198:34 D 28 '70

U.S. accedes to U.N. convention on privileges and immunities; remarks, April 29, 1970. C. W. Yost. Dept State Bul 62:671 My 25 '70

PRIX de l'Arc de Triomphe. See Horse racing —France

PRIZE contests in advertising. See Advertising —Prize contests

PRIZE fighting. See Boxing

PROBABILITIES
Math lesson from racing rats. il Sci Digest 68:90-1 O '70

Paradox of the nontransitive dice and the elusive principle of indifference. M. Gardner. il Sci Am 223:110-13 D '70
See also
Chance
Least squares
Stochastic processes

PROBATE law and practice
Time to clean up our probate courts. M. T. Bloom. Read Digest 96:112-15 Ja '70
See also
Executors and administrators

PROBLEM children
See also
Child guidance clinics
Runaway boys and girls
School children—Adjustment

Education

Cues for teaching the emotionally disturbed; turn on, tune in, drop out. J. F. Koon. Clear House 44:497-500 Ap '70

ITV turns students on. H. M. Jung. il Todays Ed 59:36-7 Ja '70

Youth in rebellion, why? interview. W. Glasser. il por U S News 68:42-6 Ap 27 '70
See also
Special classes and special schools

PROBLEM of three bodies. See Three bodies. Problem of

PROBLEM solving
Analogy: the scientist's trick for problem solving. R. Dreistadt. il Sci Digest 67:36-43 Ap '70

Boy with imagination plus. E. Hunter. il Parents Mag 45:42-3+ D '70

Cognitive model of problem-solving in chess. M. J. Scurrah and D. A. Wagner. il Science 169:209-11 Jl 10 '70

What's left when school's forgotten? process approach to curriculum development. T. Borton. il Sat R 53:69-71+ Ap 18 '70

Anecdotes, facetiae, satires, etc.

You could make a fortune in the problem business. G. Logsdon. il Farm J 94:40-1+ Mr '70

PROCEDURE (law)
Gag rule: ominous trend. D. Meade. Chr Cent 87:589-90 My 13 '70

What to do when the judge is put up against the wall. L. Nizer. il N Y Times Mag p30-1+ Ap 5 '70; Same abr. with title Order in the court! Read Digest 97:95-9 Jl '70; Discussion. N Y Times Mag p 114-15 My 3 '70
See also
Courts martial and courts of inquiry
Criminal procedure
Due process of law

PROCLAMATION of emancipation. See Emancipation proclamation

PROCTER and Gamble company
Great diaper rash; disposable diaper business. il Forbes 106:24-6+ D 15 '70

Neil McElroy of Procter & Gamble; interview. N. H. McElroy. il pors Nations Bsns 58:58-63 Ag '70

P&G; still the master marketer. por Duns 96:32-3 D '70

PROCUREMENT, Government. See Purchasing, Government

PROCUREMENT, Military. See United States —Armed forces—Procurement

PRODUCE exchanges. See Commodity exchanges

PRODUCE trade
See also
Fruit industry

PRODUCT safety, National commission on. See United States—National commission on product safety

PRODUCTION
Economics of pollution. E. L. Dale, jr. il N Y Times Mag p27-9+ Ap 19 '70

If you don't mind my saying so. J. W. Krutch. Am Scholar 39:378+ Sum '70

More productivity is a must. il Bsns W p 183 O 17 '70

Pluses in productivity and profits. Fortune 82:19 S '70

Pollution and affluence. K. Cole. Focus 20:12 Je '70

Who owns the environment? P. Schrag. Sat R 53:6-9+ Jl 4 '70
See also
Efficiency, Industrial
Gross national product
Inventories
Labor productivity

PRODUCTION, Agricultural
How green is green. Nation 211:454 N 9 '70

Third world: seeds of revolution; production explosion in the grain bowls of the world. il Time 96:24+ Jl 13 '70
See also
Crop yields
Food supply

PRODUCTION, Theatrical. See Theatrical production and direction

PRODUCTION control
How business is meeting the squeeze. il U S News 68:32-4 Mr 9 '70

PRODUCTION costs. See Cost

PRODUCTION testing of cows. See Cows— Testing

PRODUCTIVITY. See Production

PRODUCTIVITY, Labor. See Labor productivity

PRODUCTS, Commercial. See Commercial products

PRODUCTS, New
Exciting new products. C. Bilski. See issues of Popular mechanics

Good news. D. L. Gregg and D. M. Lidster. See issues of Better homes and gardens

Let the buyer be aware; untested new products. A. R. Roalman. il Todays Health 48:66-7+ Mr '70

New aerospace products. See issues of Aviation week & space technology

New products. See issues of Popular electronics

New products. See issues of Radio-electronics

New products. See issues of Science news

New products & literature. See issues of Electronics world

New products and processes. See issues of American city

Outside job fills the product gap; free-lance idea men. il Bsns W p54+ My 16 '70

Parade of new products. il U S News 68:48-9 F 2 '70

Product gallery. See issues of Popular electronics

Rush of new products for '71. il U S News 70:72-4 Ja 11 '71

PRODUCTS, Quality of. See Quality of products

PROFESSIONAL air traffic controllers organization
Air controllers may fly with the AFL-CIO. il Bsns W p 112+ My 16 '70

Controller action hurts airline revenues. Aviation W 92:26-7 Mr 30 '70

FAA may impose sanctions on controllers. Aviation W 92:36 Ap 6 '70

FAA permits controllers to take appeal to Volpe. Aviation W 92:26-7 F 23 '70

Future of air-traffic union put on line. U S News 68:44 Je 8 '70

PATCO moves seek conciliatory posture. Aviation W 92:33 Je 29 '70

Real issue in air slowdown. il U S News 68: 24-6 Ap 13 '70

PROFESSIONAL associations. See Trade and professional associations

PROFESSIONAL athletes. See Athletes

PROFESSIONAL basketball players. See Basketball players

PROFESSIONAL education
Social change and educating for the professions. A. D. Henderson. il Sch & Soc 98: 92-5+ F '70
See also
Library schools and education

PROFESSIONAL ethics
See also
Business ethics
Journalistic ethics
Literary ethics
Medical ethics
School superintendents and principals. Professional ethics for
Teachers. Professional ethics for

PROFESSIONAL football clubs. See Football clubs

PROFESSIONAL football players. See Football players

PROFESSIONAL golfers' association of America
See also
Ladies' professional golfers' association

PROFESSIONAL golfers' association tournament. See Golf—Tournaments

PROFESSIONAL patient syndrome. See Malingering

PROFESSIONAL tennis. See Tennis

PROFESSIONAL workers
Supply and demand
See also
Brain drain

PROFESSIONALISM (sports) See Amateurism (sports)

PROFESSIONS
Dreams that never fade; boyhood aspirations of prominent men. J. H. Pollack. il Nations Bsns 58:48-51 Ag '70
See also
Conservation as a profession
Occupations
Woman—Occupations

PROFESSORS. See College professors and instructors

PROFILE rocks. See Rock profiles

PROFILES. See Rock profiles

PROFIT
Bigness versus profitability. F. R. Wittnebert. il Harvard Bsns R 48:158-60+ Ja '70
Why the slide in earnings. il U S News 68:37 Je 29 '70
See also
Corporations—Finance
Risk

PROFIT sharing
Do you share the company's profits? il Changing T 24:47-50 D '70

PROGRAM music
See also
Phonograph records—Program music

PROGRAMMED instruction
See also
Computers—Educational use
Teaching machines

PROGRAMMERS, Computer. See Computer workers

PROGRAMMING (computers)
Computer software companies: how many are houses of cards? il Forbes 105:40-2 F 15 '70
Software suffers unprogrammed woes. il Bsns W p66+ Je 20 '70
See also
Applied data research, inc.

PROGRESS
See also
Science and civilization

PROGRESS, Technical. See Technological change

PROGRESSIVE education
John Dewey is alive and well in New England. R. H. De Lone and S. T. De Lone. il Sat R 53:69-71+ N 21 '70
Rise of the free school. B. B. Stretch. il Sat R 53:76-9+ Je 20 '70
What's going to happen to us individuals? address, August 14, 1970. M. Rafferty. Vital Speeches 36:752-5 O 1 '70

PROHIBITION
Texas
Texans take a shot at state's bar ban. Bsns W p28 N 14 '70
United States
Wet-dry: hawk-dove. K. Crawford. Newsweek 76:29 N 30 '70

PROINSULIN. See Insulin

PROJECT Apollo. See Space flight to the moon

PROJECT Equality. See National Catholic conference for interracial justice

PROJECT Gasbuggy. See Atomic blasting

PROJECT Head Start
Migrant youngsters: our forgotten children. Y. Postelle. il Parents Mag 45:60-3 My '70
Project Slow Down: the middle-class answer to Project Head Start. R. Fisher. Sch & Soc 98:356-7 O '70
Secretary Finch fights for Head Start. J. Lloyd. Sr Schol 96:School Teach 2 F 2 '70
Follow through programs
Follow through projects, 1970-71. il Am Ed 6:31-3 O '70
Morgan follows through; community control and Follow through, Washington, D.C. S. Moorefield. il Am Ed 6:31-3 Ja '70

PROJECT Plowshare. See Atomic blasting

PROJECT RACE. See Conservation of resources—Study and teaching

PROJECT Rulison. See Atomic blasting

PROJECT Sanguine. See Radio communication, Naval

PROJECT Stratoscope. See Balloons—Research use

PROJECT SUCCESS. See Education—Georgia

PROJECT Tektite. See Underwater laboratories

PROJECT Themis. See Research—Federal aid

PROJECT Transition. See Service men—Vocational education

PROJECT Wingspread. See Chicago—Education

PROJECTILES
See also
Ballistics

PROJECTION apparatus. See Projectors

PROJECTION cabinets. See Cabinets (furniture)

PROJECTION of transparencies. See Transparencies—Projection

PROJECTOR stands. See Stands (furniture)

PROJECTORS
Can B&H's cube gambit dent EK's carousel? H. Keppler. il Mod Phot 34:14+ Mr '70
Cube comes to the projector. L. Drukker and W. F. Wilson. il Pop Phot 66:80-1 Mr '70
Cube projector. answer to the slide-storage problem. E. H. Ortner. il Pop Sci 196:100 My '70
For Polaroid fans: now there's a sharp new projector. P. Wahl. il Pop Sci 197:53 Jl '70
Four projectors with slide preview. three with automatic focus, enlargers that project reflex target. il Pop Phot 66:96-7 Ja '70
New projector shows slides in a cube. il Pop Mech 133:50 Ap '70
New tabletop viewer shows color prints. S. M. Gallager. il Pop Mech 134:196 S '70
Slide projectors. il Consumer Rep 35:520-7 S '70
Year of the cartridge. D. Molner. Schol Teach Jr/Sr High p31 N 2 '70
See also
Moving picture projectors
Phonograph—Projector combination
Equipment
Add motion to your photo slides. W. E. Burton. il Pop Mech 133:164-7+ Ap '70
Stow-away home show center. J. Capotosto. il Mech Illus 66:116-18 Ap '70

PROKOF'EV, Sergei Sergeevich
Perlman and Ashkenazy: a stunning team for Prokofiev. P. Hart. Hi Fi sec I 20: 90 F '70

PROLACTIN. See Luteotropin

PROLINE hydroxylase. See Hydroxylases

PROMETHIUM
Action on the surface; promethium on stars. Sci N 98:429 D 5 '70
HR 465 and promethium. Sky & Tel 41:26-7 Ja '71

PROMISE of a wedding day; story. See Stern. R. M.

PROMOTERS and promoting
Chancey games in Ohio; Dean Chance enterprises. M. Cope. il por Sports Illus 32:26-8+ Mr 30 '70
Here comes the California 500. il Bsns W p70+ S 5 '70
Promoters spar for Ali's next bout. Bsns W p21 D 12 '70

PROMOTIONAL games. See Advertising—Prize contests

PROMOTIONS, School. See Grading and marking (students)

PRONGHORN hunting
Best antelope in seventy years. L. Arce. il
por Outdoor Life 145:44-5+ Ja '70
Pronghorn for a pioneer. B. Milek. il Field
& S 75:40-1+ Ag '70
PRONUNCIATION
See also
English language—Pronunciation
PROOFREADING
Proofreading may not be the oldest profession,
but . . . E. Stalcup. Pub W 198:52+ O 5 '70
PROPAGANDA
See also
America illustrated (periodical)
PROPAGANDA, Anti-Jewish. See Anti-
Semitism
PROPAGANDA, Latin American
Malvenido Rockefeller! anti-American post-
ers in Latin America. D. Horowitz. il
Ramp Mag 8:20-5 F '70
PROPAGANDA, Vietnamese
Following the script; show villages to impress
visitors. Newsweek 76:27 Jl 20 '70
PROPAGANDA in the schools
See also
Indoctrination
PROPAGATION of plants. See Plant propaga-
tion
PROPAGATION of trees. See Plant propaga-
tion
PROPANE
See also
Automobile engines—Fuel
Liquefied petroleum gas
Plants, Effect of propane on
PROPELLANTS, Rocket. See Rockets—Fuel
PROPELLERS
High performance propellers. E. H. Nabb. il
Yachting 128:64-5+ O; 68-9+ N '70
Propeller-pox; your wheels could die of it.
E. A. Zadig. il Motor B 125:172-4 My '70
See also
Airplane propellers
PROPER motions of the stars. See Stars—Mo-
tion
PROPERTY
See also
Capitalism
Church property
Mortgages
PROPERTY; story. See Gilliatt, P.
PROPERTY, intellectual
See also
Copyright
PROPERTY, Moving picture. See Moving pic-
ture properties
PROPERTY insurance. See Insurance, Property
PROPERTY tax
Bill would force state to pay in lieu taxes;
New Jersey legislation. Am City 85:40 Ag
'70
Panel hits property tax assessments. U S
News 68:67-8 Je 1 '70
PROPHECIES
See also
Astrology
Forecasts
PROPIOLALDEHYDE. See Aldehydes
PROPITIATION of witches; story. See Adams,
A.
PROPORTIONAL representation
See also
Minorities
PROPORTIONERS. See Mixers
PROPOSAL of marriage; drama. See Nolan,
P. T.
PROPOSALS of marriage. See Marriage pro-
posals
PROPRANOLOL
Improvement of learning in the aged by
modification of autonomic nervous system
activity. C. Eisdorfer and others. bibliog
il Science 170:1327-9 D 18 '70
PROPS, Moving picture. See Moving picture
properties
PROPYLENE
See also
Tricyanoaminopropene
PROSCH, Louis A.
Your traffic is a KB-50. . . il Flying 86:94+
Je '70
PROSELYTISM. See Evangelistic work
PROSPECTING
Miracle tool for prospectors. R. Burkhart.
il Sci Digest 67:45-8+ F '70
Ore search on land and in the ocean; Japan-
ese survey. S. Griffin. il Sci N 98:46 Jl 11 '70
See also
Petroleum—Prospecting

PROSPERITY
Farm wife reflects on abundance. B. P. Zim-
merman. Farm J 93:47 N '69
Paradox of prosperity; excerpt from The
passing of the modern age. J. Lukacs. Commentary 49:64-9 F '70
PROSPERO, Joseph M. and Carlson, T. N.
Radon-222 in the North Atlantic trade
winds: its relationship to dust transport
from Africa. bibliog il Science 167:974-7
F 13 '70
PROSSER, David E.
Unruly giant. il por Opera N 34:24-5 Ja 31
'70
PROSTAGLANDINS
Abortion without surgery? using prostaglan-
din F² alpha. Time 95:39-40 F 9 '70
Prostaglandin receptor site: evidence for an
essential role in the action of luteinizing
hormone. F. A. Kuehl, jr. and others. bib-
liog il Science 169:883-6 Ag 28 '70
Something for everyone. B. J. Culliton. il Sci
N 98:306-7 O 10 '70
PROSTHESIS
See also
Artificial limbs
Heart, Artificial
PROSTITUTION
Back at the Ranch; integration at bordello
in Nevada. Newsweek 75:78+ Mr 9 '70
Bring back the brothels? France considering
municipal bordellos. il Time 96:30 N 9 '70
Coffee for every taste; Rome. Time 96:35 D
14 '70
Flatfoot floozies; police technique in Wash-
ington, D.C. il Time 95:44+ My 18 '70
Flatfoot floozies; police women arrest cus-
tomers in Washington, D.C. il Newsweek
75:99 My 18 '70
Pimping game. il por Time 97:54-5 Ja 11 '71
Promiscuity and prostitution in urbanized
Indian communities. R. E. Kuttner and A.
B. Lorincz. bibliog Ment Hy 54:79-91 Ja '70

Anecdotes, facetiae, satire, etc.
Lively commerce. J. Richardson. il Harper
241:82-9 Ag '70
PROTECTION (tariff) See Free trade and pro-
tection
PROTECTION against burglary. See Burglary
protection
PROTECTION against radioactivity. See Radio-
activity—Safety devices and measures
PROTECTION from frost. See Frost protec-
tion
PROTECTION of animals. See Animals—Pro-
tection
PROTECTION of birds. See Birds—Protection
PROTECTION of cultural property. See Cul-
tural property, Protection of (internation-
al law)
PROTECTION of plants. See Plants, Protec-
tion of
PROTECTION of the president. See Presidents
—United States—Protection
PROTECTION systems, industrial. See Industry
—Security measures
PROTECTIVE mechanisms (biology) See De-
fense mechanisms (biology)
PROTEIN biosynthesis. See Biosynthesis
PROTEIN drinks. See Beverages
PROTEINS
Adenosine 3',5'-monophosphate, adreno-
corticotropic hormone, and adrenocortical
cytosol protein synthesis. M. F. Grower
and E. D. Bransome, jr. bibliog il Science
168:483-5 Ap 24 '70
Deciphering proteins. il Sci N 97:366 Ap 11 '70
Mind research: the promise and the peril;
protein synthesis in the brain. F. Warshofsky. Read Digest 96:119-23 Ap '70
News from the world of space exploration;
use of DAP I to find the primary structure
of many proteins. Space World H-1-85:49-
50 Ja '71
Non-Darwinian evolution. J. L. King and
T. H. Jukes; reply. B. Clarke. Science 168:
1009-11 My 22 '70
Partial reversion in yeast: genetic evidence
for a new type of bifunctional protein. B.
Dorfman and others. bibliog il Science 168:
1482-4 Je 19 '70
Proteins in excitable membranes. D. Nachmansohn. bibliog il Science 168:1059-66 My
29 '70; Discussion 170:1228-9, 1332-3 D 11-
18 '70
Similarity and limited multiplicity of membrane proteins from rough and smooth
endoplasmic reticulum. N. D. Hinman and
A. H. Phillips. bibliog il Science 170:1222-3
D 11 '70

PROTEINS—*Continued*
Spherical protein shell formation from an 11S subunit of bacteriophage f₂. P. O. Zelazo and R. H. Haschemeyer. bibliog il Science 168:1461-2 Je 19 '70
Sulfate-binding protein from salmonella typhimurium: physical properties. R. Langridge and others. bibliog il Science 169:59-61 Jl 3 '70
See also
Amino acids
Bacterial proteins
Blood—Proteins
Collagen
Fish protein concentrate
Food substitutes
Gluten
Histones
Insulin
Interferon
Keratin
Lipoproteins
Nucleoproteins
Proteolysis
Tryptophan
Tubulin

Analysis
Interference in the Lowry method for protein determination. J. D. Gregory and S. W. Sajdera. Science 169:97-8 Jl 3 '70; Reply. L. V. Turner and K. L. Manchester. 170:649 N 6 '70

PROTEOLYSIS
Proteolytic reaction of mammalian spermatozoa of gelatin membranes. P. Gaddum and R. J. Blandeau. bibliog il Science 170:749-51 N 13 '70

PROTEOLYTIC enzymes. See Enzymes

PROTESTANT churches
See also
Catholic church — Relations — Protestant churches
Ecumenical movement

Clergy
See Clergy

Missions
See Missions

Congo
See also
Kimbanguist church

England
See also
British council of churches

Germany (Democratic Republic)
New federation a success; Federation of Protestant churches in the German Democratic Republic. Germanicus. Chr Cent 87:1137-8 S 23 '70

Kenya
Two international confessional bodies merge in Kenya. Chr Cent 87:1059 S 9 '70

Latin America
High theology in the Andes; Fraternity of Latin American theologians. C. P. Wagner. Chr Today 15:28-9 Ja 15 '71

Portugal
Religious liberty law sought in Portugal. Chr Cent 87:986 Ag 19 '70

Spain
See also
Evangelical church in Spain

United States
Polarization within the churches. A. B. Haines. Chr Cent 87:1039-41 S 2 '70
See also
Church union—United States
National council of churches
Reformed church in America

PROTESTANT churches and race problems. See Church and race problems

PROTESTANT churches and social problems. See Church and social problems

PROTESTANT colleges. See Church colleges

PROTESTANT Episcopal church
Episcopal bishop under attack; convention of the five-county Episcopal diocese of Pennsylvania. T. W. Moore. Chr Cent 87:1363-4 N 11 '70
Episcopal church convention; with editorial comment. J. F. Politzer and R. Chandler. il Chr Today 15:33, 43-5 N 6 '70
Episcopal church's economy dismissals protested. Chr Cent 87:559 My 6 '70
Episcopal convention; violence the villain. E. M. Soukup. Chr Cent 87:1390+ N 18 '70
Episcopalians at the barricades; Houston general convention. Time 96:74 N 2 '70

Halves and the have-nots. Chr Today 15:39 Ja 1 '71
Shrinking pains; national staff laid off. Chr Cent 87:1530-1 D 23 '70

PROTESTANT missions. See Missions

PROTESTANT missions in Latin America. See Missions—Latin America

PROTESTANT monasteries. See Monasteries

PROTESTANT reformation. See Reformation

PROTESTANT theologians. See Theologians

PROTESTANTISM
See also
Evangelicalism
Fundamentalism
Reformation
Sects

PROTESTANTISM, Evangelical. See Evangelicalism

PROTESTANTS in Brazil
Brazil church surges ahead. P. Cunliffe. Chr Today 14:38 Ja '70

PROTESTANTS in Northern Ireland
Bloody Ulster: an Irishman's lament. B. Moore. il Atlan 226:58-62 S '70
Rebel in Armagh jail, the hater in the pulpit. A. Carthew. il pors N Y Times Mag p 12-13+ Ag 9 '70

PROTESTANTS in Poland
Poland's Protestants. A. Gronowicz. Chr Today 14:34-5 Ja 30 '70

PROTESTANTS in the United States
Growing up an Episcopalian. S. Bingham. Mlle 70:158+ Mr '70
Righteous empire, by M. E. Marty. Review Newsweek il 77:40-1 Ja 4 '71. K. L. Woodward
See also
WASPS (white Anglo-Saxon Protestants)

PROTESTS against Vietnamese war. See Vietnamese war, 1957- —Protests, demonstrations, etc, against

PROTESTS, demonstrations, etc.
How government would limit protesters near White House. il U S News 69:25 Jl 27 '70
How to be a demonstrator and stay out of jail. il Time 96:43 Ag 3 '70
Mayday for America; mobilizing the outraged. R. M. Brown. Commonweal 92:266-8 My 29 '70
Organizing proxy power; annual meetings under fire. R. Chandler. Chr Today 14:32-3 My 22 '70
Politics. N. Sayre. Esquire 73:82+ Mr '70
Protest and rebels. H. L. Rofinot. America 122:657-9 Je 20 '70
Protest mentality. D. E. Trueblood. Chr Today 14:14-15 Jl 17 '70
Rage against violence. K. Widmer. il Nation 211:45-8 Jl 20 '70
What's going on inside America; survey of campus dissent, antiwar protests, strike disorders, crime, pollution. il U S News 68:17-23 My 25 '70
Whose law? Whose order? Nation 211:420-1 N 2 '70
See also
Art workers coalition
Berlin (West Berlin)—Protests, demonstrations, etc.
Cambodian-Vietnamese conflict—American participation—Protests, demonstrations, etc, against
New York (city)—Protests, demonstrations, etc.
Student demonstrations
Washington, D.C.—Protests, demonstrations, etc.
Womens liberation movement

Spain
Return of the ultras? Falangists pro-Franco demonstrations. il por Time 96:18-19 D 28 '70

Vietnam (Republic)
Whiff of tear gas; disabled war veterans. il Newsweek 75:51 Ap 20 '70

PROTON accelerators. See Accelerators (electrons, etc)

PROTON magnetic resonance. See Magnetic resonance

PROTONS
Antiproton found going 'round in strange circles. G. B. Lubkin. bibliog Phys Today 23:17+ N '70
See also
Nucleons

PROTOPLASM
See also
Golgi apparatus

PROTOPLASTS
Release of protoplasts in the yeast phase of histoplasma capsulatum without added enzyme. M. D. Berliner and M. E. Reca. bibliog il Science 167:1255-7 F 27 '70

PROTOZOA
Antimycin A: Stimulation of cell division and protein synthesis in tetrahymena pyriformis. C. Elson and others. bibliog il Science 168:385-6 Ap 17 '70
Phosphonolipids: localization in surface membranes of tetrahymena. K. E. Kennedy and G. A. Thompson, jr. bibliog il Science 168:989-91 My 22 '70
Woman with a Micro-zoo. J. Fix. il por Sci Digest 67:94-6 F '70
    See also
Amebas
Bryozoa
Dinoflagellates
Euglena
Flagellates
Foraminifera
Plasmodium (parasite)
Sarcocystis

Resistance and sensitivity
Plasmodium falciparum in owl monkeys: drug resistance and chloroquine binding capacity. C. D. Fitch. bibliog il Science 169:289-90 Jl 17 '70

PROULX, E. A.
Lost friend; story. il Seventeen 29:142-3 F '70

PROUST, Marcel
Colette, Cocteau, and Proust. R. Phelps. il Mlle 72:124-5+ D '70 *

PROVENÇAL furniture, French. See Furniture, French

PROVENCAL poetry
    See also
Troubadours

PROVENCE
How to live the sweet life in the south of France. P. Campbell. il Holiday 47:52-3+ Je '70
Les Baux and the pleasures of Provence. S. Spender. il Travel & Camera 33:36-9 Ap '70

PROVIDENCE, R.I.
Theater
Family that slays together; production of Son of man and the family by the Trinity square repertory company. H. Hewes. Sat R 53:20 D 26 '70
Theater; Trinity square repertory company's production of Lovecraft's follies. H. Hewes. Sat R 53:24 Mr 28 '70

PROVIDENCE and Worcester railroad company. See Railroads, Short line

PROVINCETOWN, Mass.
Visit with the Cape Codders; excerpt from Carter's coast of New England, ed. by D. Ford. R. Carter. il Yachting 128:59+ Ag '70

Description
Pilgrims slept here too. D. Brudnoy. Nat R 22:737 Jl 14 '70

PROVINCETOWN art association
What is happening to our art colony? meeting, August 1970. K. Kuh. Sat R 53:42-3 O 31 '70

PROVING grounds
NASA is a hard act to follow; search for new Mississippi test facility tenant. il Bsns W p28 Ap 11 '70
    See also
Bombing and gunnery ranges

Russia
Moscow's better mousetrap testing new ABM system at Sary-Shagan test range. Time 96:33 O 12 '70

PROVOST, Charles H.
Build the marvelous Fold-A-Majig. H. Wicks. il por Pop Mech 135:140-5 Ja '71 *

PROWITT, Renee Brown
Seven ways to keep your child from smoking. il Parents Mag 45:42-3 Ap '70

PROXIMITY warning indicators
Anti-collision device demonstrated; low-cost infrared device. K. J. Stein. il Aviation W 93:47-50 Jl 6 '70
Proximity warning indicator measures altitude or heading. il Aviation W 93:50-1 Jl 6 '70

PROXMIRE, William
Pentagon vs free enterprise. il Sat R 53:14-17 Ja 31 '70
    about
Congress; score one for persistence. il Time 96:13-14 D 14 '70 *
Proxmire seems to have the edge. por Bsns W p78 S 26 '70 *

Report from Washington. M. Nolan. Atlan 226:6+ D '70 *
Senator William Proxmire: what makes him run? W. Connelly. por Science 168:1435-9 Je 19 '70

PRUDDEN, Bonnie
Fit by five; headstart to make your child. J. A. Segal. il Look 34:76-7+ Ap 7 '70 *

PRUDENTIAL insurance company of America
Not so dumb; move into casualty insurance. Forbes 105:25 Je 15 '70
Pru becomes larger than life. Bsns W p32+ My 30 '70

PRUDHOMME, Don
Snake. B. Lang. il pors Hot Rod 23:74-6 Ap '70 *

PRUITT-Igoe, St Louis. See Housing projects, Government

PRUNING
How to keep your trees healthy. K. F. Polscer. il Org Gard & Farm 17:38-40 F '70
How to prune and train grape vines for good looks and a good crop. il Sunset 144:182-5 F '70
Preventive pruning, called pinching. il Sunset 144:206+ Je '70
Pruning guide for fruit trees. Suc Farm 68:73 F '70
Should you stake and prune your tomato plants? K. F. Polscer. il Org Gard & Farm 17:52-3 Ap '70
    See also
Fruit trees, Training of

PRUNING apparatus and equipment
Really useful gardener gift, a pruning saw. il Sunset 145:173 D '70
Tree pruning. il Consumer Bul 53:4+ O '70

PRUSSIA
History
Creation of nobles in Prussia, 1871-1918. L. Cecil. bibliog f il Am Hist R 75:757-95 F '70

PRUYN, Dee
East Bay regional parks serve area horsemen. Parks & Rec 5:40-2 F '70

PRYBYLA, Jan S.
China's economy; experiments in Maoism. bibliog f Cur Hist 59:159-64+ S '70

PRYCE, Dick
Clearwater and smallmouth. il Field & S 75:24-5+ Jl '70
Prairie cottontails. il por Outdoor Life 146:88-9+ O '70
Spree of cats. il pors Outdoor Life 146:64-5+ Ag '70

PRYDE, Philip R.
Victors are not judged. bibliog il Environ 12:30-9 N '70

PRYER, Margaret W. See Distefano, M. K. jr, jt. auth.

PRYOR, David H.
Where we put the aged. New Repub 162:15-17 Ap 25 '70

PRYOR, Taylor Allderdice
New wave of aqua gear. il Life 68:70-3 Mr 6 '70 *

PRYOR, William A.
Free radicals in biological systems; with biographical sketch. il Sci Am 223:12, 70-6+ bibliog(p 128) Ag '70
—and others
Hydrogen atom and its reactions in solution. bibliog il Science 169:181-3 Jl 10 '70

PRYOR MOUNTAIN wild horse lands. See Wildlife sanctuaries—Wyoming

PSEUDOMONAS
Penicillin and patents; combating pseudomonas. Sci N 98:164 Ag 22 '70
Real names of Edison cylinder performers. J. Walsh. il Hobbies 75:37-9 Je '70

PSEUDOPREGNANCY. See Pregnancy in animals

PSEUDOSCIENTIFIC stories. See Science fiction

PSORIASIS
Prescribing without approval; use of methotrexate in treatment of psoriasis. Sci N 97:549 Je 6 '70

PSYCHEDELIC drugs. See Hallucinogenic drugs

PSYCHIATRIC clinics
Diagnostic intake: variation on a theme. R. A. Simons. bibliog Ment Hy 54:101-4 Ja '70
Interagency pooling of resources to establish new services. G. A. Crow. Ment Hy 54:118-22 Ja '70
    See also
Child guidance clinics

PSYCHIATRIC consultants
Role of the psychiatric consultant in the state
rehabilitation agency. R. T. Goldberg and
J. Stein. bibliog Ment Hy 54:553-8 O '70
PSYCHIATRIC consultation
How not to be a consultant. A. Hodges.
bibliog Ment Hy 54:147-8 Ja '70
Social intervention; consultation to organi-
zations. G. Rosenblum. bibliog Ment Hy 54:
393-6 Jl '70
See also
Television in psychiatry
PSYCHIATRIC foundation. See National as-
sociation for mental health, inc.
PSYCHIATRIC hospital aides. See Hospitals,
Psychiatric—Staff
PSYCHIATRIC hospitals. See Hospitals, Psy-
chiatric
PSYCHIATRIC nurses. See Nurses and nurs-
ing
PSYCHIATRIC personnel
See also
Hospitals, Psychiatric—Staff
PSYCHIATRIC research centers
Retardation research lab has total flexibility
for basic sciences; Institute for basic re-
search in mental retardation, Staten Island,
N.Y. il Arch Rec 147:157-9 Ja '70
PSYCHIATRIC residents. See Hospitals, Psy-
chiatric—Staff
PSYCHIATRIC social work
Interagency pooling of resources to estab-
lish new services. G. A. Crow. Ment Hy
54:118-22 Ja '70
PSYCHIATRIC social workers. See Social work-
ers
PSYCHIATRISTS
Do therapists play God? R. Zeligs. Ment Hy
54:161 Ja '70
Psychiatrist: activist or onlooker? discus-
sion by six psychiatrists. Ment Hy 54:191-
204 Ap '70
Psychiatrists, by A. A. Rogow. Review
Sat R 53:27-9 Mr 14 '70. G. Krupp
See also
Hospitals, Psychiatric—Staff
Lifschutz, J. E.
Psychiatric consultants
Woods, E.

Fees
See Mental health service, Cost of
PSYCHIATRY
I have a friend who ... (cont) T. I. Rubin.
il por Ladies Home J 86:38-9 D '69; 87:72
S; 44 N '70
Psychiatrist to the stars. il pors Ebony 25:74-
5+ Mr '70
Psychiatrists, by A. A. Rogow. Review
Sat R 53:27-9 Mr 14 '70. G. Krupp
R. D. Laing: in search of a new psychiatry.
J. S. Gordon. il por Atlan 227:50-3+ Ja '71
See also
American psychiatric association
Child psychiatry
Group psychotherapy
Mental hygiene
Mental illness
Neuroses
Psychoanalysis
Television in psychiatry

Bibliography
Book reviews. See issues of Mental hygiene

Terminology
Fashionable kind of slander; psychiatric jar-
gon. R. Coles. Atlan 226:53-5 N '70
PSYCHIATRY, Military
Military psychiatrist. por Time 96:52 Jl 27
'70
PSYCHIATRY and religion
Psychiatrist reflects on the changing church.
T. L. Doyle. America 122:240-3 Mr 7 '70
PSYCHOACTIVE drugs. See Psychopharma-
cology
PSYCHOANALYSIS
Ego and instinct, by D. Yankelovich and
W. Barrett. Review
Nation 210:564-6 My 11 '70. R. Sampson
Erik Erikson's eight ages of man. D. Elkind.
il N Y Times Mag p25-7+ Ap 5 '70
Freud, Jung and the collective unconscious.
D. Elkind. il pors N Y Times Mag p23-5+
O 4 '70
Freud on the couch. A. Storr. il Horizon 12:
42-7 Wint '70
Freudian psychology and ethical doctrine. M.
B. Zweig. bibliog f Am Imago 27:90-106
Spr '70
Freud's case load; theories of Benjamin Bro-
dy. Time 95:53 Je 29 '70
Potential of psychoanalytic biography; Zeligs
on Chambers and Hiss. G. Bychowski. bib-
liog f Am Imago 26:233-41 Fall '69

Profiles: E. H. Erikson. R. Coles. por New
Yorker 46:51-4+ N 7; 59-60+ N 14 '70
See also
Complexes (psychology)
Dreams
Oedipus complex
Subconsciousness

Bibliography
Reviews of current books. Am Imago 26:
295-9 Fall '70
PSYCHOANALYSIS and art
Behind the veil; drawings by J. Pollock as
an aid to psychoanalysis. C. L. Wysuph.
bibliog il Art N 69:52-5+ O '70
PSYCHOANALYSTS
See also
Erikson, E. H.
Freud, S.
PSYCHOLOGICAL apparatus
Amateur scientist; the color vision of pigeons
is tested in a Skinner box. J. S. Moran.
il Sci Am 223:124-9 O '70
PSYCHOLOGICAL games. See Games
PSYCHOLOGICAL medicine. See Psychoanal-
ysis
PSYCHOLOGICAL research
See also
Child study
Information storage and retrieval systems—
Psychology
Laboratory animals
PSYCHOLOGICAL societies
See also
American psychological association
PSYCHOLOGICAL stress. See Stress (physio-
logy)
PSYCHOLOGICAL tests
Dogmatism, religiosity and mental health in
college students. H. G. Richek and others.
Ment Hy 54:572-4 O '70
See also
Intelligence tests
Personality tests
PSYCHOLOGICAL warfare
See also
Terrorism
PSYCHOLOGISTS
See also
Hospitals, Psychiatric—Staff
Psychiatrists
Psychology as a profession
PSYCHOLOGY
Third force arises in psychology; humanistic
psychology. J. Moriarty. Sci N 98:256-7 S
19 '70
Webs of maya; with excerpts from Knots.
il Time 97:38 Ja 18 '71
See also
Adaptability (psychology)
Adjustment (psychology)
Aggressiveness (psychology)
American psychological association
Anxiety
Attention
Behavior (psychology)
Behaviorism
Child study
Complexes (psychology)
Concepts
Conflict (psychology)
Daydreams
Discrimination (psychology)
Eidetic imagery
Ethics
Experience
Generalization (psychology)
Gestalt theory
Hostility (psychology)
Hypnotism
Information storage and retrieval systems—
Psychology
Instinct
Intellect
Laughter
Motivation (psychology)
Personality
Political psychology
Preferences (psychology)
Problem solving
Psychoanalysis
Recognition (psychology)
Sex (psychology)
Sleep
Social interaction
Social psychology
Stage fright
Subconsciousness
Violence
War—Psychological aspects
Worry
also subhead Psychology under various
subjects, e.g. Woman—Psychology

PSYCHOLOGY—*Continued*

Apparatus
See Psychological apparatus

Study and teaching
Introducing students to psychology. C. Atkinson. Sch & Soc 98:164-5 Mr '70

PSYCHOLOGY, Applied
See also
Psychology, Industrial

PSYCHOLOGY, Comparative
See also
Animals—Habits and behavior

PSYCHOLOGY, Educational
Meeting students' basic concerns; views of C. Kennedy. por Sch & Soc 98:458 D '70
When youngsters cheat. L. Barney. Parents Mag 45:49-51 My '70
See also
Learning, Psychology of

PSYCHOLOGY, Industrial
Management psychologists have landed. S. Klaw. il Fortune 81:106-9+ Ap '70

PSYCHOLOGY, National. See National characteristics

PSYCHOLOGY, Pathological
Psychopathology of racism. J. Daniels. Chr Today 15:7-8 Ja 15 '71
See also
Aphasia
Autism
Malingering
Medicine, Psychosomatic
Oedipus complex
Paranoia
Psychiatry
Psychotherapy

PSYCHOLOGY, Physiological
Neural events and the psychophysical law. S. S. Stevens. bibliog il Science 170:1043-50 D 4 '70
See also
Avoidance (psychology)
Body image
Brain—Localization of functions
Conditioned responses
Movement, Psychology of
Reaction time
Reinforcement (psychology)
Sex (psychology)
Time perception

PSYCHOLOGY, Political. See Political psychology

PSYCHOLOGY, Religious
See also
Stigmatization

PSYCHOLOGY and weather. See Weather—Mental and physiological effects

PSYCHOLOGY as a profession
Academic vs. professional psychology; excerpts from address. G. W. Albee. por Sch & Soc 98:462 D '70

PSYCHOLOGY of color. See Color—Psychology

PSYCHOLOGY of gambling. See Gambling—Psychology

PSYCHOLOGY of learning. See Learning, Psychology of

PSYCHOLOGY of war. See War—Psychological aspects

PSYCHONEUROSIS. See Neuroses

PSYCHOPATHOLOGY. See Psychology, Pathological

PSYCHOPATHS. See Insane, Criminal and dangerous

PSYCHOPHARMACOLOGY
Hazards implicit in prescribing psychoactive drugs. H. L. Lennard and others. bibliog Science 169:438-41 Jl 31 '70; Discussion. 170:928-30 N 27 '70
How drugs are used to treat mental illness. Good H 171:151-3 S '70
Mood, behavior, and drugs; AAAS symposium, December 27-28, 1970. C. D. Leake. il Science 170:559-60 O 30 '70
When pills are bad medicine. V. Louirere. Nations Bsns 58:17 My '70

PSYCHOPHYSICS. See Psychology, Physiological

PSYCHOSES
Controversial drug approved; treating of manic-depressive psychosis. Sci N 97:390 Ap 18 '70
Help for the manic-depressive. por Time 95: 46 Ap 20 '70
Histochemical abnormalities of skeletal muscle in patients with acute psychoses. W. K. Engel and H. Meltzer. bibliog il Science 168:273-6 Ap 10 '70

PSYCHOSOMATIC medicine. See Medicine, Psychosomatic

PSYCHOTHERAPY
Child psychotherapy, help or hindrance? A. F. Donofrio. bibliog Ment Hy 54:510-15 O '70
Community cooperation and a shoestring budget; Rx for an activity therapy program. C. R. Gilpin and E. Neufeld. Ment Hy 54: 397-400 Jl '70
Effect of work therapy on patients' responses to other hospital therapies. M. S. Barbee and others. bibliog il Ment Hy 54:92-6 Ja '70
Hydropsychotherapy. help for the disturbed on a water couch. A. Hamilton. il pors Sci Digest 67:59-63 Je '70
TV soliloquies help young drug users. il Todays Health 48:64-5 Ap '70
Troubled child. A. Barman and L. Cohen. il N Y Times Mag p91+ N 8 '70
Whole truth, the real truth, the psychiatrist's truth. Trans-Action 7:10 Mr '70
See also
Family psychotherapy
Graphotherapy
Group psychotherapy
Moving pictures in psychotherapy
Neurotics anonymous
Psychopharmacology

PSYCHOTROPIC drugs. See Psychopharmacology

PTASHNE, Mark, and Gilbert, Walter
Genetic repressors; with biographical sketches. il Sci Am 222:12, 36-44 bibliog(p 152) Je '70

PTERANODON. See Birds, Fossil

PTERIDINES
Placental transfer of a substituted pteridine from fetus to mother. J. L. McNay and P. G. Dayton. bibliog il Science 167:988-90 F 13 '70

PUBERTY
Height and weight at menarche and a hypothesis of critical body weights and adolescent events. R. E. Frisch and R. Revelle. bibliog il Science 169:397-9 Jl 24 '70

PUBLIC address systems. See Loud speaking apparatus

PUBLIC administration
See also
Decentralization in government
Municipal government
also subhead Politics and government under names of countries, states, etc. e.g. United States—Politics and government

PUBLIC beaches. See Beaches

PUBLIC broadcasting corporation. See Corporation for public broadcasting

PUBLIC buildings
See also
City halls
Library architecture
also subhead Public buildings under names of cities, e.g. Lincoln, Neb.— Public buildings

PUBLIC colleges and universities. See Colleges and universities

PUBLIC debt (United States) See Debts, Public —United States

PUBLIC employees. See Government employees

PUBLIC finance. See Finance

PUBLIC health
See also
Air pollution
Cancer—Prevention and control
Environmental health
Medicine, Preventive
Milk hygiene
Mosquito control
Sewage disposal
Smoke prevention
Venereal diseases

Laws and legislation
See also
Food laws and legislation

Appalachian Region
Appalachia: two approaches in student summer health projects. S. Z. Goldhaber. il Science 169:746-8+ Ag 21 '70

Colorado
How I learned to live with radioactivity and love it; in Colorado. S. Gascoyne. Commonweal 92:7-9 Mr 13 '70

Congo (Democratic Republic)
Nuclear sexing in a population of Congolese metropolitan newborns. H. van den Berghe. bibliog il Science 169:1318-20 S 25 '70
See also
Indiana
Indianapolis—Public health

PUBLIC health—*Continued*

Israel

Detecting deafness early. H. Gillon. il Sci N 97:112 Ja 24 '70

Latin America

Biological control of Chagas' disease. J. Bockel. il Sci N 97:485 My 16 '70

New York (state)

Health facilities: improvement through management and money for architecture; building types study. il Arch Rec 147:151-66 Ja '70

United States

Country's no. 1 health problem; interview. R. Egeberg. il pors U S News 68:68-73 F 23 '70

Is there any way out of our health care mess? F. Bailey. il Bet Hom & Gard 48: 48-9+ N '70

U.S. health: do we face a castastrophe? J. H. Knowles. Look 34:74+ Je 2 '70

Why you really can't get good medical care. C. Remsberg and B. Remsberg. Good H 170:68-71+ F '70
See also
Indians of North America—Health and hygiene
Negroes—Health and hygiene
Nutrition problems—United States
United States—National council on health policy (proposed)
United States—Public health service
also subhead Public health under names of cities, e.g. Cambridge, Mass.—Public health

History

Mental health in and out of public health. D. A. Berlin. bibliog Ment Hy 54:288-94 Ap '70

West Virginia

Country doctor looks at conservation and health; cooperation between agencies in West Virginia. D. Hale. il pors Am For 76:16-18+ Ja '70

PUBLIC health dentistry. See Dental service

PUBLIC health service (United States) See United States—Public health service

PUBLIC health workers. See Health workers

PUBLIC high schools. See High schools

PUBLIC houses (Great Britain) See Bars and barrooms

PUBLIC houses (Ireland) See Bars and barrooms

PUBLIC houses (United States) See Bars and barrooms

PUBLIC information act. See Information, Freedom of

PUBLIC information officers

Careers in writing: government public information officer. G. L. Garrigues. Writers Digest 50:16-18 Mr '70

Local government P.I.O: a freelance job idea! T. Oglesby. Writers Digest 50:17 Mr '70

PUBLIC institutions

Inmates

See Inmates of public institutions

PUBLIC land law review commission. See United States—Public land law review commission

PUBLIC lands
See also
Wilderness areas

Alaska

Landless in Alaska. J. C. Muskrat. il Bul Atom Sci 26:12-16 Mr '70

Mexico

Forestry and the public domain; a Mexican point of view; address (cont) E. Beltran. il Am For 76:36-7+ Ja '70

United States

All we need is money; Owyhee project, Idaho. T. Trueblood. il Field & S 75:20+ My '70

Destiny of the public lands; telegram. R. M. Nixon. por Am For 76:19 Ja '70

Development and public land. il Sci N 98:5 Jl 4 '70

In the public interest; aims and objectives by American forestry association and allied conservation groups. W. E. Towell. Am For 76:6-7 Ja '70; Discussion. 76:42+ Je '70

Moving in for a land grab; Aspinall commission report. H. Peterson. il Sports Illus 33:22-4+ Jl 13 '70

Para-real estate: the handing out of resources. J. Ridgeway. il Ramp Mag 8:28-33 My '70

Private interests and public lands. R. S. Gilmour. Cur Hist 59:36-42+ Jl '70

This land is our land. D. Jackson. il Life 70: 32:43 Ja 8 '71

Will pollution win the public lands? address; with remarks by J. P. Saylor. E. C. Crafts. il por Am For 76:28-31+ Ja '70
See also
National forests
National parks and reserves—United States
United States—Public land law review commission

History

History of public land law development, by P. W. Gates. Review
Liv Wildn 34:52-5 Spr '70. H. K. Pyles

PUBLIC meetings
See also
Assembly, Right of

PUBLIC officers

At half time: shifting the bodies around; Cabinet officers and others on Nixon's drop list. il por Time 96:6-8 N 30 '70

Campus confronts the capital; cabinet officers and presidential aides listen to protests. H. Sidey. Life 68:4 Je 12 '70

Can business aid the Peace corps? il por Bsns W p 124 Ap 11 '70

Cato v. Publius in the White House; speechwriters attempting to give verbal shape to Nixon's philosophy. il pors Time 95:18 F 23 '70

Chotiner's comeback. il por Newsweek 75: 21-2 Je 22 '70

Cult of the expert; office of assistant in charge of national security. E. McCarthy. por McCalls 97:30 Je '70

First lady's lady; press secretary, C. C. Stuart. il por Time 97:43 Ja 4 '71

Good and becoming exit. E. J. McCarthy. por McCalls 97:26 Mr '70

I gave Thurmond 100 per cent loyalty and now I give Mr Nixon 100 per cent; H. Dent, the President's political coordinator. J. Boyd. il pors N Y Times Mag p 12-13+ F 1 '70

In the President's service. il Fortune 82:60-7 Jl '70

Middle American who edits ideas for Nixon; J. Ehrlichman. R. B. Semple, jr. il pors N Y Times Mag p82-3+ Ap 12 '70

New science adviser. pors Newsweek 76:63 Ag 31 '70

Nixon's White House staff: heyday of the planners? National goals research staff. A. Hamilton. Science 167:1232-4 F 27 '70

Nixon's youth corps. D. R. Maxey. il por Look 34:48-51 F 10 '70

Uncivil servants; purge of public interest types in government resource programs. D. Sanford. New Repub 162:13-14 My 16 '70

White House staff keeps growing, including regulars and phantoms. il U S News 68: 43-4 F 23 '70

Who runs Congress? congressional aides. R. Sherrill. il N Y Times Mag p52-3+ N 22 '70

Why businessmen serve in Washington. il Nations Bsns 58:36-43 Mr '70
See also
Bureaucracy
Conflict of interests (public office)
Governors
Impeachments
Negro public officers
Nuns as public officers
Political ethics
United States—Executive office of the president
United States—President's commission on personnel interchange (proposed)

Dismissal

Cold shadow on the capital. H. Sidey. Life 69:4 D 11 '70

Crucial month for Nixon; decisions pile up. il U S News 69:17-19 D 14 '70

Unfaithful servants. J. Ridgeway. Ramp Mag 9:9-10+ D '70

Families

Politics, a family affair. il Seventeen 29:170-1+ Ap '70

Sports

Parting shots; it's politics, anyone? when congressmen take on the Cabinet. il Life 68:68-9 My 29 '70

Vote getters. H. L. Masin. Sr Schol 96:22 Mr 23 '70

Czechoslovakia

Where they are now; liberal reform leaders. il Newsweek 76:34-5 Ag 24 '70

PUBLIC officers—*Continued*

Great Britain

See also
Members of Parliament

Israel

Rabin line. por Newsweek 76:29 D 28 '70

Japan

Where are they now? the Emperor's speech-writer. il pors Newsweek 76:8 Ag 24 '70

PUBLIC officers, Resignation of

Minorities: the old disappearing act. P. S. Templin. America 123:535 D 19 '70

PUBLIC opinion

Domestic origins of peace. R. Randle. Ann Am Acad 392:76-85 N '70

Opinions of mankind; influence on Spanish and Soviet governments to commute death sentences. America 124:35 Ja 16 '71

Triumph for global opinion; rescue from execution in Spain and the Soviet Union. il Time 97:18-20 Ja 11 '71

See also
Public opinion polls
Rumor
Student opinion
Vietnamese war, 1957- —Public opinion

also subhead Foreign opinion under names of countries, e.g. United States—Foreign opinion

Canada

See also
United States—Foreign opinion—Canadian

China (People's Republic)

China; misinformation breeds wrong perceptions. H. Yu. Chr Cent 87:374 Mr 25 '70

Egypt

Voices from Cairo; interviews. ed. by E. Klein. il Newsweek 75:36+ Je 29 '70

See also
Israeli-Arab war, 1967- —Public opinion

Europe

See also
United States—Foreign opinion—European

Europe, Western

Internationalism and world politics among CERN scientists; the European elite panel study. D. Lerner and A. H. Teich. il Bul Atom Sci 26:4-10 F '70

See also
United States—Foreign opinion—European

France

See also
Israel—Foreign opinion—French
United States—Foreign opinion—French

Great Britain

See also
United States—Foreign opinion—British

Greece, Modern

Conversations in Greece. T. W. Pew, jr. Nation 212:74-80 Ja 18 '71

Israel

Is Hussein necessary? il por Newsweek 75:35 Je 22 '70

Israel in siege. C. Amory. Read Digest 96:147-8+ Ap '70

Two views from the Lebanese border. M. Elkins. il Newsweek 75:40 Je 8 '70

See also
Israeli-Arab war, 1967—Public opinion

Japan

See also
United States—Foreign opinion—Japanese

Latin America

See also
United States—Foreign opinion—Latin American

Lebanon

Two views from the Lebanese border. M. J. Kubic. il Newsweek 75:40 Je 8 '70

Netherlands

See also
United States—Foreign opinion—Dutch

Northern Ireland

Two sides of a troubled Belfast street. L. Lamont. il Time 96:26 Jl 20 '70

See also
Great Britain—Foreign opinion—Irish

Poland

See also
United States—Foreign opinion—Polish

Russia

See also
United States—Foreign opinion—Russian

Sweden

Sweden's troubled mood; with views of intellectuals. R. J. Korengold. il Newsweek 75-40-2+ Mr 23 '70

Switzerland

See also
United States—Foreign opinion—Swiss

United States

Advisory committee on public opinion established by Secretary Rogers. Dept State Bul 63:654-5 N 23 '70

Agnews. New Yorker 46:19-20 Ag 1 '70

Black mood, summer 1970; survey, with views of Negro leaders. il Newsweek 75:26-8 Je 8 '70

Clean break with the past. J. Brooks. il Am Heritage 21:4-7+ Ag '70

Conservative is the way to sound; with report on R. Reagan by P. O'Neil and views of the average voter. il Life 69:24-32 O 30 '70

Fresh look at America. J. N. Wallace. il U S News 69:46-51 N 30 '70

Hard times, 1970: an oral history of the recession. S. Terkel. il N Y Times Mag p 10-11+ D 20 '70

How back is the backlash? P. Steinfels. Commonweal 93:40 O 9 '70

How the public views the schools. Sr School 95:Schol Teach 1-2 D 8 '69

Misconceptions concerning nuclear weapons. B. N. Cantrell. Chr Cent 87:1219-20 O 14 '70

New conservation poll: pollution. Nat Wildlife 8:18-19 D '69

New generation of isolationists. J. A. Johnson. For Affairs 49:136-46 O '70

Not so hawkish: results of polls on military spending. il Nation 211:354 O 19 '70

On the last frontier with VX and GB; opinions of people in Umatilla County on government's plan to store nerve gas. J. Didion. il Life 68:22 F 20 '70

On the threshold of a new decade: thoughts for 1970. E. Rabinowitch. il por Bul Atom Sci 26:2-3+ F '70

People and the press. il Newsweek 76:22-5 N 9 '70

Police violence and its public support. W. A. Gamson and J. McEvoy. bibliog f il Ann Am Acad 391:97-110 S '70

Public views its schools; survey sponsored by CFK, ltd. Sat R 53:64 O 17 '70

Report from middle America. il Sr Schol 97:8-12 O 5 '70

Shaken faith in Nixon; Fortune 500-Yankelovich survey. R. S. Diamond. il Fortune 81:60-2 Je '70

Silent generation revisited; American men and women in their thirties; Time essay. por Time 95:38-9 Je 29 '70

Silent majority. L. Carpenter. il McCalls 97:40-1+ Jl '70

Silent majority speaks out. il U S News 68:34-7 Je 8 '70

Some facts for the state of the Union; Harris poll findings on the reactions to the My Lai massacre. P. Steinfels. Commonweal 91:446 Ja 23 '70

Soundings on the right. Time 95:19 Ap 27 '70

Swing to the right? A. Etzioni. Trans-Action 7:12+ S '70; Same abr. Cur 122:11-14 O '70

Thoughts on a troubled El Dorado; Time essay. H. Grunwald. il Time 95:18-21 Je 22 '70

Two, three, many Dallases! right-wing political opinion. Nat R 22:126-7 F 10 '70

U.S. journal: Missouri; trip home with Senator T. F. Eagleton. C. Trillin. New Yorker 46:108+ My 16 '70

What business thinks; the Fortune 500-Yankelovich survey (cont) R. S. Diamond. il Fortune 81:118-19+ F; 131-2 Mr; 82:72-3 Jl '70

What the public thinks about the public schools; results of the 1970 Gallup survey. Ed Digest 36:1-4 D '70

What's bothering Americans. il U S News 69:32-6 O 5 '70

What's right, and what's wrong with America? il Sr Schol 95:6-15 S 15 '69

Will economics swing the election? Bsns W p26 O 10 '70

See also
Vietnamese war. 1957- —Public opinion

PUBLIC opinion—*Continued*

Vietnam (Democratic Republic)

See also
Vietnamese war, 1957- —Public opinion

Vietnam (Republic)

See also
United States—Foreign opinion—Vietnamese
Vietnamese war, 1957- —Public opinion

PUBLIC opinion polls
Artificial majority. T. J. Lowi. il Nation 211:
581-4 D 7 '70
Asking the right questions. Sci N 98:31 Jl 11
'70
Real majority, by R. M. Scammon and B.
J. Wattenberg. Review
Atlan 226:69-73 D '70. M. Janeway
Silent majorities and the Vietnam war. P. E.
Converse and H. Schuman. il Sci Am 222:
17-25 Je '70
Try an opinion survey; Oak Park, Ill. C. T.
Osborn. il Am City 85:80+ D '70
Why the pollsters failed; Great Britain.
Newsweek 76:58 Jl 6 '70
See also
Political forecasts

Anecdotes, facetiae, satire, etc.

Nation is moving to the left. L. J. Harrissy.
Nat R 22:260 Mr 10 '70

PUBLIC relations
How Richmond communicates. Am City 85:
120-1 Jl '70
Public relations. L. L. L. Golden. See Com-
munications issues of Saturday review
See also
Advertising, Institutional
Corporate image
Investor relations programs
School and the community
United States—State, Department of—Public
relations
also subhead Public relations under
various subjects, e.g. Libraries—Public rela-
tions

Bibliography

Books in communications. S. W. Little. See
issues of Saturday review

PUBLIC relations as a profession
Freelance job idea: public relations service.
J. J. O'Rourke. il Writers Digest 50:28-31
N '70 (to be cont)
When journalists become PR men; views of
former newsmen. N. Hill. Sat R 53:57-60
Je 13 '70

PUBLIC relations consultants
Race relations is their business. S. Friedman. il N Y Times Mag p44+ O 25 '70

PUBLIC relations directors
Playing the patsy. L. L. L. Golden. Sat R
53:62-3 Je 13 '70

PUBLIC roads, Bureau of. See United States
—Public roads, Bureau of

PUBLIC safety officers
Suburban fire-police integration a must;
Burnsville, Minn. S. R. Dorndeld. il Am
City 85:78 F '70

PUBLIC school and Catholic school relations.
See Educational cooperation

PUBLIC school libraries. See School libraries
PUBLIC school teachers. See Teachers
PUBLIC schools
See also
School management and organization

Appraisal

See Education—Evaluation

Attendance

See School attendance

Desegregation

Accountability: Right to read program and
integration vs. compensatory education.
E. Geller. Library J 95:1881 My 15 '70
Against the malingerers. il Time 96:12 Jl 20
'70
Agnew's talk with five students; text of television debate. S. T. Agnew and others. il
pors U S News 69:86-8+ O 12 '70
Ain't nobody gonna touch King Claude; Manatee school busing case. il por Time 95:
16 Ap 20 '70
All desegregation orders obeyed; then, school
chaos in Greenville, S.C. il U S News 69:
26-8 D 7 '70
America's racial crisis; symposium. Cur 118:
27-40 My '70
And we quote: President Nixon's statement
criticized in report of National commission
on civil rights. Commonweal 92:180 My 8
'70

Are courts unfair to the South? il Sr Schol
96:14-15 Mr 2 '70
At once; protest in Atlanta. il Newsweek 75:
15 Ja 26 '70
Back to school. W. F. Buckley, jr. Nat R 22:
1016 S 22 '70
Back to school. il Newsweek 76:48 O 19 '70
Bad day in Lamar; whites attacked school
buses carrying Negro children. il News-
week 75:26 Mr 16 '70
Bad side of integration. il Time 96:32 Jl 13
'70
Baton Rouge desegregates. F. Guillory. Amer-
ica 122:650-2 Je 20 '70
Benign neglect for education too; Nixon's
educational reform message. M. R. Berube.
Commonweal 92:52-3 Mr 27 '70
Bus to integration bogs down; with edi-
torial comment and report on Civil rights
act of 1964 by L. Panetta. il Life 68:22-32
Mr 13 '70
Busing quandary; situation in Charlotte, N.C.
il Newsweek 76:63 Ag 24 '70
Can we make peace inside the United States?
friction in high schools. D. Lawrence. U S
News 69:92 D 7 '70
Chaos over school busing: tale of two cities;
Charlotte, N.C. and Los Angeles. il U S
News 68:29-33 Mr 16 '70
Clarification needed. D. Lawrence. U S News
69:80 Ag 31 '70
Court says: integrate now! il Sr Schol 95:
Schol Teach 1 D 1 '69
Creed and color in the school crisis. Chr
Today 14:32-3 Mr 27 '70
Crisis in Southern schools; six governors
speak out; with interviews. il U S News
68:38-44 F 16 '70
Crossroads for desegregation. il Sat R 53:76
Mr 21 '70
D day; more southern schools desegregate.
il Newsweek 75:25 F 16 '70
Death of integration? Stennis bill. Nation
210:228 Mr 2 '70
Desegregate now; will it work? il U S News
68:4 Ja 19 '70
Desegregation blocks cited in NEA Mississip-
pi report. Library J 95:1537+ Ap 15 '70; Re-
ply. E. T. McDonald. 95:2949 S 15 '70
Desegregation: how much further? il Time
96:55-6 O 26 '70
Desegregation 1970: government moves against
recalcitrant southern school districts. News-
week 76:67-8 Jl 27 '70
Desegregation now; Court cracks down. Sr
Schol 95:21-2+ N 17 '69
Desegregation: the South is different. P. M.
Rilling. New Repub 162:17-19 My 16 '70
Desegregation: the South's tense truce. il
Time 96:39-40 S 14 '70
Desegregation: where do we go from here?
A. M. Bickel. New Repub 162:20-2 F 7 '70;
Same abr. with title Education or integra-
tion? Cur 113:31-6 My '70; Discussion. New
Repub 162:29-30 F 28; 31-8 Mr 7; 26-30 Mr
21; 25-8 Mr 28; 33-5 Ap 4 '70
Desegregation yes, integration no. Time 95:
11-12 Ap 6 '70
Desegregation's strange bedfellows; Senate
debate. il por Newsweek 75:22-3 F 23 '70
Do it; Justice department and Internal reve-
nue service move against segregated
schools. Newsweek 76:21 Jl 20 '70
End of reconstruction. il pors Time 95:12-13
Mr 2 '70
Evenhandedness at home; attack by white
extremists against school buses carrying
Negro children in Lamar, S.C. Nat R 22:
296 Mr 24 '70
Fall previews. il Sat R 53:54 Jl 18 '70
Fresh blows against segregated schools. il
U S News 69:83 Jl 20 '70
Friendly persuasion. il Newsweek 76:62 Ag 24
'70
Governors against the law; southern governors
attempt to block desegregation. il Time 95:
9-10 F 2 '70
How desegregation is working. J. B. Cum-
ming, jr. il Newsweek 76:105-7 D 21 '70
How school busing works in one town. G.
Samuels. il N Y Times Mag p38-9+ S 27 '70
How to lose your job in the Nixon admini-
stration; 1968 survey conducted by Leon
Panetta's office. Trans-Action 7:14 My '70
How to win by losing; court-ordered school
busing plan in Manatee County, Fla. Time
95:22 Ap 27 '70
I, Claudius; C. Kirk yields. Newsweek 75:
35 Ap 27 '70
Integrated, but unequal; report by civil rights
groups. Time 97:27 Ja 4 '71
Integrating friends; Office for civil rights
interprets the Nixon policy statement. J.
Osborne. New Repub 162:12-14 Ap 18 '70

PUBLIC schools—Desegregation—*Continued*
Integration in Mississippi. America 122:91
Ja 31 '70
Integration: morning after. Nat R 22:242+
Mr 10 '70
Kirk's caper. il Newsweek 75:40-2 Ap 20
'70
Latest in Congress on mixed schools. U S
News 68:88 Ap 20 '70
Lesson from the governor. Chr Today 14:25
My 8 '70
Likely soon from Supreme court: clearer
rules on school mixing. U S News 69:16
S 14 '70
Little Rock thirteen years later: how integra-
tion is working. il U S News 68:82-4 Je 22
'70
Merging city and suburban schools: the Rich-
mond story. U S News 69:24 Ag 10 '70
Midterm mixing in schools: the results and
the costs. il U S News 68:28-9 Mr 2 '70
Mixmasters. il por Time 96:20 Jl 6 '70
Nearing normal. Newsweek 76:80 S 21 '70
New desegregation targets: the North and
the suburbs. il por U S News 69:25-7 D 14
'70
New look at busing. U S News 68:63 Mr 30
'70
New nullification race; regression toward
pre-1954 levels of racial accommodation.
Chr Cent 87:283 Mr 11 '70
New realism. K. Crawford. Newsweek 75:24
Mr 9 '70
New resistance to mixed schools; several
states of the South. U S News 68:6-7 F
2 '70
Nixon goes South for integration. il por
Time 95:7-8 Ag 24 '70
Nixon on desegregation: text of statement,
March 24, 1970. R. M. Nixon. por U S News
68:30-7 Ap 6 '70
Nixon on the schools. Chr Today 14:26 Ap
24 '70
Nixon watch: chicken, southern fried. J.
Osborne. New Repub 162:13-14 F 21 '70
Nixon watch: concerning statement on school
desegregation. J. Osborne; A. M. Bickel.
New Repub 162:13-15 Ap 4 '70
Nixon watch: paying for integration. J. Os-
borne. New Repub 162:10-12 Je 6 '70
Nixon way; message. il por Newsweek 75:
28+ Ap 6 '70
Nixon's answers on desegregation. il U S
News 68:15 Ap 6 '70
Nixon's outer South strategy. Nat R 22:986+
S 22 '70
Nixon's plan to help schools integrate. il U S
News 68:70 Je 1 '70
Now, a limit on busing of pupils; U.S. ap-
peals court decision. U S News 68:47 Je 8
'70
Official policy now on South's schools. il
U S News 68:33 Ap 20 '70
Open letter to the Supreme court of the
United States; reprint from Richmond, Va,
News leader, July 22, 1970. il U S News
69:76+ Ag 10 '70
Our nation's schools: desegregation is not
enough. G. D. Fischer. por Parents Mag
45:16 S '70
Peaceful and orderly. il Newsweek 76:121 S
14 '70
President as educator. C. E. Silberman. For-
tune 81:150 My '70
President on desegregation. America 122:383
Ap 11 '70
Public school turnovers in the South. J.
Demuth. il America 123:377-9 N 7 '70
Question before High court: how much inte-
gration? il U S News 69:37-8 O 26 '70
Racism: North and South; Senator Ribicoff's
support of Stennis amendment. America
122:206 F 28 '70; Reply. C. E. Henican.
122:485 My 9 '70
Reason, not rulings, can bring racial peace.
D. Lawrence. U S News 68:96 F 16 '70
Rebellion at Lamar. il Time 95:12-13 Mr 16
'70
Requiem for a liberal dream? il por News-
week 75:18-21 Mr 2 '70
School buses roll; integrated schools in
Georgia and North Carolina. Time 96:14 S
7 '70
School desegregation problems: are federal
courts educators? address, January 3, 1970.
J. B. Williams. Vital Speeches 36:306-9 Mr 1
'70
School desegregation: some impediments and
solutions. C. A. Glatt and W. A. Gaines.
Ed Digest 35:12-15 Mr '70
School desegregation: the final breakthrough?
what is happening in the South. il U S
News 69:15-16 S 14 '70
School disruptions. Chr Today 14:21 Mr 27 '70

Second thoughts. il Newsweek 76:26+ O 26
'70
Segregation South and North. il Time 95:
14-17 F 23 '70
Sham or surrender? J. Osborne. New Repub
162:15-17 Mr 7 '70
Slowdown on desegregation; proposals of R.
M. Nixon. P. Woodring and others. Sat
R 53:57 Ap 18 '70
Southern comfort; R. M. Nixon's press con-
ference. J. Osborne. New Repub 163:13-14
Ag 1 '70
Southern governor dramatizes the push for
school integration; Governor Holton of Vir-
ginia. il por U S News 69:52 S 14 '70
Southern integrationists feel betrayed by the
North. P. Watters. il N Y Times Mag p26-
7+ My 3 '70; Discussion p83 Je 7 '70
Southern school integration rises rapidly. il
Sr Schol 96:Schol Teach 1 F 9 '70
Stennis and schools. New Repub 162:7 F 28
'70
Study of interracial conflict. G. Wittes and
S. Wittes. il Am Ed 6:7-10 Je '70
Testing time; Southern school districts. il
Newsweek 76:19-20 S 7 '70
This month's feature: Congress & federal
school racial policy. Cong Digest 49:99-
107+ Ap '70
Thurmond threatens. K. Crawford. News-
week 76:25 Ag 3 '70
Tragic failure; with remarks by militants
and liberals. S. Alsop. Newsweek 75:108 F
23 '70; Same abr. Read Digest 96:93-4 My '70
TRB from Washington: Mr Nixon's benign
neglect policy. New Repub 162:4 Mr 28 '70
TRB from Washington; the Mondale hearings.
New Repub 163:4 Jl 25 '70
Turn-around on integration. il Time 95:9-
13+ Mr 9 '70
Turn from integration. il U S News 68:29-
31 Mr 9 '70; Same abr. with title Will bus-
ing make them better? Read Digest 96:95-7
My '70
Unquiet schools; segregation disputes. New
Repub 163:8 O 3 '70
Very good day; R. M. Nixon's visit to New
Orleans to promote acceptance of school
desegregation. J. Osborne. New Repub 163:
7-9 Ag 22 '70
View from Maddox country. R. Cleghorn.
Nation 210:486-90 Ap 27 '70
What happened to one model high school;
Horace Mann school, Gary, Ind. il U S
News 68:37-40 Ap 27 '70
What the Warren court decided; excerpts
from The Warren court and the public
schools. H. C. Hudgins, jr. Ed Digest 36:
44-7 N '70
When schools reopen, tangle over busing ex-
pected. il U S News 69:11-13 Ag 24 '70
Where did everyone go to? W. Grant. New
Repub 163:20 S 5 '70
White violence in Lamar. J. Bass. New Re-
pub 162:10-12 Mr 28 '70
Year of decision for white-only schools. il
U S News 69:16-17 Jl 27 '70

Federal aid
See Education—Federal aid

Finance
See School finance

Health service
See also
School nurses

Public relations
See School and the community

Statistics
See Education—Statistics

United States
Adapting British school reforms to U.S.
needs. Sch & Soc 98:16-17 Ja '70
Can the public school survive another ten
years? G. Graham. Ed Digest 36:1-3 O '70
Can the public schools be saved? M. Polner.
Commonweal 93:15-17 O 2 '70
Carnegie public school study; crisis in the
classroom. America 123:277 O 17 '70
Crisis in the classroom, by C. Silberman.
Review
Library J 95:3946 N 15 '70
Crisis of confidence, and beyond. J. Cass.
Sat R 53:61-2 S 19 '70
Educational reform, and the role of integra-
tion. America 122:324 Mr 28 '70
End of the impossible dream. P. Schrag. il
Sat R 53:68-70+ S 19 '70
Giving Americans a choice; alternatives to
public education. M. O'Neill. America 122:
66-70 Ja 24 '70; Reply. R. E. Brady. 122:360
Ap 4 '70

PUBLIC schools—United States—*Continued*
How good are your schools? il Changing T
 24:7-10 N '70
How the public views the schools. Sr Schol
 95:Schol Teach 1-2 D 8 '69
In public schools, a crime invasion. U S News
 68:9 Ja 26 '70
Institutional reform. M. D. Fantini. Todays
 Ed 59:43-4+ Ap '70
Murder in the schoolroom; excerpts from
 Crisis in the classroom. C. E. Silberman. il
 Atlan 225:82-94+ Je; 226:83-97 Jl; 85-9+ Ag
 '70; Discussion. 226:30+ O '70
Public schools: the myth of the melting pot;
 excerpt from Cobweb attitudes: essays in
 American education and culture. C. Greer.
 Ed Digest 35:1-4 Mr '70
Race and the schools; Syracuse report. il
 Newsweek 76:80 O 19 '70
Schools for the 70's. O. Sand. il Schol Teach
 Sec Teach Sup p8-9 Ja 5 '70
Teacher opinion poll; extremist criticism of
 the schools. il Todays Ed 59:11 Ap '70
What the public thinks about the public
 schools; results of the 1970 Gallup survey.
 Ed Digest 36:1-4 D '70
What's going on in schools & colleges. See
 issues of Changing times
Why ghetto schools fail. H. M. Levin. il
 Sat R 53:68-9+ Mr 21 '70
 See also
Columbus, Ind.—Public schools
Education—United States
Equalization, Educational
Junior high schools
Rural schools—United States
School districts
School year

PUBLIC schools (endowed)

England

Fourth of June. J. A. Maxtone-Graham. il
 Travel & Camera 33:38-46 My '70

PUBLIC schools and religion
California's fourth R: Board of education
 flap. E. Plowman. Chr Today 14:37 Ja 30
 '70
Church in the courts. Chr Today 14:50 Mr
 13 '70
Facts about prayer in schools. L. Cassels.
 U S News 68:96 Mr 23 '70
Religion as an elective; Ontario. R. Brow.
 Chr Today 14:47 Ag 21 '70
Religion makes a comeback in schools
 across U.S. il U S News 68:39-40 Mr 2 '70
School prayer ban upheld. Sr Schol 96:
 Schol Teach 1 Ja 26 '70
School prayer issue: a perverse paradox. H.
 M. Engel. il Cath World 211:125-7 Je '70
Schools, songs, and supplications. J. F. Gum-
 mere. Sch & Soc 98:299-300 Sum '70
Scripture in public schools. A. Eggebroten.
 Chr Today 14:32 Jl 17 '70
What the Warren court decided; excerpts
 from The Warren court and the public
 schools. H. C. Hudgins, jr. Ed Digest 36:
 44-7 N '70

PUBLIC schools and the community. See
 School and the community
PUBLIC service advertising. See Advertising.
 Public service
PUBLIC service industries
Creeping capitalism; private operation of
 public services. il Forbes 106:22-6+ S 1 '70
PUBLIC service radio programs. See Radio
 broadcasting—Public service programs
PUBLIC services. See Municipal services
PUBLIC speaking
 See also
Audiences
Lectures and lecturing
Movement speakers bureau
Rhetoric
Speech education
Speeches, addresses, etc.
Toastmasters international, inc.
Voice
PUBLIC squares. See Plazas
PUBLIC television. See Television broadcast-
 ing, Noncommercial
PUBLIC utilities
Fifty largest utilities. il Fortune 81:212-13
 My '70
 See also
Electric utilities
Municipal services
Northern states power company

Finance

Utilities: is history repeating? Forbes 105:24
 Ap 15 '70
Utilities; with yardsticks of management performance. il Forbes 105:109-10+ Ja 1 '70;
 107:98-100 Ja 1 '71

Public relations

Utilities: is history repeating? Forbes 105:24
 Ap 15 '70

Rates

Guide to trimming electric gas, water and
 telephone costs. il Good H 171:172 N '70
Path through the maze. R. W. Dietsch. Na-
 tion 211:114-16 Ag 17 '70
 See also
Water rates

Real estate operations

Electrogas builders. Forbes 106:22-3 N 15 '70

Regulation

 See also
Public utilities—Rates

Securities

 See also
Electric utilities—Securities
PUBLIC welfare
 See also
Old age assistance

Law

Ruling that could tie up welfare aid. U S
 News 68:59 Ap 6 '70

California

Teaching how to cheat. il por Time 96:18+
 O 5 '70
 See also

New York (state)

New York (city)—Public welfare

Southern states

Looming money revolution down South. R.
 Armstrong. il Fortune 81:66-9+ Je '70

United States

Agnew explains the president's welfare plan;
 excerpts from address, March 9, 1970. S. T
 Agnew. il por U S News 68:84-5 Mr 23 '70
All it takes is money; effect of higher grants.
 Trans-Action 7:8 S '70
Behind rising alarm over welfare costs. il
 U S News 69:32 N 30 '70
Blood on the floor; Family assistance plan,
 the Administration and Congress. J. Os-
 borne. New Repub 163:10-11 D 19 '70
Champion of welfare rights. C. P. DuBose. il
 pors Ebony 25:31-4+ Ap '70
Clearing the way; plan to provide a gua-
 ranteed minimum income for all Ameri-
 cans. Newsweek 75:19-20 Mr 9 '70
Compounding the welfare mess; the Nixon
 plan. H. Hazlitt. Nat R 22:205 F 24 '70
Convert; welfare-reform bill and Wilbur Mills.
 Newsweek 75:47-8 Ap 20 '70
Creaming the poor. S. M. Miller and others.
 il Trans-Action 7:38-45 Je '70
Deeper and deeper still: Nixon's Family as-
 sistance plan. il Nat R 22:292-3 Mr 24 '70
Family assistance act; address, January 29,
 1970. G. P. Shultz. Vital Speeches 36:295-6
 Mr 1 '70
Family plan. Commonweal 92:451-2 S 18 '70
Four professors and the welfare revolution.
 L. Velie. il Read Digest 96:93-7 Ja '70
Great welfare debate. il Nations Bsns 58:
 56-7+ Ap '70
Last chance for welfare reform. America 123:
 138 S 12 '70
Minimum income for all: a step closer. il
 U S News 68:76 Ap 27 '70
More than defense. Sci N 97:146-7 F 7 '70
Nay: Nixon-Moynihan plan. Nat R 22:480-1
 My 5 '70
Nearer: aid for working poor. il U S News
 68:36 Mr 9 '70
New approach on aid to poor; Nixon amend-
 ments to Family assistance plan. il U S
 News 68:98 Je 22 '70
Nixon's Family assistance plan. H. Kasper
 and L. Hausman. New Repub 162:8-10 Mr
 28 '70
Nixon's welfare plan clears hurdle. U S News
 68:94 Mr 16 '70
Odd alliance; Moynihan and the robber
 barons. I. Mothner. il pors Look 34:18-23 Ap
 7 '70
One step we must take; Family assistance
 plan. D. P. Moynihan. il Sat R 53:20-3 My
 23 '70
Poor outlook for welfare reform. Bsns W
 p30-1 Ja 31 '70
Radical view of social welfare and mental
 health. L. Ginsberg. bibliog Ment Hy 54:
 44-9 Ja '70
Revision of welfare reform. America 122:667
 Je 27 '70
Setback for reform; Nixon's bill. Newsweek
 75:46-7 My 18 '70

PUBLIC welfare—United States—*Continued*
  Setback for welfare reform; the Family as-
    sistance plan. America 123:306 O 24 '70
  Spreading dole. Time 96:11 N 23 '70
  This month's feature: Congress & the Family
    assistance plan. Cong Digest 49:162-92 Je
    '70
  TRB from Washington:
    Nixon the socialist; Family assistance
      program. New Repub 162:6 My 2 '70
    Nixon's revolution. New Repub 163:4 S
      19 '70
    Smith experiment; proposed national
      Family allowance program. New Repub
      162:8 F 21 '70
  TRB from Washington; Family assistance
    plan. New Repub 162:8 Mr 14 '70
  Updating welfare. J. Osborne. New Repub
    162:11-13 Je 27 '70; Discussion. 163:30-3 Jl
    18; 33-4 Ag 1 '70
  Wayward welfare state; address, September
    1, 1970. R. A. Freeman. il Vital Speeches
    37:16-24 O 15 '70
  We are embarked on a great new mission of
    reform; address, July 27, 1970. E. L. Rich-
    ardson. por U S News 69:57-9 Ag 17 '70
  Welfare and muscle; Family assistance act.
    J. Osborne. New Repub 163:11-12 N 7 '70
  Welfare: back to the drawing board; House
    bill. M. Friedman. il Newsweek 75:89 My
    18 '70
  Welfare mess needs total reform. Life 69:23
    Jl 31 '70
  Welfare plan's improbable allies. Bsns W
    p35 F 28 '70
  Welfare reform again. M. Friedman. News-
    week 76:70 S 7 '70
  Welfare reform and revenue sharing. R.
    Lekachman. Duns 96:9 O '70
  Welfare: time for reform; symposium. il Sat
    R 53:19-32+ My 23 '70
  Welfare with a future. Fortune 82:54 Jl '70
  What's missing in Nixon's welfare program.
    E. Van Den Haag. Nat R 22:85-7+ Ja 27
    '70
  What's wrong with welfare; answers from
    Nixon's adviser; interview. D. P. Moyni-
    han. pors U S News 68:64-8 Je 15 '70
  When you just give money to the poor; OEO
    pilot program. F. J. Cook. il N Y Times
    Mag p23+ My 3 '70
  Why the welfare bill is stuck. il Newsweek
    76:22-3 D 7 '70
  Wilbur the shrewd. Time 95:15 Mr 23 '70
  Will money ruin the poor? Family assist-
    ance or workfare. I. Mothner. Look 34:58
    Je 2 '70
  Workfare belabored; Family assistance pro-
    gram. Time 96:17-18 O 5 '70
    See also
  Guaranteed annual income
  National welfare rights organization

  Washington (state)
  What went wrong in aid to poor; welfare of-
    ficial's report. V. Stintzi. il por U S News
    69:33-5 N 30 '70
PUBLIC works
    See also
  American public works association
  Dams
    also subhead Public works under names
    of cities, e.g. South Haven, Mich.—Public
    works
PUBLICITY
  Some tips from an editor on preparing a
    news release. G. B. Porter. il Writers Di-
    gest 50:31 N '70
    See also
  Advertising, Institutional
  Booksellers and bookselling—Publicity
  Public relations directors
  Rumor
  Television in politics
PUBLISHERS and authors. See Authors and
    publishers
PUBLISHERS and publishing
  Paper pollution. K. M. Glazier. por Wilson
    Lib Bul 44:856-7 Ap '70
    See also
  Authors and publishers
  Books—Advertising
  Books—Marketing
  Copyright
  Literary agents
  Newspaper publishers and publishing
  Review copies of books
    also names of publishers, e.g. Doubleday
    and company

  Childrens literature
  Better late than never; books about urban
    crisis. R. H. Smith. Pub W 198:125 Jl 13
    '70
  Do stores shy away from problem books?
    Pub W 197:83-5 F 23 '70

Consolidations and mergers
McGraw-Hill withdraws; Penguin goes to
  Longman. Pub W 198:247-8 Ag 31 '70
Sir Allen Lane dies, sale of Penguin quickly
  announced. Pub W 198:47-8 Jl 20 '70

Educational literature
Can creativity come to book publishing? J.
  P. Young. Pub W 198:26-30 Ag 10 '70
OE's new copyright policy. M. W. Bachrach.
  Am Ed 6:28-9 Ag '70

Employees
Dismissed Harcourt employee files unfair labor charges. Pub W 198:41 O 5 '70
Promise still unredeemed; minority groups in
  book publishing. R. H. Smith. Pub W 198:
  38 O 12 '70
Two lamentable casualties; publishing industry's intention to hire members of minority
  groups for responsible positions, and to
  help finance minority-group publishing
  companies. R. H. Smith. Pub W 198:250
  Ag 31 '70

Facsimiles
See Book rarities—Facsimiles

Fiction
Can the U.S. absorb 130 first novelists a
  year? il Time 95:75 Je 29 '70
Novel markets. Writers Digest 50:51+ Mr '70
Risking the first novel. J. Berry. Library J
  95:3219 O 1 '70

Finance
Another nice nap? national economy. R. E.
  Bye. Library J 96:49 Ja 1 '71
Big story in books is financial. il Bsns W
  p68-9+ My 16 '70
Receipts in 1969: $2.75-billion. il Pub W 198:
  28-30 O 12 '70

Foreign business
Print exporting. A. Bell. Pub W 198:pt2 184-5
  S 21 '70

History
Advent of printing in current historical literature; notes and comments on an elusive
  transformation. E. L. Eisenstein. bibliog f
  Am Hist R 75:727-43 F '70

International aspects
Overcoming barriers. R. E. Bye. Pub W 198:
  40 S 21 '70
Religious books in foreign trade. Pub W
  197:54 Mr 9 '70
Rights and permissions. P. Nathan. Pub W
  198:pt2 162-3 S 21 '70
Step toward cooperation in U.S.-U.S.S.R.
  publishing. Pub W 198:49 N 16 '70
U.S. delegation forecasts new Soviet pub-
  lishing ties. il Pub W 198:37 D 28 '70
U.S. publishing's new look in newly develop-
  ing countries; interview. E. E. Booher. il
  por Pub W 197:26-9 Ap 6 '70
    See also
Franklin book programs, inc.
International publishers association
Publishers and publishing—Translations

Microforms
Publishing scene; micropublishing. D. Dempsey. Sat R 55:39 F 21 '70

Moving picture scripts
I read the movie. D. Richie. bibliog Nation
  210:757-8 Je 22 '70

Negro literature
Two lamentable casualties; publishing industry's intention to hire members of minority
  groups for responsible positions, and to
  help finance minority-group publishing
  companies. R. H. Smith. Pub W 198:250
  Ag 31 '70

Order processing
Paying and non-paying; excerpts from address. E. Schossberger. Pub W 198:42-3 Jl
  27 '70

Paperback books
Market for paperback originals. Writer 83:
  28-30 Jl '70
Never more prosperous or interesting. Pub
  W 197:35-6 F 9 '70
New survey shows paperback growth rate.
  il Pub W 197:78-9 Je 29 '70

Poetry
Getting it all together in The rainbow box.
  M. R. Kraner. il Pub W 198:46-7 O 26 '70
Poetry as merchandise. A. Caruba; reply.
  A. Brilliant. Pub W 197:29 F 9 '70

PUCCINI, Giacomo
La Bohème. Criticism
Opera N 34:17-20 Ja 24 '70
Giri of the golden West (La fanciulla del
West) Criticism
Opera N 34:24-5 Mr 14 '70 *
Opera N il 34:17-20 Mr 14 '70 *
Sat R 53:63 F 28 '70 *
Fourth riddle. G. R. Marek. Opera N 34:24-
5 F 21 '70 *
Madame Butterfly. Criticism
Opera N il 34:17-20 Mr 7 '70 *
Massenet's Manon, and Puccini's. P. L. Mil-
ler. por Am Rec G 36:326-7 Ja '70 *
Music to my ears; concert performance of
Gianni Schicchi. I. Kolodin. Sat R 53:35
D 19 '70 *
Puccini's pot of gold. H. Bailey. Opera N 34:
16 Mr 7 '70 *
Tosca. Criticism
Opera N il 35:17-20 D 12 '70 *
Turandot. Criticism
Opera N 34:24-5 F 21 '70 *
Opera N il 34:17-20 F 21 '70 *

PUDDINGS
ABC's of steamed pudding. il Am Home 73:
68 D '70
Christmas breads and puddings. il Ladies
Home J 87:84-8 D '70
For the finish, steamed pudding. Sunset 145:
110 D '70
Snow-capped berry soup. il Sunset 145:112
Ag '70

PUEBLO architecture
Pueblos of the four corners; photographs by
W. R. Current. Arch Forum 133:44-7 S '70

PUEBLO incident, 1968
Bucher, by L. M. Bucher. Review
Newsweek 76:110+ S 14 '70. R. A. Gross
Matter of accountability, by T. Armbrister.
Review
Bsns W por p8 Ag 15 '70. D. Fausch
Pueblo variously remembered. W. A. Mc-
Whirter. por Life 69:8 Ag 21 '70
Remembering the Pueblo. por Newsweek 75:
16 Je 8 '70

PUEBLO Indians
Matter of Indian giving; question of land
rights to Blue Lake watershed. E. Shrake.
il Sports Illus 33:42-4 Ag 17 '70
See also
Tewa Indians

PUERTO RICANS in New York city. See
Puerto Ricans in the United States
PUERTO RICANS in the United States
Bicultural Americans with a Hispanic tradi-
tion. A. D. Trejo. il por Wilson Lib Bul
44:720-2 Mr '70
New York: the south Bronx project. L. Lo-
pez. il Wilson Lib Bul 44:757-60 Mr '70
Puerto Ricans. il Newsweek 75:92+ Je 15 '70
Silent minority starts to speak out. il U S
News 69:66-9 Jl 13 '70
See also
Young Lords (organization)

PUERTO RICO
See also
Airlines—Puerto Rico
Architecture, Domestic—Puerto Rico
Cost of living—Puerto Rico
Culebra Island
Education—Puerto Rico
Fishing—Puerto Rico
Hotels. taverns, etc.—Puerto Rico
Investments, Foreign (in Puerto Rico)
Music festivals—Puerto Rico
San Juan

Description and travel
Puerto Rico. B. Gillam. il Mlle 71:104-6+ My
'70
Travel scene: what's on in Puerto Rico. Bsns
W p49-50 Ja 2 '71

Economic conditions
See also
Cost of living—Puerto Rico

Industries
See also
Sugar industry

Nationalism
Puerto Rico: our backyard colony. M. Meyerson. il Ramp Mag 8:50-1+ Je 70

Photographs
When B/W is better. J. Scully. il Mod Phot
34:102-3 Ja '70

Politics and government
U.S. journal: rights of students to engage in
political activities. C. Trillin. New Yorker
45:124-6+ F 14 '70

PUERTO RICO. University
U.S. journal: rights of students to engage in
political activities. C. Trillin. New Yorker
45:124-6+ F 14 '70
PUERTO VALLARTA, Mexico
Teen travel talk; student serenade to Guada-
lajara and Puerto Vallarta. il Seventeen 29:
255 Ap '70
PUFF pastry. See Pastry
PUFFIN books. See Penguin books, ltd.
PUGET SOUND
See also
Georgia, Strait of
San Juan Islands, Wash.
PUGET SOUND live steamers (club) See Boat
clubs
PUGSLEY, William
Arrival of Miss Ruth. il por Dance Mag 44:
20-1+ D '70
**PUGWASH conferences on science and world
affairs**
On the Sochi conference. il Bul Atom Sci 26:
18-24 Ap '70
Pugwash movement; science's conscience?
C.-G. McDaniel. Chr Cent 87:1232-4 O 14
'70
PULEO, Robert
Twilight of a career; interview, ed. by S.
Jenkins, jr. por Opera N 35:16 D 12 '70
PULIN, Chuck
On the road with Mad Dogs and English-
men. il Sr Schol 97:24-5+ N 16 '70
PULITZER prizes
Front-page Fitzpatrick. il por Time 95:69 My
18 '70
Painful prize; S. Hersh awarded prize for in-
ternational reporting. por Newsweek 75:73-4
My 18 '70
PULLEN, Thomas C.
Icebreaker: saga of Northwest Passage; in-
terview, ed. by N. J. Margolis. il por U S
News 68:72-5 F 9 '70
PULLING, Pierre
Sportsmen's canoes. il Field & S 75:82 O '70
PULLMAN, Wash.
Lighting
Light for the future. J. Street. il Am City 85:
122 Mr '70
PULLMAN, Inc.
Glamour isn't everything! il Forbes 105:34 Ap
1 '70
PULMONARY hemorrhage. See Hemorrhage
PULOS, Arthur J.
Restless genius of Norman Bel Geddes. il por
Arch Forum 133:46-51 Jl '70
PULSARS
Electronic pulsarium. S. P. Maran and oth-
ers. il Sky & Tel 40:17-19 Jl '70
Glitch and antiglitch. il Sci N 98:136 Ag 15 '70
Interstellar scattering of pulsar radiation and
its effect on the spectrum of NPO532. W.
M. Cronyn. bibliog il Science 168:1453-5 Je
19 '70
Models from pulsar anomalies. D. E. Thom-
sen. il Sci N 97:626-7 Je 27 '70
Ordinary stars. white dwarfs, and neutron
stars. L. C. Green. il Sky & Tel 41:18-20
Ja '71
Pulsars today. L. C. Green. il Sky & Tel 40:
260-2 N '70 (to be cont)
Pulsars, what are they? I. Asimov. Sci Di-
gest 67:88-9 My '70
Starquake. Sci Am 22:44-5 F '70
PULSE
Slow pulse, stout heart. Sci Digest 67:54 Ap
'70
PULSE code modulation. See Radio pulse
code modulation
PULSE generators. See Signal generators
PULOWAT (island)
East is a big bird; excerpts. T. Gladwin. il
Natur Hist 79:24-35 Ap; 58-69 My '70
PULVER, Deborah
Boating with baby on board. il Motor B
125:58+ Je '70
PUMA hunting
Five-year lion hunt. T. Trueblood. il Field
& S 74:60-3+ F '70
PUMAS
American lion. M. G. Hornocker. il Natur
Hist 79:40-9+ N '70
Hail, the ferocious lion! W. L. Maughan. il
Américas 22:4-6 Ap '70
Let us now praise mountain lions; with edi-
torial comment. E. Abbey. il Life 68:3.
52B-54+ Mr 13 '70
Secrets of the mighty cougar. F. Weddle. il
Nat Wildlife 8:58-63 O '70
PUMPED-storage hydroelectric plants. See Hy-
droelectric plants

PUMPKINS
Pumpkin picking near Half Moon Bay. il Sunset 145:23 O '70
They grew pumpkins for profit. il Sunset 144:244-5 My '70

PUMPS
Floating attack pumper fights boat and dock fires in Sausalito, Calif. C. Masten. il Am City 85:58 S '70

PUNCH (beverage)
Holiday drinks; traditional wassail bowl. W. Clifford. House B 112:88+ D '70
If you'd like a bubbly punch. il Sunset 144: 142 Je '70
It's a snack in liquid form; hot milk punch. il Sunset 145:200 N '70
Julglögg-Swedish hot punch. il McCalls 98:16 D '70
Toast to safer driving. M. Solaro. il Todays Health 48:60-3 D '70

PUNGS. See Sleighs and sleighing

PUNISHMENT
How to make a difference. D. Berrigan. Commonweal 92:384-6 Ag 7 '70; Discussion. 92:431; 93:8+, 35+, 78-9 S 4. O 2-16 '70
I chose prison, by J. V. Bennett. Review Bsns W il p9-10 Ap 18 '70. R. Clark
See also
Capital punishment
Castration of criminals and defectives
School discipline
Torture

PUNISHMENT; story. See Fonger, H.

PUNISHMENT of children. See Children—Management and training

PUNITIVE expedition to Mexico, 1916. See United States—History—Punitive expedition to Mexico, 1916

PUNJAB, India

Riots
Jinxed jewel; Chandigarh, capital of Punjab. il Time 95:33 F 9 '70

PUNKE, Harold H. and Cantrell, C. H.
Libraries and education. Ed Digest 36:8-10 D '70

PUNS and punning
Test your creativity. J. E. Gibson. Sci Digest 68:23-4+ S '70

PUPFISH. See Killifishes

PUPIL (eye)
Avenging eye; pupillary dilations while watching film or TV in the Shaffer-Rossiter test. R. L. Shayon. Sat R 53:58 My 16 '70

PUPPETS and puppet plays
Dwiggins marionettes, by D. Abbe. Review Pub W il 198:44+ Ag 3 '70. P. Standard
Magic of puppetry; project in Bridgeport, Conn. inner-city schools. J. S. Zeliff. il Parents Mag 45:46-7+ Jl '70
Mini music hall; Little players theater company. il Time 97:53 Ja 4 '71
Pinocchio; dramatization of story by C. Collodi. L. Mahlmann. Plays 30:47-54 N '70
Puppet world; make puppets to act out the musical story of the Nutcraker suite. Mrs D. Jones and Mrs F. Johns. il Sch Arts 69:18-19 Je '70
Puppets are personalities. H. S. Paston. il Sch Arts 70:28-9 N '70
Puppets; fairy tale characters. R. A. Yoder. il Sch Arts 69:8-9 Je '70
Puppets of Kurt Seligmann: an homage. J. B. Myers. il Craft Horiz 30:32-5+ D '70
Shadow puppetry in a design class. R. Sylwester. il Sch Arts 69:12-14 Je '70

PUPPIES. See Dogs

PURCELL, Carl
Color after dark. il Pop Phot 67:90-5 S '70
Shooting big game with a camera. il por Pop Phot 66:98-101+ My '70

PURCELL, Edward A. jr
American jurisprudence between the wars: legal realism and the crisis of democratic theory. bibliog f Am Hist R 75:424-46 D '69

PURCELL, Gary R.
Reference books of 1969. il por Library J 95: 1437-42 Ap 15 '70

PURCELL, John Wallace
Unscarred wounded. il PTA Mag 64:18-20+ F '70

PURCHASE college. See New York (state). State university—College at Purchase

PURCHASING
See also
Buyers
Consumers
Consumption (economics)
Quality of products
Shopping and shoppers
also subhead Purchasing under various subjects, e.g. Automobiles—Purchasing

PURCHASING, Cooperative
Food shoppers buy together. il Bsns W p99+ D 5 '70
How to save 20 per cent with your own buying club. L. David. il Mech Illus 66: 41-3+ Je '70

PURCHASING, Government
House demands fly before buy. Bsns W p31 O 10 '70
Industry group asks procurement changes. C. Brownlow. Aviation W 93:15-16 Ag 17 '70
Rising electronics market expected. Aviation W 93:85 S 14 '70
See also
Contracts, Government
United States—Armed forces—Procurement
United States—Commission on government procurement
United States—General accounting office
United States—General services administration

PURCHASING, Household
Money book; excerpts from Getting the most for your money. A. Scaduto. Ladies Home J 87:147-50 Mr '70
Truth that saves money in the supermarket. V. Cadden. Redbook 135:30+ Jl '70
Twenty ways to save money at the supermarket. R. O'Brien. Read Digest 96:68-70 My '70
See also
Consumer education
Food—Prices

PURCHASING, Industrial
First blush of a buyer's market. il Bsns W p 10-11 Ja 2 '71

PURCHASING, Military
American weapons abroad: sales instead of giveaways. il U S News 69:52-3 Jl 27 '70
At year's end. Commonweal 93:339-40 Ja 8 '71
Dilemmas of the arms traffic. G. Kemp. For Affairs 48:274-84 Ja '70
President delegates certain functions under foreign military sales act; White House announcement; and executive order. R. M. Nixon. Dept State Bul 62:87-8 Ja 26 '70
Strong ECM market found abroad. B. Miller. Aviation W 93:62-3+ O 19 '70
See also
United States—Armed forces—Procurement
United States—Army—Procurement
United States—Defense, Department of—Procurement

France
Budget squeeze in France spurs talks with British on helicopters. Aviation W 92:21 Ap 13 '70

Germany (Federal Republic)
West Germany may buy 200 U.S. fighters. R. F. Coburn. Aviation W 92:103+ Ap 27 '70

Israel
Mirages' storage indicated Israeli-French talks falter. D. E. Fink. Aviation W 92:21 F 2 '70
Stacking up arms as talk runs out. il Bsns W p38 S 19 '70
Two-way affair; U.S. action on Phantoms. il Newsweek 75:47 Mr 30 '70

Latin America
Generals sharpen their swords. il Bsns W p42 Je 6 '70

Libya
Leveling and balancing; purchase of Mirage jets from France. Nation 210:130-1 F 9 '70

South Africa
Arms for the Vorster gang? T. Beeson. Chr Cent 87:836 Jl 8 '70
Passage of arms; K. Kaunda's mission to the West. il por Newsweek 76:50 N 2 '70
Pesky questions; deals with Britain. il Newsweek 76:28+ Ag 3 '70

Spain
Loan approval delay caused U.S. to lose fighter order. E. H. Kolcum. Aviation W 92:20 Ap 13 '70
Spanish-Libyan mirage sale bolsters French industry. Aviation W 92:23-4 Ja 19 '70

PURCHASING, Municipal
Clarify before you buy; Hackensack, N.J. W. Fuhro. il Am City 85:82 Ja '70
We renovated stores and print-shop operations; Des Moines. K. G. Ibson. il Am City 85:116+ Mr '70
See also
Municipal contracts

PURDIE, Wendy Campbell-. See Campbell-Purdie, W.

PURDY, James
Short visits with five writers and one friend. B. Midwood. il pors Esquire 74:150-3 N '70 *

PURGATOIRE RIVER
Requiem for a small town; Sopris, Colo. N. Wood. il Am Heritage 22:62-7 D '70

PURGES, Russian. See Communist party (Russia)—Purges

PURIFICATION of water. See Water purification

PURINES
See also
Kinins

PURITAN revolution, 1642-1660. See Great Britain—History—Puritan revolution 1642-1660

PURITANS
Rituals, the revolt against the fixed smile; Time essay; Puritans opposition to Mary Mount maypole in 1627. M. Maddocks. il Time 96:42-3 O 12 '70
See also
Pilgrim fathers

PURKINJE cells. See Nerve cells

PURKYNÉ, Jan Evangelista
Purkyne symposium. C. D. Leake. Science 167:210+ Ja 9 '70

PURLIE; musical comedy. See Musical comedies, revues, etc.—Criticisms, plots, etc.

PURO, Louis
Cliff dwellers of Las Croabas. D. Butwin. il Sat R 53:43-5 D 12 '70 *

PURPLE martins. See Martins

PURPOSE of neighborhood youth corral. See New York (city)—Parks and playgrounds

PURSLANE
See also
Portulaca
Spring beauties

PURVES, Alan C.
Of behaviors, objectives, and English. il Engl J 59:793-7 S '70

PUSEY, Nathan Marsh
Enforced conformity; address, June 9, 1970. Vital Speeches 36:588-92 Jl 15 '70

about
End of a chapter. por Newsweek 75:67-8 Mr 2 '70 *
President bows out. por Time 95:63 Mr 2 '70 *
Voices of commencement. il por Time 95:44+ Je 22 '70 *

PUSH pin studios, inc.
Louvre holds retrospective of Push pin studio's graphics. il Pub W 197:70-2 Ap 13 '70

PUSHKIN, Aleksandr Sergeevich
Echo; poem. tr. by M. Mesic. Poetry 116:343 Ag '70
Pushkin, by H. Troyat. Review
Newsweek il por 76:125-6+ N 23 '70. S. K. Oberbeck *

PUSS-in-boots; drama. See Elfenbein, J. A.

PUSSYCAT league, inc. See Womens clubs and societies

PUT and call transactions
New pizzazz in puts and calls. il Bsns W p 108+ F 21 '70

PUTNAM, George
If the silent majority could talk, what would it say? T. Ferrell. pors Esquire 73:146-51+ My '70 *

PUTNAM, Howard
Campus unrest: its cause and cure. bibliog Sch & Soc 98:372-4 O '70

PUTNAM, Patrick F.
Cal cuts down the barberians. il Sports Illus 32:22-3 Je 29 '70
College football. Sports Illus 33:78+ S 21; 60+ O 12; 51-2 O 26 '70
Don't drink the water. il Sports Illus 33:8-13 Ag 3 '70
End of a season at Syracuse. il Sports Illus 33:22-3 S 28 '70
For Mexico (and the world) il pors Sports Illus 32:18-19 Ap 27 '70
Freshman and the great guru. il pors Sports Illus 32:28-31 Je 15 '70
Meet Michigan's meanest man. il por Sports Illus 33:32-3 N 16 '70
Message from Minnesota: three dots and a dash. il Sports Illus 33:28-30+ D 14 '70
No! Not John Smith! il pors Sports Illus 33:10-13 Jl 6 '70
One round of boxing was more than enough. il pors Sports Illus 33:20-1 N 30 '70
Sam Spade goes to the dogs. il Sports Illus 33:52-4+ Jl 20 '70

They don't play no mullets down there. il Sports Illus 33:20-5 N 2 '70
Track & field (title varies) il Sports Illus 32:54-6 F 9; 48-9 F 23; 52+ Mr 9; 64+ Mr 23; 57-8 My 4; 72-3 My 11; 50 Je 1; 33:48 Jl 27 '70
Week; college football. Sports Illus 33:68+ N 23 '70
Zut! We nearly got guillotined. il Sports Illus 33:18-19 Jl 20 '70

PUTNEY synthesizer. See Musical instruments, Electronic

PUZO, Mario
Wealthy father of The godfather; interview, ed. by G. Mandel. il pors Life 69:41-4 Jl 10 '70

PUZZLE; story. See Oates, J. C.

PUZZLES
Puzzling times; hottest-selling jigsaw series. il Newsweek 76:107 N 2 '70
See also
Crossword puzzles

PYGMALION; drama. See Shaw, G. B.

PYHRR, Peter A.
Zero-base budgeting. il Harvard Bsns R 48:111-21 N '70

PYLE, Robert M.
Death row. il Audubon 72:145 N '70

PYLE, Ted
Inner-tube dog boots. il Pop Mech 133:188 F '70

PYRAMID LAKE
Here in Nevada a terrible crime. A. M. Josephy, jr. il Am Heritage 21:93-100 Je '70
They're killing Pyramid lake! D. Lynch. il Field & S 74:10-15 Ja '70

PYRAMID publications, inc.
Election set at Pyramid, Grove arbitration ends. Pub W 197:129 Je 8 '70
Pyramid charged with unfair labor practices. Pub W 198:33 Jl 6 '70
Union election set at Grove, petition for vote at Pyramid. Pub W 197:36 My 4 '70

PYRAMIDS
Exploring pyramids using cosmic rays. il Chem 43:42-3 Jl '70
Search for hidden chambers in the pyramids; adaptation of address, April 30, 1969. L. W. Alvarez and others. bibliog il Science 167:832-9 F 6 '70

Construction
New theory of pyramid building; use of weight arm. O. Tellefsen. il Natur Hist 79:10-12+ N '70; Discussion. 79:8-10+ D '70
3,000 for the seesaw? theories of O. Tellefsen. il Newsweek 76:98 N 16 '70

PYRAMIDS, Mexican. See Indians of Mexico—Antiquities

PYRAZOLE
Alcohol oxidation in rats inhibited by pyrazole, oximes, and amides. D. Lester and G. D. Benson. bibliog il Science 169:282-4 Jl 17 '70
Pyrazole and induction of fatty liver by a single dose of ethanol. G. O. Bustos and others. bibliog il Science 168:1598-9 Je 26 '70

PYRIDINE aldoxime methiodide
Double antidote. Sci N 98:137 Ag 15 '70

PYRIDOXINE. See Vitamins—Vitamin B$_6$

PYRIMIDINE metabolism. See Metabolism

PYRIMIDINES
See also
Thymine

PYRITES
Acidic mine drainage: the rate-determining step. P. C. Singer and W. Stumm. bibliog il Science 167:1121-13 F 20 '70; Discussion. 169:98, 504 Jl 3, 31 '70
Pyrrhotites: stoichiometric compounds with composition $Fe_{n-1}S_n (n \geqslant 8)$ N. Morimoto and others. bibliog il Science 168:964-6 My 22 '70

PYROXENES
Compositional zoning and its significance in pyroxenes from three coarse-grained lunar samples. R. B. Hargraves and others. bibliog il Science 167:631-3 Ja 30 '70
Lunar clinopyroxenes: chemical composition, structural state, and texture. M. Ross and others. bibliog il Science 167:628-30 Ja 30 '70
Mössbauer effect and high-voltage electron microscopy of pyroxenes in type B samples. H. Fernández-Morán and others. bibliog il Science 167:686-8 Ja 30 '70

PYROXFERROITE. See Silicates

PYRRHOTITES. See Pyrites

PYSH, E. S.
Conformations at local energy minimums for gramicidin S: optical calculations. bibliog Science 167:290-2 Ja 16 '70

Q

QABUS bin Said, sultan of Muscat and Oman
Sultan's sulky son. il por Newsweek 76:37B
Ag 10 '70 *

al-QADDAFI, Muammar
Celebrating xenophobia. il Time 96:20 S 7
'70 *
Libya's lot: half a loaf. M. J. Kubic. por
Newsweek 76:38-9 S 7 '70 *
Political jack-in-the-box. por Time 97:21 Ja
11 '71
U.S. oil companies feel the heat. por Bsns
W p42-3 Je 13 '70 *

QASSIM, Faris
Fortunes of Hussein. Nation 212:38-9 Ja 11
'71

QUACKS and quackery
Facts on food quackery. il Good H 170:6 F '70
Green wrist mania; copper bracelet fad. il
Time 96:56 Jl 6 '70
How quackery thrives on the occult. F. G.
Loyd and T. Irwin. il Todays Health 48:
20-3+ N '70
Worst of the medical swindlers: the arthritis
quacks. L. David. Read Digest 96:98-102 Ja
'70

QUADRA, Juan Francisco de la Bodega y. See
Bodega y Quadra, J. F. de la

QUAIDE, William, and others
Impact metamorphism of lunar surface materials. bibliog il Science 167:671-2 Ja 30 '70

QUAIL shooting
Be your own bird dog. D. Klepper. il Field
& S 75:46-7+ S '70
Mountains of home. C. Conley. il Field & S
75:66-7+ Je '70

QUAILS
California quail, hurry-scurry bird. G. B. Hel-
geland. il Nat Wildlife 8:20-20B O '70
If you kill Arizona's rarest bird, please re-
port at once; masked bobwhite quails. B.
Gilbert. il Sports Illus 33:85-7 N 16 '70
Pineal function and oviposition in Japanese
quail: superior cervical ganglionectomy and
photoperiod. C. L. Ralph and others. bib-
liog il Science 170:995-7 N 27 '70
See also
Cookery—Game

QUAKER action group. See Friends, Society of

QUAKERS. See Friends, Society of

**QUALIFICATIONS of librarians. See Librar-
ians—Qualifications**

**QUALIFICATIONS of teachers. See Teachers—
Qualifications**

QUALITY control
Some variable costs of ownership: repairs,
insurance, warranties; your new car. il
Consumer Rep 35:201-4 Ap 1 '70

QUALITY of products
Better appliance servicing wanted! Consumer
Bul 53:13-14 O '70
Buying guide issues, 1969-70. il Consumer
Rep 34:1-448 D '69; 35:1-439 D '70
Crushing cost of consumerism; comments of
members of the Presidents' panel. G. R.
Rosen. il Duns 95:36-7 Ap '70
GH consumer panel: how women feel about
the products they buy. il Good H 171:179-
80 O '70
Government test data are no buyer's guide.
Bsns W p26 O 31 '70
History's fourth turning point; address,
February 11, 1970. T. R. Reid. Vital
Speeches 36:369-72 Ap 1 '70
Institute report. See issues of Good house-
keeping
Let the buyer be aware; untested new prod-
ucts. A. R. Roalman. il Todays Health 48:
66-7+ Mr '70
Nothing works anymore. D. Sanford. il New
Repub 162:21-4 F 14 '70
Signs of quality in clothing. il Good H 170:
209 Mr '70
Speaker for the house. C. Montgomery. See
issues of Good housekeeping
See also
Quality control
United States—National commission on pro-
duct safety

QUALSET, C. O. and others
Mutation in internode length affects wheat
plant-type. bibliog il Science 169:1090-1 S 11
'70

**QUANTITATIVE method. See Statistical meth-
ods**

QUANTUM electrodynamics
Can equations of motion be used in high-
energy physics? P. A. M. Dirac. por Phys
Today 23:29-31 Ap '70

**QUANTUM mechanical tunneling. See Tunnel-
ing (physics)**

QUANTUM mechanics. See Quantum theory

QUANTUM theory
Chemistry by computer. A. C. Wahl. il Sci
Am 222:54-8+ bibliog(p 130) Ap '70
Quantum mechanics and reality; dilemma
of indeterminism. B. S. DeWitt. bibliog il
Phys Today 23:30-5 S '70
Three steps in the structure of matter. V. F.
Weisskopf. il por Phys Today 23:17-22+ S
'70
See also
Energy levels (quantum mechanics)
Parity nonconservation
Regge trajectories
Relativity (physics)
Statistical mechanics

QUARANTINE
Puzzle on toxicity; effect of lunar soil on
earth bacteria. Sci N 97:243 Mr 7 '70
U.S. weighs astronaut quarantine. Aviation
W 92:49-50 Je 29 '70

QUARKS. See Particles (nuclear physics)

QUARRELS
Family that fights together...fights togeth-
er. J. Viorst. Redbook 135:61+ Ag '70;
Same abr. Read Digest il 97:89-91 N '70
How to settle children's squabbles. M. R.
Weisbord. il Parents Mag 45:38-9+ Ja '70
How to stop a fight without really trying;
quarrels among brothers and sisters. H.
G. Ginott. McCalls 97:54+ F '70
When toddlers act up. C. Hotelling. il Parents
Mag 45:64-5+ Mr '70

QUARRIES and quarrying
How to doctor a quarry for landfill; Mont-
gomery County, Pa. J. A. McHenry. il Am
City 85:38 D '70

QUARRY, Jerry
Gimmick for boxing: Caucasian charisma.
J. Flaherty. pors Life 68:12 Je 12 '70 *
Return of the ringmaster. il pors Time 96:35
N 9 '70 *
Smashing return of the old Ali. M. Kram. il
pors Sports Illus 33:18-19 N 2 '70 *

QUARTERBACKS. See Football players

QUARTERMAIN, David, and others
Amnesia produced by electroconvulsive shock
or cycloheximide: conditions for recovery.
bibliog il Science 169:683-6 Ag 14 '70

QUARTETS, String. See String quartets

**QUARTETS, Vocal.   See Choral groups and
societies**

**QUARTIER de la Défense. See Paris—Metro-
politan district**

QUARTZ
Iron in synthetic quartz: heat and radiation
induced changes. A. J. Cohen and F. Hassan. bibliog il Science 167:176-7 Ja 9 '70
Quartz: preferred orientation in rocks produced by Dauphiné twinning. J. Tullis.
bibliog il Science 168:1342-4 Je 12 '70
See also
Chalcedony

QUASARS
Crowded galaxy; study of Seyfert galaxies.
il Sci N 97:552 Je 6 '70
Galaxies and quasars: puzzling observations
and bizarre theories. R. W. Holcomb. Science 167:1601-3 Mr 20 '70

Spectra

Absorption lines of quasi-stellar objects. E.
M. Burbidge and C. R. Lynds. il Sci Am
223:22-9 D '70

QUASISTELLAR objects. See Quasars

**QUATERNARY period.   See Paleobotany—
Quaternary; Paleontology—Quaternary**

QUAYLE, Theraid P.
Individualized science for the slow learner. il
Todays Ed 59:50-1 Mr '70

QUEBEC (city)
Quebec: old world flavor. J. Coyle. il Travel
& Camera 33:63 Je '70

QUEBEC (province)
Quebec: the pains of progress. il Newsweek
76:42-3 N 2 '70
See also
Insurance, Health—Quebec (province)
Longueuil

Nationalism

Terror in Quebec. America 123:366-7 N 7 '70
Testing of Pierre Trudeau. T. Buckley. il
pors N Y Times Mag p50-1+ D 6 '70
See also
Front for the liberation of Quebec

Politics and government

No to separatism. Time 95:47 My 11 '70
Pierre Trudeau's legal overkill. P. Freiberg.
Commonweal 93:292-4 D 18 '70
Quebec puts separatism to a vote. Bsns W
p48+ Ap 25 '70

QUEBEC (province)—Politics and government
—*Continued*
Temporary reprieve. il por Newsweek **75:**
60-1 My 11 '70
While Canada waited; National union party
tactics. M. M. Dorcy. America 122:525-6 My
16 '70
World around us. C. de Mestral. Chr Cent
87:772. 1495-7 Je 17. D 9 '70

Religious institutions and affairs
World around us (cont) Chr Cent 87:404-5.
878 Ap 1. Jl 15 '70
QUEBEC joinder. See Northeastern forest fire
protection compact
QUEBEC liberation front. See Front for the
liberation of Quebec
QUEEN, Errol J.
Burning out your circuits without really try-
ing. il Pop Electr 32:71 My '70
QUEEN, I.
Build: Zener power box. il Radio-Electr 41:
78-9 Jl '70
QUEEN Anne furniture. See Furniture, English
QUEEN Elizabeth (ship) See Ocean liners
QUEEN Elizabeth hotel, Montreal. See Mon-
treal—Hotels, restaurants, etc.
QUEEN Mary (ship) See Ocean liners
QUEEN'S gallery. See London—Galleries and
museums
QUEENSLAND, Australia

Industries
Our far-flung correspondents. J. Colebrook.
New Yorker 46:70+ S 5 '70
QUENNELL, Peter
Ugly, affected, disgusting fellow. il pors
Horizon 12:82-7 Sum '70
QUESTER, George H.
India contemplates the bomb. Bul Atom Sci
26:13-16+ Ja '70
Paris, Pretoria, Peking. . . proliferation? Bul
Atom Sci 26:12-16 O '70
Wars prolonged by misunderstood signals.
bibliog f Ann Am Acad 392:30-9 N '70
QUESTIONNAIRES
Drugs/teens=alcohol/parents; designing stu-
dent questionnaire. T. Lawrence and J. Vel-
leman. il pors Sci Digest 68:46-8+ O '70
Half million older Americans to tell needs in
September forums. Aging 190:3 Ag '70
Selecting the questions to be asked in sur-
veys. N. M. Bradburn. Mo Labor R 93:
27-9 Ja '70
What did he mean by etc? G. B. Harrison. il
Pub W 197:55-7 Ja 19 '70
QUETICO-Superior country. See Wilderness
areas—Minnesota
QUICHE. See Cookery, French
QUICHE Lorraine. See Cookery—Cheese
QUICK, John
Two players in the E-day action. il pors
Bsns W p30 Ap 25 '70 *
QUICK-witted Jack; drama. See Feather. J.
QUIGLEY, Carroll
Our ecological crisis. Cur Hist 59:1-12 Jl '70
QUIGLEY, Thomas E.
Repression in Brazil: protest vs. protocol.
Commonweal 93:366 Ja 15 '71
Students who came to dinner. Commonweal
91:470-1 Ja 30 '70
QUIHUIS, Lelia La Vine
Mormon items. il Hobbies 75:48-9 Ag '70
QUILLWORK. See Paper work
QUILTS
Create a quilt, big or little! il Good H 170:
110-11 F '70
See also
Coverlets
QUINACRINE. See Atabrine
QUINCY, Ill.
American city awards bring added honors.
il Am City 85:92+ Je '70
QUINCY, Mass.
Housing
Needed: more housing for the elderly. B.
Baharian. il por Am City 85:91-2 Ap '70
QUI NHON riot. See Vietnam (Republic)—
Riots
QUINLIVAN, Francis John
New American dream for blacks. America
122:498-9 My 9 '70
QUINN, John R. bp
Right to live. America 123:56-7 Ag 8 '70
QUINN, John Robert
Old man mowing graves; poem. Chr Cent 87:
568 My 6 '70
QUINONES
See also
Naphthoquinone

QUINTUPLETS
Fertility. il Newsweek 75:45 Mr 9 '70
Kienast quints. A. Lake. il Good H 171:84-
9+ S '70
QUIRK, John J. See Carey, J. W. jt. auth.
QUISLINGS. See Traitors
QUIZZES. See Information tests
QUOTAS, Immigration. See Immigration and
emigration—United States
QUOTAS, Import. See Import quotas
QUOTATION
See also
Plagiarism
QUOTATIONS
ITQ to match Roget. il Pub W 198:142-3 Jl
13 '70
Of deathless remarks; inaccuracy and incor-
rect sources of great sayings. R. Hanser.
il Am Heritage 21:54-9 Je '70
Quotable quotes. See Issues of Reader's di-
gest
See also subhead Quotations, maxims, etc
under various subjects, e.g. Fishing—Quota-
tions, maxims, etc.

Anecdotes, facetiae, satire, etc.
Well, I'll be damned! L. Rosten. Look 34:
16 F 10 '70

R

RAF. See Great Britain—Royal air force
RATE (Romero aid to elderly) project. See
Volunteer service
RBPD. See Association of American publish-
ers—Religious book publishing division
RCA corporation
Bob Sarnoff runs a new game. il pors Bsns
W p84-5+ Ja 24 '70
RCA fires a broadside at no. 1. il Bsns W p82-
3 S 19 '70

ServiceAmerica division
RCA's ServiceAmerica. W. A. Stocklin. Electr
World 84:7 Ag '70
ServiceAmerica and the independent. J. Frye.
Electr World 84:51-2 N '70
RDF (radio direction finders) See Radio in
navigation
REA express, Inc.
REA rides again on a new track. il Bsns W
p34-5 Ja 2 '71
REA tries to avoid Penn central route. Bsns
W p39 Je 27 '70
Survival of REA depends on results of CAB
probe. Aviation W 93:133 O 26 '70
REAT (radiological emergency assistance
teams) See Radioactivity—Safety devices
and measures
RFE. See Radio free Europe
RFI (radio frequency interference) See Radio
interference
RIF (Reading is FUN-damental) program. See
Childrens reading
RLDS. See Reorganized church of Jesus Christ
of Latter day saints
RNA
Aurintricarboxylic acid and initiation factors
of wheat embryo. A. Marcus and others.
bibliog il Science 167:1735-6 Mr 27 '70
Bacteriophage induced transfer RNA in
echerichia coli. V. Daniel and others. bibliog il Science 167:1682-8 Mr 27 '70
Cytokinin activity of ureidopurine derivatives related to a modified nucleoside found
in transfer RNA. W. H. Dyson and others. bibliog il Science 170:328-30 O 16 '70
Eukaryotes versus prokaryotes: an estimate
of evolutionary distance. P. J. McLaughlin
and M. O. Dayhoff. bibliog il Science 168:
1469-71 Je 19 '70
Extinction in goldfish: facilitation by intracranial injection of RNA from brains of
extinguished donors. W. G. Braud. biblog
il Science 168:1234-6 Je 5 '70
Homologous viral interference: induction by
RNA from defective particles of vesicular
stomatitis virus. T. Sreevalsan. bibliog il
Science 169:991-3 S 4 '70
Mediation of immunity to tumor isografts
in mice by heterologous ribonucleic acid.
K. P. Ramming and Y. H. Pilch. bibliog
il Science 168:492-3 Ap 24 '70
Mitochondrial RNA synthesis during mitosis.
H. Fan and S. Penman. bibliog il Science
168:135-8 Ap 3 '70

RNA—*Continued*

Nucleic acid structure function relations; United States-Japan science cooperation seminar. R. M. Bock. Science 170:351+ O 16 '70

Nucleotide sequence of an RNA from cells infected with adenovirus 2. K. Ohe and S. M. Weissman. bibliog il Science 167:879-81 F 6 '70

5S RNA synthesized by escherichia coli in presence of chloramphenicol: different 5'-terminal sequences. B. G. Forget and B. Jordan. bibliog il Science 167:382-4 Ja 23 '70

Ribonuclease V of escherichia coli: susceptibility of heated ribosomal RNA and stability of R17 phage RNA. M. Kuwano and others. bibliog il Science 168:1225-6 Je 5 '70

Secondary structure of ribosomal RNA. K. A. Hartman and G. J. Thomas, jr. bibliog il Science 170:740-1 N 13 '70

Structure of RNA in ribosomes. K. A. Hartman and others. bibliog il Science 170:171-3 O 9 '70

Triumph for a heretic. il Newsweek 76:56-7 Jl 20 '70

Trouble on the DNA front. bibliog il Chem 43:24-5 O '70

Two way street for genetics; RNA-to-DNA inversion. Sci N 98:54 Jl 25 '70

Undogmatic dogma; transfer from RNA to DNA. Sci Am 223:44 N '70

Upsetting dogma. il por Time 96:57 Jl 20 '70

Upstart RNA. Sci Am 223:82 S '70

See also
Poly I:C

RNA polymerase. See Polymerase

RNA tumor forming viruses. See Tumor viruses

ROTC. See United States—Reserve officers training corps

RTSRL. See American library association—Social responsibilities of libraries round table

RA (boat)

Life and death of the good ship Ra. N. Baker. il por Sports Illus 32:66-8+ Ap 20 '70

RA expedition, 1969

Life and death of the good ship Ra. N. Baker. il por Sports Illus 32:66-8+ Ap 20 '70

RA expedition, 1970

Heyerdahl's voyage: modern sea epic. il por U S News 69:49 Jl 27 '70

Once again for Ra. il Sci N 97:480 My 16 '70

Second time success. il Sci N 98:61 Jl 25 '70

RAAB, Earl

Deadly innocences of American Jews. Commentary 50:31-9 D '70

—See Lipset, S. M. jt. auth.

RA'ANAN, Uri

Chinese factionalism and Sino-Soviet relations. Cur Hist 59:134-41 S '70

RABB, Bert

Make mine manual. Hi Fi 20:secI 59 Ap '70

RABBIS

See also
Tanenbaum, M. H.
Women as rabbis

RABBIT cages. See Cages

RABBIT hunting

Hunting the desert cottontail. B. Milek. il Field & S 75:42-3+ S '70

Merry marathoner. B. Geagan. il Field & S 74:44-5+ Ja '70

Old-road rabbits. R. M. Gooch. il Outdoor Life 146:58-9+ D '70

Prairie cottontails. D. Pryce. il por Outdoor Life 146:88-9+ O '70

Uncle Wesley pulls his purse. R. Starnes. Field & S 74:6+ F '70

RABBITS

Amazing cottontail. J. D. Scott. il Nat Wildlife 9:20+ D '70

Cottontail rabbit facts. P. M. Kelsey. Cons 24:33 Ap '70

See also
Cookery—Game
Hares

RABBITS who changed their minds; drama. See Miller, H. L.

RABELAIS; drama. See Barrault, J. L.

RABENHORST, David W.

Super flywheel to power zero-emission car. A. P. Armagnac. il Pop Sci 197:41-3+ Ag '70 *

Wind up car. K. Hohenemser and J. McCaull. il Environ 12:14-21+ Je '70 *

RABIDEAU, S. W. and Florin, A. E.

Anomalous water: characterization by physical methods. bibliog il Science 169:48-52 Jl 3 '70

RABIES

How Matt survived rabies; case of Matthew Winkler. il Newsweek 77:59 Ja 4 '71

Recovery from rabies? il Time 97:31-2 Ja 11 '71

RABIES vaccine

Truth about rabies. D. L. Lidster. Bet Hom & Gard 48:39 S '70

RABIN, Yitzhak

Rabin line. por Newsweek 76:29 D 28 '70 *

RABINOVE, Samuel

Everybody's business, and nobody's. Chr Cent 87:843-6 Jl 8 '70

RABINOWITCH, Eugene

Jensen vs. Lewontin; a comment. Bul Atom Sci 26:25-6 My '70

On the Sochi conference. il Bul Atom Sci 26:18-24 Ap '70

On the threshold of a new decade: thoughts for 1970. il por Bul Atom Sci 26:2-3+ F '70

Twenty-five years later. il por Bul Atom Sci 26:4-6+ Je '70

RABINOWITZ, Dorothy

Activist cleric. Commentary 50:81-3 S; 28 D '70

Radicalized professor: a portrait. Commentary 50:62-4 Jl; 20 S '70

RACCOON hunting

Saddleback Bigs. L. Mueller. il Field & S 75:78-9+ My '70

Westward the raccoon. J. Stagg. il por Outdoor Life 145:56-7+ Mr '70

RACE, Walking. See Walking

RACE attitudes

Discussion effects on racial attitudes. D. G. Myers and G. D. Bishop. bibliog il Science 169:778-9 Ag 21 '70

On campus: the crisis is consciousness; University of Texas colloquium on race feelings. M. P. O'Malley. Mlle 71:48 My '70

RACE cooperation. See Interracial cooperation

RACE differences. See Racial differences

RACE discrimination

Daily irritations; black man in America. il Time 95:74+ Ap 6 '70

Eye of the storm; learning to understand race discrimination; Riceville, Ia. elementary school experiment. J. Leonard. il Life 68:16 My 8 '70

I didn't know it felt that way; project Understanding discrimination; by elementary school in Evanston, Ill. L. S. Wilson. il PTA Mag 64:20-2 Je '70

Most precious resource; Riceville, Ia. school experiment. J. Lear. Sat R 53:57 Je 6 '70

New legal weapon for blacks: monetary damages for racial discrimination. A. W. Brown, jr. Trans-Action 7:4-5 Je '70

Pigskin justice and Mormon theology. Chr Cent 87:67 Ja 21 '70

Terry funeral, America 122:30 Ja 17 '70

Who am I? The Indian sickness; the White Hawk case. R. Bongartz. Nation 210:496-8 Ap 27 '70

See also
Discrimination in education
Discrimination in employment
Discrimination in housing
International day for the elimination of racial discrimination
Negroes—Segregation
Race prejudice

RACE horses

Boom in British horses. J. Ross-Skinner. il Duns 97:44-6+ Ja '71

Commander may trail in Pimlico dust. W. Tower. Sports Illus 32:60+ My 18 '70

Even the very best can blunder; Nijinsky's defeat. W. Tower. il Sports Illus 33:56-8 O 26 '70

Happiness boys at the track; administering undetectable tranquilizer to horses. R. H. Boyle. il Sports Illus 33:20-1 O 12 '70

Horse for all seasons; 1970 horse of the year. Newsweek 76:94+ D 14 '70

In California: a colt to keep an eye on; Terlago. A. Wright. il Sports Illus 32:25 Ap 6 '70

Jacobs legacy. P. Axthelm. il por Newsweek 76:61 Ag 24 '70

Marlu has a bit of trouble. W. F. Reed. il por Sports Illus 33:22-3 Ag 24 '70

Merchandise is horses. P. Ryan. il pors Sports Illus 32:34-6+ Mr 23 '70

Mike and this horse needed each other. W. Tower. il pors Sports Illus 32:22-7 My 11 '70

Nijinsky, the $5,440,000 wonder horse. G. F. T. Ryall. il Vogue 156:158-61+ D '70

Nijinsky's last dance. il por Newsweek 76:73-4 O 19 '70

RACE horses—*Continued*
One more winner for the Derby list: Native Royalty. W. Tower. il Sports Illus 32:93-4 Ap 13 '70
Pick 'em with a pin, and don't give up on the office pool; Kentucky Derby hopefuls. W. Tower. il Sports Illus 32:24-6+ Ap 27 '70
Playing the horse market. W. Tower. il Sports Illus 33:48-9 Ag 24 '70
Plenty Old, but little else; Derby crop. W Tower. il Sports Illus 32:56 Mr 9 '70
Race track. A. Minor. See issues of New Yorker
Smiling through at (S)Miles park. J. Mann. il Look 34:46-9 Ag 11 '70
Sonny sniffs a derby, Silent Screen to Churchill Downs. W. Tower. il por Sports Illus 32:10-11+ F 16 '70
Super horse goes out to pasture; Dr Fager. B. Surface. il Read Digest 96:187-8+ Ap '70
This horse needed his owner's stamina; Silent Screen. W. F. Reed. il Sports Illus 32: 26-7 My 11 '70

RACE prejudice
How racists use science to degrade black people. C. T. Rowan. il por Ebony 25:31-4+ My '70
On stinging the ethnics. Chr Cent 87:1031 S 2 '70
    See also
Anti-Semitism
Negroes—Segregation
Racism

    Anecdotes, facetiae, satire, etc.
Parting shots; prejudice among the penguins. il Life 68:77-80 My 1 '70

RACE problems
Race and the schools; Syracuse report. il Newsweek 76:80 O 19 '70
    See also
Business and race problems
Church and race problems
Intermarriage of races
Interracial cooperation
Minorities
Race discrimination
Race relations
    also subhead Race problems under names of continents, countries, etc. e.g. South Africa—Race problems

RACE relations
Booker T. Washington in biographical perspective. L. R. Harlan. bibliog f Am Hist R 75:1581-99 O '70
Boondocks jail the future; Homer, La. N. C. Chriss. il Nation 211:495-6 N 16 '70
Can we make peace inside the United States? friction in high schools. D. Lawrence. U S News 69:92 D 7 '70
Cities: York's charrette. il Time 95:40 My 11 '70
Education in tandem: white liberal, black militant. R. Ruether. America 122:582-4 My 30 '70
Failure of black separatism. B. Rustin. il Harper 240:25-32+ Ja '70; Same abr. with title What black revolution? Cur 116:19-33 Mr '70; Discussion. Harper 240:6+ Ap '70
Growing up liberal in Atlanta. I. Allen, jr. il por N Y Times Mag p4-5+ D 27 '70 •
Humanistic tradition of Afro-American literature; address, July 2, 1970. M. Walker. il Am Lib 1:849-54 O '70
Interpreting collective violence: an argument for the importance of social structure. A. D. Grimshaw. bibliog f Ann Am Acad 391:9-20 S '70
Journey through two Americas; exploring black-white relations in Dorchester-Mattapan, Mass. Greene County, Ala. and Wichita, Kan. J. Cook and P. Hathaway. il Time 95:30+ Ap 6 '70
Melting pot: its most difficult test; the immigrant within; excerpts from The American people, with paintings by J. Lawrence. B. A. Weisberger. il Am Heritage 22:32-9+ D '70
My children have a right to feel proud. D. Gilliam. por Redbook 135:62+ Ag '70
Negro dilemma; concerning introduction to second edition of Beyond the melting pot by N. Glazer and Daniel P. Moynihan. F. S. Meyer. Nat R 22:898 Ag 25 '70
New American dream for blacks. F. J. Quinlivan. America 122:498-9 My 9 '70
Other voices, other strategies; interviews, ed. by W. Terry. J. Bond; B. Seale; W. Young, jr. il pors Time 95:23-4+ Ap 6 '70
Real anger was backstage; racial tensions during shooting of Halls of anger. B. Schulberg. il por Life 69:50-2+ Ag 21 '70

Sensitizing modules; making high school seniors aware of ghetto problems. S. S. Simon. il Schol Teach Jr/Sr High p28-9+ S 21 '70
Sister debates a brother on that black man-white woman thing; interviews, ed. by K. Mehlinger. L. Gant; D. K. Davis. il pors Ebony 25:130-3 Ag '70
Strategy for the seventies: unity, coalition, negotiation; address, July 19, 1970. W. M. Young, jr. Vital Speeches 36:732-6 S 15 '70
Suburbia reaches out; race relations program of Mt Lebanon, Pa. schools. V. A. Elliott. Engl J 59:660-4+ My '70
Teach it like it is: a stimulating game; city simulation. W. F. Harlan. Engl J 59:1146-9 N '70
U.S. journal: Luverne, Ala. G. T. Miller's plan to help Crenshaw County despite trouble with the Klan. C. Trillin. New Yorker 46:53-8 Ag 29 '70
Values as social indicators of poverty and race relations in America. M. Rokeach and S. Parker. bibliog f il Ann Am Acad 388:97-111 Mr '70
Violence in the factories. il Newsweek 75:66-7 Je 29 '70
Violent black minority. A. Hacker. il N Y Times Mag p25+ My 10; 12 My 24 '70
Walk-in exposure projects in the ghetto. M. Maruyama. Ment Hy 54:261-70 Ap '70
What now? address, July 2, 1970. J. Bond. Am Lib 1:847-8 O '70
Which way black America? Separation? Integration? Liberation? il Ebony 25:35-8+ Ag '70
White faces and white studies; courses in Afro-American history. S. Synnestvedt. Commonweal 92:182-3 My 8 '70
    See also
Black power
Interracial cooperation

    Anecdotes, facetiae, satire, etc.
Confessions of a white racist. L. L. King. il Harper 240:63-6+ Ja '70

RACE tracks
Bill Veeck is off to the races; president of Suffolk Downs. L. Merchant. il pors Look 34:68+ Je 30 '70
Delayed start, but no housing project, strike of mutuel clerks at Santa Anita park. A. Wright. il Sports Illus 32:12-13 F 16 '70
Johnny is in *agua* hot; Caliente racetrack director. A. Wright. il pors Sports Illus 33: 50-2+ Ag 3 '70
Little Joe on the big Red mile. W. F. Reed. il por Sports Illus 53:58+ O 19 '70
Season at Saratoga. J. Flaherty. il Life 69:12 Ag 21 '70
Smiling through at (S)Miles park. J. Mann. il Look 34:46-9 Ag 11 '70
Unusual twist; battle for Roosevelt raceway. il Forbes 106:43-4 S 15 '70
    See also
Speedways

    Lighting
This lighting project makes good horsesense; Hollywood park race track, Inglewood, Calif. il Am City 85:124 Mr '70

RACE walking. See Walking

RACEMIZATION
Marine sediments: dating by the racemization of amino acids. J. L. Bada and others. bibliog il Science 170:730-2 N 13 '70

RACHLEFF, Owen S.
Druids of Gaul. il Opera N 34:8-12 Ap 4 '70

RACHMANINOFF, Sergei
Records:
    Bells. Opera N 34:35 F 28 '70 •

RACIAL attitudes. See Race attitudes

RACIAL differences
Intelligence and race. W. F. Bodmer and L. L. Cavalli-Sforza. il Sci Am 223:19-29 bibliog(p 144) O '70
Jensenism: variation on a racial theme. J. Neary. il pors Life 68:58B-58D+ Je 12 '70
NAS again says no to Shockley. L. J. Carter. Science 168:685 My 8 '70

RACIAL discrimination. See Race discrimination

RACIAL extinction. See Genocide

RACINE, Jean Baptiste
Bérénice. Criticism
    New Yorker 46:98+ Je 13 '70

RACING. See Automobile racing; Bicycle racing; Horse racing; and similar headings

RACING accidents. See Automobile racing—Accidents and injuries

RACING car drivers. See Automobile racing drivers

RACING car engines. See Automobile engines

RACING car models. See Automobile models

RADIATION sickness
  Final sequel to the Lucky Dragon. il UNESCO
    Courier 23:9-10 N '70
    See also
  Atomic bomb casualty commission
RADIATION standards. See Radiation—Safety
    devices and measures
RADIATOR caps, Automobile. See Automobiles
    —Equipment
RADIATOR ornaments, Automobile. See Auto-
    mobiles—Equipment
RADIATORS, Automobile. See Automobile en-
    gines—Radiators
RADICAL left. See Right and left (political
    science)
RADICAL liberal (term)
  Politics and the name game; Time essay. M.
    Ways. il por Time 96:14-15 N 2 '70
RADICAL party. See Political parties—France
RADICAL right. See Right and left (political
    science)
RADICAL right (politics) See Right and left
    (political science)
RADICAL theology. See Theology
RADICALISM. See Right and left (political
    science)
RADICALS (chemistry)
  Free radicals in biological systems. W. A.
    Pryor. il Sci Am 223:70-6+ bibliog(p 128)
    Ag '70
RADICALS, Student. See Student militants
RADICALS and radicalism. See Right and left
    (political science)
RADIO
                History
  Question of semantics; invention of radio. F.
    Shunaman. il por Pop Electr 33:27-30 O '70
RADIO advertising
  Mammon tabernacle choir; jingles of Pepper
    & Tanner. Time 96:42+ D 21 '70
    See also
  Cigarettes—Advertising

              Cigarettes
    See Cigarettes—Advertising
RADIO aids to navigation. See Radio in navi-
    gation
RADIO alarms. See Burglar alarms
RADIO amateurs. See Radio operators, Amateur
RADIO amplifiers. See Amplifiers
RADIO antennas
  Death of Midway's antennas. H. I. Fisher. il
    Audubon 72:62-3 Ja '70
  1-2-3-4 on a mast; minimum space, multi-
    band ham antenna. il Pop Electr 33:27-30
    Ag '70
  Vertical SWL antenna, Mosley SWV-7. il Pop
    Electr 32:67-8 My '70
RADIO apparatus
  Build an SCA adapter for FM reception. V.
    Wood. il Pop Electr 33:53+ D '70
  Build the liberator; pocket-size induction
    receiver, or audio transformer. C. P.
    Troemel. il Pop Electr 33:49-52+ D '70
  New products. See issues of Popular elec-
    tronics
    See also
  Microphones
              Medical use
    See Radio in medicine
RADIO apparatus industry
    See also
  Radio shack corporation
RADIO apparatus on aircraft. See Airplanes—
    Radio equipment
RADIO apparatus on ships, boats, etc.
  Marine electronics; power & sail. il Motor
    B 125:93-9 My '70
RADIO apparatus on space vehicles. See Space
    vehicles—Radio equipment
RADIO astronomy
  Astronomy for accuracy. D. E. Thomsen. il
    Sci N 97:512-13 My 23 '70
  Curving universe; survey of radio sources.
    il Sci N 98:200-1 S 5 '70
  Galaxies and quasars: puzzling observations
    and bizarre theories. R. W. Holcomb. Sci-
    ence 167:1601-3 Mr 20 '70
  Interstellar molecules: chemicals in the sky.
    G. L. Wick. Science 170:149-50 O 9 '70
  More interstellar chemistry. Sci Am 222:49+
    Je '70
  Radio astronomy. M. Parris. il Space World
    G-4-76:32-41 Ap '70
  Radio test of relativity. Sky & Tel 40:138
    S '70
  Trying to confirm Weber waves. il Sci N 98:
    366 N 7 '70

X-ray survey of Centaurus A. E. T. Byram
  and others. bibliog il Science 169:366-8 Jl
  24 '70
  See also
Pulsars
Radio telescopes
RADIO beacons
  California sets beacon standards; aircraft
    rescue beacons. N. S. Himmel. Aviation
    W 92:68 Ap 13 '70
RADIO broadcasting

            Conversation programs
  Town meeting is not dead, it's alive and
    well on radio; over-the-air telephone con-
    versations. M. McEachern. il Todays Health
    48:32-3+ Jl '70

            Frequency modulation
    See Radio frequency modulation

            Frequency standards
    See Frequency standards

                History
  Radio. il Sr Schol 97:17 N 16 '70
  Second half century of radio. R. L. Tobin.
    Sat R 54:39-40 Ja 9 '71

                Humor
  Good sports; Boston's WBZ radio's Sports
    huddle. il Newsweek 76:53 O 26 '70

            International aspects
  Selling old news to radio stations; Voices
    across the world program. Bsns W p 134
    My 23 '70
              Licenses
    See Radio laws and regulations

              Moral aspects
  Interest on four-letter words; FCC decision
    against WUHY-FM. R. L. Shayon. Sat R
    53:50 My 2 '70

            Multiplex system
  New IC multiplex detector. K. F. Buegel. il
    Radio-Electr 41:33-5 Mr '70
  QUART, new three, four channel stereo;
    quadrature ambience with reference tone.
    M. Gerzon. il Radio-Electr 41:52-3+ D '70
  Simple SCA adapter; FM music sans com-
    mercials. W. F. Splichal, jr. il Pop Electr
    32:49-52 Je '70
  Stereo multiplex FM in 1970 cars. L. Allen.
    il Radio-Electr 41:61+ Je '70

                Music
  Country music gets soul; L. Martell at the
    Grand ole opry. il pors Ebony 25:66-8+
    Mr '70
  On the off-beat; Free music store, series of
    concerts on New York's FM radio station
    WBAI A. Rich. il Hi Fi 20:secl1 10 Ap '70
  Rock and roll Muzak; Bill Drake sound. il
    por Newsweek 75:85 Mr 9 '70
    See also
  Broadcast music, inc.

                News
  Atlanta's dynamic duo; news reporters for
    radio station WRNG. T. Levison and M.
    Silverstein. pors Time 95:73 My 4 '70
  Selling old news to radio stations; Voices
    across the world program. Bsns W p 134
    My 23 '70
                Operas
  Big broadcast; Metropolitan opera intermis-
    sion features. il Opera N 34:14-15 Ap 18
    '70
  Forty-year man; voice of opera. M. Cross.
    il pors Opera N 35:8-11 D 5 '70
  Texaco-Metropolitan opera radio network. il
    Opera N 35:12-13 D 5 '70

              Political use
    See Radio in politics

                Programs
  Iowa Sixty plus radio program now aired in
    eight states. il Aging 188:18 Je '70
  Marathon; War and peace to be read over
    WBAI radio. Newsweek 76:58 D 7 '70
  Radio. il Sr Schol 97:17 N 16 '70
  Tokyo TV records program at Iowa Dial-a-
    listener project. il Aging 191:18 S '70
    See also
  Radio broadcasting—Public service programs

              Propaganda
    See also
  Radio free Europe

RADIO broadcasting—*Continued*

Public service programs

Political schick; the Lyons radio program. J. Deedy. Commonweal 92:106 Ap 17 '70

Religious programs

Attraction of Adventism. D. Kucharsky. Chr Today 14:35 Ja 30 '70
Fairness doctrine: a stricter proposal. G. Everett. Chr Today 14:32 Jl 3 '70
God-hucksters of radio. W. C. Martin. il Atlan 225:51-6 Je '70
Problems and prospects of evangelical radio. W. R. Wineke. Chr Today 15:3-5 Ja 1 '71
Religious radio 1921-1971. Chr Today 15:5-6 Ja 1 '71
See also
Far East broadcasting company

Short wave

See Radio broadcasting, Short wave

Social aspects

Ellen Straus: the action of Call for action. il pors Vogue 155:124-5 Je '70

Stereophonic transmission

Four-channel stereo FM, from one station; quadriphonic sound. J. P. Meute. il Hi Fi 20:secI 72-3 Mr '70

Time signals

See Time signals, Radio

Far East

See also
Far East broadcasting company

United States

Radio-downhill all the way; views of G. Klavan. Nation 212:5 Ja 4 '71
Second half century of radio. R. L. Tobin. Sat R 54:39-40 Ja 9 '71
See also
United States—Federal communications commission
Westinghouse broadcasting company

Vatican

See Vatican—Radio stations

RADIO broadcasting, Short wave
English language news broadcasts: tables (cont of) English language broadcasts to North America. R. Legge. See issues of Popular electronics to August 1970

RADIO broadcasting, Stereophonic. See Radio broadcasting—Stereophonic transmission

RADIO broadcasting and Negroes
Down to fundamentals; question of WMUU's license renewal. R. L. Shayon. Sat R 53:36-7 O 31 '70

RADIO broadcasting stations. See Radio stations

RADIO circuits
IC's for microwaves. R. B. Schilling. il por Electr World 84:42-4 Jl '70
One IC replaces entire I.F. strip; new FM tuner. L. Steckler. il Radio-Electr 41:59-61 N '70

RADIO communication
See also
Intercommunicating systems
Radio in navigation
Space flight—Communication systems

Emergency use

CB radio channel 9 emergency FCC rules. Radio-Electr 41:48 D '70
EMCBT organized for mobile CB-ers. Electr World 84:11 Jl '70
New help for cars in trouble; CB channel 9 for emergency communications. R. Benrey. il Pop Sci 197:34+ O '70
Survival radio for Apollo. W. L. Blair. il Electr World 84:38-40+ N '70
See also
REACT (organization)

Interference

See Radio interference
RADIO communication, Naval
Not all is Sanguine in Wisconsin. G. Laycock. il Audubon 72:104-9 Ja '70
RADIO communication, Short wave
See also
Citizens radio service
RADIO communication, Underground
Not all is Sanguine in Wisconsin. G. Laycock. il Audubon 72:104-9 Ja '70
RADIO conductors
See also
Wave guides

RADIO control
See also
Camera shutters—Control
RADIO direction finders. See Radio beacons; Radio in navigation
RADIO emergency associated citizens teams. See REACT (organization)
RADIO engineering

Study and teaching

See also
Capitol radio engineering institute
RADIO free Europe
Voice that pierces the iron curtain. il Nations Bsns 58:70-3 Ag '70
RADIO frequency
Gigahertzian broadcasting. L. C. Tilotson. Sci Am 223:41 D '70
Millimeter-wavelength radio systems. L. C. Tillotson. bibliog il Science 170:31-6 O 2 '70

Allocation

See Radio frequency allocation
RADIO frequency allocation
Channel 9: use or abuse? G. H. Reese. il Pop Electr 32:93+ Ap '70
FCC increases frequency bands available for domestic satcoms. K. Johnsen. Aviation W 93:23-4 O 5 '70
New help for cars in trouble; CB channel 9 for emergency communications. R. Benrey. il Pop Sci 197:34+ O '70
Talk ain't cheap no more. R. Humphrey. il Motor B 125:118-19+ Ja '70
RADIO frequency interference. See Radio interference
RADIO frequency modulation
Bonus for CATV subscribers: cable FM. E. A. Lacy. il Pop Electr 34:60-2 Ja '71
Build an SCA adapter for FM reception. V. Wood. il Pop Electr 33:53+ D '70
See also
Radio stations, Frequency modulation
RADIO frequency standards. See Frequency standards
RADIO generators. See Signal generators
RADIO in aviation
See also
Airplanes—Radio equipment
Radio beacons
RADIO in education
Jovial insipid subject; method for making new words alluring to children. por Time 96:54+ Ag 10 '70
RADIO in medicine
Mechanics of medicine; automatic breathing monitor, radiosurgery, and tooth transmitter. A. S. Freese. il Pop Mech 135:92-5 Ja '71
RADIO in municipal government
Communications for the 70's and beyond; Kalispell, Mont. G. Baldwin. Am City 85:132 Mr '70
RADIO in navigation
Hand RDF/compass finds your position on land or sea. E. H. Arctander. il Pop Sci 197:79 Jl '70
Marine electronics; direction finders. il Motor B 125:95-7 My '70
Omega: a navigator's dream. C. D. LaFond. il Sci N 98:354-5 O 31 '70
Radio direction finders. il Consumer Rep 35:412-17 Jl '70
Talk ain't cheap no more. R. Humphrey. il Motor B 125:118-19+ Ja '70
Who needs a radio check? R. W. Sumner. Motor B 126:16 O '70
See also
Loran
RADIO in politics
Letter from Washington; limiting money for television and radio time. R. H. Rovere. New Yorker 46:134-5 O 24 '70
RADIO in traffic control
Automatic vehicle monitoring. W. H. Buchsbaum. il Electr World 83:42-4+ Je '70
Under-highway radio for turnpike travelers; patent granted for Turnpike radio. S. V. Jones. Sci Digest 67:87 Ja '70
RADIO industry

France

French television and the control of the news. W. B. Kerr. il Sat R 53:72+ F 14 '70
RADIO instruments
See also
Calibrators
Oscillators
RADIO interference
And now electronic pollution. il Time 96:96 O 26 '70
Dehumming small receivers. R. L. Ives. il Pop Electr 32:75-6 Ap '70

RADIO interference—*Continued*
Interference from left field. E. Arnold. il
Pop Electr 32:44-6 Mr '70
Microwave noise from rainstorms. A. A.
Penzias and R. W. Wilson. il Science 169:
583-4 Ag 7 '70

RADIO laws and regulations
CB radio channel 9 emergency FCC rules.
Radio-Electr 41:48 D '70
Fair share of air; Democrats petition for
free time for the party out of power. News-
week 76:59 Jl 6 '70
Fairness doctrine: a stricter proposal; case
affecting religious broadcasters and their
critics. G. Everett. Chr Today 14:32 Jl 3 '70
FCC adopts licensing rule. America 122:86-7
Ja 31 '70
McIntire radio stations lose licenses. Chr
Cent 87:935 Ag 5 '70
Marine communications up-to-date. R. Hum-
phrey. il Electr World 85:25-7+ Ja '71
See also
Radio frequency allocation
United States—Federal communications com-
mission

RADIO modulation. See Modulation (electronics)

RADIO operators
Chief engineer of a small radio station. K.
B. Knecht. il pors Electr World 83:37-40
My '70

RADIO operators, Amateur
Amateur radio. H. S. Brier. See issues of
Popular electronics to August 1970
Future of amateur radio. J. Frye. Electr
World 84:57-8 Ag '70
Short-wave listening. H. Bennett. See issues
of Popular electronics to August 1970
See also
REACT (organization)

Anecdotes, facetiae, satire, etc.
Ham & the lady psychologist. F. Ebel. Pop
Electr 33:60-1+ S '70

RADIO plays
Man without a country; dramatization of
novel by E. E. Hale. L. Olfson. Plays 29:
41-6 Ap '70

RADIO programs. See Radio broadcasting—Programs

RADIO pulse code modulation
Digital voice communications. S. L. Silver. il
Electr World 84:27-30+ O '70

RADIO receivers
AM clock radios. il Consumer Rep 35:638-41
N '70
Build a three-channel time receiver. C. Car-
ingella. il Pop Electr 33:33-5+ D '70
Build the original radio: crystal set. L. Buck-
walter. il Mech Illus 66:74-5+ D '70
Table radios. il Consumer Bul 53:7-12 F '70
See also
Automobiles—Radio equipment

Control
Instant-on for AC/DC radios. R. Graf and
G. Whalen. il Mech Illus 66:96-7 N '70

Frequency modulation receivers
New FM receiver pulls some switches. A.
Fisher. il Pop Sci 196:60-1 Ap '70

Maintenance and repair
Imported radio showdown. J. Darr. Radio-
Electr 41:26+ Ap '70
See also
Automobiles—Radio equipment—Maintenance
and repair
RCA corporation—ServiceAmerica division

Prices
Mysteriously high Canadian prices. il Consumer Rep 35:639 N '70

Tuning
Hi-fi product report: Kenwood KT-7000 AM/
stereo-FM tuner. il Electr World 83:6+ Ja
'70
High-quality AM section in new hi-fi receiver.
K. J. Peter. il Electr World 83:30-1 Je '70
Simple SCA adapter; FM music sans com-
mercials. W. F. Splichal, jr. il Pop Electr
32:49-52 Je '70
Sinclair Project 60 FM stereo tuner. W. Roy.
il Radio-Electr 42:82 Ja '71
Ultimate, R-E's new FM stereo tuner. K. F.
Buegel. il Radio-Electr 41:36-40+ My '70

RADIO receivers, Portable
FM/AM portable radios. il Consumer Rep 35:
516-19 S '70
General coverage receiver. Heathkit GR-78. il
Pop Electr 32:65-8 Je '70

Pleasures of portables. F. Petras. il Hi Fi
20:secI 46-52 My '70
See-through radio with falsies; GE P2760. il
Consumer Rep 35:398-9 Jl '70

RADIO receivers, Short wave
Latest turn-ons: police & firemen! L. Buck-
walter. il Mech Illus 66:61-3+ Ag '70
Single-signal S.W. receiver. L. Lisle. il Electr
World 83:64 Ap '70
V.H.F. monitor receivers. J. Frye. Electr
World 84:63-4 O '70

RADIO receivers, Stereophonic
All-in-one stereo receiver kit features plug-
in modules. H. P. Luckett. il Pop Sci 197:
128 N '70
Heathkit AR-29 AM/FM stereo receiver. M.
Gernsback. il Radio-Electr 41:32 Je '70
Hi-fi product report:
    Heath AR-29 AM/stereo-FM receiver. il
    Electr World 84:14+ O '70
    Scott model 382-C AM/stereo-FM receiver.
    il Electr World 84:18-20 Jl '70
    Sherwood SEL-200 stereo-FM receiver. il
    Electr World 84:12-13 Ag '70
How to shop for a stereo receiver. D. Law-
rence. il Hi Fi 20:50-7 S '70
Medium-power stereo receiver, Heathkit
model AR-29. il Pop Electr 32:78-9 Ag '70
New stereo receivers. J. D. Hirsch. il Electr
World 84:27-30+ D '70
Re: a case of caveat emptor; Allied radio
shack. Consumer Rep 35:662-3 N '70
Ready, world? Headset has FM stereo built
in. il Consumer Rep 35:133-4 Mr '70
Stereo receivers. il Consumer Rep 35:463-71
Ag '70
Switch your stereo speakers with this self-
balancing control. W. G. Salm. il Pop Mech
134:140-3 S '70

RADIO receivers, Superheterodyne
Technical topics. R. F. Scott. il Radio-Electr
41:71-3 Jl '70

RADIO relay systems
Millimeter-wavelength radio systems. L. C.
Tillotson. bibliog il Science 170:31-6 O 2 '70
See also
Communications satellites

RADIO remote control lawn mowers. See Lawn
mowers

RADIO reporters. See Radio broadcasting—
News

RADIO research
Experiment that saved hi-fi. D. B. Weems.
bibliog il por Pop Electr 33:29-34+ S '70

RADIO shack corporation
Re: a case of caveat emptor; Allied radio
shack. Consumer Rep 35:662-3 N '70

RADIO stations
Chief engineer of a small radio station. K.
B. Knecht. il pors Electr World 83:37-40 My
'70
Down to fundamentals; question of WMUU's
license renewal. R. L. Shayon. Sat R 53:
36-7 O 31 '70
Guerrilla war in Cairo; fight to revoke Illinois
station's license. Nation 211:516 N 23 '70
Malign neglect; bombings of Pacifica station
KPFT in Houston. Nation 211:453 N 9 '70
On the off-beat. A. Rich. il Hi Fi 20:secII
10 Ap '70
Rock and roll Muzak; Bill Drake sound. il
por Newsweek 75:85 Mr 9 '70
Sad sack in Puyallup; handling of renewal of
KAYE's license. R. L. Shayon. Sat R 53:39
Jl 11 '70
Silence in Houston; bombed radio station. il
Time 96:79 O 26 '70
Texaco-Metropolitan opera radio network.
il Opera N 35:12-13 D 5 '70
Trobriandish; WINS. R. L. Shayon. Sat R 53:
49 Ap 25 '70
Voice of protest; WNYU moratorium radio
network. il Newsweek 75:73 My 18 '70
WBAI. New Yorker 46:30 Mr 7 '70

RADIO stations, Amateur
How to talk to Vietnam, free; via MARS.
A. Lee. il Pop Mech 134:108-10 S '70
See also
Citizens radio service

Equipment
Amateur radio equipment 1970-71. H. S. Brier.
il Pop Electr 33:51-3+ Ag '70

RADIO stations, Frequency modulation
Four-channel stereo FM, from one station;
quadriphonic sound. J. P. Meute. il Hi Fi
20:secI 72-3 Mr '70

RADIO stations, Government
See also
United States—Standards, National bureau
of—Radio stations

RADIO stations, Short wave
Short-wave listening. H. Bennett. See issues
of Popular electronics to August 1970

RADIO talk shows. See Radio broadcasting—
Conversation programs
RADIO telephone
Annual catalog of five-watt CB equipment.
(cont) il Pop Electr 33:31-5+ Ag '70
How to talk to Vietnam, free; via MARS. A.
Lee. il Pop Mech 134:108-10 S '70
RADIO telephone, Portable
Briefcase phone: talk from anywhere to any-
one. il Pop Sci 196:67 F '70
RADIO telephone on motor buses
Two-way radios improve bus system twelve
ways; Dallas. W. C. Driggs. Am City 85:
146-7 My '70
RADIO telephone on ships, boats, etc.
Marine communications up-to-date. R. Hum-
phrey. il Electr World 85:25-7+ Ja '71
Marine electronics; power & sail. il Motor B
125:93-5 My '70
Ship to shore on VHF. Motor B 125:98+ Je
'70
RADIO telescopes
Attenuation on an earth-space path measured
in the wavelength range of 8 to 14 mi-
crometers. R. W. Wilson. il Science 168:
1456-7 Je 19 '70
IAU visits Jodrell Bank. L. J. Robinson. il
Sky & Tel 40:283-6 N '70
New Boon 100-meter radio telescope. O.
Hachenberg. il Sky & Tel 40:338-43 D '70
New eye on the cosmos; Effelsberg telescope.
il Newsweek 76:108+ O 12 '70
RADIO time signals. See Time signals, Radio
RADIO traffic control. See Radio in traffic con-
trol
RADIO transformers
Winding your own output transformers. E.
Francis. il Pop Electr 33:78-82 S '70
RADIO Vaticana. See Vatican—Radio stations
RADIO waves
And now, electronic pollution. il Time 96:96
O 26 '70
See also
Microwaves
Radio frequency
Wave guides
Scattering
Bistatic-radar observation of long-period, di-
rectional ocean-wave spectra with loran A.
A. M. Peterson and others. bibliog il Sci-
ence 170:158-61 O 9 '70
RADIOACTIVATION analysis
Instrumental neutron activation analyses of
lunar specimens. G. G. Goles and others.
bibliog il Science 167:497-9 Ja 30 '70
Miracle tool for prospectors. R. Burkhart. il
Sci Digest 67:45-8+ F '70
Neutron activation analysis of milligram
quantities of lunar rocks and soils. K. K.
Turekian and D. P. Kharkar. bibliog il Sci-
ence 167:507-9 Ja 30 '70
RADIOACTIVE dating
Apollo 11 lunar science conference: age mea-
surements; symposium. bibliog il Science
167:461-83 Ja 30 '70
Astronomical theory of climate change: sup-
port from New Guinea. H. H. Veeh and J.
Chappell. bibliog il Science 167:862-5 F 6 '70
Fission track ages and ages of deposition of
deep-sea microtektites. W. Gentner and
others. bibliog il Science 168:359-61 Ap 17 '70
Geochronology: recent development in the
lutetium-176/hafnium-176 dating method. A.
Boudin and S. Deutsch. bibliog il Science
168:1219-20 Je 5 '70
Potassium-argon ages of lunar rocks from
Mare Tranquillitatis and Oceanus Procel-
larum. O. A. Schaeffer and others. bibliog il
Science 170:161-2 O 9 '70
Rubidium-strontium date of possibly 3 bil-
lion years for a granitic rock from An-
tarctica. M. Halpern. bibliog il Science 169:
977-8 S 4 '70
See also
Radiocarbon dating
RADIOACTIVE fallout
Infant mortality and nuclear tests. E. J.
Sternglass; discussion. Bul Atom Sci 25:27
Je; 26-32 O '69; Cur 113:62-4 D '69; Bul Atom
Sci 26:46 Mr; 40-2+ My '70
Professor Sternglass, fallout and infant
mortality. Bul Atom Sci 26:46 Mr '70
Project Gasbuggy and catch-85. P. Metzger.
il N Y Times Mag p26-7+ F 22 '70
See also
Soils, Radioactive substances in
Physiological effects
See Radioactivity—Physiological effects
RADIOACTIVE halos. See Halos (mineralogy)

RADIOACTIVE substances
See also
Actinide elements
Americium
Promethium
Radioisotopes
Radon
RADIOACTIVE substances in soils. See Soils,
Radioactive substances in
RADIOACTIVE substances in the body
Radioactive scientist. Time 95:68 Mr 2 '70
RADIOACTIVE tracers
Composition differences at surfaces detected
by adsorption and desorption of radio-
tracers. D. A. Brandreth and R. E. John-
son. il Science 169:864 Ag 28 '70
Gallium-67 localization in rat and mouse
tumors. R. L. Hayes and others. bibliog il
Science 167:289-90 Ja 16 '70
Uranium localization on hydroxyapatite by
analysis of fission fragment tracks. R. C.
Thompson. bibliog il Science 167:1494-7 Mr
13 '70
RADIOACTIVE waste disposal
America's most radioactive city: Grand Junc-
tion, Colo. N. Wood. McCalls 97:46+ S '70
Boston worries over radioactive water. Am
City 85:26 Ag '70
Close to zero; nuclear power plants discharge
of radioactivity. Sci N 97:500-1 My 23 '70
Disposing of the waste. il Sci N 97:312 Mr
28 '70
Down to what's practicable. il Sci N 97:341
Ap 4 '70
Earthquake at Giza; Hanford atomic products
operation; with interview with G. T. Sea-
borg. S. Novick. bibliog il Environ 12:2-15
Ja '70; Same abr. with title Dangers from
radioactive wastes. Cur 118:41-5 My '70
RADIOACTIVITY
Nuclear threat inside America. J. Shepherd.
il Look 34:21-7 D 15 '70
See also
Autoradiography
Plutonium
Radon
Transmutation (chemistry)
Measurement
See also
Counters (electrons, ions, etc)
Physiological effects
A-bombed cities: twenty-five years later. K.
M. Chrysler. il U S News 69:54-6 Ag 10 '70
Catch 24,400; or, Plutonium is my favorite
element; fire at Rocky Flats plant. R.
Rapoport. il Ramp Mag 8:16-21 My '70
Fallout and Marshallese; report. il Bul Atom
Sci 26:45 Mr '70
How I learned to live with radioactivity
and love it; in Colorado. S. Gascoyne.
Commonweal 92:7-9 Mr 13 '70
How many children? with excerpts from ad-
dress, May 1969, by E. Sternglass. M. W.
Friedlander and J. Klarmann. bibliog il En-
viron 11:2-13 D '69
Infant mortality and nuclear tests. E. J.
Sternglass; discussion. Bul Atom Sci 25:27
Je; 26-32 O '69; Cur 113:62-4 D '69; Bul Atom
Sci 26:46 Mr; 40-2+ My '70
Population control through nuclear pollution,
by A. R. Tamplin and W. Gofman. Review
Environ 12:46-7 D '70. S. Novick
Professor Sternglass, fallout and infant
mortality. Bul Atom Sci 26:46 Mr '70
Radiation: the invisible casualties. J. W. Gof-
man and A. R. Tamplin. bibliog il Environ
12:12-19+ Ap '70
Rocky Flats still smolders. il Sci N 97:194
F 21 '70
See also
Fetus, Effect of radiation on the
Radiation sickness
Radiobiology
Safety devices and measures
They handle the hot stuff; Radiological emer-
gency assistance teams. N. Carlisle. il Pop
Mech 133:106-9+ F '70
RADIOBIOLOGY
Conferences
Radiation biology of the fetal and juvenile
mammal. M. R. Sikov. Science 167:1640-1
Mr 20 '70
RADIOCARBON dating
Bristlecone correction. Sci Am 223:52 Jl '70
Early holocene oöids in modern littoral sands
reworked from a coastal terrace, southern
Tunisia. F. H. Fabricius and others. bib-
liog il Science 169:757-60 Ag 21 '70
Radiocarbon dating. Chem 43:24 Jl '70

RADIOCHEMISTRY
Conferences
Physical and chemical aspects of ionization and excitation processes. F. Williams. bibliog Science 167:1522-4 Mr 13 '70

RADIOGRAPHY
N-ray, miracle tool for science and industry. A. Hamilton. il Sci Digest 68:68-72 S '70
3-D ray. Newsweek 76:85 Jl 20 '70
See also
Autoradiography
X rays

RADIOIMMUNOASSAY. See Biological assay

RADIOISOTOPES
Cosmogenic and primordial radionuclides in lunar samples by nondestructive gamma-ray spectrometry. R. W. Perkins and others. bibliog il Science 167:577-80 Ja 30 '70
Major and trace elements and cosmic-ray produced radioisotopes in lunar samples. H. Wänke and others. bibliog il Science 167:523-5 Ja 30 '70
Pattern of bombardment-produced radionuclides in rock 10017 and in lunar soil. J. P. Shedlovsky and others. bibliog il Science 167:574-6 Ja 30 '70

Decay
See also
Isotopic power generators

Medical use
Radioactive diagnosis. il Time 96:54 S 28 '70
RADIOLOGICAL emergency assistance teams. See Radioactivity—Safety devices and measures
RADIOLOGICAL physics. See Radiology
RADIOLOGY
Study and teaching
Plastic man for practice X rays. il Sci Digest 67:86-7 Je '70
RADIOLOGY, Medical
See also
American radium society
Diagnosis, Radioscopic
Society of nuclear medicine

RADIOMETERS
Use of microwave sensing grows. W. S. Hieronymus. il Aviation W 92:44-6 Mr 30 '70

RADIOTRACERS. See Radioactive tracers

RADISHES
Truth about radishes? They are accommodating. il Sunset 144:232+ My '70

RADKAI, Karen
Visconti. il pors Vogue 156:182-9+ N 1 '70

RADLOW, James
News of the mysteries; poem. Poetry 116:24-7 Ap '70

RADNOR, Jacob Bouverie, 2d earl of
From one humble servant to another; exchange of letters. il pors Am Heritage 22:112 D '70

RADOMSKI, Jack L. and Brill, Earl
Bladder cancer induction by aromatic amines; role of N-hydroxy metabolites. bibliog il Science 167:992-3 F 13 '70

RADON
America's most radioactive city: Grand Junction, Colo. N. Wood. McCalls 97:46+ S '70
Ionic radon solutions. L. Stein. bibliog il Science 168:362-4 Ap 17 '70
Radon-222 in the North Atlantic trade winds: its relationship to dust transport from Africa. J. M. Prospero and T. N. Carlson. bibliog il Science 167:974-7 F 13 '70

RADOSH, Ronald
Bare-knuckled historians. Nation 210:108-10 F 2 '70

RAEDEKE, Theodore A.
Unlocking evangelistic potential. D. Kucharsky. por Chr Today 15:43-4 Ja 1 '71 *

RAEFF, Marc
Domestic policies of Peter III and his overthrow. bibliog f Am Hist R 75:1289-310 Je '70

RAFELSON, Bob
Bob Rafelson; interview. New Yorker 46:41-2 O 24 '70

RAFFEL, Burton
Comment. R. Magowan. Poetry 116:199 Je '70 *

RAFFERTY, Max
Challenging Rafferty. il Time 96:58 N 2 '70 *
Retiring Rafferty. il por Newsweek 76:71-3 N 16 '70 *
What's going to happen to us individuals? address, August 14, 1970. Vital Speeches 36:752-5 O 1 '70

RAFFLES (night club) See Night clubs

RAFT building. See Boatbuilding
RAG dolls. See Dolls
RAGAN, Bill
I'm a rose rookie. il Org Gard & Farm 17:74-5 Je '70
RAGAN, William B. and Henderson, George
Prospects for the future of America education; excerpts from Foundations of American education. bibliog Sch & Soc 98:183-9 Mr '70

RAGETTE, Friedrich
Tower of Babel. il UNESCO Courier 23:33-4+ Ag '70

RAGS (periodical)
New eye for fashion. il Time 96:31 Ag 10 '70

RAHAMIMOFF, R. See Rotshenker, S. jt. auth.

RAHM, Neal M.
Mike Frome. M. Frome. Am For 76:3+ Je '70 *

RAHMAN, Abdul, tunku
Tunku steps down. Newsweek 76:58+ S 14 '70 *

RAHMAN, Mujibur. See Mujibur Rahman

RAHNER, Karl
Karl Rahner, an interview; ed. by W. V. Dych. America 123:356-9 O 31 '70

about
Karl Rahner; symposium, with editorial comment. il pors America 123:inside cover, 335-59 O 31 '70 *

RAHV, Philip
Critical moment. J. P. Sisk. Commentary 49:89-92 Ap '70 *

RAI, K. S. See McDonald, P. T. jt. auth.

RAIL buses. See Motor buses on rails
RAILPAX. See National railroad passenger corporation
RAILROAD crossings. See Railroads—Crossings
RAILROAD law
Emergency boards in the airline industry, 1936-69; Railway labor act's emergency dispute procedures. M. H. Cimini. il Mo Labor R 93:57-65 Jl '70
See also
United States—Interstate commerce commission
RAILROAD management. See Railroads—Management
RAILROAD models
Lot of railroad in a little space. W. C. Leckey. il Pop Mech 133:150-3+ Ja; 190-3+ F '70 (to be cont)
Sweet little Santa Fe. F. Taylor. il Pop Mech 134:112-13 N '70
RAILROAD museums
Last little red caboose going to Gettysburg; Lincoln train museum. il Hobbies 75:130 Jl '70
RAILROAD passengers. See Railroad travel
RAILROAD strikes. See Strikes—United States —Railroads
RAILROAD supplies industry
See also
Pullman, inc.
RAILROAD travel
Different America. R. McKee. il Audubon 72:9-17 Jl '70
Easy riding; trains-autos-couchettes; car on same train as owner. P. Henissart. Travel & Camera 33:16+ Ap '70
Miss your train? good trips are still left. J. A. Stowe. il Travel 133:54-9+ Mr '70
RAILROAD worms. See Beetles
RAILROADS
Cars
Different America; sightseeing from the observation car. R. McKee. il Audubon 72:9-17 Jl '70
Freight car shortage gets worse. Bsns W p78+ S 5 '70
See also
Budd company
Commuter service
Riding high on the Lindenwold line. il Nations Bsns 58:71 D '70
Consolidations and mergers
Clearer track for railroads. il Bsns W p30+ F 7 '70
Four-way merger makes America's biggest railroad; Burlington-Northern, inc. US News 68:16 F 16 '70
Getting on the route to corporate health. W. A. Lashley. il pors Nations Bsns 58:98-9 Ja '70
Jim Hill's dream; Supreme court approves merger of three northern rail lines. Newsweek 75:78+ F 16 '70

RAILROADS—*Continued*

Crossings

Rubber decks make smoother, longer-lasting railroad crossings. il Am City 85:44 F '70

Employees

Candy butcher: Samuel Jacobs, vendor on the Penn central trains. New Yorker 46:17-19 Jl 11 '70

End of the road? Congress prohibits strike. il Newsweek 75:80 Mr 16 '70

Fireman's job runs out of steam; emergency board's recommendations. Bsns W p76 Ag 15 '70

For Congress: a lonesome whistle? long fight over firemen. US News 69:60-1 Jl 20 '70

Out West with the rowdy brakeman; excerpt from Workin' on the railroad. R. Reinhardt. il Am West 7:29-37 My '70

When one work rule nearly stalled all the railroads. il US News 68:86 F 16 '70

See also
Strikes—United States—Railroads
United transportation union

Federal aid

Congress keeps brake on all rail aid. il Bsns W p 15-16 Jl 4 '70

Federal fuel for Penn central. il Bsns W p26-7 Je 13 '70

First aid for a shaky giant. il Newsweek 75:63-4 Je 22 '70

Penn central's troubles branch out. il Bsns W p92+ Je 20 '70

Rescue derailed. il Newsweek 75:62 Je 29 '70

Uncle, can you spare some millions? il por Time 95:74-6 Je 22 '70

Finance

As troubles pile up: can railroads stay in business? il US News 69:55-7 O 5 '70

Other roads on the danger track. Bsns W p39 Je 27 '70

Penn central gets its new engineers. Bsns W p20 Jl 25 '70

Freight cars

See Railroads—Cars

Freight service

Down with the freight cartel. Fortune 82:98 Ag '70

Railroads ask for help. Forbes 106:19 Jl 15 '70

Freight trains

Derailment at last chance junction? minitrain plan. il Bsns W p68-9+ Mr 28 '70

Mini-trains get a green light. il Bsns W p27-8 Je 13 '70

Government regulation

See Railroads and state—United States

History

Out West with the rowdy brakeman; excerpt from Workin' on the railroad. R. Reinhardt. il Am West 7:29-37 My '70

See also
Railroads—United States—History

Management

Derailment at last chance junction? minitrain plan. il Bsns W p68-9+ Mr 28 '70

Mini-trains get a green light. il Bsns W p27-8 Je 13 '70

When a railroad makes the rules. il Bsns W p 109-10 Ja 17 '70

Passenger service

Candy butcher: Samuel Jacobs, vendor on the Penn central trains. New Yorker 46:17-19 Jl 11 '70

On the track: the trains in Spain, etc. D. Butwin. il Sat R 54:35-6 Ja 9 '71

Story behind the commuter crisis. il Bsns W p60-6+ Mr 14 '70

What's being planned to save rail travel. il US News 68:58-9 Ja 19 '70

Where you can go by train if they change the rail map. il US News 69:56-7 D 14 '70

See also
National railroad passenger corporation
Railroads—Commuter service

High speed trains

Additional funds spur Metroliner. Aviation W 93:34 N 30 '70

Hard way to run a railroad; Metroliner experiment. il Bsns W p64-5 Ap 4 '70

Will TurboTrain survive? il Bsns W p92-3 S 19 '70

World's fastest train; the Hikari, between Tokyo and Osaka. il Travel 133:66-9 My '70

Passenger traffic

See also
Railroad travel

Rates

See also
Railroads and state—United States

Real estate operations

City in the sky; U.S. railroads interest in real estate development. Time 95:64 Mr 9 '70

Strikes

See Strikes—United States—Railroads

Train speed

See also
Railroads—Passenger service—High speed trains

Trains

Last days of the Zephyr. R. Kennedy and M. Sullivan. il Time 95:64 Mr 30 '70

Save that train; California Zephyr. New Repub 162:10 F 7 '70

See also
Railroads—Freight trains

Wages and hours

See also
Collective bargaining—Railroads

Alaska

See also
Alaska railroad
White Pass and Yukon railway

Canada

See also
Canadian national railways
White Pass and Yukon railway

Europe

On the track: the trains in Spain, etc. D. Butwin. il Sat R 54:35-6 Ja 9 '71

Europe, Western

Europe's ski safaris. il Travel 134:52-3 D '70

Railroad pass to anywhere; Europe unlimited; with report by M. Leatherbee. il Life 69:38-46B Ag 14 '70

France

Easy riding; trains-autos-couchettes; car on same train as owner. P. Henissart. Travel & Camera 33:16+ Ap '70

Hawaii

Sugar cane train; Lahaina-Kaanapali & Pacific rail road in Maui. M. R. Lee. il Travel 135:52-4 Ja '71

Japan

World's fastest train; the Hikari, between Tokyo and Osaka. il Travel 133:66-9 My '70

United States

Color them red. Newsweek 76:68+ Jl 20 '70

Lesson in transportation. Am City 85:14 Ag '70

Miss your train? good trips are still left. J. A. Stowe. il Travel 133:54-9+ Mr '70

See also
Association of American railroads
Collective bargaining—Railroads
Railroads—History
Railroads and state—United States
United States—Interstate commerce commission
also names of railroads, e.g. Illinois central railroad company

History

Sentimental journey on the Atchison, Topeka and the Santa Fe. il Am Heritage 22:40-7 D '70

RAILROADS, Magnetic. See Air cushion vehicles

RAILROADS, Narrow gage

On the Lahaina Kaanapali & Pacific. il Sunset 145:43-4 S '70

Sugar cane train; Lahaina-Kaanapali & Pacific rail road in Maui. M. R. Lee. il Travel 135:52-4 Ja '71

RAILROADS, Short line

Tiny railroad pulls a switch; demerger of Providence & Worcester railroad co. from Penn central. il Bsns W p84 My 23 '70

RAILROADS, Single rail

Tokyo monorail wins its comeback fight. il Bsns W p56 Jl 11 '70

RAILROADS and state

Canada

See also
Canadian national railways

RAILROADS and state—*Continued*

United States

After Penn central. Nat R 22:721 Jl 14 '70
All is not lost; plan for quasi-public subsidized corporation. Newsweek 75:85B My 11 '70
Are railroads doomed? il U S News 69:12-13 Jl 6 '70
Case for and against nationalization. Time 96:59 Jl 6 '70
Countdown for America's railroads; ASTRO recommendations; address, September 22, 1970. T. M. Goodfellow. Vital Speeches 37: 56-8 N 1 '70
Green signal for better rail travel. il U S News 69:24 O 26 '70
Passenger trains: rescue near? government-sponsored corporation plan. il U S News 68: 83-4 My 18 '70
Railroad reform; suggestion: government ownership of roadbeds. W. F. Buckley, jr. Nat R 22:101 Ja 27 '70
  See also
National railroad passenger corporation
United States—Interstate commerce commission

RAILS (birds)
Pointing Lab; marsh hen shooting. F. E. Hester. il Field & S 75:148-50 S '70
RAILWAY express agency, inc. See REA express, inc.
RAILWAY labor acts. See Railroad law
RAIN and rainfall
From above: heavy rains over the southeastern states. il Weatherwise 22:253 D '69
Rain by inadvertence; pollution effects. il Sci N 97:390 Ap 18 '70
  See also
Photography of rain and rainfall
Storms
RAIN clothing. See Clothing, Waterproof
RAIN forests
Vertical zonation in a tropical rain forest in Malaysia: method of study. I. Muul and L. B. Liat. bibliog il Science 169:788-9 Ag 21 '70
RAIN making
Rainfall enhancement by dynamic cloud modification. W. L. Woodley. bibliog il Science 170:127-32 O 9 '70
RAIN of fishes, insects, etc. See Fishes, insects, etc. Rain of
RAINBARRELS. See Barrels
RAINBOW trout fishing. See Trout fishing
RAINCOATS
Men's raincoats. il Consumer Rep 35:143-8 Mr '70
RAINER, Dachine
Here summer ends; poem. New Repub 162:25 F 21 '70
RAINER, John D. See Altshuler, K. Z. jt. auth.
RAINER, Yvonne
Yvonne Rainer and co. in Continuous project-altered daily; Whitney museum, NYC. N. Mason. il por Dance Mag 44:74-5 Je '70 *
RAINES, Robert A.
New-time religion. Ladies Home J 86:131 D '69
RAINEY, Sarita R.
Motivation. il Sch Arts 70:8-9 Ja '71
RAINIER, MOUNT
Mt Rainier, the live time bomb in Seattle's back yard. E. Clark. il Sci Digest 68:45-8+ Ag '70
RAINNIE, William O. and Milwee, W. I. Jr
How we raised the Alvin from 5000 feet. il pors Pop Mech 133:92-8 Ja '70
RAINSTORMS. See Storms
RAINWATER, Dorothy T.
Kaahumanu's silver spoons. il Antiques 97: 728-9 My '70
RAINWATER, Lee. See Horowitz, I. L. jt. auth.
RAINWEAR. See Clothing, Waterproof
RAISINS
  See also
Cookery—Fruit
RAJAS. See India—Nobility
RAKES, Charles D.
Touch-a-tone. il Pop Electr 32:66-72+ Mr '70
RAKESTRAW, Norris W.
Controlling breathing atmospheres. il Chem 43:18-23 O '70
RAKSTIS, Ted J.
Cheaper by the duo? il Todays Health 48:46-7+ My '70
Debate in the doll house. il Todays Health 48:28-31+ D '70
Why our kids steal. il Todays Health 48: 20-3+ D '70

RAKU glazes. See Glazes and glazing
RAKU ware. See Pottery, Japanese
RALEIGH, N.C.
Going home to Raleigh. F. Powledge. Harper 240:54-8+ Ap '70
RALPH, Charles L. and others
Pineal function and oviposition in Japanese quail: superior cervical ganglionectomy and photoperiod. bibliog il Science 170:995-7 N 27 '70
RALSTON, Mary A.
How to trade your mop for a typewriter. Todays Health 48:53-5 F '70
RALSTON Purina company
Ralston changes Foodmaker menu. Bsns W p 17 My 2 '70
RAM, Jagjivan
Untouchable with a touch. por Time 95:20 F 16 '70 *
RAMALLAH, Jordan
Time stands still in an Israeli-occupied town. J. Feron. il N Y Times Mag p30-3+ My 17 '70
RAMAN, A. S.
(ed) See Shankar, R. Ravi Shankar at home and abroad
RAMAN effect
Laser Raman spectroscopy. A. Mooradian. bibliog il Science 169:20-5 Jl 3 '70
Spin-flip Raman laser is tunable infrared source. G. B. Lubkin. bibliog Phys Today 23:57-8 Jl '70
RAMAPO, N.Y.
  Recreation
New cash control data collection system. A. Palermo. il por Parks & Rec 5:32-3 Mr '70
RAMAPO college, Mahweh, N.J.
Building a new library for a new college. A. Caruba. por Pub W 198:29-30 O 26 '70
RAMBO, F. Ralph. See Rambo, R.
RAMBO, Ralph
He thrives on history. F. L. Fox. il por Har Yrs 10:30-3 Je '70 *
RAMDOHR, Paul, and el Goresey, Ahmed
Opaque minerals of the lunar rocks and dust from Mare Tranquillitatis. bibliog il Science 167:615-18 Ja 30 '70
RAMEY, Estelle
Well, fellows, what did happen at the Bay of Pigs? And who was in control? McCalls 98:26+ Ja '71
RAMIREZ, Armando Socarras. See Socarras Ramirez, A.
RAMIREZ, José A. Rojas-. See Rojas-Ramírez, J. A.
RAMIREZ, William L.
(ed) Libraries and the Spanish-speaking. bibliog il por Wilson Lib Bul 44:714-67 Mr '70
RAMMING, Kenneth P. and Plich, Y. H.
Mediation of immunity to tumor isografts in mice by heterologous ribonucleic acid. bibliog il Science 168:492-3 Ap 24 '70
RAMO, Simon
Caution! Si Ramo at work. W. McQuade. il pors Fortune 82:104-7+ N '70 *
RAMOS, J. See Kavanau, J. L. jt. auth.
RAMPARTS (periodical)
Director resigns; letter, with reply by the editors. E. Lockwood. il Ramp Mag 9:50+ O '70
Editorial; anniversary of first issue after bankruptcy. il Ramp Mag 8:6 Ap '70
RAMSEY, Arthur Michael, abp
Archbishop Ramsey in the middle. J. Squire. Chr Cent 88:47-8 Ja 13 '71 *
Bugging the archbishop? visit to South Africa. Newsweek 76:60 D 28 '70 *
Canterbury and canonization. Chr Cent 87:782 Je 24 '70 *
Ramsey's return, or back at the palace. J. D. Douglas. Chr Today 15:41-2 Ja 1 '71 *
RAMSEY, Jarold
Giantless on the hillside; poem. Atlan 226: 58 O '70
RAMSEY, Norman F.
We need a pollution tax! il Bul Atom Sci 26: 3-5 Ap '70
RAMSEY, Paul, 1924-
Voyagings; poem. Poetry 116:12 Ap '70
RAMTHA, Battle of. See Jordan—Civil war, 1970
RAMUS, Michael
Game behind the whistle. il Sports Illus 33: 42-7 N 23 '70
RANCH life
Gambling men and honest horses; a-wintering on a Wyoming ranch. S. Hicks. il Am West 7:40-7+ N '70
Ranch vacations. B. Thomas. il Travel 133: 36-42 My '70
We did it. M. Privette. House B 112:46-7 S '70
  See also
Cowboys

RANCHES
Outdoor living on an Arizona ranch. il House & Gard 137:74-5 Je '70
Sheep station vacation; New Zealand. Travel 134:18 D '70
    See also
Ranch life
RANCHO LA BREA. See La Brea, Los Angeles
RANCK, Helen
Bush; story. Yale R 60:63-8 O '70
RAND, Paul
Paul Rand, commercial artist. P. Seitlin. il por Am Artist 34:48-53 O '70 *
RAND, Samuel J.
Computer analyzes a hydraulic colossus. il Am City 85:102+ Je '70
RAND corporation
Forecasters turn to group guesswork; Delphi technique. il Bsns W p 130+ Mr 14 '70
Research that leads to understanding. Pub W 198:53 N 16 '70
RANDALL, Charles Edgar
People-power and pollution: what can I do? il Am For 76:28-35+ O '70
RANDALL, Harold J.
Story of the Nachatank River. il Liv Wildn 34:21-3 Sum '70
RANDALL, Harrison McAllister
Obituary
    Phys Today por 23:127+ Ja '70. R. A. Sawyer
RANDALL, Margaret
Some skeleton poems, written in hiding. Nation 211:90-1 Ag 3 '70
RANDALL, Tony
Odd squad. il pors Time 96:74+ O 26 '70 *
RANDELL, Cortes Wesley
How Cortes Randell drained the fountain of youth. R. Loving, jr. il por Fortune 81:94-7+ Ap '70 *
Pied Piper of Wall Street. il por Time 95:94 Ap 13 '70 *
RANDLE, Robert
Domestic origins of peace. Ann Am Acad 392:76-85 N '70
RANDOLPH, Jennings
What's happening to Mother Earth: a warning. il por U S News 69:59-60 N 23 '70
RANDOLPH, Mass.
Smoke-out in a small town. il Todays Health 48:44-7 Je '70
RANDOLPH, Vt.
Fourth of July. il Travel & Camera 33:22-5 Jl '70
RANDOM processes. See Stochastic processes
RANDOM warp weaving. See Weaving
RANEY, Ona
Give us vine okra any time. il por Org Gard & Farm 17:74-5 My '70
You can still get the redgolds. il por Org Gard & Farm 17:94-5 S '70
RANGE finder cameras. See Cameras
RANGE finders. See View finders
RANGEL, Charles Bernard
New man from Harlem. por Time 96:19 Jl 6 '70 *
RANGERS (hockey team) See Hockey teams
RANGES. See Stock ranges
RANGES, Kitchen. See Electric stoves
RANGIA cuneata. See Clams
RANISH, N. See Ochs, S. jt. auth.
RANK, Hugh
Audience-directed writing: magazines and personae. Engl J 59:405-8 Mr '70
RANK organisation, ltd.
They saw the handwriting on the TV screen. Forbes 105:18-19 My 1 '70
RANK Xerox, ltd.
Rank Xerox: the sky's the limit. J. Ross-Skinner. Duns 95:70-1+ My '70
RANKIN, Allen
Dream called Florida. il Read Digest 96:152-8 Mr '70
Riku Ruopsa's trial by fire. il Read Digest 97:69-73 N '70
RANKIN, Bob
Trolling from an airplane. il Field & S 75:80 My '70
RANKIN, Don
Life-and-death struggle. il Outdoor Life 146:68-9 S '70
RANKING, Student. See Grading and marking (students)
RANLY, Ernest W.
Ways of violence. America 123:140-3 S 12 '70
RANSOM, David
Berkeley mafia and the Indonesian massacre. il Ramp Mag 9:27-9+ O '70

RAPAPORT, Felix T. and Dausset, Jean
Ranks of donor-recipient histocompatibility for human transplantation. bibliog il Science 167:1260-2 F 27 '70
RAPE
Can a black be acquitted? indictment of R. Holloway. N. C. Chriss. Nation 211:690-1 D 28 '70
    See also
Trials (rape)
RAPE of Tamar; story. See Jacobson, D.
RAPE trials, Military. See Courts martial and courts of inquiry
RAPHAEL
Lost masterpiece is found. il Newsweek 76:68-9 Jl 27 '70 *
RAPHAEL, Chaim
Discourses of the rabbis. Commentary 49:77-80 Ap '70
In search of Cecil Roth. bibliog f Commentary 50:75-6+ S '70
RAPHAEL, Dana
Parent and child. il N Y Times Mag p67+ F 8 '70
RAPHAEL Minichiello airplane hijacking trial. See Trials—Italy
RAPID transit. See Local transit
RAPOPORT, Roger
Catch 24,400; or, Plutonium is my favorite element. il Ramp Mag 8:16-21 My '70
Explosion in a boom town. il Sports Illus 33:26-7 S 14 '70
How I made $193.85 selling cars. Atlan 225:75-8 Ja '70
Los Angeles has a cough. il Esquire 74:83-5+ Jl '70
Nature. Sports Illus 32:54-5 Je 29 '70
No one plays in no man's land. il Sports Illus 32:20-1 Je 15 '70
RAPP, Marvin A.
Seventies; restructuring the educational system; address, November 24, 1970. Vital Speeches 37:173-7 Ja 1 '71
RAPP, Sherman E.
Wrinkles don't hurt. il Har Yrs 10:50 F '70
RARE animals
Doctor Hibben's New Mexican ark; endangered African species in desert of New Mexico. R. Gannon. il por Sci Digest 68:23-9 O '70
Environmental deterioration and declining species. J. E. Forbes. il Cons 25:21-6 Ag '70
Rarities of Ethiopia; with report by M. Mok. il Life 69:46-57 N 27 '70
Teacher tips: environmental deterioration and declining species. J. A. Weeks. Cons 25:27+ Ag '70
    See also
Ferrets
Pandas
Sea otters
RARE birds
Where have all the ospreys gone? interview, ed. by J. Hess. R. T. Peterson. il Nat Wildlife 9:36-7 D '70
Whooping promise. J. Phillips. il Sat R 53:59 O 3 '70
RARE earths. See Earths, Rare
RARE gases. See Gases, Rare
RARICK, John R.
New Jersey: the state of Mafia; attempt to discredit F. B. Lacey. F. J. Cook. il Nation 210:261-3+ My 11 '70
Rhodesia; address, March 12, 1970. Vital Speeches 36:434-7 My 1 '70
RASCHKE, Klaus
Leaf hydraulic system: rapid epidermal and stomatal responses to changes in water supply. bibliog il Science 167:189-91 Ja 9 '70
RASCOE, Judith
Church of Satan. il McCalls 97:74-5+ Mr '70
Lot of cowboys; story. Atlan 226:56-8 N '70
Odyssey of Dory Previn. por McCalls 98:6+ Ja '71
Variations on the art of wishing; poem. Atlan 226:64 Ag '70
RASH, Charles D.
Throw tall, throw wide. il Ceram Mo 18:16-18 F '70
RASHKE, Richard
Trust for black Catholics? Commonweal 92:35-7 Mr 20 '70
RASKIN, A. H.
Labor movement must start moving. il Harvard Bsns R 48:108-18 Ja '70
New York city's dailies vs. the unions: automation's armageddon. il Sat R 53:50-2 Jl 11 '70
Said Nixon to George Shultz: "I track well with you". il pors N Y Times Mag p24-5+ Ag 23 '70
Union with soul. il N Y Times Mag p24-5+ Mr 22 '70

RASMUSSEN, Howard
Cell communication, calcium ion, and cyclic
adenosine monophosphate. bibliog il Science 170:404-12 O 23 '70
—and Pechet, M. M.
Calcitonin; with biographical sketches. il
Sci Am 223:15, 42-50 O '70

RASPBERRIES
Autumn-fruiting raspberries. G. L. Slate. il
Horticulture 48:24-5+ S '70

RASPBERRY, William
Should ghettoes be accepted? Todays Ed
59:30-1+ Ap '70

RASPS. See Files and rasps

RAT control
Civil rats; results of first year of federal program. il Newsweek 76:90 S 21 '70

RATCLIFF, Carter
New informalists. il Art N 68:46-50 F '70

RATCLIFF, John Drury
Death of the Wahine. il Read Digest 97:
182-4+ D '70
How to avoid harmful stress. Todays Health
48:42-4 Jl '70; Same abr. Read Digest 97:79-82 Jl '70
I am Joe's foot. il Read Digest 97:117-20 S '70
I am Joe's hypothalamus. il Read Digest 96:
124-7 Mr '70
I am Joe's kidney. il Read Digest 96:98-102
My '70
I am Joe's man gland. il Read Digest 97:92-5
N '70

RATCLIFFE, Bill
Lichens; photographs. D. McKinley. Audubon
72:45-52 N '70
Tree is living yet! photographs. il Audubon
72:64-9 Ja '70
Winter marsh; photographs. il Read Digest
96:135-41 F '70

RATE, Hank
Deteriorating rancher-sportsman relations.
il Field & S 75:20+ S; 12+ O '70
Elk charge this bugle. il Field & S 75:54-5+
O '70
How to have a great guided hunt. il Field &
S 75:32-3+ Ag '70

RATES. See Telephone—Rates; Water rates

RATHJEN, W. F. and Sullivan, J. R.
West Indies whaling; with biographical
sketches. il Sea Front 16:130-7, 191 My '70

RATHJENS, George W. and Kistiakowsky, G. B.
Limitation of strategic arms; with biographical sketches. il Sci Am 222:16, 19-29 Ja;
6-7 My '70

RATING. See subhead Rating under various
subjects, e.g. Librarians—Rating

RATING of television programs. See Television
broadcasting—Program rating

RATIONALISM
See also
Empiricism
Enlightenment

RATLIFF, Thomas B.
Senate v. Alan and Margaret McSurely. W.
Goodman. il pors N Y Times Mag p28-9+
Ja 10 '71 *

RATNER, A. See Adamo, N. J. jt. auth.

RATNER, Milton. See Clouet, D. H. jt. auth.

RATS
Alcohol aversion in the rat; behavioral assessment of noxious drug effects. M. Nachman and others. bibliog il Science 168:1244-6 Je 5 '70
Bladder tumorigenesis. D. R. Stoltz and I. K.
Barker. bibliog Science 168:1121-2 My 29
'70
Brain norepinephrine; enhanced turnover after
rubidium treatment. J. M. Stolk and others.
bibliog il Science 168:501-3 Ap 24 '70
Cataracts produced in rats by yogurt. C. P.
Richter and J. R. Duke. bibliog il Science
168:1372-4 Je 12 '70
Catecholamine biosynthesis in brains of rats
treated with morphine. D. H. Clouet and
M. Ratner. bibliog il Science 168:854-6 My
15 '70
Copulatory behavior can inhibit pregnancy in
female rats. N. T. Adler and S. R. Zoloth.
bibliog il Science 168:1480-2 Je 19 '70
Discrimination by rats of conspecific odors
of reward and nonreward. R. R. Morrison
and H. W. Ludvigson. bibliog il Science
167:904-5 6 '70
Harderian gland; an extraretinal photoreceptor influencing the pineal gland in
neonatal rats? L. Wetterberg and others.
bibliog il Science 167:884-5 F 6 '70
Histamine production by transplantable argyrophilic gastric carcinoid of praomys
(mastomys) natalensis. S. Hosoda and others. bibliog il Science 170:454-5 O 23 '70

Hormonal effects on ontogeny of swimming
ability in the rat; assessment of central
nervous system development. S. Schapiro
and others. bibliog il Science 168:147-51
Ap 3 '70
Incubation effects in behavior induction in
rats. A. M. Golub and others. bibliog il Science 168:392-5 Ap 17 '70; Reply with rejoinder. J. A. Corson. 169:1342 S 25 '70
Monosodium glutamate; lack of effects on
brain and reproductive function in rats. N.
J. Adamo and A. Ratner. bibliog il Science
169:673-4 Ag 14 '70
Olfactory stimuli and the pseudo-extinction
effect. E. A. Wasserman and D. D. Jensen;
reply with rejoinder. M. E. Deutsch. Science 169:402 Jl 24 '70
Ontogeny of the estrogen receptor during early
uterine development. J. H. Clark and J.
Gorski. bibliog il Science 169:76-8 Jl 3 '70
Physiological responses of infant rats to separation from their mothers. H. A. Hofer.
bibliog il Science 168:871-3 My 15 '70
Rats' preference for earned in comparison
with free food. B. Carder and K. Berkowitz. 170:1273-4 F 27 '70; Discussion. 170:1229 D 11 '70

Extermination
See Rat control

RATS, Fossil. See Rodents, Fossil

RATS as laboratory animals. See Laboratory
animals

RATTAN furniture
Whatever happened to wicker? il House B
112:65-7 Je '70

RATTAZZI, Susanna (Agnelli) contessa. See
Agnelli, S.

RATTLESNAKES
Encounters with diamondbacks. A. Rutledge.
il Outdoor Life 145:78-80+ Mr '70
Rattlesnakes of Pinole. il Time 95:15 Je 29 '70

RAU, Ron
Employment for Fred. il Field & S 75:100-2
Jl '70

RAUDASCHL, Hubert
Profile of a yachtsman: Hubert Raudaschl. F.
Strebinger. il por Yachting 127:69+ My
'70 *

RAUSCHENBERG, Robert
Robert Rauschenberg. D. H. Karshan. il Art
in Am 58:48-51 N '70 *
Strong currents; show at the Pasadena art
museum. D. Davis. il por Newsweek 76:
69B Jl 27 '70 *

RAUSEO, Vic
Night at the opera. il Sr Schol 97:33-5 S 28 '70

RAVEN, Peter H.
Multiple origin for plastids and mitochondria.
bibliog Science 169:641-6 Ag 14 '70
—See Ehrlich, P. R. jt. auth.

RAVENEL, Beatrice St Julien
Public buildings of Charleston. il Antiques
97:584-9 Ap '70

RAVICH, Mikhail. See Senko, P. jt. auth.

RAVINIA festival
Ravinia; success and problems. R. C. Marsh.
il Hi Fi 20:MA14-15 N '70

RAW materials
Industrial minerals; new study of how to avoid
a supply crisis. L. J. Carter. Science 170:
147-8 O 9 '70
Red-hot economy's quest for raw material.
il Bsns W p46-7 Ja 24 '70

RAWE, Marcella
Kindly little tailor; drama. Plays 29:61-6,
74 F '70

RAY, Bill
Rarities of Ethiopia; photographs. Life 69:
46-55 N 27 '70
Soviet medicine. il Life 68:33-45 Ja 23 '70

RAY, David
Greece; Midnight diner by Edward Hopper;
poems. Poetry 115:241-3 Ja '70
This world, this growing light; poem. Nation
210:222 F 23 '70

RAY, Edward, and Cohen, R. M.
Tektite; a blueprint for cooperative undersea
scientific programs. il Bul Atom Sci 26:35-40 F '70

RAY, James Earl
Two months on the lam. W. B. Huie. il Esquire 73:104-7+ Je '70 *

RAY, Man
Remember Dada; Man Ray at eighty. S. De
Gramont. il pors N Y Times Mag p6-7+ S
6 '70 *

RAY, Satyajit
India's Chekhov. W. S. Pechter. Commonweal
93:71-2 O 16 '70 *
Profiles; city of dreadful night; Calcutta. V.
Mehta. New Yorker 46:87-90+ Mr 21 '70 *

RAYA, Joseph, abp
Hopeful voices from Israel; interview, ed. by F. D. Lueking. il Chr Cent 87:139-41 F 4 '70
RAYMAR book company
Pizzazz: Northwest wholesaler has it. il Pub W 198:31-2 O 12 '70
RAYNER, Chessy
Mica+Chessy=MAC II. il pors McCalls 97:96-101 Ad '70 *
RAYNES, Burt Franklin
Rohr breaks out. T. J. Murray. il por Duns 95:62-3 Je '70 *
RAYNOR, Jerry S.
Seed time and the catalogs. Horticulture 48:40+ D '70
RAYTHEON company
Raytheon consolidates cargo for weight break advantage. il Aviation W 93:124-5 O 26 '70
RAZA movement. See Mexican Americans
RAZAK, Tun Abdul
New man on a troubled scene. il por Time 96:35 O 5 '70 *
RAZOR blades
Crossed blades; promotional campaigns. il Newsweek 75:82 Mr 16 '70
Safety razor blades. il Consumer Bul 53:33-4 O '70
Science gives you a new edge on shaving; chrome-edged blades. H. Shuldiner. il Pop Sci 196:60-1 F '70
RAZORS
Cord-cordless electric shavers. il Consumer Bul 53:13-17 My '70
Electric shavers for the distaff side of the family. il Consumer Bul 53:18-20 Ag '70
Slant-edged razors may be worth a try. il Consumer Rep 35:75 F '70
REA, Marjorie
Mini-garden fun for a shut-in child. il Todays Health 48:66 F '70
REA express, inc.
Board to investigate air express tariffs. Aviation W 93:32 S 28 '70
REACT (organization)
New help for cars in trouble; CB channel 9 for emergency communications. R. Benrey. il Pop Sci 197:34+ O '70
Two-way REACTions. G. H. Reese. See issues of Popular electronics to April 1970
REACTANCE (electricity)
Reactance chart. il Electr World 83:57-8 Ap '70
See also
Electric resistance
Impedance (electricity)
REACTION time
How to speed up your reactions. N. Carlisle. il Mech Illus 66:60-1+ Ja '70
REACTIONARIES. See Conservatism
REACTIONS, Chemical. See Chemical reactions
REACTOR pressure vessels. See Pressure vessels
READ, David Haxton Carswell
Church to come; adaptation of address, April 9, 1970. America 122:550-4 My 23 '70
READ, Dwight W. and Lestrel, P. E.
Hominid phylogeny and immunology; a critical appraisal. bibliog il Science 168:578-80 My 1 '70
READ, Merrill S.
Malnutrition and learning. Ed Digest 35:8-11 Ad '70
READ, R. B.
Small restaurants where the San Franciscans eat. il Holiday 47:68-9+ Mr '70
READERS (books)
Basals are not for reading. F. Busch. Ed Digest 36:16-19 D '70

Anecdotes, facetiae, satire, etc.
Dick and Jane revisited; primer for non-reading inner city teen-agers. L. Israel. Sat R 53:12+ F 21 '70
READERS and libraries. See Libraries and readers
READERS' guide to periodical literature
Clinton Rossiter. W. F. Buckley. Nat R 22:775 Jl 28 '70
Reference notebook; periodicals indexed in Readers' guide. Writers Digest 50:27 F '70
READERS of newspapers. See Newspapers—Readers
READEY, Dagmar
Free trees for your borders. il Org Gard & Farm 17:50-1 N '70
READINESS for school
Good start in school. M. J. Clements. il Parents Mag 45:38-9 Ag 11 '70
Ready, set, go! New Hampshire school readiness project. D. K. Jaffe. il Am Ed 6:9-12 Ag '70
See also
Reading readiness

READING, Pa.
Streets
Self-propelled machine triples line painting. il Am City 85:42 Ag '70
READING
So you want to know more about reading? A. Berger. bibliog il por Wilson Lib Bul 45:254-69 N '70
Test yourself: what do you know about reading? J. Bloomfield. il por Wilson Lib Bul 45:242-5 N '70
See also
Books and reading
International reading association

Aids and devices
Demise of Dick and Jane; Reading systems program. il Sat R 53:59 D 19 '70
Reading industry: resources and materials. H. F. Rice. il por Wilson Lib Bul 45:298-307 N '70
See also
Teaching machines

Readiness
See Reading readiness

Remedial teaching
Citizen power; P.S. 109's man in the pin-striped suit. K. Branan. il Am Ed 6:14-17 Ad '70
If it's fun, it can't be reading! address, November, 1969. L. S. Johnson. Engl J 59:837-45 S '70
MAD magazine in the remedial English class. B. Sanders. Engl J 59:266-7+ F '70
Reading do's and don'ts. V. C. Osborne. il Todays Ed 59:48-9 Mr '70
Simplest clue. M. Medary. Horn Bk 46:635-41 D '70
We can end juvenile illiteracy. J. E. Allen, jr. Read Digest 96:157-8+ Ad '70
See also
Speed reading

Study and teaching
Barbershop reading; an insidious practice. V. G. Goldsmith. Ed Digest 35:40-1 My '70
Games that teach your children to read. il Bet Hom & Gard 48:44+ My '70
Librarian and the teaching of reading; symposium, ed. by A. Plotnik. bibliog il Wilson Lib Bul 45:239-307 N '70
Looking deep into the reading process; Targeted research and development program on reading of the USOE. M. M. Penney. il Am Ed 6:24-5 Mr '70
Partners for literacy; Literacy volunteers, inc. R. Cohen. il Am Ed 6:36 Je '70
Reading instruction in the elementary school; excerpts from address, February 1969. N. B. Smith. Todays Ed 59:42-3+ Ja '70
School where every child learns to read and loves it; individualized reading program. il Parents Mag 45:54-7 S '70
Should parents teach preschoolers to read? pro and con views. J. Beck; A. Rosenthal. Bet Hom & Gard 48:44+ My '70
Step up to reading; Huntington, W.Va. D. Marsh. il Am Ed 6:15-17 Ja '70
Washington mess. por Newsweek 76:70 O 5 '70
What do you mean, auditory perception? D. Seymour. Ed Digest 35:23-5 Mr '70
What will it be? Reading or machismo and soul? E. O. Vail. Clear House 45:92-6 O '70
Why not an intensive-gradual phonic approach? C. K. Winkley. Ed Digest 36:48-51 S '70
Why poor readers fail to improve. U S News 68:80 My 25 '70
See also
Readers (books)
Reading clinics
Reading readiness
Right to read program

Anecdotes, facetiae, satire, etc.
Son of Why Johnny can't read and what you can do about it, by Hugo Flesch, son of Rudolf Flesch, author of the father of son of Why Johnny can't read and. . . . H. Flesch por Wilson Lib Bul 45:270-1 N '70

Terminology
Up-to-date glossary of common terms used by reading instructors and informed librarians. N. B. Smith. il por Wilson Lib Bul 45:246-53 N '70

READING, Choice of. See Books and reading
READING air show. See Aviation—Exhibitions
READING aloud. See Books and reading—Reading aloud
READING by children. See Childrens reading

READING clinics
How to raise reading scores; Exemplary center for reading instruction, Salt Lake City, Utah. L. K. Chaffin. il Am Ed 6: 12-15 D '70
Juan's right to read; Whisman, Calif, reading/learning clinic. L. Goodman. il Am Ed 6:3-6 Jl '70

READING comprehension
Judgmental reading and the study of law. J. C. Johnson and H. L. Sublett, jr. bibliog Clear House 44:559-61 My '70

READING courses
Summer is for reading. P. Pine. il Am Ed 6: 26-7 Ag '70

READING disability
Hidden handicaps to learning. A. Greenblatt. il Parents Mag 45:53-5+ O '70
Some bright children can't read; with study-discussion program, by E. Harris and D. Harris. J. L. Laffey. bibliog il PTA Mag 65:9-11+, 34-5 O '70
See also
Reading—Remedial teaching

READING is FUN-damental program. See Childrens reading

READING lists
Book marks. J. W. Conner. See issues of English journal
See also
Books and reading—Best books
Childrens literature—Bibliography

READING readiness
Getting ready to read; with study-discussion program, by M. M. Conant. E. L. Cohen. bibliog il PTA Mag 65:18-20, 32 N '70
Reading readiness. D. Durkin. Ed Digest 35: 36-9 My '70
Should parents teach preschoolers to read? pro and con views. J. Beck; A. Rosenthal. il Todays Health 48:36-41+ My '70
Truth about readiness. J. S. Caldwell and S. W. Shnayer. il Library J 95:1909-10 My 15 '70

READING research
Effect of pictures on learning to read. S. J. Samuels. Ed Digest 36:48-51 N '70
In search of the impossible dream; Cleveland Heights, Ohio study. J. Lichtenstein. Ed Digest 35:34-5 My '70

READING rooms in libraries. See Libraries— Reading rooms

READY-to-cook food. See Food—Ready-to-cook food

REAGAN, Ronald
Our environment crisis. il Nations Bsns 58: 24-8 F '70
President Nixon honors President Diaz Ordaz of Mexico at a state dinner in California; remarks, September 3, 1970. Dept State Bul 63:349 S 28 '70
about
Governor v. the university. D. Neff. il por Time 95:69-70+ Mr 30 '70 *
Hottest candidate in either party. P. O'Neil. il pors Life 69:26-9 O 30 '70 *
Reagan and rhetoric. New Repub 163:10 N 7 '70 *
Reagan's bloodbath: truth and imagery. Nat R 22:445 My 5 '70 *
Riding high. il por Newsweek 75:32 Mr 23 '70 *
Ronald Reagan is giving 'em heck. S. V. Roberts. il por N Y Times Mag p42-3+ O 25 '70 *
Ronald Reagan story: scenario for a star. K. Fleming and P. Goldman. il pors Newsweek 76:28-31 N 2 '70 *
Ronnie and Jesse, by L. Cannon. Review Nat R 22:162 F 10 '70. J. Hart
Thanks to Governor Reagan. Nation 210:324-5 Mr 23 '70 *

REAL estate. See Real property

REAL estate agents
When do you need a real estate agent? il Bet Hom & Gard 48:12+ Mr '70

REAL estate business
It's not just the cities. A. Mayer. il Arch Rec 147:137-42 Je '70
It's the individual investment that counts; interview. L. A. Wien; H. Helmsley. pors Forbes 106:42-4 N 1 '70
Real estate: on the brink? il Forbes 106: 18-23 Jl 1 '70
Space preservation, taxes, planning, and talking: the crunch. R. E. Galantowicz. il Am For 76:36-8+ O '70
See also
Cabot, Cabot and Forbes (firm)
Coldwell, Banker and company
Corporations—Real estate operations
Great southwest corporation

Insurance companies—Real estate operations
Land speculation
Offices—Leasing and renting
Public utilities—Real estate operations
Railroads—Real estate operations
Webb and Knapp, inc.

Terminology
Real estate man's jargon. Sunset 145:80-1 Ag '70

REAL estate investment
Apartment houses: new home for executive cash. A. Hershman. il Duns 96:43-7 D '70
Hot sales in property shares; real estate syndication. Bsns W p34-6 N 28 '70
Real estate syndications are big-time again. Bsns W p83 N 28 '70

REAL estate investment trusts
Sorting out the real-estate investment trusts. W. Robertson. il Fortune 82:173-5 Ag '70
See also
USIF, Real estate

REAL property
Space preservation, taxes, planning, and talking: the crunch. R. E. Galantowicz. il Am For 76:36-8+ O '70
See also
Building sites
Land values

Valuation
When you may need a real estate appraiser. il Good H 170:719 Ap '70

REALISM
Realism as preached and practiced: the Russian opera dialogue. R. Taruskin. bibliog f il Mus Q 56:431-54 Jl '70

REALISM in art
Dawley re-asserts realism. R. Kolbe. il Am Artist 34:69-76 Mr '70
Nonfiction art: literalist realism. B. Rose. Vogue 156:42 Ag 1 '70
Parting shots; the camera's illusion and delusions. il Life 68:81-4 Ap 24 '70
Plight of realism today; exhibition at the Whitney museum. R. Berenson. il Nat R 22: 474-5 My 5 '70
Portrait of the artist as a wet hen. il Esquire 73:134-9 Ap '70
Presenting Duane Hanson. D. Hanson. il Art in Am 58:86-9 S '70
See also
Trompe-l'oeil

REALISM in literature
Century of American realism; interview, ed. by J. A. Garraty. A. Kazin. il Am Heritage 21:12-15+ Je '70
From now to 1984; books for children in serious times. B. Bacon. bibliog il Wilson Lib Bul 45:156-9 O '70
Here and beyond; books on today's issues for children. J. Karl. il por Wilson Lib Bul 45:149-55 O '70
Real thing: what will it be? children's books in the 1970s. A. Moxley. bibliog il Wilson Lib Bul 45:160-2 O '70
Realism in the novel. D. Goldknopf. Yale R 60:69-84 O '70

REALISM in moving pictures
Techniques of trickery. B. Nichols. Commonweal 93:375-6 Ja 15 '71

REALISM in music. See Realism

REALITY
Beyond the reality principle: illusion or new reality? L. Gordon. bibliog f Am Imago 27:160-82 O '70

REALS, Lucile Farnsworth
Bennington poodle. il Hobbies 75:80 Je '70
Silver sugar tongs by Hester Bateman. il Hobbies 75:120+ Jl '70

REAMS, Lee Roy
Pair from Applause. N. M. Stoop. il pors Dance Mag 44:42-6 O '70 *

REAPPORTIONMENT. See Apportionment (election law)

REAR view mirrors. See Automobiles—Equipment

REARDON, Dennis J.
Happiness cage. Criticism
Nation 211:414 O 26 '70 *
New Yorker 46:143 O 17 '70 *

REASON
Beyond the reality principle: illusion or new reality? L. Gordon. bibliog f Am Imago 27:160-82 O '70
Violence or reason? reprint from June 14, 1957 issue. D. Lawrence. U S News 68:92+ Je 1 '70

REASONER, Harry
Age of Reasoner. Time 96:70 N 16 '70 *

REASONING
　　See also
　Analogy
　Judgment (logic)
REAVES, John
　Gator aid. H. L. Masin. pors Sr Schol 97:26-7
　　O 26 '70 *
REAVES, Philip, pseud.
　"Shrine" of Gettysburg. il Good H 171:
　　126+ Jl '70
REAVIS, Philip
　Boating vacations abroad. il Motor B 125:
　　62-3+ My '70
REBELLIONS. See Revolutions
REBMANN, Andrew J.
　Veeder's windfall. A. A. Butkus. por Duns
　　96:59 O '70 *
REBOZO, Charles Gregory
　Nixon's friend Bebe; with editorial comment.
　　C. Leinster. il pors Life 69:3, 18B-27 Jl 31
　　'70 *
REBUILT automobiles. See Automobiles, Re-
　modeled
RECA, Maria E. See Berliner, M. D. jt. auth.
RECANATI, Raphael
　Pleasure cruise? il por Forbes 106:24-5 N 1
　　'70 *
RECEPTIONS
　　See also
　Government entertaining
RECESSION, Business. See Business depression
RÉCHAUFFÉ cookery. See Cookery—Left-
　overs
RECHNITZ, G. A. and Mohan, M. S.
　Potassium-adenosine triphosphate complex:
　　formation contant measured with ion-se-
　　lective electrodes. bibliog il Science 168:
　　1460 Je 19 '70
RECIPES. See Cookery
RECIPROCATING engines (automobile) See
　Automobile engines
RECK-MALLECZEWEN, Friedrich Percyval
　Brave old world. R. Z. Sheppard. por Time
　　96:103+ S 21 '70 *
RECLAMATION, Bureau of. See United States
　—Reclamation, Bureau of
RECLAMATION of land
　　See also
　Irrigation
　Marshes
　Terraces (agriculture)
　United States—Reclamation, Bureau of

Florida
Curing Florida's strip-mining ills. il Bsns
　W p43 Ja 2 '71

Netherlands
Landscaping the Netherlands. I. G. Simmons.
　il Am For 76:19-21+ F '70

Ohio
Returning beauty to the land; Friendship
　park in eastern Ohio. Nations Bsns 58:
　19 Ja '70
RECLASSIFICATION. See Classification
RECLUSES
　　See also
　Hermits
RECOGNITION (psychology)
　Chimp discovers its self. il Sci Digest 67:67
　　Ap '70
　Tones and numbers: specificity of inter-
　　ference in immediate memory. D. Deutsch.
　　bibliog il Science 168:1604-5 Je 26 '70
RECONNAISSANCE, Aerial. See Aerial recon-
　naissance
RECONNAISSANCE drones. See Airplanes,
　Drone
RECONSTRUCTION (Civil war)
　Public opinion and the passage of the Missis-
　　sippi black codes. M. M. Bigelow. bibliog
　　Negro Hist Bul 33:11-16 Ja '70
　　See also
　Freedmen
RECONSTRUCTION (World war, 1939-1945)
　　See also
　Crimea conference, Yalta, Russia, 1945
RECORD changers. See Phonograph—Record
　changers
RECORD photography. See Photography, Docu-
　mentary
RECORDING instruments
　Simple new amplifying device is adapted to
　　driving a pen recorder. J. B. Shackleford.
　　il Sci Am 222:130-2+ My '70
RECORDS
　　See also
　Farm records
　Police records
　Sports records
　Weather records

RECORDS, Phonograph. See Phonograph rec-
　ords
RECORDS, School. See School reports and rec-
　ords
RECREATION
　Charismatic and the playful in outdoor rec-
　　reation. R. Meyersohn. bibliog f il Ann Am
　　Acad 389:35-45 My '70
　High-rise recreation; Arlington County, Va.
　　L. Neeld. il Parks & Rec 5:50 My '70
　Recreation and parks in other lands; sym-
　　posium. il Parks & Rec 5:35-47+ Ap '70
　　See also
　Amusement parks
　Games
　Leisure
　Outdoor life
　Parks
　Physical education and training
　Play
　Playgrounds
　Recreational therapy
　Sports
　Student activities

Activities
Be in boosts recreation programs; Detroit's
　Wintercade recreation program. il Am City
　85:46 Ag '70
Social and personality correlates of outdoor
　recreation. A. L. Ferriss. bibliog f il Ann
　Am Acad 389:46-55 My '70
　　See also
　Boats and boating
　Camping—Activities
　Childrens gardens
　Picnics

Administration
Community involvement. C. M. Pendleton, jr.
　Parks & Rec 5:21-2+ O '70
Credibility gap in recreation administration
　literature. L. R. Rockwood. Parks & Rec
　5:50+ F '70
New cash control and data collection system;
　Ramapo, N.Y. A. Palermo. il por Parks &
　Rec 5:32-3 Mr '70
　　See also
　Park and recreation departments

Equipment and supplies
Mobile recreation fleet; Nassau County. J.
　W. Halper. il Am City 85:100+ S '70
Trends. il Parks & Rec 5:29-42+ My '70

Fees
Golden Eagle returns for 1971; national rec-
　reation fee system. Sunset 145:36 D '70

Finance
Economics of recreation today; U.S. annual
　expenditures. R. Kraus. il por Parks & Rec
　5:19-21+ Je '70

International aspects
Global view of parks and recreation. T. E.
　Rivers. Parks & Rec 5:21 Ap '70

Literature
Credibility gap in recreation administration
　literature. L. R. Rockwood. Parks & Rec
　5:50+ F '70

Psychological aspects
Social and personality correlates of outdoor
　recreation. A. L. Ferriss. bibliog f il Ann
　Am Acad 389:46-55 My '70
　　See also
　Recreation workers—Training

Asia
Recreation in Asia. M. H. Potter. il Parks &
　Rec 5:44-6+ N '70

Brazil
Brazil: land of contrasts. E. B. Medeiros. il
　Parks & Rec 5:36-7 Ap '70

Great Britain
Game of war. il Time 97:47 Ja 4 '71

Japan
Japan's cultural recreation. Prince Takahito.
　il por Parks & Rec 5:43+ Ap '70
　　See also
　Sports—Japan

Switzerland
Switzerland: a comprehensive youth pro-
　gram. A. Lederman. il Parks & Rec 5:44+
　Ap '70

RECREATION—*Continued*

United States

Big recreation needs; watershed projects. H. G. Uhlig. il Am City 85:59 D '70

California on wheels: I'm somebody. K. Fleming. il Newsweek 76:64-9 N 30 '70

Horses and parks; symposium. il Parks & Rec 5:29-44 F '70

Horses in California; symposium. il Parks & Rec 5:36-44 F '70

Interview with three recreation planners. H. A. Price; J. H. McCarthy; D. M. Hinchliffe. Forbes 105:202-3 Ja 1 '70

It's big business! Parks & Rec 5:25 Ja '70

Outdoor recreation. J. F. Hart and R. B. Adams. bibliog il Focus 20:8-11 F '70

Outdoor recreation economics. J. V. Krutilla and J. L. Knetsch. Ann Am Acad 389: 63-70 My '70

Recreation; address, February 9, 1970. H. D. Sessoms. Vital Speeches 36:349-52 Mr 15 '70

Where is the outdoor recreation plan? J. F. Shanklin and E. M. Fitch. il Am For 76: 28-31+ Mr '70

See also
Forest recreation
National recreation and park association
Recreation, Rural
Sports—United States
also subhead Recreation under names of cities, e.g. New York (city)—Recreation

Vietnam (Republic)

Vietnam: recreational leadership training. B. Bush. il Parks & Rec 5:40-2+ Ap '70

RECREATION, Rural

Country clubs for farmers. C. E. Ball. il Farm J 94:18-19+ Jl '70

Private enterprise reacts to recreation demands; recreation facilities provided by privately owned forest lands. E. J. Hodges. il Parks & Rec 5:36-8+ Ja '70

RECREATION and state

Outdoor recreation economics. J. V. Krutilla and J. L. Knetsch. Ann Am Acad 389:63-70 My '70

RECREATION areas

Land between the lakes. L. S. Clapper. il Nat Wildlife 8:38-41 Je '70

People, parks, and traffic. A. W. Smith. Nat Parks & Con Mag 44:2 My '70

Why not a nationwide plan for recreation? E. K. Thompson. Arch Rec 147:131 My '70

See also
National parks and reserves

Fees

See Recreation—Fees

Lighting

Lights. H. A. Oaks. il Parks & Rec 5:42-3+ Ja '70

California

Here's a hiking and fishing loop; Lakes basin recreational area. il Sunset 145:23 Ag '70

Mineral King, a fresh look. D. Anderson. il Nat Parks & Con Mag 44:8-10 My '70

Recreation for forty million people. W. P. Mott, jr. il Arch Rec 147:132-3 My '70

Trinity Lake in summer is hard to resist; Trinity national recreation area. il Sunset 145:30-1 Jl '70

Oklahoma

Planning gives big boost to recreation. Am City 85:63 S '70

Washington (state)

North Cascades, a wilderness plan. J. V. Morris. il Nat Parks & Con Mag 44:10-15 O '70

West Virginia

Hillbilly heaven; Pipestem resort area. D. Butwin. il Sat R 53:46+ N 21 '70

RECREATION buildings

Building types study. il Arch Rec 147:131-46 My '70

RECREATION centers

Ghetto youth are this doctor's bag; Washington shores association for recreation center, Orlando, Fla. il pors Ebony 25:100-2+ S '70

Hog farm becomes activities center. R. D. Espeseth. il Parks & Rec 5:38-9 O '70

Visit to the Cambridge art center; Cambridge, Mass. C. Guertin. il Sch Arts 69: 36-7 Ap '70

RECREATION conferences

Coming events. See issues of Parks & recreation

See also
National recreation and park association—Meetings

RECREATION department symbols. See Emblems

RECREATION departments. See Park and recreation departments

RECREATION education. See Recreation workers—Training

RECREATION for the aged

Easier living on less money. F. C. Weed. il Har Yrs 10:19-23 D '70

Fall River, Mass, high school pupils visit aging in new plan; Romero aid to elderly project. il Aging 188:15 Je '70

N.C. women start club based on AoA-aided senior program; Good morning club. Aging 188:14 Je '70

Time for relaxation and recreation. P. A. Dickinson. bibliog il Har Yrs 10:42-50 N '70

See also
Hobbies

RECREATION for the blind

See also
Sports for the blind

RECREATION for the handicapped

See also
Recreational therapy

RECREATION for youth. See Youth—Recreation

RECREATION in church work

See also
Church work with youth

RECREATION rooms

New party room on an older house. il Bet Hom & Gard 48:67 My '70

RECREATION workers

People. See issues of Parks & recreation

Recruiting

Black college forum gives new insights; career opportunities in parks and recreation. Parks & Rec 5:44-5 Jl '70

Manpower crises: as others see us. H. D. Sessoms. il Parks & Rec 5:39-41+ Ja '70

Recreation education: a social concern; recognition of needs of disadvantaged groups. J. F. Murphy. bibliog il Parks & Rec 9:57-8+ S '70

Supply and demand

Manpower crises: as others see us. H. D. Sessoms. il Parks & Rec 5:39-41+ Ja '70

Training

Recreation education: a social concern; recognition of needs of disadvantaged groups. J. F. Murphy. bibliog f il Parks & Rec 9:57-8+ S '70

RECREATIONAL therapy

Therapeutic program: a community responsibility. D. C. Park. Parks & Rec 5:25-6+ Jl '70

RECREATIONAL vehicle tires. See Tires, Recreational vehicle

RECREATIONAL vehicles

Best is yet to come. B. Behme. Field & S 75:104-5 Ag '70

California on wheels: I'm somebody. K. Fleming. il Newsweek 76:64-9 N 30 '70

Camping out with all the conveniences. il Sports Illus 32:32-7 Je 1 '70

Fun on wheels, on and off the highways. Bsns W p 119-20 Ap 11 '70

Ideas for RV users. C. B. Colby. il Outdoor Life 146:16+ N '70

Look at the new RVs. W. T. McKeown. il Mech Illus 66:58+ My '70

Mechanized monsters. il Time 96:41 N 23 '70

Motorized recreation vehicles: problems, and suggested solutions. D. R. Dunn. il Parks & Rec 5:10-14+ Jl '70

Recreation roundup. See issues of Popular science monthly

Recreation vehicles for today and tomorrow. J. Gartner. il Field & S 74:66-71+ Mr '70

Tricart, wild new breed of off-road vehicle. H. Shuldiner. il Pop Sci 196:44 Ap '70

We hit the RV trail! symposium. il Pop Sci 196:78-85+ Mr '70

Well traveled camera. H. Keppler. il Mod Phot 34:142+ Ap '70

Which camper fits your family? il Bet Hom & Gard 48:18+ N '70

See also
Automobile trailers
Campers and coaches, Truck
Crawler vehicles
Motor vehicles, Amphibious
Rectrans, inc.
Skyline corporation
Snowmobiles and snowmobiling

RECREATIONAL vehicles—*Continued*
Equipment
How to rig your new recreation vehicle. V. L. Oertle. il Pop Mech 133:S10+ My '70
RECRUITING for librarianship. See Librarians —Recruiting
RECRUITING of employees
Fewer jobs for the class of '70. il U S News 68:38-41 Mr 9 '70
Firm's stand on personal weakness; Pitney-Bowes screening methods. V. Louviere. Nations Bsns 58:13 Ag '70
Help wanted; must be black; College placement services program. il Bsns W p93 Ja 17 '70
Three methods of contacting employers to obtain jobs for the rehabilitated psychiatric patient. A. Loeb and others. il Ment Hy 54: 137-9 Ja '70
See also
Applications for positions
Discrimination in employment
Employment agencies
Television broadcasting—Employee recruiting programs
RECRUITING of students. See Colleges and universities—Student recruiting
RECRUITING of teachers. See Teachers—Recruiting
RECRUITING officer; drama. See Farquhar. G.
RECRUITING officer; story. See McGahern, J.
RECTRANS, Inc.
Knudsen finds a home on wheels. il por Bsns W p94 N 14 '70
RECYCLING of wastes. See Refuse, Utilization of
RED caviar. See Caviar
RED cross
Disaster relief service
Biting the hand that feeds you. Trans-Action 7:4 Ap '70
United States
Red cross national aquatic and small-craft schools. Camp Mag 42:50-1 Mr '70
See also
Red cross—Disaster relief service
RED deer hunting. See Deer hunting
RED drum fishing. See Bass fishing
RED mile track. See Race tracks
RED schoolhouse. See School buildings
RED SEA
Afar triangle. H. Tazieff. il Sci Am 222:32-40 bibliog(p 126) F '70
Red Sea hot brines. E. T. Degens and D. A. Ross. il Sci Am 222:32-42 Ap '70
See also
Suez Canal
RED sheep hunting. See Mountain sheep hunting
RED shift. See Quasars—Spectra
RED Sox (baseball) See Baseball clubs
RED tape. See Bureaucracy
RED tide
Natural gas; irritating substances in Red tide; excerpts from 1948 report. P. S. Galtsoff. il Environ 12:22-3 Mr '70
REDBUD
Now's the time to shop for and bring home a redbud. il Sunset 144:176 F '70
REDD, Virginia P.
Teaching writing in the junior high school. Engl J 59:540-7 Ap '70
REDDIG, Edward Sterling
Not with a scalpel. por Forbes 16:20 N 1 '70 *
REDDISH, Don B.
Love-in at the Utah natatorium. W. F. Reed. il por Sports Illus 32:50+ Mr 16 '70 *
REDDY, John
Bob Dylan, poet laureate of folk rock. por Read Digest 96:249-50+ Je '70
John Wayne rides again and again and again. por Read Digest 97:138-42 S '70
1776: the idea that would not let go. il por Read Digest 96:199-200+ F '70
(ed) See Socarras Ramirez, A. Stowaway
REDDY, William J. See Snyder, L. M. jt. auth.
REDEMPTION. See Salvation
REDEMPTION of Gloria Barney; story. See Soman, F. J.
REDFIELD, Alfred G. See Gupta, R. K. jt. auth.
REDFIELD, Margaret. See Ford, G. jt. auth.
REDFIELD, William C.
Espy-Redfield dispute. D. M. Ludlum. pors Weatherwise 22:224-9+ D '69

REDFORD, Robert
Oh, you Sundance Kid! L. Luckinbill. il por Esquire 74:160-3+ O '70 *
Robert Redford riding high; with report by R. Schickel. il pors Life 68:38-45 F 6 '70
REDISTRICTING. See Apportionment (election law)
REDON, Odilon
Dream world of Odilon Redon. A. Werner. il Am Artist 34:40-5+ N '70 *
REDUCING. See Corpulence
REDUCING diet. See Diet
REDUCING exercises. See Exercise
REDUCTASES
Altered dihydrofolate reductase associated with drug-resistance transfer between rodent plasmodia. R. Ferone and others. bibliog il Science 167:1263-4 F 27 '70
REDUCTION of armaments. See Disarmament
REDWOOD
Coast redwood. J. W. Wilson. Horticulture 48:44-5 Ap '70
Generous gift from Georgia-Pacific. il Am For 76:48-50 Mr '70
Redwood reflections. S. L. Keith. il Nat Parks & Con Mag 44:16-17 Ap '70
See also
Sequoia, Giant
REDWOOD NATIONAL PARK
Redwoods forever! J. Hope. il Audubon 72: 66-8+ Mr '70
REDWOOD nature trail. See Trails
REDWOOD planters. See Flower boxes, planters, etc.
REECE, Judith
American in Germany: dancing for Cranko; interview, ed. by O. Maynard. il pors Dance Mag 44:34-7 Mr '70
REED, Bob. See Hughes, J. jt. auth.
REED, David
Fedayeen: Israel's fanatic foe. il Read Digest 97:168-73 O '70
Russia turns to wheels. il Read Digest 97: 163-4+ S '70
Vietnamization, can it succeed? Read Digest 96:55-61 Ap '70
REED, Dean
Dean who? S. Turner. il por Sr Schol 96:12+ Ap 6 '70 *
REED, Dena
Lucilla's proposal; drama. Plays 30:11-20 Ja '71
REED, Donald R.
Nature and function of continuation education. Ed Digest 35:52-4 F '70
REED, Elizabeth C.
White tiger in my house. il Nat Geog 137: 482-91 Ap '70
REED, Eugenia
Grandma was a dropout. il Har Yrs 10:38-9 Ja '70
REED, Geff
Ceramics by Geff Reed. il Ceram Mo 18:23 Ap '70 *
REED, George
New planetarium in Pennsylvania. il R Pop Astron 63:14 Ag '69
REED, George W. Jr, and others
Trace elements and accessory minerals in lunar samples. bibliog il Science 167:501-3 Ja 30 '70
REED, Helen Scott Townsend
Church silver in colonial Virginia. il Antiques 97:243-7 F '70
REED, J. D.
Only bar in Dixon; poem New Yorker 46:48 O 10 '70
Organ transplant; poem. New Yorker 46:126 S 26 '70
REED, John C.
Oil & the Arctic tundra. il Nat Parks & Con Mag 44:4-7 N '70
REED, Rex
At the movies. See issues of Holiday
REED, Robert G. 3d
Children of change; address, May 7, 1970. Vital Speeches 36:713-15 S 15 '70
REED, T. Edward
Caucasian genes in American Negroes. bibliog Science 165:762-8; 166:1353, 167:1389 Ag 22, D 12 '69, Mr 6 '70
REED, William F. Jr
...And the best of them all is Archie. il por Sports Illus 33:52-5 S 14 '70
Archie and the war between the states. il pors Sports Illus 33:14-17 O 12 '70
College basketball (cont) Sports Illus 34:46 Ja 4 '71
College football. il Sports Illus 33:66+ N 16; 67-8 N 23 '70

REED, William F. Jr—*Continued*
Hambo was a family affair. il pors Sports Illus 33:24-5 S 14 '70
Harness racing (cont) il Sports Illus 32:74-6 My 25; 56+ Je 22; 52-3 Jl 13; 33:60+ O 5; 58+ O 19 '70
He whistles while he works. il pors Sports Illus 33:22-7 Ag 10 '70
Marlu has a bit of trouble. il por Sports Illus 33:22-3 Ag 24 '70
Pussycat on a quick cold rink. il pors Sports Illus 32:18-19 Mr 9 '70
Redemption after a false start. il por Sports Illus 32:26-7 Ap 6 '70
Swimming (cont) Sports Illus 32:50+ Mr 16 '70
Swimming isn't everything, winning is. il pors Sports Illus 32:26-9 Mr 9 '70
Tall story from the land of Boone. il Sports Illus 33:66-8 N 30 '70
This horse needed his owner's stamina. il Sports Illus 32:26-7 My 11 '70
Tornado with a new twist. il Sports Illus 33:16-17 Jl 6 '70
Upstaging of Pistol Pete. il Sports Illus 32:22-5 Mr 30 '70
Week. Sports Illus 33:36-8 Ag 31; 54+ S 28 '70
Week; college football. Sports Illus 33:49-50+ O 19; 52-4 O 26; 45-7 N 9; 67-9 D 7 '70
Week (football) Sports Illus 33:49-50+ O 19 '70

REED, Willis
In for two plus the title. F. Deford. il Sports Illus 32:14-17 My 18 '70 *
REED switches. See Electric switches
REEDER, Charles B.
Tall economist with a low profile. por Bsns W p74 N 28 '70 *
REEDY, George E.
Does the U.S. need a king? Look 34:32-5 Mr 10 '70
REEDY, Gerard
That obscenity report. America 123:371-3 N 7 '70
REEDY, W. A.
Georgia art potter. il pors Ceram Mo 18:19-26 Je '70
REEFS
See also
Coral reefs and islands
REEFS, Artificial
Long Island's artificial fishing reefs. C. S. Zawacki. il Cons 24:18-21 Ag '69
Old tires: a new lure for fish. V. Louviere. il Nations Bsns 58:18 O '70
REELFOOT LAKE
Legendary Reelfoot. B. Thomas. il Travel 134:40-3+ Jl '70
REELS, Fishing. See Fishing tackle
REEMTSMA, Keith
Gathering of specialists. B. J. Culliton. il pors Sci N 97:347-9 Ap 4 '70 *
REES, Martin J. and Silk, Joseph
Origin of galaxies; with biographical sketches. il Sci Am 222:12, 26-35 bibliog(p 152) Je '70
REES, Mina
Liberated all liberated. il pors Vogue 155:120 Je '70 *
Mina Rees, president-elect 1970. F. J. Weyl. bibliog por Science 167:1149-51 F 20 '70 *
REESE, G. H.
Two-way REACTions. See issues of Popular electronics to April 1970
REEVE, F. D.
Hope; Long trail; Opus aestivus; poems. Poetry 116:164-6 Je '70
REEVES, Richard
Goldilocks may not be the most exciting fellow in town but he's the only one who can win this year. il pors N Y Times Mag p7+ Je 14 '70
One Rockefeller who may make it. il por N Y Times Mag p30-1+ O 4 '70
This is the battle of the titans? il pors N Y Times Mag p23-5+ N 1 '70
REEVES, Ruth, and Knappenberger, Dorothy
Preparing a curriculum guide. bibliog Engl J 59:520-3+ Ap '70
REFEREEING (sports) See Sports officiating
REFEREES. See Umpires (sports)
REFERENCE books
Reference books for writers. R. Armour. Writer 83:23-5 F '70
See also
Biographical dictionaries
Encyclopedias
Quotations

Bibliography
Current reference books. F. N. Cheney. See issues of Wilson library bulletin
Reference books of 1969; recommendations of a committee of the Reference services division of ALA. G. R. Purcell. il por Library J 95:1437-42 Ap 15 '70
SR's semi-annual reference book roundup (cont) D. M. Glixon. il Sat R 53:35-40+ My 16; 32+ D 5 '70
REFERENCE work. See Libraries—Reference work
REFLECTING telescopes. See Telescopes
REFLECTION (optics)
See also
Light—Scattering
REFLECTION spectroscopy. See Spectrum analysis
REFLEXES
Habituation and distribution of the gill-withdrawal reflex in aplysia. H. Pinsker and others. bibliog il Science 167:1740-2 Mr 27 '70
Neuronal correlates of habituation and dishabituation of the gill-withdrawal reflex in aplysia. I. Kupfermann and others. bibliog il Science 167:1743-5 Mr 27 '70
Neuronal mechanisms of the habituation and dishabituation of the gill-withdrawal reflex in aplysia. V. Castellucci and others. bibliog il Science 167:1745-8 Mr 27 '70
REFORESTATION
Planting in Pag. J. W. Duffield. il Am For 76:22-4+ F '70
See also
Forest reproduction
REFORM
See also
Reformers
Social problems
REFORM Judaism
Cantors in Curaçao; American conference of cantors, Curaçao. il Newsweek 76:102 Jl 13 '70
Intermarriage & Jewish survival. M. Sklare. Commentary 49:51-8 Mr '70; Discussion. 49:4+ Je '70
REFORMATION
Great confrontations: Leo X and Luther. L. B. Smith. il pors Horizon 12:90-5 Spr '70

Early movements
Grass-roots reformation. W. S. Reid. Chr Today 15:6-9 O 23 '70
REFORMATORIES
Help for troubled girls; Good Shepherd home in St Paul, Minn. J. Engh. il Parents Mag 45:66-8+ Mr '70
New life for women inmates; Oakdale state reformatory for women, Dwight, Ill. il Ebony 25:105-6+ Ap '70
REFORMED church in America
Reformed church in America; weighing a wedge. A. H. Matthews. Chr Today 14:34-5 Jl 3 '70
REFORMED church in South Africa
Question for the Christian church. America 123:195 S 26 '70
REFORMED churches
Christian reformed: a classis in comtempt? 1970 synod of the Christian reformed church. J. Daane. Chr Today 14:34-5 Jl 17 '70
New reformed covenant; World alliance of reformed churches. O. W. Okite. Chr Today 14:30-1 S 25 '70
REFORMERS
Were they right? J. H. Plumb. il Horizon 12:40-1 Aut '70
REFRACTORY materials
Refractory oxide-metal composites; scanning electron microscopy and X-ray diffraction of uranium dioxide-tungsten. R. J. Gerdes and others. il Science 167:979-80 F 13 '70
REFRIGERATION and refrigerating machinery
See also
Ice—Manufacture
REFRIGERATION on boats
Galley refrigerator. C. Miller. il Motor B 126:22 S '70
Proper food preservation. E. A. Zadig. il Motor B 126:12-13+ Jl '70
REFRIGERATORS, Electric
Frostless refrigerator-freezers. il Consumer Bul 53:7-16 Je '70
Keeping food cool. il Redbook 135:90-8 Je '70
No-frost, top-freezer refrigerators. il Consumer Rep 35:606-15 O '70
Refrigerator-freezers. il Consumer Rep 34:74-86 D '69
Refrigerators: buying tips plus test results. il Changing T 24:35-8 Je '70

REFUSE collection. See Refuse and refuse disposal

REFUSE collectors strike, Great Britain. See Strikes—Great Britain

REFUSE compactors. See Refuse and refuse disposal—Apparatus

REFUSE containers. See Refuse receptacles

REFUSE grinders
Care and feeding of disposers. Sunset 145: 134-5 N '70
Food waste disposers. il Consumer Rep 35: 305-11 My '70
What you should know about garbage disposers before you buy one. S. J. Howard. il Pop Mech 133:156-9 My '70

REFUSE incinerators
Equipment that works on the refuse disposal problem. H. Kaplan. il Arch Rec 148:133-6 Jl '70
Housing development finds it pays to radicate; Youngstown, Ohio. J. P. Prosser. il Am City 85:34 Ja '70
Incinerators, environment and other radical subjects. Am City 85:8 My '70
Melting waste into urban ore; super-heater in Erie County, N.Y. Bsns W p98 Jl 25 '70
Montreal's combined incinerator-power plant. E. F. Spitzer. il Am City 85:86-9 My '70
Precision controlled flames fight air pollution. R. H. Burns and R. E. Newton. il Am City 85:98+ My '70
Promising future for underground incineration. Am City 85:48 My '70
Sea-going incineration proposed. il Am City 85:46 Mr '70
Smokeless car salvage; Cedar Rapids area. Am City 85:27 N '70

REFUSE receptacles
Bagged refuse brings better service; Rolling Meadows, Ill. J. McFeggan. il Am City 85: 69-72 Mr '70
Better refuse service with bags; use of disposable plastic garbage bags in York, S. C. R. H. Moore, jr. and J. Boland. il pors Am City 85:76+ Ag '70
New York city approves refuse sacks; plastic and paper refuse bags. Am City 85:37 Ja '70
People chose sacks over cans; Weatherford, Tex. K. E. Smith. il Am City 85:82-3 Je '70
People prefer trash bags; Malden, Mass. il Am City 85:52 S '70
Plastic containers for refuse. Sunset 145:130 O '70
Refuse-sack use rises rapidly. Am City 85:53 Ag '70
Teenagers add color to trash containers; Detroit. il Am City 85:34 Ap '70

REGAN, Donald Thomas
As they see it; interview. por Forbes 105: 48+ Ap 15 '70
Leading broker calls for new rules to aid investors; excerpts from address, September 15, 1970. por U S News 69:61-2 S 28 '70

REGATTAS
Bahamian cruise-regatta; Out island regatta, George Town, Great Exuma. P. Leslie. il Yachting 128:59+ N '70
Blues and hangovers on the Nile; Oxford and Cambridge vs Egypt. C. Freud. il Sports Illus 34:16-19 Ja 4 '71
Chesapeake appreciation day 1969; racing of oyster dredging workboats. B. Schill and B. Schill. il Motor B 125:20-1 F '70
Destination 70; a potpourri of places to go, and things to see on this year's cruise. il Motor B 125:92-3 Mr '70
Kick-off for college sailing. G. M. Hall. il Yachting 127:70-1+ Mr '70
Master mariners race; annual regatta in San Francisco Bay. W. E. Vaughn. il Motor B 125:54-6+ My '70
Mixing the seasons; autumn sailing weekend. B. Schill and B. Schill. il Yachting 128:58-9 O '70
Month in yachting. See issues of Yachting
Not much hair in the boat but plenty of ergo; Huskies of Washington, champions of Intercollegiate rowing association regatta. H. D. Whall. il Sports Illus 32:54-5 Je 22 '70
Regatta results. See issues of Yachting
Ships of the desert; Desert regatta at Lake Havasu, Ariz. L. J. Kennedy. il Motor B 126:138-40 Ag '70
Where the action is! il Yachting 128:46-51+ O '70
Year in yachting. il Yachting 129:76-83 Ja '71
See also
Rowing
Yacht racing

REGENCY furniture. See Furniture, English

REGENERATION (biology)
Regeneration of the amputated amphibian limb: retardation by hemicholinium-3. F. Hui and A. Smith. bibliog il Science 170: 1313-14 D 18 '70
Reinnervated eye muscles do not respond to impulses in foreign nerves. R. F. Mark and others. bibliog il Science 170:193-4 O 9 '70
Spinal cord regeneration. B. J. Culliton. il Sci N 98:337-8 O 24 '70

REGER, Max
Back again: Joseph Keilberth's lustrous documentation of the Hitler variations. L. Richmond. il por Am Rec G 36:332-3 Ja '70 *

REGGE trajectories
Serpukhov data are highlight at Regge-pole conference. M. Bander and G. L. Shaw. il Phys Today 23:53+ My '70

REGGIO DI CALABRIA, Italy
Italy: no saints in paradise; Reggio's rebellion. il Time 96:35 O 26 '70

REGIMENTAL bands. See Bands (music)

REGIONAL airlines. See Local service airlines

REGIONAL approach to conservation education. See Conservation of resources—Study and teaching

REGIONAL ballet companies. See Ballet companies

REGIONAL franchised basketball team. See Basketball teams

REGIONAL library associations. See Library associations

REGIONAL organizations. See International organizations, Regional

REGIONAL planning
Let's sing Auld lang syne for the upper Brandywine. L. B. Leopold. il Natur Hist 79:4-6+ Je '70
Space preservation, taxes, planning, and talking: the crunch. R. E. Galantowicz. il Am For 76:36-8+ O '70
Why and how to build another U.S.A. J Fisher. Cur 114:9 16 Ja '70
See also
Appalachian Region—Recovery program, 1965-
City planning
Ekistics
Industrial development programs
Landscape protection
Rural planning
Suburbs
Twin Cities metropolitan council
United States—Appalachian regional commission
Denmark
Planning for open space in Denmark. I. G. Simmons. il Am For 76:16-18+ F '70
United States
See Regional planning

REGISTERS of births, etc.
People of York; 1538-1812. U. M. Cowgill. il Sci Am 222:104-19+ Ja '70

REGISTRATION of voters. See Voters, Registration of

REGISTRY of ships. See Ships—Registration and transfer

REGNIER, Nita
Why has Christmas changed for me? Redbook 136:80+ D '70

REGULARS; story. See Rogin, G.

REGULATION of body temperature. See Temperature, Animal and human

REGULATION Q. See Bank deposits—Interest

REGULATORS, Voltage. See Voltage regulators

REGULATORY commissions. See Independent regulatory commissions

REHABILITATION
See also
Vocational rehabilitation
also subhead Rehabilitation under various subjects, e.g. Mentally handicapped—Rehabilitation

REHABILITATION centers
See also
Narcotic addicts—Rehabilitation
Synanon foundation, inc.

REHABILITATION of prisoners. See Prisoners —Rehabilitation

REHABILITATION of women prisoners. See Prisoners, Women

REHEARSAL bands. See Bands (music)

REHNER, Leigh
Henry Walton, American artist. il Antiques 97: 414-17 Mr '70

REICH, Bernard
United States policy in the Middle East. bibliog f Cur Hist 60:1-6 Ja '71

REICH, Charles A.
Greening of America; excerpts. New Yorker 46:42-6+ S 26 '70
about
Bag of scary mush. S. Alsop. Newsweek 76:102 N 9 '70 *
Con-manship. D. M. Alpern. por Newsweek 76:31-2 N 9 '70 *
Consciousness III. R. Starr. Commentary 50:46-54 D '70 * —
Fuzzy welcome to Cons. III. il por Time 96:12-13 N 2 '70 *
Redeeming of America according to Charles Reich. A. M. Greeley. America 124:14-17 Ja 9 '71 *

REICH, Lilly Joss
House & Garden Christmas present cookbook. il House & Gard 138:88+ D '70
Viennese pastry cookbook; excerpts. il Ladies Home J 87:104-5+ Ap '70

REICHLEY, A. James
As go the suburbs, so goes U.S. politics. il Fortune 82:104-9+ S '70
George Romney is running hard at HUD. il por Fortune 82:100-3+ D '70
Moe's boy Walter at the Court of St James's por Fortune 81:88-93+ Je '70

REICHLIN, Seymour. See Martin, J. B. jt. auth.

REICHMAN, Stella Jolles
Dining in Munich. il Travel & Camera 33:28-9+ O '70

REICHMANN, Helmut
Red baron in the wild blue yonder. R. F. Jones. il por Sports Illus 33:18-21 Jl 13 '70 *

REID, Alastair
Sporting scene. New Yorker 46:60-71 Jl 13; 60-70 Ag 29 '70

REID, Clyde H.
Some basic assumptions for continuing education. Chr Cent 87:472-4 Ap 22 '70

REID, Giorgina
Getting started in color printing for $100. il por Pop Phot 67:90-1+ D '70

REID, Joseph H.
Day care services: our best investment for the future. por Parents Mag 45:12+ Ap '70

REID, Thomas R.
History's fourth turning point; address, February 11, 1970. Vital Speeches 36:369-72 Ap 1 '70

REID, W. Stanford
Christianity: the true humanism. Chr Today 14:9-11 Je 19 '70
Easter light on history. Chr Today 14:8-9 Mr 27 '70
Grass-roots reformation. Chr Today 15:6-9 O 23 '70

REIERSON, Roy Lester
No bust, no boom. A. Hershman. por Duns 95:93-4 Je '70 *

REIF, Rita
Home (cont) il N Y Times Mag p66-7 Mr 1; 92-3 Mr 8; 82-3 Mr 22; 104-5 Ap 5; 76-7 Ap 19; 74-5 My 10; 50-1 Je 21; 36-7 Jl 19; 46-7 Ag 9; 68-9 Ag 30; 72-3 S 20; 84-5+ O 25; 98-9+ N 8 '70

REIGER, G. Wesley
Camper cruising east of the eastern shore. il Motor B 127:191-4 Ja '71

REIGER, George W.
Hustler: a new breed of Arkansas traveler. il Pop Mech 133:98-100 My '70
New York market letter. H. B. Jacobs. Writers Digest 50:10+ F '70 *

REIK, Louis, and others
Hormone-sensitive adenyl cyclase: cytochemical localization in rat liver. bibliog il Science 168:382-4 Ap 17 '70

REILLEY, Robert R. See Lowry, W. H. jt. auth.

REILLY, Christopher T. See Bird, L. P. jt. auth.

REILLY, Edgar M. Jr
Magic of metamorphosis. Cons 24:22-6+ F '70

REILLY, William L.
Campus '69; address, November 14, 1969. Vital Speeches 36:270-2 F 15 '70

REINCARNATION
Is there another life after death? cases of H. Weisz-Roos and others: psychiatric investigations by Dr I. Stevenson. E. Kinkead. il por Look 34:84-8+ O 20 '70
Tale of two lives; Bridey Murphy, incarnation of V. Tighe. il por Newsweek 76:14 N 2 '70

REINECKE, Robert D. See Eichhorn, M. M. jt. auth.

REINEMER, Vic
Budget bureau: do advisory panels have an industry bias? Science 169:36-9 Jl 3 '70

REINERT, Jeanne
Beefsteak from bean webs. il Sci Digest 68:17-22 S '70
Five unexpected new discoveries about the moon. il Sci Digest 68:9-14 N '70
Would you obey a Hitler? il Sci Digest 67:34-9 My '70

REINERT, Joe C. and Steim, J. M.
Calorimetric detection of a membrane-lipid phase transition in living cells. bibliog il Science 168:1580-2 Je 26 '70

REINFORCED concrete construction. See Concrete construction

REINFORCED plastics. See Plastics, Reinforced

REINFORCEMENT (psychology)
Rats' preference for earned in comparison with free food. B. Carder and K. Berkowitz. il Science 167:1273-4 F 27 '70; Discussion. 169:503-4; 170:1229 Jl 31, D 11 '70
Reinforcement of competing behavior during extinction. H. Leitenberg and others. bibliog il Science 169:301-3 Jl 17 '70
See also
Reward (psychology)

REINHARDT, Ad
Art; black paintings 1951-67 at the Marlborough gallery. L. Alloway. Nation 210:413 Ap 6 '70 *

REINHARDT, Richard
(ed) Out West with the rowdy brakeman; excerpt from Workin' on the railroad. il Am West 7:29-37 My '70

REINHART, Oskar, collection. See Art—Private collections

REIQUAM, Howard
Sulfur: simulated long-range transport in the atmosphere. bibliog il Science 170:318-20 O 16 '70

REIS, Herbert
U.S. discusses applicable law for outer space claims; statement, November 20, 1969. Dept State Bul 62:18-20 Ja 5 '70

REIS, Lois
1970 short story contest. Writers Digest 50:34-5 O '70

REISCHAUER, Edwin Oldfather
Danger of the Cambodian expansion; interview, ed. by R. W. McManus. Cur 120:17-21 Ag '70
Hidden crisis in Asia. Read Digest 96:77-81 F '70

REISKIND, Jonathan
Multiple mimetic forms in an ant-mimicking clubionid spider. il Science 169:587-8 Ag 7 '70

REISS, Barbara
(ed) See Dickey, J. Poet tries to make a kind of order

REISS, James
Macy's poem. New Repub 162:35 Mr 21 '70
(ed) See Dickey, J. Poet tries to make a kind of order

REISSUES of phonograph records. See Phonograph records—Reissues

REISWIG, Henry M.
Porifera: sudden sperm release by tropical demospongiae. bibliog il Science 170:538-9 O 30 '70

REITER, Howard L.
How Nixon plays his hand. Nation 210:104-8 F 2 '70
Purging the GOP. Nation 212:71-4 Ja 18 '71

REITZ, Louis P.
New wheats and social progress. bibliog il Science 169:952-5 S 4 '70

REITZE, Glenn L.
Mexico's street minstrels. il Américas 22:36-7 Ja '70

REJECTIONS, Army. See Military service—Physical and mental fitness

RELATIVE stranger; novel. See Stevenson, A.

RELATIVITY (physics)
Experimental tests of relativity. R. W. Holcomb. Science 169:40-2 Jl 3 '70
Getting within ten percent. Sci N 97:574-5 Je 13 '70
Origin of relativity. por Time 95:45 Ja 26 '70
Particles that go faster than light. G. Feinberg. il Sci Am 222:68-73+ bibliog(p 126) F '70
Particles that travel faster than light? R. G. Newton. bibliog il Science 167:1569-74 Mr 20 '70
Relativity revisited. Sci Am 223:44 Ag '70
Victory for relativity; conference on gravity at Caltech in support of Einstein's theory of relativity. il Time 96:52 N 23 '70
See also
Gravitation
Quantum theory

RELAY running. See Running

RELAYS, Time limit
Build a low-cost time delay relay. J. Stayton.
il Pop Electr 32:71 Je '70

RELFORD, Isaiah
Court-martial jurisdiction. Nation 212:69-70 Ja
18 '71 *

RELIABILITY (engineering)
See also
Space vehicles—Reliability

RELIABILITY of products. See Quality of products

RELIANCE electric company
Putting customer demands first. il Bsns W
p62-3 N 28 '70

RELIEF (sculpture)
Another relief for sculpture; illustration
board. il Design 71:19 mid-Wint '70
Transferring designs to clay for relief carv-
ing. O. Johnson. il Sch Arts 70:16-18 O
'70
See also
Rubbings

RELIEF prints. See Prints

RELIEF work
See also
Food relief
Red cross—Disaster relief service
Vietnamese war, 1957-—Relief work
also subhead Relief work under names of
continents, countries, etc. e.g. Peru—Relief
work

RELIGION
Billy Graham and civil religion. D. Kuchar-
sky. Chr Today 15:56+ N 6 '70
Does religion have a future? symposium. il
Ladies Home J 86:127-34 D '69
God's country? J. W. Montgomery. Chr To-
day 14:40 Ja 30 '70
Institutional hang-up; de-ecclesiasticiza-
tion of religion. G. Baum. Commonweal
92:212-13 My 15 '70; Reply. N. J. Rigali. 92:
423 Ag 21 '70
Religion in America; symposium. Mlle 70:
154-9+ Mr '70
Religion in the year 2000, by A. M. Greeley.
Review
Cath World 210:278-9 Mr '70. D. G. O'Shea
Sacramental humanism. P. Verghese. Chr
Cent 87:1116-20 S 23 '70; Reply. J. N. D.
Kelly. 87:1489 D 9 '70
Sixties: radical change in American religion;
symposium, ed. by J. M. Gustafson. bib-
liog f Ann Am Acad 387:1-140 Ja '70
Soft revolution explored: secular religion. S.
Keen; reply, R. G. Middleton. Chr Cent 87:
572+ My 6 '70
Toward a reconstruction of religion, by E.
Fontinell. Review
Commonweal 92:485-6 S 25 '70. W. Ar-
nold
See also
Atheism
Business and religion
Children—Religion
Christianity
Church
Faith
God
Humanism
Modernism
Mysticism
Mythology
Natural theology
Prayer
Private schools and religion
Public schools and religion
Religious liberty
Religious thought
Revelation
Revivals
Sects
Secularism
Skepticism
Television broadcasting—Religious programs
Theology
Women and religion
Worship
Youth—Religion
also subhead Religious institutions and
affairs under names of countries, states,
cities, e.g. Tokyo—Religious institutions
and affairs
Bibliography
Bibliography for Christians. Chr Today 14:
32 S 11 '70
Book briefs. See issues of Christianity today
Books to come; ed. by J. Donathan (cont)
Library J 95:2833+ S 1 '70
Books to come. Library J 96:105-7 Ja 1 '71
Contemporary issues in the spotlight. Chr
Today 14:13-20 F 13 '70
Cornucopia for bibliophiles. Chr Cent 87:
1256-8 O 21 '70

Fall book forecast. Chr Today 14:22-8 S 11 '70
Fall religious books. il Pub W 198:42-56 S
28 '70
Good books in a bad year; comp. by M. Mohs.
il Time 96:56+ D 7 '70
Religious book supplement; symposium, ed.
by R. Ortmayer. il Sat R 53:45-6+ F 28 '70
Spring religious highspots, March through
August. il Pub W 197:35-50 Mr 9 '70
Religious literature

Study and teaching
Florida's religion-social studies curriculum
project. Ed Digest 35:42-3 Mr '70
See also
Judaism—Study and teaching
Religious education

RELIGION, Comparative. See Christianity and
other religions

RELIGION, Personal. See Christian life

RELIGION, Primitive
Myth of primitive religion. M. Douglas. bib-
liog il Commonweal 93:41-4 O 9 '70
See also
Animals in religion, folklore, etc.
Oil in religion, folklore, etc.
Sun worship
Voodooism

RELIGION and communism. See Communism
and religion

RELIGION and ecology
Environmental crisis; symposium. il Chr
Cent 87:1180-92+ O 7 '70
Environmental stewardship; with editorial
comment. H. B. Kuhn. Chr Today 14:25,
46-7 My 8 '70
Man and his environment; excerpts from
address. A. Godfrey. PTA Mag 65:4-5 S '70
Theology for ecology. J. B. Shepherd. il
Cath World 211:172-5 Jl '70
Theology of ecology. il Time 95:49 Je 8 '70

RELIGION and law
Law and order. W. S. Lasor. Chr Today 14:
13-14 Ja 30 '70

RELIGION and politics. See Politics and religion

RELIGION and science
Christian roots of science. J. L. Spradley.
Chr Today 14:7-8 Mr 13 '70
Five who care. M. Mead. il Look 34:37 Ap 21
'70
Genetic engineering. J. Rohler. Chr Today 14:
50-1 Ap 10 '70
Religion and the scientific future, by L.
Gilkey. Review
Commonweal 93:377-8 Ja 15 '71. J.
Pleasants
Three Damoclean swords; annual meeting of
American association for advancement of
science. J. R. Nelson. Chr Cent 87:69-71
Ja 21 '70
Which way is right? C. F. H. Henry. Chr
Today 14:37-8 Mr 13 '70
See also
Creation
Tennessee evolution controversy

Anecdotes, facetiae, satire, etc.
Who programed that computer? Chr Cent 87:
879 Jl 15 '70

RELIGION and sex. See Sex and religion

RELIGION and social problems. See Church
and social problems

RELIGION and sociology
See also
Sociology, Christian

RELIGION and state. See Church and state

RELIGION and technology
Different 2001; excerpts from address. F. El-
der. Cath World 211:63-6 My '70
Geneva conference on technology and the
future. J. E. T. Hough. Chr Cent 87:948
Ag 5 '70
Task force probes future in technological
world. Chr Cent 87:1532 D 23 '70
See also
Computers—Religious use

RELIGION and the future conference. See Religious conferences

RELIGION and war. See War and religion

RELIGION in fiction. See Religion in literature

RELIGION in literature
Darkened sky: nineteenth-century American
novelists and religion, by J. T. Frederick.
Review
Cath World 210:273-5 Mr '70. C. J. Huels-
beck

RELIGIONS
Eastern religions: a new interest and influence. W. L. King. Ann Am Acad 387:66-76 Ja '70
Encounter, by M. Martin. Review
Cath World 211:226-8 Ag '70. J. T. Pawlikowski
Sat R il 53:50-1+ F 28 '70. H. Bowser
See also
Bahaism
Christianity and other religions
International association for the study of history of religions
RELIGIOUS architecture. See Church architecture
RELIGIOUS art. See Christian art and symbolism
RELIGIOUS books. See Religious literature
RELIGIOUS brotherhoods. See Brotherhoods
RELIGIOUS conferences
Bernard J. F. Lonergan: a name to remember. J. K. Ostling. Chr Today 14:38 Ap 24 '70
Brussels hosts the theologians; Concilium congress on The future of the church. R. A. McCormick and others. il America 123:232-4 O 3 '70
CICOP 1970: prelude to conscientization. T. M. Gannon. il America 122:214-18 F 28 '70; Discussion. 122:285, 320 Mr 21-28 '70
Delegates of four faiths hold Beirut dialogue. L. H. Dean. Chr Today 14:42-3 Ap 24 '70
First International Lonergan congress: a report. F. E. Crowe. America 122:452-3 Ap 25 '70
Future at Brussels; Concilium congress on the future of the church. G. Baum. Cath World 212:137-40 D '70
Futurists and visionaries: hope's partners; conference on religion and the future. G. Fackre. Chr Cent 87:1060-3 S 9 '70
Good News for Methodists; Good News convocation of United Methodists for evangelical Christianity. R. Chandler. Chr Today 14:23-4 S 25 '70
Liberation: word of the hour. Catholic inter-American co-operation program. America 122:288 Mr 21 '70
Lonergan explosion. M. Novak. Commonweal 92:268-70 My 29 '70; Reply. P. B. Ely. 92:351 Jl 10 '70
Lutherans and American Indians: a confrontation. E. R. Trexler. Chr Cent 87:1103-5 S 16 '70
Many whites attend black congress; first interdenominational Black congress on evangelism. J. S. Tinney. Chr Today 15:43-4 O 9 '70
Neighbors who moved in: Spanish-American congress on evangelism. W. G. Marx. Chr Today 14:60-3 S 25 '70
Pentecostals celebrate their world flame. J. S. Tinney. Chr Today 15:36 D 4 '70
Political congress; World congress on the future of the church. il Newsweek 76:62-3 S 28 '70
Rainbow for religion? Religious communication congress; with editorial comment. D. Kucharsky. Chr Today 14:25, 41 My 8 '70
Struggle for an ecological theology: a case in point; Faith-man-nature group's conference. H. P. Santmire. Chr Cent 87:275-7 Mr 4 '70
Summer is convention time. Chr Today 14:44-5 Ag 21 '70
Synagogue council head rebukes "Christians for Palestine"; pro-Arab Christian conference. Chr Cent 87:783 Je 24 '70
Theologo '70. J. Horgan. Commonweal 93:39 O 9 '70
Theology sprouts at Brussels; world congress on the future of the church. T. Beeson. Chr Cent 87:1145-6 S 30 '70
While theologians talked; congress on The future of the church. J. J. van Capelleveen. Chr Today 15:50 O 9 '70
See also
Conference of major superiors of men's institutes
Eastern Asia Christian conference
Missionary conferences
World council of churches

Africa
Africa and Afro-Americans; report of conversation between NCBC officials and members of the All Africa conference of churches. G. S. Wilmore, jr. Chr Cent 87:686 Je 3 '70; Reply. G. M. Daniels. 87:1201-2 O 7 '70

Fighting behind Che; All Africa conference of churches. O. W. Okite. Chr Today 14:50 Ap 10 '70
Report from East Africa; bishops of five East Africa countries meet. C. De Souza. il America 123:117-18 S 5 '70

Canada
Canadian evangelism conference: a first; National congress on evangelism. C. De Mestral. Chr Cent 87:1301 O 28 '70
Ottawa oscillations; Canadian Congress on evangelism. L. K. Tarr. Chr Today 14:46 Ap 10 '70
Will saints go marching out? Canadian congress on evangelism. D. Kucharsky. Chr Today 14:27-9 S 25 '70

India
India: the way to life; All India congress on evangelism. K. R. Gnanakan. Chr Today 14:38-9 F 13 '70

Korea (Republic)
Seoul brothers; world conference of the leaders of Buddhism. il Newsweek 76:59 O 26 '70
RELIGIOUS cooperation
Discoveries and dangers. R. M. Brown. por Chr Cent 87:40-5 Ja 14 '70
Livingston: Scottish venture in unity. Chr Cent 87:580-2 My 6 '70
MUST: missionary thrust or bust? R. Hull, jr. Chr Cent 87:665-7 My 27 '70; Reply. N. F. Fisher. 87:1291-4 O 28 '70
New ecumenical vehicle in southwest Pennsylvania; Christian associates. J. P. Park. Chr Cent 87:548-9 Ap 29 '70
What Luther put asunder; meeting points of Catholics and Lutherans. il Time 96:42 N 9 '70
Will Catholics recognize Protestant ministries? il Time 95:76 My 25 '70
RELIGIOUS denominations. See Sects
RELIGIOUS education
Anglican commission seeks changes in British religious education. Chr Cent 87:751 Je 17 '70
Building children's belief. D. M. Joy. il Chr Today 14:29-30 Je 19 '70
Psychosocial origins of stability in the Christian faith. B. Clouse. Chr Today 14:12-14 S 25 '70
Teaching religion in an age of scant enthusiasm. L. D. Streiker. America 123:36-8 Jl 25 '70
Value imperative. W. R. Barnhart. Chr Today 14:5 Jl 31 '70
See also
Catechetics
Catholic church—Education
Children—Religion
Church colleges
Moral education
Theological education
RELIGIOUS experience. See Experience (religion)
RELIGIOUS faith. See Faith
RELIGIOUS freedom. See Religious liberty
RELIGIOUS heritage of America, inc.
Churchman of the year. Newsweek 75:96 My 25 '70
Onward, Christian; R. Nixon Churchman of the year. J. Deedy. Commonweal 92:258 My 29 '70
RELIGIOUS institutions and affairs
Religion on the big board; religious scene in 1970. Chr Today 15:26-7 Ja 1 '71
World around us. See issues of Christian century
See also subhead Religious institutions and affairs under names of countries, states, etc. e.g. Canada—Religious institutions and affairs
RELIGIOUS intermarriages. See Marriages, Mixed
RELIGIOUS journalism. See Journalism, Religious
RELIGIOUS liberty
Case of Harry X; court rules free exercise of religion for Black Muslim ministers at California's state prisons. Newsweek 76:48 Jl 27 '70
China; Article 88 of China's constitution. H. Yu. Chr Cent 87:1302 O 28 '70
God and Zeus in Arkansas; freedom-to-worship amendment. Chr Cent 87:262 Mr 4 '70
RELIGIOUS life. See Christian life
RELIGIOUS life (Judaism) See Jewish way of life

RELIGIOUS literature
Christian use of the printed page; excerpts from address. F. E. Gaebelein. Chr Today 14:5-8 Ja 30 '70
On the religious book mart. Chr Cent 87: 229 F 25 '70
　　See also
Booksellers and bookselling—Religious literature
Christian literature
Publishers and publishing—Religious literature
Religion—Bibliography

RELIGIOUS music. See Church music

RELIGIOUS news
Dwarfed journalism; Catholic page in daily secular papers. S. J. Adamo. America 123: 160 S 12 '70

RELIGIOUS newspapers and periodicals
Church magazine market. C. Amen. Writer 83:27-8 D '70
Ecumenism and communication; cooperation among denominational journals. J. M. Bailey. Chr Cent 87:241 F 25 '70
I make a 5-figure income as a full-time freelancer in the religious field. N. Rohrer. il Writers Digest 50:33-5 Jl '70
On the need for nudging; purpose of journalistic leadership. Chr Cent 87:318-19 Mr 18 '70; Reply. D. Francis. 87:673 My 27 '70
Religious press: the printed word embattled. il Time 96:49-50 Ag 17 '70
Toward a Christian press association. Chr Cent 87:716 Je 10 '70
　　See also
Associated church press (organization)
Christianity today (periodical)
Colloquy (periodical)
Journalism, Religious
New Christian (periodical)
Watchman-examiner (periodical)

RELIGIOUS orders
Are religious orders here to stay? J. B. Sheerin. Cath World 211:242-3 S '70
Catholic church professionals. J. H. Fichter. bibliog f Ann Am Acad 387:77-85 Ja '70
Celibacy and clericalism. T. W. Guzie. Cath World 211:120-4 Je '70
Questions for pilgrims. L. Orsy. America 123: 59-63 Ag 8 '70
Religious life in low profile. K. McDonnell. il America 123:16-20 Jl 11 '70
　　See also
Conference of major superiors of men's institutes
Conference of major superiors of women's institutions of the United States of America
Franciscans
Jesuits
Malta, Knights of
Sisterhoods

RELIGIOUS persecution. See Persecution

RELIGIOUS poetry
Merton and Auden. T. Materer. pors Commonweal 91:577-80 F 27 '70; Reply with rejoinder. M. G. Walsh. 92:51+ Mr 27 '70
Poetry of Henry Vaughan. M. W. Hess. Chr Today 15:15-17 Ja 1 '71

RELIGIOUS prejudice. See Prejudice

RELIGIOUS publishers group. See American book publishers council—Religious publishers group

RELIGIOUS radio programs. See Radio broadcasting—Religious programs

RELIGIOUS revivals. See Revivals

RELIGIOUS rites and ceremonies. See Rites and ceremonies

RELIGIOUS schools. See Church schools

RELIGIOUS supplies. See Church supplies

RELIGIOUS surveys
How clergymen view hippiedom. H. M. Hacker. il Chr Cent 87:887-91 Jl 22 '70

RELIGIOUS thought
　　France
In quest of Kerygma: Catholic intellectual life in nineteenth-century France. H. W. Paul. Am Hist R 75:387-423 D '69

RELIGIOUS toleration. See Toleration

RELIGIOUS vocation. See Vocation in religion

RELISHES. See Pickles and relishes

RELYEA, Harold C.
Black power as an urban ideology. Ed Digest 35:46-9 F '70

REMARQUE, Erich Maria
Obituary
Pub W 198:37 O 12 '70

REMBRANDT Hermanszoon van Rijn
Rembrandt and his circle (cont) B. A. Rifkin. il Art N 69:58-61+ My '70 *

REMEDIAL exercise. See Physical therapy

REMEDIAL reading. See Reading—Remedial teaching

REMEDIAL teaching
　　See also
Performance contracts (education)
Reading—Remedial teaching
Tutors and tutoring

REMINGTON revolvers. See Revolvers

REMINISCENCE
Importance of childhood memories. N. M. Lobsenz. il Read Digest 97:127-30 N '70
Retrieving the past; find yourself in your photographs. R. Hattersley. il Pop Phot 67: 94-7+ Ag '70

REMODELED automobiles; Remodeled bridges; etc. See Automobiles, Remodeled; Bridges, Remodeled; etc.

REMODELING (architecture)
Westbeth's rehabilitation project: a clue to improving our cities; with statement by R. Meier. il Arch Rec 147:103-6 Mr '70

REMOTE control
　　See also
Camera shutters—Control

REMOTE control manipulators. See Manipulators

REMOTE meter reading. See Meter reading

REMOTE sensing systems
Earth resources field explored. Z. Strickland. il Aviation W 93:60-2 O 5 '70
Sensors probe earth satellite challenge. il Aviation W 92:124+ Je 22 '70
Use of microwave sensing grows. W. S. Hieronymus. il Aviation W 92:44-6 Mr 30 '70
　　See also
Earth satellite corporation

REMPEL, Henry H.
Teaching of creativity. il Design 71:20 mid-Wint '70

REMSBERG, Bonnie
(ed) See Beebe, L. Should abortion laws be liberalized?
(ed) See Brennan, R. Investigative reporter: Ray Brennan
(ed) See Fleming, J. G. Should abortion laws be liberalized?
—See Remsberg, C. jt. auth.

REMSBERG, Charles
(ed) See Beebe, L. Should abortion laws be liberalized?
(ed) See Brennan, R. Investigative reporter: Ray Brennan
(ed) See Fleming, J. G. Should abortion laws be liberalized?
—and Remsberg, Bonnie
First victims. il Good H 171:74-5+ Ag '70
Here she comes, Miss Nude America. il Esquire 73:160+ My '70
Weird Harold and the first national swingers' convention. Esquire 74:189+ D '70
Why you really can't get good medical care. Good H 170:68-71+ F '70

REMUS, Gerald J.
Storm-water retention can work. il Am City 85:68-9 O '70
To oust phosphate, add pickle liquor. il Am City 85:65 D '70

RENAISSANCE
Renaissance: maker of modern man, ed. by K. M. Setton. Review
Nat Geog il 138:588-92 O '70. F. Shor

RENAISSANCE pleasure faire. See Festivals—California

RENAL cortex. See Kidneys

RENEGOTIATION board. See United States—Renegotiation board

RENEWAL of copyright. See Copyright—Duration

RENEWAL of the church. See Church renewal

RENNELS, M. See Nelson, E. jt. auth.

RENOIR, Jean
Current cinema. P. Gilliatt. New Yorker 46: 58-60 Ag 8 '70 *

RENT
Trends in homeownership and rental costs. R. C. Joiner. il Mo Labor R 93:26-31 Jl '70
　　See also
Houses—Leasing and renting

RENTAL services. See Lease and rental services

RENTMEESTER, Co
Java; photographs. il Life 68:46-57 Je 26 '70
Jet-age scramble; photographs. Life 70:56-66 Ja 8 '71

RENTZEPIS, P. M.
Ultrafast processes. bibliog il Science 169:239-47 Jl 17 '70

RENZ, Michael
Multi-media man: William F. Nolan. il por Writers Digest 50:24-6+ D '70

REORGANIZATION, Congressional. See United
  States—Congress—Reorganization
REORGANIZATION of corporations. See Cor-
  porations—Reorganization
REORGANIZED church of Jesus Christ of Lat-
  ter day saints
  Reorganized Mormon church beset by con-
    troversy. W. D. Russell. Chr Cent 87:769-
    71 Je 17 '70
REOVIRUSES. See Viruses
REPAIR men. See Repairmen
REPAIR parts
  What you need in a roadside emergency kit.
    A. Markovich. il Pop Mech 134:120-2 Jl '70
REPAIR shops
    See also
  Automobile service stations
  Electronic service shops
REPAIRING
  Be your own Mr Fixit. R. Darling. il Har
    Yrs 10:28-9 My '70
    See also subhead Maintenance and repair
      under various subjects, e.g. Houses—
      Maintenance and repair
REPAIRMEN
  Why can't you get anything fixed anymore?
    S. Schuler. Am Home 73:32+ Je '70
REPARATIONS
    See also
  Negroes—Reparations
REPELLENTS, Animal. See Animal repellents
REPELLENTS, insect. See Insect baits and
  repellents
REPENTANCE
  America on its knees? Chr Today 14:20-1
    Je 19 '70
    See also
  Confession
REPERTORY companies. See Theater—United
  States
REPERTORY dance theatre of the University
  of Utah. See Dance companies
REPERTORY dancers of New Jersey. See
  Dance companies
REPERTORY theater. See Theater—United
  States
REPORT cards. See School reports and records
REPORTERS and reporting
  Appeal for credibility; case of New York
    times reporter. E. Caldwell. Newsweek 75:
    74 My 11 '70
  Artist as reporter. il Time 95:40 Mr 9 '70
  Coordinating the media; dragnet subpoenas
    served on C.B.S. and other news reporters.
    Nation 210:163-4 F 16 '70
  End to fishing; E. Caldwell's challenge.
    Time 96:46 N 30 '70
  Flexible guidelines. Newsweek 76:71 Ag 24 '70
  How much privilege? San Francisco court
    rules on the press's rights. il por Newsweek
    75:77-8 Ap 13 '70
  Informing by compulsion; TV reporters and
    interviewers as informers. Nation 210:133
    F 9 '70
  Investigative reporter: Ray Brennan; inter-
    view. ed. by C. Remsberg and B. Remsberg.
    il por Writers Digest 50:20-3+ F '70
  Journalist's privilege; San Francisco Court of
    appeals quashes federal subpoenas served
    on E. Caldwell. il por Newsweek 76:87 N 30
    '70
  Limit on subpoena of notes of reporters and
    authors. H. F. Pilpel and K. P. Norwick.
    Pub W 197:33-4 My 4 '70
  Newsman held immune from testifying on
    Black Panthers. Pub W 198:26 D 7 '70
  Newsmen and their confidential sources. A.
    S. Goldstein. New Repub 162:13-15 Mr 21
    '70
  Newspaper stringing as a freelance starter.
    J. L. Gillette. il Writers Digest 50:24-6 Ap
    '70
  Objectivity and the American press. il Sr
    Schol 96:2-7 F 2 '70
  Press-card disguise; police posing as news-
    men. B. J. Oudes. il Nation 211:561-4 N 30
    '70
  Privilege for the press; right of newspaper
    men to keep sources of information con-
    fidential. Nation 210:292-3 Mr 16 '70
  Promise on subpoenas. il Time 95:49 F 16 '70
  Race, riots and reporters: press coverage of
    urban disorders. T. A. Knopf. il Common-
    weal 92:336-40 Jl 10 '70; Same abr. with
    title Race and the press. Cur 121:20-5 S '70
  Reporting for court duty; subpoenas to use
    reporter's private information. il Time 95:
    52 F 9 '70
  Stronger voice for reporters. Time 95:57 My
    25 '70
  Subpoena siege: have the news media become
    too big to fight? A. M. Adelson. il Sat R
    53:106-8 Mr 14 '70

Subpoenas and sources. il Newsweek 75:55-6
  F 16 '70
Weighted news; biased news reporting, or
  propaganda. S. J. Adamo. America 122:688
  Je 27 '70
    See also
  Cambodian-Vietnamese conflict—War corre-
    spondents
  Foreign correspondents
  Government and the press
  Israeli-Arab war, 1967- —War correspondents
  Journalists
  National press club
  Negro reporters
  News
  News photographers
  Nieman fellowships
  Press conferences
  Radio broadcasting—News
  Sports journalism
  Television broadcasting—News
  United Nations correspondents association
  Vietnamese war, 1957- —War correspondents
  Women as journalists
  Women as reporters
    also names of reporters, e.g. M. Nei-
      swender
REPORTS
    See also
  Corporation reports
  Financial statements
REPOUSSÉ work
  Enameled repousse medallions. P. Rothenberg.
    il Ceram Mo 18:24-5 Mr '70
REPRESENTATIVE government and represen-
  tation
    See also
  Democracy
REPRINTS. See Books—Reprints
REPRODUCTION
  Pesticides and reproduction of birds. D. B.
    Peakall. il Sci Am 222:72-8 bibliog(p 130)
    Ap '70
  Reproductive physiology of marsupials; vivi-
    parity in therian mammals. G. B. Sharman.
    bibliog il Science 167:1221-8 F 27 '70
    See also
  Artificial insemination, Human
  Conception
  Fertility
  Fungi, Sex in
  Menstruation
  Sex determination and control

                    Research
  Psychology of human reproduction. J. Mor-
    iarty. il Sci N 98:148-9 Ag 15 '70
REPRODUCTION, Asexual
  Asexual reproduction in a sipunculan worm.
    M. E. Rice. bibliog il Science 167:1618-20 Mr
    20 '70
    See also
  Apogamy
REPRODUCTIONS of works of art
  Metropolitan museum of art's fabulous fakes.
    il Harp Baz 104:174-5 N '70
  On and off the avenue; paintings. J. Malcolm.
    New Yorker 46:68+ Je 20 '70
REPTILES
  Exhibiting reptiles. J. S. Dobbs. il Parks &
    Rec 5:23+ O '70
    See also
  Nervous system—Reptiles
  Snakes
                    Anatomy
    See also
  Cloaca (zoology)
REPTILES, Fossil
  Dentary-squamosal joint and the origin of
    mammals. H. R. Barghusen and J. A. Hop-
    son. bibliog il Science 168:573-5 My 1 '70
  Horizons for Antarctic paleontology; lystro-
    saurus fossil find. K. Frazier. il Sci N 97:
    350-2 Ap 4 '70
  Whole fossils in Antarctica. il Sci N 98:428
    D 5 '70
  World of Antarctic paleontology; Coalsack
    fossils. K. Frazier. il Sci N 97:324-6 Mr 28
    '70
    See also
  Dinosaurs
REPUBLIC of Togo. See Togo
REPUBLIC steel corporation
  How to sanitize the company image. il Bsns
    W p 116 Mr 28 '70
REPUBLICAN governors association
  Spiro Agnew on the defensive; conference at
    Idaho's Sun Valley. il por Time 96:10-11 D
    28 '70
  Sun Valley days; conference. il por Newsweek
    76:16-17 D 28 '70

REPUBLICAN party
Agnew on the warpath. B. Brower. il pors Life 69:26-31 O 16 '70
Agnew purge. Nation 211:386 O 26 '70
Agnew: purging the GOP? il pors Newsweek 76:36 O 12 '70
Agnew's task, and task force. por U S News 69:21 S 14 '70
All-Republican Senate? Jim Allison's working on it. D. R. Maxey. il por Look 34:34-6+ O 20 '70
And now, the Spiro and Martha show; G.O.P. salute to the vice president fund-raising party. J. Austin. il pors Time 96:10 N 23 '70
Black Americans want in. V. S. Baker. Nat R 22:892-3 Ag 25 '70
Coming leadership fight; Senate GOP leadership. Cato. Nat R 22:777 Jl 28 '70
Financial landslide for the G.O.P. H. E. Alexander and H. B. Meyers. il Fortune 81:104-5+ Mr '70
Future of the Republican party. F. S. Meyer. Nat R 22:1271-3 D 1 '70
Goldberg jumps in. Nat R 22:342 Ap 7 '70
GOP and God; priest influences Catholics on abortion issue in California. L. T. King. Commonweal 93:37-8 O 9 '70
GOP and the Jewish vote. Cato. Nat R 22:1044 O 6 '70
Guide for Nixon in '72; New Jersey's '69 election. il pors U S News 68:32-3 Ja 19 '70
Ike's grandson hits the '70 trail for Republicans. il por U S News 69:107 O 19 '70
Is a two-party South really here at last? il U S News 68:26-8 F 9 '70
Letter from Washington. R. H. Rovere. New Yorker 46:132+ S 26 '70
Making of a majority; excerpts from Now is the time. F. R. Harris. Harper 240:49-52 My '70
Mr Agnew and the future of the GOP. W. F. Buckley, jr. Nat R 22:324-5 Mr 24 '70
New and hungry chairman; National committee. por Time 97:13-14 Ja 18 '71
Next question; advice from the Ripon society. Newsweek 76:14 Ag 3 '70
Next round. il Time 96:22+ D 7 '70
Nixon's southern strategy; it's all in the charts. J. Boyd. il pors N Y Times Mag p25+ My 17 '70
Politics of prejudice. Nation 211:260-1 S 28 '70
Politics of resentment. M. Novak. Commonweal 92:481-3 S 25 '70; Same. Cur 123:13-18 N '70
Protracted Republican conflict. Nat R 22:718 Jl 14 '70
Purging the GOP. H. L. Reiter. Nation 212:71-4 Ja 18 '71
Republican strategy, southern fried. W. Barthelmes. Commonweal 91:420-1 Ja 16 '70
Republicans and hard hats; New York senatorial race. Nat R 22:989 S 22 '70
Rich GOP gets richer. Bsns W p 100 O 10 '70
Senator Javits reflects; senator-elect Buckley's bid to join the Republican caucus. Nation 211:677 D 28 '70
Special Spiro pin. il por Time 96:17 O 12 '70
White House hard hats. E. B. Drew. il por Atlan 226:51-7 O '70
Will Dole do it? Nat R 22:1391 D 29 '70
Will Nixon get a Senate? Nat R 22:352 Ap 7 '70
Winning in November is not enough. J. K. Galbraith. New Repub 162:13-14 Je 13 '70; Reply. G. Allott. 163:31-4 Ag 15 '70
See also
Republican governors association

REQUIEMS
See also
Phonograph records—Requiems
Video tape recordings—Requiems
RESCUE apparatus. See Life saving equipment
RESCUE beacons. See Radio beacons
RESCUE missions. See Missions—United States
RESCUE work
Face in the Mustang window. E. D. Fales, jr. il Pop Mech 134:88-94+ Jl '70; Same abr. with title Car in the river. Read Digest 97:82-6 Ag '70
See also
Drowning
First aid in illness and injury
Radar in rescue work
Space rescue work
RESEARCH
Is science stoppable? Commonweal 93:8 O 2 '70; Discussion. 93:115+, 309+ O 30, D 18 '70
See also
Balloons—Research use
Communication in science
Libraries and research
Scientists
Specialization
    also Medical research; Social science research; and similar headings

Anecdotes, facetiae, satire, etc.
Thanks a lot. il Esquire 74:58-9 Jl '70

Federal aid
Big science under fire. D. Fleming. Atlan 226:96-101 S '70; Discussion. 226:26+ D '70
Cuts begin to hurt. Sci N 97:266 Mr 14 '70
Developmental sciences: state and fate of research funding; AAAS symposium, December 27, 1970. V. H. Denenberg. il Science 170:763 N 13 '70
Federal science: differences of opinion in the highest councils. P. M. Boffey. Science 170:1383-4 D 25 '70
Future of federal contract research centers. D. C. Coddington and J. G. Milliken. bibliog f il Harvard Bsns R 48:103-16 Mr '70; Reply. 48:28+ Jl '70
Kennedy urges greater federal support for science. J. B. Phelps. il por Phys Today 23:73-4 O '70
Long slide. Sci Am 222:45 Ap '70
Mansfield amendment curb on basic research may spread. P. M. Boffey. Science 167:1473 Mr 13 '70
Mission agency support of basic research. Bul Atom Sci 26:35-7 S '70
New call for support; report of Task force on science policy. Sci N 97:478 My 16 '70
Nixon advisers call for better integrated science support. N. Gruchow. Science 168:954 My 22 '70
Nixon boosts research budget 5 per cent; NSF gets $49 million more. T. Johnides. il Phys Today 23:69+ Mr '70
Nixon budget: science funding remains tight. P. M. Boffey and others. il Science 167:845-8 F 6 '70
Nixon's budget shakes up the priorities. il Bsns W p90+ F 14 '70
Project Themis: budget cuts, critics cause phase out. J. Walsh. Science 169:749 Ag 21 '70
R&D funding: top Treasury aide decries blind faith approach. P. M. Boffey. por Science 170:512+ O 30 '70
Recession in science: ex-advisors warn of long-term effects. P. M. Boffey. Science 168:555-7 My 1 '70
Research crisis: cutting off the plant at the roots. il Time 95:45-6+ F 16 '70
Science for tomorrow. J. Lear. Sat R 53:59 My 23 '70
Science policy: budget cuts prompt closer look at the system. J. Walsh. Science 168:802-5 My 15 '70
Slump in U.S. science? Newsweek 75:109 My 11 '70

Great Britain
Unifying government research; proposed merger of National research development corporation with ten national laboratories. D. Fishlock. il Sci N 97:160 F 7 '70
See also
Great Britain—Science research council

Israel
Israel: research and education booming in a nation at war. D. S. Greenberg. il Science 168:446-51 Ap 24 '70

Italy
See also
International laboratory of genetics and biology

Japan
Japan III: industrial research struggles to close the gap. P. M. Boffey. il Science 167:264-7 Ja 16 '70

Korea (Republic)
See also
Korea institute for science and technology

Philippines
Brain drain in the Philippines: a case study. A. Muriel. Bul Atom Sci 26:33-9 S '70

United States
Basic R&D: is the U.S. falling behind? interview. P. Handler. il por Forbes 105:204+ My 15 '70
Mission agency support of basic research. Bul Atom Sci 26:35-7 S '70
Need for basic research. V. F. Weisskopf. Science 167:935 F 13 '70
R&D depression in the United States. S. Dedijer. Science 168:344-5 Ap 17 '70
Research crisis: cutting off the plant at the roots. il Time 95:45-6+ F 16 '70

RESEARCH—United States—*Continued*
Science under fire: behind the growing concern. il U S News 68:30-1 F 9 '70
See also
Colleges and universities—Research
Rand corporation
Stanford research institute
United States—National science foundation

RESEARCH, Musical. See Musicology

RESEARCH airplanes. See Airplanes, Experimental

RESEARCH and engineering council of the graphic arts industry, inc.
R&E council probes the maze of computer semantics. V. Strauss. Pub W 197:151-2+ Je 8 '70

RESEARCH centers. See Research laboratories

RESEARCH centers, Psychiatric. See Psychiatric research centers

RESEARCH in colleges. See Colleges and universities—Research

RESEARCH laboratories
Future of federal contract research centers. D. C. Coddington and J. G. Milliken. bibliog f il Harvard Bsns R 48:103-16 Mr '70; Reply. 48:28+ Jl '70
See also
Atomic research laboratories
Battelle memorial institute, Columbus, Ohio
Bell telephone laboratories
International laboratory of genetics and biology
Korea institute for science and technology

RESEARCH laboratories, Government. See Laboratories, Government

RESEARCH submarines. See Submarine research vehicles

RESEGREGATION of schools. See Segregation in education

RESERVATIONS, Airline. See Airlines—Reservation systems

RESERVATIONS, Indian. See Indians of North America—Reservations

RESERVE forces (United States) See United States—Armed forces—Reserves

RESERVE officers training corps. See United States—Reserve officers training corps

RESERVOIRS
Fabric reservoir cover stops bushels of maple seeds; Wheeling, W.Va. il Am City 85:16 D '70
Floating plywood cover keeps water fresh. G. H. Straub. il Am City 85:82-3 Ap '70
Inflated cover keeps water clean. Mount Joy, Pa. B. Wells. il Am City 85:40 Je '70
Reclaimed wastewater cleared for water-contact sports; Indian Creek reservoir. Alpine County, Calif. il Am City 85:16 Ag '70
Repair stays strong; Burkhardt street reservoir, Dayton, Ohio. il Am City 85:50 S '70
That abandoned quarry may be a water asset; Philadelphia suburban water company. J. M. Ballengee. il Am City 85:69-71 F '70
Tradition gave way to imagination; Santa Barbara, Calif. P. A. Beautrow. il Am City 85:87-9 Ag '70
Trinity Lake in summer is hard to resist; California Trinity national recreation area. il Sunset 145:30-1 Jl '70
Wood cover, rubber sidewalls; Santa Clara County, Calif. il Am City 85:66-7 Jl '70

Lining
Rubber keeps water in and debris out; Sigsbee reservoir; Erie, Pa. S. J. Prazer. il Am City 85:79-80 S '70

RESIDENCE halls. See Dormitories

RESIDENT psychiatrists. See Hospitals, Psychiatric—Staff

RESIDUAL oil. See Petroleum as fuel

RESIGNATION of Cabinet officers. See Cabinet officers, Resignation of

RESIGNATION of public officers. See Public officers, Resignation of

RESINOUS products
Slippery water; polyox. K. A. Kovaly. il Sci Digest 68:96-8 Ag '70
See also
Plasticizers
Teflon

RESISTANCE exercise. See Isometric exercise

RESISTANCE of plants to insects. See Plants—Disease and pest resistance

RESISTANCE to disease in plants. See Plants—Disease and pest resistance

RESISTANCE to government. See Government, Resistance to

RESISTANCE to insecticides. See Insects, Injurious and beneficial—Resistance to control

RESISTORS, Electric. See Electric resistors

RESNIK, Henry S.
Education. Vogue 156:302 S 1; 96 O 1; 76 N 15 '70
High school with no walls. Ed Digest 35:16-19 Mr '70
Pennsylvania advancement school; no game for radicals. il Sat R 53:49-51+ Jl 18 '70
Seismic moment in cinematic history. il Sat R 53:25-8+ Ap 4 '70
Special awareness about mankind. il Sat R 53:35-8 F 21 '70
Television. Vogue 156:108 N 1; 102 D '70
When America was singing Buddy, can you spare a dime? Sat R 53:27-30 Ap 18 '70

RESNIK, Muriel
Sex's silent majority. Vogue 157:83 Ja 1 '71

RESNIK, Regina
Musician of the month. por Hi Fi 20:MA9 O '70 *

RESOLUTIONS
See also
New Years resolutions

RESOLVING power (optics)
Is Dawes' limit out of date? R. W. Gordon. R Pop Astron 63:16-18 Ag '69

RESONANCE, Magnetic. See Magnetic resonance

RESOR, Stanley R.
United States forces in Europe; address, April 10, 1970. Vital Speeches 36:456-9 My 15 '70

RESORTS. See Health resorts, watering places, etc. Seaside resorts; Summer resorts; Winter resorts

RESOURCES, Conservation of. See Conservation of resources

RESOURCES, Natural. See Natural resources

RESPIGHI, Ottorino
Two perspectives; the Roman trilogy. G. S. Fox. Am Rec G 37:176-7 N '70 *

RESPIRATION
Bronchograms and tracheograms of seals under pressure. G. L. Kooyman and others. bibliog il Science 169:82-4 Jl 3 '70
Panting in dogs: unidirectional air flow over evaporative surfaces. K. Schmidt-Nielsen and others. bibliog il Science 169:1102-4 S 11 '70
Squeeze play; dolphin adaptation to increasing water pressure. Sci Am 222:64 Mr '70
See also
Plants—Respiration
Voice culture

RESPIRATION, Artificial
Artificial respiration for a child. C. J. Potthoff. Todays Health 48:74 F '70

RESPIRATORY apparatus
Acute respiratory failure. P. M. Winter and E. Lowenstein; reply with rejoinder. F. J. Dyson. Sci Am 222:6+ Mr '70
Race to save infant's life; Arp's machine. il pors Life 69:36-9 Jl 24 '70
See also
Iron lung
Life support systems (submarine environment)
Skin diving—Equipment and supplies

RESPIRATORY intensive care. See Hospital care

RESPIRATORY organs
See also
Gills
Lungs

Diseases
Control of acute mycoplasmal and viral respiratory tract disease. R. M. Chanock. bibliog il Science 169:248-56 Jl 17 '70
See also
Air pollution—Physiological effects
Asthma
Cold (disease)
Emphysema
Hyaline membrane disease
Lungs—Diseases
Pneumonia

RESPONSES (music)
Responsories and prosa for St Stephen's day at Salisbury. R. Steiner. bibliog f il Mus Q 56:162-82 Ap '70

RESPONSIBILITY
Campaign GM: a new pitch to university shareholders. L. J. Carter. Science 170:958-9 N 27 '70
Campaign GM: corporation critics seek support of universities. L. J. Carter. Science 168:452-5 Ap 24 '70
Campaign GM: reformers lose on vote but not on influence. L. J. Carter. Science 168:1077-8 My 29 '70
Corporate power and social duty. America 122:625 Je 13 '70
Corporate responsibility campaign. Chr Cent 87:715 Je 10 '70

RESPONSIBILITY—*Continued*
Demise of accountability; with editorial comment. J. W. Dykstra. Chr Today 14:14-16, 33 Ap 10 '70
Establishment; social responsibilities of citizens; address, April 15, 1970. C. Y. Lazarus. Vital Speeches 36:498-502 Je 1 '70
GM's ordeal may set the fashion; Campaign to make GM responsible. il Bsns W p84 My 30 '70
How social responsibility fits the game of business. J. McDonald. il Fortune 82: 104-6+ D '70
Let this madness cease; reprint. Camp Mag 42:30 Je '70
Nobody gives a damn. Bet Hom & Gard 48: 8 Jl '70; Discussion. 48:12 O '70
Responsibility; address, June 11, 1970. J. L. Davidson. Vital Speeches 36:631-2 Ag 1 '70
Responsibility is relevant; with study-discussion program. D. Harris and E. Harris. bibliog il PTA Mag 64:24-6,35-6 F '70
See also
Assistance in emergencies
RESPONSIBILITY (law) See Liability (law)
REST
See also
Sleep
REST homes. See Nursing homes
RESTAURANTS
Holiday travel handbook. See issues of Holiday
International chef. M. Woodward. See issues of Travel
Where to go for a good meal in a good place. M. Gough. il House B 112:52+ S '70
See also subhead Hotels, restaurants, etc. under names of cities, e.g. New York (city) —Hotels, restaurants, etc.

Finance
Haute cuisine customers go on a diet. il Bsns W p36+ O 31 '70

Franchise system
Food franchisers' marry-go-round. il Bsns W p 122 F 28 '70
Fried chicken that went into politics; dim future for Minnie Pearl. il Bsns W p37 S 19 '70
See also
Kentucky fried chicken corporation

Europe, Western
Europe's finest restaurants 1970. S. Spitzer and H. Spitzer. il Holiday 47:85-9 Ja '70
Trapping the truffle, jugging the hare. W. Clifford. il Sat R 53:66+ S 12 '70

France
Better mousetrap; topless customers at Pampelonne. il Newsweek 76:27-8 Ag 3 '70
See also
Lyons, France—Hotels, restaurants, etc.

Germany (Federal Republic)
Luncheon in Muenchen. P. Moor. Sat R 53: 53 Mr 14 '70

Singapore
Unbelievable coffee shop in Singapore. M. Woodward. il Travel 134:72 O '70

Switzerland
Swiss dining with a spectacular view; Schilthorn restaurant. M. Woodward. il Travel 133:75 Mr '70

United States
Dining out in America, how old ways are changing. il U S News 68:92-4 Ap 20 '70
Gourmet ashore; great waterfront restaurants: Granary restaurant; Georgetown, Md. J. W. Giles. il Motor B 126:134-5 Jl '70
Pier restaurant; Norwalk, Conn. E. Gibbs. il Motor B 126:106-7 Ag '70
Windjammer. E. Crimmin. il Motor B 125: 61+ Je '70
Guide to all-star indigestion. G. Greene. il Sports Illus 33:88-92+ O 12 '70
Holiday's choice of North American restaurants. S. Spitzer and H. Spitzer. il Holiday 48:75-82 Jl '70
Indigestion on the turnpike. G. Greene. il Life 69:12 Ag 28 '70
Random harvest of Albert Stockli; Stonehenge inn, Fairfield County, Conn. R. A. De Groot. il por Esquire 74:150-1+ O '70
RESTIF DE LA BRETONNE, Nicolas Edme
My revolution. by A. Karmel. Review
Sat R 53:36+ N 21 '70. T. Bishop *
RESTIGOUCHE RIVER
River running out of Eden. P. Ryan. il Sports Illus 32:86-9+ My 25 '70

RESTLE, Frank
Moon illusion explained on the basis of relative size. bibliog il Science 167:1092-6 F 20 '70
RESTON, James Barrett
Family planning or population control? Read Digest 97:163-4 D '70
about
Reston replies. Nat R 22:446+ My 5 '70 *
RESTON, James Barrett, Jr
Is Nuremberg coming back to haunt us? Sat R 53:14-17+ Jl 18 '70
Palace revolt? New Repub 162:9-10 Je 6 '70
RESTON, Va.
New equation: Nature center, community involvement. L. K. Daniels. il Am For 76:20-3+ N '70
RESTORATION of buildings. See Architecture —Conservation and restoration
RESTORATION of photographs. See Photographs—Conservation and restoration
RESTORATION of works of art. See Art—Conservation and restoration
RESTORE (corporation) See Bedford-Stuyvesant corporation, Brooklyn
RESTORED airplanes. See Airplanes, Restored
RESTORED automobiles. See Automobiles, Restored
RESTORED houses. See Houses, Restored
RESTORED villages. See Villages, Restored
RESTRAINT of trade
See also
Boycott
RESTREPO, Carlos Lleras. See Lleras Restrepo, C.
RESTRICTED stock options. See Stock purchase options
RESTRICTION of output. See Production control
RESTRICTIONS on travel. See Travel regulations
RÉSUMÉS of employment. See Applications for positions
RESURFACING of pavements. See Pavements —Surface treatment
RESURRECTION
See also
Jesus Christ—Resurrection and ascension
RESUSCITATION
See also
Respiration, Artificial
RETAIL advertising. See Advertising
RETAIL clerks. See Clerks (retail trade)
RETAIL credit. See Consumer credit
RETAIL trade
Beyond the retail slump. Fortune 81:16+ Mr '70
Carriage trade shops cautiously. il Bsns W p27 My 9 '70
Down and out downtown. il Time 96:87 D 7 '70
Easter buyers take a holiday. il Bsns W p27 Ap 4 '70
Exploring the un-boutique boutiques. il McCalls 97:88-93 My '70
Fifty largest retailing companies. il Fortune 81:208-9 My '70
Gray mood may last all year. Bsns W p36 Je 13 '70
Mixed basket, with peacocks; pre-Easter retail sales. Bsns W p25-6 Mr 21 '70
Style for fall is lean and anxious. il Bsns W p 16-17 Ag 15 '70
See also
Advertising
Bargain sale
Brenninkmeyer, C. and A, company
Christmas business
Department stores
Discount houses (retail trade)
Gamble-Skogmo, inc.
Kresge, S. S. company
Mail order business
Montgomery Ward and company
Returned goods
Sears, Roebuck and company
Specialty stores
Supermarkets

Finance
Distribution; with yardsticks of management performance. il Forbes 105:204-6+ Ja 1 '70; 107:124+ Ja 1 '71
Ratios of retailing; with table. Duns 96:76-7 S '70

Hours of business
See Store hours

Security measures
One in ten shoppers is a shoplifter. P. Hellman. il N Y Times Mag p34-5+ Mr 15 '70

RETAIL, wholesale, and department store union
  See also
  Drug and hospital employees union (local 1199)
RETAIL workers
  See also
  Department stores—Employees
RETARDED children. See Slow learning children
RETINA
  Induction of glutamine synthetase in embryonic retina: its dependence on cell interactions. J. E. Morris and A. A. Moscona. bibliog il Science 167:1736-8 Mr 27 '70
  Retinoscopy and eye size. M. Glickstein and M. Millodot. bibliog il Science 168:605-6 My 1 '70
  See also
  Rod and cone cells
RETIRED military personnel
  Our military retirees point the way. H. Alpert. il Har Yrs 10:6-11 Ag '70
  Perspectives of military and civilian retirement. R. Bellino. bibliog Ment Hy 54:580-3 O '70
RETIRED teachers. See Teachers, Retired
RETIREMENT
  Environment for retirement. il Har Yrs 10:19-34 Mr '70
  How to be a tough old bird. S. Costa. Har Yrs 10:46-7 Je '70
  How to live with your husband when he retires. S. Lord. Harp Baz 103:104-5 Je '70
  Inquiring about retiring; questions and answers. T. Collins. See issues of Harvest years
  News desk; retirement information. T. Schuchat. See issues of Harvest years
  Perspectives of military and civilian retirement. R. Bellino. bibliog Ment Hy 54:580-3 O '70
  Start planning your retirement right now. Changing T 24:33-5 My '70
  Time for self-expression. P. A. Dickinson. il Har Yrs 10:38-47 D '70
  What we want from the time we spend. P. A. Dickinson. il Har Yrs 10:19-23 O '70
  Where are they now? retired executives. R. Levy. pors Duns 95:40-2 Je '70
  Why not start a bank? Or a candle factory? Or make key rings? il Forbes 106:43-7 O 15 '70
  Why we spend time (the way we do) P. A. Dickinson. il Har Yrs 10:20-4 S '70
  You, too, can have a forest. D. Howlett. il Am For 76:20-3+ Ag '70
  See also
  American association of retired persons
  Pensions, Industrial
  Teachers, Retired
RETIREMENT, Places of
  Americano retires to Puerto Rico. M. Polhemus. il por Har Yrs 10:6-11+ S '70
  Best places to retire; symposium. il Har Yrs 10:35-8 Mr '70
  Environment for retirement. il Har Yrs 10:19-34 Mr '70
  For the retired, a world all their own; Sun City, Ariz; with report by P. O'Neil. il Life 68:45-50+ My 15 '70
  In search of retirement A. Phillips and L. Phillips. il Har Yrs 10:14-16 N '70
RETIREMENT housing. See Aged—Housing
RETIREMENT income
  Are you setting aside tax free retirement income as a freelancer? L. H. Houck. Writers Digest 50:32-3 D '70
RETIREMENT systems. See Pensions, Industrial
RETRIEVERS
        Training
  See Dogs—Training
RETROGRADE amnesia. See Amnesia
RETSOFF, Alexander N.
  Build bookshelf speaker system. il Radio-Electr 41:43-5 Mr '70
RETTIE, Dwight F.
  Urban conservation; adaptation of address. Parks & Rec 9:33-4+ S '70
RETURNABLE containers. See Containers
RETURNED goods
  Gift return trip. E. Bombeck. il Good H 172:48+ Ja '71

REUBEN, David R.
  Doctor David Reuben answers your questions. See issues of McCall's beginning July 1970
  Everything you always wanted to know about sex but were afraid to ask; excerpts. Ladies Home J 87:50+ Je '70
  Sexual conflicts; questions and answers. por McCalls 97:26+ Jl '70
        about
  Little Dr Reuben and his big sex book. B. Rollin. il pors Look 34:67-8 Jl 14 '70 *
  Sex: how to read all about it. il por Newsweek 76:38-9+ Ag 24 '70 *
REUM, W. Robert, and Steele, T. A. 3d
  Contingent payouts cut acquisition risks. bibliog f il Harvard Bsns R 48:83-91 Mr '70
REUNIONS, Family. See Family reunions
REUSS, Henry S.
  South African threads among the gold. Commonweal 92:32-4 Mr 20 '70
REUSSILLE, Helen
  Mailboat to Exuma. il Travel 134:52-5 N '70
REUTER-ultronic report. See Reuters news service
REUTERS news service
  Who now, Dow Jones? W. J. Slattery. Esquire 74:236-7 O '70
REUTHER, Walter Philip
  Labor loses a leader. J. Hill. Commonweal 92:260-1 My 29 '70 *
  Loss of a healer. il por Time 95:92+ My 25 '70 *
  Obituary
    Chr Cent 87:621 My 20 '70 *
    Nat R 22:553 Je 2 '70 *
    New Repub 162:7 My 23 '70. G. Tyler *
  Record wage hike for auto workers: Reuther's strategy. il U S News 68:81-2 Ap 27 '70 *
  Reuther's death creates a vacuum. il pors Bsns W p 106-8+ My 16 '70 *
  Reuther's legacy. il Newsweek 75:86+ My 25 '70 *
  Walter Reuther's untimely death. America 122:545 My 23 '70 *
  Why Reuther faces toughest bargaining test. il por U S News 68:63-4 My 4 '70
  Without Reuther: what unions and industry face. il U S News 68:55-6 My 25 '70 *
REVEL, Jean François
  De Tocqueville revisited. Newsweek 76:44-5 N 9 '70 *
REVELATION
  How do we know him? Chr Today 14:35 Ap 10 '70
  Slowly does it. V. P. McCorry. America 122: inside back cover Ap 25 '70
  See also
  Mystery
REVELLE, Roger. See Frisch, R. E. jt. auth.
REVENGER'S tragedy; drama. See Tourneur, C.
REVENUE, Municipal. See Local taxation
REVENUE bonds. See Bonds, Revenue
REVENUE sharing. See Intergovernmental tax relations
REVERIES; ballet. See Ballets—Criticisms
REVIEW copies of books
  AAP asks withdrawal of review copies ruling. Pub W 198:36-7 S 7 '70
  IRS rules review copies taxable income. S. Wagner. Pub W 198:47 Jl 20 '70
  Trade winds; taxability ruling. C. Amory. Sat R 53:14 S 19 '70
REVIEWS of books. See Book reviews
REVIEWS of moving pictures. See Moving picture plays—Criticisms, plots, etc.
REVIEWS of plays. See Dramas—Criticisms, plots, etc.
REVIVALS
  Art-gallery revival has drawing power; sight-and-sound display of Appalachian revival meetings. J. V. Lawing, jr. il Chr Today 15:38 O 23 '70
  Asbury revival blazes cross-country trail. J. Nelson and J. Rohler. Chr Today 14:46+ Mr 13 '70
  Revival at the bar; Mr Henry's in Washington, D.C. il Newsweek 76:53 S 7 '70
  See also
  Evangelistic work
REVOLTS, Student. See Student demonstrations
REVOLUTION
  Anatomy of revolution. P. W. Schmidtchen. il Hobbies 74:134-6+ F '70
REVOLUTION, Social. See Social revolution
REVOLUTIONARIES. See Revolutionists
REVOLUTIONARY actions. See Terrorsim

REVOLUTIONARY war (United States) See
United States—History—Revolution

REVOLUTIONISTS

Bombs blast a message of hate; with inter-
view with an admitted bomber. ed. by W.
Worthy. il Life 68:24-32A Mr 27 '70
Counterculture, or anticulture? F. S. Meyer.
Nat R 22:1165 N 3 '70
FBI's toughest foe: the kids. il Newsweek 76:
22-3 O 26 '70
Fleeing leftists: why they pick Algeria. il por
U S News 69:36 N 9 '70
Flowery beds of revolution. Chr Cent 87:907
Jl 29 '70
Guerrilla warfare in the U.S: FBI report.
il U S News 69:53-5 N 9 '70
Our other man in Algiers. S. De Gramont.
il NY Times Mag p30+ N 1 '70
Revolution as theatre. R. Brustein. New Re-
pub 162:13-17 Mr 14 '70; Same. Cur 118:3-8
My '70; Discussion. New Repub 162:28-31
Ap 25 '70
Revolutionaries: European vs. American. L.
Tyrmand. il N Y Times Mag p24-5+ F 15
'70; Discussion. p6+ Mr 8 '70
Revolutionists among the Chicago demon-
strators. P. R. Miller. il Bul Atom Sci 26:
16-21 F '70
Squelching revolutionaries. D. Lawrence. il
U S News 68:96 Ap 6 '70
Temptations a revolutionary encounters; ex-
cerpts from No bars to manhood. D. Ber-
rigan. Time 95:65 My 4 '70
We'll blow up the world: a nineteen-year-old
U.S. terrorist tells his story, ed. by K. Flem-
ing. il Newsweek 76:49-50+ O 12 '70
Where are the Clark Kents of yesteryear?
il Ramp Mag 9:38-42 D '70

Bibliography
Rips in the fabric of the law. S. Hyman. il
Sat R 53:21-4+ Jl 11 '70

REVOLUTIONISTS, French
Mao is watching; fashionable summer haunts
attacked. il Newsweek 76:36 Ag 10 '70

REVOLUTIONISTS, Latin American
Commune called Paradise; V. Toro and his
band of revolutionaries. il por Time 95:30
Je 1 '70

REVOLUTIONS
Are we in the middle of the second Ameri-
can revolution? symposium. il N Y Times
Mag p26-7+ My 17 '70
Bombs or Bibles? Get ready for revolution!
V. C. Grounds. Chr Today 15:4-6 Ja 15 '71
Mr Douglas' revolution. Nat R 22:481 My 5
'70
Open letter to: Norman Cousins, and others,
from the editors of National review con-
cerning Points of rebellion, by W. O.
Douglas. Nat R 22:293-4 Mr 24 '70
Revolution and social change; symposium.
Cur 118:3-22 My '70
Revolution for heaven's sake; excerpt from
One way to change the world. F. Leighton.
Chr Today 15:14-16 D 4 '70
Revolutionary war in world strategy 1945-
1969, by R. Thompson. Review
Nat R 22:1003-4 S 22 '70. J. Burnham
Sources of rebellion in western societies:
some quantitative evidence. T. R. Gurr.
bibliog f il Ann Am Acad 391:128-44 S '70
See also
Algeria—History—Revolution, 1954-1962
France—History—February revolution, 1848
France—History—Revolution
Government, Resistance to
Imaginary revolutions
Revolutionists

REVOLVERS
Cloverleaf Colt. C. Worman. il Hobbies
75:150-1 D '70
Colt Bisley model revolvers. C. G. Worman.
il Hobbies 74:152-3 F '70
1875 Remington revolver. C. G. Worman. il
Hobbies 74:150-1 Ja '70
1860 Colt .44. C. G. Worman. il Hobbies 75:158-
9 Ap '70
On the other hand. W. Page. il Field & S 74:
82-6 Ja '70

REVOLVING stage. See Opera—Stage mechanism

REWARD (psychology)
Discrimination by rats of conspecific odors
of reward and nonreward. R. R. Morrison
and H. W. Ludvigson. bibliog il Science
167:904-5 F 6 '70
Tongue cooling: a new reward for thirsty
rodents. J. Mendelson and D. Chillag. bibliog il Science 170:1418-21 D 25 '70

REWARDS, prizes, etc.
Louisville power squadron wins Chapman
award. il Motor B 125:46 Mr '70

Parting shots: orchids for eyepleasers, onions for eyesores. il Life 69:85-7 S 18 '70

Prize offers and awards. See issues of Writer
See also
Literary prizes
also names of awards, e.g. Pulitzer prizes;
also names of organizations, societies, etc.
granting awards, e.g. American forestry association; also subhead Awards, prizes, etc.
under various subjects, e.g. Landscape protection—Awards, prizes, etc.

Anecdotes, facetiae, satire, etc.
Award award. Chr Cent 87:711 Je 3 '70
LJ's non-awards. J. Berry, 3d, and others.
Library J 95:4207 D 15 '70

REX, Robert W.
Clean power from inside the earth. J. Lear.
il Sat R 53:55-6+ D 5 '70 *

REX chainbelt, inc.
Fallout from a friendly merger. Bsns W p32
O 24 '70

REXALL drug and chemical company
See also
Vanda cosmetics company

REXROTH, Kenneth
Trade winds. J. Beatty, jr. Sat R 53:18 Mr
21 '70 *

REY, José López-. See López-Rey, J.

REYES, Juan Vila. See Vila Reyes, J.

REYNAUD, David H.
Success story. il Parks & Rec 5:28-9 Jl '70

REYNER, Anthony S.
Which route for the Isthmian canal? bibliog
f il Cur Hist 58:102-6+ F '70

REYNOLDS, Fred
Sweet and swinging. See occasional issues of
American record guide to August 1970

REYNOLDS, Gary
Wasps help fight the alfalfa weevil. il Farm
J 94:20-1+ S '70

REYNOLDS, J. H. and others
Isotopic analysis of rare gases from stepwise
heating of lunar fines and rocks. bibliog il
Science 167:545-8 Ja 30 '70

REYNOLDS, Margaret
Reluctant emigrés. New Repub 162:17-19 Mr
21 '70

REYNOLDS, Mary B.
San Joaquin Valley, California: la Biblioteca
ambulante. Wilson Lib Bul 44:767 Mr '70

REYNOLDS, Richard S. 1908-
Knight in aluminum armor. il Forbes 105:
18-19 My 1 '70 *

REYNOLDS, William J.
Ten commendments for teachers of English.
Engl J 59:672-3 My '70

REYNOLDS metals company
Knight in aluminum armor. il Forbes 105:18-
19 My 1 '70

RHAPSODIES. See African violets

RHEINGOLD, Harriet L. and Eckerman, C. O.
Infant separates himself from his mother.
bibliog il Science 168:78-83 Ap 3 '70

RHEINGOLD corporation
Rheingold: growth with flavor. R. Levy. por
Duns 96:58 O '70
Rheingold's rise with the Mets. il Bsns W
p60-1 Ag 22 570

RHEOLOGY
Viscosity of the Atlantic Ocean bottom. C. H.
Cramer. bibliog il Science 167:1123-4 F 20 '70

RHESUS monkeys. See Monkeys

RHETORIC
Failure of speech in The ox-bow incident.
D. E. Houghton. Engl J 59:1245-51 D '70
Leaves from a lurid lexicon; samples. il News-
week 76:24 S 28 '70
Truth and harmony as rhetorical goals; adap-
tation of address, November, 1969. G. R.
Bramer. bibliog f Engl J 59:826-33 S '70 *

RHINE RIVER
Home on the Rhine. D. Butwin. il Sat R
53:55-7 Je 20 '70
Rhine; photographs. J. Ferri. Travel & Camera 33:20-4 O '70

RHINELANDER, John B.
Department makes determination on sea disposal of nerve agent; statement August 5,
1970. Dept State Bul 63:282-3 S 7 '70

RHINITIS in swine. See Swine—Diseases and
pests

RHINOCEROS
White rhino: the road back. D. S. Henderson. il Nat Parks 44:19-20 Mr '70

RHINOPLASTY. See Surgery, Plastic

RHO, Joon H. and others
Fluorometric examination of a lunar sample.
Science 167:754-5 Ja 30 '70

RHOADES, Jonathan
Hap i nes afloat on the Sea of Cortez. il
Sports Illus 32:64-6+ Mr 30 '70

RHOADES, Orille B.
Books reviewed. See issues of Hobbies to May 1970
RHODANINE
Rhodanine: a selective inhibitor of the multi-plication of echovirus 12. H. J. Eggers and others. bibliog il Science 167:294-7 Ja 16 '70
RHODE ISLAND
See also
Block Island
Education—Rhode Island
Fishing—Rhode Island
Hunting—Rhode Island
Libraries—Rhode Island
Music festivals—Rhode Island

Historic houses, etc.

See also
Newport, R.I.—Historic houses, etc.
RHODES, Barbara A.
Special college entry programs for Afro-Americans. bibliog Sch & Soc 98:360-2 O '70
RHODES, James Allen
Decline of Ohio. D. Hess. Nation 210:429-33 Ap 13 '70 *
Patrician and the pol. pors Newsweek 75:30 My 4 '70 *
RHODES, Joseph, jr
Agnew's pungent quotient. il por Time 95: 12 Je 29 '70 *
Establishment maverick. por Newsweek 75:58 Je 29 '70 *
Rhodes' scholarship. por Time 96:51 Ag 31 '70 *
RHODES, Lynwood Mark
Seafarers' serenity: Europe's maritime mu-seums. il Travel 133:60-4+ F '70
RHODES, Philip L.
Accomodations for the cruising boat. il por Motor B 125:128-33 Mr '70
Motorsailers. il por Motor B 125:114-15 Ja '70
RHODES, Richard
"Always on the stretch": a western voyage. il Harper 241:79-84+ N '70
Harry's last hurrah. il Harper 240:48-9+ Ja '70
Heaven on earth. il Harper 240:116-22 My '70
Ike: an artist in iron. por Harper 241:70-7 Jl '70; Same abr. Read Digest 97:121-6 S '70
Watching the animals. il Harper 240:91-4 Mr '70
RHODES scholars and scholarships
Black American in racist South Africa. S. Sanders. il pors Ebony 26:35-8+ D '70
RHODESIA
See also
Civil rights—Rhodesia
Land tenure—Rhodesia
Natural resources—Rhodesia
United Nations—Rhodesia
Zoology—Rhodesia

Economic conditions

How it goes in Rhodesia. J. Phillips. Nat R 22:894-5 Ag 25 '70
Rhodesia: penalized but prospering. il U S News 68:60 Mr 23 '70

Foreign relations

Shock of nonrecognition. Time 95:32 Mr 23 '70

History

Independent Rhodesia. A. C. Turner. bibliog f Cur Hist 58:129-34+ Mr '70
Rhodesia. T. J. Kubiak. il Focus 20:1-11 Je '70

Industries

See also
Rhodesia—Economic conditions

Native races

See also
Rhodesia—Race problems

Politics and government

Discordant election. il Newsweek 75:64 Ap 20 '70
Independent Rhodesia. A. C. Turner. bibliog f Cur Hist 58:129-34+ Mr '70
Rhodesia; U.S. foreign policy? address, March 12, 1970. J. R. Rarick. Vital Speeches 36:434-7 My 1 '70

Race problems

Bleak future for black Rhodesians. O. Eby. Chr Cent 87:899-901 Jl 22 '70
Blunt words for Rhodesia: United Methodist Bishop A. T. Muzarewa banned from tribal areas. America 123:106 S 5 '70
Dilemma in Rhodesia; bishops and the Land tenure act. America 123:79-80 Ag 22 '70

Discordant election. il Newsweek 75:64 Ap 20 '70
Ian Smith's Rhodesia; only the churches stand in the way; with editorial comment. O. W. Okite. Chr Today 14:26, 44 Je 5 '70
RHODODENDRONS
For March and April bloom, earlier rhododen-drons. il Sunset 144:195 F '70
Profuse blooming, the maddenii. il Sunset 144:235+ Ap '70
Propagation of hybrid rhododendrons. R. G. Coggeshall. il Horticulture 48:30-1+ My '70
Rhododendrons for every garden. B. Brinhart. il Org Gard & Farm 17:82-4 Ap '70
RHÔNE VALLEY
Wine-lover's tour of the Rhône. R. A. De Groot. il House B 112:80-2 Ag '70
RHUBARB
Is it time to move the rhubarb? K. L. Carl-sen. il Org Gard & Farm 17:100-1 Ap '70
RHYME. See Rime
RHYNCHOSCIARA. See Diptera
RHYNE, Charles S.
Growing law fullness of the world community; address, August 18, 1970. Vital Speeches 36: 761-4 O 1 '70
RHYTHM
See also
Musical meter and rhythm
RIBE, Fred Linden
Scyllac: toward pulsed fusion. D. E. Thomsen. il por Sci N 98:321-3 O 17 '70 *
RIBEIRO, Darcy
Third world in history; with biographical note by F. Bonilla. Trans-Action 7:6+ N '69
RIBICOFF, Abraham A.
Arab-Israeli settlement: Fulbright's proposal, and his colloquy with Senator Ribicoff. New Repub 163:22-3 O 10 '70
Do most Americans secretly want segrega-tion? por Look 34:11-13 S 8 '70
Excerpt from debate, February 9, 1970. Cong Digest 49:118+ Ap '70
Healthiest nation myth. il Sat R 53:18-20 Ag 22 '70
North is guilty of monumental hypocrisy; ex-cerpts from address, February 9, 1970. por U S News 68:32-3 F 23 '70

about

Desegregation's strange bedfellows. il por Newsweek 75:22-3 F 23 '70 *
Letter from Washington. R. H. Rovere. New Yorker 46:109 F 21 '70 *
New desegregation targets: the North and the suburbs. il por U S News 69:25-7 D 14 '70 *
Racism: North and South. America 122:206 F 28 '70 *
Ribicoff rides the tide. R. G. Sherrill. Nation 210:294-6 Mr 16 '70 *
RIBLET, Roy J. and Herzenberg, L. A.
Mouse lysozyme production by a monocy-toma: isolation and comparison with oth-er lysozymes. bibliog il Science 168:1595-7 Je 26 '70
RIBMAN, Ronald
Passing through from exotic places. Criti-cism
Commonweal 91:482-3 Ja 30 '70
RIBONUCLEASES
Ribonuclease-inhibitor system abnormality in dystrophic mouse skeletal muscle. B. W. Little and W. L. Meyer. bibliog il Science 170:747-9 N 13 '70
Ribonuclease V of escherichia coli: sus-ceptibility of heated ribosomal RNA and stability of R17 phage RNA. M. Kuwano and others. bibliog il Science 168:1225-6 Je 5 '70
RIBONUCLEIC acid. See RNA
RIBONUCLEOTIDES. See Nucleotides
RIBOSOMES. See Nucleoproteins
RICAPITO, Joseph V. See Stein, M. L. jt. auth.
RICARD (firm) See Liquor industry and trade —France
RICCARDO, John J.
Skidding Chrysler switches drivers. il por Bsns W p30-1 Ja 17 '70
RICCI, Ruggiero
Recordings. M. Mayer. il Esquire 73:44 F '70 *
RICCIARDI, Franc Mario
Kidde alumnus does his own thing. por Bsns W p36 Ja 31 '70
RICCIO, Ottone M.
Adagio; poem. Mlle 72:210 N '70
Comment. A. Brilliant. Poetry 116:127-8 My '70 *

RICE, Arthur H.
Merits of the Insite plan. il Todays Ed 59:
46-8 My '70
Squeeze the parents out of school and see
what we get. Ed Digest 36:32-3 S '70
RICE, Berkeley
Down and out along route 128. il N Y Times
Mag p28-9+ N 1 '70
RICE, Bruce
(tr) See Sartre, J. P.   Intellectuals and
revolution: interview   with   Jean-Paul
Sartre
RICE, Caroline
Men, man your needles. il Har Yrs 10:16-18
Mr '70
RICE, Charles O.
Radical Catholic; address. il por Cath World
211:156-60 Jl '70
RICE, Edward
Second chance for dropouts. Sch & Soc 98:
423-4 N '70
RICE, Helen F.
Reading industry: resources and materials.
il por Wilson Lib Bul 45:298-307 N '70
RICE, Mary E.
Asexual reproduction in a sipunculan worm.
bibliog il Science 167:1618-20 Mr 20 '70
RICE, Randall H.
Owning in partnership. il Yachting 127:92-
3+ Ja '70
RICE, Stanley
Editorial game: imagination and technology.
Pub W 197:45-6+ Ap 6 '70
RICE, Stephen. See Minton, R. jt. auth.
RICE, Susan
Blind-dating. Seventeen 29:158-9+ Ap '70
RICE, Tim
Rock passion. W. Bender. il pors Time 96:
47 N 9 '70 *
RICE, William Thomas
W. Thomas Rice of Seaboard coast line; in-
terview. il pors Nations Bsns 58:60-6 N '70
RICE
Third world: seeds of revolution; production
explosion in the grain bowls of the world.
il Time 96:24+ Jl 13 '70
Whatever happened to the promised miracle
in Asia's rice fields? il U S News 69:52
Ag 31 '70
See also
Cookery—Rice
International rice research institute
Wild rice
RICE diet. See Diet in disease
RICEVILLE, Ia.
Most precious resource; school experiment in
race discrimination. J. Lear. Sat R 53:57 Je
6 '70
RICH, Adrienne
Letters: March 1969; poem. Harper 240:95 Mr
'70
Our whole life; poem. New Repub 162:21 My
2 '70
about
Comment. M. Van Duyn. Poetry 115:433-4 Mr
'70 *
RICH, Alan
Happenings at Kent state. il Hi Fi 20:secII
27+ My '70
On the firing line. por Opera N 35:8-11 Ja 9
'71
On the off-beat. il Hi Fi 20:secII 12+ F; 10
Ap; 7 Je; 7 Ag '70
RICH, Barbarine
It's polite to slurp in Japan. il Seventeen 29:
30 Mr '70
RICH, John
All's fair for youth at Expo '70. il Seventeen
29:146-7+ Mr '70
RICH, Leslie
Creativity takes over. il Am Ed 6:16-22 D
'70
Instead of Molotov cocktails. il Am Ed 6:
11-15 Je '70
Modern industry. See occasional issues of
Dun's
RICH, Maria F.
Plus ça change: U.S. opera survey. il Opera N
35:14-16 N 21 '70
RICH, Saul, and others
Ozone uptake by bean leaves. bibliog il Sci-
ence 169:79-80 Jl 3 '70
RICH, The
See also
Capitalists
Leisure class
Millionaires
RICH in Russia; story. See Updike, J.
RICHARDS, Alice
Saturday school for future teachers. il De-
sign 71:16-19 Sum '70 *

RICHARDS, C. Arnold
How the geologist can help your city. il
Am City 85:84-6 Je '70
RICHARDS, Harold Marshall Sylvester
Attraction of Adventism. D. Kucharsky. Chr
Today 14:35 Ja 30 '70
RICHARDS, Kenneth G.
Crosby weather. bibliog il Weatherwise 22:
240-3 D '69
RICHARDS, Maxine
Fairytale Thailand. il Travel 133:42-7 Ja '70
RICHARDS, Pat
Sailing down my dirty river. il por Nat Wild-
life 8:28-9 F '70
RICHARDS, Robert R.
Education association of Norfolk. Todays
Ed 59:39 My '70
RICHARDS, Theodore William
Theodore William Richards and the periodic
table; adaptation of address, December 29,
1969. J. B. Conant. bibliog Science 168:425-
8 Ap 24 '70 *
RICHARDSON, Bernard E.
Wind is rising. bibliog il por Library J 95:463-
7 F 1 '70
RICHARDSON, Don
Rock garden in the fall. il Horticulture 48:
34-5+ O '70
RICHARDSON, Elliot Lee
Controlling local conflicts; address, April 29,
1970. Dept State Bul 62:628-31 My 18 '70
Generation gap; address, June 7, 1970. Vital
Speeches 36:583-5 Jl 15 '70; Same with title
Differing perceptions of U.S. foreign policy.
Dept State Bul 62:800-3 Je 29 '70
I want to focus on people problems; inter-
view. pors U S News 69:35-6+ D 7 '70
National foreign policy conference for edi-
tors and broadcasters; remarks, January
15, 1970. Dept State Bul 62:113-16+ F 2 '70
Office of under secretary for western hemi-
sphere affairs; statement, March 18, 1970.
Dept State Bul 62:498-9 Ap 13 '70
Strengthened programs of international co-
operation for halting the illicit supply of
drugs; address, April 2, 1970. Dept State Bul
62:544-9 Ap 27 '70
Under Secretary Richardson interviewed on
Issues and answers; transcript of program,
May 10, 1970. Dept State Bul 62:681-6 Je 1
'70
United States and western Europe; address,
January 20, 1970. Vital Speeches 36:258-60
F 15 '70; Same. Dept State Bul 62:155-9 F 9
'70
United States policy for the seabed; state-
ment, May 27, 1970. Dept State Bul 62:
738-41 Je 15 '70
U.S.-Soviet relations in an era of negotia-
tion; address, November 20, 1969. Dept
State Bul 61:584-8 D 22 '69
We are embarked on a great new mission of
reform; address, July 27, 1970. por U S News
69:57-9 Ag 17 '70
about
HEW's new secretary. il por time 95:12-13 Je
15 '70 *
Moving into chaos: new welfare chief. por
U S News 68:76 Je 22 '70 *
New man: old hand at H.E.W. il por News-
week 75:25 Je 15 '70 *
RICHARDSON, Jack
Innocence restaged. Commentary 49:20+ Mr
'70
Lively commerce. il Harper 241:82-9 Ag '70
Working theater. Commentary 50:50-2 Ag '70
RICHARDSON, James
Travel as a passport to freedom. A. Alvarez.
Sat R 54:19 Ja 2 '71 *
RICHARDSON, James F.
Historical roots of our urban crisis. Cur
Hist 59:257-61+ N '70
RICHARDSON, K. A. and others
Alpha-particle activity of Apollo 11 samples.
bibliog il Science 167:516-17 Ja 30 '70
RICHARDSON, Larry
Larry Richardson and company, 92nd St. Y,
NYC. N. Mason. Dance Mag 44:80 Ag '70 *
RICHARDSON, Tony
Current cinema. P. Kael. New Yorker 45:
66+ Ja 17 '70
RICHARDSON-Merrell, Inc.
Got a cold? What you need is... il Forbes
105:35-6 My 1 '70
RICHEK, Herbert G. and others
Dogmatism, religiosity and mental health in
college students. Ment Hy 54:572-4 O '70
RICHES, Victor W.
Systematic menu planning. Camp Mag 42:12-
13 F '70
RICHEY, David
Water temperature is fishy business. il
Field & S 75:40-1+ Jl '70

RICHIE, Donald
  I read the movie. bibliog Nation 210:757-8 Je
  22 '70
RICHIE, Jeanne
  Church, caste and women. Chr Cent 87:73-7,
  705-6 Ja 21, Je 3 '70
  Unresponsive pew. Chr Cent 86:1278-81; 87:123-
  5 O 8 '69, Ja 28 '70
RICHLER, Mordecai
  Love affair; story; excerpt from St Urbain's
  horseman. McCalls 98:92-4 Ja '71
RICHMOND, Al
  Doctor Oppenheimer's exploratorium. il Na-
  tion 211:6-9 Jl 6 '70
  Workers against the war. il Ramp Mag 9:28-
  32 S '70
RICHMOND, Doug
  Saddle up for dirt! il Pop Mech 134:138-41+
  O '70
RICHMOND, Lee J.
  Emily Dickinson's If you were coming in the
  fall: an explication. Engl J 59:771-3 S '70
RICHMOND, LeRoy
  Back again: Joseph Keilberth's lustrous doc-
  umentation of the Hiller variations. il por
  Am Rec G 36:332-3 Ja '70
RICHMOND, Va.
  How Richmond communicates. Am City 85:
  120-1 Jl '70

City planning

  Downtown Richmond makes it. il Am City
  85:140-1 Je '70

Description

  Step by step through Richmond. R. Deardorff. il Travel 134:42-7+ S '70

Education

  Merging city and suburban schools: the
  Richmond story. U S News 69:24 Ag 10 '70
  Open letter to the Supreme court of the Uni-
  ted States; reprint from Richmond, Va.
  News leader, July 22, 1970. il U S News 69:
  76+ Ag 10 '70

Galleries and museums

  Treasure house of the Confederacy. C. G.
  Worman. il Hobbies 75:150-1 N '70

Parks and playgrounds

  Playgrounds in orbit; The world above pro-
  gram. X. Morris. il Parks & Rec 5:31+ Mr
  '70
RICHTER, Curt P. and Duke, J. R.
  Cataracts produced in rats by yogurt. bib-
  liog il Science 168:1372-4 Je 12 '70
RICHTER, Les
  Rap 'n 'pinion. por Motor T 22:16+ Ja
  '70
RICHTER, Roy
  Rap 'n 'pinion. Motor T 23:14 Ja '71

about

  Car of the year; cars panel. por Motor T
  23:63 Ja '71 *
RICHTER scale. See Seismometry
RICKBORN, Harold C.
  Can your boat take a flying bridge? il
  Motor B 126:68-70+ N '70
RICKENBACKER, William F.
  Music. Nat R 22:1120+ O 20 '70
  Records (title varies) (cont) Nat R 22:579-
  80, 690-1 Je 2, 30 '70
RICKETS
  Rickets. W. F. Loomis. il Sci Am 223:76-82+
  bibliog(p 140) D '70
RICKLEFS, Robert E.
  Clutch size in birds: outcome of opposing
  predator and prey adaptations. bibliog il
  Science 168:599-600; 170:650-1 My 1, N 6 '70
RICKLES, Robert N.
  Commissioner Rickles; interview. New York-
  er 46:33-4 My 9 '70
RICKMAN, Eric
  Eric Rickman. J. Thawley. il pors Hot Rod
  23:70-2 Je '70 *
  Rooster tales. See issues of Hot rod to No-
  vember 1970
RICKSON, Fred R.
  More on eutrophication. Home Gard 58:20+
  Ja '71
RIDDELL, Nicholas
  From Teresa of Avila to Eldridge Cleaver:
  the odyssey of a radical priest. P. T. Rohr-
  bach. il por Cath World 211:116-19 Je '70 *
RIDDIFORD, Lynn M.
  Prevention of metamorphosis by exposure
  of insect eggs to juvenile hormone ana-
  logs. bibliog il Science 167:287-8 Ja 16 '70
  —See Truman, J. W. jt. auth.
RIDDLE, Lindsey G.
  Digital clock update. il Radio-Electr 41:54-
  5+ Ag '70

RIDE the Gooberville stage! drama. See Huff,
  B. T.
RIDERS to the sea; opera. See Vaughan Wil-
  liams, R.
RIDGED fields. See Terraces (agriculture)
RIDGEWAY, James
  Hard times. Ramp Mag 9:9-10+ D '70
  Para-real estate: the handing out of re-
  sources. il Ramp Mag 8:28-33 My '70
RIDING. See Horseback trips; Horsemanship
RIEGGER, Hal
  Reduction of raku glazes; excerpts from
  Raku: art and technique. il Ceram Mo 18:
  16-18 Je '70
  Hal Riegger. G. Hodge. il pors Ceram Mo
  18:13-15 Je '70 *
RIENKS, Linda
  Watercolor textiles. il pors Design 71:16-18
  mid-Sum '70
RIENOW, Leona Train. See Rienow, R. jt.
  auth.
RIENOW, Robert
  Park program: it's bigger than you think;
  address, October 1969. por Parks & Rec 5:
  27-8+ Mr '70
  Park? What good is it? poem. Parks & Rec
  5:26 Mr '70
  Age of eternal twilight. il Audubon 72:4-8
  Jl '70
RIENZO, John J. and Tarbox, E. F.
  Bipolar semiconductor IC memories. il pors
  Electr World 84:44-5 O '70
RIFKIN, Benjamin A.
  Danube mannerists. il Art N 68:56-8+ F '70
  Rembrandt and his circle (cont) il Art N 69:
  58-61+ My '70
RIFLE cartridges. See Cartridges
RIFLE sights. See Firearms—Sights
RIFLES
  Evolution in rifle stocks. W. Page. il Field &
  S 74:176-81 Ap '70
  Five times Mannlicher. W. Page. il Field &
  S 74:124-7 F '70
  Functional rifle stock. J. O'Connor. il Out-
  door Life 145:122+ Je '70
  Great .375 Magnum. J. O'Connor. il Outdoor
  Life 146:86+ N '70
  Jenks breech-loader. C. Worman. il Hobbies
  75:150-1 S '70
  One-rifle safaris. J. O'Connor. il Outdoor
  Life 145:88+ Ja '70
  Switch-barrels I have known. W. Page. il por
  Field & S 75:68-70+ D '70
  Winchester's first centennial model. C. Wor-
  man. il Hobbies 75:150-1 O '70

Manufacture

  Will the M-16 be made in Korea? il Bsns
  W p 116 O 24 '70
RIGA, Peter J.
  Green Berets. il Cath World 210:199-203 F '70
  Selective conscientious objection: progress
  report. il Cath World 211:161-5 Jl '70
RIGALI, Norbert J.
  Is theology thinking about God? Cath
  World 210:204-7 F '70
RIGDEN, John S.
  Reshaping the image of physics. bibliog il Phys
  Today 23:48-53 O '70
RIGDON, V. Bruce, and Will, J. E.
  Needed: new modes for internationalizing
  theological education. Chr Cent 87:501-5 Ap
  22 '70
RIGGING. See Masts and rigging
RIGHT and left (political science)
  Alternatives; underground media conference
  at Goddard college. R. Todd. Atlan 226:112+
  N '70
  America's other radicals: the far right. P.
  Schrag. Harper 241:35-46 Ag '70
  Amiable right. Newsweek 75:54 Mr 2 '70
  Are we moving right? W. F. Buckley, jr.
  Nat R 22:1125 O 20 '70
  Behind the terror bombings; with interview
  with J. P. Spiegel. U S News 68:15-17 Mr
  30 '70
  Bitch goddess of individualism; the new left.
  R. S. Wheeler. Nat R 22:1346+ D 15 '70
  Bombers and radicals. Chr Cent 87:1055 S 9
  '70
  Conservative and the revolutionary right. S.
  J. Tonsor. Nat R 22:1360-1 D 15 '70
  Decline of liberal politics. W. Pfaff; discus-
  sion. Commentary 49:16+ F '70
  Dissent or anarchy: common front at Buf-
  falo. H. S. Levine. il Nation 210:520-2 My 4
  '70
  Dis-United States of America? il Sr Schol
  97:14-19 S 14 '70
  FBI's J. Edgar Hoover reports on a turbu-
  lent year; excerpts from report. J. E.
  Hoover. il U S News 69:24 Jl 27 '70

RIGHT and left (political science)—*Continued*
Fight or switch? 1970 election results and the President's tactics. Nation 211:514 N 23 '70

Fortunes of the left. E. D. Genovese. Nat R 22:1266-70 D 1 '70

From Teresa of Avila to Eldridge Cleaver: the odyssey of a radical priest; N. Riddell. P. T. Rohrbach. il por Cath World 211:116-19 Je '70

Guerrilla warfare in the U.S: FBI report. il U S News 69:53-5 N 9 '70

Here is the latest radical plan; interview, ed. by G. Astor. L. Gorkin. Look 34:78 N 17 '70

Homesickness of the new left. G. Niemeyer. il Nat R 22:779-83+ Jl 28 '70

Honest, intelligible radical politics. R. Brustein. New Repub 163:15-17 S 26 '70; Same. Cur 123:20-3 N '70

How back is the backlash? P. Steinfels. Commonweal 93:40 O 9 '70

Innocence: the essence of the American heartland. E. J. Hughes. Sat R 53:25-8+ O 17 '70

Israel and the new left. S. Avineri. Trans-Action 7:79-83 Jl '70

Like fathers, like sons. N. Podhoretz. Commentary 50:21 Ag '70; Reply with rejoinder. A. Kazin. 50:28 N '70

Literature and revolution. by J. Ruhle. Review
Commonweal 92:17-18 Mr 13 '70. B. Wallenstein

Majority in both parties are against extremism; conservative trends. D. Lawrence. U S News 69:96 D 14 '70

Matzpen and its sponsors: Committee on new alternatives in the Middle East. C. Gershman. Commentary 50:52-3 Ag '70; Discussion. 50:5+ O; 14 D '70

Memories of a (latter-day) Catholic girlhood. K. Mulherin. il Commonweal 91:610-19 Mr 6 '70; Discussion. 92:77+ Ap 3 '70

Move to the right. W. F. Buckley, jr. Nat R 22:1178-9 N 3 '70

Movement seeks a mass; new left crisis. L. D. Nachman. il Nation 212:39-45 Ja 11 '71

Myth of the rad decade. P. Steinfels. Commonweal 93:62 O 16 '70

Need for politics on the left. B. Rustin. Cur 123:18-20 N '70

New blacklist; House internal security committee compilation of radical campus speakers. Time 96:28 O 26 '70

New course for the new left; excerpt from Beyond the new left. I. Howe. Sat R 53:8-11 My 30 '70

New left: a documentary history, ed. by M. Teodori. Review
Cath World 211:94-5 My '70. J. Tytell

New left reconsidered. Trans-Action 7:6+ Je '70

New reformation notes of a neolithic conservative, by P. Goodman. Review
Commonweal 93:152-5 N 6 '70. J. B. Gordon

New right credo: libertarianism. S. Lehr and L. Rossetto, jr. il N Y Times Mag p24-5+ Ja 10 '71

Nixon and the rancid right. S. Alsop. Newsweek 76:132 O 12 '70

Non-generation gap. S. M. Lipset and E. Raab. Commentary 50:35-9 Ag '70

Notes and comment: extreme-left-wing movement and current administration's response. il New Yorker 46:25-6 Je 27 '70

Notes on authority, morality, power. J. Burnham. Nat R 22:1283-9 D 1 '70; Reply F. S. Meyer. 22:1407 D 29 '70

On being deradicalized. N. Glazer. Commentary 50:74-80 O '70; Discussion. 50:30-1 O '70; 51:20-3 Ja '71

On not becoming revolutionary; excerpt from Ready for the rain. R. Gozzi, jr. il Nation 211:492-4 N 16 '70

Political terrorism: hysteria on the left. I. Howe. il N Y Times Mag p25-7+ Ap 12 '70; Discussion. p22+ My 10 '70

Politics of style; radical culture. J. Corry. il Harper 241:60-4 N '70

Politics of unreason, by S. M. Lipset and E. Raab. Review
Sat R 54:23-5+ Ja 9 '71. A. P. Sindler

Radical chic is dead. S. Alsop. Newsweek 76:120 D 14 '70

Radicalism and the skipped generation; excerpt from Toward a radical middle: fourteen pieces of reporting and criticism. R. Adler. Atlan 225:53-7 F '70

Radicals on the rampage. Chr Today 15:33-4 N 6 '70

Rally round, radiclibs. P. Steinfels. Commonweal 93:191 N 20 '70

Reaping the whirlwind: radical attack, conservative reactions. F. S. Meyer. Nat R 22:89 Ja 27 '70

Revolt of youth: where are we now? J. H. Schaar and S. S. Wolin. Cur 119:3-10 Je '70

Revolution now; radical strategy conference at University of Wisconsin. Nat R 22:716+ Jl 14 '70

Shall we let America die? both new left and conservatism threaten to liberalism. D. A. Zoll; discussion. Nat R 21:1327; 22-259-60, 311, 362+ D 30 '69, Mr 10-Ap 7 '70

Socialism of fools: the new left calls it anti-Zionism. S. M. Lipset. il N Y Times Mag p6-7+ Ja 3 '71

Split in the family? radical New York intellectuals. Nat R 22:1334-5 D 15 '70

Student revolt; the new left. C. Landauer. Yale R 60:175-84 D '70

Swing to the right? A. Etzioni. Trans-Action 7:12+ S '70; Same abr. Cur 122:11-14 O '70

Take heart from the heartland. A. M. Greeley. New Repub 163:16-19 D 12 '70

Turning off the people: the war and white ethnic groups. A. M. Greeley. New Repub 162:14-16 Je 27 '70; Same with title War and white ethnic groups. Cur 120:22-7 Ag '70

Two, three, many Dallases! right-wing political opinion. Nat R 22:126-7 F 10 '70

Unholy alliance against the campus. K. Keniston and M. Lerner. il N Y Times Mag p28-9+ N 8 '70

U.S. faces choice between anarchy and repression; address, June 1 1970. M. C. Smith. il pors U S News 68:45-6 Je 15 '70

Waltermittyization; extremism. S. Alsop. Newsweek 75:100 Mr 30 '70

War against the police: officers tell their story; testimony before Senate subcommittee. il U S News 69:82-6 O 26 '70

White left in the mother country. R. Ruether. il Commonweal 93:142-5 N 6 '70; Discussion. 93:263, 287, 363+ D 4-11 '70, Ja 15 '71

Young intelligentsia in revolt; excerpt from America: system and revolution, ed. by R. Aya and N. Miller. R. Flacks. il Trans-Action 7:46-55 Je '70

Youth and foreign policy. S. J. Kelman. For Affairs 48:414-26 Ap '70
See also
Conservatism
Liberalism
Liberty

Bibliography

American right and pamphleteering; recommendations for a radical pamphlet library. N. Kehde. il Am Lib 1:965-7 N '70

RIGHT and wrong. See Ethics

RIGHT of access to the press. See Press law

RIGHT of assembly. See Assembly, Right of

RIGHT of asylum. See Asylum, Right of

RIGHT of dissent. See Free speech

RIGHT of government employees to strike. See Strikes—United States—Government employees

RIGHT of privacy. See Privacy, Right of

RIGHT of way
See also
Trails—Laws and legislation

RIGHT to labor
See also
Discrimination in employment

RIGHT to read program
Accountability: Right to read program and integration vs. compensatory education. E. Geller. Library J 95:1881 My 15 '70

Allen's dismissal clouds right-to-read program. S. Wagner. Pub W 197:40 Je 22 '70

Federal Right to read program; summary of address, May 12, 1970. G. R. Anrig. Pub W 197:41-2 Je 1 '70

For preschoolers, the right to read; J. E. Allen's goal. W. D. Boutwell. PTA Mag 64:30 My '70

Making the right to read real. V. H. Mathews. Schol Teach Jr/Sr High p6-8 D 7 '70

Project RISE: PTA takes the lead to improve reading. W. D. Boutwell. PTA Mag 65:13-14 N '70

Right to read. P. B. Price. PTA Mag 64:15 Mr '70

Right to read leaders and a message from Louis G. Mendez, jr. director. L. G. Mendez, jr. por Wilson Lib Bul 45:240-1 N '70

Right to read pace picks up. Sr Schol 96:Schol Teach 7 My 4 '70

RIGHT to read program—*Continued*
Right-to-read project may boost U.S. book
and library programs. S. Wagner. Pub W
197:31 Mr 16 '70
Right to read, target for the 70's; address,
September 23, 1969. J. E. Allen, jr. Sch &
Soc 98:82-4 F '70; Excerpts. Ed Digest 35:
20-2 Mr '70
Right to read: what does it mean? sym-
posium, ed. by J. Veatch. bibliog il Li-
brary J 95:1899-910+ My 15 '70
Teacher and the child's right to read. W. D.
Boutwell. PTA Mag 64:12 Je '70
RIGHT wing (politics) See Right and left (po-
litical science)
RIGHTS, Bill of (United States) See United
States—Constitution—Bill of rights
RIGHTS, Civil. See Civil rights
RIGHTS of women. See Woman—Equal rights
RIHA, Thomas
Tom Cat and the Colonel. pors Time 95:13 F
9 '70
RIJKSMUSEUM. See Amsterdam, Netherlands
—Galleries and museums
RIKERS ISLAND prisons. See New York (city)
—Prisons and reformatories
RILES, Wilson C.
Challenging Rafferty. il por Time 96:58 N 2
'70 •
Remarkable Mr Riles. M. E. Leary. New Re-
pub 163:12 D 19 '70 •
Retiring Rafferty. il por Newsweek 76:71-3 N
16 '70 •
Riling Rafferty. il por Time 96:49 N 16 '70 •
Two against Rafferty. N. Melnick. New Repub
162:11-12 Mr 21 '70 •
RILEY, Bridget Louise
Perilous equilibrium. R. Hughes. il por Time
96:82-3 N 16 '70 •
RILEY, D. L. See Herzenberg, C. L. jt. auth.
RILEY, Frank
Red skis in the sunset. il Sat R 53:46+ O 24
'70
This summer it's Laguna Beach. il Holiday
47:46-9+ My '70
RILEY, James F.
Fast switch in semiconductors. il por Bsns
W p 16 S 5 '70 •
Intersil: upstart with talent. il pors Bsns W
p70+ S 12 '70 •
RILEY, James Whitcomb
Hoosier poet. B. Finnegan. il pors Hobbies
74:154-6 Ja '70
RILEY, Nord
Take me to your pichiguilas. il Outdoor Life
145:64-5+ F '70
Watch who you call birdbrain. il Outdoor
Life 145:46-7+ Ja '70
RILKE, Rainer Maria
Rest on the flight into Egypt; poem, tr. by
M. W. Hess. Cath World 212:118 D '70
RILLING, Paul M.
Desegregation: the South is different. New
Repub 162:17-19 My 16 '70
RIME
Primer on rhyme. J. Jerome. Writers Digest
50:14-16 N '70
RIMMER, Don, and Graf, R. F.
Build your own dancing light display. il
Pop Mech 134:144-6 D '70
RINDISBACHER, Peter
Frontier portfolio; paintings. Am Heritage
21:33-48 F '70
RINEHART, George
Ability grouping: out or in? il PTA Mag 65:
10-12 bibliog(p34) N '70
RINELLI, Victoria L.
Composting octogenarian. il por Org Gard &
Farm 17:54-5 My '70
RINFRET, Pierre A.
Flamboyant Pierre. por Time 96:71 Jl 13
'70 •
RING-a-day service. See Telephone in service
to the aged
RING of the Nibelung; operas. See Wagner, R.
RING-toss game. See Games
RINGLING brothers, Barnum and Bailey circus.
See Circus
RINGO, James
Intelligent trash of Jolivet and Milhaud. Am
Rec G 37:166-7+ N '70
Real thing: Satie and William Masselos. por
Am Rec G 36:692-4 My '70
RINGO, Johnny
Ringo. J. Burrows. Am West 7:17-21 Ja '70 •
RINGS
Etiquette of rings. Good H 170:138 Ja '70
Tips on removing a ring. Good H 170:196 Mr
'70

RINGWOOD, A. E. and Essene, E.
Petrogenesis of lunar basalts and the inter-
nal constitution and origin of the moon.
bibliog il Science 167:607-10 Ja 30 '70
RINHART, Floyd, and Rinhart, Marion
Tintype: tin lizzie of photography. il Mod
Phot 33:50-2 D '69
RINHART, Marion. See Rinhart, F. jt. auth.
RIO DE JANEIRO

Description
Businessman's guide to Rio de Janeiro. Bsns
W p95-6 Ja 17 '70

Prisons
See Prisons—Brazil
RIOPELLE, Arthur J.
Growing up with Snowflake. il Nat Geog
138:490-503 O '70
RIOT control
Creative restraint; riot control tactics of
Hong Kong police. il Newsweek 75:66 My
18 '70
How other nations handle riots. il U S News
68:42-3 Je 15 '70
How to keep order without killing. il Time
95:25-6 My 25 '70
Palace revolt? whether to fire weapons at
demonstrators. J. B. Reston, jr. New Re-
pub 162:9-10 Je 6 '70
Science's answer to violence: bubbles. il pors
Sci Digest 67:74-7 Ap '70
Snooping on the home front; army surveillance
of civilians. J. Hanlon. Nation 211:305-6 O 5
'70
RIOT prevention. See Riot control
RIOTS
Issueless riots. G. T. Marx. bibliog f il Ann
Am Acad 391:21-33 S '70
See also
Mob violence
Prison riots
Riot control
also subhead Riots under names of
continents, countries, cities, etc. e.g. India—
Riots
RIOTTE, Louise
Black-eyed peas, the good luck vegetable.
il Org Gard & Farm 17:73-4 Ja '70
Fall bush beans are best. il Org Gard & Farm
17:90-1 Ag '70
Figs, right from your own tree! il Org Gard
& Farm 17:31-3 My '70
Growing black walnuts from seed. il Org Gard
& Farm 17:52-3 N '70
My iris are on a great diet. il Org Gard &
Farm 17:35-7 Je '70
My roses grow vitamins! il Org Gard & Farm
17:54-7 Ap '70
Oklahoma's okay for leeks. il Org Gard &
Farm 17:52-3 F '70
Spinach: a vegetable for all seasons. il Org
Gard & Farm 17:27-9 D '70
Start tomatoes and eggplant indoors. il por
Org Gard & Farm 17:48-9 Mr '70
RIPLEY, Sidney Dillon, 1913-
Skirmish at the Smithsonian. il por Bsns
W p 128+ F 21 '70 •
RIPON society. See Political clubs and asso-
ciations
RIPP, Judith
(ed) Family movie guide. See issues of
Parents' magazine & better family living
RIPPON, Marion
Case history of a first novel: writing The
hand of Solange; with biographical sketch.
Writer 83:12-16 Mr '70
RISEBROUGH, Robert, and Brodine, Virginia
More letters in the wind. bibliog il Environ
12:16-27 Ja '70
RISHEL, Joseph J.
Rococo misto all' italiana. il Art N 69:40-3+
O '70
RISK
Odds favor the blue chips. Bsns W p88 O 10
'70
Weighing risk in capacity expansion. J. R.
Virts and R. W. Garrett. il Harvard Bsns
R 48:132-41 My '70
See also
Hedging
RISK; story. See Mackenzie, R.
RISKEN, John
Changing face of English: one school's new
program. Engl J 59:524-7 Ap '70
RISLEY, John H.
Saddled prominent. il Cons 24:29-30 Ag '69
—See Buzzard, W. H. jr
RISSHO university, Tokyo. See Colleges and
universities—Japan
RISTAU, Harland
Protocol; poem. Chr Cent 87:1214 O 14 '70
RITCH, John B. 3d
Reports: Korea. Atlan 226:6+ O '70

RITCHIE, A. Kaita, and Goldberg, A. M.
Vesicular and synaptoplasmic synthesis of acetylcholine. bibliog il Science 169:489-90 Jl 31 '70

RITCHIE-CALDER, Peter Ritchie Calder, baron
Conversion to the metric system: with biographical sketch. il Sci Am 223:15, 17-25 bibliog(p 136) Jl '70
Mortgaging the old homestead. For Affairs 48:207-20 Ja '70; Same. il Sports Illus 32:44-51 F 2 '70

RITES and ceremonies
Revival of ritual on campus. J. W. Goetz. il Cath World 212:24-8+ O '70
Rituals, the revolt against the fixed smile; Time essay. M. Maddocks. il Time 96:42-3 O 12 '70
        See also
Dancing in religion, folklore, etc.
Funeral rites and ceremonies
Marriage customs and rites

                    Japan
        See also
Harakiri

RITSOS, Giannes
Meaning of simplicity; In the barracks; Absence; Suspicious sleep; Not suspecting; Achievement; Minimum delay; poems, tr. by R. Dalven. Poetry 116:292-8 Ag '70

RITSOS, Yannis. See Ritsos, G.

RITTENHOUSE, David C.
Prisoners, patients, and public libraries. il por Wilson Lib Bul 45:490-3 Ja '71

RITTER, Tex
High noon for Tex Ritter. R. Cleghorn. il pors N Y Times Mag p 10-11+ Jl 12 '70 *

RITTER Pfaudler corporation. See Sybron corporation

RITTERBUSH, Philip C.
Conquest of Huila. il por Américas 22:19-27 Ja '70

RITUAL. See Catholic church—Liturgy and ritual; Rites and ceremonies

RITUAL D; ballet. See Ballets—Criticisms

RITZ, William C.
Photographing the lead tree reaction. bibliog il por Chem 43:28-9 S '70

RITZ in Paris. See Paris—Hotels, restaurants, etc.

The RIVALS; drama. See Sheridan, R. B. B.

RIVER; ballet. See Ballets—Criticisms

RIVER boats. See Steamships and steam boats

RIVER OF DOUBT. See Roosevelt River, Brazil

RIVER PLATE. See Plata, Rio de la

RIVER trips
Canyonlands by night; Moab, Utah boat ride. F. A. Barnes. il Travel 134:64-6 Ag '70
Creative cruising; Hudson River. R. W. Wilkie. il Yachting 127:66-7+ F '70
Cruising the high country; Grand Teton National Park Waterways. F. M. Paulson. il Field & S 75:44-5+ D '70
Double play in Minnesota. J. Seville. il Motor B 126:58-60 S '70
Enjoyable run up the Hudson River to historic West Point. B. Schill and B. Schill. il Yachting 127:62-3 Ap '70
Home on the Rhine. D. Butwin. il Sat R 53:55-7 Je 20 '70
Hoover Dam hangover; through the canyons and rapids of Colorado River. A. Schafer. il Motor B 127:62+ Ja '71
It's not called Hells Canyon for nothing. R. Bongartz. il Holiday 47:52-3+ My '70
Just bring the groceries; houseboat adventures on San Joaquin River. L. Lindquist. il Har Yrs 10:41-3 My '70
Mississippi camping. H. Fowler and C. Fowler. il Motor B 125:65-7+ F '70
Paddleboat on the Murray; Australia. R. Harrington. il Travel 135:48-51 Ja '71
Pastime returns to the coast. G. W. Capley. il Yachting 127:54-5+ My '70
River runs in the West for 1970. il Sunset 144:66+ Mr '70
Roundup on river tours. F. M. Paulson. il Field & S 74:160-2+ Ap '70
Sixteenth annual Colorado River cruise. J. Joseph. il Motor B 125:68-71 My '70
South to Arkansas. D. Duffey. il Motor B 126:52-3+ S '70
We houseboated down the mighty Miss. P. Snook. il por Nat Wildlife 8:38-42 Ag '70
White-water adventure on wild rivers of Idaho. J. Craighead and F. Craighead, jr. il pors Nat Geog 137:212-39 F '70
        See also
Canoe trips

RIVERA, Diego
Now you see him, now you don't; with poem by E. B. White. il Ramp Mag 9:33-4 S '70 *

RIVERA, Manolo
On the boards. por Dance Mag 44:20 Jl '70 *

RIVERS, Joan
What's so funny? T. Thompson. il pors Life 70:69-70+ Ja 8 '71 *

RIVERS, Larry
Strawberry cake with the psyche of a good camera. D. Shapiro. il Art N 69:30-1+ D '70 *

RIVERS, Lucius Mendel
L. Mendel Rivers. R. G. Sherrill. por Nation 210:40-7 Ja 19 '70
                about
After Rivers. Nation 212:36 Ja 11 '71 *
Mendel Rivers. por Newsweek 77:18 Ja 11 '71 *
Minority hiring under new attack. il por Bsns W p 110 Je 13 '70 *
Ol' man Rivers. C. McCarry. il por Esquire 74:168-71+ O '70 *
Sweetest finger this side of Midas; with editorial comment. M. Frady. il pors Life 68:52-52B+ F 27 '70 *
Tradeoff: a new carrier for a budget. por Bsns W p 112-13 Ap 25 '70 *
Tribune for the military. por Time 97:10-11 Ja 11 '71 *

RIVERS, Thomas E.
Global view of parks and recreation. Parks & Rec 5:21 Ap '70

RIVERS
Wild rivers. G. D. Hofe, jr. il por Parks & Rec 5:22-5+ F '70
        See also
Estuaries
Water pollution
        also names of rivers, e.g. Squannacook River
                Poetry
Remembering names of American rivers; poem. C. J. Bostelmann. il Am For 76:40-1 Ap '70
                Regulation
Crisis on our rivers. J. N. Miller and R. Simmons. il Read Digest 97:78-83 D '70
Rivers will learn to run backward. Siberian scheme. il Bsns Wp43+ Je 13 '70
        See also
Dams

RIVERSIDE COUNTY, Calif.
Vote counts by microwave. H. F. Sammis. il Am City 85:76+ Jl '70

RIVERSIDE Grand prix. See Automobile racing

RIVES, Lloyd M.
American presence. pors Newsweek 75:49-50 Je 29 '70 *

RIVIANA foods, inc.
Riviana expansion. J. Smith. il Duns 95:62+ Ap '70

RIVIERA
French Riviera in winter. D. Messinesi. Vogue 156:89+ N 1 '70

RIZER, H. Murle
California's-eye view of the ICW. il Motor B 125:72-3+ My '70
Cove hopping Havasu. il Motor B 126:48-9+ N '70

RIZER, Murle. See Rizer, H. M.

RIZZO, Eugene
(ed) See Moffo, A. Other Moffo

RIZZO, Francis
Ozymandias of opera. il por Opera N 34:13-19 My 16 '70
(ed) See Bonynge, R. Pinnacle
(ed) See Capobianco, T. Whence a production
(ed) See Sutherland, J. Pinnacle

RIZZO, Frank
City of (big) brotherly love. J. Groutt. Commonweal 92:167-9 My 1 '70 *
Philadelphia boomerang. J. Higgins. il Nation 211:332-6 O 12 '70 *
Tough vs. moderate cops. il por Bsns W p38+ D 12 '70 *

RIZZOLI, Angelo
Obituary
        Pub W 198:37 O 12 '70

RIZZUTO, Dennis
Color image builder: Dennis Rizzuto. il Pop Phot 66:77-81 Ap '70 *

ROACH, Mary Ellen
Adolescent dress: understanding the issues. Ed Digest 35:39-41 F '70

ROACHES. See Cockroaches

ROAD construction. See Highway engineering

ROAD graders. See Graders (excavating machinery)

ROAD machinery
How to purchase and maintain street equipment. R. R. Fleming. il Am City 85:96+ Ap '70
Remove old concrete the easy way. il Am City 85:88 N '70
See also
Graders (excavating machinery)

ROAD maps, guides, etc.
Aids for interstate driving. il Bet Hom & Gard 48:126 My '70
Woman beside the man behind the wheel; useful skill of map reading. D. McCluggage. il Am Home 73:24+ F '70

ROAD materials
See also
Aggregates (building materials)

ROAD runners (birds)
Roadrunners: activity of captive individuals. J. L. Kavanau and J. Ramos. bibliog il Science 169:780-2 Ag 21 '70

ROAD to Tinkhamtown; story. See Ford, C.

ROAD to Valley Forge; drama. See DuBois, G.

ROAD traffic
See also
City traffic
Electronics in traffic control
Pedestrians
Traffic engineering

Radio control
See Radio in traffic control

ROAD transport. See Transportation, Automotive

ROADRUNNERS. See Road runners (birds)

ROADS
See also
Express highways
National parks and reserves—Roads
Portages
Trails
also headings beginning Highway

Design
See also
Roads—Interchanges and intersections

Drainage
How do you drain flat land? Houston, Tex. il Am City 85:20 Ag '70

Federal aid
Coming: an expanded road program. il U S News 69:44 D 28 '70
Cracking the highway trust; proposal to broaden use of Federal highway trust fund. il por Time 95:59 Je 15 '70
1970, the year of the traveler; trust fund approach. J. Carlson. Arch Rec 148:43 D '70
320 billion dollars more for future highways? il U S News 68:34-5 Mr 2 '70
Wouldn't it be nice if everybody had a trust fund? W. F. Wagner, jr. Arch Rec 148:9 Jl '70

Interchanges and intersections
Danger: intersection. il Sci Digest 67:22 My '70
Good interchange design can make downtown viable; Milwaukee, Wis. R. C. Greaves. Am City 85:148-9 Je '70

Lighting
High lights life savers. il Am City 85:136 Je '70
High mounted lights; Illinois Division of highways. R. E. Stark. il Am City 85:140 My '70
High mounted lights in; Hennepin County, Minn. il Am City 85:114 Jl '70

Location
Placing a dollar sign on urban parks; highway location. D. G. Brauer. il Parks & Rec 5:14-16 N '70

Maintenance and repair
See also
Road machinery

Safety devices and measures
Are crowded highways getting safer? il U S News 68:50-2 F 2 '70
Finally, they really are improving our roads. A. Markovich. il Mech Illus 66:70-2+ N '70
Steel drum crash cushions life savers. il Am City 85:78 D '70
Steel drums cushion roadway collisions. il Am City 85:132 Ap '70

Superhighways
See Express highways

Alaska
Hauling and pulling in the Arctic. R. B. Weeden. il Liv Wildn 34:8-16 Sum '70

Asia
Travel notes; Asian highway. R. Joseph. Esquire 73:26+ F '70

Brazil
Highway to save the stricken Northeast; Trans-Amazon highway. il Bsns W p34-5 N 14 '70
Taming the Amazon; Transamazonic highway project. il Newsweek 76:93-4 N 2 '70

British Columbia
See Roads—Canada

California
Mattole road: Ferndale, Petrolia, and Honeydew. il Sunset 144:48+ My '70

Canada
From Prince George or from Kamloops, two routes into the Yellowhead country. il Sunset 144:44-6 My '70

Central America
See also
Pan American highway

Illinois
High mounted lights. R. E. Stark. il Am City 85:140 My '70
See also
Pan American highway

Latin America
See also
Pan American highway

New England
Road to riches? linking upstate New York and northern New England. il Time 97:62+ Ja 11 '71

New York (state)
Road to riches? linking upstate New York and northern New England. il Time 97:62+ Ja 11 '71

Pennsylvania
See also
Express highways—Pennsylvania

United States
See also
Billboards
Express highways
Pan American highway
Roads—Federal aid

Utah
Aquarius in Utah? Scenic short cut from park to park. il Sunset 145:42 O '70

ROADS, International
See also
Pan American highway

ROADSIDE improvement
Blight blossoms on the American highway; with report by J. Neary. il Life 69:26-34 Jl 24 '70
Cracking the highway trust; proposal to broaden use of Federal highway trust fund. il por Time 95:59 Je 15 '70
Freeways in and around L.A. are a big plant-testing laboratory. il Sunset 144:226-8+ Mr '70
Story framed in pines. H. R. Williams. il Am For 76:20-3 Jl '70

ROALMAN, A. R.
Baseball parks, new attractions for tourists. il Todays Health 48:42-5+ My '70
Let the buyer be aware. il Todays Health 48:66-7+ Mr '70

ROALMAN, Suzann
Earth day is coming. il Am Ed 6:3-6 Ap '70

ROAN, Barbara
Barbara Roan; the Cubiculo. J. Armstrong. Dance Mag 44:22 Ja '70

ROARK, Garland
Give your characters free rein. Writer 83: 13-15 Jl '70

ROASTING. See Cookery—Meat; Cookery—Poultry

ROBB, James A.
Microcloning and replica plating of mammalian cells. bibliog il Science 170:857-8 N 20 '70

ROBB, Lynda Bird (Johnson)
Lynda Bird Robb reports on five special young marriages, including her own. il por Ladies Home J 87:70-1 Je '70
Mothers and daughters: a new freedom to be themselves. il por Ladies Home J 87:98-9+ N '70

ROBBE-GRILLET, Alain
Narrative murder. L. Bersani. Yale R 59:376-90 Mr '70 *

ROBBERIES and assaults
Bank-heist tactic; Boston bank robbery involving Brandeis college students. il pors Newsweek 76:29-30 O 5 '70
Dostoievsky in Waltham; bank robberies by Brandeis university revolutionary students. Nat R 22:1098 O 20 '70
Gaining; way to halt stickups; exact change at gasoline stations. il U S News 68:63 Mr 30 '70
Now mail robbers plague post office. il U S News 69:42 Jl 13 '70
Oklahoma Robin Hood; bank robber C. Floyd. K. L. Steckmesser. por Am West 7:38-41 Ja '70
Parting shots; a kindly visitor to a lot of friendly banks. il pors Life 68:81 Je 12 '70
Radical bank job; series of Massachusetts bank robberies involving Brandeis students. il por Time 96:21-2 O 5 '70
Residuals for a robber; R. A. Biggs story of the Great train robbery. il por Newsweek 75:63 My 4 '70
Tempting the devil; gang of bank robbers in France. Time 96:28 N 30 '70
Truck hijacking; fastest-growing racket. il U S News 69:27-9 S 14 '70
Whatever happened to the rash of bus robberies? il U S News 68:16 F 23 '70
See also
Burglary and burglars

ROBBERSON, Elbert. See Robberson, W. jt. auth.

ROBBERSON, Winifred
Boating business. See Yachting
Water pollution and boats. bibliog il Yachting 127:70-1+ Je '70
—and Robberson, Elbert
Big dipper bilge pumps. il Yachting 127:222 F '70

ROBBIE, Joe
Rosenbloom-Robbie bowl. J. Olsen. il pors Sports Illus 33:22-4+ N 9 '70 *
Rozelle's taut ship. Newsweek 75:67+ Ap 27 '70 *
This man fired Flipper. M. Kram. il pors Sports Illus 31:76-8+ D 15 '69

ROBBINS, Ann Roe. See Lucas, D. jt. auth.

ROBBINS, Frederic John
We're not a steel company. R. Levy. por Duns 95:51-2+ F '70 *

ROBBINS, Harold, pseud.
Best-selling businessman. J. Poindexter. por Duns 95:57-8+ F '70 *

ROBBINS, Janice
Overseas study for teenagers. il Parents Mag 45:50-1+ Jl '70

ROBBINS, Jerome
Feast of Robbins. L. Lerman. il por Mlle 70:176-8 Mr '70 *
Loving couples. H. Saal. il por Newsweek 75:96-7 F 9 '70 *
People are talking about. por Vogue 155:92-3 Mr 15 '70 *
Robbins plus Chopin. W. Terry. il Sat R 53:49 F 21 '70 *

ROBBINS, Jhan
How Mr Noah T. H. Porter launched by career. Read Digest 96:115-18 Ap '70
Of miniskirts and pantyhose. il Read Digest 96:81-3 Mr '70
Pants fit now. il Todays Health 49:58-9+ Ja '71
Way back to life. il Redbook 135:76-7+ Jl '70

ROBBINS, Michael S.
Micro'lign generator. il Pop Electr 32:48-51 Ap '70

ROBBINS, Patricia
Antics; excerpts. ed. by T. Fenton. il Read Digest 96:106-7 Ja '70

ROBBINS, Richard H.
Night the peace bus left New Harley. il Cath World 210:256-61 Mr '70

ROBENZIDENE. See Guanidines

ROBERSON, John R.
Kyoto, Osaka's exotic neighbor. il Holiday 47:46-9 F '70

ROBERSON ballet school, Binghamton, N.Y. See Dance schools

ROBERT, Henry Martyn
Authors & editors. B. A. Bannon. por Pub W 197:15-16 Mr 16 '70 *

ROBERT F. Kennedy youth center, Morgantown, W.Va. See Detention homes

ROBERT Joffrey ballet. See City center Joffrey ballet

ROBERT Tannahill's collection. See Detroit institute of arts

ROBERTO Devereux; opera. See Donizetti, G.

ROBERTS, A. Hood. See Malkoc, A. M. jt. auth.

ROBERTS, Arthur H. See Tapp, J. L. jt. auth.

ROBERTS, David L. See Owen, T. jt. auth.

ROBERTS, Don
Listen, Miss, Mrs, Mr Librarian. il Library J 95:3965-7 N 15 '70
Yippie librarianship. il Am Lib 1:1046-51 D '70

ROBERTS, E. F.
Environmental lawyer urges: plead the Ninth amendment! with biographical sketch. il Natur Hist 79:2, 18-19+ Ag '70

ROBERTS, Edward Barry
Secret life of Dan Ingram; drama. Plays 29:11-19 Ap '70

ROBERTS, Edwin A. jr
Middle class does the work, pays the bills. il Todays Ed 59:20-2 Ja '70

ROBERTS, Gary L.
In pursuit of duty. il pors Am West 7:26-33+ S '70

ROBERTS, Gene
Double agent. Newsweek 76:33-4 N 23 '70 *

ROBERTS, Helen M.
Betsy Ross; drama. Plays 29:46-52 F '70

ROBERTS, Henry E. See Mims, F. M. 3d, jt. auth.

ROBERTS, John M.
Wandering sands. il Américas 22:9-14 Ag '70

ROBERTS, Millard George
Parsons college bubble, by J. Koerner. Review
Sat R 53:56 Ag 15 '70. L. B. Mayhew *

ROBERTS, Muriel
Young world of Marlo Thomas. il pors Good H 171:20-2+ Ag '70

ROBERTS, Oral
Roberts's ratings: rising. Chr Today 14:36 Ja 16 '70

ROBERTS, Patricia
Porcelains for world figures. il Design 72:26-8 Wint '70

ROBERTS, Steven V.
Better earth. il N Y Times Mag p8-9+ Mr 29 '70
Black studies: more than soul courses. Commonweal 91:478-9 Ja 30 '70
Games corporations play. Commonweal 92:142-3 Ap 24 '70
New Moon over New Orleans. Commonweal 91:501 F 6 '70
Old-fashioned at twenty-seven. il pors N Y Times Mag p45-7+ D 6 '70; 46 Ja 10 '71
Ronald Reagan is giving 'em heck. il por N Y Times Mag p42-3+ O 25 '70
Sirhan B. Sirhan literary negotiations, etc, inc. pors Esquire 74:131-4+ N '70
Why a sixty-three-year-old tycoon worth $100-million wants to run for the Senate. il pors N Y Times Mag p 10-12+ My 31 '70

ROBERTS, Thomas Bradford
Many student activists feel that middle-class society needlessly blocks personal growth. il Todays Ed 59:22-3 Ja '70

ROBERTS, Thomas D'Esterre, abp
Trying to be co-responsible: interview. ed. by J. T. Ryan. il por Cath World 211:22-5 Ap '70

ROBERTS, Wallace I.
No place to grow. il Sat R 53:62-4+ Mr 21 '70
White House and free speech. Sat R 53:26 My 2 '70

ROBERTS, William E.
Ampex record. T. J. Murray. por Duns 95:60-1 Ap '70 *

ROBERT'S rules of order. See Parliamentary practice

ROBERTSON, Frank
Cat street, Hong Kong. il Holiday 47:44-5+ F '70

ROBERTSON, Ian, and Whitten, Phillip
Black Africans in white prisons. Commonweal 93:239-41 D 4 '70

ROBERTSON, James Louis
Task ahead; address, May 14, 1970. Vital Speeches 36:520-3 Je 15 '70

ROBERTSON, Josephine
Garden in the Highlands. il Am For 76:36-9+ S '70

ROBERTSON, Oscar
Proud tower. il por Newsweek 76:92+ D 14 '70 *
Trade bait. por Newsweek 75:63 F 23 '70 *

ROBESON, Paul
Paul Robeson receives Ira Aldridge award from black history association. Negro Hist Bul 33:128 My '70 *
Paul Robeson world renowned actor, singer and scholar. G. P. McBrown. por Negro Hist Bul 33:128-9 My '70 *

ROBIE, Richard A. and others
Specific heats of lunar surface materials from
90 to 350 degrees Kelvin. bibliog il Science
167:749-60 Ja 30 '70
ROBIN, Gordon de Quetteville
Science and logistics in Antarctica. il por
Bul Atom Sci 26:90-3 D '70
ROBIN, Steve
On location with Edvard Grieg. il Dance
Mag 44:50-9 Ja '70
ROBINS, Natalie S.
M.L.K; poem. Nation 210:765 Je 22 '70
Shell; poem. Poetry 115:240 Ja '70
ROBINSON, Barbara B.
Kwan-Hi. il Todays Ed 59:18-19 N '70
ROBINSON, Betty
Checkpoint for travelers. See issues of House
beautiful
ROBINSON, Bill
Big boats take over. il Yachting 127:48-51+
Ap '70
Caribbean spectacular. il Yachting 127:74-6+
Mr '70
Editor's page. See issues of Yachting
Great yacht designers. il por Yachting 127:54-
5+ F; 66-7+ My; 128:62-3+ O '70
It took 18 years. il Yachting 128:46-8+ Ag '70
ROBINSON, Brooks
Destructive force of Robby the robber. il
pors Time 96:58 O 26 '70 *
Discord defied and deified. M. Kram. il pors
Sports Illus 33:26-8+ O 5 '70 *
One-man show. il Newsweek 76:55-6 O 26
'70 *
ROBINSON, Bruce
Return of the dropouts. il Motor B 126:44-5
D '70
ROBINSON, Carrie C.
Intellectual freedom. J. F. Krug and J. A.
Harvey. Am Lib 1:533 Je '70 *
Move to drop Robinson case refused by federal
court. Library J 95:1154 Mr 15 '70 *
NEA files suit against Alabama state educa-
tion department. Library J 95:713 F 15 '70 *
ROBINSON, Daniel N.
Critical flicker-fusion of solid and annular
stimuli. bibliog il Science 167:207-8 Ja 9
'70
ROBINSON, Donald
Danger! Hazardous materials in transit. Read
Digest 96:177-8+ My '70
(ed) Day I was proudest of my child. il Good
H 170:70-3+ Ja '70
100 most important people in the world. il
Esquire 73:104-7 Ap '70
ROBINSON, Donald W.
Police in the schools. Todays Ed 59:18-20
O '70; Same abr. Ed Digest 36:11-13 D '70
ROBINSON, Edwin Arlington
Tribute to an American poet. I. Howe. Harper
240:103-8 Je '70 *
ROBINSON, Francis
Evening of a faun. il pors Opera N 34:26-9
F 21 '70
ROBINSON, Frank
Don't be a crime target. Read Digest 97:107-10
O '70
ROBINSON, Frank, 1935-
Discord defied and deified. M. Kram. il pors
Sports Illus 33:26-8+ O 5 '70 *
Frank Robinson's cool assault on the black-
manager barrier. L. Shecter. il por Look
34:82-4+ My 5 '70 *
ROBINSON, Gail
Room at the top; interview, ed. by R.
Zachary. il por Opera N 35:12 S 5 '70
ROBINSON, James H.
Telephoto hunting simplified. il Field & S
75:154 Je '70
ROBINSON, Jerome B.
Ancient lure that stripers can't resist. il
Field & S 74:60-1+ Ap '70
Citified ducks satisfy. il Outdoor Life 146:52-
5+ N '70
Eastern homeland of the hun. il Field & S
75:136-8+ S '70
How to catch big early season trout. il Field
& S 74:58-9+ Mr '70
It's spring for smallmouths. il por Outdoor
Life 145:54-5+ My '70
New Jersey's best bet for smallmouths. il
Field & S 74:198-201+ Ap '70
Night on the ice. il pors Outdoor Life 145:
52-5+ F '70
Where little tuna hit the beach. il Field & S
75:64-5+ My '70
Whistlers like it mean. il Outdoor Life 146:84-
7+ O '70
—and Carroll, Hanson
How to think like a bass. il Field & S 75:56-
7+ N '70
Woodcock along the salmon rivers. il Field
& S 75:54-5+ S '70

ROBINSON, Joan
Making Christmas wreaths. J. Kuh. por
Ladies Home J 86:143 D '69
ROBINSON, John Arthur Thomas
In what sense is Christ unique? Chr Cent 87:
1409-12 N 25 '70
ROBINSON, Leif J.
Beyond the NGC catalogue. il Sky & Tel 39:
100-1 F '70
—See Little, R. jt. auth.
ROBINSON, Leonard Wallace, and others
New journalism. il por Writers Digest 50:32-
5+ Ja '70
ROBINSON, Louie
Eternal Mills brothers. il Ebony 25:60-3+ S
'70
Evolution of Geraldine. il pors Ebony 26:
176-8+ D '70
Jackson Five. il Ebony 25:150-4 S '70
Star couple. il pors Ebony 25:142-4+ Mr '70
Why Diana Ross left the Supremes. il pors
Ebony 25:120-6 F '70
ROBINSON, Lytle W.
Cabeza Prieta, our forgotten wilderness. il
Liv Wildn 33:25-8 Aut '69
ROBINSON, Maurice Richard
Maurice Robinson of Scholastic magazines,
inc; interview. il pors Nations Bsns 58:
54-8 D '70

about

Fifty years: oh you kid! por Sr Schol 97:2+
O 19 '70 *
ROBINSON, Michael H. and others
Attack autotomy: a defense against predators.
bibliog il Science 169:300-1 Jl 17 '70
ROBINSON, Pearl Lunt
Slaves in Egypt; poem. Chr Today 14:14 Je
19 '70
ROBINSON, Renault
Dilemma of the black cop. R. Hall. il pors
Life 69:60-60B+ S 18 '70 *
ROBINSON, Selma
Betsy McCall, my embroidery book. il McCalls
98:62-5 D '70
(ed) See Woodruff, M. Maurice Woodruff:
astrology's brightest star
ROBINSON, Wilhelmena S.
Changing the African-American image
through history. bibliog Negro Hist Bul 33:
44-6 F '70
ROBINSON Crusoe Liebowitz; story. See
Michaels, L.
ROBOTS. See Automatons
ROBOTS, Industrial. See Machinery, Automatic
ROCA, Miguel Soler. See Soler Roca, M.
ROCHA, Glauber
Way to make a future; interview, tr. by
E. Stein and ed. by G. Hitchens. il Film Q
24:27-30 Fall '70
ROCHBERG, George
Music to my ears; third symphony performed
by an instrumental ensemble of Juilliard
personnel and the Collegiate chorale. I.
Kolodin. Sat R 53:46 D 12 '70 *
ROCHE, Douglas J.
State of a diocese. America 122:366-7 Ap 4 '70
ROCHE, James Michael
Profit alone is not enough; interview, ed. by
L. L. L. Golden. Sat R 53:55 Ag 8 '70 *

about

After the courtesy, a crisis of costs. por
Fortune 81:31 Je '70 *
ROCHE, John
Toughest kid on anybody's block. C. Kirk-
patrick. il por Sports Illus 34:20-2+ Ja 4
'71 *
ROCHE, John P.
Diagnosis of the anti-Spiro jitters by a
former chairman of ADA. Nat R 22:878
Ag 25 '70
On being an unfashionable professor. il por
N Y Times Mag p30-1+ O 18; 111-12+ N
8 '70
ROCHE, Marcel
Notes on science in Cuba. il Science 169:344-9
Jl 24 '70
ROCHE, Mary
Ideas and things to bring home from Helsinki.
House & Gard 137:78+ My '70
ROCHE, William J. and MacKinnon, N. L.
Motivating people with meaningful work.
bibliog il Harvard Bsns R 48:97-110 My '70
ROCHESTER, Minn.

Hospitals
See also
Mayo clinic

Music
See also
Rochester symphony orchestra

ROCHESTER, N.Y.

Education

On the house: work-school program for dropouts: Rochester jobs inc. F. Trippett. il Look 34:66-8 D 29 '70

Explosions

It can happen anywhere; bombings. il Newsweek 76:24 O 26 '70

Housing

On the house; work-school program for dropouts Rochester jobs inc. F. Trippett:. il Look 34:66-8 D 29 '70

Parks and playgrounds

Totlots: a successful experiment. D. Warner. il Parks & Rec 5:32-3+ Jl '70

Recreation

Selling recreation; super 8 film of recreation programs. M. E. Day. il por Parks & Rec 5:27-8+ My '70

Sanitary affairs

Huge sewage outfall shipped in 80' lengths. il Am City 85:24 S '70

ROCHESTER conspiracy trial.   See Trials (conspiracy)

ROCHESTER high energy physics conferences. See Nuclear physics—Conferences

ROCHESTER symphony orchestra
Major musical precedent; totally subsidized by government. J. Gerstel. Hi Fi 20:secII 25 Ag '70

ROCHOW, W. F.
Barley yellow dwarf virus: phenotypic mixing and vector specificity. bibliog il Science 167:875-8 F 6 '70

ROCK, Arthur
Venture capitalist with a solid intuition. il por Bsns W p 102-3 My 30 '70 *

ROCK, John
Pill on trial. pors Time 95:60+ Ja 26 '70

ROCK bands. See Rock 'n' roll groups

ROCK bass fishing. See Bass fishing

ROCK carvings. See Petroglyphs

ROCK climbing. See Mountaineering

ROCK drawings. See Petroglyphs

ROCK festivals. See Music festivals

ROCK gardens. See Gardens, Rock

ROCK lyrics. See Rock 'n' roll music (songs, etc)

ROCK 'n' roll groups
Americanization of the Stones. E. Sander. il Vogue 155:170-1+ F 1 '70
Aquarius wept; Rolling Stones' Altamont concert. R. J. Gleason. il Esquire 74:84-92+ Ag '70
The band: music from home. J. Poppy. il Look 34:22-7 Ag 25 '70
Chicago. B. Scoppa. il Sr Schol 97:35 N 16 '70
Crash of the Jefferson Airplane. E. Leimbacher. il Ramp Mag 8:14-16 Ja '70
Creedence clearwater revival, energy. R. Goldstein. Vogue 155:158 My '70
Esquire's heavy 100. il Esquire 74:145-9 O '70
Good-time musicians; Delaney & Bonnie & Friends. H. Saal. il Newsweek 75:90 F 23 '70
Jackson five. E. Dunbar. il Look 34:18-21 Ag 25 '70
Jackson Five. L. Robinson. il Ebony 25:150-4 S '70
Jefferson Airplane is an unscheduled trip. C. Kentfield. il N Y Times Mag p32-4+ O 18 '70
Latin rock; Santana. il Time 96:68 S 21 '70
Loose federation. il Time 95:62 Mr 30 '70
Mick Jagger and the future of rock; Rolling Stones. il pors Newsweek 77:44-8 Ja 4 '71
Number one: Creedence Clearwater Revival; and number two: Three Dog Night. B. Scoppa. il Sr Schol 97:34-7 O 26 '70
On the road with Mad Dogs and Englishmen. C. Pulin. il Sr Schol 97:24-5+ N 16 '70
Playing it straight: Grateful Dead at the Fillmore East. Nat R 23:35+ Ja 12 '71
Rolling Stones, a play in the Apocalypse. M. Lydon. il Ramp Mag 8:26-53 Mr '70
Roots and raw feeling; England's Led Zeppelin. il Time 96:64 N 2 '70
Soul brothers; the Jackson 5. il Newsweek 75:98 Ap 20 '70
Supergroup. E. Leimbacher. Ramp Mag 8:56+ F '70
  See also
Beatles
Phonograph records—Rock 'n' roll groups

ROCK 'n' roll music (songs, etc)
At the where? rock opera Tommy at the Met. il Time 95:59 Je 22 '70
Blues for Janis. por Time 96:54 O 19 '70
Common vibration; with discography. J. Santella. il por Library J 95:3967-70 N 15 '70
Discovery through rock; with discography. B. Scoppa. il Schol Teach Jr/Sr High p 14-15 O 5 '70
Drugs and death in the run-down world of rock music; J. Hendrix and J. Joplin. A. Goldman. il pors Life 69:32-3 O 16 '70
Economics of rock. P. M. Hirsch. Nation 210:275-6 Mr 9 '70
Das hip Kapital; a critique of the youth economy. C. Karpel. il Esquire 74:184-8+ D '70
Hit it, Zubin; odd musical conjunction between rock and the classics. il por Time 95:72 Je 1 '70
How to write a rock 'n' roll song. L. Hutchinson. il Sr Schol 97:24 D 14 '70
Ignoring rock won't make it go away: Youth music institute at University of Wisconsin. E. R. Sarig. Ed Digest 35:34-7 Mr '70
Music to jangle your insides. T. McSloy. Nat R 22:680-1+ Je 30 '70
New culture. R. Goldstein. Vogue 156:99+ Ag 1 '70
Night at the opera; rock opera Tommy. V. Rauseo. il Sr Schol 97:33-5 S 28 '70
Rock criticism. B. Gewen. Commentary 49:92-6 Je '70
Rock! Is it taking teenagers? pro and con discussion. il Sr Schol 96:11-12 Mr 9 '70
Rock poetry, relevance, and revelation. H. W. English. bibliog Engl J 59:1122-7 N '70
Something is rotten in rock. E. Sander. Sat R 53:49 O 10 '70
Tribal center for the rock freaks; Fillmore East. M. Thomas. il Holiday 47:18+ F '70
Where does rock music belong in the schools? Todays Ed 59:34-6 My '70
  See also
Phonograph records—Rock 'n' roll music (songs, etc)
Radio broadcasting—Music

Periodicals
  See also
Rolling stone (periodical)

ROCK 'n' roll singers
Relics: Rock relics auction, proceeds for peace candidates. New Yorker 46:40-1 O 24 '70
Top beats the bottom: Carl Perkins and his music; excerpt from Rock folk. M. Lydon. il por Atlan 226:96-8+ D '70
Warm welcome for a human campfire; kewpie Melanie. A. Goldman. por Life 69:18 O 16 '70

ROCK 'n' roll songs. See Rock 'n' roll music (songs, etc)

ROCK opera Tommy. See Rock 'n' roll music (songs, etc)

ROCK paintings. See Cave drawings and paintings

ROCK profiles
Profiles in stone. D. Shiner. il Design 71:10-13 Spr '70

ROCK spray. See Cotoneasters

ROCKEFELLER, David
Chase gets caught in a crossfire. il Bsns W p38-9 Ja 17 '70

ROCKEFELLER, John D, Asian collection. See Art—Private collections

ROCKEFELLER, John Davison, 1839-1937
Gentlewoman and the robber baron. V. V. Hamilton. il pors Am Heritage 21:78-86 Ap '70

ROCKEFELLER, John Davison, 1906-
We need our young activists; excerpts from address, October 1968. Read Digest 97:53-7 Ag '70

  about
Spurning a giver. por Time 96:35 D 21 '70 *

ROCKEFELLER, John Davison, 1937-
One Rockefeller who may make it. R. Reeves. il por N Y Times Mag p30-1+ O 4 '70 *
Strip-mine reformer. por Bsns W p74 Ja 9 '71 *

ROCKEFELLER, Laurance S.
Laurance S. Rockefeller. Y. Fogel. il pors Parks & Rec 5:14-17+ Mr '70 *

ROCKEFELLER, Nelson Aldrich, 1908-
Governor tells of plans for environment to legislature; message. por Cons 24:12-13 F '70

  about
Countdown to November. Nat R 22:393 Ap 21 '70 *
Governor creates Department of environmental conservation; Office of parks and recreation set up in new law. por Cons 24:2-3 Je '70
Is the Rock still solid? il pors Time 96:19-20 O 19 '70 *

ROCKEFELLER, Nelson Aidrich—about—*Cont.*
Now you see him, now you don't; with poem by E. B. White. il Ramp Mag 9:33-4 S '70 *
Rock of ages. il por Newsweek 76:43-4 O 19 '70 *
This is the battle of the titans? R. Reeves. il pors N Y Times Mag p23-5+ N 1 '70 *

Visits to Latin America, 1969
Quality of life in the Americas; statement, by President Nixon with text of the Rockefeller mission report. Dept State Bul 61:493-540 D 8 '69
Rocky way to Latin liaison. D. Kurzman. il Sat R 53:30-2 Ja 31 '70

ROCKEFELLER, Winthrop
Clemency in Arkansas. por Time 97:50 Ja 11 '70 *

ROCKEFELLER Center. See New York (city) —Rockefeller Center

ROCKEFELLER foundation
Cry for courage and compassion; explaining vote at G.M.'s annual meeting; excerpts. Time 95:55 Je 1 '70
Scene of change, by W. Weaver. Review Bul Atom Sci 26:45 S '70. W. R. Gruner

ROCKET car racing. See Automobile racing

ROCKET engines
How rockets work. S. Buchanan and R. G. Cruddace. il Space World H-1-85:13-22+ Ja '71
Littlest engine. il Space World G-6-78:32-7 Je '70
See also
Space vehicles—Propulsion systems

Cooling
Small/pulsed rocket engine tested; reverse-flow, regeneratively-cooled engine. M. L. Yaffee. il Aviation W 93:53-4 O 5 '70

Design
Reusable rocket motor unveiled. M. L. Yaffee. il Aviation W 93:38-9+ Ag 31 '70

Specifications
U.S. rocket motors; tables (cont) Aviation W 92:133-6 Mr 9 '70

Testing
Hybrid rocket engine. il Space World G-7-79:28 Jl '70
News from the world of space exploration; orbiting electric rocket test. Space World G-11-83:50 N '70
Slow and steady gets its chance; electron-bombardment ion engine. il Sci N 97:169 F 14 '70

ROCKET fuel. See Rockets—Fuel

ROCKET mail
World's first steam rocket mail flight. il Space World G-9-81:35-9 S '70; Discussion. G-12-84:47-8 D '70

ROCKET propellants. See Rockets—Fuel

ROCKET propulsion
Steam propels rocket developed in Italy. il Aviation W 92:81 Ap 27 '70
See also
Rockets, Atomic powered

ROCKET research corporation
Clearing the air in the orchards; pollution-free heater. Bsns W p40+ Jl 25 '70

ROCKETS

Astronomical use
March eclipse rocket program at Wallops Island. C. A. Accardo. il Sky & Tel 39:344-9 Je '70
Observing a solar eclipse in the space age. il Space World G-6-78:4-13 Je '70

Fuel
Low-cost sounding rocket uses new fuel; hydroxyl-terminated polybutadiene. il Aviation W 93:55 Jl 20 '70
Solid propellants come of age. il Space World G-6-78:20-7 Je '70

Lightning hazards
See Aviation—Lightning hazards

Meteorological use
Kangaroo; rocket vehicle to probe atmosphere for hazardous conditions before manned launches. il Space World G-3-75:22-3 Mr '70
Steam propels rocket developed in Italy. il Aviation W 92:81 Ap 27 '70

Specifications
Leading U.S. international research rockets; tables (cont) Aviation W 92:114-15 Mr 9 '70

ROCKETS, Atomic powered
NERVA nuclear rocket reactor. il Space World G-11-83:4-10 N '70
NERVA nuclear rocket reactor program. il Space World G-7-79:30-2 Jl '70
Problems of nuclear rockets. E. Gross. il Sci N 97:440-1 My 2 '70
Propulsion for the 1980's; NERVA rocket. E. Driscoll. il Sci N 99:32-3 Ja 9 '71

ROCKETS, Sounding
Low-cost sounding rocket uses new fuel. il Aviation W 93:55 Jl 20 '70

ROCKETS, Steam
World's first steam rocket mail flight; history of the hot water rocket. il Space World G-9-81:35-9 S '70; Discussion. G-12-84:47-8 D '70

ROCKEY, Linda
Triumph of Dr Tucker. il por Todays Health 48:48-9+ N '70

ROCKFORD, Ill.

Education
We love you, Mr Tarbox; Teacher development center and demonstration school. il Life 68:76-9 Ap 24 '70

Housing
Ecstasy in Rockford; public-housing experiment aids poor to buy own houses. il Newsweek 76:61 N 30 '70

ROCKFORD college, Rockford, Ill.
Congo student mediates youth-establishment battle. il pors Ebony 25:90-2+ Je '70

ROCKOW, Bette
Glacier adventure. il Travel 134:67-71 Jl '70

ROCKS
See also
Geodes
Metamorphism (geology)
Petrology

Collectors and collecting
Mystery of rockhounding. J. R. Chenoweth. il Har Yrs 10:34-6 Je '70
Rocks of ages; collection of Arthur Court. il Esquire 73:155-9 My '70
Topaz seekers are invited; Utah's Topaz Mountain. il Sunset 144:38+ My '70

Deformation
Deformation twins in hornblende. T. P. Rooney and others. il Science 169:173-5 Jl 10 '70
Mineralogy and deformation in some lunar samples. J. A. V. Douglas and others. bibliog il Science 167:594-7 Ja 30 '70
Quartz; preferred orientation in rocks produced by Dauphiné twinning. J. Tullis. bibliog il Science 168:1342-4 Je 12 '70
Rock music; ringing rocks of Bucks County. J. Gibbons and S. Schlossman. il Natur Hist 79:36-41 D '70

ROCKS, Crystalline and metamorphic
Apollo 11 lunar science conference; fine particles, glasses, and shock effects; symposium. bibliog il Science 167:641-79 Ja 30 '70
See also
Hornblende

ROCKS, Igneous
Apollo 11 lunar science conference; papers, with editorial comment. bibliog il Science 167:447, 449-784 Ja 30 '70; Correction. 167:1759 Mr 27 '70
See also
Anorthosite
Granite
Peridotite

ROCKS, Metamorphic. See Rocks, Crystalline and metamorphic

ROCKS, Sedimentary
See also
Sandstone

ROCKS, Water in. See Water in rocks

ROCKSPRAY. See Cotoneasters

ROCKVILLE, Md.
Municipal swimming center. N. A. Ofsthun. il Parks & Rec 5:31-2 My '70

ROCKWELL, Al. See Rockwell, W. F. jr

ROCKWELL, George B.
It takes more than a banker to run a bank. il por Bsns W p38-40 N 7 '70 *

ROCKWELL, Norman
Uneasy Christmas in the birthplace of peace; painting. Look 34:18-19 D 29 '70

about
Norman Rockwell revisited. T. Buechner. il Life 69:16 N 13 '70 *
Norman Rockwell's America; excerpts from Norman Rockwell; artist and illustrator. T. S. Buechner. il por Good H 171:74-82 D '70 *

ROCKWELL, Norman K.
School mural. il Sch Arts 69:16-17 F '70
ROCKWELL, Pete
How to buy boat insurance. il Mech Illus 66:
108-9+ Mr '70
ROCKWELL, Willard Frederick, 1914-
Al Rockwell: industrialist/sportsman/con-
servationist. J. Samson. il por Field & S
74:50-2+ Ja '70
Rockwell trims North American. por Bsns W
p 112 Ja 31 '70
Warns against space cutbacks. Space World
H-1-85:48-9 Ja '71 *
ROCKWELL-Standard corporation. See North
American Rockwell corporation
ROCKWOOD, Linn R
Credibility gap in recreation administration
literature. Parks & Rec 5:50+ F '70
ROCKY MOUNTAIN goat hunting
Ghost billy of Heart Mountain. W. C. Eu-
bank. il por Outdoor Life 145:48-51+ Mr
'70
Mountain goat mysteries. V. Geist. il Field &
S 75:34-5+ Ag '70
My goat was high. L. Marvin. il Outdoor Life
146:66-7+ Ag '70
New goat country: Beartooth Mountains,
Wyo. R. A. Weidner. il por Outdoor Life
145:52-3+ Je '70
Wyoming's first Rocky Mountain goat hunt.
C. J. Farmer. il Field & S 75:56-7+ O '70
ROCKY MOUNTAIN sheep. See Mountain
sheep
ROCKY MOUNTAINS
Autumn in the Rockies. N. D. Ford. il Har
Yrs 10:30-8 Ag '70

Canadian Rockies
Adrift in the Rockies: Baghdad comes to
Jasper: Banff springs hotel and Jasper
park lodge. D. Butwin. il Sat R 53:57-9 F
28 '70
Adrift in the Rockies: Banff and the blue laws.
D. Butwin. il Sat R 53:52+ F 14 '70
ROCOCO records. See Phonograph record in-
dustry—Canada
ROD and cone cells
Visual adaptation in monkey cones: record-
ings of late receptor potentials. R. M.
Boynton and D. N. Whitten. bibliog il Sci-
ence 170:1423-6 D 25 '70
Visual cells. R. W. Young. il Sci Am 223:
80-4+ bibliog(p 144) O '70
RODALE, Jerome Irving
Mr Rodale becomes a rockhound. R. E.
Meyers. Org Gard & Farm 17:73-6 Jl '70 *
RODALE press, inc.
Rodale grants go to five students. Org Gard
& Farm 17:26-7 S '70
RODDY, Joseph
Commissar is a priest. il pors Look 34:56-8
Mr 24 '70
Jackie and Danny and sometimes Pinky. il
pors Look 34:84-6 N 17 '70
Muggeridge manhandled. por Look 34:60 Mr
24 '70
RODENT control
See also
Mice—Control
RODENTS
Tongue cooling: a new reward for thirsty
rodents. J. Mendelson and D. Chillag. bib-
liog il Science 170:1418-21 D 25 '70
See also names of rodents, e.g. Beavers
RODENTS, Fossil
Line and grade in the extinct medius species
group of sigmodon. R. A. Martin. bibliog
il Science 167:1504-6 Mr 13 '70
RODEOS
Biggest, best run and roughest rodeo in
U.S; Cheyenne frontier days. G. Cotler. il
Holiday 48:54-5+ Jl '70
Calgary stampede: drawings by Paul Hogarth;
with account by E. Whitehead. il Sports
Illus 33:34-9 Jl 13 '70
Cody, kings, & coronets; Buffalo Bill's wild
West. D. Russell. il pors Am West 7:4-10+
Jl '70
Right on cowboy! Okmulgee rodeo. il Ebony
25:115-18+ O '70
Rodeo! F. Tinker. il Travel 134.28-33 Jl '70
Rodeo: the Pendleton round-up. W. Decker.
il Travel & Camera 33:42-51 Jl '70
Why bust broncs in your dreams? youth ro-
deos. B. Scott. il Todays Health 48:30-3 N
'70
RODEOS, Photography of. See Photography of
sports
RODGERS, Dorothy, and Rodgers, Mary
Two great ways to give a good party; ex-
cerpt from A word to the wives. pors
House & Gard 138:88-9+ N '70
RODGERS, Mary. See Rodgers, D. jt. auth.

RODGERS, Mary Augusta
Marriage lesson; story. Redbook 135:80-1 Jl
'70
RODGERS, William H. Jr
Tacoma's tall stack. Nation 210:553-7 My 11
'70
RODIN, Auguste
Rodin's adventures on Mt Venus; exhibition
in London. J. Russell. il Art N 69:36-7+
Mr '70 *
RODITI, Edouard
Opinion: the art of living. por Mlle 71:18+ O
'70
RODMAN, Selden
Bolivia: friend or foe? Nat R 22:1211+ N 17
'70
Colombia's close call. Nat R 22:511+ My 19
'70
Day of the generals. il Nat R 22:1105-7 O 20
'70
October revolution in Chile? Nat R 22:1053-5
O 6 '70
RODMAN, Theodore
Handy uses of a home computer. M. Sham-
berg. il pors Life 68:48-51 Ja 30 '70
RODRIGUEZ, Alonso
Franco vs. free unions. America 122:36-7 Ja
17 '70
RODRIGUEZ, Armando
Necessity for bilingual education. bibliog il
por Wilson Lib Bul 44:724-30 Mr '70
RODS, Copper
GE dips into the copper business. il Bsns W
p40 Jl 25 '70
RODS, Fishing. See Fishing tackle
ROE, Jim
Up the scale in power. il Yachting 127:104-5+
Ja '70
ROECKER, William A.
Kingfisher; poem. Nation 210:93 Ja 26 '70
ROEDDER, Edwin, and Weiblen, P. W.
Silicate liquid immiscibility in lunar magmas,
evidenced by melt inclusions in lunar rocks.
bibliog il Science 167:641-4 Ja 30 '70
ROEDER, Kenneth D. and others
Distal lobe of the pilifer: an ultrasonic re-
ceptor in choerocampine hawkmoths. bibliog
il Science 170:1098-9 D 4 '70
ROEDING park. See Fresno, California—Parks
and playgrounds
ROETHKE, Theodore
Root of the wind; excerpts from Notebooks;
ed. by D. Wagoner. Mlle 70:92-3 Mr '70
ROGER Klein award for creative editing. See
Literary prizes
ROGERS, Archibald Coleman
Architect who supervises change. pors Bsns
W p39 Ag 22 '70 *
ROGERS, Charles M. See Davenport, R. K.
jt. auth.
ROGERS, Cornish
News editorship established. por Chr Cent
87:684 Je 3 '70 *
ROGERS, George C. Jr
History of Charleston, 1670-1860. Antiques
97:540-1 Ap '70
ROGERS, George W.
Alaska's economic resources & environmental
quality. Nat Parks & Con Mag 44:8-10 N '70
ROGERS, Howard
Nerve gas. New Repub 162:13-14 Mr 7 '70
ROGERS, John
Painting watercolors in acrylic; demonstra-
tion. il Am Artist 34:39-41 D '70
ROGERS, Millard F. Jr
Fishing subjects by Junius Brutus Stearns. il
Antiques 98:246-50 Ag '70
Nydia, popular Victorian image. il Antiques
97:374-7 Mr '70
ROGERS, Randolph
Nydia, popular Victorian image. M. F.
Rogers, jr. il Antiques 97:374-7 Mr '70 *
ROGERS, Robert E.
Report on venereal disease; ed. by E. Jacobs.
Redbook 135:26+ My '70
ROGERS, Warren
Secret link between Nixon and the New
Mobe kids. Look 34:78 Ja 27 '70
ROGERS, Will
Old cowhand; Will Rogers' U.S.A. at Wash-
ington's Ford theatre. N. MacNeil. il por
Time 96:76 S 28 '70 *
Theater; re-creation of a Chautauqua per-
formance, by J. Whitmore. H. Hewes. Sat
R 53:19 O 10 '70 *
ROGERS, William Pierce
CENTO council of ministers meets at Wash-
ington; statement, May 14, 1970. Dept State
Bul 62:711-12 Je 8 '70
Changing role of U.S; interview. il por U S
News 68:28-34 Ja 26 '70
Conversation with William Rogers; transcript
of an interview, December 23, 1969. Dept
State Bul 62:63-8 Ja 19 '70

ROGERS, William Pierce—*Continued*
Department and AID announce pledge to
U.N. population fund; statement, January
24, 1970. Dept State Bul 62:214 F 23 '70
Department gives views on trade legislation;
statement, May 13, 1970. Dept State Bul
62:700-3 Je 1 '70
Department urges liberal foreign trade pol-
icy; statement, October 12, 1970. Dept State
Bul 63:556-8 N 2 '70
Excerpt from testimony, May 13, 1970. Cong
Digest 49:267+ N '70
Federal Republic of Germany signs nuclear
nonproliferation treaty; statement, Novem-
ber 28, 1969. Dept State Bul 61:545 D 15 '69
First special session of the OAS General
assembly held at Washington; address, with
text of resolution. Dept State Bul 63:115-19
Jl 27 '70
Geneva protocol on gases and bacteriological
warfare resubmitted to the Senate; report,
August 11, 1970. Dept State Bul 63:273-5 S 7
'70
Japan is 94th nation to sign nuclear non-
proliferation treaty. Dept State Bul 62:229
Mr 2 '70
Lasting peace in the Middle East: an American view; address, December 9, 1969. Dept
State Bul 62:7-11 Ja 5 '70
Making the U.N. a more effective instrument to meet changing world needs; statement, August 6, 1970. Dept State Bul 63:220-
4 Ag 24 '70
Mexico and the United States: model for
hemisphere relations; address, May 5, 1970.
Dept State Bul 62:654-5 My 25 '70
Mr Collins becomes assistant secretary for
public affairs; remarks at swearing-in ceremony. Dept State Bul 62:142-3 F 2 '70
Mr Herter becomes special assistant for environmental affairs; remarks, January 13,
1970. Dept State Bul 62:213 F 23 '70
National foreign policy conference for editors
and broadcasters; address, January 15, 1970.
Dept State Bul 62:118-20 F 2 '70
National foreign policy conference for editors and broadcasters held at San Francisco; address, with transcript of ques-
tions-and-answers, June 29, 1970. Dept
State Bul 63:78-85 Jl 20 '70
One year in office: a conversation with the
Secretary of state; radio interview, January 14, 1970. Dept State Bul 62:124-7 F 2
'70
Our continuing commitment to western Europe; address, December 6, 1969. Dept State
Bul 61:622-5 D 29 '69
President asks Senate approval of protocol II
to Treaty for the prohibition of nuclear
weapons in Latin America; report, July 16,
1970. Dept State Bul 63:306-8 S 14 '70
President Nixon asks Senate approval of
conventions on pollution of the sea by oil;
report, May 7, 1970. Dept State Bul 62:
757-9 Je 15 '70
President Nixon ratifies nuclear nonproliferation treaty; remarks, November 24, 1969.
Dept State Bul 61:544 D 15 '69
Recent developments in U.S. foreign policy;
statement, June 9, 1970. Dept State Bul 63:
1-5 Jl 6 '70
Rule of law and the settlement of international disputes; address, April 25, 1970. Dept
State Bul 62:623-7 My 18 '70
Secretary Rogers and Secretary Laird interviewed on Issues and answers. Dept State
Bul 63:542-53 N 2 '70
Secretary Rogers' arrival remarks; Rome,
May 24; Madrid, May 28; Lisbon, May 29,
1970. Dept State Bul 62:776-7 Je 22 '70
Secretary Rogers discusses Cambodian ac-
tion in interview for television; transcript
of program. May 4, 1970. Dept State Bul 62:
646-50 My 25 '70
Secretary Rogers interviewed for German
television; transcript of interview, April
15, 1970. Dept State Bul 62:565-71 My 4 '70
Secretary Rogers interviewed for the Hearst
newspapers, January 29, 1970. Dept State
Bul 62:217-26 Mr 2 '70
Secretary Rogers interviewed on Face the
Nation; transcript of program, June 7, 1970.
Dept State Bul 62:785-92 Je 29 '70
Secretary Rogers interviewed on Issues and
answers; transcript of interview, January
18, 1970. Dept State Bul 62:148-54 F 9 '70
Secretary Rogers interviewed on national educational television; transcript of an interview, November 26, 1969. Dept State Bul
61:577-83 D 22 '69
Secretary Rogers interviewed on Today program; transcript of interview, March 17,
1970. Dept State Bul 62:440-3 Ap 6 '70

Secretary Rogers' news conference:
December 23, 1969. Dept State Bul 62:21-8
12 '70
March 23, 1970. Dept State Bul 62:477-84
Ap 13 '70
May 13, 1970. Dept State Bul 62:673-80
Je 1 '70
June 25, 1970. Dept State Bul 63:25-33 Jl
13 '70
July 15, 1970. Dept State Bul 63:125-32
Ag 3 '70
October 9, 1970. Dept State Bul 63:471-8
O 26 '70
Secretary Rogers' report on the Genocide con-
vention. Dept State Bul 62:351-2 Mr 16 '70
Secretary Rogers urges support for foreign
assistance program; statement, September
12, 1970. Dept State Bul 63:356-60 S 28
'70
Secretary Rogers visits the Philippines, South
Viet-Nam, Japan, and the United King-
dom; text of remarks and statements, June
29-July 12, 1970. Dept State Bul 63:133-49
Ag 3 '70
Secretary stresses importance of funding foreign assistance program; statement, November 24, 1969. Dept State Bul 61:593-5 D 22
'69
Seventh anniversary of the OAU; text of
message, May 25, 1970. Dept State Bul
62:752 Je 15 '70
Treaty on the nonproliferation of nuclear
weapons enters into force; remarks, March
5, 1970. Dept State Bul 62:410 Mr 30 '70
Two aspects of the search for peace; address,
April 18, 1970. Dept State Bul 62:605-8 My
11 '70
U.S. closes consulate general at Salisbury,
Southern Rhodesia; statement, March 9,
1970. Dept State Bul 62:412 Mr 30 '70
U.S. gives views on convening Conference on
law of the sea, text of note, June 12, 1970.
Dept State Bul 63:38-9 Jl 13 '70
U.S. initiative toward peace in the Middle
East; text of letter, June 19, 1970. Dept
State Bul 63:178 Ag 10 '70
U.S. mourns tragic death of Mr Mitrione,
statement, August 10, 1970. Dept State Bul
63:247 Ag 31 '70
United States comments on signing of Federal
German-U.S.S.R. treaty, statement, August
12, 1970. Dept State Bul 63:275 S 7 '70
Washington diplomatic conference approves
Patent cooperation treaty; remarks at sign-
ing ceremony, June 19, 1970. Dept State
Bul 63:44-5 Jl 13 '70

about

And now, a few words from the Secretary
of State. Time 96:10 Jl 27 '70 *
Attentive listener. il por Time 95:41 Mr 2 '70 *
Bill Rogers: at home in State. il pors News-
week 75:38+ F 23 '70 *
Getting out of Vietnam. New Repub 162:5-6
Ja 31 '70
Hunting for a policy. il por Time 95:23-4 F
23 '70 *
Living with the Nixon doctrine. il por News-
week 76:29 Jl 20 '70 *
Middle East: at last, a way out? il por Time
96:14-16+ Ag 10 '70 *
Our Middle East stance: rejected but still
valid. Life 68:28 Ja 23 '70
Phantom peace bid. il Newsweek 76:40-1 Jl
6 '70 *
Polite disengager. S. Alsop. Newsweek 76:
72 Ag 24 '70 *
Reclaiming some turf. Newsweek 75:54-5 Ja
26 '70
Secretary Rogers attends NATO ministerial
meeting, Department announcement; with
statement. Dept State Bul 61:625-6 D 29 '69
US and Israel. New Repub 162:5-6 Ja 24 '70
Who speaks for the United States? il por
Newsweek 76:31-2 Jl 27 '70 *

Visit to Africa, February 1970
On African trail with Rogers. por U S News
68:18 Mr 2 '70 *
Rogers to Africa. por Newsweek 75:48 F 16
'70 *
Secretary Rogers visits Africa; texts of remarks and statements, February 7-23, 1970.
W. P. Rogers. Dept State Bul 62:365-80 Mr
23 '70 *

ROGERS conservation education center. See
Conservation of resources—Study and teaching

ROGET, Peter Mark
Peter Mark Roget, by D. L. Emblem. Review
Nation 211:566-8 N 30 '70. R. L. Chap-
man *

ROGIN, Ellen
Gallery; photographs. il Life 69:4-5 Ag 21
'70

ROGIN, Gilbert
Regulars; story. New Yorker 46:42-5 N 7 '70
Taking stock; story. New Yorker 46:32-3 Ag 22 '70

ROGIN, Richard
Joe Kelly has reached his boiling point. il pors N Y Times Mag p 12-14+ Je 28 '70
Now it's welfare lib. il N Y Times Mag p30-1+ S 27 '70

ROHAN, Denis Michael
Eschatological stirrings: madman at the mosque? Chr Today 14:35 F 27 '70 *

ROHDE, Barbara
At Christmas I believe in mornings. Redbook 136:61+ D '70
Long live the lion; story. Redbook 135:68-9 Je '70

ROHLF, John A.
Your beef business. See issues of Farm journal

ROHLF, Robert
Fear of real costs: some financial aspects of the PLA systems study. Am Lib 1:242-4 Mr '70

ROHLFING, Duane L.
Catalytic activities of thermally prepared poly-α-amino acids: effect of aging. bibliog il Science 169:998-1000 S 4 '70

ROHM and Haas company
Vince Gregory's clear bill. il por Forbes 106: 26 N 1 '70

ROHR, Frank, jr
Great ports of call. il Travel & Camera 33: 50-4+ Ja '70
Vagabond camera. See issues of Travel, May 1970-
(ed) Water sports. See issues of Motor boating to April 1970

ROHR, John A.
Judge Wyzanski and selective conscientious objection. America 122:182-5 F 21 '70

ROHR corporation
Looking for Golliaths. il Forbes 105:62-3 Je 1 '70
Rohr breaks out. T. J. Murray. il por Duns 95:62-3 Je '70

ROHRBACH, Peter Thomas
From Teresa of Avila to Eldridge Cleaver: the odyssey of a radical priest. il por Cath World 211:116-19 Je '70

ROHRER, Norman B.
I make a 5-figure income as a full-time freelancer in the religious field. il Writers Digest 50:33-5 Jl '70
Zoning law seen banning Bible classes. Chr Today 14:37 F 13 '70

ROJAS PINILLA, Gustavo
El columpio. Nation 210:548-9 My 11 '70

ROJAS-RAMIREZ, José A. and Tauber, E. S.
Paradoxical sleep in two species of avian predator (falconiformes) bibliog il Science 167:1754-5 Mr 27 '70

ROKEACH, Milton, and Parker, Seymour
Values as social indicators of poverty and race relations in America. bibliog f il Ann Am Acad 388:97-111 Mr '70

ROLDAN, Julio
Death of a citizen; report by W. J. vanden Heuvel. J. Morgenstern. Newsweek 76:14 D 7 '70 *

ROLE playing
Accidents on purpose; Casualties union of Great Britain. D. Lampe. il Todays Health 48:34-7 S '70
Eye of the storm; learning to understand race discrimination; Riceville, Ia. elementary school experiment. J. Leonard. il Life 68:16 My 8 '70
I didn't know it felt that way; project Understanding discrimination; by elementary school in Evanston, Ill. L. S. Wilson. il PTA Mag 64:20-2 Je '70
Most precious resource; Riceville, Ia. school experiment. J. Lear. Sat R 53:57 Je 6 '70
Role playing: effective technique in the teaching of history. W. Dumas. Clear House 44: 468-70 Ap '70
Teach it like it is; a stimulating game; city simulation. W. F. Harlan. Engl J 59:1146-9 N '70

RÖLING, Bert V. A.
Peace research: the science of survival; reprint. il UNESCO Courier 23:21-2+ N '70

ROLL, Susan Kushner
Intracranial self-stimulation and wakeness: effect of manipulating ambient brain catecholamines. bibliog il Science 168:1370-2 Je 12 '70

ROLLEI (firm) See Photographic apparatus industry and trade

ROLLEI SL cameras. See Single-lens reflex cameras

ROLLER chains. See Chain gear

ROLLER skating
Don't tell your friends who won the series; World series of the Derby at Oakland and San Francisco. F. Deford. il Sports Illus 33: 56+ O 5 '70
Fifties; the Roller derby. New Yorker 46:37-8 Ap 4 '70
Going nowhere, on wheels; M. LayPort, S. Treadwell. il pors Sports Illus 32:30-2+ My 18 '70

ROLLERS, Paint. See Paint rollers

ROLLIN, Betty
Fellini: he shoots dreams on film. il pors Look 34:48-53 Mr 10 '70
How I didn't make it in the women's army of Israel. il por Look 34:68-9 F 24 '70
Little Dr Reuben and his big sex book. il pors Look 34:67-8 Jl 14 '70
Motherhood: who needs it? Look 34:15-17 S 22 '70
Steve McQueen: Mr Mansmanship. il pors Look 34:48-52 Ja 27 '70

ROLLING MEADOWS, Ill.
Bagged refuse brings better service. J. McFeggan. il Am City 85:69-72 Mr '70

ROLLING stone (periodical)
Too fast, too soon. por Newsweek 76:61 Ag 17 '70

ROLLING Stones. See Rock 'n' roll groups

ROLLS. See Bread

ROLLS-Royce (automobile) See Automobiles, Foreign

ROLLS-Royce, ltd.
Government defends Rolls. Aviation W 93:21 N 30 '70
Help for a lame eagle. il Newsweek 76:108+ N 23 '70
Price of a Rolls-Royce rescue: $144 million. il Fortune 82:31 D '70
Red ink at Rolls-Royce. Time 96:98-9 N 23 '70
Rolls develops engine trouble. Bsns W p32 Je 6 '70
Rolls gets $48-million government loan. H. J. Coleman. Aviation W 92:22 My 25 '70
Rolls-Royce reports loss, gets new loan, replaces chairman. H. J. Coleman. Aviation W 93:24 N 16 '70
Rolls-Royce's woes. il Newsweek 76:74 Ag 17 '70

ROLO, Charles J.
Stock trends (cont) por Forbes 105:61 Ja 15; 62-3 F 15; 76 Mr 15; 92 Ap 15 '70
Wall Street view. por Forbes 105:96 Je 15; 106:55 Jl 1; 54 Ag 1; 54-5 S 1; 66-7 N 1; 67 D 1 '70; 107:186-7 Ja 1 '71
What makes stock prices move? Bet Hom & Gard 43:23-4 Je '70
What's happened to the market? Bet Hom & Gard 43:28+ S '70
Why buy bonds? Bet Hom & Gard 43:32+ D '70
—and others
Some simple truths about the stock market. Bet Hom & Gard 43:28 My '70

ROLZ-BENNETT, José
Human rights, 1945-1970. UN Mo Chron 7: 78-86 Ap '70

ROMAN, Melvin
Art and social change. il Américas 22:12-20 F '70

ROMAN, Robert C.
Ruby Keeler: back to Broadway after forty years. il pors Dance Mag 44:62-7 D '70

ROMAN, Robert J.
Change can be dynamic. Clear House 44:343-6 F '70

ROMAN, Stephen Boleslav
Steve Roman's waiting game. por Forbes 106: 28-9 O 1 '70 *

ROMAN Catholic church. See Catholic church

ROMAN Catholics. See Catholics

ROMAN empire. See Rome

ROMAN remains. See France—Antiquities, Roman

ROMANCES
Africa in medieval Spanish literature: its appearance in el Caballero Cifar. M. Sampson. bibliog il Negro Hist Bul 32:14-19 D '69

ROMANI, Dorothy
Guidelines for library service to the institutionalized aging. Am Lib 1:286-9 Mr '70

ROMANONES, Aline (Griffith) condesa de
American beauty in Spain. pors Vogue 155: 102-3 Je '70 *

ROMANOV, House of
Tragic dynasty, by J. D. Bergamini. Review Nation 210:316-17 Mr 16 '70. T. H. Von Laue

ROMANSKY, Dave
Blue-collar walker. J. Gross. por Sports Illus 33:77 N 23 '70 *

ROMANTIC love. See Love

ROMANTICISM
Romantic manifesto: a philosophy of literature, by A. Rand. Review
New Repub 162:21-4 F 21 '70. P. Michelson

ROMANTICISM in moving pictures. See Moving pictures—Themes

ROME
Barbarians. R. Winston. il Horizon 12:66-81 Sum '70
See also
Agriculture—Rome

Antiquities
See also
France—Antiquities, Roman
Leptis Magna

ROME (city)

Airports
Decentralized terminal planned for Rome. R. F. Coburn. il Aviation W 92:35-6 F 16 '70

Description
She's got style: Rome. M. Cantwell. il Mlle 71:110+ Je '70
Southern boy writes home about Rome. W. P. Fox. Holiday 47:86-7+ F '70
Vittorio DeSica's Roma; interview, ed. by P. Dragadze. V. DeSica. il por Travel & Camera 33:26-34 Ap '70
When in Rome... S. E. Jones. il Nat Geog 137:741-89 Je '70

Hotels, restaurants, etc.
Little wonder hotels of Rome. P. Dallas. il Holiday 48:42-3+ Jl '70
Rome restaurants. Q. Crewe. Vogue 156:276+ S 1 '70
Rome's home-style restaurants. A. Gold and R. Fizdale. Travel & Camera 33:66-7 Ap '70

Music
Behind the scenes. J. Buckley. Hi Fi 20:21+ N '70
Caballe and the pirates. F. Nuzzo. Hi Fi 20:21 N '70
Report:
Carmen. E. Rizzo. il Opera N 34:29 My 16 '70
Off-beat performances at Teatro dell'-opera. E. Rizzo. Opera N 34:28 F 7 '70
Production of Boito's Mefistofele. E. Rizzo. il Opera N 35:25 O 10 '70
Rossini's Comte Ory. E. Rizzo. Opera N 34:33 Mr 21 '70
Teatro dell'opera productions. E. Rizzo. il Opera N 34:30-1 Mr 7 '70
Verdi's Nabucco. E. Rizzo. il Opera N 35:32 Ja 9 '71
World premiere of L'Idiota by Luciano Chailly. E. Rizzo. il Opera N 34:33-4 Ap 18 '70

St Peter's cathedral
Vatican's noisy family; Pope's general audience in St Peter's. J. Bell. il por Time 95:50+ Je 15 '70

ROMECIN, Roberto Prudencio
Potosi and Charcas. il Américas 22:2-7 Mr '70

ROMEO, Giovanni, and Migeon, B. R.
Genetic inactivation of the α-galactosidase locus in carriers of Fabry's disease. bibliog il Science 170:180-1 O 9 '70

ROMEO and Juliet; ballet. See Ballets—Criticisms

ROMEO and Juliet; drama. See Shakespeare, W.—Plays

ROMEO and Juliet; opera. See Gounod, C. F.

ROMERO aid to elderly project. See Volunteer service

ROMM, Ethel Grodzins
Swing to the right? New Repub 13:9-10 N 28 '70

ROMNEY, George, 1907-
George Romney is running hard at HUD. A. J. Reichley. il por Fortune 82:100-3+ D '70 *
Man on the spot in housing dispute. por U S News 69:25 Ag 10 '70 *
National housing policy' address, January 19, 1970. Vital Speeches 36:309-12 Mr 1 '70

ROMNEY, Lenore (LaFount)
Ahead: uphill pull for Lenore Romney. il pors U S News 69:60 Ag 17 '70 *
Lenore fights alone. A. Rothenberg. il pors Look 34:111+ O 20 '70
Real George. por Newsweek 75:21 Mr 9 '70 *
Secretary's wife. por Newsweek 76:26+ Ag 17 '70 *

ROMO, Gilda Cruz-. See Cruz-Romo, G.

RONAN, Margaret
Films (cont of) Following the films. See issues of Senior scholastic

RONAN, William John
Wholly Ronan empire. F. C. Shapiro. il pors N Y Times Mag p23-6+ My 17 '70 *

RONBERG, Gary
College basketball. Sports Illus 32:52+ Mr 23 '70
Flashing blades for a mini-mastermind. il por Sports Illus 32:20-3 Mr 2 '70
Hockey (cont) il Sports Illus 32:46-7 Ja 26; 56-7 Mr 16; 64-5 Ap 20 '70
Tea party for Bobby's Bruins. il por Sports Illus 32:18-21 My 4 '70
—See Mulvoy, M. jt. auth.

RONCONI, Luca
Orlando furioso; dramatization of poem by L. Ariosto. Criticism
Commonweal 93:276-8 D 11 '70 *
Nation 211:541-2 N 23 '70 *
New Yorker 46:141-2 N 14 '70
Newsweek 76:74 N 16 '70 *

RONDA, Gas
Gas Ronda. S. Kelly. il pors Hot Rod 23:70-2 Jl '70 *

RONDON, Cândido Mariano da Silva
River of Doubt. T. H. Brown. il pors Américas 22:15-23 O '70 *

RONK, D. E.
Here's Vietnamization. New Repub 162:13-14 Je 27 '70

RONNIE, Art
High-flying diva. il por Opera N 35:20-1 O 10 '70

ROODEN, Jan de
Reflections on the U.S. by a Dutch ceramist. il Craft Horiz 30:46-7 My '70

ROODKOWSKY, Nikita D.
Lenin (1870-1970) por Cath World 211:107-11 Je '70

ROOF gardens
Green thumb in the city. E. McDonald. il House B 112:96-7+ Mr '70
Personal garden of Ernest Beadle: small vertical garden. il House & Gard 137:116-19 Mr '70
Summer living in the city, five stories high il House B 112:60-1 Ag '70

ROOFING
Strong points of a mechanically-seamed metal roof. R. C. Schroter. il Arch Rec 148:110 D '70

ROOFS
Put your patio under cover. H. Wicks. il Pop Mech 134:162-4 Jl '70
Rigging a roof. il Arch Forum 132:64-9 Mr '70

ROOFS, Hanging. See Roofs, Suspension

ROOFS, Suspension
To Moma, from Germany; lightweight architecture of F. Otto. N. R. Piene. il Art in Am 58:118-19 My '70

ROOM air conditioners. See Air conditioning equipment

ROOM dividers. See Partitions

ROOM 8 (cat) See Cats

ROOM furnishings. See Household furnishings

ROOM service; drama. See Murray, J. and Boretz, A.

ROOMS
For mothers only: a bright new idea from P/M. J. R. Cary. il Parents Mag 45:92-5 My '70
Place to be alone; a room for the wife-and-mother. D. Hardie. House & Gard 137:70+ My '70
Twenty-five very smart rooms. P. Rumely. il Bet Hom & Gard 48:44-57+ Ag '70
Your own zone. il Seventeen 29:172-5 Ap '70
See also
Bathrooms
Bedrooms
Childrens rooms
Dining rooms
Dressing rooms
Guest rooms
House decoration
Kitchens
Living rooms
Music rooms and equipment
Outdoor rooms
Period rooms
Sewing rooms
Studies (rooms)

ROOMS, Miniature
Goodner's own miniworld. S. A. Parvin. il por Hobbies 75:144+ Mr; 144+ Ap '70

ROOMS, Remodeled. See Houses, Remodeled

ROONEY, Francis Charles, 1921-
More for Melville. A. A. Butkus. por Duns 95:64+ My '70

ROONEY, James A.
Hemolysis near an ultrasonically pulsating gas bubble. bibliog il Science 169:869-71 Ag 28 '70

ROSEN, Lawrence
"I divorce thee". il Trans-Action 7:34-7 Je
'70
ROSEN, Lillie F.
Opening night 1940; a memoir. il Dance Mag
44:34 -7 D '70
ROSEN, Maurice M.
Kidde's new boss tries to get it together.
por Bsns W p36 Ja 31 '70
ROSEN, Robert, and Madden, Stuart
Panthers go to Temple. Commonweal 93:6-7
O 2 '70
ROSEN, Seymour M.
Basic military training in Soviet schools. Sch
& Soc 98:421-3 N '70
ROSENAU, Ernest J.
Trail riders of the wilderness. il Am For
76:52-3 Mr '70 *
ROSENBAUM, Art
College football. il Sports Illus 33:48-9 O 19
'70
ROSENBAUM, H. Jon
Brazil's military regime. Cur Hist 58:73-8+
F '70
ROSENBERG, Bernard
Dictionary for the disenchanted. il Harper
241:93-5 N '70
ROSENBERG, Harold
Art world (cont) New Yorker 45:62+ Ja 24;
46:82+ F 21; 90+ Mr 28; 103-4+ My 9; 54+
Je 6; 48-52 Jl 18; 149-54 O 10; 136+ N 7 '70;
44-7 Ja 2 '71
ROSENBERG, Joe
Read the prospectus. R. Brady. por Duns 95:
103-4 My '70 *
ROSENBERG, Julius and Ethel, case
Agit-prop & the Rosenbergs; analysis of D.
Freed's play, Inquest. A. Weinstein. Com-
mentary 50:18+ Jl '70; Discussion. 50:6+
N '70
Rosenberg case: an inquest on an inquest. W.
Goodman. il pors N Y Times Mag p28-9+
My 24 '70; Reply. O. S. Marden. p80 Je 7 '70
ROSENBERG, Leon Emanuel
Finding and treating genetic diseases. por
Sci N 98:157-8 Ag 22 '70 *
ROSENBERG, Max
Educators' quiz. See issues of Education di-
gest
ROSENBLATT, Richard H. See Graham, J. B.
jt. auth.
ROSENBLOOM, Carroll
Rosenbloom-Robbie bowl. J. Olsen. il pors
Sports Illus 33:22-4+ N 9 '70 *
ROSENBLOOM, Richard S. and Shank, J. K.
Let's write off MESBICs. Harvard Bsns R
48:90-7 S '70
ROSENBLOOM, Sandi
Taxis, jitneys & poverty; adaptation of ad-
dress. il Trans-Action 7:47-54 F '70
ROSENBLUM, Gershen
Social intervention, consultation to organi-
zations. bibliog Ment Hy 54:393-6 Jl '70
ROSENFELD, M. G. and O'Malley, B. W.
Steroid hormones: effects on adenyl cyclase
activity and adenosine 3',5'-monophosphate
in target tissues. bibliog il Science 168:253-
5 Ap 10 '70
ROSENFELD, Richard S.
Student sensitivity in media production.
Clear House 44:382-4 F '70
ROSENFIELD, John M.
Boston's oriental autumn. il Art N 69:42-5+
N '70
Der ROSENKAVALIER; opera. See Strauss,
R.
ROSENSTOCK-HUESSY, Eugen
Dialogue; concerning letters on Christianity
and Judaism between E. Rosenstock-Huessy
and F. Rosenzweig. A. A. Cohen. Commen-
tary 49:90-2 Je '70 *
ROSENTHAL, Alan
Learning to lead not-so-normal lives. il To-
days Health 48:56-7+ Ap '70
Sesame street generation arrives. il Todays
Health 48:42-5+ D '70
Should parents teach preschoolers to read?
il Todays Health 48:37+ My '70
These kids don't have to run away to join
the circus. il Todays Health 48:42-7 F '70
Violence is predictable. il Todays Health 48:
56-7+ N '70
—and Kaufman, Irma
Aerosol products: caution. il Todays Health
48:36-8 O '70
ROSENTHAL, Alan (film producer)
(ed) Fiction documentary; interviews. il
Film Q 23:9-33 Sum '70
ROSENTHAL, Benjamin Stanley
Rosenthal's lament. New Repub 163:8 D 12
'70 *
ROSENTHAL, Herman
Arrogance of virtue (in old New York) R.
Starr. New Repub 163:19-21 D 26 '70 *

ROSENTHAL, M. L.
Israel of the poets. Nation 211:630-2 D 14 '70
Late at night; poem. Nation 212:27 Ja 4 '71
        about
Comment. W. Heyen. Poetry 115:426-7 Mr
'70 *
ROSENZWEIG, Franz
Dialogue; concerning letters on Christianity
and Judaism between E. Rosenstock-Huessy
and F. Rosenzweig. A. A. Cohen. Commen-
tary 49:90-2 Je '70 *
ROSENZWEIG, Rafael, and Tamarin, Georges
Israel's power elite. il Trans-Action 7:26-33+
Jl '70
ROSES
Fall care of roses. K. P. Jones. il Horticul-
ture 48:22-3+ O '70
Five-point program to keep roses blooming.
G. Ohlhus. il Home Gard 57:12-13 Jl '70
Here is Sunset's report on twenty-seven roses
new for 1970. il Sunset 144:126-7 Ja '70
How to read a rose catalog. il Home Gard 57:
26-7 F '70
I'm a rose rookie. B. Ragan. il Org Gard &
Farm 17:74-5 Je '70
It's easy with miniature roses. F. C. Loren-
zen. il Org Gard & Farm 17:62-4 F '70
Miniature roses are rewarding but are only
for the patient gardener. il Sunset 144:204
Je '70
Old fashioned roses for fall bloom. L. Bell.
il Home Gard 57:58-9 Ap '70
Roses for 1971. il Horticulture 48:18-19 Jl '70
Roses in the vegetable garden. N. P. Farris.
il Org Gard & Farm 17:46-8 My '70
Very big roses for very small gardens. H.
Mason. il Bet Hom & Gard 48:58-9 Ap '70
        See also
Conard-Pyle company
Rose hips
ROSEWALL, Ken
It almost came up roses for Rosewall. W.
Bingham. il pors Sports Illus 33:50-1 Jl 13
'70 *
Maggie and the little master. il por Time
96:53 S 28 '70 *
Sporting scene. H. W. Wind. New Yorker
46:172-4+ O 10 '70 *
Sudden death at Forest Hills; U.S. Open
tennis championships. W. Bingham. il por
Sports Illus 33:26-7 S 21 '70 *
ROSEWATER, Joseph
Monoplacophora in the south Atlantic Ocean.
bibliog il Science 167:1485 Mr 13 '70
ROSHOLT, John N. See Tatsumoto, M. jt.
auth.
ROSIENE, Alan I.
Tempera resist-plus. il Sch Arts 70:20-1 S '70
ROSNER, S. Steven
Problems and needs in rehabilitation. Ment
Hy 54:144-6 Ja '70
ROSOW report. See Labor and laboring clas-
ses—United States
ROSS, Betsy
        Drama
Betsy Ross. H. M. Roberts. Plays 29:46-52 F
'70
ROSS, Carol
Two lives of Carol Ross. L. David. por Good
H 170:65+ F '70 *
ROSS, David A. and others
Black Sea: recent sedimentary history. bib-
liog il Science 170:163-5 O 9 '70
—See Degens, E. T. jt. auth.
ROSS, Diana
Farewell, more or less, to the Supremes.
B. Farrell. por Life 68:18B F 13 '70
        about
Baby, baby, where did Diana go? pors Time
96:30-1 Ag 17 '70 *
Why Diana Ross left the Supremes. L.
Robinson. il pors Ebony 25:120-6 F '70 *
ROSS, Gilbert
Malawi: portrait of a lake. il Travel 134:34-9+
N '70
ROSS, Howard G.
Adapt oddball lenses for better tele shots. il
Mod Phot 34:82-3+ My '70
ROSS, Irwin
Chip off the old; story. Har Yrs 10:30-1 O '70
Enos Mills, Columbus on the Rockies. il por
Nat Wildlife 9:26-8 D '70
ROSS, Irwin, 1919-
Elections in plain English. Read Digest 97:
25+ N '70
High-powered boss in a hot seat. por Read
Digest 96:117-21 Mr '70
If it breathes, organize it. il Fortune 81:122-
5+ Mr '70
Irrepressible Mills B. Lane. il por Read Digest
96:17+ F '70
J. Walter Thompson is alive and well in
thirty countries. il Fortune 82:102-5+ O '70

ROSS, J. W. Jr. See Frant, M. S. jt. auth.
ROSS, Kenneth
Genesis revised. J. B. Craig. Am For 76:7
Jl '70 *
ROSS, Leonard
Regional authorities. New Repub 162:15-16
Je 20 '70
—See Kendall, D; Passell, P. jt. auths.
ROSS, Malcolm, and others
Lunar clinopyroxenes: chemical composition,
structural state, and texture. bibliog il Sci-
ence 167:628-30 Ja 30 '70
ROSS, Marianne
To the high places; story. Redbook 135:82-3
Jl '70
ROSS, Mary Ellen
Indoor vines. il Horticulture 49:28-30+ Ja '71
ROSS, Richard A.
Filling the void; the black in American lit-
erature. Engl J 59:31-3 Ja '70
ROSS, Wallace C.
How sails work. il Yachting 128:66-7+ Ag '70
ROSS, Walter Sanford
4000 kidneys later. Todays Health 48:35-6+ D
'70
How anesthesiologists save lives. il Read
Digest 96:144-8+ Mr '70
Leukemia: we're starting to use the word
cure. il Todays Health 48:49-51+ O '70;
Same abr. with title They're gaining on leu-
kemia. Read Digest 97:148-52 D '70
Man who turned sheep into gold. il por Todays
Health 48:26-9+ O '70
Nibblers' diet. il Ladies Home J 87:58-9+ Ja
'70
(ed) See Holleb, A. I. Using the cancer
cures we have now
ROSS-SKINNER, Jean
International business. il Duns 95:69-70+ Ap;
70-1+ My; 71-2+ Je; 96:57-8+ D '70
ROSS DAM. See Dams
ROSSBACH, Katherine
Ed Rossbach: a tribe of baskets. il Craft
Horiz 30:16-17 O '70
ROSSELLINI, Roberto
Current cinema. P. Gilliatt. New Yorker 46:
58-60 Ag 22 '70 *
ROSSET, Barnet Lee, 1922-
Big headlines, small profits. J. Smith. por
Duns 96:66 N '70 *
ROSSETTO, Louis, jr. See Lehr, S. jt. auth.
ROSSI, Alice S.
Job discrimination, and what women can
do about it. por Atlan 225:99-102 Mr '70
ROSSI, Giovanni B. and Friend, Charlotte
Lymphomas in mice: failure of induction
after a graft-versus-host reaction. bibliog
il Science 167:1383-5 Mr 6 '70
ROSSI, Michael
Watercolor page; with biographical sketch.
il por Am Artist 34:50-1+ S '70
ROSSI, Peter H. and Berk, R. A.
Local political leadership and popular dis-
content in the ghetto. bibliog f il Ann Am
Acad 391:111-27 S '70
ROSSIDES, Eugene T.
Foreign bank accounts; address. Vital
Speeches 36:526-30 Je 15 '70
ROSSINI, Gioacchino
La Cenerentola. Criticism
New Yorker 46:89 Ap 11 '70 *
Records:
Petite messe solennelle. Opera N 34:35
Mr 14 '70 *
ROSSITER, Clinton
Obituary
Nat R 22:775 Jl 28 '70. W. F. Buckley
ROSSMAN, Isadore J.
Two children by choice; excerpts. Parents
Mag 45:58-9+ My '70
Who should take the pill? excerpt from Two
children by choice. Parents Mag 45:54-7+
F '70
ROSSMAN, Parker
COCU and the cluster concept. Chr Cent 87:
1457-9 D 2 '70
Education in and for team ministry. Chr
Cent 87:475-7 Ap 22 '70
ROSSMANN, Michael G.
Quartet in amino acids. Sci Am 222:48 Je
'70 *
ROSSO, Wendell
Merchandise is horses. P. Ryan. il pors
Sports Illus 32:34-6+ Mr 23 '70 *
ROSS'S geese. See Geese
ROSTEN, Leo
Innocent in birdland. il Sat R 53:14-15 S 5 '70
Touch me, feel me, grunt, growl, purr; ex-
cerpt from People I have loved, known, or
admired. Sat R 53:12-13 My 30 '70
Who speaks for the young? Some startling
facts and fictions. Look 34:16+ My 19 '70

Wilbur; story; excerpt from People I have
loved, known, or admired. Ladies Home J
87:60 O '70 *
World of Leo Rosten (cont) Look 34:16 F
10; 16 Mr 24 '70
ROSTOCK. University. See Colleges and uni-
versities—Germany (Democratic Republic)
ROSTOW, Eugene Victor
Reporter at large; interview, ed. by W. Whit-
worth. New Yorker 46:30-46+ Jl 4 '70
ROSTOW, Walt Whitman
Asia; address, June 19, 1970. Vital Speeches
36:682-8 S 1 '70
What future for Asia? Read Digest 97:109-11 D
'70
ROSTROPOVICH, Mstislav
Rostropovich appeals for Solzhenitsyn; re-
print of letter to four Russian periodicals.
Sat R 53:28 N 28 '70

about

Involuntary journey; letter of criticism. pors
Newsweek 76:61 N 23 '70 *
Rostropoviches in Onegin. I. Kolodin. Sat R
53:53 S 26 '70 *
ROSWAENGE, Helge
Top tenors, on L.P. A. Favia-Artsay. pors
Hobbies 75:36 Je '70 *
ROSZAK, Theodore
Making of a counter culture; excerpts. Hori-
zon 12:20-1 Spr '70

about

Lysergic Götterdämmerung. D. L. Bromwich.
Commentary 50:56-9 D '70 *
ROTARY lawn mowers. See Lawn mowers
ROTARY tillage. See Tillage
ROTCH, William B.
News from Milford. M. L. Stein. il por Sat R
54:43-6 Ja 9 '71 *
ROTENONE
Enhancement of photoalteration of cyclodiene
insecticide chemical residues by rotenone.
G. W. Ivie and J. E. Casida. bibliog il Sci-
ence 167:1620-2 Mr 20 '70
ROTH, Arnold
Ode on a Grecian urge. il Sports Illus 32:
32-7 Ja 19 '70
Pool. il Sports Illus 33:46-51 D 14 '70
ROTH, Burnett
United States changing Mideast policy; ad-
dress, January 13, 1970. Vital Speeches 36:
442-8 My 1 '70
ROTH, Cecil
In search of Cecil Roth. C. Raphael. bibliog f
Commentary 50:75-6+ S '70 *
ROTH, Emery, and sons
One hundred buildings; high-rise office build-
ings. New Yorker 46:37 O 10 '70
ROTH, Martin
Weekend at sea; poem. Poetry 115:389 Mr
'70
ROTH, Philip
Modest proposal. il Look 34:98-100 O 6 '70

about

Beyond Portnoy. G. Wolff. por Newsweek
76:66+ Ag 3 '70 *
ROTH, Robert, and Lusnak, Karin
DNA synthesis during yeast sporulation: ge-
netic control of an early developmental
event. bibliog il Science 168:493-4 Ap 24 '70
ROTH, Robert J.
Religion and American experience. il America
124:43-4 Ja 16 '71
ROTHBLAT, G. H. and others
Desmosterol as the major sterol in L-cell
mouse fibroblasts grown in sterol-free cul-
ture medium. bibliog il Science 169:880-2
Ag 28 '70
ROTHCHILD, John
Peace corpsman into organization man. Nat
R 22:405-6 Ap 21 '70
ROTHENBERG, Al
GM's John DeLorean: powerhouse behind
the Vega. il pors Look 34:54-7 Ag 25 '70
Import invasion hits high tide. il Look 34:
30-7+ Ap 7 '70
Lenore fights alone. il pors Look 34:111+ O
20 '70
Look's fifteenth annual new car preview:
forecast '71. il Look 34:64-73+ O 6 '70
ROTHENBERG, Jerome
Connoisseur of Jews; poem. Nation 210:156
F 9 '70
ROTHENBERG, Marian S.
APS-AAPT meet in Chicago. il Phys Today
23:53-5 Ja '70
International opportunities for physicists.
il Phys Today 23:37-40+ S '70
Physicists with unusual careers. il Phys To-
day 23:23-8+ My '70

ROTHENBERG, Polly
  Brush-on enamel designs. il Ceram Mo 18:
    16-17 Ja '70
  Clay cloisonne. il Ceram Mo 18:22-3 O '70
  Decorative panels with metal. il Design 71:
    26-9 Fall '69
  Enamel inlays in wood. il Ceram Mo 18:32-3
    Je '70
  Enameled repousse medallions. il Ceram Mo
    18:24-5 Mr '70
  Hollowed-out animal sculpture. il Ceram
    Mo 18:21-3 S '70
  Making plaster bats. il Ceram Mo 18:21-3
    D '70
  Mosaic in wood. il Design 71:13-15 mid-Sum
    '70
ROTHENBERGER, Anneliese
  Music to my ears; song recital. I. Kolodin.
    Sat R 53:40 F 7 '70
ROTHKO, Mark
  Art world. H. Rosenberg. New Yorker 46:90+
    Mr 28 '70 *
  Mark Rothko, 1903-1970. Art N 69:29+ Ap
    '70 *
  Mark Rothko, 1903-1970. D. Davis. por
    Newsweek 75:98 Mr 9 '70 *
  Mark Rothko: portrait of the artist as an
    angry man. J. Fischer. Harper 241:16-17+
    Jl '70 *
  Rothko: a Venetian souvenir; exhibition at
    the Marlborough gallery. T. B. Hess. il Art
    N 69:40-1+ N '70 *
ROTHSCHILD, Miriam, and Ford, Bob
  Heart poisons and the monarch; with
    biographical sketches. il Natur Hist 79:6,
    36-7 Ap '70
ROTHSCHILD, Norman
  Are they building cameras upside down? il
    Pop Phot 66:55-7+ F '70
  B&W problems, and how to solve them. il
    Pop Phot 66:94-7+ Je '70
  Copy, correct, and crop your color slides.
    il Pop Phot 66:75-7+ Ja '70
  Filter that drives colors wild. il Pop Phot 67:
    84-9 Ag '70
  Great pictures, no! Great kids, yes! il Pop
    Phot 67:70-3+ Jl '70
  How to avoid second guessing about second
    bodies. il Pop Phot 67:78-81 S '70
  Offbeat. See issues of Popular photography
  What the eyes don't tell. il Pop Phot 66:
    64-5+ Mr '70
  Your enemy the sun. il Pop Phot 67:67-9+
    Ag '70
ROTHSCHILD, Walter C. and Möller, K. D.
  Far-infrared spectroscopy. bibliog il Phys To-
    day 23:44-9 S '70
ROTHSCHILDS; musical comedy. See Musical
  comedies, revues, etc.—Criticisms, plots,
  etc.
ROTHSTEIN, Arthur
  Critical eye. See issues of Travel & camera
  Twelve eyes on Asia. il Travel & Camera 33:
    62-7 O '70
ROTHSTEIN, Robert
  Domestic politics and peacemaking: reconcil-
    ing incompatible imperatives. bibliog f Ann
    Am Acad 392:62-75 N '70
ROTISSERIE cooking. See Cookery
ROTISSERIES. See Household appliances, Elec-
  tric
ROTMAN, Charles B.
  Camp director's role in staff orientation. il
    Camp Mag 42:11+ Ap '70
ROTOPARK. See Garages
ROTOPED. See Motor vehicles
ROTORS (helicopters) See Helicopters—Rotors
ROTSHENKER, S. and Rahamimoff, R.
  Neuromuscular synapse: stochastic properties
    of spontaneous release of transmitter. bib-
    liog il Science 170:648-9 N 6 '70
ROTTERDAM
Air pollution
  Computers v. pollution; fully automated, air-
    pollution-warning system consisting of elec-
    tric sniffers. il Time 95:84+ My 11 '70
ROTTERDAM philharmonic orchestra. See
  Orchestras
ROTTING of wood. See Wood—Decay
ROUECHÉ, Berton
  Annals of medicine (cont) New Yorker 45:60-
    3 Ja 31; 46:64-70+ Ag 22 '70
  Profiles; Stapleton, Neb. New Yorker 46:29-
    40 Ja 2 '71
ROUGH ROCK demonstration school. See In-
  dians of North America—Education
ROUGHAGE in feed. See Feeding and feeding
  stuffs—Fiber content
ROUND Britain sailing race. See Yacht racing
ROUND buildings. See Buildings, Round

ROUND table on the social responsibilities of
  libraries. See American library association
  —Social responsibilities of libraries round
  table
ROUNDS, Donald E. See Berns, M. W. jt.
  auth.
ROUNDUPS
    See also
  Rodeos
ROUNTREE, Martha
  Crusade for morality; address, June 10, 1970.
    Vital Speeches 36:597-602 Jl 15 '70
ROURKE, G. Margaret
  Medical testing. il Todays Ed 59:54-6 F '70
ROUS sarcoma cells. See Cancer cells
ROUSE, James Wilson
  Jim Rouse's satellite city. J. Peter. il por
    Look 34:55-7 F 10 '70
ROUSSEAU, D. L. and Porto, S. P. S.
  Polywater: polymer or artifact? bibliog il
    Science 167:1715-19 Mr 27 '70
ROUSSEAU, Richard W.
  Vatican and mixed marriages. Chr Cent 87:
    963-4+ Ag 12 '70
  —See Bowman, D. jt. auth.
ROUTING machines
  Make this dial-a-jig router attachment. W.
    G. Waggoner. il Pop Mech 134:188-9 O '70
ROUX, C. and others
  LSD: no teratogenic action in rats, mice, and
    hamsters. bibliog il Science 169:588-9 Ag 7
    '70
ROVAINEN, C. M.
  Glucose production by lamprey meninges.
    bibliog il Science 167:889-90 F 6 '70
ROVERE, Richard Halworth
  Letter from Washington. See occasional is-
    sues of New Yorker
ROVINSKY, Joseph J.
  How chronic health problems affect preg-
    nancy; ed. by B. R. Boylan. Redbook 135:
    14+ Je '70
ROW houses
  Future is now; clustered housing, Columbia,
    Md. N. Skurka. il N Y Times Mag p68-
    9 Ja 10 '71
  La Luz, Albuquerque, N.Mex. il Arch Rec
    147:92-3 mid-My '70
ROW spacing of plants. See Plants, Space ar-
  rangement of
ROWAN, Carl Thomas
  How racists use science to degrade black peo-
    ple. il por Ebony 25:31-4+ My '70
  Japan, all Asia watches and wonders. Read
    Digest 97:103-7 Ag '70
  Storm warnings in the Philippines. Read Di-
    gest 97:193-4+ N '70
ROWAN, Dan
  Dan Rowans: we lead an easy, entertaining
    life. il por House & Gard 138:48-51 Jl '70 *
ROWAN, Roy
  Surprises from the Yalu and beyond. il por
    Life 68:4 Je 5 '70

about
  Old friend leaves our staff. R. Graves. por
    Life 68:3 Je 5 '70*
ROWDYISM. See Vandalism
ROWE, Ernest Ras
  Question of value. Sch & Soc 98:349-51 O '70
ROWE, Sister Margaret
  Contemplative life and the sociologist. il
    Chr Cent 87:1412-16 N 25 '70
ROWING
  How I rowed across the Atlantic and found
    Florida. J. Fairfax. il Esquire 73:111-15+
    Ap '70
  Perpetual motion machine from East Ger-
    many; world championships in Canada. H.
    D. Whall. il Sports Illus 33:89-91 S 21 '70
  Quakers pull a swift one on the Charles
    Adams cup. H. D. Whall. il Sports Illus 32:
    74+ My 11 '70
  Stowing the manly oar; Columbia university.
    il Time 96:82-3 N 23 '70
    See also
  Regattas
Study and teaching
  Man your oars; workshop at Mystic Seaport.
    A. Anderson. il Yachting 129:102-3 Ja '71
ROWING coaches. See Coaches (athletics)
ROWLAND, G. Thomas. See Frost, J. L. jt.
  auth.
ROWLAND, Howard Ray
  Campus ombudsman: an emerging role. Ed
    Digest 35:28-31 F '70
ROWSON, Susanna
  Susanna Rowson and her academy. J. C. Gif-
    fen. il por Antiques 98:436-40 S '70 *
ROY, Joseph J.
  Student participation in faculty meetings.
    Clear House 44:285 Ja '70

ROYAL academy of arts, London
Royal academy Polonaise; 1,000 years of Polish art. J. Russell. il Art N 68:34-7 F '70
ROYAL American shows. See Sideshows
ROYAL ballet, Great Britain
Dame Margot; interview. M. Fonteyn. New Yorker 46:24-5 My 30 '70
Dance; performances at the Metropolitan opera house. N. Goldner. Nation 210:669-70 Je 1 '70
Dance; Ropes of time. J. Maskey. Hi Fi 20: MA11 S '70
Emotion at the ballet; Romeo and Juliet. W. Terry. il Sat R 53:58 My 23 '70
In honor of Sir Frederick; closing performance at the Metropolitan opera house. W. Terry. por Sat R 53:33 Jl 4 '70
Mixed blessings; New York visit. H. Saal. Newsweek 75:87 My 4 '70
More royal dancing. W. Terry. il Sat R 53:34 My 30 '70
Musical events:
Continuation of season at the Metropolitan opera house. W. Sargeant. New Yorker 46:148+ My 9 '70
Pas de deux par excellence: Antoinette Sibley and Anthony Dowell. O. Maynard. il pors Dance Mag 44:50-61 Ap '70
Royal ballet's New York season in retrospect. D. Hering. il Dance Mag 44:82-9 S '70
Royal magic; twelfth season in the U.S. since change of name from Sadler's Wells ballet. W. Terry. il Sat R 53:61 My 16 '70
Stars beyond. il Time 95:68+ My 25 '70
Supering with the Royal ballet. S. W. McDermott. il Dance Mag 44:62-9 Ap '70
ROYAL Canadian mounted police. See Canada —Royal Canadian mounted police
ROYAL crown cola company
Competition changes flavor, too. il Bsns W p71 Ap 25 '70
ROYAL Dutch-Shell group
Briton wins top spot in the Shell empire. por Bsns W p40 O 24 '70
Royal Dutch/Shell realigns at the top; interview. M. E. Spaght. il pors Bsns W p 102-3+ My 9 '70
ROYAL family of Great Britain. See Great Britain—Royal family
ROYAL Greenwich observatory. See Astronomical observatories—Great Britain
ROYAL Hawaiian hotel. See Honolulu—Hotels, restaurants, etc.
ROYAL Ontario museum. See Toronto—Galleries and museums
ROYAL opera, Great Britain
Boulez at Covent Garden; production of Pelléas et Mélisande. T. Heinitz. Sat R 53: 65 F 14 '70
Opera at Covent Garden: 1946-1970; comp. by S. Porter. Sat R 53:44-5 Je 27 '70
Report:
Pelléas et Mélisande. F. G. Barker. il Opera N 34:35 Ja 24 '70
Il Trovatore and two Ring cycles. F. G. Barker. Opera N 35:31 D 5 '70
World premiere of Richard Rodney Bennett's Victory. F. G. Barker. il Opera N 34:27-8 Je 13 '70
Stateside view of Webster's era. I. Kolodin. Sat R 53:46 Je 27 '70
Webster era at Covent Garden. D. Shawe-Taylor. il pors Sat R 53:43-4+ Je 27 '70
ROYAL society for the prevention of cruelty to animals
Legacy of Humanity Dick. il Time 95:28 Ja 26 '70
ROYAL warrant
By appointment. il Newsweek 76:59 Ag 10 '70
ROYALTIES
Report from Scandinavia; library royalties. D. Lattmann. Pub W 198:16 D 14 '70
ROYCE, Josiah
Religion and philosophy. M. R. Konvitz. por Sat R 53:28-30 Ja 24 '70
ROZELL, Bruce
There's nothing wrong about working for peanuts. il Org Gard & Farm 17:58-60 Ap '70
ROZELL, Margilee Johns
Crape myrtle; the shrub that laughs at drought. il Org Gard & Farm 17:84-5 N '70
Sweet banana; prince of peppers. il Org Gard & Farm 17:94-5 Mr '70
This ground cover is a blooming mulch. Org Gard & Farm 17:89 S '70
We grow burpless cucumbers. il Org Gard & Farm 17:73 Je '70
ROZELLE, Pete
Cracks in a golden egg. il por Forbes 106: 23-4 S 15 '70 *
Rozelle referees a strike settlement. il Bsns W p 19 Ag 8 '70 *
Rozelle's taut ship. Newsweek 75:67+ Ap 27 '70 *

Sporting scene. H. W. Wind. New Yorker 46:154+ D 12 '70 *
This saint has been called a sinner. M. Sharnik. il por Sports Illus 32:18-20+ Je 1 '70 *
ROZHDESTVENSKII, Robert
Some words from the author; poem. New Repub 162:34 My 9 '70
RUBBER
Air pollution and rubber. Chem 43:21 D '70
RUBBER industry and trade
Back at the plantation; Cambodia. Newsweek 76:79-80 N 30 '70
See also
Dayco corporation
Tire industry and trade
RUBBINGS
Making an impression in Mexico. P. Thomas and F. J. Thomas. il Américas 22:30-5 S '70
RUBBISH disposal. See Refuse and refuse disposal
RUBELLA
Right not to be born; refusal to grant therapeutic abortion in case of rubella baby. M. K. Sanders. il Harper 240:92-9 Ap '70
Rubella. E. Edelson. Todays Ed 59:42-3 S '70

Vaccines
Parents' magazine's awards for outstanding service to children. il Parents Mag 45:24 Ja '70
Reassurance on rubella. Time 96:54 S 28 '70
Report on Rubella vaccine. S. A. Fish and P. Feinstein. Redbook 134:29+ Ap '70
Rubella: vaccine in doubt. Newsweek 76:78 O 12 '70
RUBEN, Samuel
Titanium cuts a battery to size; small rechargeable battery. il por Bsns W p50 Ja 24 '70
RUBIDIUM in the body
Brain norepinephrine: enhanced turnover after rubidium treatment. J. M. Stolk and others. bibliog il Science 168:501-3 Ap 24 '70
RUBIES, Artificial
Making rubies by machine. Sci Digest 69: 73-4 Ja '71
RUBIN, Harold. See Robbins, H. pseud.
RUBIN, Harry
Overgrowth stimulating factor released from rous sarcoma cells. bibliog il Science 167: 1271-2 F 27 '70
about
Malignant messenger. J. Lear. Sat R 53:48 Mr 21 '70 *
RUBIN, Jerry
Indeed do it! W. F. Buckley, jr. Nat R 22: 533 My 19 '70 *
Political Portnoy. C. H. Simonds. Nat R 22: 518-19 My 19 '70 *
Stoned orphan. A. H. Norman. por Newsweek 75:106+ Ap 27 '70 *
RUBIN, Judith A.
Preparing to teach elementary art. Ed Digest 35:38-41 Mr '70
RUBIN, Larry
Discard; poem. Nation 210:120 F 2 '70
RUBIN, Maude
Time's loud alarm; poem. Farm J 94:84 Ap '70
RUBIN, Morton D.
Antarctic meteorology. il por Bul Atom Sci 26:48-54 D '70
RUBIN, Robert J. See Jaeger, R. J. jt. auth.
RUBIN, Theodore Isaac
Forever thin; excerpts. il Ladies Home J 87:59+ Ja: 60+ Mr: 94+ My '70
I have a friend who... (cont) il por Ladies Home J 86:38-9 D '69; 87:72 S; 44 N '70
If you lie about your age. por Ladies Home J 87:68 Ap '70
What gossiping reveals about you. por Ladies Home J 87:46+ F '70
What makes a man lovable? Read Digest 96: 21-4 Ja '70
RUBIN, Zick
Scientific look at romantic love. Sci Digest 67:91 My '70 *
RUBINSTEIN, Amnon
Now in Israel a fluttering of doves. il N Y Times Mag p8-9+ Jl 26 '70
Six days plus three years: Israel asks ma ihieh hassof? What will be the end? il N Y Times Mag p5-7+ My 31 '70
RUBINSTEIN, Anton Grigor'evich
In the grand manner. W. Botsford. por Am Rec G 36:690-1 My '70 *
RUBINSTEIN, Helena, inc.
Face-lift for a cosmetics maker. il Bsns W p60-1 Ag 15 '70
French perfume goes American; Rochas-Rubinstein deal. Bsns W p 132 My 23 '70

RUBSAMEN, Lou
New bathroom for old. il Mech Illus 66:90-2 D '70
RUCHELMAN, Maryon W.
Gas chromatography: medical diagnostic aid. bibliog il por Chem 43:14-19 D '70
RUCKELSHAUS, William Doyle
Policeman for pollution. il por Time 96:41-2 N 23 '70 *
RUDDLE, Frank H. See Lubs, H. A. jt. auth.
RUDEL, Reinhardt. See Taylor, S. R. jt. auth.
RUDLOE, Jack
Panacea for a salty Yankee. R. H. Boyle. il por Sports Illus 32:28-30+ Ap 20 '70 *
RUDMAN, Jeff
Opinion: politicizing the university. por Mlle 71:92+ Ag '70
RUDNER, Ruth
Let's travel: the Alpin-schule Innsbruck. il Mlle 70:124+ Mr '70
RUDNIK, Raphael
Comment. R. B. Shaw. Poetry 117:114 N '70 *
RUDOFSKY, Bernard
Covered streets? excerpts from Streets are for people. il Horizon 11:78-87 Aut '69
Invitation to Japan. il Harp Baz 103:194-5+ Mr '70
RUDOLPH, Lillian
Cinderella; poem. Ladies Home J 87:142 My '70
RUDOLPH, Mae
Sense and nonsense about growing older. Read Digest 97:23-4+ S '70
RUDOLPH, Paul Marvin
Paul Rudoph: work in progress; with introd. by M. F. Schmertz. il Arch Rec 148:89-100 N '70 *
RUDOMINO, Margarita Ivanovna
Soviet Union: of 370,000 libraries, 2.5 billion volumes, and a treasure house of foreign literature; tr. by R. A. Karlowich. il por Wilson Lib Bul 44:1022-32 Je '70
RUE, Leonard Lee
Will wild Africa survive? photographs. Nat Wildlife 8:18-19 Je '70
RUEL, Paul Durand-. See Durand-Ruel, P.
RUETHER, Rosemary
Christocentric world history. por Commonweal 93:251-3 D 4 '70
Education in tandem: white liberal, black militant. America 122:582-4 My 30 '70
Messianic core. il Commonweal 91:423-5 Ja 16 '70
White left in the mother country. il Commonweal 93:142-5, 363+ N 6 '70, Ja 15 '71
RUFF, George E.
Adaptation under extreme environmental conditions. bibliog f il Ann Am Acad 389: 19-26 My '70
RUFF, Robert Eugene
Kelp farming; with biographical sketch. il Sea Front 16:182-5, 191 My '70
RUFFED grouse shooting. See Grouse shooting
RUFFIN, Holt
Colombian gem. il Américas 22:13-17 Mr '70
RUG cleaning. See Rugs and carpets—Care
RUG hooking. See Hooking
RUGBY football
Cymru am byth! Wales-France rugby match. C. Gammon. il Sports Illus 32:58-64 F 9 '70
Farewell and come back, Fiji; Metropolitan New York rugby union All-Stars vs Fiji national team. D. Levin. il Sports Illus 33: 76+ D 7 '70
Last game Richard Burton lost. R. Burton. pors Vogue 157:102-5 Ja 1 '71
RUGER, Bill
This isn't your common everyday Vanden Plas Tourer. M. Denny. il por Motor T 22: 50-3+ D '70 *
RUGGERE, Peter L.
Target in Peru: social transformation. America 122:160-1 F 14 '70
RUGGLES, Carl
Playing and conducting that simply could not be bettered. A. Cohn. pors Am Rec G 37:148-51 N '70 *
RUGGLES, Kirk
Comment. A. Brilliant. Poetry 116:127 My '70 *
RUGS and carpets
Beautiful floor; bare floors and carpeting. W. Baldwin. House & Gard 137:12-13+ Ap '70
Carpeting. Bet Hom & Gard 48:88+ F '70
Consumer's guide to rugs & carpeting. Mech Illus 66:101 Ag '70
How GH evaluates carpets. il Good H 171:6 O '70

McCarran's magic carpet; Las Vegas airport terminal. E. A. Taylor. il por Am City 85: 82-3 N '70
Twelve great floor shows. N. Mandelbaum. il Ladies Home J 87:88-95 Ap '70
Walk-and-wear patterns. il Redbook 135:98-9+ My '70

Care
Care and cleaning of rugs and carpets. Redbook 135:45-6 S '70
Carpet cleaners. il Consumer Rep 35:114-17 F '70
Home carpet care; cleaners and shampoos. il Consumer Bul 53:33-6 My '70
Rug shampooing the easy aerosol way. E. Taylor. il Good H 171:221 O '70

Purchasing
GH selects the best carpet buys. il Good H 171:132-8 O '70
Ten-point guide to buying a good carpet. Good H 171:192 O '70
RUGS and carpets, Oriental
Egyptian carpets; exhibition at Textile museum in Washington, D.C. S. B. Sherrill. il Antiques 98:16+ Jl '70
Timeless appeal of oriental rugs. M. Dahlerus. il Good H 172:110 Ja '71
RUGSTAD, Hans E. and others
Transfer of bilirubin uridine diphosphate-glucuronyltransferase to enzyme-deficient rats. bibliog il Science 170:553-5 O 30 '70
RUKEYSER, Muriel
Iris; poem. New Yorker 46:144 My 16 '70
This morning; poem. Mlle 70:156 F '70
RULE, Betty Jo
Can man survive? il Library J 95:1448-9 Ap 15 '70
RULE, Philip C.
New fall books. America 123:236-7+ O 3 '70
You've come a long way, Bible! il America 123:433-4 N 21 '70
RULERS. See Kings and rulers
RULERS (instruments)
Mosaic ruler. R. E. Moore. il Science 167: 1385 Mr 6 '70
RULES of order. See Parliamentary practice
RUMANIA
See als
Churches—Rumania
Floods—Rumania
Transylvania
United States—Commerce—Rumania

Description and travel
Romania. J. Farb. il Travel & Camera 33: 46-52+ D '70

Economic conditions
Plus and a minus. V. Chapman. il Sr Schol 95:19 N 17 '69

Foreign relations
Rumania: the crest. il Time 95:40 Je 22 '70

Russia
See Russia—Foreign relations—Rumania

United States
See United States—Foreign relations—Rumania

Industries
See also
Airplane industry and trade—Rumania

Politics and government
What's going on now behind the iron curtain. R. A. Haeger. il U S News 69:88-9 N 9 '70

Religious institutions and affairs
Ecumenism in Sofia and Bucharest. J. R. Nelson. Chr Cent 87:437-9 Ap 15 '70
See also
Baptists in Rumania

Treaties
Russia
See Russia—Treaties
RUMMEL, Virginia C.
Crackers and cattle kings. il Américas 22:36-41 S '70
RUMOR
Funny stories. J. Beatty, jr. Esquire 74:44+ N '70
Great 1972 election rumor. P. Steinfels. Commonweal 92:407 Ag 21 '70
RUMSEY, H. Jr. See Goldstein, R. M. jt. auth.
RUMSEY, Tom
Take along the children. il pors Motor B 125: 59+ Je '70

RUMSFELD, Donald
De-escalator of the war on poverty. R. Sherrill. il pors N Y Times Mag p23-5+ D 13 '70 *
Rumsfeld on the rise. il por Newsweek 76:17 D 28 '70 *
Somebody is always offended. S. L. Greene. Nation 211:624-7 D 14 '70 *

RUNAWAY boys and girls
Case of the runaway teen-ager. B. Surface. il Read Digest 96:143-6 My '70
Runaways: a million bad trips; how youth agencies try to help. il Newsweek 76:67-8 O 26 '70

RUNCORN, S. K. and others
Magnetic properties of lunar samples. il Science 167:697-9 Ja 30 '70

RUNDLE, Frederick R.
Parking design with everyone in mind. il Am City 85:100+ Ja '70

RUNGE, Philipp Otto
Vision group from the backwater. R. Hughes. il Time 96:84-6 N 23 '70 *

RUNIA, Klaas
Evangelical responsibility in a secularized world. Chr Today 14:11-14 Je 19 '70
What do evangelicals believe about the Bible? Chr Today 15:3-6 D 4; 8-10 D 18 '70

RUNNING
And then there's Lester and Ester; California relays. P. Putnam. Sports Illus 32:50 Je 1 '70
Big man who wasn't there; M. McGrady and San Jose Invitational. P. Putnam. il por Sports Illus 32:72-3 My 11 '70
Brief, violent world of the 600; Millrose games. P. F. Putnam. il Sports Illus 32:54-6 F 9 '70
Fortune smiles on this cookie; Chi Cheng at Portland, Ore, Rose festival meet. A. Verschoth. il por Sports Illus 32:48+ Je 22 '70
It's only a transitory analogy; F. Shorter NCAA six-mile champion. S. Myslenski. por Sports Illus 33:73-4 D 7 '70
Loneliness etc; Boston marathon. il Newsweek 75:68 My 4 '70
Look who's back on the road again; J. Ryun. W. Bingham. il pors Sports Illus 33:60+ N 2 '70
Marathon and me; Boston marathon. H. Higdon. il Sports Illus 32:78-80+ Ap 6 '70
Monkey rides the easy runner; Villanova's M. Liquori. S. Myslenski. il pors Sports Illus 32:30-1+ Mr 2 '70
Neat feet with a Kenya beat; Philadelphia track classic. P. Putnam. il Sports Illus 32:18-19 F 2 '70
No! Not John Smith! national AAU track and field championship winner. P. Putnam. il pors Sports Illus 33:10-13 Jl 6 '70
Ralph the rapscallion. il por Time 95:65 F 23 '70
Revenge can be sour; M. Liquori vs K. Keino. S. Myslenski. il pors Sports Illus 32:22-5 My 25 '70
Runningest bloke alive. D. Levin. il Read Digest 96:196-200 Ja '70
Taiwan flash: Chi Cheng. il por Time 96:33 Jl 20 '70
These Mills bros. are in the record business, too; records in the 880- and 440-yard relays. P. Putnam. il pors Sports Illus 32:57-8 My 4 '70
Where are they now? the miracle at Iffley; R. Bannister. il pors Newsweek 75:13 My 11 '70

RUNNINGER, Jack
Making glasses fit your job. il Pop Sci 197:96+ Ag '70

RUNOFF
See also
Storm sewers

RUNWAYS, Airports. See Airports—Runways

RUPERT, Idaho
Town deals sternly with its own. L. Wainwright. il Life 69:40-2+ N 6 '70

RURAL life. See Country life; Farm life

RURAL planning
New life for the country; excerpts from report of Presidential task force, with editorial comment. il Farm J 94:41-3, 102 Ap '70
Up with the countryside. il Farm J 94:98 Mr '70
See also
Community development

RURAL population
Myth of urbanism. G. I. Swanson. Ed Digest 36:34-5 S '70

RURAL poverty
United States
See Poor—United States

RURAL recreation. See Recreation, Rural

RURAL schools
United States
Hitching up the small school districts; shared services. F. L. Heesacker. il Am Ed 6:18-21 Ap '70

RURAL-urban migration
Surprises from the census. il Bsns W p 16-17 Ag 8 '70

RUSH, Kenneth
New era in Europe and its meaning for America; address, October 20, 1970. Dept State Bul 63:691-7 D 7 '70

RUSH, Sue
Woodlawn: a photographic essay. M. A. Fitzharris. il Am Lib 1:892 O '70 *

RUSHER, William A.
Movies. Nat R 22:269 Mr 10 '70

RUSHMER, Robert F. and Huntsman, L. L.
Biomedical engineering. il Science 167:840-4 F 6 '70

RUSHMORE, Robert
Gounod and Georgina. pors Opera N 34:24-5 Ap 18 '70

RUSK, Dean
Honor without profit. Time 96:8 S 7 '70 *
LBJ's account of March, 1968. T. Hoopes. New Repub 162:17-19 Mr 14 '70 *

RUSKIN, Alicia E.
Art; poem. Horn Bk 46:419 Ag '70

RUSSCOL, Herbert
Music since Hiroshima: the electronic age begins. Am Scholar 39:289-93 Spr '70

RUSSEL, Patrick
New kind of French dressing. W. Johnson. il pors Sports Illus 32:12-17 F 2 '70

RUSSELL, Andy
Where the wild goose flies. il Outdoor Life 146:76-7+ Ag '70

RUSSELL, Bertrand Russell, 3d earl
On American violence. por Ramp Mag 8:54-7 Mr '70

about
Bertrand Russell, 1872-1970. por Newsweek 75:62-3 F 16 '70 *
Bertrand Russell (1872-1970): the constant critic. J. Walsh. Science 167:1110-11 F 20 '70 *
Bertrand Russell: the final passion. D. Horowitz. il pors Ramp Mag 8:36-43+ Ap '70 *
Bertrand Russell was a failure. Chr Cent 87:198 F 18 '70 *
High-minded and light-hearted. J. Bronowski. Nation 210:166 F 16 '70 *
Illustrious life of disagreements. il pors Life 68:30-3 F 13 '70
Last of the Victorian rebels. pors Time 95:22+ F 16 '70 *
Notes and comment. New Yorker 46:29 F 21 '70 *
Obituary
Chr Today 14:27-8 F 27 '70 *
Nat R 22:192 F 24 '70. P. P. Witonski *

RUSSELL, Charles Marion
Rebellious horse conquered. J. I. White. il Am West 7:18-19 Mr '70 *

RUSSELL, Charlie L.
Five on the black hand side. Criticism America 122:142 F 7 '70

RUSSELL, Dick
Cockfighting. Sports Illus 32:48-51 Mr 23 '70
Point and (sob) counterpoint. Sports Illus 32:42-3 Mr 2 '70

RUSSELL, Don
Cody, kings, & coronets. il pors Am West 7:4-10+ Jl '70

RUSSELL, Francis
Harding rides again. Nat R 22:213-14 F 24 '70
Movies. Nat R 22:797-8, 906+ Jl 28, Ag 25 '70
Sacco-Vanzetti: the end of the chapter. il Nat R 22:454-66 My 5 '70
Why Massachusetts loves the Kennedys. il Nat R 22:836-9 Ag 11 '70

RUSSELL, Franklin
Coming of the mist. il Audubon 72:16-25 N '70
Tree is living yet! il Audubon 72:64-9 Ja '70
Winter marsh. il Read Digest 96:135-41 F '70

RUSSELL, Helen Ross
Acrobats on the snow. Nat Parks 44:25 F '70
New Hampshire's eleven birches. il Nat Parks 44:23-6 Mr '70

RUSSELL, John, 1919-
Closing the gaps. il Art N 69:37-9 My '70
Francis Bacon at sixty. il por Art in Am 58:106-11 Ja '70
Introducing the National gallery of Switzerland. il Art N 69:50-1+ Ap '70
London. See issues of Art news
Mark Tobey in Basel. il Art in Am 58:134-6 N '70
New names in London: A to Z. il Art in Am 58:96-9 S '70

RUSSELL, John—*Continued*
Oxford line. il Art N 69:34-6+ O '70
Paris: unrolling the red carpet. il Art in Am 58:114-15 My '70
Richard Hamilton. il Art in Am 58:115-19 Mr '70
Rodin's adventures on Mt Venus. il Art N 69:36-7+ Mr '70
Royal academy Polonaise. il Art N 68:34-7 F '70
Seated one day at the I-Ching. il por Art N 68:52-3+ Ja '70
RUSSELL, Ken
Current cinema. P. Kael. New Yorker 46:97-101 Mr 28 '70 *
Futures, great. pors Vogue 156:92-3 Jl '70 *
RUSSELL, Lesiye
Four of a kind, yet different. pors Newsweek 75:72 Mr 23 '70 *
RUSSELL, Louis Byron, jr
Louis Russell: man with a stout heart. B. Lindeman. il pors Todays Health 48:32-4+ D '70 *
Teacher with a new heart. D. E. Steinmeier. il por Todays Ed 59:56 Mr '70 *
Transplant survival. il por Time 95:68+ Ap 27 '70 *
RUSSELL, Nina
Michael Bennett's Coco. il pors Dance Mag 44:72-8 F '70
Starbird. pors Dance Mag 44:20-1 O '70
RUSSELL, Richard Brevard
How Senate dean judges six presidents; excerpts from remarks, February 1970. il pors U S News 68:18 F 23 '70
RUSSELL, William F.
Success is a journey. il pors Sports Illus 32: 80-2+ Je 8 '70
RUSSELL Sage conference. See Educational conferences
RUSSELLVILLE, Ark.
Industry's hidden dividends. il Nations Bsns 54:82-6 O '70
RUSSETT, Bruce Martin
Boundaries of Europe. il America 122:554-5 My 23 '70
Indicators for America's linkages with the changing world environment. bibliog f il Ann Am Acad 388:82-96 Mr '70
Licensing: for cars and babies. Bul Atom Sci 26:15-19 N '70
NATO burden-sharing: its ups and downs. America 122:586-7 My 30 '70
Vietnam and restraints on aerial warfare. il Bul Atom Sci 26:9-12 Ja '70
What the hawks look to. il America 123:13-14 Jl 11 '70
RUSSIA
Russians are here! USSR photo '70. A. D. Coleman. il Pop Phot 66:88-91+ Je '70
Soviet Union, 1970; symposium. bibliog f Cur Hist 59:193-246 O '70
See also
Agricultural administration—Russia
Agriculture—Russia
Airlines—Russia
Airplanes, Military—Russia
Astronomical observatories—Russia
Automobile industry and trade—Russia
Automobile laws and regulations—Russia
Automobile touring—Russia
Ballet—Russia
Black Sea
Censorship—Russia
Children—Russia
Childrens literature—Russia
Civil rights—Russia
Civil rights organizations—Russia
Colleges and universities—Russia
Communism—Russia
Dniester River
Education—Russia—History
Foreign students in Russia
Foreign visitors in Russia
Geology—Russia
Government, Resistance to—Russia
Housing—Russia
Immigration and emigration—Russia
Investments, Foreign (by Russia)
Investments, Foreign (in Russia)
Jews in Russia
Kiev
Labor and laboring classes—Russia
Labor supply—Russia
Leningrad
Libraries—Russia
Medical service—Russia
Medicine—Russia
Merchant marine—Russia
Mines and mineral resources—Russia
Mongolia
Moving pictures—Russia
Music—Russia
Music, Popular (songs, etc.)—Russia
Nickel industry and trade—Russia
Opera—Russia

Performing arts—Russia
Periodicals—Russia
Physics—Russia
Political prisoners—Russia
Pollution—Russia
Proving grounds—Russia
Publishers and publishing—Russia
Science—Russia
Secret service—Russia
Space research—Russia
Sports—Russia
Technology—Russia
Tourist trade—Russia
Trials—Russia
United States—Economic relations—Russia
United States—Foreign relations—Russia
Water pollution—Russia
Water supply—Russia
Women—Russia
World war, 1939-1945—Russia

Air force
Russian and American pilots play chicken; maneuvers of the Sixth fleet in the Mediterranean. W. H. Honan. il N Y Times Mag p25-7+ N 22 '70

Antiquities
Russia looks to its past. J. Dornberg. il Newsweek 76:52+ S 14 '70

Armed forces
See also
Russia—Navy

Army
Life in the Soviet army. Time 95:46 My 4 '70

Census
Russia takes a census; what it shows. il U S News 68:50-1 My 18 '70

Commerce
Moscow's godsend; export of icons. il Newsweek 76:59-61 Ag 10 '70
Ostpolitik with pipes; trade deal between Soviet and West Germany. Time 95:29 F 16 '70
Rush for Soviet trade gets under way. il Bsns W p 102-4+ Ja 24 '70
Russia steps up sales to the West. il Bsns W p44 Ap 18 '70
Soviets plan Yak-40, Ka-26 sales drive in U.S, Canada. H. J. Coleman. Aviation W 92:22 My 4 '70
Soviets take a joint venture road west. il Bsns W p73-4 Je 6 '70

Cultural relations
See also
Exchange of persons programs

Defenses
Can U.S. avoid new arms race? il U S News 68:71 Mr 2 '70
Inside Russia: latest close-up; with report by K. Lachmann. il U S News 69:36-9 Jl 27 '70
Is U.S. forfeiting the arms race to Russia? il U S News 69:21-4 O 19 '70
Moscow's military machine: the best of everything. il Time 95:36-40+ My 4 '70
Russia gaining on U.S; latest authoritative report. il U S News 69:30-1 S 14 '70
Russia vs. U.S; coming crisis in arms; interview. J. S. Foster, jr. il pors U S News 69:24-6+ N 30 '70
Russians are eight feet tall, but so are we. letter to J. S. Foster, jr. J. L. Steele. il Time 96:11 Ag 3 '70; Reply. J. S. Foster, jr. 96:9 Ag 10 '70
See also
Aeronautics, Military—Russia
Atomic warfare—Defenses
Guided missiles—Defenses
Russia—Navy

Description and travel
Magnificence of Mother Russia; Kizhi Island. D. Thomas. il Holiday 48:64-5 Jl '70
Tchaikovsky's Russia: the lingering passion. S. Jacoby. il por Sat R 53:75-6+ Mr 14 '70
Through Russian snows with guide, group and camera. M. Leatherbee. il Life 68:46-9 Mr 20 '70
See also
Automobile touring—Russia

Economic conditions
B for Russia; a citizen's letter in response to L. Brezhnev's angry accusations. il por Time 95:29-30 F 23 '70
Rumors of a rift; power struggle within the Kremlin. il Time 95:24 Mr 23 '70
Russia: another setback in drive to catch U.S. il U S News 68:55-6 F 9 '70

RUSSIA—Economic conditions—*Continued*
Russia's trouble with reforms. il Time 95:
72 Ja 26 '70
Troubles and tremors. il por Newsweek 75:
33+ Ap 13 '70
See also
Communism—Russia
Labor and laboring classes—Russia

Economic policy

Birthday for Lenin and a boost for Brezhnev.
il por Time 95:30+ Ap 27 '70
Soviet dual economy. M. I. Goldman. bibliog
f Cur Hist 59:232-7 O '70
Those Soviet economic troubles are deep-
rooted. J. L. Schecter. il Fortune 81:105-6
My '70
See also
Communism—Russia

Economic relations

Russia: toward a global reach. il Time 96:29-
30 O 5 '70
See also
Russia—Commerce

India

Reporter at large; new steel plant in Bhilai,
with Soviet assistance. V. Mehta. New
Yorker 45:62+ F 14 '70

Foreign population

In the Soviet isolation ward; restrictions
against foreign residents. J. Dornberg. il
por Newsweek 76:25-6 D 28 '70

Foreign relations

Autumn chill. Newsweek 76:36+ O 26 '70
Can we trust the Kremlin? Two views. H. W.
Baldwin; H. H. Humphrey. Read Digest
96:84-92 Mr '70
Fourth dimension; U.S., China, Russia to
talk. il Newsweek 75:55 Ja 26 '70
Historian's reflections; address, March 18,
1970. R. Pipes. Vital Speeches 36:729-32 S
15 '70
If Russia would only return to God. D. Law-
rence. U S News 68:82 Mr 2 '70
Inside Russia: latest close-up; with report by
K. Lachmann. il U S News 69:36-9 Jl 27 '70
Mr Scripps said it; control of world petro-
leum; address, June 18, 1970. M. T. Hal-
bouty. Vital Speeches 36:688-92 S 1 '70
Out of all proportion; East-West relations. il
Time 96:21-2+ N 9 '70
Playing for high stakes; excerpts from
Khrushchev remembers. ed. and tr. by S.
Talbott. N. S. Khrushchev. il pors Life
69:16B-25+ D 18 '70
Question of intentions. il por Time 96:37-8 O 19
'70
Russia's foreign triumphs. H. Trewhitt; A.
de Borchgrave; J. Axelbank. il Newsweek
76:42-4 S 28 '70
Some concerns about national security; ad-
dress, June 5, 1970. I. C. Eaker. Vital
Speeches 36:701-4 S 1 '70
Soviet foreign policy: 1971. D. L. Flaherty.
America 124:6-7 Ja 9 '71
Soviet Mediterranean push deepens; with
editorial comment. E. H. Kolcum. il Avia-
tion W 92:9, 14-18 Mr 30 '70
Soviet Union, 1970; symposium. bibliog f
Cur Hist 59:193-246 O '70
See also
Cuban crisis. 1962
Military assistance, Russian
Russia—Treaties

Arab states

Into the breach? New Repub 163:5-6 S 19 '70
Middle East balance? But Russia's gain. W.
H. Dorsey, jr. New Repub 163:12-13 Ag 15
'70
See also
Israeli-Arab war, 1967- —Russian participa-
tion

Asia, Southeastern

Russians in Asia. W. Hangen. Atlan 225:30+
My '70
Soviet policies south and east of Suez. T. B.
Millar. For Affairs 49:70-80 O '70

China (People's Republic)

Bear & the dragon at war over science. J.
Critchlow. Commonweal 91:572-3 F 27 '70
Chinese factionalism and Sino-Soviet rela-
tions. U. Ra'anan. Cur Hist 59:134-41 S '70
Mideast outlook: why Russia shuns a show-
down; interview. F. D. Kohler. il por U S
News 68:25-6 Je 22 '70
Nyet means da? concerted Communist action
in Indochina. New Repub 162:9 Je 13 '70

Spoilers; Lenin's birthday celebration without
Chinese participation. il Newsweek 75:45
My 4 '70
Swapping slurs. Time 97:28 Ja 11 '71
War between Russia and China, by H. E.
Salisbury. Review
    Sat R 53:33-4 F 7 '70. T. W. Wolfe

Cuba

Meanwhile, in Cuba, increased Russian activ-
ity. Time 96:17 Jl 27 '70
New worry: Russian warships visit Cuba. il
U S News 68:81 My 25 '70

Czechoslovakia

Return engagement; visit by Brezhnev and
Kosygin. il Newsweek 75:60 My 18 '70
See also
Czechoslovakia—Occupation. 1968-

Egypt

Is the Middle East Russia's Vietnam? R.
Keatley. Cur 121:54-7 S '70
Russian influence in Egypt: a plus for the
U.S. at the moment. J. N. Wallace. U S
News 69:13 Ag 10 '70
Shoring up Sadat. il Time 96:45 D 7 '70

Europe, Eastern

Soviet aims in east Europe. V. V. Aspaturian.
bibliog f Cur Hist 59:206-11+ O '70

Europe, Western

Soviet Union and west Europe. K. L. London.
bibliog f Cur Hist 59:199-205+ O '70

Finland

Neutrality with a tilt. il por Time 96:19-20
Jl 27 '70

France

Equal time; G. Pompidou's tour. il por News-
week 76:54-5 O 19 '70
Staking a claim; G. Pompidou's visit. il
Newsweek 76:41-2 O 26 '70

Germany (Federal Republic)

Bonn's diplomatic drive to the East. il News-
week 75:45-6 Mr 16 '70
Mission to Moscow and Paris. Time 95:31 F
9 '70
Promises, promises. il Time 96:32 O 12 '70
West Germany turns to the East. M. M. Mes-
trovic. Commonweal 91:444-5 Ja 23 '70
See also
Berlin question, 1945-

Israel

Coming destruction of Israel, by M. S. Kaufmann. Review
    Sat R 53:30-1 S 5 '70. D. Kurzman

Latin America

Now Moscow finds a way to move into Latin
America. il U S News 69:25-6 O 19 '70

Middle East

Arab view; waiting for Russian rescue. J.
Law. il U S News 68:48 Mr 2 '70
Can Mideast war be averted? il U S News
69:11-13 Jl 27 '70
Is the Middle East Russia's Vietnam? R.
Keatley. Cur 121:54-7 S '70
Mideast outlook: why Russia shuns a show-
down; interview. F. D. Kohler. il por U S
News 68:25-6 Je 22 '70
Mid East: search for stability. il Time 96:
10-11+ O 5 '70
Mideast: Soviets test U.S. il U S News 69:39
S 14 '70
Russia moves deeper into Mideast conflict.
il U S News 68:54-5 Ap 6 '70
Russia's gamble in the Mideast. il U S News
69:15-16 Ag 3 '70
Russia's menacing new challenge in the
Middle East. J. Alsop. Read Digest 97:47-
51 Ag '70
Soviet interest in the Middle East. R. G.
Wesson. Cur Hist 59:212-19+ O '70
Soviet policies south and east of Suez. T. B.
Millar. For Affairs 49:70-80 O '70
Soviet role in the Middle East crisis. B.
Shwadran. Cur Hist 60:13-18+ Ja '71
Soviets testing. K. Crawford. Newsweek 76:
46 S 21 '70
Suez is the front to watch. G. W. Ball. il
N Y Times Mag p 10-11+ Je 28 '70
What is Russia up to? E. Crankshaw. Cur
121:52-4 S '70
See also
Israeli-Arab war, 1967- —Russian participa-
tion

Rumania

Reciprocal snubs. il Time 96:29 Jl 20 '70

RUSSIA—Foreign relations—*Continued*

United States

See United States—Foreign relations—Russia

History

Domestic policies of Peter III and his overthrow. M. Raeff. bibliog f Am Hist R 75: 1289-310 Je '70

See also

Russo-Japanese war, 1904-1905

Bibliography

Articles and other books received; comp. by R. V. Allen. See issues of American historical review

20th century

Lenin and education, science, culture; symposium. il por UNESCO Courier 23:4-21 Jl '70

Revolution, 1917-1921

Lenin: communism's charter myth; Time essay. por Time 95:34-5 Ap 27 '70

Lenin (1870-1970) N. D. Roodkowsky. por Cath World 211:107-11 Je '70

Lenin: his legacy. A. B. Ulam. For Affairs 48:460-70 Ap '70

Lenin's secret. J. Burnham. Nat R 22:21 Ja 13 '70

Industries

Consumers and the commissars. M. Miller. Nation 210:302-5 Mr 16 '70

See also

Automobile industry and trade—Russia

Book industries and trade—Russia

Industrial management and organization—Russia

Russia—Commerce

Intellectual life

Can Kremlin keep lid on dissenters? il U S News 69:44 N 30 '70

Crackdown; Pravda article attacks dissidents. Newsweek 76:24 D 28 '70

Discontent in Russia: threat to the Kremlin? interview. R. Conquest. por U S News 69:58-9 D 28 '70

Episode in the life of Solzhenitsyn; new Nobel laureate. J. Critchlow. por Commonweal 93:278-80 D 11 '70

Open conspiracy; presentation of Voices from the Russian underground by CBS news. R. L. Shayon. Sat R 53:62 Ag 22 '70

Poetry and power. S. Maloff. Commonweal 93: 352-4 Ja 8 '71

Rostropovich appeals for Solzhenitsyn; reprint of letter to four Russian periodicals. M. Rostropovich. Sat R 53:23 N 28 '70

Solzhenitsyn can still write, he just can't publish. N. Bethell. il N Y Times Mag p36-7+ Ap 12 '70

Televised *Samizdat*; CBS's filmed interviews of dissident intellectuals. por Newsweek 76:43 Ag 10 '70

See also

Russian literature

Military policy

See also

Preparedness, Military—Russia

Russia—Defenses

Moral conditions

Communist Kinseys; in Leningrad. il Time 95:29-30 Je 29 '70

Navy

After troop withdrawal: dependence on sea power; address, June 23, 1970. L. F. Chapman, jr. Vital Speeches 36:628-31 Ag 1 '70

As South Africa pushes for role in West's defense. il U S News 69:74-6 S 7 '70

Cutting a chain of links; Soviet naval presence in the Indian Ocean. il Time 97:41 Ja 4 '71

Full steam ahead. il Newsweek 76:57 S 14 '70

New worry: Russian warships visit Cuba. il U S News 68:81 My 25 '70

Reports: the Mediterranean. I. R. Levine. Atlan 225:4+ F '70

Russians in the Mediterranean. E. von Kuehnelt-Leddihn. Nat R 22:891 Ag 25 '70; Reply. I. C. Kidd, jr. 22:1192 N 17 '70

Russia's big red fleet. H. W. Baldwin. Read Digest 97:155-6+ N '70

Suez Canal: key to Soviet strategy in the Mideast? access to the Indian Ocean. il U S News 68:22-4 Je 22 '70

Top fleet in the Mediterranean: U.S. or Russian? il U S News 69:19 O 12 '70

Trapped ships in the Suez Canal. il U S News 69:49 Jl 20 '70

Submarine service

Another test for U.S: threat of a Russian sub base in Cuba; submarine base at Cienfuegos. il U S News 69:22-3 O 12 '70

Subs of Cienfuegos. il Time 96:20 D 28 '70

Politics and government

Are things really improving in the USSR? T. Szamuely. il Nat R 22:250-7 Mr 10 '70

Dissent and stability in the Soviet Union. D. T. Cattell. Cur Hist 59:220-5+ O '70

For sick Russia: a physicist's Rx; with excerpts from letter to Leonid Brezhnev. Newsweek 75:46 F 23 '70

Khrushchev remembers, by N. S. Khrushchev. Review

Sat R 53:21-3+ D 26 '70. H. Schwartz

Khrushchev remembers; excerpts ed. and tr. by S. Talbott. N. S. Khrushchev. il pors Life 69:32-9+ N 27; 48-54+ D 4; 54-58B+ D 11; 16B-25+ D 18 '70

Khrushchev: showdown in the Kremlin. il por Time 96:38+ D 14 '70

Letter from Dr Sakharov; democratization proposals to Russian leaders. A. D. Sakharov and others. il Newsweek 75:34-5 Ap 13 '70

Need for democratization; excerpts from letter. A. D. Sakharov and others. il Newsweek 75:34-5 Ap 13 '70

Protesters in the U.S.S.R. S. L. Levitsky. America 122:613 Je 6 '70

R for Russia; a citizen's letter in response to L. Brezhnev's angry accusations. il por Time 95:29-30 F 23 '70

Rumors of a rift; power struggle within the Kremlin. il Time 95:24 Mr 23 '70

Russia: conformity and dissent. T. Szamuely. Nat R 22:36-7 Ja 13 '70

Russia's bureaucracy, loaded with incompetents; interview. Z. Brzezinski. il pors U S News 68:71-2 Ap 20 '70

Soviet Union: leadership at the crossroads. il pors Time 95:33-6 My 4 '70

Stalin's successors. R. Conquest. For Affairs 48:509-24 Ap '70

See also

Communism—Russia

Communist party (Russia)

Population

Russia takes a census: what it shows. il U S News 68:50-1 My 18 '70

Religious institutions and affairs

Revival in Russia? D. Kucharsky. Chr Today 15:44 D 18 '70

Russian revolution yields bitter fruit. D. E. Kucharsky. Chr Today 14:42 Ap 24 '70

See also

Baptists in Russia

Orthodox Eastern church, Russian

Social conditions

Russia's drive for tourists with dollars. F. W. Rounds, jr. il U S News 68:76-9 Ja 19 '70

See also

Communism—Russia

Jews in Russia

Labor and laboring classes—Russia

Women—Russia

Social history

See also

Education—Russia—History

Social policy

Blueprint for a better system. Time 95:28 Ap 13 '70

Travel regulations

See Travel regulations

Treaties

Czechoslovakia

Soviet aims in east Europe. V. V. Aspaturian. bibliog f Cur Hist 59:206-11+ O '70

Germany (Federal Republic)

Bonn and Moscow: a treaty is signed. il Newsweek 76:28-9 Ag 24 '70

Bonn's mission to the Kremlin; renunciation of force treaty; with interview with W. Brandt, ed. by B. van Voorst and J. Moskau. il Newsweek 76:32-3+ Ag 10 '70

Brandt-Brezhnev pact. Nat R 22:878-80 Ag 25 '70

Europe: the end of World war II; Treaty of Moscow. il Time 96:17-18 Ag 17 '70

RUSSIA—Treaties—Germany (Federal Republic)
—Continued
Germany's opening to East: the meaning for
U.S. il U S News 69:37-8 Ag 24 '70
Giant step for Europe; renunciation of force
treaty with West Germany. il Newsweek 76:
44 Ag 17 '70
Good beginning. Nation 211:131-2 Ag 31 '70
New era in Europe. il Time 96:16-19 Ag 24 '70
Soviet-West German treaty; text. Cur Hist
59:233+ O '70
Stalin-Hitler pact, 1970 model? W. S.
Schlamm. Nat R 22:946-7 S 8 '70
Toward the era of negotiations; Soviet-Ger-
man Treaty of Moscow. il Time 96:14 Ag
17 '70
United States comments on signing of Fed-
eral German-U.S.S.R. treaty; statement,
August 12, 1970, with text of U.S. note.
W. P. Rogers. Dept State Bul 63:275-6
S 7 '70

Rumania
So far for so little; friendship treaty signed
with Rumania. il Newsweek 76:35-6 Jl 20 '70

United States
See United States—Treaties—Russia
RUSSIA and the United States
See also
United States—Foreign opinion—Russian
RUSSIA and the West. See World politics, 1945-
RUSSIA-United States air agreement. See Avia-
tion—International aspects
RUSSIAN architecture. See Architecture, Rus-
sian
RUSSIAN artificial satellites. See Artificial
satellites, Russian
RUSSIAN authors. See Authors, Russian
RUSSIAN cookery. See Cookery, Russian
RUSSIAN culture. See Russia—Intellectual life
life
RUSSIAN dancers. See Dancers
RUSSIAN economic assistance. See Economic
assistance, Russian
RUSSIAN humor. See Humor, Russian
RUSSIAN intellectuals. See Intellectuals
RUSSIAN Jews. See Jews in Russia
RUSSIAN literature
Fiction and policy: the hard-worked heroines.
S. Karlinsky. Nation 211:245-8 S 21 '70
See also
Authors, Russian
RUSSIAN military assistance. See Military
assistance, Russian
RUSSIAN opera. See Opera, Russian
RUSSIAN Orthodox church. See Orthodox
Eastern church, Russian
RUSSIAN Orthodox church in the United
States. See Orthodox Eastern church, Rus-
sian, in the United States
RUSSIAN poetry

Translations into English
Confessions of an old story-teller; tr. by L. G.
Leighton. K. I. Chukovskii. Horn Bk 46:577-
91 D '70 (to be cont)
Echo; tr. by M. Mesic. A. S. Pushkin. Poetry
116:343 Ag '70
How I love you; poem, tr. by the author.
V. Nabokov. New Yorker 46:44 My 23 '70
Under the skin of the Statue of Liberty; tr.
by A. C. Todd, jr. E. A. Evtushenko. il por
N Y Times Mag p34+ F 15 '70
While yet there is time, tr. by A. John-
stone. R. Rza. Mlle 70:53 Ja '70
RUSSIAN revolution. See Russia—History—
Revolution, 1917-1921
RUSSIAN soldiers. See Russia—Army
RUSSIAN space vehicles. See Space vehicles,
Russian
RUSSIAN spies. See Spies
RUSSIAN technical assistance. See Technical
assistance, Russian
RUSSIAN travel restrictions. See Travel re-
gulations
RUSSIAN underground literature. See Under-
ground literature
RUSSIANS in Egypt
Moscow-on-the-Nile. Time 95:31+ Je 22 '70
Russians in Egypt: important but invisible.
il U S News 69:20 Ag 24 '70
RUSSIANS in Germany
Memory's defense: the real life of Vladimir
Nabokov's Berlin. R. C. Williams. Yale R
60:241-50 D '70
RUSSO-JAPANESE war, 1904-1905
Germany and the Russo-Japanese war. J.
Steinberg. bibliog f Am Hist R 75:1965-86
D '70
RUST. See Corrosion and anticorrosives

RUSTIN, Bayard
Failure of black separatism. il Harper 240:
25-32+ Ja; 12+ Ap '70; Same abr. with title
What black revolution? Cur 116:19-33 Mr '70
Need for politics on the left. Cur 123:18-20
N '70
RUSTS (botany)
Bitter brew for the economy; coffee leaf rust.
il Bsns W p27 Jl 25 '70
New plant misery in Marin; hawthorn-ju-
niper rust. il Sunset 144:186-7 F '70
Self-inhibitor of bean rust uredospores;
methyl 3,4-dimethoxycinnamate. V. Macko
and others. bibliog Science 170:539-40 O 30
'70
Wheat leaf rust: control by 4-n-butyl-1,2,4-
triazole, a systemic fungicide. W. C. Von
Meyer and others. bibliog il Science 169:
997-8 S 4 '70
RUTGERS university, New Brunswick, N.J.
Academic reforms at Rutgers. Sch & Soc 98:
79-80 F '70

Livingston college
Experiment in relevance, urban studies pro-
gram at Livingston college. il Time 95:44+
Ap 20 '70
RUTH, Leo. See Farrell, E. jt. ed.
RUTHVEN, Grey
Postcard from Don Giovanni; poem. Poetry
117:190-2 D '70
Was Judas's cover blown? poem. Atlan 225:81
Je '70
RUTLEDGE, Anna Wells
Paintings in the council chamber of Charles-
ton's city hall. il Antiques 98:794-9 N '70
RUTLEDGE, Archibald
Encounters with diamondbacks. il Outdoor
Life 145:78-80+ Mr '70
Ways of the wild gobbler. il Field & S 75:84-
6+ Je '70
RUTROUGH, James E.
Building a new school plant? bibliog f Clear
House 44:378-80 F '70
RUTSALA, Vern
Unlocking the door; poem. Poetry 117:162-3
D '70
RYALL, G. F. T.
Nijinsky, the $5,440,000 wonder horse. il
Vogue 156:158-61+ D '70
RYAN, Anne
Place for everything. J. Ashbery. il por Art
N 69:32-3+ Mr '70 *
RYAN, B. F.
Mountain-building in the Mediterranean. Sci
N 98:316 O 17 '70 *
RYAN, Charlotte
Public aid for nonpublic schools? PTA votes
no. il PTA Mag 65:16-18 O '70
RYAN, Cornelius
Cornelius Ryan; interview, ed. by G. Henle.
il pors House B 112:56-9+ F '70
RYAN, Frank
Sports. R. Kahn. Esquire 74:78+ N '70 *
RYAN, John D.
Aerospace; address, September 22, 1970. Vi-
tal Speeches 37:50-2 N 1 '70
RYAN, John T.
(ed) See Roberts, T. Trying to be co-
responsible
RYAN, Kevin
From flood rescue work to snow removal.
il Am City 85:89-90 Ap '70
RYAN, Kevin A.
Schools in the 1990's. il por Sch & Soc 98:454+
D '70 *
RYAN, Michael F. and others
Flour beetles: responses to extracts of their
own pupae. bibliog il Science 170:178-80
O 9 '70
RYAN, Patricia
Earth as seen from Alaska. il por Sports
Illus 32:26-8+ My 4 '70
Golf (cont) Sports Illus 32:44-5 F 23 '70
Golf, ruffles and flourishes. il Sports Illus 32:
30-2+ Ap 13 '70
Gooey sickness smears the Gulf. il Sports
Illus 32:47-8+ Mr 30 '70
Gumshoe in a shell game. il Sports Illus
32:70-4+ Je 15 '70
In their cups. il Sports Illus 33:68-72+ N 2 '70
Little murder set to music. il pors Sports Illus
32:18-19 F 16 '70
Making of a quarterback 1970. il pors Sports
Illus 33:82-6+ D 7 '70
Man of arts and letters. il por Sports Illus
32:58-62+ Mr 16 '70
Merchandise is horses. il pors Sports Illus
32:34-6+ Mr 23 '70
River running out of Eden. il Sports Illus
32:86-9+ My 25 '70

RYAN, R. T. and Vonnegut, B.
Eyewitness tornado observations obtained with telephone and tape recorder. bibliog il Weatherwise 23:126-30+ Je '70
Miniature whirlwinds produced in the laboratory by high-voltage electrical discharges. bibliog il Science 168:1349-51 Je 12 '70

RYAN, Wayne L. and Sornson, H. C.
Glycine inhibition of asparaginase. bibliog il Science 167:1512-13 Mr 13 '70

RYAN, William Fitts
Excerpt from debate, September 17, 1969. Cong Digest 49:29 Ja '70
Excerpt from debate, May 28, 1970. Cong Digest 49:307+ D '70

RYCHETNIK, Joe
They bag live polar bears. il Nat Wildlife 8: 10-13 D '69
Whale horses of the North. il Nat Wildlife 8:44-6 Je '70

RYDER, Albert Pinkham
Student of the night. E. C. Goossen. por Vogue 156:96-7+ Ag 15 '70 *

RYDER, James A.
Shooting for the big time, and making it. il por Nations Bsns 58:102-3 Ja '70

RYDER, Mark
Goddard: genesis, transition and tradition. J. Anderson. il Dance Mag 44:36-40 S '70 *

RYDER-Great southern trucking merger. See Business consolidations and mergers

RYE, Robert O. See Schoen, R. jt. auth.

RYE
See also
Triticale

Hybrids

RYNNE, Xavier, pseud.
Papacy since Peter. il Horizon 12:60-7 Wint '70

RYSANEK, Leonie
Festive Fidelio for Beethoven's 200th. I. Kolodin. Sat R 54:16 Ja 2 '71 *

RYTHER, John H.
Photosynthesis and fish production in the sea. bibliog Science 166:72-6; 168:505 O 3 '69, Ap 24 '70

RYUKYU ISLANDS
See also
Okinawa

RYUN, Jim
Look who's back on the road again. W. Bingham. il pors Sports Illus 33:60+ N 2 '70 *

RZA, Rasul
While yet there is time; poem. tr. by A. Johnstone. Mlle 70:53 Ja '70

S

S and H green stamps. See Sperry and Hutchinson company

SABMIS (sea-based anti-ballistic missile system) See Guided missiles—Defenses

SAC. See United States—Air force—Strategic air command

SACB. See United States—Subversive activities control board

SAS. See Scandinavian airlines system

SAT (Scholastic aptitude test) See College entrance examination board—Scholastic aptitude test

SBA. See United States—Small business administration

SCAP (Supreme commander for allied powers) See Japan—History—Allied occupation, 1945-1952

SCLC. See Southern Christian leadership conference

SCM corporation
Take-over attempt was the turning point. E. E. Mead. il por Nations Bsns 58:106-7 Ja '70

SCS. See United States—Soil conservation service

SDR. See Special drawing rights

SDS. See Students for a democratic society (organization)

SEATO. See Southeast Asia treaty organization

SEC. See United States—Securities and exchange commission

SEED (special elementary education for the disadvantaged) See Socially handicapped children—Education

SEEK (search for education, elevation and knowledge) See New York (city). City university

SELA. See Southeastern library association

SEMA. See Specialty equipment manufacturers association

SERT (space electric rocket test) See Rocket engines—Testing

SFO. See San Francisco and Oakland helicopter airlines

SIECUS. See Sex information and education council of the United States

SIPC [(Securities investor protection corporation (proposed)] See Brokers—Insurance

SIPRI. See International institute for peace and conflict research

SIU. See Seafarers' international union of North America

SKAMP (station keeping and mobile platform) See Oceanographic buoys

SLA. See Special libraries association

SLAC (Stanford linear accelerator) See Accelerators (electrons, etc)

SLR cameras. See Single-lens reflex cameras

SLR lenses. See Lenses, Photographic

SMEDI (stillbirths, mummification, embryonic death, infertility) See Swine—Diseases and pests

SNAP (systems for nuclear auxiliary power) See Isotopic power generators

SODEPAX. See Joint committee on society, development and peace

SOHI. See Sponsors of open housing investment

SORC (Southern ocean racing conference) See Yacht racing

SPD (Social democratic party) See Political parties—Germany (Federal Republic)

SRI. See Stanford research institute

S. S. Kresge company. See Kresge, S. S, company

SST. See Airplanes, Supersonic

STAR (Self-testing and repairing computer) See Computers—Space flight use

STH. See Pituitary hormones

STOL airplanes. See Airplanes, Short take-off and landing

STP (drug) See Amphetamines

SU Tauri. See Stars, Variable

SUID (sudden unexplained infant deaths) See Infant mortality

SUNY (state university of New York) See New York (state). State university

SV40. See Simian viruses

SVM (student volunteer movement) See University Christian movement

SWLA. See Southwestern library association

SAAB (automobile) See Automobiles, Foreign

SAAL, Hubert
Burt Bacharach, the music man 1970. il pors Newsweek 75:50-4 Je 22 '70; Same abr. Read Digest 97:233-4+ O '70

SAAL, Rollene W.
Pick of the paperbacks. See issues of Saturday review

SAANICH INLET. See Georgia, Strait of

SAAR, John
For Cambodians, the war came like a thunderclap. il Life 69:26-30 Jl 10 '70
You can't just hand out orders. il pors Life 69:30-7 O 23 '70

SAARE, Arla
Fiction documentary; ed. by A. Rosenthal. il Film Q 23:28-33 Sum '70

SAARINEN, Aline B.
Liberated, all liberated. il pors Vogue 155:118 Je '70*

SAAVEDRA, Miguel de Cervantes. See Cervantes Saavedra, M. de

SABATINE, Onofrio
Good life on one acre, continued. il pors Org Gard & Farm 17:34-9 My '70

SABBATAI Zevi. See Shabthai Tsebi

SABBATHAIANS
Holiness of sin; tr. by H. Halkin. G. Scholem. Commentary 51:41-70 Ja '71

SABBATIANISM. See Sabbathaians

SABER saw blades. See Saws

SABIN, Walton B.
New bird ranges and environment. il Cons 24:22-3+ Je '70

SABINI, Robert C.
Cyprus plans ahead. T. J. Murray. Duns 96: 59-60 S '70 *

SABLE, Arnold P.
Whither public service in America? il Wilson Lib Bul 45:390-3 D '70

SABLEFISH
See also
Cookery—Fish

SABOTAGE
Airline risk insurance rates rise prohibitively
following bombings. Aviation W 92:234 Mr
9 '70
Closely watched planes. il Time 95:26 Mr 9
'70
Death in distant places; sabotage of Swiss
and Austrian planes. il Time 95:19 Mr 2 '70
Mid-air terrorists; bomb damage in Frank-
furt and Swissair wreckage. il Newsweek 75:
36 Mr 2 '70
New way to war on innocents; Swissair
crash. il Newsweek 75:32 Mr 9 '70
Rising terrorism in the airlanes: conference
to consider measures to deter. il U S News
68:10 Mr 9 '70
Saboteurs hit twice in one day; explosions on
Swissair and Austrian aircraft. R. F. Co-
burn. Aviation W 92:23-5 Mr 2 '70
Silence in Houston; bombed radio station.
il Time 96:70 O 26 '70
SABRE saws. See Saws
SACCHARIN. See Sugar substitutes
SACCHAROMYCES. See Yeasts
SACCO-Vanzetti case
Sacco-Vanzetti: the end of the chapter. F.
Russell. il Nat R 22:454-66 My 5 '70
SACHAROW, Alan
Mr Sacharow's funny science lab. M. Strumpf.
il pors Sci Digest 67:72-4 Ja '70
SACHS, David Peter
Work at your own risk. Sat R 53:64-5 Je 6
'70
SACHS, Joel
Hummel and George Thomson of Edinburgh.
bibliog f il pors Mus Q 56:270-87 Ap '70
SACHS, Nelly
Six poems: How long; Chorus of trees; Cho-
rus of invisible things; Chorus of the dead;
Birds; Chorus of the wanderers; tr. by R.
Mead and M. Mead. New Yorker 46:48-9 O
31 '70
SACK, E. A.
IC 12- to 6-V converter. il Electr World 83:
68-9 Ja '70
SACK, John
Corporate n*gg*r. il por Esquire 74:90-4+ Jl
'70
(ed) See Calley, W. L. jr. Confessions of
Lieutenant Calley
SACKSTEDER, Frederick H.
U.N. subcommittee discusses American Sam-
oa and Guam; statements, June 30 and
August 17, 1970. Dept State Bul 63:336-
40 S 21 '70
SACRAMENT of penance. See Confession
SACRAMENTO, Calif.

Art
Age of lucite dawns in Sacramento; sculp-
ture by B. Beasley. E. Hotaling. il pors
Art N 69:50-1+ My '70

Education
Common language; project SEED at Del
Paso Heights district. il por Newsweek 75:
57-8 My 4 '70
On making incorrigible youths corrigible;
the Sacramento opportunity school program. H. K. Parker. Ed Digest 35:22-4 My
'70

Foreign population
How Mexican-Americans view libraries. R.
P. Haro. bibliog il Wilson Lib Bul 44:736-42
Mr '70

Immigrants
See Sacramento—Foreign population

Streets
Subdrains can protect streets from seepage.
H. R. Cedergren. il Am City 85:99-100 O
'70
SACRAMENTS
Sacraments: an experiment in ecumenical
honesty, by E. J. Fiedler and R. B. Garri-
son. Review
Commonweal 91:518-19 F 6 '70. B. Cooke
Why of chrism. M. L. Tietjen. il Cath World
212:92-4 N '70
See also
Lords Supper
SACRED animals. See Animals in religion,
folklore, etc.
SACRED congregation for Catholic education.
See Congregation for Catholic education
SACRED music. See Church music
SACRIFICE, Human
Bog bodies of Denmark. il Chem 43:2 Jl '70
Most deadly games. J. H. Plumb. il Horizon
11:52-3 Aut '69
SAD Arthur; story. See Angell, R.

SADAT, Anwar
Egypt's course now: in Nasser footsteps;
with report by J. Law. il por U S News
69:41-2 O 19 '70 *
New leader and an uneasy truce. il por News-
week 76:53-4 O 19 '70 *
O Sadat, lead us to liberation. por Time 97:
26 Ja 18 '71 *
Sadat takes over in Egypt. Sr Schol 97:3-4
N 2 '70 *
Succession and stalemate. por Time 96:39 O
26 '70 *
Swift succession. il por Time 96:32+ O 19 '70 *
SADDLED prominent. See Caterpillars
SADDLER, Donald
Those were the days, my friends; interview,
ed. by O. Maynard. il pors Dance Mag 44:
38-42 D '70
SADE, Donatien Alphonse François, comte de
Never nothing. G. P. Elliott. il Harper 241:
90+ S '70 *
SADLER'S Wells ballet. See Royal ballet,
Great Britain
SADLER'S Wells opera
English Ring. E. Greenfield. Hi Fi 20:secII
27 Ag '70
Other side; production of The Valkyrie. T.
Heinitz. Sat R 53:70 Mr 28 '70
Report:
Presentation of The Valkyrie at the Lon-
don coliseum. F. G. Barker. Opera N 34:
30 Mr 28 '70
Production of The tales of Hoffman. F.
G. Barker. Opera N 35:28 O 31 '70
SADULE, Alfredo J.
In an Aztec market. il Américas 22:2-8 My '70
SAENREDAM, Pieter Janszoon
For the happy few, and gurus, too. M.
Conil-Lacoste. il Art N 69:34-5 Mr '70 *
SAFARI. See Hunting—Mozambique
SAFE boating week. See Special days, weeks,
months, etc.
SAFEGUARD missile defense system. See
Guided missiles—Defenses
SAFES
Make a picture safe. D. Shiner. il Design 72:
17-19 Wint '70
SAFETY, industrial. See Industrial safety
SAFETY belts
At last, an auto shoulder harness that's
easy to use. il Bet Hom & Gard 48:40 F '70
What every young mother should know about
auto safety; excerpt from Mothers and chil-
dren in cars. E. D. Fales, jr. il Redbook 135:
91+ S '70
SAFETY devices and measures
See also
Accidents
also subhead Safety devices and mea-
sures under various subjects, e.g. Aviation
—Safety devices and measures
SAFETY education
Accidents on purpose; Casualties union of
Great Britain. D. Lampe. il Todays Health
48:34-7 S '70
School liability and safety education. K. F.
Licht. Ed Digest 36:22-4 N '70
See also
Traffic safety—Study and teaching
SAFETY engineering
See also
Underwriters' laboratories, inc.
United States—National commission on prod-
uct safety
SAFETY eyeglasses. See Eyeglasses
SAFETY glass. See Glass, Safety
SAFETY inspection. See Automobiles—Inspec-
tion
SAFETY laws and legislation
See also
Industrial safety—Laws and regulations
SAFETY locks. See Automobile locks and
keys
SAFETY razor blades. See Razor blades
SAFETY switches. See Electric switches
SAFETYDAN escape cables. See Fire escapes,
Portable
SAFFRON
When money's no object. C. Claiborne. il N Y
Times Mag p36 Ja 3 '71
SAFIER, Daniel
Using an education model in a sheltered
workshop program. Ment Hy 54:140-3 Ja '70
SAFIRE, William
Cato v. Publius in the White House. il pors
Time 95:18 F 23 '70 *
SAFRAN, Nadav
Israeli politics since the 1967 war. Cur Hist
60:19-25+ Ja '71
SAG HARBOR, N.Y.
Reawakening: from gloom to gleam at Sag
Harbor. il House B 112:60-3 Jl '70

SAGAMORE Hill. See New York (state)—
Historic houses, etc.

SAGE, Tom, pseud.
Agog in Agaland. Nat R 22:312+ Mr '70

SAGER, Don
Comfortable pullman: administrative creativity on the siding. il Am Lib 1:587-92 Je '70

SAGINAW, Mich.
Plastic warning devices improve road safety. T. J. Brown. il Am City 85:130 Je '70

SAGOFF, Maurice
Shrinklits: Jane Eyre; Catcher in the rye; poems. Atlan 226:134 O '70

SAHAGÚN, Bernardino de
Florentine codex. H. R. Harvey. il Natur Hist 79:42-51+ D '70 *

SAHARA DESERT
Pancake oases in the desert. il UNESCO Courier 23:8-11 Je '70
Sahara grooves; this area once located at the South Pole. Sr Schol 96:15 My 11 '70
South Pole reaches the Sahara; report of symposium on the Saharan Ordovician ice age. R. W. Fairbridge. Science 168:878+ My 15 '70
This woman fights the Sahara with trees. J. Graham. il pors Sci Digest 69:20-3 Ja '71

SAID, Ahmed el ibn
Oh, that Ahmed. Poor, poor Ahmed. They're going to fry his black, skinny ass. D. Pearce. il Esquire 73:128-35+ Mr '70 *

SAID, Sami I. and Mutt, Viktor
Polypeptide with broad biological activity: isolation from small intestine. bibliog Science 169:1217-18 S 18 '70

SAIGON
Here's Vietnamization. D. E. Ronk. New Repub 162:13-14 Je 27 '70
My visit to Vietnam. N. Godfrey. il por Seventeen 29:134-5+ Je '70

Description
Saigon is bizarre center for come-and-visit war. H. Sutton. Holiday 47:12+ F '70

Economic conditions
Saigon's backfiring boom. il Time 95:31 Mr 23 '70

SAILBOAT building. See Boatbuilding
SAILBOAT masts. See Sails
SAILBOAT racing
Alone on a wide, wide sea; Sunday Times' round the world singlehanded race. E. F. Haylock. il Motor B 125:36-8+ Mr '70
Annapolis frostbiting. J. Duffet. il Motor B 126:43-5 N '70
Centerboards; excerpts from Winning. J. D. A. Oakeley. il por Yachting 128:68+ D '70
Memo from '69; ed. by F. Rohr, jr. il Motor B 125:25-40 Ja '70
On the heavy weather race; interview. ed. by E. Horan. D. Clark. il por Yachting 128:82+ Jl '70
One-design develops. B. Bentsen. il Yachting 128:70-1+ N '70
Plenty of Sunfish in the sea; Caribbean weekend. H. D. Whall. il Sports Illus 32:24-5 F 23 '70
They sail to win. See issues of Yachting to March 1970
When the wind comes up, the doctor is absent. H. D. Whall. il por Sports Illus 32:60+ Mr 30 '70
With the racing classes. ed. by E. Horan. See issues of Yachting
Yachting interviews; Brazil's Joerg Bruder. E. Horan. il por Yachting 127:61+ Jl '70
Yachting interviews, ed. by E. Horan. J. Dane, 3d il pors Yachting 127:68-9+ Je '70
You too can match race. B. Littell. il Yachting 128:73+ S '70
See also
Regattas
Yacht racing

Canada
Close-up on CORK; Canadian Olympic-training regatta Kingston. E. Horan. il Yachting 127:112-13+ Ja '70

SAILBOATS
After the sale. C. Lutz. il Yachting 127:114+ Ja '70
Beautiful Bonito. C. Conley. il Field & S 75:209 Je '70
Fireball: flat out for fun. G. Hall. il Yachting 129:72-3+ Ja '71
Flyingfish: fast but forgiving family sailing. G. Daniels. il Pop Sci 196:16 My '70
From the cockpit. R. N. Bavier, jr. See issues of Yachting
One-design sailboats. S. Etchells. il por Motor B 125:102-3 Ja '70

Sailboats. il Motor B 127:218-33 Ja '71
Sailboats and auxiliaries. il Motor B 125:214-19+ Ja '70
Sailing then and now; 1945-1970. B. Bavier. il Yachting 127:72-3+ Ja '70
Selecting sailboats for your camp. B. E. Fredrickson. il Camp Mag 42:18 Ap '70
Tempest stirs the Olympic teapot. G. M. Hall. il Motor B 125:16+ Mr '70
Unsinkable uniboat. H. Kelly. il Mech Illus 66:81-2+ Mr '70
Yachting interviews, ed. by E. Horan. J. Dane, 3d. il pors Yachting 127:68-9+ Je '70
Yachting's boat show in print. il Yachting 127:127-37+ Ja; 211-12+ F; 220+ Mr '70
See also
Catamarans
Masts and rigging
Trimarans

Design
Designs. B. D. Barker. 3d. See issues of Yachting
Introduction to sailboats. il Consumer Rep 35:280-6 My '70
New look in one-designs; Hoble Cat class. F. Miller. il Yachting 127:68-9+ Ap '70
Seven new answers to important design questions; questions and answers. S. Allan. il Motor B 127:60+ Ja '71
Shopping for the underwater boat. M. Frobisher. il Motor B 127:136-9 Ja '71
Some ripples over small sailboats; difficulty of righting self-rescuing boats. Consumer Rep 35:457-8 Ag '70
World of the flying pint; a guide to small racing-cruisers. T. Gibbs. il Motor B 125:50-3 Je '70
See also
Sloops—Design

Equipment
Gear and gadgets for the one-design. N. Freeman. il Yachting 127:64-5+ My '70
Transatlantic by Cal-20. G. Cadwalader. il Yachting 127:60-1+ Ap '70
Yachting's boat show. il Yachting 129:121-2+ Ja '71
Yachting's boat show in print. il Yachting 127:127-37+ Ja; 211-12+ F; 220+ Mr '70

Exhibitions
See Boats—Exhibitions

Leasing and renting
Profitable concession. C. J. Chamberlain. il Parks & Rec 5:29-30+ Mr '70

Materials
Revolution in sail; fiberglass auxiliaries. P. Smyth. il Motor B 126:37-41+ O '70

Specifications
What price sailing glory? T. Gibbs. il Motor B 126:52-3+ Ag '70

SAILFISH fishing
Sailfishing in southern waters. V. Evanoff. il Motor B 126:16+ N '70

SAILING
Bottoms up! excerpt from How to do practically anything. J. Goodman and A. Green. il Read Digest 97:173-6+ Ag '70
Hoist sail for family fun, and racing, too. B. Smith. il Pop Sci 196:84-5 F '70
Motor boating & sailing USA (title varies) See issues of Motor boating & sailing
Splash and go down. il Yachting 128:54-5 D '70
They sail to win. See issues of Yachting to March 1970
To the southern islands; yacht delivery service to the south. D. Humphreys. il Yachting 128:61+ O '70
See also
Navigation
Regattas
Sailboat racing
Sand yachts
Seamen

Study and teaching
Five-day switch; instruction at Annapolis sailing school. D. Heuchan. il Yachting 129:84+ Ja '71
How sails work. W. C. Ross. il Yachting 128:66-7+ Ag '70
Luff the outhaul sheet in the halyard! G. F. Hammond. il Motor B 126:42-5+ O '70
On using a land trainer. E. Horan. il Yachting 127:258 Ap '70

SAILING cruisers. See Cruisers (pleasure boats)
SAILING ships. See Sailing vessels

SAILING vessels
God bless our happy ship; aboard the three-masted bark St James, New York to San Francisco, 1900. R. A. Weinstein. il Am West 7:38-47 Mr '70
In the wake of Columbus: Windjammer cruises. S. Hart. il Travel 134:28-33+ O '70
Project Santa Maria. Travel 134:9 S '70
See also
Bounty (ship)
Sailboats
Yachts and yachting

Design
Round-the-world cruiser; cruising ketch. P. Smyth. il Motor B 126:48-51+ O '70
SAILING schools. See Sailing—Study and teaching
SAILING yachts. See Yachts and yachting
SAILOR circus, Sarasota, Fla. See Circus. Amateur
SAILORS. See Seamen
SAILPLANES. See Gliders (aeronautics)
SAILS
Guide to buying sails. H. Hild. il Motor B 127:142-3+ Ja '71
Improvements in the Moth rig. C. D. Gately. il por Yachting 128:37+ D '70
Saling on a bedsheet. M. E. Daniels. il Mech Illus 66:122-4 Mr '70
Sailmaker to the twelves; Ted Hood. B. D. Burrill. il por Yachting 128:56-7+ S '70

Maintenance and repair
Maintenance for sailors. il Motor B 125:79 Ap '70
SAINER, Arthur
Movies. Vogue 156:293 S 1 '70
SAINT ANDREWS ISLAND
Traveler's choice. F. R. Smith. Travel 133:10 Je '70
ST ANDREWS university. See Colleges and universities—Scotland
ST AUGUSTINE, Fla.

Description
Step by step through St Augustine. R. Deardorff. il Travel 134:40-5 D '70

Galleries and museums
See also
Lightner museum of hobbies
ST BONAVENTURE university, St Bonaventure, N.Y.
Bonny year for Buffalo Bob; undefeated team reaching for NCAA title. W. F. Reed. il por Sports Illus 32:16-17 Ja 19 '70
ST CHARLES COUNTY, Mo, library, St Charles
Bibliographies on social issues: Black manifesto. A. Webb. il Wilson Lib Bul 45:65-6 S '70
ST CROIX RIVER
St Croix: a national scenic riverway. U. W. Hella. il Parks & Rec 5:40-3 D '70
ST DENIS, Ruth
Arrival of Miss Ruth. W. Pugsley. il por Dance Mag 44:20-1+ D '70 *
SAINT EXUPÉRY, Antoine de
Antoine de Saint-Exupéry, by C. Cate. Review
Commonweal 93:281-2 D 11 '70. D. L. Schalk *
SAINT-GAUDENS, Augustus
Saint-Gaudens and the gilded era, by L. H. Tharp. Review
Sat R il por 53:38-9 Ja 17 '70 E. Stevens
ST GEORGE, George
1991. il Look 34:54-8+ Jl 14 '70
ST GERMAIN, Robert H. See Van Delinder, R. jr. jt. auth.
ST HELENA (island)
Edmond Halley at St Helena. J. Ashbrook. bibliog il por Sky & Tel 40:86-7 Ag '70
ST JOHN, Judith
Mrs Trimmer, guardian of education. il por Horn Bk 46:20-5 F '70
ST JOHN of Jerusalem, Order of. See Malta, Knights of
ST JOHN ISLAND
See also
Gardens—St John Island
ST JOHN'S university, Collegeville, Minn.
St John's: four years after. J. A. Scimecca; discussion. Commonweal 91:419+, 523+ Ja 16. F 13 '70
ST JOSEPH, Mo.
Fire-police communications. B. H. Jones. il Am City 85:91+ Jl '70
Troubling taste of change; John E. Fleck, police detective. D. R. Maxey. il Look 34: 70-3 Ja 13 '70

ST JOSEPH lead company
Lip service? il Forbes 105:49 Mr 1 '70
ST LAURENT, Yves Mathieu
All about Yves. H. Lawrenson. por Esquire 73:108-9+ Je '70 *
SAINT-LAURENT-DU-PONT fire. See Fires
ST LAWRENCE RIVER
See also
Nuns' Island
ST LAWRENCE SEAWAY
Dollar dilemma on the St Lawrence. il Bsns W p73+ My 23 '70
St Lawrence blues. il Newsweek 75:82+ Mr 16 '70
Seaway after ten years: busy but burdened with debt. il U S News 68:52-4 Je 1 '70
ST LEO, Fla.
This mayor is Sister. Am City 85:51 D '70
ST LOUIS
Air pollution
Rain by inadvertence. il Sci N 97:390 Ap 18 '70
Bridges
Ponte Vecchio for St Louis. B. Thorne. il Arch Forum 132:60-1 Ja '70
City planning
Mayor's tilt with the windmills; effort to salvage Spanish Pavilion. il Bsns W p 105 Ja 31 '70
Meet me in St Louis; riverfront land. il Newsweek 75:115 Ap 20 '70
Crime
Mayor, the Mob and the lawyer; two-faced crime fight in St Louis. D. Walsh. il pors Life 68:24-31 My 29 '70
Finance
Federal revenue sharing and the cities; address, October 13, 1970. A. J. Cervantes. Vital Speeches 37:33-8 N 15 '70
Hotels, restaurants, etc.
Movable feast. R. A. De Groot. Esquire 73: 36+ Je '70
Monuments, statues, etc.
Trees for the Arch. il Nat Wildlife 8:56-7 D '69
Stores
Ponte Vecchio for St Louis. B. Thorne. il Arch Forum 132:60-1 Ja '70
ST LOUIS Blues (hockey team) See Hockey teams
ST LOUIS COUNTY, Mo.
Education
Library goes to camp; Lindbergh school district. M. Petter and L. Bloomquist. Am Lib 1:166-8 F '70
ST LOUIS symphony orchestra
Music to my ears; performance in Carnegie Hall. I. Kolodin. il Sat R 53:96-7 Mr 14 '70
ST LOUIS university, St Louis, Mo.
School of divinity
School of divinity; St Louis university. A. L. Pierovich. Cath World 210:253-5 Mr '70
ST LUCIA (island)
See also
Hospitals—St Lucia (island)
ST MARGARET'S church, London. See London—Churches
ST MARK'S hospital, Salt Lake City. See Salt Lake City—Hospitals
ST MARTIN (island)
Exotic dining in St Maarten. M. Woodward. il Travel 134:23 Ag '70
ST PATRICK saves the day: drama. See DuBois, G.
ST PATRICK'S cathedral. See New York (city) —St Patrick's cathedral
ST PATRICK'S day
Drama
St Patrick saves the day. G. DuBois. Plays 29:53-62 Mr '70
ST PATRICK'S day parades. See Parades
ST PAUL
Twin Cities. J. F. Hart and R. B. Adams. bibliog il Focus 20:1-7 F '70
City planning
See also
Twin Cities metropolitan council
Education
Talent runs free at the Twin Cities institute. C. Watson. il Am Ed 6:3-6 O '70

ST PAUL—*Continued*

Lighting

Dome lighting turns night into day; Minnesota state capitol building. Am City 85: 142 S '70

Music

Report:
Carmen. P. Gainsley. Opera N 34:26 My 16 '70
Tosca. P. Gainsley. Opera N 34:33-4 F 7 '70
See also
St Paul civic opera association

Transit systems

People look at transit. H. R. Orth and W. Cherwony. il Am City 85:126+ Je '70

ST PAUL civic opera association
·Report:
Menotti's Medium and Telephone, and Antheil's Venus in Africa. P. Gainsley. il Opera N 35:31 D 12 '70
ST PAUL'S school, Concord, N.H. See Private schools
ST PETERSBURG, Fla.
Bells are ringing in St Petersburg. il Am City 85:130 Mr '70
God's waiting room. il Newsweek 75:112+ Ap 20 '70
ST PETERSBURG, Russia. See Leningrad
SAINT PIERRE and Miquelon (islands)
Contented colonies. R. Harrington. il Travel 134:60-3 Jl '70
St Pierre by air. S. Wilkinson. il Flying 87: 50-$ O '70
ST THOMAS ISLAND
Sunny and *cher.* H. Sutton. il Sat R 53:42-4 Mr 7 '70
See also
Gardens—Saint Thomas Island
ST VINCENT (island)
See also
Bequia (island)
ST VINCENT archabbey and college, Latrobe, Pa.
Architectural analogy; science center. R. Jensen. il Arch Rec 147:125-30 My '70
SAINTS
What's with the saints? V. P. McCorry. America 123:360-inside back cover O 31 '70
See also
Canonization
Doctors of the church
Herman of Alaska, Saint
Martyrs
SAIONJI, Kinkazu, prince
Noble Bolshevik. por Newsweek 76:48 S 7 '70 *
SAITO, Fred
Field day for 60,000 cameras. il Mod Phot 34:73-9 Ag '70
SAJDERA, Stanley W. See Gregory, J. D. jt. auth.
SAKHAROV, Andrei Dmitrievich
—and others
Letter from Dr Sakharov. il Newsweek 75: 34-5 Ap 13 '70
Need for democratization; excerpts from letter. Sat R 53:26-7 Je 6 '70; Same abr. with title Letter from Dr Sakharov. il Newsweek 75:34-5 Ap 13 '70
about
Blueprint for a better system. Time 95:28 Ap 13 '70 *
For sick Russia: a physicist's Rx. Newsweek 75:46 F 23 '70 *
SAKKA, Keisei
Beethoven in retrospect; Japan. Sat R 53:63-4 N 28 '70
SAKOL, Jeannie
Grit and grace of Johnny Cash. por McCalls 97:28+ Jl '70
Pussycat league. il McCalls 97:78-9+ F '70
Remarkable woman: Margaret Mead. il por McCalls 97:80-1+ Je '70
SAKOMIZU, Hisatsune
Where are they now? il pors Newsweek 76:8 Ag 24 '70 *
SAKOWITZ store. See Houston. Tex.—Stores
SAKUTARO, Hagiwara
Heavenly suicide by hanging; Third patient; Shining hand; Autumn cricket; Small town geisha; Water rite; poems, tr. by G. Wilson. Yale R 59:391-5 Mr '70
Zoo; Shadow of my former self; Hagitei inn; Early summer; poems, tr. by G. Wilson. Poetry 116:370-3 Ag '70
SALAD greens. See Greens, Edible
SALADS
Celery root, good cook's salad discovery. il Sunset 145:159 O '70

Cool salad has fruits, vegetables. il Sunset 144:171 Je '70
Fast and fancy main dish salads. il Bet Hom & Gard 48:65-6 Je '70
Fast or fancy spring vegetable salads. il Bet Hom & Gard 48:85-6 O '70
Feast of salads. il Ebony 25:150+ Je '70
Fix-ahead salads. il Farm J 94:82 Ap '70
For big groups, a big salad. Sunset 144:188-9 Mr '70
Fresh Dungeness is what makes these icy salads. il Sunset 145:108 D '70
Garden salad you can toss or mold. il McCalls 97:104 Je '70
Hostess-saving molded salads. il Bet Hom & Gard 48:121 Mr '70
How to make Chinese chicken salad. il Sunset 145:206 N '70
Jacques Pépin's salade de fruits rafraîchis. il House B 112:72-3 Jl '70
Juicy citrus with crisp apples. Sunset 144: 101 Ja '70
Salad mold with a curry flavor. il Sunset 144:183 Je '70
Salads A to Z; with recipes. D. Eby and J. McCloskey. il Bet Hom & Gard 48:76-83+ My '70
Salads or desserts. E. W. Manning. il Farm J 94:36-7 Ag '70
Salads that bear fruit. M. Happel. il Ladies Home J 87:76-7+ Je '70
Sea and garden meet; seafood salad. C. Claiborne. il N Y Times Mag p58 Ag 16 '70
Shimmering salads. il Bet Hom & Gard 48: 66-7 Ag '70
Spinach salad with a flourish. il Sunset 145: 136 O '70
Summer squash make cooling salad shells. il Sunset 145:158 S '70
Susan, our beginning cook, learns how to toss a good salad. il Good H 171:120 Jl '70
These salads start with beans. il Sunset 145: 162 D '70
This potato salad travels well. Sunset 144: 154 Je '70
Three salads at once, in one summer buffet. il Sunset 144:140-1 Je '70
Toss a mean salad. il Bet Hom & Gard 48:32 Mr '70
Turks have a different and delicious way with eggplant. il Sunset 145:150 D '70
What cucumbers are is adaptable. il Sunset 145:108 Ag '70
SALAM, Abdus
Memorandum on a world university. Bul Atom Sci 26:38-9 Mr '70
SALAMANCA
Salamanca. J. Morris. il Holiday 47:40-1+ Ja '70
SALAMANDERS
Homing behavior, orientation, and home range of salamanders tagged with tantalum-182. D. M. Madison and C. R. Shoop. bibliog il Science 168:1484-7 Je 19 '70
See also
Newts
SALAMON, Marlene
Who am I? poem. Eng J 59:409 Mr '70
SALANDINI, Victor
Breakthrough in Coachella Valley. America 122:470-1 My 2 '70
Lessons of the grape strike. America 123: 285-7 O 17 '70
SALARIES
See also
Non-wage payments
also subhead Salaries, allowances, etc. under various subjects, e.g. Office workers —Salaries, allowances, etc.
SALAZAR, António de Oliveira
Thaw in Portugal. D. L. Wheeler. For Affairs 48:769-81 Jl '70 *
Volunteer of solitude. il Time 96:25 Ag 10 '70 *
SALAZAR, Ruben
Chicano columnist. il por Newsweek 75:61 Je 22 '70 *
Death in the barrio. il Newsweek 76:35 S 14 '70 *
Killing of Ruben Salazar: nothing has really changed in the barrio. D. F. Gomez. Chr Cent 88:49-52 Ja 13 '71 *
Overkill at the Silver dollar. E. H. Lopez. il Nation 211:365-8 O 19 '70
Victim. Nation 211:197 S 14 '70 *
SALE, J. Kirk
Ted Gold: education for violence. Nation 210: 423-9, 514+ Ap 13, My 4 '70
SALEH, Dennis
Crabs; Unconscious; poems. Poetry 116:172-3 Je '70
SALEM, Mass.

History

Cargoes of splendor. V. D. Hahn and M. Evans. il Am Home 74:46+ Ja '71

SALEM, N.C. See Winston-Salem, N.C.
SALEM church dam (proposed) See Dams
SALEM witchcraft. See Witchcraft
SALES, Grover
　Herb Caen: his power is awesome. il Holiday 47:76-7+ Mr '70
SALES, Leon
　Microstripline parameters. il Electr World 83:66-7 Ja '70
SALES, Art. See Art sales
SALES, Bargain. See Bargain sales
SALES clerks. See Clerks (retail trade)
SALES promotion
　Push money=spiff=bribe. Consumer Rep 36: 24 Ja '71
　　See also
　Advertising—Prize contests
　Premiums
　Trading stamps
SALES tax
　More city sales taxes. il Am City 85:26 S '70
　　See also
　Value added tax
SALES techniques. See Salesmen and salesmanship
SALESMEN and salesmanship
　Birth of a salesman. il Nations Bsns 58:31-4 Ag '70
　Career in selling for you? D. Demske. il Mech Illus 66:45-7+ N '70
　Don't sell the buyer short; interview J. A. Howard. por Nations Bsns 58:34-5 Ag '70
　Who's who among the travelers; publishers' representatives. Pub W 197:86-103 F 9 '70
　　See also
　Automobile salesmen
　Canvassing
　Clerks (retail trade)
　Sales promotion
SALINA, Kan.
　　　　　Education
　Nostalgic reunion in Salina, Kansas. W. Friedman. il Time 96:14 Jl 13 '70
SALINE water
　　See also
　Sea water
SALINE water conversion plants
　Dry lands and desalted water. G. Young. bibliog il Science 167:339-43 Ja 23 '70; Same abr. Todays Ed 59:28-30 My '70; Reply. R. D. Gerard. Science 167:1564-5 Mr 20 '70
SALINGER, Pierre
　Gramco: the second domino. por Time 96: 79-80 O 19 '70 *
SALISBURY, Francis Markall, abp of. See Markall, F.
SALK, Jonas Edward
　Newsmakers. il pors Newsweek 75:53 Je 29 '70 *
SALLOCH, Roger
　Dissent of Roger Garaudy. New Repub 162: 17-19 Mr 7 '70
SALM, Walter G.
　Build your own blackout light. il Pop Mech 134:158-9+ N '70
　CATV is coming to your town. il Pop Sci 196:88-9+ Je '70
　For more recording fun, add a middle mike. il Pop Mech 134:130-1 Ag '70
　How to keep your tape recorder humming happily. il Pop Mech 133:160-3+ Ap '70
　New color TV cameras. il Radio-Electr 41: 30-2+ Ag '70
　New four-channel stereo techniques. il Radio-Electr 41:33-5+ O '70
　Newest improvement in hi-fi listening: now it's 4-channel stereo! il Pop Mech 133:134-8 My '70
　Public-address do's & dont's. il Radio-Electr 41:33-5 Jl '70
　Switch your stereo speakers with this self-balancing control. il Pop Mech 134:140-3 S '70
　Which mikes for what job? il Pop Mech 133: 92:5+ Je '70
SALMON
　Coho marking. Cons 25:38 Ag '70
　Danes scourge the seas; decimating migratory Atlantic salmon. G. Gammon. il Sports Illus 31:28-30+ D 15 '69
　Death by degrees for salmon; thermal pollution special studies at Bonneville. M. Davenport. Field & S 74:76-7 Ap '70
　Last chance for Atlantic salmon? A. Grahame. il Outdoor Life 145:41-3+ Je '70
　Salmon catchers make a splash; proposed ban on high-seas fishing. il Bsns W p50+ F 7 '70
　Salmon situation; excerpts from Man and the salmon. A. Netboy. il Am For 76:24-7+ Mr '70

Threat to salmon fishing; recommended ban on high seas fishing. H. J. Barnes. il Sci N 97:78 Ja 17 '70
Too much for the Columbia River salmon. E. Chaney. il Nat Wildlife 8:18-21 Ap '70
What's happening to Atlantic salmon? G. Beall. il Field & S 75:36-7+ Jl '70
　　See also
Cookery—Fish
SALMON, Cured. See Fishery products—Preservation
SALMON fishing
　Gold-plated salmon: Norway's Malangsfoss. J. A. Maxtone-Graham. il Travel & Camera 33:64+ F '70
　Kings come to the Smith. B. Nauheim. il pors Outdoor Life 146:90-3+ O '70
　Lapland salmon, at bargain prices. A. J. McClane. il Field & S 74:58-9+ F '70
　Last chance for Atlantic salmon? A. Grahame. il Outdoor Life 145:41-3+ Je '70
　Magnum salmon fishing. S. Stair. il Field & S 74:74-5+ Ap '70
　March with the kings. M. Hayden. il Outdoor Life 145:52-5+ Mr '70
　Salmon by wire. W. Davis. il Mech Illus 66: 34+ Je '70
　Salmon fishing in Scotland. E. Nabb. il Motor B 125:136-8 Je '70
　Salmon potpourri. A. J. McClane. il Field & S 75:88-90 D '70
　Sex life of the salmon is brief and terrible. W. Humphrey. il Esquire 73:123-8+ Je '70
　Ten-second salmon. N. Karas. il Field & S 74:66-7+ F '70
　Truth about New Brunswick salmon. L. J. Bashline. il Field & S 75:34-5+ Jl '70
　　See also
Fisheries—Greenland
SALMON RIVER
　River of no return. S. F. Arno. il Nat Parks 44:18-23 Ja '70
　White-water adventure on wild rivers of Idaho. J. Craighead and F. Craighead, jr. il pors Nat Geog 137:212-39 F '70
SALMON roe. See Caviar
SALMONELLA. See Bacteria, Pathogenic
SALOMON brothers and Hutzler (firm)
　Living it up in a Salomon-sized world. C. J. Loomis. il Fortune 81:72-5+ Ap '70
　Success of Salomon. Time 96:65-6 Ag 3 '70
SALPINGECTOMY. See Sterilization, Sexual
SALT
　Salt of the earth. il Chem 43:4-5 Je '70
SALT and pepper shakers
　Glass salt shakers: twelve rarities. A. G. Peterson. il(p 1) Hobbies 74:114-15+ Ja '70
SALT free diet. See Diet in disease
SALT LAKE. See Great Salt Lake
SALT LAKE CITY
　　　　　Education
　How to raise reading scores; Exemplary center for reading instruction. L. K. Chaffin. il Am Ed 6:12-15 D '70
　　　　　Hospitals
　Systems-analysis approach to hospital design; St Mark's hospital. il Arch Rec 147:112-15 Mr '70
SALT marshes
　Day the sea ran out of flounder; Hammonassett state park. S. W. Hitchcock. por(p4) Natur Hist 79:28-31+ Mr '70
　Disappearing beauty of the salt marsh; with photographs by J. Baldwin. J. Shepherd. il Look 34:24-31 Ap 21 '70
SALT rising bread. See Bread
SALT spreaders
　Easy-switch spreader removal; Milwaukee. il Am City 85:74-5 Ja '70
　Traction salt spreader serves high-accident areas; Chicago. il Am City 85:44 O '70
SALT storage
　Beehives protect snow-removal salt and prevent water pollution; Ontario. J. R. Fitzpatrick. il Am City 85:81-3 S '70
SALT tolerance of plants. See Plants, Effect of salt on
SALT water fishing
　Big fish from small boats. C. R. Meyer. il Motor B 125:68-9+ F '70
　Editorial; future of sport fishing off U.S. coastlines. B. Brister. Field & S 75:8 D '70
　Great red fleet. il Newsweek 75:73-4 F 9 '70
　Guru of Gulf Coast fishing; oceanographer N. G. Vick. D. Levin. il por Sports Illus 31: 66+ D 15 '69
　How was fishing last year? V. Evanoff. il Motor B 125:22+ F '70
　Long Island's artificial fishing reefs. C. S. Zawacki. il Cons 24:18-21 Ag '69
　Mother was a home at sea; fishing trip off coast of Florida. il Sports Illus 32:26-31 F 2 '70

SALT water fishing—*Continued*
Prince Albert's way of catching squid. S. Schlee. il por Natur Hist 79:20+ F '70
Salt water. G. Heinold. See issues of Outdoor life
Secret of offshore success. W. Davis. il Mech Illus 66:46+ O '70
Surf fishing; Michigan's newest sport. H. F. Zeman. il Field & S 74:150-3+ F '70
Tarpon, snook, and bones. J. Brooks. il Outdoor Life 146:66-7+ S '70
Ultralight in salt water. A. J. McClane. il Field & S 74:100-3+ Mr '70
With the sport fishermen. F. T. Moss. See issues of Yachting
See also
Cod fishing
Bass fishing
Bonefish fishing
Pollack fishing
Sailfish fishing
Tarpon fishing
Tuna fishing

SALTON, Gerard
Automatic text analysis. bibliog il Science 168:335-43 Ap 17 '70
On the development of libraries and information centers. bibliog il por Library J 95:3433-42 O 15 '70

SALTS, Marine. See Sea water

SALTZMAN, Murray
Will Judaism survive the seventies? il Chr Cent 87:263-6 Mr 4 '70

SALUTE to a small spender; story. See Shyer, M. F.

SALVAGE (airplanes)
Return of the Rockford. R. E. Carlin. il por Flying 87:52-7 N '70

SALVAGE (ships)
Defusing Canada's sunken time bomb; tanker Arrow. J. F. Pearson and J. Albino. il Pop Mech 134:116-20 N '70
Mysterious ships of Lake Nemi. L. S. De Camp. il Sci Digest 67:68-72 Je '70
Will the Titanic float again? il Sci Digest 69:37-8 Ja '71

SALVAGE (waste)
See also
Automobiles—Wrecking
Refuse, Utilization of
Scrap metal

SALVAT publishers. See Publishers and publishing—Spain

SALVATION
Death and transfiguration. M. O. Lee. il Opera N 34:24-5 Mr 28 '70
Evolution, revolution, or victory. H. O. J. Brown. Chr Today 14:4-6 Ap 10 '70
SALVATION: musical comedy. See Musical comedies, revues, etc.—Criticisms, plots, etc.

SALVATION army
Army to be saved; Great Britain and the U.S. il por Time 97:55 Ja 4 '71
Biting the hand that feeds you. Trans-Action 7:4 Ap '70
Breaking ranks. J. D. Douglas. Chr Today 15:58 N 6 '70
Crisis for Salvationists. Chr Cent 87:114 S 23 '70
Salvation army officer ousted in dispute over book; Secular evangelism. Chr Cent 87:1312 N 4 '70
Salvation by censorship? Mayor Brown removal. T. Beeson. Chr Cent 87:812 Jl 1 '70
Sex in the army. Chr Today 15:40-1 O 9 '70

SALVATORI, Henry
Unseen foe. pors Forbes 106:22 Ag 15 '70 *

SALZBURG
Music
Report:
Herbert von Karajan's Götterdämmerung. J. H. Sutcliffe. il Opera N 34:27 My 16 '70

SALZBURG festival
Otello: a new Karajan spectacular. G. Movshon. il Hi Fi 20:MA24-7 N '70
Report:
Productions of Mozart's Entführung aus dem serail; Beethoven's Fidelio and Verdi's Otello. J. H. Sutcliffe. il Opera N 35:25-6 O 10 '70
Those were the days. G. Breuer. il Opera N 34:6-11 My 16 '70

SALZMAN, Eric
Multi-media in South America. il Hi Fi 20:secII 10-11+ Ag '70
Theater of Igor Stravinsky. il por Opera N 35:8-15 O 10 '70

SALZMAN, Norman P. See Schneider, E. L. jt. auth.

SAMANIEGO, Manuel Bernardo Aguirre. See Aguirre Samaniego, M. B.

SAMARAS, Lucas
Autopolaroid; photographs, with interview. Art in Am 58:66-83 N '70
about
Nowhere to sit down. R. Hughes. il por Time 96:62 N 9 '70 *

SAMARIUM alloys
Permanent magnets. J. J. Becker. il Sci Am 223:92-100 bibliog(p 140) D '70

SAMEK, Karl A.
New city hall, old site. il Am City 85:90+ My '70

SAMLOFF, I. Michael, and Townes, P. L.
Pepsinogens: genetic polymorphism in man. bibliog il Science 168:144-5 Ap 3 '70

SAMMET, Rolf
Hoechst: tomorrow the world? J. Ross-Skinner. por Duns 95:71-2+ Je '70 *

SAMMIS, H. F.
Vote counts by microwave. il Am City 85:76+ Jl '70

SAMMONS, Jeffrey L.
Notes on the germanization of American youth. Yale R 59:342-56 Mr '70; Same abr. with title American youth and the Germans. Cur 119:10-14 Je '70

SAMOA, AMERICAN. See American Samoa

SAMPLING
See also
Air sampling

SAMPSON, Margaret
Africa in medieval Spanish literature: its appearance in el Caballero Cifar. bibliog il Negro Hist Bul 32:14-19 D '69

SAMPSON, Ronald V.
Power: the enshrined heresy. Nation 212:14-20 Ja 4 '71

SAMS, George, Jr
New Haven eight. Time 96:16 Ag 31 '70

SAMSON, Jack
Al Rockwell: industrialist/sportsman/conservationist. il por Field & S 74:50-2+ Ja '70
Javelina come high. il Field & S 75:68-71+ My '70

SAMSONITE corporation
Samsonite begins air delivery. Aviation W 93:105 O 26 '70

SAMUELS, Charles Thomas
Hitchcock. Am Scholar 39:295-304, 731 Spr, Aut '70
Placing Miss Porter. New Repub 162:25-6 Mr 7 '70
Sightings. Am Scholar 39:295-304, 678-82 Spr, Aut '70
(ed) See Antonioni, M. Antonioni

SAMUELS, Gertrude
How school busing works in one town. il N Y Times Mag p38-9+ S 27 '70
Pot, hard drugs and the law. il por N Y Times Mag p4+ F 15 '70

SAMUELS, H. J.
Arctic adventure. il por Outdoor Life 145:68-71+ F '70

SAMUELS, Howard Joseph
Candidates. New Yorker 46:28-30 Je 20 '70 *
Howie the horse. il por Newsweek 77:69 Ja 11 '71
No. 1 bookie makes his play. il por Bsns W p50+ N 14 '70 *

SAMUELS, Howard Joseph Jr
Fathers and sons. il pors Newsweek 75:24+ F 9 '70

SAMUELS, Nathaniel
Agriculture and foreign economic policy; address. November 19, 1969. Dept State Bul 61:569-72 D 15 '69
American business and international investment flows; address. December 11, 1969. Dept State Bul 62:33-8 Ja 12 '70; Same. Vital Speeches 36:197-200 Ja 15 '70
OECD ministerial meeting held at Paris; statement; with text of communique. May 22. 1970. Dept State Bul 62:811-14 Je 29 '70
Trade, capital, and Latin American development; address. January 19, 1970. Dept State Bul 62:179-85 F 16 '70

SAMUELS, S. Jay
Effect of pictures on learning to read. Ed Digest 36:48-51 N '70

SAMUELSON, Paul Anthony
[Column on economic questions] See issues of Newsweek
Does economics deserve a Nobel prize? M. Hudson. Commonweal 93:296-8 D 18 '70 *
Economics: Nobel prize for 1970 awarded to Samuelson of M.I.T. L. Hurwicz. por Science 170:720-1 N 13 '70 *
How the slump looks to three experts. pors Newsweek 75:78-9 My 25 '70
Laureate of new economics. por Bsns W p90 O 31 '70 *

SAMUELSON, Paul Anthony—*Continued*
Obvious Nobelist. Sci N 98:348 O 31 '70 *
Paul Samuelson. M. Friedman. Newsweek 76:
80 N 9 '70 *
Science. Time 96:39 N 9 '70 *
SAN AGUSTIN culture. See Indians of South
America—Antiquities—Colombia
SAN ANDREAS fault. See Faults (geology)
SAN ANDRÉS
Caribbean surprise: San Andrés. English
speaking since the 17th century. il Sunset
144:46+ Mr '70
SAN ANDRES ISLAND. See Saint Andrews Island
SAN ANTONIO, Tex.

Description

A few words on behalf of Texas. H. Sutton.
il Sat R 53:51-2+ My 9 '70
Saint Anthony's spring. S. Jenkins, jr. il
Opera N 34:6-11 Ap 11 '70

Education

Bilingually advantaged. J. R. Gates. il Todays
Ed 59:38-40+ D '70
San Antonio's fight against illiteracy. D.
Wright. il Am Ed 6:20-1 N '70

Fire department

Salvage what you can; fire-hydrant maintenance policy. R. P. Van Dyke. il Am
City 85:70-1 O '70

Music

Saint Anthony's spring. S. Jenkins, jr. il
Opera N 34:6-11 Ap 11 '70
SAN ANTONIO DE PICHINCHA
Feast of the sun. M. Acosta Solís. il Américas 22:24-30 O '70
SAN ANTONIO grand opera festival. See Music
festivals—Texas
SANASARDO, Paul
Pain. J. Reibstein. il pors Dance Mag 44:42-8 Jl '70 *
Saratoga school of modern dance. S. S. Mack.
il Dance Mag 44:40-1 Jl '70 *
SANASARDO, Paul, dance company. See Dance
companies
SAN BLAS Indians. See Indians of Central
America
SAN BLAS ISLANDS, Panama. See Mulatas
Islands
SANBORN, Roger
And what do you do in the winter? il Camp
Mag 42:8-10 N '70
SÁNCHEZ, Alberto
End of an exile. il pors Time 96:56 Ag 31 '70
SANCHEZ LEON, Abelardo
Poem: Why did that have to be the only answer? tr. by D. Tipton. Poetry 116:363 Ag
'70
SANCTIONS (International law)
How it goes in Rhodesia. J. Phillips. Nat R
22:894-5 Ag 25 '70
Rhodesia: penalized but prospering. il U S
News 68:60 Mr 23 '70
See also
Embargo
SANCTUARIES, Bird. See Bird sanctuaries
SANCTUARY (law) See Asylum, Right of
SAND, George, pseud.
Chopin and Sand: in the wake of that Major-can winter. R. McMullen. il Sat R 53:78-9+
Mr 14 '70 *
SAND, George X.
How to fish flies deep; excerpts from Salt
water fly fishing. Field & S 74:48-9+ F '70
How to outwit gun thieves. Field & S 75:54-5+ D '70
Mountain grouse are work. il pors Outdoor
Life 145:56-7+ F '70
Where to hunt in South Carolina. Field & S
75:134+ N '70
SAND, Ole
Schools for the 70's. il Schol Teach Sec
Teach Sup p8-9 Ja 5 '70
SAND blast
Sand blast with a tractor? Fairmount cemetery, Newark, N.J. il Am City 85:66 Je '70
SAND boxes. See Sandboxes
SAND castles; story. See Brautigan, R.
SAND casting. See Casting (sculpture)
SAND dunes
Wandering sands. J. M. Roberts. il Américas
22:9-14 Ag '70
See also
Singing sands
SAND fleas. See Beach fleas
SAND LAKE national wildlife refuge. See Wildlife sanctuaries—South Dakota

SAND sailboats. See Sand yachts
SAND yachts
Cactus to starboard. N. Levy. il Yachting
128:58-9+ D '70
SANDAGE, Allan R.
Cosmology: a search for two numbers. bibliog il por Phys Today 23:34-41 F '70
SANDBERG, W. G.
Twenty rules for whitetail. il Field & S 75:
44-5+ O '70
SANDBOXES
Raised bed continues as a sandbox. il Sunset
145:178 S '70
To foil cats, sandbox cover. il Sunset 144:132
Mr '70
SANDBURG, Carl
How to tell corn fairies if you see 'em; story.
PTA Mag 65:21 N '70
SANDEEN, Ernest
Hijack; poem. Sat R 53:38 O 3 '70
Suddenly this left-handed life; poem. Sat R
53:38 S 19 '70
SANDEEN, Ernest R.
Fundamentalism and American identity. Ann
Am Acad 387:56-65 Ja '70
SANDER, Ellen
Americanization of the Stones. il Vogue
155:170-1+ F 1 '70
Friends and neighbors alive, alive-O. il Sat
R 53:71+ Ap 25 '70
Jefferson Airplane; where we've been to-day. Sat R 53:76-7 Ja 31 '70
Joan Baez: One day at a time. Sat R 53:61 Mr
28 '70
McCartney on his own. il por Sat R 53:53-4
My 30 '70
Pop minstrelsy: madrigal blues. Sat R 53:47
Je 27 '70
Rock 1970: a level of excellence. il Sat R
53:37-9 D 26 '70
Simon & Garfunkel: the singers and the songs.
pors Sat R 53:91+ F 28 '70
Something is rotten in rock. Sat R 53:49
O 10 '70
SANDER stands. See Machinery—Stands
SANDERS, Aaron P. and others
Brain adenosine triphosphate: decreased concentration precedes convulsions. bibliog il
Science 169:206-8; 170:1431 Jl 10, D 25 '70
SANDERS, Alan J. K.
Development of transport. il Focus 20:8-11
Ja '70
Mongolia. bibliog il Focus 20:1-7 Ja '70
SANDERS, Betty
MAD magazine in the remedial English class.
Engl J 59:266-7+ F '70
SANDERS, Felicia
Nicotine cantata. Time 95:72 Je 1 '70 *
SANDERS, Charles L.
Struggle for paradise. il Ebony 25:66-8+ O
'70
SANDERS, Harland
Profiles. W. Whitworth. por New Yorker 45:
40-6+ F 14 '70 *
SANDERS, Marion K.
Addicts and zealots. il Harper 240:71-3+ Je
'70 Same abr. with title Encounter at
Phoenix house. Read Digest 97:95 D '70
Right not to be born. il Harper 240:92-9 Ap
'70
SANDERS, Noah
Pistol Pete now is up against the pros. il
pors N Y Times Mag p32-3+ O 11 '70
SANDERS, Peter L.
Robert Graves: a poet's quest for meaning.
Engl J 59:23-6 Ja '70
SANDERS, Ralph
Marketing management. See issues of Successful farming
(ed) See Jones, B. E. How I use the futures
market
SANDERS, Stanley
Black American in racist South Africa. il
pors Ebony 26:35-8+ D '70
SANDERS, Thomas G.
Church in Latin America. For Affairs 48:285-99 Ja '70
SANDERS, William Willard
Going for the jugular. il por Newsweek 76:
55 S 28 '70 *
SANDERSON, Ivan L.
Revolution in campus bookselling: second
look. Pub W 198:138-40 Jl 13 '70
SANDFLIES as carriers of infection. See Flies
as carriers of infection
SANDHILL cranes. See Cranes (birds)
SANDHOPPERS. See Beach fleas
SANDIA PEAK tramway. See Cableways
SAN DIEGO, Calif.

Air pollution

Lead aerosols in the atmosphere: increasing
concentrations. T. J. Chow and J. L. Earl.
bibliog il Science 169:577-80 Ag 7 '70

SAN DIEGO, Calif.—*Continued*

Harbor
San Diego's lively waterfront. il Sunset 145: 42-9 Ag '70

Newspapers
Censorship by harassment; underground journals. K. Widmer. Nation 210:366-9 Mr 30 '70
Not so free press; underground paper, Street journal & San Diego free press. Time 95: 38 Mr 23 '70

Parks and playgrounds
How to gamble in a low dive: Mission Bay park. L. Barry. il Pop Phot 66:24+ F '70

Police
City vs. campus violence; city police on the campus. W. J. McGill. il por Am City 85: 78+ N '70

Streets
Are crosswalks deadly? Am City 85:118 Jl '70
Slurry seal proves itself. W. M. Davis. il Am City 85:120+ S '70

SAN DIEGO-Acapulco race. See Yacht racing
SAN DIEGO COUNTY, Calif.

Religious institutions and affairs
New ecumenical organ in San Diego County. R. Ryland. Chr Cent 87:406 Ap 1 '70

SAN DIEGO state college
Layoff in California. F. K. Brose. il por Library J 95:3741-4 N 1 '70
SANDIFORD, David J. See Bertman, B. jt. auth.
SANDING blocks
Make a good boat sanding board. G. P. Manning. il Motor B 126:23 Ag '70

SANDING machines
Conical disk for scratch-free edge sanding. R. F. Finch. il Pop Sci 197:99 D '70
Sander-polishers: who needs 'em? R. J. DeCristoforo. il Pop Sci 197:80-1+ O '70

SANDOR, Gyorgy
Bela Bartok, Budapest and afterwards. il por Hi Fi 20:MA13+ S '70

SANDOVAL, Hilary, Jr
Sandoval stands siege at the SBA. por Bsns W p60+ Jl 18 '70 *

SANDS, Singing. See Singing sands
SANDSTONE
Jurassic sandstone from the tropical Atlantic. P. J. Fox and others. bibliog il Science 170: 1402-4 D 25 '70

SANDWICHES
Assemble-your-own-sandwich party. il Sunset 144:62-3 Ja '70
If you've got the bread, we've got the sandwiches. il Redbook 135:98-100+ Ag '70
Notes for the hostess. M. Hemingway. House & Gard 138:16+ Jl '70
Out of a salmon can, pleasures. il Sunset 145:164 D '70
Sandwichcraft! il Bet Hom & Gard 48:58-65+ Jl '70
Sandwiches: a hot idea; recipes. il Ladies Home J 87:78-9+ Jl '70
Stag sandwiches. il Bet Hom & Gard 48:23 F '70

SANDY, Stephen
For Mr Reed of Martha's Vineyard; poem. New Yorker 46:51 Ja 2 '71
Work; Roofs; Post card, moss garden; Suburb; poems. Poetry 116:174-7 Je '70

SANE (organization) See National committee for a sane nuclear policy
SANEL, Frances T. and Serpick, A. A.
Plasmalemmal and subsurface complexes in human leukemic cells: membrane bonding by zipperlike junctions. bibliog il Science 168: 1458-60 Je 19 '70

SAN FERNANDO, Calif.
Tennis court backboard for $100. S. Silver. il Am City 85:18 D '70
SAN FERNANDO VALLEY state college, Northridge. See California. San Fernando Valley state college, Northridge

SANFORD, David
Bad riddance. New Repub 163:14-16 D 5 '70
Chemical breakfast. New Repub 163:12-15 Ag 22 '70
Kent state gag. New Repub 163:14-17 N 7 '70
Nothing works anymore. il New Repub 162: 21-4 F 14 '70
Post office blues. New Repub 162:19-22 Mr 21 '70
Right to be seen and heard. New Repub 163: 16-17 Jl 18 '70
Unselling drugs. New Repub 162:15-16 F 28 '70

SANFORD, Jack
Memo to commencement speakers. Chr Today 14:14+ My 8 '70

SANFORD, Nevitt. See Opton, E. M. jr. jt. auth.
SAN FRANCISCO
San Francisco: a special issue; symposium. il Holiday 47:40-78+ Mr '70

Air pollution
City in danger. il Holiday 47:40-1 Mr '70

Airports
Ground equipment service chain planned by new firm. il Aviation W 92:35 Je 15 '70
San Francisco sets airport noise limit. Aviation W 93:37 D 21 '70

Anecdotes, facetiae, satire, etc.
I was born here. A. Hoppe. Holiday 47:60 Mr '70

Architecture
Beautiful building or inhuman eyesore? Transamerica's pyramidal building. il Bsns W p41 O 31 '70
Oh! San Francisco! world headquarters of Transamerica corporation. A. Zelver. il Arch Forum 132:68-71 Ja '70
Sculptural expression of tradition in San Francisco: Bank of America tower. il Arch Rec 148:126-32 Jl '70

Chinatown
Chinatown: churches and young dissenters. R. Larsen. Chr Cent 87:1542+ D 23 '70
Chinatown detail; end of special police force. il Time 96:14 S 28 '70
Chinatown in crisis. M. Yee. il Newsweek 75: 57-8 F 23 '70
Red guard on Grant avenue. S. M. Lyman. il Trans-Action 7:20-34 Ap '70
Reports: San Francisco's Chinatown. M. E. Leary. Atlan 225:32+ Mr '70

Churches
Good/bad vibes at Glide; Jesus freaks. R. L. Cleath. Chr Today 15:37 O 23 '70

City planning
Battle of the Bay. il Newsweek 76:46-7 D 28 '70
City fights for its skyline. il Bsns W p35 O 24 '70

Description
San Francisco's mystique. F. Davis. il Trans-Action 7:75-80 Ap '70

Galleries and museums
See also
M. H. De Young memorial museum, San Francisco
Palace of arts and sciences, San Francisco

Gardens
This spring-flowering marvel is the happy result of autumn planting. il Sunset 145: 194-5 O '70

Historic houses, etc.
Garden court at the Palace, now an official landmark. il Sunset 144:40 F '70

History
See also
Vigilance committees—California

Hotels, restaurants, etc.
Small restaurants where the San Franciscans eat. R. B. Read. il Holiday 47:68-9+ Mr '70
Welcome to the Hotel Miyako. R. Atcheson. il Holiday 47:86-9 Mr '70

Housing
Studio apartments, San Francisco. il Arch Rec 147:86-7 mid-My '70
Study of street life precedes town house design; Martin Luther King square. il Arch Rec 147:110-11 Mr '70

Industries
Who's in charge here? N. Von Hoffman. il Holiday 47:48-51+ Mr '70

Libraries
Slum storefront library serves San Francisco poor. il Library J 95:1793 My 15 '70

Moral conditions
Culture of civility; deviants. H. S. Becker and I. L. Horowitz. il Trans-Action 7:12-19 Ap '70
Porn capital of America. W. Murray. il N Y Times Mag p8-9+ Ja 3 '71

Music
See also
San Francisco opera company
San Francisco symphony orchestra

SAN FRANCISCO—Continued

Negroes

Game of black & white at Hunters Point. A. E. Hippler. il Trans-Action 7:56-63 Ap '70

Newspapers

See also
Bay guardian (newspaper)
San Francisco chronicle

Parks and playgrounds

Fishing on the rivers of the mind; Golden Gate angling and casting club. T. McGuane. il Sports Illus 34:40-3 Ja 4 '71

Golden Gate park centennial. J. Caverly. il por Parks & Rec 5:24-6+ O '70

Golden Gate park; everything from hippie hill to superb Oriental art. V. McHugh. il Holiday 47:61+ Mr '70

Perhaps San Francisco's greatest treat is this 100-year-old park. il Sunset 144:90-101 Ap '70

San Francisco experiment, portable parks downtown. il Sunset 145:24 Ag '70

Photographs

Light and color of a lovely city. B. Davidson. Holiday 47:42-7 Mr '70

Photography center

Photo center sets pace for nation. J. Deschin. il Pop Phot 66:34+ Ap '70

Police

We've always wanted to be cops; with report by G. Moore. il pors Life 69:32-7 N 13 '70

Politics and government

Alioto and the politics of hyperpluralism. F. M. Wirt. il Trans-Action 7:46-55 Ap '70

Popular culture

Culture and counter-culture. H. Gold. il Holiday 47:56-9+ Mr '70

Public health

Health of Height-Ashbury. D. E. Smith and others. il Trans-Action 7:35-45 Ap '70

Social conditions

Deviance and democracy in San Francisco; symposium. il Trans-Action 7:12-80 Ap '70
Who's in charge here? N. Von Hoffman. il Holiday 47:48-51 Mr '70

Social life and customs

God, gurus and Gay Guerrillas; new life-styles. R. Atcheson. il Holiday 47:52-5+ Mr '70

Stores

Shopping; from Gump's to Jax. P. J. Martineau. il Holiday 47:70-1+ Mr '70

Theater

Independent female; or, A man has his pride; text of play performed by the San Francisco Mime troupe. J. Holden. il Ramp Mag 9:20-31 D '70

San Francisco mime troupe; with text of play. D. Kolodney. il Ramp Mag 9:26-9 Ag '70

Theatre; San Francisco Mime Troupe guerrilla theatre. J. Novick. Nation 211:317-18 O 5 '70

Transit systems

Transit signs to tell it like it is. il Am City 85:102 N '70

Transportation

Commuters, ahoy! ferry system. il Newsweek 76:83-4 O 12 '70

SAN FRANCISCO and Oakland helicopter airlines
New management retrenching at SFO. R. G. O'Lone. Aviation W 92:39+ F 23 '70

SAN FRANCISCO art institute
San Francisco's art institute. R. Montgomery. il Arch Forum 132:80-5 Ja '70

SAN FRANCISCO BAY
Bay that refused to die. F. Hutchinson. il Am For 76:24-7+ Ap '70
Changing face of San Francisco Bay. il Sunset 145:72-9 N '70
Cleaning up the Coyote Point shoreline in San Francisco Bay. il Sunset 144:107-8 My '70
How to make an outfall in San Francisco Bay mud. R. G. Bezzant. il Am City 85:83-5 My '70
Victory on San Francisco Bay. J. Gooding. il Fortune 81:148+ F '70

SAN FRANCISCO BAY bridges
Golden leap. il Time 96:40 Ag 24 '70

SAN FRANCISCO BAY guardian. See Bay guardian (newspaper)

SAN FRANCISCO chronicle
Herb Caen: his power is awesome. G. Sales. il Holiday 47:76-7+ Mr '70

SAN FRANCISCO 49ers (football club) See Football clubs

SAN FRANCISCO mime troupe. See San Francisco—Theater

SAN FRANCISCO neighborhood legal assistance foundation. See Legal aid societies

SAN FRANCISCO opera company
Jenufa, the biggest hit. A. Frankenstein. il Hi Fi sec II 20:28-9+ F '70
Loose lady; Bay area opera ACTION. S. Von Buchau. Opera N 45:6-7 O 10 '70
Report:
  Cosi fan tutte. J. Rockwell. Opera N **35:** 28 D 5 '70
  Otello, Salome, Faust, and The rake's progress. J. Rockwell. il Opera N 35: 30-1 Ja 2 '71
  Productions of Siegfried, Tosca and Falstaff. J. Rockwell. il Opera N 35:27 O 31 '70
  Tristan und Isolde. J. Rockwell. Opera N 35:38 D 19 '70
Theater of Igor Stravinsky; The rake's progress to be revived. E. Salzman. il por Opera N 35:8-15 O 10 '70

SAN FRANCISCO public library
Of note: strike over. Am Lib 1:413 My '70

SAN FRANCISCO state college. See California. State college, San Francisco

SAN FRANCISCO symphony orchestra
Far out in S.F. por Newsweek 76:117 D 14 '70

SAN FRANCISCO Warriors (basketball team) See Basketball teams

SANGER, Margaret
Birth control in America, by D. M. Kennedy. Review
  Commonweal 92:299-300 Je 12 '70. W. L. O'Neill *
Faces from the past. R. M. Ketchum. il por Am Heritage 21:52-3 Je '70 *
Founding mothers. il pors Vogue 155:112-13 Je '70 *
Margaret Sanger, by E. T. Douglas. Review
  New Repub 162:22+ My 16 '70. P. Marx *

SANIBEL ISLAND
Beachcomber's paradise. H. H. Harrison. il Nat Wildlife 9:58-63 D '70

SANITARY affairs. See subhead Sanitary affairs under names of countries, states, cities, e.g. Santa Monica, Calif.—Sanitary affairs

SANITARY engineering
See also
Harbors—Cleaning
Pipe laying
Refuse and refuse disposal
Sewer cleaning
Water purification

SANITARY fills. See Filling (earthwork)

SANITATION
See also
Milk hygiene
Refuse and refuse disposal

SANJEK, Betty
Motion picture previews. il PTA Mag 65:38-40 N; 38-40 D '70

SAN JOAQUIN VALLEY library system, Fresno, Calif.
San Joaquin Valley, California: la Biblioteca ambulante. M. B. Reynolds. Wilson Lib Bul 44:767 Mr '70

SAN JOSE, Calif.

City planning

Boom town. il Newsweek 76:68+ S 14 '70
Correcting San Jose's boomtime mistakes. il Bsns W p74-6 S 19 '70

Parks and playgrounds

Community action: students in San Jose build a park in a month. il Sunset 145:86-7 O '70

Protests, demonstrations, etc.

Mr Nixon and the politics of danger. il Newsweek 76:21-2 N 9 '70

SAN JOSE, Calif, public library
San Jose: a swinger. il Library J 95:4135-6 D 1 '70

SAN JOSE state college. See California. State college, San Jose

SAN JUAN, Puerto Rico

Libraries

Bootstrap library drive succeeds in Puerto Rico; a volunteer public library. C. Lewis. il por Library J 95:1813-15 My 15 '70

SAN JUAN ISLANDS, Wash.
Exploring the San Juan Islands. J. Harpster. il Travel 133:60-5 My '70

SAN JUAN star
Another exclusive; sold to Capital cities broadcasting corp. Newsweek 76:90 Jl 13 '70

SAN LORENZO, FORT. See Fort San Lorenzo, Panama Canal Zone

SAN MARTIN, José de
Truce negotiations of San Martin. R. C. Smith, 3d. il por Américas 22:31-3 O '70 *

SAN MATEO, Calif.

Moral conditions
San Mateo: people here think race and poverty are someone else's problems. And they are. D. Jackson. il Life 69:26-7 O 2 '70

Sanitary affairs
Old digesters don't die. J. H. Jenks. il Am City 85:70-1 Ag '70

SANNES, Sanne
Sanne Sannes; with photographs. T. Galluzzo. Mod Phot 34:74-7 Ag '70 *

SANO, Bizzy Monte-. See Monte-Sano, B.

SAN QUENTIN prison. See Prisons—California

SAN RAFAEL, Calif.

Courts
Bloody breakout at San Rafael; with editorial comment. il pors Life 69:2A. 30-4 Ag 21 '70
Courthouse shoot-out. il Newsweek 76:34+ Ag 17 '70
High cost of blackmail; kidnappings and deaths of hostages. Nat R 22:880+ Ag 25 '70
Justice: a bad week for the good guys; slaying of Judge Haley. il pors Time 96:6-8 Ag 17 '70
Professor's guns; gun battle at Marin County courthouse. il por Time 96:13 Ag 24 '70

SANSBURY, Leslie
Until tomorrow; story. Good H 171:78-9 Jl '70

SANSEGUNDO, Carlos
Plastic furniture of Carlos Sansegundo. C. Southern. il Craft Horiz 30:28-31+ D '70 *

SANSOM, Andrew
Students mobilize for eco-action. Parks & Rec 5:49+ Ap '70

SANSONI (publisher) See Publishers and publishing—Italy

SANS SOUCI. See Washington, D.C.—Hotels. restaurants. etc.

SANSTEAD, Wayne
Are you politically involved? Todays Ed 59: 44-5 D '70

SANTA ANA, Calif.

Parks and playgrounds
People-planned parks. B. C. Spragg. il Am City 85:72-4 Jl '70

SANTA ANITA race track. See Race tracks

SANTA BARBARA, Calif.

Riots
Commencement at Isla Vista. Nation 210:772 Je 29 '70
Isla Vista uprising; bank burning during student riot. il Time 95:19-20 Mr 9 '70
Isla Vista war; campus violence in a class by itself. W. Griffith. il N Y Times Mag p 10-11+ Ag 30 '70; Discussion p 16 S 20 '70
Powerless students. D. Nevin. il McCalls 97:44-5+ Jl '70
Run on the bank. il Newsweek 75:23-4 Mr 9 '70
Why they burned the bank. R. Flacks and M. Mankoff. il Nation 210:337-40 Mr 23 '70

Water supply
Tradition gave way to imagination; water-storage facility. P. A. Beautrow. il Am City 85:87-9 Ag '70

SANTA BARBARA oil slicks. See Oil pollution of rivers. harbors. etc.

SANTA CATALINA ISLAND
Island kingdom of P. K. Wrigley. il Forbes 106:22-3 N 1 '70

SANTA CLARA, Calif.
Tap only the best water in your well; selective sampling of aquifers. R. R. Mortenson. il Am City 85:49-51 D '70

Sanitary affairs
One-man refuse collection crews. S. M. Cristofano. il Am City 85:86-8 Ap '70

SANTA CLARA COUNTY, Calif.
Aerospace: unemployed scientists. engineers have no place to go. J. Walsh. Science 170:1384-7 D 25 '70
Getting blue-collar workers to use buses. H. K. Evans. il Am City 85:94+ Ag '70
Wood cover, rubber sidewalls. il Am City 85: 66-7 Jl '70

SANTA CLAUS
Pictorial history of the man in the red suit. E. Sorel. il Redbook 136:104-5 D '70
See also
Nicholas, Saint

SANTA CLAUS, Calif.
Santa Claus, California. T. Tyler. por Time 96:12 D 28 '70

SANTA CRUZ campus. See California. University—Santa Cruz campus

SANTA FE, N.Mex.

Description
Santa Fe: the Southwest's most historic city. il Sunset 144:72-7 Je '70

Music
See also
Santa Fe opera company

Stores
New Mexican gadfly: John Conron; owner of store Centerline, inc. V. D. Hahn. il Am Home 73:33 Mr '70

SANTA FE opera company
Berio's Opera loses, but Open theater wins. I. Kolodin. Sat R 53:8 Ag 29 '70
Berio's Opera premiere. R. C. Marsh. il por Hi Fi 20:MA12-13+ N '70
Opera in the wilderness. M. C. Sherrod. il Holiday 47:58-9+ Je '70
Report:
Luciano Berio's Opera. J. Rockwell. il Opera 35:22 O 10 '70

SANTA makes a change; story. See Chaneles. S and Snyder, J.

SANTA Maria (ship) See Sailing vessels

SANTA MONICA, Calif.

Education
Madison plan really swings; placing of handicapped children in regular classrooms. A. A. Artuso and others. il Todays Ed 59:14-17 N '70

Sanitary affairs
Out-of-the-ordinary sewer job. il Am City 85: 84-5 Ap '70

SANTA Paula's stop-smoking cruise. See Cruising

SANTANA (rock group) See Rock 'n' roll groups

SANTANDREA, Jim
E unibus plurum, and all that. S. Nathan. il Pop Phot 67:66+ O '70 *

SANTELLA, Jim
Common vibration. il por Library J 95:3967-70 N 15 '70

SANTIAGO, Danny
The somebody; story. Redbook 134:68-9 F '70

SANTILLI, Richard A.
Monolithic LIC's for consumer products. il por Electr World 84:38-41 Jl '70

SANZ, Fernando
San Agustin. il UNESCO Courier 23:20-5 Ap '70

SÃO PAULO (city), Brazil

Economic conditions
Brazil's boom city; where things go right. il U S News 68:58-9 F 9 '70

SAPIR, Pinhas
Israel: an heir for Golda Meir. por Time 96:32 D 14 '70

SAPOTES
Sapote tree. L. E. Hoffman. Horticulture 48: 48 Mr '70

SARAH Lawrence college, Bronxville, N.Y.
Sarah Lawrence library-instructional center. R. Jensen. il Arch Rec 147:143-6 F '70

SARAH O'Loughlin Foley award. See Literary prizes

SARANDON, Susan
Five young beauties & how they get that way. il pors Mlle 72:135-41 N '70 *

SARATOGA, Calif.

Music
Report:
Production of Virgil Thomson's Four saints in three acts. J. Rockwell. Opera N 35:23 O 10 '70

SARATOGA NATIONAL HISTORICAL PARK
Living past. F. X. Kelly. il Parks & Rec 5:48-9 My '70

SARATOGA race track. See Race tracks

SARATOGA school of modern dance. See Dance schools

SARAUSA, Fermin Peraza. See Peraza Sarausa, F.

SARAVIS, C. A. and others
Rapid screening test for detecting hepatitis-associated antigen. bibliog il Science 169: 298-9 Jl 17 '70

SARAZEN, Gene
Keep your game young; ed by C. Kirkpatrick. il Sports Illus 32:20-7 F 16 '70
SARCOCYSTIS
Sarcocystis: development in cultured avian and mammalian cells. R. Fayer. bibliog il Science 168:1104-5 My 29 '70
SARCOMA
Microcytotoxicity test: detection in sarcoma patients of antibody cytotoxic to human sarcoma cells. W. C. Wood and D. L. Morton. bibliog il Science 170:1318-20 D 18 '70
Mouse lysozyme production by a monocytoma; isolation and comparison with other lysozymes. R. J. Riblet and L. A. Herzenberg. bibliog il Science 168:1595-7 Je 26 '70
SARCOMA virus. See Tumor viruses
SARDINIA
Agog in Agaland: Costa Smeralda and Porto Cervo, first of the holiday villages. T. Sage. Nat R 22:312+ Mr 24 '70
Upside-down visit. il por Time 95:53 My 4 '70
SARDIS
Croesus richer than ever. il Sci Digest 67:65 Ja '70
SARE, E. J. See Angell, C. A. jt. auth.
SARGEANT, Winthrop
Musical events. See issues of New Yorker

about

Past tense. G. Wolff. por Newsweek 76:81-2+ Jl 20 '70 *
Profiles; G. Mardersteig. por New Yorker 46: 32-6+ Jl 11 '70
SARGENT, John Singer
Watercolors of John Sargent: a brief estimate. N. Kent. il Am Artist 34:66-72+ N '70 *
SARIG, Emmett R.
Ignoring rock won't make it go away. Ed Digest 35:34-7 Mr '70
SARIN
Okinawa: the poison gas issue. E. E. Bollinger. Chr Cent 87:897 Jl 22 '70
SARMA, Padman S. and others
Feline leukemia and sarcoma viruses: susceptibility of human cells to infection. bibliog il Science 168:1098-100 My 29 '70
SARMIENTO, Domingo Faustino
Travel as a passport to freedom. A. Alvarez. Sat R 54:19-20 Ja 2 '71 *
SARNOFF, Robert W.
Bob Sarnoff runs a new game. il pors Bsns W p84-5+ Ja 24 '70
SAROYAN, William
Time of your life. Criticism
Commentary 49:20+ Mr '70 *
SARRIS, Andrew
New movie crash. Vogue 157:82 Ja 1 '71
Tomorrow's movies. Mlle 70:68+ Ja '70
SARSINI, Enrico
Male plumage; photographs with editorial comment. il por Life 69:3, 42-9 S 25 '70
SARTI, Roland
Fascist modernization in Italy: traditional or revolutionary? bibliog f Am Hist R 75:1029-45 Ap '70
SARTO, Gloria E.
Genetic counseling; ed. by S. Olds. Redbook 136:12+ D '70
SARTON, May
There. . .stood the house; excerpts from Plant dreaming deep. il por N Y Times Mag p50-1 Ag 23 '70
SARTRE, Jean Paul
Intellectuals and revolution: interview with Jean-Paul Sartre; ed. by J. C. Garot, tr. by B. Rice. il Ramp Mag 9:52-5 D '70

about

Again the days of May. il Time 95:37 Je 8 '70 *
In defense of violence. il por Newsweek 75: 57 Je 8 '70 *
Print, and be seized. il por Time 96:76+ N 16 '70 *
SASS, Herbert Ravenel
Killer! il Audubon 72:40-1 Ja '70
SATA, Lindbergh S. and others
Store-front churches in the inner city. bibliog Ment Hy 54:256-60 Ap '70
SATAN. See Devil
SATANISM
Church of Satan. J. Rascoe. il McCalls 97: 74-5+ Mr '70
Princess Leda's castle in the air. T. Burke. il Esquire 73:104-11+ Mr '70
SATANTA, Kan.
Bloody nights on the lone prairie: chicken-fighting. D. Russell. il Sports Illus 32:48-51 Mr 23 '70
SATELLITE air terminals. See Terminals
SATELLITE antennas. See Antennas (electronics)

SATELLITES
Enhanced photo shows Mars' moon. il Aviation W 92:61 My 25 '70
Oblong moon; Phobos. il Sci Am 223-50+ Jl '70
Phobos: preliminary results from Mariner 7. B. A. Smith. bibliog il Science 168:828-30 My 15 '70
See also
Artificial satellites
SATIE, Erik
Erik Satie by P. D. Templier. Review
Am Rec G por 36:744-6+ My '70. J. Ringo *
Real thing: Satie and William Masselos. J. Ringo. por Am Rec G 36:692-4 My '70 *
SATIRE
See also
Caricatures and cartoons
SATISFACTION
See also
Self realization
SATISFACTION in work. See Job satisfaction
SATO, Eisaku
President Nixon and Prime Minister Sato of Japan hold talks at Washington. Dept State Bul 61:551-8 D 15 '69
Sato talks about his country; interview. por U S News 68:56-7 F 23 '70

about

Trade squabble puts Sato on the spot. il por Bsns W p82-3 Ja 9 '71 *
U.S.-Japanese trade: Sato on a tightrope. il por U S News 69:72 N 9 '70 *
SATO, K. See Hossmann, K. A. jt. auth.
SATO, Toshio
Tokyo seminary names Sato its new president. H. Post. il Chr Cent 88:18 Ja 6 '71 *
SATTERWHITE, John H.
For authentic freedom. Chr Cent 87:236 F 25 '70
SATURDAY evening post
Born into the past. il Time 96:76 N 16 '70
Decline and fall, by O. Friedrich. Review
Bsns W p 10+ My 23 '70. S. Brown
Newsweek il 76:83-83B Jl 6 '70. R. A. Sokolov
Massmags and microcult. S. O'Connell. Nation 210:310-11 Mr 16 '70
New Post. Newsweek 76:30 N 16 '70
Post-mortem. Time 95:41-2 Je 8 '70
Resurrection of the Satevepost. por Bsns W p29-30 N 14 '70
SATURDAY review
Cartoonist Q's; use of cartoons. J. Markow. Writers Digest 50:38-9 Jl '70
Good season for the literate: SR television awards, 1970. R. L. Shayon. Sat R 53:64-5+ Ap 11 '70
Report on SR. N. Cousins. Sat R 53:28-9 N 7 '70
SR's eighteenth annual advertising awards. R. L. Tobin. il Sat R 53:59-63 Ap 11 '70
Voices from the past; excerpts from, and cover of November 16, 1929 issue. Sat R 53:36-7 Ja 24 '70
See also
Anisfield-Wolf awards
SATURN (planet)
Ammonia in the rings of Saturn. il Chem 43:24 F '70
Composition of Saturn's rings. il Sky & Tel 39:14 Ja '70; Correction. 39:80 F '70
New ring of Saturn. P. Guerin. il Sky & Tel 40:88 Ag '70
Saturn's rings: identification of water frost. C. B. Pilcher and others. bibliog il Science 167:1372-3 Mr 6 '70
SATURN V (space vehicle) See Space vehicles —Propulsion systems
SATURN launch vehicles. See Space vehicles —Propulsion systems
SAUCES
Flaming desserts; flaming fruit sauces. il Bet Hom & Gard 48:68-9 Ag '70
Pesto. il Sunset 145:56-7 Ag '70
Sauce of the Americas; guacamole. il Sunset 144:92-3 My '70
Things mother never taught you about sauces. il Ladies Home J 87:82 F '70
Zesty Mediterranean tuna sauce. Sunset 144: 164 Je '70
SAUDI ARABIA
See also
Red Sea
SAUER, Louis W.
Your child's health. See issues of PTA magazine
SAUER, R. M. and others
Demyelinating encephalomyelopathy associated with lead poisoning in nonhuman primates. bibliog il Science 169:1091-3 S 11 '70

SAUERKRAUT
Choucroute garnie. J. Jaffry. il Am Home 73:88-9 O '70
See also
Cookery—Vegetables
SAUERLAND, Caroline
Pick your own pansy seeds. il Org Gard & Farm 17:55 Je '70
SAUL, Ralph Southey
Market: time for a new broom. il pors Newsweek 76:72-3+ N 30 '70 *
SAULNIER, Raymond J.
Inflation and the prospects for prosperity. Read Digest 96:99-102 Mr '70
SAUNA
Now: prebuilt saunas that go together in an hour. il Pop Mech 133:154-7 F '70
Sauna for your home? A. Lees. il Pop Sci 196:54-7+ F '70
Sauna-steam baths show health hazard. T. Schuchat. Har Yrs 10:5 S '70
Tuck a mini-sauna into a corner, or a closet. D. Huff. il Pop Sci 197:89 S '70
SAUNDERS, Aulus Ward
Feelings and form. il Sch Arts 70:34-6 O '70
SAUNDERS, D. S.
Circadian clock in insect photoperiodism. bibliog il Science 168:601-3 My 1 '70
SAUNDERS, Josephine
Undersides of worlds; poem. Poetry 116:97 My '70
SAUNDERS, Stuart Thomas
Getting on the route to corporate health. W. A. Lashley. il pors Nations Bsns 58:98-9 Ja '70
Penn central bankruptcy express. R. Loving, jr. il pors Fortune 82:104-9+ Ag '70 *
Uncle, can you spare some millions? il por Time 95:74-6 Je 22 '70 *
SAUNDERS, W. B. company
Bro-dart sues CBS and Holt, demands sale of Saunders. Pub W 197:57 Mr 2 '70
SAUSAGE
Sausage and spice (and things not so nice) Consumer Rep 35:344 Je '70
See also
Cookery—Meat
SAUSALITO, Calif.
Floating attack pumper. C. Masten. il Am City 85:58 S '70
SAVAGE, John
Upstairs workbench/desk. il Mech Illus 66:68-9 D '70
SAVAGE, Mildred
Trade winds. C. Amory. Sat R 53:10-11 Je 20 '70 *
SAVAGE, Naomi
Ever-changing faces of Naomi Savage. J. Scully. il Mod Phot 34:80-5 Ja '70 *
SAVAGE, Robert H.
Crucial role of investor relations. il Harvard Bsns R 48:122-30 N '70
SAVAGES
See also
Cannibalism
SAVANNAH, Ga.
Monster, H. W. Jenkins. il Am City 85:146 S '70

City planning
Heart of Savannah. A. Wolff. il Am Heritage 22:54-61+ D '70

Historic houses, etc.
Heart of Savannah. A. Wolff. il Am Heritage 22:54-61+ D '70
SAVAS, Emanuel S.
Cybernetics in city hall; adaptation of address, 1968. bibliog il Science 168:1066-71 My 29 '70
SAVED; drama. See Bond, E.
SAVIN, Samuel M. See Hecht, A. D. jt. auth.
SAVING and savings
How to earn top dollar from your savings account. R. Krumme. il Suc Farm 68:G8 S '70
Penny saved is a penny; or, What you don't save won't hurt you, and why. M. S. Welch. il Redbook 134:70-1+ F '70
Public changes its saving ways. il Bsns W p34 O '70
You can save in spite of yourself. il Changing T 24:40-2 O '70
See also
Bonds
Finance, Personal
Investments
SAVINGS and loan associations
Noose tightens on housing. il Bsns W p32 Ja 17 '70
Now, a bill-paying service by S&L's. U S News 70:38 Ja 4 '71
S&Ls go slightly mod; sponsorship of savers clubs. il Bsns W p90+ Ap 13 '70
Savings-and-loan curbs, a rising controversy. U S News 69:67-8 Ag 31 '70

Savings and loans hunt for funds, and a future. il U S News 68:95-7 My 11 '70
Will variable rates cure S&Ls' woes? il Bsns W p32-3 Jl 4 '70
SAVINGS banks
Anatomy of affluence; address, November 7, 1969. A. S. Murphy. Vital Speeches 36:207-9 Ja 15 '70
See also
Savings and loan associations
SAVINGS banks, Toy. See Banks, Coin
SAVINGS bonds. See Bonds, Government
SAVINGS deposits
Those fancy-name savings accounts. il Changing T 24:45-6 Ja '70

Interest
Higher interest on savings. U S News 68:36 F 2 '70

Taxation
Tax break on new savings accounts. U S News 69:68 Ag 17 '70
SAVORY, Teo
(tr) See Eich, G. Changed landscape; Clearings in the woods
(tr) See Guillevic, E. Parallels; Right angle; Acute angle; Rectangle
SAVORY, Theodore H.
Mule; with biographical sketch. il Sci Am 223:10, 102-9 D '70
SAVOY, Judy
What's leafy, green, and to the rescue? il Todays Health 48:50-2 S '70
SAW stands. See Machinery—Stands
SAWADA, Kyoichi
Death of the daring. il pors Time 96:41 N 9 '70 *
SAWARA false cypress. See False cypress
SAWCHUK, Terry
Tip on a dead goalie. por Newsweek 75:60 Je 15 '70 *
SAWMILLS

Wages and hours
Wages in southern sawmills and planing mills. A. I. Rose. il Mo Labor R 93:49-50 N '70
SAWS
Black & Decker's new low-cost radial: I found it rugged, powerful, but noisy. W. C. Leckey. il Pop Mech 133:172-3 My '70
Chain saws. il Consumer Bul 53:25-8 N '70
Changes in chainsaws. G. L. Earle. il Suc Farm 69:B4 Ja '71
Choosing & using saber-saw blades. R. J. DeCristoforo. il Mech Illus 66:90-2+ S '70
Crosscut guide for portable saws; sure square. il Consumer Rep 35:328 Je '70
Eighteen-inch kit-built bandsaw. R. J. De Cristoforo. il Pop Sci 197:24 S '70
How to get more from your power hacksaw. P. C. Yob. il Pop Mech 134:166-7+ O '70
Look what you can do with a swivel-blade sabre saw. G. E. Daniels. il Pop Mech 134:184-6+ O '70
New bandsaw sands, too. R. J. DeCristoforo. il Pop Sci 196:22 Je '70
Now, a precision $100 radial-arm saw. R. J. De Cristoforo. il Pop Sci 196:88-9 Mr '70
Power-Mac's $140 little brother. A. Lees. il Pop Sci 197:61 S '70
Put your chain saw to work. Suc Farm 68:no3 G 16 F '70
Table saws. il Consumer Rep 35:287-93 My '70
Those incredible toothless saw blades. R. J. DeCristoforo. il Pop Sci 196:100-1+ My '70
Turning a portable saw into a table saw. il Mech Illus 66:100-1+ F '70
Two slick ways to cut wood; crouchless brush cutter and vibrationless chain saw. E. F. Lindsley. il Pop Sci 196:105 My '70
SAWS, Pruning. See Pruning apparatus and equipment
SAWYER, Mary
Mary and her little lamb. D. F. Brown. il Hobbies 75:128-9 Mr '70 *
SAWYER, Ruth

Obituary
Horn Bk 46:347 Ag '70. B. Robinson
SAX, Joseph L.
Emerging legal strategies: judicial intervention. bibliog f Ann Am Acad 389:71-6 My '70
Environment in the courtroom. il Sat R 53:55-7 O 3 '70
Legal redress of environmental disruption. Arch Forum 132:50-1 My '70
SAXBE, William B.
Excerpt from debate, September 17, 1970. Cong Digest 49:127 Ap '70

SAXE, Susan
Bank-heist tactic. il pors Newsweek 76:29-30 O 5 '70 *
Dostoievsky in Waltham. Nat R 22:1098 O 20 '70 *
Radical bank job. il por Time 96:21-2 O 5 '70 *

SAYÃO, Bidú
Fresh appeal of Bidú Sayão. G. Movshon. por Hi Fi 20:sec1 107 Je '70 *

SAYERS, Gale
Short courageous life of Brian Piccolo; excerpts from I am third, ed. by A. Silverman pors Look 34:48-51+ Ag 25 '70

SAYINGS. See Aphorisms and apothegms; Quotations

SAYLES, F. L. See Manheim, F. T. jt. auth.

SAYRE, Nora
Politics (cont) Esquire 73:82+ Mr '70
Revolt for fun and profit. il Esquire 74:70-3+ Ag '70

SCADUTO, Anthony
Money book; excerpts from Getting the most for your money. Ladies Home J 87:147-50 Mr '70

SCALDS. See Burns and scalds

SCALES (weighing instruments)
Bathroom scale called Computer; new Space-age computer scale. Consumer Bul 53:14 D '70
Bathroom scales. il Consumer Rep 36:28-31 Ja '71
Good gift for a pen pal; Danish postal scale. il Consumer Rep 34:621-2 N '69

SCALIA, Frank. See Winans, S. S. jt. auth.

SCALLOPS
See also
Cookery—Shellfish

SCALP
See also
Dandruff

SCALPING of opera tickets. See Opera tickets

SCAMMON, Richard Montgomery
Job facing Muskie. Newsweek 76:35 N 16 '70
Lindsay scenario. il pors Newsweek 76:44-5 O 12 '70
Trade winds; interview, ed. by C. Amory. Sat R 53:8+ S 26 '70
—and Wattenberg, B. J.
Strategy for Democrats; excerpts from The real majority. New Repub 163:17-21 Ag 15; 31 S 26 '70; Same abr. with title Strategy for the outs. Cur 122:14-20 O '70

SCANDALIOS, John G.
Alcohol dehydrogenase in maize: genetic basis for isozymes. bibliog Science 166:623-4; 167:1519 O 31 '69, Mr 13 '70

SCANDINAVIA
Land of the midnight fun. J. Campbell. il Sports Illus 33:50-3 N 16 '70
See also
Cruising—Scandinavia

Description and travel
Icy adventures of a viking grandson. W. Johnson. il Sports Illus 33:54-63 N 16 '70
Northland memory. C. Mitchell. il Yachting 129:66-9+ Ja '71
Scandinavian safari; American forestry association tour. W. E. Towell. il por Am For 76:40-5 D '70

SCANDINAVIAN airlines system
Computer handles twelve operations for SAS. Aviation W 92:61 F 2 '70
SAS changes bring Nilert reassignment. Aviation W 92:46 My 11 '70
SAS seeks U.S. small business traffic. R. S. Kahn. Aviation W 93:36 O 19 '70

SCANDINAVIAN furniture. See Furniture, Scandinavian

SCANDINAVIANS
Icy adventures of a viking grandson. W. Johnson. il Sports Illus 33:54-63 N 16 '70

SCANDINAVIANS in the United States
Scandinavians. il Sr Schol 96:10-11 F 2 '70

SCANLAN, Alfred L.
Chances for schism; a legal green light. America 122:150-2 F 14 '70

SCANLAN'S monthly
ACLU joins Scanlan's in dispute with printer. Pub W 198:29 N 2 '70
Censorship, north and south. Time 97:43 Ja 4 '71
Controversial Scanlan's issue may yet appear. Pub W 198:35 D 28 '70
Printer as censor. R. H. Smith. Pub W 199:37 Ja 4 '71
Scanlan's monthly and other diversions. P. Steinfels. Commonweal 92:6 Mr 13 '70
Scanlan's reviewed. L. Smith. il por Newsweek 75:66 My 25 '70

SCARAB (racing car) See Automobiles, Racing

SCARECROWS
Scarecrow crusader. il Time 96:50 N 9 '70
Theory and practice of scarecrowing. il Sunset 145:130-1 Ag '70
When shall we three meet again, in thunder, lightning, or in rain? A. Neal. il Am Heritage 21:74-7 Ap '70

SCARF, Maggie
Brain researcher José Delgado asks: what kind of humans would we like to construct? il pors N Y Times Mag p46-7+ N 15; 21+ D 13 '70

SCARLETT, W. George
Clergyman's role and community mental health. Ment Hy 54:378-81 Jl '70

SCARS
What's your trademark? occupational markings. S. P. Gerber. il Mech Illus 66:72-3+ F '70

SCARSDALE, N.Y.

Education
Local association of the month. D. G. Breslow and V. Dempsey. Todays Ed 59:56-7 F '70

SCARSDALE, N.Y. public library
They also read who roll in dough. M. A. Kateley. il por Wilson Lib Bul 45:477-81 Ja '71

SCATTERGUNS. See Shotguns

SCATTERING (physics)
Interstellar scattering of pulsar radiation and its effect on the spectrum of NP0532. W. M. Cronyn. bibliog il Science 168:1453-5 Je 19 '70
SLAC inelastic data challenges theorists. G. B. Lubkin. bibliog Phys Today 23:61 Ja '70
See also
Electrons—Scattering
Light—Scattering
Radio waves—Scattering

SCENE designers. See Designers

SCENERY

Preservation
See Landscape protection

SCENERY (television) See Television broadcasting—Setting and scenery

SCENTED candles. See Candles

SCENTS. See Odors

SCHAACK, Margaret Donald
History in houses. il Antiques 97:378-81 Mr '70

SCHAAF, Albert K.
Your money cheerfully refunded; drama. Plays 30:83-4 O '70

SCHAAF, Robert W.
Mighty theater organ sounds again. il Hi Fi 20:MA16+ O '70

SCHAAR, John H. and Wolin, S. S.
Revolt of youth. Cur 119:3-10 Je '70

SCHACHTER, Hindy
Another idea: specialized book reviewing. Writers Digest 50:19 F '70

SCHADEN, Herman
Meanwhile, back at the zoo. il Am Ed 6:18-25 Ag '70

SCHAEFER, Earl S.
Can children get smarter? PTA Mag 65:10-12+ bibliog(p35) S '70

SCHAEFER, Vincent J.
Auto exhaust, pollution and weather patterns; adaptation of testimony before subcommittee on air and water pollution, March, 1970. Bul Atom Sci 26:31-3 O '70
Condensation nuclei: production of very large numbers in country air. bibliog Science 170:851-2 N 20 '70
Escape from pollution: the Adirondacks; address June 3 1969. il Cons 24:8-11 F '70

SCHAEFFER, Francis A.
Irrationality of modern thought; excerpt from The church at the end of the twentieth century. Chr Today 15:10-14 D 4 '70
Mark of the Christian; excerpt. Chr Today 14:7-8+ S 11 '70

SCHAEFFER, Jack
Behavioral objectives in the English classroom: a model; Shane as example of unit on characterization analysis. L. Dieter. Engl J 59:1259-62+ D '70 *

SCHAEFFER, O. A. and others
Potassium-argon ages of lunar rocks from Mare Tranquillitatis and Oceanus Procellarum. bibliog il Science 170:161-2 O 9 '70

SCHAEFFLER, Willy
Goodby Billy and hello Willy. W. Johnson. il por Sports Illus 33:78-9 N 23 '70 *

SCHAFER, Ann
Hoover dam hangover. il Motor B 127:62+ Ja '71

SCHAFER, Paul W. and Chandler, J. A.
Electron probe X-ray microanalysis of a normal centriole. bibliog il Science 170:1204-5 D 11 '70

SCHALES, Franklin D.
  Wind-breaks for vegetable protection. il Org
    Gard & Farm 17:66-7 Je '70
SCHALK, Carl F.
  Shape of church music in the '70s. Chr
    Cent 87:1445-9 D 2 '70
SCHALL, James V.
  Aspects of a theology of play. il Cath World
    212:69-73 N '70
  Back to the real world. America 123:8-10 Jl 11
    '70
  Caesar as God. Commonweal 91:505-10 F 6
    '70
  War and the balance of power; address, No-
    vember 11, 1969. Vital Speeches 36:211-17 Ja
    15 '70
SCHALLER, George B.
  This gentle & elegant cat; with biographical
    sketch. il Natur Hist 79:3, 30-9 Je '70
SCHALLER, John W.
  Corporate executive and educational change
    proposals. Ed Digest 35:30-1 Ja '70
SCHANCHE, Don A.
  Panthers against the wall. il por Atlan 225:55-
    61 My '70
SCHANTZ, Grace Putnam
  Homework; poem. Chr Cent 87:133 F 4 '70
SCHAPIRO, Shawn, and Vukovich, K. R.
  Early experience effects upon cortical den-
    drites: a proposed model for development.
    bibliog il Science 167:292-4 Ja 16 '70
—and others
  Hormonal effects on ontogeny of swimming
    ability in the rat: assessment of central
    nervous system development. bibliog il Sci-
    ence 168:147-51 Ap 3 '70
SCHARDT, Arlie
  Splashy struggle for a title. il Sports Illus
    33:14-17 Ag 10 '70
SCHARLEMANN, Martin
  In the exercise of love. Chr Cent 87:807 Je 24
    '70 *
SCHARY, Dore
  Brightower. Criticism
    New Yorker 45:72-3 F 7 '70
SCHATZ, Albert, and Schatz, Vivian
  Children's gardens in New York city schools:
    an educational report dated 1897. il Org
    Gard & Farm 17:67-9 N '70
  George Washington's composting experiment.
    il Org Gard & Farm 17:86-7 Jl '70
  How soils are formed and become fertile. il
    Org Gard & Farm 17:68-72 Je '70
SCHATZ, Vivian. See Schatz, A. jt. auth.
SCHATZLEIN, Gene
  Build this Tom Thumb mini-bike. il Pop
    Mech 133:168-71 Ja '70
SCHECHTER, Alan N.
  Measurement of fast biochemical reactions.
    bibliog il Science 170:273-80 O 16 '70
—and others
  Kinetics of folding of staphylococcal nu-
    clease. bibliog il Science 167:886-7 F 6 '70
SCHECHTER, Mal
  Alive but not well. New Repub 163:15-17 Jl 11
    '70
SCHECHTER, Philip E.
  Benediction. National association for the
    advancement of colored people, June 26,
    1968. Negro Hist Bul 33:97 Ap '70
SCHECTER, Jerrold L.
  Samurai who committed hara-kiri. il pors
    Life 69:36-7 D 11 '70
  Those Soviet economic troubles are deep-
    rooted. il Fortune 81:105-6 My '70

                    about
  Jones project; preparation of reminiscences
    of N. Khrushchev for publication. R. Graves.
    il pors Life 69:3 N 27 '70 *
SCHEDULES, School
  Realistic look at the flexible schedule. R. R.
    Gard. Clear House 44:425-9 Mr '70
  Unshackled education. D. Cooper. Clear House
    45:22-5 S '70
SCHEEL, Walter
  Light touch of the genial Rhinelander. por
    Time 96:17 Ag 17 '70 *
  Technical mistake. il por Newsweek 75:61 My
    11 '70 *
SCHEFFER, Victor B.
  Can we save the great whales? il McCalls 97:
    54+ My '70
  Cliché of the killer; with biographical sketch.
    Natur Hist 79:4, 26-8+ O '70
  Year of the seal; condensation. il Read Di-
    gest 97:141-5 O '70
  Year of the whale; excerpts. il Read Digest
    96:124-8 F '70
SCHEIBER, Harry N.
  At the borderland of law and economic his-
    tory: the contributions of Willard Hurst;
    address, December 1968. bibliog f Am Hist R
    75:744-56 F '70

SCHEIE syndrome. See Metabolism, Disorders
  of
SCHEIMANN, Eugene
  Astrology-Rx for boredom? il Har Yrs 10:
    17-18 S '70
SCHELL, Harold F.
  Camping out is in for Americans seeing
    Europe. il Todays Health 48:44-7+ Mr '70
SCHELL, Orville
  Cambodian civil war. New Repub 162:12-14
    Je 6 '70
SCHEMBECHLER, Bo
  Meet Michigan's meanest man. P. Putnam.
    il por Sports Illus 33:32-3 N 16 '70 *
SCHENCK, Carl Alwin
  Cradle of forestry: where tree power
    started. H. E. Jolley. il Am For 76:16-21
    Q; 36-9 N; 36-9+ D '70 *
SCHERER, J. L.
  Good buys in used planes. il Mech Illus 66:
    55-7 Je '70
SCHERER, Leo
  Two level government, one building. il Am
    City 85:111 O '70
SCHERRER, Paul
  Obituary
    Phys Today por 23:129+ Ja '70. H. Frau-
    enfelder and R. M. Steffen
SCHERY, Robert W.
  Lawn care now pays green dividends. il Home
    Gard 57:35+ Ap '70
  Spotless summer lawn takes careful planning.
    il Home Gard 57:30-1 Jl '70
  Spring handbook on lawns. il Horticulture
    48:22-4+ Mr '70
SCHEVILL, James Erwin
  Lovecraft's follies. Criticism
    Sat R 53:24 Mr 28 '70 *
SCHICK, Allen
  Cybernetic state. il por Trans-Action 7:14-26
    bibliog(p64) F '70
SCHICK, George
  Musician of the month. D. J. Soria. il por
    Hi Fi 20:secII 14-16 Mr '70 *
SCHICK, Marvin
  Defenders of the faith. por Newsweek 76:60
    D 28 '70 *
SCHICKEL, Richard
  Freaked out on Barthelme. il por N Y Times
    Mag p 14-15+ Ag 16 '70
  Frederick Wiseman's Hospital. Life 68:9 F
    6 '70
  Life movie review. See issues of Life
  New York's Mr Urban Renewal. il pors N Y
    Times Mag p30-4+ Mr 1 '70
  Performing arts. Harper 240:97-9 Ja; 116-18+
    F; 241:34+ Jl; 44-8+ O '70
  Why it isn't easy to be a friend of the Kid.
    il Life 68:42-4 F 6 '70
SCHICKLER, Shirley
  Life is short, death is sure; excerpt from an-
    nual report. il Am Lib 1:35-8 Ja '70
SCHIEFFELIN, William Jay, 3d
  Leisurely cruising, Donzi style. il Yachting
    127:58-9+ F '70
SCHIESS, Betty
  Woman seeks Episcopal ordination. Chr Cent
    87:72 Ja 21 '70; Discussion. 87:399 Ap 1 '70 *
SCHIFF, Bennett
  How they do talk, those conceptualists. New
    Repub 162:27-8 Ap 25 '70
SCHIFF, Peter. See Trinca, J. C. jt. auth.
SCHIFF, Sheldon K.
  Community accountability and mental
    health services. bibliog Ment Hy 54:205-14
    Ap '70
SCHIKANEDER Emanuel
  One-man band. A. M. Lingg. por Opera N
    35:12-13 Ja 2 '71 *
SCHILDKRAUT, Joseph J. and others
  Norepinephrine turnover and metabolism in
    rat brain after long-term administration of
    imipramine. bibliog il Science 168:867-9 My
    15 '70
SCHILL, Bert, and Schill, Bill
  To the tip of Cape Cod. il Yachting 128:56-8
    Ag '70
  —See Schill, Bill. jt. auth.
SCHILL, Bill, and Schill, Bert
  Bugless boating. il Motor B 126:103 Ag '70
  Chesapeake appreciation day 1969. il Motor B
    125:20-1 F '70
  Dune country il Yachting 127:72-3 F '70
  Enjoyable run up the Hudson River to his-
    toric West Point. il Yachting 127:62-3 Ap '70
  Everglades. il Yachting 128:54-5 N '70
  Mixing the seasons. il Yachting 128:58-9 O '70
  Welcome aboard Aurora V. il Motor B 125:
    72-6 F '70
  —See Schill, Bert. jt. auth.
SCHILLER, Anita R.
  Disadvantaged majority. bibliog il Am Lib
    1:345-9, 644 Ap, Jl '70
SCHILLER, Marvin
  Boundaries of love; story. McCalls 97:86-7
    My '70

SCHILLER, Ronald
Best traffic court in the Nation. Read Digest
96:219-20+ Ap '70
SCHILLING, Ronald B.
IC's for microwaves. il por Electr World 84:
42-4 Jl '70
SCHILSON, Donald L. See Creason, F. jt. auth.
SCHIMMEL, Nancy. See Walter, V. jt. auth.
SCHIPOL. See Amsterdam, Netherlands—Air-
ports
SCHIPPERS, Thomas
Cincinnati kid. H. Saal. il por Newsweek 76:
124-5 O 19 '70 *
SCHIRMER, G, inc.
G. Schirmer's sells books. M. B. Tarshish.
il Pub W 197:143-4 F 23 '70
SCHISGAL, Murray
Chinese. Criticism
New Yorker 46:115 Mr 21 '70 *
Dr Fish. Criticism
New Yorker 46:115 Mr 21 '70 *
SCHISTOSOMIASIS
Swimmer's itch. G. F. Levy and J. W. Fol-
stad. bibliog il Environ 11:14-16+ D '69
SCHIZOPHRENIA
Born schizoid? research findings of Harold
E. Himwich. Newsweek 75:52 Je 8 '70
Breakdown in individuals at high risk for
schizophrenia: possible predispositional
perinatal factors. S. A. Mednick. bibliog il
Ment Hy 54:50-63 Ja '70
Genetics of schizophrenic and schizoid di-
sease. L. L. Heston. bibliog il Science 167:
249-56 Ja 16 '70
Man talk; around the bend. D. Newman and
R. Benton. Mlle 72:209 N '70
Postpartum psychiatric reactions: time of
onset and sex ratio of newborns. F. T.
Melges; reply. M. A. Taylor. Science 168:
151-2 Ap 3 '70
Prenatal and birth complications linked by
schizophrenia research. J. Moriarty and L.
Massett. il por Sci N 98:15-16 Jl 4 '70
Reticular stimulation and chlorpromazine:
an animal model for schizophrenic over-
arousal. C. Kornetsky and M. Eliasson;
reply with rejoinder. M. I. Phillips and P.
B. Bradley. Science 168:1122-3 My 29 '70
Schizophrenia, the body's chemical mistake.
H. T. Nyberg. bibliog il por Chem 43:14-17
My '70
SCHLAMM, William S.
Letter from Germany (cont) Nat R 22:946-7
S 8 '70
SCHLEE, Susan
All the fat and collage fuddy murriners;
with biographical sketch. il Natur Hist
79:4, 18-20+ D '70
Prince Albert's way of catching squid; with
biographical sketch. il por Natur Hist 79:8,
20+ F '70
SCHLESINGER, Arthur, 1917-
Amazing success story of "Spiro who?" il
por N Y Times Mag p5-7+ Jl 26 '70
Books. Vogue 155:70 Je; 156:40 Ag 15 '70
Conversations with historians; excerpts from
Interpreting American history, ed. J. A.
Garraty. il por Am Heritage 21:62-4 F '70
Lowering hemisphere. il Atlan 225:79-84+
Ja '70
Movies. See issues of Vogue
Truman's speech and Noam Chomsky. Com-
mentary 48:4+ D '69 49:4+ Mr; 14+ Je '70
Velocity of history. por Newsweek 76:32-4 Jl 6
'70
SCHLESINGER, Mike
Pot, pills and people. Camp Mag 42:10-11+
Mr '70
SCHLESWIG-HOLSTEIN
North of Hamburg. H. P. Koenig. il Travel
133:34-9+ Mr '70
SCHLIEREN apparatus
Experiments with Schlieren auras. D. L.
Heiserman. il Sci Digest 69:75-8 Ja '71
SCHLITZ, Joseph, brewing company
Schlitz brewing: always on Avis, never a
Hertz? il por Forbes 105:25 Ap 15 '70
Schlitz goes flat in Europe again. por
Bsns W p23-4 D 26 '70
That Milwaukee slogan stems from Chicago's
fire. R. A. Uihlein, jr. il Nations Bsns 58:
104-5 Ja '70
SCHLOEMER, Jo
Digging for clay. il pors Ceram Mo 18:24-5
My '70
SCHLOSBERG, Miles S. and Andrews, L. M.
Hidden costs of credit cards. Nation 210:
240-2 Mr 2 '70
SCHLOSSMAN, Steven. See Gibbons, J. jt.
auth.
SCHMERTZ, Mildred F.
Expo '70. il Arch Rec 147:115-28 Je '70
SCHMIDT, Benno Chales
Money is there. pors Forbes 106:45-6 D 1
'70 *

SCHMIDT, Ernest F.
Accounting to ACA members. por Camp Mag
42:4+ Ap '70
Day in the life of a . . . por Camp Mag 42:
4 S '70
Lawsuit against ACA. Camp Mag 42:6-7 My
'70
SCHMIDT, Helmut
Germany in the era of negotiations. For Af-
fairs 49:40-50 O '70
about
Help for the orphan army. Time 95:37 Je 15
'70 *
SCHMIDT, Marjorie G.
Bulbs from our West. il Horticulture 48:14-17
N '70
SCHMIDT, Ruth A.
Second-class citizenship in the kingdom of
God. Chr Today 15:13-14 Ja 1 '71
SCHMIDT-NIELSEN, Knut, and others
Panting in dogs: unidirectional air flow over
evaporative surfaces. bibliog il Science 169:
1102-4 S 11 '70
—See Murrish, D. E. jt. auth.
SCHMIDTCHEN, Paul W.
History in books (cont of Books) See issues
of Hobbies
SCHMITT, Henry L.
Junior yachting; first race week. il por
Yachting 128:35+ N '70
SCHMITT, Roman A. and others
Abundances of thirty elements in lunar rocks,
soil, and core samples. bibliog il Science
167:512-15 Ja 30 '70
—See Wakita, H. jt. auth.
SCHMITZ, William J. jr, and others
Bottom velocity observations directly under
the Gulf Stream. bibliog il Science 170:
1192-4 D 11 '70
SCHNADIG, Victor K.
Victorian ice water pitchers. il Hobbies 75:
121-2 Ap '70
Victorian pickle castors. il Hobbies 75:119 Mr
'70
SCHNEBELEN, Pierre
New accent on après ski. il por Bsns W p47-
8 Ja 31 '70
SCHNEIDAU, R. E.
How you can make integration work for you.
Farm J 94:H16+ Ap '70
SCHNEIDER, Alexander
Alexander Schneider's Christmas present. R.
S. Brown. il por Hi Fi 20:secII 24-5 Mr '70 *
Classical Woodstock. il por Time 97:46 Ja
11 '71
SCHNEIDER, Christian I.
Loss of soul without nature. Nat Parks &
Con Mag 44:20 Ag '70
SCHNEIDER, Edward L. and Salzman, N. P.
Isolation and zonal fractionation of meta-
phase chromosomes from human diploid
cells. bibliog il Science 167:1141-3 F 20 '70
SCHNEIDER, Gerald E. See Murphy, M. R. jt.
auth.
SCHNEIDER, Jason
Camera collector. See issues of Modern
photography
SCHNEIDER, Mark Bernard
Why our defenses are down. Nat R 22:512-13
My 19 '70
SCHNEIDER, Pierre
Henri Matisse: the further side of joy. il
Vogue 156:113-19+ D '70
SCHNEIER, Edward V.
Intelligence of Congress: information and
public-policy patterns. bibliog f Ann Am
Acad 388:14-24 Mr '70
Purity, power and politics. Nation 210:119-
21 F 2 '70
SCHNELZ, Fred C.
Save those tin cans for the garden. il Org
Gard & Farm 17:43 Je '70
SCHNETZLER, C. C. See Philpotts, J. A. jt.
auth.
SCHNITTKER, John A.
Farm payments. New Repub 162:11 Je 27 '70
SCHNITZER, Morris. See Ogner, G. jt. auth.
SCHNOOR, Jerry
Our society is a violent one; interview. U S
News 70:28-9 Ja 11 '71
SCHNORE, Leo F.
Demography and human ecology: some ap-
parent trends. bibliog f il Ann Am Acad
390:120-8 Jl '70
SCHOEBERLEIN, Marion
Look at snow; poem. Horn Bk 46:634 D '70
SCHOEN, Robert, and Rye, R. O.
Sulfur isotope distribution in solfataras,
Yellowstone National Park. bibliog il Sci-
ence 170:1082-4 D 4 '70
SCHOENBERG, Arnold. See Schönberg, A.
SCHOENBERGER, Edward T.
Slab construction using a plastic foam core.
il Ceram Mo 18:27-9 O '70

SCHOENFELD, Eugene
  Doing it in the road: folkways vs. mores.
    Ment Hy 54:450-2 Jl '70
SCHOFIELD, Brian H. and others
  Formation of virus-like particles by bone
    cells in mice with a high incidence of spon-
    taneous leukemia. bibliog il Science 168:
    588-9 My 1 '70
SCHOFIELD, Carl L.
  Water chemistry and lake productivity. il
    Cons 24:9-15+ Ap '70
SCHOFIELD, Miles
  Dragster O.D. il Hot Rod 23:94-5 Mr '70
  Wetter idea from Ford; water pumps. il Hot
    Rod 23:56-7 Ja '70
SCHOLARSHIPS and fellowships
  Foundation grants and fellowships for writ-
    ers; with list of foundations and fellow-
    ships. D. Dempsey. il Writers Digest 50:
    48-53+ Ja; 48-9 F '70
  Graduate education fellowships for Africans.
    Sch & Soc 98:337-8 O '70
    See also
  Citizens' scholarship foundation of America,
    inc.
  Institute of international education
  Nieman fellowships
  Rhodes scholars and scholarships
  Student aid

      Anecdotes, facetiae, satire, etc.
  Look over the shoulder of a scholarship
    committee chairman. R. McQueen. To-
    days Ed 59:44-6 Ja '70
SCHOLASTIC achievements. See Student
  achievements
SCHOLASTIC aptitude test. See College en-
  trance examination board—Scholastic apti-
  tude test
SCHOLASTIC aptitude tests. See Aptitude tests
SCHOLASTIC magazines, inc.
  Aladdin lamp for editors and authors. N. R.
    Ainsworth. Writer 83:28-30 Ap '70
  Founders of Scholastic honored. il Sr Schol
    96:12 F 9 '70
  Maurice Robinson of Scholastic magazines,
    inc; interview. M. R. Robinson. il pors
    Nations Bsns 58:54-8 D '70
  Presenting the 1970 Scholastic awards. il Sr
    Schol 96:11-16+ My 18 '70
  Scholastic acquires two magazines. Sr Schol
    95:Schol Teach 7 S 22 '69
  Scholastic at fifty. il Schol Teach Sec Teach
    Sup p30-1 F 2 '70
  Scholastic at fifty: more than a publisher. il
    Pub W 198:42-5 Jl 20 '70
SCHOLASTIC teacher. See Senior scholastic
  (periodical)
SCHOLEM, Gershom
  Holiness of sin; tr. by H. Halkin. Commen-
    tary 51:41-70 Ja '71
SCHOLES, William
  Kangaroos, states and conservation. Sci N
    97:564 Je 6 '70
SCHOLL, Phoebe K.
  Stimulating perception. il Sch Arts 70:12-13
    N '70
SCHOLTEN, Désirée
  Scholtens: two artist-weavers from the Neth-
    erlands. B. De Neeve. il pors Craft Horiz
    30:24-9 Ja '70 *
SCHOLTEN, Herman
  Scholtens: two artist-weavers from the Neth-
    erlands. B. De Neeve. il pors Craft Horiz
    30:24-9 Ja '70 *
SCHOLZ, Donald J.
  Corporate life was not for him. por Bsns W
    p 116 S 26 '70 *
SCHÖNBERG, Arnold
  Late Beethoven and Schoenberg by Erich
    Leinsdorf: first-rate. M. Kanny. Am Rec
    G 36:488-9 Mr '70 *
  Schoenberg for others: subscribers protest
    première in Israel of twelve-tone Violin
    concerto. por Time 97:45 Ja 18 '71 *
SCHONBERG, Harold C.
  Choreography, music, costumes, sets, etc,
    etc, by Alwin Nikolais. il por N Y Times
    Mag p56-7+ D 6 '70
  Forgotten romantics remembered. il Hi Fi
    sec I 20:87-9 Ja '70
  Man who set music free. por Read Digest
    96:110-15 Je '70
  Music. Harper 240:132+ My; 241:106+ Jl;
    132+ O; 130-2 D '70
SCHOOL administration. See School manage-
  ment and organization
SCHOOL administrators. See School superin-
  tendents and principals
SCHOOL advisory committees. See Citizens as-
  sociations
SCHOOL age
    See also
  Readiness for school

SCHOOL and social and economic problems
  Come to the Store-front learning center. T.
    Mofford and J. Mofford. il Schol Teach
    Sec Teach Sup p 13-15 F 2 '70
  End of the impossible dream. P. Schrag. il
    Sat R 53:68-70+ S 19 '70
  Secondary school as a residual agency. J.
    R. Dettre. bibliog f Clear House 44:515-18
    My '70
  Social class, college, and a dream deferred:
    College and career night at Woodrow
    Wilson high school, Bristol Township, Pa.
    T. J. Cottle. il Sat R 53:60-1+ Ja 24 '70
  Study of interracial conflict. G. Wittes and
    S. Wittes. il Am Ed 6:7-10 Je '70
    See also
  Children of migrant laborers—Education
  School and the community
  Socially handicapped children—Education
SCHOOL and the community
  Can the public schools be saved? M. Polner.
    Commonweal 93:15-17 O 2 '70
  Community involvement in change. L. L.
    Cunningham. Ed Digest 35:1-4 Ap '70
  Getting through to the establishment. M. Es-
    sex. Ed Digest 35:42-4 Ja '70
  Judicial opinion and the role of teachers:
    public school teachers as public officials.
    R. S. Vacca. bibliog Clear House 45:240-4
    D '70
  School-community relations: new issues, new
    needs; need for public relations programs.
    M. S. Norton. Clear House 44:538-40 My
    '70
  Schools and communities: a necessary rele-
    vance. R. B. Jackson. Clear House 44:488-90
    Ap '70
  Study of interracial conflict. G. Wittes and S.
    Wittes. il Am Ed 6:7-10 Je '70
  Taxpayers to the barricades. il Time 96:50 O
    12 '70
  Warner school is the place to come; Nash-
    ville, Tenn. F. Sutherland and R. W. Bo-
    gen. Todays Ed 59:48-9 F '70
    See also
  Colleges and universities—Public relations
  Community education
  Community schools
  School management and organization—Par-
    ent participation
  Teachers and the community
SCHOOL and the home
  Family relationships in the school. il Todays
    Ed 59:10-13+ D '70
  Fond farewell to back-to-school night. J. N.
    Bell. Todays Health 48:16-17+ S '70
  Home visits; classroom teachers as visitors.
    G. Horn. il Todays Ed 59:44-6 S '70
  How parents can assist local schools. il Good
    H 170:160-1 F '70
  In Roxbury, way out of a fortress. J. Kozol.
    Ed Digest 35:12-15 My '70
  Mother-child workshops. R. Herstein. il Sch
    Arts 69:18-19 Mr '70
  School records: invasion of privacy? Russell
    Sage foundation guidelines. I. McMahan.
    il Parents Mag 45:64-5+ S '70; Same abr.
    Ed Digest 36:5-7 D '70
  Squeeze the parents out of school and see
    what we get. A. H. Rice. Ed Digest 36:32-3
    S '70
  Teaching parents to teach. H. S. Resnik.
    Vogue 156:96 O 1 '70
  Wanted: R for the equitable management of
    parent-school conflict. L. Firester and J.
    Firester. Ed Digest 35:5-7 Ap '70
  When you go to see the teacher. D. S.
    Looney. Bet Hom & Gard 48:118 O '70
SCHOOL architecture. See School buildings
SCHOOL art exhibits. See Childrens art—Ex-
  hibitions
SCHOOL arts (periodical)
  School arts readers evaluate their magazine.
    Sch Arts 69:31 F '70
SCHOOL assemblies
  Subversion of the school assembly. A. W.
    Howard. Clear House 44:401-3 Mr '70
SCHOOL athletics
  High lights. H. L. Masin. il Sr Schol 96:20 My
    4 '70
  Inequities in athletics. L. J. Weber. Clear
    House 45:177-80 N '70
  Should Johnny (or Johnnie) play ball? R.
    Bugg. il Todays Health 48:56-8+ S '70
    See also
  Football
  Running
SCHOOL attendance
  Preschool enrollment. Sch & Soc 98:11-12 Ja
    '70
  Recent trends in U.S. school enrollment. C.
    E. Johnson, jr. and A. A. Zappolo. bibliog
    Sch & Soc 98:116-19 F '70
    See also
  Junior colleges—Attendance

SCHOOL boards
Big cities try a dose of smallness. Sr School 96;School Teach 1-2 My 18 '70
Can local boards survive? L. C. Rose. Ed Digest 36:19-21 N '70
Maybe you should be on the school board. il Changing T 24:31-3 Jl '70
Share the power with students; says school board members. Ed Digest 36:39-41 O '70
SCHOOL bombings. See Terrorism
SCHOOL books. See Textbooks
SCHOOL buildings
Architectural stimulus and response in a school for the mentally retarded; Wilton state school, Wilton, N.Y. il Arch Rec 147: 164-6 Ja '70
Box full of school; Latin school, Chicago. il Arch Forum 132:58-61 My '70
Building a new school plant? The first important step is educational planning. J. E. Rutrough. bibliog f Clear House 44:378-80 F '70
Building for the arts. R. Montgomery. il Arch Forum 132:80-9 Ja '70
Building process in the 1970's: the trouble with systems; Toronto's systems schools. R. E. Fischer. il Arch Rec 148:148-53 O '70
Building types study. C. W. Brubaker: H. A. Patterson, jr. il Arch Rec 148:128-34 N '70
Planning facilities for an educational program. S. J. Coffey. Clear House 45:169-73 N '70
School for small children as big as all outdoors; new Canaan country school. il Arch Rec 148:97-100 Jl '70
School that is a street; Ontario, Canada. il Arch Forum 132:50-5 Je '70
Two more for Columbus. il Arch Forum 132: 22-31 Mr '70
Ways to build mistakes out of your middle school. Ed Digest 36:11-14 N '70
What is charrette planning for schools? W. D. Boutwell. PTA Mag 65:30-1 O '70

Heating and ventilation
Round-the-clock vocational school runs on total energy. il Arch Rec 148:157-9 S '70

History
New bit of americana; little red schoolhouse. H. E. Smith. il Har Yrs 10:13 Jl '70
SCHOOL buildings, Portable

Anecdotes, facetiae, satire, etc.
Burning issue. B. Daugherty. Ed Digest 35: 35 F '70
SCHOOL bus transportation. See School children—Transportation
SCHOOL children
Drugs for learning. il Time 96:43-4 Ag 10 '70
Economic literacy of elementary school pupils. R. B. McKenzie. Ed Digest 36:41-3 N '70
Kwan-Hi. B. B. Robinson. il Todays Ed 59:18-19 N '70
Pep pills for pupils; use of stimulants to control hyperactive children in Omaha. Newsweek 76:60-1 Jl 13 '70
Pep pills for youngsters; treatment of hyperactive children in Omaha. il U S News 69:49 Jl 13 '70
Pills for classroom peace? controversy over use of drugs to improve school performance by controlling hyperactivity. E. T. Ladd. il Sat R 53:66-8+ N 21 '70; Discussion. 53:50 D 19 '70
See also
Adolescence
High school students
Intelligence tests
Problem children
Readiness for school
School lunches
Self-government in education
Teachers and students

Adjustment
Children who hate school. N. Hentoff. il Parents Mag 45:60-1+ F '70
School's role in emotional health; with study-discussion program, by E. Harris and D. Harris. A. Daniels. bibliog il PTA Mag 64: 16-18+, 33-4 Ap '70

Anecdotes, facetiae, satire, etc.
Dizzyland of show and tell. B. Moore. Todays Ed 59:57 N '70

Grading and promotion
See Grading and marking (students)

Out-of-school activities
Summer is for reading. P. Pine. il Am Ed 6:26-7 Ag '70

Punishment
See School discipline

Reading
See Childrens reading

Transportation
Bus to integration bogs down. il Life 68:22-9 Mr 13 '70
Busing quandary; situation in Charlotte. N.C. il Newsweek 76:63 Ag 24 '70
Chaos over school busing; tale of two cities; Charlotte, N.C. and Los Angeles. il U S News 68:29-33 Mr 16 '70
New look at busing. U S News 68:63 Mr 30 '70
SCHOOL children, Free food for. See School lunches
SCHOOL childrens boners. See Blunders
SCHOOL construction. See School buildings
SCHOOL counselors. See Student counselors
SCHOOL-crossing signs. See Traffic signs
SCHOOL discipline
Are student lockers offl limits to principals? H. C. Hudgins, jr. Ed Digest 36:14-15 D '70
Avoiding court cases; a guide for administrators. R. P. McAdams. jr. Clear House 45: 45-7 S '70
Controlling student conduct; National association of secondary school principals guidelines. R. L. Ackerly. Ed Digest 36: 12-15 Ap '70
Discipline in the innovative school. J. F. McCaffery and D. S. Turner. Clear House 44:491-6 Ap '70; Same abr. Ed Digest 36:16-19 O '70
Facing student unrest. R. M. Kudela. bibliog Clear House 44:547-52 My '70
Murder in the schoolroom; excerpts from Crisis in the classroom. C. E. Silberman. il Atlan 225:82-94+ Je '70
Pupil control in English and French schools. R. P. Magnuson. Ed Digest 35:25-7 My '70
School relationships; address, July 8, 1970. A. A. Berle, jr. Vital Speeches 36:715-17 S 15 '70
Teacher's guide to good discipline; six classroom techniques that also work at home. M. Bowen. il Parents Mag 45:50-2 Je '70
See also
Classroom management
SCHOOL districts
Hitching up the small school districts; shared services. F. L. Heesacker. il Am Ed 6:18-21 Ap '70
School liability and safety education. K. F. Licht. Ed Digest 36:22-4 N '70
SCHOOL drama. See College and school drama
SCHOOL employees
See also
School secretaries

Salaries, allowances, etc.
Wages of nonteaching employees in educational institutions. C. M. O'Connor. il Mo Labor R 93:54-5 Ap '70
SCHOOL enrollment. See School attendance
SCHOOL excursions
For those who look but do not see; field trip to paint seascape. T. Stevens. il Sch Arts 70:10-11 N '70
Mystery, history, and an ancient graveyard. M. G. Williams. il Todays Ed 59:42-3 My '70; Same abr. Ed Digest 36:20-1 '70
Mystery, history, and an old log cabin. H. J. Waters. il Todays Ed 59:44-5 My '70
SCHOOL exhibits
Box display. J. F. Warwick. il Sch Arts 70: 32-3 S '70
Creatively combined; fine arts festival. W. H. Kraiger. il Sch Arts 70:36-7 S '70
SCHOOL finance
Crisis in American education; address, June 19 1970. R. A. Freeman. Vital Speeches 36: 592-7 Jl '70
Poor education; Urban education task force report. New Repub 162:9-10 Mr 21 '70
Taxpayers to the barricades. il Time 96:50 O 12 '70
When the money runs out. W. E. Henry. Todays Ed 59:54-5 Mr '70
Who should finance the schools? il Sr School 95;School Teach 1 N 3 '69
Why ghetto schools fail. H. M. Levin. il Sat R 53:68-9+ Mr 21 '70
See also
Colleges and universities—Finance
Education—Economic aspects
Education—Federal aid
Education and state
Equalization, Educational
United States—President's commission on school finance

SCHOOL for scandal; drama. See Sheridan, R.

SCHOOL gardens
Children s gardens in New York city schools: an educational report dated 1897. A. Schatz and V. Schatz. il Org Gard & Farm 17:67-9 N '70

SCHOOL grading and promotion. See Grading and marking (students)

SCHOOL grounds
Gift from our seniors; landscaping. H. H. Micka. il Todays Ed 59:53 Ja '70
    See also
Campus planning

SCHOOL houses. See School buildings

SCHOOL journalism. See College and school journalism

SCHOOL laws and legislation
Equal education and the law. H. Shanks. Am Scholar 39:255-69, 727 Spr, Aut '70
    See also
Colleges and universities—Laws and legislation

California
    See also
Evolution—Laws and legislation

United States
Professional negotiations: state or federal legislation? J. W. Maguire. Sch & Soc 98: 176-7 Mr '70
With education in Washington. See issues of Education digest
    See also
Education—Federal aid

SCHOOL leaving. See Dropouts

SCHOOL legislation. See School laws and legislation

SCHOOL librarians
Din of silence; letter to the editor. P. A. Ciancione. Library J 95:708 F 15 '70
Dix on the Dix mix; letter to the editor. W. S. Dix. Library J 95:1139 Mr 15 '70
Do's and don'ts for librarians and administrators M. L. Mann. Todays Ed 59:23 O '70
Lively learning center and the alert librarian. L. G. Hunt. il por Wilson Lib Bul 45:293-7 N '70
School librarian says goodbye; letter to the editor. Am Lib 1:524 Je '70
    See also
American association of school librarians

Supply and demand
School library personnel, task analysis survey. Am Lib 1:176-7 F '70

SCHOOL librarians institutes. See Library institutes and workshops

SCHOOL libraries
Casebook of school library services; symposium; ed. by M. L. Mann. il Am Lib 1: 162-75 F '70
Crisis in the classroom, by C. Silberman. Review
    Library J 95:3946 N 15 '70
Different library, different school! City and country school library. M. B. Piel. il Pub W 198:78-81 Jl 13 '70
Generating a spirit of inquiry. F. DeHart. bibliog Am Lib 1:602-5 Je '70
Lively learning center and the alert librarian. L. C. Hunt. il por Wilson Lib Bul 45:293-7 N '70
Plan for survival. E. Geller. Library J 95: 1535 Ap 15 '70; Reply. E. B. Gild. 95:2950 S 15 '70
Reading teacher's dream come true. R. G. Stauffer. bibliog il por Wilson Lib Bul 45: 285-92 N '70
School libraries and international development; ed. by J. E. Lowrie. Am Lib 1:182-3 F '70
School library, by R. A. Davies. Review
    Library J 95:1914-15 My 15 '70. L. L. Shapiro; Discussion. 95:2950-3, 3577-9 S 15, O 15 '70
Who speaks for youth? symposium. il Library J 95:205-17 Ja 15 '70
    See also
Childrens literature
Libraries and schools
School librarians

Administration
    See School libraries—Supervisors and supervision

Audio-visual materials
    See School libraries and audio-visual materials

Automation
Automated library system: Project LEEDS; Springfield public schools, Ore. J. R. Blair and R. Snyder. il Am Lib 1:172-3 F '70

Book selection
Students, systems, and selection; address, 1969. L. O. Vinson. por Library J 95.205-7 Ja 15 '70; Reply. C. W. Koch. 95:1877 My 15 '70

Censorship
Censorship: librarians, administrators and boards. Library J 95:4309 D 15 '70
Knudson's complaint. R. Knudson. il Am Lib 1:776-8 S '70
NCA accreditation threat checks Iowa censors; Glenwood high school Library J 95:1148 Mr 15 '70

Federal aid
Accountability: Right to read program and integration vs. compensatory education. E. Geller. Library J 95:1881 My 15 '70
Ed funds threatened by veto at final hour. Library J 95:713+ F 15 '70
ESEA extended to 1973; school library program retained. Library J 95:1883 My 15 '70
Library funds rescued in second 1970 money bill. Library J 95:1542 Ap 15 '70
Media programs cited in ESEA Title I critique. Library J 95:1546 Ap 15 '70
1970 HEW funds 1st video veto; FY '71 budget: blueprint or blight? G. Krettek and E. D. Cooke. Wilson Lib Bul 44:794-5 Mr '70
1971 budget snubs libraries: 1970 bill starts again. Library J 95:1144-5 Mr 15 '70
Nixon reviews mandatory education funds. Library J 95:3583 O 15 '70
Nixon's education message shifts stand on libraries. Library J 95:1540-2 Ap 15 '70

Poetry
At the ground-breaking. . ; S. Brown. il Wilson Lib Bul 45:451 Ja '71

Services to the blind
Blind children learn to relate; Windsor Spring elementary school, Richmond County schools, Augusta. Ga. E. Johnson and T. Merriweather. il Am Lib 1:168-9 F '70

Standards
Professional development reviewed: 1969 standards for school media programs. H. Elstein and F. R. Hartz. pors Wilson Lib Bul 44:865-6 Ap '70; Reply. E. S. Borden. 45:134+ O '70
Standards for school media programs, 1920: a lesson from history. B. L. Gambee. bibliog Am Lib 1:483-5 My '70

Supervisors and supervision
Continuum: how to analyze your school environment, and loosen it up; reprint. A. Barton. bibliog il Library J 95:4317-23 D 15 '70

California
LA school librarian files unfair treatment complaint; R. K. Kwan. Library J 95:198-200 Ja 15 '70
LA teachers group appealing librarian's rights; R. K. Kwan. Library J 95:1892 My 15 '70

Iowa
NCA accreditation threat checks Iowa censors; Glenwood high school. Library J 95:1148 Mr 15 '70

New York (state)
CS takeover by school libraries recommended; study by Commissioner's committee on library development. Wilson Lib Bul 45:119 O '70
Library-A/V ties disputed in New York state; school libraries section meeting of NYLA. Library J 95:195-6+ Ja 15 '70
N.Y. report puts children services in schools; national media standards recommended as minimum. Library J 95:3945 N 15 '70
Vision transplanted: NYLA reports on lack of school-library cooperation. E. Geller. Library J 95:4307 D 15 '70
Why wait for a week? Mamaroneck avenue school, Mamaroneck; letter to the editor. M. P. Archer. Library J 95:190 Ja 15 '70

Panama
School libraries in Panama. C. V. Penna. Am Lib 1:182-3 F '70

Scandinavia
School libraries in Scandinavia. M. Nilson. Am Lib 1:183-5 F '70

Southern states
Integration scheduled for court review. Library J 95:3583-4 O 15 '70
Southern segregationism echoed in library patterns. il Library J 95:1883+ My 15 '70

SCHOOL libraries—*Continued*

Virginia

October inspiration: school libraries work! excerpt from report. I. W. Hale. il por Wilson Lib Bul 45:127 O '70

SCHOOL libraries and audio-visual materials

Media industry: its growth, structure, and role in education; address, June 1969. E. N. Nelsen. por Library J 95:1159-61 Mr 15 '70

Multimedia shelving. R. Muller. Library J 95:750 F 15 '70

Notes from a semi-darkened room; address, 1969. D. Lembo. il por Library J 95:735-7 F 15 '70

Standards for school media programs, 1920: a lesson from history. B. L. Gambee. bibliog Am Lib 1:483-5 My '70

SCHOOL libraries and Negroes

Integration scheduled for court review. Library J 95:3583-4 O 15 '70

Southern segregationism echoed in library patterns. il Library J 95:1883+ My 15 '70

Why wait for a week? Mamaroneck avenue school, Mamaroneck, N.Y; letter to the editor. M. P. Archer. Library J 95:190 Ja 15 '70

SCHOOL libraries and social and economic problems. See Libraries and social and economic problems

SCHOOL libraries and state

CS takeover by school libraries recommended; study by the New York state commissioner's committee on library development. Wilson Lib Bul 45:119 O '70

SCHOOL library supervisors. See School libraries—Supervisors and supervision

SCHOOL library surveys

School library manpower task survey available. Library J 95:1148+ Mr 15 '70

SCHOOL lockers. See Lockers

SCHOOL lunches

Hunger in the classroom. L. Velie. Read Digest 96:134-9 Mr '70

School lunch program and the NEA. G. D. Fischer and N. Kotz. pors Todays Ed 59:16-19 Ja '70

School lunch program: should it be expanded? il Good H 170:184 Ap '70

Shocking failure of the School lunch act. J. R. Komaiko. Parents Mag 45:56-9 Mr '70

SCHOOL management and organization

Big cities try a dose of smallness. Sr Schol 96:Schol Teach 1-2 My 18 '70

Black nationalism and community schools; excerpts from Community control of schools. R. C. Maynard. bibliog Sch & Soc 98:121-5 F '70

Bureaucracy and educational change. L. K. Bishop. bibliog Clear House 44:305-9 Ja '70

Child's garden of versus; community control. I. Kraft. Nation 210:790-1 Je 29 '70

City, suburbs, and education; regional government and community schools are essential; address, December 12, 1969. E. G. Olsen. Vital Speeches 36:253-6 F 1 '70

Continuum: how to analyze your school environment, and loosen it up; reprint. A. Barton. bibliog il Library J 95:4317-23 D 15 '70

Decentralization: issues and comments. D. K. Clear. bibliog Clear House 44:259-67 Ja '70; Same. Ed Digest 35:8-11 My '70

Educational structure, is it capable of innovation? S. Leles. bibliog Clear House 44: 368-72 F '70

Impact of school decentralization on collective bargaining. M. H. Moskow and K. McLennan. Mo Labor R 93:51-3 Ap '70

Limits of liberalism; liberal intellectuals and community control. L. J. Fein. il Sat R 53:83-5+ Je 20 '70

Meeting community demands for decentralization of control. R. L. Derr. Sch & Soc 98:362 O '70

Morgan follows through; community control and follow through, Washington, D.C. S. Moorefield. il Am Ed 6:31-3 Ja '70

Needed: requiem for a structure. J. M. Palardy. bibliog f Clear House 44:360-3 F '70

School reorganization and the process of educational change; adaptation of address, June 29, 1967. R. I. Miller. bibliog Sch & Soc 98: 346-9 O '70

Student unrest; structure of the public schools a major factor? N. W. Fink and B. Cullers. bibliog Clear House 44:415-19 Mr '70

See also

Colleges and universities—Administration

Courses of study

Schedules, School

School boards

School discipline

School finance

School superintendents and principals

School year

Teachers—Selection and appointment

Anecdotes, facetiae, satire, etc.

Negotiation game. il Todays Ed 59:54-5 Ap '70

Parent participation

Case for parent participation in the schools. B. Bard. il Parents Mag 45:49-51+ Mr '70

Student participation

High-school power. il Newsweek 75:63 Mr 9 '70

Student participation in faculty meetings. J. J. Roy. Clear House 44:285 Ja '70

Teacher participation

Professional negotiation. R. Perry; K. L. Law; R. Van Delinder, jr. and R. H. St Germain. Todays Ed 59:33-40 F '70

SCHOOL music

Enclave; music in school, at home and around town in Whittier, Calif. M. F. K. Fisher. New Yorker 46:35-9 O 3 '70

Where does rock music belong in the schools? Todays Ed 59:34-6 My '70

See also

Choral singing—Instruction and study

SCHOOL nurses

School nurse to the rescue. H. H. Brion. il Todays Ed 59:26-7 N '70

SCHOOL ombudsman. See Ombudsman (education)

SCHOOL organization. See School management and organization

SCHOOL phobia

School phobia and the fear of death. W. Tietz. bibliog Ment Hy 54:565-8 O '70

SCHOOL-police cooperation. See Police-school cooperation

SCHOOL prayer. See Public schools and religion

SCHOOL prayer decision. See United States—Supreme court—Decisions

SCHOOL principals. See School superintendents and principals

SCHOOL property

See also

Taxation, Exemption from

SCHOOL public relations. See School and the community

SCHOOL reports and records

Computer harvests migrant records. M. P. Pfeil. il Am Ed 6:6-9 N '70

School marks and reporting to parents. Ed Digest 36:35-7 D '70

School records: invasion of privacy? Russell Sage foundation guidelines. I. McMahan. il Parents Mag 45:64-5+ S '70; Same abr. Ed Digest 36:5-7 D '70

See also

Grading and marking (students)

SCHOOL secretaries

Anecdotes, facetiae, satire, etc.

Bad day at Wild Rose. M. Thyme. il Todays Health 48:58-9+ N '70

SCHOOL sessions. See School year

SCHOOL ships. See Training ships

SCHOOL statistics. See Education—Statistics

SCHOOL subjects. See Courses of study

SCHOOL superintendents and principals

Assistant principal: educational leader? P. J. McDonough. bibliog f Clear House 45:97-9 O '70

Black principal. J. C. James. New Repub 163: 17-20 S 26 '70

Games teachers shouldn't play with principals. E. Demsch. Clear House 45:86-8 O '70

How to obtain a principalship. W. G. Patterson. Clear House 44:310-14 Ja '70

It's not an easy life. Sr Schol 96:Schol Teach 2 S 29 '69

Job specifications for principals. G. E. Melton and J. Stanavage. Ed Digest 36:25-8 O '70

New math; suspended school superintendent in Warrensville Heights, Ohio. T. Sheridan. New Repub 163:13 S 19 '70

New roles for principals. H. Goldman. Clear House 45:135-9 N '70

New York city principals: on the razor's edge. B. Bard. il Sat R 53:58-9+ Ja 24 '70

Principal problem. il Newsweek 76:53 N 2 '70

Proverbs 7:69 let us not forsake our principals. P. A. Soderbergh. Clear House 44: 461-4 Ap '70

School principal: on the cross-fire line? W. B. Levenson. bibliog Clear House 45:216-18 D '70

SCHOOL superintendents and principals—*Cont.*
School superintendent as philosopher. J. W. Bennion. Sch & Soc 98:25-7 Ja '70
Superintendent and negotiations. A. L. Bradley. Clear House 44:278 Ja '70
Teacher opinion poll; teachers' views of the principalship. il Todays Ed 59:18 Mr '70
Twenty-five cardinal principals for the school principal. J. R. Ban. Clear House 44:441-5 Mr '70
What makes a good elementary school principal? K. Goldhammer and G. L Becker. Am Ed 6:11-13 Ap '70
  See also
Student-administrator relationships

Salaries, allowances, etc.
Salaries of school professionals. il Ed Digest 35:27-9 Ja '70

Selection and appointment
Suit seeks to smash standards; NAACP legal defense and educational fund to challenge constitutionality system of licensing principals. Sat R 53:72 N 21 '70

SCHOOL superintendents and principals, Professional ethics for
NEA expels school superintendent. Sch & Soc 98:14-15 Ja '70

SCHOOL teachers. See Teachers
SCHOOL teaching. See Teaching
SCHOOL terms. See School year
SCHOOL violence. See Violence
SCHOOL visitations. See School and the home
SCHOOL volunteer programs. See Volunteer workers in education
SCHOOL-work plan. See Education, Cooperative
SCHOOL year
Case for year-round schools. J. Engh. Redbook 134:84+ Ap '70
180 days vs. the year-round school. S. Holzman. il Schol Teach Sec Teach Sup p 18-19 Ap 6 '70
Organized camp: a laboratory for learning; 12-month school year and organized camping. J. J. Kirk. por Camp Mag 42:4 Je '70. Reply. L. V. Baldwin. 42:30 S '70
Rescheduling the school year; policy statement by NEA. Todays Ed 59:37 D '70
Should we have year-round schools? G. M. Knox. Bet Hom & Gard 43:60+ Je '70
Year-round schooling: how it really works; Atlanta. J. Barnes. por Parents Mag 45:42 My '70

SCHOOLHOUSES. See School buildings
SCHOOLS
  See also
Catholic schools
Church schools
Correspondence schools and courses
Courses of study
Education
Forestry schools and education
Private schools
Public schools
School buildings
Schools, Experimental
Summer schools

Statistics
See Education—Statistics

England
  See also
Public schools (endowed)—England

United States
Schools we want: a family dialogue. N. Hentoff; M. Hentoff. il Sat R 53:74-7 S 19 '70
  See also
Education—United States
Public schools—United States
Rural schools—United States

Wales
They called it philosophical poppycock; experiment in international education: Atlantic college at St Donat's castle. L. Jonckheere. il Schol Teach Jr/Sr High 16-17 N 2 '70
United World colleges; Atlantic college at St Donat's castle first in chain. T. Sylte. il UNESCO Courier 23:28-32 O '70

SCHOOLS, Community control of. See School management and organization
SCHOOLS, Elementary. See Education, Elementary
SCHOOLS, Experimental
Adams high: best around; John Adams high school, Portland, Ore. il Newsweek 75:68-9 F 16 '70
Free schools; New school of Decatur. J. Howard. il Life 70:45-6+ Ja 8 '71

John Dewey is alive and well in New England; free schools. R. H. De Lone and S. T. De Lone. il Sat R 53:69-71+ N 21 '70
Learning and liking it; Lincoln elementary school in Staples, Minn. C. Watson. il Am Ed 6:18-22 My '70
Magnet school; Disney experiment in elementary education, Chicago. il Newsweek 76:75 O 12 '70
Model schools: blueprint for the future. C. H. Harrison. Schol Teach Sec Teach Sup p 18-19+ Mr 9 '70
New learning center thrives in New York; John Dewey high school. W. E. Williamson. Clear House 45:26-8 S '70
Pennsylvania advancement school: no game for radicals. H. S. Resnik. il Sat R 53:49-51+ Jl 18 '70
Portland's unconventional Adams high. J. Guernsey. il Am Ed 6:3-7 My '70
Rise of the free school. B. B. Stretch. il Sat R 53:76-9+ Je 20 '70
Why must Lincoln die? experimental school being killed in Kentucky. J. Star. il Look 34:64-8 Ag 11 '70
  See also
Free universities
Philadelphia—Education
Special classes and special schools
SCHOOLS, Laboratory. See Laboratory schools
SCHOOLS, Medical. See Medical colleges
SCHOOLS, Open air. See Open-air schools
SCHOOLS and libraries. See Libraries and schools
SCHOOLS and politics. See Teachers—Political activities
SCHOOLS and social and economic problems. See School and social and economic problems
SCHOOLS for the deaf. See Deaf—Education
SCHOONMAKER, A. G, company
Loser''s victory helps contractors. Bsns W p74 O 3 '70
SCHOPF, J. William
Micropaleontological studies of lunar samples. bibliog il Science 167:779-80 Ja 30 '70
SCHOPF, James Morton
Petrified peat from a Permian coal bed in Antarctica. bibliog il Science 169:274-7 Jl 17 '70
SCHOPF, Thomas J. M. and Allan, J. R.
Phylum ectoprocta, order cheilostomata: microprobe analysis of calcium, magnesium, strontium, and phosphorus in skeletons. bibliog il Science 169:280-2 Jl 17 '70
SCHOPP, Walter W.
Electronic photoflash meter. il Electr World 83:62-3 Je '70
Small-size hi-fi stereo amplifier. il Electr World 85:34 Ja '71
SCHOTT, Adde Lou
Psychedelic ceiling. il Sch Arts 70:38 N '70
SCHOTT, Francis H.
Factors controlling inflation; address, March 19, 1970. Vital Speeches 36:561-3 Jl 1 '70
SCHOTT, Webster
Doctor Williams: beautiful blood, beautiful brain; excerpt from introd. to Imaginations. Am Scholar 39:305-9 Spr '70
Poet of the age of anxiety. il pors Life 68:52-3+ Ja 30 '70
SCHOTTE, Douglas
Eatontown caper. il por Newsweek 76:46+ Ag 24 '70 *
SCHRADER, Paul
Poetry of ideas: the films of Charles Eames. il por Film Q 23:2-19 Spr '70
SCHRAFF, Anne
Project 2469 A.D. Schol Teach Sec Teach Sup p 17-18 N 3 '69
SCHRAG, Peter
After Kent state: the first hundred days. il Sat R 53:12-15+ Ag 29 '70
America's other radicals. Harper 241:35-46 Ag '70
Decline of the WASP. il Harper 240:85-91 Ap '70
End of the impossible dream. il Sat R 53:68-70+ S 19 '70
Growing up on Mechanic street. il Sat R 53:59-61+ Mr 21 '70
Is Main Street still there? il Sat R 53:20-5 Ja 17 '70
Life on the Mississippi, 1970. il Sat R 53:19-23 D 12 '70
Out of place in America; excerpts. Sat R 53:12-13+ My 9 '70
Tennessee lonesome end. il Harper 240:59-63+ Mr '70
Who owns the environment? Sat R 53:6-9+ Jl 4 '70
SCHRAM, Frederick R.
Isopod from the Pennsylvanian of Illinois. bibliog il Science 169:854-5 Ag 28 '70

SCHRAM, Stuart R.
What makes Mao a Maoist. il N Y Times
Mag p36-7+ Mr 8 '70
SCHRAMECK, Joan E.
Crayfish swimming: alternating motor out-
put and giant fiber activity. bibliog il Sci-
ence 169:698-700 Ag 14 '70
SCHRANZ, Karl
Here comes, there goes Karl! W. Johnson.
il por Sports Illus 32:58-9 Mr 23 '70
SCHREIBER, Edward, and Anderson, O. L.
Properties and composition of lunar mate-
rials: earth analogies. bibliog il Science
168:1579-80 Je 26 '70
—and others
Sound velocity and compressibility for lunar
rocks 17 and 46 and for glass spheres from
the lunar soil. bibliog il Science 167:732-4
Ja 30 '70
SCHREIBER, Jean Jacques Servan-. See Ser-
van-Schreiber, J. J.
SCHREIBER, Jean Louis Servan-. See Servan-
Schreiber, J. L.
SCHROEDER, Duane D. and Mozen, M. M.
Australia antigen: distribution during Cohn
ethanol fractionation of human plasma.
bibliog il Science 168:1462-4 Je 19 '70
SCHROEDER, Lynn. See Ostrander, S. jt. auth.
SCHROEDER, William K.
Boy who was just there watching it and
making up his mind. J. Pekkanen. il pors
Life 68:36-7 My 15 '70 *
SCHROTH, Raymond A.
Between the lines. America 122:310-12 Mr
21 '70
Jesuit high school. Commonweal 91:472-5 Ja
30 '70
Violence and understanding: campus unrest
and the Scranton report. il Cath World
212:119-22 D '70
SCHÜBELIN, Peter
Puzzle of the A2 meson. bibliog il Phys Today
23:32-8 N '70
SCHUBERT, Carlos, and Sifontes, R. S.
Boconó fault. Venezuelan Andes: evidence of
postglacial movement. bibliog il Science 170:
66-9 O 2 '70
SCHUBERT, Franz Peter
First Steinberg-BSO recording: Symphony
no. 9 in C. M. N. Kanny. Am Rec G 36:981
Ag '70 *
On twenty-five records: forty hours of Schu-
bert lieder. P. L. Miller. il por Am Rec G
37:142-6 N '70 *
Records:
Songs. Opera N 34:36 Ja 24 '70
Stunning Schubert by Artur Rubinstein. L.
Gerber. Am Rec G 36:490-1 Mr '70 *
SCHUBERT, Gerald, and Lingenfelter, R. E.
Superheated ice formed by the freezing of
superheated water. il Science 168:469-70 Ap
24 '70
—and others
Phase change instability in the mantle. bib-
liog il Science 169:1075-7 S 11 '70
SCHUBERTH, Christopher J.
Barrier beaches of eastern America; with
biographical sketch. il Natur Hist 79:3,
46-55 Je '70
SCHUCH, Carole Tindall
Are we entertaining or educating? il Sch
Arts 69:24-6 Ap '70
SCHUCHAT, Theodor
News desk. See issues of Harvest years
With education in Washington. Ed Digest
36:55-8 O; 54-7 N; 55-8 D '70
SCHUCK, Robert F.
Revitalized curriculum for business educa-
tion. Clear House 45:32-6 S '70
SCHUELER, Robert L.
Ecology: the new religion? America 122:292-5
Mr 21 '70
SCHUESSLER, Raymond
How to sight-in a rifle. il Pop Mech 134:132-
3+ S '70
SCHUFLE, Joseph A.
Thomas Dillon: chemist & revolutionary. il
por Chem 43:18-21 Ap '70
SCHUFLETOWSKI, Frank W.
Taxonomy of words: a study in meaning.
bibliog f Clear House 44:474-8 Ap '70
SCHUH, Willi
Strauss to Schuh: letters from the last years.
R. Breuer. Sat R 53:95-6 F 28 '70 *
SCHULBERG, Budd
Real anger was backstage. il por Life 69:50-2
Ag 21 '70
SCHULDER, Diane
Women and the law; excerpt from Women's
liberation and the law. por Atlan 225:103-4
Mr '70
SCHULER, Stanley
Aerosols: $3 billion-a-year success story.
Am Home 73:34+ Ap '70
House building: dream or nightmare. Am
Home 73:40+ My '70

Instant lawns the weed-free way. il Am Home
73:22+ Ag '70
Why can't you get anything fixed anymore?
Am Home 73:32+ Je '70
SCHULITZ, Helmut C.
Message as an architectural medium il Arch
Forum 132:44-9 My '70
SCHULMAN, Joseph D. and Bradley, K. H.
Cystinosis: selective induction of vacuola-
tion in fibroblasts by L-cysteine-D-penicil-
lamine disulfide. bibliog il Science 169:595-7
Ag 7 '70
SCHULTE, E. L.
Horseshoes on the oars. Motor B 125:130-1
Je '70
SCHULTE, Elaine L.
To find the rainbow; story. Good H 172:76-7
Ja '71
What you can do for your child's school. il
Parents Mag 45:60-1+ S '70
SCHULTZ, Dodi
Your aching head. il Ladies Home J 87:56+
S '70
SCHULTZ, Jerome S. See Beck, R.E. jt. auth.
SCHULTZ, Morton J.
Automobile clinic; questions and answers.
See issues of Popular mechanics
Give your stern drive a mid-season lift. il
Pop Mech 134:123-5+ Ag '70
How the airlines hope to stop the hijackers.
il Pop Mech 133:83-5 My '70
How the jets kicked the smoking habit. il
Pop Mech 134:104-5+ Jl '70
Saturday mechanic. See issues of Popular
mechanics
Should mechanics have to have a license? il
Pop Mech 135:73-5+ Ja '71
When will you have a waterproof ignition
system? il Pop Mech 134:86-7 Ag '70
Why is your motor missing? il Pop Mech
134:124-5 Jl '70
SCHULTZE, Charles Louis
Data system for measuring and analyzing pub-
lic programs; excerpt from address, Decem-
ber 1969. Mo Labor R 93:13-15 Mr '70
SCHULZ, David
Calendar of European sporting events, 1970.
il Holiday 47:22-3 Ja '70
SCHULZ, John W.
Technician's perspective. See issues of
Forbes
SCHULZ, William
Portrait of a mobster. por Read Digest 97:
58-62 Ag '70
Shocking success story of public enemy no.
1. por Read Digest 96:54-9 My '70
Smugglers of misery. Read Digest 96:49-54
Ag '70
SCHULZE, Franz
Chaos as architecture. il Art in Am 58:88-
96 Jl '70
SCHULZINGER, Mark
Easy first step to publication: book review-
ing. Writers Digest 50:16-18 F '70
SCHUMAN, Howard. See Converse, P. E. jt.
auth.
SCHUMAN, Patricia. See Detlefsen, E. G. jt.
auth.
SCHUMANN, Maurice
Position of the U.N; address, September 18,
1970. Vital Speeches 37:5-7 O 15 '70
SCHUMANN, Robert Alexander
Horowitz vs. Rubinstein. H. Goldsmith.
il Hi Fi 20:sec1 67-8 Ag '70 *
Like a breath of fresh air: Souzay and Bald-
win. A. Sperber. Am Rec G 36:434-5 F '70 *
Schumann's die perl with Janowitz, Brilioth,
Engen, Smith. I. Kolodin Sat R 53:55 Je 6
'70 *
Songs of Robert Schumann, by E. Sams.
Review
Am Rec G por 36:722-3 My '70. E. Green-
field *
SCHUMPETER, Joseph Alois
Joseph Schumpeter. P. A. Samuelson. News-
week 75:75 Ap 13 '70 *
SCHUR, Max
Background of Freud's Disturbance on the
Acropolis. Am Imago 26:303-23 Wint '69
SCHURMANN, Franz
Cambodia: Nixon's trap. il Nation 210:651-6
Je 1 '70
SCHURR, George M.
Church colleges are peculiar institutions. Chr
Cent 87:1154-7 S 30 '70
SCHUSTER, Max Lincoln
Obituary
Pub W 199:36 Ja 4 '71
SCHUSTERMAN, Ronald J. and Balliet, R. F.
Conditioned vocalizations as a technique for
determining visual acuity thresholds in
sea lions. bibliog il Science 169:498-501 Jl
31 '70
SCHÜTZ, Heinrich
Reviews of records. A. Mendel. il Mus Q 56:
133-42 Ja '70 *

SCHUYLER, James
Paul Burlin's last paintings. il por Art N 69:28-9+ D '70
about
Freely espoused. J. Koethe. Poetry 117:54-6 O '70 *

SCHUYLER, Joseph B.
Letter from Lagos. il America 123:204-6 S 26 '70

SCHUYLER, Robert L.
Archaeology in outer space. Space World G-3-75:13 Mr '70

SCHWAB, Judith L.
I teach; poem. Chr Cent 87:1152 S 30 '70

SCHWABENLENDER, R. F.
Feedback module for motor control. il Electr World 83:66 Ap '70

SCHWABER, Paul
Manchild in the promised land: to Israel and back. Am Scholar 39:506+ Sum '70

SCHWALBERG, Bob
New SLR with 1/2,000-sec top speed. il Pop Phot 67:56+ S '70
Our men at Oberkochen. il Pop Phot 66:84-5+ Ja '70
Shifty fifty. il Pop Phot 67:72-5+ S '70
Twenty years of photoshowmanship. il Pop Phot 67:104-5+ S '70

SCHWALBERG, Carol
Discovering America. il por Travel & Camera 33:62-5+ D '70

SCHWANN, William
Twenty years of Schwann. I. Kolodin. il por Am Rec G 36:540-2 Ap '70 *
SCHWANN catalog. See Phonograph records—Catalogs

SCHWARTZ, Charles
Movement vs. the establishment. Nation 210:747-51 Je 22 '70

SCHWARTZ, Daniel
It's mountain standard time; paintings. Fortune 82:118-25 S '70

SCHWARTZ, Ed. See Schwartz, J. jt. auth.

SCHWARTZ, Elias
Heterozygous beta thalassemia: balanced globin synthesis in bone marrow cells. bibliog il Science 167:1513-14 Mr 13 '70

SCHWARTZ, Elliott
Current chronicle. Mus Q 56:119-24 Ja '70

SCHWARTZ, Francis X.
Make pavements skid resistant. il Am City 85:121+ My '70

SCHWARTZ, Harry
Covering the foreign news. For Affairs 48:741-57 Jl '70

SCHWARTZ, Herman
S.30: the seeds of repression. Nation 211:70-1 Ag 3 '70

SCHWARTZ, Jeri, and Schwartz, Ed
Mettlach masterpieces. il(p 1) Hobbies 75:64+ D '70

SCHWARTZ, Larry
Sidestepping the militants. Nation 210:273-4 Mr 9 '70

SCHWARTZ, Marvin D.
Nineteenth-century American rooms at the Metropolitan museum of art. il Antiques 98:400-9 S '70

SCHWARTZ, Marvin W.
Morocco. por Travel & Camera 33:82-3 S '70
about
When B/W is better. J. Scully. il Mod Phot 34:102-3 Ja '70 *

SCHWARTZ, Richard Jay
Helping a competitor, at a price. il pors Bsns W p48+ Ap 18 '70 *

SCHWARTZ, Robert. See Myers, S. jt. auth.

SCHWARTZ, Robert, 1938?-
Portland's unconventional Adams high. J. Guernsey. il Am Ed 6:3-7 My '70 *

SCHWARTZ, Susan-Lou
From a few minutes spent in a shaded courtyard; poem. Am Scholar 39:472 Sum '70

SCHWARTZKOPF, Gary W.
Culture and counterculture in U.S. Politics. il America 123:396-8 N 14 '70

SCHWARZ, Boris
Complete Handel for the violin. Sat R 53:84-5 F 28 '70
Virtue and virtuosity in Bach. Sat R 53:55 O 31 '70

SCHWARZ, E. J. See Larochelle, A. jt. auth.

SCHWARZ, F.A.O. (toy store) See New York (city)—Stores

SCHWARZ, Harvey F.
Decca navigation pioneer retires. Aviation W 93:33 N 16 '70 *

SCHWARZ, Meyer, and others
Insect juvenile hormone activity of selected terpenoid compounds. bibliog il Science 167:191-2 Ja 9 '70

SCHWARZKOPF, Elisabeth
Records. Opera N 34:35 F 7 '70

SCHWEID, Barry
Vietnam: shadow on the Court. Nation 211:564 N 30 '70

SCHWEIKARDT, Eric
Swift wings to bright horizons; photographs. Sports Illus 32:51-62 My 25 '70

SCHWEIKERT, Clarissa
Teaching the environment to 2,500 youngsters. il por Org Gard & Farm 17:83-5 Jl '70

SCHWEITZER, Gertrude
Island of decision; story. Good H 171:60-1 Jl '70

SCHWEITZER, Paul A.
Of many things excerpts from address. America 122:inside cover Je 13 '70

SCHWEMMER, Bruce, and others
Oxychlordane, animal metabolite of chlordane: isolation and synthesis. bibliog il Science 169:1087 S 11 '70

SCHWEPPES, ltd. See Cadbury Schweppes, ltd.

SCHWERTLEY, Donald F.
Little league can hurt kids. il Todays Ed 59:40-1 My '70

SCHWING, Pauline E.
Countdown 3-2-1-0-we're off! il Sch Arts 70:34 N '70

SCIENCE
Isaac Asimov explains; questions and answers. I. Asimov. See issues of Science digest
Physical sciences. See issues of Science news
Scene of change, by W. Weaver. Review
Bul Atom Sci 26:45 S '70. W. R. Gruner
Science: attack and defense. K. V. Thimann. Science 169:633 Ag 14 '70
See also
Communication in science
Physics
Religion and science
Scientists
Technology

Authorship
See Technical writing

Bibliography
Book reviews. See issues of Science
Book reviews. See issues of Space world
Books. See issues of Physics today
Books. See issues of Science digest
Books of the week. See issues of Science news
Books to come. Library J 95:3813-15+ N 1 '70
Books to come; ed. by J. Donathan. Library J 95:919-35+, 2552-71 Mr 1-Jl '70
Library at large. See issues of Chemistry
Reviews. See issues of Environment
Science and scientists: obligations and opportunities; excerpts from address, October 21, 1970. P. Handler. por Science 170:837 N 20 '70
Science, technology: April-September highlights. il Pub W 197:30-49 Ap 13 '70
Science, technology; some leading books scheduled for publication November 1970, through March 1971. il Pub W 198:27-40 N 16 '70
Scientific, technical, business and medical highspots; international list. Pub W 198:pt2 146-56 S 21 '70
Sci-tech books '69; one hundred outstanding titles for general library collections; comp. by D. R. Pfoutz. il por Library J 95:855-62 Mr 1 '70

Classification
See Classification of sciences

Federal aid
See Research—Federal aid

Fiction
See Science fiction

History
American science in the age of Jackson, by G. H. Daniels. Review
Trans-Action 7:58-60 Mr '70. J. L. Heilbron
Reflections: the megamachine; excerpts from The pentagon of power. L. Mumford. New Yorker 46:50-2+ O 10 '70
See also
Physics—History

Information services
Computer-based chemical information services; adaptation of address, April 1970. E. M. Arnett. il Science 170:1370-6 D 25 '70

International aspects
International challenge; adaptation of address, August 10, 1970. G. T. Seaborg. Bul Atom Sci 26:5-7 N '70

SCIENCE—International aspects—*Continued*
International opportunities for physicists. M.
S. Rothenberg. il Phys Today 23:37-40+ S
'70
U.S.-Japan scientific committee meets at
Washington; Department announcement with
text of joint communique. Dept State Bul
63:224 Ag 24 '70
US-Soviet collaboration to measure pion
charge radius. B. G. Lubkin. Phys Today
23:18-19 S '70
Yugoslav scientific delegation visits the
United States; statement. October 28, 1970.
Dept State Bul 63:698-9 D 7 '70
See also
International centre for theoretical physics,
Trieste, Italy
International geophysical year
Nuclear physics—International aspects
United Nations—Advisory committee on the
application of science and technology to
development

Juvenile literature
See Scientific literature for children

Methodology
Want to invent something? Then try using
analogy. R. Dreistadt. il Sci Digest 67:62-7
My '70

Moral aspects
See Science and ethics

Periodicals
See also
Bulletin of the atomic scientists
Science news (periodical)
Worm runner's digest

Philosophy
Reflections: the megamachine; excerpts from
The pentagon of power. L. Mumford. New
Yorker 46:48-50+ O 17 '70
Using the spirit of science; excerpts from
The crazy ape. A. Szent-Györgyi. Cur 119:
37-9 Je '70

Religious aspects
See Religion and science

Social aspects
Chandrasekhar on scientists and society. H.
Chandra. por Bul Bul Atom Sci 26:11-14
N '70
Changing dynamics in research and develop-
ment. H. Thiemann. bibliog il Science
168:1427-31 Je 19 '70
Movement vs. the establishment. C.
Schwartz. Nation 210:747-51 Je 22 '70
Reason awake: science for man, by R. Du-
bos. Review
Natur Hist il 79:68-70+ Ap '70. S. Klaw
Science and the gross national pollution. G.
M. Woodwell. Ramp Mag 8:51-4 My '70
Social relevance in the sciences. L. Massett.
il Sci N 97:391-2 Ap 18 '70
Using the spirit of science; excerpts from
The crazy ape. A. Szent-Györgyi. Cur
119:37-9 Je '70
See also
American association for the advancement of
science—Committee on science in the pro-
motion of human welfare

Study and teaching
Children can't think. A. K. Kondo. Ed Di-
gest 35:32-3 Ja '70
Egalitarian education; egg throwing experi-
ments in English secondary schools. il
Time 95:50 My 18 '70
High school science gets a face-lift. D. L.
Burleson. Sr Schol 95:Schol Teach 1 N 10
'69
Individualized science for the slow learner.
T. P. Quayle. il Todays Ed 59:50-1 Mr '70
Mr Sacharow's funny science lab. M. Strumpf.
il pors Sci Digest 67:72-4 Ja '70
Teaching of science; AAAS symposium,
December 29 1970. J. R. Mayor. il Science
170:1004-5 N 27 '70
Trends in the teaching of science. P. B.
Hounshell and E. L. West, jr. Ed Digest
35:25-8 Ap '70
See also
Botany—Study and teaching
California. University—Berkeley campus—
Lawrence hall of science
Nature study
Physics and teaching
Scientific education

Terminology
How many "graphies" do you know? quiz.
H. S. Tucker. Sci Digest 68:80+ Jl '70

Africa
Scientific safari to Africa. G. T. Seaborg. il
Science 169:554-61 Ag 7 '70

Canada
New science body for Canada; SCITEC. F.
Poland. il Sci N 97:136 Ja 31 '70
Piece of the action. il Sci N 98:462-3 D 19 '70

Cuba
Notes on science in Cuba. M. Roche. il Science
169:344-9 Jl 24 '70

India
Chandrasekhar on scientists and society. H.
Chandra. por Bul Atom Sci 26:11-14 N '70
See also
Research—Israel

Israel

Italy
Science in Italy: reform effort takes a sharp
turn leftward. D. S. Greenberg. Science
167:1704-6 Mr 27 '70

Latin America
Physics and politics in Latin America; a
personal experience. L. M. Falicov. Bul
Atom Sci 26:8-10+ N '70

Russia
Geopolitics of plate tectonics; Soviets re-
ject hypothesis. Sci N 98:29 Jl 11 '70
Rise and fall of T. D. Lysenko, by Z. A. Med-
vedev. Review
Bul Atom Sci 26:54-6 Ap '70. O. Hechtler
New Yorker 45:85-6+ Ja 24; 46:93-4 Je
13 '70. J. Bernstein

History
Lenin and the development of science. M.
Keldysh. il UNESCO Courier 23:6-11 Jl '70

South Africa
South Africa: booming nation's research
and industry benefit from close ties with
the United States. D. S. Greenberg. il
Science 169:157-63 Jl 10 '70

United States
See Science

SCIENCE (periodical)
Instructions for contributors (cont) Science
167:xviA-xviB Mr 27; 169:xv-xvi S 25; 170:
xv-xvi D 25 '70
SCIENCE advisers. See Public officers
SCIENCE and civilization
Changing dynamics in research and develop-
ment. H. Thiemann. bibliog il Science
168:1427-31 Je 19 '70
Coming of the golden age: a view of the
end of progress, by G. S. Stent. Review
Natur Hist 79:30-2 Mr '70. J. Lettvin
Crisis of transformation. J. Platt. Cur 115:3-
17 F '70
Haggerty, McElroy, Bromley stress relevance.
T. Johnides. por Phys Today 23:61-2 D '70
In defense of science; adaptation of address,
October 15, 1969. A. M. Weinberg. bibliog
Science 167:141-5 Ja 9 '70; Reply. H. E.
Thomas. 168:1042 My 29 '70
Mortgaging the old homestead. Lord Ritchie-
Calder. For Affairs 48:207-20 Ja '70; Same. il
Sports Illus 32:44-51 F 2 '70
Non-scientists dissect science; current is-
sues of impact of science on society period-
ical. UNESCO Courier 23:32 Ap '70
Painful struggle for relevancy. il Bsns W
p38-9 Ja 2 '71
Pentagon of power, by L. Mumford. Review
Nat R 23:41-2 Ja 12 '71. H. Caton
Physics & society. Phys Today 23:23-8 Ap;
23-8+ My; 21-6 Je '70
Reflections: the megamachine; excerpts from
The pentagon of power. L. Mumford. New
Yorker 46:50-2+ O 10; 48-50+ O 17; 55-8+
O 24; 50-2+ O 31 '70
Relevance of physics; adaptation of address,
June 1970. G. Holton. bibliog il Phys Today
23:40-3+ N '70
Science and immediate social goals. P. H.
Abelson. Science 169:721 Ag 21 '70
Science under fire: behind the growing con-
cern. il U S News 68:30-1 F 9 '70
Scientific revelation. K. E. Boulding. il Bul
Atom Sci 26:13-18 S '70
Today's impress & Galileo's Medicean stars.
P. W. Schmidtchen. il Hobbies 75:134-6
Ap '70
What price tomorrow? L. Hall. Am For 76:
42+ Ja '70
See also
Technology and civilization

SCIENCE and ethics
Hand and the head. P. A. Cuadra. il Américas 22:27-9 S '70
Test-tube backlash. G. E. Christianson. Commonweal 93:9-13 O 2 '70

SCIENCE and industry. See Industrial research

SCIENCE and religion. See Religion and science

SCIENCE and society. See Science and civilization

SCIENCE and sociology. See Science—Social aspects

SCIENCE and state
Changing of the guard; political consideration in the appointment of men to scientific posts. il Sci N 97:572 Je 13 '70
DuBridge's exit. Time 96:48 Ag 31 '70
Federal science: differences of opinion in the highest councils. P. M. Boffey. Science 170: 1383-4 D 25 '70
New critique of science. M. L. Perl. Cur 119: 39-43 Je '70
New policy for the government-university partnership. A. H. Dupree. Science 169: 131 Jl 10 '70
New rationale for science. A. H. Dupree. Sat R 53:55-9 F 7 '70
Nixon administration accused of downgrading science. P. M. Boffey. Science 169:265 Jl 17 '70
Point of view; excerpts from address, October 12, 1970. W. D. McElroy. por Science 170:517 O 30 '70
Quest for a science policy; Daddario report. il Sci N 98:365 N 7 '70
R&D depression in the United States. S. Dedijer. Science 168:344-5 Ap 17 '70
Recession in science; ex-advisors warn of long-term effects. P. M. Boffey. Science 168:655-7 My 1 '70
Rising debate on science policy. il por Sci N 98:57-8 Jl 25 '70
Science and the federal patron, by M. D. Reagan. Review
    Bul Atom Sci 26:45-7 My '70. W. B. Cannon
Science policy: Daddario panel urges new study changes in OST. L. J. Carter. Science 170:612-14 N 6 '70
Science under Nixon: influence has declined in national affairs. D. S. Greenberg. Science 169:1056-7 S 11 '70
    See also
Research—Federal aid
Social sciences and state
United States—National science foundation

France
Revamping priorities; new five-year plan. N. Hardy. il Sci N 97:492 My 16 '70

Great Britain
Unifying government research; proposed merger of National research development corporation with ten national laboratories. D. Fishlock. il Sci N 97:160 F 7 '70
    See also
Great Britain—Science research council

SCIENCE and the humanities
Bridge of values; adaptation of address, April 28, 1970. B. C. Keeney. Science 169: 26-8 Jl 3 '70
Humanities and the culture-hungry American. W. T. Greenleaf. il Am Ed 6:7-11 Ja '70
Poetry in a scientific world. M. Sweetkind. Engl J 59:359-66 Mr '70

SCIENCE and war. See War and science

SCIENCE as a profession
    See also
Chemistry as a profession

SCIENCE buildings, College. See College architecture

SCIENCE education. See Scientific education

SCIENCE fairs
International competition; International science fair. Sci N 97:502-3 My 23 '70
Little scientist is a dangerous thing. il Changing T 24:40-2 Ja '70

SCIENCE fiction
In defense of science fiction. Z. Sutherland. il Sat R 53:36 Ap 18 '70
One minute to now, and counting. M. Ronan. Sr Schol 97:36 N 16 '70
Pulsating disks and dials. R. Whittemore. New Repub 163:23-5 Jl 18 '70
Science fiction. A. Panshin. bibliog il por Wilson Lib Bul 44:616-20 F '70
Science fiction hall of fame, ed. by R. Silverberg. Review
    Nat R 22:1170-1 N 3 '70. T. Sturgeon
Science fiction: short story and novel. H. Harrison. Writer 83:16-18 My '70

Science fiction, the modern mythology. W. E. McNelly. il America 123:125-7 S 5 '70
Tale that wags the god. J. Blish. il Am Lib 1:1029-33 D '70

Bibliography
Basic science fiction collection. A. Panshin. por Library J 95:2223-9 Je 15 '70
Science fiction bibliography and criticism. A. Panshin. Am Lib 1:884-5 O '70
Science-fiction stories in the social studies. A. W. Wohlfeil. bibliog f Clear House 44: 300-4 Ja '70

Drama
Story machine; drama; reprint. I. Asimov. Plays 29:25-34 My '70

Periodicals
Bibliography
S/F: the other side of the coin; ed. by B. Katz. H. W. Hall. Library J 95:2240-1 Je 15 '70

Poetry
Pop epics. D. Allen. Poetry 117:115-17 N '70
Theory of the alternate universe; To the S-F woman; Escape velocity; Poster poem; poems. D. Allen. Poetry 115:219-23 Ja '70

Themes
Theme of responsibility in Miller's A canticle for Leibowitz. M. A. Bennett. Engl J 59: 484-9 Ap '70

SCIENCE in fiction. See Science fiction

SCIENCE in literature
    See also
Science fiction

SCIENCE museums
    See also
Boston museum of science
Palace of arts and sciences, San Francisco

SCIENCE news
Science month. See issues of Science digest
Science newsfront. A. Fisher. See issues of Popular science monthly, January 1970-
Science worldwide. J. F. Pearson. See issues of Popular mechanics
Search and discovery. See issues of Physics today
    See also
Medical news

SCIENCE news (periodical)
Science service: publishing pioneer in financial trouble. P. M. Boffey. Science 169:1182-4 S 18 '70

SCIENCE research council. See Great Britain—Science research council

SCIENCE service, inc.
AAAS won't absorb Science service. P. M. Boffey. Science 170:418 O 23 '70
Science service: publishing pioneer in financial trouble. P. M. Boffey. Science 169: 1182-4 S 18 '70

SCIENCE students
    See also
Science talent search

SCIENCE talent search

1970 (29th)
Climax of a search. il Sci N 97:244 Mr 7 '70
Forty winners. Sci N 97:123 Ja 31 '70

SCIENCE writing. See Technical writing

SCIENTIFIC apparatus and instruments
New products. See issues of Science news
    See also
Astronomical instruments
Chemical apparatus and supplies
Medical instruments and apparatus
Psychological apparatus
Recording instruments
Surveying instruments
    also names of scientific apparatus and instruments, e.g. Microscopes and microscopy

SCIENTIFIC conferences
Aerospace calendar. See issues of Aviation week & space technology
Calendar. See issues of Physics today
Meetings. See issues of Science
    See also
Calorimetry conference
Gordon research conferences
Pugwash conferences on science and world affairs
    also subhead Conferences under various subjects, e.g. Lunar geology—Conferences

SCIENTIFIC control corporation
Program to save Scientific control. Bsns W p36 Ja 17 '70

SCIENTIFIC education
How educated are Americans? What two surveys show. il U S News 69:62-3 Jl 20 '70

SCIENTIFIC education—*Continued*
Physics for the nonscience major; symposium. bibliog il Phys Today 23:23-9+ Mr '70
See also
Moving pictures in science education
Science—Study and teaching

SCIENTIFIC expeditions
See also
Antarctic exploration

SCIENTIFIC humor. See Humor in science

SCIENTIFIC information. See Communication in science

SCIENTIFIC information services. See Science—Information services

SCIENTIFIC instruments. See Scientific apparatus and instruments

SCIENTIFIC literature
To amend refereeing; letter, with reply by S. A. Goudsmit. J. Neufeld. Phys Today 23:9-10 Ap '70
See also
Physics literature
Publishers and publishing—Scientific literature

SCIENTIFIC literature for children
Views on science books. H. C. Stubbs. See issues of Horn book magazine

Bibliography
Annual survey of books about science for younger readers (and their parents) P. Morrison and P. Morrison. Sci Am 223:122-6+ D '70

SCIENTIFIC materialism. See Materialism

SCIENTIFIC photography. See Photography—Scientific use

SCIENTIFIC research. See Research

SCIENTIFIC societies
See also names of scientific societies, e.g. Federation of American societies for experimental biology

SCIENTIFIC terms. See Science—Terminology

SCIENTISM. See Science—Philosophy

SCIENTIST-astronauts. See Astronauts

SCIENTISTS
Lessons of the intellectual biography of science. G. Holton. Science 170:933 N 27 '70
On being a scientist. M. Wilson. Atlan 226:101-2+ S '70
Ph.D. holders in private industry. M. F. Crowley. il Mo Labor R 93:65-6 Ag '70
Science and scientists: obligations and opportunities; excerpts from address, October 21, 1970. P. Handler. por Science 170:837 N 20 '70
Test-tube backlash. G. E. Christianson. Commonweal 93:9-13 O 2 '70
See also
Dictionary of scientific biography
Negro scientists
Physicists
Specialization
Women as scientists

Pensions
Chemists formulate portable pensions. Bsns W p38 F 28 '70

Political activities
Dissent spreads to Nobelists, industrial scientists. P. M. Boffey. Science 168:1325 Je 12 '70
Harvard genetics researcher quits science for politics. J. K. Glassman. Science 167:963-4 F 13 '70; Discussion. 167:1668-9 Mr 27 '70
Internationalism and world politics among CERN scientists; the European elite panel study. D. Lerner and A. H. Teich. il Bul Atom Sci 26:4-10 F '70
Movement vs. the establishment. C. Schwartz. Nation 210:747-51 Je 22 '70
Science and politics: free speech controversy at Lawrence laboratory. P. M. Boffey. Science 169:743-5 Ag 21 '70
Science in Italy: reform effort takes a sharp turn leftward. D. S. Greenberg. Science 167:1704-6 Mr 27 '70
Scientist's role in arms control. B. T. Feld. Bul Atom Sci 26:7-8+ Ja '70
See also
Lobbying

Statistics
Foreign scientists in the United States. H. G. Grubel. il Bul Atom Sci 26:9-12 Ap '70

Supply and demand
Changing job market. P. H. Abelson. Science 168:781 My 15 '70
Employment status of recent recipients of the doctorate. F. D. Boercker and others. bibliog il Science 168:930-9 My 22 '70
Projected requirements for technicians in 1980. M. F. Crowley. bibliog f il Mo Labor R 93:13-17 My '70

Where technologists are now obsolete. il Bsns W p30 S 26 '70
Why there is a job shortage. W. R. Gruner. bibliog il por Phys Today 23:21-6 Je '70; Discussion. 23:96 Je; 9+ O '70
See also
Brain drain

SCIENTISTS, Amateur
Amateur scientist; ed. by C. L. Stong. See issues of Scientific American
Digging it; amateur archeologists. Newsweek 75:97 Mr 30 '70
Farmer-archeologist. G. Logsdon. il por Farm J 93:A4 N '69

SCIENTISTS, American
Eggomaniacs. H. Bowser. il Sat R 53:20 Jl 18 '70
Foreign scientists in the United States. H. G. Grubel. il Bul Atom Sci 26:9-12 Ap '70
New critique of science. M. L. Perl. Cur 119:39-43 Je '70

SCIENTISTS, Blacklisting of. See Blacklisting of scientists

SCIENTISTS, Chinese
See also
Tsien, H. S.

SCIENTISTS, Latin American
Migration of scientists from Latin America; adaptation of address, 1968. H. M. Nussenzveig; discussion. Science 166:820-1; 167:1669-70; 169:6 N 14 '69, Mr 27, Jl 3 '70

SCIENTISTS, Russian
See also
Kapitza, P. L.

SCIENTISTS in government
France: putting scientists into its embassies. Science 167:1230-1 F 27 '70
Movement vs. the establishment. C. Schwartz. Nation 210:747-51 Je 22 '70

SCIFRES, Bill
Goggle-eyes'll get you. il por Outdoor Life 146:82-3+ O '70
Roughing it on Smoothrock. il Outdoor Life 145:64-7+ Je '70

SCIMECCA, Joseph A.
St John's: four years after. Commonweal 91:326-7, 437-8 D 12 '69, Ja 16 '70

SCINTILLATION counters. See Counters (electrons, ions, etc)

SCISSORS and shears
Electric scissors. il Consumer Rep 35:586-9 O '70
New shears for the handyman and hobbyist. il Consumer Bul 53:28 F '70

SCISSORS-cut pictures. See Silhouettes

SCLAR, Charles B.
Shock-wave damage in minerals of lunar rocks. bibliog il Science 167:675-7 Ja 30 '70

SCLEROSIS, Multiple
Multiple sclerosis problem. G. Dean. il Sci Am 223:40-6 bibliog(p 136) Jl '70

SCOBEY, Joan. See McGrath, L. P. jt. auth.

SCOBIE, W. I.
Theater. Nat R 22:1173-4 N 3 '70

SCOFIELD, John
Gangtok: cloud wreathed Himalyan capital. il Nat Geog 138:698-713 N '70

SCOFIELD, Nanette E.
What do you want to be when you grow up? il Parents Mag 45:40-1+ Je '70

SCOOPS
Other jobs for your scoop. il Sunset 145:184 O '70

SCOPES, John Thomas
Obituary
Chr Cent 87:1342 N 11 '70
Scopes reviews the monkey trial. B. Shaw. Esquire 74:86+ N '70 *

SCOPES. See Oscillographs

SCOPES trial. See Tennessee evolution controversy

SCOPPA, Bud
Chicago. il Sr Schol 97:35 N 16 '70
Discovery through rock. il Schol Teach Jr/Sr High p 14-15 O 5 '70
Number one and number two. il Sr Schol 97:34-7 O 26 '70
—and others
DIScussions. See issues of Senior Scholastic

SCORING (sports) See Sports officiating

SCOTCH-IRISH
Melting pot: the ethnic group that blended the Scotch-Irish; excerpts from Scotch-Irish: a social history. J. G. Leyburn. il Am Heritage 22:28-31+ D '70

SCOTCH tape. See Adhesive tape

SCOTCH whiskey. See Whiskey

SCOTLAND
See also
Colleges and universities—Scotland
Cruising—Scotland
Fishing—Scotland
Gardens—Scotland
Hebrides
Holy Loch
Ness, Loch

SCOTLAND—*Continued*

Historic houses, etc.

Survival of lost causes: Traquair house. R. Kirk. Nat R 22:736 Jl 14 '70

Industries

See also
Distilleries
Electronic apparatus industry and trade—Scotland

Literary landmarks
See Literary landmarks

Religious institutions and affairs
World around us (cont) Chr Cent 87:580-2 My 6 '70
See also
Church of Scotland

SCOTLAND, Church of. See Church of Scotland

SCOTT, Adrienne. See Boyum, J. G. jt. auth.

SCOTT, Ann
Report from Detroit. il Fortune 81:71-2 F '70

SCOTT, Ann Besser
Performance of the Old Hall descant settings. bibliog f il Mus Q 56:14-26 Ja '70

SCOTT, Byron
Doctor did it. il Todays Health 48:57-9+ O '70
When a doctor needs a doctor. il Todays Health 48:54-5+ My '70
Why bust broncs in your dreams? il Todays Health 48:30-3 N '70
(ed) See Ellis, E. F. Asthma, the demon that thrives on myths

SCOTT, Carl. See Swedberg, J. jt. auth.

SCOTT, David
Incredible no-torque walking machine. il por Pop Sci 196:61-3+ Ja '70

SCOTT, David W.
American landscape: a changing frontier. il Liv Wildn 33:3-13 Wint '69

SCOTT, Douglas W.
Student activism on environmental crisis. il Liv Wildn 34:8-9 Spr '70
—See Cunningham, W. P. jt. auth.

SCOTT, Eugene L.
Forebrain and backhand. Esquire 73:141 Je '70

SCOTT, Foresman and company
Individualized approach in new reading system. Pub W 199:35-6 Ja 4 '71

SCOTT, Harold George. See Bugg, R. jt. auth.

SCOTT, Hugh
Excerpt from Senate debate, March 11 1970. Cong Digest 49:143 My '70
Scott in trouble. Cato. Nat R 21:555 Je 2 '70 *
Scott of Pennsylvania. E. Marshall. New Republ 163:11 Ag 1 '70 *

SCOTT, J. B.
Ragged edge of life. il Field & S 75:48-9 D '70

SCOTT, Jack
Coming revolt of the athletes. L. Shecter. il pors Look 34:43-7 Jl 28 '70 *
Jocks 1, war 0. il Ramp Mag 9:15-18 Ag '70

SCOTT, Jack Denton
Amazing cottontail. il Nat Wildlife 9:20+ D '70
Mighty meek. il Nat Wildlife 8:28-35 D '69

SCOTT, John T.
Report on AIP: 1969. il Phys Today 23:43-7+ Je '70

SCOTT, Ken
U.S. designer makes a splash. il por Bsns W p48-9 Mr 21 '70 *

SCOTT, Michael R.
It was great while it lasted. il por Opera N 35:14-16 D 5 '70

SCOTT, Peter Dale
Air America: flying the U.S. into Laos. por Ramp Mag 8:39-42+ F '70
Canadian chronicle. Poetry 115:353-64 F '70

SCOTT, Rachel
Firing and hiring of Fredy Jones. New Republ 163:12-15 Jl 25 '70

SCOTT, Sir Robert
China, Russia and the United States. For Affairs 48:334-43 Ja '70

SCOTT, Robert F.
Technical topics (cont) il Radio-Electr 41: 42-3 F; 59-61 My; 71-3 Jl; 67-9 S '70

SCOTT, Sir Walter, bart
Sir Walter Scott, by E. Johnson. Review Nation 211:405-8 O 26 '70. J. Farrelly * Newsweek il por 76:84A-84B S 7 '70. G. Wolff *
Sir Walter Scott, by E. Johnson, and Scott: the critical heritage, ed. by J. O. Hayden. Reviews
Sat R 53:27-9 O 10 '70. R. Alter *

SCOTT, William John, 1926-
Clean-up crusader. por Bsns W p 100 Mr 14 '70 *

SCOTT, Winfield
Thankless task of Nicholas Trist. R. M. Ketchum. il por Am Heritage 21:12-15+ Ag '70 *

SCOTT, Winfield Townley
Comment. R. Eberhart. Poetry 115:345 F '70 *

SCOTT Meredith literary agency. See Meredith, Scott, literary agency

SCOTT museum, Trinity Center, Calif. See Historical museums

SCOTT paper company
Fifty-fifty empire that Scott built. il por Bsns W p27 Ag 29 '70

SCOTTISH folk songs. See Folk songs, Scottish

SCOTTISH games. See Competitions

SCOTTISH painting. See Painting, Scottish

SCOTTISH pistols. See Pistols

SCOTTSDALE, Ariz.
Arizona's Scottsdale offers surprises. il Sunset 145:36+ N '70
Public works fire wranglers. L. B. Witzeman and M. G. Stragier. il Am City 85:108+ My '70
We automated residential refuse collection. M. G. Stragier. il Am City 85:66-7 N '70

SCOUNDRELS. See Crime and criminals

SCOUTING, Baseball. See Baseball scouting

SCOUTING, Football. See Football scouting

SCOUTS, Girl. See Girl scouts

SCOUTS and scouting
See also
Boy scouts

SCOVILLE, Herbert, Jr
Verification of nuclear arms limitations: an analysis. Bul Atom Sci 26:6-11 O '70

SCRANTON, Pa.
Concrete on steel cuts garage costs. il Am City 85:118 Jl '70

SCRANTON commission. See United States—President's commission on campus unrest

SCRAP metal
GM's new way to save scrap; reconstituted steel. Bsns W p24 Mr 7 '70
Salvage what you can; fire-hydrant maintenance policy, San Antonio, Tex. R. P. Van Dyke. il Am City 87:70-1 O '70

Prices

Steel mills fight for scrap. il Bsns W p 135 F 21 '70

SCRAP metal industry
See also
Automobiles—Wrecking
Steelmet, inc.

SCRAP metal sculpture. See Metal sculpture

SCRAPERS
Forgotten handtools: cabinetmaker scrapers. J. Burroughs. il Pop Mech 133:180-1 My '70

SCRATCHBOARD drawing
Scratchboard: a versatile graphic medium. A. Evry. il Sch Arts 70:18-19 N '70

SCREEN writers. See Dramatists

SCREEN writing. See Moving picture authorship

SCREENS (fences) See Fences

SCREENS (furniture)
Screens for the in-betweens. il Bet Hom & Gard 48:49 Ja '70

SCREENS (sun)
Shademaker and shade plants. il Home Gard 57:48-9 My '70
Shades of summer. il Bet Hom & Gard 48: 54-5 Ja '70

SCREW threads
Aluminum head savers; Phillips locking inserts. B. Lang. il Hot Rod 24:69 Ja '71
Good twist for stripped threads; Heli-Coil system. J. Davis. il Pop Sci 197:108-9 N '70

SCREWS
Primer on screws. il Mech Illus 66:68-9+ Mr '70

SCRIABIN, Alexander Nicholaevich. See Skriabin, A. N.

SCRIBERS
Tool for tracing contoured parts. M. E. Duchoviner. il Pop Sci 196:107 Je '70

SCRIBNER, Belding Hibbard
Man who said, they don't have to die. W. C. Heinz. il por Todays Health 49:26-9+ Ja '71 *

SCRIBNER, Kimball J.
Fighting the cat that threatens you from a clear blue sky. il por Pop Sci 196:60-3 My '70

SCRIMSHAW
Scrimshaw. E. W. Petley-Jones. il Antiques 98:256-62 Ag '70
Walrus and the commodore, a puzzle in scrimshaw. R. W. Updike. il Antiques 98: 263-5 Ag '70
Whittlin' on a whale. N. Levy. il Har Yrs 10:30-3 F '70

SCRIPPS college ceramics exhibit. See Pottery
  —Exhibitions
SCRIPTURE studies. See Bible study
SCROLLWORK. See Fretwork
SCUBA diving. See Skin diving
SCULLY, Celia G.
  Home is where the head is. Cath World 211:
  78-81 My '70
SCULLY, Ed
  Ed Scully on color. See issues of Modern
  photography
  Which from what? il Mod Phot 34:82-3+ F
  '70
SCULLY, Julia
  Do you see in color? il Mod Phot 34:76-81+ O
  '70
  Fritz Henle: four decades at the top. il Mod
  Phot 34:62-71+ Mr '70
  Seeing pictures. See issues of Modern photog-
  raphy
SCULPIN
  Sculpin and its imitations. D. Whitlock. il
  Field & S 75:114-16 S '70
SCULPMOBILES. See Mobiles
SCULPTORS materials. See Artists materials
SCULPTURE
  How to place and light sculpture. N. R.
  Piene. House & Gard 137:18+ F '70
    See also
  Animal sculpture
  Carving (art industries)
  Casting (sculpture)
  Ceramic sculpture
  Garden ornaments
  Masks (sculpture)
  Metal sculpture
  Monuments
  Paper sculpture
  Photosculpture
  Plaster casts
  Plastic sculpture
  Portrait sculpture
  Relief (sculpture)
  Soap sculpture
  Wood carving
    also subhead Monuments, statues, etc.
  under names of cities, e.g. St Louis—
  Monuments, statues, etc.

Competitions
  See Art—Competitions

Exhibitions
Beyond ethnography; exhibition of African
  sculpture. R. F. Thompson. il Art N 68:28-
  33+ F '70
  See also
Sculpture, American—Exhibitions

Exhibitions for the blind
Feeling sculpture; California arts commission's exhibition of sculpture for the blind.
  il Time 95:62 Je 8 '70

Private collections
  See Art—Private collections

Study and teaching
Modern sculpture in soap. L. J. Miller. il
  Design 71:30-1 Wint '69

Materials
Another relief for sculpture; illustration
  board. il Design 71:19 mid-Wint '70
Cement sculpting in high school. J. H. Vaux.
  il Sch Arts 70:24-5 N '70
Experimental sculpture; tubular packing. V.
  S. Gaston. il Sch Arts 70:20-1 O '70
From classroom grocery store to imaginary
  zoo. S. B. Severs. il Sch Arts 70:8 S '70
In space; modern sculpture made from thrown
  away parts. T. Prentiss. il Sch Arts 69:4 Je
  '70
Scrap constructions. A. D. Gernand. il Sch Arts
  70:37 O '70
Sculpture can be fun; man-made stone. H.
  Luitjens. il Sch Arts 70:28-9 O '70
Welding with wax. L. J. Miller. il Design
  71:24-5 mid-Wint '70
    See also
Papier-mâché

Technique
Doing it the hard way. il por Esquire 73:
  104-7 F '70
Portrait in steel. J. Jacquard. il pors Design
  71:16-18 mid-Wint '70
Sculptures in paper. il pors Design 71:22-4
  Wint '69
SCULPTURE, African
  Beyond ethnography; exhibition of African
  sculpture. R. F. Thompson. il Art N 68:28-
  33+ F '70
  Makonde sculpture. M. Shore-Bos. il Natur
  Hist 79:42-9 Mr '70

Millenniums of modern art; Brancusi's coun-
  terparts in African sculpture. il Life 68:
  62-6 Mr 20 '70
SCULPTURE, American
  Art in the park; Burns park, Denver. il Am
  City 85:76-7 F '70
  Charles Umlauf, sculptor of the living form.
  M. Malstrom. il por Am Artist 69:52-9+ S
  '70
    See also
Andre, C.
Beasley, B.
Boghosian, V.
Cipriano, A.
Citron, H.
King, W.
Liberman, A.
Morris, R.
Newman, B.
Oldenburg, C.
Rogers, R.
Segal, G.
Serra, R.
Whitney museum of American art, New York

Exhibitions
Maximizing the minimal; sculptor R. Morris
  and works at the Whitney. il por Time 95:
  54 Ap 20 '70
New dimensions; display at New York's Mu-
  seum of modern art called Photography into
  sculpture. il Time 95:64 Ap 13 '70
Out of the junkyard; show at Manhattan's
  Whitney museum. R. Hughes. il Time 97:
  50-1 Ja 4 '71
SCULPTURE, Ancient
  Golden hoard of the Scythians. A. Kirpich-
  nikov. il UNESCO Courier 23:18-21 O '70
    See also
Sculpture, Greek
SCULPTURE, Architectural. See Decoration
  and ornament, Architectural
SCULPTURE, British
    See also
Caro, A.
King, P.
Moore, H. S.
SCULPTURE, Central American
  Ancient Mexico and Central America; photo-
  graphs. L. Boltin. Natur Hist 79:30-5 bib-
  liog(p79) My '70
SCULPTURE, Childrens. See Childrens art
SCULPTURE, Classical
    See also
Sculpture, Greek
SCULPTURE, Dutch
    See also
Verkade, K.
SCULPTURE, Eskimo. See Eskimos—Art
SCULPTURE, French
    See also
Dubuffet, J.
Matisse, H.
Rodin, A.
SCULPTURE, Greek
  Love affair; Praxiteles' long-lost statue of
  Aphrodite. il Time 96:52+ N 23 '70
  Miss Love and Aphrodite. il Newsweek 76:
  79 N 23 '70
SCULPTURE, Italian
    See also
Lucchesi, B.
Pisano, G.
SCULPTURE, Mexican
  Ancient Mexico and Central America; photo-
  graphs. L. Boltin. Natur Hist 79:30-5 bib-
  liog(p79) My '70
SCULPTURE, Mobile. See Mobiles
SCULPTURE, Negro (American)
    See also
Patience, C. E.
SCULPTURE, Pre-Columbian
  Hello, Columbus; exhibition of sculpture of
  Middle America at the Metropolitan. K. E.
  Meyer. il Art N 69:46-9+ N '70
  San Agustin; archaeological mystery of pre-
  historic Colombia. F. Sanz. il UNESCO
  Courier 23:20-5 Ap '70
SCULPTURE, Primitive
    See also
Sculpture, African
SCULPTURE, Rumanian
    See also
Brancusi, C.
SCULPTURE, Russian
    See also
Neizvestny, E.
SCULPTURE, Spanish
    See also
Miró, J.
SCULPTURE in the home. See Art in the
  home
SCURRAH, Martin J. and Wagner, D. A.
  Cognitive model of problem-solving in chess.
  il Science 169:209-11 Jl 10 '70

SCYLLA (asteroid) See Asteroids
SCYLLAC devices. See Plasma (ionized gases)
SCYTHIANS
Golden hoard of the Scythians. A. Kirpichnikov. il UNESCO Courier 23:18-21 O '70
SEA. See Ocean
SEA-air interaction. See Ocean-atmosphere interaction
SEA anemones
Sea anemones survive oil spill. Sci Digest 68:84 O '70
SEA annelids. See Annelids
SEA-based anti-ballistic missile system. See Guided missiles—Defenses
SEA cows. See Manatees
SEA-floor spreading. See Ocean bottom
SEA food
See also
Cookery—Sea food
Fish as food
SEA food salads. See Salads
SEA ice. See Ice—Polar Regions
SEA ISLANDS
See also
Cumberland Island
SEA law. See Maritime law
SEA level
Sea level isn't level, it's hilly. B. G. Ledbetter. il Sci Digest 68:68-72 Jl '70
SEA-level canal. See Canals—Central America
SEA level changes
Interglacial high sea levels and the control of Greenland ice by the precession of the equinoxes. C. Emiliani; reply with rejoinder. J. H. Mercer. bibliog Science 168:1605-6 Je 26 '70
SEA life. See Seafaring life
SEA life park, Hawaii. See Aquariums
SEA lions. See Seals (animals)
SEA otters
Luckless sea otter. il Am Heritage 21:108-11 O '70
Sea otter returns to Canada. C. Patti. il Sea Front 16:220-2 Jl '70
SEA pens
Umbellula in its deep-sea habitat. R. H. Gilluly. il Sci N 97:586-7 Je 13 '70
SEA power
After troop withdrawal: dependence on sea power; address, June 23, 1970. L. F. Chapman, jr. Vital Speeches 36:628-31 Ag 1 '70
Attack aircraft carrier; our forward defense posture; address, March 4, 1970. T. H. Moorer. Vital Speeches 36:392-4 Ap 15 '70
Full steam ahead. il Newsweek 76:57 S 14 '70
Reports: the Mediterranean: the Sixth fleet and the Russians. Atlan 225:4+ F '70
SEA products. See Marine resources
SEA serpent
See also
Loch Ness monster
SEA shells. See Shells (conchology)
SEA travel. See Ocean travel
SEA turtles. See Turtles
SEA urchins
Alarm response of diadema antillarum. N. Snyder and H. Snyder. bibliog il Science 168:276-8 Ap 10 '70
Echinoid skeleton: absence of a collagenous matrix. L. Klein and J. D. Currey. bibliog il Science 169:1209-10 S 18 '70
Egg machine. P. T. Lindstrom. il por Natur Hist 79:52-5 F '70
Mysterious urchin. il Chem 43:28 Ap '70
SEA wasp. See Jellyfish
SEA water
Production of carbon monoxide and gaseous hydrocarbons in seawater: relation to dissolved organic carbon. D. F. Wilson and others. bibliog il Science 168:1577-9 Je 26 '70
Red Sea hot brines. E. T. Degens and D. A. Ross. il Sci Am 222:32-42 Ap '70
Why the sea is salt. F. MacIntyre. il Sci Am 223:104-15 bibliog(p 132) N '70

Pollution
See Marine pollution
SEA waves. See Waves
SEABED treaty
Ending the no-policy. il Sci N 97:526 My 20 '70
Geneva disarmament conference agrees on text of treaty banning emplacement of nuclear weapons on the seabed; statement. September 1, 1970; with revised draft treaty. J. F. Leonard. Dept State Bul 63:362-6 S 28 '70

Marine science and ocean politics. D. S. Cheever. il Bul Atom Sci 26:22+ F '70; Reply. M. Leitenberg. 26:47-8 O '70
Treading water. C. M. Eichelberger. Sat R 53:24 S 26 '70
United States and U.S.S.R. table revised draft treaty banning emplacement of nuclear weapons on the seabed; statement. April 23, 1970, with text of the revised draft treaty. J. F. Leonard. Dept State Bul 62:663-7 My 25 '70
United States policy for the seabed; statements. R. M. Nixon; E. L. Richardson. Dept State Bul 62:737-41 Je 15 '70
SEABOARD coast line railroad company
W. Thomas Rice of Seaboard coast line; interview. W. T Rice. il pors Nations Bsns 58:60-6 N '70
SEABORG, Glenn T.
Doctor Seaborg and the geologists' report; interview. Environ 12:13-15 Ja '70
From Mendeleev to Mendelevium and beyond. il por Chem 43:6-9+ Ja '70
General conference of the International atomic energy agency holds 14th session at Vienna; statement, September 22, 1970. Dept State Bul 63:485-91 O 26 '70
International challenge: adaptation of address, August 10, 1970. Bul Atom Sci 26:5-7 N '70
Our nuclear future, 1995. il por Bul Atom Sci 26:7-14 Je '70
Plutonium; address, October 5, 1970. Vital Speeches 37:69-75 N 15 '70
Scientific safari to Africa. il Science 169:554-61 Ag 7 '70
—and Bloom, J. L.
Fast breeder reactors; with biographical sketches. il Sci Am 223:10, 13-21 N '70

about
AAAS presidency: controversy flares over Seaborg candidacy. P. M. Boffey. Science 170:1177-80 D 11 '70 *
AAAS: Seaborg wins election; scientific freedom panel created. P. M. Boffey. Science 170:1283-5 D 18 '70 *
Fallout over Seaborg. il por Time 97:49 Ja 4 '71 *
In-house politics at AAAS. por Sci N 98:460-1 D 19 '70 *
Squabbling scientists. por Newsweek 76:118-19 D 14 '70 *
SEABURY, Paul
Provisionality and finality. Ann Am Acad 392:96-104 N '70
SEABURY, Samuel
Arrogance of virtue (in old New York) R. Starr. New Repub 163:20 D 26 '70 *
SEAFARERS' international union of North America
Union under fire for political spending. il U S News 69:59 Jl 13 '70
SEAFARING life
God bless our happy ship; aboard the three-masted bark St James, New York to San Francisco, 1900. R. A. Weinstein. il Am West 7:38-47 Mr '70
See also
Voyages
Whaling
SEAGOING laboratories. See Oceanographic buoys
SEAGRAM, Joseph E, and sons
CU files suits against Seagram and Hamm. Consumer Rep 35:6 Ja '70
Needs spur transoceanic flights. C. E. Schneider. il Aviation W 93:40-1+ D 14 '70
SEAGRAVE, Sterling
Reports: Burma. Atlan 225:32+ Ap '70
SEAL hunting
Arctic adventure. H. J. Samuels. il por Outdoor Life 145:68-71+ F '70
Clobbered again. il Time 95:34 Ap 13 '70
SEALE, Bobby G.
Other voices, other strategies; interview, ed. by W. Terry. il pors Time 95:23-4+ Ap 6 '70
Seize the time; excerpts. pors Ramp Mag 8:17-29 Je '70

about
Adverse to adversaries: television conversation. Sedulus. New Repub 163:29-30 Jl 11 '70 *
Behind the Chicago conspiracy trial; with editorial comment. P. Glusman. il Ramp Mag 8:7+, 39-47 Ja '70
Black Panthers and their white hero-worshipers. J. Fischer. Harper 241:18+ Ag '70; Discussion. 241:6+ O '70
Eight minus one is seven. il por Sr Schol 95:20-1 D 8 '69 *

SEALE, Bobby G.—about—*Continued*
Eighth conspirator is a prisoner of war;
excerpt from The trial. T. Hayden. il
por Ramp Mag 9:45-50 Jl '70 *
Here and now for Bobby Seale; tr. by J.
Oringer. J. Genet. Ramp Mag 8:30-1 Je
'70 *
Inside the Panthers. R. A. Sokolov. por
Newsweek 75:104+ Je 15 '70 *
Who killed Alex Rackley? il por Newsweek
75:22 Mr 30 '70

SEALS (animals)
Bronchograms and tracheograms of seals
under pressure. G. L. Kooyman and others.
bibliog il Science 169:82-4 Jl 3 '70
Conditioned vocalizations as a technique
for determining visual acuity thresholds in
sea lions. R. J. Schusterman and R. F. Balliet. bibliog il Science 169:498-501 Jl 31 '70
Harp seals; research in the zoology department of the University of Guelph, Ontario,
Canada. G. E. Toles. il Sea Front 16:66-
70 Mr '70
Protest, priorities, and the Alaska fur seal.
Audubon 72:114-15 Mr '70
Seal harems in the Pribilofs. R. K. Mathews.
il por Natur Hist 79:32-41 Ja '70
Short life of the Orkney seal. il Sci Digest
67:83-5 F '70
Year of the seal; condensation. V. B. Scheffer.
il Read Digest 97:141-5 O '70

SEAMANS, Robert C. 1918-
Public control of national security problems;
address, November 20, 1970. Vital Speeches
37:133-5 D 15 '70

SEAMANSHIP
Different world; joining Ondine's transatlan-
tic crew. B. Andre. il por Yachting 127:68-
9+ F '70
Dinghy management; excerpt from Practical
boating inland and offshore, power and sail.
W. S. Kals. il Motor B 125:102-3+ Mr '70
Shakedown cruise. J. Martenhoff. il Yachting
127:72-3+ Mr '70
Surf seamanship. il Motor B 125:70-1+ F '70
See also
Houseboats—Handling
Knots and splices
Navigation

SEAMEN
Crew for Galatea. M. Williams. il Yachting
128:63+ D '70
Different world; joining Ondine's transatlan-
tic crew. B. Andre. il por Yachting 127:68-
9+ F '70
Men of the sea; a description of a psychiat-
ric population of merchant seamen using
the M.M.P.I. L. H. Tuft and M. I. Berman.
bibliog Ment Hy 54:440-3 Jl '70
Subsidy board sinks the oversized crew; LASH
vessel. il Bsns W p 15 Ja 2 '71
See also
Maritime workers
Seafaring life
            Training
See Nautical education

SEANCES. See Spiritualism

SEAPLANE travel. See Air travel

SEAPLANES
New variants of PS-1 considered. C. Brown-
low. il Aviation W 92:52-3+ Mr 16 '70
Water birds; Lake seaplane. A. Trammell. il
Flying 86:49-53 My '70

SEAPORT museum bookshop, New York. See
Museum stores

SEAPORTS. See Ports

SEAR, Thomas R.
Stylus timer saves your records. il Pop Sci
197:81+ N '70

SEARCH and rescue operations
See also
Radar in rescue work
Vietnamese war, 1957- —Search and rescue
operations

SEARLES, John R.
More sources of free and inexpensive material.
Eng J 59:846-53 S '70
—See Blount, N. S. jt. ed.

SEARLES, Joseph L. 3d
Black capitalist; member of New York stock
exchange. por Bsns W p58 F 21 '70 *

SEARS, Peter H.
After tedious arguing; poem. Mlle 70:176 Ap
'70
Dream of the moon tree girl; poem. Sat R 53:8
Ap 11 '70

SEARS, Roebuck and company
Sears big user of Continental 747 to Hawaii.
il Aviation W 93:134 O 26 '70

SEARS, Roebuck catalog. See Catalogs, Mail
order

SEASCAPES. See Marine painting

SEASHORE
Forgotten wilds: the teeming marshes and
lagoons along California's urban coast. il
Sunset 144:46-8+ Ap '70
New fish and game law may help save our
tidepools; watching tidepools. il Sunset 144:
3-4 Mr '70
See also
Beaches
Shore protection

SEASHORE biology
Beach life at ebb tide. J. H. Loret. il Cons
24:22-8+ Ag '69

SEASHORE ecology
Beach life at ebb tide. J. H. Loret. il Cons
24:22-8+ Ag '69
Environment: journal on Jamaica Bay. A. S.
Taormina. il Cons 24:16-20 Ap '70

SEASHORE houses. See Beach architecture

SEASHORE photography. See Photography—
Marines

SEASHORE protection. See Shore protection

SEASIDE gardens. See Gardens, Seaside

SEASIDE resorts
Gathering of Europe's playgrounds. B. Gillam. il Mlle 70:259-64+ F '70

            Great Britain
Development of modern seaside resorts. C. A.
Stansfield, jr. il Parks & Rec 5:14-17+ O '70

            Ivory Coast
African Riviera. il Ebony 26:83-7 D '70

            Spain
Sotogrande: Spain's luxury resort. P. Fiori.
il Holiday 47:54-7 Ap '70

SEASONINGS
See also
Herbs

SEASONS
Hidden forest; excerpts S. F. Olson. il Nat
Wildlife 7:40-7 O '69
See also
Autumn
Summer

SEAT belts. See Safety belts

SEATON, Louis G.
One strike and you're out; interview. pors
Motor T 22:26-8+ S '70

SEATS
See also
Airplanes—Seats

SEATS, Tractor. See Tractors—Seats

SEATTLE
            Airports
New airport shows the way; Seattle-Tacoma
international airport. il Bsns W p33 D 26
'70
            Architecture
Seattle's tall one. il Arch Rec 147:129-36
Je '70
            Economic conditions
Appalachia in Seattle? il Newsweek 76:56 Ag
17 '70
Boeing cutbacks shake economy of Seattle
area. R. G. O'Lone. il Aviation W 92:14-17
Je 29 '70
Schools, housing feel Boeing pinch; with
editorial comment. R. G. O'Lone. il Avia-
tion W 93:9, 44-6 Jl 6 '70
Seattle under siege: the troubles of a com-
pany town. K. Prager. il Time 97:28-9 Ja
4 '71
            Hotels, restaurants, etc.
Great waterfront restaurants: the Windjam-
mer. E Crimmin. il Motor B 125:61+ Je '70
            Lighting
Getting the lines down effortlessly. il Am
City 85:134 Je '70
            Moral conditions
Seattle: in the last, idyllic trading post, the
blight of real depression. P. O'Neil. il Life
69:30-1 O 2 '70
            Music
Report:
World premiere of Carlisle Floyd's Of
mice and men. F. J. Warnke. il Opera
N 34:30-1 Mr 14 '70
See also
Seattle opera association
            Police
Moral career of a bum; excerpt from You
owe yourself a drunk. J. P. Spradley. il
Trans-Action 7:16-29 My '70
            Social conditions
Seattle: in the last, idyllic trading post, the
blight of real depression. P. O'Neil. il Life
69:30-1 O 2 '70
            Unemployment
See Unemployment—Washington (state)

SEATTLE eight trial. See Trials (conspiracy)
SEATTLE opera association
Floyd's Of mice and men. R. Commanday. il
Hi Fi 20:secII 28-9 Ap '70
Report:
La forza del destino. F. J. Warnke. Opera
N 34:26 My 16 '70
Madame Butterfly. F. J. Warnke. Opera
N 35:29 N 21 '70
Tales of Hoffmann. F. J. Warnke. il Opera
N 35:31 Ja 9 '71
SEATTLE Seven trial. See Trials (conspiracy)
SEATTLE-Tacoma international airport. See
Seattle—Airports
SEAVER, Nancy
Tom and Nancy Seaver. S. Davidson. il pors
McCalls 97:65-7+ My '70 *
SEAVER, Tom
Seaver prepares to strike. B. Surface. il
N Y Times Mag p36-7+ Ap 5 '70 *
Tom and Nancy Seaver. S. Davidson. il pors
McCalls 97:65-7+ My '70 *
SEAWANHAKA Corinthian yacht club. See
Yacht clubs
SEAWEED
Weed for all gardens. C. F. Bieber. il Org
Gard & Farm 17:60-1 F '70
See also
Kelp
SEAY, James
Big money comes to my hometown; poem.
Nation 210:312 Mr 16 '70
SEAY, Johnny
Willie York from Big East Fork. D. Snell.
il pors Life 69:54-8 Jl 17 '70 *
SEBASTIAN, John
Transitional sex figures. D. Newman and
R. Benton. pors Mlle 71:103 Jl '70 *
SECHZER, Jeri A.
Prolonged learning and split-brain cats. bib-
liog il Science 169:889-92 Ag 28 '70
SECKINGER, Donald S.
Initiative in learning. Sch & Soc 98:24 Ja '70
SECOND choice; story. See Hoag, M. D.
SECOND committee of the General assembly.
See United Nations—Economic and finan-
cial committee
SECOND home ownership. See Home owner-
ship
SECOND shepherd's play; drama. See Head,
F. E.
SECONDARY education. See Education, Sec-
ondary
SECONDARY schools. See High schools
SECONDHAND cameras. See Cameras, Used
SECONDHAND furniture. See Furniture, Used
SECONDHAND yachts. See Yachts, Used
SECREST, Bill
Upgraded signs give positive identity. il por
Am City 85:108+ Ap '70
SECRET agents. See Spies
SECRET life of Dan Ingram; drama. See
Roberts. E. B.
SECRET of Mike's mother; story. See Hand-
ley, D. C.
SECRET police, Russian. See Secret service—
Russia
SECRET service

Israel

Israel's early warning system in the Arab
world. P. Jacobs. il N Y Times Mag p23-
5+ F 8 '70

Russia

In the Soviet isolation ward; restriction of
news-gathering activities of western correspondents. J. Dornberg. il por Newsweek
76:25-6 D 28 '70
KGB; condensation. J. Barron. il Read Digest 97:201-15+ Ag '70
Repression with flowers; capture of A. Amal-
ric by KGB. Time 95:28 Je 1 '70
Schooling of a Soviet spy; excerpts from
KGB. J. Barron. il por Read Digest 96:225-
8+ Ap; 217-22+ My '70
Who is Mr X? S. Alsop. Newsweek 77:68 Ja
4 '71

United States

New work load for the Secret service. il
U S News 69:55 S 14 '70
State police. F. Lang. Ramp Mag 9:12-13 D '70
See also
Presidents—United States—Protection
United States—Central intelligence agency
SECRET societies
See also
Freemasons
Ku Klux klan
Mafia

Brazil

Death squads. il Newsweek 75:61+ Ap 20 '70
SECRETARIAT of the United Nations. See
United Nations—Secretariat

SECRETARIES
Girl Friday: what they're looking for. Bsns
W p 107 Je 20 '70
Girls on the bandwagon: senatorial secre-
taries. S. Davidson. McCalls 97:42-3+ Ag
'70
See also
Medical secretaries
National secretaries association
School secretaries
SECRETARIES of labor (United States)
Nixon's key man in labor crises; G. P. Shultz.
il por U S News 68:39 Ap 6 '70
SECRETARIES of state (United States)
See also
Rogers. W. P.
SECRETARIES of the treasury (United States)
See also
Connally, J.
SECRETARY General of the United Nations.
See United Nations—Secretary General
SECRETIONS
See also
Pheromones
SECTS
Pastor Paul; nondenominational Church of
Christian liberty. il por Newsweek 76:70
Jl 13 '70
Polarization within the churches. A. B.
Haines. Chr Cent 87:1039-41 S 2 '70
SECTS
See also
Friends, Society of
Hutterite Brethren
Jehovah's Witnesses
Mennonites
Mormons and Mormonism
Salvation army
Seventh-day Adventists
Shakers
Soka Gakkai (sect)
SECULAR institutes
See also
Opus Dei (secular institute)
SECULARISM
Modern schism: three paths to the secular,
by M. E. Marty. Review
Commonweal 91:538-40 F 13 '70. A. Atkins
Nymphs and shepherds. P. Hebblethwaite.
Cath World 211:55-7 My '70
SECURITIES
Odds favor the blue chips. Bsns W p88 O 10
'70
See also
Bonds
Dividends
Investment banking
Investments
Investments, Foreign
Stocks
Taxation of bonds, securities, etc.
also subhead Securities under various
subjects, e.g. Petroleum industry and trade
—Securities

Marketing

Corporate sleuths on Wall Street. J. C. Per-
ham. il Duns 95:29-31+ 9p '70
Rising attack on stock exchange insiders;
specialist system. il Time 96:58-9 Ag 10 '70
Stock market as people; interview. L. Har-
ris. il por Forbes 105:53+ F 1 '70
Turmoil in securities industry; meaning for
investors. il U S News 69:35-7 N 23 '70
Why the big traders worry industry. il Bsns
W pE2-7+ Jl 25 '70

Registration

How to sell letter stock. L. Williams. Duns
96:51-2+ N '70

Taxation

See Taxation of bonds, securities, etc.

Theft

See Securities, Theft of
SECURITIES, Tax exempt
Interest equalization tax to apply to Japanese
securities; White House announcement, with
executive order. R. M. Nixon. Dept State
Bul 62:348+ Mr 16 '70
Money crisis nears for local public works:
federal tax rules adds to the problem. il
U S News 68:73-4 My 4 '70
SECURITIES, Theft of
Bull market in stock and bond thefts; inter-
view. J. E. Hoover. il por Nations Bsns
58:28-32 Mr '70
SECURITIES and exchange commission. See
United States—Securities and exchange
commission
SECURITIES investor protection corporation
(proposed) See Brokers—Insurance
SECURITY. See International security
SECURITY, Internal. See Internal security

SEIDL, John M.
Let's compete with loan sharks. bibliog f il Harvard Bsns R 48:69-77 My '70
SEIDLER, Bea
Great homes away from home: the Ahwahnee. il Am Home 73:32-3+ Jl '70
SEIDLER, Edouard
Import report. See Issues of Motor trend
Rap 'n pinion. por Motor T 22:14 D '70
SEIDMAN, Arthur H.
Designing LC tuned circuits. il por Electr World 83:54-6 Ap '70
What's the weather going to be? il Electr World 84:31-3 N '70
SEIDMAN, Hugh
Drop the wires; poem. Nation 211:246 S 21 '70
Tale of Genji; poem. Atlan 225:56 Je '70
SEIF, Michael
Vacation home for $1200. il Mech Illus 66:80-3+ Je '70
SEIFERT, William
Test case in California. New Repub 163:8-9 O 31 '70
La SEINE (restaurant) See New York (city) —Hotels, restaurants, etc.
SEINGALT, Giacomo Girolamo Casanova de. See Casanova de Seingalt, G. G.
SEISMIC sea waves. See Tidal waves
SEISMOGRAPHS
Amateur scientist. C. L. Stong. il Sci Am 223 117-18+ Ag '70
SEISMOLOGY
Apollo 12 seismic signal: indication of a deep layer of powder. T. Gold and S. Soter. bibliog il Science 169:1071-5 S 11 '70
Crustal layer of seismic velocity 6.9 to 7.6 kilometers per second under the deep oceans. G. L. Maynard. bibliog il Science 168:120-1 Ap 3 '70
Fluid pressure variations and prediction of shallow earthquakes. A. G. Sylvester. bibliog Science 169:1231-2 S 18 '70
Kicking the gong; unexpected lunar information. Sci Am 222:49-50 Ja '70
Missile impacts as sources of seismic energy on the moon. G. V. Latham and others. bibliog il Science 168:242-5 Ap 10 '70
Passive seismic experiment. G. V. Latham and others. bibliog il Science 167:455-7 Ja 30 '70
S-48 lunar impact signal lasts four hours; new data expected. Aviation W 92:20 Ap 20 '70
Seismic data from man-made impacts on the moon. G. Latham and others. bibliog il Science 170:620-6 N 6 '70
Transversely aligned seismicity and concealed structures. C. F. Richter; reply. Z. F. Danes. Science 167:396 Ja 23 '70
SEISMOMETRY
How does the Richter scale differ from the Modified Mercalli scale. I. Asimov. Sci Digest 67:73-4 Mr '70
What is the modified Mercalli scale? I. Asimov. Sci Digest 67:81-2 F '70
SEITLIN, Percy
Paul Rand, commercial artist. il por Am Artist 34:48-53 O '70
SEITZ, Ron
Tree-trimmer; poem. Commonweal 93:98 O 23 '70
SEKYEWA, Francis M.
Rhodesian bishops: no apartheid. Commonweal 92:308-9 Je 26 '70
SELANDER, Robert K. and Yang, S. Y.
Horseshoe crab lactate dehydrogenases: evidence for dimeric structure. bibliog il Science 169:179-81 Jl 10 '70
SELBERT, Rochelle. See Anderson, R. H. jt. auth.
SELBORNE, England
Selborne nightingale; excerpt from Springtime in Britain. E. W. Teale. il Audubon 72: 58-67 S '70
SELBY, Norman. See McCoy, K.
SELDEN, William K.
Accreditation of public libraries: yes or no? por Wilson Lib Bul 45:394-8 D '70
SELDES, George
Spain: fascism gone gray. il Nation 211:77-80 Ag 3 '70
SELDES, Gilbert
Obituary
Pub W 198:35 N 9 '70
SELECTION, Natural. See Natural selection
SELECTION of teachers. See Teachers—Selection and appointment
SELECTIONS of librarians. See Librarians— Selection and appointment
SELECTIVE objectors. See Conscientious objectors
SELECTIVE service, Military. See Military service, Compulsory

SELECTAVISION. See Video recorders and recording
SELENOLOGY. See Lunar geology
SELF
Actors' search for a self. W. E. Henry and J. H. Sims. il Trans-Action 7:57-62 S '70
See also
Consciousness
Personality
SELF analysis. See Self evaluation
SELF appraisal. See Self evaluation
SELF-care. See Hospital care
SELF concept. See Self perception
SELF control
Taming the tongue. Chr Today 14:34 Mr 13 '70
SELF culture
B is for apple. G. M. White. il por Redbook 135:8+ My '70
SELF defense
Self-defense, but no kickie, no squashie; aikido. J. Bruce. Sports Illus 33:64-6+ O 26 '70
Your legal rights in the act of self-defense. Bsns W p 101 Ja 31 '70
See also
Judo
SELF defense for women
Men are full of weak points, these gals know where. K. V. Brown. il Todays Health 48: 64-6 N '70
Miss Superfist. D. Gerrity. por Atlan 225:91-3 Mr '70
SELF destruction. See Suicide
SELF discipline. See Self control
SELF disclosure. See Human relations
SELF education. See Self culture
SELF esteem. See Self love
SELF estimate. See Self evaluation
SELF evaluation
Don't tell me to be myself, that's what I want to change! A. Wood. Seventeen 29: 186+ Ap '70
Man talk: fine art of letting it all hang out. D. Newman and R. Benton. il Mlle 70:26 Ja '70
Man talk: up, up, and, especially, away! D. Newman and R. Benton. Mlle 70:74 Ap '70
Opinion: phoniness. P. Miletich. por Mlle 71:30+ Je '70
Videotape for self-evaluation. G. Mueller. il Todays Ed 59:39 Ja '70
SELF expression. See Personality
SELF-government in education
Laissez-faire curriculum in the democratic school; address, November, 1969. A. P. Lehner. Engl J 59:803-10 S '70
Participation is learning. R. S. Powell. jr. Ed Digest 35:39-42 Ap '70
Student council, elementary style. J. S. Butler. il Todays Ed 59:58-9 S '70
Student council: useful or useless? M. O. Miklos and L. D. Miklos. bibliog Clear House 45:236-9 D '70
Student council: whither goest thou? R. L. Armstrong. Clear House 44:553-5 My '70
See also
Colleges and universities—Administration— Student participation
SELF image. See Self perception
SELF improvement. See Self culture
SELF insurance. See Insurance—Self insurance
SELF knowledge. See Self evaluation
SELF love
Education and the loss of self-esteem. C. A. Tesconi, jr. bibliog f Sch & Soc 98:102-6 F '70
Give yourself a treat. F. Beck. Har Yrs 10:18 Ap '70
That old self-love. V. P. McCorry. America 123:186+ S 19 '70
What faith can do; child's faith in himself; with study-discussion program, by M. M. Conant. D. Gordon. bibliog il PTA Mag 65:6-8, 34 D '70
See also
Autism
SELF mutilation
See also
Malingering
Stigmatization
SELF perception
Developing the adolescent's self concept with literature; The loner by E. Wier. F. Fennimore. bibliog f Engl J 59:1272-5+ D '70
SELF portraits. See Photography—Portraits
SELF ratings. See Self evaluation
SELF realization
Autonomy vs. authority? W. H. Becker. il Chr Cent 87:1149-53 S 30 '70

SELF restraint. See Self control
SELF-testing and repairing computer. See Computers—Space flight use
SELIANKA. See Cookery, Russian
SELIG, Mike
Presenting Mike Selig. R. A. Ewing. il por Art in Am 58:86-7 My '70 *
SELIGMAN, Daniel
Books & ideas. Fortune 82:213-14 S '70
Cold eye on mutual funds. il Fortune 82:169-70+ O '70
SELIGMANN, Kurt
Puppets of Kurt Seligmann: an homage. J. B. Myers. il Craft Horiz 30:32-5+ D '70 *
SELIGSON, Marcia
Hollywood's hottest writer: Buck Henry. il pors N Y Times Mag p 10-11+ Jl 19 '70
Who needs etiquette? il Life 68:12 Mr 6 '70
SELIGSON, Tom. See Libarle, M. jt. ed.
SELKIRK, Helen (Hamilton) Douglas-Hamilton, countess of
Agreable voyage. M. Halliday. il pors Am Heritage 21:8-11+ Je '70 *
SELL, Kenneth W. See Green, S. S. jt. auth.
SELLERS, James
Is America moral? R. J. Neuhaus. Commonweal 92:341-3 Jl 10 '70 *
SELLERS, Peter
People inside Peter Sellers. H. Lawrenson. por Esquire 74:120-3+ N '70 *
SELLIN, Eric
African art: compositional vs. model esthetics. Yale R 59:215-27 D '69
SELLING. See Marketing; Salesmen and salesmanship
SELMAN, J. A.
He earns $30,000 a year behind the wheel. E. D. Fales, jr. il pors Pop Mech 133:79-82+ My '70 *
SELYE, Hans
How to avoid harmful stress. J. D. Ratcliff. Todays Health 48:42-4 Jl '70; Same abr. Read Digest 97:79-82 Jl '70 *
Mercury poisoning: prevention by spironolactone. bibliog il Science 169:775-6 Ag 21 '70
SELZ, Peter
West coast report (cont) il Art in Am 58:158-9 N '70
SELZER, Michael
Normalizing the Jews. H. Halkin. Commentary 51:102-4+ Ja '71 *
SELZNICK, David Oliver
Selznick. by B. Thomas. Review
Life por 68:15 Ap 24 '70. R. Lardner. jr *
SEMAK, Michael
Photographer involved with life's human drama. M. Edelson. il Pop Phot 67:98-101+ N '70 *
SEMANTICS
See also
English language—Semantics
SEMEN
See also
Prostaglandins
SEMENOV, Vladimir Semenovich
United States and Soviet Union begin third phase of strategic arms limitation talks; statement, November 2, 1970. Dept State Bul 63:652 N 23 '70
United States and Soviet Union conclude preliminary strategic arms limitation talks; statement, December 22, 1969. Dept State Bul 62:29 Ja 12 '70
United States and Soviet Union conclude second phase of strategic arms limitation talks; statement, August 14, 1970. Dept State Bul 63:245-6 Ag 31 '70
SEMICONDUCTOR memories. See Memory devices (computers)
SEMICONDUCTOR transducers. See Transducers
SEMICONDUCTORS
Amateur scientists; deposition and use of thin films; ed. by C. L. Stong. R. Baker. il Sci Am 222:143-5 Je '70
Bonds and bands in semiconductors. J. C. Phillips. bibliog il Science 169:1035-42 S 11 '70; Reply with rejoinder. L. Pauling. 170:1432 D 25 '70
C.E.T. test. D. Glass. Electr World 84:70 N '70
Charge-coupled devices would be cheap, compact. G. B. Lubkin. il Phys Today 23:17-18 O '70
Chemical bond and solid-state physics; adaptation of address, March 1969. J. C. Phillips. bibliog il por Phys Today 23:23-30 F '70
Designing solid-state stereo amplifiers. M. Horowitz. il Radio-Electr 41:38-40+ D '70
European glut in semiconductors. il Bsns W p 18-19 Ag 22 '70
Great hopes from Ovshinsky's little switches grow. L. Lessing. il por Fortune 81:110-14+ Ap '70

Ion implantation. G. L. Wick. il Science 170:425-7 O 23 '70
LSI gives semiconductors a trip; quiz. V. Bell. Pop Electr 32:32 F '70
Memory film for cameras and computers; Ovonic device. S. V. Jones. il Sci Digest 69:31 Ja '71
Negative differential conductivity. E. M. Conwell. bibliog il por Phys Today 23:35-41 Je '70
New solid-state devices evolve; electron beam semiconductors. B. M. Elson. il Aviation W 93:51+ D 7 '70
New tubes and semiconductors. Radio-Electr 41:86-7 F; 86 Mr; 76 Ap; 91 S; 91 N '70
Solid state. L. Garner. See issues of Popular electronics
See also
Diodes
Intersil, inc.
Microelectronics
National semiconductor corporation
Transistors

Conferences

Magnetic semiconductors intrigue both scientists and engineers. J. B. Goodenough. bibliog il Phys Today 23:79-81+ Je '70
SEMINARIANS
Better than looking on. J. E. Mulligan. America 122:468-9 My 2 '70; Discussion 123:69-70 Ag 8 '70
Church and office bridge a gap; Church & industry institute's internship program. Bsns W p52 S 26 '70
Lutheran seminarians advocate abolition of 4-D exemption. Chr Cent 87:470 Ap 22 '70
Parish or perish. W. J. Horvath. Chr Cent 87:790 Je 24 '70
Revolution in theology; radical Marxism on the German campuses. C. F. H. Henry. Chr Today 15:36-7 O 9 '70
Theological education 1970; symposium. Chr Cent 87:472-80+ Ap 22 '70
To save a seminarian; internship program. D. Hillis. Chr Today 14:29-30 My 22 '70
SEMINARIES. See Theological seminaries
SEMINARS
Tannenbaum and Latin America; address, January 8, 1970. G. Arciniegas. il por Américas 22:27-31 Ap '70
SEMINOLE Indians
Seminole girl; ed. by M. S. Garbarino. il Trans-Action 7:40-6 F '70
SEMPÉ, Jean Jacques
Once upon a principality. il Sports Illus 32:32-7 My 4 '70
SEMPLE, Martin
Renewal and priestly prayer. America 122:419-20+ Ap 18 '70
SEMPLE, Robert B. Jr
Middle American who edits ideas for Nixon. il pors N Y Times Mag p32-3+ Ap 12 '70
Three strategies of a master politician. il pors N Y Times Mag p32-3+ N 1 '70
SEN, Samarendranath
U.S and India join in project for instructional TV via satellite; text of letter; December 11, 1969. Dept State Bul 62:44-5 Ja 12 '70
SENATE (United States) See United States—Congress—Senate
SENATE armed services committee. See United States—Congress—Senate—Armed services, Committee on
SENATE ethics committee. See United States—Congress—Senate—Standards and conduct, Select committee on
SENATE foreign relations committee. See United States—Congress—Senate—Foreign relations, Committee on
SENATE voting. See United States—Congress—Senate—Voting
SENATORIAL candidates. See Candidates, Political
SENATORIAL secretaries. See Secretaries
SENATORS
Agnew's elastic list; radical-liberals. por Time 96:8-9 S 28 '70
Election impact: new faces in the national spotlight. il U S News 69:44-6 N 16 '70
Henry Jackson: a statesman of uncommon quality. R. K. Bennett. por Read Digest 97:110-15 Jl '70
Nixon's record is the issue; November elections. R. Sherrill. Nation 210:619-23 My 25 '70
Senate races; who won, who lost. U S News 69:23 N 16 '70
See also
United States—Congress—Senate
SENATORS (baseball) See Baseball clubs

SENDAK, Maurice
Prize is won; or, How Maurice Sendak discovered where the wild things are; address, April 4, 1970. il por Pub W 197:30-1 My 25 '70
about
In defense of the wild things. M. A. Taylor. il Horn Bk 46:642-6 D '70 *
Sendak raises the shade on childhood. S. Braun. il por N Y Times Mag p34-5+ Je 7 '70 *
SENECA Indians
Death and rebirth of the Seneca, by A. F. C. Wallace. Review
    Sat R 53:30-1 Ja 24 '70. V. Deloria, jr
SENECA ROCK
West Virginia's mountain climbing. B. Thomas. il Travel 133:28-33+ F '70
SENEGAL
    See also
United Nations—Senegal
SENESCENCE in insects. See Age (insects)
SENESCENCE in plants. See Age (plants)
SENESI, Mauro
Identity crisis Italian style. il Ebony 25:40-6 Jl '70
SENIOR centers
AoA-aided California senior center now financed by city. il Aging 187:14 My '70
Center programs in North Dakota spreading like a prairie fire. il Aging 183:4-7 Ja '70
Fourth year title III funding allotted centers in Florida. il Aging 190:19 Ag '70
Plymouth, Wis. senior center now success as city project. il Aging 190:8-9 Ag '70
Public housing center offers multipurpose program. il Aging 183:12-13 Ja '70
Senior activity program survives hurricane Camille in Biloxi, Miss. il Aging 190:6-7 Ag '70
Senior center in Spanish Fork, Utah, result of joint efforts. il Aging 193:15 N '70
STEP, senior swingers, meals are hits at Washington senior center. il Aging 188:12-13 Je '70
    See also
National institute of senior centers
SENIOR citizens clubs. See Recreation for the aged
SENIOR citizens month
1970 Senior citizens month prologue to 1971 White House conference on aging. Aging 187:3 My '70
Senior citizens month begins 1971 White House conference. T. Schuchat. Har Yrs 10: 4 My '70
SENIOR community service project. See National council on the aging
SENIOR scholastic (periodical)
Fiftieth anniversary issue. por Sr Schol 97: 2-19+ O 19 '70
SENIORITY rule. See United States—Congress—Committees; United States—Congress—House—Committees
SENIORS, High school. See High school students
SENKO, Pavel, and Ravich, Mikhail
Soviet research in Antarctica. il Sci N 98: 185-6 Ag 22 '70
SENNETT, Richard
Brutality of modern families. il Trans-Action 7:29-37 S '70
Genteel backlash; Chicago 1886; excerpts from Nineteenth century cities. il Trans-Action 7:41-50 Ja '70
    about
New longings abroad in the land. B. DeMott. Sat R 53:25-6 Jl 4 '70 *
SENOR Augusto; story. See De Ledo, L. G.
SENOR Swan/ story. See Wernicke, E.
SENSATIONS; musical comedy. See Musical comedies, revues, etc.—Criticisms, plots, etc.
SENSE of humor. See Humor
SENSE organs
    See also
Olfactory organs
    Insects
Distal lobe of the pilifer: an ultrasonic receptor in choerocampine hawkmoth. K. D. Roeder and others. bibliog il Science 170: 1098-9 D 4 '70
SENSES and sensation
    See also
Brain
Hearing
Pain
Perception
Sight
Smell
Taste
Thirst
Time perception

SENSING systems, Remote. See Remote sensing systems
SENSITIVENESS
Christian sensitivity. M. R. Chartier. Chr Today 14:9-10 Jl 3 '70
SENSITIVITY. See Sensitiveness
SENSITIVITY cards. See Greeting cards
SENSITIVITY training. See Group relations training
SENSORS, Remote. See Remote sensing systems
SENTENCE; story. See Barthelme, D.
SEOUL, Korea
    Music
Premiere by an American expatriate; J. Wade's Martyred. A. C. Heyman. il Hi Fi 20:secII 30 Ag '70
SEPARATION (chemistry)
Separating lanthanides by ion exchange chromatography. L. W. McKeen. bibliog il por Chem 43:28-31 My '70
SEPARATION (technology)
Heating of basalts with a carbon dioxide laser; vapor fractionation. M. Blander and others. bibliog il Science 170:435-8 O 23 '70
Separation of plant particles; report of meeting. C. A. Price. Science 168:282-3 Ap 10 '70
    See also
Cytology—Methodology
Dialysis
SEPARATION anxiety. See Maternal deprivation
SEPARATION of powers
What the V.P. should learn; system of checks and balances. W. Lippmann. il por Newsweek 77:19 Ja 11 '71
SEPARATIST movement, French Canadian. See Quebec (province)—Nationalism
SEPULCHRAL monuments
Graven images: sermons in stones. A. Neal. Am Heritage 21:18-29 Ag '70
Mortuary art in Charleston churches. C. V. Hershey. il Antiques 98:800-7 N '70
SEPULVEDA, José Patricio Lopez. See Lopez Sepulveda, J. P.
SEQUOIA, Giant
Giant sequoia, monarchs of the living. D. Anderson. il Nat Parks 44:14-18 My '70
Restoring fire to the Sequoias. B. Kilgore. il Nat Parks & Con Mag 44:16-22 O '70
SEQUOIA gigantea. See Sequoia, Giant
SEREBNICK, Judith, and others
(ed) Book review. See issues of Library journal
SERENGETI NATIONAL PARK. See National parks and reserves—Tanzania
SERI Indians. See Indians of Mexico
SERIAL painting. See Painting—Technique
SERIAL publications
How to computerize your serials and periodicals when you don't know how; experience of University of Alaska library. M. Matthews and S. Sherman. pors Wilson Lib Bul 44:861-4 Ap '70
Price indexes for 1970; Serial services. N. B. Brown and W. H. Huff. il Library J 95: 2428-9 Jl '70
SERIES, Book
Children's books forecast, series; comp. by P. Bragg. Pub W 198:157-63 Jl 13 '70
Peter Rabbit is alive and well, despite his age. A. Caruba. il Pub W 198:82-5 Jl 13 '70
SERIGRAPHY. See Silk screen printing
SERJEANT Musgrave's dance; drama. See Arden, J.
SERMONS
Suggestion as sermon strategy. Chr Today 14:28-9 Mr 29 '70
    See also
Preaching
SEROTA, Frederic T. and Baserga, Renato
Polyinosinic acid · polycytidylic acid: inhibition of DNA synthesis stimulated by isoproterenol. bibliog il Science 167:1379-80 Mr 6 '70
SEROTONIN
Clues from a chemical; PCPA's effects on serotonin. L. Campbell. il Sci N 98:287-9 O 3 '70
Crystal structure of serotonin picrate, a donor-acceptor complex. C. E. Bugg and U. Thewalt. bibliog il Science 170:852-4 N 20 '70
5-Hydroxytryptamine: a cytospecific growth stimulator of cultured fibroblasts. R. J. Boucek and T. R. Alvarez. bibliog il Science 167:989-9 F 6 '70
In vivo conversion of ^{3}H-L-tryptophan into ^{3}-serotonin in brain areas of adrenalectomized rats. E. C. Azmitia, jr. and others. bibliog il Science 169:201-3 Jl 10 '70

SEROTONIN—*Continued*
Pituitary serotonin content: effects of melatonin or deprivation of water. R. S. Piezzi and R. J. Wurtman. bibliog il Science 169: 285-6 Jl 17 '70

SERPENT; drama. See Van Itallie, J.-C.

SERPENT fly. See Fishing lures, flies, etc.

SERPENTS in religion, folklore, etc.
Cobra, India's good snake. H. Miller. il Nat Geog 138:392-409 S '70

SERPICK, Arthur A. See Sanel, F. T. jt. auth.

SERRA, Richard
Critic's choice. E. C. Baker. il Art N 68:26-7 F '70 *

SERRATO, José C. 1921-
Let's give foreign doctors a fair shake; ed. by W. Cole. il por Todays Health 48:36-9 F '70

SERRIN, William
Unknown who leads the Walter P. Reuther memorial strike. il pors N Y Times Mag p28-9+ S 27 '70

SERUM
Atropinesterase and cocainesterase of rabbit serum: localization of the enzyme activity in isozymes. C. Stormont and Y. Suzuki. bibliog il Science 167:200-2 Ja 9 '70
Differential reactivity of human serums with early antigens induced by Epstein-Barr virus. W. Henle and others. bibliog il Science 169:188-90 Jl 10 '70
Obstructive lung disease and α-antitrypsin deficiency gene heterozygosity. F. Kueppers and othes; discussion. bibliog il Science 167: 1015-16 F 13 '70
Soluble HL-A7 antigen: localization in the β-lipoprotein fraction of human serum. R. K. Charlton and C. M. Zmijewski. bibliog il Science 170:636-7 N 6 '70
See also
Antiserum

SERUM hepatitis. See Hepatitis

SERUM hepatitis virus. See Hepatitis viruses

SERVAAS, Beurt
Resurrection of the Satevepost. por Bsns W p29-30 N 14 '70 *

SERVAN-SCHREIBER, Jean Jacques
Express to success. il por Newsweek 76:55-6 S 28 '70 *
Flight to freedom. il por Newsweek 75:56+ Ap 27 '70 *
Letter from Paris. Genêt. New Yorker 46: 50 Jl 11 '70 *
Making of a deputy. il por Newsweek 76:48-9 Jl 6 '70 *
Man of action. por Time 96:29-30 Jl 6 '70 *
Monday of Mikis Theodorakis; reprint. J. Boetsch. il pors Sat R 53:14-15+ My 9 '70 *
Political chicken. il por Newsweek 76:50 S 21 '70 *
Politics Bordelaise. il pors Time 96:29 S 28 '70 *
Radical change. il por Newsweek 75:34 Mr 2 '70 *

SERVAN-SCHREIBER, Jean Louis
L'Express breaks with tradition. il por Bsns W p34+ S 26 '70 *

SERVANTS. See Household employees

SERVICE, Community. See Community service

SERVICE, Compulsory non-military
Real root of student disorder? S. I. Hayakawa. Read Digest 97:167-8 N '70

SERVICE, Volunteer. See Volunteer service

SERVICE industries
Address book. See Issues of House beautiful
Better appliance servicing wanted! Consumer Bul 53:13-14 O '70
How growth of services is changing America. il U S News 69:34-5 N 9 '70
There'll be less leisure than you think. G. Burck. il Fortune 81:86-9+ Mr '70
See also
Public service industries
Transamerica corporation

SERVICE men
See also
Furloughs
Gifts for service men
Military life
Soldiers
Telephone calls to service men in Vietnam

Associations, Institutions, etc.

See also
American serviceman's union

Religion

See United States—Armed forces—Religious affairs

Vocational education

Making civilians out of soldiers; Project Transition. il Bsns W p68+ S 26 '70

SERVICE men, Discharged. See Veterans

SERVICE men and narcotics. See Narcotics

SERVICE mens entertainments. See United States—Armed forces—Recreation

SERVICE mens families
Memories of divided families; with interviews with POW wives, ed. by M. Byers. il Life 69:36-40+ D 4 '70
See also
Children of service men
Service mens wives

SERVICE mens marriages. See War marriages

SERVICE mens publications
See also
Overseas weekly
Stars and stripes (newspaper)

SERVICE mens wives
Living with uncertainty: the families who wait back home; wives of US POW's in Vietnam. il pors Time 96:18-19 D 7 '70
They also serve: wives of prisoners of war, or men missing in action. P. L. Buckley. Nat R 22:786-7+ Jl 28 '70
What is Christmas to the P.O.W. wives? C. S. Wren. il Look 34:36-40 D 15 '70

SERVICE of papers. See Process

SERVICE rating of librarians. See Librarians—Rating

SERVICE stations. See Automobile service stations

SERVICEAMERICA division. See RCA corporation—ServiceAmerica division

SERVICEMEN (repairing) See Repairmen

SERVING carts
Build this handsome electric serving cart. W. C. Leckey. il Pop Mech 133:118-21+ My '70
Build your own barbecue cart. il Mech Illus 66:114-15 Ap '70
Get the party rolling! mobile servers. N. Schram. il House B 112:116-19 N '70

SERVING stands. See Stands (furniture)

SERVING tables. See Tables

SERVING trays. See Trays

SESAME street (program) See Television in education

SESKIN, Eugene P. See Lave, L. B. jt. auth.

SESSIONS, Roger
First recordings: Sessions and Lees. A. Cohn. Am Rec G 36:298+ D '69
Questions about Sessions. R. Evett. New Repub 162:40-2 My 9 '70 *

SESSLER, Gloria Jean
Orchids around the year (cont) il Horticulture 48:34-5+ Mr; 32-3+ Je; 22-3+ S '70

SESSOMS, H. Douglas
Manpower crises: as others see us. il Parks & Rec 5:39-41+ Ja '70
Recreation; address, February 9, 1970. Vital Speeches 36:349-52 Mr 15 '70

SETTERS
Pointer or setter. J. R. Falk. il Field & S 75:184-6+ O '70

SETTLE, Betty Sue
Amateur scientist. il Sci Am 222:131-4 Mr '70

SEUSS, Dr, pseud. See Geisel, T. S.

SEVAREID, Eric
Voice of reason. Time 96:9 N 2 '70

1776; musical comedy. See Musical comedies, revues. etc.—Criticisms, plots, etc.

SEVENTEEN year locusts. See Cicadas

SEVENTH-day Adventists
Adventist urgency: race and missions. R. Chandler. Chr Today 14:35-6 Jl 3 '70
Attraction of Adventism. D. Kucharsky. Chr Today 14:35 Ja 30 '70

SEVERIN, Kurt
Snake safari with camera and courage. il por Sci Digest 68:38-47 N '70

SEVERINSEN, Carl. See Severinsen, D.

SEVERINSEN, Doc
Tonight with Doc Severinsen. G. Lees. por Hi Fi 20:secI 122+ Ap '70 *

SEVERO, Richard
Horrors of heroin. Read Digest 96:72-5 Ja '70

SEVERS, Susan B.
From classroom grocery store to imaginary zoo. il Sch Arts 70:8 S '70

SEVILLE, Jack
Before you buy that boat... il Motor B 125: 144-5 Ja '70
Double play in Minnesota. il Motor B 126: 58-60 S '70
Four new ways to skin the cruising cat. Motor B 125:127 Mr '70

SEVIN. See Insecticides

SEWAGE
See also
Sewerage

SEWAGE aeration. See Sewage disposal—Aeration

SEWAGE as fertilizer

City sludge for farm fertilizer. B. Coffman. il Farm J 94:32F O '70

How to save taxes at the sewage plant; using sludge as soil conditioner. J. Olds. Org Gard & Farm 17:106-7 F '70

Pollution or profit? W. H. Fuller. Horticulture 48:22-3+ D '70

Transporting wastes to build soils. J. Olds. il Org Gard & Farm 17:43-7 D '70

SEWAGE disposal

Cleaner water hurts the builders; building ban for water pollution control. Bsns W p28-9 Je 6 '70

Coliform aerosols emitted by sewage treatment plants. A. P. Adams and J. C. Spendlove. bibliog il Science 169:1218-20 S 18 '70

Slow slogging on sewage; new technology. il Sci N 98:412 N 28 '70

Sludge and leaves; what's your community doing with them? M. Franz. il Org Gard & Farm 17:71-3 My '70

Waste-water treatment; the tide is turning. R. W. Holcomb. Science 169:457-9 Jl 31 '70

Wastewater collection and treatment. See issues of American city

What happened to the attempts to clean up the majestic, the polluted Hudson? Castleton-on-Hudson, N.Y. W. Greene. il N Y Times Mag p28-9+ My 3 '70

See also
Sewage as fertilizer
Sewage incinerators
Sewage irrigation
Trade waste disposal
Waste disposal in the ocean

Activated sludge method

Oxygen can replace aeration to lower wastewater purification costs; Unox system. il Am City 85:90 Je '70

Treating waste in greater haste; Unox process. il Bsns W p 106 N 7 '70

Aeration

Aerobics; it can solve your sewage problems, too. E. F. Lindsley. il Pop Sci 197:102-3+ O '70

Sewage plant designed for livestock wastes. B. Lovelidge. il Farm J 94:54B-54C F '70

Biological treatment

Denitrification biologically. S. Balakrishnan. bibliog il Am City 85:56-8 D '70

Chemical treatment

We don't cater to bugs; using chemical precipitation instead of biological purification; Mattabassett district, Conn. J. R. Szymanski. il Am City 85:72-5 F '70

Coagulation

Approved coagulant aids. il Am City 85:72 Ag '70

Electrolytic treatment

Electrolytic treatment permits three-way effluent reuse; Clark County, Nev. il Am City 85:22 D '70

History

All the fat and sullage fuddy murriners. S. Schlee. il Natur Hist 79:18-20+ D '70

Nitrogen removal

Denitrification biologically. S. Balakrishnan. bibliog il Am City 85:56-8 D '70

Phosphate removal

To oust phosphate, add pickle liquor; Detroit. G. J. Remus. il Am City 85:65 D '70

SEWAGE disposal plants

Combined sewers may be an advantage; Kenosha, Wis. F. I. Vilen. il Am City 85:68-70 Ja '70

How to save taxes at the sewage plant; using sludge as soil conditioner. J. Olds. Org Gard & Farm 17:106-7 F '70

New York city to use Unox system. Am City 85:24 S '70

Our neighbor the sewer plant; Kansas City, Mo. D. R. Youngquist. il Am City 85:104+ My '70

Regional authorities. L. Ross. New Repub 162:15-16 Je 20 '70

Reviving the Great Lakes; Muskegon project. J. R. Sheaffer. il Sat R 53:62-5 N 7 '70

Storm-water retention can work; Detroit. G. Remus. il Am City 85:68-9 O '70

Unoxidized nitrogen is the key; exacting standards of purity set for the Ohio River. G. Seymour. Am city 85:49 F '70

We don't cater to bugs using chemical precipitation instead of biological purification; Mattabassett district, Conn. J. R. Szymanski. il Am City 85:72-5 F '70

SEWAGE incinerators

Old digesters don't die; San Mateo, Calif. J. H. Jenks. il Am City 85:70-1 Ag '70

SEWAGE irrigation

New prospect; living-filter system of sewage disposal. L. T. Kardos. bibliog il Environ 12:10-21+ Mr '70

Reviving the Great Lakes; Muskegon project. J. R. Sheaffer. il Sat R 53:62-5 N 7 '70

SEWAGE systems. See Sewerage

SEWAGE treatment in space. See Life support systems (space environment)

SEWAGE treatment plants. See Sewage disposal plants

SEWAGE water. See Water reuse

SEWARD'S SUCCESS, Alaska

Entire city under glass. J. Davis. il Pop Sci 196:74-5 Mr '70

SEWER cleaning

Graduated weirs speed infiltration tests; method used in Cincinnati. A. D. Caster. il Am City 85:22 Mr '70

Kill roots as you clean the sewer. Am City 85:30 Je '70

Pumps speed sewer cleaning; Marion, Ohio. il Am City 85:30 My '70

SEWER inspection

Let the camera be your eyes; Paramus, N.J. J. J. Tedesco, jr. il Am City 85:86+ Ja '70

SEWER pipe laying. See Pipe laying

SEWER pipes

See also
Sewer cleaning

Maintenance and repair

Test stainless-steel tubing for aeration pipes; Houston, Tex. il Am City 85:46 O '70

SEWER revenue bonds. See Bonds, Revenue

SEWERAGE

County unifies thirty-five sewerage agencies; Washington County, Ore. R. Milbrodt. il Am City 85:64-5+ N '70

See also
Pipe laying
Storm sewers

Maintenance and repair

Gunite gives new life to an old, failing brick sewer system; Chattanooga, Tenn. W. M. Englerth. il Am City 85:101-2 Jl '70

SEWERS. See Sewerage

SEWERS, Storm. See Storm sewers

SEWING

Boutique of gifts to sew. E. D. Craster. il Bet Hom & Gard 48:60-3+ N '70

Choosing and sewing knitted fabrics. Redbook 134:66 Ap '70

It's sew easy. Ladies Home J 87:52 S '70

Look who's sewing. il Harp Baz 103:138 S '70

Men, man your needles. C. Rice. il Har Yrs 10:16-18 Mr '70

$3-billion boom in home sewing. il Bsns W p56-7 O 3 '70

See also
Curtains and draperies
Dressmaking
Needlework

SEWING cabinets. See Cabinets (furniture)

SEWING centers. See Sewing rooms

SEWING machines

New sewing machines; which one for you? C. Houck. il Parents Mag 45:51-4 Ag '70

Sewing machines. il Consumer Bul 53:33-8 D '70

Zigzag sewing machines. Consumer Rep 34:29-34 D '69

SEWING rooms

Compleat sewing center. il Bet Hom & Gard 48:12 Jl '70

Wonderful work room. J. Gillies. il Farm J 94:68-9 My '70

SEX

Everything you always wanted to know about sex but were afraid to ask; excerpts. D. Reuben. Ladies Home J 87:50+ Je '70

Sex power and the revolution. V. Eller. il Chr Cent 87:291-3 Mr 11 '70; Discussion. 87:575-6, 641, 728, 847, 1567-8 My 6, 20, Je 10, Jl 8, D 30 '70

Sexual conflicts; questions and answers. D. Reuben. por McCalls 97:26+ Jl '70

Bibliography

Facing our sexuality. America 123:565-7 D 26 '70

Research

See Sex research

SEX (biology)

See also
Hermaphroditism

SEX (psychology)
Family size and sex-role stereotypes. F. E. Clarkson and others. bibliog Science 167: 390-2 Ja 23 '70
In pursuit of the American woman; or, Gulliver at the gynecologist's. E. Grossman. il Harper 240:47-58+ F '70; Discussion. 240: 6+ My '70
   See also
Frigidity (psychology)
Oedipus complex
SEX and drug forum of San Francisco. See National sex and drug forum of San Francisco
SEX and religion
Early Christians on sex. J. J. Magee. il Cath World 211:208-10 Ag '70
Presbyterian debate over sex. J. Star. Look 34:54+ Ag 11 '70
Sex education and the church; excerpt from A time to love. L. P. Bird and C. T. Reilly. Chr Today 14:10-13 Je 5 '70
Sexuality and the United Presbyterians. Chr Today 14:21 Je 19 '70
Till death us do part! B. L. Smith. Chr Today 14:5-8+ Ja 16 '70
   See also
Sex in the Bible
SEX attractants (insects) See Insect sex attractants
SEX behavior in animals. See Sexual behavior in animals
SEX chromosomes. See Chromosomes
SEX control. See Sex determination and control
SEX crimes
   See also
Rape
SEX determination and control
Boy or girl? A new pre-birth test can tell; interview. M. M. Grumbach. il Good H 170: 139 Ja '70
Boy or girl: would you choose your baby's sex? T. Irwin. il Parents Mag 45:67-9+ N '70
Prenatal blood test predicts babies' sex. Todays Health 48:79 S '70
Where have all girlies gone? Sci Digest 67: 30 Ap '70
You can choose your baby's sex; excerpt from Your baby's sex. D. M. Rorvik and L. B. Shettles. il Look 34:88-94+ Ap 21 '70; Same abr. with title Chance to choose baby's sex. Read Digest 97:97-101 D '70
SEX differences
Is Catch-22 male chauvinist? P. Holzschlag. Commonweal 93:69-70 O 16 '70; Discussion. 93:187+ N 20 '70
Sexes: getting it all together. F. Bowers. il Sat R 54:16-19 Ja 9 '71
Women re women. E. MacCoby. Mlle 70:180-1+ F '70
SEX education. See Sex instruction
SEX hormones. See Hormones, Sex
SEX in literature
Sex and Armageddon. J. P. Sisk. Commentary 50:83-4+ D '70
Trade winds. C. Amory. Sat R 53:6 Jl 25 '70
You are the more cupcakeable for being a Cosmopolitan girl. W. F. Buckley, jr. Nat R 22:999-1000 S 22 '70
   See also
Realism in literature

   Anecdotes, facetiae, satire, etc.
Adventures of Roxanne; notes on a sensuous woman. C. Trillin. Life 69:12 N 27 '70
SEX in moving pictures
Dirty movies: hard-core and soft. D. Denby. Atlan 226:99-102 Ag '70
How skin flicks hit bible-belt Waterloo, Iowa. il Newsweek 76:28 D 21 '70
Ingrid Bergman speaks out; interview, ed. by D. Lurie. I. Bergman. il por Ladies Home J 87:141-2 O '70
Mine eyes have seen the glory; sex education documentaries. H. Alpert. Sat R 53:56 My 16 '70
Movies and the sexual revolution: should the ratings be revised? G. N. Boyd. Chr Cent 87:1124-5 S 23 '70
Obscenity in films. R. Schnickel. il Life 68: 12 Ap 10 '70
Porn and man at Yale: R. Meyer films. R. Schickel. Harper 241:34+ Jl '70
Porn capital of America; San Francisco. W. Murray. il N Y Times Mag p8-9+ Ja 3 '71
Pornography goes public; with report on attempts of clean up by Mason City, Iowa group. J. Neary. il Life 69:18-25 Ag 28 '70
Public privates; porno films from Denmark. S. Kauffmann. New Repub 163:22+ Jl 11 '70
Rich pornocopia. il Time 96:92 N 16 '70
They shoot dirty movies don't they? L. Botto. il Look 34:56+ N 3 '70

True blue. A. Keneas. il Newsweek 76:91-2 Jl 13 '70
Women in love; D. H. Lawrence's novel a classic film. J Hamilton. il por Look 34: 32-7 F 24 '70
SEX in the arts
   See also
Sex in the performing arts
SEX in the Bible
What the Bible says about sex. B. Graham. por Read Digest 96:117-20 My '70
SEX in the performing arts
Must smut smother the stage. D. Merrick. Read Digest 96:103-5 Mr '70
Pornography goes public. il Newsweek 76: 26-8+ D 21 '70
Reflections: permissiveness and rectitude. L. Tyrmand. New Yorker 46:85-96 F 28 '70
Uses of boredom. N. Cousins. Sat R 53:16 Ap 11 '70
   See also
Sex in moving pictures
SEX information and education council of the United States
Sex, SIECUS, and the schools. H. Lindsell. Chr Today 14:10-13 Ja 30 '70
Siecus-swayed librarians sought by concerned parents. Library J 95:3585 O 15 '70
SEX instruction
Cool look at sex education; symposium; with study-discussion program, by C. Smallenburg and H. Smallenburg. bibliog il PTA Mag 65:2-5, 35 D '70
Family life and sex education. bibliog Ment Hy 54:591-2 O '70
Grant v. Lee. il por Time 96:52-3 Ag 31 '70
How mothers answer: where do babies come from? R. M. Higdon. Todays Health 48:34-5+ O '70
In search of sanity: man in the middle; interview, ed. by M. Michaelson, M. M. Musselman. il por Todays Health 48:31-3+ F '70
Innovative programs in sex education; with study-discussion program, by E. Harris and D. Harris. J. L. Donaldson. bibliog il PTA Mag 64:26-8, 35-6 Ja '70; Same abr. Ed Digest 35:46-8 Ap '70
Is there a too soon? W. J. Gadpaille. il por Todays Health 48:34-5+ F '70
Latest scoop on Swedish sex. D. W. Ferm. il Chr Cent 87:45-8 Ja 14 '70; Discussion. 87: 243 F 25 '70
Library sex education: a report from Dallas; neighborhood discussions at three branches. M. Warren. Wilson Lib Bul 44:593-4 F '70
Oh! Sex education! by M. Breasted. Review Chr Today 15:33-4 D 18 '70. L. P. Bird
Preschoolers pose some tough questions. P. Thomson. il Am Ed 6:16-19 O '70
Put the hex on sex. Sr Schol 96:Schol Teach 2 My 18 '70
Right and wrong way to teach sex. B. Bettelheim. Ladies Home J 87:26-7 Ja '70
Sense about sex; excerpts from address, 1970. S. Levenson. PTA Mag 65:5 O '70
Sex ed flare-ups would ban courses, materials; discussion. Library J 94:4185; 95: 189 N 15 '69, Ja 15 '70
Sex education. D. Reuben. McCalls 98:10 Ja '71
Sex education and the church; excerpt from A time to love. L. P. Bird and C. T. Reilly. Chr Today 14:10-13 Je 5 '70
Sex education, K through 6; with study-discussion program, by E. Harris and D. Harris. D. R. Nowack and M. M. Conant. bibliog il PTA Mag 65:6-9, 33 N '70
Sex in the school: education or titillation? B. Goodheart. il Todays Health 48:28-30+ F '70
Sex mores and sex morals; with study-discussion program, by C. Smallenburg and H. Smallenburg. D. L. Farnsworth. bibliog il PTA Mag 64:2-5, 34 Ap '70
Sex, SIECUS, and the schools. H. Lindsell. Chr Today 14:10-13 Ja 30 '70
Why I'll give my daughter the pill. P. H. Wade. il por Redbook 135:30+ Je '70
   See also
Sexual behavior
SEX maniac; story. See Wolitzer, H.
SEX manuals. See Marriage—Handbooks, manuals, etc.
SEX pheromones (insects) See Insect sex attractants
SEX ratio
Postpartum psychiatric reactions: time of onset and sex ratio of newborns. F. T. Melges; reply. M. A. Taylor. Science 168: 151-2 Ap 3 '70
Sex ratio in drosophila pseudoobscura: spermiogenic failure. D. Policansky and J. Ellison. bibliog il Science 169:888-9 Ag 28 '70

SEX ratio—*Continued*
Sex ratio of newborns: preponderance of males in toxemia of pregnancy. P. Toivanen and T. Hirvonen. bibliog il Science 170:187-8 O 9 '70
Where have all girlies gone? Sci Digest 67: 30 Ap '70

SEX relations
Affair, by M. Hunt. Review
Harp Baz 103:35+ Mr '70. N. Gittelson
Can love live with indifference? il Good H 170:28+ Ja '70
Fraud in bed; with excerpt from Something in disguise. E. J. Howard. Vogue 156:98-9 S 15 '70
How important is sex in marriage? J. Brothers. il Good H 171:52+ S '70
Human sexual inadequacy, by W. N. Masters and V. Johnson. Review
Sat R 53:45 My 2 '70. J. Lear
Human sexual inadequacy; findings of the W. H. Masters-V. E. Johnson study. M. Clark. pors Newsweek 75:90+ My 4 '70
Husbands and wives talk frankly about sex. Krupp. Redbook 135:69+ Jl '70
Masters & Johnson: their new cures for sex problems. M. Weber. Ladies Home J 87:51+ Jl '70
Mlle's modest little sex survey. il Mlle 70:220-1 F '70
Priest's wise and witty view of sex without guilt. R. F. Capon. por Redbook 135:73+ My '70
Repairing the conjugal bed. il pors Time 95: 49-52 My 25 '70
Sex and marriage. W. H. Masters; V. E. Johnson. Redbook 135:82-90 S '70
Sex and the married couple; W. Master's and V. Johnson's therapy. P. Wilkes. il Atlan 226-82-4+ D '70
Sex and the married woman. W. Masters and V. Johnson. McCalls 97:68-9+ My '70
Sex games people play; excerpts from Sex in human loving. E. Berne. il Ladies Home J 87:80+ O '70
Sex, guilt and the double standard. W. H. Masters; V. E. Johnson. Redbook 135:67+ O '70
Sexual inadequacy; what can be done: Masters and Johnson write another book. W. Bradbury. il pors Life 68:42-6 My 1 '70; Same abr. Read Digest 97:63-6 Ag '70
Tell me, doctor, what about sex after my operation? W. A. Nolen. Ladies Home J 87:162-4 O '70
Too tired to love? excerpt from Women and fatigue: a woman doctor's answer. M. Hilliard. Read Digest 97:65-8 S '70
Weird Harold and the first national swingers' convention. C. Remsberg and B. Remsberg. Esquire 74:189+ D '70
What's happening to sexual privacy? F. Trippett. Look 34:50 O 20 '70
When married love is disappointing. C. Vincent. il Redbook 134:82-3+ Ap '70

SEX research
Human sexual inadequacy, by W. N. Masters and V. Johnson. Review
Sat R 53:45 My 2 '70. J. Lear
Human sexual inadequacy; findings of the W. H. Masters-V. E. Johnson study. M. Clark. pors Newsweek 75:90+ My 4 '70
Repairing the conjugal bed. il pors Time 95:49-52 My 25 '70
Sexual inadequacy; what can be done: Masters and Johnson write another book. W. Bradbury. il pors Life 68:42-6 My 1 '70; Same abr. Read Digest 97:63-6 Ag '70

SEX-role inversion. See Change of sex

SEXTON, Anne
Comment. M. Van Duyn. Poetry 115:430-2 Mr '70 *

SEXUAL behavior
Love and sex. D. Reuben. McCalls 98:26 D '70
New tyranny of sexual liberation. D. Wright. por Life 69:4 N 6 '70
Sex in human loving, by R. Berne. Review
Life 69:11 D 18 '70. D. Reuben
Sex, sex, sexzzzzzzz. R. B. Miller. Commonweal 93:192-7 N 20 '70
Sex's silent majority. M. Resnik. Vogue 157:83 Ja 1 '71
Young living; must sex be all or nothing at all? A. Wood. Seventeen 29:140+ Je '70
See also
Aged—Sexual behavior
College students—Sexual behavior
Youth—Sexual behavior

SEXUAL behavior in animals
p-Chlorophenylalanine methyl ester: an aphrodisiac. R. E. Whalen and W. C. Luttge. bibliog il Science 169:1000-1 S 4 '70
Copulatory behavior can inhibit pregnancy in female rats. N. T. Adler and S. R. Zoloth. bibliog il Science 168:1480-2 Je 19 '70

Everything you always wanted to know about your pet's sex life. F. Manolson. Ladies Home J 87:82+ N '70
Hypersexuality and behavioral changes in cats caused by administration of p-chlorophenylalanine. J. Ferguson and others. bibliog il Science 168:499-501 Ap 24 '70
Intromission pattern and species vaginal code in relation to induction of pseudopregnancy. M. Diamond. bibliog il Science 169:995-7 S 4 '70
Mating games octopi play. il Life 69:48-53 N 6 '70
Olfactory bulb removal eliminates mating behavior in the male golden hamster. M. R. Murphy and G. E. Schneider. bibliog il Science 167:302-4 Ja 16 '70
Seal harems in the Pribilofs. R. K. Mathews. il por Natur Hist 79:32-41 Ja '70
Sexual behavior of male cats after administration of parachlorophenylalanine. A. Zitrin and others. bibliog il Science 170:868-70 N 20 '70
Side effect; PCPA as aphrodisiac. Sci Am 222:44 F '70
Simulation of the mating advantage in mating of rare drosophila males. L. Ehrman. bibliog il Science 167:905-6 F 6 '70
See also
Courtship of animals
Courtship of insects

SEXUAL diseases. See Venereal diseases

SEXUAL ethics
Affair, by M. Hunt. Review
Harp Baz 103:35+ Mr '70. N. Gittelson
Civil war over smut. J. Witcover. Nation 210:550-3 My 11 '70
Communist Kinseys; in Leningrad. il Time 95:29-30 Je 29 '70
Emancipation or degradation? excerpts from The passing of the modern age. J. Lukacs. Nat R 22:833-5 Ag 11 '70
Lutheran sex code: covenant above contract. R. Chandler. Chr Today 14:32-3 Jl 31 '70
Moment of decision; new sex code for the church. Chr Today 14:26-7 Je 5 '70
Sex and Armageddon. J. P. Sisk. Commentary 50:83-4+ D '70
Why we need a new sexuality. G. B. Leonard. Look 34:54 Ja 13 '70
Young living: must sex be all or nothing at all? A. Wood. Seventeen 29:140+ Je '70
See also
Illegitimacy
Marriage
Prostitution
Sex and religion
Sex instruction
Sex relations

SEXUAL impotency. See Impotence

SEXUAL perversion
See also
Homosexuality

SEXUAL sterilization. See Sterilization, Sexual

SEYCHELLES (islands)
Seychelles. D. W. Marston. il Travel 133: 48-53 Mr '70

SEYFARTH, John T. and Canady, R. L.
Paraprofessionals: in search of an identity. il Clear House 45:221-5 D '70

SEYFERT galaxies. See Galaxies

SEYMOUR, Dan
New responsibilities of business; address, June 9, 1970. Vital Speeches 36:679-82 S 1 '70

SEYMOUR, Dorothy
What do you mean, auditory perception? Ed Digest 35:23-5 Mr '70

SEYMOUR, Whitney North, Jr
People vs. the polluters. J. Smith. Duns 96:52 D '70 *

SFORZA, Luigi Luca Cavalli-. See Cavalli-Sforza, L. L.

SGRAFFITO decoration. See Graffito decoration

SHABECOFF, Philip
You've heard of Yukio Mishima. il N Y Times Mag p6-7+ Ag 2 '70

SHABTHAI Tsebi
Holiness of sin; tr. by H. Halkin. G. Scholem. Commentary 51:41-70 Ja '71

SHACKLEFORD, J. Barry
Simple new amplifying device is adapted to driving a pen recorder. il Sci Am 222:130-2+ My '70

SHACTER, Mayer
Goblet. il por Ceram Mo 18:17-19 Ap '70

SHAD fishing
Meet the streamerettes; shad caught with light fly rod. S. R. Slaymaker, 2d. il pors Outdoor Life 145:98-100+ Ap '70

SHADE, Lucille
Make your strawberry bed last for years. il por Org Gard & Farm 17:94-5 Jl '70

SHADE
    See also
    Screens (sun)
SHADE plants. See Plants, Shade
SHADE trees. See Trees; Trees in cities
SHADEL, Jane S.
    Glass lighting devices. il Antiques 98:916-21
    D '70
SHADES. See Window shades
SHADOW puppetry. See Puppets and puppet
    plays
SHADOWGRAMS
    Photograms: non-stop imagery as art; work
    of V. Haffer. J. Deschin. por Pop Phot 67:
    20+ S '70
SHAFER, Tom
    Tom Shafer demonstrates building a jar;
    with biographical sketch. R. D Bonham.
    il pors Ceram Mo 17:14-18 D '69
SHAFFER, Anthony
    Death of a bloodsport. Harp Baz 104:122-3 N
    '70
    Sleuth. Criticism
        America 124:47 Ja 16 '71 *
        Nation 211:572 N 30 '70 *
        New Yorker 46:103 N 21 '70 *
        Newsweek 76:138 N 23 '70 *
        Sat R 53:6+ N 28 '70 *
        Time 96:100 N 23 '70 *
        Time il 95:77 Mr 30 '70 *
SHAFFER, Elaine
    Elaine Shaffer and Hermann Hesse. D. J.
    Soria. il por Hi Fi 20:secII 6-7+ Ap '70 *
SHAFFER, John H.
    Can airways handle the giant jets? interview.
    il por U S News 69:38-42 Ag 10 '70
    Technology's impact; excerpts from address.
    Aviation W 93:9 Ag 24 '70
SHAFFER, Peter
    Battle of Shrivings. Criticism
        Time 95:77 Mr 30 '70 *
SHAH, Saleem A.
    Community mental health and the criminal
    justice system: some issues and problems.
    bibliog Ment Hy 54:1-12 Ja '70
SHAHN, Ben
    Ben Shahn, photographer; excerpt from in-
    troduction. M. R. Weiss. il Sat R 53:26-7+ N
    7 '70 *
    Ben Shahn's lettering; excerpts from address.
    B. Shahn. il Pub W 198:38+ D 7 '70 *
SHAHN, Bernarda
    Ben Shahn's lettering; excerpts from ad-
    dress. il Pub W 198:38+ D 7 '70
SHAINBERG, Lawrence
    Fan's notes on the amazing Knicks. il N Y
    Times Mag p28-9+ Ja 25 '70
SHAKER architecture. See Architecture,
    American
SHAKER art. See Art, American
SHAKER churches. See Churches, Shaker
SHAKER crafts. See Arts and crafts—United
    States
SHAKER furniture. See Furniture, American
SHAKER meetinghouses. See Churches, Shak-
    er
SHAKERS
    American peaceniks, 150 years ago. D. Grum-
    bach. Commonweal 93:164-5 N 13 '70
    Milbert on the earliest Shaker community.
    il Antiques 98:516+ O '70
    On and off the avenue; Shaker museum at
    Hancock, Mass. J. Malcolm. New Yorker
    46:62-5 Ag 8 '70
    Shaker communities; Public collections of
    Shaker crafts. Antiques 98:623+ O '70
    Shaker utopia; with editorial comment. C.
    W. Upton. il Antiques 98:581, 582-7 O '70
    Shakers today. B. S. Delaney. il Antiques
    98:618-22 O '70
    See also
    Churches, Shaker
SHAKERTOWN, Ky.
    Micajah Burnett and the buildings at
    Pleasant Hill. J. C. Thomas. il por
    Antiques 98:600-5 O '70
SHAKESPEARE, Frank J. 1925-
    Static at the voice. Newsweek 76:42 N 30
    '70 *
SHAKESPEARE, William
    From postcard-length data, a wealth of im-
    ages and legends. T. Eagleton. il Common-
    weal 93:129-30 O 30 '70 *
    Bibliography
    Will the real Shakespeare please stand up?
    B. DeMott. pors Sat R 53:31-2+ N 7 '70
    Characters
    Our far-flung correspondents; from Birnam
    Wood to Dunsinane. J. McPhee. New York-
    er 46:141-7 O 10 '70

Criticism and interpretation
Blank verse and creating a character; ex-
    amples from Romeo and Juliet. J. Jerome.
    Writers Digest 50:15-19 Je '70
Shakespeare, by F. Fergusson. Review
    Sat R 53:43+ My 2 '70. B. Grebanier *
    Plays
    King Lear
Literature and the now generation. V. R.
    Mollenkott. Todays Ed 59:64-7 O '70
    Macbeth
Doing in Shakespeare; rechristened Makbeth.
    C. R. Hughes. por America 122:132 F 7 '70
    Merchant of Venice
Merchant ltd; production by the British
    national theatre company. H. Hewes. il Sat
    R 53:20 Jl 11 '70
19th century Shylock; production by Lon-
    don's National theatre. Time 95:72 My 18
    '70 *
Theatre; National theatre production in Lon-
    don. H. Clurman. Nation 211:30 Jl 6 '70
    Midsummer night's dream
Souping up Shakespeare; Peter Brook's Royal
    Shakespeare company production. C.
    Hughes. America 123:458 N 28 '70
Wizard on anti-magic. C. Porterfield. il Time
    96:72 O 19 '70
    Othello
Passion's fool; American Shakespeare festival
    production. il Time 95:48 Je 29 '70
Theatre; American Shakespeare festival
    theatre production at ANTA theatre. B.
    Gill. New Yorker 46:112 S 26 '70
    Romeo and Juliet
Blank verse and creating a character. J. Je-
    rome. Writers Digest 50:15-19 Je '70
Romeo and Juliet and the disadvantaged;
    teaching the play. J. J. Hanke. Engl J
    59:273-6 F '70 *
Romeo and Juliet; living is being relevant.
    L. W. Cohen. Engl J 59:1263-5+ D '70
    Tempest
Updating Kansas City; production by the
    Missouri repertory theatre. H. Hewes. Sat
    R 53:51 O 3 '70

Staging and acting of plays
    See also
    Shakespeare festivals
SHAKESPEARE festival, Stratford, Ontario
    Canadian capers; productions of Richard
    Sheridan's The school for scandal and Ar-
    nold Wesker's The friends. H. Hewes. Sat
    R 53:42+ Ag 22 '70
    1970 Stratford festival. R. Crinkley. Nat R 22:
    851-2 Ag 11 '70
SHAKESPEARE festivals
    Ashland will offer more Shakespeare; Ore-
    gon. il Sunset 144:83 Ap '70
    Theater; Odessa, Tex. H. Hewes. Sat R
    53:19 O 10 '70
    See also
    American Shakespeare festival theatre and
    academy, Stratford, Conn.
    Shakespeare festival, Stratford, Ontario
SHALEK, Robert J. See Brownell, G. L. jt.
    auth.
SHALER, Pa.
    Do-it-yourself solves some problems of rapid
    growth. W. L. Crawford. il Am City 85:
    90+ S '70
SHALIT, Benjamin
    Shalit case. R. Alter. Commentary 50:55-61 Jl
    '70; Reply with rejoinder. L. Bernstein.
    50:15-16 N '70 *
    Who is a Jew? il por Newsweek 75:70 F 2 '70
    Who is a Jew? il por Time 95:50-1 F 2 '70
    Who is a Jew? G. Astor. il pors Look 34:32-
    4 Je 16 '70 *
SHALIT, Gene
    Look at the movies (cont) il Look 34:68 Ja
    27; 36 F 10; 12-13 F 24; 66 Je 2; 36 Je 16; 10-
    11 Ag 25; 70 S 22; 114 O 6; 81 O 20; 45 N
    20; 12+ D 1; 84-5 D 15; 33 D 29 '70
    Rating game. il Look 34:82+ N 3 '70
    What's happening. See issues of Ladies'
    home journal
SHALLOTS
    Bountiful shallots. J. J. Meeker. il Org Gard
    & Farm 17:48-50 F '70
SHAMAN, Harvey
    Add 3-D to your photo display. il Pop Mech
    134:134-5 D '70
SHAMBERG, Michael
    Handy uses of a home computer. il pors Life
    68:48-51 Ja 30 '70

SHAME about Margaret Anne; story. See Field, L.

SHAMPOOS
Baby shampoos. il Consumer Rep 35:460-2 Ag '70

SHANE, Harold G. See Shane, J. G. jt. auth.

SHANE, Joe
Four-channel stereo. il Radio-Electr 41:45 D '70

SHANE, June Grant, and Shane, H. G.
Guidance at an early age. Ed Digest 35:21-3 F '70

SHANGHAI incident, 1932. See Chinese-Japanese war, 1931-1932

SHANK, John K. See Rosenbloom, R. S. jt. auth.

SHANKAR, Ravi
Ravi Shankar at home and abroad; interview, ed. by A. S. Raman. il por Sat R 53:46-7+ O 10 '70

SHANKLIN, John F. and Fitch, E. M.
Where is the outdoor recreation plan? il Am For 76:28-31+ Mr '70

SHANKS, Hershel
Equal education and the law. Am Scholar 39:255-69, 727 Spr, Aut '70

SHANKS, Nelson
Nelson Shanks; interview, ed. by R. Goetz. il por Am Artist 34:58-65+ N '70

SHANNON, Dell
Writing fiction today. Writer 83:11-13 O '70

SHANNON, Edith
Homework that works. il Todays Ed 59:16-19 S '70

SHANNON, James Patrick
Sense of freedom, joy and rightness. pors Time 95:54 F 23 '70 *

SHANNON airport. See Airports—Ireland

SHANNON RIVER
Slow and restful highway the Shannon. il Sunset 144:68 My '70

SHAPE perception. See Perception

SHAPIRO, David, 1947-
Faces and masks and auxiliary deceptions. il Craft Horiz 30:36-45+ D '70
Jim Dine's life-in progress. il Art N 69:42-6 Mr '70
Mr Processionary at the conceptacle. il Art N 69:58-61 S '70
Strawberry cake with the psyche of a good camera. il Art N 69:30-1+ D '70

about
Comment. J. Koethe. Poetry 117:56-7 O '70 *

SHAPIRO, David S.
Mental health professionals' hang-ups in training mental health counselors. bibliog Ment Hy 54:364-9 Jl '70

SHAPIRO, Fred C.
Arthur Goldberg, you owe me $587.50. Esquire 74:146+ S '70
Our far-flung correspondents. New Yorker 46:93-4+ My 23 '70
Profiles; T. W. Kheel. New Yorker 46:36-44+ Ag 1 '70
Wholly Ronan empire. il pors N Y Times Mag p34-6+ My 17 '70

SHAPIRO, Harvey
Feelings; poem. Nation 211:92 Ag 3 '70
Where I am now; poem. Nation 210:702 Je 8 '70

SHAPIRO, James
Harvard genetics researcher quits science for politics. J. K. Glassman. Science 167:963-4 F 13 '70; Discussion. 167:1668-9 Mr 27 '70 *

SHAPIRO, Karl
Little treasury of nonnegotiable verse. Esquire 73:131-4 My '70
Poetry wreck; address, December 8, 1969. il por Library J 95:632-5 F 15 '70

SHAPIRO, Max
Great crash in growth stocks. il Duns 97:30-2 Ja '71
Recession can't cure inflation. il Duns 96:54-6 Jl '70

SHAPIRO, Mollie
What food and oxygen is to the body, reading means to me. Wilson Lib Bul 45:469 Ja '71

SHAPIRO, Stanley
Engagement baby. Criticism
New Yorker 46:70 My 30 '70 *

SHAPIRO, Teri
Ecology begins at home; story. Redbook 136:74-5 N '70

SHAPLEN, Robert
Letter from Indo-China. New Yorker 46:130+ My 9; 125-8+ My 16; 57-70+ Jl 11; 71-82 Ag 15; 116+ D 19 '70
Letter from Saigon (cont) New Yorker 45:40-2+ Ja 31 '70
Our involvement in Laos. il For Affairs 48:478-93 Ap '70
Reporter at large (cont) New Yorker 46:162+ O 17 '70

SHARED services. See Educational cooperation

SHAREHOLDERS. See Stockholders

SHAREHOLDERS meetings. See Stockholders meetings

SHAKENOW, Arthur
Camp should be a benevolent dictatorship. por Camp Mag 42:16 Ap '70

SHARK leather
Sharkskin snaps at wider markets. il Bsns W p81 Jl 4 '70

SHARKEY, Thomas
Diabolical quiz. Read Digest 97:167+ O '70

SHARKS
Deadly sharks fed by hand. il Sea Front 16:271 S '70

SHARMAN, G. B.
Reproductive physiology of marsupials. bibliog il Science 167:1221-8 F 27 '70

SHARNIK, Morton
Downfall of a hero. il por Sports Illus 32:16-21 F 23 '70
This saint has been called a sinner. il por Sports Illus 32:18-20+ Je 1 '70
Too small to be overlooked. il pors Sports Illus 33:24-6+ N 30 '70

SHARON; story. See Spencer, E.

SHARP, Mary
Brush-on enamel designs. P. Rothenberg. il Ceram Mo 18:16-17 Ja '70

SHARP-tailed grouse shooting. See Prairie chicken shooting

SHARPE, Lawrence G. See Olney, J. W. jt. auth.

SHARPENING
How to sharpen tools. R. J. De Cristoforo. il Mech Illus 66:93-5 Ap '70
Sharpening. T. Trueblood. il Field & S 74:28+ F '70

SHARPENING jigs. See Jigs

SHATTER-proof glass. See Glass, Safety

SHATTUCK, Aaron Draper
Shattuck, the man and his art. E. P. Birk. il Antiques 97:304 Mr '70 *

SHATZKIN, Leonard
Record keeping alone isn't inventory control. Pub W 198:41-2 Ag 3 '70
Stronger books, possible savings. il Pub W 198:66-8 N 16 '70

SHAVERS, Electric. See Razors

SHAVING
See also
Razor blades

SHAVING soap and cream
Look at three hot lather shaving creams. il Consumer Bul 53:17-18 N '70

SHAW, Bernard. See Shaw, G. B.

SHAW, Bynum
Scopes reviews the monkey trial. Esquire 74:86+ N '70

SHAW, Charles
Dynamic ink drawings of Charles Shaw. il Am Artist 34:61-6 Je '70

SHAW, George Bernard
Candida. Criticism
New Yorker 46:79 Ap 18 '70 *
Devil's disciple. Criticism
America 123:104 Ag 22 '70 *
GBS/GKC, by W. B. Furlong. Review
America 123:101-2 Ag 22 '70. W. T. Noon *
How Shavian is the Pygmalion we teach? R. C. Harvey. Engl J 59:1234-8 D '70 *
Pygmalion. Criticism
Engl J 59:1234-8 D '70 *
Shaw and Chesterton, by W. B. Furlong. Review
Cath World 212:157-8 D '70. K. M. Restaino *
Shaw and the doctors, by R. Boxill. Review
Nation 210:59 Ja 19 '70. G. A. Silver
Shaw, by S. Weintraub. Review
New Repub 163:22-3 S 26 '70. A. Campbell *
Truth about Pygmalion, by R. Huggett. Review
Newsweek 76:90A O 26 '70. R. A. Sokolov *

SHAW, Herbert R.
Earth tides, global heat flow, and tectonics. bibliog il Science 168:1084-7 My 29 '70

SHAW, Irwin
Performing arts. Harper 241:26+ S '70

SHAW, Jane S.
Wackiest worm runner. il por Sci Digest 67:82-6 My '70

SHAW, Jeffrey
Inflate and float. il Life 68:76-9 Ap 10 '70 *

SHAW, Montgomery T.
Polywater discovered thirty years ago? bibliog il Science 169:705 Ag 14 '70

SHAW, Robert B.
Aubade, inside and out; Burning abortive poems; poems. Poetry 115:244-7 Ja '70
Both sides of the water. Poetry 117:108-15 N '70

SHAW, Russell
Mastering the media: the bishops go to school. il America 122:158-60 F 14 '70
SHAW festival, Niagara-on-the-Lake, Ontario.
See Drama festivals—Canada
SHAWE-TAYLOR, Desmond
Webster era at Covent Garden. il pors Sat R 53:43-4+ Je 27 '70
SHAWLS
Make a romantic shawl. il Good H 170:86-7+ Je '70
SHAWN, Ted
Remember: Jacob's Pillow was a stone. il pors Dance Mag 44:49-61 Jl '70

about

Dance magazine award, 1969. il pors Dance Mag 44:32-3+ My '70 *
Stars over Berkshires. W. Terry. il Sat R 53:38 Jl 11 '70 *
SHAWN, William
Alarms and issues. Newsweek 76:129-30 O 12 '70 *
SHAWNEE, Okla.
New lives for troubled youth; juvenile behavior council. E. Gravley. Chr Cent 87:1497-8 D 9 '70
SHAYON, Robert Lewis
Good season for the literate. Sat R 53:64 Ap 11 '70
TV-radio. See issues of Saturday review
SHCHEDRIN, Rodion
Four records, the sophisticated writing of Rodion Shchedrin. D. W. Moore. il por Am Rec G 36:410-12 F '70 *
SHE stoops to conquer; drama. See Goldsmith, O.
SHEA, Kevin P.
Blunted weapons. bibliog il Environ 12:28-35+ Ja '70
Dead stream. il Environ 12:12-15 Jl '70
Unwanted harvest. bibliog il Environ 11:12-17+ S '69
SHEA, Lynda Lee (Mead) See Mead, L. L.
SHEAFFER, John R.
Reviving the Great Lakes. il Sat R 53:62-5 N 7 '70
SHEAHAN, Franklin L. jr
Local association of the month. Todays Ed 59:53 Ap '70
SHEARER, Derek
Automated war. New Repub 162:14-15 My 30 '70
Brass image. il Nation 210:455-64 Ap 20 '70
SHEARER, Goldie
Enough life to support new fruit. il por Org Gard Farm 17:52-3 S '70
SHEARER, John C.
International talent migration and the foreign student. bibliog f Mo Labor R 93:55-9 My '70
SHEARER, Sybil
Sunbeam will outlast us all. W. Terry. por Sat R 53:42 F 7 '70
SHEARING of sheep. See Sheep shearing
SHEARS. See Scissors and shears
SHEBIB, Donald
McLuhan's child; interview. New Yorker 46:47-9 N 21 '70
SHECTER, Leonard
Coming revolt of the athletes. il pors Look 34:43-7 Jl 28 '70
Frank Robinson's cool assault on the black-manager barrier. il por Look 34:82-4+ My 5 '70
Golf's lower depths: the rabbits on tour. il pors Look 34:84+ My 19 '70
N.Y. Mets. 1970: trouble in paradise. il Look 34:76+ Ap 21 '70
(ed) See Bouton, J. My love/hate affair with baseball
SHEDLOVSKY, Julian P. and others
Pattern of bombardment-produced radio-nuclides in rock 10017 and in lunar soil. bibliog il Science 167:574-6 Ja 30 '70
SHEDS
Build this fire-wood shed. B. W. Powell. il Pop Mech 133: 164-5 Je '70
1970 workshop & garage; plus a new carport and potting shed. N. Seney and J. Pinkham. il Bet Hom & Gard 48:63 F '70
See also
Agricultural machinery—Storage
SHEED, Wilfrid
Flinty eye behind the humor. por Life 69:12 S 18 '70
TV talk (cont) Sports Illus 32:7 Mr 9; 15 Ap 13; 5 Ap 27; 33:8 Jl 6 '70

about

Max Jamison funny in his unkindness. A. Kazin. Vogue 156:34 Jl '70 *
SHEEHAN, Edward R. F.
In the flaming streets of Amman. il N Y Times Mag p26-7+ S 27 '70

Way Egyptians see Israel, Uncle Sam, the SAM's. il N Y Times Mag p28-9+ S 20 '70
Who runs Egypt? il N Y Times Mag p30-1+ N 29 '70
SHEEHAN, Ethna
Children's books at Christmastime. America 123:494-9 D 5 '70
SHEEHAN, Neil
Rush to judgment? por Newsweek 77:76-7 Ja 11 '71 *
SHEEHAN, Susan
Happy Jackie, the sad Jackie, the bad Jackie, the good Jackie. il pors N Y Times Mag p 14-15+ My 31 '70
Pro: he's a nice guy. il pors N Y Times Mag p28-9+ N 22 '70
SHEEHY, Gail
Love sounds of a wife; story. McCalls 97:91-100 Ag '70
Trade winds; interview, ed. by C. Amory. Sat R 53:16+ N 21 '70
SHEEP

Weight
See Sheep, Weight and measurements of
SHEEP, Weight and measurements of
Lamb weights still climbing. O. Bay. il Farm J 93:30F-30G O '69
SHEEP on the runway; drama. See Buchwald, A.
SHEEP shearing
How to peel a sheep. il Sci Digest 68:82-3 Ag '70
SHEERIN, John B.
Editorial. See issues of Catholic world
If you could make one change in the church, what would it be? Commonweal 92:165 My 1 '70
Israel and the Fedayeen: an exchange of letters. Cath World 21:32-3 Ap '70
SHEETS
Decorating with sheets. C. Houck. Parents Mag 45:16 Mr '70
SHEFFIELD, Harley G. and Melton, M. L.
Toxoplasma gondii: the oocyst, sporozoite, and infection of cultured cells. bibliog il Science 167:892-3 F 6 '70
SHEFFIELD watch corporation
Watch with a thousand faces. S. Margetts. il Duns 96:65-6 D '70
SHELDON, Brooke E.
Time of the Gringo. bibliog il Am Lib 1:123-7 F '70
SHELF numbers (libraries) See Libraries—Shelving systems
SHELL chemical company
Burden of proof; lack of adequate warning on DDVP resin strips. S. Novick. bibliog il Environ 12:16-29 O '70
Old shell game: No-pest insecticide strip, with DDVP. A. Wolff. il Am Heritage 21:112-13 O '70
Shell's No-pest strip; injurious effects of inhaling DDVP vapors. Consumer Rep 35:701-2 N '70
SHELL craft. See Shellwork
SHELL Italy's agricultural studies center. See Agriculture—Study and teaching
SHELL mileage marathon. See Automobile engines—Fuel consumption
SHELL museum, Mexico. See Museums
SHELL oil company
Growth despite shortage. il Time 95:91-2 My 4 '70
Shell bets a billion on Houston's boom. Bsns W p37 Je 13 '70
Shell's $25-million trip to Houston. il Bsns W p68+ S 19 '70
SHELL work. See Shellwork
SHELLEDY, Carey
Color TV antennas: how to get top performance. il Radio-Electr 41:33-6 S '70
SHELLFISH
See also
Cookery—Shellfish
Crustaceans
Lobsters
Shrimps
SHELLFISH culture
See also
Oyster culture
SHELLFISH fisheries
Australian abalone fisheries. J. Harding. il Sea Front 16:282-5 S '70
Oysters: planning the environment for an industry. D. H. Wallace. il Cons 25:28-30 O '70
Vanishing skipjack. B. Hemmig. il Sea Front 16:336-9 N '70
SHELLS (conchology)
Big shells and small shells. A. G. Melvin. il Hobbies 74:146 F '70
Mexico's new shell museum. A. G. Melvin. il Hobbies 75:146-7 N; 158-9 D '70

SHELLS (conchology)—*Continued*
Mollusk makes its shell. A. G. Melvin. il Hobbies 74:146-7 Ja '70
Shell books can help you. A. G. Melvin. Hobbies 75:147 Ap; 147+ Je '70
See also
Cowries
Mother-of-pearl

Collectors and collecting
Gumshoe in a shell game. P. Ryan. il Sports Illus 32:70-4+ Je 15 '70

SHELLS, Orchestra. See Orchestra shells

SHELLWORK
Shells: a wave of excitement. il House B 112:78-9 Je '70

SHELTER belts. See Windbreaks

SHELTERBELTS. See Windbreaks

SHELTERED workshops. See Vocational rehabilitation

SHELTERS
Easy-to-erect shelter finds many uses in parks; Papertech modules. il Parks & Rec 5:30 My '70
Four ways to hide trash cans. H. Wicks. il Pop Mech 134:168-9 S '70
Heated bus-stop shelters; Detroit. il Am City 85:126 Mr '70
Shelter: first of six rebuilt by Friends of Central park. New Yorker 46:26-7 Je 13 '70
See also
Garden houses, shelters, etc.

SHELTERS, Airplane. See Hangars

SHELTERS, Atomic bomb. See Atomic bomb shelters

SHELTON, Emma, and others
Quantitation of strain BALB/c mouse peritoneal cells. bibliog il Science 168:1232-4 Je 5 '70

SHELTON, Richard
He who remains; poem. New Yorker 46:50 N 28 '70
Rendezvous; Saturday night at the Elks' club; October; White hotel; Report of the unsatisfied lover; poems. Poetry 115:395-400 Mr '70
Reunion; poem. New Yorker 46:66 O 3 '70
Tattooed desert; poem. New Yorker 46:46 D 12 '70
Valediction; poem. New Yorker 46:32 Ag 29 '70

SHELVES
Channel modules. K. Isaacs. il Pop Sci 196:84-5 Ap '70
Clock-key and hour hand shelf. D. Shiner. il Design 71:14-15 Wint '69
Desk expander. il Mech Illus 66:106 F '70
Handsome shelves you build; ten shelf units. il Bet Hom & Gard 48:60-3+ S '70
Handy shelves you peg together. G. A. Gerber. il Mech Illus 66:138-40 O '70
Natural shelf brackets; tree fungi. D. Shiner. il Design 72:22-3 Wint '70
Shelves in a doorway. S. L. Smay. il Pop Mech 134:180 O '70

SHELVING, Library. See Library furniture and equipment

SHELVING systems (libraries) See Libraries—Shelving systems

SHEMANSKI, Frances
Pilgrims all. il Schol Teach Jr/Sr High p44-5 S 21 '70
(comp) World travel calendar, 1971. Sat R 54:37-38+ Ja 2 '71

SHENANDOAH NATIONAL PARK
Earth's words in the national parks. D. Lambert. il Nat Parks & Con Mag 44:16-22 Jl '70

SHENANDOAH VALLEY
Shenandoah, I long to hear you. M. W. Edwards. il Nat Geog 137:554-88 Ap '70

SHENGOLD, Leonard
Freud's dreams revisited. bibliog Am Imago 26:242-50 Fall '69

SHENKER, Israel
(ed) See Landon, A. M. Sage of Topeka
(ed) See Singer, I. B. Isaac Bashevis Singer scoffs

SHENKER, Morris
Mayor, the Mob and the lawyer. D. Walsh. il pors Life 68:24-31 My 29 '70 *

SHEPARD, Alan Bartlett, 1923-
Old pro gets his shot at the moon. L. Wainwright. il pors Life 69:48-50B+ Jl 31 '70

SHEPARD, Charles C.
Of mice and leprosy. il por Time 95:47-8 Mr 2 '70 *

SHEPARD, Ernest Howard
Man who drew Pooh. R. Cowley. il McCalls 97:12+ Ag '70

SHEPARD, Marietta Daniels
Reading resources and Project LEER. bibliog il por Wilson Lib Bul 44:743-50 Mr '70

SHEPARD, Ray Anthony
Non-black teacher, black literature, and black students. Engl J 59:1071-3 N '70

SHEPARD, Sam
Forensic and the navigators. Criticism
New Yorker 46:83 Ap 11 '70 *
Operation Sidewinder. Criticism
America 122:398 Ap 11 '70 *
Commonweal 92:193-4 My 8 '70 *
Nation 210:380-1 Mr 30 '70 *
New Yorker 46:115 Mr 21 '70 *
Newsweek il 75:69 Mr 23 '70 *
Sat R 53:24 Mr 28 '70 *
Time il 95:49 Mr 23 '70 *
Unseen hand. Criticism
New Yorker 46:82-3 Ap 11 '70 *

SHEPHERD, J. Barrie
Christmas: the cosmic light show. il Cath World 212:123-4 D '70
Theology for ecology. il Cath World 211:172-5 Jl '70

SHEPHERD, Jack
Disappearing beauty of the salt marsh. il Look 34:24-31 Ap 21 '70
Earth day, April 22: the fight to save America starts now. Look 34:23 Ap 21 '70
Nuclear threat inside America. il Look 34:21-7 D 15 '70
Princeton commitment: a race against mace. il Look 34:12+ Je 16 '70

SHEPHERD, James
Killer leopard of Danpur. il Sports Illus 32:18-19 Mr 2 '70

SHEPHERD, Jean
Diary of a fisherman. il por Field & S 74:88-9+ Ap '70

SHEPPARD, Carl F.
Biography of a little boat. il Yachting 128:72-3+ Jl '70

SHEPPARD, Eugenia
Big costume party. Harp Baz 103:204-5 S '70
Exciting is as exciting does. Harp Baz 103:163 O '70
Gloria, hallelujah. Harp Baz 103:142-3 F '70
Goodbye, little girl. Harp Baz 103:134-5 Ap '70
Great love stories re-written; poem. Harp Baz 103:148 Ag '70
In New York, it's Raffles. il Holiday 47:38+ Ap '70
Lions and lambs. Harp Baz 103:192 Mr '70
My best wishes for the New Year. Harp Baz 104:66 Ja '71
Toast to the host. Harp Baz 104:162-3 N '70
Vanishing Christmas person. il Harp Baz 104:106-7 D '70

SHEPPARD, George. See Shields, G. R. jt. auth.

SHERA, Jesse H.
Plus ça change. il por Library J 95:979-86 Mr 15 '70

SHERATON furniture. See Furniture, English

SHERBET. See Ice cream, ices, etc.

SHERIDAN, Richard Brinsley Butler
The rivals. Criticism
Nation 210:189-90 F 16 '70 *
School for scandal. Criticism
Nat R 22:851 Ag 11 '70 *

SHERIDAN, Robert
Membership dilemma. Am Lib 1:52-5 Ja '70

SHERIDAN, Terence
Black and blue in Cleveland. il Nation 211:48-50 Jl 20 '70
New math. New Repub 163:13 S 19 '70

SHERIDAN tanks. See Tanks, Military

SHERIFFS
Postscript to People's park; indictments of Alameda County sheriff's deputies for misusing their authority in Berkeley. Calif. Time 95:15-16 F 16 '70
Sheriffs 1970-style. il Time 96:94 N 16 '70
Where are they now? J. Clark of Dallas County, Ala. il pors Newsweek 76:16 S 21 '70

SHERIFFS deputies. See Sheriffs

SHERLOCK Holmes stories. See Doyle, A. C.

SHERMAN, Allan
Hello there, Brendan Behan Zuckerman. Read Digest 97:56-9 S '70

SHERMAN, Bennett
Is the film plane in your camera doing its job? il Mod Phot 34:80-1+ F '70
Techniques tomorrow. See issues of Modern photography

SHERMAN, Gordon B.
Separate roads for Midas and son. por Bsns W p32-3 O 10 '70 *

SHERMAN, Steve
Child's-eye view of the world. il Parents Mag 45:50 Ja '70
—See Matthews, M. jt. auth.

SHERPAS
Reporter at large; trekking expedition to base of Everest. J. Bernstein. New Yorker 46:46-8+ My 9 '70

SHERRILL, Robert G.
Birch Bayh isn't a household word, yet. il pors N Y Times Mag p28-9+ F 15 '70
De-escalator of the war on poverty. il pors N Y Times Mag p23-5+ D 13 '70
Democrats: spooked by abstractions. il Nation 211:295-302 O 5 '70
L. Mendel Rivers. por Nation 210:40-7 Ja 19 '70
Louis Kelso: nut or Newton? Nation 210:234-7 Mr 2 '70
Nixon's record is the issue. Nation 210:619-23 My 25 '70
Real Robert Finch stands up. il pors N Y Times Mag p6-7+ Jl 5 '70
Real villains. Nation 211:208-12 S 14 '70
Ribicoff rides the tide. Nation 210:294-6 Mr 16 '70
Service or efficiency? Nation 210:386-8 Ap 6 '70
Taken, by train. il Nation 210:786-8 Je 29 '70
That equal-rights amendment: what, exactly, does it mean? il N Y Times Mag p25-7+ S 20 '70
Tower of Texas is small in the saddle, but... il pors N Y Times Mag p28-9+ Ap 26 '70
We can't depend on Congress to keep Congress honest. il N Y Times Mag p5-7+ Jl 19 '70
Who runs Congress? il N Y Times Mag p52-3+ N 22 '70
Why can't we just give them food? il N Y Times Mag p28-9+ Mr 22; 34 Ap 26 '70
(ed) See Clark, R. Justice in a torn nation

about
Soldiers and the law. G. Wolff. por Newsweek 75:103+ My 11 '70 *

SHERRILL, Sarah B.
Current and coming. Antiques 97:638+, 784+; 98:16+, 156+, 296+, 480+ My-O '70

SHERROD, Margaret Carson
Opera in the wilderness. il Holiday 47:58-9+ Je '70

SHERRY, Gerard E.
Catholic press: has the wake started? America 123:91-3 Ag 22 '70

SHERWIN, J. Stephen
Via *latina* to English mastery? No; excerpt from Four problems in teaching English. Todays Ed 59:42-3 F '70

SHERWOOD, Glen
Carnage at Sand Lake. il Audubon 72:66-73 N '70

SHERWOOD, Henry A.
How toying about led to a discovery. il por Bsns W p68 O 31 '70 *

SHERWOOD, Hugh C.
Eight types of how-to articles and how to write them. Writers Digest 50:36-7+ N '70

SHERWOOD, Irene W.
Poet and the laundry list. Engl J 59:824-5 S '70

SHERWOOD, Martin
Sea of chemicals. il por Chem 43:34-6 Jl '70

SHERWOOD, Robert Emmet
Trilogy of irony; analysis of Idiot's delight. E. E. Miller. Engl J 59:59-62 Ja '70

SHETTLES, Landrum B. See Rorvik, D. M. jt. auth.

SHETZLINE, David
Discipline and anger. Writer 83:9-11+ Je '70

SHEYENNE RIVER
Next river to die. H. R. Morgan. il Nat Wildlife 8:20-1 Je '70

SHIDELER, Frank J.
Stubble-mulching moves winter wheat north. il Farm J 93:30D O '69

SHIDELER, Mary McDermott
Ancient word for modern churches. Chr Cent 87:1509-13 D 16 '70

SHIELDING (heat)
See also
Space vehicles—Shielding (heat)

SHIELDS, Gerald R. and Sheppard, George
American Indians: search for Fort Hall's library service. bibliog il Am Lib 1:856-60 O '70

SHIELDS, James T.
Limit the duck hunters? il Outdoor Life 146:47-9+ S '70

SHIFFRIN, Richard M.
Forgetting: trace erosion or retrieval failure? bibliog il Science 168:1601-3 Je 26 '70

SHIFT register. See Computers—Circuits

SHILLITO, Barry J.
Contractors claw at the money door. Bsns W p 14 Ja 2 '71 *

SHILTS, Joseph L.
Try photogrammetrisizing. il por Am City 85:66-7 D '70

SHIMODA, Takeso
Japan is 94th nation to sign nuclear non-proliferation treaty. Dept State Bul 62:228-9 Mr 2 '70

SHINE, Ted
Contributions. Criticism
Nation 210:348-9 Mr 23 '70 *
New Yorker 46:116+ Mr 21 '70 *

SHINER, Don
Artist with wood. il Design 72:24-5 Fall '70
Clock-key and hour hand shelf. il Design 71:14-15 Wint '69
Easy to make magazine rack. il Design 71:19-21 Spr '70
Horseshoe lawn furniture. il Design 71:24-6 mid-Sum '70
Make a picture safe. il Design 72:17-19 Wint '70
Natural shelf brackets. il Design 72:22-3 Wint '70
Porch for pooch. il Design 71:37 mid-Sum '70
Profiles in stone. il Design 71:10-13 Spr '70
Smart new chairs from old. il Design 72:32-3 Fall '70
Walnut, maple, pine and butternut fish. il Design 71:30-1 Spr '70
Ye olde barber pole. il Design 71:10-12 mid-Sum '70

SHINN, Roger L.
Population and the dignity of man. Chr Cent 87:442-8 Ap 15 '70
What price reversal? Cur 118:29-30 My '70

SHINNECOCK swordfish tournament. See Fishing—Competitions

SHIP and boat models
Sam Orkin's navy; working model of the dreadnought U.S.S. Pennsylvania. il por Am Heritage 21:120 Ap '70

Testing
Fine art of model testing. P. DeSaix. il Motor B 127:134-5 Ja '71
They have to come to Pete. R. W. Carrick. il por Yachting 127:52+ Je '70

SHIP building. See Shipbuilding

SHIP hijacking
Mutiny by ruse; hijacking of S.S. Columbia Eagle. il Time 95:17 Mr 30 '70
Mutiny on the Eagle. il Newsweek 75:36 Mr 30 '70

SHIP owners. See Shipowners

SHIP pilots. See Pilots and pilotage

SHIP propellers. See Propellers

SHIP propulsion
See also
Propellers

SHIP workers. See Shipworkers

SHIPBUILDING
Builder of ships goes into drydock; Verolme united shipyards, Rotterdam. Bsns W p42 F 7 '70
New shipbuilders face a battle. il Bsns W p80-1+ My 16 '70
Shipbuilders scent big revival in orders. il U S News 68:18 Je 1 '70
Shipbuilding: the inevitable boom. L. Rich. il Duns 95:70-2+ F '70
See also
Bath iron works corporation
Boatbuilding
General dynamics corporation
Hulls (naval architecture)
Litton industries, inc.
Shipworkers
United States—Maritime administration
Warships
Yacht building

SHIPLER, David K.
Moral dilemma of zoning. il Nation 211:80-3 Ag 3 '70

SHIPMENT of goods
See also
Air freight service
Forwarding companies
Freight handling
Packing for shipment
United parcel service

SHIPOWNERS
Lush era of the tanker tycoons. il Newsweek 76:94-6 O 19 '70
Oceans of wealth. il Forbes 106:24-5 Ag 1 '70
Pleasure cruise? Overseas shipholding group. il por Forbes 106:24-5 N 1 '70

SHIPPING
Billionaire sealords; avoiding taxes through flags of convenience. il Forbes 106:20-3 Ag 1 '70
See also
Panama Canal
Shipbuilding

Greece, Modern
Jackie's fabulous Greek; excerpts from Those fabulous Greeks. D. Lilly. pors Look 34:30-6+ Je 30 '70

Japan
Japanese set sail for New York. il Bsns W p32-3 D 26 '70

SHIPPING—*Continued*

United States
See also
Merchant marine—United States

SHIPPING companies
See also
Containerization (freight)
Matson navigation company
Pacific Far East line. inc.
United States lines, inc.

SHIPPING terminals. See Terminals

SHIPS
See also
Constitution (frigate)
Freight vessels
Hospital ships
Ocean liners
Sailing vessels
Salvage (ships)
Shipbuilding
Shipwrecks
Sloops
Steamships and steamboats
Tank ships
Training ships
Voyages
Warships

Crews
See Seamen

Displacement
See Displacement (ships)

Equipment
No anchor for tanker; dynamic positioning system for oil drilling ship, Naess Crusader. D. Valentry. il Sea Front 16:110-11 Mr '70

Launching
Anecdotes, facetiae, satire, etc.
Horseshoes on the oars. E. L. Schulte. Motor B 125:130-1 Je '70

Manufacture
See Shipbuilding

Registration and transfer
Billionaire sealords; avoiding taxes through flags of convenience. il Forbes 106:20-3 Ag 1 '70
U.S. waters for U.S. ships; question of waiving the Jones act. Bsns W p46 Ag 15 '70

SHIPS, Hospital. See Hospital ships

SHIPS, Model. See Ship and boat models

SHIPS, Research
Challenger sails on. il Sci N 98:159 Ag 22 '70
Finding a hole in the bottom of the sea; research vessel Glomar Challenger using scanning sonar system. M. Gruber. il Sea Front 16:309-11 S '70

SHIPS in art
See also
Marine painting

SHIPS logs. See Logbooks (ships)

SHIPTON, Clifford Kenyon
I am going off the stage of life; excerpt from Sibley's Harvard graduates. por Am Heritage 21:2 Ag '70

SHIPWORKERS
Red carpet for blue collars. Bsns W p76+ Ag 15 '70

SHIPWRECKS
Death of the Wahine. J. D. Ratcliff. il Read Digest 97:182-4+ D '70
Resurrecting the oldest known Greek ship. M. L. Katzev. il Nat Geog 137:840-57 Je '70
See also
Salvage (ships)
Titanic (steamship)

SHIPYARDS
See also
Shipbuilding

SHIRALA serpent festivals. See Festivals—India

SHIRLEY, A. Ray
Metro forestry in Atlanta: tree power. il Am For 76:8-11+ O '70

SHIRT talk; story. See Prashker, I.

SHIRTS
Breakout of the undershirt. il Time 96:41 S 7 '70
Durable-press shirts. il Consumer Rep 34:634-7 N '69
Men's T shirts. il Consumer Rep 36:25-7 Ja '71

SHNAYER, Sidney W. See Caldwell, J. S. jt. auth.

SHOCK
First aid. C. J. Potthoff. Todays Health 49:62 Ja '71
Shock room; traumatic shock treatment at Houston's Ben Taub general; with report by T. Thompson. il Life 69:24-31 N 6 '70
See also
Traumatism

SHOCK absorbers. See Automobiles—Shock absorbers

SHOCK rooms. See Hospitals—Emergency services

SHOCK waves
Transverse wave instability in a solid explosive. B. B. Dunne. bibliog il Science 167:1124-6 F 20 '70
See also
Sonic boom

SHOCKLEY, Donald G.
Alabama: down for the third time. Chr Cent 87:813 Jl 1 '70
Imprisoning the poor. Chr Cent 87:1286 O 28 '70
—and Freeman, R. L.
Johnny Cash on prison reform. Chr Cent 87:1157 S 30 '70

SHOCKLEY, William Bradford
NAS again says no to Shockley. L. J. Carter. Science 168:685 My 8 '70 *

SHOE industry. See Shoes—Trade and manufacture

SHOEMAKER, Eugene Merle, and others
Lunar regolith at Tranquillity base. bibliog il Science 167:452-5 Ja 30 '70

SHOEMAKER, Ted
AZUR: satellite landmark. il Sci N 97:208 F 21 '70

SHOEMAKER, Willie
I blew a few big ones, too; ed. by W. Tower. il Sports Illus 32:32-4+ F 9 '70
Out of the oven and into the winner's circle; ed. by W. Tower. il pors Sports Illus 32:20-5 F 2 '70

about
Shoe on the way to 6033. J. Olsen. il por Sports Illus 33:28-30+ S 14 '70 *

SHOES
Boots: questions and answers on shopping and caring for them. il Good H 171:174 D '70
Boys' shoes. il Consumer Rep 35:512-16 S '70
Buying the best sneakers for your family. il Good H 171:6 Jl '70
Going up: boot scene. il Newsweek 76:101 O 12 '70
Monsters. il Time 96:42 Jl 27 '70
Ups and downs of shoes. il Seventeen 29:28 F '70

Care
Advice on caring for boots. E. Taylor. il Good H. 170:108 Ja '70
Quick guide to shoe care. A. Holmes. il Good H 172:136 Ja '71

Storage
Projects to keep your workshop humming: roll-out shoe drawer. W. D. Kunhart. il Pop Mech 134:195 O '70

Trade and manufacture
Flat-footed shoemakers. il Forbes 106:85-6 O 16 '70
President announces assistance to footwear industry. Dept State Bul 63:91-3 Jl 20 '70
U.S. shoe imports comprise sizable market. Aviation W 93:104 O 26 '70
Where the shoe fits, or pinches; the Mills trade bill and the impact on U.S. and Italian shoemaking towns. il Newsweek 76:78 D 7 '70
See also
Beck industries, inc.
Melville shoe corporation

SHOES, Animal
Inner-tube dog boots. T. Pyle. il Pop Mech 133:188 F '70

SHOLLENBERGER, Carl A. See Lissaman, P. B. S. jt. auth.

SHOMON, Joseph James
More wildlife for urban America. il Cons 24:2-7 F '70
Nathaniel; story. il Am For 76:12-14 N '70
No time to talk. il Parks & Rec 9:37+ S '70

SHOOK, James F.
Computer-designed asphalt pavement. il Am City 85:68+ F '70

SHOOP, C. Robert. See Madison, D. M. jt. auth.

SHOOP, R. D.
Ecology book store story. il Org Gard and Farm 17:70-2 N '70

SHOOTING
Brush rifle: shooting through brush. J. O'Connor. il Outdoor Life 146:80-1 S '70
Good shot! H. G. Tapply. il Field & S 75:70 O '70

SHOOTING—*Continued*
High-flown styles of wing shooting; in six countries of Europe. T. Alexander. il Fortune 82:122-31 Ag '70
How to keep your shooter's eye sharp the year round. G. Reiger. il Pop Mech 134:116-17 D '70
Pull! shooting facilities for P&R departments. W. E. Talley. il Parks & Rec 5:18-20+ O '70
Shooter's disease; deadly flinch. W. Page. il Field & S 74:174-6+ Mr '70
Shooting. J. O'Connor. See issues of Outdoor life
Shooting; ed. by W. Page. See issues of Field & stream
Shooting off sand. W. Page. il Field & S 75:68-70 Ag '70
Shooting styles. J. O'Connor. il por Outdoor Life 145:126+ My '70
        See also
Rifles
        also Duck shooting, and similar headings

Competitions

Bad days at Black Canyon for the U.S; World shooting championships. M. Kane. Sports Illus 33:56-7 N 9 '70

SHOOTING preserves. See Game preserves
SHOP gardens. See Store gardens
SHOPE papilloma virus. See Tumor viruses
SHOPIS, Nancy M.
Beautiful onions il Home Gard 57:52 O '70

SHOPLIFTING
My niece was a shoplifter! il Good H 171:34+ Ag '70
One in ten shoppers is a shoplifter. P. Hellman. il N Y Times Mag p34-5+ Mr 15 '70
Rising wave of shoplifting and no solution in sight. il U S News 68:56-8 Mr 2 '70
Shoplifting made easy. Esquire 74:26+ Ag '70
Shoplifting: the pinch that hurts. il Bsns W p72-3+ Je 27 '70
Why our kids steal. T. J. Rakstis. il Todays Health 48:20-3+ D '70
Why so many women shoplift. D. Reuben. McCalls 97:44+ S '70
Why so many young women steal from stores. S. Blum. il Redbook 135:72-3+ O '70

SHOPPING and shoppers
How other women save money in stores; symposium. ed. by B. M. Grant. il Redbook 136:68-9+ N '70
How to be a super shopper at the supermarket. L. Lane. il Farm J 94:80+ F '70
How to hunt for bargains. il Changing T 24:7-11 Ag '70; Same abr. with title Smart shopper's guide to bargains. Read Digest 97:112-14 D '70
Meet the little lady who buys your pork. W. C. Nigut. il Farm J 94:H8-9+ Ap '70
100 ways to feed your family better, for less. R. H. Smithies. il Good H 170:141-4 My '70
Will the real American meat shopper please stand up? W. C. Nigut. il Farm J 94:B8-9 Ap '70
        See also
Christmas shopping
Computers—Shopping use
Consumers
Purchasing, Household
Returned goods

Austria

Shoppers' paradise: Vienna. S. Dummer. il Newsweek 76:38 Jl 27 '70

Germany (Federal Republic)

Is the bell tolling for blue laws? il Bsns W p39 Ap 4 '70

Hong Kong

Bargains from Mao. il Newsweek 76:60 Ag 31 '70

Mexico

Shopping tour, Guadalajara to Mexico city and back to Guadalajara. il Sunset 145:64-75 O '70

Peru

One-stop shopping in Lima, Peru. il Sunset 145:67 N '70

SHOPPING centers
Building types study. il Arch Rec 147:119-32 Mr '70
        See also
Business districts

Germany (Federal Republic)

Nordwest Zentrum: ad-hoc heart for a city? new town near Frankfurt, Germany. L. Ungers and O. M. Ungers. il Arch Forum 133:30-7 O '70

SHOPPING hours. See Store hours
SHOPWORK instruction. See Industrial arts
SHORE. See Seashore
SHORE-BOS, Megchelina
Makonde sculpture; with biographical sketch il por Natur Hist 79:4, 42-9 Mr '70
SHORE lines
Barrier beaches of eastern America. C. J. Schuberth. il Natur Hist 79:46-55 Je '70
SHORE protection
Coastal areas and seashores. W. S. Beller. bibliog f Cur Hist 59:100-4+ Ag '70
County acts to save its vanishing shorelands. K. D. Hertz. il Parks & Rec 5:48-9+ F '70
National policy for coastal management; address. October 19, 1970. E. Wenk, jr. Vital Speeches 37:177-81 Ja 1 '71
        See also
Beach erosion
SHORES, Ken
Ken Shores. R. Griffin. il Craft Horiz 30:26-9 Ag '70 *
SHORRIS, Earl
Elevation of soda pop. il por Time 96:51 O 19 '70 *
SHORT, Alison
Singing camp is a happy camp. il Camp Mag 42:11 Je '70
SHORT, Bobby
Cooking is just like making music. il pors House B 112:112+ Mr '70 *
Profiles. W. Balliett. por New Yorker 46:28-35 D 26 '70 *
SHORT, James F. Jr. and Wolfgang, M. E. (eds) Collective violence. bibliog f il Ann Am Acad 391:1-176 S '70
On collective violence: introduction and overview. bibliog f Ann Am Acad 391:1-8 S '70
SHORT, Nicholas M.
Evidence and implications of shock metamorphism in lunar samples. bibliog il Science 167:673-5 Ja 30 '70
SHORT, Robert
Birds of a feather flock to Bob. R. Blount, jr. il por Sports Illus 33:26-8+ N 2 '70 *
SHORT cake. See Shortcake
SHORT-eared owls. See Owls
SHORT line railroads. See Railroads, Short line
SHORT selling. See Stocks—Short selling
SHORT story
Beginnings. E. S. Connell, jr. Writer 83:9-11 S '70
Can you state your story in a sentence? J. D. Lucey. Writers Digest 50:27+ Je '70
First aid for story-sag. J. Z. Owen. Writer 83:14-17 O '70
In-depth market report: the lucrative confessions. L. Ellinwood. Writers Digest 51:28-30+ Ja '71
Kiss, a gun, a tear, a smile. J. McKimmey. Writer 83:15-17 S '70
Men sell confessions too! P. K. Brown. Writers Digest 50:26-8+ Ag '70
My reluctant magician. R. Powell. Writer 83:11-14+ F '70
Short short. V. Henry. Writers Digest 50:24-6 F '70
Short stories: their past, present and future. il Pub W 198:12-15 D 14 '70
Short-story workshop. J. Strong. Engl J 59:811-14+ S '70
Stories without plot. M. Granbeck. Writers Digest 50:45-6 Ja '70
Story box. D. Whitcomb. Writer 83:27 S '70
Twelve rules for story dissection. H. E. Hill. Writers Digest 50:26 F '70
What I learned from four top fiction editors M. Joerden. Writers Digest 50:24-5 S '70
Who wants to throw a cannonball? The young adult field. E. Allen. Writer 83:25-6+ O '70
Why write confessions? A. Myers and E. Jones. Writer 83:14-17 Je '70
Writing short stories; excerpts from Mystery and manners. F. O'Connor. Writer 83:17-19+ Ja '70
        See also
Fiction—Technique
Fiction in periodicals and newspapers

Study and teaching

Analysis of The prison by Bernard Malamud. D. Wechsler. Engl J 59:782-4 S '70
Question of focus; analysis of On Saturday afternoon. R. J. Levine. Engl J 59:40-2 Ja '70

SHORT story contests. See Fiction—Competitions
SHORT subject films. See Moving pictures—Short subject films
SHORT wave radio. See Radio broadcasting, Short wave

SHORT wave radio receivers. See Radio receivers, Short wave

SHORT wave radio stations. See Radio stations, Short wave

SHORTCAKE
Pastry strip shortcakes. il Sunset 144:172 Ap '70
Shortcake with a pebbled top. il Sunset 145: 115 Jl '70

SHORTER, Frank
It's only a transitory analogy. S. Myslenski. por Sports Illus 33:73-4 D 7 '70 *

SHOSTAKOVICH, Dmitrii Dmitrievich
Excellent new recordings. L. Trimble. New Repub 163:28-9 Jl 4 '70 *
Lucky 13. por Time 95:42 F 2 '70
Music to my ears; first United States performance of Symphony no. 13. I. Kolodin. Sat R 53:40 F 7 '70
Shostakovich's banned Babi Yar symphony in the original version. R. S. Brown. il por Hi Fi 20:secI 77-8 Je '70 *
Uncensored at last: Babi Yar. J. Diether. il por Am Rec G 36:944-6+ Ag '70 *

SHOTGUNS
Choosing a choke. W. Davis. il Mech Illus 66: 59+ D '70
Fancy two-barrels: double guns. W. Page. il Field & S 75:96-7+ S '70
Great dove gun. T. Trueblood. il Field & S 75:24+ S '70
Scattergun for deer? G. Laycock. il Farm J 93:C2 D '69
Snappy little 28 gauge. J. O'Connor. il Outdoor Life 146:68-70+ D '70
Specialized scatterguns; ed. by W. Page. il Field & S 75:136-42 My '70
Strange guns I have known. B. L. Spiller. il Field & S 74:80-1+ Mr '70
Today's double-barrel shotguns. J. O'Connor. il Outdoor Life 146:108+ Ag '70
What's the right shotgun for you? P. Wahl. il Pop Sci 197:84-5+ S '70

SHOVER, John L.
Three views of the western experience. Am West 7:49+ Mr '70

SHOW me where the good times are; musical comedy. See Musical comedies, revues, etc. —Criticisms, plots, etc.

SHOW-men. See Entertainers

SHOW windows
Balmy day on Herald square; Christmas display windows. D. Butwin. Sat R 53:32-3 D 26 '70

SHOWER baths
Place of the outdoor shower. il Sunset 145: 129-30 N '70

SHOWER doors. See Doors

SHOWROOMS
Objects and images: a luminous new showcase for office furniture. il Arch Rec 147:131 6 Ap '70
Singer company showroom, New York city. il Arch Rec 147:116-17 Ja '70

SHOWALTER, Dennis
Park maintenance operations. por Am City 85:84+ Mr '70

SHRAKE, Edwin
Big daddy of sport. il por Sports Illus 33:60-2+ S 7 '70
College football. il Sports Illus 33:44-5 N 9 '70
Lady was a killer. il Sports Illus 32:60-4+ Mr 9 '70
Land of the permanent wave. il Harper 240: 77-81 F '70
Matter of Indian giving. il Sports Illus 33:42-4 Ag 17 '70
Merchant of menace. il Sports Illus 32:80-4+ My 11 '70
Nature. Sports Illus 34:52-3 Ja 4 '71
Rich way to make a getaway. il por Sports Illus 33:26-33 Ag 31 '70

SHREWSBERRY, Bill
Wild Bill show; interview, ed. by J. Dianna. il pors Hot Rod 23:62-4 O '70

SHREWSBURY RIVER, N.J.
One river; development of boating. B. Robinson. il Yachting 127:82-3+ Ja '70

SHRIMP curry. See Curry

SHRIMPS
Searching the shrimp beds by sub; research submarine Aluminaut. W. W. Anderson and H. R. Bullis, jr. il pors Sea Front 16:112-19 Mr '70
Starfish eaters; painted shrimp attacking crown-of-thorns. il Time 95:73 My 25 '70
See also
Cookery—Shellfish

SHRINES
See also
Pilgrims and pilgrimages

SHRINK packaging. See Packaging

SHRINKAGE-compensating concrete. See Concrete—Expansion and contraction

SHRIVER, Donald W. Jr
He made you feel like somebody. Chr Cent 87:866-9 Jl 15 '70
Memory and a hope: Hiroshima after a quarter century. il por Bul Atom Sci 26:32-4 S '70

SHRIVER, Eunice (Kennedy)
Sargent Shriver: what happens to a man who marries a Kennedy. D. Lurie. il pors Ladies Home J 87:96-7+ Ap '70 *

SHRIVER, George H. Jr
Southern Baptists: sect or denomination? Chr Cent 87:1093-4, 1286 S 16, O 28 '70

SHRIVER, Robert Sargent, 1915-
Democratic drummer. il por Newsweek 76: 43 O 12 '70 *
Sargent Shriver: what happens to a man who marries a Kennedy. D. Lurie. il pors Ladies Home J 87:96-7+ Ap '70 *
Shriver on the road. D. Blackburn. New Repub 163:9 Jl 11 '70 *
Time for Sargent? il por Time 95:21 Ap 20 '70 *

SHRIVER, Robert Sargent, 1954?-
Busting the boys. il pors Newsweek 76:32 Ag 17 '70 *

SHROPSHIRE, England
Shropshire: by brooks too broad for leaping; with photographs by B. Glinn. il Holiday 47:32-7 Ja '70

SHRUB propagation. See Plant propagation

SHRUBS
All shrubs are hardy now. D. Foraker. il Org Gard & Farm 17:78-80 F '70
Good places to buy shrubs and trees. il Changing T 24:41-2 S '70
It's time to plant berried shrubs. Sunset 145:202-3 O '70
Start shrubs from your own cuttings. H. G. Lendle. il Org Gard & Farm 17:82-3 N '70
See also
Berry bearing plants
Hedges
Topiary work
Windbreaks
also names of shrubs, e.g. Mahonias

SHUBERT, Joseph F. and Dowlin, C. E.
Ohio's BOOKS/JOBS program. il pors Library J 95:3239-43 O 1 '70

SHUGRUE, Michael F.
Teaching English in the junior college. Ed Digest 36:51-4 O '70

SHULA, Don
Miami gets a miracle worker. T. Maule. il por Sports Illus 33:16-17 S 7 '70 *

SHULDINER, Herbert
Match wits with Danish gamemaster Piet Hein. il por Pop Sci 196:68-71 Ja '70
New cartridge super 8 projectors. il Pop Sci 196:84-7 Ja '70
Recreation roundup. See issues of Popular science monthly

SHULMAN, N. R. See Vyas, G. N. jt. auth.

SHULMAN, Robert G. See Wüthrich, K. jt. auth.

SHULTZ, George Pratt
Family assistance act; address, January 29, 1970. Vital Speeches 36:295-6 Mr 1 '70

about
Administration: George Shultz has arrived. il por Time 96:8 Ag 10 '70 *
Cautious start for OMB's Shultz. il Bsns W p 100+ Je 20 '70 *
Closing the performance gap. il pors Newsweek 75:16-17 Je 22 '70 *
Mr Shultz front and center. Newsweek 75: 18 Je 22 '70 *
Nixon's key man in labor crises. il por U S News 68:39 Ap 6 '70 *
President's (incremental) analyst. por Time 95:14-15 Je 22 '70 *
Rearranging furniture. J. Osborne. New Repub 163:8-9 Jl 4 '70 *
Said Nixon to George Shultz; "I track well with you". A. H. Raskin. il pors N Y Times Mag p24:5+ Ag 23 '70 *
White House staff. J. Osborne. New Repub 163:13-14 O 3 '70 *

SHUMAN, A. B.
It's a Maserrariac, white eyes. il Motor T 22: 48-9+ F '70

SHUMAN, James B.
Behold the hateful housefly. il Read Digest 96:49-50+ Je '70
Census '70; portrait of America. Read Digest 96:19-20+ Mr '70

SHUMAN, R. Baird
Initiation rites in Steinbeck's The red pony. Engl J 59:1252-5 D '70

SHUMAN, R. Baird—*Continued*
Portis' True grit: adventure story or *entwicklungsroman?* Engl J 59:367-70 Mr '70
Some myths that teachers live by. Ed Digest 35:32-4 F '70
—and Sublett, H. L. Jr
Realistic view of homework for the ghetto child. bibliog Clear House 45:140-5 N '70
SHUMWAY, F. Ritter
F. Ritter Shumway of Sybron corp; interview. il pors Nations Bsns 58:48-53 My '70
SHUMWAY, M.
Snail; poem. Commonweal 93:346 Ja 8 '71
SHUMWAY, Norman Edward, 1923-
Heart transplants do work. G. Astor. il por Look 34:43-4+ D 29 '70 *
SHUNAMAN, Fred
New phono pickup. il Radio-Electr 41:4+ Mr '70
One speaker stereo sound. il Radio-Electr 41:90-1 Mr '70
Question of semantics. il por Pop Electr 33:27-30 O '70
SHUSTER, E. G.
If he's hard to get along with, hire him. il Nations Bsns 55:66-8 Ag '70
SHUTDOWNS. See Factories—Shutdowns
SHUTTERS, Camera. See Camera shutters
SHUTTLE service, Airline. See Airlines—Shuttle service
SHVAREV, V. and Bulekov, V.
Automatic devices for space exploration. Space World H-1-85:33-5 Ja '71
SHWADRAN, Benjamin
Soviet role in the Middle East crisis. Cur Hist 60:13-18+ Ja '71
SHWARTZMAN phenomenon
Vascular lesions: possible pathogenetic basis of the generalized Shwartzman reaction. E. Gaynor and others. bibliog il Science 170:986-8 N 27 '70
SHWEDAGON pagoda. See Pagodas
SHYER, Marlene Fanta
But where do you get your ideas? Writer 83:19-20 My '70
Imagine two people who both wear a size eight shoe just finding each other on the street; story. Redbook 135:74-5 My '70
Just the two of us; story. Good H 171:80 S '70
Salute to a small spender; story Ladies Home J 87:86-7 Ap '70
SIBELIUS, Jean Julius Christian
Finns and Finlandia. D. Butwin. il Sat R 53:54+ Mr 14 '70 *
SIBERIA
Siberia: the endless horizon. M. McMahon. il Sr Schol 95:Schol Teach 7 N 17 '69
Siberia: the sleeping land awakes; condensation. L. Thomas. il Read Digest 97:247-55+ D '70
SIBLEY, Antoinette
Pas de deux par excellence. O. Maynard. il pors Dance Mag 44:50-61 Ap '70 *
SIBLINGS
Case for sibling rivalry. T. B. Brazelton. il Redbook 135:76-7+ O '70
My brother, the pest; sibling rivalry. G. Hechinger and F. Hechinger. il N Y Times Mag p83+ N 1 '70

Caricatures and cartoons
What is a brother? excerpts. L. P. McGrath and J. Scobey. il Good H 170:74-5 F '70
SIBSON, Robert E.
Executive pay, a time of dramatic change; excerpt from Sixth annual management compensation study. il Nations Bsns 58:89-93+ N '70
SICILIANO, Rocco C.
Piece of the action. il Nation Bsns 58:56-9 Mr '70
SICILY
See also
Art—Sicily
Catania
Antiquities
Art of Sicily. K. Kuh. il Sat R 53:16-23 O 3 '70
SICK, The
See also
Convalescence
Physicians and patients
Sick children
Sickness
SICK children
Caring for a sick-a-bed child. B. W. Howlett. il Parents Mag 45:88-90+ N '70
See also
Mentally ill children
SICKLE cell anemia. See Anemia

SICKLE-cell hemoglobin. See Hemoglobin
SICKLER, Richard C.
1820 butler's tray. il Mech Illus 66:94-5 N '70
Teflon-S makes the cutting great. il Pop Mech 133:164-6 Ja '70
SICKNESS
In sickness and in health; definitions of illness, disease and medical care. E. J. Cassell. Commentary 49:59-66 Je '70
Violence and nonviolence in the cure of disease and the healing of patients. M. Wilson. Chr Cent 87:756-8 Je 17 '70
See also
Medical service, Cost of
SICKNESS insurance. See Insurance, Health
SICRE, José Gómez-. See Gómez-Sicre, J.
SIDESHOWS
Bright lights, long nights; Royal American shows. il Forbes 105:82 Je 15 '70
SIDEWALKS, Elevated
Aerial walkways: big plans for the future. il Bsns W p48-9 D 26 '70
SIDEWALKS, Moving. See Moving platforms
SIDEY, Hugh
Nixon in a crisis of leadership. il por Life 68:28-9 My 15 '70
Parting shots. il pors Life 68:65-8 Ja 30 '70
Presidency. See issues of Life
SIDING (building)
How to repair clapboard siding. il Bet Hom & Gard 48:10 S '70
SIEBENBERG, Stanley. See Bové, J. L. jt. auth.
SIEBER, Joan E. and Crockenberg, S. B.
Teacher and the anxious child. Todays Ed 59:76-7 O '70
SIEGEL, Bob
Mosaicon. New Yorker 46:32 S 12 '70 *
SIEGEL, Dorothy
How to beat the high cost of college. il Parents Mag 45:54-5+ My '70
SIEGEL, Frank L. See Aoki, K. jt. auth.
SIEGEL, Robert
Rock; poem. America 122:334 Mr 28 '70
SIEGFRIED line. See Germany—Defenses
SIEGMAN, Judith N.
For H.K; poem. Nation 210:638 My 25 '70
SIEGMEISTER, Elie
Elie Siegmeister: a record of more than ordinary importance. A. Cohn. por Am Rec G 36:520-1 Mr '70 *
Long, long road. il por Opera N 34:26-9 Mr 14 '70
SIEHL, George H.
Our world and welcome to it! il por Library J 95:1443-7 Ap 15 '70
SIEKMAN, Philip
Europe's love affair with bigness. il Fortune 81:94-9+ Mr '70
Kodak and Polaroid: an end to peaceful coexistence. il Fortune 82:82-7+ N '70
Offshore funds are in dangerous waters. il Fortune 82:118-21+ Ag '70
Thirteen days in an instant country. il Fortune 81:43-4+ Ap '70
SIELMANN, Heinz
Looking & listening. P. Hudson. por Sr Schol 95:18-19 O 13 '69 *
SIENA, Italy
Music
North Carolina school in Italy. W. Weaver. Hi Fi 20:MA18+ N '70
SIERRA club
Less expensive Sierra club books. Sunset 144:28 F '70
Sierra club mounts a new crusade. il Bsns W p64-5 My 23 '70
Sierra club's future publishing plans. Pub W 197:68 F 2 '70
U.S. plywood's forest of trouble; sale of timber from Tongass national forest. il Bsns W p39 F 21 '70
SIERRA NEVADA (California)
Ecology of fire; excerpt from Sierra Nevada. V. R. Johnston. il Audubon 72:76-81+ S '70
Pack trip in the High Sierras. M. Carter. il Holiday 47:62-5+ My '70
SIEVERS, Harry J.
Washington front. See issues of America
SIFONTES, Ramón S. See Schubert, C. jt. auth.
SIGAL, Clancy
Looking back without anger. il Commonweal 92:186-8 My 8 '70
SIGHT
Do you have eyes in your skin? R. Hattersley. il Pop Phot 66:55-9 Mr '70
Electrophysiological evidence for binocular disparity detectors in human visual system. A. Fiorentini and L. Maffei. bibliog il Science 169:208-9 Jl 10 '70
Eye-phi and you. W. Hanson. il Pop Phot 66:60-1+ Mr '70

SILK, Joseph. See Rees, M. J. jt. auth.

SILK moths. See Moths

SILK screen printing
Photographic serigraphy. K. Christman. il Sch Arts 70:16-18 D '70

SILK tassel bushes
Coast silktassel puts on its show right through winter. il Sunset 145:186 D '70

SILKEN, Howard
They sharpen drills fast. il Mech Illus 66:96-7 Ja '70

SILKOWSKI, Daniel R.
Lord Jim: big deal. Engl J 59:780-1 S '70

SILLITOE, Alan
Comment. R. Watson. Poetry 117:209-10 D '70 *
Question of focus; analysis of On Saturday afternoon. R. J. Levine. Engl J 59:40-2 Ja '70

SILLS, Beverly
Bubbles; interview, ed. by F. Bowers. por Opera N 35:18-21 S 19 '70

about
Donizetti, Sills, and Devereux. R. Lawrence. Sat R 53:83 F 28 '70 *
Making love to the public. W. Bender. pors Time 96:86 O 26 '70 *
Music to my ears; first New York recital. R. Jacobson. Sat R 53:50 F 21 '70 *
Music to my ears; performance in Roberto Devereux. I. Kolodin. Sat R 53:41+ O 31 '70 *
Queen high. H. Saal. il por Newsweek 76:99 O 26 '70 *

SILLS, Lawrence I.
Volta River project. Focus 21:9-12 O '70

SILLS, Paul
Broadway bestiary; Story theatre. J. Kroll. Newsweek 76:88 N 9 '70 *
Story-eyed. H. Hewes. Sat R 53:58 N 14 '70 *
Story theatre. Criticism
Nation 211:506 N 16 '70 *
Theatre. B. Gill. New Yorker 46:133 N 7 '70 *

SILOS
How to convert old silos to high-moisture grain storage. Farm J 94:31 Jl '70
Low-cost silage storage ideas. D. Malena. il Suc Farm 68:49-53 Je '70
Trenches vs. uprights for high moisture milo. C. E. Ball. Farm J 93:B25 N '69
See also
Silage

SILVER, George A.
Insurance is not enough. Nation 210:680-3 Je 8 '70

SILVER, Isidore
United States Supreme court, from Bushrod Washington to Roman Hruska. Commonweal 92:224-7 My 15 '70

SILVER, Leon T.
Uranium-thorium-lead isotope relations in lunar materials. bibliog il Science 167:468-71 Ja 30 '70

SILVER, Sidney L.
Digital voice communications. il Electr World 84:27-30+ O '70

SILVER
Psyched-out in silver. A. Hershman. il Duns 96:38-41 Ag '70
See also
Silverware

Prices
Silver coins: sell 'em or save 'em? il Changing T 24:36 My '70
Silver may bounce when it's dropped. il Bsns W p23 N 7 '70
Why the silver bears won out. il Bsns W p71 Ja 9 '71

SILVER as money
U.S. gets out of the silver market. U S News 69:43 N 23 '70

SILVER certificates. See Paper money—United States

SILVER coins. See Coins

SILVER dollars. See Coins

SILVER polishes. See Polishing materials

SILVERMAN, Al
(ed) See Sayers, G. Short courageous life of Brian Piccolo

SILVERMAN, Melvin P. and Munoz, E. F.
Fungal attack on rock: solubilization and altered infrared spectra. bibliog il Science 169:985-7 S 4 '70

SILVERMAN, Paul
Party line. Sat R 53:10 S 12 '70

SILVERMAN, Phyllis Rolfe
Widow as a caregiver in a program of preventive intervention with other widows. bibliog Ment Hy 54:540-7 O '70

SILVERS, Willys K. and others
Mixed lymphocyte reactions and tissue transplantation tolerance. bibliog il Science 167:1264-6 F 27 '70

SILVERSMITHS
American silversmiths in Canada; excerpts from Loyalist silversmiths in British North America 1776-1800. J. Langdon. Antiques 97:100-1 Ja '70
See also
Bateman, H.

SILVERSTEIN, Mickie
Atlanta's dynamic duo. pors Time 95:73 My 4 '70 *

SILVERTON, Doris
Mexican maid; story. McCalls 98:82-3 O '70

SILVERWARE
American silver at the Art institute of Chicago. D. A. Hanks. il Antiques 98:418-22 S '70
Charleston silver. E. M. Burton. il Antiques 96:915-17 Je '70
Church silver in colonial Virginia. H. S. T. Reed. il Antiques 97:243-7 F '70
New catalogue of the Mabel Brady Garvan collection of silver at Yale. G. Hood. il Antiques 98:932-5 D '70
Silver: on the mark. il Vogue 156:116-17 Ag 15 '70
Silver sugar tongs by Hester Bateman. L. F. Reals. il Hobbies 75:120+ Jl '70
Victorian pickle castors. V. K. Schnadig. il Hobbies 75:119 Mr '70
See also
Pitchers
Spoons
Tableware
Tureens

Care
Tarnish-preventing silver polishes. il Good H 170:6 Mr '70
See also
Polishing materials

History
Early American official silver; excerpts from Early American silver for the cautious collector. M. G. Fales. il Antiques 97:96-9 Ja '70

SILVEX. See Herbicides

SIMENON, Georges
Letter from Paris. Genêt. New Yorker 46:77 Jl 25 '70 *
Simenon maker. S. K. Oberbeck. il por Newsweek 75:102+ Ap 27 '70 *

SIMIAN viruses
Encapsulation of free host DNA by simian virus 40: a simian virus 40 pseudovirus. D. M. Trilling and D. Axelrod. bibliog il Science 168:268-70 Ap 10 '70

SIMIC, Charles
House: Explorers; poems. Poetry 115:257-8 Ja '70

SIMIEN MOUNTAIN NATIONAL PARK. See National parks and reserves—Ethiopia

SIMKIN, Tom, and Howard, K. A.
Caldera collapse in the Galápagos Island, 1968. bibliog il Science 169:429-37 Jl 31 '70

SIMKINS, Philip
Gallery; photographs. il Life 68:8-9 My 8 '70

SIMMONS, Hal
Goosenappers. il Field & S 75:60-1+ O '70
On the upper Rio Grande. il Field & S 75:62-3+ My '70

SIMMONS, Ian G.
Landscaping the Netherlands. il Am For 76:19-21+ F '70
Planning for open space in Denmark. il Am For 76:16-18+ F '70

SIMMONS, Robert. See Miller, J. N. jt. auth.

SIMMONS company
Moving out of the bedroom. il Bsns W p98-9 D 5 '70

SIMON. See Nathan, Simon

SIMON, Arthur
Battle of Beaufort. New Repub 162:11-15 My 23 '70

SIMON, Henry William
Mostly Mozart means merry musicmaking. il Hi Fi 20:MA10-11+ N '70
Obituary
Pub W 198:33 O 19 '70

SIMON, Joanna
Joanna Simon. G. Movshon. por Hi Fi 20:secII 8-9 Ap '70 *

SIMON, Neil
Gingerbread lady. Criticism
Nation 212:29 Ja 4 '71 *
New Yorker 46:96 D 19 '70 *
Newsweek il 76:61 D 28 '70 *
Sat R 54:4 Ja 9 '71 *
Time il 96:27 D 28 '70 *
Last of the red hot lovers. Criticism
America 122:55 Ja 17 '70
Commonweal 92:38-9 Mr 20 '70 *
Nation 210:60-1 Ja 19 '70
New Repub 162:25+ F 14 '70 *
Sat R 53:28 Ja 17 '70

SIMON, Neil—*Continued*
Neil Simon: up from success. P. D. Zimmerman. il pors Newsweek 75:52-6 F 2 '70
Simple secret of Simon. T. Prideaux. por Life 68:15 Mr 6 '70
What Simon says. W. Kerr. il por N Y Times Mag p6+ Mr 22 '70 *

SIMON, Norton
Man who... A. A. Butkus. por Duns 96:36 O '70 *
Report on SR. N. Cousins. Sat R 53:28-9 N 7 '70 *
Simon says. Newsweek 75:34 Je 1 '70 *
Unseen foe. pors Forbes 106:22 Ag 15 '70 *
Why a sixty-three-year-old tycoon worth $100-million wants to run for the Senate. S. V. Roberts. il pors N Y Times Mag p 10-12+ My 31 '70 *

SIMON, Norton, inc.
At Norton Simon old ties are cut. Bsns W p37 F 28 '70
Salesman in the executive suite. A. A. Butkus. por Duns 96:34-8 O '70

SIMON, Patricia
Making of a masterpiece. il pors McCalls 98:84-5+ O '70

SIMON, Paul, 1942?-
Simon and Garfunkel, nothing gauche. R. Goldstein. Vogue 155:110 Ap 1 '70 *
Simon & Garfunkel: the singers and the songs. E. Sander. pors Sat R 53:91+ F 28 '70 *

SIMON, Ruth B.
Seismicity of Colorado: consistency of recent earthquakes with those of historical record. bibliog Science 165:897-9; 167:1519 Ag 29 '69, Mr 13 '70

SIMON, Sidney B.
Sensitizing modules. il Schol Teach Jr/Sr High p28-9+ S 21 '70

SIMON, Yves
Friend and ally. R. Speaight. por Cath World 211:268-9 S '70 *

SIMON and Schuster, inc.
Kinney national service bids to acquire Simon & Schuster. Pub W 198:29 N 2 '70
S&S asks $4-million in damages, injunctive relief. Pub W 197:127-8 F 23 '70
S&S will sue Olympia over Original seven minutes. Pub W 197:48-9 F 16 '70
Simon & Schuster & Simon. Newsweek 75: 85 My 25 '70
Simon & Schuster; policy of accepting works through agents only. H. B. Jacobs. Writers Digest 50:22 D '70

SIMONDS, C. H.
Delectations. Nat R 22:1353 D 15 '70
For now. por Nat R 23:35+ Ja 12 '71
Records. il Nat R 22:216-17 F 24 '70

SIMONDS, John O.
Miami Lakes new town. il Parks & Recc 5: 29-33 O '70

SIMONE, Nina
Nina Simone: high priestess of soul. M. Angelou. il Redbook 136:77+ N '70 *
Return of the Queen of Shebang. A. Goldman. por Life 69:11 O 2 '70 *

SIMONIS, Adrianus Johannes
More trouble in Holland. il por Time 97: 61 Ja 18 '71 *

SIMONS, Albert
Architectural trends in Charleston. il Antiques 97:545-55 Ap '70

SIMONS, Dorothy
Re-genesis; poem. Negro Hist Bul 33:17 Ja '70

SIMONS, Elwyn L. and Ettel, P. C.
Gigantopithecus; with biographical sketches. il Sci Am 222:16, 76-85 bibliog (p 146) Ja '70

SIMONS, Francis, bp
Doctrine and democracy. Commonweal 92: 479-81 S 25 '70

SIMONS, Hendrik Nicolaas Theodorus. See Heintje

SIMONS, J. A.
δ-aminolevulinic acid synthetase: induction in embryonic chick liver by glucagon. bibliog il Science 167:1378-9 Mr 6 '70

SIMONS, Mary
Looking around. por Look 34:14 F 24 '70
What the English are doing about heroin. il Look 34:47-52+ Ap 7 '70

SIMONS, Myron
Stock trends (cont) por Forbes 105:222 Ja 1; 66 F 1; 84 Mr 1; 84-5 Ap 1; 250-1 My 15; 97 Je 15; 106:68-9 Jl 15; 80-1 Ag 15; 86-7 S 15; 102 O 15; 90-1 N 15; 60 D 15 '70

SIMONS, Robert Allen
Diagnostic intake: variation on a theme. bibliog Ment Hy 54:101-4 Ja '70

SIMONSEN, Svend T.
Your best friend, the compass. il Yachting 127:72-4+ Je '70

SIMONSON, Harold P.
Huckleberry Finn as tragedy. Yale R 59:532-48 Je '70

SIMONTON, John S. Jr
Build a pink noise generator. il Pop Electr 33:61-3 D '70
Modify your electronic guitar sound. il Pop Electr 32:53+ Je '70
Thumpa-thumpa box. il Pop Electr 32:53-7 F '70

SIMPSON, Babs
Small walled garden. il House & Gard 137:60-3 F '70

SIMPSON, Elizabeth
Mother Goose lives on. il pors Am For 76:44-8 O '70

SIMPSON, Elizabeth J.
Move over, gents. il Am Ed 6:3-6 D '70

SIMPSON, George Gaylord
Ages of fossil penguins in New Zealand. bibliog Science 168:361-2 Ap 17 '70

SIMPSON, Janet M.
Vocal music teacher, pianoless. Clear House 44:271 Ja '70

SIMPSON, Jerry H. Jr
Place where I belong at. Todays Ed 59:71 S '70

SIMPSON, John
Hambo was a family affair. W. F. Reed. il pors Sports Illus 33:24-5 S 14 '70 *

SIMPSON, John, jr
Hambo was a family affair. W. F. Reed. il pors Sports Illus 33:24-5 S 14 '70 *

SIMPSON, Louis
Adam Yankev; poem. New Yorker 46:56 O 24 '70
Country house; poem. New Yorker 46:42 O 3 '70
Life, the interesting character; poem. New Yorker 46:36 My 2 '70
Vandergast and the girl; poem. New Yorker 46:62 D 5 '70

SIMPSON, Martin B. C.
Blame IBM. R. Brady. il por Duns 95:109-10 Mr '70 *

SIMPSON, P. R. and Bowie, S. H. U.
Quantitative optical and electron-probe studies of the opaque phases. bibliog il Science 167:619-21 Ja 30 '70

SIMPSON, Ralph
Ex-doughboy who can shoot with the best. J. Jares. Sports Illus 32:44 Ja 19 '70

SIMPSON, Robert H.
Hurricane peak: mid-September? interview. por U S News 69:16 Ag 10 '70

SIMPSON, Smith
New sprint in foggy bottom. Nation 210: 296-302 Mr 16 '70

SIMPSON, Wayne
Vet-rookie duo sparks Cincinnati machine. L. J. Banks. il pors Ebony 25:70-1+ S '70 *

SIMROSS, Lynn
Harness racing. Sports Illus 33:44+ Jl 27 '70

SIMS, John H. See Henry, W. E. jt. auth.

SIMULATION methods
Sulfur: simulated long-range transport in the atmosphere. H. Reiquam. bibliog il Science 170:318-20 O 16 '70
See also
Economic models
Mathematical models

SIMULATORS
World's highest-pressure chamber; diving-test chamber. S. Carpenter. il por Pop Sci 196:66-7+ Ap '70
See also
Environmental simulators
Flight simulators
Space flight simulators

SIN
America on its knees? Chr Today 14:20-1 Je 19 '70
Christ and sinners. V. P. McCorry. America 122; inside back cover Je 6 '70
Hard words; about the punishment of sin. V. P. McCorry. America 123:218 S 26 '70

SINAI (peninsula)
Wildlife of Sinai. W. Ferguson. il Audubon 72:32-41 Mr '70

SINATRA, Frank
Star time? A. Knight. Sat R 53:56 N 21 '70

SINCLAIR, Upton
Sergei Eisenstein and Upton Sinclair, ed. by H. M. Geduld and R. Gottesman. Review Newsweek il por 76:74 Ag 10 '70. G. Wolff *

SINCLAIR, Ward
Confusion in the coalfields. New Repub 163: 17-18 Jl 18 '70
—and Peters, L. K.
Cooperating teacher-student teacher as a learning team. Clear House 44:430-2 Mr '70

SINDEN, Harry
No room at the top for me; ed. by M. Mulvoy. il por Sports Illus 33:38-40+ O 19 '70
about
Penny-pinching Bruins. Newsweek 75:85 Je 1 '70 *

SINE-sweep generators. See Signal generators
SING Sing prison, Ossining, N.Y.
Parting shots. il Life 68:65-8 F 13 '70
SINGAPORE
See also
Drug trade—Singapore
Investments, Foreign (in Singapore)
Restaurants—Singapore
Tourist trade—Singapore

Economic conditions
Boom that fooled everybody. Singapore without the British. J. N. Wallace. il U S News 68:70-2 Mr 30 '70

Industries
Magnet for eager manufacturers. il Bsns W p23 Ag 8 '70
Singapore acts to cushion British withdrawal impact. C. Brownlow. il Aviation W 92:66-8 My 11 '70

Photographs
Singapore. B. Wolf. il Travel & Camera 33:52-4 Mr '70

Politics and government
Letter from Europe. A. Burgess. Am Scholar 40:119-22 Wint '70
SINGER, Arthur
National wildlife visits Arthur Singer. D. Kirkpatrick. il pors Nat Wildlife 8:58-63 D '69 *
SINGER, Bill
No hits, runs or bubbly. il por Newsweek 76: 49 Ag 3 '70 *
SINGER, C. E. and Ames, B. N.
Sunlight ultraviolet and bacterial DNA base ratios. bibliog il Science 170:822-6 N 20 '70
SINGER, Dan J.
Perilous cruise for Alaskan brown bear; re-print. il Field & S 75:200-4+ Je '70
SINGER, Daniel
American nightmare; excerpt from Prelude to revolution: France in May. Nation 210: 742-4 Je 22 '70
Death of a legendary hero. Nation 211:550-2 N 30 '70
SINGER, Isaac Bashevis
Doctor Beeber; story; tr. by the author and E. Gottlieb. New Yorker 46:38-42 Mr 7 '70
Guests on a winter night; tr. by the author and D. Straus. New Yorker 45:31-8 Ja 24 '70
Isaac Bashevis Singer scoffs; remarks, ed. by I. Shenker. Atlan 226:98-100 Jl '70
Joke; story, tr. by the author and D. Straus. New Yorker 46:36-44 Ap 11 '70
Mentor; story, tr. by the author and E. T. Beck. New Yorker 46:40-6 Mr 21 '70
On a wagon; story, tr. by the author and D. Straus. New Yorker 46:25-30 Jl 25 '70
Short visits with five writers and one friend. B. Midwood. il pors Esquire 74:150-3 N '70 *
Something is there; excerpt from A friend of Kafka and other stories. Harper 240:81-90 Je '70
Tutor in the village; story, tr. by the author and R. Gerber. New Yorker 46:32-7 Je 6 '70

about
Children's literature NBA goes to Isaac B. Singer. Library J 95:1542 Ap 15 '70 *
SINGER, J. David. See Small, M. jt. auth.
SINGER, J. R. See Morse, O. C. jt. auth.
SINGER, James
Barnacle glue; with biographical sketch. il Sea Front 16:96-103, 127 Mr '70
SINGER, Marshall
Fragments from the shooting gallery. pors Ramp Mag 8:16-18 Ap '70
SINGER, Philip C. and Stumm, Werner
Acidic mine drainage: the rate-determining step. bibliog il Science 167:1121-3; 169:98 F 20, Jl 3 '70
SINGER, Siegfried Fred
Exploring space in the seventies; adaptation of address, December 1969. il Bul Atom Sci 26:22-3 N '70
How did Venus lose its angular momentum? Science 170:1196-8 D 11 '70
Human energy production as a process in the biosphere; with biographical sketch. il Sci Am 223:38, 174-6+ bibliog(p265) S '70
Will the world come to a horrible end? bibliog Science 170:125 O 9 '70
—and Bandermann, L. W.
Where was the moon formed? bibliog il Science 170:438-9 O 23 '70

about
Astronomical mystery. Time 97:65 Ja 18 '71 *

SINGER company
Friden's new way to put data on tape. Bsns W p88 Ja 17 '70
See also
Diversified technologies, inc.
SINGERS
Debuts & reappearances; New York concerts. See issues of High fidelity and Musical America section II
Glen Campbell: the all-American country boy; interview, ed. by L. Dowty. G. Campbell. il pors Good H 170:42+ F '70
In the tenth year; Peter, Paul and Mary. A. R. Dolan. Nat R 22:208 F 24 '70
Ladies' men of music; with report by J. Bonfante. il pors Life 69:46-52+ S 18 '70
Matter of identification; singers in a photograph of the Victor male chorus. J. Walsh. il Hobbies 75:37-41+ Jl '70
Musical whirl; photographs. See issues of High fidelity and Musical America section II
Real names of Edison cylinder performers. J. Walsh. il Hobbies 75:37-9 Je '70
Rod McKuen; interview, ed. by S. Nirenberg. R. McKuen. il pors House B 112:70-1+ F '70
Take the lilies and the lace; excerpt from The Judy Collins songbook. J. Collins. il pors McCalls 97:66-7+ Ap '70
Young artists, 1970; photographs. Hi Fi 20: secII 10-13 Jl '70
See also
Beatles
Choral groups and societies
Negro singers
Opera singers
Rock 'n' roll singers
also names of singers, e.g. P. Clark
SINGH, M. P. and others
Chromosomal aberrations induced in barley by LSD. bibliog il Science 169:491-2 Jl 31 '70
SINGH, Manmohan
Regional development banks. bibliog il por(back cover) Int Concil 576:5-83 Ja '70
SINGHAL, Radhey L. and others
Cyclic adenosine monophosphate: andromimetic action on seminal vesicular enzymes. bibliog il Science 168:261-3 Ap 10 '70
SINGING
Tour of two great throats; interviews, ed. by R. Meryman. J. Sutherland; M. Horne. il pors Life 68:63-4+ Je 26 '70
See also
Diction
Embellishment (vocal music)
Voice culture

Competitions
Winners, 1970; National council's auditions finals. il Opera N 35:27 D 12 '70

Instruction and study
See Voice culture
SINGING, Congregational. See Church music
SINGING sands
Mystery of the singing sands. P. Brock. il Sci Digest 68:63-7 Ag '70
SINGING teachers
Some of my best friends are phonies. W. Alderson. il Opera N 35:8-11 D 19 '70
SINGLE-lens reflex cameras
At last, full report on Pentax 6x7 SLR. il Mod Phot 33:74+ D '69 *
B&H auto reflex 35 is Canon's automatic. il Mod Phot 34:86+ Ap '70
Exposure off? watch that diaphragm! automatic diaphragm system. N. Goldberg. il Pop Phot 66:54+ Ap '70
First look:
Petri's Ftee. N. Rothschild. il Pop Phot 66:82 Mr '70
How to solve the twelve toughest SLR problems. N. Rothschild. il Pop Phot 67: 74-7+ N '70
Keppler on the SLR. H. Keppler. See issues of Modern photography
Keppler on the SLR; all specifications subject to change without notice. H. Keppler. il Mod Phot 34:110-12 Mr '70
Lab report:
Hanimex Praktica 66. N. Rothschild. il Pop Phot 66:120+ Je '70
Miranda sensorex. E. Petersen. il Pop Phot 66:86 Mr '70
Ricoh singlex TLS. il Pop Phot 66:96-7+ F '70
Rollei SL26. M. Frank. il Pop Phot 66:88+ Mr '70
Leaf of the slit, which 2 1/4 SLR is right for you? N. Rothschild. il Pop Phot 66:63-5+ Ap '70
New SLR with 1/2.000-sec top speed: Regula reflex 2000 CTL. B. Schwalberg. il Pop Phot 67:56+ S '70

SINGLE-lens reflex cameras—*Continued*
Nikon click. N. A. Martin. il Duns 97:62-4+ Ja '71
1970-71 120 SLR roll film comparison directory. D. L. Miller. il Mod Phot 34:96-7 O '70
1970-71 SLR comparison directory. il Mod Phot 34:64-71 S '70
Pentax SL. il Pop Phot 66:94-5+ Ap '70
Readers' report: Pentax Spotmatic. il Mod Phot 34:86-7 Ag '70

SINGLE men
Eligible bachelors for 1970. il Ebony 25:112-14+ Je '70

SINGLE tax
Overdue business of tax reform. Am City 85:12 O '70

SINGLE women
New crop of eligible girls; bachelor girls of '70s. il Ebony 25:123-4+ Ap '70
Woman alone; racially mixed child adopted by single woman. E. Keiffer. il pors Good H 171:84-5+ Jl '70
Young woman's story (cont) Redbook 134:42+ Mr; 135:20+ Jl '70

SINGLETON, Henry E.
As they see it; interview. por Forbes 106:64+ N 15 '70

SINKS, Thomas A.
Individual progress: a study of seventh graders. bibliog il Clear House 44:457-60 Ap '70

SINKS
Portable sink makes hot water. H. Clark. il Pop Mech 133:159 Ja '70

SINN Fein rebellion. See Ireland—History—Sinn Fein rebellion, 1916

SINNING with Annie; story. See Theroux, P.

SINO-Japanese war, 1931-1932. See Chinese-Japanese war, 1931-1932

SINO-Japanese war, 1937-1945. See Chinese-Japanese war, 1937-1945

SIPLE, Molly
Parties without panic. House B 112:76+ N '70

SIPPEL, Robert F. and Spencer, A. B.
Cathodoluminescence properties of lunar rocks. bibliog il Science 167:677-9 Ja 30 '70

SIPUNCULAN worms. See Marine worms

SIRENS
Curiosity box. P. Franson. il Electr World 84:82-3 S '70

SIREVAG, Reidun, and Ormerod, J. G.
Carbon dioxide-fixation in photosynthetic green sulfur bacteria. bibliog il Science 169:186-8 Jl 10 '70

SIRHAN, Sirhan Bishara
R.F.K. must die! by R. B. Kaiser. Review Newsweek il por 76:114+ O 19 '70. G. Wolff *
Sat R 53:29-30+ O 17 '70. F. J. Cook *
Sirhan B. Sirhan literary negotiations, etc, inc. S. V. Roberts. pors Esquire 74:131-4+ N '70 *
Was Sirhan programmed to kill Robert Kennedy? excerpt from RFK must die. R. B. Kaiser. il por Ladies Home J 87:66+ O '70 *

SIRIO satellite. See Communications satellites, Italian

SIROTA, Hy
Chain store that dared. il Org Gard & Farm 17:66-7 Ag '70

SISARIO, Peter
Study of the allusions in Bradbury's Fahrenheit 451. Engl J 59:201-5+ F '70

SISCO, Joseph John
Assistant Secretary Sisco gives observations on the Near East; statement, April 24, 1970. Dept State Bul 62:693 Je 1 '70
Assistant Secretary Sisco interviewed on Meet the press; transcript of interview, July 12, 1970. Dept State Bul 63:150-5 Ag 3 '70
Assistant Secretary Sisco interviewed on NBC's Today. Dept State Bul 63:566-8 N 9 '70
U.S. objectives in the Middle East; address, June 30, 1970. Dept State Bul 63:175-8 Ag 10 '70

about
Bad trip. il Time 95:43 Ap 27 '70 *

SISK, John P.
Critical moment. Commentary 49:89-92 Ap '70
Future of prediction. Commentary 49:65-8 Mr; 50:6+ Jl '70
Sex and Armageddon. Commentary 50:83-4+ D '70

SISKIND, Aaron
Gallery; photographs. Life 69:6-7 S 11 '70

about
In Siskind's vision, a sense of man's impermanence. M. Mann. il Pop Phot 67:23-4+ O '70 *

SISSMAN, Louis Edward
Among schoolchildren; poem. New Yorker 46:40 D 19 '70
E-type on the interstate; poem. New Yorker 46:36 Jl 25 '70
Empson lieder: Law song; Even song; Girl song; War song; Swan song. New Yorker 46:42-3 O 17 '70
Excuse for an Italian sonnet. New Yorker 46:34 Jl 4 '70
How to write good poetry and get it published. Writer 83:18-21 O '70
Innocent bystander. Atlan 226:22-5 D '70; 227:26-8 Ja '71
Letter from coast to coast; poem. New Yorker 46:46 N 7 '70
Loss of largess: its recapture, and point after; poem. Harper 240:34 F '70
N.Y, N.Y, 1970: Cock Robbins opens in New York; First N.Y. showing; Lieder eines fahrenden Gesellen; poems. Atlan 227:48-9 Ja '71
Pursuit of honor, 1946; poem. Atlan 225:98-105 Je '70
Under the rose: a granfalloon for Kurt Vonnegut, jr; poem. Harper 241:112 S '70

about
Recurrences. X. J. Kennedy. Nation 210:378-80 Mr 30 '70 *
Urbane trash. S. M. L. Aronson. Poetry 116:40-2 Ap '70 *

SISSON, Robert F.
Wasp that plays cupid to a fig. il Nat Geog 138:690-7 N '70

SISTER Agatha and the milkman; story. See O'Connor. F.

SISTERHOODS
Demise of the IHM's. America 122:146 F 14 '70
Income and service as witness; excerpt from Religious women in the modern world. J. Tate. Cath World 211:247-50 S '70
On mystifying contemplatives. America 122:146 F 14 '70
Sister speaks up. Commonweal 91:524 F 13 '70
Sisters of the loyal opposition; new Immaculate Heart of Mary lay community. Chr Cent 87:195 F 18 '70
U.S. sisters organize. J. C. Haughey. America 122:388-90 Ap 11 '70
See also
Conference of major superiors of women's institutions of the United States of America
Contemplative orders
Nuns

SISTERS
New baby at our house; six years between first child and second. C. Lang. il por Parents Mag 45:54-5 Mr '70

SISTINE chapel. See Vatican—Sistine chapel

SITE planning. See Building sites; Housing projects—Site planning

SITES, Building. See Building sites

SITES, Industrial. See Location in business and industry

SITWELL, Dame Edith
Edith Sitwell: selected letters 1919-1964, ed. by J. Lehmann and D. Parker. Review Sat R por 54:29 Ja 9 '71. R. Halsband *

SITZ, Thomas O. and others
Equilibrium density-gradient procedure for selection of synchronous cells from asynchronous cultures. bibliog il Science 168:1231-2; 170:97 Je 5, O 2 '70

SIURU, William D. Jr. See Holder, W. G. jt. auth.

SIVERD, Clifford David
Clifford Siverd of American cyanamid; interview. pors Nations Bsns 58:58-61+ Je '70

1692 cotton mather newsreel; story. See Brautigan, R.

SIXTH committee of the General assembly. See United Nations—Legal committee

SIXTH fleet. See United States—Navy

SIXTH juror; drama. See Murray, J.

SIZE
See also
Clothing and dress—Size

SJÖSTEDT, Ulf
Egg comes first. J. Dreyfuss. il Mod Phot 34:96-9 Ja '70 *
Make light of it. J. Dreyfuss. il Mod Phot 34:80-1 Mr '70 *

SKAPURA, Robert. See Janeczko, P. B. jt. auth.

SKATERS
Little murder set to music; finalists in the U.S. figure skating championships. P. Ryan. il pors Sports Illus 32:18-19 F 16 '70

SKATING
Pussycat on a quick cold rink; L. Poulos world speed skating championship winner. W. F. Reed. il pors Sports Illus 32:18-19 Mr 9 '70
There's an undeniable link between skating and dancing! R. Brown. il Dance Mag 44:34-7 Ja '70
See also
Ice shows
Roller skating

Competitions
Little murder set to music; finalists in the U.S. figure skating championships. P. Ryan. il pors Sports Illus 32:18-19 F 16 '70

Photographs
Many-faceted champion; J. Lynn. pors Sports Illus 32:20-4 Ja 26 '70

SKATING rinks
Skating rink has translucent wall; Springfield, Mass. il Am City 85:46 Ag '70

SKELETON (invertebrates)
Coral skeletons: an explanation of their growth and structure. D. J. Barnes. bibliog il Science 170:1305-8 D 18 '70
Echinoid skeleton: absence of a collagenous matrix. L. Klein and J. D. Currey. bibliog il Science 169:1209-10 S 18 '70
Phylum ectoprocta, order cheilostomata: microprobe analysis of calcium, magnesium, strontium, and phosphorus in skeletons. T. J. M. Schopf and J. R. Allan. bibliog il Science 169:280-2 Jl 17 '70
Scleractinian coral exoskeletons: surface microarchitecture and attachment scar patterns. S. W. Wise, jr. bibliog il Science 169:978-80 S 4 '70

SKELETON clocks. See Clocks

SKELLEY, Robert C.
Woodcuts of Robert C. Skelley. N. Kent. il Am Artist 35:44-9+ Ja '71 *

SKELTON, Philip C. See Craden, M. D. jt. auth.

SKELTON, Thomas
Dream for three. D. Hering. il pors Dance Mag 44:72-6 Ap '70 *

SKEPTICISM
Filthy-minded reflections on theological method. J. Loeschen. Chr Cent 87:108-12 Ja 28 '70

SKETCH; story. See Thompson R.

SKETCHES. See Drawings

SKETCHING. See Drawing

SKEWER cookery. See Cookery

SKI clubs. See Sports clubs

SKI houses. See Vacation houses

SKI lifts
How to build a town ski slope; Manchester, Conn. W. D. O'Neill. il Am City 85:84+ Ag '70

SKI photography. See Photography of sports

SKI resorts. See Winter resorts

SKI touring. See Skis and skiing

SKI tows. See Ski lifts

SKIBOBS and skibobbing
Sitzen sie ski? F. A. Tinker. il Pop Mech 134:126-7+ N '70

SKIDDING of automobiles. See Automobiles—Skidding

SKIDMORE college, Saratoga Springs, N. Y.
Skidmore college. il Arch Rec 147:91-102 Mr '70

SKIERS
Photographs
Don't cry until it's all over; Nordic racers; photographs by N. Leifer and text by A. Verschoth. Sports Illus 34:34-9 Ja 4 '71

SKIING. See Skis and skiing

SKILLED labor
Agony of the overskilled man. Time 96:84 O 5 '70
Skills and location of defense-related workers; with tables. M. A. Rutzick. il Mo Labor R 93:11-16 F '70

SKILLED performance. See Performance standards

SKILLET cookery. See Cookery

SKILLET meals. See Cookery

SKILLICORN, Marion
French sentimentals and embroidered cards. il Hobbies 75:153 Ap '70

SKIN
Wrinkles don't hurt. S. E. Rapp. il Har Yrs 10:50 F '70
See also
Cosmetics
Sunburn

Care and hygiene
Beauty and the mask. il Ladies Home J 87:32 Ap '70
Body facial: a touching story. il Vogue 155:54 Ap 1 '70
Complexion spectrum. il Vogue 155:184-7 F 1 '70
Face facts. Mlle 71:160-1 O '70
Face to resort to: yours. il Harp Baz 103:148-9 My '70
Face up to spring. P. Van Wagenen. il Parents Mag 45:102-4 Mr '70
Food for the face. Mlle 70:90 F '70
Help is on the way; chemosurgery and dermabrasion. il Vogue 156:172 N 1 '70
How to have the kind of skin you've always wanted. il Mlle 70:92-3+ Ja '70
Mask marvels. il Mlle 70:94-6 Ja '70
Outdoor beauty. C. Bartel. il Am Home 73:16+ Ja '70
Protect your skin from the unfriendly air. C. Bartel. il Am Home 74:14 Ja '71
Set your own beauty-farm routine; programs and products. S. Lindsay. il House B 112:44+ O '70
Six ways to be kind to your skin. Har Yrs 10:11 D '70
Skin beauty under the sun. il Redbook 135:82-3+ Je '70
Total complexion care. il Good H 170:74-5+ Ja '70
What to do about cuts, blisters, and rashes. G. M. Knox. Bet Hom & Gard 48:24+ Ag '70
Your skin vs winter sun. il Vogue 156:148-50 N 15 '70

Diseases
Defect in DNA synthesis in skin of patients with xeroderma pigmentosum demonstrated in vivo. J. H. Epstein and others. bibliog il Science 168:1477-8 Je 19 '70
No sweat; ichthyosis; water dousing allows J. Borden to run. il Newsweek 75:91 My 11 '70
See also
Acne
Allergy
Angiokeratoma
Dandruff
Lupus erythematosus
Psoriasis
Schistosomiasis

Wounds and injuries
What to do about cuts, blisters, and rashes. G. M. Knox. Bet Hom & Gard 48:24+ Ag '70

SKIN, Shedding of. See Molting

SKIN cancer. See Cancer

SKIN color. See Color of man

SKIN diving
Scuba diving for fun. S. Carpenter. il por Pop Sci 196:51+ F '70
Scuba diving for live treasures. il Nat Wildlife 8:26-31 Ap '70

Equipment and supplies
Aquanaut makes diving easy. D. Fales. il Pop Mech 134:152-4 S '70
How a little fish hooked a big one; Biomarine's closed-cycle underwater breathing system. il Bsns W p88+ F 28 '70
Underwater communications. S. Carpenter. il Pop Sci 197:48-9+ Ag '70

SKIN flicks. See Sex in moving pictures

SKIN grafting. See Transplantation of organs, tissues, etc.

SKINNER, Brian J.
High crystallization temperatures indicated for igneous rocks from Tranquillity base. il Science 167:652-4 Ja 30 '70

SKINNER, Burrhus Frederic
Walden two: three? Many more? R. Todd. il por N Y Times Mag p24-5+ Mr 15 '70 *

SKINNER, Dorothy M. and Graham, D. E.
Molting in land crabs: stimulation by leg removal. bibliog il Science 169:383-5 Jl 24 '70

SKINNER, Gwen
Treacherous Tuamotus. il Yachting 127:94-6+ Ja '70

SKINNER, Jean Ross-. See Ross-Skinner, J.

SKINNER, Tom
Evangelicals and the black revolution; excerpts from address. Chr Today 14:10-12+ Ap 10 '70

about
Skinner crusade shows interracial cooperation. Chr Today 14:42-3 Je 5 '70 *

SKINNER box. See Psychological apparatus

SKINNING of deer. See Game, Dressing of

SKIR, Leo
We're freakin' on in! Mlle 71:150-1+ S '70

SKIRTS, Length of. See Clothing and dress

SKIS and skiing
Cross country. S. Wiedel. il Travel & Camera 33:32-5 D '70
Don't cry until it's all over; Nordic racers; photographs by N. Leifer and text by A. Verschoth. Sports Illus 34:34-9 Ja 4 '71
Downhill racers; wind tunnel conducted by the Canadian national ski team. il Newsweek 75:67 Mr 16 '70
Families on skis: a new fashion (Killy-approved) il pors Ladies Home J 87:78-9 N '70
Flake and the old man; T. Palmer and B. Kidd at Alpine ski racing events. R. Meryman. il pors Life 68:54-6+ Mr 6 '70
Girls from the mountain next door; photographs by Jerry Cooke. Sports Illus 32:36-41 Mr 16 '70
Goodby Billy and hello Willy; new coach for U.S. Alpine ski team. W. Johnson. il por Sports Illus 33:78-9 N 23 '70
Grab the gold and say goodby; world Alpine championship. D. Jenkins. il por Sports Illus 32:26-9 F 23 '70
Here comes, there goes Karl! Austria's superracer. W. Johnson. il por Sports Illus 32:58-9 Mr 23 '70
Kidd comes in from the old cold; world ski championship. D. Jenkins. il por Sports Illus 32:42+ F 16 '70
Mood and feeling. R. Meryman. Mlle 72:190+ N '70
Name is the name of the game; amateurism and Olympics. W. Johnson. il Sports Illus 32:12-17 Mr 9 '70
New kind of French dressing; the New naturals to World Alpine championship. W. Johnson. il pors Sports Illus 32:12-17 F 2 '70
Olympics and modern philosophy. A. Lunn. Nat R 22:840 Ag 11 '70
Ski survival for beginners. C. Howes. il Todays Health 49:35-7 Ja '71
Ski touring comes to America. P. Snook. il Nat Wildlife 8:20-3 D '69
Skiing the snows of yesteryear. L. J. Berry. il Esquire 74:154-9 N '70
Slippery days on the slopes. il por Time 95:48 Mr 23 '70
Snurfing. il Travel 134:50-1+ D '70
Some new babes in the woods; U.S. women's cross-country ski team. W. Johnson. il Sports Illus 31:72+ D 15 '69

See also
Ski lifts
Skibobs and skibobbing
Water skis and skiing

Accidents and injuries
Break a leg? Not likely. E. Bowen. Am Home 73:36+ Ja '70

Equipment
Skiing season: on the trail of new equipment. Bsns W p 103 N 7 '70
Skis & ski gear. Changing T 25:11-12 Ja '71

History
When the forty-niners went sixty. E. M. Halliday. il Am Heritage 22:75-8 D '70

Study and teaching
Jean-Claude Killy's ski kindergarten. il por Ladies Home J 87:52-3 Ja '70
Notes from the mountaintop underground. S. Mahoney. il Life 68:12 Mr 13 '70

California
What goes up must ski down; Squaw Valley resort. A. Wright. il por Sports Illus 32:28-31 F 9 '70
When the forty-niners went sixty. E. M. Halliday. il Am Heritage 22:75-8 D '70

Canada
Adrift in the Rockies: Banff and the blue laws. D. Butwin. il Sat R 53:52+ F 14 '70
Sky-high skiing in the bugaboos; photographs by J. G. Zimmerman. Sports Illus 32:38-45 Mr 30 '70
Travel notes. R. Joseph. Esquire 74:32+ N '70

Colorado
City-owned ski area; Winter park. C. W. Casewit. il Am City 85:120+ Ap '70

Czechoslovakia
Some Reds sail in the sunset; Russians at Nordic meet. A. Verschoth. il Sports Illus 32:50-1 Mr 2 '70

Europe, Eastern
Socialized Schussing: Czechoslovakia, Rumania, Yugoslavia. F. Riley. Sat R 53:50 O 24 '70

Europe, Western
Europe's ski safaris. il Travel 134:52-3 D '70

France
Skiing on the French frontier. C. Dreyfus. il Mlle 72:191+ N '70
Skiing the French Alps. P. Miller. il Travel & Camera 33:18-31 D '70
Skiing the new French Alps. F. R. Smith. il Harp Baz 104:76+ N '70
White gold in France. il Time 95:82-5 Ap 13 '70

Idaho
New direction for skiers; up; Sun Valley. H. Ehrlich. il Look 34:41-3 F 24 '70
Snowy Sun Valley. D. Taylor. il Travel 134:62-3 D '70

New York (state)
Big Vanilla adds icing. il Travel 133:72 Ja '70
Ski-center rates. Cons 25:39 D '70

Oregon
Oregon's Mount Bachelor and Hoodoo are great if you plan to take the family. il Sunset 144:52-3 Mr '70

Poland
Red skis in the sunset. F. Riley. il Sat R 53:46+ O 24 '70

Switzerland
Hard way over a high route; path across the Alps. J. Skow. il por Sports Illus 32:38-40+ Ap 27 '70
Secret Swiss ski sites. H. P. Koenig. il Travel 134:28-33 N '70

United States
Going things: ski U.S.A. S. Cuneo. Mlle 72:122-6 N '70
Travel notes. R. Joseph. Esquire 74:32+ N '70
Winter sport: learn to ski. E. Welke. il Bet Hom & Gard 48:22 D '70

Vermont
Babe in Slatland; Haystack Mountain. D. Butwin. il Sat R 53:62-3 Ja 31 '70
Scintillating Stowe. J. E. Maxwell. il Travel 134:44-51 N '70
Trashing of Vermont. C. H. Simonds. Nat R 22:1353 D 15 '70

SKLARE, Marshall
Intermarriage & Jewish survival. Commentary 49:51-8 Mr; 12+ Je '70

SKOLNICK, Jerome H. See Currie, E. jt. auth.

SKOLNICK, Sherman H.
Another death plot? por Time 95:17 Ap 20 '70 *

SKOPLJE, Yugoslavia
Profitable earthquake. il Newsweek 76:102A-102B D 14 '70

SKOVBO, Bob, pseud.
Northwest Passage; with biographical sketch. il Natur Hist 79:3, 56-65 Je '70

SKOW, Jack
If it looks like Zeus, and sounds like Zeus, it must be Robert Graves. il Esquire 74:144-5+ S '70

SKOW, John
Gossipmasters. il McCalls 97:86-7+ F '70
Hard way over a high route. il por Sports Illus 32:38-40+ Ap 27 '70

SKRIABIN, Aleksandr Nikolaevich
Fiery music of a mystic. A. Hope. il pors Life 69:72-6 O 16 '70 *
Scriabin and his demons. J. Hiemenz. por Hi Fi 20:19-20 S '70 *

SKROWACZEWSKI, Stanislaw
Fresh faces; interview, ed. by A. M. Lingg. por Opera N 34:30-1 F 21 '70

SKUNK cabbages
Skunk cabbage. P. M. Kelsey. il Cons 24:33 F '70

SKURKA, Norma
Home. il N Y Times Mag p70-1 O 4; 102-3 O 11; 80-1 N 1; 114-15 N 15; 100-1 N 22; 104-5 N 29; 122-3 D 6; 94-5 D 13; 42-3 D 20 '70; 68-9 Ja 10 '71

SKY
Far-infrared observations of the night sky. J. R. Houck and M. Harwit; reply with rejoinder. D. P. McNutt and P. D. Feldman. bibliog Science 167:1277 F 27 '70
Naked-eye sky watcher. D. B. Williams. R Pop Astron 63:26 Ag '69

SKY diving. See Parachuting

SKY lifts. See Cableways

SKY marshals. See Airplane hijacking—Prevention

SKYBUS. See Pittsburgh—Transit systems

SKYDIVING. See Parachuting

SKYJACKING. See Airplane hijacking

SKYLAB. See Space stations

SKYLINE corporation
High-altitude Skyline. Fortune 81:289 My '70

SKYNET (communications satellite) See Communications satellites, British

SKYSCRAPERS
New hot spots; dangers when a fire breaks out. il Bsns W p42 Ag 15 '70
Tall one; John Hancock center, Chicago. J. M. Dixon. il Arch Forum 133:36-45 Jl '70
View from the 92nd floor; John Hancock center. il Newsweek 75:47 F 2 '70
See also
Office buildings

SLABAUGH, W. H.
Clay colloids. il por Chem 43:8-12 Ap '70; Correction. 43:31 O '70

SLACK, Kenneth
Unity: where are we in Britain? Chr Cent 87:1281-3 O 28 '70

SLAMA, K. See Zaoral, M. jt. auth.

SLANDER. See Libel and slander

SLANG
Drug glossary. Sat R 53:21 N 14 '70
Highlighting hiplingua. Chr Cent 87:1075 S 9 '70
Inarticulate hero. A. L. Theroux. Nat R 22:199-201 F 24 '70
Rhetoric of violence. E. Goodheart. il Nation 210:399-402 Ap 6 '70; Same abr. Cur 118:9-13 My '70
Right on is off and other hiplingua news. Time 96:32 Ag 17 '70
Slang and profanity: their uses in English composition. D. P. Demarest. jr. Clear House 45:76-80 O '70
Teen-age slang: a guide for parents. Good H 170:150 Je '70
Thou shalt not. M. Mayer. Cur 117:62-4 Ap '70
See also
Americanisms (speech)

SLANSKY trial. See Trials—Czechoslovakia

SLANT-edged razors. See Razors

SLAPPEY, Sterling G.
Startling Surinam. il Travel 135:41+ Ja '71

SLATE, George L.
Apricots, nectarines and almonds. il Horticulture 48:42-3+ My '70
Autumn-fruiting raspberries. il Horticulture 48:24-5+ S '70

SLATE, Mary Ellen
Foul weather gear. il Motor B 125:111+ Mr '70
101 hints for cruising guests. il Motor B 125:123+ Mr '70
Pollution: many questions and some answers. Motor B 125:54-5 Je '70
Something for the girls. il Motor B 125:155 Ja '70
Who's on what? il Motor B 125:120-1+ Ja '70

SLATER, Harry G.
Bridging the gap; address. February 5, 1970. Vital Speeches 36:399-402 Ap 15 '70

SLATER, Philip E.
America's changing culture; excerpts from The pursuit of loneliness: American culture at the breaking point. Cur 119:15-21 Je '70

SLATTED floors (swine houses) See Swine houses—Floors

SLATTERY, William J.
Who now, Dow Jones? Esquire 74:236-7 O '70

SLAUGHTERING and slaughterhouses
Watching the animals; Des Moines slaughterhouse. R. Rhodes. il Harper 240:91-4 Mr '70
See also
Game, Dressing of

SLAVE ship; drama. See Jones, L.

SLAVE trade
Postmarked 1841: letter to former President John Quincy Adams, with editorial comment. Ka-le. Am Heritage 22:111 D '70

SLAVERY
See also
Slave trade

Brazil

Slavery in Brazil and the United States: an essay in comparative history; address. April 1969. C. N. Degler. bibliog f Am Hist R 75:1004-28 Ap '70

United States

Benjamin Banneker: he didn't fit the image. por Sr Schol 95:24 S 15 '69
Black pioneer period. L. Bennett, jr. il Ebony 25:46-8+ O '70
Road not taken. L. Bennett jr. il Ebony 25:70-2+ Ag '70

Slavery in Brazil and the United States: an essay in comparative history; address, April 1969. C. N. Degler. bibliog f Am Hist R 75:1004-28 Ap '70
World the slaveholders made, by E. D. Genovese. Review
Nation 210:56-7 Ja 19 '70. T. Nelson
See also
Abolitionists
Emancipation proclamation
Freedmen

SLAVITT, David R.
My Sony, the doctor (William J. Bryan, jr. M.D.) il Esquire 74:164-5+ O '70
What I did November 15, 1969. Esquire 73:86+ My '70
(tr) See Virgil. Two eclogues of Virgil

SLAYMAKER, S. R. 2d
Meet the streamerettes. il pors Outdoor Life 145:98-100+ Ap '70

SLED dog racing. See Dog racing

SLEDGES. See Sleighs and sleighing

SLEEP
Changes of simple and complex spike activity of cerebellar Purkinje cells with sleep and waking. N. I. Mano. bibliog il Science 170:1325-7 D 18 '70
Cortical unit activity in desynchronized sleep. R. W. McCarley and J. A. Hobson. bibliog il Science 167:901-3 F 6 '70
Evolution of sleep. T. Allison and H. Van Twyer. il pors Natur Hist 79:56-65 F '70
Facilitation of spindle-burst sleep by conditioning of electroencephalographic activity while awake. M. B. Sterman and others. bibliog il Science 167:1146-8 F 20 '70
How did you sleep last night? C. Coiro. il Har Yrs 10:22-5 Ag '70
How much sleep do you need? interview. J. Segal. il por U S News 69:30-4 D 28 '70
Light sleepers more active than long sleepers. A. J. Snider. Sci Digest 68:61 S '70
Need for sleep and dreams. J. Brothers. Good H 171:54+ N '70
Sleep and emotions; research findings of E. L. Hartmann. Time 95:53 Je 29 '70
Sleep stage characteristics of long and short sleepers. W. B. Webb and H. W. Agnew, jr. bibliog il Science 168:146-7 Ap 3 '70
Your nose is a sleep monitor. A. J. Snider. il Sci Digest 67:52-3 Ap '70
See also
Narcolepsy

SLEEP (birds)
Paradoxical sleep in two species of avian predator (falconiformes) J. A. Rojas-Ramirez and E. S. Tauber. bibliog il Science 167:1754-5 Mr 27 '70

SLEEP habits of animals. See Animals—Habits and behavior

SLEEP walking. See Somnambulism

SLEEPING bags
Air sleeping bags before using. Camp Mag 42:25 Je '70
How to pick a sleeping bag. il Changing T 24:19-20 S '70
Paper sleeping paraphernalia. J. B. Miller. il Consumer Bul 53:23-6 Ap '70
Say it's only a paper. C. Conley. il Field & S 74:185 Mr '70
Sleeping bags to dream on. il McCalls 98:46-9+ D '70

SLEEPWALKING. See Somnambulism

SLEIGHS and sleighing
Tote road and the pung. H. Krueger. il Cons 24:29-31 F '70

SLEPIAN, Edward L.
Foolproof fuel supplies. Motor B 125:14+ Je '70
Gourmet afloat. il Motor B 125:60+ Je; 126:132-3 Jl; 108-10 Ag '70
Is your head screwed on right? il Motor B 126:23+ Jl '70

SLEUTH; drama. See Shaffer, A.

SLICES. See Knots and splices

SLIDE rule
Slide rule as a frequency calculator. L. R. Bishop. Electr World 83:53 My '70

SLIDE projectors. See Projectors

SLIDES, Color. See Transparencies

SLIDING doors. See Doors, Sliding

SLIFKIN, Malcolm, and others
Growth in vitro of cells from hyperplastic nodules of liver induced by 2-fluorenylacetamide or aflatoxin B_1. bibliog il Science 167:285-7 Ja 16 '70

SLIME molds
Actomyosin from physarum polycephalum: electron microscopy of myosin-enriched preparations. V. T. Nachmias and W. C. Ingram. bibliog il Science 170:743-5 N 13 '70

SLINGS. See Bandages and bandaging
SLIP covers
How to make your own slipcovers. il Bet Hom & Gard 48:132-6 Mr '70
Slipcover on a budget with dazzling pattern on pattern. il McCalls 97:62-7 Jl '70
SLIPCOVERS. See Slip covers
SLIPHER, Vesto Melvin
V. M. Slipher's trailblazing career. J. S. Hall. il pors Sky & Tel 39:84-6 F '70 *
SLOAN, Alfred P. foundation. See Alfred P. Sloan foundation
SLOAN, Anthony, pseud.
Oedipus; adaptation of play by Sophocles. Criticism
Time 95:54 Mr 9 '70 *
SLOANE, Ruth F.
Innocent abroad. il House B 112:42+ Ap '70
SLOCHOWER, Harry
Camus' The stranger: the silent society and the ecstasy of rage; address February 9, 1969. Am Imago 26:291-4 Fall '69
SLOCUM, Michael
Why I shun headphones. Hi Fi sec I 20:59 F '70
SLOGANS
All together now; new old phrase used in ads. il Time 96:86 O 5 '70
Bring-us-together girl. il por Newsweek 75:16 Je 1 '70
That Milwaukee slogan stems from Chicago's fire. R. A. Uihlein, jr. il Nations Bsns 58:104-5 Ja '70
SLONIGER, Jerry
New boost for turbocharged cars. il Pop Sci 196:50+ My '70
SLOOPS
Clearwater's cargo is a message: stop pollution. R. Gannon. il Pop Sci 197:70-2+ Ag '70

Design
Classic boats in fiberglass. B. Cobb, jr. il Yachting 129:100-1+ Ja '71
Custom ocean racing sloop. L. J. Cross. il por Yachting 128:35+ Ag '70

Equipment
Customizing the Cal 20. L. J. Kennedy. il Motor B 125:52-5 Ap '70

Maintenance and repair
It can be done; damaged fiberglass hull made like new. R. M. Booz and T. Cobb. il Yachting 128:55-7 O '70
Long life of a great lady. W. B. Lockwood. il Motor B 125:60-1+ Ap '70
Reconstructing fiberglass. T. Cobb. il Yachting 128:154 N '70
SLOTEMAKER, Rob
School for skids. E. Dahlquist. il por Motor T 22:101-2 Ap '70 *
SLOTTEN, Ralph
Lent; poem. Chr Cent 87:317 Mr 18 '70
SLOVAK, Mira J.
Where are they now? il pors Newsweek 76:12 O 26 '70 *
SLOW learning children
Slow learner; symposium. il Todays Ed 59:42-51 Mr '70

Education
Art and the slow learner. M. G. Emlen. il Sch Arts 69:10-12 Mr '70
Reaching the unreached. B. Foy. il Todays Ed 59:44-6 Mr '70
Teaching strategies for the slow-learning social studies student. B. Davis. Ed Digest 35:43-5 Ap '70
Vocabulary for slow learners. N. J. Doemel. Engl J 59:78-80 Ja '70
SŁOWACKI, Juliusz
From the Nile to . . .; poem, tr. by R. K. Wilson. il Harp Baz 104:78-9 D '70
SLOWDOWN strikes. See Strikes
SLOYAN, Gerard S.
Is there any hope for liturgy? Commonweal 92:56-60 Mr 27 '70
SLUDGE as fertilizer. See Sewage as fertilizer
SLUM clearance. See Urban renewal
SLUMS
Ecology of a ghetto. il Time 95:48+ Ap 6 '70
Ghetto schools are different. B. E. Patrick. Nat R 22:401-4 Ap 21 '70
Local political leadership and popular discontent in the ghetto. P. H. Rossi and R. A. Berk. bibliog f il Ann Am Acad 391:111-27 S '70
New mythology of housing. A. M. Stegman. il Trans-Action 7:55-62 Ja '70
Peck of salt: a year in the ghetto, by J. T. Hough, jr. Review
America 123:547+ D 19 '70. B. N. Odell

Poverty in the urban ghetto. J. F. Bauman. bibliog f Cur Hist 59:283-9+ N '70
Separatism? We are separated and that's the cause of all our woes. W. M. Young, jr. il por Ebony 25:90-1+ Ag '70
Squatters of Miffland; report. R. Rein. il por Time 96:19 N 9 '70
Theory of the lower class: Edward Banfield, the maverick of urbanology. R. Todd. Atlan 226:51-5 S '70
Vertical ghetto; Cabrini-Green, Chicago. il Newsweek 76:76 S 7 '70
SLURRY seal. See Pavements—Surface treatment
SLUSSER, Dorothy M.
Healing narratives in Mark. Chr Cent 87:597-9 My 13 '70
SMALES, A. A. and others
Elemental composition of lunar surface material. bibliog il Science 167:509-12 Ja 30 '70
SMALL, Dorothy May
Nature's jewels; photographs. Am For 76:64-5 O; 44-5 D 5 '70
SMALL, Melvin, and Singer, J. D.
Patterns in international warfare, 1816-1965. bibliog f il Ann Am Acad 391:145-55 S '70
SMALL business
Small business eyes the four-day workweek. K. E. Wheeler. il Harvard Bsns R 48:142-7 My '70
So you'd like to go into business for yourself. il Changing T 24:43-6 F '70
Wage boom busts Japan's small business. il Bsns W p44 Ag 22 '70
See also
Franchise system

Finance
Future of minority business; interview. M. H. Stans. por U S News 69:41-2 N 23 '70
SMALL business administration. See United States—Small business administration
SMALL business investment companies
Let's write off MESBICs. R. S. Rosenbloom and J. K. Shank. Harvard Bsns R 48:90-7 S '70; Reply. M. H. Stans. 48:170-1 N '70
Piece of the action; SBA's MESBIC program. R. C. Siciliano. il Nations Bsns 58:56-9 Mr '70
Plan to utilize West coast aerospace unemployed proposed; regional investment promotion corporations to encourage establishment of new businesses. Aviation W 93:61 N 30 '70
Students flunk at new ideas; Globus, inc, offer. V. Louviere. Nations Bsns 58:14 Jl '70
Testing black capitalism. B. L. Masse. America 123:491-2 D 5 '70
See also
Chase Manhattan capital corporation
Narragansett capital corporation
SMALL colleges
Has the small college a future? H. S. Commager. il Sat R 53:62-4+ F 21 '70
Small colleges: football 1970. il Sports Illus 33:88+ S 14 '70
They don't play no mullets down there; small-college football. P. Putnam. il Sports Illus 33:20-5 N 2 '70

Finance
Small arts colleges confront crisis in science funding. J. Walsh. Science 170:611 N 6 '70
SMALL families. See Family, Size of
SMALL intestine. See Intestines
SMALL loan companies. See Finance companies
SMALL magazine editors and publishers committee. See Committee of small magazine editors and publishers
SMALL publishers company
Small publishers' company: co-op in the age of conglomerates. A. Caruba. il Pub W 198:30-1 Ag 24 '70
SMALL-town girl; story. See Cave, H.
SMALL town life. See Village life
SMALLMOUTH fishing. See Bass fishing
SMALLPEICE, Sir Basil
New bearings. por Forbes 106:31-2 Ag 15 '70 *
SMALLPOX
Case of panic; outbreak in North Rhine-Westphalia. il Newsweek 75:86 F 16 '70
Closing in on three killers. il Bsns W p 110 O 24 '70
Smallpox in the air. il Newsweek 76:121-2 N 16 '70
See also
Vaccination
SMART, Alice F.
Tropical fruits. il Horticulture 48:28-9+ N '70
SMEETON, Miles
Third time lucky (cont) Yachting 127:100-2+ Ja '70

SMITH, Herbert E.
Hall of flame. il Har Yrs 10:19 Ja '70
New bit of Americana. il Har Yrs 10:13 Jl '70
SMITH, Hilary
Back to the drawing boards. America 122:
591-2 My 30 '70
SMITH, Howard Kingsbury
Siding with Agnew. por Newsweek 75:84 Mr
9 '70
SMITH, J. W. and Kaplan, I. R.
Endogenous carbon in carbonaceous meteor-
ites. bibliog il Science 167:1367-70 Mr 6 '70
—See Kaplan, I. R. jt. auth.
SMITH, Jack
Gadgets and gilhickies. See issues of Yacht-
ing
SMITH, James Reginald
Ghetto youth are this doctor's bag. il pors
Ebony 25:100-2+ S '70 *
SMITH, Janetta
Karton kooks. il Sch Arts 69:10-11 Je '70
SMITH, Jean
At Christmas we know what we haven't got.
Redbook 136:82-3+ D '70
To be somebody someday. il por Redbook
135:86-7+ My '70
SMITH, Jean (library trustee)
Library trustee role questioned at Chicago;
summary of address, January 1970. Li-
brary J 95:839 Mr 1 '70
SMITH, Joan (Irvine)
Irvine case. il por Forbes 105:44-5+ Je 1 '70 *
SMITH, John
No! Not John Smith! P. Putnam. il pors
Sports Illus 33:10-13 Jl 6 '70 *
SMITH, John, pseud.
Power in the House. New Repub 162:10 My
30 '70
SMITH, John C.
Delectations. Nat R 22:262 Mr 10 '70
SMITH, John Gettys
Charms of Charleston. il Travel & Camera
33:28-33+ F '70
SMITH, John L.
Breaking the diploma barrier. il por Time
96:49 S 7 '70 *
SMITH, Joseph E.
Singer: a new way to make money? A.
Hershman. por Duns 95:22-3+ Ja '70
SMITH, Joseph Fielding
New prophet. pors Newsweek 75:71 F 2 '70
Prophet, seer and innovator. por Time 95:
49-50 F 2 '70
SMITH, Joseph Russell
J. Russell Smith's great organic idea. R.
Rodale. il Org Gard & Farm 17:28-33 S
'70 *
SMITH, Joseph Victor, and Mason, Brian
Pyroxene-garnet transformation in Coorara
meteorite. bibliog il Science 168:832-3 My
15 '70
SMITH, Karl E.
Lonely passion of Karl E. Smith. T. Tyler.
il por Time 96:16 Jl 20 '70 *
SMITH, Kay
From amateur to pro in the article market.
Writer 83:22-3+ Ap '70
SMITH, Ken
Suburb; poem. Nation 212:88 Ja 18 '71
SMITH, Kenneth E.
People chose sacks over cans. il Am City
85:82-3 Je '70
SMITH, Lacy Baldwin
Great confrontations: Leo X and Luther. il
pors Horizon 12:90-5 Spr '70
SMITH, Liz
Caroline Kennedy at thirteen. il por Ladies
Home J 87:84+ N '70
Great homes away from home: the Green-
brier. il Am Home 73:66+ My '70
New York life of Jacqueline Onassis. il por
Ladies Home J 87:56+ F '70
$10,000,000 jewels of Elizabeth Taylor & Jac-
queline Onassis. il pors Ladies Home J 86:
64+ D '69
SMITH, M. See Von Tigerstrom, R. jt. auth.
SMITH, Maggie
People are talking about . . . por Vogue 156:
82-3 Ag 15 '70 *
Prime of Miss Downbeat. por Time 95:72+
Ap 20 '70 *
SMITH, Margaret
Fierce lass in quest of an elusive title. G.
S. Brown. por Sports Illus 33:94-6 S 14 '70 *
Maggie and the little master. il por Time
96:53 S 28 '70 *
Sporting scene. H. W. Wind. New Yorker 46:
172-4+ O 10 '70 *
SMITH, Margaret (Chase)
Remembrance of Christmas. il House B 112:
56-7 D '70
U.S. faces choice between anarchy and re-
pression; address June 1, 1970. il pors U S
News 68:45-6 Je 15 '70
Voice of reason: call to the center; excerpts
from address. por Time 95:13 Je 15 '70

We talk to. .; interview. por Mlle 71:298
Ag '70
about
Church women united honor Margaret Chase
Smith. Chr Cent 87:659 My 6 '70 *
SMITH, Mary Alice
Obituary
Craft Horiz por 30:5 D '70. J. L. Larsen
SMITH, Merriman
Thank you, Mr Smith. por Newsweek 75:94
Ap 27 '70 *
SMITH, Morley B.
Kid crafts. il Bet Hom & Gard 48:4+ Ag '70
SMITH, Mortimer
What's ahead for our schools? il Parents
Mag 45:49-51+ S '70
SMITH, Ned
Wildlife sketchbook. See issues of National
wildlife
SMITH, Nicole Schupf, and Coons, E. E.
Temporal summation and refractoriness in
hypothalamic reward neurons as measured
by self-stimulation behavior. bibliog il Sci-
ence 169:782-5 Ag 21 '70
SMITH, Nila Banton
Reading instruction in the elementary school;
excerpts from address, February 1969. To-
days Ed 59:42-3+ Ja '70
Up-to-date glossary of common terms used
by reading instructors and informed li-
brarians. il por Wilson Lib Bul 45:246-53 N
'70
SMITH, Norma E.
Set me free; poem. Negro Hist Bul 33:41 F
'70
SMITH, Otis M.
Otis M. Smith, distinguished judge, attorney
and Michigan first. Negro Hist Bul 33:128
My '70 *
SMITH, Patrick
Still burning trees; poem. America 123:561 D
26 '70
SMITH, Patrick J.
(ed) Book reviews (cont) Hi Fi 20:secII
29:30 My; 28-30 Jl; MA29-31 S; MA30-2 N
'70
Le Comte Ory, with verve. il Hi Fi sec II 20:
26 Ja '70
How to read a libretto. il Opera N 34:13-15
Mr 7 '70
SMITH, Peter
Ten towns in New York. il Sch Arts 69:18-
19 Ap '70
SMITH, Philip M.
International cooperation in Antarctica, the
next decade. il por Bul Atom Sci 26:29-32
D '70
SMITH, R. H.
George tells it to Marvin. Nat R 23:34 Ja 12
'71
SMITH, Ralph H.
Public hearings express pros and cons of
pesticide use. il Cons 25:2-4 O '70
SMITH, Ralph Lee
Law and order 1970. il Nation 210:774-83 Je
29 '70
Wired nation. il Nation 210:582-606 My 18 '70
SMITH, Ralph Tyler
They're after Adlai. P. R. Wieck. New Repub
163:13-15 S 26 '70 *
SMITH, Ralston Fox
Day camp develops year-round operation. il
Camp Mag 42:10-11 N '70
SMITH, Ray Winfield
Computer helps scholars re-create an Egyptian
temple. il pors Nat Geog 138:634-55 N '70
SMITH, Richard J.
Spelling in the elementary school. Ed Digest
36:44-6 D '70
SMITH, Robert B.
Rebellion and repression and the Vietnam war.
bibliog f il Ann Am Acad 391:156-67 S '70
SMITH, Robert C.
Masterpieces of early American furniture
at the United States Department of state.
il Antiques 98:766-73 N '70
SMITH, Robert W.
How businessmen pitched in to save a city.
il pors Nations Bsns 58:44-8 D '70 *
SMITH, Roberta Anderson
Sack of corn candy. il Har Yrs 10:14-15 Ap
'70
To you, now. il por Har Yrs 10:42-3 S '70
SMITH, Roy C. 3d
Truce negotiations of San Martin. il por
Américas 22:31-3 O '70
SMITH, Ruth B.
(comp) Calendar of coming events. See issues
of Motor boating
SMITH, Scottie (Fitzgerald) See McLendon, W.
jt. auth.
SMITH, Sherwin D.
Study of the San Andreas fault: something
very interesting is going on deep beneath
the earth's surface. il N Y Times Mag p 16-
17+ Ja 18 '70

SMITH, Stephen Edward
Goldilocks may not be the most exciting fellow in town but he's the only one who can win this year. R. Reeves. il pors N Y Times Mag p7+ Je 14 '70 *

SMITH, Stevie
Comment. J. McGann. Poetry 117:195-7 D '70 *

SMITH, Ted
Ted Smith; the phoenix flies again. P. Garrison. por Flying 87:35-7 Ag '70 *

SMITH, Tom
North Sea. il Travel 133:28-33 Mr '70

SMITH, Tony
Sculpture by order. il por Time 96:72 S 14 '70 *

SMITH, Vertie C. See Peck, L. C. jt. auth.

SMITH, W. B.
Venus radius controversy. bibliog Science 169:1001-2 S 4 '70

SMITH, W. Eugene
Gallery; photographs. Life 69:4-7 S 4 '70

about

W. Eugene Smith, passionate involvement with Life. W. Hicks. il Mod Phot 34:88-93 Ja '70 *

SMITH, W. V.
Research management. Science 167:957-9 F 13 '70

SMITH, William Henry
Internal revenue service; address, May 12, 1970. Vital Speeches 36:660-9 Ag 15 '70

SMITH, William Jay
What train will come? poem. New Repub 162: 20-2 Ja 24 '70

SMITH ISLAND
Cruise back in time. E. Nabb. il Motor B 126: 50-3 Jl '70

SMITH-Corona-Marchant. See SCM corporation

SMITH-Haven ministries, L.I. See Church work with youth

SMITHIES, Oliver
Pathways through networks of branched DNA. il Science 169:882-3 Ag 28 '70

SMITHIES, Ronald H.
You and your diet. See issues of Good housekeeping

SMITHSONIAN institution
Skirmish at the Smithsonian. il por Bsns W p 128+ F 21 '70
Smithsonian: natural history is undernourished, panel finds. L. J. Carter. Science 169:960-3 S 4 '70

Center for short-lived phenomena

Early warning system for happenings in nature; Center for short-lived phenomena. K. Auchincloss. il N Y Times Mag p 129-32 Ap 12 '70
Lab that hops on happenings. J. F. Pearson. il Pop Mech 134:96-9+ Jl '70
Long live the short-lived phenomena. Sci Digest 67:26-7 Ap '70
Something's strange at the Smithsonian. J. O'Connell. il Sci Digest 68:78-82 O '70

Museum of history and technology

Saints and brothers; exhibit of Spanish arts in the Americas. R. E. Ahlborn. il Américas 22:6-13 S '70

SMITS, Barbara
Green Bay wildlife sanctuary. il Nat Parks & Con Mag 44:21-3 Ag '70

SMITSON, Walter S.
Foster mothers and mental patients. bibliog il Ment Hy 54:251-5 Ap '70

SMOG
Donora, Pennsylvania; smog episode of October 1948. C. Bowen. Atlan 226:27-8+ N '70
Here comes the smog. il Newsweek 76:64-5 Ag 10 '70
Let's hear it for Mr Clean. R. Starnes. Field & S 75:10+ S '70
Smog aerosol; infrared spectra. E. R. Stephens and M. A. Price. bibliog il Science 168:1584-6 Je 26 '70
Smog goes global; a bad week in the cities; power shortage in New York. il Time 96: 37-9 Ag 10 '70
See also
Los Angeles—Air pollution

SMOG; story. See Calvino, I.

SMOG control devices. See Automobile engines —Exhaust

SMOKE
See also
Cigarette smoke
Smog

SMOKE cookery. See Barbecue cookery

SMOKE prevention
Smog threat over the Thames. il Bsns W p58 O 24 '70

SMOKEY Bear. See Advertising characters

SMOKING
Case against smoking. R. M. Taylor. il UNESCO Courier 23:14-16 My '70
Caution: cigarette smoking may be hazardous to your health; smoking clinics' lack of success. Trans-Action 7:14 Jl '70
Cigar smoking kid grows up. il pors Ebony 25:58-60+ F '70
Cigarettes and cancer. G. Godber. il UNESCO Courier 23:10-13 My '70
Doctor Spence is a misocapnist. L. Witt. il pors Todays Health 48:16-17 My '70
How hypnosis may help you to quit smoking. il Good H 170:164 F '70
Kicking the habit. il Newsweek 75:80+ Mr 2 '70
Kicking the habit on the high seas; Santa Paula's stop-smoking cruise. Bsns W p31 S 26 '70
Kicking the habit; report on Santa Paula's stop-smoking cruise. B. McCabe. il Time 96: 64 D 14 '70
Kicking the smoking habit. Time 95:58 Mr 2 '70
Last gasp for cigarettes? smoking dogs research. S. M. Spencer. Read Digest 96:92-5 Ap '70
New hope for heavy smokers. O. Auerbach and S. M. Spencer. Read Digest 96:129-31 F '70
Puff is a four-letter word, says smokefighting agency. Todays Health 49:70 Ja '71
Six smoker types. A. J. Snider. Sci Digest 68:43 O '70
Smoke-out in a small town. il Todays Health 48:44-7 Je '70
Smoker's paradise; life expectancy in the U.S. Sci Am 223:53 O '70
Smoking and cancer in dogs. Time 95:48 F 16 '70
Smoking dogs: Tobacco institute tries to discount cancer studies. R. J. Bazell. il Science 170:515 O 30 '70
Those smoking statistics: fact or distortion? T. Irwin. il Todays Health 48:34-7+ Ap '70
Today's antismoking campaign will succeed. L. L. Terry. il Todays Health 48:20-2+ F '70
Tumors in smoking dogs. Sci N 97:169 F 14 '70
Weight and the weed; research at Temple university school of medicine. il Newsweek 76:62 Jl 27 '70
Women's liberation. Sci Am 223:82 S '70

History

Anticigarette crusades that failed. W. Garrison. il Todays Health 48:23-5 F '70

SMOKING accessories
See also
Ash trays

SMOKING and youth
Cigar smoking kid grows up. il pors Ebony 25:58-60+ F '70
Seminar, or suspension? Education or punishment for teen-age smokers? M. Herzog. Clear House 45:146-9 N '70
Seven ways to keep your child from smoking. R. B. Prowitt. il Parents Mag 45:42-3 Ap '70
To smoke or not to smoke; excerpts from address, March 1970. D. Patton. por PTA Mag 64:6-7 Je '70

SMOKING on aircraft
Smoking in aircraft under attack in Congress, by citizens groups. Aviation W 92:29 Ja 19 '70

SMOKY MOUNTAINS. See Great Smoky Mountains

SMOLUCHOWSKI, R.
Jupiter's convection and its red spot. bibliog Science 168:1340-2 Je 12 '70

SMOTHERS, Tom
Never gonna be a country boy again. il pors Look 34:70-4 F 24 '70

SMOTHERS brothers
Mom always loved them best. D. Brudnoy. Nat R 22:1009+ S 22 '70 *
Painful passing. R. L. Shayon. Sat R 53:48 O 3 '70 *
Return of the Smothers. Time 95:90 Mr 30 '70 *

SMUGGLING
Americans abroad; the jail scene. il Time 95: 36 Ap 13 '70
Conspiracy in Ireland; arms smuggling. S. Cronin. Commonweal 93:188-90 N 20 '70
Customs inspectors miss a lot, but don't count on it. J. Lee and B. Lee. il Holiday 47:36-7+ Ap '70
Open season on drug smugglers; with interview by W. B. Leithead, ed. by J. Fincher. R. Chelminski. il Life 68:28-35 Je 26 '70

SMUGGLING—*Continued*
Smugglers of misery; massive drug-smuggling industry. W. Schulz. Read Digest 96:49-54 Ap '70
Where smuggling is a way of life: Latin America. il Bsns W p24-5 Ag 15 '70
SMYLIE, James H.
On being Presbyterian in the South. Chr Cent 87:936-40 Ag 5 '70
SMYTH, Coke. See Smyth, J. R. C.
SMYTH, John Richard Coke
Bartlett forgeries: Coke Smyth originals. R. Davidson. il Antiques 97:202+ F '70 *
SMYTH, Paul
Portrait; poem. Atlan 225:114 My '70
SMYTH, Pete
America's cup 1970. il Motor B 126:40-3+ Ag '70
Buxom belle named Banjer. il Motor B 125:134-9+ Mr '70
History of distance racing. il Motor B 125:70-5+ Je '70
Miami's glamour boats. il Motor B 125:48-55+ F '70
SMYTHE, Linda
Capital's proud black princess. il pors Ebony 25:104-7 Jl '70 *
SMYTHE, Sandra
How to get an idea for your novel if you don't already have one. Writers Digest 50:20-2 Mr '70
SMYTHE, William D. See Miller, S. L. jt. auth.
SNACK diet. See Diet
SNACKS
After-school snacks. il Ebony 25:144A+ S '70
Off-camera snacks at TV talk shows. il McCalls 97:96-7+ F '70
What's cooking?
  A bowlful of seeds 'n raisins, homegrown, that is. M. C. Goldman. il Org Gard & Farm 17:112+ S '70
  Wise snack, no nutritional joke. G. Maddox. il Todays Health 48:60-3 Mr '70
SNAILS
That edible land snail. A. G. Melvin. il Hobbies 75:147+ My '70
SNAKE bite. See Venom
SNAKE charmers
India's incredible snake charmers. B. L. Burman. il Read Digest 97:49-50+ O '70
SNAKE RIVER
Last great dam. B. Norton. il Audubon 72:12-27 Ja '70
Wilderness and the living Middle Snake. R. Mager. il Liv Wildn 33:8-11 Aut '69
  See also
  Hells Canyon
SNAKES
How good are you as a herpetologist? quiz. J. Daugherty and M. Daugherty. il Sci Digest 67:78-9+ Ap '70
How snakes move. C. Gans. il Sci Am 222:82-6+ bibliog(p 152) Je '70
Manhattan snakes: DeKay's snake, or the northern brown snake. New Yorker 46:29-30 S 19 '70
Snake safari with camera and courage. K. Severin. il por Sci Digest 68:38-47 N '70
  See also
  Boa constrictors
  Cobras
  Rattlesnakes
SNAKES, Photography of. See Photography of reptiles
SNAKES in religion, folklore, etc. See Serpents in religion, folklore etc.
SNAPP, Thomas
July and the boat; poem. New Yorker 46:72 Je 27 '70
SNAPPING turtles. See Turtles
SNARR, Douglas T.
Cracking the highway trust. il por Time 95:59 Je 15 '70 *
SNEAD, Sam
Best in the South; interview, ed. by D. Green. il por Travel & Camera 33:46-51 F '70
SNEAKERS
  See also
  Shoes
SNEEM, Ireland
Irish sketches. J. McCarten. New Yorker 46:109-11 S 12; 127-9 O 31 '70
SNEIDER, Vern
Vin du pays: American style. il Holiday 47:60-1 My '70
SNELL, David
Willie York from Big East Fork. il pors Life 69:53-8 Jl 17 '70
SNELLING, Robert O.
Seven days to turn off turnover. il Nations Bsns 58:58-60 O '70

SNIDER, Arthur J.
Giants and midgets. il Sci Digest 69:62-6 Ja '71
Medicine. See issues of Science digest
SNIPS (tools) See Metal cutting tools
SNITZER, Milton S.
More on the Scheiber system. il Electr World 84:43 D '70
Scheiber 4-channel stereo system. il Electr World 84:43+ S '70
SNOBS and snobbishness
How to package Christmas. R. Lynes. Art in Am 58:39 N '70
People who. W. Stanton. Sat R 53:9 D 19 '70
SNODGRESS, Carrie
Five young beauties & how they get that way. il pors Mlle 72:135-41 N '70 *
SNOOK, Patrick K.
Prescott kids go wild. il por Nat Wildlife 8:4-11 F '70
Ski touring comes to America. il Nat Wildlife 8:20-3 D '69
We houseboated down the mighty Miss. il por Nat Wildlife 8:38-42 Ag '70
SNOUTERS. See Animals, imaginary
SNOW, Charles Percy, baron Snow of Leicester. See Snow of Leicester, C. P. S.
SNOW, Joel A.
IRRPOS looks for relevance to society's problems. J. B. Phelps. il por Phys Today 23:61-2 N '70 *
SNOW, Philip. See Snow of Leicester, C. P. S. jt. auth.
SNOW of Leicester, Charles Percy Snow, baron—and Snow, Philip
Hope for America. Look 34:30+ D 1 '70
  about
Strangers and brothers. R. A. Sokolov. pors Newsweek 76:88+ Ag 17 '70 *
SNOW
Deuterium content of snow cores from Sierra Nevada area. I. Friedman and G. I. Smith. bibliog il Science 169:467-70 Jl 31 '70
From snowflake to avalanche. E. R. LaChapelle. il Natur Hist 79:30-8 F '70
Snow prediction, a formidable challenge. D. B. Spiegler. bibliog il Weatherwise 23:212-20 O '70
Snowfall season of 1968-69. D. M. Ludlum. il Weatherwise 23:24-31 F '70
Snowstorm; with photographs by S. Bullaty and A. Lomeo. H. Borland. il Audubon 72:4-13 Ja '70
Winter in Yosemite; photographs. D. Muench. il Nat Wildlife 8:44-7 F '70
  See also
  Snowstorms
SNOW algae. See Algae
SNOW and ice removal
Fresh look at graders, flexible heavyweights; Duluth, Minn. il Am City 85:44 O '70
Hope for the best; plan for the worst; New York city's snow program. il Am City 85:74+ N '70
Snow and ice control. See issues of American city
Snow comes right off the cabin roof. il Sunset 144:148 Mr '70
  See also
  Airports—Snow and ice removal
  Laws and regulations
Keep snow regulations realistic. il Am City 85:20 D '70
SNOW blowers, throwers, etc.
Round up of the 1970 snowblowers. il Home Gard 57:38-41+ N '70
Safety rules for using snow throwers. il Good H 172:125 Ja '71
What you should know about the new snow throwers. E. F. Lindsley. il Pop Sci 197:16+ D '70
SNOW ecology
Life in a snowbank. R. Gilluly. il Sci N 98:80-1 Jl 25 '70
SNOW fences
Slotted windbreaks stop winter drafts. Suc Farm 68:no5 B13 Mr '70
SNOW geese. See Geese, Wild
SNOW machines
High pressure snowmaking. W. B. Hovey. il Weatherwise 23:224-7 O '70
New method of snowmaking. G. Wollin and others. il por Weatherwise 23:228-30+ O '70
SNOW melters. See Snow removal equipment
SNOW modeling
Snow modeling; fun for the entire family. il Good H 171:161 D '70
SNOW monkeys. See Monkeys
SNOW MOUNTAIN wilderness area (proposed) See Wilderness areas—California
SNOW plows
You can keep snow out of driveways; solution in Spokane. G. A. Yake. il Am City 85:63-4 Ag '70

SNOW regulations. See Snow and ice removal
—Laws and regulations
SNOW removal equipment
Flame gun for the gardener; jet rod model.
il Consumer Bul 53:20-1 Jl '70
Ice and snow melters. il Consumer Bul 53:
21-2 F '70
SNOW removal equipment. Municipal
How to keep the snow-plows moving; California division of highways. H. C. Ammon.
il Am City 85:36 F '70
Out newest snowfighter works all year; New
Canaan, Conn. L. Wood and E. Peck. il
Am City 85:54-5 D '70
Plan before you plow; Brooklyn Center, Minn.
H. Davis. il Am City 85:30 Ja '70
See also
Salt spreaders

Leasing and renting
How to use contractors for snow removal;
Baltimore County, Md. A. F. Jungers. il Am
City 85:79-81 O '70
SNOW sculpture. See Snow modeling
SNOW slides. See Avalanches
SNOW storms. See Snowstorms
SNOW surfing. See Skis and skiing
SNOW throwers. See Snow blowers, throwers, etc.
SNOW tire studs. See Tires, Automobile
SNOWBANK ecology. See Snow ecology
SNOWDEN, Donald P.
Superconducting power transmission; adaptation of address. bibliog Phys Today 23:
42-3 D '70
SNOWDON, Antony Charles Robert Armstrong-Jones, 1st earl of
Sir says: a visit with Sir Lawrence Olivier;
photographs. il pors Look 34:22-6 Ja 27 '70
Sophia Loren; photographs. il por Vogue 156:
124-36 D '70
about
Lord Snowdon on pets. il por Time 96:48 Jl
6 '70 *
Margaret and Tony, the royal black sheep.
A. Duncan. il pors Look 34:43-6+ My 19
'70 *
Princess Margaret and Lord Snowdon: their
battles royal. A. Chatsworth. pors Ladies
Home J 87:60+ Ag '70 *
SNOWFLAKES. See Snow
SNOWMOBILE camping. See Camping
SNOWMOBILE engines
Spunky, new engine for snowmobiles. M.
Lamm. il Pop Mech 135:34F+ Ja '71
Super-scavenged snowmobile engine. H. Shuldiner. il Pop Sci 197:53 D '70
SNOWMOBILE insurance. See Insurance, Motor vehicle
SNOWMOBILE racing
U.S. journal: Brainerd, Minn. fifth annual
Paul Bunyan snowmobile derby. C. Trillin.
New Yorker 45:68-71+ Ja 24 '70
SNOWMOBILE shelters. See Snowmobiles--Storage
SNOWMOBILES

Government use
New York's snow patrol. L. R. Fendrick. il
Cons 25:21-2 D '70

Maintenance and repair
Five easy steps to summerize your snowmobile. il Pop Sci 196:100-1 Ap '70
Go alone, but safely! B. Milek. il Field & S
75:40-1+ D '70
Taking care of a snowmobile. il Mech Illus
66:98-100+ D '70

Storage
Drive-thru snowmobile shelter. J. Capotosto.
il Mech Illus 66:108-10 N '70
SNOWMOBILES and snowmobiling
Cruising the Cascades. G. W. Reiger. il Pop
Mech 134:132-7+ N '70
For snowmobilers: now there's a $300 kit.
E. F. Lindsley. il Pop Sci 197:142 N '70
Forests' prime evil. Sports Illus 34:5 Ja 4 '71
Here come the '71 snowmobiles. H. Shuldiner.
il Pop Sci 197:120-1 O '70
How snowmobiles have changed! R. Gannon. il Pop Sci 197:78-9+ S '70
How to use your snowmobile. R. E. Kerr. il
Cons 25:48-9 O '70
Newest winter sport, snowmobile drill teams.
il Mech Illus 66:49 F '70
1971 snowmobile buyer's guide. B. Behme.
il Field & S 75:62-7+ O '70
1971 snowmobiles. il Mech Illus 66:102+ O '70
Pike by snowmobile. P. D. Lane. il Field
& S 75:36-7+ N '70

Sand mobile? converted snowmobile. F.
Taylor. il Pop Mech 134:82-3 Ag '70
Sap 'n snowmobiles. G. W. Reiger. il Pop
Mech 134:104-6 D '70
Shopping hints for snowmobilers. il Pop Sci
196:88-9 Ja '70
Six snowmobile emergencies. il Pop Sci 196:48
Mr '70
Snowmobile safari; Minnesota's Superior national forest. C. R. Meyer. il Field & S 74:
62-3+ Ja '70
Snowmobiles in '71. G. Reiger. il Pop Mech
134:130-3+ O '70
Snowmobiles restricted to Baxter park roads.
Nat Parks 44:27 F '70
Time to tame the abominable snowmobiler.
M. Michaelson. il Todays Health 48:46-9+
D '70
See also
Bombardier, ltd.

Accidents and injuries
Bad show out in the cold snow. J. Olsen.
il Sports Illus 32:28-30+ Mr 16 '70; Same
abr. with title Time to control snowmobiles.
Read Digest 97:174-7 D '70

Economic aspects
They put snowmobiles to work. H. Gardner.
il Mech Illus 66:66-8+ Ja '70

Safety devices and measures
Abominable snowmen. E. N. Layne. il Am
Heritage 21:113 F '70
SNOWSHOE hare hunting. See Rabbit hunting
SNOWSLIDES. See Avalanches
SNOWSTORMS
Boston's heaviest snowstorm of record. C.
H. Pierce. il Weatherwise 22:230-5 D '69
From above: Denver snowstorm 15 Oct. 1969.
il Weatherwise 22:251 D '69
Jacques frost; Europe's recent winter weather.
il Time 97:27-8 Ja 18 '71
Prairie blizzard. J. Madson. il Audubon 72:54-6+ Mr '70
Snowburst of 14 March 1969 at Fort Huachuca, Arizona. J. C. Devine. il Weatherwise
22:236-9 D '69
SNUFF
And once again, snuff's the stuff. il Bsns W
p47 Mr 14 '70
SNURFING. See Skis and skiing
SNYDER, Brad
Build this back-yard beauty. il Pop Mech 133:
110-13 My '70
SNYDER, Don
Beyond reason; photographs. Horizon 12:11-19 Spr '70
SNYDER, Helen. See Snyder, N. jt. auth.
SNYDER, Howard A.
Fellowship of the Holy Spirit. Chr Today 15:
4-7 N 6 '70
SNYDER, Jerome. See Chaneles, S.; Glaser, M. jt. auths.
SNYDER, Jim
Power of prayer and a few sharp elbows. P.
Carry. Sports Illus 32:40 F 16 '70 *
SNYDER, L. Michael, and Reddy, W. J.
Thyroid hormone control of erythrocyte 2,3-diphosphoglyceric acid concentrations. bibliog il Science 169:879-80 Ag 28 '70
SNYDER, Lewis D.
Ceramic symposium at Bechyne. il Ceram Mo
18:14-17 N '70
SNYDER, Lewis E. and Buhl, David
Molecules in the interstellar medium. bibliog
il Sky & Tel 40:267-70, 345-8 N-D '70
SNYDER, Noel, and Snyder, Helen
Alarm response of diadema antillarum. bibliog il Science 168:276-8 Ap 10 '70
SNYDER, Richard
To D.M. my writing student, upon his first
submissions; poem. Commonweal 91:430 Ja
16 '70
To the twelfth-chair cellist in the Pittsburgh symphony; poem. Commonweal 93:
249 D 4 '70
SNYDER, Ruby. See Blair, J. R. jt. auth.
SNYDER, Solomon H.
What we have forgotten about pot. il N Y
Times Mag p26-7+ D 13 '70
—See Taylor, K. M. jt. auth.
SO proudly we hail; musical comedy. See Musical comedies, revues, etc.—Criticisms, plots, etc.
SOAP
See also
Shaving soap and cream
Toilet preparations
SOAP operas. See Television broadcasting—Drama
SOAP sculpture
Modern sulpture in soap. L. J. Miller. il
Design 71:30-1 Wint '69

SOARING (aeronautics) See Gliding and soar-
ing
SOBELL, Morton
  Morton Sobell, slightly at large. R. Williams.
    Esquire 73:190-1 Mr '70 *
SOBILOFF, H. J.
  Across the storm; Journey underneath;
    Shells; poems. Poetry 115:334-6 F '70
SOCARRAS RAMIREZ, Armando
  Stowaway! ed. by D. Fodor and J. Reddy.
    il Read Digest 96:62-6 Ja '70
SOCCER
  Chelsea almost won the cup; Chelsea vs
    Leeds a tie. T. Maule. il Sports Illus 32:
    20-3 Ap 20 '70
  One replay that got away; Leeds United. T.
    Maule. Sports Illus 32:78 My 11 '70
  Pelé and pals retire the Cup; Brazilians the
    world champions of soccer. T. Maule. il
    por Sports Illus 32:24-5 Je 29 '70
  Soccer is a frenzy; World cup competition
    in Mexico. T. Maule. il Sports Illus 32:12-17
    Je 22 '70
  Soccer's wild World cup scramble. J. A.
    Michener. il Read Digest 96:173-4+ Je '70
  Something to cheer about; Brazil winning the
    World cup. il por Time 96:32 Jl 6 '79
  Special madness; Brazil wins 1970 World
    cup. il Newsweek 76:55 Jl 6 '70
  Sporting scene; World cup competition. A.
    Reid. New Yorker 46:60-71 Jl 18 '70
SOCCER players
    See also
  Best, G.
SOCIAL action
  Catholic social action: where do we go from
    here? with discussion. E. A. Marciniak.
    il America 123:511-19 D 12 '70; Discussion.
    124:29 Ja 16 '71
  Church and social action. C. Wedel. por Chr
    Cent 87:959-62 Ag 12 '70; Discussion. 87:
    1130-1 S 23 '70
  Time to meet the evangelicals? R. E. Bran-
    son; discussion. Chr Cent 87:115-16 Ja 28
    '70
SOCIAL adjustment. See Adjustment, Social
SOCIAL agencies
  Runaways: a million bad trips; how youth
    agencies try to help. il Newsweek 76:67-8 O
    26 '70
SOCIAL agencies, Voluntary
  Want to help? Here's how: directory, ed. by
    D. R. Maxey. M. M. McGlynn. Look 34:26-7
    Je 16 '70
SOCIAL and economic council of the United
  Nations. See United Nations—Economic
  and social council
SOCIAL aspects of art. See Art and society
SOCIAL behavior of animals. See Animals—
  Habits and behavior
SOCIAL change
  Are we faced with a new aristocracy? W. B.
    Cannon. Cur 124:22-6 D '70
  Bag of scary mush; views of C. A. Reich.
    S. Alsop. Newsweek 76:102 N 9 '70
  Brave new world? Consciousness III. R.
    Lekachman. Duns 96:11 D '70
  Christians and revolution. J. H. Nederhood.
    Chr Today 15:7-9 Ja 1 '71
  Clean break with the past. J. Brooks. il Am
    Heritage 21:4-7+ Ag '70
  Con-manship; Consciousness III; hopes for
    transforming American society. D. M. Al-
    pern. por Newsweek 76:31-2 N 9 '70
  Consciousness III: greening or withering? H.
    B. Kuhn. Chr Today 15:14+ D 18 '70
  Consciousness III; theories of C. A. Reich.
    R. Starr. Commentary 50:46-54 D '70
  Day of the hard-hats. Commonweal 92:283-4
    Je 12 '70
  De Tocqueville revisited; views of J.-F. Rev-
    el. Newsweek 76:44-5 N 9 '70
  Disease of the future. il Time 96:13 Ag 3 '70
  Future shock. A. Toffler. Review
    Sat R 53:39-40 D 12 '70. A. A. Rogow
  Future shock; excerpt. A. Toffler. il Horizon
    12:82-9 Spr '70
  Fuzzy welcome to Cons. III; Consciousness
    III, hoping to transform American society.
    il por Time 96:12-13 N 2 '70
  Great transition. Chr Today 14:20-1 Mr 27 '70
  Greening of a con-III-man. M. Novak. Com-
    monweal 93:245-9 D 4 '70
  Greening of America, by C. A. Reich. Review
    Bsns W il p9-10 N 7 '70. M. J. Ulmer
    Fortune 82:63+ N '70. M. Ways
    New Repub 163:21+ N 14 '70. P. Caws
    Sat R 53:24-6 D 5 '70. R. Eisner
  Here and beyond; books on today's issues for
    children. J. Karl. il por Wilson Lib Bul 45:
    149-55 O '70
  Hierarchical growth. J. Platt. Bul Atom Sci
    26:2-4+ N '70
  Ideology, interests and foreign policy in the
    1970's; address, November 18, 1970. G. C.
    Lodge. Vital Speeches 37:181-6 Ja 1 '71

Indicators of change in political institutions.
  N. E. Long. bibliog f Ann Am Acad 388:
  35-45 Mr '70
Innovation mirage; a culture based on change;
  address, September 9, 1970. J. A. Howard.
  Vital Speeches 36:743-6 O 1 '70
Issues of war and peace: Jesuit educators
  conference. A. Christiansen. America 122:
  302-3 Mr 21 '70
Jug jug jug jug jug tu-whit tu-whoo; end of
  one of the city's most pleasant ways of
  life. J. Ferris. Sat R 53:4 Jl 11 '70
Leadership; address, May 23, 1970. R. F. Delaney. Vital Speeches 36:621-2 Ag 1 '70
Living in a renaissance time. P. W. Schmidtchen. il por Hobbies 75:134-6+ Mr '70
1970 student burgesses at colonial Williamsburg; voices of today, leaders for tomorrow. il Sr Schol 96:18-19 My 4 '70
Of many things; significant student action
  against injustice. D. R. Campion. America
  122:inside cover My 23 '70
Political intelligence for America's future;
  symposium, ed. by B. M. Gross and M.
  Springer. bibliog f il Ann Am Acad 388:1-
  132 Mr '70
Redeeming of America according to Charles
  Reich. A. M. Greeley. America 124:14-17
  Ja 9 '71
Reflections: new generation in relation to
  the corporate state and the new conscious-
  ness. C. A. Reich. New Yorker 46:42-6+ S
  26 '70
Revolution and social change; symposium.
  Cur 118:3-22 My '70
Stone men to the contrary, the time to argue
  is now. B. DeMott. por Life 68:28B Ap 17 '70
Struggle for survival; looking toward the
  year 2000; address, February 18, 1970. L.
  Cherne. Vital Speeches 36:407-11 Ap 15 '70
Technology, change and the citizen; ex-
  cerpts from Technological change. E. G.
  Mesthene. Cur 119:32-6 Je '70
To heal our society's deep rifts. K. Keniston.
  Cur 123:48-56 N '70
Troubling taste of change; John E. Fleck,
  police detective in St Joseph, Mo. D. R.
  Maxey. il Look 34:70-3 Ja 13 '70
View from U.S. 80; with reports from three
  short stops. il Life 70:2-13+ Ja 8 '71
We're shy apes in a cosmic world; interview.
  A. Szent-Györgyi. por Mlle 71:238-9+ Ag '70
What role for social science elites? D. P.
  Moynihan. Cur 124:17-22 D '70
    See also
Educational sociology
Social revolution

Latin America
Encounter in Recife. B. Tyson. il pors Chr
  Cent 87:720-2 Je 10 '70
SOCIAL classes
  Environmental and genetical contributions to
    class difference: a model experiment. J. M.
    Thoday and J. B. Gibson. bibliog il Science
    167:990-2 F 13 '70
  Income and ideology. Trans-Action 7:12 N
    '69
  Last stop on the D train: in the land of the
    new racists. L. Kriegel. Am Scholar 39:272-
    88 Spr '70
  Theory of the lower class: Edward Banfield,
    the maverick of urbanology. R. Todd.
    Atlan 226:51-5 S '70
  Values as social indicators of poverty and
    race relations in America. M. Rokeach and
    S. Parker. bibliog f il Ann Am Acad 388:
    97-111 Mr '70
    See also
  Middle classes
SOCIAL clubs. See Clubs
SOCIAL columnists. See Women as journalists
SOCIAL conditions
  Crisis in development. M. S. Adiseshiah. il
    UNESCO Courier 23:4-14 O '70
    See also
  Civilization
  Social problems
SOCIAL conflict
  Agonistics: rituals of conflict. H. L. Nieburg.
    bibliog f Ann Am Acad 391:56-73 S '70
  Conflict management: preeminent challenge.
    S. Lundstedt. Ment Hy 54:584-8 O '70
  Interpreting collective violence: an argument
    for the importance of social structure. A. D.
    Grimshaw. bibliog f Ann Am Acad 391:9-20
    S '70
  Our contemporary hidden crisis; excerpt from
    Hidden crisis in American politics. S. Lu-
    bell. Cur 123:9-13 N '70
  Politics of resentment; conditions in the
    United States. M. Novak. Commonweal 92:
    481-3 S 25 '70; Same. Cur 123:13-18 N '70
    See also
  Youth-adult relationship

SOCIAL contract
Social contract, by R. Ardrey. Review
Sat R 53:32-4 O 24 '70. M. M. Tumin
SOCIAL crisis games. See Games
SOCIAL democracy. See Socialism
SOCIAL democrats (Germany) See Political
parties—Germany (Federal Republic)
SOCIAL diseases. See Venereal diseases
SOCIAL ecology. See Human ecology
SOCIAL education
Radicalizing liturgy; experiment in exposure
education. J. D. Groppe. Cath World 212:30-4
O '70
Sensitivity modules; to help tear down the
wall of unreality between school and life.
H. Kirschenbaum. Ed Digest 35:16-18 My
'70
Sensitizing modules; making high school
seniors aware of ghetto problems. S. S.
Simon. il Schol Teach Jr/Sr High p28-9+
S 21 '70
Students in the Statehouse. J. B. Arone. To-
days Ed 59:17 O '70
See also
Criminological education
Institute for the study of health and society
Sex instruction
Social sciences—Study and teaching
SOCIAL ethics
New morality and the religious communities.
J. T. Laney. bibliog f Ann Am Acad 387:
14-21 Ja '70
On the fashionable idea of national guilt.
K. R. Minogue. Am Scholar 39:211-18 Spr
'70
See also
Christian ethics
Church and race problems
Sexual ethics
Social problems
SOCIAL evolution. See Social change
SOCIAL-fascism. See National socialism
SOCIAL gerontology. See Gerontology
SOCIAL groups. See Groups (sociology)
SOCIAL history
See also
Middle classes
Urbanization
also subhead Social history under names
of countries, states, etc. e.g. Israel—Social
history
SOCIAL, humanitarian and cultural committee
of the United Nations. See United Nations
—Social, humanitarian and cultural commit-
tee
SOCIAL hygiene. See Venereal diseases
SOCIAL interaction
Indicators of the capacities for societal guid-
ance. A. Etzioni. bibliog f il Ann Am Acad
388:25-34 Mr '70
Soft revolution explored. S. Keen; reply. R.
G. Middleton. Chr Cent 87:572+ My 6 '70
See also
Group relations training
SOCIAL isolation
Monkeys as therapists; pathological behav-
ior induced by isolation. J. Moriarty. il Sci
N 98:100 Ag 1 '70
See also
Alienation (social psychology)
Loneliness
SOCIAL justice. See Social ethics
SOCIAL knowledge. See Knowledge
SOCIAL legislation
See also
Public welfare—Law
Unemployment—Relief measures

United States
See also
Consumer protection—Laws and legislation
Old age pensions—United States
Social security act, 1935
SOCIAL life and customs. See Manners and
customs; also subhead Social life and cus-
toms under names of countries, states,
and cities, e.g. Los Angeles—Social life and
customs
SOCIAL organization
Resources and social structure: some con-
ditions of stability and change. W. R.
Burch, jr. bibliog f il Ann Am Acad 389:
27-34 My '70
SOCIAL policy
See also subhead Social policy under
names of countries, e.g. United States—
Social policy
SOCIAL policy (periodical)
Déjà vu. N. Glazer. Commentary 50:60+
Ag '70; Discussion. 50:14+ D '70

SOCIAL pressure
See also
Protests. demonstrations. etc.
SOCIAL problems
Benign neglect. Am City 85:8 Ap '70
Establishment; social responsibilities of citi-
zens; address, April 15, 1970. C. Y. Lazarus.
Vital Speeches 36:498-502 Je 1 '70
Political intelligence for America's future;
symposium, ed. by B. M. Gross and M.
Springer. bibliog f il Ann Am Acad 388:1-
132 Mr '70
R&D factor. P. Steinfels. Commonweal 92:
478 S 25 '70
Solving problems in living: the citizen's view-
point. W. B. Eddy and others. bibliog il
Ment Hy 54:64-72 Ja '70
See also
Church and social problems
Crime and criminals
Discrimination
Family
Homosexuality
Illegitimacy
Juvenile delinquency
Libraries and social and economic problems
Liquor problem
Marriage
Migrant labor
Narcotic habit
Poor
Prisons
Prostitution
Race discrimination
School and social and economic problems
Slums
Suicide
Technology and civilization
Unemployment
War
Woman—Social and moral questions

Bibliography
Social indicators: selected readings. C. Agocs.
Ann Am Acad 388:127-32 Mr '70
SOCIAL problems and art. See Art and so-
ciety
SOCIAL problems in education. See Educa-
tional sociology
SOCIAL progress
See also
Social change
Social revolution
SOCIAL psychology
Collective violence; symposium, ed. by J. F.
Short, jr and M. E. Wolfgang. bibliog f il
Ann Am Acad 391:1-176 S '70
Experience of living in cities; adaptation of
address, September 2, 1969. S. Milgram. bib-
liog il Science 167:1461-8 Mr 13 '70
Perceptions, aspirations, frustrations, and
satisfactions: an approach to urban indica-
tors. R. Stagner. il Ann Am Acad 388:59-
68 Mr '70
Some pedestrian observations; Manhattan's
42nd street. il Time 95:66 My 11 '70
See also
Adjustment. Social
Alienation (social psychology)
Ethnopsychology
Family
Human relations
Hysteria (social psychology)
Morale, National
Political attitudes
Political psychology
Public opinion
Social conflict
Social interaction
Violence
War—Psychological aspects
SOCIAL reform. See Social problems; Social
revolution
SOCIAL reformers. See Reformers
SOCIAL research. See Social science research
SOCIAL responsibilities of libraries round ta-
ble. See American library association—So-
cial responsibilities of libraries round table
SOCIAL responsibility. See Responsibility
SOCIAL revolution
Against a common fate. S. Chase. il Bul
Atom Sci 26:9-10 My '70
False ideology of schooling. I. Illich. il Sat R
53:56-8+ 17 '70
Intellectuals and revolution: interview with
Jean-Paul Sartre; ed. by J. C. Garot, tr.
by B. Rice. J. P. Sartre. il Ramp Mag 9:
52-5 D '70
Needed: a new utopianism. H. Wheeler. Cur
121:30-1 S '70
New American revolution; excerpt from The
trial. T. Hayden. il Ramp Mag 9:50-8+ Jl
'70

SOCIAL revolution—*Continued*
New reformation, by P. Goodman. Review
  Sat R 53:43+ My 23 '70. H. S. Resnik
On the threshold of a new decade: thoughts
  for 1970. E. Rabinowitch. il por Bul Atom
  Sci 26:2-3+ F '70
Radical suburb and expansive man; excerpt
  from The radical suburb. J. B. Orr and F.
  P. Nichelson. Cur 122:3-10 O '70
Radical turn in theology and ethics: why it
  occurred in the 1960's. S. E. Ahlstrom. bib-
  liog f Ann Am Acad 387:1-13 Ja '70
Revolution in the university. J. Hitchcock.
  Yale R 60:161-74 D '70
Revolution of unreason. A. M. Bickel. New
  Repub 163:18-21 O 17 '70
Sex power and the revolution. V. Eller. il
  Chr Cent 87:291-3 Mr 11 '70; Discussion.
  87:575-6, 641, 728, 847, 1567-8 My 6, 20, Je
  10, Jl 8, D 30 '70
Technectronic America; excerpts from Be-
  tween two ages. Z. Brzezinski. Newsweek 76:
  36 Jl 20 '70
Third world in history. D. Ribeiro. Trans-
  Action 7:6+ N '69
Toward an ecological solution. M. Bookchin.
  il Ramp Mag 8:6-8+ My '70
Toward legalizing revolution. M. Harring-
  ton. Cur 122:28-31 O '70
What kind of revolution? D. McDonald. Cur
  121:28-30 S '70
Why Marcuse matters. J. L. Walsh. Common-
  weal 93:21-5 O 2 '70
Young people, the establishment, and the
  quality of life; excerpt from The human en-
  vironment and business. H. Ford, 2d. Read
  Digest 97:139-42 Jl '70
  See also
Counter culture
SOCIAL science research
Analytic framework for social reporting and
  policy analysis. M. Olson. bibliog f Ann
  Am Acad 388:112-26 Mr '70
Perceptions, aspirations, frustrations, and
  satisfactions: an approach to urban indica-
  tors. R. Stagner. il Ann Am Acad 388:59-
  68 Mr '70
Prospects for a social report, a review article.
  E. Clague. Mo Labor R 93:56-60 Je '70
Roundup of current research. **See issues of**
  Trans-action
Social indicators, reports, and accounts:
  toward the management of society. M.
  Springer. bibliog f Ann Am Acad 388:1-13
  Mr '70
Sociological snoopers; with reply by I. L.
  Horowitz and L. Rainwater. N. Von Hoff-
  man. Trans-Action 7:4-8 My '70
  See also
Computers—Social science use
New school for social research, New York
Political science research
SOCIAL sciences
Critique of violence, by A. Caffi. Review
  Commentary 50:45-55 S '70. L. Abel
Revolution in English social thought, 1880-
  1914. R. N. Soffer. bibliog f Am Hist R
  75:1938-64 D '70
  See also
Behavior (psychology)
Behavioral sciences
Civilization
Computers—Social science use
Forecasts (social sciences)
Human ecology
Power (social sciences)
Sociology

Bibliography
Book reviews. See issues of Trans-Action

Research
See Social science research

Study and teaching
Bridge at generation gap; EPIC project. M. E.
  Wade. il Am Ed 6:28-30 O '70
Cooperative center promotes development in
  the social studies. F. Creason and D. L.
  Schilson. Clear House 44:411-14 Mr '70
Cultural understanding; courses at Philadel-
  phia's Central high school. R. Kirk. Nat R
  22:363 Ap 7 '70
Curriculum changes in the social studies. D.
  L. Bechtel. Clear House 44:364-7 F '70
Films can end those social studies doldrums!
  R. Maynard. il Schol Teach Sec Teach Sup
  p 14-16+ Ap 6 '70
Florida's religion-social studies curriculum
  project. Ed Digest 35:42-4 Mr '70
New social studies: boon or bust? W. W.
  Goetz. bibliog Clear House 44:404-6 Mr '70
Science-fiction stories in the social studies.
  A. W. Wohlfeil. bibliog f Clear House 44:
  300-4 Ja '70
Social science laboratory. J. McLure. Clear
  House 44:407-10 Mr '70

Social studies: more of the same. D. L.
  Burleson. Sr Schol 95:Schol Teach 2 N 3 '69
Survey of the teaching of history and social
  studies in secondary schools. E. G. Kim-
  ball. Sch & Soc 98:246-9 Ap '70
Teaching strategies for the slow-learning
  social studies student. B. Davis. Ed Digest
  35:43-5 Ap '70
Topical curriculum. T. Kovach. Clear House
  44:363 F '70
Toward a mankind curriculum; from kinder-
  garten through twelfth grade. F. O. Gear-
  ing. il Todays Ed 59:28-30 Mr '70
What makes humans human? Man: a course
  of study. E. Ferber. il Am Ed 6:8-12 My '70
  See also
Citizenship, Education for
Ecology—Study and teaching
History—Study and teaching
Social education
SOCIAL sciences and state
What role for social science elites? D. P.
  Moynihan. Cur 124:17-22 D '70
SOCIAL security. See Insurance, Social
SOCIAL security act, 1935
Facts about social security; thirty-five years of
  insurance protection. R. R. Jalbert. il por
  Har Yrs 10:6-10 Jl '70
SOCIAL security administration. See United
  States—Social security administration
SOCIAL security benefits. See Insurance, Social
SOCIAL settlements
  See also
Boston—Social settlements
SOCIAL snobs. See Snobs and snobbishness
SOCIAL status
Status inconsistency theory and flying saucer
  sightings. D. I. Warren. bibliog il Science
  170:599-603 N 6 '70
  See also
Negroes—Social status
Prestige
Social classes
SOCIAL stratification. See Social classes
SOCIAL structure. See Social organization
SOCIAL studies. See Social sciences
SOCIAL thought
Revolution in English social thought, 1880-
  1914. R. N. Soffer. bibliog f Am Hist R
  75:1938-64 D '70
SOCIAL values
Bridge of values; adaptation of address, April
  28, 1970. B. C. Keeney. Science 169:26-8 Jl 3
  '70
Harmony with the life around us; adaptation
  of address. A. M. Lindbergh. il por Good H
  171:62-3+ Jl '70
Middle class. H. Fairlie. il McCalls 97:42-3+
  Jl '70
Year 2000: the future planners; address No-
  vember 8, 1969. H. D. Gideonse. bibliog f
  Vital Speeches 36:530-6 Je 15 '70
SOCIAL welfare
  See also
Family service association of America
Public welfare
United Nations—Commission for social de-
  velopment
SOCIAL work
Evolution of a Catholic worker. J. C. Cort.
  Commonweal 93:343-6 Ja 8 '71
  See also
Legal aid
Social problems
SOCIAL workers
Social worker: survival expert in urban slums;
  Woodlawn, Chicago. R. Gosswiller. il To-
  days Health 48:59-62 S '70

Training
Training child care staff: pitfalls and prom-
  ises. J. K. Whittaker. Ment Hy 54:516-19 O
  '70
SOCIALISM
Socialism and the future. R. L. Heilbroner;
  discussion. Commentary 49:14+ Ap '70
Whatever happened to socialism? M. Har-
  rington. Harper 240:99-105 F '70
  See also
Collective settlements
Communism
National socialism

Europe, Western
Future of social democracy. J. Mander. Commentary 50:57-64 S '70

Great Britain
Rise and fossilization of socialism: a lesson
  to be absorbed; address, October 14, 1970.
  C. N. Parkinson. Vital Speeches 37:149-52
  D 15 '70

SOCIALIST parties

Europe, Western

Future of social democracy. J. Mander. Commentary 50:57-64 S '70

SOCIALIZED medicine. See Medical service, State

SOCIALLY handicapped

On helping the disadvantaged. J. E. Chapman. Ment Hy 54:589-90 O '70

See also

Homeless, The

Education

Head start in legal studies for minority groups. Sch & Soc 98:135-6 Mr '70

How to catch a dogcatcher; New careers program in California. R. Moskowitz. il Am Ed 6:9-12 O '70

Underprepared college student; with editorial comment. I. Tinker. Am Ed 6:inside cover, 10-12 N '70

See also

Talent Search programs (education)

Employment

See also

COPE program

Ethnic enterprizes (firm)

Hard-core unemployed

Negroes—Employment

Opportunities industrialization centers, inc.

Recreation

Parks for all seasons, and for all people; Washington, D.C. inner city program. M. M. Boyd. il Parks & Rec 5:22-3+ My '70

SOCIALLY handicapped and libraries. See Libraries—Services to socially handicapped

SOCIALLY handicapped children

Challenge: children and youth in the 70's. J. H. Douglass. Camp Mag 42:12 Ja '70

Critical issues in research related to disadvantaged children; AAAS symposium, December 28, 1970. D. L. Peters. il Science 170:102-3 O 2 '70

Dilemma of child care. R. B. Miller. America 122:125-8 F 7 '70

How to make camping significant in the 1970's. G. Konopka. por Camp Mag 42:8-11 Ja '70

Pretty thing for me. R. M. Williams. il Sch Arts 69:40 Mr '70

Prospect street moon. T. J. Cottle. Sat R 53: 21-4+ F 14 '70

Think of these children. W. F. Mondale. New Repub 163:15-17 D 26 '70

See also

Negro children

Education

Art education for the culturally different. D. L. Barclay. il Sch Arts 69:14-17 Mr '70

Bankruptcy of compensatory education; the academic school approach. S. Gordon. Ed Digest 36:28-31 D '70

Common language; project SEED at Del Paso Heights district. il por Newsweek 75: 57-8 My 4 '70

Compensatory education; findings of the report Urban education crisis. W. D. Boutwell. PTA Mag 64:11 Je '70

Conservationists turn on for children of the concrete. A. Dennis. il Nat Parks & Con Mag 44:4-9 Je '70

Dehumanization of education of nation's poor. Sch & Soc 98:392 N '70

Denver doesn't quit on problem students. Z. Von Ende. il Am Ed 6:18-22 Je '70

Educational needs of economically deprived children. H. A. Johnson. Ed Digest 35:45-8 Mr '70

Fantasy or reality? Education in the inner city. H. E. Allen. Clear House 44:356-9 F '70

Helping the disadvantaged youth. C. J. Gehringer. Clear House 44:304 Ja '70

Hey, man, you our principal? L. L. Cunningham. Ed Digest 35:5-8 F '70

ITV in the ghetto. R. J. Meyer. Todays Ed 59:35 Ja '70

If it's fun, it can't be reading! address, November, 1969. L. S. Johnson. Engl J 59:837-45 S '70

In Roxbury, way out of a fortress. J. Kozol. Ed Digest 35:12-15 My '70

Instead of Molotov cocktails; constructive action to improve conditions in their community; New York city's Center of urban education. L. Rich. il Am Ed 6:11-15 Je '70

It's hard to come back; Liaison teacher program to help delinquent children in Milwaukee schools. M. P. Pfeil. il Am Ed 6:3-6 Je '70

Kids our high schools forget; interview. J. E. Allen. por Nations Bsns 58:70-2 Je '70

Magic of puppetry; project in Bridgeport, Conn. inner-city schools. J. S. Zeliff. il Parents Mag 45:46-7+ Jl '70

Methods, materials, and the culturally disadvantaged. E. F. DeRoche. bibliog Clear House 44:420-4 Mr '70

Moms are a must; Chicago's child-parent education centers. L. Wille. il Am Ed 6: 24-9 Ap '70

Music and dance for the disadvantaged. D. H. Clary. Ed Digest 35:50-2 Ap '70

My teacher doesn't like me. Trans-Action 7:10+ Jl '70

Nature of urban education. E. Kruszynski. Sch & Soc 98:166-8+ Mr '70

Nouns and pronouns at Carver junior high. J. P. Baute. Engl J 59:970-1 O '70

Project ASPIRE: help for hopeless kids. D. Divoky. il Schol Teach Sec Teach Sup p20-2 F 2 '70

Prospects for growth in preprimary education. J. N. Hedges. il Mo Labor R 93:40-4 Jl '70

Reaching out to Danny; Baltimore dropout prevention programs. R. H. Levine. il Am Ed 6:10-14 Jl '70

Realistic view of homework for the ghetto child. R. B. Shuman and H. L. Sublett, jr. bibliog Clear House 45:140-5 N '70

Romeo and Juliet: living is being relevant. L. W. Cohen. Engl J 59:1263-5+ D '70

Slum child. I. H. Draper. Clear House 45:48-50 S '70

Step up to reading; Huntington, W.Va. D. Marsh. il Am Ed 6:15-17 Ja '70

Student-teacher laboratory prepares a school for de facto desegregation. G. L. Downing. Clear House 45:37-40 S '70

They set their sights on careers at sea. il Ebony 26:56-8 D '70

They're on their way; Upward bound. J. Connors. il Am Ed 6:23-5 Je '70

Urban school reform: educational agenda for tomorrow's America. M. D. Fantini. Cur Hist 59:267-72+ N '70

Why must Lincoln die? experimental school being killed in Kentucky. J. Star. il Look 34:64-8 Ag 11 '70

See also

Children of migrant laborers—Education

Performance contracts (education)

Project Head Start

Talent Search programs (education)

Recreation

Guitars for everyone. S. Lesher. il Parks & Rec 5:22-4+ Jl '70

Totlots: a successful experiment in Rochester, N.Y. D. Warner. il Parks & Rec 5:32-3+ Jl '70

Washington's youth gardens. il Parks & Rec 5:47-8+ Je '70

See also

Camps for the socially handicapped

SOCIETA generale semiconduttori. See Electronic apparatus industry and trade—Italy

SOCIETIES

See also

Womens clubs and societies

SOCIETIES, imaginary. See Imaginary societies

SOCIETY, High. See Upper classes

SOCIETY, Primitive

See also

Cannibalism

Indians of North America—Culture

Nomads

Religion, Primitive

SOCIETY and art. See Art and society

SOCIETY and law. See Sociological jurisprudence

SOCIETY and music. See Music and society

SOCIETY and the arts. See The Arts and society

SOCIETY and the church. See Church and the world

SOCIETY and the individual. See Individual and society

SOCIETY and war. See War and society

SOCIETY and youth. See Individual and society

SOCIETY columns. See Newspapers—Sections, columns, etc.

SOCIETY for creative anachronism

Cult of history; Renaissance pleasure faire. il Newsweek 76:102-3 S 28 '70

SOCIETY for the advancement of education

Status of the Society for the advancement of education, 1969-70. W. E. Brickman. Sch & Soc 98:379 O '70

SOCIETY hill playhouse street theatre. See Philadelphia—Theater

SOCIETY of Friends. See Friends, Society of

SOCIETY of Jesus. See Jesuits

SOCIETY of nuclear medicine

Medical sciences. Sci N 98:70 Jl 25 '70

SOCIETY of priests for a free ministry. See
  Priests—Associations, institutions, etc.
SOCIOLOGICAL jurisprudence
  How to stop rise in crime; interview. L. Jaw-
    orski. il por U S News 69:40-3 Jl 20 '70
  Law and social action; consultation held at
    Celigny, Switzerland, July 1970. J. B.
    Kelley. America 124:41-2 Ja 16 '71
SOCIOLOGICAL research. See Social sci-
  ence research
SOCIOLOGY
  Coming crisis in western sociology, by A. W.
    Gouldner. Review
      Commentary 50:95-7 D '70. S. Rothman
      Ramp Mag 9:56-8+ D '70. J. Schevitz
    See also
  American sociological association
  Anthropology
  Civilization
  Evolution
  Family
  Groups (sociology)
  Human ecology
  Human relations
  Leisure class
  Liquor problem
  Man—Influence of environment
  Marriage
  Power (social sciences)
  Public welfare
  Social contract
  Social problems
  Social psychology
  Woman
                Study and teaching
  Potential of sociology as a liberating cur-
    riculum; excerpt from Social science in the
    schools; ed. by I. Morrissett. R. Perrucci.
    bibliog Sch & Soc 98:478-9+ D '70
  Walk-in exposure projects in the ghetto.
    M. Maruyama. Ment Hy 54:261-70 Ap '70
SOCIOLOGY, Christian
  Contemplative life and the sociologist. M.
    Rowe. Chr Cent 87:1412-16 N 25 '70; Dis-
    cussion. 88:20 Ja 6 '71
  Religion and the social sciences.   T. M.
    DeFerrari. il Cath World 212:209-10 Ja '71
  Rich country, poor country. C. Elliott. Amer-
    ica 123:455-7 N 28 '70
  Unresponsive pew. J. Richie; discussion. Chr
    Cent 86:1458+, 1549; 87:123-5 N 12, D 3 '69,
    Ja 28 '70
    See also
  Church and social problems
SOCIOLOGY, Educational. See Educational so-
  ciology
SOCIOLOGY, Rural
    See also
  Country life
  Urbanization
SOCIOLOGY, Urban
  Cities to live in; excerpts from The unheavenly
    city. E. C. Banfield. Cur 119:44-9 Je '70
  Model cities, model for failure; East New
    York section of Brooklyn. D. Stoloff.
    Arch Forum 132:78-9+ Ja '70
  Perceptions, aspirations, frustrations, and
    satisfactions; an approach to urban in-
    dicators. R. Stagner. il Ann Am Acad 388:
    59-68 Mr '70
  Unheavenly city, by E. C. Banfield. Review
    Cur 119:50-2 Je '70. R. C. Wade
  Urban Vietnamization; on developing self-
    reliant black and brown communities; ad-
    dress, November 21, 1969. B. Holman. Vital
    Speeches 36:246-50 F 1 '70
    See also
  Cities and towns
  Community power
  Urban renewal
  Urbanization
                Study and teaching
  Cornell's cultural shock treatment; course
    on Issues in the environment. il Bsns W
    p 104-5 Ja 31 '70
  Experiment in relevance, urban studies pro-
    gram at Livingston college. il Time 95:44+
    Ap 20 '70
SOCIOLOGY and science. See Science—Social
  aspects
SOCKET wrenches. See Wrenches
SOCKMAN, Ralph Washington
  Obituary
    Chr Cent 87:1059 S 9 '70
SOCOLOW, Robert. See Harte, J. jt. ed.
SOCRATES
  Hi, mistress; a remembrance of a gentle
    guide. B. Brophy. Vogue 155:92-3+ F 15
    '70
SODA bottles. See Bottles
SODA pop. See Beverages
SODEMAN, Thomas, and others
  Fine structure of the exoerythrocytic stage
    of plasmodium cynomolgi. bibliog il Sci-
    ence 170:340 O 16 '70

SODERBERGH, Peter A.
  Proverbs 7:69 let us not forsake our prin-
    cipals. Clear House 44:461-4 Ap '70
SODIUM cyclamate. See Sugar substitutes
SODIUM saccharin. See Sugar substitutes
SOEHARTO. See Suharto
SOEKARNO. See Sukarno
SOFAS
  In Hawaii, the pune'e and the big hikie'e.
    il Sunset 145:110 O '70
SOFFER, Reba N.
  Revolution in English social thought, 1880-
    1914. bibliog f Am Hist R 75:1938-64 D '70
SOFFER, Rosanne S.
  It's a small world; address, November 1969.
    Engl J 59:416-20 Mr '70
SOFIAN, Naid
  SR's 1970 Anisfield-Wolf awards. Sat R 53:
    23-4 Ap 11 '70
SOFT drink industry
  Productivity in the soft drinks industry. E.
    Adelman and C. Ardolini. il Mo Labor R
    93:28-30 D '70
    See also
  Cadbury Schweppes, ltd.
  Coca-Cola company
  Dr Pepper company
  PepsiCo, inc.
SOFT drinks. See Beverages
SOGGE, David
  Uncommon student in Africa. il Sat R 53:
    82-4 F 21 '70
SOHIGIAN, Keven
  (ed) See Uggams, L. Leslie Uggams
SOHO. See New York (city)—SoHo
SOHO artists association. See Artists colonies
SOIFER, Israel
  Doctor David Diringer and the Alphabet mu-
    seum. il por Pub W 198:48+ S 7 '70
SOIL bank. See Agricultural administration—
  United States
SOIL conservation
    See also
  Contour farming
SOIL conservation service. See United States
  —Soil conservation service
SOIL fauna
    See also
  Earthworms
SOIL fertility
  How soils are formed and become fertile. A.
    Schatz and V. Schatz. il Org Gard & Farm
    17:68-72 Je '70
    See also
  Soil productivity rating
SOIL mechanics
  Apollo 11 soil mechanics investigation. N.
    C. Costes and others. bibliog il Science 167:
    739-41 Ja 30 '70
SOIL moisture
  How to judge soil moisture. il Suc Farm
    68:B4 S '70
SOIL pollution
  Soil & fresh water: damaged global fabric.
    B. Commoner. il Environ 12:4-11 Ap '70
SOIL productivity rating
  Soil; EQ index. il Nat Wildlife 8:34 O '70;
    Same. Schol Teach Jr/Sr High pA10 O 5 '70
SOIL testing. See Soils—Analysis
SOILS
  Crop management (cont of) What's new. C.
    E. Sommers. See issues of Successful farm-
    ing
  Lunar soil. J. A. Wood. il Sci Am 223:14-23
    bibliog (p 128) Ag '70
  Some plants found to thrive in moon soil.
    il Aviation W 92:58 My 4 '70
    See also
  Clay
  Compost
  Drainage
                Analysis
  How to make an outfall in San Francisco
    Bay mud. R. G. Bezzant. il Am City 85:83-5
    My '70
  Why and how of soil testing. R. A. Miller.
    Horticulture 48:20-1+ My '70
                Composition
    See Soil fertility
                Moisture
    See Soil moisture
                Nitrogen content
  Replace nitrogen lost during rains. Suc Farm
    68:A4 My '70
                Phosphorus content
    See also
  Plants, Effect of phosphorus on

SOILS—*Continued*

Plutonium content
See Soils, Radioactive substances in

Radioactive content
See Soils, Radioactive substances in

Testing
See Soils—Analysis

Water content
See Soil moisture

SOILS, Radioactive substances in
Fire damage; aftermath of fire at Rocky Flats plutonium plant, with AEC statement. E. A. Martell and others. il Environ 12:14-21 My '70

SOKA Gakkai (sect)
Japan's new Buddhism, by K. Murata. Review
Chr Cent 87:182 F 11 '70. O. C. Thomas
New Repub 162:20-2 Ja 17 '70. A. Feldman

SOKAL, Robert R.
Senescence and genetic load: evidence from tribolium. bibliog il Science 167:1733-4 Mr 27 '70

SOKOLOV, Raymond A.
Rare Bird. il por Newsweek 76:114A-114B+ N 2 '70

SOKOLOW, Anna
Lyric theatre directed by Anna Sokolow; Edison theatre, NYC. D. Hering. Dance Mag 44:77 Je '70 *
Sokolow odyssey continued. J. Gale. il pors Dance Mag 44:42-6 F '70

SOLANAS, Fernando
Fernando Solanas: an interview; tr. by J. R. MacBean. reprinted from Cinéthique No. 3, 1969. Film Q 24:37-43 Fall '70

about
La hora de los hornos. J. R. MacBean. il Film Q 24:31-7 Fall '70 *

SOLANDRA guttata. See Cup of gold

SOLAR atmosphere. See Sun—Atmosphere

SOLAR batteries
French switch on to sun power. il Bsns W p 126+ My 9 '70

SOLAR cells
See also
Solar batteries

SOLAR corona. See Sun—Corona

SOLAR eclipses. See Eclipses, Solar

SOLAR energy
How to get sun power for New York. por Bsns W p 128 My 9 '70
On future power from the sun. il Chem 43: 25 Mr '70
See also
Solar batteries

SOLAR flares
Radioactivity induced in Apollo 11 lunar surface material by solar flare protons. H. R. Heydegger and A. Turkevich. bibliog il Science 168:575-6 My 1 '70

SOLAR furnaces
Sun power in the Pyrenees. il Time 95:52-5 My 18 '70
Sun-powered furnace. il Chem 43:23 N '70
World's biggest furnace runs on sunshine. D. Scott. il Pop Sci 196:88-9 F '70

SOLAR heating
Sunlight and bodies heat this school. il Sci Digest 69:16-17 Ja '71

SOLAR magnetic fields. See Magnetic fields (cosmic physics)

SOLAR observatories. See Astronomical observatories

SOLAR photography. See Astronomical photography

SOLAR power. See Solar energy

SOLAR radiation
Apollo 11 lunar science conference: stable isotopes, rare gases, solar wind, and spallation products. symposium. bibliog il Science 167:533-82 Ja 30 '70
Monitoring the sun's violence. D. E. Thomsen. il Sci N 98:258-9 S 19 '70
Solar activity index: validity supported by oxygen isotope dating. J. R. Bray. bibliog il Science 168:571-2 My 1 '70
Solar radiation effects in lunar samples. R. W. Hapke and others. bibliog il Science 167:745-7 Ja 30 '70
See also
Energy budget (geophysics)
Ocean-atmosphere interaction
Solar energy
Solar flares
Solar furnaces
Solar heating
Van Allen radiation belts

SOLAR system
Plutonium and formation of the solar system. Chem 43:28 Ap '70
Some mathematical curiosities embedded in the solar system. M. Gardner. il Sci Am 222:108-12 Ap '70
Through a cell of hydrogen. Sci N 99:23-4 Ja 9 '71
See also
Planets

SOLARIZATION
Is it positive or negative? A. Francekevich. il Pop Phot 66:32+ Ap '70

SOLARO, Mary
Summer sipping essentials. il Todays Health 48:50-1 Ag '70
Toast to safer driving. il Todays Health 48: 60-3 D '70

SOLARWIND; ballet. See Ballets—Criticisms

SOLBERG, Sara
J'etais jeune fille au pair a Paris (I was a mother's helper in Paris) il Seventeen 29: 144-5+ F '70

SOLDERING apparatus
How to buy a soldering iron. L. Buckwalter. il Mech Illus 66:86-8+ Je '70
Tools for electronics. T. Haskett. il Radio-Electr 41:52-6 Mr; 48-52 Ap; 48-9 My '70

SOLDIERS
See also
Women as soldiers

Civil rights
GI rights and army justice, by R. S. Rivkin. Review
New Repub 163:27-8 Ag 22 '70. P. C. Saunders

SOLDIERS, American. See United States—Army

SOLDIERS, Negro. See United States—Army—Negroes—History; United States—History—Civil war—Negro troops

SOLDIERS, Russian. See Russia—Army

SOLEDAD prison. See Prisons—California

SOLEM, Alan
Wiped out & unsung. il Nat Parks & Con Mag 44:7-8 Ag '70

SOLER ROCA, Miguel
Education revolution in Latin America. il UNESCO Courier 23:24-31 N '70

SOLERI, Paolo
Architecture; exhibition at Corcoran gallery. F. Gutheim. Nation 210:446 Ap 13 '70 *
Arcologist. D. Davis. il por Newsweek 75: 78-9 Mr 2 '70 *
Arcology: an answer for the years ahead. il Parks & Rec 5:41+ My '70 *
Arcology of Paolo Soleri. S. Moholy-Nagy. il Arch Forum 132:70-5 My '70 *
Designer in the desert. W. Karp. il por Horizon 12:30-9 Aut '70 *
Paolo Soleri, genius. J. Harithas. il por Vogue 156:96-7+ Ag 1 '70 *
Paolo Soleri thinks very big. S. D. Kohn. il por N Y Times Mag p26-7+ Jl 26 '70; Reply. J. Lobell. p30+ Ag 23 '70 *

SOLFATARAS. See Hot springs

SOLHEIM, Wilhelm Gerhard, 1924-
Secrets of Spirit cave. por Time 95:66 F 9 '70

SOLID helium. See Helium, Solid

SOLID oxygen. See Oxygen, Solid

SOLID propellants. See Rockets—Fuel

SOLID wastes. See Refuse and refuse disposal

SOLIDS
Natural coordinates for electrons in solids. J. Zak. bibliog il por Phys Today 23:51-4 F '70
See also
Thin films
Tunneling (physics)

Conferences
Inelastic behavior of solids; report of Battelle institute colloquium on the material sciences. M. F. Kanninen and others. Science 167:1761-2 Mr 27 '70

SOLIDS, Flow of. See Rheology

SOLIS, Misael Acosta. See Acosta Solis, M.

SOLITUDE
Sweet uses of solitude. J. Mills. Read Digest 96:211-12+ Je '70
See also
Loneliness

SOLKOV, Arnold
Upon first looking into Christensen's Rhetoric. Engl J 59:834-6 S '70

SOLLIDAY, S. and Bach, F. H.
Cytotoxicity: specificity after in vitro sensitization. bibliog il Science 170:1406-9 D 25 '70

SOLLIE, Finn
Political experiment in Antarctica. il Bul Atom Sci 26:16-21 D '70

SOLOMON, Solomon S. and others
Divergent biological effects of adenosine and dibutyryl adenosine 3'5'-monophosphate on the isolated fat cell. bibliog il Science 169:387-8 Jl 24 '70

SOLOMON, Stephen
Chained campuses. New Repub 163:12-13 S 19 '70
Seas. New Repub 163:21-3 O 31 '70

SOLOMON'S temple, Site of. See Jerusalem—Holy places

SOLOTAROFF, Theodore
Critical presence. J. Kroll. por Newsweek 76: 115 N 16 '70 *

SOLTI, Georg
Musical events; Chicago symphony all-Mahler program. W. Sargeant. New Yorker 45: 56-7 Ja 17 '70

about

Concerto by Levy, Solti, and Wild; the comic art of Tito Gobbi. l. Kolodin. Sat R 53:35 D 19 '70 *
Musical events; concerts in Carnegie Hall performed by Chicago symphony orchestra. W. Sargeant. New Yorker 46:135 D 19 '70 *

SOLUTION (chemistry)
Dissolving salt in benzene. il Chem 43:24 My '70
Hydrogen atom and its reactions in solution. W. A. Pryor and others. bibliog il Science 169:181-3 Jl 10 '70
Hydrogen bonding in hydrochloric acid solutions. S. C. Lee and R. Kaplow. bibliog il Science 169:477-8 Jl 31 '70
Ionic radon solutions. L. Stein. bibliog il Science 168:362-4 Ap 17 '70
Plutonium, the lively element; behavior in solutions. J. M. Cleveland. bibliog il por Chem 43:10-13 Ja '70
Redox reactions and the acid-base properties of solvents. J. A. Bishop. bibliog il Chem 43:18 Ja '70
Stable carbonium ions in solution. G. A. Olah. bibliog il Science 168:1298-311 Je 12 '70
See also
Colloids

SOLVENTS
See also
Carbon tetrachloride
Plasticizers

SOLWAY, Clifford
Turning history upside down. Sat R 53:13-15+ Je 20 '70

SOLZHENITSYN, Aleksandr Isaevich
Attack on Solzhenitsyn. por Time 96:18 D 28 '70 *
Dissent in the USSR. Nation 211:389 O 26 '70 *
Episode in the life of Solzhenitsyn. J. Critchlow. por Commonweal 93:278-80 D 11 '70 *
I accept the prize. G. Wolff. por Newsweek 76:67 O 19 '70 *
Nobel for outcast. por Sr Schol 97:5 N 2 '70 *
Nobel prize winner who deserved it. T. Foote. por Life 69:58 O 23 '70 *
Play by Aleksandr Solzhenitsyn. Criticism
Newsweek 76:85 O 26 '70 *
Time 96:77 N 2 '70 *
Prize and a dilemma. por Time 96:38-9 O 19 '70 *
Protesting spiritual murder. il por Time 95: 30-1 Je 29 '70 *
Rostropovich appeals for Solzhenitsyn; reprint of letter to four Russian periodicals. M. Rostropovich. Sat R 53:28 N 28 '70 *
Solzhenitsyn. Nat R 22:1337 D 15 '70 *
Solzhenitsyn; a candle in the wind. por Time 95:25 Mr 23 '70 *
Solzhenitsyn call still write, he just can't publish. N. Bethell. il N Y Times Mag p36-7+ Ap 12 '70 *
Solzhenitsyn wins Nobel prize in literature. Pub W 198:30-1 O 19 '70 *
Solzhenitsyn's day; joins a committee for human rights. il Newsweek 76:52+ D 21 '70 *

SOMA (drug)
Books; hypothetical identification of a drink called Soma with Amanita muscaria or fly agaric mushroom. W. Sargeant. New Yorker 46:90+ My 30 '70
Soma, by G. Wasson. Review
Atlan il 225:109-13 F '70. R. Graves

SOMALIA
See also
Education—Somalia

SOMAN, Florence Jane
Girl who believed in love; story. Good H 171: 62-3 Ag '70
Monica; story. Good H 170:66-7 Ja '70
Redemption of Gloria Barney; story. Good H 171:80-1 O '70
Spring is here! story. Good H 170:84-5 Mr '70

SOMATOLOGY
See also
Man—Constitution

SOMATOTROPHIN. See Pituitary hormones

The SOMEBODY; story. See Santiago, D.

SOMER, Hilde
Scriabin and his demons. J. Hiemenz. por Hi Fi 20:19-20 S '70 *

SOMERS, Florence
Resort luxury at a bargain. Redbook 135:162 O '70
South Carolina's 300th birthday. il Redbook 135:48+ Je '70

SOMERSON, Norman L.
Vaccine for a pneumonia. Sci N 98:317-18 O 17 '70 *

SOMETHING missing; story. See L'Heureux, J.

SOMLYO, Avril V. and others
Cyclic adenosine monophosphate; potassium-dependent action on vascular smooth muscle membrane potential. bibliog il Science 169:490-1 Jl 31 '70

SOMMER, Susan Thiemann
Monteverdi's magnificent musical drama. il Hi Fi sec I 20:102+ Ja '70

SOMMERS, Charles E.
Crop management (cont of) What's new. See issues of Successful farming

SOMMERS, Hobart Hibner
HEW official among fifty-one honored in Chicago senior hall of fame. por Aging 188: 19 Je '70 *

SOMNAMBULISM
What sleepwalking means. B. Bettelheim. Ladies Home J 87:26+ Ap '70

SON and hair; story. See Berger, T.

SON of man and the family; drama. See Taylor, T. and Hall A.

SONAR
Finding a hole in the bottom of the sea. M. Gruber. il Sea Front 16:309-11 S '70
See also
Echolocation (physiology)

SONATAS
On Beethoven's piano sonatas. I. Stravinsky. Harper 240:34+ My '70
See also
Phonograph records—Sonatas

SONDHEIM, Stephen
How two musicians live with music. il por House & Gard 138:58-9 Jl '70 *

SONG writing. See Composition (music)

SONGMY investigation. See Government investigations—My Lai massacre

SONGMY massacre. See Vietnamese war, 1957-—Atrocities—My Lai massacre

SONGS
Words without song; excerpts from address. N. Rorem. Am Rec G 36:468-9+ Mr '70
See also
Phonograph records—Songs
State songs

Interpretation, etc.
See Music—Analysis, interpretation, etc.

SONGS, American
Sentimental journey on the Atchison, Topeka and the Santa Fe. il Am Heritage 22:40-7 D '70
See also
Ballads, American
National songs—United States
State songs

SONGS, Negro. See Negro songs

SONGS, Popular. See Music, Popular (songs, etc)

SONGS, Russian
Music of dissent. il Time 96:25 S 7 '70

SONGS of birds. See Birds—Song

SONIC boom
Booms over Britain; Concorde test flights. il Newsweek 76:103 S 21 '70
FAA proposes rule to forbid overland boom. Aviation W 92:32 My 4 '70
Heat field may decrease boom of SST during overland flights. Aviation W 93:46 N 2 '70

Psychological aspects
Age and response to sonic booms. il Bul Atom Sci 26:27-8 My '70

SONIC holography. See Holography

SONNEBORN, D. W. and Hansen, H .J.
Vitamin B12 binders of chicken serum and chicken proventriculus are immunologically similar. bibliog il Science 168:591-2 My 1 '70

SONNICHSEN, C. L.
Wyatt Earp syndrome. il Am West 7:26-8+ My '70

SONOGRAPHY. See Holography

SONS and fathers. See Parent-child relationship

SOOTHSAYERS. See Fortune telling

SOPER, George Albert
　Case of the disappearing cook. M. Sufrin.
　　il pors Am Heritage 21:39-43 Ag '70 *

SOPHOCLES
　Oedipus; adaptation. See Feist, G.

about
　Self-destruction in Oedipus Rex. M. D. Faber.
　　bibliog Am Imago 27:41-51 Spr '70 *

SOPRIS, Colo.
　Requiem for a small town. N. Wood. il Am
　　Heritage 22:62-7 D '70

SORCERY. See Witchcraft

SORE throat. See Throat—Diseases

SOREL, Edward
　First in war, first in peace, first in the hearts
　　of his country club; caricature. Atlan 225:
　　64-5 F '70
　Pictorial history of the man in the red suit.
　　il Redbook 136:104-5 D '70
　Word people; drawings. il pors Horizon 12:
　　112-20 Aut '70

SOREL, Nancy
　Word people; excerpts, with drawings by E.
　　Sorel. il pors Horizon 12:112-20 Aut '70

SORENSEN, Theodore Chaikin
　Ask not what Ted Sorensen can do for
　　you . . . D. Halberstam; discussion. Harper
　　240:6+ F '70 *
　Candidates. New Yorker 46:27-8 Je 20 '70 *
　Profile in courage: Ted Sorensen's finest hour.
　　Nat R 22:345-7 Ap 7 '70 *
　Running uphill. il por Newsweek 75:19-20 Je
　　22 '70 *

SORGHUM
　Apospory in sorghum bicolor (L.) Moench.
　　W. W. Hanna and others. bibliog il Sci-
　　ence 170:338-9 O 16 '70
　　　See also
　Milo

Diseases and pests
　　　See also
　Greenbugs

Hybrids
　Forage hybrids can make top dairy feed;
　　sorghum-sudan. D. K. O'Brien. il Farm J
　　94:45 My '70

SORIA, Dorle J.
　Artist life. See issues of High fidelity and
　　Musical America section II

SORIN, Morris
　New math. T. Sheridan. New Repub 163:13
　　S 19 '70 *

SORNSON, Halvor C. See Ryan. W. L. jt. auth.

SORRENTINO, Gilbert
　Black mountaineering. Poetry 116:110-12 My
　　'70

SORROW
　　　See also
　Bereavement

SOSIN, Mark J.
　Greenland salmon. il Field & S 75:54-5+ My
　　'70

SOSNOFF, Martin T.
　Market trends. por Forbes 106:104-5 O 15
　　'70
　Stock trends (cont) por Forbes 106:56-7 Jl 1
　　'70

SOSTRE, Martin
　Anguish of Martin Sostre. W. Worthy. il pors
　　Ebony 25:122-4+ O '70 *
　Crime of Martin Sostre, by V. Copeland. Re-
　　view
　　　Nation 211:221-2 S 14 '70. P. Chevigny *

SOTER, Steven. See Gold, T. jt. auth.

SOTIRIOU, Erika
　All aboard for adventure. il Parents Mag 45:
　　44-5+ Jl '70
　How I won the war against littering. il Par-
　　ents Mag 45:68-9+ O '70

SOTOGRANDE colony. See Seaside resorts—
　　Spain

SOUFFLÉS
　Dessert soufflés you make ahead. il Sunset
　　144:178-9 Ap '70
　Onion soufflé, a last-minute flourish. Sunset
　　145:160 D '70
　Secrets of superb soufflés. il Redbook 135:
　　112-16+ S '70

SOUFFLÉS, Frozen. See Desserts

SOUL CITY, N.C.
　Soul City's need is green power. il por Bsns
　　W p 106 Ja 17 '70

SOUL culture. See Negroes—Culture

SOUL food. See Cookery, American

SOUL music. See Negro music

SOUL sister's international discotheque. See
　　Discotheques, etc.

SOULE, Gary M.
　**Neighborhood center with a difference. il
　　Parks & Rec 5:32-4 Ap '70**

SOULEN, Richard N.
　Black worship and hermeneutic. Chr Cent 87:
　　168-71 F 11 '70

SOUND
　How much do you know about the physics of
　　sound? quiz. J. Daugherty and M. Daug-
　　herty. il Sci Digest 68:74-5+ D '70
　　　See also
　Hearing
　Noise
　Plants, Effect of sound on
　Sound waves
　Ultrasonics

Apparatus
　Build a pink noise generator. J. S. Simonton,
　　jr. il Pop Electr 33:61-3 D '70
　Build IC volume expander. K. F. Buegel. il
　　Radio-Electr 41:36-9 Mr '70
　Build modular six-channel stereo mixer pre-
　　amp. G. D. Hanchett. il Radio-Electr 41:
　　36-9 O '70
　Compact stereo systems. il Consumer Rep 34:
　　222-76 D '69
　EW lab tested. See issues of Electronics
　　world
　Focus on sound. See issues of Popular pho-
　　tography
　　　See also
　Amplifiers
　Audio dealers
　Hydrophones
　Loud speaking apparatus
　Magnetic recorders and recording
　Microphones
　Moving picture cameras—Sound equipment
　Signal generators
　Sonar
　Stethoscope, Electric

Exhibitions
　Listening eye; exhibition at New York's Mu-
　　seum of contemporary crafts. A. McMillan.
　　il Craft Horiz 30:14-19 Ja '70

Charts, diagrams, etc.
　Sound. Electr World 83:38 Ja '70

Measurement
　　See Sound measurement

Recording and reproducing
　Focus on sound. See issues of Popular pho-
　　tography
　　　See also
　Audio fairs
　High fidelity sound systems—Control
　Magnetic recorders and recording
　Moving pictures, Amateur—Sound effects
　Phonograph records—Recording
　Sound—Stereophonic recording and reproduc-
　　ing

Stereophonic recording and
reproducing
　Four-channel at Westbury. I. Berger. Sat R
　　53:57 O 31 '70
　Four channel stereo. D. Lachenbruch. Ra-
　　dio-Electr 41:2+ F '70
　Four-channel stereo. J. Shane. il Radio-
　　Electr 41:45 D '70
　Four-channel stereo, problems and solutions.
　　D. von Recklinghausen. il Electr World 83:
　　33-5+ Mr '70
　Four-channel stereo, the new surround
　　sound. R. Berkovitz. il Electr World 83:39-
　　41+ F '70
　More on four-channel sound. W. A. Stock-
　　lin. Electr World 84:6-7 D '70
　Multiplying sound with a tape recorder. R.
　　Lanier. il Pop Sci 196:102-3+ My '70
　New four channel stereo techniques. W. G.
　　Salm. il Radio-Electr 41:33-5+ O '70
　New trends in sight and sound systems. R.
　　Berkovitz. il Pop Sci 197:68-9+ N '70
　Newest improvement in hi-fi listening: now
　　it's 4-channel stereo! W. Salm. il Pop Mech
　　133:134-8 My '70
　Now: four-channel records you can play on
　　any phonograph. S. M. Gallager. il Pop
　　Mech 134:56 D '70
　Stereo scene; four-channel stereo. J. G. Holt.
　　il Pop Electr 33:69-71+ N '70
　　　See also
　Magnetic recorders and recording—Stereo-
　　phonic recorders
　Stereophonic sound systems

Transmission thru water
　Underwater communications. S. Carpenter.
　　il Pop Sci 197:48-9+ Ag '70

Velocity
　Sound velocity and compressibility for lunar
　　rocks 17 and 46 and for glass spheres from
　　the lunar soil. E. Schreiber and others.
　　bibliog il Science 167:732-4 Ja 30 '70

SOUND and light programs
Sound and light and fury; Sound and light at Ford's theatre. Newsweek 76:63 Ag 3 '70

SOUND control. See Noise control

SOUND measurement
Now, a sound-level meter for $40. J. Davis. il Pop Sci 197:16 O '70

SOUND of music; musical comedy. See Musical comedies, revues, etc.—Criticisms, plots, etc.

SOUND perception
Auditory illusions and confusions. R. M. Warren and R. P. Warren. il Sci Am 223:30-6 D '70
Perceptual restoration of missing speech sounds. R. M. Warren. bibliog Science 167:392-3 Ja 23 '70

SOUND production by animals
See also
Birds—Song

SOUND production by insects. See Insect sounds

SOUND waves
News from the world of space exploration; sound heard from space. il Space World G-11-83:49 N '70
Silent sound; infrasound. Newsweek 76:62-3 Jl 27 '70

SOUNDING and soundings
See also
Depth indicators

SOUNDING rockets. See Rockets, Sounding

SOUNDPROOFING
New ideas for noise control at home. A. Lees. il Pop Sci 197:94-6 S '70

SOUP tureens. See Tureens

SOUPHANOUVONG, prince of Laos, 1902-
Brother vs. brother in Laos. il pors U S News 68:59 Mr 23 '70 *
Royal jugglers of southeast Asia. il pors Time 95:30 Mr 30 '70 *

SOUPS
Breakfast soups. il Bet Hom & Gard 48:116 Ap '70
Creamy vegetable bisques, chilled. Sunset 145:149 S '70
Favorite holiday soups and desserts; excerpts from Mastering the art of French cooking, by J. Child and S. Beck. il McCalls 98:58-61+ D '70
From Lebanon, a chewy soup. il Sunset 144:189 My '70
Great gazpacho hunt. E. J. Kahn, jr. Travel & Camera 33:50-2 Ap '70
Hearty soup is a meal in itself. il McCalls 98:74-5 Ja '71
Hearty soups & stews. Z. Coulson. il Good H 172:80-95 Ja '71
It's soup'er cool! il Ebony 25:114+ Jl '70
Ministrone in the Florentine style. il Sunset 144:190 Mr '70
Sopas de Mexico. il Sunset 145:76-7 S '70
Sorrel soups, rich and lean. M. McKendry. il Vogue 156:47+ Ag 1 '70
Things mother never taught you; cold soups. il Ladies Home J 87:80 Je '70
Think soup; *waterzooie* and *caldo xochitl.* C. Claiborne. il N Y Times Mag p73+ Ja 25 '70
Traveler's salvation: soup; with recipes. J. H. Winchester. il Travel 134:68-70+ N '70
Two glorious summer soups: gazpacho and vichyssoise. il McCalls 97:98 Jl '70
Warming bowl soup; recipes. F. M. Crawford. il Am Home 73:86-7+ O '70
Who says nuts to soup? Scotch broth and Hungarian chicken giblet soup. C. Claiborne. il N Y Times Mag p64 Mr 1 '70
Whole-meal soup, Russian *selianka.* Sunset 145:140 D '70
See also
Campbell soup company
Chowder

SOURDOUGH. See Dough

SOURDOUGH bread. See Bread

SOUSTER, Raymond
Canadian chronicle. P. D. Scott. Poetry 115:356-7 F '70 *
Comment. D. Zaiss. Poetry 116:52-3 Ap '70 *

SOUTH
American South: rise of a new confederacy. W. Hedgepeth. il Look 34:19-32+ N 17 '70
New South as census shows it; excerpts from address, October 23, 1970. G. H. Brown. U S News 69:54 N 2 '70
South and the Nation, by P. Watters. Review New Yorker 46:147-8+ O 31 '70. R. Coles
See also
Agriculture—Southern states
Confederate States of America
Crime and criminals—Southern states
Education—Southern states

Forests and forestry—Southern states
Hunting—Southern states
Negroes—Southern states
Public welfare—Southern states
School libraries—Southern states
South in literature
Wages—Southern states

Description and travel
South to spring. D. Butwin. il Sat R 53:53-4+ My 16 '70

Economic conditions
Go South, young man. Sr Schol 97:5 N 16 '70
Life on the Mississippi, 1970. P. Schrag. il Sat R 53:19-23 D 12 '70

History
John C. Calhoun: voice of the South. por Sr Schol 95:12 N 10 '69
Two southern historians: F. M. Green and D. M. Potter. G. M. Fredrickson. Am Hist R 75:1387-92 Je '70
See also
Ku Klux klan
Negroes—History
Reconstruction (Civil war)

Hotels, taverns, etc.
See Hotels, taverns, etc.—United States

Politics
Black power at the Dixie polls. il Time 95:17 Je 15 '70
Is a two-party South really here at last? il U S News 68:26-8 F 9 '70
New South creed, by P. M. Gaston. Review New Repub 163:23-5 S 26 '70. B. W. Eggler
Politics: a northern-southern strategy. por Time 96:6-8 Ag 3 '70
Republican strategy, southern fried. W. Barthelmes. Commonweal 91:420-1 Ja 16 '70
'70 political trends in the South. il U S News 69:37-40 O 12 '70
South revisited after a momentous decade. K. Fleming. il Newsweek 76:25-8 Ag 10 '70
Southern strategy. Newsweek 76:31-2 N 23 '70

Religious institutions and affairs
Anecdotes, facetiae, satire, etc.
People under glass, etc. Chr Cent 87:1523 D 16 '70

Social conditions
American South: rise of a new confederacy. W. Hedgepeth. il Look 34:19-32+ N 17 '70
More violence, more deaths. Commonweal 92:259-60 My 29 '70

Social history
See also
Slavery—United States

SOUTH AFRICA
See also
Atomic power—South Africa
Church and race problems in South Africa
Colleges and universities—South Africa
Foreign students in South Africa
Government ownership—South Africa
Investments, Foreign (in South Africa)
Kruger National park
Libraries—South Africa
Negro towns and settlements—South Africa
Negroes in South Africa
Police—South Africa
Political parties—South Africa
Purchasing, Military—South Africa
Science—South Africa
United Nations—South Africa

Antiquities
Who's who at Swartkrans. Sci Am 222:52 Je '70

Defenses
As South Africa pushes for role in West's defense. il U S News 69:74-6 S 7 '70
See also
Purchasing, Military—South Africa

Economic conditions
Foreign report; what will destroy apartheid? N. Macrae. Harper 240:30+ Mr '70; Same abr. with title What will destroy apartheid? Cur 118:57-64 My '70

Foreign relations
Money has no color; black states. il Newsweek 76:47 N 30 '70
South Africa and the wind of change. R. B. Ballinger. Cur Hist 58:165-9+ Mr '70

Industries
See also
De Beers consolidated mines. ltd.

SOUTH AFRICA—*Continued*

Politics and government

On a collision course. P. Webb. il Newsweek 75:40-9 Ap 27 '70
See also
Political parties—South Africa

Race problems

Archbishop Ramsey in the middle. J. Squire. Chr Cent 88:47-8 Ja 13 '71
Death throes of apartheid? America 123:3 Jl 11 '70
Foreign report; what will destroy apartheid? N. Macrae. Harper 240:30+ Mr '70; Same abr. with title What will destroy apartheid? Cur 118:57-64 My '70
From the UNESCO report on apartheid. Negro Hist Bul 32:22-3 D '69
No to Arthur Ashe. S. Uys. New Repub 162:17-18 F 14 '70
On a collision course. P. Webb. il Newsweek 75:40-9 Ap 27 '70
Shame city; Excelsior citizens violate immorality act. Newsweek 77:25+ Ja 4 '71
South Africa: booming nation's research and industry benefit from close ties with the United States. D. S. Greenberg. il Science 169:157-63 Jl 10 '70
South Africa: university system follows apartheid pattern. D. S. Greenberg. il Science 169:260-4+ Jl 17 '70
See also
Church and race problems in South Africa
United Nations—South Africa
United Nations—Special committee on the policies of apartheid of the government of the Republic of South Africa

Religious institutions and affairs

Moral issue for South Africa; churchmen's statement. America 122:120-1 F 7 '70
See also
Church and state in South Africa
Reformed church in South Africa

SOUTH AMERICA
See also
Latin America
Patagonia

Description and travel

Down that Pan American highway. E. A. Jahn. il Travel 133:34-9 F; 44-7+ Mr: 68-70+ Ap '70

Education

See Education—Latin America

Politics

See Latin America—Politics

SOUTH AMERICAN Indians. See Indians of South America
SOUTH AMERICAN literature. See Latin American literature
SOUTH AMERICANS. See Latin Americans
SOUTH AUSTRALIA. See Australia
SOUTH BRUNSWICK, N.J.

Education

Schools put a town on the map. C. H. Harrison. il Sat R 53:66-8+ F 21 '70
SOUTH CAROLINA
See also
Gardens—South Carolina
Hilton Head Island
Hunting—South Carolina

Churches

See Churches—United States

Description and travel

South Carolina's 300th birthday. F. Somers. il Redbook 135:48+ Je '70

Historic houses, etc.

Drayton Hall, plantation house of the Drayton family. F. D. Nichols. il Antiques 97:576-8 Ap '70
See also
Charleston, S.C.—Historic houses, etc.
Plantations

History

Mission for Mr Wedgwood; excerpts from journal, with introd. and epilogue by H. C. Wedgwood. T. Griffiths. il Am Heritage 21:64-7 Ag '70
SOUTH CAROLINA. State college, Orangeburg
Orangeburg massacre, by J. Nelson and J. Bass. Review
Nation 211:281-3 S 28 '70. J. C. Goulden
New Repub 163:26-8 N 21 '70. J. Yardley
Orangeburg relived. il Time 96:71+ O 26 '70

SOUTH DAKOTA
See also
Hunting—South Dakota
Wildlife conservation—South Dakota
Wildlife sanctuaries—South Dakota

Description and travel

South Dakota's vacation corner. W. Lane. il Travel 134:62-8 S '70
SOUTH HAVEN, Mich.

Public works

HUD aid makes the difference. A. R. Pierce. il Am City 85:80-1 Je '70
SOUTH in literature
Must the novelist crusade? E. Welty. il Writers Digest 50:32-5+ F '70
SOUTH LAKE TAHOE, Calif.

Education

Schools in a spa: unique aspects of a district serving a resort community. J. W. Myres. Clear House 45:186-8 N '70
SOUTH MIAMI, Fla.
Truck-mounted loading boom. il Am City 85:85 Ja '70
SOUTH MILWAUKEE, Wis.
Life inside a worker's idyl; report. F. Merrick. il Time 96:70-1 N 9 '70
SOUTH PACIFIC commission
President appoints Mr Marcus to South Pacific commission. Dept State Bul 63:315 S 14 '70
SOUTH POLE
See also
Antarctic exploration
SOUTH POLE, Magnetic. See Magnetism, Terrestrial
SOUTH SEA ISLANDS. See Islands of the Pacific; Oceania
SOUTH street seaport museum. See New York (city)—Galleries and museums
SOUTH VIETNAM. See Vietnam (Republic)
SOUTH WALNEY nature reserve. See Bird sanctuaries—England
SOUTHAMPTON, N.Y.
Long, glamorous summer in Southampton. P. Benchley. il Holiday 47:48-51+ Je '70
SOUTHARD, Frank A. jr
Financial setting for 1970; address, February 25-27, 1970. Vital Speeches 36:375-8 Ap 1 '70
SOUTHEAST ASIA. See Asia, Southeastern
SOUTHEAST ASIA treaty organization
Secretary Rogers' news conference of July 15, 1970. W. P. Rogers. Dept State Bul 63:125-32 Ag 3 '70
Secretary Rogers visits the Philippines, South Viet-Nam, Japan, and the United Kingdom; text of remarks and statements; with text of communique, June 29-July 12, 1970. W. P. Rogers. Dept State Bul 63:133-49 Ag 3 '70
SOUTHEASTERN conference football. See Football
SOUTHEASTERN library association
Intellectual whaaaat? SELA's 24th biennial. A. Plotnik. il Wilson Lib Bul 45:448-50 Ja '71
S.E. assn. conference meets in Atlanta. Library J 96:14 Ja 1 '71
SOUTHEASTERN regional ballet festival. See Dance festivals
SOUTHERN, Carol
Plastic furniture of Carols Sansegundo. il Craft Horiz 30:28-31+ D '70
SOUTHERN AFRICA. See Africa, Southern
SOUTHERN ASIA. See Asia, Southern
SOUTHERN Baptist convention. See Baptists in the United States
SOUTHERN Baptists. See Baptists in the United States
SOUTHERN CALIFORNIA Edison company
Worried utility asks for advice. il Bsns W p26 Mr 14 '70
SOUTHERN Christian leadership conference
SCLC: rhetoric or strategy? C. Rogers. Chr Cent 87:1032 S 2 '70
SOUTHERN consumers cooperatives
To be somebody someday. J. Smith. il por Redbook 135:86-7+ My '70
SOUTHERN cookery. See Cookery, American
SOUTHERN Methodist university, Dallas, Tex.
How to manage a professor; Alpha systems, inc. Bsns W p40 Ag 22 '70
SOUTHERN ocean racing conference. See Yacht racing
SOUTHERN PINES, N.C.
Pinehurst for golf. Southern Pines for horses. S. Birmingham. il Holiday 47:30-5+ Ap '70
SOUTHERN Presbyterian church. See Presbyterian church in the United States (South)

SOUTHERN railway company
  Southern railway: clear the tracks! il Forbes
    107:28 Ja 1 '71
  Wall Street beat. R. Brady. Duns 97:68 Ja
    '71
SOUTHERN states. See South
SOUTHERN student organizing committee
  Dixie's new left. H. E. Joye. il Trans-Action
    7:50-6+ S '70
SOUTHERN Utah state college. See Utah.
  Southern Utah state college, Cedar City
SOUTHERNERS
  Hypocrisy, southern style. B. Farber. Sat
    R 53:4 Ap 25 '70
  South and the Nation, by P. Watters. Review
    New Yorker 46:147-8+ O 31 '70. R. Coles
SOUTHWELL, John L.
  Teacher aids teacher. Clear House 45:104-6
    O '70
SOUTHWEST
  Pleasant, friendly sound of good manners.
    R. Graves. Life 68:2A Je 19 '70
    See also
  Fishing—Southwestern states
  Law—Southwestern states
  Libraries—Southwestern states
  New Mexico
SOUTHWESTERN library association
  Cooperation moves ahead in the Southwest.
    S. J. Kee. il por Library J 95:1294-7 Ap 1 '70
  Live-in in the Southwest: SWLA 1970. P.
    S. Grove. il Wilson Lib Bul 45:445-7 Ja '71
  State chapter weaknesses to be probed by
    SWLA. Library J 95:617 F 15 '70
SOUTHWESTERN regional ballet festival. See
  Dance festivals
SOUTHWICK, Charles H. and others
  Primate populations and biomedical research.
    bibliog il Science 170:1051-4 D 4 '70
SOUVANNA Phouma, prince of Laos
  Brother vs. brother in Laos. il pors U S
    News 68:59 Mr 23 '70 *
  Royal jugglers of southeast Asia. il pors Time
    95:30 Mr 30 '70 *
SOUZA, Carlito de. See De Souza, C.
SOUZA, José Patrocinio de. See De Souza, J.
  P.
SOUZAY, Gérard
  Records. Opera N 34:34 Ja 31 '70
SOVEREIGNTY
    See also
  Airspace (international law)
  State, The
SOVERN, Michael Ira
  Healer for Columbia. por Time 95:45 Ap 20
    '70 *
SOVIET-AMERICAN arms control talks. See
  Strategic arms limitation talks
SOVIET army. See Russia—Army
SOVIET government. See Russia—Politics and
  government
SOVIET literature (periodical) See Periodicals
  —Russia
SOVIET minorities. See Minorities
SOVIET UNION. See Russia
SOVIET women. See Women—Russia
SOWELL, Thomas
  Black professor says: colleges are skipping
    over competent blacks to admit authentic
    ghetto types. il N Y Times Mag p36-7+ D 13
    '70
SOWING. See Seeding
SOWINSKI, John
  Brief biography. S. Goodman. pors Dance Mag
    44:74-5 O '70 *
SOWS. See Swine
SOX, Harold C. Jr, and Mohit, Behzad
  Solid-phase radioimmunoassay of protein bio-
    synthesis. bibliog il Science 168:1467-8 Je
    19 '70
SOYBEANS
  Soybean growers try Regim-8. B. Coffman.
    Farm J 94:32F Ja '70
  Soybean seed terms you should know. C. E.
    Sommers. Suc Farm 68:B4 O '70
  Soybeans need more water than we thought.
    B. Coffman. Farm J 94:32B Ja '70
  Turn-around for soybeans. il Farm J 94:40J-
    40K Ap '70
  When should you plant soybeans? Suc Farm
    68:no3 G6 F '70
    See also
  American soybean association
  Cookery—Vegetables
  Feeding and feeding stuffs—Soybeans

Cultivation
  How the winners grow soybeans. R. D.
    Wennblom. il Farm J 94:65 Ap '70
  How to grow fifty-five bu. soybeans on 155
    acres. D. Seim. il Farm J 94:50A-50B Mr
    '70
  Is row farming outdated. J. C. Herman. il
    Suc Farm 69:A1 Ja '71

  Lodging cuts soybean yields 15 bu. per acre.
    B. Coffman. Farm J 93:30D D '69
  Weed-free soybeans average 4 bu. more. D.
    Seim. il Farm J 94:50+ Ap '70

Diseases and pests
  Who has the weediest soybeans? B. Coffman.
    il Farm J 94:29 O '70
    See also
  Nematodes

Harvesting
  How to combine two bu. more soybeans per
    acre. G. W. Wormley. il Farm J 94:28E N
    '70
  How to handle combine problems. P. B.
    Jones. il Suc Farm 68:34 Je '70

Marketing
  Did lower supports sell more soybeans? L.
    Palmer. Farm J 94:15+ Ag '70
  How promotion is selling your soybeans;
    sales in Japan. C. E. Ball. il Farm J 94:
    38-9+ My '70

Prices
  Soybean exports jump to new highs. il Bsns
    W p30 S 12 '70

Seeding
  Take care when planting soybeans. Suc Farm
    68:B8 My '70

Yield
  See Crop yields
SOYUZ (space vehicle) See Space vehicles, Rus-
  sian
SOYUZ flights. See Space flight—Manned
  flights—Soyuz flights
SPACE (architecture)
  Shelter in the woods. il Arch Forum 132:36-
    9 Mr '70
  Space shapers. B. Plumb. il Am Home 73:26+
    My '70
SPACE, Outer
  Archaeology in outer space. R. L. Schuyler.
    Space World G-3-75:13 Mr '70
  Inner and outer space. D. S. Cheever; T.
    Owen; D. L. Roberts. il Bul Atom Sci
    26:22-34 F '70
  U.S. discusses applicable law for outer space
    claims; statement, November 20, 1969. H.
    Reis. Dept State Bul 62:18-20 Ja 5 '70
    See also
  United Nations—Committee on the peace-
    ful uses of outer space

Exploration
  New horizon in space exploration. T. Owen
    and D. L. Roberts. il Bul Atom Sci 26:23-
    9 F '70
  People around the world prayed; Apollo 13
    and the future. D. Lawrence. U S News
    68:96 Ap 27 '70
  Science/the endless search. J. Lear. il Sat R
    53:39 Mr 7; 41 Mr 14 '70
    See also
  Space probes
SPACE, Personal. See Personal space
SPACE astronomy
  Astronomy developments in space. il Space
    World G-5-77:24-5 My '70
  Space astronomy plans face delay. W. J.
    Normyle. il Aviation W 92:44-6 F 2 '70
  Through space astronomy, man will study
    eras older than time. A. F. Hobbs. il Space
    World G-5-77:26-7 My '70
    See also
  Telescopes on space vehicles
  United States—National aeronautics and
    space administration—Astronomy missions
    board
SPACE biology
  Apollo 11: exposure of lower animals to
    lunar material. C. A. Benschoter. il Sci-
    ence 169:470-2 Jl 31 '70
  Germ on the moon; streptococcus mitis.
    Newsweek 75:63 Je 1 '70
  Microorganism back from the moon; strep-
    tococcus mitis. R. N. Watts, jr. Sky & Tel
    40:15 Jl '70
  Microorganisms survived lunar environment;
    streptococcus mitis found in camera. il
    Aviation W 92:22 Je 1 '70
  Reviewing space priorities. Sci N 98:93 Ag 1
    '70
  Testing man's value in space; Skylab. E.
    Driscoll. il Sci N 98:303-5 O 10 '70
SPACE committee. See United Nations—Com-
  mittee on the peaceful uses of outer space
SPACE communication. See Space flight—Com-
  munication systems
SPACE cooperation. See Space research—In-
  ternational aspects
SPACE electric rocket test. See Rocket en-
  gines—Testing

SPACE flight
Cosmonautics: a look at the future. G. Beregovoi. Space World G-6-78:30-1 Je '70
Future progress of space transportation. C. W. Mathews. il Space World G-7-79:18-21 Jl '70
Grand tour flights of 1970s to explore outermost planets. Space World G-10-82:14-15 O '70
Grand tour of the planets. I. M. Levitt. il Space World G-8-80:23-7 Ag '70
Man on an asteroid? il Chem 43:26-7 My '70
Mission to an asteroid. H. Alfvén and G. Arrhenius. il Science 167:139-41 Ja 9 '70; Discussion. 167:1758; 170:1431-2 Mr 27, D 25 '70
New horizon in space exploration. T. Owen and D. L. Roberts. il Bul Atom Sci 26:23-9 F '70
Options in space. il Sci N 98:53-4 Jl 25 '70
Putting robots on the planets. il U S News 69:45 N 30 '70
Reaching for the planets. il Sci N 97:264 Mr 14 '70
Voyage to the planets; with paintings by L. Pesek. K. F. Weaver. Nat Geog 138:147-93 Ag '70
See also
Artificial satellites
Computers—Space flight use
Ground support systems (space flight)
United States—National aeronautics and space administration

Accidents
After Apollo 13 . . . il U S News 68:19-21 Ap 27 '70
Apollo 13 accident. R. N. Watts, jr. il Sky & Tel 40:14 Jl '70
Apollo 13: the culprits. Newsweek 75:57 Je 29 '70
Apollo 13: the reason why. il Newsweek 75:61 Je 15 '70
Apollo 13: three who came back. il Newsweek 75:21-7 Ap 27 '70
Board reports. il Sci N 97:598 Je 20 '70
Four days of peril between earth and moon; Apollo 13: ill-fated space odyssey. il Time 95:14-18 Ap 27 '70
Many tests reveal mishap cause; Apollo 13. Z. Strickland. il Aviation W 92:49-50 Je 15 '70
On to Apollo 14; press conference of Apollo 13 astronauts. il Newsweek 75:70-1 My 4 '70
Oxygen reaction probable cause of crisis. E. J. Bulban. il Aviation W 92:21-3 Ap 20 '70
Post-mortem on Apollo 13. il Time 95:82-4 My 4 '70
Pre-lunch electrical overload led to Apollo 13 tank rupture. Z. Strickland. Aviation W 92:18-19 Je 8 '70
Questions left by Apollo 13. il Bsns W p25 Ap 18 '70
Review board urges re-examination of Apollo equipment. Z. Strickland. il Aviation W 92:254-7 Je 22 '70
Rupture of Apollo 13 tank laid to electrical problem. Z. Strickland. Aviation W 92:23-4 My 11 '70
Setback for Apollo. Time 95:59 Je 29 '70
Shorts in the system; Apollo 13. il Sci N 97:455 My 9 '70
13's glitch. 14's delay. il Sci N 97:571 Je 13 '70
Three astronauts tell what happened aboard the crippled Apollo 13. J. A. Lovell; J. Swigert; F. W. Haise, jr. il pors Life 68:24-33 My 1 '70
Untimely end of Apollo 13. il Sci N 97:387-8 Ap 18 '70
Vibration caused early Apollo 13 engine shutdown. Space World G-9-81:41 S '70
What really happened to Apollo 13. il Space World G-10-82:20-37 O '70
Why Apollo 13 failed. C. P. Gilmore. il Pop Sci 197:64-6+ O '70

Astronomical observations
See also
United States—National aeronautics and space administration—Astronomy missions board

Communication systems
Words from the moon: how they travel to earth. il Space World G-7-79:24-5 Jl '70

Economic aspects
Can the space program make a comeback? il U S News 70:44-6 Ja 4 '71

Finance
See also
Space flight to the moon—Finance

International aspects
Launching joint ventures in space; U.S.-Soviet cooperation. il Bsns W p86 Jl 25 '70

Link to the cosmonauts; docking agreement. Newsweek 76:100 N 9 '70
See also
United Nations—Committee on the peaceful uses of outer space

Manned flights
Space: a barrier to the species. J. P. Wiley, jr. il Natur Hist 79:70-3 Ja '70
See also
Astronauts
Space, Outer—Exploration
Space flight to Mars
Space flight to the moon—Manned flights

Accidents
See Space flight—Accidents

Extravehicular activity
See also
Space flight to the moon—Manned flights—Extravehicular activity

Soyuz flights
Back in orbit; Soyuz 9. il Time 95:43 Je 15 '70
Biomedical data collection primary goal of Soyuz 9. il Aviation W 92:17-18 Je 8 '70
Cosmonauts in quarantine following Soyuz landing. il Aviation W 92:21-2 Je 29 '70
Mahogany spaceship; Soyuz 9. il Newsweek 75:57 Je 29 '70
Soviet men in space; Soyuz 9. R. N. Watts, jr. Sky & Tel 40:14 Jl '70
Soviet space feat; its aim; Soyuz 9. il U S News 68:83 Je 29 '70
Soviets seek man's precise space role. Aviation W 93:18 Jl 20 '70
Soviets seek spacecraft, crew standards. Aviation W 92:14-15 Je 15 '70
Soyuz 9 medical reports puzzling. Z. Strickland. il Aviation W 93:51-3 N 2 '70
Soyuz 9 sets endurance record. R. N. Watts, jr. il Sky & Tel 40:83 Ag '70
Soyuz 9 sets manned endurance record, moves to lower orbit. Aviation W 92:258 Je 22 '70
Success for Soyuz; no. 9. il Time 95:59 Je 29 '70

Physiological aspects
Apollo 14 will probe light flashes. Aviation W 92:51-2 Je 15 '70
Benefits to medicine; bioastronautics. G. Gregory. il UNESCO Courier 23:16-24 Mr '70
Big booster paces Soviet manned flights. Aviation W 93:18 Jl 6 '70
Cosmonaut biomedical problems on Soyuz 9 mission detailed. Aviation W 93:19 O 12 '70
Cosmonauts experience lack of thirst; Soyuz 9. Aviation W 93:17 O 19 '70
Effects of rotating environment on future men in space. il Space World G-7-79:12-13 Jl '70
News from the world of space exploration: Orbiting primate experiment. Space World G-3-75:47-8 Mr '70
Orbiting frog otolith. il Space World G-11-83:31-7 N '70
Soviets seek spacecraft, crew standards. Aviation W 92:14-15 Je 15 '70
Soyuz 9 medical reports puzzling. Z. Strickland. il Aviation W 93:51-3 N 2 '70
Two monkeys are better than one in space; Orbiting primate experiment. J. Eberhart. il Sci N 97:251-3 Mr 7 '70
See also
Astronauts—Health and hygiene
Biosatellite program
Space flight—Radiation hazards
Space biology
Space medicine
Weightlessness

Psychological aspects
Social stresses in a flight to Mars. Space World G-8-80:41-2 Ag '70

Radiation hazards
Light in an astronaut's eye; Cerenkov radiation or cosmic-ray effects? il Sci N 97:523-4 My 30 '70
Man the experimenter; HZE particles and the brain. Sci N 98:6-7 Jl 4 '70

Safety devices and measures
Lifeboat for spacemen. il Sci Digest 67:57 Ap '70
Lunar module may become permanent Apollo lifeboat. il Aviation W 92:25-6 Ap 27 '70
See also
Space rescue work

Social aspects
Space and tomorrow's society. K. G. Harr, jr. Space World G-12-84:30-3 D '70

SPACE flight—*Continued*

Study and teaching

Aerospace education takes off. C. H. Harrison. il Schol Teach Sec Teach Sup p 10-11 Ap 6 '70

SPACE flight accidents. See Space flight—Accidents

SPACE flight in art

Space paintings by artists commissioned by NASA; portfolio. Space World G-4-76:23-30 Ap '70

SPACE flight simulators

Effects of rotating environment on future men in space. il Space World G-7-79:12-13 Jl '70

See also

Centrifuges

SPACE flight to Jupiter

News from the world of space exploration; Pioneer F. il Space World G-3-75:48-9 Mr '70

Precusors to the outer planets. il Space World G-11-83:19-20 N '70

See also

Space probes

SPACE flight to Mars

Mars or bust? pro and con discussion. il Sr Schol 95:18-19 S 15 '69

On to Mars? I. G. Barbour; reply. R. W. Graham. Chr Cent 87:88+ Ja 21 '70

Painless path to Mars. R. S. Lewis. il Bul Atom Sci 26:44-5 Ja '70

Social stresses in a flight to Mars. Space World G-8-80:41-2 Ag '70

Space odyssey of tomorrow: a trip to Mars. R. Jastrow. il N Y Times Mag p30-1+ My 10 '70

See also

Space probes

SPACE flight to Mercury

See also

Space probes

SPACE flight to the moon

How blacks view mankind's giant step. S. Morris. il Ebony 25:33-6+ S '70

Moon program's business brain trust; Apollo executive group. E Clark. il pors Nations Bsns 58:32-4+ My '70

Scientific community decries Apollo mission cancellations. Z. Strickland. Aviation W 93:55-6+ S 28 '70

Setback for future Apollo flights. il U S News 68:29 Ja 19 '70

Space goals for '70s: Nixon's timetable. il U S News 68:44-5 Ap 13 '70

Vacation trip to the moon? Space World G-4-76:17 Ap '70

See also

Space vehicles—Recovery

Cost

Lunar landing cost set at $21.35 billion. il Aviation W 92:52 Mr 2 '70

Finance

Economics of the moon shot. il Sr Schol 95:17 S 15 '69

History

Twenty years to the moon. Space World G-3-75:35-7 Mr '70

Luna flights

Buggy on the moon; Luna 17. il Newsweek 76:50 N 30 '70

Dig that rock! return of unmanned Soviet space vehicle, Luna 16. Sr Schol 97:20 O 19 '70

Giant step for Lunokhod; Luna 17 and Lunokhod I. il Time 96:63 N 30 '70

Giant step for robotkind. Sci Am 223:43 N '70

Luna first; unmanned mission of Russia's Luna 16. il Time 96:54 O 5 '70

Luna 16's successful mission. R. N. Watts, jr. il Sky & Tel 40:271 N '70

Rover initiates Soviet applied lunar work. il Aviation W 93:19-20 N 23 '70

Soviet Luna 16. Y. Marinin. Space World G-12-84:21-2 D '70

Soviet unmanned mission makes successful return; Luna 16. Aviation W 93:19 S 28 '70

Soviets call Luna 16 testbed for several new systems. il Aviation W 93:16-17 O 12 '70

Soviets plan extensive lunar exploration. il Aviation W 93:14-16 O 5 '70

Unmanned to the moon and back; Russia's Luna 16. il Sci N 98:269 S 26 '70

Voyage of Luna 16. il Newsweek 76:57 O 5 '70

Manned flights

Ax for Apollo. Newsweek 76:103 D 7 '70

Magnificent Apollos. E. K. Gann. il Flying 87:37-66+ S '70

Manned space exploration: case for Apollo; letter. A. W. England. Science 170:1033 D 4 '70

Moon, earth's book of life? Apollo lunar exploration missions. il Space World G-3-75:24-9 Mr '70

Moon shots planned for '71. il U S News 70:46 Ja 4 '71

More from the moon. Time 95:78 Je 8 '70

NASA urged to cut missions to moon. Aviation W 92:15 Je 15 '70

News from the world of space exploration; Apollo crew health program. Space World H-1-85:47-8 Ja '71

Picking Apollo goals. Sci N 98:162 Ag 22 '70

Plight of Apollo; cancellation of flight nos. 15 and 19. Newsweek 76:97 S 14 '70

Solid blow to lunar science; eliminating two Apollos. il Sci N 98:215-16 S 12 '70

Waning moon program. Time 96:45 S 14 '70

What happens next. il Sci N 97:407 Ap 25 '70

See also

Astronauts—Training

Moon—Exploration

Accidents

See Space flight—Accidents

Apollo 8 flight

First moon explorers receive the society's Hubbard medal. il Nat Geog 137:858-61 Je '70

Apollo 11 flight

Day Apollo 11 was launched. il Space World G-13-75:14-21 Mr '70

Dream fulfilled: Apollo 11. il Sr Schol 95:16+ S 15 '69

First moon explorers receive the society's Hubbard medal. il Nat Geog 137:858-61 Je '70

Of a fire on the moon, by N. Mailer. Review Nat R 23:38 Ja 12 '71. D. Brudnoy

Apollo 12 flight

Happiness is a moon walk. il Sr Schol 95:19 D 8 '69

How Apollo 12 was planned. il Space World G-2-74:4-47 F '70

Apollo 13 flight

After Apollo 13... il U S News 68:19-21 Ap 27 '70

After Apollo 13, lowered sights in space. il U S News 68:43-5 Ap 13 '70

Apollo flight: right on. il Newsweek 75:71-2 Ap 20 '70

Apollo 13 makes it back to earth. R. N. Watts, jr. il Sky & Tel 39:350 Je '70

Apollo 13: the culprits. Newsweek 75:57 Je 29 '70

Apollo 13: the mission and the meaning. F. W. Haise, jr. il por PTA Mag 65:14-16 S '70

Apollo 13: the reason why. il Newsweek 75:61 Je 15 '70

Apollo 13: three who came back. il Newsweek 75:21-7 Ap 27 '70

Apollo 13 to the highlands. E. Driscoll. il Sci N 97:353-5 Ap 4 '70

Apollo 13 weather rules altered. Aviation W 92:229 Mr 9 '70

Apollo's return: triumph over failure. il Time 95:12-14 Ap 27 '70

Aquarius and Odyssey. il Newsweek 75:62-3 Ap 13 '70

Dawning of Aquarius; Apollo 13. il Time 95:52+ Ap 13 '70

Decision time. J. Lear. Sat R 53:56 My 9 '70

Heading for the hills; Apollo 13. il Time 95:52+ Ap 20 '70

How Apollo 13 will probe the moon's interior. W. Von Braun. il Pop Sci 196:56-8+ Mr '70

Joyous triumph of Apollo 13. il Life 68:28-36 Ap 24 '70

Letter from Paris. Genêt. New Yorker 46:110 My 2 '70

People around the world prayed. D. Lawrence. U S News 68:96 Ap 27 '70

Post-mortem on Apollo 13. il Time 95:82-4 My 4 '70

Questions left by Apollo 13. il Bsns W p25 Ap 18 '70

Setback for Apollo. Time 95:59 Je 29 '70

Special report: Apollo 13; symposium, with editorial comment. il Aviation W 92:9, 14-23 Ap 20; 18-28 Ap 27 '70

Sun angle held vital to Apollo 13 landing. il Aviation W 92:67+ Ap 6 '70

13's glitch, 14's delay. il Sci N 97:571 Je 13 '70

Three astronauts tell what happened aboard the crippeled Apollo 13. J. A. Lovell; J. Swigert; F. W. Haise, jr. il pors Life 68:24-33 My 1 '70

Untimely end of Apollo 13. il Sci N 97:387-8 Ap 18 '70

What really happened to Apollo 13. il Space World G-10-82:20-37 O '70

SPACE flight to the moon—Manned flights—
Apollo 13 flight—*Continued*
What science seeks from Apollo 13. il U S
News 68:46-7 Ap 20 '70
Worth the risk? Sr Schol 96:7 My 4 '70

Apollo 14 flight

Aerospace; briefings on the upcoming
Apollo 14 mission. Sci N 99:2 Ja 2 '71
Apollo 14 plan include cart, new test gear.
Z. Strickland. il Aviation W 93:18-19 O 26
'70
Astronauts get added training due to Apollo
14 mission delays. Z. Strickland. Aviation
W 93:82-3+ N 16 '70
Modifications to spacecraft force added delay
in Apollo 14 launch. Aviation W 93:22 Jl 6
'70
On to Apollo 14. il Newsweek 75:70-1 My 4
'70
Research tradeoffs for the next Apollo. il
Sci N 97:499 My 23 '70
Site change to ease Apollo landing. Z. Strick-
land. Aviation W 93:56-7 Jl 27 '70
What goes, and who. il Sci N 97:478 My 16
'70

Apollo 15 flight (proposed)

Unknowns force Apollo 15 crew to be cautious on lunar rover. Aviation W 93:85 N
16 '70

Extravehicular activity

Apollo 12 explorers on the moon. R. Hillenbrand. il Sky & Tel 39:95-8 F '70
Apollo 13 to transmit drill sounds. Z. Strickland. il Aviation W 92:61-2 Mr 16 '70

Religious aspects

Praying the space heroes home; with editorial comment. Chr Today 14:27, 37 My 8
'70

Psychological aspects

Space: what now? Nation 210:516-17 My 4 '70

Zond flights

Optical tracking used with Soviet Zond 8.
Aviation W 93:19 N 2 '70

SPACE flight to Venus
See also
Space probes

SPACE flight training. See Astronauts—Training

SPACE medicine
Soviets seek man's precise space role. Avia-
tion W 93:18 Jl 20 '70
Space program; more time for biomedical
research? J. Walsh. Science 167:1469-71 Mr
13 '70
See also
Astronauts—Health and hygiene
Space flight—Physiological aspects

SPACE perception
Ponzo perspective illusion as a manifestation
of space perception. H. Leibowitz and others; reply with rejoinder. W. Schiff. Science
168:395 Ap 17 '70
See also
Orientation

SPACE photography
Shooting the moon. B. Sherman. Mod Phot
33:80+ D '69
See also
Earth—Photographs from space
Mars (planet)—Photographs from space

Apparatus and supplies

Moon cameras. il Space World G-4-76:18-22
Ap '70
Our camera on the moon; Apollo lunar sur-
face close-up camera. N. Rothschild. il Pop
Phot 66:100 F '70

SPACE physics. See Cosmic physics

SPACE pollution
Orbiting junkyard. D. R. Hager. il Sat R 53:
44-6 S 5 '70

SPACE probes
Lingering look at Mars; 1971 Mariner plans.
E. Driscoll. il Sci N 98:227-8 S 12 '70
Martian orbiters. Sci Am 223:80+ S '70
Pioneer-Jupiter F. il Space World G-5-77:23
My '70
Plans for pioneer flights to Jupiter. R. N.
Watts, jr. il Sky & Tel 40:82-3 Ag '70
Roster of space activity. R. N. Watts, jr. Sky
& Tel 39:81-2 F '70
Venus-Mercury flight experiments chosen.
Aviation W 93:60 Ag 10 '70

SPACE probes, Russian
Another touch of Venus; Venera 7 probe. il
Newsweek 76:42 D 28 '70
Automatic devices for space exploration;
with comments by Georgi Petrov and
Alexei Yeliseyev. V. Shvarev and V.
Bulekov. Space World H-1-85:33-7 Ja '71

SPACE radiation. See Cosmic rays

SPACE rescue work
Hottest job in the world; astronaut rescue
team. M. Caidin. il Pop Mech 133:89-92+
Ap '70
Skylab rescue capability studies pushed by
NASA. W. J. Normyle. Aviation W 92:28 Ap
27 '70

SPACE research
Aerospace. See occasional issues of Science
news
Flurry in space. Sci N 98:461 D 19 '70
See also
Artificial satellites—Use in research
United Nations—Committee on the peaceful
uses of outer space

Economic aspects

Economic efficiency of space flight. A. Yeli-
seyev. por Space World G-10-82:17-19 O '70
Space research in trouble; goal-oriented funds.
Cato. Nat R 22:665 Je 30 '70
$10 billion more for space? R. E. Lapp. New
Repub 162:16-19 F 21 '70

International aspects

British reject post-Apollo participation. D.
E. Fink. Aviation W 93:19 N 9 '70
Europeans back space cooperation. D. E.
Fink. Aviation W 93:17-18 O 5 '70
Europeans seek approval to join post-Apollo
work. D. C. Fink. Aviation W 93:20 Jl 13 '70
Getting together on space; Europe and U.S.
il Sci N 98:165-6 Ag 22 '70
International cooperation in space. A. W.
Frutkin. bibliog il Science 169:333-9 Jl 24
'70
International space station plan pushed. E.
H. Kolcum. Aviation W 93:18-19 O 12 '70
Japan asks for help. S. Griffin. il Sci N 97:
516 My 23 '70
Joining Europe in space. il Bsns W p 120+
S 26 '70
Meshing at the hardware stage. Sci N 98:365
N 7 '70
Other nations to use space station. B. M. El-
son. il Aviation W 93:50-1+ S 28 '70
Quickening pace toward space cooperation;
talks with Russians on docking compatibili-
ty. il Sci N 98:315 O 17 '70
Russians receptive to talks on space. Aviation
W 92:50 Je 29 '70
Space applications launch talks expected soon
on draft pact. Aviation W 93:18 O 5 '70
U.S.-Europe space cooperation spurred. K.
Johnsen. Aviation W 93:18-19 S 28 '70
U.S. USSR set joint space talk. E. H. Kol-
cum. Aviation W 93:16-17 O 19 '70
See also
United Nations—Committee on the peaceful
uses of outer space

Social aspects

Absolute necessity of space exploitation. K.
Ehricke. Space World G-6-78:38-9 Je '70

China (People's Republic)

China joins the space age. il Sci N 97:427-8
My 2 '70

Europe, Western

Europe tries to patch space cooperation. D.
E. Fink. Aviation W 93:25-6 N 16 '70
Europe's space dilemma. E. H. Kolcum.
Aviation W 92:11 F 23 '70
U.K. to join European space effort, balks at
launcher. D. E. Fink. il Aviation W 93:86-8
S 7 '70
See also
European launcher development organization
European space conference
European space research organization

France

Greater French space participation urged.
Aviation W 92:24 My 4 '70
Uncertainty about space; French program. N.
Hardy. Sci N 98:126 Ag 8 '70
See also
France—National center for space studies

India

India pushing for own space capability. K.
Johnsen. Aviation W 92:22-3 My 11 '70

Japan

In space at last; Ohsumi launch. S. Griffin. il
Sci N 97:232 F 28 '70
Japan asks for help. S. Griffin. il Sci N
97:516 My 23 '70
Japan sets ambitious space goals. C. Brown-
low. il Aviation W 92:73+ F 23 '70
Japan striving to solidify ranking as space
nation. il Aviation W 92:95 Mr 9 '70
Space program in Japan takes a bad trip. il
Bsns W p86 Ja 17 '70

SPACE research—*Continued*

Russia

Administering and managing the U.S. and Soviet space programs. F. D. Kohler and D. L. Harvey. bibliog Science 169:1049-56 S 11 '70

Astronautics: past and future; interview. B. Petrov. Space World G-11-83:38-9 N '70

Big booster paces Soviet manned flights. Aviation W 93:18 Jl 6 '70

Hare and the tortoise. R. Hotz. Aviation W 93:9 N 23 '70

Manned flights cut by Soviets. Aviation W 92:18 Ja 19 '70

Notes on the Soviet space program. R. N. Watts, jr. il Sky & Tel 40:350+ D '70

Reverses hamper Soviet space program. il Aviation W 92:84-5+ Mr 9 '70

Soviet space gains cited by Low to senator. Aviation W 93:20 D 7 '70

United States

Administering and managing the U.S. and Soviet space programs. F. D. Kohler and D. L. Harvey. bibliog Science 169:1049-56 S 11 '70

After Apollo 13, lowered sights in space. il U S News 68:43-5 Ap 13 '70

American space program for the 1970's. R. N. Watts, jr. il Sky & Tel 39:294+ My '70

Apollo 13: the mission and the meaning. F. W. Haise, jr. il por PTA Mag 65:14-16 S '70

Exploring space in the seventies; adaptation of address, December 1969. S. F. Singer. il Bul Atom Sci 26:2-3 N '70

Hare and the tortoise. R. Hotz. Aviation W 93:9 N 23 '70

Limited funds defer manned programs. W. J. Normyle. il Aviation W 92:63-5+ Mr 9 '70

Major decisions on space near. W. J. Normyle. il Aviation W 93:14-15 Ag 17 '70

Man vs. machines in space: what the future holds; technology applications program. il U S News 68:78-9 My 11 '70

1969, year of Apollo. il Space World G-3-75: 42-3 Mr '70

Nixon space policy lacks funding level commitment. W. J. Normyle. Aviation W 92: 19-20 Mr 16 '70

Our new worlds above: frontiers in space. il Sr Schol 96:4-7 Mr 16 '70

Space in the 1970's. Sci Am 222:54 My '70

$10 billion more for space? R. E. Lapp. New Repub 162:16-19 F 21 '70

Time to stand; excerpts from address. E. M. Cortright. Aviation W 93:9 N 2 '70

U.S. space pace slowed severely. W. J. Normyle. il Aviation W 92:16 Ja 19 '70

Von Braun: the next decade in space; interview. W. Von Braun. pors Bsns W p66-7 Jl 4 '70

Warns against space cutbacks. Space World H-1-85:48-9 Ja '71

What lies ahead in space? address, September 14, 1970. T. O. Paine. Vital Speeches 37:26-9 O 15 '70

White House study urges space advances. W. J. Normyle. Aviation W 92:20-1 Mr 23 '70

See also
Space flight
Space flight to the moon
United States—National aeronautics and space administration

SPACE sciences
See also
Cosmic physics

Study and teaching

Aerospace education takes off. C. H. Harrison. il Schol Teach Sec Teach Sup p 10-11 Ap 6 '70

SPACE scientists, Negro. See Negro scientists

SPACE shuttles. See Space vehicles

SPACE stations

Additional orbiting workshop under study at NASA center. Z. Strickland. Aviation W 92: 22 Ap 6 '70

Next big step in space: shuttlecraft, sky platforms. il U S News 69:70-1 Jl 13 '70

Other nations to use space station. B. M. Elson. il Aviation W 93:50-1+ S 28 '70

Progress report on twelve-man space station. il Space World G-12-84:14-15 D '70

Saturn V workshop. il Space World G-3-75: 6-9 Mr '70

Shuttling into space. L. B. Taylor. il Mech Illus 66:45-7+ Ap '70

Skylab, America's first space station. W. G. Holder and W. D. Siuru, jr. il Sci Digest 68:70-6 Ag '70

Skylab; our first space station. W. Von Braun. il Pop Sci 197:51-3+ S '70

Skylab: our next giant step in space. J. F. Pearson. il Pop Mech 134:107-11+ D '70

Skylab scheduled for 1972. R. N. Watts, jr. il Sky & Tel 40:146-8 S '70

Space agency urged to consider student ideas on space station. R. G. O'Lone. Aviation W 93:58 S 28 '70

Space station research. il Space World H-1-85:4-12 Ja '71

Space station '75. il Space World G-5-77:12-20 My '70

Space station to help man study his surroundings. il Space World G-3-75:4-5 Mr '70

Testing man's value in space; Skylab. E. Driscoll. il Sci N 98:303-5 O 10 '70

Toward a three-dimensional civilization; interview. K. Ehricke. il pors Space World G-12-84:4-11 D '70

Utilization of space station to be studied by NASA. W. J. Normyle. Aviation W 93:17 Ag 10 '70

Design

Design emerging for space station. Z. Strickland. il Aviation W 93:40-1+ Ag 3 '70

SPACE technology

Crisis of transition; excerpts from address. L. J. Evans. Aviation W 92:9 F 16 '70

Realizing the benefits of space technology: direct broadcast satellites; statement, May 11, 1970. W. P. Allen. Dept State Bul 63: 95-9 Jl 20 '70

Spin-off: the fruit of space research. G. Gregory. il UNESCO Courier 23:4-31+ Mr '70

Technical revolution of the 1970s; symposium, with editorial comment. il Aviation W 92: 21, 26-35+ Je 22 '70

Toward a three-dimensional civilization; interview. K. Ehricke. il pors Space World G-12-84:4-11 D '70

SPACE tug. See Space vehicles

SPACE vehicle models

Testing

NASA conducts space shuttle drop tests. il Aviation W 92:52 Je 8 '70

SPACE vehicles

Along the earth-cosmos route; transport spaceships. G. Maximov. Space World G-7-79:34-5 Jl '70

Back to Fra Mauro; changes after Apollo 13 accident. Time 95:52 My 11 '70

Everybody into space; reports on the ferry. J. Lear. il Sat R 53:41 Mr 14 '70

5:15 to orbit; reusable shuttle system. il Space World G-5-77:28-32 My '70

Grumman's earth orbital shuttle. il Space World G-5-77:21-2 My '70

NASA advances space shuttle development. Aviation W 92:21 My 18 '70

NASA plans orbital utility vehicle; space tug concept. Z. Strickland. il Aviation W 93:73+ Jl 13 '70

News from the world of space exploration; requests for quotations on space shuttle. Space World G-10-82:47 O '70

Next big step in space: shuttlecraft, sky platforms. il U S News 69:70-1 Jl 13 '70

Next giant step: space shuttles. il Time 95: 63 Je 22 '70

Orbit-to-orbit shuttle takes shape. il Space World H-1-85:38-9 Ja '71

Shuttle group readies proposal requests. il Aviation W 92:17-18 Ja 19 '70

Shuttling into space. L .B. Taylor. il Mech Illus 66:45-7+ Ap '70

Space exploration in the 70s; grand tour spacecraft. il Space World G-11-83:24-8 N '70

Space ferry wins priority. il Bsns W p49 F 7 '70

Space shuttle project faces limited funds. Z. Strickland. il Aviation W 92:87+ F 23 '70

Space tug. il Space World G-7-79:22 Jl '70

Spaceplane that can put you in orbit: space-shuttle. W. Von Braun. il Pop Sci 197:37-9+ Jl '70

Two concepts for nuclear shuttle. il Space World G-10-82:8-9 O '70

When Mars is a milk run; space shuttle program. il Bsns W p95-6 Ap 11 '70

See also
Lunar vehicles

Atomic power plants

Advanced space reactor concept. il Space World G-11-83:40 N '70

Generator for the grand tour; radioisotope thermoelectric generator. il Space World G-7-79:36 Jl '70

Nuclear shuttle concepts emerge. B. S. Elson. il Aviation W 92:64-5 My 11 '70

Providing perpetual power: radioisotope thermoelectric generators. il Space World G-12-84:36-41 D '70

SPACE vehicles—*Continued*

Control systems

See also
Inertial guidance systems

Cost

Shuttle runout set at $14 billion. W. H. Normyle. Aviation W 92:16-17 Je 8 '70

Crews

See Astronauts

Design

Apollo 14 capsule changes planned. Z. Strickland. il Aviation W 93:75 S 14 '70
Choosing shuttle options. il Sci N 98:380-1 N 14 '70
Every man an astronaut; new shuttle craft. W. Jury. il Space World G-3-75:32-3 Mr '70
Flight hardware of the Apollo/Saturn V space vehicle. il Space World G-11-83:11-17 N '70
Integrated system studies decided upon for shuttle. Aviation W 92:19 F 2 '70
NASA asks quick shuttle replies. W. J. Normyle. Aviation W 92:16-17 F 23 '70
NASA divided over space shuttle. W. J. Normyle. il Aviation W 92:18-19 Ap 13 '70
Next step in space: the shuttle. E. Driscoll. il Sci N 98:178-9 Ag 22 '70
Nuclear shuttle concepts emerge. B. S. Elson. il Aviation W 92:64-5 My 11 '70
Reusable space shuttle designs evolving. il Aviation W 92:56-7 My 4 '70
Review board urges re-examination of Apollo equipment. Z. Strickland. il Aviation W 92:254-7 Je 22 '70
Shuttle poses dominant challenge. W. J. Normyle. il Aviation W 92:96-8+ Je 22 '70
Visibility studies for space shuttle. il Space World G-7-79:8-9 Jl '70

Electronic equipment

See also
Space vehicles—Propulsion systems—Electronic equipment

Equipment

Accommodations for living in space studied by NASA. Z. Strickland. il Aviation W 92:61-2+ My 4 '70
High-resolution camera to assist Apollo 13 topographical mapping. il por Aviation W 92:19 Mr 23 '70

Escape devices

News from the world of space exploration: mini-sized escape capsules. il Space World G-10-82:48+ O '70

Fuel

See Rockets—Fuel

Landing systems

High-speed unpowered landing urged as feasible for shuttle. W. S. Hieronymus. Aviation W 93:16 O 5 '70
NASA lifting body makes first flight. Aviation W 92:21 Je 8 '70

Mars

Balsa will cushion Mars lander system. il Space World G-8-80:34-6 Ag '70

Moon

Lunar module may become permanent Apollo lifeboat. il Aviation W 92:25-6 Ap 27 '70
Support; Apollo 13 lunar module. New Yorker 46:27-8 Ap 25 '70

Launching

France seeking world use of Diamant B. D. E. Fink. il Aviation W 92:84-5+ Ap 27 '70
Lightning-warning system for NASA launches. Space World G-6-78:40 Je '70

Lightning hazards

See Aviation—Lightning hazards

Photographs

Apollo 13 damage recorded by crew. Aviation W 92:18-19 Ap 27 '70

Piloting

Crew describes Apollo crisis. Z. Strickland. il Aviation W 92:20-1 Ap 27 '70

Power supply

See also
Space vehicles—Atomic power plants

Propulsion systems

Air force gets Boeing booster. Aviation W 93:44 Ag 31 '70
Modification of Agena studied to triple payload of Nimbus. Aviation W 92:69 Ap 27 '70

New technology shuttle engine key. M. L. Yaffee. il Aviation W 93:53-5+ Ag 10 '70
News from the world of space exploration; electrochemical propulsion system. il Space World G-6-78:52 Je '70
Two-stage concept picked for Europa 3. Aviation W 92:27 My 4 '70
See also
European launcher development organization
Rocket engines
Space vehicles—Atomic power pants

Electronic equipment

Centaur gets improved avionics. B. Miller. il Aviation W 93:45-6 Ag 31 '70

Failure

Fuel pressure problem hampered Europa. D. E. Fink. Aviation W 93:21 Jl 6 '70
Old reliable in trouble; Delta booster. J. Eberhart. il Sci N 97:225 F 28 '70
Vibration caused early Apollo 13 engine shutdown; Saturn V launch vehicle. Space World G-9-81:41 S '70

Specifications

U.S. launch vehicles; International launch vehicles; tables (cont) Aviation W 92:107-8 Mr 9 '70

Testing

Steering system tested; launch stage for Titan III-C. il Space World G-5-77:46-7 My '70

Radio equipment

Survival radio for Apollo. W. L. Blair. il Electr World 84:38-40+ N '70

Recovery

Waiting for Apollo 13; aboard the Iwo Jima. B. Kocivar. il Pop Sci 197:44-6+ Ag '70

Reliability

Calculated risk; excerpts from address. J. W. O'Neill. Aviation W 92:13 My 25 '70

Safety devices and measures

See also
Space vehicles—Escape devices

Shielding (heat)

Shuttle may use low-cost ablatives. Aviation W 93:56 O 5 '70

Specifications

U.S. & international spacecraft; tables (cont) Aviation W 92:105-6 Mr 9 '70

Stability and stabilizers

Wheel may aid spacecraft; stabilization of communications satellites. il Space World G-6-78:42-3 Je '70

Testing

Flight testing of subscale shuttle urged. N. S. Himmel. il Aviation W 93:78+ Jl 13 '70

Tracking

Optical observations of Apollo 12. il Sky & Tel 39:127-30 F '70
Optical tracking used with Soviet Zond 8. Aviation W 93:19 N 2 '70

SPACE vehicles, Chinese
Chinese spaceship; conception of H. Tsien, scientist deported in 1955. J. Lear. Sat R 53:62 My 16 '70

SPACE vehicles, Russian
Docked Soyuz spacecraft are displayed in Moscow. il Aviation W 92:66 My 18 '70
Linked Soyuz spacecraft shown by Soviets at Japan's Expo 70. il Aviation W 92:70-1+ Ap 27 '70
Lunokhod 1 vehicle. Luna 17 shown on moon and in assembly. il Aviation W 93:14-15 N 30 '70
Soyuz 9 readied for launch at Tyuratam. il Aviation W 92:46-8 Je 29 '70

SPACEMEN. See Astronauts

SPACESUITS. See Astronauts—Clothing

SPACKS, Barry
Burning trash; poem. Nation 212:88 Ja 18 '71
Child Adam; poem. Poetry 117:186 D '70
E.P. in his silence; poem. New Yorker 46:46 N 28 '70
about
Comment. A. Williamson. Poetry 115:282-3 Ja '70

SPADA, Assunta R. See Friedman, J. H. jt. auth.

SPAGHETTI. See Macaroni

SPAGHT, Monroe E.
Royal Dutch/Shell realigns at the top; interview. il pors Bsns W p 102-3+ My 9 '70

SPAHN, George
Charlie Manson's home on the range. G.
Talese. il por Esquire 73:101-3+ Mr '70 *
SPAIN
California? No, the Costa Brava. il Sunset
144:120 Ja '70
See also
Andalusia
Architecture—Spain
Art—Spain
Church and state in Spain
Government investigations—Spain
Labor and laboring classes—Spain
Labor laws and legislation—Spain
Land tenure—Spain
Mancha, La
Natural resources—Spain
Pamplona
Prisoners—Spain
Prisons—Spain
Protests, demonstrations, etc.—Spain
Publishers and publishing—Spain
Purchasing, Military—Spain
Salamanca
Seaside resorts—Spain
Trade unions—Spain
Trials—Spain
Valenci

Cabinet

Scandal in the cabinet; the Matesa affair.
Newsweek 76:44-5 Jl 27 '70

Colonies

See also
Latin America—History
Spanish Sahara

Description and travel

Castle-hopping in Spain, on $5 a day! L.
Blackwood. il Schol Teach Sec Teach Sup
p 12-13 Mr 9 '70
Great gazpacho hunt. E. J. Kahn, jr. Travel
& Camera 33:50-2 Ap '70

Economic conditions

Changing course for Franco's Spain. F. C.
Painton. il U S News 69:80-2 N 16 '70
Spanish resistance grows bolder. A. Power.
Commonweal 92:332-5 Jl 10 '70

Economic history

Economic history of Spain, by J. Vicens
Vives. Review
Am Hist R 75:808-15 F '70

Foreign relations

Spain and Portugal: continuity and change.
A. P. Whitaker. Cur Hist 58:287-91+ My
'70

United States

See United States—Foreign relations—
Spain

History

Spain. P. M. Enggass. bibliog il Focus 20:1-8
My '70

Bibliography

Articles and other books received; comp.
by C. J. Bishko. See issues of American
historical review

Arab period 711-1492

Africa in medieval Spanish literature: its appearance in el Caballero Cifar. M. Sampson. bibliog il Negro Hist Bul 32:14-19 D
'69

Civil war, 1936-1939—Foreign participation

Vets. V. Hoar. Nation 210:408+ Ap 6 '70

Industries

See also
Textile machinery industry—Spain

Politics and government

Changing course for Franco's Spain. F. C.
Painton. il U S News 69:80-2 N 16 '70
Homage to the hard-liners. Time 97:34 Ja 4
'71
Opus Dei: Spain on the cross; tr. by L. Ben-
sky. Y. Le Vaillant. il Ramp Mag 8:14+
F '70
Showdown ahead for Spain. W. E. Green-
ing. il America 123:487-9 D 5 '70; Discus-
sion. 124:2, 29 Ja 9-16 '71
Spain: fascism gone gray. G. Seldes. il Na-
tion 211:77-80 Ag 3 '70
War of the succession. il Newsweek 77:24
Ja 4 '71
See also
Fascism—Spain
Spain—Cabinet

Religious institutions and affairs

World around us (cont) Chr Cent 87:307-8,
1432 Mr 11, N 25 '70
See also
Catholic church in Spain
Evangelical church in Spain
SPAIN and Latin America
Latin America and the flying buttress policy.
J. Marías. il pors Américas 22:16-20 My '70
SPALDING, Keith
Politicizing colleges; address, June 15, 1970.
Vital Speeches 36:622-5 Ag 1 '70
SPAN of life. See Longevity
SPANIARDS
See also
Basques
SPANISH AMERICAN art. See Art, Latin
American
SPANISH-AMERICAN congress on evangelism.
See Religious conferences
SPANISH AMERICAN history. See Latin
America—History
SPANISH AMERICAN literature. See Latin
American literature
SPANISH AMERICANS in the United States.
See Latin Americans in the United States
SPANISH castles. See Castles
SPANISH cookery. See Cookery, Spanish
SPANISH Evangelical church. See Evangelical
church in Spain
SPANISH Harlem. See New York (city)—Har-
lem
SPANISH language

Study and teaching

Survey of the teaching of French, Spanish,
and German in secondary schools. N. W.
Austin and J. L. D. Clark. Sch & Soc 98:
250-2 Ap '70
SPANISH peanuts. See Peanuts
SPANISH SAHARA
Hot property. il Newsweek 76:55 Jl 13 '70
SPANISH speaking students
See also
Mexican American students
SPANISH wind torte. See Meringue
SPARANO, Vin T.
(ed) Where to go. See issues of Outdoor life
SPARE parts. See Repair parts
SPARE time. See Leisure
SPAREMBLEK, Milko
Prime mover; interview, ed. by J. Boutwell.
il por Opera N 35:12-13 Ja 9 '71

about

Two by Sparemblek, Metropolitan opera. D.
Hering. Dance Mag 44:77-80 N '70 *
SPARGO, Mary
Testing paper mill sludge. il Cons 25:14-15
D '70
SPARGUR, Ronn
Can churches break the prime-time barrier?
Chr Today 14:3-4 Ja 16 '70
SPARK, Muriel
Driver's seat; story. New Yorker 46:38-48 My
16 '70
SPARK plugs
How to service sparkplugs. M. Schultz. il
Pop Mech 135:146-9 Ja '71
Wired in; distributor and spark plugs. B.
Lang. il Hot Rod 23:98-9 Je '70
Wonder where the yellow sparks went? T.
Tappett. il Mech Illus 66:94-6+ S '70
See also
Prestolite company
SPARKS, Fred
$20,000,000 honeymoon of Jackie Onassis; ex-
cerpt. il Ladies Home J 87:122-4 Je '70
SPARKS, Richard K.
How much is a Beesworth? Clear House
44:544-6 My '70
SPARN, Edwin
Mr Philby, I presume? pors Sr Schol 96:6-7
F 9 '70
Raz, dva, tri, and you're off! il Sr Schol 95:
18 N 17 '69
SPARROW, Arnold H. and others
Woody plants: changes in survival in response
to long-term (8 years) chronic gamma ir-
radiation. bibliog il Science 169:1082-4 S 11
'70
SPARROWS
Photoperiodically significant photoreception
in sparrows: is the retina involved? H. Underwood and M. Menaker. bibliog il Science
167:298-301 Ja 16 '70; Reply with rejoinder.
D. F. Lott. 169:892-3 Ag 28 '70
Thermoresponsiveness of the preoptic region
of the brain in house sparrows. S. H. Mills
and J. E. Heath. bibliog il Science 168:1008-
9 My 22 '70
Who ate those Iceland poppies? il Sunset 145:
180 D '70

SPARS. See Masts and rigging

SPARTA
Traditional enmity between Sparta and Argos: the birth and development of a myth. T. Kelly. bibliog f il Am Hist R 75:971-1003 Ap '70

SPAS. See Health resorts, watering places, etc.

SPATER, George A.
New mission for business. il Sat R 53:29-31 F 28 '70

SPATTA, George
George Spatta of Clark equipment co; interview. il por Nations Bsns 58:34-6+ Ja '70

SPAULDING, Josiah A.
Running against Teddy. il pors Newsweek 76:21-2 Ag 24 '70 *

SPEAIGHT, Robert
Friend and ally. por Cath World 211:268-9 S '70

SPEAKERS. See Loud speaking apparatus

SPEAKERS (House of representatives) See United States—Congress—House—Speakers

SPEAKING. See Voice

SPEAKING in tongues. See Gift of tongues

SPEAKING of love; story. See Groman, G.

SPECIAL classes and special schools
Cues for teaching the emotionally disturbed: turn on, tune in, drop out. J. F. Koon. Clear House 44:497-500 Ap '70
On making incorrigible youths corrigible; the Sacramento opportunity school program. H. K. Parker. Ed Digest 35:22-4 My '70
See also
Deaf—Education
Individual instruction
Slow learning children—Education

SPECIAL collections in libraries. See Libraries —Special collections

SPECIAL committee of twenty-four on colonialism. See United Nations—Special committee on the situation with regard to the implementation of the declaration on the granting of independence to colonial countries and peoples

SPECIAL committee on peace-keeping operations. See United Nations—Special committee on peace-keeping operations

SPECIAL committee on the question of defining aggression. See United Nations—Special committee on the question of defining aggression

SPECIAL days, weeks, and months
Safe boating week; proclamation. R. M. Nixon. il Motor B 125:149 Je '70
To transform the world; Week of prayer for Christian unity. R. Thomas. il Chr Cent 87:49 Ja 14 '70
United Nations day, 1970; proclamation. R. M. Nixon. Dept State Bul 63:182 Ag 10 '70
World law day, 1970; proclamation. R. M. Nixon. Dept State Bul 63:655 N 23 '70
See also names of special days, weeks, and months, e.g. National library week

SPECIAL drawing rights
Pressures on the dollar. E. H. Yeo. 3d. Nations Bsns 58:81 D '70

SPECIAL elementary education for the disadvantaged. See Socially handicapped children—Education

SPECIAL libraries association
ASIS: is it the whirlwind? overlap in memberships with SLA. T. E. Yerke. Wilson Lib Bul 45:342+ D '70
Changing face of SLA; annual conference in Detroit. K. Nyren. il Library J 95:2627-31 Ag '70
Excuse me, but your face is familiar; SLA; annual conference. A. Plotnik. il Wilson Lib Bul 45:12-13 S '70

SPECIAL missions of the United Nations. See United Nations—Special missions

SPECIAL training program (PEC) See Organization of American states—Special training program (PEC)

SPECIALISTS
Intelligence in industry: the uses and abuses of experts; excerpts from Organizational intelligence. H. L. Wilensky. bibliog f Ann Am Acad 388:46-58 Mr '70
Is management too specialized? G. Berkwitt. il Duns 95:21-3 F '70

SPECIALISTS, Stock. See Securities—Marketing

SPECIALIZATION
Planetary planning; address, November 13, 1969. R. B. Fuller. il Am Scholar 40:29-63 Wint '70 (to be cont)
See also
Specialists

SPECIALIZATION in medicine
Meet the family doctor for the 70's. M. Michaelson. il pors Todays Health 48:50-3+ My '70

SPECIALTY equipment manufacturers association
Fragmentary evidence; SEMA's new guidelines for dragster safety. B. Lang. il Hot Rod 23:82-3 Ja '70
Rap 'n 'pinion. R. Richter. Motor T 23:14 Ja '71
SEMA showtime. E. Rickman. il Hot Rod 23:126-7 Ap '70

SPECIALTY stores
More for Melville; Chess King clothing store. A. A. Butkus. por Duns 95:64+ My '70
New York summer: front-stoop fashions. J. A. Segal. il Look 34:32-4 Jl 14 '70
Nothing but pants, pants, pants; Jeans west shops. il Bsns W p51 Jl 4 '70

SPECIES
Chromosome tracers of the origin of species. H. L. Carson. bibliog il Science 168:1414-18 Je 19 '70
Continental drift and the diversity of species. Sci N 98:396 N 21 '70
Differentiation of populations; importance of gene flow. P. R. Ehrlich and P. H. Raven; discussion. bibliog Science 167:1636-7 Mr 20 '70
On killing members of one's own species; tr. by H. Zeisel. K. Lorenz. il por Bul Atom Sci 26:2-5+ O '70
State of the species; symposium. il Natur Hist 79:43-74 Ja '70
See also
Natural selection
Phylogeny

SPECIFIC heat
Specific heats of lunar surface materials from 90 to 350 degrees Kelvin. R. A. Robie and others. bibliog il Science 167:749-50 Ja 30 '70

SPECIFICATIONS
See also subhead Specifications under various subjects, e.g. Automobiles—Specifications

SPECIFICITY of enzymes. See Enzymes—Specificity

SPECK, Ross
To treat a disturbed person, treat his family. S. Davidson. il por N Y Times Mag p 10-11+ Ag 16 '70 *

SPECTOR, Robert D.
Poetry quarterly. Sat R 53:24-6 D 26 '70

SPECTOR, Sydney, and Parker, C. W.
Morphine radioimmunoassay. bibliog il Science 168:1347-8 Je 12 '70

SPECTROGRAPH
Slitless spectrograph for the flash spectrum. W. C. Atkinson. il Sky & Tel 39:318-23 My '70

SPECTROMETERS
Obtaining data on the sun by satellite; use of ultraviolet spectrometer. il Chem 43:22-3 Ja '70
See also
Mass spectrometry

SPECTROPHOTOMETERS
New products; atomic absorption spectrophotometers. il Sci N 97:230 F 28 '70

SPECTROPHOTOMETRY
Environmental mercury: rapid determination in water at nanogram levels. R. W. April and D. N. Hume. il Science 170:849-50 N 20 '70

SPECTROSCOPE
Spectroscope attachment for viewing solar prominences. J. B. Newton. il Sky & Tel 39:120-3 F '70

SPECTROSCOPY. See Spectrum analysis

SPECTRUM
Electromagnetic spectrum chart. il Electr World 83:37 Ja '70
Spectra of backscattered light from the sea obtained from aircraft as a measure of chlorophyll concentration. G. L. Clarke and others. bibliog il Science 167:1119-21 F 20 '70
See also
Stars—Spectra

Absorption spectra
Spectral reflectivity of lunar samples. J. B. Adams and R. L. Jones. bibliog il Science 167:737-9 Ja 30 '70
See also
Spectrum. Ultraviolet—Absorption spectra

Reflection spectra
Spectral reflectivity of lunar samples. J. B. Adams and R. L. Jones. bibliog il Science 167:737-9 Ja 30 '70

SPECTRUM, Infrared
Infrared emission spectra: enhancement of diagnostic features by the lunar environment. L. M. Logan and G. R. Hunt. bibliog il Science 169:865-6 Ag 28 '70

SPECTRUM, Ultraviolet
Mariner 6: origin of Mars ionized carbon dioxide ultraviolet spectrum. A. Dalgarno and others. bibliog il Science 167:1490-1 Mr 13 '70

Absorption spectra

Absorption of proteins and peptides in the far ultraviolet. A. H. Woods and P. R. O'Bar. bibliog il Science 167:179-81 Ja 9 '70
Atmospheric absorption anomalies in the ultraviolet near an altitude of fifty kilometers. A. J. Krueger; reply. J. F. Noxon. Science 168:1120-1 My 29 '70
Formaldehyde absorption coefficients in the vacuum ultraviolet (650 to 1850 angstroms) E. P. Gentieu and J. E. Mentall. bibliog il Science 169:681-3 Ag 14 '70

SPECTRUM analysis
Alpha-particle activity of Apollo 11 samples. K. A. Richardson and others. bibliog il Science 167:516-17 Ja 30 '70
Cosmogenic and primordial radionuclides in lunar samples by nondestructive gamma-ray spectrometry. R. W. Perkins and others. bibliog il Science 167:577-80 Ja 30 '70
Elemental compositions and ages of lunar samples by nondestructive gamma-ray spectrometry. G. D. O'Kelley and others. bibliog il Science 167:580-2 Ja 30 '70
Emission spectrographic determination of trace elements in lunar samples. C. Annell and A. Helz. bibliog il Science 167:521-3 Ja 30 '70
Far-infrared spectroscopy. W. G. Rothschild and K. D. Möller. bibliog il Phys Today 23:44-9 S '70
Lunar spectral reflectivity (0.30 to 2.50 microns) and implications for remote mineralogical analysis. T. B. McCord and T. V. Johnson. bibliog il Science 169:855-8 Ag 28 '70
Optical spectra of molecules at low temperature. B. Meyer. bibliog il Science 168:783-9 My 15 '70
Ultrafast processes. P. M. Rentzepis. bibliog il Science 169:239-47 Jl 17 '70
See also
Astronomical spectroscopy
Mass spectrometry
Nuclear magnetic resonance
Raman effect

SPECULATION
Everything you always wanted to know about human speculative inadequacy. M. T. Sosnoff. por Forbes 106:104-5 O 15 '70
Great crash in growth stocks. M. Shapiro. il Duns 97:30-2 Ja '71
Psyched-out in silver. A. Hershman. il Duns 96:38-41 Ag '70
See also
Commodity exchanges
Investments
Land speculation
Risk
Stock exchange
Stocks

SPECULATION in land. See Real estate business

SPEECH
See also
Children—Language
English language—Study and teaching
Language and languages
Stammering
Voice

Study and teaching

See Speech education

SPEECH, Freedom of. See Free speech

SPEECH defects
See also
Aphasia
Stammering

SPEECH education
Crisis in our cities; unit on urban problems. L. E. Swann. Engl J 59:570-2 Ap '70

SPEECH therapy
Of lollipops and larynxes; clinic at George Washington university. A. Lewis. il Am Ed 6:29-30 Jl '70

SPEECH writing. See Authorship—Collaboration

SPEECHES, addresses, etc.
Higher education as viewed by college and university presidents; inaugural addresses. R. L. Osmunson. bibliog Sch & Soc 98:367-70 O '70
See also
Baccalaureate addresses
Presidents—United States—Speeches, addresses, etc.

SPEED (drugs) See Amphetamines

SPEED boat racing. See Motor boat racing

SPEED indicators
See also
Tachometers

SPEED of computers. See Computers—Speed

SPEED reading
Look's twenty-day course in quick reading. J. I. Brown. Look 34:71+ Ja 27; 62+ F 10 '70; Same abr. with title You can read faster. Read Digest 96:169-70+ My '70
Questions asked about speed reading. A. Berger. Clear House 44:272-8 Ja '70
Speed reading. P. A. Witty. Ed Digest 35:50-1 F '70

SPEED violations. See Traffic violations

SPEEDWAYS
Auto racing's new supertrack, where the fans come first; Ontario motor speedway. B. Hartford. il Pop Mech 134:110-13+ Ag '70
Indy wheels west, fast and fancy; California 500 at Ontario motor speedway. R. F. Jones. il Sports Illus 33:30-2 S 21 '70
Motor trend interview; Ontario motor speedway. D. Lockton. pors Motor T 22:94-8+ Mr '70
Racing's most frightening corners; ed. by G. S. Brown. J. Stewart. il por Sports Illus 33:38-49 O 12 '70
Roundy-round corner; Ontario motor speedway electronic timing. S. Kelly. il Hot Rod 23:114 N '70
Top tracks. il Pop Mech 133:S44-46+ Ja '70; 135:S28-32+ Ja '71

SPEER, Albert
Long long days with the Fuhrer; excerpts from Inside the Third reich. il pors Life 68:58-58B+ Ap 24 '70

about

Albert Speer and the miracle of forgiveness. M. Barth. Chr Cent 87:1537-8 D 23 '70 *
Architect of Nazism. S. K. Oberbeck. il Newsweek 76:74-6 Ag 31 '70 *
Design for evil. D. Davis. il Newsweek 76:82 S 28 '70 *
Der Fuehrer dead center. W. H. Hale. Sat R 53:19-21+ Ag 29 '70 *
History preserved in prison and buried for years. R. Graves. por Life 68:3 Ap 24 '70 *
Hitler as architect. il Time 96:76 O 5 '70 *
In Hitler's service. L. S. Dawidowicz. bibliog f Commentary 50:85-90 N '70 *
Mephistopheles remembered. K. R. Johnson. il por Time 96:58+ S 7 '70 *
Nazi who looked away. O. Friedrich. il por Bsns W p6-7 Ag 29 '70 *
Prison of possibility. L. Kirstein. Nation 211:216-17 S 14 '70 *
Teufeldämmerung. M. L. Kahn. Nat R 22:958 S 8 '70 *

SPEHR, Paul
Feature films in your library. il Wilson Lib Bul 44:848-55 Ap '70

SPELEOLOGY. See Caves

SPELLING
Spelling in the elementary school. R. J. Smith. Ed Digest 36:44-6 D '70

Study and teaching

Generative phonology and the teaching of spelling. F. Brengelman. Engl J 59:1113-18 N '70
Practical way to teach spelling. R. I. Ammon, jr. Ed Digest 35:53-4 Mr '70

SPELLS. See Magic

SPELMAN, Franz
Munich in October. il Travel & Camera 33:30-5 O '70

SPENCE, Wayman R.
Doctor Spence is a misocapnist. L. Witt. il pors Todays Health 48:16-17 My '70 *

SPENCER, Alexander B. See Sippel, R. F. jt. auth.

SPENCER, Elizabeth
Sharon: story. New Yorker 46:36-9 My 9 '70

SPENCER, Maidee Kerr
How to help your freezer do its job. Am Home 73:84-5+ S '70

SPENCER, Steven M.
Fighting insects with insects. il Nat Wildlife 9:48-51 D '70; Same abr. with title Alternative to poisonous pesticides? Read Digest 97:57-8+ D '70
Last gasp for cigarettes? Read Digest 96:92-5 Ap '70
Marijuana: how dangerous is it? Read Digest 96:67-71 Ja '70
Snug house on the ocean floor. il Read Digest 96:116-20 Ja '70
—See Auerbach, O. jt. auth.

SPENCER-CHURCHILL, Athina (Livanos) Onassis, marchioness of Blandford. See Blandford, A. L. O. S.-C.

SPENDER, Stephen
　Les Baux and the pleasures of Provence. il
　　Travel & Camera 33:36-9 Ap '70
SPENDING. See Consumption (economics)
SPENDLOVE, J. Clifton. See Adams, A. P. jt
　auth.
SPENSER, Ian D. See Hill, R. E. jt. auth.
SPERACIO, Mario
　Halloween couplets. Good H 171:230 O '70
SPERBER, Ann
　La forza del destino. il Am Rec G 36:948-9+
　　Ag '70
　Roberto Devereux. il Am Rec G 36:660-3 My
　　'70
　Il Trovatore. il Am Rec G 36:792-4+ Je '70
SPERBER, Michael A.
　Camus' The fall: the Icarus complex. Am
　　Imago 26:269-80 Fall '70
SPERLING, Edwardine
　Conquest of space; poem. Clear House 44:
　　299 Ja '70
SPERLING, Godfrey, jr
　Breakfast with Godfrey. il Time 95:72 Mr 16
　　'70
SPERLING, Norman
　Planetarium educators conference. il Sky &
　　Tel 41:7-9 Ja '71
SPERM. See Spermatozoa
SPERMATOZOA
　Porifera: sudden sperm release by tropical
　　demospongiae. H. M. Reiswig. bibliog il
　　Science 170:538-9 O 30 '70
　Proteolytic reaction of mammalian spermato-
　　zoa on gelatin membranes. bibliog il Sci-
　　ence 170:749-51 N 13 '70
SPERR, Hans
　You don't have to be big to be fast; adap-
　　tation of address. Pub W 197:42-4 Mr 16
　　'70
SPERRY and Hutchinson company
　Green stamps get the St Louis blues. Bsns W
　　p32 Ap 25 '70
SPERRY Rand corporation
　Sperry Rand: no discards. il Forbes 107:24-5
　　Ja 1 '71
　　　　　Univac division
　United drops Univac contract for $56-million
　　data system. Aviation W 92:31 F 9 '70
SPHINX moths. See Moths
SPICA. See Stars. Double
SPICE racks
　Space-saving spice rack. P. Abbeduto. il Pop
　　Sci 197:128 O '70
SPICES
　Best ways to store herbs and spices. il
　　Good H 170:137 Ja '70
　Bokara Legendre: spice is a cliffhanger. il
　　Vogue 155:79 Je '70
　Sausage and spice (and things not so nice)
　　Consumer Rep 35:344 Je '70
　　　See also
　Curry
SPIDER lilies
　　　See also
　Basket flowers
SPIDER webs
　Freaked-out spiders. il Newsweek 76:67 Ag
　　10 '70
　Spinner. il Am For 76:24-7 Ag '70
　Turned-on spiders spin weird webs. il Sci
　　Digest 67:80-2 Ja '70
SPIDERS
　Amazing spider woman: A. Moreton photog-
　　rapher and collector. B. Strohm. il por Nat
　　Wildlife 7:12-15 O '69
　Brown recluse creeps across the country. il
　　Todays Health 48:75 F '70
　Multiple mimetic forms in an ant-mimicking
　　clubionid spider. J. Reiskind. il Science 169:
　　587-8 Ag 7 '70
　Spiders and webs. il Chem 43:4 D '70
　　　See also
　Spider webs
SPIEGEL, John P.
　Why terrorists act that way; interview. por
　　U S News 68:16-17 Mr 30 '70
SPIEGEL, Marshall
　News on wheels (cont) Sr Schol 95:20 N 10
　　'69; 96:20-1 Mr 23; 18 Ap 13; 32 My 18; 97:
　　44 S 28; 32-3+ O 26; 30 N 16; 30-1 D 14 '70
SPIEGEL, Patricia Keith-. See Keith-Spie-
　　gel, P.
SPIEGLER, David B.
　Snow prediction, a formidable challenge. bib-
　　liog il Weatherwise 23:212-20 O '70
SPIES
　Schooling of a Soviet spy; excerpts from
　　KGB. J. Barron. il por Read Digest 96:225-
　　8+ Ap; 217-22+ My '70
　Spies who came in from the sea; eight Ger-
　　mans who landed on Long Island and
　　Florida coasts in June 1942. W. A. Swan-
　　berg. il Am Heritage 21:66-9+ Ap '70

Where are the Clark Kents of yesteryear?
　il Ramp Mag 9:38-42 D '70
　　　See also
　Espionage
　Lotz, W.
　Rosenberg, Julius and Ethel, case
　Sobell, M
SPIES, industrial
　Great game of corporate espionage. J. Per-
　　ham. Duns 96:30-3+ O '70
SPIESS, Robert
　Anguilla sojourn. il Travel 134:56-61 D '70
SPIKER LaRue
　Oil discovers Maine. il Nation 210:656-8 Je 1
　　'70
SPILHAUS, Athelstan F.
　Next industrial revolution; excerpts from
　　address. Science 167:1673 Mr 27 '70; Same
　　abr. Read Digest 97:169-70 Jl '70
SPILLER, Burton L.
　Mister grouse. H. G. Tapply. il Field & S
　　75:110+ Je '70 *
　Strange guns I have known. il Field & S 74:
　　80-1+ Mr '70
SPINACH
　Spinach: a vegetable for all seasons. L.
　　Riotte. il Org Gard & Farm 17:27-9 D '70
　　　See also
　Cookery—Vegetables
SPINACH salad. See Salads
SPINAL column. See Spine
SPINAL cord
　Somatovisceral pathway: rapidly conducting
　　fibers in the spinal cord. H. L. Fields and
　　D. L. Winter. bibliog il Science 167:1729-
　　30 Mr 27 '70
　　　See also
　Meninges
SPINAL paralysis. See Paralysis
SPINDLETOP charity horse show, Beaumont,
　Tex. See Horse shows
SPINE
　　　　　　Fracture
　First aid. C. J. Potthoff. Todays Health 48:74
　　Mr '70
　　　　Wounds and injuries
　Your aching back, and what to do about it.
　　il Mech Illus 66:44-6+ Mr '70
SPINELLI, D. N. See Hirsch, H. V. B. jt. auth.
SPINNING tackle. See Fishing tackle
SPINOFF (technology) See Technology transfer
SPINS, Airplane. See Airplanes—Spinning
SPINY lobsters. See Lobsters
SPIRAL growth and movement
　Fungal endogenous rhythms expressed by
　　spiral figures. J. A. Bourret and others; re-
　　ply with rejoinder. B. M. Sweeney. Science
　　169:1229 S 18 '70
SPIRAL stairs. See Stairways
SPIRIT
　　　See also
　Consciousness
SPIRIT, Fellowship of the. See Fellowship of
　the Spirit
SPIRIT, Holy. See Holy Spirit
SPIRIT communication. See Spiritualism
SPIRITS, Alcoholic. See Liquors
SPIRITUAL healing. See Faith cure
SPIRITUAL life
　Conquest of holiness. G. Weckman. Chr Cent
　　87:595-7 My 13 '70
　Revolution for heaven's sake; excerpt from
　　One way to change the world. F. Leighton.
　　Chr Today 15:14-16 D 4 '70
　What a challenge! L. N. Bell. Chr Today 15:
　　26-7 N 6 '70
SPIRITUAL values. See Worth
SPIRITUALISM
　Bishop Pike's message from beyond the
　　grave. D. K. Pike. por Ladies Home J 87:
　　97+ N '70
　How quackery thrives on the occult. F. G.
　　Loyd and T. Irwin. il Todays Health 48:20-
　　3+ N '70
　Seances in suburbia. K. L. Woodward. il Mc-
　　Calls 97:70-1+ Mr '70
　Voices of silence. il por Time 96:68 Jl 6 '70
SPIRO, Robert G. See Beisswenger, P. J. jt.
　auth.
SPIRONOLACTONE
　Mercury poisoning: prevention by spirono-
　　lactone. H. Selye. bibliog il Science 169:775-
　　6 Ag 21 '70
SPITZ, Arnold
　Swimming isn't everything, winning is. W.
　　F. Reed. il pors Sports Illus 32:26-9 Mr 9
　　'70 *

SPITZ, Mark
Redemption after a false start. W. F. Reed. il por Sports Illus 32:26-7 Ap 6 '70 *
Swimming isn't everything, winning is. W. F. Reed. il pors Sports Illus 32:26-9 Mr 9 '70 *

SPITZER, Elroy F.
Forty years of growth in a decade. il Am City 85:115-17 Je '70
Montreal's combined incinerator-power plant. E. F. Spitzer. il Am City 85:86-9 My '70
Water rates are going up. il Am City 85:90+ O '70

SPITZER, Helen. See Spitzer, S. jt. auth.

SPITZER, Silas
Little red bottles. il Holiday 48:38-9 Jl '70
—and Spitzer, Helen
Holiday's choice of North American restaurants. il Holiday 48:75-82 Jl '70

SPITZER, Silas, and Spitzer, Helen
Europe's finest restaurants 1970. il Holiday 47:85-9 Ja '70

SPIVACK, Kathleen
Daedalus; poem. Atlan 225:126 Mr '70
In the midst of life. Poetry 116:191-3 Je '70
Tank; Snapping turtle; poems. Poetry 116:86-8 My '70

SPLASHES. See Drops

SPLICHAL, William F. jr
Simple SCA adapter. il Pop Electr 32:49-52 Je '70

SPLIT brain
Prolonged learning and split-brain cats. J. A. Sechzer. bibliog il Science 169:889-92 Ag 28 '70

SPOCK, Benjamin
[Monthly column] See issues of Redbook
about
Spock on teens. Time 96:54 N 16 '70 *

SPOILERS (airplanes) See Airplanes—Stability and stabilizers

SPOKANE, Wash.
Fuel tank filters give fire engines more pep. il Am City 85:48 N '70
You can keep snow out of driveways. G. A. Yake. il Am City 85:63-4 Ag '70

SPOKEN English. See English language—Pronunciation

SPOKEN phonograph records. See Phonograph records—Spoken records

SPOKEN tape recordings. See Tape recordings

SPOLETO festival. See Festivals—Italy

SPONG, William Belser, 1920-
Ocean resources; address, January 24, 1970. Vital Speeches 36:261-2 F 15 '70

SPONGE prints. See Prints

SPONGES
Porifera: sudden sperm release by tropical demospongiae. H. M. Reiswig. bibliog il Science 170:538-9 O 30 '70

SPONSORS of open housing investment
Ethics of residence. Chr Cent 87:1243 O 21 '70

SPONTINI, Gasparo
Napoleon of opera. R. Berges. por Opera N 34:6-7 Ap 18 '70 *

SPOON holders
Spoonholder rack for your favorite lamp. W. E. Burton. il Pop Mech 135:160-1 Ja '71

SPOONER, William Archibald
Will someone please hiccup my pat? W. S. Donald. Horizon 11:120 Aut '69

SPOONERISMS
Will someone please hiccup my pat? W. S. Donald. Horizon 11:120 Aut '69

SPOONS
Kaahumanu's silver spoons. D. T. Rainwater. il Antiques 97:728-9 My '70
Spoon-shoot. il Vogue 155:202-2+ Ap 1 '70

SPORCK, Charles E.
Confounding an industry on prices. il por Bsns W p44+ N 21 '70 *

SPORES (botany)
Self-inhibitor of bean rust uredospores: methyl 3,4-dimethoxycinnamate. V. Macko and others. bibliog Science 170:539-40 O 30 '70

SPORES, Bacterial. See Bacterial spores

SPORN, Philip
Where are they now? R. Levy. pors Duns 95:42 Je '70 *

SPOROPHYTES
See also
Apogamy

SPORT. See Sports

SPORT fishing boats. See Fishing boats

SPORT trophies. See Trophies, Sport

SPORTFISHERMEN. See Fishermen

SPORTING goods
What's new. See issues of Outdoor life

SPORTING journalism. See Sports journalism

SPORTING literature
See also
Football—Bibliography

SPORTS
Importance of play. E. Greenwood. por Camp Mag 42:8-9+ Mr '70
Outdoors with Wynn Davis. W. Davis. See issues of Mechanix illustrated
What will he think of next? enterprises of W. D. Cox. G. S. Brown. il pors Sports Illus 32:38-42+ My 4 '70
World travel calendar, 1971; comp. by F. Shemanski. Sat R 54:37-8+ Ja 2 '71
World's first peace pentathlon; super hippie D. Smith's crusade against competition. R. F. Jones. il por Sports Illus 32:50-8+ My 11 '70
See also
Athletes
College athletics
Cricket (game)
Doping in sports
Fencing
Frisbee (game)
Mountaineering
Olympic games
Public officers—Sports
Recreation
School athletics
Segregation in sports
Sports journalism
Sportsmanship
Squash (game)
Television broadcasting—Sports
Track athletics
Weight lifting
Yachts and yachting

Accidents and injuries
See also
Football—Accidents and injuries
Snowmobiles and snowmobiling—Accidents and injuries

Anecdotes, facetiae, satire, etc.
Who's next? pictorial review of sports in 1970. il Sports Illus 33:44-69 D 21 '70

Ethical aspects
Football racket; excerpt from Out of their league. D. Meggyesy. il Look 34:66+ N 17: 64-6+ D 1 '70
This saint has been called a sinner; E. Wheelwright owner of New Orleans bar with Mafia connections. M. Sharnik. il por Sports Illus 32:18-20+ Je 1 '70

History
Most deadly games. J. H. Plumb. il Horizon 11:52-3 Aut '69

Photographs
See also
Skating—Photographs

Poetry
(P)rhyme time. H. L. Masin. Sr Schol 97:32 D 14 '70

Psychological aspects
Flake and the old man; T. Palmer and B. Kidd at Alpine racing events. R. Meryman. il pors Life 68:54-6+ Mr 6 '70

Religious aspects
Are sports good for the soul? il por Newsweek 77:51-2 Ja 11 '71

Safety devices and measures
Summer sport, and how to avoid the strain of it. Bsns W p 117-18 My 9 '70

Vandalism
See Vandalism

Brazil
See also
Soccer

Canada
See also
Hockey

England
See also
Cricket (game)
Soccer

Europe
Calendar of European sporting events, 1970. D. Schulz. il Holiday 47:22-3 Ja '70

Fiji
See also
Rugby football

SPORTS—*Continued*

Japan

Frantic race for a leisurely life. il Bsns W p28-9 Ag 1 '70

See also
Baseball—Japan

Libya

Libya; the role of sports in a developing country. D. Anthony. il Parks & Rec 5: 38-9 Ap '70

Russia

Don't drink the water; U.S. track team in Leningrad. P. Putnam. il Sports Illus 33:8-13 Ag 3 '70

South Africa

See also
Segregation in sports

Spain

See also
Bullfights

Sweden

See also
Orienteering (sport)

United States

Brief search for America; observations on sports and life in four small towns. J. Underwood. il Sports Illus 32:64-8+ My 4 '70

For the record. See issues of Sports illustrated

Sports. H. L. Masin. See issues of Senior scholastic

Squinting at the stars of sport; horoscope in forecasting sports. J. Bruce. il Sports Illus 32:52-4+ Ja 19 '70

U.S.A. up, up and away; Decoration day weekend. W. Johnson. il Sports Illus 32:22-7 Je 8 '70

Who are the HUB men? sports, politics and tradition in Boston. F. Deford. il Sports Illus 33:54-6+ Jl 13 '70

Who's next? pictorial review of sports in 1970. il Sports Illus 33:44-69 D 21 '70

SPORTS car racing. See Automobile racing

SPORTS cars

Alfa Centauri. K. Ludvigsen. il Motor T 22: 30-1 Je '70

AMX/3. K. Ludvigsen. il Motor T 22:48-50+ Je '70

Corvettes in Chevy's closet are the most interesting of all! K. Ludvigsen. il Motor T 22:32-7+ Ja '70

Fly yellow; Ferrari P3. J. Lamm. il Motor T 22:38-40+ N '70

Great Corvette-Porsche controversy. C. Koch. il Motor T 22:76-8+ My '70

How to order your new Corvette. B. Sanders. il Motor T 22:40-2 Jl '70

Lamborghini Jarama. K. Ludvigsen. il Motor T 22:56-7 Jl '70

Making a sports car, Italian style; De Tomaso-Ford model. il Bsns W p87 Mr 21 '70

Motor trend interview: Paul Newman; ed. by D. Wells. P. Newman. por Motor T 22:86+ Ag '70

Never have so many spent so little and derived so much fun; Triumph Spitfire Fiat 850, Datsun 1600, MG Midget. il Motor T 22:76-8+ Ag '70

Pronounce it So-nett; Saab Sonett III. B. Sanders. il Motor T 22:28-9+ Je '70

70½ GM sports spectacular; the Firebird. il Motor T 22:28-30 Ja '70

Three's a crowd; Fiat 124, BMW 2002, Alfa Romeo Berlina. J. Brokaw; C. Koch; J. Lamm. il Motor T 22:44-7+ Jl '70

U.S. comeback for a rare car; the Morgan. il Bsns W p43 Ja 9 '71

Why the Lotus is in high gear. il por Bsns W p41 F 7 '70

See also
Automobiles, Racing

Design

Mid-engine Corvette. E. Dahlquist. il Motor T 22:56-9+ Je '70

Testing

C-111 on the wall of death; Mercedes Benz high-speed test track. G. Wilkins. il Mech Illus 66:12+ Mr '70

Five sports cars; Datsun 240Z, Opel GT, MGB GT, Porsche 914, Triumph GT6. il Consumer Rep 35:550-7 S '70

Norbye-Dunne report: at last, Detroit comes up with real sports cars. J. P. Norbye and J. Dunne. il Pop Sci 196:32+ Je '70

Old pro tries out the world's most advanced car: Mercedes' experimental mid-engine sports car. J. Fitch. il Pop Mech 133:88-91 Ja '70

SPORTS cars, Used

Purchasing

See Automobiles, Used—Purchasing

SPORTS clothes. See Clothing and dress— Sports clothes

SPORTS clubs

Buddy is everybody's buddy; manager of Chalet ski club. C. Phinizy. il pors Sports Illus 33:30-2+ D 7 '70

See also
Athletic clubs
Fishing clubs

SPORTS fans

Fanatics. P. Axthelm. il Newsweek 75:67-8 My 4 '70

Fight: fans' opinions of Muhammad Ali. New Yorker 46:16-17 D 26 '70

See also
Baseball fans
Football fans

SPORTS for the blind

Blind coach leads the way. D. P. Brewster. il pors Har Yrs 10:33-41 Jl '70

SPORTS for children

Making of a hockey slave; from the cradle to the NHL, a Canadian odyssey. L. Shecter. il Look 34:70-4 F 10 '70

SPORTS for women

See also
Bowling
Women as athletes

SPORTS hall of fame

Sports hall of fame; Yonkers, N.Y. A. Cohen. il por Parks & Rec 5:28-9 Ap '70

SPORTS humor programs. See Radio broadcasting—Humor

SPORTS in art

See also
Fishing in art

SPORTS in prison. See Prison recreation

SPORTS journalism

Black sportswriter. A. S. Young. il Ebony 25: 56-8+ O '70

Sports. R. Kahn. Esquire 74:32+ Ag '70

Super bowl. F. Bardacke. Ramp Mag 8:6 Mr '70

Writing and selling the sports and outdoor article. P. Glick; T. Wendelburg. Writer 84:26-9 Ja '71

Anecdotes, facetiae, satire, etc.

Outgoing bag. R. Angell. New Yorker 46:32-4 O 3 '70

SPORTS museums. See Museums

SPORTS officiating

Baseball, umpires, and the official scorer. R. L. Tobin. Sat R 53:85-6 S 12 '70

War games; Lakers-Hawks game referees criticized by R. Guerin. il Newsweek 75:67 Ap 27 '70

See also
Computers—Sports use

SPORTS promoting. See Promoters and promoting

SPORTS records

Full series for a fleet pair; battle for the American league batting title. W. Leggett. il pors Sports Illus 33:18-21 Ag 24 '70

Henry raps one for history; 3,000th hit. W. Leggett. pors Sports Illus 32:30-2+ My 25 '70

SPORTS vacations. See Vacations

SPORTSMANSHIP

Anecdotes, facetiae, satire, etc.

How to win at basketball: cheat. B. Cosby. il Look 34:65-7 Ja 27 '70

SPORTSWRITING. See Sports journalism

SPORULATION. See Fungi—Development

SPOT drawing. See Drawing

SPOTTSWOOD, Stephen G.

Blast from a bishop. pors Time 96:11 Jl 13 '70 *

SPOUSE for Susie Mouse; drama. See Head, F.

SPRADLEY, James P.

Moral career of a bum; excerpt from You owe yourself a drunk. il Trans-Action 7: 16-29 My '70

SPRADLEY, Joseph L.

Christian roots of science. Chr Today 14:7-8 Mr 13 '70

SPRAGG, Bruce C.

People-planned parks. il Am City 85:72-4 Jl '70

SPRAGUE, Andy

Mini steam engine made with simple hand tools. il Pop Mech 134:154-5+ Jl '70

SPRAGUE, Peter

Bowing out at thirty-one. J. Poindexter. por Duns 96:66 N '70 *

SPRAGUE, Conn.

Small towns need a good lighting, too! il Am City 85:92 Ag '70

SPRAINS
First aid. C. J. Potthoff. il Todays Health 48:84 Ap '70

SPRAY guns. See Spraying apparatus

SPRAY painting. See Paint spraying

SPRAY-steam irons, Electric. See Electric irons

SPRAYING and dusting
Custom operations pay dividends. R. Sanders. il Suc Farm 68:no4 36 Mr '70
Should you hire a custom applicator? il Suc Farm 68:no3 W16 F '70
Starting a no-spray decade, maybe. M. C. Goldman. il Org Gard & Farm 17:65-6 Ja '70
Use a sane approach to garden spraying. B. C. Kilvert, jr. il Home Gard 57:50-1 My '70
What we spray and don't spray at Sunset. il Sunset 145:62-5 Jl '70
What's new for pest control. Suc Farm 68:M1 Ap '70
Why slow down the planter with chemicals? il Farm J 94:20-1 Je '70

SPRAYING apparatus
Hot tips for using glue guns. J. Burroughs. il Pop Mech 134:188-91 S '70
How to keep a spray gun spraying. il Pop Mech 133:152-3 Je '70
Insect fogger. il Home Gard 57:12 O '70

SPREADERS, Fertilizer. See Fertilizer spreaders

SPREADERS, Lawn. See Lawn tools, equipment, and supplies

SPREADERS, Salt. See Salt spreaders

SPREADS. See Coverlets

SPRETI, Karl, graf von
Diplomats on the firing line. il por Sr Schol 96:15 Ap 27 '70 *
Helpless hostages. il Time 95:30 Ap 20 '70 *

SPRIGGS, Dillard
Oil boom? il Duns 96:36-7 N '70

SPRING
Under spring's green spell; with editorial comment by R. Graves. M. Mauney. il Life 68:3, 48-55 My 1 '70

Poetry
Great magician; poem. J. C. Spry. Am For 76:48 Ap '70
Spring bouquet. J. J. Stuart. Am For 76:57 Mr '70

SPRING beauties
Chromosomal drift, a new phenomenon in plants. W. H. Lewis. bibliog il Science 168:1115-16 My 29 '70

SPRING flowers. See Flowers

SPRING is here! story. See Soman, F. J.

SPRINGER, Axel
Ahlers affair. por Newsweek 75:68-9 F 23 '70 *
Germany's leading publishers renounce church taxation. E. E. Turner. Chr Cent 87:1164-6 S 30 '70 *

SPRINGER, John
Trade winds. C. Amory. Sat R 53:14 O 10 '70 *

SPRINGER, Michael
Social indicators, reports, and accounts: toward the management of society. bibliog f Ann Am Acad 388:1-13 Mr '70
—See Gross, B. M. jt. ed.

SPRINGER verlag. See Publishers and publishing—Germany (Federal Republic)

SPRINGFIELD, Ill.

Moral conditions
Springfield: what really upsets the Midwest most is four-letter words. J. Howard. il Life 69:28-9 O 2 '70

SPRINGFIELD, Mass.

Buildings
Skating rink has translucent wall. il Am City 85:46 Ag '70

SPRINGFIELD, Mo.
Hydraulic hammer helps improve our public image. J. Dodd. il Am City 85:66 My '70

SPRINGFIELD, Ore.
Four public agencies pool equipment maintenance. il Am City 85:105 N '70

Education
Automated library system: Project LEEDS. J. R. Blair and R. Snyder. il Am Lib 1:172-3 F '70

SPRINGFIELD, Vt.
How to keep an airport open in winter. D. Gurney. il Am City 85:56 S '70

SPRINGNATIONALS. See Automobile racing

SPRINGS, R. David. See Holder, F. W. jt. auth.

SPRINGS
See also
Hot springs

SPRINGS (mechanism)
Make your own coil springs. F. W. Schlueter. il Pop Mech 133:169+ Je '70
Making your own springs. R. Lumachi. il Mech Illus 66:71 Ag '70

SPRINGTAILS
Acrobats on the snow. H. R. Russell. Nat Parks 44:25 F '70

SPRINGTIME for Dan; drama. See Martens, A. C.

SPRINKEL, Beryl W.
Opportunity of a lifetime? interview. por Forbes 106:34 O 1 '70

SPRINKLER irrigation. See Irrigation, Overhead

SPRINKLERS
Lawn sprinklers. Consumer Rep 34:192-5 D '69
See also
Fire sprinklers

SPRINKLING systems. See Fire sprinklers

SPRITZER, Michael S.
Testing Boyle's law. il por Chem 43:29-30 O '70

SPROLL, Walter P. See Dietz, R. S. jt. auth.

SPRUILL, Leroy
Letters that legislate. Har Yrs 10:15 O '70

SPRY, James C.
Great magician; poem. Am For 76:48 Ap '70

SPURGE nettle. See Tread-softly

SPURGEON, Charles Haddon
Genius of Charles Haddon Spurgeon. J. Pitts. Chr Today 14:6-8 F 27 '70 *

SPYING. See Spies

SPYING high; drama. See Olfson, L.

SQUANNACOOK RIVER
Saving of a river. R. Donnelly. il por Outdoor Life 145:65-7+ Ap '70

SQUARES, Public. See Plazas

SQUASH (game)
Fastest game in town. R. Levy. il Duns 96:50-3 Jl '70
It's sort of like black lightning; national championships at Philadelphia. P. Wood. il N Y Times Mag p 14-16+ Mr 29 '70
Spicy day at Penn; national amateur championships at University of Pennsylvania. R. Blount, jr. il por Sports Illus 32:58-9 Mr 9 '70

SQUASH lice. See Plant lice

SQUASHES
Boy plus zucchini equals good eating and pocket money. N. W. Bubel. il Org Gard & Farm 17:90-3 Ap '70
Growing the earliest zucchini in your neighborhood. S. De Desrochers. il Org Gard & Farm 17:80-1 Ap '70
See also
Cookery—Vegetables

SQUATTERS
Had trouble with housing squatters? Am City 85:8 D '70
Squatters of Miffland; report. R. Rein. il por Time 96:19 N 9 '70

SQUAW VALLEY
What goes up must ski down. A. Wright. il por Sports Illus 32:28-31 F 9 '70

SQUIBB Beech-nut, inc.
Going first class. il Forbes 106:54 S 15 '70

SQUIDS
How to raise a squid. Sci Digest 67:69-70 Ap '70
Prince Albert's way of catching squid. S. Schlee. il por Natur Hist 79:20+ F '70

SQUIRES, Arthur M.
Clean power from coal. bibliog il Science 169:821-8 Ag 28 '70

SQUIRES, James Robert
Build the autotransformer package. il Radio-Electr 41:42-4 S '70

SQUIRREL hunting
Start from the bottoms; squirrel season in Ohio. E. A. Bauer. il Outdoor Life 146:78-9+ S '70

SQUIRREL monkeys. See Monkeys

SQUIRREL stew. See Cookery—Game

SQUIRRELS
See also
Cookery—Game

SQUIRRU, Rafael
Master draftsman. il Américas 22:31-5 Ja '70

SREEVALSAN, T.
Homologous viral interference: induction by RNA from defective particles of vesicular stomatitis virus. bibliog il Science 169:991-3 S 4 '70

SRINIVAS, M. N.
After fire, scholar faces painful reprocessing of data. J. Walsh. por Science 169:657 Ag 14 '70 *

STAATS, Elmer Boyd
Excerpt from statement, October 27, 1969.
Cong Digest 49:83+ Mr '70

about

Accounting fight flares. por Bsns W p68 Ja
24 '70
STABILATORS. See Airplanes—Stability and
stabilizers
STABILE, Jim
Roll call for carp. il Outdoor Life 146:42-3+
Jl '70
STABILITY, Boat. See Boats—Stability and
stabilizers
STABILIZATION of employment. See Employ-
ment stabilization
STABILIZATION processors. See Photography
—Processing—Apparatus and supplies
STABILIZERS, Boat. See Boats—Stability and
stabilizers
STABLES. See Barns and stables
STACHO, Maria. See Fono, P. jt. auth.
STACKELBERG, Roderick
Moral purpose of humanities programs. Engl
J 59:1141-5 N '70
STACY, Hollis
Hollis and the swinging Stacy clan. C. Kirk-
patrick. por Sports Illus 33:42-3 Ag 10 '70 *
STADE, George
Liberal education and campus activists; ex-
cerpts from address. por Sch & Soc 98:
459 D '70
STADIUMS
Baseball parks, new attractions for tourists;
with directory. A. R. Roalman. il Todays
Health 48:42-5+ My '70
Farewell to grass. il Newsweek 75:73 My 11
'70
No disgruntlements round here; Three rivers
stadium, Pittsburgh. R. Blount, jr. il por
Sports Illus 33:18-21 Ag 10 '70
Strike lays low an arena; Kansas City's twin
stadiums. il Bsns W p50 O 10 '70
Surface case of bugs in the rugs; Astroturf
surface in baseball. P. Carry. il Sports Illus
33:40-2+ S 14 '70

Lighting

Tornado fails to darken sports lighting proj-
ect; Lubbock, Tex. il Am City 85:100 N '70
STADLER, Anne
World without war; letter to editor. Com-
monweal 92:127 Ap 17 '70
STAFFEL, Bonnie
Ceramic world of Bonnie Staffel. R. D. Bon-
ham. il por Ceram Mo 18:19-23 Mr '70 *
STAFFIN, Anne
Day camp international style. il Parents
Mag 45:46-7+ Ap '70
STAFFORD, Jean
Books. See occasional issues of Vogue
Christmas books for children. New Yorker 46:
200+ D 5 '70
Love among the rattlesnakes. il McCalls 97:
68-9+ Mr '70
My (ugh!) sensitivity training. Horizon 12:112
Spr '70
STAFFORD, Jo
Funniest put-on. G. Lees. pors Hi Fi 20:120
N '70 *
STAFFORD, William
In anthropology; poem. Harper 240:49 Mr '70
On the poly sci bulletin board; poem. New
Repub 163:21 N 7 '70
Swerve; poem. New Repub 162:19 Je 13 '70
STAGE. See Acting
STAGE fright
Omygod. il Time 95:92+ Mr 30 '70
STAGE lighting
Stage lighting control system. G. Thurow. il
Pop Electr 33:65-7 Ag '70
See also
Opera—Stage lighting
STAGE names. See Pseudonyms
STAGE scenery. See Opera—Stage setting and
scenery
STAGG, Anne
House for two; great swooping arch. il
House & Gard 137:68-73+ F '70
How a talented architect stretched his build-
ing dollar. il House & Gard 137:110-15 Ap '70
Patterns. il House & Gard 137:108-15 Mr '70
STAGG, John
Westward the raccoon. il por Outdoor Life
145:56-7+ Mr '70
STAGHORN ferns. See Ferns
STAGNER, Ross
Perceptions, aspirations, frustrations, and
satisfactions: an approach to urban indica-
tors. il Ann Am Acad 388:59-68 Mr '70
STAHL, Charles R.
Bear on gold; bull on silver; interview. pors
Forbes 105:46+ Ja 15 '70

STAIGER, Ralph C.
IRA: what's in it for you? Wilson Lib Bul 45:
272 N '70
STAINED glass. See Glass painting and stain-
ing
STAINLESS steel blades. See Razor blades
STAINLESS steel tableware. See Tableware,
Stainless steel
STAINS and staining (biology)
Cones of living amphibian eye: selective
staining. A. M. Laties and P. A. Liebman.
bibliog il Science 168:1475-7 Je 19 '70
Threonine deaminase: a novel activity stain
on polyacrylamide gels. R. S. Feldberg and
P. Datta. bibliog il Science 170:1414-16 D
25 '70
STAIR, Dan
Magnum salmon fishing. il Field & S 74:74-5+
Ap '70
STAIRWAYS
Easy steps to new storage space; disappear-
ing stairs. il Mech Illus 66:90-1 Ap '70
You can build your own spiral stairs. T.
Jones. il Pop Mech 133:160-3 Ja '70
STAKES
See also
Garden stakes and staking
STAKHANOV, Aleksei Grigor'evich
Stakhanov lives. por Newsweek 76:46 O 5 '70 *
STAKING of plants. See Garden stakes and stak-
ing
STALACTITES
Stalactite growth beneath sea ice. R. A.
Paige. bibliog il Science 167:171-2 Ja 9 '70
STALCUP, Elizabeth
Proofreading may not be the oldest profes-
sion, but... Pub W 198:52+ O 5 '70
STALEY, Oren Lee
Is the NFO changing directions? interview. ed.
by L. Palmer. il por Farm J 93:28-9+ O '69
STALIN, Iosif
Death of Stalin, the menace of Beria. N. S.
Khrushchev. il pors Life 69:54-58+ D 11 '70 *
Khrushchev remembers; life with Stalin; ex-
cerpts ed. and tr. by S. Talbott. N. S.
Khrushchev. il pors Life 69:32-9+ N 27
'70 (to be cont) *
Khrushchev: the illusions of war. il pors
Time 96:38+ D 7 '70 *
Stalin the mild. il Newsweek 76:49 Jl 6 '70 *
Stalin's return. por Time 96:31 Jl 6 '70 *
STALINA, Svetlana Iosifovna
Flight from the cage. M. Drachkovitch. il
Nat R 22:40-1 Ja 13 '70 *
Free translation. por Newsweek 75:43 Mr 9
'70 *
Newsmakers. il por Newsweek 75:69 Ap 20
'70 *
Princess. P. Rahv. Commentary 49:71-2 Mr
'70 *
STALINISM. See Communism—Russia
STALKING of game. See Tracking and trail-
ing
STALL barns. See Barns and stables
STALLBAUMER, Robert, Jr
What consumers really think of beef and beef
producers. il Farm J 94:B20 S '70
STALLING of automobiles. See Automobiles—
Stopping
STALLINGS, Constance
Let's use our rights-of-way. il Read Digest
96:165-8 Ja '70
STALLONE, Carol N.
California horizons. il Art in Am 58:124-5 N
'70
STALLS, Airplane. See Airplanes—Stalling
STAMBOLIAN, Elizabeth B.
Many rivers reaching the one sea: Asian
literature in the high school. bibliog f Engl
J 59:27-30 Ja '70
STAMM, Julian L.
Camus' Stranger: his act of violence; address,
February 9, 1969. Am Imago 26:281-90 Fall
'69
Problems of depersonalization in Freud's Dis-
turbance of memory on the Acropolis. bib-
liog Am Imago 26:364-72 Wint '69
STAMMERING
New help for children who stutter. O. Men-
dels. il Parents Mag 45:80-1+ N '70
Relief for the stutterer. Time 96:42 Ag 24 '70
Stutterers, speak for yourselves. J. Mat-
thews. il Sci Digest 67:62-6 Ap '70
STAMP collecting. See Postage stamps—Col-
lectors and collecting
STAMPS, Food. See Food relief—United States
STANAVAGE, John. See Melton, G. E. jt. auth.
STANBERY, Ray C.
Thirty seconds over Toledo. Flying 87:80 Ag
'70
STANCRAFT products division. See Standard
packaging corporation—Stancraft products
division

STANDARD, Paul
Before Gutenberg: the block-book. il Pub W 198:58+ S 14 '70
Oldrich Menhart, outstanding Czech type designer; excerpts from address. il por Pub W 197:52-4 Ja 12 '70

STANDARD of living
Growth versus the quality of life. J. A. Wagar. bibliog Science 168:1179-84 Je 5 '70
See also
Budget, Household
Cost of living

STANDARD oil company
Gentlewoman and the robber baron. V. V. Hamilton. il pors Am Heritage 21:78-86 Ap '70

STANDARD oil company (New Jersey)
Jersey Standard's executive stockpile. Duns 96:29 D '70
They're holding feet to the fire at Jersey standard. D. Cortz. il Fortune 82:78-83+ Jl '70

STANDARD oil company of California
Great circle route affords access to European cities. Aviation W 93:62 D 14 '70
See also
Chevron oil company

STANDARD packaging corporation

Stancraft products division
Playing card maker does a neat trick. il por Bsns W p40+ Jl 11 '70

STANDARDS, Library. See Libraries—Standards; School libraries—Standards

STANDARDS, National bureau of. See United States—Standards, National bureau of

STANDARDS of measurement. See Weights and measures

STANDER, Lionel
Lion of the Via Veneto. il por Time 95:76 My 4 '70 *

STANDING up for Santa; drama. See Fisher, A.

STANDPIPES
Standpipe proved best; Hopkins, Minn. il Am City 85:81 Ja '70

STANDS (furniture)
Build this charming curio cabinet; étagère, or whatnot. C. Davis. il Pop Mech 134:172-4 O '70
1820 butler's tray; with fold-up stand. R. Sickler. il Mech Illus 66:94-5 N '70
Rollaway projection stand for slides or movies. H. R. Clark. il Pop Mech 134:152-4 N '70
See also
Flower stands

STANDS, Machine. See Machinery—Stands

STANFIELD, James F.
Itchetucknee, Florida's crystal river. il Nat Parks & Con Mag 44:13-16 My '70

STANFORD, Ann
Our town; poem. New Repub 162:20 Je 6 '70

STANFORD, Barbara Dodds
Affective aspects of black literature. Engl J 59:371-4 Mr '70
Fostering practical communication skills. Engl J 59:967-9 O '70
—See Stanford, G. jt. auth.

STANFORD, Gene, and Stanford, B. D.
Please don't squeeze the paperback! il Schol Teach Jr/Sr High p 12-13+ D 7 '70

STANFORD research institute
Sidestepping the militants; war research at Stanford. L. Schwartz. Nation 210:273-4 Mr 9 '70

STANFORD university, Palo Alto, Calif.
Brief encounter; K. Pitzer quits. Newsweek 76:77 Jl 6 '70
Campus politics: decentralization is pattern at Berkeley, Stanford. J. Walsh. Science 168:1187-90 Je 5 '70
Heart transplants do work; N. E. Shumway. G. Astor. il por Look 34:43-4+ D 29 '70
New order for Stanford. por Time 96:50+ O 12 '70
Overheated campuses of the Bay area. H. Wilner. il Holiday 47:72-3+ Mr '70
Physicists teach minority students. B. G. Levi. il Phys Today 23:53-6 Mr '70
Rules for political action. Sch & Soc 98:461 D '70
Stanford: why Pitzer resigned as president. P. M. Boffey. por Science 169:561-2+ Ag 7 '70
Stanford's community of consent. P. S. Stern. Nation 211:174-8 S 7 '70; Reply with rejoinder. R. M. Rosenzweig. 211:290+ O 5 '70

Graduate school of business
Lending a hand with social ills; Stanford volunteers and Committee for corporate responsibility. il Bsns W p 106+ Mr 7 '70

School of law
Stanford's dean steps down. por Time 96:69 O 5 '70

STANGL, Franz Paul
Efficiency expert. por Time 95:41 My 25 '70 *
Trial of a dutiful man. T. Land. il Nation 211:339-40 O 12 '70 *

STANHOPE, Philip Dormer, 4th earl of Chesterfield. See Chesterfield, P. D. S.

STANLEY, Anita
Constant bloom with begonias. il Org Gard & Farm 17:104 S '70

STANLEY, David
1970 books on the Bible. America 123:436-8+ N 21 '70

STANLEY cup. See Hockey

STANS, Maurice Hubert
Future of minority business; interview. por U S News 69:41-2 N 23 '70
Washington diplomatic conference approves Patent cooperation treaty; address, May 25, 1970. Dept State Bul 63:41-3 Jl 13 '70

STANSFIELD, Charles A. jr
Development of modern seaside resorts. il Parks & Rec 5:14-17+ O '70

STANTON, Edward S.
Religion (cont) America 122:472-4; 123:469-70 My 2, N 28 '70

STANTON, Frank
First amendment; address, December 15, 1969. Vital Speeches 36:234-6 F 1 '70

STANTON, John R.
Is a new approach needed? il Yachting 129: 97+ Ja '71

STANTON, Tom
Billion-dollar subsidy. Nation 211:463-4 N 9 '70
Product safety: nobody's business. Nation 211:270-2 S 28 '70

STANTON, Will
Just for laughs. Look 34:60 S 8 '70
Nicest people are married to each other; story. Good H 170:76-7 Ja '70
People who. Sat R 53:9 D 19 '70
Reaping fatherhood's rewards, at 50. il McCalls 97:50 Je '70

STANTON, William A.
Middle school years and career development. Clear House 44:531-3 My '70

STAPHYLOCOCCAL nuclease. See Nucleases

STAPLE guns
Reach for your staple gun. G. Daniels. il Pop Sci 196:114+ F '70

STAPLES, I. Ezra
Where Ethi texts fail the schools; excerpts from address. Pub W 197:43-4 Je 1 '70

STAPLETON, Neb.
Profiles. B. Roueché. New Yorker 46:29-40 Ja 2 '71

STAPP, Andrew D.
Union soldiers. R. A. Gross. por Newsweek 76:98B+ S 21 '70 *

STAR, Jack
Adlai III; his new politics startle old pros. il pors Look 34:82-4+ O 6 '70
Presbyterian debate over sex. Look 34:54+ Ag 11 '70
Virgin Islands: shame in the U.S. tropics. il Look 34:17-21 Mr 10 '70

STAR charts. See Astronomy—Charts, diagrams, etc.

STAR clusters. See Stars—Clusters

STAR of the veldt (flower) See Cape marigolds

STARBIRD, Kaye
Lion in the lei shop; story. Ladies Home J 87:135-42 S '70

STARBUCK, George
Double semi-sestina; poem. Atlan 225:77 F '70
Sad ballad of the fifteen consecutive rhymes. Poetry 115:269-73 Ja '70

STARCH painting. See Painting—Technique

STARE, Fredrick J.
Balance is all in their favor. por Life 68:38 Mr 6 '70
Breakfast, the meal you shouldn't skip. Ladies Home J 87:122+ N '70
Low calorie diet. House & Gard 137:102-3 Ja '70

STARFISHES
Acanthaster: a rarity in the past? T. F. Dana. bibliog Science 169:894 Ag 28 '70
Destruction of Pacific corals by the sea star acanthaster planci. R. H. Chesher; discussion. bibliog Science 165:645; 167:209, 1274-5; 168:607-7 Ag 15 '69, Ja 9, F 27, My 1 '70
Question of regeneration. il Sci N 97:525 My 30 '70
Starfish eaters; painted shrimp attacking crown-of-thorns. il Time 95:73 My 25 '70
Starfish threaten Pacific reefs; Acanthaster planci. J. A. Sugar. il Nat Geog 137:340-53 Mr '70

STARGELL, Willie
This big man is the cool man. R. Blount, jr.
il por Sports Illus 33:16-18 O 5 '70 *
STARK, Andrew A.
Secretariat, twenty-five years after. UN Mo
Chron 7:102-8 Ag '70
STARK, Charlotte
Those moving day blues. il Parents Mag
45:62-3+ F '70
STARK, Fortney H.
Businessmen against the war (sic) S. Weiss-
man. il Ramp Mag 9:36-7 D '70 *
Savings bonds turn political. por Bsns W p41
My 23 '70 *
STARLETS (actresses) See Moving picture ac-
tors and actresses
STARNES, Richard
[Monthly article on the outdoor life] See is-
sues of Field & stream
STARR, C. V. and company
Child of empire. il Forbes 105:40 Mr 15 '70
STARR, John T.
Corps and the environment. il Am For 76:28-31
N '70
To fit the landscape. il Am For 76:12-15+
F '70
What is a marsh worth? il Am For 76:12-
15+ Ag '70
STARR, Paul
Black Panthers and white radicals. Common-
weal 92:294-7 Je 12 '70
STARR, Ringo
Ringo goes single. J. Hamilton. il pors Look
34:40-4 F 10 '70
Y'all come hear Ringo. W. Bender. por Time
96:86+ O 26 '70 *
STARR, Roger
Aristocrat in local politics. Commentary 51:
87-91 Ja '71
Consciousness III. Commentary 50:46-54 D '70
John V. Lindsay: a political portrait. Com-
mentary 49:25-46 F '70
This is the way the world ends. il Am Heri-
tage 21:94-101 O '70
STARR, Stuart
Air-traffic control. M. S. Rothenberg. por
Phys Today 23:24-5 My '70 *
STARR, Victor P. and Gaut, N. E.
Negative   viscosity;   with   biographical
sketches. il Sci Am 223:15, 72-8+ bibliog
(p 136) Jl '70
STARS
Astronomy. J. Stokley. See fourth issue of
each month of Science news
Deep-sky wonders. W. S. Houston. See issues
of Sky and telescope
  See also
Astrology
Astrophysics
Magellanic clouds
Milky way
Occultations

Catalogs
Beyond the NGC catalogue. L. J. Robinson.
il Sky & Tel 39:100-1 F '70
Messier album. J. H. Mallas and E. Kreimer.
See issues of Sky and telescopes to September 1970
Selected objects from the Mallas Observer's
catalogue. J. H. Mallas. See issues of Review of popular astronomy to August 1969

Clusters
Globular-cluster stars. I. Iben, jr. il Sci Am
223:26-39 bibliog(p 136) Jl '70
  See also
Nebulae

Constitution
Action at the surface; promethium on stars.
Sci N 98:429 D 5 '70

Evolution
Globular-cluster stars. I. Iben, jr. il Sci Am
223:26-39 bibliog(p 136) Jl '70
Material to make stars; discovery of molecu-
lar hydrogen in space. il Sci N 97:595 Je 20
'70
Neutron stars, astronomical heavyweights.
I. Asimov. Sci Digest 68:89-90 Ag '70
Of stars and man. l. Wolfert. Read Digest 96:
49-53 My '70
Ordinary stars, white dwarfs, and nuetron
stars. L. C. Green. il Sky & Tel 41:18-20 Ja
'71
  See also
Pulsars

Motion
Barnard's star: the search for other solar
systems; stars and planets in the constel-
lation Ophiuchus. P. Van De Kamp. il
Natur Hist 79:38-43 Ap '70
Stellar rotation and atmospheric motions.
M. Hack. il Sky & Tel 40:84-6, 143-5, 208-
9 Ag-O '70

Motion in line of sight
Measuring radial velocities. il Sky & Tel 39:82
F '70

Observations
Field of Arcturus; mystery of T Bootis
and other problematical stars. J. Ashbrook.
il Sky & Tel 39:87-8 F '70

Radial velocity
See Stars—Motion in line of sight

Rotation
Stellar rotation and atmospheric motions.
M. Hack. il Sky & Tel 40:84-6, 143-5, 208-
9 Ag-O '70

Spectra
Laboratory exercises in astronomy: spec-
tral classification. O. Gingerich. il Sky &
Tel 40:74-6 Ag '70
Search for an effect of the sun on the fre-
quency of 18-centimeter radiation. J. A.
Ball and others. bibliog il Science 167:1755-
7 Mr 27 '70
Theory of stellar spectra, by C. R. Cowley.
Review
  Sky & Tel 40:227-31 O '70. D. Mihalas

Temperature
Hottest stars. l. Asimov. Sci Digest 67:80-1
Ap '70
STARS, Double
Double star measures. Sky & Tel 39:159-60 Mr
'70
Some bright visual binary stars. J. Meeus.
il Sky & Tel 41:21-5 Ja '71 (to be cont)
Spica as a double star. il Sky & Tel 40:355-6
D '70
  See also
Stars, Eclipsing binary
STARS, Dwarf
Celestial supermagnet. D. E. Thomsen. il Sci
N 98:290-1 O 3 '70
Hot white dwarf star in an eclipsing binary.
il Sky & Tel 40:89-90 Ag '70
Magnetic dwarf in Draco. il Time 96:45 S 14
'70
STARS, Eclipsing binary
Former eclipsing variable; HD 168206. Sky
& Tel 40:206 O '70
Notes for Algol watchers. J. A. Ashbrook.
il Sky & Tel 41:62-3 Ja '71
WY Geminorum as an eclipsing system. il Sky
& Tel 40:141-2 S '70
STARS, Flare. See Stars, Variable
STARS, Giant
Distribution and motions of supergiant stars.
il Sky & Tel 39:162 Mr '70
STARS, Magnetic. See Magnetism, Stellar
STARS, New
Director reports:
  On Nova Delphini. M. W. Mayall. il R Pop
    Astron 63:24 Ag '70
  More about the new star; Nova Serpentis. il
    Sky & Tel 39:334 My '70
Nova Cygni 1970. il Sky & Tel 40:81-2 Ag '70
Nova Scuti 1970. il Sky & Tel 40:272 N '70
Nova Serpentis 1970. il Sky & Tel 39:224 Ap
'70
Radio observations of new stars. Sky & Tel
40:351 D '70
STARS, Spectra
HR 465 and promethium. Sky & Tel 41:26-7
Ja '71
STARS, Variable
Chi Cygni: a famous long-period variable.
J. A. Ashbrook. il Sky & Tel 40:252 O '70
Flare star in Messier 6. G. A. Bakos. il Sky
& Tel 40:214 O '70
HBV 475: a peculiar emission star. il Sky &
Tel 39:93 F '70
Is 66 Ophiuchi a flare star? Sky & Tel 40:
206 O '70
SU Tauri: an unpredictable variable. L. J.
Robinson. il Sky & Tel 40:398 D '70
Unusual infrared object; IRC+10216. il Sky &
Tel 39:159 Mr '70
VY Canis Majoris: a unique variable. il Sky
& Tel 40:330 N '70
  See also
American association of variable star ob-
servers
Stars, Eclipsing binary
STARS and stripes. See Flags—United States
STARS and stripes (newspaper)
How the G.I.'s in Vietnam don't learn about
the war. R. Hodierne. il por N Y Times
Mag p28-9+ Ap 12 '70
STARVATION
Starvation in human pregnancy: hypogly-
cemia, hypoinsulinemia, and hyperketone-
mia. P. Felig and V. Lynch. bibliog il Sci-
ence 170:990-2 N 27 '70

STASH. See Student association for the study of hallucinogens, inc.

STATE, Heads of. See Heads of state

STATE, The
Cybernetic state. A. Schick. il por Trans-Action 7:14-26 bibliog (p64) F '70
The establishment; a lowering of our voices; address, December 2, 1969. J. V. Clyne. Vital Speeches 36:209-11 Ja 15 '70
Theory of the origin of the state. R. L. Carneiro. bibliog Science 169:733-8 Ag 21 '70; Discussion. 170:930-1 N 27 '70
    See also
Corporate state

STATE aid to education. See Education and state

STATE and art. See Art and state

STATE and environment. See Environmental policy

STATE and federal relations. See Federal and state relations

STATE and industry. See Industry and state

STATE and libraries. See Libraries and state

STATE and municipal relations
States and the urban crisis, ed. by A. K. Campbell. Review
    Sat R 53:35 Je 6 '70. J. R. Lowe

STATE and recreation. See Recreation and state

STATE and science. See Science and state

STATE and the individual. See Individual and the state

STATE birds
Our state bird, the bluebird. il Cons 24:35 Je '70

STATE bonds
Voters on spending: schools down, environment up. il U S News 69:60-2 N 16 '70

STATE candidates. See Candidates, Political

STATE colleges and universities, American association of. See American association of state colleges and universities

STATE constitutions. See Constitutions, State

STATE department (United States) See United States—State, Department of

STATE elections. See Elections—United States

STATE encouragement of science, literature and art
Composers and poodles. M. Kalmanoff. Opera N 34:6 Ap 4 '70
    See also
Art and state

STATE expenditures. See State finance

STATE finance
Money crisis nears for local public works. il U S News 68:73-4 My 4 '70
    See also
Intergovernmental tax relations
Taxation, State

STATE flowers
Flowers of the fifty; with paintings by A. O. Dowden. Audubon 72:18-27 Jl '70

STATE forests. See Forests, State

STATE governments
Nixon's strategy for '72; 1970 election results. il U S News 69:21-4 N 23 '70
Statehouses go modern. il Nations Bsns 58:24-5+ My '70
States and the urban crisis, ed. by A. K. Campbell. Review
    Sat R 53:35 Je 6 '70. J. R. Lowe
    See also
Constitutions, State
Governors

STATE hospitals, Psychiatric. See Hospitals, Psychiatric

STATE institution libraries. See Libraries, Institution

STATE labor legislation. See Labor laws and legislation—United States

STATE legislatures
    See also
Illinois—Legislature

STATE libraries. See Libraries, State

STATE library associations. See Library associations

STATE library commission, Calif. See California—State library commission

STATE library commission, Mo. See Missouri—State library commission

STATE library surveys. See Library surveys

STATE-local fiscal relations. See Intergovernmental fiscal relations

STATE medicine. See Medical service, State

STATE parks and reserves
Are campers slobs? B. Hackett. il Am For 76:36-9+ Ap '70
State parks: lands for all seasons, lands for all people; special issue. il Parks & Rec 5:13+ D '70
    See also
National conference on state parks
    also subhead Parks and reserves under names of states, e.g. California—Parks and reserves

STATE plants. See State flowers

STATE regulation of industry. See Industry and state

STATE senators. See Senators

STATE songs
Full text of Wilder address; protesting the state song: Carry me back to old Virginny. L. D. Wilder. Negro Hist Bul 33:100-1 Ap '70

STATE taxation. See Taxation, State

STATE technical services, Office of. See United States—Commerce, Department of—State technical services, Office of

STATE university of New York. See New York (state). State university

STATE university of New York at Buffalo. See New York (state). State university—Buffalo campus

STATEN ISLAND
Eighteen narcotic-addiction buildings in eighteen months. il Am City 85:152+ Je '70

Historic houses, etc.
Haunted houses of Staten Island. C. Brooks. il Travel 134:50-2+ S '70

STATES (United States)
Facts & figures of nations & states; tables. Sr Schol 95:23-5 S 22 '69
    See also
State governments

STATES, Ideal. See Utopias

STATESMEN
    See also
Heads of state
Politicians

STATIC electricity. See Electricity, Static

STATION wagons
Intermediate station wagons. il Consumer Rep 35:239-45 Ap '70
'71 wagons: big changes coming up. J. P. Norbye and J. Dunne. il Pop Sci 197:74-5 O '70
Those sensible station wagons. A. Markovich. il Pop Mech 134:134-9+ S '70

Four wheel drive
Do-anything Range Rover cruises like a sedan, clambers like a goat. D. Scott. il Pop Sci 197:84 N '70

Testing
Buick Estate wagon. il Consumer Rep 35:300-1 My '70
Norbye-Dunne report:
    Deluxe wagons. J. P. Norbye and J. Dunne. il Pop Sci 196:32+ Mr '70
    These wagons are family cars on truck chassis. J. P. Norbye and J. Dunne. il Pop Sci 196:32+ My '70
Tom McCahill tests (title varies)
    Olds Vista-Cruiser station wagon. T. McCahill. il Mech Illus 66:68-70+ My '70

Transmission
    See Automobiles—Transmission

STATISTICAL mechanics
Theorists honor Uhlenbeck with statistical-mechanics meeting. A. J. F. Siegert and C. J. Thompson. Phys Today 23:85+ F '70

STATISTICAL methods
Do managers find decision theory useful? R. V. Brown. il Harvard Bsns R 48:78-89 My '70
Management evolution in the quantitative world. R. F. Vandell. il Harvard Bsns R 48:83-92 Ja '70
    See also
Correlation (statistics)
Graphic methods
Stochastic processes

STATISTICS
Don't trust statistics. W. Parkhurst. Sci Digest 68:97-8 N '70
    See also
Census
Government statistics
Statistical methods
    also subhead Statistics under various subjects, e.g. Population—Statistics

STATUES
See also
Crazy Horse (Sioux Indian)—Statues, portraits, etc.
Monuments
also subhead Monuments, statues, etc.
under names of cities, e.g. Chicago—Monuments, statues, etc.

STATUETTES. See Figurines

STATURE
Calvin and the kiddie corps; pro basketball players. R. Blount, jr. il Sports Illus 33: 26-8+ N 16 '70

STATUS, Social. See Social status

STATUS of women, Commission on the. See United Nations—Commission on the status of women

STATUS symbols. See Prestige

STAUB, Rusty
In Montreal they love Le Grand Orange. M. Mulvoy. il pors Sports Illus 33:38-9 Jl 6 '70

STAUDACHER, Rosemarian V.
Call it sabotage! America 122:72-5 Ja 24 '70

STAUFFER, Russell G.
Reading teacher's dream come true. bibliog il por Wilson Lib Bul 45:285-92 N '70

STAVELY, Rowena
You'd never know I had skin cancer. por Har Yrs 10:44-5 S '70

STAVROPOULOS, Constantin Anghelos
United Nations and the development of international law, 1945-1970. UN Mo Chron 7: 78-84 Je '70

STAYTON, John
Build a low-cost time delay relay. il Pop Electr 32:71 Je '70

STEADY-state universe. See Cosmology

STEAK. See Cookery—Meat

STEALING
Camping security and common sense. il Pop Mech 133:S26-7+ My '70
See also
Airport thefts
Animal thefts
Art thefts
Automobiles, Theft of
Embezzlement
Firearms, Theft of
Library thefts
Securities, Theft of
Shoplifting

STEAM, Natural
Clean power from inside the earth. J. Lear. il Sat R 53:53-6+ D 5 '70
Earth's heat: a new power source. R. H. Gilluly. il Sci N 98:415-16 N 28 '70
Utilities put faith in Old Faithful; geothermal power sources. il Bsns W p50+ O 3 '70

STEAM engines, Automotive. See Automobile engines

STEAM irons, Electric. See Electric irons

STEAM power plants
Montreal's combined incinerator-power plant. E. F. Spitzer. il Am City 85:86-9 My '70
Power plants: effects of chlorination on estuarine primary production. D. H. Hamilton, jr. and others. bibliog il Science 169: 197-8 Jl 10 '70
See also
Steam, Natural

STEAM producing incinerators. See Refuse incinerators

STEAM rockets. See Rockets, Steam

STEAM tractors. See Tractors

STEAM turbines
Allis rejoins the power play; joint venture with German turbine manufacturer. il Bsns W p40 F 28 '70

STEAM vaporizers. See Vaporizers

STEAMBATH; drama. See Friedman, B. J.

STEAMBOATS. See Steamships and steamboats

STEAMED puddings. See Puddings

STEAMERS (ships) See Steamships and steamboats

STEAMSHIP lines
See also
Cunard steamship company
Ocean liners

STEAMSHIPS and steamboats
Last season on the river for the last great steamboat; the Delta Queen. il Life 69: 46-7 Jl 24 '70
Last year for the King and Queen? Sunset 144:30 Ja '70
Paddleboat on the Murray; Australia. R. Harrington. il Travel 135:48-51 Ja '71
Steam lives! Puget Sound live steamers. E. Crimmin. il Motor B 126:48-9+ S '70
Steamboat a-goin'; retirement for the Delta Queen. il Newsweek 76:108 O 19 '70
See also
Ocean liners
Ocean travel

History
Steamboat to the Rockies. W. Havighurst. bibliog il Am West 7:4-11+ S '70

STEARN, Gerald Emanuel
Rapping with the Panthers in white suburbia. il N Y Times Mag p28-9+ Mr 8 '70

STEARNS, Bob
Heat waste. il Sea Front 16:154-63 My '70

STEARNS, Junius Brutus
Fishing subjects by Junius Brutus Stearns. M. F. Rogers, jr. il Antiques 98:246-50 Ag '70

STEARNS, Marian Sherman
Early education: still in its infancy. il Am Ed 6:3-5 Ag '70

STEBBINS, Arthur L.
Little learning; Watered; poems. Nat R 22: 567 Je 2 '70

STEBBINS, Doris E.
Delphiniums for towering spikes. il Home Gard 57:28-9 My '70

STEBBINS, George Ledyard
Prospects for spaceship man; excerpts from address, 1969. il Sat R 53:48-50+ Mr 7 '70

STEBEL, S. L.
Write what you feel. Writer 83:26-7 Mr '70

STECK, Theodore L. and others
Inside-out red cell membrane vesicles; preparation and purification. bibliog il Science 168:255-7 Ap 10 '70

STECKLER, Larry
One IC replaces entire I.F. strip. il Radio-Electr 41:59-61 N '70
Stereo on wheels. il Radio-Electr 41:33-5 Je '70

STECKMESSER, Kent L.
Oklahoma Robin Hood. por Am West 7:38-41 Ja '70

STEEGMULLER, Francis
Griffe of the master; story. Atlan 226:119-20 O '70

STEEL, Ronald
Supreme commander as organization man. por Sat R 53:23-5+ Je 20 '70

STEEL
Prices
Bethlehem builds a price ceiling. Bsns W p27 F 14 '70
Countertrend in steel pricing. Bsns W p27 O 10 '70
Steel puts a hole in its new formula. Bsns W p31 Ja 24 '70
Steelmen wait out a lackluster year. il Bsns W p29 My 30 '70

STEEL, Powdered
Powdered steel: a tough customer. il Bsns W p37 Ja 2 '71

STEEL, Structural
Wages in fabricated structural steel. M. J. Tighe. il Mo Labor R 93:40-1 D '70

STEEL industry and trade
Steel: signs of springtime? il Forbes 105:24-6+ F 15 '70
Advertising
Big steel gets back into advertising. il Bsns W p96 My 30 '70
Finance
Cost-price vise squeezes steel. Bsns W p21-2 N 7 '70
Metals; with yardsticks of management performance. il Forbes 105:133-4+ Ja 1 '70; 107: 85+ Ja 1 '71
Steel is not in a spending mood. il Bsns W p33-4 S 19 '70
Wages and hours
From GM to big steel. J. Hill. Commonweal 93:238-9 D 4 '70
Pay hike for steelworkers. Bsns W p61 Ag 8 '70
Wages in fabricated structural steel. M. J. Tighe. il Mo Labor R 93:40-1 D '70
See also
Collective bargaining—Steel industry
Australia
Steel finds a gold mine Down Under. il Bsns W p58+ Mr 28 '70
India
Reporter at large; Bokaro steel project: aid from Russia rather than U.S. V. Mehta. New Yorker 45:83-4+ F 14 '70
Reporter at large; new steel plant in Bhilai, with Soviet assistance. V. Mehta. New Yorker 45:62+ F 14 '70
Japan
New Japanese giant; Nippon steel corporation. Fortune 82:176 Ag '70
Steeling for competition; steel producers Yawata and Fuji iron & steel to become Nippon steel corp. Time 95:92 Ap 13 '70

STEEL Industry and trade—*Continued*
United States
Foreign threats to a basic industry; interview. E. H. Gott. il pors U S News 69:64-8 O 26 '70
Steel braces for hedge buying. il Bsns W p 18-19 D 26 '70
Steel checking out of the supermarket. Bsns W p34+ Mr 14 '70
Steelmen wait out a lackluster year. il Bsns W p29 My 30 '70
Wary steel users run for early cover. il Bsns W p20-1 Jl 18 '70
   See also
Collective bargaining—Steel industry
United steelworkers of America
   also names of steel companies, e.g. United States steel corporation
STEEL scrap. See Scrap metal
STEEL sculpture. See Metal sculpture
STEEL service centers
   See also
Jorgensen, Earle M, company
STEEL tire cord. See Tire fabrics
STEEL workers
   See also
Steel industry and trade—Wages and hours
United steelworkers of America
STEELE, John L.
Haynsworth v. the U.S. Senate (1969) il por Fortune 81:90-3+ Mr '70
STEELE, Richard W.
Preparing the public for war: efforts to establish a national propaganda agency, 1940-41. Am Hist R 75:1640-53 O '70
STEELE, Thomas A. 3d. See Reum, W. R. jt. auth.
STEELHEAD trout fishing. See Trout fishing
STEELMET, inc.
Polish pays off for a scrap dealer. il Bsns W p 152 Mr 14 '70
STEELWORKERS union. See United steelworkers of America
STEERING gear
   See also
Automobiles—Steering gear
STEERS. See Cattle, Beef
STEERS, Nina A.
Cliché; story. Américas 22:38-42 Ap '70
STEFFEN, Robert
Crisis in agriculture. Org Gard & Farm 17:52-5 Ag '70
STEFFENSEN, D. M. See Wimber, D. E. jt. auth.
STEGENGA, James A.
(ed) Issues before the 25th General assembly. bibliog f il Int Concil 579:1-222 S '70
STEGMAN, Michael A.
New mythology of housing. il Trans-Action 7:55-62 Ja 70
STEGNER, Wallace
East Palo Alto. Sat R 53:12+ Ag 1 '70
STEICHEN, Edward
Happy birthday, Mr Steichen; interview, ed. by M. R. Weiss. il por Sat R 53:49-51 Mr 28 '70
   about
Edward Steichen. G. M. Mayer. il Mod Phot 34:82-7+ Jl '70 *
STEIG, William
Caldecott award acceptance; address, June 30, 1970. Horn Bk 46:359-60 Ag '70
   about
Newbery and Caldecott winners for 1969 books. il por Pub W 197:125-6 F 23 '70 *
Rocky! disqualification of 1969 winner because of poor taste of one of illustrations; discussion. Am Lib 1:525 Je '70 *
William Steig. R. Kraus. il por Horn Bk 46:361-3 Ag '70 *
STEIGER, William Albert
At issue: a fair approach to job safety; interview. pors Nations Bsns 58:47-9 S '70
STEIM, Joseph M. See Reinert, J. C. jt. auth.
STEIN, Arthur O. See Dawson, G. jt. auth.
STEIN, David
Forging a career. Newsweek 76:105 O 12 '70 *
STEIN, Elliott
(tr) See Rocha, G. Way to make a future
STEIN, Gertrude
Picasso; excerpt from Selected writings of Gertrude Stein. il por Vogue 157:88-9+ Ja 1 '71
   about
Americans in Paris. D. Davis. il por Newsweek 76:80-81B D 14 '70 *
Art. L. Alloway. Nation 212:61-2 Ja 11 '71 *

Exhibition preview: four Americans in Paris. J. R. Mellow. il pors Art in Am 58:84-91 N '70 *
G. Stein. F. Rose. Vogue 157:89+ Ja 1 '71 *
Patrons and roped climbers. R. Hughes. il por Time 96:76-81 D 14 '70 *
STEIN, Gertrude family collection. See Art—Private collections
STEIN, Herbert
The economy; interview. il por Forbes 105:19-20 F 15 '70
Game plan at halftime; address, September 22, 1970. Vital Speeches 37:61-4 N 1 '70
STEIN, Howard
Change and turmoil on Wall Street. il por Time 96:52-7 Ag 24 '70 *
STEIN, Jane. See Goldberg, R. T. jt. auth.
STEIN, Judy
Five passionate feminists. il pors McCalls 97:53+ Jl '70
STEIN, Lawrence
Ionic radon solutions. bibliog il Science 168:362-4 Ap 17 '70
STEIN, M. L.
First round to Agnew. Nation 211:178-81 S 7 '70
News from Milford. il por Sat R 54:43-6 Ja 9 '71
—and Ricapito, J. V.
Student revolt: Italian style. il Sat R 53:69-71+ F 21 '70
STEIN collection. See Art—Private collections
STEINBACH, Donald L.
Digital instruments you can build (title varies) il Electr World 84:28-31+ Jl; 47-50+ Ag; 50-2+ S; 41-5+ N '70; 85:35-8+ Ja '71
STEINBECK, John, 1902-1968
Journal of a novel; the East of Eden letters; excerpts. Writer 83:13-15+ My '70
   about
Initiation rites in Steinbeck's The red pony. R. B. Shuman. Engl J 59:1252-5 D '70 *
Man, a place, and a time. C. McWilliams. il pors Am West 7:4-8+ My '70 *
STEINBERG, Alfred D. and others
Tolerance to polyinosinic polycytidylic acid in NZB/NZW mice. bibliog il Science 167:870-1 F 6 '70
STEINBERG, Jonathan
Germany and the Russo-Japanese war. bibliog f Am Hist R 75:1965-86 D '70
STEINBERG, Michael
Behind the scenes. il Hi Fi 20:secI 15-16 Jl '70
STEINBERG, Saul
Artist speaks; interview, ed. by G. Glueck. il Art in Am 58:110-17 N '70
Set of rebuses. il New Yorker 46:24-7 D 26 '70
STEINBERG, Saul P.
Can Leasco come back? A. A. Butkus. il por Duns 95:69-70+ Mr '70 *
Missing millions. pors Time 96:85-6 S 14 '70 *
STEINEM, Gloria
After too much moving ... cheerful rooms to live in, a private place to work. il por House & Gard 138:52-5 Jl '70
Why we need a woman president in 1976. Look 34:58 Ja 13 '70
(ed) See Hefner, H. What Playboy doesn't know about women could fill a book
   about
Gloria, hallelujah. E. Sheppard. Harp Baz 103:142-3 F '70
What it would be like if women win; Time essay. il por Time 96:22+ Ag 31 '70 *
STEINER, George A.
Rise of the corporate planner; adaptation of address, May 1970. il Harvard Bsns R 48:133-9 S '70
STEINER, Nyle A.
Wire music. il Pop Electr 33:35+ Jl '70
STEINER, Ruth
Responsories and prosa for St Stephens's day at Salisbury. bibliog f il Mus Q 56:162-82 Ap '70
STEINER, Stan
Chicano power. New Repub 162:16-18 Je 20 '70
STEINFELS, Peter
Talk of the town. il Commonweal 91:422+ Ja 16 '70
STEINHAUSEN, M. and others
Countercurrent system in the renal cortex of rats. bibliog il Science 167:1631-3 Mr 20 '70
STEINHAUSER, Margaret N.
Art for the mentally retarded child. il Sch Arts 69:30-1 Mr '70
STEINKE, Bettina
Painter of people. F. Whitaker. il por Am Artist 35:20-7+ Ja '71 *
STEINLEY, Gary
Contemporary American novella: an existential approach. Engl J 59:52-8 Ja '70

STEINMEIER, Dorothy E.
Teacher with a new heart. il por Todays Ed 59:56 Mr '70
STEINS. See Drinking vessels
STEINWAY and sons, New York
Great Chicago piano war; World Columbian exposition. P. Hume and R. Hume. il pors Am Heritage 21:16-21 O '70
STEINWEDEL, Louis William
Eternal ghost. il Motor T 22:86-90+ Je '70
Or more precisely, the legend of Barney Oldfield. il Motor T 23:38-40+ Ja '71
Uhlenhaut. il por Motor T 22:54-6+ Ap '70
STELLA, Frank
We talk to. . ; interview. por Mlle 71:299 Ag '70

about

Art part; MOMA retrospective. D. Davis. il por Newsweek 75:98 Ap 13 '70 *
Art; retrospective at the Museum of modern art. L. Alloway. Nation 210:540-1 My 4 '70 *
Art world; retrospective at the Museum of modern art. H. Rosenberg. New Yorker 46:103-4+ My 9 '70 *
Frank Stella: perspectives; paintings at the Museum of modern art. E. C. Baker. il por Art N 69:46-9+ My '70 *
STELLAR evolution. See Stars—Evolution
STELLAR magnetism. See Magnetism, Stellar
STELLAR models. See Astronomical models
STELLAR spectra. See Stars—Spectra
STELLER'S jays. See Jays
STELZER, Irwin
As they see it; interview. por Forbes 105:46+ Ap 15 '70
STEMBERG, Tom
Discos that swing. Travel & Camera 33:16+ My '70
STEMS (plants)
See also
Petioles
STENDHAL, pseud. See Beyle, M. H.
STENNIS, John Cornelius
Excerpt from debate, February 17, 1969. Cong Digest 49:112+ Ap '70

about

Death of integration? Nation 210:228 Mr 2 '70 *
End of reconstruction. il pors Time 95:12-13 Mr 2 '70 *
Requiem for a liberal dream? il por Newsweek 75:18-21 Mr 2 '70 *
Stennis and schools. New Repub 162:7 F 28 '70 *
STENOGRAPHERS
See also
Court stenographers
STENVIG, Charles S.
God is my adviser. il por Newsweek 76:58 Jl 20 '70 *
Minneapolis librarians defeat censorship move. Library J 95:4090 D 1 '70 *
STEPANCHEV, Stephen
Teeth; poem. Nation 211:222 S 14 '70
STEPHEN, Edith
Edith Stephen theatre dance co; Brooklyn academy of music, NYC. J. Armstrong. Dance Mag 44:81 Je '70 *
STEPHEN Greene press. See Greene, Stephen, press
STEPHENS, D. R. and Lilley, E. M.
Compressibilities of lunar crystalline rock, microbreccia, and fines to 40 kilobars. bibliog il Science 167:731-2 Ja 30 '70
STEPHENS, Edgar R. and Price, M. A.
Smog aerosol: infrared spectra. bibliog il Science 168:1584-6 Je 26 '70
STEPHENS, John Lloyd
Travel as a passport to freedom. A. Alvarez. Sat R 54:18-19 Ja 2 '71 *
STEPHENS, Lisa
Gaeltacht of West Kerry; with biographical sketch. il Natur Hist 79:4, 44-90 bibliog (p 133) Ag '70
STEPHENS, Olin
Leave it to Chance. il por Time 96:75 S 21 '70 *
Olin Stephens. B. Robinson. il por Yachting 127:54-5+ F '70 *
STEPHENS, R. E.
On the apparent homology of actin and tubulin. bibliog il Science 168:845-7 My 15 '70
STEPHENS, Robert
People are talking about . . . por Vogue 156:82-3 Ag 15 '70 *
STEPS, Garden. See Garden steps
STERBA, James P.
Close-up of the grunt: the hours of boredom, the seconds of terror. il N Y Times Mag p30-1+ F 8 '70
(comp) Scraps of paper from Vietnam. il N Y Times Mag p28-9+ O 18 '70

STEREO cartridges. See Phonograph—Stereophonic pickup
STEREO headphones. See Earphones
STEREO loud speakers. See Loud speaking apparatus
STEREO shows. See Audio fairs
STEREOCHEMISTRY
Crystal and molecular structure of a thymine phototrimer. J. L. Flippen and others. bibliog il Science 169:1084-5 S 11 '70
Fourier analysis and the structure of DNA. bibliog il Science 167:1693-702 Mr 27 '70
See also
Conformational analysis
STEREOGRAPHS
See also
Stereophotography
STEREOPHONIC phonograph records. See Phonograph records—Stereophonic records
STEREOPHONIC pickup. See Phonograph—Stereophonic pickup
STEREOPHONIC radio receivers. See Radio receivers, Stereophonic
STEREOPHONIC radio transmission. See Radio broadcasting—Stereophonic transmission
STEREOPHONIC recorders. See Magnetic recorders and recording—Stereophonic recorders
STEREOPHONIC sound systems
All-in-one music centers: your best bet in hi-fi? H. Fantel. il Pop Mech 134:130-3 D '70
Compact stereo systems. il Consumer Rep 34:222-76 D '69
Consumer electronic show: observations and reservations about four-channel. I. Berger. il Sat R 53:51 Jl 52 '70
Custom-tailored stereo. L. Feldman. il Hi Fi 20:secI 42-7 Jl '70
Doing the four-channel two-step. I. Berger. Sat R 53:51+ Je 27 '70
Hi-fi product report; E-V Landmark 100 stereo compact. il Electr World 84:13-14 O '70
More on the Scheiber system. M. S. Snitzer. il Electr World 84:43 D '70
Scheiber 4-channel stereo system. M. S. Snitzer. il Electr World 84:43+ S '70
Stereo without fuss; compact systems. R. S. Lanier. il Hi Fi 20:secI 54-8 Mr '70
Wire your backyard for stereo. L. Feldman. il Hi Fi 20:secI 54-9 Je '70

Anecdotes, facetiae, satire, etc.

Fake fi. D. Williamson. Sat R 53:4+ O 10 '70

Equipment

Assemble a frequency equalizer; unity gain amplifier. G. Meyerle. il Pop Electr 33:51-9 O '70

Maintenance and repair

Get better sound from your stereo. P. Sutheim. il Radio-Electr 41:40-2 O '70
STEREOPHOTOGRAPHY
Stereo ain't dead. W. Allphin. il Mod Phot 34:80-1+ Ap '70
STEREOPTICON. See Lantern projection
STERILITY
Hope and help for the infertile. D. Rorvik. Good H 171:79+ O '70
STERILITY in insects
See also
Isolation (biology)
STERILIZATION, Sexual
At twenty-two, my husband chose sterilization. il Good H 172:39+ Ja '71
Facts about voluntary sterilization; salpingectomy and vasectomy. Good H 170:155 Je '70
One man's answer to overpopulation. il pors Life 68:42-7 Mr 6 '70
Pigeon control by chemosterilization: population model from laboratory results. J. Sturtevant. bibliog il Science 170:322-4 O 16 '70
Sterilization for both sexes; vasectomy and new gynecological technique called laparoscopy. il Time 95:38 Je 1 '70
Tax-supported sterilization wins in London despite Catholic drive. Chr Cent 87:591 My 13 '70
Trend to sterilization. Newsweek 76:90 D 21 '70
STERILIZATION of defectives, criminals, etc.
See also
Castration of criminals and defectives
STERLING, Carlos Márquez. See Márquez Sterling, C.
STERLING, Claire
Foreign report: Italy's happy Communists. Harper 240:24+ F '70
STERLING, E. M.
Myth of multiple use. il Am For 76:25-7 Je '70

STERLING, Jim
I haul corn to the elevator. il por Farm J
93:A4-31 D '69
STERLING, Kenneth, and others
Conversion of thyroxine to triiodothyronine
in normal human subjects. bibliog il Sci-
ence 169:1099-100 S 11 '70
STERLING, Manuel Márquez
Gottschalk, musical Humboldt. il por Amér-
icas 22:10-18 Ja '70
STERLING airways. See Airlines—Denmark
STERMAN, Maurice B. and others
Facilitation of spindle-burst sleep by condi-
tioning of electroencephalographic activ-
ity while awake. bibliog il Science 167:1146-
8 F 20 '70
STERN, Elizabeth, and others
Contraceptives and dysplasia: higher rate
for pill choosers. bibliog il Science 169:497-
8 Jl 31 '70
STERN, Fritz
Reflections on the international student
movement. Am Scholar 40:123-37 Wint '70
STERN, Gerd
Media in the market. D. Davis. Newsweek
76:88 N 30 '70 *
STERN, Harold
Dance marathons; look back in horror. il
Dance Mag 44:68-71 F '70
Master of jazz forms turns to TV. il pors
Dance Mag 44:44-7 Je '70
STERN, Isaac
Three men on a hobby; remarks, ed. by I.
Kolodin. il pors Sat R 53:47-9 O 31 '70
STERN, Lothar
Hybrid technology regains IC spotlight. il
Electr World 83:42-5+ F '70
STERN, Otto
Home landscape plants to give quick results.
il Home Gard 57:74-5 Mr '70 *
STERN, Paula
Womanly image. por Atlan 225:87-90 Mr '70
STERN, Peter S.
Stanford's community of consent. Nation 211:
174-8, 308 S 7, O 5 '70
STERN, Richard Gustave
Bad dreams for Carnap; poem. Am Scholar
39:677 Aut '70
Fred Hampton's apartment. Nation 210:325-6
Mr 23 '70
Memory of Forster. Nation 210:795-6 Je 29
'70
STERN, Richard Martin
Promise of a wedding day; story. Good H
170:66-7 Je '70
STERN, Sol
Oakland: that troubled town across the Bay.
il Holiday 47:74-5+ Mr '70
STERN, Walter Phillips
Return to fundamentals? il por Duns 95:73-4
Ja '70
STERN drive engines. See Motor boat engines
STERNBERG, Joseph
Project Wingspread: space-age education. il
Schol Teach Sec Teach Sup p6-8 D 1 '69;
Same abr. Ed Digest 35:16-17 Ap '70
STERNE, Hedda
Open eye. K. Kuh. il Sat R 53:53 Mr 28 '70 *
STERNER, J. F.
MOSFET utility preamp for test equipment.
il Electr World 84:62-3 Ag '70
STERNGLASS, Ernest J.
Infant mortality and nuclear tests. Bul Atom
Sci 25:18-20 Ap; 29-32 O '69; 26:40-2+ My
'70
Infant mortality; excerpts from address, May
1969. bibliog il Environ 11:9-13 D '69

about
How many children? M. W. Friedlander and
J. Klarmann. il Environ 11:3-8 D '69
Professor Sternglass, fallout and infant mor-
tality. Bul Atom Sci 26:46 Mr '70 *
STERNHELL, Carol Ruth
March in the dark. il McCalls 98:8+ N '70
Writing on the revolution. il McCalls 97:
16+ Jl '70
(ed) See Kunstler, W. M. Brief encounter
with a lawyer named Kunstler
STERNHOLD, Thomas
Sternhold and Hopkins puzzle. H. Byard.
Mus Q 56:221-9 Ap '70 *
STERNWHEELERS. See Steamships and
steamboats
STEROID hormones. See Hormones, Sex
STEROIDS
Gas chromatography: medical diagnostic aid.
M. W. Ruchelman. bibliog il por Chem 43:
14-19 D '70
See also
Dexamethasone
Lipids
Testosterone

STEROLS
Sterols in recent marine sediments. D. Atta-
way and P. L. Parker. bibliog il Science
169:674-6 Ag 14 '70
See also
Cholesterol
Desmosterol
STETHOSCOPE, Electric
Electronic stethoscope probes the unhear-
able. R. F. Graf and G. J. Whalen. il Pop
Sci 196:99-101 F '70
STETSON, John B, company
Stetson heads for the last roundup. il Bsns
W p40 D 19 '70
STETSON, Paul W.
Waterlilies around the clock. il Horticulture
48:30-3+ Ap '70
STETSON hats, inc. See Stetson, John B,
company
STETTEN, Gail. See Lederberg, S. jt. auth.
STEUBENVILLE, Ohio
True grit; air pollution. Newsweek 76:57 Ag
17 '70
Underwater pipe repair. il Am City 85:38
Mr '70
STEVE, go wash your hands! story. See Ward,
J. H.
STEVEN Institute of technology, Hoboken,
N.J.
Student-faculty common loan policy at Ste-
vens institute. J. A. McCrossan. Am Lib 1:
396-7 Ap '70
STEVENS, Denis
Music in honor of St Thomas of Canter-
bury; with list of hymns. bibliog f il Mus Q
56:311-48 Jl '70
STEVENS, Edward
When is an authority in authority? America
122:46 Ja 17 '70
STEVENS, Georgiana G.
Reports: Beirut. Atlan 225:27-8+ F '70
Reports: France and the Middle East. Atlan
226:8+ Ag; 29 O '70
What Nasser did. Atlan 227:45-7 Ja '71
STEVENS, Leonard A.
Do we need a new pledge of allegiance?
Look 34:19-21 D 1 '70
STEVENS, Robert Ten Broeck
Where are they now? il pors Newsweek 77:
10 Ja 11 '71 *
STEVENS, Roger L.
America's stake in the arts. il Sat R 53:18-
21 F 28 '70
STEVENS, S. S.
Neural events and the psychophysical law.
bibliog il Science 170:1043-50 D 4 '70
STEVENS, Sylvia G.
Masks. il Sch Arts 69:6-7 Je '70
STEVENS, Thelma
For those who look but do not see. il Sch
Arts 70:10-11 N '70
STEVENS, Wallace
Seductive gambits. R. Giannone. Nation 210:
282-4 Mr 9 '70 *
Wallace Stevens in the tropics: a conserva-
tive protest. J. Pinkerton. Yale R 60:215-27
D '70 *
STEVENS, William K.
OE: bureaucracy in trouble. Sat R 53:55 Jl
18 '70
STEVENSON, Adlai Ewing, 3d
Adlai III brand of politics. W. B. Furlong. il
pors N Y Times Mag p28-9+ F 22 '70 *
Adlai III; his new politics startle old pros.
J. Star. il pors Look 34:82-4+ O 6 '70 *
Illinois' Adlai Stevenson. il por Time 96:20-1
N 16 '70 *
Illinois: Stevenson fights TV. E. S. Gilbreth.
il Nation 211:399-402 O 26 '70 *
New Adlai. il por Newsweek 76:38+ O 12 '70 *
They're after Adlai. P. R. Wieck. New Re-
pub 163:13-15 S 26 '70 *
STEVENSON, Anne
Relative stranger; novel. Good H 170:53-5 Ja;
76-7 F '70
STEVENSON, Charles
Where you have to be retired to be hired.
Read Digest 96:21-4+ Je '70
STEVENSON, Florence
Ariadne's island. il Opera N 34:10-13 Mr 28 '70
Koanga. il Opera N 35:34-5 D 19 '70
Very special Tosca. Opera N 35:24-6 D 12
'70
(ed) See Heeley, D. Love affair
(ed) See Korjus, M. Miliza
STEVENSON, Ian
Is there another life after death? F. Kin-
kead. il pors Look 34:84-8+ O 20 '70 *
STEVENSON, James
If the president's half-hour press conference
had been allowed to go beyond half an
hour. New Yorker 46:35 D 26 '70 *
March, Saturday, 2 p.m.-3 p.m; story. New
Yorker 46:43 Mr 28 '70
Pianoforte factory revisited. il New Yorker
46:40-1 N 28 '70

STEVENSON, James—*Continued*
Waiting for Wingfield. il New Yorker 46:30-5 S 5 '70
Why I am an unsuccessful artist. New Yorker 46:47 O 31 '70
STEVENSON, John R.
Draft U.N. convention on the international seabed area; statement, August 3, 1970. Dept State Bul 63:209-10 Ag 24 '70
Extraterritoriality in Canadian-United States relations; address, September 2, 1970. Dept State Bul 63:425-30 O 12 '70
International law and the oceans; address, February 18, 1970. Dept State Bul 62:339-43 Mr 16 '70; Same. Vital Speeches 36:367-9 Ap 1 '70
Treaty on the nonproliferation of nuclear weapons enters into force; remarks, March 5, 1970. Dept State Bul 62:410-11 Mr 30 '70
United States military actions in Cambodia: questions of international law; address, May 28, 1970. Dept State Bul 62:765-70 Je 22 '70
STEVENSON, Robert E.
We're fishing from outer space. G. Lee. il por Nat Wildlife 8:36-41 F '70 *
STEVER, H. Guyford
Doctor of arts degree. Science 170:587 N 6 '70
STEW
Hearty soups & stews. Z. Coulson. il Good H 172:80-95 Ja '71
Savory stews. il Bet Hom & Gard 48:107 Ap '70
Stews from France. il Ladies Home J 87:74-5+ F '70
STEWARD, Orville M.
Bayard Cutting arboretum. il Horticulture 48:36-7 Jl '70
STEWARD, Robert
Repowering with diesels. Yachting 127:115+ Ja '70
STEWARDESSES, Air. See Airlines—Hostesses
STEWARDSHIP, Christian
On getting what one deserves. L. R. Buzzard. Chr Today 14:5 F 27 '70
What moves men as stewards? W. J. Werning. Chr Today 14:11-13 Ap 24 '70
STEWART, Alva W.
Consolidated community works better. il Am City 85:79-80 Mr '70
STEWART, David B. and others
Crystallography of some lunar plagioclases. bibliog il Science 167:634-5 Ja 30 '70
STEWART, Douglas J.
Disfranchise the old. New Repub 163:20-2 Ag 22 '70
STEWART, Ellen
La MaMa is a lady. E. Lester. il por Holiday 47:22+ My '70 *
STEWART, Fred Mustard
No loose ends. P. Nathan. Pub W 198:270 Ag 31 '70 *
STEWART, George R.
Where's that again? excerpts from A dictionary of American place-names. Am Heritage 21:116 O '70
STEWART, Jackie
Jackie Stewart; interview, ed. by E. Seidler. il pors Motor T 22:60-2 Mr '70
Racing's most frightening corners; ed. by G. S. Brown. il por Sports Illus 33:38-49 O 12 '70
about
Like a collapsed balloon. K. Prentiss. por Holiday 47:26-8 Mr '70 *
STEWART, James
Innocent revisited. il pors Time 95:54-5 Je 29 '70 *
STEWART, John
Watch your figure. Writer 83:24-7 Ap '70
STEWART, Mark A.
Hyperactive children; with biographical sketch. il Sci Am 222:12 94-8 Ap '70
STEWART, Mary
Crystal cave; story; excerpt from novel. Ladies Home J 87:65-72 Jl '70
Teller of tales. Writer 83:9-12+ My '70
STEWART, Mary Gaines
Surprising lycoris. Horticulture 48:40 S '70
STEWART, Michael
Britain, Europe and the Alliance. For Affairs 48:648-59 Jl '70
STEWART, Naomi
Bohuslan, Sweden's answer to the Riviera. il Travel 134:44-9+ Ag '70
STEWART, Ollie
Full-time freelancer. il por Writers Digest 50:23+ Ap '70
STEWART, Ramona
Authors & editors. B. A. Bannon. il por Pub W 198:17-18 Ag 17 '70 *

STEWART, Richard E.
How to pay for 15,000,000 auto accidents a year; interview, ed by J. A. Hamilton. il N Y Times Mag p32-4+ My 10 '70
STEWART, Robert H. 1925-
LTV acquires a new boss. il por Bsns W p34-5 My 23 '70 *
STEWART, Ron
Tip on a dead goalie. por Newsweek 75:60 Je 15 '70 *
STEWART, Ronald, and Mathur, S. P.
Handling hot water, with a payoff. il Cons 25:16-20 D '70
STEWART, Shirley
India? Give me exotic Iowa! il Har Yrs 10:26-9 S '70
STEWART, Thomas. See Lear, E. jt. auth.
STEWART, William S. See Hanson, G. P. jt. auth.
STEWART-GORDON, James
Great big wide and wonderful Texas. il Read Digest 96:154-61 Je '70
We're poisoning ourselves with noise. Read Digest 96:187-90+ F '70
STEWS. See Stew
STEYERT, Richard D.
Architectural economics: the concept of total cost. il Arch Rec 148:81-2 O '70
STICHT, J. Paul
Man in the mod shirt. por Forbes 105:49 F 15 '70 *
STICK insects
Chromosome number variation in a stick insects didymuria violescens (leach) E. Craddock. bibliog il Science 167:1380-2 Mr 6 '70
STICKNEY, John
Gentle poet of the young. il pors Life 69:49-52+ Ag 14 '70
STIGMATIZATION
Stigmata: a matter of mind or miracle? B. Hildenbrand. il Todays Health 48:57-9+ Ag '70
STILBESTROLS
Now, a new kind of stilbestrol. Suc Farm 68:38 Ja '70
STILL, Clyfford
Clyfford Still, 1500 rare Stills. B. Rose. Vogue 155:42 F 15 '70 *
Clyfford Still, the enigma. K. Kuh. il pors Vogue 155:180-3+ F 1 '70
STILL life painting
See also
Trompe-l'oeil
STILL life photography. See Photography—Still life
STILL point; ballet. See Ballets—Criticisms
STILLMAN, Edmund O.
Civilian sanctuary and target avoidance policy in thermonuclear war. Ann Am Acad 392:116-32 N '70
STILWELL, Joseph Warren
If Asia were clay in the hands of the West: the Stilwell mission to China, 1942-44; excerpts from Stilwell. B. W. Tuchman. il pors Atlan 226:68-84 S '70 *
Utmost try; excerpts. B. W. Tuchman. il pors Am Heritage 21:22-31+ O; 22:4-11+ D '70 *
STIMULANTS
Drugs for learning. il Time 96:43-4 Ag 10 '70
Pep pills for pupils; use of stimulants to control hyperactive children in Omaha. Newsweek 76:60-1 Jl 13 '70
See also
Amphetamines
Narcotics
STIMULATION (physiology)
Circadian rhythm of brain self-stimulation behavior. M. Terman and J. S. Terman. bibliog il Science 168:1242-4 Je 5 '70
Evoked response and behavior in cats. R. A. Hall and others. bibliog il Science 170:998-1000 N 27 '70
See also
Electronic behavior control
Electrophysiology
STIMULUS and response
Learning in the autonomic nervous system. L. V. DiCara. il Sci Am 222:30-9 bibliog (p 146) Ja '70
See also
Motor response
Reaction time
Reflexes
STINE, Charles M. A.
Encourage the seeker, and find nylon. S. Lenher. il pors Nations Bsns 58:68+ Ja '70
STINGING nettle. See Tread-softly
STINGS, Insect. See Insect bites and stings
STINNETT, Caskie
Speaking of Holiday. See issues of Holiday
STINSON, Thelma
To build nature interest, use what you have! il Camp Mag 42:13 Ja '70

STINTZI, Vernon
What went wrong in aid to poor: welfare official's report. il por U S News 69:33-5 N 30 '70
STIRLING, James
Student dorms on a Scottish coast. il Arch Forum 133:51 S '70
STIRLING homex corporation
Prebuilt homes come a long way. il Bsns W p27 Jl 18 '70
STITCHERY. See Embroidery
STIVENDER, David
First the words... il Opera N 34:24+ F 7 '70
STOA of the Basileus. See Athens, Greece— Antiquities
STOCHASTIC processes
Blood flow and diffusion through mammalian organs. J. B. Bassingthwaighte. bibliog il Science 167:1347-53 Mr 6 '70
STOCK, Dennis
California trip; excerpt. il Pop Phot 67:74-7 Ag '70
STOCK, Robert W.
Mouse stage of the new biology. il Sci Digest 67:44-7+ Ap '70
STOCK (firm) See Publishers and publishing —France
STOCK averages. See Stocks—Price indexes and averages
STOCK brokers. See Brokers
STOCK-car racing. See Automobile racing
STOCK charts. See Stocks—Price indexes and averages
STOCK control (bookstores) See Booksellers and bookselling—Stock
STOCK custodian accounts. See Custodianship accounts
STOCK dividends. See Dividends
STOCK exchange
Bear's claws have a long reach; foreign markets. il Bsns W p42+ My 16 '70
Market comment. L. O. Hooper. See issues of Forbes
Market outlook. S. B. Lurie. See issues of Forbes
Stock analysis. H. H. Biel. See issues of Forbes
Stock trends. See issues of Forbes
See also
Brokers
Computers—Investment use
Government investigations—Stock exchange
Put and call transactions
Speculation
Stocks—Marketing
United States—Securities and exchange commission

Regulation
Marginal treatment for deep ailments. il Bsns W p20 My 9 '70
Market: time for a new broom; reform proposals. il Newsweek 76:71-3+ N 30 '70
Restoring confidence. C. Morgello. il Newsweek 76:88 D 14 '70
Significance of the margin cuts. J. W. Schulz. Forbes 105:248-9 My 15 '70
Stripping secrecy from the big board; with editorial comment. il Bsns W p70-2, 94 N 28 '70
Wall Street can't cope in its present form. Bsns W p 166+ O 17 '70
Wall Street on the ropes. C. J. Loomis. il Fortune 82:62-7+ D '70

Australia
Stock market: Australia's spectator sport. il U S News 69:71 Jl 20 '70

New York (city)
As they see it; interviews. por Forbes 105: 46+ Ap 15 '70
Bear closes in on more brokers. il Bsns W p24-5 Mr 21 '70
Bears take over the stock market. il Time 95:70-1 F 9 '70
Belling the fat cats; SEC study of the impact of institutional investors on the stock market. il Newsweek 77:65 Ja 11 '71
Capital mess on Wall Street. C. J. Loomis. il Fortune 82:141+ Jl '70
Change and turmoil on Wall Street. il por Time 96:52-7 Ag 24 '70
Chinese torture in the stock market. il Time 95:87-8+ My 25 '70
Do broker exams make the grade? il Bsns W p54 D 26 '70
Gambling game that Wall Street plays; with editorial comment. il Bsns W p58-61+, 102 O 31 '70
Higher commissions? H. C. Wallich. Newsweek 75:77 Mr 30 '70
How Wall Street toes its own line. R. W. Haack. il por Nations Bsns 58:26-8+ S '70

Jawboning the market? il Time 95:82 F 16 '70
Leading broker calls for new rules to aid investors; excerpts from address, September 15, 1970. D. T. Regan. pors U S News 69: 61-2 S 28 '70
Looking around the corner. Time 95:86 Mr 16 '70
Looking for more money; trading on the exchange and Wall Street. il Time 95:82+ Mr 30 '70
Loss protection, but for whom? questioning NYSE's trust fund to aid investors. il Bsns W p28 Ag 22 '70
Making brokers toe the mark. por Bsns W p84 Jl 18 '70
Market: time for a new broom; reform proposals. il Newsweek 76:71-3+ N 30 '70
New battles boil up over the trust fund; with editorial comment. Bsns W p20-1, 92 O 3 '70
New campaign to repave Wall Street. il Time 96:73-4 N 30 '70
New York stock exchange; competition and the future; address, November 17, 1970. R. W. Haack. Vital Speeches 37:140-3 D 15 '70
No quick way out for Wall Street. il Bsns W p33 Ja 2 '71
One sunny day that routed the bear. il Bsns W p27 My 30 '70
Patient is in pain but he isn't dying. por Forbes 105:64-5 Je 1 '70
Physician, heal thyself. il Forbes 106:46+ Jl 15 '70
SEC will say no to the big board. Forbes 105: 23 Ap 1 '70
Snubbing the small investor. Duns 95:124 Mr '70
Stock-exchange head speaks out; excerpts from address, November 17, 1970. R. W. Haack. por U S News 69:76-7 N 30 '70
Stocks: greater confidence; interview. R. D. Naess. por U S News 70:30-1 Ja 4 '71
Stripping secrecy from the big board; with editorial comment. il Bsns W p70-2, 94 N 28 '70
Survey of big investors: where stock market is headed. il U S News 68:61-3 F 16 '70
To thine own self be true. Nat R 22:1200-1 N 17 '70
Trying to jawbone the stock market. il Time 95:93-4 My 11 '70
Vanishing stock market; Robert Haack proposes changes. il Newsweek 75:71-2+ F 23 '70
Wall Street. C. Morgello. See issues of Newsweek
Wall Street on the ropes. C. J. Loomis. il Fortune 82:62-7+ D '70
Wall Street won't be the same again. il Bsns W p96-100 My 23 '70
What the market says. H. Hazlitt. Nat R 22:675+ Je 30 '70
Why a broker needs a fund; membership of mutual funds in the NYSE. Bsns W p24 O 3 '70
Winds of scandal on Wall Street. il Newsweek 76:87-8+ O 12 '70
See also
Wall Street

Sydney, Australia
Mining stocks take a wild ride Down Under. il Bsns W p45 Mr 14 '70

Tokyo
Sayonara to the bears. il Bsns W p 116 Ap 11 '70

Toronto
Billion dollar windfall. by M. Schulman. Review
New Repub 162:31-3 F 14 '70. J. N. Froomkin
STOCK exchange insurance. See Insurance, Stock exchange
STOCK exchange specialists. See Securities— Marketing
STOCK locks. See Locks, Wooden
STOCK margin requirements. See Stock exchange—Regulation
STOCK market. See Stock exchange
STOCK market charts. See Stocks—Price indexes and averages
STOCK-market letters. See Investments—Advisers
STOCK option contracts. See Put and call transactions
STOCK purchase options
Are stock options dead? A. Patton. Harvard Bsns R 48:20-2+ S '70
Better than cash: new ways to pay executives. il U S News 69:31-2 Ag 24 '70
Compensation: new plans and options. Bsns W p 111 My 23 '70

STOCK purchase options—*Continued*
Flak and flap of executive stock options.
Bsns W p 109 My 2 '70
Hidden jokers in the new tax deck; Tax reform act of 1969. A. M. Louis. il Fortune 82:100-2+ Jl '70
Look twice at restricted stock! J. Perham. il Duns 96:36-8 D '70
Now they're swapping options. Duns 96:45 O '70
They're changing options, again; restricted stock option-loan plans for executives. J. Perham. Duns 95:27-9 Je '70
See also
Stock purchase warrants
Stocks—Rights

STOCK purchase warrants
New day for warrants? il Duns 95:29-31+ My '70
Wall Street:
Ma Bell goes mod. C. Morgello. il Newsweek 75:62 F 2 '70

STOCK ranges
Rangelands of the western U.S. R. M. Love. il Sci Am 222:88-94+ bibliog (p 126) F '70

STOCK salesmen. See Brokers

STOCK specialists. See Securities—Marketing

STOCK tenders. See Stocks—Tender offers

STOCK warrants. See Stock purchase warrants

STOCKBRIDGE, Mass.
Very special place; Berkshire theatre festival. il Newsweek 76:78-9 Jl 27 '70

STOCKBROKERS. See Brokers

STOCKDALE, James Bond
At least I know Jim's alive; interview, ed. by E. M. Wylie. S. Stockdale. il pors Good H 170:78-9+ F '70 *

STOCKDALE, Sybil
At least I know Jim's alive; interview, ed. by E. M. Wylie. il pors Good H 170:78-9+ F '70

STOCKER, Joseph
As-told-to article. il Writers Digest 50:20-2 Ap '70

STOCKHOLDERS
Countercurrents; stockholders vote against contributing to institutions devoted to the general welfare. L. L. L. Golden. Sat R 53:60 D 12 '70
Corporate sleuths on Wall Street. J. C. Perham. il Duns 95:29-31+ Ap '70
Fault, dear Brutus . . . por Forbes 106:54-5 O 15 '70
Management fee prompts a row. Bsns W p68 F 14 '70
People's capitalism. H. C. Wallich. Newsweek 76:70 Jl 20 '70
Plight of the small investors. il U S News 68:90-1 Ja 26 '70
Portrait of the investor. C. Morgello. il Newsweek 76:75 Jl 13 '70
Squeezing the small investor; new commission rates on transactions. il Time 95:82 F 23 '70
Stock ownership: a capital idea. Sr Schol 97:12 O 26 '70
Victims: lock, stock and over the barrel. il Newsweek 76:76 N 30 '70
See also
Employees as stockholders
Investor relations programs

STOCKHOLDERS meetings
Activist agenda for annual meetings. il Bsns W p45-6 Mr 28 '70
Activists lay plans for war on Gulf. il Bsns W p23 Ap 11 '70
Annual meeting under fire. il Newsweek 75:75-6 Ap 27 '70
Campaign GM: reformers lose on vote but not on influence. L. J. Carter. Science 168:1077-8 My 29 '70
Christian stake in dollar power. Chr Today 14:22 Je 19 '70
GM's ordeal may set the fashion; Campaign to make GM responsible. il Bsns W p84 My 30 '70
Investment showman; third annual Institutional investor conference. il Time 95:82+ F 16 '70
It's face-to-face with dissidents. il Bsns W p94+ My 2 '70
Organizing proxy power; annual meetings under fire. R. Chandler. Chr Today 14:32-3 My 22 '70
Our footloose correspondents; annual meeting of General motors corp. E. J. Kahn, jr. New Yorker 46:40-2+ Je 20 '70
Stinging the corporations. G. I. Maeroff. Nation 210:753-6 Je 22 '70
United aircraft weathers protest storm. W. H. Gregory. il Aviation W 92:24-6 Ap 20 '70

War protesters fail to appear at three stockholder meetings. Aviation W 92:24 My 11 '70
Whose business is business? student drive to persuade major corporations to become more socially responsible. R. W. Dietsch. New Repub 162:13-14 Ap 25 '70

Anecdotes, facetiae, satire, etc.
How do you face the annual meeting? il Duns 95:48-9+ Ap '70

STOCKHOLM
Gardens
Many parks and gardens of Stockholm. M. Perry. il Home Gard 57:28-30 F '70

Music
Report:
Britten's Let's make an opera! and Bengt Hallberg's Miss home alone. A. Swanson. Opera N 34:33 F 28 '70
Donizetti's Don Pasquale and Sven-Erik Bäck's Fageln. E. Redvall. Opera N 35:32 D 5 '70
Production of Brecht-Weill Aufstieg und fall der stadt Mahagonny. E. Redvall. Opera N 35:35 N 21 '70
Wagner's Götterdämmerung. A. Swanson. Opera N 34:28 Je 13 '70

Parks and playgrounds
Many parks and gardens of Stockholm. M. Perry. il Home Gard 57:28-30 F '70

Social conditions
Why are they smiling? L. Gross. il Look 34:21-7 Mr 24 '70

STOCKINGS. See Hosiery

STOCKLI, Albert
Splendid fare; excerpts. il Ladies Home J 87:114-15 N '70
about
Random harvest of Albert Stockli. R. A. De Groot. il por Esquire 74:150-1+ O '70 *

STOCKLIN, William A.
For the record (cont) por Electr World 83:6 My; 84:7 Ag; 6-9 D '70

STOCKPILING
Feather merchants. Nation 210:677 Je 8 '70
Nixon set to tap the stockpile kitty. il Bsns W p32 F 14 '70
Whatever happened to the U.S. stockpiles of critical materials? U S News 68:12 Ja 26 '70

STOCKS
Banker's stocks. R. Brady. por Duns 96:92-3 S '70
Common stocks, and common sense. Duns 96:108 O '70
Foreign resource stocks. G. J. Henry. Forbes 106:68-9 N 1 '70
Great expectations; growth stocks; table. Forbes 106:27 O 15 '70
It's a good time to buy stocks; interview. L. G. Coit. il Changing T 24:35-40 Ap '70
Loaded laggards. il Forbes 106:20-1 Jl 15 '70
New climate ahead. C. Morgello. il Newsweek 76:75 Ag 17 '70
New era opening up for investors? il U S News 68:18-20 Je 8 '70
New issues lure savings. Bsns W p 112 Mr 14 '70
No bust, no boom; views of R. L. Reierson. A. Hershman. por Duns 95:93-4 Je '70
One man's wisdom; with table. Forbes 105:194+ My 15 '70
Oversupply of stocks. il Fortune 81:171-2+ Je '70
Return to fundamentals? R. Brady. il por Duns 95:73-4 Ja '70
Run of bad luck in gambling stocks. il Time 95:81+ Ap 20 '70
Search for the new go-go stocks; interviews with Wall Street's top industry specialists, ed. by A. Hershman. il Duns 95:24-7 F '70
Sell? Now? views of K. Smilen. R. Brady. por Duns 96:74-5 Jl '70
Someone is buying; repurchased stocks. il Forbes 106:26 Ag 15 '70
Thinking about stocks; common stocks. P. A. Samuelson. Newsweek 76:59 Ag 3 '70
Why buying stocks regularly still makes sense. il Changing T 24:44 Jl '70
See also
Bonds
Computers—Investment use
Corporations—Finance
Dividends
Insurance, Stock exchange
Speculation
Stock exchange
Stock purchase options
Stock purchase warrants

STOCKS—*Continued*

Custodian accounts
See Custodianship accounts

Insider trading
How to keep up with insiders; use of SEC reports. il por Bsns W p 108+ My 9 '70
Rising attack on stock exchange insiders. il Time 96:58-9 Ag 10 '70
Texas Gulf tangle unwinds, a little. Bsns W p29-30 F 14 '70
Troubled men of Texas Gulf sulphur. N. A. Martin. il Duns 95:32-3+ Ap '70

Marketing
Bear's worst bite; over-the-counter market. C. Morgello. il Newsweek 75:88 Ap 27 '70
How to sell letter stock. L. Williams. Duns 96:51-2+ N '70
New York stock exchange; competition and the future; address, November 17, 1970. R. W. Haack. Vital Speeches 37:140-3 D 15 '70
One-man stock market; interview. D. J. Tomaso. il por Forbes 105:70-1 Mr 1 '70
Record financing: the way AT&T does it. U S News 68:92-3 Ap 27 '70
Rising fourth market. por Time 96:110 O 26 '70
Squeezing the small investor; new commission rates on transactions. il Time 95:82 F 23 '70
Tips on buying & selling stocks & bonds. il Changing T 24:35-8 F '70

Odd lots
Who says the odd-lotter is wrong? il Forbes 106:36 N 1 '70

Price earnings ratios
Great crash in growth stocks. M. Shapiro. il Duns 97:30-2 Ja '71

Price forecasting
Beating the Dow with sun power and the zodiac. il Bsns W p84-5 Ja 17 '70
Consumer and the investor are the same guy; J. King's system. por Forbes 106:43-4 S 1 '70
Stock trends the experts see. il U S News 68:74-6 My 11 '70
What experts see ahead in stocks. il U S News 69:36-3 Jl 13 '70
Which way for stocks? symposium. ed. by A. Hershman. il Duns 96:36-9 N '70

Price indexes and averages
Analyst's tip on stocks: pray. il Newsweek 75:79-80 My 18 '70
Backing and filling is better than down. il Bsns W p 19 Jl 11 '70
Barriers fall under weight of the bears. Bsns W p24 My 16 '70
Bears take over the stock market. il Time 95:70-1 F 9 '70
Building a base for a breakout. Bsns W p81 Ap 4 '70
Can stocks shake the liquidity jitters? Bsns W p42 Je 27 '70
Case of amnesia? Time 96:94 S 21 '70
Charts that show what went wrong on Wall Street. il Changing T 24:24-7 O '70
Chinese torture in the stock market. il Time 95:87-8+ My 25 '70
Comeback champions; table. Forbes 106:20 O 1 '70
Dow 1000? Forget it. por Forbes 106:51-2 S 15 '70
Forces behind stock market ups and downs. C. A. Barker. por Nations Bsns 58:27 Je 70
Gloomy feeling; a nervous market, a troubled economy. il Life 68:28-31 Je 5 '70
Hits and misses. C. Rolo. por Forbes 106:66-7 N 1 '70
Hoping fervently for a happier 1971. Bsns W p 18 Ja 9 '71
Long, deep slump. il Newsweek 75:80-1+ My 11 '70
Market finally takes the high road. il Bsns W p27-8 D 5 '70
1970: a hectic year for investors. il U S News 70:60 Ja 11 '71
Nixon bear market. il Newsweek 75:73 My 4 '70
Rally sputters into the doldrums. il Bsns W p33-4 Je 13 '70
Spreading toll of the bear market. il U S News 68:58-60 My 25 '70
State of the market still recessional. il Bsns W p38 Ja 31 '70
Stock-market slide: experts take another look. il U S News 68:81-3 Mr 23 '70
Stock market's wildest week. il Newsweek 75:71-2+ Je 8 '70

Technician's perspective J. W. Schultz. See issues of Forbes
Tranquility brings a Wall Street surge. il Bsns W p30-1 O 10 '70
Trying to jawbone the stock market. il Time 95:93-4 My 11 '70
Up the down staircase. il Fortune 81:139+ Ap 70
Wall Street:
  Back to glamour? C. Morgello. il Newsweek 76:74 S 21 '70
  Bear's worst bite. C. Morgello. il Newsweek 75:88 Ap 27 '70
  Brighter outlook. C. Morgello. il Newsweek 76:58 Jl 27 '70
  Fuel for a boomlet. C. Morgello. il Newsweek 76:95 O 12 '70
  Group is born. C. Morgello. il Newsweek 75:82 Ap 20 '70
  Look back in relief. C. Morgello. il Newsweek 77:56-7 Ja 4 '71
  New low brings new hope. C. Morgello. il Newsweek 75:75 F 9 '70
  Rally that counts. C. Morgello. il Newsweek 76:94 S 14 '70
  Shape of 1971. C. Morgello. il Newsweek 76:77 D 21 '70
  Six-month toll. C. Morgello. il Newsweek 76:66 Jl 20 '70
  Things look up a bit. C. Morgello. Newsweek 75:61 Mr 2 '70
  Those easy-money hopes. C. Morgello. il Newsweek 75:83 Mr 9 '70
  A time of despair. C. Morgello. il Newsweek 75:81 Je 1 '70
  Upside view. C. Morgello. il Newsweek 76:91 O 19 '70
  Voters' impact. C. Morgello. il Newsweek 76:94 N 16 '70
  What the rally spells. C. Morgello. il Newsweek 75:82 Je 15 '70
  When hot stocks chill. C. Morgello. il Newsweek 76:56 Ag 3 '70
Wall Street: will the rally last? il Time 95:65-6 Je 8 '70
Week the bear turned tail. il Bsns W p 18 Ag 29 '70
What happened to the stock market, and what happens next? interview. D. L. Babson. Changing T 25:25-30 Ja '71
What is the Dow worth? Fortune 82:187-8+ S '70
What makes stock prices move? C. J. Rolo. Bet Hom & Gard 48:23-4 Je '70
What stock market is saying. il U S News 69:32-4 O 12 '70
What the market says. H. Hazlitt. Nat R 22:675+ Je 30 '70
What the stock market shows. il U S News 69:36-7 D 21 '70
What's happened to the market? C. Rolo. Bet Hom & Gard 48:28+ S '70
Why the market took a nosedive. il Bsns W p 10-11 My 2 '70

Rights
When rights go wrong. il Forbes 106:60 N 15 '70

Short selling
Short of it. C. Morgello. il Newsweek 75:73 Je 8 '70
Sleeping ghost of Jesse Livemore. il Forbes 105:19-20 Je 1 '70

Taxation
See Taxation of bonds, securities, etc.

Tender offers
Morning after. il Forbes 105:15-17 F 1 '70

Valuation
See Corporations—Valuation

STOCKTON, Dave
One that got away again. D. Jenkins. il por Sports Illus 33:12-15 Ag 24 '70 *
Prize for a popcorn hitter; P.G.A. victory. il por Time 96:55 Ag 31 '70 *

STOCKTON, Peter D. H.
Lockheed threatens to die. il Nation 210:402-4 Ap 6 '70

STOCKWELL, Foster
Test tubes and scripture. Chr Cent 87:528-31 Ap 29 '70

STOCKYARDS. See Livestock markets

STOCKYARDS, Chicago. See Chicago—Stockyards

STODDARD, Charles H.
Outline for public land policy. Liv Wildn 34:30 Sum '70

STOEN, Don
Seeing with new eyes. Engl J 59:1256-8 D '70

STOENNER, R. W. and others
Cosmic ray production of rare gas radioactivities and tritum in lunar material. bibliog il Science 167:553-5 Ja 30 '70

STOERKER, C. Frederick
Open admissions: emerging concept in higher education. Chr Cent 87:1013-17 Ag 26 '70
STOESSEL, Walter John, 1920-
Memo from Warsaw: while Asia burns, talk, talk, talk. J. R. Moskin. Look 34:74-5 My 19 '70 *
STOESSINGER, John G.
(comp) Recent books on international relations. See issues of Foreign affairs
STÖHRER, Gerhard, and Brown, G. B.
Oncogenic purine derivatives: evidence for a possible proximate oncogen. bibliog il Science 167:1622-4 Mr 20 '70
STOKER, Bram
Dracula: Sabbat; dramatization. See Katz, L.
STOKES, Carl Burton
Black and blue in Cleveland. T. Sheridan. il Nation 211:48-50 Jl 20 '70 *
Black mayors. il por Newsweek 76:16-17 Ag 3 '70 *
Close-up of a city in distress: the story of Cleveland. il pors U S News 69:43-4 Ag 17 '70 *
Cop out. Newsweek 75:33+ F 16 '70 *
Fiasco in Cleveland. por Time 95:15 F 16 '70 *
Stokes' general takes his leave. pors Bsns W p62 Ag 8 '70 *
Troubles that face Carl Stokes. il por Bsns W p44+ D 19 '70 *
STOKES, William H.
Looking back; excerpts from articles. Ment Hy 54:170-1 Ja '70
STOKLEY, James
Astronomy. See fourth issue of each month of Science news
STOKVIS, Irene Ellen
(ed) First novelists (cont) il Library J 95: 516-22, 2290-9, 3309-11 F 1, Je 15, O 1 '70
STOLETOV, Vsevold
Education, key to social transformation. il UNESCO Courier 23:12-15 Jl '70
STOLIAR, Joan
Designer fuses elements in books with strong text and pictures. M. R. Kraner. il por Pub W 198:60-3 Jl 27 '70 *
STOLK, Jon M. and others
Brain norepinephrine: enhanced turnover after rubidium treatment. bibliog il Science 168:501-3 Ap 24 '70
STOLLAR, B. D.
Double-helical polynucleotides: immunochemical recognition of differing conformations. bibliog il Science 169:609-11 Ag 7 '70
STOLLEN. See Bread
STOLLEY, Richard B.
French lieutenant's woman's man. il pors Life 68:55-60 My 29 '70
Lively lady was a secret scholar. il pors Life 68:42-4+ F 20 '70
(ed) See Pompidou, G. Man from France
STOLOFF, David
Model cities, model for failure. Arch Forum 132:78-9+ Ja '70
STOLTZ, D. R. and Barker, I. K.
Bladder tumorigenesis. bibliog Science 168: 1121-2 My 29 '70
—and others
Cytogenetic studies with cyclamate and related compounds. il Science 167:1501-2 Mr 13 '70
STOMACH
Diseases
    See also
Peptic ulcers
STOMATA
Phenotypic reversion of flacca, a wilty mutant of tomato, by abscisic acid. D. Imber and M. Tal. bibliog il Science 169:592-3 Ag 7 '70
STOMMEL, Henry
Future prospects for physical oceanography. bibliog Science 168:1531-7 Je 26 '70
STOMP: musical comedy. See Musical comedies, revues. etc.—Criticisms, plots, etc.
STOMS, Richard K. and Kuerze, Edward
Build $40 X-ray detector. il Radio-Electr 42: 36-9+ Ja '71
STONE, C. Walter
AV task force survey report. Am Lib 1:40-4 Ja '70
STONE, Dana
Missing in Cambodia. il pors Time 95:43 Ap 20 '70
STONE, Elizabeth W.
Continuing education in librarianship: ideas for action. Am Lib 1:543-51 Je '70
STONE, Elly
Alive and well. pors Time 95:64-5 My 18 '70
Records. R. Courtney. Ramp Mag 9:56 S '70 *

STONE, I. F.
Law and order? or black repression? Cur 115:44-5 F '70
Toward an urban guerrilla movement? Cur 118:16-18 My '70
With atheists like him, who needs believers? interview, ed. by C. Fager. Chr Cent 87: 1313-17 N 4 '70
STONE, Jeremy J.
After Cambodia: the fight to save face. Commonweal 92:381-2 Ag 7 '70
When and how to use SALT. For Affairs 48:262-73 Ja '70
STONE, Lloyd
My special chair; poem. Good H 172:167 Ja '71
STONE, Michael
Pride and prestige: premises of policy. Chr Cent 87:286 Mr 11 '70
Project equality today. Chr Cent 87:79-82 Ja 21 '70
STONE, W. Clement
Success stories. il por Newsweek 77:77 Ja 11 '71
STONE, Ward B. and Manwell, R. D.
In competition for bird life: parasites. il Cons 24:14-17 F '70
STONE, William T.
In the Abacos. il Yachting 128:58+ N '70
Washington report. See issues of Yachting
STONE, Yvonne. See Goulding, F. S. jt. auth.
STONE
Preservation
Lalibela's ancient churches saved by a new preservative. il Sci Digest 68:84-5 Ag '70
STONE, Artificial. See Marble, Artificial
STONE age
Egyptian prehistory: some new concepts. F. Wendorf and others. bibliog il Science 169: 1161-71 S 18 '70
    See also
Man, Prehistoric
Stone implements and weapons
STONE age art. See Art, Primitive
STONE faces. See Rock profiles
STONE implements and weapons
Creativity of ancient man. E. Keller and J. Zimmerman. il Chem 43:14-17 Jl '70
Flaking stone with wooden implements. D. E. Crabtree. bibliog il Science 169:146-53 Jl 10 '70
How to make stone age tools. il por Sci Digest 67:20-1 My '70
    See also
Clubs (weapons)
Indians of North America—Implements
STONE MOUNTAIN memorial
Mountain in labor. il Time 95:66 My 18 '70
Parting shots; Dixie carves out an answer to Mt Rushmore. il Life 68:75-8 My 22 '70
STONE rubbings. See Rubbings
STONE soup; drama. See Buechler, J.
STONE tools. See Stone implements and weapons
STONEHENGE, England
Visits to Stonehenge and Herstmonceux. il Sky & Tel 40:197-8 O '70
STONEWORTS
Vacuolar perfusion technique for nitella internodal cells. T. H. Strunk. bibliog il Science 169:84-7 Jl 3 '70
STONG, C. L.
(ed) Amateur scientist. See issues of Scientific American
STONY Brook campus, State university of New York. See New York (state). State university—Stony Brook campus
STOOLS
Three footstools. il Pop Mech 133:164-7 Mr '70
STOOP, Norma McLain
Germany after the fall. il Dance Mag 44:28-42 Ag '70
To make ballet more beautiful. il pors Dance Mag 44:70-3 Ja '70
STOOPS. See Porches
STOP and shop, Inc. See Grocery trade
STOPH, Willi
Divided Germans talk at last. il pors U S News 68:37 Mr '70 *
End of an era: the German summit. il por Newsweek 75:39 Mr 30 '70 *
From bricklayer to organization man. il por Time 95:38 Mr 30 '70 *
Return engagement. il Newsweek 75:42-3 Je 1 '70 *
Two Germanys face to face. il pors Time 95:18 Mr 23 '70 *
Willy and Willi. Newsweek 75:35 Mr 2 '70 *
STOPPARD, Tom
Enter a free man. Criticism
Newsweek il 76:77 Ag 31 '70 *

STORAGE
See also
Garden houses, shelters, etc.
Shelves
also subhead Storage under various subjects; e.g. Motor fuels—Storage

STORAGE batteries
Battery: flywheel of your ignition system. C. Miller. il Motor B 126:94-8 N '70
DC-9 tests prove new battery's worth. Aviation W 93:53 Jl 20 '70
Now: atomic power to keep your heart beating. A. S. Freese. il Pop Mech 134:104-7+ S '70
Pontiac's new battery, you'll never need to fill it. J. Dunne. il Pop Sci 197:16 N '70
Titanium cuts a battery to size; small rechargeable battery. il por Bsns W p50 Ja 24 '70
See also
Electric batteries

STORAGE battery chargers
Build a better battery charger. R. F. Graf and G. J. Whalen. il Pop Sci 197:101-3+ Jl '70
Universal manganese-alkaline battery charger. H. R. Mallory. il Radio-Electr 41:52-3 Ag '70
What battery chargers can and cannot do. Good H 170:170 My '70

STORAGE cabinets. See Cabinets (furniture)

STORAGE elements (computers) See Memory devices (computers)

STORAGE in the home
Colorful storage cubes. J. Capotosto. il Mech Illus 66:80+ D '70
Extra storage in the laundry. il Sunset 145: 93 S '70
For small toys and art supplies. il Sunset 145:87 S '70
How to customize your storage space. il Bet Hom & Gard 48:14+ My '70
Linen storage, here are answers. il Sunset 144:84-5 Ja '70
More space in the kitchen. il Redbook 134: 126-7+ Mr '70
Plywood storage cabinets go high in the garage. il Sunset 145:140+ N '70
Space savers: money savers. il McCalls 98: 64-5 Ja '71
See also
Pantries
Storage walls

STORAGE shelves. See Shelves

STORAGE tanks. See Water tanks

STORAGE walls
Kitchen's pushed-out side is a new storage wall. il Sunset 144:119 Je '70
Room end becomes a storage wall. il Sunset 145:100-1 Jl '70
Study-storage wall. J. Capotosto and J. R. Connor. il Mech Illus 66:91-3 N '70
Walls that grow on you; Interlübke wall system; ed. by V. D. Hahn. il Am Home 73: 32 F '70

STORE buildings. See Stores

STORE employees. See Department stores—Employees

STORE gardens
Gardening shopkeepers. L. Burgess. il Horticulture 48:30-1 S '70

STORE hours
Is the bell tolling for blue laws? West German opposition to early closing law. il Bsns W p39 Ap 4 '70
Open and shut cases; Sunday selling. Nations Bsns 58:16 Ag '70

STORE security measures. See Retail trade—Security measures

STORE windows. See Show windows

STORES
Bright glass prism on Brattle street; Benjamin Thompson's Design research building. il Arch Rec 147:105-12 My '70
See also
Department stores
Food stores
Retail trade
Show windows
Specialty stores
Supermarkets
also subhead Stores under names of cities, e.g. New York (city)—Stores

Employees
See also
Clerks (retail trade)

Hours of opening
See Store hours

Security measures
See Retail trade—Security measures

STOREY, David
Home. Criticism
America 124:46-7 Ja 16 '71 *
Commonweal 93:373-4 Ja 15 '71 *
Nation 211:252-3 S 21 '70 *
Nation 211:605 D 7 '70 *
New Repub 163:20+ D 12 '70 *
New Yorker 46:141 N 28 '70 *
Newsweek il 76:98 N 30 '70 *
Sat R 53:16+ D 12 '70 *
Time il 96:48 N 30 '70
This sporting life. Criticism
Commonweal 93:373 Ja 15 '71 *

STORIES. See Anecdotes; Fairy tales; Fiction

STORIES of operas. See Libretto

STORKS
Stork stock low; Denmark. Sr Schol 97:4-5 D 14 '70

STORM; story. See Ellingson, M.

STORM KING hydroelectric project. See Hydroelectric plants

STORM sewers
All you see is the stream; Arlington County, Va. H. S. Hulme, jr. il Am City 85:77-8 Mr '70
Storm-water retention can work; Detroit. G. Remus. il Am City 85:68-9 O '70

STORMS
See also
Cyclones

STORMONT, Clyde, and Suzuki, Yoshiko
Atropinesterase and cocainesterase of rabbit serum: localization of the enzyme activity in isozymes. bibliog il Science 167:200-2 Ja 9 '70

STORMS
Microwave noise from rainstorms. A. A. Penzias and R. W. Wilson. il Science 169:583-4 Ag 7 '70
World war on hail. P. Friggens. il Read Digest 96:29-30+ Je '70
See also
Hurricanes
Snow
Snowstorms
Thunderstorms
Tornadoes

STORR, Anthony
Freud on the couch. il Horizon 12:42-7 Wint '70

STORR, Catherine
Lost. Mlle 70:213-15+ F '70

STORY machine; drama. See Asimov, I.

STORY telling records. See Phonograph records—Childrens records

STORY theater. See Yale university—School of drama

STORY theatre; drama. See Sills, P.

STOTLAR, David W. See Wides, J. W. jt. auth.

STOTT, William Ross
Take-charge guy in venture capital. pors Bsns W p72 O 24 '70 *

STOUFFER, Vernon Bigelow
Stouffer's double jeopardy. J. Poindexter. por Duns 96:59 O '70 *

STOUGHTENBURGH, John L.
Museum world. See issues of Hobbies

STOUGHTON family
Another Stoughton coat-of-arms. H. K. Eilers. il Hobbies 75:146-7 D '70
Stoughton coat-of-arms. H. K. Eilers. il Hobbies 75:148-9 N '70

STOUT, Jared
Keeping tabs on civilians. il Nation 211:681-3 D 28 '70

STOUT, Robert Joe
Amputee; poem. Chr Cent 88:16 Ja 6 '71
Answer; poem. Chr Cent 87:693 Je 3 '70

STOUT, Ruth
Happy mulch, organic, natch. il Org Gard & Farm 17:52-5 Jl '70
Why? And why not? il pors Org Gard & Farm 17:43-5 O '70

STOVALL, Robert
Stock trends. por Forbes 105:75 Je 1; 106:50 Ag 1; 68-9 O 1 '70

STOVES
Stoves for the homesteader. R. Bundy. il Am West 7:38-9 N '70
See also
Camp stoves
Electric stoves

STOVES, Franklin
Thank you Ben Franklin. A. Walker. il Am Home 73:60-1 Ja '70

STOWAWAYS
Stowaway! story of a teen-ager who escaped from Cuba by flying the Atlantic in the wheel well of a DC-8; ed. by D. Fodor and J. Reddy. A. Socarras Ramírez. il Read Digest 96:62-6 Ja '70

STOWE, Bill
Stowing the manly oar. il Time 96:82-3 N 23 '70 *

STOWE, David M.
COCU and N.C.C. Chr Cent 87:234-6 F 25 '70

STOWE, J. A.
Miss your train? il Travel 133:54-9+ Mr '70

STOWE, Leland
Magnificent tiger. il Read Digest 97:224-6+ Jl '70
Paper magic of origami. il pors Read Digest 97:196-200 Ag '70

STOWE, Vt.
Scintillating Stowe. J. E. Maxwell. il Travel 134:44-51 N '70

STOWELL, Earl
Lot of shop in four feet of space. il Pop Mech 133:150-3+ Mr '70

STRADIVARIUS violin. See Violin

STRAFFORD, Vt.

Historic houses, etc.
Senator Morrill's Gothic cottage at Strafford. Vermont. L. Wodehouse. il Antiques 98:237-41 Ag '70

STRAGIER, Marc G.
We automated residential refuse collection. il Am City 85:66-7 N '70
—See Witzeman, L. B. jt. auth

STRAIGHT, Elmer M. and others
Mental hospital employees and social action. Ment Hy 54:241-6 Ap '70

STRAIN gages
Earth strain measurements with a laser interferometer. J. Berger and R. H. Lovberg. bibliog il Science 170:296-303 O 16 '70

STRAINS, Muscular. See Muscles—Wounds and injuries

STRAINS and stresses
See also
Moiré method
Strain gages

STRALEY, Walter W.
Working with the unskilled; AT&T's experience; interview. il por U S News 68:88-91 Mr 9 '70

STRAM, Hank
Innovation for the fun of it. il por Time 95:35 Ja 26 '70
Pro football's dazzling new look; ed. by D. Anderson. il Look 34:27-34 S 8 '70
Wham, bam, Stram! T. Maule. il pors Sports Illus 32:10-15 Ja 19 '70

STRAND, Mark
Black maps; Seven poems. Poetry 116:178-81 Je '70
New poetry handbook; poem. Harper 240:53 Ja '70
Nine poems: Not dying; Good life; Recovery; Sleep; Guardian; Hill; Dress; Breath; Tomorrow. New Yorker 46:40-1 My 9 '70

STRANG, James Jesse
For his was the kingdom, and the power, and the glory, briefly. R. P. Weeks. il pors Am Heritage 21:4-7+ Je '70 *

STRANGE pilgrimage; story. See Waggoner, J.

STRANGE welcome; story. See Johnston, V.

STRANGWAY, D. W. and others
Magnetic properties of lunar samples. bibliog il Science 167:691-3 Ja 30 '70

STRANSKY, Thomas F.
Stransky, Wilmore; editors at large. Chr Cent 87:468 Ap 22 '70 *

STRASSENBURG, Arnold A.
Supply and demand for physicists. bibliog il por Phys Today 23:23-8 Ap '70

STRASSER, Arnold
Compensation in the construction industry. Mo Labor R 93:64-5 My '70

STRATEGIC air command. See United States —Air force—Strategic air command

STRATEGIC arms limitation talks
ABM & MIRV; in the context of SALT; address, June 12, 1970. R. Kilmarx. Vital Speeches 36:602-4 Jl 15 '70
Ambassador Smith discusses strategic arms limitation talks; December 29, 1969. G. C. Smith. Dept State Bul 62:84-6 Ja 26 '70
Arms control at the crossroads; Vienna talks. il Newsweek 75:53-4 Ap 20 '70
Arms talks: in-group debate on the technical issues. A. Hamilton. il Science 168:234-6 Ap 10 '70
At year's end. Commonweal 93:339-40 Ja 8 '71
Blue-water option; idea to propose elimination of all land-based ICBM's. S. Alsop. Newsweek 75:104 F 16 '70
Can SALT stop MIRV? R. E. Lapp. il N Y Times Mag p 14-15+ F 1 '70
Can the arms talks succeed? interview. G. Smith. il por U S News 69:62-3 D 14 '70
Can the SALT talks succeed? Cur 119:60-3 Je '70

Correcting our posture: Laird, defense and SALT. R. E. Lapp. New Repub 162:12-15 Mr 28 '70
Edge of prudent risk; excerpts from address, April 1970. M. R. Laird. Nat R 22:449 My 5 '70
Expectations from SALT. A. De Volpi. il Bul Atom Sci 26:6-8 Ap '70
Latest score in the arms race. il Bsns W p 114 Ap 25 '70
Limitation of strategic arms. G. W. Rathjens and G. B. Kistiakowsky. il Sci Am 222:19-29 Ja '70; Reply with rejoinder. J. E. Anderson. 222:6-7 My '70
Negotiate the negotiable. Nation 210:485 Ap 27 '70
Nuclear bombs for everybody: a new worry at Helsinki. il U S News 69:61-3 D 14 '70
One small step. Commonweal 92:155-6 My 1 '70
Package for SALT. Newsweek 76:33 Ag 3 '70
Progress in SALT. Newsweek 76:47-8 Jl 6 '70
SALT: a sprinkling of hope. il Time 96:24-5 Jl 20 '70
SALT and Apollo 13. S. Alsop. Newsweek 75:112 Ap 27 '70
SALT and champagne. il Newsweek 76:31-2 Ag 24 '70
SALT chips and Safeguard. R. E. Lapp. New Repub 163:14-17 Ag 15 '70
SALT in Vienna: the waltz of the powers. R. S. Lewis. il Bul Atom Sci 26:19-21 S '70
SALT: no time for dancing; Vienna conference. il Time 95:33 Ap 27 '70
SALT, part two. il Newsweek 75:56 Ap 27 '70
SALT talks: round two. A. Harrigan. Nat R 22:260 Ap 7 '70
SALT: the race to halt the arms race; sessions in Vienna. il Time 95:22-3 Ap 20 '70
SALT; the third round. il Time 96:22 N 9 '70
SALT: time to do business. B. van Voorst. il Newsweek 76:52-4 N 16 '70
Sorry history of arms control. B. T. Feld. il Bul Atom Sci 26:22-6 S '70
Strategic arms limitation talks open at Helsinki, text of message, November 17, 1969. R. M. Nixon. Dept State Bul 61:543-4 D 15 '69
Strategic arms talks; what is negotiable? A. Hamilton. Science 167:1707-8 Mr 27 '70; Reply. D. G. Brennan. 168:778 My 15 '70
TRB from Washington; a twenty-seven-minute war. New Repub 162:6 Ap 25 '70
Thoughts on Helsinki. L. L. Strauss. Nat R 22:1398 D 29 '70
Troubles of Helsinki. Nation 211:514-15 N 23 '70
Two aspects of the search for peace; address, April 18, 1970. W. P. Rogers. Dept State Bul 62:605-8 My 11 '70
Undermining of salt. Chr Cent 87:379 Ap 1 '70
United States and Soviet Union begin second phase of Strategic arms limitation talks; statement, April 16, 1970. G. C. Smith. Dept State Bul 62:572-3 My 4 '70
United States and Soviet Union begin third phase of strategic arms limitation talks; V. S. Semenov. Dept State Bul 63:651-2 N 23 '70
United States and Soviet Union conclude preliminary strategic arms limitation talks; statements, with text of communique; December 22, 1969. G. C. Smith; V. S. Semenov. Dept State Bul 62:28-9 Ja 12 '70
United States and Soviet Union conclude second phase of strategic arms limitation talks; statements at ceremonial closing, with text of communique. G. C. Smith; V. S. Semenov. Dept State Bul 63:245-6 Ag 31 '70
Was it a slip? announcement of MIRV deployment. Nation 210:354-5 Mr 30 '70
What's at stake as U.S. and Russia meet on arms. il U S News 68:61-2 Ap 20 '70
When and how to use SALT. J. J. Stone. For Affairs 48:262-73 Ja '70
Wishes aren't horses, dammit! Nat R 22:345 Ap 7 '70

STRATEGIC services, Office of. See United States—Strategic services, Office of

STRATEGY
Revolutionary war in world strategy 1945-1969, by R. Thompson. Review
Nat R 22:1003-4 S 22 '70. J. Burnham
Strategy for tomorrow, by H. W. Baldwin. Review
Nat R 22:1221-2 N 17 '70. G. F. Eliot
See also
Communist strategy
Vietnamese war, 1957- —Strategy

STRATFORD, Conn, Shakespeare festival. See American Shakespeare festival theatre and academy. Stratford, Conn.

STRATFORD, Ontario, Shakespeare festival. See Shakespeare festival, Stratford, Ontario

STRATFORD-ON-AVON
Gardens of Shakespeare's town. P. Brindley. il Home Gard 57:26-9 Mr '70

STRATMAN, Hardin
Phasing P.A. speakers. il Electr World 84: 31+ D '70

STRATOSPHERE. See Atmosphere

STRAUB, George H.
Floating plywood cover keeps water fresh. il Am City 85:82-3 Ap '70

STRAUB, Peter
Thinking about America; poem. Poetry 116: 93 My '70

STRAUS, Dorothea
(tr) See Singer, I. B. Guests on a winter night
(tr) See Singer, I. B. Joke
(tr) See Singer I. B. On a wagon

STRAUS, Ellen Sulzberger
Ellen Straus: the action of Call for action. il pors Vogue 155:124-5 Je '70 *

STRAUS, R. Peter
Is the State department color-blind? Sat R 54:12-13+ Ja 2 '71

STRAUSS, Claude Lévi-. See Lévi-Strauss, C.

STRAUSS, Levi, and company
Country pants take over the town. il Bsns W p50-2 Jl 4 '70

STRAUSS, Lewis L.
Thoughts on Helsinki. Nat R 22:1398 D 29 '70

STRAUSS, Peter
Actor in the works; interview, ed. by E. Miller. il pors Seventeen 29:140-1+ My '70

STRAUSS, Richard
Ariadne auf Naxos. Criticism
Opera N il 34:17-20 Mr 28 '70 *
Sat R 53:54 Mr 28 '70 *
Cabellé sings Salome. G. L. Mayer. il Am Rec G 36:402-4 F '70 *
Elektra. Criticism
New Yorker 46:170-1 D 5 '70 *
Sat R 53:46 D 12 '70 *
From the Arturo Toscanini society: memorable Strauss. C. J. Luten. il Am Rec G 36:330-1 Ja '70 *
Irreplaceable artifacts from musical ages past. W. Botsford. Am Rec G 36:339-40 Ja '70 *
Marschallin without marzipan. R. Freedman. il Life 68:18 Mr 6 '70 *
Records:
Der Rosenkavalier. Opera N 34:34 F 14 '70 *
Rosenkavalier (abridged) Opera N 34:36 Ja 24 '70
Richard Strauss, by N. Del Mar. Review
Am Rec G il 36:734-7 My '70. C. J. Luten *
Der Rosenkavalier. Criticism
Opera N 34:24-5 F 28 '70 *
Opera N il 34:17-20 F 28 '70 *
Der Rosenkavalier. W. Botsford. il Am Rec G 36:396-401 F '70 *
Strauss to Schuh: letters from the last years. R. Breuer. Sat R 53:95-6 F 28 '70 *
Superlative Rosenkavalier from London records. G. Movshon. il Hi Fi sec I 20:75-7 F '70 *

STRAUSS, Victor
Betwixt cup and lip. Pub W 197:263-5 Ja 26 '70
IBM selectric composition system. il Pub W 198:31-5 N 30 '70

STRAVINSKY, Igor Fedorovich
Performing arts. Harper 240:32+ F; 112-14 Ap; 34+ My; 37-8+ Je '70

about

Anniversary of a dream. D. Hamilton. il Hi Fi 20:sec1 73-4 My '70 *
Best Sacre on records today. W. Botsford. il Am Rec G 37:10-11+ S '70
Composer's workshop. S. Karlinsky. Nation 210:730-3 Je 15 '70; Reply with rejoinder. I. Stravinsky. 211:66+ Ag 3 '70 *
Excellent new recordings. L. Trimble. New Repub 163:28 Jl 4 '70 *
Music; Kipnis mime theatre's Renard and L'histoire. D. Hamilton. Nation 211:349 O 12 '70 *
Music to my ears; Stravinsky's Les noces. I. Kolodin. Sat R 53:24 O 17 '70 *
Theater of Igor Stravinsky. E. Salzman. il por Opera N 35:8-15 O 10 '70 *

STRAWBERRIES
Make your strawberry bed last for years. L. Shade. il por Org Gard & Farm 17:94-5 Jl '70
Our ten-year strawberry bed. H. Nearing and S. Nearing. il Org Gard & Farm 17:44-6 F '70
Strawberries from the barrel. V. Talbot. il Org Gard & Farm 17:82-3 F '70
See also
Cookery—Fruit

STRAWBERRY jars. See Flower boxes, planters, etc.

STREAK photography. See Photography of moving objects

STREAM gardens. See Water gardens

STREAM pollution. See Water Pollution

STREAMERS (fishing flies) See Fishing lures, flies, etc.

STREBINGER, Franz
Profile of a yachtsman: Hubert Raudaschl. il por Yachting 127:59+ My '70

STREET, James
Texas by an eyelash. D. Jenkins. il por Sports Illus 31:20-5 D 15 '69

STREET cleaning
Contract street sweeping removes more than dirt; cities in the Los Angeles area. il Am City 85:46 Je '70
No glamour, just work; cleaning New York city's arterial highways. S. Galler. il Am City 85:116+ My '70
Our crash street-cleaning program; Lynn, Mass. J. R. Casey. il Am City 85:63-5 Jl '70
Street cleaning. See issues of American city
Who loves a parade? clearing parade litter in Chicago. il Am City 85:38 Ag '70

STREET cleaning apparatus
Contract street sweeping removes more than dirt; cities in the Los Angeles area. il Am City 85:46 Je '70
Diesel engines out sweeping costs; Bakersfield, Calif. il Am City 85:54 Jl '70
Difference is inside the cab; Middletown Township, N.J. D. Jackson. il Am City 85: 52 Ja '70
Giant vacuum collects spilled dimes; Massachusetts turnpike. il Am City 85:40 S '70
Street cleaning. See issues of American city
See also
Leaf gatherers

STREET games. See Games

STREET lighting
Outdoor lighting. See issues of American city
Small towns need good lighting, too! Sprague, Conn. il Am City 85:92 Ag '70
See also subhead Lighting under names of cities, e.g. Washington, D.C.—Lighting

STREET lighting fixtures
Colonial lights for a colonial setting; Williston Park, N.Y. C. Del Vecchio. il Am City 85:110 F '70
How to choose the right light pole. R. L. Mulvany. il Am City 85:84-5 S '70
Leased street lights. il Am City 85:142 S '70
Lighting keeps downtown the focal point; Lincoln, Neb. il Am City 85:90 Ag '70
Outdoor lighting. il Am City 85:108-9 Jl '70
Wood poles with a modern appeal; Ellensburg, Wash. E. H. Knight. Am City 85:142 My '70

STREET markets, Paris. See Paris—Markets

STREET markings. See Traffic markings

STREET musicians
Mexico's street minstrels. G. L. Reitze. il Américas 22:36-7 Ja '70

STREET repairing. See Streets—Maintenance and repair

STREET shows. See Theater, Open-air

STREET signs
Street signs should be seen; College Station, Tex. il Am City 85:116 Jl '70

STREET sweeping. See Street cleaning

STREET traffic. See City traffic

STREET trees. See Trees in cities

STREET vacuum sweepers. See Street cleaning apparatus

STREETER, Donald
Early American stock locks. il Antiques 98: 251-5 Ag '70

STREETS
Covered streets? excerpts from Streets are for people. B. Rudofsky. il Horizon 11:78-87 Aut '69
Urban street; provocative forum in Minneapolis. P. Wolf. il Art in Am 58:118-23 N '70
See also subhead Streets under names of cities, e.g. Reading, Pa.—Streets

STREETS—*Continued*

Drainage

Subdrains can protect streets from seepage; Sacramento, Calif. H. R. Cedergren. il Am City 85:99-100 O '70

Intersections

Are crosswalks deadly? San Diego, Calif. Am City 85:118 Jl '70

Maintenance and repair

Businessmen transform an alley to a walkway; Lincoln. Neb. il Am City 85:40 Ap '70
Inventory your streets for better management; Waco, Tex. C. H. Hoge and J. E. Lykes, jr. il Am City 85:98+ Mr '70
Repair paving cracks faster, for less money; Minneapolis. E. Larson. il Am City 85:60 S '70
See also
Pavements—Surface treatment
Road machinery
STREIFF, Lee
Local association of the month. Todays Ed 59:14+ Mr '70
STREIKER, Lowell D.
Teaching religion in an age of scant enthusiasm. America 123:36-8 Jl 25 '70
STREISAND, Barbra
Barbra Streisand. pors Vogue 155:104-5 Je '70 *
STRELITZIA. See Bird-of-paradise-flowers
STRENGTH of materials
See also
Dispersion strengthening
STRENGTH of muscles. See Muscle strength
STREPTOCOCCUS
Cross-reactions between streptococcal M proteins and human transplantation antigens. A. A. Hirata and P. I. Terasaki. bibliog il Science 168:1095-6 My 29 '70
Germ on the moon; streptococcus mitis. Newsweek 75:63 Je 1 '70
Microorganism back from the moon; streptococcus mitis. R. N. Watts, jr. Sky & Tel 40:15 Jl '70
Microorganisms survived lunar environment; streptococcus mitis found in camera. il Aviation W 92:22 Je 1 '70
STREPTOMYCIN
He discovered healing in the soil. W. Garrison. il por Todays Health 48:42-3+ Mr '70
STRESHINSKY, Shirley G.
Happy mother's guide to successful nursing. il Parents Mag 45:52-3+ F '70
What are you worried about? Redbook 134:85+ Ap '70
STRESS (physiology)
Compensation for camp victims; determination of long-term effects of stress. H. J. Barnes. Sci N 97:604 Je 20 '70
Control of population; excerpt from The social contract. R. Ardrey. il Life 68:48-52+ F 20 '70; Same abr. with title Nature and the case for birth control. Read Digest 96:116-20 Je '70
Emotionally induced increases in effective osmotic pressure and subsequent thirst. E. Deaux and J. W. Kakolewski. bibliog il Science 169:1226-8 S 18 '70
From club to megabomb. D. Behrman. UNESCO Courier 23:22-3 Ag '70
Future shock; excerpt. A. Toffler. il Horizon 12:82-9 Spr '70
How to avoid harmful stress; Selye's stress theory. J. D. Ratcliff. Todays Health 48:42-4 Jl '70; Same abr. Read Digest 97:79-82 Jl '70
Interanimal memory transfer: results from brain and liver homogenates. B. Frank and others. bibliog il Science 169:399-402 Jl 24 '70
Mental illness' leading cause. il Sci Digest 67:55-6 Ap '70
People pollution; excerpt from The doomsday book. G. R. Taylor. il Ladies Home J 87:74+ O '70
Project: you; don't let tension destroy looks. Ladies Home J 87:121 S '70
Tektite: unique observations of men under stress. R. H. Gilluly. il Sci N 98:400-1 N 21 '70
See also
Traumatism
STRETCH, Bonnie Barrett
Rise of the free school. il Sat R 53:76-9+ Je 20 '70
STRETCH wigs. See Wigs
STRICKLAND, Charles R. See Crossman, C. L. jt. auth.
STRICKLAND, Ellen
Fall and then. .; poem. Chr Today 14:9 Ag 21 '70

STRICKLAND, Rennard, and Gregory, Jack
Nixon and the Indian. il por Commonweal 92:432-6 S 4 '70
STRICKLER, Carolyn J.
Teaching animals with electronic language. il Pop Mech 134:79-82+ D '70
STRICKLER, Martin, and La Sor, Betsy
Concept of loss in crisis intervention. bibliog Ment Hy 54:301-5 Ap '70
STRIDER, Marjorie
Moving out, moving up. Art N 69:41 Ja '71
STRIKE insurance. See Insurance, Strike
STRIKES
Waves of strikes: the industries, the issues. U S News 68:88 F 16 '70
See also
Injunctions
Labor disputes
Trade agreements

Economic aspects

Auto strike begins to cut deep. il Newsweek 76:83-4+ N 16 '70
Big auto strike; General motors workers. Newsweek 76:95-6 O 12 '70
Difference the G.M. strike makes. Fortune 82:19-20 O '70
High price of peace in Detroit. il Time 96:94-5 N 23 '70
Payless paydays take their toll. il Bsns W p 19 N 7 '70
Striking viewpoint. C. Morgello. il Newsweek 76:69 S 28 '70

Law

See Labor laws and legislation—United States

Canada

Day the Montreal police went on strike. G. Clark. il Read Digest 96:107-12 F '70
How government crackdowns helped end costly strikes in Canada. U S News 69:104 S 21 '70
London, Ontario strike ends with settlement; Public library and art museum. il Library J 95:2602-4 Ag '70

France

French have a law for it. Nat R 22:503 My 19 '70
Letter from Paris. Genêt. New Yorker 46:122-3 Ap 4 '70
Letter from Paris; new law against destructive violence. Genêt. New Yorker 46:117-19 My 16 '70

Great Britain

Bayonets baling hooks; dock strike. il Newsweek 76:44 Jl 27 '70
Behind the strike of Britain's dockers. U S News 69:76 Jl 27 '70
Blackout; electrical workers' slowdown. il Newsweek 76:44+ D 21 '70
Cracks in the glass; Pilkington strike. il Newsweek 75:74 Je 1 '70
Dark days in Great Britain; Electrical trades union slowdown. il Time 96:26-7 D 21 '70
Dock settlement; meaning for Britain. U S News 69:61 Ag 10 '70
Dock strikers deliver a punch. il Bsns W p26 Jl 25 '70
Fetid streets and fouled rivers; strike of garbagemen and sewage workers. il Time 96:28 N 9 '70
Hardly a honeymoon; nationwide dock strike. il Time 96:18 Jl 27 '70
How strike engulfed Britain in trash. il U S News 69:72-3 N 16 '70
Letter from London; slowdown by electricity-supply workers. M. Panter-Downes. New Yorker 46:55-6 D 26 '70
Stinking strike; sewage-plant workers on strike. il Time 96:52 O 19 '70
What dock strike does to Britain. U S News 69:53 Ag 3 '70

Ireland

Lots of checks, but no balances; bank strike. il Bsns W p26 Ag 22 '70

Italy

Maoists strike. il Time 95:74 Je 29 '70
Mary Simons reports on Rome's latest convenience: Dial-a-strike. M. Simons. por Look 34:14 F 24 '70

Sweden

Strikers break an old tradition. il Bsns W p44 F 14 '70

United States

Another year of crisis bargaining. il U S News 70:41-2 Ja 4 '71
Essential services. Nation 210:420 Ap 13 '70
Freedom to strike in the public interest. T. Kennedy. bibliog f il Harvard Bsns R 48:45-57 Jl '70; Same abr. with title Should we abolish all strikes? Cur 121:32-6 S '70

STRIKES—United States—*Continued*
George Meany talks about strikes, politics, the future; excerpts from press conference. G. Meany. por U S News 69:59-61 S 7 '70
Labor-management disputes; tables. See issues of Monthly labor review
Labor: the year of confrontation. Time 95: 87-8 Ap 13 '70
One answer to the strike wave? compulsory arbitration. U S News 68:85-6 Ap 20 '70
See them strike. New Repub 163:7 S 26 '70
Strike! il Sr Schol 97:9-13 N 16 '70
Strike outlook for the rest of 1970. il U S News 69:101-3 S 21 '70
Strikes this year: setting records. U S News 69:81 N 9 '70
Wages of inflation. il Newsweek 75:70-1 F 16 '70
When the public bears the burden of strikes. il Bsns W p 106 Ap 11 '70

Actors and actresses

Stage-struck; strike, closing down sixteen off-Broadway shows. Time 96:58 N 30 '70

Agricultural workers

See Strikes—United States—Farm labor

Air traffic controllers

Controller action hurts airline revenues. Aviation W 92:26-7 Mr 30 '70
Controller strike forces employe layoffs. J. P. Woolsey. Aviation W 92:30-1 Ap 13 '70

Airlines

Court vetoes antistrike tactic. Bsns W p78+ N 7 '70
Los Angeles airways costly strike ends. Aviation W 92:26 My 11 '70
Northwest, clerks union resume talks. Aviation W 93:24 O 19 '70
Post-strike service provides challenges; National airlines maintenance program. H. D. Watkins. il Aviation W 93:37+ Ag 10 '70
Rail-air clerks: long strike, and now—. U S News 69:47-8 D 21 '70
Shooting down strike pacts. Bsns W p90 O 24 '70

Artists

Pickets on Parnassus. E. C. Baker. il Art N 69:30-3+ S '70

Automobile industry and trade

As pressures rise in GM strike: some optimistic signs. il U S News 69:78-9 N 9 '70
At J&L, the auto strike hurts. il Bsns W p27 O 10 '70
Auto strike begins to cut deep. il Newsweek 76:83-4+ N 16 '70
Auto strike: what it will do to business. il U S News 69:15-17 S 28 '70
Auto strikers take the GNP for a ride. il Bsns W p 18 O 3 '70
Auto workers hear the drums again. il Time 96:69-72 S 28 '70
Big auto strike; General motors workers. Newsweek 76:95-6 O 12 '70
Cost of GM strike to the auto union. il U S News 69:90-1 O 26 '70
Costly end to a costly strike. il Newsweek 76:101-2 N 23 '70
Detroit stalemate: a blow for recovery; with editorial comment. il Bsns W p30-1, 124 S 19 '70
Difference the G.M. strike makes. Fortune 82:19-20 O '70
GM dealers sing the slowdown blues. il Bsns W p30 O 24 '70
GM strikers' mood is militant. il Bsns W p26-7 S 26 '70
GM's strike is not just a GE rerun; with editorial comment. il Bsns W p31, 118 O 24 '70
Glimmers of light in GM blackout. Bsns W p 18 N 7 '70
High price of peace in Detroit. il Time 96: 94-5 N 23 '70
How bitter will the strike be? il Newsweek 76:65-6 S 28 '70
Local 22 shows how it's done; master strike plan. il Bsns W p88+ O 24 '70
Strikers' families tell their story. il U S News 69:17-19 N 23 '70
Striking viewpoint. C. Morgello. il Newsweek 76:69 S 28 '70
UAW: getting poorer and tougher. Bsns W p75 O 31 '70
UAW's bill for repairs. B. J. Widick. Nation 211:259-60 S 28 '70
Union puts brakes on GM. il Sr Schol 97: 3 O 5 '70

Unknown who leads the Walter P. Reuther memorial strike. W. Serrin. il pors N Y Times Mag p28-9+ S 27 '70
What auto strike cost the U.S. il U S News 69:15-17 N 23 '70
Where the strike hurts. il Time 96:104 O 26 '70

Building industry

In Kansas City they couldn't go as far as they wanted. il Fortune 82:98-101 O '70
More trouble for builders: strikes go on, pay keeps rising. U S News 68:50-1 Je 29 '70
One city's ordeal by strike; Kansas City, Mo. U S News 69:64-5 S 14 '70
Strike lays low an arena; Kansas City's twin stadiums. il Bsns W p50 O 10 '70

College professors and instructors

Wisconsin: teaching assistants' strike ends in contract signing. A. Hamilton. Science 168:345-9 Ap 17 '70

Electric workers

Changing times; General electric strike. Nation 210:165 F 16 '70
Electric workers' dissent casts shadow; General electric strike. U S News 68:87 F 16 '70
Fork in the road; a postscript on the G.E. strike. J. Davenport. Fortune 81:82 Mr '70
GE and unions under pressure to settle. U S News 68:56 Ja 19 '70
GE strike as a pattern for future. U S News 68:74 Ap 13 '70
GM's strike is not just a GE rerun; with editorial comment. il Bsns W p31, 118 O 24 '70
General electric settlement; pattern for the future? il U S News 68:67-8 F 9 '70
Inflationary end to a class war. il Time 95: 71-2 F 9 '70
Less than super; settlement of General electric strike. Newsweek 75:67-8 F 9 '70
Strike hides GE's light under a bushel. Bsns W p31 Ja 17 '70

Entertainment industry

New wonder in Disneyland. il Newsweek 76: 68 S 21 '70

Farm labor

And now, lettuce. D. Henninger. New Repub 163:9-11 O 10 '70
Black eagle wins; end of grape strike. il por Time 96:10-11 Ag 10 '70
Dow on the farm; court injunction by Bud Antle inc. against the UFWOC's picketing. New Repub 163:8 D 12 '70
Eagle over the lettuce fields. N. C. Mills. Commonweal 93:140-1 N 6 '70
Grape boycott; round 2; union label grapes. New Repub 162:10 Ap 25 '70
Grape strike; and the National conference of Catholic bishops. J. Deedy. Commonweal 92:130 Ap 24 '70
Huelga! The boycott that worked. R. B. Taylor. Nation 211:167-9 S 7 '70
Lessons of the grape strike. V. Salandini. America 123:285-7 O 17 '70
Whatever happened to the grape strike and boycott? il por U S News 68:58 Ap 6 '70

Football players

Owners and players fumble on in Philly; Super bowl champs vs. College All-Stars. A. Wright. il Sports Illus 33:46-7 Ag 3 '70
Player power. il Newsweek 76:48-9 Ag 3 '70
Pro gridders cross the gold line. U S News 69:83 Ag 17 '70
Put 'er there, Judas! strike ends. Newsweek 76:79-80 Ag 17 '70
Rozelle referees a strike settlement. il Bsns W p 19 Ag 8 '70

Government employees

Changing policies in public employee labor relations; with table. J. P. Goldberg. bibliog f Mo Labor R 93:5-14 Jl '70
Crucial tests for hands off policy in strikes. il U S News 68:71-3 Ap 13 '70
Federal workers march to a new drummer. il Bsns W p40-1 Mr 28 '70
Longest strike; Maryland's Garrett County road workers. il Newsweek 76:81 N 30 '70
Recent statutes covering public employees: Hawaii and Pennsylvania statutes. J. P. Goldberg. Mo Labor R 93:31-2 D '70
Revolt of public workers. il Newsweek 75: 78A-78B My 4 '70
Right to strike in Hawaii; public employees. W. L. Abbott. Nation 210:756 Je 22 '70
See also
Strikes—United States—Municipal employeees
Strikes—United States—Postal employees

STRIKES—United States—*Continued*

Government intervention

Crisis without end; President Nixon orders 60-day cooling off period. Newsweek 76: 66+ S 28 '70

End of the road? Congress prohibits railroad strike. il Newsweek 75:80 Mr 16 '70

Labor turmoil: truce and new threats. il Time 95:8-10 Ap 6 '70

Mr Nixon's costly postage due. il Newsweek 75:23-6 Ap 6 '70

Meat industry and trade

Winners and losers; meat cutters strike against IBP. il Forbes 105:30+ My 1 '70

Migrant labor

See Strikes—United States—Farm labor

Municipal employees

Strike troubles pile up for cities and states. il U S News 68:69-70 Ap 6 '70

Musicians

Symphonic strike season. P. Hart. il Sat R 53:47-9+ S 26 '70; Discussion. 53:60-1 O 31 '70

Newspapers

How printers made a slowdown stick. U S News 68:43 Je 8 '70

Profiles: B. Powers. G. T. Hellman. New Yorker 46:53-6+ Mr 7 '70

Postal employees

Day the mail stopped. il Newsweek 75:14-17 Mr 30 '70

Economy wave stays the mails. Bsns W p31 Mr 21 '70

Even Mr Zip couldn't help. il Sr Schol 96:14-15 Ap 13 '70

Fall in for mail call; with report by reservist, F. Von Moschzisker. il Life 68:26-9 Ap 3 '70

Is America a shay or a scow? S. Alsop. Newsweek 75:100 Ap 6 '70

Mr Nixon's costly postage due. il Newsweek 75:23-6 Ap 6 '70

National humiliation. Nation 210:386 Ap 6 '70

Postal strike: the effect. il U S News 68: 16-19 Ap 6 '70

Rain, nor snow nor lousy wages. P. Steinfels. Commonweal 92:80 Ap 3 '70

Say it with flowers. Nat R 22:340-1 Ap 7 '70

Staving off the strikes. il Time 95:18 Ap 20 '70

Strike that stunned the country. il pors Time 95:10-16 Mr 30 '70

Strikes against the public: post office latest target. il U S News 68:21-2 Mr 30 '70

Untangling the mess in the post office. il Bsns W p78-80+ Mr 28 '70

When the mail doesn't go through. il Bsns W p41-2 Mr 28 '70

Railroads

Crisis without end; President Nixon orders 60-day cooling off period. Newsweek 76: 66+ S 28 '70

Day the trains stopped. il Time 96:13-14 D 21 '70

High cost of a rail truce. il Newsweek 76: 23-5 D 21 '70

Once again: threat of nationwide rail strike. il U S News 69:87-8 N 23 '70

Railroad cliffhanger. il Time 95:10-11 F 9 '70

Railroads again. il Newsweek 75:67 F 9 '70

When a railroad makes the rules. il Bsns W p 109-10 Ja 17 '70

When one work rule nearly stalled all the railroads. il U S News 68:86 F 16 '70

When railroads shut down all over the country. il U S News 69:14-15 D 21 '70

Why the railroad disputes still go on and on. U S News 69:46 D 21 '70

Teachers

Another strike technique: blockade negotiators; East St Louis, Ill. U S News 69:92 O 26 '70

As teacher strike ends first week; Los Angeles. U S News 68:84 Ap 27 '70

Children's attitudes during the New York city school strike of 1968. E. L. Fryburg. bibliog Sch & Soc 98:429-33 N '70

Library action during teachers' strike, a report; Gary, Ind. K. E. Burgess. Wilson Lib Bul 44:921 My '70

Striking proposition; Los Angeles city school system. il Time 95:54 Ap 27 '70

Teacher issues: pay, power, class size. U S News 68:86-7 Ap 20 '70

Teacher strikes. New Repub 162:8 Je 13 '70

Teacher strikes reach record heights. M. L. Hayes. Sch & Soc 98:433-4 N '70

Teachers' strike ends in lost ground; East St Louis, Ill. U S News 69:71 D 7 '70

Where school bells aren't ringing. U S News 69:103 S 21 '70

See also
Strikes—United States—College professors and instructors

Transportation workers

New curbs on transportation strikes? il Bsns W p76 Mr 7 '70

Storm signals. il Newsweek 75:67-8 Ap 6 '70

Truck drivers

Idle trucks hurt Chicago's business. Bsns W p34 Je 27 '70

Rivalry at top in truck strikes. U S News 68: 82-3 My 11 '70

Truck drivers' long dispute: costly blow to business; the Chicago situation. il U S News 68:51-2 Je 15 '70

Truck strike: a tightening vise. Bsns W p35-6 Ap 25 '70

Trucking strike hits other industries. U S News 68:84 Ap 27 '70

Wildcats at the wheel. il Newsweek 75:85B My 11 '70

STRIKING clocks. See Clocks

STRINDBERG, August
Crimes and crimes. Criticism
Newsweek 75:74 Ja 26 '70
Dance of death. Criticism
Sat R 53:12 My 16 '70 *

STRINE (dialect) See English language—Dialects

STRING ensembles
Classical Woodstock; New York's second annual Christmas string seminar. il por Time 97:46 Ja 11 '71

STRING octets
See also
Phonograph records—String octet music

STRING quartets
Guarneri quartet. S. Fleming. il Hi Fi 20: secII 8-9 Je '70
Musical events; performance of Beethoven quartets by the Juilliard string quartet. W. Sargeant. New Yorker 46:130 Ap 4 '70
Quartets by Carter; Composers string quartet in Alice Tully Hall. I. Kolodin. Sat R 53: 28 My 2 '70
See also
Phonograph records—String quartet music

STRING trios
Integrated trio goes south: Baumel-Booth-Smith trio's southern tour. R. B. Baumel. il Hi Fi 20:secII 26-7+ Jl '70

STRINGED instruments
From Apollo's lyre to Elvis' guitar; survey of plucked instruments. G. Taylor. il Hi Fi 20:secI 53-7 My '70
See also
Violin

STRINGER, W. C. and Epley, Richard
Lean pork isn't good enough; interview, ed. by B. Coffman. Farm J 94:H9+ F '70

STRINGFELLOW, William
Harlem, rebellion and resurrection. Chr Cent 87:1345-8 N 11 '70
—and Towne, Anthony
Christmas card from the FBI; statement. Commonweal 93:364 Ja 15 '71

STRIP coal mining. See Coal mines and mining—Stripping operations

STRIP films. See Film strips

STRIP mine dumps, Reclamation of. See Reclamation of land—Florida

STRIPED bass fishing. See Bass fishing

STRIPER fishing. See Bass fishing

STRIPTEASE acts. See Vaudeville

STRIX nebulosa. See Owls

STROBE units. See Photography—Electronic equipment

STROBL, Alois K.
You need good maps. bibliog il por Am City 85:83+ Jl '70

STROBOSCOPIC instrument tuners. See Tuning instruments and apparatus

STROBOSCOPIC lighting
Color organs & strobe lights enhance music. F. W. Holder. il Electr World 85:42-4+ Ja '70
Variable-rate repeating strobe light you can build. S. Daniels. il Pop Sci 196:130-1 My '70

STROCK, Carl
Long march. New Repub 162:12-13 My 9 '70

STROH, Natalie Korbel
How a diary encouraged creative writing. Ed Digest 35:54-5 Ja '70

STROHM, Bob
Amazing spider woman. il por Nat Wildlife 7:12-15 O '69

STUDENT demonstrations—*Continued*

Israel

Israel; the strange sounds of protest. R. C. Hirschfield. Commonweal 91:607-8 Mr 6 '70; Reply. J. Segal. 92:127 Ap 17 '70
See also
Israeli-Arab war, 1967—Protests, demonstrations, etc, against

Italy

Student revolt: Italian style. M. L. Stein and J. V. Ricapito. il Sat R 53:69-71+ F 21 '70

Japan

Japan II: university turmoil is reflected in research. P. M. Boffey. il Science 167:147-50+ Ja 9 '70
Japan's campus turmoil. D. Brudnoy. Nat R 22:147 F 10 '70

Mexico

Mexican students in jail. America 122:88 Ja 31 '70
Tlatelolco: massacre and aftermath. D. Peerman. Chr Cent 87:1503-6 D 16 '70

Philippines

Graduates. il Newsweek 75:38-40 Mr 9 '70
Laughing on the inside. il Newsweek 75:38 Mr 2 '70
Sacred debt. il Newsweek 75:44+ F 16 '70
Testy words in Manila. il Time 95:38 Mr 2 '70

Russia

Tourist provocateurs. Time 95:20 F 2 '70

United States

Across America; rising protest, renewed violence; demonstrations against the verdict in the trial of the Chicago seven. il U S News 68:7 Mr 2 '70
After Kent state. J. Cass. Sat R 53:71 Je 20 '70
Agnew's talk with five students; text of television debate. S. T. Agnew and others. il pors U S News 69:86-8+ O 12 '70
As senators argue on student revolt: worry, and warnings; excerpts from debate in the Senate, May 5, 1970. il U S News 68:92-6 My 18 '70
Basic cause of campus disorders. D. Lawrence. U S News 68:104 My 25 '70
Buffalo war. il Newsweek 75:33-4 Mr 30 '70
Campus crackdown; colleges strike back at violence; with interview with E. L. Chalmers, jr. il U S News 69:16-22 S 7 '70
Campus revolt: no end in sight. il U S News 68:82 Ap 13 '70
Campus revolts over? il U S News 68:53-5 F 16 '70
Can American education survive one more year like the one we have just been through? Nat R 22:722-8 Jl 14 '70
Carnival revolution; University of Michigan. M. J. Gallagher. America 122:295-8 Mr 21 '70
Commencement time: bitter protests to the end. il U S News 68:33-4 Je 22 '70
Cooling it. New Repub 162:11 My 30 '70
Courts and the child: Supreme court Tinker vs. Des Moines decision. Library J 95:216-17 Ja 15 '70
Crisis in American education; address, June 19, 1970. R. A. Freeman. Vital Speeches 36:592-7 Jl 15 '70; Excerpts. por U S News 68:72-3 Je 29 '70
Dissent and the college student in revolt. C. E. Blocker. bibliog Sch & Soc 98:20-3 Ja '70
Dissent or anarchy: common front at Buffalo. H. S. Levine. il Nation 210:520-2 My 4 '70
Ending campus myths; the findings by the Urban research corporation of Chicago. Commonweal 91:500 F 6 '70
Federal crackdown on student violence? il U S News 69:73 O 5 '70
Gentlemen songsters off on a spree; Yale May day demonstrations. il Newsweek 75:31-2 My 11 '70
Have we overlooked the obvious? campus population increase as cause of student unrest. D. Lawrence. U S News 69:96 O 5 '70
Hayakawa at Northeastern. D. Brudnoy. Nat R 22:202 F 24 '70
Indeed do it! demonstrations following J. Rubin's speech at UCLA. W. F. Buckley, jr. Nat R 22:533 My 19 '70
Inside America: as it looks to the governors. il U S News 68:24-5 My 25 '70
Kent state: another view. il Time 96:27 O 26 '70
Kunstler constituency; rioting by Columbia students. J. R. Coyne, jr. Nat R 22:467 My 5 '70

L.A.'s Scottsboro boys case. S. H. Harris. Commonweal 91:548-9 F 20 '70
Listen to youths, Hickel writes Nixon. il pors U S News 68:84 My 18 '70
Lively ivy; views of witnesses before the President's commission on campus unrest. New Repub 163:5-6 Ag 15 '70
May day; protests against Nixon's policy on Cambodia. il Newsweek 75:32-3 My 11 '70
New left v. national security: objections to research at Instrumentation laboratory of the Massachusetts institute of technology. Nat R 22:18 Ja 13 '70
No one plays in no man's land; boycott of People's park. R. Rapoport. il Sports Illus 32:20-1 Je 15 '70
Ordeal at San Francisco state college. B. Anderson. il por Library J 95:1275-80 Ap 1 '70
Peace on campuses; new survey. U S News 69:66 N 16 '70
Protest season on the campus. il Time 95:19-20+ My 11 '70
Push comes to shove: The escalation of student protest, by S. Kelman. Review
   Fortune 82:213-14 S '70. D. Seligman
Radicalizing of a guest teacher at Berkeley. J. Holt. il N Y Times Mag p30-1+ F 22 '70; Discussion. p6+ Mr 15 '70
Radicals move in; Harvard and Berkeley. il Newsweek 75:33-4 Ap 27 '70
Revolt: views from the campus. A. Goldman. il Life 68:18 My 15 '70
Spring riot season coming on strong; rise in violence on college campuses. il U S News 68:40 My 4 '70
Stop the war! open hearings on student unrest. il Newsweek 76:66-7 Jl 27 '70
Student dissent. J. J. Pietrofesa and W. H. Van Hoose. Clear House 44:395-400 Mr '70
Student protests: how far is too far? with comments. Sr Schol 95:6-13 O 20 '69
Student violence widens range. il U S News 68:24-6 Mr 16 '70
Survey of college presidents: what will happen on campus this fall. Ladies Home J 87:79+ S '70
Symbol and event. J. C. Evans. Chr Cent 87:653-4 My 27 '70
Teacher opinion poll: student unrest. il Todays Ed 59:12 S '70
Tolerance of violence on the campus. A. M. Bickel. New Repub 162:15-17 Je 13 '70
Unholy alliance against the campus. K. Keniston and M. Lerner. il N Y Times Mag p28-9+ N 8 '70
Up against the wall. R. E. Forbes. America 122:454-5 Ap 25 '70
Washington and the college campus. America 123:225 O 3 '70
Washington report; make way for the students; excerpts from report. ed. by J. Lloyd. G. R. Anrig. Sr Schol 95:Schol Teach 2 D 1 '69
What do students themselves think? Sr Schol 96:9 My 4 '70
Whatever happened to major campus agitators of recent years? il U S News 68:8 F 2 '70
Why young people protest. B. Spock. Redbook 134:46+ Ap '70
Yale proves dissent doesn't have to turn out like this. J. K. Jessup. il por Life 68:38-40 My 15 '70
See also
Cambodia—Vietnamese conflict—American participation—Protests, demonstrations, etc. against
Negro student demonstrations
United States—President's commission on campus unrest
Vietnamese war, 1957- —Protests, demonstrations, etc, against

History

Student violence: into a more dangerous era. il U S News 68:28-31 My 18 '70

Vietnam (Republic)

Viet student justice. J. Deedy. Commonweal 92:282 Je 12 '70

STUDENT employment
Employment of school-age youth; with charts and tables. A. M. Young. bibliog f Mo Labor R 93:4-11 S '70
Last-minute jobs. il Seventeen 29:126+ Je '70
Once upon a time: a fable of student power. N. Postman. il N Y Times Mag p 10-11 Je 14 '70
Pickings are slim in summer jobs. Bsns W p34-5 Je 27 '70
Psychiatric training program for high school students assigned to a geriatric service. J. H. Friedman and A. R. Spada. bibliog Ment Hy 54:427-9 Jl '70

STUDENT employment—*Continued*
Reasons for summer job crisis. il U S News 68:26-7 Je 15 '70
Scholastic achievement and part-time employment. W. A. Hammond. Clear House 44:465-7 Ap '70
Summer-job blues. il Newsweek 76:52+ Jl 27 '70
See also
College students—Employment

STUDENT exchange programs. See Students, Interchange of

STUDENT forums. See Forums (discussion and debate)

STUDENT government. See Self government in education

STUDENT housing. See College students—Housing

STUDENT life
Blowing my mind at Harvard. L. L. King. Harper 241:95-8+ O '70
On campus; drugs vs. drinking. Mlle 70:230 Mr '70
See also
College clubs and societies

History
Campus scene, by C. B. T. Lee. Review Atlan 226:133-7+ O '70. L. Kronenberger

STUDENT loans
More loan money for students, but—. il U S News 69:56 S 21 '70
Where to borrow money for college. Changing T 25:15-17 Ja '71
See also
Student aid

STUDENT lobbyists. See Lobbyists

STUDENT militants
Academia in anarchy, by J. M. Buchanan and N. E. Devletoglou. Review Nat R il 22:684-5 Je 30 '70. W. Breit
Academic freedom and academic anarchy, by S. Hook. Review Nat R 22:91-2 Ja 27 '70. R. Kirk
Advice to Princeton alumni; excerpts from address, 1970. A. Capp. il Nat R 22:994-6+ S 22 '70
Black Panthers and white radicals; notes from New Haven. P. Starr. Commonweal 92:294-7 Je 12 '70
Bombing at Wisconsin; dealing with radicals. America 123:139 S 12 '70
Campus communiqué. il Time 95:44 Ap 20 '70
Campus conflict. Chr Today 14:23 My 22 '70
Campus meets legislature. il Time 95:47 Je 8 '70
Campus revolt from an industrial relations perspective. F. H. Harbison. Mo Labor R 93:33-6 Mr '70
Campus unrest; the erosion of excellence; address, May 29, 1970. R. V. Andelson. Vital Speeches 36:619-21 Ag 1 '70
Can American education survive one more year like the one we have just been through? Nat R 22:722-8 Jl 14 '70
Candidates take second look at campus troublemakers. il U S News 69:29-30 S 28 '70
College president's open letter: "I apologize for the grotesque failure" of the campuses. M. Upton. il U S News 68:39 Je 15 '70
Democracy on the brain. K. Melvin. Nat R 22:410+ Ap 21 '70
Dink Stover in hell; drawings. Esquire 74:95-105 S '70
Dirty little war; Boston-Cambridge, April. D. Brudnoy. Nat R 22:453 My 5 '70
End of the multiversity. J. R. Coyne, jr. Nat R 22:560-1+ Je 2 '70
Extremism; student militancy. Commonweal 92:307-8 Je 26 '70
Facing student unrest. R. M. Kudela. bibliog Clear House 44:547-52 My '70
Generation gap and international development. F. Herrera. il Américas 22:13-20 Ap '70
High school revolutionaries, ed. by M. Libarle and T. Seligson. Review Trans-Action 7:63-4 S '70. L. Weiner
How to roast a marshmallow; address, April 1970. S. T. Agnew. por Time 95:20 My 11 '70
I am tired of the tyranny of spoiled brats. K. R. Toole. il pors U S News 68:76-8 Ap 13 '70; Same abr. Read Digest 96:129-32 Je '70
Kidspeak; University of Connecticut's yearbook, Nutmeg. W. F. Buckley, jr. Nat R 22:1178 N 3 '70
Kidstuff. S. McCracken. Commentary 50:100-2 O '70
Kumquat statement, by J. R. Coyne, jr. Review Nat R 22:1412-13 D 29 '70. C. H. Simonds

Kunstler constituency; rioting by Columbia students. J. R. Coyne, jr. Nat R 22:467 My 5 '70
Make war, not peace. il Time 95:27 Ap 27 '70
Of many things; unrest and dissent among collegians. D. R. Campion. America 123:inside cover Jl 11 '70
Perils of overexposing youth to college. B. Bettelheim. Ed Digest 35:35-8 Ap '70
Political terrorism: hysteria on the left. I. Howe. il N Y Times Mag p25-7+ Ap 12 '70; Discussion. p22+ My 10 '70
Real constitutional crisis. F. S. Meyer. Nat R 22:571 Je 2 '70
Real toads: real bombs and bullets on campus. Nat R 22:928-9 S 8 '70
Remembering the answers, by N. Glazer. Review Nat R 22:1409+ D 29 '70. R. Nisbet
Responsible university leadership; violence and dissent; address, September 16, 1970. R. M. Nixon. Vital Speeches 36:738-40 O 1 '70; Excerpts. il por U S News 69:27-8 S 28 '70
Revolution in the university. J. Hitchcock. Yale R 60:161-74 D '70
Revolution on American campuses: an analysis. P. J. Weber. il Cath World 210:248-52 Mr '70
Revolutionaries: a guide to who they are, what they want. il Newsweek 75:34-8 My 11 '70
Shoveling out the work of a lifetime; a lab in Wisconsin. C. Leinster. il por Life 69:38-42 S 18 '70
Student unrest and the library. M. B. Cassata. bibliog il por Wilson Lib Bul 45:78-85 S '70
Student violence widens range. il U S News 68:24-6 Mr 16 '70
Students aren't crazies; the war and the Moratorium. M. A. Tessler and R. D. Hedlund. New Repub 163:17-18 S 5 '70; Reply. H. Caton. 163:32-3 S 26 '70
Teachers' role in campus revolt. il U S News 68:36-8 Je 15 '70
Time for words is over; April moratorium. Nat R 22:448 My 5 '70
Tolerance of violence on the campus. A. M. Bickel. New Repub 162:15-17 Je 13 '70
Trouble: the high school radicals; with excerpts from The high school revolutionaries, ed. by M. Libarle and T. Seligson. E. Dunbar. il Look 34:70+ Mr 24 '70
U.S. faces choice between anarchy and repression; address, June 1, 1970. M. C. Smith. il pors U S News 68:45-6 Je 15 '70
Universities in ferment. il Newsweek 75:66-8+ Je 15 '70
War syndrome. J. Burham. Nat R 22:627 Je 16 '70
We/they: the new campus dialogue. B. F. Dick. Nat R 22:562-3+ Je 2 '70
Whatever happened to major campus agitators of recent years? il U S News 68:8 F 2 '70
Where are the Savios of yesteryear? W. Greene. il N Y Times Mag p6-9+ Jl 12 '70
Where we are. Nat R 22:549 Je 2 '70
See also
Negro student militants
Southern student organizing committee
Students for a democratic society (organization)
United States—President's commission on campus unrest

Anecdotes, facetiae, satire, etc.
Father-son rap-in. J. D. Tierney. Nat R 22:998+ S 22 '70
I am Dr Fager's night watchman. J. D. Tierney. Nat R 22:206 F 24 '70

Bibliography
Writing on the revolution. C. R. Sternhell. il McCalls 97:16+ Jl '70

France
French have a law for it. Nat R 22:503 My 19 '70
Letter from Paris; Left Bank student riots in Latin Quarter and Saint-Germain-des-Prés. Genêt. il New Yorker 46:97-8 Je 13 '70
Letter from Paris; new law against destructive violence. Genêt. New Yorker 46:117-19 My 16 '70
Mao is watching; fashionable summer haunts attacked. il Newsweek 76:36 Ag 10 '70
Reports: students in France. J. K. Glassman. Atlan 226:25-6+ S '70

STUDENT militants—*Continued*

Japan

Fly me to Pyongyang. il Newsweek 75:40+ Ap 13 '70

Red army; radical fringe. il Newsweek 75:45 Ap 13 '70

STUDENT movement

Behind the campus revolt. P. Woodring. il Sat R 53:52-3 Jl 18 '70

Campus and the student, 1970; address, May 4, 1970. W. R. Butler. Vital Speeches 36:566-9 Jl 1 '70

Confrontation tactics; letter. P. C. Roberts. Science 169:816 Ag 28 '70

Generation gap and international development: youth movement. F. Herrera. il Américas 22:13-20 Ap '70

Reflections on the international student movement. F. Stern. Am Scholar 40:123-37 Wint '70

Student revolt. C. Landauer. Yale R 60:175-84 D '70

Trade-unionization of students. I. L. Horowitz. Cur 122:55-9 O '70

Young intelligentsia in revolt; excerpt from America: system and revolution, ed. by R. Aya and N. Miller. R. Flacks. il Trans-Action 7:46-55 Je '70

Youth 'liberates' America; symposium. America 122:430-42 Ap 25, '70; Discussion. 122:429; 123:158-9 Ap 25; S 12 '70

United States

See Student movement

STUDENT newspapers. See College and school journalism

STUDENT ombudsman. See Ombudsman (education)

STUDENT opinion

Children's attitudes during the New York city school strike of 1968. E. L. Fryburg. bibliog Sch & Soc 98:429-33 N '70

Front-porch America; views of Kent state students in New York times interview. Nation 210:612 My 25 '70

Mlle's next word; our feelings as come September. . . dialogue with guest editors. il Mlle 71:203-7+ Ag '70

On campus; Women's lib. Mlle 71:104 Ag '70

Opinions of college freshmen. Sch & Soc 98:302-3 Sum '70

President is listening. il Time 96:8-9 Ag 3 '70

Student voices; what makes a social issue a library issue? ed. by E. Zaremba. il Wilson Lib Bul 45:54-61 S '70

University and society. M. Levitt. bibliog Sch & Soc 98:342-6 O '70

View through youthful eyes. L. Banks. il Fortune 81:76-7+ Ap '70

What do students themselves think? Sr Schol 96:9 My 4 '70

What do we do with our lives? letter. L. Eldredge. por Time 95:23 My 11 '70

What the kids think. il Newsweek 76:80 S 21 '70

What white students think of black studies. il Life 68:34 My 8 '70

STUDENT participation in school administration. See School management and organization—Student participation

STUDENT personnel work. See Personnel service in education

STUDENT publications. See College and school journalism

STUDENT radicals. See Student militants

STUDENT records. See School reports and records

STUDENT recruiting. See Colleges and universities—Student recruiting

STUDENT residences. See College students—Housing; Dormitories

STUDENT rights. See Students—Civil rights

STUDENT selection

Chance, or human judgment? D. Wolfle. Science 167:1201 F 27 '70; Discussion. 168:777, 1523 My 15. Je 26 '70

Should college applicants be selected by lottery? letters. A. P. Gray; A. W. Astin. Science 167:1075-6 F 20 '70; Discussion. 168:521 My 1 '70

See also

Carnegie commission on higher education

College entrance examination board

STUDENT teachers

Intern teachers for urban schools. Sch & Soc 98:74-5 F '70

STUDENT teaching

Cooperating teacher-student teacher as a learning team. W. Sinclair and L. K. Peters. Clear House 44:430-2 Mr '70

New perspective on student teaching. H. Talmage and G. E. Monroe. Clear House 44:330-3 F '70

Pass or fail credit for student teaching. S. D. Aven and E. Breazier. Clear House 44:309 Ja '70

Professionalism begins with student teaching. A. Bills. bibliog f Clear House 45:156-60 N '70

Student teaching the public school's responsibility. F. B. Dressel. Sch & Soc 98:163-4 Mr '70

See also

Teachers—Education

STUDENT teaching, Supervisors of. See Supervisors of student teaching

STUDENT tours. See Student travel

STUDENT travel

American youth in Europe '70; symposium. il Holiday 47:26-31 Je '70

For Easter, it's Nassau. L. Gauge. Travel & Camera 33:8+ F '70

Let's travel; student news, great flying. il Mlle 70:146-8+ F '70

Rude awakening; World academy's financial failure. il Newsweek 76:75 Jl 20 '70

Student travel/1970. il Sat R 53:77-87 F 21 '70

Summer '70 ; young Americans abroad. il Newsweek 76:44-8 Ag 10 '70

Ways of the young, in the wide, wide world. M. Gough. il House B 112:20-1 Jl '70

See also

Travel study courses

History

Ill conduct and manners of students on their travels abroad; with introd. by S. E. Fraser. P. D. S. Chesterfield. Sch & Soc 98:33+ Ja '70

STUDENT tutors. See Tutors and tutoring

STUDENT union buildings. See College architecture

STUDENT volunteer movement. See University Christian movement

STUDENT volunteer service. See Volunteer service

STUDENT withdrawals. See Dropouts

STUDENTS

See also

Art students

Clothing and dress—Students

College students

Foreign students in the United States

High school students

Law students

Negro students

School management and organization—Student participation

Seminarians

also Mexican students; Mexican-American students, etc.

Attitudes

Bridging the generation gap; discussion. M. K. Udall. New Repub 163:11-13 N 28 '70

Campus meets legislature. il Time 95:47-8 Je 8 '70

Cease-fire on campus. il Newsweek 76:79 O 19 '70

Does college radicalization stick? R. Kirk. Nat R 22:1058 O 6 '70

How college students feel about love, sex and marriage. M. Peters and W. Peters. il Good H 170:84-5+ Je '70

Letter to the alumni, by J. Hersey. Review Sat R 53:61-2 N 21 '70. J. Cass

Notes on the germanization of American youth. J. L. Sammons. Yale R 59:342-56 Mr '70; Same abr. with title American youth and the Germans. Cur 119:10-14 Je '70

Politics of despair; surveys of high school and college students. Sat R 53:80 S 19 '70

Silent generation meets the class of 1970. M. Gartner. il Sat R 53:52-3+ Ag 15 '70

Students aren't crazies; the war and the Moratorium. M. A. Tessler and R. D. Hedlund. New Repub 163:17-18 S 5 '70; Reply. H. Caton. 163:32-3 S 26 '70

Teachers, students, and selfishness in the seventies. V. R. Mollenkott. Chr Today 14:6-8+ Ap 10; 13-15 Ap 24 '70

Test-tube backlash. G. E. Christianson. Commonweal 93:9-13 O 2 '70

To heal our society's deep rifts. K. Keniston. Cur 123:48-56 N '70

What do they want? is school losing its meaning for students? N. P. Atkins. Ed Digest 35:19-21 My '70

What's troubling high school students? panel discussion. il Todays Ed 59:32-9 S '70

Civil rights

Hair becomes the plaintiff. il Sat R 53:73 N 21 '70

Protecting student rights. I. Glasser. Cur 115:46-54 F '70

STUDENTS—Civil rights—*Continued*
Rules of due process for college administrators. Sch & Soc 98:392-3 N '70
Students' right to criticize schools is sanctioned by Illinois appeals court. Sr Schol 96:Schol Teach 7 My 18 '70

Employment
See Students employment

Grading and promotion
See Grading and marking (students)

Political activities
Last train for peaceful politics. P. Steinfels. Commonweal 92:238 My 22 '70

Rating
Teacher perceptions of correlates of academic achievement. C. J. Dunn and G. T. Kowitz. bibliog f Sch & Soc 98:370-2 O '70

STUDENTS, Interchange of
International student: his six roles. F. Donahue. Clear House 45:51-5 S '70
New overseas study programs for future teachers. Sch & Soc 98:210+ Ap '70
See also
Foreign students in the United States

STUDENTS, Rating of. See Students—Rating

STUDENTS and teachers. See Teachers and students

STUDENTS and youth, Office of. See United States—Education, Office of—Students and youth, Office of

STUDENTS as teachers aides. See Teachers aides

STUDENTS for a democratic society (organization)
End of SDS? il Newsweek 76:55-6 N 30 '70
Enforced conformity; the big lie; address, June 9, 1970. N. M. Pusey. Vital Speeches 36:588-92 Jl 15 '70
SDS and the high schools: a study in student extremism. J. E. Hoover. il PTA Mag 64:2-5 Ja; 8-9 F '70; Discussion. 64:19-20 Mr '70
See also
Weathermen (organization)

STUDENTS poetry. See College verse

STUDENTS workshops. See Educational workshops

STUDIES (rooms)
Study-storage wall. J. Capotosto and J. R. Connor. il Mech Illus 66:91-3 N '70

STUDIOS
See also
Artists studios

STUDS, Tire. See Tires, Automobile

STUDY
See also
Courses of study
Independent study

STUDY halls
Study hall: the villain. M. Evans. Clear House 44:372 F '70

STUDY tours. See Travel study courses

STUDY-work plan. See Education, Cooperative

STUECK, Hans J.
Urban transit model. Sat R 53:62-3 D 5 '70

STUERMER, Wilhelm
Soft parts of cephalopods and trilobites: some surprising results of X-ray examinations of Devonian slates. bibliog il Science 170:1300-2 D 18 '70

STUFFING. See Cookery—Poultry

STUMM, Werner. See Singer, P. C. jt. auth.

STUMPF, Samuel Enoch
Freedom and order on the campus; adaptation of address, January 12, 1970. Sch & Soc 98:401-3 N '70

STUNT flying. See Aviation—Stunt flying

STUNT men
Ups and downs of a TV stuntman; interview, ed. by P. Hudson. F. Lerner. il Sr Schol 97:42-3 S 28 '70

STUNT motorcycling. See Motorcycling—Stunt cycling

STUNT women
Anything you can do, Mari-Lou can do better. il pors Life 69:70-3 S 25 '70

STURBRIDGE village. See Old Sturbridge village, Sturbridge, Mass.

STURGEON fishing
What, no caviar! C. Ormond. il Outdoor Life 146:60-3+ N '70

STURGES, Patricia P.
Intruders; story. il Liv Wildn 33:15-18 Aut '69

STURMAN, John A. and others
Absence of cystathionase in human fetal liver: is cystine essential? bibliog il Science 169:74-6 Jl 3 '70

STURTEVANT, Joan
Pigeon control by chemosterilization: population model from laboratory results. bibliog il Science 170:322-4 O 16 '70

STUTTERING. See Stammering

STUTTGART, Germany

Music
Report:
Leos Janáĉek's The Makropoulos case. D. Norris. Opera N 35:27 S 5 '70
Richard Strauss' Frau ohne schatten. D. Norris. Opera N 34:34 Mr 21 '70

STUTZ, Sara D.
How did you know what I wanted, mom? il Parents Mag 45:50-1+ D '70

STUTZ (automobile) See Automobiles

STYLE, Literary
Art of Herman Melville: the author of Pierre. R. J. Nelson. Yale R 59:197-214 D '69
Books. M. Muggeridge. Esquire 73:60+ Mr '70
Narrative murder. L. Bersani. Yale R 59:376-90 Mr '70
Teaching a concept of style for literature and composition. T. E. Gaston. Engl J 59:65-70 Ja '70
See also
Figures of speech
Literary criticism

STYLE in dress. See Fashion

STYLIANOPOULOS, Theodore G.
Orthodox church in America. bibliog f Ann Am Acad 387:41-8 Ja '70

STYLUSES, Phonograph. See Phonograph needles

SUBARU 360 (automobile) See Automobiles, Foreign

SUBCOMMITTEE on easing tensions in education. See United States—Education, Office of—Subcommittee on easing tensions in education

SUBCONSCIOUSNESS
Ernst Mach: the unconscious motives of an empiricist. L. S. Feuer. bibliog Am Imago 27:12-40 Spr '70

SUBCONTRACTING
See also
Contracts, Government—Subcontracting
Ethnic enterprizes (firm)

SUBJECT headings
Standardization in commercial children's cataloging: a comparative study of 100-odd titles. F. E. DeHart. il por Library J 95:744-9 F 15 '70

SUBJECTS, Literary. See Literature—Themes

SUBLETT, Henry L. jr. See Johnson, J. C; Shuman, R. B. jt. auths.

SUBLIMATION
Subliming ice surfaces: freeze-etch electron microscopy. J. G. Davy and D. Branton. bibliog il Science 168:1216-18 Je 5 '70

SUBMARINE archeology. See Archeology, Submarine

SUBMARINE bases. See Navy yards and naval stations

SUBMARINE boats
Hope for disabled undersea vessels; deep submergence rescue vehicle. C. LaFond. il Sci N 98:231-3 S 12 '70
New wave in aqua gear. il Life 68:70-3 Mr 6 '70
Rescue ship for submarines; first deep submergence rescue vehicle. il Bsns W p80 Ja 31 '70
Should your next boat be a submarine? Perry Shark Hunter. G. Reiger. il Pop Mech 134:74-7+ Ag '70
See also
Submarine vehicles

Accidents
See Submarine disasters

Design
Submarines that swim; Dermadrive project. il Mech Illus 66:90-1+ O '70

Photographs
Lockheed to sea-test navy DSRV-1 soon. il Aviation W 92:58 Mr 16 '70

Safety devices and measures
See also
Life support systems (submarine environment)

SUBMARINE boats, Atomic powered
Blue water boondoggle; projected Undersea long-range missile system to replace Polaris and Poseidon. S. D'Arazien. il Nation 211:498-500 N 16 '70
Does Russia lead U.S. in nuclear subs? il U S News 69:20-1 Ag 17 '70
Inside Holy Loch; with report by R. B. Stolley. il Life 68:66-9+ Ap 3 '70

SUBMARINE boats, Atomic powered—*Cont.*

Crews

Nuclear subs: a century after Captain Nemo. L. D. Hamilton. il Todays Health 48:26-31 Ap '70

SUBMARINE boats, Research. See Submarine research vehicles

SUBMARINE diamond mines and mining. See Diamond mines and mining, Submarine

SUBMARINE disasters
Daphné the doomed; loss of French submarine. Time 95:43 Mr 16 '70

SUBMARINE drilling. See Underwater drilling

SUBMARINE exploration. See Underwater exploration

SUBMARINE geology
Crustal layer of seismic velocity 6.9 to 7.6 kilometers per second under the deep oceans. G. L. Maynard. bibliog il Science 168:120-1 Ap 3 '70
Crustal plates in the central Atlantic. M. M. Ball and C. G. A. Harrison. bibliog il Science 167:1128-9 F 20 '70
Deep sea drilling: a giant step in geological research. A. L. Hammond. il Science 170:520-1 O 30 '70
Deep sea drilling in the South Atlantic. A. E. Maxwell and others. bibliog il Science 168:1047-59 My 29 '70
Geological history of the western North Pacific. A. G. Fischer and others. bibliog il Science 168:1210-14 Je 5 '70
Layered basic complex in oceanic crust, Romanche fracture, equatorial Atlantic Ocean. W. G. Melson and G. Thompson. bibliog il Science 168:817-20 My 15 '70
See also
Faults (geology)
Marine sediments

Conferences

Hunting clues to an ancient supercontinent. D. Behrman. il UNESCO Courier 23:28-32 Jl '70

SUBMARINE ice breaking vessels. See Ice breaking vessels, Submarine

SUBMARINE laboratories. See Underwater laboratories

SUBMARINE photography. See Photography, Submarine

SUBMARINE pilots
Booker T's yellow submarine; pilot for the International underwater contractors, inc. il Ebony 26:153-4+ D '70

SUBMARINE research. See Oceanographic research

SUBMARINE research stations. See Underwater laboratories

SUBMARINE research stations, Manned. See Underwater laboratories

SUBMARINE research vehicles
Glass submarines; future manned exploration submersibles. D. Groves. il Sea Front 16:286-90 S '70
Searching the shrimp beds by sub; research submarine Aluminaut. W. W. Anderson and H. R. Bullis, jr. il pors Sea Front 16:112-19 Mr '70
Soviet mini-submarine; MAL-3. E. P. Young. il Sea Front 16:25 Ja '70
This submarine for hire: Aluminaut. R. Gannon. il Pop Sci 196:49-51+ Ap '70

Salvage

How we raised the Alvin from 5000 feet. W. O. Rainnie and W. I. Milwee, jr. il pors Pop Mech 133:92-8 Ja '70

SUBMARINE service, Russian. See Russia—Navy—Submarine service

SUBMARINE vehicles
Sea-floor-rover, master of all trades underwater. H. Shuldiner. il Pop Sci 196:62-3 Je '70
Under the sea in a Swimmer sled. R. Gannon. il Pop Sci 197:52-3 Jl '70

SUBMARINE warfare
See also
Guided missiles—Launching from submarine boats

SUBMERGED lands
See also
Continental shelf

SUBMERSIBLE heaters. See Water heaters

SUBMERSIBLES. See Submarine research vehicles

SUBPOENAS
Appeal for credibility; case of New York times reporter, E. Caldwell. Newsweek 75:74 My 11 '70
Battling Mitchell vs. the media. Nation 210:259-60 Mr 9 '70

Coordinating the media; dragnet subpoenas served on C.B.S. and other news reporters. Nation 210:163-4 F 16 '70
End to fishing; E. Caldwell's challenge. Time 96:46 N 30 '70
Flexible guidelines. Newsweek 76:71 Ag 24 '70
How much privilege? San Francisco court rules on the press's rights. il por Newsweek 75:77-8 Ap 13 '70
Informing by compulsion; TV reporters and interviewers as informers. Nation 210:133 F 9 '70
Journalist's privilege; San Francisco Court of appeals quashes federal subpoenas served on E. Caldwell. il por Newsweek 76:87 N 30 '70
Limit on subpoena of notes of reporters and authors. H. F. Pilpel and K. P. Norwick. Pub W 197:33-4 My 4 '70
Mitchell and the media; government's right to raw news materials bearing on criminal investigations. Nat R 22:191-2 F 24 '70
Newsman held immune from testifying on Black Panthers. Pub W 198:26 D 7 '70
Policing the movement; Liberation news service. J. Deedy. Commonweal 92:2 Mr 13 '70
Promise on subpoenas. il Time 95:49 F 16 '70
Reporting for court duty; subpoenas to use reporter's private information. il Time 95:52 F 9 '70
St Gregory's revisited; harboring a criminal. J. Deedy. Commonweal 92:258 My 29 '70
Subpoenas and sources. il Newsweek 75:55-6 F 16 '70

SUBSCRIPTION television programs. See Television broadcasting—Subscription programs

SUBSIDENCES, Mine. See Mine subsidences

SUBSIDIES
Toward postal reorganization. J. G. Butler. il Chr Cent 87:104-8 Ja 28 '70
What Congress did for business. il Time 97:68-70 Ja 18 '71
See also
Agricultural administration—United States
also subhead Federal aid under various subjects, e.g. Housing—Federal aid

SUBSIDIES, Music. See Music and state

SUBSTITUTE products
See also
Food substitutes
Milk substitutes
Sugar substitutes

SUBSTITUTE teachers
Substitute's problems. H. See. Todays Ed 59:58-9 F '70

SUBSTITUTION reactions. See Chemical reactions

SUBTERRANEAN termites. See Termites

SUBURBAN life
Radical suburb and expansive man; excerpt from The radical suburb. J. B. Orr and F. P. Nichelson. Cur 122:3-10 O '70

SUBURBAN offices. See Location in business and industry

SUBURBS
Alternates to suburban sprawl: new processes, new involvement. W. F. Wagner, jr. Arch Rec 148:9-10 N '70
As go the suburbs, so goes U.S. politics. A. J. Reichley. il Fortune 82:104-9+ S '70
Battle to open the suburbs: new attack on zoning laws. il U S News 68:39-40 Je 22 '70
Flight from the cities: it's growing. il U S News 69:33 S 7 '70
Golden days are gone in suburbia. il Bsns W p34-5+ S 5 '70
Liberalism in the suburbs· squabble over proposed low-income housing project, Newton, Mass. il Newsweek 76:57 Jl 6 '70
Moral dilemma of zoning. D. K. Shipler. il Nation 211:80-3 Ag 3 '70
Revolution in suburbia? trend toward town houses and garden apartments. il Forbes 105:24-6+ Ap 1 '70
Suburbia regnant. Time 96:6 Jl 6 '70
Where the cities meet the suburbs. il Bsns W p84-6 O 17 '70

Negroes

New way to integrate the suburbs. il Bsns W p 168+ Mr 28 '70

SUBVERSIVE activities
See also
Communism—United States
Internal security
Terrorism
Treason
United States—Subversive activities control board

SUBVERSIVE activities—*Continued*
Vietnam (Republic)
Growing menace to Vietnam: red spies in the South. il U S News 69:51-2 D 21 '70
SUBWAYS
Germany ducks into subways. il Bsns W p 135 Mr 21 '70
SUCCESS
See also
Failure (psychology)
SUCCESS unlimited (periodical)
Success stories. il por Newsweek 77:77 Ja 11 '71
SUCCESSFUL farming (periodical)
New publishing plan gives you more management help when you need it. D. Hanson. il Suc Farm 68:22-3 Ja '70
Special bonus for today's dairymen; Successful dairy management section. J. R. Borcherding. Suc Farm 68:no4 E1 Mr '70
Successful beef management; special bonus for today's beefmen. D. Malena. il Suc Farm 68:no3 D1 F '70
SUCCULENT plants
Durable succulents. J. W. Wilson. il Horticulture 48:36-7 Je '70
Succulents and cactus; review. il Sunset 144:236-7 Mr '70
Succulents grow in a moss frame. il Sunset 144:74+ Ja '70
To show off succulents just put them in pots. il Sunset 144:230-1 My '70
Your garden indoors. F. S. David. il Home Gard 57:55 Jl '70
See also
Cactus
Jade plants
Sedums
SUCHOTLIFF, Leonard C. and others
Struggle for patients' rights in a state hospital. bibliog Ment Hy 54:230-40 Ap '70
SUCHY, Juliusz Katz-. See Katz-Suchy, J.
SUD aviation. See Helicopter industry and trade—France
SUDAN
See also
Arab federation (proposed)
Religious institutions and affairs
See also
Christians in Sudan
SUDAN grass
Hybrids
See also
Sorghum—Hybrids
SUDDEN death syndrome. See Infant mortality
SUDDEN luck; story. See Kaplan, J.
SUDEK, Josef
Gallery; photographs. Life 68:6-9 My 29 '70
SUELTER, C. H.
Enzymes activated by monovalent cations. bibliog il Science 168:789-95 My 15 '70
SUENENS, Léon Joseph, cardinal
Cardinal Suenens: a plea for dialogue; interview, ed. by H. Fesquet. por Cath World 211:216-20 Ag '70
about
In the steps of Pope John? T. Beeson. Chr Cent 87:1340-1 N 11 '70 *
Pope and the Cardinal. America 122:576-7 My 30 '70 *
Suenens calls for a new deal. J. A. O'Brien Chr Cent 87:818-21 Jl 1 '70 *
SUEZ CANAL
Buildup on the Suez: Soviet missiles. il Time 96:21 S 14 '70
In Israel cruel deaths, grave doubts; Israel and Russia along the canal. M. Elkins. il Newsweek 75:40-1 Je 1 '70
Ismailia childhood; Jewish members of the company. S. Eban. New Yorker 46:174-6+ D 5 '70
New missile sites threat to Israeli air supremacy. Aviation W 93:20 Ag 24 '70
Question of credence; buildup of Soviet missiles. il Newsweek 76:50-1 S 14 '70
Saboteurs of peace. il Newsweek 76:30 S 21 '70
Soviet policies south and east of Suez. T. B. Millar. For Affairs 49:70-80 O '70
Suez Canal: key to Soviet strategy in the Mideast? access to the Indian Ocean. il U S News 68:22-4 Je 22 '70
Suez Canal: the broken link. N. Mostert. il Read Digest 96:136-41 My '70
Trapped ships in the Suez Canal. il U S News 69:49 Jl 20 '70

SUEZ company. See Suez Canal
SUFFERING
Beethoven: a bicentennial tribute. F. E. Gaebelein. Chr Today 15:7-8+ D 4 '70
Costs of creativity; Beethoven's spiritual pilgrimage. Chr Cent 87:1471 D 9 '70
Inescapable fact; human suffering. V. P. McCorry. America 123:inside back cover S 12 '70
SUFFOLK Downs. See Race tracks
SUFFRAGE
See also
Voters, Registration of
Voting
Voting, Absent
Great Britain
Instant adults: teens to vote. Sr Schol 96:16 Ja 26 '70
United States
Age of Aquarius; Senate amendment to enfranchise eighteen-year-olds. Newsweek 75:30-1 Mr 23 '70
Big vote to come; youth vote; Supreme court decisions. il Time 97:24 Ja 4 '71
Congress lowers voting age. il Sr Schol 97:3 S 14 '70
Disfranchise the old; lesson of California. D. J. Stewart. New Repub 163:20-2 Ag 22 '70
Eighteen-year-old vote. Nation 212:36-7 Ja 11 '71
Eighteen-year-old vote. New Repub 162:10 My 2 '70; Reply. A. J. Mikva. 162:28-9 Je 6 '70
Generation gap; Oregon votes down lower voting age. il Newsweek 75:29 Je 8 '70
GOP and the Jewish vote. Cato. Nat R 22:1044 O 6 '70
History in an hour; 18 year old vote provision added to renewed Voting rights act of 1965. Time 95:13-14 Je 29 '70
Lower the voting age. America 122:549 My 23 '70
Lower the voting age? il PTA Mag 64:16-18+ Mr '70
Lower the voting age, why not? America 122:265 Mr 14 '70
National council supports voting rights for eighteen-year-olds. Chr Cent 87:167 F 11 '70
New constituency: eighteen-to-twenty-year group. Nation 211:2 Jl 6 '70
Now that Congress has O.K.'d the vote for eighteen-year-olds—. il U S News 68:42-3 Je 29 '70
Of many things; lowering the voting age. D. R. Campion. America 123:inside cover N 21 '70
'72 election factor; the teen-age vote. il U S News 70:16 Ja 4 '71
Splitting the difference; Supreme court ruling on youth vote. il Newsweek 77:18-19 Ja 4 '71
Teen-age vote hits snags. il U S News 69:32 N 23 '70
This month's feature: Congress & the voting-age controversy. Cong Digest 49:130-60 My '70
Vote at 18: a readers' roundup. Sr Schol 96:19 My 18 '70
Vote-at-18 campaigns grow. il Sr Schol 96:13-14 Mr 16 '70
Voting bars coming down. Sr Schol 95:Schol Teach 1 O 20 '69
Why not seventeen? proposal to lower voting age. Nat R 22:244-5 Mr 10 '70
Young at heart; bill to enfranchise 18-year-olds. il Newsweek 75:19 Je 29 '70
Youth and the vote. J. M. Carter. Ladies Home J 87:8 Ag '70
Youth is served; Senate votes to lower voting age. K. Crawford. Newsweek 75:29 Mr 30 '70
See also
Negroes—Politics and suffrage
Washington. D.C.—Politics and government
Woman suffrage—United States
SUFFRAGE amendment. See Woman suffrage—United States
SUFRIN, Mark
Case of the disappearing cook. il por Am Heritage 21:37-43 Ag '70
SUGA, Nobuo
Echo-ranging neurons in the inferior colliculus of bats. bibliog il Science 170:449-52 O 23 '70
SUGAR, James A.
Starfish threaten Pacific reefs. il Nat Geog 137:340-53 Mr '70
SUGAR
Work wonders with sugar. il Ladies Home J 87:126+ My '70
See also
Caramel
Glucose
Maple sugar

SUGAR—*Continued*

Manufacture and refining

Where sugar may turn bitter; Colonial sugar refining co. pulling out of Fiji. il Bsns W p46-7 Ap 25 '70

Physiological effects

Your family's health; sugar and the new theory about heart attacks. B. Yuncker. House & Gard 137:64-5 F '70

SUGAR bowls, etc.

Continental pewter epergnes, cruet stands, and sugar bowls. R. M. Vetter. il Antiques 98:88-93 Jl '70

SUGAR industry

Puerto Rico tries to cure sugar's ills. il Bsns W p61+ O 10 '70

Trends in output per man-hour in the sugar industry. J. W. Ferris, jr. and H. Gale. il Mo Labor R 93:32-4 Jl '70

SUGAR maple. See Maple

SUGAR refining. See Sugar—Manufacture and refining

SUGAR substitutes

After cyclamates: what's next on the FDA's food target list? K. N. Anderson. il Sci Digest 67:16-23 F '70

Aspartylphenylalanine methyl ester: a low-calorie sweetener. M. R. Cloninger and R. E. Baldwin. bibliog il Science 170:81-2 O 2 '70

Bladder tumors in rats fed cyclohexylamine or high doses of a mixture of cyclamate and saccharin. J. M. Price and others. bibliog il Science 167:1131-2 F 20 '70

Cyclamate acceptance. M. W. Wagner. bibliog Science 168:1605 Je 26 '70

Cyclamate ban. S. L. Inhorn and L. F. Meisner; discussion. Science 166:1575; 167:1436 D 26 '69. Mr 13 '70

Cyclamates: House report charges administrative alchemy at HEW. R. J. Bazell. Science 170:419-20 O 23 '70

Cytogenetic studies with cyclamate and related compounds. D. R. Stoltz and others. il Science 167:1501-2 Mr 13 '70

Diet sweeteners turn sour. Sr Schol 95:13 N 10 '69

FDA extends ban on cyclamates. T. P. Southwick. Science 169:962 S 4 '70

Fatter outlook for diet foods. il Bsns W p93+ Je 6 '70

Hazards to children's dental health: sweets and malnutrition. L. W. Sauer. il PTA Mag 64:31-2 F '70

Lessons cyclamates teach. Consumer Rep 35:59-60 Ja '70

Metabolism in the gut. Sci N 98:32 Jl 11 '70

New artificial sweeteners. il Chem 43:23-4 Je '70

Production of mouse urinary bladder carcinomas by sodium cyclamate. G. T. Bryan and E. Erturk. bibliog il Science 167:996-8 F 13 '70

Production of urinary bladder carcinomas in mice by sodium saccharin. G. T. Bryan and others. bibliog il Science 168:1238-40 Je 5 '70; Reply. L. P. Brower. 170:558 O 30 '70

Still on the block. Sci N 98:7 Jl 4 '70

Sweet news; saccharin investigation. Newsweek 76:43 Ag 3 '70

Total eclipse for cyclamates; FDA's decision. Time 96:60 Ag 31 '70

Why the ban on cyclamate sweeteners? Good H 170:137 Ja '70

SUGARBUSH VALLEY, Vt.

Flying visit. S. Wilkinson. Flying 86:128 F '70

SUGARMAN, Daniel A. and Hochstein, Rollie

How to get along with boys. il Seventeen 29:134-5+ F '70

SUGARS

See also

Lactose

SUGG, Arnold L. and Pardue, L. G.

Hurricane season of 1969. il Weatherwise 23:12-17+ F '70

SUGGESTION

Suggestion as sermon strategy. Chr Today 14:28-9 Mr 27 '69

SUGGS, Joseph E. and others

DDT metabolism: oxidation of the metabolite 2,2-bis(p-chlorophenyl)ethanol by alcohol dehydrogenase. Science 168:582 My 1 '70

SUHARTO, 1925-

President Soeharto of Indonesia visits the United States; exchange of greetings and toasts. May 26, 1970. Dept State Bul 62:743-6 Je 15 '70

about

Dukuns, bomohs and gurus. il Time 96:31 N 9 '70 *

Visit to the Netherlands, 1970

Emergency landing. il Time 96:33 S 14 '70

Overnight stay. il por Newsweek 76:60 S 14 '70

SUHOR, Charles

Case for pop scholarship: a polemic for popularizers. Engl J 59:116-18+ Ja '70

SUICIDE

Berlin syndrome. Time 95:92 Mr 30 '70

Black suicide. L. Banks. il Ebony 25:76-8+ My '70

Black suicide, by H. Hendin. Review

Trans-Action 7:85+ Jl '70. W. L. Yancey

Deaths in a youth program. E. J. Faux and B. Crawford. Ment Hy 54:569-71 O '70

Golden leap. il Time 96:40 Ag 24 '70

How to keep patients from jumping out of the window. Trans-Action 7:13 F '70

I want out; teens who threaten suicide. J. H. Pollack. il Todays Health 49:32-4+ Ja '71

No one cares; suicides at Rikers Island penitentiary. il Newsweek 75:51-2 Mr 2 '70

Peace suicides; Joan Fox and Craig Badiali of Blackwood, N.J. E. Asinof. Seventeen 29:174+ Mr '70

Racial oppression and black suicide; excerpts from Black suicide. H. Hendin. Cur 114:29-36 Ja '70

Self-destruction in Oedipus Rex. M. D. Faber. bibliog Am Imago 27:41-51 Spr '70

Suicide and civil rights. A. J. Snider. Sci Digest 67:54 Ja '70

Suicide and how to prevent it. M. O. Vincent. Chr Today 14:10-12 Ja 16 '70

Texas plane crash: nonviolent man's final act brings destruction and death. R. R. Winkelmann. Chr Cent 88:26+ Ja 6 '71

See also

Harakiri

SUICIDE prevention centers

I don't know why I'm calling, nobody can help me. B. Asbell. Redbook 135:53+ Je '70

Life you can save. C. P. Weikel. il Har Yrs 10:6-11 Ja '70

SUITE no. 3; ballet. See Ballets—Criticisms

SUITS at law. See Actions and defenses

SUK, Josef

Music to my ears; Suk by Susskind. I. Kolodin. il Sat R 53:96-7 Mr 14 '70

SUKARNO, 1901-1970

Indonesia: goodbye to *bapak*. il pors Time 95:32 Je 29 '70 *

Indonesia's Sukarno, 1901-1970. il por Newsweek 75:39 Je 29 '70 *

Obituary

Nation 211:35 Jl 20 '70 *

SUKIYAKI. See Cookery, Japanese

SULFIDES

See also

Hydrogen sulfide

Iron sulfides

SULFONYL compounds

Battle over a study; risks of oral hypoglycemic agents. Sci N 97:596 Je 20 '70

See also

Tolbutamide

SULFUR

Concentration and isotopic composition of carbon and sulfur in Apollo 11 lunar samples. I. R. Kaplan and J. W. Smith. bibliog il Science 167:541-3 Ja 30 '70

Sulfur. C. J. Pratt. il Sci Am 222:62-7+ My '70

Prices

Why sulfur hit its long slide. Bsns W p52 N 21 '70

SULFUR compounds

Sulfur: simulated long-range transport in the atmosphere. H. Reiquam. bibliog il Science 170:318-20 O 16 '70

SULFUR mines and mining

Canada

See also

Texas Gulf sulphur company

United States

See also

Freeport sulphur company

SULFUROUS hot springs. See Hot springs

SULLIVAN, Darrell T   See Widmoyer, F. B. jt. auth.

SULLIVAN, Frank

What urban redevelopment has done for Norfolk, Va. il Am City 85:60-1+ N '70

SULLIVAN, Frank, 1892-

Greetings, friends! poem. New Yorker 46:23 D 26 '70

about

Happy essence of Frank Sullivan. J. K. Hutchens. por Sat R 53:88-9 S 12 '70 *

SULLIVAN, J. R. See Rathjen, W. F. jt. auth.

SULLIVAN, James B. and Fritsch, A. J.
Getting the lead out. New Repub 163:9-10 N 21 '70

SULLIVAN, Leon Howard
Black for G.M.'s board. por Time 97:72 Ja 18 '71 *
GM's critics hail its new director. por Bsns W p 17 Ja 9 '71 *
Opening doors to opportunity. il pors Nations Bsns 58:48-9+ Ap '70 *

SULLIVAN, Leonor (Kretzer)
Excerpt from debate, July 31, 1970. Cong Digest 49:246+ O '70

SULLIVAN, Nancy
Snap judgments. Poetry 116:120-5 My '70

SULLIVAN, Nicholas
Life in the underground world. il Nat Wild-life 8:21-4 O '70

SULLIVAN, Walter
Our last great wilderness. il Am Heritage 21: 98-117 Ag '70
Writing science for the public. il por Phys Today 23:51-3 Ag '70

SULLIVAN, William H.
Department gives views on proposed congressional resolution on U.S. prisoners of war in southeast Asia; statement, May 6, 1970. Dept State Bul 62:668-71 My 25 '70
Treatment of American prisoners of war in North Viet-Nam; statement, November 13, 1969. Dept State Bul 61:596-9 D 22 '69

SULLY, Thomas
Portraits of Rebecca Gratz by Thomas Sully. H. R. London. pors Antiques 98:115-17 Jl '70 *

SULZBERGER, Cyrus Leo
Greece under the colonels. For Affairs 48: 300-11 Ja '70

SUMERIAN literature
See also
Gilgamesh

SUMMER
Summer is... H. Van Horne. il House B 112:49-9+ Je '70
Summer snapshot. J. Bishop. Read Digest 97: 77-8 Jl '70

SUMMER activities. See Vacation projects

SUMMER afternoon, summer afternoon; story. See Green, H.

SUMMER cabins. See Cabins

SUMMER camping. See Camping

SUMMER camps. See Camps

SUMMER candles; story. See Boles, P. D.

SUMMER cookery. See Cookery

SUMMER drinks. See Beverages

SUMMER furniture. See Furniture, Outdoor

SUMMER houses. See Garden houses, shelters, etc.

SUMMER jobs for students. See Student employment

SUMMER of the hero; story. See West, A.

SUMMER reading programs. See School children—Out-of-school activities

SUMMER resorts
Eighteen favorite resorts for family vacations. P. Plawin. il Bet Hom & Gard 48:109-14 F '70
Great American vacation scenes. B. Gillam. Mlle 70:258-61+ Ap '70
How to discover a resort. H. P. Koenig. il Travel 133:51-5 F '70
See also
Porto Ercole, Italy
Seaside resorts
Sun Valley, Idaho

SUMMER schools
Mexico's summer schools. Har Yrs 10:44-5 Ap '70
Study fiestas; Mexico's summer study and vacation courses. S. Hamburg. il Har Yrs 10:40-4 Ap '70
Summer school program in review. K. D. Streitmatter. Clear House 45:57 S '70
Talent runs free at the Twin Cities institute. C. Watson. il Am Ed 6:3-6 O '70
See also
School year

SUMMER vacations. See Vacations

SUMMER workshops. See Educational workshops

SUMMERALL, Henry, jr
What was the cup that Jesus had to drink? Chr Today 14:9-12 Jl 17 '70

SUMMERHOUSES. See Garden houses, shelters, etc.

SUMMERLIN, Edgar, and Cuscuna, Michael
Month's jazz. Am Rec G 36:924-5 Jl '70
—and Gerber, Leslie
In the pop bag. Am Rec G 36:602-5 Ap '70

SUMMERNATIONALS. See Automobile racing

SUMMERS, Elaine
Elaine Summers: new forms, new ideas! M. Harriton. il pors Dance Mag 44:66-73 S '70*

SUMMERS, Hollis
At the Christmas card counter; poem. Chr Cent 87:1515 D 16 '70
Staff of Durban; poem. Sat R 53:27 N 21 '70
Tour; poem. Sat R 53:61 F 28 '70

SUMMIT conferences. See International conferences

SUMNER, Lowell
Good earth and the golden rule. il Nat Parks 44:4-9 Ja '70

SUMNER, Robert W.
Who needs a radio check? Motor B 126:16 O '70

SUMTER, Fort. See Fort Sumter

SUN
Search for an effect of the sun on the frequency of 18-centimeter radiation. J. A. Ball and others. bibliog il Science 167:1755-7 Mr 27 '70
Sun, moon, and planets this month. See issues of Sky and telescope
See also
Eclipses, Solar
also headings beginning Solar

Atmosphere
Chromosphere-Corona transition region. G. W. Pneuman. il Sky & Tel 39:148-51 Mr '70

Corona
Pioneer 6: measurement of transient Faraday rotation phenomena observed during solar occultation. G. S. Levy and others; reply. K. H. Schatten. il Science 168: 365-6 Ap 17 '70
See also
Solar flares

Prominences
See also
Solar flares

SUN (newspaper)
Residuals for a robber; R. A. Biggs story of the Great train robbery. il por Newsweek 75:63 My 4 '70

SUN baths
Modern bowl for sunbathing. K. Isaacs. il Pop Sci 196:112-13+ F '70
Tan your way through winter. L. Hilts. il Todays Health 48:37-9 D '70

SUN burn. See Sunburn

SUN CITY, Ariz.
For the retired, a world all their own; with report by P. O'Neil. il Life 68:45-50 My 15 '70

SUN dials. See Sundials

SUN glasses
Clear facts about tinted eyeglasses. il Good H 170:182 Ap '70
New no-fog glasses. C. Conley. il Field & S 74:187 Ap '70
Shades. L. Hadley. il Holiday 47:46-7+ Je '70
Sunglasses for sportsmen. J. R. Gregg. il Field & S 74:50-1+ F '70

SUN in art
Seven kinds of sunburst. il Design 71:10-11+ Wint '69

SUN lamps. See Electric lamps

SUN storms. See Solar radiation

SUN tan. See Tan

SUN tan preparations. See Cosmetics

SUN VALLEY, Idaho
It's happening in Sun Valley; year-round recreational community. S. Braudy. il Am Home 73:50-3+ Ja '70
New direction for skiers: up. H. Ehrlich. il Look 34:41-3 F 24 '70
Out in Hemingway country. H. Bradshaw. il pors Field & S 75:70-1+ Je '70
Snowy Sun Valley. D. Taylor. il Travel 134:62-3 D '70

SUN worship
Feast of the sun; equatorial Indians around San Antonio de Pichincha. M. Acosta Solís. il Américas 22:24-30 O '70

SUNBURN
Sun: foe, not friend. Har Yrs 10:10 D '70
Sunburn's menace to the skin. il Consumer Bul 53:4+ Ag '70
Your skin vs winter sun. il Vogue 156:148-50 N 15 '70

SUNBURN lotions. See Cosmetics

SUND, Harald
Gallery; photographs. Life 68:8-11 My 22 '70

SUNDAES. See Ice cream, ices, etc.

SUNDAY dinner; drama. See Oates, J. C.

SUNDAY legislation
Bucking the blue laws. Chr Today 14:26 Ja 16 '70
Open and shut cases; Sunday selling. Nations Bsns 58:16 Ag '70
See also
Store hours
SUNDAY opening of libraries. See Libraries— Hours of opening
SUNDAY schools
See also
Religious education
SUNDAY supplements. See Newspapers—Magazine sections
SUNDAY telegraph
Prosecuting a leak. Newsweek 75:59+ Mr 30 '70
SUNDERLAND, John
Neurophysiology. M. S. Rothenberg. por Phys Today 23:24-5 My '70 *
SUNDIALS
About azimuth sundials. H. Egger. il Sky & Tel 40:94-5 Ag '70
Make this decorative yard ornament: armillary sphere. J. Dougherty. il Pop Mech 134:175 Jl '70
SUNDUN, Bruce G.
Bizarre case of Executive jet. il pors Bsns W p80-2+ O 24 '70
SUNFISH fishing
Behind the purple mask; the bluegill. A. J. McClane. il Field & S 75:108-11 N '70
Half a dozen for the pan; bluegills. J. Brooks. il Outdoor Life 146:88-9+ Jl '70
Where the bluegill is king. P. Barrett. il Field & S 75:34-5+ D '70
SUNFISHES
Sunfish family; and bass fishing. A. J. McClane. il Field & S 74:53-9+ Ap '70
SUNFLOWERS
Sunflowers aren't just for the birds! G. L'Allemand. il Org Gard & Farm 17:61-3 Ap '70
Winners in the 1970 sunflower contest. M. C. Goldman. il Org Gard & Farm 17:74-5 D '70
SUNGLASSES. See Sun glasses
SUNKEN treasure. See Treasure trove
SUNLIGHT
Sunlight patterns: unusual dark patches. C. J. Bowley and others; reply with rejoinder. E. P. McClain and A. E. Strong. bibliog Science 167:1757 Mr 27 '70
See also
Plants. Effect of light on
SUNNYVALE, Calif.
Computerized municipal information system. J. Gordon. il Am City 85:96-7+ Je '70
SUNRIVER, Ore.
Pollution-free paradise; with reports by B. Plumb and D. Connelly. il Am Home 74:33-9+ Ja '71
SUNSET garden. See Gardens—California
SUNSET garden contest. See Gardening—Competitions
SUNSPOTS
See also
Solar flares
SUNTAG, Murray
Expo '70. il Electr World 83:36-7 Mr '70
Radio & television news. Electr World 84:15-16 D '70; 85:5-6 Ja '71
Vacuum variable capacitors. Electr World 83:59 Ap '70
SUNTAN. See Tan
SUPAI Indians. See Havasupai Indians
SUPER 8 cameras. See Moving picture cameras
SUPER 8 film. See Moving picture films
SUPER markets. See Supermarkets
SUPER stock nationals. See Automobile racing
SUPERCHARGERS
Superchargers and turbochargers. E. Nabb. il Motor B 126:86-9 Jl '70
See also
Automobile engines—Superchargers
SUPERCONDUCTING electric transmission. See Electric transmission
SUPERCONDUCTING magnets. See Magnets
SUPERCONDUCTIVITY
How Josephson discovered his effect; adaptation of address, September 1970. P. W. Anderson. bibliog il por Phys Today 23:23-5+ N '70
Josephson detectors make astronomical observations. G. B. Lubkin. il Phys Today 23:55-6 Ap '70
Superconductivity in layered structure organometallic crystals. F. R. Gamble and others. bibliog il Science 168:568-70 My 1 '70
Superconductivity in two dimensions. D. E. Thomsen. il Sci N 97:602-3 Je 20 '70; Discussion. 98:108 Ag 8 '70
Theory versus experiment. Sci N 97:313 Mr 28 '70

Conferences
Pessimists and optimists discuss superconductivity at Stanford. B. B. Schwartz. Phys Today 23:79+ Ap '70
SUPERCONDUCTORS
Cryogenics: new superconducting materials announced at Dallas. R. W. Holcomb. Science 168:103 Ap 3 '70
Saving space with superconductors; Stanford linear accelerator. il Sci N 98:317 O 17 '70
SUPERFLUIDITY. See Fluid dynamics
SUPERGIANT stars. See Stars, Giant
SUPERHETERODYNE recievers. See Radio receivers, Superheterodyne
SUPERHIGHWAYS. See Express highways
SUPERIMPOSURES. See Photomontage
SUPERINTENDENTS, School. See School superintendents and principals
SUPERIOR, LAKE
Call it Lake inferior. G. Laycock. il Audubon 72:48-53 My '70
SUPERIOR colliculus. See Brain
SUPERIOR men. See Great men
SUPERIOR national forest, Minn. See National forests
SUPERMARKET unit pricing. See Unit pricing
SUPERMARKETS
Arden-Mayfair's busy checkout counter. il Bsns W p 126+ Je 6 '70
Blind dates in the supermarket. J. Cross. Nation 211:434-6 N 2 '70
Chain store that dared. H. Sirota. il Org Gard & Farm 17:66-7 Ag '70
Grocery bills; effect of discount pricing in Washington, D.C. D. Sanford. New Repub 163:12-14 O 17 '70
Growing into trouble; Detroit's Allied supermarkets. il Forbes 105:50 Je 15 '70
Smell it, then sell it; supermarket dating of products. New Repub 162:8-9 Ap 25 '70
Supermarket trap, by J. Cross. Review Nation 211:694-5 D 28 '70. H. Maurer
Trading stamps vs. discounts: the housewife's choice. il U S News 69:61-2 N 23 '70
Truth that saves money in the supermarket. V. Cadden. Redbook 135:30+ Jl '70
See also
Great Atlantic and Pacific tea company
SUPERNATURAL
See also
Occult sciences
SUPERNATURAL moving pictures. See Moving pictures—Horror films
SUPEROXIDES. See Oxides
SUPERSONIC air travel. See Air travel
SUPERSONIC airplanes. See Airplanes, Supersonic
SUPERSTITION
Spooked in the cradle of the deep. il Changing T 24:24 Je '70
See also
Animal lore
Astrology
Fairies
Fortune telling
Occult sciences
Witchcraft
SUPERVISORS
Communicate through your supervisors. L. I. Gelfand. Harvard Bsns R 48:101-4 N '70
SUPERVISORS, Library. See Library administration
SUPERVISORS of student teaching
Beast of burden or playboy? Which role for the student teachers' college supervisors. J. R. Cumming. bibliog Clear House 44:437-40 My '70
University supervisor: a student teacher's best friend. R. C. Jones. bibliog Clear House 44:433-6 Mr '70
SUPPERS
Après-ski supper with Killy. il Ladies Home J 86:100-1+ D '69
Breezy summer suppers. il Good H 171:88-103 Ag '70
See also
Buffet meals
SUPPLEMENTAL airlines. See Airlines—Nonscheduled operations; Local service airlines
SUPPLEMENTARY employment
How to moonlight as a freelancer. A. F. Gonzales, jr. il Writers Digest 50:28-31 F '70
Moonlighters: their motivations and characteristics; with tables. V. C. Perrella. Mo Labor R 93:57-64 Ag '70
SUPPLY and demand
See also
Consumption (economics)

SUPPLY and demand of teachers; Supply and demand of librarians; etc. See Teachers—Supply and demand; Librarians—Supply and demand; etc.

SUPPORTS, Plant. See Garden stakes and staking

SUPREME commander for allied powers. See Japan—History—Allied occupation, 1945-1952

SUPREME court of the United States. See United States—Supreme court

SUPREMES (singers) See Negro singers

SURDAM, Ronald C. See Mariner, R. H. jt. auth.

SURECK, Nancy
Return to Cozumel. il Travel & Camera 33: 10+ N '70

SURF fishing. See Salt water fishing

SURF riding
Body surfing. B. B. Smith. il Travel 134:550-3 Jl '70
Desert blooms with surf; Tempe, Ariz. il Life 68:48-9 Mr 6 '70
Shooting the big surf. D. James. il pors Travel & Camera 33:40-5 Ja '70
Surfing in the desert; Tempe, Ariz. il Parks & Rec 5:38+ My '70
Surfing on the wind; surfboard with sail. il Mech Illus 66:61 Jl '70

SURF seamanship. See Seamanship

SURFACE, Bill
Boss of the ball park. il Read Digest 97:17-25 Ag '70
Case of the runaway teen-ager. il Read Digest 96:143-6 My '70
Controversy over the pill. il por Good H 170: 64-5+ Ja '70
Growing menace of pep pills. Seventeen 29: 146-7+ My '70
Pro quarterback: toughest job in sports. il Read Digest 97:187-8+ N '70
Seaver prepares to strike. il pors N Y Times Mag p36-7+ Ap 5 '70
Super horse goes out to pasture. il Read Digest 96:187-8+ Ap '70
Thumbs down on hitchhiking! il Read Digest 96:128-31 Ja '70

SURFACE active substances
Pulmonary surfactant and evolution of the lungs. J. A. Clements and others. bibliog il Science 169:603-4 Ag 7 '70

SURFACE effect vehicles. See Air cushion vehicles

SURFACE films. See Films

SURFACE tension
Superdense water. B. V. Derjaguin. il Sci Am 223:52-64+ bibliog(p 132) N '70

SURFACE treatment of pavements. See Pavements—Surface treatment

SURFACES
Composition differences at surfaces detected by adsorption and desorption of radiotracers. D. A. Brandreth and R. E. Johnson. il Science 169:864 Ag 28 '70
See also
Thin films

SURFACTANTS. See Surface active substances

SURFING. See Surf riding

SURGEON general's advisory committee on television and social behavior. See United States—Surgeon general's advisory committee on television and social behavior

SURGEONS
Making of a surgeon; condensation. W. A. Nolen. il Read Digest 97:209-12+ N '70
Making of a surgeon; experience of W. A. Nolen. por Newsweek 76:77-8 D 14 '70
See also
Cooley, D. A.
DeBakey, M. E.
Harvey Cushing society

SURGERY
It's cut, cut, cut in the U.S.A. Trans-Action 7:6 Je '70
Tell me, doctor, what about sex after my operation? W. A. Nolen. Ladies Home J 87:162-4 O '70
See also
American college of surgeons
Cesarean section
Chemosurgery
Children—Surgery
Malpractice
Orthopedia
Surgeons
also subhead Surgery under names of organs and regions of the body, e.g. Blood vessels—Surgery

SURGERY, Cosmetic. See Surgery, Plastic

SURGERY, Military
See also
Vietnamese war, 1957- —Medical and sanitary affairs

SURGERY, Plastic
Cosmetic surgery. B. Wysor. Harp Baz 103: 94-5+ Jl '70
Cosmetic surgery comes of age; symposium. il McCalls 97:74-7 Ap '70
Cosmetics, trick or treat. Har Yrs 10:12 D '70
Diary of a face-lift. F. Evan. McCalls 97: 56+ Ap '70
Face-lifts for men. R. H. Berg. il pors Look 34:80-2+ D 1 '70
Facelift; excerpts from Plastic surgery; beauty you can buy. H. La Barre. il Ladies Home J 87:66+ Mr '70
Girl who found a face. J. L.Block. il Good H 170:30+ Ap '70; Same abr. Read Digest 97: 49-53 Jl '70
Importance of noses. S. Morini. il Vogue 156: 138-9 O 1 '70
Retreads in Rio; world capital of vanity surgery. Time 95:71 Mr 23 '70
Silicone for implantation in the body; use of dimethylpolysiloxane. il Chem 43:24 Ja '70
Transplants that help disfigured faces. M. W. Martin. il Sci Digest 68:81-3 Jl '70
Will a new nose make you happier? A. Lake. il Seventeen 29:162-3+ Ap '70

SURGERY, Primitive
See also
Trephining

SURGICAL instruments and apparatus
See also
Catheters

SURGICAL operations. See Surgery

SURGICAL research
See also
American college of surgeons

SURINAM
See also
Natural resources—Surinam

Description and travel
Startling Surinam. S. G. Slappey. il Travel 135:36-41+ Ja '71

Economic conditions
See also
Surinam—Industries

Industries
Surinam. R. Tirtha and C. Loeser. bibliog il Focus 21:1-11 S '70

SURNAMES. See Names, Personal

SURPRISE for mother; drama. See Miller, H. L.

SURREALISM (art)
Ghosts at noon; work of P. C. Curtis. il Time 96:76-7 O 5 '70
Paris: the new surrealists. C. Cutler. il Art in Am 58:129-32 Mr '70
See also
Art, Fantastic

SURRENDER. See Capitulations, Military

SURRENDER, Psychology of. See War—Psychological aspects

SURREY, Stanley S.
Value-added tax: the case against. il Harvard Bsns R 48:86-94 N '70

SURRIDGE, Robin
Doing it small. il Yachting 128:60-1+ N '70

SURTAX. See Income tax—United States

SURVEYING
See also
Building sites

SURVEYING, Aerial
See also
Photogrammetry

SURVEYING instruments
Surveyors' equipment and the western frontier. W. H. Guthman. il Antiques 98:423-7 S '70

SURVEYORS, Marine
Marine surveyor. W. Juettner. il Motor B 125:60+ F '70

SURVEYS. See Religious surveys and similar headings

SURVIVAL after airplane accidents, shipwrecks, etc.
Surviving at sea. il Mech Illus 66:78 S '70
See also
Wilderness survival

SURVIVAL after death. See Immortality

SURVIVAL and emergency equipment
Useful survival kit for auto travelers. il Sunset 144:155 Ap '70

SURVIVAL of man. See Man—Survival

SURVIVAL of the fittest. See Natural selection

SUSAN Hill is having a baby; story. See Naughton, P. J.

SUSANN, Jacqueline
Along came Joe. il por Ladies Home J 87: 74+ Ap '70

SUSPENSION, Automobile. See Automobiles—
Springs and suspension
SUSPENSION roofs. See Roofs, Suspension
SUSSEP, Peol
Case of Peol Sussep. F. W. Hatch. il Sat R
53:17 Jl 11 '70 *
SUSSKIND, Walter
Music to my ears; Suk by Susskind. I.
Kolodin. il Sat R 53:96-7 Mr 14 '70 *
SUSSMAN, Irving M.
Rise and fall of the Roman image. America
122:500-2 My 9 '70
SUTCLIFFE, James Helme
Berlin diary. il pors Opera N 35:8-13 N 21 '70
Music-lover's guide to Berlin. il Opera N
34:6-13 F 28 '70
SUTER, Carrie Rice
Black tho' I be . . ; poem. Negro Hist Bul
33:126 My '70
SUTER, J. W.
Send, we pray thee O God; excerpt from
Prayers of the spirit. il Good H 171:59 D '70
SUTHEIM, Peter
Build an equipment cart. il Radio-Electr 41:
41 S '70
Get better sound from your stereo. il Radio-
Electr 41:40-2 O '70
SUTHERLAND, Don
Added attractions. Travel & Camera 33:74-5
S '70
Movies (cont of) Movie tips for travelers. See
issues of Travel & camera
Why I film my travels. Travel & Camera 33:
77-8+ Ja '70
SUTHERLAND, Donald
Who was that guy? J. Larsen. pors Time 95:
41 F 2 '70
SUTHERLAND, Frank, and Bogen, R. W.
Warner school is the place to come. Todays
Ed 59:48-9 F '70
SUTHERLAND, Ivan E.
Computer displays; with biographical sketch.
il Sci Am 222:12, 56-60+ bibliog(p 152 Je
'70
SUTHERLAND, Joan
Pinnacle; interview, ed. by F. Rizzo. pors
Opera N 34:14-16 Ap 4 '70
Tour of two great throats; interviews, ed. by
R. Meryman. il pors Life 68:63-4+ Je 26 '70

about

Marilyn. Joan and Norma. H. Saal il pors
Newsweek 75:63 Mr 16 '70 *
Sutherland-Horne Norma. I. Kolodin. Sat
R 53:28 Mr 21 '70 *
SUTHERLAND, O. B.
(ed) See Felknor, B. L. Dream and night-
mares in the future for books
SUTHERLAND, Zena
Books for young people. See issues of Sat-
urday review
SUTPHEN, Melissa
(ed) See Orbach, J. Jerry Orbach
SUTTER, Richard P.
Trisporic acid synthesis in blakeslea trispora.
bibliog il Science 168:1590-2 Je 26 '70
SUTTMEIER, Richard P. See Orleans, L. A. jt.
auth.
SUTTON, George Miksch
Good day at Black Mesa; with paintings.
Audubon 72:58-67 Jl '70
Jenny Lind's island. il Audubon 72:14-35 S '70
SUTTON, Horace
African Riviera. il Sat R 53:37-8+ O 24 '70
Booked for travel. il Sat R 53:42-4 Mr 7; 51-
2+ My 9; 34+ Je 13; 36-7 Jl 18; 38+ S 5; 39-
41 D 19 '70
Drugs: ten years to doomsday? il Sat R 53:
18-21+ N 14 '70
Erosion of Eden. il Sat R 53:58-61+ Je 6 '70
Hawaii's Hawaii. il Travel & Camera 33:30-9
Ja '70
Is the SST really necessary? il Sat R 53:
14-17+ Ag 15 '70
Special travel correspondent. Holiday 47:14+
Ja; 12+ F; 12+ Mr; 7-8+ Ap; 8+ My; 8 Je;
12-15 Jl '70
Traveler finds his voice. Sat R 54:14 Ja 2 '71
Walking the plank at 30,000 feet. il Sat R
54:30-2+ Ja 2 '71
SUTTON, Johanna G.
Consider the confined: methods of reaching
in. il Wilson Lib Bul 45:485-9 Ja '71
SUTTON, Willie
Willie Sutton, bankers' friend. por Time 96:
106 O 26 '70 *
SUVA, Fiji
When the ship stops in Fiji. il Sunset 144:54
F '70
SUYDAM, Marilyn N.
(ed) Continuing the math revolution: ex-
cerpts from interviews. Am Ed 6:26-30 Ja
'70

SUYKER, Betty
Up the years from cassoulet. Atlan 226:110+
D '70
SUZMAN, Helen
South Africa's lonely liberal. il pors Life 68:
58C-59D My 15 '70 *
SUZUKI, David T.
Temperature-sensitive mutations in drosoph-
ila melanogaster; adaptation of address,
August 1969. bibliog il Science 170:695-706
N 13 '70
SUZUKI, Harumi. See Matsuyama M. jt. auth.
SUZUKI, Yoshiko. See Stormont, C. jt. auth.
SUZUKI, Yukihisa
Above politics: how U.S. and Japanese li-
brarians cleared the way for true profes-
sional exchange. bibliog il Wilson Lib Bul
44:1054-9 Je '70
SUZY, pseud. See Mehle, A.
SVEC, Kathryn H. and Allen, S. T.
Antibody to nuclear material eluted from
isolated spleen vessels in systemic lupus
erythematosus. bibliog il Science 170:550-1
O 30 '70
SVEHAG, S. E. and Bloth, B.
Ultrastructure of secretory and high-polymer
serum immunoglobulin A of human and
rabbit origin. bibliog il Science 168:847-9 My
15 '70
SWADOS, Harvey
City's island of the damned. il N Y Times
Mag p24-5+ Ap 26 '70
SWALLOWING
Looking into swallowing problems; barium
fudge for X-ray contrast media. J. Bockel
il Sci N 97:601 Je 20 '70
SWAMPS. See Marshes
SWAN, Jon
Invisible nation; story. Atlan 226:99-101 O '70
Mab; poem. Atlan 227:79 Ja '71
Metamorphosis; poem. New Yorker 46:33 Je
20 '70
Return; poem. New Yorker 46:62 Jl 4 '70
SWAN, Lawrence W.
Goose of the Himalayas; with biographical
sketch. il Natur Hist 79:6, 68-75 D '70
SWAN ISLANDS
U.S. and Honduras to negotiate Swan Islands
sovereignty issue. Dept State Bul 61:550 D
15 '69
SWAN lake: ballet. See Ballets—Criticisms
SWANBERG, W. A.
Spies who came in from the sea. il Am
Heritage 21:66-9+ Ap '70
SWANN, Brian
Catch; poem. Yale R 59:397 Mr '70
(tr) See Pavese, C. Untitled
(tr) See Piccolo, L. Days
SWANN, Loraine E.
Crisis in our cities. Engl J 59:570-2 Ap '70
SWANN, Peter C.
Rockefeller ceramics: China and Japan. il
Art N 69:50-1+ S '70
SWANS
How I adopted Nijinsky, my son the swan;
Peter Scott's Wildfowl trust, Slimbridge,
England. G. Cant. il Sports Illus 32:58-9 Ap
6 '70
Victory for beauty, with some human help
the trumpeter swan soars back; with edi-
torial comment by R. Graves. il Life 68:3,
48-55 Ap 10 '70
SWANSON, Gordon I.
Myth of urbanism. Ed Digest 36:34-5 S '70
SWARTZ, Roderick G.
Community finds its forum. il Am Lib 1:554-
61 Je '70
SWARTZ, W. W.
Optimizing space requirements for elevators.
il Arch Rec 147:133-6 Mr '70
SWEARINGEN, Wilna
Student writing that sells. Todays Ed 59:31
F '70
SWEARINGEN company
Swearingen revises production schedule. Avi-
ation W 92:25 My 11 '70
SWEAT, Joseph
Father Buh Buh Boo; story. Harper 241:72-
8 S '70
Renewal: Tennessee model. T. M. Gannon.
America 122:152-5+ F 14 '70 *
SWEATING. See Perspiration
SWEDBERG, Jack, and Scott, Carl
Old chiseltooth master craftsman of the
woods. il Nat Wildlife 8:10-12 Ag '70
SWEDEN
See also
Airplanes, Military—Sweden
Ballet—Sweden
Bohuslan
Childrens literature—Sweden

SWEDEN—See also—*Continued*
  Elections—Sweden
  Environmental movement—Sweden
  Morale, National—Sweden
  Political campaigns—Sweden
  Postal service—Sweden
  Taxation—Sweden
  Trade unions—Sweden

Economic policy
Coping with change. por Bsns W p29 N 7 '70

Economic relations
Europe, Western
Common market's reluctant applicant. Bsns
  W p29 N 7 '70

Foreign relations
Palme's picnic; U.S. visit. il por Newsweek
  75:44+ Je 22 '70
Sweden; neutrality, not silence; address, June
  5, 1970. O. Palme. Vital Speeches 36:578-80
  Jl 15 '70

United States
  See United States—Foreign relations—
  Sweden

Moral conditions
Latest scoop on Swedish sex. D. W. Ferm.
  il Chr Cent 87:45-8 Ja 14 '70; Discussion.
  87:243 F 25 '70

Politics and government
Sweden: antidotes to welfare. C. Eisendrath.
  Nation 211:390-2 O 26 '70
  See also
  Elections—Sweden
  Political parties—Sweden

SWEDISH cookery. See Cookery, Swedish
SWEDISH explorers. See Explorers, Swedish
SWEDISH International peace research Insti-
  tute. See International institute for peace
  and conflict research
SWEENEY, Francis
  Buildings; poem. America 122:585 My 30 '70
SWEENEY, James K.
  Small company enters the European market.
  Harvard Bsns R 48:126-32 S '70
SWEENEY, Michael
  From Dustbowl to Saigon: the "Peoples
  bank" builds an empire. il por Ramp Mag
  9:24-5+ N '70
SWEENEY, Mike
  Face to face with an actively political anti-
  pollutionist. por Seventeen 29:42 Mr '70
SWEEP generators. See Signal generators
SWEEPERS, Street. See Street cleaning ap-
  paratus
SWEEPSTAKES. See Lotteries
SWEET, Debra Jean
  Sweet 'n' sour encounter. Chr Cent 87:1547
  D 23 '70 *
SWEET, Gladys
  Murder trial of Dr Ossian Sweet; reprint.
  T. J. Fleming. il pors Ebony 25:106-8+ O
  '70 *
SWEET, Ossian H.
  Murder trial of Dr Ossian Sweet; reprint.
  T. J. Fleming. il pors Ebony 25:106-8+
  O '70 *
SWEET banana peppers. See Peppers
SWEET potatoes
  Sweet potatoes are prolific. V. Tripp. il Org
  Gard & Farm 17:86-7 Ap '70
  You can still get the redgolds. O. Raney. il
  por Org Gard & Farm 17:94-5 S '70
  See also
  Cookery—Vegetables
SWEET scented shrub
  Spice bush, subtle color, fragrance; calycan-
  thus occidentalis. il Sunset 145:199 D '70
SWEETENING agents. See Sugar substitutes
SWEETKIND, Morris
  Poetry in a scientific world. Engl J 59:359-66
  Mr '70
SWEGLE, Wayne E.
  Across the editor's desk. Suc Farm 69:20
  Ja '71
SWEIG, Martin
  Indictments for two. por Time 95:16 Ja 26 '70
  McCormack's reapers? por Newsweek 75:16 Ja
  26 '70
  Voice of the Speaker. Newsweek 76:23 Jl 20
  '70 *
SWENSON, May
  On its way; poem. Harper 241:16 O '70
SWIDLER, Leonard
  Jesus was a feminist. il Cath World 212:177-
  83 Ja '71
SWIFT, Edward F.
  Try an ice box on wheels, and change an in-
  dustry. il por Nations Bsns 58:108-9 Ja '70

SWIFT, H. F. and others
  Apollo 12 lunar module impact: laboratory
  simulation and possible downrange ballistic
  effects. bibliog il Science 169:851-4 Ag 28
  '70
SWIFT, Michael R.
  What's ahead in medicine? il Parents Mag
  45:35-7+ Ja '70
SWIFT and company
  One man's poison. il Forbes 105:56 Ap 1 '70
  Savings for you and the government. Na-
  tions Bsns 58:20 Ja '70
  Try an ice box on wheels, and change an
  industry. E. F. Swift. il Nations Bsns 58:
  108-9 Ja '70
SWIGERT, John L. 1931-
  We had no warnings, just a tremendous bang.
  il por Life 68:28-31 My 1 '70

about
  Brave men of Apollo. il pors Time 95:16-17
  Ap 27 '70 *
  See also
  Space flight to the moon—Manned flights—
  Apollo 13 flight
SWIGGETT, Hal
  Pied Piper of Texas. il Nat Wildlife 8:34-5
  F '70
SWIMMER'S Itch. See Schistosomiasis
SWIMMING
  Age of amphibians; A.A.U. national outdoor
  swimming championships. Time 96:50 S 7
  '70
  As easy as taking a stroll; ed. by C. Phinizy.
  J. E. Counsilman. il por Sports Illus 33:38-
  43 Jl 20 '70
  How to make a slow buck; marathon swim-
  ming. D. Levin. il Sports Illus 33:56+ S 7
  '70
  Impatience of Mrs Job. R. Blount, jr. il pors
  Sports Illus 33:24-9 Ag 24 '70
  Love-in at the Utah natatorium; swimming
  coach D. Reddish. W. F. Reed. il por Sports
  Illus 32:50+ Mr 16 '70
  Now look who's an old lady; D. Meyer. J.
  Kirshenbaum. il pors Sports Illus 33:18-20+
  Ag 31 '70
  Redemption after a false start: Indiana at
  NCAA swimming meet. W. F. Reed. il por
  Sports Illus 32:26-7 Ap 6 '70
  Swimming isn't everything, winning is; credo
  of A. Spitz. W. F. Reed. il pors Sports
  Illus 32:26-9 Mr 9 '70

Safety devices and measures
Be sure you'll be around to swim next year!
  install a rescue station. il Consumer Bul
  53:20 Jl '70
Water-safety rules that can save your life.
  il Good H 171:143 Jl '70

Study and teaching
Refreshing change in the ARC swimming
  program. A. W. Beck. il Camp Mag 42:18-19
  F '70
SWIMMING (animal locomotion) See Animal
  locomotion
SWIMMING clubs
  How to start a community swim club. Good
  H 171:150 Ag '70
SWIMMING coaches. See Coaches (athletics)
SWIMMING pool fences. See Fences
SWIMMING pools
  Everyone into the pool, and a pool for every-
  one; Overland Park, Kan. D. E. Pipes.
  il Am City 85:91-2 N '70
  Floating swimming pools: proposed use of
  Liberty ships around New York city. Y.
  Fogel. il Parks & Rec 5:30-1 Ap '70
  How to start a community swim club. Good
  H 171:150 Ag '70
  Municipal swimming center; Rockville, Md.
  N. A. Ofsthun. il Parks & Rec 5:31-2 My
  '70
  New York's new pool/play centers. il Arch
  Rec 148:162-3 O '70
  Swimming pools galore; King County, Wash.
  R. Sigismund. il Parks & Rec 5:35 My '70
SWIMMING pools, Home
  Get in the swim, with a family pool. J. R.
  Cary. il Parents Mag 45:62-5 Jl '70
  Pool that comes in a kit. A. Epstein. il Mech
  Illus 66:80+ Jl '70
  Pools and poolhouses. il House B 112:50-64
  Je '70
  Swim in your garden this summer. H. H.
  Fogel. il Home Gard 57:41-8 Ap '70
  Swimming pool art. il Life 69:76-80 O 9 '70
  You don't have to have a diving board to
  have interesting diving; hydro-massage
  pools. il Sunset 145:58-61 Jl '70

SWIMMING pools, Home—*Continued*

Equipment

Motorized cover rolls over swimming pool. H. F. Unger. il Pop Sci 196:98 F '70

SWIMMING suits. See Bathing suits

SWINDLERS and swindling. See Fraud

SWINE

Hog extra. See issues of Farm journal
Hog management (cont of) What's new. R. J. Fee. See issues of Successful farming
New way to get feeder pigs; feeder pig co-op. J. Russell. il Farm J 93:H10-11+ O '69
News from around the hog industry (cont of) News. See issues of Farm journal
Parting shots; the country's cops finally discover that pigs are . . . il Life 69:64-6 Jl 31 '70
Watching the animals; Des Moines slaughterhouse. R. Rhodes. il Harper 240:91-4 Mr '70

Care

Hog problems: what to do. R. J. Fee. il Suc Farm 68:48-9 O '70
How to avoid feet and leg problems. L. Lucas. il Farm J 94:H26 Mr '70
How to handle newly purchased pigs. Suc Farm 68:D6 Ag '70
Produce twice as many pigs per sow. J. Russell. Farm J 94:H7 Ap '70
Tail-biting: more trouble than you think. W. R. Prafka. por Farm J 93:H19 O '69

Confinement methods

Produce more pigs with less labor. J. Russell. il Farm J 94:H12-13 N '70
Put your confined sows on a diet. J. Russell. il Farm J 94:H10-11+ F '70
Sow confinement with a Texas twist. il Suc Farm 68:D6 N '70
Tethers: best way to handle sows? J. Russell. il Farm J 94:H10+ Ap '70
See also
Swine farrowing crates and pens

Diseases and pests

Atrophic rhinitis cause still in doubt. Suc Farm 68:no2 A14 F '70
Disease you may not recognize; sub-clinical infections. W. R. Prafka. il Farm J 94:H18-19 Ag '70
Effective TGE vaccines are here. R. Wilmore. Farm J 94:47 My '70
How to fight those costly bacterial infections; interview, ed. by R. Wilmore. N. Becker. il Farm J 94:H10-12 Mr '70
New facts about MMA. R. J. Fee. Suc Farm 68:no5 B26 Mr '70
Prompt treatment whips hog flu. W. R. Prafka. Farm J 93:H22 N '69
TGE, here are the facts. R. Fee. il Suc Farm 68:30-1 Ja '70
TGE: prevention is your only control. W. R. Prafka. por Farm J 94:H24-25 F '70
Why gilts have small litters; SMEDI virus. R. Wilmore. Farm J 94:20 Jl '70
See also
Hog cholera
Parasites—Livestock
Swine—Health certification

Feeding

Annals of medicine; case of organic mercury poisoning by pork from hogs fed surplus seed grain chemically treated. B. Roueché. New Yorker 46:64-70+ Ag 22 '70
Are you shorting your hogs on protein? R. Wilmore. Farm J 93:H7+ O '69
Feeding ideas for hogmen. R. J. Fee. il Suc Farm 68:G1 Ap '70
He pastures pigs all the way. R. J. Fee. il Suc Farm 68:32-3 My '70
High-lysine corn: boon for hogmen? J. Russell. il Farm J 94:H12-13+ S '70
Hogmen try high-lysine corn. B. Eftink. il Suc Farm 69:B8 Ja '71
New problem: hogs may need more vitamin E. Suc Farm 68:no3 A4 F '70
Other grains perform as well as corn, if you maintain amino acid levels. A. H. Jensen. il Farm J 94:H18-19 N '70
Should you feed your own soybeans? A. Oppedal. il Farm J 94:H10-11+ N '70
What are heated soybeans worth? G. R. Carlisle. il Farm J 94:H18 Mr '70
You can feed wheat. W. G. Luce il Farm J 93:H16 N '69
See also
Antibiotic feed supplements

Grading and standardization

How Roy Keppy picks a champion. J. Russell. il Farm J 94:H28 F '70
USDA feeder pig grades; USDA slaughter barrow grades. R. J. Fee. il Suc Farm 68:8 Ap '70

Health certification

Pig passports: they keep changing. il Suc Farm 68:D14-15 N '70

Marketing

Perfect hog marketing system. Farm J 94: H14+ F; H7 Mr; H16+ Ap; H7+ My; H7 Ag; H31 S '70
What makes these guys so efficient? B. Coffman. Farm J 93:H7 N '69
Who will control hog marketing. R. Wilmore. Farm J 94:B16 S '70
You can put yourself in the big boys' shoes. R. Wilmore. il Farm J 93:H8-9 N '69

Preconditioning

Pre-condition feeder pigs? J. Russell. Farm J 94:H20-1 Mr '70

Prices

How long will it last? il Farm J 94:H19 Ap '70
Market analysis. See issues of Farm journal
Price forecast. See issues of Farm journal
Short supply booms prices. il Farm J 93:H23 N '69
What can you afford to pay for feeder pigs? il Suc Farm 68:G12 My '70
What's ahead for hog prices? il Suc Farm 69:18 Ja '71

SWINE, Wild. See Woods hogs

SWINE auctions. See Auctions

SWINE breeding

Keep your farrowing house at capacity. J. Russell. Farm J 94:H12-13 Ap '70
Super pig. il Suc Farm 68:no5 22-3 Mr '70
Ten tips for more pigs. Suc Farm 68:no2 A8 F '70

SWINE cholera. See Hog cholera

SWINE farm management

He made a bankrupt system work. il Suc Farm 68:B5 O '70
Hog management ideas worth repeating. R. J. Fee. Suc Farm 69:24-5+ Ja '71
I couldn't use more live pigs! R. Wilmore. il Farm J 94:H14+ S '70
Practical pig pact. R. J. Fee. il Suc Farm 68:no5 A8 Mr '70
Successful hog management. il Suc Farm 68: D1+ Ag; D1-3+ S; D1-3+ N '70

Study and teaching

See Farm management—Study and teaching

SWINE farms

Farrowing co-ops coming on strong. J. Russell. il Farm J 94:H9+ O '70
He's big on eighty acres. R. Sanders. il Suc Farm 68:D30 O '70
Is this a good time to go into the hog business? D. Hanson. Suc Farm 68:28 O '70
Kansas hog setup planned for the future. il Suc Farm 68:D4-5 Ag '70
Pork: farming's new growth industry. J. Russell. il Farm J 94:H8-9+ My '70
Sow spreads in cow country. N. Baxter. il Farm J 94:H12-13+ F '70

Equipment

Five easy-open gates for sow feeding stalls; photographs. Farm J 94:H20 O '70

SWINE farrowing crates and pens

Easy way to keep farrowing crates disease-free: flame sterilization. B. Lovelidge. il Farm J 94:33 Ja '70
He calls it a piggy bank. il Suc Farm 68:D12 N '70
How he handles 600 sows. il Suc Farm 68: D6+ S '70
Ideas that ease your farrowing house chores. il Farm J 94:H10-11 S '70
Make money with a $1000 per sow investment? G. Lorang. il Farm J 93:H10-12 N '69
Modify open-front for low-cost nursery. J. Russell. il Farm J 94:H17 O '70
Scotland's corn belt hog farm. J. Russell. Farm J 94:50T Mr '70

SWINE house floors. See Swine houses—Floors

SWINE houses

AG college ideas worth copying. il Suc Farm 68:D8 Ag '70
Guidelines to buying packaged hog systems. A. J. Muehling. il Suc Farm 68:A10 Ja '70
Low-cost gestation barn built around feeding stalls. G. Lorang. il Farm J 94:28A N '70
Low-profile, low-cost hog house. R. J. Fee. il Suc Farm 68:no3 30-1 F '70
New twist: pie-shaped hog house. il Suc Farm 68:L4 O '70
One man looks after 1000 hogs in an hour. il Farm J 94:H8-9 Mr '70
Plan for comfort when you build. W. R. Prafka. il Farm J 94:H8-9 Mr '70

SWINE houses—*Continued*
  Southwest hogmen plan for top pork profits.
    il Suc Farm 68:D2-3 S '70
  This hog setup rates tops on all counts.
    il Suc Farm 68:D2-3 N '70
  Weaning house with all the comforts. il Suc
    Farm 68:D8+ N '70
    See also
  Swine—Confinement methods

Equipment
    See also
  Swine—Confinement methods
  Swine farrowing crates and pens

Floors
  Build slats or buy them? il Farm J 94:H35 S
    '70
  Hogs on slats: invest in new buildings or
    convert your old ones? P. Wilcox. il Farm J
    93:30B D '69
  Plywood cushions: no more knee abrasions for
    pigs. il Suc Farm 68:no4 B6 Mr '70

Heating and ventilation
  Cool or heat hogs free. R. Wilmore. il Farm J
    94:H14 O '70
  Heat in open-front unit improves health. il
    Farm J 93:H20-21 O '69
  Heated slats save more pigs; in the farrow-
    ing house. J. Russell. il Farm J 94:H15 F
    '70
  New ventilation ideas assure top perfor-
    mance in confinement. R. Wilmore. il Farm
    J 94:H8-9 Ag '70
  No bad odor in this farrowing house. R. J.
    Fee. il Suc Farm 68:no5 B22 Mr '70
SWING (golf)
  Shake before swinging. J. Nicklaus. il Sports
    Illus 32:59 Ap 27 '70
  Sorry, there is no perfect golf swing. D.
    Dempsey. il N Y Times Mag p 10-11+ Jl 26
    '70
SWINGLINE, inc.
  Forty-four years on the upswing. il por For-
    tune 81:163 Je '70
SWINGS
  Build a zoom swing. J. Hand. il Pop Sci 196:
    96-7+ Je '70
SWINNERTON, J. W. and others
  Ocean: a natural source of carbon monox-
    ide. bibliog il Science 167:984-6 F 13 '70
SWISHER, Viola Hegyi
  (ed) See Howard, B. Benn Howard and Elle
    Johnson: a dance partnership
SWISS castles. See Castles
SWISS chalet mystery; drama. See Murray, J
SWISS cookery. See Cookery, Swiss
SWISS guards of the Vatican. See Papal guards
SWISSAIR. See Airlines—Switzerland
SWITCHES. See Wigs
SWITCHES, Electric. See Electric switches
SWITCHING systems
  Great hopes from Ovshinsky's little switches
    grow. L. Lessing. il por Fortune 81:110-14+
    Ap '70
SWITCHING transistors. See Transistors—
    Control uses
SWITKES, Daniel
  Military psychiatrist. por Time 96:52 Jl 27
    '70 *
SWITZERLAND
  Nation as a park. G. M. Weinberg. Nat Parks
    & Con Mag 44:21 My '70
  Swiss sojourn. W. F. Buckley, jr. Nat R 22:
    377 Ap 7 '70
    See also
  Aeronautics, Military—Switzerland
  Airlines—Switzerland
  Airplanes, Military—Switzerland
  Appenzell
  Banks and banking—Switzerland
  Festivals—Switzerland
  Gstaad
  Hospitals—Switzerland
  National gallery of Switzerland, Winterthur
  Recreation—Switzerland
  Restaurants—Switzerland
  Skis and skiing—Switzerland

Description and travel
  Pocket notes on new Swiss-ness. D. Messi-
    nesi. Vogue 155:215 F 1 '70

History
    Bibliography
  Articles and other books received; comp. by
    A. H. Price. See issues of American his-
    torical review

Industries
  Nervous ticks. Time 95:84+ Ap 20 '70
    See also
  Airplane industry and trade—Switzerland
  Munitions industries—Switzerland

SWITZERLAND and the United States
    See also
  United States—Foreign opinion—Swiss
SWOMLEY, John M. jr
  Are parochial schools imperiled? Chr Cent
    88:40-3 Ja 13 '71
  Who wants Catholic schools? Nation 211:627-9
    D 14 '70
SYBRON corporation
  F. Ritter Shumway of Sybron corp; interview.
    F. R. Shumway. il pors Nations Bsns 58:48-
    53 My '70
SYDNEY, Australia
  Great way to explore Sydney harbour is
    by ferry. il Sunset 144:39+ Mr '70
    See also
  Stock exchange—Sydney, Australia
SYKES, Dwane
  Stalk for the book. il pors Outdoor Life 145:
    76-7+ Ap '70
SYKES, Velma West
  Why zoos? poem. Am For 76:63 Je '70
SYLTE, Tor
  United world colleges. il UNESCO Courier
    23:28-31 O '70
SYLVANIA electric products, inc.
  Why Sylvania's out of semiconductors. Bsns
    W p29 O 10 '70
SYLVESTER, A. G.
  Fluid pressure variations and prediction of
    shallow earthquakes. bibliog Science 169:
    1231-2 S 18 '70
SYLWESTER, Roland
  Shadow puppetry in a design class. il Sch
    Arts 69:12-14 Je '70
SYMBIOSIS
  Attine fungus gardens contain yeasts. S. E.
    Craven and others. bibliog il Science 169:
    184-6 Jl 10 '70
  Biochemical basis of the fungus-attine ant
    symbiosis. M. M. Martin. bibliog il Science
    169:16-20 Jl 3 '70
  Dodder weevils in simultaneous association
    with parasitic plants and their hosts. D. M.
    Anderson. bibliog il Science 168:132-3 Ap 3
    '70
  Symbiosis between euglena and damselfly
    nymphs is seasonal. R. L. Willey and others.
    bibliog il Science 170:80-1 O 2 '70
SYMBOLIC and mathematical logic. See Logic,
    Symbolic and mathematical
SYMBOLISM
  Our changing symbols; with painting by P.
    Davis. Look 34:42-3 Ja 13 '70
  Symbol and event. J. C. Evans. Chr Cent
    87:653-4 My 27 '70
    See also
  Christian art and symbolism
SYMBOLISM in art
  Effete corps of impudent snobs; nineteenth-
    century symbolist painters. G. Henry. il
    Art N 69:34-7+ D '70
  Mad world of Hieronymus Bosch; analysis
    of The garden of earthly delights. G.
    Highet. il Horizon 12:66-81, sup(folded re-
    production) Spr '70
  Symbolism, an elusive thing. R. Henkes. De-
    sign 71:32-3 Wint '69
SYMBOLISM in literature
  Rime of the ancient mariner: the agony of
    thirst. M. J. Lupton. bibliog f Am Imago
    27:140-59 Sum '70
SYMBOLS
  Pattern language; contribution of C. Alex-
    ander's center for environmental structure
    to the science of design. R. Montgomery.
    il Arch Forum 132:52-9 Ja '70
  Pax vobiscum, baby! Chr Cent 87:615 My 13
    '70
  Peace symbol; letters to editor. Cath World
    212:6 O '70
  Skirmish over Peace symbol. il Sr Schol 97:
    6 O 5 '70
  What's in a symbol; peace symbol. Time 96:6
    N 2 '70
    See also
  Emblems
SYMINGTON, Stuart
  Congress's right to know. il N Y Times Mag
    p7+ Ag 9 '70; Same abr. Cur 122:36-43 O '70
    about
  Junkets are classified; two cases of Congress
    being misled by the executive. New Repub
    162:8-9 Je 13 '70 *
  Unequal duel; Symington subcommittee
    and U.S. involvement in Morocco, Libya
    and Ethiopia. Nation 211:482-4 N 16 '70 *
SYMMETRY
  Backward run numbers, letters, words and
    sentences until boggles the mind; palin-
    dromes. M. Gardner. il Sci Am 223:110-12
    Ag '70

SYMMETRY (biology)
Inheritance of a cardiac arterial asymmetry in mice. J. H. Bruell and others. bibliog il Science 167:199-200 Ja 9 '70
Patterns of marine life. M. Gruber. il Sea Front 16:194-205 Jl '70

SYMONDS, Gardiner
Campus and the corporation; address, December 5, 1969. Vital Speeches 36:378-83 Ap 1 '70
Coming triumph over indifference; address, May 14, 1970. Vital Speeches 36:555-9 Jl 1 '70
about
Tenneco's careful diversification. por Duns 96:27-8 D '70 *

SYMONDS family
Symonds coat-of-arms. H. K. Eilers. il Hobbies 75:148-9+ My '70

SYMPATHY
Motives for witnessing, good or evil? R. K. Barrett. Chr Today 14:12-14 Jl 17 '70
Showing compassion. Chr Today 15:27 D 4 '70

SYMPHONIC poems
See also
Phonograph records—Symphonic poems

SYMPHONIES
Lucky 13; Shostakovich's Symphony no. 13 based on Babi Yar. por Time 95:42 F 2 '70
See also
Phonograph records—Symphonies

SYNAGOGUES
Congregation Beth Torah, Brooklyn, N.Y. il Arch Rec 147:98-9 Ja '70

SYNANON city, Calif.
Synanon city. R. Montgomery. il Arch Forum 133:52-5 N '70

SYNANON foundation, Inc.
Synanon city. R. Montgomery. il Arch Forum 133:52-5 N '70
They shared a victory over heroin. B. Davidson. il pors Good H 171:102-3+ O '70

SYNAPSES
Motoneuron morphology and synaptic contacts: determination by intracellular dye injection. W. J. Davis. bibliog il Science 168:1358-60 Je 12 '70
Nerve cells and behavior. E. R. Kandel. il Sci Am 223:57-67+ bibliog(p 136) Jl '70
Neuromuscular synapse: stochastic properties of spontaneous release of transmitter. S. Rotshenker and R. Rahamimoff. bibliog il Science 170:648-9 N 6 '70
Synaptic potentials recorded in cell cultures of nerve and muscle. G. D. Fischbach. bibliog il Science 169:1331-3 S 25 '70

SYNCHRONEX system. See Moving picture cameras—Sound equipment

SYNCHRONOUS electric motors. See Electric motors, Synchronous

SYNCHROTRONS. See Accelerators (electrons, etc)

SYNDICATES, Real estate. See Real estate investment

SYNGE, John Millington
Playboy of the western world. Criticism Time 97:37 Ja 18 '71 *

SYNGE, Patrick M.
Alliums for the garden. il Horticulture 49:26-7+ Ja '71

SYNNESTVEDT, Sig
White faces and white studies. Commonweal 92:182-3 My 8 '70

SYNOD of bishops, 1971
At the synod; National federation of priests' councils urge for priest representatives. Commonweal 93:36 O 9 '70

SYNTEX corporation
See also
Zoecon corporation

SYNTHESIS
See also
Biosynthesis

SYNTHESIZER, Electronic. See Musical instruments, Electronic

SYNTHETASES
s-Aminolevulinic acid synthetase: induction in embryonic chick liver by glucagon. J. A. Simons. bibliog il Science 167:1378-9 Mr 6 '70
Induction of glutamine synthetase in embryonic retina: its dependence on cell interactions. J. E. Morris and A. A. Moscona. bibliog il Science 167:1736-8 Mr 27 '70

SYNTHETIC diamonds. See Diamonds, Artificial

SYNTHETIC fibers. See Textile fibers, Synthetic

SYNTHETIC food. See Food substitutes

SYNTHETIC fur. See Fur, Artificial

SYNTHETIC grass. See Turf, Artificial

SYNTHETIC quartz. See Quartz

SYNTHETIC textile fabrics. See Textile fabrics, Synthetic

SYNTHETIC turf. See Turf, Artificial

SYON park. See Gardens—England

SYRACUSE, N.Y.
Galleries and museums
English earthenware figures in the Lake collection of the Everson museum. il Antiques 98:410-17 S '70

Politics and government
Opinion: what happened when a woman ran for mayor of Syracuse, New York. K. DeCrow. Mlle 70:34+ F '70

SYRACUSE university, Syracuse, N.Y.
End of a season at Syracuse; inability to resolve differences with black football players. P. Putnam. il Sports Illus 33:22-3 S 28 '70

School of library science
LEEP at Syracuse. J. A. McCrossan. Am Lib 1:493-4 My '70

SYRETT, H. C.
Challenges facing urban universities; adaptation of address, December 12, 1968. Sch & Soc 98:89-91 F '70

SYRIA
Army
Invasion that failed; fighting against Jordan in Ramtha. B. van Voorst. il Newsweek 76:39+ O 5 '70
Jordan's nine-day war. il Newsweek 76:36-7 O 5 '70

Politics and government
Blusterers and brinkmen. Time 96:28 O 5 '70
Golan offensive. Newsweek 75:40-2 F 16 '70
Syria and the Palestinians. il Newsweek 76:42 O 5 '70

SYRUPS
Fruit syrups convert into instant tall summer coolers. il Sunset 145:118 Ag '70

SYSTEMS analysis
Planetary planning; address, November 13, 1969. R. B. Fuller. il Am Scholar 40:29-63 Wint '70 (to be cont)
Systems approach. G. Gregory. UNESCO Courier 23:31+ Mr '70
See also
Flow charts
United States—Defense, Department of—Systems analysis, Office of

SYSTEMS engineering
Building process in the 1970's: the trouble with systems. R. E. Fischer. il Arch Rec 148:148-53 O '70
What the systems approach means to air conditioning (cont) R. E. Fischer and F. J. Walsh. Arch Rec 147:153-60 Ap '70

SYSTEMS simulation
See also
Computers—Simulation programs

SYSTEMS theory. See Systems analysis

SYVERTSEN, George
Beyond the checkpoint. il pors Newsweek 75:65 Je 15 '70 *
Twenty-three captured, one dead. il por Time 95:80 Je 15 '70 *

SYZDEK, Lawrence. See Blanchard, D. C. jt. auth.

SZABADVARY, Ferenc
Great moments in chemistry; tr. by R. E. Oesper (cont) il Chem 43:5-7 D '70

SZAMUELY, Tibor
Are things really improving in the USSR? il Nat R 22:250-7 Mr 10 '70

SZARKOWSKI, John
Bill Brandt: a haunting combination of strange and familiar. il Mod Phot 34:84-9 O '70
Ten photographers tell the story. il Art in Am 58:66-9 Mr '70

SZASZ, Suzanne
Daddy takes over; photographs. Good H 170:112-15 Ap '70

SZASZ, Thomas S.
Blackness and madness. Yale R 59:333-41 Mr '70
about
Twin to witchcraft. D. Brudnoy. Nat R 22:469-70 My 5 '70 *

SZCZEPANSKI, Jan
Barriers to change; interview, ed. by B. van Voorst. Newsweek 77:23-4 Ja 4 '71

SZELL, George
Death of a master builder. pors Time 96:46 Ag 10 '70 *
George Szell: in memoriam. H. Goldsmith. por Hi Fi 20:82-3 N '70 *
Music to my ears; all-Beethoven program in Philharmonic Hall. I. Kolodin. Sat R 53:28 Ap 25 '70 *

SZELL, George—*Continued*
Musical events: all-Beethoven program in Philharmonic Hall. W. Sargeant. New Yorker 46:150 Ap 18 '70 *
My George Szell. H. Temianka. por Sat R 53:50-1 S 26 '70 *
Obituary
Hi Fi 20:MA32 O '70
Newsweek por 76:77 Ag 10 '70. H. Saal
Opera N por 35:29 O 10 '70. G. Fitzgerald
Profiles: Cleveland orchestra. J. Wechsberg. New Yorker 46:38-42+ My 30 '70 *
Recordings. M. Mayer. Esquire 74:28 N '70 *
Size of Szell. I. Kolodin. il por Sat R 53:33-5+ Ag 29 '70 *
Szell memorial concert. B. Murray. Hi Fi 20:MA14 O '70 *
SZENT-GYÖRGYI, Albert
Third environment. Sat R 53:63 My 2 '70
Using the spirit of science; excerpts from The crazy ape. Cur 119:37-9 Je '70
We're shy apes in a cosmic world; interview. por Mlle 71:238-9+ Ag '70
SZWARC, M.
Living polymers: a tool in studies of ions and ion-pairs. bibliog il Science 170:23-31 O 2 '70
SZWEYKOWSKI, Zygmunt M.
Tradition and popular elements in Polish music of the baroque era. bibliog f il Mus Q 56:99-115 Ja '70
SZYMANSKI, John R.
We don't cater to bugs. il Am City 85:72-5 F '70
SZYMANSKY, Leon B.
Devils Postpile National Monument. il Nat Parks & Con Mag 44:4-7 S '70

T

T-groups. See Group relations training
T men. See United States—Internal revenue service
T-shirts. See Shirts
TCAP. See Tricyanoaminopropene
TEI. See Trucking employers, inc.
TFX (airplane) See Airplanes, Military—United States
TGE (transmissible gastroenteritis) See Swine—Diseases and pests
THC
Chemical basis of hashish activity. R. Mechoulam and others. bibliog Science 169:611-12 Ag 7 '70
Marihuana chemistry. R. Mechoulam. bibliog il Science 168:1159-66 Je 5 '70
Marihuana: studies on the disposition and metabolism of delta-9-tetrahydrocannabinol in man. L. Lemberger and others. bibliog il Science 170:1320-2 D 18 '70
Marijuana persistence in the body. il Sci N 98:476 D 26 '70
Metabolite of (—)-trans-Δ³-tetrahydrocannabinol: identification and synthesis. R. L. Foltz and others. bibliog il Science 168:844-5 My 15 '70
Pot facing stringent scientific examination. B. J. Culliton. il Sci N 97:102-5 Ja 24 '70
Δ¹-Tetrahydrocannabinol: structure of a major metabolite. I. M. Nilsson and others. bibliog il Science 168:1228 Je 5 '70
1-Δ⁹-Trans-tetrahydrocannabinol in pigeons; tolerance to the behavioral effects. D. E. McMillan and others. bibliog il Science 169:501-3 Jl 31 '70
TIAA-CREF. See College professors and instructors—Pensions
TMMC (tetramethylammonium manganese chloride) See Manganese chlorides
TMP. See Trimethylphosphate
TRW, inc.
Caution! Si Ramo at work. W. McQuade. il pors Fortune 82:104-7+ N '70
How TRW is bucking the recession. il Bsns W p42-4 D '70
TSH. See Thyrotropin
TVA. See Tennessee Valley authority
TWA. See Trans World airlines
TWUA. See Textile workers union of America
TABAK, May Natalie
Tamarind lithography workshop. il Craft Horiz 30:28-33+ O; 50-3+ D '70
TABARLY, Eric
Another ocean, another record. A. Colas. il por Yachting 127:74+ F '70 *

TABLE, The. See Table setting
TABLE decoration
All set for Christmas. N. Mandlebaum. il Ladies Home J 87:64-9 D '70
Party centerpieces that are really good enough to eat! M. Ying. il Good H 171:70-3+ D '70
Tables trimmed to suit the season. il Bet Hom & Gard 48:66-7+ D '70
Very merry Christmas tables. il House & Gard 138:56-9 D '70
See also
Epergnes
TABLE lamps. See Lamps
TABLE linen
Nine ways to the easy table. il House B 112:86-7 F '70
TABLE manners. See Etiquette
TABLE mats, tiles, etc.
Make it personal; placemats. il House B 112:108-9+ N '70
TABLE saws. See Saws
TABLE setting
Daring companions make lively tables. S. Lindsay. il House B 112:136-7 O '70
Eleven different ways to set the scene. il House B 112:92-7 N '70
Iridescent settings. E. D. Craster. il Bet Hom & Gard 48:64-7 N '70
Ladies' home journal open house. il Ladies Home J 87:87-97 O '70
New materials, new ideas for today's table settings. J. R. Cary. il Parents Mag 45:88-91 Ap '70
Open invitations. S. Lindsay and M. Miller. il House B 112:86-9 Je '70
Party tables fresh as all outdoors. il House & Gard 137:124-7 My '70
Set a charming table every time. il Good H 170:110-17 Je '70
Table-setting advice for the party season from a Tiffany expert; interview, ed. by V. D. Hahn. G. O. Brien. il por Am Home 73:22 N '70
Table settings for lunch around the world. il House & Gard 137:144-5 Mr '70
There's no set way to set a table. S. Lindsay. il House B 112:110-13 N '70
See also
Tableware
TABLE silver. See Silverware
TABLE ware. See Tableware
TABLES
Build a parsons table. L. Netti. il Mech Illus 66:111-13 Ja '70
Cocktail snack server. W. C. Leckey. il Pop Mech 133:166-9 F '70
Folding card tables. il Consumer Bul 53:11-13 Ja '70
Folding table for baby's bath. R. M. Glazer. il Pop Sci 197:141 O '70
For big effects: little tables. il House & Gard 137:158 Mr '70
Free tables from cable reels. D. Huff. il por Pop Sci 197:92-3 O '70
Marble-topped table you can build. F. Greenwald. il Pop Sci 196:72-3 My '70
Nesting party tables. W. C. Leckey. il Pop Mech 134:142-5+ Ag '70
Paper tables. il Consumer Rep 35:161 Mr '70
Patio table with new ideas. R. J. De Cristoforo. il Pop Sci 196:104-5 Mr '70
Ping table. J. Capotosto. il Mech Illus 66:108-9 Ag '70
Planter-coffee table, elegant today. W. C. Leckey. il Pop Mech 133:170-1 F '70
Ready-made coffee table. il Pop Mech 133:172-3 Mr '70
Real butcher block table. il Mech Illus 66:88-9 S '70
Spanish-style tile table. R. J. De Cristoforo. il Pop Sci 197:106-7 N '70
Three-legged table is wobble-proof on an uneven floor. il Sunset 145:144+ N '70
Which phone bench for your home? singleunit bench-tables. A. Lees and W. Allphin. il Pop Sci 196:86-7 Ap '70
See also
Billiard tables
Lazy susans
Stands (furniture)
TABLETS, Memorial. See Sepulchral monuments
TABLEWARE
California sets the dining scene. A. Walker. il Am Home 73:54-7 Jl '70
Case for collecting. V. D. Hahn. il Am Home 73:76-9 N '70
Changing designs for the bride's table. il House B 112:28+ Je '70
How to grace the table of the seventies. S. Lindsay. il House B 112:66-7+ Ja '70
Melamine dinnerware. il Consumer Rep 34:630-3 N '69

TABLEWARE—*Continued*
Party finery in silver & glass. il House B 112:114-15 N '70
Pattern on pattern. il Mlle 70:256-7 Ap '70
Set a striking table. il Am Home 73:82-7+ N '70
See also
Silverware
TABLEWARE, Stainless steel
Stainless-steel flatware. il Consumer Rep 34: 653-61 N '69
TABORIAN hospital. See Mound Bayou, Miss. —Hospitals
TABRAH, Frank L. and others
Antitumor activity in mice of tentacles of two tropical sea annelids. bibliog il Science 170:181-3 O 9 '70
TABS (boats)
Wonderful world of trim tabs. G. P. Manning. il Motor B 126:14+ Jl '70
TACHOMETERS
Build your own R.P.M. counter. H. McEntee. il Pop Sci 196:146-7+ Ja '70
Pocket tune-up tachometer. il Mech Illus 66: 74-5+ Ag '70
Solid-state tach & add-on speed alarm. R. M. Marston. il Radio-Electr 41:33-8 Ap '70
'Vette tach-drive cure. B. Lang. il Hot Rod 23:52 Jl '70
TACHYGLOSSUS aculeatus. See Anteaters
TACHYONS. See Particles (nuclear physics)
TACKLE, Fishing. See Fishing tackle
TACKLE boxes. See Fishing—Implements and appliances
TACOMA, Wash.
Million dollar bus trip; Tacoma centennial bus caravan. il Am City 85:108 F '70
TACOMA centennial. See Centennials
TACOS. See Cookery, Mexican
TACTICAL airlift. See Transportation, Military
TACTICAL patrol force. See New York (city) —Police
TACTILE communication. See Touch
TADPOLES
Brain enhancement in tadpoles: increased DNA concentration after somatotrophin or prolactin. R. K. Hunt and M. Jacobson. bibliog il Science 170:342-4 O 16 '70
TAEUBER, Conrad
Census '70: needed, easy, secret. il PTA Mag 64:12-14 Ja '70
TAEUBER, Irene B.
Chinese peoples. il Natur Hist 79:52-6 Ja '70
TAFT, Margery F.
Vacation in Colombia. il Américas 22:36-9 O '70
TAFT, Robert, 1917-
Ohio race: Taft vs. man with an image. pors U S News 69:52 S 28 '70 *
Patrician and the pol. pors Newsweek 75:30 My 4 '70 *
Robert Taft vs. Howard Metzenbaum. G. I. Maeroff. il pors N Y Times Mag p32-4+ O 4 '70 *
TAFT, Robert Alphonso, 1889-1953
Letter from Washington. R. H. Rovere. New Yorker 46:72+ Jl 18 '70 *
TAFT-Hartley law. See Labor laws and legislation—United States—Taft-Hartley law
TAGGART, Frank Alfred
How to build a captain's chair of Danish design. il Pop Sci 196:133-7+ Ja '70
TAGLIAVINI, Franco
Latin expression. S. Gould. por Opera N 35: 32 D 19 '70 *
TAHITI
Demography of primitive populations. N. McArthur. bibliog il Science 167:1097-101 F 20 '70
Tahiti. F. Koltun. il Mlle 71:189-90+ O '70
TAHOE, LAKE
Lake Tahoe: then & now. D. Anderson. il Nat Parks & Con Mag 44:4-11 Ap '70
Long-term efforts to clean the environment. P. H. Abelson. Science 167:1081 F 20 '70
Tahoe's king-size winter. M. Olson. il Travel 135:68-70 Ja '71
TAILS
Bloody merry and other problems; care of a dog's tail. G. B. Evans. Field & S 75:142+ N '70
TAIPEI, Taiwan
Taipei: the Chinese experience. R. Joseph. Travel & Camera 33:81 Mr '70
TAIWAN
See also
Art—Taiwan
Education—Taiwan
Investments, Foreign (in Taiwan)
Taipei
Technical assistance in Taiwan
Tourist trade—Taiwan

Description and travel
Hesitation in Haggler's alley. L. Barry. il Pop Phot 66:52+ Je '70
Taiwan; the country and its art. R. Joseph; J. L. Cohen. il Travel & Camera 33:72-5 Mr '70

Foreign relations
United States
See United States—Foreign relations— Taiwan

Industries
See also
Electronic apparatus industry and trade— Taiwan

Politics and government
Game goes on. il Newsweek 76:45 O 26 '70
When the crunch comes, can Taiwan hold together? F. Butterfield. il N Y Times Mag p 14-15+ Ja 18 '70
TAIWANESE art. See Art, Chinese
TAIWANESE technical assistance. See Technical assistance, Taiwanese
TAJFEL, Henri
Experiments in intergroup discrimination; with biographical sketch. il Sci Am 223:11, 96-102 bibliog(p 132) N '70
TAJ MAHAL
Taj Mahal: monument to love? A. Menen. il Holiday 47:64-5+ Ap '70
TAKAHASHI, Shinkichi
Spray of hot air; Canna; Sun through the leaves; Ice; poems, tr. by L. Stryk and T. Ikemoto. Poetry 116:364-7 Ag '70
TAKAHITO, prince of Japan
Japan's cultural recreation. il por Parks & Rec 5:43+ Ap '70
TAKARA company, inc.
Great barber-chair coup. il por Time 96:61 Ag 10 '70
TAKEI, Kei
Kei Takei: the Cubiculo. T. Borek. Dance Mag 44:87 Mr '70 *
TAKEO massacre. See Cambodian-Vietnamese conflict—Atrocities
TAKING some with Mister Vic; story. See Mitchell, D.
TAKING stock; story. See Rogin, G.
TAKOMA PARK, Md.
What is charrette planning for schools? W. D. Boutwell. PTA Mag 65:30-1 O '70
TAL, Moshe. See Imber, D. jt. auth.
TALARICO, Ross J.
Ungodly hour; poem. Atlan 226:81 D '70
TALBERT, William F.
Tennis: come alive with sudden death? P. Axthelm. Vogue 156:58 S 15 '70 *
—and Greer, Gordon
Tennis isn't just for kids. il por Holiday 48: 46-7+ Jl '70
TALBOT, Phillips
American posture toward India and Pakistan; address, April 1970, with questions and answers. Ann Am Acad 390:87-97 Jl '70
TALBOT, Virgil
Strawberries from the barrel. il Org Gard & Farm 17:82-3 F '70
TALBOT, William S.
American visions of wilderness; reprint. bibliog il Liv Wildn 33:14-25 Wint '69
TALBOTT, Strobe
(ed & tr) See Khrushchev, N. S. Khrushchev remembers
TALENT Search programs (education)
Small school Talent Search; University of Chicago program. Sch & Soc 98:72 F '70
Talent lies hidden in the Delta. J. H. Mulligan. il Am Ed 6:13-16 My '70
TALENTED high school students. See High school students, Mentally superior
TALES, Hasidic
In praise of the Baal Shem Tov, tr. by D. Ben-Amos and J. R. Mintz. Review
Commentary 50:88-90 S '70. A. A. Cohen
TALES of Hoffmann; opera. See Offenbach, J.
TALESE, Gay
Charlie Manson's home on the range. il por Esquire 73:101-3+ Mr '70
TALISMAN, Mark E.
Helping win elections. New Repub 162:10-12 Je 20 '70
TALK. See Conversation
TALL men. See Stature
TALLEY, William E.
Pull! il Parks & Rec 5:18-20+ O '70
TALLMAN, Frank
Gulf Hawk: great antique. il Flying 87:45-7+ Ag '70
TALLON, James
Make a reservation for trout. il Outdoor Life 146:72-3+ N '70
TALLULAH, La.
Top cop in Tallulah. por Time 95:17 Mr 2 '70

TALLY corporation
Tally forgets about glamour. il Bsns W p59+ Je 20 '70
TALMAGE, David W. See Hood, L. E. jt. auth.
TALMAGE, Harriet, and Monroe, G. E.
New perspective on student teaching. Clear House 44:330-3 F '70
TALMEY, Allene
Backaches: the real causes, what doctors can do for you. Vogue 155:108-9 Ap 15 '70
People are talking about. . . il Vogue 157: 80-1 Ja 1 '71
Tip sheet to the new season. Vogue 156:394-7 S 1 '70
(ed) See Bettelheim, B. Sex, virginity, money
—See Kendall, E. jt. auth.
TALOUMIS, George
Color in the seaside garden. il Horticulture 48:28-31+ Ag '70
Gardens of Vizcaya. il Horticulture 48:38-9 F '70
Shrubs that sport berries. il Home Gard 58: 28-9+ Ja '71
TAMARIN, Georges. See Rosenzweig, R. jt. auth.
TAMARIND lithography workshop, inc.
Tamarind lithography workshop. M. N. Tabak. il Craft Horiz 30:28-33+ O; 50-3+ D '70
TAMERLANO; opera. See Händel, G. F.
TAMPA, Fla.

Parks and playgrounds
Training school for birds; Busch gardens. W. Hartley and E. Hartley. il Sci Digest 69: 32-6 Ja '71

Sanitary affairs
How well do you program your street cleaning? N. Conaty. il Am City 85:32 N '70
TAMPA BAY oil slicks. See Oil pollution of rivers, harbors, etc.
TAMPING machines
Hydraulic hammer helps improve our public image; Springfield, Mo. J. Dodd. il Am City 85:66 My '70
TAMPLIN, Arthur R.
Gofman and Tamplin: harassment charges against AEC, Livermore. P. M. Boffey. pors Science 169:838-43 Ag 28 '70 *
Radiation risk: a scientific problem? R. W. Holcomb. Science 167:853-5 F 6 '70 *
—and Gofman, J. W.
Radiation effects controversy; with reply by T. J. Thompson and W. R. Bibb. Bul Atom Sci 26:2+ S '70
—See Gofman, J. W. jt. auth.
TAN
Let the sun shine in; treated cotton-polyester. il Life 68:52-3 My 22 '70
Sun worship. il Todays Health 48:36-9 Je '70
See also
Sun baths
TANCK, John. See Kelsey, P. M. jt. auth.
TANENBAUM, Marc Herman
Apostle to the Gentiles. il por Newsweek 76: 53 N 9 '70 *
T'ANG dynasty, 618-907. See China—History
TANGARANA; story. See Hernández, A. D.
TANGERINES
See also
Cookery—Fruit
TANGIER buzzless flies; story. See Hopkins, J.
TANGIER ISLAND
Flying visit. S. Wilkinson. il Flying 87:114 O '70
TANIMURA, Takenori, and others
Droplet countercurrent chromatography. il Science 169:54-6 Jl 3 '70
TANK ship owners. See Shipowners
TANK ships
Lush era of the tanker tycoons. il Newsweek 76:94-6 O 19 '70
U.S. waters for U.S. ships; question of waiving the Jones act. Bsns W p46 Ag 15 '70
See also
Ice breaking vessels
TANKERS. See Tank ships
TANKS
See also
Oil tanks
Water tanks
TANKS, Military
Leopard tanks roll up the sales. il Bsns W p23 O 3 '70
Soldiers; the Sheridan tank. W. Just. Atlan 226:59-68 N '70
TANNAHILL collection. See Detroit institute of arts
TANNENBAUM, Frank
Tannenbaum and Latin America; address, January 8, 1970. G. Arciniegas. il por Américas 22:27-31 Ap '70 *

TANNENBAUM, Galya
Tom Cat and the Colonel. pors Time 95:13 F 9 '70
TANNER, Marion
Real Auntie Mame. L. Hoffman. il pors Har Yrs 10:34-7 Jl '70 *
TANNINS
Botanical detective story; high-tannin foods associated with gullet cancer. il Sci Digest 68:84-6 O '70
TANSY
Tansy and yarrow, handsome, helpful herbs; pest-repellent plants. R. Tirrell. il pors Org Gard & Farm 17:106-9 Mr '70
TANTRISM
For the happy few , and gurus, too; exhibition of tantric art at the Galerie point cardinal in Paris. M. Conil-Lacoste. il Art N 69:34-5 Mr ' 70
TANTRUMS. See Temper
TANZANIA
See also
Dar es Salaam
Malawi, Lake
Marriage—Tanzania
National parks and reserves—Tanzania
Technical assistance in Tanzania
Zanzibar

Politics and government
Tanzania: commitment to self reliance. W. H. Lewis. Cur Hist 58:160-4+ Mr '70

Religious institutions and affairs
World around us. Chr Cent 87:897-8, 1106 Jl 22, S 16 '70
See also
Catholic church in Tanzania

Social life and customs
Family life in Africa: a look at another culture. M. Hope. il Parents Mag 45:46-7+ Ja '70
TANZER, Michael, and Cordell, A. J.
Price to the host country. il Nation 211:17-20 Jl 6 '70
TANZLER, Hans G. jr
Jacksonvillians like consolidated city government. il por Am City 85:79-81 Ap '70
TAORMINA, Antonius S.
Environment: journal on Jamaica Bay. il Cons 24:16-20 Ap '70
Journey down a Roman road. il Cons 24:5-7 Ag '69
TAP water. See Drinking water
TAPALPA, Mexico
If you are south of Guadalajara. il Sunset 144:62 Ap '70
TAPE
See also
Adhesive tape
Mending tape
TAPE, Magnetic. See Magnetic tape
TAPE, Masking. See Adhesive tape
TAPE cassettes. See Magnetic tape
TAPE changers. See Magnetic recorders and recording—Tape changers
TAPE controlled machine tools. See Machine tools—Control
TAPE decks. See Magnetic recorders and recording
TAPE recorders and recordings. See Magnetic recorders and recording
TAPE recordings
Auto tape tours; national parks in U.S. and Canada. il Travel 133:26 My '70
Big boom in nostalgia. R. Swathmore. il Pop Phot 67:51+ Jl '70
Soaking up law at leisure. V. Louviere. Nations Bsns 58:13 Jl '70
Tape deck. R. D. Darrell. See issues of High fidelity section I
Theater; RCA to produce plays on tape. S. Kauffmann. New Repub 163:20+ N 28 '70
Tune-up by tape. Travel 134:17 O '70
See also
Oral history

Stereophonic recordings
Tangle in tapes; sales of Ampex stereo tape recordings. il Time 95:84 F 23 '70

Unauthorized recording
See Magnetic recorders and recording—Unauthorized recording
TAPE-slide synchronizers. See Magnetic recorders and recording—Equipment
TAPED interviews. See Magnetic recorders and recording—Journalistic use
TAPER, Bernard
Serene satisfactions of a visit to Ceylon. il Travel & Camera 33:34-6+ N '70

TAPESTRY
Helena Barynina Hermarck. il por Craft
Horiz 30:20-3 Mr '70
On and off the avenue. J. Malcolm. New
Yorker 46:76 Je 20 '70
Rag tapestry. A. Wiseman. il Sch Arts 70:
35-7 Ja '71
She weaves a Shannon River view. il Sunset
144:139+ My '70
TAPESTRY weaving
Loose weaves. il Time 95:74-5 Je 1 '70
TAPP, June L. and Roberts, A. H.
Hard core unemployment. Trans-Action 7:
48-9 S '70
TAPPETT, Tom
Car care. See issues of Mechanix illustrated
TAPPLY, H. G.
Sportsman's notebook. See issues of Field
& stream
TAR pits, Los Angeles. See La Brea, Los An-
geles
TARBELL, Ida Minerva
Gentlewoman and the robber baron. V. V.
Hamilton. il pors Am Heritage 21:78-86 Ap
'70 *
TARBOX, Edwin F. See Rienzo, J. J. jt. auth.
TARBOX, Todd
We love you, Mr Tarbox. il Life 68:76-9 Ap 24
'70 *
TAREN, James A. and Gabrielsen, T. O.
Radio-frequency thrombosis of vascular mal-
formations with a transvascular magnetic
catheter. bibliog il Science 168:138-41 Ap 3
'70
TARGET ranges. See Bombing and gunnery
ranges
TARIFF
Rewards from the Kennedy round. J. F.
Ford. Nations Bsns 58:46 Ja '70
    See also
Free trade and protection

        Europe, Western
    See also
European economic community

        United States
Department gives views on trade legislation;
statement, May 13, 1970. W. P. Rogers.
Dept State Bul 62:700-3 Je 1 '70
Improving the trading opportunities of the
developing countries through generalized
preferences; statement, March 31, 1970. E.
M. Cronk. Dept State Bul 62:612-15 My 11
'70
Nixon stalls on an oil tariff plan. Bsns W
p42+ F 28 '70
Protection we can do without. Fortune 82:
97 Ag '70
Trade act of 1969; message to the Congress,
November 18, 1969. R. M. Nixon. Dept
State Bul 61:559-63 S 15 '69
Trade expansion expectations; address, No-
vember 19, 1969. C. J. Gilbert. Dept State
Bul 61:564-8 D 15 '69
Will the multinationals lose a loophole? pos-
sible repeal of section 807 of U.S. tariff code.
il Bsns W p28 My 2 '70
World of preferences. W. M. Blumenthal.
For Affairs 48:549-60 Ap '70
    See also
Free trade and protection

        History
Protectionism versus free trade; address,
September 29, 1970. J. H. Dent. Vital
Speeches 37:47-9 N 1 '70
TARIFF, Exemption from. See Duty free im-
portation
TARKENTON, Fran
Don't let your son play small-fry football. il
por Ladies Home J 87:146-7 O '70
TARNISH preventives. See Polishing materials
TARNISH removers. See Polishing materials
TAROT
Tarot. P. Friedrich. il McCalls 97:72-3+ Mr
'70
Tarots and your future. D. Powills. il Hob-
bies 75:122-4 Ag; 152-3+ S '70
TARPON fishing
New in-spot for tarpon. B. Warner. il Field
& S 74:194-7+ Mr '70
TARR, Curtis W.
Draft outlook for '70 and '71; interview. il
pors U S News 69:46-51 Jl 6 '70
From cool campus to hot seat; interview. ed.
by P. Goldberger. il por Sr Schol 97:16-17
N 2 '70
        about
Changes new draft chief sees. il por U S
News 68:79 Mr 30 '70 *
Conscripting a chief. por Time 95:13-14 Mr
23 '70 *
Greetings. por Newsweek 75:31 Mr 23 '70 *

TARRANT, John J.   See Feinberg, M. R. jt.
auth.
TARSHISH, Manuel B.
G. Schirmer's sells books. il Pub W 197:143-4
F 23 '70
Jewish bookstore-publisher: tradition, inno-
vation. il Pub W 198:45-6 S 7 '70
Odyssey of an art book dealer in New York.
il por Pub W 198:43-4 Jl 6 '70
Selling drama and film books in Manhattan.
il Pub W 197:44-6 My 25 '70
TARTS
Lime tarts are two-bite size. il Sunset 144:191
My '70
TARUSKIN, Richard
Realism as preached and practiced: the Rus-
sian opera dialogue. bibliog f il Mus Q 56:
431-54 Jl '70
TASAKI, Ichiji. See Conti, F. jt. auth.
TASTE
Taste buds don't taste. Sci Digest 67:29-30
Ap '70
TATCHELL, R. J. and Moorhouse, D. E.
Neutrophils: their role in the formation
of a tick feeding lesion. bibliog il Science
167:1002-3 F 13 '70
TATE, Allen
Sonnet: Could I be sure that I shall see the
day. New Repub 163:25 Ag 1 '70
Tate's essays. R. Howard. Poetry 116:43-5
Ap '70 *
TATE, Binnie
In house and out house. il por Library J
95:3595-8 O 15 '70
TATE, James
Professor waking; poem. Atlan 226:73 Jl '70
Saint John of the Cross in prison; poem.
Poetry 117:185 D '70
Shadowboxing; poem. New Yorker 46:40 F
28 '70
TATE, James Hugh Joseph
Philadelphia's battered mayor. il por Bsns W
p40-1 F 21 '70 *
TATE, Judith
Income and service as witness; excerpt from
Religious women in the modern world.
Cath World 211:247-50 S '70
TATE, Sharon
Sharon Tate murders. P. Maas. il por Ladies
Home J 87:52+ Ap '70 *
TATE murder case. See Murder
TATSUMOTO, Mitsunobu, and Rosholt, J. N.
Age of the moon: an isotopic study of ura-
nium-thorium-lead systematics of lunar
samples. bibliog il Science 167:461-3 Ja 30
'70
TATTILO, Adelina
Women, not girls. il por Time 97:36+ Ja 18
'71 *
TATTOOING
Pet news; dog tattooing. J. Kuh. Ladies
Home J 87:32 F '70
Tattoo renaissance. por Time 96:58 D 21 '70
TATUM, Michael
Trouble-free library planning and construc-
tion. il Am Lib 1:878-83 O '70
TAUBER, Burton R.
Satirizing the war as an investment. il Time
96:94 S 21 '70 *
TAUBER, Catherine A. See Tauber, M. J. jt.
auth.
TAUBER, Edward S. See Rojas-Ramírez, J. A.
jt. auth.
TAUBER, Maurice J. and Tauber, C. A.
Photoperiodic induction and termination of
diapause in an insect: response to chang-
ing day lengths. bibliog il Science 167:170
Ja 9 '70
TAUBES, Frederic
Brushes: their variety and uses. il Am Artist
34:24-7 Ag '70
C. L. MacNelly: portrait painter. il por Am
Artist 34:24-9+ My '70
Painting knives: variety and use. il Am
Artist 35:50-5+ Ja '71
TAUTOG fishing
Blacks. G. Heinold. il Outdoor Life 146:138-
9+ S '70
TAVASSOLI, Mehdi, and Crosby, W. H.
Bone marrow histogenesis: a comparison of
fatty and red marrow. bibliog il Science
169:291-3 Jl 17 '70
TAVERNS. See Bars and barrooms; Hotels,
taverns, etc.
TAVES, Isabella
Fired at 49. il pors Look 34:44-7+ D 1 '70
TAX administration and procedure
Internal revenue service; meeting the chal-
lenges of tax administration; address. May
12, 1970. W. H. Smith. Vital Speeches 36:
660-9 Ag 15 '70

TAX auditing
After the tax collector gets your return; questions and answers. il U S News 68:77-9 Ad 20 '70
For top brass: the purely personal audit. Bsns W p 139-40 Mr 28 '70
If your income tax return is audited. il Good H 170:198 My '70
Internal revenue service; meeting the challenges of tax administration; address, May 12, 1970. W. H. Smith. Vital Speeches 36: 660-9 Ag 15 '70

TAX collection
Mounting woes of the tax collectors; testimony before a House appropriations subcommittee. U S News 68:103 Ap 13 '70
Saying charge it to tax collector. U S News 68:91-2 Ja 26 '70
See also
Tax returns
United States—Internal revenue service
Withholding tax

TAX consultants
Happier returns. il Newsweek 75:74+ F 23 '70
Tax advice; or, How to fight the 1040. Bsns W p 121-2 Mr 7 '70
Why tax consulting is everybody's business. il Bsns W p82+ F 21 '70
See also
Block, H. and R, inc.

TAX courts
See also
United States—Tax court

TAX credits. See Investment tax credit

TAX deductions. See Income tax—Deductions

TAX evasion
Arrangement; case of S. Teshigahara in Japan. Newsweek 75:46 F 9 '70
Arrangement; the Casati case in Italy. il por Newsweek 76:52 S 21 '70
Christians and Caesar's taxes. F. Zahn. il Chr Cent 87:1349-52 N 11 '70
Foreign bank accounts: the need for legislation; address. E. T. Rossides. Vital Speeches 36:526-30 Je 15 '70
Internal revenue service; meeting the challenges of tax administration; address, May 12, 1970. W. H. Smith. Vital Speeches 36:660-9 Ag 15 '70
Johnny is in *agua* hot; Caliente racetrack director. A. Wright. il pors Sports Illus 33: 50-2+ Ag 3 '70

TAX exempt securities. See Securities, Tax exempt

TAX exemption. See Taxation, Exemption from

TAX forms
Can income tax forms ever be simplified? excerpts from address, March 18, 1970. E. S. Cohen. por U S News 68:76-7 Ap 6 '70
Foul-up over '70 tax returns. il U S News 68:17-19 Mr 23 '70
How to cope with the new tax forms. H. Ulrich. il Mech Illus 66:48-9+ Ap '70
Tax form can blow your mind; simplified form 1040. il Bsns W p27 Ap 11 '70
Tax mistakes anybody might make. il Changing T 24:7-9 F '70
What the tax people don't tell you. il Changing T 24:17-20 Mr '70
Your form 1040 is different now. il Changing T 24:17-18 Ja '70

TAX laws. See Taxation—Law

TAX loss farming. See Agriculture—Economic aspects

TAX planning
How to keep more of your profits. Farm J 93:H20 N '69
New tax wrinkles; tax-selling. C. Morgello. il Newsweek 76:84 D 7 '70
Tax reform law demands some new thinking. Bsns W p99-100 Ja 24 '70
You can protect more of those profits. il Farm J 93:B9+ N '69
See also
Estate planning

TAX reduction. See Taxation—United States

TAX reform act of 1969. See Taxation—Law

TAX relations, intergovernmental. See Intergovernmental tax relations

TAX returns
After the tax collector gets your return; questions and answers. il U S News 68:77-9 Ap 20 '70
Foul-up over '70 tax returns. il U S News 68:17-19 Mr 23 '70
How to cope with the new tax forms. H. Ulrich. il Mech Illus 66:48-9+ Ap '70
Last-minute tax tips. il Changing T 24:25-8 Ap '70
Last-minute tips for tax savings. U S News 68:26-7 Mr 30 '70

Taxes and the freelance writer. L. H. Houck. il Writers Digest 50:28-31 Ap '70
Things to do now to cut your 1970 taxes. F. K. Coffee. il Mech Illus 66:50-2+ N '70
Timely tax tips. G. Town. Har Yrs 10:22-3 F '70
See also
Confidential communications—Taxation

Auditing
See Tax auditing

TAX selling. See Tax planning

TAX sharing. See Intergovernmental tax relations

TAXATION
American taxpayers' bill: how bad is it, really? comparison with other countries. il U S News 69:72-3 S 7 '70
See also
Intergovernmental tax relations
Local taxation
Single tax
Tax administration and procedure
Taxation of bonds, securities, etc.
Value added tax
also subhead Taxation under various subjects, e.g. Corporations—Taxation

Law
Hidden jokers in the new tax deck; Tax reform act of 1969. A. M. Louis. il Fortune 82:100-2+ Jl '70
Keep an eye on the IRS; Tax reform act of 1969. il Nations Bsns 58:39-41 Jl '70
Loopholes hidden in tax reform; Tax reform act of 1969. il Bsns W p50-1 N 28 '70
Overdue business of tax reform. Am City 85:12 O '70
Tax changes for 1971: the plans taking shape. U S News 69:91-3 O 5 '70
Tax policy widening big-city blight? U S News 69:76 Ag 24 '70
Tax reform act. I. Fisher. Dance Mag 44:6 D '70; 45:83 Ja '71
See also
Taxation, Exemption from

Italy
See also
Tax evasion

Montana
Supreme court in Montana voids state tax on airline passengers. Aviation W 92:34 Ja 26 '70

New Jersey
Bill would force state to pay in lieu taxes; New Jersey legislation. Am City 85:40 Ag '70

Ohio
Where new plants don't cure tax ills. il Bsns W p89-90 Je 6 '70

Pennsylvania
Fight to repeal an insurance tax. il Bsns W p31 Mr 14 '70

Sweden
Why are they smiling? system in Stockholm. L. Gross. il Look 34:21-7 Mr 24 '70

United States
Christians and Caesar's taxes. F. Zahn. il Chr Cent 87:1349-52 N 11 '70
Federal spending: new spur to business; taxes are cut, pay rates are rising. il U S News 68:24-6 Ap 20 '70
Heller and tax reform. E. S. Herman. New Repub 161:30-1 D 6 '69; Discussion. 162: 33 Ja 3; 26+ Ja 17; 33-6 F 14; 29 F 21; 22+ Mr 14; 35-6 Ap 4 '70
How unfair are our taxes? M. J. Ulmer. il New Repub 163:17-19 N 7 '70; Discussion. 163:30 N 28; 34 D 5 '70
If you've been hoping for lower taxes—. il U S News 69:75 N 30 '70
Relief for the U.S. taxpayer. Sr Schol 96:14 Ja 26 '70
Tax aids top 44 billion dollars. U S News 68: 72 Je 15 '70
Tax dates to watch in 1970 and beyond. U S News 68:68-70 Ja 19 '70
Tax ideas in the wind and how they can affect you. il U S News 69:53-5 Jl 13 '70
Tax relief in 1971? Chances are dimming. il U S News 69:73-4 O 12 '70
Taxes & related problems; address, December 1, 1970. W. Bennett. Vital Speeches 37: 166-70 Ja 1 '71
Treasury finds many retirees overpay taxes; remedy sought. Aging 188:9 Je '70

TAXATION—United States—*Continued*
Where people's tax burdens are headed higher. U S News 69:66-8 Ag 17 '70
Where's the money coming from? Nations Bsns 58:27-9 O '70
Your chance to sound off about taxes. il Bet Hom & Gard 48:12-16 Je '70
See also
Income tax—United States
Libraries—Finance
Local taxation
Property tax
Sales tax
Tax evasion
Taxation, Exemption from
Taxation, State
United States—Internal revenue service

TAXATION, Double
United States and Belgium sign new income tax convention. Dept State Bul 63:123 Jl 27 '70
United States and Finland sign new income tax convention. Dept State Bul 62:474-5 Ap 6 '70

TAXATION, Exemption from
Muddled approach; tax-exempt status to public-interest law firms. Commonweal 93:212 N 27 '70
Segregation by tax exemption. R. Cleghorn. Nation 210:785-6 Je 29 '70
Tax blow at white private schools. U S News 68:53 Ja 26 '70
Tax exemption and political activities. Sch & Soc 98:328+ O '70
Tax exemption for private schools: what officials plan. R. W. Thrower; W. Mondale. pors U S News 69:70-4 Ag 31 '70
Tax exemptions: race and religion. America 122:576 My 30 '70
Tax status of exempt organizations; private schools, address, August 24, 1970. R. W. Thrower. Vital Speeches 37:2-5 O 15 '70
Taxing the public interest; status of public-interest law firms. Time 96:94+ N 16 '70
Will private schools no longer be private? D. Lawrence. il U S News 69:80 Ag 3 '70
See also
Church property—Taxation
Colleges and universities—Taxation
Foundations, Charitable and educational—Taxation
Securities, Tax exempt

TAXATION, Municipal. See Local taxation

TAXATION, State
Higher taxes at the state level? views of legislative and business leaders. il Nations Bsns 58:38-40 D '70
State & local taxes: how they compare, city to city. Changing T 24:46 S '70
State bite hard despite elections. il Bsns W p116+ S 19 '70
States tapping new tax sources. U S News 68:94 F 16 '70
Taming interstate taxes; income tax out-of-state businesses. Bsns W p54-6 My 2 '70

TAXATION for library service. See Libraries—Finance

TAXATION of bonds, securities, etc.
Funds; tax-equences. Forbes 106:89 S 15 '70
New tax wrinkles; tax-selling. C. Morgello. il Newsweek 76:84 D 7 '70
When to take stock losses: the impact of a new tax rule. U S News 69:72 Ag 3 '70

TAXES. See Taxation

TAXICAB drivers
Easy marks; holdups. il Time 96:84 S 21 '70
Hippie hackies: hair ruling in San Francisco. il Newsweek 75:81-2 My 4 '70
Natural phenomenon of N.Y. taxi drivers. Q. Crewe. Vogue 155:24 Mr 15 '70
Requiem for a cabbie. il Newsweek 76:83 O 12 '70
See also
Women as taxicab drivers

TAXICABS
Taxis, jitneys & poverty: adaptation of address. S. Rosenbloom. il Trans-Action 7:47-54 F '70

TAYLOR, Adele Chatfield-. See Chatfield-Taylor, A.

TAYLOR, Alvin
Vicarious murder. Time 96:61 D 21 '70 *

TAYLOR, Art
Studio on a shoestring. A. Zayat. il Pop Phot 67:108-9 D '70 *

TAYLOR, Barry N. and others
Fundamental physical constants; with biographical sketches. il Sci Am 223:15, 62-70+ O '70

TAYLOR, Carl E.
Population trends in an Indian village; with biographical sketch. il Sci Am 223:15, 106-112+ Jl '70

TAYLOR, Davida
Last flight out of Biafra. N. Cousins. Sat R 53:22+ Ja 24 '70

TAYLOR, Desmond Shawe-. See Shawe-Taylor, D.

TAYLOR, Dorice
Snowy Sun Valley. il Travel 134:62-3 D '70

TAYLOR, Douglas H. and Ferguson, D. E.
Extraoptic celestial orientation in the southern cricket frog acris gryllus. bibliog il Science 168:390-2 Ap 17 '70

TAYLOR, Elizabeth, 1912-
Choosing details that count. Writer 83:15-16+ Ja '70

TAYLOR, Elizabeth, 1932-
How do I love thee? Let me count the ways. J. Roddy. il pors Look 34:28-30 Je 16 '70 *
$10,000,000 jewels of Elizabeth Taylor & Jacqueline Onassis. L. Smith. il pors Ladies Home J 86:64+ D '69

TAYLOR, Emily
Keeping house with Emily Taylor. See issues of Good housekeeping

TAYLOR, Erle A.
McCarran's magic carpet. il por Am City 85:82-3 N '70

TAYLOR, Frank
Sand mobile? il Pop Mech 134:82-3 Ag '70
Sweet little Santa Fe. il Pop Mech 134:112-13 N '70

TAYLOR, Frank J.
You can avoid the probate trap. Read Digest 96:93-6 Je '70

TAYLOR, Fred J.
Fishing with Fred. T. Trueblood. il pors Field & S 74:20+ Ja '70

TAYLOR, George J. and Harris, W. S.
Glue sniffing causes heart block in mice. bibliog il Science 170:866-8 N 20 '70

TAYLOR, Glenhail
From Apollo's lyre to Elvis' guitar. il Hi Fi 20:secI 53-7 My '70

TAYLOR, Gordon Rattray
People pollution; excerpt from The doomsday book. il Ladies Home J 87:74+ O '70
Threat to life in the sea; excerpt from The doomsday book. Sat R 53:40-2 Ag 1 '70

TAYLOR, Harold
Inside Buckminster Fuller's universe. por Sat R 53:56-7+ My 2 '70

TAYLOR, Henry
Singing to spite this hunger. Nation 210:122-4 F 2 '70

TAYLOR, Hugh P. Jr. See Epstein, S. jt. auth.

TAYLOR, J. Allyn
Canada and change; address, September 21, 1970. Vital Speeches 37:121-4 D 1 '70

TAYLOR, James
James Taylor: sunshine and... B. Korall. por Sat R 53:83+ S 12 '70 *

TAYLOR, Jill
King of the meadow. Good H 171:137 Jl '70

TAYLOR, Kathryn S.
Success with bulbous plants. il Horticulture 48:367-7+ O '70
Summer wild flowers. il Horticulture 48:34-5+ Ag '70

TAYLOR, Kenneth M. and Snyder, S. H.
Amphetamine: differentiation by d and l isomers of behavior involving brain norepinephrine or dopamine. bibliog il Science 168:1487-9 Je 19 '70

TAYLOR, L. A. and Mao, H. K.
High-pressure polymorph of troilite, FeS. bibliog il Science 170:850-1 N 20 '70

TAYLOR, L. B. Jr
Insulin murders. Todays Health 48:50-3+ D '70
Shuttling into space. il Mech Illus 66:45-7+ Ap '70

TAYLOR, Louie S.
Gem making for the enamelist. il Ceram Mo 17:27-9 D '69

TAYLOR, Lucia. See Taylor, T. H. jt. auth.

TAYLOR, M. C. and others
Pion cancer therapy: positron activity as an indicator of depth-dose. bibliog il Science 169:377-8 Jl 24 '70

TAYLOR, Mary Agnes
In defense of the wild things. il Horn Bk 46:642-6 D '70

TAYLOR, Paul S.
Migrant mother: 1936. il Am West 7:41-5 My '70
Reclamation. bibliog il Am West 7:27-33+ Jl '70

TAYLOR, Paul, dance company. See Paul Taylor dance company

TAYLOR, Robert M.
Case against smoking. il UNESCO Courier 23:14-16 My '70

TAYLOR, Robert Scott. See Taylor, S. jt. auth.

TAYLOR, Roger
Giant killer. il por Newsweek 76:69-70 Jl 13 '70 *

TAYLOR, Ronald B.
Huelga! The boycott that worked. Nation 211:167-9 S 7 '70
Nerve gas in the orchards. Nation 210:751-3 Je 22 '70

TAYLOR, Stuart R. and Rüdel, Reinhardt
Striated muscle fibers: inactivation of contraction induced by shortening. bibliog il Science 167:882-4 F 6 '70

TAYLOR, Susie King
Teen-age Civil war nurse Susie King Taylor. il Ebony 25:96-8+ F '70 *

TAYLOR, Sybil, and Taylor, R. S.
When a boat is more than a boat. il Motor B 125:234-6 Mr '70

TAYLOR, T. G.
How an eggshell is made; with biographical sketch. il Sci Am 222:25-6, 88-95 bibliog (p 146) Mr '70

TAYLOR, T. H. and Taylor, Lucia
Don't knock park camping. il Nat Wildlife 8:46-7 O '70

TAYLOR, Telford
Of guilt and precedent. il por Time 97:10 Ja 18 '71 *

TAYLOR, Theodore
Long view. Sat R 53:44 F 21 '70

TAYLOR, Thomas F.
Jeremiah Clarke's trumpet tunes: another view of origins. bibliog f il Mus Q 56:455-62 Jl '70

TAYLOR, Timothy, and Hall, Adrian
Son of man and the family. Criticism Sat R 53:20 D 26 '70 *

TAYLOR instrument companies. See Sybron corporation

TAZIEFF, Haroun
Afar triangle; with biographical sketch. il Sci Am 222:10, 32-40 bibliog(p 126) F '70
—See Bonatti, E. jt. auth.

TCHAIKOVSKY, Peter Ilyitch
More impressive than most: the disc debut of Pinchas Zukerman. M. N. Kanny. Am Rec G 36:436 F '70 *
Must for balletomanes, especially. G. L. Mayer. Am Rec G 36:906-7 Jl '70 *
One to own, Graffman's Tchaikovsky. M. N. Kanny. Am Rec G 36:588 Ap '70 *
Rostropoviches in Onegin. I. Kolodin. Sat R 53:53 S 26 '70 *
Tchaikovsky's musical novel. P. G. Davis. il Hi Fi 20:87-8 O '70 *
Tchaikovsky's Russia: the lingering passion. S. Jacoby. il por Sat R 53:75-6+ Mr 14 '70 *
Wahnderful Tchaikovsky. Time 95:56-7 Ap 27 '70 *

TEA
Aromatic teas from wild plants. E. Gibbons. il House & Gard 138:148+ O '70
Time for tea. W. J. Thompson. il Horticulture 48:32-6 D '70
Toast to the world's no. two drink. il Changing T 24:41-2 F '70
Try tea and see; herb teas. A. Alexander. il Org Gard & Farm 17:100-1 Ag '70

TEA cups. See Cups

TEACH ins. See Teach-ins

TEACHER corps. See United States—National teacher corps

TEACHER education. See Teachers—Education

TEACHER evaluation. See Teachers—Rating

TEACHER grievances. See Teachers grievances

TEACHER librarians. See School librarians

TEACHER-pupil relations. See Teachers and students

TEACHER rating. See Teachers—Rating

TEACHER shortage. See Teachers—Supply and demand

TEACHERS
Boston story; study of schools of the Boston archdiocese. J. Deedy. Commonweal 92:178 My 8 '70
Changing the social order: the role of schooling. J. R. Burnett. Ed Digest 35:5-8 Mr '70
Crisis of confidence; Catholic teachers. il Newsweek 75:75-6 F 2 '70
Decade of crisis for education; a time for change. J. E. Patrick. Vital Speeches 36:502-5 Je 1 '70
Down on farm grew nation's no. 1 teacher. il por Sr Schol 96:Schol Teach 1-2 My 18 '70
Games teachers shouldn't play with principals. B. Demsch. Clear House 45:86-8 O '70
Getting along with reading teachers. S. I. Fenwick. il por Wilson Lib Bul 45:273-7 N '70
My special miracle. E. Vaughan. Todays Ed 59:45 N '70
Negativism and the hand that feeds us. J. M. Hansen. Clear House 45:204-6 D '70

Some thoughts about teaching and teachers; symposium il Todays Ed 59:12-18 F '70
Teacher of the year 1970. W. J. McKean. il pors Look 34:50-2+ Je 2 '70
Washington report; our all-star teachers. J. Lloyd. Sr Schol 96:Schol Teach 2 Mr 9 '70
What happened to teacher? by M. Breton. Review
America 122:346-7 Mr 28 '70. M. S. Lienert
Who is accountable? C. H. Harrison. il Schol Teach Jr/Sr High p 13+ N 2 '70
Volunteer teacher program; Archdiocese of New York. America 123:534 D 19 '70
See also
Academic freedom
American federation of teachers
Art teachers
Collective bargaining—Teachers
Dance teachers
Education
English teachers
National education association
Nuns as teachers
Priests as teachers
School and the home
Substitute teachers
Teachers unions
Teaching

Adjustment
Teacher aids teacher; orientation programs. J. L. Southwell. Clear House 45:104-6 O '70

Anecdotes, facetiae, satire, etc.
Light touch. See issues of Today's education

Appointment
See Teachers—Selection and appointment

Civil rights
Reinstatement for bearded teacher. il Sch & Soc 98:18 Ja '70

Dismissal
Case of the bearded teacher; D. Lucia. por Todays Ed 59:26-7 My '70
Davis affair. il por Newsweek 75:78 Je 22 '70
Reinstatement for bearded teacher. il Sch & Soc 98:18 Ja '70

Duties
Differentiated staffing. Ed Digest 36:22-4 O '70
High cost of non-teaching assignments. J. Canfield. Clear House 44:296-9 Ja '70

Education
Come out from under the ivy. D. Davies. il Am Ed 6:28-31 Mr '70
Developing and maintaining excellent teachers. T. P. Wilbur and D. L. Donovan. bibliog Clear House 44:501-3 Ap '70
Merits of the Insite plan; Instructional systems in teacher education. A. H. Rice. il Todays Ed 59:46-8 My '70
New overseas study programs for future teachers. Sch & Soc 98:210+ Ap '70
New teacher education program for inner-city schools. Sch & Soc 98:268 Sum '70
Preservice micro-teaching. D. B. Young. Todays Ed 59:38 Ja '70
Reorganization of Yale's teacher program; training of future high school teachers. Sch & Soc 98:208 Ap '70
Teacher education and preparation for the 21st century; adaptation of address, November 8, 1967. R. I. Miller. Sch & Soc 98:278-81 Sum '70
Teacher goes to own aid; TV and film self-evaluation. il Sr Schol 96:Schol Teach 1 F 2 '70
Touching teachers. K. Branan. il Schol Teach Jr/Sr High p20-2 S 21 '70
See also
Bank street college of education, New York
Student teaching

Education in service
Antidote: when teaching sours; National leadership methods labs. M. Manley. Clear House 45:112-15 O '70
Improved in-service: a challenge for supervisors. H. E. Turner. Clear House 45:116-19 O '70
Inservice education for secondary English teachers: so little time. . .so much to learn! R. V. Denby. Engl J 59:594-602 Ap '70
Something different in in-service education: Educational telephone network workshop. G. Hartung and R. Gelman. il Todays Ed 59:24-5 My '70
Student-teacher laboratory prepares a school for de facto desegregation. G. L. Downing. Clear House 45:37-40 S '70

TEACHERS—Education in service—*Continued*
Style of teaching and teacher evaluation;
videotape analysis. G. H. Henry. bibliog f
Engl J 59:921-7 O '70
Success with microteaching; in-service training of teachers. Sch & Soc 98:200 Ap '70

Ethics
See Teachers, Professional ethics for

Legal status, laws, etc.
Judicial opinion and the role of teachers;
public school teachers as public officials. R.
S. Vacca. bibliog Clear House 45:240-4 D
'70

Pensions
Shame of our teacher pensions. P. Friggens.
Read Digest 96:167-8+ Mr '70

Political activities
Are we politically involved? W. Sanstead. Todays Ed 59:44-5 D '70
Teacher's political role; interview, ed. by G.
D. Fischer. F. R. Harris. por Todays Ed
59:22-4 Ap '70
Teacher's political role; interview, ed. by G.
D. Fischer. R. C. B. Morton. pors Todays Ed
59:20-1+ Ap '70
Today's teacher: a new breed. G. D. Fischer.
por Parents Mag 45:34 Mr '70
See also
College professors and instructors—Political
activities

Publications
Writing for publication. J. F. Ohles. Clear
House 45:245-9 D '70

Qualifications
Developing and maintaining excellent teachers. T. P. Wilbur and D. L. Donovan. bibliog Clear House 44:501-3 Ap '70
Ph.D.'s in high schools. il Sci N 97:612 Je
27 '70
See also
College professors and instructors—Qualifications

Rating
Let's do away with teacher evaluation. C. R.
Ingils. il Clear House 44:451-6 Ap '70
Merit pay for the best teachers? G. M. Knox.
Bet Hom & Gard 48:4+ S '70
Plan for evaluation of teacher efficiency
through cooperative goal-setting. W. Fox
and R. D. Jones. Clear House 44:541-3 My
'70
Rating your school; significance of what goes
on in the teachers' room. J. M. Gray. Todays Ed 59:32-3 D '70

Recruiting
Teacher recruitment and selection in New
York city archaic and costly. I. Flinker. il
Clear House 44:483-7 Ap '70
Teachers help interview prospective teachers; Bladensburg elementary school. D. I.
Zatz. Todays Ed 59:47 F '70

Salaries, allowances, etc.
High cost of non-teaching assignments. J.
Canfield. Clear House 44:296-9 Ja '70
Merit pay for the best teachers? G. M. Knox.
Bet Hom & Gard 48:4+ S '70
Salaries of school professionals. il Ed Digest
35:27-9 Ja '70
State $ for schools; state salary supplements.
J. Duerr. Commonweal 92:243-5 My 22 '70
See also
College professors and instructors—Salaries,
allowances, etc.
Strikes—United States—Teachers

Selection and appointment
Teacher recruitment and selection in New
York city archaic and costly. I. Flinker. il
Clear House 44:483-7 Ap '70

Supply and demand
General shortage over. Sch & Soc 98:70 F '70
New era in teacher supply and demand. Todays Ed 59:51-2 Ja '70
Now: too many school teachers. il U S News
69:22-3 Jl 6 '70
Ph.D. physicists in high school jobs. Sch
& Soc 98:394-5 N '70
Prospects for growth in preprimary education. J. N. Hedges. il Mo Labor R 93:40-4
Jl '70
Supply and demand; teacher glut. il Newsweek 75:58-9 Je 29 '70
Teacher numbers game. D. Davies. Am Ed 6:
7-8 O '70

Teacher shortage turns into surplus. il Bsns
W p 18 Ag 22 '70
Too many teachers? Time 96:38 S 28 '70
See also
Teachers—Recruiting

Tenure
See also
Teachers—Dismissal

Training
See Teachers—Education
TEACHERS, New. See Teachers—Adjustment
TEACHERS, Part time
Bringing the experts to school. R. Wolkomir.
Parents Mag 45:48-9+ Ja '70
Part-time teachers. A. Groner and C. Brall.
Todays Ed 59:64-5 Ja '70
TEACHERS, Professional ethics for
Who says it's unethical? controls on behavior. E. Faulconer. il Todays Ed 59:62-
2 Ja '70
TEACHERS, Retired
Creative retirement. il Todays Ed 59:28-30
F '70
Retirement years. E. Logan. Ed Digest 36:
29-31 N '70
See also
National retired teachers association
TEACHERS aides
Little help from my friends; tutoring in Gambier, Ohio elementary schools by students
from Kenyon college. D. R. Maxey. il Look
34:22-4 Je 16 '70
Paraprofessional: slave or aide? R. J. Miltz.
Clear House 44:390 Mr '70
Paraprofessionals: in search of an identity.
J. T. Seyfarth and R. L. Canady. Clear
House 45:221-5 D '70
Statewide extension of senior teacher aides
under study in Florida. il Aging 188:16 Je
'70
Teacher aide and child care program; Pontiac, Mich. D. J. Garrison. il Todays Ed
59:32 F '70
See also
Volunteer workers in education
TEACHERS and libraries. See Libraries and
schools
TEACHERS and students
Children of the apocalypse. P. Marin. il Sat
R 53:71-3+ S 19 '70
Children who hate school. N. Hentoff. il Parents Mag 45:60-1+ F '70
Christian teacher. P. Cousins. Chr Today 15:
16-18 O 9 '70
Classroom incident. See issues of Today's education
Face of a child. H. K. Howard. Todays Ed
59:81-2 O '70
Family relationships in the school. il Todays
Ed 59:10-13+ D '70
Fostering practical communication skills. B.
D. Stanford. Engl J 59:967-9 O '70
How not to teach English in high school. E.
Luis. Engl J 59:964-6 O '70
In the beginning; beginning school meaningfully. J. Kabatznick. Engl J 59:956-9 O '70
Interaction briefs. See issues of Today's education
My teacher doesn't like me. Trans-Action
7:10+ Jl '70
Non-verbal communication and the teacher.
C. W. Garner. bibliog Sch & Soc 98:363-4 O
'70
Personal growth in the classroom: Dartmouth, Dixon, and humanistic psychology.
T. D. Klein. bibliog f Engl J 59:235-43 F
'70
Schools put a town on the map; South Brunswick, N.J. C. H. Harrison. il Sat R 53:66-
8+ F 21 '70
School's role in emotional health; with study-discussion program. by E. Harris and D.
Harris. A. Daniels. bibliog il PTA Mag 64:16-
18+, 33-4 Ap '70
Some thoughts about teaching and teachers;
symposium. il Todays Ed 59:12-18 F '70
Student attitudes toward teacher activism. J.
Blendinger. il Clear House 44:268-71 Ja '70
Student for a day; Michigan ave. school, Coos
Bay, Ore. E. Moffitt. Schol Teach Jr/Sr
High p 10-11 D 7 '70
Teacher I want to be. K. Wronski. Todays
Ed 59:47 S '70
Teachers, students, and selfishness in the
seventies. V. R. Mollenkott. Chr Today 14:
6-8+ Ap 10; 13-15 Ap 24 '70
Teachers talk too much! J. S. Cross and J. M.
Nagle. Ed Digest 35:22-4 Ap '70
Teaching the young to love. J. R. Frymier.
Ed Digest 35:9-12 F '70

TEACHERS and students—*Continued*
We/they: the new campus dialogue. B. F.
Dick. Nat R 22:562-3+ Je 2 '70
White faces and black studies. M. L. Dillon.
Commonweal 91:476-9 Ja 30 '70
Will teacher be the new drop-out? A. Beich-
man; reply. F. E. Crossland. N Y Times
Mag p21+ Ja 25 '70
  See also
Contract plan (education)

TEACHERS and the community
Advice from the top. J. Lloyd. Sr Schol 95:
Schol Teach 2 O 13 '69
Teacher and community; surveying three
worlds. M. L. Tobriner. Clear House 44:391-4
Mr '70

TEACHERS and writers collaborative newsletter. See College and school journalism

TEACHERS as authors
Case for pop scholarship: a polemic for popularizers. C. Suhor. Engl J 59:116-18+ Ja
'70

TEACHERS associations. See Educational associations

TEACHERS colleges
  See also
Teachers—Education

TEACHERS contracts
Teacher militancy and collective negotia-
tions. L. S. Vander Werf; S. M. Elkin;
J. W. Maguire. bibliog Sch & Soc 98:171-7
Mr '70

TEACHERS ethics. See Teachers, Professional
ethics for

TEACHERS grievances
Model four-stage grievance procedure. R.
Van Delinder, jr. and R. H. St Germain.
Todays Ed 59:38-40 F '70
Real heart of a negotiated agreement. K.
L. Law. Todays Ed 59:36-8 F '70

TEACHERS meetings
Faculty meetings. il Todays Ed 59:60-2 S
'70
Improving faculty meetings. B. L. Goodman.
Clear House 45:211 D '70
Student participation in faculty meetings. J.
J. Roy. Clear House 44:285 Ja '70

TEACHERS pensions. See Teachers—Pensions

TEACHERS salaries. See Teachers—Salaries,
allowances, etc.

TEACHERS strikes. See Strikes—United States
—Teachers

TEACHERS unions
Merger of NEA and AFT locals; Flint, Mich.
Sch & Soc 98:15-16 Ja '70
NUTs say nuts to small raise il Sr Schol
95:Schol Teach 1 Ja 12 '70
One big teachers' union for U.S? U S News
68:57 Ja 19 '70
Teacher militancy and collective negotiations.
L. S. Vander Werf; S. M. Elkin; J. W.
Maguire. bibliog Sch & Soc 98:171-7 Mr '70
Teachers who won't be dragooned; with-
drawal of the Detroit education associa-
tion from the Michigan education associa-
tion over agency-shop clause. R. Kirk.
Nat R 22:261 Mr 10 '70
Today chancery, tomorrow Albany; settling
with lay teachers. P. Tracy. Commonweal
91:574-5 F 27 '70
  See also
American federation of teachers

TEACHERS workshops. See Educational workshops

TEACHERS' writing competition. See Literature—Competitions

TEACHING
Give them a performance. E. G. Denholtz.
Todays Ed 59:55 O '70
Initiative in learning; teaching-learning or
telling-reciting. D. S. Seckinger. Sch & Soc
98:24 Ja '70
Open classroom, by H. Kohl. Review
  New Repub 162:24-5 My 23 '70. J. Feather-
  stone
Some myths that teachers live by. R. B.
Shuman. Ed Digest 35:32-4 F '70
Some thoughts about teaching and teachers:
symposium. il Todays Ed 59:12-18 F '70
Teacher's role in ITV. W. B. Mitchell. To-
days Ed 59:34 Ja '70
Teachers, students, and selfishness in the
seventies. V. R. Mollenkott. Chr Today 14:
6-8+ Ap 10; 13-15 Ap 24 '70
Teaching is a science, not an art. D. A. Lind-
ley, jr. Engl J 59:960-3 O '70
  See also
Academic freedom
Adult education
Audio-visual instruction
Classroom management

Colleges and universities—Teaching
Contract plan (education)
Courses of study
Discussion method (education)
Education
Education, Experimental
Individual instruction
Indoctrination
Junior colleges—Teaching
Motivation (education)
Psychology, Educational
School excursions
Teachers
Teachers—Education
Teachers—Rating

Aids and devices

Dollars and sense of the standards; School
media programs. B. Morris. il Library J 95:
1568-9 Ap 15 '70
Games students play. R. G. Shirts. Sat R 53:
81-2 My 16 '70
Instructional media. See issues of Clearing
house
Is technology a late bloomer? il Sr Schol 96:
Schol Teach 1 Mr 9 '70
Mobile educational technology; Board of edu-
cation of Baltimore County, Md. D. Merry-
man. il Am Lib 1:162-4 F '70
New educational materials. Schol Teach Jr/Sr
High p46-8 S 21; 37-8+ O 5; 32-3 N 2; 18 D
7 '70
New educational materials (cont) Schol Teach
Sec Teach Sup p26-7 F 2; 24-5 Mr 9; 29+ Ap
6; 14-15+ My 4 '70
Now curriculum. S. Boyer. Sat R 53:81 S 19
'70
Reading instruction in the elementary school;
excerpts from address, February 1969. N. B.
Smith. Todays Ed 59:42-3+ Ja '70
Schools' use of technology blasted in McMur-
rin report. Library J 95:1550 Ap 15 '70
Sesame street learning kit. il Pub W 197:32-3
Ap 20 '70
Teaching tips; suggestions sent in by teach-
ers. Schol Teach Jr/Sr High p27 O 5; 23
D 7 '70
Teaching tips; suggestions sent in by teach-
ers (cont) Schol Teach Sec Teach Sup p 10
Ja 5; 30 Mr 9 '70
When pupils don't learn, publishers don't
earn; money-back guarantees and other
offers by dealers in teaching materials. il
Sr Schol 96:Schol Teach 1 Mr 16 '70
  See also
Audio-visual aids
Computers—Educational use
Education market
Film strips
Instructional materials centers
Moving pictures in education
Tape recordings
Teaching machines
Telephone in education
Television in education

Anecdotes, facetiae, satire, etc.

Efficiency at all costs! J. Woods. Todays Ed
59:19 F '70

Bibliography

Book reviews. See issues of Clearing house
Teacher's bookshelf. Schol Teach Jr/Sr High
p49 S 21 '70
Teacher's bookshelf (cont) Schol Teach Sec
Teach Sup p26 N 3 '69, 20 My 4 '70

TEACHING, Freedom of. See Academic freedom

TEACHING as a profession
Dedicated teacher is the teaching profession's
greatest enemy. E. Edwards. Todays Ed 59:
53-4 N '70
Militancy and the profession of teaching. L. S.
Vander Werf. Sch & Soc 98:171-3 Mr '70
Professionalizing teaching; adaptation of address. H. R. Weinstock. bibliog Clear House
45:3-9 S '70

TEACHING machines
Teaching machine increases reading skill. S.
V. Jones. il Sci Digest 68:73 Jl '70
What's happening to teaching machines? il
Good H 170:181 Ap '70
  See also
Computers—Educational use
Westinghouse learning corporation

TEACHINGS of Saint Paul. See Paul, Saint—
Teachings

TEACH-ins
  See also
Environmental movement—Teach-ins

TEACUPS. See Cups

TEAGUE, Dorwin
Guadeloupe gamble. il Yachting 128:62-3+ N '70
Offbeat Caribbean: British Honduras. il Yachting 127:56-7+ Mr '70

TEAGUE, Richard A.
How the Gremlin lost its tail; interview. il Pop Mech 134:88-91+ Ag '70
1970 Gremlin; interview. por Motor T. 22:72 Mr '70

TEAL, John J. jr
Domesticating the wild and woolly musk ox. il Nat Geog 137:862-79 Je '70

TEALE, Edwin Way
Selbourne nightingale; excerpt from Springtime in Britain. il Audubon 72:58-67 S '70

TEAMS, Baseball. See Baseball clubs

TEAMSTERS union. See International brotherhood of teamsters, chauffeurs, warehousemen and helpers of America

TEAR gas
Are tear gas and herbicides permitted weapons? J. Goldblat. il Bul Atom Sci 26:13-16 Ap '70
First aid; tear gas exposure. C. J. Potthoff. Todays Health 48:64 Jl '70

TEAS. See Afternoon teas

TEATOWN LAKE reservation, Ossining. See Brooklyn botanic garden

TEATRO Colón, Buenos Aires. See Opera houses

TEBALDI, Renata
Callas and Tebaldi, yesterday and today. G. Movshon. il pors Hi Fi sec I 20:89-90 Ja '70
Records. Opera N 34:35 F 7 '70

TEBBEL, John
Can journalism schools improve the press? Sat R 53:63-5 Ja 17 '70
Do news media overplay disorder? Press power revisited. Sat R 53:53-4 Je 13 '70
Failing newspapers and anti-trust laws. Sat R 53:58-9 D 12 '70
Libraries in miniature: a new era begins. il Sat R 54:41-2 Ja 9 '71
Network television's uncertain future. Sat R 53:69-70 N 14 '70
Recruiting in the inner city. Sat R 53:54-5 Jl 11 '70
Revolution in layout. il Sat R 53:93-4 S 12 '70
Stories the newspapers do cover. Sat R 53:66-7 Ap 11 '70
Studying the mass media. Sat R 53:69-71 F 14 '70
Worst-covered stories: what's the news? il Sat R 53:111-12 Mr 14 '70

TECH art. See Art. Modern

TECHNICAL assistance
See also
Industrialization
Underdeveloped areas
United Nations—Development program

TECHNICAL assistance, American
See also
United States—Peace corps

TECHNICAL assistance, Chinese
Chinese working on the railroad; commitment in Zambia. T. Land. Nation 211:371-2 O 19 '70
Two-China war in black Africa. il U S News 69:74-6 S 14 '70

TECHNICAL assistance, Israeli
Letter from Israel: technical cooperation: Israel's way in the third world and administered territories. N. Levin. il Bul Atom Sci 26:46-52 Ap '70

TECHNICAL assistance, Russian
Our Socialist friends; aid program in Yemen. M. J. Kubic. il Newsweek 75:48 My 25 '70

TECHNICAL assistance, Taiwanese
Two-China war in black Africa. il U S News 69:74-6 S 14 '70

TECHNICAL assistance in Africa
Scientific safari to Africa. G. T. Seaborg. il Science 169:554-61 Ag 7 '70
Two-China war in black Africa. il U S News 69:74-6 S 14 '70

TECHNICAL assistance in Taiwan
Taiwan: U.S. tries one-man experiment in postpaid assistance. J. Walsh. por Science 170:835-9 N 20 '70

TECHNICAL assistance in Tanzania
Chinese working on the railroad. T. Land. Nation 211:371-2 O 19 '70

TECHNICAL assistance in Vietnam
Success story in war-torn Vietnam. il U S News 69:22-3 O 26 '70

TECHNICAL assistance in Yemen
Our Socialist friends. M. J. Kubic. il Newsweek 75:48 My 25 '70

TECHNICAL assistance in Zambia
Chinese working on the railroad. T. Land. Nation 211:371-2 O 19 '70

TECHNICAL education
Reforming vocational-technical education. Sch & Soc 98:73-4 F '70
See also
Agricultural education
Massachusetts institute of technology. Cambridge
Texas technological university, Lubbock
Vocational education

TECHNICAL literature
See also
Booksellers and bookselling—Technical literature

TECHNICAL processes in libraries. See Libraries—Technical processes

TECHNICAL writing
Business and trade journal market. O. Henry. Writer 83:24-6 Je '70
Full-time freelancing in technical writing. P. Franklin. il Writers Digest 50:20-2+ Ag '70
Tips on working as a technical writer. D. Faulkner. Writers Digest 50:23 Ag '70
Writing science for the public. W. Sullivan. il por Phys Today 23:51-3 Ag '70

TECHNICIANS, Electronic. See Electronic technicians

TECHNICIANS in industry
See also
Electronic technicians

TECHNIQUE (music) See Virtuosity in music

TECHNITROL, Inc.
Magnetic disks go to court. Bsns W p88 Ja 17 '70

TECHNOLOGICAL aids in education. See Teaching—Aids and devices

TECHNOLOGICAL change
Assessment of technology. H. Brooks and R. Bowers. il Sci Am 222:13-21 F '70
Casualties of our time. A. B. Ford. bibliog il Science 167:256-63 Ja 16 '70
Crisis of transformation. J. Platt. Cur 115:3-17 F '70
Evaluating signals of technological change. J. R. Bright. bibliog f il Harvard Bsns R 48:62-70 Ja '70
Feeling their way; technology assessment programs. Sci N 97:240-1 Mr 7 '70
Foundation for human survival; address, August 26, 1970. C. L. Hogan. Vital Speeches 36:755-8 O 1 '70
Future shock, by A. Toffler. Review
Fortune il 82:195-6 N '70. J. Zukosky
Manpower implications of computer control in manufacturing. A. S. Herman. il Mo Labor R 93:3-8 O '70
Pentagon of power, by L. Mumford. Review
Nat R 23:41-2 Ja 12 '71. H. Caton
Reflections: the megamachine; excerpts from The pentagon of power. L. Mumford. New Yorker 46:48-50+ O 17; 55-8+ O 24; 50-2+ O 31 '70
Top idea men trade ideas. il Bsns W p32-3 Ja 31 '70
Vertical is to live, horizontal is to die. R. B. Fuller; reply. J. Barzun. Am Scholar 39:514 Sum '70
See also
Technology transfer

TECHNOLOGICAL forecasting. See Forecasts (technology)

TECHNOLOGICAL innovations. See Technological change

TECHNOLOGICAL research. See Industrial research

TECHNOLOGISTS, Medical. See Medical workers

TECHNOLOGY
Human materials production as a process in the biosphere. H. Brown. il Sci Am 223:194-8+ bibliog(p266) S '70
Technical revolution of the 1970s; symposium, with editorial comment. il Aviation W 92:21, 26-35+ Je 22 '70
Technology in the manager's future; adaptation of address, June 1970. H. M. Boettinger. bibliog f il Harvard Bsns R 48:4-6+ N '70
See also
Space technology

Bibliography
Books to come. Library J 95:3813-15+ N 1 '70
Books to come; ed. by J. Donathan. Library J 95:919-35+, 2552-71 Mr 1- Jl '70
Science, technology; April-September highlights. il Pub W 197:30-49 Ap 13 '70
Science, technology; some leading books scheduled for publication November 1970, through March 1971. il Pub W 198:27-40 N 16 '70
Sci-tech books '69: one hundred outstanding titles for general library collections; comp. by D. F. Pfoutz. il por Library J 95:855-62 Mr 1 '70

TECHNOLOGY—*Continued*

Conferences

Aspen technology conference ends in chaos. V. K. McElheny. Science 169:1187 S 18 '70

Crisis in Aspen; report on conference on Technology, man and culture. M. Goldsmith. Bul Atom Sci 26:28-30+ N '70

History

Medieval uses of air. L. White, jr. il Sci Am 223:92-100 Ag '70

Origins of feedback control; water clock, the thermostat and mechanisms for controlling windmills. O. Mayr. il Sci Am 223:110-18 O '70

International aspects

Europe faces the technology gap. W. Goldstein. Yale R 59:161-78 D '69

Technological strategies and national purpose. R. Gilpin. bibliog Science 169:441-8 Jl 31 '70

Technology and international relations, 1970 and beyond; address, October 6, 1970. R. Ellsworth. Dept State Bul 63:641-7 N 23 '70

Japan

Japan: now the imitator shows the way. il Bsns W p88-9+ My 16 '70

Russia

Soviet technological threat; excerpts from address. J. S. Foster. Aviation W 92:13 Ap 27 '70

TECHNOLOGY and art. See Art and technology

TECHNOLOGY and civilization

Banality of revolt; views of Andrew Hacker and William Braden. S. M. Lipset. il Sat R 53:23-6+ Jl 18 '70

Between two ages: America's role in the technectronic era, by Z. Brzezinski. Review Nation 211:597-8 D 7 '70. P. Steinfels

Beyond survival. J. Poppy. il Look 34:30-3 Ja 13 '70

Century of mismatch, by S. Ramo. Review Bsns W p 10 Ap 25 '70. H. Wolff

Children of Frankenstein, by H. J. Muller. Review Sat R 53:32-3 Ap 4 '70. P. Woodring

Crisis in Aspen; report on conference on Technology, man and culture. M. Goldsmith. Bul Atom Sci 26:28-30+ N '70

Ecological ethic. I. G. Barbour. il Chr Cent 87:1180-4 O 7 '70

Ecology of weaponry. W. C. Clemens, jr. il Bul Atom Sci 26:27-31 S '70; Same with title Dynamics of the arms race. Cur 123:57-63 N '70

Emerging technetronic era; excerpts from Between two ages. Z. Brzezinski. Cur 124:56-64 D '70

Government interest in technology assessment grows; with editorial comment. Phys Today 23:61-2, 104 Ap '70

How I got radicalized; the making of an agitator for zero. J. Fischer. Harper 240:18+ Ap '70

Human landscape. R. Dubos. Bul Atom Sci 26:31-7 Mr '70

If you don't mind my saying so. J. W. Krutch. Am Scholar 39:202+ Spr '70

Industrial approaches to urban problems; AAAS symposium, December 28, 1970. J. Lewis. il Science 170:658-9 N 6 '70

Is our history obsolete? proposal for eliminating ethnocentrism. T. J. Knight. Ed Digest 35:28-31 My '70

Miracles, more or less. J. Ciardi. Sat R 53:6 Ag 8 '70

Myth of the machine: the pentagon of power, by L. Mumford. Review Bsns W p6 N 14 '70. R. Dubos Life 69:16 N 20 '70. H. Clurman Sat R 53:24+ D 19 '70. M. R. Konvitz

Mythos of the electronic revolution. J. W. Carey and J. J. Quirk. Am Scholar 39:219-41, 395-424 Spr-Sum '70

On controlling technology; excerpt from Reason awake. R. Dubos. Cur 119:36-7 Je '70

Pentagon of power, by L. Mumford. Review Nat R 23:41-2 Ja 12 '71. H. Caton

Pentagon of power; excerpts. L. Mumford. il Horizon 12:4-21 Aut '70

Place for snakes as well as naked lovers. G. B. Leonard. il Look 34:80-5 Ja 13 '70

Pondering the unthinkable. C. Joyner. America 123:256-8 O 10 '70

Predicting the consequences of technolgy. J. Lear. por Sat R 53:44-6 Mr 28 '70

Reason awake, by R. Dubos. Review Sat R 53:68 Je 6 '70. H. Brown

Reflections: the megamachine; excerpts from The pentagon of power. L. Mumford. New Yorker 46:50-2+ O 10; 48-50+ O 17; 55-8+ O 24; 50-2+ O 31 '70

Some kind words for a new villain; address, January 22, 1970. F. C. Foy. Vital Speeches 36:343-6 Mr 15 '70

Super technology, will it end the good life? B. Commoner. por Field & S 75:59+ Je '70

Technetronic America; excerpts from Between two ages. Z. Brzezinski. Newsweek 76:36 Jl 20 '70

Technology and growth, by E. J. Mishan. Review Bsns W p8 Ap 25 '70. L. Beman

Technology and mankind's future. R. A. Givens. America 123:254-6 O 10 '70

Technology, change and the citizen; excerpts from Technological change. E. G. Mesthene. Cur 119:32-6 Je '70

Technology's impact; excerpts from address. J. H. Shaffer. Aviation W 93:9 Ag 24 '70

Who's in charge of history? Chr Cent 87:1439 D 2 '70

Why we need new businessmen. C. Kaufmann. Look 34:76+ Ja 13 '70

Workman can master his tools. A. Maitland. Sat R 53:22 N 14 '70

Zen Buddhism and western alienation from nature. W. R. Hoyt. Chr Cent 87:1194-6 O 7 '70

TECHNOLOGY and religion. See Religion and technology

TECHNOLOGY and society. See Technology and civilization

TECHNOLOGY assessment, Office of (proposed) See United States—Technology assessment, Office of (proposed)

TECHNOLOGY planning documents. See United States—Defense Department of—Technology planning documents

TECHNOLOGY transfer

Spin-off: the fruit of space research. G. Gregory. il UNESCO Courier 23:4-31+ Mr '70

Transferring technology by transferring people. C. H. Danhof. il Mo Labor R 93:62-3 My '70

U.S. seeks to share the facts. Bsns W p58+ Mr 21 '70

TECOMATEPEC pottery. See Pottery, Mexican

TECTONICS. See Geology, Structural

TEDDY bears. See Toys

TEDESCO, James J. jr

Let the camera be your eyes. il Am City 85:86+ Ja '70

TEEN-age fatigue. See Fatigue

TEEN-age pregnancy. See Pregnancy

TEEN-age reading. See High school students—Reading

TEEN-age rooms. See Rooms

TEEN-age slang. See Slang

TEEN-age suicide. See Suicide

TEEN-agers. See Youth

TEEN-agers and smoking. See Smoking and youth

TEEN corps. See Volunteer service

TEEN tycoon; drama. See Heinzen. B. B

TEEN volunteer corps. See Volunteer service

TEETH

Dental enamel: detection of surface changes by ultrasound. S. Lees and others. bibliog il Science 169:1314-16 S 25 '70

Paint-on tooth protector. il Sci Digest 68:76 N '70

Save that tooth. Sci Digest 67:58 Ja '70
See also
Dental research

Care and hygiene

Coming: healthy teeth to last a lifetime. il Changing T 24:21-3 Mr '70

Hazards to children's dental health: sweets and malnutrition. L. W. Sauer. il PTA Mag 64:31-2 F '70
See also
Dental caries—Prevention

Diseases
See also
Dental caries

Extraction

Guilt and dental mutilation. Sci Digest 67:56 Ap '70

Transplantation

He's wearing his sister's teeth. il Todays Health 48:17 F '70

TEETH (animals)

Tooth care for your dog. D. M. Lidster. il Bet Hom & Gard 48:120+ My '70

TEETH, Artificial
Plastic teeth a success. Sci Digest 67:53 Ap '70

TEFFT, Carol
Sponge double-printing. il Sch Arts 70:12-13 D '70

TEFLON
Teflon-S makes the cutting great. R. Sickler. il Pop Mech 133:164-6 Ja '70

TEICH. Albert H. See Lerner. D. jt. auth.

TEICHERT, Curt, and others
Mixed Permian-Triassic fauna, Guryul Ravine, Kashmir. bibliog il Science 167:174-5 Ja 9 '70

TEILHARD DE CHARDIN, Pierre
On to omega! J. E. Bruns. Cath World 212:52 O '70 *
Religious aspects of cosmic consciousness. pors Chr Cent 87:1533-6 D 23 '70 *

TEIXEIRA, Charles
Murder of Jeremy Harlowe; story. il Esquire 73:101-3+ F '70

TEKTITE (underwater laboratory) See Underwater laboratories

TEKTITE project. See Underwater laboratories

TEKTITES
Fission track ages and ages of deposition of deep-sea microtektites. W. Gentner and others. bibliog il Science 168:359-61 Ap 17 '70
Microtektites and tektites: a chemical comparison. F. A. Frey and others. bibliog il Science 170:845-7 N 20 '70
Moon rock identified with tektites. Space World G-12-84:13 D '70
Tektite glass in Apollo 12 sample. J. A. O'Keefe. bibliog il Science 168:1209-10 Je 5 '70; Reply with rejoinder. E. A. King, jr. and others. 170:199-200 O 9 '70
Zircon and chromite crystals in a Muong Nong-type tektite. B. P. Glass. bibliog il Science 169:766-9 Ag 21 '70

TEL AVIV

Afro-Asian institute for labor studies and cooperation
See Afro-Asian institute for labor studies and cooperation

Galleries and museums
See also
Alphabet museum

TELECOMMUNICATION
Coming shake-up telecommunications. D. Cordtz. il Fortune 81:68-71+ Ap '70
Manufacturing by the numbers: a total systems concept of manufacturing; address, September 16, 1970. H. E. Markley. Vital Speeches 37:143-5 D 15 '70
See also
Communications satellites
Facsimile transmission
International telecommunication union
Telephone

TELEDIAGNOSIS. See Diagnosis

TELEDYNE, inc.
As they see it; interview. H. Singleton. Forbes 106:64+ N 15 '70

TELEPHONE
Big changes in TV, phones: upheaval in communications. il U S News 69:50-2 Jl 13 '70
Look, Ma Bell, no hands; vandalproof phone. il Time 95:92-3+ My 4 '70
Ma Bell takes her lumps. M. T. Bloom. Read Digest 96:206-10 Ap '70
Rising toll of the telephone hang-up. Time 95:74-5 Mr 23 '70
See also
American telephone and telegraph company
Facsimile transmission
New York telephone company
Radio telephone. Portable
TeleSession company

Answering service
Answering services have many callings. V. Louviere. Nations Bsns 58:17 S '70

Apparatus and supplies
Build Security I; scrambler system. J. Pina. il Pop Electr 32:27-33 Mr '70
Open season on telephones; interconnection devices. il Bsns W p58+ F 7 '70
They're cracking down on the telephone nuts, and you can help! J. H. Pollack. il Todays Health 48:24-7+ My '70

Computer combination
Telephone lovers, take heart. il Esquire 73:85-7 F '70

Data transmission systems
How they'll read your utility meter by phone. S. Shatavsky. il Pop Sci 196:100 Ap '70
Profitable way to translate computer talk; high speed modems. il Bsns W p 124+ My 16 '70

Emergency use
See also
Telephone in counseling

Medical applications
Physicians phone for automatic medical advice; Audio message center and telelecture. D. L. Fortney. Todays Health 48:18-19 Mr '70

Municipal use
More phones, better service, less cost; Trenton, N.J. J. Alexander, jr. il por Am City 85:137-8 O '70

Noise
Transmission delays and echoes in satellite communications. R. G. Gould. il Electr World 84:34-6+ Ag '70

Rates
Bell system kids the press. J. C. Goulden. il Nation 210:167-8 F 16 '70
Phone rate-setting raises more static. Bsns W p22 O 31 '70

Switching system
See Telephone exchanges

Wire tapping
See Wire tapping

TELEPHONE, Long distance
Transmission delays and echoes in satellite communications. R. G. Gould. il Electr World 84:34-6+ Ag '70

TELEPHONE calls
Telephonitis, the teen-age hangup. H. Arnstein. il Todays Health 48:40-1+ F '70
They're cracking down on the telephone nuts, and you can help! J. H. Pollack. il Todays Health 48:24-7+ My '70

TELEPHONE calls to service men in Vietnam
How to talk to Vietnam, free; via MARS. A. Lee. il Pop Mech 134:108-10 S '70

TELEPHONE circuits
Transmission delays and echoes in satellite communications. R. G. Gould. il Electr World 84:34-6+ Ag '70

TELEPHONE companies
Open season on telephones; interconnection devices. il Bsns W p58+ F 7 '70
Rising toll of the telephone hang-up. Time 95:74-5 Mr 23 '70
See also
American telephone and telegraph company
Bell telephone system
General telephone company of California
International telephone and telegraph corporation

Employees
Working with the unskilled. AT&T's experience; interview. W. W. Straley il por U S News 68:88-91 Mr 9 '70

Securities
Why a blue chip has been fading; AT&T's long slide. il Bsns W p26 F 7 '70

TELEPHONE directories
See also
Advertising mediums—Telephone directories

TELEPHONE employees. See Telephone companies—Employees

TELEPHONE exchanges
Loneliness of the short-distance dialer. M. Mayer. il Esquire 74:154-6+ O '70

TELEPHONE in counseling
Hotline for troubled teen-agers; Los Angeles. J. N. Bell. il Read Digest 97:41-6 N '70

TELEPHONE in education
Something different in in-service education: Educational telephone network workshop. G. Hartung and R. Gelman. il Todays Ed 59:24-5 My '70

TELEPHONE in service to the aged
New York Ring a day plan saves five lives in 2½ years; project in Nassau County. il Aging 193:19 N '70

TELEPHONE lines
Waveguides to carry phone calls. M. S. Snitzer. il Electr World 83:42 My '70

TELEPHONE numbers
Dial 686-2377 for numbers. Time 95:36 F 2 '70

TELEPHONE radio conversation programs. See Radio broadcasting—Conversation programs

TELEPHONE tables. See Tables

TELEPHOTO lenses. See Lenses, Photographic

TELEPHOTOGRAPHY
Say it with lenses. E. Wildi. il Pop Phot 67:
84-6+ S '70
Teleffects. J. Scully. il Mod Phot 34:56-65 Ag
'70
TELEPROMPTER corporation
To wire a nation. Time 95:66+ Je 1 '70
TELESCOPE lenses. See Lenses
TELESCOPE mirrors. See Mirrors for tele-
scopes
TELESCOPE mountings
Flexure of a concrete telescope pier. G. Kess-
ler. il Sky & Tel 40:235-6 O '70
Inexpensive pipe mounting. G. A. Wimer. il
Sky & Tel 39:193 Mr '70
TELESCOPES
CHT: a catadioptric Herschelian telescope
with tilted components. R. E. Cox. il Sky
& Tel 41:46-52 Ja '71
Chinese nine-inch semiportable reflector. K.
L. Liu. il Sky & Tel 40:110-12 Ag '70
Folded Herschelian off-axis reflector. J. R.
Pawlick. il Sky & Tel 39:191-2 Mr '70
Fork-mounted telescopes with dual eyepiece
positions. R. P. Jensen. il pors Sky & Tel
40:313-17 N '70
Gleanings for ATM's; ed. by R. E. Cox. See
issues of Sky and telescope
Phoenix amateur's 12½-inch Schmidt-Casse-
grain. M. Kaufman. il Sky & Tel 39:254-60
Ap '70
Pollution watching by telescope: study by P.
W. Hodge at University of Washington.
Sci N 98:300 O 10 '70
Portable 6-inch Dall-Kirkham and celestial
camera. K. Moll. il Sky & Tel 39:394-6 Je
'70
Sky's the limit with this 200-power telescope.
R. Brightman. il Pop Mech 134:166-73+ D
'70; 135:152-7 Ja '71
Spar telescope of Lockheed solar observatory.
G. A. Carroll. il Sky & Tel 40:10-13 Jl '70
Steward observatory's new 90-inch reflector.
C. M. Cardon. il R Pop Astron 63:7-9 Ag '69
Tele-topics. See issues of Review of popular
astronomy
Ten-inch Newtonian with counterpoised
canopy. E. K. Owen. il Sky & Tel 40:169-
74 S '70
236-inch Soviet reflector. V. Lutsky. il Sky
& Tel 39:99 F '70
See also
Mirrors for telescopes
Radio telescopes
Resolving power (optics)

Equipment
Easily built solar viewer. D. C. Lemmon. il
Sky & Tel 39:89 F '70
Notes on clock-drive speed controls. R. E.
Cox. il Sky & Tel 40:237-40 O '70

Mounting
See Telescope mountings
TELESCOPES on space vehicles
Covering the spectrum in space. D. E. Thom-
sen. il Sci N 98:202-3 S 5 '70
TELESCOPIC photography. See Telephotogra-
phy
TELESCOPIC sights
See also
Firearms—Sights
TELESESSION company
Conference calls become fun. il Bsns W p 101
D 5 '70
Nationwide party line. Time 97:35-6 Ja 11 '71
TELESTAR athletic club, New York. See Ath-
letic clubs
TELEVISION
Electronic wallpaper; N. J. Paik and his video
synthesizer. D. Davis. il por Newsweek 76:
54 Ag 24 '70
Nam June Paik: he composes pictures on TV.
W. F. Wilson. il por Pop Phot 66:102+
F '70
Radio & television news. F. H. Belt. See
issues of Electronics world
Television: twenty years from now. F. H.
Belt. il Electr World 83:25-9 Ja '70
Type vs tube: surviving the 70s; highlights
of panel discussion. il Pub W 197:30-1 Mr
23 '70

Social aspects
See Television broadcasting—Social as-
pects
TELEVISION, Closed circuit
Designing a small CCTV system. K. B.
Knecht. il Electr World 84:34-7+ D '70
GBC closed-circuit TV system. W. Roy. il
Radio-Electr 41:82 N '70
GE's hookup for business conferees. Bsns W
p24+ Jl 11 '70

New mini TV: your third eye. A. Fisher. il
Pop Sci 196:57 F '70
Random access to photography. H. Fried-
man. il Pop Phot 66:35-6 Je '70
TV talk. W. Sheed. Sports Illus 32:7 Mr 9 '70
TV talk:
World cup, on closed-circuit TV. W.
Sheed. Sports Illus 33:8 Jl 6 '70
See also
Television in education
TELEVISION, Color
Color TV 1971; symposium. il Radio-Electr 42:
32-51+ Ja '71
TELEVISION, Experimental
Guerrilla television. il Newsweek 76:57-8 D 7
'70
TELEVISION advertising
Brown is beautiful; Negro selling suntan lo-
tion. il Newsweek 75:92 Mr 23 '70
Buying an image on public TV; institutional
advertising on noncommercial stations. Z.
B. Grant. New Repub 163:13 N 14 '70
Caveat pre-emptor; ACT's request for free
time to expose overstated toy commer-
cials. R. L. Shayon. Sat R 54:37 Ja 9 '71
Celebrity commercials industry. S. W. Little.
il Sat R 53:55-6+ Ap 11 '70
Commercial successes. il Newsweek 76:100 O
19 '70
Inside TV view stirs media flap. Bsns W p52
Mr 14 '70
McGannon's haymaker; heavy commercial-
izing of television programming. J. Mc-
Laughlin. America 122:397 Ap 11 '70
Mea culpa campaign; General telephone com-
mercials. Time 96:67 Jl 27 '70
Now the head man's on TV. R. Levy. il Duns
95:59-61 My '70
One-eyed slicker; TV's long lasting, super
strength half-truths. D. Henninger. New
Repub 162:17-19 My 2 '70
Question of fairness; antismoking ads and
the FCC ruling. Newsweek 76:57 D 28 '70
Reviewing the commercials. M. Goodman. il
Time 96:59 N 9 '70
Selling of the candidates 1970. il Newsweek
76:34-8+ O 19 '70
Soupy road to romance; Heinz company's
ad campaign. Time 96:78 N 30 '70
Spots before our eyes. R. L. Tobin. il Sat R
53:67-8 F 14 '70
TV: living room movie course. E. Wildi. il
Mod Phot 34:100-1+ Ja '70
TV package nobody pays for; exchanging
free shows for free air time. il Bsns W p80
Ag 1 '70
Television: the splitting image. M. Mannes.
Sat R 53:66-8 N 14 '70
To wash or not to wash; equal time and
deceptive advertising. Sedulus. New Repub
163:29-30 Ag 22 '70
When advertising talks to everyone. F. Cone.
Sat R 53:56-7+ O 10 '70
You know you're not getting Maudie Frick-
ert. W. Johnson. il Sports Illus 32:30-6 Ja
26 '70
See also
Cigarettes—Advertising
Detergents—Advertising

Cigarettes
See Cigarettes—Advertising

Japan
Russians are coming? promoting Russian
products in Japan. Newsweek 75:75 Ap 13
'70

TELEVISION and children. See Television
broadcasting and children
TELEVISION and copyright. See Copyright—
Broadcasting rights
TELEVISION and libraries. See Libraries and
television
TELEVISION antennas
Antenna installer's guidebook. J. A. Gupton,
jr. il Radio-Electr 41:55-8 S; 59-62 O '70
Color TV antennas: how to get top perform-
ance. C. Shelledy. il Radio-Electr 41:33-6
S '70
How to get those blacked-out games on your
TV. L. Buckwalter. il Pop Mech 134:100-3+
N '70
No snow in June. G. Monser. il Pop Electr
32:27-9 Je '70
Small TV antennas. il Consumer Bul 53:20-1
Mr '70
UHF TV antennas, ready for your rooftop. il
Radio-Electr 41:60-2 S '70
Winegard Sensar TV antennas. il Radio-
Electr 42:26 Ja '71
See also
CATV system

Equipment
TV-FM lead-in: what kind to use? T. R.
Haskett. il Electr World 83:46-50 Ja '70

TELEVISION apparatus
See also
Cathode ray tubes
Video recorders and recording
TELEVISION apparatus industry and trade
Revolt of mama-san; boycott against buying
home-built color sets. il Time 96:90 D 7 '70
TV set tiff: Japan out of focus? Sr Schol 97:
12 S 28 '70
See also
Zenith radio corporation
TELEVISION authorship
And then there was Sidney Greenstreet. .? S.
Fickling. Writer 83:14-16 N '70
Television and film writing (cont) N. Vogel.
por Writers Digest 50:44-6 F '70
TELEVISION awards
Good season for the literate: SR television
awards, 1970. R. L. Shayon. Sat R 53:64-5+
Ap 11 '70
TELEVISION broadcasting
See also
Communications satellites
Television stations
Video recorders and recording

Advertising
See Television advertising

Animal programs
See Animals on television programs

Ballet
See Television broadcasting—Dancing

Baseball
See Television broadcasting—Sports

Business programs
Emmy for an annual meeting? live question
and answer telecast. V. Louviere. il Nations
Bsns 58:14 Jl '70

Censorship
Devil in Duval County; firing of WJXT-TV
reporter for pollution documentaries. por
Time 96:42+ Ag 17 '70
Dirty five-letter word; censoring the talk
shows. G. Ace. Sat R 53:10 Ja 24 '70
Public channels & private censors. N. John-
son. Nation 210:329-32 Mr 23 '70
Regulating the regulator; WRC-TV censors.
N. Johnson. Newsweek 76:53+ O 26 '70

Children, Effect on
See Television broadcasting and children

Childrens programs
Hot Dog, entertaining consumerism. F. Du
Plessix. Vogue 156:56 S 15 '70
Saturday morning TV is going ape; Lance
Link, secret chimp. il Life 69:62-5 O 2 '70
Time out for TV; ed. by E. Borgenicht. See
issues of PTA magazine
See also
Action for children's television (organization)
Television in education

Comedy
See Television broadcasting—Humor

Conversation programs
Adverse to adversaries. Sedulus. New Repub
163:29-30 Jl 11 '70
Can Praise ruin Dick Cavett? il pors News-
week 76:105-6 O 5 '70
David Frost rampant; Arlo Guthrie and Spiro
T. Agnew shows. Sedulus. New Repub 163:
33-4 O 10 '70
First for Cavett. il pors Time 96:74 O 26 '70
Johnny & Merv & David & Dick; or, Talk is
cheap and how it got that way. R. Schickel.
Harper 240:116-18+ Mr '70
Johnson seeks vindication. Time 95:20 F 23
'70
Late-night talker who knows how to listen:
the Dick Cavett show. J. Leonard. por
Life 68:10 F 13 '70
Listening ear; Campuses in crisis: three col-
lege presidents speak, news special. R. L.
Shayon. Sat R 53:36 My 30 '70
Memories from the Pedernales; L.B.J's talk
with W. Cronkite. H. Sidey. por Time 95:
16 F 16 '70
Would you welcome, please: Otto Friedrich?
O. Friedrich. Esquire 74:32+ D '70

Cookery programs
Cooking lessons, entertaining.   H. Resnik.
Vogue 156:102 D '70

Court proceedings
See Television broadcasting—Trials

Crime programs
Finding alternatives; a Mod squad episode.
R. L. Shayon. Sat R 53:46 Ja 24 '70
Mannix: where the action is; interview, ed.
by P. Hudson. M. Connors. il pors Sr Schol
97:40 O 26 '70
Star couple; C. Williams in the Mod squad
series. L. Robinson. il pors Ebony 25:142-4+
Mr '70

Dancing
Looking at television. M. Harriton. il Dance
Mag 44:72 Jl '70
Ritual-D: Gus Giordano company. M. Per-
rone. il pors Dance Mag 44:26-7 S '70
TV: bad ballet; superb ethnic; Canadian Cin-
derella and Camera three's Matteo and his
Indo-American dance company. W. Terry.
il Sat R 53:49+ Mr 21 '70

Documentary programs
Day in the life of the United States of America. CBS documentary. J. Leonard. il Life
69:10 S 4 '70
Eye of the storm; learning to understand
race discrimination; Riceville, Ia. elementary school experiment. J. Leonard. il Life
68:16 My 8 '70
Frederick Wiseman's Hospital. R. Schickel.
Life 68:9 F 6 '70
Hats off to NET; Who invited US? Nation
210:228-9 Mr 2 '70
Jarred halos; Banks and the poor. R. L. Sha-
yon. il Sat R 53:17 D 19 '70
Lord Snowdon on pets. il por Time 96:48 Jl
6 '70
Open conspiracy; presentation of Voices from
the Russian underground by CBS news. R.
L. Shayon. Sat R 53:62 Ag 22 '70
Potted plants, padded banks; Banks and the
poor. Sedulus. New Repub 163:27-8 N 28 '70
Siberia: the endless horizon. M. McMahon. il
Sr Schol 95:Schol Teach 7 N 17 '69
Tools for manipulation; drug-abuse pro-
grams. R. L. Shayon. Sat R 53:52 S 19 '70

Drama
Electronic globe: The Andersonville trial. R.
L. Shayon. Sat R 53:40 Je 13 '70
Forward with Forsyte. Sedulus. New Repub
163:32 N 7 '70; Reply. S. Davis. 163:35 D 5
'70
Leap year; 1970-71 season offerings. R. L.
Shayon. Sat R 53:50 O 10 '70
No. 3, and trying harder; ABC's twelve new
shows. R. Burgheim. il Time 96:79 O 5 '70
Odd couple, sparkles; Barefoot in the park,
clumpy. H. S. Resnik. Vogue 156:108 N 1 '70
Odd squad; ABC adaptation of The odd
couple. il pors Time 96:74 O 26 '70
Real scandal behind The Forsyte saga. A.
West. il Vogue 155:206-7+ My '70
Showing what's wrong: Room 222, a comedy-
drama. il Time 95:54 Mr 16 '70
Soul drama; Chicago's new series titled Bird
of the iron feather. il Time 95:59-60 F 23
'70
TV's on-again romance with medicine. J. N.
Bell. il Todays Health 48:24-9+ Mr '70
Watching it; the relevant television shows. J.
Corry. Harper 241:42+ D '70
Youth and sociology; youth-oriented shows.
Time 95:55 Mr 16 '70

Educational services
See Television in education

Employee recruiting programs
How to land a job by watching TV; Opportunity line. il Bsns W p24 My 9 '70

Experimental programming
See Television broadcasting—Programming

Fishing
See Television broadcasting—Sports

Football
See Television broadcasting—Sports

Golf
See Television broadcasting—Sports

Government programs
Advantage: Mr President; Conversation with
the President on TV. il por Time 97:36 Ja
18 '71

Hockey
See Television broadcasting—Sports

Horror programs
Turned-on vampire; Dark shadows. il Newsweek 75:102+ Ap 20 '70

TELEVISION broadcasting—*Continued*

Humor

Mom always loved them best; Smothers boys back. D. Brudnoy. Nat R 22:1009+ S 22 '70
One cheer for the conventional; McHale's navy. Sedulus. New Repub 163:30 N 14 '70
Painful passing; Smothers brothers. R. L. Shayon. Sat R 53:48 O 3 '70
Return of the Smothers. Time 95:90 Mr 30 '70
TV can be terribly vexing: My world and welcome to it to be dropped. G. Ace. Sat R 53:12 Mr 14 '70
TV's black skyrocket; M. Warren becomes director of Laugh-in. il pors Ebony 25: 113-16+ Ap '70
Tip of the tongue; My world and welcome to it. G. Ace. Sat R 53:2 Ja 17 '70

International aspects

Cracked lens? BBC-Indian dispute over TV documentary series, Reflections in a lens. Sr Schol 97:5 O 5 '70

Laws and regulations

See Television laws and regulations

Licenses

See Television laws and regulations

Moral aspects

Cultural indicators: the case of violence in television drama. G. Gerbner. bibliog f il Ann Am Acad 388:69-81 Mr '70
Fantasy-violence syndrome; Bradley S. Greenberg and Thomas F. Gordon report findings. R. L. Shayon. Sat R 53:59-60 O 24 '70
Five acts of violence per hour. R. L. Tobin. il Sat R 53:103-4 Mr 14 '70
Mannix: where the action is; interview, ed. by P. Hudson. M. Connors. il pors Sr Schol 97:40 O 26 '70
Study of TV violence: seven top researchers blackballed from panel. P. M. Boffey and J. Walsh. Science 168:949-52 My 22 '70
TV violence and sports. H. J. Cargas. America 122:610-11 Je 6 '70
Ups and downs of a TV stuntman; interview, ed. by P. Hudson. F. Lerner. il Sr Schol 97: 42-3 S 28 '70

Moving pictures

Dangerous environments; new TV movie, A clear and present danger. R. L. Shayon. Sat R 53:40 Ap 11 '70
TV or not TV? My sweet Charlie. A. Knight. Sat R 53:60 F 28 '70

Music

Switch-off television:
Switched-on symphony. M. Kastendieck. il Hi Fi 30:secII 12 Je '70

Negro programs

Black West; Black frontier series. R. L. Shayon. Sat R 53:54 N 14 '70
Changes; views of D. Carroll. R. L. Shayon. Sat R 53:46 Ap 18 '70
Soul drama; Chicago's new series titled Bird of the iron feather. il Time 95:59-60 F 23 '70
Soul opera; WTTW's Bird of the iron feather series. il Newsweek 75:68 F 23 '70

News

Agnew and the Pastore bill. S. Cupps. il Chr Cent 87:77-9 Ja 21 '70
Agnew's effect. J. Osborne. New Repub 162: 13-15 F 28 '70
Burger: no option on my face. por U S News 68:18 Mr 9 '70
Cheer leader's; ABC's Eyewitness news. J. Morgenstern. Newsweek 77:9 Ja 4 '71
Does TV news present an accurate picture? four different viewpoints. il Sr Schol 97:9-11 S 14 '70
First round to Agnew. M. L. Stein. Nation 211:178-81 S 7 '70
Freedom of the broadcast press; address. February 17, 1970. R. Frank. Vital Speeches 36: 332-6 Mr 15 '70
Good-night to all that; NBC nightly news. il Newsweek 76:60 Ag 17 '70
How well does TV present the news? H. J. Gans; reply. J. Wicklein. N Y Times Mag p 16+ Mr 1 '70
If the silent majority could talk, what would it say? views of P. Harvey and G. Putnam. T. Ferrell. pors Esquire 73:146-51+ My '70
Notes and comment: government's campaign against the news media. New Yorker 46:29-30 F 28 '70
Objectivity and the American press. il Sr Schol 96:2-7 F 2 '70
State of broadcast journalism. F. W. Friendly. Cur 114:49-54 Ja '70

State of the networks; State of the Union; post-speech coverage. Newsweek 75:74-5 F 2 '70
Tempest or a portent? R. Drummond. Cur 114:41-2 Ja '70
TV news: wrong mix. M. Wax. Nation 210: 433-5 Ap 13 '70
Troubled reflections of a TV journalist. R. Day. Read Digest 97:131-2+ N '70
Voice of reason; reply to Vice President Agnew. E. Sevareid. Time 96:9 N 2 '70
What it's like to broadcast news; excerpt from address. W. Cronkite. por Sat R 53: 53-5 D 12 '70; Reply. I. E. Fang. 54:46+ Ja 9 '71
See also
Television broadcasting—War news

Anecdotes, facetiae, satire, etc.

Till it be morrow; future goodnights from John Chancellor, Frank McGee, David Brinkley and NBC news. R. W. O'Donnell. New Yorker 46:29 Jl 4 '70

Operas

From Lizzie to Saroyan; My heart's in the highlands. P. Hudson. il Sr Schol 96:16-17 Mr 16 '70
Heart's in the highlands. F. Merkling. Opera N 34:32 Ap 4 '70
Janáček's From the house of the dead on NET: a not very memorable production. P. J. Smith. Hi Fi sec II 20:16 F '70
Musical events; NET opera production of Jack Beeson's My heart's in the highlands. W. Sargeant. New Yorker 46:108 Mr 28 '70
Musical events; NET opera production of Mozart's The abduction from the seraglio. W. Sargeant. New Yorker 46:142 O 31 '70
NET Abduction. R. D. Daniels. Opera N 35: 33 D 5 '70
Peter Grimes on NET. G. Movshon. Hi Fi 20: secII 12 Ag '70
Switch-off television:
My hearts in the highlands. J. Hiemenz. Hi Fi 30:secII 12 Je '70
TV Peter Grimes about, but without, the sea; presentation of the BBC production. I. Kolodin. Sat R 53:57 Je 20 '70

Performers

See also
Theatrical agencies
also names of televsion performers, e.g. M. Thomas

Political programs

See Television in politics

Program rating

Clean sweep? il Newsweek 76:86 N 30 '70
Dann v. Klein: the best game in town; Nielsen rating system. pors Time 95:98+ My 25 '70

Program recording

See also
Video recorders and recording

Programming

ABC tries again for top TV spot. il Bsns W p28 My 16 '70
Clean sweep? il Newsweek 76:86 N 30 '70
Group W president rocks broadcasters; proposal to let local stations program for prime time. por Bsns W p24 Ap 11 '70
How Mike Dann keeps his job at CBS. il pors Bsns W p78+ My 2 '70
McGannon's haymaker; heavy commercializing of television programming. J. McLaughlin. America 122:397 Ap 11 '70
Networks to cut prime time gladly. il Bsns W p27 N 21 '70
TV: the worst of times or the best of times? address, November 17, 1970. D. Durgin. Vital Speeches 37:186-90 Ja 1 '71
Television's avant-garde; experimental programming. D. Davis. il Newsweek 75:60-3 F 9 '70
U.S. broadcasting freedom; television's silent majority; address, June 23, 1970. J. Goodman. Vital Speeches 36:658-9 Ag 15 '70
What do we do about television? N. Johnson. il Sat R 53:14-16 Jl 11 '70

Programs

Comparative studies; Tocqueville's America and the Honor America programs. R. L. Shayon. Sat R 53:42 Jl 25 '70
Harry and Lena off the cuff! television special. il pors Ebony 25:128-9 Mr '70
How dull The advocates. Sedulus. New Repub 163:22-3 Jl 25 '70
Look and listen. P. Hudson. See issues of Scholastic teacher to May 18, 1970

TELEVISION broadcasting—Programs—*Cont.*
New season; situation comedies; variety. R.
Burgheim. il Time 96:66-7 S 28 '70
New shows. N. Vogel. por Writers Digest 50:
18-21 O '70
New TV shows, fall 1970; with Writers' guild
of America television film rates. N. Vogel.
Writers Digest 50:20-3 Je '70
Not worth a second look. Time 95:41-2 F 2
'70
Overhaul at CBS. Time 95:77 Mr 2 '70
Parade rest. Newsweek 75:72 Mr 2 '70
Seeing and believing; Metromedia's 1985. R.
L. Shayon. Sat R 53:32-3 Je 27 '70
Sight & sound. See issues of McCall's
Social season. il Newsweek 76:65 S 21 '70
Spotlight! E. Miller. See issues of Seventeen
Stroll through the wasteland. J. Leonard. il
Life 69:13 D 4 '70
Television. D. Brudnoy. Nat R 22:1009+ S
22 '70
Television. N. Compton. Commentary 48:12+
Ja; 18+ Ap '70
Television. Sedulus. See issues of New re-
public
Television (cont of) Looking and listening.
P. Hudson. See issues of Senior scholastic
Television's ten most. Time 97:53 Ja 4 '71
Time out for TV; ed. by E. Borgenicht. See
issues of PTA magazine
TV lengthens its endless summer. il Bsns
W p26 S 12 '70
TV package nobody pays for; exchanging
free shows for free air time. il Bsns W p80
Ag 1 '70
TV rehearses its fall lineups. il Bsns W p39
F 28 '70
United we fall; divided we stand; Swing out,
sweet land. R. L. Shayon. Sat R 54:59 Ja 2
'71
What you'll see on TV this fall. Changing
T 24:6 Ag '70
Woman's role on TV. J. Leonard. il por Life
69:8 D 18 '70
See also
Television broadcasting—Dancing
Television broadcasting, Noncommercial

Religious programs

Can churches break the prime-time barrier?
R. Spargur. Chr Today 14:3-4 Ja 16 '70
Euro 70 crusade: never, so many; with edi-
torial comment. D. Foster. il por Chr To-
day 14:24, 38 My 8 '70
Evangelical visibility in TV programming.
Chr Today 14:24-5 Ja 16 '70
McIntire-O'Hair debate: bruised but unbowed.
M. Moss. il Chr Today 14:42-3 Mr 13 '70
Roberts's ratings: rising. Chr Today 14:36
Ja 16 '70
Timothy Mayer; Jesus: a passion play for
Americans. New Yorker 46:33 Ap 11 '70

Setting and scenery

James Trittipo, designer for television. J.
Lovoos. il por Am Artist 34:30-5+ O '70

Social aspects

America, the violent; address, July 8, 1970.
P. L. Briand, jr. Vital Speeches 36:674-9 S
1 '70
How to talk back to your television set. by
N. Johnson. Review
New Repub 162:21-2 Mr 14 '70. R. Whit-
temore
Mass media & their impact on society. il Sr
Schol 95:4-11 D 1 '69
To youth, with love; White House conference
on the drug problem. R. L. Shayon. Sat R
53:57 N 21 '70
What do we do about television? N. John-
son. il Sat R 53:14-16 Jl 11 '70
See also
Television broadcasting and children

Sports

Cosell: milder but does he satisfy? J. Leonard.
il por Life 69:24 N 13 '70
Diary of a fisherman. J. Shepherd. il por
Field & S 74:88-9+ Ap '70
Don and Howard show. pors Time 96:59 D 14
'70
Football's long weekend; Monday night series
on ABC. P. Axthelm. il Newsweek 76:63 O
5 '70

How about a new TV deal for baseball? R.
Kahn. il Life 68:10 Mr 20 '70
TV talk:
ABC football coverage. F. Deford. Sports
Illus 33:13 D 14 '70
ABC pro football telecast. F. Deford.
Sports Illus 33:9 O 5 '70
Baseball show. W. Sheed. Sports Illus
32:15 Ap 13 '70
CBS on the Master. W. Sheed. Sports
Illus 32:5 Ap 27 '70
CBS struggled to the finish line with a
Derby show. W. Sheed. Sports Illus 32:9
My 18 '70
NBC's coverage of World series. F. Deford.
Sports Illus 33:9 O 26 '70
World cup, on closed-circuit TV. W.
Sheed. Sports Illus 33:8 Jl 6 '70
TV talk; CBS telecasts hockey. W. Sheed.
Sports Illus 32:7 F 23 '70
TV talk; Frazier-Ellis match on closed cir-
cuit. W. Sheed. Sports Illus 32:7 Mr 9 '70
TV violence and sports. H. J. Cargas. Amer-
ica 122:610-11 Je 6 '70
TV wins on points; Monday night's pro foot-
ball games. R. H. Boyle. il Sports Illus 33:
14-17 N 2 '70
TV's wild world of sports. W. Johnson. il
Read Digest 96:33-4+ Ap '70
Towering babble and (SOB) Heidi. W. John-
son. il Sports Illus 32:24-31 Ja 19 '70
You know you're not getting Maudie Frick-
ert. W. Johnson. il Sports Illus 32:30-6 Ja
26 '70

Study and teaching

High school journalism is dead! Dead! Dead!
replacement by live TV news programming
class. E. E. Balazs. Engl J 59:1283-4 D '70

Subscription programs

Latest timetable for pay TV. U S News 68:85
Mr 16 '70
To wire a nation. Time 95:66+ Je 1 '70

Test patterns

New test signal for color TV; vertical interval
reference signal. W. H. Buchsbaum. il
Electr World 84:37 Ag '70
Television's built-in test signals; vertical-
interval test signals. I. Mertes. il Electr
World 83:38-41 Mr '70

Trials

Courtroom drama; Trial: the city and county
of Denver v. Lauren R. Watson. il Time 95:
90 Mr 30 '70
Courtroom reality; NET's The city and
county of Denver vs. Lauren R. Watson.
il Newsweek 75:59 Mr 30 '70
Notorious vs. run-of-the-mill; series on
NET. R. L. Shayon. Sat R 53:40 Ap 4 '70
Television in court; the City and county of
Denver v. Lauren R. Watson. Nation 210:
421 Ap 13 '70

War news

Atrocity story; CBS replay of stabbing incident in Vietnam. il Newsweek 75:67 Je 1
'70
Blowup; CBS substantiates Vietnamese atrocity incident. R. L. Shayon. Sat R 53:16 Je
6 '70
Delayed replay; CBS replay of Bau Me stabbing incident. il Time 95:66+ Je 1 '70

World series

See Television broadcasting—Sports

France

Letter from Paris; debate between Giscard
d'Estaing and Servan-Schreiber. Genêt.
New Yorker 46:121-2 Ap 4 '70

Germany (Federal Republic)

Gangbusters, German-style; crime search
series. Time 95:53 Je 22 '70

Great Britain

Pirate television takes to the air. Bsns W
p37+ My 9 '70
See also
British broadcasting corporation

Italy

Talking like a native; TV teaching Italians
standard Italian. il Newsweek 75:57 Mr 9
'70

United States

Coming age of news monopoly. F. Cone; F.
W. Friendly. Sat R 53:56-60+ O 10 '70
How to talk back to your television set. by
N. Johnson. Review
Bsns W p8+ Mr 21 '70. N. N. Minow
Its own thing: live broadcasting. Sedulus.
New Repub 163:30-1 Ag 15 '70

TELEVISION broadcasting—United States—
—*Continued*
Network television's uncertain future. J.
Tebbel. Sat R 53:69-70 N 14 '70
On student protest, TV censorship, blacks
on TV; interview, ed by R. Hemming. D.
Cavett. por Sr Schol 95:20+ O 20 '69
Rehumanizing TV. Chr Cent 87:859 Jl 15 '70
Slouching toward Bethlehem. Sedulus. New
Repub 163:29-30 D 12 '70
TV-radio. R. L. Shayon. See issues of Sat-
urday review
Television: the splitting image. M. Mannes.
Sat R 53:66-8 N 14 '70
Well, blow my mind. Sedulus. New Repub
163:29-30 O 3 '70
Wormy norms. Sedulus. New Repub 163:29-
30 S 26 '70
    See also
American broadcasting companies
Columbia broadcasting system, inc.
National broadcasting company
Television industry—United States
United States—Federal communications com-
mission
United States—Surgeon general's advisory
committee on television and social behavior

Vietnam (Republic)
Tube takes hold; nation building by TV.
Time 96:26 N 30 '70

TELEVISION broadcasting, Noncommercial
Critics of television; address, January 15,
1970. J. W. Macy, jr. Vital Speeches 36:
286-8 F 15 '70
Forward with Forsyte. Sedulus. New Repub
163:32 N 7 '70
Greek experience; The advocates series on
public television. R. L. Shayon. Sat R 53:
40 Jl 18 '70
How dull The advocates. Sedulus. New Repub
163:22-3 Jl 25 '70
1970's big winner. il Forbes 106:38 O 15 '70
    See also
Corporation for public broadcasting
Educational broadcasting corporation
TELEVISION broadcasting and children
Five acts of violence per hour. R. L. Tobin. il
Sat R 53:103-4 Mr 14 '70
How violence affects children. il por Life 68:
57-8 Ja 30 '70
Media mystification; How mass media affects
children; edited condensation of hearing. R.
L. Shayon. Sat R 53:51 O 17 '70
Television environment. M. Davidson and
E. Borgenicht. PTA Mag 64:31-2 My '70
TELEVISION broadcasting and Negroes
Curiouser and curiouser; anti-black program-
ming bias by Alabama ETV stations. R. L.
Shayon. Sat R 53:43 Ag 8 '70
Star couple; C. Williams in the Mod squad
series. L. Robinson. il pors pors Ebony 25:
142-4+ Mr '70
    See also
Television broadcasting—Negro programs
TELEVISION broadcasting industry. See Tele-
vision industry
TELEVISION broadcasting stations. See Tele-
vision stations
TELEVISION camera tubes
Amazing see-in-the dark TV cameras. P.
Wahl. il Pop Sci 197:26+ N '70
Now electronics is breeding cross-bred com-
ponents; silicon vidicon. il Sci Digest 68:
74-5 O '70
TELEVISION cameras
How color TV works. W. Lemons. il Radio-
Electr 42:32-5 Ja '71
New color TV cameras. W. G. Salm. il Radio-
Electr 41:30-2+ Ag '70
News from the world of space exploration;
low-light-level television cameras. il Space
World G-10-82:45 O '70
TELEVISION censorship. See Television broad-
casting—Censorship
TELEVISION circuits
C.E.T. test. D. Glass. Electr World 84:67 D
'70
C.E.T. test; TV circuit analysis. D. Glass.
Electr World 84:74-5 O '70
Color TV for 1970. F. H. Belt. il Electr World
83:48-50+ F; 50-2+ Mr '70
H&V circuits; quiz. D. Glass. Electr World
83:53 Je '70
New look for television schematics. R. E.
Herzog. il Electr World 84:88 N '70
Programmed automatic fine tuning. L. Allen.
il Radio-Electr 41:57-61 F '70
Solid-state locked-oscillator FM limited/de-
tector. E. J. Jarrold. il Electr World 84:
62-4 Jl '70
TV on a chip. R. L. Goodman. il Radio-
Electr 41:69-72 Mr '70
TELEVISION commentators. See Television
broadcasting—News

TELEVISION commercials. See Television ad-
vertising
TELEVISION drama. See Television broad-
casting—Drama
TELEVISION in art education. See Television
in education
TELEVISION in criminal investigation
Gangbusters, German-style; crime search
series. Time 95:53 Je 22 '70
TELEVISION in education
At last: a TV show good for children; Ses-
ame street. E. M. Wylie. il PTA Mag 64:12-
14+ My '70
Children, television and Sesame street. B.
Spock. il Redbook 135:24+ Jl '70
Cutting oedipal ties; Sesame street. R. L.
Shayon. il Sat R 53:50 F 14 '70
Department and Nebraska ETV council to
produce educational TV series. Dept State
Bul 63:556-7 N 9 '70
Do children really learn from educational
TV? il Good H 171:182-3 O '70
From A to Z to Sesame street. S. W. Little. il
Sat R 53:62-4 My 9 '70
Improvement in teaching mathematics; using
modern mass communications techniques to
introduce the new math. Sch & Soc 98:266+
Sum '70
Instructional television; symposium. il To-
days Ed 59:33-40 Ja '70
Karton kooks; creativity through art.
Spring Branch independent school district.
Houston, Tex. J. Smith. il Sch Arts 69:10-
11 Je '70
Learning can be fun; Sesame street. C.
Terry. il Good H 170:48+ Ap '70
Marshall McLuhan lives on Sesame street.
A. Caruba. il Pub W 197:28-31 Ap 20 '70
Report card on Sesame street. J. Culhane.
il N Y Times Mag p34-5+ My 24 '70
Secrets of Sesame street. B. Baer. il Look
34:56-8+ S 22 '70
Sesame at one. il Newsweek 76:71 N 16 '70
Sesame opens up. il Newsweek 75:102 Ap 20
'70
Sesame street. New Repub 162:23-8 Je 6 '70;
Discussion. 162:30-2 Je 27 '70
Sesame street. J. G. Cooney. PTA Mag 64:
25-6 Mr '70
Sesame street and its critics. J. Cass. Sat R
53:49 D 19 '70
Sesame street generation arrives. A. Rosen-
thal. il Todays Health 48:42-5+ D '70
Sesame street; hypnotic. M. Hentoff. Vogue
155:114 F 1 '70
Sesame street opens the door. E. M. Wylie.
il Read Digest 96:112-16 My '70
Sesame street report card. Time 96:70 N 16 '70
Sesame street: what next? il Library J 95:
3958-61 N 15 '70
Success with microteaching; in-service train-
ing of teachers. Sch & Soc 98:200 Ap '70
Television: a medium in transition. R. Gil-
key. Clear House 44:510-12 Ap '70
Television as a teacher. E. Efron. Ed Digest
35:13-15 Ja '70
TV urged for mass education. Sr Schol 96:
Schol Teach 1 Ja 26 '70
TV's switched-on school; Sesame street. il
Newsweek 75:68-71 Je 1 '70
Utilizing closed circuit television; Norwalk,
Conn. N. Harding. il Am Lib 1:165-6 F '70
What educational media specialists ought to
know about CATV. Ed Digest 35:48-51 Ja
'70
Who's afraid of big, bad TV? Sesame street.
il Time 96:60-6+ N 23 '70
    See also
Television broadcasting—Study and teaching
TELEVISION in medicine
Doctor in the TV set; MGH system for tele-
diagnosis. il Life 69:77-9 N 27 '70
Five patients; excerpts. M. Crichton. Ladies
Home J 87:34+ Jl '70
TV camera shares history's spotlight; camera
used in first non-experimental color telecast
donated to Smithsonian. V. Louviere. Na-
tions Bsns 58:18 My '70
TELEVISION in meteorology
Can TV really detect tornadoes? Weller meth-
od of tornado detection. W. G. Biggs and
P. J. Waite. bibliog il Weatherwise 23:120-5
Je '70
TELEVISION in politics
Assessing the campaigners. Sci N 98:381-2 N
14 '70
Buying my time. New Repub 163:7 O 24 '70
Electronic politics; the image game. il por
Time 96:43-4+ S 21 '70
Fair fare. R. L. Shayon. Sat R 53:78 S 12 '70
Fair share of air; Democrats petition for
free time for the party out of power.
Newsweek 76:59 Jl 6 '70

TELEVISION in politics—*Continued*
First amendment; T.V. coverage, Congress and the Supreme court; address, December 15, 1969. F. Stanton. Vital Speeches 36:234-6 F 1 '70
Free and equal: political struggle for TV time. U S News 69:56-7 Jl 27 '70
Great TV squabble. America 123:138-9 S 12 '70
How Nixon changed his TV image; interview. R. E. Ailes. il pors U S News 68:68-71 F 2 '70
Larry looks at television. America 123:225-6 O 3 '70
Letter from Washington; limiting money for television and radio time. R. H. Rovere. New Yorker 46:134-5 O 24 '70
Loyal opposition; TV time for the Democrats. por Newsweek 76:73 Jl 20 '70
Madison avenue against the war. il Time 96:67 Jl 27 '70
Now is the time for all good men; proposal to prohibit all candidates from buying any TV time. America 123:6-7 Jl 11 '70
Patrician and the pol; R. Taft-J. A. Rhodes debate, Cincinnati. pors Newsweek 75:30 My 4 '70
Politics and the tube; congressional bills, FCC rulings. il Newsweek 76:70 Ag 24 '70
Punctured image; deflation of television's political image-makers. il Newsweek 76:77 N 16 '70
Right to be seen and heard: if you're a candidate. D. Zwerdling. New Repub 163:15-16 Jl 18 '70
Selling of the candidates 1970. il Newsweek 76:34-8+ O 19 '70
Selling of the President 1968, by J. McGinniss. Review
    Esquire il 73:8+ F '70. M. Muggeridge
Shrinking screen. Time 96:22 O 5 '70
Television politics; loyal opposition scramble for equal time. K. Crawford. Newsweek 76:24 Jl 20 '70
Thirty-second spot commercial. Nation 211:421 N 2 '70
Tricking the media; Nixon's Anaheim appearance. J. Deedy. Commonweal 93:186 N 20 '70
Tube power; flurry over the Fulbright amendment. por Newsweek 76:61 Ag 17 '70
TV politics: too high a price. Life 69:2 S 11 '70
Victory through TV; victory in the Ohio primary. America 122:546 My 23 '70
What wins elections today? Sr Schol 97:15-17 O 12 '70
When Nixon goes on TV: new rule on right to reply. il U S News 69:26-7 Ag 31 '70
TELEVISION in psychiatry
From couch to camera. il Newsweek 76:43 Ag 3 '70

TELEVISION industry

France
French television and the control of the news. W. B. Kerr. il Sat R 53:72+ F 14 '70

United States
How to talk back to your television set, by N. Johnson. Review
    Commentary 49:88-90 Je '70. E. J. Epstein
    New Repub 162:21-2 Mr 14 '70. R. Whittemore
Image empire, by E. Barnouw. Review
    Bsns W p6+ D 26 '70. E. A. Lewis
Making news: fight among camera crews. il Newsweek 76:65 Ag 31 '70
Troubles of television, and a coming revolution. il U S News 69:58-60 D 21 '70
TV: is the bloom off the old rose? il Forbes 106:28-30+ O 15 '70
TV: the worst of times or the best of times? address, November 17, 1970. D. Durgin. Vital Speeches 37:186-90 Ja 1 '71
TELEVISION journalism. See Television broadcasting—News
TELEVISION laws and regulations
Access to the media. Nation 210:676-7 Je 8 '70
Big changes due for TV viewers; FCC rulings. il U S News 68:85 My 18 '70
Christmas list; Pastore bill. J. Fischer; reply. J. Vacca. Harper 240:10+ Mr '70
Does a president ever get equal time? D. Lawrence. il U S News 69:84 Jl 20 '70
Fair fare. R. L. Shayon. Sat R 53:78 S 12 '70
Fair share of air; Democrats petition for free time for the party out of power. Newsweek 76:59 Jl 6 '70
Fairness doctrine; FCC's action against McIntire. Chr Today 14:17 Jl 31 '70

Frank Merriwell's way; equal time for political parties and political minorities. Sedulus. New Repub 162:30-2 Je 20 '70
Free and equal: political struggle for TV time. U S News 69:56-7 Jl 27 '70
It's junk, but is it our junk? Pastore bill. R. H. Smith. Pub W 197:61 Ja 19 '71
Loyal opposition; TV time for the Democrats. por Newsweek 76:73 Jl 20 '70
Making FCC's mission impossible. Consumer Rep 35:109-11 F '70
Not in the stars; proscriptions against the broadcast by radio and television stations of astrology material. P. Nathan. Pub W 198:41 Ag 24 '70
Now is the time for all good men; proposal to prohibit all candidates from buying any TV time. America 123:6-7 Jl 11 '70
Orderly withdrawals? question of prime time for public service use. Sedulus. New Repub 162:28 Je 13 '70
Politics and money. Commonweal 92:331-2 Jl 10 '70
Politics and the tube; congressional bills, FCC rulings. il Newsweek 76:70 Ag 24 '70
Right to be seen and heard: if you're a candidate; If you're antiwar. D. Zwerdling; D. Sanford. New Repub 163:15-17 Jl 18 '70
Television politics; loyal opposition scramble for equal time. K. Crawford. Newsweek 76:24 Jl 20 '70
Those substantial licensees; FCC's Policy statement on comparative hearings involving regular renewal applicants. R. L. Shayon. Sat R 53:38-9 F 7 '70
To wash or not to wash; equal time and deceptive advertising. Sedulus. New Repub 163:29-30 Ag 22 '70
TV: the worst of times or the best of times? prime-time access rule; address, November 17, 1970. D. Durgin. Vital Speeches 37:186-90 Ja 1 '71
When does an election start? need for the opposition to receive equal time. Nation 210:612 My 25 '70
When Nixon goes on TV: new rule on right to reply. il U S News 69:26-7 Ag 31 '70
    See also
Television broadcasting—Censorship
United States—Federal communications commission
TELEVISION news. See Television broadcasting—News
TELEVISION news photographers. See News photographers
TELEVISION plays
All around the town. E. Larson. Plays 29:63-71 Mr '70
TELEVISION program rating. See Television broadcasting—Program rating
TELEVISION programming. See Television broadcasting—Programming
TELEVISION receivers
Going tubeless: window display of Showcase '70, the Entertainment center. New Yorker 46:38-9 N 28 '70
New four-eyed TV lets you see what you're missing. D. Scott. il Pop Sci 196:67 Mr '70
RCA's new multiscreen TV lets you switch to where the action is. A. Fisher. il Pop Sci 196:48-9 Je '70
Television receivers. il Consumer Bul 53:7-13 D '70

Color receivers
See Television receivers, Color

Maintenance and repair
Case of the siamese receiver. A. Margolis. il Radio-Electr 41:59-61 D '70
C.E.T. test, TV alignment. D. Glass. Electr World 84:57 Jl '70
In the shop, with Jack. J. Darr. See issues of Radio-electronics
Kwik-fix picture and waveform charts. See issues of Radio-electronics
Replacing TV circuit breakers. J. A. Fred. il Radio-Electr 42:70+ Ja '71
    See also
RCA corporation—ServiceAmerica division
Television servicemen

Noise
Ripple and noise; unfiltered rig. J. Darr. Radio-Electr 41:24 O '70

Safety devices and measures
Know the fire safety rules for TV sets. Good H 170:147 Je '70
TELEVISION receivers, Color
Color TV. il Consumer Rep 34:270-4 D '69; 36:18-23+ Ja '71
Color TV consoles. il Consumer Rep 35:18-25 Ja '70

TELEVISION receivers, Color—*Continued*
Color TV for 1970. F. H. Belt. il Electr World
83:48-50+ F; 50-2+ Mr '70
Consumer's guide to the 1971 color TVs. il
Mech Illus 66:67 D '70
Directory of 1970 color-TV chassis; table. F.
H. Belt. Electr World 83:32-3 Ja '70
Directory of 1971 color-TV chassis; table. F.
H. Belt. Electr World 85:28-30 Ja '71
First battery color TV! A. Fisher. il Pop Sci
197:61 S '70
How color TV works. W. Lemons. il Radio-
Electr 42:32-5 Ja '71
New color-TV kit. W. Stocklin. il Electr
World 85:40-1 Ja '71
New modular color-TV receiver. E. Lemke.
il Electr World 85:32-3+ Ja '71
New modular color TV set is a solid-state
kit. il Radio-Electr 41:37-40 S '70
Product gallery; color TV kits. il Pop Electr
34:86-9 Ja '71
RCA's solid-state color chassis CTC 40. F.
H. Belt. il Electr World 83:48-50+ My '70
'70 TVs, color 'em natural. R. M. Benrey. il
Pop Sci 197:74-5+ N '70
Sony makes a new small-screen color set. il
Consumer Rep 35:72 F '70
What's new in modular and IC color TV for
'71. S. R. Prentiss. il Radio-Electr 41:62-4+
D '70

Control
Color TV by remote control. L. Allen. il Radio-Electr 42:45-9 Ja '71

Maintenance and repair
C.E.T. test. D. Glass. Electr World 84:74 Ag
'70
Case of the hot flyback. A. Margolis. il
Radio-Electr 41:58-60 Jl '70
Comb color troubles out of your hair! J. Darr.
il Radio-Electr 42:27+ Ja '71
Inside the high-voltage regulator. M. Mandl.
il Radio-Electr 41:76-9 Jl '70
Troubleshoot color TV with transistor curve
tracer. J. Williams. il Radio-Electr 41:54-6
Je '70
Vector-scope on the Quasar. S. Prentiss. il
Radio-Electr 41:88-9+ Je '70

Radiation hazards
Dubious use of a toy with TV; Winky dink
and you! Consumer Rep 35:328-9 Je '70
Radiation from color TV receivers, where lies
the danger? J. S. Paul. il Consumer Bul
53:43+ D '70
Simple field test for TV X-radiation; test of
glass for lead content. Electr World 84:65
O '70
Some observations on X-radiation. il Con-
sumer Rep 35:23 Ja '70
TV X-rays. D. Ward. il Radio-Electr 41:54-6
Ap '70

Testing
Results of Japanese tests on color-TV sets
made public. J. Yagi. il Electr World 83:
53 Ja '70
TELEVISION receivers. Portable
New pop-up TV flips its lid. il Pop Mech
133:122 Je '70
Personal TV sets. il Consumer Rep 35:154-7
Mr '70
Two-pound TV with a postage-stamp screen.
J. P. Zmuda. il Pop Sci 196:26 Ap '70
TELEVISION receivers industry. See Tele-
vision apparatus industry and trade
TELEVISION reporters. See Television board-
casting—News
TELEVISION schematics. See Television cir-
cuits
TELEVISION script writing. See Television
authorship
TELEVISION servicemen
TV-technician shortage; excerpts from ad-
dress. L. Gyarmathy. Electr World 83:32
Mr '70
TELEVISION stations
Clout bout; license challenge. R. L. Shayon.
Sat R 53:59 F 28 '70
Dynamite in pollution; Jacksonville, Fla. TV
station WJXT reports on local polluters. C.
Gillespie. Nation 211:455-7 N 9 '70; Reply
with rejoinder. J. T. Lynch. 211:674 D 28
'70
Matter of substance; policy statement on
changes in station ownership. Newsweek
75:82-3 Ja 26 '70
Mephisto and the FCC; local Jackson group offers to operate WLBT. R. L. Shayon. Sat R
53:102 Mr 14 '70
Nicholas the terrible; FCC standards for license renewal. W. F. Buckley, jr. Nat R
22:220-1 F 24 '70

People v. WPIX. Time 96:67 S 28 '70
Post script; WLBW license challenge. New
Repub 162:9-10 Mr 7 '70
Test case; hearings on license challenge
against WPIX-TV. Newsweek 76:56 S 28 '70
Today's short supply of air time. F. W.
Friendly. Cur 124:28-33 D '70
TV looks tempting to McGraw-Hill. Bsns W
p24 N 7 '70
　　See also
American broadcasting companies
Columbia broadcasting system, inc.
National broadcasting company
TELEVISION stations, Educational
Brothers and sisters; controversies over Say,
brother and In her own right. Newsweek
76:56-7 S 7 '70
Curiouser and curiouser; anti-black program-
ming bias by Alabama ETV stations. R. L.
Shayon. Sat R 53:43 Ag 8 '70
Educational windfall; KNEW-TV given to
KQED. Newsweek 75:58-9 Je 8 '70
TV news: wrong mix; KQED, San Fran-
cisco. M. Wax. Nation 210:433-5 Ap 13 '70
　　See also
Corporation for public broadcasting
Educational broadcasting corporation
TELEVISION stations, Illegal
Pirate television takes to the air; Caroline
TV flying studios off British coast. Bsns
W p37+ My 9 '70
TELEVISION test apparatus. See Testing in-
struments
TELEVISION transmission
TV signals; quiz. D. Glass. Electr World 83:
59 Mr '70
　　See also
Television, Color
TELEVISION viewing devices. See Eyeglasses
TELEVISION writing. See Television author-
ship
TELEX corporation
What makes Telex red hot? il Forbes 105:18-
19 Mr 15 '70
TELLA, Alfred J.
Wayward trail of the jobless rate. il Bsns W
p94+ Je 13 '70 *
TELLEEN, Robert
Camp director reports on Midwest training
center. il Camp Mag 42:20 Je '70
TELLEFSEN, Olaf
New theory of pyramid building; with bio-
graphical sketch. il Natur Hist 79:6, 10-
12+ N; 12+ D '70
　　about
3,000 for the seesaw. il Newsweek 76:98 N
16 '70 *
TELLER, Edward
Open arms research; defroster for the cold
war? pro and con discussion. Sr Schol 96:9-
10 My 11 '70
Proposed unilateral disarmament step. Cur
119:63-4 Je '70
Time of torment for science. il por Sci N 99:
5-6 Ja 2 '71 *
TELLING Paul; story. See Perry, W.
TEMIANKA, Henri
My George Szell. por Sat R 53:50-1 S 26 '70
TEMIN, Howard Martin
Finding a cancer clue. Time 96:41 D 21 '70 *
Teminism on the go. il Sci N 98:243-4 S 19
'70 *
Triumph for a heretic. il Newsweek 76:56-7
Jl 20 '70 *
Upsetting dogma. il por Time 96:57 Jl 20
'70 *
TEMPE, Ariz.
Computer geared to grow with a city. J.
Alexander. il Am City 85:84+ N '70
Desert blooms with surf. il Life 68:48-9 Mr
6 '70
TEMPER
Temper, temper, temper, temper, temper!
children's tantrums. A. E. Trieschman. il
N Y Times Mag p99+ Ap 12 '70
TEMPERA painting
Experimenting with tempera. C. J. Alkema.
il Design 71:26-30 mid-Wint '70
Poster paints on wrapping paper. O. John-
son. il Sch Arts 69:40-1 Ap '70
Tempera resist-plus. A. I. Rosiene. il Sch Arts
70:20-1 S '70
TEMPERAMENT
Origin of personality. A. Thomas and others.
il Sci Am 223:102-9 bibliog(p 128) Ag '70
　　See also
Man—Constitution
TEMPERANCE
　　See also
Alcohol and youth

TEMPERANCE—*Continued*

Study and teaching

Characteristics of community residents who are favorable toward alcohol education. G. Globetti and G. Pomeroy. Ment Hy 54: 411-15 Jl '70

TEMPERANCE education. See Temperance—Study and teaching

TEMPERANCE societies
See also
Woman's Christian temperance union

TEMPERATURE
See also
Boiling points
Climate
Lakes—Temperature
Stars—Temperature

Measurement
See also
Thermometers and thermometry

Physiological effects
See also
Cold—Physiological effects
Estivation
Fishes, Effect of temperature on
Heat—Physiological effects

TEMPERATURE, Animal and human
Body temperature: possible ionic mechanism in the hypothalamus controlling the set point. R. D. Myers and W. L. Veale. bibliog il Science 170:95-7 O 2 '70
Microelectrophoresis of biogenic amines on hypothalamic thermosensitive cells. A. L. Beckman and J. S. Eisenman. bibliog il Science 170:334-6 O 16 '70
Nervous control of the heart during thoracic temperature regulation in a sphinx moth. B. Heinrich. bibliog il Science 169:606-7 Ag 7 '70
Panting in dogs: unidirectional air flow over evaporative surfaces. K. Schmidt-Nielsen and others. bibliog il Science 169:1102-4 S 11 '70
Stocky folk stay warm. il Sci Digest 67:53-4 Ap '70
Thermoresponsiveness of the preoptic region of the brain in house sparrows. S. H. Mills and J. E. Heath. bibliog il Science 168:1008-9 My 22 '70
Thermosensitivity of neurons in the sensorimotor cortex of the cat. J. L. Barker and D. O. Carpenter. bibliog il Science 169: 597-8 Ag 7 '70
Thoracic temperature stabilization by blood circulation in a free-flying moth. B. Heinrich. bibliog il Science 168:580-2 My 1 '70
See also
Fever
Thermometers, Clinical

TEMPERATURE inversions
Air pollution and the temperature inversion. R. E. Falconer. il Cons 25:21-7 O '70
Teacher tips: air pollution and the temperature inversion. J. A. Weeks. il Cons 25:32-3 O '70

TEMPERATURES, Low. See Low temperatures

TEMPERED glass. See Glass, Safety

TEMPEST; drama. See Shakespeare, W.—Plays

TEMPLE, Robert W.
ABCs of front ends and steering. il Pop Mech 133:108-13+ Mr '70

TEMPLE, Shirley
United Nations conference on the human environment; statement, December 15, 1969. Dept State Bul 62:99-100 Ja 26 '70
United States comments on work of UNICEF; statement, December 2, 1969. Dept State Bul 61:642-3 D 29 '69

TEMPLE MOUNT. See Jerusalem—Holy places

TEMPLE of ten thousand Buddhas, Hong Kong. See Temples—Hong Kong

TEMPLES

Egypt

Computer helps scholars re-create an Egyptian temple. R. W. Smith. il por Nat Geog 138:634-55 N '70

Greece, Ancient

Bassae: Greece's best-preserved temple. il Holiday 47:78-9 Ap '70

Hong Kong

Up to the Temple of 10,000 Buddhas. il Sunset 144:42+ Ja '70

Thailand

Templed cities of Thailand. K. Willenson. il Travel & Camera 33:60-9 Mr '70

TEMPLES, Buddhist
See also
Borobudur, Java
Pagodas
Temples—Hong Kong

TEMPLIN, Phillip S.
Washington front. America 123:421, 499-500, 535; 124:27 N 21, D 5, 19 '70, Ja 9 '71

TEMPTATION
Temptation, A.D. 1970. V. P. McCorry. America 122:inside back cover F 14 '70

TEN THOUSAND ISLANDS
Island-hopping vacation. F. M. Paulson. il Field & S 74:53-5+ Ja '70

TEN-year-old detective; drama. See Olfson, L.

TENANCY. See Farm tenancy

TENDER offers. See Stocks—Tender offers

TENEMENT houses
See also
Slums

TENENBAUM, Samuel
School grades and group therapy. Ment Hy 54: 525-9 O '70

TENER, Morton
Camp can be much more than just fun and games. il Camp Mag 42:14 Ja '70

TENERIFE
Tenerife. J. McDonough. il Harp Baz 103:112+ Mr '70

TENNANT, G. H, company
Cleaning up by cleaning up; industrial cleaning equipment. il Bsns W p46 Ap 4 '70

TENNECO, inc.
Tenneco's careful diversification. por Duns 96:27-8 D '70
When language is a barrier; General foam's language classes. il Bsns W p 104+ F 28 '70

TENNESSEE
See also
Architecture, Domestic—Tennessee
Conservation of resources—Tennessee
Hunting—Tennessee
Negroes—Tennessee
Petroleum—Tennessee
Reelfoot Lake
Wilderness areas—Tennessee

Historic houses, etc.

See also
Knoxville, Tenn.—Historic houses, etc.

Politics and government

After the fox; Democratic senatorial primary. il por Newsweek 76:31 Ag 17 '70
Blood and Gore. P. R. Wieck. New Repub 163: 11-12 O 24 '70
Good-bye Gore? primary victory narrow. Nat R 22:934 S 8 '70
High noon for Tex Ritter. R. Cleghorn. il pors N Y Times Mag p 10-11+ Jl 12 '70
Number one target; Democratic and Republican primaries. New Repub 163:6-7 Ag 22 '70
Race in one state. il Nations Bsns 58:24-30 Ag '70
Tennessee: Gore vs. the White House. K. Leiter. Nation 211:396-9 O 26 '70

Religious institutions and affairs

Renewal: Tennessee model. T. M. Gannon. America 122:152-5+ F 14 '70

TENNESSEE evolution controversy
Evolution: still on trial after 100 years. L. S. De Camp. il Sci Digest 67:17-21 Mr '70
Scopes reviews the monkey trial. B. Shaw. Esquire 74:86+ N '70

TENNESSEE, University, Knoxville
How Nixon used the media, Billy Graham, and the good Lord to rap with students at Tennessee U. G. Wills. il Esquire 74:119-22+ S '70

TENNESSEE VALLEY authority
Roland Wank, 1898-1970. F. Gutheim. il por Arch Forum 133:58-9 S '70
TVA: coal gets cheaper, or else. il Bsns W p52 N 21 '70

TENNIS
Advantage, Mr Martin. Time 95:53 Ap 27 '70
Big cat on the prowl; Pancho Gonzales. R. H. Boyle. il pors Sports Illus 32:14-17 F 9 '70
Birth of sudden death; United States Open. il Newsweek 76:63-4 S 21 '70
Bloodthirsty tennis, anyone? D. Miles. il Sports Illus 33:32-4+ N 2 '70
Center court at Wimbledon. A. Ashe. il pors Travel & Camera 33:48-53 My '70
Confusion in the backcourt; battle between the USLTA and professional tennis. W. Bingham. il Sports Illus 32:61-2+ Ap 6 '70
Dregs in the dullest cup; Davis cup matches. G. S. Brown. il Sports Illus 33:50+ S 7 '70

TENNIS—*Continued*
Giant killer; Wimbledon tournament. il por Newsweek 76:69-70 Jl 13 '70
It almost came up roses for Rosewall; Wimbledon tennis tournament. W. Bingham. il pors Sports Illus 33:50-1 Jl 13 '70
Maggie and the little master; U.S. Open tennis championships. il por Time 96:53 S 28 '70
Pancho at forty-one. por Time 95:57 F 16 '70
Serve, backhand, volley and caviar mousse; John Gardiner's tennis ranch. A. Wright. il Sports Illus 33:70+ O 12 '70
Sporting scene; Mrs Court and Mr Rosewall. H. W. Wind. New Yorker 46:172-4+ O 10 '70
Sudden death at Forest Hills; U.S. Open tennis championships. W. Bingham. il por Sports Illus 33:26-7 S 21 '70
Tennis: come alive with sudden death? P. Axthelm. Vogue 156:58 S 15 '70
Tennis, everyone. il Esquire 73:136-7 Je '70
Tennis, everyone? J. Kraft, jr. il por Har Yrs 10:48-9 Ap '70
Tennis isn't just for kids. W. F. Talbert and G. Greer. il por Holiday 48:46-7+ Jl '70
Tennis joins the big-business set. il Bsns W p56-7 Ag 29 '70
Women's lob; Virginia slims invitational, first professional tour exclusively for women. il Time 96:78-9 D 7 '70
See also
Squash (game)
United States lawn tennis association

Accidents and injuries
Down with tennis elbow. il Esquire 73:145 Je '70

Equipment and supplies
Up from mediocrity; new gear and gadgetry. il Esquire 73:142-4 Je '70

Study and teaching
Five toughest shots in tennis. R. Laver. il Esquire 73:146-7 Je '70
Forebrain and backhand. E. L. Scott. Esquire 73:141 Je '70
How to play togetherness tennis. R. Laver. il por Ladies Home J 87:54 Ag '70

TENNIS courts
Building quality tennis courts. A. S. Alschuler, jr. il Parks & Rec 5:27-8+ O '70
Tennis court backboard for $100; San Fernando. Calif. S. Silver. il Am City 85:18 D '70

Lighting
Night tennis and basketball; Manchester, Conn. W. D. O'Neill. il Am City 85:28 N '70

TENNIS courts, Indoor
Private and public interests, keep tennis courts open year-round; Davenport racquets club. P. Conway. il Parks & Rec 5:34-5+ Mr '70

TENNIS players
Don't play with a guillotine; paying fixed expenses to top players. B. Collins. Sports Illus 32:49 Ja 19 '70
How to murder your boss; businessmen tennis players. il Esquire 73:138-40 Je '70
Women's lob; Virginia slims invitational, first professional tour exclusively for women. il Time 96:78-9 D 7 '70

TENNIS rackets
Colorful wrap for a tennis racket. il Sunset 145:104 S '70
Which tennis racket? il Changing T 24:13-14 Je '70

TENNIS ranch. See Tennis

TENNY, Ralph
Super substitution box. il Pop Electr 33:79-81 Jl '70

TENNYSON, Alfred Tennyson, 1st baron
Tennyson anyone? A. H. Leitch. Chr Today 15:48-9 D 18 '70 *

TENNYSON, Leonard B.
Britain in Europe at last? Cur Hist 58:276-80 My '70

TENSION (psychology) See Stress (physiology)

TENTH month; story. See Hobson, L. Z.

TENTING. See Camping

TENURE, Academic. See College professors and instructors—Tenure

TEOTIHUACÁN, Mexico
Solving the mystery of the Street of the dead. L. S. De Camp. il Sci Digest 68:28-33 D '70
Teotihuacán: completion of map of giant ancient city in the valley of Mexico. R. Millon. bibliog il Science 170:1077-82 D 4 '70

TERASAKI, Paul I. See Hirata, A. A. jt. auth.

TERATOLOGY. See Abnormalities (animals)

TERAYAMA, Shuji
La Marie Vison. Criticism
Vogue 156:308 S 1 '70 *

TERESA, Mother
Prize for Mother Teresa. Time 97:56 Ja 4 '71 *

TERK, Sonia Delaunay-. See Delaunay-Terk, S.

TERKEL, Studs
Hard times, 1970: an oral history of the recession. il N Y Times Mag p 10-11+ D 20 '70
Hard times remembered; excerpts from Hard times. il Am Heritage 21:36-45 Ap '70
When times were really hard; excerpt from Hard times: an oral history of the great depression. il Atlan 225:73-9+ Ap '70

TERM insurance. See Insurance, Life—Policies

TERMAN, Jiuan S. See Terman, M. jt. auth.

TERMAN, Michael, and Terman, J. S.
Circadian rhythm of brain self-stimulation behavior. bibliog il Science 168:1242-4 Je 5 '70

TERMINAL; drama. See Yankowitz, S.

TERMINAL buildings, Airport. See Airport buildings

TERMINALS
Half-mile gangplank; passenger terminal to cruise shipping. P. Blake. il Arch Forum 132:54-7 Mr '70
Suburban terminals evaluated. Aviation W 93:30 S 7 '70

TERMINATION of war. See Capitulations, Military

TERMINOLOGY. See subhead Terminology under various subjects, e.g. Politics —Terminology

TERMITES
How to keep your house safe from termites; subterranean termites. B. Ford. il Sci Digest 67:16-21 Je '70
Is the Formosan termite a threat? il Good H 170:160-1 F '70
Tackling the termite. J. H. Ingersoll. il House B 112:20+ F '70

TERMS and phrases
See also
Allusions
also subhead Terms and phrases under names of languages, e.g. English language—Terms and phrases

TERN, Jürgen
Ferment in Frankfurt. il por Newsweek 75:56 Je 29 '70 *

TERNES, Alan
Introduction to the setting and characters of the tragical farce or farcical tragedy of Victoria Bluffs, S.C; with biographica sketch. il Natur Hist 79:4, 8-10+ Ap '70

TERPENOIDS
Insect juvenile hormone activity of selected terpenoid compounds. M. Schwarz and others. bibliog il Science 167:191-2 Ja 9 '70

TERRACE gardens. See Roof gardens

TERRACES (agriculture)
Aboriginal drained-field cultivation in the Americas. W. M. Denevan. bibliog il Science 169:647-54 Ag 14 '70
See also
Contour farming
Gardens, Hillside

TERRACES (outdoor living areas) See Outdoor rooms

TERRACINA, Italy
Sunday night in Terracina. H. Kenner. Nat R 22:790 Jl 28 '70

TERRARIUMS
Not all wild pets like captivity, but some do if you treat them right. il Sunset 145:150-1 Jl '70
Woodland gardens under glass. R. M. Peters. il Home Gard 57:46-7 N '70
World under a dome; elements of a woodland environment transplanted indoors. F. Hoke. il Am For 76:12-14+ Mr '70

TERRE HAUTE, Ind.

Libraries
See also
Vigo County, Ind. public library

TERRELL, Richard L.
Boss Kettering's decision: build a better diesel. il pors Nations Bsns 58:78-9 Ja '70

TERRELL, Robert L.
Up from Uncle Tomism. Commonweal 92:87-8+ Ap 3 '70

TERRIBLE gypsy mala; drama. See Winther, B.

TERRIEN, Samuel
Demons also believe. Chr Cent 87:1481-3+ D 9 '70

TERRILL, Ross
Inscrutable West. Atlan 226:68-71 Ag '70

TERRITORIAL expansion
See also
Imperialism

TERRITORIAL jurisdiction. See Jurisdiction, Territorial

TERRITORIAL waters
International law and the oceans; address, February 18, 1970. J. R. Stevenson. Dept State Bul 62:339-43 Mr 16 '70
Politics of marine research. L. Purrett. il Sci N 99:9-11 Ja 2 '71
Testing more than the Arctic ice; Manhattan's voyages. W. Kornberg. il Sci N 97: 420 Ap 25 '70
U.S. opposes unilateral extension by Canada of high seas jurisdiction; Department statement, April 15, 1970. Dept State Bul 62:610-11 My 11 '70
United States outlines position on limit of territorial sea; Department statement, February 25, 1970. Dept State Bul 62:343 Mr 16 '70
See also
Continental shelf
Fishery laws and legislation
Maritime law

TERRITORIALISM (animals) See Animals—Habits and behavior

TERRITORY of Papua and New Guinea. See Papua-New Guinea (territory)

TERRORISM
As violence spreads U.S. goes on guard. il U S News 69:15-16 N 2 '70
Behind the terror bombings; with interview with J. P. Spiegel. U S News 68:15-17 Mr 30 '70
Biggest blast. il Newsweek 76:33 S 7 '70
Black men and bombs. il Ebony 25:134-5 My '70
Bolder cop killers hitting more often. il U S News 69:26 S 14 '70
Bomb; indictments. il Newsweek 76:14-15 Ag 3 '70
Bomb jitters. Newsweek 75:23-4 Mr 30 '70
Bomb kills physicist, damages equipment. G. B. Lubkin. il Phys Today 23:73-4 O '70
Bomb plots; warning on terror war. il U S News 69:36 O 26 '70
Bombing; a way of protest and death; bombs exploding at the Manhattan headquarters of Mobil oil, IBM and General telephone and electronics. il Time 95:8-11 Mr 23 '70
Bombs blast a message of hate; with interview with an admitted bomber, ed. by W. Worthy. il Life 68:24-32A Mr 27 '70
Brotherhood of the bomb. R. K. Bennett. Read Digest 97:102-6 D '70
City as battlefield: a global concern. il Time 96:19-22+ N 2 '70
Dealing with bombs on campus. il U S News 70:25 Ja 4 '71
Defusing the bombs. New Repub 162:5-6 Mr 28 '70
Drive to curb terror bombings. il U S News 69:33 Ag 3 '70
Fall offensive. il Newsweek 76:44 O 19 '70
FBI's toughest foe: the kids. il Newsweek 76: 22-3 O 26 '70
It can happen anywhere; bombings in Rochester, N.Y. il Newsweek 76:24 O 26 '70
Jerusalem: 1970. R. C. Hirschfield. il Cath World 212:134-6 D '70
Kidnapped diplomats: Greek tragedy on a Latin stage. M. M. Alves. Commonweal 92: 311-14 Je 26 '70
Killing cops: signs of a nationwide plot. il U S News 69:61 O 19 '70
Killing cops: the new terror tactics. il U S News 69:11-13 Ag 31 '70
Lebanon's shattered peace. L. H. Dean. Chr Today 14:36 F 27 '70
Mao is watching; fashionable summer haunts attacked by French terrorists. il Newsweek 76:36 Ag 10 '70
Militants who play with dynamite. W. Greene. il N Y Times Mag p38-9+ O 25 '70
Murder in Mississippi; condensation of Attack on terror. D. Whitehead. il Read Digest 97:191-6+ S '70
New approach. W. F. Buckley, jr. Nat R 22: 1016-17 S 22 '70
New course for the new left; excerpt from Beyond the new left. I. Howe. Sat R 53:8-11 My 30 '70
New danger in South Vietnam: anti-U.S. violence. il U S News 70:15-17 Ja 11 '71
OAS asked to consider problem of kidnaping and terrorism; statement, April 15, 1970. J. J. Jova. Dept State Bul 62:662 My 25 '70
On the Inter-American juridical level; condemning acts of terrorism; excerpts from address, August 31, 1970. G. Plaza. Américas 22:1 O '70
Parallel power: crime and revolution. J. Burnham. Nat R 22:1153 N 3 '70

Parting shots; dangers of being a diplomat in Latin America. il Life 68:81-2 Je 26 '70
Party to movement. J. Burnham. Nat R 22: 993 S 22 '70
Pattern of terror; Latin America. Time 96: 23 Ag 24 '70
Pattern of terror; Viet Cong-style terrorism in Phnom-Penh, Cambodia. il Time 96:40 D 14 '70
Playing with dynamite. il Newsweek 76:28-30 S 14 '70
Political terrorism: hysteria on the left. I. Howe. il N Y Times Mag p25-7+ Ap 12 '70
Prevalance of bombing. C. Howe. Nation 210:361-3 Mr 30 '70
Real toads: real bombs and bullets on campus. Nat R 22:928-9 S 8 '70
Rise of the dynamite radicals. il Time 96:9-10 S 7 '70
Terror bombing: rising technique of violence. il U S News 68:26-7 Mr 23 '70
Terrorism: a tale of four nations; Chile, Uruguay, Ecuador, Canada. il Newsweek 76: 35-6 N 9 '70
Terrorism for peace and justice. G. C. Zahn. Commonweal 93:84-5 O 23 '70
Terrorism in Canada; P. E. Trudeau's reaction to violence. il U S News 69:17-19 N 2 '70
Terrorism on the left. il Newsweek 75:26-30 Mr 23 '70
Terrorism rampant. Cur 124:34-6 D '70
To stop terror bombings: new laws White House asks. il U S News 68:20+ Ap 6 '70
Toward an urban guerrilla movement? J. C. Harsch; M. Lerner; I. F. Stone. Cur 118: 13-18 My '70
Unbreakable bank; attack on West coast branches of the Bank of America. il Newsweek 76:28+ N 9 '70
Violence trap; arranged bombing to catch terrorists in Miss. Nation 210:261 Mr 9 '70
Violence: worldwide problem. il U S News 69:24-6 S 28 '70
War against the police; officers tell their story; testimony before Senate subcommittee. il U S News 68:26 Mr 23 '70
War on the law. il Newsweek 76:16 Ag 31 '70
Wave of blasts; Do bombings ever pay off? il Sr Schol 96:15-16 Ap 13 '70
Week of the bombs; bombings in American cities. Nat R 22:245-6 Mr 10 '70
We'll blow up the world: a nineteen-year-old U.S. terrorist tells his story, ed. by K. Fleming. il Newsweek 76:49-50+ O 12 '70
Why they ran us out of Jenkintown. M. Moore and T. W. Moore. il pors Look 34:98 O 20 '70
Wounded soul; assassination attempt on Archbishop Makarios of Cyprus. il por Time 95:23 Mr 23 '70
See also
Kidnapping
Sabotage

TERRY, Carroll
Learning can be fun. il Good H 170:48+ Ap '70

TERRY, Charles Thaddeus
Professor Terry and the lady in brown. L. Nizer. il Read Digest 97:96-100 N '70 *

TERRY, David S.
In pursuit of duty. G. L. Roberts. il pors Am West 7:26-33+ S '70 *

TERRY, Luther Leonidas
Fluoridation: still an urgent need. por Parents Mag 45:27 N '70
Pollution: excerpts from address. il Todays Ed 59:26-9 Ja '70
Today's antismoking campaign will succeed. il Todays Health 48:20-2+ F '70

TERRY, Megan
Approaching Simone. Criticism
America 122:612 Je 6 '70 *
Newsweek il 75:64 Mr 16 '70 *

TERRY, Walter
World of dance. See issues of Saturday review

TERRY, William M.
Mr Terry named to Inter-American tropical tuna commission. Dept State Bul 63:355 S 28 '70 *

TERRY towels. See Towels

TERTIARY period. See Geology, Stratigraphic —Tertiary; Paleontology—Tertiary

TESCONI, Charles A. Jr
Education and the loss of self-esteem. bibliog f Sch & Soc 98:102-6 F '70

TESHIGAHARA, Sōfū
Arrangement. Newsweek 75:46 F 9 '70

TESICH, Steven
Carpenters. Criticism
Nation 212:60 Ja 11 '71 *

TESSLER, Mark A. and Hedlund, R. D.
Students aren't crazies. New Repub 163:17-18 S 5 '70
TEST plots. See Field experiments (agriculture)
TEST records. See Phonograph records—Test records
TEST signals, Television. See Television broadcasting—Test patterns
TEST tube babies. See Fertilization (in vitro)
TESTICLES
I am Joe's man gland. J. D. Ratcliff. il Read Digest 97:92-5 N '70
TESTIMONIALS in advertising. See Advertising—Testimonials
TESTING
NDT: will it mean flawless products for you? A. P. Armagnac. il Pop Sci 196:90-3+ Ja '70
See also
Fire testing
Moiré method
Quality of products
United States—Standards, National bureau of
also subhead Testing under various subjects, e.g. Automobiles—Testing
TESTING, Educational. See Educational tests and measurements
TESTING instruments
Amateur-built precision mirror tester. J. J. Woerner. il Sky & Tel 39:389-93 Je '70
Build dynamic diode tester. C. L. Andrew. il Pop Electr 33:53+ Jl '70
Build electronic flash tester. W. G. Eslick. il Radio-Electr 41:66 My '70
Build with IC's: color convergence generator. J. C. Votipka. i l Radio-Electr 42:50-1 Ja '71
Eico model 443 semiconductor curve tracer. il Electr World 83:54+ F '70
Heath IG-28; color bar and dot generator. J. Darr. il Radio-Electr 41:76-7 Mr '70
Hickok DMS-3200; digital measuring system. J. Darr. il Radio-Electr 41:26+ My '70
Horizontal efficiency coil checker. H. L. Davidson. il Radio-Electr 41:67-8 My '70
Multirange transistor checker. J. E. Orme. il Electr World 83:82-3 Ap '70
Portable SCR tester. il Radio-Electr 41:94-5 Mr '70
Semiconductor curve tracer, EICO model 443. il Pop Electr 32:77 Ap '70
Telvac SC-4 transistor tester. J. Darr. Radio-Electr 41:68 Ap '70
Test equipment for color. J. Darr. il Radio-Electr 42:40-4+ Ja '71
Test equipment product report. See issues of Electronics world
Testing hi-fi equipment. J. D. Hirsch. il Electr World 84:47-50+ D '70
You can improve your lathe work with indicators. W. E. Burton. il Pop Mech 133: 176-8+ My '70
See also
Antifreeze testers
Automobile engines—Testing
Calibrators
Signal generators

Leasing and renting
Instrument rental considerations. J. Frye. Electr World 84:57-8 D '70
TESTING laboratories
See also
Underwriters' laboratories, inc.
United States—Manned spacecraft center—Lunar receiving laboratory
TESTIS. See Testicles
TESTOSTERONE
Pseudohermaphrodite rat: end organ insensitivity to testosterone. C. W. Bardin and others. bibliog il Science 167:1136-7 F 20 '70
TESTS, Information. See Information tests
TESTS and scales. See Educational tests and measurements
TETANUS
Vaccination
After the nail it's too late. B. B. Smith. il Todays Health 48:30-1 Ag '70
In which I get a splinter. R. Starnes. Field & S 75:10+ D '70
TETRAHYDROCANNABINOL. See THC
TETRAHYMENA. See Protozoa
TETRAMETHYLAMMONIUM manganese chloride. See Manganese chlorides
TETRAMITUS. See Amebas
TETRAZZINI, Luisa
High-flying diva. A. Ronnie. il por Opera N 35:20-1 O 10 '70 *
TEWA Indians
Tewa world, by A. Ortiz. Review
Nation 210:504-5 Ap 27 '70. D. McNickle

TEXACO, inc.
Late tape. R. Brady. Duns 95:94 Je '70
Texaco's fire chief. A. A. Butkus. il por Duns 97:26-9 Ja '71
Texaco's master returns to the helm. il por Bsns W p36-7 S 19 '70
TEXACO opera quiz. See Radio broadcasting—Operas
TEXARKANA, Ark. and Tex.
Education
New angle on accountability. M. J. Filogamo. Todays Ed 59:53 My '70
TEXAS
See also
Airports—Texas
Architecture, Domestic—Texas
Big Thicket
Fishing—Texas
Galveston Bay
Hunting—Texas
Justice, Administration of—Texas
Music festivals—Texas
Padre Island National Seashore
Prohibition—Texas

Description and travel
Great big -wide and wonderful Texas. J. Stewart-Gordon. il Read Digest 96:154-61 Je '70

Historic houses, etc.
See also
Johnson, L. B.—Birthplace

Parks and reserves
LBJ state park. J. Barnett. il Parks & Rec 5:32-4+ D '70

Politics and government
Can a rich guy lose in Texas. W. W. Hamilton, jr. Nation 211:274-7 S 28 '70
Democratic primary, G.O.P. gain. il pors Time 95:37 My 11 '70
Hanging or drowning. New Repub 163:7-8 O 24 '70; Reply. D. Shapiro. 163:31 N 14 '70
Hot after Yarborough. R. Dugger. New Repub 162:11-12 Ap 18 '70
Politics in Texas. W. F. Buckley, jr. Nat R 22:911 Ag 25 '70
Texas politics: big names, high stakes. il U S News 69:68 O 5 '70
Unpredictable LBJ; seems like old times on the Pedernales. il por U S News 69:28 S 7 '70
Where conservatives can't lose. W. Murchison, jr. Nat R 22:1164 N 3 '70

Religious institutions and affairs
See also
Texas conference of churches

Social life and customs
Land of the permanent wave. E. Shrake. il Harper 240:77-81 F '70
TEXAS conference of churches
Agenda for a new generation. J. C. Evans. Chr Cent 87:382-3 Ap 1 '70
TEXAS eastern transmission corporation
Houston: boom in the heart of Texas. il Bsns W p86+ My 23 '70
TEXAS Gulf sulphur company
Billion dollar windfall, by M. Schulman. Review
New Repub 162:31-3 F 14 '70. N. Froomkin
Investor's silent partner. I. Ross. il Nations Bsns 58:74-6+ Je '70; Reply. W. H. Dinsmore. 58:9+ O '70
Texas Gulf tangle unwinds, a little. Bsns W p29-30 F 14 '70
Troubled men of Texas Gulf sulphur. N. A. Martin. il Duns 95:32-3+ Ap '70
Where are the fat years? il Forbes 106:40 S 15 '70
TEXAS in art
Aunt Clara's luminous world; with paintings by C. M. Williamson. il Am Heritage 21:46-56 Ag '70
TEXAS instruments, inc.
Avionics offers prime target for air cargo expansion. Aviation W 93:123 O 26 '70
TI tilts at IBM's market. Bsns W p80 Je 27 '70
Wire that slices the cost of copper: sandwich of aluminum and copper. il Bsns W p49+ My 16 '70
TEXAS international airlines
Texas airlines seeks emergency subsidy. Aviation W 93:32 D 21 '70
TEXAS technological university, Lubbock
Texas tech circulation speeded by Xerox system. il Library J 95:3729 N 1 '70

TEXAS. University
Emperor of U.T. pors Time 96:54 Ag 10 '70
On campus: the crisis is consciousness; colloquium on race feelings. M. P. O'Malley. Mlle 71:48 My '70

Austin campus

Longhorns and longhairs; football, blacks, and hippies. J. Toback. Harper 241:70-3 N '70

Art department

Saturday school for future teachers. il Design 71:16-19 Sum '70

TEXTBOOKS
Cassandra in the college market place. R. H. Smith. Pub W 198:24 N 30 '70
Gaps in minority coverage revealed in textbook survey; junior and senior high schools. Library J 95:2958 S 15 '70
Long-range prospects in book production. V. Strauss. il Pub W 198:28-31 D 14 '70
New guidelines against racism in textbooks. R. H. Smith. Pub W 198:40 D 28 '70
Textbook: a guide for its proper use. J. Hagerty. Clear House 44:410 Mr '70
Where Elhi texts fail the schools; excerpts from address. I. E. Staples. Pub W 197:43-4 Je 1 '70
See also
Booksellers and bookselling—Textbooks
Publishers and publishing—Textbooks

United States
See Textbooks

TEXTILE design
Chez Mlle: house prints. P. Bartlett. il Mlle 70:290-1 Ap '70
Dorothy Liebes. N. Znamierowski. il por Craft Horiz 30:34-41+ Ag '70
Fabrics from the forest. il por Nat Wildlife 8:28-9 Ag '70
For goodness snakes, the serpents have come. il Time 95:48 Mr 16 '70
Nature by the yard. il Home Gard 57:22-3 D '70
Textile designs with foam rubber. R. M. Koch. il Sch Arts 69:14-15 F '70
See also
Batik

TEXTILE fabrics
Choosing and sewing knitted fabrics. Redbook 134:66 Ap '70
Coming on strong: black with white. il House & Gard 137:168 F '70
Eighteenth-century English and American furnishing fashions; excerpts from Printed textiles, English and American cotton and linens, 1700-1850. F. M. Montgomery. il Antiques 97:261-71 F '70
Fabric sets the color scheme. il Good H 170:140-7+ Ap '70
How much do you know about textiles? quiz. J. Daugherty and M. Daugherty. il Sci Digest 69:80-1+ Ja '71
Irish treasury; motifs by Jack Larsen. M. Gough. il House B 112:98-101 Mr '70
What to look for in an upholstery fabric. il Good H 170:144 F '70
See also
Bleaching
Chintz
Cotton fabrics
Sheets
Weaving

Care

Laundering guide for the newer fabrics. il Good H 171:142 Jl '70
Spring-cleaning household fabrics. il Good H 170:186 My '70

Dyeing
See Dyes and dyeing

Finishing
See Textile finishing

Fireproofing
See Fireproofing of textiles

Heat transmission

Space-age fabric gives you out-of-this-world warmth. H. Shuldiner. il Pop Sci 196:48 Ja '70

TEXTILE fabrics, Bonded. See Textile fabrics, Laminated
TEXTILE fabrics, Fire resisting
Flame-retardant textiles for consumers. il Consumer Bul 53:4+ S '70

TEXTILE fabrics, Flammable
Action on flammable fabrics. Consumer Rep 35:374-6 Je '70
Fireproofing our children. C. Dishon. il Todays Health 49:38-41+ Ja '71
Preventing child burns. I. N. Holloway. il PTA Mag 64:14-15 Je '70
Spangle affair. Consumer Rep 35:30-1 Ja '70
TEXTILE fabrics, Laminated
Differences in bonded and laminated fabrics. Good H 171:154 Ag '70
TEXTILE fabrics, Synthetic
And the new fabrics. Am Home 73:72+ F '70
Fabric color impact; Celanese house showcase. il House B 112:35-41 Jl '70
Most important fibers in your house. M. Gough. House B 112:94-5+ S '70
TEXTILE fabrics, Waterproof
What you should know about the new rainwear. il Good H 170:192 Ap '70
TEXTILE fabrics, Wrinkle resistant
Durable-press shirts. il Consumer Rep 34:634-7 N '69
What you should know about no-iron fabrics and finishes. il Good H 170:158 Je '70
TEXTILE finishing
Easier living with today's fabric finishes. A. A. Latour. Good H 171:175 N '70
TEXTILE imports. See Import quotas
TEXTILE industry

Far East

Asia's great leap in textiles. J. M. Mecklin. il Fortune 82:76-83+ O '70

United States

What the U.S. textile industry really needs. R. Loving, jr. il Fortune 82:84-7+ O '70
See also
Burlington industries
Cone mills corporation
TEXTILE labels. See Labels
TEXTILE machinery industry

Spain

National scandal starts to unravel; Matesa affair. por Bsns W p56 My 23 '70
Scandal in the cabinet; the Matesa affair. Newsweek 76:44-5 Jl 27 '70
TEXTILE mills
Early New England textile village in art. R. M. Candee. il Antiques 98:910-15 D '70
Epitaph for an American landmark; Amoskeag textile mills. D. G. McCullough. il Am Heritage 21:110-13 Ap '70
TEXTILE painting
Watercolor textiles. L. Rienks. il pors Design 71:16-18 mid-Sum '70
TEXTILE printing
Textile designs with foam rubber. R. M. Koch. il Sch Arts 69:14-15 F '70
TEXTILE workers
Blacks in the mills. il Newsweek 76:88+ N 2 '70
TEXTILE workers union of America
Firing and hiring of Fredy Jones; anti-union practices of textile companies in North Carolina. R. Scott. New Repub 163:12-15 Jl 25 '70
TEXTRON, Inc.
Preparedness in Providence. Forbes 106:32-3 D 15 '70
Textron: built to diversify. Bsns W p 118+ O 17 '70
TEXTURIZING (photography) See Photomontage
TEYTE, Dame Maggie
Dame Maggie. B. Fischer-Williams. pors Opera N 34:14-16 Mr 21 '70 *
THACHER, Peter S.
Sharing the practical benefits of new technology in the peaceful uses of outer space; statement, December 11, 1969. Dept State Bul 62:67-9 Ja 19 '70
THAI dancing. See Dancing, Thai
THAILAND
Anxious Thais. il Newsweek 76:33 Ag 31 '70
Bangkok prince. A. Miller. Harper 241:32-3 Jl '70
Our Asian war widens. D. Warner. il Look 34:64-71+ My 19 '70
See also
Economic assistance in Thailand
Natural resources—Thailand
Temples—Thailand
Tourist trade—Thailand

Antiquities

Secrets of Spirit cave. por Time 95:66 F 9 '70

Armed forces

Thailand: first big test of the Nixon doctrine. il U S News 69:51-3 Ag 24 '70

THAILAND—*Continued*

Defenses

Thailand and the Cambodian conflict. K. T. Young. bibliog f Cur Hist 59:351-5+ D '70
Thailand: first big test of the Nixon doctrine. il U S News 69:51-3 Ag 24 '70

Description and travel

Fairytale Thailand. M. Richards. il Travel 133:42-7 Ja '70
Templed cities of Thailand. K. Willenson. il Travel & Camera 33:60-9 Mr '70

Foreign relations

Thailand and the Cambodian conflict. K. T. Young. bibliog f Cur Hist 59:351-5+ D '70
World's angriest man: Thannat Kohman, foreign minister. W. F. Buckley, jr. Nat R 22:46+ Ja 13 '70

History

Thailand. L. Unger. bibliog il Focus 21:1-9 N '70

Politics and government

Gloom in the land of smiles. il Time 96:22 Jl 27 '70
Prospects for the future. L. Unger. bibliog il Focus 21:9-12 N '70

THAILAND-United States air agreement. See Aviation—International aspects

THALASSEMIA. See Anemia

THALER, M. Michael
Substrate-induced conjugation of bilirubin in genetically deficient newborn rats. bibliog il Science 170:555-6 O 30 '70

THALER, Susan
He'll forget by the time he's married; story. Redbook 135:78-9 Jl '70

THALIDOMIDE children. See Deformities

THANE, Adele
Baker's neighbor; dramatization of Peruvian folk tale. Plays 30:61-6 N '70
King who was bored; dramatization of a Mexican folk tale. Plays 30:49-55 Ja '71
Little minister; dramatization of a novel by J. M. Barrie. Plays 29:83-95 F '70

THANKS. See Thanksgiving

THANKSGIVING
Every day is Thanksgiving day; reprint from December 5, 1958 issue. D. Lawrence. U S News 69:80 N 30 '70

Poetry

Where grace began. Chr Cent 87:1404 N 25 '70

THANKSGIVING day

Drama

Hooray for Thanksgiving. M. P. Churchill. Plays 30:67-8 N '70
Jonathan's Thanksgiving. A. Very. Plays 30: 38, 69-72 N '70
Many thanks. M. Hark and N. McQueen. Plays 30:39-46 N '70

Fiction

Nathaniel. J. J. Shomon. il Am For 76:12-14+ N '70

THANKSGIVING decorations. See Decoration and ornament

THANKSGIVING dinners
Choice of Thanksgivings. il Sunset 145:84-9 N '70
Picnic for Thanksgiving. E. Alston. il Look 34:82-3 N 17 '70
Six new ways with old favorites. R. Molter. il Parents Mag 45:96-9+ N '70
Thanksgiving past; reprint from an 1890 Ladies' home journal. il Ladies Home J 87:118-19+ N '70
Tradition with a twist; casseroles of rabbit and pheasant, candied cranberries. J. Hewitt. il N Y Times Mag p96 N 22 '70

Anecdotes, facetiae, satire, etc.

Thanksgiving dinner: the Pilgrims had it easy. E. Bombeck. il Good H 171:34+ N '70

THANKSGIVING in Paris, 1964; story. See McCarthy, M.

THANT, 1909-
Address by the Secretary-General at the Assembly for one Asia; April 11, 1970. UN Mo Chron 7:46-51 My '70
Address by the Secretary-General to the second World food congress; June 16, 1970. UN Mo Chron 7:132-8 Jl '70
Address by the Secretary-General to the United Nations association of Japan; April 15, 1970. UN Mo Chron 7:52-5 My '70

Human environment and world order; address, May 14, 1970. UN Mo Chron 7:69-77 Je '70
International day for the elimination of racial discrimination 21 March; message, March 21, 1970. UN Mo Chron 7:i-ii Mr '70
Introduction to the annual report of the Secretary-General on the work of the organization. UN Mo Chron 7:40-79 O '70
Man the killer of nature. il UNESCO Courier 23:46-53 Ag '70
Message for youth, 1970. UN Mo Chron 7: i-ii Jl '70
On giving the Charter a chance; address, June 26, 1970. UN Mo Chron 7:38-45 Jl '70
Quiet United Nations road to accord; June 15, 1970. UN Mo Chron 7:122-31 Ag 10 '70
Secretary-General's press conference; 22 December, 1969. UN Mo Chron 7:178-87 Ja '70
Secretary-General's press conferences; January 4 and 9, 1970. UN Mo Chron 7:34-44 F '70
Secretary-General's press conference; February 17, 1970. UN Mo Chron 7:26-36 Mr '70
Secretary-General's press conference; June 11, 1970. UN Mo Chron 7:108-21 Jl '70
Secretary-General's press conference; July 7, 1970. UN Mo Chron 7:93-101 Ag '70
Secretary-General's press conference; September 10, 1970. UN Mo Chron 7:30-9 O '70
Statements on hijacking of aircraft and safety of correspondents in war zones. UN Mo Chron 7:21-2 O '70
Statements on Palestine refugees, southeast Asia, etc. UN Mo Chron 7:44-6 Je '70
Twenty-fifth anniversary of the United Nations marked at White House dinner; exchange of toasts, July 10, 1970. Dept State Bul 63:168-71 Ag 10 '70
United Nations day, 24 October 1970; message. UN Mo Chron 7:ii-iii O '70
Universality of the U.N; address, June 26, 1970. Vital Speeches 36:652-5 Ag 15 '70; Excerpts. Cur 120:44 Ag '70

about

Secretary-General; activities during December. UN Mo Chron 7:129-32 Ja '70 *
Secretary-General; activities during January. UN Mo Chron 7:16-20 F '70 *
Secretary-General; activities during February. UN Mo Chron 7:9-11 Mr '70 *
Secretary-General; activities during March. UN Mo Chron 7:55-7 Ap '70 *
Secretary-General; activities during April. UN Mo Chron 7:21-3 My '70
Secretary-General; activities during June. UN Mo Chron 7:77-80 Jl '70 *
Secretary-General; activities during September-October. UN Mo Chron 7:21 O; 147-8 N '70
U Thant: a study in caution. il por Newsweek 76:56+ O 19 '70 *
Visits to Geneva, Washington, Ottawa and Yugoslavia. UN Mo Chron 7:67-70 Ag '70 *

THARP, Twyla
Twyla Tharp & co; Metropolitan museum of art. J. Anderson. il Dance Mag 44:90-2 Mr '70 *

THAT Franklin boy; drama. See Martens, A. C.

THATCH, Lawn. See Lawn thatch

THAT'S what happens; opera. See Krenek, E.

THAWLEY, John
Block prepping. il Hot Rod 23:72-4 My '70
Drive ya buggy. See issues of Hot rod
Eric Rickman. il pors Hot Rod 23:70-2 Je '70

THAYER, Alexander Wheelock
Beethoven's American Boswell. G. Marek. pors Hi Fi sec I 20:64-8 Ja '70

THAYER, J. A.
Group counseling. bibliog Clear House 45:100-3 O '70

THAYER, W. Paul
LTV recounts its many ills. por Bsns W p42 D 19 '70 *
New pilot at LTV. il por Time 96:64 Jl 27 '70 *
Thayer assumes leadership at LTV. Aviation W 93:60-1 Jl 27 '70 *
Tough pilot takes the stick at LTV. por Bsns W p26-7 Jl 18 '70 *

THEATER
See also
Acting
Happenings (theater)
Stage lighting
Theater, Experimental
Vaudeville

Awards

Theatre: annual awards. T. Lewis. America 122:569 My 23 '70

THEATER—*Continued*

Finance
See also
Theatrical production and direction, Cost of

Stage mechanism
See also
Opera—Stage mechanism

Stage setting and scenery
Art and English; designing sets project. T. R. Pokorny. il Sch Arts 69:40 Je '70

Canada
See also
Toronto—Theater

England
See Theater—Great Britain

France
Vocation for madness; career of A. Artaud. S. De Gramont. pors Horizon 12:48-55 Spr '70
See also
Comédie Française
Paris—Theater

Great Britain
Looking back without anger; whatever became of the angry young men? C. Sigal. il Commonweal 92:186-8 My 8 '70
Merchant ltd; production by the British national theatre company. H. Hewes. il Sat R 53:20 Jl 11 '70
National legacy: U.S. visit of Laurence Olivier's National theatre company of Great Britain. J. Kroll. Newsweek 75:56-7 F 2 '70
Sir says; interview, ed. by H. Ehrlich. L. Olivier. il pors Look 34:22-6 Ja 27 '70
Theater in England. H. Hewes. Sat R 53:20 Jl 25 '70
Theater; National theatre company production of The three sisters in the United States. S. Kauffmann. New Repub 162:31+ Mr 21 '70
See also
London—Theater

Japan
See also
Tokyo—Theater

Poland
Act of the actor; Jerzy Grotowski's Polish laboratory theatre. P. McDermott. Commonweal 91:510-13 F 6 '70
Grotowski: an unsettled American theater replies; symposium, ed. by S. W. Little. Sat R 53:20-1 F 7 '70
Grotowski revolution. C. R. Hughes. America 122:44-5 Ja 17 '70

Russia
Poet on a string; performance of Voznesensky's revue Look out for your faces. il por Time 95:27 Mr 9 '70

Spain
See also
Madrid—Theater

Turkey
See also
Istanbul—Theater

United States
Decade of engagement. E. Albee. il Sat R 53:19-20 Ja 24 '70
Emphasis. B. Diamonstein. Harp Baz 103:184-5 Mr; 98-9+ Je; 103 O '70
New life in new places for the American theater; with interview with D. Merrick. il U S News 68:80-4 My 4 '70
Oregon expands; spring season of the Angus Bowmer theatre, Ashland, Ore. and schedule of American theater company in Portland. H. Hewes. Sat R 53:20 Ap 11 '70
Special report; Barbwire theatre. P. Goldberger. il por Sr Schol 95:8-9 N 3 '69
Theater. T. Lewis. See occasional issues of America to August 22, 1970
Theater '70. R. Crinkley. Nat R 22:1308-9 D 1 '70
Very special place; Berkshire theatre festival. il Newsweek 76:78-9 Jl 27 '70
See also
Theater, Negro
also subhead Theater under names of cities, e.g. New York (city)—Theater

THEATER, Childrens
Allegorical romp; Story theatre. T. E. Kalem. il Time 96:48 N 9 '70
Story-eyed; Story theatre. H. Hewes. Sat R 53:58 N 14 '70
Theatre; Story theatre. B. Gill. New Yorker 46:133 N 7 '70

THEATER, Experimental
Act of the actor; Jerzy Grotowski's Polish laboratory theatre. P. McDermott. Commonweal 91:510-13 F 6 '70
American chickens; Commune production of Richard Schechner's Performance group. J. Kroll. Newsweek 76:61 D 28 '70
Digging it; Washington's DIG-IT troupe. il Newsweek 75:64+ Ap 27 '70
Grotowski revolution. C. R. Hughes. America 122:44-5 Ja 17 '70
Ionesco on Olympus. T. Bishop. por Sat R 53:21-3+ My 16 '70
Love play in braille; avant-garde group, The company, producing theater of touch called James Joyce memorial liquid theatre. il Time 95:68 F 23 '70
Off Broadway; New Lafayette production of The devil catchers by an anonymous hand. E. Oliver. New Yorker 46:132 D 12 '70
Theatre; San Francisco Mime Troupe guerrilla theatre. J. Novick. Nation 211:317-18 O 5 '70
Theatre; unclad bodies. H. Clurman. Nation 211:284-5 S 28 '70
Vocation for madness; career of A. Artaud. S. De Gramont. pors Horizon 12:48-55 Spr '70

THEATER, Negro
Digging it; Washington's DIG-IT troupe. il Newsweek 75:64+ Ap 27 '70
Mecca for blackness; Chicago's Affro-arts theater. il Ebony 25:96-8+ My '70
Prize winners: C. Gordone, M. Moore and C. Little. P. Garland. il pors Ebony 25:29-32+ Jl '70
Rolling thunder. por Time 95:62+ Ap 6 '70
See also
Negro drama

THEATER, Open-air
Outdoor theater in the Bay area; San Francisco Mime troupe. il Sunset 144:76 My '70
See an outdoor drama this summer. Bet Hom & Gard 48:66 Jl '70
This is street theater; Society hill playhouse street theatre. D. Kogan. il Parks & Rec 5:44-6 Ja '70
See also
Pageants

THEATER architecture. See Theater buildings

THEATER buildings
L'enfant theatre, Washington, D.C. il Arch Rec 147:114 Ja '70
Three new theaters. J. S. Margolies. il Art in Am 58:88-93 My '70
See also
Bayreuth festspielhaus
Moving picture theaters

THEATER festivals. See Drama festivals

THEATER of cruelty. See Theater, Experimental

THEATER of the absurd. See Theater, Experimental

THEATER of the living arts. See Philadelphia—Theater

THEATER of touch. See Theater, Experimental

THEATER organs. See Organ

THEATERS. See Theater buildings

THEATRICAL agencies
How to merchandise an actor on TV. J. Barthel. il por N Y Times Mag p 14+ O 25 '70

THEATRICAL photography. See Photography, Theatrical

THEATRICAL production and direction
Like father, unlike son; M. Butler, producer of Hair. il por Forbes 105:56 Je 1 '70
Oh! Hillard Elkins! C. Davis. por Esquire 74:135-7+ N '70
Parting shots: Hair, that play is sprouting everywhere. T. Prideaux. il Life 68:83-6 Ap 17 '70
Profit without honor; auditions to cast musical, Lolita. il por Time 96:42 D 21 '70
The me nobody knows; a clamorous cry from the ghetto becomes an off-Broadway hit; with report by B. Dunn. il Life 69:34-42 S 4 '70
Tokyo kid brothers: performers in Golden bat, rock revue at the Sheridan square playhouse New Yorker 46:34-6 S 12 '70
What's needed to revive Broadway; interview. D. Merrick. pors U S News 68:83-4 My 4 '70
See also
Moving picture production and direction

THEATRICAL production and direction, Cost of
Another reprise of Broadway blues. il Bsns W p34 S 19 '70

THEFT. See Shoplifting; Stealing

THEGZE, Chuck
I see everything twice. il Film Q 24:7-17 Fall '70

THEISMANN, Joe
Arms against the ogres. D. Jenkins. il Sports
Illus 33:28-30+ D 21 '70 *
Hustling the Heisman hopefuls. il Time 96:
53 N 16 '70 *
Please say it ain't so, Joe. J. Tobin. il
Sports Illus 33:64+ D 7 '70 *
Reports of li'l Joe's death were premature. P.
Putnam. Sports Illus 33:51-2 O 26 '70 *

THELEN, Herbert A.
Tutoring by students. Ed Digest 35:17-20 F
'70

THELMA; story. See Mitchell, D.

THEME writing. See English language—Composition

THEODORACOPULOS, Taki
King Hussein's ten-day war. Nat R 22:1109
O 20 '70

THEODORAKIS, Mikis
Theodorakis; interview. New Yorker 46:22-3
Ag 15 '70
about
Flight to freedom. il por Newsweek 75:56+ Ap
27 '70 *
March of the spirit; concert at London's Royal
Albert Hall. il por Newsweek 76:103 Jl 13
'70 *
Monday of Mikis Theodorakis; reprint. J.
Boetsch. il pors Sat R 53:14-15+ My 9 '70 *
Sop to the critics. il por Time 95:42 Ap 27 '70 *

THEODORE F. Jenkins memorial law library
company. See Law library company of
Philadelphia

THEODORE Hamm brewing company. See
Hamm, Theodore, brewing company

THEOLOGIANS
Barth on Tillich; neo-gnosticism. R. K.
Anderson. pors Chr Cent 87:1477-81 D 9 '70
Filthy-minded reflections on theological method. J. Loeschen. Chr Cent 87:108-12 Ja 28
'70
Tübingen revisited. G. O'Collins. America
122:275-6 Mr 14 '70
See also
Bonhoeffer, D.
Butzer, M.
Doctors of the church
Lonergan, B.
Melanchthon, P.
Rahner, K.
Seminarians

Anecdotes, facetiae, satire, etc.
Anyone for ecological theology? P. Steinfels.
Commonweal 91:576 F 27 '70

THEOLOGICAL anthropology. See Man (theology)

THEOLOGICAL degrees. See Degrees, Academic

THEOLOGICAL education
Is theology thinking about God? N. J. Rigali. Cath World 210:204-7 F '70
Theological education 1970; symposium. Chr
Cent 87:472-80+ Ap 22 '70
See also
Clergy—Education
Religious education
Theological seminaries

THEOLOGICAL school professors. See College
professors and instructors

THEOLOGICAL seminaries
Gordon-Conwell urban center future in doubt.
Chr Today 14:36 My 22 '70
Satellite abandoned; Christian missionary alliance. Chr Today 14:36-7 Je 19 '70
Seminary enrollment. il Chr Today 14:34-5
Ja 16 '70
Theological education 1970; symposium. Chr
Cent 87:472-80+ Ap 22 '70
See also
Lutheran world federation
St Louis university, St Louis, Mo.—School
of divinity
Union theological seminary, New York
Yale university—Divinity school

Cooperation
Needed: new modes for internationalizing
theological education. V. B. Rigdon and J. E.
Will. Chr Cent 87:501-5 Ap 22 '70

Curriculum
Reason for being at Union and Yale. J. E.
Dittes and C. W. Powers. Chr Cent 87:494-
501 Ap 22 '70

Germany (Federal Republic)
Revolution in theology; radical Marxism on
the German campuses. C. F. H. Henry.
Chr Today 15:36-7 O 9 '70

THEOLOGICAL seminaries, Catholic
Reforming seminaries. America 122:402 Ap 18
'70

THEOLOGICAL students. See Seminarians

THEOLOGY
Black theology and black liberation; address.
J. H. Cone. il Chr Cent 87:1084-8 S 16 '70
Black theology of liberation, by J. H. Cone.
Review
Chr Cent 87:1258 O 21 '70 J. Snider
Discoveries and dangers. R. M. Brown. por
Chr Cent 87:40-5 Ja 14 '70
God as a problem. C. F. H. Henry. Chr Today 14:32-3 F 13 '70
Harrowing of heaven. C. H. Pinnock. Chr
Today 14:7-8 Je 19 '70
Hegelian dialectic in theology. J. N. Jonsson.
Chr Today 14:3-5 Ag 21; 14-16+ S 11 '70
New theology for a new people; black theology. C. Rogers. Chr Cent 87:1080 S 16 '70
Palliative or curative? L. N. Bell. Chr Today
14:29 Ap 24 '70
Phenomenon of Bernard Lonergan. B. J.
Tyrrell. America 122:298-300 Mr 21 '70
Political gospel. F. Herzog. il Chr Cent 87:
1380-3 N 18 '70
Problem of hope; can we judge the theology
of hope an unmixed blessing? M. Daly.
Commonweal 92:314-17 Je 26 '70; Reply. G.
Willenbrink. 92:491 S 25 '70
Rahner's spiritual theology. J. T. Carmody.
America 123:345-7 O 31 '70
Toward a theology of evangelism. D. G. Miller. Chr Today 14:5-8+ My 8; 9-12 My 22 '70
Toward a theology of the black experience.
M. J. Jones. il Chr Cent 87:1088-91 S 16 '70
See also
Apocalypticism
Catechetics
Christian life
Church
Death
Devil
Freedom (theology)
God
Heresy
Man (theology)
Modernism
Mysticism
Natural theology
Religion
Religion and science
Revelation
Secularism
Skepticism

Bibliography
Wide choice in church history and theology.
G. W. Bromiley. Chr Today 14:6-8+ F 13
'70

Dictionaries and encyclopedias
On Americanizing Karl Rahner. T. E. Clarke.
America 123:337-9 O 31 '70

Study and teaching
Problems ahead for the lay theologian. R. Van
Allen. il Cath World 212:37-9 O '70
See also
Theological education
Theological seminaries

Terminology
Theological buzzwords. P. J. Henriot. Cath
World 211:180 Jl '70

THEOLOGY, Jewish. See Jewish theology
THEOLOGY, Liberal. See Modernism
THEOLOGY, Natural. See Natural theology
THEOLOGY, Pastoral. See Pastoral theology
THERAPEUTIC abortion. See Abortion
THERAPEUTIC penmanship. See Graphotherapy
THERAPEUTICS
See also
Medicine
Medicine—Practice
Occupational therapy
Physical therapy
Psychotherapy
Recreational therapy
Stimulants
THERE'S always the Bronx; story. See Wein,
B.

THERESA, Mother
Profiles; Missionaries of charity. Calcutta.
V. Mehta. New Yorker 46:97-8+ Mr 21
'70 *

THERMAL conductivity. See Heat conductivity

THERMAL fabrics. See Textile fabrics—Heat
transmission

THERMAL pollution. See Marine pollution;
Water pollution

THERMAL radiation. See Heat—Radiation and
absorption

THERMIONIC emission
Thermionic topping: a stopgap power source.
E. Gross. il Sci N 97:490-1 My 16 '70

THERMOCHEMISTRY
  See also
  Boiling points
THERMODYNAMICS
  See also
  Statistical mechanics
THERMOGRAPHY, Infrared. See Photography,
    Infrared
THERMOGRAPHY, Medical. See Photography,
    Medical
THERMOLUMINESCENCE
  Luminescence and thermoluminescence in-
    duced by bombardment with protons of 159
    million electron volts. J. A. Edgington and
    I. M. Blair. bibliog il Science 167:715-17 Ja
    30 '70
  Thermoluminescence of lunar samples. G.
    B. Dalrymple and R. R. Doell. il Science
    167:713-15 Ja 30 '70
THERMOLUMINESCENT dating. See Archeol-
    ogy—Methodology
THERMOMETERS, Clinical
  Build an electronic clinical thermometer. J.
    R. Laughlin. il Pop Electr 34:75-8 Ja '71
  Fever and fever thermometers. il Changing
    T 24:16 My '70
THERMOMETERS, Cooking
  Degrees of accuracy: a guide to thermome-
    ters. il Redbook 135:45+ Ag '70
THERMOMETERS and thermometry
  Build your own indoor-outdoor electronic
    thermometer. R. F. Graf and G. J. Whalen.
    il Pop Mech 133:150-2 F '70
  Indoor-outdoor weather thermometers. il Con-
    sumer Bul 53:30-2 N '70
THERMONUCLEAR reactions. See Nuclear fu-
    sion
THERMOREGULATORY behavior. See Temper-
    ature, Animal and human
THERMOS containers
  Cups and stuff that keep their cool. C.
    Conley. il Field & S 75:131 S '70
THEROUX, Alexander Louis
  Inarticulate hero. Nat R 22:199-201 F 24 '70
THEROUX, Paul
  Sinning with Annie; story. Harp Baz 103:
    130-1 Ap '70
THESIGER, Wilfred Patrick
  Last of the desert adventurers; excerpt from
    Restless spirit. T. S. Green. il pors Hori-
    zon 12:104-11 Spr '70 *
THEWALT, Ulf. See Bugg, C. E. jt. auth.
THIBODEAU, Jean
  Cyclamen species. il Horticulture 48:24-5 Ag
    '70
THIBODEAU, Ralph
  Beethoven's Missa solemnis. por Common-
    weal 93:328-9 D 25 '70
THICKET, Big. See Big Thicket
THIEMANN, Hugo
  Changing dynamics in research and develop-
    ment. bibliog il Science 168:1427-31 Je 19 '70
THIERRY, Pierre
  Audio-visual education in Ivory Coast. il
    Sch & Soc 98:424-6 N '70
THIEU, Nguyen-van-. See Nguyen-van-Thieu
THIEVES
  See also
  Shoplifting
  Stealing
THIMANN, Kenneth V.
  Science: attack and defense. Science 169:633
    Ag 14 '70
THIN films
  Amateur scientists; deposition and use of
    thin films; ed. by C. L. Stong. R. Baker.
    il Sci Am 222:143-5 Je '70
  Memory film for cameras and computers;
    Ovonic device. S. V. Jones. il Sci Digest 69:
    31 Ja '71
  Optical interference coatings. P. Baumeister
    and G. Pincus. il Sci Am 223:58-68+ D '70
THINGS in their proper order; story. See Ger-
    ber, M. J.
THINKING. See Thought and thinking
THIOFORMALDEHYDE. See Formaldehyde
THIOLS. See Mercaptans
THIRD class mail. See Postal service—United
    States
THIRD committee of the General assembly.
    See United Nations—Social humanitarian
    and cultural committee
THIRD party movement. See Political parties—
    United States
THIRST
  Antidotal thirst: a response to intoxication.
    D. F. Smith and others. bibliog il Science
    167:297-8 Ja 16 '70
  Tongue cooling: a new reward for thirsty ro-
    dents. J. Mendelson and D. Chillag. bibliog
    il Science 170:1418-21 D 25 '70

35mm cameras. See Cameras
THIS day of joy; story. See Aguallo, T.
THIS is my daughter; story. See Poston, P.
THIS sporting life; drama. See Storey, D.
THIS time forever; story. See Burrough, L.
THIS town needs a doctor; novel. See Block,
    L.
THODAY, J. M. and Gibson, J. B.
  Environmental and genetical contributions
    to class difference: a model experiment.
    bibliog il Science 167:990-2 F 13 '70
THOENI, Gustavo
  New kind of French dressing. W. Johnson.
    il pors Sports Illus 32:12-17 F 2 '70
THOM, Rose Anne
  Theme was variations. il Dance Mag 44:36-41
    N '70
THOMAN, Roy E.
  Persian Gulf Region. bibliog f il Cur Hist 60:
    38-45+ Ja '71
THOMAS à Becket, Saint
  Music in honor of St Thomas of Canterbury;
    with list of hymns. D. Stevens. bibliog f il
    Mus Q 56:311-48 Jl '70 *
  What of martyrdom? Chr Today 15:28 D 18
    '70 *
THOMAS, Alexander, and others
  Origin of personality; with biographical
    sketch. il Sci Am 223:12, 102-9 bibliog(p 128)
    Ag '70
THOMAS, Ann
  Psychedelic tie-dye look. il por Time 95:36-
    9 Ja 26 '70
THOMAS, Bill
  Amishville U.S.A. il Travel 134:46-51 O '70
  Big Sur cycle. il Travel 134:40-3 N '70
  Dismal delight. il Travel 133:48-51+ Ja '70
  Festival king: Ohio. il Travel 133:36-41 Ja
    '70
  Funmobiles. il Travel 134:40-3+ Ag '70
  Ghost towns; for sale! il Travel 134:34-9 O
    '70
  Grand Canyon by helicopter. il Travel 133:46-
    50 Je '70
  Legendary Reelfoot. il Travel 134:40-3+ Jl '70
  Montana's astounding earthquake area. il
    Travel 133:40-5 F '70
  Oklahoma's wee wonder. il Travel 133:40-3
    Mr '70
  Ranch vacations. il Travel 133:36-42 My '70
  Snurfing. il Travel 134:50-1+ D '70
  Super highway lakes. il Field & S 75:66-7+
    My '70
  West Virginia's mountain climbing. il Travel
    133:28-33+ F '70
  Wilderness adventure in Alaska. il Travel 133:
    34-9+ Je '70
THOMAS, Brandon
  Charley's aunt. Criticism
    New Yorker 46:48 Jl 11 '70 *
THOMAS, Carla
  B. B. and Carla. New Yorker 46:25-6 Je 13
    '70 *
THOMAS, D. Reginald
  Beyond the brick walls. Chr Today 14:40 Je
    5 '70 *
THOMAS, Dave
  Gallery; photographs. Life 68:8-11 Je 5 '70
THOMAS, David
  Onward and upward with the arts. C. Tom-
    kins. New Yorker 46:83-4+ O 3 '70 *
THOMAS, Davis
  Magnificence of Mother Russia. il Holiday
    48:64-5 Jl '70
THOMAS, Dylan
  Structure signals in The hunchback in the
    park. H. Brand. Engl J 59:195-200 F '70 *
  Williams as Thomas. R. Jacobson. por Sat R
    53:74 Ap 25 '70 *
THOMAS, Frank J. See Thomas, P. jt. auth.
THOMAS, G. J. Jr. See Hartman, K. A. jt.
    auth.
THOMAS, Gene
  Club scene. Flying 86:112 F; 25 Mr '70
THOMAS, George
  Doc and George bloom late. R. Blount, jr.
    Sports Illus 32:46 Je 29 '70 *
THOMAS, Helen
  Washington witch hunt. il por Time 96:34
    Ag 3 '70 *
THOMAS, Jack B.
  Cruelest trick-or-treat hoax. K. Engh. il
    pors Good H 171:12+ O '70 *
THOMAS, James C.
  Micajah Burnett and the buildings at Pleas-
    ant Hill. il por Antiques 98:600-5 O '70
THOMAS, John Godfrey Parry
  Day they dug up Babs. K. Prentiss. il Holi-
    day 47:62-3 F '70 *
THOMAS, Joseph
  Blood money. por Newsweek 76:77 Ag 17
    '70 *

THOMAS, Lowell, 1892-
Painful lessons of the cedars of Lebanon. il por Nat Wildlife 8:50-5 D '69
With the stone age men in New Guinea. il por Read Digest 96:154-7+ F '70

THOMAS, Lowell, 1923-
Siberia: the sleeping land awakes; condensation. il Read Digest 97:247-55+ D '70

THOMAS, Marlo
Young world of Marlo Thomas. M. Roberts. il pors Good H 171:20-2+ Ag '70 *

THOMAS, Michael
Tribal center for the rock freaks; Fillmore East. il Holiday 47:18+ F '70
Why-of all places-Ibiza? il Holiday 47:32-7+ Je '70

THOMAS, Michael, 1926?-
Cartier changes with the trend. il por Bsns W p 116 F 14 '70 *

THOMAS, Michael Tilson
With Michael Tilson Thomas, the show really goes on! interview. ed. by R. Hemming. il pors Sr Schol 97:22-4 O 26 '70

about
Bird with inward fire. il por Time 96:57 S 14 '70 *
Kid from Boston. H. Saal. por Newsweek 75:86 Ap 13 '70 *
Michael Tilson Thomas in London. D. J. Soria. por Hi Fi 20:MA7 S '70 *
Musical events: concert in Philharmonic Hall. W. Sargeant. New Yorker 46:89-90 Ap 11 '70 *
Musician of the month. J. Hiemenz. il por Hi Fi 20:secII 6-7 Jl '70 *
Newsmakers. por Sr Schol 95:15 N 10 '69 *

THOMAS, Morris Taft
Clay science and the moon. il Design 72:40-1 Wint '70
Plasticene prints. il Design 71:21 Fall '69

THOMAS, Parry. See Thomas, J. G. P.

THOMAS, Phyllis, and Thomas, F. J.
Making an impression in Mexico. il Américas 22:30-5 S '70

THOMAS, Ralph
To transform the world. il Chr Cent 87:49 Ja 14 '70

THOMAS, Theodore
Great Chicago piano war. P. Hume and R. Hume. il pors Am Heritage 21:16-21 O '70 *

THOMAS, W. H. Johnson
Seven great Charleston houses. il Antiques 97: 556-70 Ap '70

THOMASSON, Clyde. See Pittman, J. jt. auth.

THOMASSON, Ednearl
Kakes and kookies for kollege kids. J. Kuh. por Ladies Home J 87:143 S '70 *

THOMASSON, Wayman H.
Courtney Burton named to Foundation board. il por Parks & Rec 9:59+ S '70

THOMPSON, Benjamin
Bright glass prism on Brattle street. il Arch Rec 147:105-12 My '70 *

THOMPSON, Betty
D. T. Niles; world Christian. Chr Cent 87: 957 Ag 12 '70

THOMPSON, Bill
Mangoes don't grow in Brooklyn. Commonweal 93:347-50 Ja 8 '71

THOMPSON, Bob
Fall: a good time to plant. il Home Gard 57: 32-9 S '70
Four easy-to-grow fruits. il Home Gard 57: 32-3+ Ap '70

THOMPSON, Charley
Devil in Duval County. por Time 96:42+ Ag 17 '70 *
Dynamite in pollution. C. Gillespie. Nation 211:455-7 N 9 '70; Reply with rejoinder. J. T. Lynch. 211:674 D 28 '70 *

THOMPSON, Earl
Header, the rigger, the captain; story. il Esquire 74:136-7 S '70

THOMPSON, Frank B. jr
Zigzagging liquorman. G. Berkwitt. por Duns 96:52 D '70 *

THOMPSON, Geoffrey. See Melson, W. G. jt. auth.

THOMPSON, Guy A. jr. See Kennedy, K. E. jt. auth.

THOMPSON, J. Walter, company
J. Walter Thompson is alive and well in thirty countries. I. Ross. il Fortune 82:102-5+ O '70

THOMPSON, Jerry
Motor trend interview. pors Motor T 22:78+ N '70

THOMPSON, John
Books. Harper 240:94-6 Ja; 108+ Mr; 126-9 My; 241:94+ S '70
Catharsis, linguistics & all that. bibliog f Commentary 50:65-73 O '70

THOMPSON, Kay
Pooky Peckinpaugh's Christmas list; excerpt from Miss Pooky Peckinpaugh. Harp Baz 104:86-7 D '70

THOMPSON, Lawrance
Robert Frost: the years of triumph 1915-1938; excerpts. il Harp Baz 103:70-3 Jl '70

THOMPSON, Paul H. and Dalton, G. W.
Performance appraisal; managers beware. Harvard Bsns R 48:149-57 Ja '70

THOMPSON, Philip
Mary Holmes paints the figure. il por Am Artist 34:86-93 Mr '70

THOMPSON, Ralph
Imperatives in education. Clear House 44: 323-9 F '70

THOMPSON, Raymond E.
Survey of the teaching of physics in secondary schools. Sch & Soc 98:243-4 Ap '70

THOMPSON, Richard F. and others
Number coding in association cortex of the cat. bibliog il Science 168:271-3 Ap 10 '70

THOMPSON, Robert
Sketch; story. New Yorker 46:25-7 Ag 1 '70

THOMPSON, Robert C.
Uranium localization on hydroxyapatite by analysis of fission fragment tracks. bibliog il Science 167:1494-7 Mr 13 '70

THOMPSON, Robert Farris
Beyond ethnography. il Art N 68:28-33+ F '70

THOMPSON, Sir Robert Grainger Ker
Balance sheet on Cambodia; interview. il por U S News 68:31-2 Je 1 '70
On the road to a just peace. Read Digest 96:68-73 Mr '70
Question of balance. Read Digest 96:60-1 Ap '70

THOMPSON, Sada
Stage. G. Weales. Commonweal 93:48-9 O 9 '70 *

THOMPSON, Stephen
Arsenal of appeasement. Nat R 22:769 Jl 28 '70

THOMPSON, Sylvia Vaughn
Magnificent mussel. il Holiday 47:56-7+ Ja '70

THOMPSON, Theos J. and Bibb, W. R.
Response to Gofman and Tamplin: the AEC position. Bul Atom Sci 26:9-12+ S '70

THOMPSON, Thomas
Chet heads for the hills. por Life 69:33+ Jl 17 '70
Fort Worth. il Life 69:24-5 O 2 '70
Texas tornado vs. Dr Wonderful. il pors Life 68:62B-62D+ Ap 10 '70
What's so funny? il pors Life 70:69-70+ Ja 8 '71
Where were you shot? We're trying to save your life! il Life 69:28-31 N 6 '70

THOMPSON, William Hale
McAndrew case: Britain at the Chicago bar. H. K. Hutton and C. Galgoci. Sch & Soc 98:112-15 F '70 *

THOMPSON, William I.
Oxford file. R. Levy. por Duns 96:52-3 Ag '70 *

THOMS, Wayne
Bikes get bigger. il Mech Illus 66:62-4+ Je '70

THOMSON, George
Hummel and George Thomson of Edinburgh. J. Sachs. bibliog f il pors Mus Q 56:270-87 Ap '70 *

THOMSON, Grace F.
How to keep active in farming when arthritis strikes. Farm J 94:32D Ja '70

THOMSON, John R.
Talking with Cambodians. Nat R 22:788+ Jl 28 '70

THOMSON, Peggy
Preschoolers pose some tough questions. il Am Ed 6:16-19 O '70

THON, A. L.
Grow florist-size mums. il Home Gard 57:18-19+ Ap '70

THORBORG, Kerstin
Obituary
Opera N por 35:32 S 5 '70

THOREAU, Henry David
Wild apples over Indianapolis. R. Rodale. il Org Gard & Farm 17:21-4 O '70 *

THORN, Caryl A.
Computer storage & memory devices. por Electr World 84:37-9 O '70

THORNBURG, Hershel
Learning and maturation in middle school age youth. bibliog Clear House 45:150-5 N '70

THORNE, Christopher
Shanghai crisis of 1932: the basis of British policy. bibliog f Am Hist R 75:1616-39 O '70

THORNHILL, Claude
Popular records. D. Watt. New Yorker 46:75-6 Jl 11 '70 *

THORNTON, William
Tudor place. W. D. Garrett. Antiques 98:94-9 Jl '70 *

THOROUGHBRED horses. See Race horses

THORP, Gregor
Beauty is uninhabitable. il Pop Phot 67:90-3 N '70 *

THORP, Roderick, and Blake, Robert
Teen-agers speak frankly; excerpts from The music of their laughter. Ladies Home J 87:46+ Je '70

THORP, Willard L.
Foreign aid; a report on the reports. For Affairs 48:561-73 Ap '70

THORPE, MacKenzie
Wild-goose man. por Time 96:48-9 D 21 '70 *

THORSEN, Karen
Instead of the Friday night date, the Friday night identity crisis. il Life 69:38-9 N 20 '70

THOUGHT and thinking
Evaluating levels of thinking. E. D. Doak. Sch & Soc 98:177-8 Mr '70
Judgmental reading and the study of law. J. C. Johnson and H. L. Sublett, jr. bibliog Clear House 44:559-61 My '70
Philosophers as critical thinking consultants. E. D'Angelo. Sch & Soc 98:166 Mr '70
Program yourself like a computer; checklisting. J. D. Weinland. il Nations Bsns 58:31 My '70
See also
Attention
Dogmatism
Intellect
Meditation
Problem solving
Reason

THOUSAND LAKES wilderness. See Wilderness areas—California

THREAD cutting
What fun you can have cutting wood threads! R. J. De Cristoforo. il Pop Sci 196:108-10 Mr '70

THREADS, Screw. See Screw threads

THREATS
Child guerrillas? Haverhill, Mass. Time 96:81-2 N 23 '70

THREE bodies, Problem of
Some three-body atomic systems; adaptation of address, February 3, 1969. J. W. McGowan. bibliog il Science 167:1083-92 F 20 '70

THREE dimensional photography. See Stereophotography

THREE likely lads of limbo; story. See Waldron, E.

3M company
Key to success: a scrub pail. B. S. Cross. il por Nations Bsns 58:90-1 Ja '70

THREE-mile limit. See Territorial waters

THREE rivers stadium, Pittsburgh. See Stadiums

THREE sisters; drama. See Chekhov, A. P.

THREE wise men. See Magi

THREONINE
Cytokinin activity of ureidopurine derivatives related to a modified nucleoside found in transfer RNA. W. H. Dyson and others. bibliog il Science 170:328-30 O 16 '70

THREONINE deaminase. See Enzymes

THRESHOLD (perception)
Temporal summation phenomena at threshold: their relation to visual mechanisms. J. L. Zacks. bibliog il Science 170:197-9 O 9 '70

THRIFT
See also
Saving and savings

THROAT
See also
Swallowing
Diseases
Think twice about that sore throat. G. M. Knox. Bet Hom & Gard 48:16+ N '70
See also
Goiter

THROMBIN
Coagulation inhibitor elicited by thrombin. E. Marciniak. bibliog il Science 170:452-3 O 23 '70

THROTTLE. See Airplane engines—Throttle

THROUGH-lens meters. See Exposure meters

THROWER, Randolph William
Tax exemption for private schools: what officials plan. pors U S News 69:70-4 Ag 31 '70
Tax status of exempt organizations; address, August 24, 1970. Vital Speeches 37:2-5 O 15 '70

THROWERS, Snow. See Snow blowers, throwers, etc.

THROWS. See Coverlets

THRUSHES
Vespers thrust; with painting by G. Coheleach. J. J. Audubon. il Audubon 72:40-1 My '70

THRUST reversers. See Gas turbines, Aircraft —Thrust reversers

THUNDER
See also
Lightning

THUNDERBIRD graduate school of international management, Phoenix, Ariz.
Birds of a foreign feather. Forbes 106:50-1 O 1 '70

THUNDERHEAD (mountain) See Crazy Horse (Sioux Indian)—Statues, portraits, etc.

THUNDERSTORMS
Satellite observations of lightning. J. A. Vorpahl and others. bibliog il Science 169:860-2 Ag 28 '70
Thunderstorms over Oklahoma, 22 June 1969. E. Kessler. bibliog il Weatherwise 23:56-69 Ap '70
See also
Aviation—Storm hazards

THURBER, Marjorie
Santa's bag is choosing. il Todays Health 48:40-1 D '70

THURMAN, Christophe (De Menil)
Factory for living in. P. Devlin. il por Vogue 155:194-7+ Mr 1 '70*

THURMOND, Strom
Politics: a northern-southern strategy. por Time 96:6-8 Ag 3 '70 *
Thurmond threatens. K. Crawford. Newsweek 76:25 Ag 3 '70 *

THUROW, Gerald
Stage lighting control system. il Pop Electr 33:65-7 Ag '70

THURSDAY'S child; story. See Hoag, M. D.

THWING, Henry W.
Campers make more friends. il Camp Mag 42:16-18 Je '70

THYME, Mae
Bad day at Wild Rose. il Todays Health 48:58-9+ N '70

THYMINE
Crystal and molecular structure of a thymine phototrimer. J. L. Flippen and others. bibliog il Science 169:1084-5 S 11 '70

THYMUS gland
Antigen-binding cells in normal mouse thymus. F. Modabber and others. bibliog il Science 170:1102-4 D 4 '70

THYROID gland
See also
Thyroxine
Diseases
See also
Cretinism
Goiter

THYROID hormones
Thyroid hormone control of erythrocyte 2,3-diphosphoglyceric acid concentrations. L. M. Snyder and W. J. Reddy. bibliog il Science 169:879-80 Ag 28 '70
See also
Calcitonin

THYROID-stimulating hormone. See Thyrotropin

THYROTROPIN
Thyrotropin secretion in rats after hypothalamic electrical stimulation or injection of synthetic TSH-releasing factor. J. B. Martin and S. Reichlin. bibliog il Science 168:1366-8 Je 12 '70

THYROXINE
Biochemical differentiation during amphibian metamorphosis. P. P. Cohen. bibliog il Science 168:533-43 My 1 '70
Conversion of thyroxine to triiodothyronine in normal human subjects. K. Sterling and others. bibliog il Science 169:1099-100 S 11 '70

TIBBETTS, A. M.
Report from planet three: the triumph of the pseudolits. Nat R 22:841 Ag 11 '70

TIBET
Brave land lost; the tragic fall of Tibet; excerpts from From the land of lost content. N. Barber. il por Read Digest 96:205-8+ F '70

TIBETANS
See also
Sherpas

TIBOUCHINA semidecandra. See Princess flower

TICK-tack-toe, Electronic. See Electronic games

TICKELL, W. L. N.
Great albatrosses; with biographical sketch. il Sci Am 223:10, 84-93 bibliog(p 132) N '70

TICKS
Health dangers posed by ticks. Good H 170:173 My '70
Neutrophils: their role in the formation of a tick feeding lesion. R. J. Tatchell and D. E. Moorhouse. bibliog il Science 167:1002-3 F 13 '70

TICKTIN, Max D.
Abortion counseling in legal trouble. Chr Cent 87:68 Ja 21 '70
TIDAL marshes. See Salt marshes
TIDAL waves
Tidal waves. il Environ 11:49-53 Jl '69
TIDES
Clock that tells the tides. L. A. Harlow and H. R. Pfister. il Pop Sci 196:136-7+ F '70
Deep-sea tides 1250 kilometers off Baja California. J. Filloux. bibliog il Science 169:862-4 Ag 28 '70
See also
Earth tides
TIDWELL, William D.
Primeval palms. il por Time 96:46-7 S 7 '70 *
—and others
Palmoxylon simperi and palmoxylon pristina; two pre-cretaceous angiosperms from Utah. bibliog il Science 168:835-40 My 15 '70
Pre-cretaceous flowering plants; further evidence from Utah. bibliog il Science 170:547-8 O 30 '70
TIE-dyeing. See Dyes and dyeing
TIED and dyed work. See Dyes and dyeing
TIEMANN, Darwin L.
Nature's toy train, the railroad worm. il pors Nat Geog 138-56-67 Jl '70
TIEMANN, Norbert Theodore
Matter of money. Newsweek 75:44 My 11 '70 *
TIEPOLO, Giovanni Battista
Venetian virtuoso; exhibition. D. Davis. por Newsweek 75:56 Mr 30 '70 *
TIERNEY, J. D.
Father-son rap-in. Nat R 22:998+ S 22 '70
I am Dr Fager's night watchman. Nat R 22:206 F 24 '70
Women as feminists. Nat R 22:789 Jl 28 '70
TIETJEN, Mary Louise
Why of chrism. il Cath World 212:92-4 N '70
TIETZ, Walter
School phobia and the fear of death. bibliog Ment Hy 54:565-8 O '70
TIGAR, Michael
Tigar for the defense. por Time 96:55-6 D 14 '70 *
TIGER, Lionel
Male dominance? Yes, alas. A sexist plot, No. il N Y Times Mag p35-7+ O 25; 34+ N 15; 45 N 22 '70
Unchauvinist male replies; interview, ed. by R. M. Galvin. por Time 96:21 Ag 31 '70
TIGER lilies
Tiger lily treasure. H. O. Beracha. Home Gard 57:56 Ag '70
TIGERFLOWERS
Tigridias. B. Brinhart. il Horticulture 48:20-1 Jl '70
TIGERS
Big cats in trouble. J. O'Connor. il Outdoor Life 146:63-7+ O '70
Magnificent tiger. L. Stowe. il Read Digest 97:224-6+ Jl '70
Sad tale of the tiger. C. Gammon. il Sports Illus 33:42-3 Jl 6 '70
White tiger in my house. E. C. Reed. il Nat Geog 137:482-91 Ap '70
TIGHE, Virginia
Where are they now? il por Newsweek 76:14 N 2 '70 *
TIGRIDIAS. See Tigerflowers
TIJERINA, Reies Lopez
La raza, the land and the hippies. P. Nabokov. il Nation 210:464-8 Ap 20 '70
Tijerina sentenced in New Mexico. Chr Cent 87:103 Ja 28 '70
TIJUANA, Mexico
Tijuana's new ring for charros, toreros. il Sunset 145:68+ N '70
Turning off the Tijuana grass; Operation Intercept. C. Kentfield. Esquire 73:8+ My '70
TIKAL, Guatemala
Solving the mystery of ancient Tikal. S. S. McKern. il Sci Digest 69:67-71 Ja '71
Tikal: yesterday and tomorrow. D. B. Huyck. il Am For 76:34-5+ F '70
TILDEN, Paul
Last stand of the Asiatic lion. il Nat Parks & Con Mag 44:14-18 D '70
TILE, Drainage. See Drain tiles
TILE top tables. See Tables
TILES, Floor
Do-it-yourself plan. il Am Home 73:58+ My '70
Vinyl tiles. il Consumer Rep 35:100-2 F '70
TILL, J. E. and others
Repression of colony formation reversed by antiserum to mouse thymocytes. bibliog il Science 169:1327-9 S 25 '70

TILLAGE
How rotary tillage works for us. M. Welsh and S. Welsh. il por Suc Farm 68:40-1 Ap '70
One trip works up soil, puts down anhydrous. il Farm J 94:52-3 My '70
To plow or not to plow. J. I. Rodale. il Org Gard & Farm 17:96-8 O '70
Which tillage system? R. Krumme and others. il Suc Farm 68:24-5 N '70
See also
Contour farming
TILLERS. See Cultivators
TILLICH, Paul
Barth on Tillich; neo-gnosticism? R. K. Anderson. pors Chr Cent 87:1477-81 D 9 '70 *
TILLINGHAST, Charles Carpenter, 1911-
How to end skyjacking; interview. il pors U S News 69:48-52 O 12 '70
TILLINGHAST, Richard
Comment. R. Watson. Poetry 117:204-6 D '70 *
TILLOTSON, L. C.
Millimeter-wavelength radio systems. bibliog il Science 170:31-6 O 2 '70

about
Gigahertzian broadcasting. Sci Am 223:41 D '70 *
TILORONE hydrochloride. See Fluorenone
TIM, Tiny. See Tiny Tim
TIMBER
Timber; EQ index. il Nat Wildlife 8:33 O '70; Same. Schol Teach Jr/Sr High pA9 O 5 '70
See also
Lumber
Lumber industry and trade
Wood
Preservation
See Wood—Preservation
TIMBER cutting. See Lumbering
TIMBER line
Walk above the woods. R. Belous. il Nat Wildlife 8:50-4 Ap '70
TIMBER wolves. See Wolves
TIMBERDOODLE shooting. See Woodcock shooting
TIME
See also
International date line

Systems and standards
Cesium-beam atomic clock. V. Philibert. il Electr World 83:40-1+ Je '70
Using power line as accurate time standard. R. A. Anderson. il Electr World 83:46-7+ My '70
TIME (periodical)
Cover story; Russia expels correspondent S. Cloud. il por Newsweek 75:60-1 Je 22 '70
TIME, Daylight saving. See Daylight saving
TIME, inc.
Free-spending days are over. il Bsns W p52-4+ Ag 8 '70
Time for a change; sale of domestic broadcasting operation to McGraw-Hill. Newsweek 76:69 N 9 '70
TV looks tempting to McGraw-Hill. Bsns W p24 N 7 '70
See also
General learning corporation
Little, Brown and company
TIME, Reaction. See Reaction time
TIME for caring; story. See Gillette, V. M.
TIME for mom; drama. See Fisher, A.
TIME limit relays. See Relays, Time limit
TIME locks. See Locks and keys
TIME measurements
See also
Sundials
Time—Systems and standards
Timing devices
TIME of your life; drama. See Saroyan, W.
TIME payment sales. See Instalment plan
TIME perception
Of time and the child. D. Elkind. il N Y Times Mag p90+ O 11 '70
TIME sharing computers. See Computers—Time sharing systems
TIME signals, Radio
Build a three-channel time receiver. C. Caringella. il Pop Electr 33:33-5+ D '70
WWV radio time signals. S. Weed. il R Pop Astron 63:27 Ag '69
See also
United States—Standards, National bureau of —Radio stations

TIME standards. See Time—Systems and standards
TIME to keep; story. See Brown, G. M.
TIMERS. See Timing devices
TIMERSON, Robert E.
Architecture in high school. il Design 71:14-16 Fall '69
TIMES, London
Jungle drum of the British establishment; letters to the editor. A. Lewis. Esquire 74:52+ N '70
TIMES, Los Angeles. See Los Angeles times
TIMES, New York. See New York times
TIMES Mirror company
Captain bails out; acquisition of Newsday. Newsweek 75:92+ Ap 27 '70
No comment; purchase of Newsday. Time 95:38 Mr 23 '70
They found newspapers best after all. il Bsns W p42-3 D 26 '70
TIMES past; ballet. See Ballets—Criticisms
TIMING devices
Half-hour interval timer. F. H. Tooker. il Radio-Electr 41:57-8+ My '70
Once upon a time; progressive timing of race cars. il Motor T 22:82+ Je '70
Roundy-round corner; Ontario motor speedway electronic timing. S. Kelly. il Hot Rod 23:114 N '70
Stylus timer saves your records; elapsed-time meter. T. R. Sear. il Pop Sci 197:81+ N '70
Time-period module for the digital measurements lab. D. Meyer. il Pop Electr 34:63-7+ Ja '71
See also
Electric lighting—Control
TIMMINS, Ontario
Timmins: we bought everything that moved. N. A. Martin. il Duns 95:34 Ap '70
TIMMONS, Virginia G.
Clipboard. See issues of School arts
Resource materials. See issues of School arts
TIN cans
See also
American can company
TIN man (sculptured figure) See Folk art
TIN ware. See Tinware
TINDALL, Barry S.
State parks: lands for all seasons. il Parks & Rec 5:24-8+ D '70
TINDERBOX; drama. See Jones, D. C.
TINKELMAN, Murray
Illustrations of Murray Tinkelman. C. Corcos. il por Am Artist 34:20-5+ O '70 *
TINKER, Frank A.
Propane power! Should you switch to LP-gas? il Pop Mech 134:85-7+ O '70
Rodeo! il Travel 134:28-33 Jl '70
Sitzen sie ski? il Pop Mech 134:126-7+ N '70
Will you lose your right to fly? il Pop Mech 134:88-91+ O '70
TINKER, Irene
Underprepared college student. Am Ed 6:10-12 N '70
TINSLEY, David G. and Ora, J. P.
Catch the child being. il Todays Ed 59:24-5 Ja '70
TINSLEY, Russell
Hangup on javelina. il por Outdoor Life 145:66-7+ Mr '70
Now's a time for bass. il Outdoor Life 145:66-7+ F '70
TINTYPES
New tintype heroes; photographs. M. Kauffman. Sports Illus 3:26-35 Jl 6 '70
Tintype: tin lizzie of photography. F. Rinhart and M. Rinhart. il Mod Phot 33:50-2 D '69
TINWARE
Painted country tinware. M. Evans. il Am Home 73:100-2+ S '70
Tinware show at the Museum of American folk art. J. Lipman. il Life 68:10 F 27 '70
TINY Tim
Perfect mother. por Esquire 74:144-5+ D '70
TIÓ, Fernando Amiama-. See Amiama-Tió, F.
TIPPETT, Sir Michael
Music to my ears; performance of Second symphony. I. Kolodin. il Sat R 53:97 Mr 14 '70 *
Taping Tippett's Midsummer marriage. E. Greenfield. il por Hi Fi 20:22+ O '70 *
TIPTON, David
(tr) See Sanchez Leon, A. Poem: Why did that have to be the only answer?
TIPTON, Stuart Guy
Airline issues. Aviation W 93:11 D 21 '70
TIRE cord. See Tire fabrics
TIRE fabrics
Wire maker bets on a U.S. market; steel tire cord. Bsns W p49 F 28 '70

TIRE industry and trade
Rubber booms, but now it needs fresh money. il Bsns W p 142-4 Mr 14 '70
See also
Goodrich, B. F. company
Goodyear tire and rubber company

Consolidations and mergers
Dunlop, Pirelli's union of equals. il Bsns W p27 D 12 '70
International marriage; Dunlop and Pirelli. il Forbes 106:22-3 N 15 '70
One way to beat the Yanks; Dunlop-Pirelli. il Time 97:70 Ja 4 '71
Tire giant fights to keep its secrets; Goodrich vs Goodyear on Vredestein. Bsns W p44 Je 6 '70
Tire industry gets a new no. 3; Dunlop-Pirelli merger. Bsns W p 18-19 Mr 7 '70
U.S. tiremakers slug it out; Goodrich vs. Goodyear for control of Vredestein. Bsns W p37 My 9 '70
TIREDNESS. See Fatigue
TIRES, Airplane
Replaceable tire tread tested. il Aviation W 93:63 N 16 '70
TIRES, Automobile
Automobile tires. il Consumer Bul 53:24-8 Ag '70
Blue tires, red tires, cast tires! R. Guldahl, jr. il Hot Rod 24:49 Ja '71
Buyer's guide to tires; with list of brand names, types and grades. il Changing T 24:11-16 Ja '70
News: smooth-riding cordless tire, it's cast from liquid rubber! J. Dunne. il Pop Sci 196:96-7 Ap '70
Stars stayed in Alabama; Talladega. S. Kelly. il Hot Rod 23:66-8 Je '70
Studded tires take hold. M. Lamm. il Pop Mech 133:112-16+ Ja '70
Super metal's tough new job; tungsten carbide. il Bsns W p76 My 16 '70
Who makes all those brands of tires? list of approved code marks. Consumer Bul 53:18 My '70
See also
Tire fabrics
Tires, Recreational vehicle

Care
Your own wheel/tire upkeep center. R. Day. il Pop Sci 197:104+ D '70

Repairing
Some advice on the repairing of auto tires. il Consumer Bul 53:29-30 S '70

Testing
Tiresome toils of a writer; making an article exciting. M. Spiegel. Sr Schol 97:30-1 D 14 '70
TIRES, Recreational vehicle
More than you need to know about tires. B. Behme. il Field & S 75:108-12 S '70
TIROS (satellite) See Artificial satellites—Meteorological use
TIRRELL, Ruth
My peach trees take the winter. il por Org Gard & Farm 17:54-6 D '70
Not many pests in my patch. il Org Gard & Farm 17:60-3 My '70
Tansy and yarrow, handsome, helpful herbs. il pors Org Gard & Farm 17:106-9 Mr '70
Turnips, colorful root of good eating. il Org Gard & Farm 17:70-2 Jl '70
TIRTHA, Ranjit, and Loeser, Cornelius
Surinam. bibliog il Focus 21:1-11 S '70
TISI, Anthony J.
Best bartender in New York. J. Corry. por Harper 241:47-51 Ag '70 *
TISINGER, Betty
Produce prints. il Sch Arts 70:22-3 S '70
TISSUE banks
Tissue bank for exotic animals. il Sci Digest 67:25-6 My '70
TISSUE culture. See Tissues—Culture
TISSUES
See also
Connective tissues

Culture
Adenyl cyclase of cultured mammalian cells: activation by catecholamines. M. H. Makman. bibliog il Science 170:1421-3 D 25 '70
Automated continuous culture of mammalian cells in suspension. C. Peraino and others. bibliog il Science 169:104-5 Jl 10 '70
Biochemically marked lymphocytoid lines: establishment of Lesch-Nyhan cells. K. W. Choi and A. D. Bloom. bibliog il Science 170:89-90 O 2 '70.

TOFFLER, Alvin
Future shock; excerpt. il Horizon 12:82-9
Spr '70

TOGO
Republic of Togo, West Africa. R. Harrington. il Travel 133:71-3 Je '70

TOILET
See also
Baths
Manicuring

TOILET preparations
Beauty and the bath. S. Lindsay. See issues
of House beautiful
Introduction to the beauty bath. il Good H
170:122-3+ Mr '70
New bath coloring-book. R. Warfield. House
& Gard 138:28+ S '70
See also
Bath preparations
Cosmetics
Cosmetics for men
Deodorants

TOILET training. See Infants—Care and hygiene

TOILETS
New type of ball cock for toilet tanks. il
Consumer Bul 53:4+ Mr '70
Sanivac, revolutionary vacuum toilet. A. M.
Watkins. il Pop Sci 197:99+ Ag '70
Take-along comfort stations. A. J. Hand. il
Pop Sci 197:86-7 Jl '70

TOILETS for automobile campers. See Campers and coaches, Truck—Toilet facilities

TOILETS for boats. See Boats—Toilet facilities

TOIVANEN, P. and Hirvonen, T.
Sex ratio of newborns: preponderance of
males in toxemia of pregnancy. bibliog il
Science 170:187-8 O 9 '70

TOJO, Hideki
Remembrances of Tojo. il por Time 96:25 Ag
17 '70 •

TOKLAS, Alice B.
G. Stein. F. Rose. Vogue 157:89+ Ja 1 '71 •

TOKOMAK devices. See Plasma (ionized gases)

TOKYO
See also
Stock exchange—Tokyo

Hotels, restaurants, etc.
Travel tips for Expo year in Japan. P. Brooks.
House & Gard 137:60+ Mr '70

Music
Report:
Beethoven's Fidelio. S. Chizeck. il Opera
N 35:30-1 D 5 '70
Gounod's Faust. S. Chizeck. il Opera N
35:32 Ja 9 '71
Premiere of Osamu Shimizu's opera,
Daibutsu Kaigen. S. P. Chizeck. Opera
N 35:34 Ja 2 '71

Religious institutions and affairs
Tokyo seminary names Sato its new president. H. Post. il Chr Cent 88:18 Ja 6 '71

Street traffic
Power to pedestrians; banning autos in New
York and Tokyo. il Time 96:36 Ag 24 '70

Theater
Tokyo kid brothers: performers in Golden
bat, rock revue at the Sheridan square playhouse. New Yorker 46:34-6 S 12 '70

Transit systems
Tokyo monorail wins its comeback fight. il
Bsns W p56 Jl 11 '70

TOLAND, John
Fall of Japan; excerpts from The rising
sun. il Look 34:33-6+ S 22; 51-4+ O 6;
53-6+ O 20 '70

TOLANSKY, S.
Interferometric examination of small glassy
spherules and related objects in a 5-gram
lunar dust sample. il Science 167:742-3 Ja
30 '70

TOLBUTAMIDE
Debate over diabetes. Time 96:41 D 21 '70
More on tolbutamide. Newsweek 76:90 D 21
'70
Problem with drugs; harmful effects. Sci N
97:526-7 My 30 '70
Warning to diabetics. Newsweek 75:87 Je 1
'70

TOLEDO, Ohio

Galleries and museums
See also
Toledo, Ohio, museum of art

Street traffic
Federal aid for meter maids. il Am City 85:
96-7 Ag '70

Streets
Streets of glass. W. R. Malisch and others.
il Am City 85:104+ Jl '70

TOLEDO, Ohio, museum of art
Louis XIII cabinet at Toledo. R. Davidson.
il Antiques 97:893-5 Je '70
Picture tour of the Toledo museum. R. M.
Berkowitz and K. C. Lee. il Design 71:4-9
mid-Sum '70
Toledo's treasures; exhibition of accessions.
R. Davidson. il Antiques 97:352-3 Mr '70

TOLEDO BEND LAKE. See Lakes, Artificial

TOLEDO zoo. See Zoological gardens

TOLERATION
Are we too tolerant? L. Morris. Chr Today
14:48 Je 5 '70
See also
Prejudice
Religious liberty

TOLES, George E.
Harp seals; with biographical sketch. il Sea
Front 16:66-70. 127 Mr '70

TOLSTOI, Lev Nikolaevich, graf
Marathon. Newsweek 76:58 D 7 '70 •
Tolstoy in the last year of his life; excerpts,
tr. by A. Dunnigan. V. F. Bulgakov. por
Harp Baz 104:58-61 Ja '71 •

TOLSTOY, Leo. See Tolstoi, L. N.

TOLSTOY, Paul, and Paradis, L. I.
Early and middle preclassic culture in the
Basin of Mexico. bibliog il Science 167:344-
51 Ja 23 '70

TOMASO, Donald J.
One-man stock market; interview. il por
Forbes 105:70-1 Mr 1 '70

about
Rising fourth market. por Time 96:110 O 26
'70 •

TOMASSON, Verna
Women as property. New Repub 163:15-18 S
19 '70

TOMATO plants
Phenotypic reversion of flacca, a wilty mutant of tomato, by abscisic acid. D. Imber
and M. Tal. bibliog il Science 169:592-3 Ag
7 '70

TOMATOES
Everyone needs a salad tree. W. Wyman. il
Org Gard & Farm 17:49 My '70
Should you stake and prune your tomato
plants? K. F. Polscer. il Org Gard & Farm
17:52-3 Ap '70
Staking tomatoes the easy way. M. M. Crowley. il Org Gard & Farm 17:83 Mr '70
Tomatoes should be up off the ground. il
Sunset 144:193 Je '70
Worth their salt, home-grown tomatoes. G.
Abraham. il Home Gard 57:52-3 My '70
See also
Cookery—Vegetables

TOMBS
See also
Taj Mahal

TOMBS (prison) See New York (city)— Prisons
and reformatories

TOMBSTONES. See Sepulchral monuments

TOMKINS, Calvin
Equus caballus. New Yorker 45:28-9 Ja 24
'70
Mü. New Yorker 46:53 D 5 '70
Museum; story. New Yorker 46:22-4 Jl 18 '70
Onward and upward with the arts. New
Yorker 46:83-4+ O 3 '70

TOMLINSON, Charles
Movements; poem. Poetry 117:95-7 N '70

TOMLINSON, John W.
Mme X. Opera N 34:16 Ja 31 '70

TOMLINSON, Kenneth Y.
Beyond the call of duty in Vietnam. il Read
Digest 96:97-102 Je '70

TOMMY (rock opera) See Rock 'n' roll music
(songs, etc)

TOMORROW productions, Inc.
Greasepaint for GE. Newsweek 76:82-3 D 21
'70

TOMS RIVER, N.J.
First seconds count. il Am City 85:54 My '70

TONE, Aileen
Never leave me, never leave me. L. Auchincloss. il pors Am Heritage 21:20-2 + F
'70 •

TONGASS national forest, Alaska. See National forests

TONGUES. Gift of. See Gift of tongues

TONKA corporation
Tonka learns not to toy with success. il Bsns
W p38+ Ag 1 '70

TONKIN GULF incident, 1964
Letter from Washington. R. H. Rovere. New
Yorker 46:148-50+ Mr 21 '70

TONKIN GULF resolution. See United States
—Congress—Resolutions

TONSILS
If they're no use, why not yank them out? Todays Health 48:77-8 N '70
TONSOR, Stephen J.
Mess in higher education; address, October 17, 1969. Vital Speeches 36:250-3 F 1 '70
TOOKER, Frank H.
Beginner's signal generator. il Pop Electr 32:47-50 Mr '70
Build a gated 100-kHz calibrator. il Pop Electr 33:53-9 S '70
Getting to know the JK flip-flop. il Pop Electr 33:67-72+ S '70
Getting to know the UJT. il Pop Electr 32:69-73 Ap '70
Half-hour interval timer. il Radio-Electr 41:57-8+ My '70
Millivoltmeter for FET circuits. il Pop Electr 34:45-53+ Ja '71
Portable dual-range IC frequency standard. il Electr World 83:76-7 F '70
Pulsed-light darkroom timer. il Radio-Electr 41:44 S '70
SCS positive-pulse generator. il Electr World 83:78-9 Ja '70
Sensitive burglar and fire alarm. il Electr World 83:58-9 Je '70
Sensitive intrusion alarm. il Electr World 83:87 Ja '70
Silicon controlled switch multivibrator. il Electr World 83:60 Je '70
Triangular-waveform generator. il Electr World 84:79 O '70
Up-down level-sensitive trigger. il Electr World 84:69 O '70

TOOL boxes, racks, etc.
Adjustable toolholder for your Unimat. G. H. Hannon. il Pop Mech 133:175 Ja '70
Small-parts cabinets from TV dinner trays. W. E. Burton. il Pop Mech 133:199 Ap '70

TOOL catalogs. See Catalogs, Mail order

TOOL sharpening. See Sharpening

TOOLE, K. Ross
I am tired of the tyranny of spoiled brats. il pors U S News 68:76-8 Ap 13 '70; Same abr. Read Digest 96:129-32 Je '70

TOOLEY, John
Up from the ranks; interview, ed. by A. M. Lingg. por Opera N 35:13 S 5 '70

TOOLEY, Kay
Ethical consideration in the involuntary commitment of children and in psychological testing as a part of legal procedures. Ment Hy 54:484-9 O '70

TOOLPOSTS. See Lathes

TOOLS
Chemical tools for home car care. R. Day. il Pop Sci 197:120 N '70
A few basic tools and how to use them. Redbook 134:195 Ap '70
Handy homemade shop tools. W. E. Burton. il Pop Mech 133:184-5 F '70
Ingenious tools work for you beneath the sea. S. Carpenter. il por Pop Sci 196:56-7 Je '70
New twists for old tools. il Life 68:73-4 Je 26 '70
Tools for electronics. T. Haskett. See issues of Radio-electronics to June 1970
Tools for the cruising skipper. C. Miller. il Motor B 125:222-6 Mr '70
What you need in a roadside emergency kit. A. Markovich. il Pop Mech 134:120-2 Jl '70
See also
Cutting tools
Electric tools
Files and rasps
Machine tools
Stone implements and weapons
also names of tools, e.g. Wrenches

Safety devices and measures
Insulating overcoat for safer small tools; Dip'n grip. il Consumer Bul 53:4+ Je '70

Storage
See also
Tool boxes, racks, etc.

TOOMEY, Ursula
Hatheway house, and its garden. il Horticulture 48:26-7+ S '70

TOOTH decay. See Dental caries

TOPAZ
Topaz seekers are invited; Utah's Topaz Mountain. il Sunset 144:38+ My '70

TOPEKA, Kan.

Parks and playgrounds
Park maintenance operations. D. Showalter. por Am City 85:84+ Mr '70

TOPIARY work
Topiary in Britain. E. V. Malone. il Am For 76:4-5+ N '70
Witty topiary garden. H. Ladew. il House & Gard 137:88-93 Ap '70

TOPPER corporation
Hot pace in a big mini-race; great toy race between Mattel and Topper. R. H. Boyle. il Sports Illus 33:38-44 D 7 '70
TOQUE blanche (restaurant) See New York (city)—Hotels, restaurants, etc.
TORBERT, Horace Gates, 1911–
Department gives views on proposal to repeal certain congressional resolutions; text of letter to Senator. J. W. Fulbright, March 12, 1970. Dept State Bul 62:468-71 Ap 6 '70
TORCHES
See also
Flame throwers
TORCHIA-ESTRADA, J. C.
Recife school of Brazil. Américas 22:41-2 F '70
TORNABENE, Lyn
What a husband's business trips do to a marriage. Ladies Home J 87:75-6+ My '70
TORNADO detection. See Tornadoes
TORNADOES
Can TV really detect tornadoes? W. G. Biggs and P. J. Waite. bibliog il Weatherwise 23:120-5 Je '70
Eyewitness tornado observations obtained with telephone and tape recorder. R. T. Ryan and B. Vonnegut. bibliog il Weatherwise 23:126-30+ Je '70
Lubbock tornadoes: a study of suction spots. T. T. Fujita. bibliog il Weatherwise 23:161-73 Ag '70
Miniature whirlwinds produced in the laboratory by high—voltage electrical discharges. R. T. Ryan and B. Vonnegut. bibliog il Science 168:1349-51 Je 12 '70
News from the world of space exploration; satellite photographs in predicting tornadoes. Space World G-10-82:43+ O '70
Tornado at Kent, Washington, on 12 December 1969. C. Feris. il Weatherwise 23:75-7+ Ap '70
Tornado season of 1969. A. D. Pearson and R. P. Krebs. il Weatherwise 23:18-23 F '70
TORO, Victor
Commune called Paradise. il por Time 95:30 Je 1 '70 •
TORONTO
Toronto: a new dynamism. G. Hall. il Travel & Camera 33:61 Je '70
See also
Stock exchange—Toronto

Architecture
New world in the works; Ontario pavilion. il Arch Forum 133:26-9 O '70

City planning
Metro center. il Arch Rec 147:136-9 F '70

Galleries and museums
Bartlett forgeries: Coke Smyth originals; Royal Ontario museum in Toronto. R. Davidson. il Antiques 97:202+ F '70
Ontario's participatory museum; Ontario science center. il Arch Rec 148:103-8 Ag '70

Metropolitan district
Toronto's metro, it works! R. L. Clark. il Am City 85:75-8 S '70

Theater
America hurrah. . ? improvisation of Chicago 70 by the Toronto workshop company. J. Kroll. il Newsweek 75:90 Je 8 '70
Off Broadway: Chicago 70-, improvisation by the Toronto workshop company. E. Oliver. New Yorker 46:51 Je 6 '70
Theatre; Toronto workshop's production of Chicago 70 in New York. J. Novick. Nation 210:734 Je 15 '70
TORONTO art gallery
Canada's group of seven; exhibition of their work. M. Amaya. il Art in Am 58:122-5 My '70
TORONTO Maple Leafs (hockey team) See Hockey teams
TORONTO public library
Toronto's learning resources centre. il Library J 95:2422-3 Jl '70
TORPIDITY (physiology)
See also
Estivation
TORRENS, James
Dickens a century later. America 122:609-10 Je 6 '70
How dare the preacher preach? il Cath World 211:251-5 S '70
TORRES, Esequiel
Hero's welcome. Time 96:13 Ag 3 '70 •
TORRES, Juan Jose
Revolving presidency. il por Newsweek 76:60+ O 19 '70 •

TORRÈS, Tereska (Szarc)
　Woman between. G. Wolff. por Newsweek 75: 104+ Ap 27 '70 *
TORRES-GARCIA, Joaquin
　Art. L. Alloway. Nation 211:701 D 28 '70 *
TORTE. See Meringue
TORTS
　See also
　Damages
TORTURE
　Brazil: a country where Christians are outlaws. M. M. Alves. il Cath World 212:65-8 N '70
　Brazil: government by torture. Look 34:70-1 Jl 14 '70
　Brazilian torture: specifically new, specifically terrible. R. H. Bolton. Chr Cent 87: 387-8 Ap 1 '70; Discussion. 87:727-8 Je 10 '70
　From the parrots perch; atrocities against political prisoners in Brazil. il Time 96:27 Jl 27 '70
　Greek talk; case of N. Vardikos. W. F. Buckley, jr. Nat R 22:272-3 Mr 10 '70
　How one pleasant, scholarly young man from Brazil became a kidnapping, gun-toting, bombing revolutionary. S. De Gramont. il pors N Y Times Mag p43-5+ N 15 '70; Discussion. p22+ D 6; 79+ D 13 '70
　Inquisition Greek style; excerpts from Barbarism in Greece. J. Becket. il Ramp Mag 8:44-8 Ap '70
　Israel under fire. il Newsweek 75:54 Ap 20 '70
　Letter to Pope Paul; with reference to police torture in Brazil. I. Illich. Commonweal 92:428-9 S 4 '70; Reply. J. J. Kaufmann. 93:55 O 9 '70
　Notes from a Soviet asylum; excerpts. P. Grigorenko. por Time 95:40 Ap 6 '70
　People are doing...badly in Brazil. J. Armstrong. il por Chr Cent 88:14-16 Ja 6 '70
　Politics of pain. V. G. Kiernan. Nation 212: 8-14 Ja 4 '71
　Priest tells of torture. Chr Today 15:50+ O 9 '70
　Report from Greece: under the junta. N. Gage and E. Kulukundis. Am Scholar 39: 481-4 Sum '70
　Sadists in epaulets; situation in Brazil. Nation 210:645 Je 1 '70
　Torture in Brazil. R. Della Cava. Commonweal 92:129+ Ap 24 '70; Discussion. 92:307+, 378-9+, 451+ Je 26, Ag 7, S 18 '70
　Uruguay's unguents; LADOC findings. J. Deedy. Commonweal 93:362 Ja 15 '71
TORY party (Great Britain) See Conservative party (Great Britain)
TOSCA; opera. See Puccini. G.
TOSCANINI, Arturo
　Underground Toscanini. por Time 95:65 Mr 2 '70 *
TOSI, Piero
　Fantastic Tosi. A. Arbasino. il Vogue 156: 384-7+ S 1 '70 *
TOTALITARIANISM
　See also
　Fascism
TOTE bags. See Bags
TOTTEN, W. Fred
　Community education, best hope for society. bibliog il Sch & Soc 98:410-13 N '70
TOUCH
　Loving message in a touch. N. M. Lobsenz. Read Digest 96:132-4 My '70
TOUCH; musical comedy. See Musical comedies, revues, etc.—Criticisms, plots, etc.
TOUCH and see nature trail. See Washington, D.C.—National arboretum
TOUMANOVA, Tamara
　Tamara Toumanova: a unique career. V. H. Swisher. il pors Dance Mag 44:44-63 S '70 *
TOUPEES. See Wigs
TOUR de France (bicycle race) See Bicycle racing
TOUR Magne. See France—Antiquities, Roman
TOUREL, Jennie
　Teacher Tourel. E. Burns. il pors Opera N 34:20-1 Je 13 '70 *
TOURISM. See Tourist trade
TOURIST diarrhea. See Diarrhea
TOURIST trade
　Bigger exodus, at lower prices. il Bsns W p32-3 Je 13 '70
　How to measure the employment that results from tourism. E. T. O'Donnell. il Mo Labor R 93:57-9 Ap '70
　Peking on $5 a day? politics of tourism. D. Butwin. il Sat R 53:49-50+ Je 6 '70
　Stacked up over Stornoway. R. Joseph. Esquire 73:153+ Mr '70
　Tours follow historic routes taken by explorers. Travel & Camera 33:10+ Je '70

Travel notes. R. Joseph. Esquire 73:73-4+ Mr '70
Winter is less than a wonderland. il Bsns W p21 Mr 7 '70
Yankee go home and other friendly salutations; how local politics affect the American tourist. D. Butwin. il Sat R 54:28-9+ Ja 2 '71
　See also
　Travel—Economic aspects
　Travel agencies and agents
　World tourism organization

Africa
Safari for commuters. il Esquire 74:66-71 Jl '70

Bahama Islands
Black power on the beach. il Time 96:82 O 19 '70
Grand Bahama: the big binge is over. il por Bsns W p54-5+ Ag 1 '70
Mr Pindling interview. L. O. Pindling. New Yorker 46:28-30 O 3 '70

Canada
Special Canada report; where to find what you need, and what to photograph. R. Arnold. Travel & Camera 33:64+ Je '70

Carribbean Region
Dim season in the sun. il Time 95:82 Mr 30 '70

Communist countries
West made a big mistake...S. Turner. Sr Schol 95:20 N 17 '69

Europe, Western
Railroad pass to anywhere; Europe unlimited; with report by M. Leatherbee. il Life 69:38-46B Ag 14 '70

Fiji
Tourism development shapes Fiji airways' regional role. W. H. Gregory. il Aviation W 93:38-9+ D 21 '70

Florida
U.S. journal: Pinellas County; attractions. C. Trillin. New Yorker 46:52-6 Ja 2 '71

Gambia
Pink strangers: nude bathers at Gambia's beaches. il Time 96:44-5 Mr 9 '70

Georgia
Eastern gold rush. J. Bowen. il Travel 133: 48-53 My '70

Hawaii
Visitors to Hawaii up; length of stay down. Aviation W 93:30 N 30 '70

Hong Kong
Hong Kong: the best places. P. Brooks. il Travel & Camera 33:82-4 Mr '70

Ireland
Discovering Ireland. M. Gough. il House B 112:54+ Mr '70

Israel
Terrorism and tourism: the Davka syndrome. il Newsweek 75:35 Mr 9 '70

Ivory Coast
African Riviera. il Ebony 26:83-7 D '70

Latin America
Tourism: an important goal. Américas 22:1 Ja '70

Philippines
Manila; capital of many cultures. P. Brooks. Travel & Camera 33:88 Mr '70

Russia
Russia's drive for tourists with dollars. F. W. Rounds, jr. il U S News 68:76-9 Ja 19 '70

Singapore
Singapore: Asian crossroad city. T. Durdin. Travel & Camera 33:85 Mr '70

Taiwan
Taipei: the Chinese experience. R. Joseph. Travel & Camera 33:81 Mr '70
Trouble with touring Taiwan. L. Barry. il Pop Phot 66:50+ My '70

Thailand
Bangkok: a gourmet treat. K. Willenson. il Travel & Camera 33:86-7 Mr '70

TOURIST trade—*Continued*

United States
Is this your first trip to America? Advice to foreign visitors. Holiday 47:38+ My '70
Pioneer trip; Concord stagecoach along Kansas Smoky Hill trail. D. Johnson. il Travel & Camera 33:30+ Mr '70
To put your town on the map. F. L. Koltun. Read Digest 97:31-2+ S '70
Tough times after the holidays; vacation travel. il Bsns W p 18 D 26 '70
See also
Discover America travel organization
United States—Travel service

Yugoslavia
Yugoslavia: country and cuisine. H. P. Koenig. il Travel & Camera 33:74-5 F '70

TOURISTS and customs administration. See Customs service and tourists

TOURISTS bureaus. See Information services

TOURNAMENT of roses. See Pasadena, Calif.—Parades

TOURNAMENT players. See Bridge players

TOURNAMENTS
See also
Basketball tournaments

TOURNAMENTS, Bridge. See Bridge tournaments

TOURNEUR, Cyril
Revenger's tragedy. Criticism
Time 96:63 D 14 '70 *

TOURS, Package. See Travel

TOURTELLOT, Arthur B.
Rebels, turn out your dead! il Am Heritage 21:16-17+ Ag '70

TOUSSIE, Robert I.
Draft loophole. por Time 95:47 Mr 16 '70 *

TOVATT, Anthony. See DeVries, T. jt. auth.

TOWARNICKI, Frédéric de
(ed) See Lorenz, K. Z. Talk with Konrad Lorenz

TOWELL, William Earnest
Environmental concern is global. Am For 76:32-3+ Je '70
Last frontier. il por Am For 76:32-4+ Ja '70
Scandinavian safari. il por Am For 76:40-5 D '70
Score card on the environmental war. Am For 76:48-9 F '70

about
Mr Towell goes to Paris. por Am For 76:8 F '70 *

TOWELS
Disappearing dishtowel. il Sunset 145:103 S '70
Terry towels; questions and answers. Good H 170:122 Ja '70

TOWER, John Goodwin
Tower of Texas is small in the saddle, but. . . R. Sherrill. il pors N Y Times Mag p28-9+ Ap 26 '70 *

TOWER, Whitney
Horse racing. See issues of Sports illustrated
Mike and this horse needed each other. il pors Sports Illus 32:22-7 My 11 '70
One head that cost a crown. il Sports Illus 33:18-19 O 12 '70
Our joint is jumping. Sports Illus 33:22-7 N 23 '70
Pick 'em with a pin, and don't give up on the office pool. il Sports Illus 32:24-6+ Ap 27 '70
Preakness with Personality. il Sports Illus 32:26-7 My 25 '70
Saints and sidewalks. il Sports Illus 32:14-19 Je 15 '70
Sonny sniffs a derby. il por Sports Illus 32: 10-11+ F 16 '70
Two derbies down, one to go. il Sports Illus 32:22-5 Ap 6 '70

TOWER houses. See Architecture, Domestic

TOWER of Babel. See Babel, Tower of

TOWERS
See also
Babel, Tower of

TOWEY, Augustine Denis
Night walk; poem. Commonweal 92:34 Mr 20 '70

TOWING
Trailering with the new cars. B. Behme. il Field & S 75:112-15 N '70

TOWING equipment. See Automobiles—Equipment

TOWN, George
Everybody counts in 1970. il Har Yrs 10:14-15 Mr '70
Lending money to Uncle Sam. Har Yrs 10: 21+ Jl '70

Let's wipe out osteoporosis. Har Yrs 10:32-3 O '70
Should Congress flunk the retirement test? Har Yrs 10:30-1 Ja '70
Timely tax tips. Har Yrs 10:22-3 F '70

TOWN houses. See City houses

TOWN life. See City and town life

TOWN meeting
American scene: participatory democracy; Mount Vernon, Me. G. Wierzynski. il Time 95:24 Ap 13 '70
Week of group therapy for a region; Halifax, Nova Scotia. G. M. Chamberlain. il Am City 85:105-6+ O '70

TOWN planning. See City planning

TOWNE, Anthony. See Stringfellow, W. jt. auth.

TOWNEAST (shopping center) See Mesquite, Tex.—Stores

TOWNES, Philip L. See Samloff, I. M. jt. auth.

TOWNLEY, Frances W.
My friend, the goat. il Org Gard & Farm 17: 102-4+ Ja '70

TOWNS. See Cities and towns

TOWNS, Abandoned. See Abandoned towns

TOWNS, New. See New cities and towns

TOWNS, Restored. See Villages, Restored

TOWNSEND, Lynn Alfred
Chrysler's private hard times. A. M. Louis. il por Fortune 81:102-5+ Ap '70 *
Townsend takes a hard-core job. Bsns W p23-4 Mr 7 '70 *

TOWNSEND, Robert C.
Guerrilla guide for working women. McCalls 97:68-9+ S '70
P.P.A. authors' press conference; excerpts. il pors Pub W 197:27-9 Mr 23 '70
Up the organization; excerpts. il Harper 240: 73-90 Mr '70

about
Corporate guerrilla chief. il pors Bsns W p 102+ Mr 28 '70 *
How to try harder. por Newsweek 75:60-1 Mr 2 '70 *
Throw the rascal out! por Time 95:78 Mr 23 '70 *
Up the organization man. W. A. McWhirter. il pors Life 68:61-2+ Ap 17 '70 *

TOXEMIA of pregnancy. See Pregnancy, Complications of

TOXIC microorganisms. See Microorganisms, Pathogenic

TOXICOLOGY. See Poisons

TOXINS and antitoxins
Endotoxin: stimulation of bone resorption in tissue culture. E. Hausmann and others. bibliog il Science 168:862-4 My 15 '70
Germs and toxins; defining chemical warfare. Commonweal 91:523-4 F 13 '70
Ochratoxin A: inhibition of mitochondrial respiration. J. H. Moore and B. Truelove. bibliog il Science 168:1102-3 My 29 '70
Specific inhibition of nuclear RNA polymerase II by α-amanitin. T. J. Lindell and others. bibliog il Science 170:447-9 O 23 '70
See also
Antigens and antibodies
Cardenolides
Red tide
Shwartzman phenomenon

TOXOPLASMA
Toxoplasma gondii in cats: fecal stages identified as coccidian oocysts. J. K. Frenkel and others. bibliog il Science 167:893-6 F 6 '70
Toxoplasma gondii: the oocyst, sporozoite, and infection of cultured cells. H. G. Sheffield and M. L. Melton. bibliog il Science 167:892-3 F 6 '70

TOY automobiles. See Automobiles, Toy

TOY banks. See Banks, Coin

TOY industry
Danger in toyland. il Time 96:78 N 30 '70
See also
Arcade manufacturing company
Mattel, inc.
Tonka corporation
Topper corporation

TOYNBEE, Arnold Joseph
Borobudur. il Horizon 12:16-25 Wint '70
Desert hermits. il Horizon 12:22-7 Spr '70

TOYOTA (automobile) See Automobiles, Foreign

TOYOTA motor company. See Automobile industry and trade—Japan

TOYS
Choose toys for children, not for grownups! Consumer Bul 53:15-16 D '70
Crafting animals in wool. il Design 71:33-5 Sum '70

TOYS—*Continued*
Dangerous and faulty toys. B. Furness. Mc-
Calls 97:30+ Ag '70
Disappointment on Christmas morning: defective toys. Consumer Rep 34:622+ N '69
Dubious use of a toy with TV: Winky dink
and you! Consumer Rep 35:328-9 Je '70
Free-ka: howling corrugated plastic hose.
New Yorker 46:20-1 Jl 11 '70
Household toys: toys made from household
discards. E. Cain. il Design 71:30-3 mid-
Sum '70
I remember . . . Santa and the snowbound
bear. I. Donelson. il Har Yrs 10:32-3 D '70
Interesting toy: Super-eyes. il Consumer Bul
53:21 Ja '70
It says here . . ; any eight-year old can assemble it. A. B. Heath. Nat R 22:1395-6 D
29 '70
Learning to button, lace, snap, buckle. il
Sunset 144:129+ Mr '70
Made in Japan. R. Mitchell. il Natur Hist
79:60-5 O '70
Mini-truck fleet. E. Waltner and W. Waltner. il Pop Mech 134:174-5 D '70
On and off the avenue (cont) New Yorker
46:137-40+ D 12 '70
Parting shots: Teddy the enduring bear. il
Life 69:81-4 D 11 '70
Shopping guide to toys that can help children learn. il Good H 171:155-7 D '70
Toy libraries featured in preschool experiments. Library J 95:2958-9 S 15 '70
Toys of Tecomatepec. V. D. Coke. il Américas 22:36-41 Mr '70
Toys you can't buy. il Bet Hom & Gard
48:46-7+ D '70
We like these toys, and so did our children.
il McCalls 98:68-9 D '70
What's new for children. J. R. Cary. See occasional issues of Parents' magazine &
better family living
See also
Automobiles, Toy
Beanbags
Christmas gifts for children
Mattel, inc.

Anecdotes, facetiae, satire, etc.
How to assemble a Christmas toy. R. W.
O'Donnell. Sat R 53:4+ D 5 '70

Safety devices and measures
Toying around with unsafe toys. Consumer
Rep 36:4 Ja '71
See also
Toys, Hazardous
Storage
Santa toy sacks to sew. V. P. Guild. il
Good H 171:128+ D '70

TOYS, Dangerous. See Toys, Hazardous
TOYS, Hazardous
Bang, bang, you're deaf! WASP cap gun. il
Consumer Rep 35:628 N '70
Crib mobile that's not for baby: Winnie the
Pooh musical crib mobile. il Consumer Rep
35:510 S '70
Danger in toyland. il Time 96:78 N 30 '70
Dangerous and faulty toys. B. Furness. Mc-
Calls 97:30+ Ag '70
Flip, toss, you're blind! steel tipped darts.
il Consumer Rep 35:628-9 N '70
Hot Wheels can get too hot. il Consumer
Rep 34:620 N '69
In search of safer toys: Creative playthings'
rubber hedge hogs. Consumer Rep 35:132
Mr '70
Inspect that toy. J. R. Michael. New Repub
163:15 D 12 '70
It's an ill balloon that blows no good; Party
pack balloon squawkers. il Consumer Rep
35:510-11 S '70
Rhythm-band toy: not acceptable. Consumer
Rep 35:7-8 Ja '70
Squeaker squelched: Creative playthings, rubber hedge hogs. Consumer Rep 35:459 Ag '70
Toy turtle that was too tricky: Tricky Tommy turtle. il Consumer Rep 35:577-8 O '70
TRACE elements
Apollo 11 lunar science conference: trace elements: symposium. bibliog il Science 167:
485-525 Ja 30 '70
Apollo 12 lunar samples: trace element analysis of a core and the uniformity of the
regolith. R. Ganapthy and others. bibliog
il Science 170:533-5 O 30 '70
Hazards of trace elements. R. H. Gilluly. il
Sci N 97:60-1 Je 6 '70
Trace elements are for people, too; International symposium on newer trace elements in nutrition. D. Seim. Farm J 94:34
N '70
Trace elements in air and water. R. H. Gilluly. il Sci N 97:538-9 My 30 '70

TRACHTENBERG, Alan
Lost at sea. Nation 210:183-5 F 16 '70
TRACHTENBERG, Michael C. and Pollen, D.
A.
Neuroglia: biophysical properties and physiologic function. bibliog il Science 167:1248-52
F 27 '70
—See Pollen, D. A. jt. auth.
TRACK athletes, Negro. See Negro athletes
TRACK athletics
Bubbles and bounces. P. Putnam. il por
Sports Illus 32:10-13 Ja 26 '70
Cal cuts down the barberians; University of
California NCAA track and field champions.
P. Putnam. il Sports Illus 32:22-3 Je 29 '70
Don't drink the water: U.S. track team in
Leningrad. P. Putnam. il Sports Illus 33:8-
13 Ag 3 '70
Field day for Kansas; Jayhawks win NCAA
title. P. Putnam. il Sports Illus 32:64+ Mr
23 '70
Freshman and the great guru; track stars
at University of Oregon. P. Putnam. il
pors Sports Illus 32:28-31 Je 15 '70
McGrady's game, deck, deal. P. Putnam. il
por Sports Illus 32:48-9 F 23 '70
Victory over Germany but a loss to the AAU;
suspension of three of the U.S. team. P.
Putnam. il Sports Illus 33:48 Jl 27 '70
Zut! We nearly got guillotined; U.S. track
team in Paris. P. Putnam. il Sports Illus
33:18-19 Jl 20 '70
See also
Running
Walking
Weight throwing

Caricatures and cartoons
Ode on a Grecian urge; indoor track. A. Roth.
il Sports Illus 32:32-7 Ja 19 '70
TRACK type tractors. See Crawler vehicles
TRACKING and trailing
We hunted down a man-killer; grizzly. G. D.
Gosling. il por Outdoor Life 146:45-7+ N
'70
See also
Artificial satellites—Use in tracking and
trailing
TRACTION (automobiles) See Automobiles—
Traction
TRACTOR engines
See also
Diesel engines

Maintenance and repair
When your tractor engine quits. G. L. Earle.
il Suc Farm 69:B17 Ja '71
When your tractor uses too much fuel. G. L.
Earle. il Suc Farm 68:G2 S '70
When your tractor won't start. G. L. Earle.
il Suc Farm 68:A4 Ag '70
TRACTOR industry and trade
See also
Caterpillar tractor company
TRACTOR pulling contest. See Competitions
TRACTORS
Build a hydraulic lift for your tractor. M.
Orlarey. il Pop Mech 133:172-5 Je '70
Fantastic Elec-trak runs on batteries, powers
your electric tools, too. E. F. Lindsley. il
Pop Sci 196:68-70+ Je '70
Ford pushes a mini-tractor; walking tractor
for underdeveloped areas. il Bsns W p41-
2 F 21 '70
GE introduces the electric tractor. J. M. Liston. il Pop Mech 133:120-3+ Ap '70
GE's electric car that couldn't. il Bsns W
p 102 F 21 '70
Power up for more gardening with less effort.
B. C. Kilvert, jr. il Home Gard 57:32-40
Mr '70
Short cuts to a trimmer garden. W. F. Bruning. il Home Gard 57:18-19+Ag '70
Step towards a better environment, the electric tractor. il Home Gard 57:42 Jl '70
Will steam tractors stage a comeback? Suc
Farm 68:no4 D6 Mr '70
See also
Crawler vehicles

Equipment
Are you ready for twelve-row equipment?
C. E. Ball. il Farm J 94:24-5 O '70
New three-point hitches, they're fast and
easy; quick-hookup couplers. P. Jones. il
Suc Farm 68:no2 54 F '70
They customize their tractors. il Suc Farm
68:no2 A1 F '70
What you can do with power; attachments
for tractors and riding mowers. J. M. Liston. il Pop Mech 133:114-17 Ap '70

Maintenance and repair
Machinery maintenance: tractors. P. B.
Jones. il Suc Farm 68:35-7 Ja '70

TRACTORS—*Continued*

Safety devices and measures
New federal standards on tractor safety?
J. Carlson. Farm J 94:33 O '70

Seats
Tractor seat that helps take the ache out of
acres. B. Coffman. il Farm J 94:24B Ag '70

Wheels
Do more with duals. R. Gogerty. Farm J
94:521 Ap; 38 O '70

TRACTORS, Toy. See Automobiles, Toy

TRACTORS in gardening. See Tractors

TRACY, Philip
Cold night in Flint. Commonweal 91:447-50
Ja 23 '70

Getting busted in New York. Commonweal
93:371-2 Ja 15 '71

Jesus freaks. il Commonweal 93:122-5 O 30
'70

National sex and drug forum. Commonweal
93:194-5 N 20 '70

New newsreel. il Commonweal 91:532-3 F 13
'70

Today chancery, tomorrow Albany. Commonweal 91:574-5 F 27 '70

TRACY investment company
Kerkorian: goodbye to some big chips. il
Bsns W p39-40 Ja 24 '70

TRADE. See Commerce

TRADE act, 1969. See United States—Commerce

TRADE agreements
Analysis of changes in wages and benefits
during 1969. J. E. Talbot, jr. il Mo Labor
R 93:45-50 Je '70

Bishops in the vineyard. L. T. King. Commonweal 92:214 My 15 '70

Collective bargaining calendar for 1970; with
tables. H. C. Spring. Mo Labor R 93:13-26
Ja '70

Cost of getting rolling again. Bsns W p22-3
N 14 '70

Developments in industrial relations. See issues of Monthly labor review

GM settlement: impact on other industries.
il U S News 69:65-6 N 30 '70

High price of labor peace; open-end escalator clauses. Duns 96:108 N '70

Major collective bargaining agreements expiring in [month] tables (title varies) See
issues of Monthly labor review

Owners change, but not the contract. Bsns
W p30 My 16 '70

Relations between management and labor in
West Germany. E. M. Bussey. bibliog f Mo
Labor R 93:28-34 Ag '70

Rough road to GE's settlement. il Bsns W
p28-9 Ja 31 '70

Setback in the war on inflation; with editorial
comment. il Bsns W p 14-15, 116 Jl 11 '70

Tougher talk, and more to come; with editorial comment. il Bsns W p26, 104 D 5
'70

Unions keep winning more. Bsns W p50+ O
10 '70

Wage developments in manufacturing, 1969;
with tables. J. Kinyon. Mo Labor R 93:35-
9 Jl '70

Wage pressures keep building. il Bsns W p25-
6 Je 20 '70

What GM's pact means to industry. il Bsns
W p96+ N 21 '70
See also
Collective bargaining
Wages—Cost of living adjustments

TRADE and professional associations
More muscle in business' corner. Nations
Bsns 58:54-6 O '70

Tapping a lode of talent. il Nations Bsns 58:
42+ My '70
See also
Electronic service associations

TRADE journals
Beginning writer's bonanza: 2,000 trade
journals! A. S. Green. il Writers Digest
50:28-31 D '70

Business and trade journal market. O. Henry.
Writer 83:24-6 Je '70

TRADE marks and trade names
How to sanitize the company image. il Bsns
W p 116 Mr 23 '70

Name of the game. G. Lazarus. Sat R 53:60
Je 13 '70

Search for corporate identity. W. McQuade.
il Fortune 82:140-1 D '70
Story behind:
Chiquita brand bananas. il Changing T
24:44 N '70
Diners club symbol. Changing T 25:32 Ja
'71
Heinz 57. il Changing T 24:32 Ja '70
Levi's. il Changing T 24:40 Jl '70
Ralston Purina's nine-square checker-
board. il Changing T 24:30 S '70
Webster. il Changing T 24:30 Mr '70
Woolmark. il Changing T 24:44 My '70

TRADE names. See Trade marks and trade
names

TRADE regulation
See also
Export controls
Foreign trade regulation

TRADE schools
Schools that teach jobs. il Changing T 24:37-
40 Mr '70

TRADE secrets
Tire giant fights to keep its secrets: Goodrich vs Goodyear on Vredestein. Bsns W
p44 Je 6 '70

TRADE unions
Foreign labor briefs. See issues of Monthly
labor review
See also
Boycott
Collective bargaining
Government employees unions
Hiring halls
Industrial relations
Injunctions
Strikes
Trade agreements

Consolidations and mergers
Air controllers may fly with the AFL-CIO.
il Bsns W p 112+ My 16 '70

Elections
Digging into the mine workers. Bsns W p94
Mr 14 '70
What U.S. charges about mine election. il
U S News 68:54 Mr 16 '70

Ethical aspects
See Labor ethics

Finance
Slump hits union coffers. Bsns W p79 Jl 18
'70

History
American labor: the twentieth century. ed.
by J. S. Auerbach. Review
Nation 210:441 Ap 13 '70. S. Terbel
Case for independent black trade unions. O.
Bonds, jr. il por Ebony 25:142-4 Ag '70
Dreams deferred, promises betrayed. M. Du-
bofsky. Nation 210:438-40 Ap 13 '70

International aspects
Changing attitude of U.S. labor unions toward
world trade. W. C. Shelton. Mo Labor R
93:51-4 My '70
Why unions fear the multinationals. il Bsns
W p94-5+ D 19 '70
See also
International federation of chemical and gen-
eral workers' unions
International labor organization

Investments
Mutual fund for unionists only: American
union investment fund. Bsns W p71 Ja 9
'71
Unions step up mortgage buying. Bsns W
p 106 F 28 '70

Jurisdictional disputes
From fruit bowl to salad bowl. Time 96:18 S
14 '70

Law
See Labor laws and legislation—United
States

Management
Labor movement must start moving. A. H.
Raskin. il Harvard Bsns R 48:108-18 Ja '70

Membership
How trade union policy is made; excerpt
from Labor and the American community.
D. C. Bok and J. T. Dunlop. Mo Labor R
93:17-20 F '70
Picking up the pace of integration. B. L.
Masse. America 122:363 Ap 4 '70
Revolt of rank and file hits union leaders.
U S News 69:49-50 Ag 31 '70
See also
Trade unions—Negro membership

TRADE unions—*Continued*

Membership drives

ALA hard sell softens the South. il Bsns W p60+ F 21 '70

Firing and hiring of Fredy Jones; anti-union practices of textile companies in North Carolina. R. Scott. New Repub 163:12-15 Jl 25 '70

Grove and union agree to arbitration, election. il Pub W 197:55-7 Ap 27 '70

Grove fires union activists, Women's lib seizes offices. Pub W 197:38 Ap 20 '70

Grove loses arbitration; four must be rehired. Pub W 198:248 Ag 31 '70

How to keep the unions out of the plant; use of film, Labor unions in America. il Bsns W p78 Ap 18 '70

If it breathes, organize it; teamsters union philosophy. I. Ross. il Fortune 81:122-5+ Mr '70

Teamsters on campus. il Newsweek 76:52 Ag 3 '70

Union election set at Grove, petition for vote at Pyramid. Pub W 197:36 My 4 '70

Union soundly beaten at Grove press. Pub W 197:22 My 11 '70

Negro membership

Alexander's plan; Harvard minority hiring more ambitious than Philadelphia plan. il Time 95:17 F 23 '70

Case for independent black trade unions. O. Bonds, jr. il por Ebony 25:142-4 Ag '70

Integration drive fails to overcome. il Bsns W p48+ Je 6 '70

Outreach program; address, January 12, 1970. G. Meany. Vital Speeches 36:230-4 F 1 '70

Union with soul; Local 1199 of the Drug and hospital union. A. H. Raskin. il N Y Times Mag p24-5+ Mr 22 '70

Officials

How trade unions policy is made; excerpt from Labor and the American community. D. C. Bok and J. T. Dunlop. Mo Labor R 93:17-20 F '70

Labor leaders and their critics. America 122:605 Je 6 '70

Men in line to succeed Meany. il Nations Bsns 58:68-70 My '70

New crime list stirs union ire; amendment to Landrum-Griffin act barring criminals from union office. Bsns W p56 Mr 21 '70

Rising pay for labor leaders. il U S News 68:55 Ja 19 '70

Why labor can't find its young leaders. Bsns W p78 O 31 '70

Salaries, allowances, etc.

Labor chiefs settle for less. Bsns W p45 Mr 28 '70

Organizing activities

See Trade unions—Membership drives

Political activities

Bit schizoid. Nation 211:195-6 S 14 '70

Democrats: spooked by abstractions. R. Sherrill. il Nation 211:295-302 O 5 '70

Fight to keep labor Democratic. il por Bsns W p42-3 O 17 '70

Labor's political kick still there? J. Hill. Commonweal 92:133-4 Ap 24 '70

Labor's split political personality. J. Hill. Commonweal 92:382-3 Ag 7 '70; Reply with rejoinder. N. Dolan. 93:54-5 O 9 '70

Lots of labor cash for '70 election; where it's going. il U S News 69:81-2 O 19 '70

Radical strategy: don't form a fourth party; form a new first party. M. Harrington. il N Y Times Mag p28-9+ S 13 '70; Reply with rejoinder. H. Hill. p40 O 11 '70

Stoking up a drive for right-to-work; National right to work committee campaign against political activity by organized labor. Bsns W p28-9 Mr 14 '70

Troubled times for unions? A size-up by top leaders. il U S News 69:80-1 Ag 17 '70

Union-backed candidates: how they fared. il U S News 69:63-5 N 16 '70

Union under fire for political spending; largest division of Seafarers international union indicted. il U S News 69:59 Jl 13 '70

Unions gear for a November showdown. Bsns W p76 My 9 '70

Workers against the war; West coast. A. Richmond. il Ramp Mag 9:28-32 S '70

See also

American federation of labor and Congress of industrial organizations—Committee on political education

Public relations

Academic-labor alliance formally established. D. Shapley. Science 170:614 N 6 '70

Intellectuals start wooing trade unions. B. L. Masse. America 124:33 Ja 16 '71

Labor-campus link; union heads, academic leaders discuss alliance. D. Shapley. Science 170:516+ O 30 '70

Canada

See also

Strikes—Canada

Europe, Western

Labor trouble: where it's worse than in the U.S.; wage boosts. il U S News 68:86-8 My 18 '70

Germany (Federal Republic)

Relations between management and labor in West Germany. E. M. Bussey. bibliog f Mo Labor R 93:28-34 Ag '70

Great Britain

Coming struggle. Newsweek 76:27-8 D 28 '70

Disarming the stewards; shop stewards and the labor-relations law. Newsweek 76:28 D 28 '70

One more step backwards; proposed industrial relations bill. Chr Cent 87:1278 O 28 '70

Pay pressures build in Britain. Bsns W p 100 Ja 17 '70

Tories and the unions. A. Howard. New Repub 163:8-9 D 19 '70

See also

Labor party (Great Britain)

Strikes—Great Britain

Italy

Italian unions turn up the heat. il Bsns W p76 My 23 '70

Spain

Franco vs. free unions. A. Rodriguez. America 122:36-7 Ja 17 '70

Sweden

Worker participation in Swedish enterprise; excerpt from Worker participation in the enterprise: the Swedish experience. R. B. Peterson. Mo Labor R 93:48-50 Ap '70

United States

Court cases lost by unions. U S News 68:55-6 Mr 16 '70

Developments in industrial relations. See issues of Monthly labor review

Division of labor; issue of the Vietnamese war. Nation 210:707-8 Je 15 '70

Hard bargaining, more strikes; what unions see ahead. il U S News 68:62-4 Mr 2 '70

Labor and the American community. by D. C. Bok and J. T. Dunlop. Review Bsns W p 10 Ap 11 '70. E. Townsend

Labor month in review. See issues of Monthly labor review

Labor movement must start moving. A. H. Raskin. il Harvard Bsns R 48:108-18 Ja '70

Odd couple; labor support for the war. Nation 210:612-13 My 25 '70

Suffering majority. B. J. Widick. Nation 210:616-19 My 25 '70

Trade unions in the performing arts; excerpt from Labor relations in the performing arts. M. H. Moskow. il Mo Labor R 93:16-20 Mr '70

Union prospects and programs for the 1970's. A. A. Blum. bibliog f Mo Labor R 93:36-9 Mr '70

Unions aim for the blue-collar vote. il Bsns W p48+ S 5 '70

Unions face a management problem. il Bsns W p 138-9+ O 17 '70

Where is labor? il Cons 25:1 Ag '70

See also

American federation of labor and Congress of industrial organizations

Strikes—United States

United States—Labor policy

also names of unions, e.g. United mine workers of America

Bibliography

Labor's days of travail and triumph. B. B. Seligman. il Sat R 53:19-22+ S 5 '70

TRADE waste

Testing paper mill sludge. M. Spargo. il Cons 25:14-15 D '70

See also

Pollution

Refuse, Utilization of

TRADE waste disposal
Cleaning up a dirty industry; electrolytic treatment for electroplaters' waste. Bsns W p54 F 14 '70
Deep-well waste disposal needs regulation. Am City 85:30 Je '70
Economic responsibility for the by-products of production. A. V. Kneese. il Ann Am Acad 389:56-62 My '70
Field-tests oil-water separation chemical; demulsifying compound solution to problem of wastes in sanitary-sewer systems. Am City 85:50 Ja '70
Industry starts the big cleanup. J. Davenport. il Fortune 81:114-17+ F '70
Questioning deep well disposal. il Sci N 97: 314 Mr 28 '70
This company thrives on waste; Rollins-Purle industrial treatment facility for wholesale waste disposal. il Bsns W p84+ Ap 18 '70
    See also
Waste disposal in the ocean
Water pollution

TRADE winds
Radon-222 in the North Atlantic trade winds: its relationship to dust transport from Africa. J. M. Prospero and T. N. Carlson. bibliog il Science 167:974-7 F 13 '70

TRADES. See Occupations

TRADING stamps
Trading stamps vs. discounts: the housewife's choice. il U S News 69:61-2 N 23 '70
    See also
Sperry and Hutchinson company

TRAFFIC. See City traffic

TRAFFIC, Airline. See Airlines—Traffic

TRAFFIC accidents
Auto crashes and the heart; cases of injury to the aorta. il Time 96:36 Jl 27 '70
In 1970, a decrease in death on the highways. il U S News 69:39 D 28 '70
Shrine for the victims. Time 96:58 Ag 17 '70
Sound of music; when it causes auto accidents. il Good H 170:163 F '70
Summer driving: action in an emergency. Bsns W p89-90 My 30 '70
Too fast in fog; twenty-nine car collision on New Jersey turnpike. E. D. Fales, jr. il Pop Mech 134:84-9+ S '70; Same abr. Read Digest 97:180-2+ O '70
What to do if your car goes into the water. K. Anderson. il Pop Mech 134:92-5+ Ag '70
    See also
Automobile driving
Drinking and traffic accidents
First aid in illness and injury
Insurance, Automobile

Cases
    See also
Kennedy, E. M.—Accident, July 1969

TRAFFIC accidents and alcoholism. See Drinking and traffic accidents

TRAFFIC congestion. See City traffic

TRAFFIC control, Airway. See Air traffic control

TRAFFIC control, Radio. See Radio in traffic control

TRAFFIC courts
    See also subhead Traffic courts under names of cities, e.g. Chicago—Traffic courts

TRAFFIC engineering
Corridor program strikes at traffic bottlenecks; Urban corridor demonstration program. il Am City 85:122+ O '70

TRAFFIC in arms. See Munitions

TRAFFIC markings
Are crosswalks deadly? San Diego, Calif. Am City 85:118 Jl '70
Self-propelled machine triples line painting; Reading, Pa. il Am City 85:42 Ag '70
Yellow, red, orange and green pavements in accident-prone areas. il Am City 85:76 D '70

TRAFFIC regulations
    See also
Automobile laws and regulations
Computers—Traffic control use
Pedestrians
Snow and ice removal—Laws and regulations
Traffic violations

TRAFFIC research
Traffic and highway research and how it may be improved. B. D. Greenshields. bibliog Science 168:674-8 My 8 '70

TRAFFIC safety
    See also
Automobile driving
Automobiles—Safety devices and measures

Study and teaching
Lilliputian town to teach kids rules of roads; Nassau County's Eisenhower park. Am City 85:126 Mr '70

TRAFFIC safety education. See Traffic safety —Study and teaching

TRAFFIC shelters. See Shelters

TRAFFIC signals

Control
Narrow beam left-turn signals eliminate conflicts; Wichita, Kan. C. Boyle. il Am City 85:134 My '70
Six cities pilot low-cost traffic signal program; SIGOP program. Am City 85:49 Ja '70
Traffic control in a Dutch tunnel; Coen tunnel Amsterdam. il Am City 85:106 F '70

Testing
Traffic signal wind tunnel tests. il Am City 85:96+ Jl '70

TRAFFIC signs
Plastic warning devices improve road safety; Saginaw, Mich. T. J. Brown. il Am City 85:130 Je '70
School-crossing sign without words; New York city. il Am City 85:76 D '70

TRAFFIC violations
Go granny go. L. Chase. il Har Yrs 10:46-7 F '70
Great insurance debate. J. Brokaw. il Motor T 22:72-4+ Ag '70

TRAFTON, Laurence M. and Wildey, R. L.
Jupiter: his limb darkening and the magnitude of his internal energy source. bibliog il Science 168:1214-15 Je 5 '70

TRAGEDY
Between earth and heaven; Shakespeare, Doestoevsky, and the meaning of Christian tragedy, by R. L. Cox. Review
Commonweal 91:588-9 F 27 '70. S. Teselle
Huckleberry Finn as tragedy. H. P. Simonson. Yale R 59:532-48 Je '70
    See also
Catharsis

TRAGER, James
Health food: why . . . and why not. Vogue 157: 122-3+ Ja 1 '71

TRAIGER, Lynn. See Berry, B. jt. auth.

TRAIL bikes. See Motorcycles

TRAIL Blazers (basketball team) See Basketball teams

TRAIL riders of the wilderness
Trail riders of the wilderness. il Am For 76:52-3 Mr '70

TRAIL rides. See Horseback trips

TRAILER lights. See Automobile trailers— Lighting

TRAILL, R. J. and others
Garnet: first occurrence in the lunar rocks. bibliog il Science 169:981-2 S 4 '70

TRAILS
Hiking in to the McCabe lakes; Calif. il Sunset 144:68+ Je '70
Nature trails in a wild park in New York city; Inwood hill park. il Arch Rec 147:140-1 My '70
Pioneer trip; Concord stagecoach along Kansas Smoky Hill trail. D. Johnson. il Travel & Camera 33:30+ Mr '70
Red cliffs and the Colorado; trail to Corona arch in Utah. il Sunset 145:34+ Jl '70
Redbook guide to America's Heritage trails. W. Hartley and E. Hartley. il Redbook 134:35-42 Ap; 135:51-8 Jl '70
Touch and see; nature trail at the National arboretum. P. Caulfield. il Nat Wildlife 7:18-19 O '69
Walk to Wassataquoik. V. N. DeFelice. il por Am For 76:16-19+ Mr '70
Walking the Redwood nature trail in Golden Gate park's Strybing arboretum. il Sunset 144:222-3 My '70
    See also
Appalachian Trail
Oregon Trail

Laws and legislation
Let's use our rights-of-way. C. Stallings. il Read Digest 96:165-8 Ja '70

TRAIN, Russell E.
Conservation caretaker. por Time 95:46 F 9 '70
How to stop pollution; interview. il pors U S News 69:54-8 N 23 '70

about
Mr Environment. il Am For 76:5+ Je '70 •
Russell Train: Nixon's own conservationist. por Bsns W p 136+ Ap 18 '70 •

TRAIN travel. See Railroad travel
TRAINER, Daniel O. See Friend, M. jt. auth.
TRAINING, Transfer of. See Transfer of training
TRAINING airplanes. See Airplanes, Training
TRAINING camps. See Military training camps
TRAINING of birds. See Birds—Training
TRAINING of children. See Children—Management and training
TRAINING of disadvantaged workers. See Hard-core unemployed—Training
TRAINING of plants. See Plants, Training of
TRAINING ships
    They set their sights on careers at sea. il Ebony 26:56-8 D '70
TRAINING within industry program. See Employees—Training
TRAINS, Model. See Railroad models
TRAITORS
    Last of the Quislings. il por Newsweek 75: 46+ F 23 '70
    Treason and the traitor. P. Greenacre. bibliog Am Imago 26:199-232 Fall '69
TRAITS of character. See Character analysis
TRAMMELL, Archie
    Do it yourself. See issues of Flying to July 1970
TRAMMELL, G. T. See Breedlove, J. R. jr. jt. auth.
TRAMPOLINES
    Fliflises and gazip-gazaps. H. Weiskopf. il Sports Illus 32:44-6+ Je 8 '70
TRAMPS
    See also
    Homeless, The
    Vagrancy
TRAN-ba-Di
    Vietnamization of General Di. A. J. Langguth. il por N Y Times Mag p5+ S 6 '70 *
TRANE company
    Trane formula. V. Lewis. por Duns 95:61-2 Ap '70
TRAN-ngoc-Chau
    Chau affair. il por Newsweek 75:45 Mr 2 '70 *
    How to make a martyr. il por Time 95:25 Mr 9 '70 *
    Making a point. il por Newsweek 75:42 Mr 16 '70 *
    Saigon: the tail wags the dog. Nation 210: 322-3 Mr 23 '70 *
    Thieu gets his man. Newsweek 75:30 Mr 9 '70 *
TRANQUILIZING drugs
    See also
    Chlorpromazine
    Diazepam
    Phenobarbital
TRANS-ACTION (periodical)
    Sociological snoopers. N. Von Hoffman. Trans-Action 7:4+ My '70
TRANS-ALASKA pipeline system. See Petroleum—Pipe lines
TRANS-AMAZON highway. See Roads—Brazil
TRANSAMERICA corporation
    Leisure-time headaches at Transamerica. il por Bsns W p40-1+ O 31 '70
TRANS-AMERICAN championship. See Automobile racing
TRANS-AMERICAN racing. See Automobile racing
TRANSAMINASES
    Genetic polymorphisms of human mitochondrial glutamic oxaloacetic transaminase. R. G. Davidson and others. bibliog il Science 169:391-2 Jl 24 '70
    Posttranscriptional control in the steroid-mediated induction of hepatic tyrosine transaminase. I. B. Levitan and T. E. Webb. bibliog il Science 167:283-5 Ja 16 '70
TRANSATLANTIC airline service. See Airlines —International service—Transatlantic
TRANSATLANTIC airline traffic. See Airlines —Traffic
TRANSATLANTIC flights. See Aviation— Transatlantic flights
TRANSATLANTIC race. See Yacht racing
TRANSATLANTIC review
    Genre that won't die. D. Madden. New Repub 162:26-8 Je 20 '70
TRANSATLANTIC voyages. See Voyages
TRANS CARIBBEAN airways, inc.
    Captain. J Gilbert. il por Flying 86:56-61 Ja '70
    Chalk on a shoestring. por Forbes 106:47-8 Ag 15 '70
TRANSCEIVERS. See Radio telephone
TRANSCENDENCE of God
    God in an evolving world; excerpt from God within process. E. R. Baltazar. por Cath World 211:103-6 Je '70; Discussion. 211:244 S '70

TRANSCENDENTAL meditation. See Meditation
TRANSCONTINENTAL flights. See Aviation— Transcontinental flights
TRANSDUCERS
    Where electronic makers sense a bonanza. il Bsns W p 122+ My 23 '70
TRANSFER of employees. See Employees, Transfer of
TRANSFER of learning. See Transfer of training
TRANSFER of training
    Of mice and memory. il por Time 97:34 Ja 11 '71
    See also
    Interference (psychology)
TRANSFER technology. See Technology transfer
TRANSFERASES
    Amino acid transport in hepatoma cell cultures during tyrosine aminotransferase induction. E. L. Krawitt and others. bibliog il Science 169:294-6 Jl 17 '70
    Indole metabolism in the pineal gland: a circadian rhythm in N-acetyltransferase. D. C. Klein and J. L. Weller. bibliog il Science 169:1093-5 S 11 '70
    Melatonin synthesis adenosine 3',5'-monophosphate and norepinephrine stimulate N-acetyltransferase. D. C. Klein and others. bibliog il Science 168:979-80 My 22 '70
    Reduced catechol-O-methyltransferase activity in red blood cells of women with primary affective disorder. C. K. Cohn and others. bibliog il Science 170:1323-4 D 18 '70
    Substrate-induced conjugation of bilirubin in genetically deficient newborn rats. M. M. Thaler. bibliog il Science 170:555-6 O 30 '70
    Substrate stabilization, genetically controlled reciprocal relationship of two human enzymes. M. L. Greene and others. bibliog il Science 167:887-9 F 6 '70
    Transfer of bilirubin uridine diphosphate-glucuronyltransferase to enzyme-deficient rats. H. E. Rugstad and others. bibliog il Science 170:553-5 O 30 '70
TRANSFERS; drama. See Bromberg, C.
TRANSFORMERS, Electric. See Electric transformers
TRANSFORMERS, Radio. See Radio transformers
TRANSISTOR circuits
    Build the digital logic microlab. D. Lancaster. il Pop Electr 32:27-35+ Ap '70
    FET & op-amp audio circuits. N. Doyle. il Radio-Electr 41:46-9 Jl '70
    Milady's garage parking director. il Radio-Electr 41:48 D '70
    Ten emitter-coupled oscillator circuits. F. Maynard. il Radio-Electr 41:33-5 My '70
    Twenty triac circuits. R. M. Marston. il Radio-Electr 41:51-3+ Je; 49-53 Jl '70
    Up-down level-sensitive trigger. F. H. Tooker. il Electr World 84:69 O '70
    See also
    Printed circuits
    Television circuits
TRANSISTOR testers. See Testing instruments
TRANSISTORS
    C.E.T. test. D. Glass. Electr World 84:70 N '70
    Getting to know the UJT. il Pop Electr 32: 69-73 Ap '70
    How to putter with the PUT; programmable unijunction transistor. R. W. Fox. il Radio-Electr 41:50-2 O; 50-1 N '70
    Power transistors, a status report. P. Franson. il Electr World 83:25-9+ My '70
    Shakedown in transistors. A. Broy. il Duns 96:79-80+ S '70
    Solid state. L. Garner. See issues of Popular electronics
    Transistor base-emitter junctions for voltage regulation. T. J. Carmody. il Electr World 84:90 S '70
    Using silicon transistors as zeners. J. Charles. il Electr World 83:86 Ja '70

        Control uses
    FET's as audio switches. G. Neal. il Electr World 84:46+ Ag '70
TRANSIT signs. See Electric signs
TRANSITION (chemistry) See Phases (chemistry)
TRANSITION, Project. See Service men—Vocational education
TRANSITION elements. See Transition metals
TRANSITION metals
    Inversion of excited states of transition-metal complexes. G. A. Crosby and others. bibliog il Science 170:1195-6 D 11 '70
    Metallic and nonmetallic behavior in transition metal oxides. I. G. Austin and N. F. Mott. bibliog il Science 168:71-3 Ap 3 '70
    See also
    Tungsten

TRANSITRON electronic corporation
Transitron fights back. Fortune 81:180 Je '70
TRANSITS
See also
Mercury (planet), Transit of
Pluto (planet), Transit of
TRANSJORDAN. See Jordan
TRANSLATIONS and translating
Do's and don'ts for translators. S. Wilkins.
Writer 83:27 F '70
Trials of a translator; translating Günter
Grass. Time 95:73 Ap 13 '70
Up against the language barrier. il Bsns W
p 164 Mr 28 '70
See also
Publishers and publishing—Translations
Translators
TRANSLATORS
Bill of rights for wronged translators; PEN
conference, in New York. R. J. Clements.
Sat R 53:30-2 Je 20 '70
TRANSLUCENT walls. See Walls
TRANSMISSION, Automobile. See Automobiles
—Transmission
TRANSMUTATION (chemistry)
Advances in alchemy; proton decay. Sci Am
223:40-1 D '70
Fourth method; proton decay. il Sci N 98:
349 O 31 '70
See also
Alchemy
TRANSOCEANIC airline service. See Airlines—
International services—Transoceanic
TRANSOCEANIC flights. See Aviation—Trans-
oceanic flights
TRANSPAC race. See Yacht racing
TRANSPACIFIC airline service. See Airlines—
International services—Transpacific
TRANSPACIFIC airline traffic. See Airlines—
Traffic
TRANSPARENCIES
Add motion to your photo slides. W. E. Bur-
ton. il Pop Mech 133:164-7+ Ap '70
Color your slides black and white. P. Farber.
il Travel & Camera 33:92 Ja '70
Do-it-yourself developing; color slides with-
out a darkroom! D. Molner. Schol Teach
Jr/Sr High p25-6 O 5 '70
Ed Scully on color; slide file upgrading. E.
Scully. Mod Phot 34:44+ Mr '70
Freelance job idea: slide presentations. R.
Arnold. il Writers Digest 51:34-6+ Ja '71
Transparencies: the simplest teaching tool.
H. Deutsch. il Library J 95:1167-8 Mr 15 '70

Copying
Copy, correct, and crop your color slides.
N. Rothschild. il Pop Phot 66:75-7+ Ja '70
How to make accurate dupes. A. France-
kevich. il Pop Phot 67:32+ D '70
Non-silver process prints color; O/G Chroma
system. A. Francekevich. il Pop Phot 67:22+
S '70
Prints from slides in sixty sec; Polacolor.
E. Scully. il Mod Phot 34:80-1 Ag '70
Which from what? E. Scully. il Mod Phot
34:82-3+ F '70

Projection
E unibus plurum, and all that; Melandrea,
inc. multiple projection system. S. Nathan.
il Pop Phot 67:66+ O '70

Anecdotes, facetiae, satire, etc.
Nixon snaps back; reprint. Mod Phot 34:100+
F '70

Sound accompaniment
Sound-off with slides. L. Drukker. il Pop
Phot 66:76-7+ F '70
Syncro slide adds sound to your slide show.
P. Blaire. il Radio-Electr 41:73-4 Ap '70

Trimming, mounting, etc.
Copy, correct, and crop your color slides.
N. Rothschild. il Pop Phot 66:75-7+ Ja '70
TRANSPIRATION of plants. See Plants—Trans-
piration
TRANSPLANTATION of organs, tissues, etc.
Gifts of Gregory Menn. J. P. Blank. Read
Digest 97:108-12 Ag '70
Transplants that help disfigured faces. M. W.
Martin. il Sci Digest 68:81-3 Jl '70
See also
Heart—Transplantation
Immunological tolerance
Intestines—Transplantation
Kidneys—Transplantation
Liver—Transplantation
Marrow—Transplantation
Nerves—Transplantation
Teeth—Transplantation

Legal aspects
Anatomical gifts. il Time 96:59 Jl 13 '70
Transplant donation procedures; report of
meeting. R. E. Stevenson and others. Sci-
ence 168:613-15 My 1 '70
TRANSPLANTING
Fall: a good time to plant. B. Thompson. il
Home Gard 57:32-9 S '70
Go native, we did! landscaping with native
trees, shrubs and flowers. M. Enright. il
Org Gard & Farm 17:80-1 Ja '70
Save those tin cans for the garden. F. C.
Schnelz. il Org Gard & Farm 17:43 Je '70
Way with wild transplants. H. R. Berridge.
il Org Gard & Farm 17:100-1 Ja '70
See also
Tree planting
TRANSPLANTING of trees. See Tree planting
TRANSPONDERS
Air traffic control transponder identifies ra-
dar targets. D. J. Holford. il Electr World
83:36-8+ F '70
TRANSPORT, Biological. See Biological trans-
port
TRANSPORTATION
Coming revolution in transportation. F. C.
Appel. Read Digest 96:96-100 Ap '70
See also
Air travel
Carriers
Electric vehicles
Pack transportation
Roads
Urban transportation
also subhead Transportation under vari-
ous subjects, e.g. Aged—Transportation

Federal aid
See also
Local transit—Federal aid

Finance
Road-tax rebellion. J. Lear. Sat R 53:37 Jl 4
'70

Laws and regulations
White House eyes deregulation route. Bsns
W p29 N 21 '70

Research
See Transportation research

Arctic Regions
Future polar transport. A. H. Whitelaw. il
Sea Front 16:206-10 Jl '70

California
See also
Ferries

Germany (Federal Republic)
See also
Urban transportation—Germany (Federal
Republic)

Japan
Japan's secret weapon? il Forbes 105:9 Ap
15 '70
See also
Railroads—Japan

Mongolia
Development of transport. A. J. K. Sanders.
il Focus 20:8-11 Ja '70

United States
Fifty largest transportation companies. il For-
tune 81:210-11 My '70
Mass transit and the cities: mobility and place
in America's future. N. A. Owings. Cur
Hist 59:95-9+ Ag '70
Traffic and transportation. See issues of
American city
Transportation mess: some practical solu-
tions; interview. P. Cherington. por Forbes
107:170+ Ja 1 '71
Transportation needs a drastic overhaul;
with editorial comment. il Bsns W p68-9+,
116 N 14 '70
Transportation turnaround? interview, ed. by
G. R. Rosen. P. Cherington. por Duns 96:
14-16+ Jl '70
See also
Aeronautics, Commercial—United States
United States—Transportation. Department
of
Waterways—United States

Vietnam
See also
Vietnamese war, 1957- —Transportation
TRANSPORTATION, Automotive
Why America may become a parking lot. il
Bsns W p92-4 O 17 '70

TRANSPORTATION, Military
House unit weighs DOD charter policies.
Aviation W 92:27+ F 16 '70
Shrinking of U.S. tactical airlift capability
hit by House group. D. C. Winston. Aviation
W 93:16-17 Jl 6 '70
See also
Explosives—Transportation
Motor trucks, Military
United States—Military airlift command
Vietnamese war, 1957- —Transportation
TRANSPORTATION, Municipal. See Local
transit; Urban transportation
TRANSPORTATION industry. See Transportation
TRANSPORTATION of camp children. See
Camp children—Transportation
TRANSPORTATION of school children. See
School children—Transportation
TRANSPORTATION research
Why America may become a parking lot. il
Bsns W p92-4 O 17 '70
TRANSPORTATION to airports. See Airports—
Transportation problems
TRANSPORTATION workers
See also
Strikes—United States—Transportation workers
TRANSUE, Warren
How to get close to the dam fish. il Pop
Mech 134:106-8 N '70
TRANS WORLD airlines
Amenities increased by TWA in bid for 707
coach traffic. il Aviation W 93:26 N 2 '70
American, TWA report losses. il Aviation
W 92:41 Mr 23 '70
Armed courier thwarts TWA hijack attempt.
Aviation W 93:30 S 21 '70
Frustrating case of TWA flight 741. il Bsns
W p34+ O 10 '70
On returning to America. W. F. Buckley, jr.
Nat R 22:1231 N 17 '70
Overcapacity feared accompanying 747. Aviation W 92:37 F 2 '70
747 rear lounge opposed by TWA. Aviation
W 92:33 Je 8 '70
TWA asks surcharge for 747, higher tariffs
for peak seasons. H. D. Watkins. Aviation
W 92:30 Mr 23 '70
TWA blending sales drive, 747 service. H. D.
Watkins. il Aviation W 92:26-8 Mr 2 '70
TWA offers new capacity control plan. Aviation W 94:25 Ja 4 '71
TWA reserves space with IBM. Bsns W p88-9
O 31 '70
TWA schedule gets complete overhaul. il
Aviation W 93:29-30 O 12 '70
TWA seating plan suspended. Aviation W
92:29 Ja 19 '70
TWA Sun line purchase backed. Aviation W
94:25 Ja 11 '71
U.S. journal: N.Y./L.A; trip on the Boeing
747. C. Trillin. New Yorker 46:66+ Ap 4
'70
Who will pay for the burned-out 747? il
Bsns W p64+ D 5 '70
TRANSYLVANIA
Transylvania. I. J. Kappes. il Travel 133:54-9
My '70
TRAPPING
Vanishing world of trapper Joe Delia: the
Alaskan wilderness. J. Birnbaum. Time
96:48 Jl 27 '70
TRAQUAIR house. See Scotland—Historic
houses, etc.
TRASH. See Refuse and refuse disposal
TRASH can shelters. See Shelters
TRASH cans. See Refuse receptacles
TRASH mashers. See Refuse and refuse disposal—Apparatus
TRAUMATISM
Learning to be helpless. il por Sci Digest 68:
94-5 N '70
Tragedy of trauma. J. Bockel. il Sci N 98:82-
3 Jl 25 '70
See also
Shock
TRAVEL
Art of travel. S. McIlhany. Am Artist 34:5
Ap '70
Booked for travel. D. W. Butwin. See issues
of Saturday review
Checkpoint for travelers. B. Robinson. See
issues of House beautiful
Family travel. See issues of Better homes and
gardens
Far-out travel in faraway places; symposium. il Sat R 53:37-8+ O 24 '70
Holiday travel handbook. See issues of Holiday
Holiday travel horoscope. il Holiday 47:13
Ja '70
I'm saving the seventies for sentimental journeys. H. Sutton. Holiday 47:12+ Mr '70

[Month] travel in and beyond the West. See
issues of Sunset
New treats for the travel-hungry; travel
packages. il Changing T 24:25-8 Mr '70
Notes from a travel snob. G. Trotta. Harp
Baz 103:72+ My '70
Off-season choices for autumn; round-the-
world selection. B. Belford. Travel & Camera 33:61-8 S '70
Roaming the globe. See issues of Travel
South for sunshine! bargain-vacations. N. D.
Ford. il Har Yrs 10:34-41 O '70
These vacation packages save you travel
dollars. Bet Hom & Gard 48:20+ Ap '70
Travel (cont of) How to leave home and
like it. M. Gough. See issues of House beautiful
Travel as a package deal; with report on
Russian tour by M. Leatherbee. il Life
68:42-9 Mr 20 '70
Travel bazaar. See issues of Harper's bazaar
Travel digest. See issues of Travel
Travel guide. R. Joseph. See issues of Travel & camera
Travel, money, U.S. customs, and your
Health. il Consumer Bul 53:29-30 Ja '70
Travel notes. R. Joseph. See issues of Esquire
Travel: the going things; Meet-the-people
programs. S. Cuneo. il Mlle 71:106-8+ O
'70
Travel: the going things; reports of Mlle
travelers. Mlle 72:56-8+ D '70
Travel tips. Schol Teach Jr/Sr High p32
O 5 '70
Travel tips. Schol Teach Sec Teach Sup p28
Mr 9; 30 Ap 6 '70
Travel tips. L. Blackwood. Schol Teach Sec
Teach Sup p30 N 3 '69
Traveler's camera. L. Barry. See issues of
Popular photography
Way-out tripping; adventure tours of the
Chalet club and Lindblad travel, inc. il
Newsweek 76:62 Jl 13 '70
Well traveled camera. H. Keppler. Mod Phot
34:142+ Ap '70
See also
Air travel
Business travel
Canoe trips
Cruising
Customs service and tourists
Discover America travel organization
Guidebooks
Motor bus travel
Ocean travel
Presidents—United States—Travel
Railroad travel
Student travel
Tourist trade
World tourism organization
Youth hostels
also subhead Description and travel under names of countries, states, etc. e.g.
Russia—Description and travel

Bibliography
Travel books spring, summer. il Pub W 197:
37-44 F 16 '70

Economic aspects
Buy a package vacation. Bet Hom & Gard
48:18-19 Ja '70
Cost-cutting jaunts. il Seventeen 29:127 Je
'70
How to cut vacation and travel costs. il
Good H 170:145-7 Je '70
Mexico to Persia. B. Belford. Travel &
Camera 33:23-4+ F '70
Travel news. il Travel & Camera 33:11-12+
Mr; 10+ Je '70
Winter air fares: lower than ever. il Travel
& Camera 33:20+ F '70
See also
Tourist trade

Taxation
See also
Air travel—Taxation
TRAVEL (periodical)
See also
Mr Travel award
TRAVEL agencies and agents
Pastor's hobby; Krogager's Tjaereborg tours.
il pors Newsweek 76:69 S 21 '70
Rude awakening; World academy's financial
failure. il Newsweek 76:75 Jl 20 '70
Way-out tripping; adventure tours of the
Chalet club and Lindblad travel, inc. il
Newsweek 76:62 Jl 13 '70
See also
American society of travel agents
International union of official travel organizations

TRAVEL and camera (periodical)
In focus; first annual Travel photography contest results. Travel & Camera 33:4 Je '70

TRAVEL and education. See Student travel; Travel study courses

TRAVEL articles. See Periodical articles

TRAVEL clubs
If you are planning a charter flight. il U S News 68:60-2 Mr 9 '70

TRAVEL films. See Moving pictures—Travel films

TRAVEL guides. See Guidebooks

TRAVEL literature
See also
Guidebooks

TRAVEL photography
Around the world on three cameras, three lenses, 400 rolls of film and a pair of leather sandals. B. Wolf. Travel & Camera 33:89+ Mr '70
China's rear window by tour. L. Barry. il Pop Phot 66:50+ Ap '70
Color your island infra-red. H. Weber. il Travel & Camera 33:84-9+ Ja '70
Here's how to make your travel photos timeless. F. Rohr. il Travel 134:68-70 Ag '70
Include yourself in your travel photos. T. Bacon. il Pop Sci 196:74-5 My '70
Let's help ban bans; traditional ban on photography during rehearsals or performances of Lipizzaner horses, in Vienna. L. Barry. il Pop Phot 66:30+ Ja '70
Making travel films. J. Porterfield and L. Chickering. il pors Travel & Camera 33:62-7 N '70
Photo guide:
Caribbean: in the unspoiled islands. B. Binzen. Travel & Camera 33:76 Ja '70
Hawaii: the place for the image-maker. L. Jossel. Travel & Camera 33:76 Ja '70
See also
Moving pictures—Travel films

TRAVEL regulations
Kremlin will get you if you don't watch out. J. Powiansky. Nat R 22:784-5 Jl 28 '70
U.S. passports remain invalid for travel to certain areas; Department announcement, with texts of public notices by Secretary of State Rogers. Dept State Bul 62:496-7 Ap 13 '70
U. S. passports remain invalid for travel to certain areas; texts of public notices, September 29, 1970. Dept State Bul 63:699-70 D 7 '70

TRAVEL restrictions. See Travel regulations

TRAVEL study courses
All this and credits too! il Todays Ed 59:54-6 Ja '70
Beyond the classroom: life experiences in the field. G. L. Williams. Clear House 45:81-5 O '70
Making history more than old names. E. Sparn. il Sr Schol 95:14-15 S 29 '69
Summer campus on the S.S. Carina; music study-cruise. S. Willetts. il Hi Fi sec II 20:10-11 F '70
Summer overseas study-travel boom; questions and answers. il Todays Ed 59:57-9 Ja '70
Trade winds; Communications media study group. C. Amory. Sat R 53:10-11 D 19 '70
See also
American institute for foreign study

TRAVEL trailers. See Automobile trailers

TRAVEL with children
Boston stranglers; or, How to pack a pack of Cub scouts in a Bonanza. R. Peterson. il Flying 86:72-5 Ja '70
How to tote your tots. R. Hight. il Travel 134:24-5 Ag '70
Innocent abroad. R. F. Sloane. il House B 112:42+ Ap '70
Take the kids and enjoy it. Bet Hom & Gard 48:59+ Je '70
Two kids and a cat; Caribbean cruise. P. Smyth. il Motor B 126:58-60+ N '70
What every young mother should know about auto safety; excerpt from Mothers and children in cars. E. D. Fales, jr. il Redbook 135:91+ S '70
Why wait for Hawaii? il Sunset 141:46-55 Ja '70

TRAVELER and his telling; story. See Broner, E. M.

TRAVELERS
Travel, money, U.S. customs, and your health. il Consumer Bul 53:29-30 Ja '70
Yankee go home and other friendly salutations; how local politics affect the American tourist. D. Butwin. il Sat R 54:28-9+ Ja 2 '71
See also
Women as travelers

Bibliography
Travel as a passport to freedom. A. Alvarez. il Sat R 54:17-20+ Ja 2 '71

TRAVELERS checks
See also
American express company

TRAVELERS diarrhea. See Diarrhea

TRAVELERS home care. See Visiting housekeepers

TRAVELERS insurance. See Insurance, Travelers

TRAVELING bags. See Luggage

TRAVELING businessmen. See Businessmen

TRAVELING music schools. See Music schools

TRAVELING salesmen. See Salesmen and salesmanship

TRAVELS
See also
Overland journeys to the Pacific
Travel
Voyages

TRAVERS, Milton
Each other's victims; excerpts. il McCalls 97:70-1+ Je '70

TRAVERSE CITY, Mich.

Newspapers
Death at the hospital; state hospital's campaign against Weekender's advertisers. il Time 96:23 D 28 '70

TRAVERSE CITY state hospital, Mich. See Hospitals, Psychiatric

La TRAVIATA; opera. See Verdi, G.

TRAWLS and trawling
Troll for early trout. R. Cochran. il Field & S 74:52-3+ F '70
Trolling from an airplane. B. Rankin. il Field & S 75:80 My '70

TRAY stands. See Stands (furniture)

TRAYLOR, Everett
Slip cast ceramic flute. il Ceram Mo 18:26-7 Mr '70

TRAYS
1820 butler's tray; with fold-up stand. R. Sickler. il Mech Illus 66:94-6 N '70
Handsome tray for your best silverware. il Pop Mech 133:168-9 Mr '70
See also
Ash trays
Lazy susans

TREAD-softly
Nature's Christmas gifts; bull nettle. E. Gibbons. Org Gard & Farm 17:68+ Ja '70

TREADWELL, Sandy
Baseball. Sports Illus 33:44 Ag 3 '70
Boxing. Sports Illus 33:44-5 Ag 10 '70
Going nowhere, on wheels. il pors Sports Illus 32:30-2+ My 18 '70
Week; college football. Sports Illus 33:45 Ag 3; 52+ S 28; 48+ O 5; 62+ O 12; 70-1 N 16 '70

TREADWELL, Sherwood A.
Passion; poem. Chr Cent 87:1554 D 30 '70

TREASON
Treason and the traitor. P. Greenacre. bibliog Am Imago 26:199-232 Fall '69

TREASURE finders. See Metal detectors

TREASURE trove
New science of hunting underwater treasure. R. Marx. il Pop Mech 133:102-5+ Je '70

TREASURY department (United States) See United States—Treasury, Department of the

TREASURY bills. See Bonds, Government

TREATIES
How hostilities have ended: peace treaties and alternatives. Q. Wright. bibliog f Ann Am Acad 392:51-61 N '70
Rule of law and the settlement of international disputes; address, April 25, 1970. W. P. Rogers. Dept State Bul 62:623-7 My 18 '70
United States signs Convention on the law of treaties. Dept State Bul 62:639-40 My 18 '70
Why doesn't the U.S. outlaw mass murder? struggle over signing the UN genocide treaty. A. D. Morse. Look 34:40 Mr 10 '70
See also
Antarctic treaty, 1959
also subhead Treaties under names of countries, e.g. Russia—Treaties

TREATIES of alliance. See Alliances

TREATMENT of prisoners. See Prisoners—Treatment

TREATY of Moscow. See Russia—Treaties—Germany (Federal Republic)

TREBILCOCK, Dorothy
All on a summer's day. il Nat Parks & Con Mag 44:14 Jl '70

TREBLINKA concentration camp. See Concentration camps—Poland

TREE, Penelope
Penelope Tree: zapping Zambia. Vogue 157: 136 Ja 1 '71

TREE breeding
See also
Trees—Seed

TREE drawing and painting. See Trees in art

TREE farms. See Forest management

TREE ferns
Tree ferns from down under. il Sunset 145: 156-7 Jl '70

TREE ferns and tree toads
Polyploidy in the common tree toad hyla versicolor Le Conte. A. O. Wasserman. bibliog il Science 167:385-6 Ja 23 '70

TREE grafting. See Grafting

TREE lore. See Trees in religion, folklore, etc.

TREE of heaven. See Ailanthus

TREE planting
Fast and easy: bar-plant trees and vines. J. F. Bucher. il Org Gard & Farm 17:80-1 N '70
How to ball a tree. G. Hutton. il Org Gard & Farm 17:98-9 Je '70
How to replant nursery trees. Suc Farm 68:no3 52 F '70
It's the time to move small trees. il Sunset 144:135 Ja '70
Modern Johnny Appleseed; T. Bolack planting Navajo willows. V. Kraft. il por Sports Illus 33:78-9+ N 30 '70
Plant a tree in October. M. Franz. il Org Gard & Farm 17:91-2 O '70
This woman fights the Sahara with trees. J. Graham. il pors Sci Digest 69:20-3 Ja '71
Trees for the Arch; project of Future trees foundation. il Nat Wildlife 8:56-7 D '69

TREE propagation. See Plant propagation

TREE rings
Bristlecone correction. Sci Am 223:52 Jl '70

TREE seedlings
Free trees for your borders. D. Readey. il Org Gard & Farm 17:50-1 N '70

TREE tapping. See Maple sugar

TREE toads. See Tree frogs and tree toads

TREE trimmers. See Pruning apparatus and equipment

TREE trunks. See Trees

TREES
Gift wrapped in blue sky. M. Bucy. Har Yrs 10:14 D '70
Good places to buy shrubs and trees. il Changing T 24:41-2 S '70
J. Russell Smith's great organic idea; tree-crops partnership. R. Rodale. il Org Gard & Farm 17:28-33 S '70
Narrow trees. W. Flemer, 3d. il Horticulture 48:24-5+ Ap '70
Shade trees. H. Williamson. il por Am For 76:26+ O '70
Shade trees: the best choice for your area. E. McDonald. il House B 112:96-7+ S '70
Ten trees: best buys. L. V. Power. il Am Home 74:43-5 Ja '71
Tree is living yet! photographs by B. Ratcliffe. F. Russell. il Audubon 72:64-9 Ja '70
Trees for problem locations. il Bet Hom & Gard 48:82-3 Mr '70
Trees I have known. J. Stuart. il Am For 76:32-3+ Mr '70
See also
Bamboo
Chaparral
Christmas trees
Evergreens
Forest conservation
Forest ecology
Forests and forestry
Hedges
Nut trees
Sequoia, Giant
Timber line
Wood
Windbreaks
also names of trees, e.g. Elm

Diseases and pests
Saddled prominent. J. H. Risley. il Cons 24:29-30 Ag '69
Trees for people or pests? W. E. Waters and R. W. Brandt. il Am For 76:20-3+ S '70
See also
Rusts (botany)
also subhead Diseases and pests under names of trees, e.g. Beech—Diseases and pests

Planting
See Tree planting

Seed
Free trees for your borders. D. Readey. il Org Gard & Farm 17:50-1 N '70

Spraying
See Spraying and dusting

TREES, Care of
How to repair trees. il Bet Hom & Gard 48: 34 Mr '70

TREES, Dwarf
Art of bonsai trees. J. O'Connell. il Sci Digest 67:34-8 Mr '70
Making a start with bonsai. il Sunset 145 169 Jl '70
Old juniper: a bonsai, newest acquisition of Brooklyn botanic garden. New Yorker 46: 37-9 N 7 '70
With Gene Boucher after the opera: herbs and bonsai. E. McDonald. il por House B 112:167-8 F '70
See also
Fruit trees, Dwarf

TREES, Effect of air pollution on. See Plants, Effect of air pollution on

TREES, Fossil
Palmoxylon simperi and palmoxylon pristina: two pre-cretaceous angiosperms from Utah. W. D. Tidwell and others. bibliog il Science 168:835-40 My 15 '70
Pre-cretaceous flowering plants: further evidence from Utah. W. D. Tidwell and others. bibliog il Science 170:547-8 O 30 '70
Primeval palms. il por Time 96:46-7 S 7 '70

TREES, Historic
Cucumber tree mystery; cucumber magnolia of Violet Bank in Colonial Heights, Va. W. Bednarz. il Am For 76:48-50 D '70
Summer is the time to see these historic trees in Sunset's garden. il Sunset 145:132-3 Ag '70
The Woods' mighty oak; privately owned tree in Michigan Bluff, Calif. W. Fuller. Am For 76:28-9 Ag '70

TREES, Training of
See also
Fruit trees, Training of

TREES in art
Stimulating perception. P. K. Scholl. il Sch Arts 70:12-13 N '70
Trees or lollipops. R. A. Yoder. il Sch Arts 70:40-2 S '70

TREES in cities
Metro forestry in Atlanta: tree power. A. R. Shirley. il Am For 76:8-11+ O '70
Our local correspondents; ailanthus altissima; or, the tree of heaven. E. Kinkead. New Yorker 46:143-6+ O 24 '70

TREES in religion, folklore, etc.
Tales the trees could tell. G. Nicholson. il Am For 76:12-15 D '70

TREFETHEN, Florence
Mid-Pacific; poem. Poetry 115:318 F '70
Poet's workshop. See issues of Writer

TREFETHEN, James B.
Face of starvation. il Nat Wildlife 7:4-8+ O '69
Return of the white-tailed deer. il Am Heritage 21:97-103 F '70

TREIRES, James J.
Kicking the defense habit. il Nation 210: 200-4 F 23 '70 *

TREJO, Arnulfo D.
Bicultural Americans with a Hispanic tradition. il por Wilson Lib Bul 44:716-23 Mr '70

TRELAWNY of the Wells; drama. See Pinero, A. W.

TRELEAVEN, Harry
Electronic politics: the image game. il por Time 96:43-4+ S 21 '70 *

TRELFORD, Jane
Very special pair. il por McCalls 97:63-5+ Ap '70

TRELLISES
Trellis to enhance climbing plants; at Sterling Forest gardens. il Home Gard 57:50-1 Ap '70
See also
Garden stakes and staking

TRENCH silos. See Silos

TRENTON, N.J.
More phones, better service, less cost. J. Alexander, jr. il por Am City 85:137-8 O '70

TREPANNING. See Trephining

TREPHINING
Aboriginal trephination: case from southern New England? B. W. Powell. bibliog il Science 170:732-4 N 13 '70
Brain surgery in the stone age. S. S. McKern and T. W. McKern. il Sci Digest 67:32-7 F '70

TRES Vidas, Acapulco, Mexico. See Country clubs

TRESS, Arthur
Urban meadows; photographs. Sat R 53:56-7
Mr 7 '70

TREVINO, Lee
Lee Trevino, fleas and all. D. Jenkins. por
Sports Illus 32:70+ Je 8 '70 *

TREWICK, Olive
No place for women, or several? Cath World
210:216-19 F '70

TREZISE, Philip H.
Case for a positive trade policy; address,
February 27, 1970. Dept State Bul 62:
333-8 Mr 16 '70
International economic order after twenty-
five years; address, October 23, 1970. Dept
State Bul 63:569-72 N 9 '70
Outlook for energy supplies; address, Sep-
tember 24, 1970. Dept State Bul 63:479-83 O
26 '70

TRI, Do-cao-. See Do-cao-Tri

TRIAC circuits. See Transistor circuits

TRIAL by Jury. See Jury

TRIAL of A. Lincoln; drama. See Damico, J.

TRIAL of the Catonsville nine; drama. See
Berrigan, D.

TRIAL practice. See Procedure (law)

TRIAL reporting. See Newspaper court reporting

TRIALS
See also
Actions and defenses
Jury
Justice and politics
Newspaper court reporting
Television broadcasting—Trials

California
L.A.'s Scottsboro boys case. S. H. Harris.
Commonweal 91:548-9 F 20 '70
Mooney case, by R. H. Frost. Review
Am West 7:49 Ja '70. J. P. Kindregan

China (People's Republic)
Mao makes the trials run on time. R. Hughes.
il N Y Times Mag p22-3+ Ag 23 '70; Reply
with rejoinder. A. S. Whiting. p41+ N 15
'70

Connecticut
Catholic colleges on trial: Tilton v. Finch,
II. C. M. Whelan. America 122:122-4 F 7 '70
Catholic colleges pass the test; Tilton v.
Finch. C. M. Whelan. America 122:368 Ap
4 '70

Czechoslovakia
Confession, by A. London. Review
Nation 211:598-600 D 7 '70. C. L. Mark-
mann

France
In defense of violence; trial of two former
editors of La Cause du peuple. il por Newsweek 75:57 Je 8 '70

Germany (Federal Republic)
See also
Nuremberg trials

Greece, Modern
American lawyer takes notes. E. Goodman.
Nation 211:363-5 O 19 '70
Proving the wrong point; conspiracy trial of
alleged Democratic defense members.
Newsweek 75:36+ Ap 13 '70

Italy
Forget Rocinante, fly TWA; skyjacking trial
of R. Minichiello. il Time 96:32+ N 23 '70
Mama Mias didn't help; Raphael Minichiello's airplane hijacking trial. il Newsweek
76:55 N 23 '70

Japan
Speedy justice? Tokyo riot of 1952. Time
95:33 F 9 '70

New Jersey
People v. the mob; or, Who rules New Jer-
sey? F. J. Cook. il N Y Times Mag p9-11
F 1 '70
See also
Trials (extortion)

Poland
Case of the mountain climbers; trial of five
Warsaw university graduate students. J.
Burnham. Nat R 22:248, 299 Mr 10-24 '70

Russia
Involuntary journey; trial of A. Amalrik.
pors Newsweek 76:61 N 23 '70
Leningrad eleven. il Newsweek 77:29 Ja 4 '71
Let my people go; sentences passed in Leningrad on nine Jews convicted of an alleged
air hijacking; with sampling of world press
criticism. il Newsweek 77:42-3 Ja 11 '71

Opinion of mankind; Jewish hijacking case.
Nation 212:34 Ja 11 '71
Soviet Union: limited leniency; fate of the
Leningrad eleven. il Time 97:19-20 Ja 11 '71
Trial of a protester: A. Amalrik. America
123:482 D 5 '70

Spain
Burgos and Leningrad; death sentence of
Basques commuted. Nation 212:35-6 Ja 11
'71
Judgment on the Burgos trial. T. M. Gannon.
America 124:23-4 Ja 9 '71
Men of *Euskadi.* il Time 96:36 D 14 '70
Real offense; trial of Basque separatists.
Newsweek 76:57 D 21 '70.
Spain: calculated magnanimity; commutation
of condemned Basques. il Time 97:18-19 Ja
11 '71
Spain: the crackdown that failed; commuta-
tion of Basque death sentences. il News-
week 77:41 Ja 11 '71
Test of strength; Basque separatists. News-
week 76:60 D 14 '70
Trial of Basque separatists. America 123:532
D 19 '70

Tunisia
Peasants revenge; A. Ben Salah. Newsweek
75:46 Je 8 '70

United States
Can a black man get a fair trial in this country? H. Burns. il N Y Times Mag p5+ Jl
12 '70; Same abr. with title Race and fair
trial. Cur 121:12-19 S '70; Discussion. N Y
Times Mag p54 Ag 9; 21+ S 27 '70
Jails and courtrooms; techniques of judicial
security under consideration. Nation 211:
292 O 5 '70
What to do when the judge is put up against
the wall. L. Nizer. il N Y Times Mag p39-
1+ Ap 5 '70; Same abr. with title Order
in the court! Read Digest 97:95-9 Jl '70;
Discussion. N Y Times Mag p 114-15 My
3 '70

Vietnam (Republic)
Making a point; trial of Tran-ngoc-Chau. il
por Newsweek 75:42 Mr 16 '70

TRIALS (conspiracy)
After Chicago. Nat R 22:246 Mr 10 '70
Anarchy in Tacoma; case of the Seattle
Seven. por Time 96:46 D 28 '70
Assault on the courts; trials of Chicago
seven and Black Panthers. Nat R 22:189-90
F 24 '70
Behind the Chicago conspiracy trial; with
editorial comment. P. Glusman. il Ramp
Mag 8:7+, 39-47 Ja '70
Chicago fiasco. W. F. Buckley, jr. Nat R
22:273 Mr 10 '70
Chicago howler. H. Kalven, jr. New Repub
162:21-3 Mr 7 '70
Chicago seven; a sandwich with the con-
spiracy. T. W. Pew, jr. Nation 210:38-40
Ja 19 '70
Chicago trial: a loss for all. il Time 95:38-9
F 23 '70
Climax in Chicago. Newsweek 75:30+ F 23
'70
Conspiracy charges dropped against Coffin,
Godman. Chr Cent 87:655 My 27 '70
Conspiracy of clerics; Flower City conspiracy
trial, Rochester. il Newsweek 76:68+ D 14
'70
Conspiracy trial; thirteen New York Black
Panthers. il Newsweek 76:26 N 9 '70
Death machine; sentencing and jailing of the
Chicago fifteen. il Nation 212:21-2 Ja 4 '70
Double agent; thirteen Harlem Black Pan-
thers. Newsweek 76:33-4 N 23 '70
Eight minus one is seven. il por Sr Schol 95:
20-1 D 8 '69
Electric circus; pretrial hearing of the Pan-
thers charged with conspiring to bomb
public places in New York. il Time 95:14-
15 F 16 '70
Good deal; New York trio pleading guilty to
conspiracy charges. Time 95:17-18 My 18 '70
Great conspiracy trial, by J. Epstein. Review
Newsweek 76:116+ N 16 '70. R. A. Soko-
lov
Judging the Chicago trial. A. M. Bickel. bibliog f Commentary 51:31-40 Ja '71
Judgment in Chicago. il por Newsweek 75:
22-4 Mr 2 '70
Judicial process on trial; vulnerability proved
by trial of Chicago seven. il Newsweek 75:
25-6+ Mr 2 '70
Justice in Chicago: an ominous farce. Life
68:34 F 27 '70
Justice Murtagh's formula. Nation 210:260 Mr
9 '70
Many sides of the Chicago conspiracy trial.
R. Kuttner. Commonweal 93:303-4 D 18 '70
Mistrial in Tacoma; Seattle Seven. Newsweek
76:36+ D 21 '70

TRIALS (conspiracy)—*Continued*
Murtagh's formula. il Newsweek 75:22-3 Mr 9 '70
Notes and comment; dangerous precedents of Chicago seven trial. New Yorker 46:29-30 Mr 7 '70
Order in the court; New York trial of sixteen Black Panthers. il Newsweek 75:27 F 16 '70
Panthers in court. New Yorker 46:31-3 F 21 '70
Parting shots: the Chicago seven trial game: can you tell the players? il Life 68: 70-1 F 20 '70
Political meaning of Chicago. L. D. Nachman. il Nation 210:326-9 Mr 23 '70
Political trial, U.S. style; Chicago 7. Nation 210:226 Mr 2 '70
Seattle Seven. il Newsweek 76:54+ D 14 '70
Second confrontation in Chicago. J. A. Lukas. il N Y Times Mag p 10-11+ Mr 29 '70
Seize the time; excerpts. B. Seale. pors Ramp Mag 8:17-29 Je '70
Split verdict: who won? Chicago seven. il Sr Schol 96:13-14 Mr 9 '70
That riotous trial: end or beginning? Chicago conspiracy trial. Chr Cent 87:260-1 Mr 4 '70
Tigar for the defense; trial of eight Seattle liberation front members. por Time 96:55-6 D 14 '70
Too prominent to be relevant; R. Clark to testify at Chicago trial. por Time 95:42 F 9 '70
Trial; excerpts. T. Hayden. il Ramp Mag 9:10-11+ Jl '70
Unfinished business of the Chicago trial. il U S News 68:6-7 Mr 2 '70
Verdict on the Chicago seven: from court to country. il Time 95:8-11 Mr 2 '70
Voice of the Speaker; case of M. Sweig. Newsweek 76:23 Jl 20 '70
Voir dire: selecting a jury for the Panther 21 trial. New Yorker 46:38-9 O 10 '70
What, another conspiracy? the Seattle eight. B. Weiner. Nation 211:424-7 N 2 '70
When is bail excessive? Black Panthers on trial in Manhattan. Time 95:42 F 9 '70
Who is on trial in Chicago? the Chicago seven. il Newsweek 75:26-7 F 16 '70

Bibliography
Shadows cast by Chicago. H. S. Resnik. Sat R 53:27-30 D 12 '70
TRIALS (espionage)
See also
Rosenberg, Julius and Ethel, case
TRIALS (extortion)
Newark: the price of the past; H. J. Addonizio and others. por Newsweek 76:18 Ag 3 '70
TRIALS (malpractice)
White like me; J. W. Finley's suit against government for negligent use of Doriden. il por Newsweek 75:76 Je 22 '70
TRIALS (murder)
Blind justice and a deaf-mute. Time 97:51 Ja 11 '71
Enforcer; the Rackley case; McLucas trial; testimony of George Sams. Newsweek 76: 32-3 Ag 17 '70
Example of New Haven. Nation 211:196 S 14 '70
Family hour; C. Manson and others. il por Newsweek 75:22 Je 29 '70
Helter skelter; testimony of Linda Kasabian at the trial of Charles Manson. il Newsweek 76:21-2 Ag 10 '70
Here is a man who was guilty; the Manson case and reverberations of remark by President Nixon. il por Newsweek 76:24-5 Ag 17 '70
Ice him; A. Rackley case. Newsweek 76: 25 Ag 3 '70
Is Nixon guilty? consequences of remark on Manson case. W. F. Buckley, jr. Nat R 22: 910-11 Ag 25 '70
Joe and Arville; trial of Arville Garland. il Time 96:26 D 7 '70
Justice in New Haven; trial of Lonnie McLucas. il Time 96:70 S 14 '70
Linda's punishment; Charles Manson trial; testimony of L. D. Kasabian. por Newsweek 76:29+ Ag 31 '70
Manson on the stand. Newsweek 76:26+ N 30 '70
Manson scene. K. Fleming. il Newsweek 77: 19-20 Ja 4 '71
Manson's shattered defense. il Time 96:45 N 30 '70
Murder trial of Dr Ossian Sweet; reprint. T. J. Fleming. il pors Ebony 25:106-8+ O '70

New Haven eight; trial of Black Panther Lonnie McLucas. Time 96:15 Ag 31 '70
Nixon's plea: stop making heroes out of criminals; Manson case; excerpts from remarks, August 3, 1970. R. M. Nixon. il por U S News 69:70 Ag 17 '70
Of murders and messiahs; Sharon Tate murder case. Time 96:12-13 Ag 10 '70
Other end of society; trial of C. Manson. il por Time 96:12 Ag 3 '70
Verdict in New Haven; trial of Lonnie McLucas. il Newsweek 76:34-5 S 14 '70
Who am I? The Indian sickness; the White Hawk case. R. Bongartz. Nation 210:496-8 Ap 27 '70
See also
Sacco-Vanzetti case
Sussep, P.

Anecdotes, facetiae, satire, etc.
Just for laughs: the gingerbread house caper. W. Stanton. Look 34:60 S 8 '70
TRIALS (obscenity)
Dirty words smokescreen; trial of the Missouri students involved in J. Bodger incident. N. Ladof. il por Library J 95: 2424-6 Jl '70
Witness for obscenity; trial in Jackson, Miss. of theater manager and projectionist for showing The fox. J. M. Carter. Library J 95:2431 Jl '70
TRIALS (rape)
Twenty times life; sentence for Charles Callins. por Time 96:46 D 28 '70
TRIALS, Military. See Courts martial and courts of inquiry
TRIANA, Antonio
Triana! V. H. Swisher. il pors Dance Mag 44:22-6 Jl '70 *
TRIANA, José
Criminals. Criticism
New Yorker 46:83-4 Mr 7 '70 *
TRIANGLES
Elegant triangle theorems not to be found in Euclid. M. Gardner. il Sci Am 222:132-4+ Je '70
TRIASSIC period. See Paleontology—Triassic
TRIAZOLES
Wheat leaf rust: control by 4-n-butyl-1,2,4-triazole, a systemic fungicide. W. C. Von Meyer and others. bibliog il Science 169:997-8 S 4 '70
TRIBAL dolls. See Dolls
TRIBES and tribal system
Africa's divided house. il Time 95:20 Ja 26 '70
The Danakil: nomads of Ethiopia's wasteland. V. Englebert. il Nat Geog 137:186-211 F '70
TRIBOLIUM. See Flour beetles
TRIBUS, Myron
Current ecological problems; address, August 19, 1970. Vital Speeches 36:717-20 S 15 '70
Education for innovation; address, December 29, 1969. Vital Speeches 36:279-82 F 15 '70
Physical view of cloud seeding; address, April 1970. bibliog il Science 168:201-11 Ap 10 '70
about
Commerce department: Myron Tribus, top science official, resigns. J. Walsh. por Science 170:1065-6 D 4 '70 *
TRICE, Markus
Evangelist; poem. Am Scholar 39:471 Sum '70
TRICK photography. See Photography, Trick
TRICKS
Dutchman in a box. il pors Life 69:71-2 N 20 '70
TRICYANOAMINOPROPENE
Cretinism in rats: enduring behavioral deficit induced by tricyanoaminopropene. J. W. Davenport. bibliog il Science 167:1007-9 F 13 '70
TRIESCHMAN, Albert E.
Parent and child. N Y Times Mag p99+ Ap 12 '70
TRIESTE
Music
Report:
Franco Mannino's Speranza. J. Boraros. il Opera N 34:33 Ap Ap 18 '70
TRIETHYLAMINE. See Ethylamine
TRIFILO, S. Samuel
Lima through British eyes. bibliog il Américas 22:27-34 Je '70
TRIFLES (desserts) See Desserts

TRILLIN, Calvin
Adventures of Roxanne. Life 69:12 N 27 '70
Nation of shopkeepers loses three of them through contact with a nation of violence; story. Atlan 227:71-4 Ja '71
Through the muck with Myra. il Life 68:50-2 Mr 6 '70
U.S. journal (cont) New Yorker 45:68-71+ Ja 24; 124-6+ F 14; 46:120+ Mr 21; 66+ Ap 4; 92+ Ap 18; 108+ My 16; 40-2+ Je 6; 42-4+ Je 27; 32-6+ Jl 18; 53-8 Ag 29; 108+ S 19; 148+ O 17; 104+ O 31; 170+ N 21; 164+ D 12 '70; 52-6 Ja 2 '71
TRILLING, David M. and Axelrod, David
Encapsidation of free host DNA by simian virus 40: a simian virus 40 pseudovirus. bibliog il Science 168:268-71 Ap 10 '70
TRILLING, Diana
Easy rider and its critics. il Atlan 226:90-5 S '70
Female biology in a male culture; address. Sat R 53:16-18+ O 10 '70
TRIM (of boats) See Boats—Stability and stabilizers
TRIM tabs. See Tabs (boats)
TRIMARANS
Alone on a wide, wide sea; Sunday Times' round the world singlehanded race. E. F. Havlock. il Motor B 125:36-8+ Mr '70
Is this the future? pianesail. il Yachting 127:53 F '70
Multihulls. R. Harris. il por Motor B 126:108-9+ Ja '70
TRIMBLE, Lester
Music. New Repub 163:28-9 Jl 4 '70
TRIMETHYLPHOSPHATE
Mutagenicity of trimethylphosphate in mice. S. S. Epstein and others. bibliog il Science 168:584-6 My 1 '70
TRIMM, H. Wayne
Don't shoot! All hawks, owls, eagles and vultures are protected by law; drawings. Cons 24:17 Je '70
TRIMMER, Sarah (Kirby)
Mrs Trimmer, guardian of education. J. St John. il por Horn Bk 46:20-5 F '70 *
TRIMMER capacitors. See Electric capacitors
TRIMMERS, Lawn. See Lawn tools, equipment and supplies
TRINCA, John C. and Schiff, Peter
Deadly sea wasp; with biographical sketches. il pors Sea Front 16:32-40, 62-3 Ja '70
TRINI, Tommaso
At home with art: the villa of Count Giuseppe Panza di Biumo. il por Art in Am 58:102-9 S '70
TRINIDAD (island)
Caribbean mutiny. il Time 95:48 My 4 '70
Trinidad flare-up: U.S. stake there. U S News 68:66 My 4 '70
See also
Port-of-Spain
History
Loss of El Dorado, by V. S. Naipaul. Review New Yorker 46:72-6 Ag 8 '70. J. Updike
TRINIDAD and Tobago
See also
Trinidad (island)
TRINITY
Mystery of mysteries. V. P. McCorry. America 122:570-inside back cover My 23 '70
TRINITY college, Hartford, Conn.
Life sciences building designed as a wall. il Arch Rec 147:112-13 F '70
TRINITY national recreation area. See Recreation areas—California
TRINITY square repertory company. See Providence, R.I.—Theater
TRIOLET, Elsa
Letter from Paris. Genêt. New Yorker 46:50-2 Jl 11 '70 *
TRIOS, instrumental
Three men on a hobby; Stern-Istomin-Rose trio. I. Kolodin. il pors Sat R 53:47-9 O 31 '70
TRIP camping. See Camping
TRIP for wood; story. See O'Donnell, T.
TRIPE
See also
Cookery—Meat
TRIPLE crown. See Horse racing
TRIPLOIDY. See Chromosomes
TRIPODS, Camera. See Camera tripods
TRIPP, Carolyn
Woman with a Micro-zoo. J. Fix. il por Sci Digest 67:94-6 F '70 *
TRIPP, Vollie
Sweet potatoes are prolific. il Org Gard & Farm 17:86-7 Ap '70

TRIPPETT, Frank
Grenada: the nowhere island. il Look 34:28 Mr 10 '70
On the house. il Look 34:66-8 D 29 '70
Suckers. il Look 34:34-5+ My 19 '70
What's happening to sexual privacy? Look 34:50 O 20 '70
TRIPS, Student. See School excursions
TRISOMY. See Chromosomes
TRISPORIC acid
Trisporic acid synthesis in blakeslea trispora. R. P. Sutter. bibliog il Science 168:1590-2 Je 26 '70
TRIST, Nicholas Philip
Thankless task of Nicholas Trist. R. M. Ketchum. il por Am Heritage 21:12-15+ Ag '70 *
TRITICALE
Triticale. C. E. Ball. il Farm J 94:14-15 D '70
TRITIUM
Cosmic ray production of rare gas radioactivities and tritium in lunar material. R.-W. Stoenner and others. bibliog il Science 167:553-5 Ja 30 '70
Tritium and argon radioactivities in lunar material. E. L. Fireman and others. bibliog il Science 167:566-8 Ja 30 '70
TRITTIPO, James
James Trittipo, designer for television. J. Lovoos. il por Am Artist 34:30-5+ O '70 *
TRIUMPH (automobile) See Automobiles, Foreign
TRIUMPH of death; drama. See Ionesco, E.
TRIUMPHAL arches. See Arches, Triumphal and memorial
TRIVETS
Classification of trivets; heart shapes. W. Paley. il Hobbies 75:122 Mr '70
TRIVIA collecting. See Collectors and collecting
TROEMEL, C. P.
Build the liberator. il Pop Electr 33:49-52+ D '70
TROIANO, Vincent
Build a beautiful patio. il Mech Illus 66:84-6+ Jl '70
TROILITE. See Iron sulfides
TROJAN women; drama. See Euripides
TROLL, Walter, and others
Tumorigenesis in mouse skin: inhibition by synthetic inhibitors of proteases. bibliog il Science 169:1211-13 S 18 '70
TROLLING. See Trawls and trawling
TROMPE-l'oeil
Art; exhibition at the Whitney museum called The reality of appearance. L. Alloway. Nation 210:763-4 Je 22 '70
Blithe deceivers; The reality of appearance exhibition. K. Kuh. il Sat R 53:38-9 Jl 25 '70
Exhibition preview: the reality of appearance; nineteenth century trompe-l' oeil paintings at the National gallery. A. Frankenstein. il Art in Am 58:94-9 Mr '70
Just a lot of eyefoolery. il Life 68:74-7 Je 5 '70
Yankee rhyparography; exhibition of 19th century trompe-l'oeil paintings at National gallery. A. Frankenstein. il Art N 69:50-3+ Mr '70
TROPHIES, Sport
In their cups. P. Ryan. il Sports Illus 33:68-72+ N 2 '70
See also
Hunting trophies
TROPICAL fish aquariums. See Aquariums
TROPICAL fruits. See Fruit
TROPICAL islands. See Islands
TROPICAL plants
See also
Pangola grass
TROPICAL rain forests. See Rain forests
TROPICS
See also
Association for tropical biology
Caribbean Region
TROPISM
See also
Chemotropism
TROPISM (botany)
See also
Phototropism
TROST, Tom
Strategy of nonviolent direct action interpreted by Beaver 55 protesters; interview, ed. by M. Stone. Chr Cent 87:610-12 My 13 '70
TROTTA, Geri
Not to be missed. See issues of Harper's bazaar
Travel bazaar. Harp Baz 103:72+ My; 38+ Je; 46+ Ag '70; 104:112-13 Ja '71
(ed) See Preminger, I. M*A*S*H

TROTTER, F. Thomas
  Great comedians as theologians. Chr Cent 87:
    101-2 Ja 28 '70
TROTTERS. See Race horses
TROTTING races. See Harness racing
TROUBADOURS
  Troubadours. F. V. Grunfeld. il Horizon 12:
    14-27 Sum '70
TROUSERS
  Country pants take over the town. il Bsns W
    p50-2 Jl 4 '70
TROUSERS, Womens. See Clothing and dress
TROUT
  Temperature-sensitive neurons in the brain
    of brook trout. G. L. Greer and D. R. Gard-
    ner. bibliog il Science 169:1220-2 S 18 '70
  That fantastic family of trout. N. Smith. il
    Nat Wildlife 8:36-7 Ag '70
    See also
  Cookery—Fish
TROUT fishing
  Are Washington's steelhead facing disaster?
    L. Johnson. Field & S 75:46-7+ N '70
  Beer barrel brownies. C. Nansen. il Field & S
    74:82-3+ Mr '70
  Best bet for opening day. H. G. Tapply.
    il Field & S 74:92 Ap '70
  Challenge of Nova Scotia. J. Brooks. il Out-
    door Life 146:90-5 D '70
  Chug up a laker. J. O. Cartier. il Outdoor
    Life 145:58-9+ Mr '70
  Crazy way to catch lakers. W. Davis. il por
    Outdoor Life 146:78-9+ Ag '70
  Day on the Deschutes. L. Miracle. il Out-
    door Life 145:78-9+ Ap '70
  Family fishing on the Kern. J. Martin. il por
    Outdoor Life 146:56-7+ Ag '70
  Finger Lakes turnover trout. E. R. Belak,
    jr. il Cons 24:14-15 Ag '69
  First of the season. W. Davis. il Mech Illus
    66:47+ Mr '70
  Fishing in New Zealand: North Island. J.
    Brooks. il por Outdoor Life 145:56-7+ Ja
    '70
  Fur bearing trout. N. Strung. il Field & S
    74:40-1+ Ja '70
  How to catch big early season trout. J. B.
    Robinson. il Field & S 74:58-9+ Mr '70
  Ice-out lakers. J. O. Cartier. il Outdoor Life
    145:72-5+ Ap '70
  Island for summer steelhead. J. Gartner.
    il Field & S 75:22-3+ Jl '70
  Labrador's trophy trout country. B. Cairns,
    il Travel & Camera 33:50-3 Je '70
  Lunker hunters. H. G. Tapply. il Field & S
    75:68 S '70
  Make a reservation for trout. J. Tallon. il
    Outdoor Life 146:72-3+ N '70
  On the upper Rio Grande; brown and rain-
    bow trout. H. Simmons. il Field & S 75:62-
    3+ My '70
  Rainbows through the ice. H. Bradshaw. il
    Field & S 75:104-7+ D '70
  Rigging for lakers. B. Adams. il Field & S
    74:78-9+ Ap '70
  Rivière Philippe; brook trout stream in
    Quebec. B. Warner. il pors Outdoor Life
    145:48-51+ Je '70
  Small stream savvy. N. Strung. il Field & S
    75:42-3+ Jl '70
  Springtime is steelhead time. J. B. Gleason.
    il Field & S 74:42-3+ Ja '70
  Troll for early trout. R. Cochran. il Field &
    S 74:52-3+ F '70
  Trouting in solitude. M. W. Fong. il pors
    Outdoor Life 146:54-7+ S '70
  Turn left at the porcupine. J. Olsen. il
    Sports Illus 33:50-8+ Ag 24 '70
  Water all white. D. Jarden. il por Outdoor
    Life 145:45-7+ Mr '70
  Winning steelhead river. C. F. Waterman. il
    por Field & S 74:42-5+ F '70
    See also
  Char fishing
TROXLER, Robert F. and others
  Bile pigment formation in plants. bibliog il
    Science 167:192-3 Ja 9 '70
TROY, Jack
  Bird feeding stations. il Ceram Mo 18:13-15
    Mr '70
TROYANOS, Tatiana
  Greeks bearing gifts. R. Zachary. por Opera
    N 34:13 My 16 '70 *
TROYAT, Henri
  Letter from Paris. Genêt. New Yorker 46:
    128+ Ap 18 '70 *
TROYER, Will
  Izembek wilderness proposal. il Liv Wildn
    34:17-20 Sum '70
TRUAX, Hawley
  Come, now! poem. New Yorker 46:30 Ag 15
    '70
  Dayspring; poem. New Yorker 46:34 S 26 '70
  Window solstice; poem. New Yorker 46:30 Jl
    11 '70

TRUCK campers. See Campers and coaches,
  Truck
TRUCK drivers strikes. See Strikes—United
  States—Truck drivers
TRUCK farming
    See also
  Vegetable gardening
TRUCK hijacking. See Robberies and assaults
TRUCK leasing. See Motor trucks—Leasing
  and renting
TRUCKING
  He earns $30,000 a year behind the wheel.
    E. D. Fales, jr. il pors Pop Mech 133:79-82+
    My '70
    See also
  Collective bargaining—Trucking industry
  Consolidated freightways, inc.
  Motor trucks—Laws and legislation
  Pacific intermountain express company

Finance
  Trucking: passing the buck. il Forbes 105:20-
    2+ My 1 '70

Wages and hours
  Setback in the war on inflation; with editorial
    comment. il Bsns W p 14-15, 116 Jl 11 '70
  Trucking: passing the buck. il Forbes 105:
    20-2+ My 1 '70
TRUCKING employers, inc.
  Businessmen unite behind trucking pact.
    Bsns W p 16 Jl 4 '70
TRUCKS
    See also
  Motor trucks
TRUCKS, Toy. See Toys
TRUDEAU, Pierre Elliott
  Trudeau welcomes draft evaders; statement.
    Chr Cent 87:414 Ap 8 '70

about
  Canada. J. D. Hamilton. Atlan 227:86-91 Ja
    '71 *
  Canada enters the revolutionary age. il News-
    week 76:41-4+ N 2 '70 *
  Canada's P.M. is not a simple swinger nor
    a radical reformer. G. Clark. il por N Y
    Times Mag p26-7+ Ja 25 '70
  Canada's Trudeau: after the kissing stops. I.
    Mothner. il pors Look 34:47-51 F 24 '70 *
  Law, order and Trudeau. D. Coxe. il Nat R
    22:1201 N 17 '70 *
  Pierre Trudeau: counterrevolutionary. Nat R
    22:1144+ N 3 '70 *
  Politics of overreaction to seizure of hos-
    tages by the FLQ. Nation 211:418 N 2 '70 *
  Sober swinger. il pors Time 95:43-4 Ap 27
    '70 *
  Terrorism in Canada. il U S News 69:17-19
    N 2 '70 *
  Testing of Pierre Trudeau. T. Buckley. il
    pors N Y Times Mag p50-1+ D 6 '70 *
  Trudeau: a life full of contrast. por U S
    News 69:53 N 2 '70 *
  Trudeau: an enigma dispelled. il por News-
    week 76:44 N 2 '70 *
TRUDEAU, Richard C.
  Don't fight, negotiate! F. J. Monteagle. il
    Parks & Rec 9:38-9+ S '70 *
TRUDELL, Dennis
  Epilogue; Hotel in Paris; A way; Excursions;
    poems. Poetry 115:233-7 Ja '70
TRUE, D. L. and Matson, R. G.
  Cluster analysis and multidimensional scaling
    of archeological sites in northern Chile. bib-
    liog il Science 169:1201-3 S 18 '70
TRUE, Michael
  Requiem for an anarchist. Commonweal 91:
    525 F 13 '70
TRUE (periodical)
  What True's new editorial image means to
    writers. C. N. Barnard. Writers Digest 50:33
    Mr '70
TRUE-false tests. See Educational tests and
  measurements
TRUE to life (periodical) See Birth control—
  Periodicals
TRUEBLOOD, David Elton
  Life of service; excerpt from The new man
    for our time. Chr Today 14:3-5 Ja 30 '70
  Protest mentality. Chr Today 14:14-15 Jl
    17 '70
TRUEBLOOD, Elton. See Trueblood, D. E.
TRUEBLOOD, Harriet Pratt
  Eve of the wedding; story. Good H 172:72-3
    Ja '71
TRUEBLOOD, Ted, pseud.
  [Monthly article on the outdoor life] See is-
    sues of Field & stream
  Time bomb at White Clouds. il Nat Wildlife
    8:4-8 Je '70

TRUEBLOOD, Ted—*Continued*

about

Exit, laughing; is there really a Ted True-blood. E. Zern. Field & S 75:101 Je '70 *
Real Ted Trueblood. P. Barrett. por Field & S 75:42-3+ D '70 *

TRUELOVE, Bryan. See Moore, J. H. jt. auth.

TRUESDELL, Tuffy
Happy pair of hairy sports. F. Deford. il pors Sports Illus 32:52-6+ F 23 '70 *

TRUFFAUT, François
Is Truffaut the happiest man on earth? il por Esquire 74:66-7+ Ag '70
Truffaut; interview. New Yorker 46:35-7 O 17 '70

about

Current cinema. P. Gilliatt. New Yorker 46: 67-9 S 12 '70 *

TRUMAN, Harry S.
Words of warning from three presidents; excerpts from message to Congress, March 12, 1947. U S News 69:79 Jl 27 '70; Same abr. Read Digest 97:116-17 O '70

about

Harry's last hurrah. R. Rhodes. il Harper 240: 48-9+ Ja '70
Mark Twain & Harry S. Truman. C. Clemens. Hobbies 74:141+ Ja '70
Truman's speech & Noam Chomsky; with excerpts from address, March 6, 1947. A. Schlesinger, jr; discussion. Commentary 49:4+ F; 4+ Mr; 14+ My '70 *

TRUMAN, James W. and Riddiford, L. M.
Neuroendocrine control of ecdysis in silkmoths. bibliog il Science 167:1624-6 Mr 20 '70

TRUMAN, Margaret. See Daniel, M. T.

TRUMBO, Dalton
En garde, foolish world! il Esquire 74:86-9+ Jl '70

about

Additional dialogue, ed. by H. Manfull. Review
Sat R por 53:29 O 31 '70. E. Capouya *
Authors & editors. D. N. Mount. por Pub W 198:21-3 O 5 '70 *
Reclaiming a name. G. Wolff. por Newsweek 76:98+ N 9 '70 *

TRUMBULL, Van
Washington lookout. See issues of American forests

TRUMP, J. Lloyd
Model schools: blueprint for the future. C. H. Harrison. Schol Teach Sec Teach Sup p 18-19+ Mr 9 '70 *

TRUMPET music
Jeremiah Clarke's trumpet tunes: another view of origins. T. F. Taylor. bibliog f il Mus Q 56:455-62 Jl '70

TRUMPETER swans. See Swans

TRUNKS
Trunks that stay home. N. Mandelbaum. il Ladies Home J 87:110-11 N '70

TRUNKS of trees. See Trees

TRUSCOTT, Alan
Bridge. See issues of New York times magazine

TRUSCOTT, Lucian K. 3d
Body count: the degrading illusion. il Nation 211:487-9 N 16 '70

TRUSCOTT, Lucian K. 4th
Who dies in Vietnam? il Nation 211:326-7 O 12 '70

TRUSLOW, Frederick Kent
Businessman in the bush. il pors Nat Geog 137:634-75 My '70
Pileateds in a pine tree; photograph. Audubon 72:8-11 Mr '70

TRUST TERRITORY OF THE PACIFIC ISLANDS
Strategic Pacific Islands now under Older Americans act. il Aging 190:17 Ag '70
Trust Territory of the Pacific Islands. D. D. Johnson. Cur Hist 58:233-9+ Ap '70
Trust Territory of the Pacific Islands; symposium, June 3 and 11, 1970. Dept State Bul 63:251-71 Ag 31 '70
See also
Micronesia

TRUSTEES. See Trusts and trustees

TRUSTEES, Library. See Libraries—Trustees, boards, committees, etc.

TRUSTEESHIP council. See United Nations —Trusteeship council

TRUSTS, Industrial
Down with the freight cartel. Fortune 82:98 Ag '70
See also
Mass media

Law

Attack on the big boys. il Bsns W p78+ O 17 '70
Businessmen lose some immunity. Bsns W p24 N 7 '70
Changes in U.S. merger policy? U S News 69:57 N 30 '70
EEC rule, but no test yet. Bsns W p 132+ D 19 '70
FTC proposals for trustbusting. America 122:488 My 9 '70
Latest turn in trust-busting. il U S News 68:74 F 23 '70
McLaren vs. the cartels; international licensing agreements. Newsweek 75:78B+ My 4 '70
Robinson-Patman primer, by E. W. Kintner. Review
Bsns W p8 My 30 '70. G. Potvin
U.S. antitrust reaches abroad. Bsns W p 128+ D 19 '70

Europe, Western

Opening the lid on a Pandora's box; giant European tin can manufacturing combine, Europemballage. il Bsns W p38+ Ap 11 '70

United States

See also
United States—Justice, Department of—Antitrust division

TRUSTS, Investment. See Investment trusts

TRUSTS and trustees
You can avoid the probate trap; create a living trust. F. J. Taylor. Read Digest 96: 93-6 Je '70
See also
Custodianship accounts

TRUTH
Liars among us. Chr Today 14:27 F 13 '70
See also
Honesty
Lying

TRUTH in lending bill. See Consumer credit—Laws and legislation

TRUTH in lending legislation. See Consumer credit—Laws and legislation

TRYPANOSOMIASIS
Biological control of Chagas' disease. J. Bockel. il Sci N 97:485 My 16 '70

TRYPTOPHAN
Tryptophan operon: structural gene mutation creating a "promoter" and leading to 5-methyltryptophan dependence. R. Callahan, 3d. and E. Balbinder. bibliog il Science 168:1586-9 J 26 '70

TSCHUY, Théo
World council of churches and Latin America. Chr Cent 87:320-3 Mr 18 '70

TSIEN, Hsue-shen
Chinese spaceship. J. Lear. Sat R 53:62 My 16 '70 *

TSUNAMIS. See Tidal waves

TUAMOTU ISLANDS
Treacherous Tuamotus. G. Skinner. il Yachting 127:94-6+ Ja '70

TUBERCULIN
In vitro lymphocyte reactivity during depression of tuberculin hypersensitivity by 6-mercaptopurine. B. Zweiman and S. M. Phillips. il Science 169:284-5 Jl 17 '70
Tuberculin-active carbohydrate that induces inhibition of macrophage migration but not lymphocyte transformation. S. D. Chaparas and others. bibliog il Science 170:637-9 N 6 '70

TUBERCULOSIS

Prevention and control

Shot in the dark. Newsweek 76:66 Ag 10 '70

Vaccines

Double duty; Canadian research findings on BCG. Newsweek 76:83-4 O 26 '70
Shot in the dark; BCG dispute. Newsweek 76:66 Ag 10 '70

TUBEROUS begonias. See Begonias

TUBES, Copper
Tools and tricks the pros use with copper tubing. J. Burroughs. il Pop Mech 135:164-7 Ja '71

TÜBINGER, University. See Colleges and universities—Germany (Federal Republic)

TUBUAI ISLANDS
Active submarine volcanism in the Austral Islands. R. H. Johnson. bibliog il Science 167:977-9 F 13 '70

TUBULIN
On the apparent homology of actin and tubulin. R. E. Stephens. bibliog il Science 168:845-7 My 15 '70

TUCCIARONE, Wilma
Bruno LaVerdiere. il por Ceram Mo 18:14-17 S '70

TUCHMAN, Barbara W.
If Asia were clay in the hands of the West:
the Stilwell mission to China, 1942-44; excerpts from Stilwell. il pors Atlan 226:68-
84 S '70
Utmost try; excerpts. il pors Am Heritage 21:
22-31+ O; 22:4-11+ D '70

TUCHMAN, Maurice
Art and technology. il Art in Am 58:78-9
Mr '70

TUCK, James A.
Archaic Indian cemetery in Newfoundland;
with biographical sketch. il Sci Am 222:12,
112-21 Je '70

TUCKER, Beatrice
Triumph of Dr Tucker. L. Rockey. il por Todays Health 48:48-9+ N '70 *

TUCKER, Martin
Screen (cont) Commonweal 92:169-70, 223-4
My 1, 15 '70

TUCKER, Richard
Anniversary. New Yorker 45:22-4 F 7 '70
Musician of the month. por Hi Fi 20:MA9
O '70 *
Pride of the Met. pors Opera N 34:26-7 Ap
11 '70 *
Puckers for Tucker. il pors Life 68:73-4 My
15 '70 *

TUCKER, Robert L.
What every camper should know about bear.
il Field & S 74:60-1+ Mr '70

TUCKERMAN, Anne
Nigeria-Biafra and the UN. Nation 210:98-9
F 2 '70

TUCSON Ariz.
Description
Queen of the desert. E. J. Kahn, jr. Travel &
Camera 33:48-9+ N '70

TUDOR place (historic house) See Washington,
D.C.—Historic houses, etc.

TUFT, Lawrence H. and Berman, M. I.
Men of the sea. bibliog Ment Hy 54:440-3 Jl
'70

TUFTE, Obert N. See Chen, D. jt. auth.

TUGGLE, Robert A.
New audience. il Opera N 35:17-22 N 21 '70

TUGWELL, Rexford Guy
Critique on Constitution experiments. D. S.
Broder. Cur 123:24-6 N '70 *
Tugwell's constitution. por Newsweek 76:
44+ S 21 '70 *

TUITION fees. See Colleges and universities—
Finance

TULE elk. See Elk

TULIPS
Tulips, last call. il Sunset 145:240 N '70

TULLIS, Jan
Quartz: preferred orientation in rocks pro-
duced by Dauphiné Twinning. bibliog il
Science 168:1342-4 Je 12 '70

TULLY, Geri
Dangers of fad dieting. Harp Baz 103:74 F
'70
Yardstick diet. Harp Baz 103:252 Mr '70

TULSA, Okla, city-county library system
Community finds its forum. R. G. Swartz.
il Am Lib 1:554-61 Je '70

TUMBLEWEEDS
Tumbleweeds. Cons 24:13 Ag '69

TUMBLING barrels
And now, tumblestones. il Mech Illus 66:86
Ap '70

TUMOR cells
Amino acid transport in hepatoma cell cultures during tyrosine aminotransferase induction. E. L. Krawitt and others. bibliog
il Science 169:294-6 Jl 17 '70
Tumor immunity produced by the intradermal inoculation of living tumor cells and
living mycobacterium bovis (strain BCG)
B. Zbar and others. bibliog il Science 170:
1217-18 D 11 '70

TUMOR inhibitors. See Growth inhibiting substances

TUMOR viruses
Cancer viruses in primates. R. Kinard. bibliog Science 169:828-31 Ag 28 '70
Feline leukemia and sarcoma viruses: susceptibility of human cells to infection.
P. S. Sarma and others. bibliog il Science
168:1098-100 My 29 '70
Friendly virus; injections of Shope papilloma
virus to aid arginemia victims. Newsweek
76:88 S 28 '70
Immune virolysis: effect of antibody and
complement on C-type RNA virus. S.
Oroszlan and R. V. Gilden. bibliog il Sci-
ence 168:1478-80 Je 19 '70
Murine sarcoma virus: the question of defectiveness. R. Parkman and others. bib-
liog il Science 168:387-9 Ap 17 '70
New clues in the virus-cancer mystery. C. R.
Goodheart and B. Goodheart. il Todays
Health 48:32-5 Je '70

ST-feline fibrosarcoma virus: induction of
tumors in marmoset monkeys. F. Deinhardt
and others. bibliog il Science 167:881 F 6 '70
Susceptibility to an avian leukosis-sarcoma
virus: close association with an erythrocyte
isoantigen. L. B. Crittenden and others.
bibliog il Science 169:1324-5 S 25 '70
Teminism on the go. il Sci N 98:243-4 S 19 '70
Two way street for genetics; RNA-to-DNA
inversion. Sci N 98:54 Jl 25 '70
Upstart RNA. Sci Am 223:82 S '70
Whole virus from a human tumor. il Sci N
97:611-12 Je 27 '70
See also
Adenoviruses

Conferences
Cross-reactions of oncogenic viruses. L. R.
Sibal and M. A. Fink. Science 167:309+ Ja
16 '70

TUMORS
Bladder tumorigenesis. D. R. Stoltz and I.
K. Barker. bibliog Science 168:1121-2 My
29 '70
Bladder tumors in rats fed cyclohexylamine
or high doses of a mixture of cyclamate
and saccharin. J. M. Price and others. bibliog il Science 167:1131-2 F 20 '70
L-Glutamic acid decarboxylase: a new type
in glial cells and human brain gliomas. B.
Haber and others. bibliog il Science 168:
598-9 My 1 '70
Glycine inhibition of asparaginase. W. L.
Ryan and H. C. Sornson. bibliog il Science
167:1512-13 Mr 13 '70
Histamine production by transplantable argyrophilic gastric carcinoid of praomys
(mastomys) natalensis. S. Hosoda and others. bibliog il Science 170:454-5 O 23 '70
Strain C3H-A^vfB mice: ninety percent incidence of mammary tumors transmitted by
either parent. G. Vlahakis and others. bib-
liog il Science 170:185-7 O 9 '70
Tumor immunity produced by the intradermal inoculation of living tumor cells and
living mycobacterium bovis (strain BCG)
B. Zbar and others. bibliog il Science 170:
1217-18 D 11 '70
Tumors in children. L. W. Sauer. PTA Mag
65:27-8 N '70
Uterine tumors; ed. by E. Edelson. J. J.
Mikuta. Redbook 135:10+ Jl '70
See also
Angiokeratoma
Sarcoma

TUMORS, Plant
Lysopine and octopine promote crown-gall
tumor growth in vivo. J. A. Lippincott and
B. B. Lippincott. bibliog il Science 170:
176-7 O 9 '70

TUNA fish
Tainted tuna. Newsweek 76:42 D 28 '70
See also
Inter-American tropical tuna commission

TUNA fishing
But at first he did succeed; Richard Hausk-
necht's record tuna at Montauk. D. Levin.
il Sports Illus 33:82-3+ S 21 '70
Trail of the giant tuna; Notre Dame Bay,
Newfoundland. J. Brooks. il Outdoor Life
145:68-71+ Je '70
See also
Albacore fishing

TUNDRA biome program. See International biological program

TUNDRAS
Tundra biome program. J. Brown. il Science
167:1278 F 27 '70

TUNE-up meters. See Electric meters

TUNE-up-tapes. See Tape recordings

TUNE ups, Automobile. See Automobile engines—Maintenance and repair

TUNGSTEN
Refractory oxide-metal composites: scanning
electron microscopy and X-ray diffraction
of uranium dioxide-tungsten. R. J. Gerdes
and others. il Science 167:979-80 F 13 '70

TUNGSTEN carbide
Super metal's tough new job; tire studs. il
Bsns W p76 My 16 '70

TUNING
See also
Musical pitch

TUNING (radio) See Radio receivers—Tuning

TUNING instruments and apparatus
Electronic strobotuner. F. Maynard. il Electr
World 83:74-7 Mr '70

TUNISIA
See also
Architecture, Domestic—Tunisia
Peasantry—Tunisia
Trials—Tunisia

TUNISIA—*Continued*

Description and travel
To Tunisia. F. Koltun. il Mlle 71:46-9 Jl '70

Politics and government
L'affaire Ben Salah. il por Newsweek 75:45+ My 4 '70

TUNISIAN house decoration. See House decoration, Tunisian

TUNLEY, Roul
Environment crusade: your vital new cause. il Seventeen 29:158+ F '70
He brought a stream back to life. il por Read Digest 97:19-22+ Jl '70

TUNNEL effect. See Tunneling (physics)

TUNNELING (physics)
How Josephson discovered his effect; adaptation of address, September 1970. P. W. Anderson. bibliog il por Phys Today 23: 23-5+ N '70

TUNNELS and tunneling
Traffic control in a Dutch tunnel; Coen tunnel. Amsterdam. il Am City 85:106 F '70
Tunneling solves tough sewer-construction problem; Little Rock, Ark. T. W. Clapham. il Am City 85:105+ F '70

TUNNEY, John Varick
How smart do you want your child to be? McCalls 98:62+ O '70

about
California's John Tunney. il por Time 96: 20-1 N 16 '70 *
Great Tunney-Brown fight. D. Neff. il por Time 95:15 Je 15 '70 *

TUNNEY, Kieran
Open letter to Dame Margot Fonteyn. il Harp Baz 103:162-3 F '70

TUOMI, Kaarlo
Schooling of a Soviet spy; excerpts from KGB. J. Barron. il por Read Digest 96: 225-8+ Ap '70 (to be cont) *

TUPAMAROS. See Guerrillas—Uruguay

TUPPER, Barbara
Wig and I. il Farm J 94:80 Mr '70

TURANDOT; opera. See Puccini, G.

TURBINES
See also
Gas turbines, Aircraft
Steam turbines

TURBOCHARGERS. See Superchargers

TURBOCHARGERS for automobiles. See Automobile engines—Superchargers

TURBOJETS. See Gas turbines, Aircraft

TURBOTRAIN. See Railroads—Passenger service—High speed trains

TURBULENCE
Negative viscosity. V. P. Starr and N. E. Gaut. il Sci Am 223:72-8+ bibliog(p 136) Jl '70
Turbulence and swimming animals. il Sea Front 16:374-6 N '70
See also
Atmospheric turbulence

TURCO, Lewis
Mary Moody Emerson R.I.P; poem. New Repub 162:26 Ap 18 '70

TURCOTTE, Helen
Discover the Cayman Islands. il Travel 134: 44-9+ Jl '70

TURE, Norman B.
Rate structure; address, December 2, 1969. Vital Speeches 36:203-7 Ja 15 '70

TURECK, Rosalyn
First lady of Bach. H. Saal. por Newsweek 75:95+ Ap 20 '70 *

TUREENS
In the service of soup: a great collection; Campbell collection. E. Gaines. il Antiques 97:109-18 Ja '70
Silver tureens in the Campbell museum collection; excerpts from the catalogue. K. C. Buhler. il Antiques 97:904-9 Je '70

TUREKIAN, Karl K. and Kharkar, D. P.
Neutron activation analysis of milligram quantities of lunar rocks and soils. bibliog il Science 167:507-9 Ja 30 '70

TURF. See Lawns

TURF, Artificial
Artificial turfs. Ed Digest 35:42-3 F '70
Farewell to grass. il Newsweek 75:73 My 11 '70
Surface case of bugs in the rugs; Astro-turf surface in baseball. P. Carry. il Sports Illus 33:40-2+ S 14 '70

TURILLI, Rudy
Jesse James legend. P. Strickler. il pors Life 68:72 Je 12 '70 *

TURIN auto show. See Automobiles—Exhibitions

TURKEVICH, Anthony L. and others
Alpha radioactivity of the lunar surface at the landing sites of Surveyors 5, 6, and 7. bibliog il Science 167:1722-4 Mr 27 '70
—See Heydegger, H. R. jt. auth.

TURKEVICH, John, and Kim, Gwan
Palladium: preparation and catalytic properties of particles of uniform size. bibliog il Science 169:873-9 Ag 28 '70

TURKEY
See also
Americans in Turkey
Black Sea
Bridges—Turkey
Cappadocia
United Nations—Turkey

Antiquities
Archeologist; interview. I. C. Love. New Yorker 46:28-31 Mr 28 '70
Early farming village in Turkey; Çayönü Tepesi. H. Cambel and R. J. Braidwood. il Sci Am 222:51-6 Mr '70
See also
Sardis

Army
Military and politics in Turkey, 1960-64: a socio-cultural analysis of a revolution. K. H. Karpat. bibliog f Am Hist R 75:1654-83 O '70

Description and travel
Turkey; with some tips for touring Turkey by N. Liber. il Life 68:46-54 Ap 17 '70

History
Evolution of the Ottoman seaborne empire in the age of the oceanic discoveries, 1453-1525. A. C. Hess. bibliog f il Am Hist R 75: 1892-919 D '70

Politics and government
Military and politics in Turkey, 1960-64: a socio-cultural analysis of a revolution. K. H. Karpat. bibliog f Am Hist R 75:1654-83 O '70
World around us. L. Hansen. Chr Cent 87: 739-41 Je 10 '70; Reply. F. A. Stone. 87:1131 S 23 '70

Religious institutions and affairs
See also
Orthodox Eastern church in Turkey

Riots
Never mind the noise. il Time 96:20-1 Jl 27 '70

TURKEY as food. See Cookery—Poultry

TURKEY calling. See Bird calling

TURKEY carving. See Carving (meat, etc)

TURKEY hunting
Do you really want to be a turkey shooter? C. Elliott. il por Outdoor Life 145:72-5+ Mr '70
Hunting our all-American bird. L. Merovka. il Field & S 74:74-5+ Mr '70
Lord of the Cypress. J. H. Halliburton. il Outdoor Life 146:77-80+ N '70
Ways of the wild gobbler. A. Rutledge. il Field & S 75:84-6+ Je '70

TURKEYS
Marketing
Turkey carves a year-round market. il Bsns W p30 N 21 '70

TURKEYS, Wild
Wild turkey comeback. il Nat Wildlife 8: 10-11 O '70
See also
Turkey hunting

TURKISH cookery. See Cookery, Turkish

TURKS in the United States
U.N. veteran; interview. N. Eren. New Yorker 45:30-1 F 14 '70

TURN of the screw; opera. See Britten, B.

TURNBULL, James
Confrontation: battle over our forests. House B 112:54+ Jl '70

TURNER, Arthur Campbell
Independent Rhodesia. bibliog f Cur Hist 58: 129-34+ Mr '70

TURNER, Curtis
Roundy-round corner. S. Kelly. il Hot Rod 23:87 D '70 *

TURNER, Daniel S. See McCaffery, J. F. jt. auth.

TURNER, Grenville
Argon-40/argon-39 dating of lunar rock samples. bibliog il Science 167:466-8 Ja 30 '70

TURNER, Harold E.
Improved in-service: a challenge for supervisors. Clear House 45:116-19 O '70

TURNER, Ike
Ike & Tina Turner: they're too much! E. Dunbar. il pors Look 34:62-4 S 8 '70 *
TURNER, Jack
Wilderness family that helped save the swans. D. Connelly. il por Life 68:56 Ap 10 '70 *
TURNER, Mary C.
Diverse book market of Latin America. Pub W 198:pt2 170-1 S 21 '70
TURNER, Sheila
Dean who? il por Sr Schol 96:12+ Ap 6 '70
How to create an international scandal in Ulan Bator. il Sr Schol 95:18-19+ N 17 '69
Stopover in Heisinki. il Schol Teach Sec Teach Sup p22-3 Mr 9 '70
West made a big mistake... Sr Schol 95:20 N 17 '69
TURNER, Steven
Measure of dust; story. McCalls 97:82-3 Je '70
TURNER, Ted
Eagle on a wild, wet flight. H. D. Whall. il por Sports Illus 32:16-19 Mr 16 '70 *
TURNER, Tina
Ike & Tina Turner: they're too much! E. Dunbar. il pors Look 34:62-4 S 8 '70 *
Tina turns on. il pors Life 69:57-61 D 18 '70 *
TURNER, William W.
DePugh and the Minutemen: wonderland of the mind. pors Ramp Mag 8:10+ Je '70
TURNING
How to get started in wood turning. R. J. De Cristoforo. il Pop Sci 197:88-90+ D '70
Turning bowls on a table saw. R. J. De Cristoforo. il Pop Sci 197:116-18 Jl '70
TURNIPS
Turnips, colorful root of good eating. R. Tirrell. il Org Gard & Farm 17:70-2 Jl '70
TURNPIKE radio. See Radio in traffic control
TURNPIKE restaurants. See Restaurants—United States
TURNTABLES
   See also
Phonograph—Turntables
TURNTABLES, Automatic. See Phonograph—Record changers
TURTLE racing
You can enter and race your own turtle. Or you can just watch. il Sunset 145:54-5 Ag '70
TURTLES
Caretta caretta caretta: rookery rehabilitation project on Florida's Sanibel and Captiva islands. E. N. Layne. il Am Heritage 21:113-14 F '70
Green sea turtles in peril. A. Carr. il Nat Parks & Con Mag 44:19-24 Ap '70
Snapping turtle. P. M. Kelsey. il Cons 25:36 D '70
Turtles guard our garden. B. Gilford. il Org Gard & Farm 17:92-3 S '70
TURTLETAUB and the foul distemper; story. See Angell, R.
TUSCANY, William G.
Ceramic tubular trimmer capacitors. por Electr World 83:42-4 Ap '70
TUSSING, Annette
Last log drive. il Am For 76:16-19 Jl '70
TUTOR in the village; story. See Singer, I. B.
TUTORS and tutoring
Hey! I'm learning too! student tutoring. L. Blackwood. il Schol Teach Sec Teach Sup p6-8 N 3 '69
Reading and writing can be fun for the underachiever! high school students as tutors with culturally deprived elementary school students. J. P. Anderson. Engl J 59:1119-21+ N '70
Reading pays; Youth-tutoring-youth programs. M. Bonn. il Am Ed 6:26 O '70
Tutoring by students. H. A. Thelen. Ed Digest 35:17-20 F '70
TUTTLE, Helen Welch
Price indexes for 1970: U.S. periodicals. il Library J 95:2427 Jl '70
TUTTLE, Lyle
Tattoo renaissance. por Time 96:58 D 21 '70 *
TVARDOVSKII, Aleksandr Trifonovich
Truth that hurt. por Time 95:41 Mr 2 '70 *
Tvardovsky's everyman. D. Levin. Nation 211:248-9 S 21 '70 *
Writers' block. il pors Newsweek 75:38+ Mr 2 '70 *
TWAIN, Mark, pseud. See Clemens, S. L.
TWEEDY, B. G. and others
Metobromuron: acetylation of the aniline moiety as a detoxification mechanism Science 168:482-3 Ap 24 '70
TWELVE-mile limit. See Territorial waters
TWENTIETH century
   See also
Nineteen hundred and forties

TWENTIETH century-Fox film corporation
Fathers and sons. il por Newsweek 77:66+ Ja 11 '71
M*A*S*H*E*D; R. Zanuck named president. il por Time 97:62 Ja 11 '71
Zanuck: last of the red hot star-makers; interview, ed. by H. Ehrlich. il por Look 34:69-71 N 3 '70
TWIN bed bridge; story. See Hecht, F. M.
TWIN Cities metropolitan council
Where regional planners call the shots. il Bsns W p72+ F 21 '70
TWIN-lens cameras
Camera collector. J. Schneider. il Mod Phot 34:120+ O '70
Readers' report: Rolleiflex. il Mod Phot 34:104-5+ O '70
TWIN vision publishing company. See Blind, Books for the
TWO; story. See Blyth, M.
TWO by two; musical comedy. See Musical comedies, revues, etc.—Criticisms, plots, etc.
TWO days in September; story. See Dickey, J.
TWO dreams; story. See Waldron, E.
2,4-D. See Herbicides
2,4,5-T. See Herbicides
TWO in love; story. See Buck, P. S.
TWO party system. See Party government; Political parties—United States
TWO thousand (year)
Church in the year 2000; Commonweal paper; symposium; discussion. Commonweal 91:287+, 443+ N 28 '69, Ja 23 '70
Religion in the year 2000, by A. M. Greeley. Review
   Cath World 210:278-9 Mr '70. D. G. O'Shea
Struggle for survival; address, February 18, 1970. L. Cherne. Vital Speeches 36:407-11 Ap 15 '70
Year 2000: the future planners; address, November 8, 1969. H. D. Gideonse. bibliog f Vital Speeches 36:530-6 Je 15 '70
TWO thousand and forty-five (year)
Cheers and jeers; letters to the sportsmen of 2045. Field & S 75:8+ Je '70
TWO very special people; story. See Cave, H.
TWO who deserved each other; story. See Elliston, V.
TWO wives; story. See Hodge, J. A.
TWO-year colleges. See Junior colleges
TYDINGS, Joseph Davies
Excerpt from Senate debate, March 11, 1970. Cong Digest 49:144+ My '70
   about
Defying the gun lobby. Nation 211:262 S 28 '70 *
Maryland microcosm. S. Alsop. Newsweek 76:126 O 19 '70 *
Tydings of no joy. A. Campbell. New Repub 162:10 Je 27 '70 *
What the senator didn't disclose. W. Lambert. pors Life 69:26-9 Ag 28 '70 *
TYLER, Edward T.
Pill is safe; ed. by R. H. Berg. il Look 34:65-6 Je 30 '70
TYLER, Kenneth
Revival of prints. R. Hughes. il Time 97:56-7 Ja 18 '71 *
TYLER, Phil
Watercolor page; with biographical sketch. il por Am Artist 34:30-1+ Je '70
TYLER, Ralph W.
National assessment: a history and sociology; excerpt from New models for American education; ed. by J. Guthrie. bibliog Sch & Soc 98:471-7 D '70
TYMPANIC membrane
New hope for hearing; eardrum homografts. il Time 96:99 O 26 '70
TYNAN, Kathleen
Astonishing history of Moura Budberg. il por Vogue 156:162-3+ O 1 '70
Death in Venice: at the end of the path of beauty lies Eros. Vogue 156:165+ D '70
TYNAN, Kenneth
Profiles; Valencia's spring and summer ferias. il New Yorker 46:33-8+ Jl 25 '70
TYPE and typefounding
Oldrich Menhart, outstanding Czech type designer; excerpts from address. P. Standard. il por Pub W 197:52-4 Ja 12 '70
Profiles; G. Mardersteig, printer of Officina Bodoni and Stamperia Valdonega editions in Verona, Italy. W. Sargeant. por New Yorker 46:32-6+ Jl 11 '70
TYPESETTING
   See also
Phototypesetting
TYPESETTING machines
   See also
Computers—Printing use

TYPEWRITER correction tape. See Typewriter supplies

TYPEWRITER supplies
Typewriter correction tape. il Consumer Bul 53:27 F '70

TYPEWRITERS
Portable electric typewriters. il Consumer Rep 34:371-8 D '69
See also
SCM corporation

TYPHOID carriers. See Carriers of infection

TYPHOONS
See also
Cyclones

TYPOGRAPHICAL union, International. See International typographical union

TYRANNY. See Dictatorship

TYRMAND, Leopold
Renections. New Yorker 46:85-96 F 28 '70
Revolutionaries: European vs. American. il N Y Times Mag p24-5+ F 15; 12+ Mr 8 '70

about
Disillusioned wisdom. A. Hartley. Commentary 50:67-9 Ag '70 *
Home thoughts from abroad. por Time 95: 100+ Je 15 '70 *

TYROSINE aminotransferase. See Transferases

TYROSINE transaminase. See Transaminases

TYRRELL, Bernard J.
Phenomenon of Bernard Lonergan. America 122:298-300 Mr 21 '70

TYRRELL, D. A. J.
Living with a runny nose; interview. il Sci Digest 68:56-60 S '70

TYSON, Brady
Encounter in Recife. il pors Chr Cent 87:720-2 Je 10 '70

TYSON, Robert C.
Let's keep our dual system; address, March 3, 1970. Vital Speeches 36:414-16 Ap 15 '70

TYTUS, John Butler
Spare hand who went beyond the dream of Leonardo da Vinci. B. C. Huselton. il pors Nations Bsns 58:50-1 Ja '70

TZION, Ben, pseud.
On the Jewish question in the Soviet Union. il N Y Times Mag p24-5+ My 3 '70

U

U-2 incident, 1960
Francis Gary Powers tells his story; excerpt from Operation overflight. F. G. Powers. il por N Y Times Mag p36-7+ Ap 19 '70

U-8 incident. See Airspace (international law)

UAW. See United automobile, aerospace and agricultural implement workers of America

UCLA. See California. University—Los Angeles campus

UCM. See University Christian movement

UDC. See New York (state)—Urban development corporation

UFO (unidentified flying object) See Flying saucers

UFO; story. See Elizalde, F. de

UFPC. See United federation of postal clerks

UFWOC. See American federation of labor and Congress of industrial organizations—United farm workers organizing committee

UJT (unijunction transistor) See Transistors

ULMS (undersea long-range missile system) See Guided missiles—Launching from submarine boats

UMBA. See United mortgage bankers of America

UMC industries, Inc.
When a mouse tries to swallow an elephant. il Forbes 105:42+ Mr 1 '70

UMTA. See United States—Urban mass transportation administration

UMW. See United mine workers of America

UN. See United Nations

UNAF. See Universities national anti-war fund

UNCA. See United Nations correspondents association

UNCITRAL. See United Nations—Commission on international trade law

UNCTAD. See United Nations conference on trade and development

UNDP. See United Nations—Development program

UNESCO. See Unesco

UNICEF. See United Nations children's fund

UNIDO. See United Nations industrial development organization

UNRWA. See United Nations relief and works agency for Palestine refugees in the Near East

UNV. See United Nations volunteer corps (proposed)

UPS. See United parcel service

URPE. See Union for radical political economics

USAC midget race. See Midget automobile racing

USCC. See United States Catholic conference

USDA. See United States—Agriculture, Department of; United States duffers' association

USES. See United States—Employment service

USIA. See United States—Information agency

USIF, Real estate
Adverse tide hits offshore funds. Bsns W p50 O 17 '70
Bonn makes it rough for Gramco. Bsns W p84 O 10 '70
Gramco: the second domino. por Time 96: 79-80 O 19 '70
Gramco's plunge. Newsweek 76:96-7 O 19 '70
Is the game up at Gramco? with editorial comment. J. Ross-Skinner and A. Hershman. il por Duns 96:3, 28-31+ S '70; Reply with rejoinder. R. Garcia-Navarro. 96:15-16 O '70

USIS. See United States—Information service

USOE. See United States—Education, Office of

USSR (Union of Soviet Socialist Republics) See Russia

USW. See United steelworkers of America

UUA. See Unitarian universalist association

UDAIPUR, India

Hotels, restaurants, etc.
Lake Palace in Udaipur must be Asia's most exotic hotel. il Holiday 47:42-3 F '70

UDALAGAMA, D. B.
Cloud-damsels of Sigiriya rescued. il Art N 69:32-3+ Sum '70

UDALL, Morris King
Bridging the generation gap. New Repub 163: 11-13 N 28 '70

UDALL, Stewart Lee
Mining law of 1872 must be scrapped. il Nat Wildlife 8:9-11 Je '70
Seven things you can do to make America beautiful. House & Gard 137:55+ Je '70

about
Rise of American esthetic conservation. D. H. Strong. il pors Nat Parks 44:4-9 F '70 *

UDDIN, Kazi Mobin-. See Mobin-Uddin, K.

UDENFRIEND, Sidney
Nobel prize: three share 1970 award for medical research. pors Science 170:422-3 O 23 '70

UDIN, Anne
Night Higbee's put out the red carpet. il por Pub W 197:40-1 Mr 16 '70 *

UELSMANN, Jerry N.
Wynn Bullock. il Mod Phot 34:89+ My '70

UGENT, Donald
Potato. bibliog il Science 170:1161-6 D 11 '70

UGGAMS, Leslie
Leslie Uggams; interview, ed. by K. Sohigian. il pors House B 112:68-9+ F '70

UHLENHAUT, Rudolf
Uhlenhaut. L. W. Steinwedel. il por Motor T 22:54-6+ Ap '70 *

UHLIG, Hans G.
Big recreation needs. il Am City 85:59 D '70

UHSE, Beate
Riding the sex wave. Newsweek 75:108 Ap 20 '70 *

UIHLEIN, Robert August, 1916-
Schlitz brewing: always an Avis, never a Hertz? il por Forbes 105:25 Ap 15 '70 *
That Milwaukee slogan stems from Chicago's fire. il por Nations Bsns 58:104-5 Ja '70

UKRAINE
See also
Kiev, Russia

ULAM, Adam B.
Lenin: his legacy. For Affairs 48:460-70 Ap '70

ULBRICH, Mabel C.
Chemical individuality of lunar, meteoritic, and terrestrial silicate rocks. bibliog il Science 168:1375-6 Je 12 '70

ULBRICHT, Walter
Foxy Red Riding Hood. Newsweek 75:40 F 2 '70
Report on the other Germany. B. van Voorst. il por Newsweek 76:50-2 D 21 '70 *

ULCERS
See also
Peptic ulcers
ULLENSVANG, Leon P.
Food consumption patterns in the seventies;
address, November 3-7, 1969. Vital Speeches
36:240-6 F 1 '70
ULLIAN, Robert
Motherhood; story. Esquire 74:194-5 D '70
ULLMAN, Albert Conrad
Excerpt from debate, April 15, 1970. Cong Di-
gest 49:181+ Je '70
ULLMAN, Leslie
Picaro; poem. Mlle 71:196 Ag '70
ULLRICK, William C. See Leyton, R. A. jt.
auth.
ULMER, Melville J.
Depression ahead? New Repub 163:14-15 Jl 4
'70
Economic slowdown. New Repub 162:11-12 F
28 '70
How unfair are our taxes? il New Repub
163:17-19 N 7; 34 D 5 '70
Is jawboning a joke? New Repub 162:21-3
My 30 '70
Nixon's turnabout. New Repub 163:10-11 Ag
15 '70
Stabilizing the economy. il New Repub 162:
13-16 Ja 31; 163:31-2 S 26 '70
Why economists flunk out. New Repub 163:
6-7 S 19; 34 O 10 '70
ULRICH, Heinz
How to cope with the new tax forms. il Mech
Illus 66:48-9+ Ap '70
ULRICK, C. J.
Amplified zener. il Electr World 84:42+ S '70
ULSTER
See also
Northern Ireland
ULTIMATE friend; story. See Gerber, M. J.
ULTRAMICROFICHE. See Microforms
ULTRAMINIATURE cameras. See Cameras
ULTRASONIC burglar alarms. See Burglar
alarms
ULTRASONIC cleaning
New household helper you can't hear. il
Mech Illus 66:98-9 Ja '70
Put sound waves to work in your shop. P.
Wahl. il Pop Sci 196:94-5 Mr '70
ULTRASONIC waves

Dental use
Dental enamel: detection of surface changes
by ultrasound. S. Lees and others. bibliog
il Science 169:1314-16 S 25 '70

Medical use
Another space research bonus. Space World
G-6-78:45 Je '70
ULTRASONICS
Ultrasonics: the silent sound with see-
through eyes for science. A. S. Freese. il
Sci Digest 67:42-51 Mr '70
ULTRAVIOLET rays
Ultraviolet world of insects. il Sci Digest
67:84-5 Mr '70

Physiological effects
Defect in DNA synthesis in skin of patients
with xeroderma pigmentosum demonstrated
in vivo. J. H. Epstein and others. bibliog il
Science 168:1477-8 Je 19 '70
Sunlight ultraviolet and bacterial DNA base
ratios. C. E. Singer and B. N. Ames. bibliog il Science 170:822-6 N 20 '70
ULTRAVIOLET spectrometers. See Spectro-
meters
UMAG, Yugoslavia
Ulterior motive for Umag; Benvenuti-
Bethea world middle-weight champion-
ship. D. J. Hamblin. il por Sports Illus 32:
14-15 Je 1 '70
UMATILLA COUNTY, Ore.
On the last frontier with VX and GB; opin-
ions of people on government's plan to
store nerve gas. J. Didion. il Life 68:22 F
20 '70
UMBECK, Sharvy Greiner
Better management in higher education; ad-
dress, July 25, 1970. Vital Speeches 37:102-
5 D 1 '70
UMBELLULA. See Sea pens
UMBRELLA; story. See O'Sullivan, M.
UMBRELLA pine. See Pine
UMBRELLAS
Shades of summer. il Redbook 135:99-101 Je
'70
UMLAUF, Charles
Charles Umlauf, sculptor of the living form.
M. Malstrom. il por Am Artist 69:52-9+ S
'70 *

UMPIRES (sports)
Boss of the ball park; baseball umpires. B.
Surface. il Read Digest 97:17-25 Ag '70
He whistles while he works; NFL referees. W.
F. Reed. il pors Sports Illus 33:22-7 Ag 10
'70
UMPIRING (baseball) See Sports officiating
UMPIRING (sports) See Sports officiating
UN-AMERICAN activities committee. See
United States—Congress—House—Internal
security, Committee on
UNAUTHORIZED phonograph records. See
Phonograph records—Recording—Unauthor-
ized recording
UNAUTHORIZED reprints. See Copyright—Un-
authorized reprints
UNAUTHORIZED tape recordings. See Mag-
netic recorders and recordings—Unauthor-
ized recording
UNCONSCIOUSNESS. See Coma; Subconscious-
ness
UNDERACHIEVERS
Myth of underachievement. T. Gnagey. Ed
Digest 35:49-52 Mr '70
Project mobilization; program for education-
ally disadvantaged students. D. L. Carl.
Clear House 44:519-22 My '70
Reading and writing can be fun for the un-
derachiever! J. P. Anderson. Engl J 59:
1119-21+ N '70
Turning on bright underachievers; Wellesley
senior high school, Mass. W. J. Freeman
and A. C. Craig. Todays Ed 59:52-3 F '70
UNDERCOVER agents. See Police—United
States; Spies
UNDERDEVELOPED areas
Development fashions. M. Friedman. News-
week 76:82 D 21 '70
Interdependence of the world, U.S, and local
community; address, October 30 ,1970. J.
A. Hannah. Dept State Bul 63:672-7 N 30
'70
Kaleidoscope of the third world. il UNESCO
Courier 23:20-4 F '70
People versus food; excerpt from address. R.
R. R. Brooks. Sat R 53:10-14+ S 5 '70
Poor get poorer. Trans-Action 7:15 My '70
Third world in history. D. Ribeiro. Trans-
Action 7:6+ N '69

Agriculture
Green revolution can change the world. R.
Rodale. il Org Gard & Farm 17:57-63 S '70
Green revolution yields bitter fruit. Bsns W
p84 N 21 '70
Let's learn from the green revolution. R.
Rodale. il Org Gard & Farm 17:57-62 O '70

Atomic power
Super-arms for developing countries. il
UNESCO Courier 23:12-14 N '70

Birth control
Birth control for economic development? C. W.
F. Bock. Science 168:607-8 My 1 '70
Why the population bomb is a Rockefeller
baby. S. Weissman. il Ramp Mag 8:42-7
My '70
World development needs; aid to underdevel-
oped countries; address, September 21, 1970.
R. S. McNamara. Vital Speeches 37:7-14 O
15 '70

Food supply
People versus food; excerpt from address.
R. R. R. Brooks. Sat R 53:10-14+ S 5 '70

Politics
White left in the mother country. R. Ruether.
il Commonweal 93:142-5 N 6 '70; Discussion.
93:263, 287, 363+ D 4-11 '70, Ja 15 '71
UNDERGRADUATES. See College students
UNDERGROUND drainage. See Drainage
UNDERGROUND films. See Moving pictures,
Experimental
UNDERGROUND irrigation. See Irrigation,
Underground
UNDERGROUND literature
European literary scene; publication of The
monk, by Russia's Yevgenii Shiffers. R.
J. Clements. Sat R 53:33 My 2 '70
Samizdat is Russia's underground press. A.
Parry. il N Y Times Mag p64-5+ Mr 15 '70
UNDERGROUND power transmission. See Elec-
tric lines—Underground lines
UNDERGROUND press. See Newspapers—
United States; Underground literature
UNDERGROUND press, Experimental

France
See Newspapers—France

UNDERGROUND press, Student. See College and school journalism

UNDERGROUND radio. See Radio communication, Underground

UNDERGROUND television. See Television, Experimental

UNDERGROUND water. See Water, Underground

UNDERPRIVILEGED children. See Socially handicapped children

UNDERSEA long-range missile system. See Guided missiles—Launching from submarine boats

UNDERSEA mining. See Ocean mining

UNDERSEA mountains. See Ocean bottom

UNDERSEA research vehicles. See Submarine research vehicles

UNDERTAKERS and undertaking
Merchants of death. il Forbes 106:59 N 15 '70

UNDERWATER archeology. See Archeology, Submarine

UNDERWATER blinds. See Duck blinds

UNDERWATER breathing apparatus. See Diving apparatus

UNDERWATER drilling
Brines and interstitial brackish water in drill cores from the deep Gulf of Mexico. F. T. Manheim and F. L. Sayles. bibliog il Science 170:57-61 O 2 '70
Challenger sails on. il Sci N 98:159 Ag 22 '70
Deep sea drilling: a giant step in geological research. A. L. Hammond. il Science 170: 520-1 O 30 '70
Deep sea drilling in the South Atlantic. A. E. Maxwell and others. bibliog il Science 168: 1047-59 My 29 '70
Finding a hole in the bottom of the sea; research vessel Glomar Challenger using scanning sonar system. M. Gruber. il Sea Front 16:309-11 S '70
Geological history of the western North Pacific. A. G. Fischer and others. bibliog il Science 168:1210-14 Je 5 '70
Going back for more. il Sci N 97:597 Je 20 '70
Jigsaw of the primeval world; Glomar Challenger's findings. il Life 68:60-3 Ja 30 '70
Old and mobile; Glomar Challenger's eleventh voyage. Sci N 97:547-8 Je 6 '70
Probing the Atlantic's past. il Sci N 98:460 D 19 '70
Two years behind the drill; Glomar Challenger. Sci Am 223:45-6 Ag '70

UNDERWATER exploration
This submarine for hire; Aluminaut. R. Gannon. il Pop Sci 196:49-51+ Ap '70

UNDERWATER holography. See Holography

UNDERWATER laboratories
Come dive with me to Tektite II. S. Carpenter. il Pop Sci 197:54-5+ O '70
Glass submarines; future manned exploration submersibles. D. Groves. il Sea Front 16:286-90 S '70
NEMO: observation post 100 fathoms under the sea. P. Wahl. il Pop Sci 197:66 S '70
Nest of naiads; female scientists live undersea for project Tektite. il Life 69:30-1 Jl 17 '70
Revisiting the ocean floor; Tektite II. il Bsns W p74 Mr 14 '70
Room at the bottom; Tektite project. il Newsweek 76:66-7 Jl 13 '70
Scientific emphasis; Tektite II. Sci N 97:240 Mr 7 '70
Seeking oneness with the undersea world; Tektite 2. il Sci N 98:283-4 O 3 '70
Snug house on the ocean floor. S. M. Spencer. il Read Digest 96:116-20 Ja '70
Subsurface science; Tektite II project. Sci N 98:114-15 Ag 8 '70
Tektite: a blueprint for cooperative undersea scientific programs. E. Ray and R. M. Cohen. il Bul Atom Sci 26:35-40 F '70; Discussion. 26:47-8 O '70
Tektite 1, man-in-the-sea project; marine science program. H. E. Clifton and others. bibliog il Science 168:659-63 My 8 '70; Discussion. 169:1264-5 S 25 '70
Tektite: unique observations of men under stress. R. H. Gilluly. il Sci N 98:400-1 N 21 '70

UNDERWATER photography. See Photography, Submarine

UNDERWATER research. See Oceanographic research

UNDERWATER sound systems. See Hydrophones

UNDERWATER swimming. See Skin diving

UNDERWATER tools. See Tools

UNDERWATER treasure. See Treasure trove

UNDERWATER vehicles. See Submarine vehicles

UNDERWEAR
Men's knit briefs. Consumer Rep 35:434-5 Jl '70
See also
Brassieres

UNDERWOOD, Bob
Redwing black bass. il por Outdoor Life 146: 48-9+ Jl '70

UNDERWOOD, Herbert, and Menaker, Michael
Extraretinal light perception: entrainment of the biological clock controlling lizard locomotor activity. bibliog il Science 170:190-3 O 9 '70
Photoperiodically significant photoreception in sparrows: is the retina involved? bibliog il Science 167:298-301; 169:893 Ja 16, Ag 28 '70

UNDERWOOD, John
Brief search for America. il Sports Illus 32: 64-8+ My 4 '70
Mad, mad punter of Louisville. il pors Sports Illus 33:36-41 N 9 '70
(ed) See Lusteg, B. Coach wants to see you

UNDERWRITERS' laboratories, inc.
Competent product testing helps eliminate hazards. Consumer Bul 53:23-4 N '70

UNEMPLOYMENT
Foreign labor briefs. See issues of Monthly labor review
Rising spiral of unemployment. il UNESCO Courier 23:28-30 F '70
See also
Employment
Employment stabilization

Relief measures
Quacking at unemployment. P. S. Templin. America 123:499-500 D 5 '70
See also
Federal art project
Hard-core unemployed

Statistics
America's less fortunate: the long-duration unemployed; with tables. E. J. O'Boyle. Mo Labor R 93:35-43 Ap '70
Employment and unemployment development in 1969; with tables. P. O. Flaim and P. M. Schwab. bibliog il Mo Labor R 93:40-53 F '70
Unemployment by region and in ten largest states; with tables. P. M. Schwab. bibliog Mo Labor R 93:3-12 Ja '70
Unemployment: going up. il Newsweek 75:59 Mr 2 '70
Unemployment in the United States and seven foreign countries. C. Sorrentino. bibliog f il Mo Labor R 93:12-23 S '70
What the unemployment rate means. il Bsns W p84+ F 14 '70
Working women in urban poverty neighborhoods. H. M. Willacy and H. J. Hilaski. bibliog f il Mo Labor R 93:35-8 Je '70

California
Aerospace: unemployed scientists, engineers have no place to go. J. Walsh. Science 170: 1384-7 D 25 '70
Where technologists are now obsolete. il Bsns W p30 S 26 '70

Europe, Western
World experts prescribe strong medicine for inflation; OECD report. il U S News 69:17-18 D 7 '70

Latin America
Labor ministers launch attack on unemployment. Américas 22:45 Ja '70
Latin America's unemployment problem. I. Beller. bibliog il Mo Labor R 93:3-10 N '70

Massachusetts
Down and out along route 128; scientists and engineers laid off. B. Rice. il N Y Times Mag p28-9+ N 1 '70; Discussion. p48+ N 22 '70

New York (state)
Fired at 49. I. Taves. il pors Look 34:44-7+ D 1 '70

Northern Ireland
Business remains almost as usual. il Bsns W p36 Jl 11 '70
Hard times in Ulster. A. Boyd. Nation 210: 422-3 Ap 13 '70

United States
Aerospace leads jobless increase. Aviation W 92:259-60 Je 22 '70
Agony of the overskilled man. Time 96::84 O 5 '70

UNEMPLOYMENT—United States—*Continued*
Analyzing the length of spells of unemployment; with tables. H. B. Kaitz. Mo Labor R 93:11-20 N '70
As layoffs spread: where job losses are coming. il U S News 68:59-60 F 2 '70
Bigger money flow: will it stop unemployment? il U S News 69:15-17 N 30 '70
Brother, can you spare a job? Time 95:83 Ap 20 '70
Do figures lie? September rate. Newsweek 76:95 O 12 '70
Down and out along route 128; scientists and engineer laid off. B. Rice. il N Y Times Mag p28-9+ N 1 '70
4.6 million jobless. New Repub 163:9 N 14 '70
Getting harder to talk tough. Bsns W p42 F 21 '70
Impact of higher unemployment on major labor force groups. P. M. Ryscavage. il Mo Labor R 93:21-5 Mr '70
Impact on people. il Newsweek 75:75-7+ My 25 '70
Inflation feeds the jobless figure. il Bsns W p26-7 My 30 '70
Job hunters face grimmer prospects. il Bsns W p 19-20 D 12 '70
Job targets with a realistic look. il Bsns W p46-7 D 26 '70
Jobs and jawbone. Time 95:91 Je 15 '70
More cities and towns join the critical list. il Bsns W p26 Je 6; 17 Ag 22 '70
More cities join the critical list. il Bsns W p26 Je 6 '70
More unemployment ahead. il Fortune 81:20+ Mr '70
New face of unemployment. il Time 96:87 N 2 '70
No man can live with the terrible knowledge that he is not needed. E. Liebow. il N Y Times Mag p28-9+ Ap 5 '70
Out of work; conditions in the Pacific Northwest. R. Friedman. Nation 210:421-2 Ap 13 '70
Peace bonanza that went bust; cutbacks of military programs. il Bsns W p66-8 S 5 '70
Political test for policy. il Bsns W p25-6 O 10 '70
Unemployment: going up. il Newsweek 75:59 Mr 2 '70
Wayward trail of the jobless rate. il Bsns W p94+ Je 13 '70
What it is like to be laid off. il Time 95:80 F 16 '70
Where job shortage hits hardest. il U S News 68:34-6 Je 29 '70
Who are the unemployed? il U S News 69:54-7 N 16 '70
With unemployment rising faster than expected. il U S News 68:76-7 Mr 23 '70
Youth unemployment and minimum wages. T. W. Gavett. il Mo Labor R 93:3-12 Mr '70

Washington (state)
Seattle under seige: the troubles of a company town. K. Prager. il Time 97:28-9 Ja 4 '71

UNEMPLOYMENT, Technological
See also
American foundation on automation and employment
Unemployment—United States

UNEMPLOYMENT compensation. See Insurance, Unemployment

UNEMPLOYMENT insurance. See Insurance, Unemployment

UNESCO
Illiteracy, woman's worldwide burden; report. R. L. Tobin. Sat R 53:16 S 5 '70
Introduction to Unesco. il Todays Ed 59:33-49 O '70
New step against discrimination in education. Sch & Soc 98:12 Ja '70
World bank and education. Sch & Soc 98:13-14 Ja '70
See also
International book year, 1972
International centre for theoretical physics, Trieste, Italy
International education year, 1970

Headquarters
Modern art at Unesco's new building. il UNESCO Courier 23:33 Je '70
UNESCO House. See Unesco—Headquarters

UNFAIR to Goliath; revue. See Musical comedies, revues, etc.—Criticisms, plots, etc.

UNGAR, Georges
Of mice and memory. il por Time 97:34 Ja 11 '71 *

UNGEHEUER, Friedel
Czechoslovaks: between hope and fear. il Harper 241:71-7 Ag '70

Return to Frankfurt. il Harper 241:84-90+ Jl '70
Who's afraid of war? Harper 241:28-31 D '70

UNGER, Henry F.
Motorized cover rolls over swimming pool. il Pop Sci 196:98 F '70

UNGER, Joan
Four stars for hospital food? il Todays Health 49:52-4 Ja '71

UNGER, Leonard
Thailand. bibliog il Focus 21:1-12 N '70

UNGER, Sherman Edward
Turnover at the FCC. por Newsweek 76:44-5 Ag 3 '70 *

UNGERER, Miriam
Make mine amino acids. il Life 68:18 My 22 '70

UNGERLEIDER, Leslie G. and Coons, E. E.
Behavioral measure of homosynaptic and heterosynaptic temporal summation in the self-stimulation system of rats. bibliog il Science 169:785-7 Ag 21 '70

UNGERS, Liselotte, and Ungers, O. M.
Nordwest Zentrum. il Arch Forum 133:30-7 O '70

UNGERS, O. M. See Ungers, L. jt. auth.

UNGRADED classes
Away with tradition; multiunit schools in Wisconsin. D. Behrendt. il Am Ed 6:18-22 Ja '70
When teachers do their thing, it's called DS or is it? differentiated staffing. K. Branan. il Schol Teach Jr/Sr High p 10-12+ O 5 '70

UNICELLULAR organisms
See also
Amebas

UNIDENTIFIED flying objects. See Flying saucers

UNIFORM gifts to minors act. See Children—Law

UNIFORM state laws
Transplant donation procedures; report of meeting. R. E. Stevenson and others. Science 168:613-15 My 1 '70

UNIFORMS
Fancy attire for the White House guards. il U S News 68:10 F 9 '70

UNIFORMS, Police
Red, white, blue? U.S. flag either on shoulder patch or pin. Sr Schol 96:15 Mr 9 '70

UNIJUNCTION transistors. See Transistors

UNIMATE. See Machinery, Automatic

UNION annual performance trials. See Automobile engines—Fuel consumption

UNION carbide corporation
Birny Mason of Union carbide; interview. B. Mason, jr. por Nations Bsns 58:60-5 S '70

Linde division
Treating waste in greater haste; Unox process. il Bsns W p 106 N 7 '70

UNION COUNTY, N.J.

Education
Project mobilization; program for educationally disadvantaged students. D. L. Carl. Clear House 44:519-22 My '70

UNION for radical political economics
More than Marxist. M. J. Ulmer. New Repub 163:13-14 D 26 '70

UNION-management cooperation. See Employees representation in management

UNION membership. See Trade unions—Membership

UNION minière. See Mining industry and finance—Belgium

UNION of Soviet Socialist Republics. See Russia

UNION oil company of California
Luck of the drill bit. Forbes 105:16-17 Ja 15 '70
Performance tests, Detroit vs. Union oil. B. Hartford. il Pop Mech 133:94-7 Ap '70
U.S. waters for U.S. ships; question of waiving the Jones act. Bsns W p46 Ag 15 '70

UNION 76 performance trial results. See Automobiles—Rating

UNION theological seminary, New York
Reason for being at Union and Yale. J. E. Dittes and C. W. Powers. Chr Cent 87:494-501 Ap 22 '70
Stransky, Wilmore; editors at large. Chr Cent 87:468 Ap 22 '70

UNION wide collective bargaining. See Collective bargaining, Industry wide

UNIONS, Teachers. See Teachers unions

UNIONS, Trade. See Trade unions

UNIONTOWN, Pa, public library
Uniontown, Pa, Appalachian springboard. il Library J 95:4141 D 1 '70

UNIT catalog cards. See Catalog cards

UNIT pricing
Knowing what you're buying; new proposals of Ben Rosenthal. D. Sanford. New Repub 162:11-13 Ja 24 '70
$1.20 divided by 14 ounces is what? Forbes 105:55 Ap 1 '70
Price of everything. il Newsweek 75:76 Je 15 '70
Shopper's gamble; supermarket price policies. J. Cross. Nation 211:581 D 7 '70
Unit prices move onto the shelf. Bsns W p23 Je 6 '70
Unit pricing chalks up some surprises. il Bsns W p80-1 O 31 '70
Yes, but how much is it per pound? unit pricing. il Bsns W p51 Ja 31 '70

UNITARIAN churches
Changes in the black ghetto: Cleveland; white and black Unitarians form separate units. J. G. Mearns. il pors Sat R 53:13-14+ Ag 1 '70

UNITARIAN universalist association
All souls. Chr Today 14:41-2 Mr 13 '70
Resolution on environment. Liv Wildn 34:61 Spr '70
Unitarian universalists grapple with major issues. C. J. Edson. Chr Cent 87:1023 Ag 26 '70

UNITED air lines
Another airline turns innkeeper. Bsns W p50 Mr 28 '70
Dogfight downs United's top man. por Bsns W p 16 D 26 '70
Freight rise bid. Aviation W 93:27 N 23 '70
Loner who lost. pors Time 97:69 Ja 4 '71
Losses spark shakeup at United. L. Doty. Aviation W 94:24 Ja 4 '71
New boss at United: into the black? il por Newsweek 77:50 Ja 4 '71
United drops Univac contract for $56-million data system. Aviation W 92:31 F 9 '70
United move to five-abreast seats intensifies dispute in fare case. Aviation W 93:23 S 7 '70
United-pilots dispute grows; Eastern, Air West threatened. Aviation W 93:25 Ag 17 '70

UNITED aircraft corporation
United aircraft earnings rise. Aviation W 93:20 Ag 17 '70
United aircraft weathers protest storm. W. H. Gregory. il Aviation W 92:24-6 Ap 20 '70
United aircraft's secret weapon. Forbes 106: 22-3 D 15 '70

UNITED automobile, aerospace and agricultural implement workers of America
After GM: outlook for auto peace. U S News 69:72 D 7 '70
After the offer: collision course in Detroit. il Bsns W p 13-14 S 5 '70
As auto makers brace for a strike. il U S News 68:80-2 My 11 '70
Auto strike: what it will do to business. il U S News 69:15-17 S 28 '70
Auto talks take the direct route; with editorial comment. il Bsns W p 17, 100 Jl 25 '70
Auto workers' demands for 1970. il U S News 69:59-60 Jl 20 '70
Back to the big table. il Bsns W p24-5 O 10 '70
Blue collar worker's lowdown blues. il Time 96:68-72+ N 9 '70
Bugging Detroit; competition from imports. R. W. Dietsch. New Repub 162:10-11 Mr 7 '70
Carrying on for Reuther; L. Woodcock. il por Bsns W p82 My 30 '70
Cost of getting rolling again. Bsns W p22-3 N 14 '70
Cost of GM strike to the auto union. il U S News 69:90-1 O 26 '70
Deadline for auto strike: where both sides stand. il U S News 69:63-4 S 14 '70
Detroit stalemate: a blow for recovery; with editorial comment. il Bsns W p30-1, 124 S 19 '70
Different approach to auto contracts. U S News 68:64 Mr 2 '70
Farm equipment talks bog down. Bsns W p70-1 O 3 '70
Filling Walter's shoes. il por Newsweek 75: 74+ Je 1 '70
Ford settlement copies GM model. il Bsns W p 18 D 12 '70
GM and Ford take positions for July 15 wage talks. il U S News 69:65-6 Jl 6 '70
GM settlement: impact on other industries. il U S News 69:65-6 N 30 '70
GM strikers' mood is militant. il Bsns W p26-7 S 26 '70
Greek tragedy in Detroit? il Time 96:63-4 Jl 27 '70
Heading for the strike nobody wants. il por Newsweek 76:79-80+ S 14 '70

Higher wages in a poor year? U S News 68: 78 Mr 23 '70
Local 22 shows how it's done; master strike plan. il Bsns W p88+ O 24 '70
Loss of a healer. il por Time 95:92+ My 25 '70
New UAW head: a tough bargainer. por U S News 68:63 Je 1 '70
On the long, rocky road to an auto contract. Bsns W p60 Ag 1 '70
Record wage hike for auto workers: Reuther's strategy. il U S News 68:81-2 Ap 27 '70
Reuther's legacy. il Newsweek 75:36+ My 25 '70
Showdown in Detroit. Newsweek 76:65+ Jl 20 '70
Signal caller for the auto workers. por U S News 69:67 Ag 24 '70
State of auto union, assets, 129 millions. U S News 68:64 My 4 '70
Suffering majority. B. J. Widick. Nation 210: 616-19 My 25 '70
Too many layoffs for UAW fund. U S News 69:67 Jl 6 '70
Tool shops plan cut in worker benefits. U S News 70:81-2 Ja 11 '71
Top challengers at UAW. il Bsns W p 107 My 16 '70
UAW and companies state their cases. il U S News 69:52-3 Ag 3 '70
UAW fills a slot in its GM lineup. por Bsns W p25 Je 6 '70
UAW: getting poorer and tougher. Bsns W p75 O 31 '70
UAW rehearses some tough bargaining talk. il Bsns W p 124+ Ap 25 '70
UAW sees peril in foreign parts. Bsns W p80 Jl 11 '70
UAW's bill for repairs. B. J. Widick. Nation 211:259-60 S 28 '70
UAW's money and contract troubles. U S News 69:48 D 21 '70
Union puts brakes on GM. il Sr Schol 97:3 O 5 '70
Unknown who leads the Walter P. Reuther memorial strike. W. Serrin. il pors N Y Times Mag p28-9+ S 27 '70
What GM's pact means to industry. il Bsns W p96+ N 21 '70
When an auto plant closes up; Ford's Dallas plant. il Bsns W p24-5 F 14 '70
Where workers opt for a layoff; inverse seniority. il Bsns W p88+ Mr 14 '70
Why Reuther faces toughest bargaining test. il por U S News 68:63-4 My 4 '70
Without Reuther: what unions and industry face. il U S News 68:55-6 My 25 '70

UNITED brands company
Bold start for AMK and United fruit. Bsns W p22-3 Jl 4 '70
Great white empire. D. Smith. Nation 210: 687-90 Je 8 '70

UNITED Brethren. See Moravians

UNITED California bank of Los Angeles. See Los Angeles—Banks

UNITED church of Canada
Co-opting Canada; selling of Ryerson press. Commonweal 93:236 D 4 '70
Ontario; the Presbyterian and the United church surveys. J. R. Mutchmor. Chr Cent 87:429-30 Ap 8 '70

UNITED church of Christ
Gulf oil: pings over Portugal. E. E. Plowman. Chr Today 15:42 Ja 1 '71
More heat on Gulf. Commonweal 93:138 N 6 '70

UNITED farm workers organizing committee. See American federation of labor and Congress of industrial organizations—United farm workers organizing committee

UNITED federation of postal clerks
New era for federal workers: bigger unions, strike threats. il U S News 69:62-4 Ag 24 '70
United federation of postal clerks. R. R. Nelson. Mo Labor R 93:37-9 O '70

UNITED fruit company. See United brands company

UNITED Methodist church
Clash over urban ministry styles; dismissal of P. Lawson. Chr Cent 87:1507 D 16 '70
Good News for Methodists: Good News convocation of United Methodists for evangelical Christianity. R. Chandler. Chr Today 14: 23-4 S 25 '70
Methodism under siege; General conference. D. Kucharsky. Chr Today 14:36-7 My 8 '70
Methodist uproar; controversy over a radio Hanoi broadcast. J. S. Tinney. Chr Today 15:39 D 18 '70
Methodists vow new priorities; with editorial comment. D. Kucharsky. Chr Today 14:22, 31-2 My 22 '70

UNITED Methodist church—*Continued*
Mishmash and renewal: the Methodists in St Louis; special session of the United Methodist general conference. A. Geyer. Chr Cent 87:556-8 My 6 '70; Discussion. 87:846 Jl 8 '70
Sound and fury at assembly of Methodist women. B. Thompson. Chr Cent 87:773-4 Je 17 '70

Board of missions

On Dow and calico. B. Thompson. Chr Cent 86:1571-2 D 10 '69; Correction. 87:83 Ja 21 '70

UNITED mine workers of America
Boyle takes the oath; Senate labor subcommittee hearing. por Newsweek 75:72 Mr 30 '70
Coal-black shame of the UMW. T. Armbrister. Read Digest 97:135-40 O '70
Coal woes blacken utilities' outlook. il Bsns W p 18 Jl 4 '70
Coal's hollow prosperity. il Newsweek 77:51+ Ja 4 '71
Crime that shocked the Nation; the murder of J. Yablonski. D. Lawrence. U S News 68:80 Ja 19 '70
Digging into the mine workers. Bsns W p94 Mr 14 '70
It's too late for Yablonski. New Repub 162:8-9 Ja 31 '70
Jock's legacy; Justice department orders new election. Newsweek 75:80+ Mr 16 '70
Just friends; Yablonski murders. New Repub 162:10-11 F 21 '70
New questions for mine workers' head; Senate investigators about UMW's election and financial practices. U S News 68:78 Mr 23 '70
Stoking up a drive for right-to-work; National right to work committee campaign against political activity by organized labor. Bsns W p28-9 Mr 14 '70
UMW vs. Jock Yablonski's ghost. il Bsns W p38+ My 2 '70
Vindication for Jock Yablonski. Time 95:25 Mr 16 '70
What U.S. charges about mine election. il U S News 68:54 Mr 16 '70
Yablonski murders: a challenge to union leadership among mine workers. J. McGinniss. il Life 68:36-7 Ja 23 '70
Yablonski's legacy; testimony of Joseph Yablonski before Senate subcommittee. Newsweek 75:35-6 F 23 '70
Yablonski's unfinished business. R. Nader. il Nation 210:70-2 Ja 26 '70

District 50

District 50 comes to a crossroad. il Bsns W p96 Ap 4 '70
District 50 heads for further strife. Bsns W p76 My 23 '70

UNITED mortgage bankers of America
Mortgage banking: blacks share the action. il Ebony 25:80-2+ Jl '70

UNITED NATIONS
Address by the Secretary-General to the United Nations association of Japan; April 15, 1970. Thant. UN Mo Chron 7:52-5 My '70
Arms control: current prospects and problems. J. B. Wiesner. il Bul Atom Sci 26:6-8+ My '70
Can the United Nations be revived? R. N. Gardner. For Affairs 48:660-76 Jl '70; Same abr. with title Ten steps for UN reform. Cur 120:47-55 Ag '70
Celebration of twenty-fifth anniversary: Assembly adopts theme of peace, justice and progress. UN Mo Chron 7:108 Ja '70
Declaration on the twenty-fifth anniversary of the United Nations; statements, October 9 and 22, 1970; with text of resolution. S. M. Finger. Dept State Bul 63:631-5 N 16 '70
Faith of nations; summary of address at the United Nations. R. M. Nixon. il Time 96:27-8 N 2 '70
For global initiative; what the UN can do about environmental problems. R. N. Gardner. Sat R 53:41+ Jl 4 '70
How relevant is the U.N? il Life 68:48 My 8 '70; Same. Cur 120:45-7 Ag '70
Introduction to the annual report of the Secretary-General on the work of the organization. Thant. UN Mo Chron 7:40-79 O '70
Low-yield anniversary. il Time 96:36+ O 26 '70
Making the U.N. a more effective instrument to meet changing world needs; statement, August 6, 1970. W P. Rogers. Dept State Bul 63:220-4 Ag 24 '70
Making the U.N. effective. D. Lawrence. U S News 69:92 S 28 '70

Message for youth, 1970. Thant. UN Mo Chron 7:i-ii Jl '70
Notes of the month. See issues of UN monthly chronicle
Nuclear weapons for U.N? W. W. Watson. Bul Atom Sci 26:48 Mr '70
OAS permanent council honors twenty-fifth anniversary of the U.N; statement. J. J. Jova. Dept State Bul 63:637-8 N 16 '70
Objectives for the United Nations General assembly in the twenty-fifth anniversary year; address, September 30, 1970. C. W. Yost. Dept State Bul 63:437-45 O 19 '70
Peaceful competition; address, October 23, 1970. R. M. Nixon. Vital Speeches 37:66-9 N 15 '70; Same with title World interest: a generation of peace. Dept State Bul 63:601-6 N 16 '70
Poignant anniversary. Chr Cent 87:683 Je 3 '70
Politics of peace-keeping, by A. James. Review
Bul Atom Sci 26:41 Mr '70. R. A. Divine
Position of the U.N; address, September 18, 1970. M. Schumann. Vital Speeches 37:5-7 O 15 '70
President Nixon hosts dinner for U.N.'s twenty-fifth anniversary; toast at White House dinner, October 24, 1970. R. M. Nixon. Dept State Bul 63:606 N 16 '70
Quality of life; a proposed program for environmental protection. R. N. Gardner. Vital Speeches 36:466-70 My 15 '70
Quiet United Nations road to accord; June 15, 1970. Thant. UN Mo Chron 7:122-31 Jl '70
Secretary-General's press conference; February 17, 1970. Thant. UN Mo Chron 7:26-36 Mr '70
Silver anniversary. il Newsweek 76:40 O 26 '70
Twenty-fifth anniversary; arrangements for commemorative session discussed. UN Mo Chron 7:66-7 Ag '70
Twenty-fifth anniversary; committee approves preliminary plans for commemorative session. UN Mo Chron 7:6-8 Mr '70
Twenty-fifth anniversary; committee considers preparations. UN Mo Chron 7:15-21 My '70
Twenty-fifth anniversary; committee discusses participation in world youth assembly. UN Mo Chron 7:52-5 Ap '70
Twenty-fifth anniversary of the United Nations marked at White House dinner; exchange of toasts, July 10, 1970. R. M. Nixon; Thant. Dept State Bul 63:166-71 Ag 10 '70
Twenty-fifth anniversary; working group meets. UN Mo Chron 7:15-16 F '70
U.N: a quarter century of what? il U S News 68:40 Je 8 '70
U.N. at quarter-century; special issue. il Sr Schol 96:5-14 Ap 27 '70
U.N. at twenty-five. L. B. Pearson. il Sat R 53:16-18+ Je 27 '70
Unhappy birthday. B. Pilkington. Commonweal 93:174-5 N 13 '70
United Nations: a view from within, by R. Townley. Review
Bul Atom Sci 26:42-3 Mr '70. B. G. Lall
United Nations and four universal problems; address, September 10, 1970. C. W. Yost. Dept State Bul 63:414-18 O 12 '70
United Nations and the common man. N. Eren. Sat R 53:18-21 O 31 '70
United Nations and the development of international law, 1945-1970. C. A. Stavropoulos. UN Mo Chron 7:78-84 Je '70
United Nations in the coming decade; address, September 25, 1970. S. DePalma. Dept State Bul 63:454-8 O 19 '70
United Nations in the 1970's; address, October 11, 1970. S. DePalma. Dept State Bul 63:574-9 N 9 '70
United Nations; lofty intentions of twenty-five years ago. Chr Today 14:25 Ap 24 '70
United Nations: looking forward with hope. G. J. Hecht. Parents Mag 45:27 O '70
United Nations observes Lenin centenary. UN Mo Chron 7:62-4 My '70
United Nations: the crisis of authority; address, August 23, 1970. UN Mo Chron 7:86-92 Ag '70
UN anniversary: a time to move ahead. America 123:310 O 24 '70
UN at twenty-five. Commonweal 92:308 Je 26 '70
UN celebrates its twenty-fifth birthday. America 123:194 S 26 '70
UN with teeth. Commonweal 93:4 O 2 '70
U.S.-Soviet tensions and the UN. America 123:311 O 24 '70
United States and the United Nations in the 1970's; statement, February 18, 1970. C. W. Yost. Dept State Bul 62:430-4 Mr 30 '70

UNITED NATIONS—*Continued*

Universality of the U.N; giving the charter a chance; address, June 26, 1970. Thant. Vital Speeches 36:652-5 Ag 15 '70; Excerpts. Cur 120:44 Ag '70

World organization: twenty-five years. America 122:624 Je 13 '70
　See also
Food and agriculture organization of the United Nations
International court of justice, The Hague
International day for the elimination of racial discrimination
United States—President's commission for the observance of the twenty-fifth anniversary of the United Nations

Ad hoc committee on the survey program for the development of natural resources

Ad hoc committee on survey programme meets. UN Mo Chron 7:63 Ap '70

Administrative and budgetary committee

Estimates and appropriations. UN Mo Chron 7:151-5 N '70
1970 budget estimates. UN Mo Chron 7:159-71 Ja '70
U.S. discusses U.N. scale of assessments; statement, October 26, 1970. C. Pell. Dept State Bul 63:709-11 D 7 '70

Administrative committee on co-ordination

Session held in Vienna. UN Mo Chron 7:33 My '70

Advisory committee on the application of science and technology to development

Advisory committee holds thirteenth session. UN Mo Chron 7:30-2 My '70

Armed forces
Forces in Cyprus

Security council extends stationing of Peace-keeping force; with text of resolution. UN Mo Chron 7:21-8 Ja '70
Security council extends stationing of UN-FICYP; with text of resolution. UN Mo Chron 7:47-54 Jl '70
United Nations force in Cyprus extended through December 1970; statement, June 9, 1970. W. B. Buffum. Dept State Bul 63:20-1 Jl 6 '70

Assembly
See United Nations—General assembly

Budget
See United Nations—Finance

Charter

Commemorative meeting; twenty-fifth anniversary of the signing of the Charter of the United Nations, 26 June, San Francisco; messages and addresses. UN Mo Chron 7:3-45 Jl '70
Declaration on principles of friendly relations; statement, September 24, 1970; with text of resolution. R. H. Gimer. Dept State Bul 63:623-31 N 16 '70
Legacy of conscience. R. A. Graham. il America. 123:312-15 O 24 '70
On giving the Charter a chance; address, June 26, 1970. Thant. UN Mo Chron 7:38-45 Jl '70
Revision of charter; Assembly postpones consideration. UN Mo Chron 7:72 Ja '70
U.N. charter after a quarter of a century; address, with text of message from President Nixon, June 26, 1970. C. W. Yost. Dept State Bul 63:172-4 Ag 10 '70

Commission for social development

Holds twenty-first session. UN Mo Chron 7:64-7 Ap '70

Commission on human rights

Concludes twenty-sixth session. UN Mo Chron 7:69-74 Ap '70
Human rights in Israel-occupied territories, and southern Africa. UN Mo Chron 7:88-90 Jl '70
Human rights in Southern Africa and Israel-occupied territories: expert working groups meet. UN Mo Chron 7:31-2 F '70
Human rights, 1945-1970. J. Rolz-Bennett. UN Mo Chron 7:78-86 Ap '70
Twenty-sixth session begins. UN Mo Chron 7:16-24 Mr '70
United States supports creation of the post of U.N. high commissioner for human rights; statement, December 5, 1969. R. E. Hauser. Dept State Bul 62:41-4 Ja 12 '70
　See also
United Nations—Sub-commission on prevention of discrimination and protection of minorities

Commission on International trade law

International trade law: Commission holds third session. UN Mo Chron 7:41-5 My '70
International trade law: working group holds session. UN Mo Chron 7:32 F '70

Commission on narcotic drugs

Session concluded. UN Mo Chron 7:30-1 F '70
Special session begins. UN Mo Chron 7:26 O '70
Special session concluded. UN Mo Chron 7:151 N '70
U.S. proposes new U.N. action program against illicit narcotics; statement September 28, 1970. J. E. Ingersoll. Dept State Bul 63:492-7 O 26 '70

Commission on the status of women

Twenty-third session concluded. UN Mo Chron 7:35-9 My '70
Twenty-third session opens. UN Mo Chron 7:74 Ap '70

Committee for development planning

Sixth session. UN Mo Chron 7:29-30 F '70

Committee for programme and coordination

Concluded with session. UN Mo Chron 7:85-7 Jl '70
Fourth session. UN Mo Chron 7:13-14 Mr '70

Committee for the twenty-fifth anniversary

Twenty-fifth anniversary committee. UN Mo Chron 7:75-7 Jl '70

Committee of twenty-four

See United Nations—Special committee on the situation with regard to the implementation of the declaration on the granting of independence to colonial countries and peoples

Committee on disarmament

Assembly adopts twelve resolutions; with text of resolutions. UN Mo Chron 7:50-70 Ja '70
Conference of the committee on disarmament: opportunities for achievement, statement, February 17, 1970. G. C. Smith. Dept State Bul 62:354-8 Mr 16 '70
United Nations and disarmament. L. N. Kutakov. UN Mo Chron 7:56-61 My '70
U.S. reviews position on general and complete disarmament; statement, June 23, 1970. J. F. Leonard. Dept State Bul 63:198-203 Ag 17 '70

Committee on the peaceful uses of outer space

Committee adopts report. UN Mo Chron 7:16-17 O '70
Committee agrees on work programme. UN Mo Chron 7:13-14 F '70
Direct broadcast satellites; working group holds session. UN Mo Chron 7:42-3 Je '70
Legal sub-committee holds ninth session. UN Mo Chron 7:74-5 Jl '70
Peaceful uses of outer space; with text of resolutions. UN Mo Chron 7:80-6 Ja '70
Scientific and technical sub-committee holds session. UN Mo Chron 7:12-15 My '70
Sharing the practical benefits of new technology in the peaceful uses of outer space; statements, December 10-11, 1969; with text of resolution. W. B. Buffum. P. S. Thacker. Dept State Bul 62:63-9 Ja 19 '70
U.S. discusses work of U.N. Outer space committee; statement, September 1, 1970. W. P. Allen. Dept State Bul 63:398-402 O 5 '70

Committee on the peaceful uses of the seabed and the ocean floor

Committee adopts report. UN Mo Chron 7:40-3 Ag '70
Committee begins 1970 work. UN Mo Chron 7:40-3 Ap '70
Draft U.N. convention on the international seabed area; U.S. working paper submitted to U.N. seabeds committee; statements, with summary of draft convention. J. R. Stevenson; C. H. Phillips. Dept State Bul 63:209-18 Ag 24 '70
Letter from Ambassador Phillips to U.N. seabed committee chairman; May 25, 1970. C. H. Phillips. Dept State Bul 62:741 Je 15 '70
Pacem in maribus; international conference in Malta. W. Wynn. il Time 96:34-5 Jl 20 '70
Reservation of the sea-bed and ocean floor for peaceful purposes; with texts of resolutions. UN Mo Chron 7:72-80 Ja '70
Sanity from the sea? J. J. Myers. il America 123:318-19 O 24 '70
Treading water; August meeting. C. M. Eichelberger. Sat R 53:24 S 26 '70

UNITED NATIONS—Committee on the peaceful uses of the seabed and the ocean floor
—*Continued*
U.S. explains its votes on seabed resolutions; Statements, December 2 and 15, 1969; with text of resolutions. C. H. Phillips. Dept State Bul 62:89-95 Ja 26 '70
U.S. gives views on convening conference on law of the sea, text of note, June 12, 1970. W. P. Rogers. Dept State Bul 63:38-9 Jl 13 '70

Committee on trust and non-self-governing territories

See United Nations—Trusteeship committee

Conference of the committee on disarmament

See United Nations—Committee on disarmament

Development program

Department and AID announce pledge to U.N. population fund; text of announcement; with statement, January 24, 1970. W. P. Rogers. Dept State Bul 62:214 F 23 '70
Governing council holds special session on capacity study. UN Mo Chron 7:60-1 Ap '70
Second development decade; address, November 13, 1970. R. S. McNamara. Vital Speeches 37:135-40 D 15 '70
Second development decade; international strategy; statement, October 16, 1970; with text of resolution. J. K. Javits. Dept State Bul 63:607-22 N 16 '70
Underdeveloped countries: foreign aid; the Second development decade; address, July 14, 1970. C. W. Yost. Vital Speeches 36:647-52 Ag 15 '70
UNDP governing council: re-investment projects. UN Mo Chron 7:20-8 F '70
UNDP pledging conference. UN Mo Chron 7:149-50 N '70
United States supports reforms to strengthen UNDP; statement, March 18, 1970. G. A. Olds. Dept State Bul 62:582-4 My 4 '70

Documents

See United Nations—Publications

Economic and financial committee

Second committee; plans for launching the Second United Nations development decade. UN Mo Chron 7:22-4 O '70

Economic and social council

Social progress and development; with text of declaration and resolution. UN Mo Chron 7:132-42 Ja '70
See also
United Nations—Commission for social development

Meetings, 1970

First part of forty-eighth session concluded. UN Mo Chron 7:23-6 My '70
Forty-eighth session resumed. UN Mo Chron 7:57-9 Ap '70
Opens forty-eighth session. UN Mo Chron 7:28-9 F '70
Organizational meetings concluded. UN Mo Chron 7:11-20 Mr '70
Resumed forty-eighth session ends. UN Mo Chron 7:46-52 Je '70
UNDP governing council holds tenth session. UN Mo Chron 7:80-5 Jl '70

Economic commission for Africa

ECA and the paradox of African cooperation. J. S. Magee. bibliog f por Int Concil 580:5-64 N '70

Economic commission for Asia and the Far East

Twenty-sixth session. UN Mo Chron 7:26-8 My '70

Economic commission for Latin America

Committee of the whole concludes session. UN Mo Chron 7:56-7 Je '70
Concluded its sixth extraordinary session. UN Mo Chron 7:87-8 Jl '70

Eighteen-nation committee on disarmament

See United Nations—Committee on disarmament

Employees

U.N. interpreter: how to promote international understanding in five languages. E. Sparn. il Sr Schol 96:11+ Ap 27 '70
See also
United Nations—Secretariat

Fifth committee

See United Nations—Administrative and budgetary committee

Finance

1970 budget estimates. UN Mo Chron 7:159-71 Ja '70
United Nations budget estimates for 1971; statement, October 21, 1970. S. DePalma. Dept State Bul 63:701-9 D 7 '70
U.S. joins other members in support of U.N. budget; statement, December 17, 1969. J. I. Whalley. Dept State Bul 62:109-10 Ja 26 '70

First committee

See United Nations—Political and security committee

Fourth committee

See United Nations—Trusteeship committee

General assembly

Agenda of the twenty-fifth regular session of the U.N. General assembly. Dept State Bul 63:461-4 O 19 '70
Twenty-fifth president; interview. E. I. Hambro. New Yorker 46:27-9 S 19 '70
Youth, the U.N. and a split world; World youth assembly. Chr Cent 87:524 Ap 29 '70
See also
United Nations—Special committee on the situation with regard to the implementation of the declaration on the granting of independence to colonial countries and peoples

Sessions (24th)

Ambassador Yost comments on the 24th session of the U.N. General assembly; December 16, 1969. C. W. Yost. Dept State Bul 62:77-81 Ja 26 '70
Assembly decisions on economic questions. UN Mo Chron 7:150-9 Ja '70
Closing of twenty-fourth session; adopts twelve resolutions; with texts of resolutions. UN Mo Chron 7:49-128 Ja '70
24th session of the United Nations General assembly; summary of developments during the session; December 18, 1969. Dept State Bul 62:162-71 F 9 '70
United Nations calls for measures against aircraft hijacking; statement, December 12, 1969; with text of resolution. D. B. Fascell. Dept State Bul 62:69-71 Ja 19 '70

Sessions (25th)

Achievement of sorts. il por Newsweek 76:47 S 28 '70
Adoption of agenda. UN Mo Chron 7:125-6 N '70
Apartheid in South Africa: General assembly adopts resolution. UN Mo Chron 7:141-4 N '70
Commemorative session: twenty-fifth anniversary of the United Nations 14-24 October 1970; summaries of statements. October 24, 1970. UN Mo Chron 7:3-95 N '70
General debate; summaries of statements. UN Mo Chron 7:159-81 N '70
General debate; summary of statements. UN Mo Chron 7:80-130 O '70
Grateful for small favors; opening of new session. Time 96:30 S 28 '70
Issues before the 25th General assembly; ed. by J. A. Stegenga. bibliog f il Int Concil 579:1-222 S '70
Opening of twenty-fifth session. UN Mo Chron 7:8-16 O '70
Situation in the Middle East; General assembly begins debate. UN Mo Chron 7:129-36 N '70

Headquarters

United Nations headquarters accommodation; statements, December 11 and 17, 1969; with text of resolution. W. H. Ziehl; C. H. Phillips. Dept State Bul 62:102-9 Ja 26 '70
United Nations village. J. A. Munves. il Holiday 47:28-9+ Ap '70

Information centers

Secretary-General's press conference; 22 December, 1969. Thant. UN Mo Chron 7:178-87 Ja '70

International law commission

Concludes session. UN Mo Chron 7:83-4 Ag '70
Sixth committee recommendations. UN Mo Chron 7:156-7 N '70

Legal committee

Forcible diversion of civil aircraft in flight. UN Mo Chron 7:173-4 Ja '70
Principles of international law; Sixth committee adopts draft declaration. UN Mo Chron 7:28-9 O '70

Membership

Next year in New York? seating of Communist China. America 123:481-2 D 5 '70

UNITED NATIONS—Membership—*Continued*
U.S. supports admission of Fiji to the United Nations; statement, October 10, 1970. C. W. Yost. Dept State Bul 63:596-7 N 9 '70

Non-governmental organizations

Annual conference. UN Mo Chron 7:60 Je '70
Recommendations by committee. UN Mo Chron 7:15-16 Mr '70

Outer space committee

See United Nations—Committee on the peaceful uses of outer space

Political and security committee

Korean question: invitation aspects; First committee adopting resolution. UN Mo Chron 7:126-9 N '70
Strengthening of international security: Assembly adopts resolution; with text of resolution. UN Mo Chron 7:125-7 Ja '70
Strengthening of international security. UN Mo Chron 7:139-41 N '70

Privileges and immunities

Senate urged to act on convention on U.N. privileges and immunities; message, December 19, 1969. R. M. Nixon. Dept State Bul 62:61 Ja 19 '70

Public information, Office of

See also
United Nations—Non-governmental organizations

Publications

Documents relating to the commemoration of the twenty-fifth anniversary of the United Nations. UN Mo Chron 7:96-123 N '70

Bibliography

Documents; selected list. See issues of UN monthly chronicle
Publications, official records. See issues of UN monthly chronicle
United Nations documents: a selected bibliography. See occasional issues of Department of state bulletin

Publicity

See also
United Nations—Information centers

Second committee

See United Nations—Economic and financial committee

Secretariat

Secretariat, twenty-five years after. A. A. Stark. UN Mo Chron 7:102-8 Ag '70

Privileges and immunities

See United Nations—Privileges and immunities

Secretary General

President Kennedy and the Russian fable; withdrawal of troika scheme attributed to Russian fable. N. Cousins. il Sat R 54:20-1 Ja 9 '71
U Thant: a study in caution. il por Newsweek 76:56+ O 19 '70

Security council

U.S. supports Security council decision to hold periodic meetings; statement, June 12, 1970; with text of statement read by the president of the Security council. C. W. Yost. Dept State Bul 63:19-20 Jl 6 '70

Meetings, 1969

Record of the month:
Complaint by Guinea. UN Mo Chron 7: 28-49 Ja '70
Complaint by Senegal UN Mo Chron 7: 3-21 Ja '70
Cyprus. UN Mo Chron 7:21-8 Ja '70

Meetings, 1970

Record of the month:
Bahrain. UN Mo Chron 7:3-7 Je '70
Cyprus. UN Mo Chron 7:47-54 Jl '70
First periodic meeting. UN Mo Chron 7: 124-5 N '70
Namibia. UN Mo Chron 7:3-13 F; 3 Mr '70
Policies of apartheid in South Africa. UN Mo Chron 7:3-27 Ag '70
Security council approves consensus on periodic meetings. UN Mo Chron 7:54-9 Jl '70
Situation in Namibia; with text of resolutions. UN Mo Chron 7:27-37 Ag '70
Situation in the Middle East. UN Mo Chron 7:8-37 Je; 3-8 O '70
Southern Rhodesia. UN Mo Chron 7:3-35 Ap '70

Sixth committee

See United Nations—Legal committee

Social commission

See United Nations—Commission for social development

Social, humanitarian and cultural committee

Social progress and development; with text of declaration and resolution. UN Mo Chron 7:132-42 Ja '70
Third committee. UN Mo Chron 7:27-8 O '70
Violation of human rights and fundamental freedoms; with text of resolution. UN Mo Chron 7:142-50 Ja '70
Youth and human rights: Third committee concludes debate. UN Mo Chron 7:155-6 N '70

Space committee

See United Nations—Committee on the peaceful uses of outer space

Special committee of twenty-four on colonialism

See United Nations—Special committee on the situation with regard to implementation of declaration on granting of independence to colonial countries and peoples

Special committee on peace-keeping operations

Committee adopts report. UN Mo Chron 7: 17 O '70
Key requirements for U.N. peacekeeping operations; statement, December 8, 1969. C. W. Yost. Dept State Bul 62:14-18 Ja 5 '70
Peace-keeping operations. UN Mo Chron 7:103-6 Ja '70
Special committee meets. UN Mo Chron 7:39-40 Ap '70

Special committee on principles of international law concerning friendly relations and cooperation among states

Committee adopts draft declaration. UN Mo Chron 7:62-8 Je '70
Committee begins session. UN Mo Chron 7: 77 Ap '70
Declaration on principles of friendly relations; statement, September 24, 1970; with text of resolution. R. H. Gimer. Dept State Bul 63:623-31 N 16 '70

Special committee on the policies of apartheid of the government of the Republic of South Africa

Approves call to Security council. UN Mo Chron 7:39-40 Ag '70
International day for elimination of racial discrimination: commemoration by committee on apartheid. UN Mo Chron 7:35-9 Ap '70
Press communiqué adopted. UN Mo Chron 7:10-11 My '70
Special committee meets. UN Mo Chron 7:70-4 Jl '70

Special committee on the question of defining aggression

Report on the question of defining aggression. UN Mo Chron 7:174-5 Ja '70

Special committee on the situation with regard to the implementation of the declaration on the granting of independence to colonial countries and peoples

Implementation of declaration on decolonization; statement, October 12, 1970; with text of resolution. S. M. Finger. Dept State Bul 63:635-7 N 16 '70
Special committee of twenty-four; debate on territories in southern Africa, and Fiji. UN Mo Chron 7:37-40 Je '70
Special committee of twenty-four; meetings in July and August; with text of resolutions. UN Mo Chron 7:43-66 Ag '70
Special committee of twenty-four; 1970 session. UN Mo Chron 7:43-52 Ap '70
Special committee of twenty-four: tenth anniversary of the Declaration on decolonization. UN Mo Chron 7:3-10 My '70
Special committee of twenty-four. UN Mo Chron 7:59-70 Jl; 18-21 O; 144-7 N '70
Tenth anniversary of declaration on decolonization; Assembly adopts resolutions; with text of resolutions. UN Mo Chron 7:109-19 Ja '70
Tenth anniversary of U.N. declaration on the independence of colonial peoples; excerpts from address, 1970. R. Maheu. UNESCO Courier 23:14 N '70

UNITED NATIONS—Special committee on the situation with regard to the implementation of the declaration on the granting of independence to colonial countries and peoples—*Continued*

U.N. subcommittee discusses American Samoa and Guam; statements, June 30 and August 17, 1970. F. H. Sacksteder. Dept State Bul 63:336-40 S 21 '70

United Nations and decolonization. I. S. Djermakoye. UN Mo Chron 7:37-45 Mr '70

U.S. suggests fresh approach to study of decolonization; statement, April 1, 1970. S. M. Finger. Dept State Bul 62:557-60 Ap 27 '70

Special committee to investigate Israeli practices affecting the human rights of the population of the occupied territories

Assembly committee communiqué. UN Mo Chron 7:75 Ap '70

Assembly committee holds hearings. UN Mo Chron 7:39-40 My '70

Special missions

Assembly adopts convention on special missions; with text of resolution. UN Mo Chron 7:171-3 Ja '70

Convention on special missions. UN Mo Chron 7:45-65 F '70

Sub-commission on prevention of discrimination and protection of minorities

Sub-commission holds twenty-third session. UN Mo Chron 7:79-82 Ag '70

Technical assistance program

See also
United Nations—Development program

Third committee

See United Nations—Social, humanitarian and cultural committee

Treaties

See Treaties

Trusteeship committee

Decolonization: Fourth committee's recommendations approved. UN Mo Chron 7:120-4 Ja '70

Territories in southern Africa: debate in Fourth committee. UN Mo Chron 7:136-9 N '70

Trusteeship council

Annual review begins. UN Mo Chron 7:61-2 Je '70

Concludes annual session. UN Mo Chron 7:90-107 Jl '70

Trust Territory of the Pacific Islands; symposium, June 3 and 11, 1970. Dept State Bul 63:251-71 Ag 31 '70

Veto

See United Nations—Voting

Voting

Breaking a precedent; first U.S. veto. Newsweek 75:47 Mr 30 '70

U.S. vetoes Security council resolution on Southern Rhodesia; supports compromise resolution; statements, March 13, 17 and 18, 1970, with texts of resolutions. C. W. Yost; W. B. Buffum. Dept State Bul 62:501-10 Ap 13 '70

World food programme

See World food programme

Africa, Southern

United Nations, the United States, and Africa; address, September 17, 1970. D. D. Newsom. Dept State Bul 63:419-24 O 12 '70; Same. Vital Speeches 37:52-5 N 1 '70

Bahrein

Future independence of Bahrain endorsed by Security council; statement; with text of resolution, May 11, 1970. C. W. Yost. Dept State Bul 62:814-15 Je 29 '70

Security council assesses report; with text of resolution. UN Mo Chron 7:3-5 Je '70

China (People's Republic)

Next year in New York? America 123:481-2 D 5 '70

Peking duck. Nat R 22:1250+ D 1 '70

Year 1 B.C? Newsweek 76:41 N 30 '70

Cuba

U.S. asks departure of two members of Cuban mission to the U.N; Department announcement. Dept State Bul 63:483-4 O 26 '70

Cyprus

Security council extends stationing of UNFICYP; with text of resolution. UN Mo Chron 7:47-54 Jl '70

United Nations force in Cyprus extended through June 1970; statement, December 11, 1969. C. H. Phillips. Dept State Bul 62:71-3 Ja 19 '70

See also
United Nations—Armed forces—Forces in Cyprus

Fiji

U.S. supports admission of Fiji to the United Nations; statement, October 10, 1970. C. W. Yost. Dept State Bul 63:596-7 N 9 '70

Great Britain

See also
United Nations—Cyprus

Greece, Modern

See also
United Nations—Cyprus

Indochina

Secretary-General's press conference; June 11, 1970. Thant. UN Mo Chron 7:108-21 Jl '70

Israel

Security council demands withdrawal of Israeli forces from Lebanon; with text of resolution. UN Mo Chron 7:3-7 O '70

Speaker; interview. A. Eban. New Yorker 46:45-8 N 14 '70

Korea

U.N. reaffirms objectives for reunification of Korea; statements, November 11, 12 and 25, 1969; with text of resolution. W. B. Buffum; J. I. Whalley. Dept State Bul 61:609-15 D 22 '69

Korea (People's Republic)

Crew of U.S. helicopter released by North Korea; statement by United Nations command; with text of document; December 2, 1969. Dept State Bul 61:583 D 22 '69

Korean question: invitation aspects; First committee adopting resolution. UN Mo Chron 7:126-9 N '70

U.N. command in Korea submits report to the Security council; text of letter, with text of report; October 30, 1969. C. W. Yost. Dept State Bul 61:606-8 D 22 '69

Korea (Republic)

Korean question: invitation aspects; First committee adopting resolution. UN Mo Chron 7:126-9 N '70

Lebanon

Security council demands withdrawal of Israeli forces from Lebanon; with text of resolution. UN Mo Chron 7:3-7 O '70

Middle East

Arab-Israeli settlement; address, August 24, 1970; with an interchange with A. A. Ribicoff. J. W. Fulbright. New Repub 163:20-3 O 10 '70

Fulbright proposal for peace in the Mideast; abstract of address, August 24, 1970. J. W. Fulbright. il por U S News 69:43 S 7 '70

Guaranteeing a Mideast peace. D. Lawrence. U S News 69:80 S 7 '70

How U.N. has fared as peacekeeper in Mideast. il U S News 69:23 Ag 17 '70

More, the better. il Newsweek 76:58+ N 2 '70

Record of the month:
Situation in the Middle East. UN Mo Chron 7:3-8 O '70

Secretary-General's press conference; 22 December, 1969. Thant. UN Mo Chron 7:178-87 Ja '70

Secretary-General's press conference; June 11, 1970. Thant. UN Mo Chron 7:108-21 Jl '70

Secretary-General's press conference; July 7, 1970. Thant. UN Mo Chron 7:93-101 Ag '70

Security council condemns Israel for action against Lebanon; with text of resolution. UN Mo Chron 7:8-37 Je '70

Secretary-General's press conference; September 10, 1970. Thant. UN Mo Chron 7:30-9 O '70

Situation in the Middle East: General assembly begins debate. UN Mo Chron 7:129-36 N '70

Uneasy truce; General assembly debate. Newsweek 76:54+ N 16 '70

United Nations in the Middle East. H. N. Howard. bibliog f Cur Hist 60:7-12+ Ja '71

U.S. gives views in U.N. General assembly debate on the situation in the Middle East; statements, October 29 and November 4, 1970; with texts of resolution. C. W. Yost. Dept State Bul 63:656-63 N 23 '70

UNITED NATIONS—Middle East—*Continued*
War of words; General assembly debate. il
Newsweek 76:36 N 9 '70
Wrong move. Newsweek 76:42+ O 26 '70

Namibia

Assembly action; with text of resolution.
UN Mo Chron 7:108-9 Ja '70
Council for Namibia; work organized. UN
Mo Chron 7:11 My '70
Security council adopts resolutions resuming
consideration of the question of Namibia.
UN Mo Chron 7:27-37 Ag '70
Security council establishes sub-committee
of experts; with text of resolution. UN Mo
Chron 7:3-13 F '70
Security council sub-committee meets. UN
Mo Chron 7:3 Mr '70
U.N. Security council adopts new measures
concerning Namibia; statement with texts
of resolutions. W. B. Buffum. Dept State
Bul 63:284-6 S 7 '70
U.N. Security council establishes subcommit-
tee on Namibia; statement with text of
resolution. C. W. Yost. Dept State Bul 62:
359-61 Mr 16 '70

Nigeria

Nigeria-Biafra and the UN. A. Tuckerman.
Nation 210:98-9 F 2 '70
Secretary-General's press conferences; January 4 and 9, 1970. Thant. UN Mo Chron
7:34-44 F '70

Portugal

Security council asks Portugal to desist from
violations; with text of resolution. UN Mo
Chron 7:28-49 Ja '70
Security council censures Portuguese at-
tacks on Senegal; with text of resolution.
UN Mo Chron 7:3-21 Ja '70
U.S. abstains on U.N. resolution on Portu-
guese territories; statement, November 14,
1969. S. M. Finger. Dept State Bul 61:641-2
D 29 '69

Rhodesia

Security council extends sanctions; with text
of resolution. UN Mo Chron 7:3-35 Ap '70
U.S. uses veto for first time. Sr Schol 96:13
Ap 6 '70
U.S. vetoes Security council resolution on
Southern Rhodesia; supports compromise
resolution; statements, March 13, 17 and 18,
1970, with texts of resolutions. C. W. Yost;
W. B. Buffum. Dept State Bul 62:501-10 Ap
13 '70

Senegal

Security council censures Portuguese attacks
on Senegal; with text of resolution. UN Mo
Chron 7:3-21 Ja '70

South Africa

Apartheid in South Africa: General assembly
adopts resolution. UN Mo Chron 7:141-4 N
'70
Security council condemns violations of arms
embargo against South Africa; with text
of resolution. UN Mo Chron 7:3-27 Ag '70
U.S. abstains on Security council resolution
on South Africa; statement, with text of
resolution. W. B. Buffum. Dept State Bul
63:203-5 Ag 17 '70
See also
United Nations—Africa, Southern

Southwest Africa

See also
United Nations—Namibia

Turkey

U.N. veteran; interview. N. Eren. New York-
er 45:30-1 F 14 '70
See also
United Nations—Cyprus

United States

Overcoming the crisis of confidence: the U.S.
view of the United Nations; address. May
23, 1970. S. De Palma. Dept State Bul 62:
747-52 Je 15 '70
President pledges rededication of U.S. support for the U.N; exchange of letters. R.
M. Nixon. Dept State Bul 62:358-9 Mr 16
'70
U.S. stake in an effective United Nations; address, May 19, 1970. C. W. Yost. Dept
State Bul 62:705-10 Je 8 '70
United States and the United Nations. R. J.
Walton; C. M. Eichelberger. Sat R 53:19-
21+ Je 27 '70
United States and the United Nations in the
1970's; statement, February 18, 1970. C. W.
Yost. Dept State Bul 62:430-4 Mr 30 '70
UNITED NATIONS bank for reconstruction
and development. See International bank
for reconstruction and development

UNITED NATIONS center, New York. See
United Nations—Headquarters
UNITED NATIONS childrens fund
Executive board meets. UN Mo Chron 7:34
My '70
Executive board session concluded. UN Mo
Chron 7:57-9 Je '70
Peter Ustinov plays Santa to the children of
many nations. A. Levy. il pors Good H 171:
38-40+ D '70
Toward a better world for all children. C. L.
Bailey. por Parents Mag 45:30 Ag '70
UNICEF greeting cards. il UNESCO Courier
23:33 N '70
United States comments on work of UNICEF;
statement, December 2, 1969. S. T. Black.
Dept State Bul 61:642-3 D 29 '69
UNITED NATIONS conference of non-nuclear-
weapon states
Assembly adopts twelve resolutions; with
text of resolutions. UN Mo Chron 7:50-70
Ja '70
UNITED NATIONS conference on human sur-
vival
On human survival; excerpts from letter.
L. B. Pearson. Sat R 53:24+ Je 13 '70
UNITED NATIONS conference on the human
environment
EPO. A. W. Smith. Nat Parks & Con Mag
44:2 Jl '70
Human environment and world order; ad-
dress, May 14, 1970. Thant. UN Mo Chron
7:69-77 Je '70
Preparatory committee concludes first ses-
sion. UN Mo Chron 7:59-60 Ap '70
UN looks at earthman's world. A. H. Farns-
worth. Nat Parks & Con Mag 44:10 Jl '70
United Nations conference on the human en-
vironment; statement; December 15, 1969;
with text of resolution. S. Temple. Dept
State Bul 62:99-101 Ja 26 '70
UNITED NATIONS conference on the problems
of human environment (proposed) See
United Nations conference on the human
environment (proposed)
UNITED NATIONS conference on the stan-
dardization of geographical names
Ad hoc group holds second session. UN Mo
Chron 7:68 Ap '70
UNITED NATIONS conference on trade and
development
Begins tenth session. UN Mo Chron 7:78 Ag
'70
Concludes first part of tenth session. UN Mo
Chron 7:24-6 O '70
Deeds of celebration; future of internation-
al cooperation. Chr Cent 87:1277-8 O 28 '70
Ninth session concluded. UN Mo Chron 7:12-
13 Mr '70
UNITED NATIONS congress on the prevention
of crime and the treatment of offenders
Adopts declaration. UN Mo Chron 7:78-9 Ag
'70
Crime and development: disturbingly insep-
arable. L. J. Moss. Chr Cent 87:1237-8 O 14
'70
United Nations and the prevention of crime.
W. Clifford. UN Mo Chron 7:65-70 My '70
UNITED NATIONS correspondents association
Secretary-General press conference; June 11,
1970. Thant. UN Mo Chron 7:108-21 Ag 10
'70
UNITED NATIONS council for Namibia
Council for Namibia: mission to visit Africa.
UN Mo Chron 7:40-2 Je '70
Council for Namibia; mission visits Africa.
UN Mo Chron 7:37-9 Ag '70
UNITED NATIONS day. See Special days,
weeks, and months
UNITED NATIONS development decade, 2d
Preparatory committee concludes session.
UN Mo Chron 7:61-3 Ap '70
Preparatory committee concludes work. UN
Mo Chron 7:53-5 Je '70
Second chance in the 1970s. M. S. Adiseshiah.
il UNESCO Courier 23:11-14 O '70
Second committee; plans for launching the
Second United Nations development de-
cade. UN Mo Chron 7:22-4 O '70
Second development decade; preparatory
committee meets. UN Mo Chron 7:14-15
Mr '70
UNITED NATIONS educational, scientific and
cultural organization. See Unesco
UNITED NATIONS food and agriculture or-
ganization. See Food and agriculture or-
ganization of the United Nations
UNITED NATIONS fund for population ac-
tivities. See United Nations—Development
program
UNITED NATIONS general assembly. See
United Nations—General assembly
UNITED NATIONS human rights day and
week. See Human rights day and week

UNITED STATES—Air force—Procurement—
—*Continued*
Senate report blasts procurement of F-111.
D. C. Winston. il Aviation W 93:19-20 D 21
'70
USAF aircraft, missile procurement; tables.
Aviation W 92:21 Mr 23 '70

Strategic air command

Decline of U.S. bomber power. il U S News
70:49-51 Ja 11 '71
SAC reduces training schedule because of
controller slowdown. Aviation W 92:22 Ap
6 '70

American Revolution bicentennial commission

America's biggest birthday party. il U S News
69:42-4 S 28 '70
Great Scott, it's Philadelphia! il Newsweek
76:22-3 Ag 3 '70
Philadelphia: host to the spirit of '76. Bsns
W p21-2 Jl 4 '70

Anti-Communist measures

See Communism—United States—Anti-
Communist measures; United States—Foreign relations—Anti-Communist measures

Appalachian regional commission

Appalachia as a developing nation. il Bsns
W p46-7+ Jl 18 '70
Progress in Appalachia: a model for fed-
eral aid? il U S News 68:79-80 Mr 23 '70

Appropriations and expenditures

Big spender debate: Nixon vs. Congress. il
U S News 69:57 Ag 24 '70
Budget on a tightrope. il Sr Schol 96:19 Mr
2 '70
Congress's role in price rises. U S News 68:19
Je 15 '70
Control of government expenditures; address,
December 2, 1969. A. F. Burns. Vital
Speeches 36:194-7 Ja 15 '70
Dividing taxpayers' billions: another fight
brewing; use of trust funds to finance
federal programs. il U S News 69:70-1 Ag 3
'70
Double veto, a pair of cuff links. il por News-
week 76:13-14 Ag 24 '70
Federal spending: new spur to business. il
U S News 68:24-6 Ap 20 '70
Having it both ways. il por Time 96:8-9 Ag
24 '70
Less spending=fewer jobs. Sr Schol 96:14 F
9 '70
Misleading minuses. il Fortune 81:24 Je '70
Open letter to President Nixon. T. L. Kim-
ball. il Nat Wildlife 8:34-5 Ag '70
R&D factor. P. Steinfels. Commonweal 92:
478 S 25 '70
Shift in pattern of public outlays. B. L. Mas-
se. America 123:33 Jl 25 '70
To combat inflation: what Congress must
do. C. E. Walker. Read Digest 97:74-8 N '70
Very partisan session; the bill and the Pre-
sident. Newsweek 75:16+ Ja 26 '71
What hope of reforming federal spending?
K. O. Gilmore. Read Digest 97:83-7 Jl '70
Where's the money coming from? Nations
Bsns 58:27-9 O '70
Who runs the House? Nation 210:581 My 18
'70
Wouldn't it be nice if everybody had a
trust fund? W. F. Wagner, jr. Arch Rec
148:9 Jl '70
See also
Budget—United States
Government spending policy
United States—Armed forces—Appropriations
and expenditures
United States—Economic policy
also subhead Appropriations and expendi-
tures under names of government depart-
ments,e.g. United States—Air force—Ap-
propriations and expenditures

Armed forces

Armed forces reluctant retrenchment. J.
Cameron. il Fortune 82:68-73+ N '70
2.7 million troops; proposed manpower re-
duction. New Repub 163:10 N 14 '70
See also
Armed forces day and week
Courts martial and courts of inquiry
Discipline, Military
Military life
United States—Air force
United States—Army
United States—Coast guard
United States—Defense, Department of

Appropriations and expenditures

Big shifts in U.S. defense; impact of military
cutbacks. il U S News 68:30-3 F 2 '70

For defense: a shrinking share of total spend-
ing. il U S News 69:30-1 Ag 10 '70
Military spending: impact on business; inter-
view. D. Packard. il por U S News 69:44-8
Ag 3 '70
Not so hawkish; results of polls on military
spending. il Nation 211:354 O 19 '70
Power of the purse; Operation pursestrings.
Nation 210:674 Je 8 '70
What can concerned churchmen do about
the war in Indochina? J. Armstrong; G. Mc-
Govern; M. Hatfield. Chr Cent 87:622-3 My
20 '70
What cost growth in weapons costs the tax-
payer. il U S News 68:34 Ap 13 '70
What happens to the money? Nation 210:708
Je 15 '70
What the hawks look to. B. M. Russett. il
America 123:13-14 Jl 11 '70
See also
Military-industrial complex
United States—Air force—Appropriations and
expenditures
United States—Army—Appropriations and ex-
penditures
United States—Defense, Department of—Ap-
propriations and expenditures
United States—Navy—Appropriations and ex-
penditures

Barracks and quarters

What happens to the money? Nation 210:
708 Je 15 '70

Chaplains

See Chaplains, Military

Crimes and misdemeanors

See also
United States—Marine corps—Crimes and misdemeanors

Desertions

Hell, no, we won't go! deserters and draft
dodgers in Canada and Sweden. J. Cooney
and D. Spitzer; discussion. Trans-Action
7:10+ F '70
Need to hate; deserters in Canada. S. Alsop.
Newsweek 76:80 Jl 27 '70
Reporter at large; deserters in Sweden. D.
Lang. New Yorker 46:42-6+ My 23 '70
Soul Alley; home for black AWOLs and de-
serters. il Time 96:39-40 D 14 '70
They can't go home again; deserters in
Canada. S. Alsop. Newsweek 76:88 Jl 20 '70
Unilateral withdrawal of Private Weise. P.
Collier. Ramp Mag 8:4+ F '70

Equipment and supplies

Generators get in fighting trim. Bsns W p45-
6 S 5 '70
See also
Vietnamese war, 1957- —Equipment and supplies

Forces in Asia

Beyond Agnew mission: a U.S. plan for pulling back from Asia. il U S News 69:18-19
Ag 31 '70
Lowering the U.S. profile throughout Asia.
il Time 97:20+ Ja 18 '71
Sun never sets on America's empire; bases
overseas. M. T. Klare. Commonweal 92:239-
43 My 22 '70

Forces in Europe

Don't pull the GI's out of Europe; inter-
view, ed. by J. R. Moskin. W. Brandt. por
Look 34:82+ Ap 21 '70
European cuts spur service feuds. Aviation
W 93:14-15 Jl 6 '70
If U.S. pulls back from Europe. il U S News
68:78-9 Mr 16 '70
United States and western Europe; address,
January 20, 1970. E. L. Richardson. Vital
Speeches 36:258-60 F 15 '70; Same. Dept
State Bul 62:155-9 F 9 '70
United States forces in Europe; address,
April 10, 1970. S. R. Resor. Vital Speeches
36:456-9 My 15 '70
We're paying too much for NATO. C. H.
Percy. Read Digest 97:115-18 N '70
Why American GI's will stay in Europe. U S
News 68:24 Je 8 '70
Why American troops should remain in Eu-
rope. W. E. Griffith. Read Digest 96:121-5
My '70
Why U.S. will not take GI's out of Europe
now; with interview with Gen. A. J. Good-
paster. il U S News 69:59-63 D 7 '70

Forces in foreign countries

Limits to intervention. G. Allison and others.
For Affairs 48:245-61 Ja '70
Million servicemen abroad: where they are,
and why. il U S News 69:20-2 D 28 '70

UNITED STATES—Armed forces—*Continued*

Forces in Japan

U.S. steps up troop cuts in Far East. il U S
News 70:55 Ja 4 '71

Forces in Korea

Case for and against military withdrawal
from Vietnam and Korea; address, April
1970, with questions and answers. F. Greene.
Ann Am Acad 390:1-17 Jl '70
Yankees going home. il Time 96:24 Ag 3 '70

Forces in Laos

And now Laos? Commonweal 92:27-8 Mr
20 '70
In the President's words; what U.S. is doing
in Laos; statement, March 6, 1970. R. M.
Nixon. por U S News 68:86-8 Mr '70; Same
with title Scope of the U.S. involvement
in Laos. Dept State Bul 62:405-9 Mr 30 '70
Indochina not an issue? New Repub 163:7-8
N 7 '70
Lousing up Laos; analysis of President
Nixon's March 6 statement. J. Osborne.
New Repub 162:15-17 Mr 21 '70

Forces in Turkey

Problem of visibility. R. M. Fresco. Nation
211:206-8 S 14 '70

Forces in Vietnam

Another checkup on drug use by GI's. il U S
News 69:33 Ag 31 '70
Close-up of the grunt: the hours of bore-
dom, the seconds of terror. J. P. Sterba. il
N Y Times Mag p30-1+ F 8 '70; Discus-
sion. p6+ Mr 1 '70
Fresh disclosures on drugs and GI's; Senate
investigation into marijuana smoking. il
U S News 68:32-3 Ap 6 '70
Marijuana: the other enemy in Vietnam. il
U S News 68:68-9 Ja 26 '70
New GI: for pot and peace. il Newsweek 75:
24+ F 2 '70
People-to-people programs for GI's in Viet-
nam. il U S News 68:89-91 Mr 23 '70
Scraps of paper from Vietnam; comp. by J.
P. Sterba. il N Y Times Mag p28-9+ O 18 '70
Why men fight. C. C. Moskos, jr. bibliog il
por Trans-Action 7:13-23 N '69
Why more troops to Vietnam, despite pull-
backs. il U S News 68:89 My 11 '70
See also
Telephone calls to service men in Vietnam
United States—Army—Forces in Vietnam
United States—Marine corps—Forces in Viet-
nam
Vietnamese war, 1957- —American participa-
tion
Vietnamese war, 1957- —American troop with-
drawals

Forces in Vietnam—Recreation

See United States—Armed forces—Recreation

Foreign enlistments

See also
United States—Navy—Foreign enlistments

Medical and sanitary affairs

See also
Vietnamese war, 1957- —Medical and sanitary affairs

Morale

Why men fight; American combat soldiers in
Vietnam. C. C. Moskos, jr. bibliog il por
Trans-Action 7:13-23 N '69

Negroes

Black views aired before chaplains' commis-
sion. Chr Cent 87:1344 N 11 '70
See also
United States—Army—Negroes—History
United States—Marine corps—Negroes
Vietnamese war, 1957- —Negroes

Officers

Two worlds; the future officer; address,
January 17, 1970. B. K. Holloway. Vital
Speeches 36:262-5 F 15 '70
See also
Concerned officers movement

Political activities

Military life. New Repub 162:9 Ja 17 '70

Post exchanges

Military meets the Afro. L. Banks. il pors
Ebony 25:86-92 S '70

Procurement

Military procurement again facing cuts. il
Aviation W 93:10-11 D 28 '70

Military procurement; research, development,
test & evaluation; tables. Aviation W 92:16-
17 F 9 '70
Pentagon mess. Nation 211:163-4 S 7 '70
Where defense cuts hurt most. il U S News
69:40-2 O 5 '70

Public relations

Armed forces; a representative segment of
American society; address, January 31,
1970. W. C. Westmoreland. Vital Speeches
36:299-301 Mr 1 '70
Brass image. D. Shearer. il Nation 210:455-
64 Ap 20 '70
Collective security; criticism of the armed
forces; address June 15, 1970. L. L. Lemnit-
zer. Vital Speeches 36:669-71 Ag 15 '70
How it looks from the colonies. D. Brogan.
Esquire 73:68+ Mr '70
Why defense planners worry; interview. E.
G. Wheeler. il por U S News 68:34-9 Ap
20 '70
See also
United States—Armed forces—Relations with
civilians

Publications

See also
Stars and stripes (newspaper)

Race problems

See also
United States—Army—Race problems

Recreation

I get a lot more than I give. B. Hope. Read
Digest 96:177-8+ Ja '70
Miss Black America takes soul to Vietnam.
il pors Ebony 25:88-90+ My '70
This is Bob (politician-patriot-publicist)
Hope. J. A. Lukas. il pors N Y Times Mag
p28-9+ O 4 '70

Recruiting and enlistment

See also
Military service, Voluntary

Regulations

Humanizing of the U.S. military. il por Time
96:16-22 D 21 '70
Mickey Mouse war; liberalized army and navy
rules. il Newsweek 76:51-2 D 14 '70

Relations with civilians

How it looks from the colonies. D. Brogan.
il Esquire 73:54+ Ap '70
Snooping on the home front; army surveillance of civilians. J. Hanlon. Nation 211:
305-6 O 5 '70
War termination as a problem in civil-military relations. M. H. Halperin. bibliog f
Ann Am Acad 392:36-95 N '70

Religious affairs

Case of the wholly secular chapel. D. M.
Kelley. Chr Cent 87:1166-9 S 30 '70
Service academies' required chapel challenged
in court. G. Jones. Chr Cent 87:458-60
Ap 15 '70

Reserves

Who dies in Vietnam? motive for Pentagon's
switch from draft to reserve. L. K. Truscott, 4th. il Nation 211:326-7 O 12 '70
See also
United States—National guard

**Arms control and disarmament
agency**

Ninth annual report of ACDA transmitted to
the Congress; President Nixon's letter of
transmittal; with excerpts from report. R.
M. Nixon. Dept State Bul 62:585-99 My 4 '70

Army

Eyes left; J. M. O'Brien charges army with
political snooping. Newsweek 76:18 D 28
'70
Looking for trouble; court rules on army
blacklist of potential U.S. civilians. News-
week 75:35-6 My 4 '70
Making it in the U.S. army. E. L. King. New
Repub 162:19-21 My 30 '70
Military men, by W. Just. Review
Life 69:12 D 11 '70. W. McWhirter
Nerve gas disposal; how the AEC refused
to take army off the hook. L. J. Carter.
Science 169:1296-8 S 25 '70
Soldiers. W. Just. Atlan 226:59-98 O; 59-90 N
'70
Spying on civilians; monitoring of political
and social protest activities of civilians by
army intelligence. Time 95:117-18 Mr 9 '70
See also
Courts martial and courts of inquiry
Military life
Military training camps

UNITED STATES—Army—*Continued*

Appropriations and expenditures

Safeguard extension aimed at urban area protection. Aviation W 92:22-3 F 9 '70

Corps of engineers

America the raped, by G. Marine. Review Am West 7:50+ Mr '70. J. E. Illick

Cloudy Sunshine state; flirting with ecological disaster. il Time 95:48+ Ap 13 '70

Corps and the environment. J. T. Starr. il Am For 76:28-31 N '70

Corps of engineers, water, and ecology. Audubon 72:102 Jl '70

Dam outrage: the story of the army engineers. E. B. Drew. il Atlan 225:51-62 Ap '70

Dam the rivers, full speed ahead. M. Frome. Field & S 75:58-9+ O; 12+ N; 16-17+ D '70

Death row; Gillham dam project on the Cossatot River. W. Jack, jr. il Audubon 72:139 S '70

Potomac River dams; testimony and excerpts from remarks of other witnesses at Senate hearings. A. W. Smith. il Nat Parks & Con Mag 44:23-6 S '70

See also
Central and southern Florida flood control district

Corps of military police

Palace revolt; debate among the 519th MPs. J. B. Reston, jr. New Repub 162:9-10 Je 6 '70

Crimes and misdemeanors

Tragedy at Song My; the case deepens. U S News 68:28 Mr 30 '70

See also
Mutiny

Desertions

See United States—Armed forces—Desertions

Equipment and supplies

See also
Motor trucks, Military
Tanks, Military

Forces in Ethiopia

Why Pentagon has a special interest in Ethiopia: Kagnew station, Asmara. il U S News 68:48 F 23 '70

Forces in Europe

Case for GI's in Europe. il Newsweek 75:35-6 Mr 2 '70

Our uptight troops in Europe: Fulda, northeast of Frankfurt. L. Gross. il pors Look 34:14-19 S 8 '70

Forces in foreign countries

Soldiers; Military assistance officers program. W. Just. Atlan 226:72-81 N '70

Forces in Germany

Black explosions in West Germany; racial trouble of the Seventh army. il Time 96: 36 S 21 '70

Race and the GI. il por Newsweek 76:37-8 N 9 '70

Forces in Korea

Reports: Korea. J. B. Ritch. Atlan 226:6+ O '70

Forces in Vietnam

Carrot and stick; combat refusals. il Newsweek 75:45 My 25 '70

Evans nine; racial trouble in Alfa company. Newsweek 75:50 Je 29 '70

Just downright refusal; incident in war zone C. Newsweek 75:51 Ap 20 '70

Making it in the U.S. army. E. L. King. New Repub 162:19-21 My 30 '70

Troubled U.S. army in Vietnam; with report by K. Buckley. il Newsweek 77:29-31+ Ja 11 '71

Vietnam: out faster; deterioration of discipline and morale. Newsweek 76:104 D 7 '70

You can't just hand out orders; experience of a company commander in Vietnam. J. Saar. il pors Life 69:30-7 O 23 '70

See also
United States—Army—Special forces—Forces in Vietnam

Infantry

Black Buffaloes; 92nd infantry division. P. S. Cook. il Newsweek 75:45 Je 8 '70

Medical and sanitary affairs

Does our army fight on drugs? ed. by C. S. Wren. J. H. Kaplan. Look 34:72+ Je 16 '70

Military police

See United States—Army—Corps of military police

Morale

Carrot and stick; combat refusals. il Newsweek 75:45 My 25 '70

Negroes

Black explosions in West Germany; racial troubles of the Seventh army. il Time 96: 36 S 21 '70

Evans nine; racial trouble in Alfa company. Newsweek 75:50 Je 29 '70

Our uptight troops in Europe: Fulda, northeast of Frankfurt. L. Gross. il pors Look 34:18-19 S 8 '70

Race and the GI. il por Newsweek 76:37-8 N 9 '70

See also
Vietnamese war, 1957- —Negroes

Negroes—History

Black Buffaloes; 92nd infantry division. P. S. Cook. il Newsweek 75:45 Je 8 '70

Black continentals; Negro soldiers serving in the American war of independence. P. Barnett. il Negro Hist Bul 33:6-10 Ja '70

Officers

Case study of an army star; Brig. General S. B. Berry, jr. L. H. Lapham. il pors Life 69:54-6+ S 25 '70

Soldiers. W. Just. Atlan 226:59-98 O; 59-90 N '70

You can't just hand out orders; experience of a company commander in Vietnam. J. Saar. il pors Life 69:30-7 O 23 '70

Pay, allowances, etc.

Is the army a welfare state? R. Altmeyer. Nat R 22:300 Mr 24 '70

Prisons

Unlawful concert: an account of the Presidio mutiny case, by F. Gardner. Review Nation 210:628-30 My 25 '70. E. F. Sherman

Ramp Mag 8:52-3 Je '70. A. Hochschild

Procurement

Army plans 'should-cost' approach to procurements. K. Johnsen. Aviation W 92:15-16 Je 1 '70

Should-cost is the new weapons test. il Bsns W p48-9 My 30 '70

Race problems

Black explosions in West Germany; trouble in the Seventh army. il Time 96:36 S 21 '70

Race and the GI. il por Newsweek 76:37-8 N 9 '70

Recruiting and enlistment

See also
Military service, Voluntary

Regulations

See also
Soldiers—Civil rights

Relations with civilians

See United States—Armed forces—Relations with civilians

Religious affairs

Ready, aim, pray! L. Pfeffer. Commonweal 93:274-6 D 11 '70

Security agency

See United States—Army security agency

Special forces

Confessions of a Green Beret. W. Pfaff. Commentary 49:28-34 Ja '70

Special forces—Forces in Vietnam

From legend to liability: the Green Berets. il Newsweek 76:26 Ag 24 '70

Green Berets. P. J. Riga. il Cath World 210: 199-203 F '70; Discussion. 211:100, 148 Je-Jl '70

Murder case without a body; Green Beret case: I spy, but for whom? Sr Schol 95: 17 O 20 '69

Whatever happened to the Green Berets in Vietnam? il U S News 69:65 N 2 '70

Army security agency

Keeping tabs on civilians. J. Stout. il Nation 211:681-3 D 28 '70

No-wash whitewash; army intelligence spying on civilians. Nation 212:2 Ja 4 '71

Art

See Art, American

Atomic energy commission

America's most radioactive city. N. Wood. McCalls 97:46+ S '70

UNITED STATES—Atomic energy commission
—*Continued*
Catch 24,400; or, Plutonium is my favorite element; fire at Rocky Flats plant. R. Rapoport. il Ramp Mag 8:16-21 My '70
Controversial atomic energy commission. G. Alexander and H. Simmons. il Newsweek 77:37-40 Ja 4 '71
Current state of physics: AEC's view; interview. ed. by G. B. Lubkin, P. McDaniel; W. A. Wallenmeyer. il por Phys Today 23: 55-8 My '70
Fallout over Seaborg. il por Time 97:49 Ja 4 '71
Fire damage; aftermath of fire at Rocky Flats plutonium plant, with AEC statement. E. A. Martell and others. il Environ 12:14-21 My '70
Gofman and Tamplin: harassment charges against AEC, Livermore. P. M. Boffey. pors Science 169:838-43 Ag 28 '70
Job cuts at the national laboratories. Sci N 97:192 F 21 '70
Nerve gas disposal: how the AEC refused to take army off the hook. L. J. Carter. Science 169:1296-8 S 25 '70
New judge for the atom? J. Lear. Sat R 53: 39 Ag 1 '70
Nuclear fuel runs scarce. il Bsns W p84-5 Mr 21 '70
Nuclear threat inside America. J. Shepherd. il Look 34:21-7 D 15 '70
Population control through nuclear pollution, by A. R. Tamplin and W. Cofman. Review Environ 12:46-7 D '70. S. Novick
Question of jurisdiction; federal vs. state control of nuclear power plants. il Sci N 97:406 Ap 25 '70
Radiation effects controversy; with reply by T. J. Thompson and W. R. Bibb. A. R. Tamplin and J. W. Gofman. Bul Atom Sci 26:2+ S '70
Rerun on Amchitka; cannikan test. il Sci N 97:367-8 Ap 11 '70
Rocky Flats still smolders. il Sci N 97:194 F 21 '70
Visit with Paul McDaniel of the AEC; interview. ed. by G. B. Lubkin. P. W. McDaniel. il por Phys Today 23:56-7+ Ap '70
Water and air; proposed plant at Shoreham, NY. H. G. Paster. il New Repub 163:24-6 O 31 '70
What future for the AEC? H. L. Davis. Phys Today 23:80 Ag '70
Why the AEC dropped Battelle; with editorial comment. il Bsns W p 110+, 124 N 21 '70
See also
Brookhaven national laboratory
Hanford works, Richland, Wash.

Appropriations and expenditures
New weapons raise AEC budget. il Aviation W 92:44-5 F 16 '70
Paying for power, warheads. Sci N 97:148 F 7 '70

Attorney General
See United States—Justice, Department of

Boundaries
Agreement to conclude treaty to resolve boundary problems. Dept State Bul 63:296-300 S 14 '70

Budget, Bureau of the
Budget bureau: do advisory panels have an industry bias? with reply by R. P. Mayo. V. Reinemer. Science 169:36-9 Jl 3 '70
Budget bureau wields a powerful ax. il por Bsns W p80-3 Ja 17 '70
See also
United States—Management and budget, Office of

Bureau of Indian affairs
See United States—Indian affairs, Bureau of

Bureau of standards
See United States—Standards, National bureau of

Cabinet
After the off-year: the ins and outs. il Newsweek 76:30-1 N 23 '70
Benign neglect? il Newsweek 75:32 My 25 '70
Cabinet capers; liaison with the White House. J. Osborne. New Repub 162:15-17 My 30 '70
Strains in the Nixon team: is the President isolated? il U S News 68:28-30 My 25 '70
Unemployment at 33 per cent. G. Ace. Sat R 53:10+ D 12 '70
Widening cracks in Nixon's Cabinet. il Time 95:7-8 Je 1 '70
See also
Cabinet officers

Capital
See also
Washington, D.C.

Census
Census: countdown or lowdown? Sr Schol 96:11-12 Mr 23 '70
Census is over, but. . . il U S News 68:50 Ap 13 '70
Census '70: needed, easy, secret. C. Taeuber. il PTA Mag 64:12-14 Ja '70
Census '70: portrait of America. J. B. Shuman. Read Digest 96:19-20+ Mr '70
Census taker and you; what to expect. il U S News 68:32 Mr 23 '70
Count off! It's census time. il Changing T 24:35-6 Mr '70
Countdown for 1970; facts from the Current population survey. J. Lear. Sat R 53:46-7 Ap 4 '70
Counting and the costs. Nations Bsns 58: 26-7 Ap '70
Counting heads. Time 96:12 D 14 '70
Determining the labor force status of men missed in the census. D. P. Klein. il Mo Labor R 93:26-32 Mr '70
Everybody counts in 1970. G. Town. il Har Yrs 10:14-15 Mr '70
Flight from the cities: it's growing. il U S News 69:33 S 7 '70
Furor over the '70 census. il U S News 69: 28-32 Jl 27 '70
Growth and differentiation. Sci Am 223:52 O '70
Head-counting time is here again. il Bsns W p80+ F 7 '70
Losers; weepers; first figures from the 1970 census. Newsweek 76:22-3 Jl 20 '70
Muffled boom. il Sr Schol 97:10-12 S 28 '70
New South as census shows it; excerpts from address, October 23, 1970. G. H. Brown. U S News 69:54 N 2 '70
1970 census. D. Whitson. il Todays Ed 59:30-2+ Ja '70
Not really so nosy. il Time 95:19-20 Ap 13 '70
Outward bound; preliminary report of the 1970 census. il Newsweek 76:32-3 S 14 '70
Politics of population; new political alignment. Nat R 22:1040-1 O 6 '70
Portrait of a decade. D. H. Wrong. il N Y Times Mag p22-3+ Ag 2 '70
Profit from 1970 census data. A. R. Eckler. il Harvard Bsns R 48:4-6+ Jl '70
Second-guessing the census takers. il Bsns W p86 S 19 '70
Sense of the census. il Newsweek 75:80 Ap 6 '70
'70 census: how many Americans and where they are. il U S News 69:22-5 S 14 '70
Surprises from the census. il Bsns W p 16-17 Ag 8 '70
Surprises in the '70 census. il U S News 69:17 Ag 31 '70

Anecdotes, facetiae, satire, etc.
Who blew the U.S. nose count? F. Deford. il Sports Illus 33:72-3+ D 21 '70

Census, Bureau of the
Census data: tailored to suit you. Nations Bsns 58:52 Ag '70
Municipal manhunt; charges of undercounting. il Newsweek 76:77 S 7 '70

Central intelligence agency
Air America: flying the U.S. into Laos. P. D. Scott. por Ramp Mag 8:39-42+ F '70
Bad news from the CIA; Communist agents in the South Vietnamese government. Nation 211:420 N 2 '70
Clandestine militarism; Air America and the CIA. Nation 210:452 Ap 20 '70
Enemy within; report on Communist spies inside Saigon government. il Newsweek 76: 65 N 2 '70
Game of nations, by M. Copeland. Review Nation 210:759-60 Je 22 '70. D. Stewart
New Repub 162:25-6 My 23 '70. A. Campbell
Sat R por 53:39-41 My 23 '70. D. Kurzman
Intelligence establishment, by H. H. Ransom. Review
Sat R 53:24+ S 5 '70. M. Copeland
Notes and comment; C.I.A. support of opium-producing Meo tribe. New Yorker 46:31 Ap 11 '70
Who spies, and why? il Sr Schol 96:4-9 F 9 '70

Church history
In quest of America's religion. S. E. Mead. por Chr Cent 87:752-6 Je 17 '70

Civil aeronautics board
Airline secret gets hit by flak; agreement to cut competing routes. il Bsns W p74 S 26 '70
Airlines are urged to study markets. Aviation W 93:28 O 12 '70

UNITED STATES—Civil aeronautics board—
—Continued
Airlines, CAB grapple with cargo tariffs. H.
  D. Watkins. il Aviation W 93:39+ O 26 '70
Airlines tighten their seat belts. il por News-
  week 76:85 O 19 '70
Bills keep CAB's mail rate rights. Aviation
  W 92:30 Je 1 '70
Board grants tentative approval to Eastern-
  Caribair merger step. H. D. Watkins.
  Aviation W 93:30 N 16 '70
Board suspends Hawaii filings. H. D. Wat-
  kins. Aviation W 93:24-5 Jl 20 '70
Browne seeks broadened role for CAB. L.
  Doty. Aviation W 93:32-3 S 14 '70
CAB acts to halt subsidy reductions. Avia-
  tion W 92:32 My 4 '70
CAB chairman picks advisory groups. Avia-
  tion W 93:38-9 N 2 '70
CAB criticized by aide of Nader on airline
  ownership reporting. Aviation W 93:25 Ag
  24 '70
CAB girds for major fare investigation. Avia-
  tion W 92:35-6 Mr 16 '70
CAB monitoring charter crash study. Avia-
  tion W 93:21 O 19 '70
CAB orders new tariff filings. Aviation W
  93:21 Ag 3 '70
CAB studies load factor fares standard. Avi-
  ation W 93:30 D 14 '70
CAB tightens enforcement on oversales. L.
  Doty. il Aviation W 92:28 Je 29 '70
CAB to expand its investigations to East
  coast charter operators. Aviation W 92:
  39 Mr 30 '70
CAB unit expands investigation of alleged il-
  legal charter actions. Aviation W 93:29 Jl 6
  '70
CAB unit favors load factor standards. H. D.
  Watkins. Aviation W 93:28-30 Jl 27 '70
CAB unit hits affinity charter practices. J. P.
  Woolsey. Aviation W 92:38 F 2 '70; Reply.
  M. G. Manak. 92:66 Mr 2 '70
CAB wants the affinity back in flying. Bsns
  W p94+ Jl 25 '70
Carriers weigh new fare bids; CAB blocks
  summer, 747 rises. H. D. Watkins. Aviation
  W 92:34 My 18 '70
Chicago, CAB at odds over Midway. H. D.
  Watkins. Aviation W 92:53+ Ap 27 '70
Delta, National bid CAB consider alterna-
  tives to Northwest merger. Aviation W 92:
  28 F 23 '70
Disapproval of IATA vote plan by CAB
  sparks new protests. Aviation W 93:23 S 21
  '70
Dog fight over charter flights. il Bsns W
  p 128+ F 28 '70
Is there any way to run an airline? T. Alex-
  ander. Fortune 82:117+ S '70
Micronesia award creates dilemma for administration. L. Doty. Aviation W 92:27-8
  Je 1 '70
Permanent certificate awards to Atlantic
  supplementals urged. H. D. Watkins. Aviation W 94:24-5 Ja 11 '71
Protests spur CAB to delay issue of eased
  military charter rules. D. C. Winston. Aviation W 92:24 F 16 '70
Seating, fare issues speeded by CAB in tariff
  investigation. Aviation W 93:25 N 30 '70
Survival of REA depends on results of CAB
  probe. Aviation W 93:133 O 26 '70
Three-part fare review planned. H. D. Watkins. Aviation W 92:29-31 F 9 '70
TWA offers new capacity control plan. Aviation W 94:25 Ja 4 '71

Civil rights commission
See United States—Commission on civil
rights

Civilization
Agnew speaks out on terrorists vs. law and
  order; the American system; excerpts from
  address, September 2, 1970. S. T. Agnew.
  por U S News 69:49 S 14 '70
American century: myth vs. reality; interview.
  D. J. Boorstin. il por U S News 69:64-7 O
  19 '70
American institutions and ecological ideals;
  adaptation of address, December 29, 1969.
  L. Marx. bibliog Science 170:945-52 N 27 '70
America's changing culture; excerpts from
  The pursuit of loneliness: American cul-
  ture at the breaking point. P. E. Slater.
  Cur 119:15-21 Je '70
Austere and the earnestly ghastly; 19th cen-
  tury America at the Met. R. Phelps. il Life
  68:10 Je 19 '70
Bag of scary mush; views of C. A. Reich.
  S. Alsop. Newsweek 76:102 N 9 '70
Can we afford tomorrow? address, November
  19, 1970. J. I. Miller. Vital Speeches 37:
  190-2 Ja 1 '71
Con-manship; Consciousness III; hopes for
  transforming American culture. D. M. Alpern. por Newsweek 76:31-2 N 9 '70

De Tocqueville revisited; views of J.-F. Revel.
  Newsweek 76:44-5 N 9 '70
Emerging technetronic era; excerpts from
  Between two ages. Z. Brzezinski. Cur 124:
  56-64 D '70
End of the American era, by A. Hacker. Re-
  view
    Nation 211:186-8 S 7 '70. O. E. Clubb
Fuzzy welcome to Cons. III; Consciousness
  III, hoping to transform American society.
  il por Time 96:12-13 N 2 '70
Greening of a con-III-man. M. Novak. Com-
  monweal 93:245-9 D 4 '70
Greening of America, by C. A. Reich. Review
    Fortune 82:63+ N '70. M. Ways
    Nat R 22:1354-5 D 15 '70. D. Brudnoy
    Nation 212:85-7 Ja 18 '71. E. Capouya
    New Repub 163:21+ N 14 '70. P Caws
    Sat R 53:24-6 D 5 '70. R. Eisner
Honest, intelligible radical politics. R. Bru-
  stein. New Repub 163:15-17 S 26 '70; Same.
  Cur 123:20-3 N '70
In the country of the young. J. W. Aldridge;
  discussion. Harper 240:8-10 Ja '70
Massive breakdown we face. E. D. Genovese.
  Cur 120:3-6 Ag '70
Mythological and real America. E. M. von
  Kuehnelt-Leddihn. il Cath World 210:208-
  12 F '70
New longings abroad in the land; views of
  three culture critics. B. DeMott. Sat R 53:
  23-6 Jl 4 '70
New shape of America; symposium, with
  editorial comment by R. Graves. il Life
  70:1-13+ Ja 8 '71
1950 was more than twenty years ago. J.
  Didion. Life 68:20B Ja 30 '70
1970: a time of in-betweenity. Chr Cent 87:
  1551 D 30 '70
Redeeming of America according to Charles
  Reich. A. M. Greeley. America 124:14-17
  Ja 9 '71
Reflections: new generation in relation to
  the corporate state and the new consciousness. C. A. Reich. New Yorker 46:42-6+ S
  26 '70
Responsible university leadership; violence
  and dissent; address, September 16, 1970.
  R. M. Nixon. Vital Speeches 36:738-40 O 1
  '70; Excerpts. il por U S News 69:27-8 S
  28 '70
Spirit of '70: six historians reflect on what
  ails the American spirit; symposium. il
  Newsweek 76:18-34 Jl 6 '70
Supernation at peace and war, by D. Wake-
  field. Review
    Trans-Action 7:63-7 Ja '70. G. Von Der
    Muhll
Trustee of the culture; excerpt from address.
  A. MacLeish. Sat R 53:18-19 D 19 '70
Urban civilization & its discontents; theories
  of the Founding fathers. I. Kristol. Com-
  mentary 50:29-35 Jl '70; Discussion. 50:4,
  40+ N '70; 51:23-6 Ja '71
You can take Salem out of the country,
  but—. J. H. Bowden. Chr Cent 87:1562-3
  D 30 '70
    See also
Americanism
United States—Intellectual life
United States—Popular culture
United States—Social conditions

Anecdotes, facetiae, satire, etc.
Dictionary for the disenchanted. B. Rosen-
  berg. il Harper 241:93-5 N '70
Short educational dictionary. K. Amis and
  R. Conquest. N Y Times Mag p4+ Ja 10
  '71

Climate
Climatic anomaly over the United States during the 1960's. J. Namias. bibliog il Science
  170:741-3 N 13 '70

Coast guard
Above the Arctic Circle; 1969 International ice
  patrol glacier survey. D. A. Smith. il Am
  Scholar 39:434-44 Sum '70
Boat owner's safety log; U.S coast guard
  stations maintaining a continuous listen-
  ing watch on the International distress
  and calling frequency. R. Humphrey. Motor
  B 125:142-3+ Ja '70
Coast guard explains; return of Simonas
  Kudirka. W. F. Buckley, jr. Nat R 22:1421
  D 29 '70
How Simas was returned; would-be defector
  Simonas Kudirka. Time 96:11 D 28 '70
Ice survey by the U.S. coast guard. W. S.
  Carlson. bibliog il Science 168:396-7 Ap 17
  '70
Nightmare off Gay Head; case of rejected
  Lithuanian sailor, Simonas Kudirka. il
  Newsweek 76:46+ D 14 '70

UNITED STATES—Coast guard—*Continued*
No sanctuary for Simonas; case of would-be Soviet defector, Simonas Kudirka. Time 96:21-2 D 14 '70
Soviet sailor seeks U.S. haven, but loses; case of Simas Kudirka. il U S News 69:30 D 14 '70
See also
United States coast guard academy, New London, Conn.

Coast guard auxiliary
Under the blue ensign. B. Woodward. See issues of Motor boating

Colonies
See United States—Territories and possessions

Commerce
Case for a positive trade policy; address, February 27, 1970. P. H. Trezise. Dept State Bul 62:333-8 Mr 16 '70
Changing attitude of U.S. labor unions toward world trade. W. C. Shelton. Mo Labor R 93:51-4 My '70
Department urges liberal foreign trade policy; statement, October 12, 1970. W. P. Rogers. Dept State Bul 63:556-8 N 2 '70
Economic policy; who's in charge? trade bill. G. Ball. por Newsweek 76:38-9 D 14 '70
Gaudy packaging hurts the trade bill. Bsns W p21-2 D 12 '70
Is the trade bill what it seems? il Bsns W p22-3 Ag 29 '70
Mills bill; savior or disaster? il Newsweek 76:77-8 D 7 '70
President Nixon calls for passage of trade bill; text of letter, May 11, 1970. R. M. Nixon. Dept State Bul 62:697-9 Je 1 '70
Report on trade agreements program transmitted to the Congress; message, December 16, 1969. R. M. Nixon. Dept State Bul 62: 62 Ja 19 '70
Tide turns for U.S. exports. il Newsweek 76: 59-60 S 7 '70
Trade act of 1969; message to the Congress, November 18, 1969. R. M. Nixon. Dept State Bul 61:559-63 D 15 '69
Trade expansion expectations; address, November 19, 1969. C. J. Gilbert. Dept State Bul 61:564-8 D 15 '69
Trade fight is a race with time. Bsns W p26 N 28 '70
Trade: the black comedy that could come true. il Time 96:97-8 N 23 '70
United States foreign trade: January-July 1970. Dept State Bul 63:424 O 12 '70
United States international trade prospects; challenge of new world competitive forces; address, March 9, 1970. K. N. Davis, jr. Vital Speeches 36:390-2 Ap 15 '70
See also
Export controls
Export trade
Import quotas
Merchant marine—United States
Tariff—United States
Thunderbird graduate school of international management, Phoenix, Ariz.
United States—President's commission on international trade and investment policy
World trade week

China—History
Cargoes of splendor. V. D. Hahn and M. Evans. il Am Home 74:46+ Ja '71

China (People's Republic)
Restrictions eased on trade with Communist China; Department statement; December 19, 1969. Dept State Bul 62:31-2 Ja 12 '70

Communist countries
Better red than red ink? il Forbes 105:63-4+ Je 15 '70
Coexistence & commerce, by S. Pisar. Review
Bsns W il p6 O 3 '70. J. Pearson

Europe, Western
Critical period for U.S.-European trade? U S News 69:35 Jl 13 '70

Japan
Irritated friendship. Chr Cent 87:835 Jl 8 '70
Japan: a market for our fed beef? C. E. Ball. il Farm J 94:B14-15 S '70
No winners in a trade war, and one is getting started. il U S News 69:46-8 S 14 '70
Protectionist push; talks collapse. Newsweek 76:66-7 Jl 6 '70
Snag in textiles. Time 95:74 Je 29 '70
Temporizing; Japanese textiles. il Nat R 22:720 Jl 14 '70

Trade squabble puts Sato on the spot. il por Bsns W p82-3 Ja 9 '71
TV set tiff. Sr Schol 97:12 S 28 '70
U.S.-Japanese trade: Sato on a tightrope. il por U S News 69:72 N 9 '70

Mexico
U.S.-Mexico trade committee holds fifth annual meeting; joint communique, March 6, 1970. Dept State Bul 62:428-9 Mr 30 '70

Pacific countries
Pacific basin. il Forbes 106:28-31+ N 1 '70

Rumania
Communist comes to talk business. il por Bsns W p28 O 31 '70

Russia
Ford in Russia's future? il Time 95:87 Ap 27 '70
Profits and security; Soviet truck plant. Newsweek 75:73-4 My 4 '70
Rush for Soviet trade gets under way. il Bsns W p 102-4+ Ja 24 '70
Russians lay out the red carpet for Ford. il Bsns W p27-8 Ap 25 '70
Which side is Russia on? Nation 210:68 Ja 26 '70

Yugoslavia
See also
Barter

Commerce, Department of
Commerce department: Myron Tribus, top science official, resigns. J. Walsh. por Science 170:1065-6 D 4 '70
U.S. plans to increase hard sell during Paris air show in 1971. Aviation W 92:22 F 23 '70
See also
United States—Minority business enterprise, Office of
United States—National oceanic atmospheric administration

National technical information service
New information service launched by Commerce dept. Library J 95:3716 N 1 '70

State technical services, Office of
U.S. seeks to share the facts. Bsns W p58+ Mr 21 '70

Commercial policy
See United States—Economic policy

Commercial treaties and agreements
U.S. and Pakistan conclude cotton textile agreement. Dept State Bul 62:703 Je 1 '70
United States and Brazil sign cotton textile agreement. Dept State Bul 63:664 N 23 '70
United States and Hungary sign cotton textile agreement. Dept State Bul 63:271 Ag 31 '70
United States and India sign cotton textile agreement. Dept State Bul 63:559 N 2 '70
United States and Jamaica sign new cotton textile agreement. Dept State Bul 63:182 Ag 10 '70
United States and Malaysia sign textile agreements; Department announcement; with texts of notes. il Dept State Bul 63: 497-503 O 26 '70
United States and U.A.R. conclude cotton textile agreement. Dept State Bul 63:598 N 9 '70

Commission on agricultural credit
See United States—Farm credit administration

Commission on campus unrest
See United States—President's commission on campus unrest

Commission on civil rights
And we quote: President Nixon's statement on school desegregation criticized in report. Commonweal 92:180 My 8 '70
In civil rights, is U.S. falling short? conclusions of Commission report. il U S News 69:29 O 26 '70
Whose law, whose order? Commonweal 93: 139-40 N 6 '70
Within the system. Commonweal 93:115-16 O 30 '70

Commission on financial institutions (proposed)
Another stab at financial reform; with editorial comment. por Bsns W p97+, 140 Ap 18 '70
Biggest reform? il Newsweek 75:84+ Ap 20 '70

UNITED STATES—*Continued*

Commission on government procurement
New tool for cutting government costs. C. Hollifield. il por Nations Bsns 58:58-60 F '70

Commission on international trade and investment policy
See United States—President's commission on international trade and investment policy

Commission on national goals
See United States—President's commission on national goals

Commission on obscenity and pornography
Advice and dissent. Sci Am 223:42 N '70
ALA testimony presented to Commission on obscenity and pornography; statement, May 4, 1970. J. F. Krug. Am Lib 1:653-5 Jl '70
Civil war over smut. J. Witcover. Nation 210:550-3 My 11 '70
Could Danish smut laws work here? J. N. Bell. il Todays Health 48:24-9+ N '70
Court enjoins publication of obscenity report. Pub W 198:37 S 21 '70
Critics: censored! pornography report. Sr Schol 97:6 N 9 '70
Enemies of porno, and of reason: an analysis. A. Plotnik. Wilson Lib Bul 45:232-3+ N '70
Is smut good for you? il Time 96:19 O 12 '70
Kind words for the porno-researchers. E. C. Kennedy. Commonweal 93:292-3 D 18 '70
Light on the darkness of pornography. PTA Mag 65:16-17 N '70
Obscenity. S. Kauffmann. New Repub 163:22+ O 17 '70
Odd man in. por Newsweek 76:44 S 21 '70
Oldest debate; report. il Newsweek 76:37 O 12 '70
Once more, into the fray. Sci N 98:284 O 3 '70
Perspective: pornography report survives. PTA Mag 65:14-15 O '70
Platform for permissiveness. Chr Today 15: 27-8 O 23 '70
Politics of pornography; librarian's reaction to Senate's rejection of report. E. M. Oboler. il Library J 95:4225-8 D 15 '70
Porno politics. Nation 211:452-3 N 9 '70
Porno report becomes political football. S. Wagner. Pub W 198:34-5 O 12 '70
Porno report cleared for publication; with editorial comment. Pub W 198:58-60, 62 S 28 '70
Pornography and politics; draft report. il Newsweek 76:81 Ag 17 '70
Pornography report: official findings that set off a furor; excerpts from report. il U S News 69:60-4 O 12 '70
Power of pornography. Chr Today 14:35 S 11 '70
Temptations of pornography. Chr Cent 87: 1339 N 11 '70; Reply. W. D. Lockhart. 87: 1541 D 23 '70
That obscenity report. G. Reedy. America 123:371-3 N 7 '70; Discussion. 123:366, 448 N 7, 28 '70
That porno report. Nat R 22:1097 O 20 '70

Commission on population growth and the American future
Holding down the population. il Newsweek 75:86-7 Mr 30 '70

Commission on productivity
See United States—National commission on productivity

Committee for economic development
See Committee for economic development

Committee on pesticides
See United States—Council on environmental quality

Congress
Congress and the public trust, by J. C. Kirby, jr. Review
Nation 211:26-8 Jl 6 '70. S. Watzman
Leadership in the Senate; floor leaders in Congress. D. Lawrence. U S News 68:88 My 4 '70
Reprives from cynicism. Chr Cent 87:467 Ap 22 '70
Strengthening Congress in national policy-making. N. W. Polsby. Yale R 59:481-97 Je '70
See also
Congressmen
Congresswomen

Legislation—United States
Presidents—United States—Relations with Congress

Chaplains
Piety on the Potomac. Newsweek 75:64 Je 8 '70

Committees
America: today and yesterday; interview. J. W. McCormack. il pors U S News 69:58-62 Jl 27 '70
Congress: the heavy hand of seniority; Time essay. G. Clarke. Time 96:22-3 D 14 '70
Congress's nine old men; movement for reform of the chairmanship seniority system. il Newsweek 75:20-1 F 2 '70
New Congress: election produces changes in key committee posts. L. J. Carter. Science 170:715-16 N 13 '70
Parting shots; the distinguished gentlemen from yesterday. il Life 68:81-4 Ap 10 '70
Pollution: everyone's in on the act. il Bsns W p 116+ Ja 24 '70
Study of the House seniority; appointment of Chairmen of all House committees. America 122:364 Ap 4 '70
Taking the creaks out of seniority; picking chairmen. il Bsns W p52-3 My 30 '70
Winning in November is not enough. J. K. Galbraith. New Repub 162:13-14 Je 13 '70; Reply. G. Allott. 163:31-4 Ag 15 '70
See also
United States—Congress—House—Committees

Joint committee on the environment (proposed)
How Congress focuses on the environment. R. A. Carpenter. Sat R 53:43 Ag 1 '70

Joint economic committee
Congressmen who play economist. il Bsns W p 108-9 F 14 '70
New timetable for the game plan. il Bsns W p 15-16 Jl 25 '70
When economics becomes politics; midyear hearings. il Newsweek 76:51-2 Ag 3 '70

Powers and duties
Congressional presence in foreign relations. J. K. Javits. For Affairs 48:221-34 Ja '70
Groundwork; coadjutant in foreign relations. Nation 210:36-7 Ja 19 '70
In the Senate moves to end the war—. U S News 69:73 S 14 '70
Intelligence of Congress: information and public-policy patterns. E. Schneier. bibliog f Ann Am Acad 388:14-24 Mr '70
Notes and comment: power to declare war or raise armies. il New Yorker 46:31-2 My 16 '70
Powers and dominations; war power of Congress and the President. Nat R 22:550+ Je 2 '70
President's war powers: what Senate finally voted; Cooper-Church amendment. il U S News 69:29 Jl 13 '70
Reforming itself; the issue Congress won't face. E. D. Eshleman and R. S. Walker. America 122:124-5 F 7 '70
War-making machinery. R. J. Bresler. il Nation 211:105-9 Ag 17 '70
Who makes our foreign policy? R. L. Tobin. Sat R 53:28 F 14 '70

Powers and duties—History
Congress didn't make war; can it make peace? il Newsweek 75:29 Je 1 '70
President's war powers. il Time 95:36-7 Je 1 '70

Reorganization
Another step. Commonweal 93:164 N 13 '70; Reply. D. R. Asmundsson. 93:383 Ja 15 '71
Congress's nine old men; movement for reform of the chairmanship seniority system. il Newsweek 75:20-1 F 2 '70
Greening of Congress. W. Barthelmes. Nation 211:552-5 N 30 '70
Reform in Congress. Commonweal 93:84-5 O 23 '70
Stuck reform; Legislative organization act of 1970. L. L. Gapay. New Repub 163:10-11 S 5 '70
See also
Congressmen—Term

Resolutions
Department gives views on proposal to repeal certain congressional resolutions; text of letter to Senator J. W. Fulbright, March 12, 1970. H. G. Torbert, jr. Dept State Bul 62:468-71 Ap 6 '70
One-upmanship; Tonkin Gulf resolution repealed. il Newsweek 76:37 Jl 6 '70

UNITED STATES—Congress—*Continued*

Rules and practice

Breakdown in Congress; behind the drive for reform. U S News 70:18-19 Ja 11 '71
Making Congress more effective; procedure reform proposals of the Committee for economic development. R. L. Tobin. Sat R 53:22 O 31 '70
91st redeemed? K. Crawford. Newsweek 76:31 O 26 '70

Salaries

See Congressmen—Salaries, allowances, etc.

Term of members

See Congressmen—Term

Voting

How they're rated in the tight races; past performance through the eyes of ACA, ADA and COPE. il Nations Bsns 58:104-5 O '70
Matter of survival; hospital-construction bill. Newsweek 76:31 Jl 13 '70
New & responsible Congress; need for reform to force a record vote. Nation 210: 613 My 25 '70
Practical art of political arm-twisting. Changing T 24:19-20 Je '70
Rating Congress; twenty-four test votes. il New Repub 163:17-23 O 24 '70
See also
United States—Congress—House—Voting
United States—Congress—Senate—Voting

91st Congress

Anticrime pace in Congress: much talk, little action. il U S News 69:22-4 Jl 27 '70
Breakdown in Congress; behind the drive for reform; session's record. U S News 70: 18-19 Ja 11 '71
Carry-over for 92nd Congress. B. L. Masse. America 124:5-6 Ja 9 '71
Congress that couldn't make it. il Newsweek 77:17-18 Ja 11 '71
Congress: unfinished business. America 123: 84 Ag 22 '70
Rating Congress; twenty-four test votes. il New Repub 163:17-23 O 24 '70
TRB from Washington; Congress and the Court. New Repub 162:8 F 14 '70
Why the welfare bill is stuck. il Newsweek 76:22-3 D 7 '70
See also
Nixon, R.M.—Relations with Congress

91st Congress—2d session

Call for co-operation; excerpts from message to Congress, September 11, 1970. R. M. Nixon. il por U S News 69:71-3 S 21 '70
Congress. Time 95.18 My 18; 13-14 Je 29; 96:12-13 S 28; 16 O 12; 25 D 7 '70; 97:23-4 Ja 4 '71
Congress. il Newsweek 75:16+ Ja 26; 18-19 Mr 9; 30-1 Mr 23; 21 Mr 30; 26-7 Ap 6; 47-8 Ap 20; 19 Je 29; 76:31 Jl 13; 18-19 Jl 20; 21-2 Jl 27; 18 Ag 10; 18-19 S 7; 42 S 21; 29 O 5; 29-30 O 26; 17-18 N 30; 21-2 D 7; 53-4 D 14; 15-16 D 28 '70
Congress faces some long nights. Bsns W p26 N 14 '70
Congress fights, but it works. Bsns W p27-8 Je 20 '70
Congress midway. New Repub 163:9-10 Jl 18 '70
Congress: the session in between. il Time 96:8-9 N 30 '70
Congress vs Nixon; the big issues of '70. il por U S News 68:22-5 Ja 26 '70
Do-nothing Congress? The record, the outlook. U S News 69:54-5 S 28 '70
Getting the lame ducks in a row. il Newsweek 76:29-31 N 23 '70
Lame ducks limp back to Capitol hill. H. J. Sievers. America 123:452 N 28 '70
Month in Congress. Cong Digest 49:65-6, 97-8, 129+, 161 Mr-Je '70
My God, we're back to square one. Newsweek 77:14-15 Ja 4 '71
New mood in Congress; eyes fixed on next November 3. America 122:90-1 Ja 31 '70
Pace quickens in Congress, but—. U S News 69:29 O 12 '70
Politics of crime. il Time 96:16-17 O 19 '70
Problems of a lameduck session. U S News 69:20 N 23 '70
Quicker pace in Congress, but still a long way to go. U S News 69:28-9 Jl 13 '70
Reelection fever hurts major bills. Bsns W p28-9 S 26 '70
Senate: chaos at the deadline. il Time 96:6-7 D 28 '70
Staying off the strikes. il Time 95:18 Ap 20 '70
Twilight Congress. Cato. Nat R 22:1258 D 1 '70

Unsettling finale in Congress. il Time 97: 10 Ja 11 '71
Welfare reform: key issue for lameduck session of Congress. U S News 69:92-3 O 19 '70

92d Congress

Business issues the new Congress faces. il Nations Bsns 58:26-8+ D '70
Congress gets ready to battle Nixon. il Bsns W p66-70 Ja 9 '71
Congress: how the power has shifted. il Bsns W p 17-18 N 7 '70
House gets sixty newcomers. il Newsweek 76:47-8 N 16 '70
Old elephants depart. I. Dilliard. Nation 211: 677 D 28 '70
Senate: class of '70. il Newsweek 76:42-4 N 16 '70
What to expect from Congress. il U S News 70:47-8 Ja 4 '71

92d Congress—1st session

Major aerospace funding awaits Congress's return. D. C. Winston. Aviation W 93:20 O 19 '70

House

Belling the cat; proposed measures to oversee the military. Nation 210:37 Ja 19 '70
Business almost as usual. Time 96:12-13 S 28 '70
Changes in the House: a prediction. R. W. Boyd and J. T. Murphy. New Repub 163:12-14 O 24 '70
Coming upheaval in Congress. J. Fischer. Harper 241:21-2+ O '70
Congress gets ready to battle Nixon. il Bsns W p66-70 Ja 9 '71
House battle; Democratic leadership. New Repub 163:9 D 5 '70
House gets sixty newcomers. il Newsweek 76:47-8 N 16 '70
Leaderless majority; seniority in the House. L. Gapay. Nation 210:134-6 F 9 '70
Newcomers in the House. il Time 96:27-8 N 16 '70
Power in the House; caucus for military money bills proposed. J. Smith. New Repub 162:10 My 30 '70
See also
Apportionment (election law)

House—Armed services, Committee on

After Rivers. Nation 212:36 Ja 11 '71
L. Mendel Rivers: king of the military mountain. R. G. Sherrill. por Nation 210:40-7 Ja 19 '70
Ol' man Rivers. C. McCarry. il por Esquire 74:168-71+ O '70
Powerful committee post for a defense-minded congressman. por U S News 70:45 Ja 11 '71

House—Committees

Dead hand of seniority. M. J. Harrington. Nation 211:229-32 S 21 '70
Seniority, a gerontocracy. P. S. Templin. America 124:27 Ja 9 '71
Study of House seniority; appointment of chairmen of all House committees. America 122:364 Ap 4 '70
Vested seniority; selection of committee chairmen. Nation 210:356 Mr 30 '70

House—Conservation and natural resources, Subcommittee on

Problems in the environmental decade; testimony. A. W. Smith. Nat Parks & Con Mag 44:25-7 Ap '70

House—Ethics committee

See United States—Congress—House — Standards of official conduct, Committee on

House—Government operations, Committee on

See also
United States—Congress—House—Conservation and natural resources, Subcommittee on

House—Internal security, Committee on

Electronics industry gives electrifying testimony; House committee on internal security hearings. Chr Cent 87:781 Je 24 '70
Manner of speaking: defense against accusation by HISC of being a radical. J. Ciardi. Sat R 53:12+ N 7 '70
Nothing to worry about; list of guest speakers at colleges. Nation 211:580 D 7 '70
Radicals and Mr Ciardi. N. Cousins. Sat R 53:24+ D 12 '70
Revival of heresy: speakers on campuses listed. Nation 211:450-1 N 9 '70

House—Reorganization

See United States—Congress—Reorganization

UNITED STATES—Congress—*Continued*

House—*Rules and practice*

Congress: some progress toward putting House in order. J. Walsh. Science 170:45-8 O 2 '70

Congress speeds its housecleaning. Bsns W p 112 S 12 '70

Stuck reform; Legislative organization act of 1970. L. L. Gapay. New Repub 163:10-11 S 5 '70

What you don't know. New Repub 163:7 Jl 11 '70

House—*Science and astronautics, Committee on*

Davis to succeed Daddario in committee chairmanship. C. Holden. por Science 170: 1284 D 18 '70

Future of a subcommittee; subcommittee on science, research and development. Sci N 97:289-90 Mr 21 '70

Mission agency support of basic research. Bul Atom Sci 26:35-7 S '70

House—*Speakers*

America: today and yesterday; interview. J. W. McCormack. il pors U S News 69:58-62 Jl 27 '70

End of an era in Congress. pors U S News 68:35 Je 1 '70

House: changing of the guard. P. S. Templin. America 123:421 N 21 '70

House speaker; target of rebels. por U S News 68:18 Mr 2 '70

Lindsay for president; need to replace Mc-Cormack. R. Bolling. il Look 34:73-5+ My 5 '70

McCormack: a symbol retires. por Time 35: 14 Je 1 '70

Mr Speaker yields the gavel; Most likely to succeed il por Newsweek 75:26-7 Je 1 '70
  See also
United States—Congress—92nd Congress

House—*Standards of official conduct, Committee on*

We can't depend on Congress to keep Congress honest. R. Sherrill. il N Y Times Mag p5-7+ Jl 19 '70

House—*Subcommittee on science, research and development*

See United States—Congress—House—Science and astronautics, Committee on

House—*Un-American activities, Committee on*

See United States—Congress—House—Internal security, Committee on

House—*Voting*

Ambush on the Hill; Cooper-Church amendment. J. Hightower and V. Newton. Nation 211:266-70 S 28 '70

No more secrets? Sr Schol 97:5 O 5 '70

Slowly, with feeling; Cooper-Church amendment. Newsweek 76:18-19 Jl 20 '70

Standing up to be counted; proposal to abolish teller voting. Newsweek 76:18 Ag 10 '70

House—*Ways and means, Committee on*

Ways & means machine gets engine trouble; with editorial comment. il Bsns W p88+, 150 Ap 25 '70

Welfare plan's improbable allies. Bsns W p35 F 28 '70

Senate

Ambitious Senate. K. Crawford. Newsweek 76:24 Jl 27 '70

Birch Bayh isn't a household word, yet. R. Sherrill. il pors N Y Times Mag p28-9+ F 15 '70

Cooking time; question of the Cooper-Church amendment. il Newsweek 75:28 Je 1 '70

Counting out Carswell. il por Newsweek 75: 26-7 Ap 6 '70

Critics: censored! pornography report. Sr Schol 97:6 N 9 '70

End of the 91st; week's work. Time 97:23-4 Ja 4 '71

Enemies of porno, and of reason: an analysis. A. Plotnik. Wilson Lib Bul 45:232-3+ N '70

Fight for the Senate. il Newsweek 76:19-20 Jl 20 '70

How Ford put the lid on Cooper-Church. N. MacNeil. Time 96:12-13 Jl 20 '70

My God, we're back to square one. Newsweek 77:14-15 Ja 4 '71

Nixon, the Senate & the war. N. G. Levin, jr. Commentary 50:69-84 N '70

Politics of pornography; rejection of the report of the Commission on obscenity and pornography. E. M. Oboler. il Library J 95:4225-8 D 15 '70

President's candidates. il Time 96:11-12 Jl 27 '70

Republican assault on the Senate. il Time 96: 18-22+ O 26 '70

Senate: chaos at the deadline. il Time 96:6-7 D 28 '70

Senate: class of '70. il Newsweek 76:42-4 N 16 '70

Senate outcasts. Trans-Action 7:10+ N '69

Senate: unloving acts; question of the Cooper-Church amendment. por Time 95:9-10 Je 1 '70

West Virginia Byrd; replacing Edward M. Kennedy as majority whip? P. R. Wieck New Repub 163:11-13 D 12 '70

Senate—*Armed services, Committee on*

Even thinner menu for contractors. il Bsns W p30-1 Je 27 '70

Key issues face Senate defense debate. D. C. Winston. Aviation W 93:16-17 Jl 20 '70

Senate—*Ethics committee*

See United States—Congress—Senate—Standards and conduct, Select committee on

Senate—*Finance committee*

Workfare belabored; Family assistance program. Time 86:17-18 O 5 '70

Senate—*Foreign relations, Committee on*

Congressional presence in foreign relations. J. K. Javits. For Affairs 48:221-34 Ja '70

Unequal duel; Symington subcommittee and U.S. involvement in Morocco, Libya and Ethiopia. Nation 211:482-4 N 16 '70

Senate—*Government operations, Committee on*

Senate v. Alan and Margaret McSurely. W. Goodman. il pors N Y Times Mag p28-9+ Ja 10 '71

Senate—*Internal security, Subcommittee on*

Killing cops; signs of a nationwide plot. il U S News 69:61 O 19 '70

War against the police; officers tell their story; testimony before Senate subcommittee. il U S News 69:82-6 O 26 '70

Senate—*Judiciary, Committee on the*

See also
United States—Congress—Senate—Internal security, Subcommittee on

Senate—*Rules and practice*

Bayh's last stand; opponents use filibuster. por Newsweek 76:29 O 5 '70

Filibuster in the works? cloture on electoral college issue. Cato. Nat R 22:992 S 22 '70

Senate reforms from four freshmen. il Time 96:8 D 28 '70

Senate—*Standards and conduct, Select committee on*

We can't depend on Congress to keep Congress honest. R. Sherrill. il N Y Times Mag p5-7+ Jl 19 '70

Senate—*Voting*

Annals of politics; nomination of G. H. Carswell to the Court. R. E. Harris. New Yorker 46:60-4+ D 5; 53-8+ D 12 '70

Carswell rejected. Sr Schol 96:15 Ap 27 '70

Congress: score one for persistence. W. Proxmire's campaign against SST. il Time 96:13-14 D 14 '70

Four crucial nays; why they did it: Senate's vote against G. H. Carswell. il Time 95:10-11 Ap 20 '70

Looking for the outer limits; Byrd amendment voted down. il Newsweek 75:19 Je 22 '70

Margin of safety; Cooper-Hart amendment. il Newsweek 76:14-15 Ag 24 '70

Nixon crisis; advice but no consent; G. H. Carswell's defeat. il pors Newsweek 75:35-40 Ap 20 '70

Nixon 1. Senate 0; bill to limit campaign spending on TV and radio. Time 96:25 D 7 '70

No confidence on Cambodia. Time 95:15 Je 22 '70

Odd couple; amendments to the military procurement bill. il Newsweek 76:18-19 S 7 '70

Plight of the doves; defeat of the McGovern-Hatfield proposal. il Time 96:15-16 S 14 '70

Senate stammers; the Byrd amendment. K. Crawford. Newsweek 76:39 Jl 6 '70

UNITED   STATES—Congress—Senate—Voting
—*Continued*
SST hits the Senate barrier. il Newsweek 76:
83-4 D 14 '70
Uneasy riders. Chr Cent 87:1277 N 25 '70
Veto sustained: bill to limit campaign spend-
ing on TV and radio. il Newsweek 76:21-2
D 7 '70

Constitution

Critique on Constitution experiments. D. S.
Broder. Cur 123:24-6 N '70
Here is the latest radical plan; interview, ed.
by G. Astor. L. Gorkin. Look 34:78 N 17 '70
Tugwell's constitution. por Newsweek 76:44+
S 21 '70
What   the V.P. should   learn; system of
checks and balances. W. Lippmann. il por
Newsweek 77:19 Ja 11 '71

Amendments

Fifteenth amendment and black America in
the century 1870-1970. il Negro Hist Bul
33:28-31 F '70
Fifteenth amendment and the white primary.
Negro Hist Bul 33:88-9 Ap '70
How not to elect a president: Time essays;
Bayh amendment. Time 95:26-7 My 4 '70
Same justice can be both a strict and a loose
constructionist. A. Lewis. il N Y Times
Mag p30-1+ My 24 '70
Worst scandal in our history; the Fourteenth
amendment; reprint. D. Lawrence. il U S
News 68:96+ Ja 26 '70
See also
Woman—Equal rights

Bill of rights

Average citizen and freedom. J. F. Krug
and J. A. Harvey. Am Lib 1:752 S '70
Freedoms act. Nation 211:34 Jl 20 '70
Is freedom dying in America? H. S. Com-
mager. il por Look 34:16-21 Jl 14 '70
Soundings on the right. Time 95:19 Ap 27 '70

Constitutional convention (proposed)

Dirksen's ghost. New Repub 163:8 Jl 25 '70
Dirksen's ghost. G. W. Johnson. New Repub 162:14-15 Mr 7 '70
New constitutional convention? il Sr Schol 96:
7-10 Mr 23 '70

Constitutional convention, 1787

First constitutional convention. il Sr Schol
96:5-6 Mr 23 '70

Constitutional history

In pursuit of duty; in re Neagle case. G.
L. Roberts. il pors Am West 7:26-33+ S '70

Constitutional law

See also
United States—Supreme court

Consumer affairs, Department
of (proposed)

Goal for 1970: a federal consumer advocate.
Consumer Rep 35:15-17 Ja '70
Should there be a U.S. department of con-
sumer affairs? pro and con discussion. Sr
Schol 96:13 Ja 26 '70

Consumer protection and environ-
mental health service

People's protector. por Time 95:62 Mr 16 '70

Council of economic advisers

Big issue is really Nov. 3; annual Joint economic committee hearings on economic
policy. il Bsns W p32-3 F 21 '70
CEA sounds a muted alert. il Bsns W p75 Ag
15 '70
Economic report of the President and the
annual report of the Council of economic
advisers; excerpts. R. M. Nixon. il Dept
State Bul 62:240-53 Mr 2 '70
First alert; report. Newsweek 76:64 Ag 17 '70
Gradualist's dream book; profile of 1970's
economy. il Bsns W p74-5 F 7 '70
Inflation fighters see a ray of hope. il Bsns W
p 114 Ap 18 '70
Surplus to generate more capital. il Bsns W
p 104+ Mr 14 '70
Why economists flunk out. M. J. Ulmer. New
Repub 163:6-7 S 19 '70; Discussion. 163:10-11
O 3; 34 O 10; 29-31 O 24 '70

Council of social advisers (proposed)

White House advisers: Nixon cool to plans
for health, social aides. L. J. Carter.
Science 170:48-9 O 2 '70

Council on environmental
quality

Clearcutting probe sought. Am For 76:37 Jl
'70

Dodging   the   crisis; annual report. P. R.
Ehrlich   and J. P. Holdren. Sat R 53:73
N 7 '70
Enemy is us. J. Lear. il Sat R 53:58-9 Mr
7 '70
Environment report: the reality and the il-
lusion. il Sci N 98:133 Ag 15 '70
Environmental quality council. Liv Wildn 34:
60 Spr '70
EPA & NOAA or CEQ? Nat Parks & Con Mag
44:25-6 O '70
First environmental quality report. Science
169:661 Ag 14 '70
Government's plan to phase out persistent
chemicals. il Farm J 94:20-1+ Ja '70
History in making, Council on environment-
al quality. il Parks & Rec 5:13 Mr '70
I hold in my hand; noncompliance with
Environmental quality act by SST. Nation
211:292 O 5 '70
Missing ingredient; first annual report. J.
Lear. Sat R 53:43 S 5 '70
Nixon view. Time 96:37 Ag 24 '70
Russell Train: Nixon's own conservationist.
por Bsns W 136+ Ap 18 '70
Softer soap? report recommendations. il
Newsweek 76:52-3 Ag 24 '70
Stevens to direct Citizen's committee. Parks
& Rec 5:61 O '70
Tax policy widening big-city blight? U S
News 69:76 Ag 24 '70
Water quality improvement act of 1970; ex-
cerpts from text. Cur Hist 59:106-9 Ag '70

Courts

See Courts—United States

Cultural relations

For God, for China and for Yale: the open
door in action. J. Israel. bibliog f Am Hist
R 75:796-807 F '70
Japan-U.S. cultural conference holds fifth
session at Tokyo; text of communique,
March 23, 1970. Dept State Bul 62:637-9 My
18 '70
See also
Exchange of persons programs

Culture, Popular

See United States—Popular culture

Customs, Bureau of
National training center

Customs college. il Travel 134:64-7 D '70

Declaration of independence

Where are they now? the scroll at the National archives, Washington, D.C. il Newsweek 76:12 Jl 6 '70

Centennial celebrations, etc.

America's biggest birthday party. il U S News
69:42-4 S 28 '70
Festival of freedom. A. MacLeish. il Sat R
53:16 Ag 29 '70
Great birthday squabble; choice of an ex-
position site. il Time 95:14-15 Je 29 '70
Great Scott, it's Philadelphia! il Newsweek
76:22-3 Ag 3 '70
Innocent idea for a '76 fair; polis seventy
six. W. McQuade. il Life 69:10 Jl 4 '70
Philadelphia: host to the spirit of '76. Bsns
W p21-2 Jl 4 '70

Defense, Department of

Defense: Laird decentralization alters civilian
military roles. A. Hamilton. Science 167:965-
7 F 13 '70
Diplomat at the Pentagon. il por Newsweek
76:33-4+ D 13 '70
DOD panel confirms early Viet shortage;
with editorial comment. C. Brownlow. Avia-
tion W 93:11, 22-3 N 16 '70
DOD research office to broaden focus. Avi-
ation W 93:55+ Jl 6 '70
Experts plan a new Pentagon; with editorial
comment. Bsns W p64, 84 Ag 1 '70
House unit weights DOD charter policies. Aviation W 92:27+ F 16 '70
In the McNamara vein. R. Harrigan. Nat R
22:1110 O 20 '70
Is constitutional democracy doomed? W. D.
Phelan, jr. Cur 116:40-6 Mr '70
Latest ideas for a Pentagon shake-up. il U S
News 69:37 Ag 10 '70
Muddled military; proposals of the Fitzhugh
report. New Repub 163:5-6 Ag 22 '70
Shaping the amorphous lump. il por Time
96:8-10 Ag 10 '70
Study panel urges sweeping shifts in Penta-
gon; with editorial comment. C. Brownlow.
il Aviation W 93:9, 14-16 Ag 3 '70

Appropriations and expenditures

Ahead: new debate over arms funds. U S
News 68:7 Ja 19 '70

UNITED STATES—Defense, Department of—
Appropriations and expenditures—*Cont.*
Aircraft, missile funding restored by Senate group. D. C. Winston. Aviation W 93:24 D 7 '70
Billions for defense? il Forbes 106:20-1 D 1 '70
Budgeted for infinity. Nation 210:230-1 Mr 2 '70
College war labs wear camouflage. il Bsns W p36+ O 3 '70
Conferees set $66.6-billion DOD fund. Aviation W 93:18 D 21 '70
Congress requires relevance for DOD research; with editorial comment. G. B. Lubkin. il Phys Today 23:63-5, 112 F '70
Cutting the Pentagon down to size; 1970 report by MCPL. R. E. Lapp. New Repub 163:16-20 Ag 22 '70
Defense bill keyed to ABM fight; with editorial comment. D. C. Winston. Aviation W 93:9, 14-16 Jl 27 '70
Defense cuts mirage. Nation 210:323-4 Mr 23 '70
Defense fund battle seen setting pattern for 1970s. D. C. Winston. Aviation W 92:18-19 Ja 26 '70
Defense fund bid faces powerful opposition in Congress. il Aviation W 92:26-7 Mr 9 '69
Defense procurement bill voted by House unit; Senate fight seen. D. C. Winston. Aviation W 92:23 Ap 20 '70
DOD budget faces Senate floor attack. D. C. Winston. Aviation W 92:18-19 Je 29 '70
DOD emphasis swings to strategic arms. il Aviation W 92:20-1 F 9 '70
DOD fund debate centers on foreign policy matters. D. C. Winston. Aviation W 93:17-18 Ag 3 '70
Effect of federal spending on scientists and engineers; study prepared under the direction of Robert L. Aronson. Mo Labor R 93:44-5 O '70
Fate of a watchdog; A. E. Fitzgerald's concern over Pentagon wastemakers. J. Volz. Commonweal 93:341 Ja 8 '71
Future in doubt; Mansfield amendment. Sci N 97:501 My 23 '70
Holding the development line. Sci N 97:148-9 F 7 '70
House demands fly before buy. Bsns W p31 O 10 '70
House unit cuts more DOD funds; with editorial comment. D. C. Winston. Aviation W 93:9, 14-15 O 12 '70
Impact of deep cuts in defense. il U S News 68:31-3 F 16 '70
Increase in defense-related employment during Viet Nam buildup; with tables. R. P. Oliver. Mo Labor R 93:3-10 F '70
Kicking the defense habit. J. J. Treires. il Nation 210:200-4 F 23 '70
Lean times loom for suppliers. il por Bsns W p 115-16 F 28 '70
Mansfield amendment not yet dead. P. M. Boffey. Science 170:613 N 6 '70
Margin of safety; Cooper-Hart amendment. il Newsweek 76:14-15 Ag 24 '70
Mask of austerity. R. W. Dietsch. Nation 212:70 Ja 18 '71
Military maneuvers. New Repub 163:5-7 D 26 '70
Nixon contracts aerospace budget. il Aviation W 92:16-19 F 9 '70
Nixon stresses strategic buildup. il Aviation W 92:21-5 Mr 9 '70
Packard: defense on a diet; interview. ed. by A. A. Butkus. D. Packard. por Duns 96:10-14 Ag '70
Peace dividend from the Pentagon. M. R. Laird. il Nations Bsns 58:40-2+ O '70
Pentagon capitalism. by S. Melman. Review Sat R 53:26 Ag 29 '70. S. W. Clements
Pentagon's budget has a great fall. il Bsns W p76 F 7 '70
POW Congress. New Repub 163:7-9 D 5 '70
Reports: Washington. E. B. Drew. Atlan 225: 4+ My '70
Research restriction diluted; Mansfield amendment to the 1970 Military procurement authorization act. Sci N 98:332 O 24 '70
Section 203 compounds research-funding squeeze. J. B. Phelps. Phys Today 23:61-4 My '70
Senate group to restore some DOD aircraft funds. D. C. Winston. Aviation W 93:18 N 30 '70
Senate would link Mansfield amendment. NSF budget boost. J. Walsh. Science 169:1059 S 11 '70
Tradeoff: a new carrier for a budget. por Bsns W p 112-13 Ap 25 '70
Try, try again; ABM phase II and the military-hardware bill before the Senate. il Newsweek 76:18-19 Ag 10 '70

U.S. defense spending may grow. il Aviation W 92:16-17 Mr 2 '70
Who won the debate? military spending. R. F. Kaufman. Nation 210:137-42 F 9 '70
See also
Military-industrial complex

Development concept papers
Retreat from gold-plated contracts. il Bsns W p96-7 Jl 11 '70
See also
United States—Defense, Department of—Technology planning documents

Procurement
Changing marketplace. R. Hotz. Aviation W 92:11 Je 8 '70
Defense's fly before you buy policy; recommendations of the Fitzhugh report. il por Newsweek 76:53-4 Ag 10 '70
Lockheed scandal: C-5A cost overrun affair. J. G. Phillips. New Repub 163:19-23 Ag 1 '70
Lockheed's lament. il Time 95:82 My 18 '70
Major DOD procurements at war with reality. H. B. Drake. il Harvard Bsns R 48:119-40 Ja '70
Muddled military; proposals of the Fitzhugh report. New Repub 163:6 Ag 22 '70
Packard details milestone plan; excerpts. D. Packard. Aviation W 92:7 Je 15 '70
Packard urges defense decentralization; with excerpts from address. W. S. Hieronymus. Aviation W 93:7, 15-16 Ag 31 '70
TFX verdict; summary of report. Aviation W 94:7 Ja 4 '71

Public affairs, Office of
Governance of the Pentagon; excerpt from The Pentagon propaganda machine. J. W. Fulbright. Sat R 53:22-5+ N 7 '70; Reply. J. E. Greenbacker. 53:17 D 5 '70
Pentagon propaganda machine, by J. W. Fulbright. Review
Sat R 54:23-4 Ja 2 '71. E. D. Canham

Systems analysis, Office of
New mission of systems analysis. il Bsns W p70-1 Jl 4 '70

Technology planning documents
DOD technology documents planned. il Aviation W 92:62 Je 8 '70

Defenses
Can U.S. avoid new arms race? il U S News 68:71 Mr 2 '70
Correcting our posture; Laird, defense and SALT. R. E. Lapp. New Repub 162:12-15 Mr 28 '70
Dangers confronting U.S; interview. M. R. Laird. il pors U S News 68:64-8+ My 11 '70
Is U.S. forfeiting the arms race to Russia? il U S News 69:21-4 O 19 '70
Laird renews appeal for ABM, MIRA. Aviation W 92:19 My 18 '70
Missiles, troops overseas, naval forces: what Nixon defense study turned up; interview. D. Packard. U S News 69:48 Ag 3 '70
Needed: thunder from the right. Cato. Nat R 22:399 Ap 21 '70
Public control of national security problems; address, November 20, 1970. R. C. Seamans, jr. Vital Speeches 37:133-5 D 15 '70
Real race; address, 1970. R. Kilmarx. Aviation W 93:9 Ag 10 '70
Russia gaining on U.S; latest authoritative report. il U S News 69:30-1 S 14 '70
Russia vs. U.S: coming crisis in arms; interview. J. S. Foster, jr. il pors U S News 69:24-6+ N 30 '70
Russians are eight feet tall, but so are we. letter to J. S. Foster, jr. J. L. Steele. il Time 96:11 Ag 3 '70; Reply. J. S. Foster, jr. 96:9 Ag 10 '70
Some concerns about national security; address, June 5, 1970. I. C. Eaker. Vital Speeches 36:701-4 S 1 '70
Soviet power cited to aid military budget; with editorial comment. D. C. Winston. il Aviation W 92:11, 23-4 My 4 '70
We can reverse the arms race; a 10-point plan. H. F. York. il Life 69:40-1 D 11 '70
What's the cost? excerpts from address. D. Packard. Aviation W 92:9 Je 1 '70
Why defense planners worry; interview. E. G. Wheeler. il por U S News 68:34-9 Ap 20 '70
See also
Atomic warfare—Defenses
Civil defense
Guided missiles—Defenses
Stockpiling
United States—Air force
United States—Armed forces
United States—Defense, Department of

UNITED STATES—*Continued*

Description and travel

Discover America. il Pop Sci 196:74-5 My '70
Discovering America. C. Schwalberg. il por Travel & Camera 33:62-5+ D '70
Redbook guide to America's Heritage trails. W. Hartley and E. Hartley. il Redbook 134:35-42 Ap; 135:51-8 Jl '70
Travel U.S.A.; symposium. il Holiday 47:39-59+ My '70
200 attractions along the interstates. F. Welke. il Bet Hom & Gard 48:129-33+ My '70
Vacationland U.S.A. M. B. Grosvenor. il Nat Geog 137:734-40 My '70
See also
Automobile touring—United States

Diplomatic and consular service

American presence; mission to Cambodia. pors Newsweek 75:49-50 Je 29 '70
Consular posts to be closed under personnel reduction plan. Dept State Bul 61:591 D 22 '69
Is the State department color-blind? R. P. Straus. Sat R 54:12-13+ Ja 2 '71
President Nixon delineates authority of American ambassadors; letter, December 9, 1969. R. M Nixon. Dept State Bul 62:20 Ja 12 '70
U.S. journal: Grosvenor square; Protection and welfare consul. C. Trillin. New Yorker 46:108+ S 19 '70
See also
Ambassadors
United States—State, Department of

Documents office

See United States—Superintendent of documents

Domestic affairs council

Closing the performance gap; appointments. il pors Newsweek 75:16-17 Je 22 '70
Nixon: boss in a bad year. il por Time 95:12-15 Je 22 '70

Draft resisters

See Military service, Compulsory—Draft resisters

Economic conditions

Back into gear on the recovery road. Fortune 82:19 D '70
Bankers' view: a slow upturn. il U S News 69:56-9 O 26 '70
Bottoming out? Newsweek 76:45-6 Ag 24 '70
Celebration of what? il Newsweek 76:55-6 D 28 '70
Cloudy but cooler. Newsweek 76:54 Ag 10 '70
Depression ahead? M. J. Ulmer. New Repub 163:14-15 Jl 4 '70
Despite inflation, people living better. il U S News 68:85-6 F 23 '70
Don't blame the system! R. M. Christenson. Chr Cent 87:784-7 Je 24 '70
Eccles: don't blame the Fed; interview, ed. by T. J. Murray. M. S. Eccles. por Duns 96:10-12+ S '70
Economic integration and the progress of the Negro community. A. F. Brimmer. il por Ebony 25:118-21 Ag '70
Economic outlook: good or bad? America 122:645 Je 20 '70
Economic scene 1969. il Sr Schol 96:4-13 Ja 26 '70
Economic slowdown. M. Ulmer. New Repub 162:11-12 F 28 '70
Economics in the news (cont) il Sr Schol 95:17 S 15 '69; 96:19 Mr 2; 97:8-9 S 14; 14-18 S 28; 7 O 5; 12 O 26; 15 N 9; 9-13 N 16 '70
Economy. R. Lekachman. See issues of Dun's
Economy: a guide to the slump. il Time 95:84-5 Ap 27 '70
Economy: crisis of confidence. il Time 95:39-42+ Je 1 '70
The economy; interview. H. Stein. il por Forbes 105:19-20 F 15 '70
Economy: modest hopes, modest gains. il Time 96:103 O 26 '70
Economy: trying to speed up a recovery. il Time 96:63-4 Ag 3 '70
Economy turns, toward a trade war. il Time 96:62-3 Jl 27 '70
Employer bargaining: address, December 29, 1969. A. A. Hendrix. Vital Speeches 36:317-20 Mr 1 '70
First look at '71: a slow climb back; price rises by Time's Board of economists. il Time 96:76-7 O 12 '70
Game of the name. Newsweek 76:74 O 5 '70
Gloomy feeling; a nervous market, a troubled economy. il Life 68:28-35 Je 5 '70
Growth versus the quality of life. J. A. Wagar. bibliog Science 168:1179-84 Je 5 '70

How the economic issue shapes up. il Newsweek 76:71 O 26 '70
I'm glad you..; effect of economic prescriptions of R. M. Nixon. New Repub 162:8 Je 20 '70
Inflation is rolling back, at a price. il Newsweek 76:67-8 S 21 '70
Inflation's stubborn resistance. il Time 96:82-4+ D 14 '70
Insistent signals. il Time 95:84+ Mr 16 '70
Is our financial mechanism adequate for the 70s? address, April 2, 1970. A. W. Clausen. Vital Speeches 36:428-31 My 1 '70
Labor and the economy in 1969. R. W. Fisher. bibliog il Mo Labor R 93:30-43 Ja '70
Labor month in review. See issues of Monthly labor review
Lengthening shadow. Newsweek 76:73-4 N 9 '70
Leveling off. Newsweek 75:63-4 Ja 26 '70
Mood of America today. U S News 68:17-18 Ap 20 '70
New era? Duns 96:104 S '70
1970: the year of the hangover. il Time 96:52-6 D 28 '70
Our current inflation. J. R. Cammarosano. America 122:369-72 Ap 4 '70
Pause on the recovery road. Fortune 82:19-20 N '70
Pollution and the profit motive. il Bsns W p82+ Ap 11 '70
Rabbit that could turn into a tiger. il Time 96:67-8 Jl 13 '70
Rough passage. il Fortune 81:51 My '70
Sense of foreboding. il Time 95:80 My 18 '70
Side effects of planning. D. S. Ammer. il Harvard Bsns R 48:32-4+ My '70
Slump: will this bottom hold up? il Newsweek 76:51-2 Jl 27 '70
Spread of affluence. il U S News 68:16-18 Je 1 '70
Stocktaking. P. A. Samuelson. Newsweek 76:84 Jl 13 '70
Struggle to cope with recession. Time 95:79-80 F 16 '70
Technician's perspective. J. W. Schultz. See issues of Forbes
Time of contrary signs. il Fortune 81:15-16 Ap '70
To give business a boost; growing pressures on Nixon. il U S News 69:33-6 O 19 '70
Topsy-turvy ups and downs. il Newsweek 75:23-4 Je 1 '70
Trillion-dollar economy; with editorial comment. il Bsns W p65-70+. 192 O 17 '70
Turnaround. Newsweek 75:76+ Ap 27 '70
Upturn that feels like a slump. il Time 96:52-3 S 7 '70
We expect the economy to be moving upward; excerpts from news conference, July 20, 1970. R. M. Nixon. il por U S News 69:36-7 Ag 3 '70
Whatever it's called, it's a slump. il Newsweek 75:79-80 Mr 16 '70
What's going on inside America; nationwide survey. il U S News 68:21-6 My 18 '70
What's right about America; excerpts from address, June 25, 1970. R. M. Nixon. il por U S News 69:45 Jl 6 '70
When economics becomes politics; midyear hearings of the Joint economic committee of Congress. il Newsweek 76:51-2 Ag 3 '70
Where business forecasters went wrong. il U S News 68:15-16 Je 8 '70
Word for it. Newsweek 76:68 S 28 '70
See also
Business conditions
Conservation of resources
Consumption (economics)
Cost of living—United States
Finance—United States
Housing—United States
Labor and laboring classes—United States
Negroes—Economic conditions
Prices—United States
Prosperity
Strikes—United States
Unemployment—United States
Wages—United States

Economic history

At the borderland of law and economic history: the contributions of Willard Hurst; address, December 1968. H. N. Scheiber. bibliog f Am Hist R 75:744-56 F '70
Potentates, by B. B. Seligman. Review Atlan 227:92-5 Ja '71. L. Kronenberger
Progress report of the U.S. economy, 1850-present; table. Sr Schol 96:5 Ja 26 '70
Roots of the modern American empire, by W. A. Williams. Review
   Commonweal 92:94-6 Ap 3 '70. R. H. Miller
   Nation 210:214-15 F 23 '70. R. W. Van Alstyne

UNITED STATES—Economic history—*Cont.*
When businessmen sparked a revolution. il
Nations Bsns 58:52-7 Jl '70
See also
Business depression, 1929-1939
United States—Economic conditions

Economic opportunity, Office of

Bureaucratic obfuscation; emasculating the
legal services program. Nation 211:612 D 14
'70
Can handouts make better wage earners?
OEO income-maintenance program experi-
ment. il Bsns W p80-2 F 28 '70
Customers pass the test or else. Bsns W
p42 +S 12 '70; Same. Ed Digest 36:5-7 N '70
De-escalator of the war on poverty. R.
Sherrill. il pors N Y Times Mag p23-5+
D 13 '70
Exit Egeberg; and Farmer. pors Time 96:15
D 14 '70
Guaranteed income? experiment findings. R.
Lekachman. Duns 95:9 Ap '70
Health care goes into the streets. J. Bockel.
il N Y 97:276-7 Mr 14 '70
Justice for all on the defensive; future of the
Legal services program. P. R. Wieck. New
Repub 162:12 F 21 '70
Last-minute rescue for legal aid? R. M. Hall,
jr. New Repub 163:13-15 N 21 '70; Reply
with rejoinder. L. J. Churchville. 163:23-4
D 26 '70
Politics and poverty. il Time 96:66 O 26 '70
Rumsfeld on the rise. il por Newsweek 76:17
D 28 '70
Somebody is always offended; legal service
program. S. L. Greene. Nation 211:624-7
D 14 '70
Success or excess? legal services program.
Time 96:55 D 14 '70
TRB from Washington:
Smith experiment; proposed national
Family allowance program. New Repub
162-8 F 21 '70
Trying out the new plan; OEO experimental
income maintenance program. il Sci N 97:
216-17 F 28 '70
When you just give money to the poor; pilot
program. F. J. Cook. il N Y Times Mag
p23+ My 3 '70
Will work work? OEO income maintenance
programs. J. A. Hamilton. il Sat R 53:24-7
My 23 '70

Older persons advisory council

OEO names retired baseball man, thirty-four,
as advisor on aging; T. Kubek. Aging 190:
21 Ag '70

Volunteers in service to America

See Volunteers in service to America

Economic policy

Aids to fiscal and monetary policy. America
123:7 Jl 11 '70
As Nixon sees the future. por U S News 68:
17 F 2 '70
Battle against inflation; new initiatives; ad-
dress, March 9, 1970. D. S. MacNaughton.
Vital Speeches 36:437-40 My 1 '70
Bigger money flow, will it stop unemploy-
ment? il U S News 69:15-17 N 30 '70
Business questions the game plan. Bsns W p28
O 24 '70
Campaigners test their economic weapons.
il Bsns W p 15 My 2 '70
Case for a positive trade policy; address,
February 27, 1970. P. H. Trezise. Dept
State Bul 62:333-8 Mr 16 '70
Change of course; post-election cabinet meet-
ing. Newsweek 76:88 N 16 '70
Confidence factor. il Fortune 81:19 Je '70
Corporations and the cold war. ed. by D.
Horowitz. Review
Commonweal 92:321-3 Je 26 '70. R. J.
Barnet
Costly transition from a wartime to peace-
time economy; analysis of Nixon's address
on economic policy. D. Lawrence. U S News
68:88 Je 29 '70
Crucial month for Nixon: decisions pile up.
il U S News 69:17-19 D 14 '70
Doctor Galbraith? Or Dr Friedman? inter-
view. J. R. Bunting. pors Forbes 106:44+ D
15 '70
Economic issue. W. F. Buckley, jr. Nat R
22:1315 D 1 '70
Economic slowdown. M. Ulmer. New Repub
162:11-12 F 28 '70
Economy. R. Lekachman. See issues of Dun's
Economy: a switch in strategy. il Newsweek
75:71 Mr 30 '70
Economy: modest hopes, modest gains. il Time
96:103 O 26 '70
Economy: trying to speed up a recovery. il
Time 96:63-4 Ag 3 '70

Game plan at halftime; address, September
22, 1970. H. Stein. Vital Speches 37:61-4 N
1 '70
Hard going for the game plan; with editorial
comment. G. Burck. il por Fortune 81:145-6
152-5+ My '70
How many times? M. Friedman. Newsweek
76:85 N 30 '70
If Nixon had kept the jawbone. il Bsns W p93
Ja 31 '70
Inflation: a call for restraint; R. M. Nixon's
new anti-inflation policy. il por Newsweek
75:61-2 Je 29 '70
Inflation control; address, December 5, 1969.
G. Ackley. Vital Speeches 36:200-3 Ja 15 '70
Inflation or unemployment. America 123:453
N 28 '70
Inflation, unemployment, war: a Democratic
reply to Nixon; address, June 24, 1970.
M. Mansfield. por U S News 69:68-70 Jl 6
'70; Same with title Nixon's economy.
Vital Speeches 36:581-3 Jl 15 '70
Inflation's stubborn resistance. il Time 96:
82-4+ D 14 '70
Is our financial mechanism adequate for the
70s? address, April 2, 1970. A. W. Clausen.
Vital Speeches 36:428-31 My 1 '70
Letter from Washington. Cato. Nat R 22:1336
D 15 '70
Money in America: the end of the econo-
mists' dream. R. Lekachman. Harper 241:
29-34 Ag '70; Discussion. 241:9+ O '70
Mysterious American disease. S. Alsop. News-
week 75:98 F 9 '70
Nation's economic outlook: progress against
inflation; address, December 7, 1970. R. M.
Nixon. Vital Speeches 37:130-3 D 15 '70
New game plan. il por Newsweek 76:15-16 N
30 '70
Nixon eases up on the reins. Bsns W p24
Mr 21 '70
Nixon economists have a policy gap; with
editorial comment. il Bsns W p20-1, 84 Ag
1 '70
Nixon is shifting to a harder-hitting game;
with editorial comment. il Bsns W p 14-15,
92 D 12 '70
Nixon starts moves for 1971, and 1972. il por
U S News 69:9-10 D 28 '70
Nixon still sticks to the plan; with editorial
comment. il Bsns W p22-3 108 My 30 '70
Nixon: this is the critical moment; address,
December 4, 1970. R. M. Nixon. por U S
News 69:70-2 D 14 '70
Nixon's temptation to shift policy. il Time
96:86 N 16 '70
Now: drive starts to end the slump. il U S
News 68:20-1 Je 22 '70
Only way to bring inflation under control.
Bsns W p 122 Ja 24 '70
Picking up the wishbone; anti-inflation
measures of R. M. Nixon. il Time 95:10-11
Je 29 '70
Pocketbook politics. il Time 95:13-14 Je 8 '70
Political test for policy. il Bsns W p25-6
O 10 '70
President at his news conference: I do not
expect a recession; January 30, 1970. R. M.
Nixon. il por U S News 68:21 F 9 '70
President Nixon calls for passage of trade
bill; text of letter, May 11, 1970. R. M.
Nixon. Dept State Bul 62:697-9 Je 1 '70
President's post-election agenda. il Time 96:
9-11 N 23 '70
Rebuilding the economy. D. Lawrence. U S
News 69:92 N 23 '70
Recession can't cure inflation. M. Shapiro.
il Duns 96:54-6 Jl '70
Retreat on the inflation front? America 122:
364 Ap 4 '70
Return of pocketbook politics. H. Sidey. Life
68:4 Ap 3 '70
Richard Nixon, inflation fighter. il por News-
week 76:45-6 D 14 '70
Rising clamor for the jawbone. il Time 95:
88+ Ap 13 '70
Self-inflicted advice. H. C. Wallich. News-
week 77:58 Ja 4 '71
Shifting gears. H. C. Wallich. Newsweek 76:
112 N 23 '70
State of the Union; address, January 22,
1970. R. M. Nixon. il pors U S News 68:
63-7 F 2 '70; Same. Vital Speeches 36:226-9
F 1 '70; Excerpts. Dept State Bul 62:145-
7 F 9 '70
To give business a boost; growing pressures
on Nixon. il U S News 69:33-6 O 19 '70
Toward price stability; address, June 17, 1970.
R. M. Nixon. il por U S News 68:61-4 Je 29
'70; Same with title Inflation and economic
policy. Vital Speeches 36:546-9 Jl 1 '70
TRB from Washington: is Nixon smart? New
Repub 162:6 F 7 '70
TRB from Washington: Nixonomics. New
Repub 163:5 D 5 '70

UNITED STATES—Economic policy—*Cont.*
U.S. economic policy; address, May 25, 1970.
A. H. Cox, jr. Vital Speeches 36:559-61 Jl 1
'70
Very ill? Try an aspirin; analysis of Nixon's
address on the troubles of the economy.
New Repub 162:5-6 Je 27 '70
Wage and price controls? Forget about them;
address, May 19, 1970. J. N. Mitchell. il por
U S News 68:39-41 Je 1 '70
We're still cutting back; comments of mem-
bers of the Dun's presidents' panel. G. R.
Rosen. il Duns 96:27-30 Ag '70
What business can count on from Washing-
ton. il U S News 69:42-3 N 16 '70
    See also
Budget—United States
Campaign issues
Economic assistance, Domestic
Finance—United States
Government spending policy
Import quotas
Income tax—United States
Price regulation by government—United
States
Tariff—United States
Taxation—United States
United States—Appropriations and expendi-
tures
United States—Council of economic advisers
Wage-price policy

Economic relations
Economic policy: who's in charge. G. Ball.
por Newsweek 76:38-9 D 14 '70
Two vital dimensions of development:
quantity and quality; statement, July 14,
1970. C. W. Yost. Dept State Bul 63:225-34
Ag 24 '70
    See also
Economic assistance, American
United States—Commerce
United States—Commercial treaties and agree-
ments

Bolivia
Bolivia: friend or foe? S. Rodman. Nat R 22:
1211+ N 17 '70

Latin America
Ethics and the art of the possible in inter-
American relations. J. B. Housley. il Chr
Cent 87:1283-5 O 28 '70
Latin America: toward a new policy; ad-
dress, April 10, 1970. F. Church. Vital
Speeches 36:418-23 My 1 '70
    See also
Inter-American economic and social council

Poland
United States and Poland conclude new cotton textile agreement; Department announcement; with exchange of notes. Dept
State Bul 62:561-3 Ap 27 '70

Russia
Nyet to Ford's future in Russia. por Bsns W
p40 My 23 '70
Spain
U.S. and Spain hold meeting of joint economic committee; Department announcement;
with text of joint communique, January 30,
1970. Dept State Bul 62:211-12 F 23 '70

Education, Office of
Allen affair. por Newsweek 75:17-18 Je 22 '70
Education vouchers. C. Jencks. New Repub
163:19-21 Jl 4 '70
Embattled commissioner. por Newsweek 76:67
O 5 '70
Guide to OE-administered programs, fiscal
year 1970. il Am Ed 6:29-35 Je '70
Guide to OE-administered programs, fiscal
year 1971. il Am Ed 6:26-32 N '70
New programs face stricter evaluation. Am
Ed 6:36 Ja '70
OE: bureaucracy in trouble. W. K. Stevens.
Sat R 53:55 Jl 18 '70
USOE revises copyright policies. S. Wagner.
Pub W 197:46 Je 1 '70
    See also
Talent Search programs (education)
United States—National institute of educa-
tion (proposed)

Appropriations and expenditures
Book and library programs still in limbo.
S. Wagner. Pub W 197:61-2 F 9 '70
Congress votes higher USOE appropriation.
S. Wagner. Pub W 198:32 Jl 6 '70
House approves increased education spend-
ing. S. Wagner. Pub W 197:54-5 Ap 27 '70
USOE releases federal book and library
funds. S. Wagner. Pub W 198:30 N 2 '70

Educational research and develop-
ment, Bureau of
NCTE/ERIC summaries & sources; operation
evaluation. B. O'Donnell. Engl J 59:134-8
Ja '70
    See also
Eric

Libraries and educational technology,
Bureau of—Library programs,
Division of
New directions in DLP. R. M. Fry. Am Lib
1:904-7 O '70

Library programs, Division of
See United States—Education, Office of—
Libraries and educational technology, Bu-
reau of—Library programs, Division of

National center for educational
communication
OE's new copyright policy. M. W. Bachrach.
Am Ed 6:28-9 Ag '70

Students and youth, Office of
Advocate for students and young people;
establishment of an Office of students and
youth. Sch & Soc 98:18 Ja '70

Subcommittee on easing tensions
in education
Report of the Subcommittee on easing ten-
sions in education. Sch & Soc 98:306-7+
Sum '70

Employment service
Job banks: system covers forty-two cities.
U S News 69:76 Jl 27 '70

Engineer corps
See United States—Army—Corps of engineers

Environmental policy
See Environmental policy

Environmental protection agency
EPA & NOAA or CEQ? Nat Parks & Con Mag
44:25-6 O '70
Getting it all together. Sci N 98:398 N 21 '70
New judge for the atom? J. Lear. Sat R 53:
39 Ag 1 '70
Nixon proposes NOAA and EPA. L. J. Car-
ter. Science 169:266 Jl 17 '70
Policeman for pollution. il por Time 96:41-2
N 23 '70
Reshuffling the bureaucracy: Nixon proposes
pollution ocean agencies. L. J. Carter. Sci-
ence 168:1433-5 Je 19 '70
Stepped-up war on pollution. il U S News
70:20-1 Ja 11 '71
Will EPA take away your pesticides? G. W.
Wormley. Farm J 94:32 N '70

Environmental science services
administration
ESSA research flight facility's support
of environmental research in 1969. H.
A. Friedman and W. S. Callahan. bibliog
il Weatherwise 23:174-81+ Ag '70
    See also
United States—National weather service

Equal employment opportunity
commission
Equal rights for women workers: a new
push. il U S News 69:51-2 Ag 3 '70

Executive departments
Bureaucratic reshuffles. New Repub 163:7-8
Ag 1 '70
How do we get from here to there? en-
vironment control. T. H. White. il Life
68:36-40+ Je 26 '70
Praeger series contends with federal changes.
Pub W 198:40 O 5 '70
Uncivil servants; purge of public interest
types in government resource programs. D.
Sanford. New Repub 162:13-14 My 16 '70
What is to be done? Gigantism in Washing-
ton. J. F. Campbell. For Affairs 49:81-99
O '70

Executive office of the president
After the off-year: the ins and outs. il
Newsweek 76:30-1 N 23 '70
At battle stations. J. Osborne. New Repub
163:10-11 D 12 '70
Cabinet capers; liaison with the White
House. J. Osborne. New Repub 162:15-17
My 30 '70
Grand Central in the basement; the White
House office. H. Sidey. il Life 68:4 Mr 27 '70
How Nixon's White House works. il por
Time 95:15-20 Je 8 '70

UNITED STATES—Executive office of the president—*Continued*
How the White House got its new management tools; interview. R. L. Ash. il pors Nations Bsns 58:44-6 Ag '70
Ins and outs. J. Osborne. New Repub 162:11-12 My 9 '70
Is Agnew washed up? changes in the White House office. J. Osborne. New Repub 163:11-12 N 14 '70
Key men in changes at White House. il U S News 68:18-19 Je 22 '70
Men who decide what Nixon sees. il pors Bsns W p96-7 Ja 31 '70
Nixon: boss in a bad year. il por Time 95:12-15 Je 22 '70
Nixon expands the executive suite. il Bsns W p25-6 Je 13 '70
Rearranging furniture. J. Osborne. New Repub 163:8-9 Jl 4 '70
Reorganizing White House; Nixon describes the plan; excerpts from message to Congress. R. M. Nixon. il U S News 68:80-1 Je 22 '70
Reports: Washington. E. B. Drew. Atlan 225:20+ My '70
Richard Nixon's very personal White House. J. Cameron. il por Fortune 82:56-9+ Jl '70
Said Nixon to George Shultz: "I track well with you". A. H. Raskin. il pors N Y Times Mag p24-5+ Ag 23 '70
White House staff. J. Osborne. New Repub 163:13-14 O 3 '70
Who's who at the White House now. il U S News 68:26-7 Je 29 '70

Expenditures
See United States—Appropriations and expenditures

Farm credit administration
Big change in farm credit; report of Commission on agricultural credit; with editorial comment. C. W. Gifford. Farm J 94:31+, 78 My '70
New money to build feedlots; banks for co-operatives. O. Bay. il Farm J 94:B10-11+ F '70
See also
Federal land banks

Federal aviation administration
ALPA committee scores FAA all-weather landing program. B. M. Elson. Aviation W 93:27 Jl 27 '70
Awake, dreamers; increase in midair collisions. R. L. Collins. Flying 87:24 N '70
Broad impact lurks in FAA plan; proposal to redefine commercial operator. C. E. Schneider. Aviation W 93:14-15 N 23 '70
FAA acts to improve controller program. J. P. Woolsey. Aviation W 92:19 F 16 '70
FAA answers all-weather critics. C. E. Schneider. Aviation W 93:58-9 Ag 10 '70
FAA asks Senate for restoration of cuts in airport aid, research. Aviation W 93:27 Ag 10 '70
FAA asks transport certification on all new ten passenger aircraft. Aviation W 93:19 Jl 6 '70
FAA backs 747, JT9D in safety dispute. J. P. Woolsey. Aviation W 93:27-8 O 12 '70
FAA eases new attendant rule temporarily for eight airlines. Aviation W 92:36 My 4 '70
FAA issues separation standards for control of giant jet traffic. Aviation W 92:225+ Mr 9 '70
FAA may impose sanctions on controllers. Aviation W 92:36 Ag 6 '70
FAA permits controllers to take appeal to Volpe. Aviation W 92:26-7 F 23 '70
FAA proposes rule to forbid overland boom. Aviation W 92:32 My 4 '70
FAA spurns Nader unit request. C. E. Schneider. Aviation W 93:53-5 Ag 17 '70
FAA studies approved flight school revisions. Aviation W 93:81 S 21 '70
FAA to present ten-year facilities plans. Aviation W 92:24-5 Ja 19 '70
FAA, traffic controllers gear for future relations. J. P. Woolsey. Aviation W 92:30-1 My 25 '70
FAA vortex concern mounting. il Aviation W 92:31 My 25 '70
Flow control facility eases center loss. C. E. Schneider. Aviation W 93:25 S 7 '70
House unit hits FAA system management. Aviation W 92:22-3 Jl 20 '70
Lagging bureaucracy. R. Hotz. Aviation W 93:9 Jl 20 '70
Landing aids to triple under ten-year plan. P. J. Klass. Aviation W 92:29 Mr 2 '70
New office established by FAA to play key role in research; Office of systems engineering management. Aviation W 94:20 Ja 11 '71

Pilots blame FAA in jam of Washington air traffic. C. E. Schneider. Aviation W 93:21-2 Ag 31 '70
Supreme court asked to compel FAA to alter violation handling. Aviation W 93:16-17 Ag 17 '70
Traffic plan flops in Washington. J. P. Woolsey. Aviation W 93:20-1 Ag 31 '70
Wanted: black air traffic controllers. il Ebony 25:54-6+ Ap '70

Appropriations and expenditures
FAA asks $130 million more fiscal 1971 funds. D. C. Winston. Aviation W 93:15 N 23 '70
FAA budget rises steeply for airport/airway needs. J. P. Woolsey. Aviation W 92:25-6 F 9 '70
FAA plans $2.5 billion avionics growth. P. J. Klass. il Aviation W 92:203+ Mr 9 '70
Increased budget for FAA urged in ATA testimony. K. Johnsen. Aviation W 93:17 Ag 31 '70
Industry charges breach of faith in FAA funding. Aviation W 93:25 N 30 '70

Weather message switching center
Improved FAA weather services slated for November introduction. Aviation W 92:93-4 Ap 6 '70

Federal bureau of investigation
Bureau of vituperation. Time 96:11 N 30 '70
East Coast conspiracy. Time 96:25 D 7 '70
FBI's toughest foe: the kids. il Newsweek 76:22-3 O 26 '70
Guerrilla warfare in the U.S.: FBI report. il U S News 69:53-5 N 9 '70
Hoover's FBI, by W. W. Turner. Review Ramp Mag 9:54 Ag '70. A. Truskier
Italian power; demonstrations against the New York headquarters. il Newsweek 75:22 Je 22 '70
John Jay: college for cops. F. J. Cook. il Nation 211:555-8 N 30 '70
Least wanted. il New Repub 163:5-6 N 28 '70
Muckrakers' progress. Time 96:73 O 26 '70
State police. F. Lang. Ramp Mag 9:12-13 D '70
Violence trap; arranged bombing to catch terrorists in Miss. Nation 210:261 Mr 9 '70
Wanted by FBI. il Time 96:49 N 16 '70

Crime laboratory
Detectives in smocks. R. K. Bennett. Read Digest 96:201-2+ Ja '70

Federal commissions
Choosing the investigators. R. L. Shayon. Sat R 53:34 S 5 '70
See also
Commissions of inquiry
United States—Advisory council on executive organization

Federal communications commission
Act with ACT. R. L. Shayon. Sat R 53:22 Mr 7 '70
Agnew and the Pastore bill. S. Cupps. il Chr Cent 87:77-9 Ja 21 '70
Big changes due for TV viewers. il U S News 68:85 My 18 '70
Big changes in TV phones: upheaval in communications. il U S News 69:50-2 Jl 13 '70
Caveat pre-emptor; ACT's request for free time to expose overstated toy commercials. R. L. Shayon. Sat R 54:37 Ja 9 '71
CB! For better? Or worse? O. P. Ferrell. Pop Electr 33:7 O '70
Christmas list; Pastore bill. J. Fischer; reply. J. Vacca. Harper 240:10+ Mr '70
Coming shake-up in telecommunications. D. Cordtz. il Fortune 81:68-71+ Ap '70
Communications monopolies. R. H. Smith. Pub W 197:37 Ap 6 '70
Curiouser and curiouser. R. L. Shayon. Sat R 53:43 Ag 8 '70
Domestic communications satellites: FCC still looking at the options. R. J. Samuelson. Science 168:1190+ Je 5 '70
Down to fundamentals; question of WMUU's license renewal. R. L. Shayon. Sat R 53:36-7 O 31 '70
FCC increases frequency bands available for domestic satcoms. K. Johnsen. Aviation W 93:23-4 O 5 '70
FCC initiates inquiry on cables, satellites. Aviation W 92:43 Je 29 '70
FCC lets everyone in on data action. Bsns W p30 Jl 18 '70
FCC notified by five firms of domestic satcom plans. K. Johnsen. Aviation W 93:18 Ag 24 '70
FCC throws open domestic satcom field. K. Johnsen. Aviation W 92:19 Mr 30 '70
FCC tunes in Comsat again. Bsns W p30-1 Je 20 '70

UNITED STATES—Federal communications commission—*Continued*
FCC's bomb for the broadcasters. il Bsns W p25 Ap 4 '70
How CBS copes with TV pressures. il Bsns W p58-61+ Jl 4 '70
How Commissioner Johnson bugs Ma Bell. il por Bsns W p63-4 N 14 '70
Interest on four-letter words; decision against WUHY-FM. R. L. Shayon. Sat R 53:50 My 2 '70
It's junk, but is it our junk? Pastore bill. R. H. Smith. Pub W 197:61 Ja 19 '70
Kenneth Cox. Nation 210:710 Je 15 '70
Kidvid ghetto; reactions to proposal to ban commercials from children's programs. R. L. Shayon. Sat R 53:21 Je 20 '70
Making FCC's mission impossible. J. O. Pastore. Consumer Rep 35:109-11 F '70
Matter of substance; FCC policy statement on changes in station ownership. Newsweek 75:82-3 Ja 26 '70
Mephisto and the FCC; local Jackson group offers to operate WLBT. R. L. Shayon. Sat R 53:102 Mr 14 '70
New FCC tune elates cable-TV. Bsns W p38 My 23 '70
One to a customer? Newsweek 75:64 Ap 6 '70
People v. WPIX. Time 96:67 S 28 '70
Question of fairness; antismoking ads. Newsweek 76:57 D 28 '70
Right to be seen and heard: If you're antiwar; complaints against violations of the fairness doctrine rejected. D. Sanford. New Repub 163:16-17 Jl 18 '70
Sad sack in Puyallup; handling of renewal of KAYE's license. R. L. Shayon. Sat R 53:39 Jl 11 '70
Test case; hearings on license challenge against WPIX-TV. Newsweek 76:56 S 28 '70
Those substantial licensees; Policy statement on comparative hearings involving regular renewal applicants R. L. Shayon. Sat R 53:38-9 F 7 '70
Three-quarter time; FCC ruling on prime time programs. Newsweek 75:73 My 18 '70
Tube power; flurry over the Fulbright amendment. por Newsweek 76:61 Ag 17 '70
Turnover at the FCC. por Newsweek 76:44-5 Ag 3 '70
When Nixon goes on TV: new rule on right to reply. il U S News 69:26-7 Ag 31 '70
See also
Television laws and regulations

Federal highway administration
Ecology and environment; address. R. R. Bartelsmeyer. Arch Forum 132:48-9+ Je '70

Federal home loan bank board
Marshaling props for new housing. il Bsns W p34 F 28 '70
Outlook for home buyers: interview. P. Martin. il pors U S News 68:70-3 Mr 23 '70
Pumping money into housing. il Bsns W p66-7 S 26 '70
Savings-and-loan curbs, a rising controversy. U S News 69:67-8 Ag 31 '70

Federal mediation and conciliation service
Mediators tune in a new generation. il Bsns W p90-1 Ja 24 '70

Federal power commission
Gas pricing gets an update. il Bsns W p 19 Jl 25 '70
Gas shortage fuels a fight. Bsns W p22 Ag 1 '70
Hydroelectricity and your electric bill. il Consumer Rep 35:170-3 Mr '70
Power shortage gets emergency treatment. Bsns W p32 My 16 '70

Federal reserve board
Big days for the scourge of the banks. por Time 95:68-9 Ja 26 '70
Bigger money flow; will it stop unemployment? il U S News 69:15-17 N 30 '70
Burns changes the mood at the Fed. il por U S News 68:44 Je 1 '70
Burns takes over a Fed under fire; with editorial comment. il por Bsns W p31-2, 120 Ja 31 '70
Discount-rate cut; how much impact? U S News 69:66 N 23 '70
Eccles; don't blame the Fed; interview. ed. by T. J. Murray. M. S. Eccles. por Duns 96:10-12+ S '70
Economy; a switch in strategy. il Newsweek 75:71 Mr 30 '70
Economy; crisis of confidence. il Time 95:39-42+ Je 1 '70
Fed cracks Q ceiling to help the banks. Bsns W p40+ Je 27 '70

Fed feels squeeze of its own policy. il Bsns W p25 My 16 '70
Fed ruling that shook Detroit; Bank of the Commonwealth's bid to open Nassau branch and to form an Edge act corporation. il Bsns W p25-6 Ap 11 '70
Fed studies ways to even impact of monetary policy. Bsns W p58 Ap 11 '70
Fed to rule on bank growth. Bsns W p27 D 26 '70
Fed watchers spot a hint of ease; two changes in reserve requirements. Bsns W p21 Ag 22 '70
Fed's new way to play policy. il Bsns W p28 Ap 25 '70
A 500 Dow? interview, ed. by G. R. Rosen. E. Janeway. por Duns 95:10-11+ F '70
Investor's new ally. J. W. Schulz. Forbes 105:70 Je 1 '70
Let's make a deal. il Newsweek 76:78+ D 21 '70
Little trauma at the Fed. M. Seeger. Esquire 74:36+ N 1 '70
Markets dance to the new Fed tune. il Bsns W p 17-18 N 28 '70
Martin era. por Time 95:66 F 2 '70
Martin years. por Newsweek 75:59-60 F 2 '70
Monetary overheating? M. Friedman. Newsweek 76:75 Jl 6 '70
New chairman at the Fed. M. Friedman. Newsweek 75:68 F 2 '70
New Fed policy runs rough. il Bsns W p86-8 Je 27 '70
Nudge toward a lower prime. il Bsns W p24 N 14 '70
One man, one vote. por Forbes 105:24-5 Mr 1 '70
Task ahead; address, May 14, 1970. J. L. Robertson. Vital Speeches 36:520-3 Je 15 '70
Teetering between two dangers. il Time 95:87-8 My 4 '70
Topsy-turvy ups and downs. il Newsweek 75:23-4 Je 1 '70
When the Fed won the liquidity battle. il Bsns W p50+ O 24 '70
Who is making money scarce; ABC's of Federal reserve. il U S News 68:24-6 F 2 '70
Will the Fed now follow the banks? il Bsns W p32 S 26 '70

Federal trade commission
Action on flammable fabrics. Consumer Rep 35:374-5 Je '70
Beefed-up FTC gets down to work. Bsns W p50-1 O 17 '70
Burden of proof; now on advertisers. Newsweek 75:88 My 18 '70
Can FTC put a governor on Detroit? il Bsns W p31-2 F 28 '70
FTC challenges negative option mail sale. S. Wagner. Pub W 197:33-4 My 25 '70
FTC gets tough. por Time 96:80 O 19 '70
FTC hears pros and cons on negative option plans. S. Wagner. Pub W 198:21-2 N 30 '70
FTC moves to ban unordered merchandise. S. Wagner. Pub W 198:47 Jl 20 '70
FTC order against Crowell-Collier upheld. Pub W 197:43 Je 15 '70
FTC refuses to stiffen Campbell's soup order. Consumer Rep 35:456 Ag '70
FTC renews attack on door-to-door bookselling. Pub W 198:50-1 Jl 27 '70
FTC ties a can to a Zerex ad; antifreeze commercial. Bsns W p30+ D 5 '70
Further comment on negative option. C. B. Grannis. Pub W 197:45 Je 15 '70
Logical choice to head the FTC. Bsns W p21-2 Ag 15 '70
Man in he middle; C. Weinberger. il por Forbes 105:46-7 F 1 '70
Old lady's new kick. il Newsweek 76:87+ D 14 '70
One-eyed slicker; TV's long lasting, super strength half-truths. D. Henninger. New Repub 162:17-19 My 2 '70
Pollution; puffery or progress? FTC investigation into anti-pollution claims. il Newsweek 76:49-51 D 28 '70
Prize snafu in the Coke game. Bsns W p32 Jl 18 '70
Proposes cooling-off period for door-to-door sales. S. Wagner. Pub W 198:32 O 19 '70
Provisional consent order on negative option. S. Wagner. Pub W 197:76-7 Je 29 '70
Regulating the regulators. il Newsweek 76:45 Ag 24 '70
Spangle affair. Consumer Rep 35:30-1 Ja '70
Tax on mergers? interview, ed. by G. R. Rosen. C. Weinberger. por Duns 95:10-12 My '70
Things go wrong for Coca-Cola; moves on Big name bingo contest. Consumer Rep 35:578 O '70

UNITED STATES—Federal trade commission
—*Continued*
Vanity services: a consumer alert. C. B. Gran-
nis. Pub W 197:60 Mr 2 '70
Where the FTC's new chairman stands; in-
terview. C. W. Weinberger. pors Nations
Bsns 58:28-30 Ap '70
**Who wins the sweepstakes? Sr Schol 96:17
Ap 27 '70**

Federal water quality administration
Challenges federal pollution policies; with
reply by D. D. Dominick. E. E. Franchett.
Am City 85:156-7 S '70

Fiscal policy
Where's the money coming from? Nations
Bsns 58:27-9 O '70
See also
United States—Monetary policy

Fish and wildlife service
Fisheries research: rejuggling of priorities is
assailed. L. J. Carter. Science 167:1471-2
Mr 13 '70

Food and drug administration
After cyclamates: what's next on the FDA's
food target list? K. N. Anderson. il Sci
Digest 67:16-23 F '70
Apricot pit bit. por Sci N 98:55-6 Jl 25 '70
Burden of proof: lack of adequate warning on
DDVP resin strips. S. Novick. bibliog il
Environ 12:16-29 O '70
Charting a new role for embattled FDA. B. J.
Culliton. il pors Sci N 97:180-3 F 14 '70
Chemical feast, by J. S. Turner. Review
Environ il 12:40-1 O '70. D. Cottrell
Clearing out old medicines. Time 96:94 D 7
'70
**Congressman who fights for safe food. M. C.
Goldman. Org Gard & Farm 17:66-70 My
'70**
Cyclamates: House report charges adminis-
trative alchemy at HEW. R. J. Bazell. Sci-
ence 170:419-20 O 23 '70
Danger of cancer in food; controversy over
repeal of the Delaney clause. J. Carper. il
Sat R 53:47-9+ S 5 '70
Direct actionist policies food, drugs. por
U S News 69:50 Ag 17 '70
Enough to move FDA; relation of estrogen
to bloodclotting. Sci N 97:430-1 My 2 '70
Faster FDA action asked in lawsuit. T. P.
Southwick. Science 168:1560 Je 26 '70
FDA back to court; question of ineffective
drugs. Sci N 98:95 Ag 1 '70
FDA: efficiency drive stumbles over the is-
sue of drug efficacy; effects of Demulen.
T. P. Southwick. Science 169:1185-9 S 18
'70; Reply. D. C. Goldberg. 170:491 O 30 '70
FDA goes to the consumer: oral contracep-
tive warning. Sci N 97:266 Mr 14 '70
FDA: guidelines chiseled in stone; letter. R.
L. Dean. Science 169:1264 S 25 '70
FDA: new pressures, old habits bring a
change at the top. A. Hamilton. Science
167:268+ Ja 16 '70
FDA publishes a list; ineffective drugs. Sci N
98:431 D 5 '70
FDA wins round in Panalba fight. N. Gru-
chow. Science 167:1710 Mr 27 '70
Implementing a review. Sci N 98:316-17 O 17
'70
Inspect that toy. J. R. Michael. New Repub
163:15 D 12 '70
Medical devices: an unhealthy situation. Con-
sumer Rep 35:256-9 Ap '70
Nader's raiders on the FDA: science and sci-
entists misused. P. M. Boffey. Science 168:
349-52 Ap 17 '70
New broom at FDA. Sci N 97:120-1 Ja 31 '70
Out with combination drugs. Sci N 98:9 Jl
4 '70
Peculiar success of Chloromycetin. il Con-
sumer Rep 35:616-19 O '70
Road is cleared for FDA: Panalba case. Sci
N 97:242-3 Mr 7 '70
Sausage and spice (and things not so nice)
Consumer Rep 35:344 Je '70
Up against the wall, FDA! por Time 95:18+
Ap 20 '70

Foreign opinion
As others see us; comp. by N. G. Balint.
See issues of Saturday review
**Shock to foes, and friends: American in-
vasion of Cambodia. il Newsweek 75:57-8
My 18 '70**

British
American psychodrama called "Everyone
hates us." R. Conquest. N Y Times Mag
p28-9+ My 10 '70; Reply. H. Evans. p82
Je 7 '70
Hope for America. C. P. Snow and P. Snow.
Look 34:30+ D 1 '70

Minority report on U.S. violence. H. Fairlie.
Cur 114:36-40 Ja '70
Needed: a British Spiro Agnew. A. Lejeune.
Nat R 22:885 Ag 25 '70

Canadian
Murder and suicide. Nation 210:644 Je 1 '70

Dutch
Reflections on the U.S. by a Dutch ceramist.
J. de Rooden. il Craft Horiz 30:46-7 My '70

European
American nightmare; excerpt from Prelude to
revolution: France in May. D. Singer. Na-
tion 210:742-4 Je 22 '70
Newsgram. U S News 69:7-8 Ag 3 '70
Summer of Europe's content. J. Shaw. il
Time 96:24+ Ag 10 '70

French
Gloomy view of the U.S. economy. por
Forbes 105:42-3 My 1 '70

Japanese
U.S.-Japanese treaty crisis. R. Epp. bibliog
f Cur Hist 58:202-8+ Ap '70

Latin American
Malvenido Rockefeller! anti-American posters
in Latin America. D. Horowitz. il Ramp
Mag 8:20-5 F '70

Polish
Hysteria U.S.A: our action in Cambodia. W.
F. Buckley, jr. Nat R 22:645 Je 16 '70

Russian
On bearing it in the USSR; comparison with
America. W. F. Buckley, jr. Nat R 22:644-5
Je 16 '70
Roads of earth and space: impressions of So-
viet cosmonauts on U.S. tour. K. Feok-
tistov. il por Space World G-3-75:38-9 Mr
'70
Soviet portrait of America. il Time 95:30-1
F 23 '70

Swiss
View from the top; doubt about America's
effectiveness against Soviet expansionism
based on doubt about capacity to cope with
internal disorders. W. F. Buckley, jr. Nat
R 22:324 Mr 24 '70

Turkish
Problem of visibility. R. M. Fresco. Nation
211:206-8 S 14 '70

Vietnamese
Hated Americans: anti-Americanism in South
Vietnam. il Newsweek 76:39+ Ag 17 '70
New danger in South Vietnam: anti-U.S.
violence. il U S News 70:15-17 Ja 11 '71

Foreign population
See Europe, inside the USA, that is. J. Hig-
gins and S. R. Higgins. il Todays Health
48:44-7+ N '70
See also
Immigration and emigration—United States
Irish in the United States
Puerto Ricans in the United States
Turks in the United States

Foreign relations
America's mission. J. Osborne. New Repub
163:8-9 O 24 '70
Changing role of U.S; interview. W. P.
Rogers. il U S News 68:28-34 Ja 26 '70
Changing world: today's White House ap-
praisal. il U S News 69:24-5 Ag 31 '70
China, Russia and the United States; a Bri-
tish view. R. Scott. For Affairs 48:334-43 Ja
'70
Communication about foreign policy; address,
February 21, 1970. M. Collins. Dept State
Bul 62:393-6 Mr 23 '70
Congressional presence in foreign relations.
J. K. Javits. For Affairs 48:221-34 Ja '70
Conversation with William Rogers; transcript
of an interview, December 23, 1969. W. P.
Rogers. Dept State Bul 62:53-8 Ja 19 '70
Corporations and the cold war, ed. by D.
Horowitz. Review
Commonweal 92:321-3 Je 26 '70. R. J. Bar-
net
Department gives views on proposal to repeal
certain congressional resolutions; text of let-
ter to Senator J. W. Fulbright. March 12,
1970. H G Torbert. jr. Dept State Bul 62:
468-71 Ap 6 '70
Domestic politics and peacemaking: reconciling incompatible imperatives. R. Rothstein. bibliog f Ann Am Acad 392:62-75
N '70

UNITED STATES—Foreign relations—*Cont.*
Entangling alliances. D. Fromkin. For Affairs
48:688-700 Jl '70
Foreign policy: generation gap; address, December 3, 1970. F. Church. Vital Speeches
37:170-3 Ja 1 '71
Fourth dimension; U.S. China, Russia to talk.
il Newsweek 75:55 Ja 26 '70
Friends and enemies. New Repub 163:5-6 N
21 '70
Generation gap; address, June 7, 1970. E. L.
Richardson. Vital Speeches 36:583-5 Jl 15
'70; Same with title Differing perceptions
of U.S. foreign policy. Dept State Bul 62:
800-3 Je 29 '70
Grand strategy: for 1960. W. Pfaff. Commonweal 92:55 Mr 27 '70
Great retreat. J. Burnham. Nat R 22:1339 D
15 '70
Greatness at bay. W. F. Buckley, jr. Nat R
22:532-3 My 19 '70
Groundwork; coadjutant role of Congress.
Nation 210:36-7 Ja 19 '70
Henry's wonderful machine; the Kissinger
policy process. J. Osborne. New Repub 162:
11-13 Ja 31 '70
How Nixon makes the big decisions. il pors
U S News 68:42-4 F 23 '70
Ideology, interests and foreign policy in the
1970's; address, November 18, 1970. G. C.
Lodge. Vital Speeches 37:181-6 Ja 1 '71
Imperial role. G. W. Johnson. New Repub
163:9 D 12 '70
In search of a foreign policy; with views
of W. Lippmann and G. Ball. il Newsweek
76:28-34+ D 14 '70
International outlook. See issues of Business
week
International relations and the spirit of tragedy. A. N. Gilbert. Yale R 60:45-52 O '70
Letter from Washington. R. H. Rovere. New
Yorker 46:131-4 O 24 '70
Letter from Washington; Nixon in foreign
affairs. R. H. Rovere. New Yorker 46:86+
Ag 15 '70
Mr Nixon's foreign policy; report to Congress on the state of the world. H. J. Morgenthau. New Repub 162:23-5 Mr 21 '70
New empire: a star-spangled bummer. S.
Weissman. Ramp Mag 8:50-5 Ap '70
New generation of isolationists. J. A. Johnson. For Affairs 49:136-46 O '70
Nixon: a heartening progress report. il por
Fortune 82:97-8 S '70
Nixon doctrine; analysis of foreign policy
message. New Repub 162:5-6 F 28 '70
Nixon plan for U.S. in the world during the
1970s. il U S News 68:22-3 Mr 2 '70
Nixon so far. M. J. Goldbloom. Commentary
49:29-38 Mr '70
No going back. Commonweal 93:59-60 O 16 '70
No more Vietnams? address, February 4,
1970. F. A. Johnson. Vital Speeches 36:372-4 Ap 1 '70
One year in office: a conversation with the
Secretary of state; radio interview, January 14, 1970. W. P. Rogers. Dept State Bul
62:124-7 F 2 '70
Pleasures of global chess: State of the world
message. H. Sidey. il por Life 68:4 F 27 '70
Polite disengager. S. Alsop. Newsweek 76:72
Ag 24 '70
President Nixon's news conference:
January 30, 1970. R. M. Nixon. Dept
State Bul 62:173-7 F 16 '70
March 21, 1970. R. M. Nixon. Dept State
Bul 62:427-40 Ap 6 '70
July 30, 1970. R. M. Nixon. Dept State Bul
63:185-7 Ag 17 '70
Recent developments in U.S. foreign policy;
statement, June 9 1970. W. P. Rogers. Dept
State Bul 63:1-5 Jl 6 '70
Reports: Washington. H. Brandon. Atlan
225:4+ Mr '70
Responsibilities of power. H. L. Trewhitt.
Newsweek 75:39 F 23 '70
Return to confrontation; sending U.S. combat troops into Cambodia. il Time 95:22+
My 18 '70
Risks U.S. faces in foreign affairs. il U S
News 70:26-9 Ja 4 '71
Rule of thumb for politicians; metapolitical
perspective. F. X. Winters. America 123:
11-12 Jl 11 '70
Secretary Rogers interviewed for German
television; transcript of interview, April 15,
1970. W. P. Rogers. Dept State Bul 62:565-71 My 4 '70
Secretary Rogers interviewed for the Hearst
newspapers; January 29, 1970. W. P. Rogers.
Dept State Bul 62:217-26 Mr 2 '70
Secretary Rogers interviewed on Issues and
answers; transcript of interview, January
18, 1970. W. P. Rogers. Dept State Bul
62:148-54 F 9 '70

Secretary Rogers interviewed on national educational television; transcript of an interview, November 26, 1969. W. P. Rogers.
Dept State Bul 61:577-83 D 22 '69
Secretary Rogers interviewed on Today program; transcript of interview, March 17,
1970. W. P. Rogers. Dept State Bul 62:440-3
Ap 6 '70
Secretary Rogers' news conference:
December 23, 1969. Dept State Bul 62:21-8
Ja 12 '70
March 23, 1970. Dept State Bul 62:477-84
Ap 13 '70
June 25, 1970. Dept State Bul 63:25-33 Jl
13 '70
State of the Union; address, January 22, 1970.
R. M. Nixon. il pors U S News 68:63-7 F
2 '70; Same. Vital Speeches 36:226-9 F 1
'70; Excerpts. Dept State Bul 62:145-7 F 9
'70
State of the world. il por Newsweek 75:29-30
Mr 2 '70
Taking Fr Berrigan seriously. Commonweal
92:379-80 Ag 7 '70
Top dogs and underdogs. Time 96:22+ N 30
'70
Turning point? K. Crawford. Newsweek 75:
47 My 18 '70
Two aspects of the search for peace; address, April 18, 1970. W. P. Rogers. Dept
State Bul 62:605-8 My 11 '70
Under Secretary Johnson interviewed for
Voice of America; July 17, 1970. U. A. Johnson. Dept State Bul 63:188-93 Ag 17 '70
U.S. foreign policy for the 1970's, a new
strategy for peace; report to the Congress,
February 18, 1970. R. M. Nixon. Dept State
Bul 62:273-332 Mr 9 '70
U.S. foreign policy; the reasons why. R. B.
Du Boff. Commonweal 91:560-2 F 20 '70
U.S. policy: a new strategy for peace. America 122:234-6 Mr 7 '70
United States foreign policy for the 1970s;
text of introduction of message to Congress, February 18, 1970, with summaries
of report. R. M. Nixon. il por U S News
68:65-71 Mr 2 '70
What is to be done? Gigantism in Washington. J. F. Campbell. for Affairs 49:81-99
O '70
What the hawks look to. B. M. Russett. il
America 123:13-14 Jl 11 '70
Who makes our foreign policy? R. L. Tobin.
Sat R 53:28 F 14 '70
Who speaks for the United States? contradictory policy statements. il por Newsweek
76:31-2 Jl 27 '70
Words of warning from three presidents; reprint. U S News 69:80+ Jl 27 '70; Same
abr. Read Digest 97:115-17 O '70
World investment; stability; address, January 29, 1970. G. H. Weyerhaeuser. Vital
Speeches 36:312-14 Mr 1 '70
World's danger zones; U.S. appraisal. il U S
News 68:28-9 Je 29 '70
Youth and foreign policy. S. J. Kelman. For
Affairs 48:414-26 Ap '70
  See also
Cambodian-Vietnamese   conflict—American
  participation
Economic assistance, American
International security
Military assistance, American
United Nations—United States
United States—Diplomatic and consular service
United States—Information agency
United States—State, Department of

Anecdotes, facetiae, satire, etc.

Arsenal on appeasement. S. Thompson. Nat
R 22:769 Jl 28 '70
Inscrutable West. R. Terrill. Atlan 226:68-71
Ag '70

Anti-Communist measures

After ten years; excerpts from addresses and
from Congressional record, ed. by H. Dibble. C. E. Goodell. Nat R 22:948-9 S 8 '70
From John Bull to Uncle Sam: how to run an
empire. J. Aitken. il Am Heritage 21:44-5+
Ag '70
Laos; justifying involvement in Indo-China.
N. Cousins. Sat R 53:26+ Mr 21 '70
Legacy of the cold war in Indochina. T
Hoopes. For Affairs 48:601-16 Jl '70
Reporter at large: some questions about the
war; interview, ed. by W Whitworth. E.
V. Rostow. New Yorker 46:30-46+ Jl 4 '70
Stripped down: policy in southeast Asia and
Mideast. J. Burnham. Nat R 22:778 Jl 28 '70

Bibliography

Congressional documents relating to foreign
policy. See issues of Department of state
bulletin

UNITED STATES—Foreign relations—*Cont.*

Executive agreements

Advice and dissent; J. William Fulbright and the agreement with Spain. il Newsweek 76:45 Ag 17 '70

Advise and consent; proposed Case bill. New Repub 163:7 D 19 '70

History

Conversations with historians; excerpts from Interpreting American history, ed. by J. A. Garraty. R. H. Ferrell. il por Am Heritage 21:60-2 F '70

Red fascism: the merger of Nazi Germany and Soviet Russia in the American image of totalitarianism, 1930's-1950's. L. K. Adler and T. G. Paterson. bibliog f Am Hist R 75:1046-64 Ap '70; Discussion. 75:2155-64 D '70

Roots of the modern American empire, by W. A. Williams. Review
  Sat R 53:40-1 F 21 '70. D. Schoenbrun

Africa

Hunting for a policy. il por Time 95:23-4 F 23 '70

Rhodesia; U.S. foreign policy? address, March 12, 1970. J. R. Rarick. Vital Speeches 36:434-7 My 1 '70

United States and Africa in the seventies; exchange of letters; with a policy statement, March 26, 1970. W. P. Rogers; R. Nixon. Dept State Bul 62:513-21 Ap 20 '70

United States policy toward Africa; statement, May 20, 1970. D. D. Newsom. Dept State Bul 62:716-18 Je 8 '70

See also

Rogers, W. P.—Visit to Africa, February 1970

United States—State, Department of—Advisory council on African affairs

Africa, Southern

United Nations, the United States, and Africa; address, September 17, 1970. D. D. Newsom. Dept State Bul 63:419-24 O 12 '70; Same. Vital Speeches 37:52-5 N 1 '70

Asia

New American posture toward Asia; symposium, ed. by J. C. Charlesworth. bibliog f Ann Am Acad 390:1-113 Jl '70

Role of Japan and the future of American relations with the Far East; address, April 10, 1970. U. A. Johnson. Dept State Bul 62:537-42 Ap 27 '70

United States as a Pacific power. W. C. Johnstone. Cur Hist 58:193-5+ Ap '70

U.S.-Japanese treaty crisis. R. Epp. bibliog f Cur Hist 58:202-8+ Ap '70

What Agnew found in Asia; support for U.S. role there. il U S News 68:13 Ja 26 '70

What future for Asia? W. W. Rostow. Read Digest 97:109-11 D '70

See also

Agnew, S. T.—Visit to Asia

Nixon, R. M.—Visit to Asia and Rumania, 1969

United States—Foreign relations—Asia, Southeastern

Asia, Southeastern

After Cambodia: the fight to save face. J. J. Stone. Commonweal 92:381-2 Ag 7 '70

Asia; address, June 19, 1970. W. W. Rostow. Vital Speeches 36:682-8 S 1 '70

Heavy grows the crown. J. Burnham. Nat R 22:353 Ap 7 '70

Is U.S. paralyzed in southeast Asia? il U S News 68:29 Ap 13 '70

Living with the Nixon doctrine; Asian reaction. il por Newsweek 76:29 Jl 20 '70

Muskie's peace plan; views of Claiborne Peli. New Repub 163:5-6 Jl 25 '70

New multipolar balance in East Asia: implications for United States policy; address, April 1970, with questions and answers. A. D. Barnett. Ann Am Acad 390:73-86 Jl '70

Nixon doctrine. F. Lewis. Atlan 226:6+ N '70

Nixon, the Senate & the war. N. G. Levin, jr. Commentary 50:69-84 N '70

No new doctrine. New Repub 162:10 Ja 17 '70

Secretary Rogers' news conference of July 15, 1970. W. P. Rogers. Dept State Bul 63:125-32 Ag 3 '70

Southeast Asia tomorrow, by M. Gurtov. Review
  Sat R 53:35-6 Ag 8 '70. J. M. Allison

Third Indo-China war. Nation 210:418-19 Ap 13 '70

TRB from Washington: who's top briefer? New Repub 163:6 S 5 '70

United States policies in Southeast Asia. B. K. Gordon. Cur Hist 59:321-5+ D '70

Vietnam cooker. J. Osborne. New Repub 163:11-13 S 26 '70

See also

Agnew, S. T.—Visit to southeast Asia, 1970

United States—Foreign relations—Indochina

Asia, Southern

Great South Asian war. M. Klare. il Nation 210:265-73 Mr 9 '70

Cambodia

American presence. pors Newsweek 75:49-50 Je 29 '70

Cambodian confusion. Commonweal 92:107-8 Ap 17 '70

Crucial test. il Newsweek 75:37-8 Ap 27 '70

Discreet U.S. presence. il Time 96:23 Ag 3 '70

From Peking: Sihanouk talks to Americans; questions and answers. ed. by W. Attwood. Norodom Sihanouk. Look 34:102+ O 20 '70

Future of Cambodia. Norodom Sihanouk. For Affairs 49:1-10 O '70

Indochina, or Mr Nixon's dilemma. il por Newsweek 75:21-2 My 4 '70

Let my people go. Norodom Sihanouk. Nation 211:198-9 S 14 '70

U.S. and Cambodia sign agreement regulating military assistance; text of note. Dept State Bul 63:387 O 5 '70

U.S. replies to Cambodian protests over November incident at Dak Dam; excerpts from note, February 20, 1970. Dept State Bul 62:389-92 Mr 23 '70

See also

Cambodian-Vietnamese conflict—American participation

Canada

Canada. J. D. Hamilton. Atlan 227:86-91 Ja '71

Canada in search of itself. E. Cowan. Nation 210:142-5 F 9 '70

Extraterritoriality in Canadian-United States relations; address, September 2, 1970. J. R. Stevenson. Dept State Bul 63:425-30 O 12 '70

U.S. opposes unilateral extension by Canada of high seas jurisdiction; Department statement, April 15, 1970. Dept State Bul 62:610-11 My 11 '70

United States and Canada discuss Arctic research problems. Dept State Bul 62:657 My 25 '70

Chile

Chile and the US. New Repub 163:9-10 N 7 '70

China

For God, for China and for Yale: the open door in action. J. Israel. bibliog f Am Hist R 75:796-807 F '70

Making of a myth, by P. A. Varg. Review
  Am Hist R 75:1393-6 Je '70. T. J. McCormick

Utmost try; excerpts. B. W. Tuchman. il pors Am Heritage 21:22-31+ O; 22:4-11+ D '70

China (People's Republic)

Brief chat in Warsaw. Time 95:20+ F 2 '70

China and the United States: collision course? O. E. Clubb. bibliog f Cur Hist 59:153-8+ S '70

China policy. J. A. Cohen. Atlan 227:12+ Ja '71

Green tea in Warsaw; Sino-U.S. talks. il Newsweek 75:38+ F 2 '70

Memo from Warsaw: while Asia burns, talk, talk, talk. J. R. Moskin. Look 34:74-5 My 19 '70

Military saboteurs. J. C. Goulden. Nation 210:231-3 Mr 2 '70

Needed: a Washington-Peking hot line. J. Gorkin. Cur 119:58-9 Je '70

Once again in Warsaw. America 122:64-5 Ja 24 '70

Why U.S. Red China talk now. il U S News 68:35-6 Ja 26 '70

Communist countries

See also

United States—Commerce—Communist countries

Congo (Democratic Republic)

President Mobutu of the Congo visits the United States; exchange of greetings and toasts, August 4, 1970. R. M. Nixon; J. D. Mobutu. Dept State Bul 63:279-82 S 7 '70

Cuba

Blighted bloom. il Newsweek 76:62 O 12 '70

Cuba question; reply. C. F. Murphy, jr. Commonweal 91:467 Ja 30 '70

UNITED STATES—Foreign relations—Cuba—
Continued
Today's Cuba and U.S. policy. W. Jeffries.
Chr Cent 87:560-3 My 6 '70
Uptight about Cuba. E. Lamb. Nation 210:
613-14 My 25 '70

Egypt
Game of nations, by M. Copeland 3d. Review
Sat R por 53:39-41 My 23 '70. D. Kurzman

Europe
America and Europe. Z. Brzezinski. bibliog
f For Affairs 49:11-30 S 26 '70
New era in Europe and its meaning for
America; address, October 20, 1970. K.
Rush. Dept State Bul 63:691-7 D 7 '70
See also
Nixon, R. M.—Visit to Europe, 1970

Europe, Western
Our continuing commitment to western Eu-
rope; address, December 6, 1969. W. P.
Rogers. Dept State Bul 61:622-5 D 29 '69
United States and western Europe; address,
January 20, 1970. E. L. Richardson. Vital
Speeches 36:258-60 F 15 '70; Same. Dept
State Bul 62:155-9 F 9 '70
Why Europe worries about U.S. il U S News
69:32-5 Jl 13 '70
See also
Nixon, R. M.—Visit to Europe, 1970

Far East
Pacific destiny, by R. O'Connor. Review
Sat R 53:32-3 Ja 24 '70. M. Kalb
Shanghai crisis of 1932: the basis of British
policy. C. Thorne. bibliog f Am Hist R 75:
1616-39 O '70

Finland
President Kekkonen of Finland visits the
United States; exchange of remarks and
toasts, July 23, 1970. U. Kekkonen; R. M.
Nixon. Dept State Bul 63:194-7 Ag 17 '70

France
De Gaulle and three presidents. H. Sidey.
Life 69:4 N 20 '70
France and the U.S. agree to disagree. il por
Newsweek 75:17-18 Mr 9 '70
Man from France; interview, ed. by R. Stol-
ley. G. Pompidou. il pors Life 68:34-7 F 20
'70
New look at France; interview, ed. by C.
Painton. G. Pompidou. il por U S News
68:44-7 Mr 2 '70
Sauce and ceremony; President Pompidou's
three-day Washington visit. il por Time
95:18 Mr 9 '70

Germany (Federal Republic)
President Nixon and Chancellor Brandt hold
talks at Washington; exchange of greetings
and toasts, April 10, 1970. R. M. Nixon; W.
Brandt. Dept State Bul 62:573-7 My 4 '70
Real issue in Nixon-Brandt talks. il por U S
News 68:80 Ap 20 '70
Secretary Rogers interviewed for German
television; transcript of interview, April 15,
1970. W. P. Rogers. Dept State Bul 62:565-71
My 4 '70
Triumph for Brandt. por Time 95:15 Ap 20 '70
United States comments on signing of
Federal German-U.S.S.R. treaty, state-
ment, August 12, 1970 with text, of U.S.
note. W. P. Rogers. Dept State Bul 63:
275-6 S 7 '70

Great Britain
Cementing a friendship; H. Wilson's visit.
Time 95:32 F 9 '70
Interview with Britain's Prime Minister Ed-
ward Heath; ed. by J. Fromm. E. Heath.
il pors U S News 69:24-6+ D 21 '70
President Nixon and British Prime Minister
Wilson hold talks at Washington; exchange
of greetings and toasts, January 27, 1970.
R. M. Nixon; H. Wilson. Dept State Bul 62:
207-11 F 23 '70
Redefining that special relationship. il Time
95:25-6 F 2 '70

Greece, Modern
Americans bearing gifts; aid to Greece. Com-
monweal 92:330 Jl 10 '70
Bearing gifts to Greeks. Z. B. Grant. New
Repub 162:19-21 Mr 7 '70
Exile; interview. H. Vlachos. New Yorker
46:19-20 Jl 4 '70
Symbols of acceptance. Time 96:28+ S 21 '70
Uncle cries "Uncle"; arms embargo lifted by
U.S. Nation 211:356 O 19 '70
U.S. lifts partial arms embargo against
Greece; Department announcement. Dept
State Bul 63:413 O 12 '70

India
American posture toward India and Pakistan;
address, April 1970, with questions and answers. P. Talbot. Ann Am Acad 390:87-97
Jl '70

Indochina
Indochina: forging an alliance. il Time 95:27
Je 8 '70
Madness on the grand scale; address, April
2, 1970. J. W. Fulbright. New Repub 162:
19 Ap 18 '70
New hope: Asianization. il Newsweek 75:34+
Mr 30 '70
Nixon doctrine's test in Indochina. il Time
95:17-18 Ap 13 '70
Perilous path in southeast Asia. il Bsns W
p94+ Ap 25 '70
Standing pat. Newsweek 75:29 Ap 13 '70
Thieu plus two. New Repub 162:7-8 Ap 4 '70
See also
Cambodian-Vietnamese conflict—American
participation

Indonesia
President Soeharto of Indonesia visits the
United States; exchange of greetings and
toasts, May 26, 1970. R. M. Nixon; Suharto.
Dept State Bul 62:743-6 Je 15 '70

Israel
Aid to Israel. New Repub 163:7 O 3 '70
Cambodia and Israel. Chr Today 14:21-2 My
22 '70
Case for the primacy of Israel. M. Geltman.
Nat R 22:407-9 Ap 21 '70
Dilettante; Fulbright proposal. Nation 211:
166 S 7 '70
Israel against the wall. New Repub 163:5-6
S 26 '70
Middle East: new danger from old foes; So-
viet involvement in Egypt. il Time 95:23-4
Je 8 '70
Middle East on the Potomac. il pors News-
week 76:41-2 D 21 '70
New left and the Arab-Israeli conflict. M.
Harrington. Cur 118:23-6 My '70
Nixon and Israel. Nat R 22:125 F 10 '70
On ditching Israel. C. Benson. Nat R 22:
1206-10 N 17 '70; Reply with rejoinder. A.
S. Epstein. 23:12+ Ja 12 '71
Russians in Egypt. New Repub 162:9 My 16
'70; Reply. J. Hartshorne. 162:29 Je 6 '70
Strategic alternative? C. Benson. Nat R 22:
1206-10 N 17 '70
Truce survives a falling-out. il Newsweek 76:
34-6 Ag 31 '70
US and Israel. New Repub 162:5-6 Ja 24 '70
U.S. and Israel: the built-in conflict. S. Alsop.
Newsweek 76:72 Ag 3 '70
Visitors from Israel. Time 96:14 S 21 '70
Waiting for Washington to decide. il News-
week 75:39+ Je 8 '70

Japan
Behind U.S. worries over Japan; with inter-
view. E. Sato. U S News 68:56-7 F 23 '70
Hidden crisis in Asia. E. O. Reischauer. Read
Digest 96:77-81 F '70
Passing the buck to Tokyo. A. Axelbank.
Nation 211:293-5 O 5 '70
President Nixon and Prime Minister Sato
of Japan hold talks at Washington; ex-
change of greetings; toasts, remarks, Nov-
ember 19-21, 1969; with text of communique.
R. M. Nixon; E. Sato. Dept State Bul 61:
551-7 D 15 '69
Role of Japan and the future of American
relations with the Far East; address, April
1970, with questions and answers. U. A.
Johnson. Ann Am Acad 390:63-72 Jl '70
Three-power gamble: Japan, China, USA. A.
Axelbank and K. Nakamura. il Nation 211:
678-81 D 28 '70
U.S. and Japan hold meetings on environ-
mental problems; text of joint communi-
que. Dept State Bul 63:670-1 N 30 '70
U.S. and Japanese ministers hold talks at
Washington. Dept State Bul 63:34 Jl 13 '70
U.S.-Japanese treaty crisis. R. Epp. bibliog f
Cur Hist 58:202-8+ Ap '70
See also
United States—Commerce—Japan
United States—Treaties—Japan

Jordan
Bad trip; deferment of J. J. Sisco's Jor-
danian visit. il Time 95:43 Ap 27 '70
Dilemmas in the desert; unilateral military
support from the United States. Nat R 22:
1034+ O 6 '70
Middle East on the Potomac. il pors Newsweek 76:41-2 D 21 '70

Korea (People's Republic)
See also
Pueblo incident, 1968

UNITED STATES—Foreign relations—*Cont.*

Korea (Republic)

Crisis of confidence in Korea. B. Krisher. il Newsweek 76:34-5+ Jl 27 '70

Laos

Air America: flying the U.S. into Laos. por Ramparts 8:39-42+ F '70

Flank attack: chaos in Laos; clarification of policy. il Newsweek 75:33 Mr 30 '70

In the President's words; what U.S. is doing in Laos; statement, March 6, 1970. R. M. Nixon. por U S News 68:86-8 Mr 16 '70; Same with title Scope of the U.S. involvement in Laos. Dept State Bul 62:405-9 Mr 30 '70

Knee deep in Laotian war? Sr Schol 95:13 O 13 '69

Laos. N. Cousins. Sat R 53:26 Mr 21 '70

Laos and the burden of history. Chr Cent 87: 411 Ap 8 '70

Laos: another Vietnam? il Newsweek 75:38+ Mr 16 '70

Laos in the second Indochina war. A. J. Dommen. Cur Hist 59:326-32+ D '70

Laos: old war, new dispute. il Time 95:11-12 Mr 23 '70

Laos: plain (and fancy) talk. Newsweek 75: 34+ Mr 23 '70

Letter from Washington. R. H. Rovere. New Yorker 46:148-50+ Mr 21 '70

Mr Nixon's dilemma. W. F. Buckley, jr. Nat R 22:376-7 Ap 7 '70

Our involvement in Laos. R. Shaplen. il For Affairs 48:478-93 Ap '70

Pendulum of war swings wider in Laos. H. D. S. Greenway. il Life 68:32-6 Ap 3 '70

Profile leaps to view. E. Martinez. Nation 211:262-6 S 28 '70

Secret is out. America 122:291 Mr 21 '70; Reply. R. Banville. 122:661 Je 27 '70

U.S. policy's risky dead end. M. Parker. il Newsweek 75:38-9 Mr 16 '70

Vietnamization of Laos. B. Garrett. il Ramp Mag 8:36-45 Je '70

Watch on the Plain of Jars. H. Sidey. Life 68:4 Mr 20 '70

What reds are up to in Laos. il U S News 68:35-6 Mr 16 '70

Latin America

How wars end in Latin America. B. Wood. bibliog f Ann Am Acad 392:40-50 N '70

Latin America: resentful. U S News 70:29 Ja 4 '71

New realism. Nat R 22:18-19 Ja 13 '70

Rockefeller report on the Americas, by N. A. Rockefeller. Review
 Sat R 53:30-2 Ja 31 '70. D. Karzman

See also
Alliance for progress
Inter-American conferences
Inter-American relations

Mexico

Mexico and the United States: model for hemisphere relations; address, May 5, 1970. W. P. Rogers. Dept State Bul 62:654-5 My 25 '70

President Nixon and President Diaz Ordaz of Mexico, meet at Puerto Vallarta; remarks, and toasts, August 20-21, 1970; with text of joint communique, and statement concerning treaty, and declaration on the traffic in narcotics. R. M. Nixon; G. Diaz Ordaz. Dept State Bul 63:289-300 S 14 '70

President Nixon greets Mexico-U.S. interparliamentary conference; exchange of remarks, May 5, 1970. R. M. Nixon; M. B. Aguirre Samaniego. Dept State Bul 62:656-7 My 25 '70

President Nixon honors President Diaz Ordaz of Mexico at a state dinner in California; exchange of greetings and remarks, September 3, 1970. Dept State Bul 63:347-55 S 28 '70

See also
Nixon, R. M.—Visit to Mexico, 1970
United States—History—Punitive expedition to Mexico, 1916
United States-Mexico commission for border development and friendship
United States—Treaties—Mexico

Middle East

Airway war escalates; with editorial comment. il Bsns W p21-2, 134 S 12 '70

American policy toward the Middle East: address, April 1970, with questions and answers. P. T. Hart. Ann Am Acad 390:98-113 Jl '70

Arab-Israeli conflict: an American policy. J. C. Campbell. For Affairs 49:51-69 O '70

Assistant Secretary Sisco interviewed on Meet the press; transcript of interview, July 12, 1970. J. J. Sisco. Dept State Bul 63:150-5 Ag 3 '70

Back into focus; Arab-Israeli struggle. Nat R 22:17 Ja 13 '70

Big power games, small power wars. A. Perlmutter. il Trans-Action 7:70-8+ Jl '70

Can Mideast war be averted? il U S News 69: 11-13 Jl 27 '70

Congress, Vietnam, Midwest: the President's appraisal; excerpts from radio and TV interview, July 1, 1970. R. M. Nixon. il por U S News 69:20-2 Jl 13 '70

Conversation with the President; transcript of radio and TV interview, July 1, 1970. R. M. Nixon. Dept State Bul 63:101-13 Jl 27 '70; Excerpts. il por U S News 69:20-2 Jl 13 '70

Decision or drift? Nat R 22:604-5 Je 16 '70; Reply. F. S. Meyer. 22:682 Je 30 '70

Exhilaration of crisis. H. Sidey. il Life 69:2 O 2 '70

Fulbright converted? K. Crawford. Newsweek 76:34 S 7 '70

Game of nations, by M. Copeland. Review
 Nation 210:759-60 Je 22 '70. D. Stewart

Hotter and hotter. il Nat R 22:69-70 Ja 27 '70

Lasting peace in the Middle East: an American view; address, December 9, 1969. W. P. Rogers. Dept State Bul 62:7-11 Ja 5 '70

Mid East: search for stability. il Time 96: 10-11+ O 5 '70

Middle East again (still) Nat R 22:719 Jl 14 '70

Middle East cockpit; lack of attention to the developing situation. Nation 210:708-9 Je 15 '70

Middle East: showdown time. V. S. Kearney. America 124:7 Ja 9 '71

Mr Nixon makes a trip, and a point. il por Newsweek 76:22-3 O 5 '70

Movement in the Middle East? Nat R 23:20-1 Ja 12 '71

Our Middle East stance: rejected but still valid. Life 68:28 Ja 23 '70

Secretary Rogers' news conference of July 15, 1970. W. P. Rogers. Dept State Bul 63: 125-32 Ag 3 '70

Stripped down. J. Burnham. Nat R 22:778 Jl 28 '70

Suez is the front to watch. G. W. Ball. il N Y Times Mag p10-11+ Je 28 '70

U.S. objectives in the Middle East; address, June 30, 1970. J. J. Sisco. Dept State Bul 63: 175-8 Ag 10 '70

U.S, the Arabs & Israel. A. Hartley. Commentary 49:45-50 Mr '70

United States changing Mideast policy; address, January 13, 1970. B. Roth. Vital Speeches 36:442-8 My 1 '70

United States policy in the Middle East. B. Reich. bibliog f Cur Hist 60:1-6 Ja '71

While Jordan burned. il por Newsweek 76:20-1 S 28 '70

Will U.S. intervene in the Mideast? il U S News 69:18-19 S 28 '70

Zero hour for the Middle East. W. E. Griffith. Read Digest 96:49-53 Ja '70

Nicaragua

U.S. and Nicaragua agree to discuss future of Bryan-Chamorro treaty; Department announcement with exchange of notes. Dept State Bul 62:560-1 Ap 27 '70

Oman

U.S. and Oman to continue friendship and cooperation; message from sultanate of Oman and U.S. reply. Dept State Bul 63: 430 O 12 '70

Pakistan

American posture toward India and Pakistan; address, April 1970, with questions and answers. P. Talbot. Ann Am Acad 390:87-97 Jl '70

Philippines

Storm warnings in the Philippines. C. T. Rowan. Read Digest 97:193-4+ N '70

See also
United States—Treaties—Philippines

Rhodesia

Birth of a nation. il Newsweek 75:54+ Mr 16 '70

Cui bono? decision to close out the consular office. Nat R 22:297 Mr 24 '70

U.S. closes consulate general at Salisbury, Southern Rhodesia; statement, March 9, 1970. W. P. Rogers. Dept State Bul 62: 412 Mr 30 '70

UNITED STATES—Foreign relations—*Cont.*

Rumania

President Nixon meets with President Ceausescu of Romania; exchange of greetings and toasts, October 26, 1970. R. M. Nixon; N. Ceausescu. Dept State Bul 63: 648-50 N 23 '70
See also
Nixon, R. M.—Visit to Asia and Rumania, 1969

Russia

American-Soviet relations: push and pull in the power game. il Sr Schol 97:8-11+ D 7 '70
Can we trust the Kremlin? Two views. H. W. Baldwin; H. H. Humphrey. Read Digest 96:84-92 Mr '70
Clues to Soviet policy; interview, ed. by J. Fromm. M. Mackintosh. il pors U S News 69:66-9 N 2 '70
Dealing with Russia. K. Crawford. Newsweek 75:35 Ap 6 '70
Great danger from a new direction: Middle East problem. H. Sidey. Life 69:2B Jl 17 '70
Growing gulf between the big two. il Time 96:30 N 16 '70
Hostage generals: a closed case, but—. il U S News 69:34 N 23 '70
Middle East: war without end; Kosygin-Nixon correspondence. il Newsweek 75:39-40 F 16 '70
Missing element in the debate. C. Emmet. Nat R 22:678-9+ Je 30 '70
Mr Nixon makes a trip, and a point. il por Newsweek 76:22-3 O 5 '70
More, the better; Richard Nixon-Andrei Gromyko talks. il Newsweek 76:58+ N 2 '70
New climate of coexistence. A. Fontaine. Cur 122:60-4 O '70
Nixon's new drive to ward off cold war. il U S News 69:70-1 N 2 '70
Real meaning of Nixon trip. il pors U S News 69:17-19 O 12 '70
Secretary Rogers and Secretary Laird interviewed on issues and answers. W. P. Rogers; M. R. Laird. Dept State Bul 63:542-53 N 2 '70
Soviet motives and stateside suspicions. R. Gurney, jr. Commonweal 93:63-8 O 16 '70: Discussion 93:59-60, 211+ O 16, N 27 '70
U-8 incident. il Newsweek 76:60 N 2 '70
U.S. and Russia: rising tension. il U S News 70:27-9 Ja 4 '71
U.S.-Soviet relations in an era of negotiation; address, November 20, 1969. E. L. Richardson. Dept State Bul 61:584-8 D 22 '69
United States and the Soviet Union: the elusive peace. N. A. Graebner. Cur Hist 59:193-8+ O '70
Why the Kremlin is testing Nixon; interview. F. D. Kohler. por U S News 69:19-20 O 19 '70
See also
Cuban crisis 1962
Potsdam declaration, 1945
Strategic arms limitation talks
United States—Treaties—Russia

Spain

Advice and dissent; J. William Fulbright and the executive agreement. il Newsweek 76: 45 Ag 17 '70
Any port in a showdown; pact with Spain. L. Fernsworth. il Nation 211:489-91 N 16 '70
Spain: fascism gone gray. G. Seldes. il Nation 211:77-80 Ag 3 '70
Statement on U.S.-Spain agreement submitted to the Senate: August 6, 1970. U. A. Johnson. Dept State Bul 63:248-50 Ag 31 '70
U.S. and Spain sign agreement of friendship and cooperation; text of joint statement, with U.S. related letters and notes. Dept State Bul 63:237-43 Ag 31 '70

Sweden

Neutralist's equilibrium. il por Time 95:18 Je 15 '70
Swedish leader on a tightrope. il por U S News 68:58 Je 15 '70
Why Sweden is critical of U.S. role in Vietnam; interview. O. Palme. il por U S News 68:48-9 Je 22 '70

Taiwan

China policy. J. A. Cohen. Atlan 227:12+ Ja '71
Game goes on. il Newsweek 76:45 O 26 '70
Phantom Phantom jets. Nation 210:102 F 2 '70
Third party in Chinese-American relations: the need for change. J. K. Kallgren. il Bul Atom Sci 26:11-16 My '70
U.S. and Taiwan: new issues for old allies. il por U S News 68:52 My 4 '70

Thailand

World's angriest man: Thannat Kohman, foreign minister. W. F. Buckley, jr. Nat R 22:46+ Ja 13 '70

Trinidad and Tobago

U.S. Trinidad and Tobago sign new income tax convention; January 12, 1970. Dept State Bul 62:171-2 F 9 '70

Vietnam (Democratic Republic)

See also
Vietnamese war, 1957- —American participation

Vietnam (Republic)

Apprehensive allies. il Time 96:20 Jl 20 '70
David Bruce's portfolio. il por Newsweek 76: 33 Ag 3 '70
If not Thieu, who? G. Kirk. por Nat R 22: 667-9 Je 30 '70
See also
Vietnamese war, 1957-
Vietnamese war, 1957- —American participation

Yugoslavia

Exchange of toasts at Belgrade, September 30; with joint communique, October 1, 1970. Tito; R. M. Nixon. Dept State Bul 63:515-22 N 2 '70
See also
Nixon, R. M.—Visit to Europe, 1970

Foreign service

Management strategy: a program for the seventies; address, January 14, 1970. W. B. Macomber. Dept State Bul 62:130-41 F 2 '70
New sprint in foggy bottom; reform at last? S. Simpson. Nation 210:296-302 Mr 16 '70
See also
United States—Diplomatic and consular service
United States—State, Department of

Forest service

Clear cutting and conservation. il Sci N 98:430 D 5 '70
Dilemma of the Forest service. E. C. Crafts. il Am For 76:8-9+ Je '70
Fair market value. S. B. Moser. il pors Am For 76:20-3+ Ja '70
French Pete for people; Willamette national forest, Ore. A. Netboy. il Am For 76:16-18+ My '70
He remembers Pinchot; letter to the editor. A. Netboy. Am For 76:47-8 Ag '70
Mike Frome. M. Frome. Am For 76:3+ O '70
Mike Frome; criticism of the forest service. M. Frome. Am For 76:3+ Je '70
Mike Frome; lack of application of scientific forestry. M. Frome. Am For 76:3+ F '70; Discussion 76:2-4+ Je '70
Mike Frome: mismanagement of public forests. M. Frome. Am For 76:7+ D '70
Myth of multiple use. E. M. Sterling. il Am For 76:25-7 Je '70; Discussion. 76:6 S; 4 O '70
Penthouse in the wilderness; forest lookouts. P. McManus. Read Digest 96:201-2+ My '70

General accounting office

Congress rearms its own watchdog. il Bsns W p 102+ Je 20 '70
GAO attacks NASA's Saturn 5 incentives. W. J. Normyle. Aviation W 92:25-6 Ap 6 '70
GAO readies report on weapons systems. K. Johnsen. il Aviation W 92:74+ Ja 19 '70
GAO report affects contractor relations. W. J. Normyle. Aviation W 93:18-19 Jl 13 '70
Military maneuvers. New Repub 163:5-7 D 26 '70
Senate unit approves new power for GAO. Aviation W 93:77 S 14 '70

General services administration

Government test data are no buyer's guide. Bsns W p26 O 31 '70

Government

See United States—Politics and government

Government printing office

Uncle Sam's bookstores are on the move. Pub W 197:75-6 Ap 13 '70
Use of BLS survey data in wage setting at GPO; with tables. T. C. Mobley. Mo Labor R 93:66-8 Ap '70

Government publications

See Government publications

UNITED STATES—*Continued*

Health, education and welfare, Department of

Aches and pains of Robert Finch. Nation 210: 644 Je 1 '70

Cyclamates: House report charges administrative alchemy at HEW. R. J. Bazell. Science 170:419-20 O 23 '70

Exit Dr Yolles. il por Newsweek 75:91-2 Je 15 '70

Exit Egeberg; and Farmer. pors Time 96:15 D 14 '70

Finch steps down, to the White House: New man: old hand at H.E.W. il por Newsweek 75:24-5 Je 15 '70

HEW blacklists: new security procedures officially adopted. P. M. Boffey. Science Science 170:142-4 O 9 '70

HEW: blacklists scrapped in new security procedures. B. Nelson. Science 167:154-6 Ja 9 '70

HEW: the department that lost its head. J. Walsh. Science 168:1431-3 Je 19 '70

HEW: what will decentralization mean to research evaluation? J. Walsh. Science 168: 231-4 Ap 10 '70

HEW's new secretary. il por Time 95:12-13 Je 15 '70

HEW's security. B. Nelson. Trans-Action 7: 5-6 Ja '70

High-powered boss in a hot seat. I. Ross. Read Digest 96:117-21 Mr '70

I want to focus on people problems; interview. E. L. Richardson. pors U S News 69:35-6+ D 7 '70

Integrating friends; Office for civil rights interprets the Nixon policy statement. J. Osborne. New Repub 162:12-14 Ap 18 '70

Moving into chaos: new welfare chief. por U S News 68:76 Je 22 '70

New desegregation targets: the North and the suburbs. il U S News 69:25-7 D 14 '70

Real Robert Finch stands up. R. Sherrill. il pors N Y Times Mag p6-7+ Jl 5 '70

Research head for HEW. Sci N 97:596 Je 20 '70

Saving Bob Finch. J. Osborne. New Repub 162:9-10 Je 20 '70

Secretary Finch: how much is his influence waning? il por U S News 68:17 Mr 9 '70

Sex discrimination: campuses face contract loss over HEW demands. R. J. Bazell. Science 170:834-5 N 20 '70

Sickness at HEW. por Time 95:56 Je 15 '70

Social-welfare jungle: how a government department grows and grows. il U S News 69:30-4 D 7 '70

Toying around with unsafe toys. Consumer Rep 36:4 Ja '71

See also
Foster grandparent program
Project Head Start
United States—Aging, Administration on
United States—Education, Office of
United States—National air pollution control administration
United States—National institute of Mental health

Appropriations and expenditures

Acceptable compromise; health and education bill. New Repub 162:11 Mr 14 '70

After the veto. Sci N 97:121 Ja 31 '70

Another veto? Newsweek 75:21 Mr 2 '70

Battle over a billion. Time 95:8 F 2 '70

Dictating the agenda; Nixon's veto of the labor-HEW appropriations. Time 95:9-10 F 9 '70

Education and health funds: a billion dollar difference. J. Walsh. il Science 167:355-8 Ja 23 '70

HEW decentralizers exempt research. S. Z. Goldhaber. Science 168:1557 Je 26 '70

Making the veto stick. il Newsweek 75:20-1 F 9 '70

More care than research. Sci N 97:145-6 F 7 '70

1970 HEW funds 1st video veto. G. Krettek and E. D. Cooke. Wilson Lib Bul 44:794-5 Mr '70

President repeats threat to veto HEW funds. S. Wagner. Pub W 197:59 Ja 19 '70

Sordid episode. C. B. Grannis. Pub W 197: 53 F 16 '70

Historic houses, etc.

Four centuries of American style. M. Spires. il Am Home 73:39-47 F '70

See also
National trust for historic preservation

History

Conversations with historians; excerpts from interpreting American history, ed. by J. A. Garraty. H. S. Commager. il por Am Heritage 21:58-64 F '70

Paradox of American violence: a historical appraisal. H. D. Graham. bibliog f Ann Am Acad 391:74-82 S '70

Revisionism: a new, angry look at the American past; Time essay. il Time 95:14-15 F 2 '70

Spirit of '70: six historians reflect on what ails the American spirit; symposium. il Newsweek 76:18-34 Jl 6 '70

Turning history upside down. C. Solway. Sat R 53:13-15+ Je 20 '70

What America would be like without blacks; Time essay. R. Ellison. il Time 95:54-5 Ap 6 '70

See also
Cities and towns—United States—History
Education—United States—History
Frontier and pioneer life—United States
South—History
United States—Church history
United States—Economic history
United States—Foreign relations—History
United States—Social history

Bibliography

Articles and other books received; comp. by W. Gray. See issues of American historical review

Historiography

At the borderland of law and economic history: the contributions of Willard Hurst; address, December 1968. H. N. Scheiber. bibliog f Am Hist R 75:744-56 F '70

Future of the past; address, December 29, 1969. C. V. Woodward. bibliog f Am Hist R 75:711-26 F '70

Perspective. J. H. Plumb. Sat R 53:29+ Ja 31 '70

Turning history upside down; annual convention. C. Solway. Sat R 53:13-15+ Je 20 '70

Sources

Collecting for Clio; collections of the Massachusetts historical society. T. B. Adams. il Sat R 53:16-17 Je 20 '70

Study and teaching

Enigma of Negro history. L. J. Alilunas and W. Chazanof. Clear House 45:29-31 S '70; Same abr. Ed Digest 36:38-9 D '70

Innovation within the conventional school setting. R. L. Dunlap. Clear House 45:225 D '70

Toward a new American history; part of a new humanized education. C. R. Keller. Ed Digest 36:52-4 S '70

Textbooks

Civil rights and white textbooks. Negro Hist Bul 33:4-5 Ja '70

Colonial period

Political mimesis: a consideration of the historical and cultural roots of legislative behavior in the British colonies in the eighteenth century: with a comment by B. Bailyn and reply by Greene. J. P. Greene. bibliog f Am Hist R 75:337-67 D '69

Road not taken; colonies turn fateful fork by systematically dividing races. L. Bennett, jr. il Ebony 25:70-2+ Ag '70

Seek & ye shall find. P. W. Schmidtchen. il Hobbies 74:134-6+ Ja '70

See also
New England—History—Colonial period
Pilgrim fathers

Revolution

Samuel Adams: architect of Revolution. por Sr Schol 95:16 S 29 '69

When businessmen sparked a revolution. il Nations Bsns 58:52-7 Jl '70

See also
Boston massacre, 1770

Revolution—Campaigns and battles

Black continentals; Negro soldiers serving in the American war of independence. P. Barnett. il Negro Hist Bul 33:6-10 Ja '70

That bitter night in '76; famous painting Washington crossing the Delaware. B. Hibbs. il Read Digest 96:174-8 Mr '70

Revolution—Centennial celebrations, etc.

See also
United States—Declaration of independence —Centennial celebrations, etc.

Revolution—Drama

Road to Valley Forge. G. DuBois. Plays 29: 11-18 F '70

UNITED STATES—History—*Continued*

Revolution—Naval operations

Agreable voyage: invasion of England and Scotland, and defeat of H.M.S. Drake by J. P. Jones. M. Halliday. il pors Am Heritage 21:8-11+ Je '70

Revolution—Negroes

Black continentals; Negro soldiers serving in the American war of independence. P. Barnett. il Negro Hist Bul 33:6-10 Ja '70

Black pioneer period. L. Bennett, jr. il Ebony 25:46-8+ O '70

Boston massacre and Crispus Attucks. il Negro Hist Bul 33:56-7 Mr '70

Revolution—Personal narratives

Rebels, turn out your dead! detention aboard British prison ship Jersey, moored in the East River. A. B. Tourtellot. il Am Heritage 21:16-17+ Ag '70

Revolution—Prisoners and prisons

Melancholy case; order by G. Washington to hang Capt C. Asgill in reprisal for Tory atrocity. in N.J. A. L. Damon. il por Am Heritage 21:18-19+ F '70

Rebels, turn out your dead! detention aboard British prison ship Jersey, moored in the East River. A. B. Tourtellot. il Am Heritage 21:16-17+ Ag '70

1783-1812

George Washington and the new nation (1783-1793) by J. T. Flexner. Review Sat R 53:33-4 N 21 '70. M. M. Brown

War with Mexico, 1845-1848

Thankless task of Nicholas Trist. R. M. Ketchum. il por Am Heritage 21:12-15+ Ag '70

Civil war

See also
Confederate States of America
Fort Sumter
Reconstruction (Civil war)

Civil war—Medical and sanitary affairs

Nurse who outranked the general. R. Dunlop. il Todays Health 48:56-7+ My '70

Teen-age Civil war nurse Susie King Taylor. il Ebony 25:96-8+ F '70

Civil war—Negro troops

Teen-age Civil war nurse Susie King Taylor. il Ebony 25:96-8+ F '70

Civil war—Photography

Gallantry under fire. D. Vestal. il Travel & Camera 33:34-9 F '70

Civil war—Songs and music

Famous Civil war band lives again. A. Marquis. il Hobbies 75:48-9+ S '70

1865-1898

Centennial: American life in 1876, by W. P. Randel. Review
Atlan 225:95-8 Ja '70. L. Kronenberger
See also
Little Big Horn, Battle of the, 1876

European war, 1914-1918

See European war, 1914-1918—United States

Punitive expedition to Mexico, 1916

Great pursuit, by H. M. Mason jr. Review Bsns W il p6 Jl 25 '70. H. B. Gonzalez •

1918-1941

Conversations with historians; excerpts from Interpreting American history, ed. by J. A. Garraty, R. H. Ferrell. il por Am Heritage 21:60-2 F '70

1933-1945

That kind of a liberal: Franklin D. Roosevelt after twenty-five years. J. M. Blum. Yale R 60:14-23 O '70

World war, 1939-1945

See World war, 1939-1945—United States

1945-

Clean break with the past. J. Brooks. il Am Heritage 21:4-7+ Ag '70

Conversations with historians; excerpts from Interpreting American history, ed. by J. A. Garraty. A. Schlesinger, jr. il por Am Heritage 21:62-4 F '70

Great expectations, a quarter of a century later .R. Bendiner. il N Y Times Mag p36-7+ Ap 26 '70

History, Naval

See also
United States—History—Revolution—Naval operations

House of representatives

See United States—Congress—House

Housing and urban development, Department of

Breakthrough? M. Villecco and J. M. Dixon. Arch Forum 132:50-1 Ap '70

Breakthrough's progress is slow. il Bsns W p86+ N 14 '70

Furor over a drive to integrate the suburbs. il U S News 69:23-4 Ag 10 '70

George Romney is running hard at HUD. A. J. Reichley. il por Fortune 82:100-3+ D '70

Heavy fighting shakes Model cities. Bsns W p65 Ag 1 '70

Homes from production lines. il U S News 68:74-5 Mr 23 '70

HUD aid makes the difference; South Haven, Mich. A. R. Pierce. il Am City 85:80-1 Je '70

HUD chooses industrialized housing teams. il Aviation W 92:233 Mr 9 '70

Man on the spot in housing dispute. por U S News 69:25 Ag 10 '70

New government and industry partnership for building more housing. D. Pellish. il Arch Forum 133:58-61 Jl '70

Operation Breakthrough; building types study; with introd. by R. Jensen. il Arch Rec 147:137-52 Ap '70

Where housing will break new ground; Breakthrough competition. il Bsns W p32+ Mr 7 '70

Winners assembled for Breakthrough. Bsns W p35 F 28 '70

Indian affairs, Bureau of

Bureau of Indian affairs: America's colonial service. D. R. Maxey. Look 34:35 Je 2 '70

Indian reservations: should they be abolished? arguments on three sides. il Sr Schol 97: 21-3 S 28 '70

New deal coming for American Indians? il U S News 69:68-70 S 14 '70

Time to redeem an old promise. E. Fuchs. il Sat R 53:54-7+ Ja 24 '70

See also
Indians of North America—Government relations

Institute of American Indian art, Santa Fe

Industries

Are imports killing off U.S. industries? with editorial comment. il Bsns W p76-7, 100 Jl 25 '70

Modern industry. See issues of Dun's

Moon program's business brain trust; Apollo executive group. E. Clark. il pors Nations Bsns 58:32-4+ My '70

Panorama of the Nation's business. V. Louviere. See issues of Nation's business

Twelve industries moving ahead in the midst of a downturn. il U S News 68:62-3 Ap 27 '70

Who's where within the industry groups? with yardsticks of management performance. il Forbes 105:82 Ja 1 '70; 107:66 Ja 1 '71

See also
Indians of North America—Industries
Labor and laboring classes—United States
Shipbuilding
United States—Economic conditions
   also names of industries, e.g. Tobacco industry and trade
   also subhead United States under names of industries, e.g. Aluminum industry and trade—United States

Information agency

Static at the Voice; interdepartmental feud. Newsweek 76:42 N 30 '70

USIA moves to right in book selection. Library J 95:435 F 1 '70

See also
America illustrated (periodical)

Information service

Plea to investigate USIS; to; intellectual freedom committee, letter to the editor. S. Berman. Wilson Lib Bul 44:606 F '70

Insular possessions

See United States—Territories and possessions

Intellectual life

Apocalypse next exit. G. Davenport. Nat R 22:1302-4 D 1 '70

UNITED STATES—Intellectual life—*Cont.*
Changers. L. Lerman. il Mlle 71:146-9 Je '70
On being deradicalized. N. Glazer. Commentary 50:74-80 O '70; Discussion. 50:30-1 O '70; 51:20-3 Ja '71
They also read who roll in dough; observations based on activities of Scarsdale public library. M. A. Kateley. il por Wilson Lib Bul 45:477-81 Ja '71
U.S. culture moves west. il U S News 69:62-7 S 7 '70
See also
Books and reading
Education—United States
United States—Popular culture

Interior, Department of

Arrow from the chief. il pors Newsweek 76:20-1 D 7 '70
Changes at Interior. por Sci N 98:432-3 D 5 '70
Department of interior: Hickel leaves a diminished agency. L. J. Carter. Science 170:1063-4 D 4 '70
Environment man in Nixon's cabinet. il pors Bsns W p56-8+ F 14 '70
Keeping shale underwraps. C. Welles. il Nation 211:51-2 Jl 20 '70
Next Interior secretary. por Time 96:46+ D 14 '70
Odd man in. por Newsweek 75:20 Je 29 '70
Para-real estate: the handing out of resources. J. Ridgeway. il Ramp Mag 8:28-33 My '70
Secretary Hickel; interview. W. J. Hickel. New Yorker 45:24-6 Ja 17 '70
See also
United States—Fish and wildlife service
United States—National park service
United States—Outdoor recreation. Bureau of
United States—Reclamation, Bureau of

Internal revenue service

AAP asks withdrawal of review copies ruling. Pub W 198:36-7 S 7 '70
Box score on confidentiality of library circulation records. J. F. Krug and J. A. Harvey Am Lib 1:944 N '70
Card-carrying reader; probe by the IRS into what people read. New Repub 163:7 Jl 25 '70
Editor's choice; sanctity: libraries, clients, IRS, ALA. G. R. Shields. Am Lib 1:749-50 S '70
Internal revenue service; meeting the challenges of tax administration; address, May 12, 1970. W. H. Smith. Vital Speeches 36:660-9 Ag 15 '70
IRS rules review copies taxable income. S. Wagner. Pub W 198:47 Jl 20 '70
Keep an eye on the IRS; Tax reform act of 1969. il Nations Bsns 58:39-41 Jl '70
Librarian demonstrators march on IRS office. Library J 95:2749 S 1 '70
Like Jack's magic beans: controversy at the Detroit conference over IRS's inspection of private reading habits. J. F. Krug and J. A. Harvey. Am Lib 1:843-5 O '70
Litmus test of tyranny. T-men vs. librarians. W. R. Eshelman. Wilson Lib Bul 45:5-7 S '70
Loopholes hidden in tax reform; Tax reform act of 1969. Bsns W p50-1 N 28 '70
Mr 1040: row over access to tax records by C. Mollenhoff. il por Newsweek 75:34-5 Ap 27 '70
National press and television coverage: IRS incident. J. F. Krug and J. A. Harvey. Am Lib 1:1026-7 D '70
Obscenity and pornography statement further justified; incidents in Milwaukee and Atlanta. J. F. Krug and J. A. Harvey. Am Lib 1:751-2 S '70
Of note: Atlanta public library's policy on investigations by IRS and other law enforcement agencies. Am Lib 1:729 S '70
Of note: investigation of what people read by Treasury agents. G. R. Shields. Am Lib 1:633 Jl '70
Pollution politics; clampdown to stop environmentalists' class action suits. New Repub 163:5-6 O 31 '70
Putting judgment back into decisions; appraising performance. L. E. Greiner and others. il Harvard Bsns R 48:59-67 Mr '70
Reader interest in bombs checked by T-men; with editorial comment. il Library J 95:2591, 2593 Ag '70
Security leak at the 1040 level. por Bsns W p32+ Ap 18 '70
Snoopers in the public libraries. R. H. Smith. Pub W 198:33 Ag 10 '70
Tax-exempt litigation: IRS curbs draw widespread opposition. R. J. Bazell. Science 170:716-17 N 13 '70

Taxing the public interest; tax-exempt status of public-interest law firms. Time 96:94+ N 16 '70
Trade winds; taxability ruling on review copies. C. Amory. Sat R 53:14 S 19 '70
When readers become suspect. R. Cleghorn. Cur 121:42-6 S '70
Within the system. J. Lear. Sat R 53:61 N 7 '70
See also
United States—Tax court

Interstate commerce commission

Freight car shortage gets worse. il Bsns W p78+ S 5 '70
ICC sets new rules on household moving. Har Yrs 10:5 My '70
Learn the new rules on long-distance moving. il Changing T 24:13-14 O '70
Moving man cometh (maybe) proposed federal rules. il Consumer Rep 35:302-4 My '70
Nader's raiders strike again. il por Time 95:88 Mr 30 '70
Save that train; California Zephyr. New Repub 162:10 F 7 '70

John F. Kennedy center for the performing arts
See John F. Kennedy center for the performing arts, Washington, D.C.

John F. Kennedy space center

Vacation countdown. M. L. Norwood. il Travel 135:42-7 Ja '71
Weak traffic clouds fare impact. H. D. Watkins. Aviation W 93:22-3 N 30 '70

Joint chiefs of staff

Change of command. por Time 96:16 Jl 6 '70
Navy way; appointment of T. H. Moorer. il por Newsweek 75:34 Ap 27 '70
With an admiral at the defense helm. il por U S News 68:32 Ap 27 '70

Justice, Department of

Attorney General has heard it all before. L. H. Lapham. il pors Life 68:50-50B+ F 13 '70
Furor over drugs; physicians vs. the Attorney General. il Newsweek 75:65+ Mr 30 '70
Judgment on Kent state. il Newsweek 76:14 Ag 3 '70
Justice, by R. Harris. Review
Life il por 68:16 Mr 13 '70. W. Sheed Nation 211:55+ Jl 20 '70. T. I. Emerson New Repub 162:21-3 Ap 18 '70 A. M. Bickel
Sat R 53:33-4 Mr 21 '70. P. Schrag
TRB from Washington; the Justice department and school integration. New Repub 163:4 Jl 25 '70
See also
United States—Federal bureau of investigation

Antitrust division

McLaren's hatchet swings at the banks. Bsns W p24 Ap 4 '70
Mythology of antitrust. Duns 96:80 Jl '70
Should a license cut out competition? patent antitrust suit against Westinghouse. Bsns W p20+ My 2 '70
When a bank holds the purse strings; test case against Cleveland trust co. Bsns W p54 Jl 25 '70

Law enforcement assistance administration

Case of the purloined crime law. L. Velie. Read Digest 97:63-7 N '70
Cops hit the jackpot. J. C. Goulden. il Nation 211:520-33 N 23 '70

Labor, Department of

Businessman the unions like. il por Bsns W p98 Je 20 '70
Changes ahead in Washington's labor policies? interview. J. D. Hodgson. il pors Nations Bsns 58:68-72 S '70
New secretary: same strike policy. por U S News 68:86 Je 22 '70
See also
United States—Womens bureau

Federal contract compliance, Office of

Minority hiring under new attack. il por Bsns W p 110 Je 13 '70

Labor policy

Changes ahead in Washington's labor policies? interviews. E. B. Miller; J. D. Hodgson. il pors Nations Bsns 58:68-72 S '70
Hodgson: the labor outlook; interview, ed. by G. R. Rosen. J. D. Hodgson. por Duns 96:8-9+ N '70

UNITED STATES—Labor policy—*Continued*
Shopcrafts test the hands-off policy. Bsns W p32+ F 7 '70
Who cares about public interest? compulsory arbitration. D. Lawrence. U S News 69:80 D 21 '70
Wooing the labor vote. Time 96:16 S 14 '70
See also
Labor laws and legislation—United States
United States—National labor relations board

Labor statistics, Bureau of
U.S. economy in 1980: a preview of BLS projections. il Mo Labor R 93:3-34 Ap '70

Land management, Bureau of
All we need is money; Owyhee project, Idaho. T. Trueblood. il Field & S 75:20+ My '70
President's environmental crusade and the public lands. M. Frome. Field & S 74:36+ F '70
Primitive areas, a new designation under BLM; Aravaipa and Paria Canyons primitive areas, and Vermillion Cliffs natural area. B. Whitaker. il Liv Wildn 33:12-14 Aut '69
They're grabbing our hunting land; Calif.-Nevada land swap. D. Lynch. Field & S 75:12+ Ag '70

Langley research center
Langley reorganization reflects new NASA aeronautic emphasis. D. C. Winston. Aviation W 93:17-18 O 26 '70

Library of Congress
Documents expediting project
Doc ex. J. W. Brewster. bibliog il por Wilson Lib Bul 44:941+ My '70; Reply. H. S. Chona. 45:513-15 Ja '71

Legislative reference service
Expanded legislative reference service. A. Cranston. por Library J 95:2221-2 Je 15 '70
How Congress focuses on the environment; Environmental policy division. R. A. Carpenter. Sat R 53:43 Ag 1 '70
Information for decisions in environmental policy. R. A. Carpenter. il Science 168:1316-22 Je 12 '70
Technology's assessors; with letter from L. Q. Mumford. J Lear. Sat R 53:52 Ap 25 '70

Manuscript division
Outstanding collection donated to LC: Hans P. Kraus group of rare Vespucci manuscripts and other documents. Wilson Lib Bul 44:598 F '70
Quarterly notes concerning the Library of Congress manuscripts. K. V. Hostick. Hobbies 75:140 Mr; 140 Je; 110 Ag '70
Quarterly notes from the manuscript division of the Library of Congress (cont) K. V. Hostick. Hobbies 74:140 F '70

Moving picture collections
See United States—Library of Congress—National film collection

National film collection
Lost films from the National film collection. R. Koszarski. il Film Q 23:31-7 Wint '69

Special collections
Outstanding collection donated to LC: Hans P. Kraus group of rare Vespucci manuscripts and other documents. Wilson Lib Bul 44:598 F '70

Management and budget, Office of
Administration: George Shultz has arrived. il por Time 96:8 Ag 10 '70
Cautious start for OMB's Shultz. il Bsns W p 100+ Je 20 '70
Closing the performance gap; appointments. il pors Newsweek 75:16-17 Je 22 '70
Mask of austerity. R. W. Dietsch. Nation 212:70 Ja 18 '71
Nixon: boss in a bad year. il por Time 95:12-15 Je 22 '70
Nixon likes Litton's system; proposed Office of management and budget, Management information systems division. Bsns W p 162+ Mr 28 '70
Rearranging furniture. J. Osborne. New Repub 163:8-9 Jl 4 '70
White House staff. J. Osborne. New Repub 163:13-14 O 3 '70

Manned spacecraft center
Apollo center feels budget pinch; closing of one mission control room. Z. Strickland. il Aviation W 92:60-1 Ap 13 '70
Masters of Mission control; ground control of Apollo 13. il Time 95:18 Ap 27 '70

Lunar receiving laboratory
Five unexpected new discoveries about the moon. J. Reinert. il Sci Digest 68:9-14 N '70

Maps
Aids for interstate driving. il Bet Hom & Gard 48:126 My '70
Popular science 1970 travel map of the United States; with guide. il Pop Sci 196:76-80 My '70
See also subhead Maps under names of states, cities, e.g. Charleston, S.C.—Maps

Marine corps
Marines plan for Harrier introduction. W. S. Hieronymus. il Aviation W 93:55-6 S 14 '70
Next marine battle; marines leaving Viet Nam. il Time 95:17-18 Mr 30 '70

Crimes and misdemeanors
Where are they now? M. C. McKeon and the 1956 Parris Island tragedy. il pors Newsweek 76:12 Ag 17 '70

Forces in Japan
Marine doves & the baffled brass; American servicemen's union at Iwakuni, Japan. C. C. Smith. Nation 211:199-202 S 14 '70

Forces in Vietnam
As U.S. marines leave Vietnam; a closeup of one war zone; Combined-action platoons program. J. N. Wallace. il U S News 68:43-4 Ap 20 '70
Behind the battle for Khesanh. L. W. Walt. il Read Digest 96:105-11 My '70

Negroes
Rumble at Camp Lejeune. F. Lewis. Atlan 225:35-41 Ja '70

Maritime administration
Building ships Detroit-style, standardized design. il Bsns W p 106 My 30 '70

Military airlift command
Air cargo use saves money for military. C. Brownlow. il Aviation W 93:147-8 O 26 '70
House unit plans airlift proposals. Aviation W 92:22 Mr 2 '70
MAC charter purchases decline. il Aviation W 93:23 Ag 17 '70
Samaritans on wings; nurses fly transoceanic missions evacuating injured GIs from Vietnam. il Ebony 25:60-2+ My '70

Military policy
Applying Nixon's doctrine to Laos. Cur 117:47-9 Ap '70
Armed forces' reluctant retrenchment. J. Cameron. il Fortune 82:68-73+ N '70
Blindfolding the Senate; concerning views of S. Symington. Nation 211:291 O 5 '70
Change in plans for defense: its meaning. U S News 69:112 S 21 '70
Congress's right to know. S. Symington. il N Y Times Mag p7+ Ag 9 '70; Same abr. Cur 122:36-43 O '70
Governance of the Pentagon; excerpt from The Pentagon propaganda machine. J. W. Fulbright. Sat R 53:22-5+ N 7 '70; Reply. J. E. Greenbacker. 53:17 D 5 '70
In search of a foreign policy. il por Newsweek 76:28-34+ D 14 '70
Leaves fall, the blood flows. G. Wald. Sat R 53:28-9 Je 6 '70
Living with the Nixon doctrine; Asian reaction. il por Newsweek 76:29 Jl 20 '70
Military viewpoint; excerpts from address. J. Ferguson. Aviation W 92:11 Ja 19 '70
Nixon doctrine: how new is it? il Cur 117:44-7 Ap '70
Nixon stresses strategic buildup. il Aviation W 92:21-5 Mr 9 '70
Our national insecurity. R. F. Kaufman. Nation 210:186-8 F 16 '70
POW Congress. New Repub 163:7-9 D 5 '70
Shift to strategic force emphasis tied to Nixon domestic priorities. Aviation W 92:19 F 23 '70
To those who take freedom seriously. Sat R 53:24+ Ap 18 '70
Two worlds; the future officer; address, January 17, 1970. B. K. Holloway. Vital Speeches 36:262-5 F 15 '70
Ultimate pollution: war. Commonweal 92:179-80 My 8 '70

UNITED STATES—Military policy—*Continued*
Unequal duel; Symington subcommittee and U.S. involvement in Morocco, Libya and Ethiopia. Nation 211:482-4 N 16 '70
U.S. military policy. G. Allison; J. J. Stone; G. Kemp. For Affairs 48:245-84 Ja '70
See also
Military assistance, American
United States—Defenses

Militia
See also
United States—National guard

Mines, Bureau of
Bureau of mines: long search for new director ends. L. J. Carter. por Science 170:309-10 O 16 '70
Coal producers breathe easier. Bsns W p26 N 7 '70
Death by runaround. S. Cupps. il Nation 211:146-8 Ag 31 '70
Economics vs. safety. Forbes 105:25 Je 15 '70
Honeymooner. pors Forbes 106:53 D 1 '70
Merry Christmas! explosion near Hyden, Ky. Nation 212:70-1 Ja 18 '71
Setback for safety; directorship confirmation hassle. il por Newsweek 75:80+ Je 8 '70

Minority business enterprise, Office of
Let's write off MESBICs. R. S. Rosenbloom and J. K. Shank. Harvard Bsns R 48:90-7 S '70; Reply. M. H. Stans. 48:170-1 N '70
Piece of the action; SBA's MESBIC program. R. C. Siciliano. il Nations Bsns 58:56-9 Mr '70

Missions
See Missions—United States

Monetary policy
Anger at dollar imperialists. Time 95:77-8 Je 22 '70
Arthur Burns: the stage has been set for a recovery; address, December 7, 1970. A. F. Burns. por U S News 69:64-8 D 21 '70; Same with title Basis for lasting prosperity. Vital Speeches 37:162-6 Ja 1 '71
Fencing match. il por Newsweek 75:71-2 F 16 '70
For and against the use of guideposts. B. L. Masse. America 122:175 F 21 '70
How fast should money grow? views of A. F. Burns and P. W. McCracken. pors Bsns W p59-60 Ag 8 '70
Markets take Washington's hint. il Bsns W p42 Mr 28 '70
Monetary overheating? M. Friedman. Newsweek 76:75 Jl 6 '70
Money in America: the end of the economists' dream. R. Lekachman. Harper 241:29-34 Ag '70; Discussion. 241:9+ O '70
New timetable for the game plan; Joint economic committee hearings. il Bsns W p 15-16 Jl 25 '70
Pushing on a string. il Newsweek 76:80 D 7 '70
Set the dollar free. M. Friedman. Newsweek 76:98 O 19 '70
See also
Credit
United States—Federal reserve board

Moral conditions
Back to the real world. J. V. Schall. America 123:8-10, 77-8 Jl 11, Ag 22 '70
Caesar as God. J. V. Schall. Commonweal 91: 505-10 F 6 '70; Discussion. 91:526. 571+ F 13, 27 '70
Cold night in Flint. P. Tracy. Commonweal 91:447-50 Ja 23 '70
Coming home to Martha Mitchell. D. French. Commonweal 92:156-7 My 1 '70
Constitutional government under God; communism or Christianity; address, April 20, 1970. T. Anderson. Vital Speeches 36:459-66 My 15 '70
Crusade for morality; address, June 10, 1970. M. Rountree. Vital Speeches 36:597-602 Jl 15 '70
Flags and faces. R. A. Schroth. America 122: 310-12 Mr 21 '70
Flight from reason. T. Meehan. il Horizon 12:4-10 Spr '70
Growing concern over crisis in morality. il U S News 68:56-60 Je 29 '70
How to make a difference. D. Berrigan. Commonweal 92:384-6 Ag 7 '70; Same abr. Cur 122:25-7 O '70; Discussion. Commonweal 92:431; 93:3+, 35+, 78-9 S 4, O 2-16 '70
Leaves fall, the blood flows. G. Wald. Sat R 53:28-9 Je 6 '70

Let's say yes to hope; excerpt from The recovery of confidence. J. W. Gardner. Read Digest 96:74-6 Je '70
Mood back home; symposium, with editorial comment by R. Graves. il Life 69:1, 22-33 O 2 '70
New man: the compleat soldier. D. Berrigan. il Sat R 53:31-4+ F 14 '70
Notes on authority, morality, power. J. Burnham. Nat R 22:1283-9 D 1 '70; Reply. F. S. Meyer. 22:1407 D 29 '70
Pornography goes public; with report on attempts of clean up by Mason City, Iowa group. J. Neary. il Life 69:18-25 Ag 28 '70
Radical turn in theology and ethics: why it occurred in the 1960's. S. E. Ahlstrom. bibliog f Ann Am Acad 387:1-13 Ja '70
Radicals: Ilse Koch section. Nat R 22:394+ Ap 21 '70
Stone men to the contrary, the time to argue is now. B. DeMott. por Life 68:28B Ap 17 '70
See also
Crime and criminals—United States
Prostitution
Violence

Morocco air agreement
See Aviation—International aspects

National academy of sciences
See National academy of sciences

National advisory commission on civil disorders
Nation's two societies; Kerner commission report. Negro Hist Bul 33:112-14 My '70
Usefulness of commission studies of collective violence. J. S. Campbell. bibliog f Ann Am Acad 391:168-76 S '70

National aeronautics and space administration
Adapting to the environment. Sci N 98:248 S 19 '70
Can the space program make a comeback? il U S News 70:44-6 Ja 4 '71
Evolution in NASA: loss and cost of transition. R. S. Lewis. il Bul Atom Sci 26:28-9 Ap '70
Experimental civilian aircraft; new field for NASA. Sci N 98:413 N 28 '70
Future of NASA. por Time 96:44+ Ag 10 '70
GAO report affects contractor relations. W. J. Normyle. Aviation W 93:18-19 Jl 13 '70
Joining Europe in space. il Bsns W p 120+ S 26 '70
Making of an ex-astronaut, by B. O'Leary. Review
Sat R 53:31-2 My 16 '70. J. Lear
More time for science; Apollo program. Sci N 97:61 Ja 17 '70
NASA advances space shuttle development. Aviation W 92:21 My 18 '70
NASA collecting land use data on 26 cities for U.S. program. Aviation W 92:55 Je 15 '70
NASA divided over space shuttle. W. J. Normyle. il Aviation W 92:18-19 Ap 13 '70
NASA is a hard act to follow; search for new Mississippi test facility tenant. il Bsns W p28 Ap 11 '70
NASA seeks ways to handle data flood. Z. Strickland. il Aviation W 92:135+ Je 22 '70
NASA: stretching out space program. A. Hamilton. Science 167:356 Ja 23 '70
NASA to scrutinize ATS award in Apollo accident-type review. Aviation W 93:19 Jl 20 '70
Original NASA goal re-emphasized. Z. Strickland. Aviation W 93:66-7 D 7 '70
Paine resigns. Sci N 98:93 Ag 1 '70
Planning with Von Braun. por Newsweek 75:56-7 F 9 '70
Rebellion among the astronauts; excerpt from The making of an ex-astronaut. B. O'Leary. il por Ladies Home J 87:143-6 Mr '70
Reusable shuttle program paces U.S. effort in space. il Aviation W 93:17 D 28 '70
Space program: more time for biomedical research? J. Walsh. Science 167:1469-71 Mr 13 '70
Subsonic transport for 1980's. Sci N 98:478 D 26 '70
Supersalesman for space agency? por U S News 68:11 F 9 '70
Unmanned efforts assuming greater role. il Aviation W 92:69+ Mr 9 '70
See also
United States—John F. Kennedy space center
United States—Langley research center
United States—Manned spacecraft center

UNITED STATES—National aeronautics and space administration—*Continued*

Advanced research and technology, Office of

Aeronautics research growth expected. D. C. Winston. Aviation W 93:22 N 9 '70

Ames research center

NASA studying vortex, slow flight areas. R. G. O'Lone. il Aviation W 93:61+ S 21 '70
Studying the effects of gravity. E. Driscoll. il Sci N 98:77-9 Jl 25 '70

Appropriations and expenditures

Anticipating the ax. Sci N 97:60 Ja 17 '70
Apollo mission slippage weakens Senate backers of NASA funds. Aviation W 93:23 Jl 6 '70
Budgets and clues. Sci N 97:431 My 2 '70
Committee to study space cuts. Aviation W 93:16 Jl 13 '70
Curtailing field centers limits Saturn 5 options. il Aviation W 92:26-7 F 9 '70
Down in the valley. Sci N 97:149 F 7 '70
Fighting the cuts. Sci N 98:33 Jl 11 '70
House leaders concur on NASA budget. W. J. Normyle. Aviation W 92:22-3 Mr 30 '70
House probes space flight cost rises; program changes blamed. Aviation W 92:21 Mr 2 '70
House vote mirrors split on future space priorities. W. J. Normyle. Aviation W 92:28-9 My 4 '70
Limited funds defer manned programs. W. J. Normyle. il Aviation W 92:63-5+ Mr 9 '70
NASA asks Senate to restore funding. Aviation W 92:27 My 25 '70
NASA budget hits seven-year low. il Aviation W 92:16-18 F 2 '70
NASA: further cuts in university support spending. N. Gruchow. il Science 167:1107 F 20 '70
NASA plans fiscal 1972 increase. W. J. Normyle. il Aviation W 92:14-17 F 16 '70
NASA reduces manned space program. Z. Strickland. Aviation W 93:18-19 S 7 '70
Space ferry wins priority. il Bsns W p49 F 7 '70
Space in the 1970s. T. O. Paine. Aviation W 92:11 F 9 '70
Space science projects funding sought. K. Johnsen. il Aviation W 93:20-1 N 9 '70
Splits emerge on space shuttle priorities. W. J. Normyle. il Aviation W 93:17 Jl 27 '70

Art programs

Space paintings by artists commissioned by NASA; portfolio. Space World G-4-76:23-30 Ap '70

Astronomy missions board

NASA astronomy board report. il Space World G-3-75:40-1 Mr '70

Communications network

Programmers vital to success of lunar missions. Space World G-12-84:34 D '70

Electronics research center

ERC closing poses new problems. Aviation W 92:44-5 Mr 16 '70
New role for NASA research center. J. Walsh. Science 168:100 Ap 3 '70

Jet propulsion laboratory

See Jet propulsion laboratory

National agricultural library

Agricultural info network: prompt action urged. Library J 95:1423-4 Ap 15 '70

National air pollution control administration

Air control unit prods carriers on unburned jet fuel dumping. Aviation W 93:22 N 23 '70
Tacoma's tall stack. W. H. Rodgers, jr. Nation 210:553-7 My 11 '70

National bureau of standards

See United States—Standards, National bureau of

National commission on libraries and information science

Congress approves Nat'l library commission. S. Wagner. Pub W 197:19 My 18 '70
National commission bill passed from House to Senate. Library J 95:2047 Je 1 '70

National commission on product safety

Competent product testing helps eliminate hazards. Consumer Bul 53:23-4 N '70

Death in the crib; study of product hazards. Time 96:60-1 Jl 6 '70
Perspective on product safety; abridgement of chapter 1 of Commission report; with editorial comment. Consumer Rep 35:559-64 S '70
Pressure is on for safer products. il Bsns W p36-7+ Jl 4 '70
Product safety: nobody's business. T. Stanton. Nation 211:270-2 S 28 '70
What is Congress doing about safer products in your home? A. Fisher. Pop Sci 196:59+ Mr '70

National commission on productivity

Nixon sounds an inflation alert; with editorial comment. Bsns W p24-5, 126 Je 20 '70
Productivity group sticks to productivity. il Bsns W p74 Ag 15 '70
Rabbit that could turn into a tiger. il Time 96:67-8 Jl 13 '70
Warming up the first inflation alert; with editorial comment. il Bsns W p29, 102 Jl 18 '70

National commission on the causes and prevention of violence

History of violence in America, ed. by H. D. Graham and T. R. Gurr. Review
  Cath World 210:282-3 Mr '70. P. J. Riga
How to handle violence. il por Time 95:40 Ja 26 '70
Roots of violence. Sci Am 222:42 F '70
Studying the mass media; report of study groups. J. Tebbel. Sat R 53:69-71 F 14 '70
Time to act. il Ebony 25:56-7 F '70
Toward cities with fortresses; excerpts from report. Cur 114:27-9 Ja '70
Usefulness of commission studies of collective violence. J. S. Campbell. bibliog f Ann Am Acad 391:168-76 S '70

National council for development standards (proposed)

New government and industry partnership for building more housing. D. Pellish. il Arch Forum 133:58-61 Jl '70

National council on health policy (proposed)

White House advisers: Nixon cool to plans for health, social aides. L. J. Carter. Science 170:48-9 O 2 '70

National forest service

See United States—Forest service

National foundation on the arts and the humanities

Administration sees leap forward for arts. Pub W 197:62 F 9 '70
Arts and humanities: culture agency is emerging from infancy. C. Holden. il Science 170:1060-3 D 4 '70
Arts and humanities: federal money is benefiting culture. C. Holden. Science 170:1180-2 D 11 '70
Congress gives arts and letters a measure of cheer. R. H. Smith. Pub W 198:36 Ag 3 '70
Expressing the American spirit; address, December 10, 1969. R. M. Nixon. Opera N 34:6-7 Ja 24 '70
Humanities and the culture-hungry American. W. T. Greenleaf. il Am Ed 6:7-11 Ja '70
Murray Louis dance company in Chicago: residency program of the NEA. A. Barzel. il Dance Mag 44:40-3 Je '70
Story excluded from ALA #3; NEA cancels fourth edition. Pub W 198:58 S 28 '70

National guard

Double focus on Kent state: findings of grand jury at odds with those of Scranton commission. Nat R 22:1146 N 3 '70
Draft or what? Choices for spring graduates. il U S News 68:80-1 Mr 30 '70
Gag comes off Kent; grand jury's findings. New Repub 163-7 N 21 '70
Guard fired in self-defense; excerpts from Ohio grand jury report. il U S News 69:33-5 N 2 '70
Guardsmen's view of the tragedy at Kent state. W. B. Furlong. il N Y Times Mag p 12-13+ Je 21 '70
Investigations: the Kent state case. il Newsweek 75:33-4 My 25 '70
Judgment on Kent state; Department of justice summary of the FBI's report. il Newsweek 76:14 Ag 3 '70
Jury indicts twenty-five; Kent state case. Sr Schol 97:5-6 N 16 '70
Kent state continued; Justice department summary of FBI investigation. il Time 96:16 N 9 '70

UNITED STATES—National guard—*Continued*
Kent state: four deaths at noon. il Life 68:30–5 My 15 '70
Kent state gag; report of the Ohio special grand jury. D. Sanford. New Repub 163:14–17 N 7 '70
Kent state: martyrdom that shook the country; killing of four students by Ohio national guardsmen. il Time 95:12–14 My 18 '70
Kent state: what happened? contradictory judgments among the three reports. il Newsweek 76:32–3 N 23 '70
Mockery of justice; bullets fired at Kent state university. Commonweal 93:211–12 N 27 '70
My God! They're killing us; deaths at Kent state university. il Newsweek 75:31–33F My 18 '70
New verdict on Kent state; special Ohio grand jury report. Newsweek 76:25 O 26 '70
Politics of manslaughter; Kent state university. Nation 210:578–9 My 18 '70
Report on Kent state; Knight newspapers findings on killing of students. Newsweek 75:67 Je 1 '70
Reporter at large. R. Adler. New Yorker 46:40–4+ O 3 '70
Tragedy at Kent state. T. Gallagher. il Good H 171:82–3+ O '70
When the national guard is called. il U S News 68:32 My 18 '70
Who guards against the guard? il Newsweek 75:33 F My 18 '70

National heart institute
Hypertension. Todays Ed 59:48–50 Ja '70

National industrial materials commission (proposed)
Industrial minerals: new study of how to avoid a supply crisis. L. J. Carter. Science 170:147–8 O 9 '70

National institute of education (proposed)
Finding the how of learning. Sci N 97:265 Mr 14 '70
Message on education reform. R. M. Nixon. il Am Ed 6:30–4 Ap '70

National institute of mental health
Finch leaves HEW for advisor's post; Yolles out at NIMH. J. Walsh. Science 168:1327 Je 12 '70
Let's do a study; committee on TV violence. Sedulus. New Repub 163:32–3 Ag 1 '70
Pot, hard drugs and the law. G. Samuels. il por N Y Times Mag p4+ F 15 '70

National institutes of health
No doubt about suffering; crisis in organic chemistry. Sci N 97:476–7 My 16 '70

Appropriations and expenditures
Research and education in danger. il Sci N 97:58–9 Ja 17 '70

Library
Suit asks photocopying royalties. J. Walsh. Science 169:959 S 4 '70

National labor relations board
Changes ahead in Washington's labor policies? interview. E. B. Miller. il pors Nations Bsns 58:68–72 S '70
Critics slice at NLRB power. Bsns W p61 Ag 8 '70
Dark horse for the NLRB. por Bsns W p35 F 21 '70
Nixon's NLRB man rankles labor. por Bsns W p27–8 My 9 '70
Owners change, but not the contract. Bsns W p30 My 16 '70
Significant decisions in labor cases. See issues of Monthly labor review
Strike insurance; employers win. U S News 70:82 Ja 11 '71
Union contract holds when firm is sold. U S News 68:57 My 25 '70
Why NLRB is without a head. Bsns W p31 Ja 17 '70

National library of medicine
Suit asks photocopying royalties. J. Walsh. Science 169:959 S 4 '70

National mediation board
Emergency boards in the airline industry, 1936–69: Railway labor act's emergency dispute procedures. M. H. Cimini. il Mo Labor R 93:57–65 Jl '70

National oceanic and atmospheric administration
Deep six for NOAA. Sci N 97:267 Mr 14 '70
EPA & NOAA or CEQ? Nat Parks & Con Mag 44:25–6 O '70

Getting ocean sciences together. Sci N 98:59 Jl 25 '70
National policy for coastal management: protection of the environment; address, October 19, 1970. E. Wenk, jr. Vital Speeches 37:177–81 Ja 1 '71
Nixon proposes NOAA and EPA. L. J. Carter. Science 169:266 Jl 17 '70
Oceanography: a wet NASA. Will Nixon take the plunge? W. Connelly. Science 168:98–101 Ap 3 '70
Reshuffling the bureaucracy: Nixon proposes pollution ocean agencies. L. J. Carter. Science 168:1433–5 Je 19 '70
See also
United States—National weather service

National park service
Conservation hall of fame; S. T. Mather. H. M. Albright. il por Nat Wildlife 7:10–11 O '69
Environmental education; National environmental education development program. il Parks & Rec 5:42 Je '70
Future & the parks. A. W. Smith. Nat Parks & Con Mag 44:2 O '70
How to wreck a national park; overcrowding: Grand Teton National Park. C. S. Wren. il Look 34:77–8+ Je 16 '70
Interview with Horace Marden Albright. H. M. Albright. pors Parks & Rec 5:22–3+ D '70
Mike Frome. M. Frome. Am For 76:3+ Ag '70
National park service educational programs; NEED and NESA programs. Nat Parks & Con Mag 44:15 Jl '70
National park wilderness reviews (lost in the wilderness) E. M. Dickerman. il Liv Wildn 34:40–9 Spr '70

National parks and reserves
See National parks and reserves—United States

National planning
See United States—Social policy

National science foundation
Antarctic research: a pattern of science management. W. D. McElroy. il por Bul Atom Sci 26:85–8 D '70
Cambodia speech sinks nomination. J. Walsh. Science 168:1189 Je 5 '70
Creutz sees a gradual increase in NSF support of applied science; interview. E. C. Creutz. por Phys Today 23:61–3 N '70
Feeling their way; technology assessment programs. Sci N 97:240–1 Mr 7 '70
IRRPOS looks for relevance to society's problems. J. B. Phelps. il por Phys Today 23:61–2 N '70
Mission: relate science to society. il por Bsns W p72+ My 23 '70
NSF: White House nominates four to long-unfilled posts. J. Walsh. il Science 168:101–2 Ap 3 '70
New problem-oriented, interdisciplinary research program. Sch & Soc 98:201–3 Ap '70
Research priorities: new program at NSF reflects shift in values. D. S. Greenberg. Science 170:144–6 O 9 '70
Science funds: NSF survey probes effects of shifts in federal aid. D. S. Greenberg. il Science 170:609–10+ N 6 '70

Appropriations and expenditures
Daddario and Kennedy recommend boosts in NSF budget. J. B. Phelps. il Phys Today 23:61–3 Je '70
Interdisciplinary research mechanism. Sci N 97:144–5 F 7 '70
Kennedy asks more for NSF. J. Walsh. Science 168:347 Ap 17 '70
Nixon boosts research budget 5 per cent; NSF gets $49 million more. T. Johnides. il Phys Today 23:69+ Mr '70
NSF budget: House group reacts to data on plight of science. P. M. Boffey. Science 168:95–7 Ap 3 '70
Senate would link Mansfield amendment, NSF budget boost. J. Walsh. Science 169:1059 S 11 '70

National security council
Where defense priorities are set; Defense program review committee. with editorial comment. il Bsns W p34–5, 150 F 21 '70

National teacher corps
Most interns to remain in education. Sch & Soc 98:270 Sum '70

National weather service
No warning on the beach; excerpts from Hurricane. J. McCarthy. il Motor B 126:54–5+ S '70
What's the weather going to be? A. H. Seidman. il Electr World 84:31–3 N '70

UNITED STATES—*Continued*

Nationalism
Conversations with historians; excerpts from Interpreting American history. ed. by J. A. Garraty. H. S. Commager. il por Am Heritage 21:58-60 F '70

Naval air propulsion test center
Navy combines engine test units. M. L. Yaffee. il Aviation W 93:54-5+ N 9 '70

Navy
Any port in a showdown; pact with Spain; U.S. Sixth fleet. L. Fernsworth. il Nation 211:489-91 N 16 '70
Attack aircraft carrier; our forward defense posture; address, March 4, 1970. T. H. Moorer. Vital Speeches 36:392-4 Ap 15 '70
Presidential power aboard the Sixth fleet; with report by H. Sidey. il pors Life 69:38-40 O 9 '70
Reports: the Mediterranean: the Sixth fleet. I. R. Levine. Atlan 225:4+ F '70
Russian and American pilots play chicken; maneuvers of the Sixth fleet in the Mediterranean. W. H. Honan. il N Y Times Mag p25-7+ N 22 '70
Top fleet in the Mediterranean: U.S. or Russian? il U S News 69:19 O 12 '70
See also
Navy yards and naval stations
United States—Coast guard
United States—Navy department

Appropriations and expenditures
Navy asks larger aircraft, missile buys. Aviation W 92:23 F 9 '70
Navy picks up some pieces. il Bsns W p77 F 7 '70
Communication systems
Laser-beam communicator; navy ship-to-ship communications system. J. Levine. il Electr World 84:46-8 N '70
See also
Radio communication, Naval

Crimes and misdemeanors
Seaman Priest. P. M. Stern. New Repub 162:12-13 F 14 '70
Education
See also
United States naval academy, Annapolis

Foreign enlistments
They also serve; Filipinos. il Newsweek 76:32-3 N 9 '70
Procurement
Senate report blasts procurement of F-111. D. C. Winston. il Aviation W 93:19-20 D 21 '70

Navy department
Chief of naval operations
Navy way; appointment of E. R. Zumwalt. il por Newsweek 75:34 Ap 27 '70
Zinging Zumwalt, U.S.N. il por Time 96:17 N 9 '70

Office of education
See United States—Education. Office of

Officials and employees
See Government employees; Public officers

Outdoor recreation, Bureau of
Where is the outdoor recreation plan? J. F. Shanklin and E. M. Fitch. il Am For 76:28-31+ Mr '70

Patent office
U.S. patent office to be automated. Library J 95:2406+ Jl '70

Peace corps
AID-Peace corps build schools in Somalia. il Sch & Soc 98:338-40 O '70
Can business aid the Peace corps? il por Bsns W p 124 Ap 11 '70
Draft changes: troubles ahead for Peace corps, VISTA? il U S News 69:69-70 Jl 27 '70
Fresh spark plug for the Peace corps. B. Clark. Read Digest 96:20-1+ My '70
Little agency that could; Keye, Donna & Pearlstein taking over Peace corps advertising. Time 95:84 F 23 '70
New life in the peace corps. il Har Yrs 10:45 Jl '70
Peace corps and experience. Chem 43:3 Jl '70
Peace corps intrigue in the Philippines. G. H. Anderson; discussion. Chr Cent 87:184,538 F 11, Ap 29 '70

Peace corps intrigue in the Philippines. G. H. Anderson; reply. N. S. Longo. Chr Cent 87:184 F 11 '70
Peace corps: making it in the seventies. J. H. Blatchford. For Affairs 49:122-35 D '70; Same abr. with title Present status of the Peace corps. Cur 124:37-44 D '70
Peace corps physicians: reflections on the future. J. Walsh. il Science 169:1293-6 S 25 '70
Peace corpsman into organization man. J. Rothchild. Nat R 22:405-6 Ap 21 '70
Reports: Washington. E. B. Drew. Atlan 226:6+ Jl '70
Who wants the Peace corps? problems in Africa. A. Jaffe. il Newsweek 75:42+ Je 29 '70

Pesticides regulation division
See United States—Agricultural research service—Pesticides regulation division

Photographs
America. . .the beautiful? il Parks & Rec 5:18-21 Mr '70
America's everyday dreariness. Fortune 81:108-13 F '70
Environment: light and shadow. Environ 12:26-31 Ap '70
Portrait of America; prizewinning pictures in Life photography contest. Life 69:6-8+ D 25 '70
See America first. D. Plowden. il Audubon 72:46-51 Jl '70

Political history
See United States—History

Politics and government
After elections, the problems ahead. il U S News 69:17-19 N 9 '70
After ten years; excerpts from addresses and from Congressional record, ed. by H. Dibble. C. E. Goodell. Nat R 22:948-9 S 8 '70
Agnew talks about those Agnew speeches; interview. S. T. Agnew. por U S News 69:34-6 Ag 24 '70
All may yet be well. S. Alsop. Newsweek 76:106 S 21 '70
America and the new Bismarcks. P. Steinfels. Commonweal 92:215 My 15 '70
America is fed up; address, September 21, 1970. E. F. Hollings. Vital Speeches 37:37-40 N 1 '70
American notes. D. Halberstam. Harper 240:124-5 My; 241:30-1 Jl '70
As Nixon sees the future. por U S News 68:17 F 2 '70
Basic symbols of the American political tradition, by W. Kendall and G. W. Carey. Review
Nat R 22:1167+ N 3 '70. P. P. Witonski; Discussion. 22:1380-1 D 29 '70
Box score on reform. il Time 96:10-11 S 28 '70
Change in atmosphere; Nixon administration. H. Sidey. Life 69:4 S 18 '70
Changes in Nixon's political tactics? il U S News 69:11-12+ Ag 3 '70
Constitutional government under God; communism or Christianity; address, April 20, 1970. T. Anderson. Vital Speeches 36:459-66 My 15 '70
Crime & the liberal audience. J. Q. Wilson. Commentary 51:71-8 Ja '71
Crisis of confidence in our leadership. J. W. Gardner. Cur 120:6-9 Ag '70
Democratic appraisal of Nixon's record so far; interview. C. Albert. il pors U S News 69:58-61 Ag 24 '70
Does the President really know more? Time essay. Time 95:18 My 25 '70
Domestic politics and peacemaking; reconciling incompatible imperatives. R. Rothstein. bibliog f Ann Am Acad 392:62-75 N '70
Dream vs. reality. K. Crawford. Newsweek 75:23 F 2 '70
First Nixon year. K. Crawford. Newsweek 75:26 Ja 26 '70
Game plan for November. S. Alsop. Newsweek 76:80 Ag 10 '70
George Meany talks about strikes, politics, the future; excerpts from press conference. G. Meany. por U S News 69:59-61 S 7 '70
Goals: the need for priorities; address, January 7, 1970. T. J. Watson, jr. Vital Speeches 36:301-3 Mr 1 '70
Golden mean. K. Crawford. Newsweek 76:36 D 21 '70
How Nixon makes the big decisions. il pors U S News 68:42-4 F 23 '70
Idea is to cool it a little. il pors Time 96:9-10 Jl 27 '70
Ideology in America. E. C. Ladd. Review
Commentary 49:87-8 Ja '70. B. Gewen

UNITED STATES—Politics and government—
Continued
Innocence: the essence of the American heart-
land. E. J. Hughes. Sat R 53:25-8+ O 17 '70
Innovations and trends in the study of Amer-
ican politics. V. M. Goetcheus and H. C.
Mansfield. bibliog f Ann Am Acad 391:177-87
S '70
Is America a shay or a scow? S. Alsop. News-
week 75:100 Ap 6 '70
Is constitutional democracy doomed? W. D.
Phelan, jr. Cur 116:40-6 Mr '70
Kennedyism. M. Decter. Commentary 49:19-
27 Ja '70; Discussion. 49:20+ My; 17-18 Je
'70
Letter from Washington. Cato. Nat R 22:
352, 399, 505, 555,665, 777, 830, 884, 936, 992,
1044, 1150, 1258, 1336, 1391 Ap 7-21, My 19-
Je 2, 30, Jl 28-0 6, N 3, D 1, 29 '70
Letter from Washington. R. H. Rovere. See
occasional issues of New Yorker
Limits of inconsistency. N. Cousins. Sat R
53:22 O 17 '70
Looking back, and ahead; with report by
H. Hubbard. il Newsweek 75:12-15 Ja 26
'70
Mayday for America; mobilizing the outraged.
R. M. Brown. Commonweal 92:266-8 My 29
'70
Mr Nixon's home front. il por Newsweek 75:
26-8 My 18 '70
Mr Nixon's world. K. Crawford. Newsweek
75:31 Mr 2 '70
Mr President, bring us together again. D. R.
Maxey. il Look 34:15-21 Ja 27 '70
Month of crisis arrives on schedule. pors
U S News 69:13 D 21 '70
New look. il pors Newsweek 77:17 Ja 4 '71
New realism. K. Crawford. Newsweek 75:24
Mr 9 '70
Next question; advice from the Ripon
society. Newsweek 76:14 Ag 3 '70
Nixon: a heartening progress report. il por
Fortune 82:97-8 S '70
Nixon agonistes, by G. Wills. Review
Nat R 22:1112-13 O 20 '70. F. S. Meyer
Nixon and blacks: substance and symbol.
New Repub 163:7-8 Jl 18 '70
Nixon and the Lincoln approach. H. J. Sie-
vers. America 122:147 F 14 '70
Nixon enigma. K. Crawford. Newsweek 75:
28 F 16 '70
Nixon record so far: an inside appraisal; in-
terview. B. N. Harlow. il por U S News
69:74-7 Ag 17 '70
Nixon so far. M. J. Goldbloom. Commentary
49:29-38 Mr '70
Nixon supremacy. J. Kraft. Harper 240:45-51
Mr '70
Nixon's big gamble: no more rule by mi-
norities. R. Wilson. por Look 34:21-5 My
5 '70
Nixon's blueprint for a new America. il U S
News 68:66-7 F 23 '70
Nixon's first year. T. Wicker. New Repub
162:17-20 Ja 24 '70
Nixon's record is the issue. R. Sherrill. Na-
tion 210:619-23 My 25 '70
Nixon's spirit of '76. il por Newsweek 75:17-
18 F 2 '70
Nixon's turnabout. M. J. Ulmer. New Repub
163:10-11 Ag 15 '70
Notes on authority, morality, power. J.
Burnham. Nat R 22:1283-4 D 1 '70; Reply.
F. S. Meyer. 22:1407 D 29 '70
Our contemporary hidden crisis; excerpt from
Hidden crisis in American politics. S. Lu-
bell. Cur 123:9-13 N '70
Political intelligence for America's future;
symposium, ed. by B. M. Gross and M.
Springer. bibliog f il Ann Am Acad 388:1-
132 Mr '70
Politics of resentment. M. Novak. Common-
weal 92:481-3 S 25 '70; Same. Cur 123:13-18
N '70
Politics: they're off and running for 1970. il
Time 95:10-11 Ja 26 '70
Presidency. H. Sidey. See issues of Life
President needs our help because we need
his. M. Ways. Fortune 81:57-8 Je '70; Same
with title Helping the President help us.
Cur 120:9-13 Ag '70; Discussion. Fortune
82:83-4 Ag '70
President steps down, by G. Christian. Re-
view
Newsweek il por 76:68 Ag 24 '70
President's post-election agenda. il Time 96:
9-11 N 23 '70
Priorities for the seventies. R. L. Heilbroner.
Cur 116:11-18 Mr '70
Question of repression. W. Goodman. Com-
mentary 50:23-8 Ag '70; Discussion. 50:16+
N '70
Real majority, by R. Scammon and B. Wat-
tenberg. Review
Nation 211:336-9 O 12 '70. J. Newfield
Time 96:13-14 Ag 31 '70

Reports: Washington (title varies) See is-
sues of Atlantic
Revolution of unreason. A. M. Bickel. New
Repub 163:18-21 O 17 '70
Roosevelt, by J. M. Burns. Review
Sat R 53:23-6 S 12 '70. W. A. Williams
State of the Union; address, January 22, 1970.
R. M. Nixon. il pors U S News 68:63-7 F 2
'70; Same. Vital Speeches 36:226-9 F 1 '70;
Excerpts. Dept State Bul 62:145-7 F 9 '70
Summons to a new cause; R. Nixon ad-
dressing Congress. il por Time 95:7 F 2 '70
Tax-exempt foundations: their effects on na-
tional policy. I. L. Horowitz and R. L.
Horowitz. bibliog il Science 168:220-8 Ap 10
'70; Reply. F. L. Jacquette and J. A. Ker-
shaw. 168:1041-2 My 29 '70
There is a threat of losing control. il Bsns W
p 100-1 O 17 '70
'Tis the season to be jolly. S. Alsop. News-
week 76:68 D 28 '70
Top priority: renovating our ideology. G.
C. Lodge. bibliog f Harvard Bsns R 48:43-
55 S '70
TRB from Washington:
Here be ogres. New Repub 163:4 Ag 22 '70
Looking inward. New Repub 162:4 Ja 24
'70
Nixon zigzag. New Repub 163:4 Ag 1 '70
Undelivered speech; excerpts. J. Gardner. por
Time 95:16-17 My 25 '70
Unfinished business. P. Schrag. Sat R 53:
16 D 5 '70
U.S. faces choice between anarchy and re-
pression; address, June 1, 1970. M. C.
Smith. il pors U S News 68:45-6 Je 15 '70
Washington outlook. See issues of Business
week
Washington report (cont of) What's new:
Washington. See issues of Successful farm-
ing
Weatherman and Fort Sumter; wrongful use
of force against the government. H. V. Jaf-
fa. Nat R 22:1403+ D 29 '70
Weimar analogy. H. S. Levine. Nation 210
684-7 Je 8 '70
White House view: Nixon at midterm. il U S
News 70:18-19 Ja 4 '71
Who needs the liberals? views of John Ken-
neth Galbraith and Samuel Lubell. P. Kem-
ble. Commentary 50:57-64 O '70
Why an outmoded ideology thwarts the new
business conscience. G. C. Lodge. por For-
tune 82:106-7+ O '70; Same abr. with
title Top priority: renovating our ideology.
bibliog f Harvard Bsns R 48:43-55 S '70
See also
Business—Political aspects
Campaign issues
Candidates, Political
Conservatism
Democratic party
Elections—United States
Fascism—United States
Federal government
Legislation—United States
Political campaigns
Political parties—United States
Presidential campaigns
Presidents—United States
Presidents—United States—Relations with
Congress
Primaries
Republican party
Right and left (political science)
State governments
Trade unions—Political activities
United States—Cabinet
United States—Congress
United States—Constitution
United States—Executive departments
Vice-presidents—United States
West—Politics
Woman suffrage—United States
also subheads Politics, Politics and gov-
ernment under names of sections, states,
cities, e.g. South—Politics

Anecdotes, facetiae, satire, etc.
Notes and comment; an imaginary speech
on the problems of the Nation. New Yorker 46:31-2 D 19 '70
Tour of duty. J. Ciardi. Sat R 53:4+ D 19 '70

Bibliography
America in troubled times. Schol Teach Jr/
Sr High p 14-15 D 7 '70

Popular culture
America's changing culture; excerpts from
The pursuit of loneliness: American cul-
ture at the breaking point. P. E. Slater.
Cur 119:15-21 Je '70
Cultural indicators: the case of violence in
television drama. G. Gerbner. bibliog f il
Ann Am Acad 388:69-81 Mr '70

UNITED STATES—Popular culture—*Cont.*
It's a Wyeth, not a Warhol, world. W. D.
  Wells. il Harvard Bsns R 48:26-8+ Ja '70
Nostalgia. il Newsweek 76:34-8 D 28 '70
Originality and tradition in American culture.
  C. C. Mark. il UNESCO Courier 23:16-17+
  Je '70
Sacred or secular; the context of culture. B.
  Chase. il por Library J 95:3871-6 N 15 '70
  See also
San Francisco—Popular culture

Bibliography
Apotheosis of Masscult. H. S. Resnik. il Sat
  R 53:29-31+ N 21 '70

Study and teaching
Project 2469 A.D. A. Schraff. Schol Teach
  Sec Teach Sup p 17-18 N 3 '69

Population
America in 1985: an official preview. il U S
  News 69:90 O 19 '70
Holding down the population. il Newsweek
  75:86-7 Mr 30 '70
If population stops growing: impact on U.S.
  il U S News 69:80-2 S 28 '70
Nonsense explosion. B. Wattenberg. il New
  Repub 162:18-23 Ap 4 '70; Discussion. 162:
  24-6+ My 2; 44-6 My 9; 29-31 My 16 '70
Of many things; concerning views of T. C.
  Jermann. V. S. Kearney. America 123:
  inside cover Ag 8 '70
Overpopulated America. W. H. Davis; discus-
  sion. New Repub 162:28-30 Ja 31 '70
Population and national goals. il Sci N 98:
  114 Ag 8 '70
Population growth. H. C. Wallich. Newsweek
  75:70 Je 29; 76:60 Ag 10 '70
Population of the United States in 1960 and
  1969. il Aging 187:21 My '70
Third fish; why population growth is a
  problem. K. S. Norris. New Repub 162:16-
  18 My 9 '70
U.S. population growth: would slower be
  better? L. A. Mayer. il Fortune 81:80-3+
  Je '70
United States population policy, origins and
  development; address, August 21, 1970. P.
  P. Claxton, jr. Dept State Bul 63:317-26 S
  21 '70
What U.S. will be like by 1980: meaning of
  population shifts. il U S News 70:38-40 Ja
  11 '71
  See also
Birth rate—United States
Cities and towns—United States
Migration, Internal
United States—Census

Post office department
Can private enterprise save the post office?
  Sr Schol 95:12-13 S 29 '69
Mail reform moves nearer: what changes
  would mean. il U S News 68:32 Je 29 '70
Now mail robbers plague post office. il U S
  News 69:42 Jl 13 '70
Patronage privilege, and postal service. fed-
  eral corporation plan. R. L. Tobin. il Sat
  R 53:57-8 Ja 17 '70
Post office to participate in domestic Sat-
  com case. K. Johnsen. Aviation W 93:51
  D 21 '70
  See also
Postal service—United States

**President's advisory council on
  executive reorganization**
  See United States—Advisory council on
  executive organization

**President's commission for the observance
  of the twenty-fifth anniversary of
  the United Nations**
Commission for the observance of 25th anniversary of the U.N; White House announcement with executive order. Dept
  State Bul 63:180-2 Ag 10 '70
Commission on the twenty-fifth anniversary
  of the United Nations submits interim report to President Nixon. Dept State Bul
  63:390-3 O 5 '70
President appoints youth members to U.N.
  anniversary commission; statement and
  White House announcement. R. M. Nixon.
  Dept State Bul 63:393-4 O 5 '70
U.N. twenty-fifth anniversary commission
  to hold public hearings. Dept State Bul 63:
  458-9 O 19 '70

**President's commission on campus
  unrest**
Arms and the campus; report. Newsweek 76:
  44-5+ O 12 '70

Campus: bring us together; report findings.
  il Newsweek 76:24-6 O 5 '70
Campus unrest: its cause and cure. H. Putnam. bibliog Sch & Soc 98:372-4 O '70
Campus unrest: review of the Scranton commission report. J. S. Diekhoff. il PTA Mag
  65:9-12 D '70
Campus unrest; the dangers of commissions;
  address, September 5, 1970. G. Allott. Vital
  Speeches 36:758-60 O 1 '70
Campus unrest: time for action. America
  123:248 O 10 '70
Campus unrest: which tack for President's
  commission? T. P. Southwick. Science 169:
  1061-3 S 11 '70
Commissionology. Nat R 22:1036 O 6 '70
Crisis of violence. Commonweal 93:35-6 O 9
  '70
Double focus on Kent state: findings of
  grand jury at odds with those of Scranton
  commission. Nat R 22:1146 N 3 '70
Each against all? report findings and recom-
  mendations. il Sat R 53:64 O 17 '70
Epistle to the Americans; Scranton report. R.
  A. Nisbet. Commentary 50:40-5 D '70
Impact of college unrest: Scranton commis-
  sion's view. U S News 69:69 O 5 '70
Jackson-Kent killings; Scranton commission.
  Time 96:18-19 O 12 '70
Language and violence; response of S. T.
  Agnew. America 123:281 O 17 '70
Lively ivy; views of witnesses. New Repub
  163:5-6 Ag 15 '70
On campus: blame enough for all; highlights
  of report. il Time 96:16-17 O 5 '70
Pablum and poison: report findings. K. Craw-
  ford. Newsweek 76:55 O 12 '70
Presidential overkill. Nation 211:324 O 12 '70
Return to campus quiet. por Sch & Soc
  98:326 O '70
Rhodes' scholarship. por Time 96:51 Ag 31 '70
Scranton report. R. Kirk. Nat R 22:1212 N
  17 '70
Scranton report: steps to be taken. C. B.
  Grannis. Pub W 198:43 O 5 '70
Second thoughts. il Newsweek 76:27-8 S 28
  '70
Talking back. New Repub 163:7-8 O 10 '70
Time for reconciliation; report. J. Cass. Sat
  R 53:53-4 O 17 '70
Violence and understanding: campus unrest
  and the Scranton report. R. A. Schroth.
  il Cath World 212:119-22 D '70
What official report says on student deaths;
  excerpts from reports. il U S News 69:
  72-3 O 19 '70
Who's to blame? campus violence probe.
  Sr Schol 97:9-10 O 26 '70

**President's commission on
  civil disorders**
  See United States—National advisory
  commission on civil disorders

**President's commission on federal
  statistics**
Fact-crazy, theory-shy? A. Etzioni. Science
  170:391 O 23 '70

**President's commission on interna-
  tional trade and investment policy**
Mr Williams to head commission on trade
  and investment policy. Dept State Bul 62:
  699 Je 1 '70
President Nixon names commission on trade
  and investment policy. Dept State Bul 62:
  752-3 Je 15 '70

**President's commission on
  national goals**
America in 1980: a challenge now. il U S
  News 69:40 Jl 27 '70
National goals. M. Nadel. Liv Wildn 34:2 Spr
  '70

**President's commission on obscenity
  and pornography**
  See United States—Commission on obscenity and pornography

**President's commission on personnel
  interchange (proposed)**
Business and government will swap executives. Nations Bsns 58:44 Mr '70

President's commission on school finance
Message on education reform. R. M. Nixon.
  il Am Ed 6:30-4 Ap '70

**President's commission on the assassina-
  tion of President Kennedy**
Assassination of John F. Kennedy, by A.
  H. Newman. Review
  Nat R 22:606 Je 16 '70

UNITED STATES—*Continued*

President's committee on consumer interests

Why are shoppers fighting mad? Here's why! il Changing T 24:11-14 S '70

President's council on environmental quality

See United States—Council on environmental quality

President's task force on aging

Presidential task force on aging urges action now to help elderly. Aging 190:4-5 Ag '70

Public health service

Creating a doctor corps; program of Emergency health personnel act of 1970. Time 97:35 Ja 18 '71

How safe is the Nation's drinking water? with list of U.S. cities with sub-standard drinking water systems. S. Lindsay. Sat R 53:54-5 My 2 '70

See also

United States—Consumer protection and environmental health service

Public land law review commission

Capitalism v. conservation. il Time 96:54 Jl 6 '70

History of public land law development, by P. W. Gates. Review
　Liv Wildn 34:52-5 Spr '70. H. K. Pyles

Land law review stirs controversy. T. P. Southwick. Science 169:33 Jl 3 '70

Moment of truth for the public lands. M. Frome. Field & S 75:18+ Jl '70

Moving in for a land grab; Aspinall commission report. H. Peterson. il Sports Illus 33:22-4+ Jl 13 '70

One third of the nation's land; report. J. B. Craig. il Am For 76:8-11+ Ag '70

One-third of the U.S. is up for grabs. T. L. Kimball. il Nat Wildlife 9:38-40 D '70

Outline for public land policy. C. H. Stoddard. Liv Wildn 34:30 Sum '70

Powerful congressional group moves backward into the future. M. Frome. Field & S 75:38+ O '70

Scheduled grazing fee hike delayed. Nat Parks 44:29 Mr '70

This land is our land. D. Jackson. il Life 70:32-43 Ja 8 '71

This land is whose land? Aspinall report. W. K. Wyant, jr. New Repub 163:10-11 Jl 11 '70

What's involved in big dispute on public lands. U S News 69:72 Jl 6 '70

Public roads, Bureau of

Plot to pave America; highway trust fund. R. Starnes. Field & S 75:6+ N '70

Race problems

Here and now for Bobby Seale; tr. by J. Oringer. J. Genet. Ramp Mag 8:30-1 Je '70

See also

Church and race problems

Negroes

Reclamation, Bureau of

Here in Nevada a terrible crime; Pyramid Lake. A. M. Josephy, jr. il Am Heritage 21:93-100 Je '70

Relations (diplomatic)
Catholic church

See Catholic church—Relations (diplomatic)—United States

Religious institutions and affairs

Episcopalians at the barricades; Houston general convention. Time 96:74 N 2 '70

Religion in America; symposium. Mlle 70:154-9+ Mr '70

Sixties: radical change in American religion; symposium, ed. by J. M. Gustafson. bibliog f Ann Am Acad 387:1-140 Ja '70

Why churches are worried. il U S News 68:42-6 Mr 23 '70

See also

Baptists in the United States
Catholic church in the United States
Jews in the United States
Latin Americans in the United States—Religion
Lutheran church in the United States
Lutherans in the United States
Mennonites
Methodist church in the United States
Missions—United States

Mormons and Mormonism
Negroes—Religion
Orthodox Eastern church in the United States
Presbyterian church in the United States (South)
Protestant churches—United States
Shakers
United States—Church history
Unity school of Christianity
　also subhead Religious institutions and affairs under names of countries, states, cities, etc. e.g. Chicago—Religious institutions and affairs

Renegotiation board

Grumman cracks a silence barrier. Bsns W p32 Mr 21 '70

Reserve forces

See United States—Armed forces—Reserves

Reserve officers training corps

Academic world and military education; address, March 7, 1970. G. C. S. Benson. Vital Speeches 36:542-4 Je 15 '70

Behind the drive to destroy ROTC. il U S News 68:20-2 Je 29 '70

High school ROTC. Ed Digest 35:58 Mr '70

Riots

Local political leadership and popular discontent in the ghetto. P. H. Rossi and A. A. Berk. bibliog f il Ann Am Acad 391:111-27 S '70

Race, riots and reporters; press coverage of urban disorders. T. A. Knopf. il Commonweal 92:336-40 Jl 10 '70; Same abr. with title Race and the press. Cur 121:20-5 S '70

Riot season erupts, but setting changes. il U S News 69:36 Jl 20 '70

Summer: cloudy, occasional storms; possible trouble areas. il Time 95:8-10 Je 29 '70

Summer violence flares again. il U S News 69:22 Ag 10 '70

See also

Riot control

United States—National advisory commission on civil disorders

Prevention and control

See Riot control

Science and technology, Office of

Academic research: OST aide sees no shift in financial situation. D. S. Greenberg. Science 170:952-4 N 27 '70

White House study urges space advances. W. J. Normyle. Aviation W 92:20-1 Mr 23 '70

Secretary of labor

See Secretaries of labor (United States)

Securities and exchange commission

Accounting and the SEC; interview. J. J. Needham. por Duns 96:10-11+ O '70

Belling the fat cats; SEC study of the impact of institutional investors on the stock market. il Newsweek 77:65 Ja 11 '71

Challenges for the next SEC chairman. il Bsns W p28 N 21 '70

Cost overruns bring on the SEC. il Bsns W p31 Je 6 '70

Electrogas builders. Forbes 106:22-3 N 15 '70

Investor's silent partner. I. Ross. il Nations Bsns 58:74-6+ Je '70; Reply. W. H. Dinsmore. 58:9+ O '70

It's up to the SEC; regulations affecting accountants. G. R. Rosen. Duns 95:64+ Je '70

Key SEC study is under a cloud; delays in report on institutions. il Bsns W p76 D 12 '70

Lockheed objections stall SEC inquiry. D. C. Winston. Aviation W 93:21 Jl 13 '70

Lockheed stock; SEC investigation. New Repub 162:9-10 Ap 25 '70

Regulation of investments; interview. H. H. Budge. il pors U S News 69:52-6 S 7 '70

SEC to make public a portion of Lockheed's C-5A cost data. Aviation W 93:15 S 21 '70

SEC will say no to the big board. Forbes 105:23 Ap 1 '70

Seeking cures for investor anxiety. Bsns W p34 Je 13 '70

Texas Gulf tangle unwinds, a little. Bsns W p29-30 F 14 '70

Tougher SEC shuts broker Ling. Bsns W p 19 Ja 9 '71

Wall Street on the ropes. C. J. Loomis. il Fortune 82:62-7+ D '70

Senate

See United States—Congress—Senate

UNITED STATES—*Continued*

Small business administration

Sandoval stands siege at the SBA. por Bsns W p60+ Jl 18 '70

Social conditions

America, the violent; address, July 8, 1970. P. L. Briand, jr. Vital Speeches 36:674-9 S 1 '70

Another look at the American dream. R. J. Lamont. Chr Today 14:6-8 Ap 24 '70

Are we in the middle of the second American revolution? symposium. il N Y Times Mag p26-7+ My 17 '70

Bridging the gulf with dissenting youth. C. E. Goodell. Cur 122:32-4 O '70

Comes a new note of protest. B. L. Masse. America 123:445 N 21 '70

Consciousness III; theories of C. A. Reich. R. Starr. Commentary 50:46-54 D '70

Day in the life of the United States of America, CBS documentary. J. Leonard. il Life 69:10 S 4 '70

Don't blame the system! R. M. Christenson. Chr Cent 87:784-7 Je 24 '70

Executive as social activist. il Time 96:62-8 Jl 20 '70

Finding the American direction. M. Ways. il Fortune 82:70-5+ O '70; Same abr. with title What hope for the future? Cur 124:3-16 D '70

Fresh look at America. J. N. Wallace. il U S News 69:46-51 N 30 '70

Listening to America. B. Moyers. il Harper 241:47-54+ D '70

Mood back home; symposium, with editorial comment by R. Graves. il Life 69:1, 22-33 O 2 '70

Mood of America today. U S News 68:17-18 Ap 20 '70

Night thoughts of a police chief. J. P. Kimble. il Nation 210:490-2 Ap 27 '70

On the threshold of a new decade: thoughts for 1970. E. Rabinowitch. il por Bul Atom Sci 26:2-3+ F '70

Perspective. J. H. Plumb. Sat R 53:26 My 30 '70

Pessimism of Earl Warren. Chr Cent 87:652 My 27 '70

Pick any country. P. Steinfels. Commonweal 93:118 O 30 '70

Political intelligence for America's future; symposium, ed. by B. M. Gross and M. Springer. bibliog f il Ann Am Acad 388:1-132 Mr '70

Professional radical, 1970; interview, ed. by M. K. Sanders. S. Alinsky. il Harper 240:35-42 Ja '70

Rereading the Philadelphia manifesto. P. Steinfels. Commonweal 92:358 Jl 24 '70

Today's America; better or worse? symposium. il U S News 70:26-32 Ja 11 '71

Toward legalizing revolution. M. Harrington. Cur 122:28-31 O '70

Unheavenly city; views of E. C. Banfield. G. B. Porter. por Newsweek 75:56 Mr 23 '70

View of America from Lake Como. T. Griffith. Life 68:26 Je 26 '70

What's going on inside America; survey of Campus dissent, antiwar protests, strike disorder, crime, pollution. il U S News 68:17-23 My 25 '70

What's going on inside America: where things are all right; symposium. il U S News 68:15-21+ Je 1 '70

What's right about America; excerpts from address, June 25, 1970. R. M. Nixon. il por U S News 69:45 Jl 6 '70

What's worrying people. il U S News 68:18-20 F 9 '70

See also
Cities and towns—United States
Crime and criminals—United States
Divorce—United States
Immigration and emigration—United States
Labor and laboring classes—United States
Negroes
Poor—United States
Social security act, 1935
United States—Population
Women—United States
Youth—United States
also subhead Social conditions under names of sections, states, cities, e.g. New York (city)—Social conditions

Bibliography

America in troubled times. Schol Teach Jr/ Sr High p 14-15 D 7 '69

America's aches and pains; new books on contemporary themes. il Schol Teach Sec Teach Sup p 14-16 D1 '69

Home scene (cont) T. M. Gannon. America 122:476-8; 123:470-2 My 2, N 28 '70

Social indicators: selected readings. C. Agocs. Ann Am Acad 388:127-32 Mr '70

History

See United States—Social history

Social history

Banality of revolt; views of Andrew Hacker and William Braden. S. M. Lipset. il Sat R 53:23-6+ Jl 18 '70

Frontier freedoms and space age cities; excerpt. C. W. Griffin, jr. il Sat R 53:17-19+ F 7 '70

Paradox of American violence: a historical appraisal. H. D. Graham. bibliog f Ann Am Acad 391:74-82 S '70

Radicalism and the skipped generation; excerpt from Toward a radical middle: fourteen pieces of reporting and criticism. R. Adler. Atlan 225:53-7 F '70

Spirit of '70: six historians reflect on what ails the American spirit; symposium. il Newsweek 76:18-34 Jl 6 '70

Uses of violence in American history; adaptation of address, December 1969. M. Wallace. Am Scholar 40:81-102 Wint '70

See also
Business depression, 1929-1939
Education—United States—History
Negroes—History
Slavery—United States
United States—Moral conditions

Social life and customs

Nice girls don't swear? the thirties contrasted with today. N. Gittelson. Harp Baz 103:29+ My '70

Rituals, the revolt against the fixed smile; Time essay. M. Maddocks. il Time 96:42-3 O 12 '70

See also
Sports—United States
Suburban life

Social policy

Analytic framework for social reporting and policy analysis. M. Olson. bibliog f Ann Am Acad 388:112-26 Mr '70

Climbing out of the trough. Time 96:11-12 D 21 '70

Emphasis turns to the home front. il U S News 68:17 F 9 '70

Goals; the need for priorities; address; January 7, 1970. T. J. Watson, jr. Vital Speeches 36:301-3 Mr 1 '70

Mr Nixon's voluntarism. A. Etzioni. il Commonweal 91:426-30 Ja 16 '70

Needed: a new dream. N. Cousins. Sat R 53:18 Je 20 '70

Nixon turns from Chile to Chicago. il Time 97:11-12 Ja 18 '71

Our top priority: long term planning; address, June 2, 1970. W. B. Johnson. Vital Speeches 36:615-19 Ag 1 '70

Priorities for the seventies. R. L. Heilbroner. Cur 116:11-18 Mr '70

Prospects for a social report, a review article. E. Clague. Mo Labor R 93:56-60 Je '70

Social indicators, reports, and accounts: toward the management of society. M. Springer. bibliog f Ann Am Acad 388:1-13 Mr '70

Unfinished business. P. Schrag. Sat R 53:16 D 5 '70

Waking in a nightmare; excerpts from address, 1969. J. W. Gardner. Am For 76:6-7 Mr '70

Wayward welfare state; address, September 1, 1970. R. A. Freeman. il Vital Speeches 37:16-24 O 15 '70

See also
Economic assistance, Domestic
United States—Council of social advisers (proposed)

Social security administration

Life and death underground; Clay County Poor people's association holds mock trial on inadequate enforcement of the Federal coal mine health and safety act of 1969. R. Cassidy. New Repub 163:13-14 D 12 '70

Medicare kills off its cost predictor; chief actuary for Social security administration. il por Bsns W p27 Je 6 '70

Soil conservation service

Crisis on our rivers. J. N. Miller and R. Simmons. il Read Digest 97:78-83 D '70

Ditches are quicker; channelization the Soil conservation service program. W. Humphrey. il por Life 69:58-61 Ag 7 '70

Gravediggers; channelization program of the SCS. E. A. Bauer and B. East. il Outdoor Life 146:29-31+ Jl '70

UNITED STATES—*Continued*

Standards, National bureau of

Branscomb talks of NBS after his first year; interview, ed. by J. B. Phelps. L. M. Branscomb. por Phys Today 23:73-5 S '70

Dissent and reaction: vigilante activity at NBS labs in Boulder. P. M. Boffey. por Science 169:163-4 Jl 10 '70

Science takes a problem's measure. Nations Bsns 58:75 Mr '70

Radio stations

New facilities for WWVH to be activated in 1971. Electr World 84:68 N '70

State, Department of

Communication: the weak link in our foreign relations? address, October 16, 1970. W. D. Blair, jr. Dept State Bul 63:580-6 N 9 '70; Same. Vital Speeches 37:109-13 D 1 '70

Crisis spokesman. por Newsweek 76:106 O 5 '70

Mr Collins becomes assistant secretary for public affairs; Department announcement; with remarks at swearing-in ceremony. W. P. Rogers; M. Collins. Dept State Bul 62:142-3 F 2 '70

New sprint in foggy bottom; reform at last? S. Simpson. Nation 210:296-302 Mr 16 '70

Office of under secretary for western hemisphere affairs; statement, March 18, 1970. E. L. Richardson. Dept State Bul 62:498-9 Ap 13 '70

Publications. See issues of Department of state bulletin

Reclaiming some turf. Newsweek 75:54-5 Ja 26 '70

Secretary Rogers receives report of Committee to facilitate travel; Department announcement; with statement by Secretary Rogers, June 9, 1970. Dept State Bul 62:809-10 Je 29 '70

State department antiques. C. Cutler. il Art in Am 58:74-7 S '70

State looks at itself; Diplomacy for the '70s report. Time 96:15 D 21 '70

Static at the Voice; interdepartmental feud. Newsweek 76:42 N 30 '70

Wealth of eagles; the diplomatic reception rooms. il Am Home 73:63-9 N '70

What is to be done? Gigantism in Washington. J. F. Campbell. For Affairs 49:81-99 O '70

See also
National foreign policy conference for editors and broadcasters. San Francisco
National foreign policy conference for editors and broadcasters, Washington, D.C.
United States—Diplomatic and consular service
United States—Foreign relations

Advisory committee on public opinion

Advisory committee on public opinion established by Secretary Rogers. Dept State Bul 63:654-5 N 23 '70

Advisory council on African affairs

African affairs advisory council meets with Secretary Rogers. Dept State Bul 63:579 N 9 '70

International scientific and technological affairs, Office of

Mr Herter becomes special assistant for environmental affairs; Department announcement; with remarks by W. P. Rogers and C. A. Herter. Dept State Bul 62:212-14 F 23 '70

Passport division

She's the American traveler's best friend. J. Keats. Read Digest 96:39-40+ F '70

Public relations

Communicating about foreign policy; address, February 21, 1970. M. Collins. Dept State Bul 62:393-6 Mr 23 '70

Statistics

See also
United States—Census

Strategic air command

See United States—Air force—Strategic air command

Strategic services, Office of

Donovan of OSS, by C. Ford. Review
Newsweek por 75:102D+ F 23 '70. S. K. Oberbeck

Our German wehrmacht is being stopped by a shadow; excerpts from Donovan of OSS. C. Ford. il por Am Heritage 21:56-7+ F '70

Subversive activities control board

Exercise in futility. Time 95:68+ My 4 '70
Listless; Supreme court's decision. Newsweek 75:30 My 4 '70
Many lives of SACB. Nation 210:132 F 9 '70
TRB from Washington. New Repub 162:4 Mr 28 '70

Superintendent of documents

Su docs. F. J. O'Hara. bibliog il Wilson Lib Bul 44:940+ My '70

Supreme court

Advice and consent, power to select, too? D. Lawrence. U S News 68:104 Ap 13 '70

After the Carswell defeat, Nixon's new strategy; with how the Senate voted on two nominees. il por U S News 68:19-21 Ap 20 '70

Annals of politics; nomination of G. H. Carswell to the Court. R. E. Harris. New Yorker 46:60-4+ D 5; 53-8+ D 12 '70

Approaching the bench. Time 95:11 F 9 '70

Back to school. il Newsweek 76:48 O 19 '70

Berrigans' suit; liberals vs. a conservative court. J. Deedy. Commonweal 93:210 N 27 '70; Reply with rejoinder. E. B. Patterson. 93:339+ Ja 8 '71

Blackmun nomination, turning point for High court? il por U S News 68:22+ Ap 27 '70

Blackmun's baptism. il Time 96:68-9 O 5 '70

Booksellers seek support for appeal of porno bust. Pub W 198:21 N 23 '70

Bottom of the barrel, confirmation of appointments. Nation 210:164 F 16 '70

Burger/Blackmun court. J. R. Waltz. il N Y Times Mag p60-1+ D 6 '70

Burger court: a new tone. por U S News 68:36 My 25 '70

Burger court and issues it faces. il U S News 69:28 O 19 '70

Burger's court gets back to business; business issues before the Supreme court. Bsns W p72+ O 3 '70

Business and the Nixon court. F. P. Graham. il por Duns 96:40-2 O '70

Carswell file. il por Newsweek 75:29 Mr 16 '70

Carswell, ideology & the Supreme court. P. Steinfels. Commonweal 91:504 F 6 '70

Carswell in trouble. por Time 95:10 Ap 6 '70

Carswell nomination: new direction for High court. il por U S News 68:18-19 F 2 '70

Carswell on the stand. il por Newsweek 75:22-4 F 9 '70

Carswell's deed. Newsweek 75:24 F 23 '79

Choosing Supreme court judges. H. S. Commager. New Repub 162:13-16 My 2 '70

Civil rights and the Warren court. il pors Ebony 25:27-30+ F '70

Clarification needed; desegregation. D. Lawrence. U S News 69:80 Ag 31 '70

Conservative activist; A. M. Bickel on the Supreme court. por Time 96:40 Ag 17 '70

Considering the alternatives. il Time 95:53 Mr 30 '70

Counting out Carswell. il por Newsweek 75:26-7 Ap 6 '70

Deserving better; choice of a Supreme court justice. il Life 68:38 Ap 17 '70

Eight men and a chair; justices of the Burger court. il Newsweek 75:38-9 Ap 20 '70

Haynsworth to Carswell. New Repub 162:7-8 Ja 31 '70

Haynsworth v. the U.S. Senate (1969) J. L. Steele. il por Fortune 81:90-3+ Mr '70

Here comes the judge. il por Newsweek 75:19 F 2 '70

Impeaching Justice Douglas? with excerpts from address by G. R. Ford, April 15, 1970. il por U S News 68:25-6, 67-71 Ap 27 '70

Indecisive Court. C. M. Whelan. America 124:3-4 Ja 9 '71

Interview with Chief Justice Warren E. Burger. W. E. Burger. il pors U S News 69:32-6+ D 14 '70; Discussion. 70:66-9 Ja 11 '71

Is Warren G. Harding really dead? Nixon and the Court. F. M. Wilhoit. Commonweal 92:181-4 My 8 '70

Judge Carswell's bruises; Senate debate. Newsweek 75:21 Mr 30 '70

Judge Carswell's mediocrity. Nat R 22:429 Ap 21 '70

Justice Douglas and the Supreme court. America 122:464 My 2 '70

Letter from Washington. R. H. Rovere. New Yorker 46:138+ Ap 18 '70

Mediocrity factor; G. H. Carswell's nomination. il por Time 95:15 Mr 2 '70

Moment of truth; Senate reactions to Nixon-Saxbe exchange. Newsweek 75:20-1 Ap 13 '70

UNITED STATES—Supreme court—*Cont.*
More justice to come? the use of the guilty
plea. G. L. Hallworth. America 122:390-1
Ap 11 '70
Nixon makes a winning choice. il por Time
95:19-21 Ap 27 '70
Not so simple issue. Time 95:18-19 Ap 13 '70
On the bench; Nixon's criteria for choice of
a justice. il New Repub 162:7-8 Ap 25 '70
Oops! Wrong again! Chr Cent 87:131 F 4 '70
Parting shots: some better qualified Supreme
court candidates. il Life 68:67-70 Mr 27 '70
Politics of Carswell. S. Alsop. Newsweek
75:132 Ap 20 '70
Primitive relic: death sentence. E. Gertz. Na-
tion 212:48-50 Ja 11 '71
Question before High court: how much in-
tegration? il U S News 69:37-8 O 26 '70
Repairing the damage; appointment of H.
Blackmun. Time 95:17 My 18 '70
Role of the bar in selection of justices; ex-
cerpts from report by American bar associa-
tion. il U S News 68:84-7 Je 1 '70
Same justice can be both a strict and a loose
constructionist. A. Lewis. il N Y Times
Mag p30-1+ My 24 '70
Seat for mediocrity? Time 95:18-19 Mr 30 '70
Significant silence. Time 96:71 O 26 '70
Star witness. il por Newsweek 75:41+ My 11
'70
State $ for schools. J. Duerr. Commonweal
92:243-5 My 22 '70
Supreme court; address, May 1, 1970. J. N.
Mitchell. Vital Speeches 36:514-16 Je 15 '70
Supreme court and the A.B.A.; selecting Su-
preme court nominees. Time 96:43 Ag 10 '70
Third man; nominee H. A. Blackmun. il
por Newsweek 75:28-9 Ap 27 '70
Toward a Burger court. il por Time 95:50
Ap 13 '70
TRB from Washington: Congress and the
Court. New Repub 162:8 F 14 '70
TRB from Washington; the Burger court.
New Repub 163:4 O 3 '70
U.S. the law, and Chief Justice Burger. J.
Davenport. il por Fortune 82:146-50+ S '70
United States Supreme court, from Bushrod
Washington to Roman Hruska. L. Silver.
Commonweal 92:224-7 My 15 '70
Verdict against life terms; terms of Supreme
court justice. Nations Bsns 58:22 My '70
What makes a good Supreme court justice.
E. McCarthy. McCalls 97:34+ Ag '70
When senators quizzed Carswell. por U S
News 68:9 F 9 '70

Decisions
After fifteen years: seventeen days to de-
segregate. il U S News 68:53 Ja 26 '70
Backlog for lawyers; decisions on preliminary
hearings and searches. il Time 96:42-3 Jl
6 '70
Benevolent neutrality; taxation of church pro-
perty. Newsweek 75:77 My 18 '70
Big vote to come; youth vote. il Time 97:24
Ja 4 '71
Blow to unions; reverse of 1962 Decision on
no-strike agreements. Time 95:60-1 Je 15 '70
Burger challenges the Warren court. por U S
News 69:36 Jl 6 '70
Burger way. por Newsweek 75:33 Ap 6 '70
Chances for schism: a legal green light. A.
L. Scanlan. America 122:150-2 F 14 '70
Clearer track for railroads. il Bsns W p30+
F 7 '70
CO riddle; case of Elliott A. Welsh, 2d. News-
week 75:19 Je 29 '70
Conscientious objection; 1965 ruling reaf-
firmed. New Repub 163:10 Jl 18 '70
Conscription, conscience and the Court. Chr
Cent 87:908-9 Jl 29 '70
Court backing for law combatting pollution;
other decisions. il U S News 68:81 Je 1 '70
Court cases lost by unions. U S News 68:55-6
Mr 16 '70
Court says: integrate now! il Sr Schol 95:Schol
Teach 1 D 1 '69
Courts and the child: Tinker vs. Des Moines
decision. Library J 95:216-17 Ja 15 '70
Curbing the boards; reversed conviction of
D. E. Gutknecht. Time 95:11-12 F 2 '70
Defining conscientious objectors. Chr Today
14:21 Jl 17 '70
Desegregation now; Court cracks down. Sr
Schol 95:21-2+ N 17 '69
Draft is not for punishing. Sr Schol 96:13 F
16 '70
Eighteen-year-old vote. Nation 212:36-7 Ja 11
'71
End to draft as punishment. il U S News
68:9 F 2 '70
Et tu, Burger! question of offensive direct-
mail advertising. Nation 210:645 Je 1 '70
Facts about prayer in schools. L. Cassels.
U S News 68:96 Mr 23 '70

Go fight city hall; Supreme court ruling upholds Philadelphia ban. Newsweek 75:89 Je
8 '70
Half a jury is better than none; Supreme
court ruling on size of jury. Time 96:42 Jl
6 '70
How Court ruling changes draft. il U S News
68:17-19 Je 29 '70
Jim Hill's dream; approves merger of three
northern rail lines. Newsweek 75:78+ F 16
'70
Labor and the economy in 1969. R. W. Fisher.
bibliog il Mo Labor R 93:30-43 Ja '70
New 5-to-4 majority; ruling on hearsay ev-
idence. Time 96:47 D 28 '70
New ruling: order in the court means what
it says. il U S News 68:63 Ap 13 '70
New rulings on public assembly, free speech.
U S News 68:95 Je 8 '70
Nine key decisions by Supreme court. U S
News 69:79 My 4 '70
No-strike pacts now mean what they say.
Bsns W p25 Je 6 '70
No-strike reversal by Supreme court. U S
News 68:52-3 Je 15 '70
Notes and comment; decision in Dutton v.
Evans case, to admit certain kinds of hear-
say evidence. New Yorker 46:15-16 Ja 2 '71
Order in the courtroom. Time 95:51 Ap 13 '70
Point of order; ruling in the Allen case. il
Newsweek 75:21-2 Ap 13 '70
Recognizing reality. Time 96:68+ D 7 '70
Reinterpreting the draft law. Chr Today 14:
31 Jl 3 '70
Respecting the Supreme court. J. N. Mitchell.
Cur 122:34-5 O '70
Right to be nude. G. F. Will. Nat R 22:832
Ag 11 '70
Ruling that could tie up welfare aid. U S
News 68:59 Ap 6 '70
School prayer ban upheld. Sr Schol 96:Schol
Teach 1 Ja 26 '70
Seceding churches win property; with edi-
torial comment. Chr Today 14:26-7, 36 F 13
'70
Selective objectors and the Court. America
123:6 Jl 11 '70
Significant decisions in labor cases. See issues
of Monthly labor review
Splitting the difference; ruling on youth
vote. il Newsweek 77:18-19 Ja 4 '71
Supreme court already has changed. il Na-
tions Bsns 58:66-9 Je '70
Supreme court and self-restraint. America
123:423 N 21 '70
Supreme court and the idea of progress, by
A. M. Bickel. Review
   Commentary 49:94-6+ My '70. L. Friedman
   Nat R 22:414-15 Ap 21 '70. W. Berns
   Nation 211:250-2 S 21 '70. R. B. McKay
   Sat R 53:37-8+ Ap 4 '70. W. M. Wiecek
Supreme court leaves obscenity issues un-
resolved. S. Wagner. Pub W 198:50 Jl 27
'70
Supreme court reaffirms church tax exemp-
tion. Chr Cent 87:621 My 20 '70
Supreme court upholds bar to erotic mail. S.
Wagner. Pub W 197:18 My 18 '70
Tax churches? What Supreme court says.
U S News 68:105 My 18 '70
Tax exemptions: race and religion. America
122:576 My 30 '70
Trimming sails; first year of the Burger
Court. R. Shogan. il por Newsweek 76:32+
Jl 13 '70
Vietnam; shadow on the Court; refusal to
hear the Massachusetts anti-war suit. B.
Schweid. Nation 211:564 N 30 '70
Walz case; church tax exemptions. C. M.
Whelan. America 122:518-19 My 16 '70
What the Warren court decided; excerpts from
The Warren court and the public schools.
H. C. Hudgins, jr. Ed Digest 36:44-7 N
'70
Who's sincere; conscientious objectors. por
Time 95:40 Je 29 '70
Worst scandal in our history; the Fourteenth
amendment: reprint. D. Lawrence. il U S
News 68:96+ Ja 26 '70
Year of the pause. il Time 96:11-12 Jl 13 '70

**Surgeon general's advisory committee
on television and social behavior**
Choosing the investigators. R. L. Shayon.
Sat R 53:34 S 5 '70
Let's do a study; committee on TV violence.
Sedulus. New Repub 163:32-3 Ag 1 '70

Tax court
Those tax deduction blues. il Nations Bsns
58:38-40 Je '70

**Technology assessment, Office
of (proposed)**
Daddario introduces bill for technology
assessment office. J. B. Phelps. Phys Today
23:64 My '70

UNITED STATES—Technology assessment, Office of (proposed)—*Continued*
Predicting the consequences of technology. J. Lear. por Sat R 53:44-6 Mr 28 '70
Technology's assessors; with letter from L. Q. Mumford. J. Lear. Sat R 53:52 Ap 25 '70

Territories and possessions
From John Bull to Uncle Sam: how to run an empire. J. Aitken. il Am Heritage 21: 44-5+ Ag '70
See also
Guam
Micronesia
Virgin Islands

Trade policy
See United States—Commerce

Transportation, Department of
Department of its own. il Forbes 105:182-4 Ja '70
John Volpe's drive to keep America moving. il pors Nations Bsns 58:40-7 Ap '70
New role of NASA research center. J. Walsh. Science 168:100 Ap 3 '70
White House eyes deregulation route. Bsns W p29 N 21 '70
See also
United States—Federal highway administration
United States—Urban mass transportation administration

Travel regulations
See Travel regulations

Travel service
Hey, world! Look us over! il Nations Bsns 58:42-3 Ag '70

Treasury, Department of the
Battles that Connally will face. il por Bsns W p36-7 D 19 '70
Connally-Kennedy shift: its meaning. il por U S News 69:11 D 28 '70
Here come the rangers; J. B. Connally new secretary. Nat R 22:1384-5 D 29 '70
Mr Nixon enlists a Texas Democrat; the J. Connally appointment. il por Newsweek 76: 13-15 D 28 '70
President Nixon takes a Democrat. il por Time 96:8-10 D 28 '70
See also
United States—Customs, Bureau of
United States—Internal revenue service

Treaties
Treaty information. See issues of Department of state bulletin
Japan
Era of friction? demonstrations against the U.S.-Japan security treaty. il Newsweek 76:41-2 Jl 6 '70
U.S. and Japan maintain treaty of mutual cooperation and security. Dept State Bul 63: 33 Jl 13 '70
Mexico
Thankless task of Nicholas Trist. R. M. Ketchum. il por Am Heritage 21:12-15+ Ag '70
U.S. and Mexico sign treaty on archeological properties; Department announcement, with text of treaty. Dept State Bul 63:206-7 Ag 17 '70
U.S.-Mexico archeological treaty transmitted to the Senate; message. R. M. Nixon. Dept State Bul 63:587 N 9 '70
Philippines
Letter from Washington; Senate foreign relations subcommittee hearings. R. H. Rovere. New Yorker 45:63-5 Ja 17 '70
Russia
U.S. and U.S.S.R. sign exchanges agreement for 1970-1971; Department announcement with text of agreement, February 10, 1970. Dept State Bul 62:260-6 Mr 2 '70

Urban mass transportation administration
First, find the mice; UMTA policies. Newsweek 76:58+ S 28 '70
Starting signal for better trains. Bsns W p35-6 O 24 '70

Veterans administration
Hearing aids: the VA's evaluations. Consumer Bul 53:27-8 My '70
Quarter-century of the GI bill. D. E. Johnson. il Sch & Soc 98:226-8 Ap '70
VA releases more hearing-aid data. Consumer Rep 35:8 Ja '70

Veterans administration hospitals
From Vietnam to a VA hospital; assignment to neglect; with report by C. Childs. il Life 68:24D-33 My 22 '70
Growing concern over veterans' hospitals. il U S News 69:63-4 Ag 31 '70
Wounded GIs: on the care of heroes. L. Barrett. Nation 210:51-3 Ja 19 '70

Vital statistics
See also
Birth rate—United States
United States—Census

Weather bureau
See United States—National weather service

Womens bureau
Women's bureau looks to the future. E. D. Koontz. bibliog f Mo Labor R 93:3-9 Je '70

Work projects administration
See also
Federal art project

UNITED STATES air force academy, Colorado Springs
Compulsory chapel at U.S. academies. America 122:176 F 21 '70
Military academies changing their ways. il U S News 69:46-9 N 9 '70

UNITED STATES amateur championship. See Golf—Tournaments

UNITED STATES and Canada; United States and Denmark; etc. See Canada and the United States; Denmark and the United States; etc.

UNITED STATES army security agency. See United States—Army security agency

UNITED STATES-Canada cooperative fire protection. See Northeastern forest fire protection compact

UNITED STATES Catholic conference
Breaking the circle of poverty. T. M. Gannon. America 123:394-5 N 14 '70
Combating poverty. Commonweal 93:60 O 16 '70
Labor day statement, 1970. America 123:111 S 5 '70
Period of peace 1971; World day of peace observance. America 123:537 D 19 '70
Step forward, at Mundelein; first motions toward a national pastoral council. T. E. Clarke. il America 123:198-200 S 26 '70
Vocations crisis. J. Deedy. Commonweal 93: 362 Ja 15 '71
Work of depolarization. Commonweal 93: 3-4 O 2 '70
Yes, but; suggested National pastoral council. Commonweal 92:4 Mr 13 '70

UNITED STATES coast guard academy, New London, Conn.
Military academies changing their ways. il U S News 69:46-9 N 9 '70

UNITED STATES conference of mayors
Mayors sound storm warning for Nixon. U S News 68:46 Je 29 '70

UNITED STATES-Congo (Democratic Republic) air agreement. See Aviation—International aspects

UNITED STATES duffers' association
Taking the pain from the game; USDA. H. Weiskopf. Sports Illus 33:78-9 O 12 '70

UNITED STATES embassy, Amman. See Embassies (buildings)

UNITED STATES embassy, London. See Embassies (buildings)

UNITED STATES employment service. See United States—Employment service

UNITED STATES flag. See Flags—United States

UNITED STATES foreign service. See United States—Foreign service

UNITED STATES Grand prix. See Automobile racing

UNITED STATES historical documents institute
Documents institute formed to republish reference works. il Pub W 197:40-1 Ap 20 '70

UNITED STATES in art
See also
New York city in art
Texas in art
West in art

UNITED STATES industries, inc.
Conglomerate of a different color. Forbes 106:28 Ag 1 '70
Motivating the millionaires. il por Time 95: 68+ Je 8 '70
USI's mortgage trust: no money down. A. Hershman. il Duns 96:46-8+ S '70

UNITED STATES information agency. See United States—Information agency

UNITED STATES information service. See United States—Information service

UNITED STATES investment fund, Real estate.
See USIF, Real estate
UNITED STATES-Japan air agreement. See
Aviation—International aspects
UNITED STATES-Japan cooperative medical
science committee. See Medical research—
International cooperation
UNITED STATES lawn tennis association
Confusion in the backcourt. W. Bingham.
il Sports Illus 32:61-2+ Ap 6 '70
Don't play with a guillotine; paying fixed expenses to top players. B. Collins. Sports
Illus 32:49 Ja 19 '70
UNITED STATES leasing international, inc.
U.S. leasing's gamble. T. J. Murray. por
Duns 96:58-9 S '70
UNITED STATES-Lebanon air agreement. See
Aviation—International aspects
UNITED STATES lines, inc.
Kidde's seagoing days are over. Bsns W p29-
30 N 21 '70
UNITED STATES-Malaysia air agreement. See
Aviation—International aspects
UNITED STATES-Mexican boundary and water commission. See International boundary
and water commission (United States and
Mexico)
UNITED STATES-Mexico air agreement. See
Aviation—International aspects
UNITED STATES-Mexico commission for border development and friendship
U.S. and Mexico set procedures for continuing border cooperation; joint U.S.-Mexico
statement. Dept State Bul 63:121 Jl 27 '70
UNITED STATES military academy, West
Point
Compulsory chapel at U.S. academies. America 122:176 F 21 '70
Enjoyable run up the Hudson River to historic West Point. B. Schill and B. Schill.
il Yachting 127:62-3 Ap '70
Military academies changing their ways. il
U S News 69:46-9 N 9 '70
Soldiers. W. Just. Atlan 226:62-74 O '70
West Point cadets now say, "why, sir?" T.
Fleming. il por N Y Times Mag p14-18+
Jl 5 '70; Reply with rejoinder. R. B. Johnson, jr. p68 Ag 16 '70
Who would ever go to West Point today?
J. R. Moskin. il pors Look 34:31-8 O 6 '70
UNITED STATES naval academy, Annapolis
Compulsory chapel at U.S. academies. America 122:176 F 21 '70
Military academies changing their ways. il
U S News 69:46-9 N 9 '70
New broom at navy. il por Time 95:50 My
11 '70
UNITED STATES-Netherlands air agreement.
See Aviation—International aspects
UNITED STATES of Europe (proposed) See
European federation
UNITED STATES Open golf championship. See
Golf—Tournaments
UNITED STATES plywood-Champion papers,
inc.
U.S. plywood's forest of trouble; sale of
timber from Tongass national forest. il
Bsns W p39 F 21 '70
UNITED STATES police assistance program.
See United States—Agency for international
development—Office of public safety
UNITED STATES post office inspection service.
See United States—Post office department
UNITED STATES postal service (proposed)
Change at P.O. Sr Schol 97:4 S 21 '70
Post office gets a private rival. il Bsns W
p22 N 28 '70
Very special delivery. il Newsweek 76:63 Ag
17 '70
UNITED STATES power squadrons, inc.
Underway with the USPS. See issues of Motor
boating
UNITED STATES-Russia air agreement. See
Aviation—International aspects
UNITED STATES sailboat show. See Boats—
Exhibitions
UNITED STATES savings bonds. See Bonds,
Government
UNITED STATES steel corporation
Big steel gets back into advertising. il Bsns
W p96 My 30 '70
Big steel workers win a decision. Bsns W
p30 Je 13 '70
Countertrend in steel pricing. Bsns W p27 O
10 '70
Steel burns again over incentives. Bsns W
p42+ F 21 '70
UNITED STATES-Thailand air agreement. See
Aviation—International aspects
UNITED STATES travel service. See United
States—Travel service
UNITED steelworkers of America
Big steel workers win a decision. Bsns W
p30 Je 13 '70

New pattern for basic steel? Bsns W p78 N
7 '70
Next, a steel strike? il Time 96:77-8 O 12 '70
Steel burns again over incentives. Bsns W
p42+ F 21 '70
Steelworkers talk tough. por Bsns W p68 O
3 '70
Steelworkers unveil contract demands. U S
News 69:66-7 N 30 '70
United steelworkers of America. J. L. Gurney.
Mo Labor R 93:33-4 D '70
UNITED transportation union
Derailment at last chance junction? mini-
train plan. il Bsns W p68-9+ Mr 28 '70
Fireman's job runs out of steam; emergency
board's recommendations. Bsns W p76 Ag
15 '70
Mini-trains get a green light. il Bsns W p27-
8 Je 13 '70
Throttling down the rail crisis. Bsns W p78
Jl 18 '70
UNITS
Fundamental physical constants. B. N. Taylor and others. il Sci Am 223:62-70+ O
'70
UNITY (sect) See Unity school of Christianity
UNITY school of Christianity
Heaven on earth. R. Rhodes. il Harper 240:
116-22 My '70
UNIVAC division. See Sperry Rand corporation—Univac division
UNIVERSAL autograph collectors' club (international)
Autograph collectors' club celebrates 5th year.
H. M. Darvick. Hobbies 75:140-1+ D '70
UNIVERSAL declaration of human rights
Secretary-General's press conference; 22 December, 1969. Thant. U N Mo Chron 7:178-87
Ja '70
UNIVERSAL higher education. See College
education
UNIVERSAL joints (mechanics)
Amateur scientist; devices for transmitting
power mechanically; ed. by C. L. Stong. il
Sci Am 223:232+ S '70
UNIVERSAL language. See Language, Universal
UNIVERSAL Marion corporation
Using liquidation as a strategy. Bsns W p34
O 3 '70
UNIVERSAL oil products-Calumet and Hecla
merger. See Business consolidations and
mergers
UNIVERSAL postal union
International reply coupons. H. Bennett. il
Pop Electr 32:95 Mr '70
UNIVERSE
Conceptions of the universe; with paintings
by H. K. Wimmer. F. Branley. Natur Hist
79:30-5 bibliog(p90) D '70
Cosmic prison; excerpts from The invisible
pyramid. L. Eiseley. il Horizon 12:96-101
Aut '70
Edge of the universe? Newsweek 76:55 S 7 '70
Galaxies and the universe. J. H. Oort. bibliog
il Science 170:1363-70 D 25 '70
Unexpected universe, by L. Eiseley. Review
New Yorker 46:118+ F 21 '70. W. H.
Auden
See also
Cosmology
Solar system
UNIVERSITIES. See Colleges and universities
UNIVERSITIES national anti-war fund
Antiwar group raises $250,000. A. L. Hammond. Science 170:514 O 30 '70
UNIVERSITY, international. See International
university (proposed)
UNIVERSITY administration. See Colleges and
universities—Administration
UNIVERSITY athletics. See College athletics
UNIVERSITY bookstores. See College bookstores
UNIVERSITY centers for rational alternatives
Rational alternatives. Time 96:51 Ag 31 '70
UNIVERSITY Christian movement
Rise and fall of SVM. D. M. Howard. Chr
Today 15:15-17 N 6 '70
UNIVERSITY computing company
Creditor's grip on Ling and LTV. Bsns W
p54 O 17 '70
Too far, too fast. il Forbes 106:17-19 D 1 '70
UNIVERSITY drama. See College and school
drama
UNIVERSITY government. See Colleges and
universities—Administration
UNIVERSITY grants committee. See Colleges
and universities—Great Britain
UNIVERSITY investments. See Colleges and
universities—Investments
UNIVERSITY librarians. See College librarians
UNIVERSITY libraries. See College libraries
UNIVERSITY of Texas. See Texas. University

UNIVERSITY police force. See Colleges and universities—Security measures

UNIVERSITY presidents. See College presidents

UNIVERSITY presses
Be good editors by being good publishers; excerpts from address, September 13, 1970. M. Jeanneret. il Pub W 198:24-6 O 19 '70
1969 in review: book trade organizations. il Pub W 197:53 F 9 '70
University press sampler. America 122:47-53 Ja 17 '70
   See also
Association of American university presses
Chicago university press
Oxford university press
Wisconsin university press

UNIVERSITY professors. See College professors and instructors

UNIVERSITY professors, American association of. See American association of university professors

UNIVERSITY radio stations. See Radio stations

UNIVERSITY research. See Colleges and universities—Research

UNIVERSITY students. See College students

UNLEADED gasoline. See Gasoline—Additives

UNMANNED geophysical stations. See Geophysical stations

UNMARRIED mothers. See Mothers, Unmarried

UNMARRIED women. See Single women

UNORDERED merchandise. See Postal service —Unordered merchandise

UNOX process. See Sewage disposal—Activated sludge method

UNREGISTERED stocks. See Securities—Registration

UNRUH, D. R.
Pebbles; poem. Chr Today 14:11 My 22 '70
Salt; poem. Chr Today 14:10 F 27 '70

UNRUH, Fritz von
European literary scene. R. J. Clements. Sat R 53:23 S 5 '70 *

UNRUH, Jesse Marvin
Protesters, police, and politicians. Sat R 53: 31+ F 21 '70
   about
California: Jess Unruh, Populist. P. Kerby. Nation 211:393-6 O 26 '70 *
Center shifts right. J. R. Coyne, jr. Nat R 22: 1159-60 N 3 '70 *
Enough of Reagan? G. Lubenow. New Repub 162:14-15 F 14 '70 *
New Jess Unruh. D. Neff. por Time 96:17-18 S 14 '70 *
Oil on troubled waters. por Time 95:46 F 9 '70

UNSATISFIED man (periodical)
Unsatisfied newsmen. Time 96:89 S 21 '70

UNSEEN hand; drama. See Shepard, S.

UNSER, Al
Brother Al's turn in the 500. R. F. Jones. il por Sports Illus 32:30-1+ Je 8 '70 *
Mom Unser and the Indy chili caper. R. F. Jones. il por Sports Illus 32:28-9 My 25 '70 *
Why the rest of you are losers. J. Brokaw. il Motor T 23:52-7+ Ja '71 *

UNSINKABLE uniboats. See Sailboats

UNTERECKER, John
Photographs; poem. Poetry 115:330-3 F '70

UNTERMEYER, Louis
Interpretation of poetry; excerpt from The pursuit of poetry. Writers Digest 50:24-6 O '70

UNTIL tomorrow; story. See Sansbury, L.

UNTOUCHABLES
India: the politics of prejudice; long-ignored harijans. il Time 95:20-1 F 16 '70

UPDIKE, John
Bech swings? story. New Yorker 46:33-42 Mr 28 '70
Books. New Yorker 46:133-6 Ap 25 '70
Carol sing; story. New Yorker 46:36-7 D 19 '70
Deacon; story. New Yorker 46:38-41 F 21 '70
On an island; poem. Sat R 53:29 N 7 '70
Orphaned swimming pool; story. New Yorker 46:30-2 Je 27 '70
Rich in Russia; story. New Yorker 45:31-6 Ja 31 '70
Upon shaving off one's beard; poem. New Yorker 46:37 My 16 '70
   about
All the way with Updike. A. Broyard. por Life 68:12 Je 19 '70 *
Askew halo for John Updike. J. W. Aldridge. por Sat R 53:25-7+ Je 27 '70 *
Close reading and teaching; explication of Shillington. E. R. Ducharme. Engl J 59: 939-42 O '70 *

Comment. W. Heyen. Poetry 115:428 Mr '70 *
John Updike: midpoint and after. L. E. Sissman. Atlan 226:102-4 Ag '70 *
Poetry in the classroom: "Ex-basketball player." V. Busha. Engl J 59:643-5 My '70 *

UPDIKE, Richard W.
Walrus and the commodore, a puzzle in scrimshaw. il Antiques 98:263-5 Ag '70

UPDIKE, Ted
I hunted to eat. il por Outdoor Life 145:74-5+ My; 62-3+ Je; 146:56-9+ Jl; 52-5+ Ag '70

UPGREN, Arthur
Signals off. il Newsweek 75:80-1 My 18 '70 *

UPHOLSTERY fabrics. See Textile fabrics

UPJOHN company
FDA wins round in Panalba fight. N. Cruchow. Science 167:1710 Mr 27 '70
Tweedle dee. Forbes 105:65-6 Mr 1 '70

UPPER atmosphere. See Atmosphere, Upper

UPPER classes
Aristocracy is dead but society lives on. L. Auchincloss. il Holiday 47:50-1+ F '70
Those were the days, my friend; San Francisco society il Holiday 47:78 Mr '70

UPPER mantle project. See Earth—Internal structure

UPPMAN, Theodor
Chicago: Benjamin Britten's Billy Budd. J. W. Freeman. il por Opera N 35:36 D 19 '70 *
Return of Billy Budd. F. Rizzo. Opera N 35:16 O 31 '70 *

UPTON, Charles W.
Shaker utopia. il Antiques 98:582-7 O '70

UPTON, Miller
College president's open letter: "I apologize for the grotesque failure" of the campuses. por U S News 68:39 Je 15 '70

UPWARD bound (program) See Socially handicapped children—Education

URANIUM
Nuclear materials: security; address, May 25, 1970. C. Hosmer. Vital Speeches 36:635-8 Ag 1 '70
Puzzle from South Africa. Sci N 98:135 Ag 15 '70
South Africa: how valid the claim for a uranium process? D. S. Greenberg. Science 169:563 Ag 7 '70
Why uranium has run out of energy. il Bsns W p40 Ap 11 '70
   See also
Nuclear fuels

URANIUM mines and mining
Canada
   See also
Denison mines, ltd

URBAN administration. See Municipal government

URBAN coalition (organization)
Ellen Straus: the action of Call for action. il pors Vogue 155:124-5 Je '70
Is business cooling on city problems? il Bsns W p31-2 My 30 '70

URBAN corridor demonstration program. See Traffic engineering

URBAN design. See City planning

URBAN development corporation. See New York (state)—Urban development corporation

URBAN ecology. See Ecology

URBAN education. See Education, Urban

URBAN freeways. See Express highways

URBAN growth. See Cities and towns—Growth

URBAN housing. See Housing

URBAN league, National. See National urban league

URBAN life. See City and town life

URBAN parks. See Parks

URBAN poverty. See Poor—United States

URBAN redevelopment. See City planning; Urban renewal

URBAN renewal
Billions for urban renewal, but not enough to go around. il U S News 68:27-8 Ap 20 '70
Heavy fighting shakes Model cities. Bsns W p65 Ag 1 '70
Liveable cities. D. G. Alexander. bibliog f Cur Hist 59:85-90+ Ag '70
Model cities, model for failure: East New York section of Brooklyn. D. Stoloff. Arch Forum 132:78-9+ Ja '70
New architects. il Newsweek 75:59 My 4 '70
NRPA: model cities. Parks & Rec 5:53-6 Jl; 54-5 Ag '70
NRPA model cities contract ends. Parks & Rec 5:55-6 D '70
Rebuilding our cities: who wins? Who loses? slum clearance a form of black removal. il Sr Schol 97:16-21 O 26 '70

URBAN renewal—*Continued*
Resurrection; Model cities program. Newsweek 76:90 S 21 '70
Round to the mayors; federal aid bill. Newsweek 76:58-9 Jl 20 '70
See also
Business districts
City planning
Community organization
United States—Housing and urban development. Department of
Urban coalition (organization)
  also subhead City planning under names of cities, e.g. New York (city)—City planning

Michigan
See also
Pontiac, Mich.—Urban renewal

New York (state)
See also
New York (state)—Urban development corporation

Southern states
Apartheid U.S.A; Iron city; excerpts from The end of liberalism. T. J. Lowi. il Trans-Action 7:32-9 F '70
URBAN sociology. See Sociology, Urban
URBAN studies. See Sociology, Urban—Study and teaching
URBAN transit. See Local transit
URBAN transportation
Cars and cities on a collision course. A. T. Demaree. il Fortune 81:124-8+ F '70
How to move people in the cities. R. H. Gilluly. il Sci N 98:464-5 D 19 '70
Staving off auto paralysis. il Bsns W p54-6+ F 28 '70
Urban housing and transportation: a new partnership. W. Owen. bibliog f Cur Hist 59:290-5+ N '70
See also
Local transit
Moving platforms
Subways

Germany (Federal Republic)
Germany ducks into subways. il Bsns W p 135 Mr 21 '70
URBANA, Ill.
Education
Local associations of the month. J. Pittman and C. Thomasson. Todays Ed 59:80 O '70
URBANISM. See Cities and towns
URBANIZATION
Concrete cage; excerpts from Urbanization and the countryside. R. J. Benthem. il UNESCO Courier 23:54-60 Ag '70
Evolution of a super-urban nation. il Bsns W p76+ O 17 '70
Frontier freedoms and space age cities; excerpt. C. W. Griffin, jr. il Sat R 53:17-19+ F 7 '70
Lake Tahoe: then & now. D. Anderson. il Nat Parks & Con Mag 44:4-11 Ap '70
On population and environment; address, June 8, 1970. P. M. Hauser. Vital Speeches 36:696-701 S 1 '70
See also
Rural-urban migration
URBANIZED areas. See Metropolitan areas
URCHINS, Sea. See Sea urchins
URDANG, Constance
Girl; poem. New Repub 163:21 N 28 '70
URDU poetry

Translations into English
Ghazals; tr. by A. Ahmad and W. S. Merwin. Ghalib. Poetry 116:335-42 Ag '70
UREA
Discriminating disease; sickle cell anemia treated with solution of urea. il Time 96:41 D 21 '70
Healing the sickle cells. il Newsweek 76:77 D 14 '70
Hydroxyurea; suppression of two-stage carcinogenesis in mouse skin. P. C. Chan and others. bibliog il Science 168:130-2 Ap 3 '70
UREDOSPORES. See Spores (botany)
UREMIA
See also
Kidneys, Artificial
URIC acid
Uric acid=high intelligence? A. J. Snider. Sci Digest 68:63 D '70
See also
Lesch-Nyhan syndrome
URINARY organs
See also
Kidneys

Diseases
Avoiding voiding; danger; infections of the urinary tract. il Time 96:44 Ag 17 '70
URINE
See also
Urea

Analysis
Calcium oxalate; crystallographic analysis in solid aggregates in urinary sediments. F. Catalina and L. Cifuentes. bibliog il Science 169:183-4 Jl 10 '70
Spherical urine in birds; petrography. R. L. Folk; discussion. bibliog Science 169:1230-1; 170:98-9 S 18, O 2 '70

Incontinence
It wasn't me who wet. B. Bettelheim. Ladies Home J 87:62+ Mr '70
Kidneys in health and in disease; bedwetting. L. W. Sauer. PTA Mag 65:25-6 O '70
URIS, Auren
Do you need a new right hand? il Nations Bsns 58:72-4+ Jl '70
URIST, Marshall R. See Huggins, C. B. jt. auth.
UROKINASE. See Kinases
URRY, D. W. See Ohnishi, M. jt. auth.
URTAIN, José Manuel Ibar
Número uno. il por Time 95:60 Ap 20 '70 *
URUGUAY
Uruguay. T. J. King. il Travel 134:40-5 O '70
See also
Guerrillas—Uruguay
URVANT, Ellen
View from VISTA. il Am For 76:8+ S '70
URY, Claude M.
Career-related guidance for youth. bibliog il por Wilson Lib Bul 44:621-31 F '70
USDIN, Gene L. See Weihofen, H. jt. auth.
USED automobiles. See Automobiles, Used
USED boats. See Boats, Used
USED cameras. See Cameras, Used
USED car industry. See Automobile industry and trade—Used cars
USED furniture. See Furniture, Used
USED planes. See Airplanes, Used
USED yachts. See Yachts, Used
USERY, Willie J. 1923-
Architect of labor peace. por Bsns W p 114+ S 12 '70 *
USTINOV, Peter
Motor trend interview. il pors Motor T 22:98+ My '70
Peter Ustinov plays Santa to the children of many nations. A. Levy. il pors Good H 171:38-40+ D '70 *
USURY laws
Defense of usury. M. Friedman. Newsweek 75:79 Ap 6 '70
UTAH
See also
Banks and banking—Utah
Bird sanctuaries—Utah
Brigham Young university, Provo
Bryce Canyon National Park
Capitol Reef National Monument
Colleges and universities—Utah
Festivals—Utah
Geology—Utah
Great Salt Lake
Law—Utah
Monument Valley
Mormons and Mormonism
Paleobotany—Utah
Powell, Lake
Roads—Utah

Description and travel
Red cliffs and the Colorado. il Sunset 145:34+ Jl '70

Parks and reserves
Coral dunes. J. W. Krutch. il Travel & Camera 33:38-41 Jl '70
UTAH. Southern Utah state college, Cedar City
Southern Utah state college adds a jewel. il Library J 95:849-50 Mr 1 '70
UTAH Stars (basketball team) See Basketball teams
UTAH. University, Salt Lake City
Usable history for the red man; Center for studies of the American West. J. Cass. Sat R 53:69 My 16 '70

Dance theatre
See Dance companies
UTERINE tumors. See Tumors
UTERMAHLEN, Brian
You can't just hand out orders. J. Saar. il pors Life 69:30-7 O 23 '70 *

UTERUS
Diurnal variation of spontaneous uterine activity in nonpregnant primates (macaca mulatta) G. M. Harbert, jr. and others. bibliog il Science 170:82-5 O 2 '70
Ontogeny of the estrogen receptor during early uterine development. J. H. Clark and J. Gorski. bibliog il Science 169:76-8 Jl 3 '70
See also
Placenta

Surgery
Myomectomy and hysterectomy: when and why each is necessary. Good H 170:187 Ap '70

UTILITIES, Public. See Public utilities
UTILITY poles. See Electric lines—Poles
UTILITY rates. See Public utilities—Rates
UTILIZATION of land. See Land utilization
UTLEY, Freda
All-out temperament. J. Chamberlain. Nat R 22:158 F 10 '70
Personal history. H. C. Wolfe. Sat R 53:31-2 Mr 28 '70 *
UTOPIAS
End of Utopia; excerpts from Five lectures. H. Marcuse. il Ramp Mag 8:28-34 Ap '70
Needed: a new utopianism. H. Wheeler. Cur 121:30-1 S '70
Voyage to Utopia in the year 1971; Time essay. E. Warner. il Time 97:18-19 Ja 18 '71
See also
Imaginary societies
UTTAL, Leonard J.
Black maple. Horticulture 48:61-3 Mr '70
UTTAR Pradesh
See also
Almora, India
UVALDE, Tex
Side by side, and a world apart, in Uvalde, Texas; Mexican Americans. il Newsweek 75: 24 Je 29 '70
UYLENBROECK, Marcel
Old-time dialogue. Commonweal 92:355-7 Jl 24 '70; Discussion. 92:427+ S 4 '70
UYS, Stanley
No to Arthur Ashe. New Repub 162:17-18 F 14 '70
UZZLE, Burk
Gallery; photographs. Il Life 68:4-7 F 6 '70

V

VA. See United States—Veterans administration
VA hospitals. See United States—Veterans administration hospitals
VAT. See Value added tax
VD. See Venereal diseases
V-E day
V-E day: Europe's separate fates; Moscow, Bonn, Prague. il Time 95:28-30 My 18 '70
VFO (variable frequency oscillator) See Oscillators
VIC (Vision information center) See Harvard university—Medical school—Library
VOM. See Voltohmmeters
VTOL airplanes. See Airplanes, Vertical take-off and landing
VTR (video tape recorder) See Video recorders and recording
VTVM (vacuum tube voltmeters) See Voltmeters
VACATION cabins. See Cabins
VACATION houses
Benenson house, Hawley, Pa. il Arch Rec 147:82-5 mid-My '70
Custom house that budget built. il Am Home 73:52-3 Jl '70
Dome home. B. Berger. il Mech Illus 66:100+ O '70
Good life for all seasons; symposium. il Am Home 73:43-59 Ja 70
Great homes for vacation living. H. Wicks. il Pop Mech 133:132-9 Ap '70
Grey house, Wellfleet, Mass. il Arch Rec 147: 80-1 mid-My '70
Haven in New England snows; ski house of the Neil Goodwins'. B. Plumb. il Am Home 73:52-5+ D '70
Home away from home; symposium. il House B 112:29-57 Ag '70
Indoor-outdoor house. N. Skurka. il N Y Times Mag p70-1 O 4 '70
Lakefront hideaway in the Berkshires. il Am Home 73:62-5 S '70

Maybe you can afford a second home. R. Day. il Mech Illus 66:50-2+ Ap '70
Moon house; a vacation house of ideas in Tunisia; interview. G. Berthelot. il House & Gard 137:120-3 Mr '70
More weekend-house planners throw away the rule book. il Sunset 144:94-9 My '70
Need an extra house to play in? il Life 69: 66-9+ Jl 10 '70
New way to afford a second home. D Green. il Mech Illus 66:65-7+ F '70
On the up and up; Nassau tower house. il N Y Times Mag p40-1 Jl 12 '70
Outside it faces six ways into the Utah snows, inside is a grand fireplace, a sleeping balcony. il Sunset 144: 82-3 Ja '70
Package house with individuality. il Bet Hom & Gard 48:40-1 Ja '70
Prefabs: summer homes for the cost conscious. Bsns W p 105 Je 27 '70
Private residence, western North Carolina. il Arch Rec 147:46-7 mid-My '70
Retreat in the trees, ready in two weeks. il House B 112:74-9 S '70
Snow castle for skiers. il House B 112:100-7 N '70
Some weekend-house planners throw away the rule book. il Sunset 144:104-9 Ap '70
Three-family co-op in western ski country; octagonal ski house in Bear Valley, Calif. il Am Home 73:56-7 D '70
Three houses built for summer. il House & Gard 137:86-95 Je '70
Vacation home for $1200. M. Seif. il Mech Illus 66:80-3+ Je '70
Vacation homes you buy by mail. D. Huff. il Pop Sci 196:90-3 Mr '70
We did it; vacation house out of a caboose, ed. by E. Kinard. il House B 112:52+ My '70
Weekend house for entertaining; C. Owen's house on Block Island. il House & Gard 138:82-5 D '70
Weekend house must be simple to run; interview. C. Owen. por House & Gard 138: 26+ D '70
Winged weekend flight; Greenport, N.Y. il House B 112:68-71 D '70
See also
Beach architecture

Costs
Vacation home living '70. J. H. Ingersoll. House B 112:52-3+ Ag '70

Leasing and renting
Our home on Barbados; renting a house in the Caribbean. F. S. Friedman. il Travel & Camera 32:24+ Ja '70
Useful things to find out about that cottage you've rented. il Changing T 24:30 Jl '70
VACATION projects
Summer fun with the family. PTA Mag 64: 29-30 Je '70
VACATION schools. See School year; Summer schools
VACATION villages
Caribbean hideaways. G. Koretz. il Travel & Camera 33:60-3 Ja '70
Guadeloupe: French escape route for swingers; Club Mediterranee. J. Star. il Look 34:22-7 Mr 10 '70
New migratory paths; Xanadu clubs. il Harp Baz 103:52 Je '70
New spice in Creole country; Club Méditerranée on Martinique and Guadeloupe. D. Butwin. il Sat R 53:50+ Ap 18 '70
Summer of Europe's content; Club Méditerranée vacation village at Donoratico, Italy. J. Shaw. il Time 96:24+ Ag 10 '70
Sun-and-ski clubs take a single room; Club Mediterranée-Club European du Tourisme merger. Bsns W p47 Ja 24 '70
Which way back to the land? new recreation communities. R. Rodale. il Org Gard & Farm 17:57-60 D '70
VACATIONS
Advantages of making summer plans now. il Good H 170:193 Mr '70
America in search of ease. il Time 96:10-11 Jl 20 '70
Fly and drive and explore! H. Bims. il Ebony 25:156-60+ Je '70
Get away from it all, without leaving home. il Changing T 24:35-6 Ag '70
Great American vacation scenes. B. Gillam. Mlle 70:258-61+ Ap '70
Holiday on a farm. V. Block. il Parents Mag 45:42-3+ Je '70
How about a nice cool fall vacation? il Changing T 24:11-12 O '70
How to cut vacation and travel costs. Good H 170:145-7 Je '70
How to get more out of your vacation. W. Cross. Read Digest 96:113-16 Mr '70

VACATIONS—*Continued*
1970 traveler's zodiac. C. Pepper. il **Travel** 133:57-9+ Ja '70
$100 vacation $1000 entertainment. R. Varick. Har Yrs 10:30-1 My '70
100 perfect vacations. il Travel & Camera 33: 53-64 Jl '70
100 vacations in fifty states. M. Gough. House B 112:42+ Je '70
Ranch vacations. B. Thomas. il **Travel** 133: 36-42 My '70
Redbook's guide to honeymoons and other vacations. R. Deardorff. il Redbook 136:35-42 N '70
Sailing vacation for new salts. S. L. Englebardt. il Todays Health 48:36-9+ Jl '70
Sporting outing; Air France European tours. il Travel 134:16 N '70
Summer nomads; the fun and frustration of Americans on the move. il Life 69:20-46B Ag 14 '70
Swap that view; Vacation exchange club. P. Mann. Travel & Camera 33:8+ D '70
Vacationing in the great outdoors. N. D. Ford. il Har Yrs 10:6-14 F '70
Vacations abroad, with a difference. il U S News 68:58-61 Ap 27 '70
Vacations out West: 1970 style. il U S News 68:62-5 Je 22 '70
Where famous people go. B. Gillam. Mlle 71:154-6 Je '70
Where to go; ed. by V. T. Sparano. See issues of Outdoor life
Winter in Italy. W. Weaver. Harp Baz 103: 88 O '70
See also
Travel
VACATIONS, Employee
Vacation bonus, minus paycheck. Bsns W p26 Jl 18 '70
VACCA, Richard S.
Judicial opinion and the role of teachers. bibliog Clear House 45:240-4 D '70
VACCINATION
Growing controversy over smallpox vaccination. il Good H 170:195 Mr '70
Smallpox vaccinations in Africa; statement on the occasion of the 100 millionth vaccination. R. M. Nixon. Dept State Bul 61: 634 D 29 '69
Vaccine controversy. J. Bockel. il Sci N 97: 129-30 Ja 31 '70
See also
Tetanus—Vaccination
VACCINES
See also subhead Vaccines under various diseases, e.g. Tuberculosis—Vaccines
VACUUM
Vacuums, the pursuit of practically nothing. R. J. Bronikowski. il Sci Digest 67:52-6 Mr '70
VACUUM cleaners
Vacuum cleaner you hardly have to push: Hoover dial-a-matic 1170. il Consumer Rep 35:458-9 Ag '70
Vacuum cleaners. Consumer Rep 34:53-60 D '69
Vacuum cleaners. il Consumer Bul 53:18-25 O '70
See also
Hoover company
VACUUM cleaning
Central vacuum cleaning system. J. Capotosto. il Mech Illus 66:132-4 O '70
VACUUM lifter. See Hoisting machinery
VACUUM sweepers, Street. See Street cleaning apparatus
VACUUM tubes
New tubes and semiconductors. Radio-Electr 41:86 Mr; 91 S; 91 N '70
See also
Electron tubes
Klystrons
VADSTENA, Sweden

Music
Report:
Production of Chi soffre, speri by Virgilio Mazzochi and Marco Marazzoli. E. Redvall. il Opera N 35:29 O 31 '70
VAGRANCY
Moral career of a bum; excerpt from You owe yourself a drunk. J. P. Spradley. il Trans-Action 7:16-29 My '70
VAHLSING, Fred, Jr
Case of sour sugar. il por Time 95:12 F 9 '70
That mess on the Prestile. F. Graham, jr. il Am Heritage 21:106-12 F '70; Discussion. 21:94-5 Ag '70
VAHOUNY, George V. and others
Preparation of beating heart cells from adult rats. bibliog il Science 167:1616-18 Mr 20 '70

VAID, Ranjan
Girl without a country. il por Time 95:31-2 F 23 '70 *
VAIL, Edward O.
What will it be? Reading or machismo and soul? Clear House 45:92-6 O '70
VAIL, Theodore Newton
Making a business out of Mr Bell's invention. C. E. Wampler. il pors Nations Bsns 58:48-9 Ja '70
VALDEZ, George V.
Rescue on the Freeway. J. P. Blank. il Read Digest 96:73-7 My '70 *
VAL D'ISÈRE avalanche. See Avalanches
VALENCE (chemistry)
See also
Molecular orbitals
VALENCIA, Calif.
New city for the '70s. A. Flynn. il Am City 85:84+ O '70
VALENCIA, Spain
Profiles. K. Tynan. il New Yorker 46:33-8+ Jl 25 '70
VALENTI, Jack
Valenti papers. New Yorker 46:32-3 S 12 '70 *
VALENTINE, Helen
Young wife's world. See issues of Good housekeeping
VALENTINE, James W. and Lipps, J. H.
Marine fossils at Rancho La Brea. il Science 169:277-8 Jl 17 '70
VALENTINE, Jean
Comment. R. Watson. Poetry 117:206-7 D '70 *
VALENTINE, Richard J.
Build a time base calibrator. il Pop Electr 34:33-5+ Ja '71
VALENTINES
Pretty personal Valentines K. Hillyard. il Har Yrs 10:26-7 F '70
VALENTINES day

Drama
Is Cupid stupid? A. C. Martens. Plays 29:1-10 F '70
VALENTINO
Valentino's Roman roof-top. il por Vogue 155:148-53 Ap 15 '70
VALENTRY, Duane
Fish to control mosquitoes. il Sea Front 16: 231-3 Jl '70
No anchor for tanker. il Sea Front 16:110-11 Mr '70
VALIANT (yacht) See Yachts—Design
VALINOMYCIN. See Antibiotics
VALLELI, Paul A.
Astronomical league convenes in Rochester. il Sky & Tel 40:149-51 S '70
VALLEY of Fire state park. See Nevada—Parks and reserves
VALLOTTON, Félix Édouard
Félix the Nabi. H. A. LaFarge. il por Art N 69:48-9+ Ap '70 *
VALOVIC, T.
Historical Jesus tomorrow; poem. Chr Cent 87:962 Ag 12 '70
VALSE fantaisie; ballet. See Ballets—Criticisms
VALUATION
See also
Depreciation
Real property—Valuation
VALUE
See also
Cost
VALUE (philosophy) See Worth
VALUE (psychology)
Middle-class values; excerpts from article. E. A. Roberts, jr; T. B. Roberts. il Todays Ed 59:20-3 Ja '70
Values as social indicators of poverty and race relations in America. M. Rokeach and S. Parker. bibliog f il Ann Am Acad 388:97-111 Mr '70
VALUE added tax
How to revive capital spending. il Bsns W p58 Ag 22 '70
Treasury mulls a different bite; value-added concept. Bsns W p44 Ag 1 '70
Value-added tax: the case against. S. S. Surrey. il Harvard Bsns R 48:86-94 N '70
Value-added tax: the case for. D. T. Smith. il Harvard Bsns R 48:77-85 N '70
Where's the money coming from? value-added tax. il Forbes 105:20-1 F 15 '70
Will this be our next tax? value-added tax. W. Langewiesche. Read Digest 97:132-6 S '70
VALUES, Social. See Social values
VALVE train evaluator. See Automobile engines—Testing
VALVES
See also
Automobile engines—Valves

VAN ALLEN, Rodger
Problems ahead for the lay theologian. il
Cath World 212:37-9 O '70
VAN ALLEN radiation belts
Mystery of protons in space. Space World
G-12-84:16-17 D '70
VANANTWERP, Malin
Primary prevention: a challenge to mental
health associations. bibliog Ment Hy 54:
453-6 Jl '70
VANCE, Adrian
Cut loose with your Colorpack. il Pop Phot
67:98-9+ Ag '70
VANCE, Joel M.
Uncle Al's good deed. il Field & S 75:52-3+
N '70
We didn't do nothing, mom; story. Field & S
74:64-5 Mr '70
VANCIL, Richard F.
Accuracy of long-range planning. il Harvard
Bsns R 48:98-101 S '70
VANCOUVER, British Columbia
Vancouver: emerging city. J. Brooks. il
Travel & & Camera 33:60 Je '70

Architecture
Twin towers in Canada. J. S. Margolies. il
Arch Forum 132:42-7 Ap '70

Art
Vancouver: scene and unscene; interview with
artists, curators, dealers and critics; ed.
by. P. Selz. il Art in Am 58:122-6 Ja '70

Buildings
Building in the Doric tradition; MacMillan
Bloedel building. il Arch Rec 147:123-8 Ap
'70

Description
Gas of a town. D. Butwin. il Sat R 53:48+ N
28 '70

Sanitary affairs
Extra steps cut complaints. il Am City 85:68-9
Jl '70
VANCOUVER Canuks (hockey team) See Hoc-
key teams
VANCOUVER ISLAND
Quadra's and Vancouver's island. M. B. Mc-
Guire. il por Américas 22:2-8 Jl '70
VANCOUVER opera association
Report:
Production of Aida. F. B. St Clair. Opera
N 35:32 N 21 '70
Production of La Bohème. F. B. St Clair.
Opera N 34:28 Ap 11 '70
VANDA cosmetics company
Can Dart take on Avon? T. J. Murray. por
Duns 97:57-8+ Ja '71
VANDALISM
Take me out of the ball game; rowdies get
into the sports act. W. Bingham. il Sports
Illus 32:22-3 Ap 27 '70
VANDALS
Barbarians. R. Winston. il Horizon 12:66-81
Sum '70
VAN DE GRAAFF accelerators. See Accelera-
tors (electrons, etc)
VAN DE KAMP, Peter
Barnard's star: the search of other solar sys-
tems; with biographical sketch. il Natur
Hist 79:4+, 38-43 Ap '70
**VAN DELINDER, Roy, Jr. and St Germain, R.
H.**
Model four-stage grievance procedure. Todays
Ed 59:33-40 F '70
VANDELL, Robert F.
Management evolution in the quantitative
world. il Harvard Bsns R 48:83-92 Ja '70
VAN DEN BOSCH, Robert
Pesticides: prescribing for the ecosystem. il
Environ 12:20-5 Ap '70
VANDENBURGH, Mildred
I dreamed of playing the organ. il Har Yrs
10:33-4 N '70
Traveler's choice. Travel 133:22 Ap '70
VAN DEN HAAG, Ernest
Do pacifists harm peace? il Nat R 22:1344-
5+ D 15 '70
What's missing in Nixon's welfare program.
Nat R 22:85-7+ Ja 27 '70
Women: how equal? Nat R 22:945+ S 8 '70
VANDERBEEK, Stan
New talent: the computer. il por Art in Am
58:86-91 Ja '70
VANDERBILT, Amy
Monthly column. See issues of Ladies' home
journal
VANDERBILT, Byron M.
Thomas Edison: pioneer of applied chemistry.
il pors Chem 43:8-12 S '70
VANDERBILT, Gloria
Gloria, hallelujah. E. Sheppard. Harp Baz
103:142-3 F '70

Gloria the great's patchwork bedroom. il
por Vogue 155:206-9+ F 1 '70
How to turn out your own romantic wrap-
pings. il por House & Gard 138:48-51 D
'70
VANDERBILT university, Nashville, Tenn.
Academic ambassador. por Newsweek 75:69
My 25 '70
B-school for entrepreneurs of change. il por
Bsns W p82+ Ap 25 '70
VANDERBURGH County public library. See
Evansville, Ind. public library
VAN DER LINDEN, Frank
Spiro T. Agnew: vice president extraordinary.
por Read Digest 97:123-7 O '70
**VAN DER VEER, Virginia. See Hamilton, V.
V.**
VANDERVELDE, Marjorie
Pryor priority. il Travel 134:54-5+ D '70
VANDERVOORT, Paul, 2d
Calligraphy in the curriculum. il Sch Arts
70:34-6 D '70
VANDERWALL, Judith
Expo '70: Japan's world fair at Osaka. il Am
Artist 34:22-6+ Ap '70
VANDER WERF, Lester S.
Militancy and the profession of teaching. Sch
& Soc 98:171-3 Mr '70
VAN DERZEE, James
Beautiful people of James Van DerZee. il
pors Ebony 25:85-8+ O '70 •
VANDERZICHT, John R.
Race between education and catastrophe. il
Parks & Rec 5:29-32+ Ja '70
VAN DEVANTER, Ann C.
Holy family attributed to Benjamin West.
il Antiques 98:774-5 N '70
VAN DINE, Alan
Thank you, ladies; poem. Sat R 53:24 N 14
'70
VAN DORE, Wade
Robert Frost and wilderness. por Liv Wildn
34:47-9 Sum '70
VAN DOREN, Mark
Comment. R. B. Shaw. Poetry 117:115 N '70 •
VAN DUYN, Mona
Possibility after possibility. R. Howard. Na-
tion 210:536-8 My 4 '70 •
Seven women. Poetry 115:430-9 Mr '70
VAN DYKE, Knox, and others
Quinacrine: mechanisms of antimalarial ac-
tion. bibliog il Science 169:492-3 Jl 31 '70
VAN DYKE, Robert P.
Salvage what you can. il Am City 85:70-1
O '70
VANE family
Vane coat-of-arms. H. K. Eilers. il Hob-
bies 75:148 S '70
VANES. See Weather vanes
**VAN FLANDERN, T. C. See Martin, C. F. jt.
auth.**
**VAN HOOSE, William H. See Pietrofesa. J. J.
jt. auth.**
VAN HORNE, Harriet
Generation of tyrants. il Good H 170:102-3+
Mr '70
Summer is... il House B 112:48-9+ Je '70
VANISHING animals. See Rare animals
VANISHING birds. See Rare birds
VAN ITALLIE, Jean-Claude
Serpent. Criticism
Nation 210:765-6 Je 22 '70 •
New Yorker 46:90 Je 13 '70 •
VANITY. See Pride and vanity
VANITY surgery. See Surgery, Plastic
VAN MATRE, Steve
Counselor hair styles. Camp Mag 42:15-16 My
'70
VAN PELT, W. F. and others
Laser. il Radio-Electr 42:58-60 Ja '71 (to be
cont)
VANSICKLE, Reata M.
Traveler's choice. Travel 133:17 Mr '70
VAN THIEL, David H. and others
Pregnancies after chemotherapy of tropho-
blastic neoplasms. bibliog il Science 169:
1326-7 S 25 '70
**VAN TWYVER, Henry. See Allison. T. jt.
auth.**
VAN VOLKENBURG, Donald R.
Easy-to-make time/distance/speed scales. il
Motor B 126:34 Ag '70
Tin boats of Scrog Lake. il Motor B 126:52-5+
D '70
VAN WAGENEN, Pamela
Beauty scene (title varies) See issues of
Parents' magazine & better family living
Stay young and beautiful (title varies) See
issues of Parents' magazine & better fam-
ily living
VAN WICKLEN, Ellie
Doing the garden homework. il Org Gard
& Farm 17:62-5 Mr '70
Prime step in fourteen-day composting. il
Org Gard & Farm 17:40-1 D '70

VAN WORMER, Joe
Honker. il Nat Wildlife 8:12-15 O '70
North American ducks. il Nat Wildlife 7:23-
8 O '69
VAN ZANDT, Howard F.
How to negotiate in Japan. bibliog f il Har-
vard Bsns R 48:45-56 N '70
Japanese culture and the business boom.
For Affairs 48:344-57 Ja '70
VAN ZANDT, Roland
Wilson in the promise land. Criticism
New Yorker 46:49 Je 6 '70 *
Newsweek 75:90 Je 8 '70 *
VAN ZELE, Helen
African violets. il Horticulture 48:30-2 N '70
VANZETTI, Bartolomeo
See also
Sacco-Vanzetti case
VAPOR fractionation. See Separation (technol-
ogy)
VAPORIZATION
See also
Sublimation
VAPORIZERS
Vaporizers: the new safety features to look
for. D. Quentzel. il Good H 171:178+ N '70
VARADYNE, inc.
Varadyne goes the full circuit. il Bsns W
p58 Jl 18 '70
VARDAMAN, James M.
Smartest fellow around. il Am For 76:8+
N '70
VARDIKOS, Nicholas
Greek talk. W. F. Buckley, jr. Nat R 22:272-
3 Mr 10 '70 *
VARIABLE annuities. See Annuities
VARIABLE capacitors. See Electric capacitors
VARIABLE frequency oscillators. See Oscilla-
tors
VARIABLE-rate mortgages. See Mortgages
VARIABLE stars. See Stars, Variable
VARIABLE voltage transformers. See Electric
transformers
VARIAN, Elayne H.
New dealing. il Art in Am 58:68-73 Ja '70
VARIAN associates
Computers make fertile parents; instrument-
ation systems built around computers. il
Bsns W p55+ N 28 '70
VARIATION (biology)
Genetic variation of cholesterol ester con-
tent in mouse adrenals. C. H. Doering and
others. bibliog il Science 170:1220-2 D 11 '70
See also
Mosaics (biology)
VARIATION (botany)
Hydroxy-L-proline- and 2,2'-dipyridyl-induced
phenovariations in the liverwort Nowellia
curifolia. D. V. Basile. bibliog il Science
170:1218-20 D 11 '70
VARIATION (music)
See also
Embellishment (music)
VARICK, Rose
$100 vacation $1000 entertainment. Har Yrs
10:30-1 My '70
VARICOSE veins
Every woman's guide to varicose veins. P.
Ardman and H. Ardman. Ladies Home J
87:46+ My '70
VARNISH and varnishing
Expert varnishing. A. Hemenway. il Yachting
127:74-5+ Ap '70
See also
Furniture—Finishing
VARONA, José
When is a costume? il por Opera N 34:26-9 F
8 '70
VARS, Gordon F.
Student evaluation. il Clear House 45:18-21
S '70
VASARELY, Victor
Craftsman for today, dreamer for tomorrow.
il Time 95:56-8 Je 22 '70 *
Dreaming a city. D. Davis. il por Newsweek
76:87 Jl 6 '70 *
VASARY, Támas
Recordings; live concert in London. M.
Mayer. Esquire 74:238-9 O '70 *
VASCULAR lesions. See Cardiovascular sys-
tem—Diseases
VASCULAR surgery. See Blood vessels—Sur-
gery
VASCULAR system. See Cardiovascular sys-
tem
VAS DIAS, Robert
Planet/plasma; poem. Nation 210:251 Mr 2
'70
Through the automatic carwash; poem. New
Yorker 46:90 Ap 18 '70
VASECTOMY. See Sterilization, Sexual

VASES
How to turn a wood vase that holds water.
R. Capotosto. il Pop Sci 196:179-81 Ja '70
Reform art for a reform era. R. Blasberg. il
Craft Horiz 30:24-7 O '70
VASES, Greek
Some trick Greek vases. J. V. Noble. il Ce-
ram Mo 18:18-23 Ja '70
VASOPRESSIN
[8-arginine]-vasopressinoic acid; an inhibi-
tor of rabbit kidney adenyl cyclase. T.
Dousa and others. bibliog il Science 167:
1134-5 F 20 '70
Vasopressin: effect on deformability of uri-
nary surface of collecting duct cells. J. J.
Grantham. bibliog il Science 168:1093-5 My
29 '70
VASSAR college, Poughkeepsie, N.Y.
Meanwhile...back at Vassar. W. J. McKean.
il Look 34:28+ F 24 '70
VATH, William R.
Safe fireworks? There aren't any. il Todays
Health 48:50-1 Je '70
VATICAN
Vatican's second front; Latin America's chief
provider? J. Deedy. Commonweal 92:234 My
22 '70
See also
Catholic church—Relations (diplomatic)
Papacy

Finance
How rich is the Vatican? Newsweek 76:47 Ag
3 '70
Riches untold? Chr Today 14:43 Ag 21 '70
Wealthy Vatican. America 123:51 Ag 8 '70
RADIO stations
Vatican radio. R. R. Holton. Cath World
211:7-12 Ap '70

Sistine chapel
Ceiling on the wall; exhibition of photo-
graphs of the Sistine ceiling. M. R. Weiss.
il Sat R 53:50-1 D 5 '70
VATICAN broadcasting station. See Vatican—
Radio stations
VATICAN CITY
See also
Rome (city)
VATICAN council, 1869-1870
New look at Vatican I. T. Early. il Chr Cent
87:815-18 Jl 1 '70
Silent centennial. G. C. Berkouwer. Chr To-
day 14:55-6 S 11 '70
VATICAN council, 2d
John XXIII, Vatican II, and American Ca-
tholicism. E. C. Bianchi. Ann Am Acad
387:30-40 Ja '70
VATICAN council, 3d (proposed)
Myths, meaning and Vatican III. A. M. Gree-
ley. America 123:538-42 D 19 '70
VATICAN guards. See Papal guards
VATICAN radio. See Vatican—Radio stations
VAUDEVILLE
Grinding to a halt; Cincinnati's Gayety bur-
lesk. il Time 95:56 Ap 27 '70
Their hearts belong to daddy; report by
sociologists on stripteasers. il Time 96:41
Jl 6 '70
VAUGHAN, C. Edwin
Co-curricular program for higher education.
bibliog f Sch & Soc 98:29-30 Ja '70
VAUGHAN, Elaine
My special miracle. Todays Ed 59:45 N '70
VAUGHAN, Henry
Poetry of Henry Vaughan. M. W. Hess. Chr
Today 15:15-17 Ja 1 '71 *
VAUGHAN WILLIAMS, Ralph
Heirs and rebels. K. F. Reuling. il pors Opera
N 34:12-15 Ja 24 '70
Riders to the sea. Criticism
New Yorker 45:78 F 7 '70 *
VAUGHAN WILLIAMS, Ursula
Heirs and rebels. K. F. Reuling. il pors Opera
N 34:12-15 Ja 24 '70
VAUGHN, Charles L.
What you need to know before you buy a
franchise; questions and answers. por Pop
Mech 133:25-6+ F '70
VAUGHN, William E.
Master mariners race. il Motor B 125:54-6+
My '70
VAUS, Jim
Where are they now? il pors Newsweek 75:
12 Je 29 '70 *
VAUX, John H.
Cement sculpting in high school. il Sch Arts
70:24-5 N '70
VAZ, Nelson M. and Levine, B. B.
Immune responses of inbred mice to repeat-
ed low doses of antigen: relationship to
histocompatibility (H-2) type. bibliog il
Science 168:852-4 My 15 '70

VEAL
See also
Cookery—Meat
VEALE, W. L. See Myers, R. D. jt. auth.
VEATCH, Jeannette
Let's put the joy back in reading. il por Library J 95:1899-901 My 15 '70
(ed) Right to read: what does it mean? bibliog il Library J 95:1899-910+ My 15 '70
VEAZEY, George
My most unforgettable character. il Read Digest 97:145-6+ N '70
VEAZEY, Ulysse
My most unforgettable character. G. Veazey. il Read Digest 97:145-6+ N '70 *
VEECK, Bill
Bill Veeck is off to the races. L. Merchant. il pors Look 34:68+ Je 30 '70 *
Sports. R. Kahn. Esquire 74:34+ O '70 *
VEEDER industries, inc.
Veeder's windfall. A. A. Butkus. por Duns 96:59 O '70
VEEH, H. Herbert, and Chappell, John
Astronomical theory of climate change: support from New Guinea. bibliog il Science 167:862-5 F 6 '70
VEENSTRA, John G.
Microimages and the library. bibliog il por Library J 95:3443-7 O 15 '70
VEGA, Janine Pommy-. See Pommy-Vega, J.
VEGETABLE canneries. See Canneries
VEGETABLE drinks. See Beverages
VEGETABLE gardening
Presenting Thurston DeHaan, organic gardener. F. Hilliker. il pors Org Gard & Farm 17:28-31 O '70
See also
Beans
Companion crops
Peas
VEGETABLE gardening, Home
Bountiful harvest bouquet; ed. by E. Haraszty. R. E. Atkinson. il McCalls 98:50+ O '70
Doing the garden homework. E. Van Wicklen. il Org Gard & Farm 17:62-5 Mr '70
Fifty kinds of food on a city lot. H. P. Barstow. il por Org Gard & Farm 17:38-41 Jl '70
Gourmet foods for little gardens. H. F. Dale. Horticulture 48:12-14 My '70
Gourmet gardeners like 'em small! N. W. Bubel. il pors Org Gard & Farm 17:120-2 Mr '70
Imagine gardening in a new climate! E. A. Freytag. il Org Gard & Farm 17:96-9 Mr '70
No-work vegetable garden. K. McReynolds. il Org Gard & Farm 17:76-7 Ag '70
Organic gardeners grow 'em big! M. C. Goldman. il Org Gard & Farm 17:30-4 Je '70
Roses in the vegetable garden. N. P. Farris. il Org Gard & Farm 17:46-8 My '70
Should you grow your own vegetables? R. M. Carleton. il Home Gard 57:34-42 F '70
Sourdough Jack's garden bonanza. J. O'Rourke. il pors Org Gard & Farm 17:46-8 Je '70
Start tomatoes and eggplant indoors. L. Riotte. il por Org Gard & Farm 17:48-9 Mr '70
Still time to sow a tossed salad. G. Abraham. il Home Gard 57:36-7 Ag '70
To fill the freezer, plant for the insects and yourself. J. J. Dicker. il por Org Gard & Farm 17:69-71 Mr '70
Vegetables that were good to us. B. Wahlfeldt. Org Gard & Farm 17:88-9 Ap '70
Why? And why not? R. Stout. il pors Org Gard & Farm 17:43-5 O '70
See also
Childrens gardens
Cold frames
VEGETABLE glazes. See Glazing (food)
VEGETABLE protein foods. See Food substitutes
VEGETABLE salads. See Salads
VEGETABLES
Annuals and vegetables; new introductions for 1971. il Horticulture 49:18-21+ Ja '71
Vegetables that were good to us. B. Wahlfeldt. Org Gard & Farm 17:88-9 Ap '70
See also
Canning and preserving
Cookery—Vegetables
Greens, Edible
Vegetable gardening, Home
Vegetarianism
also names of vegetables, e.g. Sweet potatoes

Marketing
Boy plus zucchini equals good eating and pocket money. N. W. Bubel. il Org Gard & Farm 17:90-3 Ap '70

Storage
Expert salad storage. il Bet Hom & Gard 48:104 My '70
Use the whole outdoors for vegetable storage over winter. J. Preston. il Org Gard & Farm 17:39 S '70
Winter salad greens by the tubful. J. S. Park. il Org Gard & Farm 17:36-9 O '70
See also
Farm produce—Storage

Varieties
Growing midget vegetables. Sunset 144:197 Je '70
New fruits and vegetables. G. Logsdon. Farm J 94:50D Mr '70
VEGETABLES, Frozen
Taste test of frozen corn-on-the-cob. Consumer Rep 35:194-5 Ap '70
VEGETARIANISM
Kosher of the counterculture. il Time 96:59-60+ N 16 '70
Wow, like let's really try to win; C. Oliver's life at a commune. B. Newnham. il pors Sports Illus 33:50-4 O 12 '70
See also
Cookery—Vegetables
VEHICLES
See also
Electric vehicles
Sleighs and sleighing
VEINS
See also
Varicose veins

Surgery
See Blood vessels—Surgery
VELASCO ALVARADO, Juan
Day of the generals. S. Rodman. il Nat R 22:1105-7 O 20 '70 *
VELASCO IBARRA, José Maria
Change in the script. il por Time 96:32 Jl 6 '70 *
Supreme leader. por Newsweek 76:47 Jl 6 '70 *
VELAZQUEZ, Diego Rodriguez de Silva y
Highest ever. il Time 96:77 D 7 '70 *
World's record Velásquez. il Life 69:39 D 11 '70 *
VELIE, Lester
Case of the purloined crime law. Read Digest 97:63-7 N '70
Four professors and the welfare revolution. il Read Digest 96:93-7 Ja '70
Hunger in the classroom. Read Digest 96:134-9 Mr '70
Our food-stamp fiasco. Read Digest 96:103-7 Je '70
Poverty at the border. il Read Digest 97:92-7 Ag '70
VELLEMAN, Jim. See Lawrence, T. jt. auth.
VELVETEEN rabbit; story. See Williams, M.
VENDING machines
Vendors pull out all stops. il Bsns W p52+ Ag 15 '70

Anecdotes, facetiae, satire, etc.
Better living with machinery; excerpt from What did you have in mind? C. McDowell, jr. il Read Digest 97:113-14 Ag '70
VENEREAL diseases
Growing menace of VD. V. Block. Parents Mag 45:86-7+ N '70
In epidemic proportions. il Sci N 98:56 Jl 25 '70
Promiscuity and prostitution in urbanized Indian communities. R. E. Kuttner and A. B. Lorincz. bibliog Ment Hy 54:79-91 Ja '70
Report on venereal disease; ed. by E. Jacobs. R. E. Rogers. Redbook 135:26+ My '70
Teaching about venereal diseases. E. P. Vincent. Todays Ed 59:50-1 F '70
VD: a national emergency. il Time 96:36 Jl 27 '70
VD is on the rise again. J. E. Brody. Read Digest 97:181-2+ N '70
Venereal disease. Consumer Rep 35:118-23 F '70
Why VD is rising. Newsweek 75:65 Mr 30 '70
See also
Gonorrhea
VENETIAN cookery. See Cookery, Italian
VENEZUELA
See also
Geology—Venezuela
Petroleum—Venezuela

Industries
See also
Petroleum industry and trade—Venezuela

Native races
See Indians of South America—Venezuela

VENICE
Must Venice die? P. Moor. il Holiday 47:46-9+
Ap '70; Reply. J. McAndrew. 48:6-7 Jl '70
Venice; floods and air pollution. I. R. Levine.
Atlan 227:16+ Ja '71

Air pollution
Can Venice survive pollution? il U S News
68:72-4 Ja 26 '70

Architecture
Venice: the present: a sinking sensation. W.
Karp. il Horizon 12:73-5 Wint '70

History
Venice: the past: the most triumphant city.
J. Morris. il Horizon 12:76-91 Wint '70

Industries
New Venice; an industrial giant; Mestre-
Marghera. il U S News 68:74 Ja 26 '70

Music
Report:
Rossini's Armida. E. Rizzo. il Opera N
34:27 Je 13 '70
VENICE biennale. See Art—Exhibitions; Music
festivals—Italy
VENICE in art
Venice: the past: the most triumphant city.
J. Morris. il Horizon 12:76-91 Wint '70
VENISON
How to dress a deer. W. Davis. il Mech Il-
lus 66:76-7+ N '70
See also
Cookery—Game
VENOM
Alkaloid from fire ant venom: identification
and synthesis. J. G. MacConnell and oth-
ers. bibliog il Science 168:840-1 My 15 '70
Milking fire ants; venom is highly potent as
an antibiotic. il Newsweek 76:70 N 9 '70
Snakebite common sense. Sci Digest 67:57 Je
'70
VENTILATION
See also
Air conditioning
Barns and stables—Heating and ventilation
Dampness in buildings
School buildings—Heating and ventilation
VENTILATORS
Exhaust fans to freshen up your house. il
Changing T 24:11-12 Mr '70
VENTURE capital. See Capital, Venture
VENTURES, Joint. See Joint adventures
VENTURI, Robert
Chaos as architecture. F. Schulze. il Art in
Am 58:88-96 Jl '70 *
VENUS (planet)
Venus radius controversy. W. B. Smith. bib-
liog Science 169:1001-2 S 4 '70

Rotation
Astronomical mystery. Time 97:65 Ja 18 '71
How did Venus lose its angular momentum?
S. F. Singer. Science 170:1196-8 D 11 '70
Length of Venus' day. Sky & Tel 39:290 My
'70

Surface
Mapping the veiled planet. il Sci N 98:246 S
19 '70
New radar maps of Venus. il Sky & Tel 40:
274-5 N '70
Radar interferometric observations of Venus
at 70-centimeter wavelength. D. B. Camp-
bell and others. bibliog il Science 170:1090-
2 D 4 '70
Radar snapshot of Venus. R. M. Goldstein
and H. Rumsey, jr. il Science 169:974-7 S
4 '70
VENUS probes. See Space probes
VERBAL behavior
Evaluating levels of thinking.   E. D. Doak.
Sch & Soc 98:177-8 Mr '70
VERDI, Giuseppe
Aida. Criticism
Opera N il 35:23-6 D 19 '70 *
Opera N il 35:30-1 D 19 '70 *
Sat R 53:45 Ja 17 '70
Don Carlo. Criticism
New Yorker 46:110-11 F 21 '70 *
Opera N 34:24-5 F 14 '70 *
Opera N il 34:17-20 F 14 '70 *
Ernani. Criticism
Nation 211:350 O 12 '70 *
New Yorker 46:114 S 26 '70 *
Final moments. S. Gould. il Opera N 34:24-5
Mr 21 '70 *
Finer Forza, optional Requiems. H. Wein-
stock. Sat R 53:50 O 31 '70 *
La forza del destino. A. Sperber. il Am Rec
G 36:948-9+ Ag '70 *

Man on the thousand-lire note. W. Weaver. il
por Sat R 53:66+ Mr 14 '70 *
Masked ball (Un ballo in maschera) Criti-
cism
New Yorker 46:162 O 24 '70 *
Otello. Criticism
Sat R 53:44 Ag 8 '70 *
Recording Verdi's Requiem. D. Hamilton. il
Hi Fi 20:79-81 N '70 *
Records:
La Traviata (excerpts) Opera N 34:34
Ja 31 '70
Take notice of the words... S. Hughes. il
por Opera N 34:8-13 F 14 '70 *
La Traviata. Criticism
Opera N il 34:17-20 Mr 21 '70 *
Il Trovatore. A. Sperber. il Am Rec G 36:
792-4+ Je '70 *
Vocal gold for Trovatore. P. G. Davis. Hi Fi
20:secI 100 Je '70 *
VERDY, Violette
To be a dancer. S. J. Cohen. il por Opera N
34:26-9 Ap 18 '70 *
VERGHESE, Paul
CPC and the price of fellowship. Chr Cent
87:1353 N 11 '70
Sacramental humanism. por Chr Cent 87:1116-
20 S 23 '70
VERIN, Layna
Growing up in a kibbutz. il Parents Mag 45:
56-8+ Ap '70
VERKADE, Kees
Bronze realists. il Time 95:74 Je 1 '70 *
VERMICULITE
Vermiculite: popular plant seed-bed a danger
to the eyes. Consumer Bul 53:25 Je '70
VERMILLION Cliffs natural area. See Wilder-
ness areas—Arizona
VERMONT
See also
Architecture, Domestic—Vermont
Camps—Vermont
Education—Vermont
Environmental policy—Vermont
Gardening—Vermont
Hunting—Vermont
Music festivals—Vermont
Skis and skiing—Vermont
Sugarbush Valley

Description and travel
Vermont: of green, glory and granite. G. P.
Morrill. il Read Digest 97:145-52 Jl '70

Economic conditions
Bananas in Vermont. R. M. Klein. il Natur
Hist 79:10-12+ bibliog(p82) F; 10-12 Mr
'70

Historic houses, etc.
See also
Strafford, Vt.—Historic houses, etc.

Industries
Bananas in Vermont. R. M. Klein. il Natur
Hist 79:10-12+ bibliog(p82) F; 10-12 Mr '70;
Reply. S. E. Beall, jr. 79:8 My '70

Politics and government
Vermont Democrats: Hoff's campaign. P. R.
Wieck. New Repub 163:11-13 O 3 '70
VERNER, William K.
Wilderness and the Adirondacks, an histori-
cal view. il Liv Wildn 33:27-46 Wint '69
VERNEY, Stephen
Coventry's pilot program. T. Beeson. Chr
Cent 87:1113 S 23 '70 *
VERNIER, R. L. See Crocker, J. F. S. jt. auth.
VEROLME united shipyards. See Shipbuild-
ing
VERSCHOTH, Anita
Skiing. Sports Illus 32:50-1 Mr 2 '70
Track and field (title varies) il por Sports
Illus 32:48+ Je 22 '70
VERSE. See Poetry
VERSIFICATION
See also
Rime
VERTICAL integration of agriculture. See Con-
tracts, Agricultural
VERTICAL-interval test signals. See Television
broadcasting—Test patterns
VERTOL division. See Boeing company—Vertol
division
VERY, Alice
Jonathan's Thanksgiving; drama. Plays 30:
38, 69-72 N '70
VESCO, Robert L.
Dark horse in IOS derby. por Bsns W p23-4
Ag 29 '70 *
Prize for agility. por Time 96:98 S 21 '70 *
VESICULAR stomatitis virus. See Viruses
VESPERS thrush. See Thrushes

VESTA (asteroid) See Asteroids
VESTAL, David
Basic camera. il Travel & Camera 33:77-81
F '70
Facts about black and white film. Travel &
Camera 33:84-7 Ap '70
Gallantry under fire. il Travel & Camera 33:
34-9 F '70
VESTMENTS. See Church vestments
VETERANS
Face down: climax to the hardship tour;
undergraduate veterans of the Vietnamese
war. W. G. Pelfrey. New Repub 163:13-14
Jl 18 '70
No laurels for legionnaires. W. G. Pelfrey.
New Repub 163:18-20 N 21 '70
Scars of Vietnam. R. J. Lifton. Common-
weal 91:554-6 F 20 '70
Society and the Vietnam veteran. J. Castelli.
il Cath World 212:184-8 Ja '71
See also
Negro veterans

Associations, institutions, etc.
See also
American legion

Benefits
New law relaxes hospital rules on VA care
for older veterans. T. Schuchat. Har Yrs
10:4 D '70
See also
Veterans—Education

Education
New GI bill for Vietnam vets. Bsns W p32+
Mr 21 '70
Quarter-century of the GI bill. D. E. John-
son. il Sch & Soc 98:226-8 Ap '70
Vietnam GI bill. Newsweek 75:81 Ap 13 '70
See also
Veterans—Vocational education

Employment
Join the army, learn a trade; dubious slogan.
Trans-Action 7:8 N '69
Viet Nam war veterans, transition to civil-
ian life. E. Waldman. bibliog il Mo Labor
R 93:21-9 N '70
Who needs riflemen? Newsweek 76:61 Ag 31
'70

Vocational education
Vocational and educational guidance for vet-
erans. Sch & Soc 98:207 Ap '70
VETERANS, Disabled

Rehabilitation
Society and the Vietnam veteran. J. Castelli.
il Cath World 212:184-8 Ja '71
Wounded GIs: on the care of heroes. L.
Barrett. Nation 210:61-3 Ja 19 '70
VETERANS, Vietnamese
Rage of the wounded; trouble in South Viet
Nam. il Time 96:33 S 21 '70
VETERANS administration. See United States
—Veterans administration
VETERINARIANS
Circuit-riding veterinarians; services for feed-
lots. O. Bay. il Farm J 94:B12 Mr '70
VETERINARY hygiene
See also
Milk hygiene
VETERINARY medicine
Feedlot health. J. G. Clark. See issues of
Farm journal
Four easy ways to boost your drug bills. J. G.
Clark. Farm J 94:B10 Ap '70
Hog health. W. R. Prafka. See issues of Farm
journal
Livestock management guide; symposium. il
Suc Farm 68:47-9+ O '70
R for a sick alligator; Boston's Angell mem-
orial hospital. J. Beatty, jr. il McCalls
97:26 F '70
Tissue bank for exotic animals. il Sci
Digest 67:25-6 My '70
What today's veterinary medicine can do for
your pet. B. Ford. il Sci Digest 67:54-9 F
'70
What's new: animal health (cont) il Suc
Farm 68:C14 Je '70
What's on a dog's mind? electroencephalo-
graph for dogs. il Sci Digest 67:82-3 Mr '70
See also
Veterinarians
VETO
See also
Presidents—United States—Powers and duties
United Nations—Voting
VETRA, Vila
Indian princess from Latvia is Australian
now! J. Anderson. il pors Dance Mag 44:
65-7 Mr '70 *

VETTER, Charles T. jr
Modern communications. Vital Speeches 36:
505-12 Je 1 '70
VETTER, Robert M.
Continental pewter epergnes, cruet stands,
and sugar bowls. il Antiques 98:88-93 Jl '70
VIA, Bernard S. jr
Personnel conscience; poem. Chr Cent 87:654
My 27 '70
VIATOR, pseud.
Cuba revisited after ten years of Castro. For
Affairs 48:312-21 Ja '70
VIATRON computer systems corporation
For sale: a dream called Viatron. il Forbes
105:18-19 F 1 '70
Revamped program for volatile Viatron. Bsns
W p24-5 Ag 1 '70
Viatron fights off angry bondholders. Bsns
W p20 D 26 '70
VIBRATORS
See also
Multivibrators
VICE-PRESIDENTIAL candidates
LBJ and the Kennedys; excerpt. K. O'Donnell.
il pors Life 69:44-8+ Ag 7 '70
VICE-PRESIDENTS

United States
Our imaginary vice. G. W. Johnson. Am
Scholar 39:387-94 Sum '70
What makes a good vice-president. E. Mc-
Carthy. McCalls 98:10 O '70
VICENS VIVES, Jaime
Historical writing of Jaime Vicens Vives.
G. Jackson. Am Hist R 75:808-15 F '70 *
VICES of a perfect couple; story. See McInerny,
R.
VICK, Norman Gibbs
Guru of Gulf Coast fishing. D. Levin. il por
Sports Illus 31:66+ D 15 '69
VICKERS, Jon
Festive Fidelio for Beethoven's 200th. I.
Kolodin. Sat R 54:16 Ja 2 '71 *
VICKSBURG, Miss.

Water supply
Well supply is best for Vicksburg. L. B. Al-
len. il Am City 85:125+ My '70
VICO, Giovanni Battista
Giambattista Vico, ed. by G. Tagliacozzo and
H. V. White. Review
New Yorker 46:154+ My 9 '70. G.
Steiner *
Sat R por 53:41-2 Ap 18 '70. J. Gutman *
VICTOR, Robert C.
Sun, moon, and planets this month. il Sky
& Tel 41:65 Ja '71
VICTOR comptometer corporation
501st company. Fortune 81:178 Je '70
VICTOR male chorus. See Choral groups and
societies
VICTORIA, British Columbia

Gardens
See Gardens—Canada
VICTORIAN house decoration. See House dec-
oration, Victorian
VICTORIAN painting. See Painting, British
VICTORIAN period
Victorians unbuttoned. J. H. Plumb. il Ho-
rizon 11:16-35 Aut '69
VIDAL, Gore
Memoir in the form of a novel; story. Esquire
73:109-16 My '70
about
People are talking about ... por Vogue
156:108-9 N 15 '70 *
VIDAL, Jean
Lepenski Vir. il UNESCO Courier 23:26-31 Ap
'70
VIDEO disc. See Video records
VIDEO recorders and recording
Big boom in cartridge TV. S. M. Gallager.
il Pop Mech 135:76-80+ Ja '71
CBS' fast draw on home TV tapes. il Bsns W
p50+ Mr 28 '70
Color TV spins onto the screen; AEG-Tele-
funken's system. il Bsns W p70 Ag 8 '70
Coming through your front door: prerecorded
video cassettes. J. G. Burke and M. C.
Lux. il Am Lib 1:1069-73 D '70
For color TV: a player, recorder, do-anything
cartridge system. A. J. Hand. il Pop Sci 197:
62-3 O '70
Goldmark's variations on a video theme:
Electronic video recorder. il Fortune 81:7i
My '70
Good revolution goes on sale: Cassette TV.
E. Kerr. il Life 69:46-53 O 16 '70
Greatest thing since the nickelodeon? cart-
ridge video. il Forbes 106:13-15 Jl 1 '70

VIDEO recorders and recording—*Continued*
Here come the video phonographs! L. Buckwalter. il Mech Illus 66:45-7+ D '70
Inside portable VTR's. G. McGinty. il Radio-Electr 41:9-12+ Ag '70
New cassette videocorder will play color tapes through your TV. il Pop Sci 196:24 Ap '70
New medium, and a lot of messages. il Newsweek 76:42-3 Ag 10 '70
New trends in sight and sound systems. R. Berkovitz. il Pop Sci 197:68-9+ N '70
Now: home TV films in full color. il Pop Mech 134:144-5 S '70
Now what hath God wrought? cartridge television. R. G. Kemper. Chr Cent 87:1120-3 S 23 '70
Pick and play your own TV shows. L. Buckwalter. il Pop Mech 133:130-3 F '70
Push-button movies: the video-cassette revolution. J. Kronenberger. Look 34:94 N 3 '70
See the amazing future, beyond television, of video machines, video cassettes. H. Junker. il Vogue 157:87 Ja 1 '71
See your home movies on TV; Vidicord. D. Scott. il Pop Sci 196:23 Je '70
Tree grows in the vast wasteland; Selectra-Vision. D. M. Rorvik. Esquire 73:66+ Ap '70
Video cartridge bows, to muffled applause. il Bsns W p 100-2 N 14 '70
Video cartridges: a promise of future shock. il Time 96:40-1 Ag 10 '70
Video recording with lasers and holograms. il Hi Fi sec I 20:36+ Ja '70
Video revolution; with list of manufacturers. G. Movshon. il Sat R 53:50-2 Ag 8 '70
Video tape recorders: a help or a headache? D. E. Bumpass. Clear House 44:562-4 My '70
Video tape: this year won't quite be next year. I. Berger. Sat R 53:78+ Ja 31 '70
VideoDisc sets record for grooviness. il Pop Sci 197:32 O '70
Videofreex: an informal organization in New York. New Yorker 46:42 D 12 '70
Year of the cartridge. D. Molner. Schol Teach Jr/Sr High p31 N 2 '70

Business use
Screen tests for job seekers. V. Louviere. il Nations Bsns 58:17 S '70

Educational use
Style of teaching and teacher evaluation. G. H. Henry. bibliog f Engl J 59:921-7 O '70

Industrial use
Just the ticket for a training film. V. Louviere. il Nations Bsns 58:18 My '70
New message for the medium. N. A. Martin. il Duns 96:63-5 Jl '70

VIDEO records
Color TV spins onto the screen; AEG-Telefunken's system. il Bsns W p70 Ag 8 '70
Pictures on a record? Teldec video disc. J. W. Freeman. il Opera N 35:14-15 D 12 '70
Video records: everyone's future toy. Pub W 199:30-2 Ja 4 '71

VIDEO tape recorders and recording. See Video recorders and recording

VIDEO tape recordings
New medium, and a lot of messages. il Newsweek 76:42-3 Ag 10 '70
Veni, vidi, video. D. Davis. il Newsweek 75:98-9 Ap 13 '70
Videotape explosion R. Freedman. Life 68:22 My 15 '70
Videotape recording. E. H. Anderson. Todays Ed 59:40 Ja '70

Requiems
First video-cassette recording: Bernstein leads Verdi's Requiem. E. Greenfield. il por Hi Fi 20:secI 22+ Je '70

VIDLER, Alec R.
Remembering E. M. Forster. Chr Cent 87:894 Jl 22 '70

VIENNA
Description
Beethoven's Vienna; beuschel, backhendl, and a birthday. G. Marek. il Sat R 53:50-1+ Mr 14 '70
Beethoven's Vienna; pictures by E. Steinbicker. H. W. Heinsheimer. il Opera N 35:6-10 Ja 2 '71

Gardens
Beauty of Vienna in springtime. il Home Gard 57:45-7 My '70

History
Where were you the night of November 20, 1805? premiere of Fidelio. G. R. Marek. il Opera N 35:24-6 Ja 2 '71

Music
Behind the scenes. K. Blaukopf. Hi Fi sec I 20:25 F '70
Report:
Gottfried von Einem's The trial. J. Wechsberg. Opera N 34:33 Mr 21 '70
Productions at Redoutensaal. J. Wechsberg. Opera N 35:32 N 21 '70
Vienna opera Don Carlo. J. Wechsberg. il Opera N 35:32 Ja 2 '71
Vienna in 3/4 time, with Lehár. Stolz and Strauss. G. Jellinek. Sat R 53:46 My 30 '70

VIENNA, Congress of, 1814-1815
Reports: Europe. D. Cook. Atlan 226:22-3+ Jl '70

VIENNA festival weeks. See Music festivals—Austria

VIENNA pawnshop. See Pawnbroking

VIENNA talks. See Strategic arms limitation talks

VIENNESE pastry. See Pastry

VIERTEL, Gösta
Dirigible; comic strip. Harp Baz 104:62-5 Ja '71

VIETNAM
See also
Ecology—Vietnam

History
Thirty years of war in Viet Nam. il Sr Schol 96:8-9 Ap 13 '70

Politics and government
See also
National liberation front (Vietnam)

Religious institutions and affairs
See also
Catholic church in Vietnam

VIETNAM (Democratic Republic)
North Viet Nam: Year of the dog. il Time 95:24-5 Ja 26 '70
See also
Economic assistance in Vietnam

Army
Can South Vietnam survive after the GI's leave? S. W. Sanders. il U S News 69:72-4 S 28 '70
Reds ready for new push in Indo-China? il U S News 69:22 N 30 '70

Economic conditions
How Hanoi hangs on. il Time 96:24+ Ag 24 '70
Inside North Vietnam: a tidal wave of troubles. il U S News 69:21-2 N 30 '70

Foreign relations
Exclusive report from Hanoi; the hard-line demand: victory. J. R. Moskin. il Look 34:20-2+ D 29 '70
Hanoi's formula: how to win while losing. J. N. Wallace. il U S News 68:44-6 Ap 6 '70
Laos: another Vietnam? il Newsweek 75:42 Mr 16 '70
See also
Communist strategy

Military policy
Is Hanoi ready to end the Vietnam war? V. Zorza. Cur 120:27-30 Ag '70

Politics and government
Future of North Vietnam. A. J. Dommen. Cur Hist 58:229-32+ Ap '70
Home front. il Newsweek 75:29-30 Je 22 '70
Political processes in the two Vietnams. C. A. Joiner. bibliog f Cur Hist 59:356-61+ D '70
What's right with America; lack of liberty in North Vietnam. H. R. Perot. il por Nations Bsns 58:20-1+ Jl '70

VIETNAM (Republic)
Inoffensive Tet. il Time 95:19 F 16 '70
See also
Agriculture—Vietnam (Republic)
Americans in Vietnam
Cities and towns—Vietnam (Republic)
Communism—Vietnam (Republic)
Economic assistance in Vietnam
Elections—Vietnam (Republic)
Hué
Land tenure—Vietnam (Republic)
Missions—Vietnam (Republic)
Morale, National—Vietnam (Republic)
Phu Tam
Police—Vietnam (Republic)

VIETNAM (Republic)—See also—*Continued*
  Postal service—Vietnam (Republic)
  Prisons—Vietnam (Republic)
  Protests, demonstrations, etc.—Vietnam (Republic)
  Recreation—Vietnam (Republic)
  Saigon
  Student demonstrations—Vietnam (Republic)
  Subversive activities—Vietnam (Republic)
  Technical assistance in Vietnam
  Television broadcasting—Vietnam (Republic)
  United States—Foreign relations—Vietnam (Republic)

Army
Graduation exercise; Vietnamization for the ARVN. Nation 210:643-4 Je 1 '70
How can we lose in Vietnam, having won? P. A. McCombs. il Nat R 22:1399-402 D 29 '70
Ready or not. Newsweek 75:50-1 Ap 20 '70
Vietnamese GI: can he win his own war? C. S. Wren. il Look 34:13-21 Ag 11 '70
Vietnamization. il Nat R 22:301-4 Mr 24 '70
Vietnamization, can it succeed? D. Reed. Read Digest 96:55-61 Ap '70
Vietnamization of General Di. A. J. Langguth. il por N Y Times Mag p5+ S 6 '70
Vietnamization: policy under fire. il Time 95: 25-6 F 9 '70
Vietnamization: will it work? il Newsweek 75:31-4 F 9 '70

Forces in Cambodia
But will the ARVN withdraw? il Newsweek 75:47+ Je 1 '70
Cambodia: a cocky new ARVN. il Time 95: 30+ Je 8 '70
Cambodia and Laos. C. P. FitzGerald. Nation 210:738-9 Je 22 '70
Different scene. il Newsweek 75:35-6 Ja 8 '70

Economic conditions
After the war: a bonanza for South Vietnam. il U S News 68:34-6 Ja 19 '70
Can South Vietnam survive after the GI's leave? S. W. Sanders. il U S News 69:72-4 S 28 '70
Dubious proposition. Time 96:33 O 12 '70
Fighting slows down, but Saigon's woes increase. il U S News 69:24-5 Ag 17 '70
Revolution without plan. il Newsweek 75: 34-7 F 9 '70
Saigon in the face of an economic crisis. il Newsweek 75:37-8 Je 15 '70
  See also
  Saigon—Economic conditions

Economic policy
Inflation remains a tenacious enemy. Bsns W p40-1 O 24 '70

Foreign relations
United States
  See United States—Foreign relations—Vietnam (Republic)

Politics and government
Bad news from the CIA; Communist agents in the South Vietnamese government. Nation 211:420 N 2 '70
Enemy within; CIA report on Communist spies operating inside the government. il Newsweek 76:65 N 2 '70
Finally their own way out? il por Newsweek 75:38-9 F 9 '70
How Thieu rules. D. Luce. New Repub 162: 17-18 F 28 '70
If not Thieu, who? G. Kirk. por Nat R 22: 667-9 Je 30 '70
Letter from Indo-China. R. Shaplen. New Yorker 46:125-8 My 16; 71-82 Ag 15; 124-6+ D 19 '70
Letter from Saigon (cont) R. Shaplen. New Yorker 45:40-2+ Ja 31 '70
Name of the game; who is going to run South Vietnam? Nation 211:484 N 16 '70
Nguyen cao Ky: flying high; interview. ed. by M. Parker. Nguyen-cao-Ky. il por Newsweek 75:49 Je 1 '70
Political processes in the two Vietnams. C. A. Joiner. bibliog f Cur Hist 59:356-61+ D '70
Proposal to end the Vietnam fighting; partition of South Vietnam into political cantonments. T. H. White. Sat R 53:23-5+ Mr 21 '70
Return of lotus blossom. il Time 96:17 S 7 '70
Turmoil in Saigon. Newsweek 75:52 My 18 '70
Victory for the Buddhists. il Time 96:22 S 14 '70
Vietnamization: policy under fire. il Time 95:25-6 F 9 '70
  See also
  Elections—Vietnam (Republic)

Relief work
Beyond the call of duty in Vietnam. K. Y. Tomlinson. il Read Digest 96:97-102 Je '70
  See also
  Medical relief work—Vietnam (Republic)
  Vietnamese war, 1957- —Relief work

Riots
Bad Yankee go home; rioting in Qui Nhon caused by shooting of Nguyen van Minh. il Time 96:30 D 21 '70

Social conditions
Explosive potential; urban crisis. il Newsweek 76:31 D 28 '70
Revolution without plan. il Newsweek 75:34-7 F 9 '70

VIETNAM (Republic) and the United States
  See also
  United States—Foreign opinion—Vietnamese

VIETNAM moratorium committee. See Vietnamese war, 1957- —Protests, demonstrations, etc, against

VIETNAM victory rally. See Washington, D.C. —Parades

VIETNAMESE-Cambodian conflict. See Cambodian-Vietnamese conflict

VIETNAMESE in Cambodia
New horror in Indochina; Cambodian pogrom against country's Vietnamese minority. il Time 95:36+ Ap 27 '70

VIETNAMESE propaganda. See Propaganda, Vietnamese

VIETNAMESE refugees. See Refugees, Vietnamese

VIETNAMESE soldiers. See Vietnam (Republic)—Army

VIETNAMESE students
  See also
  Student demonstrations—Vietnam (Republic)

VIETNAMESE veterans. See Veterans, Vietnamese

VIETNAMESE war, 1957-
David Bruce's portfolio. il por Newsweek 76:33 Ag 3 '70
From the Vietnam war to an Indochina war. J. Lacouture. For Affairs 48:617-28 Jl '70
How goes the war? A colloquy in Saigon. M. Clark and others. il por Time 95:20-1 F 23 '70
Indochina not an issue? New Repub 163:7-8 N 7 '70
Korean solution for Vietnam? F. Baldwin. New Repub 163:19-21 Jl 18 '70
Letter from Indo-China. R. Shaplen. New Yorker 46:125-8 My 16; 116+ D 19 '70
Letter from Saigon (cont) R. Shaplen. New Yorker 45:40-2+ Ja 31 '70
Mr Nixon's war. New Repub 162:1+ F 14 '70
Muskie's peace plan; views of Claiborne Pell. New Repub 163:5-6 Jl 25 '70
New turn in Vietnam war. il U S News 69: 13-16 Jl 20 '70
Nixon's plan for Vietnam: the unfolding strategy. W. S. Merick. il U S News 68:20-1 Je 15 '70
Notes and comment. New Yorker 46:33-4 Ap 18 '70
Respite in the south, pressure in the north. Time 95:29 Je 15 '70
U.S. maps its progress. il Newsweek 76:32-3 O 26 '70
Vietnamization is not peace; prospects. M. Parker. il Newsweek 76:63 N 23 '70
War in Vietnam. See issues of Newsweek
Westmoreland's Vietnam visit: he liked what he saw; excerpts from news conference. W. C. Westmoreland. il por U S News 69:43 Ag 3 '70
Year of the dog. il Newsweek 75:37 F 16 '70
  See also
  Cambodian-Vietnamese conflict
  Conscientious objectors
  Libraries and the Vietnamese war
  Mines, Military
  Vietnam (Democratic Republic)—Army
  Vietnam (Republic)—Politics and government

Aerial operations
Bombers go north. il Newsweek 76:14 N 30 '70
Bombing; bombing of North Vietnam. W. F. Buckley, jr. Nat R 22:1366 D 15 '70
Daring raids in Vietnam: purpose of Nixon's move. il U S News 69:22-3 D 7 '70
Day in Laos, and an evening. W. F. Buckley, jr. Nat R 22:44 Ja 13 '70
Hitting north again. Time 96:10 N 30 '70
John Wayne in Vietnam. Commonweal 93: 267-8 D 11 '70
LBJ on the bombing halt. por Newsweek 75: 22-3 F 16 '70

VIETNAMESE war, 1957- —Aerial operations
—*Continued*
LBJ's account of March, 1968. T. Hoopes. New
  Repub 162:17-19 Mr 14 '70
Making history on the Pedernales; L. B.
  Johnson's decision to stop the bombing of
  North Vietnam. H. Sidey. il por Life 68:4
  F 20 '70
New bombing policy. il por Newsweek 76:
  21-2 D 21 '70
Nixon's new warning to Hanoi: bombing
  could be resumed; excerpts from news con-
  ference, December 10, 1970. R. M. Nixon.
  U S News 69:79 D 21 '70
North targets hit; attempt to rescue U.S.
  prisoners. Sr Schol 97:4 D 14 '70
Understanding understandings; R. M. Nixon's
  statement on bombing. Time 96:12-13 D 21
  '70
Vietnam and restraints on aerial warfare. B.
  M. Russett. il Bul Atom Sci 26:9-12 Ja '70;
  Reply. A. E. Berthoff. 26:49-50 O '70
    See also
Helicopters—Military use

Aims
  See Vietnamese war, 1957- —War aims

American participation
After pinkville, what? N. Chomsky. Cur 115:
  18-30 F '70
After the war is over. W. Lippman. il por
  Newsweek 76:32-3 D 14 '70
Agnew's talk with five students; text of tele-
  vision debate. S. T. Agnew and others. il
  pors U S News 69:86-8+ O 12 '70
All for Vietnam; excerpts from The trial. T.
  Hayden. il Ramp Mag 9:26-7+ S '70
Ambiguities of defeat. D. C. Anderson. Cur
  114:6-8 Ja '70
Belated light on Vietnam; K. P. O'Donnell's
  post-mortem on the Kennedy administra-
  tion. Nation 211:99-100 Ag 17 '70
Camelot's credibility; Kenneth O'Donnell re-
  veals plans of J. F. Kennedy. K. Crawford.
  Newsweek 76:36 Ag 17 '70
Can Vietnam go it alone? interview, ed. by
  W. S. Merick and J. N. Wallace. Nguyen-
  van-Thieu. il por U S News 68:71-5 Mr 16
  '70
Cease-fire; Hatfield-McGovern amendment to
  end the war. Commonweal 92:475-6 S 25 '70
For America; address, January 5, 1970. J. M.
  Patrick. Vital Speeches 36:341-3 Mr 15 '70
Fresh prescriptions for disengagement in
  Vietnam; three critiques; excerpts. C. Clif-
  ford; M. Bundy; J. Gardner. pors News-
  week 75:31-2 My 25 '70
From LBJ, a blast at the war's foes. U S
  News 68:18 F 16 '70
How not to fight a war; reprint. D. Law-
  rence. il U S News 68:112 My 18 '70
Invisible dead. Nation 210:484 Ap 27 '70
Klein mission. Nation 210:773 Je 29 '70
LBJ's account of March, 1968. T. Hoopes.
  New Repub 162:17-19 Mr 14 '70
Legacy of the cold war in Indochina. T.
  Hoopes. For Affairs 48:601-16 Jl '70
Lessons of the Vietnam war. W. Goldstein.
  Bul Atom Sci 26:41-5 F '70
Letter from Washington; Nixon administra-
  tion. R. H. Rovere. New Yorker 45:58+ Ja
  17 '70
Missing element in the debate; U.S.-Soviet
  relations. C. Emmet. Nat R 22:678-9+ Je 30
  '70
Mr Nixon's war. New Repub 162:1+ F 14 '70
My war, my way. New Repub 162:5-6 Je 13
  '70
Myths and realities; views of J. M. Ful-
  bright. K. Crawford. Newsweek 75:48 Ap 20
  '70
1964: exhilaration; 1968: frustration; 1970:
  hopelessness. A. J. Langguth. il N Y Times
  Mag p26-7+ O 4 '70
Notes and comment. New Yorker 46:25-6 Je
  6 '70
Old debate; application of C. Lindbergh's po-
  sition against involvement in World war II
  to involvement in Vietnamese war. W. F.
  Buckley, jr. Nat R 22:1017 S 22 '70
President Nixon's news conference of De-
  cember 8, 1969. R. M. Nixon. Dept State
  Bul 61:617-20 D 29 '69
Pride and prestige; premises of policy. M.
  Stone. Chr Cent 87:286 Mr 11 '70
Reasonable view of Vietnam. M. Mead. Red-
  book 134:48+ F '70
Reporter at large; some questions about the
  war; interview, ed. by W. Whitworth. E.
  V. Rostow. New Yorker 46:30-46+ Jl 4 '70
Set a date in Vietnam. Stick to it. Get out.
  C. Clifford. il pors Life 68:34-8 My 22 '70
Silent majorities and the Vietnam war. P.
  E. Converse and H. Schuman. il Sci Am
  222:17-25 Je '70

Thieu plus two. New Repub 162:7-8 Ap 4 '70
Vietnamese GI: can he win his own war? C.
  S. Wren. il Look 34:13-21 Ag 11 '70
Vietnamization is not peace. M. Parker. il
  Newsweek 76:63 N 23 '70
War debate rises in Congress. il U S News
  68:33 Je 15 '70
War guilt. New Repub 163:1+ D 19 '70
War: keynote for Democrats in '70? address,
  May 9, 1970. L. F. O'Brien. por U S News
  68:97-9 My 25 '70
Westmoreland appraised: questions and an-
  swers. B. Clark. Harper 241:96-101 N '70
Wet-dry: hawk-dove. K. Crawford. News-
  week 76:29 N 30 '70
Why we didn't win in Vietnam. il U S News
  68:44-5 F 9 '70
Why we fight in Vietnam; text of Vietnam in-
  formation notes no. 6, June 1967, comp.
  by the U.S. State department. il U S News
  68:84-8 Ja 26 '70
    See also
Conscientious objectors
United States—Armed forces—Forces in Vietnam
Vietnamese war, 1957- —American troop withdrawals
Vietnamese war, 1957- —Pacification programs

American troop withdrawals
After the combat troops come home. Time
  95:12 Ja 26 '70
Ahead: faster withdrawal from Vietnam; results of Laird mission. il por U S News 68:
  29-30 F 23 '70
As war rises, new pull-back of troops? U S
  News 68:82 Ap 20 '70
Case for and against military withdrawal
  from Vietnam and Korea; address, April
  1970, with questions and answers. F. Greene.
  Ann Am Acad 390:1-17 Jl '70
Ending the Vietnam war; get out now. Cur
  120:14-17 Ag '70
Ending the war. P. A. Samuelson. News-
  week 75:78 Je 1 '70
Exclusive report from Hanoi: the hard-line
  demand: victory. J. R. Moskin. il Look
  34:20-2+ D 29 '70
Finally their own way out? il por News-
  week 75:38-9 F 9 '70
Getting out of Vietnam. New Repub 162:5-6
  Ja 31 '70
Getting the boys home; McGovern-Hatfield
  amendment. New Repub 162:5-6 My 26 '70
Half step toward home. B. Pines. il Time
  95:29 Ap 13 '70
In the Senate moves to end the war—. U S
  News 69:73 S 14 '70
Indochina, or Mr Nixon's dilemma; more
  withdrawals. il por Newsweek 75:21-2 My 4
  '70
Laos, Viet Nam, & the U.S. il Sr Schol 96:5-
  10 Ap 13 '70
Letter from Indo-China. R. Shaplen. New
  Yorker 46:71-82 Ag 15 '70
Look at GI's leaving the war. il U S News
  68:76-7 Mr 16 '70
Mr Nixon's great retreat. S. Alsop. News-
  week 75:120 My 25 '70
More flimflam; analysis of President's ad-
  dress on the Vietnamese war. Nation 210:
  514-15 My 4 '70
Muskie's timetable: out of Indochina in
  eighteen months. E. S. Muskie. il N Y
  Times Mag p8-13 Jl 5 '70
Next marine battle; marines leaving Viet
  Nam. il Time 95:17-18 Mr 30 '70
Next step in Laos. W. F. Buckley, jr. Nat R
  22:376 Ap 7 '70
Nixon, the Senate & the war. N. G. Levin.
  jr. Commentary 50:69-84 N '70
Nixon's latest strategy for peace in Vietnam.
  il U S News 68:14-15 My 4 '70
Not whether, how. S. Alsop. Newsweek 76:88
  Jl 6 '70
On Vietnam: critical voices raised again. il
  U S News 68:10 F 16 '70
On violence, peace and the rule of law. R.
  Clark. For Affairs 49:31-9 O '70
Pain of Yankee going home. il Time 97:58-9
  Ja 11 '71
Peace and politics. New Repub 162:7-8 My 2
  '70
President's message on Indo-China; ad-
  dress, April 20, 1970. R. M. Nixon. por U S
  News 68:61-2 My 4 '70; Same with title Re-
  port on progress in Vietnam. Dept State
  Bul 62:601-4 My 11 '70
Prestidigitator: President Nixon's Vietnami-
  zation plan. Nation 210:162-3 F 16 '70
Progress report on our plan for peace in
  Viet-Nam; address, December 15, 1969. R.
  M. Nixon. Dept State Bul 62:1-3 Ja 5 '70
Prospect for Vietnamization. J. G. Lowen-
  stein and R. M. Moose. Cur 116:9-10 Mr '70

VIETNAMESE war, 1957- —American troop
withdrawals—*Continued*
Pull-back from Vietnam, the problems Nixon
weighed; questions and answers. il U S
News 68:27-8 Ap 27 '70
Ready or not. Newsweek 75:50-1 Ap 20 '70
Secretary Rogers' news conference of May
13, 1970. W. P. Rogers. Dept State Bul 62:
673-80 Je 1 '70
Set a date in Vietnam. Stick to it. Get out.
C. Clifford. il pors Life 68:34-8 My 22 '70
Setting a deadline for withdrawal. C. E.
Goodell. Cur 115:30-2 F '70
Showing up Agnew; McGovern-Hatfield pro-
posal. New Repub 163:7 S 5 '70
Vietnam: a crucial year. il U S News 70:
26-7 Ja 4 '71
Vietnam: out faster. S. Alsop. Newsweek 76:
104 D 7 '70
Vietnam: time to fix a date. Life 69:32
Jl 10 '70
Vietnamization: can it work? R. H. Johnson.
For Affairs 48:629-47 Jl '70
Vietnamization in the air. Time 96:33 N 2 '70
Vietnamization of General Di. A. J. Langguth.
il por N Y Times Mag p5+ S 6 '70

Anecdotes, facetiae, satire, etc.

Notes and comment: imaginary hearing on
the success or failure of the war on the
basis of effort rather than results. New
Yorker 46:47-8 D 5 '70

Art

Cuban artist views North Vietnam; silk-
screens by R. Mederos. K. Wald. il Ramp
Mag 8:21-7 Ap '70

Atrocities

After pinkville, what? N. Chomsky. Cur 115:
18-30 F '70
Another Song My? My Khe. Newsweek 75:
45 Mr 2 '70
Bloody, bloodier: documents of the Com-
munists .W. F. Buckley, jr. Nat R 22:44-5
Ja 13 '70
Case of Lieutenant Duffy. Nation 210:419-20
Ap 13 '70
Casualties of war, by D. Land. Review
Sat R 53:31-4+ F 14 '70. D. Berrigan
Horror takes the stand; National veterans'
inquiry into U.S. war crimes. J. Higgins.
Nation 212:6-8 Ja 4 '71
How relevant are the rules of war? A. Wil-
son. Cur 114:3-6 Ja '70
Massacre at Phu Thanh. il Newsweek 75:30-
1 Je 22 '70
Mere gook rule; case of J. B. Duffy. il por
Newsweek 75:30 Ap 13 '70
Night of death; massacre at Thanh My. il
Time 95:34 Je 22 '70
On American violence. B. Russell. por Ramp
Mag 8:54-7 Mr '70
One simple decision; American witnesses to
shooting of civilians by Vietcong and
North Vietnamese soldiers. C. Coe. Nat R
22:950+ S 8 '70
Psychological causes and effects of atroci-
ties. J. B. Sheerin. Cath World 211:2-3 Ap
'70
What every Vietnam veteran knows: inter-
views, with editorial comment. New Re-
pub 163:1+, 13-15 D 19 '70
What price Vietnam glory? H. Kohler. il
Chr Cent 87:113-14 Ja 28 '70

My Lai massacre

And then there were ten; new charges. News-
week 75:37+ Mr 23 '70
Calley at My Lai. il Newsweek 76:52-3 D 14
'70
Calley goes on trial. il por Newsweek 76:16-
17 N 30 '70
Calley's confessions; My Lai pretrial. por
Time 96:15 O 12 '70
Calley's defense. il Newsweek 76:25-6 D 21
'70
Carnage before noon on the Beautiful Moun-
tain. Tran-van-Dinh. Sat R 53:23-5 My 30
'70
Civilian killings in Vietnam: a congressional
report. il U S News 69:35 Jl 27 '70
Command influence; pretrial hearing. il News-
week 75:28 F 2 '70
Defendant no. 5; T. K. Willingham. por News-
week 75:52 F 23 '70
Generals accused; army investigation find-
ings. il por Newsweek 75:18-20 Mr 30 '70
Is Nuremberg coming back to haunt us? J.
B. Reston, jr. Sat R 53:14-17+ Jl 18 '70
Lieutenant Calley at bay. il por Time 96:14-
15 D 21 '70
Massacre charged to GI's. Sr Schol 95:6-8 Ja
5 '70
Mental gymnastics on Mylai. E. M. Opton,
jr. and R. Duckles. il New Repub 162:14-16
F 21 '70

Miasma of My Lai. por Time 95:16 Mr 30 '70
Mitchell case. il por Newsweek 76:30-1 O 26 '70
My Lai chain. por Time 95:13 Mr 23 '70
My Lai: did American troops attack the
wrong place? R. Hammer. il Look 34:60
F 10 '70
My Lai 4: a report on the massacre and its
aftermath: excerpts. S. M. Hersh. Harper
240:53-84 My '70; Reply with rejoinder. H.
Kamm. 241:9+ Ag '70
My Lai: the case against Calley. il por Time
96:18 D 14 '70
Mylai II. Nat R 22:341-2 Ap 7 '70
Peers report. Nation 210:354 Mr 30 '70
President Nixon's news conference of De-
cember 8, 1969. R. M. Nixon. Dept State
Bul 61:617-20 D 29 '69
Self-respect after My Lai; discussion. Chr
Cent 87:83 Ja 21 '70
Some facts for the state of the Union. P.
Steinfels. Commonweal 91:446 Ja 23 '70
Songmy inquiry. America 122:365 Ap 4 '70
Songmy: the human imperative; school li-
braries' responsibility and interest in vio-
lence. M. Braverman. il por Library J 95:
211-13 Ja 15 '70
Toward a critical social science. E. M. Op-
ton, jr. and N. Sanford. Trans-Action 7:
4-7 Mr '70
Tragedy at Song My; the case deepens. U S
News 68:28 Mr 30 '70
War crimes and individual responsibility: a
legal memorandum. R. A. Falk. Trans-
Action 7:33-40 Ja '70
Why civilians are war victims in Vietnam;
interview. R. J. Lifton. il Sci Digest 67:40-
5 My '70

Australian participation

Australia's massive moratorium. R. Mathias.
Chr Cent 7:771-2 Je 17 '70

Bibliography

Background to a tragedy. R. Halloran. Sat
R 53:25-6+ N 14 '70
Readers miscellany; a sampling of books for
special interests. J. Fletcher. Library J 95:
2446-7 Jl '70

Campaigns and battles

As war rises, new pull-back of troops? U S
News 68:82 Ap 20 '70
Behind the battle for Khesanh. L. W. Walt.
il Read Digest 96:105-11 My '70
Retreat from Ripcord. Newsweek 76:34 Ag
3 '70
Seven firefights in Vietnam. Review
Nation 212:53-5 Ja 11 '71. W. Eastlake

Cambodia

See Cambodian-Vietnamese conflict

Casualties

Am I a wife or a widow? C. S. Wren. il
Read Digest 96:93-6 Mr '70
Body count: the degrading illusion. L. K.
Truscott, 3d. il Nation 211:487-9 N 16 '70;
Reply. M. W. Clark. 212:2 Ja 4 '71
Doing what comes naturally: Dominic Scatu-
orchio who fought and died for his coun-
try. W. F. Buckley, jr. Nat R 22:584-5 Je 2
'70
First things, and last. N. Podhoretz. Commen-
tary 50:27 Jl '70; Discussion. 50:24+ O '70
From Vietnam to a VA hospital; assignment
to neglect; with report by C. Childs. il Life
68:24D-33 My 22 '70
Hey, hero! Vietnam amputees at the Oak
Knoll naval hospital. S. Kirkpatrick. il
Read Digest 97:71-5 S '70
Long return of Warrant officer Meade. J. P.
Blank. il por Read Digest 97:73-7 D '70
Mrs O'Grady is a widow; statement; ed. by
C. S. Wren. D. O'Grady. por Look 34:67
My 5 '70
Nice war; Americans killed by peasant booby
traps. Nation 211:197 S 14 '70
Sharp drop in U.S. casualties. il U S News
70:17 Ja 11 '71
Ten long minutes in Punchbowl; National
memorial cemetery of the Pacific. J. Didion.
il Life 68:26D Ap 10 '70
Vietnam: why U.S. casualties drop. il U S
News 69:14 Jl 27 '70
Who dies in Vietnam? motive for Pentagon's
switch from draft to reserve. L. K. Trus-
cott, 4th. il Nation 211:326-7 O 12 '70
Why the death toll. N. Horrock. il Newsweek
76:32 Ag 31 '70

VIETNAMESE war, 1957- —*Continued*

Censorship

Like it is; Robert Lawrence served with court martial charges. Nat R 22:74 Ja 27 '70
See also
Vietnamese war, 1957- —War correspondents

Children

Children of Vietnam–II; comp. by C. Johnes. il Ramp Mag 9:32-5 N '70

Cost

Hidden costs of the Viet Nam war. il Time 96:66 Jl 13 '70

Damage to property

See Vietnamese war, 1957- —Destruction and pillage

Destruction and pillage

Ecological effects of the war in Vietnam. G. H. Orians and E. W. Pfeiffer. bibliog il Science 168:544-54 My 1 '70; Discussion. 169:6, 1030 Jl 3, S 11 '70
Ecology of war. Sci Am 223:48-9 Jl '70
Spiking the loot; P. Arnett's report on U.S. looting in Cambodia. il por Newsweek 75:76 My 18 '70

Economic aspects

Helicopter bread line; conversion from defense production. J. C. Goulden. Nation 212:50-2 Ja 11 '71
How peace will cut employment. il Bsns W p 130 F 14 '70
Increase in defense-related employment during Viet Nam buildup; with tables. R. P. Oliver. Mo Labor R 93:3-10 F '70
Making the turn to a peacetime economy; recession in defense-related industries. S. Rose. il Fortune 82:110-13 S '70
Pain of Yankee going home. il Time 97:58-9 Ja 11 '71
Peace bonanza that went bust; cutbacks of military programs. il Bsns W p66-8 S 5 '70
Pentagon cuts: the worst is yet to come; interview. K. C. Moot. il por Bsns W p94+ S 12 '70
Vietnam pullout starts to show. il Bsns W p 102+ Je 13 '70
War and big business; views of four leaders of American corporations. L. L. L. Golden. Sat R 53:95 S 12 '70

Equipment and supplies

Automated war; use of computers and lasers. D. Shearer. New Repub 162:14-15 My 30 '70
DOD panel confirms early Viet shortage; with editorial comment. C. Brownlow. Aviation W 93:11, 22-3 N 16 '70
Photographs you haven't seen: weapons and other material uncovered in Cambodia. Cato. Nat R 22:555 Je 2 '70
Vietnam failures: a military view; Joint logistics review board report. il U S News 69:51 N 23 '70

Guerrillas

How can we lose in Vietnam, having won? P. A. McCombs. il Nat R 22:1399-402 D 29 '70

Legal aspects

For the defense: new office of inquiry to furnish free civilian defense for servicemen facing courts-martial. New Yorker 46:39-40 N 7 '70
Immoral and illegal; Massachusetts bill to test constitutionality. Nation 210:389 Ap 6 '70
Massachusetts asks: is the war legal? Sr Schol 96:16 Ap 27 '70
Outlawing the war; Massachusetts legislation. il Newsweek 75:22 Ap 13 '70
Test on Vietnam war heads for High court; state of Massachusetts challenge. U S News 68:99 Ap 13 '70
Vietnam: shadow on the Court; refusal to hear the Massachusetts anti-war suit. B. Schweid. Nation 211:564 N 30 '70
War and the law. Nation 211:355 O 19 '70
Wrath of the doves; law to outlaw war in Massachusetts. R. Donway. Nat R 22:568-70 Je 2 '70

Medical and sanitary affairs

Does our army fight on drugs? ed. by C. S. Wren. J. H. Kaplan. Look 34:72+ Je 16 '70
Highs from an explosive; intoxication from eating C-4. il Sci N 98:32 Jl 11 '70
Letter to the President; why an army neurosurgeon resigned his commission. M. H. Helfant. il Look 34:48-53 Jl 28 '70

Samaritans on wings; nurses fly transoceanic missions evacuating injured GIs from Vietnam. il Ebony 25:60-2+ My '70
See also
Veterans, Disabled—Rehabilitation

Moral and religious aspects

Churches and the Viet Nam issue. C. Kucheman. Chr Today 15:15-16 O 23 '70
Greatest victory; conscientious objector status. Chr Cent 87:99 Ja 29 '70
How the influence of many religions could stop Asia's war. D. Lawrence. U S News 69:76 Jl 6 '70
In the exercise of love; The moral aspects of war. Chr Cent 87:807 Je 24 '70; Discussion. 87:1072 S 9 '70
Is Nuremberg coming back to haunt us? J. B. Reston, jr. Sat R 53:17+ Jl 18 '70
Of many things; moral implications of the war in Indochina. D. R. Campion. America 122:inside cover Je 6 '70
Profiles; D. Berrigan and P. Berrigan. F. Du Plessix. New Yorker 46:44-6 Mr 14 '70
Vietnam and the Jewish community. B. Brickner. Chr Cent 87:531-4 Ap 29 '70
War guilt. New Repub 163:1+ D 19 '70
War, the churches, and civil religion. R. J. Neuhaus. bibliog f Ann Am Acad 387:128-40 Ja '70

Negotiations

See Vietnamese war, 1957- —Peace and mediation

Negroes

Soldier's rest; burial of Pondexteur Williams in all-white cemetery. il Newsweek 76:33-4 S 7 '70
Soul Alley; home for black AWOLs and deserters. il Time 96:39-40 D 14 '70
Terry funeral. America 122:30 Ja 17 '70

Pacification programs

ABCDs of pacification; Hamlet evaluation system. il Time 96:47-8 O 26 '70
Beware: wet paint; South Vietnamese flags painted on houses, huts, and hovels in South Vietnam. il Time 96:21 D 28 '70
But what is victory? Hamlet evaluation system, Binh Dinh province. il Newsweek 76:33 O 26 '70
Growing menace to Vietnam: red spies in the South; reassessment of Operation Phoenix by Defense department. il U S News 69:51-2 D 21 '70
In Vietnam, a new optimism. R. G. Kaiser. Read Digest 96:87-92 Ja '70
Operation Phoenix. Nation 210:230 Mr 2 '70
See also
Technical assistance in Vietnam

Peace and mediation

Amid cease-fire talks, fresh dangers in Indo-China. il U S News 69:20-1 O 26 '70
Can France and Britain help end the Vietnam war? address. A. Eden. il U S News 69:92+ Je 15 '70
Cease-fire in Indochina? Nixon's peace plan. il Sr Schol 97:9 O 26 '70
Exclusive report from Hanoi: the hard-line demand; victory. J. R. Moskin. il Look 34:20-2+ D 29 '70
Letter from Washington; Nixon administration. R. H. Rovere. New Yorker 45:58+ Ja 17 '70
Mr Nixon offers a plan for peace. il por Newsweek 76:30-1 O 19 '70
More peace signals. K. Crawford. Newsweek 76:33 N 9 '70
Nation's response to Nixon plea: divided over a call for unity. il Sr Schol 95:13-14 D 1 '69
New initiative for peace; President Nixon's plan, October 7, 1970. America 123:280-1 O 17 '70
New team takes up the quest for peace; D. K. E. Bruce and E. Bunker. pors U S News 69:38 Ag 3 '70
Nixon watch. J. Osborne. New Repub 162:11-13 My 16 '70
Nixon's new strategy in southeast Asia; will it end the war? il U S News 69:17-19 O 19 '70
Nixon's peace plan. New Repub 163:5-6 O 17 '70
Nixon's plea to end the killing. il por Time 96:15-16 O 19 '70
On the road to a just peace. R. Thompson. Read Digest 96:68-73 Mr '70
On violence, peace and the rule of law. R. Clark. For Affairs 49:31-9 O '70
Paradox of nonviolent war in Vietnam. I. de S. Pool. por Life 69:2 Jl 4 '70
President Nixon discusses reaction to peace initiative; remarks, October 8, 1970. R. M. Nixon. Dept State Bul 63:468-70 O 26 '70

VIETNAMESE war, 1957- —Peace and media-
tion—*Continued*
President Nixon interviewed for CBS tele-
vision; excerpt from interview, August 29,
1970. R. M. Nixon. Dept State Bul 63:327-9
S 21 '70
President Nixon's news conference, July 20,
1970. R. M. Nixon. Dept State Bul 63:161-
4 Ag 10 '70
President's proposals. P. Steinfels. Common-
weal 93:86 O 23 '70
President's speech. Nation 211:354 O 19 '70
Progress report on our plan for peace in
Viet-Nam; address, December 15, 1969. R.
M. Nixon. Dept State Bul 62:1-3 Ja 5 '70
Proposal to end the Vietnam fighting. T. H.
White. Sat R 53:23-5+ Mr 21 '70
Questions which tear us apart. D. Halberstam.
il Harper 240:70-2+ F '70
Secretary-General's press conference; 22 De-
cember, 1969. Thant. UN Mo Chron 7:178-
87 Ja '70
Secretary Rogers and Secretary Laird inter-
viewed on issues and answers. W. P. Rog-
ers; M. R. Laird. Dept State Bul 63:542-53
N 2 '70
Secretary Rogers interviewed on national edu-
cational television; transcript of an inter-
view, November 26, 1969. W. P. Rogers.
Dept State Bul 61:577-83 D 22 '69
Secretary Rogers' news conference of July
15, 1970. W. P. Rogers. Dept State Bul 63:
125-32 Ag 3 '70
Secretary Rogers' news conference of Octo-
ber 9, 1970. W. P. Rogers. Dept State Bul
63:471-8 O 26 '70
Signal from Moscow? the Malik proposal.
Newsweek 75:36 Ap 27 '70
Story of a peace initiative. H. Sidey. por
Life 69:2 O 16 '70
Strategy for peace in Nixon's own words;
address, October 7, 1970. R. M. Nixon. por
U S News 69:62-3 O 19 '70; Same with title
New peace initiative for all Indochina.
Dept State Bul 63:465-7 O 26 '70; Same with
title President Nixon's proposal for Indo-
china peace. Cur Hist 59:362+ D '70
U. S. reaffirms willingness to negotiate on
Viet-nam; statement, November 24, 1969.
H. C. Lodge. Dept State Bul 61:549 D 15
'69
Vietnam cooker. J. Osborne. New Repub 163:
11-13 S 26 '70
Vietcong proposal. New Repub 163:7 O 3 '70
Way out? the latest Nixon peace plan. Chr
Cent 87:1244 O 21 '70
What chance of peace? S. Alsop. por News-
week 75:92 Je 22 '70

Negotiation meetings, May 1968

Ambassador Lodge resigns as head of U.S.
delegation to Paris meetings; White House
announcement; with exchange of letters by
Lodge and President Nixon. Dept State Bul
61:549-50 D 15 '69
Americans in Paris. W. S. Just. Atlan 225:
20+ Ja '70
Bruce's debut. Newsweek 76:43 Ag 17 '70
Congress, Vietnam, Mideast: the President's
appraisal; excerpts from radio and TV
interview, July 1, 1970. R. M. Nixon. il por
U S News 69:20-2 Jl 13 '70
Gathering in praise of America. il Time 96:
9-10 Jl 13 '70
Going nowhere in Paris. G. M. Kahin. New
Repub 163:11-12 D 26 '70
Is Paris bungling? N. Cousins. Sat R 53:32 F
21 '70
Mr Habib discusses Hanoi's refusal to attend
May 6 meeting on Viet-Nam; transcript of
briefing, May 6, 1970. P. C. Habib. Dept
State Bul 62:650-1 My 25 '70
Oenologist's dilemma. Time 96:28 S 28 '70
[Plenary sessions] See issues of Department
of state bulletin
Re-enter Mme Binh; new Communist plan.
il por Newsweek 76:49 S 28 '70
Reporter at large (cont) R. Shaplen. New
Yorker 46:162+ O 17 '70
Sounds and silence in Paris. il Time 96:14-15
O 12 '70
Talking points in Paris. Time 96:48 O 26 '70
Time to ante up; 82nd session. il Newsweek
76:49 S 14 '70
Vietnamization is immoral; excerpt from
America and Russia in a changing world.
W. A. Harriman. Look 34:33+ N 17 '70
Why the Paris talks are getting nowhere. Z.
B. Grant. New Repub 163:17-19 O 10 '70

Personal narratives

Bulletins from bad guy land; excerpts from
letters. J. K. Bush, jr. por Time 95:12 Mr 23
'70

Confessions of Lieutenant Calley; interview,
ed. by J. Sack. W. L. Calley, jr. Esquire
74:113-19+ N '70
Looking back on the war; ed. by M. Parker.
P. Arnett. il por Newsweek 76:72 Jl 20 '70
My visit to Vietnam. N. Godfrey. il por Sev-
enteen 29:134-5+ Je '70
No laurels for legionnaires. W. G. Pelfrey.
New Repub 163:18-20 N 21 '70
One simple decision; American witnesses to
shooting of civilians by Vietcong and North
Vietnamese soliders. C. Coe. Nat R 22:950+
S 8 '70
Only people make you cry. I. M. Wiley.
Vogue 156:88-9+ Jl '70
War correspondent: a reappraisal. M. Herr.
il Esquire 73:95-101+ Ap '70
What price Vietnam glory? H. Kohler. il Chr
Cent 87:113-14 Ja 28 '70

Photography

Four photographers go jungle-busting; John
Saar's report. il Life 69:3 Jl 10 '70
Gallery; excerpt from War without heroes, by
D. D. Duncan. Life 69:4-5 D 18 '70
War without heroes, by D. D. Duncan. Re-
view
New Yorker 46:188+ D 12 '70. L. E. Siss-
man
Newsweek 76:89 D 7 '70. G. Wolff

Poetry

Poem with a punch line; reprint. E. Hutchins.
Chr Cent 87:1107 S 16 '70

Prisoners and prisons

Acting to aid the forgotten men; attempt to
rescue US POW's. il Time 96:15-18+ D 7 '70
At least I know Jim's alive; interview, ed. by
E. M. Wylie. S. Stockdale. il pors Good H
170:78-9+ F '70
Bill of indictment: inhuman conditions in
North Vietnam. Nat R 22:71 Ja 27 '70
Christmas package; TV film. il Newsweek 77:
20 Ja 11 '71
Colonel Borman reports on trip on behalf of
prisoners of war; transcript of news con-
ference. September 2, 1970. F. Borman. Dept
State Bul 63:344-6 S 28 '70
Colonel Borman undertakes mission relating
to prisoners of war; statement, August 7,
1970. R. M. Nixon. Dept State Bul 63:276
S 7 '70
Department gives views on proposed congressional resolution on U.S. prisoners of
war in southeast Asia; statement, May 6,
1970. W. H. Sullivan. Dept State Bul 62:
668-71 My 25 '70
Does Hanoi have a heart? D. Lawrence. U S
News 68:100 F 23 '70
Efforts to send packages to American PW's
continue; statement, February 5, 1970, by
Department press spokesman C. Bartch.
Dept State Bul 62:205-6 F 23 '70
Free them now! YAF rally on Boston Common to dramatize plight of American pris-
oners in North Vietnam. D. Brudnoy. Nat R
22:1404 D 29 '70
Freeing POWs; campaign to promote Sontay
as a success. New Repub 163:7 D 12 '70
Gamesmanship; Hanoi's high level communi-
cation. Newsweek 77:15-17 Ja 4 '71
Hanoi's pawns: the U.S. prisoners of war.
il Newsweek 76:30-1 N 30 '70
Latest on Americans held prisoner by reds.
U S News 69:23 D 7 '70
Memories of divided families; with interviews
with POW wives, ed. by M. Byers. il Life
69:36-40+ D 4 '70
Operation successful, results nil; commandoes
attempt to rescue U.S. POWs. il News-
week 76:26-8 D 7 '70
Politics of rescue. Nat R 22:1334 D 15 '70
POW Congress. New Repub 163:7-9 D 5 '70
President reaffirms U.S. concern for prisoners
in North Viet-Nam; remarks, December
12, 1969. R. M. Nixon. Dept State Bul 62:3
Ja 5 '70
Prisoners as pawns. Nation 211:610-12 D 14 '70
Prisoners of war; lest we forget; address,
September 22, 1970. F. Borman. Vital
Speeches 37:24-6 O 15 '70
Representative Leggett intervenes; Sontay
raid resolution. Nation 211:676 D 28 '70
Task group Ivory Coast; attempt to rescue
U.S. POWs. il Newsweek 76:28 D 7 '70
They also serve: wives of prisoners of war,
or men missing in action. P. L. Buckley.
Nat R 22:786-7+ Jl 28 '70
TRB from Washington; views of senators on
the Sontay rescue mission. New Repub 163:
4 D 12 '70
Treatment of American prisoners of war in
North Viet-Nam; statement, November 13,
1969. W. H. Sullivan. Dept State Bul 61:
596-9 D 22 '69

VIETNAMESE war, 1957- —Prisoners and prisons—*Continued*
U.S. prisoners of war in southeast Asia; address, September 22, 1970. F. Borman. Dept State Bul 63:405-8 O 12 '70
War claims act of 1948 extended to U.S. captives in southeast Asia. Dept State Bul 63:174 Ag 10 '70
What about the POW's? il Look 34:63 My 5 '70
What is Christmas to the P.O.W. wives? C. S. Wren. il Look 34:36-40 D 15 '70

Protests, demonstrations, etc, against

Aging Legion faces a new enemy; People's army jamboree. il Life 69:28-31 S 11 '70
All for Vietnam; excerpts from The trial. T. Hayden. il Ramp Mag 9:26-7+ S '70
Australia's massive moratorium. R. Mathias. Chr Cent 87:771-2 Je 17 '70
Battle for Berkeley. E. E. Plowman. Chr Today 14:40 My 8 '70
Cambodia: Nixon's trap. F. Schurmann. il Nation 210:651-6 Je 1 '70
Campus crisis: report to Nixon on causes of student unrest; excerpts from memoranda. A. Heard and J. E. Cheek. il pors U S News 69:28-9 Ag 3 '70
Citizens enterprise; political movements to end the war. New Repub 162:7 Je 20 '70
Clergy committee supports Moratorium fast. Chr Cent 87:351 Mr 25 '70
Clergy/lay group denounces bombing of North Vietnam. Chr Cent 87:1475 D 9 '70
College president's open letter: "I apologize for the grotesque failure" of the campuses. M. Upton. il U S News 68:39 Je 15 '70
Columbia L.S. students bus to D.C. condemn war. il Library J 95:2207 Je 15 '70
Concerned businessmen: Corporate executives committee for peace; meeting. New Yorker 46:26-7 Je 27 '70
Eric Brown; anti-war demonstration at Columbia university. New Yorker 46:30-1 Ap 25 '70
Fasting and picketing. Chr Today 14:42-4 Mr 13 '70
Few thorns among the roses; letter to Mrs Nixon from North Americans for peace in southeast Asia movement. B. Thompson. Chr Cent 87:1009 Ag 26 '70
From Hanoi: with thanks. Read Digest 96:51-5 F '70
Honoring America; political and social activist groups. New Repub 163:5-6 Jl 11 '70
Intolerant dissenters; eight Ivy league schools draft statement. Chr Today 14:28 Je 5 '70
Jane Fonda talks about. .; the G.I. coffee house movement; interview, ed. by L. Lerman. J. Fonda. pors Mlle 71:328-31 Ag '70
Jury's decision on war protesters; illegal entry and destruction of property at Dow chemical company. U S News 68:16 F 23 '70
Last train for peaceful politics. P. Steinfels. Commonweal 92:238 My 22 '70
Marine doves & the baffled brass; American servicemen's union at Iwakuni, Japan. C. C. Smith. Nation 211:199-202 S 14 '70
Military discipline; anti-war servicemen. Nation 210:548 My 11 '70
Nation's response to Nixon plea; divided over a call for unity. il Sr Schol 95:13-14 D 1 '69
New GI: for pot and peace. il Newsweek 75:24+ F 2 '70
New politics in '70; plans of Referendum '70 and Vietnam Moratorium. New Repub 162:9 Ja 17 '70
No more Vietnam; Southern Illinois university students protesting. Newsweek 75:63 Mr 9 '70
Notes from the underground; interview. D. Berrigan. New Yorker 46:20-3 Jl 25 '70
Peace suicides: Joan Fox and Craig Badiali of Blackwood, N.J. E. Asinof. Seventeen 29:174+ Mr '70
Pied Piper of the new children's crusade: A. Lowenstein. G. Astor. il por Look 34:36-8 Ag 25 '70
Pillsbury's best; Pillsbury Committee to end the war. New Repub 162:8-9 Je 27 '70
Politics and the university. J. K. Footlick. il Newsweek 75:96-7 My 18 '70
Positive spending; moratorium on buying. New Repub 162:12 My 30 '70
President designates Day of prayer for American prisoners of war, proclamation; May 6, 1970. R. M. Nixon. Dept State Bul 62:653 My 25 '70
Price of campus peace. Life 68:38 My 29 '70
Profiles; D. Berrigan and P. Berrigan. F. Du Plessix. pors New Yorker 46:44-6+ Mr 14 '70
Protestation and the elders; letter to the editor. R. V. Vaughn. Am Lib 1:112 F '70

Rally: March 12th, sponsored by Fund for new priorities in America. New Yorker 46:31-2 Mr 28 '70
Rebellion and repression and the Vietnam war. R. B. Smith. bibliog f il Ann Am Acad 391:156-67 S '70
Remobilizing for peace; the fast outside the White House. Commonweal 91:571-2 F 27 '70
Spring rerun; student antiwar conference in Cleveland. New Repub 162:10 Mr 7 '70
Sweet 'n' sour encounter; the President and D. J. Sweet. Chr Cent 87:1547 D 23 '70
Taking of Father Dan. il por Newsweek 76:37 Ag 24 '70
Toward martyrdom. il por Time 96:48 Ag 24 '70
Two gatherings: National coalition for a responsible congress; New York city bar association. New Yorker 46:22-4 My 30 '70
U.S. journal: Fort Dix, New Jersey. C. Trillin. New Yorker 46:40-2+ Je 6 '70
War casualty: Vietnam moratorium committee. il Newsweek 75:28 My 4 '70
War machine vs. the peace machinist. R. Linsley. il Esquire 73:82-3 F '70
Washington fast. New Yorker 46:32-3 Mr 7 '70
West Point cadets now say, "why, sir?" T. Fleming. il por N Y Times Mag p 14-18+ Jl 5 '70; Reply with rejoinder. R. B. Johnson, jr. p68 Ag 16 '70
What strategy for peace leadership. S. Brown. Cur 122:21-5 O '70
Workers against the war; West coast. A. Richmond. il Ramp Mag 9:28-32 S '70
Youth on the Hill; up against the marble wall anti-war activities. D. Blackburn. Nation 210:719-21 Je 15 '70
See also
Business executives move for Vietnam peace
Cambodian-Vietnamese conflict—Protests, demonstrations, etc, against
Concerned officers movement
Military service, Compulsory—Draft resisters
Universities national anti-war fund

Marches on Washington, November 1969

Night the peace bus left New Harley. R. H. Robbins. il Cath World 210:256-61 Mr '70
Peaceful crowd, a violent few. P. Goldberger. Sr Schol 95:13 D 1 '69
Secret link between Nixon and the New Mobe kids. W. Rogers. Look 34:73 Ja 27 '70

Moratorium day, October 15, 1969

On campus: is there an answer? A look at October 15. A. Ehrlich. Mlle 70:130 Ja '70
Story of the posting of the theses; M-day at Irondequoit high. R. Brookhiser. Nat R 22:196-8 F 24 '70
War over the war; with comments. il Sr Schol 95:13-15 N 3 '69

Moratoriums, rallies, etc, November 1969

Remember November. Nation 210:515-16 My 4 '70
What I did November 15, 1969. R. Drexler; D. R. Slavitt; T. Williams. Esquire 73:86+ My '70

Moratoriums, rallies, etc, April 1970

Dirty little war; Boston-Cambridge. D. Brudnoy. Nat R 22:453 My 5 '70
End of the march; New York moratorium march. M. Mohs. Time 95:27 Ap 27 '70
Radicals move in. il Newsweek 75:33-4 Ap 27 '70
Rallies, and riots; for peace. il U S News 68:73 Ap 27 '70
Time for words is over. Nat R 22:448 My 5 '70

Psychological aspects

Psychological causes and effects of atrocities. J. B. Sheerin. Cath World 211:2-3 Ap '70
Questions which tear us apart. D. Halberstam. il Harper 240:70-2+ F '70
Scars of Vietnam. R. J. Lifton. Commonweal 91:554-6 F 20 '70
Toward a critical social science. E. M. Opton, jr. and N. Sanford. Trans-Action 7:4-7 Mr '70
Why civilians are war victims in Vietnam; interview. R. J. Lifton. il Sci Digest 67:40-5 My '70

Public opinion

Division in labor. Nation 210:707-8 Je 15 '70
From Hanoi: with thanks. Read Digest 96:51-5 F '70
Mental gymnastics on Mylai. E. M. Opton, jr. and R. Duckles. il New Repub 162:14-16 F 21 '70
1964: exhilaration; 1968: frustration; 1970: hopelessness. A. J. Langguth. il N Y Times Mag p26-7+ O 4 '70

VIETNAMESE war, 1957- —Public opinion—
Continued
Turning off the people: the war and white ethnic groups. A. M. Greeley. New Repub 162:14-16 Je 27 '70; Same with title War and white ethnic groups. Cur 120:22-7 Ag '70
Vietnam and the Jewish community. B. Brickner. Chr Cent 87:531-4 Ap 29 '70
Voices from the silent majority. J. C. Goulden. il Harper 240:67-72+ Ap '70; Discussion. 241:8+ Jl '70
War and big business; views of four leaders of American corporations. L. L. L. Golden. Sat R 53:95 S 12 '70
War rallies: pro and con. il U S News 68:89 Je 1 '70
War: who wants it? Nation 210:706 Je 15 '70
What strategy for peace leadership. S. Brown. Cur 122:21-5 O '70
See also
Student opinion

Refugees
See Refugees, Vietnamese

Relief work
Modest proposal; dropping goods on southeast Asia, instead of bombs. P. Roth. il Look 34:98-100 O 6 '70
Need for a new Christian presence in Vietnam. D. Hostetter. Chr Cent 87:536-7 Ap 29 '70; Discussion. 87:826 Jl 1 '70

Search and rescue operations
Acting to aid the forgotten men; attempt to rescue US POW's. il Time 96:15-18+ D 7 '70
Daring raids in Vietnam: purpose of Nixon's move. il U S News 69:22-3 D 7 '70
Freeing POWs; campaign to promote Sontay as a success. New Repub 163:7 D 12 '70
How the raid was planned; attempt to rescue POWs. H. Sidey. Life 69:36 D 4 '70
Language of rescue missions. America 123:510 D 12 '70
North targets hit; attempt to rescue U.S. prisoners. Sr Schol 97:4 D 14 '70
Operation successful, results nil; commandoes attempt to rescue U.S. POWs. il Newsweek 76:26-8 D 7 '70
Prisoners as pawns. Nation 211:610-12 D 14 '70
TRB from Washington; views of senators on the Sontay rescue mission. New Repub 163:4 D 12 '70

Statistics
Summing up. W. F. Buckley, jr. Nat R 22:45-6 Ja 13 '70

Strategy
After pinkville, what? N. Chomsky. Cur 115:18-30 F '70
Are we and Hanoi in the same war? R. J. Barnet. Cur 116:3-9 Mr '70
Can Vietnam go it alone? interview, ed. by W. S. Merick and J. N. Wallace. Nguyen-van-Thieu. il por U S News 68:71-5 Mr 16 '70
Dangers confronting U.S; interview. M. R. Laird. il pors U S News 68:64-8+ My 11 '70
Hanoi's formula: how to win while losing. J. N. Wallace. il U S News 68:44-6 Ap 6 '70
How can we lose in Vietnam, having won? P. A. McCombs. il Nat R 22:1399-402 D 29 '70
Johnson seeks vindication. Time 95:20 F 23 '70
Nixon and Vietnam. J. Deedy. il Commonweal 91:570 F 27 '70
Nixon's dilemma; the war and the 1972 elections. Nation 211:578-9 D 7 '70
Nixon's latest strategy for peace in Vietnam. il U S News 68:14-15 My 4 '70
Nixon's new signals in Viet Nam. il Time 96:14-15 D 14 '70
On the road to a just peace. R. Thompson. Read Digest 96:68-73 Mr '70
Paradox of nonviolent war in Vietnam. I. de S. Pool. por Life 69:2 Jl 4 '70
President explains his decision on Indo-China; address, April 30, 1970. R. M. Nixon. il U S News 68:22-4 My 11 '70
Protracted war; Hanoi's policy. il Newsweek 76:60 D 21 '70
Question of balance; the process of Vietnamization. R. Thompson. Read Digest 96:60-1 Ap '70
Shift in strategy; enemy tactics. P. Brinkley-Rogers. Newsweek 76:27+ Jl 27 '70
Stepped-up war. Nation 211:674-5 D 28 '70
Summing up. W. F. Buckley, jr. Nat R 22:46 Ja 13 '70
Vietnam and restraints on aerial warfare. B. M. Russett. il Bul Atom Sci 26:9-12 Ja '70; Reply. A. E. Berthoff. 26:49-50 O '70
Vietnam and the draft; address, February 19, 1970. W. E. Hearnes. Vital Speeches 36:336-8 Mr 15 '70

Vietnamization is immoral; excerpt from America and Russia in a changing world. W. A. Harriman. Look 34:38+ N 17 '70
Why we didn't win in Vietnam. il U S News 68:44-5 F 9 '70

Television reports
See Television broadcasting—War news

Transportation
Along the infamous Ho Chi Minh trail. K. O. Gilmore. il Read Digest 97:146-50 O '70

War aims
Is Hanoi ready to end the Vietnam war? V. Zorza. Cur 120:27-30 Ag '70

War correspondents
Between the lines; report from Phnom-Penh. R. Anson. il Time 95:79 My 4 '70
Cover story; accreditation as correspondents. Newsweek 75:63 F 9 '70
Unreal MACOI. Time 95:52 F 9 '70
War correspondent: a reappraisal. M. Herr. il Esquire 73:95-101+ Ap '70

Women and the war
Am I a wife or a widow? C. S. Wren. il Read Digest 96:93-6 Mr '70
At least I know Jim's alive; interview, ed. by E. M. Wylie. S. Stockdale. il pors Good H 170:78-9+ F '70
Mrs O'Grady is a widow; statement, ed. by C. S. Wren. D. O'Grady. por Look 34:67 My 5 '70
See also
Service mens wives

Cambodia
See Cambodian-Vietnamese conflict
VIETNAMESE war and college students. See College students and war
VIETNAMESE war as a campaign issue. See Campaign issues
VIETNAMESE war brides. See War marriages
VIETTE, Andre
Outstanding daylilies. il Horticulture 48:34-5 My '70
VIETTI, Eleanor Ardel
Woman doctor is missing in action. J. C. Hefley. il Todays Health 48:38-41+ Ap '70
VIEW cameras. See Cameras
VIEW finders
Auto-focus hocus-pocus. N. Goldberg. il Pop Phot 67:70-1+ Ag '70
Do your specs and viewfinder get along. N. Goldberg. il Pop Phot 66:48+ F '70
Keppler on the SLR. H. Keppler. Mod Phot 34:16+ Ap '70
Photographic electronics '70; automatic infrared rangefinder. J. R. Free. il Radio-Electr 41:41-3 My '70
VIGILANCE committees
Citizens' war on crime; spreading across U.S. il U S News 68:55-8 Mr 23 '70; Same abr. with title America's citizen crime fighters. Read Digest 96:225-6+ Je '70
See also
Jewish defense league
Minutemen (organization)

California
San Francisco and the vigilante style. R. Olmsted. il Am West 7:6-11+ Ja; 20-7+ Mr '70
Sleeping giant stirs; Berkeley's plan. il Newsweek 75:76 Mr 16 '70

Colorado
Dissent and reaction: vigilante activity at NBS labs in Boulder. P. M. Boffey. por Science 169:163-4 Jl 10 '70
VIGILANTES. See Vigilance committees
VIGO COUNTY, Ind, public library, Terre Haute
Orbital organization. E. N. Howard. il por Library J 95:1712-15 My 1 '70
VIGREN, David D.
New space program for vacations. il Pop Sci 196:82-3+ Mr '70
What fun boating people have! il Pop Sci 196:79+ F '70
VIKING press, inc.
Journalist sues Viking, Esquire, over Calley story. Pub W 198:30 O 19 '70
VIKINGS
Seek & ye shall find. P. W. Schmidtchen. il Hobbies 74:134-6+ Ja '70
Vikings. H. LaFay. il Nat Geog 137:492-541 Ap '70
VIKINGS (football club) See Football clubs

VILA REYES, Juan
National scandal starts to unravel. por Bsns
W p56 My 23 '70 *
VILEN, Frank I.
Combined sewers may be an advantage. il
Am City 85:68-70 Ja '70
VILLA, Francisco
Great pursuit, by H. M. Mason, jr. Review
Bsns W il p6 Jl 25 '70. H. B. Gonzalez *
Papa and Pancho Villa. E. H. Lopez. il Am
Heritage 21:57-63 Ag '70 *
VILLA, Pancho. See Villa, F.
VILLAGE life
Profiles; Stapleton, Neb. B. Roueché. New
Yorker 46:29-40 Ja 2 '71
VILLAGE voice (newspaper)
Buying a voice; Taurus communications
buys controlling interest. por Newsweek
75:94 Mr 23 '70
Politics of style. J. Corry. il Harper 241:60-4
N '70
VILLAGER industries, inc.
Helping a competitor, at a price. il pors
Bsns W p48+ Ap 18 '70
VILLAGES
Early New England textile village in art. R.
M. Candee. il Antiques 98:910-15 D '70
What life is like in one little corner of China;
interview, ed. by K. Chrysler. il U S News
68:54-5 Je 22 '70
See also
Village life
VILLAGES, Models of. See Models of cities,
towns, etc.
VILLAGES, Restored
Hancock Shaker village. il Craft Horiz 30:44-5
My '70
On and off the avenue; Shaker museum.
J. Malcolm. New Yorker 46:62-5 Ag 8 '70
Restorations West. Travel & Camera 33:10+
Ap '70
See also
Henry Ford museum and Greenfield Village,
Dearborn, Mich.
Old Sturbridge village, Sturbridge, Mass.
VILLAINS. See Crime and criminals
VILLARREAL, Carlos Castaneda
First, find the mice. Newsweek 76:58+ S 28
'70 *
VILLARS, Trudy. See Bardach, J. E. jt. auth.
VILLELLA, Edward
To be a dancer. S. J. Cohen. il pors Opera
N 34:26-9 Ap 18 '70 *
VILLET, Barbara
Nobody hassles us, everybody listens. Life
68:60+ My 8 '70
VILLIARD, Paul
Bouquet for Miss Benson; excerpt from
Growing pains: the autobiography of a
young boy. il Read Digest 97:119-21 Jl '70
VILLON, Jacques, pseud.
First impressions. H. A. La Farge. il Art N
69:37+ O '70 *
VILLOT, Jean Marie, cardinal
Next Pope. J. Deedy. Commonweal 93:338
Ja 8 '71
VINCENNES university. See Colleges and univ-
ersities—France
VINCENT, Clark
When married love is disappointing. il Red-
book 134:82-3+ Ap '70
VINCENT, Edith P.
Teaching about venereal diseases. Todays Ed
59:50-1 F '70
VINCENT, Merville O.
Suicide and how to prevent it. Chr Today
14:10-12 Ja 16 '70
VINCENT, Wesley A.
Find R.M.S. values graphically. il Electr
World 84:17 Jl '70
VINCENT-BARWOOD, Aileen
Silent passage; story. Redbook 135:65-6 Ag
'70
VINEGAR
Things your mother never taught you: vine-
gar, its many lives. il Ladies Home J 87:
76 Ja '70
VINES. See Climbing plants
VINNEDGE, Harlan H.
I'd rather be hijacked. il New Repub 163:17-
19 N 28 '70
Let's hear it for pollution, if it's in Asia. New
Repub 163:14-15 O 17 '70
VINS, Georgi
Russian Baptist leader imprisoned. M.
Bourdeaux. Chr Cent 87:830 Jl 1 '70 *
VINSON, Carlos
Countdown for chucks. il Outdoor Life 145:
86-7+ Ap '70
Cow pasture buck. il pors Outdoor Life 146:
60-1+ D '70
VINSON, Lu Ouida
Students, systems, and selection: address,
1969. por Library J 95:205-7 Ja 15 '70

VINYL floor tiles. See Tiles, Floor
VIOLENCE
Academia in anarchy, by J. M. Buchanan
and N. E. Devletoglou. Review
Nat R il 22:684-5 Je 30 '70. W. Breit
Agnew's talk with five students; text of
television debate. S. T. Agnew and others.
il pors U S News 69:86-8+ O 12 '70
America as a gun culture; excerpt from
American violence, ed. by R. Hofstadter
and M. Wallace. il Am Heritage 21:4-11+ O
'70
America, the violent; address, July 8, 1970.
P. L. Briand, jr. Vital Speeches 36:674-9
S 1 '70
Anti-Nixon outburst caps a violent week. il
U S News 69:52 N 9 '70
As violence spreads in high schools . . . il
U S News 69:18-20 N 30 '70
Bombing condoned; Daily cardinal's editorial.
America 123:248-9 O 10 '70
California evil. C. Karpel. il Esquire 73:99-
100 Mr '70
Campus conflict. Chr Today 14:23 My 22 '70
Chemistry of violence. F. C. Klein. Sci Digest
68:8-12 D '70
Crisis of violence; report of the President's
commission on campus unrest. Commonweal
93:35-6 O 9 '70
Explanations and excesses. N. Cousins. Sat
R 53:20 O 10 '70
Force: a Christian option? Chr Today 14:20
Ja 30 '70
Future of American violence; excerpt from
American violence. R. Hofstadter. il Harper
240:47-53 Ap '70
Future of world politics; will there be less
violence? Cur 115:61-4 F '70
How violence affects children. il por Life 68:
57-8 Ja 30 '70
Humanism and terror, by M. Merleau-Ponty.
Review
Commonweal 93:225-6 N 27 '70. D. Howard
Life of love and freedom; wave of United
States political violence. Fortune 81:65-6
Ap '70
Minority report on U.S. violence. H. Fairlie.
Cur 114:36-40 Ja '70
New pattern of violence. il U S News 70:
23-5 Ja 4 '71
Nixon on violence: a cancerous disease; ex-
cerpts from address, September 16, 1970. R.
M. Nixon. il por U S News 69:27-8 S 28 '70
Nobody ever learned anything from violence,
except how to duck. C. Holland. Mlle 72:
177+ N '70
Protesters, police, and politicians. J. Unruh.
Sat R 53:31+ F 21 '70
Rage against violence. K. Widmer. il Nation
211:45-8 Jl 20 '70
Reagan's bloodbath: truth and imagery. Nat
R 22:445 My 5 '70
Responsible university leadership: violence
and dissent; address, September 16, 1970.
R. M. Nixon. Vital Speeches 36:738-40 O 1
'70; Excerpts. il por U S News 69:27-8 S
28 '70
Ticking of the time bomb. F. J. Cook. Nation
210:406-7 Ap 6 '70
Tooth and claw. L. Berkowitz. Trans-Action
7:59-60 Je '70
Toward peace. J. West. Redbook 135:75+ S
'70
Understanding man's aggressiveness. D.
Behrman. il UNESCO Courier 23:4-18+ Ag
'70
Uses of violence in American history; adap-
tation of address, December 1969. M. Wallace. Am Scholar 40:81-102 Wint '70
Violence as a defense against intimacy. S. H.
Kardener and M. Fuller. bibliog Ment Hy
54:310-15 Ap '70
Violence in America, by H. D. Graham and
T. R. Gurr. Review
Trans-Action 7:56-8 F '70. S. J. Mandel-
baum
Violence is predictable; episodic dyscontrol
syndrome. A. Rosenthal. il Todays Health
48:56-7+ N '70
War on violence. R. Drinnon. bibliog il Wil-
son Lib Bul 45:68-77 S '70; Reply. J. Jamie-
son. 45:236 N '70
Ways of violence. E. W. Ranly. America 123:
140-3 S 12 '70
Why blacks kill blacks; psychiatrist on ghetto
violence. A. F. Poussaint. il por Ebony 25:
143-6 O '70
Why men rebel, by T. R. Gurr. Review
Commentary 50:73-6 Jl '70. J. R. Adams
Why streets are not safe; special report on
crime. il U S News 68:15-21 Mr 16 '70
See also
Assault and battery
Terrorism
United States—National commission on the
causes and prevention of violence

VIOLENCE in art
Visions of our time; works of J. Genoves.
il UNESCO Courier 23:18-19 Ag '70
VIOLENCE in literature
Songmy; the human imperative; school li-
braries' responsibility. M. Braverman. il por
Library J 95:211-13 Ja 15 '70
Wyatt Earp syndrome. C. L. Sonnichsen. il
Am West 7:26-8+ My '70
VIOLENCE in mass media. See Mass media—
Moral aspects
VIOLENCE in moving pictures. See Moving pic-
tures—Moral aspects
VIOLENCE in television programs. See Televi-
sion broadcasting—Moral aspects
VIOLIN
First fiddles; two Stradivarius violins auc-
tioned at Sotheby's. il Newsweek 76:121 N
2 '70
Repairing
First they love the art. J. Mandelstam. il Sr
Schol 95:18-19 Ja 5 '70
VIOLIN music
Must a great violinist play in tune? R. C.
Marsh; H. Goldsmith. Hi Fi sec I 20:91 Ja
'70
See also
Phonograph records—Violin music
VIOLIN playing
See also
Ensemble playing
VIOLINISTS
See also
Lolli, A.
Maazel, L.
Perlman, I.
Ricci, R.
Zukerman, P.
VIORST, Judith
Confessions of a jealous wife. il Redbook
134:92-3+ Mr '70; Same abr. Read Digest
96:137-40 Je '70
Family that fights together. . .fights together.
Redbook 135:61+ Ag '70; Same abr. Read
Digest il 97:89-91 N '70
Lady next door; poem. McCalls 98:14 Ja '71
Pat Nixon is the ultimate good sport. il
pors N Y Times Mag p25-7+ S 13 '70
16.5 days of Christmas; confessions of a Jew-
ish mother. Redbook 136:64-5+ D '70
Who's minding the baby? il Redbook 135:
70-1+ Je '70
VIORST, Milton
Bill Douglas has never stopped fighting the
bullies of Yakima. il pors N Y Times Mag
p8-9+ Je 14 '70
Blacks who work for Nixon. il N Y Times
Mag p66-7+ N 29 '70
Friedmanism, n. doctrine of most audacious
U.S. economist. il pors N Y Times Mag
p22-3+ Ja 25 '70
(ed) See Aron, R.   There is no Raymond
Aron cult: talk with a reasonable man
VIRAL chemotherapy. See Chemotherapy
VIRAL genetics. See Microbial genetics
VIRAL hepatitis. See Hepatitis
VIRGIL
Eclogue II; poem, tr. by S. Orgel. Poetry
116:353-5 Ag '70
Two eclogues of Virgil; tr. by D. R. Slavitt.
Yale R 60:251-3 D '70
VIRGIN Mary. See Mary, Virgin
VIRGIN ISLANDS
See also
Airlines—Virgin Islands
Architecture, Domestic—Virgin Islands
Hotels, taverns, etc.—Virgin Islands
Negroes in the Virgin Islands
St Thomas Island
Description and travel
Doing it small. R. Surridge. il Yachting 128:
60-1+ N '70
Let's travel; U.S. Virgin Islands. Mlle 70:44
Ja '70
Virgin Islands. J. A. Munves. il Travel &
Camera 33:36-45 D '70
Politics and government
Struggle for paradise. C. L. Sanders. il Ebony
25:66-8+ O '70
Race problems
Struggle for paradise. C. L. Sanders. il Ebony
25:66-8+ O '70
Social conditions
Caribbean: this side of paradise: aliens. P.
Nabokov. Nation 210:332-5 Mr 23 '70
Virgin Islands: shame in the U.S. tropics;
bonded aliens. J. Star. il Look 34:17-21 Mr
10 '70

VIRGIN ISLANDS, BRITISH. See British Vir-
gin Islands
VIRGINIA
See also
Arlington County
Assateague Island
Chesapeake Bay
Colleges and universities—Virginia
Dismal Swamp
Education—Virginia
Gardens—Virginia
Hunting—Virginia
School libraries—Virginia
Shenandoah National Park
Shenandoah Valley
Smith Island
Tangier Island

Description and travel
Camper cruising east of the eastern shore.
G. W. Reiger. il Motor B 127:191-4 Ja '71
Plantation tour. N. Wood. il Travel & Cam-
era 33:65 Ap '70
South to spring. D. Butwin. il Sat R 53:53-4+
My 23 '70

Historic houses, etc.
South to spring: Monticello, Berkeley planta-
tion, and Williamsburg. D. Butwin. Sat R
53:38-9 My 30 '70
See also
Botetourt County, Va.—Historic houses, etc.
George Washington Birthplace National Monu-
ment
Monticello (historic house)
Plantations
Williamsburg

Politics and government
Shakeup in Virginia. New Repub 162:9 My
23 '70
Virginia: a state with a new style. il Bsns W
p 104+ O 17 '70
State song
See State songs
VIRGINIA CITY, Nev.
Kid on the Comstock; excerpts. J. T. Wal-
dorf. il por Am West 7:11-17 Mr '70
VIRGINITY
Christian virgins. Time 96:62 S 21 '70
Higher calling? Vatican revives rite for wom-
en. Newsweek 76:83 S 21 '70
Old hang-up; Vatican's announcement of a
rite of consecrated virginity. Commonweal
92:476 S 25 '70; Discussion. 93:183 N 13 '70
VIRTS, John R. and Garrett, R. W.
Weighing risk in capacity expansion. il
Harvard Bsns R 48:132-41 My '70
VIRTUOSITY in music
Early Gaffuriana: new answers to old ques-
tions. C. A. Miller. bibliog f por Mus Q
56:367-88 Jl '70
VIRUS diseases
War on viral diseases. A. J. Snider. il Sci Di-
gest 67:62-3 F '70
See also
Cold (disease)
Lassa fever
Virus research
Vaccines
Control of acute mycoplasmal and viral re-
spiratory tract disease. R. M. Chanock. bib-
liog il Science 169:248-56 Jl 17 '70
VIRUS diseases in plants
See also
Insects as carriers of plant disease
VIRUS research
Crib deaths; some answers to 20,000 sudden
tragedies. E. H. McGough. il Sci Digest 67:
26-30 F '70
Therapy by virus; genetic disease. il Sci N
98:198-9 S 5 '70
VIRUSES
Homologous viral interference: induction by
RNA from defective particles of vesicular
stomatitis virus. T Sreevalsan. bibliog il
Science 169:991-3 S 4 '70
Hydrocephalus in mice inoculated neonatally
by the oronasal route with reovirus type 1.
P. A. Phillips and others. bibliog il Science
168:858-9 My 15 '70
See also
Adenoviruses
Bacteriophage
Echo viruses
Fetus, Effect of viruses on the
Hepatitis viruses
Herpes simplex virus
Herpesvirus
Leukemia viruses
Simian viruses
Tumor viruses
Virus research

VIRUSES—*Continued*

Inactivation

Peroxidase-mediated virucidal systems. M. E. Belding and others. bibliog il Science 167: 195-6 Ja 9 '70

Tilorone hydrochloride: an orally active antiviral agent. R. F. Krueger and G. D. Mayer. il Science 169:1213-14 S 18 '70

Tilorone hydrochloride: mode of action. G. D. Mayer and R. F. Krueger. il Science 169: 1214-15 S 18 '70

See also
Interferon

VIRUSES, Insect

Helping nature control insects. il Sci N 98: 197-8 S 5 '70

Natural sciences; International colloquium on insect pathology. Sci N 98:194 S 5 '70

Toxic factor produced by a granulosis virus in armyworm larva: effect on apanteles militaris. H. K. Kaya. bibliog il Science 168:251-3 Ap 10 '70

VIRUSES, Oncogenic. See Tumor viruses

VIRUSES, Plant

Barley yellow dwarf virus: phenotypic mixing and vector specificity. W. F. Rochow. bibliog il Science 167:875-8 F 6 '70

VISAS. See Passports

VISCONTI, Luchino

Visconti. K. Radkai. il pors Vogue 156:182-9+ N 1 '70

Visconti in Venice. H. Alpert. il por Sat R 53:16-18 Ag 8 '70; Reply with rejoinder. L. Visconti. 53:20 D 19 '70

VISCOSITY

Negative viscosity. V. P. Starr and N. E. Gaut. il Sci Am 223:72-8+ bibliog(p 136) Jl '70

Viscosity of lunar lavas. T. Murase and A. R. McBirney. bibliog il Science 167:1491-3 Mr 13 '70

See also
Blood—Viscosity
Rheology
Surface tension

VISES

Bench vises. il Consumer Rep 35:485-8 Ag '70

VISHNEVSKII, Aleksandr Aleksandrovich

From a surgical dynasty, a dynamic surgeon general. R. Chelminsky. il pors Life 68:46-8 Ja 23 '70

VISION. See Sight

VISION information center. See Harvard university—Medical school—Library

VISITING, Hospital. See Hospitals—Visitors

VISITING housekeepers

Freelance house-sitting; Travelers home care. J. Kuh. por Ladies Home J 87:132 Mr '70

VISITOR services. See Information services

VISITORS; story. See McKimmey, J.

VISITORS, Hospital. See Hospitals—Visitors

VISTA. See Volunteers in service to America

VISTA-dome cars. See Railroads—Cars

VISTE, K. L. and others

Dimethylpropynylbenzamides: a new group of herbicides. il Science 167:280-1 Ja 16 '70

VISUAL adaptation. See Eye—Accommodation and refraction

VISUAL aids. See Audio-visual aids

VISUAL arts education. See Art education

VISUAL cells. See Rod and cone cells

VISUAL discrimination. See Discrimination (psychology)

VISUAL illusions. See Optical illusions

VISUAL instruction. See Audio-visual instruction

VISUAL perception. See Perception

VISUAL pigments

See also
Rod and cone cells

VITAL statistics

See also
Census
Population—Statistics
Registers of births, etc.
    also subhead Vital statistics under names of countries, e.g. Great Britain—Vital statistics

VITAMINS

Finding and treating genetic diseases; vitamin-dependency diseases. por Sci N 98: 157-8 Ag 22 '70

Mystery of vitamins. Newsweek 76:69 Ag 24 '70

See also
Deficiency diseases in animals
Food, Enriched

Vitamin B₆

Biosynthesis of vitamin B₆: incorporation of three-carbon units. R. E. Hill and I. D. Spenser. bibliog il Science 169:773-5 Ag 21 '70

Teratogenicity of vitamin B₆ deficiency: omphalocele, skeletal and neural defects, and splenic hypoplasia. S. D. Davis and others. bibliog il Science 169:1329-30 S 25 '70

Vitamin B₁₂

Vitamin B₁₂ binders of chicken serum and chicken proventriculus are immunologically similar. D. W. Sonneborn and H. J. Hansen. bibliog il Science 168:591-2 My 1 '70

Vitamin C

Cadmium toxicity decreased by dietary ascorbic acid supplements. M. R. S. Fox and B. E. Fry, jr. bibliog il Science 169:989-91 S 4 '70

Case of vitamin C. por Sci N 98:477 D 26 '70

My roses grow vitamins! L. Riotte. il Org Gard & Farm 17:54-7 Ap '70

Vitamin C, anyone? theories of L. Pauling. por Newsweek 76:63-4 N 30 '70

Vitamin D

Rickets. W. F. Loomis. il Sci Am 223:76-82+ bibliog(p 140) D '70

Vitamin E

Ozone and vitamin E. B. D. Goldstein and others. bibliog il Science 169:605 Ag 7 '70

VITELLO tonnato. See Cookery, Italian

VITICULTURE

Bread and wine; French bumper crop of grapes. il Time 96:92 N 2 '70

Save those grapes! H. C. Mathews. il Org Gard & Farm 17:84 Ag '70

VITREOUS state. See Glassy state

VITUPERATION. See Invective

VIVALDI, Antonio

Little Vivaldi festival. S. Fleming. Hi Fi 20: 104 S '70

VIVANTE, Arturo

Bed; story. New Yorker 46:37-9 S 12 '70

Diagnostician; story. New Yorker 46:191-3 D 5 '70

VIVATI Vivat Regina; drama. See Bolt, R.

VIVES, Jaime Vicens. See Vicens Vives, J.

VIVIAN, John

Bantys in the backyard. il por Org Gard & Farm 17:42-5 My '70

New England sodbusting, second time around. il pors Org Gard & Farm 17:32-7 Jl '70

VIVIPARITY. See Reproduction

VIVISECTION

Quandary of cats; antivivisectionist lobbying aids passage of new law in California. il Newsweek 76:103 D 7 '70

VIZCAYA gardens. See Miami, Fla.—Gardens

VIZINCZEY, Stephen

Rules of chaos; excerpts. il McCalls 97:76-7+ My; 32+ Je '70

VLACHOS, Helen

Exile; interview. New Yorker 46:19-20 Jl 4 '70

about

Lady and the colonels. S. Rousseas. Nation 211:149-50 Ag 31 '70

VLAHAKIS, G. and others

Strain C3H-A^vfB mice: ninety percent incidence of mammary tumors transmitted by either parent. bibliog il Science 170:185-7 O 9 '70

VOCABULARY

Dictionary as a tool in vocabulary development programs. W. Morris. Engl J 59:669-71 My '70

Discovering truth about words; organizing words into groups for language study. F. C. Flowers. Engl J 59:259-62 F '70

Down Giantwife: the uses of etymology. C. Laird. Engl J 59:1106-12 N '70

Techniques in vocabulary development. E. L. Dale and J. L. Milligan. Ed Digest 36:42-3 S '70

Vocabulary for slow learners. N. J. Doemel. Engl J 59:78-80 Ja '70

VOCABULARY tests

It pays to increase your word power. P. Funk. See issues of Reader's digest

Jovial insipid subject; method for making new words alluring to children. por Time 96:54+ Ag 10 '70

VOCAL groups. See Choral groups and societies

VOCAL music

See also
Phonograph records—Vocal music
Responses (music)

VOCAL ornamentation.   See Embellishment (vocal music)

VOCAL training. See Voice culture

VOCATION, Religious. See Vocation in religion

VOCATION in religion
Hard sell of vocations; Interfaith committee for religious concerns. America 123:308 O 24 '70
Latin apostolate. J. Deedy. Commonweal 93: 114 O 30 '70
Pastoral vocation in Latin America.   E. Castro. Chr Cent 88:6 Ja 6 '71
Questions without answers. V. P. McCorry. America 122:inside back cover Je 13 '70
Recruiting for religious careers. America 122: 264-5 Mr 14 '70
Vocations crisis. J. Deedy. Commonweal 93: 362 Ja 15 '71

VOCATIONAL education
Competence for all as the goal for secondary education; excerpts from address. J. E. Allen, jr. Ed Digest 36:24-7 S '70
Effective preparation for apprenticeship. R. Hammond. Mo Labor R 93:44-5 Ap '70
Manpower training goes to college; Manpower development and training act skills center in Denver. G. P. Million. il Am Ed 6:23-5 N '70
Manual high school: cutting class can get you to college. il pors Ebony 25:68-70+ My '70
Middle school years and career development. W. A. Stanton. Clear House 44:531-3 My '70
Model high school vocational program. T. L. Reddick. Clear House 45:215 D '70
More emphasis required. Sch & Soc 98:136+ Mr '70
Our neglect of vocational training. R. Kirk. Nat R 22:951 S 8 '70
PECE corps: career exploration; Georgia. M. K. Murphy. il School Teach Jr/Sr High p24-5 S 21 '70
Reforming vocational-technical education. Sch & Soc 98:73-4 F '70
Would Horatio Alger need a degree? J. W. Kuhn. il Sat R 53:54-5+ D 19 '70
Zeroing-in on a program of zero rejects. M. J. Feldman. Ed Digest 36:20-3 S '70
    See also
Agricultural education
Business education
COPE program
Education, Cooperative
Service men—Vocational education

Federal aid
Kids our high schools forget; interview. J. E. Allen. por Nations Bsns 58:70-2 Je '70
Short-term institutes for vocational educators. il Am Ed 6:35-6 Ap '70
Support for vocational-technical education. il Am Ed 6:31-2 Jl '70

Brazil
Brazil: a giant begins to stir. F. Haussman. il Sat R 53:62-3+ O 17 '70

United States
    See Vocational education

VOCATIONAL guidance
Guidance for those who guide: Kimberly-Clark's Guidance counselors' traveling workshop. Nations Bsns 58:20 Mr '70
    See also
Occupations
Veterans—Vocational education
Vocational education

VOCATIONAL literature
Career-related guidance for youth. C. M. Ury. bibliog il por Wilson Lib Bul 44:621-31 F '70

VOCATIONAL psychology
    See also
Job satisfaction

VOCATIONAL rehabilitation
Using an education model in a sheltered workshop program. D. Safier. Ment Hy 54: 140-3 Ja '70
We need sheltered workshops for former mental patients. A. H. Cristol. Ment Hy 54:444-6 Jl '70
    See also
Handicapped—Employment

VOCATIONAL schools. See Trade schools; Vocational education

VOCATIONS. See Occupations; Professions

VODKA
Vodka on the rocks: Russia's liquor problem. il Time 95:24 F 16 '70

VOGEL, Eduard
Eduard Vogel and his travels. J. Ashbrook. Sky & Tel 40:213 O '70 *

VOGEL, Manfred
Some reflections on the Jewish-Christian dialogue in the light of the six-day war. bibliog f Ann Am Acad 387:96-108 Ja '70

VOGEL, Mary
Frame opening. il Design 71:17 Fall '69

VOGEL, Nancy
New TV shows, fall 1970. Writers Digest 50: 20-3 Je '70
Television and film writing (cont) por Writers Digest 50:44-6 F; 42+ Ap; 18-21 O '70

VOGUE (French magazine) See Periodicals—France

VOHRA, Hans R.
India's nuclear policy of three negatives. il Bul Atom Sci 26:25-7 Ap '70

VOICE
Listen to my voice: is it really me? il Seventeen 29:134-5 My '70
Speaking of voices. Harp Baz 103:159 My '70

VOICE culture
Breath of life. S. Ames. il Opera N 34:6-7 Mr 21 '70
Speaking of Wagner; interview, ed. by G. Fitzgerald. L. Melchior. por Opera N 34:6-9 Mr 28 '70

VOICE teachers. See Singing teachers

VOICEPRINTS
Voiceprints not that reliable. Sci Digest 67: 41 Ja '70

VOIGHT, Jon
Voight: fresh eye on Hollywood; interview, ed. by S. Gordon. por Look 34:78 N 3 '70

VOLCANIC ash, tuff, etc.
Volcanic ash bodies and glazes. R. Behrens. il Ceram Mo 18:28 D '70

VOLCANIC glass. See Obsidian

VOLCANOES
Active submarine volcanism in the Austral islands. R. H. Johnson. bibliog il Science 167:977-9 F 13 '70
America's sleeping volcanoes. W. G. Melson. il Nat Wildlife 8:39-47 D '69; Same. Sci Digest 68:40-4 Ag '70
Exposed guyot from the Afar Rift, Ethiopia. E. Bonatti and H. Tazieff. bibliog il Science 168:1087-9 My 29 '70
Life studies flow from live volcanoes. R. H. Gilluly. il Sci N 97:411-13 Ap 25 '70
    See also
Craters
Diamond Head
Rainier, Mount

VOLDSTAD, Natalie
Our wonderful teen volunteers. il Parents Mag 46:46-7+ Ja '71

VOLES. See Mice

VOLK, Vic
Of many things. D. L. Flaherty. America 123: 161 S 19 '70 *

VOLKSWAGEN. See Automobiles, Foreign

VOLKSWAGEN foundation. See Foundations. Charitable and educational

VOLKSWAGEN of America, inc.
Rebound. il Forbes 105:60 Mr 1 '70

VOLLEYBALL
Spiking's the punch at UCLA; first college championship. J. Jares. il Sports Illus 32: 24-5 My 4 '70

VOLLMAR, Eileen B.
Chalk batik. il Sch Arts 70:28-9 Ja '71

VOLOSHEN, Nathan
Indictments for two. por Time 95:16 Ja 26 '70
McCormack's reapers? por Newsweek 75:16 Ja 26 '70

VOLPE, E. Peter, and Earley, E. M.
Somatic cell mating and segregation in chimeric frogs. bibliog il Science 168:850-2; 169: 1230 My 15, S 18 '70

VOLPE, John Anthony
NATO experts recommend international action on ocean oil spills; statement, November 2, 1970. Dept State Bul 63:666-9 N 20 '70
United States proposal on unlawful seizure of aircraft for blackmail purposes adopted by ICAO council; statement, October 1, 1970. Dept State Bul 63:449-53 O 19 '70
    about
Cracking the highway trust. il por Time 95: 59 Je 15 '70 *
John Volpe's drive to keep America moving. il pors Nations Bsns 58:40-7 Ap '70 *
Volpe rebuts critics of SST program. R. G. O'Lone. il Aviation W 92:28 Je 15 '70 *

VOLTA RIVER

Power utilization
Volta River project. L. I. Sills. Focus 21:9-12 O '70

VOLTAGE
Nomogram aids voltage-drop calculations. J. E. McAlister. il Electr World 84:46 D '70
Up-down-positive-negative. J. Darr. il Radio-Electr 41:17+ N '70

VOLTAGE converters. See Electric current converters

VOLTAGE regulators
Inside the high-voltage regulator; color TV pulse-feedback regulator. M. Mandl. il Radio-Electr 41:76-8 Jl '70
Transistor base-emitter junctions for voltage regulation. T. J. Carmody. il Electr World 84:90 S '70
Voltage regulator design nomograms. C. W. Young. il Electr World 84:32-3 Ag '70

VOLTAIRE, François Marie Arouet de
Voltaire, by T. Besterman. Review
Nat R 22:689-90 Je 30 '70. A. Bakshian, jr *

VOLTMETERS
High-impedance audio millivoltmeter. J. I. Randall. il Radio-Electr 41:92 F '70
Make your VTVM a megger too. J. Childs and J. Eskridge. il Pop Electr 33:50 Ag '70
Millivoltmeter for FET circuits. F. H. Tooker. il Pop Electr 34:45-53+ Ja '71
See also
Voltohmmeters

VOLTOHMMETERS
Assembling the Popular electronics mini-DVM. D. E. Lancaster. il Pop Electr 33:35+ S '70
Meter that doctors home appliances. E. Powell. il Pop Sci 197:110+ N '70
Solid-state V.O.M. J. Ashe and J. Eisenberg. il Electr World 83:74-5 Ja '70
Triplett 310-F solid-state vom. J. Darr. Radio-Electr 41:32 Ap '70
Tune up your car with a vom. L. E. Frenzel, jr. il Radio-Electr 41:23-5 Ad '70

VOLUME expander. See Sound—Apparatus

VOLUMETRIC analysis
Lab bench; determining the molar volume: a safe method. J. A. Douville. por Chem 43:25 Ja '70

VOLUNTARY parenthood. See Birth control

VOLUNTARY social agencies. See Social agencies, Voluntary

VOLUNTEER army. See Military service, Voluntary

VOLUNTEER fire departments. See Fire departments

VOLUNTEER service
Breaking the diploma barrier; J. L. Smith's program in Kansas City, Mo. il por Time 96:49 S 7 '70
Ellen Straus: the action of Call for action. il pors Vogue 155:124-5 Je '70
Fall River, Mass, high school pupils visit aging in new plan; Romero aid to elderly project. il Aging 188:15 Je '70
FISH volunteers in N.Y, Pa, on twenty-four hour duty to give aid. Aging 193:18 N '70
Gains without violence: people helping each other. il U S News 68:27-8 Je 1 '70
Harlem teams on top; Harlem teams for self-help, inc, K. Aylor. il Am Ed 6:32 My '70
Hempstead, N.Y, volunteer group five years old, is still expanding; Older Americans volunteers committee, Hempstead, N.Y. il Aging 191:12-13 S '70
JOY in Everett, Washington, means service to older people. il Aging 191:14-15 S '70
Loose lady; Bay area opera ACTION. S. Von Buchau. Opera N 35:6-7 O 10 '70
Mr Nixon's voluntarism. A. Etzioni. il Commonweal 91:426-30 Ja 16 '70
Mrs Leavitt lends a hand; demonstrating how to use government-issue commodities. J. E. Roper. por Read Digest 96:132-4 F '70
Off the do-gooders! student summer volunteering. J. Marks. Mlle 72:126-7+ D '70
Our wonderful teen volunteers; Huntington, L.I. N. Voldstad. il Parents Mag 46:46-7+ Ja '71
Phone calls that care; telephone reassurance services. V. Jaxon. il Har Yrs 10:38-40 My '70
Power of a woman. il Ladies Home J 87:54 Jl '70
Preservation and volunteers; reprint. Hobbies 75:76+ Je '70
Teen corps: soldiers with shovels. J. E. Roper. il por Read Digest 97:37-8+ D '70
Thoughts of a hippie sitter. M. H. Beaven. Todays Ed 59:61-2 N '70
Volunteers. D. R. Maxey. il Look 34:17-24+ Je 16 '70
See also
Community service
Health workers, Volunteer
Hospitals—Volunteer workers
Hospitals, Psychiatric—Volunteer workers

National center for voluntary action
Telephone in service to the aged
Volunteer workers in education

VOLUNTEER service, International
Ordinary guy in Ethiopia; Lalmba association. C. W. Hall. il por Read Digest 97:157-8+ Jl '70
See also
Accion international
United Nations volunteer corps (proposed)
United States—Peace corps

VOLUNTEER system, Military. See Military service, Voluntary

VOLUNTEER workers. See Volunteer service

VOLUNTEER workers in education
Citizen power: P.S. 109's man in the pin-striped suit. K. Branan. il Am Ed 6:14-17 Ap '70
Invaluable resource: the school volunteer. M. D. Caplin. bibliog Clear House 45:10-14 S '70
Moms are a must; Chicago's child-parent education centers. L. Willie. il Am Ed 6:24-9 Ap '70
What you can do for your child's school; parent volunteer groups. E. L. Schulte. il Parents Mag 45:70-1+ S '70

VOLUNTEER workers in politics. See Political campaigns

VOLUNTEERS in service to America
Draft changes: troubles ahead for Peace corps, VISTA? il U S News 69:69-70 Jl 27 '70
Narrowed VISTA. New Repub 163:7-8 Jl 25 '70
Senate v. Alan and Margaret McSurely. W. Goodman. il pors N Y Times Mag p28-9+ Ja 10 '71
View from VISTA; Appalachian volunteers in conservation programs. E. Urvant. il Am For 76:8+ S '70

VOLUNTEERS of America
Volunteers of America: seventy-five years of service. Good H 172:151 Ja '71

VOLZ, Joseph
Fate of a watchdog. Commonweal 93:341 Ja 8 '71

VOMERONASAL organ. See Olfactory organs

VON BRAUN, Wernher
[Articles on space technology and space flight] See issues of Popular science
Von Braun: the next decade in space; interview. pors Bsns W p66-7 Jl 4 '70
about
Planning with Von Braun. por Newsweek 75:56-7 F 9 '70
Supersalesman for space agency? por U S News 68:11 F 9 '70

VON BUCHAU, Stephanie
Loose lady. Opera N 35:6-7 O 10 '70
La Scala's scalpers. il Opera N 35:6-7 D 12 '70
(ed) See Burrows, S. Full force

VON DELDEN, E. K.
Bridging the gap. il Hot Rod 23:92-5 F '70
New concepts for fuelers. il Hot Rod 23:38-42 Ag '70

VON DREELE, W. H.
Albert Gore explains; Case dismissed; Yarborough bites the dust; poems. Nat R 22:496, 501, 515 My 19 '70
Areas of agreement: Dieu et mon droit; poems. Nat R 22:601, 609 Je 16 '70
Ascent from Chappaquiddick; Let's not kid ourselves; Springtime in New York; poems. Nat R 22:392, 397, 406 Ap 21 '70
At the wailing wall; Straight talk from Abe Ribicoff. poems. Nat R 22:236, 238 Mr 10 '70
Beautiful Ohio; Wool-gathering with John Lindsay; poems. Nat R 22:446, 450 My 5 '70
Biafra falls; poem. Nat R 22:73 Ja 27 '70
Bottoms up! Stamp out FAP; poems. Nat R 22:1334, 1337 D 15 '70
Byrd watching; Dump Romney? Everybody loves a monster; poems. Nat R 22:1250, 1253, 1255 D 1 '70
Dr Hyde, move over; Modest proposal; poems. Nat R 22:549, 550 Je 2 '70
El Al gets through; See Senator Mondale; poems. Nat R 22:980, 985 S 22 '70
Enormity of it all; Arthur wraps it up; poems. Nat R 22:1140, 1142 N 3 '70
Even-handed justice; poem. Nat R 22:13 Ja 13 '70
Fly backward, fly backward; Scrooge knew a thing or two; Mr Nixon's Christmas dream; poems. Nat R 22:1386, 1388, 1397 D 29 '70
Heat lightning; Calling Dr Pavlov; poems. Nat R 22:824, 827 Ag 11 '70
Here we go again; poem. Nat R 23:23 Ja 12 '71

VON DREELE, W. H.—*Continued*
High noon at the HEW saloon; Corpses on the Mekong; poems. Nat R 22:657,658 Je 30 '70
I'll give you odds; Bun in every oven; poems. Nat R 22:118, 126 F 10 '70
John F. Kennedy center for the performing arts in Washington, D.C; Blahs; Last redoubt; poems. Nat R 22:875, 877, 880 Ag 25 '70
Justice Burger decides; More free advice for Mr Nixon; poems. Nat R 22:929, 933 S 8 '70
Maryland, my Maryland; Are you there, Alice? poems. Nat R 22:1032, 1040 O 6 '70
Middle-brow me; Self diagnosis; poems. Nat R 22:186, 189 F 24 '70
Our nation's capital; poem. Nat R 22:68 Ja 27 '70
Take it off, take it all off; Epitaph; poems. Nat R 22:1199, 1203 N 17 '70
Tell me why; Margaret Mead goes to pot; poems. Nat R 22:295, 298 Mr 24 '70
They've got a little list; Final solution; Portrait of the liberal as an old man; poems. Nat R 22:768, 770, 773 Jl 28 '70
Tom Wicker isn't well; These men are dangerous; Gone are the days; poems. Nat R 22:713, 716, 719 Jl 14 '70
Tune-up time; Clap hands, here comes Humphrey; Alternative is Goldberg; poems. Nat R 22:1090, 1094, 1098 O 20 '70

VON ECKARDT, Wolf
Design for belonging. il Sat R 53:68-9 D 5 '70
Getting into the act. il Sat R 53:43-4 Jl 4 '70
Humanizing the cities. Sat R 53:72 N 7 '70
People, yes; cars, no. il Sat R 53:62-3 O 3 '70
Perils of concentration. il Sat R 53:62-3 My 2 '70
Richard Neutra: survival through design. il Sat R 53:62-3 Je 6 '70
Saving our landmarks. il Sat R 53:52-3 S 5 '70

VON ENDE, Zoe
Denver doesn't quit on problem students. il Am Ed 6:18-22 Je '70

VON HOFFMAN, Nicholas
Feedback from our readers. D. H. Wrong. Trans-Action 7:8 Jl '70 *
Sociological snoopers. Trans-Action 7:4+ My '70
Who's in charge here? il Holiday 47:48-51+ Mr '70

about
Journalistic moralizers. I. L. Horowitz and L. Rainwater. Trans-Action 7:5-8 My '70 *

VON MEYER, William C. and others
Wheat leaf rust: control by 4-n-butyl-1 2,4-triazole, a systemic fungicide. bibliog il Science 169:997-8 S 4 '70

VON MOSCHZISKER, Felix
Reservist on duty at the pigeonholes. il Life 68:29 Ap 3 '70

VONNEGUT, B. See Ryan, R. T. jt. auth.

VONNEGUT, Kurt, 1922-
Biafra. il por McCalls 97:68-9+ Ap '70
Mysterious Madame Blavatsky. il por McCalls 97:66-7+ Mr '70
Times change. por Esquire 73:60 F '70
Up is better than down; address. Vogue 156: 54+ Ag 1 '70
We talk to. . ; interview. por Mlle 71:296 Ag '70
Why they read Hesse. il por Horizon 12:28-31 Spr '70

about
Divine stupidity of Kurt Vonnegut. L. A. Fiedler. Esquire 74:195-7+ S '70 *
Happy birthday, Wanda June. Criticism
    Commonweal 93:221-2 N 27 '70 *
    Nation 211:414 O 26 '70 *
    New Repub 163:33 N 7 '70 *
    New Yorker 46:143-4 O 17 '70 *
    Newsweek il 76:123 O 19 '70 *
    Time il 96:74 O 19 '70 *
Science fiction, the modern mythology. W. E. McNelly. il America 123:125-7 S 5 '70 *
Vonnegut's gospel. Time 95:8 Je 29 '70 *

VON RECKLINGHAUSEN, Daniel
Four-channel stereo, problems and solutions. il Electr World 83:33-5+ Mr '70

VON TIGERSTROM, R. and Smith, M.
Oligodeoxyribonucleotides: chemical synthesis in anhydrous base. bibliog il Science 167: 1266-8 F 27 '70

VON TUNGELN, Annie Laurie
Your letters can help a child. Har Yrs 10:16+ S '70

VOODOOISM
Haitian voodoo. T. Desrosiers. il Américas 22:35-9 F '70

VORPAHL, J. A. and others
Satellite observations of lightning. bibliog il Science 169:860-2 Ag 28 '70

VORTEX motion
Miniature whirlwinds produced in the laboratory by high-voltage electrical discharges. R. T. Ryan and B. Vonnegut. bibliog il Science 168:1349-51 Je 12 '70

VOSBURGH, Frederick George
Frederick G. Vosburgh retires as editor; Gilbert M. Grosvenor succeeds him. M. M. Payne. il pors Nat Geog 138:838-43 D '70 *

VOSS, Norway
Traveler's choice. M. E. Lyle. Travel 133:13 Ja '70

VOTAVA, Jiri. See Weight, F. F. jt. auth.

VOTE counting machines. See Voting machines

VOTERS. See Suffrage

VOTERS, Registration of
Democratic straw; voter-registration statistics in California. M. E. Leary. Nation 211:388-9 O 26 '70
Student vote; prohibitive intervention by election boards. E. Jannson. New Repub 163: 11-12 S 19 '70
Voting in 1970: some facts and figures; comp. by R. Fisher. Todays Ed 59:64-5 S '70

VOTING
Artificial majority. T. J. Lowi. il Nation 211: 591-4 D 7 '70
Hunt for voters; 1970 elections. il Sr Schol 97:7-12 O 12 '70
Plan to pay you for voting; J. Perry's National dividend plan. D. R. Maxey. Look 34:56 D 29 '70
Statistics say the average voter is Bette Lowrey of Ohio. il pors Life 69:30-2 O 30 '70
    See also
Suffrage
United Nations—Voting
United States—Congress—Senate—Voting
Voters, Registration of

VOTING, Absent
You don't have to be at the polls to vote. Nations Bsns 58:50 O '70

VOTING, Fraudulent. See Elections—Corrupt practices

VOTING age. See Suffrage—United States

VOTING machines
Computer voting has a hole in it. Bsns W p27-8 N 14 '70
Vote counts by microwave; Riverside County, Calif. H. F. Sammis. il Am City 85:76+ Jl '70

VOTING rights act of 1965. See Election laws—United States

VOTING rights act of 1970. See Election laws—United States

VOTIPKA, John C.
Build with IC's: color convergence generator. il Radio-Electr 42:50-1 Ja '71

VOUCHER system. See Education—Federal aid

VOUGHT aeronautics company. See Ling-Temco-Vought inc.

VOW of virginity. See Virginity

VOYAGES
Bold coasts and castled islands; Gibraltar to Sardinia in Mercator. J. Hart. il Yachting 127:64-6+ Je '70
By boat around the tip of Florida. G. Reiger. il Pop Mech 133:106-9+ Je '70
Excuse me, we're looking for Bermuda. H. Harper. il Yachtng 127:60-1+ Je '70
How I rowed across the Atlantic and found Florida. J. Fairfax. il Esquire 73:111-15+ Ap '70
Land of cactus and sunshine; from Los Angeles to the Mexican border. C. Mitchell. il Motor B 125:94-9+ Mr '70
Lonely cruise on Long Island Sound. M. Lund. il Holiday 47:44-5+ Je '70
North through history aboard White Mist; following the routes of Hudson, Champlain, and Cartier. M. B. Grosvenor. il pors Nat Geog 138:1-55 Jl '70
Pacific delivery experienced circumnavigator takes a busman's holiday. J. Guzzwell. il Yachting 127:60-1+ Mr '70
Sans stove; Miami to Ottawa by outboard. J. Charleson. il por Motor B 125:68-9+ Je; 126:58+ Jl '70
Strange last voyage of Donald Crowhurst, by N. Tomalin and R. Hall. Review
    Time il por 96:101+ S 21 '70. P. Swerdloff
Third time lucky; Tzu Hang braves Cape Horn (cont) M. Smeeton. il Yachting 127: 100-2+ Ja '70
Transatlantic by Cal-20. G. Cadwalader. il Yachting 127:60-1+ Ap; 56-8+ My '70
    See also
Cruising
Northwest Passage
Ocean travel
Ra expedition, 1969
Ra expedition, 1970
Seafaring life
Whaling

VOYAGES, Imaginary
See also
Space flight
VOYAGES around the world
Alone on a wide, wide sea; Sunday Times' round the world singlehanded race. E. F. Haylock. il Motor B 125:36-8+ Mr '70
Robin sails home. R. L. Graham. il pors Nat Geog 138:504-45 O '70
Stornoway progress report. M. Peterson. il por Motor B 125:122-3+ Ja '70
Treacherous Tuamotus. G. Skinner. il Yachting 127:94-6+ Ja '70
VOYAGEURS. See French Canadians
VOZNESENSKII, Andrei
Depot of metaphors. Time 95:30 My 18 '70 *
Poet on a string. il por Time 95:27 Mr 9 '70 *
VUKOVICH, Katherine R. See Schapiro, S. jt. auth.
VULTURES
See also
Condors
VY Canis Majoris. See Stars, Variable
VYAS, G. N. and Shulman, N. R.
Hemagglutination assay for antigen and antibody associated with viral hepatitis. bibliog il Science 170:332-3 O 16 '70

W

WABCO. See Westinghouse air brake company
W. B. Saunders company. See Saunders, W. B, company
WBAI (radio station) See Radio stations
WCC. See World council of churches
WCTU. See Woman's Christian temperance union
WGBH-TV. See Television stations, Educational
WINS (radio station) See Radio stations
WJXT-TV. See Television stations
WKRO (radio station) See Radio stations
WLBT, Jackson, Miss. See Television stations
WLBW-TV. See Television stations
WMUU (radio station) See Radio stations
WNBA. See Women's national book association
WNYU (radio station) See Radio stations
WPIX-TV. See Television stations
W. T. Grant company. See Grant, W. T. company
WWVH (radio station) See United States—Standards, National bureau of—Radio stations
WACK, R. Donald
It's time to tear down the old hotel. Clear House 44:504-5 Ap '70
WACO, Tex.
Inventory your streets for better management. C. H. Hoge and J. E. Lykes, jr. il Am City 85:98+ Mr '70
WADE, James
Seoul first. il por Opera N 35:14-17 S 5 '70
about
Premiere by an American expatriate. A. C. Heyman. il Hi Fi 20:secII 30 Ag '70 *
WADE, M. Elbert
Bridge at generation gap. il Am Ed 6:28-30 O '70
WADE, Princella H.
Why I'll give my daughter the pill. il por Redbook 135:30+ Je '70
WADENA rock festival. See Music festivals—Iowa
WADKINS, Lanny
Big amateur shoot-out at generation gap. C. Kirkpatrick. il por Sports Illus 33:98+ S 14 '70 *
WADLOW, Robert Pershing
Story of a giant. P. G. Brewster. Sci Digest 69:65 Ja '71 *
WAFFLES
Breakfast favorites as desserts. Sunset 144:98 Ja '70
Corn waffles or graham waffles. Sunset 144:186 Ap '70
WAGAR, J. Alan
Challenge of environmental education. il Todays Ed 59:14-18 D '70
Growth versus the quality of life. bibliog Science 168:1179-84 Je 5 '70
WAGE agreements. See Trade agreements
WAGE bargaining. See Collective bargaining

WAGE differentials
Federal pay raise: meaning to you. il U S News 68:30-1 Ap 27 '70
WAGE payment plans
See also
Incentives in industry
WAGE-price policy
As the demand grows for wage and price controls. il U S News 68:41-2 Je 8 '70
Burns and guidelines. M. Friedman. Newsweek 75:86 Je 15 '70
Calling on Nixon for a guidepost play. Bsns W p 19 N 28 '70
Case for controls. R. Lekachman. Duns 96:13 Jl '70
Case for guideposts is still strong. Fortune 82:53-4 Jl '70
Controls may be necessary; comments by Dun's presidents' panel; with editorial comment. G. R. Rosen. il Duns 97:37-8, 80 Ja '71
Game plan loses some top fans; with editorial comment. Bsns W p32-3, 136 My 23 '70
Hard going for the game plan; with editorial comment. G. Burck. il por Fortune 81:145-6, 152-5+ My '70
High-level call for guidelines; proposals of the CED. Time 96:86 D 7 '70
How to stop inflation: stop raising wages. E. L. Dale, jr. il N Y Times Mag p 10-11+ Ja 3 '71
Imitating failure. M. Friedman. Newsweek 77:72 Ja 11 '71
Inflation showdown: new pressures on Nixon. il U S News 69:15-16 D 7 '70
Is jawboning a joke? M. J. Ulmer. New Repub 162:21-3 My 30 '70
Jawboning's a joke. E. L. Dale, jr. New Repub 162:17-19 Ap 18 '70
Mr Nixon's turn to jawbone. il Newsweek 75:75 Je 15 '70
Nixon sounds an inflation alert; with editorial comment. Bsns W p24-5, 126 Je 20 '70
Nixon's wage-price policy: will it work? il U S News 68:15-16 Je 29 '70
Political economy of prosperity, by A. M. Okun. Review
Trans-Action 7:64+ S '70. K. E. Boulding
Pressure for new steps to curb inflation. il U S News 68:37-8 Je 1 '70
Pressure mounts against hands-off policy; with editorial comment. il Bsns W p24-5, 140 Je 6 '70
Price controls. P. A. Samuelson. Newsweek 76:57 D 28 '70
Sorry record of incomes policies. Bsns W p94-5 Ja 31 '70
This month's feature: Congress and standby economic controls. Cong Digest 49:225-56 O '70
Tougher tack on inflationary hikes. Bsns W p23-4 N 21 '70
U.S. can't afford what labor wants; with editorial comment. il Bsns W p 104-8, 134 Ap 11 '70
Urging the freeze Nixon doesn't want. il Bsns W p26-7 Je 20 '70
Wage and price controls? Forget about them; address, May 19, 1970. J. N. Mitchell. il por U S News 68:39-41 Je 1 '70
Wage-price controls: the cure for runaway inflation. J. K. Galbraith. il por N Y Times Mag p24-5+ Je 7 '70
Washington shifts gears. R. Lekachman. Duns 97:9 Ja '71
Will labor lose its leverage? comments of members of the presidents' panel. G. R. Rosen. Duns 95:34-6 F '70

Canada

Canada's businessmen shoulder the load. il Nations Bsns 58:68-72 N '70
Canada's flirtation with guidelines. Bsns W p22-3 My 30 '70
Canadians slash at wage restraint. Bsns W p34-5 Jl 4 '70
How Canada fights inflation: a step beyond tight money; interview, ed. by A. Jones. pors Forbes 105:36+ Je 1 '70
Inflation guidelines fail in Canada. U S News 69:66 D 14 '70
Mailmen flout Trudeau's limit. Bsns W p 116 S 12 '70
Trudeau tries a price pause. Bsns W p39 Ja 17 '70
When other nations try wage-price restraints. U S News 68:38 Je 1 '70

Great Britain

When other nations try wage-price restraints. U S News 68:38 Je 1 '70

WAGE-price policy—*Continued*

Poland

Polish eruption: a nation in flames. il Time 96:14-17 D 28 '70

WAGES

Foreign labor briefs. See issues of Monthly labor review
See also
Bonus system
Labor cost
Non-wage payments
Overtime
Profit sharing

Annual wage

See also
Automobile industry and trade—Wages and hours
Negative income tax

Cost of living adjustments

Collective bargaining calendar for 1970; with tables. H. C. Spring. Mo Labor R 93:13-26 Ja '70
Unions' no. 1 goal now: beat the cost of living. il U S News 69:78-80 O 12 '70
Wage developments in manufacturing, 1969; with tables. J. Kinyon. Mo Labor R 93:35-9 Jl '70

Economic aspects

Econometric model of worker compensation changes. W. R. Bailey and A. Sackley. bibliog f il Mo Labor R 93:32-8 S '70
See also
Wage-price policy

Statistics

See also
Wage differentials

Women

See Equal pay for equal work

Asia

Global scramble for cheap labor. il Time 96: 91-2 S 21 '70

Europe, Western

Labor trouble: where it's worse than in the U.S. wage boosts. il U S News 68:86-8 My 18 '70

France

French shift to monthly pay. America 122: 515 My 16 '70

Great Britain

Pay pressures build in Britain. Bsns W p 100 Ja 17 '70

Japan

Global scramble for cheap labor. il Time 96: 91-2 S 21 '70

Southern states

Wages in southern sawmills and planing mills. A. I. Rose. il Mo Labor R 93:49-50 N '70

United States

Analysis of changes in wages and benefits during 1969. J. E. Talbot, jr. il Mo Labor R 93:45-50 Je '70
Cost of living inflates union wage demands. il Bsns W p84-5 F 7 '70
For wage boosts, an upward surge. U S News 69:80 N 9 '70
Hours and earnings, private nonagricultural payrolls: tables. See issues of Monthly labor review
Introducing new benchmarks. G. Storch. Mo Labor R 93:94 Jl '70
Late-shift employment in manufacturing industries; with tables. G. M. O'Connor. bibliog Mo Labor R 93:37-42 N '70
Nonagricultural employment, payroll data: tables. See issues of Monthly labor review
One reason wages will climb fast in '71. il U S News 69:55-6 D 28 '70
Out of control? wage increases. il Forbes 106: 15-16 Ag 1 '70
Record wage hike for auto workers: Reuther's strategy. il U S News 68:81-2 Ap 27 '70
Research summaries. See issues of Monthly labor review
Response to inflation alert: drive for big raises goes on. U S News 69:64-5 D 14 '70
Return of pocketbook politics. H. Sidey. Life 68:4 Ap 3 '70
To and fro in a tug of war: economic slack versus union power. il Fortune 82:24 O '70
Unions keep winning more. Bsns W p50+ O 10 '70
Using unemployment insurance wage reports as a data source. M. E. Borus. Mo Labor R 93:66-7 Jl '70

Wage-price escalator. America 122:404-5 Ap 18 '70
Who's ahead, who's behind in race with inflation. il U S News 69:33 Ag 24 '70
Who's gaining, who's losing in real pay. il U S News 68:65 Mr 16 '70
Why it's harder to get big raises. il U S News 69:42-3 N 2 '70
See also
Equal pay for equal work
Government employees—Salaries, allowances, etc.
Minimum wage—United States
Office workers—Salaries, allowances, etc.
Wages—Cost of living adjustments
also subhead Wages and hours under names of industries. e.g. Building industry —Wages and hours

WAGGONER, Jean
Strange pilgrimage; story. Américas 22:34-5 O '70

WAGGONNER, Joe David, 1918-
Excerpt from debate, September 16, 1969. Con Digest 49:15+ Ja '70

WAGGONER, William G.
Flexible-shaft machine rolls to the job. il Pop Mech 134:172-3 Ag '70
Make this dial-a-jig router attachment. il Pop Mech 134:188-9 O '70
Using a radial-arm as a routing clamp. il Pop Sci 197:109 D '70

WAGNER, Albert C.
Traveler's choice. Travel 134:12 O '70

WAGNER, Daniel A. See Scurrah, M. J. jt. auth.

WAGNER, Frank
Legsercises. il Vogue 156:78-81+ O 15 '70 *

WAGNER, Geoffrey
Of pot and pigs: the new cinema. il Nat R 22:96-7 Ja 27 '70
Plato on pop art. Nat R 22:1066-7 O 6 '70

WAGNER, John J.
Nuclear magnetic resonance spectroscopy, an outline. il por Chem 43:13-15 Mr '70

WAGNER, Kurt J.
Face-lifts for men. R. H. Berg. il pors Look 34:80-2+ D 1 '70 *

WAGNER, Mahlon W.
Cyclamate acceptance. bibliog Science 168: 1605 Je 26 '70

WAGNER, Patricia. See Chaffee, J. jr, jt. auth.

WAGNER, Richard, 1813-1883
Battle of Wagner. C. Matz. pors Opera N 34:6-7 Ja 31 '70
Bayreuth: even the kartoffelknoedel is Wagnerian. P. Moor. il por Sat R 53:52-3+ Mr 14 '70 *
Flying Dutchman (Der fliegende Holländer)
Criticism
New Yorker 45:80 Ja 31 '70
Opera N 34:17-20 Ja 31 '70
Götterdämmerung. C. J. Luten. il Am Rec G 37:4-6+ S '70 *
In the Venusberg, orgiastic abandon. G. S. Fox. Am Rec G 36:909 Jl '70 *
Karajan closes the ring. C. L. Osborne. il Hi Fi 20:77-9 S '70 *
Karajan completes the Ring. P. Moor. il por Sat R 53:63-5 Ap 25 '70 *
Music to my ears: concert version of Götterdämmerung with the New York Philharmonic. I. Kolodin. Sat R 53:40 F 7 '70
Nilsson: Venus and Elisabeth. G. L. Mayer. Am Rec G 36:522-3 Mr '70 *
Nilsson-Nilsson Tannhäuser. R. Lawrence. Sat R 53:47 My 30 '70 *
Nilsson on Wagner; interview, ed. by S. Jenkins, jr. B. Nilsson. por Opera N 35:16-18 O 10 '70 *
Parsifal. Criticism
New Yorker 46:182+ N 28 '70 *
Sat R 53:18 D 5 '70 *
Phenomenon that was Kirsten Flagstad. A. Sperber. Am Rec G 36:440 F '70 *
Records:
Tannhäuser. il Opera N 34:34 F 21 '70 *
Speaking of Wagner; interview, ed. by G. Fitzgerald. L. Melchior. por Opera N 34:6-9 Mr 28 '70 *
Wagner: the majesty that can be achieved; conducted by Wilhelm Furtwängler. M. N. Kanny. Am Rec G 37:180-1 N '70 *
Weber and Wagner at the Lincoln Center operafest. R. Jacobson. Sat R 53:35 Ag 1 '70 *
See also
Bayreuth festival

WAGNER, Robert
Chicago. Art N 69:28+ O '70; 10+ Ja '71

WAGNER, Rudolph F.
Secondary emotional reactions in children with learning disabilities. Ment Hy 54:577-9 O '70

WAGNER, Walter F. Jr
Editorial. See issues of Architectural record

WAGNER, Wolfgang
Wolfgang is not Wieland. G. Movshon. il Hi
Fi 20:MA24-6 O '70 *
WAGON models
Wagon museum is in Eugene, University of
Oregon. il Sunset 144:55 Ap '70
WAGONER, Dan
Dan Wagoner & dancers; Judson memorial
church NYC. J. Anderson. Dance Mag 44:
87 Ag '70 *
WAGONER, David
Extraordinary production of eggs from the
mouth; poem. New Repub 162:28 Ap 4 '70
Keepers; poem. Sat R 53:41 F 28 '70
Last words of the human fly; poem. Harper
241:93 S '70
On learning more new books of poems are
stolen than sold at a college bookstore;
poem. Sat R 53:74 F 28 '70
One more for the rain; poem. Mlle 71:50 Jl
'70
(ed) See Rothke, T. Root of the wind
WAGONER, Walter D. See Handspicker, M. jt.
auth.
WAGSCHAL, Peter H.
On the irrelevance of relevance. Ed Digest
35:22-3 Ja '70
WAHBA, Albert J.
Biochemist sues Ochoa and NYU. R. J. Ba-
zell. Science 170:957 N 27 '70 *
WAHINE (ferry) wreck. See Shipwrecks
WAHL, Arnold C.
Chemistry by computer; with biographical
sketch. il Sci Am 222:12, 54-8+ bibliog(p
130) Ap '70
WAHL, Paul
Amazing see-in-the-dark TV cameras. il Pop
Sci 197:26+ N '70
FLAIR, the way-out floating airport. il Pop
Sci 197:54-5+ Ag '70
5mm Magnum: hot new cartridge with a rifle
to match. il Pop Sci 197:68-9 Jl '70
How science will foil the skyjackers. il Pop
Sci 197:58-60+ N '70
NEMO: observation post 100 fathoms under
the sea. il Pop Sci 197:66 S '70
Put sound waves to work in your shop. il
Pop Sci 196:94-5 Mr '70
Science builds a guitar with the now sound.
il Pop Sci 196:93 Mr '70
They'll fly ejection seats to safety. il Pop Sci
196:60-1 Ap '70
What's the right shotgun for you? il Pop Sci
197:84-5+ S '70
Wheel-less plane lands on a cushion of air.
il Pop Sci 196:122 Je '70
WAHLFELDT, Bette
Our movable compost bin. il por Org Gard &
Farm 17:110 Mr '70
Try some peppery Hungarian peppers. Org
Gard & Farm 17:82 Ja '70
Vegetables that were good to us. Org Gard &
Farm 17:88-9 Ap '70
WAINWRIGHT, Geoffrey
Woodhenges; with biographical sketch. il
Sci Am 223:10, 30-8 bibliog(p 132) N '70
WAINWRIGHT, Loudon
Dilemma in Dyersville. il Life 68:48-50+ My
29 '70
Long Island. il Life 69:32-3 O 2 '70
Old pro gets his shot at the moon. il pors
Life 69:48-50B+ Jl 31 '70
Town deals sternly with its own. il Life 69:
40-2+ N 6 '70
WAITE, Amory H. Jr. See Waite, B.
WAITE, Bud
Submarine icebreaker for Arctic oil? J. F.
Pearson. il pors Pop Mech 133:85-9 Mr '70;
Same. Sci Digest 67:75-9 My '70 *
WAITE, Genevieve
Oh, Genevieve! E. L. Gross. pors Vogue 155:
188-91+ Ap 1 '70 *
WAITE, Paul J. See Biggs, W. G. jt. auth.
WAITING at Dachau; story. See Price, R.
WAJDA, Andrzej
Wajda redivivus. K. T. Toeplitz. il por Film
Q 23:37-41 Wint '69 *
WAKE turbulence. See Atmospheric turbulence
WAKEFIELD, Dan
Novel bites man. Atlan 226:72-8 Ag; 28 O '70;
Same. Writer 83:11-13+ N '70

about
Oversexed in Indianapolis. K. Vonnegut, jr.
por Life 69:10 Jl 17 '70 *
WAKEFIELD, Hugh
Victorian flower stands. il Antiques 98:232-
6 Ag '70
WAKEFIELD, Va.
See also
George Washington Birthplace National
Monument

WAKEMAN, Harold
Adrift with driftwood. E. Dean and J. Dean.
il por Har Yrs 10:19-20 Jl '70
WAKITA, Hiroshi, and Schmitt, R. A.
Lunar anorthosites: rare-earth and other ele-
mental abundances. bibliog il Science 170:
969-74 N 27 '70
WAKOSKI, Diane
In place of a phone call to Arabia; poem. Na-
tion 210:317 Mr 16 '70
WAKSMAN, Selman Abraham
He discovered healing in the soil. W. Garri-
son. il por Todays Health 48:42-3+ Mr '70 *
WALCOTT, Derek
Ebb; poem. Mlle 71:126 My '70

about
Dream on Monkey Mountain. Criticism
Nat R 22:1174 N 3 '70 *
WALD, George
Can corporations be tried for war crimes?
Cur 120:56-63 Ag '70
Leaves fall, the blood flows. Sat R 53:28-9
Je 6 '70

about
Angry old man. Nation 210:484-5 Ap 27 '70 *
Intellectuals start wooing trade unions. B.
L. Masse. America 124:33 Ja 16 '71 *
Labor-campus link: union heads, academic
leaders discuss alliance. D. Shapley. Science
170:516+ O 30 '70 *
WALDMAN, Diane
Holding the floor. bibliog il Art N 69:60-2+
O '70
WALDMAN, Max
Artistry of Max Waldman. R. Hattersley. il
Pop Phot 66:102-11+ Ja '70
WALDMAN, Robert H. See Henney, C. S. jt.
auth.
WALDORF, John Taylor
Kid on the Comstock; excerpts. il por Am
West 7:11-17 Mr '70
WALDORF-Astoria hotel. See New York (city)
—Hotels, restaurants, etc.
WALDRON, Eli
Three likely lads of limbo; story. New Yorker
46:38-9 Mr 21 '70
Two dreams; story. New Yorker 46:44-5 O 24
'70
WALES, Nym
Anna Louise Strong: the classic fellow-trav-
eler. New Repub 162:17-19 Ap 25 '70
WALES
See also
Government, Resistance to—Wales
Schools—Wales

Description and travel
Among the Welsh mountains. F. Mountford.
il Travel 134:50-3 Ag '70
WALINSKY, Adam
Chasing a future. il pors Time 96:20-1 O 19
'70 *
WALKER, Alice
Authors & editors. B. A. Bannon. por Pub
W 198:195-7 Ag 31 '70 *
WALKER, Barbara K.
In search of youth: a biographical quest.
Horn Bk 46:319-22 Je '70
WALKER, Biron
Think some thing you want; poem. Common-
weal 91:582 F 27 '70
WALKER, Brooks, 1928-
U.S. leasing's gamble. T. J. Murray. por Duns
96:58-9 S '70 *
WALKER, Charis Edward
To combat inflation. Read Digest 97:74-8 N
'70
WALKER, Eric Arthur
Crisis in American higher education; address,
February 7, 1970. Vital Speeches 36:362-4
Ap 1 '70
Most remarkable people; excerpts from ad-
dress. Pop Mech 134:104-5 N '70
WALKER, Howell
South Australia, gateway to the great out-
back. il Nat Geog 137:441-81 Ap '70
WALKER, J. L. Jr, and Brown, A. M.
Unified account of the variable effects of
carbon dioxide on nerve cells. bibliog il
Science 167:1502-4 Mr 13 '70
WALKER, John
How I didn't get Mr Gulbenkian's art. il por
Horizon 12:28-43 Sum '70
WALKER, John Brisben
Summer white house. E. Bluemel. il por Am
West 7:24-5 S '70 *
WALKER, John C.
Architect speaks his mind; interview. il por
House & Gard 138:58+ O '70

WALKER, Joseph A.
  Harangues. Criticism
      Nation 210:124-5 F 2 '70
      New Yorker 45:58 Ja 24 '70
      Sat R 53:30 F 14 '70 *
WALKER, Larry, and Price, Karen
  Fantasy, form and fun. il por Sch Arts 70:
      38-40 O '70
WALKER, LeBon
  Modular housing program fades away. il por
      Bsns W p55+ Mr 14 '70 *
WALKER, Leo
  Build multipurpose IC digital clock. il Radio-
      Electr 41:46-51 Ag; 97+ S '70
WALKER, Lester
  Could you bend up a chair from foamboard?
      il Pop Sci 196:106-9 F '70
  Plywood rocker-table. il Pop Sci 197:76-8 Jl
      '70
WALKER, Margaret
  Humanistic tradition of Afro-American liter-
      ature; address, July 2, 1970. il Am Lib 1:849-
      54 O '70
WALKER, Merle F.
  Image-tube observations at Cerro Tololo. bib-
      liog il por Sky & Tel 40:132-8 S '70
WALKER, Robert
  King of the talkies. Newsweek 75:69 Ja 26 '70
WALKER, Robert S. See Eshleman, E. D. jt.
      auth.
WALKER, Rube
  Say it again, Rube! W. Bingham. il Sports
      Illus 32:10-13 Je 1 '70 *
WALKER, Stuart H.
  When the wind comes up, the doctor is ab-
      sent. H. D. Whall. il por Sports Illus 32:60+
      Mr 30 '70 *
WALKER, Ted
  Boy by a river; poem. New Yorker 46:54 N
      14 '70
  Carnival; story. New Yorker 46:54-9 D 5 '70
  Celebration for autumn; poem. New Yorker
      46:44 S 26 '70
  Estrangement; story. New Yorker 46:30-5 Je
      13 '70
  Place of trees; poem. New Yorker 45:73 Ja 17
      '70
  Sunday drive to the beach; poem. New
      Yorker 45:34 Ja 31 '70
WALKING
  Back packing for pleasure, think light! S.
      Wojcik. il Cons 24:48+ Je '70
  Blue-collar walker; D. Romansky. J. Gross.
      por Sports Illus 33:77 N 23 '70
  Christmas hike. N. Smith. il Nat Wildlife
      9:47 D '70
  Creepers, floaters and squirmers; race walk-
      ing. H. Higdon. il Sports Illus 32:32-7 Ap 27
      '70
  Duffel shuffle; backpacking a heavy load. B.
      Riviere. il Field & S 75:52 Ag '70
  Hoof it to heaven; backpacking. E. A. Bauer.
      il por Outdoor Life 145:80-3+ Ap '70
  Let's travel: the Alpin-schule Innsbruck; of-
      fering hiking courses. R. Rudner. il Mlle
      70:124+ Mr '70
  Mechanics of hip-swinging. Sci Digest 67:66
      F '70
  Mighty dream come true. A. Birch. il por Har
      Yrs 10:14-15 F '70
  Pack trip in the High Sierras. M. Carter. il
      Holiday 47:62-5+ My '70
  Take the whole family on a wilderness es-
      cape. E. P. Haddon. il Todays Health 48:35-
      8 Ag '70
  This has gotta be paradise; backpacking
      trip, Montana. R. J. Whitcomb. il por Out-
      door Life 145:46-9+ My '70
  Winter walk on the Washington coast; Olym-
      pic National Park's wilderness beach. D.
      Birkner. il Nat Parks 44:23-4 F '70
      See also
  Hitchhiking
  Trails
WALKING catfish. See Catfishes
WALKING with Charlie; story. See Hayden, J.
WALKS (paths)
      See also
  Garden walks
WALKWAYS, Elevated. See Sidewalks, Ele-
      vated
WALL, Betty J. and others
  Fluid transport: concentration of the inter-
      cellular compartment. bibliog il Science
      167:1497-8 Mr 13 '70
WALL, Joseph Frazier
  Rich man's burden, and how Andrew Carne-
      gie unloaded it; excerpts from Andrew
      Carnegie. il pors Am Heritage 21:58-67+
      O '70
  What Princeton really needed; excerpt from
      Andrew Carnegie. il pors Am Heritage 21:
      91-2 Je '70
  You can take a boy out of Dunfermline..;
      excerpts from Andrew Carnegie. il por Ho-
      rizon 12:80-3 Aut '70

WALL coverings
  Easy decorating with the do-it-yourself wall
      coverings. Good H. 170:156 Ja '70
  Look of permanence. il Bet Hom & Gard 48:
      50-1+ Jl '70
  Refresher course for your house. J. R. Cary.
      il Parents Mag 45:102-5 F '70
  Wall magic with fabric. V. D. Hahn. il Am
      Home 73:68-73+ Ap '70
WALL hangings
  Loose weaves. il Time 95:74-5+ Je 1 '70
  Simple weaving to create wall hangings. M.
      P. Miles. il Sch Arts 70:20-3 Ja '71
WALL painting. See Mural painting and decor-
      ation
WALL Street
  Landlords fall prey to the Street's woes. il
      Bsns W p 17-18 My 2 '70
  Wall Street can't cope in its present form.
      Bsns W p 166+ O 17 '70
  Wall Street view. Forbes 105:96 Je 15; 106:
      55 Jl 1; 54-5 S 1; 106 O 15; 66-7 N 1; 67 D
      1 '70; 107:186-7 Ja 1 '71
WALL systems. See Walls
WALLACE, David H.
  Oysters: planning the environment for an
      industry. il Cons 25:28-30 O '70
WALLACE, George Corley
  My election is a warning; interview. por U S
      News 68:24-5 Je 15 '70
  People are upset about the economy; inter-
      view. por U S News 69:36+ N 16 '70
          about
  Alabama: down for the third time. D. G.
      Shockley. Chr Cent 87:813 Jl 1 '70 *
  Dealing with Wallace. New Repub 162:8 Je
      27 '70 *
  George does it again. Nat R 22:502-3 My 19
      '70 *
  George Wallace: moment of truth. Nat R 22:
      344-5 Ap 7 '70 *
  Here comes that man again! V. Gold. Nat
      R 22:566 Je 2 '70 *
  How George did it. il Newsweek 75:27-9 Je
      15 '70 *
  How George did it. il por Time 95:16 Je 15
      '70 *
  Letter from Washington. R. H. Rovere. New
      Yorker 46:109-10+ Je 13 '70 *
  Wallace and the shape of politics. S. Alsop.
      Newsweek 75:108 My 4 '70 *
  Wallace country. il por Newsweek 75:30+
      My 4 '70 *
  Wallace in '72. New Repub 162:7 Je 20 '70 *
  Wallace on the move. por Newsweek 75:20-1
      Mr 9 '70 *
  Wallace rides again. R. M. Williams. New
      Repub 162:12-13 Mr 21 '70 *
  Wallace runs for his political life. il pors Life
      68:36-7 My 1 '70 *
  Wallace victory; meaning for 1972. por U S
      News 68:22-4 Je 15 '70 *
  Wallace's chances against Brewer. U S News
      68:18 Mr 9 '70 *
  Wallace's Waterloo? il por Newsweek 75:42
      My 18 '70 *
WALLACE, Irving
  Author in search of a background. il pors
      Holiday 47:52-5 F '70
          about
  Each time is day one. P. Nathan. Pub W
      198:50 S 14 '70 *
WALLACE, James N.
  Fresh look at America. il U S News 69:46-51
      N 30 '70
WALLACE, Lila Acheson
  New audience. R. A. Tuggle. il Opera N 35:
      21 N 21 '70 *
WALLACE, Michael
  Uses of violence in American history; adap-
      tation of address, December 1969. Am
      Scholar 40:81-102 Wint '70
  —See Hofstadter, R. jt. ed.
WALLACE, Robert
  In the verse patch. Sat R 53:34-6 Ja 17 '70
WALLACE, Robert Keith
  Physiological effects of transcendental medi-
      tation. bibliog il Science 167:1751-4 Mr 27 '70
WALLACH, Laurence
  (tr) See Marx, H. J. Some Corelli attributions
      assessed
WALLED gardens. See Gardens
WALLENDA, Karl
  Smell of death was in the air. il pors Sports
      Illus 33:18+ Jl 27 '70 *
  Wallenda is at it again. il pors Life 69:39-40
      Jl 31 '70 *
WALLENMEYER, William A.
  Current state of physics: AEC's view; inter-
      view, ed. by G. B. Lubkin. il por Phys To-
      day 23:55-8 My '70

WALLER, R. E.
Air pollution and lung cancer. il UNESCO Courier 23:30-2 My '70

WALLICH, Henry C.
Banks need more freedom to compete. Fortune 81:114-15+ Mr '70
[Column on economic questions] See issues of Newsweek
How the slump looks to three experts. pors Newsweek 76:78-9 My 25 '70

WALLIS, C. Lamar
Confrontation in Memphis. Library J 94:4101-2; 95:189-90 N 15 '69, Ja 15 '70

WALLPAPER
Rolls; floor and wall-covering materials. il Bet Hom & Gard 48:44-5+ Ja '70

WALLS, Dwayne E.
Tobacco's double revolution. il Nation 210:113-15 F 2 '70

WALLS
Look of permanence. il Bet Hom & Gard 48:50-1+ Jl '70
Pretty, use-full walls. il Pop Mech 134:164-6 S '70
Skating rink has translucent wall; Springfield, Mass. il Am City 85:46 Ag '70
Walls that grow on you; Interlübke wall system; ed. by V. D. Hahn. il Am Home 73:32 F '70
Work wall comes apart. il Sunset 144:136 Mr '70
See also
Garden walls
Partitions, Movable
Pass-throughs
Storage walls

WALLS, Glass
How safe are glass walls and what can you do to make yours safer? il Sunset 145:62-4 Ag '70

WALNEY ISLAND
Gulls of Walney island. B. R. MacRoberts and M. H. MacRoberts. il pors(p8) Natur Hist 79:64-9 Mr '70

WALNUT trees
Growing black walnuts from seed. L. Riotte. il Org Gard & Farm 17:52-3 N '70
Why we chose black walnuts. H. G. Lendle il Org Gard & Farm 17:44-5 Je '70

WALNUTS
Growing black walnuts from seed. L. Riotte. il Org Gard & Farm 17:52-3 N '70

WALSER, Robert
Hero as zero. R. De Feo. Nation 212:92-3 Ja 18 '71 *

WALSH, Chad
Cambodia; poem. New Repub 162:24 My 16 '70

WALSH, Denny
Mayor, the Mob and the lawyer. il pors Life 68:24-31 My 29 '70

WALSH, F. J. See Fischer, R. E. jt. auth.

WALSH, James E. bp
Bishop Walsh: free at last. America 123:32 Jl 25 '70 *
Bishop Walsh released by Chinese Communists. Dept State Bul 63:114 Jl 27 '70
Pearl of great price. Chr Today 14:32 Jl 31 '70 *
Small price to pay. il por Time 96:23 Jl 20 '70 *

WALSH, Jim
Favorite pioneer recording artists. See issues of Hobbies
Through the stereoscope. il pors Hobbies 75:48-50+ Je '70

WALSH, John
Astronaut's mind. il Esquire 74:123-7+ S '70

WALSH, Joseph L.
Why Marcuse matters. por Commonweal 93:21-5 O 2 '70

WALSH, Michael J. See Davis, V. E. jt. auth.

WALSH, Moira
Films. See issues of America

WALSH, R. M.
Travel to the moon, in your car. il Pop Sci 196:84-5 My '70

WALSH, William Bertalan
Not so ugly American. America 122:288 Mr 21 '70 *

WALT, Lewis W.
Behind the battle for Khesanh. il Read Digest 96:106-11 My '70

WALT Disney productions. See Disney, Walt, productions

WALT Disney world, Fla. See Amusement parks

WALTER, Greg
Ignoble end of Elizabeth. il Life 69:32-6 S 11 '70
Navy vs. Culebra. il Life 68:47 Ap 10 '70

WALTER, Jim, corporation
Dynamic growth companies. il Nations Bsns 58:76-9 S '70

WALTER, M. R.
Stromatolites used to determine the time of nearest approach of earth and moon. bibliog Science 170:1331-2 D 18 '70

WALTER, Virginia, and Schimmel, Nancy
Looking beyond his own block. bibliog il Wilson Lib Bul 45:163-7 O '70

WALTER Kidde and company. See Kidde, Walter, and company

WALTERS, Barbara
Girl of Today; interview, ed. by S. Niernberg. pors House B 112:134-5+ O '70
How to be absolutely charming; excerpt from How to talk with practically anybody about practically anything. il McCalls 98:48+ N '70
How to cope with social disasters; excerpt from How to talk with practically anybody about practically anything. il por McCalls 98:74-5+ O '70

WALTERS, Jerry
Average deer hunt? il por Outdoor Life 146:68-9+ O '70

WALTNER, Elma, and Waltner, Willard
Mini-truck fleet. il Pop Mech 134:174 D '70

WALTNER, Willard. See Waltner, E. jt. auth.

WALTON, Elizabeth
Evaluation of children's picture making. il Sch Arts 70:6-7 N '70

WALTON, Henry
Henry Walton, American artist. L. Rehner. il Antiques 97:414-17 Mr '70 *

WALTON, Richard J.
After many a summer dies the majority. Sat R 53:19-20 Je 27 '70

WALTON, Roy A.
Universal regulated power supply. il Electr World 84:60-1 Ag '70

WALTZ, Jon R.
Burger/Blackmun court. il N Y Times Mag p60-1+ D 6 '70

WALZER, Hank. See Hawxhurst, D. jt. auth.

WALZER, Michael
Obligations of oppressed minorities. bibliog f Commentary 49:71-80 My; 50:16 Ag '70

WAMPLER, Charles Edwin
Making a business out of Mr Bell's invention. il pors Nations Bsns 58:48-9 Ja '70

WAMPLER, E. Joseph. See Faller, J. E. jt. auth.

WANG, Bob
Institutional library service at the state level. Am Lib 1:781-5 S '70

WANGERS, Jim
Rap 'n 'pinion. por Motor T 22:12 Ap '70

WANK, Roland Anthony
Roland Wank, 1898-1970. F. Gutheim. il por Arch Forum 133:58-9 S '70 *

WANKE, H. and others
Major and trace elements and cosmic-ray produced radioisotopes in lunar samples. bibliog il Science 167:523-5 Ja 30 '70

WANKEL engines. See Automobile engines

WANLESS, R. K. and others
Age determinations and isotopic abundance measurements on lunar samples. il Science 167:479-80 Ja 30 '70

WANSHEL, Jeff
Disintegration of James Cherry. Criticism New Yorker 45:76-7 F 7 '70
Newsweek 75:95 F 9 '70

WANTED: a house to haunt; drama. See Corson, H. W.

WANTING Jolinda; story. See Meyer, D.

WAR
Do pacifists harm peace? E. Van Den Haag. il Nat R 22:1344-5+ D 15 '70
How wars end; symposium, ed. by W. T. R. Fox. bibliog f Ann Am Acad 392:1-172 N '70
Modern man is obsolete; excerpts; reprint. Sat R 53:16-18+ Ag 1 '70
100 wars and other conflicts since World war II. UNESCO Courier 23:23 N '70
Patterns in international warfare, 1816-1965. M. Small and J. D. Singer. bibliog f il Ann Am Acad 391:145-55 S '70
See also
Biological warfare
Conscientious objectors
Disarmament
International security
Peace
Strategy
Vietnamese war, 1957-
War and society
Women and war

Economic aspects
See also
Businessman's educational forum
Vietnamese war, 1957- —Economic aspects

Moral aspects
See War and morals

WAR—*Continued*

Political aspects
See Politics and war

Psychological aspects
From club to megabomb. D. Behrman. UNESCO Courier 23:22-3 Ag '70
How nations take defeat. C. Barnett. Horizon 12:4-11 Sum '70
    See also
Atomic warfare—Psychological aspects
Vietnamese war, 1957- —Psychological aspects

Social aspects
See War and society

Terminology
Language and politics. E. McCarthy. por Mc-Calls 97:18+ F '70
WAR, Accidental. See Atomic weapons—Accidents
WAR, Causes of
Case for war. il por Time 95:46-7 Mr 9 '70
WAR, Ethics of. See War and morals
WAR, Laws of
How relevant are the rules of war? A. Wilson. Cur 114:3-6 Ja '70
War crimes and individual responsibility; a legal memorandum. R. A. Falk. Trans-Action 7:33-40 Ja '70
    See also
War crimes
WAR, Prevention of
Issues of thermonuclear war termination; excerpts from War termination, issues and concepts. H. Kahn. bibliog f il Ann Am Acad 392:133-72 N '70
WAR, Termination of. See Capitulations, Military
WAR aims
    See also
Vietnamese war, 1957- —War aims
WAR and civilization
Reflections: the megamachine. L. Mumford. New Yorker 46:55-8+ O 24 '70
WAR and children. See Children and war
WAR and college students. See College students and war
WAR and culture. See War and civilization
WAR and emergency legislation

Canada
Canada can, can we? New Repub 163:7-8 O 31 '70
Canada enters the revolutionary age. il Newsweek 76:41-4+ N 2 '70
Canada: the answer was murder; War measures act invoked against the FLQ. il Newsweek 76:35-6 O 26 '70
Crackdown on terrorists. il Sr Schol 97:3 N 9 '70
Law, order and Trudeau. D. Coxe. il Nat R 22:1201 N 17 '70
Pierre Trudeau; counterrevolutionary. Nat R 22:1144+ N 3 '70
Pierre Trudeau's legal overkill. P. Freiberg. Commonweal 93:292-4 D 18 '70
Testing of Pierre Trudeau. T. Buckley. il pors N Y Times Mag p50-1+ D 6 '70
WAR and emergency powers

Israel
Terrorism & preventive detention: the case of Israel. A. M. Dershowitz. bibliog f Commentary 50:67-78 D '70
WAR and libraries. See Libraries and war
WAR and literature
As the sun sets over Pinkville; war poems. J. Jerome Writers Digest 50:38-43 F '70
WAR and morals
Cambodian crisis: reason and emotion. C. E. Izard. Science 168:1157 Je 5 '70
Catch-22 and the new hero. J. Castelli. il Cath World 211:199-202 Ag '70
For men who want to be indignant. N. Cousins. Sat R 53:24 O 3 '70
Green Berets. P. J. Riga. il Cath World 210:199-203 F '70; Discussion. 211:100, 148 Je-Jl '70
    See also
Atomic warfare—Ethical aspects
Vietnamese war, 1957- —Moral and religious aspects
World war, 1939-1945—Moral and religious aspects
WAR and music. See Music and war
WAR and politics. See Politics and war
WAR and religion
American intervention and Catholic fatalism. J. B. Sheerin. Cath World 212:59-60 N '70

Coming confrontation on the church's war investments. S. C. Rose. Chr Cent 87:1209-11 O 14 '70
Need for a new Christian presence in Vietnam. D. Hostetter. Chr Cent 87:536-7 Ap 29 '70; Discussion. 87:826 Jl 1 '70
Peace of Bethlehem escapes us. B. L. Masse. America 123:535 D 19 '70
Selective conscientious objection: progress report. P. J. Riga. il Cath World 211:161-5 Jl '70
War and the balance of power; some Christian reflections; address, November 11, J. V. Schall. Vital Speeches 36:211-17 Ja 15 '70
    See also
Conscientious objectors
Vietnamese war, 1957- —Moral and religious aspects
WAR and science
Scientists' dilemma. Nation 212:68-9 Ja 18 '71
WAR and society
Is peace inevitable? by S. Genovés. Review Sat R 53:21-3 D 19 '70. M. M. Tumin
Who's afraid of war? F. Ungeheuer. Harper 241:28-31 D '70
    See also
Atomic warfare and society
WAR casualties
    See also
Israeli-Arab war, 1967- —Casualties
Vietnamese war, 1957- —Casualties
WAR correspondents
    See also
Cambodian-Vietnamese conflict—War correspondents
Israeli-Arab war, 1967- —War correspondents
Jordan—Civil war, 1970—War correspondents
Nigeria—Civil war, 1967-1970—War correspondents
Vietnamese war, 1957- —War correspondents
WAR crimes
Can corporations be tried for war crimes? G. Wald. Cur 120:56-63 Ag '70
GI's in combat: how far does just following orders go? il Sr Schol 95:9-10 Ja 5 '70
Is Nuremberg coming back to haunt us? J. B. Reston, jr. Sat R 53:14-17+ Jl 18 '70
Quality of military justice. J. W. Bishop, jr. il N Y Times Mag p32-8+ F 22 '70; Discussion. p22+ Ap 12 '70
War crimes: the circle of responsibility. R. A. Falk. Nation 210:77-82 Ja 26 '70
    See also
Vietnamese war, 1957- —Atrocities
WAR films. See Moving picture—War films
WAR games
Game of war; craze in Britain. il Time 97:47 Ja 4 '71
WAR heroes. See Heroes
WAR in art
    See also
Vietnamese war, 1957- —Art
WAR marriages
For love or money; Vietnamese-American marriages. il Newsweek 76:50-1 S 7 '70
WAR materials
    See also
Munitions
Vietnamese war, 1957- —Equipment and supplies
WAR news
How the G.I.'s in Vietnam don't learn about the war. R. Hodierne. il por N Y Times Mag p28-9+ Ap 12 '70
    See also
Nigeria—Civil war, 1967-1970—War correspondents
Television broadcasting—War news
Vietnamese war 1957- —War correspondents
WAR nurses. See Nurses and nursing
WAR objectors. See Conscientious objectors
WAR poetry
Teaching the poetry of war. S. P. Hansen. bibliog f Engl J 59:497-501 Ap '70
    See also
Vietnamese war, 1957- —Poetry
WAR powers. See Presidents—United States—Powers and duties
WAR profiteering. See Black markets; War profits
WAR profits
Myth of war profiteering. G. E. Berkley. il New Repub 161:15-18 D 20 '69; Reply. V. Perlo. 162:23-5 F 7 '70
WAR propaganda
    See also
World war, 1939-1945—Propaganda
WAR psychology. See War—Psychological aspects
WAR research. See Military research
WAR tax (United States) See Taxation—United States

WARBURG, Gerald
How two musicians live with music. il por House & Gard 138:56-7 Jl '70 *

WARD, Don
TV X-rays. il Radio-Electr 41:54-6 Ap '70

WARD, Douglas Turner
Brotherhood. Criticism
New Yorker 46:84 Mr 28 '70 *
Day of absence. Criticism
New Yorker 46:84 Mr 28 '70 *

WARD, Jack
Gallery; photographs. Life 69:4-5 O 2 '70

WARD, James D.
Manual high school: cutting class can get you to college. il pors Ebony 25:68-70+ My '70 *

WARD, Jeanne H.
Steve, go wash your hands! story. Todays Ed 59:42-3 D '70

WARD, Leo R.
Where the new liturgy limps. Commonweal 92:404-5 Ag 21 '70

WARD, Maisie
Give it a chance. America 122:589-91 My 30 '70

WARDROBES. See Closets

WARE, N. G. and Lovering, J. F.
Electron-microprobe analyses of phases in lunar samples. bibliog il Science 167:517-20 Ja 30 '70

WARE, W. Porter
Jenny Lind's 150th anniversary; concert and exhibition in London. il Hobbies 75:142-3+ O '70
Jenny Lind's 150th anniversary, 1820-1970. il por Hobbies 75:48-50 O '70 *
Rare glimpse of Jenny Lind. il por Hobbies 75:124+ O '70

WARE collection of glass flowers. See Harvard university—Botanical museum

WAREHOUSES
Warehouse too handsome to remain one; Westyard building, New York city. il Arch Rec 147:113-18 My '70

WARFEL, Alwin Harry, and Elberg, S. S.
Macrophage membranes viewed through a scanning electron microscope. bibliog il Science 170:446-7 O 23 '70

WARFIELD, Rebecca
Good looks & good health. See issues of House & garden incorporating Living for young homemakers

WARHOL, Andy
It's hard to be your own script; interview, ed. by L. Kent. Vogue 155:167+ Mr 1 '70

about

Andy Warhol disguised here as Andy Warhol. J. Perreault. il por Vogue 155:164-6+ Mr 1 '70 *
Andy Warhola, this is your life. J. Perreault. il por Art N 69:52-3+ My '70 *
Current cinema. P. Kael. New Yorker 46:132+ O 10 '70 *
Midnight snack of Andy Warhol. T. W. Moore. il Chr Cent 87:396-7 Ap 1 '70 *

WARIS, Klaus
Finland's formula for deflating inflation; interview. il por Nations Bsns 58:36-8 Ag '70

WARM-water irrigation. See Irrigation

WARNECKE, Steven
American student politics. Yale R 60:185-98 D '70

WARNER, Bob
New in-spot for tarpon. il Field & S 74:194-7+ Mr '70
Rivière Philippe. il pors Outdoor Life 145:48-51+ Je '70

WARNER, Dave
Totlots. il Parks & Rec 5:32-3+ Jl '70

WARNER, Eltinge F.
Field & stream hat trick. A. J. McClane. il por Field & S 75:72-3+ Je '70 *

WARNER, Jack Lionel
Joyous house of the Warners. il por Vogue 155:170-5 Je '70 *

WARNER, Ken
Four-barreled handgun. il Pop Mech 134:244 O '70

WARNER, Sylvia Townsend
At the stroke of midnight; story. New Yorker 46:42-8 S 12 '70
Being a lily. New Yorker 46:155-9 O 10 '70
Green torso; story. New Yorker 46:36-43 Ag 22 '70

WARNICK, Dorothy Brant
Memories in stone. il Travel 133:66-71 Ja '70

WARP weaving. See Weaving

WARRANTS, Royal. See Royal warrant

WARRANTS, Stock purchase. See Stock purchase warrants

WARRANTY
Can FTC put a governor on Detroit? proposed automobile quality control act. il Bsns W p31-2 F 28 '70
Car warranties: it pays to know what they mean. Bsns W p 110 My 2 '70
Cost of living; report on product warranties. B. Furness. por McCalls 97:28+ F '70
Detroit tries a U-turn on warranties. il Bsns W p44-5+ Jl 25 '70
Getting the most from warranties. L. M. Brown. Bet Hom & Gard 48:18 D '70
How our new warranty law would protect you. W. G. Magnuson. por Pop Sci 197:66-7 N '70
Some variable costs of ownership: repairs insurance, warranties; your new car. il Consumer Rep 35:201-4 Ap '70
Warranties: what are they worth to you? H. Shuldiner. Pop Sci 197:55-7+ N '70
Who pays the bill when your appliance breaks down? M. Spencer. Am Home 73:42+ Mr '70

WARREN, David
Workbench fit for a pro. il Pop Mech 134:162-5+ O '70

WARREN, David B.
Empire style at Bayou bend: new period rooms in Houston. il Antiques 97:122-7 Ja '70

WARREN, Donald I.
Status inconsistency theory and flying saucer sightings. bibliog il Science 170:599-603 N 6 '70

WARREN, Earl
A.C.L.U. dinner. New Yorker 46:34-5 D 19 '70 *
Civil rights and the Warren court. il pors Ebony 25:27-30+ F '70 *
Pessimism of Earl Warren. Chr Cent 87:652 My 27 '70 *
Supreme court and the idea of progress, by A. M. Bickel. Review
Nat R 22:414-15 Ap 21 '70. W. Berns *
Sat R 53:37-8+ Ap 4 '70. W. M. Wiecek *

WARREN, F. Eugene
Uncut stone; poem. Chr Today 14:12 F 27 '70

WARREN, Glenn Barton
Another new engine nudges Detroit. il Bsns W p86-7 O 24 '70 *

WARREN, James
Creepy-boppers. il Newsweek 76:103-4 D 14 '70 *

WARREN, Margaret
Literacy librarian: case studies of experiments in Dallas. il por Wilson Lib Bul 45:278-84 N '70

WARREN, Mark
TV's black skyrocket. il pors Ebony 25:113-16+ Ap '70 *

WARREN, Richard M.
Perceptual restoration of missing speech sounds. bibliog Science 167:392-3 Ja 23 '70
—and Warren, R. P.
Auditory illusions and confusions; with biographical sketches. il Sci Am 223:10, 30-6 D '70

WARREN, Robert Penn
Keys to ourselves. J. Kessler. pors Sat R 53:35-6 My 2 '70 *

WARREN, Roslyn P. See Warren, R. M. jt. auth.

WARREN, Virginia Lee
Impressions of Kay Mazzo. il pors Dance Mag 44:60-4 Ja '70

WARREN, Mich.
Furor over a drive to integrate the suburbs. il U S News 69:23-4 Ag 10 '70

WARRENSVILLE HEIGHTS, Ohio
New math; suspended school superintendent. T. Sheridan. New Repub 163:13 S 19 '70

WARS. See War

WARSAW
Music
Behind the scenes. K. Blaukopf. Hi Fi sec I 20:22+ Ja '70

WARSAW ghetto. See Jews in Poland

WARSAW pact, 1955
Europe: of defense and détente. il Time 96:24+ D 14 '70
Proposed European security conference; excerpts from Prague communiqué. Cur Hist 58:305 My '70

WARSH, Lewis
Comment. Poetry 115:440-6 Mr '70
Message; Flashing; Souffle; poems. Poetry 116:182-5 Je '70

WARSHAW, Thayer S.
Black eye in the heart. Todays Ed 59:48 My '70

WARSHIP models. See Ship and boat models

WARSHIPS
See also
Aircraft carriers
United States
Destroyers for sale: $150,000; submarines are cheaper. il U S News 68:33 F 2 '70
Return of the destroyer; contract for construction of multipurpose destroyers. il Sci N 98:7-8 Jl 4 '70
See also
Constitution (frigate)

WARSHOFSKY, Fred
Methadone: a drug to lick a drug? Read Digest 96:88-92 My '70
Mind research: the promise and the peril. Read Digest 96:119-23 Ap '70
What the moon rocks reveal. il Read Digest 97:157-60+ Ag '70

WARTS
Therapy
Warts and all. il Time 97:60+ Ja 4 '71

WARWICK, Dionne
Lifestyle. il por Am Home 73:8 O '70 *

WARWICK, James F.
Box display. il Sch Arts 70:32-3 S '70

WASH cloths. See Washcloths

WASHBURN, Frank M.
Trying sixties a prelude to the 70's. por Camp Mag 42:4 F '70

WASHBURN, Gordon Bailey
Jeweled beasts of royal hordes. il Art N 69: 28-31 Mr '70
John D. Rockefeller, III Oriental collections. il Art N 69:36-47 S '70

WASHBURN, Jerry
Trophy bucks are easy; ed. by D. Knight. il Field & S 75:36-7+ Ag '70

WASHBURN, Kermit V. jr
Three phase program starts leader training at eight years old. il Camp Mag 42:20+ F '70

WASHCLOTHS
Loos knit. A. Loos. il por McCalls 97:60+ Ap '70

WASHING compounds. See Cleaning compositions

WASHING machines
Automatic clothes washers. il Consumer Rep 34:8-14 D '69
Combination washer and dryer; Skinny mini. il Consumer Rep 36:5-7 Ja '71
Portable washing machines. il Consumer Rep 35:532-8 S '70
Washers & dryers: an up-to-the-minute report. J. R. Cary. il Parents Mag 45:95-8 Mr '70
Washing machines. il Consumer Rep 35:400-8 Jl '70

WASHING of clothes. See Laundry

WASHINGTON, Anne Blackburn
Music of the Washington family: a little-known collection. J. R. Heintze. bibliog f por Mus Q 56:288-93 Ap '70 *

WASHINGTON, Booker T. jr
Booker T's yellow submarine. il por Ebony 26:153-4+ D '70 *

WASHINGTON, Booker Taliaferro
Booker T. Washington in biographical perspective. L. R. Harlan. bibliog f Am Hist R 75:1581-99 O '70 *

WASHINGTON, George
Checking up on George; Marvin Kitman's study of wartime expense accounts. J. Iams. il Newsweek 76:55+ Ag 3 '70
From one humble servant to another; exchange of letters. il pors Am Heritage 22: 112 D '70
George Washington and the new nation (1783-1793) by J. T. Flexner. Review
Sat R 53:33-4 N 21 '70. M. M. Brown *
Melancholy case. A. L. Damon. il por Am Heritage 21:18-19+ F '70 *
Memorials
Arch. New Yorker 46:19-21 Ag 29 '70
Museums, relics, etc.
Music of the Washington family: a little-known collection. J. R. Heintze. bibliog f por Mus Q 56:288-93 Ap '70

WASHINGTON, Walter Edward
Black mayors. por Newsweek 76:18 Ag 3 '70 *
Cutting crime in nation's capital: the mayor's formula. por U S News 69:69 Ag 31 '70 *
Mayor who isn't. Newsweek 76:78-9 Ag 31 '70 *

WASHINGTON, D.C.
See also
Architecture, Domestic—Washington. D.C.
Booksellers and bookselling—Washington. D.C.
White House

Airports
Elephant that took wing; Dulles international airport. Bsns W p 138 Mr 21 '70
Pilots blame FAA in jam of Washington air traffic. C. E. Schneider. Aviation W 93:21-2 Ag 31 '70
Traffic plan flops in Washington. J. P. Woolsey. Aviation W 93:20-1 Ag 31 '70

Buildings
Watergate way. il Newsweek 75:24-5 F 16 '70

City planning
Gift for the neighborhood; church to do urban developing of their own. il Time 95:77 My 11 '70
Promises, promises; Southwest renewal project. il Newsweek 76:94+ D 14 '70

Clubs
See also
National press club

Community centers
Interview with Topper Carew; programs of the New thing art and architecture center; ed. by W. Roberts. T. Carew. il Sat R 53:46-8 Jl 18 '70

Courts
Mitchell tests the Constitution. J. R. Lundy. Nation 210:205-7 F 23 '70

Crime
About the crime bill. Cato. Nat R 22:884 Ag 25 '70
Crime-control act for capital: a model for the Nation? il U S News 69:59 Ag 3 '70
Crime crackdown. Sr Schol 97:4 S 14 '70
Cutting crime in nation's capital: the mayor's formula. por U S News 69:69 Ag 31 '70
Full of fleas; District of Columbia and the omnibus crime bill. New Repub 162:7-8 Je 27 '70
Listening to America. B. Moyers. il Harper 241:105-9 D '70
Response to fear. il por Time 96:10 Ag 3 '70
S.30: the seeds of repression; District of Columbia crime bill, with editorial comment. H. Schwartz. Nation 211:67, 70-1 Ag 3 '70
You must be out of your mind to be out alone after dark in a neighborhood like this. J. K. Batten. il N Y Times Mag p22-3+ Mr 22 '70

Description
Special travel correspondent. H. Sutton. Holiday 47:7-8+ Ap '70

Education
Morgan follows through. S. Moorefield. il Am Ed 6:31-3 Ja '70
Washington faces A possible reality; proposal of Kenneth B. Clark. Sat R 53:55 Ag 15 '70
Washington mess; reading plan of K. Clark. por Newsweek 76:70 O 5 '70

Galleries and museums
See also
Corcoran gallery of art, Washington, D.C.
National gallery of art, Washington, D.C.
Phillips memorial gallery, Washington, D.C.
Smithsonian institution

Historic houses, etc.
Frederick Douglass home fund approved for restoration use. il Negro Hist Bul 33:49 F '70
Tudor place. W. D. Garrett. il Antiques 98: 94-9 Jl '70

Hotels, restaurants, etc.
Where the elite meet; Sans Souci. il Newsweek 75:21-2 Mr 9 '70

Libraries
See also
United States—Library of Congress

Lighting
Nation's capital turns on for Christmas. il Am City 85:72+ D '70
Washington's new look at night. il U S News 69:53-5 S 21 '70

Monuments, statues, etc.
See also
Lincoln memorial
Music
Echoes from the East garden court; concert series at the National gallery of art. R. Evett. New Repub 163:24-6 Ag 15 '70
See also
Opera society of Washington

WASHINGTON, D.C.—*Continued*

National arboretum

Touch and see; nature trail. P. Caulfield.
il Nat Wildlife 7:18-19 O '69

National cherry blossom festival

Capital's proud black princess. il pors Ebony
25:104-7 Jl '70

Parades

Ill-attended victory march. America 123:277-8
O 17 '70

McIntire's victory march. R. Chandler. il Chr
Today 15:36-7 O 23 '70

Military-ecclesiastical complex. Chr Today 15:
39 O 9 '70

Parks and playgrounds

Parks for all seasons, and for all people; inner city program. M. M. Boyd. il Parks &
Rec 5:22-3+ My '70

Police

Flatfoot floozies; police women arrest customers. il Newsweek 75:99 My 18 '70

Police recruiting with an up beat. il Bsns W
p79 Ja 24 '70

What the police can, and cannot do about
crime. il Time 96:34-6+ Jl 13 '70

Politics and government

Blacker-than-thou. il Newsweek 77:27 Ja 11
'71

Blacker than thou; contestants to District
of Columbia's first non-voting delegate to
Congress. E. E. Plowman. Chr Today 15:27
Ja 15 '71

Home rule for D.C.? Nat R 22:505 My 19 '70

Mayor who isn't. Newsweek 76:78-9 Ag 31 '70

Step to equality? D.C. gets House delegate.
Sr Schol 97:22 O 19 '70

Rapid transit

See Washington, D.C.—Transit systems

Recreation

Washington's youth gardens. il Parks & Rec
5:47-8+ Je '70
See also
Washington, D.C.—Parks and playgrounds

Religious institutions and affairs

Plea for reconciliation; break between the
Archbishop of Washington and his priests.
America 122:446 Ap 25 '70; Reply with re-
joinder. J. C. Ford. 122:571 My 30 '70

Social life and customs

Menus and recipes from Washington parties.
il House & Gard 138:83+ Ag '70

Official Washington: ideas for entertaining.
il House & Gard 138:76-81 Ag '70

Random thoughts on moving to Washington from a senator's wife. L. S. Cooper.
House & Gard 138:24 Ag '70

Washington, sex, and power. J. Corry. il
Harper 241:63-8 Jl '70

Washington society isn't exactly swinging. T.
Meehan. il N Y Times Mag p30-1+ Mr 8 '70

What people are doing; that's how Washington is. House & Gard 138:33 Ag '70

Subway

Mass transit plans include handicapped. Am
City 85:54 Ap '70

Theater

L'enfant theatre. il Arch Rec 147:114 Ja '70

Lights are up at Ford's theatre. L. Aikman.
il Nat Geog 137:392-401 Mr '70
See also
John F. Kennedy center for the performing
arts, Washington, D.C.

Transit systems

End of the line. por Time 95:20+ My 4 '70
See also
Washington, D.C.—Subway

Transportation

See also
Washington, D.C.—Transit systems

Water supply

Forty years of growth in a decade; Potomac
River filtration plant. E. F. Spitzer. il Am
City 85:115-17 Je '70

Zoological park

See National zoological park, Washington,
D.C.

WASHINGTON, D.C. Federal city college

Underprepared college student; with editorial
comment. I. Tinker. Am Ed 6:inside cover,
10-12 N '70

WASHINGTON (state)
See also
Architecture, Domestic—Washington (state)
Camps—Washington (state)
Canals—Washington (state)
Fishing—Washington (state)
Gardens—Washington (state)
Geology—Washington (state)
Hunting—Washington (state)
King County
North Cascades National Park
Olympic National Park
Public welfare—Washington (state)
Rainier, Mount
Recreation areas—Washington (state)
San Juan Islands
Washington, Lake
Wilderness areas—Washington (state)
Willapa Bay

Industries

Swords into ploughshares; Hanford makes the
switch. L. J. Carter. il Science 167:1357-8+
Mr 6 '70

Parks and recreation commission

Success story: Youth development and conservation corps. D. H. Reynaud. il Parks &
Rec 5:28-9 Jl '70

Parks and reserves

County acts to save its vanishing shorelands.
K. D. Hertz. il Parks & Rec 5:48-9+ F '70

Politics and government

War is hell for Senator Jackson. B. Weiner.
por Nation 211:138-41 Ag 31 '70

WASHINGTON (state). University, Seattle

Pollution watching by telescope; study by
P. W. Hodge at University of Washington.
Sci N 98:300 O 10 '70

WASHINGTON, LAKE

Lake that came back; reclaimed from pollution. Newsweek 76:98 N 16 '70

Phosphorus, nitrogen, and algae in Lake
Washington after diversion of sewage. W.
T. Edmondson. bibliog il Science 169:690-1
Ag 14 '70

WASHINGTON COUNTY, Ore.

County unifies thirty-five sewerage agencies.
R. Milbrodt. il Am City 85:64-5+ N '70

WASHINGTON crossing the Delaware; paint-
ing. See Leutze, E.

WASHINGTON Indians. See Indians of North
America

WASHINGTON post

Editorial ombudsman. il por Newsweek 76:72
D 14 '70

Post script; WLBW license challenge. New
Repub 162:9-10 Mr 7 '70
See also
International herald tribune

WASHINGTON Senators (baseball) See Baseball clubs

WASHINGTON shores association for recrea-
tion center. See Recreation centers

WASHINGTON square, New York. See New
York (city)—Washington square

WASKISH, Minn.

Of wilderness and wolves; excerpts. P. L.
Errington. il Liv Wildn 33:3-7 Aut '69

WASKOW, Arthur I.

Community control of the police. Trans-
Action 7:4-7 D '69; 92-3 Ap '70

WASPS

Chemical defense of brood by a social wasp.
R. L. Jeanne. bibliog il Science 168:1465-6
Je 19 '70

Wasp that plays cupid to a fig. R. F. Sisson.
il Nat Geog 138:690-7 N '70

WASPS (white Anglo-Saxon Protestants)

Decline of the WASP. P. Schrag. il Harper
240:85-91 Ap '70

Disintegration of the elite. S. Alsop. Newsweek 75:108 Je 8 '70

On stinging the ethnics. Chr Cent 87:1031
S 2 '70

Reflections on Earth day; environment issue
and reassertion of primacy. N. Podhoretz.
Commentary 49:26+ Je '70

WASSAIL

Holiday drinks; traditional wassail bowl. W.
Clifford. House B 112:88+ D '70

WASSATAQUOIK STREAM

Walk to Wassataquoik. V. N. DeFelice. il por
Am For 76:16-19+ Mr '70

WASSERMAN, Aaron O.

Polyploidy in the common tree toad hyla
versicolor Le Conte. bibliog il Science 167:
385-6 Ja 23 '70

WASSERMAN, Burton

Making the gallery scene. il Sch Arts 69:
32-5 F; 36-9 Mr; 32-5 Je; 70:30-3 O '70

WASSERMAN, Edward A. and Jensen, D. D.
   Olfactory stimuli and the pseudo-extinction
   effect. bibliog Science 166:1307-9; 169:402 D
   5 '69, Jl 24 '70
WASSERMAN, Paul
   Professional adaptation: library education
   mandate. il por Library J 95:1281-8 Ap 1
   '70
—and Daniel, Evelyn
   Birth of LIST. bibliog il pors Library J 95:
   3879-83 N 15 '70
WASSERSUG, Joseph D.
   Fact and fiction about cholesterol. il Sci
   Digest 68:18-21 D '70
   What you can do about teen-age fatigue. il
   Sci Digest 67:25-8 Ja '70
WASSON, Donald
   (comp) Source material. See issues of For-
   eign affairs
WASSON, John T. See Baedecker, P. A. jt.
   auth.
WASSON, R. Gordon
   Books. W. Sargeant. New Yorker 46:93-8
   My 30 '70
WASTE, Disposal of. See Refuse and refuse
   disposal; Trade waste disposal
WASTE, Utilization of. See Refuse, Utilization
   of
WASTE disposal appliances. See Refuse and
   refuse disposal—Apparatus
WASTE disposal in the ocean
   Don't go near the water; proposed anti-
   dumping regulations. Newsweek 76:76 O 19
   '70
   Oceans: world sump. J. W. Hedgpeth. il En-
   viron 12:40-6 Ap '70
   Station 59; dumping grounds off New York
   harbor. O. Segerberg, jr. il Sea Front 16:
   223-30 Jl '70
   Study of ocean dumping of wastes transmit-
   ted to the Congress, message, October 7,
   1970. R. M. Nixon. Dept State Bul 63:669-
   70 N 30 '70
   We're making a cesspool of the sea. G. Nel-
   son. il Nat Wildlife 8:14-16 Ag '70
   See also
   Gases, Asphyxiating and poisonous—Disposal
   in the ocean
   Hazardous substances—Disposal in the ocean
WASTE disposal plants. See Refuse incinera-
   tors; Sewage disposal plants
WASTE disposers. See Refuse grinders
WASTE heat
   Can our rivers stand the heat? W. Lange-
   wiesche. Read Digest 96:76-80 Ap '70
   Finding a place to put the heat; effects on
   the ecology of bodies of water. R. H. Gil-
   luly. il Sci N 98:98-9 Ag 1 '70
WASTE in defense spending. See United States
   —Defense, Department of—Appropriations
   and expenditures
WASTE injection. See Trade waste disposal
WASTE paper
   Company thrives on a bureaucratic by-prod-
   uct; Capital reclamation corp, Washing-
   ton, D.C. V. Louviere. Nations Bsns 58:18
   O '70
   Insulate with a cool $50 million? disposal of
   worn paper money. Nations Bsns 58:41 D
   '70
   Total waste-paper reclamation and reuse is
   goal. Am City 85:52 S '70
WASTE products
   Riding on wastes; worn rubber tires and glass
   as construction materials. Time 95:62+ Mr
   16 '70
   See also
   Refuse and refuse disposal
   Waste paper
WASTE recycling. See Refuse, Utilization of
WASTE water irrigation. See Sewage irriga-
   tion
WASTE water reclamation. See Water reuse
WASTE water treatment. See Sewage disposal
WASYLUKA, Ray G.
   New blood for tired hospitals. bibliog f il
   Harvard Bsns R 48:65-74 S '70
WATCH industry and trade
   Why watchmakers are all wound up. il Bsns
   W p86-7 O 3 '70
   See also
   Sheffield watch corporation
WATCH makers. See Clock and watch makers
WATCHDOGS
   Hounds of hell; guard-dogs. il Newsweek 76:
   59 Jl 13 '70
   Intruder's worst friend. il Bsns W p 113 Je
   20 '70
WATCHES
   Those wild watches with the built-in brains.
   R. Gorman. il Pop Sci 197:80-2+ D '70

Time for Spiro; Agnew watch. il Time 96:56
   Jl 6 '70
What makes a good watch tick. il Changing
   T 24:38-40 N '70
WATCHES, Electric
   Electric timepiece on your wrist; Hamilton
   Pulsar. L. Steckler. il Radio-Electr 41:39-41
   Ag '70
   Look, little old Swiss watchmaker, no hands!
   Pulsar. A. Fisher. il Pop Sci 197:51 Jl '70
   Wrist computer tells time without hands. il
   Pop Mech 134:38 Jl '70
WATCHMAKERS. See Clock and watch makers
WATCHMAN-examiner (periodical)
   Watchman-examiner ceases publication. Chr
   Today 14:22 Mr 27 '70
WATCHTOWER Bible and tract society. See
   Jehovah's Witnesses
WATER
   Anomalous water: attempts at high-pressure
   synthesis. R. H. Wentorf, jr. bibliog Sci-
   ence 169:175-6 Jl 10 '70
   Anomalous water: characterization by physi-
   cal methods. S. W. Rabideau and A. E.
   Florin. bibliog il Science 169:48-52 Jl 3 '70
   Anomalous water: polywater or impurities?
   M. S. Rothenberg. bibliog il Phys Today
   23:17-20 O '70
   Covalent polymers of water. C. T. O'Konski.
   bibliog il Science 168:1089-91 My 29 '70
   Deryagin and the Russians; anomalous
   water. por Sci N 98:286 O 3 '70
   Doubters and Deryagin; polywater contro-
   versy. por Sci N 98:6 Jl 4 '70
   Doubts about polywater. il Time 96:46 O 19
   '70
   Mars: occurrence of liquid water. A. P. In-
   gersoll. bibliog il Science 168:972-3 My 22
   '70
   Observed diffraction pattern and proposed
   models of liquid water. A. H. Narten and
   H. A. Levy; reply with rejoinder. B. Kamb.
   bibliog Science 167:1520-1 Mr 13 '70
   On the waterfront. il Vogue 156:136-7 O 1 '70
   Polywater. E. R. Lippincott and others; discussion. bibliog il Science 167:1719-20; 168:
   151 Mr 27-Ap 3 '70
   Polywater: a hydrosol? S. L. Kurtin and
   others. bibliog il Science 167:1720-2 Mr 27
   '70
   Polywater: an attempt at synthesis in a gas
   discharge. A. G. Leiga and others. bibliog il
   Science 168:114-16 Ap 3 '70
   Polywater discovered thirty years ago? M.
   T. Shaw. bibliog il Science 169:705 My 14 '70
   Polywater: methods for identifying polywater columns and evidence for ordered
   growth. G. A. Castellion and others. bibliog il Science 167:865-8 F 6 '70
   Polywater: polymer or artifact? D. L. Rousseau and S. P. S. Porto. bibliog il Science
   167:1715-19 Mr 27 '70
   Polywater: possibility of p-electron delo-
   calization. R. P. Messmer. bibliog Science
   168:479-80 Ap 24 '70
   Proposed new structure for polywater. il
   Chem 43:22 My '70
   Proton magnetic resonance spectrum of polywater. G. A. Petsko. il Science 167:171 Ja 9
   '70
   Structure of ordinary water. H. S. Frank.
   bibliog il Science 169:635-41 Ag 14 '70
   Superdense water. B. V. Derjagin. il Sci Am
   223:52-64+ bibliog(p 132) N '70
   Symmetric hydrogen bonds give form to
   anomalous water. il Sci N 97:287 Mr 21 '70
   Theory of anomalous water. L. C. Allen
   and P. A. Kollman. bibliog il Science 167:
   1443-54 Mr 13 '70
   Vitreous water: identification and character-
   ization. C. A. Angell and E. J. Sare. bibliog
   Science 168:280-1 Ap 10 '70
   Water on the moon? E. Anders. bibliog Sci-
   ence 169:1309-10 S 25 '70
   Water: the fluid of life; Ocean space center,
   IOF's new museum. V. J. Gabianelli. il Sea
   Front 16:258-70 S '70
   What is this thing called polywater? I. Asi-
   mov. Sci Digest 67:80-1 F '70
   See also
   Drinking water
   Hot water
   Hydrologic research
   Lakes
   Sea water
   Waves

   Composition
   Mechanisms controlling world water chemistry. R. J. Gibbs. bibliog il Science 170:
   1088-90 D 4 '70
   Metamorphic waters from the Pacific tectonic belt of the West coast of the United
   States. I. Barnes. bibliog il Science 168:973-
   5 My 22 '70

WATER—*Continued*

Laws and legislation
See also
Water rights

Pollution
See Water pollution

Purification
See Water purification

Testing
Build your own portable water tester; conductivity gauge. P. Emerson. il Pop Sci 197:127-8+ S '70

WATER, Bottled
Bottled-water sales begin to sparkle. il Bsns W p44+ N 7 '70
Good taste of fresh waters. E. Alston. il Look 34:46-7 Jl 14 '70

WATER, Freezing of. See Freezing

WATER, Underground
Tap only the best water in your well; selective sampling of aquifers, Santa Clara, Calif. R. R. Mortenson. il Am City 85:49-51 D '70
See also
Wells

WATER billing. See Billing

WATER bird shooting
More tricks for waterfowl. S. M. Miller. il Outdoor Life 145:24-5+ Ja '70

WATER birds
Birds bring so much joy and excitement to our garden; interview. A. S. Hess. House & Gard 138:46+ S '70
Nevada's desert waterfowl. V. M. Carter. il Nat Parks & Con Mag 44:18-21 Je '70
Waterfowl, tame or wild in your own backyard. il Sunset 144:80-5 Je '70
See also names of water birds, e.g. Geese, Wild

WATER buffaloes
Brazil's water buffalo. D. W. Gade. il Américas 22:35-9 My '70

WATER clocks. See Clocks—History

WATER color painting
Arne Lindmark: master of the watercolor scene. M. Malmstrom. il Am Artist 35:38-43+ Ja '71
Notes on watercolor; excerpt from Starting with watercolor. R. Hilder. il Am Artist 34:20-1 S '70
Painting a watercolor in acrylic. A. J. Barbour. il Am Artist 34:48-53+ Je '70
Painting watercolors in acrylic; excerpts from Acrylic watercolor painting. W. Blake. il Am Artist 34:36-41*In* D '70
Watercolor page:
Arthur J. Barbour. A. J. Barbour. il por Am Artist 34:66-7+ F '70
Charles A. Mahoney. il por Am Artist 34:46-7+ Mr '70
Charles Demetropoulos. C. Demetropoulos. il Am Artist 34:44-5+ Ja '70
Florian K. Lawton. F. K. Lawton. il por Am Artist 34:52-3+ Ap '70
Michael Rossi. il por Am Artist 34:50-1+ S '70
Murray Wentworth. il por Am Artist 34:30-1+ My '70
Phil Tyler. P. Tyler. il por Am Artist 34:30-1+ Je '70
Rolland Golden. il por Am Artist 35:28-9+ Ja '71
Shu Dick Ju. il por Am Artist 34:50-1+ Ag '70
William James Flynn. il por Am Artist 34:60-2 D '70
William L. Ko. il por Am Artist 34:46-7+ O '70
Win Jones. il por Am Artist 34:56-7+ N '70

Study and teaching
Painting watercolor portraits. E. A. Whitney. il Am Artist 34:38-43 Ag '70

WATER cycle. See Hydrologic cycle

WATER desalting. See Water purification—Desalting

WATER drops. See Drops

WATER falls. See Waterfalls

WATER films. See Films

WATER fowl. See Water birds

WATER fronts
Cleaning
See also
Harbors—Cleaning

WATER gardens
Happy even if their feet are wet. il Sunset 144:231 Je '70

Stream. H. A. Buchanan. Good H 171:176 N '70
Very personal garden of the Thomas B. Hesses: a pond garden. il House & Gard 138:108-11 S '70
Water gardens, Japan Expo '70. il House & Gard 138:58-63 Ag '70

WATER heaters
ABCs of water heaters. R. Day. il Mech Illus 66:102-4 Ag '70
Everybody's water heater is wearing out. il Changing T 25:39-40 Ja '71
Immersion heaters; all unsafe to use. il Consumer Bul 54:24-5 Ja '71

WATER hydrants. See Hydrants

WATER in rocks
Water in the earth's mantle: melting curves of basalt-water and basalt-water-carbon dioxide. R. E. T. Hill and A. L. Boettcher. bibliog il Science 167:980-2 F 13 '70

WATER lilies
Waterlilies around the clock. P. W. Stetson. il Horticulture 48:30-3+ Ap '70

WATER mains. See Water pipes

WATER meters
See also
Meter reading

WATER mites. See Mites

WATER pipes
See also
Pipe laying

Cleaning
Pigs keep our water mains clean; Fort Worth, Tex. G. Muller. il Am City 85:112+ O '70

Freezing
Ways to thaw frozen pipes. Suc Farm 69:D8 Ja '71

Maintenance and repair
Underwater pipe repair; Steubenville, Ohio. il Am City 85:38 Mr '70

WATER pitchers. See Pitchers

WATER pollution
Calefaction of a river. D. Merriman. il Sci Am 222:42-52 My '70
Call it Lake inferior. G. Laycock. il Audubon 72:48-53 My '70
Clearwater's cargo is a message: stop pollution. R. Gannon. il Pop Sci 197:70-2+ Ag '70
Dead stream; Crooked Creek in Missouri. K. P. Shea. il Environ 12:12-15 Jl '70
Death by degree for salmon; thermal pollution special studies at Bonneville. M. Davenport. Field & S 74:76-7 Ap '70
Dirty flows the Delaware. G. Alexander. il Newsweek 76:68-73 N 2 '70
Environmental side effects of energy production. D. F. Anthrop. il Bul Atom Sci 26:39-41 O '70
Eutrophication speeded by man. R. H. Gilluly. il Sci N 98:17-19 Jl 4 '70
Fertilizers and eutrophication. W. L. Meachem. Home Gard 57:44-5 S '70
Finding a place to put the heat; effects on the ecology of bodies of water. R. H. Gilluly. il Sci N 98:98-9 Ag 1 '70
Handling hot water, with a payoff; beneficial uses of thermal discharge. R. Stewart and S. P. Mathur. il Cons 25:16-20 D '70
He brought a stream back to life; Cedar Creek, Wis. R. Tunley. il por Read Digest 97:19-22+ Jl '70
Hudson River, by R. H. Boyle. Review
Time il 95:94+ Ap 27 '70
Humic substances: fulvic acid-dialkyl phthalate complexes and their role in pollution. G. Ogner and M. Schnitzer. bibliog Science 170:317-18 O 16 '70
Joys of clear water. H. Ehrlich. il Look 34:38-45 Jl 14 '70
Just how serious is thermal pollution? G. Heinold. il por Sci Digest 68:62-6 N '70
Lake that ate too much; Lake Mendota, Wis. M. Michaelson. il Todays Health 48:42-3+ Ag '70
Lakes which produce too much; eutrophication. R. T. Oglesby. il Cons 24:18-21 Je '70
Look at water pollution across U.S; table. U S News 69:42 Ag 17 '70
Man's perpetual quest for water. R. L. Nace. il UNESCO Courier 23:4-8+ Je '70
More on eutrophication. F. R. Rickson. Home Gard 58:20+ Ja '71
Nuclear power and thermal pollution: Zion, Illinois. P. F. Gustafson. il Bul Atom Sci 26:17-23 Mr '70
Pollution problems, resource policy, and the scientist. A. W. Eipper. bibliog Science 169:11-15 Jl 3 '70
Questions phosphorus removal. Am City 85:16 Ag '70

WATER pollution—*Continued*

Sad and sorry look at pollution; ed. by E. Crimmin. E. Albert. il Motor B 126:10-12 O '70

Sailing down my dirty river; P. Seeger on the sloop, Clearwater, to point out pollution of the Hudson. P. Richards. il por Nat Wildlife 8:28-9 F '70

Scout power tidies the Hackensack; Girl scout troop 127. il Life 68:37-40 Je 12 '70

Soil & fresh water; damaged global fabric. B. Commoner. il Environ 12:4-11 Ap '70

Tempest in a nuclear teapot; thermal pollution. F. Graham, jr. il Audubon 72:12-19 Mr '70

Thermal pollution? J. Frye. il por Sea Front 16:85-95 Mr '70

Thermal pollution in the marine environment. A. C. Jensen. il Cons 25:8-13 O '70

Troubled waters. il Sr Schol 97:14-16 N 16 '70

Water pollution. H. Lieber. Cur Hist 59:23-30 Jl '70

See also

Detergent pollution of rivers, lakes, etc.
Marine pollution
Mercury pollution of rivers, lakes, etc.
Oil pollution of rivers, harbors, etc.
Sewage disposal
Trade waste

Control

Action and controversy. il Sci N 98:462 D 19 '70

Bug as garbage man. Time 96:36 D 21 '70

Chesapeake Bay fights for its life. il Bsns W p40-1+ Mr 7 '70

Cleaning up a dirty industry; electrolytic treatment for electroplaters' waste. Bsns W p54 F 14 '70

Cleaning up foul waters; proposals for pollution base and regional treatment authorities. A. M. Freeman, 3d. and L. Ross. New Repub 162:13-16 Je 20 '70

The Connecticut: priorities in conflict. E. P. Berkeley. il Arch Forum 133:28-35 S '70

Cooling it; federal policy on Lake Michigan. Newsweek 75:123 My 18 '70

Crackdown on water polluters. L. S. Clapper. il Nat Wildlife 8:14-17 F '70

Fresh water: a diminishing supply. E. S. Muskie. il Cur Hist 58:329+ Je '70

How's the fishing along your stream? L. Palmer. il Farm J 94:33 Ag '70

IJC submits report on pollution of the lower Great Lakes; Department announcement; with excerpts from IJC report. Dept State Bul 62:807-9 Je 29 '70

Ladies save the lakes; Florida lakes. H. Ehrlich. il Look 34:60-1 Ap 21 '70

Limited war on water pollution. G. Bylinsky. il Fortune 81:103-7+ F '70

Long-term efforts to clean the environment. P. H. Abelson. Science 167:1081 F 20 '70

My struggle to help the President; HRFA in Hudson River cleanup. R. H. Boyle. il Sports Illus 32:32-4 F 16 '70

Pollution with a solution; phosphate-free laundry detergents. S. Netherby. il Field & S 75:62 D '70

Pollution, your problem, too; fertilizer and erosion. R. Sanders. il Suc Farm 68:14-15 N '70

Rescuing the nation's rivers? Nixon's antipollution plan. Sr Schol 96:12 F 9 '70

That mess on the Prestile; pollution of stream running across Maine-New Brunswick border. F. Graham, jr. il Am Heritage 21:106-12 F '70; Discussion. 21:94-5 Ag '70

Thermal pollution control; letter. J. G. Muller. Science 168:421 Ap 24 '70

Unoxidized nitrogen is the key; exacting standards of purity set for the Ohio River. G. Seymour. Am City 85:49 F '70

Water pollution: control program lags as Nixon promises cleanup. L. J. Carter. Science 167:360-1 Ja 23 '70

See also

United States—Federal water quality administration

Water purification

Economic aspects

Environment dilemma. il Nations Bsns 58:50-1+ N '70

Thanks, but no thanks; federal funds, but not federal control. il Nations Bsns 58:56-7 Ag '70

History

All the fat and sullage fuddy murriners. S. Schlee. il Natur Hist 79:18-20+ D '70

Laws and legislation

Can our rivers stand the heat? W. Langewiesche. Read Digest 96:76-80 Ap '70

Crackdown on water polluters. Bsns W p28-9 Ap 4 '70

Crude on troubled waters; Chevron case. il Newsweek 75:77-8 Ap 6 '70

Harking back to 1899; waste-discharge permits. Sci N 99:8 Ja 2 '71

Lawmakers cry over spilled oil. il Bsns W p38 F 21 '70

One small step; proposed legislation to control ocean dumping. Sci N 98:318 O 17 '70

Seas; Convention on civil liability for oil pollution damage. S. Solomon. New Repub 163:21-3 O 31 '70

Toward a new water quality law; Canada's water bill. F. Poland. il Sci N 97:540 My 30 '70

Water pollution; federal legislation and programs. H. Lieber. Cur Hist 59:23-30 Jl '70

Water quality improvement act of 1970; excerpts from text. Cur Hist 59:106-9 Ag '70

Who owns the water? J. McCaull. il Environ 12:30-9 O '70

Physiological effects

Hazards of trace elements. R. H. Gilluly. il Sci N 97:560-1 Je 6 '70

Statistics

Water; EQ index. il Nat Wildlife 8:30-1 O '70; Same. Schol Teach Jr/Sr High pA6-7 O 5 '70

Canada

Legal antidote for mercury pollution. Bsns W p31 Ap 25 '70

Mad hatter's legacy; Canadian export ban on fish. Newsweek 75:72 Ap 20 '70

Mercury in Lake St Clair. Sci N 97:388 Ap 18 '70

Mercury poisoning; or, The fish you catch can kill you! Lake St Clair. J. J. Knap. Field & S 75:44-5+ Jl '70

River running out of Eden; Restigouche River. P. Ryan. il Sports Illus 32:86-9+ My 25 '70

Toward a new water quality law. F. Poland. il Sci N 97:540 My 30 '70

England

British streams are getting cleaner, slowly. P. F. Brooks. il Am City 85:78+ Jl '70

Stinking strike; sewage-plant workers on strike. il Time 96:52 O 19 '70

Japan

Fuji's frightful example. Hedoro floating in Tagonoura harbor. il Time 96:44 O 12 '70

Russia

Shortage of caviar. P. H. Abelson. Science 168:199 Ap 10 '70

Victors are not judged. P. R. Pryde. bibliog il Environ 12:30-9 N '70

Scandinavia

Stagnant sea. S. H. Fonselius. bibliog il Environ 12:2-11+ Jl '70

United States

See Water pollution

WATER polo

Splashy struggle for a title; National AAU water polo championships, Long Beach, Calif. A. Schardt. il Sports Illus 33:14-17 Ag 10 '70

WATER power

Ghana

See also

Volta River—Power utilization

WATER purification

Action needed. il Sci N 97:614 Je 27 '70

Aldrin: removal from lake water by flocculent bacteria. W. O. Leshniowsky and others. bibliog il Science 169:993-5 S 4 '70

Applies existing technology for a cleaner Lake Erie; Detroit regional system. Am City 85:18 Ap '70

Ice sandwich; functional semipermeable membrane. R. D. Miller. il Science 169:584-5 Ag 7 '70

Power plants; effects of chlorination on estuarine primary production. D. H. Hamilton, jr. and others. bibliog il Science 169:197-8 Jl 10 '70

See-through tanks save money; chemical feeding for water departments in Waynesville, N.C. and Easley, S.C. il Am City 85:81 Mr '70

See also

Filter plants
Water reuse
Water softening
Water treatment plants

Desalting

New fiber to clean water; reverse osmosis permeator. il Bsns W p83 D 12 '70

WATER purification plants. See Water treatment plants

WATER purifiers, Domestic
New water purifier. C. Conley. il Field & S 74:107 Ja '70

WATER rates
Water rates are going up. E. F. Spitzer. il Am City 85:90+ O '70

WATER requirements of plants. See Plants—Water requirements

WATER reuse
Reclaimed wastewater cleared for water-contact sports; Indian Creek reservoir, Alpine County, Calif. il Am City 85:16 Ag '70
Sewage tastes good like water should. il Time 66:44 Jl 13 '70

WATER revenue bonds. See Bonds, Revenue

WATER rights
Who owns the water? J. McCaull. il Environ 12:30-9 O '70

WATER skis and skiing
Look, mom, I'm the champ! J. Jares. il Sports Illus 33:48-9 Jl 20 '70

Safety devices and measures
Few rules take the hurt out of spills. il Todays Health 48:49 Ag '70

Study and teaching
Water skiing or bust! J. Cross. il Har Yrs 10:30-2 S '70

WATER softening
Well water ends icing problem; Poland, Ohio, water softening plant. il Am City 85:60 Ap '70

WATER sports. See Aquatic sports

WATER storage
See also
Reservoirs
Standpipes
Water tanks

WATER supply
Man's perpetual quest for water. R. L. Nace. il UNESCO Courier 23:4-8+ Je '70
Water and life. D. F. Othmer. bibliog il por Chem 43:12-17 N '70
Water supply and treatment. See issues of American city
See also
Arid regions
Boats—Water supply
Dams
Drinking water—Standards
Reservoirs
Water, Underground
Water pollution
Water purification
Water rates
Water reuse
Watersheds
Waterworks
Wells

Fluoridation
Fluoridation for all; a national priority. R. O. Egeberg. por Todays Health 48:30-1+ Je '70
Fluoridation: still an urgent need. L. Terry. por Parents Mag 45:27 N '70
Fluorides revisited. il Time 95:47 Mr 2 '70
Let's wipe out osteoporosis. G. Town. Har Yrs 10:32-3 O '70
Politics of community conflict, by R. L. Crain and others. Review
Trans-Action 7:61-2 Mr '70. W. A. Gamson
Water fluoridation benefits teeth, bones and heart. Am City 85:41 N '70

Brazil
Pantanal: 400,000 sq. km. of swampland in the Mato Grosso. N. V. Cordeiro. il UNESCO Courier 23:14-15 Je '70

California
California water plan: the most expensive faucet in the world. G. Marine. il Ramp Mag 8:34-41 My '70
Quenching California's thirst. il Time 96:55 Jl 6 '70

Illinois
Thirty-seven gallons per capita per day; rural Illinois. D. H. Stoltenberg. il Am City 85:140-1 O '70

Montana
See also
Choteau, Mont.—Water supply

Russia
Rivers will learn to run backward. il Bsns W p43+ Je 13 '70

United States
Accuses government of neglecting water supply. Am City 85:41 N '70

America's drinking water is . . .. is not safe; with editorial comment. H. J. Graeser. il pors Am City 85:8, 77-9+ Je '70
Where the water is. Cur Hist 58:328+ Je '70
See also subhead Water supply under names of cities, e.g. Choteau, Mont.—Water supply

WATER supply engineering
See also
Dams
Hydraulic engineering
Water pipes—Cleaning
Water purification
Water treatment plants

WATER tanks
Beauty, strength and efficiency; Holmdel Township, N.J. il Am City 85:20 Jl '70
See-through tanks save money; chemical feeding for water departments of Waynesville, N.C. and Easley, S.C. il Am City 85:81 Mr '70
See also
Standpipes

Maintenance and repair
Metal coatings cut tank maintenance; Cincinnati. il Am City 85:22 O '70

WATER terminals. See Terminals

WATER towers
See also
Standpipes

WATER treatment plants
Bio-disc plant confirms test data on new process; Pewaukee, Wis. il Am City 85:14 Jl '70
Challenges federal pollution policies; with reply by D. D. Dominick. E. E. Franchett. Am City 85:156-7 S '70
Read chlorine weights directly; treatment plants in Florida. il Am City 85:113-14 Ap '70
Right water psychologically; Lake Oswego, Ore. D. Seeger. il pors Am City 85:79-82 My '70
Sewage tastes good like water should. il Time 96:44 Jl 13 '70
Tour de force in water-plant design; Bollman plant, Contra Costa, Calif. S. R. Komatsu and R. W. Johnston. il Am City 85:60-2 Ag '70
Unconventional approach; water-disposal problems; Dallas, Ore. J. L. Graham and J. W. Filbert. il Am City 85:72-5 O '70
Water supply and treatment. See issues of American city
See also
Saline water conversion plants

WATER waves. See Waves

WATER wells. See Wells

WATER wheels
Garden water wheel. il Mech Illus 66:76+ Je '70

WATERCOLOR; drama. See Magdalany, P.

WATERCOLOR painting. See Water color painting

WATERFALLS
See also
Niagara Falls

Photographs
Eastern cascades. D. Smith. il Nat Wildlife 8:44-7 Ag '70

WATERFOWLERS. See Fowling

WATERFRONT restaurants. See Restaurants—United States

WATERING of gardens, lawns, etc.
Summer means watering, here are ideas. il Sunset 145:134-5 Ag '70

WATERING of plants
See also
House plants

WATERING places. See Health resorts, watering places. etc.

WATERLILIES. See Water lilies

WATERLOO, Ia.
How skin flicks hit bible-belt Waterloo, Iowa. il Newsweek 76:28 D 21 '70

WATERMAN, Charles F.
Winning steelhead river. il por Field & S 74:42-5+ F '70

WATERMAN-Bic pen corporation
Dynamic growth companies. il Nations Bsns 58:72-3+ D '70

WATERMELONS
Prepare now for big watermelons. D. Childers. il Org Gard & Farm 17:94-6 D '70
Put your melons in new ground. S. Fenell. il Org Gard & Farm 17:72-3 Ap '70
Watermelons at your back door! J. R. Coggins. il Org Gard & Farm 17:74-5 Ap '70

WATERPROOF clothing. See Clothing, Waterproof

WATERPROOF fabrics. See Textile fabrics, Waterproof

WATERS, Aaron C. See Fisher, R. V. jt. auth.
WATERS, Ethel
Ethel Waters: study in inspiration. D. Kucharsky. por Chr Today 14:44-5 Mr 13 '70 *
WATERS, Howard J.
Mystery, history, and an old log cabin. il Todays Ed 59:44-5 My '70
WATERS, William E. and Brandt, R. W.
Trees for people or pests? il Am For 76:20-3+ S '70
WATERSHEDS
Honey Hollow; Bucks County, Pa. A. Young. il Audubon 72:120 Ja '70
Jolt for Honey Hollow. E. N. Layne. il Am Heritage 21:111 Je '70
Nutrient cycles of an ecosystem. F. H. Bormann and G. E. Likens. il Sci Am 223:92-101 O '70
WATERSTON, Robert H.
Antigen competition: a paradox. bibliog il Science 170:1108-10 D 4 '70
WATERWAYS

Brazil
See also
Amazon River

Canada
North through history aboard White Mist; following the routes of Hudson, Champlain, and Cartier. M. B. Grosvenor. il pors Nat Geog 138:1-55 Jl '70
See also
St Lawrence Seaway

Europe
See also
Rhine River

South America
See also
Plata, Rio de la

United States
Coastal areas and seashores. W. S. Beller. bibliog Cur Hist 59:100-4+ Ag '70
Ocean comes to Oklahoma; Arkansas-Verdigris navigation system. C. Bakal. il Read Digest 97:121-4 N '70
Relax on Maine's inland waterways. D. Becker. il Travel 133:68-70 Je '70
Seaports for an inland empire; Arkansas River navigation project. il U S News 68:90-2 My 25 '70
Waterway that couldn't be done; Arkansas River navigation project. il Bsns W p 124-5 S 12 '70
Winter boating vacations. J. A. Emmett. il Outdoor Life 146:36+ N '70
See also
Arkansas River Waterway
Cross Florida Barge Canal
Delaware River
Houston ship channel
Intracoastal Waterway
Missouri River
National parks and reserves—Waterways
St Croix River
St Lawrence Seaway
WATERWORKS
Seven giant monuments to water; portfolio. Fortune 81:82-9 Ap '70
Water supply and treatment. See issues of American city
See also
Dams
Filter plants

Finance
See also
Water rates
WATES, Neil
Builder heaves a brick at apartheid. por Bsns W p36 S 26 '70 *
WATKINS, Arthur Martin
Sanivac, revolutionary vacuum toilet. il Pop Sci 197:99+ Ag '70
WATKINS, T. H.
Long curving shore from Alaska to Baja. il Am West 7:18-22 N '70
State of insurrection & rebellion. il Am West 7:42-7 Ja '70
WATKINS, Ted
... And a touch of pride. il por Newsweek 75:83 Mr 23 '70 *
WATKINS, Vernon
Comment. W. Heyen. Poetry 115:427-8 Mr '70 *
WATKINS, William A.
Amateur scientist. Sci Am 223:116-17 Ag '70
WATMORE, Geraldine
Girl who trains whales. il pors Sci Digest 67:58-61 Mr '70 *
WATSON, Arthur Kittredge
Off the top shelf. il por Newsweek 75:53 Mr 16 '70 *

WATSON, Catherine
Learning and liking it. il Am Ed 6:18-22 My '70
Talent runs free. il Am Ed 6:3-6 O '70
WATSON, James Alfred
Gamble finally finds a man for the top. pors Bsns W p40-1 Ja 9 '71 *
WATSON, James Dewey
Genius on the prowl. W. Bradbury. il pors Life 69:57-60+ O 30 '70 *
WATSON, Robert
Five sleepers. Poetry 117:204-10 D '70
Luxury flight from New York to Los Angeles; Radio astronomer; poems. Poetry 115:224-6 Ja '70
WATSON, Ron
On the boards. il pors Dance Mag 44:22 F '70
WATSON, Thomas John, 1914-
Goals: address, January 7, 1970. Vital Speeches 36:301-3 Mr 1 '70

about
Powerhouse growth of IBM. por Duns 96:26-7 D '70 *
WATSON, William W.
Nuclear weapons for U.N? Bul Atom Sci 26:48 Mr '70
WATT, Douglas
Popular records (cont) New Yorker 46:74-6 Jl 11; 163-4+ O 24 '70
WATT, Kenneth E. F.
Model man. il por Time 95:70 My 25 '70 *
WATTENBERG, Ben J.
Nonsense explosion. il New Repub 162:18-23 Ap 4; 46-7 My 9 '70
Trade winds; interview, ed. by C. Amory. Sat R 53:8+ S 26 '70
—See Scammon, R M. jt. auth.
WATTENBERG, William W.
Middle school as one psychologist sees it. Ed Digest 35:26-9 Mr '70
WATTERS, Pat
Southern integrationists feel betrayed by the North. il N Y Times Mag p26-7+ My 3 '70
WATTS, Charles Henry, 1926-
Problems of academic governance. Sch & Soc 98:405-8 N '70
WATTS, Donald
Short-focus 12 1/2-inch Newtonian telescope. il Sky & Tel 40:318-20 N '70
WATTS, Frances B.
Fairy ring; drama. Plays 29:80-5 Mr '70
Littlest elf; drama. Plays 30:76-7, 96 D '70
WATTS, Mabel
If you want to paint a picture; poem. Good H 171:177 N '70
WATTS, Raymond N. jr
[Articles on astronomy, space flight, etc]
See issues of Sky and telescope
WATTS, Calif. See Los Angeles
WATTS labor community action committee
... And a touch of pride. il por Newsweek 75:83 Mr 23 '70
WATTS manufacturing company
Chase capital buys into Watts. il Bsns W p24-5 My 9 '70
Minority-managed unit of Aerojet sold to Chase. Aviation W 92:64-5 My 18 '70
WAUGH, Alec
Delectations. See occasional issues of National review
WAUGH, Auberon
In London, it's Annabel's. il Holiday 47:39+ Ap '70
WAUGH, John. See Waugh, L. jt. auth.
WAUGH, Lynne, and Waugh, John
Renaissance of the Indian spirit. il Am Ed 6:15-20 Jl '70
WAVE functions
See also
Atomic orbitals
WAVE guides
Waveguides to carry phone calls. M. S. Snitzer. il Electr World 83:42 My '70
WAVE mechanics
See also
Tunneling (physics)
WAVEGUIDES. See Wave guides
WAVES
Bistatic-radar observation of long-period, directional ocean-wave spectra with loran A. A. M. Peterson and others. bibliog il Science 170:158-61 O 9 '70
Growth of a wave. F. G. W. Smith. il Sea Front 16:360-73 N '70
Simple wave. F. G. W. Smith. il Sea Front 16:234-45 Jl '70
See also
Gravity waves
Shock waves
Tidal waves

WAVES, Brain. See Brain waves

WAVES, Sound. See Sound waves

WAX, Mel
TV news: wrong mix. Nation 210:433-5 Ap 13 '70

WAX esters. See Esters

WAX modeling
Candle sculpture; using beeswax sheeting. il Design 71:30-2 Sum '70
More quillwork and waxwork; ed. by E. Gaines. il Antiques 97:272-4 F '70
Wax in the art classroom. T. A. Jambro. il Sch Arts 69:26-7 Je '70
Welding with wax. L. J. Miller. il Design 71: 24-5 mid-Wint '70

WAX painting. See Encaustic painting

WAXES
Truth about car waxes. T. Tappett. il Mech Illus 66:76-8+ Jl '70

WAXWORK. See Wax modeling

WAY it all comes loose; story. See Maloney, R.

WAY, way down South; drama. See Cable, H.

WAYMAN, Stan
Unseen glories of the reef; photographs. Life 69:50-7 O 23 '70

WAYNE, John
John Wayne rides again and again and again. J. Reddy. por Read Digest 97:138-42 S '70 *
United we fall; divided we stand. R. L. Shapon. Sat R 54:59 Ja 2 '71 *

WAYNESVILLE, N.C.
See-through tanks save money. il Am City 85:81 Mr '70

WAYS, Max
Finding the American direction. il Fortune 82:70-5+ O '70; Same abr. with title What hope for the future? Cur 124:3-16 D '70
How to think about the environment. Fortune 81:98-101+ F '70
More power to everybody. il Fortune 81:172-5+ My '70
President needs our help because we need his. Fortune 81:57-8 Je '70; Same with title Helping the President help us. Cur 120:9-13 Ag '70

WAYS and means committee. See United States —Congress—House—Ways and means, Committee on

WE didn't do nothing, mom; story. See Vance, J. M.

WE have nothing to fear; story. See Merwin, W. S.

WEALES, Gerald
Stage. Commonweal 92:193-4 My 8 '70

WEALTH
See also
Capitalists and financiers
Leisure class
Millionaires
Prosperity
Success

WEALTH, Distribution of
Resources and social structure: some conditions of stability and change. W. R. Burch, jr. bibliog f il Ann Am Acad 389:27-34 My '70
TRB from Washington. New Repub 162:8 Ap 18 '70

WEAPONS
See also
Clubs (weapons)
Firearms
Munitions

History
Preserving the Revolutionary war heritage. C. Worman. il Hobbies 75:126-7 Ag '70

WEAPONS control. See Disarmament

WEAPONS systems
Ecology of weaponry. W. C. Clemens, jr. il Bul Atom Sci 26:27-31 S '70; Same with title Dynamics of the arms race. Cur 123:57-63 N '70
GAO readies report on weapons systems. K. Johnsen. il Aviation W 92:74+ Ja 19 '70
Status of major U.S. European defense, aerospace programs (cont) Aviation W 92:14-18 Mr 9 '70
See also
Chemical and biological weapons

Cost
Cost growth detailed for major weapons. Aviation W 92:231 Mr 9 '70

WEASELS
See also
Ferrets
Wolverines

WEATHER
Circulation and weather of 1969. J. F. Andrews. il Weatherwise 23:4-11+ F '70
Ideal weather. Har Yrs 10:22-4 Mr '70

Weatherwatch. See issues of Weatherwise
See also
Climate
Cold weather
Meteorological research
Rain and rainfall
Snow

Mental and physiological effects
How the weather can affect you. il Good H 170:180 Ap '70

WEATHER and health. See Weather—Mental and physiological effects

WEATHER and plants. See Plants, Effect of climate on

WEATHER balloons. See Balloons, Meteorological

WEATHER bureau (United States) See United States—National weather service

WEATHER control
Becoming respectable. Sci N 97:365-6 Ap 11 '70
Earth sciences; Conference on weather modification. Sci N 97:384 Ap 18 '70
Physical view of cloud seeding; address, April 1970. M. Tribus. bibliog il Science 168:201-11 Ap 10 '70
Snowfall, ecology and man. Sci N 98:447 D 12 '70
Some tough westerners say: no snow job for us! Bureau of reclamation to seed Colorado clouds for snow. R. Rapoport. Sports Illus 32:54-5 Je 29 '70
Supercivilized weather and sky show. H. Lansford. il Natur Hist 79:92-7+ bibliog(p 133) Ag '70
World war on hail. P. Friggens. il Read Digest 96:29-30+ Je '70
See also
Rain making

Legal aspects
Hard questions about weather modification. K. Frazier. il Sci N 97:461-3 My 9 '70

WEATHER forecasts
Heat, smog, power crisis: where, and why. il U S News 69:14-16 Ag 10 '70
How bad a winter, long-range outlook. il U S News 69:58-9 N 30 '70
How to be weather-wise, without being a meteorologist. T. Helsiva. il Motor B 125:108-10 Mr '70
My son the rainmaker. R. Starnes. Field & S 74:28+ Ap '70
Parting shots: will it be a cold winter? il Life 69:77-80 D 4 '70
Snow prediction, a formidable challenge. D. B. Spiegler. bibliog il Weatherwise 23:212-20 O '70
Weather management (cont of) What's new. See issues of Successful farming to April 1970
Weather services: working toward worldwide forecasts. N. Gruchow. il Science 168: 352-3 Ap 17 '70
See also
Artificial satellites—Meteorological use
Computers—Meteorological use
Radar meteorology
United States—National weather service
Weather lore

WEATHER lore
How weather-wise are you? excerpt from Grab a pencil. H. H. Hart il Read Digest 97:143-4 Jl '70
Parting shots: nature's own forecasters say winter will be awful. il Life 69:77-80 D 4 '70
Shark knows where the weather is. G. Smith. il Sea Front 16:170-1 My '70

WEATHER maps
[Daily weather maps] See issues of Weatherwise

WEATHER message switching center. See United States—Federal aviation administration—Weather message switching center

WEATHER modification. See Weather control

WEATHER predictions. See Weather forecasts

WEATHER radar. See Radar meteorology

WEATHER records
Century of American weather. D. M. Ludlum. Weatherwise 23:78-83, 131-5, 187-91, 235-9 Ap-O '70

WEATHER research
Shift in scene; global atmospheric research program. il Sci N 97:342 Ap 4 '70
What's the weather report? I. Geller. il Duns 95:87-90 Mr '70
World weather program; message to Congress. R. M. Nixon. Dept State Bul 63:120-1 Jl 27 '70

WEATHER satellites. See Artificial satellites—Meteorological use

WEATHER vanes
Weathervanes. L. Burgess. il Horticulture 49:
22-3 Ja '71
WEATHERFORD, Tex.
People chose sacks over cans. K. E. Smith.
il Am City 85:82-3 Je '70
WEATHERHEAD company
Man of the year loses a stripe; G. J. Grab-
ner. Bsns W p 17 Ag 8 '70
WEATHERING
Climate and copper finishes: how to get what
you want. D. H. Thompson. il Arch Rec
148:160 S '70
WEATHERMEN (organization)
Behind a crackdown on Weathermen. il U S
News 68:42 Ap 13 '70
Bomb; indictments. il Newsweek 76:14-15
Ag 3 '70
Disruptive dozen. il Time 95:20 Ap 13 '70
Explosive words and deeds. il por Time 96:
18 O 19 '70
Fall offensive. il Newsweek 76:44 O 19 '70
House on 11th street; Greenwich Village.
New York. il Time 95:10 Mr 23 '70
Now the U.S. takes on the Chicago twelve;
indictment. il Newsweek 75:19-20 Ap 13 '70
Storm clouds for weathermen. Time 96:10
Ag 3 '70
Ted Gold: education for violence. J. K. Sale.
Nation 210:423-9, 514+ Ap 13, My 4 '70
Terrorism on the left. il Newsweek 75:27-30
Mr 23 '70
Two girls from no. 18. J. Neary. il por Life
68:26-9 Mr 27 '70
Weathermen. R. Bongartz. il Esquire 74:112-
14+ Ag '70
Weathermen and Fort Sumter; wrongful use
of force against the government. H. V.
Jaffa. Nat R 22:1403+ D 29 '70
WEATHERS, Felicia
Felicia Weathers: dauntless diva. H. Bims. il
pors Ebony 25:52-6+ My '70 *
WEATHERVANES. See Weather vanes
WEAVER, Donald E. Jr
Grand Canyon. il Nat Parks 44:10-14 Ja '70
WEAVER, Earl
Birds hop for a lively bantam. A. Wright.
il por Sports Illus 32:74-6+ Ap 13 '70 *
WEAVER, Harold D. Jr
New materials on black heritage: the un-
making of a myth. Schol Teach Sec Teach
Sup p 12-13 Ja 5 '70
WEAVER, John Carrier
Return of the native. Newsweek 76:54 N 9
'70 *
WEAVER, John D.
Good, tolerant life of the Hollywood hills. il
Holiday 47:60-3+ Ap '70
WEAVER, Kenneth F.
Voyage to the planets. Nat Geog 138:147-
93 Ag '70
WEAVER, Robert
Sketching from life. S. E. Meyer. il Am Art-
ist 34:62-7+ My '70 *
WEAVER, Robert C.
Beyond the ghetto. il por Ebony 25:148-51 Ag
'70
WEAVER, William
Arias and intermissions. il Sat R 53:42-3 S 12
'70
Beethoven in retrospect: Italy. Sat R 53:61 N
28 '70
Ireland: double image. Harp Baz 103:40-1 Jl
'70
Maggio musicale & Spoleto: both work. il
Hi Fi 20:MA30-1 O '70
Man on the thousand-lire note. il por Sat R
53:66+ Mr 14 '70
North Carolina school in Italy. Hi Fi 20:
MA18+ N '70
Winter in Italy. Harp Baz 103:88 O '70
WEAVING
Hand-woven coverlets in the Art institute of
Chicago. M. Davison. il Antiques 97:734-40
My '70
Magdalena Abakanowicz. D. Wroblewska. il
por Craft Horiz 30:18-23 O '70
Random warp weaving. il Design 71:31 mid-
Wint '70
Scholtens: two artist-weavers from the
Netherlands. B. De Neeve. il pors Craft
Horiz 30:24-9 Ja '70
Weaving with weeds. V. R. Jackson. il De-
sign 71:34-6 Wint '69
When will weaving be an art form? V. Hoff-
man. il Craft Horiz 30:18-23 Ag '70
See also
Tapestry
Tapestry weaving
Textile design

Study and teaching
Pop goes the weaving! S. Gruenberg. il Sch
Arts 70:19 Ja '71
Simple weavings to create wall hangings. M.
P. Miles. il Sch Arts 70:20-3 Ja '71

WEBB, Ann
Bibliographies on social issues. il Wilson Lib
Bul 45:65-6 S '70
WEBB, Charles
Marriage of a young stockbroker; story; ex-
cerpt from novel. il McCalls 97:108-20 Mr
'70
WEBB, Igor
Teaching poetry of the first world war; poem.
Poetry 117:33 O '70
WEBB, Kaye
Report from England. Z. Sutherland. Sat R
53:52 Ag 22 '70 *
WEBB, Thomas E. See Levitan, I. B. jt. auth.
WEBB, Wilse B. and Agnew, H. W. Jr
Sleep stage characteristics of long and short
sleepers. bibliog il Science 168:146-7 Ap 3 '70
WEBB and Knapp, inc.
Five years in the Zeckendorf labyrinth. il
pors Bsns W p98-9+ Ap 25 '70
WEBBER, Andrew Lloyd
Pop testament. H. Sall. il por Newsweek 76:
96-7 N 16 '70 *
Religious rock: première at St Peter's
Lutheran church of Decca album Jesus
Christ, superstar. New Yorker 46:39 N 7
'70 *
Rock passion. W. Bender. il pors Time 96:
47 N 9 '70 *
WEBBER, Ebbert T.
Fishing floats and currents; with biographi-
cal sketch. il pors Sea Front 16:26-31, 63
Ja '70
WEBER, Harvey
Color your island infra-red. il Travel & Ca-
mera 33:84-9+ Ja '70
WEBER, Joseph
Experimental relativity hits the big time. G.
B. Lubkin. bibliog il Phys Today 23:41+ Ag
'70 *
Gaining on gravity waves. D. E. Thomsen.
il Sci N 98:44-5 Jl 11 '70 *
WEBER, Karl Maria von
Music to my ears; concert performance of
Euryanthe. I. Kolodin. Sat R 53:48 N 14 '70 *
Records:
Der freischütz. Opera N 34:35 Mr 7 '70 *
Weber and Wagner at the Lincoln Center op-
erafest. I. Kolodin. Sat R 53:35 Ag 1 '70 *
WEBER, Larry J.
Inequities in athletics. Clear House 45:177-80
N '70
WEBER, Melva
Masters & Johnson: their new cures for sex
problems. Ladies Home J 87:51+ Jl '70
WEBER, Paul J.
Perverse observations on abortion. il Cath
World 212:74-7 N '70
Revolution on American campuses: an analy-
sis. il Cath World 210:248-52 Mr '70
WEBER, R. B.
Threatened with extinction; poem. Nation
212:94 Ja 18 '71
WEBER, Richard
American dog days; poem. Nation 211:382 O
19 '70
WEBER, Rosemary
Children's literature: books for teaching it.
Wilson Lib Bul 45:172-9 O '70
WEBORG, Jan
Gallery: photographs. il Life 68:8-11 Mr 13
'70
WEBS, Spiders. See Spider webs
WEBSTER, Sir David
Stateside view of Webster's era. I. Kolodin.
Sat R 53:46 Je 27 '70 *
Webster era at Covent Garden. D. Shawe-
Taylor. il pors Sat R 53:43-4+ Je 27 '70 *
WEBSTER, Mark
Postmaster; letter to W. Faulkner in 1924,
charging him with neglect of duties as post-
master. New Yorker 46:50 N 21 '70
WEBSTER, Mildred E.
With pride and alarm. Engl J 59:1285-8 D '70
WEBSTER'S dictionaries. See English language
—Dictionaries
WECHSBERG, Joseph
Hungary today. il Sat R 53:21-3+ N 28 '70
Letter from Berlin. il New Yorker 46:69-72
Je 27 '70
Profiles; Cleveland orchestra. New Yorker 46:
38-42+ My 30 '70
Short happy months of Mozart's Prague. il
Sat R 53:60-1 Mr 14 '70
WECHSLER, Diane
Analysis of The prison by Bernard Malamud.
Engl J 59:782-4 S '70
WECKMAN, George
Conquest of holiness. Chr Cent 87:595-7 My
13 '70
Worldly religious community. Chr Cent 87:
1513-15 D 16 '70
WEDDING march; story. See Merwin, W. S.

WEDDING meals
"Old country" weddings: Italian, Greek, Polish, and Danish; with recipes. il McCalls 97:96-103+ Je '70
WEDDING trips. See Honeymoon
WEDDINGS
Something old, something new . . . J. Morris. America 123:459-60 N 28 '70
  See also
Marriage customs and rites
Wedding meals

Caricatures and cartoons
Lohen-grins; cartoons. Read Digest 96:108-9 Je '70
WEDDLE, Ferris
Secrets of the mighty cougar. il Nat Wildlife 8:58-63 O '70
Woodland tattler. il Am For 76:5+ Ap '70
WEDEL, Cynthia C.
Church and social action. por Chr Cent 87:959-62 Ag 12 '70
WEDGEWORTH, Robert
Overdue; excerpts from The black librarian in America, ed. by E. J. Josey. por Wilson Lib Bul 45:495-7 Ja '71
WEDGWOOD, Josiah and sons, ltd.
Mission for Mr Wedgwood; excerpts from journal, with introd. and epilogue by H. C. Wedgewood. T. Griffiths. il Am Heritage 21:64-7 Ag '70
WEDGWOOD pottery. See Pottery, English
WEDNESDAY; story. See Oates, J. C.
WEED, Florence Collins
Easier living on less money. il Har Yrs 10:19-23 D '70
Nickel still goes a long way. il Har Yrs 10:19-21+ My '70
WEED, Steve
WWV radio time signals. R Pop Astron 63:27 Ag '69
WEED control
How to stop panic grass in corn. B. Coffman. il Farm J 94:40A Ap '70
  See also
Aquatic weed control

Biological control
Bugs that kill weeds. Farm J 94:32 Je '70

Chemical control
Controlling weeds in small grains. Suc Farm 68:no5 B8 Mr '70
Help still needed to control these problem weeds. il Suc Farm 68:no5 B28 Mr '70
Kill corn weeds; new sprays. D. Seim. il Farm J 94:48+ Mr '70
Top inch of soil; questions and answers. B. Coffman. Farm J 94:66 Ap '70
Weed-free soybeans average 4 bu. more. D. Seim. il Farm J 94:50+ Ap '70
Weeds are easier in January. Sunset 144:132 Ja '70
What's available for corn weed control. il Suc Farm 68:no3 W12-13 F '70
What's available for soybean weed control. il Suc Farm 68:no3 W24 F '70
  See also
Herbicides
WEED killers. See Herbicides
WEEDEN, Robert B.
Hauling and pulling in the Arctic. il Liv Wildn 34:8-16 Sum '70
Report from Alaska. il Liv Wildn 34:50-1 Spr '70
WEEDS
Do you know these weed seedlings? il Suc Farm 68:no3 48-9 F '70
In praise of weeds. L. Line. il Am Heritage 21:102-6 O '70
Make friends with your weeds. P. Young. il Org Gard & Farm 17:86-9 Ag '70
  See also
Grasses
  also names of weeds, e.g. Tumbleweeds

Biological control
See Weed control—Biological control

Chemical control
See Weed control—Chemical control

Insect control
See Weed control—Biological control
WEEGHMAN, Richard B.
Safety check. Flying 86:26+ Ap '70
WEEK of prayer for Christian unity. See Special days, weeks, and months
WEEKEND camps. See Camps
WEEKEND houses. See Vacation houses

WEEKES, Claire
Hope and help for your nerves; excerpt. Read Digest 97:138-41 D '70
WEEKLEY, Robert
Patagonian journey. il Américas 22:29-35 Mr '70
WEEKS, Edward Augustus
Peripatetic reviewer. See issues of Atlantic
WEEKS, John A.
Dynamics of the Rogers conversation education center. il Cons 25:7-9 D '70
Teacher tips: air pollution and the temperature inversion. il Cons 25:32-3 O '70
Teacher tips: environmental deterioration and declining species. Cons 25:27+ Ag '70
Teacher tips: Lake Erie: alive but changing; with glossary. Cons 25:31+ D '70
Teacher tips: metamorphosis. bibliog il Cons 24:27-8+ F '70
Teacher tips: new bird ranges and environment. bibliog il Cons 24:30 Je '70
Teacher tips: pollination. il Cons 24:32 Ap '70
WEEKS, R. A. and others
Magnetic resonance properties of some lunar material. bibliog il Science 167:704-7 Ja 30 '70
WEEKS, Ramona
Two poems: The dream; The thing. Yale R 59:249-51 D '69
WEEKS, Robert P.
For his was the kingdom, and the power, and the glory, briefly. il pors Am Heritage 21:4-7+ Je '70
WEEMS, David B.
Experiment that saved hi-fi. bibliog il por Pop Electr 33:29-34+ S '70
Frisky four speaker system. il Pop Electr 32:43-7 Ap '70
Numbers game. bibliog il Pop Electr 33:64-8 N '70
Omni-eight speaker system. il Pop Electr 32:69-73+ F '70
WEEPING atlas cedar. See Cedar
WEEQUAHIC park. See Newark, N.J.—Parks and playgrounds
WEESNER, Theodore
Irene, goodnight; story. Atlan 225:63-6 Ja '70
WEEVILS
Dodder weevils in simultaneous association with parasitic plants and their hosts. D. M. Anderson. bibliog il Science 168:132-3 Ap 3 '70
  See also
Alfalfa weevils
WEIBLEN, Paul W. See Roedder, E. jt. auth.
WEIDENBAUM, Murray L.
How to buy a cleaner environment; adaptation of address, June 16, 1970. Bul Atom Sci 26:19-21 N '70
  about
R&D funding: top Treasury aide decries blind faith approach. P. M. Boffey. por Science 170:512+ O 30 '70 *
WEIDER, Joe
Be a take-charge blaster! H. Weiskopf. il por Sports Illus 32:34-6+ Ap 6 '70 *
WEIDNER, Edward W.
Ecology: heart of our university program. il Todays Ed 59:19-21 D '70
WEIDNER, Roger A.
New goat country. il por Outdoor Life 145:52-3+ Je '70
WEIGHT, Forrest F. and Votava, Jiri
Slow synaptic excitation in sympathetic ganglion cells: evidence for synaptic inactivation of potassium conductance. bibliog il Science 170:755-8 N 13 '70
WEIGHT (physiology)
Healthy fat man. A. J. Snider. Sci Digest 68:63-4 D '70
Height and weight at menarche and a hypothesis of critical body weights and adolescent events. R. E. Frisch and R. Revelle. bibliog il Science 169:397-9 Jl 24 '70
  See also
Corpulence
Exercise
Weight watchers, inc.
WEIGHT arms. See Levers
WEIGHT lifting
Belly up to the bar, boys; superheavyweights; photographs by Neil Leifer; with account by P. Ryan. Sports Illus 33:28-33 S 7 '70
High-ho, high-ho, it's off to lift we go; World weight lifting championship, Columbus, Ohio. H. Weiskopf. il Sports Illus 33:63-4+ S 28 '70
Perils of muscle beach; weight lifter's blood pressure. il Time 96:46 Jl 20 '70

WEIGHT reducing preparations
How I broke the dangerous diet-pill habit. il
Good H 170:12+ Mr '70
WEIGHT throwing
He knows how to throw his weight around.
P. Putnam. il por Sports Illus 32:52+ Mr
9 '70
WEIGHT watchers, inc.
Story of weight watchers; excerpts, ed. by
J. R. Heilman. J. Nidetch. il pors McCalls
97:41-8 My '70
WEIGHTLESSNESS
Adjusting to space; frog otolith. il Sci N 98:
397 N 21 '70
Materials behavior experiments studied. Avia-
tion W 93:53 N 2 '70
See also
Biosatellite program
WEIGHTS and measures
One of our bouillon cubes is missing. il Con-
sumer Rep 35:248-51 Ap '70
See also
Cookery—Measurements
Metric system
WEIGL, Karl
Late romantic rediscovered: the unfashion-
able music of Karl Weigl. P. L. Miller.
Am Rec G 36:376-7 Ja '70 *
WEIGLE, R. N.
When to incorporate your farm. Suc Farm
68:no2 B6 F '70
WEIHOFEN, Henry, and Usdin, G. L.
Who is competent to make a will? Ment Hy
54:37-43 Ja '70
WEIKEL, Charles P.
Life you can save. il Har Yrs 10:6-11 Ja '70
WEIL, James L.
Comment. R. Magowan. Poetry 116:199-200
Je '70 *
WEIL, Rolf A.
Youth attitudes, 1970; address, September 8,
1970. Vital Speeches 37:55-6 N 1 '70
WEIL, Simone
Avant-garde Simone Weil. C. R. Hughes.
America 122:612 Je 6 '70 *
WEILAND, Peter
Número uno. il por Time 95:60 Ap 20 '70 *
WEILL, Daniel F. and others
Petrology of a fine-grained igneous rock
from the Sea of Tranquillity. bibliog il
Science 167:635-8 Ja 30 '70
WEILL, Kurt
Mahagonny. Criticism
New Yorker 46:97 My 9 '70
Opera N il por 34:8-12 Mr 14 '70 *
WEIMAR republic. See Germany—History—
1918-1933
WEIMARANERS. See Pointers (dogs)
WEIN, Bibi
There's always the Bronx; story. Mlle 70:102-
3 Ja '70
WEINBERG, Alvin M.
In defense of science: adaptation of ad-
dress, October 18, 1969. bibliog Science 167:
141-5 Ja 9 '70
Nuclear energy and the environment. il por
Bul Atom Sci 26:69-74 Je '70
WEINBERG, Eugene
Sounds of sickness. Time 96:57 S 21 '70 *
WEINBERG, George
Fine art of complaining; excerpt from The
action approach. Read Digest 97:81-4 S '70
WEINBERG, Gerald M.
Nation as a park. Nat Parks & Con Mag 44:
21 My '70
WEINBERG, Ruby
Evergreen cotoneasters. il Horticulture 48:32-
3+ O '70
WEINBERGER, Caspar W.
Tax on mergers? interview, ed. by G. R.
Rosen. por Duns 95:10-12 My '70
Where the FTC's new chairman stands;
interview. pors Nations Bsns 58:28-30 Ap
'70

about

Closing the performance gap. il pors News-
week 75:16-17 Je 22 '70 *
Man in the middle. il por Forbes 105:46-7 F
1 '70 *
WEINBERGER, Morris J.
Dress codes: we forget our own advice. Clear
House 44:471-3 Ap '70
WEINER, Bernard
War is hell for Senator Jackson. por Nation
211:138-41 Ag 31 '70
What, another conspiracy? Nation 211:424-7
N 2 '70
WEINER, Charles
Physics in the great depression. bibliog il
Phys Today 23:31-6+ O '70
WEINER, Sandra
Authors & editors. L. Russ. por Pub W 198:
17-19 O 26 '70 *

WEINGARTNER, Charles
Goodbye Miranda. Hello Cassandra; poem.
Engl J 59:987 O '70
WEINLAND, James D.
Program yourself like a computer. il Nations
Bsns 58:31 My '70
WEINSTEIN, Allen
Agit-prop & the Rosenbergs. Commentary
50:18+ Jl; 10+ N '70
WEINSTEIN, John N. and Caplan, S. R.
Charge-mosaic membranes: dialytic sepa-
ration of electrolytes from nonelectrolytes
and amino acids. bibliog il Science 169:
296-8 Jl 17 '70
WEINSTEIN, Robert A.
God bless our happy ship. il Am West 7:38-47
Mr '70
WEINSTOCK, Henry R.
Professionalizing teaching; adaptation of ad-
dress. bibliog Clear House 45:3-9 S '70
WEINSTOCK, Herbert
At last, Les Huguenots and Meyerbeer. Sat
R 53:75 N 28 '70
Finer Forza, optional Requiems. Sat R 53:50
O 31 '70
Jenufa ten years later. por Sat R 53:65 Mr
28 '70
Portuguese passion. Sat R 53:53 Jl 25 '70
Two (and a half) cheers for Anna Bolena.
Sat R 53:39 D 26 '70
WEIR, Dennis J.
Dennis J. Weir, library lineman. il pors Wil-
son Lib Bul 45:458-9 Ja '71 *
WEIR, Walter
Madison avenue. Sat R 52:74 D 13 '69; 53:65-6
Ja 17; 78 F 14; 113 Mr 14 '70
WEIR, William
How to use convenience foods at camp. il
Camp Mag 42:44-5 Mr '70
WEIS, Bud
Buying a used outboard motor. il Mech Illus
66:120-1+ Mr '70
WEISBERG, Barry
Raping Alaska; ecology of oil. il Ramp Mag
8:25-33 Ja '70
WEISBERG, Mary
Woman alone. E. Keiffer. il pors Good H
171:84-5+ Jl '70 *
WEISBERGER, Bernard A.
Melting pot: its most difficult test; the immi-
grant within; excerpts from The American
people. il Am Heritage 22:32-9+ D '70
WEISBORD, Marvin R.
How to settle children's squabbles. il Parents
Mag 45:38-9+ Ja '70
Now, focus on high school unrest. Ed Digest
35:5-8 Ja '70
WEISBROD, R. R.
Have you been depressed lately. Mrs Hardy?
story. Redbook 135:84-5 Je '70
WEISE, David
Unilateral withdrawal of Private Weise. P.
Collier. Ramp Mag 8:4+ F '70 *
WEISE, Donald F.
Nongrading, electing, and phasing: basics of
revolution for relevance. Engl J 59:122-30
Ja '70
WEISENBERG, Charles M.
ALA: a professional or a library association?
Am Lib 1:1060-1 D '70
Overdue. por Wilson Lib Bul 45:406-7 D '70
WEISER, C. J.
Cold resistance and injury in woody plants.
bibliog il Science 169:1269-78 S 25 '70
WEISER, Mona M.
Goodbye grandma. Har Yrs 10:13 N '70
WEISER, Morton. See Freud, E. D. jt. auth.
WEISHEIT, Eldon
Coffee at Howard Johnson's; poem. Chr Cent
87:1347-8 N 11 '70
WEISINGER, Richard S. See Woods, S. C. jt.
auth.
WEISKOPF, Herman
Be a take-charge blaster! il por Sports Illus
32:34-6+ Ap 6 '70
Fliffises and gazip-gazaps. il Sports Illus
32:44-6+ Je 8 '70
Funny ball, funny bounces. il Sports Illus
33:20-2+ Jl 20 '70
Golf. Sports Illus 33:78-9 O 12 '70
Weight lifting. Sports Illus 33:63-4+ S 28 '70
Wrestling (cont) Sports Illus 32:49-50+ F 16;
72+ Ap 6 '70
WEISMILLER, Edward
Monster poem. New Repub 162:36 My 9 '70
WEISS, Charles
Research Olympus for science teaching. il
Sci N 97:581-3 Je 13 '70
WEISS, Henry H. and Pizer, E. F.
Hospitalizing the young: is it for their own
good? bibliog Ment Hy 54:498-502 O '70
WEISS, Jeff
Jeff Weiss's plays, mad, unpredictable. J.
Gruen. Vogue 155:44 F 15 '70

WEISS, Margaret R.
Ben Shahn, photographer; excerpt from introduction. il Sat R 53:26-7+ N 7 '70
Ceiling on the wall. il Sat R 53:50-1 D 5 '70
Karsh's Japanese studies; with photographs. Sat R 53:16-18 My 9 '70
Lens at large. il Sat R 54:46-50 Ja 2 '71
Photography (cont) il Sat R 53:36-7 Jl 11 '70
(ed) See Davidson, B. At home in East Harlem
(ed) See Steichen, E. Happy birthday, Mr Steichen

WEISS, Peter
Bomb crater in the American dream. il Nation 211:302-5 O 5 '70

WEISS, R. F.
Helium isotope effect in solution in water and seawater. bibliog il Science 168:247-8 Ap 10 '70

WEISS, Theodore
Fitting revenge; Little red book; Very Tokyo; poems. Poetry 116:80-5 My '70
Heir apparent; poem. Nation 211:476 N 9 '70
Last letters; poem. New Yorker 46:38 S 5 '70

about
Cycle of sensibility. H. Carruth. Nation 212:25-6 Ja 4 '71 *

WEISS, Peck and Greer (firm)
Brave brokers take the plunge. il Bsns W p 116+ Mr 21 '70

WEISSE, Edward B.
Proposal for combating campus revolution. Sch & Soc 98:404-5 N '70

WEISSKOPF, Victor F.
Need for basic research. Science 167:935 F 13 '70
Physics in the twentieth century; adaptation of address, April 1969. Science 168:923-30 My 22 '70
Three steps in the structure of matter. il por Phys Today 23:17-22+ S '70

WEISSLER, Paul
Light truck story for 1971. il Mech Illus 66:56-8+ D '70
Steam machine to help your heart. il Mech Illus 66:68-9 Ap '70

WEISSMAN, S. M. See Ohe, K. jt. auth.

WEISSMAN, Steve
Businessmen against the war (sic) Ramp Mag 9:32-7 D '70
Why the population bomb is a Rockefeller baby. il Ramp Mag 8:42-7 My '70
—See Barkley, K. jt. auth.

WEISSMULLER, Johnny
Aaah-eeee-aaah...umgawa. J. Kirshenbaum. il pors Sports Illus 33:58-60+ Ag 17 '70 *

WEISSTEIN, Naomi
Neural symbolic activity: a psychophysical measure. bibliog il Science 168:1489-91; 170:1227-8 Je 19, D 11 '70

WEISZ, William
Apprentice president makes the grade. il por Bsns W p60+ S 19 '70 *

WEISZ-ROOS, Henriette
Is there another life after death? E. Kinkead. il pors Look 34:84-5 O 20 '70 *

WEITZ, Allan
Color and design are all around us. il Pop Phot 67:84-7 Jl '70 *

WELBOURNE, James C. jr. See Croneberger, R. B. jt. auth.

WELCH, Garth
Up on top from Down Under. N. M. Stoop. il pors Dance Mag 45:32-5 Ja '71 *

WELCH, Holmes
Deification of Mao. il por Sat R 53:25+ S 19 '70

WELCH, James
Dancing man; poem. Harp Baz 103:156 Ag '70
Only bar in Dixon; poem. New Yorker 46:48 O 10 '70

WELCH, Mary Scott
Penny saved is a penny; or, What you don't save won't hurt you, and why. il Redbook 134:70-1+ F '70

WELCH, Raquel
Raquel Welch, Mae West talk about men, morals and Myra Breckinridge; interview. ed. by J. Hamilton. il pors Look 34:44-8+ Mr 24 '70

about
Making of Raquel; TV special. M. Kasindorf. il pors Newsweek 75:91 Ap 27 '70 *
Raquel Welch retrospective exhibition 1964-1970. T. Ferrell. il pors Esquire 73:123-9 My '70

WELCOME signs. See Signs and signboards

WELDERS
Install a circuit for a 230-v. arc welder. J. Burroughs. il Pop Mech 133:178-81 F '70

WELDING, Pete
Big Bill reconsidered. il por Sat R 53:62-3 F 14 '70

WELDING
How to weld with your lathe. J. H. McVicker. il Pop Sci 196:67 Je '70

WELDON, Georgina (Treherne)
Gounod and Georgina. R. Rushmore. pors Opera N 34:24-5 Ap 18 '70 *

WELFARE, Public. See Public welfare

WELFARE federations. See Community chests

WELFARE work. See Public welfare

WELK, Lawrence
Enduringly crummy. Sedulus. New Repub 163:22-3 D 19 '70 *

WELKE, Elton
Family travel. il Bet Hom & Gard 48:141-6 Mr; 129-33+ My; 20 Ag '70

WELL drilling. See Drilling and boring (earth and rocks)

WELLER, Joan L. See Klein, D. C. jt. auth.

WELLER method of tornado detection. See Television in meteorology

WELLES, Chris
Keeping shale under wraps. il Nation 211:51-2 Jl 20 '70

WELLES, Orson
By Orson Welles: but where are we going? il pors Look 34:34-6 N 3 '70

about
Films of Orson Welles, by C. Higham. Review
Newsweek 76:64 Ag 3 '70. R. A. Sokolov *
Welles before Kane. J. McBride. Film Q 23:19-22 Spr '70 *
Welles's Chimes at midnight. J. McBride. il pors Film Q 23:11-20 Fall '69

WELLESLEY, Arthur, 1st duke of Wellington. See Wellington, A. W.

WELLESLEY, Mass.

Education
Turning on bright underachievers. W. J. Freeman and A. C. Craig. Todays Ed 59:52-3 F '70

WELLINGTON, Arthur Wellesley, 1st duke of
Wellington, by E. Longford. Review
New Yorker 46:76-8+ Je 27 '70. N. Bliven *

WELLINGTON book company
Wellington avoids bankruptcy; creditors grant extension. Pub W 198:35-6 O 12 '70

WELLMAN industries
Listening to America. B. Moyers. il Harper 241:100-5 D '70

WELLNER, Alfred M. and others
Program evaluation: a proposed model for mental health services. bibliog il Ment Hy 54:530-4 O '70

WELLS, David F.
Change and decay: Roman style. Chr Today 14:6-8 S 25 '70

WELLS, Dick
(ed) See Newman, P. Motor trend interview: Paul Newman

WELLS, H. G.
H. G. Wells, his turbulent life and times, by L. Dickson. Review
Cath World 210:234 F '70. D. Brophy *

WELLS, John M.
Immoral and illegal. Nation 210:389 Ap 6 '70 *

WELLS, Philip V.
Postglacial vegetational history of the Great Plains. bibliog il Science 167:1574-82 Mr 20 '70

WELLS, Robert
Vietnamization on Main Street: the dum-dum bullet. il Nation 211:38-41 Jl 20 '70

WELLS, William D.
It's a Wyeth, not a Warhol, world. il Harvard Bsns R 48:26-8+ Ja '70

WELLS
You can drive your own well. R. G. Christophersen. il Pop Mech 133:188-91+ Ap '70
See also
Water, Underground

WELLS, Waste disposal. See Trade waste disposal

WELS, Byron G.
How to buy audio tape. il Radio-Electr 41:43-4 O '70
How to make etchless circuits. il Radio-Electr 41:59 S '70

WELSH, Elliott A. 2d
Who's sincere? por Time 95:40 Je 29 '70 *

WELSH, Frederic S.
You press the button and we do the rest. il pors Nations Bsns 58:70-1 Ja '70

WELSH, Mitchell, and Welsh, Stanley
How rotary tillage works for us. il por Suc Farm 68:40-1 Ap '70

WELSH, Pat M.
RAP-TAG and EDP: happy marriage? Pub
W 198:46 S 21 '70
WELSH, Stanley. See Welsh, M. jt. auth.
WELSH
Cymru am byth! Wales-France rugby match.
C. Gammon. il Sports Illus 32:58-64 F 9 '70
WELTER, Paul
Put policy first in DCF analysis. bibliog f il
Harvard Bsns R 48:141-8 Ja '70
WELTY, Eudora
Jonathan Yardley: the last good one? New
Repub 162:33-6 My 9 '70 *
Must the novelist crusade? il Writers Diges{
50:32-5+ F '70
about
Eudora Welty: metamorphosis of a southern
lady writer. J. W. Aldridge. Sat R 53:21-3+
Ap 11 '70 *
WENDELBURG, Tom
Using dialogue in the outdoor article. Writer
84:27-9 Ja '71
WENDEROTH, Joseph
Diary of a dissenting priest. P. Mayer. Com-
monweal 92:78-9 Ap 3 '70 *
WENDORF, Fred, and others
Egyptian prehistory: some new concepts. bib-
liog il Science 169:1161-71 S 18 '70
WENGER, A. See Delsemme, A. H. jt. auth.
WENK, Edward, Jr
National policy for coastal management; ad-
dress, October 19, 1970. Vital Speeches 37:
177-81 Ja 1 '71
WENNER, David N.
Tracker, an ATV for all seasons. il Pop Sci
197:62-3 S '70
WENNER, Jann
Too fast, too soon. por Newsweek 76:61 Ag
17 '70 *
WENTORF, R. H. Jr
Anomalous water: attempts at high-pressure
synthesis. bibliog Science 169:175-6 Jl 10 '70
WENTWORTH, Murray J.
Watercolor page; with biographical sketch.
il por Am Artist 34:30-1+ My '70
WERBLIN, David A. See Werblin, S.
WERBLIN, Sonny
Sonny sniffs a derby. W. Tower. il por
Sports Illus 32:10-11+ F 16 '70 *
This horse needed his owner's stamina. W.
F. Reed. il Sports Illus 32:26-7 My 11 '70 *
WERBLOWSKY, Zwi
Hopeful voices from Israel; interview, ed. by
F. D. Lueking. il Chr Cent 87:139-41 F 4 '70
WERKLEY, Caroline E.
Guernseys I have loved. Esquire 74:40+ O '70
Mister Carnegie's library. il por Am Heri-
tage 21:65-8 F '70
WERNER, Alfred
Dream world of Odilon Redon. il Am Artist
34:40-5+ N '70
WERNER, David
Healing in the Sierra Madre; with biographi-
cal sketch. il pors Natur Hist 79:8, 60-7 N
'70
WERNER, Sidney C. and others
Circulating immunoglobulin M: increased
concentrations in endemic and sporadic
goiter. bibliog il Science 170:1201-2 D 11 '70
WERNICK, Robert
Dali's dollars. il pors Life 69:48-48A+ Jl 24
'70
WERNICKE, Enrique
Gardeners' affairs; story, tr. by H. E.
Francis. Harp Baz 103:131 My '70
Señor Swan; story. Harp Baz 103:130 My
'70
WERNING, Waldo J.
What moves men as stewards? Chr Today
14:11-13 Ap 24 '70
WESCHCKE, Carl L.
Shop ventures into unknown. il Pub W 197:
71-3 Mr 9 '70
WESLEYAN church. See Methodist church in
the United States
WESLEYAN university, Middletown, Conn.
Two nations at Wesleyan university. R. J.
Margolis. il N Y Times Mag p9+ Ja 18 '70;
Discussion. p 12+ F 22; 19+ Mr 8 '70
WESSEL, Morris A.
New developments in day care. il Parents
Mag 45:76-7+ N '70
WESSON, Robert G.
Soviet interest in the Middle East. Cur Hist
59:212-19+ O '70
WEST, Anthony
Books. Vogue 155:110+ Mr 1 '70
Real scandal behind The Forsyte saga. il Vo-
gue 155:206-7+ My '70
Specialists in sex: orchids. il Vogue 156:136+
D '70
Summer of the hero; story; excerpt from
David Rees, among others. McCalls 97:84-
5 S '70

WEST, Benjamin
Holy family attributed to Benjamin West.
A. C. Van Devanter. il Antiques 98:774-5
N '70
WEST, Edwin L. Jr. See Hounshell, P. B. jt.
auth.
WEST, Gordon
VHF question; letter. Yachting 127:83+ Ap
'70
WEST, Jack
Anatomy of a powerboat. il Yachting 128:52-
3+ D '70
Marine electronics, 1970 style. il Yachting
127:71-3+ Ap; 60-2 My; 128:68-70 Jl; 60-2+
Ag '70
Radar in the '70's. il Yachting 129:85-7+ Ja '71
WEST, Jerry
Long way with West, all the way with Wilt?
il pors Life 68:46-9 Mr 13 '70 *
WEST, Jessamyn
Marina Oswald Porter: seven years after
Dallas. il pors Redbook 135:57-9+ Ag '70
Mother's day; story. New Yorker 46:32-7 My
30 '70
Toward peace. Redbook 135:75+ S '70
Trade winds; interview, ed. by C. Amory. Sat R
53:8 O 24 '70
WEST, Mae
Mae West tells her secrets on staying young.
Vogue 155:28 Je '70 *
Raquel Welch, Mae West talk about men,
morals and Myra Breckinridge; interview
ed. by J. Hamilton. il pors Look 34:44-8+
Mr 24 '70
about
Unconquerable Mae. C. Beaton. pors Vogue
155:130-1 Je '70 *
WEST, Morris Langlo
Authors and editors. B. A. Bannon. por
Pub W 197:23-4 Je 22 '70 *
WEST, Nathanael
Great despiser. B. Darrach. por Time 96:
64+ Ag 17 '70 *
Nathanael West, by J. Martin. Review
Atlan 226:127-30 O '70. M. Schorer *
Commonweal 93:96-8 O 23 '70. S. Maloff *
Nation 211:120-2 Ag 17 '70. R. Gian-
none*
New Repub 162:23-4 My 23 '70. C. T.
Samuels *
New Yorker 46:185-6+ O 10 '70. L. E. Siss-
man *
Newsweek il por 75:80+ Je 29 '70. S. K.
Oberbeck *
Sat R por 53:28-9 Je 27 '70. H. Swados *
WEST, Paul
Beyond words. J. Kaplan. Commentary 51:
106-7 Ja '71
Miracle of love. R. A. Gross. Newsweek 76:
76 Ag 31 '70 *
Through the sound barrier. R. Z. Sheppard.
il por Time 96:60+ S 7 '70 *
WEST, Dame Rebecca
There is no such thing as something for
nothing. Mlle 72:74-5+ D '70
Women re women. Mlle 70:182-3+ F '70
WEST, Richard. See Fowler, J. M. jt. auth.
WEST, Ruth
Diet tips from a famous beauty spa. Ladies
Home J 87:129-30+ O '70
WEST, S. H. See Hilliard, J. H. jt. auth.
WEST
Memories of Big Country. D. Jackson. il
Life 68:40-8+ Ap 3 '70
Restorations West. Travel & Camera 33:10+
Ap '70
See also
Cowboys
Fishing—Western states
Frontier and pioneer life—United States
Geology—Western states
Irrigation—Western states
Mines and mineral resources—Western states
Negroes—Western states
Overland journeys to the Pacific
Pacific coast
Rocky Mountains
Wilderness areas—Western states
Bibliography
Current western books 1968-1969. Am West 7:
58-62 Ja '70
Western gathering. See issues of American
west
Civilization
U.S. culture moves west. il U S News 67:
62-7 S 7 '70
Description and travel
Different America. R. McKee. il Audubon
72:9-17 Jl '70
Great western bus ride. J. Kerouac. Esquire
73:136-7+ Mr '70

WEST—Description and travel—*Continued*
[Month] travel in and beyond the West. See issues of Sunset
Vacations out West: 1970 style. il U S News 68:62-5 Je 22 '70
West coast wanderings. C. Pepper. Travel 133:23 My; 21 Je; 134:23 Jl; 21 Ag '70

Economic conditions
It's mountain standard time; with paintings by D. Schwartz. J. Main. Fortune 82:118-25 S '70

History
Portraits for a western album. See occasional issues of American West
   See also
Oregon Trail

Photographs
Long curving shore from Alaska to Baja; with excerpts from Edge of a continent, by D. G. Kelley. T. H. Watkins. il Am West 7:18-31 N '70

Politics
Election outlook in Far West. il U S News 69:16-19 O 26 '70
WEST AFRICAN literature. See African literature
WEST BENGAL
Land-grab war; Naxalite movement in West Bengal. il Newsweek 76:31 Ag 3 '70

Peasantry
   See Peasantry—India
WEST CHESTER, Pa.
U.S. journal: undercover police officer, John Mervin arrested for murder. C. Trillin. New Yorker 46:42-4+ Je 27 '70
WEST Coast commodity exchange. See Commodity exchanges
WEST COVINA, Calif.
Yellow fire truck no longer curious. C. I. Brandt. il Am City 85:26 Je '70
WEST HARTFORD, Conn.

Education
Cocoon kids encounter city crises; course at Conard high school. K. Branan. il Schol Teach Sec Teach Sup p 12-13 My 4 '70
WEST in art
Bull market in Western art. il Bsns W p92-3 Je 13 '70
With pen and ink and paintbrush New Zealand's leading artist does a book on the American West. il por Sunset 145:90-3 N '70
   See also
Cowboy artists of America
WEST INDIES
   See also
Anguilla (island)
Caribbean Region
Dominican Republic
Jamaica
Leeward Islands
St Martin (island)
Virgin Islands
WEST INDIES, BRITISH
   See also
Anguilla (island)
Bahama Islands
Bequia (island)
British Virgin Islands
Grenada
Jamaica
Trinidad and Tobago
WEST INDIES, FRENCH
   See also
Guadeloupe (islands)
Martinque
WEST IRIAN
   See also
Copper mines and mining—West Irian
Jalémo

Native races
Cannibalistic revenge in Jalé warfare. K. F. Koch. il por Natur Hist 79:40-51 F '70
WEST NEW GUINEA. See West Irian
WEST POINT military academy. See United States military academy, West Point
WEST SPRINGFIELD, Mass.
Helps ease golf course maintenance problems. il Am City 85:54 Mr '70
WEST VIRGINIA
   See also
Public health—West Virginia
Recreation areas—West Virginia
Seneca Rock

Politics and government
One Rockefeller who may make it. R. Reeves. il por N Y Times Mag p30-1+ O 4 '70
WEST VIRGINIA mine disaster. See Coal mines and mining—Accidents and explosions
WESTBETH artists housing. See New York (city)—Housing
WESTBROOK, Perry D.
John Burroughs, New York's early defender of the environment. il pors Cons 25:30-2 Ag '70
WESTCHESTER classic golf tournament. See Golf—Tournaments
WESTERBECK, Colin L. Jr
Screen. Commonweal 92:390-2, 441-2; 93:20-1, 128-9, 176-7, 222-3, 302-3, 350-1 Ag 7, S 4, O 2, 30 N 13, 27, D 18 '70, Ja 8 '71
WESTERFIELD, Nancy G.
And there were shepherds; poem. America 123:560 D 26 '70
In his sameness of grace, our church, burning; poem Chr Today 14:16 My 8 '70
Sleeping with mother, in her eightieth year; poem. Commonweal 91:486 Ja 30 '70
WESTERMARK, Tory, and Gooch, B. N. S.
Basic competencies for teaching poetry. Engl J 59:517-19+ Ap '70
WESTERN air lines
American, Western in merger agreement. W. H. Gregory. il Aviation W 93:24-5 N 9 '70
Changes at Western include new look. il Aviation W 93:48-9 Ag 24 '70
WESTERN AUSTRALIA
Inside Down Under. J. Gunther. il Read Digest 97:207-10+ O '70
Winning the west in Australia. H. E. Mercer. il Travel 134:34-41 S '70
WESTERN ballads. See Ballads, American
WESTERN bancorporation
Giannini's legacy. por Forbes 105:40 Ja 15 '70
WESTERN cookery. See Cookery, American
WESTERN electric company
Flight from the cities. il Newsweek 76:58+ N 30 '70
WESTERN folklore. See Folklore—United States
WESTERN gear corporation
   See also
Airport servicecenters, inc.
WESTERN GERMANY. See Germany (Federal Republic)
WESTERN home awards
American institute of architects-Sunset magazine 1969-1970 Western home awards. il Sunset 144:78-81 F '70
More weekend-house planners throw away the rule book. il Sunset 144:94-9 My '70
WESTERN juniper. See Juniper
WESTERN music. See Folk music, American
WESTERN states. See West
WESTERN stories
Stories of the old West; written for 1904 issue. E. Hough. Field & S 75:174+ Je '70
Wyatt Earp syndrome. C. L. Sonnichsen. il Am West 7:26-8+ My '70
WESTERN union international, inc.
Getting the message across. R. Levy. il por Duns 95:43-4+ Ja '70
WESTERN union telegraph company
Can satellites replace the bike? plans for a domestic communications satellite system. il Bsns W p20 Ag 15 '70
WESTERNERS
Out West, we trust one another. B. Goldwater. por Life 69:4 O 9 '70
WESTFALL, K. F.
(ed) See Boyle I. Babies after sixty-five?
WESTFALL, Kitti
My island of life. il por Redbook 135:26+ Ag '70
WESTIN, Alan F.
Data study will watch Big Brother. por Bsns W p34 Mr 14 '70 *
WESTIN, Helen
Shopping spree; poem. Hobbies 74:76 F '70
WESTINGHOUSE air brake company
All's fair in love & war; federal court ruling on American standard-Crane battle for WABCO. il Forbes 105:26-7 Ap 15 '70
WESTINGHOUSE broadcasting company
Trobriandish; WINS. R. L. Shayon. Sat R 53:49 Ap 25 '70
WESTINGHOUSE electric corporation
McLaren vs. the cartels. Newsweek 75:78B+ My 4 '70
Should a license cut out competition? Bsns W p20+ My 2 '70
Still picking and choosing. il por Forbes 105:38-9 Mr 15 '70

WESTINGHOUSE electric corporation—*Cont.*
Westinghouse's environment school: combining business with ecology. T. P. Southwick. Science 169:453-4 Jl 31 '70
Westinghouse: the slow, thorough way. il Forbes 107:25 Ja 1 '71
WESTINGHOUSE electric nuclear energy systems Europe. See Atomic power industry—Europe, Western
WESTINGHOUSE learning corporation
High marks in the teaching business. il Bsns W p32+ My 2 '70
WESTLAKE, Donald Edwin
Authors & editors. A. P. Hackett. por Pub W 198:21-3 S 21 '70 *
WESTLEDGE (school) See Private schools
WESTLEY, Richard J.
Sticking point: religious tutelage. America 123:172-5 S 19 '70
WESTMINSTER, Colo.
Library addition has garden-like reading room. il Am City 85:81 O '70
WESTMINSTER choir
Schumann's Die Peri with Janowitz, Brilioth, Engen, Smith. I. Kolodin. Sat R 53:55 Je 6 '70
WESTMORELAND, William Childs
Armed forces; address, January 31, 1970. Vital Speeches 36:299-301 Mr 1 '70
Towards a volunteer army; address, October 30, 1970. Vital Speeches 37:98-100 D 1 '70
Westmoreland's Vietnam visit: he liked what he saw; excerpts from news conference. il por U S News 69:43 Ag 3 '70

about

Of guilt and precedent. il por Time 97:10 Ja 18 '71 *
WESTOFF, Charles F. See Bumpass, L. jt. auth.
WESTON, Brett
Gallery; photographs. Life 68:8-9 Je 12 '70

about

Brett Weston: shaping himself in his father's image. M. Mann. il Pop Phot 66:27-8+ Mr '70 *
WESTON, Christine
Magic time; story. McCalls 97:100-2 Ag '70
WESTON, Edward
Brett Weston: shaping himself in his father's image. M. Mann. il Pop Phot 66:27-8+ Mr '70 *
WESTON, John
Leap to imagination. Writer 83:12-14 Ag '70
WESTON, Paul
Funniest put-on. G. Lees. pors Hi Fi 20:120 N '70 *
WESTPORT, Conn.
In the dumps over garbage. il Bsns W p62+ S 12 '70

Education

War and pieces; student unrest becomes creative theater. C. Matheson and others. il Todays Ed 59:20-3 Mr '70
WET storage of boats. See Boats—Storage
WETLANDS
Tale of whoopers and bottles and the throwaway economy. Audubon 72:103 Jl '70
See also
Marshes
WETTERBERG, Lennart, and others
Harderian gland; an extraretinal photoreceptor influencing the pineal gland in neonatal rats? bibliog il Science 167:884-5 F 6 '70
Harderian gland: development and influence of early hormonal treatment on porphyrin content. bibliog il Science 168:996-8 My 22 '70
Harderian gland: influence on pineal hydroxyindole-O-methyltransferase activity in neonatal rats. bibliog il Science 170:194-6 O 9 '70
WEXLER, Jacqueline (Grennan)
Eclipse of authority. Ladies Home J 86:132 D '69
WEY, Ralph
Illumination in the home. il Consumer Bul 53:34-6 S '70
WEYAND, Frederick Carlton
New star in Vietnam: Weyand and Abrams? il por Newsweek 76:54 N 16 '70 *
WEYERHAEUSER, George Hunt
World investment; address, January 29, 1970. Vital Speeches 36:312-14 Mr 1 '70
WEYMOUTH, George
Coaching: the new in sport. P. Benchley. il Travel & Camera 33:40-5+ F '70 *
WEYMOUTH, Yann
Yann and Lally Weymouth. pors Vogue 155:96-7 Je '70 *

WHALEN, George J. and Graf, R. F.
Portable speaker you can plug in anywhere. il Pop Mech 134:126-9 Ag '70
—See Graf, R .F. jt. auth.
WHALEN, Grover Aloysius
Memory of Grover A. Whalen restores my faith in the art of Wetzel the tailor. J. Ferris. Sat R 53:4 Mr 7 '70 *
WHALEN, Richard E. and Luttge, W. C.
p-Chlorophenylalanine methyl ester: an aphrodisiac? bibliog il Science 169:1000-1 S 4 '70
WHALES
Can we save the great whales? blue whales. V. B. Scheffer. il McCalls 97:54+ My '70
Cliché of the killer. V. B. Scheffer. Natur Hist 79:26-8+ O '70
Girl who trains whales. il pors Sci Digest 67:58-61 Mr '70
Sing, cetacea, sing! Time 95:59+ Je 22 '70
Whale of a singer. Newsweek 75:106 Je 8 '70
Whale of a tale: a tale of a whale. il Sr School 95:14 O 13 '69
When a race breathes no more; extinction of forty-seven species of U.S. wildlife. W. J. Hickel. il Sports Illus 33:70+ D 14 '70
Year of the whale; excerpts. V. B. Scheffer. il Read Digest 96:124-8 F '70
See also
International whaling commission
WHALING
On the trail of the white whale. W. Davis. il Mech Illus 66:58-60+ Ag '70
West Indies whaling. W. F. Rathjen and J. R. Sullivan. il Sea Front 16:130-7 My '70
Whalers of Bequia. T. W. Burgess. il Nat R 22:629 Je 16 '70
Year of the whale. H. Brabyn. il UNESCO Courier 23:65-8 Ag '70
See also
Scrimshaw

History

Prince Albert's way of catching squid. S. Schlee. il por Natur Hist 79:20+ F '70
WHALL, Hugh D.
Boating (cont) Sports Illus 32:60+ Mr 30; 33:76-7 N 16 '70
Bright new Chance at the cup. il por Sports Illus 33:28-31 Jl 13 '70
Cup splashdown: Valiant and France. il Sports Illus 32:22-3 My 4 '70
Eagle on a wild, wet flight. il por Sports Illus 32:16-19 Mr 16 '70
Plenty of Sunfish in the sea. il Sports Illus 32:24-5 F 23 '70
Revolution roils the Cup. il Sports Illus 33:14-15 Jl 27 '70
Rowing. il Sports Illus 32:74+ My 11; 54-5 Je 22; 89-91 S 21 '70
Some great Dane from Tulane. il por Sports Illus 33:20-1 N 9 '70
WHALLEY, J. Irving
U.N. reaffirms objectives for reunification of Korea; statements, November 12 and 25, 1969. Dept State Bul 61:610-15 D 22 '69
U.S. joins other members in support of U.N. budget, statement, December 17, 1969. Dept State Bul 62:109-10 Ja 26 '70
WHALLON, Arthur
Indiana cabinetmakers and allied craftsmen, 1815-1860. il Antiques 98:118-25 Jl '70
WHARTON, Clifton R. Jr
Negro president at Michigan state university. por Sch & Soc 98:145-6 Mr '70 *
New boss takes over at Michigan state. il pors Ebony 25:60-2+ Jl '70 *
Ready access to higher ignorance. R. Kirk. Nat R 22:514 My 19 '70 *
WHARTON, Don
Rugged Idaho. Read Digest 97:138-44 Ag '70
WHARTON, G. W.
Mites and commercial extracts of house dust. bibliog il Science 167:1382-3 Mr 6 '70
WHARTON model. See Economic models
WHARVES
See also
Terminals
WHAT Herbert Breuer and I did to each other; story. See Oates, J. C.
WHAT is the connection between men and women; story. See Oates, J. C.
WHAT the butler saw; drama. See Orton, J
WHATCOM COUNTY, Wash.
County acts to save its vanishing shorelands. K. D. Hertz. il Parks & Rec 5:48-9+ F '70
WHATNOTS. See Stands (furniture)
WHEAT
Aurintricarboxylic acid and initiation factors of wheat embryo. A. Marcus and others. bibliog il Science 167:1735-6 Mr 27 '70
Mutation in internode length affects wheat plant-type. C. O. Qualset and others. bibliog il Science 169:1090-1 S 11 '70

WHEAT—*Continued*
Third world: seeds of revolution; production explosion in the grain bowls of the world. il Time 96:24+ Jl 13 '70
See also
Feeding and feeding stuffs—Wheat
Flour

Cultivation
How to beat wheat problems. C. E. Sommers and W. Messerly. Suc Farm 68:28-9 Ag '70

Diseases and pests
See also
Rusts (botany)

Harvesting
How to handle combine problems. P. B. Jones. il Suc Farm 68:35 Je '70

Hybrids
New wheats and social progress. L. P. Reitz. bibliog il Science 169:952-5 S 4 '70
Nobel peace prize: developer of high-yield wheat receives award. L. R. Brown. por Science 170:518-19 O 30 '70
Peace and the green revolution. il por Sci N 98:347 O 31 '70
Sowing a green revolution. por Time 96:42-N 2 '70
Wheat breeder who won the Peace prize; with editorial comment. C. P. Streeter. il pors Farm J 94:16-17+, 46 D '70
Wheat whiz wins; Nobel peace prize to N. E. Borlaug. por Sr Schol 97:8 N 16 '70
See also
Triticale

Prices
Great wheat glut; Canada. il Newsweek 75:71 Ja 26 '70

Seeding
Stubble-mulching moves winter wheat north. F. J. Shideler. il Farm J 93:30D O '69

WHEAT-free diet. See Diet in disease
WHEAT leaf rust. See Rusts (botany)
WHEAT trade
Great wheat glut; Canada. il Newsweek 75:71 Ja 26 '70
WHEATCROFT, John
Today's poetry is protest. Todays Ed 59:26-9 Ap '70
WHEELER, Bruce E.
Lincolniana in 1969. il Hobbies 74:116-19 F '70
WHEELER, Douglas L.
Thaw in Portugal. For Affairs 48:769-81 Jl '70
WHEELER, Earle Gilmore
Why defense planners worry; interview. il por U S News 68:34-9 Ap 20 '70
about
Masterful bureaucrat. il por Newsweek 75:51-2 F 23 '70 *
Wheeler: an old soldier retires. il por Newsweek 76:31 Jl 13 '70 *
WHEELER, Harvey
Needed: a new utopianism. Cur 121:30-1 S '70
Politics of ecology. il Sat R 53:51-2+ Mr 7 '70
Rise of the elders. il Sat R 53:14-15+ D 5 '70
WHEELER, Joseph Lewis
What good are public library standards? bibliog il por Library J 95:455-62, 2739 F 1, S 1 '70
WHEELER, Kenneth E.
Small business eyes the four-day workweek. il Harvard Bsns R 48:142-7 My '70
WHEELER, Richard S.
Bitch goddess of individualism. Nat R 22:1346+ D 15 '70
WHEELER, Timothy J.
Tales of Hoffman; poem. Nat R 23:18 Ja 12 '71
WHEELER, Walter, jr
More fun with camellias. il Horticulture 49:32-3+ Ja '71
WHEELER, Walter H.
Walter H. Wheeler of Pitney-Bowes; interview. por Nations Bsns 58:72-8 F '70
WHEELING, W.Va.
Fabric reservoir cover stops bushels of maple seeds. il Am City 85:16 D '70
WHEELOCK, John Hall
By daylight and in dream; poem. New Yorker 46:33 Je 27 '70
Certain hidden place; poem. Am Scholar 39:498-9 Sum '70
Last sonnet. New Yorker 46:34 Jl 11 '70
WHEELS
On the cyclical curves generated by wheels that roll along wheels. M. Gardner. il Sci Am 223:210-12+ S '70

Wheel may aid spacecraft; stabilization of communications satellites. il Space World G-6-78:42-3 Je '70
See also
Automobiles—Wheels
Flywheels
Lunar vehicles—Wheels
Tractors—Wheels
WHEELWRIGHT, Ernie
This saint has been called a sinner. M. Sharnik. il por Sports Illus 32:18-20+ Je 1 '70 *
WHEELWRIGHT, Farley W.
Changes in the black ghetto: Cleveland; white and black Unitarians form separate units. J. G. Mearns. il pors Sat R 53:13-14+ Ag 1 '70 *
WHELAN, Charles M.
Catholic colleges on trial: Tilton v. Finch, II. America 122:122-4 F 7 '70
Catholic colleges pass the test. America 122:368 Ap 4 '70
Walz case. America 122:518-19 My 16 '70
WHEN Eric loved me; story. See Aguallo, T.
WHEN will your friend be leaving, Denny? story. See Goldreich, G.
WHERE sheep may safely graze; story. See Wiser, W.
WHERRY, Don M.
Build an audio multicoupler. il Pop Electr 33:31-4 Jl '70
WHIPPLE, A. B. C.
Ugly new footprint in the sand. Life 68:20B Mr 20 '70
WHIPPLE, Dorothy Vermilya
Town that was, until ..; photographs. Américas 22:16-20 S '70
WHIRLPOOL corporation
Whirlpool tunes in the consumer; Care-a-van, musical show. Nations Bsns 58:20 Ja '70
WHIRLPOOLS
Maelstrom of the Arctic. O. Osing. il Sea Front 16:104-9 Mr '70
WHIRLWINDS
Miniature whirlwinds produced in the laboratory by high-voltage electrical discharges. R. T. Ryan and B. Vonnegut. bibliog il Science 168:1349-51 Je 12 '70
WHISKERS, Metal. See Metal crystals
WHISKEY
Bourbon: America's brandy. J. T. Elson. Travel & Camera 33:14+ F '70
Bourbon branches out across the water. il Nations Bsns 58:66-7 S '70
Fighting the Scotch tide; Scotland's finest malt whiskies. il Time 95:72 Je 8 '70
Scotch and what? H. McNulty. House & Gard 138:116+ S '70
Scotch: the Highlands' gift to all the world. J. T. Elson. il Travel & Camera 33:59-60+ My '70
Scotch whiskey, by D. Daiches. Review Sat R 53:24+ Ap 11 '70. E. Janeway
Scotch whiskey, a costly blend. A. Hershman. il Duns 95:42-3+ Ap '70
What's the new American light whiskey going to taste like? L. Dowst. il Holiday 47:44-5+ Ap '70
See also
Distilleries
WHISKEY jacks. See Jays
WHISPERS on the wind; musical comedy. See Musical comedies, revues, etc.—Criticisms, plots, etc.
WHISTLES
Aerodynamic whistles. R. C. Chanaud. il Sci Am 222:40-6 bibliog(p 146) Ja '70
See also
Sirens
WHITAKER, Arthur P.
Spain and Portugal: continuity and change. Cur Hist 58:287-91+ My '70
WHITAKER, Bob
Primitive areas, a new designation under BLM. il Liv Wildn 33:12-14 Aut '69
WHITAKER, Frederic
Bettina Steinke, a painter of people. il por Am Artist 35:20-7+ Ja '71
Marjorie Close, San Francisco realist. il por Am Artists 34:20-6+ Ja '70
WHITAKER, Johnny
For Buffy and Jody, two very special rooms. R. Fitzgerald. il por House B 112:37-41 My '70 *
WHITBREAD, Jane
(ed) See Bettelheim, B. New way to raise kids
WHITCOMB, Roberta J.
This has gotta be paradise. il por Outdoor Life 145:46-9+ My '70
WHITE, Edward M.
Writing for nobody. Ed Digest 35:32-3 Mr '70
WHITE, Elwyn Brooks
Browning-off of Pelham Manor. New Yorker 46:49 N 14 '70

WHITE, Elwyn Brooks—*Continued*
I paint what I see; poem. Ramp Mag 9:34 S
   '70
In Charlie's bar; poem. New Yorker 46:36 F
   21 '70
Laura Ingalls Wilder acceptance; address,
   June 30, 1970. il Horn Bk 46:349-51 Ag '70
WHITE, Geraldine M.
B is for apple. il por Redbook 135:8+ My '70
WHITE, Gilbert
Selborne nightingale; excerpt from Spring-
   time in Britain. E. W. Teale. il Audubon
   72:58-67 S '70 *
WHITE, Jim, and Mueller, Marti
Unknown war. Commonweal 92:476-7 S 25 '70
WHITE, John I.
Rebellious horse conquered. il Am West 7:
   18-19 Mr '70
WHITE, Joseph
Toward a black psychology. il por Ebony 25:
   44-5+ S '70
WHITE, Katharine S.
Onward and upward in the garden. New
   Yorker 46:110+ Mr 28 '70
WHITE, Ken
College stores feel the impact of tomorrow;
   excerpts from address. Pub W 197:45-6 My
   4 '70
WHITE, Leigh C.
Ode to the balsam. il Am For 76:8-10 D '70
WHITE, Lynn, jr
Medieval uses of air; with biographical
   sketch. il Sci Am 223:12, 92-100 Ag '70
WHITE, Martha S.
Psychological and social barriers to women
   in science; adaptation of address, Novem-
   ber 22, 1969. bibliog Science 170:413-16 O 23
   '70
WHITE, Merry I.
Reports: Nepal. Atlan 226:26+ Ag '70
WHITE, Patricia Holden
Pie! excerpts. il Ladies Home J 87:70-1+ Ja
   '70
WHITE, Peter T.
Behold the computer revolution. il por Nat
   Geog 138:593-633 N '70
WHITE, Philip L.
Let's talk about food. See issues of Today's
   health
WHITE, Richard
Educated man in the age of Aquarius; ad-
   dress, June 7, 1970. Vital Speeches 36:638-9
   Ag 1 '70
WHITE, Robert I.
Man in the middle. por Time 96:81 N 23 '70 *
WHITE, Ruth
Face to face with the girl behind the sword.
   por Seventeen 29:86 My '70 *
WHITE, Shari
On the boards. por Dance Mag 44:24 Ap '70 *
WHITE, Sheldon
Plus color teevee; poem. Good H 171:10 O '70
WHITE, Theodore Harold
Direct elections: an invitation to national
   chaos. por Life 68:4 Ja 30 '70
Episode in Tokyo Bay. Atlan 226:53-9 Ag '70
How do we get from here to there? il Life
   68:36-40+ Je 26 '70
Proposal to end the Vietnam fighting. Sat
   R 53:23-5+ Mr 21 '70
WHITE, William Gregg
Trucker takes to the sea and air. il por
   Bsns W p44-5+ O 3 '70 *
WHITE, William Mathews, 1939-
High flier comes back with a thud. por Bsns
   W p24 Jl 25 '70 *
WHITE alcohol. See Liquors
WHITE alder. See Alder
WHITE Anglo-Saxon Protestants. See WASPS
   (white Anglo-Saxon Protestants)
WHITE bread. See Bread
WHITE Cloud wilderness area. See Wilderness
   areas—Idaho
WHITE collar workers. See Office workers
WHITE consolidated industries, inc.
Merger of Whites eases grip on Allis. Bsns
   W p22-3 Ag 22 '70
White upon White; proposed merger. il
   Forbes 106:19-21 N 1 '70
WHITE dwarf stars. See Stars, Dwarf
WHITE fir. See Fir
WHITE House
How government would limit protesters near
   White House. il U S News 69:25 Jl 27 '70
Leak in the kitchen. Newsweek 76:101 O 19
   '70
Nixon touch in the White House. il por
   U S News 69:24-6 D 28 '70
Recollections of the fishbowl: Lady Bird's
   White House diary. por Time 96:18 N 9 '70

History
'Twas the night before Christmas .. ; fire,
   1929. R. D. Heinl, jr. il por Am Heritage
   22:105-9 D '70
Libraries
White House home library. bibliog il Pub W
   197:47-52 Mr 2 '70
WHITE House conference on aging, 1971 (pro-
   posed)
Advisory committee named for White House
   conference on aging. Aging 191:3+ S '70
Half million older Americans to tell needs
   in September forums. Aging 190:3 Ag '70
New England is first region to hold pre-
   White House parley. Aging 182:5+ D '69
1971 White House conference on aging: a
   message to older Americans. J. B. Martin.
   Aging 184:3 F '70
1¼ million older Americans speak in 6000
   White House local forums. Aging 193:4-5 N
   '70
Quotations from the commissioner. J. B.
   Martin. il por Aging 188:8 Je; 190:10-11 Ag
   '70
Stage setting for White House conference.
   R. O. Beckman. il por Har Yrs 10:42-4 Jl
   '70
This month's All-senior forums voice needs
   for 1971 conference. T. Schuchat. Har Yrs
   10:4 S '70
White House conference activities begin in
   Senior citizens month. il Aging 186:3 Ap '70
White House conference planning board
   makes recommendations on conference. il
   Aging 193:3+ N '70
WHITE House conference on children and
   youth, 1970
Adults at work; battle between organizers
   and dissidents. Newsweek 76:58-9 D 28 '70
American family: future uncertain; with com-
   ment by U. Bronfenbrenner. il Time 96:34-
   9 D 28 '70
Children's week. Newsweek 76:79 D 14 '70
Closing the generation gap: search for a na-
   tional policy; interview. S. Hess. il por U S
   News 68:56-9 F 16 '70
Continuing a tradition. R. E. Cohen. il Am
   Ed 6:7-8 D '70
Youth alienation: myths and realities; ad-
   aptation of address. S. Hess. il Parks & Rec
   5:16-20+ Ag '70
Youth conference planning under way. J.
   Lloyd. Sr Schol 96:Schol Teach 2 F 16 '70
WHITE House conference on food, nutrition and
   health
Citizens vs. hunger. il PTA Mag 64:22-4 Ja;
   30 F '70
Let's talk about food. P. L. White. Todays
   Health 48:14-15 My '70
Message from the President's nutrition con-
   sultant. J. Mayer. Todays Health 48:51 F
   '70
White House conference urges nutritional
   aids for elderly. Aging 184:19 F '70
White House panel. AoA. chart moves on nu-
   trition for aging. Aging 191:16 S '70
WHITE House conference on the drug problem.
   See Drug abuse—Conferences
WHITE House council on environmental quality.
   See United States—Council on environmen-
   tal quality
WHITE House entertaining. See Government
   entertaining
WHITE House murder case: drama. See Feif-
   fer, J .
WHITE House of the Confederacy. See Rich-
   mond, Va.—Galleries and museums
WHITE House office. See United States—Ex-
   ecutive office of the president
WHITE House pets. See Pets
WHITE House photography. See Photography,
   Journalistic
WHITE House staff. See Public officers
WHITE lies. See Lying
WHITE motor corporation
Rough-weather test. il Forbes 105:26-7 Je
   15 '70
White upon White; proposed merger. il
   Forbes 106:19-21 N 1 '70
WHITE-Negro relations. See Race relations
WHITE PASS and Yukon railway
From Skagway to Whitehorse, with your car
   on a flatcar. il Sunset 144:58+ My '70
WHITE pine blister rust. See Pine—Diseases
   and pests
WHITE racism. See Racism
WHITE rhinoceros. See Rhinoceros
WHITE sales. See Bargain sales
WHITE Sox (baseball) See Baseball clubs
WHITE tailed deer. See Deer

WHITE tailed deer hunting. See Deer hunting

WHITE-water racing. See Kayak racing

WHITE, Weld and company
Where the money talk is multilingual. il Bsns
W p76-8 Ap 4 '70

WHITEFISH fishing
Whitefish'll get you. B. W. Dalrymple. il pors
Outdoor Life 146:60-1+ Jl '70

WHITEHEAD, Charles
Education of an organic farmer. il pors Org
Gard & Farm 17:33-7 N '70

WHITEHEAD, Don
Murder in Mississippi; condensation of Attack on terror. il Read Digest 97:191-6+ S
'70

WHITEHEAD, Helen, pseud.
Opinion; the news weeklies and women. Mlle
71:36+ S '70

WHITEHORN, Ethel
Motion picture previews. See issues of PTA
magazine

WHITELAW, Aubrey H.
Future polar transport. il Sea Front 16:206-
10 Jl '70

WHITESIDE, Thomas
Annals of advertising. New Yorker 46:42-8+
D 19 '70
Department of amplification. New Yorker 46:
78+ Je 20 '70
Reporter at large. New Yorker 45:32-8+ F 7;
46:124-9 Mr 14; 64-6+ Jl 4 '70

WHITLOCK, David
Sculpin and its imitations. il Field & S 75:114-
16 S '70

WHITMAN, Ruth
Castoff skin; poem. Nation 210:245 Mr 2 '70
Nap at Sunion; Zion; poems. New Repub 162:
20, 23 Ja 17 '70

about
Comment. M. Van Duyn. Poetry 115:433-9 Mr
'70 *

WHITMORE, James
Old cowhand; Will Rogers' U.S.A. at Wash-
ington's Ford theatre. N. MacNeil. il por
Time 96:76 S 28 '70 *
Theater; performance of Will Rogers' U.S.A.
H. Hewes. Sat R 53:19 O 10 '70 *

WHITMORE, Ken
Ken Whitmore. il Pop Phot 66:66-75 F '70 *

WHITNER, Barbara
Teaching how to cheat. il por Time 96:18+
O 5 '70 *

WHITNEY, Charles A.
Forms in the sky; with biographical sketch.
il por Natur Hist 79:4, 26-31 Ja '70

WHITNEY, Edgar A.
Painting watercolor portraits. il Am Artist
34:38-43 Ag '70

WHITNEY, John O.
Better results from retail advertising. il Harvard Bsns R 48:111-20 My '70

WHITNEY, Stephen
Library system trustee. bibliog por Library
J 95:636-9 F 15 '70

WHITNEY-Fidalgo seafoods, inc.
Salmon packer hits golden run. il Bsns W
p33 Jl 25 '70

WHITNEY museum of American art, New York
Art world; annual and the Bauhaus. H. Ro-
senberg. New Yorker 46:82+ F 21 '70
Modular; exhibition of house at the Whitney
museum. New Yorker 46:27-8 O 3 '70
Out of the junkyard; sculpture exhibition. R.
Hughes. il Time 97:50-1 Ja 4 '71
Showdown at the annual; sculpture exhibi-
tion. D. Davis. il Newsweek 76:65 D 28 '70

WHITSON, Dorothy
1970 census. il Todays Ed 59:30-2+ Ja '70

WHITTAKER, James K.
Developing a unified theory of residential
treatment. bibliog Ment Hy 54:166-9 Ja '70
Training child care staff; pitfalls and promises.
Ment Hy 54:516-19 O '70

WHITTAKER corporation
Whittaker; too far too fast? T. J. Murray.
il por Duns 95:28-31+ F '70

WHITTEMORE, Reed
Foxy loxy's Christmas happiness; poem. New
Repub 163:24-5 D 5 '70
Tough martyr. New Repub 162:27-8 Ap 18 '70

WHITTEN, David N. See Boynton, R. M. jt.
auth.

WHITTEN, Phillip. See Robertson, I. jt. auth.

WHITTIER, Bob
Be your own boat tester. il Pop Mech 133:
126-9+ Mr; 156-9+ Ap; 140-3 My '70

WHITTIER, Susan
Susan; our beginning cook. See issues of
Good housekeeping

WHITTIER, Calif.
Enclave; being a non-Quaker. M. F. K. Fisher. New Yorker 46:36-42 S 5 '70
Enclave; Episcopal baptism at the age of
twelve in Quaker community of Whittier.
M. F. K. Fisher. New Yorker 46:48-50 D 12
'70

Enclave; Great London circus. M. F. K.
Fisher. New Yorker 46:175-6+ N 14 '70
Enclave; music in school, at home and
around town. M. F. K. Fisher. New Yorker
46:35-9 O 3 '70

WHITTIER college, Whittier, Calif.
Reunion with Whittier '34; President Nixon's
invitation. il por Life 69:24-5 Jl 24 '70

WHITTINGTON, Betty
Concours d'elegance. il Har Yrs 10:26-7 My
'70

WHITTON, Robert
Architect speaks his mind; interview. por
House & Gard 137:22+ Ap '70

about
How a talented architect stretched his building dollar. A. Stagg. il House & Gard 137:
110-15 Ap '70 *

WHITWORTH, William
(ed) See Rostow, E. V. Reporter at large

about
Profiles; H. Sanders. por New Yorker 45:40-
6+ F 14 '70

WHO cares? ballet. See Ballets—Criticisms

WHO killed mankind? story. See Wylie, P.

WHOLE earth catalog. See Catalogs, Mail order

WHOLE earth cooperative
Campus whole earth co-op. J. Minnich. il
Org Gard & Farm 17:73-7 S '70

WHOLE Madeline; story. See Madocs, R.

WHOLESALE price index. See Price indexes

WHOLESALE trade

Finance
Ratios of the wholesalers; with table (cont)
Duns 96:72-3 O '70

WHOLESALERS, Book. See Book jobbers

WHOOPING cranes. See Cranes (birds)

WHY is this fish smiling? story. See Ibbotson,
E.

WHYTE, Martin K.
Rural Russia today. il Trans-Action 7:26-32
Ja '70

WHYTE, William Foote
Rural Peru; peasants as activists. il por
Trans-Action 7:37-47 N '69

WHYTE, William H.
Ten ways to make your city more attractive.
House & Gard 138:100-1 S '70

WICHERS, Edward, and Peiser, H. S.
1969 table of atomic weights. il Chem 43:38-41
Jl '70

WICHERT, Edwin
Symbolizing recreation. il Parks & Rec 5:52
Ap '70

WICHITA, Kan.

Education
Local associaton of the month. L. Streiff.
Todays Ed 59:14+ Mr '70

Street traffic
Narrow beam left-turn signals eliminate conflicts. C. Boyle. il Am City 85:134 My '70

WICHITA FALLS, Tex.
Make information systems work for you. G. G.
Fox. il Am City 85:108+ Mr '70

WICK, Gerald L.
Gravitational waves; the evidence mounts. bibliog il Science 167:1237-9 F 27 '70
Parity-violating nuclear forces. bibliog il Science 168:104-5 Ap 3 '70

WICKER, Tom
Communication versus polarization. Cur 114:
48-9 Ja '70
Nixon's first year. New Repub 162:17-20
Ja 24 '70

about
Fanatics at play. W. F. Buckley, jr. Nat R
22:272 Mr 10 '70 *
March with us, Mr Wicker! Nat R 22:
1202-3 N 17 '70 *
Weatherman Wicker. Nat R 22:1039 O 6 '70 *

WICKERD, Fran. See Wickerd, R. jt. auth.

WICKERD, Ron, and Wickerd, Fran
Canterbury pilgrims today. il Travel 134:34-
9+ D '70

WICKERHAM, Lyferd J. and others
Sexual reproduction in candida lipolytica.
bibliog Science 167:1141 F 20 '70

WICKS, Harry
How to work with plastic laminates. il Pop
Mech 133:154-9+ Mr '70
(ed) See Corsak, S. Build this poolhouse for
less than $500

WIDE-angle lenses. See Lenses, Photographic

WIDES, Jeffrey W. and Stotlar, D. W.
  Urban votes. New Repub 162:9 Je 27 '70
WIDICK, B. J.
  Suffering majority. Nation 210:616-19 My 25
  '70
WIDMER, Kingsley
  Anarchism in revival. Nation 211:501-3 N 16
  '70
  Censorship by harassment. Nation 210:366-9
  Mr 30 '70
  Rage against violence. il Nation 211:45-8 Jl
  20 '70
WIDMOYER, Fred B. and Sullivan, D. T.
  Pecan tree. Horticulture 48:20-1 Mr '70
WIDOW to widow program. See Widows—Ad-
  justment
WIDOWS
  My island of life. K. Westfall. il por Redbook
  135:26+ Ag '70

          Adjustment
  Widow as a caregiver in a program of preven-
  tive intervention with other widows. P. R.
  Silverman. bibliog Ment Hy 54:540-7 O '70
WIECK, Paul R.
  Justice for all on the defensive. New Repub
  162:12 F 21 '70
  They're after Adlai. New Repub 163:13-15
  S 26 '70
  What happened to the new politics? New Re-
  pub 162:12-13 F 28 '70
WIEDEL, Suzanne
  Cross country. il Travel & Camera 33:32-5 D
  '70
  Galapagos. il Travel & Camera 33:46-9+ Je
  '70
  Isles of Greece: the Cyclades. il Travel &
  Camera 33:36-41+ O '70
WIEDER, Laurance
  Gift for some reason; poem. Poetry 115:393
  Mr '70
WIEN, Lawrence Arthur
  It's the individual investment that counts;
  interview. pors Forbes 106:42-4 N 1 '70
WIENER, Isidor
  Grand Pa Wiener, painter of many worlds. J.
  Bock. il Antiques 98:266-9 Ag '70 *
WIENER, Lily
  Hydropsychotherapy: help for the disturbed
  on a water couch. A. Hamilton. il pors Sci
  Digest 67:59-63 Je '70 *
WIER, Ester
  Developing the adolescent's self concept with
  literature; The loner. F. Fennimore. bibliog
  f Engl J 59:1272-5+ D '70 *
WIESEL, Eliezer
  Elie Wiesel: a soul on fire. C. Leviant. il Sat
  R 53:25-8 Ja 31 '70
WIESMAN, Walter
  Effective communication; address, July 1970.
  Vital Speeches 36:723-5 S 15 '70
WIESMANN, Ulrich, and Neufeld, E. F.
  Scheie and Hurler syndromes: apparent iden-
  tity of the biochemical defect. bibliog il Sci-
  ence 169:72-4 Jl 3 '70
WIESNER, Jerome B.
  Arms control: current prospects and prob-
  lems. il Bul Atom Sci 26:6-8+ My '70
WIETERS, Nelson E.
  Let's talk about a new ACA. por Camp Mag
  42:4 Ja '70
  My goals for camping: statements from
  presidential candidates. il por Camp Mag
  42:7 N '70
WIGGINS, Charles E.
  Excerpt from debate, September 17, 1969.
  Cong Digest 49:29+ Ja '70
WIGS
  All about hairpieces. il Mlle 70:210-12 F '70
  All wigged out. il Mlle 71:162-3 O '70
  City individualist with an Indian-country air;
  pin-on braids. C. Bartel. il Am Home 73:16+
  Mr '70
  Fabulous new wigs for everyone! il Red-
  book 135:80-5+ Ag '70
  Heady growth in women's wigs. il Bsns W
  p32-3 S 5 '70
  Hirsute hats for the '70s; stretch wigs on its
  way to the top. il Time 95:36 F 2 '70
  Kenneth discusses wigs. Kenneth. pors Harp
  Baz 104:121 Ja '71
  Kindest uncut of all. il Life 68:34-34B Mr 20
  '70
  Little wigs for little girls. il Life 69:34-6
  O 16 '70
  Rugs and plugs; toupees. il Time 95:50-1 Je
  8 '70
  What a wonderful beauty idea. il Harp Baz
  103:86 Mr '70
  Wig and I. B. Tupper. il Farm J 94:80 Mr '70
  Wigolution. Vogue 155:136-7 F 15 '70
  Wild wig wave. J. L. Block. Read Digest 96:
  103-5 Ja '70

          Anecdotes, facetiae, satire, etc.
  Great hair switch. E. Bombeck. il Good H
  170:16+ Ja '70
WIIK, H. B. and Ojanpera, Pentti
  Chemical analyses of lunar samples 10017,
  10072, and 10084. bibliog il Science 167:531-2
  Ja 30 '70
WIKSWO, John, and Wikswo, John, Jr
  Amateur scientist; ambitious observatory is
  built by father and son. il Sci Am 222:114-
  18+ Ap '70
WIKSWO, John, Jr.   See Wikswo, John, jt.
  auth.
WILBUR, Marion
  Easter eggs every day. il Org Gard & Farm
  17:76-9 Ap '70
  Woman can build a hothouse. il Org Gard &
  Farm 17:83-5 Ja '70
WILBUR, Richard
  Comment. M. Benedikt. Poetry 115:422-5 Mr
  '70 *
WILBUR, Thomas P. and Donovan, D. L.
  Developing and maintaining excellent teach-
  ers. bibliog Clear House 44:501-3 Ap '70
WILBUR, story. See Rosten, L.
WILCOX, David H. Jr. and Miles, W. D.
  Missing medal. bibliog il Chem 43:13 F '70
WILCOX, Frank Nelson
  Frank N. Wilcox: a review of his last book.
  N. Kent. il Am Artist 34:30-1+ Ap '70 *
WILCOX, Preston
  Kids will decide and more power to them. il
  por Ebony 25:134-7 Ag '70
WILD apples. See Apples
WILD boar hunting
  Hunting in Iran: wild boar and red sheep.
  E. A. Bauer. il por Outdoor Life 146:44-7+
  Jl '70
WILD daisies. See Fleabanes
WILD dogs
  On the hunt with the wild dogs of Africa;
  Cape hunting dogs. G. W. Frame. il Sci
  Digest 67:33-8 Je '70
WILD ducks. See Ducks, Wild
WILD flower gardens. See Gardens, Wild
WILD flowers
  Baby blue eyes, tidytips, Matilija poppy
  mariposa lily; want to have a try? il Sun-
  set 145:174-5 S '70
  Bulbs from our West. M. G. Schmidt. il Hor-
  ticulture 48:14-17 N '70
  Flowers of Rainier. D. Muench. il Nat Wild-
  life 8:22-7 Je '70
  On the trail of Connecticut's wild spring
  flowers. M. Perry. il Home Gard 57:64-5
  Ap '70
  Summer wild flowers. K. S. Taylor. il Horti-
  culture 48:34-5+ Ag '70
  There's variety in wild flowers. E. F. Stef-
  fek. il Horticulture 48:34-5+ Ap '70
  Wildflower expert speaks his mind; interview.
  G. D. Aiken. House & Gard 138:56-7 N '70
    See also
  Gardens, Wild

          Photographs
  Smokies spring; excerpts from Southern
  wilderness. E. Porter. il Audubon 72:32-9
  My '70
WILD food. See Food, Wild
WILD gardens. See Gardens, Wild
WILD geese. See Geese, Wild
WILD life. See Wildlife
WILD plants. See Plants
WILD rice
  Wild ricing: Minnesota. R. H. Hofstrand. il
  por(p8) Natur Hist 79:50-5 Mr '70
WILD rivers. See Rivers
WILD Saturday; story. See Oates, J. C.
WILD sheep. See Mountain sheep
WILD sheep hunting. See Mountain sheep hunt-
  ing
WILD turkeys. See Turkeys, Wild
WILD West shows. See Rodeos
WILDCAT hunting. See Bobcat hunting
WILDCATS. See Bobcats
WILDE, Warren E. See Gemello, L. jt. auth.
WILDER, Billy
  Private life of Billy Wilder. J. McBride and
  M. Wilmington. il por Film Q 23:2-9 Sum
  '70 *
WILDER, L. V.
  Malnourished bodies, malnourished minds.
  PTA Mag 64:10-12+ bibliog(p33) Mr '70
WILDER, Lawrence Douglass
  Full text of Wilder address. Negro Hist Bul
  33:100-1 Ap '70

WILDER, Marjorie
Comesin goes to a special launching. il Yachting 128:60-2+ D '70

WILDER, Myron
Pause; poem. Nation 211:183 S 7 '70

WILDER, Thornton Niven
Our town. Criticism
Commentary 49:20+ Mr '70 *
Commonweal 91:430-1 Ja 16 '70

WILDER award
Laura Ingalls Wilder acceptance; address, June 30, 1970. E. B. White. il Horn Bk 46: 349-51 Ag '70
Newbery-Caldecott and Ingalls awards. il Wilson Lib Bul 44:692 Mr '70
Newbery-Caldecott-Wilder awards. il Library J 95:1173 Mr 15 '70
Newbery/Caldecott/Wilder winners. Pub W 198:26 Ag 17 '70

WILDERNESS areas
Congress debates wilderness purity. Liv Wildn 34:57 Spr '70
Desert wilderness. F. R. Fosberg. il Liv Wildn 34:17-24 Spr '70
Let's stop mining in our national parks and wilderness areas; with editorial comment. R. D. Butcher. il Am For 76:11, 28-31+ S '70
Mining the public lands; Alaska and the West. E. N. Layne. il Am Heritage 21:118 Ag '70
Other side of the mountain. P. H. Oehser. il Liv Wildn 33:29-31 Aut '69
Threatened America (cont) il Life 68:52B-54+ Mr 13; 69:58-61 Ag 7 '70
Wilderness and forests tomorrow. K. P. Davis. Cur Hist 59:91-4+ Ag '70
Wilderness concept; excerpt from address, April 4, 1970. M. E. Murie. Liv Wildn 34:63 Sum '70
See also
Forests, State
Trail riders of the wilderness

Alaska

Alaskan wilderness: going, going, gone? C. Hunter. il Nat Parks & Con Mag 44:11-15 N '70
Confrontation. R. Pardo. il Am For 76:32-5+ S '70
Izembek wilderness proposal. W. Troyer. il Liv Wildn 34:17-20 Sum '70
Letter from the Arctic; Brooks Range; excerpts. S. Wright. Am Heritage 21:97 Ag '70

Arizona

Cabeza Prieta, our forgotten wilderness. L. W. Robinson. il Liv Wildn 33:25-8 Aut '69
Primitive areas, a new designation under BLM; Aravaipa and Paria Canyons primitive areas, and Vermillion cliffs natural area. B. Whitaker. il Liv Wildn 33:12-14 Aut '69

California

Hike in isn't easy, but there are rewards; Thousand Lakes wilderness area. il Sunset 144:36+ Je '70
Snow Mountain proposal; wilderness area in Mendocino national forest. Liv Wildn 34:59 Spr '70

Idaho

Idaho White Clouds: wilderness in trouble. J. H. Merriam. il Liv Wildn 34:33-7 Spr '70
Last chance for the White Clouds. M. Dahlstrom and J. Merriam. il Nat Parks & Con Mag 44:9-13 Ag '70
Time bomb at White Clouds. T. Trueblood. il Nat Wildlife 8:4-8 Je '70
White Clouds. B. Norton. il Audubon 72:111 My '70

Maine

Allagash: three years later. L. Stuart. il Parks & Rec 5:23-4+ Ap '70
Isle au Haut, Acadia's wildness area. T. E. Jones. il Nat Parks & Con Mag 44:13-17 Je '70

Michigan

Isle Royale wilderness plan, a job unfinished. G. C. Haber. il Liv Wildn 34:31-7 Sum '70
McCormick tract: new Michigan wilderness. J. Chiappetta. il por Field & S 75:76-7+ My '70
Saving the little wild places. J. D. Dingell. il Nat Wildlife 8:10-11 Ap '70

Minnesota

Mining threatens canoe area; Minnesota's boundary waters canoe area. Nat Parks & Con Mag 44:31 My '70
Of wilderness and wolves; Big Bog wilderness; excerpts. P. L. Errington. il Liv Wildn 33:3-7 Aut '69
Up on the Boundary; Boundary water canoe area, Superior national forest. G. S. James. il Am For 76:24-7+ N '70

Wilderness besieged, the canoe country of Minnesota; Quetico-Superior country. S. F. Olson. il Audubon 72:28-33 Jl '70
Wilderness challenge; proposed mining of Boundary waters canoe area; with reply by R. J. Fleming. il Liv Wildn 34:3-7 Sum '70

Montana

Trails of the Lincoln back country. G. Laycock. il Field & S 75:32-3+ Jl '70

Nevada

Magruder Corridor controversy. W. P. Cunningham and D. W. Scott. Liv Wildn 33:36-9 Aut '69

New York (state)

Saving a mountain: Clausland Mountain. E. N. Layne. il Am Heritage 21:115 F '70

Tennessee

They call it pocket wilderness; Bowaters wilderness areas. J. B. Craig. il Am For 76:22-5+ O '70

Washington (state)

North Cascades, a wilderness plan. J. V. Morris. il Nat Parks & Con Mag 44:10-15 O '70
North Cascades wilderness proposed. il Liv Wildn 34:60-1 Sum '70

Western states

Wildernesses west of the Rockies. Sunset 144: 56-7 Ap '70

WILDERNESS camping. See Camping

WILDERNESS society
For 1970 more than fifty wilderness trips. Sunset 144:58 Ap '70
KAB awards. Liv Wild 34:60 Spr '70

WILDERNESS survival
How to travel safely in the wilds. V. L. Oertle. il Pop Sci 197:82-3 Jl '70
Lost . . . and found! excerpt from Touch of wildness. L. Dietz. il Field & S 75:42-3+ Ag '70
Prescott kids go wild. P. Snook. il por Nat Wildlife 8:4-11 F '70
What would you do in a fix like this? with report by R. Woodbury. il Life 69:85-7 N 27 '70

WILDEY, Robert L. See Trafton, L. M. jt. auth.

WILDFLOWERS. See Wild flowers

WILDFLOWERS, Museum of. See Museums

WILDFOWL trust, Slimbridge, England. See Bird sanctuaries—England

WILDI, Ernst
Say it with lenses. il Pop Phot 67:84-6+ S '70
Update your movie habits. il Mod Phot 34: 94+ Ag '70

WILDLIFE
Evergreens for wildlife. N. Smith. il Nat Wildlife 8:27 D '69
Galapagos. S. Wiedel. il Travel & Camera 33: 46-9+ Je '70
Vanishing wildlife. il Time 95:52+ Je 8 '70
Wildlife of Sinai. W. Ferguson. il Audubon 72:32-41 Mr '70
See also
Zoology

WILDLIFE and pesticides. See Pesticides and wildlife

WILDLIFE conservation
Are hunters murderers? reprint of August 1948 article; with editorial comment. G. Fitz. il Outdoor Life 146:45, 46-7+ Ag '70
Face of starvation; hunting and game conservation. J. B. Trefethen. il Nat Wildlife 7:4-8+ O '69
Glossary of endangered wild animals. il Good H 171:151 Ag '70
Mike Frome. M. Frome. Am For 76:3+ My '70
Mike Frome: endangered tule elk. M. Frome. Am For 76:3 My '70; Discussion. 76:7 S; 77-9 O '70
More wildlife for urban America. J. J. Shomon. il Cons 24:2-7 F '70
Our nongame wildlife needs a helping hand. Audubon 72:103 Jl '70
Seen any wildlife lately? N. Smith. il Nat Wildlife 8:19 F '70
Washington report. L. S. Clapper. See issues of National wildlife
White rhino: the road back. D. S. Henderson. il Nat Parks 44:19-20 Mr '70
Wildlife abounding. M. Bush. Am For 76:40-1 Ja '70
Wildlife; EQ index. il Nat Wildlife 8:32 O '70; Same. Schol Teach Jr/Sr High pA8 O 5 '70

WILDLIFE conservation—*Continued*
Year of the whale. H. Brabyn. il UNESCO Courier 23:65-8 Ag '70
See also
Bird sanctuaries
Birds—Protection
Birds of prey—Protection
Game birds—Protection
Game protection
National wildlife federation
Pesticides and wildlife
Wetlands

Laws and legislation
Endangered species: Congress curbs international trade in rare animals. M. W. Oberle. Science 167:152-4 Ja 9 '70
Furs, fashion, and conservation. Vogue 156:144 S 1 '70
Survival of species; Endangered species conservation act. A. W. Smith. Nat Parks & Con Mag 44:2 Je '70

Africa
Doctor Hibben's New Mexican ark; endangered African species in desert of New Mexico. R. Gannon. il por Sci Digest 68:23-9 O '70

Africa, East
East Africa: making conservation pay. il Time 97:56-7 Ja 11 '71

Alaska
Angry men; plunder of Alaska's wildlife. B. East. il Outdoor Life 146:31-3+ D '70
Hard lessons on a far slope. E. Jensen. il Field & S 74:12+ F '70
Wildlife in Alaska. J. W. Brooks. il Nat Parks & Con Mag 44:28-30 N '70

Australia
Kangaroos, states and conservation. W. Scholes. Sci N 97:564 Je 6 '70

California
Bighorns: wild sheep of California. L. L. Lutz. il Am For 76:28-31 My; 30-1+ Je '70

Idaho
Showdown on the Salmon River range; attempt to save Idaho's bighorns. R. Woodbury. il pors Life 68:54-56A My 22 '70

New York (state)
Environmental deterioration and declining species. J. E. Forbes. il Cons 25:21-6 Ag '70
Teacher tips: environmental deterioration and declining species. J. A. Weeks. Cons 25:27+ Ag '70

South Dakota
Reporter at large; controlling the prairie dog and protecting the black-footed ferret. F. McNulty. New Yorker 46:40-2+ Je 13 '70

WILDLIFE control. See Animal populations—Control
WILDLIFE photography. See Photography of animals
WILDLIFE populations. See Animal populations
WILDLIFE sanctuaries
See also
Bird sanctuaries

Hawaii
Hawaiian Islands of birds; Hawaiian Islands national wildlife refuge. G. Laycock. il Audubon 72:44-61 Ja '70

India
Last stand of the Asiatic lion; Gir wildlife sanctuary. P. Tilden. il Nat Parks & Con Mag 44:14-18 D '70

New York (state)
Sanctuary on the subway; Jamaica Bay wildlife refuge. F. Graham, jr. il Audubon 72:54-9 My '70

South Africa
See also
Kruger National Park

South Dakota
Carnage at Sand Lake; with editorial comment. G. Sherwood. il Audubon 72:66-73, 140-1 N '70

Wisconsin
Green Bay wildlife sanctuary. B. Smits. il Nat Parks & Con Mag 44:21-3 Ag '70

Wyoming
Pryor priority; Pryor Mountain wild horse lands. M. Vandervelde. il Travel 134:54-5+ D '70

WILENSKY, Harold L.
Intelligence in industry: the uses and abuses of experts; excerpts from Organizational intelligence. bibliog f Ann Am Acad 388:46-58 Mr '70
WILENSKY, Rona W.
In my opinion. por Seventeen 29:198 Je '70
WILEY, George Alvin
Champion of welfare rights C. P. DuBose il pors Ebony 25:31-4+ Ap '70 *
WILEY, Harvey Washington
Pre-Nader raider. M. E. Duffy. por Environ 12:24-5 Mr '70 *
WILEY, Irena M.
Only people make you cry. Vogue 156:88-9+ Jl '70
WILEY, John P. Jr
Sky reporter. See issues of Natural history
Space: a barrier to the species. il Natur Hist 79:70-3 Ja '70
WILEY, Marcia
Cabin talk. See issues of Yachting
WILEY, W. Bradford
New voice on the international scene. il por Pub W 198:pt2 158-9 S 21 '70
WILHELMINA (model)
Young is knowing the beauty tricks; interview, ed. by S. Obre. pors Ladies Home J 87:64-5 F '70
WILHELMS, Fred T.
Does humanity grow in your classroom? Schol Teach Jr/Sr High p34-5 S 21 '70
WILHOIT, Francis M.
Is Warren G. Harding really dead? Commonweal 92:181-4 My 8 '70
WILINSKY, Harriet
Retailing. il Seventeen 29:130-1+ F '70
WILK, Max
Why don't you take the boy fishing? il Field & S 74:72-3+ Ap '70
WILKERSON, Cathlyn
House on 11th street. il pors Newsweek 75:29-30 Mr 23 '70 *
House on 11th street. il Time 95:10 Mr 23 '70 *
Two girls from no. 18. J. Neary. il pors Life 68:26-9 Mr 27 '70 *
WILKES, Paul
Ali MacGraw. il pors Look 34:26-30 Ag 11 '70
F. Lee Bailey, headhunter. il pors N Y Times Mag p34-5+ S 20 '70
Mother superior to Women's lib. il pors N Y Times Mag p27-9+ N 29 '70
Sex and the married couple. il Atlan 226:82-4+ D '70
Why real-life detective stories so often end with a rubber stamp. il N Y Times Mag p32-3+ Ap 19 '70
WILKIE, Richard W.
Creative cruising. il Yachting 127:66-7+ F '70
WILKINS, M. H. F. and others
Some misconceptions on Fourier analysis and Watson-Crick base pairing. bibliog Science 167:1693-4 Mr 27 '70
WILKINS, Roy
Integration. por Ebony 25:54-6+ Ag '70
Not so benign. Cur 118:30-1 My '70
WILKINS, Sophie
Do's and don'ts for translators. Writer 83:27 F '70
WILKINSON, Andrew
Concept of oracy. Engl J 59:71-7 Ja '70
WILKINSON, Martha
Oh, Prez, where is thy ring? M. Mulvoy. por Sports Illus 33:42-3 Ag 31 '70 *
WILKINSON, Stephan
Flying visit. Flying 86:128 F; 87:109 Ag; 114 O '70
Reporting points. See issues of Flying
Safety check. Flying 86:28+ My '70
WILL, George F.
Right to be nude. Nat R 22:832 Ag 11 '70
WILL, James E. See Rigdon, V. B. jt. auth.
WILL
Four essays on liberty, by I. Berlin. Review Commonweal 91:492-3 Ja 30 '70. A. Nebolsine
Yes begins with a no; theories of R. May. il por Time 95:66+ Je 22 '70
WILLAMETTE national forest, Ore. See National forests
WILLAPA BAY
Death row. R. M. Pyle. il Audubon 72:145 N '70
WILLARD, Nedd
Hidden factors in the geography of cancer. il UNESCO Courier 23:27-9 My '70
WILLATT, Norris
Wife who listened. il por Duns 95:53-4+ Ja '70
WILLCOX, Alanson F.
New professionals. bibliog Ment Hy 54:347-56 Jl '70
WILLE, Lois
Moms are a must. il Am Ed 6:24-9 Ap '70

WILLENS, Harold
Businessmen against the war (sic) S. Weissman. il Ramp Mag 9:33-4 D '70 *
WILLENSON, Kim
Templed cities of Thailand. il Travel & Camera 33:60-9 Mr '70
WILLERMAN, Lee, and others
Intellectual development of children from interracial matings. bibliog il Science 170:1329-31 D 18 '70
WILLETTS, Sandra
Summer campus on the S.S. Carina. il Hi Fi sec II 20:10-11 F '70
WILLEY, Ruth L. and others
Symbiosis between euglena and damselfly nymphs is seasonal. bibliog il Science 170:80-1 O 2 '70
WILLIAMS, A. R. and others
Hemolysis near a transversely oscillating wire. bibliog il Science 169:871-3 Ag 28 '70
WILLIAMS, Al
Constant-speed motors for tape recorders. il Radio-Electr 41:49 O '70
WILLIAMS, Albert L.
Mr Williams to head commission on trade and investment policy. Dept State Bul 62:699 Je 1 '70 *
WILLIAMS, Andy
Why I named my son after Robert Kennedy. il pors Ladies Home J 87:50+ Ja '70

about

To air is human to forgive impossible. G. Ace. Sat R 53:6 N 21 '70 *
WILLIAMS, Barbara Fischer-. See Fischer-Williams, B.
WILLIAMS, C. Dickerman
Cooper-Church amendment: is it constitutional? Nat R 22:731-3, 1069+ Jl 14, O 6 '70
WILLIAMS, Clarence, 3d
Star couple. L. Robinson. il pors Ebony 25:142-4+ Mr '70 *
WILLIAMS, Dick
Team that eats managers. M. Mulvoy. il por Sports Illus 32:20-1 Mr 16 '70 *
WILLIAMS, Don I.
How to unswamp a canoe. il Outdoor Life 146:66-7 Jl '70
WILLIAMS, Edward Bennett
There has been a terrible breakdown in criminal justice: excerpts from interview, February 15, 1970; ed. by J. McCaffrey. il por U S News 68:20-1 Mr 16 '70
What's needed to speed up justice; interview. il pors U S News 69:94-8 S 21 '70
WILLIAMS, Edward Christopher
Edward Christopher Williams: librarian's librarian; address, June 24, 1968. E. J. Josey. bibliog Negro Hist Bul 33:70-7 Mr '70 *
WILLIAMS, Elliot W.
From psychiatric aide to psychologist. bibliog Ment Hy 54:430-2 Jl '70
WILLIAMS, Ellsworth
Big loader offsets burning ban. il Am City 85:60-1 D '70
WILLIAMS, Emlyn
Williams as Thomas. R. Jacobson. por Sat R 53:74 Ap 25 '70 *
WILLIAMS, George Huntston
Loyalty and dissent: perspectives from history. America 122:669-71 Je 27 '70
WILLIAMS, George L.
Beyond the classroom: life experiences in the field. Clear House 45:81-5 O '70
WILLIAMS, Gordon
Ultimate hustle. Newsweek 76:31 N 9 '70 *
WILLIAMS, Harrison A. Jr
Franchising, solid gold or quicksilver? il Har Yrs 10:19-23 N '70
WILLIAMS, Herb
Action on the color front. il por Outdoor Life 146:72-5+ Ag '70
WILLIAMS, Hollis R.
Story framed in pines. il por Am For 76:20-3 Jl '70
WILLIAMS, Hosea
I expect more Jacksons; remarks. ed. by P. Range. por Time 95:11 Je 1 '70
WILLIAMS, James Robert
West of Out our way. F. Egan; W. H. Hutchinson. il Am West 7:18-25 My '70 *
WILLIAMS, Joan
Questions for writers. Writer 83:18-20+ D '70
WILLIAMS, John Bell
Crisis in Southern schools: interview. il por(p39) U S News 68:41 F 16 '70
School desegregation problems: address, January 3, 1970. Vital Speeches 36:306-9 Mr 1 '70
WILLIAMS, Jud
Troubleshoot color TV with transistor curve tracer. il Radio-Electr 41:64-6 Je '70
WILLIAMS, Lawrence, and Espy, H. C.
Luckiest girl in Iowa; story. Good H 171:76-7 N '70

WILLIAMS, Lynn
How to sell letter stock. Duns 96:51-2+ N '70
WILLIAMS, Margaret
Crew for Galatea. il Yachting 128:63+ D '70
WILLIAMS, Margery
Velveteen rabbit; story. il McCalls 97:84-5 Ap '70
WILLIAMS, Martin, and others
Month's jazz. Am Rec G 36:852-3 Je '70
WILLIAMS, Mason
Whimsy, philosophy, music. N. Johnson. New Repub 163:38-40 O 31 '70 *
WILLIAMS, Maxcine
Plants of the Far North. il Horticulture 48:28-30+ Jl '70
WILLIAMS, Melvin G.
Mystery, history, and an ancient graveyard. il Todays Ed 59:42-3 My '70; Same abr. Ed Digest 36:20-1 O '70
WILLIAMS, Milton
Secrets of a great party giver; with recipes. il por House & Gard 138:127-30+ N '70
Unusual party drinks from a great party giver. il House & Gard 138:126+ N '70
WILLIAMS, Norman, Jr
(ed) Zoning and planning decisions. See issues of American city
WILLIAMS, Pat
Loop has gone hoops-a-daisy. F. DeFord. il Sports Illus 32:18-19 F 9 '70 *
WILLIAMS, Patricia M.
Where have all the pandas gone? il Sci Digest 68:76-81 S '70
WILLIAMS, Ralph Vaughan. See Vaughan Williams, R.
WILLIAMS, Raymond
Saying no to Labour. Nation 210:710-12 Je 15 '70
WILLIAMS, Robert C.
Memory's defense: the real life of Vladimir Naboko's Berlin. Yale R 60:241-50 D '70
WILLIAMS, Robert Francis
Where are they now? il por Newsweek 76:8 Ag 3 '70 *
WILLIAMS, Robert H.
Morton Sobell, slightly at large. Esquire 73:190-1 Mr '70
WILLIAMS, Roger
Profits: a fruit of productivity. por Nations Bsns 58:101 O '70
WILLIAMS, Roger M.
Having fun with Florida. il Nation 211:109-14 Ag 17 '70
Wallace rides again. New Repub 162:12-13 Mr 21 '70
WILLIAMS, Roger Neville
New exodus: go north, young man. New Repub 162:15-16 My 16 '70
WILLIAMS, Ruth M.
Pretty thing for me. il Sch Arts 69:40 Mr '70
WILLIAMS, S. Irene
Survey of the teaching of mathematics in secondary schools. Sch & Soc 98:244-6 Ap '70
WILLIAMS, Samuel W.
Religion is justice. por Time 95:72-3 Ap 6 '70
WILLIAMS, Stephen F.
City as a threatened ecosystem. Arch Forum 133:48-9+ S '70
WILLIAMS, T. Harry
Exclusive interview with T. Harry Williams; ed. by P. A. Brock. por Writers Digest 50:26-7+ S '70
WILLIAMS, Ted
Ted Williams, my year. J. Underwood. Sports Illus 32:50-3+ Ja 26 '70
WILLIAMS, Tennessee
Camino real. Criticism
    America 122:140+ F 7 '70
    Commentary 49:20+ Mr '70 *
    Nation 210:93-4 Ja 26 '70
    New Yorker 45:50+ Ja 17 '70
    Sat R 53:24 Ja 24 '70
Open response to Tom Buckley. Atlan 227:34 Ja '71
Tennessee Williams survives. T. Buckley. il por Atlan 226:98-106+ N '70; Discussion. 227:34-5 Ja '71 *
WILLIAMS, Thomas
My hard hat problem, and yours. il Esquire 74:138-44 O '70
Paranoia; story. Esquire 74:128-30 N '70
What I did November 15, 1969. Esquire 73:86+ My '70
WILLIAMS, Thomas Dennis
Growing rich on the alien. Nation 211:614-17 D 14 '70
WILLIAMS, Tony
Sound of a lifetime. por Newsweek 75:96 F 9 '70
WILLIAMS, Ursula Vaughan. See Vaughan Williams, U.
WILLIAMS, William Carlos
Art is a country by itself. G. Sorrentino. Nation 211:635-6 D 14 '70 *

WILLIAMS, William Carlos—*Continued*
Art of process. A. Parsons. Nation 211:534-6 N 23 '70 *
Doctor Williams: beautiful blood, beautiful brain; excerpt from introd. to Imaginations. W. Schott. Am Scholar 39:305-9 Spr '70 *
Poet's leap into reality. W. Heyen. por Sat R 53:21-4 Ag 1 '70 *
Red wheelbarrow revisited. H. Kenner. New Repub 163:22-4 D 12 '70 *
Turns of art. M. Maddocks. Time 96:105+ S 21 '70 *
William Carlos Williams, by J. E. Breslin, and The Williams-Siegel documentary, ed. by M. Baird and E. Reiss. Reviews
  Sat R 53:31+ N 14 '70. W. Heyen *
William Carlos Williams and the old world. H. Levin. Yale R 59:520-31 Je '70 *

WILLIAMS and Wilkins company
Suit asks photocopying royalties. J. Walsh. Science 169:959 S 4 '70

WILLIAMS research corporation
Small aircraft turbofans studied. M. L. Yaffee. il Aviation W 92:43-5+ F 9 '70

WILLIAMSBURG, Va.
From Williamsburg, thirty-seven new colors in the colonial palette. R. FitzGerald. il House B 112:82-3 Mr '70

Gardens
18th century day lilies at Williamsburg. V. Blankenship. il Home Gard 57:62-3 F '70

WILLIAMSBURG student burgesses. *See* Forums (discussion and debate)

WILLIAMSON, Alan
April 5, 1968; Aubade, reconstructed in tranquility; poems. Poetry 115:259-60 Ja '70

WILLIAMSON, Audrey
Riddle of the Magic flute. il Hi Fi sec I 20: 66-9 F '70

WILLIAMSON, Clara (McDonald)
Aunt Clara's luminous world; paintings. por Am Heritage 21:47-56 Ag '70

WILLIAMSON, Dereck
Fake fl. Sat R 53:4+ O 10 '70
Shutter shudders. Sat R 53:4 D 5 '70
When your mailbox flunks. Sat R 53:20 Ag 15 '70

WILLIAMSON, Harry
Shade trees. il por Am For 76:26+ O '70

WILLIAMSON, Ruth Lundgren
All about dock lines. il Motor B 125:62-7 Je '70
Companionway. See issues of Motor boating
Getting the galley ready. il Motor B 125:76-7 Ap '70

WILLIAMSON, Wayne E.
New learning center thrives in New York. Clear House 45:26-8 S '70

WILLIAMSTOWN study of environmental problems. *See* Environmental movement—International aspects

WILLINGHAM, Thomas K.
Defendant no. 5. por Newsweek 75:52 F 23 '70 *

WILLIS, Ellen
Five passionate feminists. il pors McCalls 97: 112 Jl '70
Rock, etc (cont) New Yorker 46:112+ F 21; 155+ Ap 18; 181-2+ D 12 '70
Women and the myth of consumerism. il Ramp Mag 8:13-16 Je '70

WILLIS, Robert E.
Perennial outrage: anti-Semitism in the New Testament. Chr Cent 87:990-2 Ag 19 '70

WILLIS, Rosena J.
Obituary
  Negro Hist Bul il pors 33:130 My '70 *

WILLIS, Thomas
City of the big shoulders. il Opera N 35:8-12 O 31 '70

WILLISTON PARK, N.Y
Colonial lights for a colonial setting. C. Dell Vecchio. il Am City 85:110 F '70

WILLMER, John E.
Political evolution and the civil war. il Focus 21:7-12 D '70

WILLOUGHBY, Charles
Children's books capture college market. Pub W 197:41-2 Ap 6 '70 *

WILLOW
Planting
  See Tree planting

WILLS, Christopher
Genetic load; with biographical sketch. il Sci Am 222:26, 98-107 bibliog(p 146) Mr '70

WILLS, Garry
How Nixon used the media, Billy Graham, and the good Lord to rap with students at Tennessee U. il Esquire 74:119-22+ S '70

about
Course of Garry Wills. F. S. Meyer. Nat R 22:791 Jl 28 '70; Reply. G. Meilaender. 22: 925+ S 8 '70 *

WILLS
Just what does an executor or guardian really do? il Good H 170:178 My '70
Tips for testators. K. Donelson and I. Donelson. il Har Yrs 10:39-42 Ag '70
Who is competent to make a will? H. Weihofen and G. L. Usdin. Ment Hy 54:37-43 Ja '70
Yearend review: dusting off a man's will. Bsns W p89 D 5 '70
Your lawyer and your will. L. M. Brown. Bet Hom & Gard 48:26+ Ap '70
  See also
Executors and administrators

WILLSON, Norma
Recalcitrants. Engl J 59:105-8 Ja '70

WILLY, Joseph
Boston housing forecasts a national crisis. America 122:556-9 My 23 '70

WILMINGTON, Michael. *See* McBride, J. jt. auth.

WILMINGTON, Del.
Cooperative lighting brings the shoppers back. il Am City 85:136 S '70

WILMORE, Gayraud S. Jr
Stransky, Wilmore: editors at large. Chr Cent 87:468 Ap 22 '70 *

WILNER, Herbert
Overheated campuses of the Bay area. il Holiday 47:72-3+ Mr '70

WILNER, Isabel
For KG: poem. Horn Bk 46:74 F '70

WILSON, Andrew
How relevant are the rules of war? Cur 114: 3-6 Ja '70

WILSON, D. F. and others
Production of carbon monoxide and gaseous hydrocarbons in seawater: relation to dissolved organic carbon. bibliog il Science 168:1577-9 Je 26 '70

WILSON, Earl
Miami Beach: summer resort. il Travel & Camera 33:14+ Jl '70

WILSON, Edmund
Edmund Wilson's New republic. A. Mizener. New Repub 162:28-30 My 9 '70 *

WILSON, Flip
Evolution of Geraldine. L. Robinson. il pors Ebony 26:176-8+ D '70 *
I don't care if you laugh. por Time 96:71 O 19 '70 *

WILSON, Gill Robb
Editorial; proposed memorial aeronautical science center at the Embry-Riddle aeronautical institute. R. B. Parke. por Flying 86: 40 Mr '70 *

WILSON, Graeme
(tr) *See* Sakutaro, H. Heavenly suicide by hanging; Third patient; Shining hand; Autumn cricket; Small town gelsha water rite; Zoo; Shadow of my former self; Hagitei inn; Early summer

WILSON, H. W, company
  See also
Readers' guide to periodical literature

WILSON, Harold
President Nixon and British Prime Minister Wilson hold talks at Washington; exchange of greetings and toasts, January 27, 1970. Dept State Bul 62:207-11 F 23 '70

about
All's right with the world of Harold Wilson. A. Lewis. il pors N Y Times Mag p 14-15+ Je 14 '70 *
Britain's Wilson: how big a comeback? por U S News 68:106 My 18 '70 *
Cementing a friendship. Time 95:32 F 9 '70
Chairman Wilson. A. Howard. New Repub 162:12-13 My 30 '70 *
Charisma sweepstakes. il pors Newsweek 75: 53 Je 15 '70 *
Harold Wilson; why he's making visit to U.S. por U S News 68:10 F 2 '70
Letter from London. M. Panter-Downes. New Yorker 46:75-7 My 30; 61-2 Jl 4 '70 *
Remarkable recovery. il por Time 95:47 My 11 '70 *
Spring fever. Newsweek 75:61-2 My 11 '70 *
Tories and the unions. A. Howard. New Repub 163:8-9 D 19 '70 *
Tory, Tory, hallelujah. il por Newsweek 75: 30+ Je 29 '70 *
Up against the odds. R. J. Korengold. por Newsweek 75:36+ F 2 '70
Voyage autour de ma chambre. C. Brogan. Nat R 22:897 Ag 25 '70 *
Wilson's visit: concern, but . . . il por U S News 68:9 F 9 '70

WILSON, Hazel
Books for boys and girls. See issues of Parents' magazine & better family living
WILSON, James Q.
Crime & the liberal audience. Commentary 51:71-8 Ja '71
WILSON, James W.
Coast redwood. Horticulture 48:44-5 Ap '70
Douglas fir. il Horticulture 48:44-5+ F '70
Durable succulents. il Horticulture 48:36-7 Je '70
Monterey cypress. Horticulture 48:40-1 Jl '70
WILSON, Jane
Prologue. Bul Atom Sci 26:2-3 Je '70
WILSON, Jane S.
Concerned consumer. Bet Hom & Gard 48: 4+ Mr; 46+ Ap; 12 My; 36 S; 8+ N '70
WILSON, Jerry Vernon
What the police can, and cannot do about crime. il Time 96:34-6+ Jl 13 '70 *
WILSON, John Anthony Burgess. See Burgess, A. pseud.
WILSON, John E.
Protecting a natural beach. il Cons 24:28-31 Ap '70
WILSON, John Leonard, bp
Obituary
Chr Cent por 87:1056-7 S 9 '70. T. Beeson
WILSON, John S.
Jazz. Hi Fi 20:secI 132-3 Ap '70
WILSON, José
Kitchen secrets of five master cooks. il pors House & Gard 138:74-83 Jl '70
WILSON, Joseph Chamberlain
Welfare and pragmatism. Sat R 53:32 My 23 '70
WILSON, Kendrick R. Jr
Kendrick R. Wilson of Avco. por Nations Bsns 58:62-8 Ap '70
WILSON, Lanford
Lemon sky. Criticism
Nation 210:668 Je 1 '70 *
New Repub 162:18+ Je 13 '70 *
New Yorker 46:72 My 30 '70 *
Time 95:63 Je 1 '70 *
WILSON, Laval S.
I didn't know it felt that way. il PTA Mag 64:20-2 Je '70
WILSON, Lois E.
Contour cutting. il Sch Arts 70:36 N '70
WILSON, Lou
In-between tree. il Good H 171:60+ N '70
WILSON, Mary (Baldwin)
This Christmas night; poem. Good H 171: 186 D '70
To Robin, when a baby; excerpt from Selected poems. Good H 172:148 Ja '71

about

New literary light. pors Newsweek 76:44 O 5 '70 *
WILSON, Michael
Violence and non violence in the cure of disease and the healing of patients. Chr Cent 87:756-8 Je 17 '70
WILSON, Mildred T.
What about the middle school? Ed Digest 35: 16-17 Ja '70
WILSON, Mitchell
On being a scientist. Atlan 226:101-2+ S '70
WILSON, Peter M.
Facts and figures. Yachting 127:79+ Ja '70
Facts and the figures. Yachting 129:62+ Ja '71
WILSON, Philip
Art at auction 1968-1969; excerpts. il Antiques 97:398-401 Mr '70
WILSON, R. W.
Attenuation on an earth-space path measured in the wavelength range of 8 to 14 micrometers. il Science 168:1456-7 Je 19 '70
—See Penzias, A. A. jt. auth.
WILSON, Reuel K.
(tr) See Slowacki, J. From the Nile to . . .
WILSON, Richard
Nixon's big gamble. por Look 34:21-5 My 5 '70
WILSON, Robert
Life and times of Sigmund Freud. Criticism Vogue il 156:38+ Ag 1 '70 *
WILSON, Robert C.
New company president: ten steps to failure. il Nations Bsns 58:66-70 D '70
WILSON, Robert Rathbun
Conscience of a physicist. il por Bul Atom Sci 26:30-4 Je '70
WILSON, Sloan
Love letter to the big ditch. Motor B 126:50-1+ N '70
New hope for mechanical morons. Motor B 126:56-7 D '70
Old boats: why I love them. il por Yachting 128:60-2+ Jl '70

WILSON, Stephen C.
Gallery; photographs. Life 68:8-9 Ap 24 '70
WILSON, Tom
Look what photography's doing to greeting cards. R. Bruns. il Pop Phot 67:96-7+ O '70 *
WILSON, V. J. and Wylie, R. M.
Short-latency labyrinthine input to the vestibular nuclei in the pigeon. bibliog il Science 168:124-7 Ap 3 '70
WILSON, W. Frederic
Now everyone can make a 3-D hologram. il Pop Phot 67:82-4 N '70
WILSON, Will R.
Organized crime vs. business; interview, ed. by G. R. Rosen. por Duns 97:10-11+ Ja '71
WILSON, William K.
Record papers and their preservation. bibliog il por Chem 43:8-12 Mr '70
WILSON, William S.
Dan Flavin: flat lux. il por Art N 68:48-51 Ja '70
In the eye of the beholder. il por Art N 68: 52-3+ F '70
WILSON, Woodrow
Words of warning from three presidents; excerpts from address to Congress, April 2, 1917. U S News 69:80+ Jl 27 '70; Same abr. Read Digest 97:115-16 O '70

about

What Princeton really needed; excerpt from Andrew Carnegie. J. F. Wall. il pors Am Heritage 21:91-2 Je '70 *
WILSON in the promise land; drama. See Van Zandt, R.
WILSON library bulletin
At the newsfronts of the world; introduction: small steps and giant leaps. W. R. Eshelman. il Wilson Lib Bul 44:1020-1 Je '70
Our other customers; introduction. W. R. Eshelman. il Wilson Lib Bul 45:465-6 Ja '71
Results: WLB's cover contest for children; with portfolio of work of several of the honorable mentions. R. Bartnofsky. il Wilson Lib Bul 44:632-40 F '70
See also
John Cotton Dana publicity awards
WIMBER, D. E. and Steffensen, D. M.
Localization of 5S RNA genes on drosophila chromosomes by RNA-DNA hybridization. bibliog il Science 170:639-41 N 6 '70
WIMBLEDON tennis tournaments. See Tennis
WIMMER, Helmut K.
Conceptions of the universe; paintings. Natur Hist 70:30-4 D '70
WINANS, Sarah S. and Scalia, Frank
Amygdaloid nucleus: new afferent input from the vomeronasal organ. bibliog il Science 170:330-2 O 16 '70
WINCHESTER, Alice
Rediscovery: Parson Jonathan Fisher. il Art in Am 58:92-9 N '70
WINCHESTER, James H.
Beware those holiday accidents. Read Digest 96:155-8 Ja '70
Camping cookery. il Travel 134:64-6 Jl '70
Niagara Falls. il Travel 133:63-7 Je '70
North of Lisbon. il Travel 134:43-9 Jl '70
Tips for a safer summer. il Read Digest 97: 127-31 Jl '70
Traveler's salvation: soup. il Travel 134:68-70+ N '70
WINCHESTER rifles. See Rifles
WINCKELMANN, Johann Joachim
Winckelmann, by W. Leppmann. Review Sat R 53:32 O 10 '70. R. Payne. *
WIND, Herbert Warren
Sporting scene (cont) New Yorker 46:93-101 My 2; 60-4+ Ag 1; 172-4+ O 10; 154+ D 12 '70
WIND. See Winds
WIND breaks. See Windbreaks
WIND chill factor. See Winds
WIND chimes. See Chimes
WIND ensembles
See also
Phonograph records—Wind ensembles
WIND screens. See Windbreaks
WIND tunnels
Traffic signal wind tunnel tests. il Am City 85:96+ Jl '70
WINDBREAK fences. See Snow fences
WINDBREAKS
North side shelterbelt for our birds. N. W. Bubel. il Org Gard & Farm 17:86-8+ N '70
Plant protection from a windscreen. D. A. Butler. il Home Gard 57:50 O '70
WINDECKER, Leo
Resin in the sun. A. Trammell. il Flying 86: 36-41+ My '70 *

WINDJAMMER (restaurant) See Seattle— Hotels, restaurants, etc.

WINDJAMMER cruises. See Cruising

WINDJAMMERS. See Sailing vessels

WINDLE, William F.
Cerebral hemorrhage in relation to birth asphyxia. bibliog il Science 167:1000-2 F 13 '70

WINDMILLS
Origins of feedback control; mechanisms for controlling windmills. O. Mayr. il Sci Am 223:115-18 O '70

WINDOW air conditioners. See Air conditioning equipment

WINDOW cleaners. See Cleaning compositions

WINDOW curtains and draperies. See Curtains and draperies

WINDOW displays. See Show windows

WINDOW fans. See Electric fans

WINDOW gardening
Joy from a window greenhouse. R. M. Peters. il Home Gard 57:42-3+ S '70
See also
House plants

WINDOW shades
How to sew cafe curtains, Austrian shades, Roman shades, and swags. il Bet Hom & Gard 48:110+ My '70

WINDOWS
Adding a picture window. il Mech Illus 66: 114-17 Ja '70
See also
Automobiles—Windows
Curtains and draperies

WINDOWS, Plastic
Now you can install windows that won't break; Lexan polycarbonate plastic. E. H. Arctander. il Pop Sci 197:97 S '70

WINDS
Circulation and weather of 1969. J. F. Andrews. il Weatherwise 23:4-11+ F '70
Effect of wind sheer. A. Hemenway. il Yachting 127:62-3+ Je '70
Huachuca Mountain wind. D. L. Morgan. il Weatherwise 22:244 D '69
Ragged edge of life; chill factor. J. B. Scott. il Field & S 75:48-9 D '70
Wind chill factor. B. Kevern. il Sci Digest 68:56-9 D '70
See also
Coriolis force
Hurricanes
Tornadoes
Trade winds
Whirlwinds

WINDSHIELD defrosters. See Automobiles— Windshield defrosters

WINDSHIELD wipers. See Automobiles—Windshield wipers

WINDSOR, Charles R. See Fox, S. W. jt. auth.

WINDSOR fund. See Investment trusts

WINE
Beauty through the drinking glass. J. Larmoth. Harp Baz 103:241+ Mr '70
Choosing wines for dinner parties; excerpts from How to eat better for less money. S. Aaron. House & Gard 137:86+ F '70
Counting stars in the wines of California. Bsns W p98 S 19 '70
Good companions, appetizer foods and apéritifs. il Sunset 145:114 S '70
Guide to wine. P. Bartlett. Mlle 70:140 Ja '70
Liebfraumilch. W. Clifford. House B 112:62+ My '70
Little wines from the soul of France. J. T. Elson. il Travel & Camera 33:48-9+ Ap '70
Perspective; literature on wine. J. H. Plumb. il Sat R 53:28 Mr 28 '70
Practical man's guide to wine buying. il Changing T 23:19-22 D '69
Primer of dessert wines and cheeses. Bet Hom & Gard 48:54-5 Je '70
Rhineland is wineland. N. Hazleton. Travel & Camera 33:25-7 O '70
Twenty-question quiz on wine. House B 112: 172-3 Mr '70
Well-favored wines of Alsace. W. Clifford. House B 112:102-4 F '70
Wine in the diet. A. Gingrich. Esquire 73:6 F '70
Wine-lover's tour of the Loire. R. A. De Groot. il House B 112:74-5+ Jl '70
Wine-lover's tour of the Rhone. R. A. De Groot. il House B 112:80-2 Ag '70
Wine-tasting party. W. Clifford. il House B 112:48+ Ap '70
Wine tasting party. il Bet Hom & Gard 48: 28 Ap '70
See also
Champagne
Cookery—Wine
Viticulture

Prices
Old wine at heady prices. il Bsns W p92 Je 6 '70

Storage
Wine storage; looking for ideas? il House B 112:120-1 N '70

WINE making
California wine wizard. N. C. Gray. Am Home 73:42+ N '70
Making your own wine at home. il Sunset 145:89-90+ S '70
Potable hobby. Newsweek 76:100 S 14 '70
Vin du pays; American style. V. Sneider. il Holiday 47:60-1 My '70

WINE racks
Dowels make a wine rack. il Sunset 144:148 My '70
Harvest of portable wine racks. il House B 112:38+ N '70

WINE tasting parties. See Entertaining

WINE trade
Boom that cheers. Newsweek 76:72+ O 26 '70
See also
Wineries

WINEGARTEN, Renee
Jews in the mind of France. Commentary 50:64-8 N '70
Literary revolutionism. Commentary 49:67- 74 Je; 50:18 S '70

WINEKE, William R.
Problems and prospects of evangelical radio. Chr Today 15:3-5 Ja 1 '71

WINERIES
Vintage years for California wineries. il Bsns W p48-50 S 19 '70

WINES, James
Public art and private gallery. il Art in Am 58:74-5 Ja '70

WING, R. Cliff and Mack, P. H.
Wide open for learning. il Am Ed 6:13-15 N '70

WING shooting. See Shooting

WINGO, Walter
How to win at the bargaining table. il Nations Bsns 58:38-42 F '70

WINGS, Airplane. See Airplane wings

WINGSPREAD project. See Chicago—Education

WINICK, Charles
Drug addicts getting younger. il PTA Mag 65:6-8 bibliog(p36) S '70

WINKLEY, Carol K.
Why not an intensive-gradual phonic approach? Ed Digest 36:48-51 S '70

WINNEBAGO industries, inc.
Homes for rent, on wheels. il Bsns W p50 F 14 '70
Why Winnebago is number one. J. M. Liston. il Pop Mech 133:120-5+ My '70

WINNETKA, Ill.
Education
No place to grow; New Trier township's East and West high schools. W. Roberts. il Sat R 53:62-4+ Mr 21 '70

WINSTON, Clara
(tr) See Hesse, H. Klein and Wagner

WINSTON, Richard
Barbarians. il Horizon 12:66-81 Sum '70
(tr) See Hesse, H. Klein and Wagner

WINSTON-SALEM, N.C.
Old Salem; morning star of Moravian faith. R. Findley. il Nat Geog 138:818-37 D '70

WINTER, D. L. See Fields, H. L. jt. auth.

WINTER, Elmer L.
Generating goodwill toward the young. V. Louviere. il por Nations Bsns 58:13 Ag '70

WINTER, Peter M. and Lowenstein, Edward
Acute respiratory failure; with biographical sketches. Sci Am 221:18, 23-9 N '69; 222:6+ Mr '70

WINTER, Ruth
Fiction and fact about bats. il Sci Digest 67:31-5 Ap '70

WINTER
Winter is... J. Bishop. il Read Digest 96: 132-3 Ja '70
Winter walk. R. H. Smiley. il Horticulture 48:18-21 D '70
See also
February
Snow
Snowstorms

Photographs
May day in North Dakota; prairie blizzard. E. Bry. il Audubon 72:57-64 Mr '70

WINTER bouquets. See Flowers, Dried

WINTER camps. See Camps

WINTER cruises. See Cruising

WINTER driving. See Automobile driving

WINTER fishing. See Fishing, Winter

WINTER flowers. See Flowers
WINTER flying. See Aviation—Winter flying
WINTER garden; story. See Frame, J.
WINTER in art. See Nature in art
WINTER Olympics. See Olympic games
WINTER proofing of houses. See Houses—Maintenance and repair
WINTER protection of plants. See Plants, Protection of
WINTER resorts
  Babe in Slatland; Haystack Mountain ski resort. D. Butwin. il Sat R 53:62-3 Ja 31 '70
  Europe's ski safaris. il Travel 134:52-3 D '70
  New accent on après ski; planning Val-Thorens. il por Bsns W p47-8 Ja 31 '70
  Skiing on the French frontier. C. Dreyfus. il Mlle 72:191+ N '70
  Tahoe's king-size winter. M. Olson. il Travel 135:68-70 Ja '71
  Top ten ski resorts of France. A. Rand. il Travel & Camera 33:53-6 D '70
  White gold in France. il Time 95:82-5 Ap 13 '70
  Winter is less than a wonderland. il Bsns W p21 Mr 7 '70
  Yankeeland winter. H. P. Koenig. il Travel 134:28-33 D '70
    See also
  Aspen, Colo.
  Evergreen, Colo.
  Gstaad, Switzerland
  Squaw Valley, Calif.
  Sugarbush Valley, Vt.
  Sun Valley, Idaho
WINTER rug; story. See Brautigan, R.
WINTER sports
  See also
  Fishing, Winter
  Skibobs and skibobbing
  Skis and skiing

    Safety devices and measures
  Tips to prevent winter-sports accidents. il Good H 170:132-3 Ja '70
WINTER vacations. See Vacations
WINTERICH, John Tracy
  Obituary
    Pub W 198:249 Ag 31 '70
    Sat R 53:24 S 12 '70. R. Girson •
  Sergeant Cuff; retirement. Sat R 53:36 Je 27 '70 •
WINTERNATIONALS. See Automobile racing
WINTERS, Francis X.
  Rule of thumb for politicians. America 123:11-12 Jl 11 '70
WINTERS, Shelley
  One night stands of a noisy passenger. Criticism
    Newsweek il 77:80 Ja 11 '71 •
WINTERTHUR, Switzerland
    Galleries and museums
    See also
  National gallery of Switzerland
WINTERTHUR museum. See Henry Francis du Pont Winterthur museum
WINTHER, Barbara
  Follow the River Lai; dramatization of an Asian legend. Plays 29:53-60 F '70
  Listen to the Hodja; dramatization of a Turkish folk tale. Plays 30:33-40 Ja '71
  Old Baba Yaga; dramatization of a Russian folk tale. Plays 29:49-55 My '70
  Terrible gypsy maia; dramatization of a gypsy folk tale. Plays 29:65-70 Ap '70
WINTHER, Oscar Osburn
  Obituary
    Am Hist R 75:2166-7 D '70. P. W. Glad
WINTHROP, Henry
  Food for thoughtful environmentalists. Am Lib 1:764-7 S '70
WINTROUB, Samuel Z.
  From Maverick country. Nation 210:293 Mr 16 '70
WIRE
  New process for making wire; continuous hydrostatic extrusion. J. Holt. il Pop Sci 197:81 S '70
    See also
  Electric wire and wiring
WIRE, Aluminum
  Wire that slices the cost of copper; sandwich of aluminum and copper. il Bsns W p49+ My 16 '70
WIRE music instrument. See Musical instruments
WIRE tapping
  Defamation by wire tap; release of transcript of recorded New Jersey Mafia conversations. Nation 210:66-7 Ja 26 '70

Government and Martin Luther King. V. S. Navasky. pors Atlan 226:43-52 N '70
Legal weapon the Mafia fears most. G. Denison. Read Digest 96:81-5 Je '70
Mafia and the law; release of FBI transcripts of recorded conversations of the New Jersey Mafia. Commonweal 91:444 Ja 23 '70
New look at wiretapping; pro and con discussion. Sr Schol 96:10-11 F 9 '70
Wire tapping; constitutionality and efficiency; address, October 5, 1970. J. N. Mitchell. Vital Speeches 37:34-7 N 1 '70
WIRELESS set; story. See Brown, G. M.
WIRT, Frederick M.
  Alioto and the politics of hyperpluralism. il Trans-Action 7:46-55 Ap '70
WIRT, Sherwood E.
  Moving upon the mass media; address. Chr Today 14:3-6 My 22 '70
WISBY, Warren J.
  Secret to fish behavior. il Nat Wildlife 8:18-20 Ag '70
WISCONSIN
  Not all is Sanguine in Wisconsin. G. Laycock. il Audubon 72:104-9 Ja '70
    See also
  Agriculture—Wisconsin
  Apple River
  Education—Wisconsin
  Fishing—Wisconsin
  Hunting—Wisconsin
  Mendota, Lake
  Prisons—Wisconsin

    Description and travel
  See Europe, inside the USA, that is. J. Higgins and S. R. Higgins. il Todays Health 48:44-7+ N '70

    Politics and government
  Fight for the 69. Time 96:16-17 O 12 '70
  Proxmire seems to have the edge; W. Proxmire vs John Erickson in Senate race. por Bsns W p78 S 26 '70
WISCONSIN. University
  Acid test; course in applied security analysis and investment management. il Newsweek 77:55 Ja 4 '71
  My university, under siege! L. Palmer. Farm J 94:13 +Jl '70
  Return of the native; J. C. Weaver to become president. Newsweek 76:54 N 9 '70

    Elvehjem art center
  New museum. S. B. Sherrill. il Antiques 98:296 S '70
  On tour at the Elvehjem art center; inaugural exhibition. il Design 72:4-8 Fall '70

    Green Bay campus
  Ecology; heart of our university program. E. W. Weidner. il Todays Ed 59:19-21 D '70

    Madison campus
  At Wisconsin; shock and fear. il U S News 69:16-17 S 7 '70
  Biggest blast. il Newsweek 76:33 S 7 '70
  Bomb crater in the American dream. P. Weiss. il Nation 211:302-5 O 5 '70
  Bomb kills physicist, damages equipment. G. B. Lubkin. il Phys Today 23:73-4 O '70
  Bombing condoned; Daily cardinal's editorial. America 123:248-9 O 10 '70
  Bombings, campus disorder; interview. W. Dyke. il por U S News 69:74-9 O 5 '70
  Campus within a campus; Academic complex and art center. P. Blake. il Arch Forum 133:42-7 N '70
  Madison bombers. il pors Newsweek 76:28-9 S 14 '70
  Shoveling out the work of a lifetime. C. Leinster. il por Life 69:38-42 S 18 '70
  Uneasy return to campus. G. Wierzynski. il Time 96:65 S 21 '70
  Wisconsin; teaching assistants' strike ends in contract signing. A. Hamilton. Science 168:345-9 Ap 17 '70
  World's climate in one lab; Biotron. il Sci Digest 68:70-1 D '70

    Department of dance
  Wisconsin dance idea; 1917-1970. S. F. Enos. il Dance Mag 44:24-7+ N '70
WISCONSIN university press
  One thing and another. J. K. Hutchens. il Sat R 53:26+ Je 20 '70
WISDOM
  Christian wisdom. V. P. McCorry. America 123:274 O 10 '70
  Descent to wisdom; need for wise men; address, December 2, 1969. T. R. Peters. Vital Speeches 36:394-6 Ap 15 '70
WISE, Robert
  Wise in Hollywood. A. Knight. il por Sat R 53:22-5 Ag 8 '70 •

WISE, Sherwood W. Jr
  Microarchitecture and deposition of gastro-
    pod nacre. bibliog il Science 167:1486-8 Mr
    13 '70
  Scleractinian coral exoskeletons: surface mi-
    croarchitecture and attachment scar pat-
    terns. bibliog il Science 169:978-80 S 4 '70
WISEMAN, Ann
  Rag tapestry. il Sch Arts 70:35-7 Ja '71
WISEMAN, Denis V.
  Your voice; poem. America 122:345 Mr 28
    '70
WISEMAN, Frederick
  Frederick Wiseman; interview. ed. by D. E.
    McWilliams. il Film Q 24:17-26 Fall '70
  Frederick Wiseman's Hospital. R. Schickel.
    Life 68:9 F 6 '70
WISER, Forwood Cloud, 1921-
  Overcapacity feared accompanying 747. Avia-
    tion W 92:37 F 2 '70
WISER, William
  Change of fashion; story. Harp Baz 103:172-3
    O '70
  Empty-handed man; story. Redbook 134:98-9
    Mr '70
  Where sheep may safely graze; story. Red-
    book 135:74-5 O '70
WISTER, Owen
  Virginian rides on, and on. J. I. White. il
    Am West 7:49+ S '70 *
WISTRAND, Lila M.
  Bilingual jungle school. il Américas 22:2-8
    Ag '70
WIT and humor. See Humor
WITCHCRAFT
  Authors & editors; R. Stewart's findings on
    Puerto Rican witchcraft and the religion of
    Espiritismo. B. A. Bannon. il por Pub W
    198:17-18 Ag 17 '70
  Good witch of the West. L. Huebner. il por
    Life 68:59-61 Ag 10 '70
  Light in the heart of darkness. il Esquire 73:
    122-3 Mr '70
➤ Underlying themes in the witchcraft of seven-
    teenth-century New England; address, April
    1967. J. Demos. bibliog f Am Hist R 75:
    1311-26 Je '70
WITCOVER, Jules
  Civil war over smut. Nation 210:550-3 My
    11 '70
WITHHOLDING tax
  Pensions, annuities withholding to begin;
    plan for retirees. T. Schuchat. Har Yrs 10:
    4-5 O '70
WITHROW, Richard M.
  Cruising is where you find it. il Yachting
    128:58-9+ Jl '70
WITLOOF chicory. See Chicory
WITNESS bearing (Christianity)
  Divine imperative. L. N. Bell. Chr Today 15:
    24-5 N 20 '70
  Doctrine and democracy. F. Simons. Com-
    monweal 92:479-81 S 25 '70
  Does rejection mean failure? Chr Today 14:
    23 Je 19 '70
  Unbelief as a learning problem. Chr To-
    day 15:20-1 Ja 15 '71
  Why am I at this school? J. W. Alexander.
    Chr Today 14:12-13 S 11 '70
  Witness, A.D. 1970. V. P. McCorry. America
    122:512 inside back cover My 9 '70
  Witnessing at its best. Chr Today 14:25 F 27
    '70
WITNESSES
    See also
  Evidence, Hearsay
  Subpoenas
WITONSKI, Peter P.
  Conservative consensus. Nat R 22:1304-7 D 1
    '70
WITT, Harold
  At the end of the ride; poem. Commonweal
    92:367 Jl 24 '70
  Hippo; poem. Sat R 53:14 My 30 '70
  Opus 132; poem. New Yorker 46:117 My 2 '70
  Yet; poem. New Yorker 46:44 Ap 4 '70
WITT, Linda
  For purple mountains' travesty above pol-
    luted plain. il Todays Health 48:56-9+ D '70
  Male contraceptive: a bitter pill? il Todays
    Health 48:16-19+ Je '70
  Vote for beans. il Todays Health 48:60-3 N
    '70
  —See Olds, S. jt. auth.
WITTE, Paul W.
  Can Catholics learn anything from evan-
    gelical Protestants? Cath World 212:85-7 N
    '70; Same. Chr Today 15:12-14 D 18 '70
WITTENBORN, George
  Odyssey of an art book dealer in New York.
    M. B. Tarshish. il por Pub W 198:43-4 Jl 6
    '70 *
WITTENBURG college, Springfield, Ohio
  Phantom tackle; football team forefeits 1970
    games. Time 96:27 D 28 '70

WITTER, William D.
  Playing house. il Duns 96:38-9 N '70
WITTES, Glorianne, and Wittes, Simon
  Study of interracial conflict. il Am Ed 6:7-10
    Je '70
WITTES, Simon. See Wittes, G. jt. auth.
WITTHOLZ, Charles
  Displacement cruisers. il por Motor B 125:116-
    17 Ja '70
WITTIG, Alice
  State of the image. il Am Lib 1:710-12 Jl '70
WITTKOWER, Andrew B. See Rose, P. H. jt.
    auth.
WITTLINGER, H. A.
  IC capacitance meter. il Electr World 84:44-
    7+ S '70
  Stable one-IC reference supply. il Electr
    World 84:70 Jl '70
WITTNEBERT, Fred R.
  Bigness versus profitability. il Harvard Bsns
    R 48:158-60+ Ja '70
WITTNER, Dale
  Logjam in our courts. il Life 69:18-25 Ag 7 '70
WITTY, Paul A.
  Speed reading. Ed Digest 35:50-1 F '70
WITZEMAN, Louis B. and Stragier, M. G.
  Public works fire wranglers. il Am City 85:
    108+ My '70
WIVES
  Confessions of a jealous wife. J. Viorst. il
    Redbook 134:92-3+ Mr; Same abr. Read
    Digest 96:137-40 Je '70
  How to live with your husband when he re-
    tires. S. Lord. Harp Baz 103:104-5 Je '70
  How to train an American wife. S. De Gra-
    mont. Vogue 155:132-3+ Je '70
  Job travel isn't glamorous for him, or her.
    C. B. Howes. il Todays Health 48:27-9+ S
    '70
  Man talk; wife of Man talk. L. Newman and
    S. Benton. Mlle 70:44 F '70
  Place to be alone. D. Hardie. House & Gard
    137:70+ My '70
  When wives are attracted to other men. J.
    Brothers. Good H 170:58+ Mr '70
  Wife is. . . ; excerpts. M. Balfour. il Read Di-
    gest 96:100-1 F '70
  Young wife's world. H. Valentine. See is-
    sues of Good housekeeping
    See also
  Ambassadors wives
  Athletes wives
  Executives wives
  Housewives
  Marriage
  Married women
  Mothers
  Service mens wives
  Widows
  Woman

    Anecdotes, facetiae, satire, etc.
  How wives drive husbands crazy; excerpt
    from Penny candy. J. Kerr. il Read Digest
    97:85-7 D '70
WIXOM, Hartt
  How to find wounded deer. il Field & S 75:
    52-3+ O '70
WOBBLIES. See Industrial workers of the
    world
WODEHOUSE, Lawrence
  Senator Morrill's Gothic cottage at Strafford,
    Vermont. il Antiques 98:237-41 Ag '70
WOELFEL, James W.
  Logic of ultimate hope. Chr Cent 87:356-61,
    1041-2 Mr 25, S 2 '70
WOESTENDIEK, Bill
  Source of conflict; hiring of Kay Woesten-
    diek by M. Mitchell. il por Newsweek 75:
    63-4 My 4 '70 *
WOHLFEIL, Alan W.
  Science-fiction stories in the social studies.
    bibliog f Clear House 44:300-4 Ja '70
WOIWODE, Larry
  Beginning of grief; story. New Yorker 46:44-7
    O 17 '70
  Burning the couch; story. Atlan 226:91-4 N
    '70
WOJCIK, Sig
  Back packing for pleasure, think light! il
    Cons 24:48+ Je '70
WOKOUN, William
  Ten steps to best mike use. il Radio-Electr
    41:23-6+ Jl '70
WOLD, John S.
  Excerpt from remarks, May 25, 1970. Cong
    Digest 49:221+ Ag '70
WOLDT, Arthur, and Gavagan, J. E.
  DDT testing of lake fishes continues. il Cons
    25:28-9 Ag '70
WOLF, Bernard
  Orient; photographs. il Travel & Camera 33:
    44-59 Mr '70

WOLF, Bernard—*Continued*
Photographer speaks. Travel & Camera 33:89+ Mr '70
Serene satisfactions of a visit to Ceylon; photographs. il Travel & Camera 33:34-5+ N '70

about
Photographing people. J. Hughes. il Travel & Camera 33:90-2 Mr '70 *

WOLF, Eric R.
Algerian peasant revolt; excerpts from Peasant revolts in twentieth century. il Trans-Action 7:33-46 My '70

WOLF, F.
Anton Wilhelm Amo (Anthony William Amo) Negro Hist Bul 33:78-9 Mr '70

WOLF, Hugo
Hugo Wolf's masterful miniatures. D. Hamilton. il Hi Fi 20:85-6 O '70 *

WOLF, John B.
Palestinian resistance movement. bibliog f Cur Hist 60:26-31+ Ja '71

WOLF, Larry L. See Hainsworth, F. R; McNaughton, S. J. jt. auths.

WOLF, Peter
Urban street. il Art in Am 58:118-23 N '70

WOLFE, Alan
Hard times on campus. Nation 210:623-7 My 25 '70

WOLFE, Edgar
Scene for our time; poem. Chr Cent 87:69 Ja 21 '70

WOLFE, Frank
Fable for young grammarians. Engl J 59:569+ Ap '70

WOLFE, Randolph
Keep pornography clean. il Holiday 47:18+ Mr '70

WOLFE, Thomas
Cry of the wolf. A. H. Norman. por Newsweek 75:102+ F 23 '70 *
Motes in the eye of a mountainous man. H. T. Moore. por Sat R 53:23-4+ Mr 7 '70 *

WOLFE, Thomas K.
Fish in the brandy snifter. T. Foote. por Time 96:72-4 D 21 '70 *
Mau-mauing Wolfe. W. F. Buckley, jr. Nat R 23:51 Ja 12 '71 *
That party at Lenny's. il pors Time 95:80+ Je 15 '70 *

WOLFE, Tom. See Wolfe, T. K.

WOLFE, Winifred
Does it have to be dirty to sell? Writer 83:20-2 F '70

WOLFERT, Ira
Of stars and man. Read Digest 96:49-63 My '70

WOLFF, Anthony
(ed) American land. il Am Heritage 21:93-113 Je; 97-120+ Ag; 94-113 O '70
Caveat lector. il Am Heritage 21:106-7 O '70
Heart of Savannah. il Am Heritage 22:54-61+ D '70
Miss Stephanie Mills vs. motherhood. il por Look 34:58-9 Ap 21 '70

WOLFF, Christian
Current chronicle. J. Appleton. Mus Q 56:116-19 Ja '70 *

WOLFF, Michael
Science writing. M. S. Rothenberg. por Phys Today 23:26-7 My '70 *

WOLFF, Robert
Do students want education? M. Novak. Commonweal 92:10-13 Mr 13 '70; Reply. M. Raffini. 92:107 Ap 17 '70 *

WOLFF-Fording company
To make ballet more beautiful. N. M. Stoop. il pors Dance Mag 44:70-3 Ja '70

WOLFGANG, Marvin E. See Short, J. F. jr. jt. ed.

WOLFLE, Dael
Dael Wolfle at AAAS. P. H. Abelson. Science 168:1529 Je 26 '70 *

WOLFMAN, Augustus
Wolfman on printing. See issues of Modern photography

WOLIN, Sheldon S. See Schaar, J. H. jt. auth.

WOLITZER, Hilma
Sex maniac; story. Esquire 74:164 D '70

WOLKOMIR, Richard
Bringing the experts to school. Parents Mag 45:48-9+ Ja '70

WOLLIN, Goesta, and others
New method of snowmaking. il por Weatherwise 23:228-30+ O '70
—See Ericson, D. B. jt. auth.

WOLOSHIN, Arthur A. and Dennis, E. E.
Romance and rodomontade of comprehensive community mental health. bibliog Ment Hy 54:280-7 Ap '70
—and Goldberg, Jerome
Development of community mental health programs in the civil area. bibliog Ment Hy 54:13-19 Ja '70

WOLPERT, Bernard M.
Working library network. il Am Lib 1:570-2 Je '70

WOLTER, Adolph G.
Birth of a Sculp-mobile. il Design 71:13 mid-Wint '70
Design for living. il por Design 71:29 Wint '69

WOLVERINES
Vicious genius of the woods. G. Ott. il Nat Wildlife 8:14-16 Je '70
Wolverine: how tough? A. Russell. il Outdoor Life 145:106 F '70

WOLVES
In defense of the wolf; excerpt from The wolf. L. D. Mech. il Read Digest 97:215-18+ D '70
Of wilderness and wolves; timber wolves; excerpts. P. L. Errington. il Liv Wildn 33:3-7 Aut '69
What fate for Minnesota's wolves? L. D. Mech. il Audubon 72:78-81 N '70
Wolf. S. B. Duncan. il Nat Parks & Con Mag 44:23-4 O '70
See also
Coyotes

WOMACK, Ellie
Out of patients; poem. Good H 171:10 O '70

WOMACK, John, jr
Spoils of the Mexican revolution. For Affairs 48:677-87 Jl '70

WOMAN
Declaration of independence. E. Sheppard. il Harp Baz 103:106-7 Jl '70
Female animal. G. Eckstein. McCalls 97:20 Ag '70
On being a woman. J. Brothers. See issues of Good housekeeping
Women re women; symposium. il Mlle 70:159-63+ F '70
See also
Beauty, Personal
Education of women
Farm women
Housewives
Indians of North America—Women
Ladies
Mothers
Sex differences
Single women
Stunt women
Widows
Wives
World war, 1939-1945—Women and the war
also headings beginning Women; Womens

Aging
See Aging

Bibliography
Women, women everywhere. G. R. Smith. Pub W 197:50-1 Mr 30 '70

Crime
See also
Girls, Delinquent
Shoplifting

Defense
See Self defense for women

Education
See Education of women

Employment
Discrimination: women charge universities, colleges with bias. N. Gruchow. Science 168:559-61 My 1 '70
Equal rights for women workers: a new push. il U S News 69:51-2 Ag 3 '70
Job discrimination, and what women can do about it. A. S. Rossi. por Atlan 225:99-102 Mr '70
Midwest job conference draws women to consider human rights; conference on women's rights sponsored by National organization for women. J. Floerke. Chr Cent 87:304-6 Mr 11 '70
Move over, gents. E. J. Simpson. il Am Ed 6:3-6 D '70
Rebelling women, the reason. il U S News 68:35-7 Ap 13 '70; Same abr. with title Behind the women's-rights movement. Read Digest 97:116-18 Jl '70
Strengthening the weaker sex. Time 96:43-4 Ag 3 '70
Where the jobs are: Geneva, London, Paris, Rome. N. A. Comer. Mlle 71:114-15 Je '70
Where women man the ship; female industrial assembly line workers at Ship-a-shore co. of Mishawaka, Ind. il Bsns W p80 Jl 25 '70
Women are discriminated against [but they deserve it] N. Comer. Mlle 70:248-9+ F '70
Women at work; revolt against the kitchen. Time 95:100 My 11 '70
Women at work; symposium. bibliog f il Mo Labor R 93:3-44 Je '70

WOMAN—Employment—*Continued*
Women's gains; annual survey of employ-
ment. Newsweek 77:70 Ja 11 '71
"Women's lib" in Russia: the myth and the
reality. il U S News 69:74-5 N 16 '70
Women's liberation counts a victory; new
federal guidelines on sex discrimination. il
Bsns W p98-100 Je 13 '70
  See also
Business and professional women
Equal pay for equal work
Married women—Employment
Negro women—Employment
Woman—Equal rights
Woman—Occupations

Equal rights

Church, caste and women. J. Richie. Chr
Cent 87:73-7 Ja 21 '70; Discussion. 87:295-
6+, 705-6 Mr 11, Je 3 '70
Clash by Knight; promotion fight. por Time
96:17 O 19 '70
Equal rights for women? Things may never
be the same. il por U S News 69:29-30 Ag
24 '70
Faith of our feminists; question of ordination. il Newsweek 76:81 N 2 '70
Feminism and femininity; an assertion of
positive difference. N. R. McWilliams. Commonweal 92:219-21 My 15 '70
Fettered and stunted by patriarchy. M.
Haynes. Sat R 53:22-3+ Ag 29 '70
In my opinion: women's liberation is long
overdue. R. W. Wilensky. por Seventeen 29:
198 Je '70
It's still a man's world; with reports by seven
women who speak out. L. C. Pogrebin. il
Good H 171:73-5 N '70
Ladies' day; House approves constitutional
amendment. il por Newsweek 76:15-16 Ag 24
'70
Latest rules on jobs for women. U S News
68:87 Je 22 '70
Letter from Paris; new Law of parental authority. Genêt. New Yorker 46:12+ My 2
'70
Liberté, egalité, and maternité. G. Ace. Sat
R 53:4 S 26 '70
Men and women: equality or equity? America 123:167-8 S 19 '70
Midwest job conference draws women to consider human rights; conference on women's
rights; sponsored by National organization
for women. J Floerke. Chr Cent 87:304-6 Mr
11 '70
Mini, midi, or militant? Sr Schol 96:18 My
18 '70
New feminism: potent force in birth-control
policy. L. J. Carter. Science 167:1234-6 F 27
'70
Non humilis mulier triumpho; commencement address given by female student at
Harvard. Time 95:45 Je 29 '70
Power of a woman; the Equal rights amendment. Ladies Home J 87:50 Ag '70
Report on the status of women. S. McBee.
McCalls 97:128 S '70
Sex discrimination: campuses face contract
loss over HEW demands. R. J. Bazell. Sci-
ence 170:834-5 N 20 '70
That equal-rights amendment: what, exactly,
does it mean? R. Sherrill. il N Y Times Mag
p25-7+ S 20 '70
Visiting feminine eye; prejudice against
women. S. Chisholm. por McCalls 97:6 Ag
'70
Well, fellows, what did happen at the Bay
of Pigs? And who was in control? E. Ra-
mey. McCalls 98:26+ Ja '71
Who's come a long way, baby? with views of
L. Tiger and G. Steinem. il Time 96:16-21
Ag 31 '70
Who's she? women activists in U.S. history.
il Sr Schol 97:13-14 N 9 '70
Women: a time for change. M. Mead. Redbook
134:60+ Mr '70
Women; how equal? E. Van Den Haag. Nat
R 22:945+ S 8 '70
Women in academe. P. A. Graham. bibliog
Science 169:1284-90 S 25 '70; Discussion.
170:1258+ D 18 '70
Women re women. E. Hardwick. Mlle 70:186-
7+ F '70
Women workers and manpower demands in
the 1970's. J. N. Hedges. bibliog f il Mo
Labor R 93:19-29 Je '70
  See also
National organization for women
National woman's party
United Nations—Commission on the status
of women
Woman—Employment
Womens liberation movement

Health and hygiene

Psychiatric disorders in young women: the
public health implications. M. Mazer. bib-
liog Ment Hy 54:436-9 Jl '70
Ten questions women ask doctors most of-
ten. Good H 171:171 N '70
Your health. See occasional issues of Red-
book
  See also
Beauty, Personal
Frigidity (psychology)
Menopause
Menstruation
Pregnancy

Legal status, laws, etc.

Women and the law; excerpt from Women's
liberation and the law. por Atlan 225:103-4
Mr '70
Women's bureau looks to the future. E. D.
Koontz. bibliog f Mo Labor R 93:3-9 Je '70
  See also
Woman—Equal rights

Occupations

Conservation careers for women. A. La-
Bastille. il por Cons 24:31-4 Je '70
Girls on the bandwagon; political girls on
Capitol hill. S. Davidson. McCalls 97:42-3+
Ag '70
Long and painful record of little progress
in a man's world; the personal views of
eight women who succeeded in it. il Life
69:18-21 S 4 '70
Six ladies who can wipe you out. il Esquire
74:142-3 S '70
Women at work: anything he can do . . . il
Sr Schol 97:15 N 9 '70
Women workers and manpower demands in
the 1970's. J. N. Hedges. bibliog f il Mo
Labor R 93:19-29 Je '70
Working to a Latin beat. J. Kruger. Mlle
70:128+ Ja '70
  See also
Secretaries
Woman, Employment
  also headings beginning Women as, e.g.
Women as executives

Anecdotes, facetiae, satire, etc.

Take them they're yours; six jobs in search
of the (truly) liberated woman. il Esquire
73:63-8 F '70

Photographs

Two generations of Italian beauties. Harp
Baz 104:164-7 N '70

Professions

  See Woman—Occupations

Psychology

At my age? C. L. Miller. il Harp Baz 103:
180-3 Mr '70
Being loved is secondary to loving. F. Howe.
Mlle 72:76-7+ D '70
Crises in being female. A. J. Snider. il Sci
Digest 67:70-1 My '70
If you lie about your age. T. I. Rubin. por
Ladies Home J 87:68 Ap '70
In pursuit of the American woman; or, Gulli-
ver at the gynecologist's. E. Grossman.
il Harper 240:47-58+ F '70; Discussion. 240:
6+ My '70
Lost. C. Storr. Mlle 70:213-15+ F '70
McCall's and the new woman. D. McKinney.
Writer 83:9-11 Ag '70
On being a woman. J. Brothers. See issues
of Good housekeeping
What women think of women. J. Brothers.
Good H 170:40+ Ja '70
Whores and wars. N. Gittelson. Harp Baz
103:6+ Jl '70
Women: a house divided. M. Mead. Redbook
135:55+ My '70
Women and our plundered planet. M. Mead.
Redbook 134:57+ Ap '70
Women re women; symposium. il Mlle 70:159-
63+ F '70

Religious life

  See also
Women and religion

Rights of women

  See Woman—Equal rights

Social and moral questions

Liberated woman. M. Decter. Commentary
50:33-44 O '70
Rights of a wife and a mistress. G. Trotta.
Harp Baz 104:158-9 N '70

WOMAN—Social and moral questions—*Cont.*
Womanly image. P. Stern. por Atlan 225:87-90 Mr '70
See also
Girls, Delinquent
Prostitution
Womens liberation movement

Wages
See Equal pay for equal work

WOMAN as president. See Women as public officers

WOMAN hater; drama. See Beaumont, F. and Fletcher, J.

WOMAN in fiction. See Women in literature

WOMAN in literature. See Women in literature

WOMAN of conscience award. See National council of women

WOMAN suffrage

United States
Man whose vote gave women the vote: H. T. Burn. W. Cahn. por Look 34:60+ Ag 25 '70

WOMAN'S Christian temperance union
Onward, Christian soldiers; annual convention. il Newsweek 76:84 S 21 '70
WCTU's changing image: hatchets to house bills. Chr Today 15:49 O '70

WOMAN'S house; story. See Hoyer, L. G.

WOMEN

Africa
African women: from old magic to new power. il Time 96:28-33 Ag 31 '70
Family life in Africa; a look at another culture. M. Hope. il Parents Mag 45:46-7+ Ja '70

France
Letter from Paris; new Law of parental authority. Genêt. New Yorker 46:112+ My 2 '70
She's got style: Paris. M. Cantwell. il Mlle 71:102-3+ Je '70

Israel
How I didn't make it in the women's army of Israel. B. Rollin. il por Look 34:68-9 F 24 '70

Italy
Two generations of Italian beauties. il Harp Baz 104:164-7 N '70

Japan
See also
Geishas

Morocco
Reporter at large; honor to the bride. J. Kramer. New Yorker 46:33-6+ Ag 29; 43-8+ S 5; 112+ S 12 '70

Russia
Sex and the Russian girl. Newsweek 75:35 F 2 '70
Status of women in the U.S.S.R. E. Nash. bibliog f il Mo Labor R 93:39-44 Je '70
Women in Russia. S. Jacoby. New Repub 162:16-18 Ap 4 '70
"Women's lib" in Russia: the myth and the reality. il U S News 69:74-5 N 16 '70

United States
Face of America; six beauty types. il Mlle 71:156-9 S '70
Founding mothers. il pors Vogue 155:112-13 Je '70
How to train an American wife. S. De Gramont. Vogue 155:132-3+ Je '70
In pursuit of the American woman; or, Gulliver at the gynecologist's. E. Grossman. il Harper 240:47-58+ F '70; Discussion. 240:6+ My '70
Liberated, all liberated. il pors Vogue 155:114-23 Je '70
100 women in touch with our time. B. Diamonstein. Harp Baz 104:104-10 Ja '71
Power of a woman; Chicago woman power. il Ladies Home J 87:76 S '70
Woman's place; symposium. il Atlan 225:81-112+ Mr '70; Discussion. 225:94-7 My '70
Women at work; symposium. bibliog f il Mo Labor R 93:3-44 Je '70
Women in the '70s. il Ladies Home J 87:54 Ja '70
See also
Education of women—United States
Married women—Employment
National organization for women
Negro women
Woman—Employment
Woman—Equal rights
Woman suffrage—United States

WOMEN, Famous
GH poll: the ten most admired women. il Good H 170:10+ Ja '70; 172:10+ Ja '71
100 women in touch with our time. B. Diamonstein. Harp Baz 104:104-10 Ja '71
Wouldn't it be fun if: new images for old fashion plates. il McCalls 97:78-81 Mr '70
See also
New York university—Hall of fame for great Americans

WOMEN alcoholics. See Alcoholics

WOMEN and men
Church, caste and women. J. Richie. Chr Cent 87:73-7 Ja 21 '70
Dialectic of sex, by S. Firestone. Review
New Repub 163:24-5 N 28 '70. M. Haynes
Emancipation or degradation? excerpts from The passing of the modern age. J. Lukacs. Nat R 22:833-5 Ag 11 '70
Female biology in a male culture; address. D. Trilling. Sat R 53:16-18+ O 10 '70
Feminism and femininity; an assertion of positive difference. N. R. McWilliams. Commonweal 92:219-21 My 15 '70
Fettered and stunted by patriarchy. M. Haynes. Sat R 53:22-3+ Ag 29 '70
How to appeal to women. J. Brothers. por Mech Illus 66:35-7+ Ag '70
Is Catch-22 male chauvinist? P. Holzschlag. Commonweal 93:69-70 O 16 '70; Discussion. 93:187+ N 20 '70
It's really the men who need liberating. M. Calderone. por Life 69:24 S 4 '70
It's still a man's world; with reports of seven women who speak out. L. C. Pogrebin. il Good H 171:73-5 N '70
Jesus and the liberated woman. B. Graham. por Ladies Home J 87:40+ D '70
Jesus was a feminist. L. Swidler. il Cath World 212:177-83 Ja '71
Killing a culture; rise of unisex. il Time 96:57 O 12 '70
Liberated woman. M. Decter. Commentary 50:33-44 O '70
Mademoiselle; features and fiction special issue. il Mlle 71:57+ Jl '70
Male and female created he them. R. E. Aaseng. Chr Today 15:5-6 N 20 '70
Male dominance? Yes, alas. A sexist plot? No. L. Tiger. il N Y Times Mag p35-7+ O 25 '70; Discussion. p26+ N 15; 22+ N 22 '70
Male in crisis. Review
Sat R 53:31-3+ Je 6 '70. H. Gold
Men talk. D. Newman and R. Benton. Mlle 72:70-1 D '70
Pussycat league. J. Sakol. il McCalls 97:78-9+ F '70
Sexes: getting it all together. F. Bowers. il Sat R 54:16-19 Ja 9 '71
Sexual politics, by K. Millett. Review
Harper 241:110+ D '70. I. Howe
Life 69:8 Jl 24 '70. A. Broyard
Nat R 22:1004-5 S 22 '70. E. Van Den Haag
New Repub 163:26+ Ag 1 '70. J. Yardley; Discussion. 163:30-2 Ag 22 '70
Newsweek 76:72+ Jl 27 '70. R. A. Gross
Ramp Mag 9:51-4+ N '70. M. Tax
Sister debates a brother on that black man-white woman thing; interviews, ed. by K. Mehlinger. L. Gant; D. K. Davis. il pors Ebony 25:130-3 Rg '70
Well, fellows, what did happen at the Bay of Pigs? And who was in control? E. Ramey. McCalls 98:26+ Ja '71
What makes a man lovable? T. I. Rubin. Read Digest 96:21-4 Ja '70
What Playboy doesn't know about women could fill a book; with interview, ed. by G. Steinem. H. Hefner. il por McCalls 98:76-7+ O '70
When wives are attracted to other men. J. Brothers. Good H 170:58+ Mr '70
Why men can't say I love you. T. I. Rubin. Ladies Home J 87:36 Je '70
Woman's place; symposium. il Atlan 225:81-112+ Mr '70; Discussion. 225:94-7 My '70
Women and the church: poor psychology, worse theology. S. D. Collins. Chr Cent 87:1557-9 D 30 '70
Women re women; symposium. il Mlle 70:159-63+ F '70
Women's liberation, but how soon will it happen? N. Hentoff. Parents Mag 45:45+ D '70

Anecdotes, facetiae, satire, etc.
Parting shots; a women's lib exposé of male villainy. A. Bayer. il Life 69:62A-64 Ag 7 '70

WOMEN and peace
See also
Another mother for peace (organization)

WOMEN and politics
Crusade for morality; address, June 10, 1970. M. Rountree. Vital Speeches 36:597-602 Jl 15 '70

WOMEN and politics—*Continued*
Women and politics. M. Mead. Redbook 136:
50+ N '70
See also
Woman suffrage
Women in politics

WOMEN and the church
Church, caste and women. J. Richie. Chr
Cent 87:73-7 Ja 21 '70; Discussion. 87:295-
6+, 705-6 Mr 11, Je 3 '70
Father church and the motherhood of God;
conference at Garrison, N.Y. D. Grum-
bach. Commonweal 93:268-9 D 11 '70
Holy father church; organized Christianity
is dominated by males. J. H. Fichter. Com-
monweal 92:216-18 My 15 '70; Discussion.
92:355+; 93:134-5, 237+ Jl 24, O 30, D 4 '70
Mother church's daughters; distaff dissent.
J. R. Greisch. Chr Today 14:37-8 Je 5 '70
No place for women, or several? O. Trewick.
Cath World 210:216-19 F '70
Second-class citizenship in the kingdom of
God. R. A. Schmidt. Chr Today 15:13-14
Ja 1 '71
Sound and fury at assembly of Methodist
women. B. Thompson. Chr Cent 87:773-4
Je 17 '70
Woman's place in the church. America 122:
204 F 28 '70
Women and the church: poor psychology,
worse theology. S. D. Collins. Chr Cent 87:
1557-9 D 30 '70
Women's lib, Catholic style. J. C. Haughey.
America 123:454 N 28 '70

WOMEN and war
Women and children first; use by revolution-
ists as shields for fighters to achieve moral
disarmament of the enemy. J. Burnham.
Nat R 22:831 Ag 11 '70
See also
Vietnamese war, 1957- —Women and the war
World war, 1939-1945—Women and the war

WOMEN as air pilots
I live to fly; condensation. J. Auriol. il pors
Read Digest 97:241-4+ O '70

WOMEN as artists
Womens liberation, woman artists and art
history; symposium, with editorial comment. il Art N 69:22-49+ bibliog(p70-1 Ja
'71

WOMEN as astronauts
Women in space. Chem 43:4 O '70

WOMEN as athletes
Charged Atoms; Brooklyn's mostly black
Atoms track club for women. il Newsweek
76:42 Jl 20 '70
Girls from the mountain next door; photo-
graphs by Jerry Cooke. Sports Illus 32:36-41
Mr 16 '70
Pick up your purse, coach, and let's go;
coaching girls' basketball team. G. V. Pack-
ard. il Sports Illus 33:88-90+N 30 '70
Records are falling to a China doll; Taiwan-
ese Chi Cheng woman track athlete. il pors
Life 69:34-5 Jl 10 '70
Some new babes in the woods: U.S. wom-
en's cross-country ski team. W. Johnson.
il Sports Illus 31:72+ D 15 '69
Taiwan flash: Chi Cheng. il por Time 96:33
Jl 20 '70
Varsity girls; competitors in non-contact
sports in New York high schools. il Time
96:34 D 21 '70

WOMEN as authors
We've never asked a woman before. C. D.
Bowen. por Atlan 225:82-6 Mr '70
Women re women. H. Calisher. Mlle 70:188-
9+ F '70
See also
Detective and mystery stories—Authorship

WOMEN as automobile drivers. See Automobile drivers

WOMEN as automobile racing drivers. See Automobile racing drivers

WOMEN as college professors and instructors
Sexism on the campus: women's rights in
teaching and administrative positions. P.
Woodring. Sat R 53:80+ My 16 '70
Women in academe. P. A. Graham. bibliog
Science 169:1284-90 S 25 '70; Discussion.
170:1268+ D 18 '70
Women on college faculties; letter. B. L.
Chiñas. Science 168:917 My 22 '70

WOMEN as composers. See Women as musicians

WOMEN as consumers. See Consumers

WOMEN as doctors. See Women as physicians

WOMEN as executives
Those powerful powder puff executives; nine
top women executives. S. G. Slappey. il Na-
tions Bsns 58:80-8 N '70
See also names of women executives, e.g.
J. Evans

WOMEN as journalists
Don't quote me! excerpt. W. McLendon and
S. Smith. il Ladies Home J 87:90+ N '70
Male and female; war between the sexes in
the media. il Newsweek 75:74+ My 18 '70
Opinion; the news weeklies and women. H.
Whitehead. Mlle 71:36+ S '70
View from the masthead. A. M. Cunning-
ham. il Mlle 71:161-3 S '70
Washington witch hunt; social columnists. il
por Time 96:34 Ag 3 '70
See also
Women as reporters

WOMEN as members of Congress. See Congresswomen

WOMEN as ministers
Faith of our feminists; question of ordina-
tion. il Newsweek 76:81 N 2 '70
First woman Lutheran pastor in U.S. or-
dained. Chr Cent 87:1443 D 2 '70
Mother church's daughters; distaff dissent.
J. R. Greisch. Chr Today 14:37-8 Je 5 '70
Sensitivity or inertia? decision of the British
Methodist conference. T. Beeson. Chr Cent
87:910 Jl 29 '70
Woman seeks Episcopal ordination. Chr Cent
87:72 Ja 21 '70; Discussion. 87:399 Ap 1 '70
Women at the altar. il Time 96:71+ N 2 '70

WOMEN as musicians
Woman: artist of artist-ess? lack of women
composers. N. Rorem. Vogue 155:172-3+
Ap 1 '70

WOMEN as painters. See Women as artists

WOMEN as physicians
Bars against women. il Time 97:31 Ja 11 '71
Doctor was an adventuress; E. P. Lovejoy.
J. L. Block. il Todays Health 48:20-1+ Ag
'70
Elizabeth Blackwell: first woman doctor. por
Sr Schol 96:18 Mr 2 '70
Medical sextets; study findings of Harold I.
Kaplan. il Newsweek 76:82 O 19 '70

WOMEN as poets
Seven women. M. Van Duyn. Poetry 115:430-9
Mr '70

WOMEN as priests
Woman's place in the church. America 122:
204 F 28 '70
Women at the altar. il Time 96:71+ N 2 '70

WOMEN as public officers
Hormones in the White House; woman as
president controversy. pors Time 96:13 Ag
10 '70
How women are doing in politics. il U S
News 69:24-7 S 7 '70
Why we need a woman president in 1976.
G. Steinem. Look 34:58 Ja 13 '70
See also
Nuns as public officers

WOMEN as rabbis
Mother church's daughters; distaff dissent.
J. R. Greisch. Chr Today 14:37-8 Je 5 '70
Rabbi Sally. por Newsweek 75:89 F 23 '70
Women at the altar. il Time 96:71+ N 2
'70

WOMEN as reporters
Some of our reporters who covered Women's
lib. R. Graves. il Life 69:2A S 4 '70

WOMEN as scientists
Psychological and social barriers to women
in science; adaptation of address, November 22, 1969. M. S. White. bibliog Science
170:413-16 O 23 '70
Women in science; AAAS symposium, December 27, 1970. J. E. Simmons. Science
170:201 O 9 '70
Women in science; symposium and job mart.
N. F. Goldsmith. Science 168:1124-7+ My 29
'70

WOMEN as soldiers
How I didn't make it in the women's army
of Israel. B. Rollin. il por Look 34:68-9 F
24 '70

WOMEN as taxicab drivers
Cabbies to whistle at. il Newsweek 76:78 Ag
31 '70

WOMEN as travelers
Travel; unattached ladies. M. Gough. il House
B 112:80-1 N '70

Anecdotes, facetiae, satire, etc.
Two dames at sea. P. O'Higgins. il McCalls
97:38+ F '70

WOMEN football players. See Football players

WOMEN golf players. See Golfers

WOMEN in aeronautics. See Women as air
pilots

WOMEN in airplane racing. See Airplane racing

WOMEN in boating
Cabin talk. M. Wiley. See issues of Yachting
Companionway. R. L. Williamson. See issues
of Motor boating

WOMEN in boating—*Continued*
Women and children afloat and aground. C.
Landau. il Motor B 125:104-7 Mr '70
See also
Yachtsmans wife (periodical)

Anecdotes, facetiae, satire, etc.
Name of the game is incredible. B. Batten-
feld. il Motor B 126:56-7+ S '70
WOMEN in business. See Business and profes-
sional women
WOMEN in community service. See Community
service
WOMEN in industry. See Woman—Employment
WOMEN in literature
Fiction and policy: the hard-worked hero-
ines. S. Karlinsky. Nation 211:245-8 S 21
'70
Little Miss Muffet fights back; NOW (Na-
tional organization for women) bibliogra-
phy of children's books showing females
in non-stereotyped roles. Library J 95:3947+
N 15 '70
Through a feminist eye; childrens books.
Library J 95:4309+ D 15 '70
WOMEN in politics
Opinion. K. DeCrow. Mlle 70:34+ F '70
Power of a woman. il Ladies Home J 87:82
Ap '70
Visiting feminine eye; prejudice against wom-
en. S. Chisholm. por McCalls 97:6 Ag '70
Women on the hustings. il Time 96:11 Ag 17
'70
See also
Congresswomen
National woman's party
Women as public officers
WOMEN in publishing (organization)
McGraw-Hill picketed by women in publish-
ing. Pub W 198:35 Jl 6 '70
Publishing women form lib group. Pub W
197:129+ Je 8 '70
WOMEN in television
Woman's role on TV. J. Leonard. il por Life
69:8 D 18 '70
WOMEN in the Bible
Jesus and the liberated woman. B. Graham.
por Ladies Home J 87:40+ D '70
Jesus was a feminist. L. Swidler. il Cath
World 212:177-83 Ja '71
WOMEN medical students. See Medical stu-
dents, Women
WOMEN prisoners. See Prisoners, Women
WOMEN shoppers. See Shopping and shoppers
WOMEN tennis players. See Tennis players
WOMEN workers. See Woman—Employment
WOMEN'S amateur golf championship. See Golf
—Tournaments
WOMENS bureau. See United States—Womens
bureau
WOMENS clothes. See Clothing and dress
WOMENS clothing industry. See Clothing in-
dustry
WOMENS clubs and societies
Purr, baby, purr; Pussycat league, inc. il
Newsweek 76:84-5 S 21 '70
See also
The Links, inc.
WOMENS electric shavers. See Razors
WOMENS liberation movement
Abortion reform: the new tokenism; excerpt
from Notes (from the second year) radical
feminism (May 1970) Ramp Mag 9:19-21 Ag
'70
Ale, cheese, onions and women; McSorley's
old ale house, Manhattan. J. R. Coyne, jr.
Nat R 22:997 S 22 '70
American woman: history and HERstory.
il Sr Schol 97:7-12 N 9 '70
Business and the radicals: the women, they
want action. J. Smith. il Duns 95:46+ Je
'70
Consciousness ♀. V. Gornick. il N Y Times
Mag p22-3+ Ja 10 '71
Cutting loose. S. Kempton. Esquire 74:53-7
Jl '70
Everyone was brave, by W. L. O'Neill. Review
Cath World 212:46-7 O '70. E. Kolmer
Feminine eye. S. Alexander. por McCalls 97:
8 Je '70
Feminine eye; McCall's editor's views of
women's liberation. S. Alexander. por
McCalls 97:8+ Jl '70
Feminism moves on. il Sci N 98:199 S 5 '70
Feminist yearbook; publication of The li-
berated woman's appointment calendar and
survival handbook 1971. il Newsweek 76:
114+ N 16 '70
Five passionate feminists; symposium. il
pors McCalls 97:52-5+ Jl '70
Grove and union agree to arbitration, elec-
tion. il Pub W 197:55-7 Ap 27 '70

Grove fires union activists, Women's lib
seizes officers. il Pub W 197:38 Ap 20 '70
Grove loses arbitration; four must be rehired.
Pub W 198:248 Ag 31 '70
Help! J. Malcom. New Repub 163:15-17 O 10
'70; Discussion. 163:40-5 O 31 '70
How bosses feel about Women's lib; job pol-
icies unaffected. il Bsns W p 18-19 S 5 '70
How to unnerve male chauvinists. E. Glynn.
America 123:144-6 S 12 '70; Discussion. 123:
247 O 10 '70
Independent female; or, A man has his pride;
text of play performed by the San Fran-
cisco Mime troupe. J. Holden. il Ramp Mag
9:20-31 D '70
Ladies' day. il por Newsweek 76:15-16 Ag 24
'70
Liberated woman. M. Decter. Commentary
50:33-44 O '70
Liberating the Journal. il Newsweek 76:44 Ag
3 '70
Liberating women. il Time 95:93 Je 15 '70
Liberation struggle generates tension on
race, sex issues; interview, ed. by M. Stone.
J. Brown; P. Way; H. Fannings. il Chr
Cent 87:736-9 Je 10 '70
Male and female; war between the sexes in
the media. il Newsweek 75:74+ My 18 '70
Man talk. D. Newman and R. Benton. il Mlle
71:166 Je; 48 Ag '70
Man talk; tea and/or sympathy. D. Newman
and R. Benton. il Mlle 71:166 Je '70
Masculine mystique. G. Frazier, 4th. Mlle
71:63-4+ Jl '70
Mother superior to Women's lib; B. Friedan.
P. Wilkes. il pors N Y Times Mag p27-9+
N 29 '70
New civil rights; fem lib! M. C. Segers. il Cath
World 211:203-7 Ag '70
New feminism. L. Komisar. Sat R 53:27-30+
F 21 '70
New feminism. il Ladies Home J 87:64-71 Ag
'70; Discussion. 87:63 Ag; 69+ N '70
New feminism; with editorial comment. il
Ladies Home J 87:63, 64-71 Ag '70
New victory in an old crusade. il Time 96:10-
12 Ag 24 '70
Of many things. D. R. Campion. America 123:
inside cover O 17 '70; Reply. M. A. Gorman.
123:362 N 7 '70
On campus: Women's lib. Mlle 71:104 Ag '70
Other revolution. M. Haynes. Nation 211:632-
3 D 14 '70
Overdue; the women's liberation movement.
E. G. Detlefsen; P. Schuman; G. W. Hath-
away. il Wilson Lib Bul 44:962-5+ My '70
Profiles; founding cadre: personalities of and
dialogues among some members of a wo-
mens liberation group. J. Kramer. New
Yorker 46:52-6+ N 28 '70
Rebelling women, the reason. il U S News
68:35-7 Ap 13 '70; Same abr. with title
Behind the women's rights movement.
Read Digest 97:116-18 Jl '70
Sisterhood is powerful. S. Brownmiller. il
N Y Times Mag p26-7+ Mr 15 '70; Discussion.
p6 Mr 29; 39+ Ap 5 '70; Same abr. Cur
117:28-38 Ap '70
Very volcanic. il Newsweek 76:47 Ag 31 '70
What are you supposed to do if you like
children? A. Bernays. por Atlan 225:107-9
Mr '70; Same. Cur 117:38-43 Ap '70
What shall we tell our children? M. Mead.
Redbook 135:35+ Je '70
What's happened to Eve? address, September
10, 1970. L. Bushnell. Vital Speeches 36:749-
52 O 1 '70
Who wants equality? women in Wyoming. S.
Hunsucker. Nation 211:465-8 N 9 '70
Who's come a long way, baby? with views of
L. Tiger and G. Steinem. il Time 96:16-21
Ag 31 '70
Who's so liberated? Why? S. Beauman. il
Vogue 156:382-3+ S 1 '70
Woman-power. il Time 95:59 Mr 30 '70
Woman power; feminists storm headquarters
of Ladies' home journal. il Newsweek 75:61
Mr 30 '70
Woman's place. S. North; A. Bernays; B. De-
Mott. pors Atlan 225:105-12+ Mr '70
Women's lib: a second look. Time 96:50 D 14
'70
Women's lib, Catholic style. J. C. Haughey.
America 123:454 N 28 '70
Women's lib, continental style. il Time 96:23-
5 Ag 17 '70
Women's lib in Iberia. T. Goslin. Chr Cent 87:
1432 N 25 '70
Women's lib loves you. A. Gross. il Mlle 70:
232-3+ F '70
Women's lib: the idea you can't ignore. S.
Burnham. il Redbook 135:78-9+ S '70
Women's lib: the war on sexism; with views
of social scientists. H. Dudar. il Newsweek
75:71-6+ Mr 23 '70

WOMENS liberation movement—*Continued*
Women's lib watching. W. F. Buckley, jr. Nat R 22:964-5 S 8 '70
Womens liberation: a woman's view; a man's view. E. Steinberg; J. Starke. Sr Schol 97: 16-17 N 9 '70
Women's liberation, but how soon will it happen? N. Hentoff. Parents Mag 45:45+ D '70
Women's liberation counts a victory; new federal guidelines on sex discrimination. il Bsns W p98-100 Je 13 '70
Women's liberation, the time is now. M. Hentoff. Parents Mag 45:44+ D '70
Women's liberation, woman artists and art history; symposium, with editorial comment. il Art N 69:22-49+ bibliog(p70-1) Ja '71
See also
Women in publishing (organization)

Anecdotes, facetiae, satire, etc.
Parting shots; a women's lib exposé of male villainy. A. Bayer. il Life 69:62A-64 Ag 7 '70
Quiz: are you ready for liberation? Mlle 70: 236+ F '70
Spiro and the rotten kids; Spiro Keats, bartender and his philosophy. K. Nyren. Library J 95:2403 Jl '70
Women as feminists. J. D. Tierney. Nat R 22: 789 Jl 28 '70

Caricatures and cartoons
Women's liberation in historical perspective; cartoons. J. Noonan. Cath World 212:95-6 N '70

Drama
Doll's house 1970. C. B. Luce. il pors Life 69:54-6+ O 16 '70

Marches, rallies, etc.
Coming Wednesday: a herstory-making event. J. Klemesrud. il N Y Times Mag p6+ Ag 23 '70
Gals on the move. il Sr Schol 97:12-13 S 28 '70
Liberation. New Yorker 46:26-9 S 5 '70
March in the dark. C. R. Sternhell. il McCalls 98:8+ N '70
When the women struck for equality. il U S News 69:26-7 S 7 '70
Women arise; with statements by successful women. il Life 69:16B-21 S 4 '70
Women on the march. il Time 96:12-13 S 7 '70
Women who know their place; Women's strike for equality. il Newsweek 76:16-18 S 7 '70

WOMEN'S national book association
President of NOW socks it to WNBA. Pub W 199:34-5 Ja 4 '71
WOMENS organizations. See Womens clubs and societies
WOMENS reformatories. See Reformatories
WOMENS shoes. See Shoes
WOMENS studies. See Colleges and universities—Curriculum
WOMEN'S wear daily
Out on a limb with the midi. il por Time 96: 76-81 S 14 '70
Women's wear sets the line. il Newsweek 75: 72-3 Mr 16 '70
WOMETCO enterprises, inc.
How to make escapism pay. il Bsns W p 112+ Jl 11 '70
WON ton. See Cookery, Chinese
WONDER
Sense of wonder in a changing world. D. Goldman. Nat Parks & Con Mag 44:25-6 Je '70
WONG, Bing Low. See Charm, S. E. jt. auth.
WOOD, Abigail
Young living; questions and answers. See issues of Seventeen
WOOD, Beatrice
Ceramics of Beatrice Wood. R. Bryan. il por Craft Horiz 30:28-33 Mr '70 *
WOOD, Bryce
How wars end in Latin America. bibliog f Ann Am Acad 392:40-50 N '70
WOOD, David
Inland cruising. il por Yachting 127:82-3+ My '70
WOOD, Don E. See Netz, D. J. jt. auth.
WOOD, Edmund C.
When men were iron. S. Iselin. il Yachting 128:58+ S '70 *
WOOD, Frank H. E.
Heaven can wait; I hope. Chr Cent 87:269-70 Mr 4 '70
WOOD, Fred H.
Non-graded, multi-directional approach to the study of foreign languages. bibliog f Clear House 44:279-85 Ja '70

WOOD, George
The Woods' mighty oak. W. Fuller. il Am For 76:28-9 Ag '70 *
WOOD, John A.
Lunar soil; with biographical sketch. il Sci Am 223:12, 14-23 bibliog(p 128) Ag '70
—and others
Lunar anorthosites. bibliog il Science 167: 602-4 Ja 30 '70
WOOD, Lawrence, and Peck. Ernest
Our newest snowfighter works all year. il Am City 85:54-5 D '70
WOOD, Marion N.
Eating well on a wheat-free diet. il Todays Health 48:60-3 F '70
WOOD, Nancy
America's most radioactive city. McCalls 97:46+ S '70
Requiem for a small town. il Am Heritage 22:62-7 D '70
WOOD, Norton
Bermuda golf. il Travel & Camera 33:48-53 S '70
Breakfast ride. il Travel & Camera 33:10+ Jl '70
From a Carolina kitchen. Travel & Camera 33:68 F '70
James River plantations. il Travel & Camera 33:55-9 Ap '70
WOOD, Peter
In this corner, the official heavyweight champ. il pors N Y Times Mag p52-3+ N 15 '70
It's sort of like black lightning. il N Y Times Mag p 14-16+ Mr 29 '70
WOOD, Vincent
Build an SCA adapter for FM reception. il Pop Electr 33:53+ D '70
Numitron readout. il Pop Electr 32:73-5 Mr '70
WOOD, William C. and Morton, D. L.
Microcytotoxicity test: detection in sarcoma patients of antibody cytotoxic to human sarcoma cells. bibliog il Science 170:1318-20 D 18 '70
WOOD
Inside wood; excerpts. W. M. Harlow. il Am For 76:24-7 S '70
Wood: the oldest material. J. H. Ingersoll. House B 112:124-5+ O '70
See also
Driftwood
Lignin
Lumber industry and trade
Timber
Trees

Diseases and pests
See also
Termites
Wood—Decay

Preservation
How rotten can you get? W. P. Ferren. Motor B 126:66-9+ O '70
WOOD, Irradiated
Atomic wood, for stomping on. H. Friedman. il Mech Illus 66:72-3 D '70
WOOD boats. See Boats—Materials
WOOD carving
Chromatic wood sculpture of Mortimer Borne; interview. M. Borne. il Natur Hist 79:28-33+ N '70
Makonde sculpture. M. Shore-Bos. il Natur Hist 79:42-9 Mr '70
Root art. M. Dunn. il Design 71:14-16 Spr '70
Thirty-year sculpture project; limewood triptych. M. B. Kane. il Am Artist 34:38-43+ Ja '70
Walnut, maple, pine and butternut fish. D. Shiner. il Design 71:30-1 Spr '70
See also
Fretwork
WOOD chests. See Chests
WOOD cuts. See Wood engravings
WOOD decaying fungi
How rotten can you get? W. P. Ferren. Motor B 126:66-9+ O '70
WOOD engravings
Artist with wood; F. Campbell's wood-inlay pastime. D. Shiner. il por Design 72:24-5 Fall '70
Simple way to do large woodcuts. A. Geisert. il Sch Arts 70:14-15 D '70
Woodcuts of Robert C. Skelley. N. Kent. il Am Artist 35:44-9+ Ja '71
WOOD fastenings. See Fastenings
WOOD finishing
Paint or stain, or nothing? for exterior wood. J. H. Ingersoll. il House B 112:126-7+ My '70
See also
Furniture—Finishing

WOOD inlay. See Inlay
WOOD lots. See Woodlots
WOOD mosaics. See Mosaics
WOOD preservation. See Wood—Preservation
WOOD pulp and paper mill waste. See Trade waste
WOOD rot fungi. See Wood decaying fungi
WOOD sculpting. See Wood carving
WOOD sheds. See Sheds
WOOD thrushes. See Thrushes
WOOD turning. See Turning
WOOD working. See Woodworking
WOODALL, Martha
Pigeon man; story. Mlle 71:251 Ag '70
WOODBURY, Mary
God in small letters; poem. Chr Cent 87:1247 O 21 '70
WOODBURY, Richard
Showdown on the Salmon River range. il pors Life 68:54-56A My 22 '70
Survival is a mental attitude. il Life 69:88 N 27 '70
WOODCARVING. See Wood carving
WOODCHUCK hunting
Chucking the chucks. W. Davis. il Mech Illus 66:63+ S '70
Countdown for chucks. C. Vinson. il Outdoor Life 145:86-7+ Ap '70
WOODCOCK, Leonard
Carrying on for Reuther. il por Bsns W p82 My 30 '70 *
Filling Walter's shoes. il por Newsweek 75:74+ Je 1 '70 *
Heading for the strike nobody wants. il por Newsweek 76:79-80+ S 14 '70 *
New UAW head: a tough bargainer. por U S News 68:63 Je 1 '70 *
Signal caller for the auto workers. por U S News 69:67 Ag 24 '70 *
Unknown who leads the Walter P. Reuther memorial strike. W. Serrin. il pors N Y Times Mag p28-9+ S 27 '70 *
WOODCOCK shooting
This is the timberdoodle. C. E. Heacox. il Outdoor Life 146:76-7+ O '70
Woodcock along the salmon rivers. J. B. Robinson and H. Carroll. il Field & S 75:54-5+ S '70
WOODCUTS. See Wood engravings
WOODEN, John
UCLA: simple, awesomely simple. C. Kirkpatrick. Sports Illus 33:39-43 N 30 '70 * ·
WOODEN boats. See Boats—Materials
WOODEN bullets. See Bullets
WOODFORD, Elizabeth M.
What to plant for the birds. il Horticulture 49:38+ Ja '71
WOODHENGES. See Great Britain—Antiquities
WOODLE, Allan S.
Knot that everyone ties backwards. il Motor B 126:16 Jl '70
WOODLEY, Richard
Cappital punishment. il Esquire 74:160-1+ N '70
WOODLEY, William L.
Rainfall enhancement by dynamic cloud modification. bibliog il Science 170:127-32 O 9 '70
WOODLOTS
Finding your forest. R. W. Brenberger. il Am For 76:44-5 F '70
Trees for people; questions and answers. K. B. Pomeroy. il Am For 76:8+ Ap; 28-9+ Je '70
Your woodlot: worth more than ever. G. Logsdon. Farm J 94:50N Mr '70
WOODMAN, Elizabeth and Woodman, George
Ceramist's odyssey of clay: Italy. il Craft Horiz 30:18-19 My '70
WOODMAN, George. See Woodman, E. jt. auth.
WOODPECKERS
Apartment: with photographs by F. K. Truslow. L. de K. Lawrence. Audubon 72:4-11 Mr '70
Pileated woodpecker: king of the feathered woodchoppers. R. L. Kapral. il Cons 25:5+ O '70
WOODPILES
My woodpile is a shelter; harboring chipmunk, steller jay, deermouse. V. B. Scheffer. il Home Gard 57:14-15 Ja '70
WOODRING, Paul
Editor's bookshelf (cont) Sat R 53:62-3 Ja 24; 52-3 Jl 18; 74+ N 21; 60-1 D 19 '70
Higher education in this decade. Ed Digest 36:20-3 D '70

Retrospect and prospect. Sat R 53:66 S 19 '70
View from the campus (cont) Sat R 53:80+ My 16 '70
—and others
Education in America. See issues of Saturday review
WOODROW, Alain
Excommunication of Roger Garaudy. Commonweal 92:28-30 Mr 20 '70
Taking sides: Mauriac, polemicist. por Commonweal 93:322-3 D 25 '70
WOODRUFF, Maurice
Horoscopes. See issues of McCalls
Maurice Woodruff: astrology's brightest star; interview, ed. by S. Robinson. il por McCalls 97:76-7+ Mr '70
WOODRUM, Lon
Convert. Chr Today 14:17 Je 5 '70
Diabolical didactics. Chr Today 15:36 N 6 '70
WOODS, A. H. and O'Bar, P. R.
Absorption of proteins and peptides in the far ultraviolet. bibliog il Science 167:179-81 Ja 9 '70
WOODS, Bruce
To a friend's wife; poem. McCalls 98:34 O '70
WOODS, Earl
Psychiatrist to the stars. il pors Ebony 25:74-5+ Mr '70 *
WOODS, June
Efficiency at all costs! Todays Ed 59:19 F '70
WOODS, Stephen C. and Weisinger, R. S.
Pagophagia in the albino rat. bibliog il Science 169:1334-6 S 25 '70
WOODS hogs
Perfect sow, almost. R. Wilmore. il Farm J 94:H9+ S '70
WOODS HOLE, Mass, oceanographic institution
Ocean pollution. New Yorker 45:27-30 Ja 31 '70
WOODWARD, Bliss
Under the blue ensign. See issues of Motor boating
WOODWARD, Comer Vann
Future of the past; address, December 29, 1969. bibliog f Am Hist R 75:711-26 F '70
WOODWARD, Kenneth L.
Berrigans in prison. Commonweal 92:428-30 S 4 '70
Seances in suburbia. il McCalls 97:70-1+ Mr '70
WOODWARD, Marc
International chef. See issues of Travel
WOODWARD, R. B. See Hoffmann, R. jt. auth.
WOODWELL, George M.
Effects of pollution on the structure and physiology of ecosystems. bibliog il Science 168:429-33 Ap 24 '70
Energy cycle of the biosphere; with biographical sketch. il Sci Am 223:33, 64-74 bibliog (p262) S '70
Science and the gross national pollution. Ramp Mag 8:51-4 My '70
WOODWORK
See also
Fretwork
WOODWORKING
Nakashima, the craftsman. il por Life 68:74-7 Je 12 '70
What fun you can have cutting wood threads! R. J. De Cristoforo. il Pop Sci 196:108-10 Mr '70
See also
Cabinet work
Drilling and boring (woodwork)
Joints (carpentry)
Planes and planing
Turning
Wood carving

Projects

Build this handsome electric serving cart. W. C. Leckey. il Pop Mech 133:118-21+ My '70
Compleat sewing center. il Bet Hom & Gard 48:12 Jl '70
Five weekend workshop projects. il Pop Mech 133:134-8 Je '70
Four popular woodworking projects. W. C. Leckey. il Pop Mech 133:166-76 F '70
Four projects you can finish in a weekend. il Pop Mech 133:182-5+ Ap '70
Four things to make for a home shop: sanding spindles, squaring guide, whatnot tray and holding edge for square. il Pop Sci 196:138-9 Ja '70
Great projects to keep your workshop humming. il Pop Mech 133:164-79 Mr '70
Modern bowl for sunbathing. K. Isaacs. il Pop Sci 196:112-13+ F '70
They're fun to make! crystal ball lamp, dice game, tabletop bookrack, doggie reminder. il Pop Mech 134:150-3 Ag '70
Three pop-together home accessories; wine rack, pipe rack, and lamp. A. J. Hand. il Pop Sci 197:90-1+ N '70
Three smart ideas for your home; wall lamp, wood patio, and mirror shelf. il Pop Sci 196:92-3 Ap '70

WORLD conference on religion and peace. See Peace conferences
WORLD congress on the future of the church. See Religious conferences
WORLD cooperation. See International cooperation
WORLD council of churches
Anticipating Addis Ababa. T. Beeson. Chr Cent 87:1473-4 D 9 '70
Faith and order: facing forward. Chr Cent 87:955 Ag 12 '70
Faith and order: fifty years of service. America 123:81 Ag 22 '70
Geneva conference on technology and the future. J. E. T. Hough. Chr Cent 87:948 Ag 5 '70
Grants for guerrillas generate grumbles. Chr Today 15:39 O 9 '70
Greece: the right to spread good news. Chr Today 15:29 Ja 1 '71
Guns for God. Time 96:74 O 5 '70
Hard times for the WCC; financial crisis. T. Beeson. Chr Cent 87:1008 Ag 26 '70
Law and social action; consultation held at Celigny, Switzerland, July 1970. J. B. Kelley. America 124:41-2 Ja 16 '71
Next WCC head: likely and unlikely prospects. T. Beeson. Chr Cent 88:4-5 Ja 6 '71
On pious horror: allocation of funds for antiapartheid and liberation groups. Chr Cent 87:1111 S 23 '70; Reply. J. Richie. 87:1357 N 11 '70
Peril and promise of wider ecumenism; Ajaltoun meeting. Chr Cent 87:524-5 Ap 29 '70
Syncretism and the quest for interiority. P. Verghes. Chr Cent 87:1529-30 D 23 '70
WCC in the U.S: what of the future? S. Cunneen. Chr Cent 87:707-8 Je 3 '70
WCC racism grants issue still smolders. Chr Today 15:44-5 N 20 '70
World council of churches and Latin America. T. Tschuy. Chr Cent 87:320-3 Mr 18 '70
See also
Joint committee on society, development and peace
WORLD court. See International court of justice, The Hague
WORLD crafts council
WCC conference in Dublin. P. Hogan. il Craft Horiz 30:46-9 D '70
World crafts council. J. N. White. Craft Horiz 30:7 Mr '70
WORLD cup matches. See Golf—Tournaments
WORLD cup soccer celebrations. See Celebrations
WORLD federation of diamond bourses
See also
Diamond dealers club, inc (New York)
WORLD food congress. See Food and agriculture organization of the United Nations
WORLD food programme
Intergovernmental committee approves projects. UN Mo Chron 7:29-30 My '70
UN and the power of food; progress report on the World food programme. R. L. Tobin. Sat R 53:20 Ja 31 '70
WORLD food supply. See Food supply
WORLD government. See International organization
WORLD history
Imperialism. G. Lichtheim. bibliog Commentary 49:42-75 Ap; 33-58 My '70
World of nations: problems of political modernization, by D. A. Rustow. Review
Trans-Action 7:66-7 Ja '70. E. A. Nordlinger
Bibliography
Continuing revolution: new books about world history and politics. il Schol Teach Sec Teach Sup p24 F 2 '70
WORLD language. See Language, Universal
WORLD law. See International law
WORLD law day. See Special days, weeks, and months
WORLD maps
Economic map of the world. il Sr Schol 95:18-19 S 22 '69
World and how we abuse it. il Nat Geog 138:782-3, sup(folded map) D '70
World: polar projection. Sr Schol 95:22 S 22 '69
WORLD opinion. See Public opinion
WORLD organization. See United Nations
WORLD Pentecostal conference. See Religious conferences
WORLD politics
History of the cold war, by A. Fontaine. Review
Nation 210:411-12 Ap 6 '70. D. F. Fleming
See also
International relations

WORLD politics, 1945-
Coexistence and commerce, by S. Pisar. Review
Sat R 53:29-31+ S 19 '70. D. Schoenbrun
Current documents. See issues of Current history
Future of world politics; will there be less violence? Cur 115:61-4 F '70
New look at France; interview, ed. by C. Painton. G. Pompidou. il por U S News 68:44-7 Mr 2 '70
Nonalignment and the great powers. L. Mates. For Affairs 48:525-36 Ap '70
Of many things; Decade of development. D. R. Campion. America 123:inside cover O 24 '70
Playing for high stakes; excerpts from Khruschev remembers, ed. and tr. by S. Talbott. N. S. Khruschev. il pors Life 69:16B-25+ D 18 '70
Soviet motives and stateside suspicions. R. Gurney, jr. Commonweal 93:63-8 O 16 '70; Discussion. 93:59-60, 211+ O 16, N 27 '70
U.S. and world affairs annual, Directions '70-'71. il Sr Schol 97:6-24 S 21 '70
U.S. & world affairs annual, 1969-70 edition. il Sr Schol 95:5-25 S 22 '69
U.S.-Soviet tensions and the UN. America 123:311 O 24 '70
Worldgram: from the capitals of the world. See issues of U.S. news & World report
See also
Balance of power
Communist strategy
Current events
International relations
WORLD publishing company
Corpus authors asked to forego advances, take royalty. Pub W 197:56 Mr 9 '70
New president at World; bookseller joins sales force. il Pub W 197:60 Ja 19 '70
New World's creative director builds a '70s image and sales, too; interview, ed. by M. R. Kraner. M. Charles. il por Pub W 198:48-50 D 28 '70
WORLD revolution. See Social revolution
WORLD rowing championships. See Rowing
WORLD series (baseball)
Flying start for the big bad Birds; Baltimore Orioles vs Cincinnati Reds. W. Leggett. il Sports Illus 33:14-17 O 19 '70
Heroes a la mode. H. L. Masin. il Sr Schol 97:19 O 12 '70
One-man show; Baltimore Orioles win. il Newsweek 76:55-6 O 26 '70
Sporting scene (cont) R. Angell. New Yorker 46:110+ O 31 '70
That black and orange magic; Orioles vs Cincinnati Reds. W. Leggett. il Sports Illus 33:22-4+ O 26 '70
WORLD shooting championships. See Shooting—Competitions
WORLD ski championship. See Skis and skiing
WORLD social conditions. See Social conditions
WORLD tourism organization
Landmark for world travel. W. D. Patterson. Sat R 53:27 O 24 '70
WORLD tours
See also
Voyages around the world
WORLD trade. See Commerce
WORLD trade corporation. See International business machines corporation
WORLD trade week
World trade week, 1970; proclamation, May 4, 1970. R. M. Nixon. Dept State Bul 62:703 Je 1 '70
WORLD travel photo contest. See Photography—Competitions
WORLD unity. See International organization
WORLD university. See International university (proposed)
WORLD war, 1914-1918. See European war, 1914-1918
WORLD war, 1939-1945
After twenty-five years: memory of two dictators. il pors Time 95:54 My 4 '70

Aerial operations
See also
Dresden—Air raids
Great Britain—Royal air force
Hiroshima

Anecdotes, facetiae, satire, etc.
War as theater of the absurd. J. Fischer. Harper 240:18+ Mr '70

Atrocities
Lammerding affair. il por Time 97:22 Ja 11 '71
Wartime journals of Charles A. Lindbergh; excerpts. C. A. Lindbergh. il pors Am Heritage 21:114-15 O '70
See also
World war, 1939-1945—Jews

WORLD war, 1939-1945- —*Continued*

Bibliography
World war II: a survey of recent writings. L. Morton. bibliog Am Hist R 75:1987-2008 D '70

Campaigns and battles
Pacific
See also
Pearl Harbor, Attack on, 1941
World war, 1939-1945—Japan

Western
See also
Arnhem, Battle of, 1944
Berlin, Battle of, 1945
World war, 1939-1945—France

Compensation of non-combatants
Compensation for camp victims: Danish law. H. J. Barnes. Sci N 97:604 Je 20 '70

Diplomatic history
See also
Crimea conference, Yalta, Russia, 1945
World war, 1939-1945—Peace and mediation

Jews
Destruction of the Dutch Jews, by J. Presser. Review
Commentary 49:77-80 Ja '70; H. Boas. Reply with rejoinder. R. M. W. Kempner. 50:14-15 Jl '70
Dietrich Bonhoeffer, by E. Bethge. Review
Sat R 53:17-22 My 30 '70. D. Berrigan
Efficiency expert: Treblinka, Nazi death factory, Poland. por Time 95:41 My 25 '70
Out of place in America; excerpts. P. Schrag. Sat R 53:12-13+ My 9 '70

Moral and religious aspects
Wartime journals of Charles A. Lindbergh; excerpts. C. A. Lindbergh. il pors Am Heritage 21:114-15 O '70
Wartime journals of C. A. Lindberg. Review
Nat R 22:1213-14 N 17 '70. J. Chamberlain

Peace and mediation
Secret attempts to surrender; excerpts from The rising sun. J. Toland. il Look 34:33-6+ S 22 '70
See also
V-E day

Personal narratives
Great patriotic war; excerpts from Khrushchev remembers, ed. and tr. by S. Talbott. N. S. Khrushchev. il Life 69:48-54+ D 4 '70
Khrushchev: the illusions of war. il pors Time 96:38+ D 7 '70
Reflections: experience as schoolboy pacifist to RAF Bomber command collision expert. F. J. Dyson. New Yorker 46:44-6+ F 21 '70
Wartime journals of C. A. Lindberg. Review
Nat R 22:1213-14 N 17 '70. J. Chamberlain
Wartime journals of Charles A. Lindbergh; excerpts. C. A. Lindbergh. il pors Am Heritage 21:32-7+ O '70

Prisoners and prisons
See also
Concentration camps

Propaganda
Preparing the public for war: efforts to establish a national propaganda agency, 1940-41. R. W. Steele. Am Hist R 75:1640-53 O '70

Psychological aspects
See also
World war, 1939-1945—Propaganda

Public opinion
Preparing the public for war: efforts to establish a national propaganda agency, 1940-41. R. W. Steele. Am Hist R 75:1640-53 O '70

Strategy
Papers of Dwight David Eisenhower, ed. by A. D. Chandler, jr. and S. E. Ambrose. Review
Sat R 53:23-5+ Je 20 '70. R. Steel

War criminals
See also
Nuremberg trials

Women and the war
Pilgrim's progress: adjustment to home life by an American exchanged prisoner of war from Hong Kong. E. Hahn. New Yorker 46:26-30 Ag 15 '70

China
If Asia were clay in the hands of the West: the Stilwell mission to China, 1942-44; excerpts from Stilwell. B. W. Tuchman. il pors Atlan 226:68-84 S '70

England
See World war, 1939-1945—Great Britain

France
Collapse of the Third republic, by W. L. Shirer. Review
Nat R il 22:268-9 Mr 10 '70. G. F. Eliot; Reply. B. H. Smith. 22:578-9 Je 2 '70
Lammerding affair. il por Time 97:22 Ja 11 '71

Germany
See also
Dresden—Air raids

Great Britain
People's war, by A. Calder. Review
New Yorker 45:74+ Ja 17 '70. G. Steiner
Reflections: experience as schoolboy pacifist to RAF Bomber command collision expert. F. J. Dyson. New Yorker 46:44-6+ F 21 '70

Italy
Our German wehrmacht is being stopped by a shadow; excerpts from Donovan of OSS. C. Ford. il por Am Heritage 21:56-7+ F '70

Japan
Fall of Japan; excerpts from The rising sun. J. Toland. il Look 34:33-6+ S 22; 51-4+ O 6; 53-6+ O 20 '70
Japan strikes: 1941; prophesies in books by H. C. Bywater. W. H. Honan. il por Am Heritage 22:12-15+ D '70
Remembrances of Tojo. il por Time 96:25 Ag 17 '70 *
Rising Sun, by J. Toland. Review
Bsns W il p 10 D 5 '70. G. Ringwald
See also
Japan—History—Allied occupation, 1945-1952

Surrender
Conspiracy to continue the war; excerpts from The rising sun. J. Toland. il Look 34: 53-6+ O 20 '70
Episode in Tokyo Bay. T. H. White. il Atlan 226:53-9 Ag '70
Secret attempts to surrender; excerpts from The rising sun. J. Toland. il Look 34:33-6+ S 22 '70

Russia
Great patriotic war; excerpts from Khrushchev remembers, ed. and tr. by S. Talbott. N. S. Khrushchev. il Life 69:48-54+ D 4 '70
Khrushchev: the illusions of war. il pors Time 96:38+ D 7 '70

United States
Old debate: application of C. Lindbergh's position against involvement in World war II to involvement in Vietnamese war. W. F. Buckley, jr. Nat R 22:1017 S 22 '70
Pilgrim's progess: adjustment to home life by an American exchanged prisoner of war from Hong Kong. E. Hahn. New Yorker 46:26-30 Ag 15 '70
Wartime journals of Charles A. Lindbergh. Review
Sat R por 53:31-2+ O 3 '70. B. Goldwater
See also
Japan—History—Allied occupation, 1945-1952

WORLD weather program. See Weather research

WORLD weather watch. See Weather forecasts

WORLD without war council of the United States
World without war; letter to editor. A. Stadler. Commonweal 92:127 Ap 17 '70

WORLD youth assembly
No end of ideology. Chr Cent 87:984 Ag 19 '70
Peace, anyone? il Newsweek 76:33 Jl 27 '70
Professional youths. Time 96:21-2 Jl 27 '70
U.S. discusses preparations for World youth assembly; statement, with text of Ambassador Yost's note, June 2, 1970. S. M. Finger. Dept State Bul 62:782-3 Je 22 '70
What generation gap? Sr Schol 97:6 S 14 '70
World youth assembly; adopted reports of meeting at United Nations headquarters, July 1970. UN Mo Chron 7:109-38 Ag '70
Youth has its day at the UN. B. Pilkington. Commonweal 92:405-6 Ag 21 '70
Youth, the U.N. and a split world; World youth assembly. Chr Cent 87:524 Ap 29 '70

WORLD'S Christian endeavor union
Christian endeavor: comeback trail? D. E. Kucharsky. Chr Today 14:43 S 11 '70

WORLDS Columbian exposition, 1893. See Chicago—Worlds Columbian exposition, 1893
WORLDS fair, Osaka. See Osaka, Japan—Worlds fair, 1970
WORLEY, James
Jesus as Sisyphus; poem. Chr Cent 87:230 F 25 '70
Second becoming; poem. Chr Cent 87:1062 S 9 '70
Soldiersong. Chr Cent 87:1342 N 11 '70
Sub rosary; poem. Chr Cent 87:1478 D 9 '70
Sunday morning; poem. Chr Cent 87:1211 O 14 '70
Teacher to pupil; poem. Chr Cent 87:1156 S 30 '70
Tired teacher's view from the rear of the classroom; poem. Chr Cent 88:41 Ja 13 '71
WORLEY, William
Good property maintenance needs a good property manager. Camp Mag 42:22+ F '70
WORM runner's digest
Wackiest worm runner. J. S. Shaw. il por Sci Digest 67:82-6 My '70
"When I get through explaining this to you, you will know even less than before I started" J. V. McConnell. il Horizon 12:112-13 Sum '70
WORMAN, Charles G.
Firearms. See issues of Hobbies
WORMS
See also
Annelids
Earthworms
Marine worms
Nematodes
WORMS, intestinal and parasitic
Worms like dairy cows too N. Reeder. il Farm J 94:D8+ Je '70
See also
Lungworms
WORRY
What are you worried about? S. Streshinsky. Redbook 134:85+ Ap '70
See also
Anxiety
WORSHIP
Black worship and hermeneutic. R. N. Soulen. Chr Cent 87:168-71 F 11 '70 •
New unity in the new city; shared religious facilities, Columbia, Md. America 123:370 N 7 '70
See also
Church attendance
Church music
Prayer
WORSHIP of the sun. See Sun worship
WORSTER, Steve
Woo of Texas is upon you. D. Jenkins. il Sports Illus 33:18-19 O 19 '70 •
WORSTHORNE, Peregrine
On looking back at Cambodia; reprint. Nat R 22:825 Ag 11 '70
WORTH, C. Brooke
Allure of the mosquito. il Audubon 72:60-2+ My '70
Last days of polyphemus. il Audubon 72:22-30 Mr '70
WORTH, Helen, cooking school. See Cookery—Study and teaching
WORTH, Irene
Private masterpiece. por Time 95:70 Je 22 '70 •
WORTH
Income and service as witness; excerpt from Religious women in the modern world. J. Tate. Cath World 211:247-50 S '70
Question of values and vulgarity. R. Graves. Life 69:1 Jl 4 '70
Recovery of purpose. Chr Today 14:21 Ja 30 '70
See also
Social values
WORTHAM, Robert
You can create period styling with stock moldings. il Pop Mech 133:166-8 Je '70
WORTHY, William
Anguish of Martin Sostre. il pors Ebony 25:122-4+ O '70
WOUK, Herman
Ashes & the gold. il Ladies Home J 87:68+ O '70
WOULD-be swingers; drama. See Greth, R.
WOUNDED, Vietnamese war. See Vietnamese war, 1957- —Casualties
WOY, James B.
(comp) Business books of 1969. il por Library J 95:863-6 Mr 1 '70
WRAGGE, Clement Lindley
Tropical disturbance Eline, 1898. E. B. Buxton. il por Weatherwise 23:222-3+ O '70 •
WRAPPING of packages
Christmas wrappings with a double life. il Ladies Home J 86:86-7+ D '69
Christmas wrap-up. S. Lindsay. il House B 112:54-5 D '70

How to turn out your own romantic wrappings. G. Vanderbilt. il por House & Gard 138:48-51 D '70
Stitches in burlap. il Sunset 145:68-9 D '70
Workshop Christmas wrap-ups. R. E. Hawkins. il Pop Sci 197:86-7 D '70
See also
Packing for shipment
WREATHS, Christmas. See Christmas wreaths
WRECKING
See also
Automobiles—Wrecking
WRECKS. See Shipwrecks
WREN, Christopher S.
Am I a wife or a widow? il Read Digest 96:93-6 Mr '70
How to wreck a national park. il Look 34:77-8+ Je 16 '70
Moog is more than a vogue. il por Look 34:24+ Ap 7 '70
Ross Perot: billionaire patriot. il pors Look 34:28-32 Mr 24 '70
Vietnamese GI: can he win his own war? il Look 34:13-21 Ag 11 '70
What is Christmas to the P.O.W. wives? il Look 34:36-40 D 15 '70
(ed) See Kaplan, J. H. Does our army fight on drugs?
—and English, Margaret
Murder New Jersey style. il Look 34:43-7 Mr 10 '70
WRENCHES
How to spot good wrench assortments. il Mech Illus 66:76-7+ My '70
Tools for electronics (cont) T. Haskett. Radio-Electr 41:52-6 F '70
Tools for electronics; nutdrivers. T. Haskett. il Radio-Electr 41:48-52 My; 56-60 Je '70
WRENN, Marie-Claude
Furious young philosopher who got it down on paper. il pors Life 69:22-3 S 4 '70
WRENN, Roger
Ceramic stitchery. il pors Design 71:38-41 mid-Sum '70
Flowers from beads. il pors Design 71:26-9 Spr '70
WRESTLING
Down with masked villains! birth of professional collegiate wrestling. J. Jares. il Sports Illus 32:60-1 Ap 27 '70
Good littler man wins big; L. Owings vs D. Gable in NCAA championships. H. Weiskopf. Sports Illus 32:72+ Ap 6 '70
Happy pair of hairy sports; middleweight wrestling champion and a wrestling bear. F. Deford. il pors Sports Illus 32:52-6+ F 23 '70
This soufflé always falls; Cal Poly the best small-college team. H. Weiskopf. Sports Illus 32:49-50+ F 16 '70
See also
Judo
WRIGGINS, W. Howard
Presence in southern Asia of outside powers; address, April 1970, with questions and answers. Ann Am Acad 390:48-62 Jl '70
WRIGHT, Alfred
. . . And a mighty Met is he! il por Sports Illus 33:22-4+ S 7 '70
Birds hop for a lively bantam. il por Sports Illus 32:74-6+ Ap 13 '70
In California: a colt to keep an eye on. il Sports Illus 32:25 Ap 6 '70
Johnny in agua hot. il pors Sports Illus 33:50-2+ Ag 3 '70
Pro basketball. il Sports Illus 32:42-4+ Mr 16 '70
Pro football. Sports Illus 33:46-7 Ag 3 '70
Tennis. Sports Illus 33:70+ O 12 '70
La vie en rose. il Sports Illus 34:56-65 Ja 4 '71
What goes up must ski down. il por Sports Illus 32:28-31 F 9 '70
You win! You're fired! por Sports Illus 33:34-6+ S 7 '70
WRIGHT, Charles David
Nightletter; Epithalamion; Entries; Salt; Night piece; poems. Poetry 116:186-90 Je '70
WRIGHT, Derek
New tyranny of sexual liberation. por Life 69:4 N 6 '70
about
Price of friendship. Time 95:54 Je 8 '70 •
WRIGHT, Doris
San Antonio's fight against illiteracy. il Am Ed 6:20-1 N '70
WRIGHT, Dorothy
Try a quest. Engl J 59:131-3+ Ja '70
WRIGHT, G. T.
Villanelle; poem. Nation 211:440 N 2 '70
WRIGHT, Grady
Christmas is his best crop. il Farm J 94:22-3+ D '70 •

WRIGHT, H. Elliott
Movies (title varies) (cont) Chr Cent 87:274,
367+ Mr 4, 25 '70
(ed) See Bethge, E. Aftermath of Flossenburg: Bonhoeffer, 1945-1970

WRIGHT, James
Echo for the promise of Georg Trakl's life;
poem. New Yorker 46:125 N 21 '70
Eclogue at Nash's grove. Harper 240:114 Je
'70

WRIGHT, John David
Conglomerates will come back; interview.
pors Forbes 107:111 Ja 1 '71

WRIGHT, John Joseph, cardinal
Religion in tomorrow's world; interview, ed.
by A. Kucherov. il por U S News 69:56-61
Ag 31 '70

about

Wright's writ. il por Newsweek 75:88-9 F 23
'70 *

WRIGHT, Joseph, 1734-1797
English painter of light. E. P. Birk. Antiques
97:164 F '70 *
Midlander. il Time 95:64-5 Ap 13 '70 *

WRIGHT, Joseph, 1756-1793
Joseph Wright's portrait of Frederick Muhlenberg. M. H. Fabian. il por Antiques 97:
256-7 F '70 *

WRIGHT, Phyllis, and Zimmerman, D. R.
Medicine today. See issues of Ladies' home
journal

WRIGHT, Quincy
How hostilities have ended: peace treaties
and alternatives. bibliog f Ann Am Acad
392:51-61 N '70

WRIGHT, Ralph
Robot crib 1970; poem. America 123:561 D 26
'70

WRIGHT, Richard
Black fiction: a second look. C. Mason. pors
Life 68:18 My 8 '70 *
Richard Wright reappraised. S. E. Hyman.
Atlan 225:127-8+ Mr '70 *
White trap: a motif; Native son. D. M. Don-
lan. Engl J 59:943-4 O '70 *

WRIGHT, Roe M.
In memoriam. por PTA Mag 65:26 D '70 *

WRIGHT, Russell
Town plan of Charleston. Antiques 97:542-4
Ap '70

WRIGHT, S. Harry
Trust territory of the Pacific Islands; statements, June 3 and 11, 1970. Dept State Bul
63:251-4, 265-6 Ag 31 '70

WRIGHT, Samuel
Last frontier. il pors Am West 7:32-7 N '70
Letter from the Arctic; excerpts. Am Heri-
tage 21:97 Ag '70

WRIGHT, Sylvia Hart
Pre-college program for the disadvantaged. il
por Library J 95:2884-7 S 15 '70

WRIGHT, Tennant C.
Revolution in Belize. America 122:219-20 F
28 '70

WRIGHT of Derby. See Wright, J. 1734-1797

WRIGLEY, Philip Knight
Island kingdom of P. K. Wrigley. il Forbes
106:22-3 N 1 '70 *

WRINKLE resistant textile fabrics. See Textile
fabrics, Wrinkle resistant

WRINKLES. See Skin

WRITERS. See Authors

WRITERS colonies. See Authors colonies

WRITERS conferences. See Authors conferences

WRITER'S digest (periodical)
Winners: Writer's digest creative writing
awards. Writers Digest 50:34-7+ O '70
Writers: 1920-1970; with editorial comment. C.
Canfield. il Writers Digest 50:16-17, 25-9+
Ja '70

WRITING
See also
Autographs
Calligraphy
Cryptography
Penmanship
Picture writing

WRITING (authorship) See Authorship; Creative writing

WRITING (composition) See English language
—Composition

WROBLEWSKA, Danuta
Magdalena Abakanowicz. il por Craft Horiz
30:18-23 O '70

WRONG, Dennis H.
Case of the New York review. Commentary
50:49-63 N '70
Feedback from our readers. Trans-Action 7:8
Jl '70
Portrait of a decade. il N Y Times Mag p22-
3+ Ag 2 '70

WRONSKI, Kendrick
Teacher I want to be. Todays Ed 59:47 S '70

WROUGHT iron work. See Ironwork

WU, Annie
On the highway; poem. Ment Hy 54:539 O '70
Three children of a mad woman; poem. Ment
Hy 54:160 Ja '70

WUERTH, Dietrich P.
Hybrid integrated circuits. il por Electr
World 84:52-3 Jl '70

WULFF, V. J. and Mendez, C.
Visual receptor potential: modification by
injected current in the limulus lateral eye.
bibliog il Science 168:1351-3 Je 12 '70

WUNDERLICH, Fritz
Records. Opera N 34:35 F 7 '70

WUNDERLICH, Paul
Beauty in the bizarre. il Time 95:74-5+ Ap
27 '70 *

WUNTCH, Thomas, and others
Lactate dehydrogenase isozymes: further kinetic studies at high enzyme concentration.
bibliog il Science 169:480-1 Jl 31 '70

WUORINEN, Charles
Musician of the month. il por Hi Fi 20:
MA8-9 S '70 *

WUPPERTAL, Germany

Music

Report:
Krzysztof Penderecki's The devils of
Loudun. H. Koegler. Opera N 34:29 My
16 '70
Lortzing's Undine and Dvořák's Rusalka.
H. Koegler. Opera N 34:26 Je 13 '70
Report: production of Fidelio. H. Koegler.
Opera N 34:35 Ja 24 '70

WURLITZER, Rembert, inc.
First they love the art. J. Mandelstam. il
Sr Schol 95:18-19 Ja 5 '70

WURLITZER organ. See Organ

WURSTER, Charles F.
DDT in mother's milk. Sat R 53:58-9 My 2 '70
Product pushers vs. the people. por Field
& S 75:6(+ Je '70

WURSTER, Doris H. and Benirschke, K.
Indian muntjac, muntiacus muntjak: a deer
with a low diploid chromosome number.
bibliog il Science 168:1364-6 Je 12 '70

WURSTER, William W.
Three architects speak their minds. pors
House & Gard 137:14+ Je '70

WURTMAN, Richard J. and others
L-Dihydroxyphenylalanine: effect on S-adenosylmethionine in brain. bibliog il Science
169:395-7 Jl 24 '70
—See Piezzi, R. S. jt. auth.

WÜTHRICH, Kurt, and Shulman, R. G.
Magnetic resonance in biology. bibliog il
pors Phys Today 23:43-50 Ap '70

WYANT, Rowena
Business failures. See issues of Dun's

WYANT, William K. jr
Consumer be damned. New Repub 162:11-12
Mr 7 '70
Oil rush. New Repub 162:19-21 F 14 '70
This land is whose land? New Repub 163:
10-11 Jl 11 '70

WYCHE, Zelma Charles
Top cop in Tallulah. por Time 95:17 Mr 2
'70 *

WYCKOFF, Charles W. and Leavitt, P. R.
Eclipse photography with a new color film.
il Sky & Tel 40:72-3 Ag '70

WYDEN, Barbara W.
Overweight? A fresh look at the problem.
Read Digest 97:129-32 D '70
Parent and child. il N Y Times Mag p89-
90+ S 13 '70

WYER, John
Captain Cool strikes again. G. S. Brown. il
por Sports Illus 32:26-9 Ja 26 '70

WYETH, Andrew
Presidential choice. il por Time 95:62-3+ F
23 '70 *
World of Wyeth; exhibition in Boston. D.
Davis. il por Newsweek 76:54-7 Ag 24 '70 *
Wyeth country. M. Evans. il Am Home 73:
74-82+ O '70 *

WYETH, Jamie
Portrait of Den-Den. il por Newsweek 75:
73 Ap 27 '70 *

WYLE, Edith
Folk art and fine food. V. D. Hahn. il pors
Am Home 73:46-7 Jl '70 *

WYLIE, Chalmers P.
Excerpt from debate, July 31, 1970. Cong Digest 49:239+ O '70

WYLIE, Evan McLeod
ARENA breaks the adoption barrier. il Read
Digest 97:19-20+ N '70
At last: a TV show good for children. il PTA
Mag 64:12-14+ My '70

WYLIE, Evan McLeod—*Continued*
Disgrace of our divorce laws. il Good H 170:
98-9+ Ap '70
Sesame street opens the door. il Read Digest
96:112-16 My '70
Up the executive ladder. il Good H 171:78-9+
S '70
(ed) See Stockdale, S. At least I know Jim's
alive
WYLIE, Max
When faced with grief. Read Digest 97:
103-5 N '70
WYLIE, Philip
Who killed mankind? story. Todays Health
48:20-5 O; 38-40 N '70
WYLIE, R. M. See Wilson, V. J. jt. auth.
WYLLIE, Peter J. See Lambert, I. B. jt. auth.
WYMAN, Donald
Flowering dogwood. il Horticulture 48:44-5
My '70
White fir. il Horticulture 48:44-5 S '70
WYMAN, Karen
Awake and sing. il pors Time 96:41 Jl 27
'70
WYMAN, William
William Wyman: the rebel in the conserva-
tive. I. Horovitz. il por Craft Horiz 30:10-
15+ O '70 *
WYMAN, Wilma
Everyone needs a salad tree. il Org Gard &
Farm 17:49 My '70
WYNAND, Derk
(tr) See Chatard, J. La houle à bout-portant;
Briser le silence; Élans du jour; Chaque
trace d'envol; Oublier tout
WYNDHAM, Lee
Heroes and villains in stories for children and
teenagers; excerpt from Writing for children
and teenagers. il Writers Digest 50:32-3+ N
'70
WYNDHAM, Robert J.
Cactus you can eat. il Org Gard & Farm 17:
102 Jl '70
Choose plants that will grow for you! il Org
Gard & Farm 17:102-3 S '70
Plants that don't get thirsty. Org Gard &
Farm 17:97 D '70
WYNN, Barbara L.
Oakland, California: la Biblioteca latino amer-
icana. il Wilson Lib Bul 44:751-6 Mr '70
WYNN, Richard
Collective bargaining vs. collective gaining.
Ed Digest 36:13-16 S '70
WYNN, Wilton
Boxing. Sports Illus 33:80-2 N 16 '70
Zombanakis plan to counter capital outflow.
il por Fortune 82:39+ Jl '70
WYOMING
See also
Fishing—Wyoming
Hunting—Wyoming
Paleobotany—Wyoming
Wildlife sanctuaries—Wyoming
Yellowstone National Park

Social conditions
Who wants equality? women of Wyoming. S.
Hunsucker. Nation 211:465-8 N 9 '70
WYSE, Lois
I love you better now: Cool lady; I'll meet
you at 5 at the Plaza; Nobody is born free;
Reflections on a birthday; Just because I
look positive doesn't mean I am positive;
English lesson; poems; excerpts. il Ladies
Home J 87:44 Je '70
Mrs Success; excerpt. il Ladies Home J 87:
50+ O; 58+ N '70
WYSOR, Bettie
Cosmetic surgery. Harp Baz 103:94-5+ Jl
'70
Face America loves. il Harp Baz 103:106-8
F '70
WYSUPH, C. L.
Behind the veil. bibliog il Art N 69:52-5+ O
'70
WYSZYŃSKI, Stefan, cardinal
Polish politics. il pors Newsweek 75:110+ Mr
16 '70 *
WYZANSKI, Charles Edward, 1906-
Judge Wyzanski and selective conscientious
objection. J. A. Rohr. America 122:182-5,
319 F 21, Mr 28 '70 *

X

X RAY crystallography. See Crystallography—
X ray studies
X RAY diagnosis. See Diagnosis, Radioscopic
X-RAY interferometry. See Interferometry

X RAYS
See also
Crystallography—X ray studies
Radiography

Archeological use
Radiography: new tool for retrieving the
wealth of the pharaohs. S. S. McKern.
il Sci Digest 68:8-13 Jl '70

Diffraction
Electron population parameters from least-
squares refinement of X-ray diffraction data.
P. Coppens and others. bibliog il Science
167:1126-8 F 20 '70

Measurement
X-ray survey of Centaurus A. E. T. Byram
and others. bibliog il Science 169:366-8 Jl 24
'70

Physiological effects
Radiation phobia. T. R. Bledsoe. Nat R 22:361
Ap 7 '70
Response of olfactory bulb neurons to X-rays
as a function of nasal oxygen concentration. G. P. Cooper. bibliog il Science 167:
1726-7 Mr 27 '70

Therapeutic use
See also
Cancer—Therapy
XANADU clubs. See Vacation villages
XANTHIUM. See Cockleburs
XENON arc lamps. See Electric lamps, Arc
XENON compounds
Xenon hexafluoride: structure of a cubic
phase at —80°C. R. D. Burbank and G. R.
Jones. bibliog il Science 168:248-50 Ap 10
'70
XERODERMA pigmentosum. See Skin—Dis-
eases
XEROGRAPHY. See Copying processes
XEROX corporation
Copy war. Time 95:92 My 4 '70
Technology machine at Xerox. Duns 96:28 D
'70
Two gee-whiz giants go at each other. il
Bsns W p70-1+ Je 13 '70
Xerox vs. IBM. il Newsweek 75:74 My 4 '70
Xerox's new anti-IBM machine. Bsns W p42+
My 23 '70
See also
Rank Xerox, ltd.
XYLOPHONE
See also
Metallophone

Y

YAF. See Young Americans for freedom (or-
ganization)
YASD. See American library association—
Young adult services division
YMCA. See Young mens Christian association
YABLONSKI, Joseph A.
Crime that shocked the Nation. D. Lawrence.
U S News 68:80 Ja 19 '70
Dead man's finger. il por Newsweek 75:22 F
2 '70
Fifth suspect. Newsweek 75:24 Mr 9 '70 *
Hand from the grave. il Time 95:11 F 2 '70
It's too late for Yablonski. New Repub 162:8-
9 Ja 31 '70
Jock's legacy. Newsweek 75:80+ Mr 16 '70 *
Just friends. New Repub 162:10-11 F 21 '70 *
Murder with a union link? U S News 68:6
Ja 19 '70
Vindication for Jock Yablonski. Time 95:25
Mr 16 '70 *
Yablonski murders. il Life 68:36-7 Ja 23 '70
Yablonski's legacy. Newsweek 75:35-6 F 23
'70 *
Yablonski's unfinished business. R. Nader. il
Nation 210:70-2 Ja 26 '70
YACHT building
Those were the days; mass-produced luxury
yachts in July 1929. J. A. MacDonald. il por
Yachting 127:50-2+ F '70
Welcome aboard Aurora. V. B. Schill and B.
Schill. il Motor B 125:72-6 F '70
YACHT clubs
Long tradition; New York YC cruise. E.
Horan. il Yachting 128:63-6 Jl '70
Yachtsmen of Seawanhaka are different from
you and me. J. Culhane. il N Y Times
Mag p30-1+ S 13 '70
YACHT compass. See Compass

YACHT decoration
Below decks. il Motor B 127:144-7 Ja '71
How to decorate a dreamboat. il House & Gard 138:144-7 O '70
Your boat's interior; excerpts from The woman's guide to boating & cooking. R. Lawrence. il Yachting 127:103+ Ja '70

YACHT models. See Ship and boat models

YACHT racing
Aboard a defender: Intrepid veterans tell of their roles in the 1967 campaign. B. Monte-Sano; W. E. Tobin, 3d. il Yachting 128:52-3+ S '70
America's cup; an incredible series. B. Robinson; B. Bavier. il Yachting 128:46-52+ N '70
America's cup: hanging by a thread? C. S. Booz, jr. il Motor B 126:46+ Ag '70
America's cup news. See issues of Yachting
America's cup 1970. P. Smyth. il Motor B 126:40-3+ Ag '70
America's cup preview: here they come! il Yachting 127:50-1+ Je '70
America's cup report: a close call for the cup. G. F. Hammond. il Motor B 127:25-40 Ja '71
America's cup trials. il Life 69:26-31 S 4 '70
Another ocean, another record; Transpac race. A. Colas. il por Yachting 127:74+ F '70
Apres vous, Gretel; selecting a challenging yacht for the America's cup. C. Mitchell. il Sports Illus 33:12-15 S 7 '70
Aussies and French hook up; America's cup international race-off. C. Mitchell. il Sports Illus 33:14-15 Ag 31 '70
Bermuda race summaries & awards. Yachting 128:49 Ag '70
Big boats take over; 1970 Southern ocean racing conference, with editorial comment. B. Robinson. il Yachting 127:39, 48-51+ Ap '70
Caribbean spectacular; Round Grenada race. B. Robinson. il Yachting 127:74-6+ Mr '70
Cast of characters; America's cup scene in ten pages of pictures. il Yachting 128:62-71 S '70
Challenger from France; M. Bich and America's cup. il por Bsns W p36-7 Ag 15 '70
Charisma wins Bayview classic; Mackinac event. G. E. Van. il Yachting 128:44+ S '70
Charlie Morgan: the Dixie gambler, America's cup. R. Marston. il Motor B 126:65-70+ Ag '70
Congressional cup to California youngster again. B. D. Barker, 3d. il Yachting 127:48+ My '70
Cruising to the cup. W. Juettner. il Motor B 126:44-7+ Jl '70
Deep water racing. B. D. Barker, 3d. See issues of Yachting
Different world; joining Ondine's transatlantic crew. B. Andre. il por Yachting 127:68-9+ F '70
Dismasting story; Bermuda race. B. D. Barker, 3d. il Yachting 128:42+ Ag '70
Dora takes Chicago race in gale; Mackinac race. il Yachting 128:44+ S '70
Down to the sea in $; America's cup trials. W. Johnson. il Sports Illus 33:16-21 Ag 17 '70
Eagle on a wild, wet flight; American Eagle champion of the Southern ocean racing conference. H. D. Whall. il por Sports Illus 32:16-19 Mr 16 '70
End of a quest; America's cup trials. il Newsweek 76:74 S 7 '70
Ensenada mob scene. L. J. Kennedy. il Motor B 126:56-7+ Jl '70
Fetching Bermuda: how meteorology and oceanography helped Robin win in 1968. J. Chase. il Yachting 127:56-7+ Je '70
First guns in a sea war; Valiant, Intrepid and Heritage in America's cup race. H. D. Whall. il Sports Illus 32:18-19 Je 22 '70
French challenge; America's cup. B. Bich. il Motor B 126:44-5+ Ag '70
From the committee boat; organization behind the America's cup races. B. D. Barker, 3d. il Yachting 128:75+ S '70
Full sail ahead; preliminary trials for U.S. contenders for the America's cup. il Time 95:62 Je 22 '70
Gallic challenger; the France. il por Newsweek 76:68 Ag 10 '70
Great grab bag. B. Robinson. il Yachting 127:46+ Je '70
Great round Britain sailing race. E. F. Haylock. il Motor B 126:38-42+ N '70
Gretel to the challenge. il Time 96:50 S 7 '70
Grim week for a battling lady; Australia's Gretel II. C. Mitchell. il Sports Illus 33:24-5 S 28 '70
How science is putting the wind in our sails. A. M. Geer and A. J. Hand. il Pop Sci 197:76-7 S '70

How to lose the Bermuda race. A. Zich. il N Y Times Mag p8-9+ Ag 2 '70
Incredible shebang; Gretel II's victory over Intrepid. il Time 96:51 O 5 '70
Intrepid indeed. por Time 96:39 Ag 3 '70
It took 18 years; Bermuda race. B. Robinson. il Yachting 128:46-8+ Ag '70
L'Allegro wins Mazatlan race; Los Angeles to Mazatlan race. A. Lockabey. il Yachting 129:61 Ja '71
Leave it to Chance; architect of Intrepid. il por Time 96:75 S 21 '70
Magoon Hennessy victor. J. Smith. il Yachting 128:45 S '70
Memo from '69; ed. by F. Rohr, jr. il Motor B 125:25-40 Ja '70
Month in yachting. See issues of Yachting
NYYC cruise. B. D. Barker, 3d. il Yachting 128:46+ S '70
No cup for the lady; with editorial comment. C. Mitchell. il Sports Illus 33:10, 12-15 O 5 '70
Powerboat race to Bermuda; contest may be revived. B. B. Brown. il Yachting 127:69-71 My '70
Racing clinic. See issues of Yachting
Regatta results. See issues of Yachting
Revolution roils the Cup; the observation trials of the America's cup race. H. D. Whall. il Sports Illus 33:14-15 Jl 27 '70
Shepherding the races; San Diego to Acapulco. L. J. Kennedy. il Motor B 125:144-9 My '70
Some great Dane from Tulane; Douglas cup collegiate match-racing championship in California. H. D. Whall. il por Sports Illus 33:20-1 N 9 '70
SORC's most challenging competition. R. Marston. il Motor B 125:28-30+ Ap '70
Southern circuit; Southern ocean racing circuit. M. W. Johnson. il Motor B 125:66-7+ My '70
Swap-boat series sailing; NAYRU championships. G. Hall. il Yachting 128:63+ Ag '70
To the onion patch again; prospects for the 1970 Bermuda race. il Yachting 127:58-9+ Je '70
¿To windward to Mexico? Galveston-Vera Cruz race. B. Robinson. il Yachting 128:56-7+ Jl '70
Triumphant youngsters; congressional cup. L. J. Kennedy. il Motor B 125:56-7+ Je '70
Victory at sea; America's cup. il Newsweek 76:64+ O 5 '70
Vincit qui patitur; America's cup race. Time 96:41 O 12 '70
What really goes on? America's cup behind-the-scenes. R. N. Bavier, jr. il Yachting 128:50-1+ S '70
With the racing classes, ed. by E. Horan. See issues of Yachting
Year in yachting. il Yachting 129:76-83 Ja '71
See also
Computers—Sports use
Navigation—Competitions
North American yacht racing union
Sailboat racing

Accidents and injuries
Incident from the Venice race. M. W. Johnson. Motor B 125:186-7 My '70

History
History of distance racing. P. Smyth. il Motor B 125:70-5+ Je '70
How the cup was won... and held. il Yachting 128:72+ S '70
Strange end of Shamrock IV. B. Day. il Yachting 128:59+ S '70
When men were iron. S. Iselin. il Yachting 128:58+ S '70
Where do old cup boats go? R. W. Carrick. il Yachting 128:60-1+ S '70

Rules
IOR snowballs; International offshore rule handicapping formula. P. R. Smyth. Motor B 125:164+ Ja '70

YACHTS

Chartering
Chartering in the Mediterranean. L. Elliot. Motor B 125:63+ My '70
Million dollar honeymoon. G. E. Miller. il Motor B 125:64-5+ My '70
Sailing vacation for new salts. S. L. Englebardt. il Todays Health 48:36-9+ Jl '70
Thoughts on bareboating. B. Bavier and others. il Yachting 128:66-7+ N '70
Yachting on a rowboat budget. B. McKeon. il Mech Illus 66:73 N '70

Crews
See Seamen

Decoration
See Yacht decoration

YACHTS—*Continued*

Design

America's cup; Gretel II and Intrepid. il por Newsweek 76:60-3 S 21 '70
And all they need is a tall ship. T. Gibbs. il Motor B 125:170-2 Je '70
Bright new Chance at the cup. H. D. Whall. il por Sports Illus 33:28-31 Jl 13 '70
Buxom belle named Banjer. P. Smyth. il Motor B 125:134-9+ Mr '70
Choice for offshore. R. H. Heacock. il Yachting 127:106-7+ Ja; 62-4+ F '70
Cup splashdown: Valiant and France; new America's cup boats. H. D. Whall. il Sports Illus 32:22-3 My 4 '70
Design showcase. il Motor B 125:156-63 Ja '70
Designing and building for offshore. E. Hiscock. il Yachting 127:76-7+ Ap '70
Designs. B. D. Barker, 3d. See issues of Yachting
Full sail ahead; contenders for the 1970 America's cup. il Time 95:62 Je 22 '70
Gallic challenger; the France. il por Newsweek 76:68 Ag 10 '70
Great yacht designers. B. Robinson. il por Yachting 127:54-5+ F; 66-7+ My; 128:62-3+ O '70
His southern belle; C. Morgan's Heritage. R. Marston. il Motor B 126:65-70+ Ag '70
History of distance racing. P. Smyth. il Motor B 125:70-5+ Je '70
How science is putting the wind in our sails. A. M. Geer and A. J. Hand. il Pop Sci 197: 76-7 S '70
Intrepid 1970: the designer's view. B. Chance, jr. il Yachting 129:94-6+ Ja '71
Is a new approach needed. J. R. Stanton. il Yachting 129:97+ Ja '71
Leave it to Chance; architect of Intrepid. il por Time 96:75 S 21 '70
Marlowe 48. W. Juettner. il Motor B 126:62-3+ D '70
One man's million-dollar gamble: Heritage to race for the America's cup. il por Life 68:56-8 My 15 '70
Welcome aboard Aurora. V. B. Schill and B. Schill. il Motor B 125:72-6 F '70
Welcome aboard Hedonist. E. F. Haylock. il Motor B 125:78-80+ Je '70
Yachting interviews: Bruce King; ed. by B Crabtree. B. King. il Yachting 127:77+ Mr '70
See also
Sloops—Design

Equipment

In the Herreshoff tradition. il **Yachting 127:** 68 My '70
12-meter gear, 1970 style; look at cup boat equipment. S. Colgate. il Yachting 129:92-3 Ja '71
Yachting's boat show. il Yachting 129:121-2+ Ja '71
Yachting's boat show in print. il Yachting 127:127-37+ Ja; 211-12+ F; 220+ Mr '70

Exhibitions

See Boats—Exhibitions

Finance

See Boats—Finance

Launching

Now let's not go overboard. il Motor B 126: 140-1 Jl '70

Materials

Down to the sea in cement. R. Brigham. il Life 69:70-3 S 11 '70
Old boats: why I love them. S. Wilson. il por Yachting 128:60-2+ Jl '70
Quest for lightness. E. Hall and K. T. Marshall. il Yachting 128:54-5+ S '70

YACHTS, Historic
Where do old cup boats go? R. W. Carrick. il Yachting 128:60-1+ S 19 '70

YACHTS, Remodeled
Pipit becomes a yawl. S. C. Henkel. il Yachting 129:108-9+ Ja '71

YACHTS, Used
Love affair, almost. K. S. Kynell. il Yachting 127:56-7+ F '70

YACHTS and yachting
America's cup news. See issues of Yachting
Aussie bid. W. Hood. il Yachting 127:54-5+ Je '70
Calendar of coming events; comp. by R. B. Smith. See issues of Motor boating
Calendar of major power and sail events. See issues of Yachting
Lilac time. R. Starnes. Field & S 75:8+ O '70
Long tradition; New York YC cruise. E. Horan. il Yachting 128:63-6 Jl '70
Motor boating & sailing USA (title varies) See issues of Motor boating & sailing

Motor boating USA. See issues of Motor boating
New life for Felicity Ann. D. C. McGregor. il Yachting 128:64-5+ Ag '70
News from yachting centers. See issues of Yachting
Offbeat Caribbean: British Honduras. D. Teague. il Yachting 127:56-7+ Mr '70
Old boats: why I love them. S. Wilson. il por Yachting 128:60-2+ Jl '70
Postwar yachting 1945-1970; symposium. il Yachting 127:66-83+ Ja '70
Racing-cruising auxiliaries. A. Gurney. il por Motor B 125:104-5 Ja '70
Southern circuit; Southern ocean racing circuit. M. W. Johnson. il Motor B 125:66-7+ My '70
Southern yachting: special report. il Yachting 128:53-67+ N '70
Twelve-meter story. R. W. Carrick. il Yachting 128:50-2+ Ag '70
Where are all the twelves? M. P. Copp. il Motor B 126:62-4+ Ag '70
Yachting's boat show in print. il Yachting 127:127-37+ Ja; 211-12+ F; 220+ Mr '70
Yachtsman's guide. T. Bottomley. Motor B 127:163-78+ Ja '71
Year in yachting. il Yachting 127:84-91 Ja '70
See also
Boats and boating
Cruisers (pleasure boats)
Cruising
Lloyd's register of American yachts
Marinas
Sailing
Seamanship
Sloops
Voyages
Yacht racing

Bibliography

Book notes and reviews. K. Aamodt. See issues of Yachting

History

There have been some changes. il Yachting 127:66-9 Ja '70

Laws and regulations

See Boats and boating—Laws and regulations

YACHTSMANS wife (periodical)
Something for the girls. M. E. Slate. il Motor B 125:155 Ja '70

YADDO (writers and artists colony) See Authors colonies

YADVEN, Art
Captain. J. Gilbert. il por Flying 86:56-61 Ja '70

YAGI, James
Results of Japanese tests on color-TV sets made public. il Electr World 83:53 Ja '70

YAKE, Glen A.
You can keep snow out of driveways. il Am City 85:63-4 Ag '70

YALE college. See Yale university

YALE drama school. See Yale university—School of drama

YALE school of drama repertory theater. See Yale university—School of drama

YALE university
And now Yale. il Time 95:59 My 4 '70
Behind the turmoil at Yale. il U S News 68:41-2 My 11 '70
Black Panthers and white radicals. P. Starr. Commonweal 92:294-7 Je 12 '70
Gentlemen songsters off on a spree; May day demonstrations. il Newsweek 75:31-2 My 11 '70
Girls at Yale. P. Goldberger. il Todays Ed 59:50-1 O '70
How Brewster does it at Yale. il por Newsweek 75:68-9 Je 15 '70
Letter to the alumni, by J. Hersey. Review Atlan 226:120+ N '70. R. Gilman Sat R 53:61-2 N 21 '70. J. Cass
Mathematics at Yale: new mathematics building. E. P. Berkeley. il Arch Forum 133:62-5 Jl '70; Discussion. 133:64-6 O '70
New catalogue of the Mabel Brady Garvan collection of silver at Yale. G. Hood. il Antiques 98:932-5 D '70
New Haven: the missing context. A. R. Dolan. Nat R 22:502 My 19 '70
New Haven under siege; rally in support of eight Black Panthers. P. Goldberger. Sr Schol 96:18 My 18 '70
Panther and bulldog. il por Newsweek 75: 52+ My 4 '70
Politics of academia. K. Brewster, jr. Sch & Soc 98:211-14 Ap '70
Reorganization of Yale's teacher program. Sch & Soc 98:208 Ap '70

YALE university—*Continued*
Trial itself put on trial; Yale student strike and rally. America 122:487 My 9 '70
U.S. journal: New Haven annual bladder-ball game and other traditions. C. Trillin. New Yorker 46:170+ N 21 '70
When the Panther came to Yale. R. Brustein. il N Y Times Mag p7-9+ Je 21 '70; Reply with rejoinder. K. Keniston. p2+ Jl 12 '70
Yale & female. B. Baer. il Look 34:24-7 F 24 '70
Yale and the deadly danger. S. Alsop. Newsweek 75:124 My 18 '70
Yale proves dissent doesn't have to turn out that way. J. K. Jessup. il por Life 68:38-40 My 15 '70
Yale's new dean. por Time 95:66 Mr 23 '70

Divinity school
Reason for being at Union and Yale. J. E. Dittes and C. W. Powers. Chr Cent 87:494-501 Ap 22 '70

Libraries
Yale catalog study yields rich data. Library J 95:3720 N 1 '70

School of art and architecture
Too much form, too little function? il Time 95:58 Mr 16 '70

School of drama
Yale's story theater. T. Prideaux. il Life 69:20 S 18 '70

YALIN-MOR, Nathan
Where are they now? il pors Newsweek 76:14 N 9 '70 *
YALTA conference. See Crimea conference, Yalta, Russia, 1945
YAMORI, Yukio, and others
Norepinephrine metabolism in brainstem of spontaneously hypertensive rats. bibliog il Science 170:544-6 O 30 '70
YAMS
See also
Cookery—Vegetables
YANG, Suh Y. See Selander, R. K. jt. auth.
YANGTAOS
To our West coast from New Zealand, here comes the kiwi vine. il Sunset 144:56-7 Ja '70
YANKEES (baseball) See Baseball clubs
YANKEES. See New Englanders
YANKELOVICH, Daniel, inc.
Sampling with seniors. R. Levy. por Duns 96:50-1 D '70
Self-portrait of the chief executive; the Fortune 500-Yankelovich survey. R. S. Diamond il Fortune 81:181+ My '70
Shaken faith in Nixon; Fortune 500-Yankelovich survey. R. S. Diamond. il Fortune 81:60-2 Je '70
What business thinks; the Fortune 500-Yankelovich survey (cont) R. S. Diamond. il Fortune 81:118-19+ F; 131-2 Mr; 82:72-3 Jl '70
YANKOWITZ, Susan
Terminal. Criticism
America 123:65-6 Ag 8 '70 *
Nation 210:765-6 Je 22 '70 *
Newsweek il 75:89 My 4 '70 *
Sat R 53:12 My 2 '70 *
YANNACONE, Victor John, jr
People need advocates. il Am For 76:20-3+ Ap '70
YARBOROUGH, Ralph Webster
Democratic primary, G.O.P. gain. il pors Time 95:37 My 11 '70 *
Hot after Yarborough. R. Dugger. New Repub 162:11-12 Ap 18 '70 *
YARBROUGH, Lee Roy
Fading hero strikes back. K. Chapin. il por Sports Illus 33:62-3 O 19 '70 *
Lee Roy pulls the string. il por Motor T 22:94-5 D '70 *
Winning with restrictions. S. Kelly. il por Hot Rod 23:74-6 D '70 *
YARD lighting. See Lighting, Outdoor
YARD of sun; drama. See Fry, C.
YARDS. See Home grounds
YARHAM, E. R.
Forest scene in Norway. il Am For 76:28-30+ F '70
YARMUTH, Stanley
Wild ride of Stanley Yarmuth. il pors Bsns W p41 Ag 8 '70 *
YARN animals. See Toys
YARROWS
Tansy and yarrow, handsome, helpful herbs; pest-repellent plants. R. Tirrell. il pors Org Gard & Farm 17:106-9 Mr '70

YARWOOD, C. E.
Man-made plant diseases. bibliog Science 168:218-20 Ap 10 '70
YASMIN, princess
Yasmin Aga Khan. pors Vogue 155:94-5+ Je '70 *
YASMINEH, Walid G. See Yunis, J. J. jt. auth.
YASTRZEMSKI, Carl
Full series for a fleet pair. W. Leggett. il pors Sports Illus 33:18-21 Ag 24 '70 *
YATES, Brock
Box? Bar of soap? No, it's a car. il por Sports Illus 33:16-17 Jl 20 '70
Motor sports. il por Sports Illus 32:52-3 Je 29; 33:56-8 N 2 '70
New kind of wheel at GM. il pors Sports Illus 31:39-42+ D 15 '69
YATES, Elizabeth
Day the library closed its doors. Am Lib 1:179-80 F '70
YAZOO CITY, Miss.

Education
Yazoo: notes on survival. W. Morris. il Harper 240:43-50+ Je '70
YEAR round school. See School year
YEARBOOKS, College. See College annuals
YEAST bread. See Bread
YEASTS
Attine fungus gardens contain yeasts. S. E. Craven and others. bibliog il Science 169:184-6 Jl 10 '70
Colcemid sensitivity of fission yeast and the isolation of colcemid-resistant mutants. S. Lederberg and G. Stetten. bibliog il Science 168:485-7 Ap 24 '70
Saccharomyces cerevisiae: a diffusible sex factor. W. Duntze and others. bibliog il Science 168:1472-3 Je 19 '70
Sexual reproduction in candida lipolytica. L. J. Wickerham and others. bibliog Science 167:1141 F 20 '70
YEATS, William Butler
He kept a sword upstairs. C. Molesworth. Nation 212:58+ Ja 11 '71 *
Let a thousand blooms. J. Hollander. Poetry 117:43-5 O '70 *
Yeats, by H. Bloom. Review
Sat R 53:37-9 Je 20 '70. H. T. Moore *
YEE, Min
Chinatown in crisis. il Newsweek 75:57-8 F 23 '70
YEHOSHUA, A. B.
Facing the forests; story. Esquire 74:101-3 Jl '70
YELISEYEV, Alexei. See Eliseev, A.
YELLEN, Dwight
Look at mass marketing in the 1970s. Pub W 198:31-2 Ag 24 '70
YELLOW dwarf virus. See Viruses, Plant
YELLOW-fever mosquitoes. See Mosquitoes
YELLOWHEAD highway. See Roads—Canada
YELLOWS (plant disease)
Plant-pathogenic mycoplasma like organism; maintenance in vitro and transmission to zea mays L; corn stunt. T. A. Chen and R. R. Granados. bibliog il Science 167:1633-6 Mr 20 '70
YELLOWSTONE NATIONAL PARK
Managing the Yellowstone elk. G. F. Cole. il Nat Parks & Con Mag 44:20-2 S '70
Parks are for people? J. Hope. il Audubon 72:68-70+ Jl '70
Sulfur isotope distribution in solfataras, Yellowstone National Park. R. Schoen and R. O. Rye. bibliog il Science 170:1082-4 D 4 '70
There's a water-level way to explore Yellowstone and Grand Teton Parks. il Sunset 144:44-6 Je '70
YEMEN
See also
Technical assistance in Yemen
YEN, Harry S. C.
Fragile beauty all about us. il Nat Geog 138:784-95 D '70
YEO, Edwin H. 3d
Pressures on the dollar. por Nations Bsns 58:81 D '70
YERKE, Theodor B.
ASIS: is it the whirlwind? Wilson Lib Bul 45:342+ D '70
YERMAKOV, Nicolas V.
Cannons to the right and left. Nat R 22:567 Je 2 '70
YESHIVA university, New York
Articulated library. il Arch Forum 133:56-9 N '70
YEVTUSHENKO, Yevgeny Aleksandrovich. See Evtushenko, E. A.

YOUNG, Andrew J. 1932-
Mediator. por Time 96:17 O 5 '70 •
YOUNG, Barbara
Our garden in the city. il Horticulture 48:
24-5+ Je '70
YOUNG, Charles E.
Chancellor in a crossfire. il por Time 95:63
My 18 '70 •
YOUNG, Chester W.
Voltage regulator design nomograms. il Electr
World 84:32-3 Ag '70
YOUNG, David B.
Preservice micro-teaching. Todays Ed 59:38
Ja '70
YOUNG, David P.
Comment. R. Watson. Poetry 117:207-8 D
'70 •
YOUNG, Edgar P.
Soviet mini-submarine. il Sea Front 16:25 Ja
'70
YOUNG, Gale
Dry lands and desalted water. bibliog il Sci-
ence 167:339-43 Ja 23 '70; Same abr. Todays
Ed 59:28-30 My '70
YOUNG, Gene
Trade winds. C. Amory. Sat R 53:6 S 5 '70 •
YOUNG, Gordon
Pollution, threat to man's only home. il Nat
Geog 138:738-81 D '70
YOUNG, Graham
Everything's coming up diamonds. il Pop
Mech 133:116-19+ Mr '70; Same. Sci Digest
68:68-73 O '70
YOUNG, John Humphrey
How Canada fights inflation: a step beyond
tight money; interview, ed. by A. Jones.
pors Forbes 105:36+ Je 1 '70
YOUNG, John P.
Can creativity come to book publishing? Pub
W 198:26-30 Ag 10 '70
YOUNG, Kenneth Todd
Any answers must involve all of southeast
Asia. il Life 68:40-1 My 8 '70
Thailand and the Cambodian conflict. bib-
liog f Cur Hist 59:351-5+ D '70
YOUNG, Mahonri Sharp
Mormon art and architecture. il Art in Am
58:66-9 My '70
YOUNG, Otis B.
He helps jockey the jumbo. il pors Ebony
25:54-6+ S '70 •
YOUNG, Otis E. Jr
Fire in the hole! excerpts from Western min-
ing. bibliog il Am West 7:15-19 Jl '70
YOUNG, Peggy
Make friends with your weeds. il Org Gard &
Farm 17:86-9 Ag '70
Mushrooms; with biographical sketch. il
Natur Hist 79:3, 66-71 Je '70
YOUNG, Pete
Waltermittyization. S. Alsop. Newsweek 75:
100 Mr 30 '70 •
YOUNG, Peter
Dissent cannot be shot down or arrested. il
por Life 68:61+ My 1 '70

about

Scouting both sides of an angry border. R.
Graves. pors Life 68:3 Je 12 '70 •
YOUNG, Richard W.
Visual cells; with biographical sketch. il Sci
Am 223:15, 80-4+ bibliog(p 144) O '70
YOUNG, Robert M.
Current trends in construction. See issues of
Architectural record to June 1970
YOUNG, Roberta
When is a social issue a school library is-
sue? Wilson Lib Bul 45:62 S '70
YOUNG, Russell G.
We did it; ed. by C. L. Miller. il House B 112:
57-8+ Ap '70
YOUNG, Sally
This tigress burned very bright. C. Goren.
il Sports Illus 33:73-4 N 16 '70 •
YOUNG, Stephen M.
Great public servant. Nation 210:772 Je 29
'70 •
YOUNG, Walter
Walter Young, landscape painter. N. Kent.
il por Am Artist 34:42-7+ D '70 •
YOUNG, Whitney Moore, 1921-
Other voices, other strategies; interview, ed.
by W. Terry. il pors Time 95:23-4+ Ap 6
'70
Racism in white America; excerpts from Be-
yond racism; building an open society.
Read Digest 96:167-72 F '70
Separatism? We are separated and that's the
cause of all our woes. il por Ebony 25:90-1+
Ag '70
Strategy for the seventies; address, July 19,
1970. Vital Speeches 36:732-6 S 15 '70

about

New look. il pors Newsweek 77:17 Ja 4 '71 •
Whitney Young: black leader or "Oreo
cookie"? T. Buckley. il pors N Y Times
Mag p32-3+ S 20 '70; Reply with rejoinder.
A. P. Randolph and others. p62+ O 18 '70 •
YOUNG, William C.
Education for the 70's. Clear House 44:387-90
Mr '70
YOUNG adults literature
Aladdin lamp for editors and authors. N. R.
Ainsworth. Writer 83:28-30 Ap '70
Outlook tower; books of interest to high-school
students. M. S. Cosgrave. See issues of Horn
book
See also
Young adults reading

Bibliography
Adult books for young adults; ed. by R. Minudri (cont) Library J 95:259-62, 792-8,
1210-16, 1659-65, 1969-75, 2318-20, 2545-50,
3076-8+, 3649-55, 4065-70, 4385-90 Ja 15, F
15, Mr 15, Ap 15, My 15, Je 15-Jl, S 15, O
15, N 15, D 15 '70
Best books for spring 1970; ed. by L. N.
Gerhardt and others. Library J 95:1913 My
15 '70
Books for young people. Z. Sutherland. See
issues of Saturday review
Children's books for spring. Z. Sutherland.
il Sat R 53:70 My 9 '70
Christmas books for children. J. Stafford.
New Yorker 46:218-20 D 5 '70
From movies to music. il Schol Teach Sec
Teach Sup p 18-19 D 1 '69
Twenty-two choice teen books announced by
ALA. Library J 95:1894 My 15 '70

Technique
Who wants to throw a cannonball? The young
adult field. E. Allen. Writer 83:25-6+ O '70
YOUNG adults reading
Recalcitrants. N. Willson. Engl J 59:105-8
Ja '70
What the kids are reading. J. Seelye. New
Repub 163:23-6 O 17 '70
YOUNG Americans for freedom (organization)
Cannons to the right and left; long haired
members of YAF. N. V. Yermakov. Nat R
22:567 Je 2 '70
Free them now! YAF rally on Boston Com-
mon to dramatize plight of American pris-
oners in North Vietnam. D. Brudnoy. Nat
R 22:1404 D 29 '70
Reunion in Sharon; YAF 10. C. S. Horn. Nat
R 22:1056-7 O 6 '70
YOUNG Lords (organization)
From rumble to revolution: the Young Lords;
Chicago and New York city. F. Browning.
il Ramp Mag 9:19-25 O '70
Lording it over the church; Puerto Rican
group called the Young Lords. il Chr Today
14:31 Ja 30 '70
Lords leave, litter lingers. E. E. Plowman.
Chr Today 15:45 Ja 1 '71
Right on with the Young Lords. J. Yglesias.
il N Y Times Mag p32-3+ Je 7 '70
Young Lords and the Spanish congregation.
D. M. Kelley. Chr Cent 87:208-11 F 18 '70
YOUNG mens Christian association
Chicago YMCA senior transport serves 1606.
aids 48 agencies. il Aging 186:7-8 Ap '70
YOUNG militants
Bitch goddess of individualism. R. S. Wheeler.
Nat R 22:1346+ D 15 '70
Bridging the gulf with dissenting youth. C.
E. Goodell. Cur 122:32-4 O '70
Counter-establishment; seven you can trust,
none over thirty. J. Kronenberger. il Look
34:68-73 D 15 '70
Editorial. Ramp Mag 8:2+ My '70
Honest, intelligible radical politics. R. Bru-
stein. New Repub 163:15-17 S 26 '70; Same.
Cur 123:20-3 N '70
Houston's MAYO clinic: complicated chemis-
try; Mexican-American youth organization.
R. Durham. Chr Today 14:42-3 My 8 '70
How radicals make money. il Time 95:52 Je
22 '70
In the Nation: our kids on West 11th street.
Nat R 22:344 Ap 7 '70
Militants who play with dynamite. W. Greene.
il N Y Times Mag p38-9+ O 25 '70
New faces of 1970; the Chicago seven and
their engagements. il Newsweek 75:33-4 Ap 6
'70
Notes of a young radical; arts festival at
Columbia university to benefit political pris-
oners. G. H. C. Knox. il Sat R 53:48-51+
Ag 15 '70
Paul Goodman vis-à-vis; interview, ed. by
H. S. Resnik. P. Goodman. Sat R 53:44 My
23 '70

YOUNG militants—*Continued*
Radical chic is dead. S. Alsop. Newsweek 76:120 D 14 '70
Radicals: Ilse Koch section. Nat R 22:394+ Ap 21 '70
Revolution as theatre. R. Brustein. New Repub 162:13-17 Mr 14 '70; Same. Cur 118:3-8 My '70; Discussion. New Repub 162:28-31 Ap 25 '70
Rhetoric of violence. E. Goodheart. il Nation 210:399-402 Ap 6 '70; Same abr. Cur 118:9-13 My '70
We'll blow up the world: a nineteen-year-old U.S. terrorist tells his story, ed. by K. Fleming. il Newsweek 76:49-50+ O 12 '70
See also
Student militants
Young Lords (organization)
YOUNG people. See Youth
YOUNG women
Four girls who say they are found. il Mlle 70:216-17+ F '70
Top people: the Mlle awards; twenty-five great hopes for the '70s. il Mlle 70:56-9 Ja '70
YOUNGBLOOD, Charles E.
As they see it; interview. por Forbes 105:53 Ap 15 '70
YOUNGQUIST, Duane R.
Our neighbor the sewer plant. il Am City 85:104+ My '70
YOUNGSTOWN, Ohio

Sanitary affairs
Housing development finds it pays to radicate. J. P. Prosser. il Am City 85:34 Ja '70
YOUR halo is showing; story. See Hoag, M. D.
YOUR money cheerfully refunded; drama. See Schaaf, A. K.
YOUTH
Youth: a new stage of life. K. Keniston. Am Scholar 39:631-54 Aut '70
See also
Adolescence
Boys
Children
Church work with youth
College students
Discipline
High school students
Hippies
Libraries—Services to young people
Negro youth

Attitudes
Communes and the work crisis; rebellion against the work ethic. L. M. Andrews. Nation 211:460-3 N 9 '70
Dozen duds in the canons of youth. A. Herzog. Ed Digest 36:37-40 N '70
Generation gap; free-market system. H. C. Wallich. Newsweek 76:98 O 12 '70
Hamelin to be revisited. P. W. Schmidtchen. il Hobbies 75:134-6+ My '70
Life problems and interests of adolescents; replication of 1935 and 1957 studies. W. H. Lowry and R. R. Reilley. bibliog il Clear House 45:164-8 N '70
New youth poll; Life-Louis Harris poll. il Life 70:22-7+ Ja 8 '71
Sex, virginity, money; interview, ed. by A. Talmey. B. Bettelheim. Vogue 156:94-5+ Ag 1 '70
Which would you pick up? Guess again; findings of University of Dayton study. il Life 68:61-2 Mr 13 '70
Youth alienation: myths and realities; adaptation of address. S. Hess. il Parks & Rec 5:16-20+ Ag '70
Youth attitudes, 1970; address, September 8, 1970. R. A. Weil. Vital Speeches 37:55-6 N 1 '70

Conduct of life
Autonomy vs. authority? W. H. Becker. il Chr Cent 87:1149-53 S 30 '70
Generation without fathers; Christian leadership of tomorrow. H. Nouwen. Commonweal 92:287-94 Je 12 '70; Reply. J. L. Kater, jr. 92:403+ Ag 21 '70
Spock on teens. Time 96:54 N 16 '70
Street kids; excerpt. L. Cole. Harp Baz 104:168 N '70
See also
Counter culture

Employment
Employment of high school graduates and dropouts; with tables and charts. H. Hayghe. Mo Labor R 93:35-42 Ag '70
Employment of school-age youth; with charts and tables. A. M. Young. bibliog f Mo Labor R 93:4-11 S '70
Jobs for boys and girls? B. P. McCarthy. il Parents Mag 45:42-3+ Ja '70

Would lower pay mean more jobs? question of a minimum wage for teen-agers. U S News 68:23 Mr 30 '70
Young workers: growing problem for unions. il U S News 68:81-3 Ja 26 '70
See also
Student employment

Health and hygiene
Teen-age hotline to help. Sci Digest 67:58 Ja '70
What teen-age medicine can do for you; adolescent clinics. A. Lake. il Seventeen 29:132-3+ Je '70
What you can do about teen-age fatigue. J. D. Wassersug. il Sci Digest 67:25-8 Ja '70

Management and training
Why parents should take a firm stand. B. Bettelheim. Ladies Home J 87:16+ Jl '70
Young people who hate the police. B. Bettelheim. Ladies Home J 87:52+ F '70
See also
Camp discipline
Discipline

Political activities
Closing the generation gap: search for a national policy; interview. S. Hess. il por U S News 68:56-9 F 16 '70
Patriot and protestor: can young people today be both? excerpts from panel discussion. il Sr Schol 95:14-16+ O 20 '69
Pixie power in Amsterdam. il Time 95:37 Je 15 '70
Revolt of youth: where are we now? J. H. Schaar and S. S. Wolin. Cur 119:3-10 Je '70
Revolutionists among the Chicago demonstrators. P. R. Miller. il Bul Atom Sci 26:16-21 F '70
Right on with the Young Lords. J. Yglesias. il N Y Times Mag p32-3+ Je 7 '70
Youth and foreign policy. S. J. Kelman. For Affairs 48:414-26 Ap '70
Youth on the Hill: up against the marble wall; anti-war activities. D. Blackburn. Nation 210:719-21 Je 15 '70
Youth to the rescue? G. A. Nelson. Cur 114:24-6 Ja '70

Reading
See Young adults reading

Recreation
Dialogue on leisure; PTA seminar. E. R. Walsh. il PTA Mag 65:24-5 D '70
Program called Workreation; Oakland park dept. boys program. W. P. Mott. Parks & Rec 5:72 Je '70

Religion
Dreambeat Down Under; Australian Christian endeavour convention. F. J. Nile. Chr Today 14:38-9 F 27 '70
Of many things; approach of youth toward the churches. D. R. Campion. America 122: inside cover Ap 11 '70
Protestant hangups with the counter-culture. R. L. Johnson. Chr Cent 87:1318-20 N 4 '70
Some words on the generation gap. R. Haughton. Cath World 211:5-6 Ap '70
West coast youth: spiritual revolution. R. Klein. il Chr Today 14:36 Je 19 '70
Youth 'liberates' America; symposium. America 122:430-42 Ap 25 '70; Discussion. 122-429, 123:158-9 Ap 25, S 12 '70

Sexual behavior
What kids still don't know about sex. T. Fleming and A. Fleming. il Look 34:59-60+ Jl 28 '70; Same abr. Read Digest 97:153-6 D '70

Suicide
See Suicide

Unemployment
See Unemployment—United States

China (People's Republic)
Rusticating the rebels. Time 96:22+ Jl 27 '70

Europe, Eastern
Surprises in the East. il Time 96:30 Ag 24 '70

Great Britain
Instant adults: teens to vote. Sr Schol 96:16 Ja 26 '70
Walk on London's wild side. D. Moraes. il N Y Times Mag p 100+ S 13 '70
Young men seeing visions. D. Martin. il Chr Cent 87:1063-6 S 9 '70

Israel
Six days plus three years: Israel asks, *ma ihieh hassof?* What will be the end? A. Rubinstein. il N Y Times Mag p5-7+ My 31 '70

YOUTH—*Continued*

Netherlands

Pixie power in Amsterdam. il Time 95:37 Je 15 '70

Poland

Threshold of change. il Time 96:35-6 N 16 '70

United States

All hail Andy Barker. Sat R 53:26 Ag 8 '70

America's young people. Chr Today 14:22-3 Je 19 '70

As I see youth today; interview. M. Haworth. Todays Ed 59:46 Ja '70

Banality of revolt; views of Andrew Hacker and William Braden. S. M. Lipset. il Sat R 53:23-6+ Jl 18 '70

Brave new world? Consciousness III. R. Lekachman. Duns 96:11 D '70

Children of the apocalypse. P. Marin. il Sat R 53:71-3+ S 19 '70

Communicating with today's youth; address. May 11, 1970. M. Collins. Dept State Bul 62:694-6 Je 1 '70

Consciousness III; theories of C. A. Reich. R. Starr. Commentary 50:46-54 D '70

Counter-establishment; seven you can trust, none over thirty. J. Kronenberger. il Look 34:68-73 D 15 '70

Faith, rebirth and renewal. P. B. Price PTA Mag 64:15 Ap '70

For now. C. H. Simonds. por Nat R 23:35+ Ja 12 '71

Greening of America, by C. A. Reich. Review
  Bsns W il p9-10 N 7 '70. M. J. Ulmer
  Nat R 22:1354-5 D 15 '70. D. Brudnoy
  Sat R 53:24-6 D 5 '70. R. Eisner

In the country of the young. J. W. Aldridge; discussion. Harper 240:8-10 Ja '70

In the country of the young, by J. W. Aldridge. Review
  Bsns W p 10+ Mr 14 '70. G. Koretz
  Commonweal 92:276-8 My 29 '70. H. R. Wolf

Is the corporation next to fall? A. G. Athos. bibliog f il Harvard Bsns R 48:49-61 Ja '70

New American revolution; excerpt from The trial. T. Hayden. il Ramp Mag 9:50-8+ Jl '70

1970: a time of in-betweenity. Chr Cent 87:1551 D 30 '70

Notes asides; letter to W. F. Buckley with comments by members of editorial board. T. McSloy. Nat R 22:347-51 Ap 7 '70

Peace in Middle Earth; escapist trend. D. Kolodney. il Ramp Mag 9:35-8 O '70

Rearing rads, rebs, & regulars; with study-discussion program. J. Katz. bibliog il PTA Mag 64:8-10, 33 Ap '70

Redeeming of America according to Charles Reich. A. M. Greeley. America 124:14-17 Ja 9 '71

Teen-agers speak frankly; excerpts from The music of their laughter. R. Thorp and R. Blake. Ladies Home J 87:46+ Je '70

Teenager's world: 1920's-1960's. il Sr Schol 97:3-19 O 19 '70

Trusting those under thirty. il Nations Bsns 58:22 F '70

We need our young activists; excerpts from address, October 1968. J. D. Rockefeller, 3d. Read Digest 97:53-7 Ag '70

We won't cop out. J. Nogg. por Redbook 134:42+ Mr '70

What the young want to live with. M. Gough. House B 112:48-9+ Jl '70

When the young teach and the old learn. il Time 96:35-40 Ag 17 '70

Who speaks for the young? Some startling facts and fictions. L. Rosten. Look 34:16+ My 19 '70

Whole world is watching, by M. Gerzon. Review
  Trans-Action 7:68-9 S '70. C. M. Curtis

Whose country is America? excerpt from First things, last things. E. Hoffer. il N Y Times Mag p30-1+ N 22 '70; Discussion. p34+ D 13 '70

Woodstock and beyond, why? E. Kiester, jr. il Todays Health 48:20-5+ Jl '70

Youth 'liberates' America; symposium. America 122:430-42 Ap 25 '70; Discussion. 122:429, 123:158-9 Ap 25, S 12 '70
  See also
College students
Counter culture
Dating
High school graduates
Volunteer service
White House conference on children and youth, 1970 (proposed)
Youth market
Youth movement—United States

YOUTH-adult relationship

Different-and the same; excerpt from radio series The Overstreet outlook. B. W. Overstreet. PTA Mag 64:19 Je '70

Drugs are your problem. D. C. King. America 122:497-8 My 9 '70

Hamelin to be revisited. P. W. Schmidtchen. il Hobbies 75:134-6+ My '70

I am tired of the tyranny of spoiled brats. K. R. Toole. il pors U S News 68:76-8 Ap 13 '70; Same abr. Read Digest 96:129-32 Je '70

Kids are children. R. Starnes. Field & S 75:6+ My '70

View through youthful eyes. L. Banks. il Fortune 81:76-7+ Ap '70

Youth 'liberates' America; symposium. America 122:430-42 Ap 25 '70; Discussion. 122:429, 123:158-9 Ap 25, S 12 '70
  See also
Generation gap

YOUTH and alcohol. See Alcohol and youth

YOUTH and drugs. See Narcotics and youth

YOUTH and moving pictures. See Moving pictures and youth

YOUTH and narcotics. See Narcotics and youth

YOUTH and society. See Individual and society

YOUTH associations

Motivated to be better; youth-serving agencies. A. E. Iverson. il Todays Ed 59:34-5 Mr '70
  See also
Young Americans for freedom (organization)

YOUTH conferences
  See also
World youth assembly

YOUTH development and conservation corps. See Washington (state)—Parks and recreation commission

YOUTH forums. See Forums (discussion and debate)

YOUTH group achievement awards

Parents' magazine's sixteenth annual youth group awards. il Parents Mag 45:70-2+ O '70

YOUTH hostels

Holiday guide to European youth hostels. J. Fraser. il Holiday 47:38-9 Je '70

YOUTH in moving pictures

Last great show on earth. C. Karpel. il Esquire 74:59 Ag '70

Stanley Kauffmann on films; youth films. S. Kauffmann. New Repub 162:20+ Je 27 '70

YOUTH in opera. See Characters in opera

YOUTH market

Das hip Kapital. C. Karpel. il Esquire 74:184-8+ D '70

Distillers worry about the youngsters. il Bsns W p 126+ Mr 7 '70

Economics of rock. P. M. Hirsch. Nation 210:275-6 Mr 9 '70

Is youth dead? il Newsweek 75:66 Ap 13 '70

Promoters follow the sun and fun trail. Bsns W p26 Mr 21 '70

Rap 'n' pinion. J. Passino. por Motor T 22:24 Jl '70

Why youth needs a new definition. il Bsns W p34-5 D 12 '70
  See also
National student marketing corporation

YOUTH movement
  See also
Counter culture
Student movement
World youth assembly

China (People's Republic)

Making of a Red guard: comp. by M. London and T. Lee; discussion. N Y Times Mag p20 F 1 '70

United States

  See Youth—United States

YOUTH opportunity program. See New York (state)—Labor, Department of—Youth opportunity program

YOUTH rodeos. See Rodeos

YOUTH-serving agencies. See Social agencies

YOUTH volunteer service. See Volunteer service

YU, Hwa
China. See issues of Christian century

YUCATAN
  See also
Arts and crafts—Yucatan
Cozumel Island

YUCHI Indians
Ancient landings in America; findings of C. H. Gordon. J. Lear. il Sat R 53:18-19+ Jl 18 '70

YUGOSLAVIA
See also
Catholic church—Relations (diplomatic)—Yugoslavia
Church and state in Yugoslavia
Conglomerate corporations—Yugoslavia
Dalmatia
Economic assistance in Yugoslavia
Pag (island)
Skoplje
Tourist trade—Yugoslavia
Umag

Antiquities

Animal remains from Lepenski vir. S. Bökönyi. bibliog il Science 167:1702-4 Mr 27 '70
Lepenski Vir: Europe's oldest settlement on the banks of the Danube. J. Vidal. il UNESCO Courier 23:26-31 Ap '70

Description and travel

Journey. M. Cantwell. il Mlle 71:184-5+ S '70
Rift in the curtain. C. Mitchell. il Yachting 128:50-2+ Jl; 53-5+ Ag '70
Yugoslavia; change within tradition. H. P. Koenig. il Travel & Camera 33:52-63 F '70
Yugoslavia: six republics in one. R. P. Jordan. il Nat Geog 137:589-633 My '70

Economic conditions

Mr Nixon: meet Tito, unorthodox red. U S News 69:24 O 5 '70

Foreign relations
Italy
See Italy—Foreign relations—Yugoslavia
United States
See United States—Foreign relations—Yugoslavia

Foreign service

Yugoslavs appoint science attaché. T. P. Southwick. Science 169:1062 S 11 '70

Nationalism

After Tito. K. Huszar. il por Newsweek 76:36+ D 7 '70

Politics and government

After Tito. K. Huszar. il por Newsweek 76:36+ D 7 '70
Collectivizing the presidency. por Time 96:32+ O 5 '70
Mr Nixon: meet Tito, unorthodox red. U S News 69:24 O 5 '70
Tito the elder. W. F. Buckley, jr. Nat R 22:696-7 Je 30 '70

Religious institutions and affairs

World around us. Chr Cent 87:403 Ap 1 '70

YUGOSLAVS
Yugoslavia: six republics in one. R. P. Jordan. il Nat Geog 137:589-633 My '70

YULETIDE. See Christmas

YUMA, Ariz.
In Arizona's southwest corner, consider a stopover in sunny Yuma. il Sunset 144:42-4 Mr '70

YUNCKER, Barbara
Keep up with medicine. See issues of Good housekeeping
Your family's health; sugar and the new theory about heart attacks. Home & Gard 137:64-5 F '70

YUNG, Robert
Expo '70, the curtain goes up. Travel & Camera 33:23-6 Mr '70

YUNGAY, Peru
Town that was, until May 31, 1970. il Américas 22:16-20 S '70

YUNICK, Henry. See Yunick, S.

YUNICK, Smokey
Say, Smokey; questions and answers. See issues of Popular science monthly
Smokey answers your eight most-asked auto questions. il pors Pop Sci 196:58-9+ F '70

YUNIS, Eduardo J. and Lee, R. E.
Tubules of globoid leukodystrophy: a right-handed helix. bibliog il Science 169:64-6 Jl 3 '70

YUNIS, Jorge J. and Yasmineh, W. G.
Satellite DNA in constitutive heterochromatin of the guinea pig. bibliog il Science 168:263-5 Ap 10 '70

YURCHENCO, Henrietta, and others
Folk music. See issues of American record guide

YURIKO
Yuriko and dance company; 92nd street Y. NYC. M. Marks. Dance Mag 44:81-2 Je '70 *

YUZAKI, Minoru
Japan: to count the dead. il Time 96:27 Ag 10 '70 *

Z

ZPG (zero population growth) movement. See Birth control

ZABAGLIONE. See Desserts

ZABRISKIE, J. B. and others
Lymphocytic responses to streptococcal antigens in glomerulonephritic patients. bibliog il Science 168:1105-8 My 29 '70

ZACHARY, Ralph
Latin expression. il por Opera N 35:32-3 D 19 '70
Little project. il Opera N 35:26-9 Ja 9 '71
Sin city comes to Fun city. il por Opera N 34:8-12 Mr 14 '70
(ed) See Blegen, J. Virtuoso
(ed) See Carson, C. Best foot forward
(ed) See Robinson, G. Room at the top

ZACHER, Gerd
Organ as synthesizer. il por Time 95:60 Je 8 '70 *

ZACHRY, Juanita
Entire town in one obsolete missile site. il Am City 85:87 Jl '70

ZACK, David
Ceramics of Robert Arneson. il Craft Horiz 30:36-41+ Ja '70
Nut art in quake time. il Art N 69:38-41+ Mr '70
San Francisco (cont) Art N 68:24 Ja '70

ZACKS, James L.
Temporal summation phenomena at threshold: their relation to visual mechanisms. bibliog il Science 170:197-9 O 9 '70

ZADE, Wayne
Lover on trial; Conclusion of love; poems. Poetry 117-188-9 D '70

ZADIG, Ernest A.
Basic position finding. il Motor B 125:30-2+ Je '70
Here they are: results of the $25,000 anti-car-theft competition. il por Pop Sci 196:72-3+ Je '70
Let a robot do your steering. il Motor B 126:48-9+ Jl '70
Pencil piloting. bibliog il Motor B 125:118-22 Mr '70
Powerboat hull design. il Motor B 127:130-3 Ja '71
Propeller-pox. il Motor B 125:172-4 My '70
Proper food preservation. il Motor B 126:12-13+ Jl '70

ZAFFARONI, Alejandro
Alza's big promise. por Duns 97:53 Ja '71

ZAFRED, Mario
Man of Rome; interview, ed. by E. Rizzo. por Opera N 34:29 F 14 '70

ZAFRULLA KHAN, Sir Muhammad
Contribution of the principal judicial organ of the United Nations to the achievement of the objectives of the organization. UN Mo Chron 7:139-46 Jl '70

ZAHL, Harold A.
1937, a new device to detect aircraft. il Electr World 83:48-9+ Mr '70
Tube behind the army's SCR-268 radar. il Electr World 83:37-9+ Je '70

ZAHL, Paul A.
Seeking the truth about the feared piranha. il por Nat Geog 138:714-33 N '70

ZAHN, Franklin
Christians and Caesar's taxes. il Chr Cent 87:1349-52 N 11 '70

ZAHN, Gordon C.
Berrigans: radical activism personified. pors Cath World 212:125-30 D '70
Terrorism for peace and justice. Commonweal 93:84-5 O 23 '70

ZAISS, David
Comment. Poetry 116:51-7 Ap '70
Too many ducks; Wong's short visit: In the white giant's mouth; Special delivery of celebrants; poems. Poetry 116:6-11 Ap '70

ZAK, Joshua
Natural coordinates for electrons in solids. bibliog il por Phys Today 23:51-4 F '70

ZAKARIASEN, William
Duet of the century. il pors Hi Fi 20:secI 52-6 Jl '70
Siegfried waltz? il Hi Fi 20:secI 66-70 Mr '70

ZAKROFF, Pete
Parthenon made of paper. il Design 71:40-1 Sum '70

ZAKY, Abdel Rahman
Cairo. il UNESCO Courier 23:10-16 Ap '70

ZALAMEA, Luis
Brazil's Senhor Jose. il por Américas 22:8-12 Mr '70
Pocket-size Panama. il Travel 134:72 S '70

ZALEZNIK, Abraham
Power and politics in organizational life. il Harvard Bsns R 48:47-60 My '70

ZAMANTAKIS, Mark S.
Vocational ceramic training in Japan. il Ceram Mo 17:12-13 D '69

ZAMBIA
See also
Copper industry and trade—Zambia
Government ownership—Zambia
Hunting—Zambia
Investments, Foreign (in Zambia)
Malawi, Lake
Technical assistance in Zambia

Description and travel
Penelope Tree; zapping Zambia. P. Tree. Vogue 157:136 Ja 1 '71

Economic policy
Zambia. S. Meisler. Atlan 226:32+ S '70

Foreign relations
Zambia's foreign policy. B. V. Mtshali. bibliog f Cur Hist 58:148-53+ Mr '70

ZAMFATIN, Evgenii Ivanovich
Icebreaker. S. K. Oberbeck. por Newsweek 75:92C-92D+ Ap 13 '70 *
Prophet, victim and exile. T. Szamuely. Nat R 22:1222-3 N 17 '70 *

ZAMYATIN, Yevgeny. See Zamfatin, E. I.

ZANDONAI, Riccardo
Records:
Francesca da Rimini. Opera N 34:35 F 28 '70
Return of Magda Olivero. P. G. Davis. Hi Fi 20:secI 77-8 Mr '70 *

ZANE, Maitland
Living together in California. il Nation 211:360-3 O 19 '70
Turning on in society. il Nation 211:595-6 D 7 '70

ZANI, William M.
Blueprint for MIS. il Harvard Bsns R 48:95-100 N '70

ZANUCK, Darryl Francis
Zanuck: last of the red hot star-makers; interview, ed. by H. Ehrlich. il por Look 34:69-71 N 3 '70
about
Fathers and sons. il por Newsweek 77:66+ Ja 11 '71 *

ZANUCK, Richard Darryl
Fathers and sons. il por Newsweek 77:66+ Ja 11 '71 *
M*A*S*H*E*D. il por Time 97:62 Ja 11 '71 *

ZANZIBAR
Take us from this place; forced interracial marriages. Newsweek 76:62+ O 12 '70

ZAORAL, M. and Slama, K.
Peptides with juvenile hormone activity. bibliog il Science 170:92-3 O 2 '70

ZAPATA, Emiliano
Zapata and the Mexican revolution, by J. Womack, jr. Review
Trans-Action 7:69-72 S '70. K. M. Coleman *

ZAPATA Norness, inc.
Why it's no longer viva Zapata. il Bsns W p40+ Ap 4 '70

ZAPPA, Frank
Hit it, Zubin. il por Time 95:72 Je 1 '70 *

ZAPPOLO, Aurora A. See Johnson, C. E. jt. jt. auth.

ZAREMBA, Elaine
(ed) Student voices. il Wilson Lib Bul 45:54-61 S '70

ZATZ, David I.
Teachers help interview prospective teachers. Todays Ed 59:47 F '70

Die ZAUBERFLÖTE; opera. See Mozart, J. C. W. A.

ZAWACKI, Chester S.
Long Island's artificial fishing reefs. il Cons 24:18-21 Ag '69

ZAYAT, Albert
Studio on a shoestring. il Pop Phot 67:108-9 D '70

ZBAR, Berton, and others
Tumor immunity produced by the intradermal inoculation of living tumor cells and living mycobacterium bovis (strain BCG) bibliog il Science 170:1217-18 D 11 '70

ZEBRAS
What is the zorse? offspring of zebra mother and horse father. il Sci Digest 67:39 Mr '70

ZECKENDORF, William, 1905-
Black and the red. R. Z. Sheppard. por Time 96:92 S 14 '70 *
Five years in the Zeckendorf labyrinth. il pors Bsns W p98-9+ Ap 25 '70 *
Man who lost the Midas touch. G. Williams. por Bsns W p7 Ag 22 '70 *

ZEFFIRELLI, Franco
Music to my ears. I. Kolodin. Sat R 53:21 Ja 24 '70

ZEIK, Michael
Must Christians be anti-Semitic? Commonweal 91:557-8 F 20 '70
Who is a Jew? Commonweal 92:114-17 Ap 17 '70

ZEILLER, Warren, and Compton, G. W.
Rare gift from the sea. il Sea Front 16:322-7 N '70

ZEISEL, Hans
(tr) See Lorenz, K. On killing members of one's own species

ZEISER, Sue. See Nystrand, M. jt. auth.

ZEISS optics symposium. See Photographic optics

ZEITLIN, Maurice
Inside Cuba: workers and revolution; excerpt from Revolutionary politics and the Cuban working class. il Ramp Mag 8:10-11+ Mr '70
Rights of a gadfly. Nation 211:165 S 7 '70 *

ZELAZO, Peter O. and Haschemeyer, R. H.
Spherical protein shell formation from an 11S subunit of bacteriophage f_2. bibliog il Science 168:1461-2 Je 19 '70

ZELIFF, Jane Seely
Is there a generation gap? poem. Good H 171:11 S '70
Magic of puppetry. il Parents Mag 45:46-7+ Jl '70

ZELIGS, Dorothy F.
Moses in Midian: the burning bush. bibliog Am Imago 26:379-400 Wint '69

ZELIGS, Rose
Do therapists play God? Ment Hy 54:161 Ja '70

ZELNICK, Robert
Oil rush of '70. il N Y Times Mag p26-7+ Mr 1 '70

ZELVER, Alvin
Oh! San Francisco! il Arch Forum 132:68-71 Ja '70

ZELVER, Patricia
On the desert; story. Atlan 226:76-81 D '70

ZEMAN, Henry F.
Surf fishing; Michigan's newest sport. il Field & S 74:150-3+ F '70

ZEN art. See Art, Buddhist

ZEN Buddhism
Making brain waves; findings of Japanese scientists. il Newsweek 75:92-3 Mr 23 '70
Zen Buddhism and western alienation from nature. W. R. Hoyt. Chr Cent 87:1194-6 O 7 '70

ZEN diet. See Diet

ZENDEGUI, Guillermo de
Great Haitian epic. il pors Américas 22:2-11 Je '70
Portobelo. il Américas 22:20-30 Ag '70
Promised land. il Américas 22:2-8 O '70
See the Americas first. il Américas 22:18-28 Mr '70

ZENER diodes. See Diodes

ZENITH radio corporation
Zenith fills the rooms at the top. il Bsns W p62-3 My 16 '70

ZEOLITES
Alkalinity and formation of zeolites in saline alkaline lakes. R. H. Mariner and R. C. Surdam. bibliog il Science 170:977-80 N 27 '70

ZEPHYR (train) See Railroads—Trains

ZEPPELINS. See Airships

ZERN, Ed
Exit, laughing. Field & S 75:101 Je '70

ZERNER, Henry
Masques and massacres. il Art N 68:59-61+ F '70

ZERO gravity. See Weightlessness

ZICH, Arthur
How to lose the Bermuda race. il N Y Times Mag p8-9+ Ag 2 '70

ZIDE, Larry
Are cassettes fulfilling their promise? il Hi Fi 20:73-7 N '70
Sound ideas. See issues of American record guide

ZIDOCK, Alex, jr
Nick Marchetti's spaghetti boats. il pors Motor B 125:14+ Ap '70

ZIEHL, Wilbur H.
United Nations headquarters accommodation; statement, December 11, 1969. Dept State Bul 62:102-7 Ja 26 '70

ZIGGURATS
See also
Babel, Tower of

ZILINSKY, Ursula
Novelist as village idiot. Writer 83:24-6 D '70

ZIMMERMAN, Blanche Perkins
Farm wife reflects on abundance. Farm J 93:47 N '69

ZIMMERMAN, David R.
Death comes to the peregrine falcon. il N Y Times Mag p8-9+ Ag 9 '70
—See Wright, P. jt. auth.

ZIMMERMAN, Irene
National bibliographer in exile: Fermín Peraza Sarausa of Cuba, 1907-1969. il pors Wilson Lib Bul 44:1060-3 Je '70

ZIMMERMAN, Joan
Strange world of helium. bibliog il Chem 43: 14-17 F '70

ZIMMERMAN, Joseph F.
Indianapolis consolidates. Am City 85:76 Ja '70

ZIMPEL, Lloyd
Hard-core jobs; are there any left? Chr Cent 87:941-2 Ag 5 '70

ZINACANTAN, Mexico
Zinacantan: a Maya community in the highlands of Chiapas, by E. Z. Vogt. Review
Natur Hist 79:66-72 F '70. H. R. Harvey

ZINACANTECOS. See Indians of Mexico

ZINDEL, Paul
Effect of gamma rays on man-in-the-moon marigolds. Criticism
Commonweal 93:49 O 9 '70 *
Life il por 69:8-9 Jl 4 '70 *
Nation 210:476 Ap 20 '70 *
New Yorker 46:82+ Ap 18 '70 *
Newsweek 75:64 Ap 27 '70 *
Sat R 53:12 My 2 '70 *
Time 95:51 Ap 20 '70 *
Man with a bag of marigold dust. T. Prideaux. il por Life 69:8-9 Jl 4 '70 *

ZINNAMON, Jerry
Diary of a dead Bavarian. Esquire 74:68+ D '70

ZINNES, Harriet
Geneva: a single gull; poem. Nation 211:152 Ag 31 '70

ZINNIAS
Zinnias go on and on and cost so little! H. Mason. il Bet Hom & Gard 48:86-7 Mr '70

ZINSSER, William Knowlton
Funniest college on earth. il Life 68:62-6 F 20 '70
Johnson Smith catalogue. il Life 69:12 Jl 24 '70
Movies Nixon shouldn't see. il Life 69:59-60 Jl 4 '70
Notes on a new style for Agnew. Life 69: 29 O 16 '70
Old word freak's first trip. il Life 69:16-17 S 25 '70
Parting shots. il Life 68:63-6 Ja 23 '70
Walt Disney's psychedelic Fantasia. il Life 68:15 Ap 3 '70
What happened when Refractory & brake ran afoul of the U.S. godwit lobby; a fantasy. il Life 68:42-3 Ap 24 '70

ZIOLKOWSKI, Korczak
How to carve a mountain. J. M. Liston. il por Pop Mech 133:76-9+ Je '70
Man and his mountain. il por Design 71:22-3 mid-Wint '70 *

ZIONISM
Anti-Zionism, anti-Semitism and the Christian mind. A. T. Davies. Chr Cent 87:987-9 Ag 19 '70; Discussion. 87:1228+ O 14 '70
Audacious struggle; Russian anti-Zionist drive. il Time 95:24+ Mr 23 '70
Matzpen and its sponsors. C. Gershman. Commentary 50:52-3 Ag '70; Discussion. 50:5+ O; 14 D '70
Normalizing the Jews; theories of M. Selzer. H. Halkin. Commentary 51:102-4+ Ja '71
Nyet is no answer; anti-Zionist drive in Russia. il Newsweek 75:48 Mr 23 '70
Zionism for the 70's. R. Alter. bibliog f Commentary 49:47-57 F '70; Reply with rejoinder. G. Steiner. 49:4+ My '70
See also
Israel
Jewish-Arab relations
Jews

ZIONS Utah bancorporation. See Banks and banking—Utah

ZIRIN, Harold
Big Bear solar observatory. il Sky & Tel 39: 215-19 Ap '70

ZISES, Alvin
CNA: there's leverage in leasing. A. Hershman. por Duns 95:42-4 My '70 *

ZISSELMAN, Susan
Sight and insight. Opera N 34:6-7 F 14 '70

ZITKO, Howard John
Battle for earth; address, August 1, 1970. Vital Speeches 36:692-6 S 1 '70

ZITRIN, Arthur, and others
New York's mental hygiene law: a preliminary evaluation. bibliog Ment Hy 54:28-36 Ja '70
Sexual behavior of male cats after administration of parachlorophenylalanine. bibliog il Science 170:868-70 N 20 '70

ZMIJEWSKI, Chester M. See Charlton, R. K. jt. auth.

ZMUDA, Joseph P.
Convert to LP gas. il Pop Sci 197:43-5 Jl '70
Homebuilt steam car takes to the road! il Pop Mech 135:114-16+ Ja '71
New: a catalytic converter that really cleans up auto exhaust. il Pop Sci 197:47-9 D '70
New gas cuts smog, cleans engine, too! il Pop Mech 133:44+ Ap '70

ZNAMIEROWSKI, Nell
Dorothy Liebes. il por Craft Horiz 30:34-41+ Ag '70

ZODHIATES, Spiros
Greece: the right to spread good news. Chr Today 15:29 Ja 1 '71 *

ZODIAC
Revised zodiac. il Time 96:44 N 23 '70

ZOECON corporation
When it arrives, it will be a killer; hormone analog as ultimate insecticide. il Bsns W p 136+ Je 6 '70

el-ZOGHBY, Gamal
Designed for contemplation. il Craft Horiz 30:12-19+ Mr '70

ZOLL, Donald Atwell
Shall we let America die? Nat R 21:1261-3; 22: 259-60, 362+ D 16 '69, Mr 10, Ap 7 '70

ZOLOTH, Stephen R. See Adler, N. T. jt. auth.

ZOMBANAKIS, Minos
Zombanakis plan to counter capital outflow. W. Wynn. il por Fortune 82:39+ Jl '70 *

ZOND flights. See Space flight to the moon—Zond flights

ZONING
Alternates to suburban sprawl: new processes, new involvement. W. F. Wagner, jr. Arch Rec 148:9-10 N '70
Color zoning white. il Time 96:51 S 7 '70
Cracking the suburbs. R. W. Dietsch. New Repub 163:8 S 5 '70
Mobile homes granted residential zoning; Lincoln, Neb. Am City 85:34 S '70
Zoning is a three-dimensional word; changes in New York city. E. P. Berkeley. il Arch Forum 133:48-51 N '70
Zoning; the new battleground; excerpts. C. Funnyé. Arch Forum 132:62-5 My '70

ZONING law
Battle to open the suburbs: new attack on zoning laws. il U S News 68:39-40 Je 22 '70
Moral dilemma of zoning. D. K. Shipler. il Nation 211:80-3 Ag 3 '70
Zoning law seen banning Bible classes. N. B. Rohrer. Chr Today 14:37 F 13 '70

ZOO, Central park. See New York (city)—Parks and playgrounds

ZOOLOGICAL exhibitions, Traveling. See Exhibitions, Traveling

ZOOLOGICAL gardens
Château menagerie; Château de Thoiry menagerie, France. il Time 96:36 Jl 20 '70
Dublin treat: the Phoenix park zoo. il Sunset 144:35 Mr '70
Escape; zoo escapes of birds and animals. New Yorker 46:23-5 Ag 8 '70
Exhibiting reptiles. J. S. Dobbs. il Parks & Rec 5:23+ O '70
New zoos. il Newsweek 75:58 Je 1 '70
P.O.N.Y. farm, where city youngsters have fun sharing the care of animals; corral in New York city dock district. il por Good H 170:52-3+ Mr '70
Things are changing at the zoo, too. il Changing T 24:24-5 F '70
Zoo-a-go-go; traveling zoo. M. D. Craden and P. C. Skelton. il Parks & Rec 5:25+ Ap '70
Zoo environment: man made; Cleveland, Ohio. P. Van Dijk. il Am City 85:26 Jl '70
See also
New York zoological park

Buildings
Free as a bird; birdhouses of the National zoological park. Washington, D.C. R. W. Elder. il Parks & Rec 5:33 Ja '70

Employees
Meanwhile, back at the zoo; MDTA course for upgrading zookeepers. H. Schaden. il Am Ed 6:18-25 Ag '70

ZOOLOGICAL research
See also
Fishery research

ZOOLOGICAL specimens

Collection and preservation
Panacea for a salty Yankee; collecting marine creatures for scientific study. R. H. Boyle. il por Sports Illus 32:28-30+ Ap 20 '70